WHO'S
WHO
AMONG
AFRICAN
AMERICANS

WHO'S WHO AMONG AFRICAN AMERICANS

24TH EDITION

Introductory Essay by
Jessie Carney Smith
University Librarian and
William and Camille Cosby Professor in the Humanities
Fisk University

Edited by
Kristin B. Mallegg

Who's Who Among African Americans, 24th Edition

Project Editor: Kristin Mallegg

Editorial: Katherine H. Nemeh

Editorial Support Services: Natalyia Mikheyeva

Composition and Electronic Prepress: Gary Oudersluys

Manufacturing: Rita Wimberley

For product information and technology assistance, contact us at **Gale Customer Support, 1-800-877-4253.**
For permission to use material from this text or product, submit all requests online at **www.cengage.com/permissions.**
Further permissions questions can be emailed to **permissionrequest@cengage.com**

While every effort has been made to ensure the reliability of the information presented in this publication, Gale, a part of Cengage Learning, does not guarantee the accuracy of the data contained herein. Gale accepts no payment for listing; and inclusion in the publication of any organization, agency, institution, publication, service, or individual does not imply endorsement of the editors or publisher. Errors brought to the attention of the publisher and verified to the satisfaction of the publisher will be corrected in future editions.

EDITORIAL DATA PRIVACY POLICY: Does this product contain information about you as an individual? If so, for more information about our editorial data privacy policies, please see our Privacy Statement at www.gale.cengage.com.

Gale
27500 Drake Rd.
Farmington Hills, MI, 48331-3535

ISBN-13: 978-1-4144-4849-7
ISBN-10: 1-4144-4849-X

ISSN 1081-1400

Printed in the United States of America
1 2 3 4 5 6 7 13 12 11 10 09

Advisory Board

Lerone Bennett, Jr.
Author and Historian
Executive Editor Emeritus, Ebony

Dr. Carla Hayden
Director
Enoch Pratt Free Library

Vivian D. Hewitt
Former Librarian
Carnegie Endowment for International Peace

Jessie Carney Smith
University Librarian
Fisk University

Roslyn M. Brock
Vice Chairman
NAACP National Board of Directors

Contents

Foreword

When national news correspondent William C. "Bill" Matney became founding editor of *Who's Who Among Black Americans* in 1976, he noted with pride that it contained the "largest total of biographical entries of high achieving Blacks ever published in one volume." There were 10,000 entries in that inaugural edition. Although he cast his net widely, doubtless he knew that he had but touched the surface of accomplished blacks who deserved such recognition. His work showcased blacks from a variety of professions, ranging from those in government to those in civic affairs, from civil rights to the arts, from sports to the theater, from religion to science, and so on. Since his pioneering work, the world has seen African Americans, as black Americans are popularly known now, swell the ranks of achievers in these fields and also excel in newer fields barely known when Matney pioneered, such as computer forensics, hospitalist, computational biologist, and behavioral geneticist.

From Matney's 10,000 entrants in 1976, over thirty years later the list now exceeds 20,000 African American achievers. The compilation itself is a history of a people. While the pioneers on whose shoulders they stand—Ida Wells Barnett, Mary McLeod Bethune, W.E.B. Du Bois, Frederick Douglass, Martin Luther King Jr., Booker T. Washington, and other prominent members of the race who have completed their journeys, it is enlightening to see others of achievement as well. For some—particularly those bound by the restrictions of race and gender— upward mobility was a struggle; for others—those who lifted the historic and traditional barriers of oppression, progress was smooth and seamless in the transition from the unknown to the known.

We must know our achievers to know our astounding history, who made it, and who lived it. Years ago bibliophiles Arthur A. Schombug and Charles L. Blockson, who had a curiosity about their history early on, were told by one of their teachers that blacks had no history. Their teachers lacked knowledge of black history or they would have known at least the pioneers and other movers and shakers of that time. It is scholars like Schomburg and Blockson who know our history and culture as well as they know those who make history and preserve culture, such as those listed in the limited biographical directories that stood alone for so long.

For African American women and those sympathetic to their plight, this work is especially significant. They, too, are great trailblazers who made their way when there was no way for women or blacks. When Monroe Majors, a physician

and biographer who compiled the seminal work *Noted Negro Women,* asked abolitionist Frederick Douglass to suggest the names of women who should be included in his book, Douglass replied "We have many estimable women of our variety, but not any famous ones." And so he sent no names, not even Sojourner Truth or Harriet Tubman. Fortunately, the twenty-three editions of *Who's Who Among African Americans* never discriminated against women. Thus, we find women like Johnetta Betsch Cole and Ruth Simmons filling the spot that Mary McLeod Bethune and other pioneer black women educators would have filled if this work had existed in an earlier time. Similarly, women civil rights leaders Eleanor Holmes Norton and Mary Berry are modern versions of Sojourner Truth and Harriet Tubman. This biographical compilation helps to dispel two notions: that "blacks have no history" and that there are no famous black women in our culture.

The compilation of this edition is a chronicle of an astounding history. The memberships and affiliations of the entrants give an historical context to African American achievement that spans much of the twentieth century and the beginning of the twenty-first. We need the additional insights into the professional and personal lives that the entries include, such as board memberships, honors, awards, publications, and often identification of a number of African American firsts, whether the first editor of a particular newspaper or first president of an organization. The Historically Black Colleges and Universities (HBCUs) are well represented in the listings, for the entrants are asked to identify the institutions from which they graduated. Similarly, members of Greek-letter organizations may marvel at the achievements of their members who identify their sororities or fraternities.

For African Americans, doubtless most will turn the pages to Barack Obama and rejoice in seeing his entry updated, listing him now as our first African American President. Notwithstanding the grim realities of some public rejection and accompanying ugly reactions to his leadership, his accomplishments are refreshed, as they should be. Such reactions do not remove the facts or change his historic accomplishment. Nor does this change the fact that he descended from racially-mixed heritage, translated by American standards and traditions as "black," since one parent was African. Obama's election transcended race and, in the infancy of his run for the presidency, his primary supporters were from upper-middle-class American society and represented all races. He functions, however, as the President of all Americans. While many of the entrants in this work share their fame as educators, writers, politicians, and scientists, Obama stands without peer. President Obama can increase his knowledge about who we are and how much we have accomplished if he will examine the copy of *Who's Who Among African Americans* included in the Presidential Collection at Camp David.

Preparing the various editions of Who's Who's that identify African American men and women of action has been a monumental task and an enormous challenge. There is always the fear that someone of great accomplishment has been overlooked. Thus, as comprehensive as it tries to be, *Who's Who Among African Americans,* like other biographical directories, rarely includes all deserve an entry. Our task as scholars and culture keepers is to make certain that, as far as possible, we cast big nets in multiple arenas and come closer to capturing many more notable achievers in our culture.

Jessie Carney Smith
University Librarian and
William and Camille Cosby Professor in the Humanities
Fisk University

Introduction

Now in its twenty-fourth edition, *Who's Who Among African Americans (WWAFA)* is your guide to more than 20,000 men and women who have changed today's world and are shaping tomorrow's. The biographical entries you will find on these pages reflect the diversity of African-American achievement by documenting the contributions of leaders in all fields of endeavor. Together these entries make *Who's Who Among African Americans* the most comprehensive publication devoted to recording the accomplishments of African Americans.

Compilation Methods

The selection of *WWAFA* listees is based primarily on reference value. In order to identify noteworthy new achievers and monitor significant events in the lives of current listees, the editorial staff scans a wide variety of books, magazines, newspapers, and other material on an ongoing basis. Associations, businesses, government offices, and colleges and universities were also contacted for their suggestions. Users, current listees, and members of the *WWAFA* Advisory Board continue to provide their recommendations as well.

These candidates become eligible for inclusion by virtue of positions held through election or appointment to office, notable career achievements, or outstanding community service. Black persons who are not American citizens are considered eligible if they live or work in the United States and contribute significantly to American life. Such broad coverage makes *Who's Who Among African Americans* the logical source for you to consult when gathering facts on a distinguished leader or a favorite celebrity, locating a colleague, contacting an expert, recruiting personnel, or launching a fund-raising effort.

Once this identification process is complete, we make an effort to secure information directly from biographees. In absense of this, we gather information from reliable sources. Those candidates whose achievements merit inclusion proceed through the remaining stages of entry compilation.

In an almost simultaneous process, current listees receive copies of their entries from the most recent edition in which they appeared. They then update their biographies as necessary to reflect new career positions, address changes, or recent awards and achievements.

Sometimes potential and current listees decline to furnish biographical data. Recognizing that this does not satisfy your need for comprehensiveness, we have compiled selected entries from a variety of secondary sources to help ensure that the people you want to see in *WWAFA* are indeed listed. These entries are marked by an *asterisk (*)*, indicating that the listees have not personally provided or reviewed the data, but you still benefit from having basic biographical information at your fingertips.

Important Features

To complement its thorough coverage, *Who's Who Among African Americans* uses these important features to help you locate the information you need:

- **Boldface Rubrics** allow quick and easy scanning for specifics on personal data, educational background, career positions, organizational affiliations, honors and awards, special achievements, military service, home address, business address, and telephone number.

- **Obituaries Section** provides you with entries on recently deceased newsworthy African Americans. This section provides a full entry plus date and place of death, when available.

Indexing

Who's Who Among African Americans features two indexes, both of which make quick work of your searches:

- **Geographic Index.** Locate biographees by specific city, state, and country of residence and/or employment. (Only those listees who agree to allow their addresses to be printed in the directory will appear in this index.)

- **Occupation Index.** With more than 150 categories, this index allows you to identify listees working in fields ranging from accounting to zoology.

Acknowledgments

The editors wish to thank the Advisory Board members whose names appear at the front of this volume for their advice and encouragement as we compiled this edition of *Who's Who Among African Americans.*

We would also like to thank the many individuals and organizations who nominated achievers for consideration in this edition.

Available in Electronic Formats

Licensing. Who's Who Among African Americans is available for licensing. The complete database is provided in a fielded format and is deliverable on such media as disk or CD-ROM. For more information, contact Gale's Business Development Group at 1-800-877-GALE, or visit our website at http://gale.cengage.com/bizdev.

Online. WWAFA is accessible online as part of the Gale Biographies (GALBIO) database accessible through LexisN-exis, P.O. Box 933, Dayton, OH 45401-0933; phone: 937-865-6800; toll-free: 800-227-9597.

Suggestions Welcome

Comments and suggestions from users on any aspect of *WWAFA* are cordially invited to write:

The Editor

Who's Who Among African Americans

Gale

27500 Drake Road

Farmington Hills, MI 48331-3535

Key to
Biographical Information

❚1❚ MATNEY, WILLIAM C., JR. [In Memorium]

❚2❚ Federal official (retired), communications consultant. ❚3❚ **Personal:** Born Sep 02, 1924, Bluefield, WV; died June 13, 2001, La Plata, MD; son of William C Matney Sr and Jane A Matney; widowed; children: Alma, Angelique, William III. ❚4❚ **Educ:** Wayne State Univ, 1940-42; Univ of Michigan, BA, 1946. ❚5❚ **Career:** The Michigan Chronicle, reporter, sports editor, city editor, mng editor, 1946-61; Detroit News, reporter, writer, 1962-63; WMAQ-NBC, TV and radio reporter, 1963-65; NBC Network Television, correspondent, 1966-72; ABC Network News, correspondent, 1972-78; Who's Who among Black Americans, founding editor, 1974-88, consulting editor, 1988-93; US Bureau of the Census, sr public affairs coord, 1979-93. ❚6❚ **Orgs:** Mem, Big Ten Championship Track Team, 1943; pres, Cotillion Club, 1962-63; mem, NAACP, AFTRA; Alpha Phi Alpha; Natl Acad of Television Arts and Sciences. ❚7❚ **Honors/Awds:** Natl Achievement Award, Lincoln Univ, 1966; Man of the Year, Intl Pioneers, 1966; Sigma Delta Chi Citation, 1967; Outstanding Achievement Citation (Emmy), Natl Acad of Television Arts and Sciences, 1967; Natl Award, Southern Press Inst, 1976; Hon Dr Jour, Benedict Coll, 1973; Outstanding TV Correspondent, Women in Media, 1977; Outstanding Natl Corres Serv Award, Michigan Minority Business Enterprise Assn, 1977; Natl Advisory Comm, Crisis Magazine, NAACP, 1981-91. ❚8❚ **Special Achievements:** First Black exec sec, Michigan State Ath Assn, 1950-61; First Black reporter, Detroit News, 1960-63; First Black network news correspondent, NBC-News, 1965-70; First Black correspondent permanently assigned to the White House, Washington NBC News, 1970-72. ❚9❚ **Military Serv:** USAAF, 1943-45. ❚10❚ **Business Addr:** Former Sr Public Affairs Specialist, US Bureau of the Census, Washington, DC 20233.

Description

❚1❚ Name of biographee.

❚2❚ Occupation.

❚3❚ Personal data.

❚4❚ Educational background.

❚5❚ Career information.

❚6❚ Organizational affiliations.

❚7❚ Honors/Awards.

❚8❚ Special Achievements.

❚9❚ Military Service.

❚10❚ Home and/or business address and telephone number (at listee's discretion).

Biographees are listed alphabetically by surname. In cases where the surnames are identical, biographees are arranged first by surname, then by first and middle names, and finally by suffixes such as Jr., Sr., or II, III, etc. Surnames beginning with a prefix (such as Du, Mac, or Van), however spaced, are listed alphabetically under the first letter of the prefix and are treated as if there were no space. Other compound surnames, hyphenated names, and names with apostrophes, likewise, are alphabetized as if there were no space or punctuation. Surnames beginning with Saint, Sainte, St., or Ste. appear after names that begin with Sains and before names that begin with Sainu.

Abbreviations Table

AK	Alaska	KS	Kansas	PA	Pennsylvania
AL	Alabama	KY	Kentucky	PR	Puerto Rico
Apr	April	LA	Louisiana	PUSH	People United to Save
AR	Arkansas	MA	Massachusetts		Humanity
Aug	August	Mar	March	RI	Rhode Island
AZ	Arizona	MD	Maryland	SC	South Carolina
CA	California	ME	Maine	SCLC	Southern Christian Leader-
CO	Colorado	MI	Michigan		ship Conference
CT	Connecticut	MN	Minnesota	SD	South Dakota
DC	District of Columbia	MO	Missouri	Sep	September
DE	Delaware	MT	Montana	TN	Tennessee
Dec	December	NC	North Carolina	TX	Texas
Feb	February	NH	New Hampshire	UT	Utah
FL	Florida	NJ	New Jersey	VA	Virginia
GA	Georgia	NM	New Mexico	VI	Virgin Islands
HI	Hawaii	Nov	November	VT	Vermont
IA	Iowa	NUL	National Urban League	WA	Washington
ID	Idaho	NV	Nevada	WI	Wisconsin
IL	Illinois	NY	New York	WV	West Virginia
IN	Indiana	Oct	October	WY	Wyoming
Jan	January	OH	Ohio		
Jul	July	OK	Oklahoma		
Jun	June	OR	Oregon		

Biographies

A

AARON, HENRY LOUIS (HANK AARON)
Baseball player, executive. **Personal:** Born Feb 5, 1934, Mobile, AL; son of Edwin Caldwell and Pearl Caldwell; married Barbara Lucas, Oct 1, 1953 (divorced 1971); children: Gail, Hank, Lary, Gary (deceased) & Dorenda; married Billye Williams, Nov 12, 1973; children: Ceci. **Educ:** Josephine Allen Inst, attended 1951. **Career:** Professional baseball player (retired), baseball executive; Mobile Black Bears, right fielder; Indianapolis Clowns, Negro Am League, prof baseball player, right fielder, 1952; Milwaukee Braves, Eau Claire, right fielder, 1954-65, vpres player develop, 1975-76; Atlanta Braves, right fielder, 1966-74; Atlanta Nat League Baseball Club Inc, farm syst dir, 1976-90, vpres, spec asst pres, 1990, sr vpres & mem bd dirs, currently; Hank Aaron Automotive Group Inc, pres, currently; 755 Restaurant Corp, owner,currently; CNN Airport Network, vpres bus develop, currently; Medallion Financial Corp, bd dirs, 2004-. **Orgs:** Sponsor, Hank Aaron Celebrity Bowling Tourn for Sickle Cell Anemia, 1972; Negro Am Leagues Indianapolis Clowns; pres, No Greater Love 1974-; natsports chmn, Nat Easter Seal Soc, 1974; nat chmn, Friends Fisk Athletes; state chmn Wis Easter Seals Soc, 1975; Atlanta Comt Progress, 2004. **Honors/Awds:** Most Valuable Player Award, Nat League, 1957; Gerogia Sports Hall of Fame, 1975; Gold Glove Awards; MLB Hall of Fame, 1982; Presidential Citizens Medal; Presidential Medal of Freedom, 2002; Hank Aaron State Trail, Milwaukee, Wisc, named in honor, 2006. **Special Achievements:** Hank Aaron BMW ranked 87, BE Top 100 Auto Dealers, 2001; One of Most Influential Atlantans, Atlanta Bus J, 2004; Broke Babe Ruth's home run record April 18, 1974; holds 18 major league records; holds 9 Nat League records; coauthor autobiography, I Had a Hammer, Harper, 1991; dedicated, Hank Aaron-Chasing the Dream, to Baseball Hall of Fame, 2009. **Business Addr:** President, Co-founder, Hank Aaron Automotive Enterprises LLC, 4171 Jonesboro Rd, Union City, GA 30291-2251, **Business Phone:** (770)969-0755.

ABADEY, NASAR
Musician. **Educ:** State Univ NY, Buffalo; Howard Univ; Univ DC. **Career:** Songs: "Mirage", Amosaya Records; "Better Days", Karen Francis& Virgo Rising Records; "Secrets of the Soul", Sendy Brown& Po Tolo Music; "Steppin' Out", Sandra Y. Johnson& SYJ Productions; "Finally", Sharon Clark; "Rising Day Star", Malachi Thompson & Delmark Records; "NewStandards", Malachi Thompson & Delmark Records; "Spirits", Malachi Thompson & Delmark Records; "The Jaz Life", Malachi Thompson & Delmark Records; "47th Street", Malachi Thompson & Delmark Records; "Freebop Now!", Malachi Thompson & Delmark Records; "Timeline", Malachi Thompson & Delmark Records; "Songbook", Gerry Eastman & WMC Records; "Native Son",Gerry Eastman & WMC Records; "My Real Self", Gerry Eastman & WMC Records; "Today's Nights", Joe Ford & Mesa Records; "Yoka Boka", Jeff Majors; "Keyto Nowhere", Brother Ah & Sounds of Awareness & Divine Records; "FreeSpirits", BIRTHRIGHT& Freelance Records; "Breathe of Life", BIRTHRIGHT&Freelance ecords; "Timbre Tambre", Rey Scott & Planetary Lights Records; "Sweet Heritage", Jaman Quartet & Mark Records. Brown Univ, artist inresidence, 1981-82; Young Audiences, Wash, DC, 1984-2004; Levine Sch Music, artist in residence, 1988-90; Creative Arts Performance, 1989-93; Birthright, band co-founder & co-leader; Prince George's Arts Coun &Thelonious Monk Inst Jazz, teacher & performer, 1995-99; Smithsonian JazzCamp, artist in residence, 2001-02; Savoy Elem Sch, Wash, DC, artist inresidence, 2004; John Hopkins Univ, Peabody Inst, fac, 2006-07; Supernova, band founder, leader, currently. **Orgs:** Panelist, Mid Atlantic Arts Found; Nat Endow-ment Arts & Humanities; DCComn Arts; bd mem, Wash Area Lawyers Asn; artist-in-residence, Honda Dream Lab Proj, Wash, DC; Int Asn Jazz Educr; Int Musicians Union Local, #161-710, Wash, DC. **Honors/Awds:** Creative Artist Performance Serv Award, NY State composition.

ABBOTT, LEANDRA
Public utility executive. **Career:** Cosmopolitan mag, staff mem; Newsweek mag, reporter, 1967-69; Community News Serv, reporter; Zambia Times, reporter; Consol Edison NY Inc for community rels & corp philanthropy, asst vpres electric opers, currently. **Orgs:** Exec vol, United Way NY; Am Asn Blacks in Energy. **Honors/Awds:** All-Star, NY Women's Agenda, 1994; Lifetime Service Award, Consol Edison Inc, 2001. **Special Achievements:** First black female staff in Cosmopolitan Magazine. *

ABDUL, RAOUL
Writer, editor, singer. **Personal:** Born Nov 7, 1929, Cleveland, OH; son of Abdul Hamid and Beatrice Shreve. **Educ:** Acad Mus & Dramatic Art Vienna, Austria, dipl; Harvard Summer Sch, addn studies, 1966; New Sch Social Res; Cleveland Inst Music; NY Col Music; Mannes Col Music; Salzburg Mozarteum, Salzburg, Austria, dipl, 1988. **Career:** Cleveland Call & Post, journalist, 1947-51; Coffeehouse Concerts, Harlem, founding dir; 3000 Years of Black Poetry, co-ed, 1970; Magic of Black Poetry, ed; Kennedy Ctr Performing Arts, lectr; Lincoln Ctr Performing Arts, lectr; Harvard Univ, lectr; Atlanta Univ, lectr; Univ Conn, lectr; Howard Univ, lectr; Columbia Univ, lectr; Harlem Sch Arts, fac; Amsterdam News, music critic; Books: Blacks in Classical Music, 1977; Famous Black Entertainers of Today. **Orgs:** Founder, Liedklasse Raoul Abdul/Kelley Wyatt. **Honors/Awds:** Key to City of Cleveland, Mayor Ralph Perk, 1974; Nat Asn Negro Musicians Distinguished Serv Award, 1974, 1978; Harold Jackman Memo-rial Committee Award, 1978; Black Pride New York, 2002. **Special Achievements:** TV & radio guest appearances; lieder recitals in Austria, Germany, Holland, Hungary, US & Canada. **Home Addr:** 535 W 23rd St Suite 58B, New York, NY 10011-1102, **Home Phone:** (212)929-0307. *

ABDUL-JABBAR, KAREEM (FERDINAND LEWIS AL-CINDOR, JR.)
Athletic coach, basketball player, writer. **Personal:** Born Apr 16, 1947, New York, NY; son of Ferdinand Alcindor and Cora Alcin-dor; children: Amir; children: Adam; married Habiba Abdul (divorced 1978); children: Habiba, Sultana, Kareem & Amir. **Educ:** Univ Calif, Los Angeles, BA, hist, 1969. **Career:** Basketball player (retired), basketball coach, author, producer; NBA Milwaukee Bucks, 1969-75; Los Angeles Lakers, 1975-89, spec asst coach, 2005-; Alchesay High Sch, White Mountain Apache Reservation, asst coach, 1999; Los Angeles Clippers, asst coach; Ind Pacers & Seattle Supersonics, player consult; USBL Okla Storm, coach, 2002; NY Knicks, player consult & scout; Phil Jackson, spec asst; Los Angeles Lakers, special asst coach, 2006-; Producer: co-exec producer, "The Vernon Johns Story", 1994; On the Shoulders of Giants, 2007; Books: Giant Steps: An Autobiography of Kareem Abdul-Jabbar, 1983; Kareem, 1990; Black Profiles in Courage: A Legacy of African American Achievement, 1996; A Season on the Reservation: My Sojourn with the Mountain Apaches, 2000; Brothers in Arms: The Epic Story of the 761st Tank Battalion, 2004; On the Shoulders of Gi-ants: My Journey Through the Harlem Renaissance, 2007. **Honors/Awds:** MVP of NCAA Tournament; MVP 6 times; All Star Team 14times; Rookie of the Year, 1970; Maurice Podoloff Cup, 1971-77; The Jackie Robinson Award for Athletics for career accomplishments as NBA's Most Valuable Player, Sports Il-lustrated Sportsman of the Year, 1985; Elected to Naismith Memo-rial Basketball Hall of Fame, 1995; One of 50 Greatest Players in NBA History, 1996; NBA Hall of Fame; Top 75 NBA Players of all time, SLAM Mag, 2003. **Special Achievements:** First basketball player ever to be a recipient of the National Sports Awards presented by President Bill Clinton in 1993; Film appear-ances: Game of Death, Airplane, The Fish that Saved Pittsburgh, Fletch; TV shows: "Mannix", "Different Strokes", "Full House?". **Business Phone:** (310)426-6000.

ABDUL-KABIR, JAMAL. See WYATT, S MARTIN, III.

ABDULLAH, DR. LARRY BURLEY
Dentist. **Personal:** Born Apr 17, 1947, Malvern, AR; children: Zakkiyya, Jeffery, Kerry, Larry II & Najla. **Educ:** Univ Ariz, BS, 1968; Meharry Dent Col, DDS, 1972; Govs State Univ, MHA, 1996. **Career:** Pvt prac, dent surgeon. **Orgs:** Guardian PPO; Am Dent Asn, 1974-, Chicago Dent Soc, 1974-, Ill Dent Asn, 1974-, Acad Gen Dent, 1974-, Am Straight Wire Orthodontic Soc, 1982-; Health Volunteers Overseas, 1994-. **Honors/Awds:** Fel, Acad Gen Dent, 1987. **Home Addr:** 22715 Torrence Ave, Chicago Heights, IL 60411. **Business Addr:** Dentist, Private Practice, 7013 S Western Ave, Chicago, IL 60636, **Business Phone:** (773)476-0600.

ABDULLAH, DR. MAKOLA
Educator. **Educ:** Howard Univ, BS, 1990; Northwestern Univ, MS, civil engineering, 1991, PhD(civil engineering), 1994. **Career:** Northwestern Univ, Dept Civil Engineering, res & teach-ing asst, 1990-94; Chicago State Univ, Dept Chem & Phys, adj prof, 1994-96; Jackson & Tull Chartered Engrs, Washington, DC, proj mgr, 1994-96; Fla Agr & Mech Univ, div engineering tech, asst prof, 1996-98, Dept Civil Engineering, asst prof, 1998-2002, assoc prof, 2002-, dir diversity prog, dean & dir, currently. **Orgs:** Nat Soc Black Engrs; Am Soc Civil Engrs; Tau Beta Pi Engineer-ing Hon Soc. **Honors/Awds:** Teaching Assistant Of The Year, Nat Soc Black Engrs, 1993; CAREER Award Recipient, Nat Sci Found, 1997; Graduate Teacher of the Year, Fla Agr & Mech Univ, 2002; Outstanding Grantsmanship Award, Fla Agr & Mech Univ, 2003; Teacher of the Year, Fla Agr & Mech Univ, 2004; Golden Key, Nat Hon Soc. **Special Achievements:** Served on several NSF Grant Review Panels, author of several journal papers. **Business Phone:** (850)561-2644.

ABDULLAH, MUSTAFA
Executive. **Career:** Original Afro Wear Inc, co-founder, 1996-. **Business Addr:** Co-Founder, Original Afro Wear Inc, 1560 E 61st St Suite 2 E, Chicago, IL 60637-3049.*

ABDULLAH, RABIH FARD
Football player. **Personal:** Born Apr 27, 1975, Martinsville, VA; son of Shahid; married Nichole. **Educ:** Lehigh Univ, BA, intl bus, 1998. **Career:** Tampa Bay Buccaneers, running back, 1999-2001; Chicago Bears, running back, 2002-03; New England Patriots, running back, 2004. *

ABDULLAH, SAMELLA BERRY
Educator, psychotherapist, consultant. **Personal:** Born Mar 9, 1934, Chicago, IL; daughter of Samuel and Addie Berry; divorced; children: Tracey Everett-Carter, Dr Makola M & G Noora. **Educ:** Howard Univ, BS, 1955, MSW, 1959; Heed Univ, PhD, 1978. **Career:** Legal Aid Soc, social worker, 1962-63; Northwestern Univ Med Sch, instr, 1964-69; City Chicago, Ment Health admin, 1973-77; Abdullah & Assocs, owner & chief therapist, 1979-; Ill Sch Prof Psych, prof, 1987-95; FL A&M Univ, adj prof, 2001; Afi Coun Assoc, Clin soc work & therapist, currently. **Orgs:** Nat Asn Black Social Workers, 1969-; life mem, Nat secy, Asn Black

Psychologists, 1986-88, Nat pres, 1998-99, nat bd dir, 1985-87, 1996-97; co-founder, Chicago Coalition Against Violence Inst; Nat Asn Social Workers; partner, Alliance for Childhood; Am Psychol Asn; ed bd, Ethical Human Psychol & Psychiatry. **Honors/Awds:** Community Service Award, Asn Black Psychologists, 1985-87; Cultural Diversity Award, Nat Coun Schs Psych, 1991-92; scholarship, Ill Nat Asn Black Social Workers, 1999. **Special Achievements:** Author: A Cultural Competency Guideline, 1993; PTSD: A Diagnosis for Victims of the African Holocaust, 1995; Transracial Adoption Is Not Solution to America's Problems, 1996; Transracial Adoption & Genocide, 1986; Mammy-ism: A Diagnosis of Psychological Misorientation, 1998; Conducting Research with People of African Heritage, 2000. **Business Addr:** Clinical Social Work, Therapist, Afi Counseling Associates, 345 Off Plz 2892 E Pk Ave Suite 1 C, Tallahassee, FL 32301, **Business Phone:** (850)339-3723.

ABDULLAH, SHARIF (VAUGHN ALLEN GOODWIN)
Public speaker, businessperson, philanthropist. **Personal:** Born Jan 1, 1968, Philadelphia, PA; son of Alfred and Mary; divorced. **Educ:** Temple Univ, Philadelphia, PA; Morehouse Col, Atlanta, GA; Lancaster Univ; Islamic Teaching Ctr. **Career:** Temple Univ, Philadelphia, PA, asst dean students, 1988-89; Am Friends Serv Comt, student consult; Vine Memorial Baptist Church, Philadelphia, PA, youth minister; Morehouse Col, Du Bois Hall, resident asst; Am Family Financial Servs, mortgage financial planner, currently; Ummah Int Found: A Muslim Investment Group, ceo & founder. **Orgs:** Exec mem, Youth Sect, Dem Socialists Am; founder & pres, Temple Progressive Nat Asn Advan Colored People, 1988; speechwriter & speaker, Jesse Jackson Campaign, 1988; founder & chmn, Student Coalition Racial Equality; Martin Luther King Int Chaplain Asst; Int Asn Fin Planning; Islamic Soc North Am; Metro-Atlanta Chamber Com; Speakers Bur; Consumer Credit Coun Serv Metro Atlanta; Ga Bankers Asn. **Honors/Awds:** Seniors of Pennsylvania Service Award, Outstanding Service, 1989; Outstanding Scholastic Achievement, 1985; ACTSO Winner, Nat Asn Advan Colored People, 1985-86; Oratorical Contest Winner, Black History Month, 1985; License, Nat Baptist Conv, 1990; Certificate of Outstanding Service, African Fel Fund; Certificate of Achievement, Islamic Teaching Ctr ISNA. **Special Achievements:** Contributing author and editor: Towards 2000: Young African-American Males in the 21st Century, 1994. **Home Addr:** 6901 Roosevelt Hwy, College Park, GA 30337, **Home Phone:** (404)767-5536. **Business Phone:** (404)814-1660.

ABDULLAH, TALIB
Chief executive officer, screenwriter. **Personal:** Born Aug 7, 1973, Rochester, NY. **Career:** Producer, currently; Tv series: "Being Bobby Brown", 2005; TZA Assocs, pres & chief exec officer, currently. **Orgs:** Chair, exec team, Nat Young Adult Asn.

ABDULLAH-MUSA, OMALAWA
Architect. **Personal:** Married Melissa Glasgow. **Educ:** City Col Ny. **Career:** Magnusson Archit & Planning PC, architect, currently. **Business Addr:** Architect, Magnusson Architects & Planning PC, 853 Broadway Suite 800, New York, NY 10003, **Business Phone:** (212)253-7820.*

ABDULMAJID, IMAN
Fashion model, actor, chief executive officer. **Personal:** Born Jul 25, 1955, Mogadishu, Somalia; married Spencer Haywood, 1992 (divorced 1987); children: Zulekha; married David Bowie; children: Alexandria Zahra Jones. **Educ:** Univ Nairobi, Kenya, polit sci. **Career:** Wilhelmina Model Inc, 1975; Vogue, model, 1979; Film: The Human Factor, 1979; Jane Austen in Manhattan; 1980; Out of Africa, 1985; No Way Out, 1987; House Party 2, 1991; Star Trek VI: The Undiscovered Country, 1991; Exit to Eden, 1994; The Deli, 1997; Omikron: The Nomad Soul, 1999; Project Runway Canada, 2009; TV series: "Miami Vice", 1985; "Heart of Darkness", 1994; Iman Cosmetics, chief exec officer & founder, currently. **Special Achievements:** Feb 29, 1980 declared Iman Day in NYC; appeared in music video for Micheal Jackson's "Remember the Time", 1992; documentary creator, Somalia Diary, 1992; autobiography, I Am Iman, 2001. **Business Phone:** (212)560-9906.

ABDUL-MALIK, DR. IBRAHIM
Consultant, counselor. **Educ:** CCNY, BS, 1952, MA, 1954; Harvard Univ, EdD, 1971. **Career:** Teacher & asst prin & staff developer, 1954-65; Bank St Col, dir EducResource Ctr, 1965-68; Harlem Sch NYC, prin, 1968-69; New York City Urban Educ, dir Develop Div Ctr, 1971-72; New York City Bd Educ, vice chmn Bd Examiners, 1972-74, educ planner, 1974-76, sci assoc, 1976-79; UNESCO, overseas sci adv, 1979-81; curriculum spec col & univ fac; educ coun, admin, res, writer, health counr & pract & nutritional consult; Ctr Higher Sec Educ, prin; Ctr Empowerment and Personal Growth, dir, currently. **Orgs:** Bd dir, Harlem Neighborhood Asn; 1968-70; Community Serv Soc; Family Life Educ Comn, 1966-70; Nat Asn Bilingual Educ; Am Asn Sch Personnel Admin; Intl Coun Educ Teaching; Kappa Delta Pi; Phi Delta Kappa; Imams Coun New York, gen secy, currently. **Honors/Awds:** Recipient, National Science Foundation Fellow. **Special Achievements:** Book: "The Joys and Rewards of Prayer-A Guide for Beginners, A Reminder for Believers".

ABDUL-RAHMAN, TAHIRA SADIQA
Real estate agent. **Personal:** Born Dec 15, 1947, Shreveport, LA; daughter of Albert Maurice Moody Sr and Estella Martin; married Mustafa Abdul-Rahman; children: Jamilla, Zainab, Naeema, Ibn & Ismail. **Educ:** Howard Univ, BA, 1968; Howard Univ Sch Soc Work, MSW, 1970; Adams Inst Mkt Shreveport, LA, attended 1990; Baker's Prof Real Estate Col, Shreveport, LA, attended 1990. **Career:** New Careers Prog, specialty instr, 1970-71; Parent & Child Ctr, supvr, 1971-72; Morgan Univ, assoc prof, 1972-74; Assoc Comm Training Inc, dir homemaker prog, 1984-87; Marak Realty, Shreveport, LA, realtor & assoc, 1986-90; Family Ctr Asn Community Training Inc, dir, 1987-88; Tahira & Assoc Realty, Shreveport, LA, realtor & owner, 1990-. **Orgs:** Pres, PTA West Shreveport Elem Sch, 1982-84; exec bd mem, Dist Parent Teachers Asn, 1984-85; guest columnist, Shreveport Sun, 1985-87; vpres, PTA Booker T Wash High Sch, 1986-87; steering comt, YMCA Annual Awareness Banquet, 1986; guest speaker, Annual Luncheon Sr Citizens Union Mission Baptist Church, 1987; Delta Sigma Theta Sorority Inc, Polit Action Community Delta Sigma Theta Sor Inc; pres, Booker T Wash High Sch Alumni Found, 1990-; chairperson, fundraiser comt, Nat Asn Women Bus Owners, Shreveport Chap, 1991-; pres, Shreveport/Bossit Chap Women's Coun Realtors, 2001-; pres-elect State Chap Women's Coun Realtors, 2004. **Honors/Awds:** Certificate of Appreciation, W Shreveport Sch, 1980-87; Honorary Life Member, La State PTA, 1984; Outstanding Leadership Award, W Shreveport Sch PTA, 1984; Outstanding Realtor/Asniate, Marak Ralty, 1988; Emerging Young Leader, YWCA Allendale Br, Shreveport, 1989; Outstanding Service Award, BTW Alumni Found, 1990; Outstanding Leadership, 1995; Business Award, Shreveport African-Am Chamber Community. **Business Addr:** Owner, Tahira & Associates Realty, 449 Stoner Ave, Shreveport, LA 71101-4120, **Business Phone:** (318)425-2707.

ABDUL-RAUF, MAHMOUD (CHRIS WAYNE JACKSON)
Basketball player, clergy. **Personal:** Born Mar 9, 1969, Gulfport, MS. **Educ:** LA State Univ, attended 1989. **Career:** Basketball player, Imam; Denver Nuggets, guard, 1990-95; Sacramento Kings, 1996-98; Fenerbahce, EuroLeague, 1998-99; Vancouver Grizzlies, 2000-01; Ural Great basketball team, Russia, 2003-04; Sedima Roseto, Italy, 2004-05; Aris Thessaloniki, Greece, 2006-07; Masjid al-Haqq, imam, currently; Al Ittihad Jeddah, 2008-. **Honors/Awds:** NBA, All-Rookie second team, 1991; NBA, Most Improved Player, 1993. **Special Achievements:** NBA Draft, First round pick, No 3, 1990.

ABDUL-WAHAD, TARIQ (OLIVIER SAINT-JEAN)
Basketball player. **Personal:** Born Nov 3, 1974, Val de Marne, France; son of George Goudet and Luc Saint-Jean; married Khadijah Ibn-Lahoucine; children: Amine, Hind & Anas. **Educ:** Univ Mich, 1995; San Jose State Univ, attended 1997. **Career:** Alm Evreux, France, 1990-93; Sacramento Kings, forward & guard, 1997-99; Orlando Magic, 1999-2000; Denver Nuggets, 2000-01; Dallas Mavericks, 2001-05. **Orgs:** Seed Acad. **Honors/Awds:** First round, Sacramento Kings, NBA Draft, 1997; Elu All-American Most Valuable Player, 1996-97. **Special Achievements:** First player to be born and raised in France and play in the National Basketball Association. *

ABDUR-RAHIM, SHAREEF
Basketball player, president (organization). **Personal:** Born Dec 11, 1976, Marietta, GA; son of William and Aminah; married Delicia; children: Jabri & Samiyah. **Career:** Vancouver Grizzlies, forward, 1996-2001; Atlanta Hawks, 2001-04; AVF Inc (now Abdur-Rahim Enterprises), Atlanta, GA, pres, 2003-; Portland Trail Blazers, 2004-05; Sacramento Kings, forward, 2005-. **Orgs:** Founder, Future Found, 2001-. **Honors/Awds:** John Wooden Award; Conf Player of the Year; All Rookie Team, NBA, 1997; Rookie of the Month, 1996-97; gold medal, basketball, Olympics, 2000; Player of the Week, NBA, 2001; NBA All-Star team, 2002. **Special Achievements:** NBA Draft, First round pick, No 3, 1996. **Business Addr:** Professional Basketball Player, Sacramento Kings, 1 Sports Pkwy, Sacramento, CA 95834, **Business Phone:** (916)928-6900.

ABDUS-SALAAM, SHEILA
Judge. **Personal:** Born in Washington, DC. **Educ:** Barnard Univ, BA, 1974; Columbia Univ, JD, 1977. **Career:** NY State Atty Gen's Office, Civil Rights Bur, lawyer; NY State Atty Gen's Office, Real Estate Fin Bur, lawyer; City NY, Dept Contract Compliance, gen coun; NY City Civil Ct, lawyer; NY State Supreme Ct, justice, 1993-. **Orgs:** Chair, Women's Housing & Econ Develop Corp, currently; vchair, Columbia Law Sch, currently. **Business Addr:** Justice, New York State Supreme Court, 71 Thomas St Rm 307, New York, NY 10013, **Business Phone:** (646)386-3804.

ABE, DR. BENJAMIN OMARA A
Educator. **Personal:** Born Nov 19, 1943, Gulu, Uganda; married Joan B White; children: Daudi John & Peter Okech. **Educ:** Carleton Col, BA, social anthrop, 1968; Wash State Univ, MA, anthrop, 1970; Faith Grant Col, LLD. **Career:** Trans World Trading Corp, pres & chmn brd, 1974-75; BAS Assoc Int, managing gen partner, 1975-; N Seattle Community Col, East African Study Tour Prog,dir, 1978-, Anthrop Dept, prof, 1970-; phys anthropologist, currently. **Orgs:** Am Anthrop Assn; pres, Soc Anthrop Community Cols, 1999-2000; hon consult for Uganda to Wash St; vpres, bd mem, UNAA; founder, chmn, African Chamber Of Commerce; mem, Univ Dist Rotary Club Of Seattle; vol, Polio immunization works & clean water Proj in Ethiopia. **Business Addr:** Professor, North Seattle Community College, Math Science & Social Sciences Division, 9600 Col Way N, Seattle, WA 98103-3599, **Business Phone:** (206)526-7012.

ABEBE, RUBY
Civil rights activist. **Personal:** Born Apr 19, 1949, Waterloo, IA; children: Yeshimebet Marie, Tsehaynesh Eugena & Saba DyAnn. **Educ:** Univ IA, BA, 1972; Univ Northern. **Career:** Nat Black Repubans, IA, state chair, 1984-; Govt Branstad Black Adv Bd, ad hoc, 1985; Sr Vol Prog, adv bd, 1985; Iowa Civil Rights Comn, comnr, 1986-94; Dept Agri, citizen adv to secy, 1991; Iowa City, civil rights coordr, 1994; Water 1st, owner, currently. **Orgs:** ABC; comnr, State IA Family Youth & C; Abebe Int; Adv Bd Blacks, State IA; IA City UN Asn USA; Affirmative Action Adv Bd, Oakdale Med Classification Ctr, Black Resource Guide. **Business Addr:** Owner, Water 1st, 621 Independence Ave, Waterloo, IA 50703.

ABEL, RENAUL N.
Administrator, executive director, manager. **Personal:** Born Dec 28, 1940, Philadelphia, PA; son of William J and Revender C Strother; married Patricia Fenner, Aug 24, 1964; children: Sean Abel, Damien Abel. **Educ:** Cent State Univ, Wilberforce, OH, BS, Biol, 1962; OH State Univ, Columbus, OH, 1972. **Career:** Anheuser-Busch Inc, Newark, NJ, Columbus, OH, asst plant mgr, mgr beer packaging & shipping, mgr packaging, mgr warehouse & shipping, asst mgr indust rels, coord tech serv opers dept, qual control lab supvr, Tampa, FL, beer packaging & shipping mgr, asst plant mgr, plant mgr, dir dispute resolution prog, 1965-. **Orgs:** bd mem, Greater Tampa Urban League; Pinellas Co Urban League, Boy Scouts Am, Gulf Ridge Coun, Hillsborough Community Col Found;Pebble Creek Civic Asn; Master Brewers Asn; Beer & Beverage Packaging Asn; Boys & Girls Clubs Am; Greater Tampa Chamber of Com; mentor, Hillsborough Community Col, Minority Affairs; bd mem, Tampa Marine Inst Inc, 1991-; chmn, bus retention comn; Greater Tampa Chamber Com Comt 100, 1991-; bd mem, Univ S Fla Inst Black Life, 1984-; minority devel coun, Greater Tampa Chamber of Commerce, 1991-. **Honors/Awds:** Outstanding Participant, Greater Tampa Urban League, 1987, 1988; Leadership Award, Boy Scouts of Amer, Gulf Ridge Council, 1988; Support Award, Univ of S Florida Inst on Black Life, 1989; Executive of the Year, Greater Florida Minority Development Council, 1990. **Military Serv:** AUS, spec weapons instr, first lt; spec weapons detatchment comdr. **Business Phone:** (314)765-6565.*

ABERCRUMBIE, DR. PAUL ERIC
School administrator. **Personal:** Born Jun 14, 1948, Cleveland, OH; son of Margaret Louise Taylor-Nelson; married Claudia Marie Colvard, Jun 14, 1987; children: Paul II & Erica Marie. **Educ:** Eastern Ky Univ, BA, 1970, MA, 1971; Univ Cincinnati, PhD, 1987. **Career:** Princeton City Sch Dist, adv specialist, 1971-72; Univ Cincinnati,resident counr, 1972-73, spec serv counr, 1973-75, dir, ethnic progs & african-am cult & res ctr, 1975-, asst adj prof, currently; pres, John DO'Bryant Nat Think Tank Black; founder, Black Man Think Tank. **Orgs:** Omicron Delta Kappa Hon Soc, Univ Cincinnati, 1974; Omega Psi Phi Frat Inc; bd mem, Dr Martin Luther King Jr Coalition; coach, Athletic Asn; Nat Asn Advan Colored People; exec bd mem, Dr Martin Luther King Jr Coalition,1980-. speaker, EASFAA . **Honors/Awds:** Outstanding Young Men Am, US Jaycees, 1978 & 1980; Dr Martin Luther King Jr Award of Excellence, Alpha Phi Alpha Frat Inc, 1980; Community Leader sof the World, Am Biographical Inst, 1985; Golden Key, Nat Hon Soc, 1987;Black Educator of the Year, US Peace Corps, 1987; Presidental Award of Excellence, United Black Fac & Staff Asn, 1988; Black Achiever, YMCA,1989; Outstanding Fac Mem Quarter, Univ Cincinnati Morta Bd, 1989. **Business Addr:** Director of Ethnic Programs, University of Cincinnati, African-American Culture & Research Center, 555 Steger Student Life Ctr, PO Box 210092, Cincinnati, OH 45221-0092, **Business Phone:** (513)556-6008.

ABERNATHY, ELOISE (ELOISE ALEXIS)
Administrator, vice president (organization). **Educ:** Spelman Col, BA, Eng; Vanderbilt Univ, MA, higher educ admin. **Career:** Spelman Col, dir alumnae affairs & annual giving, vpres instnl advan, currently. **Orgs:** Jr League Atlanta; Alpha Kappa Alpha Sorority Inc; Nat Alumnae Asn Spelman Col. **Business Phone:** (404)270-5040.

ABERNATHY, RALPH DAVID
State government official, executive, business owner. **Personal:** Born Mar 19, 1959, Montgomery, AL; son of Ralph David II and Juanita Odessa; married Annette; children: Ralph David IV & Christiana. **Educ:** Morehouse Col, ling, 1981. **Career:** Ga Gen Assembly, state rep, 1988-92, state sen, 1992-98; Ga State Prison, staff, 2000-01, 2002-03; Ga House Representatives, 38th Dist, sen; Clean Air Industs, owner & chmn. **Orgs:** Vice chmn, Senate Retirement Comn; vice chmn, Ins & Labor Comn; chmn,

Interstate Coop; Legis Black Caucus & Policy Comn, Senate Dem Caucus; chmn, Sunshine Litigation Study Comn; Senate Electrology Study Comn; bd dirs, Consumer Credit Coun Serv; bd dirs, Big Brothers/Big Sisters; Underground Adv Comn.

ABERNATHY, RONALD LEE
Basketball coach. **Personal:** Born Dec 13, 1950, Louisville, KY; son of Juanita Abernathy and Ben W Abernathy. **Educ:** Morehead State Univ, BA Soc, 1972; LA State Univ, MA, admin, 1979. **Career:** Shawnee HS Louisiana KY, head basketball coach, 1972-76; LSU Baton Rouge, asst basketball coach 1976-83, assoc head coach, 1983-89; Belgium All-Star Team, Namur Belgium, head basketball coach, 1981; LA Assoc Basketball Coaches All-Star Game, exec dir, 1981; S&R Oilfield Serv Co, pres 1981-;Tenn State Univ, head basketball coach, 1989; Lane Col, athletic dir, currently, head basketball coach, currently. **Orgs:** Nat Asn Basketball Coaches, 1976-; dir & lead singer, Gospel Chorus Gr Salem Baptist Church, 1954-76; lead singer, Young Adult Choir Shiloh Baptist Church, 1976-; bd mem, Morehead Rec Comns, 1971-72; big brother prog, Family Court Baton Rouge, LA, 1982; asst basketball coach, Nat Asn Basketball Coaches All-Star Game, 1982; LA Pageant Judges & Entertainers Asn 1983-. **Honors/Awds:** Teacher of the Year, Shawnee HS Louisville KY, 1976; High School Coach of the Year, Louisville Urban League, 1976; Runner-up State of KY High School Coach of the Year 1976; Houston Post Top Ten Assistant Coaches America, 1980; Final Four Basketball Team Philadelphia, PA coach 1981; LA's 10 Best Dressed Men, 1983; LA's Most Eligible Bachelors, 1983; Baton Rouge's Most Fashionable Man, 1983; Final Four Basketball Team Dallas, TX coach, 1986; Recruiter of the Year, Sporting Mag. **Special Achievements:** First black appointed to full time coaching position LSU. **Business Addr:** Athletic Director, Head Coach, Lane College, 545 Lane Ave, Jackson, TN 38301, **Business Phone:** (731)426-7500.

ABERNATHY, TENISHA. See TAYLOR, TENISHA NICOLE.

ABIBIO, NANA ESSIE. See JEFFRIES, DR. ROSALIND R.

ABIF, KHAFRE KUJICHAGULIA
Librarian, library administrator. **Personal:** Born Jun 6, 1966, McKeesport, PA; son of Jackie and Barbara J Page; divorced; children: Amenhotep Kazembe Ture Abif. **Educ:** Florida A&M Univ, attended 1989; Univ Pittsburgh, BA, 1992, MLS, 1993. **Career:** District Columbia Pub Libr, c librn, 1993-95; Montclair Pub Libr, youth serv librn, 1995-98; Mt Vernon Pub Libr, head, c serv, 1998-99; Brooklyn Pub Libr, mgr, c serv, 1999-2001; C Defense Fund/Haley Farm, dir Langston Hughes Libr, dir, currently. **Orgs:** Pub Libr Asn, 1996-; Asn Libr Serv C, 1996-; ALA, Black Caucus exec bd, 1996-98; 1999-2001; Spectrum Initiative Steering Comm, 1997-2000; C Book Coun, 1997-99, 1999-2001; Global Awareness Team, 1998, Coun, 2001-05. **Honors/Awds:** Miracle Award, Family & Children's Services, Miracle Makers Inc, 1999. **Business Addr:** Director, Langston Hughes Library, Children's Defense Fund, 1000 Alex Haley Lane, PO Box 840, Clinton, TN 38152, **Business Phone:** (865)457-6466.

ABNEY, ALBERT
Commissioner. **Career:** City Planning Comn, comnr, NY, 1996-01. *

ABNEY, ROBERT
Playwright, school administrator, television producer. **Personal:** Born Jul 2, 1949, Washington, Afghanistan; son of Robert Abney Sr and Willie Mae Carson. **Educ:** DC Teachers Col, BS, educ psychol, 1972. **Career:** First Georgetown Adv DC, vpres, 1981-82; Windstar Ltd, DC, pres 1981-; Washington, DC, advert consult, 1982-; Creative Connection, DC, dir mkt & advert, 1982-83; Channel 48 Cable TV, Vol's Forum, host, independent video producer, 1985-; DC Pub Schs, coord home study prog, 1987-. **Orgs:** Chmn, SNEA Human Rels Coun, Nat Educ Asn, DC, 1970-71; Clearing house mgr, DC Pub Lib Comt Info Serv DC, 1976-81; consult, US Dept Comn DC Pub Sch Syst, 1983-; pres, Amidon Ele PTA, 1984-86; Int Platform Asn; Nat Leadership Conf; Honor Book; bd dirs, Southwest Neighborhood Assembly; bd dirs, Southwest House, 1989-90. **Honors/Awds:** Special Award, 1969; Award for Artistic Achievement, 1978; Riggs National Bank Community Achievement Award, 1990, 1991. **Special Achievements:** Jaycee's Vol Citation, 1969, Headstart Volunteer Citation, 1977-84. **Home Addr:** 421 Gallatin St NW, Washington, DC 20011. **Business Addr:** Coordinator, DC Public Schools, Home Study Program, 4th Eye St Southwest, Washington, DC 20024, **Business Phone:** (202)724-8618.*

ABRAHAM, CLIFTON EUGENE
Football player. **Personal:** Born Dec 9, 1971, Dallas, TX. **Educ:** Fla State Univ, attended 1994. **Career:** Tampa Bay Buccaneers, 1995; Chicago Bears, 1996; Carolina Panthers, 1997, Los Angeles Extreme, XFL, 2001. **Honors/Awds:** All-Am Honorable Mention, 1993; 1st Team All-Am, 1994; All-Am Honorable Mention, united press int, 1994; 1st Team All-Am, Associated Press; Walter Camp; Football News; The Sporting News, 1994. *

ABRAHAM, DONNIE
Football player, businessperson. **Personal:** Born Oct 8, 1973, Orangeburg, SC; married Tunisia; children: Devin Isaiah, Alivia, Micah. **Educ:** E Tenn State Univ, BS, bus mgt. **Career:** Tampa Bay Buccaneers, defensive back, 1996-01; NY Jets, defensive back, 2001-05; bus exec, 2005-. **Special Achievements:** Southern Conf finalist; NFC Defensive Player of the Week, 1999. *

ABRAHAM, JEANETTE
Chief executive officer, business owner. **Educ:** Wayne State Univ, BA, interdisciplinary studies; Cent Mich Univ, MA, human resources. **Career:** Gen Motors Corp, staff; JMA Logistics, LLC, founder; Detroit Heading LLC, pres, chief exec officer & owner, 2000-. **Orgs:** Nat Asn Black Automotive Suppliers. **Special Achievements:** Top Black Technology Entrepreneurs, 2006. **Business Addr:** Owner, Chief Executing Officer, Detroit Heading LLC, 6421 Lynch Rd, Detroit, MI 48234-4140, **Business Phone:** (313)267-2240.

ABRAHAM, SHARON L
School administrator, executive director. **Educ:** Univ Mich, BA, 1980, MBA, 1984, PhD. **Career:** City of Detroit, urban renewal asst, 1980-82; Int Bus Mach, mkt rep, 1984-87; Ameritech, mgr, 1987-94; Oakland Univ, Off Diversity & Compliance, dir, 1996-2002, Pub Sch Academics & Urban Partnerships, dir, 2002-04; Eastern Mich Univ, dir diversity, 2006-. **Orgs:** Arbitrator, Better Bus Bur, 1989-94; finance comm chair & vice bd chair, Head Start Agency, 1989-94; Nat Black MBA Asn, 1990-; vol coordr, Heidelberg Proj, 1995-97; Leadership Detroit XIX, 1997; Leadership Oakland IX, 1998-. **Honors/Awds:** Research Award, Mich Col & Univ Personnel Asn, 1999-; Diversity Champion, Birmingham Bloomfield Taskforce Race Rels, 2000. **Home Addr:** 26336 Lathrup Blvd, Lathrup Village, MI 48076. **Business Addr:** Director of Diversity, Eastern Michigan University, 11 Welch Hall, Ypsilanti, MI 48197, **Business Phone:** (734)487-1849.

ABRAHAM, TAJAMA
Basketball player, basketball coach. **Personal:** Born Sep 27, 1975, St Croix, VI; children: Naja & Patrick II. **Educ:** George Washington Univ, BA, sociol, 1997. **Career:** Basketball player (retired), basketball coach; Sacramento Monarchs, ctr, 1997; Detroit Shock, 1998; prof player France & Italy; George Wash Univ, admin asst, 1999-2001; asst coach basketball, currently; Univ Richmond, asst coach, 2001; Va Commonwealth Univ, coach, 2002-04; US VI Nat Team, team captain, asst coach, 2002. **Honors/Awds:** GWU Female Athlete of the Century, 2000; Hall of Fame, George Wash Univ, 2004. **Special Achievements:** Univs all-time leading scorer; all-time leading rebounder. **Business Addr:** Assistant Coach, George Washington University, Athletic Department, 2121 1st St NW, Washington, DC 20052, **Business Phone:** (202)994-6505.

ABRAHAMS, ANDREW WORDSWORTH
Physician. **Personal:** Born Oct 8, 1936, Kingston, Jamaica. **Educ:** Columbia Univ, BS, 1961; NY Med Col, MD, 1966. **Career:** Kings Co Hosp, physician, 1973-. **Orgs:** Med dir, Bur Alcoholism, New York, 1970-72; founder dir, Bedford Stuyvesant Alcoholism Treat Ctr, 1972; New York affiliate Nat Coun Alcoholism, 1972; lect consult, Nat Coun Alcoholism, 1972, med consult, Comm Health Facil; bd mem, NY State Asn Coun Alcoholism, 1975; mem, NY State Senate Legis Adv Comm, 1976. **Honors/Awds:** Certificate of Appreciation, Bedford Alcoholism Treat Ctr; Certificate of Appreciation, NY State Asn Alcoholism Coun; Am Fedn Labor & Congress Indust Orgn, NY. *

ABRAHAMS, ANTHONY D.
Executive. **Educ:** Va State Univ, BS; Harvard Bus Sch, MBA. **Career:** Coopers & Lybrand LLP, auditor; Peabody & Co, investment banker, 1990-95; Ernst & Young LLP, finance exec, 1995-98; Lucents New Ventures Group, chief financial officer, 1998-; New Venture Partners LLC, chief financial officer & partner, 2001-. **Orgs:** Technol Ventures Incubator; Stevens Inst Technol. **Business Phone:** (908)464-0900.*

ABRAMS, KENNETH RODNEY
Marketing executive. **Personal:** Born Dec 31, 1970, Baltimore, MD; son of Titus Robertson and Sheila Abrams-Jones; married Denise Reid, May 21, 1994; children: Khalil. **Educ:** Towson State Univ, BS, 1992. **Career:** Baltimore Orioles, comn rels rep, 1992-95; Trahan, Burden & Charles, acct exec, 1995-97; Baltimore Ravens, proms & advert mgr, 1997-; Corp Commun Partnerships Mgr, dir Community Relations, currently. **Orgs:** United Negro Coll Fund, MD, publicity chair, 1995-97; Woodholme Found, celebrity auction chair, 1996-97; Advert Asn Baltimore, diversity comn, 1995-97. **Honors/Awds:** Black Achiever Award, Druid Hill YMCA, 1993. **Special Achievements:** Coordinate Stars Early Black Baseball event 1993 MLB All-Star Game. **Home Addr:** 3824 Collier Rd, Randallstown, MD 21133, **Home Phone:** (410)922-1186. **Business Phone:** (410)547-8100.

ABRAMS, KEVIN R.
Football player. **Personal:** Born Feb 28, 1974, Tampa, FL. **Educ:** Syracuse Univ, attended 1996. **Career:** Football player (retired); Detroit Lions, corner back, 1997-99. **Honors/Awds:** All-American, 1995-96. *

ABRAMSON, JOHN J., JR.
Government official. **Personal:** Born Aug 26, 1957, Brooklyn, NY; son of John J and Norine; divorced; children: John III, Jason, Monae', Kiara. **Educ:** Univ Del, BS, 1979; New Hampshire Col, MS, 1991; The Union Inst, PhD, 1996. **Career:** Gov VI, energy dir, 1981-87; Legis VI, chief staff, 1987-89, 1991-92, consult Sen Judy M Gomez, 1992-94, supvr elections, 1995-; Energy Resources Int, Caribbean rep, 1988-90; Pvt Indust Coun, inr, consult, 1989-90; US Small Bus Admin, documents examr, 1990; Election Syst VI, supvr elections, 1995-. **Orgs:** Resource Conservation & Develop Coun, chair, 1988-90; VI Tourism Awareness Link, 1988-90; VI Bd Educ, cot & parental com chair, 1986-88; Int Basketball Fed, 1986-93; Opp Fraternity, chapter pres, 1985-89; VI Dept Health, adv bd chair, 1983-84. **Honors/Awds:** Man of the Year, Opp Fraternity, 1983; Distinguished Political Achievement Award, 1985; Terrance Todman Scholarship for Int Affairs, 1990; Outstanding Service Award, US Small Bus Admin, 1990. **Special Achievements:** Certified Legal Asst, 1985, Cert Parliamentarian, 1989. **Home Addr:** PO Box 55, Frederiksted, Virgin Islands of the United States 00841-0055, **Home Phone:** (340)772-4066. **Business Addr:** Supervisor, Election Syst VI, Lagoon Complex, PO Box 1499 Kingshill, St Croix, Virgin Islands of the United States 00851-1499, **Business Phone:** (340)773-1021.*

ABSTON, NATHANIEL, JR.
Clinical psychologist. **Personal:** Born Jul 18, 1952, Mobile, AL; son of Minnie L Abston and Nathaniel Abston Sr; married Elverna McCants; children: Jamila Aziza, Khalid Amir. **Educ:** Univ S Ala, BA, 1975, MS, 1978; Univ Southern Miss, PhD, 1984. **Career:** Mobile Youth Ct, stud social worker, 1971-74; Mobile Ment Health Ctr, counr, 1974-76; Univ S Ala, lectr, 1978-; Va Outpatient Clin, Mobile, Ala, staff clin psychol, 1984-; licensed psychol, Miss, 1984-; Licensed Psychol, Ala, 1998-; Gulf Coast Vet Health Care Syst, Biloxi, MS, staff psychol; Univ S Ala, prof Psychol, currently. **Orgs:** Alpha Phi Alpha Fraternity; Am Psychol Asn; Ala Psychol Asn; Miss Psychol Asn; Urban League Mobile. **Honors/Awds:** Psi Chi Hon Psychol Club, Univ S Ala Chap, 1975-; USA Res Grant Award, Univ S Ala, 1978-79. **Special Achievements:** Several scientific publications & presentations. **Business Addr:** Staff Psychologist, VA Med Ctr, Psych Serv (116B), Gulfport, MS 39501.*

ACKERMAN, PATRICIA A.
Educator. **Personal:** Born Feb 6, 1944, Cleveland, OH; daughter of Amos Abraham (deceased) and Minnie Ruth Glover; divorced. **Educ:** Ohio Univ, Athens, OH, BA, Eng, 1966; Cleveland State Univ, OH, MEd, admin, 1974; Kent State Univ, OH, PhD, admin, 1983. **Career:** Cleveland Bd Educ, OH, teacher, 1966-72 (retired); Beachwood Bd Educ, OH, teacher, 1972-74; Lima City Schs, OH, dean girls, 1974-75; Cleveland Heights-Univ Heights Bd Educ, OH, coordr, 1975, high sch asst prin, 1975-87, prin Taylor Acad, 1987, exec dir curric/instr (retired); Nat Alliance Black Sch Educr, pres, 1987-89; Chalkdust Inc, Founder, pres & chief exec officer, currently. **Orgs:** Nat Alliance Black Sch Educ, 1987-89; Leadership Cleveland, 1988-89; mem, Bd Trustees, Ohio state Univ, 2004. **Honors/Awds:** George A Bowman Fel, Kent State Univ, 1981; Commendation, Int Asn Bus Communicators, 1982; African-Am Educr Year, African Am Mus, Cleveland, OH, 1988; Distinguished Alumna, Cleveland State Univ, 1990; Distinguished Educr, Cleveland State Univ Black Fac/Staff, 1991; President's Social Responsibility Award, Kent State Univ, 1993. **Special Achievements:** First African-American woman & first K-12 educator to chair the board of Ohio University. **Home Addr:** 456 Rushmore Dr, Richmond Heights, OH 44143. *

ACKORD, MARIE MALLORY
Educator. **Personal:** Born Jan 5, 1939, Bronwood, GA; daughter of Clarence Mallory and Lula Perry Mallory; married Ronald A, Sep 14, 1983; children: Monique Patrice Campbell. **Educ:** Bethune-Cookman Col, BS, math, 1960; Nova Univ, Ft Lauderdale, FL, MS, 1982. **Career:** Carver High Sch, Naples, FL, 1960-64; Dunbar High Sch, math teacher, 1964-66; N Ft Myers High Sch, math teacher, 1966-70, 1973; Dunbar Middle Sch, head math dept & teacher, 1970-73; varsity cheer leading, sponsor, 1976-77; Ft Myers Comm Relations Commin, commr; Sch Bd Lee County, N Ft Myers, FL, human rel specialist, 1980-83, math teacher, 1983-. **Orgs:** Sch Community Adv Com; NCTM Fla Math Teachers; Lee County Teachers Math, Delta Sigma Theta Inc; secy, Fort Myers Alumnae Chap Delta Sigma Theta, 1975-77; past charter pres, vpres, Ft Myers Alumnae Chap Delta Sigma Theta; Nat Asn Advan Colored People; adv bd, Dunbar Day Care; depelections clerk, Lee County, 1987-; Phi Delta Kappa Educ Fraternity; NCNW; treas, Ft Myers Alumnae Chap Delta Sigma Theta, 1991-; consumer mem, State Fla, Agency Health Care Admin, bd clin social work, Marriage & Family Therapy & Mental Health Coun, 1991-98; secy, Caribbean Continental Social Club; bd mem, Clavary Am Methodist Episcopal Church. **Honors/Awds:** Elected Beta Kappa Chi, 1960; Teacher of the Month, N Ft Myers High Sch, 1976; Nom Lee Co Woman of the Year, 1976-77; Zeta Phi Beta Minority Woman of the Year; Cert of Appreciation from Gov Bob Graham, 1986; Staff Member of the Month, N Ft Myers High Sch, 1990, 1995. **Home Addr:** 1921 SE 8th St, Cape Coral, FL 33990. **Business Phone:** (813)995-2117.*

ACKRIDGE, FLORENCE GATEWARD
Administrator. **Personal:** Born Jun 14, 1939, Philadelphia, PA; married John C; children: Anthony, Antoinette & Angelo. **Educ:**

Temple Univ, BSW, 1977. **Career:** Norris Brown & Hall, legal secy, 1965-68; Rentex Systems, off asst, 1968-69; Philadelphia Urban Coalition, secy, 1969-71; Rebound Med Group, clerical supvr, 1971-73; YMCA, Youth Leadership Inst, prog coordr, 1973-74; Philadelphia City, Dept Human Serv, social worker, currently. **Orgs:** Vol, Consult Prisoners Rights Coun; social worker, Walton Village; Nat Coun Black Child Develop; Black Social Workers Alliance; W Oak Lane Comn Group; Black & Non-White YMCA; Model Legis Plan Com Model Judicial Plan Comn; vol, Christian St YMCA Mem Drive. **Honors/Awds:** Trophy Outstanding Service. **Special Achievements:** Volunteer Service to Community, Temple Univ. **Business Addr:** Social Worker 2, Department of Human Services, IAR Unit 19, 1515 Arch St, Philadelphia, PA 19102, **Business Phone:** (215)683-5987.

ACOSTA NESMITH, WINIFRED L
U.S. attorney. **Personal:** Married Kimblin NeSmith. **Educ:** Univ Fla, BA, 1992, JD, 1995. **Career:** Fla Atty Gen Off, Jacksonville, asst statewide prosecutor; Third Judicial Circuit in Lake City, asst state atty; US Attys Off Northern Dist Fla, asst US atty, currently. **Orgs:** Vpres planning, Nat Black Prosecutors Asn, regional dir. **Honors/Awds:** Received numerous awards from high school, church, family & civic organizations. **Special Achievements:** First African American to receive the honor from Mayor Garth "Sonny? Nobles with the Live Oak "key to the city? and a proclamation; recognized as the "Executive Board Member of the Year? for outstanding service. **Business Addr:** Assistant US Attorney, US Attorneys Office, Northern District of Florida, 111 N Adams St 4th Fl, Tallahassee, FL 32301, **Business Phone:** (850)216-3832.

ACREY, AUTRY
School administrator. **Personal:** Born Mar 20, 1948, Frederick, OK; son of William and Mildred Thomas. **Educ:** Jarvis Christian Col, BS, educ, 1970; Tex Christian Univ, MA, 1972; N Tex State Univ. **Career:** Jarvis Christian Col, Hawkins, Tex, instr hist, 1973-76, asst dean,1976-79, asst prof, 1976-, assoc dean, 1981-89, vpres acad affairs, 1994, Instnl Res, Planning, & Assessment, Off Pres, actg dir, currently, Instnl Res & Planning, regist, currently. **Orgs:** Dir, Consortium Res Training, 1974-76; secy, Mu Rho Lambda Chap, Alpha Phi Alpha, 1978; dir, Coop Educ, 1981-; dir, East Tex Res Coun, 1983-84. **Honors/Awds:** Outstanding Teacher, Jarvis Christian Col, 1975; Outstanding Member, Mu Rho Lambda Chap, Alpha Phi Alpha, 1979. **Home Phone:** (903)769-2972. **Business Addr:** Registrar, Acting Director, Jarvis Christian College, Institutional Research & Planning, PO Box 1470, Hawkins, TX 75765, **Business Phone:** (903)769-5737.

ADAIR, ALVIS V.
Educator. **Personal:** Born Jul 19, 1940, Hare Valley, VA; son of Eddie Adair and Sereta Adair; married Deloris (deceased); children: Almaz & Poro. **Educ:** Va State Col, BS, 1962, MS, 1964; Univ Mich, PhD, psychol, 1971; Monrovia Col Liberia W Africa, LLD, 1973. **Career:** US Peace Corps, teacher & community develop, 1965-68; Allen Univ, assessor & dir spec experimental progs, 1968-69, asst prof, 1971, assoc prof, 1972, chmn, soc res, 1973, pres, 1977-79; Howard Univ, asst to dean res develop, 1979-84, Sch Soc Work, Coun Int Prog, dir, prof, currently. **Orgs:** Bd mem, Social Work Abstracts; Hill crest C Ctr; DC Comn Aging; hon mem, Cross roads Africa, 1966; State Planning Comn White House Conf Families & Aging, 1980-81; co-chairperson, Asn Black Psychologists; trustee, St Paul AME Church; Asn Univ Prof, Social Workers, Black Soc Workers, Psychologists; chmn, DC Nursing Home Adv Comn, 1988-90; DC Bd Psychol, 1990-; Bd Psychol DC. **Honors/Awds:** Outstanding University Professor, 1972, 1974; Outstanding Educator of America, 1974; Outstanding Young Men America, 1974; Service Award, Fed City Col, Chap Black Soc Workers, 1974. **Special Achievements:** Author, 'Desegregation: The Illusion of Black Progress', Univ Press Am, 1984. **Home Addr:** 711 Quackenbos St NW, Washington, DC 20011. **Business Addr:** Professor, Howard University, School of Social Work, 601 Howard Pl NW, Washington, DC 20059, **Business Phone:** (202)806-7300.

ADAIR, ANDREW A.
Chief executive officer, lawyer. **Personal:** Born Aug 5, 1933, Chicago, IL; children: Andrew Jr & Suzanne. **Educ:** Morehouse Col, BS, 1965; Univ Toledo Col Law, JD, 1969. **Career:** Nat Urban League, assoc dir, field oper, 1971-72, assoc dir progs, 1973-74,dir, Mauy Develop Ctr, 1975-79, actg gen coun, 1978-79, dir cent region, 1979-. **Orgs:** Legal couns Ctr Stud Rights Dayton, 1969-70; bd mem, Human Rights Comn Dayton, 1969-71; bd mem, ACLU Dayton Chap, 1969-71; Ind Bar Asn; Fed Bar US Dist Ct; Nat Bar Asn, 1971; secy, nat coun exec dir, Nat Urban League, 1971-72; nat adv & coun, Nat Coun Urban League Guilds, 1972-79; bd mem, Coun Econ Educ NY, 1975-78; Am Bar Asn, 1976. **Military Serv:** AUS, cpl, 1953-55; Korean Serv Medal. **Business Addr:** Director Central Region, National Urban League, 36 S Wabash Ave, Chicago, IL 60603.

ADAIR, GWEN (GWEN FARRELL)
Judge. **Personal:** Daughter of Lovie Yancey. **Career:** Athletic Comn, referee & judge, 1980-; actress. **Orgs:** Calif Referees Asn. **Honors/Awds:** Inducted into the Calif Boxing Hall Fame, World Boxing Hall Fame, 2006. **Special Achievements:** First African Am & only woman referee to officiate a world championship heavyweight bout; Films: Lady Sings the Blues; The Poseidon Adventure; Billy Jack Goes to Washington, 1977; TV appearance: "MASH". **Business Addr:** Referee, Judge, Athletic Comn, 1424 Howe Ave Suite 33, Sacramento, CA 95825-3217, **Business Phone:** (916)263-2195.*

ADAIR, JAMES E.
Educator. **Personal:** Married Marjorie P Spellen; children: Andrea Denice & Tonja Michelle. **Educ:** Fort Valley State Col, BS. **Career:** Adair's Art Gallery Atlanta, dir, 1963-64; Barber-Scotia Col Concord, art instr, 1964-66; Parks Jr High Sch, Atlanta, art instr, 1967-69; MorrisBrown Col Atlanta, art lectr, 1970-. **Honors/Awds:** Executed murals, Ft Valley State Coll, 1962; Annual Negro Exhibition 1stPlace Award, 1969; Fine Arts Gallery Atlanta, 1964, 1968. **Military Serv:** USNR. **Business Addr:** Art Lecturer, Morris Brown College, 643 Martin Luther King Jr Dr, Atlanta, GA 30314, **Business Phone:** (404)739-1012.*

ADAIR, ROBERT A.
Physician. **Personal:** Born Jun 27, 1943, New York, NY; married Ella; children: Kai, Robert A. **Educ:** Univ Penn, BA, 1965; Howard Univ Med Sch, MD, 1969; Met Hosp, med intern, 1970; Dept Health New York City, pub health residency, 1972; Columbia Univ, MPH, 1972. **Career:** Staten Community Col, adj prof, 1970; E Harlem Alcoh Anony Asn, spec consult, 1970; NY City Dept Health, actg dist health officer Cent Harlem, 1970-71; Bd Educ Harlem Pub Sch, consult, 1970-71; Narcot Addict & Ven Dis Mt Morr Presb Chap, spec consult, 1970-72; Morrisania Youth Ctr & box tm, consult physician, 1970-72; NY City Dept Correc, physician, 1971; WNBC-TV, med consult & co-prod 4 TV films, 1971-72; Pub Health Nurses New Pub Health, sch syst, spec consult & instr, 1971-72; Sydenham Hosp NY City, dir ambul serv, 1972; Manhattanville Col, spec health course on pub health, 1972; pvt pract, physician, 1980-; Holy Name Hosp, med dir community rels, 2002. **Orgs:** fel Am Pub Health Asn, 1969; NY Co Med Soc; NY State Med Soc; Nat Med Asn; Black Am Med & Dent Asn Stud; Black Caucus Health Workers; Am Med Asn; med adv bd, Found Res & Educ Sick Cell Dis; sec adv counc, Pres Med Bd NY City Health & Hosp Corp; bd pres, med bd Sydenham Hosp; bd dir, Physic Inc; chmn, Health Comn 10 Black Men; consult Health Dept Englewood NY; admis com Bio-Med Prog City Col, NY, 1973-; Nat Asn Advan Colored People; Harlem Alli May Org Task Force; Duke Elling Jazz Soc; elder Mt Morris Unit Presby Chap; sub-area health plan body mod cit; fin com Mt Morris Fed Cred Un; bd trust Mary Holmes Col; bd trust, Harl Interf Couns Serv; First Aid Com Red Cross Asn; adv coun, NY UrbanLeague Manhat; bd, dSherm Terr Corp; Am Soc Bariatric Physicians. **Honors/Awds:** Woodrow Wilson Acad Scholar, 1961-65; dipl, Nat Med Bd, 1970; bd Elig Am Acad Pub Health & Prevent Med, 1972; chmn, Prevent Med Sect Nat Med Conv, 1973; hon disc, 1974. **Special Achievements:** author of several publications. **Business Addr:** physician, Private Practice, 1086 Teaneck Rd, Teaneck, NJ 07666, **Business Phone:** (201)837-2111.*

ADAMS, DR. AFESA M.
Educator. **Personal:** Born Feb 20, 1936, Greenwood, MS; daughter of Annie Miller and Eddie; married Allan Nathaniel, Jul 19, 1975; children: Suzanne Bell-Brown, Steven A Bell & David C Bell. **Educ:** Weber State Col, BS, 1969; Univ Utah, MS, 1973, PhD, social psychol, 1975. **Career:** Univ Fla, asst prof, behav studies, 1974-79, actg chair, behav studies,1976-78, assoc prof, psychol, 1976-80; Univ Utah, dept family & consumer studies, chair, 1980-83, assoc vpres, acad affairs, 1984-89, assoc prof, family & consumer studies, adj assoc prof, dept psychol; Univ N Fla, Col Arts & Sci, dean, 1989-93, prof psychol, 1993, Fla Inst Educ, sr res assoc, currently, prof emer psychol, currently. **Orgs:** Am Psychol Asn; Utah Coun Family Rels; Nat Coun Negro Women Inc; Southeastern Psychol Asn; Am Psychol Asn; bd dirs, Gainesville Womens Health Ctr; adv bd, State Utah, Div C, Youth & Families Day Care, 1980-83; Gov's Comm Exec Reorganization, 1983-85; Gov's Task Force, study financial barriers health care, 1983-84, employer sponsored child care, 1984; several publ & papers; bd dirs, Daniel Memorial Inst Inc, 1989; bd dir,1993, pres, bd dir, 1997-98, Jacksonville Community Coun Inc; bd dirs,Hubbard House Progs Spouse Abuse, 1992-94; Advocates Better Jacksonville,1989-, bd dirs, Jacksonville Art Mus, 1990-93; Jacksonville Womens Network, 1989-; adv coun, Raines High Sch, 1989-; Andrew Jackson High Sch,accreditation team, 1989-; chair, Implementation Community: JCCI Young Black Males Study, 1989-; Nat Coun Family Rels, 1989-; Popular Culture Asn, 1989-; Am Asn High Educ, 1989-93; Leadership Jacksonville Class,1994; bd dirs, LJ, 1994-95; bd dirs, Fla Theatre, 1994-, vpres, 1996-; UNFNW Link: A Serv Learning Monitoring Prog, 1995-; Phi Kappa Phi. **Honors/Awds:** Community Service Award, Beehive Lodge, Elks, 1986; Community Service Award, United Way, Great Salt Lake Area, 1986; Hall of Fame, Granite High Sch, 1987-88; Civil Rights Worker of the Yr, NAACP SL Br, 1988; Distinguished Alumni Award, 2006. **Special Achievements:** Featured in State Off Educ Equity Unit film, Bldg Legacy: Contemp Pioneering Women, 1988. **Business Addr:** Senior Research Associate, Professor Emeritus of Psychology, University of North Florida, Florida Institute of Education, 12000 Alumni Dr, Jacksonville, FL 32224-2678, **Business Phone:** (904)620-2496.

ADAMS, ALBERT W. See Obituaries section.

ADAMS, ALICE OMEGA
Physician. **Personal:** Born Apr 28, 1951, Washington, DC; children: Sharon, Leslie Wilbanks. **Educ:** Univ DC, BS, 1974; Howard Univ Grad Sch, PhD, 1979; Howard Univ Col Med, MD, 1984. **Career:** Univ DC, teaching asst, 1972-74, asst prof, 1979-81; Childrens Hosp Nat Med Ctr, res assoc, 1975-77; Howard Univ, grad teaching asst, 1976-79, med stud tutor, 1978-79, asst prof neurol, 1985-; Children's Hosp, med tech 1977-81; Howard Univ Hosp, resident physician internal med, 1984-85. **Honors/Awds:** Outstanding Achievement, DC Med Chirolurgical Soc, 1983; Outstanding Achievement, Howard Univ Dept of Internal med, 1984; Outstanding Achievement, Alpha Omega Alpha Honor Med Soc, 1984. **Business Addr:** Assistant Professor, Howard University Hospital, 2042 Georgia Ave NW Suite 5b05, Washington, DC 20060.*

ADAMS, ANNE CURRIN
Educator, social worker. **Personal:** Born Jun 28, 1942, Hackensack, NJ; daughter of Charles Colbert Currin and Etta Greer Currin; married Thomas E; children: Tracey Anne. **Educ:** Keuka Col, NY, BA, 1964; Rutgers Univ, Grad Sch Social Work, MSW, 1970, PhD, educ & sociol. **Career:** YWCA, prog dir youth & teenagers, 1964-66; NJ Bur Children's Serv,caseworker, activities dir, 1966-70; Newark NJ Bd Educ, sch social worker, 1970-72; Newark Engineering Col, adminr asst to eop dir, 1971-72; Rutgers Grad Sch Social Work, asst prof, 1972-86, consult, trainer human serv delivery, 1986-; Brandeis Univ, Ctr Youth & Communities, sr prog assoc, 1994-. **Orgs:** Shiloh Baptist Church, Cascade, VA; Nat Coun Negro Women. **Honors/Awds:** Outstanding Student Award, Rutgers GSSW, 1969; Excellence in Education Award, Paterson Alumnae Chap, Delta Sigma Theta Sorority, 1989. **Special Achievements:** Publ: Book Review Int Social Welfare Journal, 1980; co-author "Characteristics and Consequences of a Time-Limited Writing Group in a Academic Setting" in Social Worth With Groups, Vol. 8, No. 2, 1985; Article "Field Training for Social Work Students in Maternal and ChildHealth"; co-author, Nourish & Publish: An Academic Women's Self-HelpEffort in Affilia, Journal of Women an Social Work, Vol. 1, No. 3, Fall, 1986; co-author, Group Approach to Training Ethnic-Sensitve Practitioners,in C Jacobs & D Bowles, ed. Ethnicity & Race, Critical Concepts in Social Work, National Asn Social Workers, 1988; author, "Outrageous Leadership, "CYD Journal, summer 2000.

ADAMS, ARMENTA ESTELLA (ARMENTA ADAMS HUMMINGS)
Pianist. **Personal:** Born Jun 27, 1936, Cleveland, OH; daughter of Albert and Estella Mitchell; married Gus Lester, Feb 1, 1973 (divorced); children: Amadi, Gus Jr, Martin & Marcus. **Educ:** New Eng Conserv, Preparatory Div, 1953; Juilliard Sch Music, BM, MM, 1960; London, England, post-grad Study, 1963. **Career:** Juilliard Sch Preparatory Div, piano teacher, 1967-69; Harlem Sch Music, piano teacher, 1968-69; Fla A&M Univ, piano fac, 1965-66; Urban Arts Winston-Salem, artist-in-residence, 1983-84; Winston-Salem State Univ, instrument fac, 1984-85; NC A&T Univ, piano fac, 1987-88; Gateways Music Festival, founder & artistic dir, 1993-; Univ Rochester, Eastman Sch Music, distinguished community mentor, assoc prof music, 1994-. **Honors/Awds:** First prize, Musicians Club, NY, 1956; John Hay Whitney grant; Martha Baird Rockefeller grant; First prize, Nat Asn Negro Musicians; Special prize, Int Competition Leeds England; grant, Int Inst Educ; Freida Loewenthal Eising Award; Musical Am Musician of the Year Award; Special Prize, Leeds Int Competition. **Special Achievements:** Recording: Music That Feeds The Soul, extensive concert tours throughout the world US State Dept 1963-67, performance at Univ MD Int Piano Festival Great Performer Series 1985. **Business Addr:** Artistic Director, Founder, Gateways Music Festival Inc, 26 Gibbs St, PO Box 58, Rochester, NY 14604, **Business Phone:** (585)232-6106.

ADAMS, BENNIE
Basketball executive. **Personal:** Born Apr 8, 1967, New Orleans, LA. **Career:** NBA, official, currently. **Business Addr:** Official, National Basketball Associaiton, Olympic Tower, 645 5th Ave 15th Fl, New York, NY 10022-5986, **Business Phone:** (212)826-7000.*

ADAMS, BETTY PHILLIPS
Foundation executive, consultant, president (organization). **Personal:** Born Apr 9, 1944, Washington, DC; daughter of Charles Willis Phillips III and Mary Ellen Russell Phillips; divorced. **Educ:** Howard Univ, BA; Stanford Univ, Grad Sch Bus, MS. **Career:** Nat Urban League, vpres admin; Nat Urban League, Nat Planning & Eval, dir; Jackie Robinson Found, pres, chief exec officer & sr adv; Nat Asn Advan Colored People Legal Defense & Educ Fund & Fedn Protestant Welfare Orgn, consult, 2003-. **Orgs:** Bd Dir & Exec Comt, Nat Black Leadership Comn AIDS; vpres, YWCA New York City; Spelman Corp Women's Round table; YWCA Acad Achievers; Rockefeller Found fel; Sloan fel. **Honors/Awds:** Rev Dr Martin Luther King Jr Living the Dream Award, New York Gov, 1998; Seagrams Vanguard Award. **Home Addr:** 2166 Broadway, New York, NY 10024, **Home Phone:** (212)362-5721. **Business Addr:** Consultant, National Association for Advancement of Colored People, Legal Defense & Educational Fund, 99 Hudson St Suite 1600, New York, NY 10013, **Business Phone:** (212)965-2200.

ADAMS, BILLIE MORRIS WRIGHT
Pediatrician, administrator. **Personal:** Born in Bluefield, WV; married Frank M Adams; children: Frank M Jr. **Educ:** Fisk Univ, BS, 1950; Ind Univ, MA, zool, 1951; Howard Univ, MD, 1960; Am Bd Pediat, Dipl, 1964. **Career:** Oper consult, Sickle Cell Comprehensive Ctr, Univ Ill Coll Med; clin asst prof, Dept Pediat, Univ Ill Col Med; Links Inc; Cook Co Hosp Hekutoen Inst, rotating intern, 1960, pediat residency, 1961-63, hematol fel, 1963-65, res assoc hematol dept, 1965-67; Martin Luther King Ctr, pediatrician, 1967-68; Pediat Hematol Clin Mercy Hosp, pediat hematologist, actg br chief; Pediat Asn, pvt practice physician, currently; Health Power Infant & Child Health Channel, ed, currently; Univ Ill, coordr, 2006-. **Orgs:** Nat Med Asn, 1962; Pediat Asn, SC; Am Acad Pediat, 1963; Am Soc Hematol, 1968; Chicago Pediat Soc; Alpha Gamma Pi, 1972; appl chairperson, State Ill Comt Sickle Cell Anemia, 1972; med adv comt, Planned Parenthood, 1972-75; Cook Co Physicians Asn, 1974-; med adv comt, Chicago Bd Health's C & Maternal Comn; Am Med Asn; Chicago Inst Med; Chicago Med Asn; Ill State & Med Soc; bd dir, Midwest Asn; Art Inst Chicago; Lyric Opera Guild; bd mem, Ounce Prev; Delta Sigma Theta; bd dir, S Side Community Art Ctr; Friends Carter G Woodson Libr; exec comt, Ounce Prev; Robert Taylor Boys & Girls Clubs; Bronzeville C Mus; bd dirs, Michael Reese Health Trust; past pres, Chicago Pediat Soc; gardner trustees, Michael Reese Health Trust, 2004-; chmn, Nat Med Asn. **Honors/Awds:** Archibald Hoyne Award, Chicago Pediat Soc; Grace James Award, Nat Med Asn; Honoree, Alpha Gamma Pi , 1973; PUSH Woman of the Year, 1975; Congress District Award in Medical, 1985; United Negro College Fund Star, 1986; Pediatrician of the Year, Ill Chap Am Acad Pediat, 1997; Public Service Award, Chicago Med Soc, 1999. **Special Achievements:** First to win Cong Dist Awd in Med, 1985; one of the Best Doctors in America and honored at the University of Illinois at Chicago in 2005/2006. **Business Addr:** Co Ordinator, University Of Illnois, 1301 W Green St, Urbana, IL 61801, **Business Phone:** (217)333-1216.*

ADAMS, DR. CAROL LAURENCE
Government official, sociologist. **Personal:** Born May 11, 1944, Louisville, KY; divorced; children: Nia Malika Augustine. **Educ:** Fisk Univ, BA, 1965; Boston Univ, MA, 1966; Univ Chicago; Union Grad Sch, PhD, 1976. **Career:** Northeastern Ill, Univ Ctr Inner City Studies, asst dir, 1969-78; Neighborhood Inst, dir res & planning, 1978-81; Loyola Univ, dir Afro-Amer studies, assoc prof sociol, 1981; Chicago Housing Authority, dir resident prog, 1997; Int House Blues Found, exec dir, 1997; Ill Dept Human Serv,secy, 2003-. **Orgs:** Nat Asn Blacks Criminal Justice, African Heritage Studies Asn; Am Sociol Asn; bd mem, Ebony Talent Creative Arts Found, Asn Advan Creative Musicians; bd dir, Cable Access Corp; Nat Coun Black Studies, Ill Coun Black Studies. **Honors/Awds:** Phi Beta Kappa Fisk Univ, 1965; George Edmund Hayes Social Sci Award, Fisk Univ, 1965; Community Achievement Award, Hubame Assoc; Leadership in Ed Award, YMCA Metrop Chicago; Govrs Award Arts; Black Bus Award, Black Book Dir; Achievement Award, Ill Bd Higher Educ. **Home Addr:** 6929 S Crandon 3A, Chicago, IL 60649. **Business Addr:** Secretary, Sociologist, Illinois Department Human Service, c/o Alexander Tennant Treas, 100 S Grand Ave E, Springfield, IL 62762.*

ADAMS, CECIL RAY
Banker. **Personal:** Born Feb 15, 1948, Crockett, TX; son of Leo and Verna Davis (deceased); married Myra Bliss Adams, Oct 30, 1971; children: Jennifer, Kraig, Andrew. **Educ:** Univ N Tex, Denton, TX, BA, Polit Sci, Econ, 1970; Univ Houston, TX, MS, accountancy, 1982. **Career:** First City Nat Bank, Houston, TX, vpres, 1973-85, sr vpres, 1985-86; Union Bank, Los Angeles, CA, vpres, 1986-88; Unity Nat Bank, Houston, TX, pres & chief exec officer, 1988-90; Imperial Bank, Costa Mesa, CA, vpres, 1990-95; Community Bank of the Bay, Oakland, CA, pres/chief exec officer, 1995; Founders National Bank, sr vpres & chief operating officer, 1991-01; Pacific Mercantile Bank, 2004. **Orgs:** Bd mem, Hester House Community Ctr, 1978-80; bd mem, Houston Sun Literacy Acad, 1988-90; bd mem, S Cent YMCA, 1988-90; bd mem, Professions & Finance Assocs, 1990-93; bd mem, Nat Monetary Fund. **Honors/Awds:** Bank of the Year, Black Enterprise Mag, 1990; Founders Award, YMCA, 1990. **Military Serv:** AUS, specialist 4, 1971-73. *

ADAMS, DR. CHARLES GILCHRIST
Clergy. **Personal:** Born Dec 13, 1936, Detroit, MI; son of Charles Nathaniel and Clifton Verdelle Gilchrist; married Agnes Hadley Adams, 1987; children: Tara Hancock Adams-Washington & Charles Christian Adams. **Educ:** Fisk Univ, Nashville, TN, 1956; Univ Mich, Ann Arbor, MI, BA, 1958; Harvard Divinity Sch, Cambridge, MA, MDiv, 1964. **Career:** Concord Baptist Church, Boston, MA, pastor, 1962-69; Hartford Memorial Baptist Church, Detroit, MI, sr pastor, 1969-; Boston Univ; Andover Newton Sch Theol; Cent Baptist Sem, Kans City; Lliff Sch Theol, Denver, CO; Ecumenical Theol Sem, Detroit, MI. **Orgs:** Pres, Detroit Br, NAACP, 1984-86; pres, Black Alumni-Nat Asn Harvard Divinity Sch, 1988-94; pres, Progressive Nat Baptist Conv, 1990-94; cent comn, 1991, planning comm, 1994, World Coun Churches; Nat Coun Churches, 1992; ed columnist, Mich Chronicle; chair, Ecumenical Urban Strategy Comn; bd trustee, Morehouse Col, Atlanta; bd trustee, Morris Col, Sumpter, SC; mem bd dir, First Independence Bank, Detroit, MI; Phi Mu Alpha; Omega Psi Phi. **Honors/Awds:** Doctor of Divinity, Morehouse Col, 1984; Doctor of Laws, Dillard University, 1985; Doctor of Humanities, University of Michigan, 1986; Doctor of Humane Letters, Marygrove Col, 1985; Doctor of Divinity, Morris Col, 1980; Ebony Magazine, 15 Greatest Black Preachers, 1993-94; Top 100 Influential Black Americans, 1990-94; Harvard Divinity School, Rabbi Marvin Katzenstein Award, 1992. **Special Achievements:** Spoke before United Nations, 1989; World Congress of the Baptist World Alliance, Speaker, 1990; Seventh General Assembly of the World Council of Churches, speaker, 1991; Spoke before President Clinton at the White House, 1992; cited as one of Americas 15 greatest Black preachers, Ebony Mag. **Business Addr:** Pastor, Hartford Memorial Baptist Church, 18900 James Couzens Hwy, Detroit, MI 48235.

ADAMS, DR. CLARENCE LANCELOT, JR. See Obituaries section.

ADAMS, CURTIS N.
Dentist. **Personal:** Born Mar 28, 1931, Waycross, GA; married Jean; children: Cheryl, Curtis Jr. **Educ:** SC State Col, BS, 1954; Howard Univ, attended 1958, DDS, 1962; Provident Hosp, attended 1963. **Career:** Pvt Pract, Baltimore, med, 1963-68; Provident Hosp, staff-oral surg, 1963-; Rosewood St Hosp, staff, 1964-68; Provident Compreh Neigh Health Ctr, dent clin super, 1968-; Work Incentive Prog, lectr, 1970-71; Provident Hosp Compl, lectr, 1970-71; Pvt Pract, dentist, 1968-. **Orgs:** Chmn, Health Task Force, 1969-71; treas med, Staff Provident Hosp, 1970-73; treas, NW Civic Forum, 1971-73; pres elect, MD Dent Soc, 1971-73; pres, MD Dent Soc, 1971; organizing comt, Harbor Nat Bank, 1973; md, State Bd Dent Examr, 1991-95; Northeast Regional Bd, 1991-; pres, Heritage United Church Christ; 1994-; chmn med audit, Provident Hosp Complex; mem patient care comt, Provident Hosp; Utilization Comt Provident Hosp; mem med exec comt, Provident Hosp; Nat Dent Asn, SC State Univ; Am Dent Assn; Nat Dent Asn; md, Dent Soc; md, St Dent Asn; Alpha Phi Alpha Fraternity; Chi Delta Mu Fraternity; NW Civic Forum; Model Cities Policy Steering; bd mem, Provident Hosp Med Staff; bd dir, Health & Welfare Coun Ctr, MD; bd dir, Community Col Allied Health Fields. **Honors/Awds:** Alumnus of the Year, SC State Col. **Business Addr:** Dentist, Pvt Practice, 2300 Garrison Blvd Suite 290, Baltimore, MD 21216.*

ADAMS, DEBORAH ROSS
Judge. **Educ:** Univ Mich, BA, 1975; Georgetown Univ Law Ctr, JD, 1979. **Career:** City Detroit Law Dept, sr asst corp coun, 1983-94; Mich 36th Dist Ct, magistrate, 1994-97; 3rd Circuit Ct, Mich, judge, 1997-. **Orgs:** State Bar Mich; Wolverine Bar Asn; NAACP; Georgetown Law Alumni Asn; Tabernacle Missionary Baptist Church, Detroit; Campaign Steering Comt, United Way Community Serv. **Business Addr:** Judge, 3rd Circuit Court, 2 Woodward Avenue, Detroit, MI 48226, **Business Phone:** (313)224-5261.*

ADAMS, DON L.
Financial manager, basketball player. **Personal:** Born Nov 27, 1947, Atlanta, GA; married Mary Wilson; children: Don Jr & Damar. **Educ:** Northwestern Univ, attended 1970. **Career:** Basketball player (retired); consultant : San Diego Houston Rockets, 1970-71; Atlanta Hawks 1971-71; Detroit Pistons, 1972-75; St Louis Spirits, 1975; Buffalo Braves, 1975-77; Sagemark Cosult Linc Fin, MI, investment adv, currently . **Orgs:** Northwestern Univ MEN Club; 4x4 Golf Club; TPC of MI. **Honors/Awds:** Co MVP Northwestern Univ; All-Rookie Team, 1971; Won 2 TPC. *

ADAMS, EDWARD B.
Consultant. **Personal:** Born Jan 31, 1939, New York, NY; son of Clarence L Sr and Erna C A; married Mary Louise; children: Jennifer, Edward Jr & Michelle. **Educ:** NY Univ, BIE, 1959; Brooklyn Polytech Inst, grad study; Stanford Univ, Sloan fel, 1974. **Career:** IBM Corp Co, buying mgr, indust engineering mgr, plant mgr, dir site opers, mgr external progs, regional corp comm rels mgr, consult; EB Adams & Assoc, owner; N Austin Med Ctr, chmn; Citizens Cent Tex Health. **Orgs:** Chmn, Austin Urban League; chmn brd, regents Tex State Tech Col Syst; chmn, Brackenridge Hosp Brd; trustee & chmn, Huston Tillotson Col; vice chmn, govt rels, Greater Austin Chamber Comm; gov, Austin Comm Found; chmn brd trustees, N Austin Med Ctr; brd dir, KLRU-TV; exec Comm, Tex Work force Investment Coun; Sigma Pi Phi; fel, Stanford Sloan, 1973-74; judge, Tex Womens Hall Fame; Treas, Citizens Cent Tex Health; bd mem, Capital Tex Broadcasting; brd dir, Tex Taxpayers & Res Assn; pres, Tex Educ; govr, Austin Community Found; bd mem, Tex Higher Educ Corrd Brd. **Honors/Awds:** Whitney Young Award, Austin Area Urban League, 1989; Dr Humane Letters, Huston-Tillotson Col, 1989; Communicator of the Year Award, Tex Sch Pub Rels Assn, 1992; Austin Comm Found Serv C & Families Award, 1998; Tex Bus & Educ Coalition Award, 1998. **Home Addr:** 7308 Valbrun Dr, Austin, TX 78731. **Business Addr:** Owner, EB Adams & Associates, LLC, 7308 Valburn Dr, Austin, TX 78731.

ADAMS, EDWARD ROBERT
Lawyer. **Personal:** Born Nov 1, 1943, Jamaica, NY; son of Anna Mae Nelson. **Educ:** Queens Col, BA, 1971; Rutgers Univ, Sch Law, JD, 1977. **Career:** NY State Dept Law, asst atty gen, 1996-. **Orgs:** Macon B Allan Black Bar Asn, 1979-; NY Co Lawyers Asn, 1980-; past chair, Third World Lawyer's Caucus, 1981-; bd dir, BRC Human Serv Corp, 1982-; NY City Community Bd 12, chair laws comn, 1984-89; regional rep, Nat Bar Asn, 1988-; Metrop Bar Asn, 1989-; comn mem, NY Comn Qual Care Mentally Disabled, 1993-. **Honors/Awds:** Two Student Achievement Awards, Queens Col, 1971. **Special Achievements:** Ran for US Congress for the 15th District of NY, 1996. **Military Serv:** AUS, signal corp, sp-4, 1963-66. **Home Addr:** 100 W 93rd St, New York, NY 10025, **Home Phone:** (212)316-4842. **Business Addr:** Assistant Attorney General, New York State Department of Law, 120 Broadway Suite 25, New York, NY 10271, **Business Phone:** (212)416-8080.*

ADAMS, DR. ELAINE PARKER
School administrator. **Educ:** Xavier Univ La, BA, 1961; La State Univ, MS, 1966; Univ Southern Calif,PhD, 1973; Harvard Univ, Mgt Develop Prog, 1986, Inst Educ Mgt, 1989. **Career:** Orleans Parish Sch Syst, librn, teacher, 1961-68; Xavier Univ, New Orleans, La, ref librn, 1966-67; Grossmont Union HS Dist, dist catalog librn, 1971; Upper St Clair Sch Dist, librn, 1972-73; Univ Md, vis asst prof, 1973; Univ Southern Calif Health Sci Campus, media specialist, 1974-75; Tex Southern Univ, coord learning resource ctr, 1976-80; Getty Oil Co Res Ctr, supvr libr serv, 1980-83; Prairie View A&M Univ, assoc vpres, acad serv & planning, 1983-85, vpres stud affairs, 1985-89; TexHigher Educ, Coord Bd, asst comnr, 1989-91; Houston Community Col Syst, NE, pres, 1991-96, vice chancellor, 1997-99; Houston Comm Col-SW, psychol prof, adj fac, 2006-; Advocacy Inc, bd mem, currently. **Orgs:** Alpha Kappa Alpha Sor, 1967-; Am Libr Asn, 1970-, chairperson, Calif Librns Black Caucus, Southern Area, 1975; area rep, Youth Understanding Int Stud Exchange, 1979-82; Spec Libr Asn, 1981-84; rec secy, Nat Coalition 100 Black Women Houston, 1984-86; Nat Asn Women Deans, Adminr & Counr, 1985-; Nat Asn Stud Personnel Admin, 1986-89; inst rep, Prairie View A & M Univ Army, ROTC Adv Camp, 1986; Am Asn Higher Educ, 1987-; accreditation team mem, Middle States Asn Col & Univ, 1987-91; bd mem,Black Caucus, 1989-; pres, Xavier Univ Alumni Asn, 1989-91; bd trustees, Xavier Univ, 1990-95; accreditation team mem, Southern Asn Col & Sch, 1991-; Am Coun Educ, Comn Leadership, 1994-96; pres, Houston YWCA; presiding officer, Tex Traumatic Brain Injury Adv Coun. **Honors/Awds:** Marguerite Bougere Award, Deep S Writers & Artists Conf, 1965; fel HEA-Title II USC, 1968-71; contrib, Media & Young Adult Series, 1977-84;co-ed, Media & Young Adult, Chicago Ala, 1981; Meritorious Service Award, Asn Black Social Workers Tex, 1988; Victor J Labat Alumna of the Year,Xavier Univ, 1992; School of Library & Information Science Alumna of the Year, La State Univ, 1992; Makeda Award, Nat Coalition 100 Black Women,1993; Award for Excellence in Teaching, Syst Fac Asn, 2001; Outstanding Service Learning Faculty Award, SW Col, 2003. **Home Addr:** 10906 Holly Springs Dr, Houston, TX 77042. **Business Phone:** (713)718-5625.

ADAMS, EUGENE BRUCE
Funeral director. **Personal:** Born May 6, 1953, Atlanta, GA; son of John Wesley (deceased) and Eunice Hines; children: Amari Alexander. **Educ:** Morehouse Col, Atlanta, BA, Business Admin, 1971-74, BS, biol, 1980-82; Gupton Jones Col Mortuary Sci, attended 1974-75. **Career:** Guyton Bros Funeral Home, co-owner, 1974-78; Sellers Bros Funeral Home, gen mgr, 1978-84; Williams & Williams Funeral Home, gen mgr, 1984-86; Speed & Smart Funeral Home, gen mgr, secy corp, 1986-. **Orgs:** Kappa Alpha Psi Fraternity Inc, 1973-; Epsilon Nu Delta Mortuary Fraternity, 1975-; Nat Funeral Dir & Morticians Asn, 1975-; vpres, First District Ga Funeral Serv Practictioner Asn, 1986-; pres, Ga Funeral Serv Practitioners Asn, 1992-. **Honors/Awds:** Boy Scouts of America, Eagle Scout, 1970. **Special Achievements:** Appointed by Governor Ga, Joe Frank Harris, Ga State Bd Funeral Serv, 1984, pres, 1988-90; appointed by Govenor GA, George Busbee, Juvenile Justice Comt, 1980-84. **Business Addr:** General Manager, Secretary, Speed and Smart Funeral Home Inc, 224 Houston St, Savannah, GA 31401, **Business Phone:** (912)236-0307.

ADAMS, EUGENE WILLIAM
Educator, college teacher. **Personal:** Born Jan 12, 1920, Guthrie, OK; son of Clarence Leon and Lucille Evelyn Owens; married Myrtle Louise Evans Adams, Jul 25, 1956; children: Eugene W Jr, Clyde, Michael. **Educ:** Wichita State Univ,attended 1941; Kansas State Univ, DVM, 1944; Cornell Univ, MS, 1957, PhD, 1962. **Career:** US Dept Agr, St Louis, MO, pub health vet, 1944-51; Tuskegee Univ, prof, vice provost & dir, 1951-89, prof emer, currently; Ahmadu Bello Univ, Zaria, Nigeria, prof, 1970-72. **Orgs:** Nat Resources Res Coun, NIH, 1974; Africa Bur Steering Comt Agr Educ, USAID, Africa Bur, 1984; Adv Panel, Off Technol Assessment, 1987; chair, Trustee Bd Southeast Corsortium Inter Develop, 1987-89; bd dirs, Inst Alternative Agr, 1990; Sigma Xi, Kappa Alpha Psi; Phi Zeta; Phi Boule. **Honors/Awds:** Distinguished Teaching Award, Vet Med Norden Drug Co, 1956; Bd Cert, Col Vet Pathologists, 1964; Vet Prototype Nine Black Am Doctors, Robert C Hayden & J Harris, Addison-Wesley Publ Co, Boston, 1976; Distinguished Fac Achievement Award, Tuskegee Univ, 1979. **Military Serv:** USAF, capt, 1949-56. **Business Addr:** Professor Emeritus, The Tuskegee University, 1866 Southern Lane, Decatur, GA 30033.*

ADAMS, EULA L.
Executive. **Personal:** Born Feb 12, 1950, Tifton, GA; son of Thelma Billington; married Janet C, May 19, 1973; children: Kevin B. **Educ:** Morris Brown Col, BS, 1972; Harvard Bus Sch, MBA, 1976. **Career:** Deloitte & Touche, partner, 1972-91; First Data Corp, First Data Teleservices subsi, exec vpres finance & admin, 1991-94, exec vp & gen mgr, 1994-97, sr exec vp & chief operating officer, 1997-98, First Data Merchant Serv, pres, 1998-00, First Data Resources, sr exec vpres, 2000-03; Storage Technol Corp, vpres, global serv, 2003; NetBank, bd dirs, 2003-; Sun Microsystems Inc, Data Mgt Group & Delivery Serv, vpres, 2005-; MasterCard Int, bd dirs; Wells Fargo Merchant Servs, bd dirs; Pay By Touch, bd dirs, currently. **Orgs:** bd mem, treas, Cong Black Caucus Found, 1993-; bd mem, treas, Southern Ed Found, 1988-; Am Inst CPAs, 1974-; Colo Soc CPAs, 1991-; Am Heart Assn, bd mem, treas, 1991-93; Denver Zool Soc, bd mem, 1994-; USO of GA, bd mem, treas, 1988-91; United Way of CO, bd mem, 1993-. **Honors/Awds:** 100 Black Men of Am; Best & Brightest Young Men in Am under 35; Ten Outstanding Young Atlantans under 35; one of the 50 most powerful black executives, Fortune, 2002. **Military Serv:** Georgia Air Nat Guard, sergeant, 1972-78. **Business Addr:** Board of Directors, Pay By Touch, 101 2nd St Suite 1100, San Francisco, CA 94105, **Business Phone:** (415)281-2200.*

ADAMS, FLOYD, JR.
Editor. **Personal:** Born May 11, 1945, Savannah, GA; son of Floyd Sr and Wilhelmina; children: Kenneth & Khristi. **Educ:** Armstrong Col, BA, bus. **Career:** Savannah Herald, pres gen mgt & editor; Savannah City Coun, councilman & alderman-at-large; Savannah Mayor Pro-Tem, mayor, 1996-03. **Orgs:** Pvt Indust Coun; The GA Munic Asn; The GA Black Elected Officials Asn; Finance & Inter-Government Rels Comt Nat League Cities; Pvt Indust Coun; Georgia Black Elected Officials Asn; Nat Black Coun Local Elected Officials; Georgia Municipal Asn; Savannah's Printers Asn; NAACP; Savannah Br; Prince Hall Masons. **Special Achievements:** First African-Am to be elected mayor of Savannah; first African-Am to win alderman-at-large post 1 in his own right; first African-Am mayor pro-tem of Savannah. cand for GA Dist 12 Race 2002.

ADAMS, FLOZELL
Football player. **Personal:** Born May 18, 1975, Chicago, IL. **Educ:** Mich State Univ. **Career:** Dallas Cowboys, guard & offensive tackle, 1998-. **Orgs:** Active in numerous charities. **Honors/Awds:** Big Ten Offensive Lineman of the Yr; All-Am hons; Lombardi Award. **Business Addr:** Professional Football Player, Dallas Cowboys Football Club, 1 Cowboys Pkwy, Irving, TX 75063, **Business Phone:** (972)556-9900.*

ADAMS, GREGORY ALBERT
Lawyer. **Personal:** Born Jun 10, 1958, Atlanta, GA; son of Enoch Q Sr and Emily E Jackson; married Wanda C Adams, Oct 27, 1984. **Educ:** Ga State Univ, Atlanta, GA, BS, criminal justice, 1981; Univ Ga, Sch Law, Athens, GA, JD, 1983. **Career:** Ga State Univ, Atlanta, GA, supvr, 1977-81; Inst Continuing Judicial Educ, Athens, GA, researcher, 1983-84; Dekalb Co Solicitor, Decatur, GA, asst solicitor, 1984-87; Dekalb County Juv Ct, asst dist atty, 1987-94, judge, chief judge, 1994-; State Ga, Super Ct, Stone Mountain Judicial Circuit, judge, currently. **Orgs:** Alpha Phi Alpha Fraternity Inc, 1980-; Asn Trial Lawyers Am, 1984-88; State Bar Ga, 1984-; Dekalb Lawyers Asn, 1984-; pres, Scarbrough Square Homeowners Asn, 1986-87; Dekalb County, Nat Asn Advan Colored People, 1987-; Dekalb Lawyers Asn, 1987-88; bd mem, Decatur-Dekalb Bar Asn, 1988-89; parliamentarian, Alpha Phi Alpha Fraternity Inc, 1988-90; vpres, Dekalb Jaycees, 1989-; Chief Justice Comn Prof, 1994-; pres, DeKalb Bar Asn, 1994-95; Rotary Int, 1995-; bd chmn, Leadership DeKalb, 1996. **Honors/Awds:** Serv Award, Dekalb Br Nat Asn Advan Colored People, 1988; Merit Award, Dekalb Lawyers Asn, 1988; Legion of Honour, Dekalb-Atlanta Voters Coun, 1988; Outstanding Pub Serv, Dunwoody Rotary Club, 1990-. **Business Addr:** Judge, State of Georgia Superior Court, Stone Mountain Judicial Circuit, 556 N McDonough St, Decatur, GA 30030, **Business Phone:** (404)371-2836.*

ADAMS, GREGORY KEITH
Meeting planner. **Personal:** Born Apr 9, 1958, Philadelphia, PA. **Educ:** Rutgers Univ, Econs & Bus, 1981. **Career:** Hyatt Hotels Corp, sales mgr, 1981-83; Westin Hotels Corp, sales mgr, 1983-85; Radisson Corp, asst dir sales, 1985; NAACP, nat conf dir, 1985; Bayard Rustin Alliance, founder & exec dir; Gay & Bi Equal Rights & Liberation, media dir, 1993; Westchester Co, bldg inspector planning, 2003-. **Orgs:** Greater Wash Soc Assoc Execs; Nat Assoc Exposition Mgrs; Omega Psi Phi Frat; Prince Hall Master Mason; bd mem, Nat Coalition Black Meeting Planners; steering comm, Baltimore Black Enterprise Prof Exchange; bd mem, Port Chester Carver Ctr. **Home Addr:** 2019 Madison Ave, Baltimore, MD 21217. **Business Addr:** Building Inspector, Westchester Co, Department Planning, 148 Martine Ave, White Plains, NY 10601, **Business Phone:** (914)995-8353.

ADAMS, H. LESLIE (HARRISON LESLIE ADAMS)
Composer. **Personal:** Born Dec 30, 1932, Cleveland, OH; son of Harrison Leslie Sr and Jessie B Manease. **Educ:** Oberlin Col, BME, 1955; Calif State Univ, Long Beach, MA, 1967; Ohio State Univ, PhD, 1973. **Career:** Soehl Jr High Sch, vocal music instr, 1962-63; Karamu House, assoc musical dir, Cleveland, OH, 1964-65, composer-in-residence, 1979-80, resident composer, 1980-82; N Mex Sec Sch, vocal music supvr & choir dir, 1966-67; Kaleidoscope Players, musical dir, 1967-68; Fla A & M Univ, Tallahassee, asst prof music, 1968; Kans Univ Lawrence, assoc prof music, dir Univ choir, dir choral clin, 1970-78; Univ Kans, assoc prof, 1970-79; Yaddo Artist Colony, Rockefeller Found, 1977, composer fel, 1980-84; Accord Associates Inc, founder & pres, 1980-86, exec vpres& composer in residence, 1986-92; Cuyahoga Community Col, guest composer, 1980; Martha Holden Jennings Found, artist in residence, 1981-83; Cleveland Music Sch Settlement, resident composer, 1982-84; Haridan Enterprises, pres & artist in residence, 1993-97; Creative Arts Inc, pres & artist-in-residence, 1997-; Univ Md, College Park, Guest composer, 2000; Shasta College, Shasta, California Guest composer, 2000. **Orgs:** Phi Kappa Phi, 1965-; Phi Kappa Lambda 1972-; Phi Mu Alpha Sinfonia, 1973-; Phi Delta Kappa, 1974-; Am Composers Alliance, 1984-; Am Organists Guild, 1992-; Pi Kappa Lambda; Am Choral Dir Asn. **Honors/Awds:** Winner, composition competition, Nat Asn Negro Women, 1963; Nat Award, Choral Arts, Inc, 1974; Competition Award, Nat Choral Comp, 1974; Nat Endowment for the Arts, 1979; Fellowship Award, Rockefeller Found, 1979; Yaddo Artists Fellowship Award, 1980-84; KC Composers Forum winner choral composition competition, 1974; Cleveland Orchestra Commissioned Composer, 1995. **Special Achievements:** Works performed by the Cleveland Orchestra, Buffalo Philharmonic,Indianapolis Symphony, Detroit Symphony, Savannah Symphony, OH Chamber Orchestra; Robert Page Singers & Orch; Springfield Symphony, Prague Radio Symphony, New York City Opera Company, compositions Symphony No 1, A Kiss In Xanadu (ballet), Ode to Life (orch), Hymn to Freedom, Piano Concerto, Sonata for Violin & Piano, Sonata for Horn & Piano, Sonata for Cello & Piano, Etudes for Piano, Love Expressions (orch), Five Millay Songs, African American Songs, The Wider View, The Righteous Man-Cantata to the Memory of Dr ML King, Blake (opera), numerous other works for solo and ensemble vocal & instrumental groups, works Published by American Composers Edition, New York except Etudes for Solo Piano, String Quartetin D Flat, pub by Art Source Publishing, Cleveland, OH. **Business Addr:** President, Artist-in-residence, Creative Arts Inc, 9409 Kempton Ave, Cleveland, OH 44108-2940.

ADAMS, HARRISON LESLIE. See ADAMS, H. LESLIE.

ADAMS, DR. HOWARD GLEN
Educator. **Personal:** Born Mar 28, 1940, Danville, VA; married Eloise Christine Davis; children: Stephanie Glenn. **Educ:** Norfolk State Univ, BS, 1964; Va State Univ, MS, 1970; Syracuse Univ, PhD,1979. **Career:** Norfolk City Pub Schs, biol/gen sci teacher, 1964-70; Norfolk State Univ,alumni affairs dir, 1970-73; vpres stud affairs, 1974-77; Nat Consortium GEM, exec dir, 1978-95; GEM National Institute on Mentoring, found dir; H G Adams & Assocs Inc, founder & pres, currently. **Orgs:** Comn serv bd, YMCA, 1979-85; bd trustees, Meadville/Lombard Theol Sch,1980-87; corp adv bd, Nat Assoc Equal Opportunity Higher Educ, 1981-;consult, Black Collegian Publications, 1984-91; coun economic Priorities, bd dirs, 1986-93; US Cong Task Force Women, Minorities & the Handicapped Sci & Tech, 1987-90; Col Indust Partnership Div, Am Soc Engineering Educ, bd dirs, 1988-; Nat Adv Coun Environ Tech Transfer, US Environ Protection-Agency, 1988-90; Sci & Engineering Rev group, Waste Policy Inst, US Dept Energy, 1990-; Women in Engineering Prog Advocates Network, Wash, DC,1990-92; Col Engineering, Univ Mich, Nat Adv Comn, 1992-95. **Honors/Awds:** Nat Teachers Sci Fel, 1964-65; Nat Alumni Serv Award, Norfolk State Alumni, 1974; Torch Bearers Award, Nat Soc Black Engineers, 1986;Promotion Higher Educ Award, US Black Engineering Mag, 1987; Reginald H Jones, Distinguished Service Award, Nat Action Coun Minorities Engineering Inc, 1987; Centennial Medallion, Am Soc Engineering Educ, 1993; Recipient of the Presidential Awards for Excellence in Science, Mathematics, Engineering and Mentoring, 1996. **Special Achievements:** Author, Successfully Negotiating the Graduate School Process: A Guide for Minority Students; Mentoring: An Essential Factor in the Doctoral Process for Minority Students; Focusing on the Campus Milieu: A Guide for Enhancing the Graduate School Climate; Making the Grade in Graduate School: Survival Strategy 101. **Business Addr:** Founder, President, HG Adams & Associates Inc, 361 Willow Glenn Ct, PO Box 7495, Marietta, GA 30065.

ADAMS, JAMILE. See ADAMS, NICK.

ADAMS, JAN R.
Writer, surgeon. **Educ:** Harvard Univ; Ohio State Univ; Univ Mich, plastic & reconstructive surg training; Lenox Hill Hosp, residency, gen surg. **Career:** Lenox Hill Hosp, chief surg resident; UCLA Sch of Med, Plastic & Reconstructive surg, clin instr; Everything Women of Color Should Know About Cosmetic Surg, auth, 2000; Beverly Hills, CA, Plastic surg, currently. **Orgs:** Aesthetic Plastic Surgery, 1992. **Special Achievements:** First univ trained aesthetic plastic surgeon in the US; Author, "THE DECISION TO HAVE an elective cosmetic surgical procedure is never an easy one.", St Martin's Press. **Business Addr:** plastic surgeon, 450 North Bedford Drv, Beverly Hills, CA 90210.*

ADAMS, JEAN TUCKER
Government official. **Personal:** Born in Baltimore, MD; children: Stuart Randall, Scott Hamilton. **Educ:** Coppin State Teachers Col, BS, 1958; Univ MD, MSW, 1972. **Career:** Baltimore City, teacher, 1958-64; Health & Mental Hygiene Juvenile Serv Admin, asst reg dir, 1965-76; Pvt pract, psychotherapist, 1975-; Off Mayor Baltimore MD, dep dir, 1976-80; State House Gov Off, exec asst. **Orgs:** Consult, Pvt Pub, 1975-; Nat Asn Soc Workers, 1975-; legislative adv, Exec & Prof Women's Coun MD, 1980-; vpres, United Serv Orgn, 1982-; bd mem, Sudden Infant Death Syndrome Inst, 1983-. **Honors/Awds:** Mayor's Citation, Baltimore City, 1979; Governor's Citation, State MD, 1984; Scroll Appreciation, Wiesbaen Germany Military Comn, 1984; Social Worker of the Year, Nat Asn Soc Workers, 1984. *

ADAMS, JOHN HURST
Clergy. **Personal:** Born Nov 27, 1927, Columbia, SC; son of Avery Adams and Charity Nash Adams; married Dolly Jacqueline Desselle; children: Gaye Desselle, Jann Hurst, Madelyn Rose. **Educ:** Johnson C Smith Univ, AB, hist, 1948; Boston Univ Sch Theology, STB, 1952, STM, 1956; Union Theol Sem NYC; Payne Theol Sem, DD, 1956; Wilberforce Univ, LLD, 1956; Paul Quinn Col, HHD, 1972; Harvard Univ. **Career:** Clergy (retired); Bethel African Methodist Episcopal Church, Lynn, MA, pastor; Payne Theol Sem, seminary teaching faculty, 1952-56; Paul Quinn Col Waco, pres, campus pastor, 1956-62; First African Methodist Episcopal Church, Seattle, sr pastor, 1962-68; Grant African Methodist Episcopal Church, Los Angeles, CA, sr pastor, 1968-72; African Methodist Episcopal Church, sr bishop, 1988-04. **Orgs:** Chmn bd, Paul Quinn Col; chmn, Comn Higher Educ Am Church; dir, Am Income Life Ins Co; chmn, Am Church Serv & Develop Agency, 1978; dir, The Fund Theol Educ; vpres, Nat Black United Fund; chmn, The Congress Nat Black Church; dir, chmn, Interdenominational Theol Ctr; Allen Univ; Edward Waters Col; Morris Brown Col; chmn bd trustees, Atlanta Univ Ctr; founder & chmn emeritus, Congress Nat Black Churches; initiator exec mgt training, Black Church Leaders; chmn, Inst Church Admin & Mgt; Joint Ctr Political & Econ Studies; Transafrica; Nat Black United Fund; King Ctr Develop Bd; Alpha Phi Alpha Fraternity. **Honors/Awds:** Man of the Year, B'nai B'rith NW, 1964; Man of the Year, Urban League, Seattle & NW Area, 1965. *

ADAMS, JOHN OSCAR
Executive. **Personal:** Born Apr 3, 1937, Chattanooga, TN; son of John M and Queen M. **Educ:** Wayne State Univ, BS, 1962; Loyola Univ, JD, 1970. **Career:** Detroit Publ Sch, instr, 1962-64; Pasadena City Col, lectr, 1964-65; IBM LA, mgr, sys engr, instr, 1964-70; IBM Corp Hq, atty antitrust, 1970-72; US Senate Small Bus Comm, minor coun, 1972-75; City Los Angeles, dep city atty, 1975-76; Wallace & Wallace, spec coun, 1975-80; Adams Industries Inc, Calif, pres, bd chmn, 1978-82; atty at law, 1982-; art dealer, 1985-; judge pro term, 1995-; US Bankruptcy Ct, Cent Dist Calif, bd mediators, currently; Adams & Alexander, partner, currently. **Orgs:** Former chmn & mem bd dirs, Hollywood Chamber Com; bd dirs, Hollywood Arts Coun; Supreme Ct; Calif, NY, Wash DC Bar Asns; former mem, Hollywood Kiwanis; former mem, bd regents, Loyola Marymount Univ; Cent Dist Consumer Bankruptcy Attorneys Asn. **Honors/Awds:** Special Achievement Award, Los Angeles Urban League, 1970; Saturday Review Commen Issue, 1975; Men of Achievement. **Special Achievements:** Author, "Notes of an Afro-Saxon", "Future Hope for the US". **Military Serv:** USN, Southern Pacific Fleet, 1958-62. **Home Addr:** 8880 Appian Way, Los Angeles, CA 90046, **Home Phone:** (323)650-8879. **Business Addr:** Managing Partner, Adams & Alexander, 8383 Wilshire Blvd Suite 919, Beverly Hills, CA 90211, **Business Phone:** (323)966-5533.

ADAMS, JONATHAN, III
Actor. **Personal:** Born Jul 16, 1967, Pittsburgh, PA; married Monica Farrell, Jan 1, 1994; children: Sydney. **Educ:** Carnegie-Mellon Univ. **Career:** Theater: "Danger: Memory"; "The Taming of the Shrew"; "A Midsummer Night's Dream"; "Cymbelline"; Film: Two Evil Eyes; Heartstopper, 1991; TV Series: "Frasier"; "City of Angels"; "Walker, Texas Ranger"; "Felicity"; "The American Embassy", 2002;"American Dreams", "Bones"; NBC, 2004; "The Unit", 2006; "The Closer", 2007; "Navy NCIS: Naval Criminal Investigative Service"; 2007; "Women's Murder Club", 2007-08; "Boston Legal", 2008; "The Cleaner", 2009; "The Philanthropist", 2009. *

ADAMS, JOSEPH LEE
Educator. **Personal:** Born Jan 5, 1944, Kansas City, MO; son of Joseph L Adams Sr and Thelma V O; children: Joseph III & Patrick. **Educ:** Univ Mo, BA, Kans City, 1970, MA, 1971; Wash Univ, St Louis, post grad,1979. **Career:** IBM, data ctr suprv, 1968-70; Univ Mo, Kans City, teaching asst, 1970-71; Univ City, councilman, 1974-95, mayor, 1995-; Meramec Comm Col, assoc prof hist; St Louis Community Col, prof hist, currently. **Orgs:** Soc Hist Asn, Nat League Cities; bd dir, Mo Mcpl League, vpres, 1998-99, pres, 1999-2000; St Louis Cty Municipal League; Episcopalian Church, Univ Democrats; Mo Comn Intergovernmental Coop, 1985-; steering comttransportation community, Nat League Cities, 1982-; vchmn, Transportation& Commun Steering Comt, 1988; chmn, Telecommunication Subcommit-

tee Transportation & Commun, Nat League Cities, 1991; bd dirs, Nat League Cities, 1991-93, adv coun, 1993-, vchair, 1997; bd dirs, Citizens Modern Transit, 1994-97; adv coun, Nat League Cities, 1993. **Special Achievements:** First African-American to serve on the City Council and the first to beelected Mayor. **Military Serv:** USAF, sgt, 1962-66. **Home Addr:** 924 Wild Cherry Lane, University City, MO 63130, **Home Phone:** (314)862-7877. **Business Addr:** Mayor, City of University City, 6801 Delmar Blvd, 300 S Broadway, University City, MO 63130, **Business Phone:** (314)862-6767.

ADAMS, DR. JULIUS GREGG
Educator. **Personal:** Born Oct 4, 1957, Buffalo, NY; son of Peter William and Evelyn; married Carmon Grigsby, Jul 29, 1991. **Educ:** St Univ NY, Buffalo, BA, educ psychol, 1978, MA, psychol, 1985, PhD, Educ Psychol, 1988. **Career:** St Univ NY Col, Fredonia, Sch Educ, assoc prof & dir, 1997-2001; Univ Bufflalo, assoc dean teacher educ, 2006; Ralph C Wilson Jr Sch Educ, St John Fisher Col, assoc dean, 2006-. **Orgs:** Western New York Educ Serv Coun. **Honors/Awds:** State University of New York Chancellor's Award for Excellence in Teaching. **Business Addr:** Associate Dean, St John Fisher College, Ralph C Wilson Jr School of Education, 3690 E Ave R WILSN 205C, Rochester, NY 14618, **Business Phone:** (585)899-3813.

ADAMS, KATHERINE
President (Organization). **Personal:** Born Oct 16, 1952, Pittsburgh, PA; married Herman L Jr (divorced); children: H Dean Adams. **Educ:** Malone Col, commun, 1972; Kent State Univ, commun, 1974; Cleveland State Univ, commun; Wayne State Univ, BA, 1993. **Career:** WJKW-TV Storer Broadcasting, desk asst, 1974-75, reporter trainee, prod asst, 1976-77, news anchor, reporter, host, 1977-82; WDIV, news anchor; Katherine Enterprises Inc, owner, 1989-; A&M Automotive Transp, pres, 2000-. **Orgs:** Comn comnr, Cleveland Chap, Nat Asn Advan Colored People; hostess, Focus Black-Pub Serv Prog; City Cleveland Comm Rels Bd; adv bd, Salvation Army Hough Multi Purpose Ctr. **Honors/Awds:** Salute to Black Clevelanders Award, Greater Cleveland Interchurch Coun, 1980; Emmy Award. **Business Addr:** President, A & M Automotive Transport Company LLC, 645 Griswold Suite 1300, Detroit, MI 48226.

ADAMS, KATHY J
President (Organization), television journalist. **Career:** WDIV Channel 4, TV news anchor; Katherine Enterprises Inc, owner, 1989-; A & M Automotive Transp, pres, currently. **Honors/Awds:** Emmy Award winning journalist.

ADAMS, KAWEEDA G.
School principal, educator. **Educ:** Univ New Orleans, BA; Univ Nev, Las Vegas, MEd. **Career:** O'Callaghan Mid Sch, asst prin; Duane D Keller Mid Sch, asst prin; Bob Miller Mid Sch, Clark County, prin; Clark County Sch Dist, dir instr & facil admin, currently; Regis Univ, Denver, CO, fac, currently. **Orgs:** Alpha Kappa Alpha Theta, Las Vegas Chap.

ADAMS, LEHMAN D., JR.
Dentist. **Personal:** Born Feb 19, 1925, Mansfield, LA; married Gloria Estelle Williams; children: Troy S, Traci L. **Educ:** Wilberforce Univ, BS, 1945; Ind Univ Sch Dent, DDS, 1949; Ind Univ, grad study, 1951. **Career:** Pvt Pract, Ind, dentist, 1999. **Orgs:** Nat Dent Asn; Am Dent Asn; Ind Dent Soc, Ind Implant Soc; Midwest Soc Periodontia; Am Analgesia Soc; Acad Gen Prac; various other prof orgns; pres, Wis Educ Career Access Network Found; chmn, life mem, Comn Nat Asn Advan Colored People; bd dirs, Indianapolis Br Nat Asn Advan Colored People; bd dirs, Indianapolis Nat Bus League; treas, bd dir, OIC; Indianapolis C C; bd dir, Summit Lab, 1959-72; bd dir, Midwest Nat Bank, 1975; Alpha Phi Alpha, Chi Delta Mu, Omicron Kappa Upsilon (hon); Witherspoon Presb Ch; pres, bd trustees, Citizens Gas & Coke Utility. **Honors/Awds:** Freedom Award, Nat Asn Advan Colored People Nat Off, 1973; Man of the Year, Alpha Phi Alpha, 1958. *

ADAMS, LEON
Administrator. **Career:** Ohio Civil Rights Comn, mediation adminr, currently. *

ADAMS, LEONARD E, JR.
Contractor. **Career:** Adams Home Improvement, owner, currently. **Home Addr:** 4625 Brandon Ridge Dr NE, Marietta, GA 30066, **Home Phone:** (770)924-1062. **Business Addr:** Owner, Adams Home Improvement, 4625 Brandon Ridge Dr NE, Marietta, GA 30066, **Business Phone:** (770)924-1062.

ADAMS, LILLIAN LOUISE T.
Educator. **Personal:** Born Aug 8, 1929, Greenwood, SC; married David H; children: Hannah Iula, David Jr & Debra. **Educ:** Fisk Univ, AB, 1951; SC State Col, MEd, 1970. **Career:** Gordon High Sch, teacher, 1951-53; Lincoln High Sch, 1955-57; Willow Creek Elem, 1957-68; Harllee Elem Sch, 1968-. **Orgs:** Florence Co Educ Asn; Asn Classroom Teacher; Cumberland United Methodist Church; chmn, Stewardship Comn. **Honors/Awds:** Pres, Am Legion Aux; Teacher Month, 1974; Dist Teacher of the Year, 1975. **Home Addr:** 600 W Sumter St, Florence, SC 29501. **Business Addr:** Teacher, Harllee Elem School, 408 E Pine St, Florence, SC 29501.*

ADAMS, LUCINDA WILLIAMS
Educator, athlete. **Personal:** Born Aug 10, 1937, Bloomingdale, GA; daughter of David Williams and Willie M; married Floyd, Sep 1959 (deceased); children: Kimberly. **Educ:** Tenn State Univ, BS, 1959, MS, 1961; Univ Dayton, attended 1979; Ohio State Univ, attended 1984. **Career:** Educator (retired); Dayton Pub Schs, teacher, 1960-73, curric supvr, 1975,assoc dir; Dayton Div Parks & Recreation, recreation leader, 1968-70; Natl Assoc for Sports & Physical Edn, pres, 1994-. **Orgs:** AKA Sorority, Inc, 1958-; pres, Midwest Dist Assn Health, Phys Educ, Recreation, Dance, 1958-, 1990; Ohio Assn Health, Phys Educ, Recreation,Dance, 1970-; Phi Delta Kappa, 1979; Am Alliance Health, Phys Educ, Recreation & Dance, 1983-; adv brd, Univ Dayton Phys Educ, 1983-; Ohio Spec Olympic Brd, 1989-; Dayton Chap Ronald McDonald's Charities Brd, 1991; pres, Natl Assn Sports & Phys Educ, 1994; US Olympian Soc. **Honors/Awds:** Three Gold Medals, Pan-American Games, 1958; Gold Medal, Rome Olympic, 1960; Geo Hall of Fame, Savannah, 1968; Hall of Fame, Tenn State Univ, 1983; Lifetime Achievement Award, Ohio Prof & Amateur Athletics Comt; Presidential Award, Am Alliance Health Phys Educ Recreation & Dance; Georgia Hall Of Fame, 1994. **Special Achievements:** Co-author, "Standards for Elementary Health Education", 1992; author, "An Olympic Experience", 1988. **Home Addr:** 5049 Coulson Dr, Dayton, OH 45417. *

ADAMS, MELBA K.
Dentist. **Career:** Pvt Pract, dentist, currently. **Home Addr:** 1213 Hermann Dr Suite 265, Houston, TX 77004. **Business Addr:** Dentist, 1213 Hermann Dr Suite 265, Houston, TX 77004.*

ADAMS, NELSON EDDY
Association executive. **Personal:** Born Aug 11, 1945, Southport, NC; married Yvonne McKenzie; children: Nelson Demond, Marius Anton. **Educ:** Cape Fear Tech Inst, rec admin, 1972, nondestructive testing, 1973; Convair Sch, Nondestructive Testing, 1974; Southeastern Comt Col, police sci, 1975; Northwestern Univ, super police personnel, 1976. **Career:** Brown & Root Const Co, qual control inspector, 1974; Brunswick Co Sheriff's Dept, jailer patrolman sgt detective, 1974-80; Int Longshoremans Asn, pres. **Orgs:** Steward Mt Carmel AME Church; Pythagoras Lodge No 6 F&AM; Southport Lions Club; city alderman Southport Bd Aldermen 2nd 4 year term; former adv, NAACP Youth Coun, 1967-69. **Honors/Awds:** Cert Appreciation pres elect S Brunswick Middle Sch PTO, 1982-83; Cert of Appreciation pres S Brunswick Middle Sch PTO, 1984. *

ADAMS, NICK (JAMILE ADAMS)
Comedian, writer. **Personal:** Married. **Career:** TV series: "BET Live", writer; Book: Making Friends with Black People, 2006. **Business Addr:** Writer, Claudia Menza Literary Agency, 1170 Broadway Suite 807, New York, NY 10001, **Business Phone:** (212)889-6850.*

ADAMS, OLETA
Singer, songwriter. **Personal:** Born in Seattle, WA; married John Cushon, 1996. **Career:** Tears for Fears's Seeds of Love album, backup singer, 1989; opened tour for Michael Bolton, singer, 1992; solo Albums: Going on Record, 1983; Circle of One, 1990; Evolution, 1993; Movin On, 1995; Come Walk with Me, 1997; All the Love, 2001; Ultimate Collection, 2004, Christmas Time with Oleta, 2006; Lets Stay here, 2009; William Morris Agency, singer, cur. **Special Achievements:** Debut album, Circle of One, earned a certified gold record, 1991. **Business Addr:** Singer, William Morris Agency, 1 William Morris Pl, Beverly Hills, CA 90212, **Business Phone:** (310)859-4000.*

ADAMS, PAUL
Military pilot. **Personal:** Born in Greenville, SC. **Career:** Military pilot (retired); USAF, pilot, 1942-45, Pacific Air Div, Hickam Field, Honolulu, HI, supply officer, 1945-63; Lincoln High Sch, Lincoln, NE, shop teacher, 1963-84. **Orgs:** Kiwanis Builders Club; exec bd, Mad Dads. **Special Achievements:** Former Tuskeegee Airman. **Military Serv:** USAF, lt col, 1942-45. *

ADAMS, RICHARD MELVIN (RICK ADAMS)
School administrator. **Personal:** Born May 13, 1951, Pittsburgh, PA; son of Richard M Sr and J Marion; married Judy Duck; children: Amena C & Marcus T. **Educ:** Bowdoin Col, AB, govt & afro-am studies, 1973; Univ Pittsburgh, Grad Sch Pub & Int Affairs, attended 1974; Jones Int Univ, Master Bus Commun, 2005. **Career:** GMAC, field rep, 1974-75; Homewood-Brushton Community Improv Asn, field rep, 1975-76; Operation Better Block Inc, community develop specialist, 1976-85; Community Col Allegheny County, asst exec dean, 1985-97, asst pres, 1998, actg asst dean recruitment & outreach, currently. **Orgs:** Primary Care Health Serv Inc, vice chair, 1978-2000, pres, 2000-; bd mem, Dist I Pittsburgh Pub Schs, 1985-; reg vice chair, Nat Asn Neighborhoods, 1985-; bd mem, NE Region Coun Black Am Affairs, 1985-; bd dirs, Am Asn Sch Administrators; NAACP, Operation PUSH, TransAfrica; state chmn, Pa Nat Rainbow Coalition, 1986-; convener, W Pa Black Polit Assembly. **Honors/Awds:** Named one of 200 Most Influential Pittsburghers, Pittsburgh Press, 1983. **Home Addr:** 700 N Sheridan Ave, Pittsburgh, PA 15206. **Business Addr:** Assistant Dean of Recruitment & Outreach, Community College of Allegheny County, Allegheny Campus, 701 N Homewood Ave, Pittsburgh, PA 15208, **Business Phone:** (412)310-1600.

ADAMS, RICK. See ADAMS, RICHARD MELVIN.

ADAMS, ROBERT EUGENE
Educator. **Personal:** Born May 14, 1946, Richmond, VA; son of Thomas S and Daisy W; married Kathye J Gary, Dec 2, 2000; children: Shannon Marie. **Educ:** Norfolk State Univ, AS, 1969; Va State Univ, BS, 1972, MEd, 1990. **Career:** Imperial Plz, asst food serv mgr, 1972-73; Marriott Corp, mgr food serv, 1973-82; Creative Cuisine, owner/mgr, 1982-88; Northern Va Community Col, instr restaurant mgt prog, 1989-90; Va State Univ, instr, recruiter, 1990-2000; Morris Brown Col, instr, bus & hospitality admin dept, 1992-, interim chmn, 1994-96. **Orgs:** Am Dietetic Asn; Coun Hotel, Restaurant & Instnl Educ; Omega Psi Phi Frat, Psi Alpha Alpha Chap; secy, Int Food Execs Asn; Hist & Predominantly Black Col & Univs. **Honors/Awds:** Manager of the Year, Marriott Corp, 1980; Meritorious Service Award, Omega Psi Phi Fraternity Inc, 1982; Hospitality Diamonds of the Future, 1994; Va State Univ, Friend Human Ecol, 1995; Member of the Year, IFSEA, 1996 & 1997; Morris Brown Col, Outstanding Contributions Serv, Learning Prog, 1996. **Home Addr:** 5112 Hunterest Dr SW, Mableton, GA 30126.

ADAMS, ROBERT HUGO
Editor, publisher, writer. **Personal:** Born Dec 6, 1943, Washington, DC; son of Gerald H and Ella Mary Hodge; divorced; children: Tiffany K Adams. **Educ:** DC Teachers Col, Wash, DC, BS, 1967; Univ Hawaii, Honolulu, 1973. **Career:** Xerox Corp, Honolulu, HI, salesman, 1973-74; KGMB Radio & TV, Honolulu, salesman, writer, 1974-75; H R Adams & Assoc, Honolulu, owner, 1975-76; CS Wo Furniture, Honolulu, salesman, 1976-78; Levitts Furniture, Garden City, NY, salesman, 1978-80; New York Amsterdam News, Harlem, NY, acct exec, bus ed, 1980-81; Minority Business Review, Hempstead, NY, ed, publisher, 1981-; Econ Forum, ed; Articles: White House Conf of Small Business, 1986; African-Americans abused by corporations & agencies, 1988; Books: 15 Years of Minority Business Development, 1995; When WBLS Comes to Harlem, New York Times. **Orgs:** Omega Psi Phi Fraternity, 1962-; Asn Minority Enterprises New York, 1980-; Nat Minority Bus Coun, 1981-; Minority Bus Enterprise Week Planning Comn, 1984-; Nat Asn Minority Contractors, 1986-; New York Region Small Bus Admin Adv Coun, 1988-; mentor, Small Bus Enterprise Ctr, State Univ New York, Old Westbury, 1988-; adv, New York State Sci & Technol Prog, 1988-; Procurement Task Force, 100 Black Men Nassau/Suffolk, 1989-; chmn, Street Fair, Celebrate Hempstead 350th Anniversary; Congregational Church South Hempstead; bd dir, Uniondale Hispanic Civic Asn, 2000-; bd dir, The 100 Black Men Long Island; 2003-06. **Honors/Awds:** Writing Excellence Award, Advertising Club of New York, 1980; Outstanding Journalism Award, Assn Minority Enterprises of New York, 1983; Regional Minority Advocate of the Year, Minority Business Devel Agency, US Dept Commerce, 1987; Service Award, Equal Opportunity Commn Nassau County, 1988; African American Achievement Award, New York Million Dollar Boys Club, 1988; African Amerocan Award, United New Jersey Minority Business Brain Trust, 1989; began publishing first newspaper dedicated to minority business success, Minority Business Review, 1981; resulting in funding for the Apollo Theater, 1982; series of radio interviews, MBR Forum, 1989; Media Award, Natl Minority Bus Council, 1995; Business Advocacy Award, Brooklyn Minority Business Development Center, 1995; Media Advocacy Award, US Dept Commerce, Minority Business Develop Agency, NY Region, 1995; Certificate of Recog, Incorporated Village Hempstead & Town Hempstead, 1995. **Military Serv:** AUS, capt, 1968-72. **Business Addr:** Editor, Publisher, Minority Business Review, 236 Fulton Ave Suite 201, Hempstead, NY 11550, **Business Phone:** (516)486-4211.

ADAMS, RUSSELL LEE
Educator. **Personal:** Born Aug 13, 1930, Baltimore, MD; son of James Russell and Lilly B Adams; married Eleanor P; children: Sabrina & Russell. **Educ:** Morehouse Col, BA, minor hist & sociol, 1952; Univ Chicago, MA, polit sci, 1954, PhD, polit sci, 1971. **Career:** Cook County probation officer, 1958-64; NC Cent Univ, asst prof & chairperson dept polit sci, 1965-69; Newark-New Castle-Marshalton McKean Sch Dist, Jackson Pub Schs, consult, 1969-70; Fed City Col, assoc prof & actg chairperson div humanities, 1969-71; Howard Univ, Dept Afro-Am Studies, prof & chair, 1971-2005, prof emer, 2005-; Univ Pittsburgh, Ctr Deseg, consult, 1976-. **Orgs:** Chmn, Comm Status Blacks Prof Am Polit Sci Asn, 1974-77; Nat Asn Advan Colored People; bd ed, Prince Georges County, Curr Eval Pool, 1976-; consult, Wilmington DE Pub Schs, 1977; lectr & consult, US Info Agency, 1977; Nat Conf Black Polit Scientists; Nat Asn Study Afro-Am Life & Hist. **Honors/Awds:** George Washington Honor Medal, 1966. **Special Achievements:** Author of Great Negroes Past & Present, 1963-69, 1972, Leading American Negroes, 1965, Perceptual Difficulties Dev Political Science Varia, Spring 1976, publisher of

Black Studies Movement, Assessment Journal of Negro Education, 1977. **Home Addr:** 2414 Fairhill Dr, Suitland, MD 20746. **Business Addr:** Professor Emeritus, Howard University, Department of Afro-American Studies, 2400 6th St NW Founders Lib Rm 316, Washington, DC 20059-0002, **Business Phone:** (202)806-7242.

ADAMS, SAM AARON
Football player. **Personal:** Born Jun 13, 1973, Houston, TX; son of Sam Adams Sr. **Educ:** Tex A&M Univ, agricultural economics. **Career:** Seattle Seahawks, defensive tackle, 1994-99; Baltimore Ravens, defensive tackle, 2000-01; Oakland Raiders, defensive tackle, 2002; Buffalo Bills, defensive tackle, 2003-05; Cincinnati Bengals, defensive tackle, 2006; Everett Hawks, Nat Indoor Football League, owner; Denver Broncos, defensive tackle free agent, 2007-. **Honors/Awds:** Pro Bowl alternate, 1997; Hall of Fame, Texas A&M, 2001. **Business Phone:** (303)649-9000.*

ADAMS, SAMUEL LEVI, SR.
Educator, journalist. **Personal:** Born Jan 25, 1926, Waycross, GA; son of Joe Nathan (deceased) and Viola Virgil (deceased); married Elenora Willette Grimes; children: Carol W, Bruce L & Samuel L Jr. **Educ:** WVa State Col, BA 1948; Wayne State Univ, AB, 1950; Univ Minn, MA, 1954. **Career:** Educator, Journalist (retired); Atlanta Daily World, reporter, 1954-56; Des Moines Regis, copy ed, 1956-57; Gibbs-St Petersburg Jr Col, dir pubrels, 1958-60, part-time teacher, 1960-64; St Petersburg Times, reporter,1960-65; Univ Wis, Russell Sage Fel Behav Sci Writing, 1965-66; SouthernRegional Coun, dir res, 1965-66; Wis St Jour, corr, 1966-67; St PetersburgTimes, investigative reporter, 1967-68; Univ Wis, vis prof, 1968-69; UnivS Fla, asst prof, 1969-71; Dem Nat Comm, asst dir Minorities Div & asstpress sec, 1970-72; Univ KS, assoc prof jour, 1972-00; Hampton Univ, visprof jour, 1982-83; Univ Wis, vis prof jour, 1985-87; Univ KS Sch Jour &Mass Commun, prof emer. **Orgs:** Founder, dir Continuing Acad Cult Enrich Prog, 1962-64; First vpres,Greater St Petersburg Coun Churches, 1963-65; prog dir div & jointsessions San Diego Conv, 1974; Asn Educ Journ Head Minorities Div,1974-75; dir Gannett-AEJ Proj Enrichment of Jour Educ, 1975-80; pres & bdchmn, Nat Youth Commun Inc, 1977-82; dir, The Newspaper Fund's NatMinority Internship Prog, 1979-80; KU Tenure Study Task Force; Task ForceUniv Outreach; Minority Affairs Adv Bd; Am Asn Univ Prof; bd dir & educresource chmn, Jones Holloway-Bryan Found, 1986-; consult commun, AmnestyInt USA, 1988-92. **Honors/Awds:** Regional Award, Nat Conf Christians & Jews, 1962; Pulitzer Prize Award-,nominee in journ, 1964-65; Lane Bryant Awards, semi-finalist outstandingvolunteer serv, 1966; Hampton Jr Col Award, 1966; Green EyeshadeSweepstakes Award, Sigma Delta Chi Atlanta, 1969; state, local & regionalawards, jour; Award for Distinguished Serv to Journalism NC A&T State Univ1978; Distinguished Vis prof Hampton Univ, 1981-82; Ida B Wells Award,1983; "Blackening in the Media," in NUL's State of Black America, 1985;"Highways to Hope," in St Pete Times and Hohenburg's The New Front Page,1965; Partners in Progress Award, Nat Asn Black Journalists, 1990; Nat AsnBlack Journalists, Lifetime Achievement Award, 1997; United Minority MediaAsn, Distinguished Serv Journalism Award, 1996; UMMA Hall Media Fame,1998; Ida B Wells Award, 2002. **Military Serv:** AUS, field artillery survey & chem warfare specialist, 1950-52. **Home Addr:** 1304 McDonald St, Waycross, GA 31501. *

ADAMS, SHEILA J
Association executive. **Personal:** Born Jun 1, 1943, Cincinnati, OH; married Jan 1, 1963 (divorced); children (previous marriage): Ariana; married Alexander, Jan 1, 1992; children: Derek & Brian. **Educ:** Univ Cincinnati, BA, sociol. **Career:** Association exec (retired); City Cincinnati, Employ & Training div, chief planner, 1971-81; Pvt Indust Coun, pres, 1982-89; Urban League Greater Cincinnati, pres & chief exec officer, 1990-2003. **Orgs:** Bd mem, Key Bank, ChoiceCare Found; Downtown Cincinnati Inc; United Way Found; Cincinnati Youth Collaborative; Advocates Youth Educ; Family & C First Exec Comn; Black Career Women Inc; Cincinnati Links; Delegate Pres Clinton Summit Am Future, 1997; dir emer, Health Found Greater Cincinnati. **Honors/Awds:** Notable Black Alumni, Univ Cincinnati, 1984- 1997; Hall of Fame, Withrow High Sch, 1991; Delta Sigma Theta Econ Empowerment Award, 1995; Gem Award, Asn Women Commun Cincinnati Chap, 1997; Dr MLK Jr Dream Keeper Award, 1998; Distinguished Black Women Award, Black Women Sisterhood Action, 1999; Bridges Award, Cincinnati Bell Bldg, 2000; Joseph A Hall Award, Promoting Diversity.

ADAMS, SHEILA MARY
Consultant. **Personal:** Born Jun 7, 1947, Chicago, IL; daughter of Frank Ricks and Delores Lawrence Wasmund; married Alvin, Oct 23, 1968; children: Lara, Kristina, Stefani & Susan. **Educ:** De Paul Univ, Chicago, IL, BA, music, 1979; Off Ministry Formation, Chicago, IL, lay ministry, 1983. **Career:** Chicago Police Dept, Chicago, IL, junior clerk, 1968-71; US Treas Dept, Chicago, IL, clerk, 1973-74; Archdiocese Chicago, IL, elem teacher, 1979-90, Off Black Cath Ministries, exec 1990-91, Off Ethnic Ministries, 1991-2000, african am consult, 1991-98, dir African Am Ministry, 1998; Off Black Cath, african am consult, currently, BlackCatholicChicago.org, co founder & events ed, currently. **Orgs:** Regional coordr, Nat Black Cath Cong VII, VIII, IX, 1990-2002; chair, Bishop's Nat Adv Coun, 1989; Bishop's Nat Adv Coun, 1985-90; chair, Spirituality Com Archdiocesan Pastoral Coun, 1986-88; delegate; Nat Black Cath Cong VI, 1987; Cong VII, 1992; Cong VIII, 1998; Nat Asn Black Cath Adrs, secy, 1996-99; dir, Off Black Cath; dir, African Am Ministries. **Honors/Awds:** Archdiocesan Honoree, Fr Augustus Tolton Hon Award, 1987-88, Sr Thea Bowman Award, 1994; Dei Gloriam Award, 1999. **Business Addr:** African American Consultant, Office of Black Catholics, Archdiocese of Chicago, 155 E Superior St 2nd Fl, PO Box 1979, Chicago, IL 60611.

ADAMS, STEPHAN
Entrepreneur. **Educ:** Univ Calif, Berkeley, BS; Wright Inst, phD, psychol. **Career:** Adamation Inc, pres & chief exec officer, founder, 1984-. **Business Addr:** President, Chief Executing Officer, Adamation Inc, 1940 Webster St Suite 250, Oakland, CA 94612, **Business Phone:** (510)452-5252.*

ADAMS, T. PATTON
Government official, consultant, executive director. **Personal:** Born Feb 16, 1943, Columbia, SC; married Jacquelyn Hackett Culbertson; children: Thomas, John & Lucas. **Educ:** Wash & Lee Univ, BA, 1965; Univ SC, JD, 1968. **Career:** Columbia Zoning Bd Adjustments, bd mem, 1974-76; City Columbia, SC, city coun member, 1976-86, mayor, 1986-90; Army SC secy, civilian aide, 1986-2001, civilian aide emer, 2001-05; SC Comn Indigent Defense, exec dir, 2005-; pvt consult. **Orgs:** SC Bar Asn; Richland Co Bar Asn; SC Chamber Com; Columbia Visitors & Conv Bur; Nat Asn Criminal Defense Lawyers, Nat Legal Aid & Defender Asn; Am Legion; SC Off Indigent Defense; SC Veterans Mem Pk Comn. **Honors/Awds:** Distinguished Service Award, Munic Asn SC, 1987; Nat Distinguished Service Award, Asn AUS; States Order of the Palmetto. **Military Serv:** AUS, lt, 1961-65, capt, 1969-70; Bronze Star. **Business Addr:** Executive Director, South Carolina Commission on Indigent Defense, 1330 Lady St Suite 401, Columbia, SC 29201, **Business Phone:** (803)734-1343.

ADAMS, V TONI
Executive. **Personal:** Born Dec 13, 1946, Oakland, CA; married James L Robinson; children: Karla, Doyle, Todd & Vikki. **Educ:** Mills Col, BA, 1968; Oxford Univ, Eng, attended 1976; Calif State Univ, MPA, 1976; Golden Gate Univ, DPA. **Career:** UC Berkeley, cont ed spec, 1968-77; City Oakland, spec asst to mayor, 1977-84; Builders Mutual Suriety Co, chief finance officer, 1982-83; Alameda Co Off Educ, bd chmn & dir stud progs & serv, currently. **Orgs:** Grand juror, Alameda County Super Ct, 1973-74; bd dir, Calif Alcoholism Found, 1975-77; Alameda County Juvenile Delinquency Prev, 1976-78; bd mem, Displaced Homemakers Ctr, 1983-; bd dir, Oakland Conv Ctr Mgt Inc, 1983-; past pres, Oakland Conv & Visitors Bur; bd mem, Nat Forum for Black Pub Adminrs; vpres tourism, Nat Asn Black & Minority Chamber Com. **Honors/Awds:** Outstanding Service Education, Col Bounders Oakland, 1979; Outstanding Young Women of America, 1981,1983; Dick Spees Award for Tourism Promotion, 2005. **Business Phone:** (510)670-7747.

ADAMS, VASHONE LAVEY
Football player. **Personal:** Born Sep 12, 1973, Aorora, CO. **Educ:** Eastern Mich. **Career:** Cleveland Browns, defensive back, 1995; Baltimore Ravens, 1996; New Orleans Sts, 1997; Kansas City Chiefs, 1998; Dallas Cow boys, 1999. *

ADAMS, DR. VERNA MAY SHOECRAFT
School administrator. **Personal:** Born Jul 1, 1928, Toledo, OH; daughter of John Henry and Ogrietta Lee; married Fred (deceased); children: Jacqueline O Redd, Fred A Jr, Douglas F & Cynthia V McBride. **Educ:** Toledo Univ, St Francis Col, Ft Wayne, IN, BS, 1962, MS, educ, 1964; Ball State Univ,Muncie, IN, EdD, 1979. **Career:** Educator (retired); Ft Wayne Comm Schs, teacher, 1961-67, guid couns,consult teacher, 1966-68, elem teacher, 1967-71, elem prin, 1971-80, dirtitle I prog, 1980-82, Supplemental Instructional Prog, dir, 1982-89; StFrancis Col, Ft Wayne, IN, instr, lectr, 1964-74; Whitney Young Elem Sch,prin; Harmar Elem Sch, fac; Croniger Elem Sch, fac; Smart Elem Sch, prin. **Orgs:** Bd dirs, Parkview Hosp; bd dirs, Fort Wayne Found; bd dirs, Fort WaynePhilharmonic; Fort Wayne Philharmonic Outreach Comm; develop comm, TurnerChapel AME; trustee, Int Links Inc; NAACP, Urban League, Phi Delta KappaFt Wayne Chapter; Nat Alliance Black Sch Educ; cofounder, Fort WayneAlliance Black Sch Educ. **Honors/Awds:** Woman of the year, Ft Wayne Urban League, 1964; Woman of the year, KappaAlpha Psi Ft Wayne, Alumni Chap, 1976; Verna M. Adams educ financial asst prog excellence teacher educ, Lincoln Nat Bank & Fort Wayne Comm Sch,1989; Verna M. Adams Scholarship, FWCS, named in honor, 1989; Woman of the year, Zeta Phi Beta, Ft Wayne Chap; Service Award in the field of educ, DrMartin Luther King Jr Club Comm, 2002. **Special Achievements:** Scholarship named Verna M Adams Educ Financial Asst Prog for Excellence inTeacher Educ, First African-Am woman fac mem, St. Francis College, 1964;First African-American woman prin, Ft. Wayne Community Sch, 1971; FirstAfrican American woman director in the FWCS department of instruction,1980; First African American woman elementary consultant teacher for FWCS,1987. **Home Addr:** 3524 Autumn Lane, Fort Wayne, IN 46806.

ADAMS, WILLIE, JR.
Mayor, gynecologist. **Personal:** Born in Apalachicola, FL. **Educ:** Fla A&M Univ; Meharry Med Col, Nashville, med degree; Hurley Hosp, internship; Emory Univ, Sch Med, residency. **Career:** Pvt pract, Obstet & Gynec, 1973; Dipl Am Bd of Obstet & Gynec; Am Col Obstet & Gynec; Gov's Coun Maternal & Infant Care; City Albany, mayor, 2004-; Ga Dept Community Affairs, bd dir, 2005-. **Orgs:** Pres, Stud Govt Asn, Fla A&M Univ; founder & dir, First Nat Bank S Ga; Albany Dougherty Inner City Authority; Dougherty County Bd Educ; Dougherty Aviation Comn; Ga Chamber Com; Phi Beta Sigma Fraternity; Adv Bd Salvation Army; bd dir, Mag Mutual Ins Co; Shiloh Baptist Church; Am Asn Gynec Laparoscopists; Am Med Asn; Am Fertil Soc; Ga State Med Soc. **Honors/Awds:** Honored by: Albany State Univ; Dept Army; Kiwanis Club. **Military Serv:** USAR, second Lt, Lt Colonel (retired). **Home Addr:** 320 W Second Ave, Albany, GA 31701, **Home Phone:** (229)439-7721. **Business Addr:** Mayor, City of Albany, Office of the Mayor, 222 Pine Ave, PO Box 447, Albany, GA 31702-0447, **Business Phone:** (229)431-3244.*

ADAMS, YOLANDA
Gospel singer. **Personal:** Born Aug 27, 1962, Houston, TX; married Tim Crawford, 1997 (divorced); children: Taylor Ayana; married Frank Fountain; children: 1. **Educ:** Teaching degree & cert; Howard Univ, divinity stud. **Career:** Gospel music rec artist, 1987-; Albums: Just as I Am, 1987; Through the Storm, 1991; Save the World, 1993; Bring It to Jesus, 1993; More Than a Melody, 1995; Yolanda.Live in Washington, 1996; Songs From the Heart, 1998; Mountain High Valley Low, 1999; The Best of Yolanda Adams, 1999; Christmas with Yolanda Adams, 2000; The Experience, 2001; Believe, 2001; The Praise and Worship Songs of Yolanda Adams, 2003; Day by Day, 2005; The Essential Yolanda Adams, 2006. **Honors/Awds:** Soul Train Music Award, More Than Melody, 1995; Grammy Nomination, Yolanda.Live in Washington, 1996; Two Stellar Gospel Awards, 2002; Grammy Award, Be Blessed, 2006; Gospel-Indust Stellar Awards; Grammy Award, Victory, 2007. *

ADAMS-DUDLEY, LILLY ANNETTE
Educator, consultant. **Personal:** Born Jun 7, 1950, Lochgelly, WV; daughter of James Alfred Adams Sr and Jerlena Paulanne Williams; married Jerry Lee Dudley Sr; children: Jerry Jr. **Educ:** Canisius Col, BA, 1972, MA, 1976, MS, 1984. **Career:** Hampton City Schs, Eng teacher, 1972-73; Buffalo Pub Schs, Eng teacher, 1974-75; Canisius Col, lang arts specialist, 1975-78, asst dir, 1978-80, writing lab instr, 1982-84, reading & study skills instr, 1981-, dir canisius opportunity progs educ, 1980-, consult on self-esteem devel & multiculturalism in workplace, assoc dean & dir, canisius opportunity progs educ, currently. **Orgs:** Policy bd mem, Consortium Niagara Frontier, 1980-; treas & campus rep, AJCU Conf Minority Affairs, 1980-81; Buffalo/Rochester regional rep, HEOP Prof Orgn, 1980-; Am Asn Black Women Higher Educ; Am Soc Training & Devel; Am Asn Univ Women; Nat Asn Female Execs; seminar developer & co-leader Today's Prof Woman, Developing Attitudes for Success; Self-Esteem & Your Success; Prof Black Women & Success; Am Soc Prof & Exec Women, 1986-. **Honors/Awds:** Martin Luther King Jr Full Academic Scholarship, 1968-72; Canisius Col Di Gamma Honor Soc, 1983; workshop given: Managering the Multicultural Workforce 1989; Management Award for Western NY, YWCA, 2004. **Business Phone:** (716)888-2575.

ADAMS-ENDER, CLARA LEACH
Military leader, entrepreneur. **Personal:** Born Jul 11, 1939, Willow Springs, NC; daughter of Otha Leach and Caretha Bell; married F Heinz, 1981; children: Sven Ingo. **Educ:** NC A&T Univ, BS, nursing, 1961; Univ Minn, MS, med surgical nursing, 1969; Army Command & Gen Staff Col, master's, military arts & sci, 1976. **Career:** AUS, beginning 1963, Fort Belvoir, commanding gen, Military Dist, Wash, DC, dep commanding gen, 1991-93; Georgetown Univ, adj prof; Oakland Univ, adj prof; CAPE (Caring About People with Enthusiasm) Assocs Inc, founder, pres & ceo, currently. **Orgs:** Fel, Am Acad Nurses; Defense Adv Comt Women Servs, 1994-; military aide-de-camp, State Va, 2003-. **Honors/Awds:** Distinguished Serv Medal; Legion of Merit; Meritorius Serv Medal; Cross of Honor in Gold, German Army; Lifetime Achievement Award, Nat Black Nurses Asn. **Special Achievements:** Co-author: My Rise to the Stars: How a Sharecropper's Daughter Became an Army General, 2002; one of the highest ranking African-American women in U.S. Army history. **Business Addr:** President, Chief Executive Officer, Caring About People with Enthusiasm (CAPE) Associates Inc, 3088 Woods Cove Lane, Woodbridge, VA 22192, **Business Phone:** (703)497-3088.*

ADAMS-GASTON, DR. JAVAUNE
Executive director, educator. **Educ:** Univ Dubuque; Loras Col, Masters degree, Psychol; Iowa State Univ, PhD, Psychol. **Career:** Univ Md, staff psychologist coun ctr, Dept Intercollegiate Athletics, asst athletic dir, Undergrad Studies, assoc dean, Letters & Sci Dept, dir, Univ Career Ctr, exec dir, currently, Coun & Personnel Serv Dept, affil asst prof, vpres, currently.

ADAMS-MAILLIAN, AUBREY
Public relations executive. **Career:** Essence Mag, dir corp pub rels; Andrea Jovine's fashion line, pub rels dir.

ADAMS PECK, DR. DOROTHY
Administrator. **Career:** AME Church, sr bishop, currently; Women's Missionary Soc, pres, currently. **Orgs:** Bd mem Bread the World. **Business Addr:** President, Women's Missionary Society, 1134 11th St NW, Washington, DC 20001, **Business Phone:** (202)371-8886.

ADDAMS, ROBERT DAVID
Lawyer, college teacher. **Personal:** Born Feb 12, 1957, Chicago, IL. **Educ:** Princeton Univ, AB, 1978; Columbia Univ Grad Sch Jour, MSJ, 1980; Columbia Univ Sch Law, JD, 1982. **Career:** Goodman, Eden, Millender & Bedrosian, assoc atty, 1982-86; Nat Conf Black Lawyers, assoc dir, 1986; City Col NY, revson prof, 1986-87; Asn Legal Aid Atty, exec dir, 1986-92; Inst Mediation & Conflict Resolution, dir & pres, currently; Brooklyn Col, vis distinguished prof, Belle Zeller, 1994-. **Orgs:** State Bar Mich, 1982-92; Nat Lawyers Guild, 1982-86; Am Bar Asn, 1982-84; Nat Bar Asn, 1982-84; Wolverine Bar Asn, 1982-86; bd dirs, Nat Conf Black Lawyers, 1985-87; Metrop Black Bar Asn, 1992; bd dirs, NY State Mediation Asn, 1993-94. **Honors/Awds:** Sr Thesis Prize, Dept Afro-Am Studies, Princeton Univ, 1978. **Business Phone:** (212)643-0711.*

ADDEI, ARTHELLA HARRIS
School administrator. **Personal:** Born in St Louis, MO; daughter of Jesse K and Iona L; married Kwabena A, Nov 28, 1970; children: D'Asante. **Educ:** Harris Teacher Col, St Louis, MO, BA; Columbia Univ NYC, MA; CUNY, MS; Long Island Univ, prof dipl educ admin supervision. **Career:** New Perspectives WWRL Radio NYC, producer & moderator; Essence Mag, contributing ed; NY Pub Schs, guidance counr; Manpower Prog NYC, supvr counr; St Louis Pub Sch, teacher; Community Sch Dist 19 NY Pub Schs, dist supvr; NY Pub Sch System, prin; Ethan Allen Elem Sch, prin; Dept Sch Admin, adj prof, currently. **Orgs:** Mayor's Task Force/Early Childhood, 1989-90; prog chairperson, NY St Div Youth Adv Brd & Youth Serv Action Team; Alpha Kappa Alpha Sor; Women's Aux Nassau Co Med Soc AMA; Women's Auxiliary Nat Med Assn; CSA Coun Supvrs& Admins, NY City; NYESPA Prins Assn. **Honors/Awds:** Hon Education Fraternity, Kappa Delta Pi, 1962; Award for Serv Recognition, Westbury Mothers Group Westbury Long Island, 1974; Community Service, Assn Study African-Am Life & Hist, 1974; Featured Administrator,NY Brd Educ Newsletter, Impact Star, Winter, 1991; Administrator of the Year, Community Sch Dist 19, Brooklyn, NY, 1993; Featured Alumnus in the Intl House World Newsletter, November, 1996. **Home Addr:** 475 Glen Cove Rd, Roslyn, NY 11576.

ADDERLEY, HERB ANTHONY
Football player, executive. **Personal:** Born Jun 8, 1939, Philadelphia, PA; son of Charles and Rene White; married Bell; children: Toni. **Educ:** Mich State Univ, BS, educ, 1961. **Career:** Football player (retired), executive; Green Bay Packers, cornerback, 1961-69; Dallas Cowboys, 1970-72; Giant Step Rec Co, vpres. **Orgs:** Charter mem, Sigma Chap Omega Psi Phi Fraternity. **Honors/Awds:** Super Bowl, 1967, 1968, 1971; All-Star Game, 1963-67; Pro Bowl, 1963-67; Inducted into Football Hall of Fame, 1980; Green Bay Packer Hall of Fame. **Military Serv:** AUS, 1962-66.

ADDERLY, T. C., JR.
Manager. **Personal:** Born in Miami, FL; son of Bertha L. and T.C. Sr; children: Beth, Andrew, Janine, Ashlee. **Educ:** Miami Dade Community Col, Miami, FL, AA, 1980; Univ Miami, Miami, FL, Masters, bus, 1991. **Career:** Fl Power & Light, Miami, FL, human res mgr, 1969-91; pres, Y's Men Intl, 1979-83; City Miami Beach, Dept Human Res, FL, human res dir, 1992-. **Orgs:** Bd Mem & vice chmn, Family Christian Asn Am Inc, 1979-; mentor chmn, Ocean Reef Mentor Prog, 1986-91; Amigos De Ser, 1983-; scholar chmn, Miami dade Chamber Com, 1981-. **Honors/Awds:** Am's Best & Brightest Young Bus & Prof, Dollars & Sense, 1989; Leadership Miami, Greater Miami, Chamber, 1980; Membership Chmn App Award, Family Christian Asn Am Inc, 1990; Black Achiever, Family Christian Asn Am Inc, 1984. **Business Addr:** Human Resoures Director, City of Miami Beach, Human Resources Dept, 1700 Convention Ctr Dr, Miami Beach, FL 33139, **Business Phone:** (305)673-7524.*

ADDERTON, DONALD V
Editor. **Educ:** Shaw Univ, Raleigh. **Career:** Sun Herald; Delta Democrat Times; Hattiesburg Am, asst managing ed, 2004-. **Orgs:** Vpres, Miss Freedom Info; bd dirs, Assoc Press Managing Ed. **Business Addr:** Assistant Managing Editor, Hattiesburg American, 825 N Main St, Hattiesburg, MS 39401, **Business Phone:** (601)584-3061.

ADDISON, ADELE
Singer. **Personal:** Born Jul 24, 1925, New York, NY; married Norman Berger (died 2005). **Educ:** Westminster Choir Col, BMus, 1946; Berkshire Music Ctr; Univ Massachussets, dhv, 1963. **Career:** Town Hall New York City, recital debut, 1952; State Univ NY, voice teacher; Eastman Sch Music, voice teacher; Aspen Music Festival & Sch,voice teacher; Aspen Music Festival, fac artist, 1956; New Eng City Ctr Wash Opera Co; orchestral & engagements w/symphonies Boston, Cleveland; NY Philharmonic, Nat Chicago, Pittsburgh, Indianapolis, LA, SF; World Premiere performances Incl John La Montaigne's Fragments, Song of Songs w/New Haven Symphony, 1959, Porgy & Bess Original Film Soundtrack, 1959; Foss' Time Cycle w/NY Philharmonic, 1960; Poulenc's Gloria w/Boston Symphony, 1961; Philharmonic Hall Lincoln Ctr, soloist, 1962; US, Can, Soviet Union, recital tours, 1963; Aspen Music Inst, pvt voice lessons, 1975; Foss, Time Cycle; Phorion; Song of Songs, 1997; Mahler, Symphonies Nos 2,5 & 8, 1997; Bach Clavierubung Part 3 (ii), 1999; Bach, Mass in Bminor, 1999; Bach, St Matthew Passion, 1999; Debussy, Le Martyre de St Sebastien, 1999; Handel, Messiah, 1999; Handel, Ode for St Cecilia's Day, 1999; The Essential Beethoven, 1999; Albums: Porgy & Bess, 1958;Beethoven, Symphony No 9, 1988; Beethoven, Symphony No 9 Fidelio Ov, 1991; Beethoven, Symphonies & Overtures, 1992; Gershwin, 1994; Vaughan Williams, Orchestral Works, 1994. **Orgs:** Am Acad Teachers Singing; chmn, Voice dept, Manhattan Sch Music. **Honors/Awds:** Honorary doctorate, Manhattan Sch Music, 2001. **Home Addr:** 98 Riverside Dr, New York, NY 10024. *

ADDISON, CAROLINE ELIZABETH
College teacher, dean (education). **Personal:** Born Nov 14, 1938, Brooklyn, NY; married Wallace O Kelly Peace; children: Douglas K & Rock P. **Educ:** Bronx Community Col, AAS, 1964; Long Island Univ, BSN, 1972, MS, 1974; New York Univ, MPA, 1976; Walden Univ, PhD, 1978; Wayne State Univ, EdD, 1986. **Career:** St Joseph's Col, dean fac, 1976-78; Passaic Community Col, dir nursing & allied health prog, 1978-80; Va State Univ, dean & dir nursing, 1980-81;Univ Detroit, dir & chair nursing educ, 1981-; Univ Phoenix, Mich Campus, dir. **Orgs:** Nat League Nursing, 1964-, Am Nursing Asn, 1964-, Mich Asn Cols Nursing, 1981-; Mich Holistic Asn, 1983-; League Women Voters, 1984-; Wellness Network, 1986. **Special Achievements:** Selected Factors Related to Admission and Retention of Adult Registered Nurses. **Home Addr:** 29264 Franklin Hills Dr, Southfield, MI 48034-1149.

ADDISON, JAMES DAVID
Business owner, automotive executive. **Personal:** Born Jan 8, 1949, Shelby, NC; son of Inez Mildred and Jimmie Lee; married Marie Yolene Pierre, Mar 27, 1982; children: Jessica Marie & Jennifer Maureen. **Career:** Addison Auto Parts, pres, 1987-. **Business Addr:** President, Addison Auto Parts, 3908 Pennsylvania Ave SE, Washington, DC 20020, **Business Phone:** (202)581-2900.

ADDISON, RAFAEL
Basketball player, college teacher, basketball coach. **Personal:** Born Jul 22, 1964, Jersey City, NJ. **Educ:** Syracuse Univ, BA, commun, 1986. **Career:** Phoenix Suns, 1986-87; Livorno, Italy, 1987-91; NJ Nets, 1992-93; Benetton, Italy, 1993-94; Detroit Pistons, 1994-95; Charlotte Hornets, 1995-97; Snyder High Sch, head basketball coach, 2002-05; Jersey City St Univ, currently. **Orgs:** Vol, Spec Olympics; Fannie Mae Found; US Olympic Basketball Team, 1982. **Honors/Awds:** Victor Hanson Medal of Excellence, Syracuse Univ; Most Valuable Player,Catholic Youth Orgn; inducted, Hudson Co Sports Hall of Fame, 2004; Syracuse All Century Team, 2000. **Special Achievements:** Pub speaker. **Business Phone:** 888-441-6528.*

ADDISON, TERRY HUNTER, JR.
School administrator. **Personal:** Born May 15, 1950, Memphis, TN; son of Terry Sr and Carsaunder Goosby; married Michele Ann Walker, Mar 9, 1985; children: Terry III & Matthew Kenneth. **Educ:** Univ Minn, Minneapolis, BA, 1971, MA, 1973. **Career:** ABC Prog Carleton Col, instr, 1972; Macalester Col, Eng Dept, instr, 1972; Augsburg Col, Minority Prog dir, 1972-73; Minneapolis Urban League St Acad, instr, 1979-81; Macalester Col, coord minority prog, 1981-84; Univ Rhode Island, dir minority student serv, 1984; Multicultural Student Serv, dir, 1984-93; Ctr Non-Violence, Counseling Ctr, asst dir, dir, 1993-95; Kent County YMCA, Greater Providence YMCA, assoc exec dir, 1995-97; Intown Providence YMCA, Greater Providence YMCA, exec dir, 1997-00; Johnson & Wales Univ, dean of students; Brown Univ, assoc dean student life, currently. **Orgs:** Bd Dir, Leadership RI; bd dirs, Sojourner House; Omega Psi Phi Frat; Urban League, NAACP; Asn Prof YMCA, 1976-; Kent County YMCA, bd dir, 2000-; Nat Asn Sch Personnel, NASPA, 2000; Asn Student Judicial Affairs, 2001; Warwick City Affirmative Action Equal Employment Opportunity, comnr. **Honors/Awds:** Positive Image Award, Minneapolis Urban League, 1984; Henry L Williams Memorial Award, Univ Minnesota; Awareness Award, 1987, Leadership Award, 1989, USN Recruiting Dist, Boston; Leadership Rhode Island, Lambda Class, 1991; Inductee Golden Key Nat Honor Soc, 1992; Inductee Order of Omega Nat Honor Soc, 1992; Leadership RI, David L Sweet Award, 1996; Man of the Year, Omega Psi Phi, Sigma Nu Chap, 2000. **Military Serv:** USMC, pfc, 1976-77. **Business Addr:** Associate Dean, Brown University, Office of Students Life, 20 Benevolent St, Providence, RI 02912, **Business Phone:** (401)863-9579.*

ADDY, TRALANCE OBUAMA
Executive. **Personal:** Born Aug 24, 1944, Kumasi, Ghana; son of Matthew Biala Addy (deceased) and Docea L Baddoo Addy (deceased); married Jo Alison Phears, May 26, 1979; children: Nii Mantse, Miishe, Dwetri, Naakai. **Educ:** Swarthmore Col, BA, chem, BS, mech eng, 1969; Univ Mass, Amherst, MSME, PhD, 1974; Harvard Bus Sch, advan mgt prog, 1987. **Career:** Scott Paper Co, Philadelphia, PA, sr res proj eng, 1973-76, res scientist, 1976-79, prog leader, 1979-80; Surgikos Inc, Johnson & Johnson, Arlington, TX, dir appl res, 1980-85, dir technol venture develop, 1986-88, ASP div, vpres, gen mgr, 1988-95, ASP, pres, 1995-98, int vpres, 1998-01; Plebys Int LLC, founder, pres & chief exec officer, currently. **Orgs:** Teacher, Upward Bound, 1967-73; Am Soc of Mech Eng, 1979-; Am Asn Advan Sci, 1983-; Black & Jewish Dialogue Dallas, 1986-92; chmn, co-chmn, Surgikos United Way Campaign, 1985-86; fel, AIMBE, 1997; bd dirs, United Way; bd mem, Sickle Cell Disease Asn Am; adv bd, Univ NC, Kenan-Flagler Bus Sch, Ctr Sustainable Enterprise; Johnson & Johnson, Global Mgt Comn; Sigma Xi. **Honors/Awds:** Johnson & Johnson Entrepreneurial Achievement Award, 1986; One of 125 Alumni to Watch, Univ Mass, Amherst, 1988; inventor on 12 US patents. **Special Achievements:** First person to receive both BA & BS degrees simultaneously from Swarthmore; author, several publ nonconventional food resources & prod. **Business Addr:** Founder, President & Chief Executive Officer, Plebys International LLC, 9 Orchard Rd Suite 111, Lake Forest, CA 92979, **Business Phone:** (949)716-5792.*

ADEGBILE, DR. GIDEON SUNDAY ADEBISI
Physician. **Personal:** Born May 18, 1941, Iree, Nigeria; son of Rev John and Sarah; children: Lisa, Titilayo & Babalola. **Educ:** Va Union Univ, BS, cum laude, 1966; Meharry Med Col, MD, 1971. **Career:** Good Samaritan Hosp, intern, 1971-72; Drexel Health Ctr, community health physician, 1972-73; PEG Inc, emergency physician, 1972-75; Wright State Univ, Sch Med, clinic instr, 1975-79, from asst clinic prof to clinic prof, 1979-92; pvt practice, physician, 1973-; Free Pke Med Ctr, Gen & Family Practice, currently. **Orgs:** Pres, Gem City Med Dental & Pharm Soc, 1978-80; chmn bd, Dayton Contemp Dance Co, 1978-80; chmn, Horizon Med Prog, 1978-; trustee, Montgomery County Med Soc, 1978; bd mem, Adv Ment Health Bd, Good Samaritan Hosp & Health Ctr, 1979-85; chmn, Long Term Care Commuity Region II Med Review Corp, 1979-81; secy, Buckeye Med Asn, 1980-82; House Delegate Nat Med Asn, 1980-91; chmn, Qual Assurance Comt, St Elizabeth Med Ctr, 1980-82, 1984; bd mem, Region II Review Corp, 1981-84, exec bd mem, 1982-84; med dir, Christel Manor Nursing Homes; Am Acad Family Physicians; Ore Acad Family Physicians; Ohio State Med Asn; Nat Med Asn; Montgomery County Med Soc; Nat Asn Advan Colored People; Alpha Phi Alpha Fraternity; Sigma Pi Phi Fraternity; Dem Bapt; Miami Valley Racquet Club; bd mem, Dayton Area Health Plan, 1985-92; pres, Selectmen, 1986-87; secy, Montgomery County Med Soc, 1987; chmn, Dept Family Practice, GSH & Health Ctr, 1987-88; chmn, Credentials & Accreditation Comt, St Elizabeth Med Ctr, 1987-88, 1995-96, chief staff, 1993-94, bd mem, PHO, 1994-; pres, Buckeye Med Asn, 1987-89; med dir, Dept Archaeol & Hist Preserv, 1994-, bd mem, Dayton Area Am Red Cross, 1994-. **Honors/Awds:** Certificate of Appreciation, Christel Manor Nursing Home, 1977. **Business Addr:** Physician, Free Pike Medical Center, Private Practice, 4001 Free Pke, Dayton, OH 45416.

ADELEKAN, TAHIRA GITTENS
Executive. **Career:** C Hosp Philadelphia, behavioral pediatric fel, currently. **Orgs:** Rep, Res Action Group; Comm Interns & Residents; Team of Scientists & Health Care Profs Investigating Down Syndrome. **Honors/Awds:** Doris Millman Award for excellence, State Univ NY Health Sci Ctr. **Business Addr:** Developmental & Behavioral Pediatric Fellow, Childrens Hosp Philadelphia, Childrens Seashore House, Child Develop Prog Rm 5, 34Th St Civic Ctr Blvd, Philadelphia, PA 19104, **Business Phone:** (215)590-7057.*

ADESUYI, DR. SUNDAY ADENIJI
Educator. **Personal:** Born Jun 27, 1948, Igbajo, Oyo, Nigeria; son of Jacob Owolabi and Mary Ojuolape. **Educ:** Howard Univ, Wash, DC, BS hon, 1974, PhD, 1980. **Career:** Howard Univ, Chem Dept, teaching asst, 1974-75, teaching fel, 1974-78, instr, 1978-79; St Paul's Col, Sci & Math Dept, asst prof, 1979-83, Pan-Hellenic, coun, 1986-2001, 2002-, interim provost, acad vpres, actg pres, 1988, interim vpres, Acad Affairs & provost, 1999-2000, Dept Natural Sci & Math, prof & chair, 2001-, fac, Athletics Rep, currently; Med Col Va, Dept Pharmacol, res assoc, 1983-84. **Orgs:** Pres, Grad Student Asn, 1976-78; exec bd mem, US Student Asn, 1977-78; co-chmn, Teaching Effectiveness Sub Comn; Howard Univ's Steering Comn Self-Study, 1977-79; coordr, Sci & Math Fair, St Paul's Col, 1980-82; Am Chem Soc, 1976-; coordr, Annual Project, Serv Elderly People, Lawrenceville, VA, 1981-; found & adv, Xi Rho Chap, Phi Beta Sigma, 1983-; adv, Sci & Math Club, St Paul's Col, 1984-; fac rep to bd trustees, St Paul's Col, 1985-88, 1996-98; adv, Pan-Hellenic Coun, St Paul's Col, 1986-; adv, Int Stud Asn, St Paul's Col, 1986; Presidential Search Comn, St Paul's Col, 1986; chmn, Provost Search Comn, St Paul's Col, 1987; Steering Comt, Self-Study, St Paul's Col, 1987-80, 1998-; chmn, Inst Purpose Comn, Self-Study, St Paul's Col, 1987-80, chmn, Educational Prog Comn, 1998-; chmn, Athletic Comn, St Paul's Col, 1988-; fac Athletic Chair, CIAA, 1988-; vpres, Northern Div, CIAA, 1992-94; Southern Asn Col & Sch Vis Team Erskine Col, 1992; Miles Col, 1993; Campbellsville

Col, 1994; Berea Col, 1995; Anderson Col, 1997; Our Lady Lake Col, 1998; deacon, trustees bd, First Bapt Church; Sigma Pi Phi Fraternity, CIAA Basketball Tournament Comn, 1990; parliamentarian, CIAA Fac Athletics Rep Assoc, 1994-, pres, 1997-; mem bd dirs, Nat Asn Med Minority Educrs Inc, 1994-98; chair, Nat Comnunications, ed-in-chief newsletter, 1994-98; SACS Vis Team to Huston-Tillotson Col, 2000; pres, CIAA Conf, 2002-; Div II Mgt Coun, Nat Collegiate Athletic Asn, 2002-; admin review sub Comn, Nat Collegiate Athletic Asn, 2002-, initial eligibility waiver review Comn, 2002- res comn, 2002-; vis team to Erskine Col, Southern Asn Col & Sch, 2002. **Honors/Awds:** Most Outstanding Graduate Student, Grad Student Asn, Howard Univ, 1978; Presial Silver Award, Howard Univ Stud Asn, 1978; Appreciation Award, Sophomore class, St Paul's Col, 1979-80; Student Merit Award, Student Body, St Paul's Col, 1982, 1983; Most Outstanding Dept Faculty Member, Sci & Math Club, St Paul's Col, 1982; 1 Supporter Award, Tennis Team, St Paul's Col, 1982; Appreciation Award, Sr Class, St Paul's Col, 1983; Presidential Medal, Outstanding Contributions to St Paul's Col, 1988; Excellence in Academy Advising Award, St Paul's Col, 1990; Sears-Roebuck Faculty of the Year, 1990-91; UNCF Distinguished Leadership Award, 1991, Meritorious Service Award, 1992; Sunbelt Video Sports & CIAA Partnership Award, 1993; CIAA Outstanding Service Award, 1994; Appreciation Award, SPC Athletic Dept, 1995; Certificate Of Appreciation, St Paul's Col, 1998; Appreciation Award, US Dept Com, 1999; 20-yr Service Award, St Paul Col, 1999; 15-Yr Service Award as Dept Chair, St Paul Col, Dept Natural Sci & Math, 1999; Certificate Of Appreciation, UNCF, 1999, 2000; Leadership & Encouragement Award, St Paul's Col, Upward Bound Prog, 2000. **Home Addr:** PO Box 71, Lawrenceville, VA 23868. **Business Addr:** Professor, Chairman, St Pauls College, Department Natural Sci & Math, 115 College Dr, Lawrenceville, VA 23868, **Business Phone:** (434)848-6484.

ADEYEMI, BAKARI (DESMOND MURRAY)
Educator. **Personal:** Born Apr 21, 1960, Queens, NY; son of James Murray and Elizabeth; married Sandra Alexander-Murray, Jun 29, 1997; children: Deyami Murray & Alexis Alexander-Murray. **Educ:** State Univ NY New Paltz, BA, 1982. **Career:** New Paltz Sch Dist, teacher, 1985-87; DJ Realization & DJ Unique, mgr; Marist Col, asst dir HEOP prog, 1987-90, asst dir field experience, 1990-, Affirmative Action adv comm chmn, currently; Blue Ice Entertainment, chief exec officer. **Orgs:** Promotions dir, Ambiance Productions; adv bd, Poughkeepsie Jour, multi cult affairs community; pub rels chair, African Am Mens Asn; founding mem, Simba, 1991-; co-founder, Poughkeepsie Unity B-Ball Classic, 1985; Order Feather Fraternity; Order Bonnet Fraternity. **Honors/Awds:** Educator of the Year, Inroads Inc; honoree, 3rd Annual Prestige Award; A Partner in Education Award honoree, Inroads Inc; Distinguished Service Award, Marist Col. **Home Addr:** 9 Waldorf Pl, Poughkeepsie, NY 12601, **Home Phone:** (845)473-7370. **Business Addr:** Assistant Director of Field Experience, Marist College, 3399 N Rd, Poughkeepsie, NY 12601, **Business Phone:** (845)575-3547.

ADEYIGA, DR. ADEYINKA A.
Educator, college administrator. **Personal:** Born Jan 20, 1948, Irolu, Nigeria; son of Alhaja Oladunni Apadiya-Osinbowale and Alhaji Adeyiga Osinbowale; married Abidemi Adibi, Dec 11, 1975; children: Adeleke, Adebunmi & Adetayo. **Educ:** Tenn Tech Univ, Cookeville, BS, 1974; Univ Mont, Columbia, MS, 1976; Okla State Univ, Stillwater, PhD, 1980. **Career:** Okla State Univ, Fluid Properties Res Inc, res asst, 1979-80; EI DuPont De Nemours Co, res engr, 1981-82; Shell Petroleum Develop, reservoir engr, 1982-84; Va State Univ, asst prof, 1984-85; Hampton Univ, assoc prof chem engineering, head engineering, prof chem engineering & dir DOE-Massie Chair Excellence, currently. **Orgs:** Chief consult, Padson Engineering Co, 1983-84; Engineering Deans Coun HBCU, 1986-; State Va Engineering Dean Coun, 1986-; Am Inst Chem Engrs; Am Chem Soc; AAAS; Omega Chi Epsilon; Soc Petrol Engrs; Am Soc Engineering Educ. **Honors/Awds:** US Black Engineer Career Communication Group Award, 1987. **Special Achievements:** He has authored and/or co-authored over 45 publications in this field; Vapor-liquid equil co-efficient for acid gas constituents and physical solvents, 1980; equilibrium constants for physical solvents in naturalgas, 1980; a manual of chemical engineering labs, 1988; evaluation of on-board hydrogen storage for aircraft, 1989; catalytic gasification ofcoal chars by non-transition metal catalyst, 1986. **Business Addr:** Professor of Chemical Engineering, Director, Hampton University, School of Engineering & Technology, Olin Engineering Bldg Suite 318, Hampton, VA 23668, **Business Phone:** (757)727-5289.

ADEYIGA, DR. OLANREWAJU MUNIRU
Physician. **Personal:** Born Sep 30, 1949, Irolu, Nigeria; married Mosekunola Omisakin; children: Adebowale, Oladunni, Adeniyi & Temitope. **Educ:** Southern Ill Univ, Edwardsville, BA, 1973, MSc, 1975; Howard Univ, Col Med, MD, 1979. **Career:** SIP Prog, Southern Ill Univ, vis lectr, 1976-77; Howard Univ Hosp, instr, attending, 1985-86; Columbia Hosp Women, attending 1985-; Wash Hosp Ctr, attending, 1985-; Group Health Asn, physician; Howard Univ Hosp, Dept Obstet & Gynec, dir & asst prof, currently, interim chair, 2002-. **Orgs:** AMA, 1976-, ACOG, 1986-. **Honors/Awds:** Dipl, Nat Bd Med Exam, 1981, Am Bd Obstet/Gynec, 1986; Fel, Am Col Obstet/Gynec, 1987. **Business Addr:** Professor, Interim Chair, Howard University Hospital, Department of Obstetrics & Gynecology, 2041 Georgia Ave NW Suite 3200, Washington, DC 20060, **Business Phone:** (202)865-4164.

ADIELE, DR. MOSES NKWACHUKWU
Executive director, government official. **Personal:** Born Jun 22, 1951, Umuahia, Nigeria; son of Robert and Virginia; married Vickie I Eseonu Adiele, Jul 7, 1984; children: Elizabeth, Bobby & Casey. **Educ:** Ga Inst Tech, BSHS, 1976; Howard Univ, MD, 1980; Johns Hopkins Univ, MPH, 1981; Uniformed Serv Univ Health Sci, Bethesda, MD, cert armed forces combat casualty care course, 1990; Acad Health Sci, San Antonio, TX, cert officer advan course, 1990; Fort Leavenworthe, Kansas, AUS command & gen staff officer course, 1993. **Career:** Baltimore City Health Dept, pub health clinician, 1980-81; Howard Univ, med house officer residency family pract, 1981-84; Richmond City Health Dept, asst dir pub health, 1984-86; VI State Health Dept, dist health dir, 1986-90; Va Dept Med Assistance Serv, Richmond, dir med support, 1990-; Dipl Nat Bd Med Examr, Fed Licensure Examr Med Bd. **Orgs:** Pres, bd dirs, Asn African Physicians N Am, 1981-84; prof mem, fel Am & VI Asn Family Physicians, 1982-; bd adv, Int United Black Fund, 1984-89; Richmond Med Soc, 1984-90; VI Pub Health Asn, 1984; Richmond Acad Med, 1986-90; US Mil Res Officers Asn, 1988-; Am Col Physician Exec, 1998-; fel Am Col Med Qual; fel Am Col Prev Med. **Honors/Awds:** Outstanding Resident Physician Award, Howard Univ Hosp, 1982; Who Most Exemplifies a Family Physician Award, Howard Univ Hosp, 1982; Mead-Johnson Sci Presentation Award, 1983; Outstanding Serv Award, Richmond Redevelop & Housing Authortiy, 1984; Physician Recognition Award, Am Med Asn, 1984, 1989, 1991, 1997, 2000; Outstanding Serv Award, Richmond Area High Blood Pressure Ctr, 1985, 1986; Community Serv Achievement, City Richmond, 1989. **Military Serv:** AUS Res, lt col, 1996-; Cert Achievement, 1988; Army Serv Ribbon, 1988; Nat Defense Serv Medal, 1991; Southwest Asia Serv Medal, 1991; Army Command Combat Patch, 82 Airborne Div, 1991; comdr, 348th Gen Hosp, AUS Res, 2000-. **Business Addr:** Director, Virginia Department of Medical Assistance Services, Div Prog Opers, 600 E Broad St Suite 1300, PO Box 24826, Richmond, VA 23219, **Business Phone:** (804)786-8052.

ADJAYE, DAVID
Architect. **Educ:** South Bank Univ, BA, 1990; Royal College of Art, M.Arch, 1993. **Career:** Architect, Chassay Architects, 1988-90; David Chipperfield Architects, 1991; Eduardo Souto de Moura Architects, 1991; in partnership with William Russell as Adjaye & Russell, 1994-00, founded Adjaye Assoc, London, 2000-. **Orgs:** Trustee, Architectural Education Trust; board member Greenwich Dance Agency; advisor, LDA Thames Gateway Design Panel; fellow, Royal Academy; Trustee, South London Gallery; Honrary Fellow of the American Institute of Architecture. **Honors/Awds:** RIBA, Bronze Medal, 1993. **Special Achievements:** Independent Sunday, London newspaper, "Most Fashionable architect of the moment", 2002; Elektra House, finalists in the 2002 World Architecture Awards, sponsored by World Architecture; youngest architects ever invited to participate in the Intl Architecture biennale in Venice; selected to design the Natl Museum of Af Am History and Culture in Washington, DC, 2009. **Business Addr:** 415 Broadway, 3rd Floor, New York, NY 10013, **Business Phone:** (212)965-8420.*

ADKINS, LEROY J
Law enforcement officer. **Personal:** Born Jun 17, 1933, St Louis, MO; son of Alfred J and Fannie E; married Glenda J Watt, Jan 19, 1957; children: Kevin L & Alfred J. **Educ:** Forest Park Community Col, AA, 1976; Columbia Col, attended 1978; Webster Univ, MA, 1979. **Career:** Law Enforcement Officer (retired); St Louis Police Dept, dep chief, 1958-92; St Louis Homicide Div, comdr, capt; St Louis Airport Police Dept, chief, 1992-96. **Orgs:** Local treas, Nat Orgn Black Law Enforcement Exec, 1976-; Omega Psi Phi, 1980-; Int Asn Chiefs Police, 1984-; Mo Police Chiefs, 1992-; Newstead Missionary Baptist Church. **Honors/Awds:** Letter of Commendation, St Louis Jr Chamber Com, 1968; Letter of Commendations, Grand Jury Asn St Louis, MO, 1968; Jr Chamber Commerce Law Enforcement Award; Outstanding Police Officer in Metro St Louis, 1971; Letters of Commendation, Chief Detectives; Humanitarian Award, Cong Racial Equality, St Louis, MO, 1974; Outstanding Police Work, Am Legion Cert Achievement, 1976; Recipient ten Letters Commendations, Chief Police, Except Performance Duty; Citizenship, Fourth Ward Adv Coun, 1982; St Louis Argus Newspaper Award, Distinguished Public Service, 1982; St Louis American Newspaper Salute to Excellence Award, 1992; Home Founders Award, Annie Malone C's, 1992; Hall of Fame, Sumner High Sch, 1994; Noble's Robert Lamb Humanitarian Award, 1995. **Special Achievements:** First Black to be in charge of the Homicide Department for the St Louis Police Department. **Military Serv:** USN, petty officer, 1950-54. **Home Addr:** 4892 San Francisco Ave, St Louis, MO 63115, **Home Phone:** (314)382-9045.

ADKINS, ROD, II. See ADKINS, RODNEY C.

ADKINS, RODNEY C (ROD ADKINS, II)
Computer executive. **Personal:** Born Aug 23, 1958, Augusta, GA; son of Archie and Wauneta; married Michelle, Dec 17, 1983; children: Rodney II & Ryan. **Educ:** Ga Inst Technol, BSEE, 1981; Rollins Col, BA, 1982; Ga Inst Technol, MSEE, 1983. **Career:** IBM, exec asst dir planning, 1990-91, exec asst vpres systs, 1991-92, mgr, ps/2 desktop develop, 1992-93, mgr, mobile computing opers, 1993-94, dir com desktop develop, 1994-95, vpres com desktop develop, 1995-96, vpres & gen mgr, desktop systs, 1996-98, svpres, currently; UNIX Systs, vpres & gen mgr, 1998-2001; Pervasive Computing, vpres & gen mgr, 2001-. **Orgs:** Life mem, Kappa Alpha Psi, 1979-; chmn, 1994-95, Micro Channel Developers Asn, bd dirs, 1995-96; exec sponsor, Nat Soc Black Engrs, 1995-98; bd dirs, Southeastern Consortium Minorities Eng, 1996-98; bd govs, IBM Acad Technol, 1996-98; Peopleclick Inc, 2000-; bd dirs, Ga Tech Res, 2001-; bd dirs, Ga Tech, 2003-. **Honors/Awds:** Black Engineer of the Year, Professional Achievement Indust, 1996; Outstanding Young Engineering Alumni, Ga Tech, 1996; A New Generation Leader, Edges Group, 1996; Lifetime Achievement in Industry, NSBE Golden Torch, 2001. **Special Achievements:** Fortune Top 50 Most Powerful Black Executives, 2002. **Business Addr:** Senior Vice President, International Business Machine, 294 Rte 100, MD-3122, Somers, NY 10589, **Business Phone:** (914)766-3130.

ADKINS, WILLIAM
Automotive executive. **Personal:** Born in Chicago, IL. **Educ:** Bus Col, Univ Md, accounting. **Career:** First Nat Bank; Gen Motors Corp, Finance Div; Pontiac Motors, serv & part & sales mgr; Adkins Chevrolet Buick Oldsmobile, owner, 1985; Adkins & Asn, owner, 1989; Ford Motor Co, consult; Gen Motor Corp, consult; Volkswagen Am, consult; Palanker Chevrolet-GEO, pres, 1994-05. **Orgs:** Suffolk Co Community Col; Harbor Country Day Sch; Gen Motors Minority Dealers Asn; Greater NY Dealers asn; Long Island United Way; Nat Advan Asn Colored People; prin, Day Prog; active supporter, United Negro Col Fund; bd trustee, Island Aquarium. **Honors/Awds:** Martin Luther King Jr Commission Public Service Award, Suffolk Co; Medals of Honrary Award, Ellis Island; Times Qual Dealer Award, 1998. *

ADOLPH, GERALD STEPHEN
Management consultant. **Personal:** Born Dec 30, 1953, New York, NY. **Educ:** MIT, BS, chem Eng, 1976, BS, mgt, 1976, MS, chem eng, 1981; Harvard Bus Sch, MBA, 1981. **Career:** Polaroid, engr 1976-81; Booz Allen & Hamilton, assoc, 1981-83, sr assoc 1983-85, prin 1985-88, partner, 1988-99, sr partner, 1999-, sr vpres, currently. **Orgs:** Corp adv bd chair, Univ Mich Bus Sch; bd dirs, chair, Exec Leadership Coun; bd dir, Nat Am Advan Colored People Legal Defense Fund; bd dir, Hellen Keller Worldwide; bd mem, Archbishop's Leadership Proj; bd mem, Nat Am Advan Colored People Legal Defense & Educ Fund. **Business Addr:** Senior Vice President, Booz Allen Hamilton, 101 Pk Ave 20th Fl, New York, NY 10178, **Business Phone:** (703)902-5000.

ADOM, EDWIN NII AMALAI
Psychiatrist. **Personal:** Born Jan 12, 1941, Accra, Ghana; son of Isaac Quaye and Juliana Adorkor Brown; married Margaret Odarkor Lamptey, May 28, 1977; children: Edwin Nii Nortey Jr, Isaac Michael Nii Nortei. **Educ:** Univ Pa, BA, 1963; Meharry Med Col, MD, 1968; Royal Soc Health, Eng, FRSH, 1974; Am Bd Psychiat & Neurol, dipl, 1978. **Career:** Pa Hosp, internship, 1968-69; Thomas Jefferson Univ, residency, 1969-72; W Philadelphia Consortium, staff psychiatrist, 1972-; Univ Pa Sch Med, fac, clin asst prof psychiat, 1972-74; State Pa, cons psychiatrist, Bur Visually Handicap & Blindness, 1974-, Bur Disability Determination, 1975-; Parents Preparing Parenthood, Philadelphia, PA, cons psychiatrist, 1975-76; Grad Hosp, Philadelphia, cons psychiatrist, 1976; St Joseph Hosp, Philadelphia, cons psychiatrist, 1976-80; Stephen Smith Home Aged, Philadelphia, cons psychiatrist, 1976-80; Mercy Douglas Human Serv Ctr, Philadelphia, cons psychiatrist, 1977-79; St Ignatius Home Aged, Phildelphia, cons psychiatrist, 1978-85; Philadelphia Psychiat Ctr, attend psychiatrist, 1987-; Horizon House Rehabilitation Ctr, Pa, cons psychiatrist, 1987-89; Hosp Univ Pa, cons psychiatrist, 1989-; W Philadelphia Community Mental Health Consortium, Philadelphia, PA, med dir, 1991-. **Orgs:** Am Psychol Asn; Nat Med Asn; MSEP; Black Psych Am, World Fedn Mental Health; Royal Soc Health; NY Acad Sci, 1987-; Am Acad Psychiat & the Law, 1990-; Am Soc Clin Psychopharmacology. **Honors/Awds:** Fel, Royal Soc of Health of Eng; Citizens Citation Chapel of 4 Chaplins Philadelphia; fel, Thomas Bond Soc of Pa Hospital, 1994; African-Am Wall of Fame, 1995; Black Ams Achievement, 1995; Astra Merck & the Med Soc of Eastern Pa Excellency Award for Mentorship, 1995. **Special Achievements:** Nation's first black blind physician and psychiatrist. **Business Addr:** Medical Director, West Philadelphia Community Mental Health Consortium, 255 S 17th St Suite 2704, Philadelphia, PA 19103-6228, **Business Phone:** (215)545-5116.*

ADONA, ALISA
Photographer. **Career:** Tilford Art Group, Photographer, currently. **Orgs:** Break the Cycle. **Special Achievements:** "CUBA, Reflections of Life" series; "Lost Tribe" photographic exhibition. **Business Phone:** (323)461-5050.*

ADRINE, RONALD BRUCE
Judge. **Personal:** Born Apr 21, 1947, Cleveland, OH; son of Russell T Adrine(deceased); divorced. **Educ:** Wittenberg Univ, at-

tended 1966; Fisk Univ, BA, hist, 1969; Cleveland Marshall Col Law, JD, 1973. **Career:** Cuyahoga County, asst pros atty, 1974-77; Adrine & Adrine, partner, 1977-78; US House of Reps, staff coun, 1978-79; Adrine & Adrine, partner, 1979-82; Cleveland Munic Ct, judge, 1981-, chmn & secy, currently. **Orgs:** Trustee, Urban League Greater Cleveland, 1972; comn, Cuyahoga Metro Housing Auth, 1981; Mayor's Citizen Charter Rev Comn, 1983; African Am Leadership Network; African Am Family Cong; cofounder, Black Male Agenda Ohio Inc; Nat Leadership Inst Minorities Ohio Inc; bd trustees, Shaker Heights High Sch Alumni Asn; bd trustees, Opportunities Industrialization Coun; bd trustees, Ohio Community Corrections Orgn; bd trustees, Norman S Minor Bar Asn; bd trustees, Exodus Prog; bd trustees, Transitional Housing; bd trustees, Proj Second Chance; adv bd, Resocializing African Am Males; Omega Psi Phi Fraternity; bd trustees, Harambee Servs Black Families; Fisk Alumni Asn; bd trustees, Cleveland Bar Asn; Cleveland-Marshall Law Alumni Asn; Cleveland State Univ Alumni Asn. **Honors/Awds:** Man of the Year, Omega Psi Phi Fraternity fourth Dist, 1983. **Special Achievements:** First chmn, Cleveland Domestic Violence Coordinating Coun. **Home Addr:** 13515 Drexmore Rd, Cleveland, OH 44120. **Business Addr:** Judge, Cleveland Municipal Court, Justice Center, 1200 Ontario Ave Suite 15A, PO Box 94894, Cleveland, OH 44101-4894.

AGEE, BOBBY L.
Funeral director, county commissioner. **Personal:** Born Oct 28, 1949, Maplesville, AL; son of Clara M; married Emily Wilson, Apr 28, 1968; children: Anthony, Antionette, Bobby II, Ahzeezee, Ngozi, Jabari & Awlahjaday. **Educ:** Ky Sch Mortuary Sci, KY, mortician, 1973; Sch Govt Serv, Auburn, AL, attended 1989-; Ala Co Comnrs Col, Ctr Govt Serv, Auburn Univ, attended 1992. **Career:** Agee Bros Funeral Home, Clanton, AL, owner, 1975-; Chilton Co Comnr, comnr, 1989-92; Chilton Co Ala, conventioneer, currently. **Orgs:** Chmn, W End Park Bd, 1989-; Zoning Bd City Clanton, 1989-; vice chmn, Middle Ala Area Agency Aging, 1992-; 4-H & FHA Bd Chilton, Co, 1990-; deacon, Union Baptist Church, 1983-; Clanton Evening Lions Club, 1986-89. **Honors/Awds:** Certificate of Merit, Booker T Wash Bus Col, 1988; Certificate of Merit, Auburn Univ, 1989; Certificate of Merit, Middle Ala Area Agency Aging, 1990; Certificate of Merit, Clanton Evening Lions Club, 1988. **Military Serv:** AUS, SP/4, 1971. **Business Addr:** Mortician, Owner, Agee Brothers Funeral Home, 907 Samaria Rd, PO Box 851, Clanton, AL 35045.*

AGEE, THOMAS LEE
Football player. **Personal:** Born Feb 22, 1964, Chilton, AL; married Anchylus. **Educ:** Auburn Univ, criminal justice. **Career:** Football player (retired); Seattle Seahawks, 1988; Kansas City Chiefs, 1989; Dallas Cowboys, running back, 1990-94. **Orgs:** Speaker, Fel Christian Athletes & Athletes Action groups, Ala.

AGGREY, O. RUDOLPH
Ambassador, executive. **Personal:** Born Jul 24, 1926, Salisbury, NC; son of J E Kwegyir and Rose Douglass; married Francoise C Fratacci; children: Roxane Rose. **Educ:** Hampton Inst, BS, 1946; Syracuse Univ, MS, 1948. **Career:** Ambassador (retired); United Negro col Fund, publ asst, 1947-50; Cleveland Call & Post, news reporter, 1948-49; Chief Defender, corresp, 1948-49; Bennett Col, publ dir, 1950; Dept State Lagos, Nigeria, vice consult & info officer, 1951-53; USIA, Lille, France, asst pub affairs officer, 1953-54; USIA, Paris, France, asst cult officer & dir cult ctr, 1954-60; Dept State, dep pub affairs adv African Affairs, 1961-64; Voice Am, chief French batch, 1965; Am Embassy Kinshasa Zaire, first secy & dep pub affairs, 1966-68; US Info Agency, prog mgr motion picture & TV serv, 1968-70; Dept State, dir off West African Affairs, 1970-73; US, ambassador to Senegal & The Gambia, 1973-77, ambassador to Romania, 1977-81; Georgetown Univ, dept State Foreign Affairs, Sr Fel, res prof diplomacy & res asn; Georgetown Univ, 1981-83; Bur Res & Intelligence Dept State, spec asst, 1983-84; intl rels consult, 1984; Howard Univ, Patricia Robert Harris Pub Affairs Prog, dir, 1987-90; Howard Univ Press, dir, 1988-90, consult, 1990-94. **Orgs:** bd dirs, Asn Black Am Ambassadors, Wash Asn Diplomatic Studies; consult, Dept State Nat Geog, Howard Univ, USAID, 1984-87; Phelps-Stoke Fund, 1990-; Atlantic Coun USA, exec comn; Soc Prodigal Sons State NC; Fed City Club; Alpha Phi Alpha; Sigma Delta Chi; Alpha Kappa Mu; Sigma Pi Phi. **Honors/Awds:** Meritorious & Super Service Awards, USIA, 1950, 1955; Honorable mem, French Acad Jazz Paris, 1960; Alumni Award Hampton Inst, 1961; Harvard Univ, fel, Ctr Intl Affairs, 1964-65; Presidential Meritorious Award, US Govt, 1984; Syracuse Univ Chancellor's Medal, 1984; FL A&M Univ Meritorious Achievement Award, 1985; Distinguished Achievement Award, Dillard Univ, 1987; LLD, Livingstone Col, 1977; Grand Officer, Senegalese Nat Order Lion; Am Acad Diplomacy. **Special Achievements:** Author of comprehensive study leading to establishment of Howard Univ's Ralph J Bunche Intl Affairs Ctr, 1987. *

AGNEW, RAYMOND MITCHELL, JR.
Football player. **Personal:** Born Dec 9, 1967, Winston-Salem, NC; married Katherine; children: Ray III, Malcolm Lamar & Keenan. **Educ:** NC State Univ, BA, History. **Career:** New Eng Patriots, defensive end, 1990-94; NY Giants, 1995-97; St Louis Rams, defensive tackle (retired), 1998-01, dir player develop & teampastor, 2001-04; sports editor, Sch's newspaper. **Orgs:** NatHonor Society. *

AGUIRRE, MARK ANTHONY
Basketball player, basketball coach. **Personal:** Born Dec 10, 1959, Chicago, IL; married Angela Bowman, 1988; children: 4. **Educ:** De Paul Univ, attended 1982. **Career:** Basketball player (retired), coach; Dallas Mavericks, 1981-89; Detroit Pistons, 1988-93; Los Angeles Clippers, 1993-94; Life Cast, chmn & chief exec officer, 1999-2001; Ind Pacers, spec asst, 2001-02, asst coach, 2002-03; NY Knicks, asst coach, 2004-08. **Orgs:** Big Bros & Big Sisters. **Honors/Awds:** NBA Player of the Month; Dallas Pro Athlete of the Year; USBWA Col Player of the Year Award, 1980. **Special Achievements:** First Maverick to participate in the All-Star game as reserve; has appeared on the cover of The Sporting News, NBA Today, Basketball Digest.

AGURS, DONALD STEELE (SIMON FRY)
Journalist. **Personal:** Born Jun 1, 1947, Rock Hill, SC; married Brenda Louise Crenshaw; children: Renda & Chris. **Educ:** Howard Univ, attended 1967 & 1977; DC Teachers Col, attended 1971; Fed City Col, attended 1972. **Career:** Westinghouse Broadcasting Co, newsman, 1970-71; WHUR-FM, newsman/producer, 1972; WSOC Radio & TV, newsman, 1973; 236 Housing Proj, admin, 1973-75; WGIV, newscaster, 1975; WHUR-FM, NBN, White House, corresp, 1975-78; Sheridan Broadcasting Network, White House, corresp. **Orgs:** PAG, 1973-74; Bd dir, Mecklenburg Co Pub Access, 1974-75; Am Fedn TV & Radio Artists; Nat Asn Black Journalists; Wash press Club, Cong Corresp Asn; White House Corresp Asn; Nat Asn Advan Colored People; Laytonsville Golf Club; Pinetuck Golf Club. **Honors/Awds:** Special Award, Asn Press, 1972. **Special Achievements:** Birthday Spec, WHUR Martin Luther King Jr, 1976. **Military Serv:** AUS, sp4, 1967-70; AUS, instr, 1969-70. **Home Addr:** 315 T St NW, Washington, DC 20001.

AGWUNOBI, ANDREW C.
Executive, activist, chief executive officer. **Personal:** Born in Scotland, United Kingdom; married Elizabeth Nega; children: Hannah. **Educ:** Howard Univ Hosp, pediatrician, 1995; Stanford Grad Sch Bus, MBA, 1999. **Career:** Qual Life Health Serv, 1995-97; Harvard Vanguard Med Assocs, chief & instr, 1997-98; S Fulton Med Ctr, chief operating officer, chief exec officer & pres, 2001; Grady Health Syst, pres & chief exec officer, 2003-; St Joseph Health Syst, exec vpres & chief operating officer, currently. **Orgs:** Bd adv & bd dir includes: Ga State Univ Col Health & Human Sci; The Ga Chamber Com; 191 Club Bd Gov; Cent Atlanta Progress Inc; Atlanta Regional Health Forum Inc; Nat Asn Pub Hosp & Health Syst; The Arthur M Blank Family Found & Better Beginnings Adv Coun; Atlanta Fulton Family Connection; The Metro Atlanta Chamber Com; The Ga Hosp Asn Bd; The Ga Alliance Community Hosp; Am Col Healthcare Execs; The Ga Asn Healthcare Execs; Partners Int Develop; The Hosp Exec Coun; Leadership Ga Class 2005; 100 Black Men Atlanta; Rotary Club Atlanta; fel Acad Pediatrics; chmn bd & opers adv, Health-e-Sta Adv Bd. **Honors/Awds:** Cert distinguished acad achievement, Howard Univ Hosp, 1995; Cert Excellence Award, Qual Life Health Serv, 1997; Roselyn Kolodny Award, Harvard Vanguard Med Assocs, 1998; Cert Serv Excellence, Harvard Vanguard Med Assocs, 1999; Chief Exec Officer Circle Excellence Award, S Fulton Med Ctr, 2003; 40 Under 40 Rising Stars, Ga Trend mag ann, 2002; 2002 Up & Comers Award Rising Stars in Health Care Mgt, Modern Healthcare's ann, 2002; Speaker of the Yr, Atlanta Peachtree Rotary, 2004; Trailblazer Award, The Atlanta Bus League, 2005. **Special Achievements:** featured in Atlanta Business Chronicle, as one of the "Most Influential Atlantans"; featured in Atlanta Magazine's "Atlanta's Top 40 Most Influential People"; featured in one of Georgia Trend magazine's 2005 "100 Most Influential Georgians" & "Who's Who in Black Atlanta"; one of the youngest CEOs of a large public and teaching hospital in the nation. **Business Addr:** Executive Vice President, Chief Operating Officer, St Joseph Health System, 500 S Main St Suite 1000, PO Box 14132, Orange, CA 92863-1532, **Business Phone:** (714)347-7500.*

AHANOTU, CHIDI OBIOMA
Football player. **Personal:** Born Oct 11, 1970, Modesto, CA; son of Austin; children: Ijechi Woodrow & Mayan. **Educ:** Univ Calif. **Career:** Tampa Bay Buccaneers, defensive end, 1993-00; STL, 2001; BUF, 2002; SFO, 2003; Miami dolphins, 2004; Tampa Bay Buccaneers, 2004 . **Orgs:** Active with Big Bros & Big Sisters, Save a Child & Ahanotu Found. *

AHART, THOMAS I
Executive. **Personal:** Born Apr 3, 1938, Detroit, MI; son of Greek and Eula; married Menda Britton; children: Pamela M & Thomas B. **Educ:** Wayne State Univ, BA, 1962. **Career:** Networks Solutions, Customer Opers, supvr; A & M Group, pres, 1987-98; Dyma Assocs, pres, 1978-87; Nat Min Purch Coun, exec dir, 1977-78; Am Bankers Asn, dir, 1970-77; Ford Motor Co, indust rel adminr, 1967-70; Nations Bus Group, nat proj dir, proj dir emerging markets, currently. **Orgs:** Omega Psi Phi 1962-; consult, Control Data Corp 1984; consult, Export-Import Bank US, 1985; dir, Crispus Attucks Inst, 1990; pres, S Lakes HS PTA, 1992; consult, US Com Dept, 1995-; chmn, Hughes PTA Human Rels. **Special Achievements:** Numerous publications including "Bankers and Urban Affairs,"; "Future of Comm Bnkg Praeger," 1976; "Poems" Rustlings, Reston Publishers, 1975. **Home Addr:** 12385 Copenhagen Ct, Reston, VA 20191, **Home Phone:** (703)620-3875. **Business Addr:** Project Director of Emerging Markets, Nations Business Group, 8206 Leesburg Pke Suite 301, Vienna, VA 22182, **Business Phone:** (703)821-6600.

AHMAD, JADWAA
Lawyer. **Personal:** Born Jul 23, 1935, Detroit, MI; married Ruth Joyce; children: Jamar H, Jadwaa W, Jamil O. **Educ:** W Mich Univ; E Mich Univ, BS, 1957; Detroit Col Law, JD, 1970. **Career:** City Detroit, jr chemist, 1957-59; Stroh Brewery Co, Detroit, chemist, 1959-70; Wayne City Neighborhood Legal Serv, atty trainee, 1970-71; Gragg & Gardner Detroit, atty, 1970-72; Terry Ahmad & Bradfield Detroit, atty; pvt pract atty, currently. **Orgs:** Legal Frat Sigma Nu Phi; Kappa Alpha Psi; State Bar Mich; Wolverine Bar Asn; Nat Bar Asn; Detroit Bar Asn; Am Bar Asn; House Coun PEACE, 1972-. **Honors/Awds:** NAACP Recipient of Scholastic Awards, E Mich Univ, 1954-57. **Military Serv:** AUS, pvt, 1958. **Business Addr:** Attorney, Jadwaa Ahmad, 126 Massachusetts St, Highland Park, MI 48203-3539.*

AHOTO, YAO
Entrepreneur, business owner, business owner. **Career:** Karibu Books, co-owner, 1993-. **Orgs:** Hurston-Wright Found, Nat Med Asn, Nat Coun Negro Women. **Special Achievements:** Nation's largest Black black store chain. **Business Addr:** Co-owner, Karibu Books Bowie, Town Center, 15624 Emerald Way, Bowie, MD 20716, **Business Phone:** (301)352-4110.*

AIKEN, CAROL ANN. See AMIN, KARIMA.

AIKEN, KIMBERLY CLARICE
Columnist, fashion model. **Personal:** Born Oct 11, 1976, Columbia, SC; daughter of Charles and Valerie; married Haven Earl Cockerham Jr, 1998; children: Russell. **Educ:** Univ NC; Univ SC; NY Univ, grad. **Career:** Miss Am, 1994; Ernst & Young LLP, pub acct; Pageantry Mag, columnist, currently; Aikens Community Care Home Inc, founder, currently; Homeless Educ & Resource Orgn, founder, pres, currently; image consult & speaker. **Orgs:** Delta Sigma Theta Sorority Inc; HERO; Habitat for Humanity. **Honors/Awds:** Order of the Palmetto; Miss America, 1993; Miss Columbia; Miss SC. **Special Achievements:** First African American to win the Miss SC contest, 1993; Fifth African American to win the Miss America pageant; recognized by People Magazine as one of the "Fifty Most Beautiful People in the World. **Business Addr:** Founder, President, Aikens Community Care Home Inc, 216 Cora Dr, Columbia, SC 29203, **Business Phone:** (803)754-4468.

AIKEN, WILLIAM
Executive. **Personal:** Born Mar 11, 1934, New York, NY; son of Eugene Aiken Sr and Ida Brown; married Joyce Blackwell Aiken; children: Adrienne, William Jr, Candice, Nicole, Sharla. **Educ:** City Col, BBA, 1963; Baruch Col, MBA, 1970. **Career:** NY State Ins Dept, state ins examiner, 1963-67; Arthur Young & Co, sr acct, 1967-72; Aiken & Wilson CPA, 1972-78; NY City Human Resources Admin, asst dep comnr, 1978-80; Main Hurdman, NY, partner, 1980-87; KPMG Peat Marwick Main & o, New York, NY, partner, 1987-88; Medger Evers Col, adj prof; Long Island RR Co, Jamaica, NY, vpres finance. **Orgs:** Bd chmn, Nat Asn Black Accountants, 1971-73; NY State Bd Pub Accountancy, 1974-; Coun Am Inst Cert Pub Accountants, 1975-78; NY Soc Cert Pub Accountants; Accountants Club Am; 100 Black Men; comn mem, Ins Cos & Agencies Acct; NC Agr & Tech Univ, Cluster Prog; bus develop coun, NC Cent Univ; Nat Bus League Comn Nat Policy Rev; Nat Urban League Black Exec Exchange Prog; bd dir, Nat Asn Black Accountants; Westchester Minority Bus Asst Org; Ethical Fieldson Fund; Studio Mus Harlem; treas, Assoc Black Cities, 1990-. **Honors/Awds:** Achievement Award, Jackson State Chapter, Nat Asn Black Accountants, 1972; Ebony Success Libr, 1974; Annual Achievement Award, Nat Asn Black Accountant, 1975. **Special Achievements:** Auth: The Black Experience in Large Public Accounting Firms, 1971; First black to receive appointment to New York State Bd for Public Accountancy in 1974. **Military Serv:** USMC, sgt, 1953-56. **Business Addr:** President, New York State Society of Certified Public Accountants, 530 Fifth Avenue, New York, NY 10036.

AIKENS, ALEXANDER E
Banker, educator. **Personal:** Born Feb 22, 1949, Chicago, IL; son of Alexander E Aikens Jr and Ruth Lane; married Jean Murgida, Nov 5, 1988; children: Talia C & Felicia. **Educ:** Brandeis Univ, BA, econ, 1971; Northeastern Law Sch, JD, 1974; Harvard Bus Sch, Prof Mgt Develop Prog, 1986. **Career:** Chase Manhattan Bank, NA, New York, NY, second vpres, 1974-80; The First Nat Bank Boston, Boston, MA, group sr credit officer, Global Banking Group, 1987-91; Div Exec Multinational, 1992-95; Bank Boston, Emerging Markets Investment Banking, managing dir; Brandeis Univ, Int Bus Sch, adj prof, 2000-. **Orgs:** Mass Bar Asn, 1974; bd mem, Boston Acoustics, 2001-04; trustee, Wheecock Col; bd dirs, Pension Retirement Investment Mgt Bd, Commonwealth Mass. **Business Phone:** (781)736-2250.

AIKENS, DR. CHESTER ALFRONZA
Lawyer, dentist. **Personal:** Born Feb 8, 1951, Quitman, GA; son of Augustus Davis Aikens Sr and Lucile Balloon; married E Jean

Johnson Aikens, Aug 4, 1974; children: Chester Alfronza Aikens II & Chae Rashard Aikens. **Educ:** N Fla Jr Col, AA, 1970; Fla State Univ, BS, 1973; Howard Univ, DDS, 1977; Fla Coastal Sch Law, JD, 1999; Jacksonville Univ, MBA, 1999. **Career:** AUS Ft Benning, GA, dentist, 1977-79; Dept Prof Regulations, dent exam, 1978-89; Marchand & Brown Dent Pract, dentist, 1979-80; Fla Army Res Nat Guard, dentist; Pvt Pract, dentist, 1980-; The Fla Bar, atty, 2002-. **Orgs:** House delegates Nat Dent Asn, 1980-; pres, Jacksonville Chap Fla Med Dent & pharmaceut Asn, 1983-85; bd dirs, Joseph E Lee Child Develop Ctr, 1983-; dent examr, Fla Dept Prof Regulation, 1985-; Northwest Coun Chamber Com, 1985; bd dirs, Jacksonville Urban League, 1986-, YMCA, John Weldon Johnson Br, 1986-; pres, Howard Univ Alumni Assoc Jacksonville Chap, 1986-; bd dirs, The Midal Touch Daycare Ctr, 1986-; Parliamentarian Nat Dent Asn, 1988; chmn, Jacksonville UNCF Telethon Campaign, 1988-89; bd chmn, Jacksonville Urban League, 1988-89; bd mem, Metro Bd Dir, Jacksonville YMCA, 1989; pres, Nat Dent Asn, 1994; Wash DC Bd Dent, 1994; fel, Int Cong Oral Implantologists, 1995; fel, Am Col Dent, 1995; Fla Bar, 2002-; Wash DC bar. **Honors/Awds:** Polemarch's Award, Kappa Alpha Psi Frat Jacksonville Chapter, 1983; President's Achievement Award, Fla Med Dent & Pharmacist Asn, 1986; Community Service Award, Mother Midway AME Church, 1986; Service Award, Jacksonville Urban League, 1986; Greek of the Year, Jacksonville Panhellenic Coun, 1988; Professor Man of the Year, Greater Grant Mem AME Church, 1989; Award Appreciation, Edward Waters Col Alumni Asn, 1989; Performed the role Rev Perlie in the prod of Perlie, 1989; Howard University Col of Dental Alumni Award, 1991; WSVE Businessman of the Year, 1994; Outstanding Alumni Award, Fla State Univ Black Alumni, 1994; Community Service Award, Mt Vernon Baptist Church, 1995; Community Service Award, Alpha Kappa Alpha, Pi Eta Chap, 1995; Sire Archon, Sigma Pi Phi Fraternity Gamma Beta Bowle, 1993 & 1994; Outstanding Leadership Award, 1994. **Military Serv:** AUS, capt, 1977-79; Dedication to Others Award, 1977; Fla Army Res Nat Guard, maj, 1980. **Home Addr:** 4196 Old Mill Cove Trl W, Jacksonville, FL 32277. **Business Addr:** Dentist, Attorney, 305 Union St E, Jacksonville, FL 32202-2748, **Business Phone:** (904)358-3827.

AIKENS-YOUNG, DR. LINDA LEE
Educator. **Personal:** Born Nov 5, 1950, Conyers, GA; daughter of Willie Melvin Lee and Genoulia Minter Lee; married W Roger; married William Roger, Apr 14, 1990; children: Konswello & Jimmneka Aikens. **Educ:** Spelman Col, Atlanta, GA, BA, 1972; GA State Univ, Atlanta, GA, MA, elem educ, 1975, specialist, elem educ, 1976, specialist, educ admin, 1979, PhD, 1988. **Career:** Rockdale County Schs, Conyers, GA, headstart, summers, 1972-77, classroom teacher, 1972-81, lead teacher, 1981-89; Conyers Middle Sch, asst prin, 1989-91; Salem High Sch, asst prin, 1991-92; CJ Hicks Elem Sch, prin; Brenau Univ, asst prof educ, currently. **Orgs:** Wesley Chapel United Methodist Church; bd dir, Ga Asn Educr, 1979-82; exec comt, Rockdale County Democratic Party, 1980-; state dir, Nat Educ Asn Bd Dirs, 1983-89; trustee, Nat Educ Special Servs, 1986-92. **Honors/Awds:** Outstanding Young Educator, Flat Shoals Elementary, 1978-79, 1980-81; Delegate, NEA Conventions, 1979-; Delegate, Nat Democratic Conventions, 1984, 1988; Featured in "Planning for Your Retirement," Black Enterprise, April 1990; "Should the SAT Be Eliminated," Nat Educ Asn Now Magazine, 1990; Lifetime Achievement Award, Nat Asn Mem Ins Educ, 1992. **Business Addr:** Assistant Professor of Education, Brenau University, School of Education, 500 Washington St SE, Gainesville, GA 30501, **Business Phone:** (770)534-6220.

AIRALL, DR. GUILLERMO EVERS
Dentist, college teacher. **Personal:** Born Apr 17, 1919, Paraiso, Panama; son of Josiah C Sr (deceased) and Rosetta Letitia Christian; married Clara; children: Zoila, Angela & Sheldon. **Educ:** Panama Univ, BS, 1946; Howard Univ, DDS, 1953. **Career:** Pub Health Detroit, dentist, 1953; AUS, dentist, 1953-74; 252nd Med Detachment Thailand, comdr, 1963-64; Temple Univ, Philadelphia, asst prof, 1978-82; dentist, pvt pract, 1972-. **Orgs:** Pres, Little League BB, Ger, 1969-71; vpres, Boy Scout Ger, 1969-71; pres,Lions Club Willingboro, NJ, 1979-80; Burlington Chamber Com, 1982-; admin bd & stewardship bd, United Methodist Church, 1983-; vpres & pres elect, Chi Delta Mu Fraternity Philadelphia, 1984-; chmn, Church & Soc, 1988; co-chmn, outreach, St Paul United Methodist Church, 1989; vpres elect & pres, Chi Delta Mu Fraternity, Nu Chap, Philadelphia 1984-87; Alpha Phi Alpha Fraternity Kappa Iota Lambda Chap, Willingboro, NJ, 1989-. **Military Serv:** AUS, col 21 yrs; Nat Defense Serv Med w/Oak Leaf Cluster; Meritorious Unit Emblem; Cert Achievement & Cert Appreciation; Armed Forces Res Medal. **Business Addr:** Dentist, Private Practice, 28 Windsor Lane, Willingboro, NJ 08046-3413.*

AIRALL, ZOILA ERLINDA
School administrator. **Personal:** Born Jan 21, 1951, Washington, DC. **Educ:** Douglass Col Rutgers Univ, BA, 1973; Columbia Univ Teachers Col, MA, 1974, EdM, 1975; Univ PA, PhD, anthrop educ, 1996. **Career:** Pemberton Twp HS, guid counr, 1975-81; Zurbrugg Hosp, ment health therapist, 1981; Bethany Col, dir coun, 1981-; Univ PA, asst dean residence, 1984-88, assoc dir, 1988-96; Bryn Mawr Col, dir instrnl diversity, 1996-2002; Duke Univ, asst vpres campus life, 2002-. **Orgs:** Pres, basileus Beta Theta Omega-Alpha Kappa Alpha, 1978-; organist, Cove United Presbyterian Church, 1983-; Fels Menniger Found, 1984. **Honors/Awds:** Grad Fellowship Columbia Univ, 1973 & 1974; Keynote Speaker Annual Breakfast, Bethany Col, 1984; Outstanding Young Women publication, 1984. **Business Phone:** (919)684-3737.

AKANDE, BENJAMIN OLA
Educator. **Personal:** Son of Samuel Ola Akande; married Bola. **Educ:** Wayland Baptist Univ, BS, Bus Admin; Univ Okla, MA, PhD (Econ); John F. Kennedy Sch Govt Exec Prog, Harvard Univ, Post Doctrol. **Career:** Wayland Baptist Univ, dean, Sch Bus, Tx, 1995-2000; Wayland's pres, spec asst, 1998-2000; Univ Okla; Dallas Baptist Univ; Univ Cent Okla; Okla City Univ & DeVry Inst; World Bank, econ consult; United Nations Develop Prog, econ consult; Webster Univ, Sch Bus & Technol, dean & prof, 2000-; bd dir, Newberry Group; Xiolink Corp; Private Bank of St Louis. **Orgs:** Bd mem, Pvt Bank St. Louis; The World Affairs Coun; St. Louis Chap; Mary Inst & Saint Louis Country Day Sch. **Special Achievements:** One of St. Louis 40 under 40, the top 40 leaders under 40 years old who have demonstrated resolve and leadership in the St. Louis community. **Business Addr:** Professor, Dean, Webster University, Sch Bus & Technol, 470 E Lockwood Ave, St Louis, MO 63119, **Business Phone:** (314)968-5951.

AKBAR, DR. NA (LUTHER B WEEMS)
Educator, founder (originator). **Personal:** Born Apr 26, 1944, Tallahassee, FL; son of Bessie G Weems and Luther B Weems; married Renee V Beach; children: Shaakira, Mutaqee & Tareeq. **Educ:** Univ Mich, BA, 1965, MS, 1969, PhD, 1970. **Career:** Morehouse Col, assoc prof & dept head, 1970-75, chmn; Norfolk State Univ, assoc prof, 1977-79; Fla State Univ, vis prof, 1979-81, Dept Psychol, clin fac, 1981-; J Black Psychol, assoc ed, 1980-85; J Black Studies, ed bd, 1981-95; Mind Prod & Assocs, pres, 1980-; author, 1985-. **Orgs:** Bd mem, Off Human Develop Am Muslim Mission, 1975-77; bd mem, Nat Black Child Develop Inst, 1978-81; bd dir, Nat Asn Black Psychologists, 1983-84, 1986-89, pres, 1987. **Honors/Awds:** Annual Member Award, Asn Black Psychologists, 1980; Martin Luther King Jr Distinguished Scholar Award, Fla State Univ, 1983; Distinguished Black Psychologists, Nat Asn Black Psychologists; DHL, Edinboro Univ Pa; DHL, Lincoln Univ. **Special Achievements:** Authored Chains & Images Psychol Slavery, 1984; Visions Black Men, 1991; The Community of Self, Know Thy Self; Oprah Winfrey Show; The Geraldo Show; one of the world's preeminent psychologists & a pioneer in the development of an African-centered approach in modern psychology, Essence Magazine. **Home Addr:** 503 Famcee Ave, Tallahassee, FL 32310, **Home Phone:** (850)574-9039. **Business Addr:** Founder, Mind Productions & Associates, 324 N Copeland St, PO Box 11221, Tallahassee, FL 32304, **Business Phone:** (850)222-1764.

AKINS, DANIEL L.
College teacher. **Educ:** Howard Univ, BS; Univ Calif, Berkeley, PhD, phys chem, 1968. **Career:** Fla State Univ, Inst Molecular Biophys, post-doctoral assoc, 1968-69, vis asst prof chem, 1969-70; Univ S Fla, from asst prof to assoc prof, 1970-77; Nat Bur Stds, Laser Chem Sect, guest scientist, 1977-79; Nat Sci Found, Dynamics Prog, phys chem subsection, prog dir chem dynamics, 1977-79; Polaroid Corp, sr scientist, 1979-81; City Univ NY, City Col, prof phys chem., 1981-, Ctr Anal Struct & Interfaces, dir, 1988-, distinguished serv prof chem, 1996-. **Orgs:** Am Chem Soc; Soc Appl Spectros; Sigma Pi Sigma Physics Soc, 1962; Phi Beta Kappa, 1963; Soc Sigma Xi, 1963. **Honors/Awds:** Bausch and Lomb Science Award, 1959; Howard University Competitive Scholarship; Howard University Sophomore Chemistry Award; American Institute of Chemists Award, 1963; Distinguished Lecturer, Sigma XiLectrs, 1996-98; Presidential Award, Excellence in Science, Mathematics & Engineering Mentoring, 2000. **Special Achievements:** Has been published in numerous professional journals, has extensively lectured at conferences & universities, both national & international.

AKINYEMI, DR. NURUDEEN B
College teacher, educator. **Educ:** State Univ NY, Buffalo, BA, 1985; Southern Univ, Baton Rouge, MA, 1986; Univ SC, PhD, 1994. **Career:** Kennesaw State Univ, Dept Polit Sci & Int Affairs, assoc prof & comt chair, currently, Ctr African & African Diaspora Studies, asst dir, currently. **Business Addr:** Associate Professor of Political Science, Committee Chair, Kennesaw State University, Department of Political Science and International Affairs, SO 5052 1000 Chastain Rd, PO Box 2302, Kennesaw, GA 30144-5591, **Business Phone:** (770)499-3346.

AKOREDE, AYO
Educator. **Personal:** Born Jan 24, 1971, Nigeria; son of Sholape and Salawadeen; children: Sholape. **Educ:** Nova Univ, BS, 1993; Nova Southeastern Univ, MBA, 1995, Mgt Info Sys, 1995. **Career:** St Attorney's Off, legal asst, 1993-94; Nova Southeastern Univ, grad asst, 1993-95; Savannah St Univ, stud affairs adv, 1995-; asst dir & event coordr. **Orgs:** Adv, Peer Counselor Org, 1995-; adv, Phi Alpha Delta, 1996-; volunteer, Union Mission, 1995-; Nat Orientation Dir Asn, 1998-; Nat Acad Advising Asn, 1998-; adv, Savannah St Univ, Stud Govt Asn, 1999-; Nat Asn Stud Affairs Personal, 1999-2000; Savannah Chatham County Coun DisabilityIssues, 1999-. **Honors/Awds:** Governor's Award, 1998; Student Government Award Advisor of the Year, 1998-99.

ALBERS, KENNETH LYNN
Actor, movie director. **Personal:** Born Jan 24, 1944, Macomb, IL; son of Mildred and Clarence; married Catherine, Dec 24, 1987; children: Elizabeth & Matthew. **Educ:** Ill Wesleyan Univ, BFA, 1967; Univ Minn, MFA, 1969. **Career:** LaCross Community Theater, managing dir, 1969-71; Case Western Reserve Univ, assoc prof, 1971-84; Cleveland Play House, actor & dir, 1974-82; Milwaukee Repertory Theater, actor & dir, 1984-94; Freelance, actor & dir, 1974-97; Oregon Shakespeare, actor & dir, 1997-. **Honors/Awds:** Six Cleveland Critics Circle Awards; IL Wesleyan, Alumni Award, 1985; LA Ovation Award, 1995; Dramalogue Award, 1996. **Special Achievements:** Worked with deaf theater companies including Natl Theater of the Deaf and Deaf West Theater Co. **Business Addr:** Actor, Oregon Skakespeare Festival, 15 S Pioneer St, PO Box 158, Ashland, OR 97520, **Business Phone:** (541)482-2111.*

ALBERT, CHARLES GREGORY
Lawyer. **Personal:** Born May 12, 1955, Chicago, IL; son of Essie L and Eugie. **Educ:** Princeton Univ, AB, 1976; Harvard Law Sch, JD, 1979. **Career:** Bell Boyd & Lloyd, assoc, 1979-86, partner, 1987-92; Albert Whitehead PC, atty, 1992-. **Orgs:** Dir, Better Boys Found, 1986-, Young Execs Politics, 1986-, Project Skil, 1986-90; St. Gregory's Episcopal Choir Sch, 1990-; Ill Asn Defense Trial Coun; Cook County; Chicago and Am Bar asns; Nat Asn Railroad Trial Counsel. **Business Addr:** Lawyer, Albert Whitehead PC, 10 N Dearborn St Suite 600, Chicago, IL 60602, **Business Phone:** (312)357-6300.

ALBERT, DONNIE RAY
Opera singer. **Personal:** Born Jan 10, 1950, New Orleans, LA; son of Etta Mae Hatter; married Gwendolyn Veal; children: Dimitri Rholas & Domenic Raoul. **Educ:** La State Univ, BM, 1972; Southern Meth Univ, MM, 1975. **Career:** Wolf Trap Co, 1974-77; Southern Opera Theater & Memphis Opera Theater, 1975-76; Houston Grand Opera, singer, 1976-77; Affiliate Artist, 1978-83; Chicago Lyric Opera, 1979; Baltimore Opera Co, 1984, 1988; Boston Concert Opera, 1979; New York Opera, 1979-80, 1990; Ft Worth Opera, 1980-81; San Francisco Opera, 1985; Theater der Stadt Heidelberg Bremen & Saarbrucken, 1985-86; Can Opera, 1986; Houston Grand Opera, 1986-87; Theater des Westens, Berlin, 1988-89; Florentine Opera Co, 1989; many other major orchestras throughout North America; Miami Opera, 1990; Salome, Sao Paulo, Brazil, 2004; Dallas Opera's LA VIDA BREVE, 2004; Austin Lyric Opera, FLYING DUTCHMAN, 2004; Opera Pacific, I PAGLIACI, 2004; Florentine Opera, IL TROVATORE, 2004. **Orgs:** Am Guild Musical Artists; Actor's Equity; Am Fedn TV & Radio Artists; artist in residence, Ctr Black Music Res, 1989-. **Honors/Awds:** Shreveport Symposium Award, 1973; Grant Nat Opera Inst, 1976; First Place, Metro Opera, Nat Coun SW Region, 1975; Grammy Award for Best Opera Rec, 1977. **Business Phone:** (212)397-7915.

ALBRIGHT, GERALD ANTHONY
Singer. **Personal:** Born Aug 30, 1957, Los Angeles, CA; son of Mattie Pearl Albright and William Dudley Albright; married Glynis, Dec 21, 1981; children: Selina Marie & Brandon Terrell; married Glynis. **Educ:** Univ Redlands, BS, bus mgmt, 1979. **Career:** Studio rec musician, 1980-; Atlantic Rec, rec artist, 1987-99; Albums: Just Between Us, 1988; Bermuda Nights, 1989; Live At Birdland West, 1991; Smooth, 1994; Giving Myself to You, 1995; Live To Love, 1997; Groovology, 2002; Kickin' It Up, 2004; New Beginnings, 2006; "Sax for Stax", 2008; "Gerald Alston Sings Sam Cooke", 2008. **Orgs:** Hon spokesperson, Inst for Black Parenting, beginning 1989; mem, Alpha Phi Alpha Fraternity, 1978-. **Honors/Awds:** Best Jazz Artist Award, Black Radio Exclusive, 1988; Recognition Award, Boy's Club of Am, 1991. **Special Achievements:** Film Score, Devlin; performance, Passenger 57; two-time Grammy Award nominee, 1989, 1990; performance, Hank Gathers Story, 1991-92; performer dat Pres Bill Clinton's Inaguration Ceremony, 1993. **Business Addr:** Singer, C/o Concord Music Group Inc, PO Box 15096, Beverly Hills, CA 90209.*

ALBRIGHT, DR. ROBERT, JR.
School administrator. **Personal:** Born Dec 2, 1944, Philadelphia, PA; married Linda Diane Pittman; children: Keia Lorriane & Lance Robert. **Educ:** Lincoln Univ, AB, 1966; Tufts Univ, MA, 1972; Kent State Univ, PhD, 1978. **Career:** School administrator (retired); Lincoln Univ, dir, 1969-71, vpres, 1972-76; Va Union Univ, dir upward bound morton; Consortium RR Morton Memorial Inst Wash, dir, 1977-79; US Dept Ed Wash, spec asst asst secy, 1979-81; Univ NC Charlotte, vice chancellor, 1981-83; Harvard Univ Summer Inst Cambridge, MA, instr; Johnson C Smith Univ Charlotte, pres, 1983-94, pres emer, Currently; The NC Consortium, Chmn Bd Dirs; Educ Testing Serv, exec vpres, 1983-94. **Orgs:** Consult, US Off Ed, Wash, 1970-79, PA Dept Ed, Harrisburg, 1972-79, Res Triangle Inst; ed, Stud Serv Issues Probs & Opportunity J, 1983; Urban League, 1983; bd visitors, Univ NC, 1983; Rotary; bd dir, Duke Power Co; bd dirs, Nat Bank NC; bd

trustees, Educ Testing Serv; bd trustees,Southern Educ Found; bd dirs, trustee, Warren Wilson Col; Southern Educ Found; Educ Develop Ctr; bd dir, United Negro Col Fund; Nat Consortium Educ Access; bd Visitors, Lenior-Rhyne Col; trustee, Educ Testing Serv; chmn, bd dirs, NC Consortium Int & Intercultural Educ; State Department Task Force. **Honors/Awds:** Sec's Cert Appreciation, US Dept Educ, 1981; Distinguished Service Award, Nat Advan Asn Colored People; Hope Award, Mult Sclerosis Soc; President's Award, NASPA; W K Kellog Leadership Fel, Nat Asn Equal Opportunity Higher Educ, 2003. **Special Achievements:** First African Am to serve as the Chmn of the Bd of Dirs of the Am Coun of Educ; Fulbright Scholar, 1984; Publ numerous articles relating to higher education. **Business Addr:** President Emeritus, Johnson C Smith University, 100 Beatties Ford Rd, Charlotte, NC 28216.

ALBRIGHT, WILLIAM DUDLEY
Executive, executive director. **Personal:** Born Dec 1, 1949, Los Angeles, CA; son of William Dudley Sr and Mattie Pearl Dabner; divorced; children: Anterine Penee Albright & Jackson. **Educ:** Univ Redlands, Redlands, CA, BS, chem, 1971; Calif State Univ Dominguez Hills, CA, MBA, 1974. **Career:** Aerospace Corp, El Segundo, head personnel & security, 1972-78; MITRE Corp, McLean, corporate dir human resources mgt, dir, qual work life & benefits, 1978-, dir human resources mgt, 1999. **Orgs:** Life mem, Alpha Phi Alpha Fraternity Inc, 1968-; bd mem, Grad Eng Minorities Inc, 1981-. **Honors/Awds:** Outstanding Young Man of America, US Jaycees, 1985; HR Leadership Award for Greater Washington, DC Area, 2003. **Home Addr:** 821 Still Creek Lane, Gaithersburg, MD 20878-3218, **Home Phone:** (301)258-1352. **Business Phone:** (703)983-6000.

ALCINDOR, FERDINAND LEWIS, JR. See ABDUL-JABBAR, KAREEM.

ALDREDGE, PROF. JAMES EARL
Educator. **Personal:** Born May 1, 1939, Gilmer, TX; married Daisy Rae. **Educ:** Fresno City Col, AA, bus, 1959; Calif State Univ, BA, therapeutic recreation, 1964, MPA Pub Admin, 1976; Golden Gate Univ, PhD (pub admin), 1985. **Career:** Fresno Cty Econ Opportunities, prog coord 1965; City Fresno, city mgr, 1985-89; Calif St Univ, prof, 1990-2002, Cent Valley Health Policy Inst, adv coun, currently, prof emer, 2002-. **Orgs:** Bd mem, Fresno Cty United Way, CA State Univ, Fresno; vice chair, St Agnes Med Ctr, Fresno; bd trustee, Calif Sch Prof Psychol. **Honors/Awds:** Alumnus of the Year, Col Health & Human Serv, Calif St Univ, 1996. **Home Addr:** 5555 N W Ave, Fresno, CA 93711, **Home Phone:** (559)431-4137.

ALDRIDGE, ALLEN RAY
Teacher, football player. **Personal:** Born May 30, 1972, Houston, TX; son of Allen Sr. **Educ:** Univ Houston, BA, sports admin. **Career:** Football player (retired), teacher; Denver Broncos, linebacker, 1994-97; Detroit Lions, 1998-2001; Houston Texans, 2002; George Bush High Sch, teacher, currently; Philadelphia Eagles, vol asst coach. **Orgs:** Fel Christian Athletes; vol, Pontiac Rescue Mission. **Honors/Awds:** Defensive MVP, Blue-Gray All-Star game, 1993; Championship Game Defensive MVP, 1999. **Business Phone:** (281)634-6060.

ALDRIDGE, DR. DELORES PATRICIA
Educator, sociologist. **Personal:** Born Jun 8, 1941, Tampa, FL; daughter of Willie L and Mary Ellen; married Kwame Essuon, Jun 17, 1972; children: Kwame G Essuon & Aba D Essuon. **Educ:** Clark Col, BA, 1963; Atlanta Univ, MSW, 1966; Univ Ireland-Dublin, certchild psychol, 1967; Purdue Univ, PhD, sociol, 1971; Univ Ghana-Legon, attended 1972; Bryn Mawr, advan cert educ mgt, 1980. **Career:** Tampa Urban League, assoc dir, 1966; St. John God Bros Child Guid Clin, supvr & family therapist, 1966-67; Comprehensive Community Ment Health Ctr, actg chief social work, 1967-68; Purdue Univ, Dept Sociol, teaching asst, 1968-70; Greater Lafayette Community Ctrs Inc, dir community develop div, 1969, exec dir, 1969-71; Emory Univ, Dept Sociol, asst prof, founding coordr, 971-75, Inst Lib Arts, adj prof, 1973-75, assoc prof, coordr Black Studies, 1976-78, Ctr Res Social Change, res assoc, 1977-85, assoc prof sociol, 1978-87, prof social, 1988-, Grace Towns Hamilton prof sociol &african Am Studies, 1990-, Clin Eval Serv, Prog Res Women's Health Care, assoc dir, 1994-; Summer Nat Defense Educ Act fel, 1969; Am Forum Int Study fel, 1972; Spelman Col, vis lectr, 1972-74; USDA Forest Service-,policy analyst, 1980-81; Nat Coun Black Studies, dir res component grants, 1988-93; State Ga, Social & Econ Contrib Women Ga, proj dir, 1997-; Univ Ghana, vis distinguished prof, 1997-. **Orgs:** Delta Sigma Theta Sorority; Asn Social & Behav Scientists; Int Black Women's Cong; Asn African Am Life & History; Nat Coun Black Studies; Asn Black Sociologists; Societas Doctas; Care Int-Atlanta; Decatur Alumnae Chapter Delta Sigma Theta Sorority'Ga; Ankh Maat Wedjau Honor Soc; Int Black Women's Cong; Am Sociol Asn; Southern Sociol Soc. **Honors/Awds:** W E B Du Bois Distinguished Scholar Award, Asn Social & Behav Scientists, 1986; Distinguished Alumni Award, Purdue Univ, 1988; Presidential Award, Nat Coun Black Studies, 1989; Oni Award, Int Black Women's Cong, 1990;Thomas Jefferson Award, Emory Univ, 1992; World lifetime Achivement Awards, Governing Bd Ed Am Biographical Inst, 2003; A Wade Smith Award, Asn Balck Sociologist, 2003; Delores P.Aldridge Excellence Awards, Off Multicultural Affairs, 2003; African American Culture and Philosophy Award, African Am Studies & Res Ctr, Purdue Univ, 2004; Southern Sociological Society Charles S Johnson Award, 2006. **Special Achievements:** Foremost Women of the 20th Century, 1985; Honored as one of eight individuals considered illustrative of Emory's Great faculty from 1836 to the present by the Delegate Assembly of the Emory National Alumni Association on November 14, 1992; numerous television and radio shows on women, families, intergroup relations, & African American Studies; published & edited numerous articles & books. **Business Addr:** Professor, Emory University, Department of Sociology, 228 Tarbutton Hall 1555 Pierce Dr, Atlanta, GA 30322, **Business Phone:** (404)727-0534.

ALDRIDGE, KAREN BETH (KAREN B ALDRIDGE-EASON)
Government official, association executive. **Personal:** Born Oct 19, 1952, Flint, MI; daughter of Avery Aldridge and Mildred Light Aldridge; married Spencer Sims (divorced 1988). **Educ:** Univ Mich, Ann Arbor, MI, BA, 1980; Western Mich Univ, Kalamazoo, MI, MPA, 1985. **Career:** Nat Baptist Foreign Mission Bd, Liberia, West Africa, prin & mgr, 1975-77; Mich State Senate, Lansing MI, legis asst, 1977-83; Mich Dept Com, Lansing, MI, sr budget analyst, 1984-87, acting budget dir & dep budget dir, 1987-88; City Flint, MI, budget dir, 1988-92; Mich Dept Mgt & Budget, dir off health & human servs; Charles Stewart Mott Found, found liaison, Off Gov Jennifer M Granholm, State Mich (formerly prog dir, Flint Area prog). **Orgs:** Treas, bd, mem, Am Soc Publ Admin, Flint & Saginaw Valley Chap, 1983-; bd mem, 1989-, treas, Visually Impaired Ctr, 1990-91; adv bd mem, Baker Col, 1989-; bd mem, Int Inst Flint, 1990-; dir, Youth Div, Nat Baptist Congress. **Honors/Awds:** Woman of the Year, Wolverine State Congress, 1977; Fel, Educ Policy Fel Prog, Inst Educ Leadership, 1986-87. **Business Addr:** Foundation Liaison, Program Director, Charles Stewart Mott Foundation, 503 S Saginaw St Suite 1200 Mott Foundation Bldg, Flint, MI 48502-1851, **Business Phone:** (810)238-5651.

ALDRIDGE, MARKITA
Basketball player. **Personal:** Born Sep 15, 1973; daughter of Adele Aldridge. **Educ:** Univ NC, Charlotte, attended 1996. **Career:** Portland Power, guard, 1996-97; Colo Xplosion, 1996-97; Philadelphia Rage, 1997-98; Columbus Quest, 1998-99; Wash Mystics, 1999-01; Atlanta Justice, 2000-01; Charlotte 49ers, 2008. **Orgs:** Founder, Markita Aldridge Found. **Honors/Awds:** Most Valuable Player, Univ NC. *

ALDRIDGE-EASON, KAREN B. See ALDRIDGE, KAREN BETH.

ALERS, ROCHELLE
Executive, writer. **Personal:** Born Aug 7, 1943, New York, NY; daughter of James A and Minnie L Ford; divorced; children: Noemi V. **Educ:** John Jay Col Criminal Justice, CUNY, BA, 1974. **Career:** Empire State Med Equipment Dealers Asn, exec asst, 1987-91; Nassau County Dept Drugs & Alcohol Addiction Serv, community liaison specialist, 1991-. Author: "Careless Whispers," 1988, "Happily Ever After," 1994, "My Love's Keeper," 1991, "Holiday Cheer-First Fruits," 1995, "Hideway," 1995, "Careless Whispers," reprint, 1996, "Home Sweet Home," 1996, "Vows," 1997, "Reckless Surrender," 1997, "Hidden Agenda," 1997, "Love Letters-Hearts of Gold," 1997, "Careless Whispers," reprint, 1998, "Heaven Sent," 1998, "Gentle Yearning," 1998, "Harvest Moon", 1999, "Just Before Dawn", 2000, "Private Passions", 2001, "No Compromise", 2002, "Renegade", 2003, "Hideaway Saga", 2004, "All My Tomorrow", 2005, "A Younger Man", 2005, "Beyond Business", 2005, "Best Kept Secrets", 2006 "Stranger In My Arms", 2007, "Hideaway Legacy", 2007. **Orgs:** Freeport Exchange Club, 1990-; co-founder, pres, Women Writers Color, 1990-94; Long Island Quilters Soc, 1996. **Honors/Awds:** Archdiocese Rockville Ctr, Pope Pius X, 1997, Gold Pen Award, 2000; Vivian Stephens Award for Excellence in Romance Writing, 2001; Heart & Soul online mag, The Top Five Most Popular African-Am romance writers, 1999; Emma Award; Romantic Times Career Achievement Award; Zora Neale Hurston Literary Award.

ALEX, GREGORY K.
Clergy, administrator. **Personal:** Born Nov 30, 1948, Seattle, WA; son of Joseph P and Delores; married. **Educ:** Univ Wash, BA, urban planning/archit, 1971, MA, theol, 1996. **Career:** Housing & Urban Develop, Wash DC, urban planner, 1971-75; Seattle Housing Authority, dir target proj prog, 1975-78; A & R Imports Inc, pres, 1978-80; Matt Talbot Ministry, Seattle, WA, minister & dir, 1985-. **Orgs:** Yale Univ Black Environ Studies Team Curric Comn; comnr judo, Goodwill Games, 1988-90; African Am Reach & Teach Health Ministry. **Honors/Awds:** Outstanding Achievement Award, Housing & Urban Develop, 1972; Outstanding Achievement Award, Univ WA; Black Athletic Alumni Award, 1971; Master TKD, Chang Moo Kwan, Seoul, Korea, 1989; Fran Nordstrom Vol Year, King County Boys & Girls Clubs, 1986; Community Serv Award, Downtown Human Serv Coun, 1986. **Business Addr:** Minister, Director, Matt Talbot Center, 2312 3rd Ave, Seattle, WA 98121-1712, **Business Phone:** (206)723-9395.*

ALEXANDER, DR. A MELVIN
Dermatologist. **Personal:** Born Feb 4, 1943, Cleveland, OH; son of Alvin Melvin and Grace; married Leslie Gaillard; children: Hollie C & Allison L. **Educ:** Hillsdale Coll, BS, 1965; Howard Univ Col Med, MD, 1968. **Career:** US Army Med Ctr Okinawa, chief dermatology serv, 1972-74; Howard Univ, asst prof, 1975-80; Shaw Health Ctr, dermatology consult, 1977-78; Alexander Dermatology Ctr, PC, sr res assoc, dir 1978-. **Orgs:** Consult, Am Safety Razor Co, 1980-82; chmn, dermatology section Nat Medial Assoc, 1985-87; consult, United Parcel Service, 1992-; Gillette Research Inst, 1993-; Black Entertainment TV, 1993-. **Honors/Awds:** Upjohn Award for Excellence in Research, Howard Univ; contributor "Conn's Current Therapy," 1983, 1984; author of several published professional articles. **Military Serv:** AUS. **Home Phone:** (410)464-5656. **Business Addr:** Physician, 11085 Little Patuxent Pkwy, Columbia, MD 21044, **Business Phone:** (301)596-4187.

ALEXANDER, ARIKA
Marketing executive. **Personal:** Born in Bronx, NY. **Career:** Reach Media Inc, mkt mgr, currently. **Orgs:** ASD. **Business Addr:** Affiliate Marketing Manager, Reach Media Inc, 13760 Noel Rd Suite 750, Dallas, TX 75240, **Business Phone:** (972)789-1058.

ALEXANDER, BILLYE J.
Executive. **Educ:** Univ Pac, Stockton, BA, fr. **Career:** Executive (retire); Sears, Roebuck & Co, exec, 1970, Weberstown Mall Store, div mgr, 1971, dist gen mgr, 1992, NW Region, sr vpres commun, 2002, Midwest Region, vpres & gen mgr, 2003, Dept Multicultural Mkt, vpres, 2004. **Orgs:** John McLendon Memorial Minority Blue Ribbon Comn. **Special Achievements:** One of the 25 Influential Black Women In Business, 2003. *

ALEXANDER, BLAIR E
Executive. **Career:** Oper Urgent Fury, plt ldr; United Negro Col Fund Spec Progs Corp, Dept Defense Tech Asst Prog, prog dir, currently. **Military Serv:** AUS, lt. **Business Phone:** (703)205-7631.

ALEXANDER, BRENT
Football player. **Personal:** Born Jul 10, 1971, Detroit, MI; married Mari; children: Corey & Myles. **Educ:** Tenn State Univ. **Career:** Football player (retired), NY Giants, 2004-06; Arizona Cardinals, defensive back, 1994-97; Carolina Panthers, 1998-99; Pittsburgh Steelers, 2000-03; New York Giants, 2004-05. *

ALEXANDER, REV. CEDRIC V
Chief executive officer, chairperson. **Educ:** Howard Univ, BA, int rels; Univ Calif, PhD. **Career:** First AME Church, pastor; Seventeenth Episcopal Dist, exec asst; Col Financial Planning, adj fac mem; Am Express Financial Advisors, staff; Waddell & Reed, staff; Primerica Financial Serv, staff; Robert Van Securities, sr vpres & chief compliance officer; Demanco Brokerage Serv Inc, founder, chmn & chief exec officer, currently. **Orgs:** Orange County Bar Asn; Richard Banyard Inns Ct; Nat Bar Asn; Financial Planning Asn; Nat Asn Black Accountants; Calif Conf Ministerial Alliance, AME Church; Int Fraternity Delta Sigma Pi. **Business Addr:** Chairman, Chief Executive Officer, Demanco Brokerage Services Inc, PO Box 71761, Oakland, CA 94612-2006, **Business Phone:** (510)435-1780.

ALEXANDER, DR. CHARLES
College administrator. **Career:** UCSF Sch Dent, assoc dean admiss & stud affairs, 2003-06. *

ALEXANDER, CHARLES FRED, JR.
Football player. **Personal:** Born Jul 28, 1957, Galveston, TX; married Yvette; children: Nicole. **Educ:** La State Univ, attended 1979. **Career:** Football player (retired); Cincinnati Bengals, running back & fullback, 1979-85. **Honors/Awds:** All-Am, La State Univ; Only La State Univ player to ever account for 4000 or more yards in a career.

ALEXANDER, CLIFFORD L., JR.
Management consultant, lawyer. **Personal:** Born Sep 21, 1933, New York, NY; married Adele Logan; children: Elizabeth, Mark Clifford. **Educ:** Harvard Univ, BA, 1955; Yale Univ, LLB, 1958; Malcolm X Col, LLD, hon, 1972; Morgan State Univ, LLD, hon, 1972; Wake Forest Univ, LLD, hon, 1978; Univ Md, LLD, hon, 1980; Atlanta Univ, LLD, hon, 1982. **Career:** NY Co, asst dist atty, 1959-61; Manhattanville Hamilton Grange, exec dir, 1961-62; HARYOU Inc, exec dir, 1962-63; pvt pract, atty, 1962-63; Nat Security Coun, staff mem, 1963-64; Pres Lyndon, Johnson, dep spec asst, 1964-65, assoc spec coun, 1965-66, dep spec coun, 1966-67; Equal Employ Opportunity Comn, chmn, 1967-69; Arnold & Porter, partner, 1969-75; TV news, Wash, DC, commentator, 1972-76; Howard Univ, prof law, 1973-74; DC, mayor, 1974; Verner, Liipfert, Bernhard, McPherson & Alexander, partner, 1975-76; Dept Army, secy, 1977-80; Alexander & Assocs Inc, WA, pres & founder, 1981-; consult, Maj League Baseball; IMS Health, bd dirs, 1998-02. **Orgs:** Chmn, US Equal Employ Opportunity Comn, 1967-69; pres Comn Income Maint Progs, 1967-68; pres Comn Observation Human Rights, 1968; bd dirs, Mex-Am Legal Def & Educ Fund; Nat Asn Advan Colored People Legal & Educ Fund; bd overseers, Harvard Univ, 1969-75; trustee, Atlanta Univ; host & co-producer, TV prog Cliff Alexander, Black on White,

1971-74; chmn, The Comm for Food & Shelter Inc; chmn, Dance Theatre Harlem, 1995-; dir, Penn Power & Light Co; dir, Dreyfus Third Century Fund, Dreyfus Gen Money Mkt Fund, Dreyfus Common Stock Fund, Dreyfus Govt Sec Fund, Dreyfus Tax Exempt Fund, MCI Corp; adj prof, Georgetown Univ; prof, Howard Univ; mem, Am & DC Bar Asns; dir, Equitable Resources Inc. **Honors/Awds:** Ames Award, Harvard Univ, 1955; Named Hon Citizen Kans City, MO, 1965; Frederick Douglass Award, 1970; Outstanding Civilian Serv Award, Dept Army, 1980; Distinguished Publ Serv Award, Dept Def, 1981. **Special Achievements:** Rep pres, Kingdom of Swaziland, 1968; first African-American Secretary of the Army. **Military Serv:** AUS, 1958-59, secy, 1977-81. **Business Addr:** President, Founder, Alexander & Associates Inc, 400 C St NE, Washington, DC 20002, **Business Phone:** (202)546-0111.*

ALEXANDER, CORNELIA
Beautician, government official, public speaker. **Personal:** Born in Winona, MS; daughter of George Thompson and Emma Trotter Thompson; married John Alexander Sr (died 1979); children: Margaret Alexander McLaughlin, John Jr, Leslie B Hardy, Charles, Carl E Hardy & Constance E Hardy Atkins. **Educ:** Vestal Labs, Cert, 1969; Youngstown State Univ, Cert, 1977. **Career:** Alexander's Garage, off mgr, 1959-77; Salem City Hosp, laundry mgr, 1965-80; Mary Kay Cosmetics, beauty consult, 1979; NCSC Sr Aide Prog, sr aide, 1982-83; Salem City Coun, coun woman, 1984-89; pub speaker, 1986; Columbiana County Recorder's Off, dep recorder, 1982. **Orgs:** Mt Zion AME Church, 1957-82; Salem YWCA, 1968-; dir, Salem YWCA, 1971-75; dem precinct comn, 1980; Bus & Prof Women, Lisbon, OH, 1981-83; Am Cancer Soc, 1982-83; Believer's Christian Fel, 1982-; spec exec, Salem YWCA, 1982-85; bd dir, Mobile Meals Salem, 1978; chmn, Fed & State Funding Comn City Coun; served on 9 coun comn; Columbiana County Community Corrections Planning Bd, 1984; vpres, pres, Human Serv Dept Adv Bd, 1991; Salem Bus & Prof Women Orgn; corresp secy, Salem Women's Aglow, 1992; Salem Area Habitat Housing Humanity, bd mem, vpres, 1992-95; Salem Sr Citizens Orgn; pres, Salem Women's Dem Club; Salem Hist Soc; E Liverpool African Am Hist Mus; sr companion vol, Dept Eldercare, State of Fla, 1998-. **Honors/Awds:** Senior Citizen of the Year, Columbiana County, 1992; Community Service Award, Fed Prison Bd; Black Achievers Award, State Rep, 2000. **Special Achievements:** First among 3 nominees Chosen as Democrats of the Year, 1985; First African American to obtain a seat on the City Coun of Salem; "Local Heroes/They Made a Difference in 1992", The Vindicator, Jan 3, 1992; Salem News, June 8, 1992, May 17, 1993; Ohio's Heritage, Autumn 1994; Yesteryears, January 14, 1995.

ALEXANDER, CORY LYNN
Basketball player. **Personal:** Born Jun 22, 1973, Waynesboro, VA. **Educ:** Univ Va, BA, psychol. **Career:** San Antonio Spurs, guard, 1995-98; Denver Nuggets, 1997-2000; Orlando Magic, 2000-01; Roanoke Dazzle, 2002-03; Virtus Roma, 2003-04; Charlotte Bobcats, guard, 2004-05.

ALEXANDER, DAWN
Marketing executive. **Educ:** Oberlin Col, BA, 1982; Harvard Univ JFK Sch Govt, cert, 1985; Yale Sch Mgt, MBA, 1987. **Career:** Morgan Stanley, syst analyst, 1982-84, data ctr oper supvr, 1984-85; Drew-Dawn Enterprises, pres, 1984-85, chair & chief exec officer, 1997-; DFS Dorland Worldwide, asst acct exec, 1986; Pepsi-Cola Co, from asst assoc to sr assoc, mkt mgr, 1987-90; Colgate-Palmolive, prod mgr, 1990-91; Uniworld Group, acct supvr, 1991, regional acct dir, 1991-92, vpres mgt supvr, 1992-95; Compuserve, sr prod mgr, 1995-96, promotions group mgr, 1996-97; IBM, sr prod mgr, 1997; Image Mkg Solutions Inc, pres, 1996-; Aether Systs, dir mkt, 2000-01; SecureNet Solutions Inc, vpres sales & mkt, currently; Univ Md, Univ Col, adj fac mem, bus & mgt unit, currently. **Orgs:** Alumni admis rep, Oberlin Col, 1982-; Nat Black MBA Asn, 1986-; bd mem, Dance Theatre Workshop, 1993-95; chairperson, Oberlin African Am Alumni Group, 1996-; bd mem, Oberlin Col Alumni Asn, 1996-; Women Sports Found, 1996-01; Women Basketball Coaches Asn, 1996-01; bd mem, Gateway, Ga AV Revitalization Corp, 1999-00; Am Mkt Asn; Am Advert Fedn & Advert Club Metrop DC; bd mem, Rockville Chamber Com, 1999-00; comnr, chair, develop comt, Montgomery Co Celebration, 2000. **Special Achievements:** Served as first vice president of Maryland InfraGard chapter. **Business Addr:** Vice President of Sales & Marketing, SecureNet Solutions Inc., 761 Silver Spring Ave Suite B, Silver Spring, MD 20910, **Business Phone:** (301)565-0001.*

ALEXANDER, DERRICK L.
Football player. **Personal:** Born Nov 13, 1973, Jacksonville, FL. **Educ:** Fla. **Career:** Football player (retried); Minnesota Vikings, defensive end, 1995-98; cleveland browns, 1999. **Honors/Awds:** Inducted into the Florida State Hall of Fame, 2007. *

ALEXANDER, DERRICK SCOTT
Football player, businessperson. **Personal:** Born Nov 6, 1971, Detroit, MI. **Educ:** Univ Mich, sports mgt. **Career:** Football player (retired); Cleveland Browns, wide receiver, 1994-95; Baltimore Ravens, 1996-97; Kansas City Chiefs, 1998-01; Minnesota Vikings, 2002; bus exec, currently. *

ALEXANDER, DOROTHY DEXTER
Educator. **Personal:** Born Jun 17, 1929, Chattaroy, WV; daughter of William (deceased) and Georgia (deceased); married Robert D, May 22, 1956 (deceased); children: Robert D Jr & Doncella Darice. **Educ:** WVa State Col, BS, 1950; Pikeville Col, 1957; Marshall Univ, attended 1962; Ohio State Univ, attended 1964. **Career:** Educator (retired); Mingo County Educ Bd, social studies & music teacher, 1950-63; Franklin County Child Welfare Bd, OH, teacher, 1963-66; Educ Bd, Columbus, OH, vocal music teacher, 1966-88; Shiloh Baptist Church, minister music, 1992-97; mgr, Greater Columbus Conv Ctr, currently. **Orgs:** Local vpres, Ark Sorority Inc, 1950, 1984, local secy music, 1982-92, chair awards luncheon, 1983; Mid-Ohio & Franklin County Health Planning Fedn, 1979-80; collector, UNF, 1979-88; pres, Aesthetics Social Club, 1980-84; accompanists, Columbus Boychoir, 1985-88; community rept, educonsort, Franklin County Child Develop Coun, 1988-92; regional music dir, Great Lakes, 1990; chair scholarship comt, Lunch Bunch, 1991-92; NCW, 1989-; Nat Coun Negro Women; Nat Asn Advan Colored People; Federated Women's Club; Esther Chap No 3, OES PHA; Friends Arts Community Enrichment; dir sr choir, Shiloh Baptist Church. **Honors/Awds:** Outstanding Accompanists, Columbus Boy choir, 1986; Human Service Award, Ark Sorority Inc, 1988; Outstanding Director Messiah, Trinity Baptist Church, 1987; Inducted into the Board Sponsors, More house Col, 1995; OH Senior Citizens Hall of Fame, OH Dept Aging, inducted, 2001; Lady of Distinction, Gospel Excellence, 2001; Heroine of the Year, 2002. **Special Achievements:** Local Music Dir of Pre-Convention Musical for the 93rd annual Lott Carey National Music Convention, 1989; director of Shiloh-Trinity Baptist Churches Presentation of "Excerpts from Handel's Messiah," 1986-89;collaborated with a Franklin County Commission to develop a reading system for Educable Retarded Children, Library of Congress, 1971; composed hymn for 125th Anniversary of Shiloh Baptist Church "Steadfast Faith"; coordinator, Annual Martin Luther King Jr. Birthday Breakfast, Columbus,OH, 2001-03; Composed music for Alpha Sigma Omega, 2003. **Home Addr:** 2187 Liston Ave, Columbus, OH 43207. **Business Addr:** Manager, Greater Columbus Convention Center, 400 N High St, Columbus, OH 43215, **Business Phone:** (614)827-2500.

ALEXANDER, DREW W.
Physician, educator. **Personal:** Born Dec 21, 1948, Peoria, IL. **Educ:** Earlham Col, BA, 1970; Med Col Ohio, MD, 1973. **Career:** Albert Einstein Col Med, resident & intern, 1973-76; Univ Tex, Health Sci Ctr, Dallas, adolescent med fel, 1976-77, asst prof pediat, 1977; W Dallas Youth Clinic, health team leader, 1977; Southwestern Med Sch, asst dean, community affairs, currently; Adolescent Health Assoc, physician, currently. **Orgs:** Educ comt, Soc Adolescent Med, 1976-; asst med dir, Dallas City Juvenile Detention Clin, 1977-; consult, Multidisciplinary Adolescent Health Training Proj, 1977-; admissions comn, Univ Tex, Dallas, 1978-; coordr, Minority Affairs, 1979-; vol, Big Brothers & Big Sisters, 1976-; bd mem, Child Care Asn Metrop, Dallas, 1978-. **Business Addr:** Assistant Dean Community Affairs, UT Southwestern Medical School, 5323 Harry Hines Blvd, Dallas, TX 75390-9003, **Business Phone:** (214)648-2509.*

ALEXANDER, DR. EDWARD CLEVE
Scientist, educator. **Personal:** Born Nov 20, 1943, Knoxville, TN; son of Robert W and Gladys Clardy; married Edwina Carr; children: Everett, Erika & Efrem. **Educ:** City Col, New York, BS, 1965; State Univ New York, Buffalo, PhD, 1969. **Career:** Iowa State Univ, post doctoral fel, 1969-70; Calif Univ, San Diego, Third Col Sci & Technol Prog, asst prof chem & coordr, 1970-78; Calif State Univ, Los Angeles, lectr, 1978-82, vis assoc prof; BOOST Prog, San Diego, supvr dept math & sci, 1982-89; US Navy Broadened Opportunity Officers Selection & Training Prog, supvr math & sci; consult; San Diego Mesa Col, chmn chem, 1995-, chair of chairs, 1996-99, prof chem, Bridges Prog Dir, currently. **Orgs:** Consult, NIH; Am Chem Soc, 1965-; Minority Bio med Support Br, 1974-78; bd dir & exec bd, San Diego Urban League, 1972-76; IBM, San Jose, CA, 1976. **Honors/Awds:** Thirty Five Year Distinguished Service Award, Am Chem Soc, 2000. **Special Achievements:** Published & presented over 25 papers in fields of chem research & higher edu; published 4 coll chem instruction packets; reviewer & editor of over 20 Col chem textbooks. **Home Addr:** 3381 Lone Jack Rd, Encinitas, CA 92024. **Business Addr:** Professor, Bridges Prog Director, San Diego Mesa College, Chemistry Department, I-214 7250 Mesa Col Dr, PO Box K-202, San Diego, CA 92111, **Business Phone:** (619)388-2618.

ALEXANDER, ERIKA
Administrator. **Career:** Marriott Corp, brand vpres. *

ALEXANDER, DR. ESTELLA CONWILL
Educator, poet. **Personal:** Born Jan 19, 1949, Louisville, KY; children: Patrice Sales & Dominic. **Educ:** Univ Louisville, BA, 1975, MA, 1976; Univ Iowa, PhD 1984. **Career:** Univ Iowa, instr/dir black poetry, 1976-79; Grinnell Col, asst prof, 1979-80; Ky State Univ, prof eng; poet, currently; Hunter Col City Univ NY, prof eng. **Honors/Awds:** Recording Motion Grace Gospel Recordings, 1983; Ky Arts Coun Grant, 1986; Art Grant, Ky Found Women, 1986.

ALEXANDER, F S JACK
State government official, commissioner. **Personal:** Born Dec 7, 1930, Iola, KS; son of James Floyd and Agnes Marie Stewart; married Tillie Marie Simon; children: Patricia M, Jack Jr, Stephanie R & Terrell L. **Educ:** Washburn Univ, BA, 1954. **Career:** Commissioner (retired), state government official; Topeka Bd Educ, stockroom mgr, 1948-51 (retired); Goodyear Tire & Rubber Co, qual control, 1951-85; Topeka City, water commr, 1973-85; State Kans Oilfield & Environmental Geol, consult, 1985-86; dept health & environ, 1986-90; Gov Legis Affairs, 1990-91; Kansas Corp Comn, comnr, 1991-96; State Fire Marshal, 2004-. **Orgs:** Ex-com & bd, NLC, 1975-85; Econ & Com Develop Comn, 1975-85; vpres, Topeka United Way Bd, 1975-85; pres, Topeka City Comn, 1975-85; trustee, St Vail Hosp Bd, 1976-85, 1992-; State Water Authority, 1981-86; exec comn, NAACP; past pres, Kans League Munic, 1983-84. **Honors/Awds:** Pub Serv Shawnee Co Comm Asst, 1972-83; Outstanding Public Officer Award, Topeka Comm Develop, 1976; Award, USA 501 Dir Assoc, 1977; Award, Reg 7 Comm Action 1979. **Military Serv:** USN, radiomen second class, 1952-56. **Home Addr:** 2509 Fillmore St, Topeka, KS 66611, **Home Phone:** (785)232-5715. **Business Addr:** State Fire Marshal, Kansas State Fire Marshal, 700 SW Jackson St Suite 600, Topeka, KS 66603, **Business Phone:** (785)296-3401.

ALEXANDER, FLEX
Comedian, actor. **Personal:** Married Shanice Wilson; children: Imani Shekinah. **Career:** Films: Juice, 1992; Money Train, 1995; City of Industry, 1997; The Sixth Man, 1997; Modern Vampires, 1998; She's All That, 1999; Out Cold, 2001; Out Cold, 2001; Sweet Oranges, 2003; Her Minor Thing, 2005; Love. & Other 4 Letter Words, 2006; Snakes on a Plane, 2006; The List, 2006; TV Series: "One on One", actor & co-exec producer, 2001-06; "Gas", 2004; "Man in the Mirror: The Michael Jackson Story", 2004;"Waiting for Huffman", 2005; "One on One, One Oh Oh", 2005; "House Dad", 2005; "Money's Tight & So Are My Abs", 2005; "Cuts", 2005; "Keeping It Real", 2005; "Missing the Daddy Express", 2006; "Nice Girls Don't Get the Corner Office ", 2007; "Love & Other 4 Letter Words ", 2007; "The Hills Have Eyes II ", 2007; "Deep Freeze", 2007; "CSI: Miami", 2007.

ALEXANDER, GARY ROBERTS
Basketball player. **Personal:** Born Nov 1, 1969, Jacksonville, FL. **Educ:** Univ Southern Fla, attended 1992. **Career:** Maccabi Haifa, 1992; Miami Heat, 1993; Elecon Desio, Italy, 1993-94; Cleveland Cavaliers, 1994; Strasbourg IG, 1994-95; Besiktas Istambul (Turkey), 1996-97; Breogan Lugo, Spain, 1996-98; SSA Trefl Sopot, Poland, 1997, 2001-02; BCM Gravelines, France, 1998-2001; Caceres, Spain, 2001-02; STB LeHavre, 2003-04; Roanne, France, 2004-06.

ALEXANDER, HARRY TOUSSAINT
Judge, lawyer. **Personal:** Born Jul 22, 1924, New Orleans, LA; married Beatrice Perkins; children: Normastel Agnes, Harry Jr, Beatrice, Louis. **Educ:** Xavier Univ, BS, 1949; Georgetown Univ Sch Law, JD, 1952. **Career:** Attorney, associate judge (retired); Georgetown Univ, res asst, 1951-52; Off Price Stabilization, atty adv, 1952-53; pvt pract atty, 1953-; US Atty District of Columbia, asst, 1953-61, spec atty, 1961-64, staff asst criminal div, 1964-65; US Dept Justice, atty, 1961-66; Super Ct, Washington, DC, assoc judge, 1966-76; Howard Univ Sch Law, adj prof, 1970. **Orgs:** Judicial Conf DC; Cardoza Comt Judicial Conf, Am Bar Asn; Youth Coun, New Orleans, La; vpres, Nat Fedn Cath Col Students La Region; US Nat Students Asn; treas, Nat Asn Advan Colored People; recording secy, Washington Bar Asn, 1955-60; pres, NW Boundary Civic Asn, 1958-60; comt mem, Abolition Mandatory Capital Punishment, DC, 1959-62; nat vpres, Xavier Univ Alumni Asn, 1960-62; Scouters Int Rep St Gabriels Cath Church, 1963-65; Interreligious Comt Race Rels, 1963-66; vice chmn, BSA, 1966; Nat Conf Christians & Jews, 1965-70; Family & Child Servs, Washington, 1971; United Nat Bank Washington, 1977; pres, Nat Asn Advan Colored People, DC, 1977; Phi Delta Phi Int Legal Fraternity; Alpha Delta Int Legal Fraternity. **Honors/Awds:** Dr Cruezot Award; Frederick W Shea Award; Outstanding Service, DC C C; Certificate of Degree Strategic Air Command 1973; Outstanding Community Service Award, 1975; William H Hastie Award, Nat Conf Black Lawyers, 1976; Harry Toussaint Alexander Day DC Council; Martin Luther King Jr Outstanding Service Award, Howard Univ Sch Law, 1977. **Special Achievements:** Author: The Black Judge as a Change Agent, The Administration of Criminal Justice, ed Lee Brown, 1974; Published "Appeals in Fed Jurisdiction" NBA 1960, "Curbing Juvenile Delinquency with Adequate Playground Facilities" 1957, "The Nature of Our Heritage" 1950-51, "The Unconstitutionality of Segregation in Ed" 1950-51, "Due Process Required in Revocation of a Conditional Pardon" 1950-51, "The Antislavery Origins of the Fourteenth Amendment", "Convention Coverage" Assoc Negro Press Inc 1947, Xavier Herald 1946-49;TV appearances The Admin of Juv Criminal Justice; radio appearances The Admin of Cinal Juv Justice. **Military Serv:** USN, 1943-46. *

ALEXANDER, HUBBARD LINDSAY
Football coach. **Personal:** Born Feb 14, 1939; married Gloria; children: Todd, Chad & Bard. **Educ:** Tenn State Univ. **Career:** Tenn State Univ, coach, 1962; high sch coach, nine seasons, Memphis, TN; Vanderbilt Univ, asst coach, 1974-78; Univ Miami,

tight ends football coach, 1979-84, wide receivers, 1985-88; Dallas Cowboys, receivers coach, 1989-97, 2000; Minn Vikings, receivers coach, 1997-99; New Orleans Saints, receivers coach, 2001-04; Melrose High Sch, football head coach, 2006-. **Business Phone:** (901)416-5974.

ALEXANDER, JAMES, JR.
Lawyer. **Personal:** Born Oct 7, 1945, Charlotte, NC. **Educ:** Columbia Col, Columbia Univ, BA, 1967; Case W Res Univ, JD, 1970; Nat Col Crim Defense Lawyer, cert, 1974. **Career:** Reginal Heber Smith Fell, Cleveland, 1970-72; Hough Area & Develop Corp, Cleveland, gen couns, 1971-72; Cuyahoga Co, asst co pro secy, 1972; Tolliver Nimrod & Alexender, atty, 1972-75; Hardiman Alexander Buchanan Pittman & Howland Co LPA, atty; Daryl E Pittman & Assoc. **Orgs:** Cleveland Bar Asn; Am Acad Trial Layers; Nat Bar Asn; Cuyahoga Bar Asn; Nat Conf Black Lawyers Asn; pres, Hough Community Coun; treasurer, Columbia Univ Club, Cleveland, 1972; mem bd trust, Un Torch Serv; Fed Community Plan Bd; Goodrich Soc Settle Bd; vpres, Legal Aid Soc Cleveland; pres, Hough Area Develop Corp. **Honors/Awds:** President Award, 1972; Martin Luther King Award.

ALEXANDER, JAMES ARTHUR
School administrator, executive director. **Personal:** Born Aug 22, 1953, Memphis, TN; son of Calvin and Katherine; married Vicki Marshall, Oct 7, 1978. **Educ:** Yale Univ, BA, 1975, JD, 1978. **Career:** Lord Bissell & Brodk, assoc atty, 1978-84; Chicago State Univ, exec asst to pres, 1985-86, vpres, admin, 1986-89; Ill State Univ, vpres, bus & finance, 1989-93; Govs State Univ, 1993-99; Admin & Planning, Univ Park, IL, vpres; Nat Louis Univ, exec vpres, 2001-02, 2003-; Inner City Teaching Corps, exec dir, 2003-. **Orgs:** Am Bar Asn; CBA; CCBA; NACUBO; Leadership Greater Chicago, NACUA. **Home Addr:** 6818 S Euclid Ave, Chicago, IL 60649, **Home Phone:** (773)363-8883. **Business Addr:** Executive Director, Inner City Teaching Corps, 3141 W Jackson Blvd, Chicago, IL 60612, **Business Phone:** (773)265-7240.*

ALEXANDER, JAMES BRETT
Journalist. **Personal:** Born Nov 19, 1948, Boston, MA. **Educ:** Northeastern Univ, BA 1971. **Career:** NE Univ, Div Instr Community The Urban Confrontation, producer, dir 1968; Northeastern's radio, prod dept; CBS News Prods, exec producer; CBS corp diversity comm; Christian Sci Monitor Boston, staff writer, 1968-71; Random House Inc Lang Arts Div, ed asst, 1972-73; Manhattan Community Col, dir, publs New York City, 1973-74; NY Post, staff reporter, journalist, 1994. **Orgs:** The Experiment in Int Living, 1969-; The Am Forum for Intl Study; The Boston Black United Front, 1969-70; The Int Peace Acad, 1972-; The Sixth Pan-African Congress; dir, publ No Am Reg Ford Found Fel, 1966-69; Ford Found grants, 1966. **Honors/Awds:** Nieman fel, Harvard Univ; Martin Luther King fel, Univ Denver, 1971-72; Nat Asn Black Journalists Award.

ALEXANDER, JAMES EDUARD (JIM ALEXANDER)
U.S. attorney. **Career:** Adams & Alexander, atty, currently. **Business Addr:** Attroney, Adams & Alexander, 272 S Los Roberts, Pasadena, CA 91101-2872, **Business Phone:** (626)798-0888.*

ALEXANDER, JIM. See ALEXANDER, JAMES EDUARD.

ALEXANDER, JOHN WESLEY, JR.
School administrator, college teacher. **Personal:** Born May 17, 1938, Salem, OH; son of John Wesley and Virgina. **Educ:** Southern Colo State Col, AA, 1958; Boston Univ, BS, math, 1961; Bowling Green State Univ, MA, 1965; Boston Univ, EdD, math educ, 1985; Calif Coast Univ, MBA, 1987, PhD, mgt sci & opers res, 1989. **Career:** Model Cities Col Consortium, acad dean, 1969-70; W African Reg Math Prog, math adv, 1970-77; Ed Develop Ctr, consult ed, 1977-78; Boston Univ, asst, 1977-78; CT Mutual Life Ins Co, acturial analyst, 1978-81; Futures Group, chief statistician, 1981-82; Wentworth Inst Tech, prof math, 1982-84; Col Arts & Sci, dean, 1984-90; Univ DC, Dept Math, chmn, 1992-94; Nat Acad Sci, Bd Math Sci, prog officer, 1995-96, dir bd, 1996-97; Spelman Col, chair & prof math, 1998-02; Miami Dade Community Col, prof, 2005-. **Orgs:** Fel Bowling Green State Univ, 1964-65; Campaign chairperson, United Combined Health Appeal, CT Mutual Life Ins Co, 1981; pres, Nat Asn Mathematicians, 1994-; pres, Nat Asn Math, 1994-. **Honors/Awds:** Athletic scholar, Southern Colo & Boston Univ, 1956-60; Award of Excellence, Conn Mutual Life Ins Co, 1981. **Home Addr:** 9739 Country Meadows Lane Apt 2A, Laurel, MD 20723. *

ALEXANDER, JOSEPHINE
Registered nurse. **Personal:** Born in Tuskegee, AL; daughter of P Alexander and Daisy Menefee. **Educ:** Tuskegee Univ, Tuskegee, BSN, 1958; Univ Calif, Los Angeles, MN, 1972. **Career:** Veterans Admin Med Ctr est Los Angeles, staff nurse, 1958-60, nurse mgr, 1960-72, psychiat clin specialist, 1972-, primary adult care nurse practr, 1977-. **Orgs:** Life mem, Chi Eta Phi; Am Nurses Asn; Nat League Nursing; Nat Coun Negro Women; historian, 1974-84, first vpres, 1980-84, pres, 1985-89, Chi Eta Phi; Sigma Theta Tau Hon Soc; ANA Found; Black Women Forum; asst parliamentarian, Tuskee Nat Alumni Asn Inc, currently. **Honors/Awds:** Outstanding Leadership Award, Chi Eta Pi, Southwest Region, 1987; Outstanding Service Award, Tuskegee Univ Alumni Asn, Los Angeles Chap, 1988; Black Woman Achievement Award, NAACP Legal Defense & Educ Fund, 1989. **Home Phone:** (323)734-0288. **Business Addr:** Clinical Nurse Specialist, Veterans Administration Medical Center, Brentwood Div, Wilshire & Sawtelle Blvds, Los Angeles, CA 90073.

ALEXANDER, HON. JOYCE LONDON
Judge. **Personal:** Born Sep 1, 1946?; daughter of Oscar London and Edna London. **Educ:** Howard Univ, BA; New England Law Sch, JD, 1972; North eastern Univ Law Sch, LLD; Bridgewater St Col, LLD; Suffolk Univ, LLD; NC Cent Univ, LLD. **Career:** Greater Boston Legal Assistance Proj, staff atty, 1972-74; Reginald Heber Smith Community, law fel; Youth Activ Comn, legal coun, 1974-76; Tufts Univ, asst prof, 1974-75; MA Bd Higher Educ, gen coun, 1976-79; WBZ-TV Boston, on-camera legal ed, 1978-79; US Dist Ct, Dist Mass, magistrate judge, 1979-. **Orgs:** Urban League Eastern MA, pres emer, Nat Coun US Magistrates, First Circuit dir; chair, MA Black Judges Conf; chair, Nat Bar Asn Judicial Coun; bd mem, Joint Ctr Polit & Econ Studies, Wash, DC; bd overseers, Boys & Girls Club Greater Boston; Alpha Kappa Alpha Sorority Inc. **Honors/Awds:** William Robert Ming Award, NAACP; Equal Justice Award, Nat Bar Asn; William Hastie Award, Nat Bar Asn; Raymond Pace Alexander Award, Nat Bar Asn; C Francis Stadford Award, Nat Bar Asn; Martin Luther King Jr Drum Major for Justice Award, Southern Christian Leadership Conf, 1985; Thurgood Marshall Award, Natl Bar Asn, 2004. **Special Achievements:** Ten Outstanding Young Leaders of Massachusetts, Boston Jaycees, 1980; One of Ten Outstanding Young Women in American; honored as a "Living Legend",Museum of Afro-American History, 2004; New England Law Review dedicated its entire summer edition; First African-American Chief United States Magistrate Judge; First African-American woman Chief Judge of any court in Massachusetts. **Business Addr:** Magistrate Judge, US District Court District of Massachusetts, John Joseph Moakley US Courthouse, 1 Courthouse Way Suite 2300, Boston, MA 02210, **Business Phone:** (617)748-9238.

ALEXANDER, JULIUS
Executive. **Educ:** Morehouse Col, BA, eng. **Career:** Lockheed Martin Corp, chief instr; Aviation Career Enrichment Inc, founder, chief exec officer & chief instr, 1980-. **Honors/Awds:** Community Service Award, 2007.

ALEXANDER, KELLY MILLER, JR.
Funeral director. **Personal:** Born Oct 17, 1948, Charlotte, NC; son of Kelly and Margaret; divorced; children: Kelly M III. **Educ:** Univ NC, BA, Polit Sci, 1970, MPA, 1973. **Career:** NC Personnel Dept, admin intern, 1971-72; Charlotte Area Fund, planner, 1972-74; Alexander Funeral Home, vpres, 1973-94, vpres & chief finance officer, 1994-. **Orgs:** Exec vpres, US Youth Coun, 1976-85; trustee, Nat Asn Advan Colored People Spec Contrib Fund, 1985-98; pres, NC Nat Asn Advan Colored People, 1985-96; chmn, Mothers of Murdered Offspring, 2003-; past vpres, Nat Asn Advan Colored People; chmn, Nat Asn Advan Colored People Econ Develop Fair Share Community. **Honors/Awds:** UNCF Labor Dept Res Grant, 1977. **Business Addr:** Vice President, Chief Finance Officer, Alexander Funeral Home Inc, 1424 Statesville Ave, Charlotte, NC 28236, **Business Phone:** (704)333-1167.

ALEXANDER, KHANDI
Actor. **Personal:** Born Sep 4, 1957, New York City, NY. **Educ:** Queensborough Community Col. **Career:** Films: Street walkin, 1985; A Chorus Line, 1985; Maid to Order, 1987; CB4,1993; Joshua Tree, 1993; Menace II Society, 1993; What's Love Got to Do with It, 1993; Poetic Justice, 1993; House Party 3, 1994; Sugar Hill, 1994; Greedy, 1994; No Easy Way, 1996; Thick as Thieves, 1998; There's Something About Mary, 1998; Fool Proof, 2002; Emmett's Mark, 2002; Dark Blue, 2002; First Born, 2006; Rain, 2006; TVseries: "The Motown Revue Starring Smokey Robinson", 1985; "Shameful Secrets", 1993; "To My Daughter with Love", 1994; "Terminal", 1996; "Spawn", 1997; "Soul Sacrifice", 1998; "Kids", 1997; "TV Episode Twins", 1997; "Bill Moves On", 1998; "X-Chromosome", 1999; "Cosby-The Awful Truth", 1999; "Partners", 1999; "The Corner", 2000; "Third Watch", 2000; "Life's a Bitch", 2003; "Perfect Strangers", 2004; "CSI: Miami", 2002-09. **Honors/Awds:** Black Reel for Network/Cable-Best Actress, 2001; 36th Annual Image Awards, Nat Asn Advan Colored People; Image Award, 2005. **Business Addr:** Actress, CBS TV Network, 51 W 52nd St, New York, NY 10019, **Business Phone:** (212)975-4321.*

ALEXANDER, LARRY
President (Organization), chief executive officer. **Career:** Westin Hotels & Resorts, 1973-93; Westin Hotel, managing dir, 1993; Detroit Metro Sports Comn, founder; Detroit Metro Conv & Visitors Bur, pres & chief exec officer, currently. **Orgs:** exec comt, owners adv comt & bd dirs, Metrop Detroit Conv & Visitors Bur; bd dirs, Mich Hotel, Motel & Resort Asn; Greater Detroit Chamber Com; Kidney Found Mich; Detroit Riverfront Conservancy; Auto Nat Heritage; Super Bowl XL Host Comt; The Parade Co; New Detroit Inc. **Special Achievements:** Appointed by Mich Govt John Engler to the White House Conf on Travel & Tourism, 1995; appointed by Detroit Mayor Dennis Archer to serve on the Detroit Master Plan Task Force, 1994; listed in Who's Who in Civic Service. **Business Phone:** (313)202-1800.*

ALEXANDER, LAURENCE BENEDICT
Journalist, educator. **Personal:** Born Oct 31, 1959, New Orleans, LA; son of Dorothy Alexander and Garland Alexander; married Veronica Wicker, Aug 13, 1988; children: Brandon Keith, David Laurence & Tyler Christian. **Educ:** Univ New Orleans, BA, 1981; Univ FL, MA, 1983; Tulane Univ, Sch Law, JD, 1987. **Career:** Times-Picayune, New Orleans, staff writer, 1981, 1982-85; Houma Courier, staff writer, 1982; Univ New Orleans, dir, jour prog, asst prof, jour, 1987-88; Temple Univ, dir, news ed sequence, asst prof, commun, 1988-91; Philadelphia Inquirer, summer copy ed, 1989-92; Univ Fla, asst prof, jour, 1991-94, chmn, jour, 1994-98, assoc prof, 1994-2003, prof, jour, 2003-, interim assoc dean, currently. **Orgs:** Am Bar Asn, 1987-; La State Bar Asn, 1987-; Asn Educ Jour & Mass Commun, 1989-; Soc Prof Journalists, 1989-; Nat Asn Black Journalists, 1989-; Int Commun Asn, 1992-; mwm, 1995-2001, chmn, 2000-01, AEJMC Prof Freedom & Responsibility Comt; mem, 1997-, chmn & bd dir, 2001-, Campus Commun Inc. **Honors/Awds:** Deadline News Writing Award, Press Club New Orleans, 1985; Selected Teaching Fel, The Poynter Institute, 1989; AEJMC, AHANA Research Grant, 1990; AEJMC/ACEJMC Baskett Mosse Award, 1994; Florida Blue Key Distinguished Faculty Award, 2001; UF Distinguished Alumni Professor, 2001-03; Freedom Forum Journalism Teacher of the Year, 2002; Joseph C Beckham Dissertation of the Year Award, Edu Law Assn, 2007. **Special Achievements:** Major works published: The Tulane Maritime Lawyer, 1987; The Black Law Journal, 1989; Newspaper Research Journal, 1992, 1994, 1995, 1996; Western Journal of Black Studies, 1992; Commun & the Law, 1993, 1996; Journalism Educator, 1994; Notre Dame Journal of Legislation, 1997; Free Speech Yearbook, 2000; Visual Commun Quarterly, 2001; Yale Law and Policy Review, 2002. **Business Addr:** Professor, Interim Associate Dean, University of Florida, Department of Journalism, 3052 Weimer, PO Box 118400, Gainesville, FL 32611, **Business Phone:** (352)392-0448.

ALEXANDER, DR. LENORA COLE
Executive. **Personal:** Born Mar 9, 1935, Buffalo, NY; daughter of John L and Susie Stamper; married Theodore M Sr (died 2001). **Educ:** State Univ Col, Buffalo, NY, BS, 1957; State Univ NY, Buffalo, NY, med, 1969, PhD, educ admin & policy & orgn develop, 1974. **Career:** State Univ NY, res asst, 1968-69, asst vpres stud life, 1969-73; Am Univ, vpres stud life, 1973-77; Univ DC, vpres stud affairs, 1978-81; US Dept Labor, dir womens bur, 1981-86; George Mason Univ, commonwealth vis prof pub admin, 1986-89; LCA & Assocs Inc, pres, 1989-; US Agency Int Develop, Off Human Resources, Div Labor Rels, staff, 1990-; Univ Md, adj prof, 2004-; Inst Women, bd dir, currently. **Orgs:** Delta Sigma Theta Sorority, 1976-; bd dirs, DC Chamber Com, 1979-81; US Rep Working Party Role Women Econ, Orgn Econ Develop & Coop Paris France, 1981-86; Alpha Kappa Alpha Sorority Inc 1982; adv comt mem, Women Veterans Affairs US Vet Admin, 1983-86; us rep, Conf Int Comn Status Women Cartegena Colombia, 1983; bd mem, Girl Friends Inc, 1983-; conf, Vienna Austria, 1984; US Del UN Decade Women Conf Nairobi Kenya, 1985; bd dirs, Jerusalem Int Forum Am Israel Friendship League, 1987-89; Defense Adv Comt Women Servs, 1989-92; DC Bd Elections & Ethics, 1998-2000, 2003-; DC Bd Elections & Ethics, 2000-; bd dirs, McAuley Inst; bd dirs, Found Except C; Adv bd, Black Women's Fashion Mus; bd dir, IWPR. **Honors/Awds:** Special Citation Award, Comn Women's Affairs Off Gov Puerto Rico, 1982; Salute for Contributions Award, Club Twenty Wash, 1983; Distinguished American and Humanitarian Coahoma, Jr Col, 1983; Distinguished Alumnus Award, State Univ NY, 1983; Pauline Weeden Maloney Award, Nat Trends & Serv, Links Inc, Philadelphia, 1984; Gratitude for Success Award, Unit Church Usher's League, Chicago, 1984; Distinguished Service Citation, Nat Black MBA Asn Inc, Wash, 1984; Outstanding Women Award, Progressive DC Chap Federally Employed Women Washington, 1984; Outstanding Political Achievement Award, Nat Asn Minority Polit Women, 1985; Woman Achievement Award, Women's City Club Cleveland 1986; Outstanding CareerWoman Award, Alpha Phi Alpha. **Home Addr:** 3020 Brandywine St NW, Washington, DC 20008, **Home Phone:** (202)686-0512. **Business Addr:** Board of Directors, Institute for Women, 1707 L St NW Suite 750, Washington, DC 20036, **Business Phone:** (202)785-5100.

ALEXANDER, LIVINGSTON
Administrator. **Personal:** Married Evelyn; children: Erika, Jason & Alicia. **Career:** Western Ky Univ, from asst prof psychol to prof; Troy State Univ, vpres acad affairs; Ga Southern Univ, dept head; Kean Univ, Union, NJ, vpres for acad affairs & prof psychol, provost; Univ Pittsburgh Bradford, pres, currently. **Orgs:** Fac mem & seminar leader, Am Coun Educ. **Special Achievements:** Numerous publications & presentations. **Business Addr:** President, University of Pittsburgh Bradford, Office of the President, 1234 Cathedral of Learning, Pittsburgh, PA 15260, **Business Phone:** (814)362-7501.

ALEXANDER, LIYONGO PATRISE
Football player. **Personal:** Born Oct 23, 1972, Galveston, TX. **Educ:** Univ louisiana, attended. **Career:** Football player (retired);

Wash Redskins, linebacker, 1996-98; Philadelphia Eagles, 2000; Orlando Rage, Xtreme Football League, 2001; Dallas Desperadoes, Arena Football League, 2002-03; Austin Wranglers, 2004. *

ALEXANDER, LYDIA LEWIS
School administrator. **Personal:** Born Aug 21, 1938, Bessemer, AL; daughter of Clinton E and Flora Laird; married Judson T Alexander Sr, Dec 29, 1961 (died 1980); children: Judson T Jr. **Educ:** Talladega Col, Talladega, AL, BA, Hist, 1958; Ind Univ, Bloomington, IN, MAT, 1964; Auburn Univ, Auburn, AL, EdD, 1972. **Career:** Wenonah High Sch, Birmingham, AL, Eng instr, 1959-66; Lawson State Jr Col, Birmingham, AL, speech & Eng instr, 1966-70; Auburn Univ, Auburn, AL, asst prof, sch educ, 1972-74; Univ Ala, Birmingham, asst prof, sec educ, 1974-79, asst vpres, 1980-84, biomed sci prog dir, 1982-84, dir gen studies, 1984-89, asst dean, 1989-94, assoc prof educ leadership, currently. **Orgs:** Pres, Univ Ala Birmingham Faculty & Staff Benevolent Fund Coun, 1990; pres, Birmingham Chap The Links, 1988-89; pres, Omicron Omega Chap, Alpha Kappa Alpha Sorority, 1978-82; nat pres, The Holidays, 1987-91; Asn Supv & Curriculum Develop; Am Asn Col Teacher Educ. **Honors/Awds:** Outstanding Soror in the Southeast Region, Alpha Kappa Alpha, 1988; Soror of the Year, Omicron Omega Chapter, Alpha Kappa Alpha, 1987, 1993; Educator of the Year, Univ Ala Birmingham Chap, Omega Psi Phi Fraternity, 1990; Woman of Distinction, Iota Phi Lambda Sorority, Birmingham Chap, 1979. **Special Achievements:** Book: Wearing Purple, 1996. **Business Phone:** (205)934-4011.*

ALEXANDER, MARCELLUS WINSTON
Executive, president (organization). **Personal:** Born Oct 3, 1951, Austin, TX; son of Juanita Smith and Marcellus Sr; married Linda Carter Alexander, Sep 20, 1975; children: Ehrin, Andrea & Marcellus III. **Educ:** Southwest Tex State Univ, San Marcos, Tex, BS, 1973; Western Med Col, PhD, 1995. **Career:** Am Broadcasting Co, Detroit, MI, gen sales mgr, 1982-84, vpres & gen mgr, 1984-86; Silver Star Commun, Detroit, Mich, chief operating officer, part owner, 1986; Group W Broadcasting, Philadelphia, PA, sta mgr, 1987-89; Group W Broadcasting, Baltimore, MD, vpres & gen mgr, 1989-98; Nat Asn Broadcasters TV, exec vpres, pres, currently; NAB Educ Found, pres, 2004-. **Orgs:** Nat Asn Black Journalists, 1987-; bd mem, Baltimore Urban League, 1989-; bd mem, Advert Asn Baltimore, 1989-; bd mem, Kennedy Inst, 1989-; bd mem, Advert & Prof Club, 1989-. **Honors/Awds:** Distinguished Black Marylander, Towson State Univ, 1991; Humanitarian Award, Juv Diabetes Asn, 1991. **Business Addr:** President, National Association of Broadcasters Television, 1771 N St NW, Washington, DC 20036, **Business Phone:** (202)429-5300.

ALEXANDER, OTIS DOUGLAS
Librarian, executive director. **Personal:** Born Jun 1, 1949, Norfolk, VA; son of Gilbert and Vivian Bell. **Educ:** Fed City Col, Washington, DC, BA, urban studies & music, 1972, MSc, media sci, 1974; Ball State Univ, Muncie, IN, MLS, libr sci, 1983; Atlanta Univ, GA, attended 1982. **Career:** Dept Educ, VI St John, interant librn, 1976-77; Bur Libr Mus & Archeol Serv, Christiansted St Croix US VI, juvenile serv librn, 1977-78; Cuttington Univ Col Liberia W Africa, asst librn & lectr c, 1978-79; Dept Educ VI, info spec, 1979-83; Atlanta Univ, scholar, 1982; fel USDOE, 1982-83; Bur Libr & Mus, head librn, 1983-85; St Dunstan's Episcopal Sch, St Croix VI, lit teacher, 1985-90; St Theatre Dance Ensemble, fdr/drr, 1986-00; Dept Educ VI, Sec Music, 1990-01; Howard Reed Int Scholar, 1992; Southeastern Univ, Randolph E Meyer Mem Libr, dir; Danville Pub Libr, dir, currently. **Orgs:** Dir, St John Ethnic Theatre, 1976-77; Children's Theatre, St Croix, 1977-78; dir, performer Cuttington Cult Troop West Africa, 1978-79; Am Libr Asn, 1983-; artistic dir, St Theatre 1986-97; bd dirs, Univ DC Alumni Asn, 1991-93; chap adv, Phi Delta Kappa; Am Fedn Teachers; St Croix Fedn Teachers; Omega Psi Phi Fraternity. **Special Achievements:** African Heritage Dancers & Drummers, Washington, DC, professional dancer, 1973-76; DFA in music performance, 2003; Publs, "Librarianship in a Developing Nation" Bur of Libr Mus & Archael Servs, "Media-Children-Reading" Personality & Instrl Strat Thesis 1974; publ book reviews "They Came Before Columbus," "The Red Wind," "Where Did I Come From?", "Sturdy Black Bridges," "When Harlem Was In Vogue"; Awds, Fellowship USDOE 1982-83, Scholarship Atlanta Univ 1982; Howard Reed International Scholarship, 1992; The Encyclopedia As An Information Source, A Study of the Usefulness & Objectivity of Selected Encyclopedias as Perceived by School & Public Librarians in Muncie IN 1983; "Arthur Shomburg Alfonso and his Contributions to Black Culture" in St Croix Avis; Virgin Islands and Caribbean Comm, (joint author), 1988; "Writers in the Comm," 1984; author, "Helping Cool Black Males," 1991, "An Unfinished Agenda: Aiding Hispanic Students," 1990, "Education Also Requires Curiosity and Exploration," 1990, VI Daily News; "A Love for the Arts is the Best Lesson We Can Teach Our Youth," 1992; "Teach the Children in A Way In Which They Love Learning," 1995; "Home School and Community Should Help Young Black Males," 1996; "Students Need Community's Help Getting Over Hurdles to Success," 1996; Changing A Society at Risk, 1998; Empower Teachers for Reform, 1998; Enlightenment Depends on Order of Schools, 1999; Changing Negative Behavior is a Mission of the System, 2000; co-author, Berkley: the Other Side of Town, 2000; co-author, Jumpin' de Broom, 2001. **Military Serv:** USMC, res, 1967-69. **Home Addr:** 609 Obendorfer Rd, Norfolk, VA 23523. *

ALEXANDER, PAMELA GAYLE
Judge. **Personal:** Born Sep 25, 1952, Minneapolis, MN; daughter of Robert W Bellesen and Frances L Smith; married Albert G Alexander, Jan 16, 1982; children: two. **Educ:** Augsburg Col, BA, 1974; Univ Minnesota Sch Law, JD, 1977. **Career:** Neighborhood Justice Ctr & the Legal Rights Ctr, Law Clerk, 1974; First Bank, Minneapolis, trust adminr, 1977-78; Legal Rights Ctr Inc, criminal defense atty, 1978-81; Hennepin Co Atty Off, prosecutor criminal div, 1981-83; State Minneapolis, co ct judge, 1983-86; Hennepin Co Dist Co, dist ct judge, 1986-96, asst chief judge, 1996-98; Juvenile Div, Hennepin Co Dist Ct, dis ct judge, currently. **Orgs:** Charter mem, former vpres, Minnesota Minority Lawyers Asn; trustee, Greater Friendship Missionary Bapt Church, 1980-84; Nat Bar Asn Judicial Coun; parliamentarian, treas Minneappolis & St Paul Links; chmn governance comt, exec comt, Minneapolis Found; bd dir, Emma Howe Memorial Found Esther V Crosby Girl Scout Comt. **Honors/Awds:** Special Recognition Award, Phi Beta Sigma Frat, 1982; Constance B Motley Award, TCBWTC Comn, 1982-83; Community Service Award, Inner City Youth League, 1983, Loft Teen Ctr, 1983; Distinguished Service Award, Hennepin Co Atty Off, 1983; Community Service Award, Kappa Alpha Psi Fraternity, 1992; BIHA The Comm Award, 1993; Omega Citizen of the Year Award, 10th Dist, 1993; Chauncey Eskridge Distinguished Barrister Award, Southern Christian Leadership Conf, 1993; Freedom Fund Award, Nat Asn Advan Colored People, Minneapolis br, 1993; Humanitarian Award, Metrop Community Col, 1995; Profiles in Courage Award, Minnesota Minority Lawyers Asn, 1995; Esther V Crosby Award, Greater Minneapolis Girl Scouts; Jurist Award, Nat Bar Asn Women Lawyers Div, 1997; Woman of the Year Award, Iota Phi Lambda; Star Performer Award, Hennepin County, 1998; Torchbearer's Award, Rainbow Push Coalition, 2000; Profiles in Courage Award, Nat Bar Asn, 2001. **Business Addr:** Judge, Hennepin County District Court, 626 S 6th St, Minneapolis, MN 55415.*

ALEXANDER, PRESTON PAUL
Labor relations manager. **Personal:** Born Apr 20, 1952, Bronx, NY; son of Preston Sr and Sylvia; married; children: Drew Philip & Jason Ross. **Educ:** Fairleigh Dickinson Univ, BA, psychol, 1973, MPA, 1980. **Career:** Teaneck Vol Ambulance Corps, Sunday evening crew chief, 1972-; Midlantic Nat Bank Citizens, internal auditor, 1973-74; Fairleigh Dickinson Univ Cent Admis, dir admis rel, 1974-79; Nat Asn Col Admis Counr, vpres human rel, 1978-79; Citibank NA, dir human resources, 1979-89; Alexander's Surgical Supply Co, co-owner 1989-91; Joseph E Seagram & Sons Inc, human resources dir, 1993-98; Oxford Health Plans, regional dir human resources, 1998-99; Pitney Bowes Inc, vpres, human resources, 1999, vpres workforce rel, 2003. **Orgs:** Soc Human Res Mgt; bd trustees, Shelter Our Sisters. **Honors/Awds:** Outstanding Distinguished Service Award, Fairleigh Dickinson Univ, 1978. **Business Addr:** Vice President Workforce Relations, Pitney Bowes Inc, 1 Elmcrotf Rd, Stamford, CT 06926, **Business Phone:** (203)351-7514.

ALEXANDER, RICHARD C.
Association executive, military leader. **Personal:** Born Jun 26, 1935, Cleveland, OH; married LaVera; children: Jeff, Ronald, Gail. **Educ:** Franklin Univ, BA; Ohio Nat Guard Officer Cand Sch, attended 1965; Army Command & Gen Staff Studies Course, 1977; Army War Col, 1983; Air Defense Sch, Air Defense Officer Basic Course; Mil Police Sch, Missile Site Security Course; Missile & Munitions Command Sch, Officer Maintenance Mgt Course; Air Defense Sch, Air Defense Officer Advan Course; Air Defense Sch, Air Defense Missile Staff Officer Course; Finance Sch, Internal Review Course; Defense Race Rels Inst, Defense Race Rels Instrocos Course; Nat Defense Univ, Res Components Nat Security Course. **Career:** military leader (retired), executive; US Marine Corps, 1954; Army Nat Guard, second lt, 1965, first lt, 1967, capt, 1969, maj, 1973, lt col, 1978, brig, 1988, maj gen, 1992-98; Ohio Nat Guard, adj gen; Dept Defense Res Forces Policy Bd, 1993-96; Nat Guard Asn US, pres, 1996-98, exec dir, 1999-. **Orgs:** Nat Asn Advan Colored People. **Special Achievements:** First African-American president and executive director of NGAUS. **Military Serv:** Army Nat Guard, 1965 -98; Meritorious Serv Medal; Army Commendation Medal; Army Achievement Medal; Good Conduct Medal-Marine Corps; Army Research Component Achievement Medal; Nat Defense Serv Medal; Humanitarian Serv Medal ; Armed Forces Res Medal; Army Serv Ribbon; Army Res Component Overseas Training Ribbon; Defense Super Serv Medal; Legion Merit; Ohio Award Merit; Gen Raymond S McLain Medal, Assn of the AUS. **Business Addr:** Executive Director, National Guard Association of the United States, 1 Massachusetts Ave NW, Washington, DC 20001, **Business Phone:** (202)789-0031.*

ALEXANDER, ROBERT I. See Obituaries section.

ALEXANDER, S TYRONE
Executive. **Career:** Highmark Blue Cross, Human Resources & Admin Servs, exec vpres & sr vpres, currently. **Orgs:** Bd mem, Penn Workforce Invest Bd; bd dir, Inst Supply Mgt. **Honors/Awds:** Circle of Hope Award, 2006. **Business Addr:** Senior Vice President, Highmark Blue Cross Blue Shield, Human Resources Administrative Services, 120 Fifth Ave Suite 3012, Pittsburgh, PA 15222-3099, **Business Phone:** (412)544-4017.

ALEXANDER, VIC
Vice president (Organization). **Personal:** Married Rose Cornell. **Educ:** Cent Mich Univ, grad; Univ Cincinnati, attended. **Career:** Cent Mich Univ, commun coordr; Local Union No 87, United Steel Workers Am, Delphi Chassis Automotive, vpres, currently. **Business Addr:** Vice President, United Steel Workers of Amercia, Delphi Chasis Automotive, 21 Abbey Ave, Dayton, OH 45417, **Business Phone:** (937)268-6646.*

ALEXANDER, VINCENT J.
Teacher, executive, chief executive officer. **Personal:** Born Oct 19, 1958, Fort Wayne, IN; son of John and Dorothy Logan; married Gail, Feb 1, 1990; children: Vince II, Colin & Gavin. **Educ:** Vincennes Univ, AS, 1979; Ind State Univ, BS, 1981. **Career:** WMRI-WGOM, Marion, radio announcer & reporter, 1982-85; Chronicle-Tribune, sports writer, 1985-90; J-Gazette, sports writer, 1990-; High Sch, sports ed, 1990-97; Sports Page Mag, founder, 1997; It's All Good Inc, pres, chief exec officer, 1997-99; Indianapolis Pub Schs, teacher; Indianapolis Public Sch, Dept Educ, teacher; Julian Coleman Middle Sch, eng teacher, currently. **Honors/Awds:** Gen Salute Alumni Award, Outstanding Grad Wayne High Sch, 1993; Soc Prof Journalists Award, 1999. **Special Achievements:** 2nd Place, APME Sports Writing Contest, 1996. **Business Addr:** English Teacher, Julian Coleman Middle School, Indianapolis, IN.*

ALEXANDER, WALTER GILBERT, II
Dentist. **Personal:** Born Jul 6, 1922, Petersburg, VA. **Educ:** Rutgers Univ, BS, mech eng, 1943; Howard Univ, DDS, 1952. **Career:** Douglas Aircraft Co LA, designer, 1943; pvt pract, S Orange NJ, dentist, 1952-; NJ Col Med & Dent, post grad fac, 1967, clin asst prof, 1969. **Orgs:** Am Nat Dent Asn; NJ Dent Asn; Commonwealth, Essex Co Dent Soc; Urban League; life mem, Nat Asn Advan Colored People; NJ St Bd Dent, 1972-76; pres, NJ St Bd Dent, 1976; Am Asn Dent Examiners; Northeast Regional Bd Dent Examiners; Tau Beta Pi, Omicron Kappa Upsilon; Episcopalian; Howard Univ Alumni Asn. **Business Addr:** Dentist, 555 Ctr St, South Orange, NJ 07079.*

ALEXANDER, WARDINE TOWERS
Health services administrator. **Personal:** Born Jul 26, 1955, Birmingham, AL; daughter of Ward Towers Jr and Thelma Otey Towers; married Gregory Bernard Sr, Sep 6, 1975; children: Gregory Bernard II. **Educ:** Univ Ala, Birmingham, AL, BS, 1978. **Career:** Am Red Cross, Birmingham, AL, ref lab technologist, 1977-84, asst dir, tech serv, 1984-90, dir hosp serv, 1990-; Hosp/Tech Serv, reg mgr, 1994-; Am Red Cross Blood Servs, educ mgr; BioLife Plasma, training supvr, currently. **Orgs:** Am Asn Blood Banks, 1977-; Ala State Asn Blood Banks, 1977-; Am Soc Med Technologist, 1977-; Am Soc Clin Pathologist, 1977-; publicity comt chair, Alpha Kappa Alpha Sorority Inc, 1982-; pres, Ala State Asn Blood Banks, 1994-95. **Special Achievements:** "Stored Red Cells," Am Red Cross Publication, 1979. **Business Addr:** Training Supervisor, BioLife Plasma, Birmingham, AL.

ALEXANDER, WILLIE
Football player, executive, insurance executive. **Personal:** Born Sep 21, 1949, Montgomery, AL. **Educ:** Alcorn A & M Univ, BBA. **Career:** Football player (retired), executive; Houston Oilers, cornerback, 1971-79, career consult, 1981-86, dir player rels, 1987; W J Alexander & Assocs PC, founder & pres, 1980-. **Orgs:** Nat Adv Coun, Univ Houston; chair, Greater Houston Partnership Educ. **Business Phone:** (713)802-0900.

ALEXANDER-WHITING, HARRIETT
Educator. **Personal:** Born in Charlotte, NC; daughter of James Alexander Sr; married Robert W. **Educ:** Northern IL Univ, BS, 1968; Kent State Univ, MA, 1970. **Career:** Va Regional Med Prog, asst allied health off, 1971-72; Emory Univ, instr, 1972-74; Ala Inst Deaf & Blind, Talladega Col, prog coord/supv teacher, 1974-80, asst vis prof, 1976-79; Gallaudet Univ, speech lang path & coord of commun unit & lab, 1980-84, prog supvr, 1985-96, asst dir, support serv, 1996, dir, student serv team, currently. **Orgs:** Am Speech Language & Hearing Assoc, 1971-; bd trustees, Ala Assoc Retarded Citizens, 1977-79; Nat Accreditation Coun Site Team, 1978; Nat Task Force Deaf-Blind US Dept Educ, 1979; Nat Comn Develop Disabilities; Am Speech Language & Hearing Asn, 1980-82; Middle States Accreditation Team, 1983; task group, Mayor's Comn Early Childhood, 1987; Nat Comm Deafness Am Speech Language & Hearing Asn, 1987-90; Conf Educators & Admin Serving Deaf, 1992-; Gallaudet Univ, Child Development Ctr Adv Coun, 1993-2000; Nat Task Force Equity in Testing, 1997-. **Honors/Awds:** Outstanding Young Women America, 1979. **Home Phone:** (301)262-6675. **Business Addr:** Director, Student Services Team, Gallaudet University, 800 Florida Ave NE, Washington, DC 20002-3695, **Business Phone:** (202)651-5050.

ALEXANDRE, JOURNEL
Physician. **Personal:** Born Jul 14, 1931, Arcahaie, Haiti; children: Cibe, Colette. **Educ:** Lycee Toussaint Louverture, BS, 1952; Univ

Mex, MD, 1960. **Career:** St Joseph Hosp, Physician; Mercy Cath Med Ctr, Physician; Montgomery Hosp, Valley Forge Med Ctr, Physician; Scarborough Gen Hosp, internship, 1960-61; Mercy Douglass Hosp, resid, 1961-65; Montgomery Hosp, 1965-66; pvt pract, physician. **Orgs:** Penn & Montgomery Co Med Soc, 1967; dipl, Am Bd Surgery, 1968; Int Col Surgeons; fel Am Col Surgeons, 1969. **Business Addr:** Physician, Private Practice, 1033 W Germantown Pike, Norristown, PA 19403, **Business Phone:** (610)539-8500.*

ALEXIS, DR. CARLTON PETER
Physician, administrator. **Personal:** Born Jun 29, 1929, Port of Spain, Trinidad and Tobago; married Ogbonia M; children: Carla, Anthony & Lisa. **Educ:** NY Univ, BA, 1953; Howard Univ, MD, 1957; Haiti, DHC, 1972; Georgetown Univ, DSc, 1980. **Career:** Physician; Administrator (retired); Walter Reed Army Hosp, intern, 1957-58; Bronx VA Hosp, res int med, 1961-63; Georgetown Univ Hosp, fel endocrinol, 1963-64; Freedmens Hosp, pres med-dent staff, 1968-69; Howard Univ, instr prof med, 1964; HowardUniv, vpres health affairs, 1969, exec vpres, interim pres, 1989. **Orgs:** Nat Med Asn; Am Med Asn; Am Col Phys; Am Soc Int med; Asn Acad Health Ctr; Med Soc DC; Med Chirurgical soc DC; chmn, Gov Bd, DC Gen Hosp; Mayors TaskForce Reorganization, Dept Human Resources DC; adv comn community, IRS; Mayors Comn Drug Abuse; Ed Bd Jour Med Educ; fel, Am Col Physicians. **Honors/Awds:** Elected Alpha Omega Alpha; Outstanding Teacher, Howard Univ, Col Med, 1966. **Military Serv:** Med Corps, second lt to capt, 1956-61. **Business Addr:** 9800 Buccaneer Mall Suite 8, St Thomas, VA 00802.*

ALEXIS, DORIS VIRGINIA
Administrator. **Personal:** Born Jul 10, 1921, Brooklyn, NY; married Joseph Alexis; children: Neal Howe, Priscilla Rand. **Educ:** Hunter Col, NY, attended 1946; Univ Calif, LA, CA, attended 1960; Univ Calif, Davis, Cert Program Mgmt, 1976. **Career:** Calif Dept of Motor Vehicles, dep dir, 1977-83, first woman and first career, dir, 1977-; National Traffic Safety Inst, Senior Consult. **Orgs:** Bd trustees, Sacramento Safety Cncl, 1978-79; bd dir, Amer Asn of Motor Vehicle Admin, 1979-; bd dir, Sacramento Safety Cncl, 1979-; pres, bd trustees Commonwealth Equity Trust, 1979-; mem Women's Forum, 1977-; bd dir, YWCA, 1978-; NAACP, 1978-; Urban League, 1978-; Adv Coun, Californians for Drug Free Youth. **Honors/Awds:** planning & implementation, DVM Child Care Cntr for children of State Employees, 1975; Grand Masters Award, MW Prince Hall Grand Lodge F and AM; Honoree Coalition of Women in State, Svc; 1st CA Official, nominated, membership Women's Forum. *

ALEXIS, ELOISE. See ABERNATHY, ELOISE.

ALEXIS, DR. MARCUS
Educator. **Personal:** Born Feb 26, 1932, Brooklyn, NY; married Geraldine M. **Educ:** Brooklyn Col, AB, econ, 1953; Mich State Univ, MA, econ, 1954; Univ Minn, PhD, econ, 1959. **Career:** Macalester Col, asst prof, 1957-60; DePaul Univ, assoc prof, 1960-62; Univ Rochester, assoc prof, prof, 1962-70; Univ Calif, Berkeley, vis prof, 1969-71; Northwestern Univ, prof econs & urban affairs, 1970-85; US Interstate Com Comn, comnr, 1979-81; Univ Ill, Chicago Col Bus Admin, dean, 1985-90; Northwestern Univ, vis prof econ & mgt, 1990; J L Kellogg Prof; Fed Res Bank Chicago, dep chmn, 1986-90, chmn, 1991; Northwestern Univ, bd trustees, prof econs, prof mgt & strategy, 1991; Kellogg Sch Mgt, prof econ & mgt strategy, bd trustees prof econs, prof emer mgt & strategy, currently. **Orgs:** Pres & bd dir, Urban League Rochester, 1966-69; Nat Bd Am Mkt Asn, 1968-70; chmn, Caucus Black Economists, 1969-71; Increasing Supply Minority Economists Am Econ Asn, 1970-73; nat bd dirs, PUSH, 1972-73; chmn, Status Minorities Prof Am Econ Asn, 1974-80; Minorities Sci Nat Res Coun Nat Acad Sci, 1975; trustee, Macalester Col, 1983-88; educ policy bd rev, Rev Black Polit Econ 1984-; chair econ policy task force, Joint Ctr Polit Studies 1985-; trustee, Teachers Ins & Annuity Asn, 1987-; Beta Gamma Sigma; Order Artus; bd economists, Black Enterprise mag; Ed Bd, Econ Perspectives; ed bd, Rev Econ Lit; Ed Bd, Rev Black Polit Econ; bd trustee, Kellogg Sch Mgt. **Honors/Awds:** Ford Found Fel, Harvard Univ & Mass Inst Technol, 1961-62; Samuel Z Westerfield Distinginguished Achievement Award, Nat Econ Asn, 1979; Outstanding Achievement Award, Univ Minn, 1981; Caribbean American Intercultural Organization Scholar Award, 1981; President Award, Minority Trucking & Transp Develop Coun, 1981; University Teacher's Honor Roll, Chicago Tribune, 1992; Prentice-Hall Economics Hall of Fame. **Special Achievements:** Published numerous articles including "Relocating Core Competencies: The Case of Banking and Financial Services", Strategic Int, 1996. **Business Addr:** Professor Emeritus of Management & Strategy, Kellogg School of Management, Department Management & Strategy, Leverone 608 & Andersen 321, 2001 Sheridan Rd, Evanston, IL 60208, **Business Phone:** (847)491-3300.

ALFONSO, PEDRO
Executive. **Personal:** Born Jun 28, 1948, Tampa, FL; son of Eugenio and Florencia Alfonso; married Kimberley, Sep 25, 1993; children: Gabrielle & Alexandra. **Educ:** Howard Univ, BA, 1973. **Career:** IBM Corp, systs engr, 1969-75; Seymore Systs, mkt mgr, 1975-76; Gen Elec Co, acct mgr, 1976-79; Dynamic Concepts Inc, pres & chief exec officer, 1979-. **Orgs:** Past pres & bd mem, DC Chamber Com, 1985-2001; past chair & bd mem, YMCA Metrop, 1990-; bd mem, Leadership Wash, 1987-90; co-founder & bd mem, DC Techno Coun, 1998-2000; bd & exec comm, Federal City Coun, 1995-; bd & exec comn, Nat Small Bus United, 1995-; bd trustees, Southeastern Univ, 1995-; bd dir, Georgetown Hosp, 1999-; BICSI; bd mem, Greater Southeast Community Hosp. **Honors/Awds:** Entrepreneur of the Year, Nat Black MBA Asn, 1987; Nat Award of Excellence, US Small Business Administration, 1990; Howard Univ, Alumnus of the Year, 1994; Office of the President, Appointment to White House Conference on Small Business, 1995; Business Leader of the Year, DC Chamber of Commerce, 1999. **Business Addr:** President, Chief Executive Officer, Dynamic Concepts Inc, 2176 Wisconsin Ave NW, Washington, DC 20007, **Business Phone:** (202)944-8787.

ALFORD, BRENDA
Association executive. **Personal:** Born Jan 27, 1947, Atlanta, GA; daughter of James and Rosette. **Educ:** TN State Univ, BS, 1969; Univ Pittsburgh, MSW, 1975. **Career:** fel, Nat Inst Mental Health Fellowship, 1973-75; City Houston, prog mgr human res, 1975-78; US Dept Health & Human Servs, pub health adv, 1978-83; Am Asn Black Women Entrepreneurs Inc, nat pres & exec dir, 1982-; RABA Inc, exec vpres, 1981-84; Brasman Health & Bus Res, pres, 1985-. **Orgs:** Nat Asn Soc Workers, Am Pub Health Asn, treas, Wash Urban League Guild, 1980-82; Silver Spring Chamber Comt, Fedn Republican Women, Nat Asn Small Res Co. **Honors/Awds:** edited, Predicted Kilograms Quantities Med & Res Needs Controlled Substances, 1980-81. **Business Phone:** (301)230-5583.*

ALFORD, BRIAN WAYNE
Football player. **Personal:** Born Jun 7, 1975, Oak Park, MI. **Educ:** Purdue. **Career:** Football (retired); NY Giants, wide receiver, 1998-99; Miami Dolphins,wide receiver, 2000; Ind Firebirds, OS, 2003; Grand Rapids Rampage, OS, 2006. **Honors/Awds:** Most Valuable Player, Purdue, 1996. **Special Achievements:** Ranked Second in the Big Ten & twenty second in the NCAA in pass receptions; Ranked Second in Purdue career receiving touchdowns.

ALFORD, HARRY C.
Executive. **Career:** exec, var orgn: Procter & Gamble, Johnson & Johnson & Sara Lee Corp; US Chamber Com, bd dir, currently; Nat Black Chamber Com, pres, chief exec officer & co-founder, currently. **Orgs:** Nat Adv Coun; Small Bus Admin; bd dirs, Studs Free Enterprise. **Honors/Awds:** Bus Advocate Yr, US Dept Com's, 1991; honored Af Ams Corp Responsibility New York; named cult Ambassador by US State Dept; DC's most influential small bus advocates. **Special Achievements:** ranked No 5 on its "Power 30" list Wash, Small Bus mag; place at the table in the White House and at the top levels of Corporate America. **Business Addr:** President, Chief Executive Officer, National Black Chamber of Commerce, 1350 Conn Ave NW Suite 405, Washington, DC 20036, **Business Phone:** (202)466-6888.*

ALFORD, THOMAS EARL
Librarian. **Personal:** Born Mar 5, 1935, McKeesport, PA; son of Horace and Della Slade; married Kay Alice Taylor Alford, Aug 26, 1962; children: Thomas E Jr, Elaine Kay. **Educ:** Eastern Mich Univ, Ypsilanti, MI, BS, 1958; Univ Mich, Ann Arbor, MI, MALS, 1964. **Career:** Mideastern Mich Libr Cooper, Flint, MI, coordr, young adult serv, 1967-69; Berrien Co Libr League, Benton Harbor, MI, dir, 1969-74; Benton Harbor Pub Libr, dir, 1969-74; Libr Cooper Macomb, Mt Clemens, MI, dir, 1974-80; Macomb Co Libr, Mt Clemens, MI, dir, 1974-80; Los Angeles Pub Libr, Los Angeles, CA, asst city librn, 1980-; Queens Borough Pub Libr, dep lib dir, cust serv, currently. **Orgs:** Am Libr Asn, 1960-; co-chair, Mich Delegation White House Conf Libr Info & Servs, 1979-80; Mich Libr Asn, 1960-80; Calif Libr Asn, 1980-. **Honors/Awds:** Librn, Libr USA NY World Fair, 1964; Author, chapter, Black Librarian Am, Scarecrow, 1970, What Black Librarian Are Saying, Scarecrow, 1972, Libraries Political Process, Scarecrow, 1980. **Military Serv:** AUS, First Lt, 1958-61. **Business Addr:** Deputy Director, Queens Borough Public Library, 89 11 Merrick Blvd, Jamaica, NY 11432, **Business Phone:** (213)612-3333.*

ALFORD JOSEPH, TAROME
Educator. **Personal:** Born May 3, 1960, Milwaukee, WI; son of Joe and Joyce Alford; married Milva McGhee, Jun 5, 1999. **Educ:** Univ Wisconsin-Oshkosh, BA, BS, 1982; Southern Ill Univ Carbondale, MA, 1985. **Career:** Univ Wis-Oshkosh, resident asst, 1980-82; Southern Ill Univ, Carbondale, grad asst, 1982-84; Cornell Col, residence hall dir, 1984-85; Univ Nebr, residence hall dir, 1985-88; SUNY, Col New Paltz, asst dir residence life, 1988-89; Eastern Conn State Univ, assoc dir housing & res life; Texas A&M Univ, Kingsville, dir housing; Cent Conn State Univ, dir residence life, currently. **Orgs:** NASPA Region I, Conf Planning Comm, 1989-92; chair, NTWK Edu Equity & Ethnic Diversity, 1989-92; chair, Elections & Nominations Comm, 1992-94, Regional Liaison Minority Undergrad Fel Prog, 2002-; ACPA, Comm on Multical Affairs, 1990-92; ACUHO-I, Multical Affairs Comm, 1993-; Nat Chair, Membership Comm, 1994-96; Foundation Bd Trustee, 1996-99. **Honors/Awds:** Professionals Achievement Award, Conn ASN Affirmative Action, 1993; Martin Luther King Jr Distinguished Service Award, ECSU, 1993; NASPA Region I Continuous Service Award, 1995; Foundation of Excellence Award, ACUHO, 1999. **Special Achievements:** Fourteenth Annual Communications CNF, Presenter, 1985; Regional Entry Level Institute (RELI), 2001. **Business Phone:** (860)832-1660.

ALFRED, DR. DEWITT C., JR.
College teacher, psychiatrist. **Personal:** Born Oct 12, 1937, Chattanooga, TN; son of Dewitt Clinton and O'Teele Eloise (Nichols); married Marion Leticia Bottoms, Aug 22, 1959; children: Leticia O'Teele Alfred Garrick & Dewitt Clinton Alfred III. **Educ:** Morehouse Col, BS, 1956; Howard Univ, MD, 1960. **Career:** Homer G Philips Hosp St Louis, internship, 1960-61; Wash Univ St Louis,asst res psychiat, 1961-62; USAF Reg Hosp, gen med officer, 1962-64;Walter Reed Gen Hosp, resident psychiatrist, 1964-67; USAF Area Med Ctr,asst chief psychiat, 1967-68; USAF Regional Hosp, chief psychiat, 1968-71; Grady Mem Hosp, prof psychiat, 1971-84; Morehouse Sch Med, prof emer,currently. **Orgs:** Fel Am Psychiat Asn; diplomate, Am Bd Psychiat & Neurol; dir, InpatientPsychiat & asst chief psychiat Malcolm-Grow USAF Area Med Ctr Andrews AFB,1967-68; Dept Ment Health USAF Reg Hosp Sheppard AFB Tex & Reg ConsultPsychiat USAF Surgeon Gen, 1968-71; dir Inpt Psych & Asst supt Psychiat &Grady Mem Hosp Atlanta, GA, 1971-73; staff psychiatist Emory Univ Clinic &Emory univ Hosp, 1971-; Dept Psychiat Grady memorial Hosp Atlanta 1973-; Am Med Asn; Nat Med Asn; Am Acad Psychiat & Law; Southern Psychiat Asn; Soc USAF Psychiatrists; Black Psychiatrists Am; trustee GA Psychiat Asn, 1979-82; founding chmn, psychiat dept, Morehouse Sch Med, 1984-; dir, Morehouse Med Assocs, 1985-93; Nat Ment Health Coun, 1992-. **Honors/Awds:** Young MD of the Year, Atlanta Med Asn, 1976; Pub Service Award, MentHealth Asn, Metro Atlanta, 1989; Solomon Carter Fuller Award, 1994. **Business Addr:** Psychiatrist, Morehouse School of Med, Department Psychiat & Behavioral Sci, 75 Piedmont Ave NE Ste 800, Atlanta, GA 30350, **Business Phone:** (770)394-6007.*

ALFRED, RAYFIELD
College teacher, firefighter. **Personal:** Born Jul 11, 1939, Ville Platte, LA; married Cynthia A Patterson; children: A LaChelle, Shaun C, Raphael W & Jonathan K. **Educ:** Univ Va, attended 1975; Univ DC, AA, 1977, BS, 1981; Okla State Univ, attended 1981, 1983; US Fire Acad, attended 1983, 1984. **Career:** College teacher (retired); Univ DC, asst prof, cardiopulmonary resuscitation, 1980-81; DC Fire Dept, consult, pub info officer, fire chief, 1988-94. **Orgs:** Instr trainer, Am Heart Assoc, 1977; adv neighborhood comm, DC Govt, 1981-84; adv sub comt of facilities, bd trustees, Univ DC, 1982-83; prof adv comt, Greater SE Comm Hosp, 1983-85; emergency cardiac comm, Am Heart Asn, 1983-84; bd dirs, Leadership Wash; bd dirs, Anthony Bowen, YMCA; bd dir, DC Street Acad; chmn bd, Greater DC Cares; Nat Fire Protection Asn. **Honors/Awds:** Certificate of Honor Mention DC Fire Dept, 1967; Certificate of Appreciation, DC Dental Soc, Am Red Cross, 1978-83; Certificate of Appreciation, Am Heart Asn, 1982-83; Silver Medal for Valor, DC Fire Dept,1984. **Special Achievements:** First African-American fire chief in Jacksonville, Florida. **Military Serv:** AUS, sgt, 3 yrs; Hon Discharge, 1958-61. *

ALI, DR. FATIMA (ANN LOUISE REDMON)
Educator. **Personal:** Born Apr 20, 1925, Indianapolis, IN; daughter of Theophilus Adams (deceased) and Eugenia Dudley Adams (deceased); married LeRoy Redmon (deceased); children: Lydia Ann. **Educ:** Purdue Univ, BS, 1946, MS, 1960, PhD, 1970. **Career:** School administrator (retired); Gary Pub Sch, teacher, counr, 1948-65; Purdue Univ, teaching asst, 1959-60, NDEA summer fel, 1962, asst dir, NEDAsummer fel, 1964; psychol teacher, prin, prof, clinician, psychotherapist,adminr, dean women, dir; Black Studs Affairs, 1965-70, EOP summer fel,1966-67; Univ Calif Berkeley, assoc coord Afro-Am Studies, dean women,1970-71; Cailf State Univ, asst prof educ psychol, Hayward, 1971-74; Contra Costa Co Hosp, clin psychol, 1971-75; Am Muslim Mission, natlminister educ & dir educ, 1974-79; Pueblo House, clin dir, 1980-83; Reading Res Coun, co founder, 1981; Burlingame CA, chief executiveofficer, 1982; Davis Res Found, vpres, 1988; Univ Santa Barbara, prof,educ psychol, CA, 1982; consult, currently. **Orgs:** Consult, Serene Comm Sch Sacramento, CA, 1972; Cailf State Dept PubHealth, 1972-73; trustee, Cailf Unified Sch Dist, Benicia, 1973-75; CailfState Dept Educ, 1972; Contra Costa Co CETA Prog, 1978; instr, IN St Deptof Pub, 1978; consult, US Dept of Educ, 1979; Jenkins Homes for DisabledC, Oakland, 1981-82; CA Pub Lib Adult Literacy Prog, 1984; mem, Assn Clearning disabilities, The Common Wealth Club CA, CA Alliance Black; educr, Alpha Kappa Alpha Sorority, ssn Humanistic Psychol, 1985; adv coun, Intl Biog Ctr, Cambridge, Eng, 1988; dep gov & res bd advisors, Am BiolInst, 1988. **Honors/Awds:** Distinguished Leadership Award, Am Biol Inst, 1987; Int Leaders inAchievement Award, Intl Biol Ctr, Cambridge, Eng, 1987. **Special Achievements:** First African-American woman to earn a PhD, Purdue Univ. **Business Addr:** Consultant, Reading Research Council Dyslexia Correction Center, 1601 Old Bayshore Hwy Suite 260, Burlingame, CA 94010, **Business Phone:** (650)692-8990.*

ALI, GRACE L.
Executive, chief financial officer. **Personal:** Born May 27, 1952, Georgetown, Guyana; daughter of Joseph Moore and Victoria Nurse Moore; married Oscar, Jun 16, 1973; children: Asgar & Rasheed. **Educ:** Univ Mass, Amherst, Mass, BBA, 1973; Univ Miami, Miami, Fla, MBA, 1987. **Career:** Peat, Marwick, Mitchell, New York, NY, internal analyst, 1973-76; Peat, Marwick, Main, Miami, Fla, sr auditor, 1976-79; Air Fla Syst, Miami, Fla, asst controller, 1979-80; Air Fla Europe, London, Eng, vpres finance, 1980-83; Univ Miami, Miami, Fla, asst controller, 1983-89; Fla Memorial Col, Miami, Fla, vpres bus & fiscal affairs, 1989; Fla A&M Univ, vpres fiscal affairs; Miami-Dade Pub Schs, chief financial officer, 2007-. **Orgs:** Am Inst CPAs, 1984-; Fla Inst CPAs, 1984-; bd mem, 1987-, comt chmn, 1987-89, Fla Inst CPAs-South Dade; mem finance comt, United Way Dade Co, 1990-. **Honors/Awds:** CPA, State Fla, 1984; Service Award, Town Crawley Eng, 1983; Outstanding Professional, Phi Beta Sigma, 1983; Outstanding Comt, FICPA-South Dade, 1988, 1989; Service Award, Fla Memorial Col, 1990. **Home Addr:** 10920 SW 125 St, Miami, FL 33176, **Home Phone:** (305)251-4791. **Business Addr:** Chief Financial Officer, Miami-Dade County Public Schools, 1450 NE 2 Ave Suite 456, Miami, FL 33132, **Business Phone:** (305)995-2532.

ALI, DR. KAMAL HASSAN
Educator. **Personal:** Born Sep 3, 1944, Springfield, MA; son of Stella Abrams Bridges-Marshall and Edwin Harold Marshall Sr; married Ayesha Ali, Apr 1, 1966; children: Ahmed Hassan, Quesiyah Sana & Ibrahim Suhnoon. **Educ:** Hunter Col, attended 1964; New York Univ, 1965; Univ Mass, Amherst, MEd, 1977, EdD, 1981. **Career:** Human Resources Admin, sr human resource specialist, 1967-71; Harlem East-Harlem Model Cities, proj liason, 1971-74; Univ Mass, Amherst, grad res & teaching asst, 1974-78; Vantage Consult, Hartford, Conn, training prog developer, 1978-79; Westfield State Col, dir, minority & bilingual voc teacher educ prog, 1980-81, dir minority affairs, 1981-, asst dean acad affairs, prof, World Lang, Multicultural & Gender Studies, currently. **Orgs:** Vpres, Islamic Soc Western Mass, 1983-; chmn, bd dir, 1984-86, chmn, New Bldg Comm, 1986-, Dunbar Community Ctr; Ya-Sin Mosque's Dar ul-Islam movement; Ludlow Correctional Facil, Mass, first Imam, currently. **Honors/ Awds:** Producer, host, cable TV prog "Col Journal," Springfield, Mass, 1983-; author, "Islamic Education in the United States: An Overview of Issues, Problems & Possible Approaches," 1984, "The Shariah and Its Implications to Muslim School Planning," 1986, Am J Islamic Social Studies. **Home Addr:** 698 Alden St, Springfield, MA 01109. **Business Addr:** Assistant Professor, Westfield State College, World Languages, Multicultural & Gender Studies, Wilson Hall 235, Westfield, MA 01086, **Business Phone:** (413)572-5388.

ALI, LAILA
Television show host, boxer. **Personal:** Born Dec 30, 1977, Miami Beach, FL; daughter of Muhammad and Veronica Porche Anderson; married Curtis Conway, Jul 22, 2007; married Johnny McClain, Aug 27, 2000 (divorced 2005). **Educ:** Univ Southern Calif Bus Sch, Santa Monica Col, BA, bus mgt. **Career:** Boxer (retired), TV show host; Nail Salon, owner; prof boxer, 1999-2007; CBS? The Early Show, health & lifestyle correspondent, 2007-; NBC's "American Gladiators", co-host, 2008-. **Orgs:** Founder, Reach Found. **Honors/Awds:** Female Athlete of the Year, Black Sports Agents Asn, 2001; Super Middleweight champion, Women's InterNat Boxing Asn, 2002; Super Middleweight champion, Int Women's Boxing Fedn, 2005. **Special Achievements:** Won debut bout against April Fowler, Oct 15, 1999; undefeated in first 10 matches w/8 knockouts; appeared in TV commercials & numerous magazines; co-author, Reach; Film: All You've Got, 2006. **Business Addr:** Co-Host, NBC, 30 Rockefeller Plaza, New York, NY, NY 10112, **Business Phone:** (212)664-4444.

ALI, MAAJID F.
Clergy. **Career:** Masjid Jihad, imam, currently. **Business Addr:** Imam, Masjid Jihad, 117 E 34th St, Savannah, GA 31401-8101, **Business Phone:** (912)236-7387.*

ALI, MUHAMMAD (CASSIUS MARCELLUS CLAY, JR.)
Boxer, activist, social worker. **Personal:** Born Jan 17, 1942, Louisville, KY; son of Cassius Marcellus Clay Sr and Odessa Grady Clay; married Belinda Boyd, Aug 17, 1967 (divorced 1977); children: Maryum, Jamillah, Liban & Muhammad Jr; married Veronica Porsche, Mar 13, 1977 (divorced 1986); children: Hana, Khaliah, Miya & Laila; married Yolanda, Nov 19, 1986; children: Asaad Amin & Rasheda; married Yolanda "Lonnie", Nov 19, 1986; children: Asaad. **Career:** Boxer (retired), polit activist, lect, philanthropist; prof boxer, 1960-81; Muhammad Ali Ctr, founder & owner, 2005-; Muhammad Ali Enterprises LLC, partner, 2006-. **Orgs:** World Community Islam; conducts missionary work; World Organization for Rights, Liberty & Dignity. **Honors/Awds:** Light heavyweight champion, AAU, 1959, 1960; 6 Golden Glove Titles in Kentucky; Light heavyweight champion, Golden Gloves, 1959; Heavyweight champion, Golden Gloves, 1960; Gold Medal, light heavyweight div, Olympics, 1960; World Heavyweight championship, 1964-67, 1974-78, 1978-79; inducted into US Olympic Hall of Fame, 1983; honored for long, meritorious service to boxing, WBA, 1985; elected Intl Boxing Hall of Fame, The Ring, 1987; Spirit of America Award, 1991; Jim Thorpe Pro Sports Award, Lifetime Achievement Award, 1992; Essence Award, 1997; recipient of the World Sports Awards of the Century, 1999; Sportsman of the Century, Sports Illustrated, 1999; Personality of the Year Award, BBC Sports, 1999; Messenger of Peace, UN, 1998-2008; Presidential Citizen's Medal, presented by President Clinton, 2001; Presidential Medal of Freedom, presented by George Bush, 2005; Otto Hahn Peace Medal in Gold, UN Asn Germany, Berlin, 2005; Lifetime Achievement Award, Amnesty International; Kentuckian of the Century, State of Kentucky; Louisvillian of the Century, Advertising Club of Louisville; XNBA Human Spirit Award. **Special Achievements:** Film Appearances: Buck White, 1969; Requiem for a Heavyweight, 1962; The Greatest, 1977; Body and Soul, 1977; Doin' Time, 1985; When We Were Kings:The True Story of the Rumble in the Jungle, 1996; TV includes: Tomorrow's Champions, 1950s; Muhammad Ali, animated series, 1977; Freedom Road, 1979; Muhammad Ali: The Whole Story, 1996; Muhammad Ali Museum, Louisville Galleria, 1995; film, Ali, based on his life, 2001; author, The Greatest: My Own Story, 1975; named to the list of the Greatest Chicagoans of the Century; Olympic Torch bearer, 1996; author, Muhammad Ali: His Life and Times with Thomas Hauser; honor of lighting the flame at the 1996 Summer Olympics in Atlanta, Ga. **Business Addr:** Founder, Owner, Muhammad Ali Center, 144 N 6th St, Louisville, KY 40202, **Business Phone:** (502)584-9254.

ALI, RASHEEDAH ZIYADAH
Administrator, automotive executive. **Personal:** Born Jul 3, 1950, Springfield, IL; daughter of Zeddie L and Montez R McIntosh (deceased); married Rahman Munir Ali, Jun 15, 1970; children: Jamillah, Sakinah & Rahman II. **Educ:** Sangamon State Gerontology Seminars, cert,1976, 1977, 1978; United Way, counselors training cert, 1986. **Career:** Springfield Fair Housing Coalition, vpres, pres, 1987; Imani Inc, chmn & owner, currently. **Orgs:** Bd mem, Advocates Health; adv coun mem, bd mem, Community Action Agency, 1986; vol, Community Energy Systems, 1986, Access Housing, 1986, People Progress; chmn bd, Imani Inc; exec bd mem, Sangamon Co Democrat Minority Caucus; comnr, Springfield Human Rels Comn. **Honors/Awds:** Fair Housing Award, City Springfield, 1990; Humanitarian Award, Ill Munic Human Rels Asn Community Serv, 1992. **Business Addr:** Owner, Imani Inc, 908 S Wirt Ave, Springfield, IL 62703-1930, **Business Phone:** (217)523-8978.*

ALI, RASHIED (ROBERT PATTERSON)
Musician, drummer. **Personal:** Born Jul 1, 1935, Philadelphia, PA; son of Randolph Patterson and Dorothy Mae Christopher; married Patricia Bea Wyatt; children: Akeela, Annik. **Educ:** Wm Pa Bus Inst, Philadelphia, attended 1953; Granoff Music Sch, attended 1955. **Career:** John Coltrane Combo, 1965; Survival Rec, leader; Funkyfreeboppers; Ali's Alley Jazz Club, owner; Survival Rec & Studio. **Home Addr:** 77 Greene St, New York, NY 10012. *

ALI, SHAHRAZAD
Writer, executive. **Personal:** Born Feb 5, 1949, Cincinnati, OH; daughter of Lucy Marshall and Harry Levy; married Solomon Ali, 1967 (died 1985); children: three; married Yahya Ali, 1996. **Educ:** Xavier Univ, Cincinnati, OH; Georgia State Univ, Atlanta, GA. **Career:** Cincinnati Herald, Call & Post, Cincinnati Enquirer and Hi-Lites Magazine, feature contributing editor, 1966-71; medical transcriptionist, 1977-83; Clark Col, assistant to vice pres, 1983-85; Civilized Publications, Atlanta, GA, 1985-; Ali's Unlimited Accessories, executive assistant, 1986-89; Temple Univ, PASCEP Program for Independent Publishing, teacher, 1987. **Orgs:** Advisory board mem, Ford Recreation Center, Philadelphia, PA, 1988-89; advisory board mem, Pennsylvania Board of Probation and Parole, Philadelphia, PA, 1988-89; public relations director, Mayor's Commission on Women, Philadelphia, PA, 1987-88; published author, Moonstone Black Writers Association, Philadelphia, PA, 1987-88. **Honors/Awds:** Alpha Phi Alpha Literary Award, 1987; Mayor's Proclamation for Writing, New Orleans, LA, 1987, Detroit, MI, 1990; Third Place, Top Georgia Authors of Atlanta Public Library, 1985; author, How Not to Eat Pork, 1985; author, The Blackman's Guide to Understanding the Blackwoman, 1990, #1 book on Black Best Selling List for 40 weeks, 1990; The Blackwoman's Guide to Understanding the Blackman, 1992; Blackman's Guide on Tour Video, 1992; Are You Still a Slave?, 1994; Things Your Parents Should Have Told You, 1998; Urban Survival for the Year 2000/Y2K, 1999; honorary doctoral, journalism, UHURU Univ, 1995. **Special Achievements:** Promotional activities include appearances on Donahue, Geraldo, Sally, Montel, Larry King, Jerry Springer, Ricki Laker, Judge for Yourself, Gordon Elliot, Rolonda, Our Voices-BET, Tony Brown's Journal; author: How To Tell If Your Man Is Gay or Bisexual, 2003. **Business Addr:** Writer, Civilized Publications, 2023 S 7th St, Philadelphia, PA 19148, **Business Phone:** (215)339-0062.*

ALI, TATYANA MARISOL
Singer, actor. **Personal:** Born Jan 24, 1979, Atlanta, GA; daughter of Sheriff Ali and Sonia Enieda. **Educ:** Harvard Univ, anthrop, 2002. **Career:** Theatre performance: Fences, 1987; Orfeo del Campo; Sugar Hill; TV Series: "Sesame Street", 1984-88; "Star Search"; "Brains & Brawn", co-host, 1993; "Fresh Price of Bel Air", 1998; "413 Hope Street"; "Living Single"; "In the House"; Albums: Everytime; Boy You Knock Me Out; Day dreaming; Kiss the Sky; TV movies: "Fall Into Darkness"; "Foster's Field Trip"; Films: Eddie Murphy Raw; Jawbreakers; Brother, 2000; National Lampoon Presents Dorm Daze, 2003; Nora's Hair Salon, 2004; Back in the Day, 2005; Glory Road, 2006; The List, 2007; Hotel California, 2008; Privileged, 2009; MJJ Music, vocal artist, currently. **Honors/Awds:** Junior Vocalist Champion, 1987; BET Awards, 2005. **Special Achievements:** Appeared on Star Search & won twice receiving a 4 star rating when she appeared for a 2nd time; ranked 6th in Billboard 100 Hot Singles; Ranked seventy fourth in VH1 100 Top Child Stars, 2005; Gold Album: "Daydreamin". *

ALICE, MARY (MARY ALICE SMITH)
Actor. **Personal:** Born Dec 3, 1941, Indianola, MS. **Career:** Theatrical appearances: A Rat's Mass, 1969; The Duplex, 1972; Miss Julie,1973; House Party, 1973; Black Sunlight, 1974; Terraces, 1974; Heaven andHell's Agreement, 1974; In the Deepest Part of Sleep, 1974; Cockfight,1977; Nongogo, 1978; Player No 9, Spell No 7, NY Shakespeare Festival,1979; Zooman and the Sign, 1980;; Open Admissions Long Wharf Theatre,1982; A Raisin in the Sun, 1984; Glasshouse, 1984; Take Me Along, 1984;Fences, Goodman Theatre, Chgo, 1986; 46th St Theatre, NYC, 1987; TheShadow Box, 1994; Films: The Education of Sonny Carson, 1974; Sparkle,1976; Teachers, 1984; Brat Street, 1984; To Sleep With Anger, 1990;Awakenings, 1990; Bonfire of the Vanities, 1990; A Perfect World, 1992;Life with Mikey, 1993; The Inkwell, 1994; Heading Home, 1995; Bed ofRoses, 1996; Down in the Delta, 1998; Catfish in Black Bean Sauce, 1999;The Wishing Tree, 1999; The Photographer, 2000; Sunshine State, 2002; TheMatrix Revolutions, 2003; The Matrix Recalibrated, 2004; The Burly ManChronicles, 2004; TV films: "The Sty of the Blind Pig", 1974; "Just an OldSweet Song", 1976; "This Man Stands Alone", 1979; "Joshua's World", 1980;"The Color of Friendship", 1981; "The Killing Floor", 1984; "ConcealedBurmies", 1984; "Charlotte Forten's Mission: Experiment on Freedom", 1984;"The Women of Brewster Place", 1989; "Laurel Avenue", 1993; "The Mother",1994; "The Vernon Johns Story", 1994; TV series: "Sanford and Son", 1972;"A Different World", 1988-89; "I'll Fly Away", 1991-93; "Oz", 2002; "Lineof Fire", 2004; "The Jury", 2004; "Kojak", 2005. **Orgs:** Am Fedn TV & Radio Artists; Screen Actors Guild; Actor's Equity Asn. **Honors/Awds:** Obie Award, Village Voice, 1979; Antoinette Perry Award; Drama Desk Award,1987; Tony Award, 1987; Emmy Award, 1993; Nominated for Black Reel Award, 2004. **Special Achievements:** Tony Award nominee, Having Our Say: The Delany Sisters' First 100 Years. **Business Phone:** (310)275-0172.*

ALICE, MILLER
Executive director. **Career:** Bd Elections & Ethics, exec dir, currently. **Business Addr:** Executive Director, Board of Elections & Ethics, 441 4th St NW Suite 250N, Washington, DC 20001, **Business Phone:** (201)727-2525.*

ALI-JACKSON, KAMIL
Government official. **Personal:** Born Mar 4, 1959, El Paso, TX; daughter of John Ali and Ruth; married Michael S Jackson, Aug 31, 1985; children: Ross, Kendall & Kamryn. **Educ:** Princeton Univ, AB, 1981; Harvard Law Sch, JD, 1984. **Career:** McCarter & English, assoc, 1984-86; Pepper, Hamilton & Scheetz, assoc, 1986-90; Merck & Co Inc, dir, Corp Licensing, 1990; Endo Pharmaceuticals Inc, assoc gen coun & vpres; Caresoft Inc, gen coun; Dr Reddy's Lab Inc, assoc gen coun & vpres legal; Ception Therapeutics Inc, gen coun, currently. **Orgs:** Nat Bar Asn, 1986-92; Philadelphia Bar Asn, 1986-92; Pa Bar Asn; bd mem, Zoning Hearing. **Business Addr:** General Counsel, Ception Therapeutics, 101 Lindenwood Dr Suite 400, Malvern, PA 19355, **Business Phone:** (610)640-2940.

ALLAH, RAKIM (WILLIAM MICHAEL GRIFFIN, JR.)
Rap musician. **Personal:** Born Jan 28, 1968, Long Island, NY. **Career:** Eric B & Rakim, group mem; All-Pro Football 2K8, com spokesman, currently; Albums: Paid in Full, 1987; Follow the Leader, 1988; Let the Rhythm Hitem, 1990; Dont Sweat the Technique, 1992; The 18th Letter, 1997; oh mygod; The Master, 1999; The Seventh Seal, 2009; Holy Are You, 2009. **Honors/ Awds:** The Greatest MCs Of All Time, #4 MTV. **Special Achievements:** Raekwon of the Wu-Tang Clan dedicated a tribute to Rakim entitled "Rakim Tribute"; Tupac Shakur also pays tribute to Rakim in a song called "Old School". **Business Phone:** (212)373-0600.*

ALLAIN, STEPHANIE
Movie producer. **Personal:** Born Oct 30, 1959. **Educ:** Univ Calif, Santa Cruz, BA, lit & creative writing. **Career:** Creative Artists Agency, staff reader; Jim Henson Pictures, pres prod, 1997-; Columbia Pictures, vpres prod; Homegrown Pictures, independent producer, 2003-; Films: Buddy, 1997; The Adventures of Elmo in Grouchland, 1999; Muppets from Space, 1999; Good Boy!, 2003; Biker Boyz, 2003; Hustle & Flow, 2005; Something New, 2006; Black Snake Moan, 2006. **Special Achievements:** Nominated for Black Reel Awards and Black Movie Awards. *

ALLEN, ALEX JAMES, JR.
Judge. **Personal:** Born Dec 8, 1934, Louise, MS; married Nancy Ann Green; children: Alex III, Michael P, Derek J. **Educ:** Wayne

State Univ, BA, 1964; Detroit Col Law, JD, 1969. **Career:** Total Action Against Poverty Med Div, admin asst, 1966-68; Comn C & Youth, City Detroit, asst dir, 1968-71; Stone Richardson & Allen PC, atty, 1971-82; 36th Dist Court Detroit, MI, judge, 1981-90, chief judge, 1990-95; Detroit Area Agency Aging, chmn, 1999-. **Orgs:** Omega Psi Phi; Nat Asn Advan Colored People; Founders Soc Detroit Inst of Arts; State Bd Mich; Am Judges Asn; Mich Dist Judges Asn; bd dir, Mich Black Judge Asn. **Military Serv:** USAF, s/sgt, 1954-57. **Home Addr:** 1943 Hyde Park Dr, Detroit, MI 48207. **Business Addr:** Chairman, Detroit Area Agency Aging, 1333 Brewery Park Blvd, Detroit, MI 48207.

ALLEN, BENJAMIN P., III
Financial manager. **Personal:** Born Feb 27, 1942, Washington, DC; son of Benjamin (deceased) and Elizabeth (deceased); married Francesca M Winslow; children: Nicole & Camille. **Educ:** Howard Univ, BS, 1963; Rutgers Univ, MBA, 1976. **Career:** Marine Midland Bank, proj officer, 1970-78, from asst br mgr to br mgr,1978-84, opers, 1985, corp mgr employee rels, 1986-87, asst vpres br mgr,1987-88; Riggs Bank NA, vpres, pvt banking officer, 1988-89, vpres br mgr,1990-91, vpres, regional mgr, 1992-97; Prudential Securities, financialadvisor, 1997-99; Br Banking & Trust, financial ctr, mgr, vpres, financialctr leader & br mgr, 1999-. **Orgs:** Treas Edges Group, 1984-88; Urban Bankers Coalition, 1984-88; Nat Black MBA Asn, 1984-88; vestry mem, St Andrews Church, 1985; Wash Urban Bankers Asn, 1988-; treas, Edges Group, Metrop Wash DC Chapter, 1989-; bd dirs, Mentors, 1989-94. **Honors/Awds:** Black achiever, Harlem Br YMCA, 1974. **Military Serv:** USAR-MSC Col (retired); AUS Achievement Award, 1983; Meritorious Service Medal, 1989, Oak Leaf Cluster, 1994. **Home Addr:** 5451 Ashleigh Rd, Fairfax, VA 22030. **Business Addr:** Branch Manager, Branch Banking & Trust Co, 8200 Greensboro Dr, McLean, VA 22102, **Business Phone:** (703)442-4035.*

ALLEN, BERNESTINE
Government official. **Personal:** Born Aug 20, 1944, Soperton, GA. **Educ:** Ft Valley State Col, BS, 1967; Northeastern Univ, MA, 1968. **Career:** Dept Labor, Wash, econ analyst, 1967; NSF grant, 1967; Gen Elec Co, financial analyst, 1968-69; Dept Transp, Wash, economist, 1969-71; Airport & Airway Cost Allocation Study, economist asst dir, 1971-73; Int Aviation Policy, economist, 1973-75; Dept Transportation, int transportation specialist, 1975-80, sr int transp specialist, 1980-87, int coop div & secretarial chief, 1987-95, int coop & trade div chief, 1995-97, deputy dir & acting dir off int transp trade, 1997-2000, dir office int transp, 2000-. **Orgs:** Am Econ Asn; Am Fedn Govt Employees, 1970-72; Nat Econ Asn; Am Acad Polit & Soc Sci; Bus & Prof Women's League; DC Asn Retarded Citizens; pres, Delta Sigma Theta Inc, 1966-67, 1972-74; exec comt, March Dimes, Nat Capital Area Chap, 1988-91; bd dirs, DST Telecommunications Inc, 1976-81; Garfield Home Sr Citizens; Proj Women; Women Ex-Offenders Prog, 1973; Nat Coun Negro Women; NAACP; Nat Urban League; exec bd, financial secy, Nat Pan-Hellenic Coun Inc, 1991-95; Int Freedom Found. **Honors/Awds:** Alpha Kappa Mu Nat Honor Soc, 1965; Wall St Journal Scholastic Achievement Award, 1967; Outstanding Service in Government, Dollars & Sense Mag, 1990; Silver Medal for Meritorious Professional Achievement, 1990. **Business Addr:** Director, US Department of Transportation, Office of International Transportation & Trade, 400 7th St SW, Washington, DC 20590.

ALLEN, BETTIE JEAN
Executive. **Personal:** Born Oct 21, 1926, Springfield, IL; divorced. **Educ:** Springfield Col; Lincoln Col Law, Univ IL; Sangamon State Univ. **Career:** YWCA Kenya, int div, vol, 1967-68; Springfield Human Rel Comn, exec dir, 1969-70; entrepreneur, 1970-74; Assoc Gen Contractors Illinois, training dir, 1971-72; State of Illinois, Capital Devel Bd, coord. **Orgs:** Pres, Nat Asn Advan Colored People; Serv Bur Colored C; supvr, Zion Bapt Church Sch; trustee bd mem, YWCA, 1954-70; bd mem, United Way; RR Relocation Auth. **Honors/Awds:** Webster Plaque Award, Springfield Nat Asn Advan Colored People, 1957; Achievement Award, Urban League, 1964; Affirmative Action Award, 1975; Breadbasket Commercial Achievement Award, 1977. *

ALLEN, BETTY. See Obituaries section.

ALLEN, BILLY R.
Consultant. **Personal:** Born Mar 16, 1945, Crossroads, TX; son of Fannie M; married Clare Dickerson Allen, Aug 14, 1971; children: Sheldon C, Sean L, Kristy B. **Educ:** Univ N Tex, BA, 1968. **Career:** New York Life Insurance, field underwriter, 1970-72; Pitney Bowes, account representative, 1971-73; Minority Search Inc, pres, chief exec off & chmn, 1975-. **Orgs:** DFW Airport Bd, comt chmn, 1988; Nat Recreation & Park Asn, vice chmn, 1986-92; Concord Missionary Baptist Church, elder, currently; The Dallas Assembly; The Dallas Black Chamber Com; Comt 100; Univ N Tex, bd visitors, 1990; Soc Int Bus Fel, 1986. **Honors/Awds:** Willow Award, Dallas Black Chamber, 1986; Outstanding Ex-Stud, Henderson Co Jr Col, 1985; Nat Asn Community Leadership Orgn, Distinguished Leadership Award, 1986; Dallas Chamber Com, 1976; YMCA Achievement, 1984. **Home Addr:** 830 Misty Glen Ln, Dallas, TX 75232, **Home Phone:** (214)374-8607. **Business Addr:** Chairman, Chief Executive Officer, Minority Search Inc, 777 S RL Thronton Freeway Suite 105, PO Box 764241, Dallas, TX 75203, **Business Phone:** (214)948-6116.*

ALLEN, BLAIR SIDNEY
Educator. **Personal:** Born Aug 7, 1952, Abington, PA; divorced; children: Thageron. **Educ:** Pa State Univ, BS, biophysics, 1974; Univ Calif, Berkeley, MS, biophysics, 1979. **Career:** Educator(retired); Bio physics Dept, Pa State Univ, PA, 1973; Presbyterian Univ Pa, Med Ctr, res teacher, 1980-81; Harcum Jr Col, instr sci. **Orgs:** Pres, Res Inst Technol Inc, 1978-, Opport Coun Eastern Montgomery County, 1980-82; Grad Fel & Minority Fel, 1974-79; fel, Nat Adv Study Inst, 1981; fel, Fac Summer Inst, 1983; Nat Asn Advan Colored People Amber Br, 1984-85. **Honors/Awds:** First Prize Chem, Montgomery & DE Valley Sci Fairs, 1970; Scholarship, Pa Senatorial Scholar & Grad, 1970-74.

ALLEN, DR. BRENDA FOSTER
Educator. **Personal:** Born Jan 24, 1947, Gloucester, VA; married Robert P; children: Tameka D. **Educ:** Va State Univ, BS, 1969; NC State Univ, MS, 1976, Ed.D, 1985. **Career:** Cornell Univ, Coop Exten Serv, youth develop specialist, 1971-72, county 4-H agent, 1969; Nat 4-H Found, Div Leadership Develop, prog specialist, 1972-75; NC State Univ, Sch Educ, res asst, 1975-76, Div Stud Affairs, coordr, 1976-80, asst dir, 1980-83, Off Provost, coordr, 1983-85, Agr Exten Serv, prog specialist, 1985-; Col Textiles, coordr African-Am Advising, currently. **Orgs:** NC State Univ, grad stud's assoc adult educ exec bd; Nat 4-H Found, staff develop & training comt, volunteers' forum planning comt; Task Force Prog Develop 4-H volunteers; Nat Teen Leaders' Symposium Planning Comt; Am Home Econs Asn; Nat 4-H Asn; Kappa Omicron Phi; Image NC State Univ Seminars, facilitator, 1979-80, task force mem, 1978-79; Outstanding Young Women of Am, 1980; NCSU comt Recruitment & Retention Black Studs, 1982-83; Gov's Conf Women & Economy, facilitator, 1983; Shaw Univ Sem Ext Prog, teacher, 1984-86, Youth Motivation Task Force, 1985-86; NC Home Econs Ext Prog Comn, 1983-84; NC 4-H Volunteer Task Force, 1986; NC Home Econ Volunt Task Force, 1986; Epsilon Sigma Phi, Nat Hon Extension Fraternity, 1989. **Honors/Awds:** Publications, "Making Incentives Work for You", 1976; "Competencies Needed by 4-H Volunteers for the Effective Use of Incentives - A Needs Asessment Study", 1976; "Criteria for Selection, Evaluating or Developing Learning Modules", 1976, "Are Your Reading Habits a Liability?", 1977; "Video tapes Help University Students Learn How to Learn", 1981; "Build Up One Another", 1986; "Women, Builders of Communities and Dreams", 1986; "Rural Minority Women As Community Volunteers", 1986; NC Coordinator, Women and Chronic Disease Teleconference, 1988; received Infant Mortality Grant from United Church of Christ, 1989. **Home Addr:** 2025 Rabbit Run, Raleigh, NC 27603. **Business Addr:** Coordinator of African-American Advising, North Carolina State University, College of Textiles, 2401 Research Dr, PO Box 8301, Raleigh, NC 27695.*

ALLEN, BYRON (BYRON ALLEN FOLKS)
Entertainer. **Personal:** Born Apr 22, 1961, Detroit, MI; married Jennifer Lucas, Sep 1, 2007; children: Chloe Ava. **Career:** TV Series: Director: "The American Athlete",1996; "Global Business People", 1999; "Every Woman", 2000; "Recipe TV Featuring the World's Greatest Chefs", 2002; "Beautiful Homes & Great Estates", 2002; "Urban Style", 2003; "Designers Fashions & Runways", 2004; The Best of Comics Unleashed with Byron Allen, 2008; "Real People", host, 1979-84; exe prod: "Every Woman", 2000; "Beautiful Homes & Great Estates", 2002; "Designers Fashions & Runways", 2004; "Comics Unleashed", 2006; Are U Serious?: Best of Shawn Morgan, 2008; "ES.TV HD", 2009; "The Byron Allen Show," 1989-92; "Comics Unleashed", currently; Film: America's Sweethearts, 2001; Entertainment Studios, chmn & Chief Exec Officer, 2004-. **Business Addr:** Chairman, Chief Executive Officer, Entertainment Studios, 9903 Santa Monica Blvd Suite 418, Los Angeles, CA 90212, **Business Phone:** (310)277-3500.*

ALLEN, CAROL WARD
Executive director. **Career:** Oakland Port Authority, pres; Laney Col, Community Servs Off, dir, 1993. **Orgs:** Senior Volunteers Prog, supvr; California Comn Status Women, past-pres; Bay Area Women Enterpreneurs, found & pres; Child Abuse Prevention, bd mem; Oakland Lyric Opera, bd mem; Bay Area Dance Series, bd mem; Phi Theta Cappa Honorary Soc, Laney Col, adv; Nat Women's Political Caucus; Black Women Organizers Political Action; Nat Organization Women; Emily's List, listee; Bay Area Rapid Transit (BART), bd dirs. **Special Achievements:** First African American female to head the Oakland Port Authority. **Business Addr:** Director, Laney College, Community & Informational Service, 900 Sallon St, Oakland, CA 94607, **Business Phone:** (510)834-5740.*

ALLEN, CAROLE GENEVA WARD
Educator. **Personal:** Born Jan 14, 1943, Phoenix City, AL. **Educ:** Calif State Univ, San Jose, BA, 1965, MA, 1973; Univ Calif, attended 1970; Int Comm Col, PhD; Univ Ile-Ife Nigeria, attended 1970; Univ Sci & Tech, attended 1970; Kumasi Ghana Forah Bay Col, Sierra Leone, attended 1970; Sorbonne, attended 1963. **Career:** Andrew Hill High Sch, 1965-69; airline stewardess, 1966-68. Calif Col Arts Cabrillo Col, 1970; Laney Col, ethnic studies, chairwoman, 1970-; Goddard Col, mentor consult teacher for masters degree stud, 1973-74; Oakland Bd Port Commissioners, pres, 1990-92; San Francisco Bay Area Rapid Transit Dist, bd dir, 1998-. **Orgs:** Bay Area Black Artists, 1972-; Nat Conf Artists, 1973-74; Bay Area Rapid Transp Admin, vice chairperson; Fruitvale Policy Comt, chair personl Oakland Airport connector Liaison Comt; Metrop Transp Comn AB 842; Alameda County Trap Improve Authority. **Honors/Awds:** Purchase Award, 27th Annual SF Art Festival, 1973; Outstanding Black Woman Award, Alpha Phi Alpha, 1974; Thirty Most Influential African Americans, City Fight Mag; C.J. Walker Business and Community Recognition Award, National Coalition of 100 Black Women, 2005; COMTO Award. **Special Achievements:** Publ Images of Awareness Pan Africanist Mag, 1973; Afro-Am Artists Bio-Biographical Dir Theres Dickason, 1973; black artist on Art Vol 2 by Samella Lewis Ruth Waddy, 1970. **Business Addr:** Board of Director, Laney College, 900 Fallon St, Oakland, CA 94607-4808.

ALLEN, CATHY H.
Executive. **Educ:** Stephen F Austin State Univ, BBA, 1981, MEd, 1989. **Career:** Tex Tech Univ, vice chancellor community & multicultural affairs; Covenant Health Syst, pres, currently. **Orgs:** Bd dir, Tex Ct Appointed Spec Advocates; historian & regional dir, Leadership Texas Alumnae Asn; treas, Lubbock Housing Finance Corp; vice chair, Grants Comt, LISD Found Excellence; Backpack Buddies, Jr League Lubbock; past chair, Women Excellence Comt, YWCA. **Honors/Awds:** Mentor of the Year, Texas Tech Univ, 2005; Women of Distinction, Girls Scouts of Caprock Council. **Business Addr:** Board of Director, Court Appointed Special Advocates, 1501 W Anderson Lane Suite B2, Austin, TX 78757, **Business Phone:** (512)473-2627.*

ALLEN, CHARLES CLAYBOURNE
Consultant. **Personal:** Born Sep 21, 1935, Newport News, VA; son of John C and Margaret C; married Sallie Tucker; children: Charles II, John IV & Sallie Monique. **Educ:** Hampton Inst, BS, archit, 1958; Columbia Univ, MSUP, 1963. **Career:** Clarke & Rapuano Inc, urban planner, 1963-68; Dept Develop & Planning Gary, dir, 1968-74; The Soul City Col, vpres, gen mgr, 1974-75; Wendell Campbell Assoc Inc, sr vpres, 1975-88; Newport News, Dept Planning & Develop, dep dir, VA, 1988-91; consult, urban planning, 1991-; Newport News City Coun, mem, 1992-; City Newport News, Vice Mayor, 1996-. **Orgs:** Bd mem, 1979-82, charter mem, Am Planning Asn 1979-; charter mem, Am Inst Cert Planners, 1979; bd mem, Am Soc Planning off, 1971-73; Am Inst Planners, 1977-78; chmn, joint AIP & ASPO Comn Min Affairs, 1973-78; pres, Nat Asn Planners, 1976; Kappa Alpha Psi Fraternity, 1955; Lambda Alpha;Commonwealth Va Adv Comn Inter governmental Rels, 1997-; chair, ACIR Comt Visual Quality; Transp Comn Hampton Roads, 1999-; Hampton Roads Planning Dist Comn, 1994-; bd mem, Hampton Roads; Virginia Municipal League, General Laws Comt; Visual Quality Comt. **Honors/Awds:** Dept Head of Year, City Gary, 1973; Outstanding Govt Award, Gary Jaycees, 1974; Meritorious Serv Award, Gary Chapter Frontiers, 1974; City Counr, Gary City Co, 1974; Outstanding 20 Year Alumnus, Hampton Inst, 1978; Outstanding Person, DuPage Co, NAACP, 1978; Award of Achievement, Hampton Newport News, Alumni Chap, Kappa Alpha Psi Fraternity, 1992; Distinguished Citizen Award, Zeta Lambda Chap, Alpha Phi Alpha Fraternity, 1992. **Military Serv:** ROTC Comn, 1958; AUS, 2nd Armored Div, lt, 1958-60; USAR, capt, 1960-67; USANG, capt, 1966-68. **Business Addr:** Vice Mayor, South District 3 Seat A, Newport News, 2400 Wash Ave, Newport News, VA 23607, **Business Phone:** (757)926-8634.*

ALLEN, CHARLES EDWARD
Real estate developer, executive. **Personal:** Born Feb 22, 1948, Atlanta, GA; son of Charles Sr and Ruby Collins; married Elizabeth Ann Glover, Jul 6, 1972 (divorced); children: Charles Phillip, David Kennedy, Rebecca Ann. **Educ:** Morehouse Col, Atlanta, GA, BS, finance, 1970; Univ Chicago, IL, MBA, 1972. **Career:** First Nat Bank, Chicago, Ill; Bank Calif, vpres & mgr, 1976-78; First Bank Nat Asn, pres & chief operating officer, 1978-80; United Nat Bank, WA, DC, exec vpres & chief admin officer, 1980-81; First Ind Nat Bank, pres & chief exec officer, 1981-88; MIG Realty Adv, vpres & regional mgr, 1988; Graimark Realty Adv Inc, co-founder, pres, chmn & chief exec officer, currently. **Orgs:** Bd dirs, AAA Mich & Affil Ins Co; former corp dir, Blue Cross/Blue Shield Mich; past pres, Nat Bankers Asn; former dir, Mus Afro-Am Hist; former chmn bd, Benedict Col; former dir, 7th Fed Res Bank, Detroit Br; bd mem, Preferred Provider Orgn Mich; Mutual Funds Nationwide Ins Co; Detroit Econ Club; United Negro Col Fund. **Honors/Awds:** Black Achiever's Award, 1976; Outstanding Young Men of America, YMCA, 1981; Alpha Theta GPD Sorority, 1981; Citizen of the Year, Hartford Ave Baptist Church, 1982; Boy Scouts Am, 1984; Mayor's Award Merit, 1984; America's Best & Brightest Young Men & Women, 1987; During tenure, First Ind Natl Bank featured as Bank of the Year, Black Enterprise Mag, profiled in Minority Bus Entrepreneur Mag; Outstanding Business Leader, Northwood Univ, 2003. **Special Achievements:** First African American elected AAA Chairman from Michigan Chronicle. **Home Addr:** 8162 E Jefferson Ave Apt

15B, Detroit, MI 48214. **Business Addr:** Chairman & President, Chief Executive Officer, Graimark Realty Advisors Inc, 500 River Pl Dr Apt 5105, Detroit, MI 48207.*

ALLEN, CHARLES EDWARD
Manager, public relations executive. **Personal:** Born Jul 21, 1973, New Orleans, LA; son of Charles E Allen Jr and Rosemarie. **Educ:** Xavier Univ La, BS, biol, 1995; Tulane Univ, MSPH, 1998. **Career:** New Orleans Public Sch Syst, substitute teacher, 1995-97, admin asst, 1997; La Off Pub Health, asst prog coordr, 1998, admin intern, 1998; Tulane Xavier Univ, Ctr Bioenvironmental Res, educ & outreach coord, 1999-, pub rel off, 2000-, prog mgr, currently, asst dir, external rels, currently. **Orgs:** Captain, Times-Picayune Christmas Doll & Toy Fund, 1987-; Knights Peter Claver, 1994-; commt co-chair, Omega Psi Phi, Rho Phi chap, 1995-; La Environ Roundtable, 1999-; vpres, Holy Cross Neighborhood Asn. **Honors/Awds:** Cert Merit, New Orleans City Coun, 1996, 1997, 2000; Brother of the Year, Omega Psi Phi, Rho Phi chap, 1997; Excellence in Total Quality Mgt, John McDonogh Sr HS, 1997; Dean's Leadership Award, Tulane Univ Sch Public Health, 1998; Certificate of Merit, Jefferson Parish Off Environ Affairs, 2000, 2001. **Business Addr:** Program Manager, Assistant Director, Tulane University, Center Bioenvironmental Research, Health & Environment Research Bldg, 1430 Tulane Ave SL 3, New Orleans, LA 70112, **Business Phone:** (504)988-6612.

ALLEN, CHERYL L
Judge. **Personal:** Born Dec 16, 1947, Pittsburgh, PA; daughter of Robert and Corrine Davis; married Jim Skipwith (divorced); children: Jason, Justin & Frederick. **Educ:** Penn State Univ, Pittsburgh, PA, BS, elem educ, 1969; Univ Pittsburgh, PA, grad studies, 1972, JD, 1975. **Career:** Pittsburgh Pub Schs, Pittsburgh, PA, teacher, 1969-72; Col Arts & Scis, Univ Pittsburgh, acad adv, 1973-75; Neighborhood Legal Servs, Northside Office, staff atty, 1975-76; PA Human Rels Comn, asst gen coun, 1976-77; Allegheny County Law Dept, asst county solicitor, 1977-90; self-employed lawyer, 1980-90; Allegheny County Disadvantaged & Women's Bus Enterprise Appeal Bd, admin hearing officer, 1988-90; Allegheny County Common Pleas Court, Criminal Div, judge, 1990-92; Allegheny Co Crt Pleas, Family Div Juvenile Sec, judge, 1992-99; supv judge, 1999-2003; judge, 2003-; Point Park Univ, Criminal Justice Dept, assoc prof, 2000-06. **Orgs:** Bd mem, Pittsburgh Leadership Found; bd mem, Communities in Schools; bd mem, Child Watch; bd mem, Lydia's Place; bd mem, Theotherapy; mem, Faith, Law & Morality Committee the Nat Cncl Juvenile/Family Court Judges; mem, Juvenile Court Judges Comn, PA Comn on Crime & Delinquency. **Honors/Awds:** Message Carriers 1st Annual Tree of Hope in Life Award, 2003; Jubilee Intl Ministries-Catalyst for Change Award; Every Child Permanency Award; Rankin Christian Center-Community Unity Service Award; Sojourner Award; 3 Rivers Youth Nellie Leadership Award; Pennsylvania Commission for Women's History Month Award; Second Chance Inc, Woman of Standard Award. **Special Achievements:** The first black woman to serve on the state Supreme Ct; Univ PA Women's Law Asn Women Yr; University of Pittsburgh's Alumni of the Year. **Business Addr:** Judge, Allegheny County Court Common Pleas, Family Division Juvenile Section, 3333 5th Ave, Pittsburgh, PA 15213, **Business Phone:** (412)578-8261.

ALLEN, CHRIS
Health services administrator. **Educ:** Wayne State Univ, BA, jour, 1976; Univ Mich, MA, health serv admin, 1980. **Career:** Detroit Osteopathic Hosp Corp, Oak Park, MI, exec asst; Detroit Osteopathic Hosp, Highland Park, MI, adminr; Hurley Med Ctr, Flint, MI, asst dir; Detroit Med Ctr, Hutzel Hosp, exec vpres & Chief Exec Officer; Family Road Care Ctrs, pres & Chief Exec Officer, 1995-. **Orgs:** Bd dirs, Christus Health, 1999-; bd dirs, Sisters Charity Health Care Sys; Nat Arthritis & Musculoskeletal & Skin Diseases Adv Coun, NIH, 2000-; bd dirs, Am Nat Red Cross, currently. **Business Addr:** President and Chief Executive Officer, Family Road Care Centers, 19440 Bretton Dr, Detroit, MI 48223, **Business Phone:** (313)535-6009.*

ALLEN, CLAUDE A
Government official, health services administrator. **Personal:** Born in Philadelphia, PA; married Jannese; children: Claude III & Lila-Cjoan. **Educ:** Univ NC, BA, 1982; Duke Univ Law Sch, Masters Law, int & comparative law, JD, 1990. **Career:** Off Atty Gen, coun gen, dep atty gen, 1995-97; Va state govt, secy health & human resources, 1997; US Dept Health & Human Serv, dep secy, 2001; White House, Domestic Policy, asst to pres. **Orgs:** Durham Guardian Ad Litem Program; bd dir, CARAMORE; Legal Coun Elderly & Street Law Program, DC; bd dir, Peacemaker Ministries Inc.

ALLEN, CLYDE CECIL
Marketing executive, president (organization). **Personal:** Born Jan 29, 1943, Youngstown, OH; son of Eugene and Frances; married Gayle Thigpen; children: Michael Clyde & Brett Donaldo. **Educ:** Kent State Univ, BS, microbiol, 1965; Rutgers Univ, MS, ind rels, 1977. **Career:** Schering Corp, sr microbiologist, 1965-70, personnel admin, 1970-72; Ind Community Ctr, exec dir, 1972-74; Johnson & Johnson, sr personnel admin, 1974-75, sr comps admin, 1975-76, mgr, human resource planning, 1976-78; M & M Mars Inc, dir, compensation & benefits, 1978-80; JE Seagram Inc, corp mgr eeo, 1980-83, dir community rels, 1983-87, dir pub rels & event mkt, 1987-; Allen & Partners Inc, pres, 1994-, exec dir, 2003-. **Orgs:** EDGES NY, NJ, 1972-; Am Comps Asn, 1976-; chair US Comt on Civil Rights NJ, 1968-; Employer Asn, NJ, 1976-; Port Auth Airport Rev, Coun, 1972-74; pres, Frontiers Int Inc, 1974-; chair, Plainfield Econ Dev Comt, 1975-85; founder dir, Youth Leadership Club Inc, 1968-72; vchmn, Bd dir, Union Co OIC, 1973-75; bd dir, Negro Ensemble Co, 1989-92; trustee, Jack & Jill Am Found, 1989-92; Sigma Pi Phi Fraternity, Mu Boule Chap; chair bd, Nat Asn Mkt Developers, 1994-; chair, Nat United Merchants Beverage Asn, Corp Adv Bd, Black Chamber Com Nothern, 2001-. **Honors/Awds:** Outstanding Service Award, Frontiers Int, 1978; Malcolm X Award, YLC Inc, 1971; Outstanding Service Award, Elizabeth YMCA, 1970; Blackbooks Bus & Prof Award, 1989; Community Service Award, Pres Reagan; Pinnacle Award, Harbor Pub Co, 1990; Most Outstanding Marketeer Award, Nat Asn Market Developers, 1987; Still Award, NJ Minority Braintrust, 1989; Man of the Year, Nat Asn Negro Bus & Prof Women, 1986; Outstanding Corporate Exec, Black Pages, 1989; ELKS Lovejoy Award, 1994; PRAME Award Outstanding Marketer, 1995; CLYDE Award MOBE, 1993; "Those Who Make a Difference", Nat Urban Affairs Coun, 1990; Kent State Social Responsibilty Award, 1995; Social Responsibility Award, Kent STate Univ; Corporate Award, Nat Newspaper Publishers Asn. **Business Addr:** President, Founder, Executive Director, Allen & Partners Inc, 620 Sheridan Ave, Plainfield, NJ 07060, **Business Phone:** (908)561-4062.

ALLEN, DEBBIE (DEBORRAH KAYE ALLEN)
Actor, singer, dancer. **Personal:** Born Jan 16, 1950, Houston, TX; daughter of Arthur Allen and Vivian Ayers; married Winfred Wilford, Jun 22, 1975 (divorced 1983); married Norman Nixon, Apr 27, 1984; children: Vivian Nicole & Norman Jr. **Educ:** Howard Univ, Sch Fine Arts, BA, hons, speech & drama, 1971. **Career:** Works: Ti-Jean & His Brothers, 1972; Purlie, 1972; Raisin, 1973; Ain't Misbehavin', 1978; The Illusion & Holiday, 1979; West Side Story, 1980; Louis, 1981; The Song is Kern!, 1981; Parade of Stars Playing the Palace, 1983; Sweet Charity, 1986; JoJo Dancer, 1985; "Fame", choreographer, 1982-87; "A Different World", 1988-93; "In the House", 1995; "The Debbie Allen Show", 1989; Amistad, exec producer, 1997; Harriet's Return, play, 1998; Ragtime; Michael Jordan: An American Hero, 1999; The Old Settler, 2001; Debbie Allen Dance Acad, Los Angeles, CA, founder & owner, 2001-; C's Musical, Pearl, writer, dir & choreographer, 2003; "All of Us", 2004; Tournament of Dreams, 2006; Tournament of Dreams, 2007; Confessions of an Action Star, 2008; Next Day Air, 2008; Fame; 2009; Director: Girlfriends; Everybody Hates Chris; Life Is Not A Fairy Tale; That's So Raven; A Different World; The Fresh Prince of Bel-Air; Family Ties; "The Game", 2008. **Orgs:** Actors Equity Asn; Screen Actors Guild; Am Fedn TV & Radio Artists; founder, Debbie Allen Dance Inst; Delta Sigma Theta Sorority Inc. **Honors/Awds:** Drama Desk Award, Outstanding Featured Actress in a Musical, West Side Story, 1980; Antoinette Perry Award, 1986; Tony Award nomination, Best Actress, Sweet Charity, 1986; Essence Awards, 1992, 1995; Career Achievement Award, Acapulco Black Film Festival, 1998; Lifetime Achievement Award, Am Women Radio & TV, 2001; Strong, Smart & Bold Award, Girls Inc Greater Houston, 2002; Emmy Award. **Special Achievements:** Choreographer for the Academic Awards, 1991-94, author of Brothers of the Knight & Dancing in the Wings, Penguin Putnam Publ. **Business Addr:** Owner, Debbie Allen Dance Academy, 3623 Hayden Ave, Culver City, CA 90232, **Business Phone:** (310)280-9145.

ALLEN, DOZIER T., JR.
Government official. **Personal:** Born Jan 10, 1931, Gary, IN; married Arlene McKinney; children: 4. **Educ:** Los Angeles Jr Col; Ind Univ; Valparaiso Univ. **Career:** Allen Enterprise, vpres, 1957-67; N west Ind Urban League, field rep, 1968-69; Gary City Coun, vpres, 1970; Gary, IN, city coun man at large, 1968-72; Dozier T Allen Jr Enterprise, pres; Double AA Inc, pres; Lake Shore-Birch Inc, pres; Mach Investors Inc, vpres; Downtown Deli-Mart, proprietor; Calumet Township, trustee, 2000-02; deputy mayor, 2006. **Orgs:** Chmn, First Cong Dem Dist, 1971; founder & chmn bd dir, N west Ind Sickle Cell, 1971-73; Nat PTA; Nat Roster Black Elected Officials; Nat Black Caucus Local Elected Officials; Ind Black Caucus; In Township Trustee Asn; Northwest Ind Urban League; Gary Toast masters Int; life mem, Nat Asn Advan Colored People, Gary Br; charter mem, Gary Hum Rel Comn; bd mem, Gary Marona House Drug Abuse; pres, Lake Co Ment Health Bd; Am Pub Welfare Asn; contrib mem, Dem Nat Comn; Ind Township Trustee Asn; Lake Co Bd Educ; Downtown Gary Merchant's Asn; Chancellor's Asn Ind Univ; Nat Sheriff's Asn; asst chief, Lake Co Sheriff's Police Res Unit. **Honors/Awds:** Sponsors Award, Gary Greens Pop Warners Football League, 1974; Boss Century Award, 1974; Mexican American Award, 1974; NAACP Ovington Award; NAACP Humanitarian Award; Honorary Doctorate of Business Administration & Humanities. *

ALLEN, DR. EDNA ROWERY
School administrator. **Personal:** Born Jul 20, 1938, Carrollton, AL; married Robert H; children: Robin, Dawn & Robert Jr. **Educ:** Lincoln Univ, BS, Bus Educ, 1960; Univ Ill, MS, Counr Educ, 1970; Edward sville Ill, attended 1974; McMurray Col, Dr Humanities, 1983. **Career:** Rock Jr Higher Sec Sch, teacher, 1962-70, counr, 1970-71; E St Louis Libr Bd, dir gifted prog, 1971-. **Orgs:** Chmn, social action, Delta Sigma Theta Sorority Inc; bd dirs, Nat Asn Gifted C, 1973-83; bd dirs, E St Louis Pub Libr, 1974-83; bd trustees State Comn, Col E St Louis, 1975-78, 1985-99; pres, St Ann's Sodality St Patrick's Ch; vpres, Concerned Citizens Comn; chmn, social action, Top Ladies Distinction; chmn, Status Women Comn; Top Ladies Distinction; Phi Delta Kappa. **Honors/Awds:** Service Award, State Comn Col, 1978; Merit Award, ML King Jr High Sch, ESt Louis, 1979; Recognition Award, Delta Sigma Theta Sorority Inc, 1984; Hon Doctorate, Mac Murray Col, Jacksonville, Ill, 1983. **Military Serv:** Those Who Excel" IL Office of Educ, 1978. **Home Addr:** 664 N 33rd St, East St Louis, IL 62205. **Business Addr:** Vice Chairman, E St Louis Board of Education, 8740 State St Suite 200, East St. Louis, IL 62201.

ALLEN, EUGENE, JR.
Executive. **Personal:** Born Nov 7, 1937, Chicago, IL; son of Eugene Sr and Pearl; married Ledell Fields, Apr 16, 1961; children: Sheryl, Karla, Nicole, Eugene III. **Educ:** Ill Inst Technol, BS, 1970; Univ Chicago Grad Sch, MBA, 1976. **Career:** Sherwin-Williams Co, paint technologist, chemist, 1963-67; Libby McNeil & Libby, materials mgr/engr, 1967-69; Avon Products, Inc, div mgr, 1969-76; Hub States Corp, sr vpres, 1976-79; Clinitemp Inc, pres, 1979-81; Aquamint Labs, Inc, pres, 1981-; Allen Chem, Inc, pres, 1989-; Consol Cleaning Systs, Inc, pres, 1990-; Allen Industs Inc, chmn, pres & chief exec officer, 1981-. **Orgs:** chmn bd, Indianapolis Bus Develop, 1986-90; bd mem, Jr Achievement, 1986-96; bd mem, Dist Export Coun, 1979-91. **Military Serv:** AUS, sgt, 1961-63. **Business Addr:** Chairman, President, Allen Industries Inc, 6874 Hawthorn Park Dr, Indianapolis, IN 46220-3909, **Business Phone:** (317)595-0730.*

ALLEN, GEORGE MITCHELL
Executive. **Personal:** Born Nov 14, 1932, Boston, MA; married E Louise Peek, Jun 5, 1954; children: Leslie. **Educ:** Massachusetts Univ, Ext Courses; US Army Career Ext Courses. **Career:** Special Asst to Gov, 1970-74; Commonwealth MA, dep commr veterans serv; Intergovernmental Relations, notary pub 1972; Dept Army, fed women's prog mgr, equal employ opportunity officer; Freedom Link, pres & chief exec officer, currently. **Orgs:** Real estate broker; town rep Stoughton MS; past pres, Roxbury Med Tech Found, 1971-73; external adv bd Minorities Educ Advan; Ms Col Pharm, 1972-; nat pres African Am Veterans; Ms Joint Ctr Polit Studies; vpres, Blacks Govt AZ Chapt; pres, Nat Asn Advan Colored People, Greater Huachuca Area Br; arbitrator & mediator, Az Ct Syst. **Military Serv:** AUS, sgt first class, 20 yrs retired; Army Commendation Medal; many serv medals Japan, Korea, Germany; Cert Commendation Mil Serv & Community Agencies. **Business Addr:** President, Freedom Link, PO Box 1381, Sierra Vista, AZ 85635, **Business Phone:** (520)458-7245.

ALLEN, GLORIA MARIE
Physician. **Personal:** Born in Washington, DC; daughter of Archie and Viola Childs; married William Henry Toles; children: William Henry III, Allen Wesley. **Educ:** Howard Univ, BS, 1947; Howard Univ Med Sch, MD, 1951. **Career:** Harlem Hosp, asst attend physician, 1954-56; Jamaica Hosp NY, asst attend physician, 1963-; Carter Comm Health Ctr, chief pediat, 1974-85; Linden Cs Servs, pvt med pract, 1985-. **Orgs:** Med Soc Co Queens, 1964-; secy, Empire State Med Asn, 1975-; treas & charter mem, Susan S McKinney Smith Med Soc, 1976-; bd dirs, Queens Urban League, 1970-; nom comt, Young Men's Christian Asn New York, 1974-75; chmn, Merrick Young Men's-Young Women's Christian Asn Day Care Ctr, 1975-77; past pres, Omega Wives Long Island, 1964-; Delta Sigma Theta Sorority, 1964-. **Honors/Awds:** Woman's World Award, Bethel Temple, 1958; Senior Youth Community Award, Queens Young Women's Christian Asn, 1973; Community Award, Queens Fresh Air Fund, 1978; Appointed by Mayor Koch, Comnr Comn Status Women, NY, 1979. **Home Addr:** 10427 192 St, Jamaica, NY 11412. **Business Addr:** Physician, Linden Childrens Services, 14504 97th Ave, Jamaica, NY 11435-4426.*

ALLEN, DR. HARRIETTE INSIGNARES
Educator, journalist, government official. **Personal:** Born Oct 24, 1943, Savannah, GA; daughter of Caleb H and Louise Bias; married Warren Joseph Allen II, Jan 1, 1968 (divorced 1973); children: Tracy Marcette & Heather Lenae; married Jorge Isaac Insignares, Jan 1, 1981 (divorced 1984); children: Jorge Eric & Juan Carlos Antonio. **Educ:** Fisk Univ, BA, 1964; Univ Wis, MST, 1972; George Peabody Col Teachers, Vanderbilt Univ, PhD, Eng Edu, 1980. **Career:** S Am Columbia, Foreign Exchange, teacher eng, 1964-65; Chicago Bd Educ, spanish resource consult, 1965-68; Wis St Univ, asst proj dir tutorial prog, 1970-72; Fisk Univ, poet-story teller, 1973-; Univ Tenn, poet-in-residence, 1977-79; Tenn St Univ, prof jour, speech, theater & educ, 1977-, asst prof commun, 1979, ambassador letters, 1977-, prof commun, currently; Volunteer St Community Col, adj prof, 2000; USForest Serv, Res Info Off, info specialist. **Orgs:** Int Soc Poets; mem bd dir, Nat Asn Preservation & Perpetuation Storytelling; Nat Asn Black Journalists; Soc Prof Journalists; Christian Writers Network; co-dir, Consortium Doctors, Links Inc; Tenn Commun Asn; vpres, Fisk

Univ Alumni Asn; charter mem, Theta Alpha Phi; Pi Kappa Delta, Phi Delta Kappa, Golden Key; Alpha Kappa Alpha; Nat Theatre Asn; Black Theatre Asn SCETC; Nat Asn Preservation & Perpetuation Storytelling; Theta Alpha Phi Hon Forensic Fraternity; Ga Soc Poets; Nat Soc Pub Poets; originator, Ballad Folk Theatre Art; star Jubas Jubilee Folktale Traveling Ensemble Co. **Honors/Awds:** Governor's Outstanding Tennessean Award, 1980; Award for Distinguished Achievement in the Arts, Eta Phi Beta, 1990; Award, Nat Asn Negro Bus & Prof Women's Clubs, 1990; Adjutant General's Distinguished PatriotMedallion, 1991; Trailblazer Award, Consortium of Doctors, 1993; Outstanding Achievement Award, Gannett, 1993; Governor's Distinguished Achievement Award, 1995; proclamation for excellence and achievement in writing, 1995; David Eshelman Outstanding Nat Adviser Award, Soc ProfJourn, 1997; Jour Teacher of the Year Award, Nat Broadcasting Soc, Tenn State Univ, 1998; InterNat Poet of Merit Medallion, Int Soc Poets, 1999. **Special Achievements:** First black storyteller, Nat Storytelling Fest Jonesboro, TN; first Black to receive Gov Spotlight Awd; first Black poet to be read into the Congressional Record; author "Genesis & Jubas Folk Games"; first poet tobe publ in Attica Rebirth Newspaper of Attica Prison.

ALLEN, HERBERT J.
Educator. **Personal:** Born May 19, 1922, Jersey City, NJ; son of Benjamin and Jeanetta Casey; divorced; children: Deborah. **Educ:** Univ Cincinnati Teachers Col, BS, 1946; Case Western Res Univ, MSSW, 1948; Nat Cincinnati, admin & mgmt Training Prog. **Career:** Ohio State Univ, Sch Soc Work, clin instr; Cincinnati Gen Hosp, sr caseworker; Montgomery City Child Welfare Bd, supvr, 1952-64; Barney C MedCtr, dir social serv, 1964-66; Good Samaritan Hosp, dir soc serv, 1966-67; Univ Cincinnati Med Ctr, adj assoc prof, dir soc work, 1970-89; Human Resources, asst adminr, 1990-. **Orgs:** Acad Cert Soc Workers; past pres, Ohio Valley Chap Nat Asn Soc Workers, 1972-74; past pres, Miami Valley Chap Dayton Nat Asn Social Workers, 1969; trustee, Cent Community Health Bd Hamilton City Inc, 1976-77; chmn, Community Action Comn, 1974-77; Soc Serv, Asn Gr Cincinnati; past pres, Child Health Asn; pres, Mt Auburn Health Ctr, 1975-; Manpower Serv AdvCoun City Cincinnati, 1975-; Cincinnati Gen Hosp Med Audit Comt, 1975; ColMed Expanded Deans Conf, 1977; pres, Ohio Valley Chap; soc dir, Hosp SocWork Depts. **Honors/Awds:** Certificate of Outstanding Social Worker Year, Nat Asn Soc Workers, 1973; Award Gold Medal, Cincinnati Gen Hosp Emp Arts & Crafts, 1973; CertificateLeadership Training Prog, Soc Workers Mental Health Nat Asn Soc Workers, 1974; nominee, Soc Worker Year, 1974; Certificate of Appreciation, Mt Auburn Community Coun, 1975; Certificate of Appreciation, Lincoln Heights Health Ctr Inc, 1975; Merit Award Gold Medal, 1975; nominee,Outstanding Citizen Award, 1976; University of Cincinnati Humanitarian Award, 1990; Community Service Award, Kappa Alpha Psi, Cincinnati AlumniChapter, 1990. **Military Serv:** AUS, sgt, 1942-45. **Home Addr:** 144 Dorsey St, Cincinnati, OH 45202. *

ALLEN, HERMAN
Dentist. **Career:** Pvt pract, dentist, currently. **Business Addr:** Dentist, 2323 NW 19 St Suite 1, Fort Lauderdale, FL 33311, **Business Phone:** (954)484-8780.*

ALLEN, JACOB BENJAMIN, III
Counselor. **Personal:** Born Sep 20, 1927, Raleigh, NC; son of Jacob Benjamin Jr and Fannie Williams; married Shirley K Allen, Nov 24, 1961. **Educ:** Shaw Univ, attended 1955; Springfield Col, grad cert, 1962. **Career:** NC Dept Voc Rehab, Human Resources Dept; NC Dept Mental Health; Patterson Ave Br Young Men's Christian Asn; Voc Eval Facil, voc rehab counr, currently. **Orgs:** Nat Black Achievers Asn; Raleigh Mayor's Eastside Neighborhood Task Force; Shaw Univ Alumni Asn; NC Rehab Counr Asn; AEAONMS Inc, Prince Hall Shrine; comdr chief, Boyer Consistory No 219; United Supreme Coun Ancient & Accepted Scottis Rite Masonary 33 Degree; chair, exec bd, Garner Rd Family Young Men's Christian Asn; NC State Employees Asn; ruling elder, Davie St Presbyterian Church; potentate, Kabala Temple No 177, AEANMS Inc. **Special Achievements:** Achieved independent status as a counselor. **Military Serv:** USY, staff sgt, 1950-52; Korean Serv Medal, UN Serv Medal. *

ALLEN, JAMES
Football player. **Personal:** Born Mar 28, 1975, Wynnewood, OK. **Educ:** Univ Okla. **Career:** Football player (retired); Chicago Bears, running back, 1998-2001; Houston Texans, running back, 2002.

ALLEN, JAMES H.
Auditor, executive. **Personal:** Born Apr 20, 1934, Farmville, VA; married Angelene Elliott; children: James Jr, Anita, Edward. **Educ:** Johnson C Smith Univ, AB, 1960; Rutgers State Univ, MBA, 1976. **Career:** Progressive Life Ins Co, debit mgr, 1960-62; Jet-Heet Creative Mfg, perpetual inventory control clerk, 1962-64; Wyssmont Engr Co, asst off mgr, 1964-68; Bendix Corp, expeditor, 1968-69; State NJ Div Taxation, field auditor; JAMCAR Int, chief exec officer, currently. **Orgs:** Passaic Co Bd Realtors; Am Soc Notaries; Fed Govt Accts Asn; Nat Asn Black Accts; Nat Asn Black MBA's; Nat Asn MBA; exec pres, Delta Mu Lambda Chap Alpha Phi Alpha; pres, Clavary Baptist Church; Fed Credit Union; exec bd mem, Paterson Br Nat Asn Advan Colored People; Paterson Financial Aid Corp; Am Legion Post 268. **Honors/Awds:** Faithful Service Award, Nat Asn Advan Colored People, 1968; Outstanding Alumnus, Johnson C Smith Univ Alumni Asn Reg I, 1971; Johnson C Smith Univ Gen Alumni Asn Dedicated Serv, 1973; State NJ Outstanding Performance Award, 1971.

ALLEN, JAMES TRINTON
Government official. **Personal:** Born Oct 31, 1924, Michigan City, MS; married Magnolia Hudson; children: James Jr, Charles Banks, Sam, Margie Ree Holcomb, Melvin, Helen Ruth Thomas & Auther Wayne. **Career:** Elected official, currently. **Orgs:** Masonic 68, 1979. **Special Achievements:** First African American constable of Benton County, MS. **Home Addr:** 961 Allen Corner Rd, Lamar, MS 38642.

ALLEN, JERRY ORMES
Lawyer. **Personal:** Born Dec 16, 1953, Cleveland, OH; son of Luther Ormes Allen and Netty L Cooper; married Jacqueline L Allen, Oct 10, 1987; children: Danielle Y & Jerry Ormes II. **Educ:** Capital Univ, BA, 1975; Capital Univ Law Sch, JD, 1984; NY Univ Law Sch, LLM, taxation, 1987. **Career:** Chief Coun, IRS, staff atty, 1984-86; Bricker & Eckler, partner, atty, 1987-. **Orgs:** Nat Bar Asn; Am Bar Asn; Ohio Bar Asn; Columbus Bar Asn; bd pres, Martin Luther King Arts Complex; past trustee, bd mem, Columbus Zoo; bd mem, Hospice Riverside Hosp; bd mem, Greater Columbus Arts Coun. **Special Achievements:** Author, "Taxation of Investment Income From Offshore Trusts and Other Foreign Entities," Offshore Finance USA, 1999; "Residency of Asset Protection Trusts: IRS Issues New Regulations," Offshore Finance USA, 1999; "Look Before You Leap - The Tax Consequences of Golden Parachute Payments," International Legal Strategy, 2000; " Solving The Low Income Tax Credit Housing Partnership Dilemma," Exempt Organization Tax Review, 2005. **Business Addr:** Partner, Bricker & Eckler, 100 S 3rd St, Columbus, OH 43215-4291, **Business Phone:** (614)227-8834.

ALLEN, DR. KAREN
Administrator. **Personal:** Born Aug 31, 1956, Ypsilanti, MI; daughter of George Moses Jr and Claudia M Moses. **Educ:** Andrews Univ, 1983; Univ Ill Chicago, PhD, nursing sci, 1992. **Career:** US Ctr Substance Abuse Treatment, res consult; Univ MD, asst & assoc prof; Andrews Univ, prof, chair nursing dept & dir grad progs, currently. **Orgs:** Pres, Int & Nat Nurses Soc Addictions, 1996-2000; fel, Am Acad Nurses; Sigma Theta Tau Int Nursing; Phi Kappa Phi, Nat Honor Soc. **Honors/Awds:** Dean's Award for Scholary Activity, Univ Ill, Chicago, Col Nursing, 1992; Distinguished Alumna Award, Univ Ill, Chicago, Col Nursing, 1995; Nightingale Nursing Admin/Leadership Award, Oakland Univ Sch Nursing; Carol E Franck Nursing Leadership Award, Mich Nurses Asn, 2003; 2004 Innovator Award, Women's Substance Abuse Treatment, US Ctr Substance Abuse Treatment. **Special Achievements:** First African Am Pres Nat & Int Nurses Society on Addictions; Edited Text: "Nursing Care of the Addicted Client," cited as suggested reading in the 1997-98, Joint Community Comprehensive Accreditation Manual for Behavioral Health Care.

ALLEN, KAREN B.
Manager. **Career:** Comerica Bank, vpres & civic affairs mgr, currently. **Special Achievements:** First vice president of Civic Affairs in Comerica Bank history. **Business Addr:** Vice President of Civic Affairs, Comerica Bank, 188 N Old Woodward, Birmingham, MI 48009-3371, **Business Phone:** (248)544-9955.*

ALLEN, LARRY CHRISTOPHER, SR.
Football player. **Personal:** Born Nov 27, 1971, Los Angeles, CA; married Janelle; children: Jayla & Larry Jr. **Educ:** Sonoma State Univ. **Career:** Football player (retired), Dallas Cowboys, guard, 1994-05; 2008; San Francisco 49ers, guard, 2006-07. **Honors/Awds:** NFL 1990s All-Decade Team, All-Rookie Team, 1994; Pro Bowl, 1995-07; Strongest Man Award, ESPN, 2006. *

ALLEN, LECESTER L.
School administrator. **Personal:** Born Feb 27, 1944, Pickens, AR; son of Joe and Rebecca; married Mattie, Aug 31, 1968; children: Dana Nicole, Aaron Matthew. **Educ:** Wayne State Univ, BS, 1966, pursuing MA. **Career:** Do Re Mi Learning Ctrs & Acad Detroit Sch, pres & chief exec officer, currently. **Orgs:** pres, Mich Asn Childcare Ctrs, 1974-80; pres, Optimist Club Cent Det, 1976-77; pres, Don Bosco Home Boys, 1982-86; chmn summer funding comn, United Comn Servs, 1979-82; pres, Booker T Wash Bus Asn, 1980-82; co-chair/funding mem, Citizens Better Gov, 1982-; Mich State Job Training Coun, appt Govr Mich, 1983-85; pres, The Lawton Sch; pres, Charter Sch Admin Serv. bd mem, nominating com Metropolitan YMCA, 1988-. **Honors/Awds:** Minority Bus Excellence Award, Sate Mich, 1977; Distinguished Detroit Citizen, City Clerk, City of Detroit, 1981; Advocate of the Year, Small Bus Admin, 1982; Outstanding Educr Entrepreneur, Success Guide Mag, 1991; Outstanding Educ Businessman, Ala A&M, 1995. **Special Achievements:** Opened first pre-school computer lab in Detroit, 1983; Served as member of Michigan Dept of Commerce Minority Business; City of Detroit, Private Industry Council for Job Training, 1982; Special Commendation, Gov William Milliken, MI Conference on Small Businesses, 1981; Conducted workshops for new & prospective child care centers. **Business Addr:** President, Chief Executive Officer, Do Re Mi Learning Centers & Academy of Detroit Schools, 20755 Greenfield Rd Suite 300, Southfield, MI 48075, **Business Phone:** (248)569-7787.*

ALLEN, MARCUS LEMARR
Football player, sports manager. **Personal:** Born Mar 26, 1960, San Diego, CA; son of Harold and Gwen Allen; married Kathryn. **Educ:** Univ Southern Calif. **Career:** Football player (retired), sports executive; Los Angeles Raiders, running back, 1982-92; Kansas City Chiefs, 1993-97; CBS Sports, commentator, studio analyst; NFL Network, analyst, currently. **Orgs:** Spokesperson, Ronald McDonald Children's Charities. **Honors/Awds:** Col Player of the Year, Walter Camp, Maxwell Club & Football News, 1981; Heisman Trophy, 1981; Pro Bowl, 1982, 1984, 1985, 1986, 1987, 1993; Most Valuable Player, Super Bowl, 1983; Most Valuable Player, Prof Football Writers Asn & Asniated Press; Player of the Year, Sporting News & Football News; Col Football Hall of Fame, 2000; Offensive Player of Year, UPI; NFL Hall of Fame, 2003; Price water house Coopers Doak Walker Legends Award, 2007. **Special Achievements:** Executive producer for a film, Searching for Angela Shelton, 2004.

ALLEN, MARK
Government official, executive. **Personal:** Born Mar 18, 1962, Chicago, IL; son of Minor Sr and Ollie; children: DaNia & Markus. **Educ:** Western Ill Univ, BA, 1986. **Career:** Citizen Action-Midwest Acad, asst, nat co-dir, 1986-87; Push Excellence, Chicago Off, project dir, 1987-88; Jesse Jackson for Pres 88, nat youth coordr & nat field staff, 1988; Oper Push, interim chief staff & spec projects coordr, 1988-89; Chicago Urban League, voter educ & govt rels specialists, 1989-92; Chicago Rehab Network, field coordr, 1993; Ill Dept Human Rights, human rights investr, 1994-; Rainbow & PUSH, field dir, 1995-2003; Chicago Communicator, independent consult newspaper columnist; AJ Wright & Assocs Ltd, field dir, currently. **Orgs:** Task Force Black Political Empowerment, 1986-; founder & pres, Black Leadership Devel Inst, 1989-; local coordr, Nat Coalition Black Voter Participation, 1989-; vice chair, Chicago Sch Bd Nominating Comn, 1989-; Kappa Alpha Psi Fraternity, 1987; Black elected Officials Ill, 1990-; Chicago Urban Policy Inst, 1991. **Honors/Awds:** Community Service Award, Monroe Found, 1994; America's Best and Brightest, Dollars & Sense Mag, 1989; Man of the Year, United Am Progress Asn, 1989; Kool Achiever Awards, Chicago Area Finalist, 1990; Outstanding Young Men of America. **Special Achievements:** "Voices of the Electorate," Nat PBS TV Documentary on 92 Presidential Elections; Analyst, Live Broadcast "Front and Center" Chicagoland TV News on Urban Violence, 1994; co-host/urban affairs correspondent, "Omnibus Roundtable," Chicago Cable Access; motivational speaker/trainer. **Home Phone:** (773)925-4797. **Business Addr:** Field Director, AJ Wright and Associates Ltd, 1634 E 53rd St Suite 174, Chicago, IL 60615, **Business Phone:** (773)268-6526.

ALLEN, MARTHA
State government official. **Educ:** Chicago Teachers Col, BS; Northwestern Univ, Medill Sch Jour, MS, jour. **Career:** Chicago pub sch, teacher; Chicago Reporter, journ, 1985-86; Channel 2 Anchorman Walter Jacobson, investigative prod, 1986-89; Channel 2 Political Ed Mike Flannery, political prod, 1989-92; Dept C & Family Servs, Chief Commun, 1993-97; Ill Dept Human Serv, press secy, 1997-99, dept C & Family Servs, dir external affairs, 1999, chief staff, 2001-. **Orgs:** Nat co-chair, Am Pub Human Serv Asn's Child Welfare Task Force, 2000. *

ALLEN, MARVA
Executive, vice president (organization). **Personal:** Born Feb 21, 1954, Sav-LaMar, Jamaica; daughter of Enid Moulton and Hedley Moulton; divorced; children: Kenneth R. **Educ:** Staffordshire Gen Infirmary, England, BS, nursing, 1975; Univ Mich, BS, biol, 1979; Univ Detroit, MS, bus & health admin, 1982. **Career:** Univ Mich Hosp, nurse, 1975-76; Upjohn Pharmaceut, res, 1977-80; Girlstown Found, med coordr, 1980-82; Universal Solutions Inc, exec vice pres & co-founder, 1983-. **Orgs:** Nat Asn Women Bus Owners; bd trustee, St Francis Assisi Sch; Eastern Mich Univ, Hospitaliy Comt; Women Corp Bds Comt. **Honors/Awds:** 40 under 40, Crain's Bus, 1993; Honorary Award, Int Black Women's Cong, 1998; Outstanding Accomplishment in Community, Lynx, Ann Arbor chap, 1999; Diamond Award, Mich Minority Bus Develop Coun, 2000; Marketing Opportunities in Business & Entertainment Award, 2001. **Special Achievements:** Numerous mag publ; Auth of romance novels: Protogee, 1993; Camouflage, 2000. **Business Addr:** Executive Vice President, Co-founder, Universal Solutions Inc (USI), 2126 N Monroe, Monroe, MI 48162, **Business Phone:** (734)243-7922.

ALLEN, MAXINE BOGUES
School administrator. **Personal:** Born Jul 31, 1942, Portsmouth, VA; daughter of Raymond A Bogues (deceased) and Essie M

Kemp; married George Stanley; children: Vanya A Belk. **Educ:** Norfolk State Univ, BS, 1966; Hampton Univ, MA, 1972; Va Polytech Inst & State Univ, EdD, 1976. **Career:** School Administrator (retired); Portsmouth City Schs, math dept, head, 1966-74; Norfolk State Univ, prof math, 1976-79, dir, instnl res & planning, 1980, dir, inst res AA/EEO, 1980-86, exec asst, pres, dir instr sch, 1986-87, assoc vpres acad affairs, 1987. **Orgs:** Alpha Kappa Alpha Sorority, 1974; consult, A&T Univ, 1978-79; consult, Inst Serv Educ, 1982; bd trustees, SE Univ Res Assoc, 1984; pres, Suffolk Chap Links Inc, 1985-92; bd dirs, WHRO Educ TV, 1986-92; vice chair schbd, Suffolk City, 1986-92; The Moles Inc, 1990-. **Honors/Awds:** Presidential Citation, Asn Equal Opportunity, 1988; Administrator of the Year, Norfolk State Univ, 1996. **Home Phone:** (727)595-7378.

ALLEN, DR. MITCHELL
Educator. **Educ:** Univ Houston, EdD, 1978. **Career:** Tex Southern Univ, Col Sci & Technol, prof & interim dean, currently. **Orgs:** Am Coun Indust Arts Teacher Educ; Am Design & Drafting Asn; Epsilon PiTau; Nat Asn Indust Technol; Alief YMCA Bd Managers; trustee, Gamma Pi Chapter - Epsilon Pi Tau; Strategic Planning Steering Comt, Tex Southern Univ. **Honors/Awds:** Certificate of Appreciation, Welch Sci Fair Judge.

ALLEN, NANCY A.
Executive. **Career:** Urban Solutions Inc, founder, dir & pres, currently. **Orgs:** prog chair, Fashion Extravaganza, March of Dimes; exec dir, Charles H Wright Mus African Am Hist; NY Asn HIV over Fifty. **Honors/Awds:** Volunteer Award, March of Dimes, 2005. *

ALLEN, OTTIS EUGENE
School administrator, educator. **Personal:** Born Feb 2, 1953, Fletcher, NC; son of Georgia Bradley Allen and Eugene Allen; married Vanessa R Northcutt; children: Dawn, Ottis III & Eboni. **Educ:** Appalachian State Univ, BA, 1975, MA, 1976; Univ SC, addn studies Ed TV; Spartanburg Methodist Col, addn studies Comput Sci. **Career:** Coun Ministries United Methodist Ch SC, field coord, 1981; Radio Shack Corp, salesman, 1982-; Spartanburg Methodist Col, dir, audio-visual serv, assoc librn & dir multimedia serv, currently. **Orgs:** SC Libr Asn, 1977-; Piedmont Libr Asn, 1980-; Mt Moriah Baptist Church, 1980-; chmn, Sound Comm Mt Moriah Baptist Church, 1983-2004; bd trustees, Mt Moriah Baptist Church, 1983-; United Way Allocation Community Spartanburg, 1986-; Epsilon Nu Chap Omega Psi Phi Fraternity, 1987-; Spartanburg Human Rels Community, 1999; vchmn bd, Zoning appeals, Spartanburg, SC, 2002. **Honors/ Awds:** Trustee of the Year, Mount Moriah Baptist Church, 1990; Omega Man of the Year, Epsilon Nu Chap Omega Psi Phi Fraternity Inc, 1990, 1992; Superior Service Award, Epsilon Nu, 1998. **Home Addr:** 208 Sheffield Dr, Spartanburg, SC 29301. **Business Addr:** Associate Librarian, Director Multimedia Services, Spartanburg Methodist College, 1000 Powell Mill Rd, Spartanburg, SC 29301, **Business Phone:** (864)587-4213.

ALLEN, PERCY
Hospital administrator, executive. **Personal:** Born Apr 7, 1941, New Orleans, LA; son of Esther Anderson and Percy Sr; married Zennia Marie McKnight; children: Merrily Marie Littlejohn & Percy III. **Educ:** Delgado Trade & Tech Inst, attended 1965; Oakland Univ Rochester Mich, BA, Econ, 1973; Cornell Univ Grad Sch Bus & Pub Admin, MPA, 1975. **Career:** Executive, Hosp Administrator (retired); Gr New Mt Moriah Baptist Church, Detroit, Mich, youth dir, summer camp founder & dir, 1968-73; Chrysler Corp, Detroit, Mich, qual control supvr, 1968-70; Oakland Univ, Rochester, Mich, residence hall dir, 1972-73; Cornell Univ, Ithaca, NY, prog consult, 1973-75; Parkview Memorial Hosp, Fort Wayne, Ind, asst hosp adminr, 1975; Sinai Hosp, asst adminr; Univ Hosp Brooklyn, chief exec officer & vpres hospital affairs, 1989-; Bon Secours Baltimore Health Syst Inc, chief exec officer. **Orgs:** First vpres, Ft Wayne Urban Leag, 1976-; bd mem, Am Cancer Soc, 1977-; exec comt, NE Ind Emergency Med Serv Comn, 1977-; Emrgcy Med Serv Comn Ind Hosp Asn, 1978-; first vpres Allen Co Oppor Indstrlztn Ctr, 1978-; bd mem, United Way Allen Co, 1979-; Counc Health Care Dlvry Syst Ind Hosp Asn, 1979-; past pres, Nat Asn Health Serv Execs; fel, Am Col Healthcare Execs; prog develop comt mem, Greater New York Hosp Asn; bd mem, Col South Brooklyn Houses Inc. **Honors/Awds:** Outstanding Leadership Service, Oakland U Rochester Mich, 1971-73; appreciation service fdr & dir smmr cmpng prgm Mt Moriah Bapt Ch Detroit, 1973; recog first empl postn Union Bapt Ch Ft Wayne Ind, 1976; cert appreciation, Sickle Cell Found, 1979. **Military Serv:** USAF, E-4, 1959-64.

ALLEN, PHILIP C.
Manager. **Personal:** Born Nov 20, 1936, Pittsburgh, PA; son of Elmer and Vivian A Taylor; divorced; children: Lauretta L, Wanda I, Karl C, Phylis D, Michelle L, Sylvia D, Arthur K, Marlyn L, Tracy, David, Brandy, Philip M. **Educ:** Univ Pittsburgh, BBA, 1958; retail mgt sch, 1960; systems eng sch (IBM), 1962; banking mgt sch Brown Univ, attended 1966; Dale Carnegie training, 1967; advanced audit sch, Inst Internal Auditors, 1972; Univ Pittsburgh, MEd, 1977. **Career:** May Co-Kaufmanns Dept Store, asst buyer, 1959-60; IBM Corp, systems engr, 1960-65; Dollar Savings Bank, internal auditor, 1965-67; PPG Ind, sr EDP auditor, 1967-73; Comm Col Allegheny Co, dir internal audit. **Orgs:** Basileus Omega Psi Phi, 1962; treas, Bidwell Cultural & Training Ctr, 1969; treas, Pro-Sports Orgn; chmn, US Bond Dr CCAC, 1976; vpres, CCAC Credit Union; bd mem, United Way Am; v chmn, Allegheny YMCA, 1978-80; NAACP; Am Mgt Assn; Inst Internal Auditors; EDP Auditors Found; pres, CCAC Credit Union; bd mem, United Negro Col Fund. **Honors/Awds:** Distinguished Service Award, United Way, 1977-79; Distinguished Service Award, YMCA, 1978-79; Cert Data Processing Auditor CDPA, EDP Auditors Found, 1979; certified info systems auditor, CISA, 1982. *

ALLEN, QUINCY L
Executive. **Personal:** Born Mar 28, 1960, Quonset Point, RI. **Educ:** Northeastern Univ, BS, elec eng, 1982; Univ Rochester, MBA, 1993. **Career:** Xerox Corp, elec engr, 1982, Worldwide Customer Serv Strategy, vpres, 1999, North Am Serv & Solutions, sr vpres, 2001, corp vpres, 2004-, vpres, Xerox Prod Syst Group, pres, 2004-; Gateway Inc, bd dir, 2006-. **Orgs:** Compensation Comt; Corp Governance & Nominating Comt. **Business Addr:** Board of Directors, The Gateway Inc, 7565 Irvine Ctr Dr, Irvine, CA 92618, **Business Phone:** 800-846-2000.*

ALLEN, RAY
Basketball player. **Personal:** Born Jul 20, 1975, Merced, CA; children: Tierra. **Educ:** Univ Conn, attended 1996. **Career:** Milwaukee Bucks, 1996-2003; Team USA 2000 Olympics, mem; Seattle SuperSonics, guard, 2003-07; Boston Celtics, 2007-. **Orgs:** Founder, Ray Hope; All-Star Adv Coun. **Honors/Awds:** USA Basketball's Male Athlete of the Year, 1995; Big East Player of the Year, 1996; Olympic Gold Medal, 2000; NBA, Three-Point Shootout Champion, 2001; Joe Dumars Sportsmanship Award, 2003. **Special Achievements:** Movie: He Got Game, 1998. Named Sporting News "Good Guy" in 2000 & 2001. **Business Addr:** Professional Basketball Player, Boston Celtics, 226 Causeway St 4th Fl, Boston, MA 02114, **Business Phone:** (617)854-8000.

ALLEN, ROBERT
Law enforcement officer. **Career:** City Indianapolis Police Dept, asst police chief, currently. **Business Addr:** Assistant Police Chief, City of Indianapolis Police Department, 50 N Ala St, Indianapolis, IN 46204, **Business Phone:** (317)327-3911.

ALLEN, ROBERT L
Editor, writer, teacher. **Personal:** Born May 29, 1942, Atlanta, GA; son of Robert Lee and Sadie Sims; married Janet Carter, Jun 11, 1995; children: Casey Douglass; married Pamela Parker, Aug 25, 1965 (divorced). **Educ:** Univ Vienna, attended 1962; Morehouse Col, BS, 1963; Columbia Univ, attended 1964; New Sch Social Res, New York, NY, MA, 1967; Univ Calif, San Francisco, PhD, 1983. **Career:** Guardian Newsweekly NYC, staff reporter, 1967-69; San Jose State Col, asst prof new col & black studies dept, 1969-72; Black Scholar Mag, ed; Mills Col, Oakland, CA, from lectr to asst prof ethnic studies, 1973-84; Guggenheim fel, 1978; Wild Trees Press, gen mgr, 1984-90; Black Scholar, sr ed, 1990-; African-Am & Ethnic Studies, Univ Calif-Berkeley, vis prof, 1994-2003, African Am Studies & Ethnic Studies, adj full prof, 2003-. **Orgs:** Vpres, Black World Found; Am Sociol Asn; Am Hist & Cult Soc; Asn Black Sociologists; Pac Sociol Asn; Coun Black Studies; Bay Area Black Journalists; bd mem, Oakland Men's Proj; bd mem, San Francisco Book Coun. **Honors/ Awds:** Winner American Book Award, 1995. **Special Achievements:** Author of "Black Awakening in Capitalist Amer" Doubleday, 1969, "Reluctant Reformers, The Impact of Racism on Amer Social Reform Movements" Howard Univ Press, 1974, contributor to periodicals, author of The Port Chicago Mutiny, Warner Books, 1989, co-editor of Brotherman Ballantine, 1995, co-author of Strong in the Struggle: My Life as a Black Labor Activist, 2001, co-author of Honoring Sergeant Carter, HarperCollins, 2003, One of 12 honorees of the San Francisco Public Library's Long Walk to Freedom living-history exhibition, 2003. **Business Addr:** Adjunct Professor, University of California, African American Studies & Ethnic Studies, 688 Barrows Hall, Berkeley, CA 94720, **Business Phone:** (510)642-6378.

ALLEN, ROSCOE
Business owner. **Career:** Roscoe Allen Co, owner & pres, currently. **Honors/Awds:** Georgia Small Business Person of the Year, 1998; Nat Small Business Person of the Year, 1998; Cong Rec Recognition; Featured in numerous books and magazines including Black Enterprise Mag & Ga Trend. **Military Serv:** USMC, serv disabled veteran. **Business Addr:** Owner, President, Roscoe Allen Co, 213 Alapaha Hwy, PO Box 796, Ocilla, GA 31774-2339, **Business Phone:** (229)468-9540.

ALLEN, S MONIQUE NICOLE
Publisher. **Personal:** Born Dec 20, 1964, New York, NY; daughter of Charles and Sallie Tucker. **Educ:** Princeton Univ, Princeton, NJ, AB, 1986. **Career:** Tucker Publs Inc, Lisle, IL, ed, 1989-. **Orgs:** Recording secy, The Links Inc. **Business Addr:** Editor, Tucker Publications, 5823 Queens Cove, PO Box 580, Lisle, IL 60532, **Business Phone:** (630)969-3809.

ALLEN, SAMUEL WASHINGTON (PAUL VESEY)
Poet, educator, writer. **Personal:** Born Dec 9, 1917, Columbus, OH; son of Alexander Joseph and Jewett Washington; divorced; children: Marie-Christine Catherine. **Educ:** Fisk Univ, AB, 1938; Harvard Law Sch, JD, 1941; New Sch Soc Res, grad study, 1947; Sorbonne, 1950. **Career:** New York, dep asst dist atty, 1946-47; USAF, Europe, historian, claims officer & civilian atty, 1951-55; New York, gen pract, 1956-57; Tex Southern Univ, assoc prof, 1958-60; US Info Agency, asst gen coun, 1961-64; US Community Rels Serv, chief coun, 1965-68; Tuskegee Inst, prof humanities, 1968-70; Wesleyan Univ, vis prof, 1970-71; Boston Univ, Col Arts & Sci, prof eng, 1971-81, prof emer, 1981-; Poems: Presence Africaine, 1949; Elfenbeinzahne, 1956; Ivory Tusks & Other Poems, 1968; Poems from Africa, ed, 1973; Paul Vesey's Ledger, 1975; Every Round, 1987. **Orgs:** Vpres & bd dirs, Southern Educ Found, Atlanta, 1969-76; bd dir, Afrikan Heritage Inst, Roxbury, MA, 1974-78; bd dir, Old S Meeting House, 1984-2000; bd, New Eng Mus African-Am Hist, 1986-2000; bd mem, Boston Partners Educ, 1986-91; comnr, Mass Hist Comn, 1986-92; bd dirs, Blackside, 1988-97; African Studies Asn; NY Bar Asn; New Eng Poetry Club. **Honors/Awds:** NEA Award for Poetry, 1979. **Special Achievements:** Translated Orphee Noir (Jean Paul Sartre), 1960. **Military Serv:** AUS, 1st lt, 1942-46. **Home Addr:** 1155 N Miranda St D7, Las Cruces, NM 88005. *

ALLEN, SANFORD
Violinist. **Personal:** Born Feb 26, 1939, New York City, NY; married Madhur Jaffrey. **Educ:** Juilliard Sch Music; Mannes Col Music. **Career:** Rutgers Univ, Livingston Col, fac mem; NY Philharmonic, violinist, 1962; Columbia Co's Leaf Peeper Series, Clarion Concerts, dir, currently. **Orgs:** Adv panel, NY State Arts Coun; vice chmn adv comm, High Sch Performing Arts Fed Music Clubs Award; exec bd, Kennedy Ctr Nat Black Music Colloquium & Competition; juror, Sphinx Orgn. **Honors/Awds:** Koussevitzky International Recording Award, High Fidelity Mag, 1974. **Special Achievements:** First Black musician ever to become a regular member of the NY Philharmonic, 1962; has appeared in var: Quebec, Baltimore, Detroit Symphonies, NY Philharmonic; recorded Cordero Violin Concerto with Detroit Symphony on Black Composers Series; gave a premiere performance of Sir Roland Hanna's Sonata for Violin and Piano at the Kennedy Center in Washington. **Business Addr:** Director, Columbia County's Leaf Peeper Series, Clarion Concerts, Chatham, NY.*

ALLEN, SAUNDRA C
Chairperson. **Career:** Coun DC, Comt Human Serv, chairperson, 2003. **Business Phone:** (202)724-8045.

ALLEN, SHIRLEY JEANNE
Educator. **Personal:** Born Dec 19, 1941, Tyler, TX; daughter of Theressa Carter McDonald and Ralph C; divorced. **Educ:** Talladega Col, Music, 1960; Jarvis Christian Col, Hawkins, TX, Music, 1963; Gallaudet Col, Wash, DC, BA, Eng Lit, 1966; Howard Univ, Wash, DC, MA, Couns, 1972; Univ Rochester, EdD, Coun, 1992. **Career:** Educator (retired); Rochester Inst Technol, assoc prof gen educ, 1973-2001; Gallaudet Col, Wash, DC, couns instr, 1967-73; US Peace Corp, classification clerk, 1964-65; US IRS, ed clerk; US Post Office, dist clerk, 1966-67. **Orgs:** Nat Asn Deaf; Conf Am Instr Deaf; Nat Asn Women Educ; Nat Black Deaf Advocates. **Honors/Awds:** National Deaf Woman of the Year, Quota Int, 1993; Inducted into the Jarvis Christian College Pioneer Hall of Fame, 1994; Black Deaf Advocates Achievement Award, Calif State, Dept Rehab & Los Angeles, 1994; Special Achievement Award, Campbell Alumni Asn. **Special Achievements:** Author: "What are the factors considered in the selection of vocationalgoals by persons—with differing degrees of hearing ability?", 1972; Received BA, MA, & EdD after becoming deaf, 1962; The first Black deaf female to earn a doctoral degree, 1992; one of the 20 most influential black deaf persons in America, 2003.

ALLEN, STANLEY M.
Airplane pilot. **Personal:** Born Dec 6, 1941, Washington, DC; married Josita E Hair; children: Khyron Shane, Kesha Lynette. **Educ:** Howard Univ, BA, 1965. **Career:** Howard Univ Football, co-capt, 1964; Eastern Airlines Inc, airline pilot. **Orgs:** Airline Pilots Asn; sr class pres ,Fairmont Heights High Sch, 1960. **Honors/Awds:** Md State High Hurdles Champion, 1960. **Military Serv:** USAF, capt, 1965-70. **Business Addr:** Airline Pilot, Eastern Airlines Inc, Washington, DC 20001.*

ALLEN, TAJE LAQAYNE
Football player. **Personal:** Born Nov 6, 1973, Fairburn, GA; married Gladys. **Educ:** Univ Tex, sports mgt. **Career:** St Louis Rams, defensive back, 1997-2000; Kansas City Chiefs, corner back, 2001-02. *

ALLEN, TERRELL ALLISON, III
Association executive. **Personal:** Born Feb 10, 1959, Washington, DC. **Educ:** Howard Univ, BS, elec engineering, 1982; Univ Pa, MBA, finance, 1987. **Career:** Eastman Kodak Co, coop educ stud, 1978-81; Howard Univ, electronics lab asst, 1980-82; Commonwealth Edison Co, gen engr, 1982-85; Coopers & Lybrand, consult; Nat Black MBA Asn, pres. **Orgs:** Vpres, Phi Beta Sigma Fraternity Inc Alpha Chap, 1981-82; comt chmn, Chicago Jr Asn Com & Indust, 1982-85; sci club dir, Chicago Adopt-A-Sch Prog, 1982-85. **Honors/Awds:** Outstanding Young Men America, 1984;

Leadership Award, Johnson & Johnson Family Co, 1985. **Business Addr:** President, National Black MBA Association, PO Box 1384, Philadelphia, PA 19105.

ALLEN, TINA
Sculptor, painter (artist). **Personal:** Born Dec 9, 1949, Hempstead, NY; daughter of Gordon Powell and Rosecleer; married Roger; children: Koryan, Josephine & Tara. **Educ:** Sch Visual Arts, BFA; Univ Southern Ala, BFA, 1978; Pratt Inst, advan studies; Univ Venice, Italy, advan studies. **Career:** Sculptor, currently. **Orgs:** Bd dirs, Am Lung Asn Los Angeles Co; hon mem Art 200; Black Art Nat Diaspora; bd dirs, Int Ctr African Am Asian Rels; bd dirs, Los Angeles Support Comt ANC. **Honors/Awds:** Urban League Award, 1988; Genesis-Generation Spirit, 1989; Artist's Salute to Black History Month, 1995; Thurgood Marshall Lifetime Achievement Award; Dorthy C Height Lifetime Achievement Award; Commerce Secretary Ron Brown Lifetime Achievement Award; Essence Award; Stellar Award; Fannie Lou Hammer Award. **Business Addr:** Sculptor, Allen Studio, 369 S Doheny Dr Suite 401, Beverly Hills, CA 90212, **Business Phone:** (818)920-5108.

ALLEN, TREMAYNE
Football player. **Personal:** Born Aug 9, 1974, Nashville, TN. **Educ:** Univ Fla, BS, bldg construct. **Career:** Football player (retired) Chicago Bears, tight end, 1997-98; Scottish Claymores, tight end, 2000-01; Los Angeles Xtreme Roster, tight end, 2001. *

ALLEN, TY W
Executive. **Personal:** Born Jun 27, 1961, Denver, CO; son of Elijah and Carleen Matis. **Educ:** Univ Colo, Denver, CO, eng, polit sci, 1979-83. **Career:** Burlington Northern Air Freight, sales, 1982-85; C F Air Freight, sales, 1985; Worldwide Air Freight, pres, 1985-88; AFI Int Forwarding, founder, 1988-. **Business Addr:** Founder, Director, AFI International Forwarding Inc, 700 S Colorado Blvd, Denver, CO 80206, **Business Phone:** 888-276-4405.

ALLEN, DR. VAN SIZAR
School administrator. **Personal:** Born Apr 2, 1926, Edwards, MS; son of Van and Edna Sizar; married Mary Frances Cartwright, Dec 1, 1990; children: Van S Jr & Nathaniel B. **Educ:** Tougaloo Col, BA, 1950; Univ Mich, MS, 1952; Yale Univ, Cert, 1955; Univ NC, MPH, 1962, PhD, 1969. **Career:** School Administrator (Retired); Univ Mich, John Hay Whitney Opportunity fel, 1950; Bennett Col, assoc prof, 1952-68; Guilford Co Anti-Poverty Prog, dep dir, 1966-68; Southern Regional Educ Bd, assoc dir, inst higher educ opportunity, 1969-71; TACTICS, exec dir, 1971-80; Tougaloo Col, vpres acad affairs, 1980-85; Paul Quinn Col, vpres acad affairs, 1985-87, 1989-90, vpres & ceo, Waco Campus; Central Tex Cancer Network Prog, dir, 1988-89. **Orgs:** Pres, Tougaloo Col Nat Alumni Asn, 1978-80; chmn, Tougaloo Col Nat Alumni Fundraising Campaign, 1980-84; Am Asn Univ Prof; Beta Kappa Chi Scientific Soc; Nat Inst Sci; AAAS; John Hay Whitney Opportunity Fel Org; Phi Delta Kappa Nat Educ Fraternity; NC Community Develop Asn; Omega Psi Phi Frat; Sigma Pi Phi Frat; Nat Asn Advan Colored People; SOPHE. **Honors/Awds:** Centennial Award Distinguished Service, Tougaloo Col, 1970, Alumnus of the Year, 1977; Presidential Citation, Wash, DC, 1979; Meritorious Service, TACTICS Prog, 1980; Outstanding Service Award, Greensboro, NC, Pub Housing Auth, 1981; Alumni Club Award, Tougaloo Community, 1984; Outstanding Commitment Strengthening Black Cols & Univ NAFEO, 1987. **Special Achievements:** Numerous publications & book reviews. **Military Serv:** USN, third class petty officer, 1944-46; Asiatic Theater Ribbon, Good Conduct Ribbon. **Home Addr:** 225 Garrison St, Waco, TX 76704.

ALLEN, W GEORGE
Lawyer. **Personal:** Born Mar 3, 1936, Sanford, FL; son of Lessie Mae Williams and Fletcher; married Enid Meadows; children: Timothy, Frederick, Amy & Jonathan. **Educ:** FL A&M Univ, BA (Hon), polit sci, 1958; Univ FL Law Sch, JD, 1962. **Career:** FL Human Rels Comn, comnr; Pvt Pract, atty, 1963-. **Orgs:** Comn Fla Ethics Comt; Fla Adv Comn, US Civil Rights Comn, Govs prop Rights Study Community; pres elect, Nat Bar Asn, 1974-75, pres, 1975-76; pres, Fla Bar Asn, 1988-89; Broward City Bar Asn; Am Trial Lawyers Asn; Fla Acad Trail Lawyers; Broward Criminal Defense Asn; Nat Asn Crim Defense Lawyers; Nat Asn Advan Colored People; Alpha Phi Alpha Fraternity Inc, Elks; YMCA; Fla A&M Univ Alumni Asn, State FL; bd dir, Univ Fla Found Inc; Urban League Broward Co; bd trustee, Fla A&M Univ, 2005. **Honors/Awds:** Distinguished Alumnus Award, Univ Fla, 2000; Silver Medallion Award, Nat Conf Community & Justice, 2001; Hall of Fame, Nat Bar Asn, 2003. **Special Achievements:** First black to graduate from the Univ of Florida. **Military Serv:** AUS, first lt spec agt CIC, 1958-60. **Business Addr:** Attorney, 800 SE 3rd Ave, Fort Lauderdale, FL 33316-1152, **Business Phone:** (954)463-6681.

ALLEN, WALTER R
Educator. **Personal:** Born in Allendale, SC; married Mary Clay; children: Walter Jr, Jeffrey & Brian. **Educ:** Beloit col, BA, Sociol, 1971; Univ Chicago, MA, Sociol, 1973, PhD, Sociol, 1975; Univ NC, Sch Pub Health, Postdoctoral Study, 1978. **Career:** Shoals High Sch, asst prin; Univ Georgia, asst prof; Faulkner State Jr Col, Dept Fine Arts, art instr, currently; Univ NC, Dept Sociol, from instr to asst prof, 1974-79; Duke Univ, vis fac, 1976; Univ Zimbabwe, vis fac, 1984-88; Univ Mich, Ctr Afroamerican & African Studies, assoc dir, 1987-89, Dept Sociol & Ctr Afroamerican & African Studies, from asst prof to prof, 1979-91; Univ Zimbabwe, sr fulbright lectr, 1984, 1987-88; Wayne State Univ, vis fac, 1988; Univ Ill Urbana-Champaign, Allerton Lectr, 1988; Univ Calif Los Angeles, Dept Sociol, prof, 1988-, Sch Med, assoc dir, Robert Wood Johnson clin scholars prog, 1993-97, Inst Social Sci Res, dir, 1998-, Grad Sch Educ & Info Studies, Dept Educ, Allan Murray Cartter prof, 2004-; Howard Univ, vis fac, 1975, 1997-2001; consult. **Orgs:** NIH, 1978-79; coun, Am Sociol Asn, 1991-94; elected mem, Sociol Res Asn, 1991-; pres, Asn Black Sociol, 1992-93; Am Educ Res Asn, 2000; Kappa Alpha Psi; Phi Delta Kappa; Kappa Kappa Psi; Thirty second Deg Mason; Am Psychol Asn; Nat Asn Musicologists; educr, Haile Selassie Ethiopia; social psychologist, musician & adminr, Hundred Percenters Orgn; Hill First Baptist Church; Nat Asn Advan Colored People; Free Lance Musician. **Honors/Awds:** Achievement Award, Kappa Alpha Psi; Hundred Percenters Award; Educators Award; Phi Delta Kappa Award; Nat Asn Musicologists; Kappa Kappa Psi Award; Distinguished Leadership Award, United Negro Col Fund, 1985; Faculty Recognition Award, Univ Mich, Ann Arbor, 1987; Distinguished Scholar Award, Am Educ Res Asn, 1987; Research Excellence Award, Am Educ Res Asn, 1993; Distinguished Career Award, Asn Black Sociologists, 1995; Harriet & Charles Luckman Distinguished Teaching Award, Univ Calif Los Angeles, 1996; Ellis Joseph Distinguished Scholar Award, Univ Dayton, 1997; Special Merit Award, Asn Study Higher Edu, 2002; DuBois-Johnson-Frazier Award, Am Sociol Asn, 2002. **Special Achievements:** Contributed numerous publications. **Military Serv:** AUS, 1951-53. **Home Addr:** 220 Swanson Dr, Athens, GA 30606, **Home Phone:** (706)546-9160. **Business Addr:** Professor, University of California, Graduate School of Education & Information Studies, 264 Haines Hall, PO Box 951551, Los Angeles, CA 90095-1551, **Business Phone:** (310)206-7107.

ALLEN, WILL D.
Football player. **Personal:** Born Aug 5, 1978, Syracuse, NY; son of Will Allen Sr and Carolyn; married Roshonda; children: Jasmine, Will Jr & Blake. **Educ:** Univ Syracuse, econ. **Career:** New York Giants, defensive Back, 2001-05; Miami Dolphins, 2006-. **Orgs:** The Ronald McDonald House, Giants Fund Golf Outing; Nat Football Found. **Honors/Awds:** First-team All-Big East, 2000; Jim Thorpe Award semi-finalist, 2000. **Business Addr:** Professional Football Player, Miami Dolphins, 7500 SW 30th St, Davie, FL 33314, **Business Phone:** (954)452-7000.*

ALLEN, DR. WILLIAM BARCLAY
Educator. **Personal:** Born Mar 18, 1944, Fernandina Beach, FL; son of Rev James P and Rosa Lee Johnson; married Carol Michelle Pfeiffer; children: Danielle Susan & Bertrand Marc. **Educ:** Pepperdine Col, BA, 1967; Claremont Grad Sch, MA, 1968, PhD, 1972. **Career:** Sears, Roebuck Inc, Calif, Elec Supplies, sales & asst mgr, 1965-66; Radio Sta KMPC, Hollywood, news ed, 1966-68; Fernandina Beach High Sch, instr Am hist, phys sci, & bus math, 1968-69; Pepperdine Col, Am Polit Theory, instr, 1969; Univ de Rouen, lectr, 1970-71; Fulbright fel, 1970-71; Am Univ Sch Gov & Pub Admin, asst prof, 1971-72; Harvey Mudd Col, from asst prof to prof, 1972-92; St John's Col Grad Inst, vis tutor 1977-; Liberty Fund Inc, Bicentennial Series, prog admin & co-organizer, 1982-90; Earhart Found res grant, 1986-87; Pac Res Inst Pub Policy, mem Civil Rights Task Force, 1988-90; US Comn Civil Rights, chmn, 1988-89; Bicentennial Educ Grant Prog, Comn Bicentennial US Const, 1988-89; Mich State Univ, James Madison Col, dean, 1993-98, prof polit sci, 1993-, dir Prog Pub Policy & Pub Admin, 1998-; State Coun Higher Educ Va, dir, 1998-99;Yorktown Univ.com, adj prof, currently; sr fel, Inst Responsible Citizenship, currently. **Orgs:** NUmerous memships in various organizations including Claremont Rotary, 1980-86; pres, Claremont Unified School Dist Bd, 1981-84; bd mem, Calif Assembly Fel Prog, 1982-92; prog dir, Liberty Fund Inc, 1982-89; chmn, Calif Scholars Reagan, 1984; bd mem, LeRoy Boys Home; Nat Coun Humanities, 1984-87; Am Polit Sci Kellogg Nat fel, Kellogg Found, 1984-87; Asn; Academie Montesquieu; Chair US Comn Civil Rights, 1987-92; US Civil Rights Comn, Calif State Adv Comt, 1985-87; trustee, Hoover Inst, Stanford Univ, 1995-98; chmn emer, George Wash Soc, Calif; dir Youth Ministry, Westwood Baptist Church, Richmond, Va, 1998-2000; co-chair, anniversary Comt, 2003,co-chair, Stewardship Comt, 2003, trustee, 2005-, Union Missionary Baptist Church, Lansing, Mich; Pi Sigma Alpha, Sigma Alpha. **Honors/Awds:** Numerous honors, awards & grants including; Prix Montesquieu Acad France, 1986; res grant, Earhart Found, 1986-87; LID, Pepperdine Univ, 1988; Templeton Honor Roll, 1997; Fulbright Sr Specialists Roster, 2002-07; Booker T Washington Legacy Award, Heartland Inst, Chicago. **Special Achievements:** Numerous publications and books including, Montesquieu, The Federalist-Anti federalist Dispute, 1972; Jesus Walked on Water: George Washington Built on Land, manuscript under review for publication; The Essential Anti federalist: Second Edition, 2002; Habits of Mind: Fostering Excellence and Access in Higher Education, 2003; George Washington: A Collection, editor and Introduction, 2003; "Jesus Walked on Water; George Washington Built on Land", 2004; "The Beauty of Common Sense", 2005. **Military Serv:** USATC 1968,col's Orderly. **Business Addr:** Professor, Michigan State University, Department of Political Science, 307 S Kedzie Hall, East Lansing, MI 48824-1032, **Business Phone:** (517)432-9967.

ALLEN, DR. WILLIAM HENRY
Dentist, educator. **Personal:** Born Jan 27, 1917, New Orleans, LA; son of William H and Victoria; married Martha Mae Mosley (deceased). **Educ:** Tougaloo Col, AB, 1938; Meharry Med Col, DDS, 1943; Univ Mich, attended 1944. **Career:** Meharry Med Col, instr, 1943-44, Sch Dent, asst prof dent mat, prosthetics & clin dent, 1945-47, actg dean, 1946-47, dir, dean, dent educ, 1949-50, dean, 1950-71, prof prosthetics, dir div dent technol, 1947-86, vpres, prof emer prosthodontics, 1986-. **Orgs:** Pres, Capitol City Dental Soc, 1958-59; dent training comt Nat Inst Dent Res, 1971-; Coun Nat Bd Dent Examr; Tenn Nat Dent Assoc, Am Asn Dent Sch; Am Fund Dent Educ; regional med adv comt, fel AAAS; Al State Dent Soc; Am Assoc Cleft Palate Rehab; Am Asn Dent Sch; Nashville Dent Soc; Am Asn Endodontists; Kappa Sigma Pi; Kappa Alpha Psi; Omicron Kappa Upsilon; Chi Boul Frat; Dent Mat Group Asn; Int Asn Dent Res. **Home Addr:** 4213 Ashland City Hwy, Nashville, TN 37218. **Business Addr:** Professor Emeritus, Meharry Medical College, School of Dentistry, 1005 DB Todd Blvd, Nashville, TN 37208, **Business Phone:** (615)327-6000.*

ALLEN, DR. WINSTON EARLE
Executive. **Personal:** Born 5283, New York, NY; married Ruby; children: Vaughn, Julie. **Educ:** NY Univ Wash Square Col Arts & Sci, BA, 1955; City Col NY, MA, 1958; Fordham Univ, PhD, 1971. **Career:** NY City Bd Educ, teacher econ, 1956-68; Fordham Univ, asst prof 1970-72; George Wash Univ & American Univ, adj prof mgt sci dept, 1974-75; Creative Investor Serv Inc, pres; Xerox Corp Educ Planning & Develop, mgr, 1972-82; Innovative Health Prod Inc, founder, 1993-. **Orgs:** bd mem, US comn UNICEF, 1972-82; phi delta kappa prof frat; bd dirs, sunrise rotary westport, ct; chmn, westport conservation comn, 1989-93; zoning bd appeals, westport, CT; pres elect, westport rotary, 1997-98; Rotary District Governor, 2000-01. **Honors/Awds:** Paul Harris Fellow Award, Rotary Int; inventor patented hydrotherapy prod, Hydrotone. **Business Phone:** (203)227-4897.*

ALLEN-HOWARD, MARQUITA W.
Municipal government official, police officer. **Career:** City NY, Dept Invest, dep inspector gen, currently. **Business Addr:** Deputy Inspector General, City of New York, Department of Investigation, 80 Maiden Lane 16th Fl, New York, NY 10038, **Business Phone:** (212)825-2467.*

ALLEN-JONES, PATRICIA ANN
Journalist. **Personal:** Born Nov 9, 1958, Pittsburg, CA; daughter of William J and Bettye J; married George Wallace Jr, May 25, 1991. **Educ:** Calif State Univ, BA, 1981. **Career:** Neighbor News, reporter, 1981-83; Suncoast News, reporter, 1983-84; Fla Sentinel Bulletin, reporter, 1984-86; Leesburg Com Newspaper, reporter, 1986-88; Herald-Tribune Newspaper, reporter, 1988-. **Orgs:** St Martha's Cath Church, 1988-; Adult Black Achievers, 1992-. **Honors/Awds:** Media Award, Eastern Seal Soc SW Fla, 1992. **Business Addr:** Reporter, Herald-Tribune Newspaper, 1741 Main St, Sarasota, FL 34236, **Business Phone:** (941)361-4880.

ALLEN-MEARES, PAULA G
Educator, school administrator. **Personal:** Born in Buffalo, NY; daughter of Joseph N Allen and Mary T Hienz; married Henry, Jun 8, 1974; children: Tracey, Nichole & Shannon. **Educ:** State Univ New York, Buffalo, NY, BS, 1969; Univ Ill, Urbana-19Champaign, Jane Addams Sch Social Work, MSW, 1971, PhD (social work & educ admin), 1975; Univ Ill, MSW, child welfare, 1971; Harvard Univ, Mgt Inst, Boston, MA, cert, 1990, Grad Sch Mgt Develop Prog, cert, 1990; cert, 1994; UM Bus Sch, Mgt Mgr, Cert, 1993. **Career:** Facilty Univ Ill Sch Social Work, Urbana-Champaign, IL, 1978-84, assoc prof, 1983-89, dir doctoral prog, 1985-89; Univ Mich, Sch Social Work, dean, 1993-, Norma Radin Col prof social work, currently, prof educ, currently. **Orgs:** Chair, Comn on edu, Nat Asn Social Workers, 1982-88; ed chief, J Social Work Edu (CSWE), Nat Asn Social Workers, 1989-93; elected mem, steering comm, Group for the Advan Doctoral Edu, 1987-88; Bd dirs, Coun Social Work Edu, 1989-91; commun Bd mem, Nat Asn Social Workers, 1990-. **Honors/Awds:** Medallion Honors, Univ Ill Urbana-Champaign, 1990, Participant Comm Instnl Coop Develop Seminar, 1989-90; Delta Mu Nat Social Work Honor Soc; Delta Kappa Gamma Intl Honor Soc Women Educr. **Business Addr:** Dean, Professor, University Michigan, Sch Social Work, 1080 S Univ Rm 4728 SSWB, Ann Arbor, MI 48109.

ALLEN-NOBLE, PROF. ROSIE ELIZABETH
School administrator. **Personal:** Born Jun 22, 1938, Americus, GA; daughter of Velma Douglas and Ulysses Grant Allen; married Apr 1963 (divorced); children: Antoinette Celine Noble-Webb. **Educ:** Albany State Col, BS, 1960; Atlanta Univ, MS, 1967; Rutgers Univ, MS, 1974, DEd, 1991. **Career:** Rutgers Univ, instr, 1970-76; Seton Hall Univ, vis asst prof, 1972-78; Univ Med & Dentist, NJ, instr, 1972; Univ Med & Dent, NJ, consult, 1972-; So-

roptomist Int, 1974-; Fairleigh Dickinson Univ, asst prof, 1974-80; Upsala Col, Sci Enrichment Prog, dir, 1976; Montclair State Col, Health Careers Prog, dir, 1979; Med Col Ga, Spec Acad Progs, assoc dean, currently, Dept Cellular Biol & Anat, assoc prof, 2004-; Univ Conn, consult & evaluator, 1981-83; Hobart William Smith Col, consult, 1983; Long Island Univ, 1984; Wichita State Univ, 1984; Univ Med & Dent NJ, Sch Health Related Professions, consult, 1986-; Gwynedd-Mercy Col, consult, 1987-. **Orgs:** Alpha Kappa Alpha Sorority, 1959; Am Asn Univ Women, 1969-; NJ Chap Albany State Col Alumni Asn, 1974; Nat Asn Med Minority Educ, 1980; Omicrom Xi Omega, 1984; Evaluation Comt Higher Educ Middle State Asn Evaluation Team, 1984; Nat Asn Pre-Prof Advs, 1984; nat treas, Nat Asn Med Minority Educ Inc, 1984; NE regional dir, Nat Asn Med Minority Educr, 1988-90, bd dir, 1990. **Honors/Awds:** Merit Award for Outstanding Service, Montclair State Col, 1982 & 1987; Outstanding Leadership & Service, Upsala Col, 1982; NSF Grants; Outstanding Service Award, Montclair State Col, 1984-85; Numerous Fed, State & Private Found Fellowship Grants over the past 20 years. **Home Phone:** (706)721-2522. **Business Addr:** Asoociated Dean for Special Academic Programs, Associate Professor, Medical College of Georgia, 1120 15th St, Augusta, GA 30912, **Business Phone:** (706)721-2522.

ALLEN-RASHEED, JAMAL RANDY
Association executive, judge. **Personal:** Born Dec 15, 1953, Memphis, TN; married Jacquline Carlotte Gipson; children: Randy D. **Educ:** Southern Ill Univ, Carbondale, BS, 1980; Prairie View A&M Univ, MA, 1986. **Career:** KEWC-AM/FM Radio, disc jockey & reporter, 1975-76; WPHD-NBC TV, news asst, 1979-80; Black Observer Newspaper, managing ed, 1979-80; WLS-ABC Network, prod engr, 1980; Lackland Tailspinner Airforce Pub, reporter, 1981; Forward Times Newspaper, asst circulation mgr, 1982-83; Sam Houston State Univ/Housing, pub rels dir, 1983-84; Martin Luther King Jr Ctr Nonviolent Social Change Inc, community develop asst, 1984; Tex Dept Corrections, correctional officer, 1984-86; Dallas County Adult Probation, adult probation officer, currently; Dallas County Juv Prog, admin; state dir. **Orgs:** Alpha Epsilon Rho Hon Radio/TV, 1978-80; nat bd dirs, Alpha Phi Alpha Frat Inc, 1978-79; Sigma Delta Chi Prof Journalist, 1979-80; pub rels dir, Black Affairs Coun SI U-C, 1979-80; founder & dir, Martin Luther King Jr Inst Afro-Am Studies/Soc Change, 1985-86; bd dirs, Hillvale Educ Asn Substance Abuse, 1986-; Blacks Soc, Blacks Journ, Blacks Criminal Justice; 32 Degree Ancient & Accepted Scottish Rite Masonary Prince Hall Affiliation; John M Harlan Alumni Asn; dep supreme master, Knight KOP Prog. **Honors/Awds:** Outstanding Serv Midwest Region, Alpha Phi Alpha, 1979; Outstanding Service Board Directors, Alpha Phi Alpha, 1979; Outstanding Service Black Affairs Coun, SIU-C, 1980; Cert Training Nonviolent Social Change, Martin Luther King Jr Ctr Nonviolent Social Change Inc, 1984; Int Distinguished Young Leaders, 1987; Outstanding Am. **Military Serv:** USAF, airman first class, 2 yrs; Basic Training Leadership Award. **Business Addr:** Adult Probation Officer, Dallas County Adult Probation, 414 S RL thornton, Dallas, TX 75203, **Business Phone:** (214)521-0224.

ALLENSWORTH, JERMAINE LAMONT
Baseball player. **Personal:** Born Jan 11, 1972, Anderson, IN. **Educ:** Purdue Univ. **Career:** Pittsburgh Pirates, outfielder, 1996-98; Kans City Royals, 1998; NY Mets, 1998-99; Boston Red Sox, outfielder, 2000; Milwaukee Brewers, outfielder, 2004; Joliet Jack Hammers, 2004-05; Gary South Shore Rail Cats, 2006; Schaumburg Flyers, 2008; free agent, currently. **Honors/Awds:** Big Ten Conference All-Star OF, 1993; Pacific League All-Star OF, 1996. **Special Achievements:** He was portrayed by Tracy Morgan in a 1997 episode of Saturday Night Live. *

ALLEYNE, EDWARD D.
Clergy. **Personal:** Born Jun 14, 1928, Brooklyn, NY. **Educ:** Catholic Univ Am, BA, 1956. **Career:** Clergy (retired); Mother Savior Sem, instr, 1960-67; var parishes Diocese Camden, assoc pastor, 1968-84; St Monica's Church, pastor, 1984; Queen Heaven Church, pastor. **Orgs:** Diocesan Bd Educ, 1969-; Dir, Parkside Cath Ctr, 1971-75;Diocesan Ecumenical Comn, 1971-; Camden Region Moderator Diocesan PTA, 1971-; Diocesan Campaign Human Develop Comn, 1971-; Diocesan Soc Justice Comn, 1972-; financial coordr, Consol Cath Sch, Camden, 1972-75.

ALLIGOOD, DOUGLASS LACY
Executive. **Personal:** Born Feb 15, 1934, St Louis, MO; son of Forest D and Countess M Murphy; divorced; children: Donna L Johnson, Craig F, Debra Alligood-White & Douglas L Jr; married. **Educ:** Bradley Univ Peoria, IL, BFA, 1956. **Career:** Seymour, Leatherwood & Cleveland, Inc, Detroit, staff artist & copywriter, 1956; Radio Sta WCHB, Detroit, MI, merch dir, 1959-62; Batten, Barton Durstine & Osborn Inc, Detroit, acct exec, 1962-64, sr acct exec, 1964-71; RCA Corp, NY, dir corp adv, 1971-83; UniWorld Group Inc, New York, NY, pres, 1983-84; BBDO Worldwide Inc, sr vpres spec mkt, 1984-; A P Phillips lectr, Univ Fla, 1989. **Orgs:** Dir adv coun, Int Film & TV Festival NY, 1976-; dir & speaker, Advert Educ Found, 1985-; Am Asn Advert Agencies EOO Comn, 1986-93; chmn adv coun, Ethnic Perspectives Comn, 1991-93; chmn, Health Watch Info & Prom Serv, 1995-99; life dir, Advert Coun; chmn, BBDO Diversity Coun, 2006; bd dirs, BBDO, 2006. **Honors/Awds:** Five To Watch Award, Am Women Radio & TV, Detroit, 1964; CEBA Advert Campaign Awards, 1980-82; Black Achievers in Industry, Harlem Br YMCA Greater New York 1990; BBDO Founders Award, 1993; Bradley University Centurion, 1994; 2-Year Service Award, Adv Coun, 1996; Institute Award, Nat Eagle Leadership, 1998; Distinguished Service Award, Health Watch, 1999; Mediaweek "All Star-Research", 1998; AAF Diversity Achievement Award, 2005; BBDO Dillon Prize, 2007. **Special Achievements:** An Analysis of Black Audience Primetime Network Viewing Preferences, 1984-; Media Opportunities Newsletter, 1991; Special Markets Media Guidebook, 1993; An Analysis of Hispanic Audience Primetime Network Viewing Preferences, 1993-; Spindex Media Star, Advertising Age, 1997-00; Crains Top 100 Minority Executive, 1998, 2003; co-author of "Color Television: Fifty Years of Images of African Americans and Latinos on Prime Time Television, 2005. **Military Serv:** USAF, capt, 1956-59. **Business Addr:** Senior Vice President, Horizontal Markets, Chairman, Diversity Council, BBDO Worldwide Inc, 1285 Ave of the Americas, New York, NY 10019-6028, **Business Phone:** (212)459-5000.

ALLISON, E. LAVONIA
Executive. **Career:** Durham County Govt, chmn durham commt affairs black people, currently. **Honors/Awds:** Humanitarian Award, NAACP, 2006. *

ALLISON, FERDINAND V., JR.
Chief executive officer. **Personal:** Born Jan 15, 1923, Emporia, VA; son of Ferdinand Vincent Allison Sr (deceased) and Elizabeth R; married E Lavonia Ingram; children: Karen Michele Allison-Davis & Ferdinand Vincent Allison III. **Educ:** Hampton Inst, BS, 1948; New York Univ, MBA, 1952. **Career:** Chief Executive Officer (retired); Army Air Force, inventory clerk,squadron clerk, 1943-46; Hampton Inst, budget clerk, 1948-50, invoice auditor, 1952-53; Mutual Savings & Loan Asn, dir, pres, 1953, chmn, ceo. **Orgs:** Dir, Nat Bus League; dir, past pres, chmn, Durham Bus & Prof Chain Inc;past dir, John Avery Boys Club; exec comt, chmn, Durham Co CommunityAffairs Black People; life mem, NAACP; Omega Psi Phi; AS Hunter Lodge 825F&AM; Durham Chap Hampton Inst Nat Alumni; Durham C of C; trustee, White Rock Bapt Ch; Rotary Club Durham; bd dir, exec comt, Savings & Community Bankers Am; Found Better Health Durham; bd mem, NC Alliance Community FinInst; dir, exec, comt, Nat Bus League; trustee, White Rock Baptist Church; Rotary Club Durham; past chmn, vchmn Am League Fin Insts. **Military Serv:** USAC, 3 yrs. **Home Phone:** (919)682-5219.

ALLISON, VERNE
Singer. **Personal:** Born Jun 22, 1936, Chicago, IL. **Career:** Dells, tenor vocalist; Albums (with Dells): There Is, 1968; Love Is Blue, 1969; The Dells' Musical Menu/Always Together, 1969; The Dells' Greatest Hits, 1970; Like It Is, Like It Was, 1971; Freedom Means, 1971; Sweet As Funk Can Be, 1972; The Dells Sing Dionne, 1972; Give Your Baby a Standing Ovation, 1976; The Dells, 1973; The Mighty Mighty Dells, 1974; The Dellsvs. The Dramatics, 1975; The Dells' Greatest Hits Volume 2, 1975; We Got To Get Our Thing Together, 1975; No Way Back, 1976; They Said It Couldn't Be Done But We Did It, 1977; Love Connection, 1977; New Beginnings, 1978; Face to Face, 1979; I Touched a Dream, 1980; Whatever Turns You On, 1981; One Step Closer, 1984; The Second Time, 1988; On Their Corner, 1992; I Salute You, 1992; Dreams of Contentment, 1993; Bring Back the Love:Classic Dells, 1996; I Touch a Dream/Whatever Turns, 1998; Reminiscing, 2000; Open Up My Heart: The 9/11 Album, 2002; Hott, 2003; (with MichaelRoss): We Finally Meet, 1995; Last Love Letter, 1996. **Orgs:** The Dells. **Business Addr:** Singer, The Original Dells Inc, 10112 S La Salle St, Chicago, IL 60628, **Business Phone:** (708)474-1422.

ALLISON, VIVIAN
Executive. **Personal:** Born Aug 27, 1936; widowed; children: one (deceased). **Educ:** Fisk Univ, attended 1953; Wayne Co Gen Hosp, med technol internship, 1959; Wayne State Univ, BS, chem, 1958. **Career:** Robeson-Tubman Community Devel Corp, 1970-79, bd dirs, 1979-85, chairperson, 1981-85; Off US Congman John Conyers, cong asst, 1980-93; Off Wayne County Exec William Lucas, exec asst, 1983-86; Mich Dept Licensing & Regulation, admin asst to dir, 1987-90; City Detroit, Consumer Aff Dept, dep dir, 1991. **Orgs:** Nat Asn Advan Colored People; Am Med Technologists; Nat Asn Black Substance Abuse Workers; Nat Clearinghouses Licensure, Enforcement & Regulation; Int Asn Transp Regulators; Greenacres-Woodward Civic Asn; Nat, State, 14th Dist Democratic Party. **Honors/Awds:** Outstanding Community Serv, Congressman John Conyers, 1969; Community Service in Substance Abuse, Governor William Milliken, 1972; Cert of Appreciation as Member of the Selective Service System, Pres Gerald R Ford, 1974; Spirit of Detroit, Detroit City Coun, 1982; Mother of the Year, State Rep Teola Hunter, 1990. **Home Addr:** 20159 Warrington, Detroit, MI 48201, **Home Phone:** (313)863-8127. *

ALLOTEY, VICTOR
Football player, entrepreneur. **Personal:** Born Apr 8, 1975, Brooklyn, NY. **Educ:** Univ Ind. **Career:** Football, Founder & President: Buffalo Bills, guard, 1998; Kans City Chiefs, 2001-04, free agent; CK Entertainment Productions Inc, found & pres, currently. *

ALLOY, DR. VALERIE
Psychologist. **Personal:** Married Phillip; children: 1. **Educ:** Univ Toledo, MA, PhD, clinical psychol; Ohio Univ, MEd, BA. **Career:** Pvt prac, psychol, currently; State Ohio, counr; Ohio Dept Mental Health Recovery Demonstration Grant, project mgr & consult. **Orgs:** Nat bd, Women's Philanthropy Inst, 2003-; Catherine Eberly Ctr Women; minoriy Asn comt, Am Heart Asn. **Business Addr:** National Board, Women's Philanthropy Institute, 550 WN St Suite 301, Indianapolis, IN 46202-3272, **Business Phone:** (317)278-8990.

ALLSTON, THOMAS GRAY, III
Executive, consultant. **Personal:** Born Jul 13, 1954, Stoneham, MA; son of Thomas G II and Zeola Belle. **Educ:** Hampton Inst, BA, eng, 1977; Hampton Univ, bus mgt, 1994. **Career:** Burson-Marsteller, New York, asst acct exec, 1977-78; Hampton Inst Univ, asst dir pub rel, 1979-85; Hill Knowlton Inc, acct exec, 1985-87; Renaissance Comm, vpres, 1987-91; Allston Commun Inc, Newport News, pres, ceo, 1991-; Hampton Univ, internal consult, 1991-. **Orgs:** Calvary SDA Church, 1973-; life mem, Alpha Phi Alpha Fraternity Inc, 1974-; Nat ampton Alumni Asn, 1977-; Pub Rel Soc Am, 1977-. **Honors/Awds:** Outstanding Communications Achievement, John W Hill Award, Hill & Knowlton, 1986. **Business Phone:** (804)888-6583.

ALLY, DR. AKBAR F.
Educator. **Personal:** Born Aug 23, 1943, Wismar, Demerara, Guyana; son of Beraspratt and Lucille Ward; married Ellen Mason, Dec 22, 1967; children: Antonius & Kristina. **Educ:** St Lawrence Univ, BA, 1967; Hunter Col, MA, 1972; Univ Wis, Milwaukee,PhD, 1981. **Career:** Chase Manhattan Bank, New York, NY, int adjuster, 1970; Metrop Life Ins,New York, NY, claims adjuster, 1970-72; Brooklyn Col, Brooklyn, NY, lectr, 1973-75; Bronx Community Col, New York, NY, lectr, 1975; UnivWis-Milwaukee, dir & coordr, 1975-82; Univ Wis-Madison, asst dean, 1982-89, asst vice chancellor, 1989-2001; emer asst vice chancellor, 2002-. **Orgs:** Caribbean Hist Soc, 1972-; Nat Asn Advan Colored People, Madison, 1985-; Madison Urban League, 1985-. **Honors/Awds:** Fulbright Hays Award, US State Dept, 1963-67; New York State Education Scholarship, NY, 1971-72; Professional Development Certificate, Harvard Univ, MA, 1991; Professional Development Certificate, Univ Wis, Madison,WI, 1986. **Business Addr:** Emeritus Assistant Vice Chancellor, University of Wisconsin-Madison, Bascom Hall 500 Lincoln Dr Suite 121, Madison, WI 53706, **Business Phone:** (608)262-3571.

AL-MATEEN, DR. CHERYL SINGLETON
Physician, educator. **Personal:** Born Aug 26, 1959, Washington, DC; daughter of Israel Benjamin and Carole Waters; married Kevin Bakeer; children: Benjamin & Katherine. **Educ:** Howard Univ, Col Liberal Arts, BS, 1981, Col Med, MD, 1983. **Career:** Howard Univ Hosp, transitional Med internship, 1983-84; Hahnemann Univ Hosp, psychiat residency, 1984-87; Hahnemann Univ Hosp, Philadelphia, Pa, child psychiat residency, 1987-89; Med Col Va, VCU sch med, asst prof, 1989-96, assoc prof psychiat, 1996-, clerkship dir, currently. **Orgs:** Vpres, admin Howard Univ Col Med Class 83, 1982-; ed-in-chief Spectrum, APA/NIMH fel Newsletter, 1986-87; component mem, Am Psychiat Asn, 1985-98, 2001-; Am Acad Child & Adolescent Psychiat, 1987-. **Honors/Awds:** Serv Citation, Howard Univ Col Med Fac, 1983; Nat Inst Ment Health fel; Am Psychiat Asn, 1985-87. **Business Addr:** Associate Professor, Virginia Commonwealth University, Department of Psychiatry, School of Medicine, PO Box 980489, Richmond, VA 23298, **Business Phone:** (804)828-3129.

AL-MATEEN, DR. K BAKEER
Physician. **Personal:** Born Aug 31, 1958, Pasadena, CA; son of Eddie Jr and Margaret Janet Strain; married Cheryl Singleton; children: Benjamin. **Educ:** Univ Calif, Davis, attended 1980; Howard Univ, Col Med, MD, 1984; Va Commonwealth Univ, MS, 1999. **Career:** Pres, Howard Univ, Col Med; St Christopher's Children Hosp, PA, pediatric resident; Med Col Va, Dept Neonatology, asst prof pediat, dir, Neonatal ECMO prog; Swift Creek Pediatrics, Physician, currently. **Orgs:** Chesterfield Co Republican Comt. **Honors/Awds:** Malcolm X Scholar & Service Citation, Howard Univ, Col Med, 1984. **Home Addr:** 5306 Clipper Cove Rd, Midlothian, VA 23112. **Business Addr:** Physician, Swift Creek Pediatrics, 13700 St Francis Blvd Suite 501, Midlothian, VA 23114, **Business Phone:** (804)378-4420.

ALOMAR, ROBERTO
Baseball player. **Personal:** Born Feb 5, 1968, Ponce, Puerto Rico; son of Sandy Alomar Sr. **Career:** Baseball player (retired); San Diego Padres, 1988-90; Toronto Blue Jays, 1991-95; Baltimore Orioles, 1996-98; Cleveland Indians, 1999-2001; New York Mets, 2002-03; Chicago White Sox, 2003, 2004; Ariz Diamondbacks, 2004; Tampa Bay Devil Rays, 2005. **Honors/Awds:** Silver Slugger Award, 1992, 1996, 1999, 2000; ALCS MVP, 1992; All-Star Game MVP, 1998; 10 Gold Glove Awards.

ALOMAR, SANDY (SANTOS ALOMAR CONDE, SR.)
Baseball player, athletic coach. **Personal:** Born Oct 19, 1943, Salinas, Puerto Rico; married Maria; children: Sandia, Sandy Jr &

Roberto. **Career:** Baseball player (retired), coach; Milwaukee Braves, infielder, 1964-67; New York Mets, infielder, 1967, Willie Randolph's bench coach, 2004-05, 2008-, first base bench coach, 2005-07, third base coach, 2007-08; Chicago White Sox, 1967-69; Calif Angels, infielder, 1969-74; New York Yankees, 1974-76; Tex Rangers, infielder, 1977-78; Puerto Rican Nat Team, coach, 1979-84; San Diego Padres, third base coach, 1986-90; Cleveland Indians, coach, 1990; Iowa Pac Coast League, interim mgr, 1991; Latin Am coordr, 1991-94; mgr rookie-level affiliate, Ft Myers, 1995-96; roving minor league instr; SanJuans, gen mgr, 1999-2000; Chicago Cubs, bullpen coach, 2000-01, first base coach, 2002; Colo Rockies, third base coach, 2003-04. **Orgs:** Chicago Cubs Orgn, 1991-2003. **Honors/Awds:** Pioneer League Player of the Year, 1962. **Business Phone:** (718)507-8499.

ALOMAR, SANDY
Baseball player, athletic coach. **Personal:** Born Jun 18, 1966, Salinas, Puerto Rico; son of Sandy Sr; married Christie Solis (divorced); children: Marcus Xavier & Marissa Daniele; married Kelly Donovan (divorced); children: 1; married Margred; children: Leanna April, Brianna Maria & Isabela Simone. **Career:** Baseball player (retired), athletic coach; San Diego Padres, prof baseball player, 1988-89, Cleveland Indians, prof baseball player, 1990-2000; Chicago White Sox, 2001-02, 2003-04, 2006; Colorado Rockies, 2002; Tex Rangers, 2005; Los Angeles Dodgers, 2006; NY Mets, 2007, catching instr, 2008-. **Honors/Awds:** Minor League Co-Player of the Year, Sporting News, 1988, Minor League Player of the Year, 1989; Player of the Year, Pac Coast League, 1989; American League Rookie Player of the Year, 1990; Gold Glove, American League, 1990; American League Rookie of the Year, Baseball Writers Asn Am, 1990; MLB All-Star Game MVP, 1997. **Home Addr:** PO Box 367, Salinas, PR 00751.

ALONZO, JENNY
President (Organization). **Career:** Nat Asn Multi-Ethnicity Commun, pres, bd chair, mem bd dirs, currently. **Business Addr:** Board of Directors, National Association for Multi-Ethnicity in Communications, 336 W 37th St Suite 302, New York, NY 10018, **Business Phone:** (212)594-5985.*

ALSTON, BETTY BRUNER
Educator. **Personal:** Born Jul 5, 1933, Concord, NC; daughter of Buford Sr and Ethel Torrence; married Henry Clay; children: Henry Clay Jr & Terry Verice. **Educ:** Barber-Scotia Col, BS, 1955; A&T State Univ, attended 1957; Appalachian State Univ, attended 1969. **Career:** Educator (retired); PTA/Odell Elem Sch, secy, 1979; PTSA/Northwest Middle Sch, secy, 1980, 1981; Northwest High Sch Booster Club, secy, 1982, vpres, 1983; Briarwood, Sch teacher, 1983-93. **Orgs:** NC Asn Educrs; elder, organist First United Presbyterian Church; bd dir,Stonewall Jackson Sch, 1988, adv Coun, 1988, vice chair, 1991, Cabarrus County Bd Educ; second vpres, Democrat Womens Orgn, 1989; Concord, Cabarrus Chamber Com, pres club, 1994; chmn, Cabarrus County Bd Educ,1993-94; pres, Democratic Women, 1993; adv coun, Stonewall Jackson Sch,1995; bd trustees, Barber-Scotia Col, 1995; ambassador, Cabarrus Regional Chamber Com, 1996; bd mem, Am Red Cross, Cabarrus County chp, 2000. **Honors/Awds:** Alpha Kappa Alpha; Cabarrus County Sch Bd; Northwest HS Bd Dirs;Outstanding Achievement Educ & Comm Serv Omega Psi Phi Frat, 1986; Service to the Welfare of the Community W Cent Cabarrus Optimist, 1986; IntLeaders in Achievement, 1989; Citation of the Year Award, DistinguishedBarber-Scotia Alumni, 1994; President's Club of the Year Award, Cabarrus Chamber Commerce, 1995; Woman of the Year, nominated, Int Biographical Ctr, 1999-00; honorary mem, Int Biographical Ctr Adv Coun, 2000. **Special Achievements:** Publication-Poem-Teachers' Invitation to Writing 1983; appointed by Gov Jim Martin to serve on the Cabarrus Co Resource Council of Mt Pleasant Prison Unit, 1986; publ Invitation to Writing/Charlotte-Mecklenburg School System. **Home Addr:** 1216 Crossbow Circle, PO Box 5091, Concord, NC 28027, **Home Phone:** (704)782-2571.

ALSTON, DERRICK SAMUEL
Basketball player. **Personal:** Born Aug 20, 1972, Bronx, NY. **Educ:** Duquesne Univ. **Career:** Philadelphia 76ers, ctr, 1994-95; Atlanta Hawks, ctr, 1996-97; Boston Celtics, 2002; Ural Great Perm, forward; Caprabo Lleida, 2003-04; Turk Telekom BK, Ankara, Turkey, currently; NBL, New Zealand Breakers, currently. **Business Addr:** Professional Basketball Player, Turk Telekom BK, Ankara, Turkey.

ALSTON, FLOYD WILLIAM
School administrator, association executive. **Personal:** Born Oct 23, 1925, Brooklyn, NY; married Marilyn Deloris Baker; children: Craig E F & Marilyn Suzanne. **Educ:** Temple Univ, BS, bus admin, 1970; Fels Inst St & Local Govt, Univ Pa; Franklin Sch Sci & Arts, cert. **Career:** Sch administrator, association executive (retired); Philadelphia Housing Authority, housing mgr, 1958-68; Core St Bank NA, vpres community rel; First Pennsylvania Bank, vpres; HOPE Develop Corp, pres, 1968-73; Berean Federal Savings Bank, vice chair; Philadelphia Tribune Newspaper, treas & bd mem; Philadelphia Bd Educ, pres; Beech Interplex Inc, pres & chief exec officer, 1990. **Orgs:** Pres, Union Benevolent Assoc Found, 1979-; pres, JM Nursing Serv, 1980-85; vpres, Philadelphia Housing Develop Corp, 1982; pres, Comt Serv Planning Coun, 1982-84; nat vpres, actg exec dir, Frontiers Int Inc, 1984-; Philadelphia Tribune Charities, 1980-83; pres & dir, Tucker House Nursing; bd mem, Avenue of the Arts; treas, African Am Hist & Cultural Mus. **Honors/Awds:** Tribune Charities Chairman Award, Philadelphia Tribune Charities, 1983; Don Alexander Award, Nat Bankers Asn, 1978; DHL, Temple Univ, 2008. **Special Achievements:** Prentice-Hall article published "Helping Troubled Employees" 1978. **Military Serv:** USMC, sgt 1943-46, 1950-51. **Home Addr:** 108 Sedgwick St, Philadelphia, PA 19119, **Home Phone:** (215)848-5379.

ALSTON, GERALD
Singer. **Personal:** Born Nov 8, 1951, Henderson, NC; son of John and Geraldine Boyd; married Edna Chew, Jun 26, 1982; children: Kyle & Tod M. **Educ:** Kittrell Col. **Career:** New Imperials, mem; The Manhattans, lead singer, 1971-88; Motown band, singer; Albums: Where Did We Go Wrong, 1986; Gerald Alston, 1988; Open Invitation, 1990; Always in the Mood, 1992; First Class Only, 1994; Songs:"Devote All My Time"; "Stay the Night"; "Send for Me"; "Hell of a Situation"; "Getting Back into Love"; "Tell Me This Night Won't End";"Take Me Where You Want To"; "You Laid Your Love"; "Slow Motion". **Honors/Awds:** Grammy Winner for Shining Star, 1980. **Special Achievements:** Nominee, Am Music Award, 1980. *

ALSTON, DR. KATHY DIANE
Physician. **Personal:** Born Mar 29, 1958, Staten Island, NY. **Educ:** Univ Va, BA, 1980; Howard Univ Col Med, MD, 1984. **Career:** Martin Luther King Gen Hosp, physician, currently. **Orgs:** Asn Black Women Physicians, 1985-86; dorm coun, Joint Coun Interns & Residents, 1986-87. **Honors/Awds:** Nat Health Serv Corp Scholarship, 1980-83. **Home Addr:** 1540 Hunting Ave, McLean, VA 22102-2914. **Business Addr:** Physician, Martin Luther King Gen Hosp, 12021 So Wilmington Ave, Los Angeles, CA 90059.

ALSTON, KWAKU
Photographer, business owner. **Personal:** Born Feb 19, 1971, Philadelphia, PA. **Educ:** Rochester Inst Technol, BFA, 1994. **Career:** The New York Times Mag, rep music, entertaiment & adv; Kwaku Alston Photog Inc, Owner, currently. **Business Addr:** Owner, Kwaku Alston Photographer Inc, 1346 Abbot Kinney Blvd, Venice Beach, CA 90291, **Business Phone:** (310)392-9957.

AL'UQDAH, WILLIAM MUJAHID
Lawyer. **Personal:** Born Oct 29, 1953, Cincinnati, OH; son of William Henry Jones Sr and Helen G Jones; married Deborah, Oct 30, 1976; children: William M Ibn III, Shareefah N & Nadirah A. **Educ:** Univ Cincinnati, BS, 1982; Salmon P Chase Col Law, JD, 1987. **Career:** Hamilton Co Welfare Dept, prog adminr, 1974-88; Hamilton Co Prosecutors Off, asst dist atty, 1988-94; WCIN 1480 AM Radio, sports dir & air personality, 1992; Harmon, Davis & Keys Co, LPA, sr assoc, 1994-96; Lawson & Gaines, atty. **Orgs:** Pres, Black Law Student Asn Am, 1985-86; first exec dir, Black Male Coalition, 1988-89; Cincinnati Bar Asn; pres, Ohio Rep Coun, Cin, 1990. **Honors/Awds:** Scholarship, Black Prof, 1986. **Special Achievements:** When Going Gets Tough, Central State Univ Symposium, Welfare Reform, 1982; The Good, The Bad, and The Ugly, Criminal Justice State of Cincinnati, sponsored by Cincinnati Urban League, 1995. **Military Serv:** AUS, Infantry, Ohio Army Nat Guard, capt, 1979, Ohio Commendation Medal, 1990. **Home Phone:** (513)221-0690.

ALVES, PAGET L.
Executive. **Educ:** Cornell Univ, BS, indust & labor rels; Cornell Law Sch, JD. **Career:** IBM Corp, atty & sr mgr; Centennial Commun Corp, pres & chief oper officer; Sprint Commun, Bus Serv Group, pres sales & support, 1996-00; PointOne Telecommun, pres & chief exec officer, 2000-05; GTECH Holdings Corp, dir, 2005-; Strategic Markets, pres, currently. **Orgs:** Bd mem, Higher M-Pact. **Special Achievements:** "Top 50 Blacks in Corporate America", Black Enterprise, 2000. **Business Addr:** Director, GTECH Holdings Corp, 55 Technol Way, West Greenwich, RI 02817, **Business Phone:** (401)392-6980.

ALWAN, MANSOUR
Government official, engineer. **Personal:** Married; children: 5. **Career:** Chesilhurst, NJ, mayor, 1975-83, Electronic engr & consult, currently. **Orgs:** Adenu Allah Arabic Asn; Coalition Youth & Family Develop. **Honors/Awds:** Certified Network Administrator.

AMADO, JOSEPH S.
Executive, vice president (organization). **Personal:** Born in Yonkers, NY. **Educ:** Winston-Salem State Univ, BA. **Career:** Nestle; Philip Morris USA, comput analyst, 1986; Philip Morris USA, Louisville, Ky, systs supvr, 1989; Philip Morris USA, Louisville, Ky, info technol mgr, 1992; pioneer Philip Morris USA SAP Competency Ctr, 1994; pioneer Philip Morris USA SAP Competency Ctr, info technol dir info servs sales orgn, 1997; pioneer Philip Morris USA SAP Competency Ctr, info technol dir opers, 1998; Philip Morris USA's IT Orgn, exec sponsor, Col recruiting efforts, currently; Philip Morris USA, vpres, chief info officer, 2000-. **Orgs:** Bd dir, Greater Richmond Technol Coun; bd dir, Greater Richmond Chamber Found; bd dir, FRIENDS; bd dir, Asn Children, Richmond, VA; trustee, bd dir Winston-Salem State Univ, currently. **Business Addr:** Vice President, Chief Information Officer, Philip Morris USA, 120 Park Ave, New York, NY 10017, **Business Phone:** (212)880-5000.*

AMAKER, HAROLD TOMMY
Basketball coach, basketball player. **Personal:** Born Jun 6, 1965, Falls Church, VA. **Educ:** Univ Harvard, econ. **Career:** Basketball player (retired); Duke Univ, asst coach, 1988-97; Seton Hall Univ, head men's basketball coach, 1997-01; Univ Mich, head men's basketball coach, 2001-07; harvard Univ, coach, 2007-. **Orgs:** Black Coaches Asn. **Honors/Awds:** Gold Medal, FIBA World Basketball Championship, 1986; Gold Medal, World Championships, 1986; National Defensive Player of the Yr, 1987; Dr Martin Luther King Jr Awd, N Ward Ctr, 1998; Metro Coach of the Yr, 2000; Duke Circle of Honor. **Special Achievements:** First winner of the Henry Iba Corinthian Award. **Business Addr:** Head Coach, Harvard Uniersity, Men's Basketball Team, Holyoke Center 3rd Fl, 1350 Massachusetts Ave, Cambridge, MA 02138, **Business Phone:** (617)495-1000.*

AMAN, MARY JO
Educator. **Personal:** Born Sep 6, 1938, Postsmouth, OH; daughter of Ronald F and Goldia M Parker; married Mohammed, Sep 15, 1972; children: David. **Educ:** Fisk Univ, BA, 1960; Clark Atlanta Univ, MSLS, 1962. **Career:** Brooklyn Pub Libr, asst coordr, children's serv; Viking Press, dir, libr prom; Naussau Libr Syst, coordr, children's servs; Univ Wis, Milwaukee, bus librn, 1983-86; head, curric collection, 1986-98; outreach specialist, 1998-2001, dir, tech stud affairs, 2001, sr outreach specialist, Div Outreach & Continuing Edu, currently. **Orgs:** Am Libr Asn, 1962-; Wis Lib asn, Am libr Asn Coun, 1996-2000. **Business Addr:** Director, Senior Outreach Specialist, University Wisconsin-Milwaukee, Division Student Affairs, 2200 E Kenwood Blvd, PO Box 413, Milwaukee, WI 53201-0413, **Business Phone:** (414)229-1122.

AMAN, DR. MOHAMMED M.
School administrator, educator, library administrator. **Personal:** Born Jan 3, 1940, Alexandria, Egypt; son of Mohammed and Fathia Ali al-Maghrabi; married Mary Jo Parker, Sep 15, 1972; children: David. **Educ:** Cairo Univ Egypt, BA, 1961; Columbia Univ, MS, 1965; Univ Pittsburgh, PhD, 1968; NY Univ, post graduate studies. **Career:** Univ Pittsburgh, res asst, 1965-66; Duquesne Univ Pittsburgh, ref libr, 1966-68; Pratt Inst NY, asst prof; St Johns Univ NY, asst prof to assoc prof, 1969-73, dir & prof, 1973-76; Long Island Univ, Greenvale Long Island NY, dean & prof, 1976-79; Univ Wisc-Milwaukee, Sch Info studies, dean & prof, 1979-2002, dean emer & prof, 2002-; IT2000 MITEC Progs, prin investr & dir, 2000-05. **Orgs:** Egyptian Am Scholars Asn, 1971-; info mgt consult, UNIDO, 1978-; UNESCO, 1982-, US-AID, 1984-96; chmn, Int Rels Comt, Am Lib Asn, 1984-86; Asn Lib & Info Sci Ed, 1985-86; Am Soc Info Sci Int Rel Comt; chair, Int Issues Info Spec Interest Group; life mem & founding exec bd mem, NAACP 1984-; bd mem, Wisc African Relief Effort, 1986-89; bd mem, Wisc African Hist Soc Mus, 1988-91; Audience Develop Comt, Milwaukee Art Mus; founder, Milwaukee Leader's Forum, 1991-; bd mem, Am Black Holocaust Mus, 1998-2001; bd mem, Coun Eyptian-Am Rels, 2000-; bd mem, Clarah Mohammad Sch. **Honors/Awds:** Beta Phi Mu Int Lib & Info Sci Honor Soc; Award of Appreciation, Black Caucus Am Lib Asn, 1986; Award of Service, Asn Lib & Info Sci Educ, 1988; UNESCO consult on the Revival of the Alexandrian Lib Proj, 1988-01; John Ames Humphry OCLC-Forest Pres Award, Am Lib Asn, 1989; WLA Special Service Award, 1992; Leadership Award, Black Caucus Am Lib Asn, 1994; Award of Excellence, Black Caucus of The ALA, 1995; Prof Kaula Medal & Citation, 1996; Librarian of the Year, WLA, 1998; Appreciation Award, African Am Fac & Staff Asn, 2002; Award of Appreciation, Kuwait Authority Applied Educ & Training, 2005; Award from UWM African American Faculty & Staff Association (AAFSA). **Special Achievements:** Contributing consult: Int Lib Rev, 1969-91; Librarianship in the Third World, 1976; Arab Serials & Periodicals, 1979; Cataloging & Classification of Non-Western Lib Material, 1980; Cataloging & Classification of Non-Western Lib Material, 1980; Developing Comput Based Lib Syst, 1984; Online Access to Database 1984; Info Servs, 1986; UNESCO consult Revival of the Alexandrian Lib Proj, 1988-01; Urban Lib Mgt, 1990; The Gulf War in World Lit, 1990-2000, 2004; author, ed-in-chief, Digest of Middle E Studies (DOMES), 1991-; Info Tech, 1999; use of Internet in Libs & Info Ctrs, 2000; Info Tech in Libs, 2005. **Business Addr:** Dean Emeritus, Professor, University of Wisconsin-Milwaukee, School of Information Studies, Bolton Hall Rom 560, Milwaukee, WI 53201, **Business Phone:** (414)229-3315.

AMARO, RUBEN, SR.
Baseball manager, baseball executive, baseball player. **Personal:** Born Jan 7, 1936, Veracruz, Mexico; married Judy, 1988 (divorced); children: David & Ruben Jr; married Lilia, 1988; children: Luis Alfredo & Ruben Andres. **Career:** Baseball player (retired), baseball coach (retired), baseball exec; St Louis Cardinals, 1958; Philadelphia Phillies, shortstop, 1960-65, coach

minor leagues, 1970-71, scout, 1972-74, Latin Am, coordr, asst to Dallas Green, Minor Leagues of Scouting, dir, 1974-77, scout develop supvr, 1977-79, minor league coach, 1980-81, scout, 1982; NY Yankees, shortstop, 1966-68; Calif Angels, shortstop, 1969; Chicago Cubs, coach, 1982-87, caribbean area scout, 1988; Detroit Tigers, scout, 1989-96; Chicago Cubs, minor league mgr. **Orgs:** Mem of Chicago Cubs. **Honors/Awds:** Nat League Gold Glove, shortstop work, 1964. **Special Achievements:** Guided Zulia to Venezuelan League title, Caribbean World Series Championship. *

AMBEAU, KAREN M
Marketing executive. **Personal:** Born Jul 4, 1956, Berkeley, CA; daughter of Mildred Anthony and Lucien; married Michael McClendon, Aug 7, 1983. **Educ:** Tuskegee Univ, Tuskegee, AL, BSEE, 1981. **Career:** Pacific Gas & Electric, Hayward, CA, acct rep, 1981-. **Orgs:** McGee Ave Church Educ Aid, 1982-; corresp sect, Delta Sigma Theta Sorority, 1987-89, chairperson & fundraiser, 1990; Bus Prof Women's Club, 1987-90; dir, All Seasons Youth Ski Club. **Honors/Awds:** Outstanding Young Careerist, Bus & Prof Womens, 1987; Miss Tuskegee, Tuskegee Univ, 1977. **Business Addr:** Marketing Supervisor, Pacific Gas & Electric Co, 245 Market St Rm 385 E, San Francisco, CA 94105-1126.

AMBERS, MONIQUE
Basketball player, basketball coach. **Personal:** Born Dec 21, 1970, Hayward, CA; daughter of Robert and Linda. **Educ:** Ariz State Col, BS, child develop, 1993. **Career:** Basketball player (retired), basketball coach: George Wash Univ, asst coach, 1994-97; Phoenix Mercury, forward, 1997; Sacramento Monarchs, forward, 2002, asst coach, currently. **Business Addr:** Assistant Coach, Sacramento Monarchs, 1 Sports Pkwy, Sacramento, CA 95834, **Business Phone:** (916)928-0000.*

AMBROSE, ASHLEY AVERY
Football player. **Personal:** Born Sep 17, 1970, New Orleans, LA; married Monica. **Educ:** Miss Valley State. **Career:** Indianapolis Colts, defensive end, 1992-95; Cincinnati Bengals, 1996-98; New Orleans Saints, 1999, 2003-04; Atlanta Falcons, 2000-02. **Honors/Awds:** All-Pro Team, Assoc Press, 1996; AFC Defensive Back of the Year, NFL Players Assn, 1996. *

AMBROSE, ETHEL L.
Government official, social worker. **Personal:** Born Dec 18, 1930, Perryville, AR; divorced; children: Ethel M Harris, Derek S Brown & Lakeitha Brown. **Educ:** Highland Park Community Col, attended 1975; Southeastern Univ, BS, sociol,1980. **Career:** Government official, social worker (retired); Univ Mich, licensed social worker, 1973; City Highland Park, spec asst mayor, 1969-76; Detroit Adult Ed, substitute teacher, 1978-79; Diversified Health Ctr, social worker, 1979-80; Alpha Annex Nursing Ctr, social worker. **Orgs:** Citizen Interest Scholar Comt, 1967-; life mem, Highland Park Caucus Club,1973-; bd pres, Wayne Metrop Community Servs Agency, 1983-84; trustee,Highland Park Bd Ed/ Community Col, 1983-; pres, ACCT Minorities Affairs/Cent Region, 1984-; Nat Polit Cong Black Women, 1984; sr aide, Healthier Black Elders Ctr, Mich Ctr Urban African Am Aging Res, Wayne State Univ.

AMDERSON, GARY
Artistic director, theatrical producer. **Educ:** Wayne State Univ, BFA, MFA, directing. **Career:** Plays: Woza Albert; Zooman & the Sign; Pill Hill; The Piano Lesson; Buses; I Am A Man; Two Trains Running; Plowshares Theatre Co, co-founder & producing artistic dir, 1989-; BTN's Black Voices, ed, 1990-94; Nat Conf African Am Theatre, 1991-92; Theatre Commun Group, vpres, 2004-06, bd dir, currently. **Orgs:** Dana Found. **Honors/Awds:** Detroit Free Press's Lawrence DeVine Award, 2000; Michiganian of the Year Award, Detroit News, 2003. **Business Addr:** Co-Founder, Producing Artistic Director, Plowshares Theatre Company, 2870 E Grand Blvd Suite 600, Detroit, MI 48202-3146, **Business Phone:** (313)872-0279.*

AMENKHIENAN, DR. CHARLOTTE
Counselor. **Personal:** Born Nov 15, 1958, Warri, Bendel, Nigeria. **Career:** VA Polytech Inst & State Univ, staff counr, currently.

AMERICA, RICHARD F.
Educator. **Personal:** Son of Richard F Sr and Arline America; married Diane Salin. **Educ:** Pa State Univ, BS, 1960; Harvard Univ, MBA, 1965. **Career:** Univ Calif, Lectr & Dir; Visiting Lectr at Stanford Business Sch; Georgetown Univ, McDonough Sch Bus, exec prof lectr, currently.

AMIE, GWEN E
School administrator. **Personal:** Born May 5, 1956, Las Vegas, NV; children: Justina. **Educ:** Univ Nev, Las Vegas, BS, Ed, 1978, master in coun, 1982; Nat Univ, MAdmin, 1986. **Career:** CCSD, math teacher, 1979-85, counselor, 1985-92, dean of students, 1992-97, asst principal, 1997-; Nat Bowling Asn Inc, chairperson, 2003; Sierra Vista High Sch, asst prin, currently. **Orgs:** Delta Sigma Theta, 1976-; Western regional tournament comn, Nat Bowling Asn, 1980-, nat scholarship chair, 1999-; Western States Golf Asn, 1986-; Nat Asn Secondary Sch Prin, 1992-; Clark Co Asn Sch Admin, 1992-; debutante advisory comn, Les Femmes Douzer, 1996-; bd mem, Southern Nev Bowling Asn, 2000-. **Honors/Awds:** Service Award, Delta Sigma Theta, 1982; Leadership Support Award, Las Vegas Indian Educ, 1992; Big Dog Award, Las Vegas Stealth Track Club, 1996. **Business Addr:** Assistant Principal, Sierra Vista High School, 8100 W Robindale Rd, Las Vegas, NV 89113, **Business Phone:** (702)799-6820.

AMIJI, HATIM M.
Educator. **Personal:** Born Jun 11, 1939, Zanzibar. **Educ:** London, BA, Hons, 1964; Princeton Univ, MA, PhD. **Career:** Trinity Coll Nabingo, Uganda, lectr, 1964; Princeton Univ, lectr, 1969-70; Nairobi Univ, Kenya, res assoc hist, 1967-68; Boston Univ, lectr, Dept Hist & Centre African Studies, 1972; Univ Mass, assoc prof hist. **Orgs:** Sec gen Zanzibar Youth League, 1960; dir, African Studies Workshop WorldAffairs Coun, Boston, 1972; mem, Middle Eastern Studies Assoc; fel, African Acad; African Studies Assoc, US; ed bd, Gemini Rev; founder & mem, Pan-African Univ Org. **Honors/Awds:** E African Railways & Harbours Res Award, 1963; Rockefeller Found Fellow,1965-67; Princeton Univ, Fel, 1969-70; Zanzibar Govt Scholar, 1961-64; Superior Merit Awd Univ MA. **Special Achievements:** Auth: The Bohras of East Africa. **Business Addr:** Associate Professor, University of Massachusetts, Department of History, Harbor Campus, Boston, MA 02125.

AMIN, KARIMA (CAROL ANN AIKEN)
Educator, storyteller, writer. **Personal:** Born Jun 1, 1947, Buffalo, NY; daughter of Harvey and Bessie Mabry; married; children: Abdur Rahman, Takiyah Nur & Sabriyah. **Educ:** State Univ NY, Buffalo, BA, eng, 1969, MEd, urban educ, 1974. **Career:** Buffalo Pub Schs, teacher, lang arts sec, 1969-92, multicultural lit specialist, 1992-94; prof storyteller & auth, 1994-. **Orgs:** Treas & secy, Taara Zakkiyya Islamic Strhd, 1975-82; Nat Coun Teachers Eng, 1982-86; bd dir, Afro-Am Historical Asn Niagara Frontier, 1984-86; co-founder, Spin-a-Story Tellers Western NY, 1984-; Nat Storytelling Network, 1984-; Nat Asn Black Storytellers, 1985-; We All Storytellers, 1987-; Nat Comn Storytelling, 1987-90; Comn Preservation Multicultural Lit Am, 1988-90; consult, Project Reach, 1989-; bd dirs, Epic Nat, 1994-; nat adv bd, MacMillan McGraw-Hill Publ, 1994-96; 50 Women Vision Inc, 1996-; Tradition Keepers: Black Storytellers WNY, 1996-; bd dir, Squeaky Wheel Media Arts Org, 1999-; bd mem, Crossroads Storytelling Ctr, 2003-. **Honors/Awds:** Black Educators of the Year, Black Educators Asn WNY, 1977; Teacher of Tomorrow Award, Buffalo Bd Ed, 1978; William Wells Brown Award, Afro-Am Historical Asn, 1984; Award, Eng Speaking Union WNY, 1986; Achievement Award, Nat Asn Negro Bus & Prof Women's Clubs, 1994; Apple for the Teacher Award, Iota Phi Lambda Sorority Inc, Beta Phi Chap, 1994; Community Service Award, Alpha Kappa Alpha, 1997; Outstanding Artist Award, Alpha Kappa Alpha, 2000; Community Leadership Award, Niagra Univ, 2001; Daisy Lampkin Award, Links Inc Eastern Region, 2001; Uncrowned Queen Award, Pan-Am Exposition, 2001; Storytelling World Winner Award, 2006. **Special Achievements:** Co-wrote Black Lit for HS Studs, NCTE, 1978; Publ: You Can Say That Again!, Galactic Multimedia, 1994; Brer Rabbit, Dorling-Kendersley, 1999; contributor, African Am Children's Stories: A Treasury of Tradition and Pride, 2001; My First Treasury: Grandma Loves You, 2003. **Home Addr:** 103 Fernhill Ave, Buffalo, NY 14215. **Business Addr:** Story Teller, PO Box 273, Buffalo, NY 14212, **Business Phone:** (716)834-8438.

AMMONS, DR. JAMES H.
Educator. **Personal:** Son of James Henry and Agnes Ammons; married Judy Riffin; children: James III. **Educ:** Fla A&M Univ, BS, polit sci, 1974; Fla State Univ, MS, pub admin, 1975,PhD, govt, 1977. **Career:** Univ Cent Fla, asst prof pub policy & admin, 1977-83; Fla A&M Univ, asst prof polit sci, 1983-84, asst vpres acad affairs, 1984-89, assoc vpres, dir, 1989-93, prof, 1993-95, provost, vpres acad affairs, 1995; Univ Wis, Madison, Booth Ferris fel, 1993; NC Cent Univ, chief adminr, chancellor, 2001-07; Florida A&M Univ, chancellor, currently. **Orgs:** Fel Am Coun Educ, 1986-87; CIGNA Found, 1986-87; Comn Col Southern Asn Col& Sch; Am Asn State Col & Univ Task Force; Joint Comn Accountability Reporting; chair compliance & report comt, Comt Col Coun Advan & Support Educ. **Honors/Awds:** Named Distinguished Alumni, Fla A&M State Univ, 1999; Citizen of the Year,Beta Phi chap, Omega Psi Phi, Durham, 2002. **Business Addr:** Chancellor, North Carolina Central University, Hoey Admin Bldg 1801 Fayetteville St, Durham, NC 27707, **Business Phone:** (919)530-6104.

AMORY, REGINALD L
Educator, engineer, chairperson. **Personal:** Born Jul 17, 1936, Peekskill, NY; married Marion Rose Boothe; children: Reginald & Susan. **Educ:** New York Univ, BCE, 1960; Clarkson Univ, MCE, 1963; Rensselaer Polytech Inst, PhD, 1967. **Career:** Throop & Feiden, engr, 1960-61; Abbott, Jerkt & Co, engr, 1961-63; RPI, tech asst, 1963-64, instr, 1965-66; NC Agri & Tech Univ, dean, 1968-74; Northeastern Univ, Dept Civil Eng, asst prof, 1966-68, prof, 1974-; Morgan State Univ, Dept Civil Eng, prof & chair, currently. **Orgs:** Consultant to numerous organizations including: GE Co; MSF; B&M Tech Servs; US Dept Energy; Education Develop Corp; Nat Acad Engineering; SC Commn Higher Educ; Tenn State Univ; Mobil Oil Co; Robert Charles Assoc; proj bd, vpres, exec bd, Am Soc Engr Educ; fel Am Soc Civil Engrs; Int Asn Bridge & Structural Engrs; Nat Soc Prof Engrs; AAAS; bd trustees, St Augustine's Col; adv bd, Nat Urban League; Sigma Psi Phi; Lambda Alpha Int Hon Soc. **Honors/Awds:** Excellence Award, NC A&T State Univ, 1972; Engineer of Distinction, Joint Eng Coun, 1973; Alumni Achievement Award, RPI, 1977; University of Cambridge, visiting scholar, 1983; Alcoa Foundation Professorship, Northeastern Univ; Nat Science Honor Society; Maryland Civil Engineering Educator of the Year Award, 1999. **Special Achievements:** First African-American to receive a Ph.D. in engineering from Rensselaer Polytechnic Institute. **Business Addr:** Professor, Chair, Morgan State University School of Engineering, Department of Civil Engineering, 1700 E Cold Spring Lane, Baltimore, MD 21251, **Business Phone:** (443)885-4220.

AMOS, DONALD E
Lawyer. **Personal:** Born Aug 2, 1953, Buffalo, NY; son of Edward Amos Jr and Ann; divorced; children: Sharnele, Lauren & Amber. **Educ:** Chicago State Univ, BS, 1975; DePaul Univ, JD, 1984. **Career:** US EPA Off Inspector Gen, spec agent, currently. **Business Addr:** Special Agent, US EPA Off Inspector General, Washington, DC 20024, **Business Phone:** (703)347-8741.

AMOS, JOHN
Actor. **Personal:** Born Dec 27, 1939, Newark, NJ; son of John Amos Sr and Annabelle P; married Noel J Mickelson, Jan 1, 1965 (divorced 1975); children: 2; married Elisabete De Sousa; children: 2; married Lillian Lehman, Feb 12, 1978 (divorced 1979); children: 2. **Educ:** Colo State Univ. **Career:** Social worker; advert copywriter; TV series: "Mary Tyler Moore", 1970-77; "The District", 2000; "All About the Andersons", 2003; "Men in Trees, 2006; "My Name Is Earl", 2008; films: Touched by Love, 1980; The Beastmaster, 1982; Am Flyers, 1985; Coming to Am, 1988; Lock Up, 1989; Die Hard 2, 1990; Ricochet, 1991; Clippers, 1991; Mac, 1992; Night Trap, 1993; The Black Cat, 1993; Hologram Man, 1995; For Better or Worse, 1996; A Woman Like That, 1997; The Player's Club, 1998; All Over Again, 2001; The Watermelon Heist, 2003; My Baby's Daddy, 2004; Lichnyy nomer, 2004; Boy s tenyu, 2005; Voodoo Moon, 2005; Dr. Dolitttle 3, 2006; Ascension Day, 2007; Tamales and Gumbo, 2008. **Honors/Awds:** Golden Gloves boxing champion; Groundbreaking Show, 2004; Impact Award, 2006; Anniversary Award, TV Land Awards, 2007. **Business Addr:** Actor, c/o Michael Mesnick & Associates, 11300 Olympic Blvd Suite 610, Los Angeles, CA 90064.*

AMOS, KENT B.
Association executive. **Personal:** Born May 21, 1944, Washington, DC; son of Benjamin F and Gladys C; married Carmen. **Educ:** DE State Col, BS, 1970. **Career:** Xerox Corp, sales mgr, 1975-76, area mgr, 1976-77, mgr ISG Affirm Action, 1977-78, dir corp affirm action, EEO, 1978-82; pres, The Triad Group; Community Acad Pub Charter Sch, founder & acad leader, currently; Urban Family Inst, pres & founder, currently. **Orgs:** Alpha Kappa Mu Nat Hon Soc, 1968-69; Corp Few, 1971-79; Big Bros, 1971-74; Inside & Outside, 1972-; bus consult, Cong Black Caucus, 1975-79; Bus Policy Rev Comn, 1977-79; NAACP; Nat Urban League; Nat Coun Negro Women; Del State Col Alumni Asn; Coolidge High Sch Alumni Asn; Omega Psi Phi; bd dirs, Boys & Girls Club of Greater Wash, 1990-; adv bd mem, I Have a Dream Found, 1990-. **Honors/Awds:** Black Hist Week Awards, WMAL Radio & TV Sta, 1974; Merit Awards for Job Performance, Xerox Corp; Pres Sales Recognition Award, Xerox Corp; Chair's Award, Cong Black Caucus, 1979; Nat Asn Equal Oppportunity Higher Educ; Legacy Award, Nat Coun Negro Women; Image Award, NAACP; Whitney Young Award, Urban League; Roy Dykes Mem Award, Xerox Corp; Citizen of the Yr, Omega Psi Phi; Man of the Yr, Shiloh Baptist Church; Alumnus of the Century, Delaware State Col; Alumnus of the Yr, Calvin Coolidge High Sch; Alumnus of the Yr, Del State Col; scholar funds created in his name at Calvin Coolidge High Sch & Del State Col; Annual Serv Youth Award, Big Brothers Nat Capea, 1990; Thanksgiving Tuesday Award, Distinguished Community Serv, Catholic Univ Am & Madison Natl Bank, 1990. **Military Serv:** AUS, lt, 1964-71; numerous Vietnam Decorations, 1970. **Business Phone:** (202)234-5437.*

AMOS, RALPH
Executive director. **Educ:** Ohio State Univ, BS, 1986; Ohio Univ, MPA, 2004. **Career:** Ohio State Univ, Alumni Asn, staff, 1990-98; Ohio Univ, Off alumni rel, asst vpres & exec dir, 1998-2007; Univ Calif, Los Angeles, Alumni Asn, exec dir, 2007-, External Affairs, asst vice chancellor alumni rel, 2007-. **Business Phone:** (310)794-2345.

AMPREY, WALTER G
Executive, consultant. **Personal:** Born Dec 13, 1944, Baltimore, MD; son of Joseph L Sr and Marion A; married Andrea Marie Qualls; children: Kimberley & Keli. **Educ:** Morgan State Col, BA, 1966, MS, hist & soc sci, 1971; John Hopkins Univ, MS, educl admin & supv, 1977; Temple Univ, PhD, 1984. **Career:** Woodlawn Senior High Sch, from asst prin to prin, 1973-84; Calverton Jr High Sch, Woodlawn Senior High Sch, from asst prin to prin,

1973-84; Calverton Jr High Sch, teacher, 1966-71; Walbrook Sr High Sch, teacher, 1971, sch admin, 1971-73, asst prin, 1973-78, prin, 1978-84; Greenwood Baltimore County Pub Schs, dir, chief negotiator, office staff rels, 1984-85; Baltimore County Pub Schs, div f physical facil, assoc supt, 1985-90, assoc supt, div staff & community res, 1991, supt, pub instr, 1991; 4GL Sch Solutions, sr adv, currently; Nat Sch Conf Inst, nat vpres; KimKeli Group, pres; Defywire, chmn, currently; Wireless Generation Inc, adv bd; Amprey & Assoc, pres; KimKeli Group, pres, currently. **Orgs:** Bd dirs, Municipal Employees Credit Union; bd dirs, Nat Aquarium, Baltimore; bd trustees, Baltimore Mus Art; bd trustees, NW Hosp Ctr; Md State Teachers Asn; exec, Nat Asn Black Sch; admin, Nat Asn Sec Sch Admin; Asn Supv & Curric Developers; admin, Am Asn Sch; Phi Alpha Theta; Omega Psi Phi, grand keeper records & seal, 1982-84; bd dirs, Nat Ctr Educ Res & Technol, 2004-; New Shiloh Baptist Church, Baltimore, MD; bd mem, Assoc Black Charities; bd trustees, Villa Julie Col. **Honors/Awds:** Omega Man of the Year, Omega Psi Phi, 1971; Maryland Superintendent of the Year, 1994-95. **Business Addr:** Chairman, Defywire Inc, 11800 Sunrise Valley Dr Suite 1135, Reston, VA 20191.

AMPY, DR. FRANKLIN R.
Educator. **Personal:** Born Jun 22, 1936, Dinwiddie, VA; son of Preston Ampy and Beatrice Tucker Ampy. **Educ:** Va State Col, Petersburg, BS, 1958; Ore State Univ, Corvallis, MS, PhD, biostatistics & genetics, 1962; Univ Calif, post doctorate, 1970. **Career:** Am Univ Beirut, asst prof, Lebanon, 1962-68; Univ Calif, Davis, postdoctorate, 1968-70, Educ Oppor Prog, assoc dean, 1970-71; Howard Univ, assoc prof zoology, Wash, 1971-, acting chmn zoology, 1973-75, 1984-86; Ore State Univ, Corvallis, res asst, 1958-62; Howard Univ, prof biol, 2003-, Interim Chmn, currently. **Orgs:** Evaluator, Va Talent Search, 1980-; consult, Nat Inst Health, 1981, 1983; treas, Howard Chapter Am Assoc Univ Prof, 1983-84; Project Thirty, Carnegie Found NY, comm. **Honors/Awds:** Geneticist World Poultry Con Kiev Russia, 1966; Faculty Fellow NASA Am Moffett Fields, 1976; Fulbright Nominee, Nat Coun Scholars 1984-85. **Business Addr:** Professor, Interim Chairman, Howard University, Department of Biology, 415 Col St NW, Washington, DC 20059, **Business Phone:** (202)806-6952.

ANASAZI, TYR. See COBB, KEITH HAMILTON.

ANCRUM, ALBERTA E.
Municipal government official, police chief. **Career:** City NY, Dept Invest, spec investgr, 2001, Inspector Gen Office, dep inspector gen, chief staff, currently. **Business Addr:** Chief of Staff, Office of the Inspector General, City of New York, Department of Investigations, 80 Maiden Lane 16th Fl, New York, NY 10038, **Business Phone:** (212)825-2467.*

ANDERS, KIMBLE LYNARD
Football player, football coach. **Personal:** Born Sep 10, 1966, Galveston, TX. **Educ:** Univ Houston, attended. **Career:** Football player (retired), football coach; Kans City Chiefs, running back, 1991-00; Avila Univ, running back coach; Mid America Nazarene Univ, running back coach, 2006; head football coach, Northeast H.S, 2009-. **Honors/Awds:** Unsung Hero achievement award, 1997. *

ANDERS, RICHARD H.
Educator. **Personal:** Born Jul 29, 1925, Arcadia, FL; son of James Anders and Nettie Anders; married Charlotte King; children: Kenneth, Keith & Rosalind. **Educ:** Fla A&M Univ, BS, 1947; Ind Univ, MS, 1963. **Career:** Dunbar High Sch, Ft Myers, athletic dir coach, 1947-48; Richardson HighSch, Lake City, 1948-69; Part time city recreation asst, 1968-; ColumbiaHigh Sch, suprv educ health, 1973-75, dir, 1970-. **Orgs:** Vpres, Columbia Educ Asn, 1974-75; secy, Gateway Serv Unit, Fla Educ Asn,1974-75; adv bd, N Cent Fla Phys Educ Clin, 1970-; CEA Exec Bd; pres, Fla A&M Alumni Gateway Chap Lake City, 1974-; Polemarch GainesvilleAlumni,Chap Kappa Alpha Psi Frat, 1968-69, 1972-73, pres, 1989-91; Lake City Optimist Club; Emerg Med Training Comt; Versiteers Soc Club; Masonic Fraternal Order Shiloh 619; chorister New Bethel Bapt Ch; pres, 1990-; Columbia County Sch Bd, chmn, 1988, 1992-. **Honors/Awds:** Football Championships, 1947, 1951, 1953, 1959, 1963-65; runner up, 1955-56,1961-62; Coach of Yr Awd, 1963, 1966; Life Mem Award, FL Athletic Coaches Asn 1970; Fla Interscholastic Coaches Asn Award, 1967; Music DirTrophy, 1974; Versiteers Presidential Award, Versiteers Club, 1987-89; SABO Serv Award, Sothern Asn Basketball Official, 1991; Educ AchievementAward, NAACP, 1985; Achievement Award, Girl Scout Troop 117, 1989; Kappa Founders Day Award, Kappa Alpha Psi Fraternity, 1991. **Business Addr:** Intramural Director, Columbia HS, Lake City, FL 32055.*

ANDERSON, ABBIE H.
Military leader, administrator. **Personal:** Born Jun 3, 1928, Terrell, TX; son of James C and Abbie Gill; married Frances R Morgan; children: Donna R, Rosalind T, Abbie H Jr & Michael EC. **Educ:** Tuskegee Inst, BS, 1953; Lincoln Univ, MO, MEd, 1966. **Career:** Brigade exec officer; Vietnamese Chief of Reg Forces, Popular Forces, dist sr adv; asst prof military sci; mem gen staff, chief auto weapons sec; marksmanship Unit, co comdr; rifle platoon leader & weapons & platoon leader, co exec officer; US Army, ret Lt Col sect leader; NY Life Ins Co, ins salesman; Terrell Ind Sch Dist, pres, currently. **Orgs:** Dallas Asn Life Underwriters, 1971-; pres, Am Heart Asn Kaufman County, 1983-85; Nat Asn Advan Colored People; treas, Tuskegee Alumni Club Dallas,; sch bd mem, Terrell Ind Sch Dist; bd mem, Rosehill Water Coop; Cath Ch; Omega Psi Phi Frat; grand knight Father Vincius Coun 6887 Knights Columbus; chmn bd, Jackson Comm Hosp; bd mem, Terrell Comm Hosp. **Honors/Awds:** Rookie of the Year, NY Life Ins Co. **Military Serv:** AUS, lt col, over 24 years; Repub of Vietnam Campaign Medal; Meritorious Serv Medal; Bronze Star; Combat Infantryman's Badge; Armed Forces Honor & Medal First Class Vietnam; Army Occup Medal, Ger; Nat Def Medal & First Oak Leaf Cluster; Armed Forces Res Medal; Vietnam Serv Medal. **Business Addr:** President, Terrell Independent School District, 700 N Catherine St, Terrell, TX 75160.*

ANDERSON, REV. DR. AL H
Entrepreneur, marketing executive. **Personal:** Born May 1, 1942, Winston-Salem, NC; son of Albert H Sr and Gladys H; married Jeanette Robbins, Nov 25, 1971; children: April & Albert H. **Educ:** Morehouse Col, BS, 1964; Rutgers Univ, 1971. **Career:** C&S Nat Bank, mgt trainee, 1967-68; Citizens Trust Bank, vpres, 1968-70; Entreprises Now Inc, exec dir, 1970-72; Anderson Commun, chief exec officer, foundER & chmn, 1971-. **Orgs:** Vpres, Black Pub Rels Soc; African-Am Mkt & Media Asn; Nat Asn Mkt Developers; pres, Am Med Team Africa; chmn & founder, Black Health Now. **Honors/Awds:** Outstanding Agency Award, honorary Doctorate Degree, AAF. **Special Achievements:** Speaker at numerous seminars, univs & confs. creator of the three award winning nationally syndicated programs: "Inspirations Across America", a two-hour weekly program of contemporary gospel music which is currently aired in more than 107 cities; "Focus on Women" a daily program that addresses issues affecting African-American women; & "Power Minutes". **Business Addr:** Cheif Executive Officer, Chairman, Founder, Anderson Communications Inc, 2245 Godby Rd, Atlanta, GA 30349, **Business Phone:** (404)766-8000.

ANDERSON, ALFRED ANTHONY
Executive. **Personal:** Born Aug 4, 1961, Waco, TX. **Educ:** Baylor Univ. **Career:** Minn Vikings, running back, 1984-92; Gen Nutrit Ctr, owner, 1993-; AAA Sports Mgt, pres. **Orgs:** Arlington S Rotary Club; Optimist Club; Baylor Alumni Orgn. **Honors/Awds:** Played in NFC Championship Game, post-1987 season; NFC Offensive Rookie of the Year, 1984-85. **Business Addr:** President, AAA Sports Management, 4101 W Green Oaks Blvd Suite 305, No 531, Arlington, TX 76016.*

ANDERSON, DR. AMEL
School administrator. **Personal:** Born Nov 17, 1936, Hazlehurst, MS; children: Reynaldo, Terrence & Robert. **Educ:** Jackson State Univ, BS, 1962; Univ Houston, MS, 1969; Va Polytech Inst & State Univ, EdD, 1976. **Career:** Sch administrator (retired); Va Polytech Inst State Univ, res asst, 1975-76; Univ Md Div Agr & Life Sci, asst to the provost, 1976-86; Univ Md, Jr Sci & Humanities Symp, asst dean. **Orgs:** NSF fel, Univ Houston, 1967; vol & instr, Receiving Home C Wash, DC,1977-79; pres, Jackson State Univ Alumni Chap, 1978-79; pres, PTA Happy Acres Elem Sch, 1978-80; Md Asn Coun & Develop, 1980-81. **Honors/Awds:** Civitan Jackson, MS, 1960. **Military Serv:** USAF, capt, 1964-75.

ANDERSON, AMELIA VERONICA
Marketing executive. **Personal:** Born Mar 13, 1947, New York, NY; daughter of Howard A and Bernardine Turbee Grissom. **Educ:** Bernard M Baruch Col, BBA, 1969. **Career:** Bloomingdales, dept mgr & personnel rep, 1967-74; Essence Mag, dir sales prom & merchandising, 1974-83; Playboy Enterprises Inc, Games Mag, prom mgr, 1983-84, Playboy Mag, prom mgr, 1985-87; Mary Gilliatt Interiors Ltd, design asst & off mgr, 1987-88; Anderson-Rooke Designs, partner, 1988-90; AVA Co, owner, 1991; Times Mirror mag, promotion mgr, corp sales, 1993-96; Creative Health Concepts, mkt dir. **Honors/Awds:** CEBA Award Excellence, 1980; Outstanding Achievements Commun, BESI Inc, 1982; CEBA Award Merit, 1983; CEBA Award Excellence, 1983. *

ANDERSON, ANTHONY
Actor. **Personal:** Born Aug 15, 1970, Los Angeles, CA; son of Dora; married Alvina; children: 2. **Educ:** Hollywood High Sch Performing Arts Ctr; Howard Univ. **Career:** Films: Life, 1999; Trippin', 1999; Liberty Heights, 1999; Romeo Must Die, 1999; Big Momma's House, 2000; Urban Legends: Final Cut, 2000; Me Myself & Irene, 2000; Kingdom Come, 2001; See Spot Run, 2001; Exit Wounds, 2001; Two Can Play That Game, 2001; Barbershop, 2002; Kangaroo Jack, 2003; Cradle 2 the Grave, 2003; Malibu's Most Wanted, 2003; Scary Movie 3, 2003; My Baby's Daddy, 2004; King's Ransom, 2005; The Departed, 2006; The Last Stand, 2006; Transformers, 2007; Steppin: The Movie, 2009; TV series: "Hang Time", 1995; "All About the Andersons", 2003; "Veronica Mars", 2005; "The Shield", 2005; "Campus Ladies", 2006; "'Til Death", 2006; "K-Ville", 2007; "Samantha Who?", 2008; "Law & Order", 2008-09. **Honors/Awds:** Acapulco Black Film Festival, Rising Star Award, 2001; Black Movie Award, 2005; National Board Review Award, 2006. **Home Addr:** 17133 Albers St, Encino, CA 91316. **Business Addr:** Actor, William Morris Agency, 17328 Ventura Blvd, PO Box 185, Encino, CA 91316.*

ANDERSON, ANTONIO (ANTONIO KENNETH ANDERSON)
Football player. **Personal:** Born Jun 4, 1973, Brooklyn, NY. **Educ:** Syracuse Univ. **Career:** Football player (retired), football player coach; Dallas Cowboys, defensive tackle, 1997-98; Dallas Cowboys Hempstead High Sch, Long Island, NY, coach, 2004-. **Honors/Awds:** All Rookie, Pro Football Weekly, 1997. *

ANDERSON, ARNETT ARTIS
Dentist. **Personal:** Born Apr 1, 1931, Georgia; married Delores C Perry; children: Angela C, Andrea C. **Educ:** Savannah State Col, BS, 1953; Grad Sch, Howard Univ, attended 1957; Howard Univ, DDS 1962; Univ Mich, MS, 1965. **Career:** Inst Health, nutrit & endocrinol res, 1956-58; Howard Univ, cardiovasc res part-time, 1960-62, pedodontics & instr, 1962-63; Children's Orthodontic Clin, Livonia, MI, dir, 1964-65; Howard Univ Col Dent, assoc prof, 1965-69; Pvt Pract, Wash DC, dentist, 1966-. **Orgs:** Orthodontic consult, Community Group Health found, St Elizabeth Hosp Wash, DC; NE Regional Bd Dent Examr; DC Bd Dent Examr; Am Asn Orthodontists; Middle Atlantic Soc Orthodontists; Am Col Dent; Am Asn Dent Examr; Nat Dent Asn; Am Dent Asn; Int Asn Dent Res, Am Soc Dent C; Robert T Freeman Dent Soc; SW Neighborhood Assembly; Alpha Phi Alpha Fraternity; Omicron Kappa Upsilon Nat Hon Dent Soc; Sigma Xi Hon Sci Soc; Beta Kappa Chi; Alpha Kappa Mu. **Honors/Awds:** Best Thesis Award, Univ Mich Sch Orthodontics, C Edward Martin Award, 1965; First Place, Int competition Dent Res Edward H Hetton Award, 1966. **Military Serv:** AUS. **Business Addr:** Dentist, 635 G St SW, Washington, DC 20024.*

ANDERSON, AVIS OLIVIA
Educator. **Personal:** Born Aug 27, 1949, Vivian, WV; daughter of Harvey Fails and Naomi T Fails; married Weldon Edward Anderson. **Educ:** Bronx Community Col, AAS, 1970; Herbert H Lehman Col, BS, 1971; Hunter Col, MS, 1973; New York Univ, PhD, 1986. **Career:** Bronx Community Col, Col lab tech, 1971-72; Herbert H Lehman Col, adjunct instr, 1972-73; LaGuardia Community Col, full time instr, 1973-75; asst, assoc, full prof ,1975-. **Orgs:** Morrisania Educ Coun, 1972-; exec bd mem, Bus Educ Assoc, 1978-; pres, Col Bus Educators, 1981-82; Charismatic Prayer Group, 1985-; Conf Coordr, SUNY Off Tech & Secretarial Educators, 1986-87; 2nd vpres, Bus Educ Assoc, 1986-87; past pres, Gregg Shorthand Teachers Assoc, 1986-87. **Honors/Awds:** Outstanding Administrator, Morrisania Educ Coun, 1980; Service Award, Business Educ Assoc, 1987. **Business Addr:** Professor, LaGuardia Community College, Department Computer Information Systems, 31 10 Thomson Ave, Long Island City, NY 11101, **Business Phone:** (718)482-7200.*

ANDERSON, BARBARA LOUISE
Librarian, social worker. **Personal:** Born in San Diego, CA; daughter of Lorenzo and Louise Morgan. **Educ:** San Diego State Col, BS, 1954; Kans State Teachers Col, MS, LS, 1955. **Career:** Librarian (retired); LA Pub Libr, br young adult librn, 1956-59; San Diego Pub Libr, ref young adult librn, 1959-64; AUS Europe, admin librn, 1964-69; Serra Regional Libr Systs, San Diego, ref proj coordr, 1969-70; Riverside Pub Libr, head reader serv, 1971-74; San Bernardino Co Libr, dir, 1974-94. **Orgs:** Am CA Libr Asns; NAACP, Alpha Delta Chi; bd dirs, YWCA, San Bernardino, 1989-; pres, Calif Soc Librns, 1974-75; delegate, OCLC, Users Coun, 1983-88; deleg, White House Conf Info Sci, 1979-; bd dir, Inland Empire Sumphony, 1982-83; vol, Riverside Co Archives Comn, 1997-; pres, Black Art & Cult Club, Lake Elsinore; Riverside Co Libr adv comt, 1998-; Recording Blind & Dyslexic, 1992-; vpres, 1997-, sunshine chair, NAACP; Riverside Co Libr Adv Comt, 1998-99; Lake Elsinore Woman's Club; bd mem, Riverside Mental Health; bd mem, Calif Youth Authority Libr Asn; past chair, Inland Libr Syst Admin Coun; bd mem, Univ Southern Calif Sch Lib & Info, Nat Coun Negro Women Serv; past pres, Am Asn Univ Women. **Honors/Awds:** Citizen Achievement, San Bernardino League Women Voters, 1990; Honoree, Black Art & Cult Club Lake Elsinore, 1988; Blacks Govt, Riverside City Col, 1972; Resolutions CA State Senate, 1994; San Bernardino Co Bd Supvrs, 1994; US House Reps, 1994. *

ANDERSON, DR. BARBARA STEWART JENKINS
Pathologist, educator. **Personal:** Born in Chicago, IL; daughter of Carlyle F and Alyce Walker; married Sidney B Jenkins, Sep 22, 1951 (divorced); children: Kevin C Jenkins, Judith Jenkins Kelly MD, Sharolyn Jenkins Sanders, MarcJ Jenkins & Kayla S Jenkins French; married Arthur E Anderson (deceased), Sep 30, 1972 (died 2002). **Educ:** Univ Mich, BS, 1950; Wayne State Med Sch, MD, 1957. **Career:** Wayne Co Hosp, 1966-70; Detroit Gen Hosp, dir clinical lab; Wayne State Med Sch, assoc prof, 1970-, staff pathologist; DMC Univ Labs, admin med dir, Detroit Receiving Hosp, chief pathol, 1988, Assoc Med Dir; Wayne State Univ, prof & vice chmn clinical path. **Orgs:** Wayne Co Med Soc, MI State Med Soc, Am Med Asn, Detroit Med Soc, Wolverine Med Soc,

Nat Med Soc, Col Am Path; Am Soc Clinical Pathol; Minority Recruitment Comt, Wayne Med Sch; Careers Club HS Studs; elected, Alpha Omega Alpha, 1956. **Honors/Awds:** Alexander McKenzie Campbell Award, 1957; Pathfinders in Medicine Award, Wayne State Univ, 2004. **Home Addr:** 6920 Nashway Dr W, West Bloomfield, MI 48322, **Home Phone:** (248)661-3650. **Business Addr:** Clinical Associate Professor, Medical Laboratory Sciences, Wayne State University, Department Of Pathology, School Of Medicine, 540 E Canfield Ave, Detroit, MI 48201, **Business Phone:** (313)577-1104.*

ANDERSON, BELINDA C.
College president. **Educ:** Radford Univ, BS, 1976, MA, hist, 1977; Va Tech Univ, EdD. **Career:** Portsmouth pub sch syst, teacher; Norfolk pub sch syst, teacher; Radford Univ, dir acad advising serv; Norfolk State Univ, Sch gen & Continuing Educ, dean & prof; VA Union Univ, vpres acad affiars, 2000-2003, interim pres, 2003-2004, pres, 2004-. **Honors/Awds:** Outstanding alumnus of the yr, Radford Univ, 2001. **Special Achievements:** First female President of Va Union Univ. **Business Phone:** (804)257-5600.*

ANDERSON, BENJAMIN STRATMAN, JR.
Physician, chairperson. **Personal:** Born Feb 23, 1936, Dothan, AL; son of Benjamin Anderson Sr and Lula Sutton; married Sandra C Wright, Jun 15, 1962 (died 1995); children: Benjamin III, Kevin, Carita. **Educ:** Fisk Univ, BS, 1957; Meharry Med Col, MD, 1962; Am Bd Family Pract, dipl, 1975, re-certified, 1981, 1987, 1995. **Career:** Polk Gen Hosp, staff pres, 1969-70, 1978-79, 1988-89, 1991-93; GA State Med Asn, exec bd, 1973-; fel Am Acad Family Physicians, 1979; Polk Co Bd Health, 1979-; chmn, 1985-; GA Bd Human Resources, secy, 1972-86; med dir, Brentwood Park Nursing Home, 1988-93; Coosa Valley Residential Substance Abuse Prog, dir med servs, 1989-02; Polk County Emergency Med Servs, med dir, 1977-99; Anderson Med ctr, physician, currently. **Orgs:** Life mem, Kappa Alpha Psi Fraternity, 1970-; adv coun, Cedartown City Comn, 1970-86; health serv dir, proj Head start, Tallatoona EOA Inc, 1974-79; life mem, Nat Asn Advan Colored People, 1975-; vice speaker House Delegates GA Acad Family Physicians, 1975-77; bd dirs, Cedartown Little League, 1976-85; consult & preceptor, Polk Co Primary Care Proj, 1981-83; Cedartown Comm Relations Coun, 1986-; Wayside Inn Alcohol & Drug Residential Rehab Prog, consult, 1986-92; bd dirs, GA Asn Minority Entrepreneurs, 1988-90; Am Soc Addiction Med, 1989-03; Cedartown Recreation Comn, 1990-95; bd advs, Columbia/Polk Gen Hospital, 1996-, chair, 1998-. **Honors/Awds:** Service Award, Atlanta Med Asn, 1973; Service Award, GA State Med Asn, 1975; President's Award, GA County Welfare Asn, 1982; Businessman of the Yr, Northwest GA Minority Business Asn, 1986; Community Service Award, Polk County Nat Asn Advan Colored People, 1987; Community Service Commendation, GA House Reps, 1988; Service Award, Polk Co EMS, 1999. **Home Addr:** PO Box 508, Cedartown, GA 30125. **Business Phone:** (770)748-3006.*

ANDERSON, BERNADINE M.
Beautician. **Personal:** Born Dec 1, 1942, New York, NY; daughter of Benjamin Tonsler and Sarah Brown; divorced; children: Sherri Bruce, Jacqueline Brown,. **Educ:** NY Univ, BA, 1963. **Career:** Cicely Tyson, head make-up artist, 1979-81; Jane Fonda Movies, 20th Century Fox, personal make-up artist, 1980-84; Stevie Wonder, head make-up artist, 1981-82; Eddie Murphy Movies, Paramount, head make-up artist, 1985-94; Lionel Ritchie, head make-up artist, 1986-87; Laurence Fishburne, Touchtone, personal make-up artist, 1990-93; Angela Basset Movies, Paramount, head of dept, 1994-95. **Orgs:** IASE Local 706, SAG-SEG, 1970-. **Honors/Awds:** Academy Awards, Emmy Nomination, Am 4 times, 1987-89; Academy Award Nomination, Filmmakers Acad, Best Make-Up, 1990; Inductee, Black Filmmakers Hall Fame, 1991. **Special Achievements:** Roots, 1976; A Soldiers Story, 1982; Another 48 Hours, 1985; Whats Love Got To Do With It, 1991; Bad Company, 1993. **Business Addr:** Make-up Artist, Self Employed, 4559 Don Richardo Dr, Los Angeles, CA 90008, **Business Phone:** (213)296-5891.*

ANDERSON, DR. BERNARD E.
Educator. **Personal:** Born in Philadelphia, PA; son of William and Dorothy Gideon; children: Melinda D & Bernard E II. **Educ:** Livingstone Col, BA, econ, 1959; Mich State Univ, MA, econ, 1961; Univ Pa, PhD, bus & appl econ, 1969. **Career:** US Bur Labor Statist, economist, 1963-66; Wharton Sch, Univ Pa, from asst prof indust to assoc prof indust, 1969-75, prof, 1978-83, Whitney M Young term prof, 2001-, pract prof mgt, currently; MDRC Corp, brd dir, 1977-93, vice chair, 1988-93; Swarthmore Col, lectr; Rockefeller Found, dir socialsci, 1979-85; Woodrow Wilson Sch, Princeton Univ, vis fel, 1985; Provident Mutual Life Ins Co, brd dirs, 1988-; Urban Affairs Partnership, mng partner; US Dept Labor, asst secy, 1994-2001; Overseas Pvt Investment Corp, brd dir, 1995-; Anderson Group, pres; US Dept Labor, asst sec for the emp standards admin. **Orgs:** Philadelphia Urban League, 1970-76; former pres, Nat Econ Assn 1970-; bd mem, NAACP Spec Contrib Fund, 1976-80; brd trustees, Livingstone Col,1980-94; brd econs, Black Enterprise Mag, 1981-93; consult, Ford Found,1985-93; Natl Comn Jobs & Small Bus, 1986; United Bank Philadelphia; bd mem, Lincoln Univ Brd Trustees, 1987-93, chmn, 1989-93; chmn, Palnter gove Coop Authority; co-chmn, Northeast Region SigmaPi Phi Fraternity. **Honors/Awds:** Shaw Univ, hon doctorate degree, 1984; Livingstone Col, hon doc deg, 1996; Benedict Col, hon doc degree, 2001; Samuel Z Wester field Award, Natl Econ Assn, 2002-03; Tuskegee Univ, hon doc deg, 2005. **Military Serv:** AUS, nco, 2 yrs; Good Conduct Medal. **Business Addr:** Assistant Sec Employment Standards Admin, US Department of Labor, Francis Perkins Bldg 200 Constitution Ave NW, washington, DC 20210.

ANDERSON, BETTY KELLER
Journalist, editor. **Personal:** Born Dec 13, 1951, Pineville, LA; daughter of Arthur D Keller Sr and Helen L Keller; divorced; children: Tamara Renee & Travis Randolph. **Educ:** Univ NMex, Albuquerque, NM, BA, jour, 1973. **Career:** Albuquerque Jour, summer intern, 1971; Tacoma News Tribune, reporter/copy ed, 1974-85; Houston Chronicle, copy ed, 1985-86; Seattle Times, copy/design ed, 1986-. **Orgs:** Pres, Black Journalist Asn Seattle, 1988-90; dep regional dir, Region 10, Nat Asn Black Journalists, 1990-91; regional dir, NABJ, 1991-93; supvr, Editing & Publ Ministry, Tacoma Christian Ctr, 1994-. **Honors/Awds:** fel, Editing Prog Minority Journalists, Inst Jour Educ, 1984. **Home Addr:** 6514 N Pkwy, Tacoma, WA 98407, **Home Phone:** (253)756-1051. **Business Addr:** Copy Editor, The Seattle Times, 1120 John St, Seattle, WA 98109, **Business Phone:** (206)464-2111.

ANDERSON, BRYAN N.
Executive. **Personal:** Born Jun 18, 1955, New Haven, CT. **Educ:** Univ Conn, attended 1977. **Career:** Sen Weicker, staff asst; Vir Legis Improv Proj, St Thomas, US Vir, proj dir; admin asst cheif dep Minority Leaders, Conn state senate; Harlem mayor; Hamden CT, constable, 1973-80; Pace Advert, coordr client serv. **Orgs:** Bd mem, State Bd Higher Educ; dist leader, Hamden Rep Town Comn; Hamden Arts Coun; Hamden League Women Voters; Ripon Soc Nat Gov Bd. **Honors/Awds:** Hamden Outstanding Youth Awd, 1971; Comm Involvement Awd, Greater New Haven Urban League, 1973.

ANDERSON, CADILLAC. See ANDERSON, GREGORY WAYNE.

ANDERSON, CAREY LAINE, JR.
Architect. **Personal:** Born Jan 12, 1950, Louisville, KY; married Karen Elizabeth White; children: Latrice Elizabeth. **Educ:** Univ Ky, BArch, 1973. **Career:** Arrasmith Judd Rapp & Assoc Architects, architect draftsman, 1973-77; Robert F Crump Architects, proj architect, 1977-78; City Louisville Pub Works Dept, city architect, 1978-79; Larry E Wright & Assocs Architects, assoc/proj architect, 1979-80; Anderson C L Archit LLC, architect, 1980-. **Orgs:** prog chmn, Cent Ky Chap Am Inst Architects; Construct Specif Inst; Ky Soc Architects; Nat Asn Advan Colored People; Phi Beta Sigma Fraternity Inc; adv bd, Greater Louisville CVB; Louisville Urban League, currently. **Special Achievements:** First Black Architect License in Kentucky in 1977; first Black Architect to establish architectue firm in Kentucky. **Business Addr:** Architect, Anderson C L Architecture LLC, 455 S 4th St Suite 949, Louisville, KY 40202-2593.*

ANDERSON, CARL EDWARD
Judge, business owner. **Personal:** Born Jan 8, 1939, Pendleton, SC; son of Wilhelmina and Amos; married Etta Humphrey, Feb 26, 1972; children: Carl Wendell. **Educ:** Tri Co Tech Col, criminal justice, 1975; SC Criminal Justice Acad. **Career:** Sangamo Elec Co, 1965-70; Anderson County Sheriffs Dept, 1970-89; Anderson County Summary Ct, chief magistrate, judge, 1989-2000; CEAS Investigative Agency, owner, currently. **Orgs:** Tri County Judicial Asn; SC Summary Ct Educ Comn; Anderson Jr Assembly Adv Bd; SC Summary Court Asn; SC Human Affairs Comnr; SC Asn Legal Investigators. **Special Achievements:** First black chief magistrate, Anderson County, 1991; first black capt, Anderson Count Sheriff Department, 1988; First black officer, Anderson County Sheriff Department, 1970. **Military Serv:** AUS, lcpl, 1963-65. **Business Addr:** Owner, CEAS Investigative Agency, 201 N Main St, Anderson, SC 29621-5610, **Business Phone:** (864)261-7775.

ANDERSON, CARL EDWIN
School administrator, government official. **Personal:** Born Sep 29, 1934, St Louis, MO; son of Raymond W and Elizabeth Hooper; married Ida Bass Anderson, Jun 19, 1954; children: Carl Jr, Rhonda L Anderson-Speight, Sherri Anderson-Cherry. **Educ:** Southern Ill Univ, BA, 1956, MS, 1958; Univ Md, EdD, 1969. **Career:** School Adminstrator, Govement official (retired); Howard Univ, dir stud activities, 1960-64, assoc dean stud, 1964-69, actg dean stud, 1969, vpres stud affairs, 1969-90; consult; US House Rep, Post Office & Civil Serv Comn, prof staff, 1991-95. **Orgs:** Bd dir, Am Asn Univ Admin; Southern Ill Univ Found; Howard Univ Found; Nat Asn Stud Personnel Admin; Am Asn Counseling & Develop; Nat vpres Stud Affairs Org; evaluator, Middle States Asn & Sec Sch & Col; Nat Urban League; Nat Asn Advan Colored People; pres, Kappa Scholar Endowment Fund; Kappa Alpha Psi Frat; Sigma Pi Phi Frat; bd dir, William L Clay Scholar & Res Fund, 1988-; Nat Asn Personnel Workers; Eastern Asn Col Deans. **Honors/Awds:** Distinguished Alumni Achievement Award, Southern Ill Univ, 1972; Lamont Lawson Award Outstanding Contrib, Kappa Alpha Psi Frat, 1984; Serv Southern Ill Univ; Admin of the Year Stud Coun, Howard Univ; Scott Goodnight Award for Outstanding Performance as a Dean, Nat Asn Stud Personnel Adminr, 1990; John E King Award Outstanding Contrib Higher Educ, Southern Ill Univ, 1990; Golden Key Honor Soc; Diamond Honoree, Am Col Personnel Asn; Outstanding Leader Educ Distinguised Alumni Achievement Award, Univ Md, 2003. **Home Addr:** 2100 Yorktown Rd NW, Washington, DC 20012. *

ANDERSON, DR. CAROL BYRD
Economist, educator. **Personal:** Born Jun 7, 1941, Kansas City, MO; daughter of Hartwell and Elmira; married Winston Anthony; children: Laura Elisabeth & Lea Elmira. **Educ:** Col St.Teresa, BA, 1962; Boston Col, MA, 1964, PhD, 1969. **Career:** Economist, educator, banker (retired); Bur Labor Statist, gen economist, 1963-64; Fed Res Boston, economist, 1969-70; First Nat Bank Chicago, staff officer, 1970-75; Howard Univ Wash, DC, assoc prof, 1975-76; Fed Res Wash, DC, economist, 1976-86. **Orgs:** Am Econ Asn, 1960-; Social Econ, 1960-; Nat Econ Asn, 1975-; trustee, Col St Teresa, 1975-81. **Honors/Awds:** Woodrow Wilson Scholar Award, 1962; Award, Chicago Jr Chamber Com, 1972.

ANDERSON, DR. CAROLYN
Administrator. **Educ:** Morgan State Univ; Johns Hopkins Univ; NC State Univ. **Career:** North Lake Col, asst dir, human resources; Broome Community Col, dean acad serv div; Cincinnati State Tech & Community Col, exec vpres, actg pres, currently. **Business Addr:** President, Cincinnati State Technical & Community College, 3520 Central Pkwy, Cincinnati, OH 45223-2690, **Business Phone:** (513)569-1515.

ANDERSON, DARREN HUNTER (DARREN HUNTER ANDERSON)
Football player. **Personal:** Born Jan 11, 1969, Cincinnati, OH; married Robyn. **Educ:** Univ Toledo. **Career:** Football player (Retired); Tampa Bay Buccaneers, defensive back, 1992-93; New England Patriots, 1992; Kans City Chiefs, 1994-97; Atlanta Falcons, 1998.

ANDERSON, DR. DAVID ATLAS
Educator, storyteller. **Personal:** Born Apr 28, 1930, Cincinnati, OH; son of Willie David Anderson and Mary Alice Anderson; married Ruth Joanine; children: David M, Kenwood M & Joanine C. **Educ:** Rochester Inst Tech, BFA, 1960; Syracuse Univ, MA, 1962; Union Inst, PhD, educ admin, 1975. **Career:** Urban League Rochester, deputy exec dir, 1967-70; State Univ NY, Brockport, lectr Afro-Amer studies; Rochester Inst Tech, vis asst prof 1981-, dir parent educ; Rochester City Sch Dist, Storyteller, currently; Tex Educ Agency, cheif coun; teacher, African American Studies. **Orgs:** Assoc Comn Health, Univ Rochester Med Sch, 1970-82; vpres, Mental Health Asn, 1980-86; Correctional Inst, Sonyea & Oatka, NY, 1983-85; bd dirs, Rochester Mus & Sci Ctr, 1986-90; Nat Asn Black Storytellers, 1988-89; chmn, Rochester-Monroe County Freedom Trail Comn. **Honors/Awds:** Community Leadership Award, Urban League Rochester, 1982; Outstanding Community Serv, Health Asn Rochester, 1984; Distinguished Volunteer, Mental Health Asn Rochester 1986; Zora Neale Hurston Award, 2000. **Special Achievements:** Author of award winning books: The Origin of Life on Earth: an African Creation Myth, 1991; The Rebellion of Humans: an African Creation Myth, 1991; Kwanzaa: an Everyday Resource and Instructional Guide, 1992. **Military Serv:** USAF staff sgt 6 yrs. **Home Addr:** 181 Royleston Rd, Rochester, NY 14609, **Home Phone:** (585)482-5192. **Business Phone:** (585)262-8100.

ANDERSON, DAVID TURPEAU
Judge. **Personal:** Born Aug 9, 1942, Cincinnati, OH; son of Florida Turpeau and Randall Hudson; children: David M & Daniel M. **Educ:** Univ Cincinnati, BS, 1963; George Wash Univ, JD, 1972. **Career:** Congressman Robert Taft Jr, congressional staff asst, 1967-69; HUD, asst congressional relations, 1970; Am Hosp Assn, asst for legislation, 1971-73; Stanley, Durham & Johnson, assoc, 1972-76; City Philadelphia, asst city solicitor, 1976-81; US Dept Housing & Urban Develop, chief admin judge, 1981-, chmn, currently. **Orgs:** Nat Press Club; Philadelphia Bar asn; BCA Judges asn; Inter-Am Bar asn; Sr Executives asn. **Business Addr:** Cheif Administrative Judge, US Department of Housing & Urban Development, 1707 H St NW 11th Fl Rm 2131 HUD Bldg, Washington, DC 20004, **Business Phone:** (202)254-0000.

ANDERSON, DEREK
Basketball player. **Personal:** Born Jul 18, 1974, Louisville, KY. **Educ:** Univ Ky, pharmacy, 1997. **Career:** Cleveland Cavaliers, guard, 1997-99; Los Angeles Clippers, 1999-2000; San Antonio Spurs, 2000-01; Portland Trail Blazers, guard, 2001-05; Houston Rockets 2005-06; Miami Heat, Guard, 2006; Charlotte Bobcats, 2006-08; free agent, currently. **Special Achievements:** First Player in the league waived using the so-called "luxury tax amnesty clause" of the 2005 NBA collective bargaining agreement. *

ANDERSON, DERRICK RUSHON
Clergy. **Personal:** Son of Bishop Hermon L and Ruth R; married Margaret R, Mar 11, 1973; children: Michael, Rashana Benjamin

& Adria. **Educ:** Hampton Univ, BA, 1973; Livingstone Col, Hood Theol Sem, MDiv, 1983; Asbury Theol Sem, DDiv, 1995. **Career:** Jefferson County Circuit Ct, ct clerk, 1973; Louville Home Fed, br mgr, 1973-80; Soldier's Memorial AME Zion Church, youth pastor, 1980-81; Bethel AME Zion Church, 1981-82; Shady Ridge AME Zion Church, 1982-86; East Stonewall AME Zion Church, sr pastor, 1986-96; St Paul AME Zion Church, pastor, 1996-. **Orgs:** Jeffersontown Chamber Com, 1978-80; bd mem, Uptown Homeless Shelter, 1990-91; co-founder & bd mem, Ministry Recovery, 1990-91; bd mem, Human Servs Coun, 1992-94. **Home Addr:** 1901 Chicago Blvd, Detroit, MI 48206, **Home Phone:** (313)865-8502. **Business Addr:** Pastor, St Paul AME Zion, 11359 Dexter Ave, Detroit, MI 48206-1424, **Business Phone:** (313)933-1822.

ANDERSON, DOREATHA MADISON
Manager. **Personal:** Born Apr 3, 1934, Lynchburg, VA; widowed; children: Wanda M Taylor, Rae L. Madison, Raymond B Madison Jr, (deceased) Doretha L Madison,Dr. Octavia D. Madison-Colmore. **Educ:** Va Sem Col, BS, 1968; Va Union Univ, BA, 1984. **Career:** Juvenile Detention Home, youth care worker, 1968-82; Bags Unlimited Inc, pres, 1982-; NAACP, finance chmn, 1982-84; Comm Educ Employment Svcs, prog mgr, 1985-86; Youth Development Svcs, prog mgr, 1986-. **Orgs:** Diamond Hill Baptist ch; Usher Bd; Ch Aid; recording secy, Daughter Elk Chap 181 IPOEW, 1975-82; Eastern Star, 1980-82; pres, Missionary Circle; asst treas, Variety Garden Club Hill City Chap; Am Bus Women Assoc, 1983; United Way 1986; Nat Assoc Female Exec Inc, 1986. *

ANDERSON, DORIS J.
Educator, counselor. **Personal:** Born Oct 16, 1933, Reagan, TX; married Franklin D; children: Deborah, Daryl F & Caleb. **Educ:** BA, 1962; MEd, 1966. **Career:** Teacher, 13 yrs; Bastian Sch, counr. **Orgs:** Nat Educ Asn; Tex State Troopers Asn; Tex Classrm Teachers Asn; HTA; APGA; TVGA; Am Sch Counr Asn; Nat Voc Guid Asn; Am News Women's Club; Tex Pecan Growers Asn; TACES; HSCA; treas, Houston Teachers Asn, 1974-75; pres, Houston Sch Counr Asn, 1975; Ct Vol WICS Vol; Sigma Gamma Rho Sor, 1962; Phi Delta Kappa, 1975; Nat Coun Negro Women. **Honors/Awds:** Sigma Woman of Year 1975; Outstanding Serv Award, Houston Teachers Asn, 1975. *

ANDERSON, EDDIE LEE, JR.
Football player. **Personal:** Born Jul 22, 1963, Warner Robins, GA. **Educ:** Ft Valley State Univ. **Career:** Football player (retired); Seattle Seahawks, defensive back, 1986; Los Angeles Raiders, 1987-94; Oakland Raiders, safety, 1995-97. **Special Achievements:** Hold the team record for longest interception return with a 102 yarder against Miami, 1992. *

ANDERSON, ELIZABETH M
Association executive, government official. **Personal:** Born in Paris, TX; daughter of Walter Mason and Emma McClure; married Rev Harold, Oct 3, 1941; children: Andrew Anderson, Patricia Anderson Roper, Theresa Anderson Danzy & Portia Anderson Tucker. **Educ:** Draughon Bus Col, attended 1955-58; Tulsa Univ, attended 1969-74. **Career:** Okla Tax Comn, Tulsa, OK, dir personnel-supvr acct; Anderson Amusement Corp, Tulsa, OK, dir personnel. **Orgs:** Nat Asn Advan Colored People Tulsa Chap, 1949-89; Tulsa Urban League, 1950-89; past pres, Jack & Jill Am, Tulsa Chap, 1952-71 & 1984-86; exec bd, Tulsa Pastor's Wives Coun; nat bd, Nat Coun Negro Women, Wash, DC; nat coun, Assault Illiteracy, New York City; exec bd, YWCA, Tulsa, OK; southern regional dir, Eta Phi Beta Sorority; nat pres, Eta Phi Beta Sorority, chief exec officer, vpres. **Home Addr:** 1724 Mohawk Blvd, Tulsa, OK 74110.

ANDERSON, ELMER
Baseball player. **Personal:** Born Aug 21, 1941, Detroit, MI; son of Rosie Lee. **Career:** Sebring Industrial Co, block fitter; Detroit Motor City Red Caps, Outfielder, 1959-67; Wess Springs, block fitter; Detroit Diesel, 1967-97; Int African Am Sports Hall of Fame, founder. **Honors/Awds:** Presocos Award, World Sports Humanitarian Hall of Fame; "Key to the City", 1989; Gold Cast Fist Award, International Boxing Hall of Fame, 1994; Detroit Ring 32 Award, International Veterans Boxing Association, 1995; Valuable Employee Award, General Motors, 1970. **Business Phone:** (208)343-7224.

ANDERSON, EUGENE
Government official, executive. **Personal:** Born Mar 9, 1944, Diffee, GA; son of Velver Sr and Velma; married Mamie Jewel Sapp, Dec 3, 1966; children: Timothy E, Tamara E & Melanie J. **Educ:** Wichita Tech Inst, radio & telephone commun, 1971. **Career:** State Kans, state rep, 1973-76; Congressman Dan Glickman, dist aide,1976-78; Kans Comn Civil Rights, chairperson, 1979-83;K Black Dem Caucus, S, secy, 1982-85; Rollin & Smokin Bar-B-Que Hut, owner & operator; Kans Legis, sen, rep, currently. **Orgs:** Pres, Optimist Club NE Wichita, 1974-75; treas, State Dem Party, KS,1985-87; Masonic Lodge, Nat Asn Advan Colored People; Fed & State Affairs; Confirmations Comt, Ed Comt, Pub Health & Welfare Comt, Midwestern Conf Coun State Govts, Adv Coun Aging, Legis Ed Planning Comt. **Honors/Awds:** Sommunity Service Award, Police Neighborhood Serv Ctr, 1976; Coach of the Year Award. **Military Serv:** AUS, sp5, 1962-65, Parachutist Badge. **Home Addr:** 1832 N Poplar, Wichita, KS 67214. **Business Phone:** (785)296-3296.

ANDERSON, FLIPPER. See ANDERSON, WILLIE LEE, JR.

ANDERSON, FRED
Music director. **Personal:** Born Jun 3, 1962, Lima, OH; son of Lucious Upshaw and Mary Anderson. **Educ:** Northeastern Bus Col, attended. **Career:** Mid Bus Inc, production, currently; Rudolph Foods, processing, currently. **Orgs:** New Morningstar Church, choir dir. **Home Addr:** 473 E 4th St, Lima, OH 45804. **Business Addr:** Production, Mid Bus Inc, 505 E Jefferson St, Bluffton, OH 45817-1398, **Business Phone:** (419)358-2500.

ANDERSON, GARRET JOSEPH
Baseball player. **Personal:** Born Jun 30, 1972, Los Angeles, CA; married Teresa Arciniega, Feb 20, 1993; children: Brianne & Bailey. **Career:** California Angels, 1994-96; Anaheim Angels, outfielder, 1997-2004; Los Angeles Angels of Anaheim, 2005-08; Atlanta Braves, outfielder, 2009-. **Orgs:** Boy Scouts Am recruiting campaign & Responsible Fatherhood Campaign; Calif Dept Social Serv; LA City Championship baseball team, 1989. **Honors/Awds:** All-LA City & All-League preparation honors, 1989-90; Am League Rookie Player of the Year, The Sporting News, 1995; Topps Rookie All-Star Team, 1995; World Series Champion, 2002; Most Valuable Player, MLB All-Star Game, 2003. **Business Addr:** Baseball Player, Atlanta Braves, Turner Field, 755 Hank Aaron Dr, Atlanta, GA 30315, **Business Phone:** (404)522-7630.*

ANDERSON, GARY WAYNE
Football player. **Personal:** Born Apr 18, 1961, Columbia, MO; married Ollie; children: Antisha & Gary Jr. **Educ:** Univ Ark, attended 1983. **Career:** Football player (retired); Tampa Bay Bandits, 1983-85; San Diego Chargers, running back & wide receiver, 1985-88; Tampa Bay Buccaneers, running back,1990-93; Detroit Lions, 1993. **Honors/Awds:** All-Rookie First Team, UPI, Football Digest & Pro Football Writers. *

ANDERSON, GEORGE A.
Executive. **Personal:** Born Nov 15, 1923, Chicago, IL; married; children: George Jr. **Educ:** Howard Univ; Roosevelt Univ; Central YMCA Col, Chicago. **Career:** Draper & Kramer, br off mgr, vpres; Lake Meadows Apts Chicago, mgr. **Orgs:** Chicago Real Estate Bd; Nat Real Estate Bd; Inst Real Estate Mgt; Apt Bldg Owners & Mgrs Asn; S Side Planning Bd; supports La Rabida C Hosp; Jane Dent Home for the Aged. *

ANDERSON, GEORGE ALLEN
Lawyer. **Personal:** Born Sep 11, 1941, Zanesville, OH; son of Louis B and Cenna M; married Brenda, Sep 28, 1962; children: Kim & George A Jr. **Educ:** South Carolina State Univ, BA, 1962, JD, 1965. **Career:** Aiken-Barnwell CAC Inc, chief exec officer, 1966-, exec dir, currently; Anderson & Assocs Aiken PA, owner, currently. **Orgs:** Am Bar Asn; Nat Bar Asn; Southeastern Lawyers Asn; South Carolina Bar Asn; Lower Savannah Coun Governments; Zoning Bd Adjustments, City Aiken; Cumberland AME Ch, Aiken; Aiken County Bar Asn; SC State Col Alumni Asn. **Honors/Awds:** Sch Law Award, SC State Col. **Business Addr:** Owner, Anderson & Assocs of Aiken PA, 302 Pk Ave SE Suite 2, Aiken, SC 29801-4508, **Business Phone:** (803)648-0797.

ANDERSON, GLENN B.
College teacher. **Personal:** Married Karen; children: Danielle & Jamaal. **Educ:** Gallaudet Col, BA; Univ Ariz, MS; NY Univ, PhD, 1982. **Career:** LaGuardia Community Col, prog coordr; NY Univ, assoc res scientist; Univ Ark, Rehab Res & Training Ctr, prof & dir training, 1982-; consult, currently; Gallaudet Univ Bd Trustees, Chair. **Orgs:** Chmn, Gallaudet Univ Bd Trustees; Nat Coun Disability; Ark Rehab Coun; coord, RSA-funded deafness rehabilitation Counspecialization; mem, nat adv Coun rehabilitation cultural diversity proj; mem, Arkansas Rehabilitation Coun. **Special Achievements:** Has numerous publications & has conducted more workshops & invited presentations. **Business Phone:** (501)686-9691.

ANDERSON, DR. GLORIA L.
Educator. **Personal:** Born Nov 5, 1938, Altheimer, AR; daughter of Charley Long (deceased) and Elsie Foggie Long (deceased); divorced; children: Gerald L. **Educ:** AM&N Col, BS, 1958; Atlanta Univ, MS, 1961; Univ Chicago, PhD, 1968. **Career:** SC State Col, instr, 1961-62; Morehouse Col, instr, 1962-64; Univ Chicago, teaching & res asst, 1964-68; SC State Col, summer sch, prof, 1967; Lockheed GA Corp, NSF res fel 1981, res consult, 1982; Air Force Rocket Propulsion Lab, SCEEE fac res fel, 1984; Morris Brown Col, assoc prof & chmn, 1968-73, Callaway prof & chmn, 1973-84, acting vpres, acad affairs, 1984-85, dean acad affairs, 1985-89; UNCF, Distinguished Scholar, 1989-90; Morris Brown Col, Fuller E Callaway, prof chem, 1990-, interimpres, 1992-93, dean sci & technol, 1996-; Am Inst Chemists, cert prof chemist, 1992-; Morris Brown Col, Dept chem, Fuller E Callaway prof & chmn, 2003, fac rep bd, 2004. **Orgs:** Fel, Am Inst Chemists; fel, Am Chem Soc; fel, Ga Acad Sci; fel, NY AcadSci; AASI; Nat Sci Teachers Asn; Am Asn Univ Profs; Delta Sigma ThetaSorority Inc; Nat Inst Sci; Atlanta Univ Sci Res Inst; Nat Asn Educ Broadcasters; Nat Asn Advan Colored People; educ consult, US Dept Educ, 1976-88; ad hoc technol review group, Nat Cancer Inst, 1986; NIADA, contract reviewer, 1990-91. **Honors/Awds:** Alpha Kappa Mu Natl Honor Soc; Beta Kappa Chi Sci Honor Soc; Alpha KappaMu Honor Trophy Col All Expense Scholar Highest Average in Freshman Class, 1955; appointed by Pres Nixon, bd Corp Pub Broadcasting, 1972; honored byAtlanta Chap, AR AM&N Coll Nat Alumni Asn, 1973; honored by Atlanta Chap-Delta Sigma Theta Sor Inc as one of 25 Atlanta Deltas, "Breaking NewGround", 1974; Fel Mem Am Biographical Inst, 1977; gov's appointee PubTelecommunications Task Force, 1980; Arkansan of Achievement in Educ, 1985; United Negro Col Fund Distinguished Scholar, 1985; National Alumni Award, 1986; All-Star Excellence in Education Award, Univ Arkansas, PlineBluff Alumni, 1987; 30 other honors and awards. **Special Achievements:** Author of numerous science publications; "Atlanta's Best and Brightest Scientists", Atlanta Mag, 1983. **Business Addr:** Fuller E. Callaway Professor, Morris Brown College, Department of Chemistry, 643 Martin Luther King Jr Dr, Atlanta, GA 30314.*

ANDERSON, GRANVILLE SCOTT
School administrator. **Personal:** Born Jul 25, 1947, Honolulu, HI; son of Granville P and Olga Edna Jones; married Jennifer Sachie Kato, Sep 13, 1986. **Educ:** Queensborough Community Col, AAS, 1971; Ruskin Col, Oxford, Eng, cert, 1970; Queens Col, BA, 1972. **Career:** City Univ NY, exec asst, 1972-82, exec officer, 1982-87, coordr res found, 1987-90, dep dir admis, 1990-; Town Squash Inc, squash prof, 1980-. **Orgs:** Univ Chancellor's Scholar Study UK, 1969-70; Oscar Wilde Speaker's Tour Belfast, N Ireland, 1969; adminr, CUNY Pamela S Galiber Scholar Fund, 1976-86; exec bd, Metro Squash Racquets Asn, 1977-80; Sports Mgt Consult, 1977-; chmn, Referees Comm MSRA, 1978; pres, Queensborough Community Col Alumni Asn, 1979-86; NY Aikido Club, 1990-. **Honors/Awds:** John F Kennedy Award, 1968. **Special Achievements:** Nationally ranked amateur squash player US Squash Racquets Assoc. **Home Phone:** (212)674-7063. **Business Addr:** Deputy Director Admissions, City University of New York, Off Finacial Aid, 1114 Ave of the Americas, New York, NY 10036-7703.*

ANDERSON, GREGORY WAYNE (CADILLAC ANDERSON)
Basketball player. **Personal:** Born Jun 22, 1964, Houston, TX; married Tammie; children: Greg Jr, Geia, Gabrielle & Geremy. **Educ:** Univ Houston, TX, 1987. **Career:** Basketball player (retired); San Antonio Spurs, ctr forward, 1987-89; Milwaukee Bucks, ctr forward, 1989-90; NJ Nets, ctr forward, 1991; Denver Nuggets, ctr forward, 1991-92; Phonola Caserta, Italy, ctr forward, 1992-93; Detroit Pistons, ctr forward, 1993-94; Atlanta Hawks, ctr forward, 1994-95; San Antonio Spurs, ctr forward, 1995-97; Atlanta Hawks, ctr forward, 1997-98. **Honors/Awds:** NBA All Rookie Team, 1988.

ANDERSON, HAROLD A.
Manager. **Personal:** Born Oct 12, 1939, New York, NY; married Alice Campbell; children: Joi, Dwight. **Educ:** Morehouse Col, attended 1963; Queens Col, BA, 1966; NY Univ, attended 1969. **Career:** Nat Urban League Black Exec Exchange Prog Coord, vis prof; singer; rec artist; song writer; NY Life Ins Co, pub rels asst, 1967-69; Interracial Coun Bus Opers, dir pub rels, 1969-70; ITT News Serv, writer, 1970-74; ITT News & Pub Affairs, adminr, 1974-76; ITT, mgr pub affairs, 1977-86; NY Pub Libr, Schomburg Ctr Res Black Cult, pub rels officer, 1986-, dir pub rels, 2000. **Orgs:** Provide Addict Care Today; Rutgers Minority Invest; Harlem Consumers Educ Coun; Nat Urban Affairs Coun; Pub Rels Soc Am; 100 Black Men; OIC NY Tech Adv Comm; Nigerian Am Friendship Soc; Youth Motivation Task Force Living Witness Prog; consult, Nat Urban League; Col Awareness Prog; bd mem, Harlem YMCA, Greater NY; award comm, CBS TV's "Living The Dream" Awards; hon mem, YMCA Black Achiever Indust; Citations US Dept Treas; save our scholar comm, Dillard Univ Louise Wise Serv. **Special Achievements:** Black Achiever, ITT, 1976. **Business Addr:** Director, Public Relations Officer, New York Public Library, Schomburg Ctr Res Black Cult, 515 Malcolm X Blvd, New York, NY 10037-1801.*

ANDERSON, HELEN LOUISE
Consultant, executive. **Personal:** Born Feb 23, 1941, Luxora, AR; daughter of Mack and Ruby Lee Evans Nunn. **Educ:** Syracuse Univ, attended 1961; Fashion Inst Tech, attended 1967. **Career:** Eastern Airlines, flight attendant, 1965-67; Fashion Barn, exec vpres, 1967-88; Anderson & Assoc Financial Consult Inc, pres, region deleg, 1988-. **Orgs:** Dir, bd mem, Fred J Rogers Memorial Found; mem, Princess Grace Found, exec Women NJ; Coalition 100 Black Women; Cornell Univ Medical Sch Comm for the Benefit Minority Stud, BRAG; Nat Asn Black Journalists; bd dirs, Fashion Barn 1987-; bd mem, Support Network Inc; bd dir, Can Pension Benefits Inst. **Honors/Awds:** Twin Award, Nat Bd of the YWCA, 1986. **Business Addr:** President, Delegate, Anderson & Associates Financial Consulting Inc., 2624 Windsor St, Halifax, NS, Canada B3K 5C8.

ANDERSON, HENRY L N
School administrator. **Personal:** Born May 23, 1934, Ogeechee, GA; son of Egister Lee and Louise Burns Lonon; married Margie

N Johnson, Nov 1998; children: Brenda Ivelisse, Ileana La Norma & Henry Lee Norman. **Educ:** Earlham Col, Richmond, IN, 1954; Cheyney Univ, Pa, BSEd, 1957; Univ Calif, Los Angeles, EdD, 1972; Yale Univ, MAR, 1973. **Career:** Los Angeles County Schs, teacher, 1961-66; Los Angeles Unified Schs Dist, instr & adminr, 1967-68; Univ Calif, Los Angeles, dir, Dept Spec Educ Progs, assoc dir, 1968-69; Loyola Univ, Grad Sch Educ, asst prof, 1968-72; Eval & Mgt Int Inc, dir, chairperson, chief exec officer, 1971; Calif St Univ Grad Sch Educ, supvr stud teachers, 1972-73; Windsor Univ, Los Angeles, CA, vpres, 1973-75; Fruitarian & Wellness, lectr; financial consult; real estate developer & entrepreneur; African-Am Community Trust, chief exec officer; Lonon Classic Motorcars, chief exec officer; City Univ Los Angeles, pres & chancellor, currently. **Orgs:** Yale Club Southern Calif; life mem, Nat Asn Advan Colored People; life mem, Univ Calif Los Angeles Alumni Asn; founder, Organic Wellness Crusade Network; pres, Phi Delta Kappa. **Honors/Awds:** Four Honorary Doctorates; Hall of Fame, Cheyney Univ PA, 1984; Danford Foundation Honoree, Honor Roll, 1953; Nominee, Nobel Prize; Recipient of Renaissance Award, 1991. **Special Achievements:** You and Race, 1960; "No Use Cryin' ", 1961, Revolutionary Urban Teaching, 1973, Helping Hand: 8-Day Diet Programs, 1986, A Guide to Healthy Living, 1990, produced and hosted an award-winning TV talk show on wellness, Ihre Gesundheit in Ihrer Hand, 1992, Organic Wellness Fasting Technique, 1992, African: Born in America, 1993, developed over 25 years, and sole producer of HARA, recipient of gift of 10,000 acres in Igueben, Edo St, Nigeria, as international home site for Anderson-Imahe Wellness Villages, organized YIEWth (Young International Entrepreneurs in Wellness), author of the Nature and Purpose of Disease: Definitive Guide for Peoples with Melanin,2001. **Military Serv:** AUS, corporal, 1953-60. **Home Addr:** 4647 Presidio Dr, Los Angeles, CA 90008-4825, **Home Phone:** (323)296-1566. **Business Addr:** President, Chancellor, City University Los Angeles, c/o EMI Inc, 3960 Wilshire Blvd Suite 501, PO Box 45227, Los Angeles, CA 90045-5227, **Business Phone:** (310)671-0783.

ANDERSON, HOWARD D.
Executive. **Personal:** Born Feb 28, 1936, Lumpkin, GA; son of James M and Lila; married Susan Benson. **Educ:** Morehouse Col, BA, 1968; Univ Iowa Sch Law, 1969. **Career:** US Post Office, clerk, 1957-66; Merck, Sharpe & Dohme, sales rep, 1969-70; Univ Chicago, staff writer, 1970-72; Sickle Cell Dis Asn Ill, pres, 1972-; Midwest Asn Sickle Cell Anemia, pres, currently. **Orgs:** bd mem, Chicago Regional Blood Prog, 1979-84; second vice chair, Sickle Cell Disease Asn Am, 1994-95, third vice chair, 1990-91, bd sec, 1971-85, treas, 1986-88; chmn, Nat Vol Health Agencies Ill, 1985-93; secy, Combined Health Appeal, 1991-. **Honors/Awds:** Beautiful People Award, Chicago Urban League; Chicago Reg Blood Prog; Fred Hampton Scholar Fund; Black Woman's Hall of Fame Foundation; League Black Women, 1992. **Military Serv:** AUS, sp-4, 1958-60; Lett Commendation. **Business Addr:** President, Sickle Cell Disease Association Of Illinois, 200 N Mich Ave Suite 605, Chicago, IL 60601-5980, **Business Phone:** (312)345-1100.*

ANDERSON, J MORRIS
Television producer, entrepreneur, publisher. **Personal:** Born Jul 6, 1936, Greenville, SC; divorced; children: J Morris Jr, Gracelyn, Aleta & Kathy. **Educ:** Amer Univ, BA, 1961. **Career:** Miss Black Am Beauty Pageant, founder, 1968-; Little Miss Black Am, staff; Tiny Miss Black Am, staf; Miss Black Am Teenager, staff; Miss Black Am, staff; Mrs Black Am, staff; Miss Third World, founder & exec producer. **Orgs:** Pres, Success Seekers Sem; chmn & founder, Black Am Radio & TV Network; chmn, Miss Black Am Beauty Ctrs; exec dir, Rehab Inst Am; founder, J Morris Anderson Asn Investments Stocks & Bonds; Omega Psi Phi; bd mem several public orgns. **Honors/Awds:** Received over 50 awards & citations. **Special Achievements:** Author "Recipes for Black Togetherness", "The Seeds of Positivity", "The Secrets of Mind Control" Vol 1-12. **Business Addr:** Founder, Miss Black America Pageant, PO Box 25668, Philadelphia, PA 19144.

ANDERSON, JAMAL (JAMAL SHARIF ANDERSON)
Football player, television sportscaster. **Personal:** Born Sep 30, 1972, El Camino Real, CA; son of Zenobia. **Educ:** Utah Univ. **Career:** Football player (retired); Atlanta Falcons, running back, 1994-2001; ESPN, NFL Analyst, currently. **Honors/Awds:** Pro Bowl, 1998. *

ANDERSON, JAMES
Business owner, consultant. **Career:** Bank Ann Arbor, bd dir, 2004-; Anderson Assocs, owner & pres, currently. **Orgs:** Bd trustees, Washtenaw Community Col; Washtenaw Tech Mid Col; bd dirs, NEW Ctr; bd dirs, Ann Arbor Chamber Com; Ann Arbor Area Bd Realtors, 2006-; Another Ann Arbor. **Business Addr:** President, The Anderson Associates, 2160 Huron Pkwy, Ann Arbor, MI 48104, **Business Phone:** (734)677-4300.

ANDERSON, JAMES
Executive, vice president (organization). **Educ:** Denison Univ, BA. **Career:** The Carsey-Werner Co, vpres publicity & pub rel, sr vpres, publicity & pub rel; Turner Broadcasting Syst Inc, staff, currently. **Business Addr:** Staff, Turner Broadcasting System Inc, Cartoon Network, 1 CNN Ctr, Atlanta, GA 30303, **Business Phone:** (404)885-4205.

ANDERSON, DR. JAMES ALAN
Educator, school administrator. **Personal:** Born Dec 13, 1948, Washington, DC. **Educ:** Villanova Univ, BA, 1970; Cornell Univ, PhD, 1980. **Career:** Xavier Univ, asst prof psy chol, 1976-80, chmn dept psychol & assoc prpsychol, 1980-83; Ind Univ PA, assoc prof psychol 1983-87, prof psych, 1987-92; NC State Univ, Undergrad affairs, vice provost, 1992-2003; Tex A& M Univ, Off Inst Assessment & Diversity, assoc provost & vpres, 2003. **Orgs:** Asn Black Psychologists 1982-; Asn Black Women Higher Educ, 1983-; Am Fedn Teachers 1983-; dir, Benjamin E Mays Acad Scholars IUP, 1985-; ed Benjamin E Mays Acad Scholars Monograph Series, 1986-; Am Psychol Soc; Nat Asn Develop Educ. **Honors/Awds:** Grant to Develop Res Modules in Psychology Nat Sci Found, 1976; Danforth Fellow 1980; grant Cross-Cultural Res, Dillard Univ, 1982; Research Travel Award, Int Congress of Psychol, 1984; Distinguished Black Alumni, Villanova Univ, 1987; Distinguished Black Pennsylvanian, 1988.

ANDERSON, JAMES R., JR.
Educator. **Personal:** Born Feb 25, 1922, Brazil, IN; son of James R and Eva Roberts; married Fern Gabenez Turner; children: James III, Reginald H, Stephen E, Pamela S & Carla J. **Educ:** Ind Univ, BS, social serv, 1952; Am Soc Serv, attended 1954; Mich Sch Pub-Health, attended 1968. **Career:** Ind State Dept Public Welfare, child welfare consult, 1954-55; Va Hosp Indianapolis, clin social worker, 1955-60; VA Hosp Dearborn MI, chief patient sect social serv, 1960-61; Wayne State Univ Sch Social Work, asst prof & assoc prof, 1963-68; Univ Wash, assoc prof sch socialwork, 1968-90; asst to the dean for health sci & coord health care concentration, adj assoc prof health serv sch pub health & comm med, assoc prof emer, 1991-. **Orgs:** Consult, Multiple Sclerosis Soc King Co, 1976-79; adv com, AMSA Found, Interdisciplinary Team Proj, 1977-79; consult, ID Migrant Health Coun,1979-81; bd dir, pres, vpres, Seattle Urban League, 1971-73; adv comt,Midwifery Proj Group Health Coop of Puget Sound, 1979-82; bd dirs, Chr Prog Com African Am Community Health Network, 1996-. **Military Serv:** AAF, t/sgt 1941-45; ETO Ribbon w/9 clusters. **Home Addr:** 4081 224th Lane SE Apt 203, Issaquah, WA 98029.

ANDERSON, JOHN C., JR.
President (organization), air force officer. **Personal:** Born Aug 12, 1917, Dwiggins, MS; son of John C Anderson Sr and Carrie Hicks; married Celestyne L; children: Corrie Reginald. **Educ:** Univ Toledo, OH, AB, 1940; Golden Gate Law Sch, JD, 1953; Univ CA, postdoctoral studies. **Career:** Civil Serv, LeCarne, OH, fed employee, 1941; Golden Gate Mutual Ins Co,1946-47; Civil Serv, Oakland, CA, fed employee, 1946-52; Naval Supply Ctr,Oakland, CA, 1952-53; Alameda Co Probation Dept, sr dep probation officer,1953; City Col, San Francisco, CA, criminol instr, 1976; Bd PeraltaCommunity Col, trustee (retired), emer, currently. **Orgs:** Bd trustees, Peralta Community Col Dist, 1971-92; bd trustees, Beth EdenBaptist Church; pres, Beth Eden Housing Inc; Omega Psi Phi Frat; Monarch#73 Prince Hall Masons; Bay Area Urban League; Oakland Br Nat Asn AdvanColored People; pres, E Oak Sr Ctr; comnr, Coun on Aging, City of Oakland,CA, 1994-95; pres, E Oakland Sr Citizens, Inc, 1993-95. **Honors/Awds:** Men of Tomorrow, Oakland Man of Yr, Beth Eden Baptist Church, 1962; OmegaCit of Yr, Sigma Iota Chap Omega Psi Phi, 1971; Minister's DistinguishedServ Award, 1978; Coun of Black Am Affairs Award, Western Region, 1989;Pub Sch Serv Award, 20 years, 1991; Peralto Col Found Award, 1991; ColAlameda Serv Award, 1992; Cert Honor & Appreciation, Vista Col, 1992; HonTrustee Award, Beth Eden Baptist Church, 1992. **Military Serv:** OH NG, pvt, 1938-40; AUS, m/sgt, 1942-46; USAF, Tuskegee AirmanAward, 1991.

ANDERSON, JOSEPH B., JR.
Administrator. **Personal:** Born in Topeka, KS. **Educ:** US Military acad, BS, 1965; Univ Calif, Los Angeles, attended 1973; US Army & Gen Staff Col, attended 1984. **Career:** General Motors Corp, plant mgr, dir, gen dir, 1979-92; Composite Energy Mgt Systs Inc, pres & chief exec officer, 1994; Chivas Industs LLC, chmn & chief exec officer, 2002; TAG Holdings LLC, chmn & chief exec officer, currently; Valassis, bd dir; Quaker Chemical Corp, bd dir; ArvinMeritor Inc, bd dir; Sierra Pacific Resources, bd dir; Rite Aid Corp, bd dir. **Orgs:** Original Equipment Suppliers Asn; Soc Automotive Engineers Found; Soc Automotive Engineers Int; Nat Asn Black Automotive Suppliers; adv bd, Horizons Upward Bound. **Honors/Awds:** Honorary Doctor of Management Degree, Kettering University, 2007. *

ANDERSON, JULIUS J.
Administrator. **Educ:** Ivy Tech Col, attended 1984. **Career:** JJ Electric, owner; Ball State Univ, supvr, currently; Muncie Educ Bd, vpres, pres, currently. **Orgs:** Habitat Humanity; Am Heart Asn. **Honors/Awds:** Distinguished Alumnus Award, Ivy Tech Col, 2006.

ANDERSON, KARL EVAN. See EVANZZ, KARL ANDERSON.

ANDERSON, KATHLEEN WILEY
Government official. **Personal:** Born May 22, 1932, Kansas City, KS; married Harvey L (deceased); children: Harvey, H Delon & Doryanna. **Educ:** Univ Kans, Lawrence, KS, BS, 1954, MS, 1955; Univ Southern Calif, MPA, 1974; Wharton Sch, Univ Pa, attended 1979. **Career:** Government official (retired); Kansas City, high sch teacher, 1954-56; Sch Deaf, teacher, 1958-63; Calif Inst Women, adminr, 1963-74, supt, 1976-80; Correctional Training Facility, assoc supt act dep supt, 1974-76; CalifInst Men, supt. **Orgs:** United Black Correctional Workers Asn; Calif Black Correctional Coalition; Nat Advan Asn Colored People; Am Correctional Asn; Alpha Kappa Alpha Sor; Eastern Star; Links Inc; guest instr, Simon Fraser Univ Banbury British Columbia, Wharton Sch; instr, Int Women Corrections. **Honors/Awds:** Ford Found Fellowship Fisk Univ, Univ Kans, 1948-55; Ina B Temple Fellowship, Univ Kans; Notable Women, 1977-87; Inductee, Hall of Fame, African-Am Criminal Justice. **Special Achievements:** First female correctional admin in a male facility; first black female correctional supervisor in CA. **Home Addr:** 4795 Boyd Ct, Riverside, CA 92507. *

ANDERSON, KEISHA (KEISHA DAWN ANDERSON)
Basketball player. **Personal:** Born May 17, 1974. **Educ:** Univ Wis. **Career:** Chicago Xplosion, guard, 1997; Wash Mystics, 2000; Atlanta Justice, 2000-01; Charlotte Sting, 2001-02; Springfield Spirit, 2002-03; DallasFury, 2004; Chicago Blaze, guard, 2004; San Antonio Silver Stars, 2005. **Honors/Awds:** Kodak All-Am, 1996-97; first team All Big 10, 1996-97. *

ANDERSON, KEISHA DAWN. See ANDERSON, KEISHA.

ANDERSON, KENNETH RICHARD
Electrical engineer. **Personal:** Born Aug 4, 1936, Philadelphia, PA; son of William and Dorothy; married Dorothy, Apr 17, 1987; children: Pamela, Veronica. **Educ:** Drexel Univ, BSEE, 1968; Cent MI Univ, BA, 1975, MA. **Career:** Retired: Inselek, mgr test engr, 1971-75; Aeroneutronic Ford, super comp engr, 1975-76; RCA Gov Systems Div, mgr rel & test, 1976-79; Siemens RTL, mgr IC design & test, strategic planning, analysis & design mfg syst; Widener Univ, adj prof, 1982. **Orgs:** Bd mem, Willingboro NJ Sch Dist, 1971-74; pres, IEEE Comp Soc, 1988-90, 2nd vpres chmn, technical activities, 1987, governing bd, 1979-; pres, IEEE Comp Soc, 1989, governing bd, 1999-00; Asn Dept Heads Comp & Info Sci & Eng. **Honors/Awds:** Distinguished Service Award, US Jaycees, 1972; Computer Society Meritorious Service Awards, 1981-85. **Military Serv:** AUS, specialist 4, 2 yrs. *

ANDERSON, KENNY
Basketball player, basketball coach. **Personal:** Born Oct 9, 1970, Queens, NY; children: Christenese; married Tami Akbar Anderson (divorced); children: Lyric Chanel & Kenni Lauren. **Educ:** GA Tech, attended 1993. **Career:** Basketball player (retired), basketball coach; NJ Nets, guard, 1991-95; Charlotte Hornets, 1995-96; Portland Blazers, 1996-97; Boston Celtics, 1998; Atlanta Hawks, 2004; Los Angeles Clippers, prof basketball player, 2004-05; Zalgiris Kaunas, point guard, 2005-06; Conn Basketball Asn, Atlanta Krunk, head coach, 2007-. **Orgs:** Kenny Anderson Found. **Honors/Awds:** NBA All-Star, 1994; Silver medal with Team USA, Goodwill Games, 1990. **Special Achievements:** NBA Draft, First round pick, No 2, 1991. **Business Addr:** Head Coach, Atlanta Krunk Wolverines, 643 Martin Luther King Jr Dr, Atlanta, GA 30314, **Business Phone:** 800-201-9919.*

ANDERSON, KERNIE L.
Executive, media executive. **Personal:** Born Jun 5, 1940, Harrisburg, PA; son of George P and Fannie R; married Althmeana C Coachman, Mar 10, 1973; children: Shama. **Educ:** Howard Univ, attended 1963; Univ MAR, Korean Extension Sch, 1967. **Career:** WQMR AM & WGAY FM, 1963-68; Ed Winton & Asn, WOCN AM & FM, gen mgr & prog dir, 1968-76; WWBA AM & FM, consult & troubleshooter, 1969-75; WCGL AM, gen mgr, 1976-77; KDIA, gen mgr, 1977-81; WBMX AM & FM, gen mgr, 1981-88; WIZF FM, vpres & gen mgr, 1988-89; WDAS AM & FM, vpres & gen mgr. **Orgs:** bd, Greater Philadelphia C C; bd, NCP; Nat Adoption ctr; Oper PUSH; Philadelphia Indust Develop Corp; Police Athletic League Philadelphia; bd, Philadelphia Radio Orgn; Urban League; bd, Utility Emergency Serv Fund; American Civil Liberties Union; Am Red Cross, Southeastern Pennsylvania Chap; Int Visitors Coun; Nat Adoption Ctr; Nat Coun Chiristians & Jews; Philadelphia Indust Develop Corp; Police Athletic League; Soul C Chicago, Youth Choir; United Way southeastern Pa; Utility Emergency Serv Fund. **Military Serv:** AUS, 1966-67. *

ANDERSON, LEON H.
Executive, educator. **Personal:** Born Sep 22, 1928, Jacksonville, FL; married Mary T Taylor; children: Lisa, Leon R, Leah & Lori. **Educ:** Morris Col, BA, 1956; Columbia Univ, MPA, 1963. **Career:** Teacher, executive (retired); Corbett High Sch, teacher, 1956-58; Morris Col, teacher, 1958-59; Saltertown Elem Sch, prin, 1958-61; Moore Elem Sch, prin, 1961-64; Ninth Ave High Sch, prin, 1964-65; Los Pinos Job Corps Ctr, Cleveland, Nat Forest, dep dir educ, 1964-65; USDA Forest Serv, SanFrancisco, educ specialist, 1965-69; USDA Forest Serv Wash, educ specialist, 1969-70; USDA, Mo, liaison officer, 1970-72; USDA, Human Resource Prog, asst dir, 1972-74, dir, 1974. **Honors/Awds:** Superior Service Award, USDA,1972; Superior Service Award,

Lincoln Univ,1974. **Military Serv:** AUS, cpl, 3 yrs. **Home Addr:** 12320 Millstream Dr, Bowie, MD 20715, **Home Phone:** (301)262-9606. *

ANDERSON, LESLIE BLAKE
Lawyer. **Personal:** Born Sep 14, 1966, Port Jefferson, NY; daughter of Alphonso and Andrea. **Educ:** Univ Endinburgh, Scotland, 1986; State Univ NY, Albany, BA, 1987; Albany Law Sch, JD, 1990. **Career:** Suffolk Co Dist Atty, asst dist atty, dist ct bur, 1991-92, case adv bur, 1993, major crime bur, 1993-97, chief, Gang Invests Unit, 1998-02; Suffolk County Dist Atty, atty, currently. **Orgs:** NY Dist Attys Asn, 1991-; Boy Scouts Am, Eagle Scout comm, 1993-; Suffolk Co Human Rights Comn, comnr, 1996; African-Am Adv Bd, Cong man Rick Lazio, 1996; E Coast Gang Investrs Asn; parliamentarian & coun, Long Island Headstart, bd dirs; Opportunities Industrialization Ctr, Inc, exec bd. **Honors/Awds:** Suffolk Co Exec, Advocate Award, 1996; Nat Asn Advan Colored People Advocacy Award, 1997; Cong Recognition Awards, 1997, 1998; Republican of Distinction, Afro-Am Republican Club, 1997; Suffolk Co Police Depart Guardians, Guardian of the Yr, 1999; Zonta Woman of the Yr, 1999. **Business Addr:** Attorney, Suffolk Co Dist Atty, Veterans Memorial Hwy, Hauppauge, NY 11788, **Business Phone:** (516)360-4161.*

ANDERSON, LOUISE PAYNE
Educator, advocate. **Personal:** Born Oct 18, 1923, Cannelton, WV; daughter of Andrew Payne Sr and Nancy Elizabeth Johnson Payne; married William Alexander, Feb 14, 1946 (deceased); children: Patricia C Petty & Cheryl Oni Plear. **Educ:** Bluefield State Col, BS, 1945; WV Col, MA; WV Univ. **Career:** Teacher, Advocate (retired); Pentagon, sec, 1946; Kanawha County Schs, teacher, 1947-85. **Orgs:** Beta Beta Omega Chap Alpha Kappa Alpha Sorority, 1943-; clerk, Bethel Bapt Ch, 1955-; counr, Mt Olivet Dist Asn; Delta Kappa Gamma, 1972-; Nat Asn of Univ Women, 1973; pres, Montgomery Br NAACP; auditor, Mt Olivet Women's Missionary Conv, 1983-; pres, Wash High Alumni Asn, 1985-; counr, WV State Baptist Asn; bd dir, Wash High Community Educ Ctr; NAACP, 1989; Alpha Kappa Alpha Sorority Inc; WVa Coalition Minority Health, 1995; pres, WHS Alumni Asn. **Honors/Awds:** Kanawha County Teacher of the Year, Kanawha Co Bd of Educ, 1982-83; Living the Dream Award, Martin Luther King Comn, 1986; Excellence in Teaching, WVa State Col, 1982; Community Service Award, Omega Psi Phi Frat, WVa Inst of Tech, 1988; Noell Award, United Teaching Profession, Kanawha Teachers Assn, 1981; Human Relations Award, Mary L Williams Memorial Comt, WV Educ Assn, 1980; Commercial Teacher of the Year, Bluefield State High Sch, 1957; Citation in Recognition of Significant Contribution as Sponsor of East Bank High, FTA; Received Certificate of Honor, Golden Circle Soror, Alpha Kappa Alpha & Educ, 1994; Ettie Mayham Brown, WVEA Minority Affairs Comt for Community Growth & Contributions, Oct 1, 1993. **Special Achievements:** First African-Am to serve as a dept head at E Bank High Sch; Delta Sigma Theta Inc, Charleston Inst Alumnae Chapter; organizer of non profit WHS Community Educ Ctr; sponsor of the organization supporting the project, grand opening, Nov 11, 1989; Helped to organize a Black Caucus within the WVa Educ Assn; first chairperson, 1972. **Home Addr:** PO Box 6, Cannelton, WV 25036, **Home Phone:** (304)442-8603.

ANDERSON, MADELINE
Television producer, administrator. **Personal:** Born in Lancaster, PA; daughter of William and Nellie; married Ralph Joseph Anderson; children: Adele, Rachel, Laura, Ralph Jr. **Educ:** New York Univ, BA, 1956. **Career:** WNET-TV, film ed, assoc producer, producer & dir, 1964-69; CTV Workshop, supv ed & prod dir, 1971-75, TV producer, 1985-87; Onyx Prod, pres, 1975-; Infinity Factory Educ Develop Ctr, exec producer, 1976-77; Off Black Ministry, Diocese Brooklyn/Queens, assoc dir, 1995-2000; TV series: "Al Manaahil", 1986; Movies: Integration Report 1, 1961; I Am Somebody. **Orgs:** Bd trustees, Int Film Seminars, 1974-77; film panelist & bd mem, NY Coun Arts, 1975-79; Nat Acad TV Arts & Sci; bd mem, Women Make Movies, 1986-88; bd mem, NY Film Coun. **Honors/Awds:** Woman of the Year, Sojourner Truth Festival Arts, 1976; Grand Prize, Media Women, 1977; Grants, NYSCA, WNET Doc Fund, Nat Endowment Arts & Am Film Inst; Indie Award, 1985; Lifelong Achievement Award, Asn Independent Video & Filmmakers; Unsung Heroine of Local 1199, 1969; Office of Black Ministry Diocese of Brooklyn, 1995; Humanitarian Award, NAWBPW Baisley Park Club, 1999; Gallery of the Greatest, Miller Brewing Co, Year 2000 Calendar; Award for Outstanding Contributions As A Documentary Filmmaker, African-Am Cinema Conf, 2000; Award for Willingness to Share Love & Knowledge of Black Catholic Heritage, Kuienga Youth Diocese Brooklyn. **Special Achievements:** First African-American woman to executive produce a TV series; inducted into the Black Filmmakers Hall of Fame, 1992; became the first African-American woman to executive produce a television series with Infinity Factory. **Home Addr:** 83 Sterling St, Brooklyn, NY 11225. *

ANDERSON, DR. MARCELLUS J., SR. See Obituaries section.

ANDERSON, DR. MARJORIE
Public relations executive. **Personal:** Born in Detroit, MI. **Educ:** Univ Detroit, BBA. **Career:** US Govt, EEO counselor, staff adv; D-Sace Charm Sch Comn, pub rel; Urban League Youth Assembly, pub rel dir; St Paul's Ch, pub rel dir; Afboney Mod & Fin Sch, pub rel dir; CANAC, pub rel dir. **Orgs:** Bd mem, Det Soc Adv Cultur & Educ; bd mem, Fisher YMCA; pres, FEMS Fisher YMCA; corr secy, media coord Det Urban League Guild; Red Cross vol; coordr, child hops Sickle Cell Anemia prog; columnist Spirit Det Tarcom Newspaper; bi-centennial chmn, Det Urban League Guilds Fund Raising Proj; nat historian Gamma Phi Delta Sor Inc; ed chief, Basileus Delta Nu Chap GPD Sor; youth dir, Delta Nu's Rosebud Youth Group; US Govt coord, Equal Oppty Day Upward Mobility Race Relat Unit Found Progs. **Honors/Awds:** Commission Service Award, GPD Sor, 1976; Commission Service Award, Det Urban League; Most Value Member Award, Urban League Guild, 1976; President of the Year, Gamma Phi Delta, 1973; Nat Pres, Outstanding Basileus GPD, 1974; Bi-Centennial Award, Delta Nu's Youth Group 1976.

ANDERSON, MARLON ORDELL
Baseball player. **Personal:** Born Jan 6, 1974, Montgomery, AL; married Shadia; children: Zoe, Hannah & Caleb. **Educ:** Univ S Ala. **Career:** Philadelphia Phillies, second baseman, 1998-2002; Tampa Bay Devil Rays, 2003; St Louis Cardinals, 2004; New York Mets, 2005, 2007-09; Wash Nationals, 2005; Los Angeles Dodgers, 2006-07, free agent, currently.

ANDERSON, MARSHA C
Educator. **Career:** Abraham Baldwin Agr Col, dir stud support serv, currently. **Business Phone:** (229)391-5160.

ANDERSON, MARVA JEAN
Government official, president (organization). **Personal:** Born May 9, 1945, Morrilton, AR; children: Tamikko Afresa Green. **Educ:** Los Angeles Trade Tech Col, AA, 1970; Calif State Univ, Dominguez Hills, BA, 1973; Univ Calif Los Angeles, MSW, 1978. **Career:** Communicative Arts Acad, admin asst, 1972-76; Spec Serv Groups, asst dir prog develop, 1976-82; YWCA Women Shelter, dir, 1982-84; Los Angeles County Dept C Serv, spec asst, 1984. **Orgs:** Vpres, 1980-81, pres, 1982-83, treas, 1984-87, Nat Asn Black Social Workers Los Angeles Chap; nat rep, Nat Asn Black Social Workers, 1984-87; comt mem, Image Awards, 1984-86, bd mem, 1987; Nat Asn Advan Colored People Hollywood Chap, 1984-86; vpres,Jenesse Inc, 1986-88; Asn Black Social Workers Greater Los Angeles, 1976-; bd mem, Jenesse Domestic Violence Shelter, 1985-; Lambda Kappa Mu Sorority, 1990-; sponsor, Black Women's Forum, 1990-. **Honors/Awds:** Plaque of Appreciation, Asn Black Social Workers Los Angeles, 1983; Recognition & Appreciation for Contribution to XXIII Olympics, Los Angeles Olympic Organizing Comn, 1984; Certificate of Commendation, Los Angeles City Councilman Robert Farrell, 1984; Leadership Award, Los Angeles Brotherhood Crusade, 1985; Plaque of Recognition, Calif Asn Black Social Workers, 1986.

ANDERSON, MARY ELIZABETH
Government official, educator. **Personal:** Born in Andersonville, VA. **Educ:** Va Union Univ, BS; Chicago Col Com; Am Univ; US Dept Agr Grad Sch. **Career:** Off Educ, fiscal officer, 1965-70, women's prog coordr, 1975-; Union High Sch, teacher; Va Union Univ Rept Women's Nat Adv Coun, counr, 1976-; Health, Educ & Welfare, specialist, 1970-. **Orgs:** Affil Nat Alliance Black Sch Educs; life mem, Nat Asn Advan Colored People exec bd mem, 1975-77; DC Women's Polit Caucus; Friends Frederick Douglass Mus African Art; Alpha Kappa Alpha. **Honors/Awds:** Spec Citation US Civil Serv Comn, 1973; Citation of Appreciation, Nat Asn Advan Colored People, 1974; Outstanding Service Award, Nat Asn Advan Colored People, 1976. **Special Achievements:** Published book Sex Equality in Education; Co-Author for the book of History of US Office of Education & Feild Services. **Business Addr:** Specialist, United States Department of Health Education & Welfare, 400 Maryland Ave SW, Washington, DC 20202.

ANDERSON, MICHAEL WAYNE
Public relations executive. **Personal:** Born Feb 24, 1942, Wilmington, DE; married Yvonne Gloria Copeland; children: Kima-Joi Michaele. **Educ:** CA State Univ, BS, LA, 1973. **Career:** YMCA Youthmobile Metro Los Angeles, dir, 1971-73; A Better Chance Inc, western states reg dir, 1973-, recruitment coordr, currently; Crenshaw Branch YMCA Metro Los Angeles, exec dir, 1975-77; Calif FAIR Plan Asn, mgr public affairs, 1977. **Orgs:** Calif Arson Prevent Comt, 1977-80; pres, Los Angeles chap, Nat Asn Mkt Developers, 1978-80; San Francisco Arson Task Force, 1979-80; chmn, speakers bur Pub Club Los Angeles, 1979-80; eligible comt chmn, Pub Rel Soc Am, 1980; res secy, PIRATES, 1980; bd dirs, Angeles Girl Scout Coun, 1980; pres, Toastmasters Int, 1980; Los Angeles Mayor's Arson Suppression Task Force; Los Angeles Chap, Nat Asn Advan Colored People; Los Angeles Chap Urban League; Crenshaw Neighbors. **Honors/Awds:** Certificate of Appreciation, County Los Angeles, 1972, 1974; Certificate of Appreciation Los Angeles Jr C C, 1974; Distinguished Toastmaster Toastmasters Int, 1977; Speaker's Award,Western Ins Info Serv, 1978-80. **Military Serv:** AUS, E-4, 1964-66. **Business Addr:** Recruitment Coordinator, A Better Chance Inc, c/o Univ Southern Calif, Tyler bldg 100, Los Angeles, CA 90089-0911, **Business Phone:** (213)743-2674.

ANDERSON, MILLER R.
Social worker. **Personal:** Born in Chicago, IL. **Educ:** Ill State Univ, BS; Univ Ill, MSW, 1984. **Career:** Ill Dept C & Family Serv, case mgr; Children's Home & Aid Soc Ill; Chicago Youth Ctrs, pres & chief exec officer, 2000-. **Honors/Awds:** City Partner Award, Univ Ill, 2003.

ANDERSON, MONROE
Writer. **Personal:** Born Apr 6, 1947, Gary, IN; married Joyce Owens; children: Scott, Kyle. **Educ:** Ind Univ, Bloomington, BA, jour, eng lit, 1970. **Career:** Newsweek magazine; Chicago Tribune, polit columnist; Nat Observer, staffwriter, 1970-72; Ebony Mag, asst ed, 1972-74; Post-Tribune, 1969; Columbia Col-Chicago, 1984-88; Mayor's Office, press secy, 1988-89; WBBM-TV, dir sta serv & community affairs, host, exec prod,1989-02; N'DIGO, ed; Savoy Mag, ed, 2003-2004. **Orgs:** NABJ; past dir, Region V; Ill Broadcasters assoc; IL Arts Found; Keep Chicago Beautiful; Gilda's Club; Nat Acad of TV Arts and Sci, Chicago Chapt. **Honors/Awds:** AP IL St Award, 1976; Chicago Trib Edward Beck Spcl Award, 1976; First Place Inland Press Award, 1977; Jacob Scher Award, 1979; Best Comm Serv Award, UPI, 1980; Outstanding Print Jour Award, Chicago Assoc of Black Journalists, 1981; Outstanding Print Jour Award, DuSable Mus, 1982; Outstanding Commentary Chicago Assoc of Black Journalists, 1985; Media Award, NY State Bar Assoc, 1986. **Special Achievements:** Co-auth, Brothers, 1988; contribr, Restoration, 1989; Chicago Elects a New Daley, 1991. *

ANDERSON, MOSES B.
Clergy. **Personal:** Born Sep 9, 1928, Selma, AL. **Educ:** St Michael's Col, BA, philosophy, MAT, sociol, 1961; St Edmund Sem; Xavier Univ, Theol, 1968. **Career:** Clergy (retired); Our Lady Consolation Parish, assoc pastor, 1958-59; St Michael col, lect, 1959-61; St Catherine, Parish, pastor, 1961-64; St Michael Col, assoc prof theol, 1964-71; Xavier Univ, Notre Dame Sem, dir religious affairs & assoc prof, 1971-81; All Saints Parish, pastor, 1981; Titular Bishop Vatarba; Detroit, auxiliary bishop, 1982-03; Precious Blood Parish Detroit, Pastor, 1992. **Honors/Awds:** Doctor Humane Letters, St Michael Col, 1984; Kansas Neumann Col, LLD, 1985; Honorary Doctor of Humanities, Madonna Col, 1989. **Special Achievements:** Ordained priest, 1958. *

ANDERSON, NATHANIEL
Educator, school administrator. **Personal:** Born Sep 15, 1950, St Louis, MO; son of Noble and Rosie; married Tanya E, Aug 1, 1981; children: Shunique Oliver & Nichelle Womack. **Educ:** Eastern Ill Univ, BS, recreation, 1973, MS, educ, 1977; Southeast MO State Univ, specialist, educ, 1991; Ill State Univ, doctorate, education admin, 1998. **Career:** Decatur Recreation Dept, park leader, 1977; MacArthur High Sch, counselor & teacher, suspension counr, phys ed instr, football & track asst coach, 1977-82; Stephen Decatur High Sch, dean stud, 1982-88; Cairo High Sch, prin, 1988-90; Dwight D Eisenhower High Sch, prin, 1990-93; Rock Island & Milan Dist 41, high sch prin, asst supt, 1993-98; Bd Educ Sch Dist 189, supt, 1998; Univ Ill Springfield, vis asst prof, asst prof educ leadership, currently. **Orgs:** Bd dirs, Eastern Ill Univ Alumni Asn, 1992-93; adv bd, Educ Admin Comt, Eastern IL Univ, 1992-93; dir, Decatur Parks Found, 1992-93; bd mem, Decatur Respect, 1992-93; bd dirs, West End Coalition, 1992-93; secy & treas, vpres, Big 12 Athletic Conf, 1992-93; Rock Island Youth Concerns Group Comn, 1992-93; bd dir, Bethany Home, 1992-93; bd dir, Quad Cities Scholars, 1992-93; Ill Asn Sch Adminrs; Nat Asn Secy Sch Principals; Ill Principals Asn; Asn for Supv & Curriculum Develop; Phi Delta Kappa; Ill High School Asn; Omega Psi Phi Fraternity; Nat Asn Advan Colored People; John C Ellis Masonic Lodge; Eastern IL Club-Athletic Boosters; founder, Base Runners Athletic Team; Optimist Int, Rock Island, IL; Nat Asn Black Sch Educrs; Mt Zion Baptist Church, East St Louis. **Honors/Awds:** Kodak, All Am Col Div Football Team, 1972; AP, All Am Col Div Football Team, 1973; Jaycees, Outstanding Young Men of Am, 1973; Community Contrib Citation, City of East St Louis, 1976; citation, CETA Summer Youth Prog, 1982; Great Teacher Citation, EIU Dept of Education Psychol, 1984; Eastern IL Athletic Hall of Fame, 1986; Citizen of the Yr Award, Omega Psi Phi Frat, 1988; Volunteer Award, Ill High School Asn, 1990; President's Award in Educ, Nat Asn Advan Colored People, Decatur Branch, 1992; Education Award, Anna Waters, 1995; Excellence in Education Award, Rock Island Rotary, 1995. **Business Addr:** Assistant Professor of Educational Leadership, University of Illinois, Brookens 390 1 Univ Plz, Springfield, IL 62703, **Business Phone:** (217)206-6600.

ANDERSON, NELISON. See ANDERSON, NICK.

ANDERSON, NICHOLAS CHARLES
Association executive. **Personal:** Born Feb 7, 1953, Gaston County, NC; son of Nicodemus (deceased) and Fannie Mae Moses; married Darlene Davis (divorced 1990); children: Takecia Kamari, Brandye Nicole & Michelle Darlene; married Marionette, Jun 25, 1994. **Educ:** Cent Piedmont Community Col, Charlotte, NC, 1971-72; Wayne State Univ, Detroit, MI, BA, 1981. **Career:** Am Tobacco Co, sales rep, 1974-76, dist sales mgr, 1976-81; Com Freddie G Burton Jr, legis aide, 1983-87; Detroit Urban League, pres & chief exec officer, 1987-94, 1997-; City Detroit, Dept Human Servs, exec dir, 1994-97. **Orgs:** Youth prog dir, Detroit Br, Nat Asn Advan Colored People, 1981-83, Midwest region III, dir, 1983-87; Econ Club Detroit, 1988-; bd dirs, Oper ABLE, 1990-

97; adv bd, NBD Community Develop Corp, 1990-95; bd dirs, CATCH, 1991-; bd dirs, Mich Black Caucus, 1991-96; trustee, Mich Non-Profit Forum, 1991-; Detroit Compact Community Partners Comn; Detroit Pub Sch City-Wide Community Orgn; secy & trustee, Luellen Hannah Found; bd trustees, chair, Pub Responsibility Comn, Henry Ford Health Syst; bd dir, Health Alliance Plan; vice chmn, bd dir, Schs 21st Century; bd Police comnr, Testimonial Resolution, 1994; bd dirs & pres, WSU Alumni Asn 1996-97; Detroit Bd Educ, 1997-98; chmn bd, Health Alliance Plan, Detroit. **Honors/Awds:** Regional III Service, Nat Asn Advan Colored People, 1988; Man of the Year, Minority Women's Network, 1992. **Special Achievements:** Co author "The State of Black Michigan: 1993". **Home Addr:** 18232 Fairfield St, Detroit, MI 48221, **Home Phone:** (313)342-5907. **Business Addr:** President, Detroit Urban League, 208 Mack Ave, Detroit, MI 48201, **Business Phone:** (313)832-4600.*

ANDERSON, NICK (NELISON ANDERSON)
Basketball player, basketball executive. **Personal:** Born Jan 20, 1968, Chicago, IL; son of Robert Anderson and Alberta; children: Joshua. **Educ:** Univ Ill, Champaign, IL, 1989. **Career:** Basketball player (retired), basketball executive; Orlando Magic, forward-guard, 1989-99, Sacramento Kings, 1999-2001; Memphis Grizzlies, 2001-02; mem community rels dept, 2006-. **Honors/Awds:** Rich and Helen DeVos Community Enrichment Award, 1996. **Business Phone:** (407)916-2400.

ANDERSON, NORMAN
Administrator. **Educ:** NC Cent Univ; Univ NC, Greensboro, NC, PhD, clin psychol. **Career:** Duke Univ Med Sch, prof; Harvard Sch Pub Health, Dep Health & Soc Behav, prof, currently. **Orgs:** Fel, AAAS; Am Psychol Asn; Asn Psychol Sci; Soc Behavl Med; Acad Behav Med Res; past-pres, Soc Behav Med; past-pres, Bd Dirs, Steven Spielberg's Starbright Found, Los Angeles; chair, Nat Acad Sci, Panel Future Res Race, Ethnicity & Health Later Life; founding dir, Off Behav & Social Sci Res, 1995-2000; exec vpres & chief exec officer, Am Psychol Asn, currently. **Special Achievements:** Numerous publications including Editor-in-Chief, The Encyclopedia of Health and Behavior, Author, Emotional Longevity: What Really Determines How Long You Live, Editor-in-Chief of APA's flagship journal, American Psychologist; Firat African American Chief Executive Officer of American Psychological Association. **Business Addr:** Professor, Harvard School of Public Health, Department of Health & Social Behavior, 677 Huntington Ave, Boston, MA 02115, **Business Phone:** (617)432-1135.

ANDERSON, NORMAN B
College teacher, executive, psychologist. **Educ:** NC Cent Univ, clin psychol, Durham; Univ NC, Greensboro, master's & doctoral degrees, Brown Univ, clin psychol internship. **Career:** Duke Univ, assoc prof; Nat Inst Health, assoc dir; prof, Harvard Univ Sch Pub Health, 2000-02; Am Psychol Asn, chief exec officer & exec vpres, 2003-. **Orgs:** Bd dir, Am Pyschol Asn Coun Rep. **Business Phone:** (202)336-5700.

ANDERSON, PATRICIA HEBERT
Activist, executive. **Personal:** Born Aug 28, 1945, Houston, TX; daughter of Emma Jean Pope and Aldaah Augusta; married Rev Adolphus Anderson Jr, Jun 28, 1964 (deceased); children: Renee, Reginald, Adolphus III, Ruthalyn, Victor, Albert, Michael & Miriam. **Educ:** Tex Southern Univ, attended 1963, MS, 1997, doctoral student; Gulf Coast Bible Col, AA Theol, 1975; COGIC, nat evangelist prog, 1987; Union Baptist Bible Col & Sem, BTh, 1992; Arts & Sci Social Work, TSU, attended 1995; Union Baptist Sem & Bible Col, Coun & Rel Ed, master's degree, 1995. **Career:** Harris City Democratic Exec Comn, precinct comnr, 1976-; Glen Manor Weyburn Pl Civic Col, pres, 1979-; Gulf Coast Community Serv, sec, bd dir, 1980; North Forest ISD, sec, bd dir, 1981; Nat Black Caucus Sch Bd, sec, 1982, 1984, bd dir, 1984; Pleasant Green Bapt Church, active church musician; Star Faith Grand Chap, OES 55 grand musician; North Forest Sch Dist, trustee; North Forest Sch Dist Bd Educ, pres, 1988-89; Harris County Dem Party, precinct chair, currently. **Orgs:** Community coordr, NE Community Proj Fund, 1972; chairwoman, New Hope Baptist Church Missionary Affairs, 1975; pres, Glen Manor Weyburn Pl, 1979-; alt person, City Comnr Jim Fontero, 1980; sec, Gulf Coast Community Serv, 1981; bd dir, BATTS, 1982; admin asst, City Comn EA Squattylyons, 1982; Harris County Black Elected Officers, 1986; bd mem, Evangelistic Bible Days Revival Church; secy, Nat Caucus Black Sch Bd Members, 1986-; Houston Cent Young Women Christian Coun, 1987-89; bd mem, Greater Park Hill Church God Christ Evangelical Bd, 1987-; pres, Sewing Circle, 1988-; pres, Young Women Christian Coun, 1988-; Houston Cent Dist Church God Christ; Mt Sinai Grand Lodge, AF&AM, grand matron; Greater Park Hill Church God Christ. **Honors/Awds:** Community Service Award, City Houston Mayor Whitmire, 1983; Hon, Nat Black Caucus Sch Bd Mem, 1983; Woman of the Year, New Hope Baptist Church, 1983; Honor Award, Gulf Coast Community Serv, 1983; High Achievement, NE Community Proj, 1984; Merit of Achievement, Legis Black Caucus State Rep Harol Dutton, 1986; Mother of the Year, New Hope Baptist Church, 1986; Outstanding Black Elected Official, Wayside Church of Christ, 1986; Juneteenth Freedom Award, Nat Am Advan Colored People, 1987; Nat Dean's List, Tex Southern Univ, 1989-90; Outstanding Leadership, Bd Educ, North Forest ISD, 1992; TSU, Deans List, Nat, 1993-95. **Home Addr:** 7539 Carothers St, Houston, TX 77028, **Home Phone:** (713)631-8213. **Business Addr:** Precinct Chair, Harris County Democratic Party, 7539 Carothers St, Houston, TX 77028, **Business Phone:** (713)631-8213.

ANDERSON, PERRY L
Law enforcement officer. **Career:** Miami Police Dept, chief; Cambridge Police Dept, comnr, currently. **Orgs:** Pres, Nat Orgn Black Law Enforcement Off. **Special Achievements:** The second black chief of the Miami Police Department. **Business Addr:** Commissioner, Cambridge Police Department, Office of the Commissioner, 5 Wern Ave, Cambridge, MA 02139, **Business Phone:** (617)349-3378.*

ANDERSON, RACHEL
Educator. **Career:** Kent State Univ, Off Adult Serv, co-pres & dir, currently, life coordr, currently. **Business Phone:** (330)672-7933.

ANDERSON, RACHELL
Educator, administrator. **Educ:** Philander Smith Col, BA; Sangamon State Univ, MA; Northern Ill Univ, MS;Adler Sch Prof Psychol, PhD. **Career:** Pvt clin pract, 1974-; Univ Ill, Human Services prog, chair, 1999-2006, Women & Gender Studies, assoc prof & dept chair, currently. **Orgs:** Cent Ill Soc Adlerian Psychol; Cent Ill Psychol Soc; Am Asn Black Psychologists; AM Psychol Asn; Nat Org Human Serv. **Honors/Awds:** The Committee for Children's Award for 25 years of dedicated services on the Family Stress team; Who's Who Among America's Teachers; Who's Who Among Outstanding Americans. **Special Achievements:** Publ: "Before Our Eyes,", The Legacy Continues: Writing Healing Stories".

ANDERSON, RICHARD CHARLES
Lawyer. **Personal:** Born Nov 25, 1945, Vallejo, CA; son of Walter and Margaret; married Rosalynn Anderson, Jan 26, 1974; children: Walter. **Educ:** Kennedy-King Jr Col, AA, 1972; Univ Chicago, BA, 1973; Northwestern Univ, Sch Law, JD, 1977. **Career:** CNA Ins Co, acct exec, 1980-81; Cook County State's Atty, asst state's atty, 1981-84; Pvt Pract, atty law, 1984-86, 1995-; Chicago Housing Authority, dep gen coun, 1986-95. **Orgs:** Volunteers for Housing, chmn, 1971-76. **Special Achievements:** Regenald Heber Smity Community Lawyer Fellowship, 1977; published article, "I Love My Son Walter As He Is," in Exceptional Parent Magazine, 1991; published article, "Walter At 10," in book entitled Uncommon Fathers Reflections on Raising a Child with a Disability, Woodline House, 1995. **Military Serv:** AUS, spec 5, e-5, 1967-69; Purple Heart, 1968. **Home Addr:** 518 W 62nd St, Chicago, IL 60621-3206, **Home Phone:** (773)994-5154. *

ANDERSON, RICHARD DARNOLL
Football player. **Personal:** Born Sep 13, 1971, Olney, MD; married; children: Richie II & Reginald. **Educ:** Pa State Univ. **Career:** Football player (retired), Football coach; New York Jets, running back, 1993-2002; Dallas Cowboys, running back, 2003-04, coach, 2007; New York Jets, asst wide receivers coach, 2005-06; free agent, currently. **Honors/Awds:** NFLPA Byron Whizzer White Award, 2000; Maryland Player of the Year, USA today. Pro Bowl, 2001.

ANDERSON, RONALD EDWARD, SR.
Manager. **Personal:** Born Aug 4, 1948, Indianapolis, IN; married Dolores Jean Benson; children: Ronald Jr. **Educ:** TN State Univ, BS, 1970; Univ Evansville, attended 1976, Cent Mich Univ, attended 1986. **Career:** State Farm Fire & Casualty Ins, admin & tech trainee, 1971-72, sr claim rep, 1973-75, claim specialist, 1975-80, claim supt, 1980-85; State Farm Mutual Ins Co, claim specialist, 1985-; Anderson Financial Servs, owner, currently. **Orgs:** Trustee, New Hope Bapt Chap, Evansville, IN, 1974-80; bd dir, Transit System, Evansville, 1976-78; bd dir, Carver Comn Orgn, Evansville, 1976-80; vice pole march, Evansville Alumni Chap Kappa Alpha Psi, 1977-79; chmn finance comn, Evansville Black Expos, 1979; sec & treas, Flint Alumni Chap Kappa Alpha Psi, 1982-86. **Honors/Awds:** Good Neighbor of the Year Award, IN Regional Off State Farm Ins Co, W Lafayette, IN, 1978. **Military Serv:** AUS Reserves, cpt, 6yrs. **Business Addr:** Owner, Anderson Financial Services, 2775 Karoc Ct, Simi Valley, CA 93063.*

ANDERSON, RONALD GENE
Basketball player. **Personal:** Born Oct 10, 1958, Chicago, IL. **Educ:** Calif State Univ, Fresno, attended 1984. **Career:** Cleveland Cavaliers, 1984-86; Ind Pacers, 1986-88; Philadelphia 76ers, 1988-93; NJ Nets, 1993-94; Wash Bullets; 1993-94; Maccabi Natanya, Israel, 1995-96; Le Mans SB, 1996-97. **Honors/Awds:** NBA rookie named to league's All-Star team.

ANDERSON, ROSALAND GUIDRY
Manager. **Personal:** Born Jan 27, 1959, Lake Charles, LA; daughter of Calvin and Theresa; married David T Anderson Jr, Feb 12, 1978; children: David III & Theresa Camille. **Educ:** Tex Southern Univ, BS, math, 1978; Univ Houston, MS, math, 1979. **Career:** IBM, systs engr, 1988-90, systs eng mgr, 1990-94, solution serv mgr, 1994-95, availability serv mgr, 1995-97, AS/400 area mgr, nat bp prog mgr, 1999-. **Orgs:** Jack & Jill Am, nat recording sec, 1985-; Leadership Tex Alumni; bd mem, Bexar County Oppor Industrialization Ctr, 1987-; bd mem, Catholic Families & Charities, 1987-; bd mem, UT Pre Freshman Engineering, 1987-; jr counr girls, Knights St Peter Claver, 1987-. **Honors/Awds:** Eagle Award, IBM, 1979, Regional Awards, 1983, 1985, 1987; BCOIC, Top Citizens Award, 1992; Profiles in Leadership Award, Mission City Business & Professional Women, 1999. **Home Addr:** 15507 Dawn Crest, San Antonio, TX 78248. **Business Addr:** National Business Partner Program Manager, IBM Corp, 911 Central Pkwy N Suite 100, San Antonio, TX 78232, **Business Phone:** (210)403-1014.

ANDERSON, RUTH BLUFORD
Educator. **Personal:** Born Oct 28, 1921, Braden, OK; daughter of Roy and Josie Blocker Knowles; married Everett McKinnis (divorced 1959); married James C Anderson Jr; children: Eugene McKinnis, Carl, Valerie (deceased), Glennis Anderson Mines, Dennis,James Anderson & Keith McKinnis. **Educ:** Lincoln Univ, Jeff City, MO, 1941; Univ Calif, Berkeley, BA, 1946; Columbia Univ, NY, MSW, 1956; Univ Chicago, Summer Inst, SSA, 1971; Smith Col, Northampton, MA, 1982. **Career:** Westchester County, Welfare Dept New York, staff, 1956; Black Hawk Co Welfare Dept, dir, 1963-67; Wartburg Col, IA, asst prof social work, 1967-69; Univ Northern Iowa, from asst prof to assoc prof,1969-86, prof 1986-93, Dept Soc Work, actg head, 1988-90, prof emer, 1989-; Black Hawk Co, bd supervisors, 1988-91, chmn, 1990. **Orgs:** Community Gov Branstads Long Term Care, 1984; N E Iowa AIDS Coalition,1987; Nat Asn Black Soc Workers, 1989; Nat Asn Advan Colored People, 1990;mem bd dir, NE Co Substance Abuse, 1990; Golden Life mem, Delta Sigma Theta Sorority; Univ Northern Iowa Emer Asn; Iowa Coalition Community Orgn; Iowa Mental Health Asn. **Honors/Awds:** Iowa Women's Hall of Fame, 1982; Women of Achievement, Networking Together IX,1988; DHL, Simpson Col, 1990; Soc Worker of the Year, IA, 1991; Great Delta Teacher of the Year, Delta Sigma Theta Sorority, 1992; Kirk Strong Award, Gov Conf on Substance Abuse, 1992; IA African-Am Hall of Fame Inductee, 1996. **Special Achievements:** First African-American woman to be elected to an at-large seat on the Black Hawk County Board of Supervisors; Articles on Blacks & Substance Abuse; author of From Mother's Aid Child to University Professor: An Autobiography of an American Black Woman, 1985. **Home Addr:** 1503 Newell St, PO Box 1692, Waterloo, IA 50707. *

ANDERSON, S. A.
Executive. **Personal:** Born May 31, 1935, Ennis, TX; married Betty; children: Monetta Kaye, Madeline Joyce & Arthur Girard. **Educ:** Prairie View Agr & Mech Univ, BS, 1956; Atlanta Univ; Tex Southern Univ; Univ Okla. **Career:** Pemberton High Sch, Marshall, TX, teacher & coach, 1958-69. **Orgs:** Nat Urban League; E Tex Coaches & Officials Asn, 1958-69; Asn Black Soc Workers; Order Arrow Boy Scouts Am, 1962; Am Soc Pub Admin; Tex Asn Comm Action Agencies; chmn, NAACP, 1970-75; Nat Asn Comm Develop; exec dir, Nat Comm Action Agency Asn; bd dir, E Tex Legal Serv Corp; Alpha Phi Alpha Frat; SW Baseball Umpires Asn; Am Asn Retired Persons. **Honors/Awds:** Man of Year, Reg Fels Club, 1970, 1975; NSF Grants, 1960, 1962-64, 1967; Excellence Awards, E Tex Coaches & Officials Asn, 1964, 1968; Service Award, Zeta Phi Beta, 1972; Service Award, Phi Beta Sigma, 1971; Service Award, AKA, 1976; Outstanding Achievement Award, Tex State Conf, NAACP, 1971. **Military Serv:** AUS, capt, 1956-58; Sr Parachutist Badge.

ANDERSON, SHANDON RODRIGUEZ
Basketball player. **Personal:** Born Dec 31, 1973, Atlanta, GA; son of Willie and Dorothy; children: Kori, Dorothy & Willie. **Educ:** Univ Ga, attended 1996. **Career:** Utah Jazz, forward, 1996-98; Houston Rockets, guard, 1999-2001; NY Knicks, forward guard, 2001-04; Miami Heat, guard, 2004-06; free agent, currently. **Orgs:** Founder & pres, Shandon Anderson Found, 2003-. **Business Addr:** Founder, The Shandon Anderson Foundation, 595 Piedmont Ave NE Suite 320-115, Atlanta, GA 30308, **Business Phone:** (786)777-4328.

ANDERSON, STEVE
Football player. **Personal:** Born May 12, 1970, Monroe, LA. **Educ:** Grambling State Univ. **Career:** Football player (retired); New York Jets, wide receiver, 1994; Ariz Cardinals, 1995-96.

ANDERSON, TALMADGE
Educator. **Personal:** Born Jul 22, 1932, Hazlehurst, GA; son of Viola Lee Baker; married Cerci Lee (divorced); children: Rose, Ramona, Talmadge, Rhunell & Raul. **Educ:** Savannah State Col, BS, 1953; Atlanta Univ, MBA, 1958. **Career:** Educator (retired); Lane Col, Dept Bus, chmn, 1958-59; Allen Univ, asst prof, 1959-62; St Augustine's Col, asst prof & chmn, 1963-65; Bethune-Cookman Col, assoc prof, 1966-67; WVa Inst Tech, asst prof, 1968-70; Western J Black Studies, founder & ed; Wash State Univ, assocprof bus adminr, dir assoc prof mkt & black studies, assoc prof bus adminr, 1998-2005, Dept Comp Am Cultures & Mkt, prof emer, currently. **Orgs:** Adv bd mem, Employ Security Comn Wash, 1975-77; exec bd mem, Nat CounBlack Studies, 1975-; exec coun mem, Asn Study African Am Life & Hist,1977-86.

Honors/Awds: Hundred Most Influential Friends Award, Black Jour, 1977; Certificate of Achievement, Africa-Hamline Univ, 1978; Frederick Douglass Scholar Award, 1986. **Special Achievements:** Author: Black Studies: Theory, Methods & Cultural Perspectives, 1990; Introduction to African American Studies, 1993. **Military Serv:** AUS, sgt, 1953-56. **Business Addr:** Professor Emeritus, Washington State University, Department of Comparative American Cultures and Marketing, PO Box 641045, Pullman, WA 99164-1045, **Business Phone:** (509)335-2447.

ANDERSON, DR. THOMAS JEFFERSON
Composer, educator. **Personal:** Born Aug 17, 1928, Coatesville, PA; son of Thomas J and Anita Turpeau; married Lois Ann Field; children: T J III, Janet & Anita. **Educ:** WVa State Col, BM, 1950, DMus, 1984; Pa State Univ, MEd, 1951; Univ Iowa, PhD, compos, 1958; Holy Cross Col, DMA, 1983. **Career:** Opera: Soldier Boy, Soldier, 1972; Treemonisha; High Pt City Pub Sch, teacher, 1951-54; W Va State Col, instr, 1955-56; Langston Univ, prof & chmn, 1958-63; Tenn State Univ, prof music, 1963-69; Atlanta Symphony Orchestra, composer-in-residence, 1969-71; Morehouse Col, Danforth vis prof music, 1971-72; Tufts Univ, prof music & chmn, 1972-80, Austin Fletcher prof music, 1976-90, Austin Fletcher prof emer music,1990-; Univ Salvador, artistic residency, 1988; DeKalb Univ, Dept Fine Arts, prof, 1998. **Orgs:** Fel Mac Dowell Colony, 1960-83; fel Yhaddo, 1970-77; founder & pres, Black Music Caucus MENC; bd mem, Elma Lewis Sch Fine Arts, 1975-; chair, Comt Status Minorities, Col Music Soc, 1976-80; Harvard Musical Assn, 1976-; hon mem, Phi Beta Kappa, 1977; Music Coun Arts & Humanities, 1978-81; St Botolph Club, 1980; adv brd, Meet The Composer, 1980; fel John Simon Guggenheim Found, 1989; bd mem, Harvard Musical Assn, 1989. **Honors/Awds:** Copley Foundation Award, 1964; Fromm Foundation Award, 1964-71; Honorary degree, Northwestern Univ, 2002; Honorary Doctor of Music degree, Bates Col, Lewiston, Maine, 2005. **Special Achievements:** Over 50 published compositions; 60th Birthday Concert, Videmus, Harvard University, 1989; Anderson was singularly honored when Bruce Alfred Thompson devoted his Ph.D. dissertation at Indiana University to an analysis of his works. **Home Addr:** 34 Grove St, Medford, MA 02155. **Business Phone:** (404)299-4136.*

ANDERSON, TONY
Insurance executive. **Personal:** Born Jun 14, 1947, Dillon, SC; son of Mary Agnes; married Westley A Smith, Oct 22, 1983; children: Christopher & Natasha. **Educ:** Western Conn State Col, Danbury, Conn, BA, 1979; Univ New Haven, W Haven, Conn, MBA, 1989. **Career:** N J Natural Gas Co, duplication clerk, Asbury Park, 1968-72; City Trust, Bridgeport, Conn, comput operator, 1972-76, security trader, 1976-80; Equitable Life Assurance Soc, NYC, security trader, 1980-81, mgr, money mkt trading, 1981-82, asst treas, 1982-83, asst vpres, 1983-88, vpres, 1988-; Equitable Credit Union, NYC, dir, 1988. **Orgs:** NASD, 1977-; dir, Equitable Credit Union, 1988-. **Honors/Awds:** Ford Found Scholar, 1976. **Military Serv:** USAF, E-4, 1965-68. **Business Addr:** Vice President, Equitable Financial Co, 787 7th Ave Suite 41N, New York, NY 10019, **Business Phone:** (212)554-3100.

ANDERSON, TONY
Executive. **Personal:** Born Oct 29, 1950, Washington, DC; son of William Anderson and Frances; married Antoinette, Dec 5, 1981; children: Angela, William, Nathan, Aja. **Career:** Track Recording Studio, recording engr, 1971-73; Warner Elektra Atlantic Distribution, mktg coordr, 1974-75; Jonas Cash Promotions, independent promotion rep, 1975-82; Motown Records, nat R&B promotion dir, 1982-85; Arista Records, vpres, R&B promotion, 1985-91; Mercury Records, exec vpres & gen mgr, 1991-93; Columbia Records, svpres & black music. **Honors/Awds:** One of the Top 50 Black Entertainment Power Brokers, Black Enterprise Magazine, 1994; Joe Medlin Contributors Award, International Asn African Am Music, 1995; Black Entertainment & Sports Lawyers Asn Hall of Fame, 1993. *

ANDERSON, TYFINI CHENCE
Manager. **Personal:** Born Jan 9, 1978, Cincinnati, OH; daughter of Edward and Avis. **Educ:** Wilberforce Univ, BS, psychol. **Career:** Volunteers Am, case mgr, 2000-. **Orgs:** Alpha Kappa Mu Hon Soc; Wilberforce Book Club, 1997; pres, Imani Dance Troope, 1998-99; vpres, Kappa Theta Epsilon Honor Society, 1999-00. **Honors/Awds:** Belle Hogan Roberts Award, Wilberforce Univ, 1999; Employee of the Month, Volunteers Am, 2000. **Business Addr:** Case Manager, Volunteers of America, Ohio River Valley Inc, 1931 S Gettysburge Ave, Dayton, OH 45408, **Business Phone:** (937)262-8876.

ANDERSON, BISHOP VINTON RANDOLPH
Bishop, clergy. **Personal:** Born Jul 11, 1927, Somerset, Bermuda; married Vivienne Louise Cholmondeley, 1952; children: Vinton R Jr, Jeffrey Charles, Carlton Lawson & Kenneth Robert. **Educ:** Wilberforce Univ, BA; Payne Theol Sem, MDiv, 1952; Kans Univ, MA, philos; Yale Univ Divinity Sch; Urban Training Ctr Christian Missions. **Career:** Clergy (retired); itinerant deacon, 1951; itinerant elder, 1952; St Mark AME Church, pastor, 1952-53; Brown Chapel AME Church, pastor, 1953-55; St Luke AME Church, Lawrence, pastor, 1955-59; St Paul AME Church, Wichita, pastor, 1959-64; St Paul AME Church, St Louis, pastor, 1964-72; presiding bishop, chief pastor: 9th Episcopal District, AL, 1972-76; 3rd Episcopal Dist, OH, W Va, W Pa, 1976-84; Off Ecumenical Rel & Develop, staff, 1984-88; 5th Episcopal Dist, bishop, 1988-2004. **Orgs:** Del, World Methodist Coun & Conf, 1961-; World Coun Churches; first vpres, World Methodist Coun, N Am Region; gov bd, Nat Coun Churches; chair, Faith & Order Comn; vpres, Cong Nat Black Churches; vpres, Consultation Church Union; United Methodist Church, Gen Comn Christian Unity & Inter religious Concern; Schomburg Ctr Res Black Cult; Nat Asn Advan Colored People; Urban League; ecumenical officer & pres, N Am Jurisdiction World Coun Churches. **Honors/Awds:** Religion Award, Ebony Mag, 1988, 1991; American Black Achievement Awards, 1991; Distinguished Alumni Honoree, Nat Asn Equal Opportunity Higher Educ, 1988; Honorary Doctorate Degree, Paul Quinn Col; Honorary Doctorate Degree, Wilberforce Univ; Honorary Doctorate Degree, Payne Theol Sem; Honorary Doctorate Degree, Temple Bible Col; Honorary Doctorate Degree, Morris Brown Col; Honorary Doctorate Degree, Interdenomi Nat Theol Ctr; Honorary Doctorate Degree, Eden Theol Sem. **Special Achievements:** First black American to be elected a president of the World Council of Churches; Developed: church hymnal, The Bicentennial Edition, first AME Book of Worship; Edited: The Connector; produced, edited: A Syllabus For Celebrating The Bicentennial; numerous articles in publications of the AME Church. **Home Addr:** 22 W Sherwood Dr, Saint Louis, MO 63114, **Home Phone:** (314)427-2711.

ANDERSON, WARREN E
Executive, president (organization). **Educ:** Univ Mich, BS, 1974, MS, 1976. **Career:** Acct exec; nat & local sales mgr; gen sales mgr; Anderson-Dubose Co, gen mgr, chief exec officer & pres, currently. **Orgs:** Young Presidents; Playhouse Sq Found; Cuyahoga Community Col Found; Leadership Cleveland; Shoreby Club; President's Coun. **Honors/Awds:** NE Ohio Entrepreneur of the Year. **Business Addr:** President, Chief Executive Officer, Anderson Dubose Co, 6575 Davis Indust Pkwy, Solon, OH 44139, **Business Phone:** (440)248-8800.

ANDERSON, WILLIAM
Educator. **Personal:** Born Aug 30, 1932, Selma, AL; son of William James Anderson Sr and Minnie B; married Peggy Rambo, 1980; children: Bridgette Anderson Lucas, Barbara Erwin & William Harrington. **Educ:** Ala State Col, BS, 1959; Layton Sch Art, Univ Wis, BFA, 1962; Instituto Allende, San Miguel, Mexico, MFA, 1968. **Career:** Univ Wis, prof, 1963-64; Alcorn Col, prof, 1964-69; Knoxville Col, fac, 1970-71; Univ Tenn, fac, 1970-71; Savannah State Col, fac, 1971-80; Dallas County Performing Arts Ctr, 1981-82; Ala Arts Coun, 1982-90; pvt instr,1982-90; Morehouse Col, assoc prof, bus admin, assoc prof, photogr, profart, currently. **Orgs:** C-Natural Music Club, WI, 1957-; Ga Art Asn, 1970-; Savannah Art Asn,1971-80; Telfair Acad Art, 1971-80; Nat Conf Artists. **Honors/Awds:** Grant, Ga Coun for Art, 1987; Purchase Award, 2nd place, Atlanta Life Ins Co, 1987, 1st place, 1991; Hiram Walker Grant for Photography, 1996. **Special Achievements:** Bust Dr. Albert Schweitzer, Gabon, West Africa, 1962; Sculpture Technique Form Content textbook, 1st ed, 1989, 2nd ed, 1993; Solo exhibit, Wadsworth Atheneum, Hartford, CT, 1994; African Am Art & Artists, pg 219, 1994; James Porter Annual Colloquium, Howard Univ, 1996, 1998; portfolio of 12 black & white photographs is in the permanent collections of the J. Paul Getty Photog Museum, Los Angeles & the Bodleian Libr, Oxford Univ, Oxford, Eng. **Home Addr:** 1997 King George Lane, PO Box 310025, Atlanta, GA 30331-4929, **Home Phone:** (404)349-1432. **Business Addr:** Professor of Art, Morehouse College, Department of Arts & History, Wheeler Hall 101 830 Westview Dr SW, Atlanta, GA 30314, **Business Phone:** (404)681-2800.

ANDERSON, WILLIAM A.
Physician. **Personal:** Born Jul 21, 1921, Atlanta, GA; son of Will and Mary; married Joyce McIntosh; children: Serena, Cheryle Posey & William A III. **Educ:** Tuskegee Inst, BA, 1942; Univ Mich Med Sch, MD, 1953. **Career:** Pvt Pract, dermatologist, 1957-; Div Virus, Rsch Cornell Univ Med Col, res fel, 1957-61; Whitehall Labs NYC, assoc med dir, 1965-69; Counr, Essex Co Med Soc, NJ, 1983-85; Weill Med Col Cornell Univ, clin assoc prof dermat, currently; NY-Presbyterian Hosp, assoc attending dermatologist, currently. **Orgs:** Fel Am Acad Dermatol, 1959-; pres, Metro Derm Soc, NY, 1962; pres, NJ Dermatological Soc, 1963; consult, Nat Acad Sci, Nat Res Coun, 1965; Nat Med Asn; officer, Essex Co Med Soc NJ, 1989-91. **Special Achievements:** Author, articles on clinical dermat, immunol, virology. **Military Serv:** AUS, cpl, 4 yrs; Combat Med Badge, 1945. **Business Addr:** Clinical Associate Professor, Weill Medical College of Cornell University, 525 E 68th St, New York, NY New York, **Business Phone:** (212)746-1067.*

ANDERSON, DR. WILLIAM A
Educator. **Personal:** Born May 28, 1937, Akron, OH; children: 1. **Educ:** Ohio State Univ, PhD, 1966. **Career:** Kent State Univ, instr, 1961-62; Disaster Res Ctr Ohio State Univ, res asst, 1966-69; Minority Fel Prog, Am Sociol Asn, dir, 1974-75; Ariz State Univ, assoc prof to prof, 1969-76; Nat Sci Found, prog dir, 1976; World Bank, Infrastucture Div, Disaster Mgt Facility, sr adv, 1999-2001; Nat Academies & Nat Res Coun, Earth & Life Studies Div, assoc exec dir, currently, natural disasters roundtable, dir, currently; Off Sci & Technol Policy, staff. **Orgs:** Nat Acad Sci Panel Pub Policy Implications Earthquake Prediction, 1974-; Nat Acad Sci Ad Hoc Comm Minorities Sci 1975; Am Sociol Asn; Pac Sociol Asn. **Special Achievements:** Co-author of numerous research monographs, reports and articles including Future Directions and A History of Social Science Earthquake Research: From Alaska to Kobe.

ANDERSON, WILLIAM GILCHRIST
Physician, surgeon. **Personal:** Born Dec 12, 1927, Americus, GA; son of John D Sr and Emma G; married Norma Dixon Anderson, Nov 23, 1946; children: A Laurita Faison, W Gilchrist II, V Jeanita Henson, Frank L, Darnita Dawn & Anderson-Hill. **Educ:** Alabama State Col, BS, 1949; Univ Osteopathic Med, DO, 1956; Art Ctr Hosp, attended 1984. **Career:** Art Center Clin Group, staff surgeon, 1967-71; Zieger Clin Group, attending surgeon, 1971-74; Detroit Surgical Asn, sr attending surgeon & consult, 1974-84; Mich Healthcare Corp, exec vpres & chief medical officer, 1984-86; Detroit Osteopathic Hosp, dir government affairs, 1986-92; Detroit Riverview Hosp, dir med educ, 1992-; Kirksville Col Osteopathic Med, assoc dean, 1996-; Detroit Osteop & Riverview Hosp, physician, currently. **Orgs:** YMCA, dir, 1970-; Univ Osteopathic Med, dir, 1974-; Citizens Trust bank, dir, 1974-; Wayne County Osteo Asn, dir, 1968-, pres, 1977, exec dir, 1993-; Mich Asn Osteo Physicians, dir, 1975-, pres, 1981; Am Osteopathic Asn, delegate, 1980-, trustee, 1981-, pres, 1994-95. **Honors/Awds:** Patenge Meritorious Service Award, Mich State Univ, 1982; Phillips Meritorious Service Award, Ohio Univ, 1986, Doctor of Humane Letters, 1990; Doctor of Humane Letters, Univ New England, 1992; Doctor of Science, W VA Sch Osteo Med, 1993; Doctor of Humane Letters, Univ Osteo Med, 1994; Distinquished Service Award, Am Osteopathic Asn, 2001. **Special Achievements:** Publications: Abnormal Uterine Bleeding after Tubal Ligation, MI Journal of Osteo Med, 1957; Von Redklinghausen's Disease of the Mesentery, MI Journal of Osteo Med, 1965; Choledocholithiasis After Cholecystectomy, Journal of AOA, 1973; Osteopathic Physician Looks at Quality, DO Magazine, 1984. **Military Serv:** USN, petty officer, 1944-46. **Home Addr:** 24535 N Carolina, Southfield, MI 48075. **Business Phone:** (313)499-4000.

ANDERSON, WILLIE AARON
Football player. **Personal:** Born Jul 11, 1975, Whistler, AL. **Educ:** Auburn Univ, Mkt educ. **Career:** Cincinnati Bengals, tackle, currently. **Honors/Awds:** NFL All-Rookie Team, Football News, 1996; NFL All-Rookie Team, Col & Pro Football Newsweekly, 1996; Pro Bowl, Cincinnati Bengals; 4-time Pro Bowler & 3-time first-team All-Pro. **Special Achievements:** Wears biggest shoe size (19-EEE) in Bengals history. **Business Addr:** Professional Football Player, Cincinnati Bengals, 1 Paul Brown Stadium, Cincinnati, OH 45202, **Business Phone:** (513)621-3550.*

ANDERSON, WILLIE LEE, JR. (FLIPPER ANDERSON)
Football player. **Personal:** Born Mar 7, 1965, Paulsboro, NJ. **Educ:** Univ Calif, Los Angeles. **Career:** Los Angeles Rams, wide receiver, 1988-94; Indianapolis Colts, 1995; Washington Redskins, 1996; Denver Broncos, 1997; Yes to Life Ministries, clergy. **Honors/Awds:** NFL Record, 1989; NFC Championship Game, 1989. **Business Phone:** (510)706-0259.

ANDERSON-BUTLER, CAROLYN
Dean (education). **Educ:** Morgan State Univ, BA; Johns Hopkins Univ, MLA, MS; NC State Univ, EdD. **Career:** Broome Community Col, dean acad serv, 2001-. **Business Addr:** Dean of Academic Services, Broome Community College, PO Box 1017, Binghamton, NY 13902, **Business Phone:** (607)778-5210.

ANDERSON JANNIERE, IONA LUCILLE
Educator. **Personal:** Born Aug 28, 1919, Brooklyn, NY; daughter of Oliver Ashby and Clarine Ashby; married Ivan Lloyd Janniere, Jun 17, 1988; children: Wendie Anderson Peterson, Robert. **Educ:** Hunter Col, BA 1942; NY Univ, MA, 1959; Heed Univ Fla, PhD, 1976. **Career:** Educator (retired); Bd Educ NY City, teacher common branches, 1945-69; Bank St Col NY City, field rep, 1969-70; Brooklyn Col CUNY, asst prof educ, 1969-74; City Univ NY Medgar Evers Col, assoc prof educ, 1974-85; Manatee Cot Col, inr, 1990-97; writer/financial planner; Modern Woodmen Ins Co. **Orgs:** Educ consult Richmond Col, City Univ NY, 1973-75; chairperson, NE Flatbush Comm Coalition, 1977; community rep, NY City Planning Bd 17, 1978-83; evaluator Early Childhood Prog Bd, Educ Dist 73, 1979-80 & Dist 9, 1974-76; consult Eng a Stand Dialect Bd Educ NY, 1983; reading consult Houghton Mifflin Pub Co, 1983-84; bd, East NY Develop Corp, 1984-85; early childhood consult, PS Dist 17, NY, 1984-85; financial planner Krueger Assoc, N Port, Fla, 1986-87; Am Asn Univ Women, 1987-; J com, Bethune Cookman Chorale Women's Coalition SW Fla, 1990-; Equity by 2000, 1988-; Planning and Zoning Adv Brd N Port, 1988-91; Charter Bd N Port, vice-chair, 1991-97; North Port High Sch Adv Bd; Big Brothers Big Sisters, mentoring prog; Boys & Girls Club; volunteer & rep, Sarasota County Coalition Prev Substance Abuse; Univ South Fla res proj; Venice Women's All; Women's Resource Ctr; SW FL Peace Coalition. **Honors/**

Awds: Fanny Lou Hamer Award, Medgar Evers Col, 1983; Sojourner Truth Award, Nat Bus & Prof Women, 1984; Special Award NY State Tesol, 1985; ESL Students in the Mainstream publ in Integrative Approaches to ESL Teaching & Learning, 1986; Womens Inner Circle of Achievement, 1991; Women of Today, 1992; Women of Change, Am Asn Univ Women, 1991; Women of Distinction, Sarasota County, 1999. **Special Achievements:** Published many articles, the latest on Ebonics, 1997. **Home Addr:** 5893 Mayberry Ave, North Port, FL 34287. *

ANDERSON SAMKANGE, TOMMIE MARIE. See SAMKANGE, TOMMIE MARIE.

ANDRADE, MERY
Basketball player. **Personal:** Born Dec 31, 1975. **Educ:** Old Dominion Univ, BA, health & phys educ, 1999. **Career:** Cleveland Rockers, forward, 1999-2002; Charlotte Sting, forward, 2004-06; pro basketball player, currently. **Honors/Awds:** Defensive Team, 1997-98; Women's Basketball Jour, Defensive All-Am, 1998-99; Kodak Dist, All-Am, 1998-99; Colonial Athletic Assn, Defensive Player of the Year, 1998-99; CAA, Co-Player of the Year, 1998-99, All-Tournament Team, 1997-99; All-CAA, First Team, 1998-99. *

ANDREW, MILTON
School principal. **Educ:** Dillard Univ, BA; Wayne State Univ. **Career:** Wilkins Elem Sch, prin, 2002-. **Business Addr:** Principal, Wilkins Elementary School, 12400 Nashville St, Detroit, MI 48205-3848.

ANDREWS, ADELIA SMITH
Executive. **Personal:** Born Nov 7, 1914, New Orleans, LA; daughter of Christopher Columbus and Adelia Beatty; married Joseph H; children: Yolanda Reed & Joseph Reginald. **Educ:** Prof Secretaries Int; Cert Prof Secy, 1978. **Career:** Whiteway Cleaners & Dyers, secy, 1933-36; St Calif, sec, 1936-42; LosAngeles County Probation Dept, secy, 1942-44; A-Z Steno Serv, sec bookkeeper, 1946-49; Los Angeles Urban League, admin asst, 1949-53; Watkins Entrepreneurs Inc, admin asst, 1953-63; Calif Mus Sci & Indus, admin asst, 1963-84; Caribbean C space, St Croix US VI, admin asst, 1985-. **Orgs:** Los Angeles Urban League, Prof Secretaries Int, 1971-; proj dir, CMSI Black Achievement Exhibit, 1973-78; bd mem, C Space, 1979-; Asn Women Pepperdine Univ; Cong Calif Sr, 1991-. **Honors/Awds:** Twenty Five year pin State of Calif, 1982.

ANDREWS, DR. ADOLPHUS. See Obituaries section.

ANDREWS, CARL R.
Association executive. **Personal:** Born Apr 20, 1926, Williamsport, PA; son of Carl M and Georgie Bannister; married Jeanette M White, May 1, 1955; children: Carl R Jr, Keith R, Cheryl Y. **Educ:** Lycoming Col, attended 1948; Howard Univ, attended 1950; Howard Univ Sch Soc Work, attended 1952; Rutgers Univ, adj urban fel prog, 1964; Yale Univ Drug Dependence Inst, attended 1971. **Career:** Boys' Club Newark, NJ, club dir, 1952-66; Boys' Club Am Nat Prog & Training Serv, asst dir, 1966-73; Boys' Club Asn, Indianapolis, IN, exec dir, 1973-89; hon dir, Boys & Girls Clubs Indianapolis, IN, currently. **Orgs:** Kiwanis Int; Ind Juvenile Justice Task Force; Witherspoon Presbyterian Church; Alpha Phi Alpha Fraternity; Exec Serv Corps; Boys & Girls Clubs, Indianapolis; Nat Scholastic Hon Soc. **Honors/Awds:** New Jersey Afro-American Newspaper Award, 1959; Man of the Week Award, Prudential Ins Co, 1966; Midwest Region Heart & Soul Award, 1978; Paul Lemmon Administrator of the Year Award, 1977; President Award, E Orange Comm Day Nursery, 1973; Career Award, Kiwanis Club, Indianapolis, 1980; Sagamore Wabash, State Indiana, 1989; Lifetime Achievement Award, Exec Serv Corps. **Military Serv:** USN, 1944-46. **Business Addr:** Honorary Director, Boys & Girls Clubs of Indianapolis, 300 E Fall Creek Pkwy N Dr Suite 400, Indianapolis, IN 46205, **Business Phone:** (317)920-4700.*

ANDREWS, CHARLES CLIFTON
Media executive. **Personal:** Born Dec 16, 1939, San Antonio, TX; son of Charles Clifton; married Thelma W; children: Charles III & Michael. **Educ:** Lincoln Univ, attended. **Career:** Inner City Broadcasting Corp, pres, 1982-. **Orgs:** Bd mem & secy, AfriCom Telecommunications Ltd, 1990-; bd dirs, San Bernardino Child Advocacy Prog. **Honors/Awds:** Outstanding Texan Award. **Business Addr:** President, Inner City Broadcasting Co, 217 Alamo Plz Suite 200, San Antonio, TX 78205, **Business Phone:** (210)271-9600.

ANDREWS, DONNOVAN
Executive. **Educ:** St Bonaventure Univ, BS, polit sci, jour & mass commun; Univ Pa, Wharton Exec Educ Prog, cert finance & acct. **Career:** DDB Worldwide; Compaq, Lockheed-Martin, Reuters; McDonalds; Tanqueray; Fast Co; Bank Am; FortuneCity Inc, dir bus develop; Ziff Davis Publ, dir bus develop; Performance Bridge Advert, pres, currently. **Orgs:** Advert Club New York; co-founder & bd mem, Xenium Found; founder, Red Wagon Found. **Business Phone:** (212)533-9500.*

ANDREWS, ELEANOR
President (Organization). **Educ:** California State Univ; Univ Alaska. **Career:** State of Ak, Dep Comnr & Comnr Admin; Municipality Anchorage, Dir Human Resources; Andrews Group Inc, pres & chief exec officer, currently. **Orgs:** Bd dir, 2002; bd officer, Anchorage Chamber Com, Anchorage Neighborhood Housing Serv, Anchorage Municipal Housing Asn; adv bd, Univ Alaska, Small Bus Develop Ctr. **Honors/Awds:** YWCA Woman of Achievement Award, 1994; ATHENA award, 1995; Small Bus Admn, Small Bus Person of the Yr Alaska, 1998. **Business Addr:** President, Chief Executive Officer, Andrews Group Inc, 2627 C St 99503, PO Box 241845, Anchorage, AK 99524-1845, **Business Phone:** (907)276-1454.*

ANDREWS, EMANUEL CARL
Government official, politician. **Personal:** Born Sep 9, 1956, New York, NY. **Educ:** Medgar Evers Col, BA, 1978; Albany State Univ, MA, 1981. **Career:** Black & Puerto Rican Caucus NYS Legislature, asst exec dir, 1980-81; US Congressman Major Owens, spl asst, 1982-84; NY State Assembly, special asst state assembly; Gov Rel NYS Sen Minority, dir; NYS house race, cand, 2006; US Congressman. *

ANDREWS, REV. FRAZIER L.
Clergy. **Personal:** Born May 3, 1933, Mobile, AL; married Lula Tillett. **Educ:** Ala State Univ, BS, 1955; Va Union Grad Sch Religion, M Div, 1958; Columbia Pacific Univ, PhD, philos, 1993. **Career:** First Baptist Church, Hertford, NC, pastor, 1957-68; First Baptist Church, High Point, NC, minister, 1968-, Sr pastor, currently; Shaw Univ, teacher. **Orgs:** Treas, High Point Church Housing Inc; founder & pres, Antil Enterprise Inc; Head Start Pol Co Bd, Guilford County; ESAA Adv Com; High Point City Schs; exec bd, Model City Comn; former bd mem, SCLC; pres, Minister's Conf High Point; chmn, High Point Bus Develop Corp; pres, Brentwood Shop Ctr; Legal Aid Bd & Fam Serv Bur; co-spon, London Wood Dev low-mid-inc Housing Develop; former mem, NC Good Neighbor Coun; pres, Hert ford Movement. **Honors/Awds:** Pastor of Year, Hertford, NC, 1966; holds several Hon Degrees. **Business Addr:** Minister, First Baptist Church, 701 E Washington Dr, High Point, NC 27260, **Business Phone:** (919)882-9229.

ANDREWS, GEORGE G., III
Executive. **Educ:** Morehouse Col, BS, bus admin; Clark Atlanta Univ; Banking Sch S. **Career:** Nat Bank GA, area br mgr; United Way Coordr; Capitol City bank & Trust Co, founder, treasr & dir; Capitol City Bancshares, pres, dir, cheif financial officer & cheif exec officer, currently. **Orgs:** Nat Bankers Asn; Independent Community Bankers Am; United Way; bd mem, Atlanta Workforce Develop Agency; Community Bankers Asn GA; West End Merchant Asn. **Business Phone:** (404)752-6067.*

ANDREWS, JAMES E.
Educator, psychologist. **Personal:** Born Aug 6, 1943, Pensacola, FL; son of Emma and C Andrews; married Pat; children: Lisa, Marcus. **Educ:** Compson Col, AA, 1970; CA State Dom Hill, BA, 1972; UCLA, MA, 1974; Nova Univ, PhD, 1977. **Career:** Compson Unified Sch, psychologist, 1973-75; consult, Dept Rehabilitation, 1975-; Pomona Unified Sch, psychologist, 1975-79; Psychol Assessment Lab, owner, 1977-; Mt San Antonio Col, psychologist, 1979-; consult, Calif Poly 1981-. **Orgs:** Pres, Southern Calif Asn Black Psychologists, 1975-76. **Special Achievements:** Published book Theories of Child Observation, 1974; published several articles on children and learning. **Military Serv:** AUS, sp/4, 2 yrs. *

ANDREWS, JAMES EDWARD
Labor activist, president (organization), chief executive officer. **Personal:** Born Sep 29, 1948, Norlina, NC; son of Merlin and Bettie Hargrove; married Audrey P; children: Timothy, Annisha & LaTonya. **Career:** Perfect Packed Prod Co, Henderson, NC, 1971-75; NC State AFL-CIO, proj outreach dir, 1975-84, actg secy & treas, 1984, secy & treas, 1985, chief exec officer, 1991, pres, 2002-; Nat A Philip Randolph Inst grant. **Orgs:** Pres, Warren County Nat Asn Advan Colored People, 1971-75; exec bd mem, NCAPRI, 1975-; exec comt & bd mem, Nat APRI, 1978-; regional rep, APRI southern Region, 1978-; pres, NC State AFL-CIO, 1997-; OPEIU. **Honors/Awds:** Tar Heel of The Week, News & Observer; recipient of the Purple Heart. **Special Achievements:** First full-time elected African-American state federation president in the country's history; A Vietnam veteran. **Military Serv:** AUS, E-5, 1969-70, Purple Heart. **Home Addr:** 1309 Lions Way, Raleigh, NC 27604. **Business Addr:** President, North Carolina State AFL-CIO, 1408 Hillsborough St, PO Box 10805, Raleigh, NC 27605.

ANDREWS, JAMES F. See Obituaries section.

ANDREWS, JUDIS R
Lawyer. **Personal:** Born Aug 27, 1941; married Cheryl D. **Educ:** Ariz State Univ, JD, 1972. **Career:** AZ Civil Rights Comn, asst dir, 1964-67; Phoenix Col, instr, 1967-68; Ariz State Univ, adminstrv asst to pres, 1968-69; Joshua M Bursh II firm Cunningham Goodson Tiffany & Weltch, law clerk, 1968-69; Pvt Pract, atty, currently. **Orgs:** Pres, Negro Polit Action Asn Ariz State, 1966-67; dir, Summer Youth Proj, Phoenix, OIC, 1969; dir, Spec Serv Maricopa Co Community Action Prog, 1969; spec asst to dir, Housing Ariz State Univ, 1969-70; dir, Progs & Opers Seattle Oppors Indus Ctr Inc, Seattle, 1972-73; founding mem, first secy to bd dir, Wm F Patterson Lodge IBPOE No 47; founding mem & initial bd mem, Civil E Neighborhood Coun; Nat Asn Advan Colored People Youth Pres Pinal Co; chmn, CORE, vice chmn, secy, treas; pres & founder, 50 Bus Man Club; Omega Psi Phi Frat Ariz State Univ Scholar Comn; bd dir, AZ Comn Post Sec Educ, 1974-75; bd dir, Ariz State Alumni Asn, 1975. **Honors/Awds:** Scholar Award, Martin Luther King Ctr Disadvantaged Youth Seeking Educ Oppors; Man of Year, 50 Bus Man Club, 1967-68; Man of Year, Negro Polit Action Asn Ariz, 1968. **Business Addr:** Attorney, 710 W Roosevelt, Phoenix, AZ 85007-2104, **Business Phone:** (602)253-2013.

ANDREWS, MARK ALTHAVEAN
Singer, actor. **Personal:** Born Nov 9, 1978, Baltimore, MD; son of Alonzo and Carolyn Andrews; children: Shaione. **Educ:** Baltimore City Col, attended. **Career:** Mem group Dru Hill; Albums Dru Hill: Dru Hill, 1996; Enter the Dru, 1998; Solo Albums: Unleash the Dragon, 2000; Return of the Dragon, 2001; TV Series: Sisqo's Shakedown, 2000; Linc's, 2000; "Sabrina, the Teenage Witch", 2001; Films: Get Over It, 2001; Snow Dogs, 2002; Pieces of April, 2003; Surf School, 2006; Singles: "It's All About Me", 1998; "Got to Get It", 1999; "Thong Song", 2000; "Unleash the Dragon", 2000; "What These Bitches Want", 2000; "Incomplete", 2000; "How Many Licks", 2000; "Lap Dance", 2001; "Can I Live", 2001; "Dance For Me", 2001; "Who's Ur Daddy", 2007; "Gone Country", 2008; "Last Dragon Promo", 2008; Dragon Music Group, owner, currently. **Honors/Awds:** Numerous awards including 3 Grammy awards, 2 Radio Music Awards, 6 Billboard awards, a Source award, MTV Video Music Award & World Music Award. **Business Addr:** Singer, c/o Richard De La Font Agency Inc, 4845 S Sheridan Rd Suite 505, Tulsa, OK 74145, **Business Phone:** (918)665-6200.*

ANDREWS, MELANIE
College administrator. **Career:** Compton Community Col, bd mem, currently.

ANDREWS, NELSON MONTGOMERY
Statistician. **Personal:** Born Jul 9, 1951, Winston-Salem, NC; son of Frances and Clem Sr; married Sharon Millicent Parrish; children: Elenora & Ava. **Educ:** Johnson C Smith Univ, physics, math, 1969-73; Purdue Univ, statist, MSD, 1977. **Career:** BF Goodrich, statistician, 1977-78; Bell Labs, NJ, statistician, 1978-82; Bellcore Community NJ, statistician, 1982-84; GTF Deer Valley Ariz, sr orgn statistician, 1985-87; NEC America Inc, mgr, quality statist, presently. **Orgs:** Phi Beta Sigma Frat, 1971-; participant, Gistault Inst Career Develop Prog, 1978; career recruiter, Bell Labs, Bellcore, NJ, 1980-84; Affirmative Action Educ Career Developer, 1982-84; charter mem, Boule, Sigma Pi Phi Frat, 1986-. **Honors/Awds:** pres, Beta Kappa Chi, Phi Beta Sigma, Johnson C Smith Univ; speaker on statist abstracts, Joint Statist Meeting, 1986; speaker, Int Commun Meeting, Tokyo, Japan, 1987. **Business Addr:** Statistician, NEC America Inc, 6555 N State Hwy 161, Irving, TX 75039-2402, **Business Phone:** (214)262-2000.

ANDREWS, PHILLIP
Executive. **Personal:** Born Jun 8, 1963, Hempstead, NY; son of Frank and Daphine; married Chriscelle S Seldon; children: Phillip, Chriscelle Seldon II. **Educ:** Intl Career Inst, paralegal diploma, 1985; John Jay Col Criminal Justice, 1990. **Career:** NYC Dept Correction, correction officer, 1984-; The Hair Cut Hut, vpres, 1990-; Envogue I Beauty Salon, co owner; C & B Bks Distrib, Pub Rels Dir, 2002-. **Orgs:** Chair, Majestic Eagles Long Island, Speaker's Bur, 1990-; Black Unity Day Comt, 1990-91; chair, One Penny a Day Self Help Movement, 1991-; bd mem, Roosevelt Chamber Com, 1992-; bd mem, Roosevelt Kiwanis Club, 1992-; 100 Black Men Nassau & Suffolk Inc; Barber Culture Asn Long Island Queens, vpres, cosmetologist; exec comt, Hempstead Nat Asn Advan Colored People; bd mem, West Indian Am COC; ed bd, Econ Forum Newspaper; West Indian American COC; Nassau County Coun Chambers. **Honors/Awds:** First Annual Entrepreneur's Award, Village Hempstead, 1991; First Annual AFA Entrepreneur Award, Black Unity Comt, 1991; Excellent Duty, NYC Dept Correction, 1992; Award of Appreciation for Outstanding Contribution, Oper Get Ahead, 1992; AFA Human Relations Award, Roosevelt High Sch, 1991; Black Entrepreneurs Award, 1993; Award of Appreciation, Oper Get Ahead, 1993; Certificate of Appreciation, Long Island Cares Inc, 1993; The Haircut Hut Small Businessman of the Year, Nassau County Coun Chambers, Roosevelt COC, 1995; New York State Assembly Certificate of Merit, 1995; Outstanding Youth Advocate Award, LI Youth Found, 1996; Small Businessperson of the Year, West Indian Am Chamber Com, 1998. **Special Achievements:** Mind Development Series, poetry, 1990; The COT Reporter, staff writer, 1990-91. **Business Phone:** (718)602-7797.*

ANDREWS, REAL (ANTONIO CAMERON DAVIS)
Actor. **Personal:** Born Jan 31, 1963, British Columbia. **Career:** General Hospital, 1963; "Days of Our Lives", 1965; "Step by Step", 1994; Family of Cops, 1995; "Side Effects", 1995; Mad Dog Time, 1996; "Viper",1996; "Nash Bridges", 1996;

"Highlander"; The End of Innocence, 1996;Expect No Mercy, 1996; Balance of Power, 1996; "The Sentinel", 1996; Port Charles, 1997-03; "Soldier of Fortune", 1997; "Breach of Faith: Family of Cops II", 1997; "PSI Factor: Chronicles of the Paranormal", 1997; Lookin 'Italian, 1998; "The Girl Next Door", 1998; "Beyond Belief: Fact or Fiction"; "Port Charles", 1998; "General Hospital", 2002-03; "As the World Turns", 2003-04; Lost in Plainview, 2004; Blood, 2004;"Law & Order", 2006; "Damages", 2007; Films: Iceman, 1984; Wild Thing, 1987; Born on the Fourth of July, 1989; Under Surveillance, 1991; No Escape, No Return, 1993; Rocky V; Expect No Mercy, 1995; Simon Says, 1998; As the World Turns, 2003-04; Lost in Plainview, 2005; The Picture of Dorian Gray, 2006. **Honors/Awds:** Trained as 100-meter sprinter for the 1984 Olympics. **Business Addr:** Actor, CBS Television Network, 51 W 52nd St, New York, NY 10019, **Business Phone:** (212)975-3247.*

ANDREWS, SHARONY S
Painter (Artist), journalist, writer. **Personal:** Born Jan 28, 1967, Miami, FL; daughter of Estela Meyers and Garcia; married Grant Green Jr. **Educ:** Univ Miami, BS, polit sci & broadcast jour, 1989; Univ NC, Greensboro, Masters in Dance & Related Studies. **Career:** Miami Herald, reporter, 1989-92; Detroit Free Press, reporter & asst nat ed, 1993, writer, 1997-, painter, 1997-; Columbus Ga Ledger-Enquirer, bus ed; Books: Cuttin the Rug Under the Moonlit Sky, 1997; Essence mag, freelancer, currently. **Orgs:** Alpha Kappa Alpha Sorority, 1986-; vpres print, S Fla Asn Black Journalists, 1991-92; Jour & Women's Symp, 1992-. **Honors/Awds:** Greater Miami Achievers Goldendrum Scholar, Univ Miami, 1985; Soc Professional Journalists Scholar, 1985; Scholar, Alpha Kappa Alpha, Gamma Zeta Omega Chap, 1985; Grant Green, Rediscovering the Forgotten Genius of Jazz Guitar, 1999. **Special Achievements:** Paintings exhibited in various galleries included: Peligro Gallery, Red Piano Too Gallery, Zeitgeist Gallery & House of Blues.

ANDREWS, WILLIAM PERNELL
Educator, psychotherapist, manager. **Personal:** Born Mar 24, 1947, Richmond, VA; son of William and Rena Thompson; married Michele Evans Andrews, Dec 10, 1983; children: Oronde K, Joshua T, Kayla S. **Educ:** Cambridge Col, EdM, 1989. **Career:** Boston City Hosp, staff psychologist narcotics addiction, 1981-83; Mass Dept Corrections, clin coordr, psychologist, 1983-92; Roxbury Youth Works Inc, exd, 1992-93; Dimock Comn Health Ctr, dir family coun, 1993-95; Northeastern Univ, JDOAAI, asst dir, 1995-; Bur Substance Abuse Serv, Dept Pub Health, regional mgr, currently. **Orgs:** Am Counselors Asn, 1986-92; Am Ment Health Counselors Asn, 1986-92. **Honors/Awds:** Outstanding Young Men in Am, US Chamber Com, 1980; Black Rose Award, 1996. **Special Achievements:** Papers/Presentations: "Treatment of Families in Urban County," 1995; "Beyond Stereotyping - Historic Media Presentation," 1994; "New Horizons - A Conceptual Model for Treatment," 1992; "Racial/Cultural Issues in Corrections," 1985; "African Philosophical Foundations," 1982. **Military Serv:** USAF, tech sgt, 1966-70, 1976-86. **Home Phone:** (617)244-1095. *

ANDREWS, WILLIAM PHILLIP
Executive. **Personal:** Born Jan 9, 1938, Kansas City, MO; son of William and Florence; married Dolores Caesar, Mar 31, 1961; children: Phillip, Steven, Jeffrey. **Educ:** Lincoln Univ, Jefferson City, MO, BS, 1961. **Career:** Anheuser-Busch Inc, Houston, TX, ethnic sales mgr, 1967-. **Orgs:** Kappa Alpha Psi, 1958-. **Honors/ Awds:** Distinguished Service Award, Lincoln Univ, Jefferson City, MO, 1989. **Military Serv:** AUS, 1st Lt, 1961-63; USFF Fort Sam Houston, San Antonio, TX, 2nd Lt Cmdr, 1961. *

ANDREWS-MCCALL, DR. MAXINE RAMSEUR
Educator. **Personal:** Born in Fayetteville, NC; daughter of Patsy Evans and Emory Adolphus; children: Sabrina Andrews Molden, Gigi & Thurman J III. **Educ:** Fayetteville State Univ, BS, 1956; NC Central Univ, MEd, 1963; E Carolina Univ, EdS, 1975; Univ NC, Greensboro, EdD, 1985. **Career:** Educator (retired); Cumberland County Schs, teacher, 1956-66, sch social worker, 1966-69; Elizabeth City State Univ, title III coord, 1969-71; Fayetteville State Univ, adj prof, 1985, asst prof & coord sec educ, coord educ admin & curriculum instruction, dir, teaching fellows prog, Mc Callcoord, master sch admin degree prog, 1999; coord, MSA Prog, 1996-99, adjunct prof, 1999-; Cumberland County Schs, elem supvr, 1971-84, supvrsec educ, 1984-90. **Orgs:** Nat Educ Asn; Asn Supervision & Curriculum Div; NC Asn Educrs; Phi Delta Kappa; NC Asn Admin; Delta Sigma Theta Sor; NC Historical Preservation Soc; Fayetteville State Alumni Asn; pres, 1987-90, sec, 1988-91, NC Asn Supervision & Curriculum Develop; Master Sch Admin, Fay State Univ, coord, 1997-. **Honors/Awds:** Distinguished Alumnae Fayetteville State Univ, Nat Asn Equal Opport Higher Educ, 1986. **Special Achievements:** Sincerely Yours Writing & Specialty Services, 1986. **Home Phone:** (919)423-1727. **Business Addr:** Facilitator, Adjunct Professor, Educational Administration, Fayetteville State University, 1200 Murchison Rd, Fayetteville, NC 28301, **Business Phone:** (910)672-1111.

ANDRIA, HALL. See Obituaries section.

ANDUJAR, JOAQUIN
Baseball player. **Personal:** Born Dec 21, 1952, San Pedro de Macoris, Dominican Republic; married Walkiria; children: Jesse Joaquin. **Career:** Basebell player (retired); Houston Astros, Pitcher, 1976-81, 1988; St. Louis Cardinals, 1981-85; Oakland Athletics, 1986-87; Houston Astros, 1988. **Honors/Awds:** All-Star, 1977, 1979, 1984, 1985; World Series Champion, 1982; Gold Glove Award, Nat League, 1984; NL Comeback Player of the Year, Nat League, 1984. **Special Achievements:** First twenty game winner. **Home Addr:** 400 Randall Way Suite 106, Spring, TX 77388.

ANGELOU, DR. MAYA (MARGUERITE ANNIE JOHNSON)
Writer, poet, playwright. **Personal:** Born Apr 4, 1928, St Louis, MO; daughter of Vivian Baxter Johnson and Bailey Johnson; married Tosh Angelos, 1973 (divorced); children: Guy Johnson; married Paul Du Feu (divorced); children: 1. **Career:** Author, poet, playwright, stage & screen producer, dir, actress, 1954-; Southern Christian Leadership Conf, coordr, 1959-60; Arab Observer Egypt, assoc ed, 1961-62; Univ Ghana, asst adminr, 1963-66; African Rev, ed, 1964-66; Calif State Univ, Wichita State Univ, Wake Forest Univ, Dept Humanities, vis prof, 1974; Wake Forest Univ, distinguished vis prof, 1974; Wichita State Univ, distinguished prof, 1974; Calif State Univ, Sacramento, distinguished vis prof, 1974; Reynolds prof Am studies, 1981-; Poetry: Just Give Me a Cool Drink of Water 'fore I Diiie, 1971; Oh Pray My Wings Are Gonna Fit Me Well, 1975; Poems, 1981; Shaker, Why Don't You Sing?, 1983; Now Sheba Sings the Song, 1987; I Shall Not Be Moved, 1991; On the Pulse of Morning, 1993; Life Doesn't Frighten Me, 1993; The Complete Collected Poems of Maya Angelou, 1994; Phenomenal Woman: Four Poems Celebrating Women, 1995; A Brave & Startling Truth, 1995; Amazing Peace, 2005; Recordings: Miss Calypso, 1957; For the Love of Ivy, 1968; The Poetry of Maya Angelou, 1969; Women in Business, 1981; Georgia, Georgia, 1972; All Day Long, 1974; Been Found, 1996; Plays: Cabaret for Freedom, 1960; The Least of These, 1966; Gettin' up Stayed on My Mind, 1967; Ajax, 1974; Moon on a Rainbow Shawl, 1988; King, 1990; "Sisters, Sisters", 1982; Tv documentaries: "Black, Blues, Black", 1968; "Assignment America", 1975; "The Legacy", 1976; "The Inheritors", 1976; "Trying to Make It Home", 1988; "Maya Angelou's America: A Journey of the Heart? "Who Cares about Kids, Kindred Spirits, Maya Angelou: Rainbow in the Clouds,& To the Contrary?; Other: I Know Why the Caged Bird Sings, 1970; Gather Together in My Name, 1974; Singin' & Swingin' & Gettin' Merry Like Christmas, 1976; The Heart of a Woman, 1981; All God's Children Need Traveling Shoes, 1986; Mrs. Flowers: A Moment of Friendship, 1986; Wouldn't Take Nothing for My Journey Now, 1993; My Painted House, My Friendly Chicken, & Me, 1994; Kofi & His Magic, 1996; A Song Flung Up to Heaven, 2002; Hallelujah! The Welcome Table: A Lifetime of Memories & Recipes, 2004; Angelina of Italy, 2004; Mother: A Cradle to Hold Me, 2006. **Orgs:** Am Fed TV & Radio Artists; bd trustees, Am Film Inst, 1975-; Directors Guild Am; Actors' Equity; Women's Prison Asn; Harlem Writer's Guild; The Nat Comn Observance Intl Women's Year; Horatio Alger Asn Distinguished Americans; Nat Soc Prev Cruelty C; adv bd, Bennett Col; adv bd, First Commercial Bank; Nat Soc Collegiate Scholars; Clinton Global Initiative. **Honors/Awds:** Rockefeller grant, 1975; Ladies Home Journal Award, 1976; Golden Eagle Award, 1977; North Carolina Award in Literature, 1987; American Academy of Achievement's Golden Plate award, 1990; Langston Hughes Award, City Col NY, 1991; Essence Woman of the Year, 1992; Horatio Alger award, 1992; Woman in Film award, 1992; Grammy award for best spoken word album, 1994; Spingarn Award NAACP, 1994; Frank G. Wells Award, 1995; Nat Award, Southern Christian Leadership Conf Los Angeles & Martin Luther King Jr Legacy Asn, 1996; W K Kellogg Found, expert-in-residence Prog, 1997; Cultural Keepers Award, Black Caucus Am Libr Asn, 1997; Christopher Award, 1998; Award, Tubman African Am Mus, 1999; Sheila Lifetime Achievement Award for Literature, 1999; Sheila Lifetime Achievement Award for Literature, 1999; Nat Arts & Humanities Medal, 2001; Quills Award for Poetry, 2006; John Hope Franklin Award, 2006; Mother Teresa Award, 2006; Emmy award; Nat Book Award; Pulitzer Prize; Hon degrees: Smith Col, Northampton, Mass, 1975; Mills Col, Oakland, Calif, 1975; Lawrence Univ, Appleton, Wis, 1976; 32 Honorary Degrees. **Special Achievements:** Pulitzer Prize Nomination for "Just Give Me A Cool Drink of Water 'fore I Diiie," 1972; Tony Award Nomination for "Look Away," 1975; One of the Women of the Year in Communications, Ladies Home Jour, 1976; Emmy Award Nomination for her performance in "Roots," 1977; Horatio Alger Awards Dinner Chairman, 1993; wrote and presented a poem for President Clinton's Swearing-In Ceremonies, 1993; named UNICEF National Ambassador, 1996; Named one of the top 100 best writers of the 20th Century, Writer's Digest, 1999; Grammy nomination for Best Spoken Word Album for Hallelujah! The Welcome Table, 2004. **Business Addr:** Writer, Lordly & Dame Inc, 51 Church St, Boston, MA 02116, **Business Phone:** (617)482-3593.

ANGLEN, REGINALD CHARLES
Journalist, public relations executive. **Personal:** Born Feb 20, 1952, Cleveland, OH; son of Howard and Barbara. **Educ:** Ohio State Univ, BA, 1989; Columbus Tech Inst, grantsmanship cert. **Career:** Ohio State Sch Blind, pub rels dir, 1973-75; St Stephen's Community House, caseworker, 1979-85; OH State Univ, commun specists, Pub Rels Coordr, 1989-. **Orgs:** Phi Beta Sigma Fraternity, 1972-; Nat Asn Black Journalists, 1989-; Columbus Asn Black Journalists, 1989-; Columbus Area Leadership Prog. **Honors/Awds:** Delegate, White House Coun Youth, 1970; Friend of Education Award, CEA, 1996. **Special Achievements:** 1 of 5 Outstanding Ohioans, Ohio Jaycees, 1974; 1 of 10 Outstanding Young Man, Columbus Citizen Journal, 1974. **Home Addr:** 2525 Avalon Pl, Columbus, OH 43219. **Business Addr:** Public Relations Coordinator, Ohio State University, Office University Communication, 1125 Kinnear Rd Suite 102 Rm 102, Columbus, OH 43216, **Business Phone:** (614)292-4272.

ANISE, LADUN OLADUNJOYE E
Educator. **Personal:** Born Mar 24, 1940. **Educ:** Albion Col, BA, 1967; Syracuse Univ, MA, 1968, PhD, polit sci, 1970; Univ Pittsburgh, MA, 1975. **Career:** Syracuse Univ, African Studies-Minority Studies, lectr, 1968-70; Syracuse Univ, Educ Policy & Resource Develop Ctr, res assoc, 1969-70; Univ Pittsburgh, asst prof, 1970-75, assoc prof; Univ Ife Nigeria, vis sr lectr, 1979-83; Hill Dist Catholic Sch Syst & Educ Develop Ctr, Pittsburgh, Pa, consult, 1972-75; African Studies Group, coordr, 1982-88, Black Studies Dept, chmn (summers), 1987-89. **Orgs:** Current Issues Comt African Studies Asn, 1968; Am Polit Sci Asn; Nat Orgn-Black Polit Sci; African Heritage Studies Asn; Nat Acad Social Sci. **Honors/Awds:** ASPAU Achievement & Scholastic Award, 1967; Omicron Delta Kappa, 1967;Maxwell Fellowship Award, 1967-70; Woodrow Wilson Fellowship Award, 1970;Meritorious Achievement Award, Univ Pittsburgh, 1974. **Home Addr:** 4259 Minn St, Pittsburgh, PA 15217, **Home Phone:** (412)521-9531. *

ANOKWA, KWADWO
Chairperson, educator. **Educ:** Univ Wis, Milwaukee, BA, 1975; Univ Wis'Madison, MA, 1977; Mich State Univ, PhD, 1991. **Career:** Butler Univ, Dept Jour, prof jour & Eugene S Pulliam Sch, dir, currently.

ANSA, TINA MCELROY
Editor, writer, novelist. **Personal:** Born Jan 1, 1949?, Macon, GA; daughter of Walter J and Nellie McElroy; married Jonee Ansa. **Educ:** Spelman Col, attended 1971. **Career:** Spelman Col, writer-in-residence, 1990; DownSouth Press, 2007-; Atlanta Const, copy desk, copy ed, makeup ed, layout ed, entertainment writer, features ed & news reporter; Charlotte Observer, ed & copy ed; freelance journalist; newspaper columnist; Brunswick Col, Emory Univ, Spelman Col, writing workshop instr; Sea Island Writers Retreat, writer, currently; novels: Baby of the Family, 1989; Harcourt Brace Jovanovich, 1989, 1993; Ugly Ways, 1993; The Hand I Fan With, 1996; Doubleday, 1996; You Know Better, 2002; William Morrow, 2002; Taking After Mudear, 2007; Short Story: Willie Bea and Jaybird: A Love Story. **Orgs:** S African African-Am SisterLove Sisters Sharing Book Program; adv comt mem, Ga Ctr Book; host comt mem, Flannery O'Connor Awards; founder, Good Lil' Sch Girl Found. **Honors/Awds:** Ga Auth Serv Award, 1989; Stanley W Lindberg Award, 2005; Int Lit Hall of Fame Writers African Descent, Gwendolyn Brooks Ctr, Chicago State Univ. **Special Achievements:** First black woman hired by The Atlanta Const; produced and directed the 1989 Georgia Sea Island Festival. **Business Addr:** Writer, Novelist, Sea Island Writers Retreat, PO Box 20602, St Simons Island, GA 31522.*

ANTHONY, BERNARD WINSTON
Manager. **Personal:** Born Mar 20, 1945, St Maurice, LA; son of Lee and Ica O Wade; married Marion D Sherman Anthony, Nov 28, 1987; children: Alaric B, Timothy W, Corwin S, Shelley D, Christopher M, Dante Harris, Tanesha M Harris. **Educ:** Bakersfield City Col, Bakersfield, CA, AA; Fresno City Col, Fresno, CA, 1992; Merced Col, 1996; CA State Bakersfield, 1996. **Career:** Pacific Gas & Electric Co, Bakersfield, CA, supt gas & elec construct, maintenance & opers, 1965. **Orgs:** Teacher, trustee, deacon, coordr, dir, St Peter Miss Baptist Church, 1965-; pres, Black Employees Asn, Bakersfield, 1983-; Black Employees Asn, Fresno, 1986-; Nat Asn Advan Colored People, Fresno, 1987-; mentor, facilitator, Fresno Unified Sch Dist, 1988-; tax preparer, Enrolled Agents Am, 1988-; Black Employees Asn, Yosemite Div, adv; mentor & dir, Tassel Prog Merced High Sch Dist, 1992-; Pres, Nat Asn Advan Colored People, currently. **Honors/Awds:** Community Service Award, Pacific Gas & Elec Co, 1989-90; Service Award, Fresno Unified Sch Dist, 1989-90. *

ANTHONY, BRENDA TUCKER
Executive. **Personal:** Born in Java, VA; daughter of James P and Beulah E; married Edward French Anthony, Nov 28. **Educ:** Central State Univ, BS, 1969; Univ Dayton, MBA, 1974. **Career:** NCR Corp, financial analyst, 1969-76; Gen Motors Corp, acct, 1976-87; Johnson Energy Co, finance mgr, 1987-90; EFA & Assoc Inc, comptroller. **Orgs:** AKA, 1967-; NCP, 1969-; Central State Univ Alumni Asn, 1969-; Nat Black MBA Asn, 1970-; Nat Asn Female Exec, 1973-; Nat Coun Negro Women, 1974-.

ANTHONY, CLARENCE EDWARD
Consultant, mayor, president (organization). **Personal:** Born Oct 10, 1959, Belle Glade, FL; son of Bill and Irene; children: Reidel V. **Educ:** Palm Beach Jr Col, AA, 1979; Fla Atlantic Univ, BA, soc sci, 1981, MPA, pub admin, 1982. **Career:** S Fla Water Mgt Dist, intern res asst; Treas Coast Regional Planning Coun, regional planner; Comnr Ken Adams Dist V, admin asst; Dept Equal Op-

portunity, dir; Palm Beach Co Bd Comnrs, county comnr; Anthony & Assocs, pres; mayor, South Bay Fla, 1984-03, 2006-; PBS&J, sr vpres, dir govt rels & assoc bd mem, chief mkt officer, 2007-. **Orgs:** Pres, Fla Atlantic Univ Alumni Asn; bd dirs Big Brothers & Big Sisters; Dist IX Mental Health Drug Abuse Planning Coun; bd dirs Leadership Palm Beach County; bd of dirs Hispanic Human Resources, Glades Area Retarded Citizens; mem FL League of Cities Urban Admin Comm; bd dirs FL Inst Govt; pres & founder, FAU Black Alumni Asn; Omega Psi Phi Fraternity; chmn, Fla League of Cities Finance and Taxation Comm; bd mem Palm Beach County Area Planning Bd; pres, Nat League of Cities; PBS&J's Corp Diversity Adv Coun; The PBSJ Found Inc. **Honors/Awds:** 30 Leaders of the Future, Ebony Mag, 1988; Fla Jaycees Mayor of the Yr Award, 1989-90; Nat Leadership Award, Nat Forum Black Pub Adminrs, 2006; McKnight Found Black Doctoral Fel; FAU Distinguished Alumnus Award; Distinguished Alumnus Award, Palm Beach Jr Col; Environ Growth Mgt Grad Fel; Phi Theta Kappa Scholarship; Intl Youth in Achievement; Outstanding Young Men in America Award; Outstanding Community Leaders in America Award. **Business Addr:** Chief Marketing Officer, PBS&J, 3230 W Commercial Blvd, Fort Lauderdale, FL 33309-3400, **Business Phone:** (954)733-7233.*

ANTHONY, DR. DAVID HENRY
Educator. **Personal:** Born Apr 28, 1952, Brooklyn, NY; son of David H Jr and Carolyn; married Allison Anitra Sampson; children: Adey Tabita Frances & Djibril Senay Frederick William. **Educ:** NY Univ, AB, 1972; Univ Wis-19 Madison, MA, hist, 1975, DPhil, hist, 1983. **Career:** Dept St, Fulbright fel & res assoc, 1976-77; Univ Dar es Salaam Tanzania, res assoc, 1976-77; Clark Univ, vis prof, 1979; Coppin St Col, instr hist, 1980-84; Towson St Univ, Hist Dept, vis prof, 1982-83; Univ Ore, Eugene, asst prof hist, 1984-88; Univ Calif, Presidents humanities fel, 1990-91; Univ Calif, Oakes Col, Santa Cruz, provost, 1996-2002, asst prof, Dept Hist, assoc prof, currently. **Orgs:** Curr spec, Madison Metro Sch Dist, 1977-78; consult, Swahili AnteiroPietila Helen Winternitz, 1980; Fulbright Alumni Asn, 1981-; res affil,Univ Fla Ctr African studies, 1982; judge, Gr Baltimore Hist Fair, 1982-84; Phi Alpha Theta, 1983-. **Honors/Awds:** Fulbright Hays Award, Fulbright Found, Dept State, 1976-77. **Special Achievements:** Author, Max Yergan: Race Man, Internationalist, Cold Warrior, New York: New York Univ Press, 2006; published numerous articles in Jour and Periodicals including: "Islam in Dar es Salaam, Tanzania," Studies in Contemporary Islam 4:2, 2002; "Max Yergan Encounters South Africa: Theological Perspectives on Race," Jour of Religion in Africa 34:3. 2004; "Unwritten History: African Work in the YMCA of South Africa," History in Africa: A Journal of Method 32, 2005; "African Film Festivals in Focus,"Documentary Box: Jour of the Yamagata International Documentary FilmFestival No 24, 2005; "The Evolution of Southern Africa: Travelogue," indiasporamagazine.com, 2005. **Business Addr:** Associate Professor, University of California, Department of History, 532 Humanities 1, Santa Cruz, CA 95064, **Business Phone:** (831)459-4028.

ANTHONY, EMORY
Judge. **Personal:** Born Jan 1, 1953, Birmingham, AL; married; children: 2. **Educ:** Miles Sch Law, attended. **Career:** Jefferson County District Attorney Off, prosec, 1979; Mun judge to Mayor Bernard Kincaid; Birmingham Munic Court, judge; defensive lawyer; Guster Law Firm LLC, mentor, currently; Metropolitan Development Board Birmingham City, brd mem; Housing Authority Birmingham City, brd mem, currently. **Orgs:** Deacon, Tabernacle Baptist Church. **Business Addr:** Mentor, Guster Law Firm LLC, 505 20th St N, Birmingham, AL 35203, **Business Phone:** (205)581-9777.

ANTHONY, ERIC TODD
Baseball player. **Personal:** Born Nov 8, 1967, San Diego, CA. **Career:** Baseball player (retired); Houston Astros, TX, outfielder, 1989-93; Seattle Mariners, 1994; Cincinnati Reds, 1995-96; Colo Rockies, 1996; Los Angeles Dodgers, 1997; Yakult Swallows, 1998. **Honors/Awds:** Most Valuable Player, Southern League, 1989.

ANTHONY, GREGORY C (G-MONEY GREG)
Basketball player. **Personal:** Born Nov 15, 1967, Las Vegas, NV. **Educ:** Univ Portland; Univ Nevada, Las Vegas, attended 1991. **Career:** Basketball player (retired), game analyst; New York Knicks, guard, 1991-95; Vancouver Grizzlies, 1995-97; Seattle Supersonics, 1997-98; Portland Trailblazers, free agent, 1998-2001; Chicago Bulls, 2001; Milwaukee Bucks, guard, 2001-02; ESPN, analyst, NBA coverage, currently.

ANTHONY, JEFFREY CONRAD
Consultant. **Personal:** Born Jun 3, 1949, Washington, DC. **Educ:** Georgetown Univ, BA, 1976. **Career:** Nat Endowment Arts, sr prog specialist, 1980-85; Brooklyn Acad Music, dir comn rels, 1985-86; Freelance Consult, independent prod consult; JBV Prod, partner, currnetly. **Orgs:** Assoc producer, Capital City Jazz Festival Wash DC, 1982-85; assoc mem, Smithsonian Inst; Nat Assoc Jazz Educrs; bd mem, New Music Distrib Servs; assoc mem, Mgt Nat Jazz Serv Orgn. **Honors/Awds:** Certificate of Merit Outstanding Young Men American, 1983; Sustained Superior Performance, Nat Endowment Arts, 1984; Special Act & Service Award, 1984; Certificate of Appreciation, 1985. **Special Achievements:** producer "Dance Africa" Brooklyn NY, 1986; assoc producer "Black Family Reunion Celebration," Wash DC, Atlanta GA, Los Angeles CA, Detroit MI, 1986-87; producer "1st Annual DIVA Found Awds" Kennedy Center, Wash DC, 1987. **Military Serv:** USMC, sgt E-5, 3 1/2 yrs; Silver Star, Bronze Star, Purple Heart (2), Vietnamese Serv, Vietman Campaign Medal, Nat Defense Medal, Good Conduct Medal, Vietnamese Cross Gallantry. **Home Phone:** (718)783-7333. **Business Addr:** Partner, JBV Production, 427 3rd St NW, PO Box 2928, Washington, DC 20002, **Business Phone:** (202)723-1483.

ANTHONY, REIDEL CLARENCE
Football player. **Personal:** Born Oct 20, 1976, Pahokee, FL. **Educ:** Univ Fla. **Career:** Tampa Bay Buccaneers, wide receiver, 1997-02; free agent; Wash Redskins, wide receiver, 2002; Trinity Catholic High Sch, receivers coach, 2009-. *

ANTHONY, VERNICE DAVIS
Chief executive officer. **Personal:** Born in Mobile, AL; widowed. **Educ:** Wayne State Univ, BS, nursing, 1970; Univ Mich, MPH, 1976. **Career:** MI Dept Public Health, dir, 1991-95; John Health Syst, Corp Affairs & Community Health, sr vpres, 1995-2002; St. John Health Syst, sr vpres; Western Mich Univ, 2001; Greater Detroit Area Health Coun Inc, pres & chief exec officer, 2002; Western Mich Univ, trustees & chair, Greater Detroit Area Health Coun, pres & chief exec officer, currently. **Orgs:** Molina Healthcare Inc. **Honors/Awds:** Distinguished Alumni Award, Univ Mich Sch Pub Health, 1994; Named Detroit's Most Influential Women, 1997 and 2008.

ANTHONY, WENDELL
Clergy, association executive, activist. **Personal:** Born Jan 1, 1950, St Louis, MO; son of James and Ida; divorced; children: Tolani, Maia. **Educ:** Wayne State Univ, BA, polit sci, 1976; Marygrove Col, MA, pastoral ministry, 1974; black theol, Univ Detroit. **Career:** Detroit Black News & Detroit Black J Pub TV News Show, commentator, 1972-76; WNEC 4 Radio, news commentator; Community Health Forum TV Show, Channel 62, host, 1985-86; "A New Vision", radio prog, WCHB Radio, host & producer; Fel Chapel, assoc pastor, 1983-86, pastor, 1986; Isuthu Inst & Intonjane Inst, founder, currently; lectr, motivationalist & writer; Holt, Rinehart & Winston Publ Inc, educ consult; Fel Chapel Health Clinic, Cape Coast, Ghana, W Africa, founder, 1996; Detroit Br Nat Asn Advan Colored People, pres, currently. **Orgs:** New Detroit Inc; Mich Coalition Human Rights & Minority State Health Policy Adv Bd; chmn, Interfaith Coun Religious & Civic Leaders; trustee, Gen Retirement Syst Bd, City Detroit; chmn, New Stadia Develop Task Force Comerica Park & Ford Field; co-chmn, Detroit Comm, Amalgamated Clothing & Textile Workers Union; founder, Fannie Lou Hamer Polit Action Comn; co-chmn, City Detroit Million Man March Comn; Detroit Bldg Authority, 1994; founder, Detroit Relief Effort Aid Mozambique, Zimbabwe & S Africa; co-chair, Detroit Fair Banking Alliance. **Honors/Awds:** Named as Nana Kwamina Amoesi, II, 1992; Int Freedom Award; Unity Award, Cong Black Caucus; Spirit of Detroit Award; State Mich Spec Tributes; Frederick Douglass Speakers Award; President's Special Citation, Nat Asn Advan Colored People; Malcolm X Award, Nat Black United Fund Detroit Chap; Martin Luther King, Jr. Commemorative Award; Human Touch Award, Zeta Phi Beta Sorority Inc; Brotherhood Award, Booker T Wash Bus Asn; Civic Activist Award, Phi Beta Sigma Fraternity Inc; Black Star of Ghana Award, Ghanaian Community Asns; Walter P Reuther Award for Distinguished Service; Michiganian of the Year Award, Int United Auto Workers; Champion of Hope Award, Nat Kidney Found Mich; Outstanding Achievement Award, Anheuser-Busch Co; Human Service Award, SHAR Founds ; Ben Richard Coleman Award, Phylon Soc Wayne State Univ; St Anthony's Keep the Dream Alive Award; Urban Bankers Award for Justice; Metro Detroit APRI-CBTU Community Service Award; nominated to the NAACP Nat Bd Dirs. **Special Achievements:** Guest columnist, Mich Chronicle; Invited by the Government of Angola in Southwest Africa to conduct a fact-finding mission of the South African Military's invasion. Special delegation of the National NAACP leadership to visit South Africa, 1994. **Business Addr:** President, Detroit Branch-NAACP, 2990 E Grand Blvd, Detroit, MI 48202, **Business Phone:** (313)871-2087.*

ANTHONY-PEREZ, DR. BOBBIE M.
Educator, psychologist. **Personal:** Born Nov 15, 1923, Macon, GA; daughter of Solomon Richard Cotton Sr (deceased) and Maude Alice Lockett Cotton (deceased); widowed; children: Freida M Chapman. **Educ:** Univ De Paul, BS, 1953, MS, 1954, MA, 1975; Univ Ill, Urbana, MS, 1959; Univ Chicago, PhD, 1967. **Career:** Chicago Pub Sch, math teacher, 1954-68; Univ Chicago, math consult, 1965;Worthington Hurst, psychiat Head Start, 1971-72; Howard Univ, Inst UrbanAffairs res coordr, 1977; Chicago State Univ, acting coordr black studies,1981; Chicago State Univ, prof psychol, 1968-95, coordr black studies,1990-94, prof emer, currently. **Orgs:** Local rep, Midwestern Psychiat Asn, 1979-97; Am Educ Ress Asn, 1980-; chpbus relations, Chatham Avalon Pk Comm Coun, 1982-; conf presenter, Int Asn Appl Psychol, 1974, 1982, 1986, 1988; conf presenter, Int AsnCross-Cultural Psychol, 1986, 1988, 1990, 1992, 1994; Asian Regional,1992; communs chair, Communs Ingleside Whitfield Parish, 1989-91, 1994-96;presenter, United Am Prog Asn, 1980-; asst secy & bd mem, Chicago Chap,Asn Black Psychologists, 1990-92, pres, 1995-96; Int Cong Psychol, confpresenter, 1992; Midwestern Educ Res Asn, conf presenter, 1989, 1990,1992; Nat Coun Teachers Math; Pi Lambda Theta; Educ Hon Asn; Asn BlackPsychologists, Midwestern Educ Res Asn; elder, Int Asn Black Psychol,1994-; life mem, DODO chap Tuskegee Airmen; feature writer & reporter,DODO newsletter, 1998-; vpres, Ladies Aux, Tuskegee Airmen, 2000-01;chair, mem & Outreach, United Methodist Women Ingleside Whitfield Parish,2000-; chair, Friends of Blackwell, Blackwell Mem Church, 2000-. **Honors/Awds:** Outstanding community service, Chicago Area Asn Black Psyhcologists, 1983;Appreciation Service, Young Adults of Ingleside Whitfield Parish, 1984;Cert for serv & support, 1984, Distinguished bd mem, 1988, Chatham BusAssn; ed, Torch Newsletter of the Chatham Avalon Pk Comm Cou, 1985-01;many plaques & certificates for services to students and for Black studiesteaching & curriculum development; visited all 7 continents in 10 1/2months to study cultural factors through ethnography; Faculty of the YearAward, Stud Govt Asn, 1980, 1988, 1990, 1995, Prof Advancement Award,1989, Faculty Achievement Merit Award, 1986, 1988, 1991, Chicago StateUniv; Woman of the Year, United Am Progress, 1991-92; Community ServiceAward, Chatham Avalon Pk Comm Serv, 2001; President's Award, TuskegeeAirman, 2000, 2002. **Special Achievements:** Publication in the areas of cultural studies, Black Am Issues,gender issues, mathematics, spelling, multicultural curricula, testdevelopment, 1968-96. **Business Addr:** Professor Emeritus of Psychology, Chicago State University, PO Box 19104, Chicago, IL 60619.*

APEA, JOSEPH BENNET KYEREMATENG
Executive, president (organization). **Personal:** Born Aug 19, 1932, Aburi, Ghana; son of Madam Nancy Ofeibea Norman and Nana Esumgyima II Omanhene of Ejisu; married Agnes Johanna Hinson; children: Kathleen Kyerewa, Adwoa Ofeibea, Abena Otwiwa & Akua Nyam. **Educ:** IL Inst Tech, BSCE, 1968; Univ IL, Arch. **Career:** Westen hoff & Novic Inc, Chicago, civil engr, 1961-64; Kaiser Engrs, Chicago, struct engr, 1964-65; Sargent & Lundy Engrs, Chicago, struct engr, 1965-72; Samuels, Apea & Assoc, Inc, pres, 1972-80; Joseph Apea & Assocs Inc, Consult Engrs, pres, 1981-86; Apian International Ltd, Chicago, IL, pres, 1986-; Cosmic Petrol Inc, pres & financier, African countries, currently. **Orgs:** Nat Soc Prof Engrs; Am Soc Civil Engrs; IL Asn Struct Engrs; Framework reconstruction Ghana Citizens Org USA & Canada; chmn, DBE/WBE Adv Coun IL Dept Transp, 1986-88. **Special Achievements:** Positive attitude toward progress, The Talking Drums, UK, 1985. **Business Addr:** President, Westaf Investment Inc, 2650 Wern Ave, Park Forest, IL 60466.*

APPLEBY-YOUNG, SADYE PEARL
Educator. **Personal:** Born Dec 18, 1927, Gainesville, GA; married Harding B; children: Sybil Bernadette, Harding G, Angela & Gregory. **Educ:** Tuskegee Inst, BS, 1945; Cornell Univ, MS, child develop, 1946; Ga State Univ, PhD, educ & psychol, 1974. **Career:** Educator (retired); Univ Ark Pine Bluff, div dir, 1946-57; NC Cent Univ Durham, interim div dir, 1958-60; Spelman Col Atlanta, Ga, dept chmn, 1961-78; Morris Brown Col, div dir, educ & psychol, 1978-89. **Orgs:** Alpha Kappa Mus Nat Hon Soc, 1943-; secy, Pi Lambda Theta Hon Soc, 1978; fac secy, Omicron Delta Kappa Nat Hon Leadership Soc, 1983-89; St Paul Cross Roman Cath Church; rep, Cath Sch Bd Educ; Acad Coun Work Related, Morris Brown Col. **Honors/Awds:** Moton Scholar Tuskegee, Inst Tuskegee, Al, 1945; Alpha Kappa Mus Nat; Frederick Patterson's Winner Oratory Tuskegee Inst, 1945; All Expense Fel Gen Educ Bd Cornell Univ, 1945.

APPLETON, CLEVETTE WILMA
Social worker. **Personal:** Born in Louisville, KY; daughter of Cleve and Wilma Henry. **Educ:** Ky State Univ, BA, 1971; Ky Sch Social Work, Univ Louisville, MSSW, 1974. **Career:** Neighborhood Youth Corp, teacher asst, 1966-67; Louisville Free Pul Libr, clerk, 1968-70; Ky Dept Human Resources, soc worker, 1971-73; Metro Soc Serv Dept, stud soc worker, 1974; Bridgehaven, stud soc worker, 1974; Ky Dept Human Resources, soc worker grad I, 1975-77; River Region Serv, sr social worker, 1977-78; Univ Louisville Sch Med, sr social worker, 1978-91; Bryce Hosp, social worker II, 1991-92; Indian Rivers Community Ment Health, Ment Retard Ctr, asst trainer, 1993. **Orgs:** Coun Nephrology Soc Workers Network 9; Nat Kidney Found Metro Louisville. **Honors/Awds:** Nat Hon Soc Sec Schs, 1965; Maude Ainslie Scholar, 1967; Miss Wesley Club, Ky State Univ, 1971; Ky Dept Human Resources, Grad Sch Stipend, 1973. **Business Phone:** (205)345-6016.

APPLEWHAITE, LEON B.
Lawyer. **Personal:** Born Sep 4, 1927, Brooklyn, NY; married Louise J Harley. **Educ:** NY Univ, BA, 1948; Brooklyn Law Sch, JD, 1951; Brooklyn Univ Law Sch, LLM, 1961. **Career:** Social Security Admin, claims authorizer, 1955-59; Judge Francis E Rivers, legal secy, 1959-63; NY State Comn Human Rights, field rep; NY State Bd Mediation, labor arbit & mediator, 1964-67; NY State Workmen's Comp Bd, assoc coun, 1967-68; NY State Pub Employee Rels Bd supv mediator regional rep; atty, currently. **Orgs:** Asn Bar City NY; Nat Acad Arbitrators; Indus Rels Res

Asn; Nat Bar Asn; Am Arbit Asn; Soc Prof Dispute Resolution. **Military Serv:** AUS, 1952-54. **Business Addr:** Attorney, 1110 Fidler Lane, Silver Spring, MD 20910-3425.*

ARAMBURO, SOPHIE WATTS
Executive, teacher. **Personal:** Born Nov 23, 1931, New Orleans, LA; daughter of George Victor Watts and Eugenia Robinson Watts; married Alvin Noel Aramburo Sr, Jun 26, 1954; children: Alvin N, Sue A, Anthony J, Sheryl A Boudy & Alden G. **Educ:** Xavier Univ, BA, 1951, IST for Black Catholic Studies, attended 1991; Tulane Univ, MEd, 1967. **Career:** Executive, Teacher (retired); Orleans Parish Sch Bd, teacher, 1951-66, rdg specialist, 1967-70, high school rdg teacher, 1970-76, team assoc/proj real, 1976-77; Southern State Univ LA, rdg lab teacher/asst prof, 1977-85; Archdiocese New Orleans, LA, exec/assoc dir. **Orgs:** Past La State pres, depy, grandlady, financial secy, Knights Peter Claver, Ladies Aux Ct 21, 1950-; chair nat trends comt, Links Inc, Crescent City Chapter, 1984-; secy adv bd, Crescent House (Home for Battered Women); Nat Asn Black Cath Adminr, 1990-; Cursillo Movement, New Orleans; regional coord, Nat Black Catholic Congrss-Region V, 1990-. **Honors/Awds:** Papal Award, Pro Ecclesia et Pontifice, 1976; Silver Medal, Nat Court, LAKPC, 1979; Lady of the Year, New Orleans Central Comm, KPC, 1976; St Louis Medallion, 1994. **Home Addr:** 2533 Orbit Ct, Harvey, LA 70058-3013.

ARAUJO, DR. NORMAN
Educator. **Personal:** Born Mar 22, 1933, New Bedford, MA; son of Julia Coracao Araujo and Jose Joao Araujo; married Barbara Cartmill, 2000. **Educ:** Harvard Coll, AB, 1955; Universite d'Aix-Marseille, Certificat d'etudes litteraires, 1956; Harvard Univ, AM, 1957, PhD, 1962. **Career:** Univ Mass-Amherst, asst prof, 1962-64; Boston Col, asst prof, 1964-68, assoc prof fr, 1968-. **Orgs:** Modern Lang Asn Am, 1976-; chief advisor Cape Verdean News. **Honors/Awds:** Fulbright Fellowship (France); Nat Defense Act Fellowship (Portugal). **Special Achievements:** Book "A Study of Cape Verdean Literature," 1966; book "In Search of Eden, Lamartine's Symbols of Despair and Deliverance," 1976; Article "Emile Augier," in Magill's Critical Survey of Drama 1986; "Theophile Gautier," in Magill's Critical Survey of Literary Therory, 1988; "The Language of Business and the Business of Language," in Becque's Les Corbeaux, French Review, 63 (1989), pages 66-77; "Prosaic Licence and the Use of the Literary Past in Daudet's La Chevre de M Seguin," Forum for Modern Language Studies, 27:3, p 195-208, 1991; "Petrus Borel," Dictionary of Literary Biography, Ed Catharine Savage Brosman, vol 119; Nineteenth-Century French Fiction Writers: Romanticism and Realism, 1800-1860, p 49-61, 1992; 3 articles in Encyclopedia of Literary Critics & Criticism, 1999. **Business Addr:** Associate Professor, Boston College, 140 Commonwealth Ave Lyons Hall 304, Chestnut Hill, MA 02467, **Business Phone:** (617)552-3820.

ARBERRY, MORSE
Chief executive officer, real estate executive, government official. **Personal:** Born Mar 1, 1953, Berkeley, CA; married Carol I Daniels. **Educ:** Cent Ariz Col, AA; Northern Ariz Univ, BS, eng; Univ Nev, Las Vegas, MBA. **Career:** Assembly man, business executive; Nev Legis Coun Bur, Carson City Nev, state assemblyman, Dist 7, 1985-2005; Nev Assembly, Legis Comn, mem, 1987-2005; Nev Assembly, Interim Finance Comt, vice chair, 1993-95, 1997-99, 2001-03, 2005-07; chair, 1995-97, 1999-2001, 2003-05, co-chair, 1995-96; Clark Co Assembly, democrat, currently; Mortgage Co, pres & chief exec officer, currently. **Orgs:** Nat Asn Advan Colored People; Nat Black Caucus State Legislators; Clark Co Cent Dem Comt; Western Legis Conf; Coun State Governments; Nat Conf State Legislatures; Jodie Cannon Prince Hall Mason; Dr Martin Luther King Jr Comn; Order Elks Lodge; Order Eastern Star; Opportunity Village Bd; West Charleston Lions Club; Lied Discovery C's Mus Bd; Am Legis Exchange Coun; Urban Chamber Com, Las Vegas; Las Vegas Chamber Com; Gov's Comn Martin Luther King Jr Holiday; Valley Hosp Bd Gov; Nat Asn Mortgage Brokers; chmn, KCEP Radio Sta; Dem Club N Las Vegas. **Business Phone:** (702)562-2323.

ARBUCKLE, JOHN FINLEY, JR.
Financial manager. **Personal:** Born Jan 16, 1938, Peoria, IL; son of Florence E Netter and John F Sr; married Janet M Johnson, Feb 7, 1959; children: Elana L Arbuckle & Andrea D Parker. **Educ:** Bradley Univ, attended 1956, 1985; Life Underwriter Training Coun, grad,1962; Peoria Chamber of Com, leadership Sch, grad, 1977; Am Bankers Asn,Grad Sch, Univ Okla, 1985. **Career:** Retired: Chicago Metropolitan Mutual Assurance, asst dist mgr, 1958-66; Metropolitan Life Ins Co, sales consult, 1966-75; First of Am Bank, bus lender & vpres, 1975-97; AT & Investor Serv, sr investment analyst, 1997; Farmers Home Fire Ins Co, chmn. **Orgs:** Pres, Minority Bus Mgt Conf Bd, 1990-; proj mgr, Ctr for Study, Res &Learning, 1981-; past pres, Florence Crittenton Home, 1980; Phoenix Bus Awareness Asn, 1992-93; corp mem, Peoria Area Chamber of Com, 1975-; Illinois Valley Yacht & Canoe Club, 1970-; life mem, NAACP, 1984-; Sons of Union Vets of the Civil War, 1976-77; past pres, South West Kiwanis Club; bd mem, Peoria Pub Sch Dist 150. **Honors/Awds:** Inducted, African-Am Hall of Fame Mus Inc, 1992; Man of the Yr, Peoria-Dist Met-Life, 1969. **Special Achievements:** Chmn, Am Freedom Train, City of Peoria, 1974-75; Chicago Urban Lie,article on "Negro New Breed," 1962. **Military Serv:** USAF, ROTC, Bradley Univ, 1956-58; Precision Drill Team. **Business Addr:** Chairman, Farmers Home Fire Insurance Company, 122 South Jefferson St, Lewisburg, WV 24901-1315, **Business Phone:** (304)645-1975.*

ARBUCKLE, RONALD LEE
Engineer, police officer. **Personal:** Born Jul 13, 1945, Newark, NJ; son of Robert Lee and Mary Alice White; married Helena Yvonne Patrick, Sep 9, 1967 (divorced); children: Ronald L Jr. **Educ:** Rutgers Univ, Newark, NJ, 1973; AT&T Corp Schs; Newark Police Acad, NJ Inst Real Estate. **Career:** AT&T, Edison, NJ, customer eng, 1963-; Newark Spec Police, Newark, NJ, pres, 1971 (retired); Sweet Temptations Lingerie Co, East Orange, NJ, sales, 1986-88; Maylock Realty Corp, Newark, NJ, sales, 1987-. **Orgs:** Pres, Fed Afro Am Police Officers, 1976-99; bd dirs, Theater Universal Images, Newark, NJ, 1985-; pres, Newark Spec Police Asn, 1988-94; vpres, Neighborhood Housing Servs Newark, 1988-91; conf chairperson, Nat Black Police Asn, Northeast Region, 1988-92. **Honors/Awds:** Class A Valor Award, Newark Spec Police Asn, 1978; Member of the Year, Nat Black Police Asn, Northeast Region, 1985; Rookie of the Year, Sweet Temptations, 1986; Member of the Year, Newark Spec Police Asn, 1988; Outstanding Service Award, Nat Black Police Asn, Northeast Region, 1990. **Home Addr:** 21 Porter Ave, Newark, NJ 07112, **Home Phone:** (973)923-2453. **Business Addr:** Agent, Maylock Realty Corporation, 252 Chancellor Ave, Newark, NJ 07112, **Business Phone:** (973)923-6200.

ARBUCKLE ALSTON, PAMELA SUSAN
Dentist. **Personal:** Born Mar 12, 1955, Oakland, CA; daughter of Ruby Arbuckle. **Educ:** Laney Col, AS, 1975; Univ Calif, AB 1977, BS, DDS, 1982, MPP, 1984. **Career:** Univ Calif, teaching asst, 1982-83; Cong Res Serv, policy analyst summer, 1983; San Francisco Gen Hosp, staff dentist, 1983-91; Alameda Cty Health Care Serv Agency, Central Health Ctr, staff dentist, 1983-; Johnson, Bassin & Shaw Inc, consult, jobs corps health support proj, 1987-95; Prison Health Serv Inc, 1988-96; San Francisco Community Provider, dental consult, AIDS proj, 1990-93; Humanitas, Inc, Job Corps Health Support Proj, consult. **Orgs:** Secy, Nat Dental Soc Bay Area, 1983-84; comnr, Emeryville Community Develop Adv Comn, 1983-85; bd mem, Holy Names HS Alumnae Bd, 1983; Alameda City Bd Suprvs Subcomm on Dental Health, 1983-85; prog comm mem, Bay Area Black Consortium Quality, 1983-85; ed, Network Black Health Prof newsletter, 1984-85; bd mem, Berkeley Head Start Health Adv Bd, 1984-85; vpres, Calif Chap Nat Dental Asn, 1985; counr, UC CA Alumni Asn, 1984-87; bd mem, City Berkeley Maternal Child & Adolescent Health Bd, 1985-86, Univ Calif Black Alumni Club; Nat Asn Advan Colored People, 1985. **Honors/Awds:** Regents Scholar, Univ Calif, 1978-84; Williard Fleming Scholar, Univ Calif, 1979; Community Dentistry Serv Award, Univ Calif, 1982; Cert Appreciation SF Area Health Educ Ctr, 1984; Rosalie Stern Award, Community Serv, Univ Calif, 1990; Pub Health Hero Award, Univ Calif, Berkeley Sch Pub Health, 1999. *

ARCHAMBEAU, LESTER MILWARD, III
Football player. **Personal:** Born Jun 27, 1967, Montville, NJ; married Kathleen; children: Lester IV, Kellyn & Carsyn. **Educ:** Stanford univ, BS, Industrial Engineering. **Career:** Green Bay Packers, defensive end, 1990-92; Atlanta Falcons, defensive end, 1993-99; Denver Broncos, defensive end, 2000; Miami Dolphins, agent. **Honors/Awds:** SuperBowl, 1999. *

ARCHAMBEAU, SHELLYE L.
Chief executive officer, executive director. **Personal:** Born Jul 6, 1962, Washington, DC; daughter of Lester and Mera; married S Clarence Scott, Aug 25, 1984; children: Kethlyn, Kheaton. **Educ:** Univ Pa, Wharton Sch, BS, 1984; IBM Bus Mgt Inst, 1995. **Career:** Keystone Service Syst Inc, 1989-, chair finance comt, 1991-93, vice chair bd, 1993; NorthPoint Communications, chief mkt officer & exec vpres, 2000-01; Loudcloud Inc, chief mkt officer & exec vpres sales, 2001-02; MetricStream Inc, Wharton Econ Summit, chief exec officer, 2002-; Arbitron Inc, dir, 2005-; Blockbuster Inc, E-Com Div, pres; IBM, various exec sales & mkt positions. **Orgs:** bd dir, Nation's Capital Girl Scout Coun, 1995-97; Nat Asn Women Bus Owners, 1995-97; Coun Foreign Rels, 1997-; Am Chamber Com, Tokyo, Japan, 1998-99; Girls Inc, 2000; trustees, Coun Women, Univ Pa; Mentium, 2001-; USPS, mktg adv bd, 2002; Info Technol Sr Mgt Forum; Forum Women Entrepreneurs; Women's Coun Bd Trustees Univ Pa. **Honors/Awds:** Hall of Fame Inducted, Nat Asn Negro Bus & Prof Women, 1997; the Top 25 'Click & Mortar' Exec in the Co, 2000; numerous other awards. **Home Addr:** 4016 Purdue Ave, Dallas, TX 75225. **Business Addr:** Chief Executive Officer, MetricStream Inc, 3000 Bridge Pkwy, Redwood Shores, CA 94065, **Business Phone:** (650)620-2900.*

ARCHER, DR. CHALMERS, JR.
School administrator, educator. **Personal:** Born Apr 21, 1938, Tchula, MS; son of Chalmers Archer Sr (deceased) and Eva Alcola Rutharford Archer (deceased). **Educ:** Saints Junior Col, Assoc, art; Tuskegee Inst, Ala, BS, 1972, MEd, 1973; Auburn Univ, Ala, PhD, 1979; Univ Ala, Post Doctorate Cert, 1979; MIT, Cambridge Mass, Cert, 1982. **Career:** School administrator, Educator (retired); Saints Jr Col, asst to the pres, 1968-70; Tuskegee Inst, asst vres & asst prof, 1970-83; Northern Va Community Col, admin & prof, 1983-2000, prof emer, 2000-; past Jackson Advocate, contributing editor. **Orgs:** Nat Asn Col Deans, Registrars & Admissions Officers; Phi Delta Kappa; Kappa Delta Pi; APGA; NAACP, lifetime mem; charter mem, Kiwanis Int Macon Col; AAUP; AACRAO; Southeastern Assoc Community Col; Cooperative Educ; vpres, Saints Jr Col Alumni; past bd mem, Nat Consortium for the Recruitment of Black Students from Northern Cities; past chmn, St Ala's Steering Comm for Advanced Placement High Sch Studs; consult, Dept Educ on Retention, 1990-92. **Honors/Awds:** Hon Doctorate of Letters, Saints Jr Col, Lexington, Mass, 1970; Phi Delta Kappa Award for Leadership; Exemplary Res & Prog Develop, 1981; cited for community contribution; lectured at Cambridge Univ, England, and five major univs on teaching and learning inter disciplinary studies, 1988-89; architect of Comp Counseling Ctr & Weekend Col Tuskegee Inst; Architect of Reading & Language Arts Special Emphasis Curriculum for public schs; developed successful multi-level Educ Alliance to Adv Equal Access with public schs; participated in President-elect Clinton's "A Call for Reunion" Opening Ceremony; President Clinton's Task Force, Americans for Change, charter member; Democratic Nat Committee; Clinton/Gore Rapid Response Team; received the Miss Inst Arts and Letters Award for non-fiction, 1992. **Special Achievements:** Author: Growing Up Black in Rural Mississippi, 1992; ON the Shoulders of Giants in progress; Growing up With the Green Berets, Feb, 1999; author, Green Berets In the Vanguard: Inside Special Forces, 1953-63, 2000. 22 educational & other publications. **Military Serv:** USY Green Berets-Airborne; distinction of saving life of first Am injured in Vietnam, 1957; Attempted to save life of first Am killed, 1956. **Home Addr:** 4522 Commons Dr Suite 40, Annandale, VA 22003-4959. **Business Addr:** Professor Emeritus, Northern Virginia Community College, Alexandria Campus, 3001 N Beauregard St, Alexandria, VA 22311.

ARCHER, DENNIS WAYNE
Lawyer. **Personal:** Born Jan 1, 1942, Detroit, MI; son of Ernest James and Frances Carroll; married Trudy DunCombe, Jun 17, 1967; children: Dennis Wayne Jr & Vincent DunCombe. **Educ:** Western Mich Univ, BS, 1965; Detroit Col Law, JD, 1970, LLD, 1988; Univ Detroit Sch Law, LLD, 1988, John Marshall Law Sch, LLD, 1991. **Career:** Gragg & Gardner PC, trial lawyer, 1970-71; Hall Stone Allen & Archer,trial lawyer, 1971-73; Detroit Col Law, Detroit MI, assoc prof, 1972-78; Charfoos Christensen & Archer, trial lawyer, 1973-85; Wayne State Univ Law Sch, Detroit MI, adj prof, 1984-85; Mich Supreme Ct, assoc justice, 1985-93; Dickinson Wright PLLC, partner, 1991-93, chmn, 2002-; City Detroit, mayor, 1994-2001; Am Bar Asn, pres, 2003-04. **Orgs:** Pres, Nat Conf Democratic Mayors, 1996-99; pres, Nat Bar Asn; Am Judicature Soc; pres, State Bar Mich; Wolverine Bar Asn; Detroit Bar Asn; fel, Intl Soc Barristers; Old Newsboys Goodfel Fund, 1980-97; Alpha Phi Alpha; The Fel Am Bar Asn; life mem, NAACP; bd dir, MI Cancer Found, 1985-92; bd trustees, Olivet Col, 1991-94; US Conf Mayors, 1994; Nat Conf Black Mayors, 1994; Intergovernmemtal Policy Adv Comt US Trade Rep, 1994; Nat Comt Crime Control & Prev, 1995; Dem Conv Platform Comt, 1996; vicechair, Nat League Cities, Comt & Econ Develop Policy Comt, 1997; Brookings Inst, 1997; Nat Res Coun, Steering Comt Harnessing Technol Am Econ Future, 1997; US Dept Housing & Urban Develop, Joint Ctr Sustainable Communities, 1998; Fannie Mae, Nat Adv Coun, 1998-99; Compuware, 2001-; pres-elect, 2002, pres, 2003, Am Bar Asn; chmn & bd dir, Detroit Regional Chamber, 2006-07. **Honors/Awds:** Distinguished Achievement Award, NAACP Detroit Br, 1985; Spirit of Excellence Award, Am Bar Asn, 1996; Newsmaker of the Year, Engr News-Record mag, 1998; Public Official of the Year, Governing mag, 2000; Distinguished Achievement Award, Tuskegee Airmen Natl Hist Mus, 2001; Award of Excellence; 25 most dynamic mayors in America. **Special Achievements:** Author: Blackballed-A Case Against Private Clubs Barrister 1983; Named one of the 100 Most Influential Black Americans, Ebony magazine 1984; citedin Nat Law Journal as one of the 100 most powerful attorneys in the US, 1985; Most Respected Judge in Michigan, Michigan Lawyers Weekly, 1990. **Business Addr:** Chairman, Dickinson Wright PLLC, 500 Woodward Ave Suite 4000, Detroit, MI 48226-3425, **Business Phone:** (313)223-3500.

ARCHER, DR. JUANITA A.
Physician, educator. **Personal:** Born Nov 3, 1934, Washington, DC; daughter of Roy E Hinnant and Anna Blakeney; married Frederick; children: Frederick II. **Educ:** Howard Univ, Wash, DC, BS, 1956, MS, 1958, MD, 1965. **Career:** Freedman's Hosp, intern, 1965-66; Howard Univ, resident, 1966-68, fel, 1970-71, instr, 1971-75, Diabetes Investigative Group, dir, Endocrine Metabolic Lab, 1972-, Endocrine & Metabolic Dis Sect, asst prof med, 1975-79, assoc prof med, 1980-. **Orgs:** DC Med Soc; Am Diabetes Asn; Sigma Xi; Beta Kappa Chi; Am Fedn Clin Res; Endocrine Soc; NY Acad Sci; Delta Sigma Theta; Gen Clinical Res Comt NIH, 1976-86; Biohazards & Biosafety Comt, Howard Univ; consult, Arizona Research Coun, 1986, 1987. **Honors/Awds:** Josiah Macy Faculty Fel, 1974-77; Physician's Recognition Award, 1983-86; Nat Podiatry Med Award, 1989; Am Red Cross Award, 1988; Physicians Recognition Award, Am Med Asn; Moses Wharton Young Research Award, 1988; Public Relations Award, Howard Univ Hosp, 1990. **Special Achievements:** Numerous publications

including: P Gorden & J Roth, Defect Insulin Binding Receptors Clin Invest 55, 166-175, 1975; with R Knopp, J Olefsky, C RShuman, "Clinical Diabetes Update 11" Upjohn Monograph, 1980. **Home Addr:** 4305 Ranger Ave, Marlow Heights, MD 20748. **Business Addr:** Associate Professor, Howard University Hospital, 2041 Georgia Ave NW Suite 5000, Washington, DC 20060.*

ARCHER, LEE A., JR.
Army officer. **Educ:** Delehenty Inst. **Career:** Army officer (retired); Camp Wheeler, Ga, instr, 1942; Tuskegee Army Airfield, Acting Sergeant, 1942, second Lt , 1943; 302nd Fighter Squadron & 332nd Fighter Group, Italy, 1944; Tuskegee Army, lt Coronal, 1970. **Honors/Awds:** Distinguished Flying Cross, Air Medal, 18 Oak Leaf Clusters.

ARCHER, MICHAEL EUGENE
Singer. **Personal:** Born Feb 11, 1974, Richmond, VA; married Angie Stone; children: Michael Jr & Imani. **Career:** Albums: Brown Sugar, 1995; Live at the Jazz Cafe, 1998; Voodoo, 2000; YODA: The Monarch of Neo-Soul, 2007; The Best So Far, 2008. **Honors/Awds:** Two Grammy Awards, 2000. **Special Achievements:** Named in the list of 50 Bands To See Before You Die in Q magazine in 2002. *

ARCHER, SUSIE COLEMAN
Educator, administrator. **Personal:** Born Mar 29, 1946, Pembroke, KY; married Dennis Archer. **Educ:** BS, 1968; MA, 1969; Vanderbilt Univ, PhD. **Career:** Austin Peay State Univ, supvr women's dormitories, 1969-74, tchr, 1969-75; Univ Md, European Br, W Berlin, Ger, instr, 1975-77; Salt Lake City Sch Dist, supvr counr, 1978-80; UT Tech Col, Salt Lake, dir regis & admin, 1980-87; Vanderbilt Univ, assoc univ registrar, 1987-, asst to the provost & dir, currently. **Orgs:** Fac adv, Phi Alpha Theta, 1971-72; fac adv, Sr Classical League, 1973-; Altrusa Club, 1979; bd dir, Travelers Aid Soc, 1979-; Acad Governance Comt; Discrimination & Unfair Grading Practices Comm; Affirmative Action Comm; Comt Revise Prom & Tenure Policies; Comn Union Women's Rights; Middle Tenn Educ Asn; APSU Women's Club; fac adv, Alpha Mu Gamma; fac adv, Circle K; fac adv, Alpha Phi; fac adv, Int Students Asn; Am Asn Collegiate Registrars & Admis Officers, 1980-; pres, UT Asn Collegiate & Admis Officers, 1985-86; Tenn Southern Asn Collegiate Registrars & Admis Officers, 1987-; pres, Southern Asn Col Registrars & Admis Officers. **Honors/Awds:** Outstanding Student in French, 1967; Outstanding Student in History, Phi Alpha Theta, 1968; Rene Descartes Medal in French Literature, 1968; APSU Grad Assistantship, 1968; Alpha Mu Gamma's Scholarship to participate in experiment in Intl Living Vanderbilts Chancellors Fellowship for Grad Study, 1972-73. **Business Addr:** Assistant to the Provost, Director, Vanderbilt University, Provost & Vice-Chancellor Acad Affairs Office, 512B Kirkland Hall, PO Box 7745 Sta B, Nashville, TN 37240.

ARCHER, TRUDY DUNCOMBE
Judge, mayor. **Personal:** Married Dennis W, Jun 17, 1967; children: Dennis Wayne Jr & Vincent DunCombe. **Educ:** Eastern Mich Univ, BS; Wayne State Univ, Masters Educ Guid & Coun; Detroit Col Law, JD. **Career:** Detroit, mayor; Mich, 36th Dist Ct, judge, 1989-2006. **Orgs:** Pres, Am Bar Asn.

ARCHIBALD, B. MILELE
Lawyer, educator. **Personal:** Born Jul 4, 1945, New York, NY; married Faruq Muhammad; children: Nyota. **Educ:** Bronx Comm Col, AAS, 1968; Hunter Col, New York, NY, BA, 1973; Univ Calif, Berkeley, JD, 1976. **Career:** Chief Judge DC, Court Appeals, law clerk, 1976-77; Fed Trade Comt, WA, staff atty, 1977-78; Overseas Pvt Investment Corp, spec asst pres; Womens Health Ctr, dir; Alamance Community Col, Small Bus Ctr, dir, 2002-. **Orgs:** Washington DC Bar Asn, 1977-; Nat Asn Black Women Atty, 1978; bd mem, Womens Resource Ctr. **Business Addr:** Director, Alamamce Community College, Small Business Center, BC-101, 1247 Jimmie Kerr Rd, Graham, NC 27253-8000.

ARCHIBALD, NATHANIEL (TINY ARCHIBALD)
Basketball player, basketball coach. **Personal:** Born Sep 2, 1948, New York, NY; son of Big Tiny and Julia. **Educ:** Univ Tex, El Paso, attended 1970; Fordham Univ, MA, 1993. **Career:** Basketball player (retired), basketball coach; Cincinnati Royals, basketball player, 1970-76; NY Nets, basketball player, 1976-77; Buffalo Braves, basketball player, 1977-78; Boston Celtics, 1978-83, Milwaukee Bucks, 1983-84; Univ Ga, asst basketball coach; Univ Tex, El Paso, asst basketball coach; Harlem Armory Homeless Shelter, athletic dir, 1991; Nat Basketball Develop League, head coach, 2001. **Orgs:** Alpha Phi Alpha Fraternity Inc. **Honors/Awds:** All-NBA Second Team, 1972, 1981; All-NBA First Team, 1973, 1975, 1976; Comeback Player of Year, NBA, 1979-80; NBA Champion, 1981; Six-time All-Star, All-Star Game MVP, 1981; Naismith Memorial Basketball Hall of Fame, 1991; One of 50 Greatest Players in NBA History, 1996. **Business Phone:** (410)554-0040.

ARCHIBALD, TINY. **See ARCHIBALD, NATHANIEL.**

ARCHIE, SHIRLEY FRANKLIN
Association executive, educator. **Personal:** Born Apr 15, 1944, Philadelphia, PA; married Robert Lewis Archie Jr; children: Keita T, Kweli I. **Educ:** Cheyney State Col, BA, 1966; Howard Univ, attended 69; Temple Univ, Urban Educ, 1981. **Career:** DC School System, educator, 1967-70; Philadelphia Sch System, educator, 1976-; Temple Univ, instr, 1983-85; Sigler Travel Serv Inc, travel consult; nat asn Bench & Bar Spouses, nat pres. **Orgs:** Links Inc; Alpha Kappa Alpha; Jack & Jill Am; Women's Leaders Team, African-American Inst Zimbabwe; bd dir, Girl Scouts Am; bd trustees, Springside Sch; comn Camden City, Comn Women, 1983; comn Philadelphia, Major's Comn Women, 1985. **Honors/Awds:** Distinguished Service Award, Girl Scouts Am, 1982; Commendation Outstanding Teacher, Philadelphia Systems, 1982, 1984; Teacher of the Year Delaware Valley, Daily News & Inquirer, 2002. **Business Addr:** Educator, School District of Philadelphia Education Center, 440 N Broad St, Philadelphia, PA 19130, **Business Phone:** (215)400-4000.*

ARCHIE-HUDSON, MARGUERITE
School administrator. **Personal:** Born Nov 18, 1937, Yonges Island, SC; married Hudson (divorced). **Educ:** Talledega Col, BA, psychol, 1958; Harvard Univ, MA, educ & coun, 1962; Univ Calif, Los Angeles, PhD, higher educ admin, 1980. **Career:** Burke High Sch, Charleston, SC, counr, 1958; Inst Psychol Servs, IL Inst Technol, psychometrist, 1959-69; City Chicago, test writer, 1960; Univ Chicago, Lab Sch, counr, 1962-66; Upward Bound, Occidental Col, dir, 1966-68; Locke High Sch, Los Angeles, dir col coun, 1968-71; Calif State Univ, dir Educ Opportunities Prog, 1971-72; US Congresswoman, Yvonne Brathwaite Burke, dist staff dir, 1972-78; Dept HUD, Los Angeles, 1978-79; office CA Assemblyman Willie Brown, staffer, 1980; Free All, TV host, 1980-98; Calif State Govt, Assemblywoman District 48, 1990-96; Talladega Col, pres, 1998-2001; Col Charleston, dept polit sci, asst prof, 2002-. **Orgs:** Bd trustees, Los Angeles Community Col Dist; vpres, Calif Mus Sci & Indust Found; bd trustees, Los Angeles SW Col Found; bd trustees, Jenesse Ctr; Crystal Stairs, bd trustees; State Bar CA; Delta Sigma Theta Sorority; chairperson, March Dimes, Talladega; United Way. **Special Achievements:** First female prexy of Talledega College, 1998; First African American woman to head a four-year institution in the State of Alabama. **Business Addr:** Assistant Professor, College of Charleston, Department polit sci, 66 George St, Charleston, SC 29424, **Business Phone:** (843)953-8138.

ARD, REV. ROBERT
Clergy. **Career:** Christ Church San Diego, pastor, 2002. **Orgs:** Bd dir, Ecumenical Coun San Diego County; exec bd, Interfaith Comt Worker Justice. **Business Addr:** Pastor, Christ Church San Diego, 1355 Fern St, San Diego, CA 92101, **Business Phone:** (619)264-7240.

ARDREY, DR. SAUNDRA CURRY
Educator. **Personal:** Born Aug 26, 1953, Louisville, GA; daughter of Earle and Estella; married William McCarty Ardrey. **Educ:** Winston-Salem State Univ, BA, 1975; Ohio State Univ, MA, 1976, PhD, 1983. **Career:** Univ NC, Chapel Hill, vis lectr, 1979-80; Univ Ky, Jefferson Community Col, instr, 1980-81; Furman Univ, asst prof, 1983-88; Western Ky Univ, Dept Govt, from asst prof to assoc prof, 1988-99, spec asst to provost fac recruitment, 1999-2000, Dept Govt, head, 2000-, Dept Polit Sci, head & dir, currently. **Orgs:** Am Polit Sci Asn, 1975-87; Nat Conf Black Polit Sci, 1978-; Southern Polit Sci Asn, 1983-87; Am Asn Univ Prof, 1983-85; bd mem, Greenville City Urban League, 1983-87; Greenville City United Way, 1983-84; exec community mem, Greenville City Dem Party, 1984-85; pres, Greenville City Young Dem, 1984-85; Alpha Kappa Alpha Sorority, 1989-; Nat Asn Advan Colored People, Bowling Green Br, 1990-; pres, Bowling Green NOW. **Honors/Awds:** Outstanding Achievement in Service Award, Western Ky Univ, 1990; Outstanding Paper Award, Nat Conf Black Polit Scientists, Annual Conf, 1994; Outstanding Educator of the Century, 1999. **Business Addr:** Director, Department Head, Western Kentucky University, Department of Political Science, 300 Grise Hall 1 Big Red Way, Bowling Green, KY 42101, **Business Phone:** (270)745-4558.

ARDS, DR. SHEILA DIANN
Educator. **Personal:** Born Jun 30, 1960, Houston, TX; daughter of James Ed and Rosie M; married Samuel L Myers Jr, Aug 21, 1982; children: Andrea & Angela. **Educ:** Univ Tex, Austin, 1981; Carnegie Mellon Univ, MS, pub mgt, 1983, PhD, pub policy, 1990. **Career:** Urban Institute, research scholar; Univ Md, asst prof; Univ Minn, assoc prof, Humphrey Inst Pub Affairs, assoc vpres community partnerships & develop, 2002-06; Benedict Col, vpres, community develop, currently, Dept Soc Sci & Criminal justice, assoc prof, currently, Ctr Excellence, dir, currently. **Orgs:** Pi Sigma Alpha Exec Coun, 1995-; bd dirs, Nat Leadership Inst, 1995-; pres, Nat Conf Black Political Scientists, 1997; vpres, APPAM, 1998; pres, Nat Economic Assoc, 2004. **Honors/Awds:** Bush Faculty Development Fellowship, 1993-94, Minority Faculty Research Award, 1996-97, Univ Minn; Twin Award, Girl Scouts, 1998. **Special Achievements:** "The Effects of Sample Selection Bias on What We Know About Child Abuse", 1978, "Efforts of Sample Selection Bias on Racial Differences in Child Abuse", 1999, Child Abuse & Neglect. **Business Addr:** Vice President, Director, Benedict College, 1600 Harden St, Columbia, SC 29204, **Business Phone:** (803)256-4220.

AREMU, ADUKE
Writer, educator, television producer. **Personal:** Born in New York City, NY; daughter of Robert and Frances Holmes; married W Calvin Anderson, Nov 23, 1998; children: Hakim Salih James. **Educ:** Hunter Col, BA, speech & theatre, 1968, MS, educ, 1973; Col New Rochelle, supv & admin; New York Univ, PhD, theatre. **Career:** Essex County Col, prof, 1974-79; Urban Coalition, consult, 1979; New Dove Promotions Inc, chief exec officer, 1981-; Borough Manhattan Community Col, prof, 1981-83; Sch Syst New York City, 1981-99; Col New Rochelle, prof, 1985-87; Medgar Evers Col, prof, 1993-98; Sch Syst New Rochelle, NY, 1999-. **Orgs:** Zeta Phi Beta Sorority, 1975-; chief exec officer, New York Youth Consortium Inc, 1985-; Hunter Col Alumnus Asn; Audelco NY, 1998-; Stud Empowerment Prog, 1999-; Educ Comt, NAACP, 1999-. **Honors/Awds:** Theatre Award, Audelco, 1979; Woman of the Year, Caribbean-American Chamber Com, 1998; Creativity Award, Kwanzaa Found New York, 1998. **Special Achievements:** Published: "Hannibal and The Culture Carnival", 1995; Reaching Out With Love, 1981; Plays: "Kwanzaa-A Musical Play", 1996; "The Liberation of Mother Goose", 1977; "Babylon II", 1981; "Bum Sonata", 1991. **Business Phone:** (914)576-0983.

ARGRETT, LORETTA COLLINS
Government official. **Personal:** Married Vantile E Whitfield; children: Lisa & Brian. **Educ:** Howard Univ, BS, 1958; Inst Fur Organische Chemie, Technische Hochschule; Harvard Law Sch, JD, 1976. **Career:** US Cong, Joint Comt on Taxation, atty; Wald, Harkrader & Ross, atty, partner; Howard Univ Sch Law, prof; US Justice Dept, Tax Div, asst atty gen, 1993-99; consult, currently. **Orgs:** Vis comt mem, Harvard Law Sch, 1987-93; Amn Bar Found, fel, 1993-; legal ethics comt mem, Dist Columbia Bar, 1993-97; adv comt mem, Univ Baltimore Law Sch, Graduate Tax Prog, 1986-; Am Bar Asn, standing comn ethics & prof responsibility, 1998-; joint comn, Am Bar Asn, currently; bd dirs, Am Bar Retirement Asn, currently; elected mem, Am Law Inst. **Honors/Awds:** Outstanding Service & Achievement in Field Law, Greenwood Voters League, 1994; Lifetime Achievement Award for Black Alumni, 1997; Chief Counsel's Award, 1999; Special Recognition for Contributions to the Tax System, ABA Sec Taxation, 2000; Charlotte E Ray Award, Nat Bar Asns Women Lawyers Div, 2004; Margaret Brent Women Lawyers Achievement Award, 2005. **Special Achievements:** First African American woman in the history of the Justice Department to hold a position requiring Senate confirmation; First African American member of the staff of the Joint Committee on Taxation of the US Congress. **Business Addr:** Board of Directors, ABA Commission, 321 N Clark St, Chicago, IL 60610, **Business Phone:** (312)988-5715.

ARGRETTE, JOSEPH
Executive, president (organization), chief executive officer. **Personal:** Born Apr 1, 1931, New York, NY; son of Joseph Jr and Mariah Tucker Dawson; children: Kendelle Ruth. **Educ:** Long Island Univ, Brooklyn, NY, BS, MS, 1954. **Career:** Argrett Enterprises Corp, New York, NY, pres, 1977-; Riverside Hosp-,Bronx, NY, dir voc coun; Fed Govt Off Equal Opportunity, Off Inspections,Washington, DC, dir region 2; Nat Alliance Businessmen, Washington, DC,dir community rels; Stone Craft Int, New York, NY, pres; JMA Concrete Construct Co Inc, pres & chief exec officer, currently. **Orgs:** Asn Gen Contractors Am, 1980-89; dir, vpres, emer bd, Nat Asn Minority Contractors, 1985-89; dir, Gen Bldg Contractors-Asn Gen Contractor; exec comt mem, Gen Contractors Asn, NYC; Eagle Scout, Boy Scouts Am. **Honors/Awds:** Outstanding Minority Contractor, NY State Dept Environ Conserv, 1984; Outstanding Member Award, Nat Asn Minority Contractors, 1987;Distinguished Service Award, Asn Minority Enterprises NY, 1987; Contractor of the Year Award, Westchester Minority Contractors Westchester, NY, 1988. **Business Addr:** President, Chief Executive Officer, JMA Concrete Construct Company Inc, 213-08 920 Lester Ave, Queens Village, NY 11429, **Business Phone:** (914)777-6400.

ARKHURST, JOYCE COOPER
Librarian. **Personal:** Born Oct 20, 1921, Seattle, WA; daughter of Felix and Hazel James; married Frederick Arkhurst, Oct 3, 1959; children: Cecile Arkhurst. **Educ:** Univ Washington, Seattle, BA, 1944; Columbia Univ, MLS, 1957. **Career:** Librarian (retired); New York Pub Libr, children's librn, 1947-58; Chicago Pub Lib, children's librn, 1967-69; Fieldston Sch, Bronx, NY, librn, 1971-74; Elisabeth Irwin Sch, New York, NY, 1978-83; New York City Bd Educ, libr teacher, 1983-93. **Orgs:** Delta Sigma Theta Sorority, 1943-; NAACP, 1984-88; Am Libr Asn, 1983-85; Schomburg Corp, 1988-; New York Black Librns Caucus, 1983-; Countee Cullen Libr Support Group, 1988-; Am Asn Univ Women, 1991-. **Honors/Awds:** Mortar Bd, Sociology Honorary, Univ Washington, 1944; author, The Adventures Spider, 1964, More Adventures Spider, 1971. *

ARMANO, KWADWO J.
Lawyer. **Educ:** St Louis Univ, Sch Law. **Career:** Armano Law Office, atty, currently. **Business Phone:** (314)721-5211.*

ARMISTEAD, MILTON
Lawyer. **Personal:** Born Jun 19, 1947, Indianpolis, IN; son of Mitchell and Margarette; children: Jeff & Milton. **Educ:** Pasadena City Col, AA, 1967; San Jose State Col, BA, 1969; Univ Southern Calif, MS, 1972, JD, 1974. **Career:** Pvt Pract, atty, currently.

Orgs: Pres, Wiley Manual Law Soc, 1979-; corresp, Sacramento Observer, 1981; Calif Trial Lawyers Asn; Defense Res Inst, 1983; pres, Toastmasters Capital Club, 1984; bd dir, Sacramento Claims Asn, 1984; vpres, Sacramento Black Chamber Comn, 1985-; chmn, Vols Am, 1985; Black Ins Prof Asn, 1985. **Honors/Awds:** Best Speaker Toastmasters, 1984; Competent Toastmaster Award, 1987. **Home Phone:** (916)773-9290. **Business Addr:** Attorney, 2377 Gold Meadow Way Suite 100, Gold River, AR 95661, **Business Phone:** (916)257-1525.*

ARMOUR, DR. CHRISTOPHER E
Physician. **Personal:** Born Nov 1, 1959, Columbus, GA; son of John Henry Crowder Armour III and Mildred L; married Jacqueline L, Dec 16, 1984; children: Jonathan R & Kristen M. **Educ:** Univ Ga, BS, 1982; Morehouse Sch Med, MD, 1987. **Career:** Southwest Hosp, med resident physician, 1987-90; Smyrna Medfirst, med dir & physician, 1990-94; Aetna Healthways Family Med Ctr, staff physican, 1995-; Wellstar Physician Group, 1998; Pkwy Med, physician; The Southeat Permanente Med Group, 2003-. **Orgs:** Am Acad Family Physicians, 1990-; Ga Acad Family Physicians, 1990-; Nat Med Asn, 1991-; AMA, 1994. **Home Addr:** 2725 Thornbury Way, College Park, GA 30349. **Business Addr:** Physician, Kaiser Permanente, 1175 Cascade Pkwy, Atlanta, GA 30311, **Business Phone:** (770)941-7090.

ARMOUR, DR. LAWRENCE
Educator. **Career:** Southern Univ, New Orleans, asst prof & dir, post baccalaureate cert, currently. **Business Phone:** (504)286-5042.

ARMSTEAD, JESSIE WILLARD
Football player. **Personal:** Born Oct 26, 1970, Dallas, TX; married Channon; children: Jessica & Jaya. **Educ:** Univ Miami, Fl, criminal justice. **Career:** Football player (retired); NY Giants, linebacker, 1993-2001; Wash Redskins, 2002-03; Carolina Panthers, linebacker, 2004. **Orgs:** Founder, Armstead Found; mem, NY community; Wash Community. **Honors/Awds:** Natl Football Conf Spec Teams Player of the Week, 1993; Nat Football Conf Spec Teams Player of the Month, 1993; Rookie of the Year, NY Giants, 1993; Defensive Most Valuable Player, 1996; Most Valuable Player, 1997; Pro Bowl, 1997-2001; Nat Football Conf Defensive Player of the Month, 1999; Nat Football Conf Defensive Player of the Week; Top 25 team hon, USA Today; Jessie's Giant Hoop Team. **Special Achievements:** TV appearence: Pros vs Joes, Spike TV, 2008. *

ARMSTEAD, RON E.
Social worker, city planner. **Personal:** Born Apr 12, 1947, Boston, MA; son of Leemon Smith and Ruby Smith; children: Tod, Kaili, Ronni. **Educ:** Boston Univ Metro Col, attended 1974; Boston State Col, BA (with honors) 1979; Harvard Univ, Graduate Sch Design, cert, 1983; Mass Inst Technol, Cambridge MA, MCP, 1989. **Career:** Teen Educ Ctr, educ counr, 1970-73; Model Cities Admin, community planner, 1970-74; Vet Ctr Vet Admin, readjustment counr, social worker, 1979-87; Amistad Asn, pres; Cong Black Caucus Vet Braintrust, exec dir, currently. **Orgs:** bd dirs, William Joiner Ctr Study War & Social Consequences; conf issue coordr Speakers Conf on Vietnam Vet; co-chmn, Nat Black Vet Working Group; coord, Mass Black Vet Think Tank Group; Soc Traumatic Stress Studies; Nat Asn Black Social Workers; Asn Study Afro-Am Life & Hist, 1985-; pres, bd dirs, Vet Benefits Clearinghouse Inc, 1975-85; Nat Asn Social Workers, 1980-, Sen John F Kerry's Black Adv Comt, 1989; consult, Secy Jesse Brown's Adv Comt Minority Veterans. **Honors/Awds:** Commendation, Vet Admin, 1982; Commendation, Gov Michael L Dukakis, 1983; Salute Award, Chelsea Soldiers Home, 1986; fel Mass Inst Technol, 1987; Scholar Award, Mass Inst Technol, 1987; Cert Award, Mass Off Affirmative Action, 1989; coordinated Black Vet Workshops at Cong Black Caucus Legis Weekends, 1985, 1987, 1988; presented Stress & Trauma Workshops, Nat Asn Black Social Workers Conf, 1987-89; Spec Cong Recognition Award; Boston Neighborhood Fels Award; Outstanding Veterans Achievement Award; Drylongso Award. **Military Serv:** USN, E-4 1966-69; Vietnam Campaign Medal, Vietnam Serv Medal 3/16 Bronze Star, Nat Service Defense Medal.

ARMSTEAD, WILBERT EDWARD, JR.
Administrator. **Personal:** Born Jun 23, 1934, Baltimore, MD; son of Wilbert Edward and Mary Josephine Hill; married Erma Shirley Cole; children: Barbara E, Valerie, Sheryl J, Joann C, Jeri L Connelly & Angela M Bernard. **Educ:** Johns Hopkins Univ, BA, Elect Engr, 1955. **Career:** RCA Missile & Surface Radar, assoc mem engr staff, 1955-58, mem engr staff, 1958-62, sr mem engr staff, 1963-74, unit mgr, 1974-86; GE, Moorestown, NJ, mgr, 1986-93; Martin Marietta Principal Prog, ctr specialist, 1993-95; Lockheed Martin GES, prog mgr, 1995-. **Orgs:** Vpres, 1979, pres, 1980-86, Moorestown Township Bd of Educ; Community Serv Club Blue Chips, 1975; Ed Comn, Baptist Ch Moorestown, 1977, NJ State Fed Colored Women, 1981; pres & newsletter ed, Moorestown Improvement Asn; bd trustees, Burlington City Family Serv; advisory bd, Moorestown Citizens; Low and Moderate Income Housing, 1994-97; Moorestown Zoning Bd; Republican Committeeman, 10th District, Moorestown NJ, 1997-. **Honors/Awds:** Citizen of the Year, Moorestown NJ Combined Serv Clubs, 2000; Star of Excellence Award Citizen of the Year, Lockheed Martin Corp, Naval Electronics and Surveillance Systems Div, 2000. **Military Serv:** AUS, Corp Engrs, 2nd lt; NJ Nat Guard, AABN, 2nd lt. **Business Addr:** Program Manager, Lockheed Martin, Mail Stop 116 302, PO Box 1027, Moorestown, NJ 08057.*

ARMSTER-WORRILL, CYNTHIA DENISE
School administrator, educator. **Personal:** Born Aug 7, 1960, Tokyo, Japan; daughter of Dorothy L and Franksin; married Conrad W Worrill, Mar 7, 1987; children: Sobeenna Armster Worrill. **Educ:** Emporia State Univ, BS, 1982, MS, 1983. **Career:** Emporia State Univ, job develop coordr, 1982-83; Northern Ill Univ, counr,minority prog, 1983-85; George Williams Col, dir acad support, 1985; Chicago State Univ, dir freshmen serv, 1986-; City Col Chicago, assoc vice chancellor stud affairs, currently. **Orgs:** Chair, Minority Personnel Concerns Comn, 1984-85; prog chair, 1985-86, mem chair, 1986-87, Am Col Personnel Asn; rec secy, Alpha Kappa Alpha Sor Inc, 1986-87; Nat Black United Front, 1986-87; YWCA Chmn, Monarch Awards Found, 1989. **Honors/Awds:** Outstanding Black Woman Black Stud Union NIU, 1984. **Home Addr:** 7414 S Chappel 2nd Fl, Chicago, IL 60649. **Business Addr:** Associate Vice Chancellor of Student Affairs, City Colleges of Chicago, 226 W Jackson Blvd 9th Fl, Chicago, IL 60606, **Business Phone:** (312)553-3449.

ARMSTRONG, B. J.
Basketball player, executive, vice president (organization). **Personal:** Born Sep 9, 1967, Detroit, MI; married. **Educ:** Univ Iowa, Iowa City, IA, 1985. **Career:** Basketball player (retired); Chicago Bulls, guard, 1989-95, 1999-2000; Golden State Warriors, guard, 1995-97; Toronto Raptors, 1995; Charlotte Hornets, guard, 1997-98; Orlando Magic, 1999; Chicago Bulls, 1999-2000, asst gen mgr, 2000-03, gen mgr, 2003, spec asst exec vpres basketball oper, 2005; ESPN, basketball analyst, 2005-; Wasserman Media Group LLC, vpres basketball mgt, currently. **Honors/Awds:** NBA Championship, Chicago, 1991-93; NBA All-Star, 1994. **Special Achievements:** NBA Draft, First round pick, #18, 1989.

ARMSTRONG, BRUCE CHARLES
Football player. **Personal:** Born Sep 7, 1965, Miami, FL; married Melinda Yvette; children: Candace Lynne & Nicholas Charles. **Educ:** Univ Louisville, polit sci. **Career:** New England Patriots, tackle, 1987-2001; salon, owner, currently. **Honors/Awds:** Pro Bowl, 1990-91, 1994, 1995-97; 1776 Quarterback Club of New England, Rookie of the Year, 1987; All-American honorable mention. *

ARMSTRONG, DARRELL (DARRELL EUGENE ARMSTRONG)
Basketball player. **Personal:** Born Jun 22, 1968, Gastonia, NC; married Deidra; children: Arkia, Mayliah & Darrell Jr. **Educ:** Fayettville State Univ, attended 1991. **Career:** Global Basketball Asn, 1991-92, 1992-93; CBA, Capitol Reign Pontiacs, 1992-93; USBL, Atlanta Trojans, 1992-94; Coren Orense, Spain, 1994-95; Orlando Magic, guard, 1995-2003; New Orleans Hornets, guard, 2003-04; Dallas Mavericks, guard, 2004-06; Ind Pacers, 2006-07; NJ Nets, 2007-. **Orgs:** Pres, Darrell Armstrong Found, currently. **Honors/Awds:** Alumni Hall of Fame, Boys & Girls Clubs Am, 1998; Rich and Helen DeVos Community Enrichment Award, 1998, 2000; NBA Sixth Man of the Year, 1999; NBA Most Improved Player, 1999; Hometown Hero Award, 1999. **Business Addr:** Professional Basketball Player, New Jersey Nets, 390 Murray Hill Pkwy, East Rutherford, NJ 07073, **Business Phone:** (201)935-8888.

ARMSTRONG, EARL M.
Physician. **Educ:** Univ Chicago, Chicago, IL. **Career:** Johns Hopkins Hosp, Baltimore, MD, internship, 1974-76, residency, 1976-78; Providence Hosp, physician; Wash Hosp Ctr, physician, currently. *

ARMSTRONG, ERNEST W., SR.
Educator, real estate agent. **Personal:** Born May 1, 1915, Soper, OK; son of Giles and Vinnie; divorced; children: Earl M & Everett W. **Educ:** Dillard Univ, AB, 1942; Howard Univ, MDiv, 1946, MA, 1947; Univ Heidelberg Germany, cert, 1954; Univ OK, MEd, 1969; Santa Barbara Univ, PhD 1974; Prince Georges Community Col, AA 1979, 1981. **Career:** Educator, Real estate agent (retired); Nat YMCA, NY Army-Navy Dept, student sec, 1944-45; Howard Univ, 1946-48; Shiloh Baptist Church, asst pastor, 1946-48; Savannah State Col, Col chaplain/asst prof social sci, 1948-49; Triton Community Col, Reiver Grove IL, counselor/instr, 1969-70; Enon Baptist Church, Baltimore, MD, asst pastor, 1970-72; Catonsville Community Col, counr, 1970-72; Livingstone Col, Salisbury NC, counr, 1972-73; Annapolis MD Senior High Sch, counr, 1973-77; real estate broker, 1977-92. **Orgs:** Am Pub Gardens Asn; Am Col Personnel Asn; AAMFC; MPGA; MCPA; Nat Asn Black Psychol; Omega Psi Phi Frat; Prince Hall Masons thirty third degree; US Chess Fedn. **Honors/Awds:** Publ Army Chaplain in Korea "The Oracle" Omega Psi Phi Frat Inc 1952; Distinguished Alumni Award, Dillard Univ, 1983; honorary doctorate degree, Faith Grant College, 1995. **Special Achievements:** Published autobiography, The Joy of Living at 85, 2000; Omega Man of the Year Frankfort, Germany/Theta Rho Tau Chap 1962; Mason of the Year, 1962; OK Prince Hall Grand Lodge. **Military Serv:** AUS chaplain 1948-69, retired col 1969; received: BSM, KSM; NDSM; NDSMw/st OLC; UNSM, 1O/S Bar: AFRM w/10 year Dev. **Home Addr:** 4046 Hilton Rd, Baltimore, MD 21215-9123, **Home Phone:** (410)367-9123. *

ARMSTRONG, EVELYN WALKER
Librarian. **Personal:** Born in Philadelphia, PA; daughter of Jay D and Laurena. **Educ:** Howard Univ, BA, 1949; Drexel Univ, MS, 1956; Temple Univ, grad sch bus admin, 1976. **Career:** Librarian (retired); Sharp & Dohme Inc, from asst librn to assoc librn, 1953-57, chief librn 1957-66; Drexel Univ, Grad Sch Libr Sci, adj fac, 1963-66; Merck Sharp & Dohme Res Lab, mgr libr serv, 1966-81; Drexel Univ, Grad Sch Libr Sci, vis lectr 1975-80; Merck Sharp & Dohme Res Lab, dir lit resources ctr, 1981-92. **Orgs:** Past sec & exec bd mem Sci Tech Div, Rankin Fund Comm; Elect & Nom Comm, Spec Libr Coun Philadelphia, 1956-75; chmn, Pharm Div, 1963-64; Prof Studies Comm, 1965-67; Am Soc Info Sci, 1965-73; past adv bd mem & sec, Spec Interest Group & Biol Chem Elect & Nom Comm; 1965-73; mem comm, Spec Libr Asn, 1972-73; Adv Comm Libr & Med Curric, Montgomery County Community Col, 1973-77; chmn, Regis Comm, Montreal Drug Info Asn, 1973; Adv Comm Accreditation, Drexel Univ Grad Sch Libr Sci, 1974-75; conf comm mem, Boston, 1974; Div Chem Info, Am Chem Soc; steering comm mem Sci Info Subsection, Pharmaceutical Mfrs Asn, 1976-81; bd mem Montgomery County Emergency Se 1988-90; adv bd mem Drexel Univ Col Info Studies, 1989-; Big Sisters Montgomery County, 1989-; Jenkintown PA Libr Bd, 1993-97; Philadelphia Futures, Sponsor a Scholar Prog, Sponsor & Mentor, 1998-; JD & Laurena Walker Found, founder. **Honors/Awds:** Black Achiever, YMCA; Drexel 100 Honoree, Drexel Univ Centennial, 1992; Harriet E. Worrell Award, Drexel Univ, 2000; Award for minority graduate student Library Science, Dexrel Univ, 2005. **Home Phone:** (215)576-0263.

ARMSTRONG, JANET (JAZZ ARMSTRONG)
Fashion designer. **Career:** Polo Jeans Co, sr dir tech design, currently. **Business Addr:** Senior Director of Technical Design, Polo Jeans Company, 115 5th Ave 4th Fl, New York, NY 10003, **Business Phone:** (212)780-6100.*

ARMSTRONG, JAZZ. See ARMSTRONG, JANET.

ARMSTRONG, JOAN BERNARD
Judge, teacher. **Personal:** Born in New Orleans, LA; married Andrew; children: David M, Anna K. **Educ:** Xavier Univ, BA, 1963; Loyola Univ Sch Law, JD, 1967; Nat Col Juv Justice, col cert, 1974. **Career:** Orleans Parish, teacher; Orleans Parish Juv Ct, judge, 1974-84; 4th Circuit Ct Appeal, judge, 1984-. **Orgs:** Pres, Community Rels Coun, 1972-74; pres, La League Good Govt, 1972-74; Vis Comm Loyola Univ; charter mem, Nat Asn Women Judges; trustee, Loyola Univ S; Bar Asn; Am Red Cross; Legal Aid Bur; La Asn Ment Health; Crisis Care Ctr. **Honors/Awds:** Outstanding Young Woman, New Orleans Jaycees, 1974; hon mem, Alpha Kappa Alpha, 1974; Silver Bowl Award, Greyhound Co; Clay Award, The C Bureau, New Orleans; Special Jurist Award, Nat Bar Asn. **Business Phone:** (504)412-6001.*

ARMSTRONG, JOE
Legislator (U.S. state government). **Personal:** Born Nov 30, 1956, Knoxville, TN; married LeTonia Armstrong; children: 3. **Educ:** Univ Tenn, BS, 1981. **Career:** Knox County, TN, comnr, 1986-88, vice chair 1982-88; Tenn Gen Assembly, Tenn House Rep, currently. **Orgs:** Chmn, House Health & Human Resources Comt; House Calendar & Rules Comt; House Finance Comt; vice Chair, Tenn House Dem Caucus; exec comt mem, Nat Black Caucus State Legislators; bd mem, Nat Dem Leadership Found; Nat Ins Asn; life mem, NAACP; life mem, Omega Psi Phi Frat; Knoxville Urban League; Tenn Black Alumni Asn; Univ Tenn Alumni Asn. **Honors/Awds:** Legislator of the Year Award, County Officials Asn Tenn, 2002; Hardest Working Volunteer Award, Tom Joyner Found, 2004; Humanitarian Award, Nat Conf Community & Justice, 2004; Health Disparities Leadership Award, NBCSL/NBCHL, 2005; Legislator of the Year Award, Tenn Men's Health Network, 2005. **Business Addr:** State Representative, House of Representatives, 25 Legis Plz, Nashville, TN 37243, **Business Phone:** (615)741-0768.

ARMSTRONG, KEVIN
Executive. **Educ:** Rutgers Univ; Rutgers Univ Law Sch, JD. **Career:** Prudential Securities, mgt; Thomson McKinnon Securities Inc, mgt; NY Stock Exchange, sr mkt analyst; Nat Asn Securities Dealers, sr compliance examr; First Mich Corp, vpres, dir compliances; Fleet Financial Group, sr vpres, functional dir compliance, 1998; US Bancorp, PowerTrack, vpres, sr vpres & gen mgr, currently. **Orgs:** NJ State Bar Asn; Pa State Bar Asn; Am Bar Asn; Nat Bar Asn; Bond Mkt Asn; Securities Indust Asn. **Honors/Awds:** Honored by USAF, 2004. **Business Phone:** (612)872-2657.

ARMSTRONG, REGINALD DONALD, II
Editor. **Personal:** Born Jul 28, 1958, Long Beach, CA; son of Reginald D and Marie Roque; married Sandra Achue Armstrong,

Dec 21, 1985; children: Omari Hasan, Sarou Bakila. **Educ:** Univ Calif San Diego, LaJolla, CA, attended 1977; Morehouse Col, Atlanta, GA, attended 1977; Univ SC, Columbia, BA, 1979. **Career:** Nat Asn Advan Colored People/Crisis Mag, Brooklyn, NY, ed asst, 1983-85; Village Voice, New York, NY, asst ed, 1985-88; Times Mirror/Sports Inc, New York, NY, copy chief, 1988-89; Gen Media/Omni, asst managing ed, 1989; Emerge Mag, New York, NY, asst managing ed, 1989. **Orgs:** Nat Asn Black Journalists, 1990-. **Home Addr:** 930 St Nicholas Ave, New York, NY 10032, **Home Phone:** (212)283-1529. **Business Phone:** (212)941-8811.*

ARMSTRONG, RICH
Executive, president (organization). **Career:** Sara Lee Foods US, pres & chief exec officer Galileo Foods, 2000, pres supply chain, 2001-. **Business Addr:** President Supply Chain, Sara Lee Foods, 10151 Carver Rd, Cincinnati, OH 45242, **Business Phone:** 888-863-2975.*

ARMSTRONG, ROBB
Cartoonist or animator, illustrator. **Personal:** Born Mar 4, 1962, Wynnefield, PA; son of Dorothy (deceased); married Sherry West; children: Tess, Rex Alexander. **Educ:** Syracuse Univ, BFA, art. **Career:** Various ad agencies, art dir; syndicated cartoonist, 1988-; Savannah Col of Art & Design, visiting professor, 1997; United Media, syndicated Cartoonist, currently. **Orgs:** Syracuse Univ Alumni Bd. **Honors/Awds:** Religious Public Relations Council, Wilbur Award, 1995; Nestle, Men of Courage Award. **Business Addr:** Cartoonist, United Media, 200 Madison Ave, New York, NY 10016, **Business Phone:** (212)293-8500.*

ARMSTRONG, SAUNDRA BROWN
Judge. **Career:** US Dist Ct, Northern CA, fed judge, 1991-. **Orgs:** Consumer Product Safety Comn, 1983-90. **Business Addr:** Federal Judge, US District Court of Northern California, 3rd Fl Courtroom 3, Oakland, CA 94612, **Business Phone:** (510)637-3562.*

ARMSTRONG, TYJI (TYJI DONRAPHEAL ARMSTRONG)
Football player, executive. **Personal:** Born Oct 3, 1970, Inkster, MI; married Jeannie. **Educ:** Univ Miss. **Career:** Football player (retired), executive; Tampa Bay Buccaneers, tight end, 1992-95; Dallas Cowboys, 1996; St Louis Rams, 1998; Chicago Enforcers, 2000-01; Jakona Rhodesian Ridgebacks, owner, currently. **Business Phone:** (813)746-1103.

ARMSTRONG, VANESSA BELL
Gospel singer. **Personal:** Born Oct 2, 1953, Detroit, MI; children: 5. **Career:** Gospel vocalist, Albums:Peace Be Still, Onyx, 1983; Chosen, Onyx, 1984;Vanessa Bell Armstrong, Jive Novus, 1987; Wonderful One, Jive Novus, 1990;The Truth About Christmas, Jive Novus, 1990; Something on the Inside, JiveNovus, 1993; The Secret Is Out, Verity, 1995; Desire of My Heart: Live in Detroit, Verity, 1998; A Brand New Day, Tommy Boy, 2001; Walking Miracle, EMI Gospel, 2007; actress, Don't Get God Started; The Women of Brewster Place; compilations: The Best of Vanessa Bell Armstrong, Verity, 1999; Sing To Glory. Sony MBG, 2005; Praise & Worship, Verity Legacy, 2006. **Orgs:** Sigma Gamma Rho Sorority, Inc. **Honors/Awds:** Best Soul Gospel Performance, Female for Peace Be Still, 1983; Best Soul Gospel Performance, Female for Chosen, 1985; Best Soul Gospel Performance,Duo, Group, Choir or Chorus for Choose Ye, 1986; Best Soul Gospel Performance, Female for Pressing On, 1988; Gospel Music Hall of Fame, 2001. **Business Addr:** Gospel Vocalist, EMI Gospel, 101 Winners Circle, PO Box 5085, Brentwood, TN 37024, **Business Phone:** (615)371-6800.*

ARMSTRONG, WILLIAM
Automotive executive. **Career:** Armstrong Toyota, pres, 1994-; Hollywood Ford, pres, currently.

ARMSTRONG, WILLIAM F.
Government official. **Personal:** Born Aug 13, 1942, York, PA; son of Jesse C and Mary L; married Carolyn Ann Armstrong, Jul 19, 1964; children: Nadine M Walker, Paulette Armstrong, Darnell L Armstrong, DeAnna R McKoy, Darleen L Smith, Daryl J Armstrong (deceased). **Educ:** Univ Md, Eastern Shore, BS, 1970; Catholic Univ Am, MA, 1971; CPM; APP. **Career:** Univ Md, Col Park, Dept Procurement & Supply, asst dir & mgr, MBE progs, 1982-98; Prince George's County govt, Off Cert Svc, dep dir, 1998-. **Orgs:** Nat Asn Purchasing Mgt; Purchasing Mgt Asn Md; Md Pub Purchasing Asn; Nat Inst Govt Purchasing; Nat Asn Black Procurement Profs; Univ Syst Md Found. **Honors/Awds:** Recruiter of the Year, NABPP, 1990-91; Walter Kirkman Award, NABPP, 1995; Stanley D. Zemansky Award, Md Pub Purchasing Asn, 1996. **Military Serv:** USAF, 1961-66, Good Conduct Medal. **Business Phone:** (301)883-6450.*

ARMSTRONG BUSBY, DELIA BLISS
Educational consultant. **Personal:** Born Nov 28, 1945, Los Angeles, CA; daughter of Willard and Zeltee; married Ronald, Dec 1968; children: Aaron Busby, Preston Shelton. **Educ:** CA State Univ, Los Angeles, attended 1967; Univ Colo Springs, MA, attended 1977. **Career:** Colo Springs Pub Schs, educr, 1970-94; Ctr Qual Schs, consult, 1995-97; Denver Pub Schs, consult, 1997-99; Mitchell High Sch, prin; Milwaukee Pub Schs, consult, 2001; Alliance Qual Pub Sch, founder. **Orgs:** Urban League, bd mem, vp, 1990-98; Nat Asn Advan Colored People; bd, Boys & Girls Club; bd, Girl Scouts; bd, Tutmuse Acad; bd, Colo Springs D 11, 1999-00; Bd vp, Pikes Peak Commnunity Col; bd, D-11, 2001. **Honors/Awds:** Milken Found, Educ Leadership, 1990; State Colo, Educ Cert, 1990-93; Drug Free Communities, Educ cert, 1990; SW Regional Drug Free Schs, 1993. **Special Achievements:** Absence Addiction Work Book, 1995. **Business Addr:** Absence Addiction Achievement Services, 2236 Monteagle Ave, Colorado Springs, CO 80909.*

ARNELLE, HUGH JESSE
Lawyer. **Personal:** Born Dec 30, 1933, New Rochelle, NY; son of Lynn and Hugh; married Carolyn; children: Nicole, Paolo & Michael. **Educ:** Pa State Univ, BA, 1955; Dickinson Sch Law, JD, 1962; admitted to pract CA, PA, US Supreme Ct. **Career:** AU State Univ, All-Am Basketball, 1952-54; Nat Basketball Asn, Ft Wayne Piston, 1955-56; Nat Football League Baltimore Colts, 1957-58; Dept Labor, atty, 1962-63; Peace Corps, assoc dir, 1963-65, dir, 1965-66, staff, 1966-67; FPC, asst to gen coun, 1967-68; Morrison Foerster Holloway, atty, 1971-73; US Dist Ct, asst fed pub defender; pvt pract, 1973-85; fac, Hastings Law Sch Criminal Trial Advocacy, 1977; Arnelle & Hastie, civil litigation & pub finance atty, sr partner, 1985-97; FPL Group Inc; Waste Mgt Inc, dir, 1992; Textron Corp, dir; Armstrong World Indust Inc, dir; Eastman Chem Co Inc, staff; Gannett Co, dir; Union Pac & Resources Inc, staff; Metrop Life Series Fund, dir, 2002-; URS Inc, dir, 2004-. **Orgs:** IDEA Inc Chas F Kettering Found, 1968-69; Col Civil Trial Advocacy, 1976; Hall Fame NY, 1977; comnr, San Francisco Redevelop Agency; bd dir, San Fransisco Boys Club, 1981; Am Bd Criminal Trial Lawyers, 1982; exec comnr, bd trustees, San Francisco World Affairs Coun, 1983; bd trustee, PA State Univ; vice chmn, PA State Bd Trustees, 1993; vice chmn, PA State Univ Bd Trustees, 1993; Nat Football Found Hall Fame, 1993; PA State Univ; dir, Renaissance Fund PA State Univ; Charles Houston Bar Asn; Nat Bar Asn; Bar Pa; Bar US Supreme Ct; dipl, Hastings Law Sch; Nat Panel Arbit, Am Trial Lawyers Asn; Westchester Co Hall Fame; pres, Afro-Am Hist Soc; bd dir, San Francisco Opportunity; bd dir, Bay Area UNICEF; Univ Governance. **Honors/Awds:** Honory mention, All-Am Football, 1953-54; Dr Martin Luther King Jr Medal for Outstanding Professional Service, George Washington Univ; 1995; Lion's Paw Award, Dr laws, Dickinson Sch Law. PA State, 2000. **Special Achievements:** Ranks among the top 10 bond council in the state. **Business Phone:** (415)774-2700.

ARNETTE, EVELYN
President (Organization), entrepreneur. **Educ:** Wells Col, NY, BA; Mercer Univ Atlanta, MBA, mkt. **Career:** BellSouth, staff sales & customer serv; A Customer's Point View Inc, founder & pres, 1997-. **Orgs:** Delta Sigma Theta Sorority. **Honors/Awds:** Creative Style Award, Atlanta Bus League, 2001. **Business Addr:** Founder, President, A Customers Point of View Inc, 815 Pavilion Ct, McDonough, GA 30253, **Business Phone:** (770)288-2717.

ARNEZ, DR. NANCY L.
Teacher, lecturer, school administrator. **Personal:** Born Jul 6, 1928, Baltimore, MD; daughter of Emerson Milton Levi and Ida Barbour Rusk; divorced. **Educ:** Morgan State Col, AB, 1949; Columbia Univ, MA, 1954, EdD, 1958; Harvard Univ, post doctoral, 1962; Loyola Col, attended 1965. **Career:** Teacher, lecturer (retired), Sch Admin; Baltimore Pub Sch, Eng teacher,1949-58, dept head, 1958-62; Morgan State Col, dir stud teaching, 1962-66; Northeastern Ill Univ, assoc prof & asst dir, Ctr Inner City Studies,1966-69; prof & dir Ctr Inner City Studies, 1969-74, co-founder, Cultural Linguistic, Follow Through Early Childhood CICS, 1969-74; Pub Sch Systs, Black Female Supt, 1982; Howard Univ Sch Educ, assoc dean, beginning, 1974, acting dean, 1975, prof, dept chair, 1980-86, 1976-9. **Orgs:** Congress African People, 1968-70; Am Asn Sch Admin, 1968-87; Black Child Develop Inst DC, 1971-74; Asn African Historians Chicago, 1972; Asn Study Afro-Am Life & Hist, 1972-77; bd dir, memship secy, African Heritage Studies Asn, 1973-77; Nat Alliance Black Sch Educators; Am Asn Sch Admin Resolutions Community, 1973-75; African Info Ctr Catalyst Chicago,1973-77; bd dir, DuSable Museum Chicago, 1973-74; Black Women's ComnDevelop Found, DC, 1974; Phi Delta Kappa Howard Univ Chap; Am Asn Col Teachers Educ, 1977; Nat Coun Negro Women, 1977; ed bd, 1975-78; ed bd, JNegro Educ, 1975-80; prof, ed bd, Am Asn Sch Adminr, 1981-84; ed, NatAlliance Black Sch Educators Newsbrief, 1984-86; DC Alliance Black Sch Educator, 1984-86, pres, 1986-88. **Honors/Awds:** Association African Histroy Service Award, 1972; Alpha Kappa Alpha SorService Award, 1971; Howard Univ distinguished faculty research award, 1983; outstanding res award, Phi Delta Kappa's biennial, 1985. **Home Addr:** 3122 Cherry Rd NE, Washington, DC 20018. *

ARNOLD, ALISON JOY
Lawyer. **Personal:** Born Apr 26, 1960, Seattle, WA; daughter of James A and Janice M Arnold. **Educ:** Brown Univ, AB, 1982; Wesleyan Univ, MA, 1988; Univ Pa Law Sch, JD, 1991. **Career:** Univ Mich, res scientist, 1983-84; Bristolmyers, Squibb, res scientist, 1984-88; Fish & Neave, assoc, 1991-2000, partner, 2000-; King & Spalding LLP, patner & atty; Univ Pennsylvania Law Sch, assoc ed. **Orgs:** Am Bar asn; mem, Nat Bar asn; Am Intellectual Property Law asn; Federal Circuit Bar asn. **Special Achievements:** Numerous articles published in scientific journals. **Business Addr:** Partner, Fish & Neave, 1251 Ave of the Americas, New York, NY 10020.

ARNOLD, ALTON A., JR.
Educator. **Personal:** Born Aug 10, 1932, Little Rock, AR; married Ramona L Worlds; children: Anita Alton III & David. **Educ:** Philander Smith Col, BA, psych, 1953; Univ Ark, ME Elem Ed, 1954; Univ Calif Los Angeles, MA, 1972; Univ LA, EdD Ed, 1976. **Career:** City LA, juvenile hall couns, 1955-56; LA Unified Sch Dist, elem teacher,1956-69, Div Career & Continuing Ed, 1970-72, adult Sch 1972-; Arnolds Shell Serv Shell Oil Co, owner, 1959-65; Pepperdine Univ, adj prof ed, 1975-76; Jordan-Locke Comm Adult Sch, prin, 1976-. **Orgs:** Alpha Phi Alpha Beta Chi Chap, 1950; Phi Delta Kappa Ed Soc, 1967; chmn, bd dir, LA City, Model Cities Model Neighborhood Prog, 1972-76; LA City Econ Housing Develop Corp, 1975-77; S Cent Community Child Care Ctr,1979-80; Calif State Voc Educ Comn, 1980. **Honors/Awds:** Alpha Kappa Mu Nat Hon Soc, 1951; Fellowship Ford Found, 1953-54; HEW Fellowship, US Dept of HEW, 1970-72; Resolution LA City, 1975; Citizens Part Award, Model Neighborhood Prog LA City, 1976. **Military Serv:** AUS, 1953-54; Good Conduct Medal; Marksman Medal. **Business Addr:** Principal, Jordan-Locke Comm Adult School, 325 E 11th St, Los Angeles, CA 90061.*

ARNOLD, CLARENCE EDWARD, JR.
School administrator. **Personal:** Born May 18, 1944, Eastville, VA; son of Clarence Edward Arnold Sr and Nicey Press; married Katreena Davenport, Dec 23, 1989; children: Sherri Mignon & Chelsea N Davenport (stepdaughter). **Educ:** Va State Univ, BS, 1970, MEd 1973; Howard Univ, 1979; Univ Va, 1990. **Career:** Petersburg High Sch, home sch coordr, 1970-71; McGuffy Educ Ctr, teacher, 1971-72; 16th Dist Ct Serv Unit, counr juvenile & domestic rel 1973-74; Va St Univ, teacher educ, TV prodn & photographer, 1977-78; J Sargeant Reynolds Community Col, instr & coordr audio visual serv dept, 1974-80; CE Arnold Photographic Serv, freelance photographer, 1980-81; Va St Univ, instr & coordr mass communs prog, 1981-88; Danville Conn Col, dir, Learning Resource Ctr, 1988-91; Chancellor's fel, Va Conn ClearingSystem, 1990-91; Univ Va, doctoral internship, 1991, fel, 1991-93. **Orgs:** Vpres, Richmond Br Nat Asn Advan Colored People, 1976-82; bd dir, VA StateConf Nat Asn Advan Colored People, 1976-82; Community Col Asn Instr &Technol, 1976-80; Va Television Reps Higher Educ, 1976-80; Black AdvisoryCoun, WTVR TV AM & FM, 1979-83; Va Educ Asn; Va State Univ Educ Asn, 1981-88; pres, Richmond Media Soc, 1986-87; mem, Va Community Col Asn, 1988-; mem, Va Lib Asn, 1988; Nat Educ Asn; Kappa Alpha Psi Frat Inc; Asn Educ Communs & Technol; Va Educ Media Asn. **Honors/Awds:** R P Daniel Award & Trophy for Outstanding Mil Leadership & Scholastic Achievement in ROTC, Va State Univ, 1966; Grant NDEA Educ Media Instr for Trainers of Teachers, Va State Univ, 1972-73; Black Arts Award for VisualArts, BOTA, 1981; Chancellor's Fel, Va Conn Clearing System, 1990-91; Univ Va, Fel, 1991-93. **Military Serv:** AUS, 1968-70; Reserves, Capt, 1970-79; Recipient Bronze Star/CIB, Vietnam Commendation Medal, Vietnam Serv Medal, Natl Defense Serv Medal, Expert Marksman Badge. **Home Phone:** (804)977-3814.

ARNOLD, DAVID
Opera singer. **Personal:** Born in Atlanta, GA; son of Charles. **Educ:** Ind Univ, BA, 1968, MA, 1970; New Eng Conserv, artist dipl, 1974. **Career:** Temple Univ, artist-in-residence, currently; Performances: Opera Co, Boston; Metrop Opera; Boston Symphony; New York Opera; Eng Nat Opera; Komische Opera Berlin; Am Symphony; San Francisco Opera; Am Composer Orchestra; Atlanta Symphony; Wolf Trap Festival; Baltimore Symphony; Chatauqua Festival; Spoleto Festivals; Nashville Symphony; Tanglewood Festival; Chicago Symphony; Cincinnati May Festival; Concertge bouw; Tulsa Opera; Musica Sacra New York; Boston Baroque; Handel & Haydn Soc, Boston;Am Symphony New York; Metrop Opera, baritone singer; Komische Opera,Berlin, leading baritone; Recordings: "Gurrelieder"; "The Magic World";"Full Moon in March"; "Walpurgisnacht"; "Beethoven Ninth Symphony"; "Mozart Requiem"; "Haydn's Lord Nelson Mass". **Honors/Awds:** Metrop Auditions Winner; Sullivan Foundation Music Award; New York Opera Gold Debut Award, 1980. **Special Achievements:** Guest appearances at the White House on the occasion of a state dinner honoring Prime Minister Margaret Thatcher and at musical events for President Clinton. **Business Addr:** Grant House, 309 Wood St, Burlington, NJ 08016.*

ARNOLD, ETHEL N.
Executive. **Personal:** Born Dec 20, 1924, Stillwater, OK; married; children: Nishua Bell, Renay Thigpen, Booker Jr, Myron & Geino. **Educ:** Langston Univ, ICS Bus Col; Northwestern Col, BBA. **Career:** Cleve Cell & Post, news columnist; Picker Corp, tax specialist, 1968; Harshaw Chem, asst tax mgr, 1970; Diamond Shamrock, accts asst, 1973; Ohio Cell Podiatry Med, dir com-

munity relations, 1976-84; Avant-Garde ModelsInc, Modeling Sch & Agency, owner; R & E, pres & owner. **Orgs:** Nat pres, Nat Asn Career Womens Civic Club, 1964-88; chmn, Nat Asn Negro Bus Prof Womens Club, Cleveland, 1984-85; Human Res Comn. **Honors/Awds:** Liberty Bell Award Mayor Philadelphia, 1972; cong placque award, Univ SHouse Rep, 1977; comn serv award, Ohio Cell Podiatry Med, 1977; Bell Air Civic Club, 1978; Mayor Cleveland, 1977. **Business Addr:** President, R & E, 14402 Kinsman, Cleveland, OH 44120.

ARNOLD, JAHINE AMID
Football player. **Personal:** Born Jun 19, 1973, Rockville, CT. **Educ:** Fresno State Univ. **Career:** Football player, (retired); Pittsburgh Steelers, wide receiver, 1996 & 1998; Green Bay Packers, 1999; Tampa Bay Storm, 2002; Los Angeles Avengers, 2003; Austin Wranglers, 2004. *

ARNOLD, JOHN RUSSELL, JR.
Executive. **Personal:** Born Sep 13, 1954, Detroit, MI; son of John Russell Sr and Christene Ford; married Cheryl Anne Young, Jul 7, 1984 (divorced); children: John R III. **Educ:** Univ Detroit & Mercy, 1971-75; Univ Mich. **Career:** WABX, disc jockey, 1972-73; WERD, prog dir, 1973-74; WCHB, music dir, 1974-87; WFXY, prog dir, 1987-88; WCXI/WWWW, dj, staff announcer, 1988-89; Barden Cable, advert sales, 1988-90; WCHB, host & exec producer, 1989-97; Detroit Bell Broadcasting Syst, founder; Metro Detroit Broadcasting Corp, The John Arnold Show, host, currently; Univ Mich, lectr. **Orgs:** Inkster, MI City Planning Comnr, 1990-94; founder, Black Men Inc, 1992-; founder, Black Women Inc, 1992-; Talk Radio Host Am, 1994-; Talkers, 1995-; Am Asn Talk Show Host; Nat Asn Broadcasters; Blacks Advertising, Radio & TV; Mich Asn Teachers; Mich Asn Broadcasters; Ad Crafters; Thursday Luncheon Group; Booker T. Wash Businessmen's Asn. **Honors/Awds:** BART, Talk Show Host of the Yr, Detroit, 1995-97. **Special Achievements:** Youngest Disc Jockey in the World, Major Mkt, 1969, 1970; Pres Clinton's Bi-Continent Summit Economic with S Africa, 1996. **Business Addr:** Doctoral Candidate, KCP Fellow, University of Michigan-Dearborn, 3032 CB, **Business Phone:** (313)583-6378.

ARNOLD, LIONEL A.
Educator. **Personal:** Born Aug 30, 1921, Greenville, PA; son of J P Arnold and Gertrude Dowe. **Educ:** Thiel Col, BA 1943; Anderson Col, B Th, 1944; Oberlin Grad Sch, MA, BD, 1947; Harvard Univ, STM, 1955; Drew Univ, PhD, 1969. **Career:** LeMoyne-Owen Col, Col pastor, 1947-64, dean, 1964-71; OK State Univ, prof humanistic studies & eng, 1971-86, prof emer. **Honors/Awds:** DHL, Thiel Col Greenville, PA, 1964. **Home Addr:** 2132 W University Ave, Stillwater, OK 74074. *

ARNOLD, MONICA DENISE
Singer. **Personal:** Born Oct 24, 1980, Atlanta, GA; daughter of MC Arnold Jr and Marilyn Best; married Rodney R Hill, Jan 1, 1997; children: Rodney Ramone Hill III & Romello Montez. **Career:** Rowdy Rec, 1993; Albums: Miss Thang, 1995; The Boy is Mine, 1998; All Eyezon Me, 2002; After the Storm, 2003; The Makings of Me, 2006; Songs: "For You I Will"; "Don't Take It Personal", 1995; "The Boy is Mine", 1998;"Angel of Mine", 1999; "So Gone", 2003; Films: Boys and Girls, 2000; ATL, 2006; Pastor Brown, 2009; TV Series: "Living Single", 1996; "Love Song", 2000; "Felicity", 2001; "American Dreams", 2003; "Keyshia Cole: The Way It Is", 2006-08; "The Single: Monica", 2008. **Honors/Awds:** Billboard Music Awards, 1996, 1998; Grammy Award, 1999. **Special Achievements:** Became the youngest recording act to ever have two consecutive chart-topping hits on the U.S. Billboard Top R&B Singles chart; nominated for numerous awards. **Business Addr:** Vocalist, c/o Arista Records, 6 W 57th St 5th Fl, New York, NY 10019.*

ARNOLD, NANCY
Registered nurse. **Career:** Fairlane Nursing Ctr, Regist Nurse, 2003; John J Pershing VA Med Ctr, dir, currently. **Honors/Awds:** Nursing Award Excellence, 2003. **Business Addr:** Director, John J Pershing VA Medical Center, Hwy 67 N, Poplar Bluff, MO 63901, **Business Phone:** (573)686-4151.*

ARNOLD, RUDOLPH P
Lawyer, banker. **Personal:** Born May 24, 1948, Harlem, NY; married Linda J Kelly; children: Preston & Rebecca. **Educ:** Howard Univ, BA, 1970; Univ Conn, JD, 1975; New York Univ, LLM, 1976. **Career:** Aetna Life & Casualty, 1971-72; Legal Aid Soc Hartford City, atty, 1976-81; Arnold & Hershinson, atty, 1982-84; Arnold & Assoc, atty, 1985-, vpres, pres, currently; Soc Savings Bancorp Inc, dir & chmn, 1991-93. **Orgs:** Conn Bar Asn; Hartford Bar Asn; Pub Int Lawyer-Law, 1974; bd dir, Urban League, 1977-79; dep mayor, Hartford City Coun, 1979-83; Nat Bar Asn, 1980-; bd dir, World Affairs Ctr, 1983-88; chmn, Hartford Community TV, 1986-89; bd dir, Soc Savings, 1987-93; Am Bar Asn; lifetime mem, Nat Asn Advan Colored People; dir, Nat Coun Int Visitors, 1989-92; bd dirs, Hartford Pub Libr, 1994-; Nat Asn Bond Lawyer; Nat Asn Securities Prof; George Crawford Law Soc; Nat Campaign Human Develop; Hartford World Affairs Coun; bd mem, Farmington Ave Alliance; Conn Nat Asn Housing & Redevelopment Off; Community Partners Action & FannieMae Con Partnership Adv Comt. **Honors/Awds:** Pro Bond Award, Hartford County Bar, 1991. **Special Achievements:** Author, What You Should Know About Evictions, 1981. **Home Addr:** 132 Terry Rd, Hartford, CT 06105, **Home Phone:** (203)233-1431. **Business Addr:** Attorney, President, Arnold & Associates, 80 Cedar St, Hartford, CT 06106, **Business Phone:** (860)728-0037.*

ARNOLD, WALLACE C.
Executive, army officer. **Personal:** Born Jul 27, 1938, Washington, DC; son of George W and Lydia Gibson; married Earlene Costner Arnold, Jan 21, 1961; children: Sheila, Stephanie. **Educ:** Hampton Inst, BS, indust educ, 1960; George Wash Univ, Wash, DC, MA, personnel mgt & admin, 1965; Naval War Col, Newport, RI, 1977. **Career:** Army officer (retired), exec; AUS, major gen, 1961-95, Wash, DC, mil asst & exec officer, off under secy army, 1979-81, USA Europe, inspector gen, VII corps Europe, 1981-82, comdr, 69th air defense artil brigade, 1982-84, dir/officer personnel & admin for Europe, 1984-87, Ft Bragg, NC, commanding gen, 1st ROTC reg, 1987-90, Ft Monroe, VA, commanding gen, ROTC cadet command, 1990-93, Wash, DC, asst dep chief staff for Personnel, major gen, 1995; Info Technol Solutions Inc, exec vpres & chief Admin off, 1995; Comput Sci Corp, Hampton, Va, regional dir bus develop; Hampton Univ Tech Data Mgt Lab, dir; Cheyney Univ Penn, interim pres, currently. **Orgs:** chmn, Boy Scout Dist, Boy Scouts of Am Coun, Raleigh, NC, 1987-90; deacon, Second Baptist Church, Falls Church, Va, 1977-81; chmn, budget comm, Second Baptist Church, Falls Church, Va, 1977-81; pres, Northern VA Chap Nat Hampton Univ Alumni Assn, 1979-81; chmn, European Sch Coun, DOD Dependent Sch Syst, 1984-87; past pres, Hampton Rotary Club; Commonwealth Va Comn Vet Affairs; Base Closure Task Force; Ft Monroe Credit Union; bd dirs, Piney Woods Sch. **Honors/Awds:** Hampton Univ Outstanding Alumni Award, 1985; Roy Wilkins Meritorious Serv Award, NAACP Inc, 1990; Hon Doctor of Law Degree Campbell Univ, Buies Creek, NC, 1990; Douglas MacArthur Distinguished Serv Award, Assn US Army; Paul Harris Fel, Rotary Intl. **Military Serv:** AUS Command & Gen Staff Col, Ft Leavenworth, KS, 1970-71; Distinguished Service Medal; Defense Superior Service Medal, Legion Merit, Bronze Star Medal, Meritorious Service Medal, Army Commendation Medal; Parachutist Badge; Army Staff Identification Badge. **Business Addr:** Interim President, Cheyney University of Pennsylvania, 1837 Univ Cir, PO Box 200, Cheyney, PA 19319-0200, **Business Phone:** (610)399-2275.*

ARNSTRONG, TYJI DONRAPHEAL. See ARMSTRONG, TYJI.

ARNWINE, BARBARA
Activist, lawyer, executive director. **Personal:** Born in Claremont, CA; daughter of Vera Pearl Carter-Arnwine; children: Justin Daniel Almiri. **Educ:** Scripps Col; Duke Univ Sch Law, grad, 1976. **Career:** Durham Legal Assistance Prog, Reginald Huber Smith fel, 1976-79; NC Legal Serv, 1979; Boston Lawyers Comm Civil Rights, exec dir, 1989; Lawyers Comm Civil Rights Under the Law, exec dir, 1989-; Network Black Women for Justice, founder, currently. **Orgs:** Leader, Nonpartisan Election Protection Coalition, 2004. **Honors/Awds:** Charlotte E Ray Award, Nat Bar Assn, 2002; Equal Justice Award, Nat Bar Assn, 2002; Numerous awards from Nat, regional & local civil rights organizations. **Special Achievements:** Nat Convenor, Nat Conf on African American Women, Washington, DC, 1995 & 2000; TV & Radio appearance; First African-American woman to lead the Lawyers' Comm for Civil Rights Under Law. **Business Addr:** Executive Director, Lawyer, 1401 New York Ave NW Suite 400, Washington, DC 20005, **Business Phone:** (202)662-8600.

ARRINGTON, HAROLD MITCHELL
Physician. **Personal:** Born Apr 9, 1947, Detroit, MI; son of Robyn and Irene. **Educ:** Adrian Col, BS, 1968; Univ Mich Med Sch, MD, 1972; Am Bd Obstetrics & Gynec, dipl, 1978. **Career:** Wayne State Univ Hosp, resident obstetrics/gynec, 1972-76; pvt pract, obstetrics/gynec, MI, 1976-; Planned Parenthood League Inc, med dir, 1976-93; Detroit Bd Educ, med dir, 1978-93; Mich State Surgeon, 1998-. **Orgs:** fel Am Coll Obstetrics/Gynec, 1980; Iota Boule Sigma Pi Phi, 1988-; NAACP; LPN Adv Comt, Am Med Asn; Nat Med Asn; Nat Guard Asn US; fel Int Col Surgeons. **Special Achievements:** Commercial instrument pilot's license, 1979. **Military Serv:** USNG, 207th Evacuation Hosp, col, 1972-; Army Nat Guard Med Corps, col, 1972-; 207th Evacuation Hosp, Mich Army Nat Guard, comdr, 1992; Officer Charge Am personnel, King Fund Mil Complex, Dhahrar, Kingdom Saudia Arabia, Oper Desert Shield/Storm, col. *

ARRINGTON, LLOYD M., JR.
Executive. **Personal:** Born Dec 12, 1947, Montgomery, AL; son of Lloyd and Annie; children: Briana, Bianca. **Educ:** Fisk Univ, BA, 1970; Stanford Univ, MBA, 1973. **Career:** T J Watson Fellow, Fisk Univ, 1970-71; C E Merrill Fellow, Stanford Univ, 1972-73, COGME Fellow, 1971-73; Bankers Tr NY Corp, asst treas, 1973-77; Asn Integration Mgt, proj dir, 1974-75; Pfizer Inc, mgr strategic planning, 1978-79; US Small Bus Admin, asst adv, 1979-81; US Dept Comt MBDA, chief capital develop, 1981-82; Arrington & Co, pres; Econ Develop Finance Corp, investment assoc, 1988-90, vice pres, 1990-92; pres, 1992-; Econ Develop Corp, pres, 1990-; Columbia Capital Group, pres. **Orgs:** Chmn, MD Small Business Develop Finance Authority, 1986-93; Nat Black MBA Asn; Omega Psi Phi; WA Soc Investment Analyst. **Home Addr:** 1602 Pebble Beach Dr, Mitchellville, MD 20721. *

ARRINGTON, JUDGE MARVIN S., SR.
Lawyer, judge. **Personal:** Born Feb 10, 1941, Atlanta, GA; son of George Robert and Maggie Andrews; children: 2. **Educ:** Clark Atlanta Univ, BA, 1963; Emory Univ Sch Law, JD, 1967. **Career:** Atlanta Bd Aldermen, mem, 1969-73; Ga Sen Leroy Johnson, staff; Arrington & Hollowell law firm, sr partner; Fulton County Superior Ct, judge, 2002-. **Orgs:** Nat Bar Asn; Am Bar Asn; State Bar Ga; Lawyers Club; Gate City Bar Asn Hall Fame; Kiwanis Int; pres, Atlanta City Coun; Big Bethel African Methodist Episcopalian Church; Soc Intl Bus Fels. **Honors/Awds:** The Chief Justice Robert Benham Award for Community Service, Ga Bar Asn; Distinguished Alumnus, Emory Univ; Gold Medal, Emory Univ; President's Award, Clark Atlanta Univ; Georgia's 100 Most Influential People, Georgia Trends Mag; PhD, Morris Brown Col. **Special Achievements:** One of the first two black students to undertake full-time studies at the Emory University School of Law, 1965. **Business Phone:** (404)730-6907.

ARRINGTON, DR. PAMELA GRAY
Vice president (Organization), college teacher. **Personal:** Born Feb 28, 1953, Montgomery, AL; daughter of Willis E Gray; married Richard Arrington III; children: Gray, Julian & Justin. **Educ:** Spelman Col, BA, 1974; Univ Mich, MA, 1975; George Mason Univ, DA, 1987, PhD, 1993. **Career:** Talladega Col, counr, 1976-77; Northern VA Community Col, counr, 1977-80, coordr affirmative action & grants devel, 1980-88; Bowie State Univ, Human Resource Devel, prof, 1988-; Coppin State Univ, dir Off Planning & Accreditation, chief of staff, 2005-, assoc vpres Planning & Accreditation, 2004-. **Orgs:** ASTD, OD; HRD Profs Network, Wash Metro Area; Am Asn Univ Prof; dir, Nat Retention Proj, Am Asn State Cols & Univs, 1993-; Alpha Kappa Alpha Sorority; HBCU Summit Steering Comt, 2006; mem, NCAA. **Honors/Awds:** Honor Scholar, Spelman Col, 1972-74; Psi Chi Spelman Col, 1974; Grad Scholar, Univ Mich, 1974-75; Pi Lambda Theta, 1975; Leaders for the 80's FIPSE/Maricopa Cols, 1983; Phi Delta Kappa, 1983; Grad Res Ast & Scholar, George Mason Univ, 1984-86; Fac fel, Dept Defense, Off Secy Defense, Civilian Personnel Policy, 1989-91. **Business Addr:** Chief of Staff, Associate Vice President, Coppin State University, Planning & Accreditation, 2500 W N Ave, Baltimore, MD 21216-3698, **Business Phone:** (410)951-3000.

ARRINGTON, RICHARD, JR.
Mayor. **Personal:** Born Oct 19, 1934, Livingston, AL; son of Richard Sr and Ernestine; married Rachel; children: Anthony, Kenneth, Kevin, Angela & Erika Lynn. **Educ:** Miles Col, BA, 1955; Univ Detroit, MS, 1957; Univ Okla, PhD, 1966, PhD, zool, biochem; Harvard Univ, Univ Mich, Postdoctoral Work, Higher Educ Admin. **Career:** Miles Col, prof, 1957-63; Univ Okla, spec instr, 1965-66, prof, 1966-; Univ Ala, assoc prof, part-time, 1971-72, chair, Natural Scis Dept; Miles Col, counr men, 1962-63, dir summer sch & actg dean, 1966-67, dean Colacad, 1967-70; Ala Ctr Higher Educ, dir, 1970-79; City Birmingham, AL, mayor, 1979-99; Univ Ala, Ctr Urban Affairs, vis prof, currently. **Orgs:** Birmingham City Coun, 1971-75; Am Inst Biol Sci; Okla Acad Sci; AAAS; Am Soc Zoologists; Phi Sigma Nat Biol Soc; Soc Sigma Xi; Am Asn Col Deans; adv bd, Family Coun Asn Jefferson County; Alpha Phi Alpha; bd trustee, Univ Ala. **Honors/Awds:** Ortenburger Award for Outstanding Work in Biology, Univ Okla, 1966; Man of the Year, Alpha Phi Alpha, 1969; Achievement Award for Outstanding Community Service, Alpha Phi Alpha, 1971; Man of the Year Award, Ala Fedn Civic Leagues, 1971; Community Civic Service Award, Druid Hill-Norwood Civic League, 1972; Charles A Billups Community Service Award, 1972; Community Achievement Award, 1972; Distinguished Alumni Award, Miles Col Alumni Asn, 1972; Freedom Achievement Award, Emancipation Asn, 1973; Public Service Award, Birmingham Chap Delta Sigma Theta, 1974; Outstanding Educator Award, Friends Miles Col, 1973; Presidential Commendation Award, Miles Col Alumni Asn, 1974; Distinguished Community Service Award, Birmingham Oppor Indust, 1974; Alabama Administrator of the Year, Alabama Society of Public Administrators, 1982; number-one leader in Birmingham by polls of corporate and civic leaders, TheBirmingham News and The Birmingham Post-Herald, 1984 and 1990; one of the Top 20 City Officials in the nation by U.S. News & World Report; one of the 100 Most Influential Black Americans from 1980-2000 by Ebony Magazine; one of the Nation Best Mayors,U.S. News & World Report, 1987; Most Distinguished Mayor, National Urban Coalition, 1988. **Special Achievements:** First African American to be elected as mayor of Birmingham, Alabama. **Business Addr:** Visiting Professor, University of Alabama, 1715 9th Ave S, AB 340, Birmingham, AL 35294-1270.*

ARRINGTON, WARREN H., JR.
President (Organization). **Personal:** Born Jul 10, 1948, Raleigh, NC; son of Warren H Arrington and Lois B; married Annie Hilliard, Aug 4, 1979; children: Janssen, Jamaine, Jarrodd. **Educ:** Livingstone Col, BS, math, 1970; Hardbarger Bus Col, acct & bus, 1979; NC State Univ, Sociologists. **Career:** Arrington Warren H Jr Enterprises Inc, pres, 1985-. **Orgs:** Piedmont Minority Supplier

Develop Coun, 1990-91; exec bd, Minority Bus Enterprises Input Comt, 1991-; vpres, Livingstone Col Alumni Asn; dir, Touch-A-Teen Found Wake Co, 1985-; bd dirs, The Greater Raleigh Chamber Com, 1993-96; vpres, small bus bd, 1994-; adv bd, MCI small bus ctr, 1994-; state dir, Touch-A-Teen Found of NC, 1993-; bd trustees, Livingston Coll & Hood Theological Seminary. **Honors/Awds:** Outstanding New Vendor of the Year, Piedmont Minority Supplier Develop Coun, 1987; Vendor of the Year, Carolina Minority Supplier Develop Coun, 1989; Minority Vendor of the Year, Piedmont Minority Supplier Develop Coun, 1989; Supplier Distributor Firm of the Year, Minority Bus Develop Ctr, 1991; Progress Business Award, Durham Bus & Prof Chain, 1992; Service to Mankind Award, Capital City Sertoma Club, 1990-91; Centennial Award, The Greater Raleigh Chamber Com, 1992; "Triangle Future 30," 1993; Outstanding County Dir, Touch-A-Teen Found NC, 1989; "1994 Fast Fifty", Peat Merick Triangle Business Journal, 1994; MBE, Entrepreneur of the Year, Service of the Year, 1996; Triangle, Future 30 award, 1997; Triangle Pinnacle Business Award, 1999. **Home Phone:** (919)848-1346. **Business Addr:** Arrington Warren H Jr Enterprises Inc, 3200 Glen Royal Rd Suite 105, Raleigh, NC 27617-7419.*

ARRINGTON-JONES, LORRAINE
Association executive. **Personal:** Married Robert Cannon Sr. **Career:** People For Econ Reform, chief exec officer. **Business Addr:** Chief Executing Officer, People For Economic Reform, 1350 Moore St, Toledo, OH 43608, **Business Phone:** (419)727-4245.*

ARROYO, PROF. MARTINA
Opera singer, educator. **Personal:** Born 1936, New York, NY; daughter of Demetrio and Lucille Washington; married Michel Maurel. **Educ:** City Univ, Hunter Col, BA, romance lang, 1954; Marinka Gurewich, pupil; Mo Martin Rich, pupil; Joseph Turnau, pupil; Rose Landver, pupil; Kathryn Long Course Metro Opera, studies. **Career:** Opera: Aida; Madame Butterfly; Un Ballo Maschera; Cavalleria Rusticana; La Forza del Destino; Macbeth; Don Giovanni; La Gioconda; Trovatore; Andrea Chenier; Metrop Opera; Vienna State Opera; Paris Opera; Covent Garden, London; Teatro Colon, Buenos Aires; Hamburg Staatsoper; La Scala, Milan; Munich Staatsoper; Berlin Deutsche Opera; Rome Opera; San Francisco, Chicago & all major opera houses; soloist NY, Vienna, Berlin, Royal/London, Paris Philharmonics, San Francisco, Pittsburgh, Philadelphia, Chicago, Cleveland Symphonies; Ind Univ, Bloomington, prof emeritus. **Orgs:** Former trustee Nat Endowment Arts; trustee, Carnegie Hall; trustee emerita, Hunter Col Found; fel Am Acad Arts & Sci; pres, Martina Arroyo Found, Inc; bd dirs, The Metrop Opera Guild; Ambassador Arts, WA; bd dirs, The Collegiate Chorale; bd overseas mem, Harvard Col Cambridge. **Honors/Awds:** Outstanding Alumna; Dr Honoris Cause of Human Letters, Hunter Col; The President Award, Lehman Col CUNY; Distinguished Professor, Indiana Univ; Distinguished Achievement, Opera Index New York; Verdi Medal, Amici di Verdi London and many more. **Special Achievements:** First soprano in thirty years to sing three opening nights for the Met, 1970, 1971 & 1973, co-authored the Task Force report of music education in the United States, published by the NEA, Washington, DC, has made more than 50 recordings for EMI, Decca, Philips etc., has thaught at University of California Los Angeles, Louisiana State University Baton Rouge, Wilberforce University Ohio, School of Music, Bloomington among others. **Business Addr:** President, Martina Arroyo Foundation, Inc., PO Box 2015 Radio City Sta, New York, NY 10101-2015, **Business Phone:** (212)315-9190.

ARTERBERY, DR. V. ELAYNE
Educator, oncologist. **Educ:** Stanford Univ, Palo Alto, BS; Univ Mich, MD, 1988. **Career:** Memorial Sloan Kettering Cancer Ctr, residency prog; Johns Hopkins Hosp, Dept Radiation Oncology, Baltimore, clinician; Karmanos Cancer Ctr, assoc prof radiation Oncol & interim assoc chair, currently; Wayne St Univ, affil; Swedish Tumor Inst, vis prof; Gershenson Radiation Oncology Ctr, dir prostate brachy therapy, currently; Wayne St Univ Sch Med, dir, currently. **Orgs:** Detroit Symphony Orchestra; Univ Mich Med Ctr Alumni Soc; Am Brachy therapy Soc.

ARTERBERY, VIVIAN J.
Executive. **Educ:** Howard Univ, BA, 1958; Univ Southern Calif, MLS, 1965. **Career:** Space Tech Labs; Aerospace Corp, CA, 1960-79; Rand Corp Santa Monica, libr dir, 1979-86, corp, secy, 1988-; US Nat Comn Libr & Info Sci, exec dir, 1986-88; RAND Corp, corp secy, currently. **Orgs:** Consult, US Off Educ, 1974-76; pres, Special Libr Asn, 1984-85; SLA rep, Am Libr Asn US Dept Educ Accreditation Proj, 1985-86; adv bd mem, Calif Libr Asn Counr & Univ Southern Calif Libr Sch; bd dir, Santa Monica YMCA; treas, Nat Conf Christians & Jews, Santa Monica Chap; Santa Monica YWCA, bd dirs; bd dirs, Santa Monica Col Found, 1995-99; adv bd, Salvation Army, 1996-98; Links Inc; Alpha Kappa Alpha. **Honors/Awds:** Presidents Award, Spec Libr Asn, 1986; Fel Spec Libr Asn, 1988. **Business Addr:** Corporate Secretary, Rand Corp, 1700 Main St, PO Box 2138, Santa Monica, CA 90407-2138.*

ARTEST, RONALD WILLIAM, JR.
Basketball player. **Personal:** Born Nov 13, 1979, Queensbridge, NY. **Educ:** St John's Univ, mathematics. **Career:** Chicago Bulls, 1999-02; Indiana Pacers, defense, 2002-06; Sacramento Kings, guard, 2007-08; Houston Rockets, 2008-09, Los Angeles Lakers, guard, 2009-. **Business Phone:** (310)426-6000.*

ARTHUR, GEORGE KENNETH
Administrator. **Personal:** Born Jun 29, 1934, Buffalo, NY; son of William E and Jayne M Potter; married Frances Bivens Arthur, Jun 19, 1960; children: George K Jr, Janice M, Hugh. **Educ:** Empire State Col, Polit Sci, 1977. **Career:** Retired: Erie Cty Bd Suprvs, supvr, 1964-67; City Buffalo, councilman, 1970-77; city Buffalo, councilman large, 1978-84, pres, common coun, 1984. **Orgs:** Bd dir, Better Bus Bureau, Buffalo Philharmonic Orch, Kleinhans Music Hall, NAACP Life Mem; Jr Warden St John Lodge 16; First Shiloh Baptist Church. **Honors/Awds:** Man of the Year, The Buffalo Club, 1970; Man of the Year, Afro Police, 1973; Medgar Evers Award, NAACP, 1984; Jackie Robinson Award, YMCA, 1985. **Military Serv:** AUS, corpl, 1953-55. **Home Addr:** 154 Roebling Ave, Buffalo, NY 14215, **Home Phone:** (716)896-6188. *

ARTIES, LUCY ELVIRA YVONNE
Educator. **Personal:** Born in Pittsburgh, PA; daughter of William Walter Eugene Jr and Catherine Lillian Holland (deceased). **Educ:** Oakwood Col, Huntsville, AL, 1958; Univ DC, BA, 1972; Howard Univ, Wash DC, 1974; George Wash Univ, 1984; Univ DC, 1989. **Career:** Dept Navy, pres spec, 1964-69; Fed City Col, Wash DC, staff asst, 1969-72; Dept Housing & Urban Develop, Wash DC, educ specialist, 1973-74; Wash DC Pub Sch, educr, 1974-; Kinder-Care Learning Ctr, Bowie, MD, teaching, 1991-92. **Orgs:** Oakland Col Alumni Assoc, 1958-; Univ DC Alumni Assoc, 1981-; Wash DC Chamber Com, 1985; DC/DECA DC Pub Sch, 1985; secy, Wash Metrop Area, 1991-; chaplain, Botsmota Club, 1992-. **Honors/Awds:** Certificate of Appreciation, Govt State MD; Graduate School Award, George Wash Univ, 1982-83; Meritorious Award, Wilson Sr High Sch, 1982; Certificate of Merit, Spingran Sr High Sch, 1984; Certificate ofAppreciation, McFarland Jr High Sch, 1988-89; Certificate of Appreciaion, DC Ct Syst, 1987; Appreciation, Breath Life, SDA Church, 1993; Outstanding Art Dedicated Service, Breath life, SDA Church, Bd Ushers, 1993; Certificate of Merit, Spingarn Sr High School 1984; Certificate ofAppreciation, McFarland Jr High School, 1988-89; Certificate of Appreciation, DC Ct Syst, 1987; Appreciation, Breath Life, SDA Church, 1993; Outstanding Art Dedicated Service, Breath Life, SDA Church, BoardUshers, 1993. **Special Achievements:** Mayor of District of Columbia in 1981. **Business Addr:** Teacher, Our Lady of Lourdes Catholic School, 7500 Pearl St, Bethesda, MD 20814, **Business Phone:** (301)654-5376.

ARTIES, WALTER EUGENE, III
Television producer, administrator, musician. **Personal:** Born Nov 12, 1941, Pittsburgh, PA; married Beverly Ruth Deshay. **Educ:** Faith Col, Birmingham, LHD, 1977. **Career:** Walter Arties Chorale La, dir & arranger, 1961-71; Little Richard Gospel Singer Penniman, arranger, 1961-63; Webber Button Co, off head, 1961-71; Billy Graham Crusades Asn Minneapolis, guest tenor soloist; KHOF-TV & FM Radio, comm serv dir, 1971-74; Breath Life Telecast, prod coordr & founder, evangelism & field serv dir; Voice Prophecy, mgr & treas, currently; Adventist Media Ctr, human resources dir, Simi Valley, CA, currently. **Orgs:** Baseball partic La, Dept Rec Univ, SDC Chap, LA, 1966-67; bd trustees, 7th Day Adventist Radio & TV Film Ctr, Thousand Oaks, CA, 1974-; exec mem, N Am Adv Comm, Wash, DC; SDA Radio Film Ctr, Thousand Oaks, CA, 1974-; bd dir, RV Opers, Thousand Oaks, CA, 1974-; singing partic, World Evangilization Lusanne Switz, 1974. **Honors/Awds:** Outstanding Music Accomplishment Award, Grant Theol Sem Birmingham, 1977; Musical Contributions Singing Award, Port Albernia, BC, Canada, 1977; Outstanding Production Coordination Award, Breath Life Comm, Wash, DC, 1980; Religion in Media Award. **Business Addr:** Manager, Treasurer, Voice of Prophecy, 101 W Cochran St, Simi Valley, CA 93065.*

ARTIS, ANTHONY JOEL
Musician, bass guitarist. **Personal:** Born Jan 11, 1951, Kokomo, IN; son of Myrle E and Yvonne S; married Iris Rosa; children: Andre Antonio & Claudia Lizet. **Educ:** Miami Univ Oxford OH, B Environ Design, 1975. **Career:** Musician & instrumentalist bass guitar various groups in IN & OH, 1967-; percussionist, 1990-; various architects in IN & OH, draftsman & designer, 1974-79; Artis Environ, owner, 1979-; Group "Directions" jazz & fusion, 1985-92; GRPs Invisible Art, 1992-; Sancocho, 1994-; Coal Bin Prods, owner, 1992-. **Orgs:** Youth adv coun Ctr Leadership Devel, 1979-; speaker & mem, Exhib Comt Minorities Eng, 1979-82; Meridian Kessler Neighborhood Asn, 1981-; Nat Trust Hist Preserv, 1983-; vol staff, Indianapolis City Ctr, 1983-84; Indianapolis Chamber Com, 1984-; bd dir, Neighborhood Housing Serv Indianapolis, 1985-87; bd devel corp, Meridian-Kessler Neighborhood Asn, 1996-; Creative Renewal Arts Fel. **Honors/Awds:** Governors Trophy Indianapolis 500 Festival Parade Float Design Team Indiana Black Expo 1982; Black Achiever in Sci, C Mus, IN, 1989. **Business Addr:** Musician Drum-Maker Instructor, 3946 Guilford Ave, Indianapolis, IN 46205, **Business Phone:** (317)925-4823.

ARTIS, JENNIFER
Executive director. **Career:** St James Hosp & Health Ctrs, dir pub affairs, currently; Star columnist, currently. **Business Addr:** Director of Public Affairs, St. James Hospital and Health Centers, 1423 Chicago Rd, Chicago Heights, IL 60411, **Business Phone:** (708)756-1000 Ext 6009.*

ARTISON, RICHARD E.
Law enforcement officer, educator. **Personal:** Born Jun 9, 1933, Omaha, NE; married Charleszine; children: Lisa (Von), Richard Jr & Kelli. **Educ:** Drake Univ, sociol & psychol, attended 1954; Univ NE Law Sch, attended 1955; Cornell Univ, Ed, pub mgt, 1974. **Career:** US Army Counter Intelligence, spec agent, 1955-58; Omaha NE Police Dept, police officer, 1958-62; US Treas Secret Serv, spec agent, 1963-67; Milwaukee Off Secret Serv, spec agent in-charge, 1974-83; Milwaukee County, sheriff, 1983-9; Penn St Univ, Dept Justice, trainer, currently. **Orgs:** Exec bd mem, Milwaukee City Boy Scouts; bd dir, Boys & Girls Clubs Greater Milwaukee; past pres, Fed Officials Asn; past vpres, Milwaukee Frontiers Int; Milwaukee City Metro Police Chiefs; charter mem, Fed Criminal Invest Asn. **Honors/Awds:** Exemplary Achievement Kappa Alpha Psi; High Quality Award, US Treas Dept; Law Enforcement Exec of the Yr Award, Wisc Atty Gen, 1992. **Military Serv:** AUS, spec agent, 3 yrs.

ARTISST, ROBERT IRVING, SR.
Educator. **Personal:** Born Jul 13, 1932, Washington, DC; children: Tawnya Alicia, Robert Irving II & Kevin Frederick. **Educ:** Howard Univ, BA, 1959, MA, 1969; Univ DC, MA, 1971. **Career:** Educator (retired); Appalacian Reg Comm, pub info & visual specialist,1966-71; Urban Inst, dir pub, 1972-71; Nat Asn Black Manufacturing Inc,exec liaison officer, 1972-73; Cooperative Extension Serv WTI, pub info &comm coord, 1973-76; Univ Wash DC, assoc prof media; Mary Mount Univ, prof. **Orgs:** Comm Adv, Neighborhood Comn, 1975-85; vice chmn, Neighborhood PlanningCoun, 1976-79;pres, Brookland Civic Asso Inc, 1977-84; vpres DC Citizensfor Better Pub Ed 1977-84; comm Dept C Human Rights Comn, 1978-84; chm bd,DC Capitol Head Start, 1983-85; comnr, Democratic Clinton Delegate, 1988-. **Honors/Awds:** Special Accomadation, Mayor of the City for Services, 1976-77, speccitation 1978-79; Special Award, Youth Operation Rescue, 1982-84;President Special Award for Citizen Service, 1993; Special Award by PhiDelta Kappa. **Special Achievements:** Ed & Writer, Handbook for Teachers of Adult, 1971-72. **Military Serv:** AUS, 5 yrs; Wings/Calvary Star-Airman Star, 1954. *

ARTOPE, WILLIAM
Executive, advertising executive. **Personal:** Born Apr 2, 1943, New York, NY; son of James and Warnetta Mays; married Linda Young Artope, Nov 2, 1979; children: Westley, Tamara, George & William. **Educ:** NY Univ; RCA Inst Technol, electronics. **Career:** Columbia Prep Sch, teacher, 1965-69; J Walter Thompson, producer, 1970-79; W B Donner & Co, exec producer, 1980-81; DDB Chicago, exec producer, 1981; Wild-Eyed Entertainment, exec producer, currently. **Orgs:** Chapter Chief, Nichiren Shoshu Soka Gakkai Am. **Honors/Awds:** Clio Award, 1974, 1979. **Business Addr:** Executive Producer, Wild Eyed Entertainment, 3959 Flower St, Los Angeles, CA 90037-1310, **Business Phone:** (213)741-9301.

ASANTE, KARIAMU WELSH
Educator, choreographer. **Personal:** Born Sep 22, 1949, Thomasville, NC; daughter of Harvey Farabee and Ruth Hoover; married Molefi K Asante; children: Daahoud, Khumalo. **Educ:** State Univ NY Buffalo, BA, 1972, MA, 1975; NY Univ, doctorate, arts, 1992. **Career:** Black Dance Workshop, choreographer, 1970-77; Ctr Positive Thought Buffalo, NY, artistic dir, 1971-81; Kariamu & Co, choreographer, 1977-84; Nat Dance Co Zimbabwe Harare, artistic dir, 1981-83; Temple Univ, prof & choreographer, 1987; Univ Zimbabwe, Fulbright scholar, 1990-92, Temple Univ, prof dance, 2001. **Orgs:** Dir, Mus African Am Art & Antiquities 1978-; ed bd, Jour Black Studies, 1982-; panel mem, Buffalo Arts Coun, 1983-85; panel mem, NYS Coun Arts Spec Arts Serv, 1984-85; consult, Nat Dance Co Zimbabwe, 1984-; dir, Inst African Dance Res & Performance, Temple Univ, 1985-; Commonwealth Pa Coun Art, dance panel, 1991-93. **Honors/Awds:** Nat Endowment for the Arts Choreography Fellowship, 1973; NYS Creative Artist Service Award, 1974; Choreographer Award, Clark Ctr Performing Arts, NY, 1977; Choreographers Fellowship, NYS Creative Artist Service Award, 1978; Fulbright Scholars Fellowship, Harare, Zimbabwe, 1982-83; Minority Choreographers Fellowship, NY State Coun Arts, 1984; Pew Fellow, 1996; Guggenheim, 1997; co-ed, The African Culture, Rhythms of Unity, 1985; Dance Hist Fellowship, Commonwealth PA Cou Arts, 1988; ed, The African Aesthetic: Keeper of the Traditions, Greenwood Press, 1989; ed, Jour African Dance, 1989; Annual Creative Achievement Award, Temple Univ, 1994. **Special Achievements:** Guest editor, Sage: The Scholarly Journal on Black Women, 1992; author: African Dance; Zimbabwean Dance; Dictionary of African Dance. **Business Addr:** Professsor, Director, Temple University, Department of African American Studies, 810 Gladfelter Hall, 1115 W Berks St, Philadelphia, PA 19122, **Business Phone:** (215)204-8491.*

ASANTE, DR. MOLEFI KETE (ARTHUR L SMITH, JR.)
Educator. **Personal:** Born Aug 14, 1942, Valdosta, GA; son of Arthur L Smith Sr and Lillie B Wilkson; married Kariamu Welsh;

married Ana Yenenga Asante; children: Kasina Eka, Daahoud Ali & Molefi K Jr. **Educ:** Southwestern Christian Col, AA, 1962; Okla Christian Col, BA, 1964; Pepperdine Univ, MA, 1965; Univ Calif, Los Angeles, CA, PhD (commun), 1968; Cath univ, dipl, 2002; L' Universite Catholique de l'Ouest, Angers, Dipl French, 2002. **Career:** Calif State Polytechnic Col, instr, 1967; Calif State Univ, Northridge, instr, 1968; Purdue Univ, Dept Commun, asst prof, 1968-69; Pepperdine Univ, vis prof, 1969; Univ Calif, LA, asst prof, 1969-71,Ctr Afro-Am Studies, dir, 1970-73, assoc prof speech, 1971-73; Fla State Univ Tallahassee, vis assoc prof, 1972; State Univ NY, Buffalo, prof & chair commun dept, 1973-82; State Univ NY, Buffalo, Dept Black Studies, prof & chair, 1977-79; Ctr for Positive Thought Buffalo, curator; Univ Ibadan, Univ Nairobi, external examiner, 1976-80; Zimbabwe Inst Mass Communs, fulbright prof; Howard Univ, vis prof, 1979-80, 1995; Temple Univ, chmn african am studies, 1984-96, prof African-Am studies, 1984-. **Orgs:** Spec Black Rhetoric County Probation Dept, LA, 1969-; bd eds, Black Man Am; adv bd, Black J; Int Soc Gen Semantics; Int Asn Symbolic Analysis; Int Commun Asn; Western Speech Asn; Central State Speech Asn; S Speech Asn; Nat Asn Dramatic & Speech Arts; Int Scientific Comn FESPAC, 1986-87; chairperson, IMHOTEP 1987-; pres, Nat Coun Black Studies, 1988-; vpres, African Heritage Studies Asn, 1989-; pres, Asn Nubian Kemetic Heritage, 1995-2003; pres & chairperson, African Writers Endowment Found, 2000-. **Honors/Awds:** Ehninger Award for Outstanding Rhetorical Scholar, NCA, 2003. **Special Achievements:** Author of 40 books; consulting ed for books; Christian Ed Guild Writer's Awards, 1965; LHD Univ New Haven, 1976; Outstanding Community Scholar, Jackson State Univ, 1980; author, 'The Afrocentric Idea', 1987; Afrocentricity, 1987; Kemet, Afrocentricity and Knowledge, 1990; Historical & Cultural Atlas African-Ams, 1991; African Am Hist: A Journey of Liberation, 1995; Love Dance, 1996; African Intellectual Heritage, 1996; African American Names, 1998; Egyptian Philosophers, 2002; Egypt v Greece in the American Academy, 2003; Erasing Racism, 2003; Encyclopedia of Black Studies, 2005; Handbook of Black Studies, 2006; Race, Rhetoric and Identity, 2006; The History of Africa, 2007. **Business Addr:** Professor, Temple University, Department of African American Studies, 1115 W Berks Mall 615A Gladfelter Hall, Philadelphia, PA 19122, **Business Phone:** (215)204-4322.

ASBURY, WILLIAM W
School administrator. **Personal:** Born Feb 22, 1943, Crawfordville, GA; son of William J and Ida B McLendon; married Leslee Diane Swift, Mar 30, 1968; children: Keleigh, Kristin & Kimberly. **Educ:** Kent State Univ, Kent, OH, BS, 1966, MA, 1973. **Career:** NFL Pittsburgh Steelers, 1966-69; Sanford Rose Assoc, Akron, OH, senior consult, 1969-70; City Akron, OH, contract compliance off, 1970-74; Kent State Univ, Kent, OH, dir human resources, 1974-76; Penn State Univ, Univ Park, Pa, affirmative action off, 1976-83, exec asst pres, 1983-87, vpres stud affairs, 1987; vpres stud affairs emer, 2003-. **Orgs:** Pres, 1991-92, exec Coun secy, NASULGC Student Affairs Coun; Am Asn Higher Educ; Nat Asn Student Personnel Administrators; past pres, Penn Black Conference Higher Education; mem, Forum on Black Affairs, Penn State Univ; hon mem, Nat Residence Hall Honorary; Quarterback Club; hon chmn, Penn State 4-H Ambassador Prog; life mem, Kent State Univ Alumni asn; past pres, Kiwanis Club State Col; past mem, NASPA Found, past mem, bd dir, Special Olympics. **Honors/Awds:** Kent State Univ Hall of Fame, 1981; hon mem, Golden Key Nat Honor Soc, 1983; Cultural Diversity Equity Award, PSU Forum Black Affairs, 1990; Distinguished Pres Kiwanis Club State Col, 1991; Special Achievement Award, Kent State Alumni Assn, 1991; 4-H Clover Award, Benjamin Rush Award, 1992. **Home Addr:** 119 Wildernest Lane, Port Matilda, PA 16870, **Home Phone:** (814)238-3246. **Business Addr:** Vice President of Student Affairs Emeritus, Pennsylvania State University, 206 Old Main Bldg, University Park, PA 16802, **Business Phone:** (814)865-0909.

ASEME, KATE NKOYENI
Surgeon. **Personal:** Born Nov 20, 1944, Nigeria; daughter of Justice; married Larry Winborne, Apr 1, 1977; children: Jeffrey, Isah Paul, Heidi S. **Educ:** Bennett Col, BS, 1967; Howard Med Sch, MD, 1970. **Career:** Surgical & Med Assoc, Hattisburg, pvt pract, 1977-98; Hattisburg Clinic, group pract, 1998-01; Forest Gen Hosp, med dir, trauma servs, 2000-, med dir, surgery servs, 2001-. **Orgs:** Fel, Am Col Surgeons, 1981-; fel, Int Col Surgeons, 1981; Southern Med Asn; Miss State Med Asn; S Miss Med Soc; bd trustees,Forest General Hosp, 1990-93; Miss State Bd Health, 1995-01; community bd, Bancorp S, 1996-; risk mgt comm, Med Asn Miss, 1997-; Am Med Asn; Eagle Club; Int Col Surgeons; Univ Southern Miss; Miss bank. **Home Addr:** 416 Bay St, Hattiesburg, MS 39401, **Home Phone:** (601)544-3464. **Business Addr:** Physician, Hattiesburg Clinic, 415 S 28th Ave, Hattiesburg, MS 39401, **Business Phone:** (601)264-6000.*

ASH, RICHARD LARRY
Hotel executive. **Personal:** Born Mar 23, 1959, Newark, NJ; son of Richard Jr and Daisy Pugh; married Kathy W (divorced 1985); children: Alexandra Erin. **Educ:** Snow Col, Ephraim, UT, attended 1983; Rutgers Univ, Newark, NJ, attended 1985. **Career:** McDonald's Corp, crew person, 1978-80, restaurant mgr, 1983-85; Ana Serv, Bedminster, NJ, banquet sized catering mgr, 1985-87; Chelsea Catering, Newark Airport, NJ, asst food prod mgr, 1987-89; Marriott/Host, Newark Airport, NJ, asst food & beverage mgr, 1989-90; Harrisburg Hilton & Towers, PA, dir human resources, 1990-. **Orgs:** Nat Job Corps Alumni Asn, 1982-; vpres, Nat Asn Black Hospitality Professionals, 1988-. **Honors/Awds:** Numerous National & Regional Debate Awards, 1980-83; Silver Hat Award, McDonald's Corp, 1984. **Business Addr:** Director Human Resources, Harrisburg Hilton and Towers, MHM Inc, 1 N 2nd St, Harrisburg, PA 17101.*

ASHBURN, VIVIAN DIANE
Executive. **Personal:** Born Oct 7, 1949, Kansas City, KS; daughter of Alvin M Patterson and Margaret V Patterson; married Richard R Ashburn, Jun 30, 1972; children: Aaron Cedric, Joseph Elliott. **Educ:** Ohio State Univ, BA, indust rels, 1972; IBM Systems Eng Inst, attended 1974. **Career:** Int Bus Mach, syst engr, 1972-77; Ashburn Pizza Dominos, vpres, 1977-85; Stark Tech Col, 1984-88; Univ Akron, lectr, 1990-; VDP Assocs Inc, pres, 1990-. **Orgs:** Alpha Kappa Alpha Sorority, 1970-; vpres, Black Data Processing Assocs, 1986-; ch air, prog planning, Portage Pvt Indust Coun, 1985-; exec dir, Franklin Mills Mediation Coun, 1989-91; bd mem, W VIZ Radio, 1987-88; Minority Bus Coun, Ohio Chap, 1989-91. **Honors/Awds:** Systems Eng Symposium, IBM Corp, 1977, 1979; Minority Contractor of the Year, US Dept Agr, 1989; Nat Bus Partner, 1990-. **Home Addr:** 305 E Archwood Ave, Akron, OH 44301, **Home Phone:** (330)773-4494. **Business Addr:** President, VDP Assocs Inc, 2633 State Rt 59 Suite B, Ravenna, OH 44266, **Business Phone:** (216)384-7169.*

ASHBY, ERNESTINE ARNOLD
Educator. **Personal:** Born Aug 20, 1928, Washington, DC; widowed; children: Ira Von. **Educ:** Cortez Peters Bus Sch, bus cert, 1947; Coppin State Teachers Col, BS,1950; Univ Md, MEd 1967; Walden Univ, PhD. **Career:** Baltimore City Pub Sch, teacher, 1950-69; Accomack County Sch Syst, reading specialist. **Orgs:** Bd dir, Emmanuel Christian Community Sch Fed Credit Union Adv Coun, 1954-57; mgr, Furniture Exchange United Appeal Orgn Community Chest, 1955-57; YWCA; Nat Asn Advan Colored People. **Honors/Awds:** Literary Guild Award; Certificate of Achievement, Small Bus Mgt; Voluntary Service Award, PTA. **Home Addr:** 13204 Nandua Rd, Painter, VA 23420, **Home Phone:** (757)442-5711.

ASHBY, LUCIUS ANTONE
Executive, consultant, certified public accountant. **Personal:** Born Feb 1, 1944, Des Moines, IA; son of Lucius A Sr and Ruth M Moore; married Victoria Lacy; children: Felecia & Armand. **Educ:** Univ Colo, Denver, BS, bus maj acct, 1969; Harvard Univ, OPM 10, 1985. **Career:** Great Western Sugar Co, mgt trainee prog, 1968-69; Arthur Andersen & Co, sr acct, 1969-72; Ashby Armstrong & Co, managing partner, 1973-91; Ashby Jackson Inc, investor, consult, chmn bd, 1991-; Software Develop Co, consult & investor; DECIS, co-founder, mkt mgt software serv, DC; Jackson, Ashby & Goldstine PC, cert pub acct & partner, 2003-. **Orgs:** Numerous memverships including past treas, Colo State Dem Party; Am Inst CPA's; bd dirs, Colo Soc CPAW's Denver Partnerships; Asn Black CPA Firms; Leadership Denver Asn; Salvation Army, 1975-; bd dirs, Downtown Denver Inc; chmn bd, Colo Invesco Inc, 1988-; Rotary Club Denver Club 31, 2003-. **Honors/Awds:** Barney Ford Eastside Action Movement Award, 1975; Achievement Award, Nat Asn Black Accountants, 1979; Entrepreneur Award, United Negro Col Fund, 1980; Colorado Gospel Music Academy Award. **Military Serv:** AUS, sp-5, e-5,1961-64. **Home Addr:** 3861 S Rosemary Way, Denver, CO 80237, **Home Phone:** (303)773-3665. **Business Addr:** Partner, Certified Public Accountant, Jackson, Ashby & Goldstine PC, 655 Broadway Suite 565, Denver, CO 80203, **Business Phone:** (303)825-4072.

ASHBY, REGINALD W.
Executive. **Personal:** Married Ernestine C Arnold; children: Eugene Paula, Iravon. **Educ:** Morgan State Col, cert bus admin. **Career:** Life Ins Career, 1936-; Universal Life Ins Co, Norfolk, agent, 1969-; Accomack Co, pres, VA. **Orgs:** Veterans Foreign Wars; Nat Asn Advan Colored People; Neighborhood Boys Club, Baltimore, 1963; Grand Jury, Baltimore, 1968-69. **Military Serv:** AUS, 1946. **Business Addr:** Agent, Universal Life Insurance Company, 2802 Va Beach Blvd, Norfolk, VA 23504.*

ASHE, CLIFFORD
Clergy. **Personal:** Married Audree; children: 5. **Educ:** Mich State Univ, BA; Philadelphia Col Bible; Geneva Col. **Career:** Willie Richardson Christian Stronghold Baptist Church, Philadelphia, Pa, associate minister 1982- 87, fulltime staff, 1987-91; Geneva Col, adj prof; DaySpring Ministries, sr pastor & founder, 1992-. **Honors/Awds:** DDiv, 2005. **Business Phone:** (717)939-9500.

ASHFORD, EVELYN
Businessperson, athlete. **Personal:** Born Apr 15, 1957, Shreveport, LA; daughter of Samuel and Vietta; married Ray Washington, Jan 1, 1978; children: Raina Ashley Washington. **Educ:** Univ Calif Los Angeles. **Career:** Athlete (retired), businessperson; track & field runner; businessperson, currently. **Orgs:** Bd dirs, US Anti-Doping Agency (USADA), 2003-. **Honors/Awds:** World Cup Champion, 1979; two Olympics gold medals, 1984; Vitalis Award for excellence in track-and-field, 1987; One Olympic Gold medal, one silver medal, 1988; One Olympic gold medal, 1992; Nat Track and Field Hall of Fame, 1997. **Special Achievements:** First Black woman to carry the American flag during an Olympic opening ceremony, 1988; one of the first women to receive an athletic scholarship from UCLA. **Business Addr:** Board of Directors, United States Anti-Doping Agency (USADA), 1330 Quail Lake Loop Suite 260, Colorado Springs, CO 80906-4651, **Business Phone:** (719)785-2000.

ASHFORD, JOHN
Business owner, artist. **Personal:** Born in Silver Spring, MD. **Educ:** Va Commonwealth Univ, BFA. **Career:** Artist, painter; Tv Series: "For Your Love"; "Malcolm & Eddie", "The Parkers"; John Ashford Art Collection, owner, currently. **Special Achievements:** Numerous exhibits across the US; Painted portraits of numerous musicians, including: Miles Davis, Bob Marley, Tupak Shakur, Notorious BIG. **Business Addr:** Artist, The John Ashford Art Collection, 340 Franklin Ave, PO Box 8321, New York, NY 11238, **Business Phone:** (212)386-2163.

ASHFORD, L JEROME
Executive. **Personal:** Born Aug 7, 1937, Woodville, MS; son of Mazie Iola Moore and Littleton Perry; married Joyce Linebacker, Jan 1, 1956; children: Wesley Jerome, Maurice Eugene, Dwayne Perry & Jerome; married Alicestine D, Sep 6, 1984. **Educ:** Boston Univ, Boston, Mass, BS, 1968; Univ Southern Calif, Los Angeles, Calif, MPA, 1979. **Career:** Nat Assn Community Health Ctr, Wash, DC, exec dir, 1973-78; US Dept Health & Human Serv, Wash, DC, sr research fel, 1978-82; IPM Health Plan, Vallejo, Calif, pres, 1982-88; Kaiser Permanente,Colorado Region, Denver, Colo, health plan mgr, 1988-90; Kaiser Permanente, Southern Calif Region, Pasadena, Calif, vpres & health plan mgr, 1990-94; Univ Miss, Sch Med, Int Acad Health Mgt Informatics, dir, 1999; Univ Miss adj prof, health Mgt & informatics, currently; Ashford Miller Moore Health Care Consult, pres, currently. **Orgs:** USC Alumni asn; Los Angeles March Dimes, Bd directors; NAACP, life mem. **Business Addr:** Adjunct Professor, University Missouri -Columbia School of Medicine, The Acadamy off Departmentt of Health Management & Informatics, 304 Clark Hall, Columbia, MO 65211, **Business Phone:** (573)882-3931.

ASHFORD, MARY E
Educator. **Personal:** Born Jul 15, 1945, Barnwell, SC; daughter of Bernice Wright; married Jesse, Jun 21, 1964; children: Angela & Eric. **Educ:** Austin Community Col, AA, 1974; Huston-Tillotson Col, BA, 1981; Univ Tex, MLS, 1995. **Career:** Austin ISD, teacher, 1981-87; Huston-Tillotson Col, dir, alumni affairs, 1992-. **Orgs:** NAACP, 1981-; Nat Coun Negro Women, 1990-; Asn Prof Fundraisers, 2000-; Travis County Hist Comm, 2000-02; pres, Sigma Gamma Rho sorority, 2002-. **Honors/Awds:** Women Who Can Award, Nat Women Achievement, 1992; President's of Huston-Tillotson Col Award, 1996; Certificate of Congressional Recognition, 1996; Mentoring Award, AISD, 1996-97. **Business Phone:** (512)505-3074.

ASHFORD, NICKOLAS
Songwriter, singer, actor. **Personal:** Born May 4, 1942, Fairfield, SC; married Valerie Simpson; children: Nicole. **Career:** William Morris Agency, singer & songwriter; Sugar Bar, restaurateur; Songs: "You're All I Need to Get By", 1969; "Let's Get Stoned"; "Ain't No Mountain High Enough"; "Your Precious Love", 1996; "I'm Every Woman", 2000; "Ain't Nothing Like the Real Thing; "California Soul", 2003; "Solid", 2004; "Ain't No Mountain High Enough", 2005; Albums: Musical Affair; Is It Still Good to Ya; Stay Free; High Rise; Love or Physical; Films: New Jack City, 1991; A Fight for Jenny. **Honors/Awds:** Has been collected 22 gold and platinum records and more than 50 ASCAP Awards. **Special Achievements:** Performance at Nelson Mandela's 70th birthday celebration in London in 1988; Singing for President Clinton at the 52nd Presidential Inauguration in 1992; Performance at the White House for the CISAC 39th World Congress. **Business Phone:** (212)586-5100.

ASHHURST-WATSON, CARMEN
Executive, activist, movie producer. **Career:** Filmmaker; fundraiser; Def Jam Records & Rush Communs, pres & chief operating officer, 1992; Hip Hop Indust, exec. **Honors/Awds:** Black Radio Exclusive President's Award. **Special Achievements:** One Hundred Most Promising Black Women in Corporate America, Ebony Mag; Selling My Brothers, writer.

ASHLEY, DWAYNE
President (Organization), executive. **Educ:** HBCU Wiley Col, BS; Univ Pa Fel Sch Govt, Master's Degree, Govt Admin; Univ DC, Hon Doctorate Law, 2001. **Career:** Thurgood Marshall Scholar Fund, pres, currently. **Orgs:** Bd Dirs, The Gallup Organization; Exec Dir & Chief Prof Officer, 100 Black Men Am Inc; United Negro Col Fund & United Way; Bd Dirs Newark Pub Library. **Honors/Awds:** Phi Beta Sigma Fraternity's Image Award, 2003. **Business Addr:** President, Thurgood Marshall Scholar Fund, 80 Maiden Ln Suite 2204, New York, NY 10038, **Business Phone:** (212)573-8888.*

ASHLEY, MAURICE
Chess player. **Personal:** Born Mar 6, 1966, St Andrew, Jamaica; children (previous marriage): Nia; married Michele. **Educ:** City

Col NY. **Career:** Prof Chess Grand Master, currently; Raging Rooks Harlem, coach, 1991; Dark Knights, coach, 1994-95; Commentator: Man vs Machine chess match, 1996, Kasparov vs Deep Blue chess rematch, 1997. **Orgs:** Founder, Harlem Educational Activities Fund Inc. **Honors/Awds:** Nat Jr High Sch Championships, 1991; Nat Champions, 1994, 1995; Grandmaster of the Year award, US Chess Fed, 2003. **Special Achievements:** Designer, award-winning instructional CD-ROM; Maurice Ashley Teaches Chess; became the first and only African-American to attain the coveted title of International Grand Master of Chess in 1999; first African-American International Grandmaster includes Time magazine, USA Today, New York Times, Sports Illustrated, London Times, Ebony, Investors Business Daily, New York Daily News, Jet, New York Newsday, New York Post,Emerge & a host of other papers around the world served by the Associated Press & Reuters; TV shows: Charlie Rose Show, CBS News This Morning,National Public Radio, Today New York (W-NBC), CNN, Bloomberg Radio & a number of radio shows around the US; Authored essay :The End of the Draw Offer?. **Home Phone:** (718)528-3006. **Business Phone:** (212)663-9732.

ASHLEY-WARD, AMELIA
Editor, publisher, business owner. **Career:** Sun-Reporter, owner, publ & editor-in-chief, currently. **Orgs:** Nat Newspaper Publ Asn; bd mem, San Francisco Nat Asn Advan Colored People; life mem, Nat Coun Negro Women; life mem Nat Asn Advan Colored People. **Honors/Awds:** Alumnus of the Year, San Jose State Univ; Woman of the Year, Calif State Senate; Photojourn Award, Nat Newspaper Publs Asn (The Black Press of America), 1980; Feature Writing Award, NNPA, 1981; Publ of the Year, NNPA, 1998. **Business Phone:** (415)671-1000.*

ASHMORE, DARRYL ALLAN
Football player. **Personal:** Born Nov 1, 1969, Peoria, IL. **Educ:** Northwestern Univ, bus. **Career:** Football player (retired); Los Angeles Rams, tackle, 1993-94; St Louis Rams, 1995-96; Wash Redskins, 1997-98; Oakland Raiders, 1998-01. **Honors/Awds:** Scholar Athlete of the Year, tri-county area. *

ASHTON, VIVIAN CHRISTINA R.
Government official, executive. **Personal:** Born Aug 14, 1910, Spokane, WA; daughter of Elijah J Reynolds (deceased) and Madeline D Mackingham Reynolds (deceased); married Lawrence Thomas Ashton (deceased). **Educ:** Wash Lee Col, US Armed Forces, Cert, 1945; Howard Univ, sociol, 1982; Berne-19Davis Bus Col, Cert, 1948; Ohio State Univ, sociol, 1950. **Career:** The Wee-Angels Inc, chmn, 1959-85; NOW, lobbyist, 1975-76; Adv Comn, 5D DC Govt, comnr, 1981-85; League Women Voters, speaker, 1983-85. **Orgs:** Col Charles Young Chap 3 DAV, 1945-95; Prince Hall No five OES Masonic Order, 1950-95; pub rels, Club Int, 1960-80; chair, crime comm, Brookland Civic Asn, 1980-85; community liaison, DC Comm Humanities Coun, 1981; chair, Hist Comm ANC-5C, 1981-85; Panel Comment Pres Reagan's Add Nation, 1981; group leader, Solidarity Club, St Anthony's Church, 1991. **Honors/Awds:** Letter of Appreciation, Mayor Walter Wash, 1975; Cert of Appreciation, Spingarn Moreland Res Ctr, 1975; Award, Active Bicentennial Prog, 1976; Cert of Appreciation, DC City Coun, 1985; DC Talent Search, first Pl, Adult Singer "Summer Time," 1989; Cert of Appreciation-Exemplary Acts Serv, MW Prince Hall Grand Masonic Lodge, FAAM-PHA, Wash DC, 1990; res, compiler, presenter, ed, Masonic Hist Landmark Appln for Woodlawn Cemetary, 1990-92; Humanities Award, MW Prince Hall Grand Masonic Lodge, FAAM-PHA, Wash DC, 1994; inducted, Ronald Wilson Reagan Founder's Wall. **Military Serv:** sp E-2 personnel serv, 1943-45; Women's Army Corps, WWII; WWII Victory Medal, Am Campaign Medal. *

ASKA, JOSEPH (JOE ASKA)
Football player. **Personal:** Born Jul 14, 1972, St. Croix, Virgin Islands of the United States; married. **Educ:** Cent Okla. **Career:** Football(retired), Oakland Raiders, running back, 1995-97; Indianapolis Colts, 1999; New YorkNJ Hitmen, 2001. *

ASKEW, BONNY LAMAR
Government official, association executive. **Personal:** Born Mar 4, 1955, Rome, GA; married Adrianne Denise Smith. **Educ:** US Naval Acad, 1973; West Ga Col, BA, polit sci, 1977. **Career:** South Rome Comm Assoc, co-founder, 1979; 2nd Ward City of Rome, comnr, 1983-84; GA Kraft Co, laborer, 1977-; Rome Coun Human Rels, vchmn; Univ Ga, Alumni Asn, dir, currently. **Orgs:** Thankful Baptist Church; S Rome Comm Asn; Starlight Lodge 433 FAAYM; comt mem, Ga Munic Asn Comm Develop, 1983-84; comt mem, Nat League Cities Comm Develop, 1983-84; Nat Black Caucus local elected official, 1983-84; Ga Assoc Black Elected Off, 1983-84. **Business Addr:** Director, University of West Georgia Alumni House, 1601 Maple St, Carrollton, GA 30118, **Business Phone:** (678)839-6582.

ASKEW, VINCENT JEROME
Basketball player. **Personal:** Born Feb 28, 1966, Memphis, TN. **Educ:** Memphis State Univ. **Career:** Basketball player (retired), basketball coach; Philadelphia 76ers, 1987-88; Savannah Spirits (CBA), 1987-88; Bologna Arimo (Italy), 1988-89; Albany Patroons (CBA), 1988-91; Golden State Warriors, 1990-92; Sacramento Kings, 1992; Seattle Supersonics, 1993-96; Denver Nuggets, 1996-97; NJ Nets, guard, 1996-97; Ind Pacers, guard, 1996-97; Portland Trailblazers, guard, 1997-98; Tacoma Navigators, Am Basketball Asn, head coach; Albany Patroons, head coach, 2007-. **Honors/Awds:** Most Valuable Player, Continental Basketball Asn, 1990, 1991. **Business Phone:** (518)694-7160.

ASKINS, KEITH BERNARD
Basketball player, basketball coach. **Personal:** Born Dec 15, 1967, Athens, AL. **Educ:** Univ Ala, attended 1990. **Career:** Basketball player (retired), Coach; Miami Heat, guard-forward, 1990-99, asst coach, 1999-, advan scout, 2000-02. **Honors/Awds:** Leadership Award, 1994-95, 1995-96. **Business Addr:** Assistant Coach, Miami Heat, 601 Biscayne Blvd, Miami Arena, Miami, FL 33132, **Business Phone:** (786)777-4667.

ASMA, THOMAS M
Artist. **Educ:** Layton Sch Art, attended 1968; Col Lake Co, Liberal Arts, 1975; Univ Ill, attended 1976. **Career:** Layson Prods, commercial artist, 1970-71; Carlson Studios, commercial artist, 1971-72; Lake County Regional Planning Comn, planning tech, 1972-73; Lake County Safety Comn, graphic artist, 1973-74; BALL Corp, palletizer gen factory, 1976-78; Kitchens Sara Lee, prod sanitation, 1978-80; Am Heritage Indust, custom artist, 1980-. **Business Addr:** Custom Artist, Am Heritage Indust, 3400 W Grand Ave, Waukegan, IL 60085.*

ASOM, MOSES T.
Scientist. **Personal:** Born Jul 27, 1958, Gboko Benue, Nigeria; son of Asom Ikyutor and Lydia. **Educ:** Univ DC, BSc, physics, 1980; Howard Univ, MSc, 1982, PhD, elec eng, 1985; Univ Pa, Wharton Sch, MBA, 1994. **Career:** Univ DC, Wash, instr, 1984; Howard Univ, Wash, res asst, 1981-85; AT&T Bell Labs, Murray Hill, NJ, MTS, 1986-89; AT&T Bell Labs, SSTC, 1990-94; AT&T Microeletronics, Asia/Pac, Japan & S Am, mgr, 1994; Lucent New Ventures Group, dir; SyChip Inc, co-founder & sr vpres mkt & bus develop, currently. **Orgs:** Comn mem, Educ Affairs, Am Soc Mat; Inst Elec & Electronics Engrs; Am Phys Soc; Nat Tech Asn; Am Vacuum Soc; Mat Res Soc; Nat Orgn Adv Black Chemists & Chem Engrs. **Honors/Awds:** NASA-HBCU, NASA, 1989; Black Engineer of the Year, 1989; 2 patents awarded. **Special Achievements:** Holds 3 patents; publ & presented over seventy tech papers & seminars. **Business Addr:** Co-founder, Senior Vice President Of Marketing and Business Development, SyChip Inc, Pkwy Centre II, 2805 N Dallas Pkwy Suite 400, Plano, TX 75093.*

ATCHISON, DR. CALVIN O.
Executive. **Personal:** Born Sep 15, 1920, Millry, AL; married Amanda Rosetta McFadden; children: Antoinette & Calvin II. **Educ:** Ala A&M Col, BS, 1944; Columbia Univ, MA, 1949; Ind Univ, EdD, 1958. **Career:** Charlotte City Schs, sch psychol, 1949-53; TN State Univ, assoc prof, 1953-58, prof & coord graduate studies & res, 1958-64, prof psychol & asst grad dean, 1964-67, acting dir res & develop, 1968-69, develop officer, 1969-72, vpres res planning & develop, 1972-; TN State Univ Found, exec dir, 1986-; Metrop Nashville Head Start Admin, vice chmn, 2003-. **Orgs:** Am psychol Assn; Soc Study Projective Tech; Psy Chi; Nashville Mental Health Assn; Better Bus Bureau Nashville; Metro Nashville Housing & Urban Devel; Coun Advan & Study Educ. **Honors/Awds:** Danforth Teacher, 1956-57; Outstanding Educator, 1972-73; Admin Year, 1985. **Military Serv:** USN Yeoman, 2nd Class, 1944-46. **Business Addr:** Vice Chairman, Metrop Clerk's Off, 225 Polk Ave, Nashville, TN 37203.*

ATCHISON, LEON H.
Executive. **Personal:** Born Feb 27, 1928, Detroit, MI; son of A R and Rosy Lee; children: Aleta, Terrance, Erika. **Educ:** Mich State Univ, BA, 1960, MA, 1962. **Career:** US Congressman John Conyers, admin asst, 1965-71; Univ Detroit, dir urban studies, 1971-74; dir purchasing, 1974-75; dir parks & recreation, 1975-79; Mich Consol Gas Co, dir civic & govt affairs, 1979-94; Ultimed HMO Mich, vpres pub affairs, 1994-. **Orgs:** Bd gov, Wayne State Univ, State Wide Election, 1970-78; bd dir, Cent Bus Dist, 1981; Am Asn Blacks Energy; bd dir, Greater Detroit Chamber Com, 1987-. **Honors/Awds:** Man of the Year Award, Nat Asn Negro Bus & Prof Women's Clubs, 1976; Outstanding Service Award, United Cerebral Palsy Asn, 1978; Testimonial Resolution Outstanding Public Service, Detroit City Coun, 1979; Proclamation, Outstanding Public Service, Mayor Detroit City, 1979. **Military Serv:** USN 3/c petty ofcr 1945-47; Good Conduct Medal, S Pacific Ribbon. **Business Addr:** Vice President for Public Affairs, Ultimed HMO Michigan, 2401 20th St, Detroit, MI 48216.*

ATCHISON, LILLIAN ELIZABETH
Educator, librarian. **Personal:** Born in Meridian, MS; daughter of Robert W Hilliard and Danella Gardner Hilliard; married Guy R Atchison, Feb 5, 1948. **Educ:** Harris Stowe State Col, St Louis, MO, BA; Univ Ill, Urbana, IL, MA, ed, 1948; Washington Univ, St Louis, MO, BS, 1968; Univ Ill, Urbana, IL, MS, libr sci, 1971. **Career:** Librarian (retired); Educ, St Louis, MO, teacher, libr consult, 1966-71; Univ City Sch Dist, Univ City, MO, librn K 12, 1972-98. **Orgs:** Bd mem, Sigma Gamma Rho Sorority, Inc, 1963-65; north central secy, Nat Asn Univ Women, 1953-63; leader, Wyoming Trekkers, Girl Scouts Greater St Louis, 1973-74; bd mem, MO Asn Sch Librns, 1985-89; Kappa Delta Pi, Univ Illinois, 1948; Beta Phi Mu, Univ Illinois, 1972. **Honors/Awds:** Woman of the Year, Greyhound, 1974; Service Certificate Award, MO Asn Sch Librns; Arts Award, Sigma Gamma Rho Sorority, Inc, 1991; Alpha Zeta Chapter, Iota Phi Lambda Sorority, Inc, Apple Teacher Award, 1992; Community Service Awards, Zeta Sigma Chapter, Sigma Gamma Rho Sorority Inc, 1996. *

ATKINS, BRENDA JOYCE
School administrator. **Personal:** Born Jan 25, 1954, Washington, DC. **Educ:** Loyola Marymount, BA, 1975; Georgetown Univ Law Ctr, JD, 1978. **Career:** Lawy Com Civil Rights Educ Proj, researcher, 1976; US Dept Justice, Tax Div, law clerk, 1977; White House Off Coun, pres, law clerk, 1977-78; Am Crim Law Rev, managing ed, 1977-78; Georgetown Univ Law Ctr, asst dean, 1978-. **Orgs:** Nat Conf Black Lawyer; Nat Bar Asn. **Special Achievements:** Author, US Tax For & For Tax Art, 1980.

ATKINS, DR. CARL J
Educator, arts administrator, musician. **Personal:** Born Jul 4, 1945, Birmingham, AL; son of James Spencer and Kathryn Watson Woods; married Deborah Little Atkins, May 17, 1981; children: Kathryn-Louise & Leslie Stevens-Atkins Dowdell. **Educ:** Cent State Col, Wilberforce, OH, 1963; Ind Univ, Bloomington, IN, BM, 1967; New Eng Conserv, Boston, DMA, MM, 1975; Univ Rochester, Eastman Sch, Rochester, NY, DM, 1982. **Career:** Am Nat Opera Co, Boston, MA, orchestra, 1967-68; New Eng Conserv Boston, MA, fac, 1968-78; Univ Rochester Eastman Sch, conducting fel, 1978; Hochstein Music Sch, Rochester, NY, dean, 1979-81; Univ Rochester, Rochester, NY, asst prof, 1981-84; David Hochstein Mem Music Sch, Rochester, NY, pres, 1984-91; Rochester Philharmonic Orchestra Inc, pres & chief exec officer, 1991-93; Carl Atkins & Assoc, pres, 1993-; Thelonious Monk Inst Jazz New England Conserv, Boston, MA, dir, 1995-; Rochester Inst Tech, Rochester, NY, Dept Fine Arts, prof, currently. **Orgs:** Am Fedn Musicians, 1960-; Col Band Dirs Nat Asn, 1981-; Nat Guild Comm Schs Arts. **Honors/Awds:** Grant for Research, Black Marching Music, NEA, 1977; Alabama Jazz Hall of Fame, 1984. **Home Addr:** 53 Mt Morency Dr, Rochester, NY 14612-3631. **Business Addr:** Professor, Rochester Institute of Technology, Department of Fine Arts, 1 Lomb Memorial Dr, Rochester, NY 14623-5604, **Business Phone:** (585)475-2411.

ATKINS, CAROLYN VAUGHN
Educator, psychologist. **Personal:** Born Sep 29, 1930, St Louis, MO; daughter of George Louis Sr (deceased) and Eva Merritt (deceased); divorced. **Educ:** Fisk Univ, Nashville; Morgan State Univ, Baltimore, BS, 1951; Southern Ill Univ, Edwardsville; Wash Univ, St Louis, MA, 1968; Cent Mo State Univ, Warrensburg, MS, 1981; St Louis Univ, PhD, 1993. **Career:** Ment Health Ctr St Clair Co, counseling psychologist, 1968-72; St Louis City Jail, consult res eval & planning, 1972-73; State Correctional Ctr Women, supt 1974-76; Div Corrections, prog specialist, 1976-77, human res officer, 1977-78; Div Probation & Parole Interstate Compact Admin, chmn & dir bd probation & parole, 1978-85; KLUM 98.9 FM, hostess, Criminal Justice Radiogram; Lincoln Univ, prof criminal justice, 1986. **Orgs:** Am Corrections Asn; Mo Corrections Asn Del Assmebly; former secy & pres, Acme Art & Culture Club; bd chmn, Wesley Cent-Lincoln Univ; various off Union Memorial United Meth Church, 1968-80; Psi Chi Southern Ill Univ,1969; chmn, Soc Action Ment Health St Louis Alumnae Chap, 1971-74; pres, Mo Chap Nat Assoc Blacks Criminal Justice, 1979-80; Mo reclamation coord Delta Sigma Theta Sorority, 1990, pres Jefferson City Alumni Chap,1988-90; Scholarship & Standards, 1991-95; Child Abuse & Neglect ReviewBd; State Mo, 1988; Nat Advan Asn Colored People; adv, Alpha Theta Chap;Delta Sigma Theta Sorority, 1988-00; Inst Review Bd, Memorial Hosp,Jefferson City, Mo. **Honors/Awds:** Sigma Gamma Rho Community Service Award, St Louis, 1977; Community Service Award & Distinguished Women, Tea Union Memorial United Methodist Church, 1978; Missouri Distinguished Citizen Award, Union Memorial United Methodist Church, 1979. **Home Phone:** (573)893-7948. *

ATKINS, CHUCK
Executive. **Career:** Clear Channel Commun, oper mgr & prog dir, currently.

ATKINS, DAVID. See SINBAD in the Obituaries section.

ATKINS, EDMUND E.
City planner. **Personal:** Born Dec 6, 1944, Winston-Salem, NC; married Vera Clayton; children: Damien. **Educ:** Grinnell Col, BA, 1966; Univ Oklahoma, MRCP, 1972. **Career:** San Francisco Redev Agency, asst planner, 1969; Oakland Model Cities, chief phys planner, 1970-71; US Dept HUD, urban planner, 1971-74; City Berkeley, city planner, 1974, Consulate Gen Rio de Janeiro, Brazil, Consul Gen, currently. **Orgs:** Assoc mem, Am Inst Planners; vpres, Nat Asn Planners; pres, Bay Area chap New Niagra Movement Demo Club; treas, Oakland Citizens Comt Urban Renewal, 1976-; Alameda Co Human Serv Coun, 1976-; CA Land

Use Taks Force; life mem, NAACP; vpres, Youth Coun. **Military Serv:** AUS, Reserves, 1968-74. **Business Addr:** Consul General, Rio de Janeiro Consulate, Av Presidente Wilson 147 Castelo, 20030-020 Rio de Janeiro, Brazil, **Business Phone:** (552)13823-2000.*

ATKINS, EDNA R.
Lawyer. **Personal:** Born Jan 22, 1945, Sicily Island, LA. **Educ:** Univ Omaha, BA, 1967; Creighton Law Sch, JD, 1970. **Career:** Legal Aid Soc Omaha, Coun Bluffs Inc, staff atty, 1970-; State Nebr County Ct 4th Judicial Dist Douglas County, judge, currently. **Orgs:** NE State Bar Assoc, Nat Bar Asn; Am Bar Asn; Nat Asn Black Women Attny; Nat Asn Advan Colored People, 1970; gen counsel, CARE Prog Inc, 1973. **Business Addr:** Judge, State Nebraska County Court 4th Judicial District Douglas County, 1701 Farnam St, Omaha, NE 68183.*

ATKINS, ERICA (ERICA CAMPBELL)
Gospel singer, actor. **Personal:** Born Jan 1, 1972?, Inglewood, CA; daughter of Eddie and Thomasina; married Warryn Campbell, May 1, 2001; children: 1. **Career:** TV show: "What's Hot in Music", 2000, "Trackers", 2000, "Whassup with Heyyy?", 2000, "The Parkers", 2000, "An Evening of Stars: A Celebration of Educational Excellence", 2001, "Top of the Pops", 2001, "The Big Bitter Shower Episode", 2003, "Half & Half", 2003, "Gospel Fest 2004", 2004, "Living It Up with Patti La Belle", 2004, "Tavis Smiley", 2005, "Episode #35.2", 2005, "Soul Train", 2005, "It's Showtime at the Apollo", 2005; "BET Awards", 2006; "21st Annual Stellar Gospel Music Awards", 2006; "22nd Annual Stellar Gospel Music Awards", 2007; "Tavis Smiley", 2005-09; Movies: Sister Act II: Back in the Habit, 1993. **Orgs:** Duo Mary Mary. **Honors/Awds:** New Artist of the Year & Contemporary CD of the Year, 2001; 4 Stellar awards. **Special Achievements:** Wrote songs appearing on secular and sacred CDs & on Dr. Dolittle & ThePrince of Egypt soundtracks.

ATKINS, FREDD G
City commissioner. **Personal:** Born Jun 19, 1952, Sarasota, FL; son of Glossie; married Sheila Hammond; married Luethel Chochran Atkins, Oct 1985 (divorced); children: Carol, Nilaja, Amina, Baraka, Dumaka & Zakia. **Educ:** Manatee Jr Col, soc welfare, Bradenton, FL, AA, 1979; Univ Southern Fla, interdisciplinary soc scis, Sarasota, FL, BA. **Career:** Storefront Newtown Community Ctr, Sarasota, FL, asst dir, 1982-85; Genus Enterprises, Inc, Sarasota, FL, dir mkt, 1985-87; City Sarasota Comn, FL, comnr, 1985-95, Dist 1, vice mayor, 2003-; Cent Life Ins, Tampa, FL, vpres, 1988-89. **Orgs:** Nat Black Family Found; Nat Forum Black Administrs; NAACP, Sarasota chap; Southwest Fla Regional Planning Coun; Fla League Cities; founder & former pres, Newtown Little League; founding mem, Greater Newtown Community Redevelop Corp; pres, Booker High Sch Boosters; chair, Booker Middle Sch Adv Comt;, Southwest Fla Regional Planning Coun; Metropo Planning Organ; econ develop bd, Sarasota County; Tourist Develop Counc; Urban Admin Comt; bd trustees, Out Door Acad, former educ chmn, Sarasota County NAACP; Fla Adv Counc HUD. **Honors/Awds:** Political Academic Award, Kappa Alpha Psi, 1987; Martin Luther King Award for Service to Youth, 1988; NAACP Achievement Award, 1988; Human Rights and Achievement Award, InterdenomiNat Ministerial Alliance, 1988. **Home Addr:** 1598 29th St, Sarasota, FL 34234, **Home Phone:** (941)358-5851. **Business Addr:** Vice Mayor, Commissioner, City Sarasota, Dist 1, 1565 First St Rm 101, PO Box 1058, Sarasota, FL 34230, **Business Phone:** (941)954-4115.

ATKINS, HANNAH DIGGS
State government official, educator. **Personal:** Born Nov 1, 1923, Winston-Salem, NC; daughter of James T Diggs and Mabel Kennedy Diggs; married Charles N, May 24, 1943 (deceased); children: Edmund, Valerie & Charles Jr; married Everett P O'Neal, Jun 1993 (deceased). **Educ:** St Augustine's Col, Raleigh, NC, BS, 1943; Univ Chicago Grad Libr Sch, BLS, 1949; Oklahoma City Univ Sch Law, 1964; Univ Oklahoma, MPA, 1989; Harvard Univ, John F Kennedy Sch Govt; prog sr exec; Univ Texas, Lyndon B. Johnson Sch Public Affairs, Exec Leadership Dev Prog, cert. **Career:** State Government official (retired), educator; Winston-Salem J/Sentinel, reporter, 1945-48; Atkins High Sch, teacher, 1945-48; Meharry Med Col, biochem res asst, 1948-49; Fisk Univ, ref librn, 1949-50; Kimberly Park Elem Sch, sch librn, 1950-51; Oklahoma City Pub Libr, br librn, 1953-56; Oklahoma State Library, ref librn, 1962-63, chief gen ref div & actg law librn, 1963-68, instr libr sci, 1967-68; Oklahoma City Univ, instr law, 1967; Oklahoma State Rep, 1969-80; Oklahoma Dept Human Serv, asst dir, 1983-87; State Oklahoma, state cabinet secy human resources, 1987-91; Univ Cent Oklahoma, prof, 1991-92; Oklahoma State Univ, prof, 1992-93; Univ Okla, vis prof. **Orgs:** Exec bd, Sunbeam Home & Family Serv, Nat Asn Advan Colored People; pres, Vis Nurses Asn; Govt Comn Status Women; bd mem, Women Exec State Govt; nat bd mem, Trans-Africa; pres, Oklahoma Chap Am Soc Pub Admin; bd mem, Nat Am Civil Liberties Union, Nat Black Child Develop Inst; founder & pres emer, Nat Art Asn, Oklahoma City; chair, Oklahoma Adv Comt, US Community Civil Rights; vpres, Oklahoma City Chap People; secy, Oklahoma Sister Cities; mem, Exec Comt, Oklahoma Chap UNA/USA. **Honors/Awds:** Outstanding Woman of the Year, Oklahoma Soroptomist Int, 1965; Woman of the Year, Theta Sigma Phi, 1968; Outstanding Sororority & Nat Founders Service Award, Alpha Kappa Alpha Midwest Region; Distinguished Service Award, Nat Links Inc, 1972; Hibler Award Distinguished Service, 1973;Finer Womanhood Award, Zeta Phi Beta; National Public Citizen, Nat Asn Social Work, 1975; Oklahoma Woman's Hall Fame, 1982; Afro-American Hall of Fame, Oklahoma, 1983; Phi Beta Kappa; DHL, Benedict Col; Hannah Atkins Endowed Chair of Public Service, Oklahoma State Univ, 1990; Phi Beta Kappan Year, Oklahoma Chap, Phi Beta Kappa,1990; Humanitarian Award, Oklahoma Chap, Nat Conf Christians & Jews, 1990; Distinguished Service State Government Award, Nat Gov's Asn, 1990; Trailblazers Award, Oklahoma Hist Soc, 1997; Keeper of the Dream, Ebony Tribune, 1997; Constitution Award, Rogers Univ, 1998; Honorary Doctorate, Univ Oklahoma, 1999; Honorary Doctorate, Oklahoma State Univ, 2000; Oklahoma Hall Fame, 2000. **Special Achievements:** First African American woman to be elected to the Oklahoma House of Representatives. **Home Addr:** 3701 Int Dr Apt 601, Silver Spring, MD 20906. **Business Phone:** (405)325-3811.*

ATKINS, JAMES
Football player. **Personal:** Born Jan 28, 1970, Amite, LA; married Nicole, May 28, 1995. **Educ:** Univ La Lafayette. **Career:** Football player (retired); Seattle Seahawks, tackle, 1994-97; Baltimore Ravens, 1998-99; Detroit Lions, 2000. *

ATKINS, JEFFREY. See JA RULE.

ATKINS, MARYLIN E.
Judge, lawyer. **Personal:** Born Jan 1, 1946?, Detroit, MI. **Educ:** Saginaw Valley State Univ, BA, psychol, 1973; Univ Detroit Sch Law, JD, 1980. **Career:** Mich Employment Security Comn, asst dir labor rels, 1977-80; Mich Legislative Serv Bur, staff atty, 1980; US Dist Ct, Eastern Dist, asst atty gen, 1980-83, Worker's Compensation Appeal Bd, mem, 1983-85, chair, 1985-91; State Mich, 36th Dist Ct, magistrate, 1994-99, chief judge pro tem, 1999, chief judge, 2000-; bd dirs, Eastern Wayne Div, Am Heart Asn. **Orgs:** Wolverine Bar Asn; State Bar Mich; Mich Black Judges Asn; Detroit Bar Asn; Nat Asn Advan Colored People; Optimist Club; bd dirs, Interim House, YMCA; adv bd, Benjamin E. Mays Male Acad; Kiwanis Club 1 Detroit. **Business Addr:** Chief Judge, State of Michigan, 36th District Court, 421 Madison Ave, Detroit, MI 48226, **Business Phone:** (313)965-8736.*

ATKINS, PERVIS R., JR.
Executive, football player, actor. **Personal:** Born Nov 24, 1935, Ruston, LA; son of Pervis and Mattie; children: Gerald, Christine, Gregory & Gayle. **Educ:** NMex State Univ, BA, socio, 1962. **Career:** Football player (retired), executive, actor; Los Angeles Rams, wide receiver, 1961-63; Wash Redskins, wide receiver, 1964-65; Oakland Raiders, wide receiver, 1965-66; KIIX, TV sports commentator; TV Series: "Police Woman", 1975-77; "Desperate Miles", 1975; "Ellery Queen", 1976; "Delvecchio", 1977; ABC-TV, dir develop motion pictures; Artist Career Mgt, vpres; Atkins & Assocs, owner, currently. **Orgs:** Pop Warner Football League; Kwanza Adv Bd. **Honors/Awds:** Consensus, All Am Football, 1960 & 1961; Outstanding Citizen of Ruston, LA 1961; Inducted in College Football Hall of Fame, 2009. **Military Serv:** USMC, sgt, 1954-57; Commendation for Meritorious Service, United ServOrgns, 1971. **Business Addr:** Owner, Atkins & Associates, 303 S Crescent Heights Blvd, Los Angeles, CA 90048, **Business Phone:** (323)658-1025.*

ATKINS, RICHARD
Executive, architect. **Personal:** Born Feb 9, 1949, Stephens, AR; son of Robert and Clemmine Ferguson; married Diane Williams, Sep 1, 1971; children: Gregory & Gary R. **Educ:** Forest Pk Community Col, 1971; Wash Univ, 1970; Howard Univ, BA, Arch, 1975; Lindenwood Col, MBA, 1982. **Career:** Stottler, Stagg & Assoc, engr technician II, 1972-74; Gordon H Ball Inc, engr technician & draftsman, 1974; Itzig Heine Construct, engr technician & draftsman, 1974-75; Peckham-Guyton Inc, architect-in-training, 1975-77; JG Randle & Assoc, project architect, 1977-78; Environmental Seven Ltd, office mgr, project architect, 1978-80; TDP & St Louis Inc, Chief Archit, owner, pres, 1980-. **Orgs:** Nat Orgn Minority Architects; pres, 100 Black Men St Louis; mem, Scholar found, currently; Boy Scouts Am, Chmn, 1991. **Honors/Awds:** Man of the Year, 100 Black Men St Louis Chap, 1992, 1997. **Business Addr:** Owner, President, TDP/St Louis Incorporation, 3101 Olive St, St Louis, MO 63103-1212, **Business Phone:** (314)533-1996.

ATKINS, RUSSELL
Writer, composer. **Personal:** Born Feb 25, 1926, Cleveland, OH; son of Perry Kelly and Mamie Belle Kelley. **Educ:** Cleveland Sch Art, scholar, 1943-44; Cleveland Music Sch Settlement, prischolar, 1943; Cleveland Inst Music, attended 1944-45; Pvt Music Study, 1950-54. **Career:** Editor, poet, writer & composer; Free Lance Mag, ed & co-founder 1950-79;Univ Iowa, Iowa Workshop, affil, 1953-54; Sutphen Sch Music, asst dir,1957-60; Poets & Lecturers Alliance, lectr, 1963-65; WVIZ- TV, consult,1969-72; Karamu Writers Conf, consult, 1971; Karamu House, writing instr,1972-86; Cleveland Bd Educ, consult, 1972-73; Cuyahoga Community Col, writer-in-residence, 1973; Ohio Prog Humanities, instr, 1978; writer,currently; Books: A Podium Presentation, 1960; Phenomena, 1961; Objects,1963; Objects 2, 1963; Heretofore, 1968; Presentations, 1969; Sounds &Silences: Poetry for Now, 1969; Here in The, 1976; Celebrations, 1977; Whichever, 1978; Juxtapositions: A Manifesto, 1991; Contributor to anthologies including The Garden Thrives, 1996; Voices of Cleveland, 1996;Beyond the Reef, 1991; Letters to America, 1995. **Orgs:** Bread Loaf Writers Conf, 1956; Artists-in-Schs Prog, Ohio Arts Coun & Nat Endowment Arts, 1973-; lit adv panel, Ohio Arts Coun, 1973-76; Cleveland State Univ Poetry Forum; Coord Coun Lit Mag, Nat Endowment Arts; Int Platform Asn, 1976-77; trustee, Poets League Greaster Cleveland, 1978;Comt Small Mag Ed & Publishers; Poets League Greater Cleveland. **Honors/Awds:** Honorary PhD, Cleveland State Univ, 1976; Individual Artist grant, Ohio Arts Coun, 1978. **Home Addr:** 6005 Grand Ave, Cleveland, OH 44104, **Home Phone:** (216)431-7116.

ATKINS, SHARIF
Actor. **Personal:** Born Jan 29, 1975, Pittsburgh, PA; son of David and Jacqueline. **Educ:** Northwestern Univ, BA, 1997. **Career:** TV Series: "The More You Know", 1989; "Turks", 1999; "Early Edition",1999; "That's Life", 2001; "The District", 2001; "Arli$$", 2002; "Hawaii",2004; "ER", 2001-04; "Eve", 2005; "The 4400", 2005; "Numb3rs", 2007;"Close to Home", 2007; "Raising the Bar", 2008; "My Manny", 2009; "Criminal Minds", 2009. Films: Light It Up, 1999; The Big Time, 2002; Something for Nothing, exec producer, 2004; Paved with Good Intentions, 2006; Privacy Policy, 2007. **Business Addr:** Actor, NBC Productions, 30 Rockefeller Plz, New York, NY 10112.

ATKINS, THOMAS IRVING
Lawyer. **Personal:** Born Mar 2, 1939, Elkhart, IN; son of Rev Mrs N P Atkins; married Sharon Annette Soash (divorced); children: Todd, Thomas Jr, Trena. **Educ:** Indiana Univ, BA, 1961; Harvard Univ, MA, 1963; Harvard Law Sch, JD, 1969. **Career:** Boston NAACP, exec secy, 1963-65; Boston City Coun, Boston city councilman, 1968-71; Exec Off Communities & Develop, secy, 1971-75; NAACP, gen coun, 1980-84; Pvt Pract, atty, currently. **Orgs:** ABA; Nat Bar Asn; Massachusetts Bar Asn; bd dir, Pub Broadcasting Serv, 1972-74; vice chmn, Fed Reserve Bank Boston, 1980-85; Harvard Univ, bd overseers. **Honors/Awds:** Honorary PhD, Northeastern Univ, 1974; Honorary LLD, New England Sch Law, 1982. **Business Addr:** Attorney, Private Practitioner, 135 Eastern Pkwy, Brooklyn, NY 11238, **Business Phone:** (718)638-4153.*

ATKINS, TINA (TRECINA EVETTE CAMPBELL)
Gospel singer. **Personal:** Born Jan 1, 1975?, Inglewood, CA; married Teddy Campbell; children: Laiah Simone & Meela Jane. **Career:** Mary Mary, gospel duo; Albums: THankful, 2000; Incredible, 2002; Heaven, 2005; The Real Party, 2005; Mary Mary, 2005; A Mary Mary Christmas, 2006; The Sound, 2008. **Honors/Awds:** Grammy Award, 2000; Four Stellar awards, including New Artist of the Year & Contemporary CD of the Year, Thankful, 2001; Dove Award; American Music Award; Best Inspirational/Christian Contempary Artist, 2005; Nominee, Favorite R&B/Soul or Hip-Hop New Artist Award, 2001; Best Gospel Artist Award, 2009.

ATKINSON, CURTIS L.
State government official, teacher. **Personal:** Born Sep 12, 1934, Brunswick, GA; son of Israel; married Melvis Evans. **Educ:** Howard Univ, attended 1954; Fort Valley State Col, BS, 1956; Columbia Univ, attended 1969. **Career:** Teacher, state government offical (retired); teacher, 1956-69; US Senate, staff, 1969-80; State Ga, asst secy of state. **Orgs:** Exec comn, Ga Spec Olympics, 1984-85; bd dir, Ga Alliance C, 1980-; bd dir, Southeast Regional & SERO & Nat Scholarship Serv, 1980-; chmn & sec, State's Econ Develop Task Force, 1983-; bd dir, Fort Valley St Col Found,1983-; trustee & bd, CME Church; Eta Lambda & Alpha Phi Alpha. **Honors/Awds:** Roy Wilkins Award, Georgia Nat Asn Advan Colroed People, 1983; Public ServAward, Alpha Phi Alpha, 1983; Outstanding Georgian, Fort Valley State Col,1984; Community Serv Award, Ga Coun Deliberation, 1984; Honor, Ga YoungFarmers Asn, 1985; Leadership Award, Metro Atlanta Chap, Farnham Vol ServCoun Nat Alumni Asn, 1985; Political Leadership Award, Bronner Bros Int, 1984. **Military Serv:** AUS, 1st Lt, 1951-53.

ATKINSON, EUGENIA CALWISE
Administrator. **Personal:** Born Jan 16, 1943, Laurens, SC; married Richard W Atkinson; children: Najuma, W Omari, Akilah, Jamila. **Educ:** Youngstown State Univ, ABA, 1971; Hiram col, BA, 1989. **Career:** Hon Natlaniel R Jones Judge US Dist Court, sec, 1960-63; Youngstown Sheet Tube Co, supvr sec-steno pool, 1969-74; Youngstown Area Com Action Coun, admin asst, 1974-76, dir WIC prog, 1976-79; Western Reserve Transit Auth, pres bd trustees; Youngstown Civil Serv Comn, chmn; Metro Housing Authority, dir admin, exec dir, currently. **Orgs:** bd trustees, Youngstown State univ, 1989; OHI mlk Holiday cms; Scholarship com chmn, Youngstown Chap OH Black Womens Leadership Caucus, 1977-80; pres, YWCA, 1981-81; Leadership Warren-Youngstown Alumni Assn; Yo Alumnae Chapter Delta Sigma Theta; Nat Afro-Amer Mus Plng Coun, 1978-80; bd trustee,

Career Develop Ctr Women, 1979-80; Youth Area Urban league; NAACP. **Honors/Awds:** Dedication Commitment Award, Freedom Inc Youngstown OH, 1972; Outstanding Admin Performance, OH Dept Health Cols OH, 1978; Downtown Improvement Com Service, Youngstown Bd Trade, 1980. **Business Addr:** Executive Director, Metro Housing Authority, 131 W Boardman St, Youngstown, OH 44503, **Business Phone:** (330)744-2161.*

ATKINSON, LEWIS K.
Physician. **Personal:** Born Nov 3, 1924, Georgetown, SC; children: 6. **Educ:** Howard Univ, BA, 1950, MD, 1956. **Career:** Wash Hosp Ctr, attending physician; Howard Univ Hosp, attending physician, instr med, 1961-; Pvt pract, physician. **Orgs:** Nat Med Asn; Medico-Chirurgical Soc DC; Howard Univ Med Alumni Asn; Daniel Hale Williams Reading Club; DC Med Soc; Am Diabetes Asn; Am Soc Clin Endocrinol; Am Col Endocrinol; Am Col Physicians; Am Soc Internal Med; Am Med Asn. **Military Serv:** AUS, s/sgt, 1943-46. *

ATKINSON, REGINA ELIZABETH
Social worker. **Personal:** Born May 13, 1952, New Haven, CT; daughter of Samuel Griffin and Virginia Louise Atkinson Griffin. **Educ:** Univ Conn, BA, 1974; Atlanta Univ, MSW, 1978. **Career:** Palm Beach Co Health Dept, med social worker, 1978-81; Glades Gen Hosp, dir social serv, 1981-95; Palm Beach County Community Servs, sr servs, case mgr, 1996-. **Orgs:** AHA Soc Hosp Soc Work Directors; Comn Action Coun; Fla Pub Health Asn Inc; Glades Area Asn Retarded Citizens; Nat Asn Black Social Workers Inc; Nat Asn Social Workers Inc; Fla Asn Health & Social Serv; The Nat Chamber Com Women Inc; Nat Asn Female Exec; Area Agency Aging Adv Coun, Nat Asn Advan Colored People. **Honors/Awds:** American Legion Award; Whitney Young Fellowship; DHEW Pub Health Serv Scholarship. **Home Addr:** 525 12 SW 10th St, Belle Glade, FL 33430. **Business Addr:** Case Manager, Palm Beach County Community Services, 2916 State Rd 15, Belle Glade, FL 33430, **Business Phone:** (561)992-4808.

ATLAS, DR. JOHN WESLEY
Educator. **Personal:** Born Aug 15, 1941, Lake Providence, LA; married Arthurlean Johnson; children: Mavis, Candace, Jamila & Amina. **Educ:** Grambling Col, BS, 1963; Wayne State Univ, MEd, 1968, EdD, 1972. **Career:** LA Schs, music teacher, 1963-65; Detroit Pub Schs, music teacher, 1965-67, guidance counr, 1967-70, asst prin, 1970-72; Gov State Univ, prof, 1972-73; Oakland Univ, assoc prof, 1973. **Orgs:** Am Personnel & Guidance Asn; Asn Non-White Concerns Personnel & Guidance; Omega Psi Phi Frat; Topical Conf Career Educ for Handicapped Indiv, 1979. **Special Achievements:** Publ "Consulting, Affecting Change for Minority Students" Jour ofNon-White Concerns in Pers & Guidance Wash, DC 1975; publ "Effects ofCrystal & Bolles on Vocational Choice" Jour of Emp Counsel Wash, DC 1977;publ "Career Planning Need of Unemployed Minority Persons" Jour of EmpCounseling Wash, DC 1978; book chap "The Role of Counseling & Guidance inFacilitating Career Educ Needs of Handicapped". *

ATTAWAY, JOHN DAVID
Educator. **Personal:** Born Jan 30, 1929, Chicago, IL; son of Allen Attaway Sr and Pearl Holloway; married Paquita Anna Harris. **Educ:** Cent State Col, BS, 1950; Babson Col, MBA, 1956; George Washington Univ, DBA, 1979. **Career:** US Dept Com, secy's staff, policy analyst, 1970-72; US Gen Servs Admin, Off Civil Rights, exec dir, 1973; US Dept Labor OFCCP, chief policy & procedures, 1984; Univ DC, Dept Bus Mgt, prof, 1984-97; Univ MD Univ Col, prof, 1997-. **Orgs:** Kappa Alpha Psi, 1948-; pres, Attaway Assocs, 1978-; chmn, The Dr Chester E Harris Med Stud Fund Inc, 1978-; Sigma Pi Phi, Epsilon Boule, 1985-. **Honors/Awds:** Grass Roots Award, Outstanding Civic Work, DC Fedr Civic Asns Inc, 1970; Public Service Award, Gen Serv Adminr, 1976. **Military Serv:** AUS, battalion commdr, 3rd Armored Div. **Home Addr:** 3127 Appleton St NW, Washington, DC 20008. **Business Phone:** (301)282-3718.*

ATTLES, ALVIN A., JR.
Basketball coach, basketball player, basketball executive. **Personal:** Born Nov 7, 1936, Newark, NJ; married Wilhemina Rice; children: Alvin III & Erica. **Educ:** NC A&T Univ. **Career:** Basketball player (retired); Philadelphia Warriors, 1960-62; San Francisco Warriors, 1962-71; Golden State Warriors, guard, coach, 1970-83, gen mgr, 1983-89, vpres & asst gen mgr, currently. **Honors/Awds:** Warriors all-time winningest coach; NBA Championship, 1974-75; two divtitles, 1974-76; inducted, Bay Area Sports Hall of Fame, 1993. **Special Achievements:** First African-American coaches in the NBA. *

ATWATER, STEPHEN DENNIS
Football player. **Personal:** Born Oct 28, 1966, Chicago, IL; married Letha; children: Stephen Jr, DiAndre & Paris. **Educ:** Univ Ark, BS, bus admin, 1989. **Career:** Football player (retired) Denver Broncos, safety, 1989-98; NY Jets, 1999-2000. **Honors/Awds:** All-SW Hons; All-American Hons; Pro Bowl, 1990-98; NFL 1990s All- Decade Team; Ring of Fame at Invesco Field at Mile High; Super Bowl championship, 1997-98; Broncos Ring of Fame, 2005.

ATWATER, DR. TONY
Educator. **Personal:** Born Jan 1, 1952, Nashville, TN. **Educ:** Va Western Community Col, AAS, 1972; Hampton Univ, BA, mass media arts, 1973; Mich State Univ, PhD, commun res, 1983; Harvard Univ, Grad Sch Educ, mgt develop prog cert, 1995, inst mgt leadership educ cert, 2001, inst educ mgt cert, 2002; Carnegie Mellon Univ, HJ Heinz Sch Pub Policy & Mgt, col mgt prog, 1996. **Career:** WTOY Radio, Roanoke, VA, asst news dir & reporter, 1971-72; WSLC Radio, Roanoke, VA, news reporter, 1973-74; WPVR-FM Radio, Roanoke, VA, news dir, 1975-76; WSET-TV, Lynchburg, VA, assignment ed, news reporter, 1976-78; Va Polytech Inst & State Univ, Blacksburg, VA, radio & TV specialist, 1978-79; Mich State Univ, teaching asst & instr, 1982-82, from asst prof to assoc prof, 1983-91, asst dir, 1988-91; Rutgers Univ, New Burnswick, NJ, chairperson & prof, dept jour & mass media, 1991-94; Univ Conn, spec asst to provost & vpres acad affairs, 1994-95; Univ Toledo, prof commun & assoc vpres acad affairs, 1995-99; Northern Ky Univ, dean, col prof studies & educ, 1999-2001; Youngstown State Univ, provost vpres acad affairs, 2001-05; Ind Univ Pa, pres, currently. **Orgs:** Am Asn Higher Educ; Int Commun Asn; Broadcast Educ Asn; Soc Prof Journalists; Ky Gov Task Force on Youth & Substance Abuse Prev; bd trustee, Northwest Ohio Pub TV Found; Leadership Cincinnati, 2000-01; adv bd, KeyBank, OH; Youngstown Bus Incubator; past pres, Asn Educ Jour & Mass Commun; adv bd, Pa Econ League Southwestern Pa; bd dir, Int Stud Exchange Prog; Am Coun Edu's Comn Lifelong Learning; bd dir, Ind County Chamber Com; Ind County Ctr Econ Opers; Rotary Club Ind; Greater Ind Revitalization Steering Comt; Ind County Tourist Bur Bd. **Honors/Awds:** Received numerous awards including: Baskett Mosse Faculty Award, AEJMC, 1987. **Special Achievements:** Published approximately thirty refereed journal articles on mass media.

AUBERT, ALVIN BERNARD
Educator, poet, short story writer. **Personal:** Born Mar 12, 1930, Lutcher, LA; son of Lucille Roussel Aubert and Albert Aubert; divorced; children (previous marriage): Stephenie; married Bernadine Tenant; children: Miriam & Deborah (deceased). **Educ:** Southern Univ, BA 1959; Univ MI, MA 1960; Univ Ill, post-grad study, 1963-64, 1966-67. **Career:** Educator (retired); Woodrow Wilson Nat Fel,1959-60; Southern Univ, instr, 1960-62, asst prof, 1962-65, assoc prof, 1970-74, prof, 1974-79; Nat Endowment for the Arts Creative Writing Fel Grant,1973, 1981; CCLM Editors Fel, 1979; Univ OR, prof, summer, 1970; State Univ NY, Fredonia, assoc prof, 1970-74, prof, 1974-79; Obsidian, ed & publ, 1975-85; Wayne State Univ, prof 1979-93, Ctr Black Studies, interim dir,1988-90, Dept African Studies, interim chmn, 1990-93. **Orgs:** Book rev, Lib Jour, 1972-74; eval, NY State Poets in Schs, 1974; adv ed, Drama & Theater Mag, 1973-75; adv ed, Black Box, 1974; adv ed, Gumbo, 1976-78; adv ed, Collaloo, 1977; ed & pub, Obsidian, Black Literature in Rev, 1975-85; Col Lang Asn; bd dir, Coord Coun Lit Mags, 1983-86; Black Theater Network; Modern Lang Asn Am; Nat Coun Teachers Eng; African Heritage Studies Asn; Nat Coun Black Studies. **Honors/Awds:** Liberal Arts Scholarship, 1957-59; Bread Loaf Scholarship in Poetry, Bread Loaf Writers' Conf, 1968; A Directory of Am Poets; Black Am Writers Past & Present; Contemporary Poets of the English Lang; The Callaloo Award, Callaloo Mag, 1988; The Oxford Companion to African Am Lit; Writer's Voice Award, YMCA, 2000; Activist for the Humanities Award, Xavier Univ of LA, 2001. **Special Achievements:** Poetry books, "Against the Blues" 1972; "Feeling Through" 1975; "New andSelected Poems" 1985; "If Winter Come: Collected Poems" 1994; "HarlemWrestler" 1995; play "Home From Harlem," 1986; "Piney Brown" 1996; listedBroadside Authors & Artists. *

AUBESPIN, MERVIN R.
Journalist. **Personal:** Born Jun 30, 1937, Opelousas, LA; son of Henry and Blanche Sittig Earsery; divorced; children: Eleska. **Educ:** Tuskegee Inst, BS, 1958; Ind State Univ, postgrad, 1960; Columbia Univ, attended 1972; Univ Louisville, KY, postgrad work, 1973. **Career:** Journalist (retired); Courier Jour, artist, 1965-72, dir minority recruitment, spec asst exec ed, reporter, 1972-84; Louisville Times, artist, dir minority recruitment, spec asst exec ed; The Courier-Jour Newspapers, assoc ed develop; Nat Asn Black Journalists, pres, 1983-85, vpres & reg dir; Courier Jour, assoc ed develop, 1969-02. **Orgs:** Pres & founder, Louisville Asn Black Commun, 1979-80; dir reg, 5 Nat Asn Black Journalist, 1979-81; bd mem, Overseers Bellarmine Col, 1980-81; vpres, 1981-83, pres, 1983-, Nat Asn Black Journalist; Minorities Comn Am Soc Newspaper Ed, 1985; chair, Minorities Comn & Human Resource Comn; The Am Soc & Newspaper; co-chn, Indust Wide Minority Issues Steering Comt, 1985-; chmn, Ida B Wells Jury, 1986-88; bd mem, Mid Am Press Inst, 1995; Sch Journ, Howard Univ, Univ KY, Western KY Univ; adv bd, Black Col Commun Asn. **Honors/Awds:** Leadership Award, W End Cath Coun, 1970; Unity Award, Econ Reporting Lincoln Univ, 1980; Outstanding Achievement Award, Louisville Br Nat Asn Black Journalist, 1980; Louisville Man Year Award, Louisville Defender Newspaper, 1980; Unity Award, Civil Rights Reporting Lincoln Univ, 1981; Outstanding Achievement Award, Nat Asn Black Journalists, 1981; Achievement Award, Nat Asn Advan Colored People, 1981; Special Achievement Award, Reporting Concerns Blacks; Leadership Award, Louisville Asn Black Communicators, 1981; Meritorious Service Award, Southern Reg Press Inst, 1985; Distinguished Service Award, Inst Journ Educ, 1985; Mary HDunn Lecturship, Univ Ill; Ida B Wells Award, Nat Asn Black Journalists, 1990; Distinguished Service Award, Asn Sch Jour & Mass Commun, 1991; Mervin Aubespin Award, Black Col Commun Assn, 1991; Nat Asn Black Journalist Region VI, Hall Fame, 1994; E Ky Jour, Hall Fame, 1995. **Special Achievements:** First African American hired as a news artist by the Courier-Journal in 1967. **Military Serv:** AUS, E-4, 2 yrs. **Home Addr:** 733 Southwestern Pkwy, Louisville, KY 40211. *

AUDAIN, LINZ
Educator, lawyer, physician. **Personal:** Born Jul 13, 1959, Port-au-Prince, Haiti; daughter of Fenelon B and Georgette Nicoleau. **Educ:** Southern Col, BA, 1979; Univ Miami, MBA & MA, 1981; Florida Intl Univ, MSM, 1982; Univ Chicago, JD, 1987; Duke Univ, PhD, 1991; Howard Univ, MD, 1997; George Wash Univ, internal med, resident. **Career:** Var univs, part time instr econ, 1981-86; Hartunian, Futterman & Howard, atty & assoc, 1987-88; Loyola Univ Chicago, instr econ, 1988-89; Wash Col Law, The Am Univ, asst & assoc prof law, 1989-95; The Mandate Corp, chief exec officer, 1992; Northwestinternists com. **Orgs:** Am Bar Asn; Ill Bar Asn; Nat Bar Asn; Hispanic Nat Bar Asn; Law & Soc Asn; Am Econ Asn; Am Soc Law & Med; Radio & TV News Dir Asn; Am Law & Econs Asn; Am Med Asn; Nation Med Asn. **Special Achievements:** Publications: Co-author, Business Statistics of the United States, Bernan Press, 2001; Foreign Trade of the United States, Bernan Press, 2001; Cocain use as an Abdominal Pregnancy Risk Factor, Journal of Natl Med Assn 1998; Gender and Trauma in the Near-Death Experience: an Epidemiological and Theoretical Analysis, Journal of Near-Death Studies; NDE's and a Theory of the Extraneuronal Hyperspace, Journal of Near-Death Studies. CLS, Feminism, L & Ec and the Veil of Intellectual Tolerance, Hofstra Law Review; The Econs of Law-Related Labor vs Judicial Careers, Amer Univ Law Review, 1992; Of Posner & Newton & Twenty-First Century Laws: and Econ, Loyola Law Review, 1990; Critical Cult Law & Econs, Ind Law Jour, 1995; Prof of the Yr, Am Univ, 1995. *

AUGMON, STACEY ORLANDO
Basketball player. **Personal:** Born Aug 1, 1968, Pasadena, CA; son of Vernett. **Educ:** Univ Nev, Las Vegas, attended 1991. **Career:** Basketball player (retired), basketball coach; Atlanta Hawks, forward, 1991-96; Detroit Pistons, 1996; Portland Blazers, 1997-2001; Charlotte Hornets, guard & forward, 2002; New Orleans Hornets, guard & forward, 2003-04; Orlando Magic, forward, 2004-06; Denver Nuggets, player develop coach, 2007-. **Honors/Awds:** Bronze Medal, Olympic Games, US Basketball Team, 1988; NBA All-Rookie first team, 1992. **Special Achievements:** NBA Draft, First round pick, No 9, 1991. **Business Addr:** Player Development Coach, Denver Nuggets, 1000 Chopper Circle, Denver, CO 80204, **Business Phone:** (303)405-1100.

AUGUSTE, DONNA M.
Businessperson, chief executive officer, social worker. **Personal:** Born Sep 11, 1958, Beaumont, TX; daughter of Willa Mae Fruge. **Educ:** Univ Calif, Berkeley, BS, elec eng & comput sci, 1980; Carnegie-19 Mellon Univ, grad studies, comput sci, 1984. Aspen Inst, Henry Crown Fel Prog. **Career:** Intelli corp, engr, 1986-90; Apple Comput, eng mgr, 1990-93; US W Advan Technologies, sr dir, multimedia systs eng & develop, 1994-96; Freshwater Software Inc, found & chief exec officer, 1996-2001; Leave Little Rm Found, found & chief exec officer, 2001-; LLR Gospel Music, founder, pres & chief exec officer, currently. **Orgs:** Inst Elec & Electronic Engrs Internet Comput Ed Bd; Colo Comn Sci &Technol. **Honors/Awds:** Outstanding Women in Business Award, Denver Bus Jour, 2000; Lifetime Contribution Award, Colo Women Technol, 2000; Women in Technology Inter Nat Hall of Fame; Outstanding Woman in Technology Award, Golden Torch, 2001; Colorado Woman Technologist of the Year, World Wide Web Radio Show; Black Pioneer in Business Award Honorees, Colorado Black Chamber Com, 2003. **Business Addr:** Founder, Chief Executive Officer, Leave Little Room Foundation, 9350 Paradise Lane, Broomfield, CO 80020, **Business Phone:** (303)449-5024.

AUGUSTINE, HILTON H
Chief executive officer, chairperson. **Personal:** Married; children: 4. **Career:** Int Bus Mach, mfg mgr, 1985-88; Global Mgt Syst Inc, chmn & chief exec officer, 1988-. **Business Addr:** Chairman, Chief Executive Officer, Global Management System Inc, 2201 Wisconsin Ave Suite 300, Washington, DC 20007, **Business Phone:** (202)471-4674.

AUGUSTINE, MATTHEW
Executive. **Educ:** Univ La-Lafayette; Harvard Univ, Cambridge, MBA. **Career:** RBA Bd Bus, secy; Eltrex Industs Inc, chief exec officer & pres, 1976-. **Orgs:** Regional vice-chair & dir, Bus Coun NY State Inc. **Special Achievements:** Co is ranked 95th on Black Enterprise's list of Top 100 Indust/Serv Co, 1993. **Military Serv:** USMC, 1966-68. **Business Phone:** (585)454-6100.*

AUGUSTUS, FRANKLIN J P
Airplane pilot. **Personal:** Born Mar 6, 1950, New Orleans, LA; son of Henry Jr and Annie Cooper; children: Brandi Augustus. **Educ:** NC State Univ; AUS, Military Police, MPI, CID Narcotic Agent; NCSBI Sch & Conf. **Career:** Terrebonne Parish Sheriff's Off, reserve dep, instr acad; New Orleans Recreation Dept, LA, head martial arts dept; Franklin JP Augustus Detective Agency

Inc, New Orleans, LA, pres; Orleans Parish Civil Sheriff's Off, reserve duty; Super Air Shows Int Inc, New Orleans, LA, pres. **Orgs:** Pres, Black Wing Pilots Asn; Experimental Aircraft Asn, New Orleans & Slidell Area Chapters of the Experimental Aircraft Asn, Negro Airmen Int, Int Aerobatic Club, Int Coun Air Shows; charter, Cajun Chapter No 72 Int Aerobatic Club, Crescent City Aviators; accident prevention counr, FAA, 1985-. **Honors/Awds:** Aerobatic license, FAA Unlimited Low Level; private license earned 1977; commercial license earned 1978; flight instructor certificate, 1979; certified in scuba, NOSD School, 1977-; Master of Martial Arts; movie stuntman; logged over 8000 flight hours. **Military Serv:** AUS, sgt. **Business Phone:** (504)897-2718.

AULD, ALBERT MICHAEL
Artist. **Personal:** Born Aug 15, 1943, Kingston, Jamaica; married Rose A Powttatan; children: Ian, Alexei & Kiros. **Educ:** Howard Univ, BFA, 1966, MFA, 1980. **Career:** Lindo, Norman, Craig & Kummel, designer illusr, 1966-67; Nat Ed Assoc, designer illusr, 1967-73; US Dept Agr Grad Sch, instr, 1967; Sidwell Friends Sch, art teacher, 1973-77; Howard Univ, Dept Art, lectr, 1977-82; Dist Columbia Pub Schs, 1982-; Auld Powhatan, co-founder; writer & researcher on Indigenous Caribbean cultures; Vietnam Metro Sta, 1982; Chickhnominy Tribal Ctr; Jamestown Festival Park, VA, sculptural installations, 1995. **Orgs:** Co-founder & dir, A & B Assoc Adv, 1973-79; co-founder & dir, Opus 2 Gallery, 1973-77; self-syndicated published comic strip, writer & illusr, 1967-72; freelance Ill designer, The Design Co, 1977-; cultural chmn, Caribbean Am Intercutl Orgn, 1975-79; Africobra Nat Artists Coop, 1977-; Int Sculpture Conf, 1983-; Nat Art Educrs Asn, 1984-; Artists Equity, Nat Conf Artists, 1986-; mem bd dirs, Fondo del Sol Museum & Cultural Ctr, 1986-; chmn, Humanities Bd Fondo del Sol Museum, Wash DC; chmn, Visual Arts Dept, Duke Ellington Sch Arts. **Honors/Awds:** Research Grant, Cafrit Z Found; Research Grant, DC Comm Arts. **Special Achievements:** Published articles: "Taiano Survival In Caribbean: A Focus on Jamaica," "Dead Languages?", article on Africobra Artists Black Colegian 1967-, exhibited widely as a sculptor 1967-, Folkloric Article titled Ananesem pub in Jamarca Journal 1983, lectured on African Retentions in Ams Oberlin, Smithsonian Inst, Nat Conf Artists, NY Univ, Bronx Museum, NBCHs Tony Brown at Daybreak, local & overseas radio networks, Sculptural Works acclaimed by NY Times, Wash Post, Wash Times, lecturer on Indigenous people Caribbean, Howard Univ, NY Museum Natural History, etc. **Home Addr:** 1519 Monroe St NW, Washington, DC 20010.

AUSBROOKS, BETH NELSON
Educator. **Personal:** Born May 18, 1930, Philadelphia, PA; daughter of Phoebe Novotny Nelson and David Nelson; children: Dawna Rogers & Gregory Rogers. **Educ:** Howard Univ, BA, WA, DC, 1952, MA, 1956, PhD, 1971. **Career:** Howard Univ, Wash, DC, assoc prof, 1971-72; Univ NC, Chapel Hill, assoc prof, 1972-74; Univ Md, Baltimore, MD, assoc prof, 1974-75; Univ DC, Dept Urban Affairs, Social Sci & Social Work, prof, 1975-. **Orgs:** Minority Group Review Comt, Nat Inst Mental Health, 1975-79; Bd Dirs, Provident Hosp, Baltimore, MD, 1980-83; resident adv bd, DC Dept Housing, 1987-; extramural assoc, Nat Inst Health, 1999; Am Polit Sci Orgn; CounUniv Inst Urban Affairs; Am Sociol Asn; Nat Conf Black Polit Scientists, UDC Chap, Phi Delta Kappa. **Honors/Awds:** Scholar-In-Residence, Fanon Res Ctr, Martin Luther King Med Sch, Los Angeles, CA, 1983. **Home Addr:** 4986 April Day Garth, Columbia, MD 21044, **Home Phone:** (301)596-3869. **Business Addr:** Professor, University of the District of Columbia, Department of Urban Affairs & Social Science & Social Work, 4200 Conn Ave NW Bldg 41 Room 400-05, Washington, DC 20008, **Business Phone:** (202)274-5795.

AUSBY, ELLSWORTH AUGUSTUS
Artist, educator. **Personal:** Born Apr 5, 1942, Portsmouth, VA; married Jemillah; children: Amber, Andra, Dawn, Kalif. **Educ:** Pratt Inst, 1961; Sch Visual Art, BFA, 1965. **Career:** Sch Visual Arts, instr, 1979-; One man shows: Cinque Gallery, 1970; Artist House, 1973; Soho Ctr Visual Arts, 1975; Reviews: "Art in Am", 1970; "Barbra Rose", 1970; "Henri Ghent", 1974; "Black Creations", 1972; "The Sch Weekly News by April Kingsley", 1975; NY Coun Arts, CAPS fel painting, 1980. **Honors/Awds:** Federal Artist Grant, CETA Title VI, 1978. **Special Achievements:** American representative at "FESTAC" 2nd world Black Arts & Cultural Festival Lagos, Nigeria, 1977; exhibit the US Mission to the United Nations, 1978; "Rock Paper Scissors" Port of Auth Publ Works Proj, "Space Odyssey" mural Howard Johnsons Queens Village, NY, 1980; "Universal Units" exhibition at the Afro-American Historical & Cultural Museum, Philadelphia, 1979; "Afro-American Abstraction", Long Island, NY. **Business Addr:** Instructor, School of Visual Arts, 209 E 23 St, New York, NY 10010-3994.*

AUSTIN, DR. BOBBY WILLIAM
School administrator, writer, lecturer. **Personal:** Born Dec 29, 1944, Bowling Green, KY; son of Herschel and Mary E; married Joy L Ford; children: Sushama Meredith Cleva, Julian Sanjay Ford, Leah Mary Sajova & Aviana JoyLalita. **Educ:** Western Ky Univ, BA, econs & sociol, 1966; Fisk Univ, MA, sociol, 1968; McMaster Univ, PhD, 1972; Harvard Univ, dipl, 1986. **Career:** Univ DC, exec asst to the pres, asst bd trustees; Georgetown Univ, asst prof, 1971-72; Georgetown summer term, Dept Sociol, chmn, 1972; Nat Urban League, Urban League Review, founder & ed; Austin Ford Assocs, pres; W.K.Kellogg Found, prog dir, 1986-98; Village Found, pres & chief exec officer, currently. **Orgs:** Nat Coun Accreditation Teachers Educ; Am Soc Asn; Groves Conf Marriage & Family; Alpha Phi Alpha Frat; Nat Cong Black Prof; Voice; Alphi Phi Omega Nat Serv Fraternity; Peoples Congregational Church; Hannover Proj, Ger; Acad Coun UN Systs; Global Co-Operation Better World; UN Asn, DC Chap; Mahatma M.K. Gandhi fel, Am Acad Polit & Social Sci; fel Kellogg Nat; Nat Housing Trust; Nat Inst Urban Wildlife. **Special Achievements:** Author of numerous publications; paper presented at the Association for the Study of Afro-American Life & History, New York, 1973; Smithsonian Inst, 1976; published National Black Opinion ACRA Inc, 1977; co-author of Repairing the Breach; listed in Who's Who in Black America, Outstanding Young Men of America and Men of Achievement. *

AUSTIN, CARRIE M.
Government official. **Personal:** Married Lemuel (died 1994); children: 7. **Career:** US Rep Mel Reynolds, dep dist dir second Cong dist; City Chicago,alderman, 34th ward, 1994-; State Cent comt woman, 2000-. **Orgs:** Logos Baptist Assembly Church; Committee mem on Finance, Budget, Zoning, Housing, Energy. **Special Achievements:** Selected as one of Chicago's 100 Most Influential Women. **Business Addr:** Alderman 34th Ward, City of Chicago, 507 W 111th St, Chicago, IL 60628, **Business Phone:** (773)928-6961.

AUSTIN, DALLAS
Executive. **Personal:** Born Dec 29, 1970, Columbus, GA. **Career:** Rowdy Records, pres/chief exec officer, 1992-; Albums: "Push the Button", Sugababes; "Ugly", Sugababes; "Trick Me", Kelis; "Blowin Me Up", JC Chasez; "Keep It Down", Kelis; "Secret", Madonna; "Sanctuary", Madonna; "Don't Stop", Madonna; "Survival", Madonna; "The Power of Good-Bye, Dallas' Low End Mix" Madonna; "Your Honesty", Madonna; "In Demand", Texas; "Stuck", Stacie Orrico; "Secrets", Eternal; "Cool", Gwen Stefani; "Crash", Gwen Stefani; "Danger Zone", Gwen Stefani; "Hit 'Em Up Style, Oops, Blu Cantrell?; "Don't Let Me Get Me", P!nk; "Just like a Pill", P!nk; "Left Outside Alone", Anastacia; "Sick & Tired", Anastacia; "Creep", TLC; "Case of the Fake People", TLC; "Unpretty", TLC; "Silly Ho", TLC; "If They Knew", TLC; "Shout", TLC; Warner Bros Studios, producer, currently. **Honors/Awds:** Named Billboard Producer of the Year, 1991. **Special Achievements:** Wrote and produced the following: TLC's "Creep," Madonna's "Secret," Monica's "Don't Take It Personal"; producer of the film Drumline for 20th Century Fox, 2002. **Business Phone:** (818)954-3000.

AUSTIN, DR. DEBRA
Chancellor (education), college administrator. **Educ:** Mich State Univ, BA, eng; Univ Fla, MA, eng; Fla State Univ, Master's Degree, bus admin; Fla State Univ, Doctorate, Higher Educ; Flagler Col, Hon Doctorate. **Career:** Lake-Sumter Community Col, eng instr; Tallahassee Community Col; Florida State Univ, asst vpres acad affairs & provost; State Univ System Fla,chancellor, 2003-05; Fla A & M Univ, provost & vpres acad affairs, 2005-; chancellor col univ, 2003-. **Orgs:** Bd dirs, Tallahassee Mem Health Care, 2003-04. **Business Addr:** Provost & Vice President of Academic Affairs, Florida A&M University, Office of the Provost and Vice President for Academic Affairs, Foote-Hilyer Administration Ctr Suite 301, Tallahassee, FL 32307, **Business Phone:** (850)599-3276.

AUSTIN, DORIS
College president. **Career:** Tallahassee Community Col, interim pres, currently. **Business Addr:** Interim President, Tallahassee Community College, 444 Appleyard Dr, Tallahassee, FL 32304.

AUSTIN, DR. ERNEST AUGUSTUS
Physician, educator. **Personal:** Born Nov 26, 1932, Brooklyn, NY; son of Augustin Austin and Elrica Mildred Davidson; married Margaret P Byrd, Aug 24, 1957; children: Vivian, Jean & Alan. **Educ:** St Johns Univ, BS, 1953; Howard Univ, MD, 1957. **Career:** Physician, Educr(retired); Suny, clin instr surg, 1962-69; Fordham Hosp, chief surg, 1966-69; Bowman Gray Sch Med, asst prof surg, 1969-72;Reynolds Meml Hosp, dir surg, 1969-72; Univ MD Sch Med, asst prof surg, 1972-79; Provident Hosp, chief surg, 1972-73; Univ MD Inst Emergency MedShock Traum Ctr, chief surg & traumatology, 1974-76, 1978-79; Univ MD Hosp, dir emergency serv, 1977-78; Cooper Med Ctr Camden NJ, chief traumatology, dir emergency med serv, 1979-84; CMDNJ-Rutgers Med Sch, assoc prof surg,1979-84; Prudential Insurance, Horsham, PA, dir med serv, 1989-92,1994-97; Intracorp, Plymouth Meeting, PA, sr physician adv, 1992-93. **Orgs:** Founding mem, Am Trauma soc; bd dir, Am Cancer Soc Forsyth Unit NC; bddir, Nat Found Forsyth-Stokes Chap NC; bd dir, Am Trauma Soc MD Chapt; dipl Am Bd of Surg; fel Am Col Surgeons. **Honors/Awds:** Z Smith Reynolds Found Grant; ed bd, "Trauma: Clinical Update for Surgeons", 1983-86; vis prof & lectr, numerous universities & hosps, US & Canada; "Thoracic Injuries," Camden County Med Soc, 1982; "Left Atrial Rupture Secondary to Blast Injury," Journal Med Soc of NJ, 1985. **Special Achievements:** Published 2 articles in Journal: "Royal Col Surgeons", 1975; pub "Critical Care Med Journal", 1979; author & publisher, "The Black Amer Stamp Album", 1988. **Home Addr:** 131 Paisley Pl, Hainesport, NJ 08036, **Home Phone:** (609)265-2928. *

AUSTIN, ISAAC EDWARD
Basketball coach, basketball player. **Personal:** Born Aug 18, 1969, Gridley, CA; married Denise, Dec 24, 1992. **Educ:** Ariz State Univ, attended 1991. **Career:** Basketball Player (retired), Basketball Coach; Utah Jazz Ctr, 1991-93; Philadelphia 76ers, 1993-94; Tuborg Izmir, Turkey, 1995-96; Miami Heat, 1996-97, 1998; Los Angeles Clippers, 1997; Orlando Magic, 1998-99; Wash Wizards Ctr, 1999-2000; Vancouver Grizzlies Ctr, 2000-01; Memphis Grizzlies Ctr, 2001-02; Utah Snowbears, coach, 2004-05. **Honors/Awds:** NBA Most Improved Player, 1996-97.

AUSTIN, JAMES N, JR. **See AUSTIN, JIM.**

AUSTIN, JIM (JAMES N AUSTIN, JR.)
President (organization). **Personal:** Married Gloria. **Career:** Am Express, mgr; Austin Co, owner & pres, currently. **Business Addr:** Owner, President, Austin Co, 2401 Scott Ave, Fort Worth, TX 76103-2228, **Business Phone:** (817)923-9305.

AUSTIN, JOYCE PHILLIPS
Lawyer. **Personal:** Born Sep 10, 1923, New York, NY; daughter of Fitzgerald and Kathleen Miller; married Rodman W Austin, Mar 20, 1945 (deceased). **Educ:** Hunter Col, BA, 1943; Fordham Univ Sch Law, JD, 1945. **Career:** Lawyer (retired); Off Price Stabilization, atty adv, 1951-53; NY State Dept Comn, exec secy, Women's Coun, 1956-57, asst dep comnr, 1957-59; City NY, asst mayor, 1959-65; Off Econ Opportunity, exec asst regional dir, 1966-68; Sheltering Arms C Serv, asst dir, 1968-75; Fedn Protestant Welfare Agencies Inc, exec vpres, 1975-86. **Orgs:** Episcopal Diocese NY, Bishop's Cross, 1983; trustee, Helen Keller, Worldwide; bd mem, Consortium Endowed Episcopal Parisher; Am Bar Asn; NY Lawyers Asn; Fordham Law Alumni Asn; Nat Asn Advan Colored People; Nat Coun Negro Women; Union Black Episcopalians; Cosmopolitan Club; Nat Arts Club. **Honors/Awds:** Keystone Award, Fedn Protestant Welfare Agencies, 1986; Hall of Fame, Hunter Col; John H Finley Award, City Col Alumni Asn. **Home Addr:** 510 E 23rd St, New York, NY 10010, **Home Phone:** (212)674-2903. *

AUSTIN, LUCIUS STANLEY
Newspaper editor. **Personal:** Born Jul 3, 1960, Batesville, MS; son of Sherman E Sr and Glennie V Cox; married Laurie Scott, May 25, 1991; children: Rebekah Hope & Joshua T S. **Educ:** Jackson State Univ, attended 1982; Univ Memphis, BA, journ, 1982; Univ Mo, jour, 1987. **Career:** The Belleville News Democrat, reporter, 1983-84; The St Louis Am, city ed, 1984-85; The Kansas City Times, copy ed, 1985-86, makeup ed, 1986-87; The Kansas City Star, asst bus ed, 1987. **Orgs:** Alpha Phi Alpha Fraternity, 1980-; Nat Asn Black Journalist, 1983-; Kans City Asn Black Journalist, 1985-; Soc Am Bus Ed & Writers, 1992-.

AUSTIN, MARY JANE
School administrator. **Personal:** Born Apr 24, 1935, Orange, NJ; daughter of George W Jr and Louise Margaret Street; married Harry Lester, Dec 21, 1957; children: Sharon Milora & Sherrill Ruth. **Educ:** Newark State Col, BS, 1957; Kean Col, grad work, 1978; Bank St Col Parsons Sch Design, MS, 1983. **Career:** Educator (retired); Elizabeth Pub Sch, art educr, 1953-79; Roosevelt Jr Sch, art consult, 1970-73; Elizabeth Bd Educ, layout artist, 1973-78; William F Halloran Alternative Sch Gifted & Talented, art educr, 1979-87; Irvington Bd Educ, supvr art educ, 1987. **Orgs:** Arts Educr NJ; Nat Art Educ Asn, 1979-86; Independent Orders Foresters, assoc supv & curric develop; Asn Supv & Curric Devel, 1987-89; treasr, Citizen Awareness Group/ Cranford, 1989-90; chairperson, Women's Day, 1989-90; Prin Supvr Asn. **Honors/Awds:** Scholarship Artist, Inst Stockton Col NJ Coun Arts, 1980-81; Art Educator Award, Nat Coun Negro Women Inc, 1981; Governors Award, Govr Teacher Grant NJ State Dept Educ, 1987. **Home Addr:** 15 Wall St, Cranford, NJ 07016.

AUSTIN, PATTI
Singer. **Personal:** Born Aug 10, 1950, Harlem, NY; daughter of Edna and Gordon Austin. **Career:** Albums: End of A Rainbow, 1976; Havana Candy, 1977; Live at the Bottom Line, 1979; Body Language, Every Home Should Have One, 1981; In My Life, 1983; Patti Austin, 1984; Getting Away With Murder, 1985; The Real Me, 1988; Love Is Gonna Getcha, 1990; Carry On, 1991; Live, 1992; That Secret Place, 1994; In & Out of Love, 1998; Street of Dreams, 1999; On the Way to Love, 2001; For Ella, 2002; Avant Gershwin, 2007; TV shows: The Kennedy Center Honors: A Celebration of the Performing Arts, 2001; Pyramid, 2003; Apollo at 70: A Hot Night in Harlem, 2004; Q Prod Inc, currently; Compliations: The Very Best Of Patti Austin, 2001; Collection, 2002; Baby Come To Me & Other Hits, 2003; Intimate Patti Austin, 2007. **Honors/Awds:** Grammy Award for Best Jazz Vocal Album for Avant Gershwin at the 50th annual Grammy Awards. **Special Achievements:** Appeared in several television shows, theatre performances, and stage productions; studio sessions include collaborations with Harry Belafonte, Paul Simon, George

Benson, Quincy Jones, Roberta Flack, Steely Dan, numerous others; duet with James Ingram "Baby Come to Me" topped the charts at #1 USA, #11 UK along with being the theme song to TV soap opera General Hospital, 1983; "How Do You Keep The Music Playing" from the movie Best Friends, nominated for best song Oscar; Nominated for a Nat Asn Advan Colored People Image Award in the category of Outstanding Jazz Artist.

AUSTIN, RAYMOND DEMONT (RAY AUSTIN)
Football player. **Personal:** Born Dec 21, 1974, Lawton, OK. **Educ:** Univ Tenn. **Career:** NY Jets, defensive back, 1997-98; Chicago Bears, defensive, 1998. **Special Achievements:** Acted in 11 commercials. *

AUSTIN, DR. WANDA M
Engineer. **Personal:** Born in New York, NY; daughter of Murry Pompey and Helen; married Wade Austin Jr; children: 2. **Educ:** Franklin & Marshall Col, BA, math, 1975; Univ Pittsburgh, MS, Systs Engineering & math, 1977; Univ Southern Calif, PhD, Systs Engineering, 1987. **Career:** The Aerospace Corp, gen mgr, electronic systs div, 1979-; Engineering & Tech Group, sr vpres, 2001-03; Nat Systs Group, sr vpres, 2004-07, pres & chief exec officer, currently. **Orgs:** Fel Am Inst Aeronaut & Astronaut, 1980-; Nat Acad Engineering, 2008-. **Honors/Awds:** Herndon Black Image Award, Aerospace Corp, 1984; Outstanding Business & Professional, Dollars & Sense, 1993; Outstanding Achievement, Women Aerospace, 1996; Service & Leadership Award, Int Coun Systs Engineering, 1996; Upward Mobility Award, Soc Women Engrs, 2002; Nat Reconnaissance Office Gold Medal, 2004; Women in Technology InterNat Award, 2007. **Special Achievements:** Publ: Austin W & Khoshnevis B, Qualitative Modeling Using Natural Language: An Application in Systems Dynamics; Qualitative Simulation Modeling & Analysis, Springer Verlag, Spring, 1991; First female, first black sr vpres Aerospace Corp's Engineering & Technol Group, 2001; First female, first black President and CEO of major Aerospace company. **Business Addr:** President, Cheif Executive Officer, The Aerospace Corporation, 2350 E El Segundo Blvd, El Segundo, CA 90245-4691, **Business Phone:** (310)336-5000.

AUTRY, DARNELL
Football player. **Personal:** Born Jun 19, 1976, Tempe, AZ. **Educ:** Northwestern Univ. **Career:** Football player (retired); Chicago Bears, running back, 1997; Philadelphia Eagles, running back, 2000. *

AVANT, CLARENCE
Music producer, executive, president (organization). **Personal:** Born in Greensboro, NC. **Career:** Albums: Save the Children, 1973; Joey, 1977; Jason's Lyric, 1994; Motown Records, chmn, 1993; Avant Garde, pres, currently; Interior Music Publ, pres, currently. **Orgs:** Int Mgt Bd, Polygram; Nat Asn Advan Colored People Legal Defense Fund; Pepsi-Cola African-Am Adv Bd. **Honors/Awds:** Lifetime Achievement Award, 1996; Honorary Doctorate, Morehouse Col; Nat Asn Advan Colored People Legal Defense & Educ Fund Awards. **Business Addr:** President, Interior Music Publishing, Los Angeles, CA.

AVENT, JACQUES MYRON
Government official, manager. **Personal:** Born Nov 13, 1940, Washington, DC; son of Charles Alexander Sr (deceased) and Virginia Hartwell (deceased); married Loretta Taylor Avent; children: James E. **Educ:** Howard Univ, BS, 1963. **Career:** Nat Asn Regional Couns, field dir, 1969-71; Nat Urban Coalition, asst dir field opers, 1971-72; NLC USCM, prog mgr, 1972-74; League CA Cities, spec proj assoc, 1974-75; Human Serv Inst, exec dir, 1975; NLC, asst dir mem serv, 1976-77, dir off membership serv, 1977-86; Security Pac Nat Bank, vpres munic finance, 1986-88; City Phoenix, exec asst to city coun, 1989-90, exec asst to city mgr, 1990-92, dep city mgr, 1992-. **Orgs:** Urban Exec Prog, Sloan Sch MIT, 1973; Am Soc Pub Admin, 1978-; bd mem, Nat Forum Black Pub Admin, 1983-; secy, Nat Forum Black Pub Admin, 1985; mem dir, Nat League Cities, Nat Forum Black Pub Admin; bd mem, Phoenix Lisc; adv bd, Phoenix Salvation Army; bd mem, Valley Sun United Way; Cent Ariz Chap, NFBPA; ICMA. **Business Addr:** Deputy City Manager, City Phoenix, 200 W Washington St 12th Fl, Phoenix, AZ 85003.*

AVERY, BYLLYE Y
Association executive, college teacher. **Educ:** Talladega Univ, BA, 1959; Fla State Univ, MEd, 1969; Univ Fl, PhD, 1969; State Univ NY, attended 1990; Bowdoin Col, DHL, 1993; Bates Col, LLD, 1995. **Career:** Avery Inst Social Change, founder; Gainesville Women's Health Ctr & Birthplace, co-founder; Nat Black Women's Health Proj, founder & pres, 1981-91; Columbia Univ, Ctr Bioethics, external adv bd; Mailman Sch Pub Health, clin prof pop & family health, currently. **Orgs:** Fenway Health Ctr, Boston, 2002; bd mem, Global Fund Women; bd mem, Int Women's Health Coalition; bd mem, Boston Women's Health Book Collective; bd mem, Adv Comt Kellogg Int Fel Prog; bd visitors, Tucker Found, Dartmouth Col; Dana Farber Cancer Adv Bd; Charter Adv Comt, Off Res Women's Health, NIH; vis fel, Harvard Sch Pub Health; Am Pub Health Asn; Nat Women's Health Network. **Honors/Awds:** Essence Award, 1989; Gustav O Lienhard Award, Acad Sci Inst Med, 1994; Pres Citation, Am Pub Health Asn, 1995; New Horizons Award, Bus & Prof Women, 1998; Leadership Award, Univ Fla Sch Med, 1998; Grassroots Realist Award, Ga Legis Black Caucus; Dorothy I Height Lifetime Achievement Award; hon degree, Thomas Jefferson Univ; hon degree, Gettysburg Col; hon degree, Bowdoin Col. **Special Achievements:** Author, An Altar of Words: Wisdom, Comfort, and Inspiration for African American Women.

AVERY, CHARLES E
Photographer, writer. **Personal:** Born Jan 1, 1938?. **Educ:** Sch Visual Arts, attended 1964; Germain Sch Photog, attended 1968; Essex Co Col, attended 1974. **Career:** Piscataway Libr, sr asst librn bookmobile, 1988; Piscataway Dept Public Works, traffic asst, 1989; author currently; Books: Everybody Has Feelings/ Todos Tenemos Sentimientos. **Military Serv:** AUS, pfc, 1956-58; Good Conduct Award, 1958. **Business Phone:** (206)323-2187.

AVERY, JAMES L.
Actor. **Personal:** Born Nov 27, 1948, Atlantic City, NJ; married Barbara. **Educ:** Univ Calif, BA, Drama & Literature. **Career:** Fresh Prince of Bel Air, 1990-96; Sparks, 1996; Pepper Ann, 1997; Going Place, 1997; Soul Food, 2000; The Division, 2001; films: Fletch, 1985; Three for the Road, 1987; Night flyers, 1987; Body Cound, 1987; License to Drive, 1988; The Linguini Incident, 1991; Little Miss Millions, 1993; The Brady Bunch Movie, 1995; Spirit Lost, 1996; 12 Bucks, 1998; Out in Fifty, 1999; After Romeo, 1999; Dancing in September, 2000; Honeybee, 2001; Dr Dolittle 2, 2001; Chasing Sunsets, 2001; Wheelmen, 2002; Nancy Drew, 2002; "That '70s Show", 2004; "NYPD Blue", 2004; "Charmed", 2004; "Girlfriends", 2004; "All of Us", 2004; "The Closer", 2005; Think Tank, 2006; Restraining Order, 2006; "The Closer", TNT series; Who's Your Cadd?, Divine Intervention, 2007; "Eli Stone", "His Good Will", "Live with It", 2008; Steppin: The Movie, Let the Game Begin, 2009. **Honors/Awds:** Emmy Award. **Military Serv:** USN, Vietnam War, 1968-69. **Business Phone:** (310)859-0625.*

AVERY, JAMES S
Executive. **Personal:** Born Mar 24, 1923, Cranford, NJ; son of John Henry and Martha Ann Jones; married Joan Showers; children: Sheryl & James Jr. **Educ:** Columbia Univ, BA, 1948, MA, 1949. **Career:** Executive (retired); Cranford NJ H S tchr, 1949-56; Esso Standard Oil, Humble Oil, comt, Retired. rel coord 1956-68; Humble Oil, Exxon Co USA, pub rel mgr, 1968-71; Exxon Co USA, pub affairs mgr, 1971-81, sr pub affairs consult, 1986. **Orgs:** Vice chmn, Nat Campaigns UNCF, 1962-65; vice chmn & chmn, Vpres Task Force Youth Motivation, 1964-67; nat pres & bd chmn, Nat Asn Market Developers, 1964-67; grand basileus, Omega Psi Phi Frat, 1970-73; bd trustees, NY & NJ State Councs Econ Educ, 1975-86; vice chmn, Philadelphia Reg Intro Minorities Engr, 1977-94; vice chmn, Am Pet Insts Offshore Sub-Comt, chmn, NY St Pet Coun, 1978-79; Coun Munic Performance, 1981-83; bd trustees, NJ State Higer Educ Stud Assistance Authority; NJ State Educ Opportunity Fund; bd trustees, Lincoln Univ; Omega Psi Phi Fraternity. **Honors/Awds:** Co-author, 'Book of American City Rankings', 1983; article, 'energy development', NY State Coun for The Soc Studies, 1978; article, 'on oil decontrol', NY State Council on Econ Educ, 1985; several major articles have been published in pamphlet, 1968-72. **Military Serv:** AUS, corp 3 yrs. **Home Addr:** 389-B Orrington Lane, Monroe Township, NJ 08831. **Business Addr:** District Representative, Omega Psi Phi Fraternity Inc, 389B Orrington Lane, Monroe Township, NJ NJ 08831, **Business Phone:** (609)409-1365.

AVERY-BLAIR, LORRAINE
Banker. **Personal:** Divorced; children: Nina, Lanita, Martina. **Educ:** Univ Wis. **Career:** First Financial Bank, sr vpres, currently. **Orgs:** Pres, bd dirs, Woodland Girl Scouts Coun; pres & bd mem, WI Automated Clearing House, WACHA; bd chair, EFTI & Access 24 ILL Regional Electronic Funds Network; bd vis, Univ WI, Stevens Point; adv comn, Tyme Regional Electronic Funds Network; pres, Zonta, Central WI Chap; United Way Campaign for Portage County, chair; Accountability Measures, governor's task force, Univ WI, 1993-. **Honors/Awds:** Am Best & Brightest Bus Women, Dollars & Sense Mag, 1993; Outstanding Women Color Educ Award, Univ Wis. *

AVILES, DORA
Educator. **Personal:** Born Oct 12, 1960, Puerto Cortes, Honduras; daughter of Juan Aviles; widowed; children: Karima Raimundi, Atrion Raimundi & Crayg Springer. **Educ:** Lehman Col. **Career:** Bronx Community Col, Stud Govt Activies, secy, 1991-93; Citizen's Adv Bur, head teacehr infant, toddler rm, 1995-2000; City Univ NY, Lehman Col, Res Found, admin asst, asst educ, res asst. **Orgs:** Network Orgn Bronx Bus Women, 1995-; bd mem, NW Bronx Neighborhood Orgn, 1997-; bd mem, Youth Comt, 2000-02, Bronx Community Bd-7; COBRA, 2000-; bd mem, Truman High Leadership Team, 2000-02; bd mem, PS 94 Leadership Team, 2000-02. **Honors/Awds:** Community Service Award, Bronx Community Col; United HS Parents Federation Award; Service Award, Parents Asn; Recognition Award, Bronx Community Bd-7. **Home Addr:** 3351 Reservoir Oval W Suite 2A, Bronx, NY 10467, **Home Phone:** (718)325-1825.

AWKARD, LINDA NANLINE
Lawyer. **Personal:** Born Nov 21, 1948, Harrisonburg, VA; daughter of Joseph C Jr and Julita C; married Edward C Maddox Jr, Oct 6, 1989; children: Edward C Maddox III. **Educ:** Fla State Univ, BA, BS, chem, 1970; Fordham Univ Sch Law, JD, 1978, Harvard Law Sch, grad cert, 1982. **Career:** Pan Am Airways, int flight attendant, 1970-79; Legal Servs Corp, spec asst pres, 1979-83; Awkard & Assocs, owner, pres, 1984-. **Orgs:** NY State Bar Asn, 1979-; Am Bar Asn, 1979-; comt mem, Nat Bar Asn, 1979-; Nat Bus League, 1984-. **Honors/Awds:** NBL Merit Citation, Nat Bus League, 1991. **Special Achievements:** Founder of one of the few minority and female owned law firms in the US specilizing in commercial transactional law with emphasis on financing of automobile, marine vehicle, and commercial real estate development transactions; first female to serve as general counsel of the 93 year-old Natl Bus League; first African-American to graduate from Florida State Univ with a degree in chemistry and mathematics. **Home Addr:** 12608 Tartan Lane, Fort Washington, MD 20744, **Home Phone:** (301)292-9181. **Business Addr:** President, Awkard & Associates, 1101 30th St NW Suite 500, Washington, DC 20007, **Business Phone:** (202)333-2106.

AXAM, JOHN ARTHUR
Consultant, librarian. **Personal:** Born Feb 12, 1930, Cincinnati, OH; married Dolores Ballard, Sep 20, 1958. **Educ:** Cheyney State Univ, BSE, 1953; Drexel Univ, MSLS, 1958. **Career:** Free Library Philadelphia, librn, 1958-64, head, stations dept, 1964-78, area adminr, 1978-91; Employment Relations and Strategies Unit, consultant, 2003. **Orgs:** Am Libr Asn; Pa Libr Asn; United Way Southern Pa; United Methodist Church; Public Lib Asn Goals, Guidelines and Standards Committee, 1971-77; Marketing of Public Lib Serv Comm, 1983-84; Pennsylvania Library Asn, Alternative Educ Prog Section, pres, 1980; Pennsylvania Library Asn. **Honors/Awds:** Various articles, Library Prof Publ; Chapel of the Four Chaplains Award; Cert Merit, Pa Libr Asn, 1988; Harry Hosier Award, Black United Methodist Preachers. *

AYCOCK, ANGELA LYNNETTE
Basketball player. **Personal:** Born Feb 28, 1973, Dallas, TX; daughter of Charles Williams and Albertine Aycock. **Educ:** Univ Kans. **Career:** Basketball player (retired); Seattle Reign, guard, 1996; SC Alcamo-Banca Don Rizzo; Nun, Russian Orthodox Church, currently. **Honors/Awds:** Kodak All-American, 1995; USBWA All-American, 1995.

AYERS, GEORGE WALDON, JR.
Dentist. **Personal:** Born Sep 23, 1931, Lake City, FL; married Marjorie; children: Dwayne, Marva, Damian, Donald. **Educ:** Fla A&M Univ, BS, 1956; Meharry Med Col, Sch Dent, DDS, 1966. **Career:** Alachua Co Health, 1969-70; Sunland Ctr, dent dir, 1972-. **Orgs:** Alachua Co Dent Soc, Cent Dist Dent, Fla Dent Asn, Am Dent Asn, Fla Pub Health Asn & S Asn Int Dentist. **Military Serv:** Sgt, 1951-54; capt, 1966-68; Serv Medal; Korean War. **Business Addr:** Dental Director, Sunland Center, Waldo Rd, PO Box 1150, Gainesville, FL 32602.

AYERS, RANDY
Basketball coach. **Personal:** Born Apr 16, 1958, Springfield, OH; married Carol; children: Ryan & Cameron. **Educ:** Miami Univ, Ohio, attended 1978 & 1981. **Career:** Basketball player (retired), basketball coach; Played professional basketball, Reno, NV; Miami Univ, grad asst; US Mil Acad, West Point, coach; Ohio State Univ, basketball coach; Philadelphia 76ers, asst coach, 1998-2003, head coach, 2003-04; Orlando Magic, asst coach; Wash Wizards, asst coach, 2007; Philadelphia 76ers, asst coach, 2009. **Honors/Awds:** Ohio Player of the Year; Coach of the Year, Big Ten, 1991, 1992; Big Ten Champions, Ohio State Buckeyes, 1991, 1992; Nat Coach of the Year, Asniated Press, 1991; National Coach of the Year, Black Coaches Asn, 1991. **Business Addr:** Assistant Coach, Philadelphia 76ers, Wachovia Center, 3601 South Broad Street, Philadelphia, PA 19148.

AYERS, ROY
Musician. **Personal:** Born Sep 10, 1940, Los Angeles, CA. **Career:** Ubiquity, founder; musician, currently; Evolution: The Polydor Anthology, two-cd compilation, 1995; Smooth Jazz, 1999; Albums: West Coast Vibes, 1963; Stoned Soul Picnic, 1968; Ubiquity, 1971; Change Up The Groove, 1974; Mystic Voyage, 1975; Vibrations, 1976; Red, Black & Green, 1976; Everybody Loves The Sunshine, 1976; You Send Me, 1978; No Stranger To Love, 1979; Love Fantasy, 1980; Music Of Many Colors, 1980;

Africa -Centre Of The World, 1981; Mahogany Vibe, 2004; Sunshine Man, 2005; Virgin Ubiquity II, 2005; Virgin Ubiquity Remixed, 2006; Perfection, 2006. *

AYERS, HON. TIMOTHY F.
Mayor, insurance agent. **Personal:** Born Nov 19, 1958, Springfield, OH; son of Franklin R and Betty R; married Lisa J Henry-Ayers, Aug 31, 1985; children: Katheryne "Lindsay" Ayers. **Educ:** Capital Univ, Columbus, OH, Polit Sci, 1981. **Career:** Ohio House Reps, Columbus, OH, legislative page, 1979, legislative message clerk, 1980-84; Ohio House Campaign Comn, Columbus, OH, 1982; Clark County Community Action Corp, Springfield, OH, 1984-86; City Springfield, OH, mayor, 1984-90; Licensed insurance agent, OH; Reach Out Youth Inc, Springfield, OH, foster care social worker; Equitable, Springfield, OH, agent; N Nashville Community Develop Corp, exec dir, 2000. **Orgs:** bd mem, Am Red Cross; Truman Kennedy Club, Clark County Democratic Exec Comm. **Honors/Awds:** Outstanding Young Man in America, 1984, 1985. *

AYERS-ELLIOTT, CINDY
Executive. **Personal:** Born Aug 12, 1956, Ashland, MS; daughter of Annie Mae Ayers Jackson; children: Lagrand & Eric. **Educ:** Rust Col, Holly Springs, Mass, BA, 1984; Univ Mass, Boston, Mass, MBA, 1987. **Career:** Sen Campaign, Jackson, Mass, field coordr, 1984-85; Gov Off, Jackson, Mass, prog specialist, 1985-86, nat rural fel, 1986-87; State Treas Off, Jackson, Mass, admin asst, 1987-94; Grigsby Brandford & Co Inc, vpres; Chapman Capital Mgt Inc, vpres mkt, 1994; Sun-Delta Capital Access Ctr Inc, pres, currently. **Orgs:** Nat delegate, Dem Nat Conv, 1984-96; nat comt woman, Miss Young Democrats, 1986; track delegate, Dem Nat Conv, 1988; state coordr, Presidential Election, 1988; treas, Young Democrats Am, 1989-; vice chairperson, bd dir, Miss Home Corp, 1989; chairwoman, First Am bank; founder, Miss First African-Am Bank; Nat Bankers Asn; Miss Bankers Asn; Nat Asn Advan Colored People; Nat Rural Fel; vice chair, Delta Found; vice chair, Miss Home Corp, 1990; Leadership Jackson Class, 1991. **Honors/Awds:** Nat Rural Fel, Nat Urban Fel, New York, 1987; Mississippi Head Start, Head Start Asn, 1988; Spec Recognition, Miss Dem Party, 1988; Spec Recognition, Nat Bankers Asn, 1990; Award of Merit, First Am Bank, 1990; Top 50 Women in Business, Miss Bus J, 2002. **Home Addr:** 4945 S Dr, Jackson, MS 39209, **Home Phone:** (601)922-8395. **Business Addr:** President, Sun-Delta Capital Access Ctr Inc, 819 Main St, Greenville, MS 38701, **Business Phone:** (662)335-5291.

AYERS-JOHNSON, DARLENE
Government official. **Personal:** Born Feb 28, 1943, Oakland, CA; daughter of Ernest and Thelma; married Perry Oliver, Dec 27, 1981; children: Cynthia Maria Ayers. **Educ:** Holy Names Col, 1981-84; Golden Gate Univ, 1991-. **Career:** Standard Register Co, Oakland, group exec, mkt, 1972-85; Bermuda Bus Machines & Gen Mgr, A F Smith Trading Ltd, mkt mgr, 1985-88; AMBER Printing Co, ceo & owner, 1989-91; Friends of Faith Inc, exec dir, 2004-07; Interagency Support Div, Dept Gen Servs, dep dir, chief dep dir. **Orgs:** Ford's Consumer Appeals Bd; Emergency Bus Enterprises Comn, speaker of house, 1992; Port Oakland Comt Admin, Aviation, Exec & Pub Art, first vpres, currently. **Honors/Awds:** Woman of the Year Award, State Calif, 1992; Federated Republican Women; Postal Comn; Nat Asn Women Bus Owners Award. **Business Addr:** First Vice President, Port of Oakland, Board of Commissioners, 530 Water St, Oakland, CA 94607, **Business Phone:** (510)627-1100.

AZIBO, DR. DAUDI AJANI YA
Educator. **Educ:** PhD. **Career:** Fla A&M Univ, Dept Psychol, prof. **Orgs:** Eval Rev Panel, Off Asst Secy Planning & Eval. *

AZIZ, KAREEM A
School administrator, executive director. **Personal:** Born Dec 15, 1951, Dayton, OH; married Nini Oseye; children: Jinaki Milele & Atiba Erasto. **Educ:** Cent State Univ, BA, 1975; Univ Dayton, MPA, 1976; Morgan State Univ, Doctoral Stud, 1982-. **Career:** Comprehensive Manpower Ctr, admin asst exec dir, 1975-77; Clark Co Employ & Training Off, coord comm PSE prog, 1977-78; YMCA Springfield OH, exec dir, 1978-80; YMCA Baltimore, MD, exec dir, 1980-81; Sojourner Douglass Col, Inst Res & Planning, coord, 1981-, dir, currently; Co Investr, Minority Univ Space Interdisciplinary Network, NASA, currently. **Orgs:** Co chair, Nat Communs Community Nat Black Independent Political Party, 1983-; Consult, New Day Asn, 1985. **Honors/Awds:** "Key Statistics About Minorities in the Dayton Area" Dayton Human Relations Council 1973. **Business Addr:** Director, Sojourner Douglass College, Institute Research training, 500 N Caroline St, Baltimore, MD 21205, **Business Phone:** (410)276-0306.

AZIZ, SAMIMAH
Executive. **Personal:** Born Oct 19, 1960, New York, NY; daughter of Larry and Marion Williams; married; children: 2. **Educ:** SE Mo State Univ, Cape Girardeau, Mo, attended 1978-80; Howard Univ, Wash, DC, BA, hist, 1984; Webster Univ, St Louis, Mo, educ prog, 1991. **Career:** Howard Univ Student Asn, Wash, DC, prog dir, 1983-84; Nat Archives/Archives Tech, Wash, DC, 1983-84; KITS, Washington, DC, travel consult/tour guide, 1984, 1985; DC Pretrial Agency, Wash, DC, pretrial officer, 1985-88; Akbars Books-N-Things, St Louis, MO, cost svc mgr/co-owner, 1988; Cousin Trips, dir, currently. **Orgs:** Ubiquity, 1983-; Multicultural Publishers Exchange, 1990-; Nation Islam, 1963-; African Am Asn Book Sellers, Writers & Publishers, 1990-. **Business Addr:** Director, Cousin Trips, 5200 Dallas Hwy Suite 200, PO Box 244, Powder Springs, GA 30127, **Business Phone:** (678)549-4775.

AZOULAY, KATYA GIBEL. **See GIBEL MEVORACH, KATYA.**

B

BAAKO, SEKOU MOLEFI. **See JACKSON, ANDREW PRESTON.**

BAAQEE, SUSANNE INEZ
Dentist. **Personal:** Born Nov 24, 1952, Boston, MA; daughter of Inez Sabree and Everett Sabree; married Melvin Bilal; children: Shakir, Aneesah, Mikal. **Educ:** Simmons Col, BS, 1974; Tufts Dent Sch, DMD, 1978; Harvard Sch Dent Implantology, 1987; Simmons Grad Sch Mgt, MBA, 1995. **Career:** Children's Hosp Med Ctr, hemat asst, 1972-75; Roxbury Community Health Clinic, family dentist, 1979-81; Harvard Biol Labs, res asst, 1974; Implant & Family Dent Prac, dentist, 1980-. **Orgs:** MASJID Al-Quaran, 1965-; Mass Women's Dent Soc, 1975-; Mass Dent Soc, 1979-; Am Dent Asn, 1979-; bd mem, Dorchester Coun Serv, 1983-86; New Eng Soc Clinical Hypnosis, 1985-; treas, Amerislamic EID Asn, 1983-87; vpres, Mattapan Community Concern Group, 1984; Am Acad Implant Dent, 1987-. **Honors/Awds:** Girl of the Year Award, 1970; Scholastic Achievement, Nat Honor Soc, 1967-70; Alpha Kappa Alpha, 1975-77; Links Soc, 1976-78; HAJJ, 1980, 1990. *

BABATUNDE, OBBA
Actor. **Personal:** Born Jan 1, 1951?, Jamaica Queens, NY; married. **Educ:** Brooklyn Col. **Career:** Metrop Brass Ensemble; Negro Ensemble Theater, performer; Harriet Tubman Sch, teacher & admin, 1974-76; Theater: Guys and Dolls, 1976; Timbuktu, 1977-78; Dream girls, 1982; Golden Boy, 1984; Grind, 1985; Jelly's Last Jam, 1991; Chicago, 1997-98; TV series: "All My Children", 1987; "Dawson's Creek", 1999-2000; "Soul Food", 2000; "Half & Half", 2002-; "One Life To Live", 2005; TV movies: "MANTIS", 1994; "The Cherokee Kid", 1996; "The Tomorrow Man", 1996; "Miss Evers' Boys", 1997; "Temptations", 1998; "Introducting Dorothy Dandridge",1999; "The Apartment Complex", 1999; "Redeemer", 2002; "The Great Commission", 2003; Films: Short Eyes,1977; Married to the Mob, 1988; Miami Blues, 1990; Silence of the Lambs,1991; Dead Again, 1991; Importance Of Being Earnest, 1992; Undercover Blues, 1993; Philadelphia, 1993; Conversations, 1994; A Reason to Believe, 1995; Born To Be Wild, 1995; Carpool, 1996; Multiplicity,1996; That Thing You Do!, 1996; Fatal Pursuit, 1998; Life, 1999; The Visit, 2000; How High, 2001; John Q, 2002;The Wild Thorn berrys Movie (voice), 2002; MVP, 2003; The Great Commission,2003; After the Sunset, 2004; The Manchurian Candidate, 2004; Kangaroo Jack, 2004; After The Sunset, 2004; Material Girls, 2006; The Celestine Prophecy, 2006; The Black Man's Guide To Understanding Black women, 2006; Stage: "Secret Place", 1970; "Timbuktu!", 1978; "Sing Happy", 1978; "Liza Minnelli in Concert", 1979; "Baryshnikov on Broadway", 1980; "Esau, Reggae: A Musical Revelation", 1980; "Dreamgirls", 1981-85; "Grind",1985; "ittle Ham", 1987; "Golden Boy", 1989; "The Roar of the Greasepaint, Smell of the Crowd", 1989; "Blues in the Night", 1991; Album: "Dream girls", 1982; Song: "Throw Down", 1985. **Orgs:** Bill Picket All Black Rodeo. **Special Achievements:** Earned Emmy and Cable ACE Award nominations for his role as "Willie Johnson" in HBO's "Miss Evers' Boys," and a NAACP Image Award nomination for his portrayal of "Harold Nicholas" in HBO's "Introducing Dorothy Dandridge"; was nominated for Broadway's 1982 Tony Award as Best Actor. **Business Addr:** Actor, c/o Stone Manners, 8436 W 3rd Suite 740, Los Angeles, CA 90048, **Business Phone:** (323)655-1313.*

BABB, DR. VALERIE M
Educator. **Personal:** Born May 6, 1955, New York, NY; daughter of Dorothy L and Lionel S Duncan. **Educ:** Queens Col, City Univ NY, New York, NY, BA, 1977; State Univ NY, Buffalo, NY, MA, 1981, PhD, 1981. **Career:** Georgetown Univ, Washington, DC, from asst prof to prof; Middlebury Col, Bread Loaf Sch English, faculty, currently; Univ Ga, Franklin Col Arts & Sci, prof eng, currently; Langston Hughes Review, ed, currently. **Honors/Awds:** Award for Academic Excellence, Seek Program, City Univ NY, 1985; Mt Zion United Methodist Church Award. **Special Achievements:** Black Georgetown Remembered: A Documentary Video, 1989; Books: Whiteness Visible: The Meaning of Whiteness in American Literature & Culture, NYU Press, 1998; Ernest Gaines. **Business Addr:** Professor, University of Georgia, Department of English, 312 Holmes Hunter Acad Bldg, Athens, GA 30602-6205, **Business Phone:** (706)542-1261.

BABBS, DR. JUNIOUS C., SR.
Educator. **Personal:** Born Aug 15, 1924, Arkansas; married Bobbie; children: Junious C Jr, Dwayne (deceased) & Jade. **Educ:** BS, MS, EdS, 1971; EdD, 1984. **Career:** Cotton Plant Pub Schs, coach, sci teacher, rec dir, prin, supt sch; educ consult; motivational speaker, 1989-; Little Rock Sch Dist, asst supt,assoc supt, currently. **Orgs:** Chmn bd trustees, Ash Grove Bapt Church; secy, ECOEO; County Health Comn; City Adv Comn; City Coun; chmn, Finance Comn; NEAAA, AEA, State Prin Orgn Admin; NCA State Comm; Adv Coun Sec Ed, City Extension Bd; dir, Cotton Plant Clinic; Ariz State Admin Assn, 32 Deg Mason, NAC; bd dir, DAD; secy, Mental Health Bd; deacon Ash Grove B Church; State Adv Comt Chap II State Bonds & Facil Comn; Chair, Woodruff Co Local Planning Group, Arkansas DeptHuman Servs; mem, bd dirs, Wilber D Mills Ed coop; State Health Comn; Dr Martin Lihing Comn, govt appointment, 1993; Nat Community Serv Comn, govt appointment, 1993; dir, Little Rock Rotary Club, 2002-03. **Honors/Awds:** Coach of the Year, 1953, 1956, 1960-62; Biology Teacher Award, 1960-61; Man of the Year Award, 1969, 1973; State Service Chapter I Award, 1990; Service Award, City Cotton Plant, 1989; Man of the Year Award, Am Biographic Inst, 1990; Distinguished Service Award, North Arkansas Services, 1994. **Home Addr:** 400 Gum St D 10, Cotton Plant, AR 72036. *

BABER, DR. CEOLA ROSS
Educator. **Personal:** Born Nov 30, 1950, Selma, AL; married Willie L; children: Lorenzo DuBois, Tylisha Marie & Cheickna St Clair. **Educ:** Calif State Univ, Sacramento, BA, 1972; Stanford Univ, MA, 1975; Purdue Univ, PhD, 1984. **Career:** Sequoia Union High Sch Dist, teacher, 1974-78; Tuskegee Univ, proj coordr, instr, 1979-80; Purdue Univ, res assoc, 1980-81, grad asst, 1982-84, dir, asst prof, 1984-89; Univ NC, Greensboro, Sch Educ, Sec Social Studies Licensure Prog, from asst prof to assoc prof, 1989-2005, coordr, 1989-, from actg assoc dean to assoc dean, 1998-, Currently. **Orgs:** Am Asn Col Teacher Educ; Am Educ Res Asn; Nat Asn Multicultural Educ; Nat Coun Social Studies; Phi Delta Kappa; Kappa Delta Pi Int Educ Hon Soc; Delta Kappa Gamma Int Educ Soc. **Honors/Awds:** Distinguished Women of Color Award, Consortium Doctors, 1991; UNCG Alumni Teaching Excellence Award, Jr Faculty Recipient, 1993. **Home Addr:** 1512 Forest Hill Dr, Greensboro, NC 27410. **Business Addr:** Assosiate Professor, University of North Carolina-Greensboro, Department of Curriculum & Instruction, 1000 Spring Garden St 301 A Curry Bldg, PO Box 26170, Greensboro, NC 27402-6170, **Business Phone:** (336)334-4667.

BABERO, DR. BERT BELL
Scientist, educator. **Personal:** Born Oct 9, 1918, St Louis, MO; son of Andras and Bertha; married Harriett King; children: Bert Jr & Andras Fanfiero. **Educ:** Univ Ill, BS, 1949, MS, 1950, PhD, 1957. **Career:** Arctic Health Res Ctr, AK, med parasitologist, 1950-55; Ft Valley State Col, GA, prof zool, 1957-59; Southern Univ, Baton Rouge, LA, prof zool, 1959-60; Educ Emergency Sci Skeme, Lagos, Nigeria, lectr zool, 1960-62; Sch Med Univ, Baghdad, Iraq, parasitologist, 1962-65; Univ Nev Las Vegas, prof zool, 1965-87; Grambling State Univ, prof zool, 1987-89; Univ Nev Las Vegas, prof emer zool, 1987-. **Orgs:** Am Soc Parasitologists, 1951-; Am Microscopial Soc, 1951-; Hon Soc Phi Sigma Biol Soc; Helm Soc Wash, 1951-; Am Soc Parasitol, 1951; Wildlife Disease Soc, 1955-; Alpha Phi Alpha Fraternity, 1957-; pres, Sigma Xi Hon Sci Soc Local Chap, 1966-72; Phi Kappa Phi, 1966-; NV St Equal Rights Comt, 1967-68; fel, trop med La State Univ Med Sch, 1968; pres, 1975, hon life mem, 1982, Rocky Mt Conf Parasitologists; coun, Rep Am Soc Parasitologists, 1981-85. **Honors/Awds:** Hall of Fame, DuSable High Sch Chicago, 1985; Man of the Year, NAACP, Las Vegas, 1968. **Special Achievements:** Hundred science publications in Parasitology journals of many countries,described 21 new species. **Military Serv:** AUS, T4, 1943-46; 3 overseas serv Bars; Am Campaign Medal; Asiatic Pac Campaign Medal; Bronze Star; Good Conduct Medal; WWII Victory Medal. **Home Addr:** 2202 Golden Arrow Dr, Las Vegas, NV 89109. **Business Addr:** Emeritus Professor of Zoology, University Nev-Las Vegas, 4505 Maryland Pkwy, Las Vegas, NV 89154, **Business Phone:** (702)895-3011.

BACKSTROM, DON
Investment banker. **Personal:** Born Jun 4, 1941, Los Angeles, CA; son of Walter and Julia Carter; married Jacquelyn Webster Backstrom, Oct 5, 1969; children: Kellye Dion Backstrom. **Educ:** Am Inst Banking, Los Angeles, CA, cert, 1975; El Camino Community Col, Torrance, CA, attended 1975; Calif State Univ, Dominguez Hills, CA, attended 1978. **Career:** Bank Am, Los Angeles, CA, bank mgr, 1964-73; Bank Finance, Los Angeles, CA, bank mgr, 1973-75; Home Bank, Compton, CA, bank mgr, 1975-76; Imperial Bank, Los Angeles, CA, vpres, 1976-77; Mechanics Bank, bank mgr, 1977-78; State Calif, Sacramento, Los Angeles, mgr CAL-VET housing program, 1978-84, Calif State Treasurer's Office, exec dir CIDFAC, 1984-91;Salomon Smith Barney, Harris Upham & Co Inc, vpres, public finance div, 1991-98; John Nuveen Co, 1998-99; Chapman Co, 1999; Backstrom Mccarley Berry & Co LLC, managing dir & prin, currently. **Orgs:** Dir, Calif Statewide Cert Develop Corp, 1988-. **Military Serv:** USAF, E-4, 1960-64.

BACKUS, BRADLEY
Executive. **Personal:** Born Sep 12, 1950, Kings County, NY; son of Thomas and Bernice Smith; married Stephanie George (divorced); children: Crystal Olivia Backus. **Educ:** Lincoln Univ,

Oxford, Penn, BA, 1972; George Washington Univ, Nat Law Ctr, JD, 1975. **Career:** Executive (retired); Metrop Life Ins Co, New York, advan underwriting consult, 1977-80, dir estate planning, 1980-82, sr bus & estate consult, 1983-93, agency mgr training, field mgt training. **Orgs:** Pres, Bedford-Stuyvesant Lawyers Asn, 1980-81; bd mem, Bedford-Stuyvesant Community Legal Serv Corp, 1980-89; pres, Metrop Black Bar Asn, 1986-89; vpres, MBBA Scholarship Fund, 1987-; bd mem, Comt Modern Cts, 1988-; comnr, NY State Judicial Comn Minorities, 1988-90; comnr, NY City Korean Vet Memorial Comn, 1988-90; comnr, NY State Comn Improve Availability Legal Serv, 1988-90; regional dir, Nat Bar Asn, 1990-91 & 1994-; bd mem, The Legal Aid Soc, 1988-. **Honors/Awds:** Black Achievers in Industry, 1994. *

BACOATE, MATTHEW, JR.
Executive. **Personal:** Born Feb 10, 1931, Asheville, NC. **Educ:** Med Admin Sch, attended 1951; Univ SC, USAFI, bus admin, 1955; Western Carolina Univ, Bus Admin, 1971; NC State Univ CEU's, 1975. **Career:** Executive (retired); Asheville Chamber Com, gen mgr; Afran Inc, gen mgr; Asheville Comun Enter Inc, gen mgr; M Bacoate Disposable's Inc, pres; Western Mtn Sci Inc, pres. **Orgs:** NC Minority Bus Comn, 1969; appeal officer, Asheville City Schs Free Lunch Prog, 1969-95; adv comt, Sen Robert Morgan, 1974, 1980; steering comt, Gov Jim Hunt, 1976-92; bd dir, NC Economic Dev, 1977; Small Bus Adv Coun, 1978; bd dir Gov Western Residence Asn, 1978; Pvt Indust Coun, 1979, 1988; NC Small Bus Advocacy Coun, 1979; Employ Security Adv Coun, 1979; Cent Asheville Optimist Club, 1979; steering comt, Martin L King Prayer Break; Daniel Boone Coun Boy Scouts Am, 1978; bd mem, Asheville Area Chamber Com, 1981; adv coun US Small Bus Admin, 1981; chmn bd, Victoria Health Care Ctr, 1981-; co-founder, Black Bus & Prof League, 1983; adv comt, AB Tech Small Bus, 1986; Senator Terry Sanford Adv Comn, 1986; Smky Mountain Minority Purchasing Coun, 1986; City of Asheville Minority Bus Comn, 1989; chmn, Minority Loan Pool, 1990; Buncombe County Sheriffs Transition/Review Comn, 1990; chmn, Minority Loan Pool, 1990; bd dirs, Pack Place Inc, 1991; NC Sheriff Asn, 1991; bd dir, YMI Cultural Ctr, 1987, chmn, 1992; chmn Bd, YMI Community Develop Corp, 1992; bd dir, Western NC Regional Econ Develop Comn, 1993; chmn bd, Black Mountain Ctr Found, 1994; founder & co-chmn, Comt Prog; bd vis, Western Carolina Univ; Comm Int & Comt WLOS-TV; bd dir Asheville Chap Am Red Cross; bd dir Comn Mus Fire Equip. **Honors/Awds:** Look Mag Recognition, 1970; Nat Audiance, Exemplifying Accomplishments, documentary "Help" ABC, 1970; Appreciation Serv Phalany Frat, Market St YMCA, 1972; Asheville Jaycees, Boss of the Year, 1976; Cert Appreciation Asheville Buncombe Tech Inst, 1977; White House invitation, Pres Jimmy Carter, 1979; Cert Recognition, City Winston-Salem, NC, 1980-; Award Ashville Area Chamber Com, 1981; Cert Recog, Western Carolina Univ, 1983; Outstanding Serv Inducted Chamber Echoes Cent Asheville Optimist, 1984; Cert City Asheville, 1988; Buncombe County Sheriff Dept, Outstanding Serv Award; Outstanding Serv Recognition, City Asheville, 1993; Appreciation Leadership/Dedication to the Region, Advantage West WNCREDC, 1993-97; Appreciation Outstanding Leadership, Black Mountain Ctr Found, 1995-96. **Military Serv:** Army Med Corps, 1951-56. *

BACON, ALBERT S.
Dentist. **Personal:** Born Mar 1, 1942, LaGrange, GA; son of Albert Stanley Bacon Sr and Julia Spain. **Educ:** Howard Univ, BS, 1963, DDS, 1967; cert Orthodontics, 1971. **Career:** Va Hosp, staff dentist, 1969; pvt pract, 1970; Community Group Health Found, staff dentist, 1970; Howard Univ, asst prof, 1971; pvt pract orthodontics, 1971-; Dept Comm Dentistry, acting chmn, 1972; Univ Dent Assocs, chief dent, currently. **Orgs:** Am Nat Soc MD Dental Asn; Robert T Freeman Dental Soc; Am Asn Orthodontists; Middle Atlantic Soc Orthodontists; Am Acad Group Dental Pract; Chi Delta Mu Frat; Young Adults Wash; St Albans Soc; Canterbury Club; Howard Univ Alumni Asn. **Business Phone:** (202)291-5000.*

BACON, BARBARA CRUMPLER
School administrator, administrator. **Personal:** Born Sep 7, 1943, Youngstown, OH; daughter of Robert Crumpler and Jessie McCray Irby; married Oscar (divorced 1992); children: Robert, Jessica. **Educ:** Youngstown State Univ, BA, Sociol, 1980; Univ Akron Sch Law, Akron, OH, 1990. **Career:** Smithsonian Inst, EEO spec, 1972-78; Mahoning City Transitional Homes, affirm action consult, 1980, instr, 1980-81; Youngstown State Univ, asst to the pres for affirm action. **Orgs:** Bd mem, Assoc Neighborhood Ctrs, 1984-92, YWCA, 1985-92; Links Inc, 1985-; bd mem, Gateways to Better Living, 1985; Design Rev Comn; bd mem, Help Hotline; bd mem, Burdman Group. **Honors/Awds:** Distinguished Serv Award, Youngstown State Univ, 1995. *

BACON, CHARLOTTE MEADE
Educator. **Personal:** Born in Alberta, VA; daughter of Ollie (deceased) and Pinkie Manson (deceased); married Edward D Bacon Jr; children: Judith, Edward P, Susan & Detrick. **Educ:** Hampton Inst, BS, 1946; Univ Pittsburgh, MEd, 1952. **Career:** Educator (retired); Great Aliquippa YWCA, prog comn, 1965-72; Aliquippa Ed Assoc, record secy, 1969-72; Aliquippa Br Am Asn Univ Women, corres secy, 1971-73; Aliquippa Sch Dist, teacher. **Orgs:** Delta Sigma Theta Sor; Nat Educ Asn Retired Teachers; PA St Educ Asn Retired Teachers; Triumph Baptist Church; Nat Asn Advan Colored People; World Affairs Coun Pgh; life mem, New Sheffield PTA; women's hist speaker, PA Dept Educ Speaker's Bur Black Hist; Aliquippa Negro Bus & Prof Women'sClub, 1960-89; pres, Aliquippa Negro Bus & Prof Women's Club, 1960-62, 1963-77; pres, PA State Fed Negro Women's Clubs, 1969-73; vchmn, MayorsComm Civil Rights, 1972-77; dir, Aliquippa Nat Asn Advan Colored People Creative Dramatics Club, 1972-76; bd dirs, 1976 & 1982, spl task force, 1978-83, interim adminr, 1992-, Sewickley Comn Ctr; chmn, Consumer Affairs, 1976-80; Sewickley Int Toastmistress Club, 1976-82; pres, Aliquippa Br Am Asn Univ Women, 1977-79; Nat Asn Colored Womens Clubs; edchairperson, NE Fed Womens Clubs; Sewickley NYPUM Prog Comn, 1979-82; 3rdvpres, Prog Comm, 1979-82; third vpres, Aliquippa Elem School PTA, 1980-81; chairperson, Women's Hist 1980-90; first vpres, Aliquippa NBPWClub, 1980-90; Commun Comm Nat Asn Negro Bus & Prof Women's Clubs, 1985-89; Black Womens Pol Crusade Pgh, 1987-90; Black Womens Pol Crusade Pgh, 1987-90; exec bd, Northeastern Fedn Negro Women, 1987-; Pa State Minority Recruitment Comn, 1987-91; Hist Modern Club Aliquippa PA, 1987-90; chaplain, Daniel B Mathews Hist Soc, 1987-89; pres, Willing Workers Mission Soc, 1988; sec vpres, Aliquippa AAUW, 1988-90; Adult Literacy Coun Beaver County; rec secy, N Central Dist NANBPWC, 1988-90;exec bd, Nat Asn Colored Women's Clubs, 1988-; pres, Hawthorne ClubSewickley, 1989-; pres, FFUTURE Assocs, 1989; exec bd, chairperson, Black Family & Homeless, 1990. **Honors/Awds:** Woman of the Year, Aliquippa NBPW Club, 1970; Commission Involvement Award, Delta Sigma Theta, 1971; Bict Int Biog, 1971-76; Notable American of the Bicent Era,1976; Sojourner Truth Award, Nat Asn NBPW Clubs, 1976; Pa Woman of the Year, Aliquippa Br AAUW, 1981; Distinguished Serv Award, Pa State Fed Negro Womens Clubs Inc, 1983; Appreciation Award, Beaver-Castle Girl Scout Coun, 1985; Aliquippa Elem Sch PTA Scholarship Award, 1986; Teacher of the Year, Aliquippa Sch Dist, 1987; Woman of the Year Award, Beaver Castle Girl Scout Coun, 1989; Hall of Fame Award, Pa State Fedn Negro Women, 1990; Merit Award, Northeastern Fed Women's Clubs, 1990. **Special Achievements:** Listed in the 498 Hardworking Women PA, 1987; Co-author of Four Drummers, poetry book, 1989. *

BACON, DR. GLORIA JACKSON
Poet, physician, singer. **Personal:** Born Sep 21, 1937, New Orleans, LA; daughter of Henry and Vina V; married Frank C Bacon Jr; children: Constance Jackson, Judith Jackson, Phillip, Geoffrey & Stuart. **Educ:** Xavier Univ, BS, 1958; Univ Ill Col Med, MD, 1962, Sch Pub Health, MPH, 1984. **Career:** Altgeld Inc, founder/dir, 1970-2001; Health & Hosp Governing Comn, Cook County, med dir, 1979; Clinic Assocs Chicago Ltd, pres, 1982; Provident Hosp & Med Ctr, vpres, 1985; Metro Care HMO, med dir, 1986-87; TCA Healthier health-care ctr, founder; Chicago Orchestra Hall, soloist; ETA Theater soloist, currently. **Orgs:** Bd trustees, Fisk Univ, 1980-85; Gannon & Proctor Comn, 1982-83; Nat Med Asn; Robert Wood Johnson Found; fel Am Acad Family Physicians; bd trustees, Univ Ill, 1990-97; steering comt, Lincoln Net; pres, Altgeld Community Found; founder, Clinic Altgeld Inc, med dir. **Honors/Awds:** Woman of the Year, PUSH, 1975; Candace Award, Nat Coalition 100 Black Women, 1984; UIC City Partner Award, 1998. **Special Achievements:** Publ: "Is Love Ever Enough?" A Finial Press Champaign IL, 1987.

BACON, RANDALL C.
Government official. **Personal:** Born Oct 2, 1937, Youngstown, OH; divorced; children: Randy, Keith & Kevin. **Educ:** Los Angeles City Col, AA, 1958; CA State Univ, BS, 1962; Univ Southern CA, attended 1964; Loyola Law Sch, attended 1966. **Career:** LA County Social Servs, fiscal officer, 1965-69; LA County Pks & Rec, chief dep dir, 1969-74; LA County Admin Off, div chief, 1974-79; San Diego Co, asst chief admin off, 1979-81, dir social serv, 1981; City LA, dept gen serv, gen mgr; African Am Male Acheivers Network Inc, chair, Emer, currently. **Orgs:** Black Leadership Coun San Diego; chmn, 44th Cong Dist Adv Bd; past pres, Kappa Alpha Psi Frat, 1985; chmn, CA Welfare Dirs Asn, 1985; pres, Nat Forum Black Pub Adminr, 1993-95. **Honors/Awds:** National Public Service Award, 1987; Marks of Excellence Award, Forum Black Pub Adminrs, 1990. **Special Achievements:** Published article "A Model Program for all California," Pub Welfare Mag, 1986. **Business Phone:** (310)412-2680.*

BACON, DR. ROBERT JOHN
Psychiatrist. **Personal:** Born Nov 20, 1948, Houston, TX; son of Robert Bacon Sr and Bernice; children: Robyn, Kristen & Angelle. **Educ:** Lake Forest Acad, IL, attended, 1963; Stanford Univ, BA, hist, 1970; George Wash Univ Med Sch, attended, 1970-71; Meharry Med Col, MD, 1975; Howard Univ Hosp, 1975-77; Univ Tex, Houston, resident, 1977-78. **Career:** Univ Tex Health & Sci Ctr Psychiat, Hermann Hosp, Geriatric, head, 1977-78; Harris County MHMRA, Harris County Forensic Treatment Unit, clin consult, 1979-81; Tex Med Found, physician adv, 1982-88; Univ Tex-Houston, clin asst prof, 1984-90; Ben Taub Gen Hosp, dir psychiat emergency serv, 1984-88; Baylor Col Med, clin asst prof, asst prof psychiat, 1984-90; Tex Dept Corrections, consult, 1985-86; Riverside Gen Hosp, Total Care/Stress Unit, psychiat sect chief, dir, 1987-90; The Chrysalis Ctr, Cheml Dependency Treatment, med dir, 1989-90; Charter Counsel Ctr Pasadena, med dir, 1990; Charter Hosp Kingwood, clin dir adult psychiat, 1989-94; NBA Aftercare Network Team, network provider, 1989-93; Houston Recovery Campus, Day Treatment, physician, 1992-; CHOICES Prog, acupuncture consult, 1992-; Comprehensive Therapies & Servs, psychiat med dir, 1994-; Friends Mind, psych med dir, 1997-; Silveridge Community Care Ctr, psych med dir, 1998; Glory Partial, psych med dir, 1998; Waymaker, psych med dir, 1998; pvt pract, currently. **Orgs:** Clin consult Harris Co Forensic Treatment Unit, 1979-81; Sum Arts; Am Bd Qual Assurance & Utilization Review Physicians, diplomat; Am Psychiatric Asn; Harris County Psychiat Soc; Tex Med Asn; Harris County Med Soc; Med Forum. **Honors/Awds:** Riverside Hospital Black Achievement Awards; Physicians Recognition Award, 1989. **Special Achievements:** Developed the Therapeutic Community of Howard Univ Hosp, Dept Psychiat, 1975-76; article: "The Single Parent-Helping the Children Adjust", Your Health, Texas Health Plan, June 1980; "Providing Mental Health Services with Meager Resources: The Experience of Riverside General Hospital", presented at annual meeting of Black Psychiatrist Assn, Bahamas, 1986; seminars: "Coping with Stress: Teenagers, Drugs and Suicide", Natl Medical Assn, 1981; "Job Stress", US Customs Service, Federal Woman's Program, 1979; symposiums: On Family Therapy, Washington Institute of Psychiatry, Washington, DC, 1977; On Psychiatric Problems of College Students, Conf of College Health Administrators, TX Southern Univ, 1980. **Business Phone:** (713)655-9410.

BACON, WILLIAM LOUIS
Surgeon. **Personal:** Born Dec 3, 1936, Austin, TX; son of William and Louise; married Donna Marie Harbatis; children: Tyra, William II, Donna, Mary Schroeder, Jesse, Louise, Jonathan & Nicholas. **Educ:** Morehouse Col, 1956; Meharry Med Col, 1962. **Career:** Fitzsimons Gen Hosp, intern, 1962-63; Ireland Army Hosp, prespec surg, 1963-64; Brooke Army Med Ctr, ortho, 1964-67; Wash, DC, course dir, 1972-74; Miami, surg, 1975-; pvt pract, physician; Metrop Nashville Gen Hosp & Meharry Med Ctr, chief orthop surg, chief orthop & rehab, currently. **Orgs:** Cert Am Bd Ortho Surg, 1970; Am Col Surg, 1971; Am Acad Ortho Surg, 1972; guest lectr, Univ Miami, 1976; staff consult, Friedman's Hosp & Howard Univ; staff mem, Mt Sinai Med Ctr, Cedars Leb Hosp, Vict Hosp, Jack Mem Hosp; mem bd, Cedars Leb Hosp; Dade Co Med Asn, FL Med Soc, Am Med Asn, Miami Ortho Soc, FL Ortho Soc; recert Am Bd Ortho Surg, 1983; Soc Black Am Surg. **Honors/Awds:** Merit Service Medical, 1970, 1974; Examiner, Am Bd Ortho Surg, 1978-84. **Military Serv:** AUS, 1962-74; AUS Reserves, Col, 1975-; Army Commendation Medal, 1972; Meritorious Service Medal, 1970, 1974; USAR, 324th Gen Hosp , comdr, 1983-86; Persian Gulf Medal, 1992. **Business Addr:** Physician, Meharry Medical College, Department of Orthopedic Surgery, 1005 DB Todd Blvd, Nashville, TN 37208, **Business Phone:** (615)327-4663.*

BACON-BERCEY, JUNE
Meteorologist, lecturer, consultant. **Personal:** Born Oct 23, 1932, Wichita, KS; married George W Brewer; children: two daughters. **Educ:** Univ Clif Los Angeles, BS, 1954, MS, 1955; Univ So CA, MPA, 1979. **Career:** Nat Meteorol Ctr, 1956-62; Sperry Rand Corp, 1962-69; NBC, 1970-73; lectr, 1974-75; Nat Weather Serv, 1975-78, 1982-89; Nat Oceanic & Atmospheric Agency, chief adminr television activities,1979-81; consult & educr, 1990-. **Orgs:** bd mem women & minorities, Am Meteorol Soc, 1975; chair, N Calif Chap,1985; Women in Sci & Eng; Am Geophys Union; Am Asn Pub Admins; NY Acad Sci. **Honors/Awds:** Seal of Approval, Am Meteorol Soc, 1972; Cert of Recognition for Sustained Superior Performance, NOAA, 1982-84; Outstanding Contrib to Furthering the Mission of NOAA, NOAA, 1984-92; Minority Pioneer for Achievements in Atmospheric Sci, Nat Sci Found & Nat Aeronauts & Space Admin, 2000. **Special Achievements:** The First African American woman to earn a meteorology degree in the 1950s;The first female broadcaster in the country in Buffalo, New York, 1970. *

BADEJO, DIEDRA L.
Administrator, educator. **Career:** Kent State Univ, Dept Pan-African Studies, assoc dean, prof & dept chmn, currently. **Orgs:** Bd mem, Nat Coun Black Studies; ACE Fellow program, Kent state univ. **Special Achievements:** One of 37 scholars chosen to serve in the ACE Fellow program. **Business Addr:** Department Chairman, Professor Pan-African Studies, Kent State University, Department of Pan-African Studies, 117 Ritchie Hall, PO Box 5190, Kent, OH 44242-0001, **Business Phone:** (330)672-0142.

BADGER, BRENDA JOYCE
Counselor. **Personal:** Born May 10, 1950, Camden, AR; daughter of Woodrow Hildreth and Lizzie Mae Frazier Hildreth; married David Badger, Feb 27, 1982; children: Kreya Jackson & Keith Jackson. **Educ:** Wayne State Univ, BS, criminal justice, 1982, MA, guidance & coun, 1987. **Career:** Wayne County Community Col, secy, 1970-92; Community Informant, ed, columnist, 1988-; Pontiac/Hazel Park Schs, part-time adult educ counr, 1988-89; "Did You Know?" producer, host, 1989-; Lawrence Technol Univ, counr, 1991-, dir, HELP prog, 1994-; Am Couns Asn, Red Cross, disaster ment health counr/instr, 1992-. **Orgs:** Am Coun Asn,

1985-; founder, pres, Spirit, Ambition, Vigor, & Enthusiasm SAVE, 1986-; Juv Teen & Violence Comt, Detroit City, 1986-; Asn Marriage & Family Coun, 1992-; Am Col Coun Asn, 1992; mem sch bd, Detroit Acad Schs, Westland Sch, 1996-; bd trustees, Cent Mich Univ, 2001. **Honors/Awds:** WJLB-FM Radio, Strong Achiever Award, 1991. **Special Achievements:** Author, "Teachers Still Work Miracles," Detroit Free Press, 1984; State Counseling Licensee, 1991; "Did You Know?" song, 1992; licensed counselor, selected nationwide for training, 1992; "The Alto," poem, 1993; wrote a proposal for the Buddy System, which was approved for funding. **Business Addr:** Counselor, Lawrence Technological University, 21000 W 10 Mile Rd CAAC-West Bldg, Southfield, MI 48075-1058, **Business Phone:** (248)204-4113.

BADGER, DR. LEONARD MICHAEL
Dentist. **Personal:** Born Oct 17, 1962, Jacksonville, FL; married Madelyne Woods, Nov 10, 1998; children: Montana S Williams & Michael Bryce. **Educ:** Fla A&M Univ, BS, 1985; Meharry Med Col, DDS, 1990. **Career:** Dentist, pvt pract, currently. **Orgs:** Nat Dent Asn; Am Dent Asn; Acad Gen Dent; Fla Dent Asn; Kappa Alpha Psi Frat; Dent Soc Greater Orlando; Am Acad Implant Dent. **Honors/Awds:** Fel Acad Gen Dent, 1999. **Military Serv:** AUS, first lt, 1984-86.

BADGER, LLOYD, JR.
City council member. **Personal:** Born May 25, 1950, Hilton, GA. **Educ:** Rochester Inst Technol, Indust Mgt, 1972. **Career:** Self-employed salesman; City Hilltonia, city coun mem, mayor, 1989-91; City Sylvania, city coun mem. **Orgs:** Johnson Grove Baptist Ch; Nat Advan Assoc Colored People; Optimist Club, Masons. *

BADGETT, EDWARD
City manager. **Personal:** Born May 22, 1935, Cleveland, OH; son of Edward Daniel and Margurite Rogers Lowe; married Erbetine Jackson, Dec 18, 1955; children: Edward Ronald, Evelyn Denise & Evette Marie. **Educ:** Univ Akron, OH, BA, 1965, MA, 1971. **Career:** City Flint, Flint, MI, dir, dept community develop, 1974-77; US Dept Housing & Urban Develop, Kansas City, MO, regional dir, community planning & develop, 1978-80; City Austin, TX, asst city mgr, 1980-82; City Berkeley, CA, asst city mgr, 1982-84; City Commerce, TX, city mgr, 1984-86; City Forest Hill, TX, city mgr, 1986. **Orgs:** Trustee, Historic Savannah Found, 1972-74; Int City Mgt Asn, 1975-; trustee, Mich beethoven Soc Found, 1975-77; Nat Forum Black Pub Adminr, 1985-; bd mem, Tarrant County Red Cross, 1990-. **Honors/Awds:** Eagle Scout, Cleveland Council, BSA, 1950; Image Award, Akron Branch, NAACP, 1968, 1969; Image Award, Phoenix Branch, NAACP, 1978; Distinguished Service Award, City of Austin, TX, 1982; Honorary Order of Kentucky Colonels, Commonwealth of Kentucky, 1990. **Military Serv:** USN, Petty Officer first Class, 1953-57; received Korean Presidential Citation. *

BADU, ERYKAH (ERICA ABI WRIGHT)
Singer, actor, songwriter. **Personal:** Born Feb 26, 1971, Dallas, TX; daughter of Kolleen Wright; married The DOC; children: Puma & Mars Merkaba; children: Seven & Sirius. **Educ:** Grambling State Univ, dance & theatre. **Career:** S Dallas Cult Ctr, drama & dance teacher; Erykah Free, founder & drama teacher, 1993-; Universal Rec, currently; Albums: Funky Cousins; Baduizm, 1997; Live, 1997; Mama's Gun, 2000; Worldwide Underground, 2003; Songs: "On & On", 1997; "Next Lifetime", 1997; "Other side of the Game", 1997; "Apple Tree", 1997; "Tyrone", 1997; "Southern Gul", 1999; "Bag Lady", 2000; "Didn't Cha Know?", 2000; "Cleva", 2001; "Love of My Life", 2002; "Danger", 2003; "Back in the Day", 2004; "The Wire", 2008; Films: Blues Brothers, 2000, 1998; The Cider House Rules, 1999; House of D, 2004; Dave Chappelle's Block Party, 2006; Before the Music Dies, 2006; Say My Name, 2009. **Orgs:** Beautiful Love Inc Non Profit Develop. **Honors/Awds:** Soul Train Lady of Soul Awards, Best New Artist, Best Album, Best Single, Best Song, 1997; Blockbuster Awards, Favorite Female New Artist, Favorite Female R&B Artist, 1997; American Music Awards, Favorite New Artist Soul &Rap, Favorite Soul Album, 1998; Outstanding New Artist, Outstanding Female Artist, NAACP Image Awards, 1998; Danish Grammy Awards, Best International Newcomer, Best International Female Artist, 1998; Soul Train Music Awards, Best R&B/Soul Single-Female, Best R&B & Soul Album-Female, Best R&B & Soulor Rap Album of the Year, Best R&B/Soul or Rap New Artist, 1998; Black Reel Award, 2000, 2003. **Special Achievements:** People magazine's 50 Most Beautiful People, 1999; VH1's 100 Greatest Women of Rock N Roll. **Business Addr:** Singer, Universal Records, 1325 Avenue of the Americas, New York, NY 10019, **Business Phone:** (212)373-0600.*

BAETY, EDWARD L.
Lawyer, judge. **Personal:** Born Mar 13, 1944, Jacksonville, FL; married. **Educ:** Morris Brown Col, BS, 1965; Howard Univ Sch Law, JD, 1968. **Career:** Atlanta Leg Aid Soc, staff atty, 1968-71; Equal Employ Opportunity Comn, dist coun, 1971-72; Hill Jones & Farr, assoc coun, 1972-74; Hill Jones & Farr, part, 1974-76; City Ct Atlanta, assoc judge 1976, chief judge, currently. **Orgs:** Atlanta Bar Asn; Gate City Bar Asn; State Bar Asn Ga; Atlanta Bus League; Vol Leg Serv Atty; pres, Atlanta Spart Ath Club; vpres, Phi Beta Sigma Fraternity Inc; Black Consort. **Military Serv:** AUS, spec-5. **Business Addr:** Chief Judge, City Ct Atlanta, 104 Trinity Ave SW, Atlanta, GA 30303-3686.*

BAEZA, DELLA BRITTON
President (organization). **Personal:** Born in Pittsburgh, PA; married Mario L; children: 3. **Educ:** Princeton Univ, BA; Columbia Law Sch, JD, 1978. **Career:** Covington & Burlington Law Firm, atty; Am Broadcasting Companies Inc,coun; AJM Rec LLC, pres; Hillside Broadcasting LLP, AJM Records, pres; pres; Jackie Robinson Found, pres & chief exec officer, 2004-. **Orgs:** Chair, Dance Theatre Harlem Bd Dirs; consult, Nat Black Archives Film &Broadcasting, Ford Found Proj; Inwood Settlement House; Nat Urban League Black Exec Exchange Prog; NY Times Instnl Task Force. **Special Achievements:** Among 25 Influential Black Women in Bus, 2005; the fourth individual to hold the position in the Foundation's 33-year history. **Business Addr:** President, Chief Executive Officer, Jackie Robinson Foundation, 75 Varick St 2nd Fl, 1 Hudson Sq, New York, NY 10013-1917, **Business Phone:** (212)290-8600.

BAFFOE, NANA KWAME, II. **See KIRKLIN, DR. PERRY WILLIAM.**

BAGBY, RACHEL L.
Educator, writer, composer. **Personal:** Born Feb 11, 1956, Philadelphia, PA; daughter of William H and Rachel Edna Samiella Rebecca Jones; married Martin Neal Davidson, Oct 3, 1987. **Educ:** NC AT&T State, Greensboro, NC, 1974; Univ Pittsburgh, Pittsburgh PA, BA(summa cum laude), 1977; Stanford Law Sch, Stanford, CA, JD, 1983. **Career:** V Pitssburgh, Chancellor's Teaching Fel, 1975; Wall Street Jour, San Francisco, CA, writer, 1979; Stanford, CA, freelance composer & writer, 1979-; Philadelphia Community Rehab Corp, Philadelphia, PA, asst dir, 1980-82; Stanford Univ, African & Am Studies, prog coordr, 1983-85; Comm Black Performing Arts, Stanford, CA, prog coordr, 1983-85; Martin Luther King Jr, Papers Proj, Stanford, CA, assoc dir, 1985-; Bobby McFerrin's Voicestra, San Francisco, CA, composer & performer, 1989-; Outta Box Recs,pres, 1989, Vallecitos Mountain Refuge, bd dir, 2000-; Satyana Inst, consult, currently; Composer: "Grandmothers' Song?; "A Power of Numbers?; "Healing the Wounds", 1989; "Daughters of Growing Things?; "Reach Across the Lines?. **Orgs:** Calif Lawyers Arts, 1982-; consult, Calif Arts Coun, 1984-86; consult, Nat Black Womens Health Prog, 1986-; co-dir, Woman Earth Inst, 1986-; bd, Ctr Contemplative Mind & Soc; bd, Vallecitos Mountain Refuge. **Honors/Awds:** Chancellor's Teaching Fellowship, V of Pittsburgh, 1975. **Special Achievements:** Admitted into master class with Bobby Mc Ferrin, Omega Inst, 1988, composed and recorded "Grandmothers' Song", theme for a documentary on Alice Walker; chapters published in anthologies: "A Power of Numbers," Healing the Wounds, 1989, "Daughters of Growing Things," Reweaving the World: The Emergenance of Econ feminish, 1989, composed, recorded and produced anti-racism tape "Reach Across the Lines," on self-owened independent label, 1989, author of Divine Daughters: Liberating the Power and Passion of Women's Voices. **Business Addr:** Board of Directors, Vallecitos Mountain Refuge, 1219E Gusdorf Road, PO Box 3160, Taos, NM 87571, **Business Phone:** (505)751-9613.

BAGLEY, GREGORY P.
Engineer. **Personal:** Born Sep 19, 1930, New York, NY; son of Garrett P and Carrie A; married Helen Smith; children: Gregory Jr, Carole, John. **Educ:** Johns Hopkins Univ, BES, 1958; Adelphi Univ, MS, 1969. **Career:** Engineer (retired); Hazeltine Corp, elec engr, 1958-62; Sperry Gyroscope Cty, sr elec engr, 1962-68; Assoc Univ Brookhaven Nat Lab, res engr I, 1968-93. **Orgs:** Secy, bd deacons Union Baptist Church Hempstead, 1962-98, Sunday Sch Supt, 1985-96; vpres, Franklin PTA, 1972-73; bd Park Lake Develop Fund Corp, 1970-98; African Scientific Inst. **Honors/Awds:** Tau Beta Pi, Eta Kappa Nu Hon Engr Soc. **Military Serv:** USAF, a & 1c, 1950-53. *

BAGLEY, DR. PETER B E
Educator, conductor (music). **Personal:** Born May 22, 1935, Yonkers, NY; married Bythema Byrd; children: Margaret R. **Educ:** Crane Sch Music, SUNY & Potsdam, BS, 1957; Ind Univ, Sch Music, MM, chorus conductor, 1965, DM, chorus conductor, 1972. **Career:** Greenwich Conn Pub Sch, vocal music teacher, 1957-61; First Baptist Church, dir music, 1964-66; New Paltz Concert Choir & Chamber Singers,conductor, 1966-; All State Choruses W Va, 1970-71, New Hampshire, 1972,Connecticut, 1976, Vermont, 1978; New England Festival Chorus, guest conductor, 1980; SUNY New Paltz, assoc prof music, 1966; Univ Conn, prof music, prof emer music, currently. **Orgs:** Am Choral Dir Assn; Am Choral Found; Music Edn Natl Conf; Music Library Assn; Natl Assn Afro Am Edn; NY Sch Music Assn; Am Choral Dirs Assn. **Honors/Awds:** Connecticut Choral Educator of the Year, Conn chap, 1990. **Home Addr:** 206 Foster Dr, Willimantic, CT 06226, **Home Phone:** (860)456-8761. **Business Addr:** Professor emeritus of Music, Special Assistant to the Dean, University of Connecticut, Department of Music, 1295 Storrs Rd Suite 1012, Storrs, CT 06269-1012, **Business Phone:** (860)486-2000.

BAGLEY, STANLEY B.
Chaplain. **Personal:** Born Sep 7, 1935, Trenton, NJ; son of Dr Semuel M and Leomae Walker; married Ruth McDowell; children: Bernard, Sharon, Bryant, Brett. **Educ:** Morehouse Col, BA, 1958; Crozer Theol Sem, BD, 1961; Ashland Theol Sem, MDiv, 1973; Univ OK, grad study, 1967; Century Univ, PhD, 1994; Asn Mental Health Clergy, certified prof mental health clergy, 1976; Department VA Nat Black Chaplin Asn, certified clinical chaplain, 1996. **Career:** Galilee Bapt Ch Trenton NJ, asst pastor, 1961-65; Calvary Bapt Ch, pastor, 1965-67; Bapt Campus Ministry Langston Univ, dir, 1967-70; Hough Ch, minister educ comn, 1970-71; VA Medical Ctr Brecksville OH, chaplain, 1971-; Lakeside Bapt Ch E, Cleveland OH, pastor, 1972-79. **Orgs:** E Cleveland Ministerial Alliance, 1975; Asn Mental Health Clergy, bd certified chaplain, 1974; Ohio Health Care Chaplains; Am Protestant Hosp Asn; Col Chaplains; chmn, Evangelism Com Bapt Minister's Conf Cleveland OH; Dept Metropolitian Ministry Cleveland Baptist Asn; life mem & golden heritage life mem, NAACP; Omega Psi Phi Fraternity Inc; Am Asn Christian Counrs; Asn Christian Marriage Counrs; Dept Veterans Affairs, Nat Black Chaplains Asn, certified clinical chaplain, 1996. **Honors/Awds:** Christian Leadership Citation, Bapt Student Union Langston Univ, 1969; Outstanding Young Man, Outstanding Am Found, 1970; 33 Degree Free Mason; United Supreme Council 33 Degree Ancient & Accepted Scottish Rite Freemasonry Prince Hall Affiliation; loaned executive, VAMC Combined Federal Campaign, 1988; Crozer Theological Seminary, Crozer Scholar, 1989, 1995. *

BAGNERIS, MICHELE. **See BEAL BAGNERIS, MICHELE CHRISTINE.**

BAILER, BONNIE LYNN
Art consultant. **Personal:** Born Oct 11, 1946, New York, NY; daughter of Lloyd Harding and Maryelyne Matthews; children: Miles Bailer Armstead. **Educ:** Queens Col, City Univ New York, BA, 1968, MS 1975; Columbia Univ Sch Law, attended. **Career:** Foreign Lang Dept, New York City Pub Sch System Jr High Sch, acting chmn, 1970-75; Yellow-Go-Rilla Prod Ltd, vpres, 1975-77; Manhattan Borough pres campaigns, polit campaign admin, 1977; Nat Asn Advan Colored People, mem consult, 1978-79; Talkshop Foreign Lang Prog C, founder & pres, 1981-; Gilbert Jonas Co Inc, prof fund raiser, vpres, 1979-86; United Nations Asn USA, dir capital campaign, 1986-88; Bailer Studios, artists agent & prof fund raising consult, 1988-; Jones, Day, Reavis & Pogue, legal intern, 1991-. **Orgs:** Bd mem, Morningside Montessori Sch, 1979-82, The Grinnell Housein Defense Corp, 1984-; cert building mgr, City New York, 1979; pres, coordr, Annual Westside Community Conf, 1979-; consult, Minisink City Mission Soc, 1984; comn mem, Cathedral Sch, 1984-; Nat Asn Female Exec; Nat Asn Advan Colored People; Nat Soc Fundraising Exec; Women Fin Develop, Planned Giving Group; Black Law Students Asn, Columbia Univ, 1989-. **Business Addr:** Consultant, Bailer Studios, 42 W 38th St, New York, NY 10018, **Business Phone:** (212)354-2729.

BAILEY, DR. ADRIENNE YVONNE
Association executive, educator. **Personal:** Born Nov 24, 1944, Chicago, IL; daughter of Leroy and Julia Spalding. **Educ:** Mundelein Col, BA, 1966; Wayne State Univ, MEd, 1968; Northwestern Univ, PhD, 1973. **Career:** Chicago Bd Educ, Deneen Elementary Schl, teacher Social Studies, English, French, Math 1966-67; So Shore YMCA, Chicago, neighborhood youth corps supvr, 1967; Circle Maxwell YMCA, Chicago, prog coordr, 1967-68; Detroit Bd Educ, substitute teacher, 1968-69; Govt Off Human Resources, Chicago, educ coord, 1969-71; Northwestern Comn Educ Proj, Northwestern Univ, univ coordr, 1972-73; Chicago Comn Trust, Chicago, sr staff assoc, 1973-81; Col Bd, New York, NY, vpres acad affairs, 1981; educational consult currently. **Orgs:** IL State Bd Educ, 1974-81; Nat Assn state Bds Educ; steering comn, 1974-79, exec comn, 1975-77, 1978-79, comn, 1981, Educ Comn States;bd dir, Assn Black Found Exec, 1975-87; Nat Assessment Educ Prog Policy Comn, 1976-80; task force Desegregation Strategies Project, 1976-81; policy comn Sch Educ Northwestern Univ; bd trustees, Hazen Found, New Haven CT, 1977-87; Career Develop Advisory Comn Nat Urban League; visiting comn Grad Sch Educ Harvard Univ, 1977-83; bd trustees, So Educ Found, Atlanta GA; Nat Task Force State Efforts Achieve Sex Equity, 1980-83, chmn, advisory comn Coun Found Internship & Fellowship Prog Minorities & Women, 1980-82; adv comn, Inst Educ Finance & Govt Stanford Univ, 1980-85; adv panel Phi Delta Kappa Gallup Poll Pubs Attitudes Toward Pub Educ, 1984; bd dir, Coun Found, 1986; META, 1986; ed bd, The Kappan (Phi Delta Kappan); co chmn, Governor's Adv Comn Black Affairs, NY, Educ sub-Comt; bd dir, The Negro Ensemble, NY; bd trustees Marymount Col, 1988-89; bd trustees, The Found Ctr. **Honors/Awds:** MDEA Inst french, Univ ME, 1966; TTT Fellowship, Northwestern Univ, 1971-73; Image Award, League Black Women, 1974; Recognition Award, Black Achiever Indust YMCA Metro Chicago, 1974; 1 of 100 Outstanding Black Women in America Award, Operation PUSH 1975; 1 of 10 Outstanding Young Persons Award, IL Jaycees, 1975; Community Motivation Award, HU MA BE Karate Assoc, 1975; 1 of 10 Outstanding Young Citizens Award, Chicago Jaycees 1976; Distinguished Service Award, Ed Comn State 1977; outstanding Achievement Award, YWCA Metro Chicago, 1978; Kizzy Award, Outstanding Contributions, 1979; Salute IL Serv, Federal Savings & Loan Bank, 1980; Meritorious Service Award, Educ Comn State NAEP, 1980; Human Relations Award, IL Educ Assn, 1980; Cert

Recognition, Phi Delta Kappa NW Univ Chap, 1980; Merit Award, NW Alumni Assn, 1981; Diamond Jubilee Recognition, Phi Delta Kappa 1981; Agenda for Action, Educ Leadership, 1984; Top 100 Black Bus & Prof Women, Dollars & Sense Magazine, 1985; Special Service Award, Nat Alliance Black Sch Educr, 1987. *

BAILEY, ANTOINETTE M.
President (organization), teacher. **Personal:** Born Oct 4, 1949, St Louis, MO; daughter of Jack D and Margurie Brown; married George E, Jul 10, 1988; children: Dara Braddock & Errin Braddock. **Educ:** Southern Ill Univ, BA, 1972; Mich State Univ, MA, 1973. **Career:** Mich St Univ, grad asst, 1973-75; E Lansing High Sch, MI, teacher, 1973-74; Panama Canal Co, Balboa Heights, CZ, EEO specialist investr, 1976-77; Narcotics Serv Coun, St Louis, super counr, 1978-80; Mo Div Vocational Rehab, Olivette, sr counr deaf, 1980-84; McDonnell Douglas Corp, St Louis, dir training & devt, 1984-, vpres community rels; Boeing-McDonnell Found, pres, currently; Boeing Co, Community & Educ Rels, vpres, pres, currently. **Orgs:** Bd mem, Urban League Metrop St Louis; bd mem, Regional Com & Growth Asn. **Honors/Awds:** Nat Inst Ment Health Fel, 1972-75; Counselor of the Year, Mo Nat Rehab Asn, 1983; Presenteeism Award 1, McDonnell Douglas, 1985-86, 1986-87; Leadership Award, YMCA, 1988; Leadership St Louis Participant, Class, 1991-92. *

BAILEY, ARTHUR
Government official, gospel singer. **Personal:** Born in Wilkinsburg, PA; son of William Henry and Winifred Townsend. **Educ:** Pittsburgh Acad, 1949; Carnegie Inst Tech, 1955; Dept Agr Grad Sch Wash DC, 1956; Dept Interior, mgt training prog, 1956. **Career:** Downtown Chorale, singer, tenor, 1949-58; Dept Interior Bur Mines, admin asst, 1956-58, purchasing agent, 1958-60; Holmes & Narver Inc, secy, 1964-65; NASA Pasadena, CA, contract asst, 1966-68; Social Security Admin, claims rep, 1968-73, field rep, 1974-81, claims rep, 1981-93, social ins specialist, 1993-. **Orgs:** Actor Pittsburgh Playhouse, 1958-59; field rep journalist, pub speaker Social Security Admin, 1974-83; dir pub, rel Black Porsche Inc, 1976-78; Parliamentarian, 1979-82, historian, 1983-84; BPI, 1973-; Porsche Club Am, 1981-; bd dirs, 1986-88, treas & bd dirs, 1989-90, secy, & bd dirs, 1991-92, Fed Employees West Credit. **Honors/Awds:** Sustained Superior Performance Award, Corps of Engrs, 1960-61; Outstanding Performance Award, Social Security Admin Huntington Park, CA, 1976; Superior Performance Award, Social Security Admin Los Angeles, CA, 1984; Outstanding Performance Award, Univ Village Office, Los Angeles, CA, Social Security Admin, 1988; Public Service Award in Recognition of 40 years of service in the govt of USA, Commr of Social Security, Baltimore, MD, 1988; Outstanding Performance Award, 1992, Social Security Admin, Univ Village Off, Pittsburgh, PA; Outstanding Performance Award, University Village Office, Los Angeles, CA, 1992-93. **Military Serv:** USAF, sgt, 1945-46. **Business Addr:** Social Insurance representative, Social Security Administration, 1115 W Adams Blvd, Los Angeles, CA 90007.

BAILEY, BEN E. See Obituaries section.

BAILEY, CARLTON WILSON
Football player. **Personal:** Born Dec 15, 1964, Baltimore, MD. **Educ:** Univ NC, BA, sociol, 1988. **Career:** Buffalo Bills, linebacker, 1988-92; NY Giants, 1993-94; Carolina Panthers, 1995-97. *

BAILEY, CAROL A
Air traffic controller. **Career:** Fed Aviation Admin, Detroit Metropolitan Air Traffic Control, supervisory air traffic control specialist, 1991. **Orgs:** Prof Women Controllers. **Special Achievements:** First African American female supervisory air traffic control specialist at the Detroit Metropolitan Air Traffic Control. **Business Addr:** Supervisory Air Traffic Control Specialist, Detroit Metrop Air Traffic Control, Bldg 801 Suite 104, Detroit, MI 48242, **Business Phone:** (313)955-5000.

BAILEY, CLARENCE WALTER
Executive. **Personal:** Born Sep 25, 1933, Longview, TX; married Mavis Lean Blankenship; children: Sherry Lenel Smith. **Educ:** Wiley Col, BS, 1954; Drake Univ, MS, 1959. **Career:** Baileys Ins Co, mgr, 1966-. **Orgs:** dir, Oil Belt Asn Life Underwriters, 1967-; Life mem, Million Dollar Round Table, 1973-; mem, Civitan Club, 1978-; dir, Jr Achievement, 1984-; secy, LISD Sch Bd, 1984-; dir, Good Shephard Med Ctr, 1983-; bd trustees, Wiley Col, 2000-03. **Honors/Awds:** Top ten prod, President Coun NWL, 1971-; Outstanding Citizen Award, NAACP, 1978; Silver Beaver Award, BSA, 1980; Phi Delta Kappa, 1981-; Hon Doctorate Degree, Wiley Col, 1995. **Military Serv:** USAF, sgt, 1954-57. **Home Addr:** 2307 Lilly St, Longview, TX 75602. **Business Addr:** Divisional Sales Manager, Bailey's Insurance Company, 2411 S Eastman Rd, PO Box 7406, Longview, TX 75607.*

BAILEY, CURTIS DARNELL
Consultant, educator. **Personal:** Born May 21, 1954, Philadelphia, PA; son of Helena Bailey. **Educ:** Temple Univ, BA, 1976; Clark/Atlanta Univ, MBA, 1978. **Career:** Benton & Bowles Inc, asst account exec, 1978-79; Atochem Corp, advertising mgr, 1979-84; DuPont Co, mkt commun specialist, 1984-87; mkt & commun consult, 1987; Rowan Univ, prof mgt/mkt, 1990-93; Eastern Col, prof fast-track MBA prog, 1997-. **Orgs:** Kappa Alpha Psi Fraternity, 1983-. **Honors/Awds:** Bell Ringer Award, Best Newsletter Bus & Prof Advertising Asn, 1982 & 1983; Top Ten Readership Ad Award, Chem Processing Mag, 1983 & 1985; fac fel, State Nj, Dept Higher Educ, 1993. **Home Addr:** 1601 E Mt Pleasant Ave, Philadelphia, PA 19150.

BAILEY, DARLYNE
Educator. **Educ:** Lafayette Col, BA; Columbia Univ, MS, soc work; Case Western Res Univ, PhD, orgn behav. **Career:** Case Western Reserve Univ, Mandel Sch Appl Social Scis, dean & prof, 1994-2002; Columbia Univ, Teachers Col, interim pres, 2003, vpres acad affairs & dean, 2006; Col Education & Human Development, dean, 2006-08; Bryn Mawr Coll, dean, prof, Graduate Sch Social Work,Social Research, special asst to pres community partnerships, currently. **Orgs:** Bd mem, Lorraine Monroe Leadership Inst. **Honors/Awds:** George Washington Kidd Award 1836, Lafayette Col; Group XIII Fel, WKKellogg Nat Leadership Pro. **Special Achievements:** Author: Strategic Alliances Among Health and Human Services Organizations:From Affiliations to Consolidations; Managing Human Resources in the Human Services. **Business Addr:** Dean & Vice President for Academic Affairs, Columbia University, Teachers College, 122 Main Hall 525 W 120th St, PO Box 164, New York, NY 10027-6696, **Business Phone:** (212)678-3050.

BAILEY, D'ARMY
Circuit court judge. **Personal:** Born Nov 29, 1941, Memphis, TN; son of Walter L Sr and Will Ella; married Adrienne Marie Leslie; children: Justin, Merritt. **Educ:** Southern Univ, attended 1962; Clark Univ, BA, 1964; Boston Univ Sch Law, attended 1965; Yale Univ, LLB, 1967. **Career:** author; guest speaker; Law Student Internship Program, Southern Program Coordinator, 1966; Law Students Civil Rights Res Coun, New York, NY, dir, 1967-68; San Francisco Neighborhood Legal Assistance Found, staff atty, 1968-70; Field Found NY, prog adv, 1970; city coun, Berkeley, CA, 1971-73; pvt pract, Memphis, TN, atty, 1974-90; Memphis Light, Gas & Water Division, Memphis, Tennessee, Board Commissioner (Appointed by Mayor), 1988 - 1990; circuit ct judge, currently. **Orgs:** La Coordr, Nat Asn Advan Colored People, 1965; exec mem, Book & Gavel Soc; Yale Law Sch, 1966-67; Equality Comt, Am Civil Liberties Union, 1967-68; Staff atty, Neighborhood Legal Assts Found, 1968-70; nat dir, Law Stud Civil Rights Res Cou, 1967-68; Coun Legal Ed Prof Resp, 1969-70; bd dir, Vollitine Boys Club, 1974-76; pres, Bd dirs, Lorraine Civil Rights Museum Found Inc, 1982-91; Tenn Comn Humanities, 1984-88; founder, Nat Civil Rights Museum, Memphis; Tenn Historical Comn, 1990-. **Special Achievements:** Books: The Role of Race in the Memphis Courts, Washington and Lee Law Review, 1994; Mine Eyes Have Seen, Dr Martin Luther King Jr's Final Journey, Towery Press, 1993; Inequities of the Parole System in CA, Howard Univ Law Journal, 1972; Trying to Make it (The Law) Real Compared to What, Univ of Toledo Law Review, 1971; Equal But Separate, Civil Liberties, 1969; Enjoining the Enforcement of the State Criminal Statutes Which Abridge First Amendment Freedoms, Harvard Civil Rights, Civil Liberties Law Review, 1967; Mystery Train, screen actor; How Stella Got Her Groove Back, screen actor; People Vs. Larry Flynt, screen actor. **Home Phone:** (901)327-5544. **Business Addr:** Circuit Court Judge, Shelby Co Courthouse, 140 Adams Ave Rm 324, Memphis, TN 38103, **Business Phone:** (901)545-4022.*

BAILEY, DR. DERYL
Educator. **Educ:** Campbell Univ, BS, 1982, MED, 1984; Univ Va, EDS, 1995, PhD, 1999. **Career:** Sec sch counr; Univ Ga, Col Educ, Dept Coun & Human Develop Serv, dir, 1989-, asst prof, 1995-2005, assoc prof, 2005-; Univ N Fla, vis asst prof, 2002; Univ Buffalo, vis asst prof, 2003, 2005. **Orgs:** Am Coun Asn; Asn Specialists Group Work; Asn Counr Educ & Supvn; AsnMulticultural Coun & Develop; founder & dir, Empowered Youth Progs; Am SchCounAsn; Asn Counselor Educ & Supv; Southern Asn Counr Educ & Supv;Ga Sch Counr Asn; Asn Specialists Group Work; CounAsn Humanistic Educ & Develop; Int Asn Counseling. **Honors/Awds:** Group Work Pract Award, Asn Specialists Group Work, 2000-01; MulticulturalProg Award, Nat Asn Multicultural Educ, 2004; 'Ohana Honors Award,Counselors Social Justice, 2004; Martin Luther King Jr Community Service-Award, Athens Area HumanRights Comn, 2004; Community Service Award, KappaAlpha Psi Fraternity, Inc, 2004; Helping Hands Award, 2005; Super CitizenAward, 2005; Outstanding Teaching Award, Univ Gia Student Asn, 2006;Outstanding Mentoring Award, Univ Ga Grad Sch, 2006; Mary Smith ArnoldAnti-Oppression Award, American Counseling Asn, 2007; African AmericanMale Initiative Best Practices Leadership Award, Univ Syst Ga, 2007;Community Service Award, Nat Orgn Black Law Enforcement Executives, 2007. **Special Achievements:** Co-author of Survival of the Fittest: Navigating Your Way Through theCounselor Education Graduate School Experience, Charles C Thomas Publishers. **Business Phone:** (706)583-0126.

BAILEY, DIDI GISELLE
Psychiatrist. **Personal:** Born Mar 14, 1948, New York, NY; daughter of William Buster and Gertha Jones Smith; divorced; children: Jordan Eleanor Pete. **Educ:** Howard Univ, BS, 1968, MD, 1972; Howard Univ Hosp, attended 1975. **Career:** DC Govt, forensic psychiatrist, 1974-79, med consult disability dept, 1979-80; pvt pract, psychiatrist, 1975-; State CA, med consult disability dept, 1981-85. **Orgs:** adv bd, Alameda County Mental Health, 1981-89; pres, Nat Coalition Black Women Physicians Asn, 1990-93; counr, Golden State Med Asn, 1990-93; mem exec comt, Sinkler Miller State Med Asn, 1991-92. **Honors/Awds:** Commendation, Alameda Co Bd of Supvrs, 1989. **Business Addr:** Psychiatrist, 2730 Adeline St, Oakland, CA 94607, **Business Phone:** (415)353-5050.*

BAILEY, DORIS JONES
Association executive, activist. **Personal:** Born May 16, 1927, Port Chester, NY; daughter of Robert Leon and Alice M Randall; married Alfred K Bailey, May 31, 1964; children: Alethia Joy Streeter. **Educ:** Immanuel Lutheran Col, Assoc Degree, educ, 1947. **Career:** Dept Army-Pentagon, clerk; NY State, secy; NY Bd Cop Educ Serv, soc worker asst, admin asst. **Orgs:** Pres, Immanuel Lutheran Col Alumni Asn, 1985-; pres, Port Chester Rye Nat Asn Adv Colored People, 1990-; bd mem, Carver Community Ctr, 1990-; bd mem, Coun Community Serv, 1992-; mus adv comt mem, State Univ NY, 1992-; Sno-burners, Ski & Sports Asn. **Home Addr:** 325 King St, Port Chester, NY 10573, **Home Phone:** (914)937-6613. *

BAILEY, DUWAIN
Administrator. **Personal:** Born May 29, 1957, Chicago, IL; son of McWillie and Arlena Sanders; married Jocelyn Kyle Bailey, Jul 16, 1983; children: Branden, Kyle. **Educ:** Southern Ill Univ, Carbondale, IL, BA, 1980. **Career:** State Ill, Springfield, IL, tech mgr/safety proj mgr, 1980-84, tech mgr III/pub transp mgr, 1984-85; City Chicago, Chicago, IL, sr budget analyst, 1985-87, finance mgr, 1987-88, deputy comnr; Chicago Housing Authority, dir opers, currently. **Orgs:** Asst financial secy, Phi Beta Sigma Fraternity-Upsilon Sigma, 1991-; chmn, social action comt, Phi Beta Sigma Fraternity-Upsilon Sigma, 1990-; treas, bd dirs, Nat Forum Black Pub Adminr, Chicago Chapter, 1989-; advisor, South Shore High Sch Clg Club; Apostolic Church of God; partic, Chicago Asn Com & Indust Youth Motivation Prog. **Honors/Awds:** Pan-Hellinic Member of the Year, 1977; Kathie Osterman Award, Outstanding Exec Employee, 2006. **Business Addr:** Director of Operations, Chicago Housing Authority, 60 E Van Buren, Chicago, IL 60605-1207.*

BAILEY, EUGENE RIDGEWAY
Military leader. **Personal:** Born Oct 1, 1938, Painter, VA; son of James Hatton and Alma Cleo Jacobs; married Juanita Hicks Bailey, Aug 28, 1961; children: Denise, Duane. **Educ:** Va State Univ, Petersburg, VA, BS, 1960; US Int Univ, San Diego, CA, MA, 1976, DBA, 1986. **Career:** Military leader (retired); USS Fort Fisher, LSD-40, San Diego, CA, exec officer, 1977-79; Amphibious Squadron, San Diego, CA, chief staff, 1979-81; USS Racine, LST-1191, Long Beach, CA, commanding officer, 1981-83; Telecommunications, CMD, Wash, DC, div dir, 1983-85; USS Juneau, LPD-10, San Diego, CA, commanding officer, 1985-87; Naval Recruiting HDQ, Arlington, VA, dep, 1987-89; Naval Educ & Training Support Ctr, San Diego, CA, captain/commanding officer; Eugene R Bailey & Assoc, founder. **Orgs:** Greater San Diego Chamber Com; Nat Naval Officers Asn, 1977-91; Calif Continuing Milit Educrs Asn, 1990-91; bd dir, Jackie Robinson, YMCA, San Diego, 1987-91. **Military Serv:** US Navy, Capt, 1961-91; Legion of Merit 1989, Meritorious Serv 1987. **Business Addr:** San Diego, CA 92119, **Business Phone:** (619)463-7671.*

BAILEY, PROF. GARY
Social worker, educator. **Personal:** Born Oct 9, 1955, Cleveland, OH; son of Samuel Jr and Lucille Bailey; married Richard D McCarthy. **Educ:** Tufts Univ, BA, 1977; Boston Univ, Sch Social Work, MSW, 1979. **Career:** Social worker, 1979-84; Family Serv Asn Greater Boston, unit suvr, 1984-92; Univ Mass, Col Pub & Commun, lectr, 1984-93; Family Serv Greater Boston, Serv Older People, asst dir, 1986-90, Special Projects, dir, 1990-91, dir boston social serv, 1991-93; Boston Univ Sch Social Work, adj asst prof, 1989-, coordr, 1990-92, adj prof pub health, 1993-; Parents & C Serv, exec dir, 1993-99; Simmons Col Sch Social Work, adj assoc prof, 1994-99, vis prof, 1999-2002, asst prof, 2002-05; Simmons Col Sch Social Work, asst prof & coord racism & oppression sequence, currently; PARC, Inaugural Chair, 2006. **Orgs:** Past Pres, AIDS Action Community Inc, 1992-; treas, Nat Asn Social Workers, Wash, DC; Wang Ctr Performing Arts, 1994-; Phillips Brooks House Asn, Harvard Univ, 1996; pres & bd dir, Nat Asn Social Workers, 2003-05; bd mem, Leadership Coun, United Way Mass Bay; bd mem, Comnrs Prof Adv Comt, Mass Dept Soc Serv; bd mem, Mass Dept Mental Health Prof Adv Comt, Child & Adolescent Serv; Mass Education Finance Authority; Design Indust Found AIDS; Wang Ctr Performing Arts; mem & bd dir, Community Benefits Adv Bd, Children's Hosp; mem rels comt, Tufts Health Plan; United Homes C Dorchester; Nat Asn Social Workers Washington; Black Admin Child Welfare; Asn Black Social Workers, Mass Chap. **Honors/Awds:** Social Worker of the Year, Nat Asn Social Work Mass Chap, 1988; Boston Gerontology Center Community Award, Univ Mass, 1993; Congressman Gerry Studds Visibility Award, 1944; Alumni Asn Award, Boston Univ Sch Social Work, 1995; Multicultural AIDS

Coalition Wayne S Wright Advocacy Award, 1996; Visibility Award, Fenway Community health Ctr, Congressman Gerry Studs, 1996; Social Work Pioneer, NASW,2005; Legacy of Caring Award, Devereux -Massachusetts, 2007. **Special Achievements:** Named a Social Work Pioneer by the NASW Foundation; In 2008 was the Cecil and Ida Green Honors Professor, at Texas Christian University; received the State Directors Award for Excellence in Social Work Leadership from the South Carolina Office of Public Health. **Business Addr:** Assistant Professor, Simmons College, School of Social Work, Rm P-404J 300 The Fenway, Boston, MA 02115, **Business Phone:** (617)521-3977.

BAILEY, DR. GRACIE MASSENBERG
School administrator. **Personal:** Born Feb 25, 1936, Waverly, VA; daughter of Maxine Stith and Ernest R; married Erling Sr (divorced); children: LaVetta B Goldsborough & Erling Jr. **Educ:** Va State Col, BS, 1958; Va St Col, comput mgt, 1969, MEd, 1970; VaPolytech Inst & State Univ, DEd 1983. **Career:** VA St Col, sec 1958-62; Amelia City Sch Bd, teacher, 1958-60; HartfordVariable Annuity Life Ins Co, salesperson, 1960-79; Sussex City Sch Bd, teacher, 1961-63; Dinwiddie City Sch Bd, bus educ teacher, 1963-74; Richard Bland Col, dir personnel, assoc prof bus, asst to pres AA/EEO,1974, registr, 1986-88, assoc provost stud serv, 1988-90, assoc provost, 1990, assoc prof emer, currently. **Orgs:** Sussex Ed Assoc, 1961-63; Dinwiddie Ed Assoc, 1963-74; sec, treas Erling-Baily Elect Contr, 1966-85; Am Bus Women Assoc Dinwiddie Charter Chap, 1971-84; Am Asn Univ Profs, 1974-79; Am Asn Affirmative Action, 1976-; Advcoun Educ Computing for the St of Va, 1976-80; Col & Univ Personnel Assoc, 1978-; Nat & Va Asn Women Higher Ed 1978-; recording sec Va Admis Coun on Black Concerns, 1984-; Human Rights Comn Hiram Davis Med Ctr, 1986-; Va Assoc Col Registrars & Admis Officers, Southern Asn Col Registr & Admis Officers; Am Asn Col Registr & Admis Officers, 1986-; vpBudget, Allocation & Fund Raising, UnitedWay Serv, 1988-89; chairperson Sside Opers Bd, 1990; chairperson, Girl Scouts Va, 1991-94; Petersburg Festival Chorus Inc, bd mem, 1990-. **Honors/Awds:** Salutatorian Sussex City Training Sch, 1954; Cert & Plaque Apprec Future Bus Leaders of Am, 1972-74; Achievement Awards Dinwiddie Ed Assoc,1973-74; Outstanding Ed Am, 1975. **Business Addr:** Associate Professor Emeritus, Richard Bland Coll, 11301 Johnson Rd, Petersburg, VA 23805, **Business Phone:** (804)862-6100.*

BAILEY, HARRY AUGUSTINE, JR.
Government official, educator, editor. **Personal:** Born Dec 19, 1932, Fort Pierce, FL; son of Harry Augustine and Ruth; married Mary L, Aug 5, 1952; children: Harry III & Larry B. **Educ:** Fla A&M Univ, BA, 1954; Univ Kans, MA, 1960, PhD, 1964. **Career:** Government official (retired), educator (retired), editor; Univ Kans, asst instr, 1960-62, asst instr, Western Civilization, 1962-64, instr sociol, 1964; Temple Univ, Dept Polit Sci, from asst prof to prof, 1964-75, Dept Polit Sci, chmn, 1970-73, prof & dir, Masters Prog Pub Admin, 1975-80, chmn grad studies, 1985-90; Charles Merrill Publ, Negro Polit Am, ed, 1967; Book: The Politics of the Southern Negro, rev auth; Charles Merrill Publ, co-ed, Ethnic Group Polit, 1969; J Polit, ed bd, 1975-76; Moore Publ Co, ed, Classics Am Pres, 1980; Dorsey Press, co-ed, Am Pres, 1988; FE Peacock Publ, co-ed, State & Local Gov & Polit, 1993. **Orgs:** Am Polit Sci Asn; Am Soc Pub Admin; C Study Pres; Pi Sigma Alpha; Pa Polit Sci & Pub Admin Asn, 1970-72; pres, Pa Polit Sci Asn, 1970; vpres, Northeastern Sci Asn, 1971-72; pres, bd gov, Temple Univ Fac Club, 1972-73; Danforth Asn, 1975-81; chmn, Civil Serv Comn, City Philadelphia, 1983-91; Zoning Bd Adjust, City Philadelphia, 1992-. **Honors/Awds:** Leonard D White Award, Com Am Polit Sci Asn, 1974-75; Lindback Distinguished Teaching Award, 1978; Great Teacher's Award, Temple Univ, 1992. **Military Serv:** AUS, second lt, 1954-55, first lt, 1955-57.

BAILEY, HILTRON
Photographer. **Educ:** Hope Int Univ, attended; Penn Valley Community Col, attended. **Career:** Photo-journalist, Eurweb, currently; freelance photogr, currently. **Home Phone:** (213)272-3677. **Business Addr:** Photographer, Eurweb.com, PO Box 412081, Los Angeles, CA 90041, **Business Phone:** (323)254-9599.

BAILEY, DR. JOSEPH ALEXANDER, II
Educator, physician. **Personal:** Born Jul 22, 1935, Pine Bluff, AR; son of Joseph A Sr and Angeline Elaine Davis; children: Ryan, Jana, Joseph III, Johathan, Jerad & Jordan. **Educ:** Univ Mich Ann Arbor, undergrad, 1955; Morehouse Col, BS, 1957; Meharry Med-Sch, MD, 1961; Am Bd Ortho Surgeons, dipl, 1971. **Career:** Los Angeles Co Hosp, internship, 1961-62; Hahnemann Hosp Phil, PA, chiefres, 1964-66; St Hosp Crippled C, PA, chief researcher, 1966-67; HospJoint Dis, NY, sr researcher, 1967-68; Med Gen John Hopkins Hosp, fel,1968-69; Ortho Sur John Hopkins Hosp, Baltimore, fel, 1968-69; Univ Calif,Riverside, asst clin prof, clin instr, 1986-; San Bernardino Co Gen Hosp,assoc staff, prof; St Calif, independent med examr; St Benardines Hosp,assoc staff; Univ New Am Communities Prog, endowed chair. **Orgs:** Fel Am Col Surgeons, 1971-; chief gen secy, Acad Ortho-Neuro Soc; dir & instr, Life Skills Courses, Los Angeles Conserv, currently; Omega Psi Phi Fraternity, 1954. **Honors/Awds:** Eagle Scouts Award, Boy Scouts Am, 1953; Community Leadership Award, Noteworthy Am, 1978; Black Voice News Award, 1985; Humanitarian Award, 2001. **Special Achievements:** Listed in Best Doctors of America, 1979; Authored: Disproportionate Short Stature Diagnosis and Management, 1973; The Handbook for Worker's Compensation Doctors, 1994; Medical Legal Dictionary, 1996; Rational Thinking, 1997; Preparing to Prepare, 2000. **Military Serv:** USAF, capt, 1962-64. **Business Phone:** (951)827-1012.

BAILEY, KENETTA
Executive, vice president (organization). **Educ:** Northwestern Univ, BS, MS, MBA, mkt & strategy. **Career:** Golin/Harris Communications, sr acct exec; Allstate Ins Co, Ill, corp rels rep; Pepsi-Cola Co, mkt mgr; Kraft Foods, brand mgr, 1997; BMG Entertainment, dir youth mkt progs, RCA Recs, sr dir strategic bus, 1999-2002; vpres strategic mktg, 2002-04; BMG Music, VPres Strategic Mkt, 2004-06; NBC Universal's Telemundo Network, group mkt dir; Women's Entertainment TV, sr vpres mkt, 2006-. **Orgs:** Women Cable Telecommunications; Nat Asn Multi-Ethnicity Communications; Cable & Telecommunications Asn Mkt. **Honors/Awds:** Forty Under 40, Network J. **Business Addr:** Senior Vice President of Marketing, Women's Entertainment TV, 200 Jericho Quadrangle, Jericho, NY 11753.

BAILEY, LEE
President (Organization). **Career:** Radio programming, 1970; Disc jockey; EURweb, founder, currently; Lee Bailey Communs Inc, pres, currently. **Business Addr:** President, Lee Bailey Communications Inc, 3151 Cahuenga Bl W Suite 200, PO Box 412081, Los Angeles, CA 90068-1768, **Business Phone:** (213)969-0011.

BAILEY, LINDA F (LINDA F GLOVER)
Government official. **Personal:** Born Oct 1, 1951, Emerson, AR; daughter of Edmond Glover and Alberta Washington Glover; married Fred E, May 19, 1979; children: Janelle Nicole & Jocelyn Briana. **Educ:** S Ark Univ, Magnolia, AR, BME, 1973; Univ Mo, Kansas City, MO, MPA, 1978. **Career:** Social Security Admin, Kansas City, MO, Social Ins Claims Examiner, 1973-79; Small Bus Admin, Kansas City, MO, equal opportunity officer, 1979-82, bus develop spec, 1982-90, asst dist dir bus dev, 1990-94, chief, 1994, econ develop specialist, currently. **Business Addr:** Economic Development Specialist, Assistant District Director, Small Business Administration, 323 W 8th Suite 501, Kansas City, MO 64105-1500, **Business Phone:** (816)374-6762 Ext 223.

BAILEY, MONA HUMPHRIES
School administrator, consultant. **Personal:** Born Dec 14, 1932; married William Peter Bailey; children: Peter Govan & Christopher Evans. **Educ:** Fla A&M Univ Tallahassee, BS, chem, 1954; OR State Univ Corvalis, MS, Sci Educ, 1962; Univ Wash, PhD. **Career:** Meany-Madrona Middle Sch, Seattle Wash, prin, 1970-73; Univ Wash, instr, 1973-74; Eckstein Middle Sch, Seattle Wash, prin appointee, 1974-75; Wash State Supt Pub Instuction, asst supt, 1974-86; Seattle Public Sch, Dist Asst Supt, 1986-90; Seattle Pub Sch, Deputy Supi, 1990-94; Nat Fac Western Region, dir, 1995-98; Forest Ridge Sch Sacred Heart, head, 1998-2000; Univ Wash, Ctr Educ Renewal, sr assoc, currently; independent consult, currently. **Orgs:** Comn mem, Gov's Comn Criminal Justice, 1974-; bd trustees, Pac Sci Ctr, Seattle, 1975-;Bd dirs, Totem Girl Scout Coun Seattle, 1977-; chmn, adv comn, Seattle Oppors Industrialization Ctr, 1978; adv bd, United Negro Col Fund Inc, Seattle, 1978-; Delta Sigma Theta Sorority, Inc, 17th Nat Pres, 1979-83; nat pres, Delta Sigma Theta, 1980; pres, Delta Res & Educ Found, 2002-06; Delta Sigma Theta Sorority, Inc; Nat Network Sacred Heart Sch; Forest Ridge Sch; Assoc, Pac Sci Ctr Found; Nat Bd TransAfrica; Mary McLeod Bethune Memorial Mus Found; Am Civil Liberties Union Nat Adv Comt; Wash State Vendor Rates Adv Comt; bd, Wash State Crime & Delinquency; bd, Seattle's Univ Prep Acad; bd, Pac Sci Ctr; City Seattle Adv Comt, African Am Heritage Mus; Bd Dir, Wash Special Olympics; Pac Sci Ctr Found Adv Comt; Chair, State Bd Wash MESA Prog, currently. **Honors/Awds:** Disting Serv Field of Educ Inner City Award, Carnation Co, 1973-74; Achievement Award, Les Dames Bridge Club Seattle, 1974; Distinguished achievement Service to Youth Award, Links Inc, Twentieth Nat Asn Seattle, 1976; Distinguished Comm Service Award, Benefit Guild Seattle, 1978; Meritorious Achievement Award, Florida A & M Univ; Centennial Medallion, Florida A & M Univ. **Special Achievements:** Hundred most influential FAMUANS of the century. **Home Addr:** 4708 E Mercer Way, Mercer Island, WA 98040, **Home Phone:** (206)232-9451. **Business Addr:** Senior Associate, University of Washington, Center for Educational Renewal College of Education, 315A Miller Hall, PO Box 353600, Seattle, WA 98195-3600, **Business Phone:** (206)543-6230.

BAILEY, MYRTLE LUCILLE
Business owner. **Personal:** Born Jul 11, 1954, St Louis, MO; daughter of George Wendell and Mildred Turrentine; married R Mark Odom, Oct 18, 1986; children: Jared Michael. **Educ:** Dillard Univ, BA, psychol, 1976; St Louis Univ, Cert, applied gerontol, MA, urban affairs, 1977. **Career:** Cent Med Ctr, dir mkt, 1977-80; Greater St Louis Health Systs Agency, planning assoc, 1980-81; Catalyst, consult, 1981-84; Women's Self Help Ctr, bd drs; Harris-Stowe Col, dirpub rels, 1984-87; Real Estate agt; Catalyst Pub Rels Inc, cheif exec officer, 1987-;Coldwell Banker Gundaker CWE, owner, currently. **Orgs:** Bd mem, Paraquad, 1992-; pres, City-wide fed Republican Women, 1992-; bd mem, Catholic cms on Housing, 1990-; bd mem, Provident Sch, 1990-; St Louis Convention & Vis, 1991-; RCGA St Louis, 1992-; exec comt, Nat Asn Advancement Colored People, 1992-. **Honors/Awds:** Silver Microphone Award "We Wish to Plead Our Own Cause", 1989; Appreciation Student Gover, Harris Stowe State Col, 1987; Outstanding Business Man, St Louis Develop Agency, 1992. **Special Achievements:** Annie Malone Children's Home, Special Contribution, 1990; Lincoln Univ Student Gov Asn, Participation-YMTF, 1988; Dedication & Service Alumni Asn, 1987. **Business Phone:** (314)535-7535.*

BAILEY, PHILIP
Singer. **Personal:** Born May 8, 1951, Denver, CO; married Krystal. **Career:** Phoenix Horns, vocalist; Earth Wind & Fire, singer, 1972-84 & 1987-; Albums: "Last Days & Time", 1972; "Head to the Sky", 1973; "Open Our Eyes", 1974; "Another Time", 1974; "That's the Way of the World", 1975; "Spirit", 1975; "Gratitude", 1975; "Continuation", 1983; "All 'N All", 1977; "Sing a Song", 1977; "I Am", 1979; "Faces", 1980; "Raise!", 1981; "Secret Messages", 1982; "Powerlight", 1983; "Electric Universe", 1983; "Philip Bailey: The Wonders of His Love", 1984; "Triumph", 1986; "Inside Out", 1986; "Touch the World", 1987; "Family Affair", 1989; "Chinese Wall", 1990; "Heritage", 1990; "Millennium", 1993; "Philip Bailey: Best of Gospel Collection", 1991; "Philip Bailey", 1994; In the Name of Love, 1997; "Life Love", 1998; "Dreams", 1999;; Take Two, 2001; Soul on Jazz, Heads Up Records, 2002. **Honors/Awds:** Grammy for Best R&B Vocal Performance By a Duo, Group or Chorus (With Earth, Wind & Fire), 1975, 1978, 1979, 1982; Grammy for Best R&B Instrumental Performance (With Earth, Wind and Fire), 1978, 1979; Grammy Award for Gospel Male, 1986. **Special Achievements:** Actor in film Full Metal Jacket, 1987 & on the TV show Matlock portraying Pvt. Bobby Thomas. **Business Addr:** Singer, c/o Bret Steinberg, Creative Artists Agency, 2000 Ave of the Stars, Los Angeles, CA 90067, **Business Phone:** (424)288-2000.*

BAILEY, DR. RANDALL CHARLES
Clergy, educator. **Personal:** Born May 26, 1947, Malden, MA; son of Charles C and Lorraine Margolis; married Dorothy Jean Lewis, Apr 7, 1973; children: Omari & Imani Akilah. **Educ:** Brandeis Univ, Waltham, BA; Univ Chicago, IL, AM, Emory Univ, Candler Sch Theol, Atlanta, GA, MDiv, 1979; Emory Univ, Atlanta, GA, PhD, relig, 1987. **Career:** PCSAP Loop Col, Chicago, Ill, dir educ prog, 1972-73; Shelby County Develop Coord Dept, Memphis, TN, assoc dir, 1973; Atlanta Univ Sch Social Work, Atlanta, GA, asst prof, 1973-81; First Cong Church, UCC, Atlanta, GA, asst minister, 1980-81; Interdenominational Theol Ctr, instr, 1981-87, asst prof, 1987-90, assoc prof, Atlanta, GA, 1990-, Andrew W Mellon prof Hebrew Bible, currently; fel, United Negro Col Fund, 1984-85. Memphis Theol Sem, adj prof, 2005-06. **Orgs:** Black Theol Proj, 1986-; co-chair, Afro-Am Theol & Biblical Hermeneutics Soc Biblical Lit, 1987-94; co-chair, Unity/Renewal Study, COFO/NCCCUSA, 1988-92; Div Educ & Min/NCCCUSA, 1988-91; Bible Translation & Utilization Comm DEM/NCCCUSA, 1988-, Soc Study Black Relig, 1988-; mem exec bd, NCCCUSA; consult, Balm in Gilead Inc; ed bd, Semeia Jour. **Honors/Awds:** Distinguished Service Award, Atlanta Nat Assn Black Social Workers, 1978. **Special Achievements:** Author: "Wash Me White as Snow: When Bad is Turned to Good, Race, Class and the Politics of Bible Translation," Seneia 76, 1996; "The Redemption of Yhwh: A Literary Critical Function of the Songs of Hannah and David," Biblical Interpretation, 1995; "'Is That Any Name for a Nice Hebrew Boy?' - Exodus 2:1-10: The De-Africanization of an Israelite Hero," The Recover of Black Presence: An Interdisciplinary Exploration, Abingdon, 1995; "They're Nothing but Incestuous Bastards: The Polemical Use of Sex and Sexuality in Hebrew Canon Narrative," Reading From This Place: Social Location and Biblical Interpretation in the United States, Fortress, 1994; "And Then They Will Know That I Am YHWH: The P Recasting of the Plague Narratives," JITC, 1994; "What Price Inclusivity?: An Afrocentric Reading of Dangerous Biblical Texts," Voices from the Third World, 1994; "Cobb Clergy's Gay Stance Loses Punch in Biblical Debate," Atlanta Journal/Constitution, p F2, June 26, 1994; "A De-politicized Gospel: Reflections on Galatians 5:22-23," Ecumenical Trends, 22 No 1, Jan 1993; "Doing the Wrong Thing: Male-Female Relationships in the Hebrew Canon," We Belong Together: The Churches in Solidarity with Women, Friendship Press, 1992; David in Love and War: The Pursuit of Power in a Samuel 10-12, Sheffield, 1990; numerous other publications. **Business Addr:** Andrew W Mellon Professor of Hebrew Bible, Interdenominational Theological Center, 700 Martin Luther King Jr Dr SW, Classroom Bldg 308B, Atlanta, GA 30314-4143, **Business Phone:** (404)527-7754.

BAILEY, RICHARD
Historian. **Personal:** Born Oct 29, 1947, Montgomery, AL; son of Raymond and Lottie; married Judy, Feb 14, 1987; children: Judy, Valerie, Richard Jr., Karen. **Educ:** Ala State Univ, BS, 1971, MEd, 1972; Atlanta Univ, MA, 1973; Kans State Univ, PhD, 1984. **Career:** Hist Res Agency, Maxwell AFB, AL, tech info specialist, 1982-83; Extension Course Inst, Gunter AFB, AL, educ specialist, 1983-85; Air Univ Press, Maxwell AFB, AL, res writer spec,

1986-. **Orgs:** pres, Phi Delta Kappa, 1985-; Ala Hist Asn, 1986-; Ala Hist Comn, 1995. **Honors/Awds:** Maxwell Air Force Base Angel Award, 1994, State Volunteer of the Year, 1991; National Volunteer of the Year, 1991. **Special Achievements:** Neither Carpetbaggers nor Scalawags: Blacks Officeholders during the Reconstruction of Alabama, 1867-1878, 1991, reprint, 1997. They Too Call Alabama Home: African American Profiles, 1800-1999, 1999. **Business Addr:** Researcher, Maxwell Air Force Base, 172 W Selfridge St, Montgomery, AL 36112.*

BAILEY, ROBERT MARTIN LUTHER (ROBERT BAILEY)
Football player, businessperson. **Personal:** Born Sep 3, 1968, Barbodas, West Indies; married Wylidra; children: Kharee. **Educ:** Miami, Fla, BS, science. **Career:** Football player (retired); Los Angeles Rams, defensive back, 1991-94; Wash Redskins, 1995; Dallas Cowboys, 1995; Miami Dolphins, 1996; Detroit Lions, 1997-99, 2001; Baltimore Ravens, 2000; sports marketing business, currently. **Orgs:** Spokesperson, Save the Earth Found. **Special Achievements:** The only current Lion to have won Super Bowl titles with two different teams. *

BAILEY, ROBIN
Administrator. **Career:** Am Postal Workers Union, admin asst. **Business Addr:** Administrative Assistant, American Postal Workers Union, 1300 L St NW, Washington, DC 20005.

BAILEY, RONALD W
Planner, consultant. **Personal:** Born May 21, 1938, Chicago, IL; son of Claude Bailey and Leona Z Smith Alexander; married Florentine Kelly; children: Darlene Bailey, Ronald Jr & Charles. **Educ:** Univ Wis, BS, 1962; Northeastern IL Univ, MEd, 1972; Univ Mich, mgt obj, 1978; John Marshall Law Sch, Community Law Cert, 1979; Loyola Univ, master's of jurisprudence, child & family law, 2001. **Career:** Dayton YMCA, Dayton, youth prog dir, 1964-67; Off Econ Opportunity, Dayton, exec dir, 1967-70; Chicago Youth Ctrs, assoc exec dir; Northeastern Ill Univ, instr; United Way Chicago, planner; City Chicago, child care mgr; Cook Co Ill, manpower planner; United Way Dade Co, sr consult, prog mgr, Community Renewal Soc; State Ill, DCFS, Governors State Univ, caseworker trainer; Lancaster County Planning Comn, exec dir, currently. **Orgs:** Chicago Urban League, 1970-88; co-founder, chmn, Chicago Black Child Develop, 1978-; Black Child Dev Inst Wash, 1978-, Chicago Blacks Philanthropy, 1984-, Asn Black Fund Raising Execs, 1984-; People United Save Humanity, 1984-88; Asn Black Fundraising Execs, 1986-88; vpres, Roosevelt PTA; Steering Comm Neighborhood Capitol Budget Group; Chicago Coun Urban Affairs, Chicago Workshop Econ Dev, Chicago Mgt Assistance Prog; bd mem, Provident St Mel Develop Corp, 1990-; bd mem, Provident St Mel Sch, 1990-; Village Bellwood, Ill, bd health; Canaan AME Church, steward; bd mem, Chicago Area Tech Assist Providers; bd mem, LEAD; coord, Black Caucus, Family Resource Coalition, Chicago; Statewide Family Preserv, Statewide Task Force, Ill Dept C & Family Serv; consult, Ill Dept C & Family Serv; consult, Fishers Men Proj, a male mentoring prog, Chicago; consult, Project 2000, Governors State Univ, Ill; consult, Coun Accreditation Serv Families & C Inc. **Honors/Awds:** Superior Supervisor Award, SCOPE, 1969-70; Executive of the Year, Chicago Youth Center, 1980. **Military Serv:** AUS, Corp, 2 yrs; Good Conduct Medal, Expert Marksman, 1962-64. **Home Addr:** 125 Rice Ave, Bellwood, IL 60104, **Home Phone:** (708)544-5140. **Business Addr:** Executive Director, Lancaster County Planning Commission, 50 N Duke St, Courthouse, PA 17608-3480, **Business Phone:** (717)299-8333.

BAILEY, SHARON BROWN
Administrator. **Career:** Western Interstate Comn Higher Educ, policy assoc, 2002-. **Orgs:** Pres, Int Black Women's Cong; past mem, Denver Sch Bd. **Business Addr:** Policy Associate, Western Interstate Commission for Higher Education, 2520 55th St, PO Box 9752, Boulder, CO 80301-9752, **Business Phone:** (303)541-0200.

BAILEY, THOMAS R., JR.
Economics historian. **Educ:** Harvard University, BA, 1976; MIT, PhD. **Career:** Columbia University—Teachers College, Director of the Institute of Education and the Economy (IEE), 1992; National Center for Postsecondary Research (NCPR), Director, 2006; Columbia University-Teachers College, George and Abby O'Neill Professor of Economics and Education. **Orgs:** 100 Black Men of America. **Special Achievements:** Wrote "The Double Helix of Education and the Economy", "Manufacturing Advantage", "Working Knowledge: Work-Based Learning and Education Reform", and "Defending the Community College Equity Agenda". *

BAILEY, THURL LEE
Television broadcaster, songwriter, basketball player. **Personal:** Born Apr 7, 1961, Seat Pleasant, MD; married Sindi; children: 3 (divorced); children: Thurl Jr, Tevaun & Chonell (Stanley). **Educ:** NC State, commun, 1983. **Career:** Basketball player (retired), broadcast analyst, songwriter; executive; Utah Jazz,forward, 1983-91 & 1998-99, broadcast analyst, currently; Minnesota Timber wolves, 1991-94; Italian League, 1995-98; Univ Utah, broadcast analyst, currently; inspirational speaker, currently; Album: Faith In Your Heart, songwriter; The Gift of Christmas; I'm Not The Same, songwriter, 2002; Big TLC, founder; Big T Productions, chmn; Fertile Earth, chmn; FourLeaf Films, chmn. **Honors/Awds:** J Walter Kennedy Citizenship Award, NBA, 1989; Community Service Award,Utah Asn Gifted Children's; Exemplary Manhood Award, Sigma Gamma Chi Fraternity; American Champion Award, Great Salt Lake Coun Boy Scouts Am; All Star Games Most Valuable Player, Italian League, 1998; Pearl Award, 2000; Best New Artist of the Year. **Special Achievements:** Utah Symphony, guest coordr, 1990. **Business Addr:** Broadcast analyst, Utah Jazz, 301 W S Temple, Salt Lake City, UT 84101-1216, **Business Phone:** (801)325-2500.

BAILEY, WELTMAN D., SR.
Dentist. **Personal:** Born Jan 26, 1927, Harveil, MO; married Margaret Barber; children: Sandra, Weltman Jr, Peter, Robert. **Educ:** Univ Wiscon, BS, 1950; Meharry Med Col, DDS, 1956; Univ Mo, MPA, MPH, 1973. **Career:** Pvt Pract, dentist, 1958-; Staff numerous hosps health ctr. **Orgs:** Trustee, Baptist church, 1967-; Rehab Inst; Reg Health Welfare Coun, 1969-70; bd dirs, Mid-Am Comprehensive Health Planning Agency, 1970-71; med adv bd, Mo Div Family Health, 1974-; fel Royal Soc Health; Acad Gen Dent; Alpha Phi Alpha Fraternity; YMCA; Urban League; Nat Am Dent Asn; Am Pub Health Asn; Am Soc Pub Admin; Nat Rehab Asn; Am Asn Hosp Dentists. **Military Serv:** AUS, 1945-47. **Home Addr:** 10433 Grand Ave, Kansas City, MO 64114. **Business Addr:** Dentist, Private Practice, 2514 E 27 St, Kansas City, MO 64127.*

BAILEY, WILLIAM H. (BOB BAILEY)
Association executive. **Personal:** Born Feb 14, 1927, Detroit, MI; married Anna L Porter; children: John Robert, Kimberley Ann. **Educ:** Morehouse Col, BA, 1947. **Career:** Records:"Danny Boy"; "The Worst Blues I Ever Had"; "Blue and Sentimental"; Count Basie Orchestra, featured vocalist, 1946-50; Las Palmas Theatre, Hollywood, CA, entertainer, musical comedy, 1950-51; Natl & Intl Supper Club, tours, 1951-54; Moulin Rouge Hotel, producer, prod singer, entertainer, 1955; Las Vegas ABC, CBS, PBS Affil, co-producer, master of ceremonies, 1955-65, 1985; Las Vegas Sun, newspaper columnist, 1955-57; KTNV-Channel 13, 1957; Channel 8, 1961; First Securities Investment, broker, owner, 1962-72; Sugar Hill, Club, founder, 1964-89; Pan-Afro Auditorium, 1965; Channel 13, newscaster, 1965-71; Manpower Serv Las Vegas, dir, 1971; New Ventures "503", Cert Devel Co & New Ventures Inc, pres, exec dir; NEDCO Inc, pres, exec dir, 1972-; Minority Bus Develop Agency, US Dept Com, dep dir; New Ventures Inc, Nev Bus Inst, pres. **Orgs:** Local chmn, Urban Renewal Adv Comn, 1956; Las Vegas Bd Realtors, Ctr Bus & Econ Res, Univ Nev Las Vegas, Southern Nev Econ Devel Coun; exec bd mem, Southern Nev "Special Impact Area"; Online Exec Develop Prog, pres Prospectors; exec bd mem, Las Vegas C of C; mem, White House Small Bus Conf, 1980, 1986; mkt assoc, SW Equal Opportunity Bd, Officers Asn, Nev Minority Purchasing Council, Las Vegas Press Club; exec bd mem Nat Asn Advan Colored People, Southern Christian Leadership Conf; hon mem, Nev Asn Latin Am; Uptown Kiwanis Club, Alpha Phi Alpha, 33 Degree Mason; exec bd mem, Nat Asn Black & Minority CC; chmn, Nev Inst Bus. **Honors/Awds:** Recipient of over 150 awards from nat, state, local gvts & private sector organizations; "Bob Bailey Day" Proclaimed for 30 Yrs Serv in State of NV; Nat Univ, DHL, 1987. **Special Achievements:** Develop Las Vegas first dance program for teens; Named among First 100 Persons Who Shaped Southern Nevada. **Business Addr:** Deputy Director, US Dept Com, Minority Bus Develop Agency, 1401 Constitution Ave NW, Washington, DC 20230.*

BAILEY-THOMAS, SHERYL K.
Publisher, executive, chief executive officer. **Personal:** Born Jul 29, 1958, Palmer, AK; daughter of Algian R and Evelyn D; children: Mykal Jabari Thomas. **Educ:** Univ Alaska, AAS, electronics technol, 1978, BA, bus mgt, 1988; MED,counsel & guidance sec educ, 1998; adult educ & career develop, MA, 1998. **Career:** National Weather Serv, technician, 1979-80; Multi vision Cable TV, AV technician, 1980-85; State of Alaska, AV technician, 1988-; Abram Abraham Prod & Mgt Inc, pres & ceo. **Orgs:** Founder, organizing comt, UCAAN; BIG, 1990-92. **Special Achievements:** FCC, Radio-Telephone License, 1978; Anchorage Gazette, The African-Am Voice of Alaska, assoc ed, 1992-93; African-American in Alaska, a Black Community Booklet & Calendar of Events, publ, 1990-93; Alaska Resource Guide, 1994-99. **Home Addr:** PO Box 201741, Anchorage, AK 99520-1741.

BAIN, ERLIN. See IFALASE, DR. OLUSEGEN.

BAIN, LINDA VALERIE
Management consultant. **Personal:** Born Feb 14, 1947, New York, NY; daughter of Carlton L and Helen Boyd; married Samuel Green, Mar 21, 1986. **Educ:** City Col NY, BA, 1974. **Career:** NYS Dept Labor, secy, 1965-66; NY City Dept Soc Serv, exec secy, 1966-70; Manhattan St Hosp, prog coordr, 1970-73; Nat Coun Negro Women's Ctr Educ & Career Advan, assoc dir, 1973-79; Donchian Mgmt Serv, sr consult, 1980-85; Bain Assoc Inc, pres, 1985-. **Orgs:** Nat Asn Female Exec, 1980; Am Soc Training & Develop, 1981; Nat & NY Org Develop Network, 1981; bd dir, NY Friends Alvin Ailey, 1985; chairperson, bd dirs, The Friendly Pl, 1989; Corp Women's Network; The Books Kids Found, 1992. **Honors/Awds:** Coalition of 100 Black Women, 1971; Mary McLeod Bethune Achievement Award, Nat Coun Negro Women. **Home Addr:** 23 W 104th St, New York, NY 10025, **Home Phone:** (212)864-5812. **Business Addr:** President, Bain Associates Inc, 23 W 104th St, PO Box 20789, New York, NY 10025, **Business Phone:** (212)864-5811.

BAINES, HAROLD DOUGLAS
Baseball player, athletic coach. **Personal:** Born Mar 15, 1959, Easton, MD; married Marla Henry; children: Antoinette, Britni, Harold Jr & Courtney. **Career:** Baseball player (retired), baseball coach; Chicago White Sox, outfielder, 1980-89, 1996-97, 2000-01; Texas Rangers, outfielder, 1989-90; Oakland Athletics, outfielder, 1990-92; Baltimore Orioles, outfielder, 1993-95, 1997-99, 2000; Cleveland Indians, outfielder, 1999; Chicago White Sox, bench coach, 2004-05, first base coach, currently. **Orgs:** Cook County Teen Democracy; Nat Asn Down Syndrome. **Honors/Awds:** Six-time American League All-Star; every January nineth is Harold Baines Dayin St. Michaels. **Home Addr:** PO Box 10, Saint Michaels, MD 21663. **Business Addr:** First Base Coach, Chicago White Sox, Comiskey Pk 333 W 35th St, Chicago, IL 60616, **Business Phone:** (312)674-1000.

BAINES, HENRY T., SR.
Executive. **Personal:** Born in Wilson, NC. **Educ:** Howard Univ sch divinity, MA; united technol seminary dayton Ohio, DMin. **Career:** Baines Stop Shop & Save Food Mkts, pres & chief exec officer, currently. **Honors/Awds:** Co No 9 on the Black Enterprise List of Top 100 Indust Co, 1992. **Business Addr:** President, Chief Executing officer, Baines Stop Shop & Save Food Markets, 200 S Arlington Ave Suite 300, Baltimore, MD 21223-2672, **Business Phone:** (410)783-8180.*

BAINES, DR. TYRONE RANDOLPH
Association executive. **Personal:** Born Feb 22, 1943, Exmore, VA; son of Hilton Baines and Clarease Dillard Baines; married Shereatha; children: Tyrone R II & Tonita. **Educ:** Morgan State Univ, AB, 1965; Univ Pa, MSW, 1967; Univ Md, MA, 1971, PhD, 1972. **Career:** Association Executive (retired); Community Progs Inc, consult, 1971-72; Md Sch Syst, consult, 1972; Fed Exec Inst, sr fac mem, 1974-75; NC Cent Univ, dir pub admin, 1975-78, dir publ admin prog, 1979-82, exec asst chancellor, 1985-88, sr fel, currently; W K Kellogg Found, Battle Creek, MI, prog dir; Kellogg Youth Initiatives Prog, Battle Creek, MI, dir. **Orgs:** Omega Psi Phi Fraternity, 1965-; Social worker Children's Serv Inc, Philadelphia, PA, 1967; capt, AUS Med Serv Corp 1967-69; consult, US Congress House Rep, 1969-70; grad teaching asst, Univ Md, 1969-70; personnel rels spec, Off Econ Opport, 1970-71; exec coun, Nat Asn Schs Pub Affairs & Admin, 1985; bd trustees, Durham Acad, 1986; ed bd, Political Sci, Southern Review Pub Admin, 1986; Citizens Adv Comm for Durham Bd Educ, 1987; Nat Forum Black Pub Adminrs, 1989-; bd trustees, Mt Zion AME Church, 1989-; bd dir, Nat Inst for Pub Mgt; bd dirs, Battle Creek YMCA, 1990-. **Honors/Awds:** Superior Performance Duty Award, 1969; Nat Award, Conf Minority Pub Admin, 1975; Fellowship, Harvard Univ Inst Educ Mgt, 1977; Phelps-Stokes Fund West Africa Seminar, 1977; Am Coun on Educ Fellow, Educ Admin, 1978; Certificate of Recognition US Dept Labor, Atlanta Reg, 1979; Kellogg Nat Fellow Kellogg Found, 1982-85; honorary doctor humane letters, Medgar Evers Col, 1997; honorary doctor of public service, Bowie State Univ. **Military Serv:** AUS, capt, 1967-69; Outstanding Achievement Award, 1969.

BAIOCCHI, REGINA HARRIS
Composer, writer, poet. **Personal:** Born Jul 16, 1956, Chicago, IL; daughter of Elgie Jr and Lanzie Mozelle Belmont; married Gregory, Jul 12, 1975. **Educ:** Roosevelt Univ, BM, 1978; Ill Inst Technol, 1986; NW Univ, 1992; NY Univ,pub rels cert; De Paul Univ, MA, music, 1995. **Career:** Composer, numerous pieces for instrument and voice, 1978-; Dunbar Voc HS, teacher, 1979; St Bride's Jr HS, teacher, 1979-81; St Thomas the Apostle Jr HS, teacher, 1983-86; Telaction Corp, audio quality control analyst & writer, 1986-89; Catholic Theo Union, pub rels dir, 1989-94; Steppen wolf Theater, composer & dir, 1997; Ravinia Music Festival, Music Illumination Prog, artistic dir, 1997-99; Roots & Wings concert, artist dir, 1998; East West Univ, lectr, 2000-, Dept Eng &Comm, instr, part-time fac, currently; composer, poet & writer-,currently; poems: Teeter Totter, Ghetto Child, Chicago Tribune Mag; short story: Mama's Will, 1988; novel: Indigo Sound, 2003; numerous music compositions, 1978-; Compositions: Two Piano Etudes, 1978; Chase For Wind Sextet, 1979; Realizations 1979; Father, We Thank You, 1986; Two Zora Neale Hurston Songs, 1989; Miles per Hour, 1990; We Real Cool, 1990; Autumn Night, 1991; Foster Pet, 1991; Crystal Stair, 1991; Orchestra Suite, 1991; Shadows, 1992; Legacy, 1992; A Few Black Voices, 1992; Bwana's Libation, 1992; Sketches for Piano Trio, 1992; Mason Room, 1993; Much in Common, 1993; Ain't Nobody's Child, 1993; Teddy Bear Suite, 1994; QFX, 1994; Liszten, My Husband Is Not a Hat, 1994; Three Pieces For Greg, 1994; Deborah, 1994; Best

Friends, 1994; Ancestor's Medley, 1994; Much In Common, 1994; After The Rain, 1994; Say No To Guns, 1994; Good New Falls Gently, 1995; Darryl's Rose, 1995; Friday Night, 1995; Dream hoppers, 1997;Gbeldahoven: No One's Child, 1997; African Hands, 1997; Nikki Giovanni, 1997; Skins, 1997; Muse, 1997; Message To My Muse, 1997; Dream Weaver 1997; Azuretta, 2000; Ask Him, 2000; Cycles, 2000; HB4A, 2000; Lovers & Friends, 2000; Psalm Cat, 2000; Litany for Hale Smith, 2000. **Orgs:** Am Soc Composers, Authors & Publ; Nat Endowment Randolph St Gallery; IllArts Coun. **Honors/Awds:** Poets & Patrons Award; McDonald's Literary Achievement Award, 1988; Illinois Arts Council grant, 1995; Chicago Music Assn Award, 1995; Art Institute of Chicago grant, 1997; NEA Regional Artists Prog grant, 1997. **Business Addr:** Part-time Faculty, East-West University, English & Communications Department, 816 S Michigan Ave, Chicago, IL 60605, **Business Phone:** (312)939-0111.

BAIRD, SR. ANITA PRICE
Executive director. **Personal:** Born Feb 8, 1947, Warrensburg, MO; daughter of Robert Price Jr and Marcella Hill Price. **Educ:** DePaul Univ, BA, sociol; Loyola Univ-Chicago, Mundelein Col, MA, relig studies. **Career:** Archdiocese Chicago, St Sabina Church, Chicago, IL, word ministry team leader, exec asst archbishop; St Paul, regional super, Chicago, currently; St Louis communities Daughters Heart Mary, dir, 2000-; Archdiocese Chicago's Office Racial Justice, dir, 2000-. **Orgs:** Nat Black Sisters Conf, 1982-, pres, 2001-03. **Honors/Awds:** NBC-5 Jefferson Award; Harriet Tubman Award, NBSC; Dominick's Fresh Spirit Award. **Business Addr:** Director, Archdiocese Chicago, Office of Racial Justice, 155 E Superior St, Chicago, IL 60611, **Business Phone:** (312)751-8336.

BAIRD, DR. KEITH E.
Educator, college teacher. **Personal:** Born Jan 20, 1923; children: Diana Baird N'Diaye & Marcia Baird-Johnson. **Educ:** Columbia Univ, BS, 1952; Union Grad Sch, PhD, 1982. **Career:** Educator (retired); Freedom ways, assoc ed & writer, 1961-85; Hunter Col, prof & dir afro-am studies, 1969-70; Ford Found, travel sem grant, 1969; Hofstra Univ, prof humanities, 1970-73; State Univ NY, Old West bury, prof humanities, 1973-75; State Univ NY, Buffalo, chair, african am studies, assoc prof anthrop, 1975-; Univ Jena, US GOR Friendship Comt, summer scholar grant, 1981; Clark Atlanta Univ, Dept Soc Sci, prof. **Orgs:** Assoc fel, Ctr Afro-Am Studies, Atlanta Univ, 1973-; consult, Gullah Lang, Sea Island Ctr, 1977; State Univ NY Chancellor's Task Force Afro Studies,1984; pres emer, NY African Studies Asn; assoc ed, Freedom ways; ed bd, J Black Studies, African Urban Quart; co-founder, Kush Mus African & African-Am Art & Antiq; Hutkaptah Soc. **Special Achievements:** Publ: Names from Africa, Johnson Publ Co, 1972. **Home Addr:** 2289 Venetian Dr SW, Atlanta, GA 30311-3310, **Home Phone:** (404)753-9948. *

BAISDEN, MICHAEL
Radio host, writer. **Personal:** Born Jun 26, 1963, Chicago, IL; divorced; children: 1. **Career:** Writer, motivational speaker & talk show host; Books: Never Satisfied: How & Why Men Cheat, 1995; Men Cry in the Dark, 1997; The Maintenance Man: It's Midnight, Do You Know Where Your Woman Is?, 1999; God's Gift to Women, 2002; Chicago Transit Authority, train driver, 2003; writer, 1993-2001; Legacy Publ, ceo, 2001; Tribune Broadcasting, TV Talk Show Talk or Walk, host, 2001; Tribune Entertainment, radio host, 2001; 98.7 KISS FM, noon drive-time host, 2003; ABC Radio Network, radio host, 2004-; Legacy Publ & Happilysingle.com, founder. **Orgs:** Founder, The Michael Baisden Foundation Literacy & Technol. **Business Addr:** Radio Host, ABC Radio Network Inc, Michael Baisden Show, 13725 Montfort Dr, Dallas, TX 75240, **Business Phone:** (972)991-9200.*

BAITY, GAIL OWENS
Manager. **Personal:** Born May 20, 1952, New York, NY; daughter of Ruth Owens and George A Owens; married Elijah A Baity, Apr 20, 1985; children: Allen J. **Educ:** Spelman Col, BA Psych 1974; Univ WI, Madison, MA Indust Relations 1976. **Career:** Corning Consumer Prod Div, prdn suprv 1978; Corning Info Serv Div, personnel dev spec 1978-80; Elmira Col, instr 1980; Corning R&D Div, personnel suprv 1980-82; Corning Consumer Products Div, personnel suprv 1982-83; Corning Personnel Div, human resource consultant; Corning Glass Works, human resource consult, 1983-87. **Orgs:** Consult Career Devel Council 1982-; vice pres Soc of Black Professional 1982,86; treas Elmira Corning NAACP 1982-83; mem Soc of Black Profl, Elmira/Corning NAACP; chairperson policy comm Corning Children's Ctr 1986-87; mem, Organizational Development Network (ODN), 1988-; mem, American Society of Education and Training (ASTD), 1987-; mem, National Black MBA Association, 1987-; board mem, Career Development Council, 1988-; board mem and chair person personnel policy comm, Corning Children's Center, 1986-. **Home Addr:** 39 Forest Hill Dr, Corning, NY 14830. **Business Addr:** Human Resources Consultant, Corning Glass Works Houghton Pk, Corning, NY 14831.*

BAJOIE, DIANA E
Legislator (U.S. state government). **Educ:** Southern Univ, BA. **Career:** La House Reps, pub serv, 1976; adult educr; La State Senate, state rep, 1976-91, sen, 1991, pres pro tempore, 2004, sen dist five, currently. **Orgs:** Founder & chmn, La Legis Black Caucus, La Legis Women's Caucus; pres, Nat Org Black Elected Legis Women. **Honors/Awds:** Named Susan G Komen Beast Cancer Survivor of the Year, 2000; Mayor's Medal of Honor, 2002; Pfizer Visionary Leadership Award, 2002; La Social Workers Public Servant of the Year Award, 2003; Legislator of the Year Award, Nat Black Caucus State Legislator, 2005; Nat Leadership Award, 2007; Citizens Against Crime Award, 2007; Ochsner Clinic Foundation Award for Distinguished Leadership Award. **Special Achievements:** First African-Am woman ever elected to the La Senate, 1991; The first woman ever elected to the leadership post in the La Senate, 2004. **Business Addr:** Senator, Louisiana State Senate, District Five, 4129 Liberty St, PO Box 15168, New Orleans, LA 70175, **Business Phone:** (504)568-7760.

BAKER, ALTHEA
Judge, lawyer, educator. **Personal:** Born Dec 24, 1949, San Francisco, CA; daughter of Vernon Ross and Ethel Ross; divorced; children: Chase Brendan Mitchell. **Educ:** Pepperdine Univ, BA, 1970, MA, clin psychol, 1974; Loyola Univ, Sch Law, JD, 1984. **Career:** Licensed marriage family child therapist, 1976-84; La Community Cols, prof, coun & psychol, 1975-89; Law Off Althea Baker, atty, 1984-93; Los Angeles Community Cols, trustee, 1989-01; La Super Ct, judge pro team, Sylmar Juvenile Courthouse Dept 275, referee. **Orgs:** Black Women Lawyers Los Angeles; Mediator & arbit, 1990-01; bd mem, Southern Calif Mediation Asn, 1990-92; Pepperdine Univ Grad Sch Educ & Psychol Bd, 1990-92. **Honors/Awds:** Delores Award, Distinguished Service Psychology, Pepperdine Univ, 1990; Outstanding Pro-Bono Service, Calif State Bar Asn, 1990. **Business Addr:** Referee, Los Angeles Super Court, Sylmar Juvenile Courthouse, 16350 Filbert St, Sylmar, CA 91342, **Business Phone:** (818)364-2187.*

BAKER, ANITA
Songwriter, singer. **Personal:** Born Jan 26, 1958, Detroit, MI; married Walter Bridgforth, Dec 31, 1988; children: Walter Baker Bridgforth & Edward Carlton Bridgforth. **Career:** Vocalist, several Detroit bars & nightclubs; lead vocalist, Chap Eight, 1978; receptionist, Detroit law firm; Albums: The Songstress, 1983; Rapture, 1986; Giving You The Best That I Got, 1988; Compositions, 1990; Rhythm of Love, 1994; Fireside Love Songs, 2003; My Everything, Blue Note Records, 2005; Christmas Fantasy, 2005; Why Did I Get Married?, 2007; Live Performances: with singer AlJarreau, Montreaux Jazz Festival, Switzerland, 1988; Bermuda Music Festival, 2004; The BET Honors, actress, 2009. **Honors/Awds:** NAACP Image Award, Best Female Vocalist & Best Album of the Year; Grammy Awards, best female singer & best song Giving You the Best That I Got, 1989; Grammy Awards: Best Rhythm & Blues Vocal Performance - Female won, 1995; Best Rhythm & Blues Album Nominee, 2005; Best Traditional R&B Vocal Performance, nominee, 2005; Best Traditional R&B Vocal Performance, Nominee, 2006. **Business Phone:** (212)253-3000.

BAKER, DR. BERYLE I.
Educator. **Educ:** Univ Madras, International studies; Norfork State Univ, VA, BA, hist; Cent Mo State, Med; Auburn Univ, Ala, Ed.D. **Career:** Ga Perimeter Col, assoc prof educ, prof educ, currently.

BAKER, BEVERLY POOLE
Lawyer. **Personal:** Born Jan 14, 1944, Birmingham, AL; daughter of Grafton C and Minda Ingersoll; married James K, Nov 1968 (died 2003); children: Paige, Paula & Leslie. **Educ:** Univ Ala, Birmingham, BA, Urban Studies, summa cum laude, 1982; Cumberland Sch Law, Birmingham, AL, JD, 1985. **Career:** McMillan & Spratling, Birmingham, AL, atty, 1985-86; Haskell Slaughter & Young, Birmingham, AL, atty, 1986-2002; Miller, Hamilton, Snider & ODOM LLC, Birmingham, AL, Atty, 2002-. Deakins, Nash, Smoak & Stewart PC, lawyer & arbitrator, currently. **Orgs:** Am Bar Asn, Standing Comt Lawyers' Pub Serv Responsibility; co-chair, Equal Opportunity Comt Litigation Sect; Nat Bar Asn; Nat Asn Bond Lawyers; Ala State Bar Asn, ADR Comt; Magic City Bar Asn; Birmingham Bar Asn; bd dirs, alumni coun, Leadership AL; Leadership Birmingham; Jefferson County Med Examr Comn; Res Coun Ala; adv bd, Cumberland Sch Law; Birmingham Leadership Coun, Univ Ala,; arbitrator, Am Arbitration Asn; arbitrator, Nat Arbitration Forum; arbitrator, Nat Arbitration Mediation. **Honors/Awds:** Dean's Award, Univ Ala, 1981, 1982; Perceptions and Propinquity on Police Patrol, SE Sociological Asn, 1982; Fel, Am Asn Univ Women, 1984; Privacy in a High-Tech World, 1985; The Age Discrimination in Employment Act and Termination of the Public Sector Employee, Ala Bar Inst Sem, 1989; Basic Wage and Hour Law in AL, NBI, 1996; Employment Arbitration Basics for Legal Services Professionals, Ala State Bar Asn, 2004. **Home Addr:** 224 Cahaba Lake Circle, Helena, AL 35080. **Business Addr:** Lawyer, Arbitrator, Ogletree, Deakins, Nash, Smoak & Stewart, PC, 1819 5th Ave N 1000 1 Federal Pl, Birmingham, AL 35203, **Business Phone:** (205)328-1900.

BAKER, C C
School administrator. **Career:** Ala State Univ, pres, 1991-94. *

BAKER, CAROLETTA A
Administrator. **Career:** Wake County Pub Sch Syst, Elem Sch Serv, Spl Educ Serv Dept, sr adminr elem, currently. **Orgs:** Wake County Bd Educ.

BAKER, DARRYL BRENT, SR.
Executive. **Personal:** Born May 5, 1955, Detroit, MI; son of Elliott D Sr. and Mary L Scott; children: Darryl Jr, Donnathon, LaKeisha. **Educ:** General Motors Inst Tech, attended 1973; Mott Community Col, AS, 1983; Univ MI, 1988; Baker Col, BA, bus leadership, MBA. **Career:** Stockbroker & financial consult, General Motors, Flint, Metal Fab, machinist, machine repairer, 1977-; Baker Financial Serv, owner, pres, chief exec officer, 1992-; video & youth music, producer. **Orgs:** Owner income tax serv, 22 yrs; Ebony and Ivory Enterprises investment consult serv, 8 yrs; cub scout & boy scout leader dist exec Boy Scouts, 1975-77; football & basketball coach Primary Sch, 1981-82; Order of the Arrow; life mem, NAACP; exec bd mem, unit chmn UAW Local 659, 1993-01; mgr Little League & Pee Wee League Baseball Teams, 1987; exec bd mem, vp, The Black Caucus of Genessee Cty; exec bd mem, Millionth Man; chmn, UAW Black Leadership Caucus, Local 659, 1993-01; Genessee Cty Bd Canvassers; Vernon Chapel AME Ch; pres, Nat Asn of Black Acct, Flint, 2000. **Honors/Awds:** Scouting Wood Badge Award; Business Award, Top Gun, 1989; Life Accident Health Insurance License and Securities Series 7, Investment License, 1988; Flint Journal, Top 10 Personality of Flint, 1994. **Business Phone:** (810)232-0522.*

BAKER, DAVE E.
Educator, baseball executive. **Personal:** Born Jun 18, 1943, Manhattan, KS; married Janice; children: Sherri Ann. **Educ:** Emporia St Col, BS, phys educ, 1968, MS, phys educ, 1969. **Career:** Emporia St Col, phys educ, grad asst, asst baseball coach, 1969; Lib Community Jr Col, head track coach, asst basketball coach, instr phys educ, 1970; Creighton Univ, instr phys educ, asst basketball coach, asst baseball coach, 1971-75, head baseball coach, 1972-. **Orgs:** Phi Delta Kappa; Nat Collegiate Athletic Asn; Col World Ser Games Comm, 1972-75. *

BAKER, DAVID NATHANIEL
Musician, composer, educator. **Personal:** Born Dec 21, 1931, Indianapolis, IN; married Lida Margret Belt; children: April Elaine. **Educ:** Sch Jazz, Lenox, MA; Ind Univ, Bloomington, BME, MME, BM 1953, MM, 1954; New Eng Conserv Music. **Career:** Boston Sym Evansville, IN Philharmonic, soloist; Indianapolis Sym, guest conductor; Indianapolis Civic Orch, guest conductor, Ind Univ Sym, guest conductor; George Russell Sextet, mem; Ind Univ, Jazz Dept, chmn, Sch Mus, distinguished prof, currently; Smithsonian Inst, artistic dir & conductor, sr consult music progs, currently. **Orgs:** Chmn, Nat Endowment Arts; bd dir, Nat Music Coun; AAUP; Nat Asn Negro Musicians; Nat Coun Arts; pres, Nat Jazz Serv Org; chmn, Jazz Studies Dept, Ind Univ Sch Music. **Honors/Awds:** Recipient, Dizzy Gillespie Scholarship, 1959; Nominee, Pulitzer Prize, 1973; Nominee, Grammy; Nat Asn of Jazz Educators Hall of Fame Award, 1981; President's Award, Ind Univ, 1986; Arts Midwest Jazz Masters Award, 1990; Governor's Arts Award, State Indiana, 1991; Nat Endowment for the Arts Jazz Master Award; Oberlin Col, hon doctorate; Wabash Col, hon doctorate; The Third inductee to their Jazz Education Hall of Fame, 1994; lifetime achievement, Down Beat mag; American Jazz Masters Award, Nat Endowment Arts, 2000; The Indiana Historical Society's Living Legend Award, 2001; The James Smithson Medal, Smithsonian Inst, 2002. **Special Achievements:** Toured Europe with Quincy Jones, 1961, author of 70 books on music improvisation, has more than 400 articles and 75 recordings to his credit; Books: A Comprehensive Method of Study for All Players, 1969; Techniques of Improvisation, 1971; with L. Belt and H. Hudson, The Black Composer Speaks, 1978. **Business Addr:** Distinguished Professor, Chairman of the Jazz Department, Indiana University, School of Music, 107 S Indiana Ave, Bloomington, IN 47405-7000, **Business Phone:** (812)855-8546.

BAKER, DELBERT WAYNE
Editor, educator. **Personal:** Born Jan 25, 1953, Oakland, CA; son of Paul Thomas and Amelia A; married Susan M Lee Baker; children: David Mathias, Benjamin Joseph, Jonathan Michael. **Educ:** Oakwood Col, BA(cum laude), ministerial theol, 1975; Andrews Univ Sem, Masters, divinity, 1978; Howard Univ, PhD, commun, 1992. **Career:** pastor, MI, VA, OH, 1975-85; Messsage Mag, ed chief, 1985-92; Howard Univ, instr, 1990-91; consult, 1990; Loma Linda Univ, from asst to pres, dir diversity, assoc prof, 1992-01; Oakwood Col, pres, 1996-. **Orgs:** Clergy's Black Caucus, 1985; bd mem, Rev & Herald Pub Asn, 1985; bd mem, San Mars C Home, 1986-89; bd mem, Human Rels Coun Gen Conf of Seventh-day Adventist Church, 1987; contribr video, Africa Continent of Explosive Growth, 1987; Asn Latin Am Stud, 1993; Black Fac Forum, 1993; Hisp Fac Forum, 1995. **Honors/Awds:** Alumnus of the Yr, Oakwood Col, 1985; Ed Jour Awards, Ed Int, 1988-90; White House Spec Comt on HBCUs, 2006. **Special Achievements:** Auth: The Unknown Prophet, 1986; From Exile to Prime Minister, 1988; Profiles of Service, 1990; Communication and Change in Religious Organization, 1992. **Home Addr:** 2141 Hill Ct, Colton, CA 92324. *

BAKER, DUSTY
Baseball manager, baseball player, broadcaster. **Personal:** Born Jun 15, 1949, Riverside, CA; son of Johnnie B Sr and Christine; married Melissa; children: Natosha & Darren. **Educ:** Am River Jr Col, Sacramento, CA. **Career:** Baseball player (retired); Atlanta

Braves, outfielder, 1968-75; Los Angeles Dodgers, outfielder, 1976-83; San Francisco Giants, outfielder, 1984; Oakland Athletics, outfielder & first baseman, 1985-86; Minnesota Twins, 1990; San Francisco Giants, mgr, 1993-2002; Chicago Cubs, mgr, 2003-06; ESPN analyst, MLB Postseason; Cincinnati Reds, mgr, 2008-. **Orgs:** US marine corps. **Honors/Awds:** All-Star & Silver Slugger teams, Sporting News, 1981; Golden glove award, 1981; Silver Slugger awards, 1981-82; Nat League All-Star Team 1981-82; National League Manager of the Year, 1993, 1997, 2000. *

BAKER, FLOYD EDWARD
Dentist. **Personal:** Born Mar 28, 1920, Auxvasse, MO; married Gertrude Andrews; children: Floyd E Jr, Teressa. **Educ:** Lincoln Univ, MO, BS, 1943; Meharry Col Dent, DDS, 1946; Inst Grad Dent, attended 1956. **Career:** Mercy Douglas Hosp, staff dentist, 1954-74, co-chair oral surg, 1970-74; New Era Dent Soc, bd mem, currently. **Orgs:** Zone vpres, Nat Dent Asn, 1958-80; Mt Airy Presby Church, 1964-87; treas, Bravo Investment Corp, 1964-87; registr, Am Dent Asn; Philadelphia County Dent, 1978-85; Special Olympics, 1983-87. **Honors/Awds:** Forty Year Plaque, Omega Psi Phi Fraternity, 1984; Alumni of Year Award; Presidential Citation, 1984; Life Mem, Pin Am Dent Asn, 1985. **Military Serv:** AUS, Dent Corps, capt, 1946-48. **Business Addr:** Dentist, 1826 W Girard Ave, Philadelphia, PA 19130-1516.*

BAKER, GAIL F.
Vice president (organization), college administrator, educator. **Educ:** Northwestern Univ Medill Sch Jour, BS, jour, 1976; Roosevelt Univ, MS, mkt commun, 1980; Univ Mo-Columbia, PhD, jour, 1991. **Career:** Chicago Daily Defender, reporter & ed; IBM; Int Harvester; Univ Mo-Columbia, Advert Dept, chmn & dir, Knight Found Off Minority Recruiting& Retention, 1991-95; Univ Fla, Col Jour & Commun, assoc prof & dir pubrels dept, 1995-2005, vpres pub rels, spec asst to pres diversity,2004-05; Univ Nebr, Omaha, Col Commun, Fine Arts & Media, dean, 2006-. **Orgs:** Chmn, Pub Rels Soc Am, Mem Col Fellows, Multicultural Commun Sect. **Honors/Awds:** Professional of the Year Award, Fla Pub Rels Asn, 1999. **Special Achievements:** Auth: Advertising & Marketing to the New Majority; Co-auth: Exploding Stereotypes: Milestones in Black Newspaper Research. **Business Addr:** Dean, University of Nebraska, College of Communication, Fine Arts & Media, Off Dean, 6001 Dodge St WFAB 314, Omaha, NE 68182, **Business Phone:** (402)554-2232.

BAKER, GREGORY D.
Executive. **Personal:** Born Mar 2, 1948, Kansas City, MO; son of Richard A and Lacy B; married Janet L Carlson, Jun 6, 1986; children: Kimberly R, Timothy P, Chad G, Sydney L, Aaron Mitchell. **Educ:** Rockhurst Univ, BA, liberal arts, 1974; Univ Ky, cert rational behav therapist ; Univ Kans, MPA, 1981. **Career:** DC Refugee State, coordr; Community Develop Int Bus, mgr; Chamber Com Greater Kans City, MO; Kans City Minority Developer Supplier Coun, pres; Miss Gas Energy, vpres, community leadership; LeadTeam LLC, founding chief exec officer; Minority Bus Capital Corp, chmn, currently; Kans City Mgr Off, asst city mgr, currently. **Orgs:** pres, Kans City Consensus, 1981; vpres, Jr Achievement, 1991-; bd dirs, Leukemia Soc, 1991-; bd dirs, Truman Med Ctr, 1990-; bd dirs, CORO, Metrop Orgn Counter Sexual Assault; bd dirs, Citizens Asn; bd mem, Metrop Energy Ctr; bd mem, Metrop Community Col Trust Fund. **Honors/Awds:** Top 100 Most Influential Black Am, Kans City, MO, 1994; Up & Comers Award, 1994; Eagle Leadership Award, Career Focus Mag, 1994. **Special Achievements:** Omni Award, "Project Restart" Vocals, 1992; Emmy Award, Song "Remember Me KC," 1997. **Military Serv:** USAF, A first class, 1967-69. **Home Addr:** 11200 Summit, Kansas City, MO 64114. **Business Addr:** Assistant to City Manager, Kansas City Manager Office, 29th Fl City Hall, 414 E 12th St, Kansas City, MT 64106, **Business Phone:** (816)513-3554.*

BAKER, GWENDOLYN CALVERT
President (Organization), educator, socialist. **Personal:** Born Dec 31, 1931, Ann Arbor, MI; daughter of Burgess Edward and Viola Lee; married James Grady (divorced 1978); children: JoAnn, Claudia, James Jr. **Educ:** Univ Mich, Ann Arbor, MI, BS, elem educ, 1964, MA, educ admin, 1968, PhD, educ, 1972. **Career:** Ann Arbor Pub Schs, Ann Arbor, MI, teacher, 1964-69; Univ Mich, Ann Arbor, MI, asst/assoc prof, 1969-76, dir affirmative action, 1976-78; Nat Inst Educ, Wash, DC, chief, minorities & women's prog, 1978-81; Bank St Col, New York, NY, vpres & dean grad & c's progs, 1981-84; Young Women's Christian Asn USA, New York, nat exec dir, 1984-93; US Comn UNICEF, pres, CEO, 1993-97; Calvert Baker & Assocs, pres, 1997-; Am Educ Res Asn, dir soc justice, 2005. **Orgs:** Pres, NY City Bd Educ; Alpha Kappa Alpha Sorority; Am Asn Univ Women; bd, Nat Coalition 100 Black Women; bd, 1984, US Olympic Comt; bd, US Comn UN Develop Fund Women; NYC Women's Forum; NY Alliance Black Sch Educr; Women's City Club NY. **Honors/Awds:** Hon Degrees: Medgar Evers Col, City NY, 1990, Univ Mich, 1996, 1997, King's Col, 1994, Southeastern MA Univ, 1989, Bentley Col, 1995, Fairleigh Dickinson Univ, 1994; Old Masters Award, Purdue Univ, 1985; Willystine Goodsell Award, Am Educ Res Asn & Women Educrs, 1985; Salute to America's Top 100 Black Business and Professional Women, 1986; Distinguished Alumna, Univ Mich Educ Alumni Soc, 1987; Strength of the City Awards, 1989; Chicago State Univ, 1995. **Business Addr:** President, Calvert Baker & Associates Inc, New York, NY 10128, **Business Phone:** (212)472-6022.*

BAKER, HENRY W., SR.
Educator. **Personal:** Born Apr 26, 1937, Valdosta, GA; son of Herbert and Amie Lee Harrell; married Rubye Veals, Jan 29, 1969; children: Henry W II, Michael De Leon, Debra Marie, Edith Marie & Brittnye Nicole. **Educ:** Alcorn State Univ, BS, 1964, Grad Study, 1983; William Paterson Col, MA, 1992. **Career:** Anchorage Jr HS, 1964-67; Natchez, MI, teacher & coach phys educ; EastsideHigh Sch, Paterson, NJ, phys educ teacher & basketball coach, 1967-80;Passic Co Col, Paterson, NJ, head basketball coach, 1978-83; Eastside HighSch, head coach girls tennis team & coord phys educ, 1983-84; PassaicCounty Community Col, head basketball Coach, 1979-91; Eastside High Sch, head track coach (boys), 1988-89, co ord of physical education, 1989-91, head coach, boys baskeball & track, 1991-; John F. Kennedy High Sch, lead teacher. **Orgs:** Dir, Martin Luther King Comm Ctr, Paterson, 1970-76; founder/dir, BlackYouth Orgn, Paterson 1971-77; pres, Passaic Co Planned Parenthood Inc, 1976-79; vpres, Children Youth Serv, Paterson, NJ, 1986-; vpres, Afrikan Amer Men Interested in Neighborhood Develop Inc, 1986-. **Honors/Awds:** Comm Serv Award, Master Barber's Asn Unit 9, 1975; Youth Serv Award, NewPolitical Alliance, Paterson, 1975; Basketball Coach Yr, NY Daily News,1975; Coach Yr, Basketball Passaic Co Asn, 1976; Coach Yr, Girls Track Passaic Co Coaches Asn, 1977-80; Jr Col Coach Yr 1985-86; Jr Col 100 Victory Club Award, Garden State Athletic Conf, 1990. **Business Addr:** Lead Teacher, Boys Varsity Basketball Coach, John F. Kennedy High School, Eastside High School, 61 Preakness Ave, Paterson, NJ 07501.*

BAKER, DR. HOUSTON ALFRED, JR.
Educator. **Personal:** Born Mar 22, 1943, Louisville, KY; son of Alfred Sr and Viola Elizabeth Smith; married Charlotte Pierce; children: 1. **Educ:** Howard Univ, BA, 1965; Univ Calif, MA, 1966, PhD, 1968; Univ Edinburgh, Scotland, doctoral work, 1968. **Career:** Howard Univ, instr, 1966; Yale Univ, instr, 1968-69, asst prof, 1969; Ctr Advan Studies, Va Univ, from assoc prof to prof, 1970-73, dir, Dept Afro-Am Studies, 1974-77; Univ Penn, prof eng; Duke Univ, Susan Fox & George D Beisher, prof eng & african am studies; Modern Language Assn, Pres, 1992; Vanderbilt Univ, distinguished univ prof & prof Eng, currently. **Orgs:** MLA Exec Coun; assoc editor, BALE; com on Scholarly Worth, Howard Univ Pres; pres, Modern Lang Asn. **Honors/Awds:** Numerous honorary degrees from American Cols and universities. **Special Achievements:** He has authored a number of critical and scholarly books and studies of Afro-American literature and culture, including: Blues, Ideology & Afro-American Literature; Workings of the Sprit: The Poetics of Afro-American Women's Writing; Modernism & the Harlem Renaissance; Black Studies, Rap & the Academy. Workings of the Spirit: Poetics of Afro-American Women's Writings, 1991. **Business Addr:** Distinguished University Professor, Professor of English, Vanderbilt University, English Department, 223 Buttrick Hall, PO Box 1654 Sta B, Nashville, TN 37235, **Business Phone:** (615)343-7355.

BAKER, JACQUELINE
Educator. **Personal:** Born Jun 13, 1952, Cleveland, OH; daughter of Ora Lee and R C Baker; divorced; children: Jody James, Dayairre Zeleeka. **Educ:** Univ Minn, BS, arts, 1984; Univ St Thomas, MA, educ, 1998. **Career:** Fed Res, banker, 1973-89; NW Airlines, 1989-94; Minn Pub Schs, 1994-. **Honors/Awds:** Academic Achievements, Omicron Nu Honor Soc, 1980. **Home Addr:** 2823 Lyndale Ave N, Minneapolis, MN 55411-1449. *

BAKER, KIMBERLEY RENEE
Journalist. **Personal:** Born Sep 26, 1965, Houston, TX; daughter of Melvin Lavoisier and Diane Denise Randolph. **Educ:** Univ Tex Austin, Austin, BA, jour, 1988. **Career:** Bellaire Texan, Houston, community reporter, 1981-84; Houston Sun, Houston, gen assignments intern, 1987; Amarillo Globe-News, Amarillo, lifestyles reporter, 1988-93; City Austin, media prog mgr; Tex Dept Econ Develop Bus, community assistance & small bus, currently. **Orgs:** Issue staff, Daily Texan, UT-Austin, 1984-87; publ liaison, Afro-Am Cult Comm, UT-Austin, 1984-88; chairwoman commun week, Commun Coun, UT-Austin, 1985-88; second vpres, Delta Sigma Theta Sorority, UT-Austin, Amarillo, 1987-; Nat Asn Black Journalists, 1987-88, 1990-94; bd mem, Tex Stud Publ, UT-Austin, 1987-88; community serv reporting, United Way, 1988-93; Provisional Class Jr League Amarillo, 1993; Nat Asn Black Journalists; Asn Women Commun. **Honors/Awds:** Texas Student Publication Board Award, UT-Austin, 1987-88; Plaque for helping the handicapped, Goodwill Indust, 1988-93; Opportunity Symposium Series Award, Austin, 1992, 1993; Hon Big Sisters, Big Brothers/Big Sisters, 1993-94; Outstanding Alumnus, Delta Sigma Theta Sorority, Amarillo Alumnae, 1993-94. **Home Addr:** 1415 Marsh Harbour Dr, Round Rock, TX 77033, **Home Phone:** (512)990-7911. **Business Addr:** Community Assistance & Small Business, Texas Department of Economic Development Business, 1700 N Cong Ave Suite 200, Austin, TX 78711-2728, **Business Phone:** (512)936-0211.

BAKER, LAVOLIA EALY
Insurance executive. **Personal:** Born Nov 11, 1925, Shreveport, LA; married Luchan G; children: Paul, Ronald & Luchan Jr. **Educ:** Univ Calif, Berkeley, Sch Bus, attended 1968; Contra Costa, AA, 1970;Golden Gate Univ, 1972-74; Univ San Francisco, BS, 1998. **Career:** L Baker Ins, owner & mgr, 1974, fire & casualty ins broker, currently. **Orgs:** Founder, Church By the Side of the Road, 1955; Chairperson, Oakland Metro Enterprises; chmn, WAPAC; BOWOPA & E Bay Area Dem Club, 1972; dir, Sojourner Truth Housing Corp, 1974; dir, San Francisco Indep Agents Asn,1975; dir, Black Brokers & Agents Asn; vpres, Nat Asn Negro Bus & Prof Womens Club; pres, bd chmn, Alpha Phi Alpha Wives Aux; life mem, Nat Asn Advan Colored People; Bay Area Urban League. **Honors/Awds:** Bus Woman of the Year. **Business Addr:** Fire, Casualty Insurance Broker, 1320 Va St, Berkeley, CA 94702-1426.

BAKER, MAXINE B
Executive, association executive. **Personal:** Born Feb 29, 1952, Homestead, PA; daughter of Evan Posey and Maxine Reynolds; married Mark McIntosh; children: Morgan & Jill. **Educ:** Emerson Col, BS, speech commun; Univ Md, grad study; Southeastern Univ, grad study. **Career:** Business executive (retired), association executive; Pac Consults, asst vpres admin; Urban Inst, mgr staff support serv; Freddie Mac Corp, vpres admin & corp properties, vpres human resources, dir admin serv, mgr procurement & regional admin serv, contracts & budget admin, vpres community rels, 1997-2007; African American Nonprofit Network, pres, 2008-. **Orgs:** Pres & chief exec officer, Freddie Mac Found. **Business Addr:** President, African American Nonprofit Network, 1201 15th St NW Suite 420, Washington, DC 20005, **Business Phone:** (202)973-2510.

BAKER, MYRON TOBIAS (MYRON BAKER)
Football player. **Personal:** Born Jan 6, 1971, Haughton, LA. **Educ:** La Tech. **Career:** Football Player (Retired); Chicago Bears, linebacker, 1993-95; Carolina Panthers, 1996-97.

BAKER, ROBERT N.
Executive. **Personal:** Born Sep 15, 1943, Cleveland, OH; son of Ora Lee Pettit Baker and R C Baker; divorced; children: Schaaron, Brionne. **Educ:** Univ Minnesota, extension division. **Career:** Werner Continental Transportation, central dispatcher, 1969-73; Glendenning Motorways, manager of linehaul transportation, 1973-77; Gateway Transportation, manager labor & industrial relations, 1977-82; Regency Air Freight, Inc, co-owner, 1982-83; Baker Motor Freight, Inc, owner, 1983-86; Astro Air Express, Inc, regional vice pres, 1986-89; Shippers Air Freight Express Inc, owner, ceo, 1989-99. **Orgs:** Better Business Bureau, Detroit, Michigan, arbitrator, 1986-89; Better Business Bureau, Minnesota, senior arbitrator, 1989-. **Honors/Awds:** BBB, Minnesota, senior arbitrator, 1990. **Military Serv:** AUS, PFC, 1961-67; Mortar Gunner 81mm, Emer Med Care, Sharpshooter, 5 ton truck. **Home Addr:** 4018 Dupont Ave N, Minneapolis, MN 55412, **Home Phone:** (612)588-8115. *

BAKER, ROLAND CHARLES
Executive. **Personal:** Born Aug 12, 1938, Chicago, IL; married Addie Scott; children: Scott, Stephen, Stefanie. **Educ:** Univ CA, BS, Bus Admin, 1961; Univ CA, MBA, 1962; CPA licensed CA, 1971; Chartered Life Underwriter. **Career:** N Am Rockwell Corp, CA, budget admin, 1962-64; Ampex Corp Culver City, financial analyst, 1964-65; Beneficial Standard Life Ins Co, staff asst & controller, 1965-67, mgr corporate acct, 1967-68, asst controller, 1968-69, vpres & controller, 1969-71, admin vpres & controller, 1973-75, sr vpres, 1975-77; Colonial Penn Ins Co & Colonial Penn Franklin Ins Co & Colonial Penn Life Ins Co, exec vpres bd dirs; Colonial Penn Group Inc, sr vpres, 1977-80; The Signature Group, chmn & chief exec officer; Quanta Capital Holdings Limited, bd dir. **Orgs:** CA Soc CPA's & AICPA; bd dir, Philadelphia Zool Soc, 1979-80; bd dir, Fund Open Society OPEN, 1979-; com mem, Central Allocations Com United Way Fund, 1979-. **Honors/Awds:** Fellow, Life Mgmt Inst, 1971; CLU Bryn Mawr, PA, 1976. **Military Serv:** USMCR, 1962-67. **Business Addr:** Board of Director, Quanta Capital Holdings Limited, 48 Wall St 14th Fl, New York, NY 10005, **Business Phone:** (212)373-1800.

BAKER, SHANA V
Transportation consultant. **Personal:** Born Feb 27, 1971, Baltimore, MD; daughter of Gordon and Vera Baker. **Educ:** Bethune-Cookman Col, BA, 1993; Univ Akron, MA, 1995. **Career:** Akron Metropolitan Regional Transit Authority, transportaton planner, 1995-96; Federal Hwy Admin, transp planner, scenic byway dir, 1996-. **Orgs:** Alpha Kappa Alpha Sorority, Inc; Women's Transportation Seminar, Am Planning Asn.

BAKER, SHARON SMITH
Government official. **Personal:** Born Oct 13, 1949, Boston, MA; daughter of Howard William and Elnora Clark; married Donald Baker, May 20, 1972. **Educ:** NC Central Univ, Durham, NC, BA, 1971; NC Central Univ Law Sch, Durham, NC, JD, 1975; Duke Univ, durham, NC, 1975. **Career:** Paul C Bland Law Firm, Durham, NC, paralegal, 1978-81; City Durham, Durham, NC, affirmative action dir CETA, 1979-80, admin asst II, 1982-85, asst

to city mgr, 1985-87; Pub Tech, Inc, Wa, DC, membership officer, 1987-88; City Durham, Durham, NC, dir employ & training; On Point Res, owner, currently. **Orgs:** VPres, N C Triangle Area Chapter Nat Forum Black Pub Adminrs, 1989-91; Nat Asn Aadvan Colored People, Durham, N C, 1985-; NC Black Child Develop, 1990-91; NC Job Training Adminrs Asn, vpres, 1992-94; parish coun bd mem, Holy Cross Catholic Church, 1989-. **Honors/Awds:** Award of Merit, NCCU Law Sch, 1975; Leadership Award, Negro Coun Bus & Prof Women, 1983; Appreciation Award, Durham Human Rels Comn, 1987. **Business Addr:** Owner, On Point Research, 106 W Geer St, Durham, NC 27701-2219, **Business Phone:** (919)688-2386.*

BAKER, SHAUN
Actor. **Personal:** Born in New York, NY; married Julie, Jan 1, 2003; children: 2. **Career:** Films: When the time comes, 2000; Banged Out (voice), 2002; Full Clip, 2004; Blowing Smoke, 2004; Cuttin Da Mustard, 2008; There But Not There, 2009; TV Series: "Living Single", 1994-97; "VIP", 1998-2002. *

BAKER, THURBERT E.
Lawyer, government official. **Personal:** Born Dec 16, 1952, Rocky Mount, NC; son of Mary Baker High; married Catherine; children: Jocelyn, Chelsea. **Educ:** Univ NC, Chapel Hill, BA, 1975; Emory Univ Sch Law, attended 1979. **Career:** US Environmental Protection Agency, lawyer; Governor Miller, asst admin house fl leader; Ga, atty gen, 1997-. **Orgs:** Ga Bar Asn; Kiwanis; Nat Med Soc-Emory Univ; Perimeter Col Bd; adv, Harrell Ctr Stud Domestic Violence, Univ S Fla; adv, State Bar Ga bd Gov; Judicial Nominating Cms; exec comt, pres, chmn, Nat Asn Attys Gen, 2006-07; Am Bar Asn House Del; mem coun, Foreign Rels; DeKalb County Libr Bd; trustee, Ebenezer Baptist Church; mem bd, Nat Med Soc Emory Univ & DeKalb Col Found; Emory Law Sch Coun; Bd Visitors, Emory Univ; mem bd governors, State Bar Ga; Judicial Nominating Comn. **Special Achievements:** In 2003, Black Enterprise Magazine named him one of America's top black lawyers. **Business Addr:** Attorney General, Office of the Attorney General of Georgia, 40 Capitol Sq SW, Atlanta, GA 30334, **Business Phone:** (404)656-3300.*

BAKER, VERDENIA C. See CRUTCHFIELD-BAKER, VERDENIA.

BAKER, VIN
Basketball player, president (organization). **Personal:** Born Nov 23, 1971, Lake Wales, FL; son of James. **Educ:** Univ Hartford, mass commun, 1993. **Career:** Milwaukee Bucks, forward, 1993-97; Seattle SuperSonics, 1997-2002; Boston Celtics, 2002-04; NY Knicks, 2003-04; Houston Rockets, 2004-05; NY Knicks, forward, 2004-05; Los Angeles Clippers, forward, 2005-06; MN Timberwolves, 2006; Stand Tall Found, founder; Vin Baker Enterprises, pres, currently. **Honors/Awds:** NBA All-Rookie Team, 1994; NBA All-Star, 1995-98. **Special Achievements:** NBA Draft, first round, eighth pick, 1993. **Business Addr:** President, Vin Baker Enterprises, PO Box 179, Old Saybrook, CT 06475, **Business Phone:** 877-395-1383.

BAKER, WILLIE L., JR.
Labor activist, executive. **Personal:** Born May 21, 1941, Sanford, FL; son of Willie Sr and Ila Jessie Harris; married Madeline Dennis, Jan 26, 1966 (deceased); children: Kim, Keith. **Educ:** Univ Md Eastern Shore, Princess Anne, BA, 1965. **Career:** United Food & Com Workers, Local 56, Bridgeton, NJ, rec sect, 1974-80, asst bus agt, 1974-85, legis, S Jersey, 1974-85, vpres, 1980-85; United Food & Com Workers Int Union, Wash, DC, int vpres, 1985, dir, Civil Rights & Community Rels Dept; Coalition Black Trade Unionists, exec vpres, currently. **Orgs:** Bd mem, Community Serv Comn AFL-CIO, 1986-95; Univ Md Eastern Shore Nat Alumni Asn, 1987-91; former vpres, Consumer Fedn Am Exec Comn, 1990-95; Nat Asn Advan Colored People; Coalition Labor Union Women; bd mem, Food Res & Action Ctr; bd mem, TransAfrica; vice chmn, Labor Roundtable Nat Black Caucus State Legislators; Dem Nat Comm, 1990-95. **Honors/Awds:** Presidential Citation, Nat Asn Equal Opportunity Higher Educ, 1981; Alumnus of the Year Award, Univ Md Eastern Shore, 1986; Retiree of the Year, UFCW Minority Coalition, 2006. **Business Addr:** Executive Vice President, Coalition of Black Trade Unionists, PO Box 66268, Washington, DC 20036-6268.*

BAKER-KELLY, DR. BEVERLY
Lawyer, educator. **Personal:** Born Nov 2, 1942, Detroit, MI; daughter of Robert Edwoods and Cornelia Lewis; married A Paul Kelly, Jun 25, 1966; children: Traci Allyce Kelly & Kara Gisele Kelly. **Educ:** Howard Univ, attended 1962; Univ Mich, BA, 1964; Columbia Univ, MA, 1966, MEd, 1970, Sch Int Affairs, Cert African Studies, 1970, Edd, 1973; Univ Calif, Berkeley, JD, 1976; Harvard Univ, MA, 1977, Phd, 1978; Johns Hopkins Univ, attended 1986; London Sch Econ, attended 1992. **Career:** Columbia Univ, co-dir, African-Am Summer Studies Prog, 1970; Univ Windsor, sociol instr, 1971-73; Greenberg & Glusker, law clerk, 1974; Dunn & Cruthcer, law clerk, 1975; Legal Aid Soc, law clerk, 1976; Calif St Univ, assoc prof, 1976-82; Mayr, Galle, Weiss-Tessback, und Ben Ibler, Attorneys Law, stagiaire, 1978-79; UNESCO, stagiaire, 1979-80; Univ Md, AUS Bases, lectr & facilitator, 1980; Southern Poverty Law Cent, assoc, 1981; Univ Calif, Dir Acad Support Prog, lectr, 1982-84; Res Mgt Servs, partner & dir, Int Law Div, 1984-86; Focus Int Consultancy, dir, 1986-93; Pvt Immigration Law Pract, 1991-93; Howard Univ, vis assoc prof, 1993-; Golden Gate Univ, Sch Law, 1996, 1997; Int Criminal Tribunal Rwanda, dep registr, 1998-2000; Focus Legal Consultancy, lawyer, 1991-; Golden Gate Univ, adj fac, currently. **Orgs:** Union Int Des Advocates; vpres & bd dir, Boalt Hall Fund Diversity, 1988-91; chair, Nat Bar Asn, Int Law Sect, 1994-96, currently; Comn Judicial Nominees Eval, 2001-; deleg, African Judicial Network, Bamako, Mali, 2003. **Honors/Awds:** Presidential Award, Natl Bar Assn, 1992, 1993 & 1995. **Special Achievements:** Editor: Assoc Ed, California Law Review; Articles Editor, Black Law Journal; Co-author: "The African-American Encyclopedia of Education", 1994; "A Study of the Degree of Trans nationalization of College & Non-College Educated Blacks", Columbia Univ; "Housing Conceptions & Satisfactions of Residents in Federally Subsidized Lower-Middle Income Housing", Harvard Univ; "US Immigration: A Wake up Call", Howard Law Journal, 1995; Participant, Fulbright Seminar for Intl Law Professors on McDougal-Lasswell Jurisprudence. **Home Addr:** 2983 Burdeck Dr, Oakland, CA 94602, **Home Phone:** (510)530-9331. **Business Addr:** Adjunct Faculty, Golden Gate University, School of Law, 536 Mission St, San Francisco, CA 94105-2968, **Business Phone:** (415)442-6600.

BAKER-PARKS, SHARON L
Social worker. **Personal:** Born Jan 18, 1958, New York, NY; daughter of Willie Baker Jr (deceased) and Lee Baker (deceased); married Brainard J; children: Kendra. **Educ:** Univ NC Charlotte, BA, sociol, Afro-Am & African studies, 1979; Columbia Univ, Sch Social Work, MSW, 1983; Baruch Col, Sch Continuing Studies, cert bus, 1986. **Career:** Steinway Child & Family Developmental Ctr, social worker, 1983-84; South Bronx Ment Health Coun Inc, psychiat social worker 1984; Bedford Stuyvesant Community Mental Health Ctr Inc, psychiat social worker & recreation coord, 1985; Victim Serv Agency, casework supvr, 1985-86; Bronx-Lebanon Hosp Ctr, psychiat social worker, 1986-89; New York Bd Educ, sch social worker, 1989-. **Orgs:** Delta Sigma Theta Sorority, Inc, 1977-; Nat Asn Social Workers, NYC Chap, 1981-; Workshop Bus Opportunities Alumni Asn, 1985-; Girl Scout Coun Greater NY; Volunteer Troop Leader, 1996-. **Honors/Awds:** NY State Certification in Social Work (CSW), 1986; NY State Sch Social Work, License, NY City Sch Social Work, Lic, Sch Social Work Specialist Credential. **Home Addr:** 880 Colgate Ave Suite 11L, Bronx, NY 10473. **Business Addr:** School Social Worker, New York Bd Education, 1070 Castle Hill Ave, Bronx, NY 10472.

BAKR, RASHIDA ISMALI ABU
Career: WEB Du Bois Foundation, 1999.

BALDON, JANICE C.
Lecturer, college teacher. **Personal:** Born Jun 5, 1955, Louisville, KY; daughter of Virgil Baldon and Willana. **Educ:** Univ Louisville, bus sci com, 1977; Bellarmine Col, bus, 1987. **Career:** DuPont Dow Elastomers, off coord, 1978-; Univ Louisville, lectr econs, 1990-. **Orgs:** Nat Coun Negro Women, 1994; Million Man March Comt Adv; Alpha Kappa Alpha; Ky Alliance Against Racism/Repression. **Honors/Awds:** Black Achievers, 1996. **Special Achievements:** Assisted in establishing higher educ in underserved minority area, col in nontraditional locations, 1993. *

BALDWIN, ARTHUR L
Manager. **Career:** Nat Energy Technol Lab, US Dept Energy, regional mgr, currently. **Business Addr:** Regional Manager, US Dept Energy, Nat Energy Technology Laboratory, 626 Cochrans Mill Rd, Pittsburgh, PA 15236-0940, **Business Phone:** (412)386-6011.

BALDWIN, CAROLYN H.
Executive. **Educ:** Fisk Univ, BA, econs, bus admin; Univ Chicago, MBA. **Career:** Citibank, NA, acct officer, sr acct officer; Coca-Cola Co, sr financial analyst, treasury specialist, asst treasurer & mgr, Latin Am treas serv, vpres; Coca-Cola Financial Corp, pres, 1997-00; Schweppes Beverages, Human Resource dir, 1999; Coca-Cola N Am, Finance, Info Systems, Human Resources & Tech, human resources dir, Global Mkt Div, Human Resource dir, vpres, human resources; Global Tech Financial, chmn, ceo; ReliaStar Financial Corp, dir; RARE Hospitality Int Inc, bd dir, chmn, ceo. **Orgs:** Leadership Atlanta, Soc Int Bus Fels; dir, Exec Leadership Found; dir, Consumer Credit Counseling serv; vchmn, Teachers Retirement System Ga; bd trustees, Fisk Univ. **Honors/Awds:** Woman Yr, Women Looking Ahead Magazine, 1999; Nat Women Achievement Award, 2000; Industrious Achievement Award, Delta Sigma Theta, Atlanta Suburban Alumna chp, 2001; Alumna of the Year, Fist Univ, 2002; Antioch Anchor Award, Corp Antioch Baptist Church, 2002; one of 20 Extraordinary Women in Atlanta, Bus-to-Bus magazine, 2002. *

BALDWIN, CYNTHIA A.
Judge, educator. **Personal:** Born Feb 8, 1945, McKeesport, PA; daughter of James A Ackron (deceased) and Iona Meriweather Ackron (deceased); married Arthur L Baldwin, Jun 17, 1967; children: James A, Crystal A. **Educ:** Pa State Univ, Univ Park PA, BA, eng, 1966, MA, eng, 1974; Duquesne Univ Sch Law, Pittsburgh PA, JD, 1980. **Career:** Pa State Univ, McKeesport, PA, asst dean stud affairs, 1976-77; Neighborhood Legal Serv, McKeesport PA, staff atty, 1980-81; Off Atty Gen, PA, dep atty gen, 1981-83, atty-in-charge, 1983-86; Palkovitz & Palkovitz, McKeesport PA, atty; Duquesne Univ Law, Pittsburgh PA, adj prof, 1984-86, vis prof, 1986-87, adj prof, 1989-99; Allegheny Co Ct Common Pleas, Family Div & Part-time Civil Div, judge, 1999-; bd of dirs, Duquesne Univ, 1996-; Pa State Univ, vice chmn bd, 2001-03, chmn bd; Supreme Ct Pa, justice, 2006-. **Orgs:** Exec comt mem, Homer S Brown Law Asn, 1980-97; Allegheny Co Bar Asn, 1980-; vpres & bd dir, Neighborhood Legal Serv Asn, 1986-88; pres-elect, Pa State Alumni Asn, 1987-88; vice chair & bd dir, Greater Pittsburgh YMCA, 1987-89; Greater Pittsburgh Comn Women, 1987-89; Pa Bar Asn, 1988-; Pa Bar Asn House Delegates, 1988-99; pres, Pa State Alumni Asn, 1989-91; vice chair & gubernational appointee, Pa State, 1995-; bd trustees, Pa State, 2004-07; Pa Comn Crime & Delinquency. **Honors/Awds:** Tribute to Women Award in the Professions, YWCA, 1987; Humanitarian Service Award, Pa State Forum Black Affairs, 1989; Whitney M Young Jr Service Award, Boy Scouts Am, 1991; Women's Equality Day Recognition Plaque, Greater Pittsburgh Comn Women, 1990; Inducted into MCK Sch Hall of Fame, 1990; Distinguished Alumna, Pa State Univ, 1995; Distinguished Daughters of Pennsylvania Award, Gov Tom Ridge, 1996; Woman of the Year in Law & Government, Pittsburgh, 1998; Honorary Doctor of Laws, Point Park Col, 1999; Espirit C's Service Award, Ment Health Asn, 2003; Sylvia H. Rambo Award, Dickinson Sch law, 2007. **Special Achievements:** First black woman elected to the Allegheny Co, PA, bench for a ten-year term; first black woman installed as pres of Pa State Alumni Asn. **Business Addr:** Justice, Supreme Court of Pennsylvania, 200 N Third St, PO Box 1106, Harrisburg, PA 17108-1106, **Business Phone:** (717)772-3771.*

BALDWIN, GEORGE R.
Lawyer. **Personal:** Born Oct 4, 1934, Brunswick, GA; children: Kirk, Goldie. **Educ:** Lincoln Univ, BA, econs, 1955; Brooklyn Law Sch, LLB, JD, 1964; NY Univ Law Sch, LLM, 1976. **Career:** Pvt Pract NYC, atty, 1966-67; Danch, Rivers & Baldwin Westbury, NY, partner, 1967-71; Legal Aid Soc NYC, atty-in-charge Comn Defender Off, 1971; atty, currently. **Orgs:** Nat Bar Asn; Nat Conf Black Lawyers; 100 Black Men Inc; JFK Dem Club; Metro AME Church. **Military Serv:** AUS, 1957-59. **Business Addr:** Attorney, 78 80 Mott St Suite 300, New York, NY 10013.*

BALDWIN, JAMES, JR.
Baseball player. **Personal:** Born Jul 15, 1971, Southern Pines, NC; children: James III. **Career:** Chicago White Sox, pitcher, 1995-01; Los Angeles Dodgers, 2001; Seattle Mariners, 2002; Minnesota Twins, 2003, New York Mets, pitcher, 2004; Baltimore Orioles, 2005; Texas Rangers, 2005; Toronto Blue Jays, 2006. **Honors/Awds:** American League Rookie Pitcher of the Year, The Sporting News, 1996; American League All-Star, 2000. *

BALDWIN, LEWIS V
Educator, writer, clergy. **Personal:** Born Sep 17, 1949, Camden, AL; son of L V and Flora Bell; married Jacqueline Loretta Laws-Baldwin, Sep 29, 1979; children: Sheryl Boykin-Robinson. **Educ:** Talladega Col, BA, 1971; Colgate-Rochester, black church studies, 1973, MDiv, theol, 1975; Northwestern Univ, PhD, hist christianity, 1980. **Career:** Wooster Col, vis asst prof relig, 1981-92; Colgate Univ, asst prof philos & relig, 1982-84, vis asst prof, church hist, 1983-84, Colgate-Rochester Divinity Sch; Vanderbilt Univ, asst prof relig studies, 1984-90, assoc prof, 1991-2000, prof relig studies, 2001-, dir, african am studies. **Orgs:** Nat Asn Advan Colored People, 1980-; Soc Study Black Relig, 1981-; Am Acad Relig, 1981-; Am Soc Church Hist, 1981-; Southern Christian Leadership Conf, financial supporter, 1986-. **Honors/Awds:** Outstanding Young Man of America, US Jaycees, 1975, 1980, 1985, 1990; Book Award, Am Theological Libr Asn, 1981; MBA Book Award, Mid-West Publishers' Asn, 1992. **Special Achievements:** Books published: Freedom is Never Free: A Biographical Profile of E D Nixon Sr, 1992; To Make the Wounded Whole: The Cultural Legacy of M L King Jr, 1992; There is a Balm in Gilead: The Cultural Roots of M L King Jr, 1991; The Mark of a Man: Peter Spencer and the African Union Methodist Tradition, 1987; Invisible Strands in African Methodism: The AUMP and UAME Churches, 1805-1980, 1983; Toward the Beloved Community: Martin Luther King Jr and South Africa, 1995. **Home Addr:** 651 Harpeth Bend Dr, Nashville, TN 37221. **Business Addr:** Professor, Vanderbilt University, Department of Religious Studies, 2301 Vanderbilt Pl, PO Box 351585, Nashville, TN 37240-1121, **Business Phone:** (615)322-6358.

BALDWIN, LOUIS J
Executive. **Personal:** Born in New York, NY. **Educ:** Ithaca Col, BA, bus admin, 1970. **Career:** Ithaca Col, asst dir admis, 1970-72; Am Arbitration Asn, asst dir, 1972-73; Union Carbide Corp, adminr, recruitment & placement, 1974-77; Allied Corp, supvr employee rels, 1977-83; Staten Island Cable, mgr human resources, 1984-85; Amerada Hess Corp, personnel admin, 1985-86; Time Warner Cable, mgr human resources, 1986-91; Cablevi-

sion NY, dir human resources, 1992-99, employee rels, area dir, 1999-2005; Seeking Opportunity, Human Resources Mgt, 2005-. **Orgs:** Adv, Jr Achievement New York, 1976; EDGES Group Inc 1977-; Nat Asn Advan Colored People, 1978-; bd mem, Forum Advan Minorities Eng, 1980-82; loaned exec, United Way, 1982; Nat Asn Minorities Cable, 1984-; secy/bd mem, Harlem Dowling, Westside C & Family Ctr Serv, 1986-; New York Urban League, 1986-; One Hundred Black Men Inc, 1990-; bd dirs, Ithaca Col Alumni, 1996-99.

BALDWIN, MITCHELL CARDELL
Systems analyst, president (organization). **Personal:** Born Aug 22, 1958, Birmingham, AL; son of Bernard and Ezell Caldwell Barnes. **Educ:** Jacksonville State Univ, Jacksonville, AL, BS, comput sci, 1980. **Career:** Am Intermedial Resources, Birmingham, AL, comput prog, 1980-82; Fed Reserve Bank, Birmingham, AL, comput analyst, 1982-84; Alabama Power Co, Birmingham, AL, systs analyst, 1984-; Smart Talk with MCB, pres, currently. **Orgs:** Founder, chmn bd, CHAMP Inc, 1989-; educ comt, AABE. **Honors/Awds:** 200th Point of Light, Pres George Bush, 1990; KOOL Achiever finalist, Brown & Williamson, 1990; People Who Make the Difference finalist, Helene Curtis, 1990; Volunteer of the Year, Gov Guy Hart, 1990; Outstanding Community Servs, Hayes Middle Sch PTA, 1990. **Special Achievements:** Author, Surviving Corporate Downsizing With Dignity and Grace!. **Business Addr:** President, Smart Talk with M.C.B., PO Box 11404, Birmingham, AL 35202-1404, **Business Phone:** (205)970-0828.

BALDWIN, OLIVIA MCNAIR
Government official. **Personal:** Born Mar 30, 1943, Cleveland, OH; daughter of Merdic McNair Jr and Carrie Mae Head McNair; married Otis L, Apr 14, 1962; children: Omar L Baldwin. **Career:** Government official (retired); St Lukes Hosp, Cleveland, OH, food serv supvr, 1962-65; Sumby Hosp, River Rouge, MI, purchasing asst, 1965-66; City Detroit, Detroit, MI, typist, 1970-75, asst market master, 1975-90; Mich Real Estate agt, 1998-. **Orgs:** Order Eastern Star, 1980-; Ways & Means Comt, Am Bus Womens Asn, treasr, 1990-; second vpres, Local 808-M, SEIU, 1989-. **Honors/Awds:** First female asst market master, first female market master, City Detroit, Bureau Markets; Unity Bap Church, Sr Ursher Bd, Busy Bee.

BALL, BRENDA LOUISE
Insurance executive. **Personal:** Born May 26, 1951, Springfield, OH; daughter of John W and Virginia L Davis; married Richard Nixon, Jan 2, 1981; children: Majenni Nixon & Johnathan Nixon. **Educ:** Sinclair Community Col, ABA, 1971; Univ Cincinnati, BBA, 1973; State Mich, Cert Pub Accountants, 1975; Univ Detroit, MBA, 1988. **Career:** Arthur Andersen & Co, sr auditor, 1973-78; Ford Motor Co, fin analyst, 1978-79; Fed-Mogul Corp, bank & pension fund mgr, 1979-81, staff controller, 1982-86, internal audit, 1986-88; Blue Cross & Blue Shield Mich, vpres & controller, 1988-94, vpres & dep treas, 1995-96, vpres & treas, 1996-2003, Ronrich Corp, exec vpres fin, currently. **Orgs:** Fin Execs Inst; Econs Am, bd dirs; Liberty BIDCO, bd dirs; Richard Austin Scholar Comn, Wayne State; United Way, Community Servs Community Priority Review Comt; Nat Asn Black Accts; Univ Detroit-Mercy, bd dirs; Luella Hannan Mem Found, bd dirs; Vista Maria, adv & fin comts; Am Hear Asn, women & heart disease comt; Leadership Detroit, trustee; invest comt, Wayne State Univ Found; bd trustees, Kettering Univ. **Honors/Awds:** 'Nat & Local Achievement Awards', Nat Asn Black Accts; Wall Street Journal Award; Links Inc, Scholar; Ford Found, Scholar. **Business Addr:** Executive Vice President of Finance, Ronrich Corporation, 22400 Lucerne Dr Suite 201, Southfield, MI 48075, **Business Phone:** (248)448-8400.

BALL, CLARENCE M.
Nursing home administrator, chief executive officer. **Personal:** Born Dec 23, 1949, New Braunfels, TX; son of Clarence and Clarice Coleman; married Charlesetta Owens, Aug 20, 1970; children: Sean Terrell, Kevin Denard & Cherise Montre. **Educ:** Tex A&M Univ, Kingsville, TX, 1970; SW Tex State Univ, San Marcos, TX, BA, 1972; N Tex State Univ, 1974. **Career:** Vari-Care Inc, Rochester, NY, adminr, 1974-84; Ball Healthcare Servs Inc, Mobile, AL, pres & chief exec officer, 1983-, Currently. **Orgs:** Ala Nursing Home Asn, 1988-; pres, Am Col Nursing Home Adminrs, 1982; pres, Montgomery Area Coun Nursing Home Adminrs, 1980; bd mem, Young Men's Christian Asn, Mobile, AL, 1987-; second vice chair, Alabama St Port Authority, 2000. **Honors/Awds:** Small Business of the Month, Mobile Area Chamber Com, 1987; Alumnus of the Year Award, N Tex State Univ, 1989; Minority Business Service Award, Mobile Minority Bus Ctr, 1990; Community Service Award, Mobile Chap, Nat Asn Black Social Workers, 1990; Benefactor of Youth Award, Mobile Young Men's Christian Asn, 1990.

BALL, DREXEL BERNARD
College administrator. **Personal:** Born Apr 30, 1948, McClellanville, SC; son of Lucille Ball Garrett; married Brenda Petty, Feb 16, 1975; children: Tyler Anderson. **Educ:** Morehouse Col, Atlanta, Ga, BA, 1972; NC A&T State Univ, Greensboro, NC,MS, 1986. **Career:** Greensboro Daily News, Greensboro, NC, reporter, 1972-82; NC A&T State Univ, Greensboro, NC, asst dir pub rel, 1982-89; Delaware State Univ,Dover, DE, dir pub rels, 1989-92, exec asst pres, 1992-2006; Lincoln Univ Commonwealth Penn, Off Commun & Pub Rel, dir, 2006-08; Exec vpres, Claflin Univ, currently. **Orgs:** Pres, Gate City Morehouse Alumni Chap, 1985-89; Sigma Delta Chi; Nat Asn Black Journalist; Steering Comt, Delaware Chicken Festival, 1991; PR Specialist, Cent Delaware United Way Campaign, 1991; chmn, Dev Comt, Dover Arts Coun; co-dir, Col Proj, Dover Art League. **Business Addr:** Executive Vice President, Claflin University, 400 Magnolia st, Orangeburg, SC 29115, **Business Phone:** 800-535-5000.

BALL, JANE LEE
Educator. **Personal:** Born Jun 2, 1930, Springfield, OH; daughter of Henry and Luella Simpson; married Wilfred R Ball, Apr 1, 1958; children: Janet, Carol B Williams, Wendy B Felder, Wilfred Cristan. **Educ:** Wilberforce Univ, OH, attended 1947; Cent State Univ, Wilberforce, OH, BSEd, 1949; Howard Univ, WA DC, MA, 1951; Wash Univ, St Louis, MO, 1957; Ohio State Univ, Columbus, OH, 1967. **Career:** Educator (retired); Southern Univ, Baton Rouge, LA, instr, asst prof, 1951-58; Alcorn Col, Lorman MS, asst prof, 1959-60; Ohio State Univ, Columbus, OH, instr, 1961, 1964-65; NC Cent, Durham, asst prof, 1963-64; Wilberforce Univ, OH, instr, asst prof, assoc prof, prof, 1966-96, cordr acad affairs, 2000; Wiljaba Publ Co, owner, 1989-91; emer prof Eng, Wilberforce Univ, currently. **Orgs:** AME Church, 1945-; Alpha Kappa Mu Hon Soc, 1948-; Delta Sigma Theta Sorority, 1949-; Col Lang Asn, 1955-; Wilberforce Univ Fac Asn, 1975-80, 1989-96. **Honors/Awds:** Teacher of the Month, 1982, Wilberforce Univ Faculty Merit Award, 1980, 1985, 1991, 1995, Wilberforce Univ. **Special Achievements:** Co-auth, Col Writing, 1977; auth, articles in Humanist, 1980, Critical Survey of Short Fiction; Auth, "Virginia Hamilton," "Gordon Parks," in Dictionary of Literary Biography, 1984; The Black Experience Perpetual Calendar, 1989; auth, articles on Joan Collins, Anne Rice, Beacham's Popular Fiction in America, 1990; auth, articles on Erskine Caldwell, Hamlin Garland, Research Guide/Biog & Criticism, 1985; auth, A Flea in Your Ear (teacher's manual), 1996; auth, After the Split (Wilberforce Univ Hist), 2001. *

BALL, JANET M
Executive director. **Educ:** Univ Ariz, MA, libr sci, 1995. **Career:** Circulation clerk; inter libr loan clerk; libr asst; asst libr dir; libr mgr; libr dir; Ariz State Libr, continuing educ coordr & Archives & Pub Rec Libr Develop Div consult; Copper Queen Libr, Bisbee, AZ, librn, facilitator & dir, currently. **Special Achievements:** Published a regional magazine in northeastern Arizona, written for encyclopedias. **Business Phone:** (520)432-4232.

BALL, JERRY LEE
Entrepreneur, football player. **Personal:** Born Dec 15, 1964, Beaumont, TX; married Michelle; children: Faren, Lindsey & Halle. **Educ:** Southern Methodist Univ. **Career:** Football player (retired), business owner; Detroit Lions, nose tackle, 1987-92; Cleveland Browns, 1993-94, 1999; Los Angeles Raiders, 1994; Oakland Raiders, nose tackle, 1995-96; Minn Vikings, nose tackle, 1997-98, 1999; Ice Box Sportswear Inc, pres & owner, currently. **Orgs:** Omega Psi Phi Fraternity Inc. **Honors/Awds:** Pro Bowl, 1989-91. **Business Phone:** (313)963-4433.

BALL, RICHARD E.
Educator, economist, lawyer. **Personal:** Born Jul 18, 1918, Springfield, MA; married Edwinton Raiford. **Educ:** NY Univ, BS, 1946, MBA, 1948; Brooklyn Law Sch, LLB, 1954, JD, 1967. **Career:** NY City Housing Authority; Dept Welfare; NY City Bd Educ; St Augustine'sCol, chmn & prof; NC Cent Univ, bd trustees & actg pres & bus mgr; Nat Asn Advan Colored People, atty & legal ed, coun & consult; Episcopal Church, lay reader. **Orgs:** Masons, shriners; Consistory; life mem, Alpha Phi Alpha; life mem, Am Nat Bar Asn; NC, MA, State Bar Asn; Nat Mgt Asn; pres, Alpha Phi Lambds Chap. **Honors/Awds:** Cand, Super Court Judge. **Business Addr:** Odd Fellows Bldg Suite 304, Raleigh, NC 27601.

BALL, RICHARD ERWIN
Zoologist. **Personal:** Born Sep 24, 1946, Zanesville, OH; son of Evelyn T; divorced; children: Jennifer Giodano, Michael Ball. **Career:** Paradise Park, opers mgr, 1969-76; Honolulu Zoo, animal keeper I, 1976-88, working foreman II, 1988-90, animal specialist III, 1990-. **Orgs:** Am Zoo Asn; Am Asn Zoo Keepers; Sierra Club. **Business Addr:** Mammal Specialist, Curator, Honolulu Zoo, 151 Kapahulu Ave, Honolulu, HI 96815, **Business Phone:** (808)971-7193.*

BALL, ROGER
Vice president (organization). **Personal:** Born Feb 19, 1961, Ashtabula, OH; son of E Peter Ball and Helen R; married Trenisha G Moore, Mar 19, 1989; children: Demetrius A D & Quinton T. **Educ:** Am Bankers Asn, bank mkt, 1984; Ohio State Univ, BS, 1985; Ohio Univ, MBA,1994. **Career:** Evcor Bus Syst, govt acct mgr, 1986-87; TBS, Ohio, nat acct mgr, 1987-88; Dispatch Consumer Serv Inc, acct exec, 1988-89; B&B Comput Serv Inc, founder & owner, 1986-96; Leaf Productions, exec vpres, currently. **Orgs:** Omega Psi Phi Frat; OSU, Black Alumni Soc, treas & steering comt, 1991; OSU Advocate, 1991; Nat Black MBA Asn. **Honors/Awds:** Outstanding Community Serv, Columbus City Coun, 1985; Community Service, Ohio House Representatives, 1986; Student Leadership, Ohio State University, 1985, Pace Setter Award, 1985. **Special Achievements:** Volunteer speaker for OSU Young Scholars Program, 1992. **Business Phone:** (614)447-2100.*

BALL, WILFRED R.
Educator. **Personal:** Born Jan 3, 1932, Chicago, IL; son of Wilfred Sr and Mary Sanders; married Jane Lee, Apr 1, 1958; children: Janet, Carol, Wendy, Cris. **Educ:** Morehouse Col, BS, 1952; Atlanta Univ, MS, 1955; Ohio State Univ, PhD, 1965. **Career:** Educator (retired). Southern Univ, instr, 1955-60; Alcorn Col, asst prof, 1960-61, 1968-69; Knoxville Col, assoc prof, 1969-70; Wilberforce Univ, assoc & prof, 1972, Natural Sci Div, chair, 1991-96. **Orgs:** Fel, Nat Sci Found, 1960-62; Beta Kappi Chi Honor Scientific Soc; Beta Beta Beta Biol Soc; Kappa Alpha Psi Fraternity. **Honors/Awds:** President's Award for Outstanding Teacher, Wilberforce Univ, 1985. **Home Addr:** 1395 Corry St, Yellow Springs, OH 45387. *

BALL, WILLIAM BATTEN
Accountant, lawyer. **Personal:** Born Aug 28, 1928, San Antonio, TX; son of William Henry (deceased) and Lillian Edna Young Ball (deceased); married Charlie Mae Cooper, Nov 9, 1956; children: Jeffrey Christopher, Kathleen Lorraine & William Eric. **Educ:** Woodrow Wilson Jr Col, Chicago, IL, 1944-45; Roosevelt Univ, Chicago, IL, BS, Commun, 1955, MBA, 1960; Chicago Kent Col Law, IL Inst Technol, Chicago, IL, JD, 1968. **Career:** IRS, revenue officer 1955-57; Supreme Life Ins Co, acct, jr exec, 1957-59; State IL Dept Labor, auditor, 1959; IRS, agent, 1959-67, appellate appeals officer, 1967-86; mgt coordr, 1972-73; atty, pvt pract, 1986-. **Orgs:** Cook Co Bar Asn; Nat Bar Asn; chmn, admin bd, St Mark United Meth Church, 1973-77; troop committeeman, BSA; order Arrow Nat Fraternity Scout Honor Campers; Order Brotherhood; Kappa Alpha Psi Fraternity Inc; bd dir, Community Ment Health Coun, 1982-87; Chicago Bd Educ: Westcott Local Sch Coun, 1989-93, chmn, Bylaws Comm, Subdist Coun Rep, 1989-93. **Honors/Awds:** Various Awards & Honors, BSA; Outstanding Performance Award, IRS; master's thesis, Insurance Co Annual Statement Prep & Instrs, Roosevelt Univ, 1960; Silver Beaver Award, Chicago Area Boy Scouts Coun, 2000. **Special Achievements:** Chicago, Sch Reform Act, created by Illinois State Legisative. **Military Serv:** AUS, cpl, 1951-53. **Business Addr:** Attorney at Law, 8355 S Perry Ave, Chicago, IL 60620, **Business Phone:** (312)874-1863.

BALLARD, ALLEN BUTLER
Educator. **Personal:** Born Nov 1, 1930, Philadelphia, PA; son of Allen Sr and Olive Robinson; divorced; children: John & Alayna. **Educ:** Kenyon Col, BA, 1952; Univ Bordeaux, attended 1953; Harvard Univ, MA, 1957, PhD, 1962. **Career:** City Col NY, asst prof, assoc prof, 1961-69, dean fac, 1973-76; St Univ New York, Albany, NY, prof hist, polit sci & Afro-Am studies, 1986-. **Orgs:** Ford Found; Nat Humanities Ctr; Moton Ctr Grants; Fulbright Scholar, France, 1952-53. **Honors/Awds:** First Novelist Award, Black Caucus, ALA, 2001; DHL, Tuskegee Univ, 2001; DHL, Kenyon Col, 2002. **Special Achievements:** Author: The Education of Black Folk, Harper & Row, 1974; One More Days Journey, McGraw-Hill, 1984; Where I'm Bound, Simon & Schuster, 2000. **Military Serv:** AUS, corporal, 1953-55. **Home Addr:** 15 Cobble Ct, Clifton Park, NY 12065. **Business Addr:** Professor, State University of New York, Department of History, 1400 Wash Ave, Albany, NY 12222, **Business Phone:** (518)442-5407.

BALLARD, DR. BILLY RAY
Physician, educator, dentist. **Personal:** Born Aug 15, 1940, Bossier City, LA; married Rose M Carter; children: Rachel & Percy. **Educ:** Southern Univ, BS, 1961; Meharry Med Col, DDS, 1965, MD, 1980. **Career:** Meharry St Univ NY, Hubbard Hosp, Buffalo, NIH fel, 1965-67; NIH Am Cancer Soc NIH fel, Buffalo, 1967-69; NIH fel, NCI, Roswell Park, Buffalo, 1967-70; State Univ NY, Buffalo, Dept Oral Path, asst prof oral path, 1971-74; Univ Miss Med Ctr, Dept Path, assoc prof, 1982, dir minority student affairs, 1982; Surgical Pathology & Cytopathology fel, 1982-85; Meharry Med Col, assoc prof path, 1974-82; assoc prof & chmn oral path, 1981-82, Grad Med Col, assoc dean, prof & dept chair, currently; Am Soc Clin Pathologists fel, 1986-; Col Am Pathologists fel, 1986-. **Orgs:** Lay reader & vestry St Philips Episcopal Church; Nat Asn Advan Colored People; Urban League, Am Acad Oral Path, Am Asn Dent Schs; Am Asn Med Col; Am Dent Soc; AMA; Am Soc Clin Pathologists; Am Soc Cytol; Cent Miss Med Soc; Int Acad Path; Int Asn Dent Res, Miss Med & Surg Asn; bd dir, Miss Div Am Cancer Soc. **Honors/Awds:** Bd Cert, Am Bd Dent. **Business Addr:** Professor, Department Chair, Meharry Medical College, 1005 Dr D B Todd Blvd, Nashville, TN 37208.

BALLARD, BRUCE LAINE
Physician, psychiatrist. **Personal:** Born Dec 19, 1939, Waverly Hills, KY; married Eleanor Glynn Cross; children: Tracy, Timothy. **Educ:** Yale Univ, BA, 1960; Columbia Univ, Col Physicians & Surgeons, MD, 1964. **Career:** Harlem Hosp Ctr, Dept Psychiat,

assoc dir training, 1970-76; NY Hosp-Westchester Div, assoc dir, adult out patient dept, 1976-81; Weill Med Col, Cornell Univ, assoc dean stud affairs & equal opport progs, 1981-, assoc prof clin psychiat, 2001. **Orgs:** chmn, selection/adv comn, APA-Nat Inst Ment Health fel prog, Am Psychiat Asn, 1974-80, fel, 1976; chmn, comn black psychiatrists, 1982-86; Am Psychiat Asn Assembly Rep, 1994-02; chair, Group Stud Affairs, Asn Am Med Cols, 1992-93; fel, NY Acad Med; bd mem, NY Community Trust. **Honors/Awds:** Alumni Fel, Weill Med Col, 2001; Distinguished Life Fel, Am Psychiat Asn, 2003. **Military Serv:** USAF, capt, 1968-70, commendation medal, 1970. **Business Addr:** Associate Dean for Student Affairs and Equal Opportunity Programs, Associate Professor of Clinical Psychiatry, Weill Medical College Cornell University, 445 E 69th St Rm 110, New York, NY 10021.*

BALLARD, GREGORY
Basketball player, basketball coach. **Personal:** Born Jan 29, 1955, Los Angeles, CA; married Donna; children: Lawrence, Gabrielle & Gregory Jr. **Educ:** Univ Ore. **Career:** Basketball Player (Retired); Basketball Coach; Wash Bullets, prof basketball player, 1977-85; Golden State Warriors, 1985-87; Ill Messagero Roma, 1987-90, asst coach, 1990; CBA; Seattle Supersonics, 1988-89; Burghy Roma, Italian League, intl scout; Dallas Mavericks, asst coach; Minn Timberwolves, asst coach, 1994-03; MikeWoodson; Atlanta Hawks, asst coach & player develop, 2004. **Honors/Awds:** NBA Champions, 1978; Univ of OR, Hall of Fame, inductee; OR Hall of Fame, inductee, 1996. **Special Achievements:** Selected by Montreal Expos (MLB), 1973. *

BALLARD, DR. HAROLD STANLEY
Physician, college teacher. **Personal:** Born Nov 25, 1927, New Orleans, LA; son of Dan and Lillie; married Gail; children: Harold Jr & Kevin. **Educ:** Univ Calif, AB; Meharry Med Col, MD. **Career:** Brooklyn Hosp Ctr, resident; Queens Hosp Ctr, resident; Vet Affairs Med Ctr, resident; Natl Heart Lung & Blood Inst, consult; NY Va Hosp, asst chief, physician; Columbia Univ, Dept Clin Med, Div Hemat & Oncol, prof, currently. **Orgs:** NIH Coun Thrombosis; Am Heart Assn; Am Brd Int Med; chmn policy brd, Hemat Oncol Natural Hist Study Sickle Cell Anemia; Cent Tex Med Found. **Honors/Awds:** Award For 20 Year service Epidemiology & Health Promotion NCYUD, 2004. **Special Achievements:** Published approximately 30 scientific articles. **Business Addr:** Professor, Columbia University, Department of Clinical Medicine, 350 First Ave Apt 7F, New York, NY 10010.

BALLARD, JAMES M., JR.
Psychologist. **Personal:** Born May 19, 1938, Petersburg, VA; married Natalie Dandridge; children: Tresa Melinda, James, III. **Educ:** Va State Col, BS, 1963, MS, 1964; Ind Univ; George Wash Univ; Univ Minn, PhD, soc psychol, 1971. **Career:** Mid-Level Community Clinical Psychol Prog, dir; Howard Univ, assoc prof; Univ Man, assoc prof; Bowie State Col, first dir Inst Res & Eval; Crownsville State Hosp, staff psychol; Behav & Soc Systs Inc, founder & pres; Pvt Prac, Psychiatrist, currently. **Orgs:** SE Psychol Asn; Am Educ Res Asn; Asn Black Psychologists; pres, Eta Eta Lambda Chap Alpha Phi Alpha Frat; Psi Chi Psychol Hon Soc, 1964. **Honors/Awds:** Cited for Service, Inspiration & Support, Nat Asn Advan Colored People; Certificate of Appreciation, 1974. **Military Serv:** USAF E-3, 1955-59. **Business Addr:** Psychiatrist, Behavioral and Social Systems Inc, PO Box 43, Arnold, MD 21012.*

BALLARD, MYRTLE ETHEL
Government official. **Personal:** Born Apr 20, 1930, Shreveport, LA; daughter of Henry Jr and Roxanna Turner Gammage; married Thomas A Ballard, Jun 8, 1952; children: Thomas A Ballard Jr, Roxane R Johnigan, Michael S Ballard & Alexandria Alicia Ballard. **Educ:** Saint Mary's Col, Moraga CA, BA, Pub Mgt, 1978. **Career:** Government official (retired). Calif State Employment Devel, Oakland, CA, office mgr, 1967-2003; Northern Alameda County, mandated partner. **Orgs:** Secy, Int Asn Personnel Security, 1971-73; secy, Black Personnel Mgt Asn, 1972-75; pres, Calif State Employees Asn, 1973-75; secy, Moneyworks; bd mem, Calif Coun Children & Youth, 1973-75; bd mem, Lincoln Child Ctr, 1975-; bd chairperson, Sickle Cell Anemia Res & Educ, 1982-84; regional dir, Zeta Phi Beta Sorority, 1986-92; loan exec, United Way, 1988; bd mem, Lincoln Child Ctr, 1990-, chair, regional exec bd, 1992-96; bd mem, Bay area consortium Qual Health Care; Staff Pastor Parish comt Taylor Mem United Methodist Church, 2003-; regional bd mem, Panhellenic coun; chair, Nat Trustee Bd; Zeta Capital Campaign. **Honors/Awds:** Cert Appreciation, Sickle Cell Anemia Res, 1984; Zeta of the Year, Zeta Phi Beta Sorority, 1986; Those Who Care Award, Zeta Nu Chapter, Zeta Phi Beta, 1987; Noble Citizen, Phi Beta Sigma Fraternity, 1989; Outstanding State Employee of the Year, 1992. **Home Addr:** 2239 Dexter Way, Hayward, CA 94541, **Home Phone:** (510)538-0584.

BALLARD, SHAREESE RENEE
Singer. **Personal:** Born Jan 1, 1978?, Philadelphia, PA. **Educ:** Temple Univ, Philadelphia. **Career:** Album: How I Do, 2001; Singles: Golden Boys, 2001; Ice King, 2001; They Say Vision, 2002; Sittin' Back, 2002; There's No Way, 2007; Black Girls Rock!, 2009; Party Robot, 2009. **Business Addr:** Recording Artist, c/o MCA, 100 Universal City Plz, Universal City, CA 91608.

BALLARD, WALTER W.
Dentist. **Personal:** Born Feb 12, 1928, Toledo, OH; son of Walter W and Edna F; married Joanne Marie Brown; children: Patricia Joan, Walter III. **Educ:** Bowling Green State Univ, BA, 1956; Notre Dame Univ, MS, 1961; IN Univ, DDS, 1963. **Career:** Professor (retired), practitoner: CO Univ, asst prof & oper dentist, 1979-80; gen pract, currently. **Orgs:** Am Dent Asn; Nat Dent Asn; Chicago Dental Soc; IN Dent Asn, 1963-80; CO Dent Asn, 1966-80; pres, trustee, Southeastern CO Dent Asn, 1974-75; chmn, Coun Jud Affairs, CDA, 1979-84; pres, Pueblo Symphony Asn, 1979; 32nd degree, Worshipful master Eureka 2 PHA F&AM, 1979; shriner, Dentist Am Soc Forensic Odontol, 1971; fel, Pierre Fouchard Soc, 1974; fel, Acad Gen Dent, 1978; fel, Am Col Dentists, 1979; dist gov, 1978-79, intl dir, 1984-86, Lions Club Intl; Kappa Alpha Psi Fraternity; The Intl Asn Lions Clubs. **Honors/Awds:** Ambassador of Goodwill, 1985, Melvin Jones Fellow, 1986, Lions Club Intl; Pueblo Image Award, Pueblo, CO, Chamber Com, 1984; 33 Degree Mason, 1996. **Military Serv:** USNR, lt, 1946-73. *

BALLENTINE, KRIM MENELIK
Military leader, politician. **Personal:** Born Oct 22, 1936, St Louis, MO; son of Habib Dickey and Rose Mae Grimes; married Rosalie Erica Simmonds; children: Taraka T, Jabriel S. **Educ:** Wayne State Univ, BS, 1980; Univ Va, Quantico Continuing Educ Prog, cert, 1980; Univ VI, MA, educ coun, 1999. **Career:** Military leader (retired), politician; Pinkerton Nat Detective Agency, spec investr, 1958-60; St Louis Airport Police, patrolman, 1960-66; US Marshals Serv, chief dep, 1966-94; St Thomas-St John Crime Comn, exec dir, 1984-85; ICOP Investigations, exec officer, 1984-; Minority Bus Develop Ctr, bus counr, 1987-88; CBS Affil, talk show radio host, 1987-88; Univ VI, teacher, 1996; VI Police Dept, asst comnr; Repub Party, Washington, DC, politician, currently. **Orgs:** Charter mem, Nat Orgn Black Law-Enforcement Exec; Int Asn Chiefs Police; Mo Peace Officers Asn; FBI Acad Asn; Rotary Int; life mem, Disabled Am Veterans; Int Platform Asn; Int Asn Law Enforcement Intelligence Analysts; Northeast Regional Boy Scout Comt; VI Republican Territorial Comt; chmn, Governors Comn Crime & Violence, Criminal Justice Inst; hon mem, Mark Twain Soc. **Honors/Awds:** Alumni, Wayne State Univ; Silver Beaver, 1983. **Special Achievements:** Author of Krim's Simplistic Philosophies published by Vantage Press Inc. **Military Serv:** USAF & AUS, 18 yrs; Army Achievement Medal. **Business Addr:** Politician, Republican Party, 310 1st St SE, Washington, DC 20003.*

BALL-REED, PATRICE M.
State government official. **Personal:** Born Sep 16, 1958, Chicago, IL; daughter of Arthur and Portia; married Roy L Reed, Jul 16, 1983; children: Candace, Alexis, William. **Educ:** Trinity Col, grad; John Marshall Law Sch, JD, 1984. **Career:** Wash, Kennon, Hunter & Samuels, law clerk, 1984-85, assoc atty, 1985-88; Patricia Banks & Assocs, independent contractor, 1988-89; Cook County State's Atty Off, asst state's atty, 1989, dep supvr Real Estate Property Tax Unit, sr trial supvr child support enforcement div, dep atty gen child support, 2003-. **Orgs:** Assembly, family sect coun, women & minority participation comt, Bd Govs, Bar Publ bd, Ill State Bar Asn; Women's Bar Asn; bd dirs, Black Women Lawyer's Asn Greater Chicago, treas, scholar found; Cook County Bar Asn; Nat Polit Women's Caucus; bd dirs, John Marshall Alumni Asn; registered agent, treas, Nat Black Prosecutors Asn; Scholar Ill Residents Trinity Col. **Honors/Awds:** Distinguished Service Award, John Marshall Law Sch; received a number of awards including the Board of Governors Award from the Illinois State Bar Association, 2000. **Special Achievements:** Discovery Checklist for child support, Illinois Inst Continuing Legal Educ publ, 1993 & 1994. **Business Addr:** Board of Governors, Illinois State Bar Association, 424 S 2nd St, Springfield, IL 62701, **Business Phone:** (217)525-1760.*

BALMER, HORACE DALTON, SR.
Executive, police detective. **Personal:** Born May 28, 1939, Norfolk, VA; son of Martha W; children: Pamela Walker & Horace D Balmer Jr. **Educ:** Norfolk State Univ, attended 1959; VA State Univ, attended 1960. **Career:** Police Detective(retired), executive; NY City Police Dept, detective, 1965-85; Showman's Realty, proprietor & pres, 1985-97; Nat Basketball Asn, asst dir security, 1985-86, dir security, 1986-89, vpres, dir security, sr vpres, currently. **Orgs:** Nat Org Black Law Enforce Execs; Int Soc Black Security Execs; Int Asn police Chiefs; NY City Police Dept Guardians Asn; Nat Asn Advan Colored People; Omega Psi Phi; Guardians Asn, 1985-87; Drug Enforcement Agency, 1986. **Honors/Awds:** 8 awards from New York City Police Dept, Elmcor Youth Org, 1987; Guardian Person of the Year Award, 1990; Sports Executive of the Year Award, The Wheelchair Charities, 1992; Executives Achievement Award, New York Chap Nat Org Black Law Enforcement, 1993. **Special Achievements:** first African-Am Sergeant to supervise detectives in the Bronx. **Business Addr:** Senior Vice President, National Basketball Association, Olympic Tower, 645 Fifth Ave Suite 10, New York, NY 10022.*

BALTHROPE, DR. JACQUELINE MOREHEAD
Educator. **Personal:** Born in Philadelphia, PA; married Robert G Balthrope Sr (deceased); children: Robert G Jr, Yvonne G & Robin B. **Educ:** Cent State Univ, BS, 1949; Case Western Res Univ, MA, 1959; honors PhD: John Carroll Univ, Bowling Green State Univ, Cleveland State Univ, Kent State, post-grad work. **Career:** Cleveland Call Post, free-lance writer & columnist; Chicago Defender, freelance writer & columnist; Pittsburgh Courier Afro-Am, free-lance writer &columnist, 1960-69; Cleveland Pub Sch Syst, teacher & supvr student teachers; Cleveland Bd Educ, Oliver Hazard Perry Elem Sch, prin; Consult,educ. **Orgs:** Hon mem, Entre Nous Club; officer, Royal Hearts Bridge Club; The Pair Ables Vol Homes Aged & Juvenile; active mem & officer, Alpha Kappa Alpha Soc, 1946-; Delta Kappa Gamma Soc, 1972; Eta Phi Beta Soc, 1972; Nat SorPhi Delta Kappa, 1960; Nat Coun Negro Women; Cleveland Chap The CaratsInc; Cleveland Squaws; The Jr League; local, state, nat Elem Sch Prin; active church worker, St John AME Ch; vol Heart, Cancer, March Dimes; UNICEF; Mental Health; United Negro Col Fund; Girl Scouts Campaigns; Retarded Child; active mem & officer, League Women Voters; NAACP; YWCA; Phillis Wheatley Asn; Forest Hosp; Urban League & Guild; Phi Delta Kappa Nat Frat; organizer Top Ladies Distinction; Chums Inc; Project Friendship; Pi Lambda Omega; Am Assoc Univ Women. **Honors/Awds:** Received scholastic, citizenship, civic & religious awards; Cleveland Teacher of the Year; Outstanding Black Women Cleveland OH; America's Outstanding Community Worker; Nat Honor Soc.

BALTIMORE, CHARLI (TIFFANY LANE)
Rap musician. **Personal:** Born Aug 16, 1974, Philadelphia, PA; children: India & Sianni. **Educ:** Pierce Col, fine arts. **Career:** Singles: "Money", 1998; "Feel It", 1998; "Stand Up", 1999; "Everybody Wanna Know", 2000; "Diary", 2002; "Hey Charli", 2002; "Come Test Us",2007; "Lose It", 2008; "P.S.", 2008. **Honors/Awds:** Grammy Award nominee, Best Female Rap Solo Performance, 2002.

BALTIMORE, AMBASSADOR RICHARD LEWIS, III
School principal, administrator. **Personal:** Born Dec 31, 1947, New York, NY; son of Richard Lewis Baltimore Jr and Lois Madison Baltimore; married Eszter Anna, Dec 4, 1993; children: Krisztina, Josephine, Natalie & Vanessa. **Educ:** MacMurray Col, attended 1967; George Wash Univ, BA, 1969; Harvard Law Sch, JD, 1972. **Career:** Dept State, foreign serv officer; US Embassy Lisbon, Portugal, polit/econ officer, 1973-75; US Embassy, Pretoria, S Africa, polit officer, 1976-79; Dept State, spec asst to state secy, 1979-81; US Embassy Cairo, Egypt, polit officer, 1981-83; US Embassy, Budapest, Hungary, polit chief, 1984-87, dep chief Mission, 1990-94; Bur Near E & S Asian Affairs, dep dir, Off Regional Affairs, 1987-88, dir, 1988-90; sr polit adv asst sec European/Canadian affairs, 1994-95; Sr Seminar, class pres, 1995-96; US Embassy, San Jose, Costa Rica, dep chief Mission, 1996-99; US Consulate Gen, Jeddah, Saudi Arabia, coun gen, 1999-2002; Sultanate Oman, ambassador, 2002-06; US Embassy, Kabul, Afghanistan, counr rule law, 2006; Int Consult Blue City, Oman, 2007-; SASLO Legal Training Ctr, prin (retired), 2009-; SASLO Law Office, consultant, sr mgr, 2008-. **Honors/Awds:** Salgo Award, Political Reporting, 1986; Group Honor Award, 1997; Meritorious Honor Award for Rule of Law performance in Afghanistan, 2006. **Special Achievements:** First Black Political Officer to serve in apartheid South Africa.

BALTIMORE, ROSLYN LOIS
Executive. **Personal:** Daughter of Richard Jr and Lois; married John Ervin; children: Richard. **Educ:** Boston Univ, AB, 1964; Harvard Grad Sch Educ, EdM, 1970; Harvard Bus Sch, MBA, 1972. **Career:** Paul Sack Prop, asst develop, 1972-73; Wells Fargo Bank, asst vpres, 1973-77; RL Baltimore Co, pres, 1977-; San Francisco Planning Comn; Baltimore Mortgage Co Inc, owner, pres, 1989-; Crescendo LLC, real estate developer, 2005-. **Orgs:** Bd mem, Reality House W, 1978-; dir, Bay Area Rapid Transit; Access Appeals Bd, 1983-; pres, Handicapped Access Appeals Bd, 1985; hon mem, Sigma Gamma Rho, 1986; SF Planning Comn, 2000. **Honors/Awds:** Business Woman of the Year, Savvy Mag, 1984; proclamation, Mayor San Francisco, 1985; Key to the City, Evansville, Ind, 1985. **Business Addr:** President, RL Baltimore Co, Crescendo LLC, PO Box 193422, San Francisco, CA 94119, **Business Phone:** (415)242-7888.

BALTON, JUANITA J.
Educator. **Educ:** EdD. **Career:** Educator (retired). **Orgs:** Women's Fund Greater Birmingham; hon mem, Alys Stephens Ctr Performing Arts. *

BALTON, KIRKWOOD R.
Executive. **Personal:** Born Jun 9, 1935, Birmingham, AL; son of William (deceased) and Gertrude; married Juanita Jackson, Jul 13, 1957; children: Adriene Yvette. **Educ:** Miles Col, BS, 1957; Stamford Univ, MBA, 1970. **Career:** Bradford Indust Ins Co, bookkeeper, 1957-59; Booker T Wash Ins Co, bookkeeper, internal auditor, admin asst to pres & vpres, 1959-73, exec vpres, mem bd dir, 1973; A G Gaston Construct Co Inc, pres, 1988-01; Zion Memorial Gardens; New Grace Hill Cemetery; L & K Elecc Supply Co LLC; J & B Mgt & Elec Supply Co Inc; J & B Med Supply Co, chmn & pres, currently. **Orgs:** Birmingham Area Chamber Com; Our Lady Queen Univ Cath Church; Rotary Int; Leadership Birmingham Class, 1986-87; bd dir Alpha Phi Alpha Fraternity; A

G Gaston Boys Club Inc, chairman, Colonial Bank; 101 Black Men; Leadership AL, 1994-95; Bus Coun Ala; Univ Ala; Birmingham Health Servs Found; United Way Cent Ala; Ala Asn Minority Contractors; red bd, NCCJ; Am Red Cross; bd & pres, Birmingham Civil Rights Inst; bd mem, Birmingham Mus Arts. **Honors/Awds:** Honorary Doctor Humanity, Bham Easonian Baptist Bible Col, 1995; DHL, Miles Col, 2000. **Special Achievements:** Black Enterprise's list Top Insurance Com, ranked at fourth position in 1999, 2000. **Business Addr:** President, Birmingham Civil Rights Institute, 520 16th St N, Birmingham, AL 35203.*

BAMBAATAA, AFRIKA (KEVIN DONOVAN)
Disc jockey, music producer. **Personal:** Born Apr 10, 1960, South Bronx, NY. **Career:** Founding mem, Bronx River Proj; albums: Return to Planet Rock, 1999; Hydraulic Funk, 2000; Theme Of The United Nations w/ DJ Yutaka, 2000; Electro Funk Breakdown, 2001; Looking for the Perfect Beat: 1980-85, 2001; Lovage: Music To Make Love To Your Old Lady By, 2001; Dark Matter Moving at the Speed of Light, 2004; Metal, 2005; Metal Remixes, 2005. **Honors/Awds:** The Source Hip-Hop Music Award; Pioneer Award, 1999. *

BANDELE, ASHA
Writer. **Personal:** Born Jan 1, 1970?; married Rashid. **Educ:** City Univ, New Sch Social Res, NY, BA; Bennington Col, MFA. **Career:** Essence mag, writer, 2000-04, ed, currently; Columbia Univ, Revson fel, 2004-; author: Absence in the Palms of My Hands (poetry), 1996; The Prisoner's Wife: A Memoir, 2000; Daughter, 2003; Brown Sugar 4: Secret Desires, 2005; The Subtle Art of Breathing, 2005. **Orgs:** Dep dir, Pub Policy Drug Policy Alliance. **Business Addr:** Writer, c o Charles Scribners Sons, 300 Park Ave S 9th Fl, New York, NY 10010.*

BANDELE, DR. SAFIYA
College administrator. **Career:** Medgar Evers Col, Ctr Women's Develop, dir, currently. **Honors/Awds:** New York City Ellen Lurie Award, Community Serv Soc; Malcom X Award, E Orgn; Outstanding Service Award, Black Veterans Social Justice; Outstanding Women's Leadership Award, State Sen Velmanette Montgomery; Community Service Award, Haitian Health Ctr; Presential Award, Medgar Evers Col. **Business Addr:** Director, Medgar Evers College, Center for Women's Development, 1650 Bedford Ave Bedford Campus Rm B-2032, Brooklyn, NY 11225-2010.

BANDO, THELMA PREYER
Educator, dean (education). **Personal:** Born Mar 11, 1919, Philadelphia, PA; daughter of Katherine Person Preyer Perry and Henry J Preyer; married McDonald M, Dec 27, 1947 (deceased). **Educ:** Howard Univ, BA, 1935; VA Sem & Col, LHD; Columbia Univ, MA, 1939; Univ PA, postgrad, 1940; Temple Univ, postgrad, 1955. **Career:** Educator, Dean (retired); Bishop Col, Educ Dept, chmn, 1939-40; Dudley High Sch, Eng Dept, chmn, 1940-41; Morgan State Univ, assoc prof, 1942-55, dean, 1942-77, asst dean women, 1996; Va Seminary, Lynchburg, asst dean women & head educ. **Orgs:** Pres, Morgan Univ Bredgettes, 1943-; Col Woman's Asn; Alpha Kappa Alpha; nat pres, Chi Delta Mu Wives, 1949-53; Gov's Comn Status Women; pres, Women's Med Auxil, Baltimore, MD; comnr, Baltimore City Comn Women; pres, Philomathian Club; bd mem, Pickersgill, Park Ave Lodge; comt mem, Baltimore Symphony Orchestra, 1990-. **Honors/Awds:** Received 2 major proclamations in Baltimore, MD; At Morgan Univ founder of Women's Week, Charm Club, Mentor Syst, Col Canteen; City Coun Award; Morgan State Univ Meritorious Award; Morgan Heritage Award, Morgan State Univ, 1991; Recognition Award, Distinguished Serv as Pres of the Phelomathians, 1994; Thelma Preyer Bando Lounge was dedicated in the Harper-Lubman Residence Hall, Morgan State Col, 1994. **Special Achievements:** Auth: Handbook for Col Res Hall Dir; Guide for Off Campus Housing; Handbook for Mentors. **Home Phone:** (410)466-7432. *

BANFIELD, ANNE L.
Public relations executive. **Personal:** Born May 27, 1925, Detroit, MI; married William J; children: DuVaughn, Bruce & William Credric. **Educ:** Detroit Inst Com Sec Sci, attended 1945; Wayne State Univ; HP Col, Univ MI, Wayne Community Col. **Career:** US Army Signal Corps, tech sec & chief engr; Dr HM Nuttall, med sec; Julian Rodgers & Julian Perry, legal sec; Anne's Secretarial Serv, self-employed; YWCA, sec exec dir; Detroit Inst Com, asst adminr officer, asst mgr; MI Chronicle, pub rels dir; Anna Lue Enterprise, pres, currently. **Orgs:** Bd mem, Nat Media Women; bd mem, Mayor's Keep Detroit Beautiful Community; Women's Econ Club Detroit; Women's Conf Concerns; Women's Community United Negro Col Fund; bd mem, Randolph Wallace Kidney Found; Urban League; Nat Tech Asn Auxiliary; Concerned Boaters.

BANFIELD, DR. EDISON H
Surgeon. **Personal:** Born Jun 25, 1924, Baltimore, MD; married Julia; children: Ava, Yvonne, Stephen & Edison, Jr. **Educ:** Howard Univ, BS (cum laude), 1950, MD, 1954. **Career:** Baylor Col Med, instr surg; pvt pract physician & surgeon, currently. **Orgs:** Fel, Am Col Surgeons, 1963. **Military Serv:** AUS, cpl, 1943-46. **Home Addr:** 3423 N MacGregor, Houston, TX 77004. **Business Phone:** (713)528-5375.

BANKETT, WILLIAM DANIEL
Government official. **Personal:** Born Dec 8, 1930, Oak Grove, VA; son of William Rich and Edna Weeden Rich; married Evelyn Robinson Bankett, Jun 25, 1955; children: Wendell, Kevin. **Educ:** West Va State Col, Inst WV, BS, 1954; George Wash Univ, WA DC, 1958; Hampton Inst, Hampton VA, 1961; Massachusetts Inst Technol, Boston, MA, cert Urban Exec, 1972. **Career:** Nat Security Agency, WA DC, 1954-55; Dept Agr, Minneapolis, MN, exam, 1955-57; Westmoreland Co Sch, Oak Grove VA, prin, 1957-62; Prince William Co Schs, Manassas VA, prin, 1962-67; Southeast House, WA DC, exec dir, 1967-68; Southwest Community House, WA, DC, exec dir, 1968-70; Redevelop Land Agency, H St area dir, Dept Housing & Community Develop, spec asst, 1970-; chief exec officer, Dan Man Mustangs Inc, 1973-. **Orgs:** Vpres, Elem Prins Asn, 1960-65; Mayor's Econ Task Force, 1970-78; VOICE, 1970-79; Anacostia Econ Develop Corp, 1970-80, Marlton Swim Asn, 1972-; Mustang Club Am, 1980-; Dept Housing & Community Develop Asn, 1985-; vpres, Johnson Alumni Asn 1986-. **Honors/Awds:** Outstanding Member Award, Am Cancer Soc, 1985-87; Presidential Award, Am Cancer Soc, 1988; Platinum Award for going 266% above the quota, DC One Fund, 1988. **Special Achievements:** Author, "Schools Without Grades," Virginia Educ Jour, 1967. **Military Serv:** AUS, corporal, 1945-47; Good Conduct, Sharp Shooter, 1946. *

BANKHEAD, PATRICIA ANN
Educator. **Personal:** Born Dec 30, 1947, Los Angeles, CA. **Educ:** Calif State Univ, Los Angeles, BS, sociol, 1972; Pepperdine Univ, MS, sch mgt, 1976; San Jose State Univ, cert aerospace educ, 1983. **Career:** Los Angeles Unified Sch Dist, elem teacher, 1973-76; Calif Lutheran Col, lectr, 1977; Los Angeles Southwest Col, instr, 1977-80; Los Angeles Unified Sch Dist, prog coordr, 1977-80; State Calif, mentor & teacher, 1984-87. **Orgs:** Sponsor Black Women's Forum, Los Angeles, 1980-87; adv bd, United Negro Col Fund, 1981-87; official hostess, City of Los Angeles, 1983-87; Nat Asn Advan Colored People, 1984-87; Mentor Adv Bd, LA Unified Schs, 1984-87; Calif Aerospace Asn, 1985-87; Delta Kappa Gamma Int, 1987; Nat Coun Negro Women, 1987; mayor, City of Inglewood, Human Affairs Comn, 2003-06. **Honors/ Awds:** Black College Fair Black Women's Forum, 1981; selected for Public Service TV spot State of CA Dept of Educ, 1986; Letter of Appreciation, Serv Supt of Educ State of CA, 1986; Certificate of Appreciation, Mayor of Los Angeles for 200 service hrs; Letter of Recognition, Master Teacher, City of Los Angeles. **Business Addr:** Mentor Teacher, State of CA, Los Angeles Unified School District, 1745 Vineyard Ave, Los Angeles, CA 90019.

BANKS, ALICIA
Columnist, executive, radio producer. **Personal:** Born Aug 10, 1963, Chicago, IL. **Educ:** Univ Ill, Urbana-Champaign, BA, speech commun pre-law, 1984; Univ Ark, Little Rock, MA, interpersonal & orgn & commun, 2001. **Career:** WUHS Radio, gen mgr, announcer, newscaster, 1979-80; WPGU Radio, vocal prod talent, copy writer, 1980-82; WBML Radio, founder, gen mgr, prog dir, host, producer, dj, sales agent, 1982-84; WRFG Radio, producer, host, dj, engr, non-profit fund raiser, subscription sales, 1989-96; WIGO Radio, producer, talk show host, copywriter, vocal prod talent, sales agent, 1993-95; Friends Mag, columnist, 1994-96; WGST Radio, talk show host, 1995-96; Hues Mag, columnist, 1996; KPFA/KPFB/KFCF Radio, producer, host, engr, 1996-98; Eloquent Fury Website, webmaster, columnist, 1994-; KABF Radio, producer, currently. **Honors/Awds:** Trailblazer Award, Univ Ill, Urbana-Champaign, 1996; various leadership, alumni awards, 1980-86; Outstanding Young Woman of Am, 1986; Senior 100 Award, UIUC, 1984; Young Woman of Am Leadership Award, UIUC, 1982. **Special Achievements:** Eloquent Fury; Les Chanteueses Africaines, 1989; has been featured in many publications. **Business Addr:** Producer, KABF, 2101 S Main St, Little Rock, AR 72206, **Business Phone:** (501)372-6119.

BANKS, ANDREW J.
President (organization). **Educ:** Cleveland State Univ, BA, econ; Baldwin Wallace Col, MBA, bus admin. **Career:** Mgt consult div Deloitte & Touche, mgr, 1986; LTV Steel, bus systs analyst; Caterpillar Tractor Co, planner; Mid-America Consult Group Inc, chmn, pres & chief exec officer, currently. **Orgs:** Trustee, Kent State Univ. **Business Addr:** President, Chief Executive Officer, Mid-America Consult Group Inc, 25800 Sci Pk Dr Suite 225, Beachwood, OH 44122, **Business Phone:** (216)292-2800.

BANKS, ANTHONY LAMAR. See BANKS, TONY.

BANKS, BEATRICE
Executive. **Personal:** Born Jul 24, 1936, Uniontown, AL; daughter of Robert. **Educ:** Wayne State Univ, BS, 1963. **Career:** Detroit Bd Educ, teacher; Residential & consumer Serv, adv, 1963-71, asst supv 1971-72; Detroit Wayne Div Customer Mkt Serv, asst mgr, 1972-74, mgr, 1974-75, dir mkt serv, 1975-79; Detroit Edison Co, Customer & Mkt Serv, Macomb Div, dir, 1979-84; Detroit Edison Co, asst mgr, 1980-. **Orgs:** Women's Econ Club; Eng Soc Detroit; Greater Detroit C C; Project Pride Board; Corp Urban Forum; bd dir, Don Bosco Home Boys;Mich Civil Rights Comn; Dearborn & Greater Detroit Chambers Com; exec comt, NAACP; Booker T. Washington Bus Asn; Am Asn Blacks Energy; adv bd, Horizon Upward Bound; adv bd, Black Family Develop. **Honors/Awds:** Headliner Award, Women Wayne State Univ, 1976; YMCA Minority Achievement Award, 1982. *

BANKS, CARL E.
Football player, broadcaster. **Personal:** Born Aug 29, 1962, Flint, MI. **Educ:** Mich State Univ, attended 1984. **Career:** Football player (retired), broadcaster; NY Giants, 1984-92, radio broadcast analyst, 2007-; Wash Redskins, 1993; Cleveland Browns, 1994-95; NY Jets, dir player develop, 1993-97; Banks Commun, chmn; GIII Apparel Group, pres sports lic; Sirius NFL Radio, host, currently; WFAN, host currently. **Honors/Awds:** NFC Championship Game, 1986; Pro Bowl, 1987. **Business Phone:** (201)935-8111.

BANKS, CARLTON LUTHER
Accountant. **Personal:** Born Apr 9, 1958, Bronx, NY; married Creecy Seymore; children: Regina & Attallah. **Educ:** Morgan State Univ, BA, polit sci, 1980; NY Univ, dipl direct mkt, 1986; Columbia Univ, MS, real estate develop, 1999. **Career:** TroCar Realty Inc, vpres, 1981-85; Greek Gallery, pres; NY Life Ins Co, registered financial advisor, 1988-; Talented Tenth Invests Inc, chief exec officer, prin, currently; Global Financial Network, bd mem, currently. **Orgs:** Omega Psi Phi Fraternity, 1977; Direct Mkt Club, NY, 1986; Nat Asn Advan Colored People, 1987; Keeper fin, 1987. **Business Addr:** Principal, Talented Tenth Investments Inc, 676 Riverside Dr Apt 10A, PO Box 606, New York, NY 10031-5535, **Business Phone:** (212)281-1833.

BANKS, CAROLINE LONG
City council member, executive. **Personal:** Born Oct 30, 1940, McDonough, GA; daughter of Ralph A and Rubye Carolyn Hall; divorced; children: April Lynn & James H Jr. **Educ:** Clark Col, Atlanta GA, BA, 1962; Univ HI, 1963; Ga State Univ, MA, 1973. **Career:** HI Bd Educ, eng teacher, 1963-64; Atlanta Bd Educ, eng teacher, 1967-69; Rich's Depart Store, Corp Credit Servs, from mgt trainee to mgr, 1973-89; Atlanta City Coun, 1980-, pub safety comn, finance comn, chair, 1992, comn coun, exec, & community develop comns, city council woman, currently; Minority Training & Assistance Partnerships Inc, chief exec officer, 1990-. **Orgs:** Atlanta League Women Voters, 1980-; bd dirs, Black Women's Coalition, 1980-; Ga Coalition Black Women, 1980-; Nat League Cities, 1980-, bd dirs, 1981-, adv coun, 1990-; Delta Sigma Theta Sorority Inc, Golden Life mem, 1980-; Nat Black Caucus Local Elected Off, 1981-, bd dirs, 1981-, pres, 1992; Ga Munic Asn, 1980-, bd dirs, 1990-92, domestic violence task force, 1990-92; Nat Forum Black Pub Adminrs, 1983-; Nat Purchasing Coun; Atlanta Regional Minority Purchasing Coun; Atlanta Chamber Com. **Honors/Awds:** Bronze Woman of the Year, Iota Phi Lambda, 1980; Cummings Forsyth Optimist Club & Forsyth Co Sch Syst, 1987; Outstanding Community Awards, Human Econ Love Plan Atlanta Jamaican Asn, Gamma Theta Chap, 1987; Outstanding Contribution, Port-of-Spain People-to-People Exchange, 1987; Outstanding Achievement Award, Clark Col, 1988. **Special Achievements:** First African-Am woman appointed to Atlanta City Coun, 1980; Democratic Nat Part Conv delegate, 1984; panelist, Nat Congress of Black Women, 1989; panelist, Atlanta Historical Soc Educ Series: 150 Years of Key Civil Rights Decisions, 1990; First African American woman to serve on the city's Board of Aldermen. **Business Addr:** City Councilwoman, Atlanta City Council, 55 Trinity Ave SW Suite 2900, Atlanta, GA 30303, **Business Phone:** (404)330-6030.

BANKS, CECIL J.
Lawyer, business owner. **Personal:** Born Sep 27, 1947, Des Moines, IA; married Dr Margot H; children: Kimberly, Imani & Jamaal. **Educ:** Sophia Univ, Tokyo, Japan; Duquesene Univ, BA, 1970; Univ Pittsburgh, Grad Sch Pub & Int Affairs, MPA, 1974; Rutgers Univ Sch Law, JD, 1976. **Career:** Mc Carter & Enguisir Esq, assoc, 1976; Newark Bd Educ, gen coun, 1978-82; City of Orange, legis coun, 1980-84, city atty, 1984; Sills Beck Cummis, Zuckerman Radin Tischman & Epstein, partner; City of Orange, atty, currently; Banks Erlanger, partner, currently. **Orgs:** Bd trustees, United Commun Corp; chmn & founder, Young Lawyer's Com Essex Co Bar Asn; bd dir, NAACP; mem, Nat Bar Asn, Am Bar Asn & Nat Asn Bond Lawyers; bd mem, Nat Asn Sch Law Attorneys; bd dir, Community Coop Develop Found, Bridgeport, CT; pres, Advice & Consent US Senate bd dir African Develop Found; bd dirs, United Hosps Found; legis coun, Orange City Coun, 1980-84; active democrat fund raiser, 1996. **Honors/Awds:** Service Award, United Commun Corp; Service Award, United Clergy Oranges. **Business Addr:** Owner, Banks Erlanger, 1 Gateway Ctr, Newark, NJ 07102.*

BANKS, CHARLIE
Chief executive officer, business owner. **Personal:** Born Aug 11, 1931, Little Rock, AR; son of George Banks and Lela Ervin Williams; married Mary Caster Catherine, Sep 13, 1969; children: Charles, Lamarr & Daphne. **Educ:** Chicago Tech Col, BSEE, Chicago, Ill, 1955; Western State Univ, Law, Fullerton, Calif,

1975. **Career:** Rockwell Int, Downey, Calif, engineering, logistics, 1960-75; Rockwell Int, Pittsburgh, Pa, purchasing mgr, 1975-79; Gould Inc, Rolling Meadows, Ill, purch dir, 1979-83; Mitchell S Watkins Assoc, Chicago, Ill, vpres, 1981-83; City Chicago, Chicago, Ill, first dep PA, 1983-85; Prod Dynamics Chicago Inc, Ill, pres, 1985-, owner, currently. **Orgs:** Omega Psi Phi, 1959-; Am Mgt Asn, 1960-75; Purch Mgt Asn, 1975-79. **Honors/Awds:** Black Enterprise Top 100, Black Enterprise Mag, 1990-91; Chicago Crains, Crains, 1990-91; Booker T Wash Found, 1990. **Military Serv:** USAF, airman first class, 1949-53. **Business Phone:** (773)375-2600.

BANKS, CHRIS (WARREN CHRISTOPHER BANKS)
Football player. **Personal:** Born Apr 4, 1973, Lexington, MO. **Educ:** Kans Univ. **Career:** Denver Broncos, guard, 1996-99; Atlanta Falcons, guard, 1999-2001. **Orgs:** Mem of Super Bowl XXXIII championship team, 1998. *

BANKS, DWAYNE MARTIN
Educator. **Personal:** Born Apr 7, 1961, Newport News, VA. **Educ:** Norfolk State Univ, BS, 1985; Old Dominion Univ, MEd, 1992. **Career:** NEA, Crittenden Mid Sch, technol teacher, currently. **Orgs:** Bd mem, SCA, 1986-87; PTA, 1986-87; Alpha Phi Alpha Fraternity Inc. **Honors/Awds:** Deans List, Norfolk State Univ, 1985; Asn Supv & Curriculum Develop, 1992-; Staff Develop Coun, 1994. **Home Addr:** 604 S Ave, Newport News, VA 23601. **Business Addr:** Technology Teacher, Crittenden Middle School, Technol Educ, 6158 Jefferson Ave, Newport News, VA 23605, **Business Phone:** (757)591-4900.*

BANKS, ELLEN
Artist. **Personal:** Born Jan 1, 1938?, Boston, MA. **Educ:** Mass Col Art, BA; Sch Mus, fine arts. **Career:** Dunbarton Galleries, painter & exhibits, 1962; Boston Mus Fine Arts, 1970; Smith-Mason Gallery, 1971. **Orgs:** Nat Ctr Afro-Am Artists. **Honors/Awds:** Prix De Paris, 1967. **Home Addr:** 4260 58th St, San Diego, CA 92115.

BANKS, ERNEST
Baseball player, orator, executive. **Personal:** Born Jan 31, 1931, Dallas, TX; son of Essie and Eddie; married Liz Ellzey, Jan 1, 1997; married Marjorie, 1997 (divorced); children: Jan, Jerry, Joey & Lyndel. **Career:** Baseball player (retired), orator, executive; Negro Am League, 1950-53; Kans City Monarchs, 1950, 1953; Chicago Cubs, infielder, 1953-71, first base coach, 1954-71, minor league instr; Seaway Nat Bank, exec; New World Van Lines, spokesman & consult, 1984; Ernie Banks Int, founder & pres; Ernie Banks Live Above & Beyond Found, founder & chmn, currently; All Am Speakers Bur, speaker, currently. **Orgs:** Bd mgr, Chicago Met YMCA; bd mem, Chicago Transit Auth; bd mem, LA Urban League. **Honors/Awds:** Most Valuable Player Award, Nat League, 1958, 1959; played 13 All-Star Games; Golden Glove Award, 1960; Texas Sports Hall of Fame, 1971; Nat Baseball Hall of Fame, 1977. **Special Achievements:** First black to play with the Chicago Cubs; Autobiography, Mr Cub. **Military Serv:** AUS, 1951-52. **Business Addr:** Motivational Speaker, All American Speakers Bureau, 6123 Farrington Rd, Chapel Hill, NC 27707, **Business Phone:** (919)403-7004.

BANKS, EUGENE LAVON. **See BANKS, GENE.**

BANKS, FRED L.
Judge, businessperson. **Personal:** Born Sep 1, 1942, Jackson, MS; son of Violet Mabery and Fred L; married Pamela Gipson, Jan 28, 1978; children: Rachel, Jonathan & Gabrielle. **Educ:** Howard Univ, BA, Accounting, 1965; Howard Univ Sch Law, JD, 1968. **Career:** Nichols Attys & Pred, partner, 1968-84; Miss House Rep, Judiciary Comt, 1976-85; Banks Owens & Byrd Attys, 1985; Circuit Ct Dist Miss, circuit judge, 1985-91; Miss Supreme Ct, justice, 1991-2000, presiding justice, 2000-01; Phelps Dunbar LLP, partner & atty, 2001-. **Orgs:** Pres, State Mutual Fed Savings & Loan Asn, 1979-89; Miss Bd Bar Admis, 1978-80; nat adv, Community Educ Disadvantaged C, 1978-80; nat bd dir, NAACP, 1982-, Jackson Goodwill Industries, 1985-91; Community Found Greater Jackson, 2000-; Phi Beta Sigma, Beta Gamma Boule. **Honors/Awds:** Numerous civic awards from national state and local organizations. **Home Addr:** 976 Metairie, Jackson, MS 39209, **Home Phone:** (601)354-0786. **Business Addr:** Partner, Attorney, Phelbs Dunbar LLP, 111 E Capitol St Suite 600, Jackson, MS 39201-2122, **Business Phone:** (601)360-9356.

BANKS, GENE (EUGENE LAVON BANKS)
Basketball player, basketball coach. **Personal:** Born May 15, 1959, Philadelphia, PA; married Belle. **Educ:** Duke Univ, BS, 1981. **Career:** Basketball player (retired), basketball coach; San Antonio Spurs, 1981-85; Chicago Bulls, 1985-87; Arimo Bologna, 1988-89; Maccabi Rishon LeZion, Israel, 1990-92; Bnei Herzeliya, 1992-93; Hapoel Gvat & Haemek, 1993-94; Bluefield State Col, Lady Blues, head basketball coach. **Honors/Awds:** Rookie of the Year award, 1978; Walter Kennedy Citizenship Award, 1984; inducted Duke Basketball Hall of Fame, 1994. **Special Achievements:** Film appearance, Eddie, 1996. *

BANKS, GEORGE S.
Chief executive officer, executive, president (organization). **Personal:** Born in Liberia. **Educ:** Univ Liberia, Liberia, Training & Cert, 1990; Community Col RI Providence, RI, AA, arts gen studies, 1992; Johnston Police Dept, Johnston, RI, Criminal Justice Internship, 1993; RI Col Providence, RI, BA, justice studies & criminal justice, 1994; George Washington Univ, Wash, DC, Web Mgmt Grad Cert Prog. **Career:** Liberian News Agency, Liberia, News Reporter, 1981-83; Welcome to Liberia Mag, publ, 1983-85; Interim Nat Assembly, Liberia, Admin Secy, chmn com tlabor, 1985-86; spec asst to Sr Senator Montser rado County & Chmn Banking,Currency, 1986-90; Guardsmark Inc, Boston, MA, security officer & site supvr, 1990-92, asst to br mgr, 1993, inve str, 1995, acct supvr, 1995-96;security officer; Super Ct, Wash, DC, Regist Pvt Criminal Justice Act Inve str, 1996-99; Sentry Security Int Inc, pres & cheif executive officer,1999-. **Orgs:** White House Community Empowerment; Black Enterprise Inc; pres, bd dirs, St James Int Community Church USA; Am Soc Ind Security; mem, Comnon African Affairs, Gov dist of Columbia. **Business Addr:** President, Chief Executive Officer, Sentry Security International Inc, 7705 Georgia Ave NW Suite 212, Washington, DC 20012, **Business Phone:** (202)291-8030.

BANKS, HAYWOOD ELLIOTT
Lawyer. **Personal:** Born Dec 3, 1922, Suffolk, VA; son of William Henry and Rosa Coston; married Barbara Farthing, Jun 12, 1946; children: Bobby Darnell & Linda. **Educ:** A&T Col NC, 1941; Ky State Col, 1943; St Louis Univ Law Sch; Lincoln Univ Sch Law, LLB, 1949. **Career:** Shobe Lunderman & Banks, law partner, 1949-52; Cincinnati Ordinance Dist, lawyer army, 1952-58; Nat Labor Rels Bd, lawyer, 1958-83; pvt lawyer, labor rels consult, 1983-. **Orgs:** Nat Asn Advan Colored People; Bus & Labor Comt, 1958-; Nat Bar Asn. **Military Serv:** Med Corps, Dent Lab Tech, tech grade 5, 1943-46. **Home Addr:** 13810 Franklin Ave Apt 11N, Flushing, NY 11355. **Business Addr:** Private Attorney, Labor Relations Consultant, PO Box 661, Flushing, NY 11355, **Business Phone:** (718)445-4583.*

BANKS, JAHSHUWAN-JESSEAN
Educator. **Career:** Clark Atlanta Univ, psychol prof, 2004. **Business Addr:** Professor of Psychology, Clark-Atlanta University, 223 James P Brawley Dr SW, Atlanta, GA 30314, **Business Phone:** (404)880-8000.*

BANKS, DR. JAMES ALBERT
Writer, educator, college teacher. **Personal:** Born Sep 24, 1941, Marianna, AR; son of Matthew and Lula Banks; married Cherry Ann McGee, Feb 15, 1969; children: Angela Marie & Patricia Ann. **Educ:** Chicago City Coll, AA, 1963; Chicago St Col, BEd, 1964; Mich State Univ, MA, 1967, PhD, 1969. **Career:** Joilet Ill Pub Schs, teacher, 1965; Francis W Parker Sch, teacher, 1965-66; Univ Wash, Seattle, from asst prof to assoc prof, 1969-73, prof educ, 1973-, chmn curriculum & instruction, 1982-87, Ctr Multicultural Educ, dir, 1992-; Univ Wash, Seattle, WA, assoc prof, 1971-73, prof educ, 1973-, chmn, dept curric & instr, 1982-87, Kerry & Linda Killinger prof diversity Studies & dir ctr multi cultural Educ, currently; Nat Acad Educ,Spencer Fel, 1973; Univ Mich, vis prof educ, 1975; Kent St Univ, distinguished scholar lectr, 1978; Univ Ariz, vis prof, 1979; Univ Guam,vis prof, 1979; Va State Univ, eminent scholar lectr, 1981; British Acad,UK, vis lectr, 1983; Ind Univ, Bloomington, vis prof, 1983; Monash Univ,Australia, vis prof educ, 1985; Humboldt State Univ, vis prof, 1989; CalifState Univ, Fullerton, distinguished vis lectr, 1989; Univ NC, ChapelHill, vis prof, 1989; Syracuse Univ, Harry F & Alva K Ganders MemorialFund Distinguished Lectr, 1989; Univ Minn, Twin Cities, James J Hill visprof, 1991; Howard Univ, Charles F Thompson Lectr, 1995; Columbia Univ,Teachers Col, Sachs Lectr, 1996; Fla State Univ, Mack & Effie CampbellTyner Eminent Scholar, 1998; Books: Teaching Strategies for Ethnic-Studies, 7th Edition; Multicultural Education: Issues & Perspectives,fourth ed; Cultural Diversity & Education: Foundations, Curriculum &Teaching, fourth Edition; An Introduction to Multicultural Education,third ed; Multicultural Education, Transformative Knowledge, & Action;Educating Citizens in a Multicultural Society; Diversity & CitizenshipEducation: Global Perspectives; Race, Culture, & Education: The SelectedWorks of James A. Banks; Teaching Strategies for Ethnic Studies, fourthed, 1987; Multiethnic Educ Theory & Practice, second ed, 1988;Multicultural Education: Issues & Prespectives, 1989; fel, Ctr AdvanStudies Behavioral Sci, Stanford, Califonia, 2005-06. **Orgs:** Nat Defense Educ Act; Spencer fel, Nat Acad Educ, 1973-76; bd dir, NatCoun Social Studies, 1973-74, 1980-85, chmn task force, Ethnic Studies Curriculum Guidelines, 1975-76, vpres, 1980; Nat Adv Coun Ethnic HeritageStudies, 1975-79; pres, 1982; Nat fel, W K Kellogg Found, 1980-83;Rockefeller Found fel, 1980; bd dirs, Social Sci Educ Consortium, 1976-79;bd dir, Asn Supervision & Curriculum Develop, 1976-79; vpres, 1980, preselect, 1981, pres, 1982, bd dirs, 1980-84, Nat Coun Social Studies; pres,Am Educ Res Asn, 1997-98; bd mem, Nat Res Coun; bd mem, Inst Med, Nat AcadSci. **Honors/Awds:** Hon mem, Golden Key Nat Hon Soc, 1985; Distinguished Scholar MinorityEduc, Am Educ Res Asn, 1986; LHD, Bank St Col Educ, 1993; LD, Univ Alaska,Fairbanks, 2000; Jean Dresden Grambs Distinguished Career Award, Nat CounSocial Studies, 2001; LHD, Univ Wis-Parkside, 2001; LHD, DePaul Univ,Chicago, 2003; LHD, Lewis & Clark Col, 2004; Social Justice in EducationAward, Am Educ Res Asn, 2004; Distinguished Alumni Award, Col Educ, MichState Univ, 2004; UCLA Medal, Univ Calif, Los Angeles, 2005; LHD, GrinnellCol, 2006. **Business Addr:** Professor, Director, University Washington, Center for Multicultural Education, College of Education, 110 Miller Hall, PO Box 353600, Seattle, WA 98195, **Business Phone:** (206)543-3386.

BANKS, JEFFREY
Fashion designer. **Personal:** Born Nov 3, 1953, Washington, DC. **Educ:** Pratt Inst, attended 1973; Parsons Sch Design, BFA, 1975. **Career:** Ralph Lauren Polo, design asst to pres, 1971-73; Calvin Klein & Calvin Klein Ltd, design asst to pres, 1973-76; Nik-Nik Clothing & Sportswear, designer, 1976-78; Jeffrey Banks Ltd, 1978-; Alixandre, designer, 1980; Merona Sports, head designer, 1980; Parson's Sch Design, design critic; Jeffrey Banks Int, 1980-; Haggar Clothing Co, design consult, 2004-. **Orgs:** Designers Collective; sr bd mem, Fashion Inst Technol; mem exec bd, Coun Fashion Designers of Am. **Honors/Awds:** Coty Fashion Critics Award, Men's Furs; Special Coty Award, Men's Furs, 1977; Harvey's Bristol Cream Tribute to Black Designers, Excellence in Men's Wear Design, 1978-80; Special Coty Award, Menswear, 1982; Cutty Sark Award, Outstanding US Designer, 1987. **Business Addr:** Designer, Haggar Clothing Co, 2nd Colinas Crossing, 11511 Luna Rd, Dallas, TX 75234, **Business Phone:** (214)352-8481.*

BANKS, JUNE SKINNER
Pathologist. **Personal:** Born Jun 5, 1936, Norfolk, VA; daughter of Solomon Kermit and Gaynell Clanton; married John L Banks, Jan 27, 1962 (died 2001); children: Junelle Letha. **Educ:** Fisk Univ, BA, Eng, 1956; NY Univ, MA, speech educ, 1966; Old Dominion Univ; Norfolk State Univ; Univ Va. **Career:** Pathologist (retired); Am Military Secondary Sch, Eng Dept, chair, 1968-69; Old Dominion Univ, instr, 1969-70; JRE Lee High Sch, eng teacher, 1956-57; Norfolk Pub Schs, eng teacher, 1957-67, speech & lang pathologist, 1967-93, speech eligibility liaison, 1989-93, teacher spt, 1993-95. **Orgs:** Nat mem-at-large & found bd, The Links Inc, 1990-94; trustee bd, Mt Zion Baptist Church, Norfolk, 1993-; local bd, Coalition 100 Black Women, 1992-94; local social action comn, Delta Sigma Theta Sorority Inc, 1991-2002; parlimentarian, Dejouir Inc, 1988-90; Moles Inc, 1981-94, vpres, Norfolk Chap, 1990-94; pres, Chums Inc, Norfolk Chap, 1998-2002; chair, Nat Nominating Comn, 2002; chair, Nat Scholar Comt, 2002; local pubity dir, Chums Inc, 1994-96; Am Speech & Hearing Asn; chair, Speech & Hearing Asn VA, Multicultural Interest Group, 1994-95; Pinochle Bugs Inc, 1971-; vpres, VA Br Chap, 2002-; Nat Hon Soc. **Honors/Awds:** Professional Award, Norfolk Metropolitan Club, Nat Asn Negro Bus & Prof Women's Clubs, Inc; Apple for Teacher Award, Iota Phi Lambda Sorority, 1989; Distinguished Service Award, Links Inc, 1984; Nat Serv Award, Dejouir Inc, 1996. **Home Addr:** 1052 Lockwood Ct, Virginia Beach, VA 23464, **Home Phone:** (757)424-2591.

BANKS, DR. LAURA NOBLES
School administrator. **Personal:** Born Jun 29, 1921, Tucson, AZ; daughter of James Nobles Sr and Missouri Johnson Nobles; married Jack Leonard Banks (deceased), Jun 6, 1950 (died 1998). **Educ:** Univ Ariz, BS, 1943, MA, 1966, EdS, 1970, EdD, 1981. **Career:** Sch Administrator (retired); Univ Ariz, 5 summers, asst teacher workshops; Cavett Elem Sch, elem teacher & prin; Tucson Pub Sch Dist No 1, coord reading progs K-12; Mari Mac Corp, pub rels dir; LNB Enterprises, pres & owner, currently; Jack's Original Bar-B-Q, Tucson, AZ, owner, 1950-92; Links Inc, parliamentarian & nat sec, 1970-76, nat rec secy, 1974-78; adv coun, Col Social & Behav Scis, Univ Tex San Antonio, 1999-2002; coordr, Neighborhood Youth Corp; Peace Corp lectr, dist reading coordr & prin, Univ Ariz. **Orgs:** Nat Coun Women Admin; TEA; AEA; Nat Educ Asn; chairperson, Elem Prin Group; Ariz Admin Asn; Golden Heritage mem, Nat Asn Elem Prin; nat bd, YWCA, 1965-76; Nat Asn Advan Colored People; pres, Tucson Urban League, 1979-81; Palo Verde Ment Health Found; bd dir, Alumni Bd Univ Ariz; organizer, pres local chap, far western reg dir, nat secy & nat prog chmn, past local pres, Alpha Kappa Alpha; Nat Coun Negro Women; Model Cities Neighborhood Housing Task Force; bd mem, Coun United Way; Pima Col Exec Comm Comm Affairs; adv bd, Resources Women, bd dirs, 1984-94; pres, Women at the Top, 1985-94; hon Soroptomist Int; bd dirs, Univ Ariz Pres Club, Comm Housing Resource Bd; Rotary Int; community adv bd, Tucson Jr League, 1990-94; Tucson Rotary Club, 1990-94; planned giving com, Univ Ariz Black Alumni, 1992-94; Coalition 100 Black Women-San Antonio, TX. **Honors/Awds:** Shriners Award of Excellence in Education; Successful Business Award, Nat Asn Advan Colored People; Certificate of Merit, Black Econ Develop; Women on the Move Recognition, Outstanding Life time Achievement Award, YWCA; Pioneer in Education Award, Links; Distinguished Citizen Award, Univ Ariz; Inductee, Ariz Restaurant Hall Fame, 1994; US Distinguished Service Award, 2002; Laura Nobles Banks New Elementary School Tuscon, AZ, named in honor, 2002; Distinguished Service Award, Univ Ariz Col Educ, 2002; Black Alumni Phenomenal Women Award, Univ Ariz; Robert L Horn Award. **Special Achievements:** Was selected as the first African American Assistant Superintendent in TUSD. **Home Addr:** 9438 Gray Sage, Helotes, TX 78023, **Home Phone:** (210)695-3424. **Business Phone:** (520)750-1280.

BANKS, DR. LULA F.
Government official. **Personal:** Born Feb 23, 1947, Tallahassee, FL; daughter of Harry E Banks Sr and Elizabeth Gaines Richard-

son; divorced; children: Felicia A Williams & Deanna M Williams. **Educ:** Tallahassee Community Col, FL, AA, 1985; Fla State Univ, Tallahassee, FL,BS, 1992; Fl A&M Univ, Tallahassee, MEd, FL, 1995; Argosy Univ, Sarasota, FL, EdD, 2004. **Career:** Harris Corp, Melbourne, FL, 1978; Indian River Co Sch Bd, Vero Beach, teacher adult educ, 1978; Brevard Co Sch Bd, Melbourne, FL, teacher adult educ, 1979; Leon Co Bd Comnrs & Leon Co Sch Bd, Tallahassee, FL,purchasing agent, 1980-85, purchasing dir, 1985-90; City Tallahassee,purchasing adminr, 1990-96; Pinellas County BOCC, purchasing depart, dir,1996-2001; Hillsborough County BOCC, Dept Procurement Serv, Dept Purchasing, dir, 2001-. **Orgs:** Exec mem, Small Bus Week Comn; Nat Inst Govt Purchasing, FL Asn Pub ProfPurch Officers; Am Soc Pub Admin; COMPA/ASPA; Nat Forum Black Pub Admin &grad Exec Leadership Inst, 1994; PACE, Sch-to-Work Comn, Workforce Dev Bus& Ed Comn, Leadership Pinellas Alumni; NIGP Nat Ed Comn; NFBP Nat Prog Comn; Delta Sigma Theta Sorority; Tampa Bay Area NIGP Chapter; FL State Univ Black Alumni. **Honors/Awds:** Chairman's Award-MEDCOP of Tampa Bay, Public Admin-FL State Univ;Certificate of Outstanding Performance for Excellence in Government-Hillsborough County; Certificate of Extra Mile Award-Hillsborough County; Certificate of Leadership & Excellence-NIGP. **Business Addr:** Director, Department of Purchasing, Hillsborough County, Department of Procurement Services, County Ctr 18th Fl, 601 E Kennedy Blvd, Tampa, FL 33602, **Business Phone:** (813)272-5790.

BANKS, MANLEY E.
Executive. **Personal:** Born Oct 12, 1913, Anniston, AL; married Dorothy M Jones; children: Manley E Jr & Jacquelyn A. **Educ:** Ala State Univ, BS, 1937; Howard Univ, LLB, 1949. **Career:** Perry Co Sch Union town AL, asst prin coach, 1937-42; Afro Cab Co Inc Enterprises, co-founder & vpres, 1946-51; teacher, 1949-52; Banks Bicycle Shop, owner, currently. **Orgs:** Treas deacon clerk, United Church Christ, 1949-69; mem, Human Rels Coun, 1964-70; adv bd, City Water & Sewer Bd, 1965-; dist adv bd, Salvation Army, 1972-; elected chmn, City Water & Sewer Bd, 1976; mem, Alpha Phi Alpha Fraternity Inc; mem, Boy Scout Coun Exec Bd; mem legal adv, Calhoun County Improv Asn; NAACP. **Special Achievements:** First Black appointed to the City Advisory Board. **Military Serv:** AUS, sgt, 1942-45. **Business Addr:** Owner, Banks Bicycle Shop, 112 W 10 St, Anniston, AL 36201.*

BANKS, MARGUERITA C.
Journalist. **Personal:** Born Sep 13, 1946, New York, NY; married Alfred Quarles. **Educ:** Notre Dame Col, Cleveland, BA, Eng & Fr Lit, 1967. **Career:** Journalist (retired); Cleveland Press, reporter, 1967-69, ed comm page, 1969-70; WEWS-TV Scripps Howard Broadcasting, gen assignment reporter & consumer troubleshooter, host "Black on Black", 1970-87; WEWS-TV Scripps Howard Broadcasting, co-host Ed Five, 1986-87. **Orgs:** exec bd mem, Am Sickle Cell Anemia Assoc, 1972-; adv bd mem, Notre Dame Col, 1978-; exec bd mem, Harambee Serv Black C, 1979-; past bd trustee, Big Bros Greater Cleveland; past bd trustee, Urban League Cleveland; past bd trustee, Blacks Commun, NE Young Women's Christian Asn; Womens Equity Action League, Sigma Delta Chi; ed, Gamma Phi Delta Sor; former ballet & mod dance teacher, local art ctrs; leadership Cleveland Class. **Honors/Awds:** Most Interesting People, Cleveland Mag, 1979; numerous Community Service Awards: pamphlet "Buying Used Cars", City Cleveland Off Consumer Affairs; "Punk Kids" series made into film, comm groups, Cuyahoga Cty Juvenile Ct, 1979; Woman of the Year, Notre Dame Col, 1982; Female Broadcaster of the Year, Nat Asn Career Woman's Civil League, 1982; Career Woman Achievement Award, Young Women's Christian Asn, Cleveland, 1985; numerous press awards, Press Club Cleveland & Women Communs Cleveland Chap; Notre Dame College Award for Excellence in Communication, 2007. *

BANKS, PATRICIA
Lawyer, judge. **Personal:** Born Feb 6, 1949, Marianna, AR. **Educ:** Univ Ill, BA, 1969; Univ Wis, JD, 1972. **Career:** US Dept Labor Chicago Region, 1972-73; Leadership Coun Met Open Comt, atty, 1973-74; Sears Roebuck & Co, 1974-78; pvt pract atty, 1978-; State Ill, Cook Co Circuit Ct, judge, currently. **Orgs:** Nat Bar Asn; Cook Co; Delta Sigma Theta Sorority; Ill Judicial Coun; recording secy & treas, Nat Judicial Coun Nat Bar Asn; chair, Judicial Coun, Nat Bar Asn, 2002-03. **Honors/Awds:** League Black Women Award, US Marine Corps, 1974; Meritorious Service Award, Cook Co. **Special Achievements:** One of the ten Outstanding Young Citizens, Chicago-Chicago Jaycees, 77. **Business Addr:** Judge, State of Illinois, Cook County Circuit Court, Richard J Daley Ctr, 50 W Wash St Suite 2505 Rm 1001, Chicago, IL 60602, **Business Phone:** (312)603-4347.*

BANKS, PAULA A.
Executive. **Personal:** Born in Chicago. **Educ:** Loyola Univ; Univ Ill; Harvard Univ, Int Advan Mgt Prog. **Career:** Sears, Roebuck & Co, dir pub rels, human resources dir, mgr, labor rel, store operations & merchandising mgr; Global Social Investment, BP, vpres, 1996-; PepsiCo Inc, sr vpres global diversity & orgn partnership. **Orgs:** Bd, Fisk Univ; pres, Exec Leadership Coun; corp adv bd, Conf Bd. **Honors/Awds:** Outstanding alumnus, Harvard Univ. **Special Achievements:** First African American president of the Amoco Foundation Inc, highest ranking black female in Amoco Corp. **Business Phone:** (914)253-2000.*

BANKS, PERRY L
Executive. **Personal:** Born Apr 15, 1955; son of Josie Greer and Walter; married Shirley, Jul 30, 1985; children: Patrice & Chinua. **Educ:** Shaw Bus Col, Detroit, MI, 1976; Nat Inst Technol, Detroit, MI, AS, 1981. **Career:** Gen Tel AE, Northland, IL, test engr II, 1981-84; Rotelcom Bus Systs, Rochester, NY, technician, 1984-86; Telecommunications Bank Inc, Rochester, NY, pres & chief exec officer, 1986-. **Orgs:** Trustee, Greater Rochester Metro Chamber Com, 1990-92; vpres, Black Bus Asn Chamber Com, 1991-. **Honors/Awds:** Super Performance Cert, 89th Army Res Corp, 1986; Up & Coming Entrepreneur Award, Minority Enterprise Develop Comn, 1988; Spec Recognition for Entrepreneurial Spirit & Leadership Comm, 1989; Administrator Award Excellence, US Small Bus Admin, 1990; Service Award, Minority Enterprise Develop Comn, 1990. **Business Addr:** President, Chief Executive Officer, The Telecommunication Bank Inc, 274 N Goodman St, Rochester, NY 14607, **Business Phone:** (585)442-2040.*

BANKS, PRISCILLA SNEED
Federal government official. **Personal:** Born Jul 13, 1941, Washington, DC; daughter of Mabel Sneed and Excell Sneed; widowed; children: Monica Banks Greene. **Educ:** Am Univ. **Career:** Low Income Housing, tech instr; Low Rent Occupancy; US Dept Housing & Urban Devel, task force desegregate pub housing, housing prog specialist; Anti-Drug Prog Pub Housing; Civil Rights Act 1964 & Title VIII, 1988; US Dept Housing & Urban Develop, housing specialist, currently. **Orgs:** Nat Asn Advan Colored People; Wash Urban League; Nat Welfare Mothers; Nat Asn Housing & Redevelopment Officials. **Honors/Awds:** Public Service Awards; Miss Houisng & Urban Develop, 1972; Special Achievement, 1975-76 & 1978; Sustained Superior Performance, 1969 & 1980; 2nd Highest Award, US Dept Housing & Urban Develop, 1984; Outstanding Performance Award, 1984. **Special Achievements:** Assumed the role of the Vidor Housing Authority Chairperson & appointed to oversee the Authority's day-to-day operations; On Jan 14, 1994, four months after taking over the complex four black families moved into the all-white project. **Business Addr:** Housing Specialist, US Department of Housing and Urban Development, 451 7th St SW, Washington, DC 20410, **Business Phone:** (202)402-4224.

BANKS, RICHARD EDWARD
Lawyer. **Personal:** Born Jan 5, 1960, St Louis, MO; son of Vincent A and Laura M Gillispie; children: Jessica Ruth & Richard Edward Jr. **Educ:** Howard Univ, BBA, 1982; Tex Southern Univ, JD, 1986. **Career:** State Farm Ins Co, St. Louis, MO, claims atty, 1986-88; Vickers, Moore & Wiest, St. Louis, MO, assoc atty, 1988-89; Banks & Assoc, managing partner, St. Louis, MO, 1989-, Pvt Pract, atty, currently. **Orgs:** Bd mem, Urban League St Louis; MO Trial Lawyers Asn, 1989-; MO & Ill Bar Asn, 1988-; Bar Asn Metrop St. Louis, 1988-; Chicago Bar Asn, 1989-; Am & Nat Bar Asn, 1988-; MO Bar Disciplinary Bd, 1995-. **Honors/Awds:** 50 Leaders of the Future, Ebony Mag, 1990; Leaders Conf, C's Defense Fund, 1990; Judicial Selection Comt, MO Bar, 1990; Outstanding Business Leader Award, St Louis Sentinel Newspaper, 1996; Trailblazer Award, St Charles Lwanga Cath Ctr; Corporate Citizen Award, Better Family Life; Martin Luther King Outstanding Businessman of the Year Award. MO Governor's Office. **Home Addr:** 8000 Maryland Ave, Saint Louis, MO 63105, **Home Phone:** (314)721-4040. **Business Addr:** Attorney, Counselor at Law, Banks & Associates, Grand Cent Bldg 1000 St Louis Union Station Suite 101, St Louis, MO 63103, **Business Phone:** (314)721-4040.

BANKS, RONALD
Executive, president (organization). **Personal:** Born Jun 19, 1951, Chicago, IL; son of Geneva Martin Banks and Earl Banks; married Vera D Lott; children: Janel & Lauren. **Educ:** Loyola Univ, Chicago, BA, 1973. **Career:** Montgomery Ward Chicago, buyer, 1973-82; Sherwin Williams Co Cleveland, buyer, 1982-84; Parks/Carver Tripp Cos, regional vpres 1984-91; Marketing 2000, pres, 1991-. **Business Addr:** President, Marketing 2000 Inc, 1939 Miller Ct, Homewood, IL 60430, **Business Phone:** (708)922-0391.

BANKS, RONALD TRENTON
Educator, school administrator. **Personal:** Born Sep 20, 1947, Knoxville, TN; son of Ralph Banks and Clara Banks; children: Rashondra Trenia & Brianna Jene. **Educ:** Tenn State Univ, BS, 1970, MS, 1976; Meharry Medical Col, Cert Mental Health, 1971. **Career:** Meharry Medical Col, mental hlth tech trainees, pres, 1970-71; Kentucky State Police, drug & alcohol consult, 1976; Kentucky State Univ, founder & dir, Dial A Job prog, co-chair rotating staff adv bd, vpres, 1983-84, career planning & placement, assoc dir, career planning & Placement, dir, currently; Kentucky Teachers Network, 1984-85; Coop Educ Handicap Comt, nat co-chairperson, 1985-86. **Orgs:** Frankfort Comn, dir crisis serv, 1977-; Kappa Alpha Psi; United Way, 1978; YMCA, Sr Citizens, Blind, Juvenile Deliq Mental Health Volunteer, 1978; Coop Educ Asn Kentucky, Awards Comn, 1988-89; Coop Educ Asn; bd dir, YMCA, 1992-. **Honors/Awds:** Most Loyal Coop Co-ord, KY, 1982; Staff Award, KY Student Govt, Kentucky State Univ, 1983; Coop Educ Appreciation Award, Kentucky State Univ, 1983 & 1984; Most Outstanding Coop Educ Coord, State Kentucky, 1987; Kentucky Colonel, 1987; State "B" Kentucky Racquetball Champion, 1997, Kentucky Racquetball Asn, 1987; State "B" Senior Runner Up, Kentucky Racquetball Asn, 1988; producer, Street Life of Drugs on a Col Campus, 1989; Martin Luther King Equality Award, 1992 & 1994; COT Action Volunteer of the Year, 1992; Gold Medal Racquetball, State of KY, 1994; Gold Medal Racquetball, State of KY, Bluegrass Champ, 1998; Silver Medal Racquetball, Bluegrass Games, 1999; Gold & Silver Medal, Racquetball, State of KY, Bluegrass Champ, 2000. **Home Addr:** 177 Winding Way Dr, Frankfort, KY 40601. **Business Addr:** Director Career Counseling, Kentucky State University, 400 E Main St, Frankfort, KY 40601.

BANKS, SHARON P
Lawyer, educator. **Personal:** Born Sep 21, 1942, Washington, DC. **Educ:** Morgan State Col, BA, 1964; Howard Univ Law Sch, JD, 1967. **Career:** Neighborhood Legal Serv Prog, 1967-72; pvt pract, atty, 1972-; Howard Univ, part-time teacher, 1969-72, full-time teacher, 1972-, Off Pres, sr assoc gen coun, currently. **Orgs:** DC Bar Asn; Howard Univ Law Alumni Asn; bd dir, DC ACIU; Kappa Beta Pi Legal Sorority. **Business Addr:** Senior Associate General Counsel, Howard University, Office of the President, 2400 6th St NW Suite 321, Washington, DC 20059, **Business Phone:** (202)806-2650.

BANKS, DR. TAZEWELL
Educator. **Personal:** Born Jan 7, 1932, Washington, DC; son of Cora Page and Seldon Banks; married Myrtle Marie Trescott; children: Andrea, Gregory & Kelley. **Educ:** Howard Univ, BS, Chem, 1953; Howard Med Col, MD, 1957. **Career:** Vet Affairs Med Ctr, resident; Wm Beaumont Army Med Ctr, resident; Howard Med Col, clin instr, 1966-68, from asst prof to assoc prof, 1968-76, prof med, vol fac, 1976-. **Orgs:** Bd dir, Wash Heart Asn, 1983-87; Phi Beta Kappa Howard Univ, 1953; Alpha Omega Alpha Howard Med Col, 1957; Asn Black Cardiologists, chair, nutrition comt; Chmn, Stud Res Comn, Wash Heart Asn. **Honors/Awds:** Meritorious Serv, DC Gen Hosp, 1970; Citizens Adv Comn DC Bar, 1972-76; Outstanding Teacher Stud Coun Award, Howard Med, 1977; Golden Apple Award, Wash Heart Asn, 1983; Outstanding Physician Award, DC Gen Hosp, 1985-86. **Special Achievements:** Published over 50 articles on cardiovascular diseases; Presented over 300 talks on cardiovascular diseases. **Military Serv:** AUS, Med Corps capt, 1956-61. **Home Addr:** 1925 Varnum St NE, Washington, DC 20018. **Business Addr:** Professor of Medicine, Volunteer Faculty, Howard Medical College, Wash DC Gen Hosp, 520 W St NW, Washington, DC 20059, **Business Phone:** (202)806-6270.

BANKS, TONY (ANTHONY LAMAR BANKS)
Football player. **Personal:** Born Apr 5, 1973, San Diego, CA; married Yolanda. **Educ:** Mesa Community Col, Mich State. **Career:** St Louis Rams, quarterback, 1996-98; Baltimore Ravens, quarterback, 1999-2000; Wash Redskins, quarterback, 2001; Dallas Cowboys, quarterback; Houston Texans, quarterback, 2002-05. **Honors/Awds:** Super Bowl champion. *

BANKS, TYRA LYNNE
Actor, fashion model, television broadcaster. **Personal:** Born Dec 4, 1973, Inglewood, CA; daughter of Don and Carolyn London-Johnson. **Career:** TV series: "Fresh Prince of Bel-Air", 1993; "Felicity", 1999; Mad TV, 2000; Life-Size, 2000; America's Next Top Model, 2003; American Dreams, 2004; All of Us, 2004; The Tyra Banks Show, 2007; Entertainment tonight, 2 2006-09; Films: Higher Learning,1995; A Woman Like That, 1997; Love Stinks, 1999; Coyote Ugly, 2000; Love& Basketball, 2000; Life-Size, 2000; Love & Basketball, 2000; Halloween:Resurrection, 2002; Eight Crazy Nights; 2002; Halloween Resurrection,2002; Larceny, 2004; Mr Woodcock, 2007;Songs: "Shake Ya Body," 2003; TVseries: "America's Next Top Model", 2003; Marple: The Body in the Library"2004; "The Tyra Banks Show," 2005-; Nike, fashion model; Pepsi, fashionmodel; Tommy Hilfiger, fashion model; Ralph Lauren, fashion model; Dolce &Gabbana, fashion model; Swatch, fashion model; Cover Girl, fashion model;Ty Ty Baby Prod, founder & chief exec officer, currently; CW TV Network,talk show host, currently. **Orgs:** Spokesperson, Ctr C & Families; founder, T-Zone. **Honors/Awds:** Michael Award, 1997; Won, Teen Choice Award, 2007, 2008; Won Daytime Emmy Award, 2008. **Special Achievements:** Listed in "50 Most Beautiful People in the World", People mag, 1994, 1996;first African-American model on cover of Sports Illustrated & theVictoria's Secret catalog, 1997; author of Tyra's Beauty Inside & Out,Harper Collins, 1998; first black woman to sign for a cosmetic company atthe age of 23; one of only four African Americans and seven women to haverepeatedly ranked among the world's most influential people by Timemagazine.

BANKS, VANITA M.
President (organization), lawyer. **Career:** National Bar Association, Pres, 2002. *

BANKS, WALDO R., SR.
Educator, association executive. **Personal:** Born Mar 30, 1928, Beaumont, TX; married Anice D; children: Monica Diane, Natalie

Anice, Waldo R. **Educ:** Bishop Col, BA 1951; Prairie View Univ, attended 1952; Tex Southern Univ, MA 1957; Ind Univ, EdS 1964; Claremont Grad Sch Educ, PhD 1975. **Career:** Educator (retired), association executive: S Park Ind Sch Dist, psychol consult instr, 1952-54; Orange Ind Sch Dist, psychol consult instr, 1954-56; Tex Southern Univ, instr coun, 1957-58; Ind Univ, admins researcher, 1958-59; Knoxville Col, dean, dir & asst prof, 1959-61; Gary Public Sch, dir scholar, 1961-65, dir consult, 1961-65; Los Angeles Bd Educ, instr & couns, 1965-66; Calif State Univ, consult; Los Angeles City, Human Rel Bur, asst prof couns & dir, 1965-67; PACE Proj, prof researcher writer, 1967-69; Compton Unified Sch Dist, adminr & dir, 1967-75; Univ Calif Los Angeles, instr, 1971-76; Global Oil Co Inc, pres, 1975-77; Imperial Health Ctr Inc, dir, 1975-77; Natl Employ Ctr, pres, 1975-77; Am Educ Found, pres, 1970-80; Dept Health, Educ & Welfare, consult. **Orgs:** Am Soc Mil History Los Angeles; Nat Adv Counc Educ Prof Devel; mem, Harry Walker Inc; Am Prog Bur; UN Speaker Bur; mem, Am Asn Col Registr & Admis Officers; Am Asn Col & Univ Deans; Am Asn Sec Sch Prin; Am Asn Sch Admin; Am Asn Univ Profs; Am Col Personnel Asn; Am Fed Teachers; Am Jr Col Asn; Am Personnel & Guidance Asn; Am Polit Sci Asn; Am Sociol Soc; Am Psychol Asn Boys Club Am; BSA; BPOE; Calif Asn Prog Dem; Calif Fed Teachers; Calif Person & Guid Asn; Calif State Teachers Asn; Intl Platform Asn; Masonic Lodge; NAACP; Nat Adv Coun EPDA; Nat Cong Parents & Teachers; NEA; Nat Urban League; Phi Delta Kappa; S Christian Leadership Conf; YMCA. **Honors/Awds:** Dr Joseph J Rhoads Schlrshp, Grant Bishop Col, 1946-50; Admin Res Grant, Ind Univ, 1957-58; educ grant, Claremont Grad Sch Educ, 1972-74; pres USA appointee Nat Adv Coun Educ Prof Devel, 1972-75; grant Nat fel Fund Atlanta, 1974-75; numerous publications, research programs and projects; Nat Prof Serv Citation Pres Ford USA. *

BANKS, WARREN CHRISTOPHER. **See BANKS, CHRIS.**

BANKS, WILLIAM JASPER, JR. (WILLIE J BANKS)
Physician, educator. **Personal:** Born Jul 4, 1944, Richmond, VA; son of W J Banks and C E Banks. **Educ:** VA Univ, BS, 1965; VA Commonwealth Univ, MS, 1966; Howard Univ, MD, 1970; Univ Edinburgh McMasters Col, MA, 1986. **Career:** DC Gen Hosp, med officer, 1977-, vpres med staff, 1981-82; Howard Univ Hosp, chief orth clinics, 1979-; Howard Univ, instr surg, 1977-80, sec div orth surg, asst prof surg, 1980, assoc prof; Veterans Admin Hosp, chief Dept Orthop; pvt pract, currently. **Orgs:** Fel Am Col Surgeons, Am Acad Ortho Surgeons, Int Col Surgeons; Am Med Asn; DC Med Soc; Southern Med Soc; Arlington Hosp Found; Intl Oceanog Found; secy, Capital City Orth Found; fel Royal Col Surgeons Edinburgh, Nat Geographic Soc Navl Inst; Southern Orth Soc, Eastern Orth Soc, Sigma Xi, Am Asn Advan Sci; NY Acad Sci; Am Philosophical Soc; Pan Am Orth Group; Soc Clin Investrs. **Honors/Awds:** Hon fel JF Kennedy Libr; Community Serv Silver Spring Boys Club; "Complications of Amputatim" Ortho Update Series; Osteoporosis Int Conf Metabolic Bone Dis-Rome Spec Citation Southern Poverty Law Ctr; Osteomyelitis A New Look At An Old Problem Jour of Diseases of Children. **Military Serv:** USN, rear adm; Legion of Merit, Presidential Citation, Vietnam Medal. *

BANKS, DR. WILLIAM MARON
Educator. **Personal:** Born Sep 22, 1943, Thomasville, GA; son of William and Hattie; children: David, Tracey, Trey & Shane. **Educ:** Dillard Univ, 1963; Univ Ky, EdD, 1967. **Career:** Attebury Job Corps Ctr, supr counr & psychol, 1967; Howard Univ, counr psychol, 1967-70, dept chairperson, 1972-75; Univ Calif, Berkeley, CA, prof, 1970, provost, 1988-89, prof emeritus, african am studies, currently. **Orgs:** Soc Psychol Study Soc Issues; Soc Study Soc Probs; Am Personnel & Guid Asn; chairperson, Univ Calif Afro-Am Studies Consortium, 1979-81; Asn Black Psychologists; fel, Nat Humanities Ctr; fel, Ctr Advan Study Social and Behavioral Sci. **Honors/Awds:** Summer Scholars Award, US Civil Serv Comn; Univ Calif Regents Fel; Instructional Improve Grant; num scholarly articles & monographs pub on effects of racial differences in psychotherapy & counseling; American Book Award, 1996. **Special Achievements:** Published, Black Intellectuals. **Business Addr:** Emeritus Professor, University of California Berkeley, Department of African American Studies, 660 Barrows Hall 6th Fl, Berkeley, CA 94720-2572.

BANKS, WILLIE ANTHONY
Baseball player. **Personal:** Born Feb 27, 1969, Jersey City, NJ. **Career:** Minn Twins, pitcher, 1991-93; Chicago Cubs, 1994-95; Los Angeles Dodgers, 1995; Fla Marlins, 1995; Philadelphia Phillies, 1995-97; NY Yankees, 1997-98; Boston Red Sox, 2001-02; The Newark Bears, 2004, 2005-; Triple Crown Baseball Academy, instr, currently.

BANKS, WILLIE J. **See BANKS, WILLIAM JASPER, JR.**

BANKSTON, ARCHIE M
Lawyer, executive. **Personal:** Born Oct 12, 1937, Memphis, TN; son of Archie M Sr and Elsie Shaw; married Emma Ann DeJan; children: Alice DeJan & Louis Shaw. **Educ:** Fisk Univ, BA, 1959; Wash Univ Sch Law, LLB 1962; Wash Univ Grad Sch Bus Admin, MBA, 1964. **Career:** General Foods Corp, asst div counsel, 1964-67, prod mgr Maxwell House Div, 1967-69; Pepsico Inc, asst sec & corp counsel 1969-72; Xerox Corp, div counsel, 1972-73; Consolidated Edison Co NY, sec & asst gen counsel, 1974-89; sec & assoc gen counsel 1989, secy, 1997-2002; The Col New Rochelle, exec-in-residence, 2002-. **Orgs:** Phi Delta Phi Legal Fraternity, 1960-; Securities Indu Comm; advisory group, NY Chapter, Corp Practices Comn; budget comm., Am Soc Corp Sec, 1974-; Stockholder Relat Soc NY; Am Bar Asn; NY State Bar Asn; Asn Black Lawyers Westchester Co; dir, Beth Israel Med Ctr NYC; Mental Health Asn Westchester Co; Am Mgmt Asn; Assoc Black Charities; trustee, Col New Rochelle; 100 Black Men Inc; Beta Zeta Boule; Alpha Phi Alpha Fraternity; Westchester Clubmen. **Honors/Awds:** Recipient Black Achievers in Industry Award Harlem Branch YMCA, 1971; Merit Award for Black Exec Exchange Program Nat Urban League, 1974; distinguished service commendation award, Mental Health Assn, 1987; Corp Award, Red Cross, 2001; Bracebridge H Young Distinguished Service Award, Am Soc Corporate Secretaries, 2001. **Special Achievements:** First Black atty/product mgr Gen Foods, 1964-67; First Black Sr Exec Officer Consolidated Edison, 1974; First Black Corp Sec of a major US Co, 1974. **Business Addr:** Executive-in-Residence, The College of New Rochelle, 29 Castle Pl, New Rochelle, NY 10805, **Business Phone:** (914)654-5000.

BANKSTON, CHARLES E.
Automotive executive. **Career:** Village Ford Lewisville Inc, owner, chief exec, 1996-. **Special Achievements:** Co ranked No 65, Black Enterprise magazine's list of top 100 auto dealers, 1992; B.E. Auto Dealer 100 - top-ranking African American-owned automobile dealership, 2001. **Business Phone:** (972)221-2900.*

BANKSTON, MICHAEL KANE
Football player. **Personal:** Born Mar 12, 1970, East Bernard, TX; married Kimberly; children: Michael Jr & Mikaela. **Educ:** Sam Houston State Univ, bus mgt, 1995. **Career:** Football player (retired); Phoenix Cardinals, defensive tackle, 1992-93; Ariz Cardinals, defensive end, 1994-97; Cincinnati Bengals, 1998-2000; Wash Redskins, defensive end, 2001. *

BANNER, DR. WILLIAM AUGUSTUS
Educator. **Personal:** Born Sep 18, 1915, Philadelphia, PA; son of Zacharias and Nannie Beatrice Perry; married Beatrice V Suggs; children: Beatrice Anne & William Perry. **Educ:** Pa State Univ, BA, 1935; Yale Univ, MDiv, 1938; Harvard Univ, MA, 1944, PhD, 1947. **Career:** Univ RI; Bennett Col, philosophy instr, 1938-43; Howard Univ Sch Divinity, asst assoc prof, 1945-55, Col Liberal Arts, assoc prof philosophy, 1955-58, prof, graduate prof, 1981-85; Smith Col, visiting lec, 1958-59; Yale Univ, visiting prof, 1964-65; Univ Rochester, distinguished visiting prof, 1970; Col Liberal Arts, assoc dean, 1971-75; Howard Univ, dept philosophy, chmn, 1976-81; Folger Inst, lecturer, 1984-85; Howard Univ libr, currently. **Orgs:** Am Philos Asn; Nat Humanities Faculty; Guild Scholars Episcopal Church; fellow, Soc Religion High Educ; Harvard Club. **Honors/Awds:** Doctor of Humane Letters, Howard Univ, 1988; Excellence at Howard Award, Howard Univ, 1999. **Special Achievements:** Books : Ethics, An Introduction to Moral Philosophy, 1968; Moral Norms and Moral Order, The Philosophy of Human Affairs, 1981; contributor Greece, 478-336 BC, 1982; The Path St Augustine, 1996. **Business Addr:** Professor, Howard University, Howard University Libraries, 500 Howard Pl NW, Washington, DC 20059, **Business Phone:** (202)806-7234.*

BANNERMAN, ALFRED
Neurologist. **Career:** Jamaica Hosp Med Ctr, neurologist; pvt pract, currently. **Business Addr:** Neurologist, Private Practice, 8906 135th St S, Jamaica, NY 11430.*

BANNERMAN-RICHTER, GABRIEL
Educator. **Personal:** Born Oct 28, 1931, Oyo, Nigeria; married Jane Harvey-Ewusie; children: Anna, Jessica, Gabriel Jr, Matilda & Elizabeth. **Educ:** Calif State Univ, BA, 1969, MA, 1970; Univ Calif, Davis, attended 1972. **Career:** Sacramento City Col, instr, 1969-80; Univ Calif, Davis, instr, 1972-75;Univ Cape Coast Ghana, vis assoc prof, 1976-77; Calif State Univ,Sacramento, prof eng & ethnic studies, prof emer, 1996-2001. **Orgs:** Pub Gabari Pub Co, 1982-. **Honors/Awds:** NEH Scholar, NEH Inst, Univ Ind, 1985. **Special Achievements:** Author, "Practice of Witchcraft in Ghana", 1982; "Don't Cry My Baby, Don't Cry", 1984; "Mmoetia, The Mysterious Dwarfs", 1985. **Home Addr:** 3612 21 Ave, Sacramento, CA 95820.

BANTON, LINDA WHEELER
Executive, vice president (organization). **Personal:** Born Mar 28, 1948, Akron, OH; daughter of James and Jane Wheeler; divorced; children: Brooks. **Educ:** Univ Akron, BS, bus admin, 1979; John F. Kennedy Sch Govt, Harvard, attended 1998. **Career:** Goodyear Aerospace, bus devel rep, 1980-85; Sunohio Co, govt laison mgr, 1985-86; Honeywell, sr mkt rep, 1986-88; Alliant Techsyst, mgr govt relations, 1988-92; Lockheed Martin, vpres legis affairs, 1992-99; Honeywell, vpres aerospace govt relations, 1999; Russell Reynolds Assocs Aerospace & Defense Pract, sr exec search consult; Lockheed Martin, vpres legis affairs, currently; Henry L. Stimson Ctr, bd dirs, currently. **Orgs:** Women in Gov Relations, secy, 1988-; Wash Indust Roundtable, 1996-; Aerospace Indust Asn, Wash rep, 1999-; Electronic Indust Alliance, bd govs, 1999-. **Special Achievements:** Jazz singer; fluent in Spanish. *

BANTON, WILLIAM C., II
Military leader, physician. **Personal:** Born Nov 9, 1922, Washington, DC. **Educ:** Howard Univ, Col Liberal Arts & Sci; Howard Univ Col Med, MD, 1946; John Hopkins Univ Sch Hygiene & Pub Health, attended 1970; St Louis Univ Sch Med; USAF Sch Aviation Med; USPHS; Sch Aerospace Med; USN Med Sch; Armed Forces Inst Pathol; Wash Univ Sch Med; Def Atomic Support Agy; Sch Aerospace Med; Boston U; Harvard U; Tufts Univ Sch Med; Indust Col Armed Forces. **Career:** Homer G Phillips Hosp, 1946-47; Robert Koch Hosp, 1947-49; USAF Gen Hosp, 1950-52; Mitchell AFB NY, med officer internal med; 2230th AFR Floyd Bennett Naval Air Sta, flight surgeon, 1951-52; St Louis Health Div Chest & TB Svc; pvt pract internal med; 8711th USAFG Hosp Scott AFB, comdr & flight surgeon, 1954-71; Hq USAF/SG Forrestal Bldg Wash, asst surgeon gen, 1971-; served short active duty tours So Vietnam, 1968-69; City St Louis, health comnr; Dept Community Health & Med Care, St Louis County, Mo, dir; St Louis Univ Sch Med, asst clin prof internal med; pvt pract, currently. **Orgs:** Reserve Officer's Asn; Air Force Asn; life mem, Alpha Phi Alpha; Chi Delta Mu; Howard Univ Alumni Asn; life mem, NAACP; bd dir, Koch Welfare Asn; Friends City Art Mus St Louis; Nat Geog Soc; St Louis Zoo Asn; John Hopkins Univ Alumni Asn; Homer G Phillips Hosp Intern Alumni Asn. **Honors/Awds:** Promoted Brigadier Gen Apr 6 1973; recipient WW II Victory Medal; Am Campaign Medal; Nat Def Serv Medal; Good Conduct Medal; Expert Marksman Medal; Armed Forces Longevity Serv Award; Award Forces Res Medal; S Vietnam Campaitn Medal. **Military Serv:** AUS, 1st lt, 1946; USAFR, capt, 1950. *

BAPTISTA, HOWARD
Association executive. **Personal:** Born Nov 24, 1930, Nantucket, MA; married Margarit Von Steiger; children: Mark, Kim, Kevin, Stephan. **Educ:** Bryant Col, BA, 1956; NY Univ, MA, 1960. **Career:** Altman's Dept Store, jr exec; NY City Housing Auth, 1959-60; NY Bd Educ, 1960-62; Bedford Redevelop Auth, from exec dir to dir. **Orgs:** Vpres, SE Bank & Trust Co; incorporator, NB Inst Savs Bank; dir, Vol Am; Comn Coun; United Fund; New Eng Coun NAHRO. **Honors/Awds:** Eqalitarian Award, NAACP. **Military Serv:** AUS, cpl. *

BAPTISTE, HANSOM PRENTICE, JR.
Educator, college teacher, teacher. **Personal:** Born Jan 18, 1939, Beaumont, TX; married Mirabelle; children: 7. **Educ:** Lamar State, Col, BS, 1961; Univ Calif, attended 1962; Univ Notre dame, attended 1964; Ind Univ, Math, 1966, EdD, 1968. **Career:** Cuero Independent Sch Dist, 1961-63; Beaumont Independent Sch Dist, teacher, 1963-65; Ind Univ, asst prof, 1968-72; Off Educ Title III, grant training fac, doctorate level, 1973-75; Univ Houston, Dept Educ Admin, assoc prof. **Orgs:** Many workshops & seminars, 1971-75; Ind Univ Alumni Asn; Nat Sci Teachers Asn; Nat Cong Parents & Teachers; Phi Delta Kappa. **Honors/Awds:** Valedictorian Scholar, 1957-58; Outstanding Teacher Award, 1969-70. *

BAQUET, DEAN
Editor. **Personal:** Born Jan 1, 1957. **Career:** States-Item & Times-Picayune, New Orleans; Chicago Tribune, chief investigative reporter, assoc metrop ed, reporter, 1984-90; New York Times, investigative reporter, 1990-95, nat ed, 1995-2000; Los Angeles Times, managing ed, ed, 2005-. **Honors/Awds:** Pulitzer Prize, Chicago City Coun, 1988. **Business Addr:** Editor, Los Angeles Times, 202 W 1st St, Los Angeles, CA 90012, **Business Phone:** (213)237-5000.

BARAKA, AMINA (SYLVIA ROBINSON)
Writer. **Personal:** Married Amiri Baraka; children: 5. **Career:** Writer, currently; Blue Ark: Word Ship, ensemble mem, currently; Kimako's Blues People, co-dir, currently. **Business Phone:** (201)242-1346.

BARAKA, IMAMU AMIRI (EVERETT LEROI JONES)
Educator, poet, writer. **Personal:** Born Oct 7, 1934, Newark, NJ; son of Coyette LeRoi and Anna Lois Russ Jones; married Hettie Robinson Cohen, Oct 13, 1958 (divorced 1965); children: Kellie Elisabeth & Lisa Victoria Chapman; married Bibi Amina, Jan 1, 1966; children: Obalaji Malik Ali, Ras Jua Al Aziz, Shani Isis, Amiri Seku & Ahi Mwenge. **Educ:** Howard Univ, BA, Eng, 1954; Columbia Univ, MA; Rutgers Univ, attended 1952. **Career:** Educator, retired, Writer, Poet; Totem Press, founder, 1958; New Sch Social Res, New York, NY, instr, 1961-64; writer, 1961-; John Whitney Found fel, 1962; Univ Buffalo, vis prof, 1964; Columbia Univ, vis prof, fall 1964, 1966-67; San Francisco State Univ, lectr, 1966-67; Yale Univ, vis prof, 1977-78; George Washington Univ, vis prof, 1978-79; State Univ NY, Stony Brook, asst prof to assoc prof, 1980-84, prof Afro Am studies,1985-99; Plays: A Good Girl Is Hard To Find, 1958; Dante, 1961; Dutchman & the Slave, 1964; The Toilet, 1964; The Syst of Dante's Hell, 1965; Guggenheim fel, 1965-66; The Baptism: A Comedy in One Act, 1966; Slaveship,

1967; Arm Yourself, or Harm Yourself! A One-Act Play, 1967; Four Black Revolutionary Plays: All Praises to the Black Man, 1969; J-E-L-L-O, 1970; What Was the Relationship of the Lone Ranger to the Means of Prod: A Play in One Act, 1978; The Sidnee Poet Heroical in Twenty-nine Scenes, 1979; Primitive World, 1984; Gen Hag's Skeezag, 1992; Poetry: April 13, 1959; Spring & So Forth, 1960; The Dead Lecturer, 1964; Black Art, 1966; A Poem for Black Hearts, 1967; Black Magic, 1969; It's Nation Time, 1970; Spirit Reach, 1972; Afrikan Revolution: A Poem, 1973; Spring Song, 1979; In the Tradition: For Black Arthur Blythe, 1980; Reggae or Not!; Poems: Preface to a Twenty Volume Suicide Note, 1961; Black Magic, 1969; It's Nation Time, 1970; Hard Facts, 1975; Transbluesency: The Selected Poems of Amiri Baraka/LeRoi Jones, 1995; Wise Why's Y's: The Girot's Tale, 1996; Euologies, 1996; Funk Lore: New Poems, 1984-95, 1996; Somebody Blew Up America & Other Poems, 2003; William Morrow & Co, author; Harper Collins Publ, author, currently; Nonfiction: Cuba libre, 1961; Blues People, 1963; Home: Social Essays, 1966; Black Music, 1968; Trippin: A Need for Change, co-author, 1969; A Black value System, 1970; Raise Race Rays Raze, 1971; Strategy And Tactics Of An Pan African Nationalist Party, 1971; Beginning Of National Movement, 1972; Kawaida Studies: The New Nationalism, 1972; Afrikan Free School, 1974; Crisis In Boston!!!!, 1974; National Liberation And Politics, 1974; Toward Ideological Clarity, 1974; The Creation Of The New Ark, 1975; Spring Song, 1979; Daggers And Javelins, 1984; The Autobiography Of Leroi Jones/Amiri Baraka, 1984; The Artist And Social Responsibility, 1986; The Music: Reflections On Jazz And Blues, 1987; A Race Divied, 1991; Conversations With Amiri Baraka, 1994; Digging: Afro Am Be/At Am Classical Music, 1999. **Orgs:** Founder, Black Community Dev & Defense Org, 1968; Black Acad Arts & Letters; secy gen, co-gov, Nat Black Polit Assembly; chmn, Cong African People; United Bros; All African Games; Pan African Fedn; African Liberation Day Support Comt; Polit Prisoners Relief Fund; IFCO Int Force. **Honors/Awds:** Longview Best Essay of the Year Award for Vuba Libre, 1961; Obie Award for Dutchman, 1964; Nat Endowment Arts Grant, 1966; Poetry Award, Nat Endowment Arts, 1981; New Jersey Council of the Arts Award, 1982; American Book Award, 1984; Before Columbus Found Award, Confirmation: An Anthology of African-Am Women, 1984; Drama Award, 1985; Langston Hughes Medal, 1989; Ferroni Award & Foreign Poet Award, Italy, 1993; Playwright's Award, Black Drama Festival, 1997; Wallace Stevens Poetry Prize, Univ Conn, 1998; NJ poet laureate, 2002-03. **Special Achievements:** Films: One P.M, 1972; Fried Shoes Cooked Diamond, 1978; Black Theatre: The Making of a Movement, 1978; Furious Flower: A Video Anthology of African American Poetry 1960-95, Volume II: Warriors, 1998; Bulworth, 1998; Pinero, 2001; Strange Fruit, 2002; Ralph Ellison: An American Journey, 2002; Chisholm 72: Unbought & Unbossed, 2004; Keeping Time: The Life, Music & Photography of Milt Hinton, 2004; Hubert Selby Jr: It'll Be Better Tomorrow, 2005; 500 Years Later, 2005; The Ballad of Greenwich Village, 2005; The Pact, 2006; Retour a Goree, 2007; Polis Is This: Charles Olson and the Persistence of Place, 2007; Revolution 67, 2007; Turn Me On, 2007; Oscene, 2007; Corso: The Last Beat, 2008; The Black Candle, 2008; Ferlinghetti: A City Light, 2008; Motherland, 2009. **Military Serv:** USAF, gunner, 1954-57. **Business Addr:** Writer, Poet, HarperCollins Publishers, 10 E 53rd St, New York, NY 10022, **Business Phone:** (212)207-7000.

BARANCO, GORDON S.
Judge. **Personal:** Born Feb 25, 1948, Oakland, CA; son of Arnold and Lillian; married Barbara N Gee; children: Lauren Barbara Gee Baranco, Brandon Michael Gee Baranco. **Educ:** Univ Calif, BA, 1969, JD, 1972. **Career:** San Francisco, asst dist atty, 1974-77; Neighborhood Legal Asst, managing atty, 1977-80; Oakland, asst city atty, 1980; Oakland Municipal Ct, judge, 1980-84; Alameda Co Super Ct, judge, currently. **Orgs:** vice chair, Access & Fairness Advisory Comt, currently. **Honors/Awds:** Judicial Distinguished Service Award, Alameda County Bar Asn, 2002 . **Business Addr:** Judge, Superior Court of California, Co Alameda, 1221 Oak St Dept 15, Oakland, CA 94612.*

BARANCO, GREGORY T.
Automotive executive, president (organization). **Career:** Baranco Lincoln-Mercury Inc, chief exec, Duluth, GA, Baranco Pontiac-GMC Truck-Subaru Inc, Decatur, GA, Acura Tallahassee, Tallahassee, FL; Baranco Automotive Group, pres, currently. **Orgs:** Bd mem, Morehouse Sch Med; Nat Minority Supplier Develop Coun; former pres, Gen Motors Minority Dealers Asn; bd dir, Kaiser Found Health Plan Ga; Metrop Atlanta Automobile Dealers Asn; Ga Automobile Dealers Asn; DeKalb Chamber Com; pres coun, Spelman Col; Atlanta Bus League; Ga Res Alliance. **Honors/Awds:** Quality Dealer Award, Time Mag. **Special Achievements:** Auto 100 listing, Baranco's three auto dealerships, Black Enterprise, 1991. *

BARANCO, JUANITA P.
Vice president (Organization), executive, attorney general (u.s. federal government). **Personal:** Born Jan 1, 1949?, Washington, DC. **Educ:** La State Univ, BS. **Career:** Legal Coun, co-owner; State GA, asst atty gen; Fed Res Bank Atlanta, bd dirs; Baranco Automotive Group, exec vpres & chief operating officer, 1978-; John H. Harland Co, dir; First Union Bank, dir; Clark Atlanta Univ, chair, currently; Ga Power Co, bd dir, currently; Southern Co, bd dir, currently; CoxRadio, bd dir, currently. **Orgs:** past chair, Bd Regents Univ Syst, GA; chmn, DeKalb Co Educ Task Force; mem, Ga State Bd Educ, 1985-91; chmn, Educ Comn, 1996 Olympics; exec comt mem, Ga Chamber Com; bd mem, Sickle Cell Found Ga; Am Bar Asn; State Bar Asn Ga; State Bar Asn La; Gov's Human Rels Comt; Clark Atlanta Univ's Nat Bus Adv Bd; bd mem, DeKalb Chamber Com; Delta Sigma Theta Sorority; bd trustees, Clark Atlanta Univ. **Honors/Awds:** Enterpreneur of the Year, Atlanta Bus League; Entrepreneurial Excellence, Dow Jones Co; Trumpet Award, Turner Broadcasting Systs; DECCA Award, Atlanta Bus Chronicle; Women of Achievement Award, YWCA; Atlanta Life Award, Atlanta History Ctr's Defining Women. **Special Achievements:** First African-American Female Chair, Bd of Regents; 100 Most Influential Georgians, Trend Magazine; Finalist for the 2003 Time Magazine Quality Dealer Award. **Business Addr:** President, Chief Operating Officer, Baranco Automotive Group, 7060 Jonesboro Rd, Morrow, GA 30260-2905, **Business Phone:** (770)968-5252.*

BARANCO, RAPHAEL ALVIN
Dentist. **Personal:** Born Nov 19, 1932, Baton Rouge, LA; married Terry Bryant; children: Angela, Rachel, Raphael. **Educ:** Xavier Univ, BS, 1956; Meharry Med Col, DDS, 1961. **Career:** Jersey City Med Ctr, intern, 1961-62; Meharry Med Col, Nashville, instr prosthetic dent, 1963-64; Va Hosp, Tuskegee, AL, dir clin dent, 1964-68; Individual Pract, dent, 1968-. **Orgs:** Lafayette Coun Human Rels, 1968-; Sheriff's Adv Comn, 1968-; pres, bd dirs, Holy Family Sch, 1971-; chmn, Lafayette Parish Comt Action Coun, 1971; NAACP; Alpha Phi Alpha; Alpha Phi Omega; Chi Delta Mu; Am Dent Asn; Lafayette Parish Sch Bd; Lafayette Parish Coun Govt; bd dirs, Tri-Parish Comt Action Agency; United Givers Fund. **Military Serv:** AUS, 1953-55. **Business Addr:** Dentist, Individual Practice, 701 N Pierce St, Lafayette, LA 70501.*

BARBER, ATIIM KIAMBU. See BARBER, TIKI.

BARBER, HARGROW DEXTER
Oral surgeon. **Personal:** Born Aug 29, 1956, Alameda, CA; son of Hargrow Dexter Sr and Jessie Singleton; married Kimberly Higgins DDS. **Educ:** Univ Calif, BA, 1978; Meharry Med Col, DDS, 1983. **Career:** Pvt pract, dentist, 1983-85; Highland Gen Hosp, oral maxillofacial surgeon residency, 1985-89; Cooper Univ Hosp, physician surg, currently; Oral Surg Residency Highland Hosp, 1989. **Orgs:** Nat Dent Asn, 1979-; Am Acad Oral Med, 1983; Calif Dent Asn, 1986; Am Asn Oral & Maxillofacial Surgeons, 1986; Md State Dent Asn, 1988; Am Dent Asn, 1986-; Am Dent Soc Anesthesiol, 1989. **Honors/Awds:** Outstanding Achievement Award, Am Acad Oral Med, 1983; Honor Scholarship Award, Meharry Medical Col Sch Dent, 1983; Hospital Dentistry Award, Meharry Medical Col, 1983; Golden State Achievement Award, 1988. **Special Achievements:** Second black person accepted into the Oral and Maxillofacial Residency Program at Highland General Hospital in its fifty year history; published "Double Degree Oral Surgeons," Journal of Oral and Maxillofacial Surgery, Oct 1989, and "Orbital Infections," Journal of Oral and Maxillofacial Surgery, Nov 1989. **Business Addr:** Physician Surgery, Cooper University Hospital, 2 Plaza Dr Suite 203, Sewell, NJ 08080.*

BARBER, JAMAEL ORONDE. See BARBER, RONDE.

BARBER, JAMES W.
Educator. **Personal:** Born Sep 17, 1937, Alexandria, VA; married Doris; children: Laura & Tracy. **Educ:** BS, 1964; MS, 1975. **Career:** High Meadows Conn State Treatment Ctr, dir educ & group life; Ala Ctr Higher Educ, sr group training consult, 1972; Southern Conn State Univ, fac, exercise & sci, 1969-70, dir comm & minority affairs, 1976-81, dir, AAIEEO, 1981-89, dir stud support Serv, 1989-, Women's Track & Field, headcoach, currently. **Orgs:** Awards chair, New Haven Scholar Fund Inc; Nat Asn Advan Colored People; bd dirs, Regional Workforce Develop; bd dirs, Enterprise Empowerment Zone; dir, AAIEEO, 1981-89; dir, Stud Support Serv, 1989-. **Honors/Awds:** African American Distinguished Service Award, Southern Conn State Univ, 1997. **Home Addr:** 65 Vista Terr, New Haven, CT 06515, **Home Phone:** (203)397-3391. **Business Addr:** Director of Student Support & Services, Southern Connecticut State University, 501 Crescent St Engleman Hall Room 34, New Haven, CT 06515, **Business Phone:** (203)392-6814.

BARBER, DR. JANICE DENISE
Dentist. **Personal:** Born Nov 6, 1952, Alameda, CA; daughter of Hargrow and Jessie Singleton; married Russell J Frazier. **Educ:** Mills Col, BA, 1974; Meharry Med Col Dental Sch, DDS, 1979. **Career:** Hubbard Hosp, gen pract resident, 1981-82, asst instr in hosp dentistry, 1981; NY City, assoc dentist, 1983-86; Sydenham NFCC/Harlem Hosp, attending dentist, 1984-86; Harlem Hosp, clin fl coordr, 1985-86; Oakland, CA, assoc dentist, 1986-; Highland Gen Hosp, 1990; pvt pract, currently. **Orgs:** Delta Sigma Theta; Acad Gen Dentistry; Am Dental Asn. **Honors/Awds:** Employee of the Year, Harlem Hosp Dental Clin, 1985; Employee of the Month, Harlem Hosp, 1985; Attending of the Year Dental Clinic, Harlem Hosp, 1986. **Special Achievements:** Abstract: "The Mental Foramen Injection", The NY J Dentistry, 1983; "Cosmetic Dentistry" Harlem Hosp Ambulatory Newsletter, 1986. **Business Addr:** Physician, 5325 Broder Blvd, Dublin, CA 94568, **Business Phone:** (925)551-6706.

BARBER, MICHAEL LENARD (MIKE BARBER)
Football player. **Personal:** Born Nov 9, 1971, Edgemore, SC. **Educ:** Clemson Univ. **Career:** Football Player (Retired); Seattle Seahawks, linebacker, 1995-97; Indianapolis Colts, linebacker, 1998-99. *

BARBER, MIKE. See BARBER, MICHAEL LENARD.

BARBER, ORNETTA M
Consultant. **Personal:** Born Mar 14, 1949, St Louis, MO; daughter of James Ornett and Edna Morales; married R Gregg Dickerson, Feb 24, 1990. **Educ:** Calif State Univ, Los Angeles, BA, radio & tv broadcasting, 1978. **Career:** Greater Los Angeles Community Action Agency, community activist; KHJ Tv, Frankly Female, assoc prod, 1977-86; Elektra & Asylum Records, Natl Mkt Res, sr dir, 1979-86; WEA Corp, Black Music Mkt, nat dir, 1986-87, vpres, 1987; Hidden Beach Recordings, consult, currently; Witha-Song Inc, pres, currently. **Orgs:** Thurgood Marshall Scholar Fund, 1990-; Inst Black Parenting, 1989-; Yes Jobs Prog, 1987-; Nat Assoc Rec Arts & Sci, 1979-; Avalon Carver Community Ctr, 1976-; Westminster Neighborhood Assoc, 1976-; 331 Found, 1991-; chair, Int Asn African-Am Music, 1993; Nat Asn Black Female Execs Music & Entertainment. **Honors/Awds:** Original 13 Award, Jack the Rapper, 1990; Women's Networking Award, Impact Mag, 1990; Heritage Award, Black Radio Exclusive, 1991; Black Woman Achievement, Nat Am Advan Colored People Legal Defense Fund, 1991. **Special Achievements:** Best & Brightest 100 Women in Corporate America, Ebony Mag, 1990. **Business Addr:** President, WithaSong Incorporated, Sherman Oaks, CA 91401, **Business Phone:** (818)264-3144.

BARBER, RONDE (JAMAEL ORONDE BARBER)
Football player. **Personal:** Born Apr 7, 1975, Montgomery County, VA; son of James Barber JB and Geraldine Brickhouse Barber; married Claudia; children: Yammile Rose & Justyce Rosina. **Educ:** Univ Va, BA, com, 1997. **Career:** Tampa Bay Buccaneers, defensive back, 1997, starting right corner back, 1998, corner back, currently. **Orgs:** Phi Eta Sigma Honor Soc, Virginia. Fel Christian Athletes; Phi Eta Sigma Hon Soc, VA; co-chair, Read Across Am Day, 2005. **Honors/Awds:** Best Sportscast, Assoc Press; Soc Prof Journalist Award; 50 Most Beautiful People, People Mag, 2001; Women's Sexiest Male Athletes, Sports Illustrated, 2001; NFL's 100 Best Players, The Sporting News, 2003; inductee, Univ Va Hall of Fame, 2005; Super Bowl XXXVII ring, 2003. **Special Achievements:** Co-host, Sunday Sports Extra, WFLA News Channel; co-auth: By My Brother's Side, 2004; Game Day, 2005. **Business Addr:** Professional Football Player, Tampa Bay Buccaneers, 1 W Buccaneer Pl, Tampa, FL 33607, **Business Phone:** (813)870-2700.*

BARBER, SHAWN WILLIAM
Football player, television show host. **Personal:** Born Jan 14, 1975, Richmond, VA. **Educ:** Univ Richmond. **Career:** Football player; show host: Wash Redskins, linebacker, 1998-01; Philadelphia Eagles, linebacker, 2002,2006; Kansas City Chiefs, linebacker, 2003-05; Houston Texans, linebacker, currently; Comcast Sports Network, fantasy analyst. **Business Addr:** Professional Football Player, Houston Texans, Two Reliant Pk, Houston, TX 77054, **Business Phone:** (832)667-2000.*

BARBER, TIKI (ATIIM KIAMBU BARBER)
Football player, radio broadcaster. **Personal:** Born Apr 7, 1975, Roanoke, VA; son of James Barber and Geraldine Brickhouse; married Ginny Cha, May 15, 1999; children: Atiim Kiambu Jr & Chason. **Educ:** Univ Va. **Career:** Football player (retired), sports broadcaster; New York Giants, 1997-06; OBeverages, partner & investor; LLCWFAN & WCBS, New York, 2007; NBC News corres; analyst NBC's Football Night In America; Tiki Ventures. **Orgs:** Bd, MMRF; chmn, co-founder, Tiki Ventures, LLC. **Honors/Awds:** Three ProBowls, 2004-06. **Special Achievements:** Wrote a book "My Life and the Game Beyond ", 2007. **Business Addr:** Chairman and Co-founder, Tiki Ventures LLC, 546 Fifth Ave 6th Fl Circle, New York, NY 10036, **Business Phone:** (212)869-1100.*

BARBER, VAUGHN J
Lawyer. **Career:** Pvt Pract, atty, currently.

BARBER, WILLIAM, JR.
Construction worker. **Personal:** Born Jan 4, 1942, Morristown, NJ; married Anita C; children: William III. **Educ:** Univ Nebr, BE, 1967. **Career:** Town Morristown, recreational dir; M&M Mars, employ & comm rels rep; NJ Morris Cath HS, wrestling coach, coach, 1967-73; Urban 4H, social comt worker, 1967-73; Morristown Neighborhood House, social rec dir, 1967-; Int Harvester, sales trainee, sch comt worker, social case & guid counr, 1967-73; Barber Maintenance Cleaning Contractor, pres; AT&T, mgr bldg opers, mgr pub rels, bldg serv; Passaic Tech Voc Educ, intervention instr, phys health educ instr; St Clare Riverside Med Ctr, ment health counr; Passaic Juv Detentions, phys ed teacher, 1990, 1998.

Orgs: Counr After Care Clinic Drug Rehab Regions Clergy Coun; chmn Juv Conf Bd; Morristown YMCA; Morris Community Col; Plainfield Nat Asn Advan Colored People, 1974, Human Civil Rights Comn; Morristown Kiwanis Club, Morris City Nat Asn Advan Colored People, 1980; Morristown Mem Hosp; parole bd State NJ; Int Group Friendship Force; Morris Habitat Humanity; NJ Sch Soc Workers Coun; Hands Across Morristown; SCI Club; Charles Menninger; Notary Pub NJ; Radio History Soc. **Honors/Awds:** Jaycees Distinguished Serv Award, 1969; Outstanding Citizen 4-H Club Award, 1970; Morris County Human Resource Award, 1978; Nat Asn Advan Colored People Comm Serv Award; Comm Serv Award Ike Martin Book of Honors, 1987. **Special Achievements:** First black wrestling coach; First black volunteer fireman in Morristown; Developed a private library with antique radios. **Business Addr:** Instructor, Passaic Co Tech Institute, 45 Reiwhardt Rd, Wayne, NJ 07470, **Business Phone:** (201)790-6000.*

BARBOZA, ANTHONY
Photographer, artist. **Personal:** Born May 10, 1944, New Bedford, MA; son of Anthony and Lillian Barboza; married Laura Carrington, Jul 15, 1985; children: Leticia, Laryssa, Danica, Alexio, Lien. **Career:** Began photog career Kamoinge Workshop, under dir photogr, Roy DeCarava, 1964; Anthony Barboza Photographer, com photogr, currently. **Honors/Awds:** Achievement Award, Cape Verdean Film Festival, 1998; awarded New York State Council on the Arts grants, 1974 ,1976, National Endowment for the Arts grant, 1980, New York Foundation for the Arts grant, 2002. **Special Achievements:** Art Pubs: Day in the Life of Israel, Viking, 1994; African-Ams, Viking, 1993; Songs of My People, Little Brown, 1992; Flesh & Blood; Picture Project, 1992; Shooting Stars: Stuart, Tabori & Chang, 1992; numerous others; Books: "Black Borders," "Piano For Days," "Black Book of Lists," NYU Press, 1998; Exhibs: Brooklyn Mus of Art, Committed to the Image A Half Century of Black Photog, 2001; Day in the Life of Africa, 2002; Day in the Life of Armed Forces Around the World, 2003; Songs of My People, Time Life Tour, 1990; Cinque Gallery, NY, 1990; Drew Univ, One-Man Show, 1989; numerous others; TV Com, Miles Davis Present Van Liquor, It's A Miracle!, Dentsu Advertisting, Dentsu of Japan, 1984; Permanent Collections, Mus of Modern Art; Studio Mus of Harlem; Newark Art Mus; Howard Univ; Orleans Pub Libr; Univ of Ghana; Univ of Mexico; Lectures & Grants at various schs, 1965-; Documentary, Ken Burn's Jazz, PBS, 2001. **Business Addr:** Photographer, Anthony Barboza Photographer, 13 Laight St Third Fl, New York, NY 10013, **Business Phone:** (212)925-7991.*

BARBOZA, STEVEN ALAN
Writer. **Personal:** Born Jul 20, 1952, New Bedford, MA; son of Lillian Barros Barboza and Anthony Canto Barboza; married Regina Lewis, Aug 8, 1992. **Educ:** Boston University, BA, 1976; Columbia University Gradute School Journalism, MSJ, 1979. **Career:** Writer, currently. **Special Achievements:** Books include: I Feel Like Dancing, American Jihad: Islam After Malcolm X, Door of No Return, numerous magazine and newspaper articles. **Home Phone:** (212)995-5921. *

BARCLIFF, MELVIN
Rap musician. **Personal:** Born Jul 12, 1973, Norfolk, VA. **Career:** Vocalist, 1997-; Albums: Welcome to Our World, 1997; Tim's Bio: Life From Tha Bassment, 1998; Indecent Proposal, 2001; Under Construction, 2003; Singles: "Beep Me 911", 1997; "Up Jumps Da Boogie", 1997; "Luv 2 Luv URemix", 1997; "Here We Come", 1998; "We At It Again", 2000; "Drop", 2001; "All Y'all", 2002; "Cop That Disc", 2003; "Indian Flute", 2003; Respect M.E., 2006; Shock Value, 2007. **Orgs:** DeVante Swing's Swing Mob. **Business Addr:** Rap artist, c/o WEA Corp, 111 N Hollywood Way, Burbank, CA 91505, **Business Phone:** (818)843-6311.

BARDEN, BELLA MARSHALL
Executive, president (organization). **Personal:** Daughter of Lillian Clarice; married Don H. Barden; children: one. **Career:** Mayor's Off, Detroit, MI, finance dir; Barden Cos, Waycor Develop Inc, pres; Barden Int Inc, pres, currently. *

BARDEN, DON H.
President (organization), chief executive officer, business owner. **Personal:** Born Dec 20, 1943, Detroit, MI; son of Milton Sr and Hortense Hamilton; married Bella Marshall, May 14, 1988; children: Keenan. **Educ:** Cent State Univ, attended 1964. **Career:** Record Store, owner, 1960-67; newspaper owner, 1972; Lorain County Times, partner, 1974; Lorain City Coun, coun mem, 1972-75; Don H Barden Inc, pres, 1976-81; WKYC-TV, talk-show host, 1977-80; Barden Cable vision, chief exec officer, 1982-94; Majestic Star Casino LLC, mgr, chmn, pres & chief exec officer, 1993-; Barden Cos, chief exec officer & pres, 1994-; Majestic Investor Capital, dir; Barden Miss, pres & chief exec officer investor & mgr, currently; BDI, chmn & pres, 1993-; Majestic Star, chmn, pres & chief exec officer, 1993-; Majestic Investor Capital, chmn, pres & chief exec officer, 2001-; Barden Colo, pres & chief exec officer investor & mgr, 2001-; Barden Nev, pres & chief exec officer investor & mgr, 2001-. **Orgs:** Exec, Dem Party; Ed Task Force; dir, Detroit Symphony Orchestra, 1986-, Nat Cable TV Assoc IOB, 1985-; dir, MI Cable TV Assoc, 1987-, dir, First Independence Nat Bank, 1987-; dir, Metrop Detroit Conv Bur, 1988-; chmn bd dir, Booker T Wash Bus Asn. **Honors/Awds:** Trumpet Award, Turner Companies, 2004; Entrepreneur Yr, 2004. **Special Achievements:** First African American cable-company owner; only African American to own gaming casino in Las Vegas; Listed in Black Enterprise magazine; One of the Seven Living Legends, Mayor Kwame Kilpatrick & Detroit City Coun, 2004. **Home Addr:** 18240 Fairway Dr, Detroit, MI 48221. **Business Phone:** 888-225-8259.

BAREFIELD, DR. JAMES E
Chemist. **Career:** Los Alamos Nat Labs, Anal Chem, laser chemist, currently. **Business Addr:** Laser Chemist, Los Alamos National Laboratory, Chemistry Division, PO Box 1663 MS J565, Los Alamos, NM 87545, **Business Phone:** (505)665-5195.

BAREFIELD, MORRIS
Educator, high school teacher. **Personal:** Born Aug 15, 1939, Madison, IL; son of William Barefield and Pearlie McClelland; married Lun Ye Crim, Aug 18, 1963; children: Erik & Myla. **Educ:** Southern Ill Univ, BS, 1961, MS, 1965. **Career:** Educator (retired); Eisenhower High Sch, Blue Island Ill, instr, 1961-64; Richard High Sch, Oak Lawn, IL, instr, 1964-66; New Trier E High Sch, instr, 1966-2006; Chicago Land Jewsih High Sch, instr, 2006. **Orgs:** Instructional Affairs Comt Nat Coun Teachers Math, 1969-72, NEA, Ill Educ Asn; treas, secy, New Trier Educ Asn, 1971-74; Glencoe Concerned Parents Asn; dir, stud prog, Rights & Responsibilities New Trier HS, 1973-75; guest speaker, Nat Coun Teachers Math, 1972, regional speaker, 1971-72; fac coun pres, New Trier HS, 1987-88; New Trier Educ Asn, pres, 1993-. **Honors/Awds:** Award for Outstanding Effort in Human Rels, Ill Educ Asn, 1974. *

BAREFIELD, OLLIE DELORES
School administrator, educator. **Personal:** Born Dec 19, 1930, Teague, TX; married Henry B Barefield Sr; children: John Anthony. **Educ:** Huston-Tillotson Col, BA, 1950; Univ Northern Colo, MA, 1966, EdS, 1970. **Career:** Teague Independent Sch Dist, Eng teacher, 1950-55; Bur Indian Affairs, Ariz, Bilingual teacher, 1955-60; Denver Pub Schs, elem teacher, 1960-70, elem prin. **Orgs:** Am Asn Univ Women, 1980, Ministers Wives Asn, 1980; Nat Asn Elem Prin,1980; bd dir Nat Asn Advan Colored People, Denver, 1980; Delta SigmaTheta, 1980, Nat Coun Negro Women, 1980; guest lectr, Rocky Mountain BookFestival, 1970. **Honors/Awds:** Teacher of the Year, Denver Pub Schs, 1969; Distinguished Teacher Award,1969; Woman of the Year, Kappa Omega Chi Beauticians Sorority, 1980. **Home Addr:** 2979 Monaco Pkwy, Denver, CO 80207. *

BARFIELD, CLEMENTINE
Association executive, executive director. **Personal:** Born Aug 19, 1950, Lexington, MS; daughter of Tolbert and Malinda Baugh; married John J Barfield, Apr 4, 1967 (divorced); children: John, Ollie, Malinda, Derick (deceased), Roger. **Educ:** Wayne State Univ, Detroit MI, BS, 1981. **Career:** Save Our Sons & Daughters, Detroit, MI, founder & pres, 1987-. **Orgs:** Am Humanics, Wayne State Univ; comnr, Detroit City Coun-Youth Adv Commn; bd mem, Proj Start; bd mem, Mich Victim Alliance; Nat Org Victim Assistance. **Honors/Awds:** Community Service Award, Nat Asn Negro Prof & Bus Women, 1987; Nat Black Journalist, 1987; Community Serv Award, Am Muslim Community, 1987; Community Serv Award, Univ Detroit, 1987; Black Prof Award, Michelob Beer, 1988; hon doc Marygrove Col, Detroit MI, 1988; Victims Advocacy Award, Pres Ronald Reagan, 1988; Special Tributes, City Detroit & State Mich; Status Women Awards, Top Ladies Distinction; Pub Citizen of the Yr Award, Nat Asn Social Workers, 1989. **Business Phone:** (313)361-5200.*

BARFIELD, DEBORAH DENISE
Journalist. **Personal:** Born Jul 6, 1963, St Albans, NY; daughter of William and Carrie Montgomery. **Educ:** Univ Md, Col Pk, MD, BS, Col Journalism, 1985. **Career:** Black Explosion, Col Park, MD, reporter, 1983-85; Star-Democrat, Easton, MD, sportswriter, 1985-87; Times Herald Record, Middletown, NY, reporter, 1987-89; Providence Journal-Bulletin, reporter, 1989-, Newsday, wash corresp, 2004. **Orgs:** Nat Assoc of Black Journalists, 1987-; Sigma Circle of Omicron Delta Kappa, 1984-; Sigma Delta Chi, Society of Professional Journalist, Univ of Md, 1983-85. **Honors/Awds:** Best in Show, "How Far Have We Come," Maryland, Delaware, DC Press Asn, 1985; NAACP Service Awards, 1987-88. **Business Addr:** Correspondent, Newsday, 235 Pinelawn Rd, Melville, NY 11747-4250.*

BARFIELD, JON E.
Executive. **Personal:** Born Jan 1, 1951?; son of John W; married Betty; children: Jon, Aaron. **Educ:** Princeton Univ, BA, 1974; Harvard Law Sch, JD, 1977. **Career:** Univ Mich, janitor, 1954; Janitorial Serv, 1954-59; Sidley, corp & security law; Austin, corp & security law; Brown & Wood, Chigago, IL, corp & security law; Barfield & Assoc, consult; Barfield Co, chiec exec & pres; Princeton Univ, Janitorial Serv, charter trustee emer, 1975; Bartech Group, chmn & pres, 1995-; Nat City Corp, bd dir; Tecumseh Prod Com, bd dir; BMC Software, bd dir; Granite Broadcasting Corp, bd dir; Pantellos Group Ltd Partnership Inc, dir. **Orgs:** Ypsilanti Chamber Com; bd mem, Eastern Mich Univ Col Bus; Nat Tech Servs Asn; bd trustee, Kettering Univ; bd trustee, Detroit Renaissance. **Honors/Awds:** Tree of Life Award, Jewish Nat Fund, 1992. **Military Serv:** AUS. **Business Phone:** (734)953-5050.*

BARFIELD, DR. RUFUS L.
Educator. **Personal:** Born Nov 14, 1929, Hickman, KY; married Emma Crawford; children: Rufus Jr, Sheila & Joselyn. **Educ:** Ky State Univ, BA, 1952; Univ Ky, MA, 1956; Univ Cincinnati, MEd, 1966; Ohio State, adv grad work, 1967; Miami Univ, PhD, 1972. **Career:** Educator (retired); Rosenwald High Sch, KY, teacher, 1952-55; Lincoln Heights Schs, OH, teacher, 1955-56; Hoffman Schs, Cincinnati, OH, teacher,1956-64; Schiel Schs, Cincinnati, OH, teacher, 1964-66, asst prin, 1966-69; Colum Schs, prin, 1969; Burton Schs, Cincinnati, OH, prin, 1969-71; Ky State Univ, admin asst pres, 1972-74; Acad Affairs Univ AR, vice chancellor, 1977-78; Acad Affairs Ky State Univ, vpres, 1974-77; Montgomery Co Pub Sch, pup personnel admin. **Orgs:** Nat Educ Asn; Am Asn Sch Admin; Phi Delta Kappa; Nat Orgn Legal Prob Educ; Soc Res Admin; Ky Coun Higher Educ; Comn Higher Educ Ky comn child servs. **Honors/Awds:** Merit Award Service, YMCA, 1964; Certificate Award for Outstanding service, Corryville Community Coun, Cincinnati, 1967. **Military Serv:** AUS, 1953-54. **Home Addr:** 11801 Chantilly Lane, Bowie, MD 20721. *

BARGONETTI, JILL (DR. JILL BARGONETTI-CHAVARRIA)
Biologist, educator. **Personal:** Born in New York; daughter of Arthur Bargonetti and Adah Askew; married Nicholas Chavarria, 1991; children: Carlo & Miles. **Educ:** State Univ NY Purchase, BA, 1985; NY Univ, MS, 1987, PhD, molecular biol, 1990; Columbia Univ, postdoctoral work, 1994. **Career:** City Univ NY, Hunter Col, Assistant biol prof, 1994-99, Associate prof 1999-2006, Professor, 2007-cancer researcher, currently. **Honors/Awds:** Presidential Early Career Award for Scientists & Engineers, 1997; Cathy Keeton Mountain Top Award, NAACP NY Branch, 1997; Felix Gross Endowment Award, 1998; NY Voice Award, 1998; Research Award, NIH/SCORE, 2000; New York Mayor's Award, 2001; Outstanding Woman Scientist Award, Asn Women Sci, 2001. NYU and SUNY Purchase Distinguished Alumni Award 2005. **Special Achievements:** Numerous publ including, "Mdm2 Associates with Chromatin in the Presence of p53 and is Released to Facilitate Activation of Transcription", Cancer res, 2006; "Phospholipase D Elevates the Level of MDM2 and Suppresses DNA Damage-Induced Increases", 2004. **Business Addr:** Professor of Biology, Hunter College, Department Biology, 695 Pk Ave Rm 903B, New York, NY 10021, **Business Phone:** (212)650-3519.

BARGONETTI-CHAVARRIA, DR. JILL. See BARGONETTI, JILL.

BARHAM, WILBUR STECTSON
Executive. **Personal:** Born in Como, NC; son of Lincoln and Jessie Mae Cowper; married Sonia Arlene Guy, May 16, 1981. **Educ:** NC Cent Univ, Durham, NC, BSC, 1977; Univ Wis, Madison, Madison, WI, MBA, 1980. **Career:** Prudential Ins Co, Wash, DC, assoc investment mgr, 1980-83; Ky Fried Chicken, Hanover, MD, real estate mgr, 1983-88; Cardinal Industs, Glen Burnie, MD, real estate rep, 1988; HMS Host Corp, Bethesda, MD, dir, govt affairs, 1988-. **Orgs:** Nat Forum Black Pub Adminr; First Baptist Church, Glenarden, MD; Airport Mny Adv Coun. **Home Addr:** 1214 Kings Heather Dr, Bowie, MD 20721. **Business Addr:** Director Government Affairs, HMSHost Corp, 6600 Rockledge Dr, Bethesda, MD 20817-1109, **Business Phone:** (301)380-3768.*

BARISFORD, ROBERT. See BROWN, BOBBY.

BARKER, JUDY
Executive. **Career:** Key Bank Found, cleveland, OH, sr vpres, chairwoman; Avon products, global vpres; KeyCorp, Cleveland, OH, sr vpres, civic affairs & corp contrib, currently. **Orgs:** Pres, Avon Prod Found; Borden Found; United Negro College Fund; Paine Col; Women's Forum & Project People Found, NY. **Honors/Awds:** DHL, Xavier Univ; Women of Achievement Award, YMCA; National Council of Negro Women Award, Wash, DC; Role Model Image Award, Bennett Col; Citizens Union Leadership Award, New York; Ohio State University Distinguished Citation of Community Service Award; 50 Top Black Executives in Corporate America, Ebony Mag; 10 Top Corporate Women Power Players, Ebony Mag. **Special Achievements:** First African-American woman to become president of an international corporation's philanthropic foundation. *

BARKLEY, CHARLES WADE
Basketball player, television sportscaster. **Personal:** Born Feb 20, 1963, Leeds, AL; son of Frank and Charcey Glenn; married Maureen, Jan 1, 1989; children: Christiana. **Educ:** Auburn Univ. **Career:** Basketball player (retired), sports commentator; Philadelphia 76ers, forward, 1985-92, Phoenix Suns, 1992-96; US Olympic Basketball team, 1992, 1996; Houston Rockets, 1996-

99; TNT, NBA sports commentator, 2001-. **Honors/Awds:** NBA All-Star, 1986-97; NBA All-Star MVP, 1991; NBA Most Valuable Player, 1992-93; Olympic Gold Medalist, 1992 & 1996; One of 50 Greatest Players in NBA History, 1996; Naismith Memorial Basketball Hall of Fame, 2006. **Special Achievements:** Films: Hot Shots!, 1991; Look Who's Talking Now, 1993; Forget Paris, 1995; Space Jam, 1996; He Got Game, 1998; Jackie's Back!, 1999; The Year of the Yao, 2004; Author: I May Be Wrong, But I Doubt It, 2002; Who's Afraid of a Large Black Man, 2005. **Business Addr:** Sports Commentator, Turner Network TV, 1050 Techwood Dr NW, Atlanta, GA 30318, **Business Phone:** (404)885-4538.

BARKLEY, MARK E.
Government official. **Personal:** Born Oct 2, 1932, Alpine, AL; son of Simon W Stamps and Ruby Bledsoe; married Arrie Ann Morton, Oct 3, 1959. **Educ:** Ala State Univ, BS, 1957; Ohio State Univ, 1960; Atlanta Univ, 1963; Wash Univ, DSC, 1976; Oper Res, Comput Sci, Stats, 1976. **Career:** AVSCOM Dir, S & CA, mathematician, 1969-70; AVSCOM Dir, S&CA & P&P, oper res analyst, 1970-72; AVSCOM Dir, Plans & Anal, supr oper res analyst, 1972-77; AVSCOM BLACK HAWK, Proj Mgr, supr oper res analyst, 1977-86; Prog Innovators Inc, St Louis, pres, vpres, 1973-; Chm, bd dirs, 1972-. **Orgs:** Asn Comp Mach, 1968-; Oper Res Soc Am, 1972-; Nat Sci Found fel, Ohio St Univ, Columbus, OH; secy, bd dirs, Gateway Fed Employees CU, 1976-87, chmn, bd dirs, 1987-91; Soc Logistics Engrs, 1977-; Army Aviation Asn Am, 1972-; deacon, Antioch Bapt Church, St Louis, MO, 1972; Cedar VlyEst Trustees, 1983-; Free & Accepted Masons, AL, 1960; Beta Kappa Chi Sci Honor Soc, 1956-. **Honors/Awds:** Hons grad, Ala St Univ, 1957; long term training, USAF & AUS, 1967-68, 1975; commanders award for civil service, TSARCOM St Louis, MO, 1983; Exceptional Performance Award, AVSCOM BLACK HAWK Proj Mgr, 1984. **Military Serv:** AUS, pfc, 1953-55; Armed Forced Exped Medal; Overseas Service Medal, 1955-54. **Home Addr:** 104 Camden Cir, Madison, AL 35758. *

BARKLEY, RUFUS, JR.
Fashion designer. **Personal:** Born Jan 11, 1949?, New York, NY; son of Rufus Sr and Sally Virginia Motron. **Educ:** Parsons Sch Design, NY City 1970. **Career:** Teal Traina, New York, designer; Oscar de la Renta Int, asst designer; Geoffrey Beene Bag & Beene Shirt Bazaar, NY City, designer, 1973-74; Mollie Parnis Boutique & Couture NY City, asst designer, 1975-78; Beldoch Industs, NY City, designer Pierre Cardin blouses, 1982-83; Sherry Cassin & Co Ltd, freelance fashion illusr, currently; Rhode Island Sch Design, adj fac, currently. **Honors/Awds:** Don Simonelli Crit Award; JC Penney Sports Award; participant, Ebony Fashion Fair, 1969-79. **Special Achievements:** "New Face of '72," article in Women's Wear Daily, 1972; dress design, Bazaar Mag, 1972; "Soul on Seventh Ave," article in Time magazine, Aug 7, 1972; 'Designer of the Month', Essence Mag, 1972; dress design, cover of Cosmopolitan mag, 1973. *

BARKSDALE, CHUCK
Singer. **Personal:** Born Jan 11, 1935, Chicago, IL. **Career:** The Marquees, mem; The Cats & the Fiddle, mem; The Dells, mem, currently; Albums (With the Dells): Oh What a Night, 1957; It's Not Unusual, 1965;There Is, 1968; Love Is Blue, 1969; The Dells' Musical Menu/Always Together, 1969; The Dells' Greatest Hits, 1970; Like It Is, Like It Was,1971; Freedom Means, 1971; Sweet As Funk Can Be, 1972; The Dells Sing Dionne, 1972; Give Your Baby a Standing Ovation, 1976; The Dells, 1973;The Mighty Mighty Dells, 1974; The Dells vs. The Dramatics, 1975; The Dells' Greatest Hits Volume 2, 1975; We Got To Get Our Thing Together,1975; No Way Back, 1976; They Said It Couldn't Be Done But We Did It,1977; Love Connection, 1977; New Beginnings, 1978; Face to Face, 1979; I Touched a Dream, 1980; Whatever Turns You On, 1981; One Step Closer, 1984; The Second Time, 1988; On Their Corner, 1992; I Salute You, 1992; Dreams of Contentment, 1993; Bring Back the Love: Classic Dells, 1996; I Touch a Dream/Whatever Turns, 1998; Reminiscing, 2000; Open Up My Heart: The 9/11 Album, 2002; Hott, 2003. **Honors/Awds:** Rock & Roll Hall of Fame, The Dells, 2004. **Business Addr:** Singer, The Original Dells Inc, PO Box 1113, Harvey, IL 60426, **Business Phone:** (708)474-1422.

BARKSDALE, LEONARD N
Clergy, lawyer. **Personal:** Born Nov 11, 1948, Galveston, TX; son of Leonard N II and Joan Pendergraff; married Gladys Glass Barksdale, Aug 10, 1974; children: Lea N & Anita J. **Educ:** Univ Houston, BA, 1969; Houston Grad Sch Theol, MA; Thurgood Marshall Sch Law, JD, 1974; Col Biblical Studies, Houston, ABS; Dallas Theol Sem, CGS. **Career:** Boys Scouts Am, Eagle Scout, 1964; United States Judge Advocate Gen, Pentagon, Wash, DC, legal intern, 1972; Reginald Legal Aid Soc, Louisville, atty, 1974; Houston Legal Found, atty, 1975; Houston Community Col, law instr, 1975-85; Col Biblical Studies-Houston, chmn bd trustees; pvt pract law, sr atty, 1976-; Fifth Ward Missionary Baptist Church, minister, 1992-, pastor, currently. **Orgs:** Omega Psi Phi, 1970-; State Bar Tex, 1974-; Phi Alpha Delta, 1974; The Nat Bar Asn, 1975-; secy, Houston Lawyers Asn, 1975-; vpres, Cent High Sch Alumni Asn, 1988-; bd dir, Houston Habitat Humanity,1988-92; Nat Asn Advan Colored People, 1990-. **Honors/Awds:** Heber Smith Fellow, 1974-75; Leadership Award, Boy Scouts Am, 1987; Men on the Move in the 90's, Sigma Gamma Rho Sorority, 1992. **Special Achievements:** Scout show chairman, W L Davis Dist of Boy Scouts of America, 1980-81; continuing legal education lecturer, Gulf Coast Black Women Lawyers Association, 1992; frequent speaker at church, civic & legal functions. **Business Phone:** (713)675-5111.

BARKSDALE, MARY FRANCES
Manager. **Personal:** Born Apr 5, 1934, Richmond, IN; daughter of Charles and Mary Ardelia Mitchell; married Wayne Edward Barksdale, Apr 18, 1953; children: Wayne E Jr, Stacey L McCampbell, Vickki A Morgan. **Educ:** Earlham Col, 1953; Ind Univ, attended 1981. **Career:** Manager (retired); Int Harvester Co, employ asst, 1969-74, employ supvr, 1974-77, labor rels supvr, 1977-80, human resources mgr, 1981-83; Navistar Int Corp, compensation & develop mgr, 1984-90, mgr human res, 1990-99. **Orgs:** Bd mem, Parkview Memorial Hosp, 1970-73, 1974-77, 1985-91, 1995-98; bd adv, Ind Univ, Purdue Univ, 1976-89; bd mem, Urban League, Ft Wayne, 1979-85; Links Inc, mem, 1979-92, pres, 1989-91; bd sch trustees, E Allen Co Schs, 1979-92; bd mem, United Way Allen Co, 1983-86; Leadership Ft Wayne, bd mem, 1983-91; Fort Wayne Mus Art, bd mem, 1991-93; Local Educ Fund, bd mem, 1989-93; Fort Wayne Med Found, bd mem, 1992-95; Foellinger Found bd mem, 1997-; Midwest Alliance Health Educ, 1997-. **Honors/Awds:** Commander of the Garrison Award Community Service, Robert E Armstrong Mayor, City Ft Wayne, 1979; Recognized for Community Service, Kappa Alpha Psi Fraternity, 1981; Community Service to City of Ft Wayne, Gent's Club, 1983; Humanitarian Award, Fort Wayne Urban League, 1985; Helene Foellinger Award, Outstanding Contributions, 1989; Fort Wayne Rotary, Paul Harris Fel, 1992; Executive Director Award, Fort Wayne Urban League, 1994. **Home Addr:** 3424 Mono Gene Dr, Fort Wayne, IN 46806.

BARKSDALE, ROSA KITTRELL
Executive. **Personal:** Born Apr 5, 1936, Mt Vernon, NY; daughter of Fred and Edna; married Leroy, Oct 15, 1977; children: Marion R Davis Jr & Kellye Jan Davis. **Educ:** Long Island Hosp, Sch Nursing, 1957; Col New Rochelle, BA, 1974. **Career:** NY Bd Ed, nurse, drug abuse & health teacher; Gould Statham, sales rep; Abbott Labs, prof hosp rep; Barksdale Home Care Serv Inc, founder, chief exec officer, 1982-. **Orgs:** NY Health Care Facilities Workers Compensation Trust, chair, bd trust, 1998-; Visting Nurse Serv Westchester, adv bd; Col New Rochelle, bd trustees; Westchester Black Nurses Asn; NY Asn Health Care Providers; Westchester HELP Mt Vernon; Delta Sigma Theta; Mt Vernon High Sch, adv coun mem; Westchester/Putnam Workforce, investment bd, chair, youth coun; Am Red Cross Westchester, bd mem; Nat Conf for Community & Justice, bd dir; African Am Chamber Com, Westchester/Rockland County; Westchester Alumnae Chapter Delta Sigma Theta Sorority Inc. **Honors/Awds:** Excellence in Enterprise Award, Monroe Col, 1992; Black Entrepreneur Award, 1992; The Monroe Col Excellence in Enterprise Award, 1992; Community Service Award, Chabad Lubavitch Westchester Cty; Community Service Award, Int Health Prof Network, 1996; Sister Int Asantewa honoree, 1996; WEST COP Corp Achievement Award, 1996; Omega Phi Psi, Perseverance Award, 1997; Nat Asn Negro & Prof Women's Club, Achievement Award; YWCA of White Plains, Women in Bus Award; African Am Chamber Com, Westchester Business Person of the Year; Weste County Red Cross, Jerome P Holland Power of Humanity Entrepreneurial Award, 2001; Corporate Community Service Award, Am Lung Asn Hudson Valley, 2003; Community Service Award, NAACP Westchester County, 2006. **Special Achievements:** The first African American Female Home Licensed Home Health Care Agency in Westchester County; Network Jnl, named one of 25 Influential Black Women in Business, 2000. **Home Addr:** 2 Greens Way, New Rochelle, NY 10805, **Home Phone:** (914)632-0278. **Business Addr:** Chief Executive Officer, Barksdale Home Care Services Corp, 327 5th Ave, Pelham, NY 10803, **Business Phone:** (914)738-5600.

BARKSDALE, WAYNE E., JR.
Executive. **Educ:** Purdue Univ, BS, indust mgt. **Career:** Weil-McLain, dir mfg opers, 1996-99, vpres opers, 1999-. **Business Phone:** (219)879-6561.*

BARLEY, TRACY HICKS
Lawyer. **Personal:** Born in Roanoke Rapids, NC; married Lesley; children: Leslie. **Educ:** Winston-Salem State Univ, BA, eng, 1983; NC A&T State Univ Grad Sch, adult educ, 1990; NC Cent Univ Sch Law, JD, 1993. **Career:** Tracy Hicks Barley & Assocs, P.A., atty, currently. **Orgs:** Union Baptist Church Durham; bd mem, Women In Action, Inc., pres, N Cent Legal Assistance Prog; Legal Aid NC Durham Adv Bd; comnr, NC Social Serv Comn; Delta Sigma Theta, Inc; legal coun, Winston-Salem State Univ, currently.

BARLOW, REGGIE DEVON
Football player, football coach. **Personal:** Born Jan 22, 1973, Montgomery, AL. **Educ:** Ala State Univ. **Career:** Football player (retired); football coach; Jacksonville Jaguars, wide receiver, 1996-00; Tampa Bay Buccaneers, widereceiver, 2002-03; Oakland Raiders; Ala State Hornets, head coach, currently. **Honors/Awds:** Super Bowl ring for Super Bowl XXXVII award, winner. *

BARLOW, WILLIAM B.
Educator, college teacher, consultant. **Personal:** Born Feb 25, 1943, Fort Rucker, AL; son of John Earl and Dorothy Goodman; divorced. **Educ:** San Francisco State Univ, BA, 1968; Univ Southern Calif, Santa Cruz, MA, 1974, PhD, 1983. **Career:** Mount Vernon Col, asst prof, 1976-80; Howard Univ, prof, 1980; Univ Miss, Nat Endowment Humanities fel, 1986; Schomburg, Nat Endowment Humanities fel, 1991-92; Smithsonian Inst, Blues Found, consult; Pacifica Radio, music programmer & producer; Barlow Systs, currently. **Orgs:** Union Dem Commun Steering Comt, 1977-; Int Asn Study Popular Music Steering Comt, 1989-; Int Asn Mass Commun Res, 1986-. **Special Achievements:** Looking Up at Down: The Emergence of Blues Culture, 1989; From Cakewalks to Concert Halls, 1992; co-author with Jan Dates, Split Image: AFAs in the Mass Media, 1990. **Military Serv:** USY, sp-4, 1964-66. **Home Addr:** 19 E Curtis Ave, Alexandria, VA 22301, **Home Phone:** (703)519-7894. **Business Phone:** (817)735-4277.*

BARNARD-BAILEY, WANDA ARLENE
Social worker. **Personal:** Born Jan 29, 1962, Norfolk, VA; daughter of James Webster and Wilhelmina Phillips; married Kevin Bernard, Feb 15, 1992. **Educ:** Univ NC, Chapel Hill, BA, 1984, MSW, 1986; PhD, social work. **Career:** Albemarle Home Care, hospice social worker coordr, 1986-87; Currituck Co bd Educ, alcohol/drug & dropout prev coordr, 1987-92; Navy Family Advocacy Prog, clin social worker, 1992-, regional dir, 2001. **Orgs:** Nat Asn Social Workers, 1984-; bd dir, NC Dropout Prev Asn, 1987-92; NC Sch Social Work Asn, 1987-92; bd dir, Albemarle Home Care Hospice, 1988-92; bd dir, Am Cancer Soc, 1988-92; bd, Albemarle Hopeline, 1991-92; dep city mgr, Va Local Govt Mgt Asn. **Honors/Awds:** Volunteer Award, Currituck Co Schs, 1988-91. **Home Addr:** 306 Cedar Rd, Chesapeake, VA 23322-4607, **Home Phone:** (757)382-6166. **Business Addr:** Regional Director, Navy Family Advocacy Program, 6500 Hampton Blvd, Norfolk, VA 23508, **Business Phone:** (757)444-2230.

BARNER, SHARON R
Executive. **Educ:** Syracuse Univ, BS, (cum laude), 1979; Univ Mich, JD, 1982. **Career:** Foley & Lardner LLP, Chicago, Ill, partner & chair intellectual property litigation, currently. **Orgs:** Ill State Bar asn, Nat Bar asn, Fed Am Bar asn; bd, Grateful Hand Found. **Business Addr:** Partner, Chair, Intellectual Property Litigation Practice Group, Foley & Lardner LLP, 321 N Clark St Suite 2800, Chicago, IL 60610, **Business Phone:** (312)832-4569.

BARNES, ADIA OSHUN (ADIA OSHUN BARNES)
Basketball player, radio broadcaster. **Personal:** Born Feb 3, 1977, San Diego, CA; daughter of Pete and Patricia Mcrae. **Educ:** Uni Ariz, sociol, 1998. **Career:** Sacramento Monarchs, 1998; Minnesota Lynx, forward, 1999; Cleveland Rockers, 2000-01; Seattle Sonics & Storm, forward, 2002-05; Houston Comets, forward, 2005-06; Broadcaster, 1150 AM KKNW, 2007-. **Orgs:** Girl Power; Barnes Found; Adia's Dreams in Action. **Honors/Awds:** Pac-10 Freshman of the Year, 1994-95; Pac-10 Player of the Year, 1997-98; UA Sports Hall of Fame, 2003. **Business Addr:** Broadcaster, 1150 AM KKNW radio, 3650 131st Ave SE Suite 550, Bellevue, WA 98006, **Business Phone:** (425)373-5536.*

BARNES, ANNE T.
Executive. **Personal:** Born Mar 10, 1940, Pitt County, NC; children: Darryl, Anita. **Educ:** Corrine Brooks Hair Design Inst, dipl, cosmetology, 1958; Norfolk State Univ, BA, 1964; Nat Beauty Culturist League Inc, BA, 1965, MA, 1969; Va Union Univ Sch Theol, cert, 1979; Gulf Coast Sem, Bachelor Theol, 1985. **Career:** LaBaron Hairstyling Salon, stylist, 1958-61; Bett's Hairstyling Salon, stylist, 1961-67; Anne's Beauty Acad, pres, 1975; Anne Barnes Inc, pres, 1967; MAKUBI II Corp, currently. **Orgs:** Bd dirs, Tidewater Tele Adv Coun; assoc min, Garretts Community Church; bd dirs, 100 Black Women Coalition; bd mem, United Christian Front Brotherhood; bd mem, Hal Jackson Talented Teen; Nat Beauty Culturists League, 1959-; bd mem, Church St Merchant Assoc, 1982-; bd mem, Nat Teachers Educ Coun, 1983-. **Honors/Awds:** Businessperson of the Year, TABCA, Norfolk; Award of merit, STOIC, Norfolk, 1981; Outstanding Citizen Award, Iota Phi Lambda Sor Inc, 1984; Black Businesswoman of the Year, Norfolk J & Guide Newspaper, 1984; Outstanding Businessperson of the Year, WRAP radio st, Norfolk, 1984. **Home Addr:** 1506 Covel St, Norfolk, VA 23523-1808. **Business Addr:** President, MAKUBI II Corporation, 701 Tidewater Dr, Norfolk, VA 23504, **Business Phone:** (757)622-7721.*

BARNES, ANTHONY L.
Entrepreneur, government official, real estate agent. **Career:** Realtor, 1983-; Anthony L Barnes & Assocs, pres & chief exec officer, 1989-. **Orgs:** Chmn, bd dir, Water Works & Sewer Bd, Birmingham, 1991-; Metrop Develop Bd. **Business Addr:** President, Chief Executive Officer, Barnes & Associates, 660C Univ Blvd, Birmingham, AL 35233, **Business Phone:** (205)328-3330.*

BARNES, DR. BOISEY O
Educator, cardiologist. **Personal:** Born May 16, 1943, Wilson, NC; married Bernadine. **Educ:** Johnson C Smith Univ, BS 1964;

Howard Univ, MD 1968. **Career:** Howard Univ Hosp, dir, noninvasive echocardiography lab, 1974-77, dir, Cardiac Clinic, asst prof med, 1976-77; Am Heart Asn, lectr, 1975-77; Shaw E Corp, staff; Boisey O Barnes, pres; Pvt Pract, cardiologist, currently. **Orgs:** Pres, Beta Kappa Chi Hon Soc, 1963-64; DC Med Soc Diplomate Am Bd Int Med, 1972; past keeper records & seals, Omega Psi Phi Frat, 1975-77; Am Inst Ultrasound, 1975-77; Am Soc Echocardiography, 1977; adv bd, Anacostia Cong Hghts Sect Red Cross, 1977. **Honors/Awds:** Outstanding Young Men American, 1970. **Special Achievements:** Honorary Mention Department Prize International Medicine & Pediatrics, Howard Univ, 1968; publ "Echocardiographics Findings in Endocarditis in Heroin Addicts" Amer Journ Card 1977; "Echocardiography Abstracts, Echocardiography in Hypertensive Patients" "Echocardiography in Amyloidosis". **Business Addr:** Physician, 413 G St SW, Washington, DC 20024, **Business Phone:** (202)554-2679.

BARNES, DR. DELORISE CREECY
Educator, consultant. **Personal:** Born Apr 2, 1947, Hertford, NC; daughter of William O and Easter Lillian; married James M, Jun 8, 1968; children: Victor, Timothy, Stephen & Jonathan. **Educ:** Livingstone Col, BS, 1969; Univ Tenn, MS, 1970, EdD, Voc Tech Educ, 1978; Univ Tenn, Knoxville-19 US Office Educ Fel, 1976. **Career:** Creecy's Poultry Farm, owner, 1962-65; Oak Ridge Pub Health & Welfare Dept, analyst, surveyor summer, 1965; Eureka Ctr Roane County Schs, head office admin, 1970-75; Oak Ridge Schs, adult ed instr, 1973-76; Roane State Community Col, prof bus, 1975-. **Orgs:** Advisor, Phi Beta Lambda RSCC 1976-; appt Gov TN mem, Sec TN Commiss for Human Develop, 1977-79; consult, Univ Tenn, Ctr Govt Training, 1980-87, Knoxville Prof Sec Int, 1983-87, Oak Ridge Schs, 1983-88, Martin Marietta Energy Syst Inc 1984-; pres, Alpha Kappa Alpha Xi Iota Omega; chmn-organized, Homework Hot Lines Oak Ridge Schs, 1986-87; Nat Bus Educ Asn, 1969-, Am Bus Comn Asn, Delta Pi Epsilon, resource person, Youth Enrichment Ctr; bd dir, Big Brother/Big Sisters, 1985-88; secy, Crown Monarch, auxillary Girls Club, 1988-; legis liaison chmn, Tenn Bus Educ Asn, 1988-; pres, Oak Ridge Chap AKA Sorority, 1990-92; pres, Tenn Chap Am Asn Women Community Cols; first vpres, Monarch Inc. **Honors/Awds:** USOE grant, Univ Tenn, Knoxville, 1975-77; Grant for a Model Office, Univ Tenn, 1976; led a round table discussion at NBEA conv; Dedicated Prof, Phi Beta Lambda, RSCC chap, 1988; Publication Award, Writing Ctr, RSCC, 1989; Leadership Award, AKA Sorority Inc, 1990; Businesswoman of the Year Award, Bus & Prof Women's Orgn, 1989; Consortium of Doctors Honoree, Ga Univ Syst, 1991. **Special Achievements:** Changes in Business Education Programs in Tennessee public senior high schools since the passage of the National Vocational Education Act of 1963, 1978; Publ six articles in major publs between 1979-84; "Mobilizing for the Minority Teacher Educ Shortage" in The Balance Sheet, SW Publ, 1988; numerous other articles; presented papers at Am Bus Commun Asn, SE & Midwestern regionals, 1989. **Business Addr:** Professor, Roane State Community College, Office of Admin Information Technology, 276 Patton Lane, Rockwood, TN 37854, **Business Phone:** (865)882-4600.*

BARNES, DIANE
Police officer. **Personal:** Born Jul 4, 1961, Ridgeland, SC; daughter of Leroy and Sally Mae Barnes; children: Trameka Lashond Wade. **Educ:** Miami Dade Community Col N, Miami, FL, criminal justice; Nova Seastern Univ, elem educ, 1996. **Career:** Johnson Model City Ins, Miami, Fl, ins underwriter, 1977-79; Metro-Dade Police Dept, Miami, Fl, loan servicing clerk, 1979-80, police record specialist, 1981; City Miami Police Dept, Miami, Fl, commun oper, 1981-84, police officer, 1984-. **Orgs:** Head Orgn Newsletter, Miami Community Police Benevolent Asn, 1985-; exec bd mem, Miami Community Police Benevolent Asn, 1985-; pres, Miami Community Police Benevolent Asn, 1985; Nat Black Police Asn, 1985-; Fla Women Law Enforcement, 1990-. **Honors/Awds:** Training Adverse Award, Basic Law Enforcement Classes, 1987-89; President's Award, Miami Community Police Benevolent Asn, 1990-91; Community Service Award, People United Lead Struggle, 1990. **Home Phone:** (305)433-9587. **Business Addr:** Police Officer, Miami Police Department, 400 NW 2nd Ave, Miami, FL 33128, **Business Phone:** (305)579-6624.

BARNES, DR. ELSIE M.
College administrator, educator. **Educ:** NC A&T Univ, BS, polit sci; Ind Univ, MA, teaching polit sci; Lehigh Univ,DA; Univ NC, pub admin. **Career:** Norfolk State Univ, vpres acad affairs & prof polit sci, currently. **Orgs:** Instrnl Progs Adv Comt, State Coun Higher Educ Va; Am Soc Pub Admin; AmPolit Sci Assn; Conf Minority Publ Adminr; ad brd, Va Correctional Enterprises; pres & bd mem, Va Beach HOME Inc. **Business Addr:** Acting Vice President of Academic Affairs, Professor of Political Science, Norfolk State University, Department Acad Affairs, 460 Harrison B Wilson Hall 700 Pk Ave Suite 460, Norfolk, VA 23504, **Business Phone:** (757)823-8408.

BARNES, ERNIE, JR.
Artist, football player. **Personal:** Born Jul 15, 1938, Durham, NC; son of Ernest Barnes Sr and Fannie Mae Geer; married Bernadine C Gradney, Dec 1984; children: Deidre, Michael, Sean, Erin, Paige. **Educ:** NC Cent Univ, BA, 1960. **Career:** Baltimore Colts, offensive guard, 1959; San Diego Chargers, offensive guard, 1960-63; Denver Broncos, offensive guard, 1963-64; NY Jets, off artist, 1966; Am Football League, off artist, 1966; Creator: Super Comedy Bowl, 1969-70; The Co Art, artist, founder & pres, 1970-; Summer Olympic Games, off sports artist, 1984. **Orgs:** Screen Actors Guild; Nat Football League Players Asn. **Honors/Awds:** Sport Artist of the Year Award, Am Sport Art Mus & Archives, 1984, 2004; Sports Artist of the Year, US Sports Acad, 1985; Honoree, Mus African Am Art, 1988; Honorary DFA, NC Cent Univ, 1990. **Special Achievements:** Paintings featured 4 seasons, "Good Times"; from Pads to Palette, WRS Publ, 1994; "A Life Restored" comn by Kanye West, 2005. **Business Addr:** Owner, The Company of Arts, 8613 Sherwood Dr, West Hollywood, CA 90069, **Business Phone:** (310)652-2941.*

BARNES, FANNIE BURRELL
Librarian. **Personal:** Born in New Orleans, LA; married Richard Alexander Barnes; children: Erica Arnetta, Maria Monique. **Educ:** Dillard Univ, AB, 1945; Atlanta Univ, MS, 1950. **Career:** Gilbert Acad New Orleans, teacher eng, 1945-49; Atlanta Univ, asst libr summer, 1950-67; Claflin Col Orangeburg, SC, head libr, 1950-54; Clark Col Atlanta, head libr, 1954, teacher C lit; Atlanta Pub Libr Bookmobile, C libr summer, 1961. **Orgs:** Am Libr Asn; Nat Educ Asn; Nat Asn Advan Colored People; Alpha Kappa Alpha.

BARNES, JOHNNIE DARNELL
Football player. **Personal:** Born Jul 21, 1968, Suffolk, VA. **Educ:** Hampton Univ. **Career:** Football player (retired); San Diego Chargers, wide receiver, 1992-94; Pittsburgh Steelers, 1995. *

BARNES, JOSEPH NATHAN
Lawyer. **Personal:** Born Nov 29, 1950, Hermondale, MO; son of John Wesley and Lillie Mae; children: Julius. **Educ:** Ibadan Univ Nigeria, Cert Int Econs, 1971; Antioch Col, BA, finance & com, 1973; Univ Pa, MBA, 1977, Sch Law, JD, 1977. **Career:** Spearman & Sterling, assoc atty, 1977-81; Zimet Haines Moss & Friedman, assoc atty, 1981-82; Barnes & Williams, partner, 1982-85; Barnes & Darby, partner, 1985; Barnes, McGhee, Neal, Poston & Segue, founding partner, currently. **Orgs:** Fel, Nat Fel Found, 1973 & 1974; Nat Bar Asn, 1981-87; dir, Black Entertainment & Sports Lawyers Asn, 1983-88; bd mem, Urban League Manhattan Br, 1985-87; Metro Black Bar Asn, 1986-87, Nat Asn Securities Profs, 1986-87; NY chmn, telethon United Negro Col Fund 1986, 1987, 1988; Nat Asn Advan Colored People. **Honors/Awds:** Rockefeller Grant, 1968 & 1973. **Special Achievements:** First Black NY Law firm listed in Directory of Municipal Bond Dealers, 1987. **Home Addr:** 150 W End Ave Suite 19M, New York, NY 10023. **Business Addr:** Founding Partner, Barnes, McGhee, Neal, Poston & Segue, 888 7th Ave Suite 1809, New York, NY 10019-3201, **Business Phone:** (212)944-1095.*

BARNES, DR. LEONARD C.
Educator, administrator. **Career:** Southern Univ, Shreveport Campus, chancellor, 1970-87, chief exec officer, vpres & chancellor emer, currently. **Orgs:** Bd mem, Shreveport Found; bd mem, La Community & Tech Col Syst. **Honors/Awds:** All-American running back, 1941-42, 1946; inducted, Sports Hall of Fame, Southern Univ, 1989; inducted, Southwestern Athletic Conference Hall of Fame, 1994. **Business Addr:** Chancellor Emeritus, Southern University, Shreveport Campus, 3050 Dr Martin Luther King Jr Dr, Shreveport, LA 71107.*

BARNES, LIONEL, JR.
Football player. **Personal:** Born Apr 19, 1976, New Orleans, LA. **Educ:** Univ La, Monroe. **Career:** St Louis Rams, defensive tackle, 1999; Indianapolis Colts, 2000-01; Jacksonville Jaguars, defensive end, 2003-04. *

BARNES, MARTIN G.
Mayor. **Personal:** Born Mar 5, 1948, Paterson, NJ; married Diane Judith Grant; children: Gregory, Antoinette & Marcus. **Educ:** Seton Hall Univ, BS Edn. **Career:** Sterling Drug Co, sales & mgr 1968-72; HUD Target Proj Prog, coord dir, 1975-77; Barnes Assoc Bus Mgt Consult, pres 1975-; RP Vivino Esq, priv investr, 1975-; Passaic Co Dept Youth Serv, dir, 1977-79; City Peterson, coun pres, 1991-93; Hacken sack Mea dowlands Develop Comn, dir admin, 1990-94; elected City Coun pres, 1991-93; mayor, 2002. **Honors/Awds:** Outstanding Young Man Concerned Citizens of Paterson, 1976; Hon Mem, Brosin Blue 1976; Man of the Year, Tom brock Col, 1977. *

BARNES, MATTHEW MOLENA
Community activist. **Personal:** Born Jan 28, 1933, Homer, LA; son of Matthew Molena Sr and Addie Mae; married Clara Mae Lee Barnes, Dec 3, 1958 (died 1990); children: Danette LaTrise Barnes Perry. **Educ:** Contra Costa Community Col; Calif State Univ; Hayward Univ; The Univ Calif. **Career:** Mare Island Naval Shipyard, marine machinist, 1951-55, machinist, 1955-63, foreman machinist, 1963-64, equipment spl, 1964-65, engr tech methods & stand, 1965-66, foreman machinist, 1966-73, eng tech prev maint, 1973-81, prog mgr, 1981-88; Greater Richmond Community Devlop Corp, Nat Asn Advan Colored People, pres, currently, community activist, currently; past supt, Sunday Sch. **Orgs:** Mare Island Super Asn; Super Toastmasters Club; pres, Richmond Br, Nat Asn Advan Colored People, past vpres, Northern Area Conf, officer, Calif State Conf; choir bd, Stewarts Davis Chapel CME Church; past chmn, Scholar Com Davis Chapel CME Church; Richmond City Human Rel Speakers Bur; chmn bd, Richmond City Youth Serv Bur; Shipyard Comdr Equal Employment Opp Adv Com; pres, The Original 21'ers Club; staff mem, state assembly mem Bob Campbell. **Honors/Awds:** First Black Supervisor Mare Island Naval Shipyard. **Military Serv:** AUS, 2 yrs; Army, res, 21 yrs, master sgt (retired). **Business Addr:** Community Activist, President, National Association for the Advancement of Colored People, PO Box 2402, Richmond, CA 94802.

BARNES, MELODY
Government Official. **Personal:** Born Apr 29, 1964. **Educ:** Univ of North Carolina, BA, 1986; received her law degree from the Univ of Michigan. **Career:** Served as Assistant Counsel to the House Judiciary Subcommittee on Civil and Constitutional Rights, where she helped enact into law the voting rights Improvement Act of 1992; Dir of Legislative Affairs for the US Equal Employment Opportunity Commission; Chief counsel to Sen. Edward M. Kennedy, 1995-2003; Exec VP for policy at the Center for American Progress, headed by John D. Podesta; Dir of White House Domestic Policy Council, 2009-. **Orgs:** Member of the New York State and District of Columbia bar associations; member of the board of dir of The Constitution Project, EMILY'S List, and The Maya Angelou Public Charter School. **Business Addr:** The Domestic Policy Council, The White House, 1600 Pennsylvania Ave, NW, Washington, DC 20500.*

BARNES, MILTON, JR.
Automotive executive. **Educ:** Xavier Univ; Univ Cincinnati. **Career:** Yorba Linda, dealer; Gen Motors Co; Classic Chevrolet, pres & cheif exec officer, 1999-. **Orgs:** Nat Automobile Dealers Asn Acad, 1999-. **Business Addr:** President, Chief Executive Officer, Classic Chevrolet, 1001 N Weir Canyon Blvd, Anaheim, CA 92807, **Business Phone:** (714)283-5400.*

BARNES, N KURT
Executive. **Personal:** Born Jan 11, 1947, Washington, DC; son of Norman H and Doris Boyd. **Educ:** Yale Col, BA, econ, 1968; Harvard Univ, MA, 1973. **Career:** Rand Corp, assoc economist, 1968-73; Fortune Mag, assoc ed, 1973-75; Time Inc, financial analyst, 1975-77; Inco Limited, financial analyst, dir investor rels & pres, 1977-98; Marquest Investment Coun Ltd, chmn, 1989-91; Morgan Stanley Dean Witter Investment Mgt, vpres, 1999-; Hale House Ctr, chief financial officer, 2002; Amnesty Int USA, interim dep exec dir; Episcopal Church USA, treas & chief financial officer, 2003-. **Orgs:** Treas, Hale Found 1974-; Friends Legal Defense Fund; treas, Episcopal Charities NY. **Honors/Awds:** John Hay Whitney Fel, 1970-71; Harvard Graduate Prize Fellowship, 1971-73. **Home Addr:** 1 Sherman Sq, New York, NY 10023. **Business Addr:** Treasurer, Chief Financial Officer, The Episcopal Church Center, 815 Second Ave, New York, NY 10017, **Business Phone:** (212)922-5296.

BARNES, PAUL DOUGLAS
Government official. **Personal:** Born Dec 20, 1946, Henderson, TN; married Faye L Rainey; children: Richard, Michael & Felica. **Educ:** Lane Col, BS, 1968; Univ Southern Calif, MPA, 1977; Harvard Univ. **Career:** Soc Sec Admin, Columbia, TN, claims rep, 1968-70, admin officer, 1970-73, prog analyst, 1973-77, area dir, 1977-79, regional comnr, 1990-96; Social Security Admin, Dep Comnr Human Res, 1997; Social Security Admin, Atlanta, regional comnr, 2002-. **Orgs:** Am Soc Pub Admin; Omega Psi Phi; Nat Asn Advan Colored People; chmn, Atlanta Fed Exec Bd, 2004; United Methodist Church. **Honors/Awds:** Special Achievement Award, 1971 & 1974; Superior Performance Award,1975-92; Leadrship Award, Social Security Admin, 1992; Meritorious Service Award, Pres Bush, 1992; Distinguished Executive Award, Pres Clinton, 1995; Federal Executive of the Year, 1997; Meritorious Service Award, Pres Clinton, 1998; Federal Hispanic Heritage Month Excellence Award, 1999; Distinguished Executive Award, Pres Clinton, 2000; National Public Service Award, NAPA, ASPA, 2001; Roger Jones Award, Am Univ, 2001; Equal Employment Opportunity Award, Secy Dept Health & Human Servs; first recipient of the Social Security Commissioner's Personal Achievement Award, 2002; Commissioner's Trailblazer Award for "Successfully guiding the Social Security Administration in the implementation of the electronic Disability Process through exemplary Initiative, Leadership, Determination and Practicality", 2005. **Business Addr:** Regional Commissioner, Social Security Administration, Atlanta Fed Ctr, 61 Forsyth St SW Suite 20T45, Atlanta, GA 30303-8920.*

BARNES, QUACY (QUACY TIMMONS)
Basketball player. **Personal:** Born Sep 26, 1976; daughter of John and Sonia Wright; married Desmond; children: Trenell Domonic Bell. **Educ:** Indiana Univ, phys educ, 1998. **Career:** Basketball player (retired), basketball coach; Sacramento Monarchs, 1998; Cleveland Rockers, 1999; Seattle Storm, 2000-01; Phoenix Mercury, ctr, 2002; Ind Womens Basketball, asst coach; Eastern Ill Univ Panther Athletics, asst coach, 2006-. **Business Addr:** Assistant Coach, Eastern Illinois University Panther Athletics, Department of Athletics, 600 Lincoln Ave, Charleston, IL 61920, **Business Phone:** (217)581-6014.*

BARNES, RONALD LEWIS
Chief executive officer. **Personal:** Born May 2, 1951, Farmville, NC; son of Carlillia Bethea Barnes; married Dannie Edwina, Aug 28, 1976; children: Tiffany Monique. **Educ:** NC A&T State Univ, BS, econ, sociol, 1972; Trinity Univ, MS, urban studies, 1974. **Career:** ATE Mgt Serv Co Inc, assoc, 1973-74; Greater Lynchburg Transit Co, dir mktg, pre & plan, 1974-76; B'ham & Jefferson Cty Transit Authority, asst resident mgr, 1976-80; Transit Mgt Wayne & Oakland Ctys, Inc, gen mgr, 1980-81; Western Reserve Transit Authority, exec dir, gen mgr, 1981; Madison Metro Transit, gen mgr, 1982-88; Gr Cleve Regional Transit Authority, deputy gen mgr, 1989-; Cent Ohio Transit Authority, pres & chief exec officer, currently. **Orgs:** Conference Minority Transit Officials; Am Public Transit Asn Scholarship Found; Western Reserve Historical Soc; Greater Cleve Coun Boy Scouts Am; pres, Black Professionals Asn Charitable Found; Nat Forum for Black Public Administrators; Blacks In Mgt; dir, Prof on the Move. **Honors/Awds:** United Negro Col Fund, Distinguished Service Citation, 1979; ATE, President Award, 1987; Conference of Minority Transit Officials, Executive of the Year, 1992; Dollars & Sense Magazine, America's Best & Brightest Business & Professional Men Award, 1993; NC A & T State Univ Alumni, Distinguished Service Award, 1994. **Business Addr:** President, Chief Executive Officer, Central Ohio Transit Authority, 1600 McKinley Ave, Columbus, OH 43222-1093, **Business Phone:** (614)275-5800.

BARNES, STEPHEN DARRYL
Lawyer. **Personal:** Born May 29, 1953, Los Angeles, CA; son of John J and Marian E. **Educ:** Univ Southern Calif, BA, 1978; Harvard Law Sch, JD, 1981. **Career:** Covington & Burling, assoc, 1981-86; Weissmann Wolff et al, assoc, 1986-87; Strange & Nelson, partner, 1987-89; Bloom, Hergott, Cook, Diemer & Klein, partner, 1989-; Barnes Morris Klein Mark Yorn Barnes & Levine, partner, 2002-, atty, currently. **Orgs:** Local Spiritual Assembly Baha'i Faith, 1981-; Calif Bar Asn; Am Bar Asn. **Business Addr:** Attorney, Partner, Barnes Morris Klein Mark Yorn Barnes & Levine, 1424 2nd St 3rd Fl, Santa Monica, CA 90401, **Business Phone:** (310)319-3900.

BARNES, THOMAS V.
Mayor. **Personal:** Born Apr 23, 1936, Marked Tree, AR; son of Ollie Garfield and Thelma Louise Brooks; married Francis Jean Carroll; children: Paul Matthew. **Educ:** Purdue Univ, BS, 1958; DePaul Univ, JD, 1972; AUS Command & Gen Staff Col. **Career:** Pvt pract, atty, Gary, IN 1972-88; City Gary, mayor, 1988-95. **Orgs:** Life mem, NAACP; founding mem, James G Kimbrough Law Asn; life mem, Res Officers Asn; AMVETS; Lions Clubs Intl, Dunes Chap; hon bd dir, Brother's Keeper; St Monica-Luke Cath Church; Alpha Phi Alpha. **Military Serv:** USAR, col, JAGC; Meritorious Serv Medal, 1985.

BARNES, VIVIAN LEIGH
Government official. **Personal:** Born Aug 9, 1946, Wilkinson, WV; daughter of James Wilder and Margaret Lawson Anderson; married Leroy P, Mar 9, 1974; children: Charles Pershon, Jamila Kali & Nathifa Oni. **Educ:** Delta Col; SaginaWVAlley State Univ, BA, sociol, commun, 1996. **Career:** Greater Omaha Community Action Youth Prog, asst dir, 1969-71; Opportunity Indust Ctr, exec secy, 1974-76; Delta Col, Univ Ctr, admin sec, 1977-79; Buena Vista Charter Twp, twp clerk, 1980-90, trustee, 1991-92. **Orgs:** Exec bd mem, Saginaw City Dem Party, 1980-, vice chair, Mich Dem Black Caucus, 1980-; alt delegate, Mich Dem State Cent, 1980-; comnr, Mich Econ & Social Opportunities Comn; bd mem, Saginaw County Community Action Agency. **Honors/Awds:** Community Service Delta Col Black Honors Award, 1983. **Home Addr:** 151 Barbara Lane, Saginaw, MI 48601-9469. *

BARNES, WILLIAM L.
Lawyer. **Personal:** Born Nov 28, 1936, Benton Harbor, MI; married Patricia Jean; children: Barbara. **Educ:** Los Angeles City Col, AA, 1962; Van Norman Univ, BS, 1965; Univ Southern Calif, JD, 1969. **Career:** Litton Syst, analyst, 1963-65; Northrop Corp, buyer & contracts admin, 1965-69; workmen's comp specialist, 1969-71; Fibre-Therm, gen coun & vpres; Barnes & Grant, atty, 1971-. **Orgs:** Nat Bar Asn; Am Bar Asn; Nu Beta Epsilon Nat Law; Am Trial Lawyers Asn; Calif Lawyers Criminal Justice; Los Angeles Trial Lawyers Asn; Kappa Alpha Psi; Shriners, Free Mason Scottish Rite. **Honors/Awds:** Scholarship, Balwin-Wallace Col, 1953. **Military Serv:** USAF, sgt, maj co-pilot B-47E SAC, 1957; Outstanding Crew Chief, 1955.

BARNES, WILLIE R.
Lawyer. **Personal:** Born Dec 9, 1931, Dallas, TX; married Barbara Bailey; children: Michael, Sandra; Traci, Wendi, Brandi. **Educ:** Univ Calif, Los Angeles, BA, polit sci, 1953, sch Law, JD, 1959. **Career:** State Calif, Dept Corps, various atty positions, 1960-68, supvr corps coun, 1968-70, asst comnr, 1970-75, comnr corps, 1975-79; Univ Calif, Los Angeles, Alumni Asn, gen coun, dir, 1983-86; Manatt Phelps Rothenberg & Phillips, sr partner, 1979-88; Wyman Bautzer, Kuchel & Silbert, sr partner, 1989-91; Katten, Muchin, Zavis & Weitzman, sr partner, 1991-92; Musick, Peeler & Garrett LLP, sr partner, 1992-. **Orgs:** Exec comt, Bus & Corps Sec, 1970-86; vpres, dir, Univ Calif, Los Angeles, Law Alumni Asn, 1973; Comn Real Estate Franchises Mutual Funds; chmn, SEC Liasion Comn, 1974-78; chmn, Real Estate Investment Comn, 1974-78; pres, Midwest Securities Community Asn, 1978-79; first vpres, N Am Securities Admin Asn, 1978-79; co-managing ed, Calif Bus Law Reporter, 1983; exec comn, Corp & Commercial Law Sec, Beverly Hills Bar Asn; bd govs, Century City Bar Asn, 1982-84; vice chmn, Comn Corp; vice chmn, Oil Investment Comn; active leadership directing Securities Reg Prog Calif; vice chair, exec comt, Bus Law Sec, Calif State Bar, 1983-86; Corp Banking & Bus Law, Fed Regulation Securities, Commodities, Franchises & State Regulation Comts; Am Bar Asn; chmn, bd trustees, Wilshire United Methodist Church, 1986-91; chmn, Knox Keene Health Care Service Plan Comn, 1976-79; chmn, Leveraged Real Estate Task Force, 1985-86; Calif Senate Comn CRE Governance; Independent Comn Review Los Angeles Police Dept; advy bd, Inst CRE Coun. **Honors/Awds:** Certificate of Appreciation, Practicing Law Inst, 1973; Law School, Alumnus of the Year, Univ Calif Los Angeles, 1976; Resolutions of Commendation, Calif State Senate & Assembly, 1979. **Special Achievements:** Major role in developing uniform standards for real estate progs on nationwide basis; Acknowledged expert in real estate & oil & gas securities. **Military Serv:** USY, pfc, 1954-56. **Business Addr:** Partner, Musick Peeler & Garrett LLP, 1 Wilshire Blvd Suite 2000, Los Angeles, CA 90017-3321.*

BARNES, WILSON EDWARD
Military leader, marshal. **Personal:** Born Jun 9, 1938, Richmond, VA; son of Ora Henderson; married Barbara Jones; children: Kaye, Lynette & Kimberly. **Educ:** Va State Univ, BS, Biol, 1960, MS 1971; Univ Southern Calif, Doctoral Studies. **Career:** Military leader (retired), Marshal (retired); AUS 18th Battalion 4th Training, comdr, 1976-78; Richmond Recruiting Battalion, comdr, 1978-80; Area IV First ROTC Region, comdr, 1982-84; Hq Dept Army ROTC Study Group, dir, 1984-86; US Cent Command, Dep J-1, col, 1986-88. Fla Supreme Ct, marshal, 2001-05. **Orgs:** Asn AUS; Va State Univ Alumni Asn; NAACP; Retired Officer's Asn; Urban League. **Military Serv:** AUS, col, 1960-88; ARCOM; Bronze Star; Meritorious Service Medal; Defense Meritorious Service Medal.

BARNES, YOLANDA L.
Government official. **Personal:** Born Aug 15, 1961, Cleveland, OH; daughter of Ellis Clancy and Henrietta; married James A Barnes, Dec 24, 1985; children: Alayna. **Educ:** Cleveland State Univ, BA, 1983; Cleveland Marshall Col Law, JD, 1987. **Career:** Ohio Bur Worker's Compensation; Indust Comn OH; Ohio Atty Gen Off, asst atty gen, appellees Indust Comn, Ohio. **Orgs:** Ohio State Bar Asn, workers' compensation comm. **Honors/Awds:** Lloyd O Brown Scholar, 1986. **Special Achievements:** Defense litigation, jury trials; appellate pract; mediation, negotiation. **Business Addr:** Assistant Attorney General, Ohio Atty Gen Off, 150 E Gay St Fl 18, Columbus, OH 43215-5148, **Business Phone:** (614)466-6696.*

BARNETT, DR. ALVA P.
Educator. **Personal:** Born May 4, 1947, Jacksonville, FL. **Educ:** Bethune-Cookman Col, BA, 1969; Univ Pittsburgh, MSW, 1971, MPH, 1978, PhD, 1981. **Career:** N Cent Comm MH-MR Ctr Crisis Ctr, asst adm dir, 1971-72, soc work supvr, 1970-75; admin dir, 1972-75; dir consult soc serv, 1975-76; Univ NebrOmaha, assoc prof, currently. **Orgs:** Res consult & prog evaluator, Maternal & Child Health County, Health Dept,PA; United Methodist Community Ctrs Inc; bd dirs, Social Settlement Asn Omaha, 1982-; Chas Drew Health ctr, 1986-, Head Start Child Develop Corp, 1986-. **Honors/Awds:** Listed in Dictionary Inter Nat Biography, 1983; Visiting Scholar Quantitative Methods in Social Research, Michigan University, Ann Arbor1984; Two book chapters & Two articles published. **Business Addr:** Associate Professor, University of Nebraska at Omaha, School of Social Work, Annex 40, 6001 Dodge St, Omaha, NE 68182-0001, **Business Phone:** (402)554-2921.

BARNETT, AMY
Editor. **Career:** Essence Mag, ed, 1999-00; Teen People, managing ed, 2003; Time Inc, managing ed, currently. **Business Addr:** Managing Editor, Time Inc, Time Warner Inc, 1 Time Warner Ctr, New York, NY 10019-8016, **Business Phone:** (212)484-8000.*

BARNETT, CARL L
Automotive executive. **Career:** Paris Ford Lincoln & Mercury, owner; Gulf Freeway Pontiac GMC Truck, pres; Barnett Auto Group, pres, currently. **Orgs:** Bd dirs, Houston Automobile Dealers Asn; bd dirs, Nat Automobile Dealers Asn. **Special Achievements:** Black Enterprises list of top 100 auto dealers, ranked 34, 1994, 31, 1999,18, 2000. **Business Addr:** Owner, Paris Ford Lincoln Mercury, 3411 NE Lp 286, Paris, TX 75460, **Business Phone:** (903)784-2566.

BARNETT, ETHEL S.
Government official. **Personal:** Born Mar 7, 1929, Macon, GA; widowed; children: Prentis Earl Vinson. **Educ:** Pioneer Bus Sch, 1950; Cheyney State Col. **Career:** Government official (retired); Supreme Lib Life Ins Co, ins agent, 1954-55, City Philadelphia Police Dept, officer, 1961-71; Commonwealth Pa, civil serv comnr; State Civil Serv Comn, chmn, 1991-98. **Orgs:** Bd dir, Women Greater Philadelphia, 1978-; consult, PECO Elec Co, 1979-; first Black reg dir, Pa Fedn Dem Women; nat dir, Educ Dept, 1978-; Int Personnel Mgr Asn; PUSH; Elks; Nat Asn Advan Colored People; Nat Asn Female Execs; nat dir resource develop, Am Found Negro Affairs, 1972, 1976, 1978, 1987, 1992, 1998, vpres, treas. **Honors/Awds:** Community Service Award, N Philadelphia Chap, Nat Asn Advan Colored People, 1973; Humanitarian Award, Bell Tel Co Pa, 1976; Outstanding Woman of the Year, Bright Hope Bapt Church, 1977; Patriots Bowl, City Philadelphia, 1980. **Special Achievements:** First Black regional director to Pennsylvania Federation of Democratic Women. *

BARNETT, FRED LEE
Football player, restaurateur. **Personal:** Born Jun 17, 1966, Shelby, MS. **Educ:** Ark State Univ. **Career:** Football player (retired), Restaurateur; Philadelphia Eagles, wide receiver, 1990-95; Miami Dolphins, wide receiver, 1996-97, restaurant, owner, currently. **Honors/Awds:** Pro Bowl, 1992. *

BARNETT, KEN
Business owner. **Personal:** Married Helene Morgan. **Career:** Lagniappe Bed & Breakfast, innkeeper, currently. **Business Phone:** (504)899-2120.

BARNETT, LORNA
Chiropractor. **Personal:** Born Sep 5, 1951, Trinidad, Trinidad and Tobago; daughter of Theodora J Barnett; children: Ki Joy, Sophia, Angelika Morris. **Educ:** Brooklyn Col, attended 1978; Pratt Inst, attended 1987; NY Chiropractic Col, DC, 1991. **Career:** New York Tel, supvr, comput opers, 1982; self-employed, massage therapist & chiropractor, currently. **Orgs:** NYZS; NY Chiropractic Coun. **Business Phone:** (718)399-1709.*

BARNETT, ROBERT
Government official. **Personal:** Born Apr 21, 1938, Fayetteville, GA; son of Robert and R C Hightower; married Bessie Pearl Burch, Nov 7, 1964; children: Robert Terrance. **Educ:** Morris Brown Col, BA, 1961; Ga State Univ, MA. **Career:** Atlanta Housing Authority, admin intern, 1966-67, bus relocation adv, 1967-69, proj coordr, 1969-71, asst dir redevelop, 1971-75, dir redevelop, 1975-; HUD, Atlanta, GA, regional rehab mgt officer, 1981-; Barnett & Assocs, PA, pres & owner, currently. **Orgs:** Basketball & football referee, S Conf Official Asn, 1965-; Nat Asn Housing & Redevelop Officials, 1966-; Ford Fel Scholar, Ga State Univ, 1970; Resurgens, 1971-; vice chmn, Salvation Army Adv Coun, 1974-; Leadership Atlanta, 1978-; first vpres, W Manor Elem Sch PTA, 1979-; bd trustees, Morris Brown Col, 1989-; pres, Morris Brown Col Athletic Found, 1985-; pres, Capitol City Officials Asn, 1980-. **Honors/Awds:** Annual Housing Award, Interfaith Inc, Atlanta, 1976; Certificate of Appreciation for Outstanding Performance, Atlanta Housing Authority, 1977; Hall of Fame, inductee Morris Brown Col, TAY Club, 1978; Federal Employee of the Year, Civic & Community Servs, Fed Exec Bd, 1989; Atlanta Univ Ctr Hall of Fame, Extra Point Club Inc, 1990. **Military Serv:** AUS, cpl; Certificate for Outstanding Service & Achievements, 1964. **Home Addr:** 3317 Spreading Oak Dr SW, Atlanta, GA 30311. **Business Addr:** President, Principal Owner, Barnett & Associates PA, 1000 N Ashley Dr, Tampa, FL 33602, **Business Phone:** (813)224-9510.

BARNETT, DR. SAMUEL B.
Educator. **Personal:** Born May 5, 1931, Philadelphia, PA; son of Solomon and Jennie; married Dorothy; children: Diane, Avonna, Christopher, Samuel, Donna & Betty. **Educ:** Temple Univ, AA, BS; Kean Col, MA; Rutgers Univ, EdD; Univ Pa, Fels Inst; Woodrow Wilson Sch Princeton Univ, Southeastern Univ, PhD, 1979. **Career:** City Philadelphia, PA, police officer, 1957-62; Philadelphia Area Delinquent Youth Prog, proj dir, 1965-67; German town Settlement, Philadelphia, PA, youth work counr, 1965-68; State Pa, parole officer, 1967-68; Social Learning Lab Educ Testing Serv, prof assoc res div, 1968-82; Veterans Admin, Philadelphia, PA, benefits counr, 1985-86(retired). **Orgs:** Am Personnel & Guidance Asn; Am Soc Criminol; Nat Coun Measurement Educ; Nat Asn Blacks Criminal Justice Syst; bd dirs, Timberlake Camp Charities Inc. **Honors/Awds:** Chamber of Commerce Award, City Philadelphia; Pop Warner All-American Football Player, 1950; Police Dept Commemdation Bravery, City Philadelphia, 1959, Badge & Key Award, 1959; Award for Outstanding ServiceYouth, 1967. **Military Serv:** AUS, 1946-49; R A, Korea, 1951-53; Paratrooper Badge; Combat Infantry mans Badge; Several other military Awards. *

BARNETT, TEDDY
Accountant. **Personal:** Born Mar 12, 1948, Freeport, NY; married Carol Ann Grier; children: Joell Carol, Jason Theodore, Jordan Dai. **Educ:** Boston Univ, BS, 1970. **Career:** Price Waterhouse & Co, sr acct, 1970-75; Bedford Stuyvesant Restoration Corp, dir int audit, 1976-78, dir fin admin, 1978-79, vpres fin & admin, 1980-81, exec vpres, 1981-82, pres, 1982. **Orgs:** Bd dirs, Enock Star Restoration Housing Develop Fund; Stearns Park Civic Asn; Nat Asn Accountants; Nat Asn Black Accountants; bd dir Brooklyn Arts Coun; Am Red Cross, Greater NY Brooklyn Chap. **Honors/Awds:** Black Achievers in Industry Award, 1974; American Achievement Award, Key Woman 1984.

BARNETT-REYES, SAUNDRA
Psychiatrist. **Career:** St Joseph's Hosp Health Ctr, psychiat, currently. **Orgs:** Am Bd Psychiatry & Neurol. **Business Addr:**

Psychiatry, St Josephs Hosp Health Center, 301 Prospect Ave, Syracuse, NY 13203, **Business Phone:** (315)448-5111.*

BARNEY, LEMUEL JACKSON (LEM BARNEY)
Executive, football player, baptist clergy. **Personal:** Born Sep 8, 1945, Gulfport, MS; son of Lemuel Barney Sr and Burdell; married Jacci; married Benny; married Martha; children: Lemuel III & LaTrece. **Educ:** Jackson State Univ, BS, 1967. **Career:** Football player (retired), clergy; Detroit Lions, cornerback, 1967-77; Black Entertainment TV, sports analyst, 1992; MichCon, community activities specialist, 1992-93; Mel Farr Automotive Group, finance dir, 1993-2001; Springhill Missionary Baptist Church, baptist minister, currently. **Orgs:** Kappa Alpha Psi Fraternity Inc; bd dir, Prison Fellowship Ministries. **Honors/Awds:** Defensive Rookie of the Yr, 1967; Elected to Pro Football Hall of Fame, inducted, Aug 1, 1992; elected to Afro-Am Sports Hall of Fame, inducted, March 2, 1992. **Special Achievements:** Warner-Lambert Celebrity Super Bowl Classic, golfer, 1992.

BARNEY, WILLIE J
Executive, president (organization). **Personal:** Born Oct 10, 1927, Parkdale, AR; married Hazel Willis; children: Ronald, Reginald, Raymond & Reynaldo. **Career:** WISEC C, pres, founder, 1967-70; Consol Record Distrib, pres, 1968-; Pyramid Int, pres 1953-66; Barney's Records Inc, pres, 1953-96. **Orgs:** Sr warden Masons Masonic Chicago, 1959-69; Westside Bus Asn, 1973-75; mkt & com Black Music Asn, 1978-; treas, Operation Brotherhood, 1979-. **Honors/Awds:** Businessman Award, FORUM, 1975; Service Award, Lu Palmer Found & Fernwood Meth Ch, 1976; Service Award, CBS Records, 1978. **Military Serv:** AUS, pvt. **Business Addr:** President, Barney, 3145 W Roosevelt Rd, Chicago, IL 60612-3939, **Business Phone:** (773)521-6300.

BARNWELL, ANDRE
Educator, fashion designer. **Educ:** Howard Univ, BA. **Career:** Andre Barnwell Frangrances Inc, pres & designer, currently; The Fashion Inst Design & Merchandising, adj prof, currently. **Business Phone:** (562)529-5955.

BARNWELL, HENRY LEE
Clergy. **Personal:** Born Aug 14, 1934, Blountstown, FL; married Shelie Yvonne Whiley; children: Aubrey, Cassandra, Timothy, Darlene. **Educ:** Univ MD; Ariz Col, BA, 1978; St Stephens Col, MS, 1979; Carolina Christian Univ, doctorate ministry, 1984; Grand Canyon Col; Talbot Theol Sem, Biola Univ; Lacy Kirk Williams Minster's Inst, Bishop Col. **Career:** USAF, flight examr, 1954-70, recruiter, 1971-74; Maricopa City Personnel, admin aide, 1977-80; Bishop Can & 1st State Bishop Ariz, pastor, currently. **Orgs:** Chmn, Evangelism Bd Area I AB PSW, 1970-83; exec bd mem, Phoenix AZ PUSH Inc, 1979-; chaplain, Juv Dept Corrections, 1980-; exec bd mem, Phoenix OIC, 1980-; moderator, Area I Am Baptist Pac SW, 1984-; pres, Interdenominational Ministerial Alliance, 1984-; reg dir, Nat Evangelism Movement, 1984-; relig adv coun mem, Maricopa City Sheriff Dept, 1984-; Libr Cong. **Honors/Awds:** Community Serv Award, Williamsfield AFB, 1975-78; Hon Citizen of Tucson City, 1980; Outstanding Citizen Award, Citizens Phoenix, 1982; Appreciation Award, 82nd Flying Training Wing, 1984; Floyd Adams Community Serv Award, Phoenix OIC; Relig Award, Maricopa County Br, Nat Asn Adv Colored People; Recognition Christian Serv Award, Nat Evangelism Workshop. **Military Serv:** USAF, E-7 sgt, 1954-74; Airmans Medal, Air Force Commendation. **Home Addr:** 11633 N 49th Dr, Glendale, AZ 85304. *

BARR, LEROY
Police officer. **Personal:** Born Jul 1, 1936, New York, NY; married Virginia; children: Denise, LeRoy Jr & Nicole. **Educ:** John Jay Col, AA, 1970, BS, 1971; New York Univ, MA, 1973. **Career:** Youth House Girls, couns, 1959-64; New York City Bd Educ, teacher,1971-73; Brooklyn Col, coun, 1973; New York City Police Dept, supvr. **Orgs:** Asn Black Psychologists; 100 Black Men; Am Personnel & Guid Asn; Am Acad Prof Law Enforce; dir, Black Family & marriage Coun, 1976-. **Military Serv:** Sgt 1954-57. **Business Addr:** Supervisor, NY City Police Department, 1 Police Plz, New York, NY 10038.

BARR-BRACY, ADRIAN (ADRIAN E BRACY)
Vice president (organization), sports agent. **Personal:** Married Vernon; children: Donovan. **Educ:** Morgan State Univ, Baltimore, BA, acct; Nova SE Univ, Fort Lauderdale, Fla, MBA. **Career:** The Baltimore Sun, acct, 1983-86; Athletic player (retired), Athletic director; Wake Forest Univ, sports marketer and acct exec, 1989, dir community programs, 1991-94, asst athletic dir, 1995-99; Bowie State Univ, athletics dir, 2000-02; NC A&T State Univ, athletics dir, 2002-04. **Honors/Awds:** St. Louis Business Journals Most Influential Business Women Award, 2006; YWCA Metro St. Louis Leader of Distinction Award in Corporate Management, 2006; 50 Most Powerful Black Women in Business, 2006. *

BARR-DAVENPORT, LEONA
President (Organization). **Personal:** Married Jewel L Davenport. **Educ:** Benedict Col, BS; MBA. **Career:** Atlanta Bus League, pres & chief exec officer, currently. **Orgs:** Antioch Baptist Church N. **Honors/Awds:** Keeper of the Dream Award, 1997; Ordinary Women with Extraordinary Talents Award, 1998; President's Award, Concerned Black Clergy, 2000; Community Achievement Award; Pinnacle Leadership Award, Fortitude Educ & Cult Develop Found, 2002; Advocacy Award, Nat Asn Minority Contractors. **Business Addr:** President, Chief Executive Officer, Atlanta Business League, 931 Martin Luther King Dr, PO Box 92363, Atlanta, GA 30314, **Business Phone:** (404)584-8126.

BARRETT, AUDRA (AUDRA BARRETT SHIVERS)
Business owner. **Personal:** Born Mar 12, 1967, Richmond, VA; daughter of William and Barbara; married Roderic A Shivers, May 27, 1999. **Educ:** Southern Ill Univ, BS, jour, 1989. **Career:** Richmond-Times Dispatch Newspaper, advert rep, 1989-90; Pharmaceut Mfrs Am, commun asst, 1992-93; Paralyzed Veterans Am, communs asst, 1993-98; communs consult, 1998-99; Howard Univ, staff writer, 1999-2002; Barrett Books, lit agt, 1999-. **Orgs:** Black Pub Rels Soc, 1996-98; dir, Marlborough Condominium Bd, 1997-2002, pres, 2002-; Women's Nat Book Asn, 2001-02; Nat Asn Black Journalists, 2002-03. **Honors/Awds:** Outstanding Intern, The Voice Newspaper, 1988. **Special Achievements:** Selected as county correspondent for the Washington Afro Newspaper, 1998. **Business Addr:** Literary Agent, Barrett Books, 12138 Central Ave Suite 183, Mitchellville, MD 20721, **Business Phone:** (301)627-2104.

BARRETT, IRIS LOUISE KILLIAN
Executive, founder (originator). **Personal:** Born Aug 28, 1962, Hickory, NC; daughter of James C and Dorothy Booker; married Jathan. **Educ:** Univ NC, BSPH, 1984; Duke Univ, MBA, 1986. **Career:** Duke Univ Fuqua Sch Bus, grad fel, 1984-86; Am Med Int, summer assoc, 1985; Corning Cable Systs, training specialist, 1986-88, prod supvr, 1988-89, supvr training dept telecommuns cable plant, 1989-92, qual & educ mgr, 1992-97, Wildacres Leadership Initiative Friday Fel, 1997-99; Corning Cable Systs, staffing & develop, mgr, 1997-2001, human res dir, cable div, 2001; The Word is My Life Training Ministry, founder & owner, currently. **Orgs:** Am Bus Women's Asn, 1990-94; Grace Pentecostal Holiness Church, 1994-; bd mem, Econo Force, 1994-00; Catawba Valley Community Col; bd mem, Chamber Com, 1995-97; vol, Hospice, 2000-; bd dir, Grace Church, 2001-. **Honors/Awds:** Girl Scout Woman of Distinction Award, 1999; Outstanding Business Woman of Catawba County, 1993. **Business Addr:** Founder, Owner, "The Word is My Life" Training Ministry, PO Box 1771, Hickory, NC 28601, **Business Phone:** (828)327-7848.*

BARRETT, JACQUELYN H
Sheriff. **Personal:** Born Jan 1, 1950; daughter of Cornelius Harrison Sr and Ocie P Harrison; married Gene Washington; children: Kimberly & Alan. **Educ:** Beaver Col, criminal justice; Clark-Atlanta Univ, master's degree, sociol; Arcadia Col, LLD, 2001. **Career:** Ga Peace Officer Stand & Training Coun, 10 yrs; Fulton County Pub Training Safety Ctr, 5 yrs; Fulton County, sheriff, 1992-2004. **Orgs:** Pres, Nat Orgn Black Law Enforcement, 1997-98. **Honors/Awds:** Jean Young Community Service Award; Trumpet Award, Turner Broadcasting System, 1998; Martin Luther King Jr Drum Major for Justice Award; Triple Crown award, 2003. **Special Achievements:** The nation's first African-American female sheriff, Fulton County, 1992.

BARRETT, JAMES A.
Association executive. **Personal:** Born Dec 2, 1932, Cleveland, OH; married Edith Ransby; children: Zina, Jurena. **Educ:** Ky State Univ; Cleveland State Univ. **Career:** E Cleveland City, app city commnr, 1969, elected, 1970-72; E Cleveland Civil Serv, app commnr, 1972-76; E Cleveland Pub Libr, app trustee, 1974-80; Blue Cross NE Ohio, rep labor affairs. **Orgs:** E Cleveland Cits Adv Comn, 1968-69; former bd mem, E Cleveland, YMCA 1972-73; trustee, E Cleveland PA, 1974; past pres, Chamber Mayfair League. **Business Addr:** Representative Labor Affairs, Blue Cross Northeast Ohio, 2066 E 9th St, Cleveland, OH 44112.

BARRETT, MATTHEW ANDERSON
Executive. **Personal:** Born Nov 13, 1947, Roanoke, VA. **Educ:** Va Commonwealth Univ, BS, bus admin, 1974. **Career:** Univ Ford Motor Co, salesman, 1969-70; Standard Drug Stores Inc, asst mgr, 1970-72; Va Commonwealth Univ, comput prog, 1972-76; Seminary Walk Unit Owners Asn, pres, 1986-89; 3M Co, account rep, currently. **Orgs:** Speaker, Richmond Pub Sch Speakers Bur, 1970-74; big brother Big Brothers Richmond, 1970-75; treas, Huntington Club Condominiums, 1980-84; aircraft Owners & Pilots Assoc, 1981-; scuba diver NAUI, 1982-; Seminary Walk Condominium Asn, pres, 1986-90. **Honors/Awds:** Salesman of the Year, 3M Co, 1979-80, Apogee Award, 1989; Prod Award, 3M Co, 1979; Salesman of the Year, 1987. **Business Addr:** Account Representative, 3M Company, 1101 15th St NW, Washington, DC 20005.*

BARRETT, DR. RONALD KEITH
Psychologist, educator. **Personal:** Born Aug 17, 1948, Brooklyn, NY; son of Cyril and Dorothy. **Educ:** Morgan State Univ, Baltimore, BS, psychol, 1970; Univ Pittsburgh, MS, social psychol, 1974, PhD, social psychol, 1977. **Career:** Calif State Univ, Dominguez Hills, asst prof psychol, 1977-78; Open Soc Inst, consult; Philadelphia Co coroner's offs, consult; Mayor's Off City, Baltimore, consult; Loyola Marymount Univ, Dept Psychol, Los Angeles, from asst prof to assoc prof, 1977-96; Acad Int Educ via Univ Bonn, Germany, assoc prof psychol 1995; Loyola Marymount Univ, Dept Psychol, Los Angeles, prof, psychol, 1996-. Loyola Marymount Univ, Dept African Am Studies, Los Angeles, actg chair, 2004-. **Orgs:** Asn Death Educ & Counseling; Int Asn Trauma Counrs; Int Work Group Death, Dying & Bereavement; Asn Black Psychologists; Am Psychological Asn; Asn Traumatic Stress Specialists; Psi Chi Nat Honor Soc Psychol. **Honors/Awds:** Elected Psi Chi Natl Honor Soc, Psychol, 1969; Optimist Club, Man of the Year, 1991; Lay Man of the Year 1991; numerous scholarly publs & citations. **Special Achievements:** Author, "Urban Adolescent Homicidal Violence: An emerging public health concern", 1986, "Urban Adolescent Homicidal Violence: An emerging public health concern", 1993, "Contemporary African-American Funeral Rites and Traditions" In DeSpelder & Strickland's, 1995, "It's How You Play the Game: Amazing things happen when a community reaches out to youth who are at risk", 1996, "Sociocultural Considerations for working Blacks Experiencing Loss and Grief", 1998, "Unresolved Grief and Urban Youth Violence", 2000, "Recommendations for Culturally Competent End-of-life Care Giving", 2001, "Can We Provide Better Aftercare to Blacks?". **Home Addr:** 240 W Queen St Suite 3, Inglewood, CA 90301, **Home Phone:** (310)677-8414. **Business Addr:** Professor Of Psychology, Loyola Marymount University, Univ Hall 4763 1 LMU Dr, Los Angeles, CA 90045, **Business Phone:** (310)338-2995.

BARRETT, SHERMAN L.
Educator. **Personal:** Born Aug 15, 1945, Charleston, SC; children: Larry. **Educ:** Aurora Col, BA, educ, 1967; Adelphi Univ, attended 1966; Univ Wis, Milwaukee, attended 1983. **Career:** MTEA, negotiations, 1969-72; WEA, credentials, 1970-72; NEA, deleg, 1970-72; Milwaukee Recreation, playground ctr dir, 1967-81, basketball coach,1972-85; A L Williams, dist dir, 1985; Milwaukee Pub Schs, teacher, currently. **Orgs:** Vpres, Black Teachers Org, Milwaukee, 1970-72. **Home Addr:** 1626 W Capitol Dr, Milwaukee, WI 53206. **Business Phone:** (414)475-8393.

BARRETT, REV. WALTER CARLIN
Clergy. **Personal:** Born Sep 30, 1947, Richmond, VA; son of Walter Carlin Sr and Elizabeth Norrell. **Educ:** St John Vianney Sem, dipl; St Mary's Sem Col, Catonsville, BA, Philos; St Mary's Sem & Univ, Baltimore, MDiv, Theol. **Career:** Roman Cath Diocese Richmond, priest, 1975-; St Mary's Cath Church, assoc pastor, 1975-77; St Gerard's Cath Church, Roanoke VA, pastor, 1977-85; Basilica St Mary, Norfolk, VA, rector, 1985-2000; Holy Rosary Cath Church, Richmond, VA, pastor, 2001-. **Orgs:** Nat Asn Advan Colored People; Nat Black Cath Clergy Caucus; Black Cath Comn; Black Cath Clergy Conf; Diocesan Pastoral Coun; Diocesan Priest Coun; founder, Richmond Black Cathc Caucus, 1971-74; Exec Comn Priests Coun. **Honors/Awds:** Winner Diocese & Deanery Pub Speaking Contest Richmond Area, 1965; Recognized for Outstanding Service, Roman Catholic Diocese, Richmond 1985; St Mary's a Minor Basilica, 1991; Named "Prelate of Honor", 1996. **Special Achievements:** Only predominately African-American Roman Catholic Church in US with this distinction. **Business Addr:** Pastor, Holy Rosary Catholic Church, 3300 R St, Richmond, VA 23223, **Business Phone:** (804)222-1105.

BARRINGTON, DR. EUGENE L.
Educator. **Educ:** Rutgers Univ, M.Ed; Syracuse Univ, M.Ph, PhD. **Career:** Tex Southern Univ, assoc prof pub admin, currently. **Orgs:** Adv bd, Southern Conf African Am Studies Inc, currently. **Business Addr:** Associate Professor of Public Administration, Texas Southern University, Department of Public Affairs, 3100 Cleburne St, SPA/COLABS Bldg Faculty Suite 402Z, Houston, TX 77004, **Business Phone:** (713)313-7385.

BARROIS, LYNDON J.
Administrator, cartoonist or animator. **Personal:** Born Jun 6, 1964, New Orleans, LA. **Career:** TV series: The PJs, dir, 1999; Film: Parasite Eve, 1998; Kung Pow: Enter the Fist, 2002; Scooby-Doo, 2002; The Matrix Reloaded, 2003; The Matrix Revolutions, 2003; The Karate Dog, 2004; I, Robot, 2004; The Matrix Recalibrated, 2004; Elektra, 2005; The Lion, the Witch & the Wardrobe, 2005; appy Feet, 2006; Night at the Museum, character supvr, 2006; Happy Feet, 2006; Rhythm & Hues, animator supvr, currently. **Business Addr:** Animator Supervisor, Rhythm & Hues, 5404 Jandy Pl, Los Angeles, CA 90066, **Business Phone:** (310)448-7500.*

BARRON, REGINALD
Automotive executive. **Career:** Barron Chevrolet-Geo Inc, Danvers, Mass, chief exec officer, 1984-. **Orgs:** Bd mem, Judge Baker Children's Ctr. **Honors/Awds:** Auto 100, Barron Chevrolet-Geo, Black Enterprise, 1991. **Business Addr:** Chief Executive Officer, Barron Chevrolet-Geo Inc, 90 Andover St, Danvers, MA 01913, **Business Phone:** (508)388-0861.

BARRON, WENDELL
Automotive executive. **Personal:** Married Marta; children: Elena, Randall, Steven. **Educ:** Howard Univ, BS, mech eng, 1966.

Career: Fotor Motors, Buffalo, NY, engr, Dearborn, MI; Campus Ford Inc, Okemos, MI, chief exec officer & pres, 1986-. **Orgs:** pres, Mich Automobile Dealers Asn, 1997; bd mem, Sparrow Hosp. **Business Addr:** Chief Executive Officer, President, Campus Ford Inc, 1830 W Grand River, Okemos, MI 48864, **Business Phone:** 888-719-9553.*

BARROS, DANA BRUCE
Business owner, basketball player. **Personal:** Born Apr 13, 1967, Boston, MA; married Veronica; children: Jordan. **Educ:** Boston Col, MA, 1985. **Career:** Basketball player (retired), business owner; Seattle Supersonics, guard, 1989-93; Philadelphia 76ers, 1993-95; Boston Celtics, 1995-2000, 2004; Detroit Pistons, 2001-02; Dana Barros Sports Complex, owner; Celtics, Media Relations, Currently. **Honors/Awds:** NBA Draft, First round pick, 1989; NBA Most Improved Player, 1995; NBA All-Star Game, 1995. **Business Addr:** Owner, Dana Barros Sports Complex, 31 Oxford Rd, Mansfield, MA 02048, **Business Phone:** (508)337-3100.

BARROW, JOE LOUIS
Executive. **Personal:** Born May 28, 1947, Mexico City, Mexico; son of Joe Louis and Marva Spaulding; married Susan. **Educ:** Univ Denver, BA, 1968. **Career:** United Bank Denver, trust off, asst vpres, 1968-76; US Dept Energy, Off Commercialization Conserv, Solar Energy, dir, 1978-81; Wood Bros, vpres, corp mkt, 1981-82, vpres reg mkt, dir, 1982-85; Ronald H Brown, dir special projects, sr adv; IZZO Systs, pres & chief exec officer; World Golf Found, The First Tee, exec dir & chief executive officer, currently; World Golf Found, sr vpres, currently. **Orgs:** IZZO Systs Inc; IZZO Ltd, UK; Franklin & Eleanor Roosevelt Inst; Planned Parenthood the Rocky Mountains; Nat Golf Found, bd mem, Colo Golf Asn, bd mem; Am Jr Golf Asn; Planned Parenthood Fed Am; Mile High United Way; Univ Denver; Colo Health Facilities Finance Authority; Urban League Colo; Big Brothers Metro Denver; Piton Found Community Dev Project; Denver Metro Chamber Comm. **Special Achievements:** Published, "Joe Louis: 50 Years An American Hero," McGraw-Hill, 1988. **Business Phone:** (904)940-4300.

BARROW, MICHEAL COLVIN
Football player, football coach. **Personal:** Born Apr 19, 1970, Homestead, FL; married Shelley; children: Mikenzi & Caleb. **Educ:** Univ Miami, acct, 1992. **Career:** Football player (retired), coach; Houston Oilers, linebacker, 1993-96; Carolina Panthers, 1997-99; New York Giants, 2000-03; Wash Redskins, 2004; Dallas Cowboys, 2005; Univ Miami, coach, 2007-. **Honors/Awds:** Starting linebacker on national championship teams at Miami in 1989 and 1991; All-America as a senior in 1992; Seventh in voting for the Heisman Trophy in 1992; Second-round draft choice of the Houston Oilers in 1993. *

BARROW, REV. WILLIE T.
Association executive, activist. **Personal:** Born Dec 7, 1924, Burton, TX; married Clyde (deceased); children: Keith (deceased). **Educ:** Univ Monrovia, Monrovia, Liberia, DD. **Career:** First Black Church God Portland, OR, organizer; Malcolm X Col, bd dir, 1976; Vernon Pk Church God, assoc min/bd trustees; Rev Jackson Pres Campaign, nat dep campaign & mgr; Oper PUSH, Chicago, IL, chmn bd; Rainbow/PUSH Coalition Inc, co-chairperson, chmn emer, currently; Vernon Park Church of God, minister justices, currently. **Orgs:** Chairperson, Nat World Peace Coun; Nat Polit Congr Black Women; Nat Urban League, 1943; Nat Coun Negro Women, 1945; commr, Int Women's Yr, 1978; vice chair, Nat Polit Congress Black Women; bd dir, Doctors Hosp Hyde Pk; bd trustees, Bennett Col; bd dirs, Core Found. **Honors/Awds:** Human Serv Award, Chicago Firefighters; Woman of the Yr, City Chicago, 1969; Image Award, League Black Women, 1972; DHL, Bennett Col, 1991; DDiv, Southern Calif Sch Ministry, 1992; Adv Award, Willie T Barrow Wellness Ctr Doctors Hosp, 1998; History Makers Award, Christian Women's Conf, 1998; Trailblazer Award, Ameritech, 1998; Hall of Fame Award, Victor Goodell Memorial Golf Classic, 1998; Legend Award, Rainbow/PUSH Coalition, 1998; Humanitarian of the Year Award, Indo-Am Democratic Org, 1999; Who's Who in Chicano Bus, Crain's Mag, 1999; Dr, Adler Sch; Willie Barrow St, Named in Honor. **Business Addr:** Chairman Emeritus, Rainbow/PUSH Coalition Inc, 930 E 50th St, Chicago, IL 60615-2702, **Business Phone:** (773)373-3366.

BARROWS, PROF. BRYAN H
School administrator, playwright. **Personal:** Born May 21, 1952, Bryan, TX; son of Mable Dolores Sadberry and Bryan H Jr; married Delia De la Cerda, Sep 5, 1992; children: Jerry, Gerald, Marshal & Michelle. **Educ:** Del Mar Col, AA, 1972; Tex A & I Univ Corpus Christi, BA, 1974, MA, 1976. **Career:** HIALCO OIC Inc, counr, off mgr, EEO dir, pub info dir, 1979-81; Amoco Prod Co, admin analyst, 1981-85; Chem Dependency Unit, pub info dir, 1984-85; City CC, counr, 1985; Nueces County MHMR, asst personnel dir & staff develop dir, 1985-86; Del Mar Col, asst prof speech commun, 1985-92; prof speaker, 1988-; Prairie View A&M Univ, pub info dir, 1992, Later PVAMU press officer; N Harris Col, prof speech commun, currently, managing ed, N Star News, 2001-; Author: The Humanities, 2007. **Orgs:** Comn chair, Coastal Bend Pub Rels Asn, 1984-92; Int Community Asn, 1985-92; Speech Community Asn, 1985-91; bd dir, Black United Fund Texas; Del Mar Commun Club, founder/sponsor, 1987-91; Spectrum Comt, Channel 16 PBS, 1989-91; NAACP, 1990-91; adv, N Star News Club. **Honors/Awds:** CC Chamber Com, Leadership Corpus Christi Grad Cert, 1978; Outstanding Young Men of America, US Jaycees, 1983 & 1988; Houston Defender Editorial Achievement Award, Houston Defender Newspaper, 1986; East Campus Teacher of the Year, Del Mar Col Stud Body, 1989 & 1990; Nat Inst Staff Develop, Nat Award Teaching Excellence, Del Mar Col, 1991; Cleo Glenn Johnson Humanitarian Award, 1999; Faculty Excellence Award. **Special Achievements:** Star Film Festival; Excellence in Local TV Award—presented by CC Arts Council to Spectrum TV Show KEDT; presented the Austin Metropolitan Business Resource Center's "Men of Valor" award; US-Philippine Military Award for Merit, 1973; Okinawa Marine Command Commendation, 1973; Plaque for Meritorious Service to US Command, Japan/US Naval Group. **Home Addr:** 7711 Ashton Dr, Houston, TX 77095. **Business Addr:** Professor of Speech Communications, Managing Editor, North Harris College, 2700 WW Thorne Blvd, Houston, TX 77073-3499, **Business Phone:** (281)765-7808.

BARRY, HARRIET S.
Executive. **Educ:** Northwestern Univ, MBA. **Career:** Gen Foods, mkt & brand mgt; Kimberly Clark; Soft Sheen Corp, dir mkt; Urban Ministries Inc, gen mgr, currently, Communion Source, pres, currently. **Business Addr:** General Manager, Urban Ministries Inc, Communion Source, 1551 Regency Ct, Calumet City, IL 60409, **Business Phone:** (708)868-7100.*

BARRY, MARION SHEPILOV
Mayor, politician. **Personal:** Born Mar 6, 1936, Itta Bena, MS; son of Marion S and Mattie; married Effi Slaughter, 1978 (divorced 1992); children: Marion Christopher; married Cora Lavonne Masters, 1993. **Educ:** Le Moyne Col, BS, 1958; Fisk Univ, MS, org chem, 1960; Univ Kans, attended 1961; Univ Tenn, chem studies, 1964. **Career:** Pride Inc, dir opers, 1967; Pride Econ Enterprises, co-founder, chair, dir, 1968; Wash DC Sch Bd, mem, 1971-74; Wash City Coun, mem-at-large, 1975; Wash, DC, mayor, 1979-90, city councilman, 1992-94; City Washington, DC, mayor, 1994-98; Coun DC, council member, Comt Finance & Rev, chair. **Orgs:** Pres, Wash DC Bd Educ, 1972-2006; first nat chmn, SNCC; Third World Coalition Against War; Alpha Phi Alpha Fraternity; pres, Nat Conf Black Mayors; Nat Asn Advan Colored People. **Special Achievements:** Film appearance: Slam, 1998.

BARRY, REV. RICHARD L.M.
Church historian. **Career:** St Agnes Episcopal Church, rector; Historic St Agnes Episcopal Church, rector. *

BARTEE, KIMERA ANOTCHI
Baseball player, athletic coach. **Personal:** Born Jul 21, 1972, Omaha, NE. **Educ:** Creighton Univ. **Career:** Baseball player (retired), Athletic coach; Detroit Tigers, outfielder,1996-99; Cincinnati Reds, 2000; Colo Rockies, 2001; Pittsburgh Pirates, Delmarva Shorebirds, field coach, 2004-207, outfield & base running coordr, coach, 2007-. **Business Addr:** Outfield & Baserunning Coordinator, Pittsburgh Pirates, 600 Stadium Circle, Pittsburgh, PA 15212, **Business Phone:** (412)323-5000.

BARTHELEMY, SIDNEY JOHN
Mayor, executive. **Personal:** Born Mar 17, 1942, New Orleans, LA; son of Ruth Fernandez and Lionel; married Michaele Thibodeaux, 1968; children: Cherrie, Bridget & Sidney Jr. **Educ:** Epiphany Apostolic Jr Col, attended 1963; St Joseph Sem, BA, philos, 1967; Tulane Univ, MSW, 1971. **Career:** Total Community Action, admin asst, 1967-68, asst dir, 1969; Adult Basic Educ Prog, guidance counr & interim dir, 1968-69; New Careers Prog, asst dir, 1969; Parent-Child Ctr, dir, 1969-71, dir social serv, 1971-72; Labour Educ Advancement Prog, Urban League, coordr, 1969-72; City New Orleans Welfare Dept, dir, 1972-74; Xavier Univ, assoc prof sociol, 1974-86; La Legis, St senator, 1974-78; New Orleans City Coun, councilman-at-large, 1978-86; City New Orleans, mayor, 1986-94; Nat Asn Reg Coun, pres, 1987-88; Dem Nat Party, vice chmn voter registration, 1988-89; Nat League Cites, second vpres, 1988; La Conf Mayors, second vpres, 1989-93; Kennedy Sch Gov, Tulane Univ Sch Pub Health & Univ New Orleans Col Educ, adj prof; HRI Properties, dir gov affairs, vpres gov rel, currently. **Orgs:** Vpres, Comm Org Urban Polit; Orleans Parish Dem Exec Comt; chmn, Youth Assistance Coun; bd dir, Cent City Fed Credit Union; bd dir, Family Serv Soc; bd dir, St Bernard Neighborhood Comt Ctr; Comm Serv Ctr; City Park Comn; Dem Nat Comn; Labor Educ Advancement Prog, La Conf Mayors; La Munic Asn; Miss-La-Ala Transit Comn; Nat Asn Advan Colored People; Nat Asn Black Mayors; Nat Asn Co Officials; Nat Asn Reg Couns; Nat Black Couns Local Elected Officials; Nat Inst Educ; New Orleans Asn Black Soc Workers, US Conf Mayors; first vpres, 1989-90, pres, 1990, Nat League Cities. **Honors/Awds:** Purple Knight Award, Best All Around Stud, 1960; Outstanding Alumnus, Tulane Univ; Social Worker of the Year, La Chap, Nat Asn Soc Workers, 1987; American Freedom Award, Third Baptist Church Chicago, 1987; American Spirit Award, USAF Recruiting Serv, 1989; Daniel E Byrd New Orleans Nat Asn Advan Colored People Award, 1990; Nat League of Cities Leadership Award, 1994. **Business Addr:** Vice President of Government Relations, HRI Properties, 909 Poydras St Suite 3100, New Orleans, LA 70112, **Business Phone:** (504)566-0204.

BARTLEY, WILLIAM RAYMOND
Physician. **Personal:** Born Dec 9, 1944, Daytona Beach, FL; married Freddye; children: Diallo, Rashida. **Educ:** Knoxville Col, BA, 1968; Meharry Med Col, attended 1975. **Career:** Equal Opportunity Agency, staff; Little Rock Va Hosp, Lee Co Co-op Clinic, part time staff; Erlanger Hosp, intern, 1975; USAF Sch Aerospace Med, 1976; USAF, flight surgeon; US Public Health Service; Alton MultiSpecialists, internist; Pvt pract, Internal Med, currently. **Orgs:** Little League Sports. **Honors/Awds:** Nat Med Fels Award, 1970-72. **Military Serv:** USAF, capt, 1976-. **Business Addr:** Physician, Alton MultiSpecialists, 1 Professional Dr, Alton, IL 62002.*

BARTON, RHONDA L
Engineer, lawyer. **Personal:** Born Dec 10, 1966, Wilmington, DE; daughter of Lyndon and Olive. **Educ:** Howard Univ, Wash, DC, BS, mech eng, 1989; Univ Md, Sch Law, JD, 1998. **Career:** Pacific Gas & Electric Co, San Francisco, gas distribution engr, 1989; Arent Fox, assoc patient pract, currently. **Orgs:** Nat Soc Black Engrs Alumni Ext, 1989-; Pacific Coast Gas Asn, 1991-; Am Intellectual Property Law Asn. **Business Phone:** (202)857-6000.

BARTON, WAYNE DARRELL
Chief executive officer, law enforcement officer. **Personal:** Born Feb 21, 1961, Fort Lauderdale, FL; son of Burnett and Willie; children: Tarsheka D & Sharque. **Educ:** Palm Beach Jr Col, attended 1992. **Career:** Police Officer (Retired), Social Worker; Boca Raton Police Dept, police aid, 1980-81, police officer, 1981; Barton's Boosters, founder & chief exec officer, currently. **Orgs:** Salvation Army; March Dimes; Child Watch; Visions 2002; Boca Raton Jaycees; founding mem: I Have Dream Found; Law Day Found; numerous others. **Honors/Awds:** Numerous Awards & Honors including Meritorious Award, Atty Gen State Fla, 1988; Officer of the Year Award, Boca Raton Rotary Club, 1988; Certificate of Appreciation, Ala Gov, 1989; Unsung Hero Award, Vision Mag, 1991; Outstanding Community Service Award, St Paul AME Church, 1992; Book of Golden Deeds Award, Nat Exchange Club, 1992. **Business Addr:** Chief Executive Officer, Founder, Barton Boosters, 269 NE 14th St, Boca Raton, FL 33432, **Business Phone:** (561)620-6203.

BARTOW, DR. JEROME EDWARD
Executive. **Personal:** Born in Orange, NJ; married Louise Tolson; children: Sharon B Mitchell & Jerome E Bartow Jr. **Educ:** Va State Univ, AB, 1951; Columbia Univ, MA, 1955, EdD, 1968. **Career:** Executive (retired); Various insts higher educ, 1955-64; New York Tele Co, various positions, 1965-69; ITT World Headquarters, mgr exec placement, 1969-74, dir employee rel operations, 1974-77, dir, personnel/indust rel, 1977-79, dir admin bsns systems & community group, 1979; Hartford Inst Group, sr vpres & dir admin, 1979-95. **Orgs:** Chmn, exec adv comt, BEEP Nat Urban League, 1980-93; past mem, bd trustee, Nat Urban League; past mem bd, regents Univ Hartford; past mem, bd visitors, Univ Conn; founding charter mem, bd dirs, Exec Leadership Coun. **Honors/Awds:** Cert Merit, Va State Univ, 1983; Cert Merit, Ft Valley State Col, 1981; Hon Dr Humane Letters, Va State Univ, 1991-; McGannon Award, Nat Urban League, 1987; Whitney M Young Jr Medallion, 1994; Heritage Award, Exec Leadership Coun, 1996. **Military Serv:** AUS, lt, 1951-53.

BARZEY, DR. RAYMOND CLIFFORD, II
Government official. **Personal:** Born in New York, NY; son of Raymond C and Elva Waters. **Educ:** City Col City Univ New York, BA, 1967; Atlanta Univ, MS, 1968; State Univ New York, MA, 1970; New York Univ, PhD, 1980; Seton Hall, JD, 1983. **Career:** Sterns Dept Store, asst buyer, 1965-67; MN Mining & Mfg, prod analyst,1968-71; Urban Develop Corp, assoc economist, 1971-73; Housing Develop Corp, asst exec dir, 1974; Urban Develop Corp, assoc economist, 1975; Harlem Urban Develop Corp, dir commercial develop, 1976; Co La, sr budget analyst; City Univ New York, Baruch Col, New York, adjunct asst prof,1981-87; New York off Econ Develop, 1982; NJ Dep Atty Gen, asst chief,1983-. **Orgs:** Am Assn Univ Profs; Am Econ Assn; Am Inst Planners; Am Libr Assn; Am Soc Planning Officials; Nat Assn Housing & Re development Officials; Nat Econ Assn Amnesty Int; Hosp Audience; Nat Trust Historic Preserv; Nat Urban League; 100 Black Men; Am Bar Assn, NJ Bar Assn; Assn City New York; New York County Lawyers Assn. **Honors/Awds:** Martin Luther King Scholarship, New York Univ, 1975-77. **Home Addr:** 65 W 90th St, New York, NY 10024. **Business Phone:** (609)984-3900.*

BASHFUL, DR. EMMETT WILFORT
Chancellor (education). **Personal:** Born Mar 12, 1917, Oscar, LA; son of Charles and Mary Walker; married Juanita Jones, Aug 16, 1941; children: Cornell J Morean. **Educ:** Southern Univ Baton Rouge, BS, 1940; Univ IL, Urbana, MA, 1947, PhD, 1955. **Career:** Allen Parish Sch, LA, teacher, 1940-41; Fla A&M Univ, prof, 1948-58, Polit Sci Dept, head, 1950-58; Southern Univ,

Baton Rouge, LA, prof, 1958-59; Southern Univ New Orleans, LA, dean, 1959-69, vpres, 1969-77, chancellor, 1977-87, chancellor emer, currently. **Orgs:** Bd mem, Metrop Area Comm; bd mem, World Trade Ctr; adv bd, Goodwill Ind; bd dir, Comn Alcoholism Greater New Orleans United Way Agency; bd mem, New Orleans Chapter, Nat Conf Community & Justice; bd dir, Frey Found; chmn, Southern Univ New Orleans Found. **Honors/Awds:** Silver Beaver Award, Boy Scouts of Am, 1967; Volenteer Activist Award, 1976; Alumni Achievement Award, Col Liberal Arts & Sci, 1991; Leadership Award, Nat Asn Equal Opportunity Higher Educ, 2002. **Special Achievements:** First African Americans to receive a graduate degree in Political Science from University of Illinois; Author, The Fla Supreme Ct, A Study in Judicial selection, 1958; One of the Ten Outstanding Citizens of New Orleans by the Institute for Human Understanding. **Military Serv:** AUS, first lt, 1942-46. **Home Addr:** 5808 Lafaye St, New Orleans, LA 70122. **Business Addr:** Chancellor Emeritus, Southern University of New Orleans, 31 McAlister Dr, PO Box 1692, New Orleans, LA 70118, **Business Phone:** (504)865-6100.

BASIL, RICHARD
Football coach, football player. **Personal:** Married Mary Diase. **Educ:** Savannah State Univ. **Career:** Football player, Football coach (retired); Detroit Tigers, quarterback, 1988-89; Johnson C Smith & Tenn State, asst coach, 1994-06; Savannah State Univ, asst coach, 1993-95; head coach, Savannah State Univ, 2003-05. **Honors/Awds:** Offensive Player of the Year honors, SIAC, 1988; George H. Hopson Offensive Back of the Year, 1988. *

BASKERVILLE, DR. CHARLES ALEXANDER
Educator. **Personal:** Born Aug 19, 1928, Queens, NY; son of Charles H and Annie M Allen; married Susan; children: Mark, Shawn, Charles & Thomas. **Educ:** City Col, BS, 1953; New York Univ, MS, 1958, PhD, geol, 1965. **Career:** NY Dept Transp, 1953-65; City Univ, New York, prof, 1965-70, Sch Gen Studies, dean, 1970-79, prof emer, 1982; McFarland-Johnson, soils engr,1967; Madigan-Hyland Engrs, sr soils engr, 1968; US Geol Survey, proj Geologist Geol Risk Assessment Br, 1979-90; Cent Connecticut State Univ, City Col New York, dept phys & earth sci, prof, dept chmn, 1992-94, prof emer, currently; George Mason Univ, vis prof geol; Univ Ariz, Dept Hydrology & Water Resources, prof environ geochem; New York State, Dept Environ Protection's Water Tunnel Project, consult; Argonne Nat Lab, US Environ Protection Agency, Proposal Review Panel & Radioactive Waste Panel, staff; Asn Ground Water Scientists & Engineers, Darcy distinguished lectr; Waterloo Ctr Groundwater Res, Scientific & Indust Adv Comt, staff. **Orgs:** Nat adv comm, Minority Participant Earth Sci & Mineral Engr US Dept Interior, 1972-75; Asn Engr Geol, 1973; Tech Session subcomt, Nat AEG Conv, 1976; chmn, Marliave Scholar Comm, 1976-77; adv comm, Earth Sci, Nat Sci Found, 1989-91; Minority Grad Fel Prog, 1979-80; Geol Soc Wash; panelist, Nat Sci Found Grad Fel Prog; Sigma Xi; chmn educ & training subcomt, US Nat Comm Tunnelling Tech Nat Acad Eng, Nat Res Coun; consult,IBM; consult, Madigan Hyland Praeger Cavanaugh Waterbury, 1969; consult, St Raymond's Cemetery, 1970-76; consult, Consolidated Edison Co; consult, Eastmore Construct Co; consult, New York Corp Coun; New York Acad Sci; fel, Geol Soc Am Ad Hoc Comm Minorities Geosciences; chmn, E B Burwell Awards Comt; rep, US Nat Comm tunneling technol, 1991-94; NY Dept Transp Construct Proj Expert Witness; NY Dept Law expert witness; Nat Res Coun; ed review bd, Groundwater; bd dir, Asn Ground Water Scientists & Engr. **Honors/Awds:** Founders Day Award, New York Univ; 125th Anniversary Medal, City Col; Award for Excellence in Engineering Geology, Nat Consortium Black Prof Develop; Black Achievers in Science, Museum Sci & Indust, Chicago, IL. **Special Achievements:** US delegate to the Beijing International Colloquium on Tunneling & Underground Works, Beijing, People's Republic of China, 1984, presented & published numerous scientific papers, guest lecturer to schools & colleges. **Business Addr:** Professor, Cent Connecticut State University, Department of Physics & Earth Sciences, 5th Fl Copernicus Hall 1615 Stanley St, New Britain, CT 06050, **Business Phone:** (860)832-3188.

BASKERVILLE, LEZLI
Association executive, u.s. attorney. **Personal:** Born in Montclair, NJ; daughter of Charles W. and Marjorie. **Educ:** Douglass Col, BA; Howard Univ Sch Law, JD, 1979; Benedict Col, LLB. **Career:** Congressional staffer; DC Ct Appeals, law clerk; pvt pract, lawyer; The Baskerville Group, founder & mem; The Col Bd, Wash Off, chief exec officer, vpres govt rels, 1999-03; Nat Asn Equal Opportunity Higher Educ, pres & chief exec officer, 2004-. **Orgs:** Nat legis coun, Nat Asn Advan Colored People; exec dir, Nat Black Leadership Roundtable; mem, Nat Appellate Litigation Team, Lawyers Comt Civil Rights Under the Law; nat co-chair, Pathways Col Network; The Douglass Soc. **Special Achievements:** Mem, NAFEO brief writing teams in the landmark Supreme Ct affirmative action cases of Bakke, Weber & Fullilove; primary ed, Nat Dialogue Stud Financial Aid; first woman president of the National Association for Equal Opportunity in Higher Education; Top 10 Black Women in Higher Education, AOL Black Voices; Top 100 Most Influential Association Leaders, Ebony Mag. **Business Addr:** President, Chief Executive Officer, National Association for Equal Opportunity in Higher Education, 209 3rd St SE, Washington, DC 20003, **Business Phone:** (202)552-3300.*

BASKERVILLE, PENELOPE ANNE
Labor relations manager. **Personal:** Born Jul 9, 1946, South Orange, NJ; daughter of Robert L and Yolanda Reaves; divorced; children: Dylan Craig, Ailey Yolanda. **Educ:** Brown Univ, BA, 1968. **Career:** NJ Div Civil Rights, field rep, 1975-77; NJ Dept Pub Advocate Off Citizen Complaints, field rep, 1977-80; Princeton Univ, personnel admin, 1980-86; Peterson's Guides Inc, personnel mgr, 1986-89; Rider Col, benefits mgr, 1989; Summit Bank, benefits spec, 1998, cebs, 2005-. **Orgs:** Brown Univ Alumni Sch Comt, 1971; pres, Bd Trustees Princeton Nursery Sch, 1977-82; Intergovernmental Drug Comn; Corner House, 1982-94; Bd Educ Princeton Region Sch, 1982-85, ET Byrd Scholar Fund, 1983-87; bd trustees Princeton YWCA, 1985-90; NAACP Legal Defense Fund, Princeton comn, 1992; Princeton Young Achievers, bd mem, 1993. *

BASKERVILLE, RANDOLPH
Lawyer, district court judge. **Personal:** Born Jul 22, 1949, Henderson, NC; married Sarah McLean; children: Latoyia, Nathan. **Educ:** Fayetteville State Univ, BS, 1971; NC A&T State Univ, MS, 1972; NC Cent Univ Sch Law, JD, 1976. **Career:** Admin Off Courts, asst, 1979-84; Dept Social Serv, staff atty, 1985-86; pvt pract, lawyer, 1985; Judicial Dist 9B, dist judge, 2005-. **Orgs:** NC Bar Asn, 1977-; Nat Bar Asn, 1977-; dir, YMCA, 1984-85; Am Cancer Soc, 1984-; pres, Charles Williamson Bar Asn, 1985-86; dir, NCNB Bank, 1985-; dir, C of C, 1986-; NC Asn Trial Lawyers; Vance County Bar Asn. **Honors/Awds:** Outstanding Young Dem, Vance County, 1983; Contrib to Planning, YMCA Henderson/Vance, YMCA, 1983; Outstanding Contrib to Ninth Dist, Ninth Judicial Dist Bar, 1984; Outstanding Contrib to Black, Comn Vance Cty Black Leadership Caucus, 1984. **Business Addr:** District Court Judge, District 9B, Admin Off Courts, PO Box 2448, Raleigh, NC 27602-2448.*

BASKERVILLE, SAMUEL J., JR.
Physician. **Personal:** Born Mar 2, 1933, Charleston, WV; son of Samuel Baskerville Sr and Geraldine. **Educ:** Howard Univ Wash, DC, BS, 1953; Meharry Med Col, MD, 1958. **Career:** Detroit Receiving Hosp, intern, 1958-59; Kern Co Gen Hosp, res internal med, 1959-62, chief res internal med, 1961-62; Mercy Hosp Bakersfield, CA, chief staff, 1973, bd dirs, 1979-81, 1986-90. **Orgs:** bd dirs, Kern Co Med Soc, 1964-67; Calif Med Asn, 1964; Am Med Asn, 1964; Nat Med Asn, 1967; Am Soc Internal Med, 1968; Omega Psi Phi Fraternity; Kern Co Sheriff's Adv Coun, 1988-90. **Honors/Awds:** Civil Serv Comn Kern Co, 1969-77; Kern Co Heart Asn, 1991. **Military Serv:** USAF, Med Corps, capt, 1962-64. *

BASKETT, KENNETH GERALD
Army officer, educator. **Personal:** Born Nov 18, 1942, Kansas City, MO; son of W Cletus Baskett and Rosella Kelly King; divorced; children: Charmel, Adrienne & Tiffany. **Educ:** Tuskegee Inst, BS, acct, 1972; Alabama A&M, MS, personnel mgt, 1975; Command & Gen Staff Col, Masters, 1979. **Career:** Professor (retired); Ala A&M Univ, asst prof, 1972-75; Lincoln Univ, prof, 1982-85; Lt Col USA, educr. **Orgs:** Bd mem, Optimist Club Jefferson City, 1982-85; Atlanta City Country Club; Alpha Phi Alpha Frat, 1989; pres, Pi Gamma Lambda Chap, Alpha Phi Alpha Frat Inc. **Honors/Awds:** Numerous awards for combat service, Vietnam, 1968-69; Number One Bus Manager, Tuskegee Inst, 1970-72. **Military Serv:** AUS, infantry Lt col, 22 yrs; Air Medal, Bronze Star, 3 Meritorious Service Awards, 1966-86; capt & co comdr, Vietnam, 1968-69; Retired 1986. **Home Addr:** 4584 Jamerson Forest Pkwy, Marietta, GA 30066, **Home Phone:** (770)928-1630.

BASKETTE, ERNEST E., JR.
Association executive. **Personal:** Born Apr 24, 1944, Lumpkin, GA; son of Ernest E and Julia Williams; married Stephanie R Bush-Baskette; children: Damien B Baskette. **Educ:** City Col-CUNY, New York, NY, BA, 1972; Hunter Col, New York, NY, Master's Urban Planning, 1974. **Career:** Town Islip, Islip, NY, urban planner, 1974-75; City New Rochelle, New Rochelle, NY, urban planner, 1975-77; NHS Newark, Newark, NJ, exec dir, 1977-80; Neighborhood Housing Serv Am, sr vpres, 1980-. **Orgs:** Bd mem, SEW & Lorraine Hansbury Theatre, 1985-87. **Military Serv:** USAF, 1961-65. **Business Addr:** Senior Vice President, Neighborhood Housing Services of America Inc, 1970 Broadway Suite 470, Oakland, CA 94612, **Business Phone:** (510)832-5542.*

BASKIN, ANDREW LEWIS
College teacher. **Personal:** Born Feb 28, 1951, Maryville, TN; son of Eloise and Jimmy; married Symerdar Lavern Capehart; children: Thalethia Elois & Thameka La Cape. **Educ:** Berea Col, BA, hist, 1972; Va Tech, MA, Am hist, 1975. **Career:** Ferrum Col, asst prof, 1975-83; Berea Col, dir Black Cult Ctr, 1983-, dir, 1983-95; ed, "The Griot: The Journal of African American Studies", 1986-; Appalachian Col Asn, fel, coordr, 1995-2000; Berea Col, Gen & African & African American Studies, assoc prof, 2000-, interim dir Black Studies, 2002-04. **Orgs:** Phi Alpha Theta, 1975-; bd dir, Mt Maternal Health League, 1984-86; treas, Coun So Mts, 1983-84; bd dir, Berea Col Credit Union, 1985-91; bd dir, Kentucky Humanities Coun, 1990-97; chairperson bd dir, Kentucky Humanities Coun, 1995-97; bd ed, Berea Independent Sch Syst, 1991-99, chairperson, 1996-99; vchmn, Kentucky African Am Heritage Comn, 1994-2006; chair bd dir, Kentucky River Foothills Develop Corp, 1994-97; Phi Kappa Phi, Berea Col, 2002; bd trustee, Lincoln Foundation, 2008-. **Honors/Awds:** Hurt Faculty Achievement Award, Ferrum Col, 1976; James B St Award, Am Hist, Berea Col, 1972; Elizabeth Penny Miles Award, Community Serv, Berea Col, 2002; Seabury Award for Excellence in Teaching, Berea Col, 2004. **Home Addr:** 105 Cherry Rd, Berea, KY 40403, **Home Phone:** (859)986-1430. **Business Addr:** Associate Professor, Berea College, Department of African & Afro American Studies & General Studies, Hafer-Gibson Room 113, CPO 1715, Berea, KY 40404, **Business Phone:** (859)985-3393.

BASKINS, LEWIS C.
Executive, dentist. **Personal:** Born Jul 16, 1932, Springfield, AR; married Amanda J; children: Duane, Brian, Kevin, Holli. **Educ:** AR AM & N Col, BS, 1956; Univ Ill, DDS, 1961. **Career:** Fuller Products Co, vpres; Dentist. **Orgs:** Pres, Chicago Chap AR AM & N Alumni; mem Am, Chicago, Lincoln Dental Soc; Omega Psi Phi Fraternity; Mt Zion Baptist Church. **Military Serv:** AUS, sp3, 1953-55. **Business Addr:** 701 W 111th St, Chicago, IL 60628.*

BASRI, GIBOR
Educator, scientist. **Personal:** Born May 3, 1951, New York, NY; married Jessica Broitman; children: Jacob. **Educ:** Stanford Univ, BS, 1973; Univ Colo, PhD, Astrophysics, 1979. **Career:** Univ Colo, res asst, 1974-79; Univ CA, postdoctoral fellow, 1979-82, asst prof, 1982-87; Univ Calif Berkeley, assoc prof, 1988-94, prof, 1994-, vice chancellor, Equity & Inclusion, 2007-. **Orgs:** Am Astron Soc 1979; Int Astron Union, 1984; Astron Soc Pac, 1984. **Honors/Awds:** Miller Research Professorship, 1997; Sigma Xi Distinguished Lecturer, 2000; Chancellors Award for Advancing Inst Excellence, 2006. **Special Achievements:** UC Berkeley's first vice chancellor for equity and inclusion (VCEI). Many articles Astrophysical Jour, 1979-. **Home Addr:** 2940 Forest Ave, Berkeley, CA 94705. **Business Addr:** Vice Chancellor, University California, 102 Calif Hall MC 1508, Berkeley, CA 94720-1508, **Business Phone:** (510)642-7294.

BASS, ANTHONY
Football player. **Personal:** Born Mar 27, 1975, South Charleston, WV. **Educ:** Bethune-Cookman. **Career:** Minn Vikings, defensive back, 1998-99, corner back. *

BASS, DR. FLOYD L.
Educator. **Personal:** Born Aug 11, 1921, Sullivan, IN; married Hazel B Huddleston; children: Floyd L Jr, Eileen C, Marc C & Lisa C Ealum. **Educ:** Ind State Univ, BS, 1948, MS, 1950; Univ Colo-Boulder, EdD, 1960. **Career:** LeMoyne Col, dean, 1960-63; Ala State Univ, dean, 1963-64; City Col NY,admin intern w/pres, 1964-65; NC Cent Univ, prof educ, 1965-68; Univ Conn, prof educ, 1968, prof emer, educ leadership. **Orgs:** Dir, The Ctr Black Studies, Univ Conn, 1969-; pres, Northeastern Chap Conn Affil ADA, 1982-84; pres, Willim antic Rotary Club, 1983-85; grand historian Grand Encampment Knights Templar, 1985, 1987; pres, Conn Order High Priesthood, 1985,86; accreditation team mem, Nat Coun for Accreditation Teacher Educ, 1983, 1984, 1985, 1986, 1987; fel John Jay Whitney. **Military Serv:** USN, 3rd class, petty off, 1945-46.

BASS, HARRY S.
Educator. **Personal:** Born Apr 15, 1954, Farmville, VA; son of Harry S Bass, Sr. **Educ:** Va Union Univ, BS, 1976; Atlanta Univ, MS, 1979, PhD, 1985. **Career:** Notre Dame Univ, fel, 1985-86; Mehary Med Col, fel, 1986-89; Va Union Univ, assoc prof, 1989-, chair, div of nat sci, 1990-93, chair, dept biol& natural sci & math, 1993-, admin dir, currently. **Orgs:** Am Parasotology Soc, 1980; Transactions Am Microscopic Soc, 1980; AAAS, 1989; dir, Mid-Eastern Alliance Minority Participation. **Honors/Awds:** Tribute of Appreciation, EPA, 1998; Certificate of Appreciation, GEM, 1998; MARC-VUU, Award of Appreciation, 1998. **Special Achievements:** Author of numerous articles. **Home Addr:** PO Box 25596, Richmond, VA 23260. **Business Addr:** Chair, Associate Professor, Virginia Union University, Department of Natural Sciences and Mathematics, 1500 N Lombard St, Ellison Hall Room 220B, Richmond, VA 23220, **Business Phone:** (804)257-5612.

BASS, DR. HERBERT H.
Educator, consultant. **Personal:** Born Dec 26, 1929, Warsaw, NC; married Carrie L Ruff; children: Lori. **Educ:** Shaw Univ, BA, 1955; Antioch Univ, MEd, Counseling 1972; Union Grad, PhD, 1980. **Career:** Supreme Liberty Life Co, ins agent, 1956; Philadelphia Sch Dist, teacher,1957; City Philadelphia, gang control worker, 1959; Pa Dept Pub Asst,social worker, 1960; Philadelphia Dept Welfare, recreation supvr, 1960;Philadelphia Sch Dist, counr special educ, 1961; Provident Life Ins Co,consult, 1965; Leeds & Northrup Co, coord counseling, 1968-. **Orgs:** Vice chmn & trustee, New Bethlehem Bapt Church; comnr, Boy Scouts Am; CounExceptional C; Nat Advan Asn Colored People; YMCA. **Business Addr:** Coordinator of Counseling, Leeds & Northrup Co, Sumneytown Pike, North Wales, PA 19454.*

BASS, JAMES F
Superior court judge. **Career:** Chatham County, Ga, super ct judge, currently. **Business Addr:** Superior Court Judge, Chatham

County, Eastern Judicial Circuit, 421 Chatham County Courthouse, 133 Montgomery St, Savannah, GA 31401, **Business Phone:** (912)652-7154.

BASS, JOSEPH FRANK
Administrator. **Personal:** Born Jan 10, 1938, Phenix City, AL; married Jenean Brantley; children: Terence, Steven, Sandra. **Educ:** Hartnell Col, AA, 1958; Carnegie-Mellon Univ, Cert Transp, 1972; Univ Santa Clara, Cert Mgt, 1977; Harvard Univ, cert state & local govt, 1981. **Career:** City Salinas, engineering draftsman, 1958; City San Jose, civil engr, 1962, sr civil engr, 1967, prin civil engr & head transp planning, 1975-80, dir dept traffic, 1980-92. **Orgs:** Regis civil engr CA, 1966; Inst Traffic Engrs, 1970; Am Pub Works Assn, 1975; regis traffic engr CA, 1977; NAACP, 1980; Black Coalition Local Govt Employ, 1980; No CA Coun Black Prof Engrs, 1980; 100 Black Men 1990. *

BASS, KEVIN CHARLES
Baseball player. **Personal:** Born May 12, 1959, Redwood City, CA; married Elaine; children: Garrett Charles, April Brittany & Justin Charles. **Career:** Baseball player (retired); Milwaukee Brewers, outfielder, 1981-82; Houston Astros, outfielder, 1982-89, 1993-94; San Francisco Giants, outfielder, 1990-94; New York Mets, 1992; Baltimore Orioles, 1995. **Honors/Awds:** Led Astros pinch hits, 1981, 1983; Nat League All-Star Team, 1986. *

BASS, DR. LAURENT
President (Organization). **Educ:** DVM. **Career:** RLM Vet Serv, pres, 2002-. **Business Addr:** President, RLM Veterinary Services, 2805 N State Hwy 3, North Vernon, IN 47265, **Business Phone:** (812)346-8008.*

BASS, LEONARD CHANNING
Physician. **Personal:** Born Jul 23, 1941, Live Oak, FL; married Janet. **Educ:** Meharry Med Col, MD, 1966. **Career:** Genessee Hosp, intern, 1967; Pvt Pract, physician, 1969-; Plantation Med Hosp, Dept Family Pract, chief serv, 1986-90. **Orgs:** Fla Med Dent & Pharm Asn; Nat Med Asn; Fla Med Asn; Broward Co Med Soc; pres, Fla State Med Asn; vpres, Am Heart Asn, 1976; Fla bd Med, 1982-86; life mem, Alpha Phi Alpha Frat. **Honors/Awds:** Distinguished Service Award, Med Fla Dent & Pharm Asn, 1977; co-chmn, prof conf Am Heart Asn, 1976; Vietnam Commendation Medal, USAF; fel, Am Bd Family Pract. **Military Serv:** USAF MC, capt, 1967-69. **Business Addr:** Physician, 2323 NW 19th St Suite Three, Fort Lauderdale, FL 33311.*

BASS, MARSHALL BRENT
Consultant, executive. **Personal:** Born in Goldsboro, NC; son of Estella and Marshall; married Celestine Pate; children: Brenda & Marsha. **Educ:** Univ Md, College Park, BS. **Career:** RJ Reynolds Tobacco Co, mgr personnel develop, 1968-70; RJ Reynolds Industs, corp mgr, 1970-76, corp dir 1976-82, vpres, 1982, sr vpres, 1986-91; RJR Nabisco, retired sr vpres, 1991; Marshall B Bass & Assocs, pres, 1997-. **Orgs:** Bd dirs, Piedmont Fed Savings & Loan Asn; former mem, Nat Comn Working Women; former bd dirs, Winston-Salem/Forsyth Co, YMCA; indust adv coun, Nat Newspaper Publishers Asn; bd visitors, NC Cent Univ; chmn, bd dirs, Winston-Salem State Univ Found; former mem, bd trustees, NC A&T State Univ; Phi Beta Sigma Frat Inc; Gamma Kappa Boule Sigma Pi Phi; sr warden St Stephen's Episcopal Church; lay leader chalice bearer Episcopal Diocese NC; bd trustees, NAACP Spec Contribution Fund; chmn, bd trustees, St Augustines Col, Raleigh; chmn, Adv Bd Consortuim, Grad Studies Mgt; bd dirs, Piedmont Triad Horizon; chair, bd trustees, Vorhees Col. **Honors/Awds:** Black book Nat Outstanding Business & Professional Award, 1984; Several Honorary Degrees: Doctor of Civil Law, St Augustines Raleigh; Doctor of Humane Letters, Florida A&M Univ, Tallahasse, Fla; Doctor of Divinity, Tenn Sch Relig, Detroit, Mich Div; LLD, Dr of Humane Letters, NC Cent Univ, St Augustine Col, Raleigh, NC, King Memorial Col, Columbia, SC, Livingston Col, Salisbury NC, Winston Salem State Univ. **Military Serv:** AUS, officer, 1945-68; chief of army promotions, 23 yrs; Legion of Merit; 3 Commendation Medals; Purple Heart; Combat Infantry man's Badge. **Home Addr:** 3726 Spaulding Dr, Winston-Salem, NC 27105, **Home Phone:** (336)724-6852. **Business Addr:** President, Marshall B Bass & Associates, 1324 Ashley Sq, PO Box 24388, Winston-Salem, NC 27114-4338, **Business Phone:** (336)659-7898.

BASS, PATRICK HENRY
Book editor. **Career:** New York Times, ed; Wash Post, ed; Entertainment Weekly, ed; Essence Commun, book ed, currently; Blacxk Issues Book Review; Quarterly Black Rev Books; Am Visions; Black Enterprise; Notorius; Time Out New York; YSB; BET Weekend; Like A Mighty Stream: The March on Washington, August 28, 1963, author; Treasures African American Traditions, Journeys & Icons, author. *

BASSARD, YVONNE BROOKS
Administrator, health services administrator. **Personal:** Born Oct 27, 1937, Oakland, CA; married Edward Lee Jr; children: Edward Lee Jr, Margot Denise Walton, Daryl Lamont, Alicia Yvonne. **Educ:** Patten Bible Col, BS, theol, 1973; St Stephens Col, MA, health sci, 1975, PhD, 1978. **Career:** Parks AFB Hosp, nurse, 1956-57; Eden Hosp Castro Valley, CA, nurse, 1960-62; St Rose Hosp, Hayward, CA, nurse, 1962-63; Patten Sch Religion, sch nurse, 1976-; Bassard Rehab Hosp, owner, admin & nurse, 1963-2007. **Orgs:** Am Col Nursing Home Adminr, 1976-; Lic Voc Norses League, 1977-; Consumer Aging Comn, Calif Asn Health Fac, 1978-80; Smithsonian Inst. **Honors/Awds:** Heart Award Patten Bible Coll 1969. *

BASSETT, ANGELA
Actor. **Personal:** Born Aug 16, 1958, New York, NY; daughter of Betty; married Courtney Vance, 1997. **Educ:** Yale Univ, BA, 1980, MFA, 1983. **Career:** Films include: City of Hope, 1991; Boyz N the Hood, 1992; Malcolm X, 1992; The Jacksons, 1992; Passion Fish; What's Love Got to Do With It?, 1993; Waiting to Exhale, 1995; Contact, 1997; How Stella Got Her Groove Back, 1998; Music From the Heart, 1999; Supernova, 2000; Boesman & Lena, 2000; The Score, 2001; Sunshine State, 2002; Masked & Anonymous, 2003; HBO movie, Unchained Memories: Readings from the Slave Narratives, reader, 2003; tv movie: Ruby's Buckey of Blood, 2001; The Rosa Parks Story, 2002; Plays: Joe Turner's Come & Gone; Macbeth; Sunshine State, 2002, Masked & Anonymous, 2003, Mr 3000, 2004, Mr. & Mrs. Smith, 2004; Authorized Personnel Only: Part 1, 2005; Mr & Mrs Smith, 2005; Akeelah & the Bee, 2006; TV Series: "The Index", 2005; "The Descent", 2005; "Search & Rescue", 2005; "Before the Flood", 2005. **Honors/Awds:** Acapulco Black Film Festival, Best Actress Award for How Stella Got Her Groove Back; Image Award for Outst&ing Lead Actress in a Motion Picture, 1999; Image Award for Outst&ing Lead Actress in a Motion Picture, 2000; Black Reel Award for Network/Cable-Best Actress, 2002; Image Award for Outst&ing Actress in a Television Movie, Mini-Series or Dramatic Special, 2002; Image Award for Outst&ing Supporting Actress in a Motion Picture, 2002; Black Reel Award for Network/Cable-Best Actress, 2003; Black Reel Award for Theatrical-Best Actress, 2003; Image Award for Outst&ing Supporting Actress in a Motion Picture, 2003; Image Award for Outst&ing Actress in a Television Movie, Mini-Series or Dramatic Special, 2003. **Business Addr:** Actress, c/o Ambrosio Mortimer, 1127 High Ridge Rd Suite 119, Stamford, CT 06905-1203.

BASSETT, DENNIS
Executive. **Personal:** Born Dec 12, 1947, Gary, IN; son of Leonard Sr. and Ruby; married Carmen Johnson, Dec 30, 1969; children: Dennis LaShun, Dawn Lashae. **Educ:** Knoxville Col, BA, Eng, 1970; Pa State Univ & Univ Chicago, exec mgt progrs. **Career:** Eastman Kodak, Wash DC, sales mgr, 1980, Chicago IL, dist sales mgr, 1982, Rochester NY, program dir, worldwide training, 1985, 1st black staff asst sr vpres, 1986, Mid Atlantic, regional sales mgr, 1987, Restructuring Proj, proj leader, 1989, dir intercultural develop progs, 1990-94; Bausch & Lomb Corp, regional dir, 1994, vpres field sales, conact lens div, 1995, leader collab sales & commun, dir. **Orgs:** pres, Network Nstar, Black Networking Org Ek, 1992; bd dirs, Kappa Alpha Psi, Rochester Chap; Bd dir, Monroe Community Col Found, 2002; chmn, OMNI; Health assoc Inc; Rochester Community Found. **Honors/Awds:** Man of the Yr, Kappa Alpha Psi, Alumni Chap, 1992. **Business Addr:** Board of Directors Members, Monroe Community College Foundation, Damon City Campus, 228 E Main St, Rochester, NY 14604, **Business Phone:** (585)262-1500.*

BASSEY, MORGAN
President (Organization), chief executive officer. **Educ:** Purdue Univ, BS; Univ Colo, MBA, MS, finance; Univ Denver Col Law, JD. **Career:** Harvestons Securities Inc, pres & chief exec officer, 1993-, City & C Denver, Single Family Mortgage Financing, cofinancial adv, currently. **Orgs:** co-chair, Nuisance Abatement Ordinance Oversight Comt. **Business Phone:** (303)832-8887.*

BATAILLE, JACQUES ALBERT
Physician. **Personal:** Born Jul 11, 1926. **Educ:** Faculty Med Haiti, MD, 1953. **Career:** Physician (retired); Provident Hosp, jr asst, 1955-56; Homer G Phillips Hosp, 1956-57; Cumberland Hosp, res, 1957-58; Albert Einstein Med Col, 1958-59; Port-Au-Prince, pvt pract, 1960-69; Muscatatuck State Hosp, staff physician 1971-73, med dir 1974; Pvt Pract, physician 1974-77; Sharon Gen Hosp, 1974. **Orgs:** Am Med Asn; Nat Asn Advan Colored People; Shenango Valley C of C; Mercer Co Heart Asn; PA med Soc; Smithsonian Inst. **Honors/Awds:** Sharon Gen Hosp Continuing Educ Award, Am Med Asn; Am Citizen, 1973. **Home Addr:** 1808 Mcdowell St, Sharon, PA 16146, **Home Phone:** (724)981-1981. *

BATCH, CHARLIE (CHARLES D DONTE BATCH)
Football player. **Personal:** Born Dec 5, 1974, Homestead, PA. **Educ:** Eastern Mich Univ, BA, criminal justice. **Career:** Detroit Lions, quarterback, 1998-01; Pittsburgh Steelers, quarterback, 2002-. **Orgs:** Spokesman, Canned Food Dr; founder, Best of the Batch Found, 2000. **Honors/Awds:** All-Mid Am Conf first-team; James M Bingo Brown Award, 1995; All-State third-team; Fabulous 22, Pittsburgh Press, 1991; Mel Farr Rookie of the Yr Award, Detroit Lions, 1998; first Jerome Bettis Award. **Business Addr:** Professional Football Player, Pittsburgh Steelers, 3400 S Water St, Pittsburgh, PA 15203-2349, **Business Phone:** (412)432-7800.*

BATCHELOR, ASBURY COLLINS
Executive. **Personal:** Born Nov 26, 1929, Leggett, NC; married William Ethel Stephen; children: Marlon Diane Whitehead. **Educ:** A&T Univ Greensboro, NC, attended 1956; NC Cent Univ Durham, NC, attended1957; AUS Intelligence Sch, attended 1958. **Career:** NC Mutual Life Ins Co, agent, 1957-61, sales mgr, 1961-80; Western Dist Union, dir training, 1970-; Rocky Mount Develop Corp, secy, 1973-; NC Mutual Life Ins Co, asst agency dir, 1980-. **Orgs:** Chmn & treas, Rocky Mount Opportunity Industrializ Ctr, 1974-; Am Legion Post, 1965; chmn pub rel, Big Brothers/Big Sisters, 1978; Rocky Mount Rotary Club, 1979. **Honors/Awds:** Man of the Year Award, Mt Lebanon Masonic Lodge, 1960; Staff Manager of the Year, NC Mutual Life Ins Co, 1963; Appreciation Award, Coastal Plain Heart Fund Asn, 1968; Citation for Meritorious Service, Am Legion Post, 1979. **Military Serv:** AUS, sgt, 27 yrs; Good Conduct Medal, 1953. **Business Addr:** Assistant to Agency Director, North Carolina Mutual Life Insurance Company, Mutual Plz, Durham, NC 27701.

BATEMAN, CELESTE
Publicist, business owner. **Personal:** Born Sep 1, 1956, Newark, NJ; daughter of William and Elma; married Carter Mangan, May 10, 1986; children: Jamil & Carter Jr. **Educ:** Rutgers Univ, BA, Theatre Arts and Speech, 1978; Montclair State Univ, MA, Comm arts. **Career:** New Community Corp, Newark, NJ, prog dir, 1978-79; Port Authority New York & New Jersey, secy, 1981-84; The Newark Museum, Newark, NJ, prog coordr, 1984-87; City of Newark, Div Recreation/Cultural Affairs, Newark, NJ, cultural affairs supvr, 1987-97; Celeste Bateman & Assoc, pres, 1997-. **Orgs:** Alpha Psi Omega, 1978; Alpha Epsilon Rho, 1978; selection comm mem, Newark Black Film Festival, 1984-87; mem, Friends Newark Symphony Hall, 1985-88; mem adv coun, Newark Symphony Hall, 1987-89; ex-officio mem, Newark Festival People; mem, Am For The Arts, 1987-96; bd dir, WBGO-FM Jazz Radio, 1989-95; mem, Asn Am Cultures, 1987-90; Asn Performing Arts Presenters, 1984-87; bd dir, Newark Jazz Festival, 1991-96; exec dir, Newark Arts Coun, 1997-99; bd mem, Governors Sch, NJ, 1991-92. **Honors/Awds:** NAACP Image Award, 2003. **Special Achievements:** Author: We have Got the Victory; Fall Back and Let the Universe Catch You. **Business Addr:** President, Celeste Bateman & Associates, 9 11 Crawford St Suite 3, PO Box 4071, Newark, NJ 07114-4071, **Business Phone:** (973)705-8253.

BATEMAN, PAUL E
Lawyer. **Personal:** Born Feb 28, 1956, Highland Park, IL; son of Joel and Tyree; married Sylvia L Bateman, Aug 19, 1978; children: Paul Jr, Philip & Preston. **Educ:** Ill State Univ, BS, 1976; Univ Mich, JD, 1980. **Career:** Nat Labor Rels Bd, trial atty, 1980-84; Friedman & Koven, assoc, 1984-86; Sachnoff & Weaver, shareholder, 1986-93; Burke, Warren & MacKay, shareholder, 1993; Littler Mendelson PC, shareholder, currently, atty, currently. **Orgs:** Am Bar Asn, 1980-; US Ct Appeals, First, Fourth, Eighth, Ninth, Tenth, Eleventh & DC Circuits, 1981; adv bd, Civic Fedn Chicago, 1989-; regional liasion, Univ Mich Black Law Alumni, 1991-; cubmaster, Boy Scouts Am, 1992-. **Special Achievements:** Illinois Institute of Continuing Legal Education, Age Discrimination, 1996; Investigations, Testing & Privacy, 1990; Bateman is recognized as a Leading Illinois Attorney in the employment law field. **Business Addr:** Shareholder, Attorney, Littler Mendelson PC, 200 N La Salle St Suite 2900, Chicago, IL 60601-1014, **Business Phone:** (312)372-5520.

BATES, ARTHUR VERDI
Lawyer, musician. **Personal:** Born Jan 16, 1916, New Haven, CT; son of Arthur D and Beulah Hay; married Ruthann Brennan (deceased); children: Jean & Arthur Jr. **Educ:** Lincoln Univ, BA, 1937; Howard Univ Sch Law, JD, 1940; Brooklyn Law Sch, LLM, 1956. **Career:** Lawyer (retired), Musician; Musician; Pvt practice, atty, 1948-67; The Legal Aid Soc, sr family law specialist, 1986; legal consult. **Orgs:** APA; SPP; vchmn bd, past pres, Lincoln Civic Asn, 1971-75; consult, Cent Brooklyn Coord Coun, 1975-; Brooklyn Legal Serv Corp, 1977-. **Military Serv:** AUS, 1st lt, 4 1/2 yrs; Bronz Star Medal, Cmbt Inf Bdg 1945. *

BATES, BARBARA ANN
Executive, fashion designer. **Personal:** Born in Chicago, IL; children: 2. **Career:** First Nat Bank Chicago, secy; corp secy, 1986; Bates Design Inc, chief exec officer & pres, 1986-. **Orgs:** Founder, Bates Found. **Special Achievements:** Has designed clothes for Oprah Winfrey, Hammer, Whitney Houston, the Winans, Isiah Thomas, and other celebrities. **Business Phone:** (312)427-0284.*

BATES, CLAYTON WILSON, JR.
Educator, electrical engineer. **Personal:** Born Sep 5, 1932, New York, NY; son of Clayton and Arline; married Priscilla Suzanne Baly; children: Katherine Arline, Christopher Thomas & Naomi Elizabeth. **Educ:** Manhattan Col, BEE, 1954; Brooklyn Polytech Inst, MEE, 1956; Harvard Univ, ME, 1960; Wash Univ, St. Louis, PhD, physics, 1966. **Career:** RCA, elect engr, 1955; Ford Inst Co, 1955; Sylvania Elec Prod, 1955-57; AVCO, 1960; Varian Assoc, sr res engr, 1966-72; London Univ, visiting prof, 1968; Princeton Univ, visitng fel, 1978-79; Stanford Univ, elec eng & material sci eng, emriti prof, 1972-94; Howard Univ, Assoc Dean Graduate Educ & Res, prof, 1984-. **Orgs:** Optical Soc Am; sr mem, Inst Elec & Electronics Engrs, 1980; fel, Am Phys Soc, 1982; AAAS; Am

Asn Univ Profs; Soc Photo-Optical Instr Engrs; Sigma Xi; Eta Kappa Nu; Sigma Pi Sigma; Am Ceramic Soc; chmn, Affirm Action CommSch Engr, fac, adv Soc Black Scientists & Engrs, resident fel, 1973-76,Stanford Univ; past mem, bd dir, Jr Achievement; past mem, Nat Acad Sci Eval Panel; NSF; Demeter Agency San Francisco. **Honors/Awds:** Sabbatical Award Varian Asn, 1968; published 100 articles & scientific journals, 75 presentations in scientific meetings; Distinguished Engineer, Tau Beta Pi, 1976; Distinguished Faculty Author Award, Howard Univ, 2003. **Special Achievements:** Publ: Detection of optical radiation in the 8-12 m range using Ag -Cu InSe2 composites, 1996; Factors affecting the optical behavior of metal-semiconductor composites, 1997; Preparation of metal-semiconductor composite films by chemical spray pyrolysis, 1997; Micro structural and electronic transport properties Pt-Si films, published in Materials Letters, May 1999; The use of reliability factors in analyzing powder patterns in Pt-Si sputtering targets and subsequent films, 1998. **Business Addr:** Professor, Howard University, Department of Electrical & Computer Engineering, 2400 6th St NW, Washington, DC 20059, **Business Phone:** (202)806-6147.

BATES, ELIAS. See DIDDLEY, BO in the Obituaries section.

BATES, GEORGE ALBERT
Lawyer, manager, consultant. **Personal:** Born May 30, 1954, Charlottesville, VA; son of Otto L and Lucy H. **Educ:** Princeton Univ, BA, 1976; Univ Va, JD, 1980; Mediate Tech Inc, Gen Mediation Cert, 1994. **Career:** Princeton Univ Food Serv, asst mgr, 1972-76; Univ Va, grad asst track coach, 1976-80; State Farm Ins Co, automobile liability underwriter, 1976-77; US Dept Labor, law clerk-judge Roy P Smith, 1980-81; Univ Va, assoc dean off afro-am affairs, 1987; Gen Coun N Am Van Lines, norcross trans, 1990-94; Law Off George A Bates, proprietor, 1983-2005; EEO & Diversity consult, mediator. **Orgs:** Alpha Phi Alpha Fraternity, 1977-05; bd mem, Old Dominion Bar Asn, 1985-05; pres, Coop Exten Serv Bd Va State Univ, 1985-96; Cent Va Minority Bus Asn, 1987-05. **Honors/Awds:** NJ State Col Champ Triple Jump Winner, 1973-76; Track Team Keene-Fitzpatrick Award, 1975; Co-Capt Track Team, Princeton Univ, 1976; Heptagonal Track Meet All-Ivy, Triple Jump, 1975; Affairs Warrior Award, Univ Va Off Afro-Am, 1987; Humanitarian Service Award, Va State Univ, Coop Exten Serv, 1987; Humanitarian Service Award, Saint Paul's Col, 1988. **Special Achievements:** Co-ed/Prof Kenneth R Redden, "Punitive Damages" Michie Co, 1980; Organized the first legal advocacy workshop for the Old Dominion Bar Assn, 1988; Organized the first Employment Law Seminar for the NAACP, 1993; Journalist for five local newspapers & manuscript in progress on "The History of Bid Whist"; mem of the Ministerial Training Program, Charlottesville Church of Christ-Worldwide Bible Way, 1997. **Home Addr:** 644 Maxfield Rd, Keswick, VA 22947. **Business Addr:** Consultant, 644 Maxfield Rd, Keswick, VA 22947, **Business Phone:** (804)293-8724.

BATES, KAREN GRIGSBY
Journalist, writer. **Personal:** Married Bruce W Talamon; children: 1. **Educ:** Wellesley Col, BA; Univ Ghana; Yale Univ, Sch Orgn & Mgt, post-grad coursework. **Career:** NY Times, staff; Wash Post, staff; Essence & Vogue, journalist; Los Angeles Times, contrib columnist; ABC's Nightline, host; CBS Eve News, guest; People mag, writer & news reporter; Nat Pub Radio, corresp, 2002-; Tavis Smiley Show, alt host, 2002-, Day to Day, corresp, 2003-. **Special Achievements:** First correspondent and alternate host for The Tavis Smiley Show; co-author: Basic Black: Home Training for Modern Times, 1996; Author: Plain Brown Wrappers, 2001; Contributor: Mothers Who Think: Tales of Real-Life Parenting, 1999; Gumbo: An Anthology of African American Writing, 2002. **Business Addr:** Correspondent, National Public Radio, 635 Massachusetts Ave NW, Washington, DC 20001.

BATES, LIONEL RAY, SR.
Diver. **Personal:** Born Oct 21, 1955, New Orleans, LA; married Karen M; children: Nicole M & Lionel R Jr. **Educ:** Com Dive Ctr, Cert, air/mixed gas, 1979. **Career:** Anatole's Garage, auto mechanic 1965-78; Sub-Sea Int, tender, 1979-80, com diver. **Orgs:** Bible stud & minister Inst, Divine Metaphysical Res Inc, 1980-. **Honors/Awds:** People & Places, Ebony Mag, Jan, 1984. **Special Achievements:** First Black to Graduate from Cmmercial Dive Center, 1979; First Black to do saturation diving to depth of 450 feet, 1985.

BATES, LOUISE REBECCA
Executive, business owner. **Personal:** Born Sep 16, 1932, Cairo, IL. **Educ:** Wilson Jr Col, AA, 1957. **Career:** Executive (retired); Gold Blatt Bros Inc, clerk & buyer, 1952-75; Evans Inc, buyer, 1976-77; Louise Bates Jewelry Store, mgr, pres & owner. **Orgs:** Nat Asn Advan Colored People, Oper Breadbasket Urban League; WTTW TV; United Negro Col Fund; pres, Jr Hostess Coun & Ed newsletter USO; vol,work Better Boys Found hostess Kup's Purple Heart Cruises; vol work & guest lectr, Audy Juvenile Home Prog & Chicago Pub Sch. **Honors/Awds:** Cert Leadership, Hon Leadership Women in Econ Cult & Civic Life Metro Chicago Community, YWCA of Chicago 1972; Woman of the Day, 1975; Citation of Merit in Recog of Outstanding Contribution to Community, WAIT Radio St; Nathan Award for Outstanding Buyer of the Year, Goldblatts 1975.

BATES, MARIO DONIEL
Football player. **Personal:** Born Jan 16, 1973, Tucson, AZ. **Educ:** Ariz State Univ. **Career:** Football player, free agent (retired); New Orleans Saints, running back, 1994-97; Ariz Cardinals, 1998-99; Detroit Lions, running back, 2000. *

BATES, MICHAEL DION
Football player. **Personal:** Born Dec 19, 1969, Tucson, AZ; married Kethera. **Educ:** Univ Ariz. **Career:** Seattle Sea hawks, wide receiver, 1993-94; Cleveland Browns, 1995; Carolina Panthers, kick returner, 1996-00; Wash Redskins, 2001; Dallas Cowboys,2003; New York Jets, 2003. **Honors/Awds:** Olympic bronze medal, 1992; NFL 1990s All-Decade Team, 5 time Pro Bowl selection, 1996-2000. *

BATES, NATHANIEL RUBIN
Government official, politician. **Personal:** Born Sep 9, 1931, Cason, TX; son of Viola Hill; married Shirley Adams; children: Michael (deceased), Gale, Larry & Steven. **Educ:** San Francisco State Col, BA, 1963; Calif State-Hayward, teachers cert, 1975. **Career:** City of Richmond, councilman, 1967-, mayor, 1971-72, vice mayor, 1975-76, 2000-01, mayor, 1976-77, unit superv probation dept Alameda Co, 1963-93; State Senator Dan Boatwright, Contra Costa Co, CA, field rep. **Orgs:** Pres, E Bay Div League CA Cities, 1972-73; US Conf Mayors, 1972-74; Bay Area Sewage Serv Agency, 1973-; bd dir, Nat League Cities, 1973-75; vchmn, Human Resources Comn; chmn, Contra Costa Co Mayors Conf; Richmond Port Auth, 1976-; Richmond Housing Auth, 1976-; Richmond Redevel Comn, 1976-; bd dir, League CA Cities; Black Probation & Parole Asn; Nat Black Elected Officials Adv Bd; Nat Coun Alcoholism Contra Costa Co; Regional Coun Criminal Justice; Adv bd Mt Diablo Coun Boys Scouts Am, Camp Fire Girls, Richmond Boys Club; pres, Richmond Democratic Club, 1986-89; bd dirs, El Sobrante Girls Club, 1986-89; West Co Young Men Christain Asn, 1986-89; Salesian Boys Club, 1986-87; Nat Black Conf League Elected Officials; Citizen Civic Club. **Honors/Awds:** Father of the Yr, Easter Hill Doris Cluster, 1988; Richmond Democratic Club Honors, 1990; Bethel Temple POA Church Honors, 1990; Resolution Honors, Senator Dan Boatwright, 1983, 1988, 1990-97; Resolution Honors, Assembly man Bob Campbell, 1983, 1988, 1990; Don Bosco Award, 2004. **Home Phone:** (510)237-3905. **Business Addr:** Councilmember, Richmond City Hall, 1401 Marina Way S, Richmond, CA 94804, **Business Phone:** (510)620-6500.

BATES, PERCY
School administrator, educator. **Personal:** Born Jul 8, 1932, Pensacola, FL; son of Gladys Travis Graves and Percy; married Cheryl Proctor, Sep 12, 1962; children: Allison & Nathan; married. **Educ:** Cent Mich Univ, Mt Pleasant, MI, BS, 1958; Wayne State Univ, Detroit, MI, MA, 1961; Univ Mich, Ann Arbor, MI, PhD, psychol, 1968. **Career:** Univ Mich, Ann Arbor, MI, from asst prof to assoc prof educ, 1965-73, assoc prof & chairperson, 1969-73, asst dean, 1973-80, dir div, 1984-87, prof educ, currently, Sch Educ, dir progs educ opportunity, 1987-; US Dept Educ, Wash, DC, dep asst secy/dir, 1980-81. **Orgs:** Numerous memberships including chair, Nat Alliance Black Sch Educ; Tech Assistance Parent Progs, 1986-; co-chair, TAPP Select Comt, 1986-; chair, Perry Nursery Sch, 1987-; chair, Higher Educ Comn, Nat Alliance Black Sch Educators, 1989-93; Nat Coun Proj Equal Educ Rights, 1991-; exec bd, Father Patrick Jackson House, Ann Arbor, Mich, 1997-; Secy Education's Title IX Comn Opportunities Athletics, 2002-03; Am Asn Ment Retardation; Am Educ Res Asn; Am Psychol Asn; Coun Exceptional C; Mich Psychol Asn. **Honors/Awds:** President's Service Award, NABSE, 1983; Title IV, Desegregation Assistance Ctr Awards, 1999-2002; Dwight D Eisenhower Higher Educ Prof Develop Grant, Family Math, Family Sci, Playtime Is Sci, 2000-01; Kellogg Found Closing the Achievement Gap, 2001-02. **Special Achievements:** Numerous publications including, "Desegregation: Can We Get There From Here?", 1990; "Proceedings of the Magnet School/Title IV Desegregation Programs,", 1993; "Controlled Choice: A New and Effective Desegregation Method,", 1995. **Military Serv:** AUS, Corporal, 1952-54. **Home Phone:** (734)665-8341. **Business Addr:** Professor of Education, University of Michigan, 2244 Pinegrove Ct, Ann Arbor, MI 48103, **Business Phone:** (313)763-9910.

BATES, ROBERT E., JR.
Manager. **Personal:** Born Oct 12, 1934, Washington, DC; son of Robert E and Alice M; married; children: Dawne E Bates Collier, Brandon R, Hillman M. **Educ:** Univ IL, AB, 1955. **Career:** US Census Bur, statistician, 1958-69 (retired); US Off Econ Opportunity, mgt info analyst, 1967-69; Sen Edward Kennedy, legis aide, 1969-77; Mobil Oil Corp, mgr govt rels. **Orgs:** bd dirs, Am Lung Asn, 2005-; bd mem, Everybody Wins. **Military Serv:** AUS, 1st lt, 1955-58. **Business Phone:** (212)315-8700.*

BATES, WILLIAM J
Architect. **Personal:** Born Oct 5, 1952, Canonsburg, PA; son of George C and Laura Ethel Andersen; married Margaret M McDermott, Oct 27, 1977; children: Meaghan A, Owen P & Nora K. **Educ:** Univ Notre Dame, BA, Notre Dame, IN, 1975. **Career:** Shields Construct Co, Pittsburgh, PA, designer, 1975; Celento & Edison Archits, Pittsburgh, PA, intern archit, 1976, partner, 1978-84; Selck Minnerly Group Inc, Pittsburgh, PA, proj archit, 1976-78; Westinghouse Electric Corp, Pittsburgh, PA, consult, 1984-88, design mgr, 1988-93; PNC Bank, Pittsburgh, PA, vpres, 1993-95; Fore Systs Inc, Pittsburgh, PA, dir, real estate & facilities, 1995-99; Marconi Inc, vp, real estate & bldg servs, 1999-2002; Eat'n Park Hospity Group, Eat N? Park Restaurants, vpres, real estate & bldg servs, 2002-. **Orgs:** Pres, Pittsburgh Archits Woskshop, 1980-85; Partnerships Educ Speakers Bur, 1980; founder, Allegheny Trails Archit Career Explorer Post, 1983; pres, Pittsburgh chap Am Inst Architects, 1987; pres, Pa Soc Architects, 1991; chmn, Minority Resource Comt Am Inst Architects, 1990; Allegheny County Airport Develop Comn, 1989-91; Leadership Pittsburgh, 1989; organizer, Intl Remaking Cities Conf, 1988; Allegheny County Parks Comn, 2002-; bd mem, Allegheny Land Trust; Am Inst Architects, tres, 2007-. **Home Addr:** 57 Marlin Dr W, Pittsburgh, PA 15216, **Home Phone:** (412)341-2640. **Business Addr:** Vice President, Eat N? Park Restaurants, Real Estate & Bldg Servs, 285 E Waterfront Dr, PO Box 3000, Pittsburgh, PA 15230, **Business Phone:** (412)461-2000.

BATES, WILLIE EARL
Executive. **Personal:** Born Feb 19, 1940, Shaw, MS; son of Magnolia Gossett; married JoEllen; children: Roman Earl II & Patrice Simone. **Educ:** Tenn State Univ, BS, 1963. **Career:** Universal Life Ins Co, salesman, asst mgr, dist mgr, asst vpres, dir ordinary mkt. **Orgs:** Capital Investment Club; Met Bapt Church; Omega Psi Phi; chmn bd dir, Goodwill Boys Club, 1989-91; vice basileus, Omega Epsilon Phi Chap, 1989-91; bd dir, Jr Achievement, 1984-91. **Honors/Awds:** Manager of the Year, 1968; Cox Trophy, Nat Ins Asn, 1969; Omega Man of the Year, Omega Psi Phi, 1989. **Business Addr:** Director of Ordinary Marketing, Universal Life Insurance Company, 480 Linden Ave, Memphis, TN 38126.*

BATES, YASMIN T.
Banker, vice president (organization). **Educ:** Univ Ill, BS, bus admin. **Career:** Harris NA, com banking trainee, 1976, banking officer, Cash Mgt Sales & Consult, team leader, asst vpres, 1981, sect mgr sales & consult; Harris NA, Metrop Banking Div, vpres & div admin, 1991; Harris Chicago Community Bank, pres, 1994; Harris Bank's City Region, pres, 1998; Harris Trust & Savings Bank, Chicagoland, S Div, exec vpres, 2003-. **Orgs:** Bd mem, Chicago Equity Fund; Community Investment Corp; Glenwood Sch Boys; Network Real Estate Prof; Univ Ill Bus Adv Coun; Univ Chicago's Vis Forum; Urban Bankers Forum Chicago; Spec Allocations Comm, United Way Chicago; Comprehensive Housing Affordability Strategy Comt, Chicago City; Fannie Mae Nat Adv Bd; Am Bankers Asn; Community Develop Comt. *

BATES-PARKER, LINDA
Educator. **Personal:** Born Feb 23, 1944, Cincinnati, OH; married Breland K; children: Robbin & Brandon. **Educ:** Univ Dayton, BS, Eng, 1965, grad teaching assistantship, 1968; Univ Cincinnati, MA, Eng, 1970; Harvard Univ, Mgt Develop Prog, 1992. **Career:** Procter & Gamble, mkt res, 1966-67; Shillito's Dept Store, training coordr, 1968-70; Univ Cincinnati, head counr, asst to dean, 1970-75, asst to VProvost, Stud Affairs, 1975-76, assoc dir, career planning & placement, 1975-81, assoc vprovost, Career Develop Ctr, dir, currently, distinguished teaching fel, adj prof, currently; Black Career Women, pres & founder, 1977-. **Orgs:** Bd mem, Cincinnati Local Develop Corp; bd mem, WCET Educ TV, 1973-74; Pres Comn Domestic Affairs, 1975; commentator, OH Valley Kool Jazz Festival, 1975; coordr, Prof Develop Sem Black Women, 1977; Cincinnati Charter Bd Com, 1980-81; Mayor's Comt Rels Comt, 1980; Chest Eval Comn, 1980; hon mem, Soc Black Engrs, 1980; Am Personnel & Guidance Asn, 1980-81; (UC) vpres, Midwest Asn Col & Employers, 2002-03; Am Red Cross Bd, 2002-04; Col Placement Coun; women's com, Cincinnati Symphony Orch; Midwest Col Placement Asn; Jr Alliance for Soc, Civic Action; United Black Fac & Staff Asn; Asn Women Adminr; Middle Mgrs Asn; adv bd, Greater Cincinnati Women's Chamber Com. **Honors/Awds:** Career Woman of Achievement Award, YWCA, 1982; Women in Communications Advocate Award, 1982; Woman of the Year, Cincinnati Enquirer, 1983; cover story, Elancee Mag, Sept, 1984; Ethelrie Harper Award Cincinnati Human Rels Comn, 1984; Nat Diversity Champion Award, Working Mother Mag, 2000; Global Citizen Award, Greater Cincinnati InterNat Hall of Fame, 2004; Acad Fels, 2005; Distinguished UC Alumna Award; Distinguished Professor Award, Univ Cincinnati. **Special Achievements:** Top 100 Black Business & Professor Women in America, Dollars & Sense Magazine, 1985; First Black Woman Hired in Market Research for the Procter & Gamble Company. **Business Addr:** President, Founder, Black Career Women, 3696 Dogwood Lane, Cincinnati, OH 45213, **Business Phone:** (513)531-1932.

BATH, DR. PATRICIA E.
Physician, ophthalmologist, educator. **Personal:** Born Nov 4, 1942, New York, NJ; daughter of Rupert and Gladys; married Beny J Primm; children: Eraka. **Educ:** Hunter Col NY, BA, chem, 1964; Howard Univ Med Col, MD, 1968; NY Univ, specialty training; Columbia Univ, specialty training. **Career:** Sydenham Hosp NYC, asst surg, 1973; Flower & Fifth Ave Hosp NYC, asst-surg, 1973; Metro Surg NYC, asst surg, 1973-74; NY Med Col Dept Ophthalmol, clin instr, 1973-74; UCLA Ctr for Health Scis, asst attend, 1974-93; UCLA Sch Med, asst prof opthal, 1974-93;

Charles R Drew Postgrad Med Sch, asst prof opthalmol, 1974-, asst prof surg, 1974-; Martin L KingJr Gen Hosp Los Ageles, dir clin serv & asst chief, Div Ophthal, 1974-; Univ Nigeria Med Sch, visit prof surg, 1976-; Jules Stein Eye Inst DeptOphthal, prog dir ophthalmic asst, 1977-93; Charles R Drew Postgrad MedSch Los Angeles, asst prof dept community med int health sect; UCLA MedCtr, chair, ophthal residency training prog, 1983; Dept Ophthal, UCLA Med Ctr, chair, 1983-86; Howard Univ Hosp, prof telecommunications; St George's Univ, Grenada, prof telecommunications; Howard Univ Sch Med, dir telemedicine prog, 2001-. **Orgs:** NSF, 1959; Med Soc Co of NY; Am Med Asn, 1973-75; Nat Med Asn 1973-; Am Soc Contemp Ophthal, 1974-; Am Pub Health Asn, 1975-; Int Agency Prev Blindness, 1975-; Soc Eye Surg Int Eye Found, 1976-; fel, Am Col Surgeons,1976-; fel, Am Acad Ophthal & Otolaryngology, 1976-; pres, Am Inst Prevent Blindness, 1976-; White House consult, Nat & Int Blindness Prevention Prog USA, 1977-78; consult, Fed Drug Admin Ophthalmic Devices Panel, 1979-. **Honors/Awds:** Merit Award, Mademoiselle magazine, 1960; Scholarship Alpha Kappa Alpha-Sor, 1965; NIH Fel, 1965; NIMH Fel, 1965; NIMH Fel, 1966; Fel Dept HEWChildrens' Bur, 1967; NIH Fel Dept Ophthal Howard Univ, 1968; Outstanding Student Endocrinology, Dept med, Howard Univ, 1968; Outstanding Student Pulmonary Diseases, Dept Med, 1968; Outstanding Student Ophthalmology Prize, Dept Surg, 1968; Hunter College Hall of Fame, 1968; Howard UnivPioneer Academic Med, 1993; Int Women in Med Hall of Fame; Am Med Women's Asn, 2001. **Special Achievements:** First African American woman doctor to receive a patent for a medical invention; first African-American woman surgeon at the UCLA Medical Center; Dr. Patricia Bath was the first woman opthalmologist to be appointed to the faculty of the University of California at Los Angeles School of Medicine Jules Stein Eye Institute. *

BATHER, PAUL CHARLES. See Obituaries section.

BATINE, RAFAEL
Lawyer. **Personal:** Born Jul 20, 1947, Santurce, PR; married Patricia Estelle Pryde; children: Rafael Pablo. **Educ:** St John's Univ, Col Bus Admin, BS, 1969; St John's Univ, Sch Law, JD, 1974. **Career:** Westbury Pub Sch, NY, math teacher, 1969-73; Covington Howard Hagood & Holland, NY, law clerk, 1973-74; Queens Dist Attys Off, asst dist atty, 1974-75; Rutledge Holmes Willis Batine & Kellam NY, pvt law pract, 1975-78; Ga Off Fair Employ, gen coun, 1978-79; US Dept Labor, Off Solicitor, atty, sr trial atty, currently. **Orgs:** Martin Luther King Scholar, St John's Univ, Sch Law, 1971-74; Admitted pract law, NY, 1975, US Supreme Ct, 1977, GA, 1983. **Business Addr:** Senior Trial Attorney, United States Department of Labor, Office of the Solicitor, Sam Nunn Atlanta Fed Ctr, 61 Forsyth St SW Rm 7T10, Atlanta, GA 30303-8916.*

BATISTE, KIM
Baseball player. **Personal:** Born Mar 15, 1968, New Orleans, LA. **Career:** Baseball player (Retired); Philadelphia Phillies, 1991-95; San Francisco Giants, 1996; Atlantic City Surf, 1999, 2003.

BATTEAST, ROBERT V.
Executive. **Personal:** Born Jan 1, 1931?, Rosetta, MS. **Educ:** Ind Univ. **Career:** S Bend Develop Corp, vpres; Batteast Construct Co Inc, pres, currently. **Orgs:** Dir, First South Bank; Off Bldg Comn, Ind State. **Business Addr:** President, Batteast Construct Co Inc, 430 E LaSalle Ave, South Bend, IN 46617.*

BATTEN, REV. GRACE RUTH
Clergy, chairperson. **Personal:** Born Mar 22, 1943, Harbeson, DE; children: Earl William Jr. **Educ:** Del Tech & Comn Col, AAS, 1976; Burke Bible Col, BTh, 1977; Wilmington Col, BS, 1986. **Career:** Adult Educ Satellite Prog, admin; Nat Youth Conf, educ chair, 1980-84; Mt Sinai Farm Develop Comn, chair, 1985-87; Mt Zion Holy Church Inc, pastor & pres admin, currently; Mt Zion Bible Inst, founder & dir, 1988-; Milton Pub Libr, vpres, currently. **Orgs:** Nat Coun Negro Women; bd mem, Del Asn A & C Educ; coun woman & secy, Milton Town Coun; Am Soc Notaries; vchmn, Sussex Co Red Cross; Nat Asn female Execs; bd mem, People Place II Coun Ctr; vmayor, Milton Town Coun. **Honors/Awds:** Big Sister of the Year, Sussex Co Br, 1981; Outstanding Citizen Award, Milton Chamber Com, 1983; Cert Appreciation, Vica Sussex Voc Tech Ctr, 1986. **Special Achievements:** 1st black coun woman/secy Milton Town Coun; 1st black vice mayor, Milton Town Coun. **Business Addr:** Bishop, Mount Zion Holy Church, 325 Front St, Milton, DE 19968.*

BATTIE, TONY (DEMETRIUS ANTONIO BETTIE)
Basketball player. **Personal:** Born Feb 11, 1976, Dallas, TX. **Educ:** Tex Tech, communications. **Career:** Denver Nuggets, ctr-forward, 1997-98; Boston Celtics, ctr-forward, 1998-04; Cleveland Cavaliers, ctr-forward, 2004; Orlando Magic, ctr-forward, 2005-09; New Jersey Nets, currently. *

BATTIES, DR. PAUL TERRY
Physician, cardiologist. **Personal:** Born Jul 22, 1941, Indianapolis, IN. **Educ:** Ind Univ, AB, 1962; Ind Sch Med, MD, 1965. **Career:** Detroit Gen Hosp, internship, 1965-66; Wayne State Univ, resident internal med, 1966-69, chief med resident, 1969; Univ KY, Cardiology Fel, 1971-73; pvt pract, physician . **Orgs:** founding mem, bd dir, Asn Black Cardiologists; past bd, Marion Co Heart Asn; pres, Aesculapian Med Soc, 1982-84; past chmn, Hypertension Comn; Kappa Alpha Psi Frat; Univ United Meth Ch; Ind Soc Int Med; pres, Am Heart Asn, 1990; Am Med Asn; Ind State Med Asn; life mem, Nat Advan Asn Colored People. **Honors/Awds:** Distinguished Citizens Award, Ind, 1976. **Military Serv:** USAF, Maj, 1969-71. **Business Addr:** Cardiologist, 1633 N Capitol Ave Suite 510, Indianapolis, IN 46202, **Business Phone:** (317)924-1001.*

BATTIES, THOMAS L.
Chief executive officer, president (organization). **Career:** Enterprise Fed Savings Bank, pres & ceo, 1999-03; Independence Fed Savings Bank, actg pres & ceo, 2003-2006. **Business Phone:** (202)628-5500.*

BATTISTE, AUDREY ELAYNE QUICK
Librarian. **Personal:** Born Aug 24, 1944, Norfolk, VA; daughter of Oscar S Quick Jr and Geneva Shokes Quick; married Eugene Wilson Tyler (divorced 1986); married Auggeretto Battiste. **Educ:** SC State Univ, Orangeburg, SC, BS, 1965; John Carroll Univ, Cleveland Heights, OH, attended 1966; Univ Okla, Norman, OK, attended 1965; Atlanta Univ, Atlanta, GA, MSLS, 1968. **Career:** Librarian (retired); Dept Welfare, Bronx, NY, caseworker, 1966-67; Bristol Myers Res Labs, E Syracuse, NY, librn, 1968-70; Atlanta Pub Libr, Atlanta, GA, librn, 1972-74; SC State Col, Orangeburg, SC, instr, 1975; Atlanta Fulton Pub Libr, Atlanta, GA, libr adminr, 1977-90, mgr human resources, 1997-99; Fulton County Superior Ct, Atlanta, GA, proj dir, 1990-97. **Orgs:** Treas, bd dirs, ACIP, 1985-87; chair, nominations comt 1985-90, chair, prof develop comt 1984-86, Black Caucus, AL; nat vpres, 1986-89, nat pres, 1989-93, SC State Univ Nat Alumni Asn; pres, bd dirs, Atlanta Coun Int Prog, 1987-89; bd dir, SC State Univ Educ Found, 1989-; African Am Family Hist Asn; vol, Fulton County Juvenile Ct, Citizens Rev Panel. **Honors/Awds:** Bulldog Award, SC State Univ Almni Asn. **Home Addr:** 1421 S Gordon St SW, Atlanta, GA 30310. *

BATTLE, BERNARD J. See Obituaries section.

BATTLE, CONCHA Y. See BATTLE, DR. CONCHITA Y.

BATTLE, DR. CONCHITA Y (CONCHA Y BATTLE)
Administrator, public speaker. **Personal:** Born Feb 8, 1963, Philadelphia, PA; daughter of Turner C Battle, III and Yvonne M Minnick; children: Amethyst Jai Battle. **Educ:** Talladega Col, BA, 1987; Jacksonville State Univ, MPA, 1981; Univ PA, EDD, 1999. **Career:** Talladega Col, dir equal opp employ, 1991-92, instr, 1990-92, acting dept head/asst dir teacher ed prog, 1990-92; Univ PA, research assist, 1994-95; Philadelphia Sch Readiness Proj, research assoc prog develop, 1995-96; Lincoln Univ, assist vp Acad Affairs, 1997-98; Univ MD, assist dir admin, acad achievement progs, 1998-2001; CA State Univ, Northridge, dir advising resource ctr & eop, 2002-CA State Libr, assembly speaker, 2004-. **Orgs:** Phi Delta Kappa; NACADA; Am Asn Higher Ed; Am Asn Univ Prof; Am Coun Ed; United Negro Col Fund; Coun Opportunity Ed; Nat Asn Women Ed; Nat Asn Equal Opp Higher Ed; Nat Consortium Sports Asn, Nat Acad Advising Asn. **Home Phone:** (805)527-4270.

BATTLE, GLORIA JEAN
County government official. **Personal:** Born May 23, 1950, Deerfield Beach, FL; daughter of Joyce and Eugene Battle. **Educ:** Bennett Col, Greensboro NC, BA, 1972; Howard Univ, Wash DC, MUS, 1976; Fla State Univ, Tallahassee FL, 1985-. **Career:** Social Systs Intervention, Wash DC, res analyst, 1973-76; Mark Battle Asn, Wash DC, consult, 1976; Child Advocacy Inc, Ft Lauderdale, FL, planner, 1977-79; Fla Int Univ, Miami Fla, dir, 1979-80; Broward County Govt, Ft Lauderdale FL, dir human rels div, 1981-. **Orgs:** Pres, Nat Asn Human Rights Workers, 1981-, pres Deerfield Child Develop Ctr, 1981-82; first vpres, Nat Asn Advan Colored People, N Broward Chapter, 1984-85; Int Asn Human Rights Off; Community Housing Resource Bd, 1983-86; Forum Black Pub Admin, 1984-. **Honors/Awds:** Davison-Foreman Scholarship, Bennett Coll, 1971; NIMH Fellowship, NIMH, Howard Univ, 1973; McKnight Fellowship, McKnight Found, 1985; Global Woman of the 80s, Charmettes, 1987; Liberty Bell Award, Broward County Bar Asn, 1989. **Business Addr:** Director, Broward Co, Hum Rights Div, 115 S Andrews Ave Rm A640, Fort Lauderdale, FL 33301.*

BATTLE, JACQUELINE
Banker. **Personal:** Born Sep 7, 1962, Columbus, GA; daughter of Myrtis Mahone Porter; married Gregory, Nov 26, 1982; children: Gregory II & James. **Educ:** Columbus Col, Columbus, Ga, 1982; Tuskegee Inst, Tuskegee, Ala, attended 1984. **Career:** Atlantic Mortgage, Columbus, Ga, loan off, 1983-84; Money Express, Columbus, Ga, pres, 1985-. **Orgs:** Am Bus Women's Asn; Coordr Sus Women's Commn; clerk, Seventh-day Adventist Church; dir, Children of Praise; Am Bus Women; Criminal Justice Club; Columbus Chamber Com. **Honors/Awds:** Future Leader of America, Ebony Magazine, Nov, 1989; leader of teen support group; Million Dollar Club. **Home Addr:** 210 Whipoorwill Lane, Columbus, GA 31903, **Home Phone:** (404)689-9770. **Business Addr:** President, Money Express Inc, 2310 N Lumpkin Rd, Columbus, GA 31903, **Business Phone:** (404)689-8209.

BATTLE, JOE TURNER
Government official. **Personal:** Born Aug 25, 1941, Atlanta, TX; married Barbara L; children: Joe D & Kim C. **Educ:** Dept Defense Race Rel Inst, Cert, 1975; CA State Univ, Dominguez Hill, BS, Bus Admin, 1985. **Career:** Off Training Sch Ft Sill, staff instr, 1967-68; Schweinfurt Ger, equal oppurtunity educ co, 1975-77; Lynnwood Unified Sch Dist, pres sch bd mem,1983-85; Lynnwood Unified Sch Dist, Personnel Comn, Vice Chairperson, Chairperson, pres, 1998-. **Orgs:** Chairperson, mem Lynnwood Sch Site Coun, 1980; Lynnwood USD Adv Coun, 1980-81; S Cent Area Adv Coun Catholic Youth Org, 1981-85; pta legis rep, Lynwood PTA Coun, 1983-84; Cerritos Area Trustees Assoc, 1981-85. **Military Serv:** AUS, sgt, 1st class, 21 yrs; Bronze Star, Meritorious Service Medal, Combat Infantry Badge, 3 Commend Medals, 5 Campaign Stars Vietnam, Vietnam Cross Galantry. **Business Addr:** Chairperson, Lynwood Unified School District, 11321 Bullis Rd, Lynwood, CA 90262, **Business Phone:** (310)886-1600.*

BATTLE, PROF. JUAN
Educator. **Educ:** York Col Pa, AS, law enforcement, 1988, BS, corrections & sociol, 1989;Univ Mich, MA, sociol, 1991, PhD, sociol, 1994. **Career:** City Univ New York, Hunter Col & Grad Ctr, prof sociol, currently. **Orgs:** Pres, Asn Black Sociologists, 2006-07; Nat Gay & Lesbian Task Force; Ctr Lesbian & Gay Studies; Am Sociol Asn. **Honors/Awds:** Fulbright Sr Specialist; "Ten Black Men Transforming The World", ARISE Mag. **Special Achievements:** Numerous publications in many academic journals, his work has been highlighted in popular national magazines, radio shows and newspapers; among these have been Black Entertainment Television (BET), Essence magazine, and The Advocate magazine. **Business Addr:** Professor, City University of New York Graduate Center, Department of Sociology, 365 5th Ave, New York, NY 10016-4309, **Business Phone:** (212)817-8775.

BATTLE, KATHLEEN
Opera singer. **Personal:** Born Aug 13, 1948, Portsmouth, OH. **Educ:** Univ Cincinnati Col Conserv, BA, 1970, MA, 1971. **Career:** Requium, Cincinnati May Festival, singer, 1972; Festival of Two Worlds in Spoleto, Italy, performer, 1972; NY Metrop Opera, singer, 1980-94; regular guest soprano with orchestras in NY, Chicago, Boston, Philadelphia, Cleveland, Paris & Berlin & at major opera houses including the Metrop, Paris, Vienna & the Royal Opera/Covent Garden; Albums: Christmas Celebration, 1986; Sings Mozart, 1995; So Many Stars, 1995; Angels' Glory, 1996; Greatest Hits, 2002; Kathleen Battle, 2002; Classic Battle: A Portrait, 2002; First Love, 2004; Best of Kathleen Battle: 20th Century Masters/The Millennium Collection, 2004. **Honors/Awds:** Nat Achievement Scholar; Salz burg Recital; Candace Award, Nat Coalition100 Black Women, 1992; Hall of Fame, NAACP Image; five-time Grammy Award winner; Emmy Award, 1991; Honorary Doctorate, Univ Cincinnati; Honorary Doctorate, Westminster Choir Col; Honorary Doctorate, Ohio Univ; Honorary Doctorate, Xavier Univ; Honorary Doctorate, Amherst Col; Honorary Doctorate, Seton Hall Univ; NAACP Image Hall Of Fame, 1999.

BATTLE, MARK G.
Association executive, educator, social worker. **Personal:** Born Jul 28, 1924, Bridgeton, NJ; son of Edward M. Battle (deceased) and Mary Noble Battle (deceased); children: Erica, Kewana, Marcus. **Educ:** Univ Rochester, BA, 1948; Case Western Res, MSSA, 1950; Kings Pt Fed Exec Inst, cert, Fed Prog Mgt, 1966. **Career:** Association executive, Educator, Social worker (retired); Lower N Ctr, Chicago, 1952-60; Franklin Settlement, exec dir, 1960-64; Bur Work Training Prog USDOL, admin, 1964-69; US Dept Labor, consult; Mark Battle Assn, chmn bd dir, 1969-83; Howard Univ Sch Social Work, prof & chmn, 1971-85; Nat Asn Social Workers, exec dir, 1984-92; Univ Md, vis prof, 2002. **Orgs:** admin, Bur Work Training Progs, USDOL, 1964-69; mem, House Delegates CSWE; mem, Am Soc Pub Admin; Am Pub Welfare Asn, 1975-85; Nat Urban League; mem, bd dir Wash Coun Agency, 1981-85; life mem, Nat Conf Social Welfare; Nat Non-Profit Risk Mgt Inst Bd, 1990; bd dirs, Coun Int Progs; Nat Asn Social Workers (NASW); Friendly Inn Settlement House. **Honors/Awds:** James M Yard Brotherhood Award, NCCJ, 1957; Distinguished Alumni Award, Case Western Res SASS, 1986; President Award, NASW, 1989; Exemplary Leadership & Service Award, NASW, 1992; Lifetime Achievement Award, NASW, 2002. **Military Serv:** USN V12, midshipman, 1943-46. *

BATTLE, MAURICE TAZWELL
Administrator. **Personal:** Born Aug 7, 1927, Oberlin, OH; son of Turner R and Anne Evelyn McClellan; married Esther Coleman Battle, Jun 7, 1948; children: Carla M, Maurice T Jr, Renee E, Michael C. **Educ:** Oakwood Col, Huntsville Al, BA, 1948; Union Theological Seminary, Birmingham, AL, LLD, 1974. **Career:** adminr (retired); Sierra Leone Mission Seventh-day Adventists, Sierra Leone, W Africa, pres, 1958-59; W African Union Seventh-

day Adventists, Accra, Ghana, W Africa, departmental dir, 1959-66; Northern European div Seventh-day Aventists, Watford, Herts, England, departmental dir, 1966-70; General Conference Seventh-day Adventists, Wash, DC, assoc dept dir Northern Europe regional office, 1970-75; Afro-Mideast div Seventh-day Adventists, Beirut, Lebanon, secy, 1975-77; World Headquarters Seventh-day Adventists, Silver Spring, MD, assoc secy, 1977-01. **Orgs:** mem bd dirs, pres, Rotary Club of Silver Spring. **Honors/Awds:** Special Award, Serv Humanity . **Special Achievements:** Author, Your Friends the Adventists, 1960. *

BATTLE, ROXANE
Television news anchorperson. **Personal:** Born in St Paul, MN; children: 1. **Educ:** Univ Minn, BA, jour; Univ Mo, Columbia, MA, jour. **Career:** KOMU-TV, Columbia, MO; WJXT-TV, Jacksonville, FL; WDAF-TV, Kans City, MO; KARE-11, Minneapolis, MN, gen assignment reporter, 1992, KAFE KARE, host, weekend anchor, 1998-2000, KARE 11 Today Show, co-host, anchor, 2000-. **Honors/Awds:** Nominee, Emmy Awards. **Special Achievements:** Has been featured in Working Mother and Ebony magazines. **Business Addr:** Reporter, Kare-11, Gannett Broadcasting-Nbc, 8811 Hwy 55, Minneapolis, MN 55427, **Business Phone:** (763)546-1111.

BATTLE, DR. STANLEY F
President (Organization). **Personal:** Born Jun 12, 1951, Springfield, MA; son of Henry and Rachel Williams; married Judith Lynn Rozie, Nov 1, 1975; children: Ashley Lynn. **Educ:** Springfield Col, BA, 1973; Univ Conn, MSW, 1975; Univ Pittsburgh, MPH, 1979; PhD, 1980; Harvard Univ, Inst Educ Mgt, attended 2002. **Career:** Univ Minn Sch Social Work, asst prof, 1980-84; Boston Univ Sch Social Work, assoc prof, 1984-87; Sch Med (Pediatrics), sr res, 1984-89; Univ Conn, Sch Social Work, prof, 1987-93, Sch Med-Community Med, sr lectr, 1987-93, assoc dean res & devel, 1991-93, Sch Allied Health, adj prof, 1996-98; Eastern Conn State Univ, assoc vpres acad affairs, 1993-98; Schs Social Welfare & Educ, sullivan spaights distinguished profship, 1998-2001; Univ Wis-Milwaukee, vice chancellor student & multicultural affairs, 2000-03; Coppin State Univ, pres, 2003-; chancellor of North Carolina Agricultural & Technical State Univ. **Orgs:** Chair, Univ Planning Coun, Coppin State Univ, currently. **Honors/Awds:** 2005 Legacy Laureate Alumni Award, Univ Pittsburgh; 2005 Champions fo Courage, FOX 45/WB 54TV, Baltimore; 2003-04 Recipient for Outstanding Support, Coppin State Student Senate Asn; 2002 AKA, Epsilon Kappa Omega Trailblazer Award; 2001 Mentoring Award, St. Mark AME Church; 1999 African American Heritage Award, Univ Wis-Whitewater; 1998 Endowed named scholarship, Eastern Conn State Univ; 1996 Martin Luther King, Jr. Community Service Award, Eastern Conn State Univ. **Business Addr:** Chancellor, North Carolina Agricultural & Technical State University, 1601 East Market St, Greensboro, NC 27411, **Business Phone:** (336)334-7500.

BATTLE, THOMAS CORNELL
Librarian, administrator. **Personal:** Born Mar 19, 1946, Washington, DC; son of Thomas Oscar and Lenora Thomas; divorced; children: Brima Omar, Idrissa Saville, Mensah Lukman. **Educ:** Howard Univ, BA, 1969; Univ MD, MLS, 1971; George Wash Univ, PhD, 1982. **Career:** Fed City Col, Sr Media Intern, 1969-71; DC Pub Libr, readers adv, 1971; MSRC, ref librn, 1972-74; Sierra Leone Lib Bd, exchange librn, 1972-73; Howard Univ, Moorland Spingarn Res Ctr, cur manuscripts, 1974-86, dir, 1986-. **Orgs:** Councillor at large, 1980-83, treas, 1983-85; African Am Mus Asn; bd mem, mus City Wash, 1978, 1981-90; chair, task force minorities, Soc Am Archivists, 1982-86; bd mem, Wash, DC, Nat History Day, 1983-85; exec bd, Black Caucus Am Libr Asn, 1980-92; chair, nominating comn; chair, African & Caribbean Task Force Black Caucus Am Libr Asn, 1980-82; bd mem, DC Libr Asn, 1978-80; consult, Nat Park Serv, 1983-85; Am Library Asn; mem, Mid-Atlantic Regional Archives Conf; field reviewer & panelist, Nat Endowment humanities, 1976-; bylaws comt, Metro Wash Caucus Black Librns, 1982-83; prog comn, 1986, nominating comn, 1987, Mid Atlantic Regional Archives Conf; prog comn, Soc Am Archivists, 1987. **Honors/Awds:** Title IIB Higher Educ Acct fel, 1970-71; Beta Phi Mu Iota Chap, 1971; Certified Archivist, Academy Certified Archivists, 1989; author of: "Howard University: Heritage and Horizons," Academic Affairs Bulletin, Howard Univ, v. 2, no. 1, February, 1977; "Research Centers Document the Black Experience," History News, February, 1981; "Behind the Marble Mask," The Wilson Quarterly, New Year's, 1989. **Business Addr:** Director, Howard University, Moorland-Spingarn Research Center, 500 Howard Pl NW, Washington, DC 20059, **Business Phone:** (202)806-7240.*

BATTLE, TURNER CHARLES, III
Association executive, educator. **Personal:** Son of Turner and Annie Evelyn McClellan; married Carmen H Gonzalez Castellanos; children: Anne E (McAndrew), Turner IV, Conchita, Carmen Rosario. **Educ:** Oakwood Col, BA; Temple Univ, MFA; Columbia Univ; NY Univ; Columbia Pacific Univ; Wiley Col, HHD. **Career:** Oakwood Col, instr; USN Dept, auditor & acct; Philadelphia Sch Dist, teacher; Elmira Col, asst prof; Moore Col Art, assoc prof; La Salle Col, dir spec progs; Higher Educ Coalition, exec dir; NY Univ, assoc prof; Westminster Choir Col, assoc prof; United Negro Col Fund Inc, asst exec dir, corp sec; Educ Develop Serv, pres. **Orgs:** Oakwood Col Alumni Asn; Temple Univ Alumni Asn; vis comn educ, Metro Mus Art; Am Soc Assoc Exec; Sierra Club; mem, Am Mus Nat Hist; Smithsonian Inst; Am Asn Higher Educ; Phi Delta Kappa. **Home Addr:** 1519 W Turner St, Allentown, PA 18102. *

BATTLES, SHERYL Y
Executive. **Career:** Pitney Bowes Inc, vpres, corp commun, currently. **Business Addr:** Vice President of Corporate Communications, Pitney Bowes Inc, 1 Elmcroft Rd, Stamford, CT 06926-0700, **Business Phone:** (203)351-6808.

BATTS, ALICIA
Lawyer. **Educ:** Harvard Col, BA, soc studies, 1987; Columbia Univ Law Sch, JD, 1990. **Career:** Howrey Simon Arnold & White LLP, antitrust & com litigator; Skadden, Arps, Slate, Meagher & Flom LLP, antitrust & com litigator; Federal Trade Comnr Mozelle W. Thompson, atty-adv, 1998-2000; Foley & Lardner's Litigation Dept, partner, 2000-04; Dickstein Shapiro Morin & Oshinsky, Litigation & Dispute Resolution Group, atty & partner, 2004-. **Orgs:** Am Bar Asn, DC Bar Asn; vice chair, Am Bar Asn Antitrust Sec Bus Torts & Civil RICO Comt; ed bd, Antitrust Law Jour; bd dirs, Appleseed Found. **Special Achievements:** Listed in Black Enterprises Americas Top Black Lawyers; Author: "Prudence is the Best Policy for Standard-Setters", Merger Review in a Sluggish Economy. **Business Phone:** (202)420-2200.

BAUDUIT, HAROLD S
Lawyer. **Personal:** Born Aug 27, 1930, New Orleans, LA; children: Lianne & Cheryl. **Educ:** US Naval Acad, BS, eng, 1956; Univ Colo, MA, Econs, MS, mgt, JD, Law. **Career:** Martin Luther King Jr fel; Woodrow Wilson Nat fel Found, 1969-71; Univ Colo, instr bus law, 1969-76, atty fac, 1972-76, Econs & Black Studies, asst prof, law pract, beginning 1983; pvt pract, atty, currently. **Orgs:** Sigma Iota Epsilon Hon Mgt Fraternity, Univ Colo, 1969-72; Community Corrections Bd, beginning 1997. **Military Serv:** USAF, capt retired, 1956-69. **Business Addr:** Attorney, 2760 Iliff St, Boulder, CO 80303-7020, **Business Phone:** (303)494-4080.

BAUGH, EDNA Y
Lawyer, administrator. **Personal:** Born Aug 22, 1948, Orange, NJ; daughter of George W and Pauline E. **Educ:** Hartwick Col, BA, 1970; Vermont Law Sch, JD, 1983. **Career:** City East Orange, corp trial coun, 1986-94; Medvin & Elberg, assoc atty, 1988-98; Ruters Law Sch, asst dir clin admin, 2004-; Stephens & Baugh LLC, managing mem & co-chairperson, 2000-. **Orgs:** Nat Bar Asn, 1986-; Garden State Bar Asn, 1986-; Essex-Newark Legal Servs, bd sec, 1993-; Girl Scout Coun Greater Essex & Hudson Counties, 1986-, pres, 1995-2001; Essex County Col Bd Trustees, 1997-; NJ State Bar Asn; Essex County Bar Asn. **Honors/Awds:** Alumni Asn Award, Vermont Law Sch, 1983; Hartwick Col, 1993; Outstanding Alumna Award, Essex County Bar Asn Spec Merit Award, 2002; Womens in Real Estate Award, Ruters Law Sch, 2004. **Business Addr:** Co-Chairperson, Managing Member, Stephens & Baugh, 2040 Millburn Ave Suite 305, Maplewood, NJ 07040-3716, **Business Phone:** (973)762-9400.

BAUGH, FLORENCE ELLEN
Administrator. **Personal:** Born Feb 2, 1935, Beaver Dam, KY; daughter of William C Jackson and Glendora Fant Birch; married Dallas A Baugh, Aug 31, 1953 (deceased); children: Delandria, Dallas, Christopher, Orville, Lynne. **Educ:** Millard Fillmore Col, SUNY, BA; Empire State Col; CCAP certif, 1995; CCAP certif renewed, 2003. **Career:** Comm Action Org, Erie Co, comn aide, 1965-70; YWCA, dir racial justice pub affairs, 1971-72; Comn Action Org, Erie Co, dir, neighborhood servs dept, 1972-01, New Venture Housing Inc, mgr, 1988-01; dir, Sr Serv & Community Rels Dept, 2001-04. **Orgs:** Trustee, Sheehan Mem Emer Hosp, 1974-86, D'Youville Col; Buffalo Bd Educ, 1973-89; dir pres, Ellicott Houses Inc; Univ Buffalo CAC; bd mem, We NY Art Inst; Coun Grt City Sch Bds, sec treasurer, 1978-89; Governor's appointee, Dist Judicial Review Comn; organist, clerk, trustee, Providence Bapt Ch; Pres, Coun Great City Sch, 1988-89; pres, State Univ Buffalo CAC; bd mem, EPIC; Erie County Dept Social Serv Adv Bd, comnr, 1991; Concerned Citizens Against Violence Coalition, 1991; co-chmn, Irene Bellamy Scholarship Fund; Nat Black Child Develop Inst; Nat Caucus & Ctr Black Aged Inc; Nat Museum Women Arts; State Univ Buffalo Community Adv Coun, 1989-91; EPIC Nat Bd Dirs, 1989-92; trustee, Theodore Roosevelt inaugural site; Cert Housing Counselor, 1995; Cert Community Action Prof, 1995; bd trustees, Villa Marie Col, 1995; bd dirs, City Buffalo, Enterprise Zone, 1995; Buffalo & Erie County Workforce Develop Bd, 2002. **Honors/Awds:** Commisson Service Award, Afro-American Policeman's Asn, 1972; Buffalo Chapter Negro Business & Professional Women Commission Service Award, 1973; Black Educators Association Education Service Award, 1974; Citizen of the Year, Buffalo Evening News, 1975; Woman of the Year, Nat Org PUSH, 1975; Buffalo Urban League Family Life Award, 1976; President Distinguished Medal, Buffalo St Teacher Col, 1978; University Alumni Award, Univ Buffalo, 1982; Nat Conf Christians & Jews Educatin Award, 1982; Medal Excellence, NY State Univ, Bd Regents, 1984; Week of the Young Child, honorary chmn; Vernie Mulholland Friend of Ed Award, Delta Kappa Gamma, 1986; Distinguished citizen award, St Univ Syst of NY St, 1986; Empire State Fed of Women's Clubs Commission Service Award; honorary doctorate degrees: Canisius Col, 1976; Medaille Col, 1989; YMCA Community Service Award, 1989; Western NY Women Hall of Fame, 1994; Buffalo Queens, 2001; Southern Christian Leadership Conference Community Service Award, 2004. **Special Achievements:** Appointed Governor Cuomo NY State Sch & Bus Alliance; Conducted numerous Training Sessions as Rep State CSBG NY Bd dirs; Conducted Training Seminar State SC Dept Social Serv; Conducted Training Seminar Little Rock, Arkansas Pub Sch Parents; Participated Mem Long Range Comt People Inc, 1990; Canisius Col Sports Comt; Appointed Honorable Michael A Telesca, Chief Judge, United States District Court, Merit Selection Comt interview & recommend candidate position US Magistrate Judge Western Dist NY, 1994.

BAUGH, HOWARD L.
Pilot, executive, salesperson. **Personal:** Born Jan 20, 1920, Petersburg, VA; son of William H (deceased) and Carrie Rawlings (deceased); widowed; children: Howard, David, Richard. **Educ:** Va State Col, BS, 1941. **Career:** Pilot (retired), Sales Adminstrator (retired); US Army Air Corp, fighter pilot, 1942-47; USAF, pilot admin instr, 1947-67; Eastman Kodak Comp, admin sales, 1967-84. **Orgs:** Tuskegee Airmen Inc, 1985-; Retired Officers Asn, 1985-. **Honors/Awds:** Outstanding Unit Award, USAF; Honoree, Strong Men & Women Excellence Leadership Ser, Dominion, 2006. **Military Serv:** AUS, AirCorps; USAF, lieutenant, col, 1942-67; Distinguished Flying Cross, 1943-44; Air Medal w/ 3 oakleaf clusters, 1943-44; French Legion of Honor, French Govt, 2004; Am Campaign Medal; European-African-Middle Eastern Campaign Medal w/Bss; WW II Victory Medal; Nat Defense Serv Medal w/One BSS; Air Force Commendation Medal. **Home Phone:** (804)794-1620. *

BAUGH, PROF. JOYCE A.
Political scientist. **Personal:** Born Jul 19, 1959, Charleston, SC; daughter of Jeff and Ella Jones; married Roger D Hatch, Nov 23, 1989. **Educ:** Clemson Univ, Clemson, SC, BA, 1981; Kent State Univ, Kent, OH, MA, 1983, PhD, 1989. **Career:** Kent State Univ, Kent, OH, grad asst, 1982-83, teaching fellow, 1984-88; Cent Mich Univ, Mt Pleasant, MI, from asst prof to assoc prof, 1988-98, Dept Polit Sci, chairperson, 1995-2001, prof, 1998-; Saginaw News, guest columnist, 2005. **Orgs:** Secy, Womens Aid Serv, 1990-2004; secy, Midwest Women's Caucus Polit Sci, 1990-91; Affirmative Action Coun, Cent Mich Univ, 1990-95; bd dirs, Cent Mich Univ Fac Asn, 1991-95, 2000-04; co-chairperson, Affirmative Action Coun, 1992-94; exec bd, Cent Mich Univ Acad Senate, 2004-05. **Honors/Awds:** Harry S Truman Scholar, Truman Found, 1979; Outstanding Graduate Student Teaching Award, Kent State University, 1984; selected to receive 2009 Excellence in Teaching award from Central Michigan University's College of Humanities and Social and Behavioral Sciences. **Home Addr:** 711 Hopkins Ave, Mount Pleasant, MI 48858, **Home Phone:** (989)773-2589. **Business Addr:** Professor, Central Michigan University, Department of Political Science, 247 Anspach Hall, Mount Pleasant, MI 48859, **Business Phone:** (989)774-3475.

BAUGH, LYNNETTE
Executive. **Personal:** Born Feb 22, 1949, Charleston, WV. **Educ:** W Virginia State Col, BA, 1971; Univ Pittsburgh, MPA, 1972. **Career:** City Chicago Pub Works Dept, planning anal, 1973-74; IL Dept Local Govt Affairs, area rep, 1974-76; IL Dept Local Govt Affairs, area supvr, 1976-77; Tacoma Inter Govern Affairs Off, dir; City Tacoma Comn Develop Dept, asst dir, 1978-; Dept Public Utilities, mgt anal, 1984-89, Customer Finance & Admin Serv, asst dir, 1989-. **Orgs:** Title 9 Sex Equity Adv Comt; bd mem, Pierce Co Growth Policy Asn; exec com & vpres, NAHRO Puget Sound Chap NAHRO; bd mem, Tacom Urban League; NAACP; vpres, Tacoma Alumnae Chap Delta Sigma Theta Sorority; Delta Sigma Theta Sorority, 1968-; Altrusa Int; Kiwannianne; APPA Comn Perform Mgt; Women Govern; Acct Adv Comt; Tacoma Rotary Club; vice chmn, 1989-91, chmn, 1991-93, APPA Perform Mgt Comt; RK Mellon Fels. **Special Achievements:** named Wash Potential Black Leader 1980's NW Conf Black Pub Officials. **Business Addr:** Assistant Director, Tacoma Public Utilities, PO Box 11007, Tacoma, WA 98411.*

BAUGH, REGINALD F.
Executive, physician. **Personal:** Born Jun 12, 1956, Grand Forks, ND; son of Gerald R and Virginia; married Bobbie Hafford Baugh, Jun 5, 1981; children: Brandon, Aaron. **Educ:** Univ IA, BS, 1977; Univ MI, Med Sch, MD, 1981; Nat Bd Med Examiners, Dipl; Am Bd Otolaryngol, Dipl. **Career:** Kansas City Veteran's Hosp, chief otolaryngol, 1988-90; Univ Kans Med Sch, asst prof, 1988-90; Kaiser Permanente, chief otolaryngol, 1990-93, res mgt, dir, 1991-93; Henry Ford Health Syst, med dir, hosp utilization, 1993-; clin res improv, med dir, 1995-98, clin serv, med dir, 1996-; Tex A&M Health Sci Ctr Col Med, prof surg; Scott & White, Div Otolaryngol, dir, 2005-; New Grace Apostolic Church, deacon & Sunday Sch teacher. **Orgs:** Am med Asn; coun, AMAP Performance Measurement Comn; House Delegates, Am Med Group Asn; pres, treas, Nat Med Assn, Otolaryngol Sect; Mich State Med Soc; Mich Inst Med Qual; chair, Reimbursement Comt, Am Acad Otolaryngol; Aetna US Healthcare, MI, Credentialing/Performance

Management Comt, Qual Oversight Comt; trustee, Onika Ins Co; trustee, Henry Ford Health Syst/Henry Ford Med Group/Herny Ford Hosp; Am Col Physician Exec; treas, Barnes Soc; Walter P. Work Soc; exec comt, Healthy Detroit. **Honors/Awds:** Joseph F. Dwyer Memorial Award, 1986, 1987; Merit Scholar, Kaiser Family Found, 1981; Outstanding Service Award, Am Acad Otolaryngol. **Special Achievements:** Co-authored "Epiglottis In Children: Review 24 Cases," Otolaryngology Head & Neck Surgery, vol 90, 1982; "Adult Supraglottitis Early Age," Southern Med Journal, vol 80, 1987; "Lymphangiomatosis Skull Manifesting with Recurrent Meningitis & Cerebrospinal Fluid Otorrhea," Otolaryngology Haed & Neck Surgery, vol 103, 1990; numerous other publications; presented: "An Objective Method Prediction Tracheosophageal Speech Production", Am Speech-Language Hearing Assn, 1986; "Tonsicillar Abscess", Nat Med Assn, 1989; "Accelerated Fractionation Radiation Therapy & Concurrent Cisplatin Chemotherapy in Advanced Squamous Cell Cancers Head & Neck", Int Congress Radiation Oncology, 1993; numerous other presentations, posters, exhibits, seminars and abstracts; America's Top Physicians" Otolarynology, Consumers Research Council of America. **Business Addr:** Director, Scott & White, Division of Otolaryngology, 2401 S 31st St, Temple, TX 76508.*

BAULDOCK, GERALD
Writer, chemical engineer, inventor. **Personal:** Born Aug 5, 1957, Trenton, NJ; son of Dalbert and Ora; married Alveria; children: Gerald Jr, Justin & Jacob. **Educ:** Bucknell Univ, Lewisburg, PA, BS, chem engineering, 1979; Villanova Univ, Philadelphia, PA, MS, chem engineering, 1986. **Career:** Rohm & Haas, Bristol, PA, process engr, 1979-90; B-Dock Press, Willingboro, NJ, pres; B-Dock Educ Products, chief exec officer & vpres, currently; Sybron Chemicals, Birmingham, NJ, sr process engr; WL Gore & Assocs, process engr; Author: Reaching for the Moon; Say It Loud. I'm Smart, Black & Proud, 2003; "Racial Profiling in Kindergarten!", "Arrested by Officer Dan Polo Jr!", Kids for Chemistry; Inventor, Kids for Chemistry The Game, the PI Wheel, The CosSin Calculator, The Cylinder Calculator. **Honors/Awds:** Achievement Award, Optimist Club Philadelphia, 1990; Achievement Award, Bus Women Atlantic City, 1990; The Carl T Humphrey Memorial Award, Villanova Univ, 1992. **Business Addr:** Chief Executive Officer, Vice President, B-Dock Educational Products, PO Box 8, Willingboro, NJ 08046, **Business Phone:** (609)871-3932.

BAUTISTA, DANNY (DANIEL ALCANTARA BAUTISTA)
Baseball player. **Personal:** Born May 24, 1972, Santo Domingo, Dominican Republic. **Career:** Detroit Tigers, outfielder, 1993-96; Atlanta Braves, 1996-98; Fla Marlins, 1999-2000; Ariz Diamondbacks, 2000-04; Tampa Bay Devil Rays, left-forward, 2005; York Revolution, Atlantic League of Professional Baseball. **Honors/Awds:** World Series championship ring, 2001. *

BAXTER, A. D.
Educator. **Career:** Univ Tenn, Nat Asn Advan Colored People, chap adv, currently.

BAXTER, DR. CHARLES F., JR.
Physician. **Personal:** Born Apr 23, 1959, Brooklyn, NY; son of Charles F Sr and Bernice Kinand. **Educ:** City Col NY, BS, 1981; Meharry Med Col, MD, 1986. **Career:** Col of Physicians & Surgeons of Columbia Univ, assoc fell surg; Columbia Univ Col Physicians & Surgeons, surg resident; Harlem Hosp Ctr, surg resident, 1986-92; Sloan-Kettering Mem Hosp, New York, NY, surg pres oncol, 1989; McHarry Med Col, vis instr, dept anat, 1990; Portsmouth Naval Hosp, staff gen surgeon, 1990-94; USS George Wash, ship surgeon, 1992-94; US Naval Hosp, Yokosuka, Japan, staff gen surgeon, 1995-. **Orgs:** Am Med Asn; Am Chem Soc; The New York Acad Sci; Asn Mil Surgeons US; Am Col Surgeons, Cand Group; Med Soc New York State; Am Asn Clinical Chem; Nat Naval Officers Asn; Nat Naval Inst. **Honors/Awds:** Baskerville Chemical Award, City Col New York, 1981; Navy Commendation Medal, 1994. **Military Serv:** Navy, Med Corp, LCDR. *

BAXTER, FRED. See BAXTER, FREDERICK DENARD.

BAXTER, FREDERICK DENARD (FRED BAXTER)
Football player, founder (originator). **Personal:** Born Jun 14, 1971, Brundidge, AL; son of Brittany and Kellan; married Lisa. **Educ:** Auburn Univ. **Career:** Football player (retired); NY Jets, tight end, 1993-2000; Chicago Bears,2001-02; New Eng Patriots, 2002-03. **Orgs:** Founder, Fred Baxter Found, 2000. **Honors/Awds:** NY Jets, Most Valuable Player, 1996; Super Bowl, New England Patriots, 2003. *

BAXTER, NATHAN DWIGHT
Educator, school administrator. **Personal:** Born Nov 16, 1948; son of Belgium Nathan and Augusta Ruth Byrd; married Mary Ellen Walker, May 10, 1969; children: Timika Ann, Harrison David. **Educ:** Lancaster Theol Sem, 1976, Doctor Ministry, 1985; Dickenson Col, Doctor Sacred Theol; St. Paul's Col, Doctor Divinity. **Career:** St Paul's Col, chaplain & prof religious studies; Lancaster Theol Sem, dean & assoc prof church ministry; Episcopal Divinity Sch, adm dean & assoc prof pastoral theol, 1990-92; Wash Nat Cathedral, dean, 1991-03; St James Episcopal Church, rector; Episcopal Diocese Cent Pa, bishop, 2006-. **Orgs:** Bd, Episcopal Cathedral Telecommunications Network; Metrop Dialogue WA; bd, Riggs Nat Bank; bd, Faith's Politics Inst; Am Soc Order St John Jerusalem; Urban League; Epsilon Boule Sigma Pi Phi; life mem, Nat Asn Advan Colored People. **Honors/Awds:** Charles E Merrill Fellow, Harvard Univ Divinity Sch, 1998. **Special Achievements:** Guest on "30 Good Minutes," Tony Brown's Journal, "Both Sides with Jesse Jackson," "The O'Reilly Factor," "Good Morning America," "The Brian Lamb Show". **Military Serv:** AUS; Combat Medic Badge; Vietnam Cross Gallantry, 1969. **Business Addr:** Bishop, Episcopal Diocese of Central Pennsylvania, 101 Pine St, PO Box 11937, Harrisburg, PA 17108.*

BAXTER, HON. WENDY MARIE
Judge. **Personal:** Born Jul 25, 1952, Detroit, MI; married David Ford Cartwright Jr; children: Samantha. **Educ:** Eastern Mich Univ, BBA, 1973; Univ Detroit Sch Law, JD, 1978. **Career:** Gen Motors, oil lease analyst, 1977; Wayne Cty Criminal Bond, investigator, 1978; Recorder's Ct, ct docket admin, 1979; State Appellate Defender's Off, atty 1980; Pvt pract, atty 1982; Thirty Sixth Dist Ct, judge; Recorder's Ct, Detroit, judge; Wayne Co Circuit Ct, judge; Third Circuit Ct judge, currently. **Orgs:** Women Lawyers Asn, 1981; bd dirs, Wolverine Bar Asn, 1981; rules & forms comt woman, Dist Judges Asn, 1982; seventh dist prog dir, Nat Asn Women Judges, 1985; pres, Asn Black Judges Mich, 1986; Nat Asn Advan Colored People; Nat Bar Asn; Mich Asn Black Judges; State Bar Mich; Jim Dandies Ski Club. **Honors/Awds:** Spirit Detroit Detroit City Coun, 1981; Adoptive Parent Detroit Pub Sch, 1985. **Business Addr:** Judge, 3rd Circuit Court, Two Woodward Ave, Detroit, MI 48226, **Business Phone:** (313)224-5261.

BAYE, BETTY WINSTON
Writer, columnist. **Personal:** Born in Brooklyn, NY; daughter of George Washington Winston and Betty Jane Brown Winston. **Educ:** Hunter Col, City Univ NY, BA, commun; Columbia Univ Grad Sch Jour, MA. **Career:** The Courier-Journal, general assignment reporter, 1984, ed writer & columnist, currently. **Orgs:** Nieman Fellow, Harvard Univ, 1990-91; Trotter Group. **Business Addr:** Editorial writer, Columnist, The Courier-Journal, 525 W Broadway, PO Box 740031, Louisville, KY 40201-7431.

BAYE, PROF. LAWRENCE JAMES J
Educator. **Personal:** Born Oct 10, 1933, Houston, TX; son of Frank Claude and Bernice Margrett Navy; children: Elizabeth Lenoa & Ursula Frances. **Educ:** Tex Southern Univ, BS, 1956, MS, 1957; Univ Tex, Austin, PhD, chem, 1963. **Career:** Educator (retired); Univ Tex, Austin, Post Doctoral Res, 1964; Univ Tenn, Knoxville, Post Doctoral Res, 1966; Tex Southern Univ, asst prof chem, Houston, 1961-64; Knoxville Col, assoc prof & head, Dept Chem, TN, 1964-67; Houston-Tillotson Col Austin, prof chem, Tex, 1967. **Orgs:** Am Chem Soc; Sigma Xi; Beta Kappa Chi; Nat Org Prof Adv Black Chemists & Chem Eng, 1980-; Black Citizens Task Force, 1978-; Phi Beta Sigma Fraternity, 1955-. **Honors/Awds:** Recepient Robt A Welch Found Res Grants; NASA Grant Fluorocarbon Polymer Res, 1995-97. **Special Achievements:** Author of 14 publications, J Am Chem Soc & other Major Chem J, 1956. **Home Addr:** 1729 E 38th 1 2 St, Austin, TX 78722-1211. *

BAYLISS, JOCELYN KELLY
Engineer. **Educ:** Univ Tenn, BS, 1991. **Career:** Corning Cable Systs, engr, 2001. **Orgs:** Nat Soc Black Engrs. *

BAYLOR, DON EDWARD
Baseball player, baseball manager, athletic coach. **Personal:** Born Jun 28, 1949, Austin, TX; son of George Baylor and Lillian Brown Baylor; married Rebecca Giles, Dec 27, 1987; children: Don Jr; married Jo Cash, Jan 1, 1970 (divorced 1981); children: Don Jr. **Educ:** Jr col, Attended. **Career:** Baseball player (retired), sports coach, sports mgr; Baltimore Orioles,1970-75; Oakland Athletics, 1976, 1988; Calif Angels, 1977-82; NY Yankees, 1983-85; Boston Red Sox, 1986-87; Minn Twins, 1987; Milwaukee Brewers, hitting coach, 1990-91; St Louis Cardinals, hitting coach, 1992; Colorado Rockies, mgr, 1993-98; Atlanta Braves, hitting coach, 1999; Chicago Cubs, mgr, 2000-02; NY Mets, bench coach, 2003-04; Seattle Mariners, hitting coach, 2005; The Mid-Atlantic Sports Network, Nats Xtra, co-host, currently. **Orgs:** Cystic Fibrosis Found, 1979. **Honors/Awds:** Sporting News Minor League Player of the Yr, 1970; Am League Most Valuable Player & the Sporting News Player of the Yr, 1979 three-time mem of The Sporting New Am League Silver Slugger Team; Am League All-Star team, 1979; Roberto Clemente Award, 1985; Am League career record for being hit by apitch (267 times) & the Am League career record for being hit by a pitch the most times in a single season (35); career totals of 338 home runs, 1,276 RBI's & 285 stolen bases; played in seven Am League Championship Series & holds LCS record for most consecutive game with at least one hit(12); played in World Series in his final three seasons with Boston, 1986; Minn, 1987; Oakland, 1988, hitting .385 & a home run in the 1987 series to help the Twins win the World Championship; Nat League Mgr of the Yr, Baseball Writers of Am, 1995. **Special Achievements:** Author: Don Baylor, Nothing But the Truth: A Baseball Life, with Claire smith, 1989.

BAYLOR, ELGIN GAY
Sports manager, basketball coach, administrator. **Personal:** Born Sep 16, 1934, Washington, DC; married Elaine; children: Krystle. **Educ:** Col Idaho, 1955; Seattle Univ, 1958. **Career:** Basketball player (retired), basketball coach, basketball exec; Minneapolis Lakers, player, 1958; New Orleans Jazz, asst coach, 1974-77, coach, 1978-79; Los Angeles Clippers, exec vpres & gen mgr, vpres basketball opers & gen mgr, 1986-2008. **Honors/Awds:** NBA's seventh all-time leading scorer; Rookie of the Year, 1959; Co-MVP of the All-Star Game; Basketball Hall of Fame, 1976; NBA Executive of the Year, 2006.

BAYLOR, EMMETT ROBERT, JR.
Government official. **Personal:** Born Oct 18, 1933, New York, NY; son of Emmett (deceased) and Lilliam (deceased); married Margaret, Mar 1, 1937; children: Kathryn R, Gladys E, Emmett R III & Steven G. **Educ:** Wayne County Community Col, pub admin; Mercy Col, pub admin, 1991. **Career:** Maidenform Inc, sales rep, 1963-75; Metrop Life Ins, rep, 1975-79; City Detroit, dir detroit house correction, 1977-85; Mich Dept Corrections, warden/dep warden, 1985-93; Scott Correctional Facility, dep warden, 1992; City Detroit, exec asst mayor, public safety dir. **Orgs:** THE Asn, 1968-; Detroit Chap, TransAfrica, 1970-; founder Soc Detroit Inst Arts, 1970-; Wardens & Superintendents N Am, 1985-93; Am Correctional Asn, 1985-93; Am Jail Asn, 1985-93; Mich Correctional Asn, 1985-93; Nat Asn Advan Colored People. **Honors/Awds:** Outstanding Accomplishment Award, Metrop Life Ins, 1976; Dedication Award, St Scholatica/Benedictine High Sch, 1983; Mich Correctional Prison Mgt Leadership Award, 1991; MDL 21 Visionaries & Architect Award, 1993; Unsung Hero Community, Corinthian Baptist Church, 1994. **Home Phone:** (313)835-1154.

BAYLOR, ERNESTEIN WALKER. See Obituaries section.

BAYLOR, HELEN
Gospel singer. **Personal:** Born Jan 8, 1953?, Tulsa, OK; married James; children: 4. **Career:** Toured with muscial Hair, 1970; R&B group Side Effect, 1976; Albums: Highly Recommended, 1990; Look A Little Closer, 1991; Start All Over,1993; Live Experience, 1995; Love Brought Me Back, 1996; Live, 1999; My Everything, 2002; Diadem Music, 2003; MCG Records, 2006. **Orgs:** Adv coun, Elizabeth Home Unwed Mothers, 2000-; bd mem, St Dominic's Home Unwed Mothers, 2000-; Crenshaw Christian Ctr; fel Inner-City Word Faith Ministries. **Honors/Awds:** Soul Train Lady Soul Award, Best Gospel Album, 1995; 3 Stellar Awards; 4 Grammy nominations; 2 Dove Awards; honarary doctorate, Friends Int Christian Univ, 1995. **Special Achievements:** Ordained to Christian ministry, 1993. **Business Addr:** Singer, MCG Records, PO Box 2154, Alpharetta, GA 30023, **Business Phone:** (770)667-4970.

BAYLOR, MARGARET
Government official. **Personal:** Born Jan 1, 1937. **Educ:** Detroit Col of Law. **Career:** 36th Dist Ct, magistrate, currently. **Orgs:** Asn Black Judges Mich; Wolverine Bar Asn. **Business Addr:** Magistrate, 36th District Court, 421 Madison St Suite 2027, Detroit, MI 48226-2358, **Business Phone:** (313)965-5025.*

BAYLOR, SANDRA JOHNSON
Executive. **Educ:** Southern Univ, BS, elect eng; Stanford Univ, MS, elect eng; Rice Univ, PhD, elect eng. **Career:** Int Bus Mach Corp, Thomas J Watson Res Ctr, mgr & res staff mem, 1988-, WebSphere Database Develop Silicon Valley Lab, mgr, 2001; Int Bus Mach Linux Technol Ctr, mgr, 2002. **Special Achievements:** Holds 10 patents. **Business Addr:** Manager, International Business Machinery Linux Technology Center, International Business Machinery Res Div, PO Box 704, Yorktown Heights, NY 10598.

BAYNE, CHRIS (CHRISTOPHER OLIVER BAYNE)
Football player. **Personal:** Born Mar 22, 1975, Riverside, CA. **Educ:** Fresno State Univ. **Career:** Atlanta Falcons, defensive back, 1997-98; Scottish Claymores, 2000; LasVegas Outlaws, 2001; Fresno Frenzy, 2002; Hamilton Tiger-Cat, 2003. *

BAYNE, CHRISTOPHER OLIVER. See BAYNE, CHRIS.

BAZIL, RONALD
Educator. **Personal:** Born Mar 10, 1937, Brooklyn, NY; married Bonnie; children: Lance & Tami. **Educ:** Springfield Col, BS, 1958; Brooklyn Col, MS, health, phys edu & recreation, 1964. **Career:** US Mil Acad, coach; Adelphi Univ, dir inter col athel, 1972-, assoc dean studs, 1970-72, dean mem, 1969-70, asst dean stud, 1968-69; Health Educ, teacher, 1959-68; Tulane Univ, head coach, 2002. **Orgs:** Exec coun, ECAC; pres exec coun, ICA; Concerned City Westbury, NCAA Men's & Women's Track and Field Committee, 1994. **Honors/Awds:** Indoor coach of the Year, USTFF, 1974; Cross Country Coach of the Year, Dist II, 1993. **Military Serv:** AUS, reserve sp4, 1958-63. *

BAZILE, LEO
Administrator. **Career:** City Coun Dist 7, Oakland, CA, coun mem, 1983-92; City of Oakland, Calif, vice mayor; Friendly Cab,

Oakland, CA, gen mgr, 2002; Oakland, CA, atty; chmn, Oakland Bus Develop Corp; chmn, Community Econ Develop Adv Comn, Oakland; Harrison, Taylor & Bazile Law Pract, partner, currently. **Orgs:** State Bar mem, 1977-01; mem, Community Policing Adv Bd; mem, City Loan Rev Comt, Oakland. *

BEACH, GEORGE
Advertising executive. **Personal:** Born Aug 14, 1936, New York, NY; son of James H. and Ethel McKinnon. **Educ:** Univ the Arts Philadelphia, BA; Simon Gratz High Sch, BFA, 1954. **Career:** Artist Guild Delaware Valley, pres, 1967; Beach Advert & Beach Graphics, chmn & chief exec officer, 1974-. **Orgs:** Am Numis Asn; Found, Af Am Commemorative Soc; bd, Alliance Aging Res, The Philadelphia Af Am Mus, Hist Philadelphia Inc, The Philadelphia Conv & Visitors Bur, The Nat Arthritis Found, The W Philadelphia Cult Alliance, The Univ Arts. **Honors/Awds:** Awards: Addy, Neographic; Art Director Club awards; Printing Indust Am, best category award. **Special Achievements:** First African Am pres of the Artist Guild of Delaware Valley. **Business Addr:** Chairman, Chief Executive Officer, Beach Advertising & Beach Graphics, Beach Advertising & Beach Graphics, 1613 Spruce St, Philadelphia, PA 19103, **Business Phone:** (215)735-4747.*

BEACH, MICHAEL ANTHONY
Actor. **Personal:** Born Oct 30, 1963, Roxbury, MA; married Tracey; children: 4. **Career:** Films: Streets of Gold, 1986; Lean On Me; One False Move; White Man's Burden; Waiting to Exhale, 1995; A Family Thing, 1996; Soul Food, 1997; Johnny Skid marks, 1998; Dr Hugo, 1998; A Room Without Doors, 1998; Asunder, 1998; Made Men, 1999; Crazy As Hell, 2002; First Sunday, 2008; Hell Ride, 2008; Stargate: The Ark of Truth; 2008; Play Dead, 2009; Pastor Brown, 2009; TV movies: "Ms Scrooge", 1997; "Ruby Bridges", 1998; "Critical Assembly", 2003; TV series: "ER", 1996-97; "Spawn", 1997; "Third Watch", 1999; "Justice League Unlimited", 2006; "Brothers & Sisters", 2006; "Shark", 2007; "Stargate: Atlantis", 2007; "Numb3rs", 2009; "The Cleaner", 2009; Relative Stranger, 2009. **Honors/Awds:** Volpi Cup for Best Ensemble Cast, 1993; Special Award for Best Ensemble Cast, 1994; Golden Globe Award, 1994; Image Award for Outstanding Actor in a Drama Series, 2003. **Special Achievements:** Nominated for Image Awards, Black Film Award and Black Reel Awards. **Business Addr:** Actor, c/o Paradigm, 10100 Santa Monica Blvd 25th Fl, Los Angeles, CA 90067, **Business Phone:** (310)277-4400.*

BEACH, WALTER G., II
Executive. **Personal:** Born in Cataula, GA; married Marian C; children: Pennie, Pamela, Walter III, Bradford. **Educ:** Univ WI, BS, educ, 1975; Marquette Univ Law Coloquium, attended 1975; Univ WI Law Sch. **Career:** Restaurant owner, 1963-64; news dir; spec agent ins; Harambee Newspaper, managing ed; Milwaukee Torch Newspaper, adv mgr; Echo Mag, feature writer; Dept Store, acting asst mgr; Channel 18 (TV), news reporter; The New Image Concept Inc, pres & founder,; WAWA AM & FM Radio, news & pub affairs dir, currently. **Orgs:** chmn, State Polit Action; pres, Criminal Justice Asn Univ WI; chmn, NAACP; bd mem, State Police Examining Bd;TV producer & vice chmn, Soc Black Drama Heritage; co-founder, Comt Twenty-One; Steering Comt Model Cities; Midtown Kiwanis Club; Sickle Cell Anemia Found. **Honors/Awds:** Man of the Year, 1971; Youth Image Maker, 1973; Congress Award, 1974. **Military Serv:** AUS; USN; Nat Guard. **Business Addr:** News and Public Affairs Director, WAWA AM & FM Radio, PO Box 2385, Milwaukee, WI 53212.

BEADY, DR. CHARLES H, JR.
School administrator. **Personal:** Born in Adel, GA. **Educ:** Michigan State Univ, BA, advertising, MA, urban counseling, PhD, counsr educ. **Career:** Morgan State Univ, asst prof; Johns Hopkins Univ, postdoctoral res, Inst Urban Res, sr res scientist; Johns Hopkins Univ, res affil, Ctr Social Orgn Sch, prof cartoonist; Piney Woods Country Life Sch, provost, 1984, pres, 1985-. **Honors/Awds:** Distinguished Alumni Award, Mich State Univ, 1995; Fraternity's Humanitarian Award, Kappa Alpha Psi, 1996. **Special Achievements:** President of one of six historically black boarding school in US; He was instrumental in constructing two new girls dormitories and has helped to increase the school's endowment from $17.5 million to $30 million in 15 years; National support of many celebrities, including Oprah Winfrey, Charles Schulz, Morgan Freeman, Denise Graves, Paul Warfield and Yolanda King. **Business Addr:** President, Piney Woods Country Life School, 5096 Hwy 49 S, PO Box 9998, Piney Woods, MS 39148, **Business Phone:** (601)845-2214.

BEAL, ANNE
Pediatrician. **Educ:** Brown Univ, AB; Cornell Univ Med Col, MD; Columbia Univ, MPH. **Career:** Albert Einstein Col Med, intern, resident; Montefiore Med Ctr, Bronx, NY, intern, resident, NRSA fel; Mass Gen Hosp, Ctr Child & Adolescent Health Policy, health serv researcher, Gen Pediat, pediatrician, Multicultural Affairs Off, assoc dir; Harvard Med Sch, instr pediat; Essence Mag, Am Baby Show, ABC News & NBC News, med corresp, currently; Commonwealth Fund, sr prog officer, asst vpres, currently. **Orgs:** Am Acad Pediat; co chair, Nat Qual Forum. **Special Achievements:** Auth: The Black Parenting Book: Caring for Our Children in the First Five Years; The Changing Face of Race: Risk Factors for Neonatal Hyperbilirubinemia, 2006; numerous prof articles in Pediat, Ambulatory Pediat, Health Affairs, etc. **Business Addr:** Assistant Vice President, The Commonwealth Fund, Program Quality Care Underserved Populations, 1 E 75th St, New York, NY 10021, **Business Phone:** (212)606-3800.

BEAL, BERNARD
Investment banker. **Educ:** Carleton Col, BA; Stanford Univ Sch Bus, MBA, 1979. **Career:** Shearson Lehman Hutton Inc, Munic & Corp Finance Div, sr vpres; MR Beal & Co, owner, founder, chmn & chief exec officer, currently. **Special Achievements:** Listed as one of 25 "Hottest Blacks on Wall Street" and company ranked third on BE Investment Bank list, Black Enterprise, 1992, ranked #6, 2000. **Business Addr:** Chief Executing Officer, M R Beal & Co, 110 Wall St 6th Fl, New York, NY 10007, **Business Phone:** (212)983-3930.*

BEAL, LISA SUZANNE
Association executive, administrator. **Personal:** Born Sep 2, 1963, Paris, France; daughter of James Thomas and Francis Yates. **Educ:** Hampton Univ, BS, 1987. **Career:** Geo Recource Consultants, info specialist, 1990-92; Am Trucking Asn, environ specialist, 1992-95; Hazardous Waste Mgt Asn, mgr transp & safety, 1995-96; Interstate Sanit Comn, compliance inspector; Interstate Nat Gas Asn Am, dir environ & construct policy, 1996-. **Orgs:** EnvironMentors; Nat Coun Sci & Environ; secy, INGAA Found Inc; Women's Coun Energy & Environ; Am Asn Blacks Energy. **Home Addr:** 51A G St SW Suite A, Washington, DC 20024, **Home Phone:** (202)554-7915. **Business Addr:** Director, Environment & Construction Policy, Interstate Natural Gas Association of America, 10 G St NE Suite 700, Washington, DC 20004, **Business Phone:** (202)216-5935.

BEAL BAGNERIS, MICHELE CHRISTINE (MICHELE BAGNERIS)
Lawyer. **Personal:** Born Mar 7, 1959, Los Angeles, CA; daughter of M Meredith and Rohelia; married Jules S Bagneris III, Aug 30, 1986; children: Monet Christine, Jules S IV, Mariana. **Educ:** Stanford Univ, AB, 1980; Boalt Hall Sch Law, Univ Calif, Berkeley, JD, 1983. **Career:** Richards Watson & Gershon, atty, 1983-92, partner, 1992-; City Monrovia, CA, city atty, 1992; Pasadena City, atty, currently. **Orgs:** Asst secy, Los Angeles Urban League Bd, 1985-91; State Bar Comn Human Rights, 1987-90; bd mem, San Fernando Legal Serv Corp, 1989-; LA City Atty Criminal Justice Panel, 1991-; dir missionary educ, AME Church, S Calif Conf Women's Missionary Soc, 1992-93; Langston Bar Asn; Black Women Lawyers Los Angeles. **Special Achievements:** Stanford Univ, international political economy participant, 1979. *

BEALS, YVONNE
Government official. **Personal:** Daughter of Melvin L and Marietta; married Vincent Rogers, May 19, 2001. **Educ:** Calif State Univ, BS, criminal justice, MS, pub admin & pub policy. **Career:** City Calif, legis secy & dist field rep; City Pittsburg Calif, coun mem,2000-04, mayor, 2003; Exec Bd Yahweh Enterprises, chief financial officer;Food Bank Contra Costa & Solano, community rels mgr & dir, currently. **Orgs:** Co-chmn, Black Am polit Asn Calif; Kennedy-King Memorial Col Scholar Fund Ltd; Sigma Gamma Rho; exec br secy & exec comt mem, E County br, Nat Asn Advan Colored People, bd mem, 4AC. **Special Achievements:** First African American woman to be elected to the city council; first Black female mayor of the 100-year-old city, Pittsburg, CA. **Business Addr:** Community Relations Manager, Director, Food Bank of Contra Costa and Solano, PO Box 271966, Concord, CA 94527-1966.

BEAMON, ARTHUR LEON
Lawyer. **Educ:** USAF Acad, BS, 1965; George Wash Univ, MA, 1970; Univ Chicago Law Sch, JD, 1972; Harvard Univ Prog Instr Lawyers, cert, 1981. **Career:** FDIC, atty, 1972-78, sr atty, 1978-80, coun, 1980-84, asst gen coun, 1984-89, assoc gen coun, 1989-. **Orgs:** Bd mem, treas, 1996-; rep, Ad Hoc Homeowners Asn Comn, 1997-; Tuckerman Sta Condominium Asn; outreach comm, St Mark Presbyterian Church; Dist Bar Asn; Am Bar Asn; Nat Bar Asn. **Honors/Awds:** Sustained Superior Performance Awards, 1980-97; Annual Performance Bonus Awards, 1989-97. **Business Phone:** (202)898-3707.

BEAMON, BOB (ROBERT A BEAMON)
Executive. **Personal:** Born Aug 29, 1946, New York, NY; son of Naomi Brown; married Milana Walter Beamon, 1994; children: Deanna. **Educ:** Adelphi Univ, BA, cult anthrop, 1972. **Career:** Youth Serv/Metro-Dade, dir, 1982-95; Bob Beamon Commun Inc, pres, 1995-; artist & neckwear designer, 1996-; Fla Atlantic Univ, dir Athletic Develop, currently. **Orgs:** Chair, S Fla Inner City Games, 1994-96; Orange Bowl Community, 1994-; pres, US Olympic Comt Alumni, 1996-; bd of trustees, United Way, Dade City. **Honors/Awds:** NCAA Long Jump/Triple Jump Champion, 1967; Olympic Long Jump Record, Still Standing, 1968; Gold Medal, Int Olympic Comt, 1968; Hall of Fame, US Olympic Comt, 1992; Humanitarian, Miami Children's Hosp, 1995; Humanitarian, UNESCO, 1996; Golden Olympian, Xerox, 1996; New York Black 100. **Special Achievements:** Motivational Speaker, 1972-; Children's Advocate, 1972-; Olympian Producer; author: The Man Who Could Fly, 1999. **Business Addr:** Director of Athletic Development, Florida Atlantic University, 777 Glades Rd, Boca Raton, FL 33431.*

BEAMON, ROBERT A. See BEAMON, BOB.

BEAMON, TERESA KRISTINE NKENGE ZOLA. See ZOLA, NKENGE.

BEAN, BOBBY GENE
Librarian, educator. **Personal:** Born Jan 15, 1951, Houlka, MS; son of Dan (deceased) and Mary Bess (Deceased); married Mattie Marie Kitchen, Aug 25, 1974; children: Bobby Gene II. **Educ:** Southeast Mo State Univ, BSE, 1974; Southern Ill Univ, MSE, 1979, EDS, 1981; Lael Univ, EDD, 1983; Atlanta Univ, MSLS, 1987; Inter denominational Theol Ctr, MDiv, 1989; Univ Sarasota, EDD, cand, 1998. **Career:** Sikeston Pub Sch, high sch librn asst, 1972-73; E St Louis Pub Sch, 6thgrade teacher, 1974-82, Jr high math teacher, 1982-83, Jr high librn, 1983-87; Atlanta Pub Sch, John Hope Elem, media specialist, 1988-; Atlanta Univ Ctr, R W Woodruff Libr, ref librn, 1988-; Interdenominational Theol Ctr, instr, 1992-, Therrell High, Crim Eve Col, media specialist, 2003; C.H. Mason Theol Sem, instr, currently. **Orgs:** Atlanta Univ, Beta Phi Mu Libr Sci Hon Fraternity, 1987; ITC, Dean's List, 1988-89; United Negro Col Fund Scholar, 1989; Theta Phi, 1989; Am Libr Asn; Ga Libr Asn; Am Asn Sch Librn; Ga Chaplain Asn. **Honors/Awds:** Honorable Mention Those Who Excel, Sch Media Serv, 1987; Research Board Advisor, Am Biog Inst, 1990; Distinguished Leadership Award, ABI; Man of Achievement Award, Am Biographical Inst. **Special Achievements:** Author of the book - This is The Church Of God in Christ.

BEANE, DOROTHEA ANNETTE
Educator. **Personal:** Born Mar 30, 1952, Plainfield, NJ; daughter of Floyd and Mary. **Educ:** Spelman Col, attended 1972; Drew Univ, BA, 1974; Rutgers-19Newark Col Law,JD, 1977. **Career:** US Dept Justice, Civil Div, Torts Branch, trial atty, 1977-81; Law Firm Robinson & Geraldo, assoc atty, 1981-82; US Dept Justice, asst US atty;Stetson Univ Col Law, asst prof, 1990-95, prof, 1996-, Law Tribunal proj dir, 2004-, Inst Caribbean Law & Policy, co-dir, currently. **Orgs:** Am Bar Asn, 1990-; fac adv, Black Law Stud Asn, 1990-; acad master, Sarasota County Am Inns Ct, 1990-; house rep, Asn Am Law Sch, 1991; rep, Stetson Univ Sen, 1992-; Am Col Legal Med, 1992-. **Honors/Awds:** Atty General's Special Achievement Award, US Dept Justice, 1986; Women's Singles Table Tennis Championship of Jacksonville, FL, 1988-89; US Marshal's Service Letter of Appreciation, 1990; US Postal Service Letter of Appreciation, 1990; Special Achievement Award (Sustained Superior Performance of Duty); Stetson University College of Law Teaching Excellence Award, 2005. **Special Achievements:** Published numerous articles & publications. **Home Addr:** 7912 Sailboat Key Blvd, South Pasadena, FL 33707. **Business Addr:** Professor, Stetson University College Law, 1401-61st St S Room 211, Saint Petersburg, FL 33707-3299, **Business Phone:** (727)562-7800.

BEANE, PATRICIA JEAN
Educator, secretary (organization). **Personal:** Born Jan 13, 1944, Massillon, OH; married Frank Llewellyn; children: Frank Clarence II & Adam Tyler. **Educ:** Ashland Col, OH, BS, 1966. **Career:** Akron City Schs, teacher 1966-67; Massillon City Schs, teacher, 1967-. **Orgs:** NEA, 1966-76, 1979-; Ohio Educ Asn, 1966-76, 1979-; E Cent Ohio Teachers Asn, 1966-76, 1979-; Massilon Educ Asn, 1966-76, 1979-; Akron Symphony Chorus, 1966-67; Canton Civic Opera Chorus, 1969-79; secy, bd trustees, Massillon YWCA, 1972-76; Massillon Bus & Prof Women, 1977-; Massilon Bus & Prof Women, 1977-80; Ohio Asn Colored Women's Clubs, 1978-; Nat Asn Colored Women's Clubs, 1978-; Doris L Allen Minority Caucus, 1984; bd trustees, Massillon Youth Ctr, 1984; regional & local women's clubs, secy, bd trustees, Massillon pub library, currently. **Honors/Awds:** Guest soloist with various choirs. **Home Addr:** 1134 3rd St SE, Massillon, OH 44646. **Business Addr:** Secretary & Board of Trustees, The Massillon Public Library, 1134 3rd St SE, Massillon, OH 44646, **Business Phone:** (330)833-4560.

BEANE, ROBERT HUBERT
County government official. **Personal:** Born Mar 4, 1947, New York, NY; son of Sidney and Lorraine Braithwaite; divorced; children: Craig J. **Educ:** Fordham Univ Col Lincoln Ctr, BA, 1974, Fordham Univ Grad Sch Social Serv, MSW, 1976. **Career:** Mt Vernon Community Action Group; Westchester Community Opportunity Prog, exec dir 1970-73; Westchester Urban Coalition, prog dir, 1973-74; Alcohelp Prog, res & eval specialist, 1974-76; Westchester County, prog specialist, 1976, Dept Mental Health, ctr adminr, 1976-79, asst to comnr, 1979-83, dir community serv, 1983-00. **Orgs:** Community Protection Human Sub NY Med Col, 1980-96; trustee, City Yonkers Bd Educ, 1983-93, vpres, 1988-90, pres, 1992-93, 1995-97; Youth Shelter Prog Westchester, 1996. **Honors/Awds:** Alpha Sigma Lambda, 1974; MLK fellow, Woodrow Wilson Found, 1975-76; COT Service Award, NCP, 1991. **Military Serv:** USAF, AFC. *

, BEAR, MIKE. See BROWN, MICHAEL.

BEARD, BUTCH (JR.)
Basketball player, basketball coach. **Personal:** Born May 5, 1947, Hardinburg, KY. **Educ:** Louisville Col, attended 1969. **Career:** Basketball player, head coach (retired); Atlanta Hawks, player, 1969-70; Cleveland Cavaliers, player, 1971-72, 1975-76; Seattle Supersonics, player, 1972-73; Golden State Warriors, player, 1973-74; New York Knicks, player, 1975-78, asst coach, 1978-82, broadcaster, 1982-87; Atlanta Hawks, broadcaster, 1987-88; New Jersey Nets, asst coach, 1988-90; Howard Univ, head coach, 1990-94; New Jersey Nets, head coach, 1994-96; Dallas Mavericks, asst coach, 1996-98; Morgan State Bears, head coach, 1998-2006. **Honors/Awds:** NBA All-Star Game, 1972; MEAC Coach of the Year.

BEARD, DARRYL H., CPP, C
Executive, security consultant. **Educ:** John Jay Col Criminal Justice, NY, BS, criminal justice, 1992; Seton Hall Univ, S Orange, NJ, MA, 1999. **Career:** Integrated Security & Training Consult Inc, vice chmn; Williams Associates LLC, prin security consult, currently. **Orgs:** Am Soc Indust Security; Int Asn Black Security Professionals; Prof Security Consults Int; Trans-Continental Pub Safety Consults; John Jay Col Alumni Asn; Seton Hall Univ Alumni Asn. **Honors/Awds:** Outstanding Young Man of America Award, 1996; Walter Lawson Award, Nat Orgn Black Law Enforcement Execs, 2001; Regional Award of Achievement, Am Soc Indust Security, 2002; Vanguard Award, Brother Officers Law Enforcement Soc, 2002. *

BEARD, JAMES WILLIAM
Lawyer, educator. **Personal:** Born Sep 16, 1941, Chillicothe, OH; married Gail LaVerne Rivers; children: James III, Ryan Jamail & Kevin Jarrard. **Educ:** Hardin-Simmons Univ, BS, 1967; Tex Southern Univ, JD, 1973; Univ Tex, LLM, 1976. **Career:** Tex Southern Univ, Thurgood Marshall Sch Law, spec admin asst to dean, 1976-79, assoc dean acad affairs, 1979-80, assoc prof law, 1974-, dir fed tax clin, 1984-92; pres, Earl Carl Inst Legal & Social Policy Inc, 2002-. **Orgs:** Nat Asn Advan Colored People, 1968-; bd governors & chmn, Sect Taxation, Nat Bar Asn, 1983-86; Texas Coalition Black Dem, 1986; legal adv, S Union Civic Club, 1987-91; election judge, Briargate Community Improvement Asn, 1991-92; coordr, Studs Tax Testimonies Hearings Before Comt Ways & Means, House Rep, 1991; Bus & Prof Men's Club, 1991; chair, Legal Address Comt, Fort Bend Co Nat Asn Advan Colored People, 1991; founder, DAD's Club, Mo City Middle Sch, FBISD, 1993-94; Tex Hosp Licensing Adv Coun, 1994; founder, E Fort Bend Alliance Educ, 1994-95; Am Bar Asn; State Bar Tex; bdgovs, Nat Bar Asn; trustee, Houston Legal Found; bd dirs, Texas War Drugs. **Honors/Awds:** Outstanding Young American, 1977. **Special Achievements:** Published numerous books. **Military Serv:** USAF, A/2c, 1959-63. **Business Addr:** Associate Professor of Law, Texas Southern University, Thurgood Marshall School of Law, Thurgood Marshall Law Sch Bldg 3100 Cleburne St, Houston, TX 77004, **Business Phone:** (713)313-7111.

BEARD, DR. LILLIAN MCLEAN
Physician, educator. **Personal:** Born Jan 1, 1943, New York, NY; daughter of Woodie McLean and Johnie Wilson; married DeLawrence Beard. **Educ:** Howard Univ, Col Lib Arts, BS, 1965, Col Med, MD, 1970. **Career:** C Hosp, Nat Med Ctr, pediat internship, residency, fel, 1970-73, Child Develop, dir, consult, 1973-75; Howard Univ Col Med, asst prof, 1979-; George Wash Univ, Sch Med, Dept Pediats, assoc clin prof, 1982-; pvt pract, pediatrician, 1973-; child & adolescent health consult; Good Housekeeping Magazine, "Ask Dr Beard" column, authored, 1989-95, contributing ed; Carnation Nutrit Prod, Communs consult, 1991-; ABC TV-7, med health expert, currently; Newschannel 8, med health expert, currently; C Pediatricians & Assocs, sr physician, 2002-. **Orgs:** Fel Am Acad Pediat; Nat Med Asn; Am Medical Women's Asn; Med Soc Dist Columbia; Links Inc; Girl Friends. **Honors/Awds:** 8 awards, Am Med Asn; Outstanding Young Women For Yr, 1979; Diplte, Nat Bd Med Examrs; Diplte, Am Bd Pediat; Physician Recognition Awards, Am Med Asn; Hall Fame Award, Nat Med Asn, 1994; Distinguished Alumni Leadership Award, Nat Asn Equal Opportunity Higher Educ; Howard Univ Charter Day, 1996; Women Courage, 1998; 1998 Global Initiative for Telemedicine Award of Merit, Nat Med Asn, 1998. **Home Addr:** 10517 Alloway Dr, Potomac, MD 20854. **Business Addr:** Associate Clinical Professor, Pediatrics, George Washington Univeristy, School of Medicine and Health Sciences, Wash. D.C., 2300 1 st NW, Washington, DC 20037, **Business Phone:** (202)994-3727.

BEASLEY, AARON BRUCE
Football player. **Personal:** Born Jul 7, 1973, Pottstown, PA. **Educ:** WVa Univ. **Career:** Football player (retired); Jacksonville Jaguars, defensive back, 1996-01; New York jets, 2002-03; Atlanta Falcons, corner back, 2004; co-found, Fever energy drink co. **Honors/Awds:** All-American, 1995; WVU Sports Hall of Fame, 2009 . *

BEASLEY, ANNIE RUTH
Educator. **Personal:** Born Oct 6, 1928, Nashville, NC; daughter of Lucious and Lillie Alston. **Educ:** Shaw Univ, Raleigh, BA, 1949; NC Cent Univ, MA, 1958. **Career:** Educator (retired); Civil Serv, file clerk, 1951-53; S Nash Sr High Sch, teacher, 1956-90; Town Sharpsburg NC, coun woman, 1981-83; Town Sharpsburg NC, mayor, 1983-; Nash County Econ Dev Comm, exec comt mem. **Honors/Awds:** Leader, Am Sec Educ, 1972; Teacher of the Year, Nash County Teachers, NC, 1973-74; Human Relations Award, Nash County Teachers, NC, 1978-79. **Home Addr:** 101 Dawes Dr, PO Box 636, Sharpsburg, NC 27878. *

BEASLEY, ARLENE A (PHOEBE BEASLEY)
Executive, artist. **Personal:** Born Jun 3, 1943, Cleveland, OH; divorced. **Educ:** Ohio Univ, BA, 1965; Kent State Univ, grad study, 1969. **Career:** Cleveland Bd Educ, teacher, 1965-69; Sage Pub, artist, 1969-70; KFI & KOST Radio, acct exec, 1970; solo exhibitions, artist, 1976-; Los Angeles Co Arts comn, pres, 2002-03; Phoebe Beasley Art Studio, artist, currently. **Orgs:** Bd trustees, Savannah Col Art & Design; adv bd, New Regal Theater, Chicago; bd dirs pres & hon bd trustees, Museum African-Am Art; curric adv bd, Calif State Univ, Long Beach; county comnr, Pvt Indust Coun; exec adv bd, United Negro Col Fund, Los Angeles; bd dir, Story Proj Found; bd mem, Prologue Soc Los Angeles; bd dir, Story Project Found; bd, Transportation Found Los Angeles. **Honors/Awds:** Merit Award, Am Women Radio & TV, 1975, Achievement Award, Genii Award; Woman of the Year, Los Angeles Sentinel, 1989; Black Women of Achievement Award, NAACP Legal Defense & Educ Fund, 1991; Medal of Merit, Ohio Univ, 2003; Honorary Doctorate of Fine Arts, Ohio Univ, 2005. **Special Achievements:** First African-American female president, American Women in Radio & TV, 1977-78; "Clinton Inaugural" artwork, has been accorded the coveted Presidential Seal, Clinton presented prints of this work to Ambassadors of the Diplomatic Corps at a formal ceremony at Georgetown University; only artist to twice receive the Presidential Seal, selected to design the prestigious International Tennis Trophy and Medal, 1984 Summer Olympic Games; named Official Artist, 1987 Los Angeles Marathon, chosen to design the national poster, Sickle Cell Disease Campaign, Inauguration of former President Bush, artwork, official poster, 1989, "Morning Glory," Paramount Television pilot, artwork, 1989, Oprah Winfrey, series of lithographs, and paintings based on television mini-series "The Women of Brewster Place", artist, private collections for: Andre and Linda Johnson-Rice, Robert and Nancy Daly, Joel and Marlene Chaseman, Attorney Tyrone Brown, Attorney Reginald Govan, Edward and Bettiann Gardner, William and Carol Sutton-Lewis, Maya Angelou, Anita Baker, Gordon Parks, Oprah Winfrey, numerous others; numerous institutional collections, one-woman exhibits and group exhibitions, commissioned: 20th Anniversary of Essence Magazine, artwork, poster, 1990, was named the "Official Artist" for.the Democratic National Convention/ 2000. **Home Addr:** 6110 El Canon, Woodland Hills, CA 91367, **Home Phone:** (818)888-5525. **Business Addr:** Artist, Phoebe Beasley Art Studio, 6110 El Canon, Woodland Hills, CA 91367, **Business Phone:** (818)888-5525.

BEASLEY, CORA THOMAS
Educator. **Personal:** Born Mar 16, 1945, Oktaha, OK; daughter of Clarence Weldon; married Billy G Beasley, Aug 16, 1968. **Educ:** Langston Univ, BS, 1967; Northeastern Okla State Univ, MED, 1980. **Career:** Educator (retired); Idabell (Riverside) Schs, instr, 1967-68; Muskogee Pub Schs, instr, 1969-97. **Orgs:** Okla State Home Asn, 1967-; Okla Educ Asn, 1967-; secy, Alpha Kappa Alpha Sor, 1970-80; treas, Muskogee Ed Assn, 1980; secy, Goodwill Industries, 1984; financial secy, Nat Sorority of Phi Delta Kappa, 1985; Nat Educ Asn; pres, Okla Baptist State Conv (collate dist), 1991. **Honors/Awds:** Zeta Phi Beta, All Greek, 1990. **Home Addr:** 1303 S 38th St, Muskogee, OK 74401, **Home Phone:** (918)683-6154. *

BEASLEY, EDWARD
City manager. **Personal:** Born in Omaha, NE; son of Edward Jr and Bessie Chandler. **Educ:** Pittsburgh State Univ, Pittsburgh, PA, 1977; Loyola Univ, BA, Polit Sci, 1980; Univ Mo, Kans City, MO, MPA, 1983; Pioneer Community Col, Kans City, MO, 1984. **Career:** Jolly Walsh & Gordon, Kans City, MO, legal clerk, 1982-84; Fed Govt, Wash, DC, aid, Senator Thomas Eagleton, 1983; City Kans, MO, mgmt trainee, 1984-85; City Flagstaff, Flagstaff, AZ, admin asst city mgr, 1985-88; Wyandotte County Kansas City, asst county adminr; Pinal County, asst county mgr; City Eloy, city mgr; City Eloy, city mgr, 1988-; City Glendale, city mgr, 2002-. **Orgs:** Bd dir, Am Cancer Soc, Pinal County, AZ; bd mem, United Way Northern Ariz, 1988, bd mem, Center Against Domestic Violence, 1988; bd mem, Impact Crisis Funding, 1988; Int City Mgrs Asn; bd dir, Nat Forum for Black Pub Admin; vpres, ICMA Mountain Plains Region, currently. **Honors/Awds:** Lincoln J Ragsdale Outstanding Director Award; John J Jack Debolske Professional Excellence Award, Ariz City & Co Mgt Asn, 2001; 100 Black Men of Phoenix Inc; African Am Achievement Award; Work Force Diversity Prof Develop Award, Int City Mgrs Asn, 2004; Martin Luther King Leadership Diversity Award; Roy Wilkins Freedom Award, Maricopa Co Nat Asn Advan Colored People, 2005. **Business Addr:** City Manager, City of Glendale, 5850 W Glendale Ave, Glendale, AZ 85301-2563, **Business Phone:** (623)930-2870.

BEASLEY, DR. EULA DANIEL
Educator. **Personal:** Born Sep 16, 1958, Oxford, NC; daughter of Benjamin Daniel III and Helen Pettiford Daniel; married Robert, Jun 25, 1983; children: Lydia & Benjamin. **Educ:** Univ NC, Chapel Hill, NC, BS, pharm, 1981; PharmD, 1983. **Career:** Orange-Chatham Comprehensive Health Serv, Carrboro, NC, proj pharmacist, 1983-84; Univ NC, Chapel Hill, NC, clinical asst, prof, 1983-84; Wash Hosp Ctr, Wash, DC, clin pharmacist, 1984-85, 1987, clin serv mgr, 1990, clin coordr med; Howard Univ, Col Pharm, Wash, DC, asst prof, 1985. **Orgs:** Phi Lambda Sigma Pharmacy Leadership Soc, 1978; Rho Chi Pharmacy Hon Soc, 1980; Fac rep, Stud Info Network, 1986-89; Am Soc Hosp Pharmacists, 1981; DC Soc Hosp Pharmacists, 1985-. **Honors/Awds:** Nat Achievement Scholar, 1976; James M Johnston Scholar, 1976. **Special Achievements:** "Sickle Cell Anemia" in Pharmacotherapy, co-author with C Curry; A Pathophysiologic Approach, CT: Appleton & Lang, 2nd edition, 1992. **Home Addr:** 232 Mowbray Rd, Silver Spring, MD 20904, **Home Phone:** (301)384-1388. *

BEASLEY, FREDERICK JEROME
Football player. **Personal:** Born Sep 18, 1974, Montgomery, AL; married Jackie; children: Frederick Jerome Jr. **Educ:** Univ Auburn, psychol. **Career:** San Francisco 49ers, 1998-05; Miami Dolphins, practice/squad member, 2006; Washington Redskins, practice/squad member, 2007; free agent, currently. **Honors/Awds:** Pro Bowler Selection Once, 2003; All Pro Selection Twice, 2002-03. **Special Achievements:** Two-time All-State honoree & one-time AAU National decathalon champion;named an All-American by Parade Magazine. *

BEASLEY, JAMAR
Soccer player. **Personal:** Born Oct 11, 1979, Fort Wayne, IN. **Career:** New England Revolution, 1998-2001; Chicago Fire, 2001; Italian club, Puteolana, 2002; Indiana Blast, 2003; Charleston Battery, 2003; Milwaukee Wave United, 2004; Kansas City Comets, forward, 2003-05; US Nat Futsal Team, 2004; St Louis Steamers, 2005-06; major indoor soccer league, Detroit Ignition, 2006-08; Rockford Rampage, Mid, currently. **Honors/Awds:** MLS Player of the Week, 2000; Most Improved Player, Kansas City Comets, 2003-04. **Business Phone:** (248)436-1116.*

BEASLEY, JESSE C.
Optometrist. **Personal:** Born Mar 11, 1929, Marshall, TX; married Ruth Adella Evans; children: Jesse II, Joseph, Janice. **Educ:** La City Col, AA, Ophthal Optics, 1952; La Col Optom, OD, 1956; Univ Calif, MPH, 1971. **Career:** Assoc Pract, 1957; Pvt Pract, optometrist, 1957-; Manchester Optom Ctr, optometrist, 2001. **Orgs:** CA Optom Asn; Optom Health Ctr; Optom Vision Care Coun; Comp Health Planning Comt Southern Calif Optom Soc; Am Optom Comt; Div Pub Health Optom; Am Pub Health Asn; Los Angeles Optom Soc; Calif Optom Asn; Am Optom Asn. **Special Achievements:** Has published & presented many papers on optometry; ; Appointed to Calif State Bd of Optometry by Gov Edmund G Brown Jr 1978-86; elected bd pres Calif State Bd Optometry 1982,84. **Military Serv:** USAAF, Corp Sgt, 1946-49. **Business Addr:** Optometrist, Manchester Optom Eye Care Ctr, 10024 S Vermont Ave 2, Los Angeles, CA 90044.*

BEASLEY, DR. PAUL LEE
School administrator. **Personal:** Born Jan 10, 1950, East Point, GA; married Pamela Simmons; children: Deanna Estella & Erin Michelle. **Educ:** Earlham Col, BA, 1972; Trenton State Col, MEd, 1973; Univ Tenn, EdD, 1988. **Career:** Trenton State Col, dormitory dir, 1973-74; Emory Univ Upward Bound, dir, 1974-75; US Off Educ, educ prog specialist, 1975-78; Univ Tenn Chattanooga, dir spec serv, 1978-89; Univ SC, TRIO, dir, 1989-. **Orgs:** State rep, SE Asn Educ Opportunity Prog Personnel, 1979-; comm chmn, Tenn Asn Spec Prog, 1978-; usher & bd mem, First Baptist Church Chattanooga, 1979-; Toastmasters Int, 1979-; pres, SAE-OPP, 1989-91. **Honors/Awds:** Outstanding Young Men of America, 1979; Outstanding Upward Bounder, US Off Educ, 1976; Award for Distinguished Service, SE Asn Educ Opportunity Prog Personnel, 1977; Walter O Mason Award, Coun Opportunity Educ, 2003; Paul L Beasley Leadership Award, named in honor. **Business Addr:** Director, University of South Carolina, TRIO, BTW Auditorium USC, Columbia, SC 29208, **Business Phone:** (803)777-7000.

BEASLEY, PHOEBE. See BEASLEY, ARLENE A.

BEASLEY, THURMOND
Dentist. **Educ:** Meharry Med Col, DDS, 1971; Harvard Univ, MD, anesthesiol, 1974. **Career:** Union Co Gen Hosp, staff anesthesiologist; Pvt pract, dentist & anesthesiologist, currently. **Orgs:** Southern Conf Dent Deans & Examr; Am Dent Asn; Am Soc Dent Anesthesiologists; MS Dent Asn; MS Dent Soc; Am Asn Dent Examr; pres, MS State Bd Dent Examr, 2004-05. **Business Phone:** (662)844-6414.*

BEASLEY, ULYSSES CHRISTIAN, JR.
Lawyer. **Personal:** Born Jan 14, 1928, Arkansas City, AR; married Rose Jeanette Cole; children: Gayle, Mark & Erika. **Educ:** Fresno City Col, attended 1951; Fresno State Col, attended 1953; San Francisco Law Sch, attended 1965. **Career:** Fresno Co, Welfare Dept, social worker, 1953-54; Fresno Police Dept, police officer, 1954-59; Welfare Dept Contra Costa Co, soc worker, 1959;

State Calif, investr, 1959-66; Dist Atty Off, Santa Clara County, dep dist atty. **Orgs:** Vpres, Nat Asn Advan Colored People, San Jose Br; bd dir, Santa Clara Youth Village; Black Lawyers Asn. **Military Serv:** USN, 3rd Class Petty Officer, 1945-48; Good Conduct Medal. **Home Addr:** 332 Avenida Arboles St, San Jose, CA 95123.

BEASLEY, VICTOR MARIO
Lawyer. **Personal:** Born Feb 13, 1956, Atlanta, GA; son of Willie J and Mary L Ferguson; married Linda Kaye Randolph; children: Cea Janay. **Educ:** Morehouse Col, BA, 1979; GA Inst Tech, attended 1975, GA State Col Law, attended 1985. **Career:** City Atlanta Planning Bur, planning asst, 1977-78; Atlanta Bur Corrections, sgt/officer, 1980-83; Atlanta Municipal Ct, clerk/bailiff, 1983-85; Atlanta Pub Defender's Off, resr, investr, 1985-; SOAR Songs Inc, Douglasville, pres, 1989-; State Ga Bd Pardons & Paroles, parole officer, 1991. **Orgs:** Region I mem, Morehouse Col Alumni Asn, 1985; publisher, songwriter, Broadcast Music, Inc, 1989-. **Honors/Awds:** Scholarship, Atlanta Fellows & Interns, 1977-78. **Home Addr:** 217 Lakeridge Dr, Temple, GA 30179-4304. **Business Addr:** Parole Officer, Georgia State Board Pardons Paroles, 8687 Hospital Dr, Douglasville, GA 30134.*

BEATTY, BRYAN E., SR.
Secretary general. **Educ:** State Univ NY, Stony BrooK, BA, 1980; NC State Bur Invest Acad, Salemburg, NC, 1981; Univ NC, Sch Law, JD, 1987. **Career:** NC Dept Crime Control & Pub Safety, secy, currently; Gov Terrorism Preparedness Task Force, chmn. **Business Addr:** Secretary, North Carolina Department of Crime Control & Public Safety, Administration Division, 4701 Mail Service Ctr, Raleigh, NC 27699-4701, **Business Phone:** (919)733-2126.*

BEATTY, CHRISTINE
Social worker, government official. **Educ:** Howard Univ, BA, social work, 1993; Wayne State Univ, MA, social work, 1996. **Career:** Orchards C Serv; Judson Ctr; Ninth Dist State House campaign, mgr, 1996; City Detroit, Mayor Off, dist dir, legis chief staff, dep campaign mgr, chief of staff, 2002-. **Orgs:** Mayor's Cabinet, 2002-. **Honors/Awds:** Michigan's Most Influential Women, Crain's Detroit Bus. **Business Addr:** Chief of Staff, City Detroit, Mayor Office, Two Woodward Ave, Detroit, MI 48226, **Business Phone:** (313)224-3400.*

BEATTY, MARTIN CLARKE
Athletic coach, educator. **Personal:** Born in New Haven, CT; son of Eunice Clarke and Raszue Willis; married Barbara Conger, Jun 6, 1990. **Educ:** Middlebury Col, BA, art hist, Middlebury, VT, 1984. **Career:** Trinity Col, Hartford, Conn, grad fel, 1985-87; Middlebury Col, asst coach, 1987, Cook Commons Fac Head, head coach, 1988-. **Orgs:** Fac adv, Middlebury Col Activities Bd, 1987-88; Minority Issues Group,1989-; African-Am Alliance, Commons Fac Assoc; Community Rel Adv Sexual Harassment. **Honors/Awds:** Coach of the Year, US Track Coaches Asn, NCAA Division III New Eng, 1998, 2000; men's coach of the year, New Eng Small Col Athletic Conf. **Home Addr:** 629 Happy Valley Rd, Middlebury, VT 05753, **Home Phone:** (802)388-9931. **Business Addr:** Head Coach, Middlebury College, M&W Track & Field, Memorial Field House 200A, Middlebury, VT 05753, **Business Phone:** (802)443-5956.

BEATTY, OTTO, JR.
State government official, lawyer. **Personal:** Born Jan 26, 1940, Columbus, OH; son of Otto Beatty Sr and Myrna Beatty; married Joyce; children: Otto III & Laurel. **Educ:** Howard Univ, Wash, DC, BA, bus admin, 1961, MA bus admin; Ohio State Univ,Columbus, OH, JD, 1965. **Career:** Ohio House Reps, state rep, 1980-99; Beatty & Roseboro, Columbus, OH, founder & sr partner; Otto Beatty Jr & Assocs, owner, 2004-; Black Elected Democrats of Ohio, atty. **Orgs:** Am Arbitration Asn; Am Bar Asn; Am Trial Lawyers Asn; Black Elected Democrats Ohio; Columbus Area Black Elected Officials; Ohio State Consumer Educ Asn; Nat Bar Asn; Nat Asn Advan Colored People; Oper PUSH; Nat Conf Black Lawyers, Columbus Chap; Columbus Apt Asn; Chamber Com; Hunger Task Force Ohio; Ohio Alliance Black Sch Educrs; Nat Black Programming Consortium; Black Chamber Com; Columbus Asn Black Journalists; Ohio Asn Real Estate Brokers; Eastern Union Missionary Baptist Asn; pres, Franklin Co Trial Lawyers Asn; chmn, Ohio Comn Minority Health; Nat Asn Defense Lawyers. **Honors/Awds:** Citizens for Jesse Jackson Special Achievement Award; Outstanding Leadership Award, Columbus State Community Col; Outstanding Service Award,Family Missionary Baptist Church; Outstanding Services Award, Franklin Co Childrens Service Award; 10 Outstanding Young Men Award, Jr Chamber Com Ohio; Meritorious Service Award, The Ohio Acad Trial Lawyers; Community Service Award, Ohio Minority Bus; Cert Appreciation Dedicated Serv, Upward Bound Prog; Outstanding Legislator Award; Outstanding Local Trial Bar Asn, Continuing Legal Educ; Outstanding Work sites Award. **Business Addr:** Attorney, Owner, Otto Beatty Jr & Associates, 233 S High St Suite 300, Columbus, OH 43215, **Business Phone:** (614)221-2400.

BEATTY, ROBERT L.
Executive. **Personal:** Born Sep 10, 1939, Turin, GA; married Marion L Bearden; children: Tara Patrice. **Educ:** Univ Md, BA, mkt, 1961; Northwood Inst, spec dipl, mkt, 1969. **Career:** WB Doner & Co, Detroit, audio/vis dir, 1965-72; Grey Advert NY & Detroit, acct supvr, 1972-75; Ross Roy Inc, Detroit, vpres/acct supvr, 1975-. **Orgs:** Adcraft Club Detroit, 1970-; exec bd com mem, Nat Asn Advan Colored People Detroit Br, 1977-; adv bd chmn, Mich Cancer Found, 1978-; com mem, New Detroit Inc, 1978-. **Honors/Awds:** CLIO Award, Nat CLIO Adv Comn, 1978. **Military Serv:** AUS, sgt, 1958-61; Good Conduct European Command Award. **Business Addr:** Vice President, Account Supervisor, Ross Roy Inc, 2751 E Jefferson, Detroit, MI 48204.

BEAUBIEN, GEORGE H.
Executive director. **Personal:** Born Nov 10, 1937, Hempstead, NY; married Lois Ann Lowe; children: Jacqueline II. **Educ:** Compton Col, AA, 1956; Pepperdine Col, BA, 1958. **Career:** Golden State Mutual Life Ins Co, staff mgr, 1960-64; IBM Corp, legal mkt rep, 1964-65, mkt mgr, 1965-71; Self-Employed, gen ins agency all line sins, 1971-76; Mayor's Off, Small Bus Asst, exec dir, 1976-85; A & S Resources Inc, pres, 1985. **Orgs:** Dir, pres, Alpha Phi Alpha Fraternity; dir, La fire Dept Recruitment Prog; consult, Nat Bank United Fund Wash, DC, Norfolk; chmn bd, La Brotherhood Crusade, 1968; pres, New Frontier Dem Club, 1969; pres, La Bd Fire Comnr,1973-77. **Honors/Awds:** Resolution Appreciation, La City Coun; Top Rookie Salesman of Year, IBM Corp, 1971; Certificate Accomplish, IBM Corp, 1972-74; Executive of the Year, La Brotherhood Crusade, 1976.

BEAUCHAMP, PATRICK L.
Executive, president (organization), chief executive officer. **Career:** Beauchamp Distributing Co, Compton CA, chief exec officer & pres, 1973-. **Business Addr:** President, Chief Executive Officer, Beauchamp Distributing Company, 1911 S Santa Fe Ave, Compton, CA 90221, **Business Phone:** (310)639-5320.*

BEAUVAIS, GARCELLE
Actor. **Personal:** Born Nov 26, 1966, St Marc, Haiti; daughter of Axel Jean Pierre and Maria Claire Beauvais; married Daniel Saunders (divorced); children: Oliver; married Michael Nilon, May 12, 2001; children: Jax & Jaid. **Career:** Eileen Ford modeling agency; tv guest appearances: "Miami Vice"; "The Cosby Show"; "Family Matters"; "Dream On"; "The Fresh Prince of Bel-Air"; "Hangin' with Mr Cooper"; "Models Inc"; tv series: "The Jamie Foxx Show",1996; "Opposite Sex", 2000; "NYPD Blue", 2001; "Curb Your Enthusiasm", 2004; "Life with Bonnie", 2004"; "Eyes", 2005; "The Cure", 2007; tv movies: Second String, 2002; The opposite Sex, 2003; films: Manhunter, 1986; Coming to America, 1988; Every Breath, 1993; Wild Wild West, 1999; Double Take, 2001; Bad Company, 2002; Barbershop 2: Back in Business, 2004; 10.5: Apocalypse, 2005; American Gun, 2005; I Know Who Killed Me, 2007; Women in Trouble, 2009; "Maneater", 2009. **Honors/Awds:** Emmy award, Outstanding Supporting Actress Drama Series, 1993. **Business Addr:** Actress, c/o United Talent Agency, 9465 Wilshire Blvd Suite 405, Beverly Hills, CA 90212, **Business Phone:** (310)273-6700.*

BEAVER, JOSEPH T, JR.
Publisher, writer. **Personal:** Born Sep 22, 1922, Cincinnati, OH; son of Joseph and Eva; married Helen Mae Greene; children: Joseph T III, James Paul, Northe Lejana Olague & Wendla Tarascana Helene Coonan. **Educ:** Univ Cin, lib arts, 1940-41; Univ Wis Ext, econ, 1947; Univ Teuerife Spain, econ geog, 1951; Foreign Serv Inst, languages labor confs pub speech consular officers courses 1954, 1960-61, 1964-68, sr exec seminar course, 1967; Col Desert Palm Desert CA, jour micro-macro econ, 1978-79. **Career:** US foreign serv, 26 years; Spanish interpreter; Int Rev Third World Cult & Issues, publ, ed. **Orgs:** Life mem NAACP; bd mem, Western States Black Res Ctr; bd mem, Coachella Economic Develop Corp; Palm Springs Chamber Com; Citizens Freedom; affirmative action cr Coalicion Politica de la Raza; DEMAND; founder Friends Jesse Jackson Coalition, 1985; exec dir, Black Hist & Cult Soc Coachella Valley; lectured on foreign policy Africa & Latin Am; chmn, Martin Luther King Commemoration Comm Palm Springs; pres, Jesse Jackson Demo Club Coachella Valley; Col Desert Adv Comt; Educ Alert Comt; Coachella Valley African Am Chamber Com; honorary mem, Greater Palm Springs Hispanic Chamber Com; Col the Desert Extended Opportunity Prog Serv, EOPS, co-chair; Col Desert Diversity Task Force; bd dirs Black Am Cinema Soc; ed bd, Desert Sun; bd dirs, Palm Springs Convention Ctr; Friends Cuba, Coachella Valley Br, organizer; Coachella Valleywide Kwanzaa Celebration Ceremonies, co-pres, 1993-94; bd dirs, Cabazon Indian Cult Ctr, 1996; "Que Nuevas" Newspaper, advisory bd, 1997. **Honors/Awds:** Meritorious Honor Award 1965; Trophy for Editorial Excellence in Journalism Col of Desert CA 1978; Named Exec Dir Black Historical & Cultural Soc Coachella Valley Palm Springs, CA 1984; Certificate of Appreciation for Significant Serv to the Comm & in observation of Black History month County of Riverside; recipient, Buffalo Soldiers Trophy, Edwards A F Base 1991; First Corechella Valley Hispanic Recognition Award, 1997; Kwanzaa Plaque, 1998; International Film Festival Trophy, 1998; Baha'i Models of Unity Award, 1999; Leadership & Perserverence Plaque, NAACP, 2001. **Military Serv:** USMC, sgt 1943-46. **Home Phone:** (760)327-4983. **Business Addr:** Publisher, Editor, International Review of 3rd World Culture, PO Box 1785, Palm Springs, CA 92263, **Business Phone:** (619)327-4983.

BEAVERS, NATHAN HOWARD, JR.
Clergy, executive, u.s. attorney. **Personal:** Born Aug 6, 1928, Alexander City, AL; married Velma C; children: Vincent, Norman, Stephany, Rhonda, Lyrica. **Educ:** Howard Univ Sch Law, JD, 1952; Hamma Sch Theol, MDiv, PhD, 1975. **Career:** Gen Pract, civil & criminal law, 1955-62; Ohio Eagle Newspaper, 1963-65; Cleveland, real estate develop & gen contr & consult, 1966-71; FHA St Univ Col, Buffalo, Nat Acad Sci, lectr, 1969; Affil Contractors Am Inc, founder & nat exec dir, 1971-; Faith Baptist Church, co-pastor, Springfield, 1974-. **Orgs:** Pres, Beta Chap, 1949; founcer & pres, Omicron Lambda Alpha Chap, 1950; Sigma Delta Tau Legal Fraternity, 1951; founder & pres, Zeta Delta Lambda Chap, Alpha Phi Alpha Fraternity, 1957; pres, Soc Registered Contractors, 1968-70; World Bank, 1973; consult, Urban League, 1973-75; Planned Parenthood, 1975; Prince Hall Masons, Shriners, Knights Pythias, Elks, Am Legion; charter mem, Frontiers Int; bd dir, YMCA; Nutrit Elderly. **Honors/Awds:** First & Outstanding FHA, Multi-Fam Housing Proj, HUD, 1968; Outstanding Businessman of the Yr, Urban League, 1969; Outstanding Serv Affil, Contractors Am, 1971-72; Outstanding Serv, Mayor Roger Baker, 1976; Outstanding Contrib, Minority Econ Develop, State Ohio, 1977. **Military Serv:** USAF, capt, 1955. *

BEAVERS, ROBERT M.
Executive, chairperson, chief executive officer. **Personal:** Born Jan 1, 1944?; married; children: 4. **Educ:** George Washington Univ, Wash & Jefferson Col, BS, elec eng. **Career:** McDonald's Corp, Oakbrook, IL, part-time crew employee, 1963, restaurant mgr, area supvr, oper mgr, dir opers, asst lic dir, sr vpres & dir, 1998; Best Harvest Bakeries, chmn & chief exec officer, 2000-; Best Diamond Packaging, chmn & chief exec officer, 2003-; Beavers Holdings, chmn & chief exec officer, 2008-. **Orgs:** Nicor Inc, Chicago, 1992-; Zool Asn; vis trustee, Hinsdale Hosp; bd adv, NC A&T Col; Howard Univ Sch Bus; Nat Asn Educ Progress. **Honors/Awds:** Distinguished Service Award. **Special Achievements:** First African American member of McDonald's Board of Directors. **Business Addr:** Chairman, Chief Executive Officer, Best Harvest Bakeries, 530 S 65th St, Kansas City, KS 66111, **Business Phone:** (913)287-6300.

BECHET, RONALD (RON J BECHET)
Artist, educator. **Personal:** Born Jul 22, 1956, New Orleans, LA; son of Ronald Bechet Sr and Yvonne. **Educ:** Univ New Orleans, BA, 1979; Yale Univ, MS, 1982. **Career:** Southern Univ New Orleans, prof fine arts; Xavier Univ, Dept Art, chairperson, asst prof, prof fine arts & artist, currently. **Business Addr:** Professor, Artist, Xavier University of Louisiana, Art Department, 1 Drexel Dr, NewOrleans, LA 70125, **Business Phone:** (504)520-7553.

BECK, COREY LAVEON
Basketball player. **Personal:** Born May 27, 1971, Memphis, TN. **Educ:** Univ Ark, attended 1995. **Career:** Basketball player (retired); Charlotte Hornets, guard, 1995-98; Detroit Pistons, guard, 1998-99; Fila Biella, guard, 2001; Euro Roseto, 2001. **Honors/Awds:** NCAA Champion, Ark Razorbacks, 1994; CBA Champion, Sioux Falls Sky force, 1996; CBA, Defensive Player of the Yr, All-Defensive Team, 1996-97. *

BECK, HERSHELL P.
Government official. **Personal:** Born Dec 19, 1940, Carthage, TX; married Ida Mae Reese; children: Lorengo Raoul, Jackie Deshun. **Educ:** Tyler Barber Col, attended 1960. **Career:** Poney League, coach, 1977-83; Boy Scouts, leader, 1977-85; Planning & Zoning Comm, mem, 1978-80; Human Develop Corp, bd mem, 1980-84; City Carthage, mayor pro tem, 1998. **Orgs:** Comm City Carthage, 1980-; Turner Alumni Asn, 1980-; exec bd, Turner Alumni Asn, 1980-; mayor pro tem City Carthage, 1983-; bd mem, Develop Block Grant Rev Comm, 1983-; bd mem, E Tex Reg Community, 1984-. **Honors/Awds:** Plaque HUDCO, 1980; Cert Gov Tex, 1984. **Home Addr:** 402 Highland St, Carthage, TX 75633. *

BECK, SAUL L.
Government official. **Personal:** Born Jul 11, 1928, Greenwood, MS; married Elaine; children: 5. **Educ:** Chicago Tech Col. **Career:** City Councilman, 1964-72; E Chicago Heights Ill, mayor, 1973-, city councilman, 1991-95; Sch Dist No 169, Ford Heights, Ill, dir bldg &grounds; Ford Heights, IL, mayor, currently. **Orgs:** Int Brotherhood Elec Workers; Ill Bd Community & Econ Develop; bd mem,Prairie State Jr Col; educ counr mem, Natl Conf Black Mayors, 1976; IllChap Nat Conf Black Mayors; del Dem Nat Conv NY, 1980; bd dir, Ill Munic League; NBC LEO; Nat Asn Advan Colored People; PUSH. **Honors/Awds:** Appreciation Award Order of Eastern Star; Humanitarian Award Fel for Action; Community Serv Award, CEDA. **Business Addr:** Mayor, Ford Heights, 1343 Ellis Ave, Ford Heights, IL 60411, **Business Phone:** (708)758-3131.*

BECKER, ADOLPH ERIC
School administrator. **Personal:** Born Mar 16, 1925, East Rutherford, NJ; married Dorothy; children: Linda & Adolph II. **Educ:** Univ Southern Calif, BA, 1952, MS, 1956. **Career:** Jordan Locke

Comm Adult Sch, prin, 1974-77; Watts Branch NAACP, Paramed Occupational Ctr, first on site adminr, 1977; Abram Friedman Occupation Ctr, prin, 1977-83; Crenshaw-Dorsey Communlty Ad Sch, prin, 1983-90; Youth Intervention Prog Family Preserv Agency, chairperson, 1992-. **Orgs:** Alpha Phi Alpha Frat, 1950; Nat Asn Pub Continuing & Adult Educ, 1958-74; Crenshaw Neighbors Inc, 1964-; co-founder, owner, dir, producer, Dorothy, Argo Ctr Cult Arts, 1969-74; chmn, Adult HS Com Nat Asn Pub, 1975-77; dir, Nat Coun Urban Adminr Adult Educ, 1975-; chmn, Curr Coun La City Sch, 1976-77; Phi Delta Kappa, 1977-; charter mem, vpres & prog chmn, Watts Willowbrook Rotary Club Int Inc; Adult Sch Prins Asn & Guid Coun La; chmn, Scope & Sequence Com Curric Coun La City Sch; comm rep, Policy Planning Coun, La County Head start Grantee Prog, 1994-; res & eval comn, La County Headstart, 1994-; chairperson, Acad Comn, La County Probation Dept. **Honors/Awds:** Nat Med Asn Found Inc Award, 1972; Co-Recipient, Bahai Human Rights Award,1972; Best Principal of the Year Award, Watts Star Rev News, 1975; Community Service Award, La Urban League, 1984; Principal of the Year Award, Youth Intervention Prog, 1988; Certificate of Appreciation, La County Probation Dept, 1994. **Military Serv:** AUS, Transp Corps WWII, Europe, 1943-45. **Home Addr:** 4296 Don Luis Dr, Los Angeles, CA 90008-4217.

BECKER-SLATON, DR. NELLIE FRANCES
Educator, writer. **Personal:** Born Aug 31, 1921, Providence, RI; daughter of Nell Frances Occomy and Leslie Earle; married William H, Sep 27, 1950; children: Glenn, Shell & Baxter. **Educ:** NY Univ, BS, occup ther, 1946; CA State Col, LA, teachers credential, 1952; Pepperdine Univ, MA, 1975; Claremont Grad Univ, PhD, 1988. **Career:** Hines Va Hosp Chicago, IL, Sawtelle Va Hosp, Los Angeles, Ca, occup therapist, 1947-50; Calif Eagle, family edit, 1948-51; prof writer, 1950-; Pittsburgh Courier, contrib writer, 1951-52; La Unified Sch Dist Reg D,multicultural adult educ teacher, 1972-77; Frances Blend Sch Visually Handicapped, sci coordr, 1973-75; Westminster Elem Sch, multicultural coordr, 1978-79; Walgrove Elem Sch & Charnock Elem Sch, integration coordr, 1979-80; Los Angeles Unified Sch Dist, educ prof writer; West minister Elem, 1980-97; Oral His Proj, City Inglewood, CA, consult & instr, 1998-2001. **Orgs:** Dir, Comm Sci Workshops, 1960-69; pres, Int Scribbles West, 1960-65; Chap 587 Coun Excep C; bd mem, Los Angeles Reading Asn; Am Folklore Soc; Los Angeles Calif Geneal Soc; EDUCARE; Lings Soc Am; Alpha Kappa Alpha Sorority Inc; Comm Work West minster Presb, 1973; co-founder, ADADS Assoc,1982; Western Folklore Soc; Nat Asn Prof Process Servers; SCCLYP; Afro-Am Geneal Soc, Southern CA; Los Angeles Urban League; co-founder & pres, Asn Pan African Doctoral Scholars, 1981-92; Resolution Comm Work Los Angeles City Coun, 1985; Comm Work Nat Asn Col Women; Daughters Am Revolution; Hollywood Chap Calif, 1996; Int PEN; ANASCA, 1999-. **Honors/Awds:** Women of the Year, Los Angeles Sentinel Newspaper, 1962; Sci Auth Radio Station K DAY, 1965; Author Writers Award, Our Auth Study Club, 1966; Senate Resolution State California, 1990; Oral History Award City Inglewood CA, 2001; International Educators Hall Fame, 2001. **Special Achievements:** Author of Bacteria & Viruses Prentice Hall, On My Own Harcourt Brace-Jovanovich, U.S. Congressional Recognition Community Work, 2001. **Home Addr:** 2409 Carmona Ave, Los Angeles, CA 90016.

BECKETT, EVETTE OLGA (EVETTE BECKETT-TUGGLE)
Marketing executive. **Personal:** Born Sep 1, 1956, Glen Cove, NY; daughter of Arthur Dean Beckett and Ollie Leone Hall Beckett; married Reginald Tuggle; married J Barrington Jackson (divorced); children: Lauren. **Educ:** Tufts Univ, BA, 1978; Columbia Univ Grad Sch Bus, MBA, 1981. **Career:** Random House Inc, prod asst, 1978-79; Bankers Trust Co, corp lending officer, 1981-82; Avon Prod Inc, merchandising planner, 1982-84, asst merchandising mgr, 1984-85, merchanding mgr, 1985-86, mgr fragrance mkt, 1986-89; dir fragrance mkt, 1989-92; gen mgr, Speciality Gift Bus, 1992-; Nassau County Off Econ Develop, exec dir, currently. **Orgs:** Nat Asn Female Exec, 1986-87; bd mem, Coalition Black Prof Orgn, 1986-87; Cosmetic Exec Women, 1987; prog chmn, NY Chap Nat Black MBA Asn, 1987; vpres, oper, Nat Black MBA Asn, New York Chap, 1987-88; bd dir, C House, 1988-; prog chmn, 1987-, bd dir, 1990-, 100 Black Women Long Island; bd dir, Glen Cove Boys & Girls Club 1990-; Long Island Women's Agenda; Women Econ Developers Long Island; Alpha Kappa Alpha Sorority; Theta Iota Omega. **Honors/Awds:** Billie Holiday Performing Arts Award, Tufts Univ, 1978; Outstanding Volunteer Award, Avon Products Inc, 1984; Top 100 Black Bus & Prof Women, Dollars & Sense Mag, 1988; Black Achievers Award, Harlem YMCA, 1989; Crain's NY Bus 40 People Under 40 to Watch in the 1990's; On The Move, Fortune Mag, 1990; Essence Mag 10 Corp Women, 1991; Marketer of the Month Sales & Marketing Management, 1991. **Business Phone:** (516)571-0578.

BECKETT, JUSTIN F.
Association executive, founder (originator), chief executive officer. **Personal:** Born Apr 5, 1963, Boston, MA; son of Herbert and Eleanor. **Educ:** Duke Univ, BA, polit sci & hist, 1985. **Career:** E F Hutton, acct exec, 1985-86; NCM Capital Mgt Group, Inc, exec vpres, 1986; New Africa Advs, pres & chief exec officer, 1992-; Sloan financial group, exec vpres, principal; Fluid Audio Networks, chief exec officer & founder, currently. **Orgs:** Nat Investment Mgrs Asn, secy & treas, 1988-92; Nat Asn Securities Profs, 1988-; Southern Univ New Orleans, adjunct prof, 1989-92; Nat Minority Suppliers Develop Coun, advocacy comn, 1989-93; Duke Univ Black Alumni Connection, 1990-; Elizabeth City State Univ, trustee, 1992-94. **Honors/Awds:** Atlanta Coast Conf, ACC Honor Roll, 1985; Acad All Conf Football Team, 1985; Nat Minority MBA, Asn Ron Brown Award, 1997. **Business Phone:** (310)665-9878.*

BECKETT, SYDNEY A.
Educator, executive. **Personal:** Born Nov 20, 1943, Philadelphia, PA. **Educ:** Temple Univ, BA, 1965, MEd, 1967, PhD. **Career:** Philadelphia Sch Dist, elem teacher, 1965-66; IBM, mkt support rep, 1967-73; Pa Comm Status Women, comnr appointed Govn, 1972-; EI Dupont, training & develop, 1974; Silver Horse Artists Creations, artist. **Orgs:** Bd dir, Alumni Asn, Temple Univ, 1967; bd dir, SW Belmont Young Women Christian Asn, 1970; Am Soc Training & Develop, 1974; Phi DeltaGamma; Am Asn Univ Women, 1977; Delta Sigma Theta Sor, 1962; bd mem, Philadelphia Singers. **Honors/Awds:** Outstanding Woman of the Year, Temple Univ, 1970; Community Service Award, IBM, 1970-72; Dale Carnegie Inst 2 awards; Sr Recognition Award of Pres & Faculty; Outstanding Sr Templar Yearbook; Greek Woman of Year, Temple Univ; Vol Serv Award; Treble Clef Alumnae Award. **Business Addr:** Artist, Silver Horse Artists Creations, 2118 Co Hwy 33, Cooperstown, NY 13326.*

BECKETT-TUGGLE, EVETTE. **See BECKETT, EVETTE OLGA.**

BECKFORD, ORVILLE
Automotive executive. **Career:** Orville Beckford Ford-Mercury Inc, chief exec officer, principal & dealer, 1987-. **Business Addr:** Chief Executive Officer, Principal, Orville Beckford Ford-Mercury Inc., 6400 Hwy 90 W, Milton, FL 32570, **Business Phone:** (850)623-2234.

BECKFORD, TYSON CRAIG
Fashion model, actor. **Personal:** Born Dec 19, 1970, Bronx, NY. **Career:** Ralph Lauren, lead model, actor; "Make Me A Supermodel", host, currently; Bethann Hardison/Bethann Mgt Co Inc, model, currently; Films: Punks; Boricua's Bond, 2000; Zoolander, 2001; Shottas, 2002; Pandora's Box, 2002; Gully, 2002; Biker Boyz, 2003; Gas, 2004; Searching for Bobby D, 2004; Into the Blue, 2005; Dream Street, 2006; Kings Of the Evening 2008; Hotel California; 2008; TV Shows: "Superbikes", "Americas Next Top Model"; "Project Runaway"; "Candy Girls"; Music Videos: "Unbreak My Heart"; "Ice Cream", "21 Questions"; "Toxic". **Honors/Awds:** Hottest Male Model, Man of the Year, VH-1, 1995. **Special Achievements:** First African American to be featured with Ralph Lauren/Polo; 50 MostBeautiful People in the World, People Magazine, 1995; appeared on variousmagazines: Essence & Paper; Vogue; GQ; Details; Men's Health; Vibe & TheNY Times; TV appearances include Toni Braxton; Mia X; Notorious BIG-;Shaquille O'Neal; Jay Leno; Oprah; Rosie O'Donnel; Vibe; The Magic Hour;Good Morning Am; Keenan Ivory Wayans; Mad TV; Nickelodeon; EntertainmentTonight; E! Entertainment; Video Soul; Teen Summit. **Business Addr:** Model, c/o Bethann Management, 36 N Moore St, New York, NY 10013, **Business Phone:** (212)925-2153.*

BECKHAM, BARRY EARL
Publisher, writer, educator. **Personal:** Born Mar 19, 1944, Philadelphia, PA; son of Mildred Williams and Clarence; married Betty Louise Hope, Feb 19, 1966 (divorced 1977); children: Brian Elliott & Bonnie Lorine; married Monica L Scott, Oct 23, 1997; married Geraldine Lynne Palmer, 1979 (divorced 1983). **Educ:** Brown Univ, AB, 1966; Columbia Univ law sch, attended. **Career:** Prof (retired), founder, pres & writer; Chase Manhattan Bank, pub rels, consult, 1966-67, urban affairs assoc, 1969-70; Nat Coun YMCAs, pub rels assoc, 1967-68; Western Elec Co, pub rels assoc, 1968-69; Brown Univ, vislect, 1970-72, asst prof, 1972-78, assoc prof eng, 1979-87, dir grad creative writing prog, 1980-87; Gary Lives, Writer, 1973; Hampton Univ, prof, 1987(retired); Publ: My Main Mother, 1969; Runner Mack; Double Dunk, 1972; Will You Be Mine; Beckham's Guide to Scholarships for Black & Minority Students; The Col Selection Work book; The Black Students guide to col, 1982; The Col Selection Workbook, 2nd ed, 1987; You Have a Friend: The Rise & Fall & Rise of Chase Manhattan Bank, serialized on Internet, 1998; Plays: Garvey Lives! 1972; Articles: "Listen to the Black Graduate, You Might Learn Something", Esquire, 1969, "Ladies & Gentlemen, NoSalt-Water Taffy Today", Brown Alumni Monthly, 1970, & "Why It Is Right to Write", Brown Alumni Monthly, 1978; Ed: The Black Student's Guide to Cols, 1997; The Black Student's Guide to Scholarships, 1999; Beckham Publ Group, pres, 1989-, founder, currently; Nat Endowment Arts, fel. **Orgs:** Bd dirs, Authors Guild; Authors League Am; bd dirs, PEN; Rhode Island Coun Arts, lit panel; judge, Hurston Wright Found, 2005. **Special Achievements:** One of the judges of the 2005 Hurston Wright Foundation Award for the best novel by an African American. **Home Addr:** 13619 Cedar Creek Lane, Silver Spring, MD 20904, **Home Phone:** (301)384-1118. **Business Addr:** Founder, President, Beckham Publications Group, PO Box 4066, Silver Spring, MD 20914, **Business Phone:** (301)384-7995.

BECKLES, BENITA HARRIS
Human services worker. **Personal:** Born Feb 21, 1950, Chicago, IL; daughter of Felicia Mason Williams; married Lionel L, Jun 27, 1981; children: Lionel E & Jefferson. **Educ:** Hampton Univ, BA, 1971; George Washington Univ, MA, 1977. **Career:** Potential Plus, human potential consult, 1996; Detroit Pub Libr, employee develop coordr, 1998-; Tuskegee Airmen Inc; White House fel. **Orgs:** Delta Sigma Theta Sorority, Inkster Alumni Chap. **Special Achievements:** Auth: Back to Basics Life Strategies for Success. **Military Serv:** USAF, mil personnel officer, 1972, Support Group Comdr, col, 1981-; Joint Service Commendation Medal, 1980; Meritorious Service Medal, 1990, 1999. **Home Addr:** 18810 Alhambra, Lathrup Village, MI 48076. **Business Addr:** Coordinator, Detroit Public Library, 5201 Woodward Ave, Detroit, MI 48202, **Business Phone:** (313)833-1000.

BECKLES, IAN HAROLD
Football player, broadcaster. **Personal:** Born Jul 20, 1967, Quebec;married Dayle; children: Zayna, Marques. **Educ:** Waldorf JC, Ind. **Career:** Tampa Bay Buccaneers, guard, 1990-96; Philadelphia Eagles, 1997-99; NY Jets, 1999; Denver Broncos, 2000; WDAE Radio, sportscaster. **Special Achievements:** Selected 52nd Greatest player in Buccaneer history in 2007. **Business Phone:** (813)832-1000.*

BECKLEY, DR. DAVID LENARD
College president. **Personal:** Born Mar 21, 1946, Shannon, MS; married Gemma Douglass; children: Jacqueline & Lisa. **Educ:** Rust Col, BA 1967; Univ Miss, MEd, 1975, PhD, 1986. **Career:** Rust Col, purchasing agent, 1968-69, dir pub rels, 1967-77, dir develop, 1977-81, interim provost, 1984, dir advan, 1984, pres currently; Wiley Col, pres, 1987-93. **Orgs:** Bd dir, Holly Springs Miss Chamber Com, 1980-86; consult, UN Negro ColFund, Lilly Endowment, 1981-84; secy, Indust Develop Authority, MarshallCity, 1985-87. **Honors/Awds:** Kappan Year, Phi Delta Kappa Educ Frat, 1984; Omega Man Year, Omega Psi Phi Frat Phi Rho Chap, 1983. **Military Serv:** AUS, pub rels, 1969-71; AUS, E-5 2 yrs; Army Commdtn Vietnam Srvc Corp1969-71. **Home Addr:** PO Box 481, Holly Springs, MS 38635. **Business Phone:** (662)252-8000.

BECKWITH, REV. DR. MICHAEL BERNARD
Clergy, executive. **Career:** Agape Int Spiritual Ctr, founder, spiritual dir & sr minister, currently; Ernest Holmes Inst Sch Ministry, dir, currently. **Orgs:** Asn Global New Thought. **Honors/Awds:** Africa Achievement Peace Award, 2004; Humanitarian Award of the Nat Council for Community & Justice; United World for the InterNat Protection of Children's Rights "Prime Minister of the Children's Diplomatic Corp" Award; Inducted into the Martin Luther King, Jr Board of Preachers of Morehouse Col; Excellence in Spiritual Leadership and Community Development Award; Congress of Racial Equality award as one of the top ten ministers in Los Angeles; Martin Luther King Peace Award. **Special Achievements:** Auth: Inspirations of the Heart; Forty Day Mind Fast Soul Feast, A Manifesto of Peace; Living from the Overflow. **Business Phone:** (310)348-1250.

BECOTE, FOHLIETTE W
Banker, executive. **Personal:** Born Dec 28, 1958, Burgaw, NC; daughter of Arlander and Ola Mae; married Lawen J Becote II, Aug 28, 1988. **Educ:** Univ NC, Chapel Hill, NC, BA, 1981; NC Cent Univ, Durham, NC, MBA, 1985. **Career:** NC Cent Univ, Durham, NC, grad asst, 1983-84; Mechanics & Farmers Bank, Durham, NC, analysis clerk, 1983-84, asst comptroller, 1984-87, asst vpres & asst comptroller, 1987-88, vpres & comptroller, 1988-96, sr vpres/comptroller, 1996-2000, sr vpres, chief financial officer & corp secy, 2000-; M&F Bancorp Inc, secy & treas, currently. **Orgs:** Leadership Durham Alumni Asn, 1990-; secy, Bankers Educ Soc Inc, 1987-88; treas, Salvation Army Adv Bd, 1985-88; treas, Durham Child Advocacy Comn, 1987-88; Nat Asn Accts, 1986-90; Univ NC Educ Found; Univ NC Gen Alumni; Alpha Kappa Alpha; Delta Sigma Pi Alumni; Wake County Ind Facilities & Pollution Control Financing Authority. **Honors/Awds:** 100 Most Promising Black Women in Corp Am, Ebony, 1991; YWCA Women of Achievement Award, YWCA, 1985. **Business Addr:** Senior Vice President & Chief Financial Officer, Corporate Secretary, Mechanics & Farmers Bank, 2634 Chapel Hill Blvd, PO Box 1932, Durham, NC 27702-2800, **Business Phone:** (919)687-7835.

BECTON, LT. GEN. JULIUS WESLEY, JR.
School administrator. **Personal:** Born Jun 29, 1926, Bryn Mawr, PA; son of Julius Wesley Becton Sr and Rose Inez (Banks) Becton; married Louise Thornton, Jan 29, 1948; children: Shirley McKenzie, Karen Johnson, Joyce Best, Renee Strickland & J WesleyIII. **Educ:** Prairie View A&M Col, BS, Math, 1960; Univ Md, MA, Econ, 1966; AUS Command& Gen Staff Col; Armed Forces Staff Col; Nat War Col, 1970. **Career:** Military service (retired), dir, educ administrator; First CavalryDiv, commanding gen, 1975-76; AUS, Oper Test & Eval Agency, commandinggen, 1976-78; VII US Corps, commanding gen, 1978-81; USA Train-

ing DctrnCommand, dep commanding gen & the Army inspector training, 1981-83; Agencyfor Int Develop, Office Foreign Disaster, Asst dir, 1984-85; Fed EmergencyMgt Agency, dir, 1985-89; Prairie View A&M Univ, pres, 1989-94; DC PubSchs, supt, pres, 1996-98. **Orgs:** Dir, Nat Asn Uniformed Serv, 1969-71; vpres, US Armor Asn, 1982-91; TheRet Officers Asn, 1983-85; Fairfax Coun Red Cross, 1983-84; USO World BdGov, 1985-90; Am Red Cross bd gov, 1986-90; bd trustees, Valley Forge MilAcad & Jr Col, 1988-90; bd, Fund for the Improv Post-Sec Educ, 1990-93; bddirs, Marine Spill Response Corp, 1990-2001; vchair & dir, Southern-Regional Educ Bd, 1991-94; Community Col Southern Asn Col & Schs, 1991-94;bd dir, Nat Asn Equal Oppor Higher Educ, 1992-94; bd dir, Wackenhut Corp,1993-2002; adv coun, The Citadel Bd Visitors, 1994-99; bd dirs, GenDynamics, 1997-2002; bd adv, First Cavalry Div Asn; bd visitors, DefenseEqual Opportunity Mgt Inst; five star coun mem, Libr Cong Veterans HistProj; adv bd, Resolution Trust; Long Range Planning & Oversight Comn, FedDist Ct, Knight v Ala; bd dir, Greater Wash Urban League; vchair countrustees, Asn AUS; bd trustees, George C Marshall Found; Am BattleMonument Comn, 2001-05; FAMU Bd Trustees, 2001-04; bd dir (retired), IllTool Works Inc, 2002. **Honors/Awds:** Top Hat Award, Courier Inc, 1973; Prairie View A&M Univ, Distinguished Graduate, 1975; Rock of Year, Rocks Inc, 1983; GE Rush Award, Nat Bar Asn, 1984; Dist Honor Award, Agency for Int Develop, 1986; Hon Degrees: Huston-Tillotson, 1982, Muhlenberg Col, 1988, Prairie View A&M Univ, 1994,The Citadel, 1997; Dickinson College, 2009. **Military Serv:** AUS, lt gen, 39 Yrs; DSM, SS 2, LOM 2, DFC, BSN 2, AM 4, PH 2, ACM 2,Knights comdr Cross FRG. **Home Addr:** 7737 Jewelweed Ct, Springfield, VA 22152, **Home Phone:** (703)644-5771.

BECTON, RUDOLPH
Businessperson. **Personal:** Born May 21, 1930, Eureka, NC; married Annie Veronia Wilson; children: Karen L. **Educ:** Green County Training Sch, Diploma, 1950; Harris Barber Col Diploma, 1956; Sampson Tech Inst Cert, 1979; NC Agr Exten Cert, 1984. **Career:** UNC Chapel Hill, emergency medical serv, 1976 & 1978; James Sprunt Inst, communi & patrol, 1978; Winston Salem State Univ, hair styling & cutting tech, 1979; James Sprunt Tech Col, fire apparatus & house practice, 1983; Becton Barber Shop, owner & operator, currently. **Orgs:** Humanitarian Magnolia Civic League, 1968-73; comt mem, Farmer's Home Admin, 1970-73 & 1977-80; Human Relations Duplin Co Good Neighbor Coun, 1973; town commissioner, Town Magnolia; volunteer fireman & rescue, Town Magnolia; bd mem, Duplin & Sampson Mental Health; mayor pro team, Town Magnolia; bd mem, Magnolia Fire Dept; pres, Dupenza; Pres, Magnolia Civic League. **Honors/ Awds:** Trailblazer Boy Scouts Am, 1968; Distinguished Citizen, Crouton III Boy Scouts of Am, 1979; Good Conduct Medal. **Military Serv:** AUS, PFC, The Quartermaster Corps; Honorable Discharge; Two Battle Stars. **Business Addr:** Owner, Becton Barber Shop, PO Box 86, Magnolia, NC 28453.*

BEDELL, DR. FREDERICK DELANO
School administrator. **Personal:** Born Apr 13, 1934, New York, NY; married Gail Smith; children: Karin, Kevin & Keith. **Educ:** NY Univ, BS, 1957, MA, 1965; Univ MA, EdD, 1984. **Career:** Rockaway Beach, chief life guard, 1953-56; White Plains Pub Schs, 1957-68, asst prin, 1968-69, asst supt Pub Serv, 1984-; Bd Coop Educ Serv, prin,1969-76; NY State Div Youth, dir educ, 1983-84; NY State Dept Corrections, asst comnr & dir Correctional Industs,1983-84; Del-K Educ Consult Serv,pres, 1993. **Orgs:** Chmn, Equal Opportunity Educ Comt, White Plains Teacher Asn,1966-68; deputy mayor & village trust Ossining,1973-76; vice chmn, Ossining Urban Revewal Bd, 1973-76; vpres Cage Teen Ctr; bd mem, St Mary's Field Sch; sec, treas & bd dir, High Meadow Coop; NY State Cong Parents & Teachers. **Honors/Awds:** Jaycees Award. **Business Addr:** President, Del-K Educ Consult Serv, 8 Rolling Brook Dr, Clifton Park, NY 12065.*

BEDOYA, ADRIANA. See SYKES, WANDA.

BEE, QUEEN. See JONES, KIMBERLY DENISE.

BEHRMANN, SERGE T.
Executive. **Personal:** Born Jun 9, 1937, Port-au-Prince, Haiti; married; children: Rachelle, Daphne, Serge J, Alex & Sophia. **Educ:** Col Simon Bolivar, 1955; Wis Univ, struct fabricating eng, 1973; Purdue Univ, struct fabricating eng, 1974. **Career:** Feinstein Iron Works, 1959-66; Behrmann Iron Works, structural fabricator. **Orgs:** Pres, Ferrum Realty Corp, New York. **Business Addr:** Structural Fabricator, Behrmann Iron Works Inc, 832 Dean St, Brooklyn, NY 11238.

BELAFONTE, HARRY (HAROLD GEORGE BELAFONTE, JR.)
Singer, television producer, actor. **Personal:** Born Mar 1, 1927, Harlem, NY; son of Malvene Love Wright and Harold George Belafonte Sr; married Marguerite Byrd, Jan 1, 1948 (divorced 1957); children: Adrienne & Shari; children: David & Gina. **Educ:** Manhattan New Sch Soc Res Dramatic Workshop, 1948. **Career:** Broadway appearances: Almanac, 1953, Three for Tonight, 1955; Films: Bright Rd, 1952; Carmen Jones, 1954; Island in the Sun, 1957; The World: the Flesh & the Devil, 1958; Odds Against Tomorrow; 1959; The Angel Levine, 1969; Buck & the Preacher, 1971; Uptown Saturday Night, 1974; White Man's Burden, 1995; Fidel, 2001; XXI Century, 2003; Conakry Kas, 2003; Ladders, 2004; Mo & Me, 2006; Bobby, 2006; TV: "TV Specs", prod; "A Time of Laughter", 1967, "Harry & Lena", 1969; "Tonight with Belafonte",1960; "Strolling Twenties TV", prod; "Beat St", coprod, 1984; "Tanner on Tanner", 2004; "That's What I'm Talking About", 2006; Belafonte Enterprises Inc, pres, currently. **Orgs:** Bd dir, Trans Africa Forum Bd. **Honors/Awds:** Tony Award, 1953; Emmy Award, 1960; Honorary Doctor of Humanities, Park Col, 1968; Honorary Doctor of Arts, New Sch Social Res, 1968; Martin Luther King Jr Nonviolent Peace Prize, 1982; ABAA Music Award, 1985; Grammy Award, 1985; Honorary Doctorate, Spel man Col, 1990; Nat Medal of Arts Award, White House, 1994; Freedom in Film Award, 2000; Bishop John T Walker Distinguished Humanitarian Service Award, Africare, 2002; Humanitarian Award, BET, 2006; Hollywood Film Award, 2006. **Special Achievements:** Received an appointment to UNICEF as a goodwill ambassador in 1987. **Military Serv:** USN, 1943-45.

BELAFONTE, SHARI (SHARI BELAFONTE HARPER)
Actor, fashion model. **Personal:** Born Aug 22, 1954, New York, NY; daughter of Harry and Marguerite Byrd; married Robert Harper, May 21, 1977 (divorced 1988); married Sam Behrens, Dec 31, 1989. **Educ:** Hampshire Col; Carnegie-Mellon Univ, BFA, 1977. **Career:** Actress, producer, photographer, writer & fashion model; Hanna Barbera Prod, publicist asst; fashion model; TV series: Hotel, 1983-88; The Midnight Hour, 1985; French Silk, 1994; The Heidi Chronicles, 1995; "Babylon 5: Third space", 1998; Loving Evangeline, 1998; "The Octopus Show", 2000; "The District", 2001; "Nip/Tuck", 2008. Photographer: The Big Empty, 2003; Betrunner, 2004; Betty's Treats, producer, 2004; Lonesome Matador, 2005. Films: Feuer, Eis & Dynamit, 1990; Harlequin's Loving Evangeline, 1998; Mars, 1998. **Special Achievements:** Appeared on more than 200 magazine covers. **Business Phone:** (213)462-7274.*

BELARDO DE O, LILLIANA
Senator (u.s. federal government), politician. **Personal:** Born Jan 11, 1944, Christiansted, Virgin Islands of the United States; daughter of Gil Belardo Sanes and Paula Mendez Agosto; married Humberto, Jan 30, 1986; children: Carlos Gill Ortiz. **Educ:** Inter-Am Univ, BA, 1963; Univ Mich, MSW, 1969; Calif State Univ; NY UnivPuerto Rico Exten; Univ Miami, doctoral study. **Career:** Dept Social Welfare, social worker, 1964, probation worker, 1970; Dept Social Welfare Girls Training Sch, dir, 1971; State Calif, youth authority worker, 1975; Dept Educ, sch guid counr, 1976; Legis VI, legislator, 1981, sen; Republican Party VI, nat comt woman, currently. **Orgs:** Bd dir, Am Red Cross, St Croix Chap; League Women Voters; St Croix Lioness Club; Asn Social Workers Bus & Prof Women. **Military Serv:** AUS, Nat Guard, capt, 5 yrs; dir, Selective Serv US VI. **Home Addr:** 53 Dlagr Princess Cisted, PO Box 3382, St Croix, Virgin Islands of the United States 00820. **Business Addr:** National Committee Woman, The Republican Party of the Virgin Islands, 6067 Questa Verde, St Croix, Virgin Islands of the United States 00820-4485, **Business Phone:** (340)332-2579.

BELCHER, JACQUELYN M.
School administrator, president (organization). **Educ:** Marymount Col, BS, nursing; Univ Wash, MA, psycho-social nursing & psychol; Univ Puget Sound, JD; Inst Mgt Lifelong Educ. **Career:** Minneapolis Community Col, pres; Ga Perimeter Col, pres, 1995-05, pres emer, 2005-. **Orgs:** Exec coun & chair, AACC; bd dirs, Metro Atlanta Chamber Com; Metro Atlanta Boys & Girls Clubs; Atlanta Bus League; Carter Ctr; Seamless Educ Comt; vice chair, Ga Human Rels Comn; vice chair, KnowledgeWorks Found. **Honors/Awds:** Altanta's 30 Most Prominent Female Prof, Bus-To-Bus Mag, 1998; Mildred B Bulpitt Woman of the Year Award, AAWCC, 1996; Outstanding Alumnus, Marymount Col, 1990; Woman Achievement Award, Quota Club, 1989; Woman of the Year, Girl Scouts Am, 1989; Am Jurisp Award, Univ Puget Sound, 1983. **Special Achievements:** First African American woman to head a University System of Georgia institution; first African-American to have head a Coll/Univ in GA that is not historically black. **Business Addr:** President Emeritus, Georgia Perimeter College, 3251 Panthersville Rd, Decatur, GA 30034.*

BELCHER, DR. LEON H.
Educator. **Personal:** Born Aug 8, 1930, Mineral Springs, AR; married Mary S Randall; children: 2. **Educ:** Univ Ark, BS, 1955, MS, 1957; Univ Northern Colo, PhD, 1961. **Career:** State Ark, teacher, jr high sch counr, 1955-60; Ala A&M Univ, Dean Studs, prof, 1961-66; Princeton Univ, res psychologist, 1966-67; Tex Southern Univ, dir testing, dir inst res, prof, 1967-71, Dept psychol & philos, prof & chair, currently. **Orgs:** Alpha Kappa Mu, 1955; Phi Delta Kappa, 1960; Am Psychol Asn; Am Personnel & Guid Asn; Am Educ Res Asn; Am Col Personnel Asn; ed bd, Col Stud Personnel J; ed bd, Asn Inst Res; Tex State Bd Examiners; Cultural Affairs Comt, Houston Chamber Com; Houston Coun Boys Scout Am. **Honors/Awds:** Wall Street Journal Student Award, 1955; Post Doctoral Research Fellowship Award, HEW, 1966. **Military Serv:** AUS, 1952-54. **Home Addr:** 4305 Fernwood Dr, Houston, TX 77021. **Business Addr:** Professor, Chair, Texas Southern University, Department of Psychology & Philosophy, 3100 Cleburne St ED B02A, Houston, TX 77004-4501, **Business Phone:** (713)313-7011.

BELIZAIRE-SPITZER, JULIE
Social worker. **Personal:** Born Dec 23, 1969, New York, NY; daughter of Gabriel and Simone; married Andrew, Sep 11, 1999; children: 3. **Educ:** Albany Univ-SUNY, BA; Hunter Col-CUNY, MSW. **Career:** Citizens Advice Bur, prog dir, HRAP, 1997, asst dir, Homeless Prev, 1998, prog dir, sr servs, 1999-, Citizens Adv Bur, acting dir, 2001-. **Orgs:** Zeta Phi Beta, 1990-; bd dirs, Bronx Regional Inter-Agency Council on Aging (BRICA), 2000. **Business Addr:** Program Director - Homelessness Prevention Program, Citizens Advice Bureau, CAB Community Center, 1130 Grand Concourse 3rd Fl, Bronx, NY 10456, **Business Phone:** (718)293-0727.*

BELL, ALBERTA SAFFELL
Publisher. **Personal:** Born Sep 25, 1944, Knoxville, TN; daughter of Alfred J Saffell Sr and Mildred J; married C Gordon Bell, Oct 25, 1985 (deceased); children: Tiffany M & C Gordon II. **Educ:** Tenn State Univ, BS, 1966, MS, 1968; Howard Univ, DDS, 1976. **Career:** Nashville Pub Sch; Massachusetts Newspapers, Publs, 1992; Gardner News, vpres, 1989-92, publ & pres, 1992-. **Orgs:** Vpres, Heritage State Park Friends, 1988-; trustee, Gardner Mus, 1989-; bd mem, Montachunett Girl Scout, 1990-; trustee, Citchburg State Univ, 1991-; publs, Massachusetts Newspapers, 1992-. **Military Serv:** AUS, major, dent corp, 1976-86. **Business Addr:** President, Publisher, The Gardner News, 309 Central St, PO Box 340, Gardner, MA 01441-0340, **Business Phone:** (978)632-8000 Ext 16.

BELL, DR. CARL COMPTON
Psychiatrist, medical researcher. **Personal:** Born Oct 28, 1947, Chicago, IL; son of William Yancey Bell Jr and Pearl Debnam; married Phyllis W Bell; children: Briatta & William. **Educ:** Univ Ill, Chicago Circle, BS, biol, 1967; Meharry Med Col, MD, 1971; Ill State Psychiat Inst, Chicago, psychiat residency, 1974. **Career:** Goldberger Fel, 1969; Matthew Walker Comp Health Ctr, Meharry Med Col, bio statistician, 1970-72; Ill Dept Ment Health, resident physician, 1971-74; pvt pract, psychiatrist, 1972-; Jackson Park Hosp, consult, 1972-74; Chicago Med Sch, clin instr psych, 1975; Psychiat Emergency Serv Prog, dir, 1976-77, assoc dir, div behav & psychodynamic med, 1979-80; Human Correctional & Serv Inst, staff psychiatrist, 1977-78; Chatham Avalon Ment Health Ctr, staff psychiatrist, 1977-79; Chicago Bd Educ, staff psychiatrist, 1977-79; Community Ment Health Coun, day treatment ctr, staff psychiatrist, 1977-79, med dir, 1982-87, pres & chief exec officer, 1987-; Univ Ill, Sch Med, clin prof, clin psych, 1983-; WVON-AM, Chicago, IL, radio talk show host, 1987-88; WJPC-FM, The Black Couch, radio talk show, 1992-93; Univ Ill, Sch Pub Health, prof, 1995, Sch Med, clin prof psychiat & pub health, currently; Community Ment Health Coun, pres & chief exec officer, currently. **Orgs:** Am-Indian Asian-Pacific Am/Black & Hispanic Core Ment Health Discipline Adv Comn, Howard Univ Sch Social Work, 1980-83; Nat Comn Correctional Health Care, 1983, chmn, 1992; chmn, Nat Med Asn Sect Psych, 1985-86; bd dir, Am Asn Community Ment Health Ctr Psychiatrists, 1985-89; dipl, bd examr, Am Bd Psychiat & Neurol; Shorei Goju Karate Soc-Rank 6th Degree Black Belt; Black Belt Med Soc Physicians Martial Arts Asn; secy, treas, Nat Coun Community Ment Health Ctr, 1986-87; Am Psychiat Asn; Am Col Psychiat, 1987; bd dirs, IL, Coun against Handgun Violence, 1990-; co-investigator, African-Am Youth Proj, Univ Il Sch Pub Health, 1994-; ed bd, Jour Infant, Child & Adolescent Psychother, 1997-; IL State Attorney's Comn Violent Young Offenders, 1998; ed adv bd, Clin Psychiat News, 2000; Univ IL, Pres's Distinguished Speakers Prog, 2000; Am Psych Asn; Nat Inst Ment Health, res planning work groups for DSM V, 2000-02; Inst Med, Bd Neuroscience & Behav Health Study Psychopathology & Prev Adolescent & Adult Suicide, 2000-02; Am Col Psych Bd Regents, 2006-11; NIMH Nat Ment Health Adv Coun, 2008-11. **Honors/ Awds:** Citation of Merit, Disabled Am Veterans, 1971; Mosby Scholar Book Award, Scholastic Excellence in Med, Meharry Med Col 1971; Falk Fel, Am Psychiatric Asn Participate Coun Nat Affairs, 1972, 1973; Plaque, IL Shaolin Karate & Kung-Fu Asn, 1975; Certificate of Appreciation, Chatham-Avalon Community Mental Health Ctr, 1979; Gamma TN Chap Alpha Omega Alpha, 1980; Scholastic Achievement Award, Chicago Chap, Nat Asn Black Social Workers 1980; Monarch Award Medicine, Alpha Kappa Alpha, 1986; Ellen Quinn Memorial Award for Outstanding Individual Achievement in Community Mental Health, 1986; Social Action Award, Chicago Chap Black Social Workers, 1988; Mental Health Award, Englewood Community Health Org, 1988; EY Williams Distinguished Senior Clinical Scholar Award, Sect Psychiat & Behav Sci Nat Med Asn, 1992; Am Asn Community Psychiatrists' Annual Award of Excellence in Community Mental Health, 1992; Outstanding Young Doctor Award, Dollars & Sense Mag, 1991; Alumnus of the Year, Meharry Med Col 20 Year Reunion, 1991; President's Commendation for work on violence, Am Psychiat Asn, 1997; Blanche F Ittleson Award for lifetime contributions, Am Orthopsychiatric Asn, 1999. **Special Achievements:** Creator & producer of animation "Book Worm," PBS

1984; Top Doctor, Chicago magazine, 2001, 2007. **Military Serv:** USNR, lt comdr, 1975-76. **Business Addr:** President, Cheif Executive Officer, Community Mental Health Council & Inc, 8704 S Constance Ave, Chicago, IL 60617, **Business Phone:** (773)734-4033.

BELL, CHARLES SMITH
Educator. **Personal:** Born May 21, 1934, Capeville, VA; son of James A Bell Sr and Martha Robinson; married Sallie Annette Parker; children: Charlette LaVonne, Mia Sallie & Angel Monique. **Educ:** Va Union Univ, BS, biol, 1957, 1970; Old Dominion Univ, attended 1972; Norfolk State Univ. **Career:** Educator (retired); Northampton Co Sch Bd, teacher, 1960-90; Dist Dep, Grand MW Prince Hall Masons Inc, 1960-85; Northampton Co Bd Super, Eastville Magisterial Dist, teacher. **Orgs:** Exec bd, Northampton Co Br Nat Asn Advan Colored People, 1960-85; Northampton Co Voter's League, 1960-85; Northampton Ed Asn, 1960-85; Va Ed Asn, 1960-85; Nat Ed Asn, 1960-85; Eastern Shore VA & MD Baptist Asn, 1960-85; master, chmn bd of deacons, First Baptist Church Capeville, 1960-85; chmn, scholar comm, Club Chautauqua, 1961-85; chaplain, Northampton Co Bd of Super, 1982-85; chmn, Accomack-Northampton Co Planning Dist Comn. **Honors/Awds:** Teacher of the Year, Northampton High Sch, 1980-82. **Military Serv:** AUS, staff sgt, 1957-59; Soldier of the Month; vice comdr, Post 400 Am Legion. *

BELL, CHRISTOPHER
Clergy. **Career:** Naperville Christian Church, pastor, currently.

BELL, COBY ERIK
Actor. **Personal:** Born May 11, 1975, Orange County, CA; son of Michel; married Aviss Pinkney; children: Serrae, Jaena, Quinn & Eli. **Educ:** San Jose State Univ. **Career:** TV series: "Smart Guy", 1997; "ER: Good Touch, Bad Touch", 1997; "Buffy the Vampire Slayer: Reptile Boy", 1997; "LA Doctors", 1998; "ATF", 1999; "Third Watch", 1999; "Weakest Link", 2001; "Half & Half", 2005; "CSI: Miami", 2007; "The Game", 2006-09. Film: "Drifting Elegant", 2006; Showdown at Area 51, 2007; Ball Don't Lie, 2008; Flowers and Weeds, 2008. **Business Addr:** Actor, c/o NBC, 30 Rockefeller Plz, New York, NY 10112.*

BELL, DARRYL M.
Actor. **Personal:** Born May 10, 1963, Chicago, IL. **Educ:** Syracuse Univ, attended 1986. **Career:** TV series: "A Different World", 1987-93; "Homeboys In Outer Space", 1996; "Cosby", 1997; "For Your Love", 1999; "Beverly Hills S.U.V.", 2004; "Househusbands of Hollywood", 2009. Films: School Daze, 1988; Mr. Write, 1994; New Jersey Turnpikes, 1999; Brother, 2000. **Orgs:** Alpha Phi Alpha Fraternity; mem, fictional fraternity. **Special Achievements:** Was awarded the Chancellor's Citation from Syracuse for prominent alumni. **Business Addr:** Actor, 1750 S Hauser Blvd, Los Angeles, CA 90019.*

BELL, DEREK NATHANIEL
Baseball player. **Personal:** Born Dec 11, 1968, Tampa, FL. **Career:** Toronto Blue Jays, outfielder, 1991-93; San Diego Padres, 1993-94; Houston Astros, 1995-99; NY Mets, outfielder, 2000; Pittsburgh Pirates, outfielder, 2001. **Honors/Awds:** InterNat League Most Valuable Player Award; Minor League Player of the Year, Baseball Am Mag.

BELL, DERRICK ALBERT
Educator, writer, lawyer. **Personal:** Born Nov 6, 1930, Pittsburgh, PA; son of Derrick and Ada; married Janet Dewart, Jun 28, 1992; married Jewel Hairston, Jun 20, 1960 (died 1990); children: Derrick III, Douglass & Carter. **Educ:** Duquesne Univ, AB, 1952; Univ Pittsburgh Law Sch, LLB. **Career:** US Dept Justice, 1957-59; Pittsburgh Br, NAACP, exec secy, 1959-60; NAACPLegal Defense & Educ Fund, staff atty, 1960-66; Dept Health Educ &Welfare, deputy asst to secy civil rights, 1966-68; Western Ctr Law & Poverty, dir, 1968-69; Harvard Law Sch, lectr law, 1969, prof, 1971-80; Univ Ore, Sch Law, dean, 1981-85; Harvard Law Sch, prof of law 1986-92; NY Univ Sch Law, vis prof law, 1991-. **Orgs:** Bar mem, DC, PA, NY, CA, US Courts Appeals 4th, 5th, 6th, 8th, & 10thCircuits, US Supreme Ct; Fed Dist Ct. **Honors/Awds:** Tougaloo Col, hon degree, 1983; Northeastern Univ Law Sch, hon degree, 1984; Teacher of the Year, Soc Am Law Teachers, 1985; Mercy Col, hon degree, 1988; Allegheny Col, hon degree, 1989; Howard Univ, 1995; Pace Univ Law Sch, hon degree, 1996; Metropolitan Col, 2003. **Special Achievements:** Author: And We Are Not Saved, The Elusive Quest for Racial Justice, 1987;Faces at the Bottom of the Well: The Permanence of Racism, 1992;Confronting Authority: Reflections of an Ardent Protester, 1994; GospelChoirs, Psalms of Survival in an Alien Land Called Home, 1996; AfrolanticaLegacies, 1998; Race, Racism and American Law, 4th ed, 2000; editor,Shades of Brown, New Perspectives on School Desegregation; Ethical Ambition: Living & Life of Meaning and Worth, 2002; Silent Covenant, 2004; Race, Racism and American Law, 2008; First tenured black professor at the Harvard Law School. **Military Serv:** USAF 1952-54. **Home Addr:** 444 Cent Pk W Suite 14B, New York, NY 10025. **Business Addr:** Visiting Professor, New York University School of Law, 40 Washington Sq S 308B, New York, NY 10012, **Business Phone:** (212)992-6235.

BELL, DORIS E.
Educator, school administrator, nurse. **Personal:** Born Nov 25, 1938, Oak Ridge, MO; daughter of James W Lenox and Oma A Wilson Lenox; married Charles A Bell, Aug 31, 1963 (deceased). **Educ:** Harris Teacher's Col, AA, 1957; Homer G Phillips Hosp Sch Nursing, diploma, 1960; WA Univ, BSN, 1963, MSN, 1965; St Louis univ, PhD, 1979. **Career:** Barnes Hosp, staff nurse, 1960-63; St Luke Hosp, staff nurse, 1963; MSR Baptist Hosp, staff nurse, 1964-65; KAS Neurological Inst, dir, nursing inservice, 1965-69; Marymont Col, psychiatric nurse inr, 1967-68; Res Hosp, mental health crd, 1969-70; SIUE Sch Nursing, psychiatric nurse inr, 1970-72, inr, crd, psychiatric mental health nursing, 1972-73, asst prof, 1973-81, assoc prof, 1981-88, prof, nursing, 1988-04, chairperson area II nursing; St Louis Univ Med Sch, visiting fac, 1981-04; East Central COT Col, inr, 1981-04; Southern Ill Univ Edwardsville, prof nursing. **Orgs:** Am Asn Personnel & Guidance; Am Asn Univ Prof's; Am Nurses' Asn; Nat League Nursing; Sigma Phi Omega; Black Nurses' Asn; MSR Nurses' Asn; Sigma Theta Tau, Delta Lambda Chapter; Asn Black Fac Higher Educ; numerous others. **Honors/Awds:** Vernice E Walter Award, Outstanding Student Gerontology, 1985; Fellow, Ill Comt Black Concerns Higher Educ, Acad Admin, 1985-86; Outstanding Alumni, Homer G Phillips Sch Nursing, 1987; Certificate of Appreciation, Proj GAIN, 1989; Ill Student Nurses Bd, Award, 1989; numerous others. **Special Achievements:** Author: "Elderly Abuse," 1986; "Primary Prevention in Psychiatric-Mental Health Nursing," 1987; "Psychiatric Nursing Review," MSR Nurses League Nursing State Bd & Review Manual, 1989; numerous others. **Military Serv:** USF, major, 1973-85. *

BELL, EDNA TALBERT
Government official. **Personal:** Born Mar 9, 1944, Detroit, MI; daughter of Theodore and Edna Rush; children: Alisha, Sonja. **Educ:** Wayne State Univ, BS, 1989. **Career:** Mich Bell Phone Co, mgr; Wayne County Govt, comnr, 1999. **Orgs:** Chair, Environ Task Force, Southeastern Mich Coun Gov; vice chair econ & sustainable leadership team, Nat Asn Counties; Nat Orgn Black County Officials; bd dir, Boscoe Home Boys; Nat Alliance of Black Educr; Nat Asn Negro Bus Prof Women; Optimist Club Cent Detroit; bd dir, Metro Detroit YWCA. **Honors/Awds:** Nat Caucus Black Sch BDM's, 1990-91; Optimist New Club Bldg Comt Award, 1991-92; Detroit Street Law Project Award, 1991; Detroit Public School Region 3 Board Award, 1980-82; Receipient of PRS's Point of Light, 1996. **Special Achievements:** Congressional Black Caucus Foundation's 22nd Annual Legislative Conference, 1992. *

BELL, ELDRIN A.
Civil servant, government official. **Personal:** Born Mar 1, 2009, Georgia; children: Terry,Elizabeth, Terry,Ashley, Michael, Val, Albert,Adrion,Allyson,Gregory & Justin. **Educ:** Morris Brown Col, Atlanta, GA; Ga State; Atlanta Univ; Harvard Univ Law Sch; Northwestern Univ Traffic Inst. **Career:** Police Chief (retired), government officer; Atlanta Police Dept, police chief, 1990; Clayton County Bd Comnrs chmn. **Orgs:** Gate City Bar Asn; Nat Org Black Law Enforcement Officers; Ga Int Law Enforcement Exchange; Clayton County NAACP; Govs Martin Luther King Holiday Comn; minister, Salem Baptist Church, Atlanta. **Honors/Awds:** Executive of the Year; elect, Delegate for the Kerry & Edwards 2004. **Business Addr:** Chairman, Clayton County Board of Commissioners, Clayton County Administration Annex 1, 112 Smith St, Jonesboro, GA 30236, **Business Phone:** (770)477-3208.

BELL, ELLA L. J. EDMONSON
Educator. **Career:** Belk Col Business Admin; Univ N Carolina, Charlotte, Sloan Sch Mgt; Massachusetts Institute of Technology; Yale's Sch Management; Univ Massachusetts Amherst.; Assoc Prof Business Administration, Tuck Sch Business, Dartmouth, currently. *

BELL, ELMER A.
Executive director. **Personal:** Born Nov 17, 1941, Gurdon, AR; married Jo Ann Miller; children: Elmer II. **Educ:** Univ Ariz, BS, 1964. **Career:** Univ Ariz, counr, 1964; Pine Bluff Pub Sch, teacher; Off Econ Opport, Pine Bluff, field rep, asst dir, exec dir. **Orgs:** Licd prof, funeral dir, bd mem, bd sec, Housing Develop Corp Ariz Inc; Royal Knight Soc; life mem, Kappa Alpha Psi Frat keeper records; St John Meth Ch; bd dir, Am Red Cross; bd mem, Big Bros Am. **Honors/Awds:** Certificate Of Merit, Ariz OEO Training Sch; Volt Tech Inst; Develop Assoc Inc; Community Service Award, 1974. *

BELL, GEORGE
Administrator. **Personal:** Born in Pittsburgh, PA; children: George Jr, Christian & Kofi. **Educ:** Cheyney State Col, BS; Univ Detroit, MA. **Career:** Friends Select Sch Phila, teacher; Philadelphia Pub Schs, teacher; Harvou-Act Inc NYC, acting dir; United Ch of Christ, asst to dir & prog coord comn for racial justice; Shaw Col, chmn, div soc sci; Mayor City Detroit, exec asst. **Orgs:** Dir, Child & Family Ctr, City Detroit; chmn, Reg One Bd Educ, City of Detroit; pres, Central Bd Educ, City of Detroit; chmn, bd trustees, Wayne Co Comm Col.

BELL, GEORGE ANTONIO (JORGE ANTONIO BELL MATHEY)
Baseball player. **Personal:** Born Oct 21, 1959, San Pedro de Macoris, Dominican Republic; married Marie Louisa Beguero; children: Christopher & George Jr. **Career:** Baseball player (retired); Toronto Blue Jays, outfielder, 1981, 1983-90;Chicago Cubs, outfielder, 1991; Chicago White Sox, 1992-93. **Honors/Awds:** Labatts Blue MVP; Blue Jays Minor League Player of Month, 1983; Most Valuable Player, Am League; Am League Most Valuable Player, Baseball Writers Asn Am, 1987; Am League All-Star Team, 1987, 1990.

BELL, GORDON PHILIP
Financial manager. **Personal:** Born Jan 1, 1961?, Brooklyn, NY; son of Betty Ann Bell and Elver Joseph Bell, Jr; married Sherrie Curette Bell, Sep 19, 1998; children: Dandridge Bell, Elver Bell III. **Educ:** Harvard Col, AB, 1983; Univ Mex, rotary scholar, 1984; Harvard Bus Sch, MBA, 1988. **Career:** Lehman Brothers, trader, 1988-90; Prudential Capital Corp, vres, 1990-93; UCP, asset mgr, prin, 1993-97; JP Morgan, client adv, 1997-98; Citigroup/ Salomon Smith Barney, dir, portfolio mgr, 1999-; Insts & High Net-worth Persons Pvt Portfolio Group, vpres & portfolio mgr, currently. **Orgs:** Asn Investment Mgt & Res, 1993-; NY Soc Security Anal, 1993-; bd, Literary Partners, 1998-; bd, Rudel Scholar Fund, 1998-; bd, Gen Hosp, 2003-. **Honors/Awds:** 40 Achievers Under 40, Network J, 2001. **Special Achievements:** Chartered Financial Analyst Designation, 1993. **Business Addr:** Vice President, Portfolio Manager, Citi Group, Salomon Smith Barney, 399 Park Ave 4th Fl, New York, NY 10022, **Business Phone:** (212)559-0880.*

BELL, GREG
Labor activist. **Career:** Bakery, Confectionery, Tobacco Workers & Grain Millers Int Union, Local 232, financial secy, 2004; Am Postal Workers Union, Am Fedn Labor & Congress Indust Orgn, dir indust rel, 2004-. **Business Addr:** Director Industrial Relations, American Postal Workers Union, 1300 L St NW, Washington, DC 20005, **Business Phone:** (202)842-4273.*

BELL, H. B.
Educator, school superintendent. **Personal:** Born Apr 13, 1938, Larue, TX; married Susie Alice Davis; children: Diedrae Carron, Dionica Britte. **Educ:** Prairie View A&M Univ, BA, 1961, MEd, 1967; E Tex State Univ, EdD, 1981. **Career:** Retired (educator); Rust Col, asst dean, men eng teacher, 1961-63; Dallas Independent Sch Dist, teacher sr high eng, 1963-68, asst prin, 1968-73, educ planner, 1973-74, dir teacher educ ctr, 1974-76, dep assoc supt, personnel devel, 1976-78, dep assoc supt, spec funds acquisition & monitoring, 1978-82, asst supt subdist II, 1982-85, asst supt elem instr, 1985-, assoc supt alternative prog, 2002-05. **Orgs:** Tex Educ Agency Eval Team evaluating Univ Tex Austin's Prog, 1977; presented paper Competency-Based Teacher Educ Dallas Assoc Teacher Educrs Conf Atlanta, GA, 1977; Southern Assoc Eval Team LG Pinkston HS, 1977; adj prof, E Tex State Univ, Dept Admin & Supv, 1985,86; Dallas Sch Admin Assoc, Nat Assc Sec Sch Prins, Nat Coun Teachers Eng, Young Men's Christian Assoc Mooreland Br, Nat Asn Advan Colored People Dallas Br, Alpha Phi Alpha Frat; bd dirs, Alpha Merit Group, Woodstream Property Asn; Nat Asn Admin State & Fedr Educ Progs; Am Asn Sch Admin. **Honors/Awds:** Disting Alumnus Prairie View A&M Univ, 1977; Outstanding Urban Educator Dallas Independent Sch Dist, 1982; Distinguished Alumnus, E Tex State Univ, 1983; Outstanding Admin Leadership Educ Dallas Independent Sch Dist, 1984; Outstanding Black Texan's Award, Tex House Rep Austin, 1987; 5 publications. **Home Addr:** 6626 Harvest Glen, Dallas, TX 75248. *

BELL, HAROLD KEVIN
Radio host, association executive. **Personal:** Born May 21, 1938, Washington, DC; son of Alfred and Mattie; married Hatti Thomas, Nov 28, 1968. **Educ:** Winston-Salem State Univ, attended 1963. **Career:** United Planning Orgn, 1964-66; DC Recreation Dept, Roving Leader Prog, 1966-69; Dept Defense, sports & recreation specialist, 1969-71; Proj Build, job placement specialist, 1971-74; WOOK Radio, sportscaster & talk show host, 1974-78; Anheuser-Bush, mkt & sports rep, 1978-80; Nike Shoes, sports promotions rep, 1980-82; WUST Radio, sports dir & talk show host, 1986-94; WINX Radio, sportscaster & talk show host, currently; Kids in Trouble, pres, currently. **Orgs:** Founder, Hillcrest C's Ctr Saturday Prog, 1969; coordr, Send A Kid To Camp, 1970; founder, first halfway house for juvenile delinquents on a military base, "Bolling Boys Base", 1971; media coordr, NAACP, 1976; consult, SE Youth Develop Prog, 1979; consult & celebrity fund raiser, United Negro Col Fund, 1980; bd mem, Nat Jr Tennis League, 1982; bd mem, Sonny Hill/John Chaney Summer League, 1984; bd mem, DC Sch Syst Community Task Force, 1988. **Honors/Awds:** Cited in Congressional Record by Rep Louis Stokes, 1975; Washingtonian of the Year, Wash Mag, 1980; Cited for Work with the Youth, President Richard M. Nixon, 1970; Founder of First Half Way House, Dept Defense, 1971; Community Person of the Year, Phi Delta Kappa, Howard University, 1988; Image Award, Pioneering/San Francisco, 1995. **Special Achievements:** Media pioneer & first African-American to host and produce own radio sports talk show in Washington, DC, 1974, first to host and produce own TV sports special on NBC affiliate WRC-TV4, 1975, first sports media personality to create a media roundtable to discuss current issues in the sports world, by inviting radio, TV, and print media personalities to participate on "Inside Sports," once monthly, cited in Congressional record by Sen Bob Dole,

1994, included in the Richard M. Nixon Library in Yoba Linda, CA. **Home Addr:** 2322 Wood Bark Lane, Suitland, MD 20746, **Home Phone:** (301)568-8036. **Business Addr:** President, Kids in Trounle, 2322 Wood Bark Lane, Suitland, MD 20746.

BELL, HUBERT THOMAS
Government official. **Personal:** Born Jul 9, 1942, Mobile, AL; son of Hubert Thomas Sr and Theresa; married Satwant Kaur, Aug 9, 1975; children: Naydja Maya, Nileah Shanti, Anthony Anand & Andrew Amrit. **Educ:** Ala State Univ, Montgomery, AL, BS, 1965. **Career:** Agt incharge, Vice Presidential Protective Div; Agt in charge, Honolulu, Hawaii, Field Office; US Secret Serv, Wash, DC, Off Invests, dep asst dir, Off Protective Operations, asst dir, Off Inspection, exec dir, Work Force Planning & diversity mgt; Progressive Govt Inst, Nuclear Regulatory Comn, inspector gen, 1996-. **Orgs:** Kappa Alpha Psi Fraternity, 1963-; vpres, VA chap, Region II, 1977-; Intl Assn Chiefs Police, 1988-; pres, Fraternal Order Police, 1991; pres, Natl Org Black Law Enforcement Execs, 1994-95; brd dirs, Natl Ctr Missing &Exploited C; past natl pres, Natl Org Black Women Law Enforcement; Nat Assn Regulatory Utility Comners. **Home Addr:** 5906 Reservoir Heights Ave, Alexandria, VA 22311, **Home Phone:** (703)671-2556. **Business Addr:** Inspector General, US Government Nuclear Regulatory Commission, 11545 Rockville, Rockville, MD 20852, **Business Phone:** (301)415-5930.

BELL, JAMES A.
Educator. **Personal:** Born in Charleston, SC; married Sidney Silver; children: J Yvonne. **Educ:** Hampton Univ, BS, 1951; NY Univ, MA, 1961. **Career:** Educator (retired); Hampton Univ, asst prof, 1952-70, dir, career planning & placement, 1970-94. **Orgs:** Am Soc Eng Educ; pres, Va Col Placement Asn, 1980-81; bd dirs, Southern Col Placement Asn, 1980-82; exec bd, Episcopal Diocese Southern Va, 1984-86. **Honors/Awds:** Certificate, Va Col Placement Asn, 1975 & 1981; Certificate, Alpha Phi Alpha Fraternity, 1980; Certificate, NASA, 1980. **Military Serv:** AUS, corp, 1943-46; European Service 2 Stars; Good Conduct Medal; WWII Victory Medal.

BELL, JAMES A.
Executive. **Educ:** Calif State Univ, Los Angeles, BA, acct. **Career:** Rockwell, 1972 dir acct, 1984; Boeing Rocketdyne unit, Space Sta Elec Power Syst, dir bus mgt; Boeing Corp, vpres contracts, 1996, sr vpres & corp controller, 2000-03, actg chief financial officer, 2003-04, chief financial officer & exec vpres finance, 2004-, interiem pres & chief exec officer. **Orgs:** Joint Leadership Coun; bd dirs, Dow Chem Co; Joffrey Ballet; Chicago Urban League; World Bus Chicago; Chicago Econ Club; New Leaders New Schs. **Business Addr:** Chief Financial Officer, Executive Vice President of Finance, Boeing Company, World Headquarters, 100 N Riverside, Chicago, IL 60606, **Business Phone:** (312)544-2000.*

BELL, JAMES L., JR.
Civil engineer. **Personal:** Born Aug 4, 1921, Buffalo, NY; son of James L Sr (deceased) and Madie G Nelson (deceased); married Jessal Holland Bell, Jun 1957 (divorced); children: James L III. **Educ:** Howard Univ, BSCE, 1954; Univ Buffalo, Cert Mech Engineering, 1949; Dept Transp Wash DC, cert bridge inspector, 1973. **Career:** Civil engineer (retired). Tenn Valley Authority, civil engr, div power opers, 1954-63, mech engr & asst mech maint supvr, Widows Creek Steam Plant, 1963-64, prin civil engr, div oil spill prev & control coordr, 1964-67; Tenn Valley Authority Office Power, chief bridge inspector, 1967-82. **Orgs:** Chattanooga Engr Club; chmn, Fellowship Comt, Equal Empl Opport, United Way Comt chmn; Tenn Valley Authority Engrs Asn; Am Soc Civil Engr, Chattanooga Br, Tenn Valley Sect past pres; Am Concrete Inst; Physiography Judge Chattanooga Area Regional Sci & Engineering Fair; engineering career guid couns, Chattanooga HS; chmn, Credit Com & bd dirs, Chattanooga Tenn Valley Authority Employees Fed Credit Union; Tenn Valley Authority Chattanooga Community Rels Comt; past keeper records & seals 5th dist Omega Psi Phi Frat Inc; past basileus, Kappa Iota Chap, Omega Psi Phi Frat Inc; Dist Comnr, Cherokee Area Coun Boy Scouts Am; chmn, Planning Comn; Chattanooga Br Nat Asn Advan Colored People; bd dir, Chattanooga Hamilton Co Speech & Hearing Ctr & chmn, Indust Audiol Com; Ruling Elder Renaissance Presb Ch; past pres, Chattanooga Chap Pan-Hellenic Coun Inc; Boy Scout Adv; Alpha Phi Omega Frat Boy Scouts Am; past dist comnr, Cherokee Area Coun; mem-at-large, Merit Badge Coun; Chmn Vet Comt, Chattanooga Nat Asn Advan Colored People; Chattanooga Area Urban League; bd dirs & bd secy, Chattanooga, Hamilton County Air Pollution Control Bur; bd mem, Interfaith Elderly Assistance Agency, 1989-; Chattanooga Afro-Am Museum; Chattanooga Sr Neighbors; bd mem, Chattanooga Memorial Soc. **Honors/Awds:** Silver Beaver Award; Arrowhead Honor Commissioners Key Award, Order Arrow; 35 yr Vet Award; People-to-People Award, Nat Engr Week Comt, 1984; Citation Plaque, Chattanooga State Tech Community Col, 1977; Service Recognition Plaque, Fairview Presbyterian Church, 1987; Recognition Plaque, Alpha Phi Omega Fraternity, 1978; Recognition/Certificate, Chattanooga Br, Am Soc Civil Engrs, 1984. **Military Serv:** AUS, capt, 1942-46; South-West Pac Campaign, Philippine Liberation, World War II Victory, Asiatic-Pac Campaign with one star, Army Occupation. **Home Addr:** 606 Mooremont Terr, Chattanooga, TN 37411-2924. *

BELL, HON. JANET SHARON
College administrator. **Personal:** Born Jun 27, 1947, Chicago, IL; divorced; children: Lenny. **Educ:** Chicago State Univ, BS, educ, 1972; Ill State Univ, MS, educ, 1978. **Career:** Chicago Pub Sch, teacher, 1972-74; State Farm Ins, coordr, 1974-76; Ill State Univ, acad adv, 1981, counr spec serv prog, 1981-86, asst coordr minority stud serv, 1986-88, asst dir, financial aid off, 1988-92. **Orgs:** Ill Asn Educ Opportunity Prog Personnel, 1977-86; Mid-Am Asn Educ Opportunity Prog Personnel; vpres, Asn Black Acad Employ, 1985-87; Mid W Asn Stud Fin Aid Adminr; chmn, Community Rels Comt, Ill Asn Fin Aid Adminr, 1990-92; co-chair, Ill Coun Col Attendance, Prof Develop Comt; Ind State Bar Asn. **Home Phone:** (309)663-5629. *

BELL, JIMMY
Educator. **Personal:** Born Jan 4, 1944, Indianola, MS; married Clara Mcgee; children: Sonya, Arlinda, Meredith & Rasheda. **Educ:** Miss Valley State Univ, BS, 1966; Miss State Univ, MA/ABD, 1969; NY Univ Albany, 1978. **Career:** Jackson State Univ, Dept Criminal Justice, asst prof, 1970, criminal justice coordr, 1972-80, prof & interim chmn, currently; Lexington Books DC Health, writer, 1977-79. **Orgs:** Nat fel, Nat Inst Ment Health, 1966-70; dir res proj, SCAN Indianola MS, 1969; consult, Nat Inst Law Enforcement, 1975-77; consult, IT&T, 1970; consult lectr, Jackson Police Dept, 1974-80; chmn, Dept Sociol, Miss Valley State Univ, 1969; chmn, Black Caucus Southern Sociol Soc, 1973; exec comm mem, Nat Asn Blacks Criminal Justice, 1973-76. **Honors/Awds:** Personality of the Society, 1977; Nominee, Outstanding Young Men ofAmerica, 1979. **Special Achievements:** First Black Recipient of MA Degree at Mississippi State University 1968. **Business Addr:** Chairman, Criminology Professor, Jackson State University, Department of Criminal Justice, 1400 Lynch St, PO Box 18830, Jackson, MS 39217, **Business Phone:** (601)979-2626.

BELL, JOSEPH N.
Executive. **Personal:** Born Aug 15, 1948, Wilmington, NC; married Carolyn. **Educ:** Shaw Univ, BS, 1970; Univ GA; Armstrong St Col; Am Inst Banking; BSA. **Career:** Shaw Univ, hd lncch, 1970; Cental Trust Co, sr anal, 1971; Carver State Bank, exec vpres. **Orgs:** Dir, Savannah Area C C; dir, Savannah Bus Leag; dir, Savannah Trbn; Am Cancer Soc; Grnbr C Ctr; Cit Adv Com Chthm Urban Trans; Chthm Co Assn Rtrd C; Savannah Area Mnrty Cntrctrs; Better Bus Bureau; NAACP; Omega Psi Phi Frat; dcn tst Cnnrs Temp Bapt Ch. **Honors/Awds:** Man of the Year, Shaw Univ, 1969. **Business Addr:** executive vice president, Carver State Bank, 701 W Broad st, PO Box 2769, Savannah, GA 31402, **Business Phone:** (912)233-9971.*

BELL, KARL I.
Banker. **Personal:** Born Jan 29, 1960, Atlanta, GA; son of Henry and Naomi Bell; married Pamela, Nov 19, 1989; children: Alexis, Kristina, Cameron. **Educ:** Morehouse Col, BA, 1981; Univ Wisc-Madison, MBA, 1983; Grad Sch Banking, 1997. **Career:** Lockheed Co, Georgia, 1981; IBM Corp, 1982; NBD Bank, 1983-. **Orgs:** pres, Urban Bankers Forum, 1994-; Detroit Econ Develop Task Force, 1994-95; dir, Morehouse Alumni Asn, Detroit, 1988-90; bd dirs, Southfield Symphony Orchestra, 1987-88; trustee, New Detroit Inc, 1996-98; Mich Metro Girl Scout Coun, finance comn, 1997. **Honors/Awds:** Fellow, Consortium for Grad Sch Study, 1981; Student of the Year, Trust Co Bank, 1981; Banking School Fellow, Nat Asn Urban Bankers, 1994. **Business Phone:** (313)225-3368.*

BELL, DR. KATIE ROBERSON
Librarian, educator. **Personal:** Born Jun 14, 1936, Birmingham, AL; daughter of Alex and Blanche Davis; married Leroy Bell Jr; children: Cheryl Kaye, Mada Carol & Janel E, Janet E. **Educ:** Ala State Col, BS, 1956, EdS 1977; Wayne State Univ, MSLA, 1973; Univ AL, PhD, 1982. **Career:** Educator, Librarian (retired); Tuskegee Inst HS, libr, 1956-59; Parker HS, asst libr, 1959-70, libr, 1970-73; AL State Univ, asst ref libr, 1973-74, coordr, user serv, 1974-75, coordr, libr educ, 1975-; So AL Reg Inserv Educ Ctr, dir, 1985; AL State Univ, prof libr educ, 1985; Montgomery City-Co Pub Libr, trustee, currently. **Orgs:** Consult, ESAA Task Force ASU & Mobile Sch Syst, 1979-82; Comt Tutorial Prog & links Inc, 1982-84; evaluator Nat Coun Accreditation Teacher Educ, 1983-; bd mem, pres elect AL Instructional Media Asn, 1984-; counr, Nu Epsilon Chap Kappa Delta Pi, 1984-; evaluator S Asn Schs & Cols, 1985-; bd mem, Montgomery Comn Coun United Way, 1985-; area dir, The Links, Inc., southern area dir, 1991-94. **Honors/Awds:** Certificate Honor, Birmingham Classroom Teachers Asn, 1970; Educator of the Year Area of Instructional Leadership, Univ AL, 1981; Identification Activities Staff Capstone Journal, 1982; Develop Progs Sec Educ Teachers; Women Distinction Luncheon, 2005. **Business Addr:** Trustee, Montgomery City County Public Library, PO Box 1950, Montgomery, AL 36102, **Business Phone:** (334)240-4300.*

BELL, KENDRELL ALEXANDER
Football player. **Personal:** Born Jul 2, 1980, Augusta, GA; son of CB Jim Marsalis; married Tahira Locke. **Educ:** Univ Ga, child & family develop. **Career:** Pittsburgh Steelers, linebacker, 2001-04; Kans City Chiefs, linebacker, 2005-. **Honors/Awds:** Named NFL Defensive Rookie of the Year, Asniated Press, 2001. **Business Addr:** Player, Kansas City Chiefs, 1 Arrowhead Dr, Kansas City, MO 64129.

BELL, KENNETH M.
Educator, city council member. **Personal:** Born Apr 17, 1941, Bayboro, NC; married Geraldine P; children: Kenneth Jr, Sonji & Marcel. **Educ:** Livingstone Col, BA, 1964; NC State Univ; Duke Univ, MEd, 1975. **Career:** NC Manpower Devel Corp Bayboro, dep dir; Pamlico Jr High Sch, teacher, social studies, sch guidance counsr; Ashley Assocs, gen partner; Mt Shiloh Baptist Church, New Bern, NC, minister, 1990-. **Orgs:** Nat Asn Advan Colored People, 1964-; pres, Local NC Teachers Asn, 1966; NCEd Asn; Asn Classroom Teachers; Nat Educ Asn; founder, City Youtharama Prog, 1966; dir, Local ABC-TV Gospel Music Show, 1972-73; chmn exec bd, Pamlico Co Voter League, 1974-; bd comnr, Democratic Party Nominee Pamlico Co, 1982. **Special Achievements:** First black elected in Pamlico City as town alderman, 1969; Audition for Dick Cavett Show, 1971. Recognised in Pamlico County Centen Cele Year book as one of most outstanding blacks in Pamlico County. **Business Addr:** Guidance Counselor, Pamlico Jr High School, 15526 Nc Hwy 55, Bayboro, NC 28515-9400.

BELL, LAWRENCE A.
Government official, president (organization). **Educ:** Univ Md, College Park, BA. **Career:** Baltimore City Coun, pres, 1995-99; Radio 860 AM WBGR, The Lawrence Bell Show, host, currently. **Orgs:** Founder & pres, Nat Black Anti-Defamation League; Baltimore Worldwide Speakers Bur. **Special Achievements:** Ebony Magazine named Bell as one of "30 leaders of the future", 1988;Youngest person ever elected as City Council President. **Business Phone:** 800-999-9999.

BELL, LAWRENCE F.
Business owner. **Personal:** Born Dec 1, 1958, Philadelphia, PA; son of Marian Green and Furman Bell. **Educ:** Temple Univ, PA, BBA, 1979; Wharton Sch, Univ Pa, MBA, 1989. **Career:** Mellon Bank, sr auditor, 1979-81; PPG Indust, sr auditor, 1981-87; IU Int, audit supvr, 1987-88; Wharton Sch, sr consult, 1988-89; Bell & Associates, owner, 1989; Pepsi Cola, finance mgr, 1991-94. **Orgs:** Treas, Uptown Community Resource Ctr, 1987; mgr, W Philadelphia Enterprise Ctr, 1989-, partnership, 1995; treas, W Philadelphia Neighborhood Enterprise Ctr, 1990. **Honors/Awds:** Black Accountant's Entreprenuer of the Year, 1991.

BELL, LEON
Clergy, manager, business owner. **Personal:** Born Jul 14, 1930, Liberty, MS. **Educ:** Miss Bapt Sem, ThB, 1957; Jackson State Univ, BS, 1959; Wheaton Col, pursued grad studies, 1966; Univ Southern Miss, MS, coun & Eng, 1969; Univ Southern Miss, post-grad studies, Eng & writing. **Career:** Springhill Priestly Chap Fairview Bapt Church, Pilgrim Br Bapt Church, Monticello First Bapt, pastor, 1954-68; Miss Baptist Sem, state dirvacation Bible schs, 1958-59; MS Bapt Sem, dean cent ctr, 1959-67; Jackson State Univ, chaplain 1965-69, dir stud actvts, 1967-69, relig adv, instr, 1969-75; Jackson Dist Mission Bapt Asn, moderator, 1976-82; Hyde Park Bapt Churches, pastor, 1967-91; New Mount Zion Baptist Church, pastor, 1969-;Miss Baptist Cong Christian Educ, instr bible hist; Bell's Robes & Worship Aids, proprietor & mgr, currently. **Orgs:** Chmn, Jackson Bicent City-wide Simultan Rev, 1976; org Bell's All-Faith Lit Supplies, 1975; chmn, Curric Com Convert Natchez Jr Col into four yrs Bible Col, 1976; moderator, Jackson Dist Mission Bapt Asn, 1976-82, 1994-96; Jackson Ministrial Allian; bd mem, MS Bapt Sem; 1st vpres, Gen Bapt State Conv MS; Dir, Youth Oratorical & Musical Contest, Gen Missionary Bapt State Conv Miss, 1993-; asst Dir, Oratorical Contest, Nat Baptist Conv, USA Inc, 1980-94; VFW; Nat Asn Advan Colored People; Masons; Smithsonian Inst; bd mem, Southern Christian Leadership Conf, Jackson MSchap, 1995-; Metropolitan Ministerial Fel Jackson MS, instr homiletics,1996-. **Honors/Awds:** Ambass Life Mag, 1966; Miss Baptist Sem, Honorary DDiv, 1973; Most Outstanding Minister Community Affairs, Jackson Mississippi Chap Nat Bus League, 1985. **Special Achievements:** Auth & publ, Top Notch Introductory Essays all Occasions, 1983 (revised1987); Prog Outlines Spec Occasions Church, 1987. **Military Serv:** AUS, 1952-54. **Home Addr:** 4322 Beacon Pl, Jackson, MS 39213. *

BELL, DR. MARION L
Executive. **Educ:** EdD. **Career:** Bennett Col, Nat Alumnae Asn, pres, currently; United Negro Col Fund, vpres pub rels, 2006-. **Business Addr:** President, Bennett College, National Alumnae Association, 8757 Castle View Ave, Las Vegas, NV 89129, **Business Phone:** (702)255-6987.

BELL, MELVYN CLARENCE
Executive. **Personal:** Born Dec 13, 1944, Los Angeles, CA; married Eliza Ann Johnson. **Educ:** Calif State Univ, Los Angeles, BS, 1971; Univ Southern Calif, MBA, 1973. **Career:** Security Pac Nat Bank, vpres, 1971; KFOX Radio Inc, co-owner & vpres,1979; Los Angeles Community Develop Bank; Comerica Bank-Calif, Long Beach, Calif, vpres. **Orgs:** Univ Soc Cal MBA Asn; Nat Asn Black MBAs; Kappa Alpha Psi Fraternity; Nat Asn Advan Colored

People; Los Angeles Urban League; Los Angeles Black Bus Mens Asn; bd dirs, Los Angeles Soc Area Boys Club; pres, Kappa Alpha Psi Fraternity Upsilon Chap Los Angeles. **Military Serv:** USN, yeoman 3rd, 1966-68. *

BELL, MICHAEL P
Firefighter. **Personal:** Born 1955, Louisiana; son of Norman and Ora. **Educ:** Univ Toledo, BA, 1978. **Career:** Toledo Fire Dept, Water Rescue Diver, Fire Recruiter, Paramedic Shift Supr & Training Officer, Training Capt, 1980-90, chief, 1990-2007; Ohio Fire Dept, ohio fire marshall, 2007-. **Orgs:** True Vine Baptist Church Toledo; Joint Terrorism Task Force, Lucas Co, OH, 2001-. **Honors/Awds:** President's Recognition Award, Int Asn Fire Chiefs, 2000; Woodward HS Hall of Fame; Boys and Girls Club of Toledo's Hall of Fame. **Special Achievements:** Selected to carry the Olympic Torch in June 1996 through the City of Toledo as a community leader; first African-American to be appointed to the position of Chief in the history of the Toledo fire service. **Business Addr:** Fire Marshall, Ohio Fire Dept, 8895 East Main Street, Reynoldsburg, OH 43068.

BELL, MYRON COREY
Football player. **Personal:** Born Sep 15, 1971, Toledo, OH; children: Myron Jr & Kennedy. **Educ:** Mich State Univ. **Career:** Football player (retired); Coach: Pittsburgh Steelers, defensive back, 1994-97,2000-01; Cincinnati Bengals, 1998-99; North side Christian Acad, asst coach,currently.

BELL, NAPOLEON A.
Lawyer. **Personal:** Born Jun 17, 1927, Dublin, GA; son of Arthur L and Ethel L; married Dorothy J Lyman; children: Kayethel, Napoleon II. **Educ:** Mt Union Col, BA, 1951; Western Reserve Univ Law Sch, JD, 1954. **Career:** Indust Commn of OH, att examr 1955-58, comnr, 1989-91; Bd Tax Appeals, chmn 1971-74; Beneficial Acceptance Corp, pres & chmn bd; Bell White Saunders & Smallwood, atty; Gov's Off, Columbus, OH, coun gov, 1988-89. **Orgs:** 5th Ward Community, 1963; Franklin Co Dem exec comn, 1965; bd dir, treasurer, pres, Columbus Urban League, 1965-72; chmn, Concerned Cit Columbus Comn, 1969; Dem Party Struct & Del Selection Comn, 1969; Bd dir, Columbus Area C C, 1970-73; Dem State exec comn, 1971; bd dir, Mt Union Col; chmn, United Negro Col Fund state, 1972; Columbus Bar Asn; special coun Atty, Gen State, OH, 1972-74; bd dir, Cent Ohio Boy Scouts; life mem, Nat Advan Asn Colored People; bd dir, pres, Columbus State Comn Col, 1994-95; Ohio Bd Tax Appeals, 2002. **Honors/Awds:** Award of Merit, Ohio Legal Ctr; Man of Yr Award, Kappa Alpha Psi, 1964; Award of Merit, Mahoning Co Youth Club, 1964; Award of Merit, United Negro Col Fund; Mt Union Col Alumni Chair Award, 1967; Government Community Service Award, 1974; Silver Anniversary Honoree Col Athletic's Top, Nat Collegiate Athletic Asn 10, 1976. **Military Serv:** AUS, 1946-47. *

BELL, NGOZI O
Executive, executive director. **Personal:** Born May 10, 1967, Enugu, Nigeria; daughter of E Obikwerc; married Durane A, Jan 1, 1991; children: Yamira & Zaneta. **Educ:** Univ Port Harcourt, Nigeria, BS, physics & electronics, 1988; Fla State Univ, Col Eng, MS, elec eng, 1992. **Career:** Fla A&M Univ, Col Eng, res asst, 1990-92; RW Beck, consult engr, 1993-95; AT&T Bell Labs, Lucent Technol, design engr, 1995-97, mkt mgr, 1997-2000; Agere Systs, optical networking solutions group, sr marketing mgr, 2001, Access & Transp Group, segment mgr, 2002, Enterprise & Networking Div, dir mkt, currently. **Orgs:** Zita Sigma Hon Soc, 1984-88; vpres, Nat Asn Physics Studs, 1985-86, pres, 1986-88; chair, Sch Involv Lucent Tech, 1996-97; co-chair, Lucent Diversity Comt, 1997-; bd mem, Camp Place, Allentown, 1997-. **Honors/Awds:** Appreciation Award, UNCF, Region Bd Dirs, 1997. **Special Achievements:** Tech publications, 10 Points to Ponder on Echo Cancellation in Communications System Design, December 1998; Int Fashion Designer, fashion shows, October 1997, December 1997, 1994. **Business Addr:** Director of Marketing, Agere Systems Inc, Enterprise and Networking Division, 1110 American Pkwy NE, Allentown, PA 18109, **Business Phone:** (610)712-4323.

BELL, RICKY
Singer, entertainer. **Personal:** Born Sep 18, 1967, Roxbury, MA; son of Daniel and Dorothy. **Career:** Albums: Hey There Lonely Girl; School; One More Day; I'm Still In Love With You; New Edition, 1984; All for Love, 1985; Christmas All Over the World, 1985; Heart Break, 1989; Poision, 1990; WBBD-Boot city, 1991; Above the Rim, 1993; Hootie Mack, 1993; Ricardo Campana, 2000; BBD, 2001; When Will I See You Smile Again; Songs: "The Album", 2000; "Spanish Fly"; "Please Don't Cry"; "Pretty Little Girl"; " Bobby"; New Edition, founder &singer, 1983-; Bell Biv Devoe, soloist; Featured songs: Candy; Phenomenon; CD Baby, 2000; So So Def/Geffen, 2008. **Honors/Awds:** Recipient of the Golden Note Award at ASCAP's, 2008. **Special Achievements:** Debut album Poison reached Billboard's Top Ten, 1990. **Business Phone:** (818)777-4000.*

BELL, RICKY
Football player. **Personal:** Born Oct 2, 1974, Columbia, SC. **Educ:** NC State Univ. **Career:** Jacksonville Jaguars, defensive back, 1996; Chicago Bears, defensive back, 1997; Calgary Stampeders, 2001; Ottawa Renegades, 2002; Winnipeg Blue Bombers, 2003-04; Major League Baseball, 2005-06; Georgia Force, Defensive Back, 2008-. **Honors/Awds:** Grey Cup championship, calgary, 2001. *

BELL, DR. ROBERT L.
Physician, educator. **Personal:** Born May 10, 1934, Bastrop, TX; married Mattye M; children: Allison E & Millicent P. **Educ:** Tex Southern Univ, BA, 1953; Univ Tex, MA, 1955, PhD, 1961; Univ Tex Sch Pub Health, MPH, 1980. **Career:** Va Hosp Waco, clin psychologist, 1961-66; Baylor Univ, adj prof psychol,1965-66; Va Hosp, psychologist, 1966-72; Rice Univ, consult, 1970-72; Va Hosp Houston Drug Abuse Prog, asst dir, 1970-72; Tex Southern Univ, assoc prof, 1972; Riverside Gen Hosp Drug Abuse Prog, psychologist, 1972; Coun Ctr Vassar Col, clin psychologist, 1972-73; Rice Univ Houston, dir stud advising & prof psychol, 1973-79, adj prof, 1979-80; Pvt Pract, clin psychol, currently. **Orgs:** Asn Black Psychologists; Am Psychol Asn; SW Psychol Asn; Tex Psychol Asn; Houston Psychol Asn; Am Group Psychotherapy Asn; Houston Group Psychotherapy Soc; SW Inst Personal & Organizational Develop; Nat Inst Applied Behav Scis; Alpha Phi Alpha Fraternity; Ethnic Arts Ctr Hope Develop Inc. **Honors/Awds:** Super Performance Award, Vets Admin, 1964; Special Service Performance Award, Vets Admin, 1968; Cattell Fund Award, Am Psychol Asn, 1969; Outstanding Alumnus Award, Tex Southern Univ, 1972. **Home Addr:** 11410 Ribstone Dr, Houston, TX 77016. **Business Addr:** Clinical Psychologist, 11410 Ribstone Dr, Houston, TX 77016.

BELL, ROBERT MACK
Judge. **Personal:** Born Jul 6, 1943, Rocky Mount, NC. **Educ:** Dunbar High Sch, Baltimore, MD; Morgan State Col, AB, hist & polit sci, 1966; Harvard Univ Law Sch, JD, 1969. **Career:** Piper & Marbury, assoc, 1969-74; Dist Ct MD, judge, 1975-80; Md Ct Appeals, judge, 1991-96, chief judge, 1996-; Md Judicial Conf, Judicial Coun, Chair, 2000. **Orgs:** Bd dir, Villa Julie Col; bd dir, Legal Aid Bur; grader MD St Bar Examr, 1973-75; bd dir, Afro Am Newspaper, 1973-74; bd dir, Neighborhood Adolescent & Young Adult Drug Prog Inc, 1974-75; Grievance Comt, exec comt & chmn Baltimore City Bar Asn; Md State Bar Asn; chmn, Bar Asn; Bail Bond Comn, 1973-77. **Honors/Awds:** Distinguished Performance & Accomplishment Award, Morgan Alumni, 1975; Distinctive Achievement Award, Phi Alpha Theta, 1976; Community Serv Award, Hiram Grand Lodge AF & AM, 1976. **Business Addr:** Chief judge, Md Ct Appeals, 634 Courthouse E, 111 N Calvert St, Baltimore, MD 21202.*

BELL, ROBERT WESLEY
Construction worker. **Personal:** Born Apr 10, 1918, Bethlehem, GA; married Louvenia Smith. **Educ:** Welders & Mech Sch, 1940. **Career:** Afro-Am Life Ins Co, agent, 1955-75; State Ga, selective serv, 1972-, first black dist commander Am Legion 1973-74, first black chmn c & youth div Am Legion, 1974-80; Econ Opportunity Atlanta, mem fin comn, 1980-84; Buford city Sch, elected mem bd educr, 1981-85; People's Bank Buford, first black mem bd dir, 1983-85; Bell Brothers Construct Co, part owner; Buford City Sch, vice chmn bd educr. **Orgs:** Deacon bd Poplar Hill Baptist Church, 1940-85; church clerk, Poplar Hill Baptist Church, 1950-85; supt, Sunday Sch Poplar Hill Baptist Church, 1950-85; asst clerk, Hopewell Baptist Asn, 1974-85; staff mem, Boys State Am Legion, 1976-85; appt mem, Planning & Zoning City Buford, 1979-85; chmn, Boy Scouts State Ga, 1980-82; Gwinnett Clean & Beautiful Citizens Bd Gwinnett Cty, 1980-83; am chmn, Am Legion State Ga, 1982-85. **Honors/Awds:** National Achievement Award, Nat Am Legion, 1966; Man of the Year, Buford Comm Orgn, 1974; Gwinnett Clean & Beautiful Award, Gwinnett Cty Citizens Bd, 1980. **Military Serv:** AUS, master sgt, 1943-46; Asiatic Pacific Serv Medal, World War II Victory Medal, Am Serv Medal, European-African Middle East Serv Medal 2 Bronze Stars. **Home Addr:** 201 Roberts St, Buford, GA 30518.

BELL, ROSALIND NANETTE
Marketing executive, vice president (organization). **Personal:** Born Dec 1, 1958, Panama City, FL; daughter of Stanley J and Bettye Price; married Jacob R Miles III, Oct 25, 1986. **Educ:** Wash Univ, BA, bus, 1980; Northwestern Univ, MBA, 1981. **Career:** Dow Chemical, Merrell Dow Pharmaceutical, sales, asst prod mgr, 1981-84; Kraft Foods, Dairy Group, asst prodmgr, assoc prod mgr, 1984-86; Pillsbury Co, assoc prod mgr, pizza new prod develop, 1986-88, sr mkt mgr, 1991-95, grp mktg, 1996-97; Gillette, Lustrasilk div, from assoc prod mgr to sr product mgr, acting dir, 1988-91; Cultural MGR, Exchange Gallery, managing dir, 1991; Six Flags Amusement Parks, vp mkt, 1997-98; Avado Brands Inc, vpres mkt, 1998-99; optel inc, vpres mkt, 1999; Urban cool network inc, dir, 1999, mkt consul, 2000-. **Orgs:** Jr League, Minneapolis; Nat assn Black MBA, 1981-87; Minneapolis & St Paul Chap Links; Ordway Theater Advisory comn; Family & Children's Serv; Hennpin Unit AM Cancer soc. **Honors/Awds:** Award of Distinction, CEBA, 1992. **Business Addr:** Director, Urban Cool Network Incorporation, 1401 Elm St, Dallas, TX 75626, **Business Phone:** (214)752-5818.*

BELL, ROSEANN P.
Educator. **Personal:** Born May 2, 1945, Atlanta, GA; divorced; children: William David. **Educ:** Howard Univ, BA, 1966; Emory Univ, MA, 1970, PhD, 1974. **Career:** US Civil Serv Comn, typist, 1964-66; Atlanta Pub Sch Syst, instr, 1966-70; var part-time teaching positions; freelance educ manuscripts, 1970-; Spelman Col, asst prof, 1970-; Atlanta Voice Newspaper, columnist, 1971; Nat Inst Humanities Fels, 1971-73; Nat Fel Fund Fels, Ford Found, 1973-74; Cornell Univ, Afro-Am Studies Dept, asst prof; Univ Miss, Dept Eng, assocprof, currently. **Special Achievements:** Author of numerous published articles; Erotique Noire/Black Erotica, EDITOR. **Business Addr:** Associate Professor, University Mississippi, Department English, University, MS 38677-9701.*

BELL, ROUZEBERRY, JR.
Dentist. **Personal:** Born Jul 13, 1934, Pittsburgh, PA; married Alice McGhee; children: Cheryl, Karen, Jeffrey. **Educ:** Univ Pittsburgh, BS, pharma, 1959; Howard Univ, DDS, 1970. **Career:** Univ Hosp Cleveland, 1959-66; Wash Hosp Ctr, pharmacist, 1966-70; St Lukes Hosp, intern, 1970-71; Hough Norwood Family Care Ctr, staff dent, 1971-75; Pvt Pract, dent, 1973-; KW Clement Family Care Ctr, dent dir, 1975-94. **Orgs:** Big Bros Am, 1966-; Forest City Dent Soc, 1970-; Dept Comm Dent Case Western Res Univ, 1975-; bd dir, Forest City Dent Indep Prac Asn, 1976-; Cleveland Dent Soc; Ohio St Dental Asn; Nat Dent Asn; Am Dent Asn; Buckeye St Dent Asn; bd med, adv comt, Am Cancer Soc, Cuyahoga County Unit, 1991. **Honors/Awds:** Fel, Dept Anesthesiology St Luke's Hosp, 1971. **Military Serv:** USN, hosp man third class, 1952-55. **Business Addr:** Dentist, 5 Severance Circle Suite 413, Cleveland, OH 44118, **Business Phone:** (216)291-1305.*

BELL, SANDRA WATSON
Executive, vice president (organization). **Personal:** Born May 30, 1955, San Francisco, CA; daughter of Adell Rogers Watson; married Phillip Bell; children: Phillip Jr & Lauren. **Educ:** San Jose State Univ, San Jose, Calif, BS, bus admin, 1976. **Career:** Fairchild, Mountain View, Calif, mgr system software, 1976-83; Masstor Systems, Santa Clara, Calif, vpres human resources & admin, data ctr, 1983, pres. **Special Achievements:** Exec Prog for Smaller Cols, Stanford Univ, Grad Sch Bus. **Home Addr:** 120 Tehama Ct, San Bruno, CA 94066. **Business Phone:** (408)988-1008.

BELL, SHEILA TRICE
Lawyer, executive, vice president (organization). **Personal:** Born Aug 25, 1949, Pittsburgh, PA; daughter of William Benjamin and Mildred Moore; married Howard W Bell Jr, Jun 7, 1971; children: Mayet Maria, Annora Alicia, William Howard. **Educ:** Wellesley Col, BA, 1971; Harvard Law Sch, JD, 1974. **Career:** Pine Manor Jr Col, fac mem, 1972-74; Hutchins & Wheeler, assoc lawyer, 1973-77; Pvt Legal Prac, atty, 1977-79; Fisk Univ, univ coun, 1979-83; J Col & Univ Law, ed bd, 1982-83; Northern Ky Univ, actg univ coun & affirmative action officer, 1984-85, univ legal coun, 1985; Bell & Trice Enterprises Inc, exec vpres, currently. **Orgs:** Equal Rights Amendment Comn Commonwealth, MA, 1976; bd mem, Family & C Serv, Nashville, TN, 1981-83; Mayor's Spec Task Force Union Sta, Nashville, TN, 1982-83; vpres, Links Inc, Cincinnati Chap, 1984-89; Jack & Jill Inc, Cincinnati Chap, 1984-90; bd mem, Nat Asn Col & Univ Attys, 1985-88; bd mem, Prog Cincinnati, 1986-88; bd mem, Bethesda Hosp Inc, 1990-; MA, TN, KY Bars; Am Bar Asn; US Dist Ct, MA; Mid Dist TN & Eastern Dist KY, US Ct Appeals Sixth Circuit. **Honors/Awds:** YWCA Career Woman Achievement, YWCA, Cincinnati, OH, 1988. **Special Achievements:** Publication: "Protection and Enforcement of College and University Trademarks"; co-author w/Martin F Majestic J College & Univ Law, Vol 10, No 1, 1983-84. **Home Addr:** 800 McCeney Ave, Silver Spring, MD 20901-1453. **Business Addr:** Executive Vice President, Bell Trice Enterprises Inc, Washington, DC 20001.*

BELL, THEODORE JOSHUA
Financial manager. **Personal:** Born Jan 8, 1961, Berkeley, CA; son of Theodore J and Beverly Russ. **Educ:** St Mary's Col, BA 1983; Calif Sch Arts & Crafts, attended 1984; Heald Bus Col, Oakland, diploma career bus, 1985; Berkeley Sch Comput Graphics, attended 1989. **Career:** Marriott Boykin Corp, graphic illusr banquet waiter, 1981-85; Equitec Financial Group, acct, 1985-88; McCue Systs Inc, prod support analyst, 1994-, sr bus analyst, currently; First Am Title Inc, escrow acct. **Orgs:** Donator/supporter, St Mary's Col Alumni, 1983-; illusr/vol, Work Love Prog, 1984-85; admin mem, Heald Col Bus Club, 1985; adv viewer, Kron TV Adv Bd, 1985-; supporter, Nat Urban League, 1986-; organizer & developer, TBELL Visual, 1988-; facilitator & speaker, Excel Net Customer First Prog, 1990-. **Honors/Awds:** Berkeley Marriott Employee of the Year Award, 1984; Commitment to Excellence Equitec Award, 1986; Investment in Excellence Award, Equitec Financial Group, 1986; Customer First Award, First Am Title, 1990; 100 Steps Award, First Am Title, 1990. **Home Addr:** 2777 Pk St, Berkeley, CA 94702, **Home Phone:** (510)841-1614. **Business Addr:** Senior Business Analyst, McCue Systems Inc, 111 Anza Blvd Suite 310, Burlingame, CA 94010-1932, **Business Phone:** (650)348-0650.

BELL, THERON J.
Management consultant, manager. **Personal:** Born Jun 2, 1931, Junction City, KS; married Sonya M Brown; children: Kirk, Mark, Joy Pinell, Kimberly Good, Margo Goldsboro, Michele Brown.

Educ: Wayne State Univ, attended 1951. **Career:** AK Railroad Housing Dept, janitor, 1951-53; US Army Corps of Engs, acct, 1953-55; Masseyl Bell Trucking Co, partner, 1953-55; Westward Motor Co, bus mgr, 1955-60; Blue Largo & Easy St nightclubs, partner, 1958-60; Independent Ins Agency, 1960-61; N Am Life & Casualty Co, agent, 1961-63; Fed Automotive Servs, bus mgr, 1963-66; Calif Govt Ronald Reagan's cabinet, 1967-69; Calif Off Econ Opportunity, dir, 1967-69; Volt Info Sci, dir govt relations, 1969-70; Chrysler Motors Corp, exec, 1970-72; Action Agency, various exec, 1972-81; Minority Bus Devel Agency, US Dept Com, dep dir, 1981-89; Va Dept Labor & Indust, commissioner, 1994-98; Walcoff & Assocs, bus devel mgr, 1992-94; US Dept Interior, Off Surface Mining, asst to dir, 1989-91; Va Employment Comn, chief dep commissioner, 1998-99; adv to Co Lt Gov Joe Rogers, 1999-00; AARP, CO state office, state coord for cot operations, 2000-01; US EPA, cot relations coord, 2001-02. **Orgs:** Calif Asn Health & Welfare, 1967-69; Calif Job Training & Placement Coun, 1968-69; Erie Cty NY Environ Mgt Coun, 1970-71; bd dir, Lafayette Fed Credit Union, 1976-81; Alexandria VA Human Rights Comn; Fed Interagency Comn Fed Activities Alcohol Abuse & Alcoholism; Alexandria VA Republican City Comn, CA Republican State Cent Comt; life mem, Republican Nat Comn; Alexandria VA Republican City Comn; Navy League of the US, Am Legion, dir, Fredrick Douglass Coalition; VA Emergency Response Coun, 1994-99; Commonwealth of VA Competition Coun, 1995-99; bd dir, Latin Am Res & Serv Agency, 2000-02; bd dir, CO Republican Bus Coalition, 2000-02. **Honors/Awds:** Top Producer for One Year, consistently among the top producers for N Am Life & Casualty Co San Francisco. **Military Serv:** AUS, pvt 8 mo. **Home Addr:** 8465 S Holland Way Suite 102, Littleton, CO 80128, **Home Phone:** (720)981-2101. *

BELL, THOM R.

Songwriter, performing arts administrator. **Personal:** Born Jan 27, 1941, Philadelphia, PA; married Sybell; children: Cybell, Mark, Thom Jr. **Career:** Chubby Checker, conductor, arranger & band leader, 1962-65; Cameo Parkway Rec, musician, 1966-68; Recordings: Closer Than Close; Gentlemen of Soul, 2003-; Gamble Huff & Bell, managing partner, currently; Philadelphia Int Rec, producer, currently; songs: "La La Means I Love You"; "Didn't I Blow Your Mind This Time". **Orgs:** Pres, Mighty Three Music; Am Fedn Musicians; Thom Bell Songwriter Workshop. **Honors/Awds:** Ten BMI Awards; Grammy Award; 2 Number One Producers Awards; 2 Business Awards, Billboard Mag; 2 Number One Songwriter Awards, Billboard Mag; 2 Number One Producers Awards, Northern Ariz Trail Runner's Asn. **Special Achievements:** 2 Grammy nominations; 45 Gold Albums & 45's. **Business Addr:** Producer, Philadelphia International Records, 309 S Broad St, Philadelphia, PA 19107.

BELL, TOM, JR.

Lobbyist, educator. **Personal:** Born Oct 2, 1941, Gilbertown, AL; son of Tom and Lular Mae; married Judith Pullin Bell, Jul 7, 1962; children: Victor Thomas, Vaughn Edward, Vernon Christopher. **Career:** American Steel Foundry, union time study, 1959-76; United Steel Workers, casual staff, 1976-77; Ohio AFL-CIO, dir, Compensation & Civil Rights, 1977; Cousins Properties Incorporated, Chmn, Pres & Chief Exec Officer, currently. **Orgs:** Bureau Worker's Compensation, Labor-Govt-Mgt Comn, 1980-92; Indust Comn Adv Comt, 1990-; Ohio Supreme Ct, Continuing Legal Educ Comt, 1989-91; trustee, chmn, Christ Mem Baptist Church, 1989-90; pres, United Steelworkers Local 2211, 1976-77; pres, Alliance AFL-CIO Central Labor Coun, 1975-77. **Honors/Awds:** Labor Award, Coalition Black Trade Unionist, 1991; Exemplary Service Award, A Philip Randolph Inst, 1990; Organization Award, Ohio Rehabiliation Asn, 1990; Elk of the Year, Cantell Elks Past Exalted Ruler, 1977. **Business Phone:** (404)407-1000.*

BELL, VICTORY

Executive, government official. **Personal:** Born Mar 7, 1934, Durant, MS; son of Gladys Thompson Parker and Bea; married Carol Banks, Nov 21, 1981; children: Jeffrey, Gregory, Victor, Michele McAlister, Caryle Farrar & Bradley Farrar. **Career:** Ill Bell, Rockford, IL, installer tech, 1953-70, asst mgr, 1956-86; City Coun, alderman, 1971-; Cwans Corp, pres, Rockford, IL, 1986-. **Orgs:** Region coordr, Ill Statewide Black Caucus, 1990-; bd mem, Winnebago Co Health Dept, 1990-; bd mem, Southwest Ideas Today & Tomorrow, SWIFTT, 1990-; pub rep, US Census, 2000; App mayor's, Econ Develop Comn C C; mem, Pilgrim Baptist Church; Na Asn Advan Colored People; Rockford Citizen Adv Bd Sch; chmn, Coun Sub Comm Soc Serv Prog; chair, Community Develop Comn, Rockford; vice chmn, Fair Housing Bd, Planning & Develop Comm, currently. **Honors/Awds:** Man of the Year Recognition, Nat Coun Negro Women, 1975; Man of the Year, Polit Christian Union Baptist Church, 1976; Rockford Set Aside Ordinance Minority Statewide Contractors, 1987; Sr Alderman Yr, Allen Chapel (AME), 1989; Father of the Year, Ethnic Heritage Orgn, 1999. **Special Achievements:** The first African Am elected Alderman, 1971; one of 1000 most influential leaders 20th century, Rockford, IL, 1999. **Business Addr:** Vice Chairman, Fair Housing Board, 425 E State St, Rockford, IL 61101, **Business Phone:** (815)987-5600.

BELL, VIVIAN

Broker. **Career:** Alpha-Omega Properties, broker, currently. **Business Addr:** Broker, Alpha-Omega Properties, 3131-F E 29th St, Bryan, TX 77802, **Business Phone:** (979)774-7820.

BELL, WILLIAM A.

Government official. **Educ:** Univ Al, Birmingham, MA, Psychol & Guidance Counseling; Miles Law Sch, Doctorate Jurisprudence. **Career:** Birmingham City Coun, Pres; Dist 5 City Coun, Councilor, currently. **Business Phone:** (205)254-2678.*

BELL, WILLIAM JERRY

Government official. **Personal:** Born Apr 18, 1934, Chicago, IL; son of William and Kathlyn. **Educ:** Univ Ill, Roosevelt Univ, BS, Com, 1958; Univ Chiago, PA. **Career:** Ill Bur Budget, sr budget anal, 1969-72, (retired); Ill Dept Labor, mgmt specialist, 1972-75, financial res, 1975-79, asst comm, unemploy ins; IDES, doc control mgr, 1980-90. **Orgs:** Bell & Assoc Ins Agency, 1970-83; consult, Small Bus Asn, 1968-69; bd mem, Southside Comt Art Ctr, 1985; adv, Univ IL Sch Art & Design, 1981-83; founder & chmn bd, Talent Asst Prog, 1976-77; bd dir, Citizenship Educ Fund; Rainbow & Push.

BELL, WILLIAM MCKINLEY

Secretary of the navy, administrator. **Personal:** Born Aug 31, 1926, Grand Rapids, MI; son of William M (deceased) and Mentie N Moore (deceased); married Patsy Ann Kelley, Oct 1, 1955. **Educ:** Univ Mich, BA, 1948, MBA, 1954. **Career:** Johnson Publ Co, salesman & merchandising rep, 1956-57; William M Bell & Assoc, pres, 1958-75; Equal Employ Opportunity Comn, consult, 1975-76; Bold Concepts, Inc, pres, 1976-82; Legal Serv Corp, legis asst dir. **Orgs:** Omega Psi Phi Fraternity, 1947; Univ Mich, Sch Bus Alumni Asn, 1982; Shiloh Baptist Church, 1986-. **Honors/Awds:** Optimist of the Year, Optimist Club, 1981; Special Tribute Award, State Mich, 1981. **Military Serv:** AUS, 1950-52; USN, staff asst secy, 1982-87. **Home Addr:** 1515 S Jefferson Davis Hwy Apt 1303, Arlington, VA 22202.

BELL, WILLIAM VAUGHN

Engineer. **Personal:** Born Jan 3, 1941, Washington, DC; son of William B Bell and Willie M Mullen; married Judith Chatters; children: William V II, Tiffany A, Anjanee N & Kristen V. **Educ:** Howard Univ, BSEE, 1961; NY Univ, MSEE, 1968. **Career:** Martin Marietta Corp, jr engr, 1961; US Army Electronics Command, proj engr, 1963-68; IBM Corp, mgr, 1968-83, tech asst, 1983-85, elect engr, 1985-96, sr engr, 1996, City Durham, mayor, currently-; United Durham Inc/Community Develop Corp, exec vpres & coo, 1996-. **Orgs:** Inst Electrical & Electronics Engrs, 1961-; pres, bd dir, UDI/CDC, 1970-83; bd dir, NC Sch Sci & math, 1979-; city comn, Durham City Bd Comn, 1972-; Durham Bd County Comner, 1972-94, 1996-2000; chmn bd, Durham City Bd Comn, 1982-94; dir, Durham Chamber Comm, 1982-; bd trustees, Durham County Hosp Corp, 1984-; adv bd, Duke Univ Hosp, 1987-; Mutual community Savings Bank, chair; Triangle Transit Authority. **Honors/Awds:** Community Service Award, State NC, 1981; Outstanding Citizen, Durham Comt Affairs Blacks, 1985; Community Service Award, Durham Chap Kappa Alpha Psi, 1985; Outstanding Alumnus, Howard Univ Club Res Triangle Park, 1985; Outstanding Citizen Award, Omega Psi Phi, Durham NC, 1986; Alumni Award for Distinguished Post-Graduate Achievement, Howard Univ, 1988; Service to Mankind Award, James E Shephard Sertoma Club, 1989. **Military Serv:** AUS, Signal Corp, first lt, 1961-63. **Home Addr:** 1003 Huntsman Dr, Durham, NC 27713-2384, **Home Phone:** (919)544-5597. **Business Addr:** Mayor, City Durham, Off of the Mayor, 101 City Hall Plz, Durham, NC 27701, **Business Phone:** (919)560-4333 Ext 269.

BELL, WINSTON ALONZO

Pianist, educator. **Personal:** Born Mar 24, 1930, Winchester, KY; son of Edward C and Margaret Hansbro; married Marlita Peyton; children: Taimia Danielle, Chase. **Educ:** St Louis Institute Music, St Louis, MO, 1947; Fisk Univ, BA, 1951; Univ Michigan, Mus, 1955; Columbia Univ, EdD, 1963; Gen Theol Seminary, StB, 1964; studied Cincinnati Conservatory Music, Wells Theol Col Wells England, Oxford Univ, Catholic Univ, UCLA, Univ Louisville. **Career:** NY City Sch Syst, teacher, 1955-60; Elizabeth City State Univ NC, instr piano, 1953-55; Music Studio Nyack NY, pianist & teacher, 1955-60; St Augustine Chapel NYC, curate, 1963-64; St James Less Jamaica NY, rector, 1964-71; Exec Enterprises, Winsont Salem, NC, found & Chief Exec Officer, 1984. Winston Salem State Univ NC, chmn dept music, 1972-; real estate broker, 1981-; Livingstone Col, adj lect, African-Am Studies, currently. **Orgs:** Organist Holy Family Catholic Church; bd dir, Winston Salem Symphony, Piedmont Opera Society; Suzuki Assoc Am, MENC, Phi Mu Alpha Sinfonia, Omega Psi Phi Frat, Col Music Soc; Reynolda House Chamber Music Soc; Knights Columbus; One Hundred Black Men. **Honors/Awds:** Rockefeller Theol Fellowship, Fisk Univ; Honor Graduate, Piano Recitals Winchester KY, Louisville, Washington, San Juan, New York, Norfolk, Virginia Beach, Winston-Salem, St Louis, Ft Knox, Santo Domingo, Elizabeth City, London, Oxford, Paris, Heidelberg, Rome, Brussels. **Military Serv:** AUS, spl serv, pfc, 1951-53. **Business Addr:** Chairman, Winston-Salem State University, Dept Music, Columbia Heights, Winston-Salem, NC 27101, **Business Phone:** (336)750-2520.*

BELL, YVONNE LOLA

Restaurateur, talk show host. **Personal:** Born Dec 25, 1953, New York, NY; daughter of Henry and Gladys Greene. **Career:** Flowers by Yvonne, owner & mgr, 1980-84; Pesca Restaurant, mgr, 1981-84; Ribbons & Rolls, owner & mgr, 1982-84; Lola Restaurant, owner & mgr, 1985-91, LolaBelle Restaurant, owner & mgr, 1992-94; Valentine's Day "Live Your Fantasy" night, theater show; hostess, Caribbean/soul food restaurant, currently. **Special Achievements:** Starting a TV cooking talk show, "Lunch with Lola". **Business Addr:** Owner, Manager, LolaBelle Restaurant, 206 E 63rd St, New York, NY 10021.

BELLAMY, ANGELA ROBINSON

Government official. **Personal:** Born Nov 25, 1952, Miami, FL; daughter of Leon Giddings and Helen Peavy; married Gregory Derek, Dec 23, 1978; children: Gregory Robinson & Evan Matthew Robinson. **Educ:** Fisk Univ, TN, BA, 1974; Vanderbilt Univ, Owen Grad Sch Mgt, TN, MBA, 1976; Harvard Univ, John F Kennedy Sch Govt, Prog Sr Execs State & Local Govt, 1986; Nat Forum Black Adminrs Exec Leadership Inst, cert, 1991. **Career:** Government official (retired); City Miami, admin asst, 1976-77, personnel officer, 1977-78, sr personnel officer, 1978-79, personnel supr human resources, 1979, asst city mgr, 1979-81, asst dir human resources, 1981-84, dir, personnel mgt, 1984, asst city mgr, 1988, dir, dept human res, 2002; The Links Inc, pres, 2008-. **Orgs:** Sec, IPMA S FL Chapt, 1978, vpres, 1979; co-ch host comn, IPMA Int Conf, 1983-84; area coord, FL Pub Personnel Asn, 1984-85; chair, IPMA Human Rights Comn, 1985-86; Nat Forum Black Pub Admin; IPMA Nomination Comm, 1987; pres, Delta Sigma Theta, Dade Co Alumnae Chapter, 1991-93; Soc Human Resource Mgt; Personnel Asn Greater Miami; Int Found Employee Benefit Plans; Am Mgt Asn; Int City Mgt Asn; Fla Pub Personnel Asn. **Honors/Awds:** Greater Miami, Outstanding & Most Influential Blacks, 1986; Award Outstanding Achievement Personnel Assoc Greater Miami, 1987; Mayor's Commendation, City of Miami, 2002. **Home Phone:** (305)233-7074.

BELLAMY, BILL

Comedian, actor. **Personal:** Born Apr 7, 1965, Newark, NJ; married Kristen Baker. **Educ:** Rutgers Univ, BS, econs, 1988. **Career:** Rep, Tobacco sales; MTV Jams, deejay; TV credits include, Martin; Russell Simmons' Def Comedy Jam; The Bill Bellamy Show; Men, Women & Dogs; Fastlane; Cousin Skeeter; "Caerdydd", Amy Coyne, 2006; "October Road", 2007; film: Who's The Man?; Love Jones; The Brothers; Any Given Sunday, 1999; Buying the Cow, 2002; How to Be a Player, 1997; Host, MTV Jams; The Real Mario Grey, 2005; Never was, Getting Played, 2005. **Honors/Awds:** Image Award for Outstanding Performance in a Youth or Children's Series/Special, 1998; Image Award for Outstanding Actor in a Drama Series, 2002; Teen Choice Award for Choice TV Actor - Drama/Action Adventure, 2002. *

BELLAMY, EVERETT

Educator, school administrator. **Personal:** Born Dec 29, 1949, Chicago, IL; son of William T and Emma M; divorced. **Educ:** Univ Wis, BS, 1972, MS, 1974; Cleveland State Univ JD, 1980; Cleveland-Marshall Col Law. **Career:** Univ Wis, grad asst; Cleveland State Univ, cord stud activ; Charles Hamilton Houston Pre-Law Inst, instr & asst exec dir; Georgetown Univ Law Ctr, sr asst dean & adj prof, currently. **Orgs:** Phi Alpha Delta Law Fraternity Int, 1980-; chairperson, Natl Conf Black Lawyers, DC Chap, 1981-83; Am Bar Assn, 1984-; Nat Bar Assn, 1986-; mem, Hon degrees Commt Georgetown Law; fac adv, Moots Court George Town Law. **Honors/Awds:** Honors Cert, Montgomery County, MD, 1996; Presidential Award, The Natl Bar Assn, 2004. **Special Achievements:** The Status of the African American Law Professors, 1990; Academic Enhancement and Counseling Programs, 1991; Where We Stand: African American Law Professors Demographies, 1992. **Home Addr:** 11706 Sherbrooke Woods Lane, Silver Spring, MD 20904, **Home Phone:** (301)622-2416. **Business Addr:** Assistant Dean, Adjunct Professor of Law, Georgetown University Law Center, 600 New Jersey Ave Room 352, Washington, DC 20001, **Business Phone:** (202)662-9039.

BELLAMY, IVORY GANDY

Educator, health services administrator. **Personal:** Born Feb 21, 1952, Tuscaloosa, AL; daughter of Iverson Sr; married Kenneth; children: Cinnamon & Cecily. **Educ:** Stillman Col, BA, 1974; Fla Int Univ, Miami; Nova Univ. **Career:** Dade County Pub Schs, instr, 1978-79; Miami Dade Community Col, prog coordr, 1979-85; Univ Miami, prog dir Minority Admis, 1985-89; Fayette County Schs, teacher, 1990-. **Orgs:** Southern Asn Admis Counrs; bd dirs, Rainbow House, 1991-. **Honors/Awds:** Alpha Kappa Mu. **Business Addr:** Teacher, Flat Rock Middle School, Department of English, 325 Jenkins Rd, Tyrone, GA 30290.

BELLAMY, JAY

Football player. **Personal:** Born Jul 8, 1972, Perth Amboy, NJ. **Educ:** Rutgers State Univ, sociol. **Career:** Seattle Sea hawks, defensive back, 1994-2000; New Orleans Saints, 2001-. **Business Addr:** Professional Football Player, New Orleans Saints, 5800 Airline Dr, Metairie, LA 70003, **Business Phone:** (504)733-0255.*

BELLAMY, VERDELLE B.
Administrator, nurse. **Personal:** Born Mar 15, 1928, Birmingham, AL; daughter of Zephry Brim and Gladys Stovall Brim; married Monroe, Mar 17, 1950; children: Michael. **Educ:** Tuskegee Univ, BS, 1958; Emory Univ, Atlanta GA, MSN, 1963; GA State Univ, Atlanta GA, cert community geront leadership, 1984. **Career:** Tuskegee Univ, Tuskegee Inst AL, clinical assoc, 1957-58; Grady Mem Hosp Sch Nursing, Atlanta GA, instr, 1958-62; VA Med Ctr, Atlanta GA, coordr & supvr, 1963-82, assoc chief nurse, 1983-, bd dir, 1984-; Ga State Univ, mem bd counr, geront, 1985-. **Orgs:** Am Nurses Asn; Nat League Nursing; Am Cancer Soc; state co-ordr black family, Nat Coun Negro Women, 1987-89; NAACP; Nat Parliamentarian Asn; bd dir, Georgia Nurses Asn, 1971-74; Georgia League Nursing; charter mem, Century Club, Am Nurses Found, 1983; Emory Univ Alumni Asn; Tuskegee Univ Alumni Asn; Top Ladies Distinction; bd dir, 1980-, nat secy, 1984-86, vpres, 1986-, Nurses Orgn Vet Admin; Supreme Basileus & nat pres, Chi Eta Phi Sorority, 1973-77; Sigma Theta Tau; nat exec bd, 1979-86, 1988-, nat secy, 1988-, Delta Sigma Theta; southern regional dir, Delta Sigma Thete Sorority, 1982-86; nat secy, Delta Theta Sigma Sorority Inc, 1988-92; charter mem, Thousandair Club, NAACP, 1991. **Honors/Awds:** Outstanding Service Award, Am Nurses Asn, 1973; Mary McLeod Bethune Illuminated Scroll, Nat Coun Negro Women, 1976; Distinguished Ludie Andrew Service Award, Nat Grady Nurses Conclave, 1977; Human Rights Award, Am Nurses Asn, 1977; Negro Women service award, Nat Med Asn and Nat Coun, 1979; US Congressional Rec achievement, 1980; Distinguished Tuskegee Inst Alumni Merit Award, 1981; NAACP "Unsung Heroine" Award, 1981; Excellence Health Care Professions Award, 1983, special achievement & community service award, 1984, Black Nurses Asn; Mary Mahoney Award, Am Nurses' Asn; Distinguished Alumni Citation of the Year Award, Nat Asn Equal Opportunity Higher Educ, 1985; NAACP FreedomHall Fame Award, 1986; Veterans Admin Leadership Award, 1988; Federal Employee of the Year Award, 1988; America's Top 100 Black Bus & Prof Women, Dollars & Sense Mag, 1988; Am Acad Nursing, Fel, 1993; Ludie Andrew's Award, GA Nurses Asn, 1995. Emory Medal, Emory Univ, 2005. **Special Achievements:** First African-American graduated from Emory Univ; presented one of two Emory Medals for 2005. **Business Addr:** Associate Chief, Medical Center Atlanta, Department Veteran Affairs, 1670 Clairmont Rd, Decatur, GA 30033, **Business Phone:** (404)321-6111.*

BELLAMY, WALTER JONES
Basketball player. **Personal:** Born Jul 24, 1939, New Bern, NC; son of Walter Bellamy Sr and Theo Jones; married Helen Ragland; children: Derrin. **Educ:** Ind Univ, BS, 1961. **Career:** Basketball Player (retired); Chicago Packers, 1961-62; Chicago Zeyphers, 1963; Baltimore Bullets, 1963-65, NY Knicks, 1965-68; Detroit Pistons, 1968-70; Atlanta Hawks, 1970-74; New Orleans Jazz, 1974. **Orgs:** NBA Player Rep, 1971-74; vpres, Nat Basketball Players Asn, 1972-74; Senate Doorkeep GA Gen Assembly, 1977-81; Atlanta Police Athletic League; Alpha Phi Omega Serv Frat; Alpha Phi Alpha Frat; Ind Univ Alumni Club Adv Bd; Atlanta Urban League; SCLC; bd dr, Nat Asn Advan Colored People; founder & pres, Men Tomorrow Inc; vpres, Shaw Temple AME Zion Church; SW Youth Bus Org; pres, Camp bellton-Cascade Yasmen Int; bd trustee, Gate City Nursey; bd trustee, Friends S west Hosp; co-chair, Atlanta Labor Day Weekend Football Classic. **Honors/Awds:** Rookie of the Year, NBA, 1961-62; Atlanta Hawks MVP, 1971-72; Atlanta Salutes Walt Bellamy, 1974; All-Am mem, Olympic Basketball Team, 1960; Olympic gold medalist, 1960; Hall of Fame, US Olympic, 1984; Hall of Fame, Ind Univ, 1984; Hall of Fame, NC Sports, 1984; Naismith Memorial Basketball Hall of Fame, 1993. **Special Achievements:** Nineth NBA Player to reach 20,000 point career mark.

BELLAMY, WERTEN F W
Lawyer. **Educ:** Princeton Univ, BA, 1986; Univ Va Law Sch, JD, 1989. **Career:** Merck & Co Inc, atty, joint ventures & technol licensing; Wyeth-Ayerst Pharmaceut, atty, corp trans & technol licensing; Celera Genomics Group, Group Coun; Blackwell Igbanugo PA, adv, currently, chmn & shareholder, currently. **Orgs:** Chmn, Lewis & Munday Corp & Technol Pract Group, 2002-. **Honors/Awds:** Chairman's Award, Nat Bar Asn, 1999; Excellence in the Corporate Practice Award, Am Corp Coun Asn, 2000. **Business Addr:** Chairman & Shareholder, Advisor, Blackwell Igbanugo PA, 555 13th St NW Suite 410, Washington, DC 20004, **Business Phone:** (202)624-1564.

BELLE, ALBERT JOJUAN
Baseball player. **Personal:** Born Aug 25, 1966, Shreveport, LA; son of Albert Belle Sr and Carrie Jean Giles; married Melissa; children: Cecila Marie. **Educ:** LA State Univ, BA, acct, 1987. **Career:** Baseball player (retired); Cleveland Indians, outfielder, 1989-96; Chicago White Sox, 1997-98; Baltimore Orioles, 1999-2000. **Honors/Awds:** AL Silver Slugger Award, 1993-96, 1998; Sporting News Player of the Year, 1995; Baseball Digest Player of the Year, 1995; Louisiana Sports Hall of Fame, 2005. **Special Achievements:** First player to ever hit 50 HR and 50 Doubles, 1995. *

BELLE, CHARLES E
Executive. **Personal:** Born Sep 2, 1940, Chicago, IL; son of Charles Douglas and Ella; married Rita Cummings, Aug 23, 1980; children: Cynthia Maureen & Charles Escobar. **Educ:** Roosevelt Univ, BSBA, 1963; Harvard Grad Sch Bus, MBA, 1973. **Career:** Harvard Univ, COGME fel, 1971-73; Drexel Burnham Lambert Inc, asst vpres, 1973-80; Brookings Inst, econ journalist, 1978; Nat Endowment Humanities, journalist, 1979; Prudential Bache Securities Inc, vpres & investment mgt adv, 1989; A G Edwards & Sons Inc, investment broker. **Orgs:** Bus ed, Nat Newspaper Publ Asn, Wash, DC 1973-; prof lectr, Golden Gate Univ, San Francisco, 1975-80; chmn, Mayors Adv Comm Community Develop San Francisco, 1983-85; bd dir, San Francisco Conv & Vistors Bur; bd gov, The Nat Conf Christians & Jews, Northern Calif Region; dir, Australian Am Chamber Com. **Honors/Awds:** Best Column, John Ryan Motoring Press Asn, 1993-94, 1998-99. **Home Addr:** 270 Francisco St, San Francisco, CA 94133.

BELLE, JOHN OTIS
Educator. **Personal:** Born Jun 8, 1922, Fort Worth, TX; married Joe Helen Hall. **Educ:** Huston-Tillotson Col, BA, 1948; Our Lady the Lake, MEd, 1956; Univ Tex. **Career:** Rosewood Elem Sch, teacher, 1948-56; Sims Elem Sch, prin, 1956-72; Austin Independent sch dist, asst dir, 1972. **Orgs:** Tex Asn Supv & Curric Devel; Tex Asn Gifted C; Tex Elem & Prin Asn; Tex State Teachers Asn; Nat Elem Prin Asn; NEA; Austin Asn Pub Sch Adminr; Kiwanis Int; Nat PTA Commn reg vpres Tex Cong of PTA; bd mem, Austin Energy Comn; Curric Adv Comt KLRN-TV; Nat Asn Advan Colored People; Austin Urban League; bd dir, Austin Sym Soc; trustee, Ebenezer Bapt Ch; adv bd Prog, Teenage Parents; Omega Psi Phi Frat; Phi Delta Kappa Educ Frat; exec comt, Huston Tillotson Col Alumni Asn; life mem, Nat & Tex PTA. **Honors/Awds:** Distinguished Service Award, Jack & Jill of Am; Outstanding Accomplishment in Educ; Zeta Phi Beta Sor; Distinguished Service Award, Delta Sigma Theta Sor; Certificate of Appreciation; Child & Family Service Award Am; Sch Dist Officials. **Military Serv:** AUS, sgt, 1943-46. **Business Addr:** Assistant Director, Austin Independent School District, 1607 Pennsylvania Ave, Austin, TX 78702.

BELLE, REGINA
Singer, actor. **Personal:** Born Jul 17, 1963, Englewood, NJ; daughter of Eugene Belle and Lois Belle; married John Battle, Jan 1, 1991; children: Winter, Sydni Milan, Tiy Chreigna, Jayln Nuri & Nyla. **Educ:** Manhattan Sch Music, opera & class music; Rutgers Univ, acct & hist. **Career:** Singer, currently; Albums: All By Myself, 1987; Stay With Me, 1989; Better Together: The Duet Album, 1992; Passion, 1993; Reachin Back, 1995; Baby Come to Me, 1997; Believe In Me, 1998; This Is Regina!, 2001; Dont Let Go, 2002; Lazy Afternoon, 2004; Love Songs, 2006; Love Forever Shines, 2008; Singles : You Got the Love, 1986; Show Me The Way, 1987; So Many Tears, 1987; Without You, 1988; How Could You Do It To Me, 1988; All I Want Is Forever, 1989; Make It Like It Was, 1990; This Is Love, 1990; What Goes Around, 1990; If I Could, 1993; The Deeper I Love, 1994; Oooh Boy, 2001; For the Love of You, 2004; God Is Good, 2008. **Honors/Awds:** Grammy Award for Pop Duo & Group, 1993; Grammy Award; Oscar, 1994. **Special Achievements:** Headliner, Avery Fisher Hall, NY; Am Music Awards, nomination, Best R&B Female Singer, 1991. **Business Phone:** (201)722-1500.

BELLEGARDE-SMITH, DR. PATRICK
Educator. **Personal:** Born Aug 8, 1947, Spokane, WA; son of Jasper Benton and Simone Cecile Smith. **Educ:** Syracuse Univ, BA, polit sci, 1968; Am Univ, MA, latin am area studies, 1970, PhD, int studies, 1977. **Career:** Howard Univ, Dept Fr & Span, lectr, 1977; consult, Moorland-Springarn Res Ctr, Howard Univ, 1980; bd dir, Third World Conf Found, Chicago, 1983-84; Bradley Univ, Inst Int Studies, assoc prof, 1978-86, tenured, 1983-84; Univ Wis, Milwaukee, Dept Africology, assoc prof africology, 1986-2005, chair 1987-90, 1994-95, & 2005-06, prof africology, 2005-; mem & exec bd, Nat Coun Black Studies, 1991-92 & 1996-97; bd mem, Haitian Inst Cultural & Sci Res, 1991-; Ctr Black Studies, Univ Calif, Santa Barbara, scholar-in-residence, instr & vis prof, Dept Religious Studies, 2000- 01; assoc ed, J Haitian Studies, 2001-. **Orgs:** Founding mem, Ill Coun Black Studies, 1979; founding mem, Progressive Latin Am Network, 1985; founding mem, Nat Cong Black Fac, 1988; founding mem, Brasilian Studies Asn, 1993; founding mem, Cong Santa Barbara, 1997; Am Asn Univ Profs; African Studies Asn; life mem, Caribbean Studies Asn; Nat Coun Black Studies; Nat Conf Black Polit Scientists; life mem, Asn Caribbean Historians; Latin Am Studies Asn; Scholarly Asn Study Haitian Vodou; vpres, Gens de la Caraibe; Haitian Studies Asn; Am Asn Religion. **Honors/Awds:** Barnett J Frank Award, Outstanding Social Science Student, Univ Virgin Islands, 1964-66; published numerous books and articles. **Business Addr:** Professor of Africology, University of Wisconsin-Milwaukee, Department of Africology, Mitchell Hall 221 PO Box 413, Milwaukee, MI 53201, **Business Phone:** (414)229-6099.

BELLINGER, HAROLD
School administrator, educator. **Personal:** Born Mar 28, 1951, New York, NY; son of Lionel Jordan and Naomi Jordan; divorced. **Educ:** State Univ NY, Farming dale, AAS, 1972; Rochester Inst Technol, BS,social work, 1974; Univ Pittsburgh, Masters Pub & Int Affairs, 1975; New York State Exec Chamber/NYS Affirmative Action Progs, Cert Completion, 1982. **Career:** Legis Comn Expenditure Rev, sr assoc, 1976-79; New York State Senate Finance Comm/Minority, legis budget analyst, 1979-81; New York State Dept Corrections, bus affairs & contract compliance mgr, 1981-82; New York State Correctional Indust, Indust asst dir mkt sales, 1982-84; Econ Opportunity Comn Nassau County, asst dir Youth proj, 1984-85; State Univ New York, asst pres affirmative action, 1985-89; Nassau Community Col, affirmative action & diversity, 1989-, asst pres, currently. **Orgs:** Assn Minority Bus Enterprises, 1981-82; Albany Chamber Com, 1981-82; course instr, New York State Budget Process sponsoring w/AL 1982; UN Assn USA/Mid-Long Island Chap, 1986-91; Minority Access Licensed Professionals, Long Island Regional Comt, 1986-90; brd dir, Econ Opportunity Comn Nassau County, 1984-89; 100 Black Men Nassau, Suffolk Chap, 1991-96, 2001-; brd dir, Urban League Long Island, 1991-93; Am Assn Affirmative Action Officers, 1996. **Honors/Awds:** Urban Fellowship Award, City Rochester, 1973-74; Univ Pittsburgh Grad Stud Award Pub & Int Affairs Fel, 1974-75; Ford Found Undergrad Scholar Award;State Univ New York Off Special Programs 1977; fel community col develop,Kellogg found, 1991-92; US Pres, Vol Action Award, nominated, 1991. **Business Addr:** Assistant to the President, Nassau Community College, 1 Educ Dr Tower Bldg Room 818, Garden City, NY 11530-6793, **Business Phone:** (516)572-7747.

BELLINGER, LUTHER GARIC
Executive director. **Personal:** Born Apr 24, 1933, Blackville, SC; divorced; children: Luther Garic Jr. **Educ:** John C Smith Univ, BS, 1955; Notre Dame Univ, MA, 1965; Teamers Sch Religion, DHL, hon, 1968; Universal Bible Inst, PhD, hon, 1978. **Career:** Edgefield SC, teacher, 1959; Mecklenburg Sch Sys, Charlotte NC, teacher, 1959-63; S Bend Ind Comm Sch Corp, teacher, 1963-65; Bendix Corp, Detroit, mgr equal employ off prog, 1965-70; Mich Lutheran Col, part-time counr, 1968-69; McDonnell Douglas Corp, corp dir equal employ off prog, dir community affairs. **Orgs:** Co-founder, St Louis Equal Employ Off, Group 1972-; bd dirs, United Negro Col Fund, 1972-75; bd dir, Loretto Hilton Repetory Theater, 1977-; secy, Mo Health Educ Facilities Auth, 1978-80; Pilgrim Congregational Church; Macedonia Baptist Church. **Honors/Awds:** Scholar NSF, 1961-63; Distinguished Service Award, Commonwealth Va Govt Linwood Holton, 1971; honorary Texas Citizen Award , 1974; Recognition for Exceptional Service to others, 1981. **Special Achievements:** Author: "A Guide to Slang" 1963; co-author primer for parents "An Internationally Circulated Tabloid on Modern Mathematics" 1964. **Military Serv:** AUS, 1956-58. *

BELLINGER, REV. MARY ANNE ALLEN (BIBI TALIBA MSHONAJI)
Consultant, clergy, administrator. **Personal:** Born Jul 16, 1939, Cincinnati, OH; daughter of George W Allen and Mary Jane Banks Allen; divorced; children: Georgiana, Teresa Lynn, Lawrence Wesley, Maurice & Sheila Renee Kinnard. **Educ:** Andover Newton Theol Sch, Boston, MA, MDiv, 1981. **Career:** Wellesley Col, Wellesley, MA, asst chaplain, 1975-80; Andover Newton Theol Sch, Boston MA, adj fac, 1978-80; ordained Baptist clergywoman, 1980; Big Bethel AME Church, assoc pastor, 1984-85; ordained itinerant elder AME church, 1984; St Stephens AME Church, pastor, 1985-87; Grady Memorial Hosp, chaplain intern, 1986-87; Newberry Chapel AME Church, pastor, 1987-89; VISION House Inc, group home, founder & dir, 1987-; Atlanta Voice Newspaper, columnist/ed, 1988-89; elected Atlanta Bd Educ, vpres large rep, 1989-93; Think About This Inc, Atlanta, GA, pres, 1994; Atlanta Pub Sch, substitute teacher, 1994-96; Black Women Church & Soc, prog assoc, 1997-; Interdenominational Theol Ctr, proj coordr, 1997-2000; consult, currently. **Orgs:** SE regional vpres, Partners Ecumenism Nat Coun Churches 1984-90; fac, first Year Class, AME Church Ministerial Preparation, 1987-89; bd dir, Christian Coun Metrop Atlanta, 1987-91; chairperson, Ecumenical Celebrations/Church Women United, 1987-88; chairperson, Racial Justice Working Group, Nat Coun Churches Sea Islands Comt, 1989-92; secy, Racial Justice Working Group, Nat Coun Churches, 1988-92; Ga Network Against Domestic Violence, 1988-89; Nat Asn Advan Colored People; Concerned Black Clergy Atlanta; secy, bd dirs, Exodus, Atlanta Cities Schs; adv comt, Success Six Atlanta United Way, 1990-94; Atlanta Fulton Comn C & Youth, 1990-96; judge, organizing comt, Hearts for Youth Salute, 1990-96; parliamentarian, Beulah Baptist Church Gospel Choir; asst minister, Beulah Bapt Church, Vine City; assoc, First African Presbyterian Church, 1998-. **Honors/Awds:** Black Women in Ministry, Boston Ecumenical Comn, 1980; Boston YMCA Black Achiever Award, Boston YMCA, 1980; Salute to Women of the Clergy, Eta Phi Beta Sorority, Gamma Theta Chapter, 1988; Woman of the Year, Religion, Iota Phi Lambda Sorority, 1991; Women in Leadership Scholarship Award, Asn Theo School, 2000. **Business Addr:** Consultant, 6232 Austin Dr, Mableton, GA 30126-4308, **Business Phone:** (770)819-2647.

BELL-SCOTT, PATRICIA
Writer, educator, editor. **Personal:** Born Dec 20, 1950, Chattanooga, TN; daughter of Louis Wilbanks and Dorothy Graves. **Educ:** Univ Tenn, Knoxville, BS, 1972, MS, 1973, PhD, 1976.

Career: Univ Tenn, Child & Family Study, fac, 1974-76, asst dir black studies & asst prof, 1976-79; JFK Sch Govt Harvard, Pub Policy Prog, fel & res assoc, 1979; Psychol Women Quarterly, New Directions Women, guest ed, 1982-83, J Nat Asn Women Deans & Admins, ed, 1979-81; Wellesley Col Ctr Res Women, res assoc, 1980-84; Mass Inst Technol, asst equal opportunity officer, 1982-84; J Negro Educ, ed bd, 1983-; Women of Power, A J Feminism & Power, staff, 1984; Univ Conn, Sch Family Studies, assoc prof, 1985-91; Univ Ga, Dept Child & Family Studies, Women's Studies Prog & Psychol Dept, prof, 1991-, adj prof, 1999. **Orgs:** Chair, Nat Coun Family Rels, Family Action Sect, 1974-76, nominating comt, 1991-92; chairwoman, AWA, Black Women's Community Comn, 1975-77; bd mem, Black Community Develop Inc, Knoxville, 1975-77; social action comt mem, Delta Sigma Theta, Alumnae Chap, Knoxville, 1977-78; co-convener, Coordinating Coun, Nat Women's Studies Asn, 1977-78; Consult Women's Prog Off Educ, 1978; nat exec bd, Nat Asn Women Deans Adminr & Counrs, 1978-80; consult, Nat Adv Comn Black Higher Educ, 1979; vpres, Nat Asn Women Deans & Admins, 1980-82; bd mem, Col Express Found, 1989-; contributing ed, Ms Mag, 1995-. **Honors/Awds:** Citation for Outstanding Service, UTK Chap Mortar Bd, 1977; Regional Finalist White House Fel Prog, 1977-78; Cited for Outstanding Service to the University of Tennesse, Knoxville Black Studs Asn, 1978; Award for Outstanding Contribution to Feminist Scholarship, Nat Inst Women Color, 1982; Fourth Curriculum Materials Award, Women Educrs, 1983; Distinguished Educator in Connecticut Award, Conn Chap Coalition 100 Black Women, 1986; Citation of Outstanding Contribution to the Psychology of Black Women, Div 35, Am Psychol Asn, 1988; Esther Lloyd-Jones Distinguished Service Award, Nat Asn Women Deans, Counrs, 1989; Letitia Woods Brown Memorial Book Prize, Asn Black Women Historians, 1992; Women of Achievement Award, Nat Asn Women Educ, Ethnic Women's Caucus, 1992; Archive of Achievement Alumnae Award, Univ Tenn, 1994; Cited at 20th Anniversary of the Wellesley Col Center for Research on Women, 1995; Centennial Leader Award, Univ Tenn, 1997. **Special Achievements:** Author of over 25 arts and four books. **Business Addr:** Professor, University of Georgia, Department of Child & Family Development, Dawson Hall Benson Bldg 1200 S Lumpkin St, Athens, GA 30602-3622, **Business Phone:** (706)542-4831.

BELL-TAYLOR, WILHELMINA
Entrepreneur. **Educ:** Univ Pittsburgh, BA. **Career:** Betah Assocs Inc, founder, chmn & chief exec officer, 1988-. **Orgs:** Women Press Orgn; Nat Asn Women Bus Owners; Exec Comt; BB&T Bank Community Adv Bd; Montgomery Co Md; Nat Contract mgt Asn. **Business Addr:** Founder, President, Betah Associates Incorporated, 7910 Woodmont Ave Suite 600, Bethesda, MD 20814, **Business Phone:** (301)657-4254.

BELMEAR, HORACE EDWARD
School administrator. **Personal:** Born Dec 12, 1916, Bardstown, KY; son of Horace and Julia; married Geraldine; children: Dianne, Derrick, Michael & Tracy. **Educ:** WVa State Col, BA, 1940; WVa Univ, MS, physical educ, 1948, MA, 1951; UnivIll; Univ Pittsburgh. **Career:** School administrator (retired); Dunbar High Sch, teacher & coach, 1946-55; AUS Missile Secy, dir educ, 1964-69; Univ Pittsburgh, instr; Allegheny County Community Col, dir admis, 1969-71; WVa Univ, admis officer, asst dean admis, 1971-93; foreign stud admis, dir, 1971; black student advisor, 1971-93. **Orgs:** Omega Psi Phi Frat; Nat Advan Asn Colored People; Human Rel Bd Fairmont WVa; chmn, Affirmative Action Comn WVa Univ; myriad community orgn; WVa Univ Sch Physical Educ. **Honors/Awds:** Hall of Fame, WVa Univ Sch Phys Educ; Outstanding Service, WV Univ Students; Spec recognition from President's African Am Vis Comm, Ann Horace & Geraldine Belmearr New Stud & Fac Reception; Outstanding Personin History Award; The Distinguished WVa Award; inductee, Hall Fame Stud Affairs; WVa Coach of the Year; inductee, WVa State Col Sports Hall Fame; Outstanding Alumnus Award, WVa Univ Sch Physical Educ. **Military Serv:** US, Naval Air Station, Pensacola, Fla, spec 1st class. *

BELSER, JASON DAKS
Football player, athletic director. **Personal:** Born May 28, 1970, Kansas City, MO; son of Caesar. **Educ:** Univ Okla, BA. **Career:** Football Player (Retired); Indianapolis Colts, defensive back, 1992-2000; Kansas City Chiefs, 2001-02;NFL Players Asn, regional dir, currently. **Orgs:** mem NFL Plyoff Team, 1995. **Honors/Awds:** Unsung Hero Award, NFL Players Asn, 1996, 1997. **Business Addr:** Regional Director, NFL Players Association, 2021 L St NW, Washington, DC 20036, **Business Phone:** (202)463-2200.*

BELSON, JERRY
Manager, government official. **Personal:** Born Mar 1, 1949, Lafayette, LA; son of Joseph and Elrose; married JoAnn St Clair, Apr 25, 1970; children: Dedrick, Abayomi, Farisa, Aisha & Jonathan. **Educ:** Southern Univ, BA, 1970; Sulross State Univ, BS, 1983. **Career:** Amistad Nat Recreation Area, dist ranger, 1973-85; Tuskegee Inst NHS, supt, 1985-87; Nat Park Serv, Ft Frederica Nat Monument, supt, 1987-89, MLK Nat Hist Site, supt, 1989-91, Yosemite Nat Park, deputy supt, 1991-94, Southern Arz Group, gen supt, 1994-95, Atlanta, dep regional dir, 1995-96, regional dir, 1996-. **Orgs:** Bd mem, Trust Pub Land, 1990-92; bd dir, Nat Assoc Interpreters, 1992-; bd dir, Atlanta Conv & Viss Bur, 1992-95; bd dir, Atlanta Olympic Comt, 1995-96; bd mem, Round table Assoc, 1996-98. **Honors/Awds:** Meritorious Service, Nat Park Serv, 1995. **Military Serv:** AUS, sgt, E-5, 1970-74. **Home Addr:** 3060 Birchton St, Alpharetta, GA 30022, **Home Phone:** (770)650-2096. **Business Addr:** Regional Director, US National Park Service, Atlanta Regional Office, 100 Alabama St SW 1924 Bldg, Atlanta, GA 30303, **Business Phone:** (404)562-3182.

BELTON, C RONALD
Chief executive officer, president (organization). **Personal:** Born Aug 28, 1948, Jacksonville, FL; son of Clarence A Jr and Bettye Ruth Taylor. **Educ:** Hampton Inst, BS, Sociol, 1970. **Career:** Jacksonville Urban League, assoc dir 1970-76; Tucker Brothers, mortgage broker 1972-; Merrill Lynch Inc, sr fin consult 1976-96; St. Johns Investment Mgt Co Inc, vpres; Riverplace Capital Mgt Inc, exec vpres, prin, compliance officer, chief exec officer & pres, Riverlpace Analytics LLC, currently. **Orgs:** Chmn bd, Jacksonville Urban League, 1983-84; life NAACP; Nat Eagle Scout Asn; chmn, Jacksonville Downtown Develop Authority, 1987-90; bd gov, Jacksonville Chamber Com 1988-91; bd, Jacksonville Symphony Asn, 1988-91; adv bd, Univ N Fla Sch Bus, 1988-91; fin comt, Jacksonville Community Found, 1990-92; Sigma Pi Phi Fraternity; State Bd Community Cols; bd trustees, Memorial Hosp Jacksonville, 2003-, chmn bd, Boys & Girls Club Northeast Fla. **Home Addr:** 2970 St Johns Ave, Jacksonville, FL 32205, **Home Phone:** (904)388-2582. **Business Addr:** Chief Executive Officer, President, Riverplace Analytics LLC, Riverplace Capital Management Inc, 1301 Riverplace Blvd Suite 2130, Jacksonville, FL 32207, **Business Phone:** (904)346-3460.

BELTON, HOWARD G.
Educator, administrator. **Personal:** Born Mar 22, 1934, Muskogee, OK; son of Louis and Jonella; married Ann Rempson; children: Consandra Denise & Sheryl Anne. **Educ:** Mich State Univ, BA, MS. **Career:** Mich Dept Social Serv, case worker, 1960-64; Lansing Mich Sch Dist,teacher, 1964-69; Mich Educ Asn, human rel consult, 1969-72; Nat Educ Asn, orgn specialist, 1972-73, dir employee rels, 1973-85, dir internal opers; HG Belton Photography. **Orgs:** Nat Asn Advan Colored People; Chicago Chap Oper PUSH; Urban League, Proj Equality; Prof Photographers Soc Greater Wash, currently. **Honors/Awds:** Lansing Mich Jaycees Outstanding Teacher Award. **Home Addr:** 14017 Breeze Hill Lane, Silver Spring, MD 20906, **Home Phone:** (301)460-0760. *

BELTON, ROBERT
Lawyer, educator. **Personal:** Born Sep 19, 1935, High Point, NC; son of Daniel and Mary L; married Joyce B Martin; children: R Keith & Alaina Yvonne. **Educ:** Univ Conn, BA, 1961; Boston Univ Sch Law, JD, 1965. **Career:** NAACP, Legal Defense & Educ Fund Inc, civil rights atty asst coun, 1965-70; Chambers Stein & Ferguson Charlotte NC, partner, 1970-75; Vanderbilt Univ, Sch Law, fair employ clin law prog, dir & instr, 1975-77, assoc prof law 1977-81, prof law, 1982-; Dept Labor, Off Fed Contracts Compliance Progs, consult, 1979-80; Harvard Law Sch, visiting prof law, 1986-87; Univ NC Sch Law, Chapel Hill, NC, visit prof law, 1990-91; counsel, Harris v Forklift Sys, 1993; NC Cent Univ Law Sch, Charles Hamilton Houston Distinguished vis prof, 1997. **Orgs:** Bd dir, ABAR III, 1979-81; comt prof develop, 1986-89, comt chair, 1987-90, exec comt, Amn Asn Law Schs, 1991-94; consult, TN Community Human Develop, 1976-; edal bd Class Action Reports, 1978-89; consult, Equal Employ Opportunity Community Trial Advocacy Training Progs, 1979-; consult, Pres Reorgn Proj Civil Rights, 1978; mem exec bd, Nat Employment Lawyers Asn, 1995-2002; NC Asn Black Lawyers; Am Bar Asn; TN Bar Asn, NC State Bar Asn; Am Law Inst, 1996-; Alpha Phi Alpha; Chi Boule; 100 Black Men Middle TN; mem, Steering Comt, US Ct Appealse Sixth Circuit's Gender Fairness Task Force & Racial Fairness Task Force; fel, Col Labor & Employment Lawyers; Napier-Looby Bar Found. **Honors/Awds:** NC Legal Defense Fund Dinner Committee Plaque, 1973; Clyde C. Ferguson Award, Minority Sect, Am Asn Law Sch, 2003; Napier-Looby Lifetime Achievement Award, Napier-Looby Bar Found, 2004; Nat Bar Asn Presidential Award, 2006. **Special Achievements:** His 2004 casebook on employment discrimination law is the first to extensively integrate critical race and feminist theory in a published set of teaching materials on employment discrimination law. Published: "Remedies in Employment Discirmination Law", Wiley, 1992; "Discrimination in Employment ", West Publ, 1986; "Mr Justice Marshall and the Sociology of Affirmative Action", 1989; "Reflections on Affirmative Action after Johnson and Paradise", 1988. **Home Addr:** 505 Belgrave Pk, Nashville, TN 37215, **Home Phone:** (615)292-5213. **Business Addr:** Professor, School of Law, Vanderbilt University, 131 21st Ave S Rm 276, Nashville, TN 37203-1181, **Business Phone:** (615)322-2856.

BELTON, SHARON SAYLES
Government official, college administrator. **Personal:** Born Jan 1, 1951, Minnesota; daughter of Bill and Marian; married Steven Belton; children: 3. **Educ:** Macalester Col. **Career:** Minn Dept Corrections, parole officer; Minn Prog Victims Sexual Assault, asst dir; Minnapolis City Coun, coun mem; City Minneapolis, mayor, 1994-2001; Univ Minn, Hubert H Humphrey Inst Pub Affairs, Roy Wilkins Ctr Human Rels & Social Justice, sr fel, currently. **Orgs:** Minneapolis Youth Coord Bd; Bd Estimates & Taxation; Heritage Bd; past pres, Harriet Tubman Shelter Battered Women; past pres, Nat Coalition Against Sexual Assault; Metrop Task Force Develop Disabilities; bd mem, Minneapolis Youth Diversion Prog; Minn Women Elected Officials; Children's Theater & Turning Point; bd mem, Bush Found, 1991-; bd mem, United Way Minneapolis, 1997-. **Honors/Awds:** Alumni Hall of Fame, Boys & Girls Club, 1996; Harvey Award, 1998; nat honoree, Nat Polit Caucus Black Women, 1999; Trailblazer Award, Alpha Kappa Alpha, 1999; Gertrude E. Rush Distinguished Service Award, Nat Bar Asn; Rosa Parks Award, Am Asn Affirmative Action. **Special Achievements:** Author of resolution passed by Minneapolis City Council mandating the divestment of city funds in South Africa; Only African American and the only female mayor in the city's 140 year history. **Business Phone:** (612)625-0315.

BELTON, Y MARC
Vice president (Organization), executive. **Personal:** Born in West Hempstead, NY. **Educ:** Dartmouth Col, BS, econ & environ studies, 1981; Univ PA, Wharton Sch Bus, MBA, mkt & finance, 1983. **Career:** Gen Mills, mkt asst, 1983, vpres, 1991; New Ventures, pres; Gen Mills Inc, Canada, pres, Worldwide Health, Brand & New Bus Develop, sr vpres, 1994, exec vpres, currently. **Orgs:** Leadership bd, Promise Keepers, 1995; bd dir, Guthrie Theater & Urban Ventures, 2004; Exec Leadership Coun; Audit Comt, Finance Comt, Compensation Comt & Governance Comt, Navistar Int; bd trustee, NW Bible Col; co-chair, Capital Campaign, Minneapolis Salvation Army. **Special Achievements:** One of corporate Americas most powerful African American executives by Fortune and Black Enterprise magazines. **Business Addr:** Executive Vice President, Worldwide Health Brand & New Business Development, General Mills Inc, 1 Gen Mills Blvd, PO Box 9452, Minneapolis, MN 55426, **Business Phone:** (763)764-7600.

BEMBRY, JERRY E
Journalist. **Personal:** Born Sep 18, 1962, Brooklyn, NY; children: Ashley. **Educ:** Ohio Wesleyan Univ, BA, journ, broadcasting, 1984. **Career:** Courier-News, reporter, 1984-85; Baltimore Sun, reporter, 1985-99; ESPN The Magazine, gen ed, 1999-. **Orgs:** Nat Asn Black Journalists, 1984-; past pres, Asn Black Media Workers, 1985-. **Honors/Awds:** Award for Series News, SPJ, 1988; Award for Local Govt, 1988; Award for Feature Writing Sports, 1999; Feature Writing Award, Pro Basketball Writers Asn, 1999. **Business Addr:** General Editor, ESPN The Magazine, 19 E 34th St Suite 7, New York, NY 10016-1000, **Business Phone:** (212)515-1000.

BEMBRY, LAWRENCE
Government official. **Personal:** Born Nov 29, 1946, Columbus, OH; son of Richard and Willie B Matthews; married Carol Flax, Oct 14, 1984; children: Steve Lakin, Lisa Lee Steptoe, Ross Lakin & Laura Jean. **Educ:** Am Int Col, BS, indust mgt, 1967; Univ Delaware, 1973; Lewis & Clark Univ, attended 1991. **Career:** US Merit Systs Protection Bd, admin dir, 1979-82; US Equal Employ Opportunity Comm, admin mgt dir, 1982-85; Dept Agriculture, Equal Opportunity dir, 1985-86, dir, 1986-89, dep regional forester, 1989-91, natural resources prog dir, 1991-94; Bur Land Mgt, serv ctr dir, 1993-95, spec asst dep dir, 1995-98, sr adv dir, 1998-, dir serv ctr, currently. **Orgs:** Tau Epsilon Phi Fraternity, 1963; B'nai B'rith, 1982-93; Hebrew Educ Alliance; HEAR Now, chief financial officer, 1994-99. **Honors/Awds:** Presidential Rank Awards, 1986, 1988, 1989; Meritorious Service Awards, US Merit Syst Protection Bd, USAF & US Dept Interior. **Business Addr:** Director Service Center, US Bur Land Mgmt, 303 W Colfax Ave, Denver, CO 80204, **Business Phone:** (303)534-0412.

BEMPONG, DR. MAXWELL A
Educator. **Personal:** Born Sep 14, 1938, Oda, Ghana; married Jacqueline B; children: Jeffrey Eugene & Kwabena Alexander. **Educ:** Michigan State Univ, BS, MS, PhD, 1967. **Career:** Mich State Univ, res asstship, 1965-67; Univ Nevada Reno, teaching fel, 1970; J Basic & Applied Sci, Nat Inst Sci Transactions, ed-in-chief; Norfolk State Univ, dir biomed res, head interim, chair, Dept Biol, prof biol, currently. **Orgs:** Fel, Phelps-Stokes Found, 1962-64; fel, Cocoa Mkt Bd, 1964-67; Am Genetic Asn; Am Col Toxicol; AAAS; Environ Mutagen Soc; Torrey Botanical Club; Nat Inst Sci; Sigma Xi; Beta Kappa Chi; Alpha Pi Zi. **Honors/Awds:** Outstanding Fac Award, Commonwealth Va, 1990. **Home Addr:** 3746 Brennan Ave, Norfolk, VA 23502. **Business Addr:** Professor, Norfolk State University, Department of Biology, 700 Pk Ave, 113 WSB, Norfolk, VA 23502, **Business Phone:** (757)823-2911.

BENDOLPH, LAURIE
Executive. **Career:** Charter Capital LLC, owner & partner, 1998-.

BENDY, MELINDA
School administrator. **Career:** McAuliffe Elem Sch, prin, dir, currently. **Business Addr:** Director, McAuliffe Elementary School, 13540 Princedale Dr, Dale City, VA 22193-3845, **Business Phone:** (703)680-7270.

BENEFIELD, MICHAEL MAURICE, JR.
Government official. **Personal:** Born Jan 22, 1968, Washington, DC. **Educ:** Univ NC, Chapel Hill, BA, 1990. **Career:** US Sen

William V Roth Jr, staff asst, 1990-91; New Castle Co Chamber Com, mgr city & state govt rels, beginning 1991; DOL/Div Employ & Training, US Dept Labor, dir, currently. **Orgs:** Bd dirs, Christina Educ Endowment Fund, 1992; adv coun, Pub Allies Del. **Business Addr:** Director, DOL/Div of Employment & Training, 4425 N Mkt St, Wilmington, DE 19809-0828, **Business Phone:** (302)761-8000.

BENET, ERIC (ERIC BENET JORDAN)
Singer. **Personal:** Born Oct 15, 1966, Milwaukee, WI; married Halle Berry, 2001 (divorced 2005); children: India; married Halle Berry, 2001. **Career:** Vocalist; Benet, mem, 1990-96; solo artist, 1996-; Albums with Benet: Benet, 1992; Solo Albums: True to Myself, 1996; Let's Stay Together, 1996; Spiritual Thang, 1996; Femininity, 1997; True To Myself, 1997; A Day in the Life, 1999; Georgy Porgy, 1999; Spend My Life With You, 1999; When You Think Of Me, 2000; Glitter, 2001; Love Don't Love Me, 2001; I Wanna Be Loved, 2005; Hurricane, 2005; Pretty Baby, 2006; Where Does The Love Go, 2006; TV Episode: "For Your Love," 1998-2002; Burden of Truth, 2000; Half & Half, 2002-; The Big Who's Wooing Who Episode, 2005. **Honors/Awds:** Three Wisconsin Area Music Industry Awards, 2000. **Special Achievements:** Nominee, Grammy Award, 2000. **Business Addr:** Recording Artist, Warner Brothers Records, 3300 Warner Blvd, Burbank, CA 91505, **Business Phone:** (818)846-9090.

BENFORD, EDWARD A
Executive, president (organization). **Career:** Benford & Assoc Inc, mgr, 1989-, pres, currently. **Business Addr:** President, Benford & Associates Inc, 3000 Town Ctr Suite 1333, Southfield, MI 48075, **Business Phone:** (248)351-0250.

BENFORD-LEE, ALYSSIA
Executive. **Educ:** Florida A&M Univ, BA, acct. **Career:** Deloitte & Touche LLP, sr auditor; Motorola Inc, regional adv bd; Benford Brown & Assocs LLC, co-founding partner, currently. **Orgs:** Am Inst Cert Pub Acct, The Ill CPA Soc; Nat Asn Black Acct. **Business Addr:** Managing Partner, Benford Brown & Assocs LLC, 400 N Schmidt Rd Suite 210, Bolingbrook, IL 60440, **Business Phone:** (630)679-9424.

BENHAM, DR. ROBERT
Judge. **Personal:** Born Sep 25, 1946, Cartersville, GA; son of Clarence and Jesse Knox; married Nell Dodson; children: Corey Brevard & Austin Tyler. **Educ:** Tuskegee Univ, BS, polit sci, 1967; Univ Ga, JD, 1970; Univ Va, LLM, 1989. **Career:** State Ga, spec asst attorney gen, 1978-84; Ga Ct Appeals, judge, 1984-89; Ga Supreme Ct, judge, 1989-; Ga Supreme Ct, chief justice, 1995-2001. **Orgs:** Bd dirs, Cartersville Chamber Com, 1976; bd chmn, Coosa Valley APDC, 1978; pres, Cartersville Bar Asn, 1981-82; vpres, Ga Conf Black Lawyers; bd mem,Fed Defender Prog, 1983-84; Am Judicature Soc; Ga Hist Soc; pres, Bartow County Bar Asn; Gov's Southern Bus Inst; pres, Soc Alternative Dispute Resolution; Nat Criminal Justice Asn; Ga Bar Found; Lawyers' Club Atlanta;Nat Asn Court Mgt; Nat Conf Chief Justices; Ga Asn Trial Lawyers; Alpha Phi Alpha; Am Soc Writers on Legal Subjects. **Honors/Awds:** Outstanding Service Award, Cartersville Bar Asn, 1984; Dent Award, Ga Asn Black Elected Officials, 1986. **Special Achievements:** First black appointed to Ga State Ct of Appeals, 1984; First black named to Ga Supreme Ct, 1989. **Military Serv:** AUS reserve capt, 1970-77. **Business Addr:** Justice, Supreme Court of Georgia, 244 Wash St Room 572, Atlanta, GA 30334, **Business Phone:** (404)656-3470.

BENJAMIN, ALBERT W.
Educator. **Personal:** Born in New York, NY; son of Alfred W and Olivia E; married Goldie Benjamin; children: Albert II, Scott, Candace. **Educ:** Brooklyn Col, BA, 1953, MS, 1958, Columbia Univ, prof dipl, 1964, Fordham univ, PhD, 1976. **Career:** City NY Bd Educ, teacher, 1953-60, asst prin, 1964-68, exec asst to asst supt, 1964-69; consult, 1968-; Exp Elem Prog, cent coordr, 1969-72; Career Educ, Develop & Implementation, dir , 1972-73, prin, 1973-78; Bd Examiners, supv asst examr, 1978-90; Brooklyn Col, adj prof, 1980-; Bur Teacher Test Develop & ADM, dir, 1990-02. **Orgs:** Alpha Phi Alpha, 1952; Phi Delta Kapa, 1963; Kappa Delta Pi, 1971; NY Acad Pub Educ, 1974; life mem, NCP. **Honors/Awds:** Fellow, Ford Found, 1968; Certificate of merit, Coun Supervisors/Adminr, 1983; Educator of the Year, Asn Teachers NY, 1985; Outstanding Educator, Bd Examiners Personnel, 1989; Educator of the Year, Asn Black Educr NY, 1990; Certificate of merit, Am Fedn Sch, 1991; Outstanding Educator, NY Elem Sch Principals, 1991; Outstanding & Dedicated Service, Brooklyn Oldtimer's Found, 1996. **Military Serv:** AUS, Korean War. **Home Addr:** 17234 133rd Ave Apt 11C, Jamaica, NY 11434. *

BENJAMIN, ARTHUR, JR.
Executive. **Personal:** Born Feb 8, 1938, Wagener, SC; married Dorothy Carrington; children: Lisa Simone, Cecily Lyn, Stacy Elisabeth. **Educ:** Nat Bus Col, jr acct cert, 1955; Tenn State Univ, BS, 1959; Univ Colo, attended 1960; NY Univ, attended 1964. **Career:** Franklin Book Progs, sr acct, 1962-67; Am Home Prod Corp, asst comptroller, 1967-68; Whitehall Labs, asst treas, 1968-72; ITT, sr financial analyst, 1972-77; Wallace & Wallace Ent, vpres & comptroller, 1977-82; Unity Broadcasting Network, vpres finance. **Orgs:** Chmn bd Queensborough Soc Prev Cruelty C, 1981-83; pres, Jamaica Serv Prog Older Adults, 1979-81. **Honors/Awds:** Black Achievers Harlem Br YMCA, 1978; Tenn State Univ Sch Bus Award, 1978. **Military Serv:** AUS, 3 Yrs. **Home Addr:** 115101 222nd St, Cambria Heights, NY 11411. *

BENJAMIN, COREY DWIGHT
Basketball player. **Personal:** Born Feb 24, 1978, Compton, CA. **Educ:** Ore State Univ, attended 2000. **Career:** Chicago Bulls, guard, 1998-01; Atlanta Hawks, guard, 2002-03; Charlotte Bobcats, guard, 2004-05; NBA Develop League Enterprises LLC, D-League; Benfica, Portugal; Guaynabo, Puerto Rico, forward, 2007. **Honors/Awds:** Pac-10, All Freshman Team, 1997; All Pac, Hon Mention All Am, 1998. *

BENJAMIN, DONALD S.
Educator, artist. **Personal:** Born Feb 13, 1938, New Orleans, LA; married Tritobia Hayes; children: Zalika Aminah, Aminah Liani, Anwar Saleh. **Educ:** So Univ, BS, 1961; Howard Univ, MFA, 1972. **Career:** AUS Engineering Sch, artist & illus, 1961-63; Bailey's Cross Roads, asst art dir, 1964-67; Defense Comm Agy, illus, 1964-67; Naval Observ, AV specialist, 1967; PTAI & CDC S Vietnam, consult, 1967-69; freelance writer, artist, cons, 1969-71; Comm Control Exp Sch, coordr, 1973; Wash Tech Inst, res coordr, 1974-75; James Mason's Univ, Black Studies Prog, media & res assoc, 1980-81; Donald Benjamin Artist Diversified & Assoc, freelance visual commun arts, consult & culturalist, 1982-87; Saints Missionary Found, dir, Memorial Rebirth Prog, currently. **Orgs:** Co-founder, dir, Nat Consortium Multi-Ethnic Studies & Cultural Exchange; exec charge prod, Diva Found; founder, Lemeul Pa Ctr Consortium Training & Prod, 1988-90; activity dir, Wheel-in-Wheel Summer Youth Prog. **Honors/Awds:** Artist, exhibitions include: Tribute Caribbean Independence Martin Luther King Library, Wash, DC, 1977; Madam's Organ Gallery Exhibition Adams Morgan Comm 1977; 1st Annual Kappa Alpha Psi Scholarship Benefit 1977; Black Caucus Annex Exhibit of Washington Area Artists 1975-77; Project director EXPO '76; Compared to What Inc 1974; assisted research that resulted in the placement of the first slave memorial in America which was located at Mount Vernon, home of George Washington; conducting research to isolate, identify and give high profile to 100 Black Historical sites in the south-eastern quadrant of the United States of America; provides guidance and support to reestablish the 1936 National Memorial to the Progress of the Colored Race in America and the Rebirth of Elder light foot Solomon Michaux; research efforts resulted in the placementan historical marker in the National Colonial Parkway, at Williamsburg opposite Jamestown Island. *

BENJAMIN, FLOYD
Executive. **Personal:** Married Floretta; children: Floyd Jr. **Educ:** NC Cent Univ, BS biol, MS microbiol. **Career:** Pasadena Res Lab, CEO; Akorn Inc, ceo, vice chmn. *

BENJAMIN, MICHAEL
Health services administrator. **Personal:** Married Marva P. **Educ:** Tex Southern Univ, Houston, BA, psychol; Yale Univ, MA, health adminr. **Career:** Nat Asn counties, human serv lobbyist, prog dir mental health & alcohol abuse prevention; Nat Inst Mental Health, health scientist adminr; Community mental health ctr, exec dir; Employee Assistance Profs Asn, chief operating officer; US Dept Health & Human Serv, Substance Abuse & Ment Health Serv Admin; Inst Ment Health Initiatives, exec dir; Nat Coun Family Rels, Minneapolis, MN, exec dir, currently. **Orgs:** Bd mem, Child Care Works; Univ Minn Family Social Sci Adv Bd; adv bd mem, NC A&T State Univ Human Environ & Family Sci Adv Bd. **Special Achievements:** Published articles on mental health; The Role of Leadership in Addressing Issues of Race and Ethnicity: Cultural Competence as a Framework and Leadership Strategy, co-author, 2004. **Business Addr:** Executive Director, National Council on Family Relations, 3989 Cent Ave NE Suite 550, Minneapolis, MN 55421, **Business Phone:** (763)781-9331.

BENJAMIN, DR. REGINA M
Physician, founder (originator). **Personal:** Born Oct 26, 1956, Mobile, AL; daughter of Millie and Clarence. **Educ:** Xavier Univ, BS chem, 1979; Morehouse Sch Med, 1982; Univ Ala, Birmingham, 1984; Med Ctr Cent GA, Macon GA, Residency, 1987; Tulane Univ, MBA, 1991. **Career:** Bayou La Batre city, pvt pract; Bayou La Batre Rural Health Clin, founder & chief exec officer, 1990-; Kellogg-Nat fel, 1993-96; Univ S Ala, Col Med, Mobile, AL, assoc dean rural health, admnr, currently. **Orgs:** Bd mem, Bd Health, Mobile County Health Dept, 1992-97; Ala Bd Censors MASA, bd med examr, bd pub health, 1992-97; Gov's Health Care Reform Task Force, 1994-95; past vice chair, Gov's Comn Aging, 1994-95; adv comt, Clin Lab Improv, 1994-; bd trustees, AMA, 1995-; past pres, Educ & Res Found, Coun on Ethical & Judicial Affairs, currently; Coun Grad Med Educ, 1997; pres, bd dirs, Mobile County Med Soc, 1997; pres, Med Asn State Ala, 2002-; Nat Acad Sci Inst Med; Dipl, Am Bd Family Pract; fel, Am Acad Family Physicians; past bd mem, Physicians Human Rights; exec comt, Forum Med Affairs. **Honors/Awds:** Angel in a White Coat, New York Times, 1995; Nelson Mandela Award for Health and Human Rights, 1998; honored by The Nat Gov Asn (NGA) in the pvt citizen category at its 95th annual meeting in Indianapolis, 2003; Rockefeller Next Generation Leader. **Special Achievements:** First physician under age 40 and the first African-American woman to be elected to AMA's board trustees; Time Magazine, 50 Future Leaders Age 40 & Under, 1994; ABC World News Tonight with Peter Jennings, Person of the Week, 1995; CBS This Morning, Woman of the Year, 1996; National Forum, The Phi Kappa Phi Journal, "Feeling Poorly: The Troubling Verdict on Poverty & Health Care in America", Summer 1996; Am Med Assn Bd of Trustees first African-Am woman to be elected. **Business Addr:** Founder, Chief Executive Officer, Bayou La Batre Rural Health Clinic, 13833 Tapia Lane, Bayou La Batre, AL 36509, **Business Phone:** (334)824-4985.

BENJAMIN, RONALD
Auditor, accountant. **Personal:** Born Dec 31, 1941, New York, NY; married Carmen E Hodge; children: Nicolle, Danielle & Christopher. **Educ:** Bronx Community Col, AAS 1966; Pace Col, BBA 1968; Bernard M Baruch Col, MBA 1974. **Career:** Main LaFrentz & Co CPA's, sr acct, 1968-71; Union Camp Corp, sr auditor, 1971-74; Ross Stewart & Benjamin PC CPA's, dir, 1974-; Bronx Lebanon Hosp, vice chmn & treas, currently; Hostos Comm Col, adj prof; NY Soc State Cert Public Accountants, treas, 1999; Mitchell & Titus LLP, partner, currently. **Orgs:** NY State Health Care Trustees, 1999; Am Inst Cert Public Accountants; NY St Soc Cert Public Accountants; NJ Soc Cert Public Accountants; co-founder Nat Asn Black Accts; William Patterson & Essex Co Col. **Military Serv:** USAF, e-3, 1960-64. **Business Addr:** Partner, Mitchell & Titus LLP, 1 Battery Pk Plz 27th Fl, New York, NY 10004-1461, **Business Phone:** (212)709-4530.

BENJAMIN, ROSE MARY
Government official, vice president (organization). **Personal:** Born Apr 28, 1933, Pueblo, CO; married Orville B; children: Darryl Kevin, Darwin Craig, Duane Carter & Benjamin Jr. **Career:** Educator (retired);Inglewood Unified Bd Educ, pres, 1982; Southern Calif Regional Occup, clerk, v pres, 1983-84; Calif Urban Assn Sch Dist, secy exec brd, 1985; Inglewood Sch Brd, v pres,1988. **Orgs:** Chmn, Coaltition Black Sch Bd, 1983-84; dist chairperson coalition,Advocating Reform Educ, 1984; secy exec, March Dimes Bd Dir, 1984; rep,March Dimes, Inglewood Coun PTA, 1984; brd dir, Centinela Child GuidClinic, 1984; comt mem, Calif Sch Brd. **Honors/Awds:** Salute to Women, Mornig side News Advertiser, 1970; Martin Luther King Award, Holy Faith Episcopal Church, 1970; Comm Contrib, Inglewood Neighbors, 1973; Commendation Centinela & Prof Bus Women, 1983; Hon Serv, Calif Cong PTA, 1985; Hall of Fame Award, Calif Sch Brd, 1985. **Home Addr:** 8711 3rd Ave, Inglewood, CA 90305.

BENJAMIN, DR. TRITOBIA HAYES
School administrator, educator, art historian. **Personal:** Born Oct 22, 1944, Brinkley, AR; married Donald S Benjamin; children: Zalika Aminah, Aminah Liani & Anwar Salih. **Educ:** Howard Univ, BA, 1968, MA, 1970; Univ Md, Col Park, PhD, 1991. **Career:** Georgetown Univ, instr, 1970; Howard Univ, instr, 1970-73, Art Dept, from asst prof to assoc prof, 1973-93, Cafritz guest lectr, 1978, prof art, 1993-, Col Arts & Sci, Div Fine Arts, dir art gallery, currently, assoc dean, currently; Afro-Am Inst, African Artists Am, guest curator; NEH, fel, 1984-85. **Orgs:** Nat Conf Artists; Col Art Asn; Smithsonian Nat Assocs; Studio Museum, Harlem; Nat Museum Am Art; cultural consult, Wash-Moscow Cult Exchange, Moscow, Russia, 1989. **Honors/Awds:** Recipient, Nat Endowment for the Humanities, Fellowships-in-Residence Col Teachers, 1975-76, Spencer Foundation Research Award, Howard Univ Sch Educ, 1975-77; honorary member, Eta Phi Sigma, 1986; PEW Humanities Fellowship Grant, humanities Fel Prog Pvt Black Cols, United Negro Col Fund, 1986-87; Faculty Research Grant in the Social Sciences, Humanities, and Education, Off VP Acad Affairs, Howard Univ, 1988-89. **Special Achievements:** Author of "Color, Structure, Design: The Artistic Expressions of Lois Mailou Jones," The International Review of African-American Arts, 1991, biographies on: "Selma Hortense Burke, American Sculptor," and "Lois Mailou Jones, American Painter," Black Women in America, An Historical Encyclopedia, Brooklyn, New York: Carlson Publishing Inc, 1992, biography on: "Annie EA Walker, Painter," Dictionary of American Negro Biography, New York: WW Norton Publishing, 1993, Two summer publications: Haitian Art Newsletter, Africa Reports Magazine, The Life & Art of Lois Mailou Jones, San Francisco: Pomegranate Artbooks, 1994. **Business Addr:** Associate Dean, Professor, Howard University, College of Arts and Sciences, 2455 6th St NW, Washington, DC 20059-0002, **Business Phone:** (202)806-6700.

BENNETT, AL
Automotive executive. **Personal:** Married Yvonne. **Career:** Al Bennett Inc, Flint MI, chief exec. **Business Addr:** Chief Executive, Al Bennett Ford Inc, 6206 Kings Crown Rd, Grand Blanc, MI 48439, **Business Phone:** (313)789-1511.

BENNETT, ANN. **See NESBY, ANN.**

BENNETT, ARTHUR T
Judge. **Personal:** Born Feb 3, 1933, Corapeake, NC; married Josephine Adams. **Educ:** Norfolk State Col, cert, 1957; Howard

Univ, BA, 1959; Howard Univ, Sch Law, LLB & JD, 1963; Univ Houston, Nat Col Dist atty, grad, 1972. **Career:** BL Hooks, AW Willis Jr, RB Sugarmon Jr & IH Murphy Memphis, Tenn, assoc atty, 1963-65; pvt pract, atty, 1964; Nat Col Dist Atty, faculty adv, 1973; Shelby Co, Tenn Gen Sessions Ct, judge, 1976; State Tenn, Criminal Ct, 30th Judicial Dist, Shelby Criminal Justice Complex, judge, 1976-. **Orgs:** Memphis & Shelby Co Bar Asn; Nat Bar Asn; legal dir & exec bd mem, Nat United Law Enforcement Officers Asn; Nat Asn Advan Colored People; bd dirs, Memphis Br, Nat Asn Advan Colored People; Memphis Chap Asn Study Afro-Am Life & History; Title XX State Adv Coun Dept Human Servs; Nat Dist Atty Asn. **Honors/Awds:** King of Cotton Makers Jubilee, Memphis 1974; Nat Historical Honor, Soc Phi Alpha Theta, 1959; Nat Forensic Honor, Soc Tau Kappa Alpha, 1959. **Military Serv:** AUS, 1953-55. **Business Phone:** (901)545-5858.

BENNETT, BETTY
College administrator. **Educ:** MSN. **Career:** Savannah State Univ, Harris-McDew Stud Health Services, admin dir, currently. **Business Phone:** (912)356-2217.*

BENNETT, BRANDON (BRANDON PURRELL BENNETT)
Football player, physical anthropologist. **Personal:** Born Feb 3, 1973, Greenville, SC. **Educ:** Univ SC. **Career:** Football player (Retired), Physical Education Teacher; Cincinnati Bengals, running back, 1998-2003; Carolina Panthers, running back, 2004; Off Season player, Tampa Bay Buccaneers, 2004; Bethlehem Baptist Church Christian Academy, Simpson, South Carolina. *

BENNETT, BRANDON PURRELL. See BENNETT, BRANDON.

BENNETT, CHARLES JAMES
Manager. **Personal:** Born Aug 17, 1956, Shreveport, LA; son of Charles Bennett Sr and Emma M Fountain. **Educ:** Wiley Col, Marshall, TX, BA, Educ. **Career:** Coors Brewing Co, Golden, CO, field mgr, 1979-, dir, environ affairs, currently. **Orgs:** Bd dirs, Brass Found, 1989-; recruitment comt, Chicago Urban League, 1989-; bd, Coors African Am Asn; NCP; comt mem, S Side Br. **Honors/Awds:** Being Single Magazine Pinnacle Award, Achievement Bus & Prof Excellence, 1988; Chicago Race for Literacy Campaign, Chicago Pub Schs. **Special Achievements:** America's Best & Brightest Business and Professional Men, Dollars & Sense Mag, 1989.

BENNETT, CORNELIUS O'LANDA
Football player. **Personal:** Born Aug 25, 1965, Birmingham, AL; son of Lino Bennett. **Educ:** Univ Ala. **Career:** Football player (retired); Buffalo Bills, linebacker, 1987-95; Atlanta Falcons, 1996-98, Indianapolis Colts, linebacker, 1999-2000. **Honors/Awds:** Pro Bowl, 1988, 1990-93; Lombardi Award; SEC Player of the Year hons, 1986; Vince Lombardi Trophy, 1986; Rookie of the Year, Sports Illustrated, 1990; Super Bowl, 1990-93; NFL 1990's All-Decade Team, 1990; College Football Hall of Fame, 2005; Alabama Sports Hall of Fame. **Special Achievements:** First-team All-Pro selection, 1988, 1991-92; All-America Selection, 1984-86. *

BENNETT, COURTNEY AJAYE
Educator. **Personal:** Born Nov 17, 1959, New York City, NY. **Educ:** HS Music & Art, dipl, music, 1976; Wagner Col, BS, 1980. **Career:** Health Ins Plan Greater NY, mkt rep, 1983; Ralph Bunch Sch, sci coord, teacher. **Orgs:** Partner, JBR Discount Corp; bd dir, Sigma Phi Rho Frat, 1978-80; mem, 100 Young Black Men, 1985; founder, Phoenix Sorority, 1994; chair, Harlem Tobacco Community Action Bd. **Honors/Awds:** Music scholar, Wagner Coll Parker scholar, 1977 & 1978; Outstanding Young Man of Am, US Jaycees, 1982; Outstanding serv, Sigma Phi Rho Frat, 1983.

BENNETT, DAINA T
Writer. **Educ:** SW Tex State, jour. **Career:** Chelsea House, Scholastic Publ; Educ Mat distribrs, chief exec officer, currently. **Orgs:** Co-chair, African-Am Parent Coun, 1987-91; chair, African-Am Community Improv Found, 1991-92; bd mem, Country Doctor, 1991-92. **Special Achievements:** State of Wash, designed & implemented multiculture mat prog, 1989; Seattle Sch Dist, multiculture mat, 1992. **Home Addr:** 5550 17th Ave S, Seattle, WA 98108, **Home Phone:** (206)763-1036. **Business Phone:** (206)853-8230.

BENNETT, DEBORAH MINOR
Consultant, executive. **Personal:** Born Aug 13, 1951, Long Branch, NJ; daughter of Leonard and Caroline; married Harvey. **Educ:** Montclair State Col, BA, 1973, MA, 1976; NY Univ, Doctoral cand; Stevens Inst Tech, org development coursework. **Career:** Neptune Sr HS, humanities instr, 1974-75; Webster Hall Res Hall Montclair State, dir, 1975-76; Upward Bound, dir, 1976-78; Stevens Tech Enrichment Prog, dir, 1978-83; Chicago Area Pre-Col Eng Prog, exec dir; WBDC's Child Care Bus Initiative, coordr, 2000-02; Right Source Inc, pres, currently. **Orgs:** Bd mem & treas, Asn Equality & Excel Educ; bd mem, NJ Asn Black Educrs; bd mem, Educ Opportunity Fund Dir Asn; steering comt, Nat Asn Multicultural Eng Prog Advocate Inc; dir, Nat Asn Pre-Col; Asn Supvr & Curric Develop; Coalition Keep Sch Open; bd mem, Ill Fair Schs Coalition Blacks Develop; pres, Partners Profit; Youth move Christ; vice chmn, Chicago Inst Urban Poverty; Haye's Educ Leg Adv Coun; represented Women's Business Development Center, 2007; vice-chair, bd mem, Chicago Inst Urban Poverty; Sustain, an environmental communications group. **Special Achievements:** Published Article, "Overcoming Barriers"-Winning The Retention Battle, NSBE Journal, Dec 85/Jan 86. Published article, "Case for Retention Programs". **Home Addr:** 1423 E 68th St, Chicago, IL 60637, **Home Phone:** (773)324-1833. **Business Addr:** President, The Right Source Inc, 1423 E 68th St Suite 3, Chicago, IL 60637, **Business Phone:** (773)324-1834.

BENNETT, DEBRA QUINETTE
Editor. **Personal:** Born Feb 10, 1958, New York, NY. **Educ:** Wagner Col, BA, Eng (dean's list) 1980. **Career:** Asn Ship Brokers & Agts, asst exec dir, 1980; Newsweek Mag, res & reporter, 1981-82; Mamaroneck Daily Times, reporter, 1981; Sci Am mag, proofreader & copy ed. **Orgs:** Managing ed, Sigma Phi Rho Frat Newsletter, 1981-; sunday sch teacher, Grace Episcopal Church, 1984-; Zeta Phi Beta Sorority Inc. **Honors/Awds:** Dean's List Wagner Col, 1980; Zeta Lady Award for Scholarship & Service, Zeta Tau Alpha Frat Delta Epsilon Chap, 1980. **Home Addr:** 16010 89th Ave Suite 12M, Jamaica, NY 11432, **Home Phone:** (718)658-8290. **Business Addr:** Editor, Scientific American Magazine, 415 Madison Ave, New York, NY 10017, **Business Phone:** (212)451-8200.

BENNETT, DELORA
Executive. **Career:** Genesis Personnel Serv Inc, pres & chief exec officer, 1984-. *

BENNETT, DELORES
Community activist, social worker. **Personal:** Born in Clarksville, TN; daughter of Will Henry Caudle and Carrie B Barbee-Caudle; married Eugene Bennett Sr, Oct 12, 1951; children: Ronda J Bennett, Eugene Bennett Jr, Mary Bennett-King & Esther M Bennett. **Career:** Founder & exec dir, Northend Youth Improv Coun, 1964-; Wayne Co, Mich, Wayne Co comnr, 1978-82. **Orgs:** Bd trustees, Henry Ford Hosp; chair by-laws comm, Detroit Health Dept Substance Abuse Adv Coun; bd dir, United Community Serv; lifetime mem, Nat Asn Advan Colored People; bd assembly, United Found; mem, Detroit Rctrn Partners. **Honors/Awds:** Resolution Service, Detroit Bd Educ, 1982; Proclamation of Dolores Bennett Day, Mayor City Detroit, 1982; Michigan State Senate Resolution, MI State Senate, 1982; Jefferson Award, Am Inst Pub Serv, 1987; Michiganian of the Year, The Detroit News, 1988; Mental Health Clothing Drive, Northend Youth Improv Coun; Operation Green Thumb, Northend Youth Improv Coun; Jobs for Youth Conference, Northend Youth Improv Coun; Northend Youth Improv Coun Youth Against Drugs; America's Award Hero, Positive Thinking, 1990; WWJ Radio 95 Citizen, WWJ Radio, 1990.

BENNETT, DONNELL, JR.
Football player. **Personal:** Born Sep 14, 1972, Fort Lauderdale, FL. **Educ:** Univ Miami, FL. **Career:** Kans City Chiefs, running back, 1994-2000, Wash Redskins, running back,2001. *

BENNETT, EDGAR, III
Football coach, football player. **Personal:** Born Feb 15, 1969, Jacksonville, FL; son of Juanita; married Mindy; children: Edgar IV & Elyse Morgan. **Educ:** Fla State Univ, BA, polit sci. **Career:** Football player (retired), football coach; Green Bay Packers, running back, 1992-97; Chicago Bears, running back, 1998-99, Green Bay Packers, dir player develop & dir player prog, 2001-04, running backs coach, 2005-. **Orgs:** March of Dimes, 2003; Fund C with Cancer. **Honors/Awds:** Inducted Hall of Fame, Green Bay Packers, 2005; Nice Guy Award, Doug Jirschele Sports Awards Banquet in Clintonville, 2006; Florida State Athletic Hall of Fame. **Business Phone:** (920)496-5700.*

BENNETT, GORDON D.
Bishop, school principal, clergy. **Educ:** Loyola Univ, Los Angeles, CA; Jesuit Sch Theol, Berkeley, CA, MDiv, 1975; Loyola Marymount Univ, MEd; Gonzaga Univ, BA, philos. **Career:** Loyola High Sch, Los Angeles, CA, prin, 1980-88, pres, 1996-98; Diocese, Mandeville, Jamaica, bishop, 2004-; St Ignatius Col Prep, San Francisco, CA, asst prin campus ministry; Jesuit Novitiate Santa Barbara & Culver City, CA, rector & master novices; Diocese, Baltimore, MD, auxiliary bishop. **Business Addr:** Bishop, Diocese, 59 Main St, PO Box 8, Mandeville, West Indies, **Business Phone:** (876)962-1269.*

BENNETT, IVY H.
Marketing executive. **Personal:** Born Oct 30, 1951, Waterbury, CT. **Educ:** Hampton Univ, BA, 1973; Univ Mich, Ann Arbor, MPH, 1975; Harvard Bus Sch, MBA, 1982. **Career:** Quaker Oats Co, brand mkt assoc, 1982-84; Kraft Foods, mkt brand mgr, 1984-89; Allstate Ins Co, asst vpres mkt, 1989; Univ Chicago Hosp, vpres & cheif mkt officer, 2002-; Harris Bank, sr vpres advert res mkt serv, 2006-. **Special Achievements:** Charted Property Casualty Underwriter, CPCW, insurance designation, 1995. **Business Addr:** Senior Vice President, Harris Bank, 111 W Monroe St, Chicago, IL 60603, **Business Phone:** (312)461-6475.*

BENNETT, DR. JAMES L.
College administrator. **Educ:** Mankato State Univ, BA; Macalester Col, MA; Univ Wash, PhD, higher educ, 1988. **Career:** Metrop Community Col, Minneapolis, St Paul, Minn; Bellevue Community Col,counr, Minority Affairs Prog, 1978, Eng-as-a-Second Lang & Lang Arts, instr, dean instr, 1990-, vpres equity & pluralism, 2006-. **Orgs:** Chmn, Task Forces Developmental Educ; Wash Voc Techn Coun; Joint Comt Assessment; pres-elect, bd dirs, Nat Coun Black Am Affairs, currently; Western Region Coun Black Am Affairs; United Way King County Employ Impact Coun; Lake City Rotary; N Seattle Boys & Girls Club. **Special Achievements:** First Vice President for Equity and Pluralism at Bellevue Community College. **Business Addr:** Vice President for Equity & Pluralism, Bellevue Community College, 300 Landerholm Circle SE, Bellevue, WA 98007-6484, **Business Phone:** (425)564-2300.

BENNETT, JOSSELYN
Executive director. **Educ:** Capital Univ, social work; Ohio State Univ, MSW. **Career:** Proj Linden Coun Ctr, exec dir; Evangelical Lutheran Church Am, 1988-91, Age-Span Ministries, dir, 1991-2003, dir educ & prog resources, Div Church Soc, currently, dir poverty ministry, currently. **Orgs:** Am Soc Aging; Nat Coun Churches Christ Comt on Justice for C; Comt Human Sexuality & Family Ministry; past chair, Deleg Coun NICA, 1996-19, secy, 2003-05. **Honors/Awds:** Spirituality & Aging Award, Nat Interfaith Coalition on Aging, 2005. **Special Achievements:** Manual published on aging ministry for Lutheran congregations and clergy and the subsequent training of local leaders.

BENNETT, JOYCE ANNETTE
Research scientist. **Personal:** Born Apr 18, 1941, Columbia, NC; daughter of Henry and Polly Bryant; married Robert L Bennett, Oct 6, 1960; children: Roderick, Roberta, Rhonda J Banks, Juancara, Robert, Chet. **Educ:** WA Tech Inst, AA, acct, 1974; Univ DC, BBA, acct, 1989. **Career:** Raleigh Haberdasher, acct technician, 1970-72; Riggs Nat Bank, bank teller, 1972-73; Fed Res Bd, statist asst, 1973-79, sr statist asst, 1979-94, res asst, 1994-; Bennett Beauty Inst Inc, Sch Cosmetology, Barbering & Manicuring, owner, currently. **Orgs:** chair, Greater Mount Calvary Holy Church, trustee bd, 1985-; Women Virture, 1992-; Pastor's Aid, 1985-. **Business Addr:** Research Assistant, Board of Governors of the Federal Reserve Board, 20th St Constitution Ave NW, B2219 A, Washington, DC 20551, **Business Phone:** (202)452-3000.*

BENNETT, KANYA A
Government official. **Educ:** Univ Ill, Urbana-Champaign, BS, Jour; Univ NC Law Sch, JD, 2002. **Career:** US Dept Educ, law clerk; NC Jour Law & Technol, student ed, 2001-02; Charter High Sch, tutor; US House Rep Comt Judiciary, Wash, DC, minority legal coun, currently. **Orgs:** Cong Fel, Cong Black Caucus Found. **Business Addr:** Minority Legal Council, US House Representatives Committee Judiciary, 2142 Rayburn House Off Bldg, Washington, DC 20515, **Business Phone:** (202)225-6504.

BENNETT, KAREN
President (Organization). **Career:** Metro Ther Providers Inc, owner & pres, 1990-. **Honors/Awds:** Small Business Innovator of the Year Award, Black Enterprise Mag, 2003. **Special Achievements:** One of the top three finalists in the Black Business Enterprises competition held in Tennessee.

BENNETT, LERONE, JR.
Writer, editor, historian. **Personal:** Born Oct 19, 1928, Clarksdale, MS; son of Lerone Sr and Alma Reed; married Gloria Sylvester, 1956 (died 2009); children: Alma Joy, Constance, Courtney & Lerone III. **Educ:** Morehouse Col, BA, 1949. **Career:** Editor, writer, journalist; Atlanta Daily World, journalist, 1949-52; Jet, city ed, 1952-53; Ebony, assoc ed, sr ed, 1953-87, exec ed, 1987-2005, exec ed emer, 2005-; Northwestern Univ, vis prof hist, 1968-69; Books: Pioneers in Protest, 1968; What Manner of Man: A Biography of Martin Luther King, Jr., 1976; Before the Mayflower: A History of Black America, 1984; Shaping of Black America: The Struggles & Triumphs of African Americans, 1619-90s, 1993; Forced Into Glory: Abraham Lincoln & the White Dream, 2000; Great Moments in Black History: Wade in the Water, 2000; Black Voices: An Anthology of African-American Literature, 2001. **Orgs:** Sigma Delta Chi; Kappa Alpha Psi; Phi Beta Kappa; trustee, Chicago Hist Soc, Morehouse Col, Columbia Col. **Honors/Awds:** Patron Saints Award, Soc Midland Authors, 1965; Book of Year Award, Capital Press Club, 1963; DHum, Wilberforce Univ, 1977; Academic Institute Litearture Award, AAAL, 1978; DLitt, Marquette Univ, 1979; LHD, Univ Ill, 1980; LHD, Lincoln Col, 1980; LHD, Dillard Univ, 1980; DLitt, Morgan St Univ, 1981; DLitt, Voorhees Col & Morgan St Univ, 1981; DLetters,Morris Brown Univ, 1985; DLetters, SC Univ, 1986; DLetters, Boston Univ, 1987; named to Pres Clinton's Comn Arts & Humanities; Trumpet Award, Turner Broadcasting Syst, 1998; Lifetime Achievement Award, Am BookAwards, 2002. **Military Serv:** AUS, first sgt, 1951-52. **Business Addr:** Executive Editor

Emeritus, Johnson Publishing Co, 820 S Mich Ave, Chicago, IL 60605, **Business Phone:** (312)322-9200.

BENNETT, LONNIE M
Automotive executive. **Career:** Champion Ford, Champion Mitsubishi, Rountree Hyundai, pres & dealer, currently; Rountree Olds-Cadillac Co Inc, pres & ceo, currently. **Orgs:** Comm One Hundred; adv bd, Cadillac; GM Minority Asn. **Special Achievements:** Black Enterprise's list of Top 100 Auto Dealers, ranked no 11, 2000. **Business Addr:** President, Chief Executive Officer, Rountree Olds-Cadillac Company Inc, 8750 Bus Pk Dr, Shreveport, LA 71105, **Business Phone:** (318)798-5565.*

BENNETT, MARIAN C
Lawyer, government official. **Educ:** Harvard Univ, BA, hist, 1966; Univ Penn Law Sch, JD, 1972. **Career:** Nat Labor Rels Bd, investr, field atty; US Dept Energy, various positions; Off Inspector Gen, sr atty; US Info Agency, inspector gen, 1993-96; Off Civil Rights, Transp Security Admin, atty, currently, dir, currently. **Special Achievements:** First African American inspector general of the US Information Agency, 1994.

BENNETT, MARION D.
Clergy, legislator. **Personal:** Born May 31, 1936, Greenville, SC; married Gwendolyn; children: Marion Jr, Karen. **Educ:** Morris Brown Col, AB; Interdenom Theol Ctr, MDiv; Univ NV, Atlanta Univ, Switzerland Ecumenical Inst. **Career:** NV State, legislator, civil rights leader; Zion United Meth Church, Las Vegas, NV, pastor. **Orgs:** NV Legislature; bd dir, Black Meth Church Renewal; chmn, Health & Welfare Comn; Legislative Functions & Rules Comn; pres, Las Vegas Br NAACP, 1963-67, 1971-73, vpres, 1967-69, treas, 1969; chmn, bd dir, Oper Independence, 1969-71; treas, Econ Bd Clark Co, NV, 1969; dem, ACLC. **Business Addr:** Pastor, Zion United Methodist Church, 2108 Revere St, North Las Vegas, NV 89030, **Business Phone:** (702)648-7806.*

BENNETT, MAYBELLE TAYLOR
City planner. **Personal:** Born Oct 19, 1949, Washington, DC; daughter of Ruby Elizabeth Mills Taylor and Raymond Bernard Taylor; married Robert Alvin Bennett, Apr 17, 1971 (divorced); children: Rebeccah Leah. **Educ:** Vassar Col, Poughkeepsie, NY, AB, 1970; Columbia Univ, New York, NY, MSUP, 1972. **Career:** Lagos State Develop & Property Corp, Lagos, Nigeria, town planning officer, 1972-75; Joint Ctr Polit Studies, Wash, DC, proj mgr, 1975-78; Working Group Community Develop Reform, dir res, 1978-81; Nat Comn Against Discrimination Housing, asst dir prog serv, 1982-84; DC Zoning Comn, chairperson, 1997-98; Coalition Human Needs, dir res, 1984-91; Howard Univ, Off Pres, asst community rels & planning, 1991-; Howard Univ, dir community rels, 1996-. **Orgs:** Alpha Kappa Alpha Sorority, 1968; Lambda Alpha Land Econs Soc, 1986-; Leadership Wash, 1991-; Eckankar, 1994. **Honors/Awds:** Maryland Vassar Club Scholar, Maryland Vassar Club, 1966; Carnegie-Mellon Fel Grad Studies, Carnegie-Mellon Found, 1970-71; HUD Work-Study Fel Grad Study, US Dept HUD, 1971-72; William Kinne Fellows Travel Fel, Columbia Univ Sch Archit, 1972. **Special Achievements:** Author, Community Development Versus Poor Peoples' Needs: Tension in CDBG, 1981, Citizen-Monitoring-A How-To Manual: Controlling Community Resources through Grass Roots Research & Action, 1981, Private Sector Support for Fair Housing: A Guide, 1983, Block Grants: Beyond the Rhetoric, An Assessment of the Last Four Years, 1986 & 1987, Block Grants: Missing the Target, An Overview of Findings, 1987. **Home Addr:** 2806 2nd St SE, Washington, DC 20032. **Business Addr:** Director, Howard University Community Association, Community Advisory Committee, 2731 Georgia Ave NW, Washington, DC 20059, **Business Phone:** (202)806-4771.

BENNETT, MICHAEL
Boxer. **Personal:** Born Mar 26, 1971, Charlotte, NC; son of Calvance and Aileen Brock. **Educ:** Univ NC, BS, Finance, 2000. **Career:** Boxer (retired); Bank Am, banking assoc, 1999-2000; prof boxer, 2001-03. **Honors/Awds:** Champion, Nat Police Force Athletic League, 1993, 1996, 1998; Silver medal, US Nat Championships, 1997, 1998, gold medal, 1999; Nat Golden Gloves, champion, 1998; champion, US Challenge, 1999; National Amateur Heavyweight Boxing Champion, 2000. *

BENNETT, MICHAEL
Football player. **Personal:** Born Aug 13, 1978, Milwaukee, WI. **Educ:** Univ Wis, consumer sci. **Career:** Minn Vikings, running back, 2001-05; New Orleans Saints, 2006; Kansas City Chiefs, running back, 2006-.Tampa Bay Buccaneers, 2007-08; San Diego Chargers, 2008-. **Orgs:** Twin Cities community. **Honors/Awds:** Pro Bowl, 2002. **Business Addr:** Professional Football Player, San Diego Chargers, PO Box 609609, San Diego, CA 92160-9609.*

BENNETT, PATRICIA A.
Judge. **Personal:** Divorced; children: Shandra Elaine. **Educ:** Col Guam Agana GU, 1961; Riverside City Col CA, 1970; Univ Calif, BA, 1973; Hastings Col Law San Francisco, CA, 1976. **Career:** Judge (retired), attorney; State Ohio, Dept Finance, asst supr pay roll div, 1962-66; UCR Computing Ctr, prin clk, 1967-71; Stanislaus Co Dist Attorney's Off, legal researcher, 1974; State Calif, Dept Water Resources, legal researcher, 1975; Contra Costa County, Dist Attorney's Off, Martinez, Calif, law clerk, 1976-77; State Pub Utilities Comm, atty, 1978-88; Calif Pub Utilities Comn, administrative law judge; atty, Tenn, currently. **Orgs:** Urban League Guild, 1970; Univ Calif Riverside Stud Coun, 1971-72; vol, San Francisco Co Legal Asst Prog, San Bruno, Calif, 1973; Coun Legal Educ Opportunity Scholar, 1973-76; vol, San Francisco Int Visitors, 1980-83; Assembly man Walter Ingalls, Sacramento, Calif, Polit Sci Intern, 1973; Nat Dist Atty Asn Intern, 1974; Charles Houston Bar Asn, 1976-; Nat Bar Asn, 1979-. **Honors/Awds:** CLEO, 1973-74. **Home Addr:** 2701 Maxwell Ave, Oakland, CA 94619.

BENNETT, PATRICIA W
Educator. **Personal:** Born Aug 31, 1953, Forest, MS; daughter of J C Watkins and Velma Watkins; married. **Educ:** Tougaloo Col, BA, 1975; Miss Col Sch Law, JD, 1979. **Career:** Small Bus Admin, atty, 1979-80; Miss Atty Gen, spec asst atty gen, 1980-82; District Atty Hinds County, asst dist atty, 1982-87; US Atty, asst US atty, 1987-89; Harvard Law Sch Trial Advocacy Prog, vis prof, 1990, 1993, & 1995; Univ Ark Sch Law, Little Rock, Summer Trial Advocacy Prog, vis prof, 1991, 1992, 1993, 1994 & 1996; Emory Univ Sch Law Trial Techniques Prog, vis prof, 1992, 1993, 1995, 1996, 1999 & 2000; Nat Inst Trial Advocacy (NITA), instr, 1993-; Miss Col Sch Law, prof law, currently. **Orgs:** Secy, Cent Miss Legal Services Corp Bd, 1989-; Smith Robertson Mus Bd, 1992; YMCA Bd Dirs, 1991-; comnr, Miss Bd Bar Comners, 1992; Governor, Fifth Circuit Federal Bar Asn, 2001-; pres, Hinds County Bar Asn, 2001-02; Miss Bar Asn,; Am Bar Asn; Magnolia Bar Asn; Miss Women Lawyes Asn; Metro Jackson Black Women Lawyers Asn. **Honors/Awds:** Woman of Achievement, Mississippi Women for Progress, 1988; Professionalism in the Field of Law Award, Miss Col Sch Law, 1990; Jack Young Legal Award, 1997; Lawyer of the Year Award, Miss Col Alumni Asn, 2001; Outstanding Service Award, Hinds County Bar Asn, 2002-03; Susie Blue Buchanan Lifetime Achievement Award, Mississippi Bar, Women in the Profession Committee, 2002; Outstanding Woman Lawyer of the Year Award, Mississippi Women Lawyers Asn, 2002; Appreciation Award for Service as Trustee, Mississippi Bar Foundation, 2003; Distinguished Board Service Award, Fifth Circuit Bar Asn, 2004. **Military Serv:** AUS, capt, 1984-92; several certs & medals during six yr tenure. **Business Addr:** Professor, Mississippi College School of Law, 151 E Griffith St, Jackson, MS 39201-1391, **Business Phone:** (601)925-7154.

BENNETT, ROBERT A.
Educator, writer, clergy. **Personal:** Born Jan 11, 1933, Baltimore, MD; son of Robert (deceased) and Irene Julie Harris (deceased); married Marceline M Donaldson; children: Elise Frazier, Mark Bennett, Malica Aronowitz, Ann Bennett, Michelle Aronowitz, Jacqueline Aronowitz. **Educ:** Kenyon Col, AB, 1954; Gen Theol Sem, NYC, STB, 1958, STM, 1966; Harvard Univ, PhD, 1974. **Career:** Educator (retired). Episcopal Diocese MAR, ordained priest, 1959; Episcopal Theol Sch/Divinity Sch, instr, asst prof, 1965-74, prof, 1974-94; Int Theol Ctr, Atlanta, vis prof, 1973-77; Boston Univ Sch Theol, vis prof, 1975, 1982; Princeton Theol Sem, vis prof, 1975, 1983, 1986; Harvard Divinity Sch, vis prof, 1976; Hebrew Univ, Jerusalem, Israel, fld arch staff supvr, 1984; Episcopal Divinity Sch, prof Old Testament, 1974-94. **Orgs:** Trustee, bd mem, Int Theol Ctr, Atlanta, 1973-77; vice-chair, Standing Lit Comn Episcopal Church, 1982-; Nat Coun Churchs Christ, 1982-; final selection comt, Fund Theol Educ, 1984-. **Honors/Awds:** Phi Beta Kappa, Kenyon Col, 1953; Fulbright Scholar, Univ Copenhagen, Denmark, 1954-55; Visiting Research Scholar, Am Res Ctr, Cairo, Egypt 1979-80; Research Scholar, Univ Khartoum, Sudan 1980; Israel Hebrew Univ 1984. **Special Achievements:** Author: "Africa & the Biblical Period," Harvard Theological Review, 1971; "The Bible for Today's Church," Seabury Press, 1979; "Howard Thurman & the Bible," God & Human Freedom, 1983; "Black Episcopalians," The Episcopal Diocese of Massachusetts 1784-1984, 1984; "Black Experience and the Bible," African American Religious Studies, Duke Univ Press, 1989; "Africa," Oxford Companion to the Bible, Oxford Univ Press, 1993; "The Book of Zephaniah," The New Interpreter's Bible, vol 7, Abington Press, 1996. **Home Addr:** PO Box 380367, Cambridge, MA 02238-0367. *

BENNETT, DR. SYBRIL M.
Television journalist, educator. **Educ:** Marquette Univ, BA, 1990; Loyola Univ, Chicago, Ill, Med, 1993; Vanderbilt Univ, PhD, higher educ admin, 1999; Harvard Univ, Mgt Develop Prog, 2007. **Career:** WISN-TV, assignment desk news trainee, 1989-90, assoc producer, 1991; WBBM-TV, desk asst & fill-in assignment ed, 1993-94; WTVF-News Channel 5, assoc producer & weekend assignment ed, 1994-95, freelance news writer & assignment ed, 1995-98, 1999-2000; Vol State Community Col, adj prof, 1995-98; Tenn State Univ, adj prof, 1995-97, MARC Prog, res assoc, 1997-99; Vanderbilt Univ, res asst, 1995-96, teaching asst, 1996, Media Rels, spec asst vice chancellor & sr pub officer, 1998-99; Middle Tenn State Univ, asst prof elec media jour, 1999-2000, sr pub affairs officer; Black Collegian & Music & Ministry Mag, freelance writer, 1999-2001; WNPT-PBS affil, producer & reporter, 1999-2000, Telethon vol host, 2003-; News Channel 5 Network, gen assignment reporter & anchor, 2000-03, freelance reporter, 2003-; Belmont Univ, New Century Jour Prog, asst prof jour, 2003-07, exec dir, 2003-, assoc prof jour, 2007-; Coop Ctr Study Abroad, study abroad instr, 2006. **Orgs:** Nat Asn Black Journalists; Broadcast Educ Asn; Radio & Tv News Dirs Asn;Soc Prof Journalists; bd mem, Nashville Area Chapter Am Red Cross, 1995-97, comt mem, pub rels, 1999-2000; chair, Grad Stud Higher Educ Fac Search Comt, 1998; bd dirs, Vanderbilt Univ Stud Commun, Inc, 2003-; Grant Comt, Fifteenth Ave Baptist Church Child Learning Ctr, 2003-05; coordr, Belmont-Nashville Asn Black Journalists, 2004-05; Nashville Conv & Visitors Bur, 2004; adv bd, Greater Nashville Chapter MBA Asn, 2005; R. H.Boyd Leadership Soc, 2005; Rotary Club, 2006; Leadership Nashville Alumni Asn, 2006-; Nashville Area Chapter Nat Asn Advan Colored People, 2007. **Honors/Awds:** Student Leadership Award, Marquette Univ, Multicultural Ctr, 1987-89; Outstanding Senior Award, Marquette Univ, 1990; Senior Award, Marquette Univ, Off Student Affairs, 1990; Service Award, Nat Asn Advan Colored People, Murfreesboro, TN, 1995; Service Award, Comt Ethnic Participation, Asn Study Higher Educ, 1996; Service Award, Nashville Area Chapter Am Red Cross, 1997; NATAS Emmy Award, 2001, 2002; The Tennessean, 2005. **Special Achievements:** Published books & articles; Author: The Color-Full Alphabet Book.

BENNETT, TOMMY
Football player. **Personal:** Born Feb 19, 1973, Las Vegas, NV. **Educ:** Univ Calif, Los Angeles. **Career:** Ariz Cardinals, defensive back, 1996-2000; Detroit Lions, safety, 2001-02. *

BENNETT, TONY LYDELL
Football player. **Personal:** Born Jul 1, 1967, Alligator, MS. **Educ:** Univ Miss. **Career:** Football player (retired); Green Bay Packers, defensive end, 1990-93; Indianapolis Colts, 1994-97.

BENNETT, WILLIAM RONALD
School administrator. **Personal:** Born Jan 1, 1935, Parkersburg, WV; son of William D and Pearl C; married Sarah L Clarkson; children: Denise Renee, Diane Elizabeth & Douglas Eugene. **Educ:** Hampton Univ, BS, 1956; John Carroll Univ, MEd, 1972. **Career:** Cleveland Clnc, res teacher, 1960-62; Cleveland Bd Educ, sch admin,1962-72; Mount Vernon Nazarene Univ, registr & assoc prof educ, 1968-91, assoc prof emer educ, 1991-; Cleveland State Univ, dir financial aid, 1972. **Orgs:** Dir, Inroads N E Ohio Inc, 1983-; pres, Friendly Town Inc, 1983-; CEEB Comm Pre Col Guidance & Coun, 1984-; pres, Nat Asn Stud Fin Aid Admin, 1984-85; treas, Inner City Renewal Soc, 1985; trustee, Antioch Baptist Church, 1985-88; pres, Midwest Asn Stud Fin Aid Admin, 1988-89. **Honors/Awds:** Man of Year, Alpha Phi Alpha Fraternity, 1982, 1986, 1988; Distinguished Services Award, Nat Asn Stud Financial Aid Adminr; Alan Purdy Distinguished Service Award, Nat Asn Stud Financial Aid Adminr. **Business Addr:** Associate Professor Emeritus of Education, Mount Vernon Nazarene University, 800 Martinsburg Rd, Mount Vernon, OH 43050, **Business Phone:** (740)392-6868.

BENNETT-ALEXANDER, DAWN DEJUANA
Educator, lawyer. **Personal:** Born Jan 2, 1951, Washington, DC; daughter of William H Sr and Ann Pearl Frances Liles; divorced; children: Jenniffer, Anne Alexis & Tess. **Educ:** The Defiance Col, 1970; Fed City Col, BS, sociol, 1972; Howard Univ, Sch Law, JD, 1975. **Career:** Oreg State Dept Justice, Solicitor's Off, Law Clerk, 1974; DC Court Appeals, law clerk, Hon Julia Cooper Mack, 1975-76; White House Domestic Coun, from asst to assoc dir & coun, 1976-77; US Fed Trade Comn, lawclerk, 1977-78; Antioch Sch Law, instr, 1979-81; Fed Labor Rels Authority, atty, adv, 1981-82; Univ N Fla, assoc prof, bus & employment law, 1982-87; McKnight Found, Fla Endowment Fund, McKnight Jr fac award fel, 1984; Fla Pub Employee Rel Comn, labor arbitrator, 1985-91; Employ Law & Diversity Consult, consult, 1985-; Terry Found, Terry fel Excellence res & teaching, 1991; Selig Found, Selig fel for Excellence res & teaching, 1992; Seed Grant Award, Consortium on Multi Party Dispute Resolution, 1992; Practical Diversity, consult, 1998-; BJD Consult Diversity Consult, consult, 1993-98; Univ Ga, assoc prof, legal studies, 1988-; Prac Diversity, founder, 1998-. **Orgs:** Pres, Southeastern Acad Legal Studies Bus, 1992-93; co-chair, Am Acad Legal Studies Bus, Employment Law Sect, 1992-94; Ga Polit Action Comt PAC,1993-94; Natl Coun Negro Women, 1983-; Natl Org Women, 1985-; treas, GA Now,1993-95; DC Bar, 1979-; bd mem, Friends Athens Creative Theater, 1990; bd mem, Consumer Credit Coun Servs NE Fla, 1983-84; bd mem, Girls Clubs Jacksonville Inc, 1983-85; Beta Gamma Sigma Nat Hon Soc, 1992. **Honors/Awds:** Fulbright, Council On the Exchange Of Scholars, 2000. **Special Achievements:** Employment Law Bus, Irwin Pub, 1995; The Legal, Ethical & Regulatory Pres,Southeastern Acad Legal Studies Bus, 1992-93; co-chair, Am Acad Legal Studies Bus, Employment Law Sect, 1992-94; Ga Polit Action Comt PAC, 1993-94; Natl Coun Negro Women, 1983-; Natl Org Women, 1985-; treas, GA Now, 1993-95; DC Bar, 1979-; brd mem, Friends Athens Creative Theater, 1990; brd mem, Consumer Credit Coun Servs NE Fla, 1983-84; brd mem, Girls Clubs Jacksonville Inc, 1983-85; Beta Gamma Sigma Nat Hon Soc, 1992. **Business Addr:** Associate Professor, Employment Law & Legal Studies, Terry College of Business University of Georgia, Department of Legal Studies, 202 Brooks Hall, Athens, GA 30602-6255, **Business Phone:** (706)542-3438.

BENNETT-MURRAY, JUDITH
Registered nurse. **Educ:** CUNY, NY City Technical Col, AAS, RN; CUNY, Hunter Col, BSN, MSN; Columbia Univ Teachers Col, MEd. **Career:** Nassau Community Col, assoc prof, currently. **Orgs:** Co chair, Alpha Phi Chapter. **Honors/Awds:** Shirley Chisolm Award, Brooklyn Mus, 2000; award for Excellence in Nursing Education. **Business Addr:** Associate Professor, Nassau Community College, 1 Educ Dr, Garden City, NY 11530-9793, **Business Phone:** (516)572-7501.*

BENNING, DR. EMMA BOWMAN
Educator. **Personal:** Born Oct 5, 1928, Columbus, GA; daughter of Ralph Bowman and Tinella Bowman; married Calvin C, 1946; children: Sheryl Ann Benning-Thomas, Nathaniel A & Eric A. **Educ:** Cleveland State Univ, Cleveland, OH, BS, MEd; Case Western Reserve Univ, Cleveland, OH; Kent State Univ, Kent OH; LaSalle Univ, Mandeville, LA, PhD. **Career:** Educator (retired). Cleveland Pub Schs, Cleveland, OH, prin; Benjamin Franklin Elem, 1975-77, prin, planner, 1979, dir, elem schs, 1979-80, cluster dir, 1980-85, area supt, 1985-87, asst supt curric & instr, 1987-90; Cleveland State Univ, supvr teachers; Cleveland State Univ, supvr stud teachers. **Orgs:** Trustee, bd dirs, Children's Serv, 1969-96; pres, bd dir, Karamu House, 1976-80; pres, Ludlow Community Asn, 1979-80; vpres, Jack & Jill Am Found, 1977-85, nat pres, 1985-96; Shaker Heights; Human Rels Comn, 1991-96; Delta Sigma Theta; Nat Sorority Phi Delta Kappa; The Links Inc; Imani Temple Ministries; trustee, Rainbow Babies & Children's Hosp; vpres, bd trustees, Shaker Heights Pub Libr, currently; women's coun, Cleveland Mus Art. **Honors/Awds:** Outstanding AME Woman of the Year; Good Neighbor Award; Outstanding Contributions to Jack & Jill of American Foundation; Outstanding Achievement Award, Cleveland Pub Sch; Good Neighbor Award, City Cleveland. **Special Achievements:** Community Hero Torch Bearer for the 1996 Olympic Torch Relay; Education Fellow, Educ Policy Fellowship Program; Author: Early Learning Laboratory Curriculum Guide, Curricula Guides for Major Subject Areas, Cleveland Public Schs; Early Learning Lab Curriculum Guide; Early Childhood Educ Guide Supplement; Educ Prog Guide for Inner City and EMR Children; Parent Guide, Getting Into the Equation, AAAS. **Home Addr:** 3143 Ludlow Rd, Shaker Heights, OH 44120, **Home Phone:** (216)991-2563. **Business Addr:** Board of Trustee, Shaker Heights Public Library, 16500 Van Aken Blvd, Shaker Heights, OH 44120, **Business Phone:** (216)991-2030.*

BENOIT, DAVID
Basketball player. **Personal:** Born May 9, 1968, Lafayette, LA; married Aline; children: Deseree & David Jr. **Educ:** Tyler Jr Coll. **Career:** Basketball player (retired), basketball coach; Utah Jazz, forward, 1991-96; NJ Nets, forward, 1996-98; Orlando Magic, forward, 1998; Utah Snowbears, forward, 2001; Shanghai Sharks, forward, 2002-03; Sunrockers, forward, 2003-04; Saitama Broncos, forward, 2005-07, head coach, 2007-.

BENOIT, EDITH B.
Manager. **Personal:** Born Mar 7, 1918, New York, NY; married Elliot; children: Barbara & Lloyd. **Educ:** Hunter Col, AB, 1938; Harlem Hosp Sch Nursing, RN, 1942; Teachers Col Columbia Univ, MA, 1945, prof dipl, 1959. **Career:** Harlem Hosp, instr & supvr & asst supt nurses, 1942-51, dir nursing serv, 1967; VA Hosp Brooklyn, NY, supvr & instr & asst chief nurse res & coordr, 1951-64; VA Hosp E Orange, NJ, assoc chief nursing serv educ, 1964-65; VA Hosp Bronx, NY, asst chief nursing serv, 1965-67. **Orgs:** Am Nurses Asn, 1942; chmn, NY State Asn Comn Study Nurse Practice Act, 1970; asst prof, Columbia Univ; adj asst, prof Pace Univ; bd dirs, Nat League Nursing; Open Curric Comn, NLN, 1972; Hunter Col Alumnae Asn; membd dir, Nat League Nursing, 1973-77; bd mgrs, Minisink Town House, NY City Mission Soc, 1972-77. **Business Addr:** Director, Harlem Hospital, Nursing Service School Nurse, 506 Lenox Ave, New York, NY 10037.

BENSON, DR. ANGELA
Educator, writer. **Personal:** Born in Alabama. **Educ:** Spelman Col, BS, math, 1982; Ga Inst Tech, MS, Indust Engineering, 1982, MS, operations res, 1984, MS, human res develop, 1997, PhD, instrnl tech, 2001; Univ Ga, doctorate instrnl technol. **Career:** AT&T Bell Lab, systs engr, 1982-90; Bell S Telecommunications Indust, res engr, 1990-95; Univ Ill, urbana campaign, asst prof educ technol dept human resource educ, 2001-06; Univ Manchester, sch educ, Manchester, UK, hon res fel & fac humanities, 2006; Univ Ala, assoc prof instrnl technol, 2006-; Novels: Bands of Gold, 1994; For All Time, 1995; Between the Lines, 1996; A Family Wedding, 1997; The Way Home, 1997; The Nicest Guy in America, 1997; Second Chance Dad, 1997; Awakening Mercy, 2000; Abiding Hope, 2001; The Amen Sisters, 2005; The Pastors Wife, 2005. **Orgs:** Acad human ers develop; Am Educ Res Asn; Ed Bd, J Res Technol Educ, 2002-; reviewer, Human Res Develp Review, 2002-; HRE Dept Adv Comt, 2003-; Asn Advan computing Educ; early career scholar award comt, Acad human Res Develop, 2004-; pres & training performance div, Asn Educ Commu & technol, 2005-; Educ Technol Bd, Univ Ill, Urbana Champaign, 2005-. **Honors/Awds:** Distinguished Contribution Award, AT&T Bell lab, 1984, Exceptional Contribution Award, 1987, Dept Recognition Award, 1991-93, Deptl Head Award, AT&T Bell lab, 1993; Individual Performance Award, 1998, 2000; Christy Award, Christian Booksellers Asn; Most Outstanding Doctrol Student, Dept Instrnl Technol, UGA, 2001; Emma Award, Romance Slam Jam Mag, 2002; Spitze & Mather Faculty Excellence Award, Univ Ill Urbana Campaign Col Educ, 2005. **Business Phone:** (205)348-7824.

BENSON, DARREN
Football player. **Personal:** Born Aug 25, 1974, Memphis, TN. **Educ:** Trinity Valley Community Col; Ark State Univ. **Career:** Football player (Retired); Dallas Cowboys, defensive tackle, 1995-98.

BENSON, GEORGE
Jazz musician, actor, singer. **Personal:** Born Mar 22, 1943, Pittsburgh, PA; married Johnnie; children: Keith Givens (deceased), Robert, Marcus, Christopher, George Jr & Stephen. **Career:** Pittsburgh night club, singer & dancer; Verve Music Group, guitarist, performer, singer, composer, currently; Composer: The Greatest; The Switchor How to Alter Your Ego, 1974; Saturday Night Live, 1977; Mike Hammer, 1986; Albums: George Benson/Jack McDuff, The New Boss Guitar, 1964; Benson Burner, Its Uptown, 1965; The George Benson Cookbook, Willow Weep for Me, 1966; Blue Benson, 1967; Giblet Gravy, Goodies, 1968; Shape of Things to Come, Tell It Like It Is, The Other Side of Abbey Road, 1969; I Got a Woman & Some Blues, 1970; Beyond the Blue Horizon, 1971; White Rabbit, 1972; Jazz on a Sunday Afternoon, Vol. 1, Jazz on a Sunday Afternoon, Vol. 2, Witchcraft, 1973; Body Talk, 1974; Bad Benson, 1975; Good King Bad, Benson & Farrell, Breezin, 1976; In Concert-Carnegie Hall, In Flight, 1977; Space Album, Weekend in L. A., 1978; Livin Inside Your Love, Take Five, 1979; Cast Your Fate to the Wind, Give Me the Night, 1980; GB, The George Benson Collection, 1981; In Your Eyes, Pacific Fire, 1983; 20/20, Live in Concert, 1984; The Electrifying George Benson, 1985; While the City Sleeps, 1986; Collaboration (with Earl Klugh), 1987; Twice the Love, 1988; Tenderly, 1989; Big Boss Band, 1990; Midnight Moods, 1991; The Essence of George Benson, 1992; Love Remembers, 1993; The Most Exciting New Guitarist on the Jazz Scene, 1994; The Best of George Benson, 1995; California Dreamin, Lil Darlin, That's Right, 1996; Standing Together, Masquerade, 1998; The Masquerade Is Over, 1999; Live at Casa Caribe, Absolute Benson, 2000; All Blues, 2001; Blue Bossa, 2002; After Hours, 2002; Irreplaceable, 2003; The Greatest Hits of All, 2003; Golden Legends Live, 2004; Jazz After Hours with George Benson, 2005; Best of George Benson Live, 2005; Givin It Up, 2006; Live from Montreux Immortal, 2007; Songs And Storie, 2009; Singles: Supership, 1975; This Masquerade, Breezin, 1976; Everything Must Change, Nature Boy, Gonna Love You More, The Greatest Love of All, 1977; On Broadway, Lady Blue, 1978; Love Ballad, Unchained Melody, 1979; Give Me the Night, Love X Love, 1980; Love All the Hurt Away, Turn Out the Lamplight, Whats On Your Mind, Turn Your Love Around, 1981; Never Give Up on a Good Thing, 1982; Inside Love (So Personal), Lady Love Me (One More Time), Feel Like Makin' Love, In Your Eyes, 1983; Late At Night, 20/20, 1984; Beyond The Sea (La Mer), I Just Wanna Hang Around You, New Day, 1985; Kisses in the Moonlight, Shiver, 1986; Teaser", 1987; Let's do it again, Twice the Love, 1988; Standing Together, 1998; Cell Phone, 2004. **Honors/Awds:** Grammy Award for Record of the Year, 1976; Grammy Award for Best Record of Year, 1977; Grammy Award for Best Instrumental Performance, 1977; Grammy Award for Best Pop Instrumental Performance, 1984; Grammy Award, Best R&B Male Vocal Performance, 1980; Grammy Award, Best R&B Instrumental, 1980; Grammy Award, Best Jazz Vocal Performance, 1980; Grammy Award, Best Pop Instrumental, 1983; Multi-platinum Album: Breezin; Platinum Albums: Give Me the Night, In Flight, Weekend in LA; Gold Albums: 20/20, In Your Eyes, Livin Inside Your Love, The George Benson Collection, Collaboration; Honorary Doctorates in Music, Berklee Sch of Music, Morris Brown Col; recipient of a "Hollywood Walk of Fame" star; World Music Award, Legend Award, 2003. **Business Addr:** Jazz Musician, Verve Music Group, 1755 Broadway Fl 3, New York, NY 10019, **Business Phone:** (212)331-2000.

BENSON, GILBERT
Administrator, counselor. **Personal:** Born Nov 1, 1930, Paterson, NJ; son of Walter Benson and Hattie Benson; widowed; children: Michelle & Gilda. **Educ:** Howard Univ Wash, DC, BS; William Paterson Col Wayne, NJ, MA. **Career:** A(retired) Family Planning Admin Youth Serv, welfare caseworker & youth worker, 1960-74; Passaic Community Comn Col, EOF counr & admin; Coun Probs Living, counr & adminr; Bergen County Shelter Homeless, supvr; Paterson Bd Educ, East side HS, Paterson, NJ, counselor; jazz vocalist. **Orgs:** Chmn, Paterson NAACP; affirm action chmn, NJ State NAACP; chmn, Paterson Coalition Media Changes; chmn, Passaic Co Citizens Vs Passaic Co Vocational Sch Bd; now Theater Paterson, NJ; Black Male Caucus Paterson, NJ; Omega Psi Phi Fraternity, 1985; delegate assembly, Nat Educ Asn, 1987-90; past chmn, Greater Paterson Arts Coun. **Honors/Awds:** Comn Serv Award NAACP; Salute Black Men & Women Duke Ellington Award Arts, 1985; Coun Serv Award, Passaic County Col, 1976; Adminrs Merit Award,Passaic County Co, 1978; JFK High Sch Award Contribution Arts, 1990. **Military Serv:** USAR, Capt, 1956-58.

BENSON, HAYWARD J., JR.
President (organization), chief executive officer, business owner. **Personal:** Born Aug 29, 1936, Mt Dora, FL; son of Hayward J Sr and Emily Smith; married Mattie Jo Alexander; children: Stephan & Cameron. **Educ:** Fla A&M Univ Tallahassee, Florida, BS, elem educ, 1958; Univ Ariz Tucson, Arizona, MEd, educ, 1965; Univ Fla, cert admin & supv, 1968; Fla Atlantic Univ Boca Raton, Florida, EdD, 1984. **Career:** Sch Bd St Lucie County Ft Pierce, Fla, teacher, 1958-59; Fla Educ Syst, educr & admin, 1958-83; Broward County Sch Bd, teacher, 1961-65, ITV Utilization, specialist, 1966, prin, 1968-70; Comprehensive Planning Equal Opportunities, exec dir, 1971-75, dir, 1975-83; Broward County Bd County Comnrs, dir, 1983-89; Nova Univ, adj prof, 1975; Broward County Sch Bd, admin asst to supt sch, 1977-83; Broward County Govt, Pub Serv Dept, dir, 1983; Lauderhill City, counman, 1982-84; Nat Alliance Black Sch Educ, prof & vpres; Airocar Inc, chief exec officer; Airocar Inc, Gray Line Ft Lauderdale, vpres, 1990-91, chief exec officer, 1991-93, pres, 1993-95; Universal Meeting Makers Inc, owner & pres, 1995-2000; Broward County Charter Rev Comn, 2006-08; City Lauderhill, Fla, comnr & dep vice mayor, 2006-; Southeastern Consult Group, dir, currently; Equal Access Sch Bd, classroom teacher, sch prin & dir; Ben-Alex Group Inc, owner, pres & chief exec officer, currently. **Orgs:** Fla Asn Health & Social Serv; Broward County Human Rels Div; State Univ Syst EEO Adv Comn Bd Regents, Dem Exec Comn; bd dir, Areawide Coun Aging; Am Red Cross; chmn, bd dir, Nova Univ Clin; pres, Fla Asn Community Rels; libr adv bd, Boward County, 2004-; City Nat Bank Miami; Estates Inverrary Home Owners Asn; Inverrary Home Owners Asn; bd dir, Am Cancer Soc, Broward County; comnr, Fla Comn Tourism. **Honors/Awds:** Teacher of the Year Award, BCTA, 1966, Distinguished Serv Award, 1967; Certificate of Recognition Award, Sch Bd Broward County, 1971; Human Rels Award, FEA, 1972; Community Service Award, LINKS Proj Pioneer, 1975; Numerous other awards & citations for professional & community services. **Military Serv:** USAR, capt, 1959-65; AUS, 2nd Lt QMC, Fort Lee, Virginia. **Home Addr:** 4410 NW 67 Terr, Lauderhill, FL 33319. **Business Phone:** (954)730-3015.

BENSON, JAMES RUSSELL
Educator, administrator. **Personal:** Born Jan 19, 1933, Marks, MS; son of Escar and Tressie V; married Madgeolyn Warren; children: Barry Ray, Agnela Davis. **Educ:** Ala State Univ, BS, 1963; Claremont Grad Col, MA, 1972, PhD, 1977. **Career:** Radio Sta WRMA Montgomery, Ala, news dir, 1960-63; Urban League, dir teen post, 1963-64; Lincoln High Sch, human rels dir, 1964-66; Gow-Dow Experience, pres, 1968-; Pomona Unified Sch Dist, dir music; Calif Polytech, Pomana; Palomares Jr High Sch, vice prin. **Orgs:** bd dirs, JoAnn Concert Dance Corp, 1984-85; bd dirs, Nat Asn Advan Colored People, 1986-87; dir, MESA, 1986-87; chmn, ACT-CO/Acad Excellence Prog, 1989-91; Nat Alliance Black Sch Educators. **Honors/Awds:** Teacher of the Year, Pomona Unified Sch Dist, 1982-84; Langston Hughes Art Award, Nat Asn Advan Colored People, Pomona, 1985; Bravo Award, La Music Ctr, 1985-86; Contemporary African-American Achievement Award, Pomona Alliance Black Sch Educators, 1990. **Military Serv:** AUS, Sp4, 2 yrs; High Hon Trainee.

BENSON, LILLIAN
Movie editor. **Career:** Film: Alma's Rainbow, 1994; The Promised Land, 1990; The Revolutionary War, 1995; A Century of Living, 1999; Soul Food, 2000; The Old Settler, 2001; Smothered: The Censorship Struggles of the Smothers Brothers Comedy Hour, 2002; Eyes on the Prize, LightWave Pictures, dir, 2004; Au Pair Chocolat, 2004; All Our Sons: Fallen Heroes 9 & 11, 2004; Troop 1500, 2005; Life Is Not a Fairytale: The Fantasia Barrino Story, 2006. **Orgs:** Am Cinema Ed. **Honors/Awds:** The Promised Land, Emmy Nomination, News & Documentary, 1990. **Special Achievements:** First African-American woman elected to the American Cinema Editors Assn, 1991. **Business Phone:** (310)315-7130.

BENSON, RUBIN AUTHOR
Graphic artist, educator, executive. **Personal:** Born Feb 8, 1946, Philadelphia, PA; son of Calvin and Mable S Skinner; married Janet Wicks, Jul 10, 1978; children: Rubin, Heather & Badeerah. **Educ:** Cheyney Univ, Cheyney, PA, BS, 1969; Univ Pa, Philadelphia, PA, 1971; Parsons Sch Design, New York, NY, 1972. **Career:** Philadelphia Sch Dist, Philadelphia, PA, graphic arts teacher, 1969-; Philadelphia Int Recs, art dir, 1982-84; First Impressions Design Group, Philadelphia, PA, pres, currently. **Orgs:** Judge, CEBA Awards, 1980-. **Honors/Awds:** Award of Distinction, 1983, 1984 & 1985; Award of Excellence, 1986. **Business Addr:** President, First Impressions Design Group, 4920 Hazel Ave, Philadelphia, PA 19143, **Business Phone:** (215)472-1660.*

BENSON, SHARON MARIE
Administrator. **Personal:** Born Apr 20, 1959, Chicago, IL. **Educ:** Ill State Univ, BS, 1981, MS, 1983. **Career:** Ill State Univ, res asst, 1982-83; Goodwill Indust, voc coordr, 1983-84; Opers Training Inst, job skills developer, 1984-85; SAMCOR Develop Corp, adminr small bus ctr; Westside Small Bus Develop Ctr, bus consult, 1985-. **Orgs:** MED Week Steering Comt, 1985-; Chicago Asn Neighborhood Develop, 1986-; Task Force Small Bus Needs, 1986. **Business Addr:** Administrator Small Business Center, SAMCOR Development Corporation, 4 N Cicero Ave Suite 38, Chicago, IL 60644.

BENSON, WANDA MILLER
Publisher. **Personal:** Born Jul 15, 1956, Washington, DC; daughter of William Miller and Rosetta; married Steve Benson, Jul 15, 1986; children: Brandon, Connor. **Educ:** Tenn State Univ, BA, 1980. **Career:** IRS, union rep, 1975-86; Contempra Brides, publ, 1986-. **Orgs:** NAACP Personnel Comt, 1995-96. *

BENT-GOODLEY, DR. TRICIA
Educator. **Personal:** Born in New York, NY; married. **Educ:** Univ Penn, MSW; Columbia Univ, PhD. **Career:** Family violence prev programs, Harlem, USA & Jamaica, New York, dir, clinician; Harlem & Queens County, admin & practitioner; Howard Univ, Sch Social Work, assoc prof currently. **Orgs:** Coun on Social Work Education; Nat Asn Black Social Workers; Nat Asn Social Workers; Am Public Health Asn; Alpha Kappa Alpha Sorority, Incorporated. **Honors/Awds:** Samuel Fels Fellow; HISTP Program Fellow; Child & Family Scholars Fel. **Special Achievements:** She has published in a number of areas, including social policy, domestic violence, child welfare, social work entrepreneurship and African American social welfare history. **Business Phone:** (202)806-4729.

BENTLEY, HERBERT DEAN
Executive. **Personal:** Born Dec 9, 1940, DeSoto, MO; married Judy Ann Lazard; children: Herbert, Karthryn & Karyn. **Educ:** Harris Teachers Col, AA, 1958; Southern Ill Univ, BS, 1966; Am Mgt Asn, cert syst design, 1972. **Career:** New Age Fed Savings & Loan Asn, managing officer. **Orgs:** Pres, PAS Mgmt Systs Inc; bd dir, Gateway Nat Bank, 1973-; bd dir, New Age Fed Savings & Loan Asn, 1974-; bd dir, Nat Asn Black Acct, 1974-75; bd mem, Nat Asn Black Acct, 1975-; bd dir, Inter racial Coun Bus Opportunity, 1974-; bd dir, Ctr Med Ctr, 1976-; bd dir, Christian Med Ctr, 1976-; bddir, Opportunity Industrialisation Ctr, 1976-; bd dir, Minority Bus Forum Asn, 1976-; St Louis Tax Task Force Cong US, 1977. **Honors/Awds:** Public Service Award Small Bus Admin, 1977. **Business Addr:** Managing Officer, New Age Federal Savings & Loan Association, 1401 N Kings Hwy, Saint Louis, MO 63113.*

BENTON, ADRIENNE R.
Executive. **Educ:** Rutgers Univ, BA; Univ Ala, MS, Birmingham; Seton Hall Univ, pre-legal studies; Dr. Martin Luther King Jr Ctr, non-violent soc change, Atlanta. **Career:** New Media & Technol, dir, 2003; WebCTel LLC, sr exec vpres, 2003. **Orgs:** Am Col Healthcare Exec; Nat Asn Health Serv Exec; Men Color Against AIDS; S End Hist Soc; Bd Dir; Lena Park Community Develop Corp; The Boston Coalition of Black Women; Adv Bd, Fleet Bank's Women's Entrepreneurs Connection; Nat Asn Recording Arts & Sci; co-chair, Women's Dinner Party. **Honors/Awds:** Nifty Fifty Award, Nat Found Teaching Entrepreneurship, 2006; TheUnityFirst.com; African-Am Newswire Leadership Excellence Award, Bus World Summit, 2005; Entrepreneurial Achievement Award, Global Diversity Group, 2005. **Business Phone:** (617)876-1756.*

BENTON, GEORGE A.
Executive. **Personal:** Born May 15, 1933, Philadelphia, PA; married Mildred Hogans; children: Anthony, Ondra. **Career:** Pro boxer, 1949-70; Smokin' Joe Frazier, boxing trainer. **Honors/Awds:** Outstanding Coach Award; John F.X. Condon Award, 1989-90. **Special Achievements:** Inducted in PA Hall of Fame 1979; International Boxing Hall of Fame, 2001. **Military Serv:** AUS Pfc served 2 years 14th Div Korea 1957. **Business Addr:** President, Hardknocks Inc, 2830 N Bailey St, Philadelphia, PA 19132.

BENTON, JAMES WILBERT, JR.
Lawyer. **Personal:** Born Sep 16, 1944, Norfolk, VA; son of James W (deceased) and Annie Scott; married; children: Laverne Aisha. **Educ:** Temple Univ, AB, 1966; Univ Va Law Sch, JD, 1970. **Career:** Hill Tucker & Marsh attys, Richmond, VA, partner, 1970-85; Court Appeals Va, Richmond, VA, judge, 1985-. **Orgs:** Former bd mem, Friends Asn C; bd mem, Am Civil Liberties Union, Va; Va State Educ Ast Authority; Nat Advan Asn Colored People; former bd mem, Neighborhood Legal Aid Soc; ichmond Traffic Safety Comn; former bd mem, Va Educ Loan Authority; bd mem, Va Arts Comn; bd mem, Va Ctr Performing Arts. **Business Addr:** Judge, Court of Appeals of Virginia, 109 N 8th St, Richmond, VA 23219-2321, **Business Phone:** (804)371-8428.*

BENTON, LEONARD D
Association executive, consultant. **Personal:** Born Jul 1, 1939, Chickasha, OK; married Barbara Y Pointer; children: Quincy L. **Educ:** Grambling Col, BS, 1961; Ill Wesleyan Univ, MS, 1964; Univ Pittsburgh, MPA, 1975. **Career:** Pub Sch Shreveport, La & Chicago, instr, 1961-65; Urban League, assoc dir, 1967-69; Urban League Job Ctr, dir, 1969-70; Southern Regional Off Nat Urban League, dir, 1986-88; Urban League, Okla City, pres; educ consult, currently. **Orgs:** NSF, 1962-64; chmn, Nat Black Luth Lay Comn; exec secy, Coalition Civil Leadership Okla City; polemarch, Kappa Alpha Psi Frat Inc; gen mgr, SW Urban Develop Corp; secy coun, exec dirs, Southern Region; Nat Urban League; chmn, Soc Ministry Okla Dist Luth Church. **Honors/Awds:** Service to Mankind Award, Seroma Club, Okla City, 1975. **Business Addr:** Consultant, 3201 E Forest Pk, Oklahoma City, OK 73121.

BENTON, NELKANE O
Executive. **Personal:** Born Jun 15, 1935, New York City, NY; married Thomas J Hill; children: Donna M. **Career:** KABC & KLOS Radio, dir pub affairs; Bing Crosby, pub rel, record promo; STEP Inc, counr; NKB Prod Hollywood, exec dir; KABC-AM/ KLOS-FM Am Broadcasting Corp, dir community rel, dir, ombudsman ser; KABC Talk radio, asst dir, dir, community rel, currently. **Orgs:** KABC Radio Edn; bd mem, bd dir, Consumer Credit Coun, LA; bd dir, La Beautiful, Community Resources Develop; Pacific Bell Consumer Adv Panel, Southern Calif Gas Go Black Adv Panel. **Honors/Awds:** Unity Award for Human Rel, 1974; Mayor's Award Pub Serv, 1974; Outstanding Awards, Pres Carter, Senator Alan Cranston, Supvr Kenneth Hahn, State Senator Nate Holden 1976; Outstanding Employee Am Broadcasting Co, Los Angeles Mayor Tom Bradley 1977,78; La County Media Volunteer Award, 1990; United Way Media Award for Public Service, 1989-90; 'The Nat Broadcasting Asn Award for Outstanding Community Relations', Crystal Award, 1989-90; Community Relations Award, Am Cancer Soc, 1993-94. **Business Addr:** Director of Community Relations, American Broadcasting Company Inc, Radio KABC-AM KLOS FM, 3321 S LaCienega Blvd, Los Angeles, CA 90016, **Business Phone:** (310)840-4900.

BENTON, PHYLLIS CLORA
Entrepreneur. **Personal:** Born Dec 4, 1947, Portland, OR; daughter of William T Benton Sr and Theresa. **Educ:** Portland State Univ, BS, 1970, MSW, 1972, Cert Black Studies, 1974. **Career:** State Oregon, C's Servs Div, social worker, 1976-77; US DHSS Social Security Admin, claims rep, 1977-80, Off Civil Rights, investr, 1980-84, Off Child Support Enforcement, prog specialist, 1984-93; Midnight Ramble Video, owner, 1992-. **Home Addr:** 1810 NE Jarrett St, Portland, OR 97211-5522, **Home Phone:** (503)287-0319. **Business Addr:** Owner, Midnight Ramble Video, PO Box 11522, Portland, OR 97211-0522, **Business Phone:** (503)287-0319.

BENYARD, WILLIAM B
Computer scientist. **Personal:** Born Nov 6, 1948, Detroit, MI; son of Willie and Frances Wilcher Tidwell; married Regenia Christine Powell, Aug 4, 1984; children: Erica, Brian, Clarence & Ian; married Regenia Jackson, Aug 4, 1984. **Educ:** Delta Col, Univ Ctr, MI, 1978; Wayne State Univ, Detroit, MI; Ind Univ, South Bend, IN. **Career:** Dow Chem USA, Midland, MI, oper analyst, 1974-80; Am Natural Serv Co, Detroit, MI, prod control analyst; Mich Consolidated Gas Co, Detroit, MI, programmer analyst, 1980-82; AM Gen Corp, South Bend, IN, MIS analyst, 1982-85; Genesis Info Systs, Akron, OH, independent contractor, 1985; Premark Int Food Equip Group, Troy, OH, sr analyst, 1986-87; Advan Programming Resolutions Inc, Dublin, OH, MIS consult, 1987-88; Dayton Bd Educ, OH; Metters Industs, sr syst programmer opers facilitator, sr prin comput analyst; Bilgen Group, Real Estate Investments & Mkt & Distrib, partner, 1988-. **Orgs:** Nat rec secy, Black Data Processing Assocs, 1982-86; founder, Dayton Chapter, Black Data Processing Assocs, 1988-90; pres, Princeton Park Neighborhood Asn, 1989-; Nat Asn Advan Colored People, Dayton Chapter, 1984; Equity Lodge, 121 PHFAU, 1990. **Honors/Awds:** Founders Award, Black Data Processing Asns, 1989. **Home Addr:** 123 Briar Heath Circle, Dayton, OH 45415-2601, **Home Phone:** (937)276-3916.

BENYMON, CHICO (THERON 'CHICO' BENYMON)
Actor, rhythm and blues singer. **Personal:** Born Jan 1, 1969?, Amityville, NY. **Career:** Tra-Knox, group mem; TV Series: "Moesha", 2000, 2001; "Half & Half", 2002-06; "Life Is Not a Fairytale: The Fantasia Barrino Story", 2006; Media Blitz, 2007; The Truth Hurts, 2007; "The Game", 2007; Films: Ali, 2001; Love on Layaway, 2005; Where Is Love Waiting, 2006; Nite Tales: The Movie, 2008; See Dick Run, 2009; Steppin: The Movie, 2009; Albums: Born to Reign Introducing Tra-Knox; Songs in films: Men in Black II; Black Suits Coming. **Special Achievements:** Nominated for Image Awards. **Business Addr:** Actor, United Paramount Network, 11800 Wilshire Blvd, Los Angeles, CA 90025, **Business Phone:** (310)575-7000.*

BENYMON, THERON 'CHICO'. See BENYMON, CHICO.

BERAKI, DR. NAILAH G
Physician. **Personal:** Born Jun 17, 1951, New York, NY; daughter of Ina L Green; children: Omar Jackson. **Educ:** San Diego State Col, BA, psychol, 1981; Mueller's Col Wholistic Med, 1987; Lehman Col, BS, health edu, 1998; Mercy Col, MS, oriental med, attending. **Career:** Muwasi Wholistic Health Healing Arts, practioner, massage therapist, currently; Skakeray Health & Wellness Collaborative, owner, currently. **Orgs:** Int Massage Asn; Int Reflexology Asn; Nat Black Iridologist Asn; Asn Rebirthers Int; Soc Pub Health Educrs, Greater New York Chap; Nat Acupuncture Detox Asn. **Honors/Awds:** Kentucky Colonel, honored for service. **Business Addr:** Massage Therapist, Muwasi Wholistic Health Healing Arts, 100 Benchley Pl Suite 6L, Bronx, NY 10475, **Business Phone:** (917)805-6475.

BERGER, NATHANIEL
Architect. **Personal:** Married Lady Washington-Berger. **Educ:** Carnegie Mellon Univ, BA, archit, Pittsburgh, Pa. **Career:** Design Experience Includes: projs NASA, IBM Corp, AUS Corps Engrs, U.S. Dept State - Off Foreign Bldg Opers, USN, Intel Corp, Motorola Semiconductor; JMGR Inc, partner, currently; Am Inst Architects, dir pub awareness, currently; Pbs & J, prog mgr, currently. **Orgs:** Am Inst Archit; bd dir, Asn Atlanta chap. **Special Achievements:** First African American to be named a partner with JMGR Inc, the oldest architectural and engineering design firm in Memphis. **Business Phone:** (770)933-0280 Ext 2643.

BERGER, SHIRLEY A
Police officer. **Career:** Nat Black Police Asn, Detroit Chap, chair, currently. **Business Addr:** Chair, National Black Police Association, Detroit Chapter, 1300 BeauBine Rm 700, Detroit, MI 48226.

BERHE-HUNT, ANNETTE
Librarian. **Personal:** Born in Batesville, MS; daughter of Roland Cole and Adelle Toliver Cole. **Educ:** Jackson State Univ, Jackson, MS, BS, 1974; Atlanta Univ, Atlanta, GA, MLS, 1979. **Career:** Quitman Co Pub Schs, Marks, MS, teacher, 1974-77; Lemoyne-Owen Col, Memphis, TN, Hollis F. Price Libr, librn, 1979-, dir libr, currently. **Orgs:** Tutor, Memphis Literacy Coun, 1982-86; Young Women Christian Asn, 1982-90; Tenn Libr Asn, 1986; Am Libr Asn, 1987-; treas, Les Gemmes Inc, 1989. **Honors/Awds:** Archival Training Inst, Nat Historical Pub & Record Comn, 1982. **Home Phone:** (901)368-5158. **Business Addr:** Director Library, Lemoyne-Owen College, The Hollis F Price Library, 807 Walker Ave, Memphis, TN 38126, **Business Phone:** (901)435-1000.

BERKLEY, DR. CONSTANCE E GRESHAM
Educator, poet. **Personal:** Born Nov 12, 1931, Washington, DC; married; children: Robert & Richard. **Educ:** Columbia Univ, BA, 1971, MA, 1972; NY Univ, Dept Near Eastern Lang & Lit, PhD, 1979. **Career:** Educator (retired), Poet; Fordham Univ, Black Drama, 1971-72; Vassar Col,lit lectr, 1972-75, Prog Africana Studies, lectr Africana Studies, prof emer, currently; Ramapo Col, African lit, 1976; Fordham Univ, asst prof, African/Afro-American & Islamic lit, 1979. **Orgs:** Harlem Writer's Guild, 1961-; contributing editor, Am Dialog, 1967; bd dir, Nat Coun Soviet Am Friendship, 1968; NEC Dramatists Workshop Affiliate, 1969-;, "Islam in Africa", CBS/NYU Sunrise Semester Program", 1400 Years Islam", 1980; guest lecturer guest lecturer, New School for Social Research, 1980-81; New York State Coun the Arts, lecturer; Intl Poetry Society; Asn Study Afro-Am Life & History; Middle Eastern Studies Asn African Literature asn; New York African Studies asn. **Honors/Awds:** Poetry published in several anthologies; Black American Writers Past & Present; Fisk University, Biography of Living Black Writers. **Special Achievements:** One of the founders of the Sudan Studies Assn, 1981; Editor of the SSA Newsletter; Specialist in the literature of the famous Sudanese writer, Tayeb Salih; Invited participant in special tribute to Tayeb Salih at Asilah's 17th Season in Asilah Morocco, 1994; Fulbright Lecturer at Ahfad Univ for Women, Omdurman, Sudan, 1990; Author of numerous articles concerning Sudanese literature. **Home Phone:** (845)485-2435. **Business Addr:** Professor Emeritus, Vassar College, Prog Africana Studies, 124 Raymond Ave, PO Box 739, Poughkeepsie, NY 12604, **Business Phone:** (845)437-7487.

BERNARD, DONALD L
Artist, educator. **Personal:** Born Nov 26, 1942, Baton Rouge, LA; son of Matthew L D and Doris Lillian; divorced; children: Alecia C Bernard. **Educ:** Los Angeles City Col attended 1968; Calif State Univ La, BA, 1974, MFA, 1997; Otis Parsons, 1982; Grossmont Col, Polaroid Workshop, 1999. **Career:** Artist/Photographer: "A Certain Beauty," pub Los Angeles Times, 1985; publication & exhibit, The History of Black Photographers from 1840-: Reflections in Black, 2000; publication & exhibit, Committed to the Image: Contemporary Black Photographers, 2001; City Los Angeles, graphic designer/photographer, 1971-2000; San Bernadino Valley Col, part-time photography instr, 1999; Calif State Univ Los Angeles, part-time visual literacy instr; elementary Sch Children, teacher, 2000-08. **Orgs:** Exposure Group, Washington, DC, 2007-08; Los Angeles Photography Ctr, 1981-87; co-founder, Black Photographers CA, 1984-86; co-founder, Black Gallery, 1984-86; San Francisco Cameraworks, 1998-99; Friends Photography, 1999; San Diego Mus Photography, 1999; FNFOCO, 1999-2000. **Honors/Awds:** First Place, Los Angeles County Fair, Open Category; Photo Contest Award, EV Camera, 1983; Photo Contest Award, Los Angeles Downtowner, 1984; Annual Award, Black Students Calif State Univ, Los Angeles, 1993; Presidents Award, Calif State Univ, Los Angeles, 1996; Black History Artist, Los Angeles, 2008. **Military Serv:** AUS, PFC, 1961-63.

BERNARD, HAROLD O.
Educator, physician. **Personal:** Born Jan 5, 1938; married Clara; children: Harold, Emily & Warren. **Educ:** St Mary's Col, attended 1955; Fisk Univ, attended 1960; Meharry Med Col, attended 1964; Univ Manitoba, attended 1968. **Career:** Hubbard Hosp, intern, 1964-65, resident, 1965-68; Emory Univ, Dept obstet & gynec assoc, 1968-71; Meharry Med Col, asst prof, assoc prof obstet & gynec, Assoc Dean, 1990-2001; dir grad med educ, prof emer, currently. **Orgs:** Am Bd Ob-Gyn; fel Am Col Ob-Gyn; Morgagni Soc; consult, Maternal & Infant Care Proj, Grady Hosp; Maternal & Child Health Family Planning, Meharry Med Col; Nat Med

Asn; RF Boyd Med Soc; Vol State Med Asn; Atlanta Med Soc; Gia State Med An; Tenn State Med Found; YMCA Century Club; Beta Kappa Chi; Alpha Omega Alpha. **Honors/Awds:** Professor of the Year, 1975. **Home Addr:** 4608 Mountain View Dr, Nashville, TN 37215, **Home Phone:** (615)254-7634. **Business Addr:** Professor Emeritus, Meharry Medical College, 1005 D B Todd Blvd 4220 Harding Rd, Nashville, TN 37208, **Business Phone:** (615)327-5809.

BERNARD, LINDA D.
Association executive. **Career:** Wayne Co Neighborhood Legal Serv, project mgr, dir, pres & ceo, 1999-. **Orgs:** vpres Nat Asn Women Lawyers; Founding mem, State Bar's Delivery Legal Serv Comt. **Business Phone:** (313)874-5820.*

BERNARD, DR. LOUIS JOSEPH
Surgeon, educator. **Personal:** Born Aug 19, 1925, Laplace, LA; son of Edward (deceased) and Jeanne Vinet (deceased); married Lois Jeanette McDonald, Feb 1, 1976; children: Marie Antonia Bernard Jenkins & Phyllis Elaine Bernard Robison May. **Educ:** Dillard Univ, BA, 1946; Meharry Med Col, MD, 1950. **Career:** Hubbard Hosp Nashville, intern, 1950-51, resident, 1954-58; Memorial Ctr NY Col, resident, 1956-57; pract, med spec surg, Okla City, OK, 1959-69; Nashville 1969-; Univ Okla, clin asst prof surg, 1959-69; Meharry Med Col, interim dean, 1987-; Tenn Div Am Cancer Soc, pres, 1987-88; Sch Med, dean, 1987-90; Health Services, vpres, 1988-90; Drew Meharry & Morehouse Consortium Cancer Ctr, dir, 1990-96, assoc prof; Meharry Med Col, vice chair, surg dept, 1969-73; Sch Med, prof, chmn, surg dept, 1973-87; Sch Med, assoc dean, 1974-81. **Orgs:** Nat Cancer Inst Res Fel, 1953-54; Am Cancer Soc Clin Fel, 1958-59; bd dir, Tenn Div Am Cancer Soc; fel, Am Col Surgeons; fel, Southeastern Surgical Cong; Nashville Acad Med; Tenn Med Asn; Nat Med Asn; Soc Surgical Oncologists; Okla Surgical Asn; Okla City Surgical Asn; Comn Cancer Am Col Surgeons, 1974-84; Alpha Omega Alpha; Alpha Phi Alpha; Sigma Pi Phi; Am Asn Cancer Educ. **Honors/Awds:** St. George Award, 1985; Distinguished Prof Surgery Emer, 1990; Louis JBernard Neighbors Life Award, 1992; Humanitarian Award, Nat Am Cancer Soc,1993; Margaret Hay Edwards Achievement Medal, Am Asn Cancer Educ, 1996. **Military Serv:** AUS, first lt, 1951-53. **Home Addr:** 156 Queens Lane, Nashville, TN 37218. *

BERNARD, MICHELLE DENISE
Lawyer. **Personal:** Born Jul 30, 1963, Washington, DC; daughter of Milton D and Nesta Hyacinth Grant; married Joe Johns; children: Logan Christopher & Avery. **Educ:** Howard Univ, Wash, DC, BA, philos & polit sci, 1985; Georgetown Univ Law Ctr, Wash, DC, JD, 1988. **Career:** Wash Perito & Dubuc, Wash, DC, atty, 1988; Patton Boggs LLP, partner, currently; Independent Womens Forum, sr vpres, pres & chief exec officer, currently. **Orgs:** Am Bar Asn, 1988-; Nat Found Black Pub Adminrs, 1990-; Md Chamber Com, 1990-. **Honors/Awds:** 'Award for outstanding contribution to the Law Center Academic Program', Georgetown Univ Law Ctr, 1988. **Special Achievements:** Authored numerous articles including: Qui Tam Litigation Under the Civil and Criminal False Claims Act, Complex Crimes Journal (Annual Update of the Complex Crimes Committee of the Litigations Section of the American Bar Association) (December 1994); RICO and the "Operation Management" Test: The Potential Chilling Effect on Criminal Prosecutions , 28 U. Rich. L. Rev. 669 (May 1994) (co-author, Ira H. Raphaelson); Financial Institution Fraud: Congress Still Struggles to Respond Consistently , 2 Bank Fraud (ABA White Collar Crime Committee, Section of Criminal Justice) (Summer-Fall 1993) (co-author, Eva Marie Shivers); and Maryland Environmental Law, Federal Publications (1990 & Supp 1991) (contributing author).; featured in several publications, including: Fast Company magazine, The Legal Times, The New York Daily News, The Washington Business Journal, The Washington City Paper, The Washington Lawyer, The Washington Post, The Washington Post Sunday Magazine, and The Washington Times and also featured in the Observer and the Gleaner, two of Jamaica 's leading national newspapers; television and radio appearances include America's Black Forum, BBC Radio, CNBC's The Dennis Miller Show, C-SPAN's Washington Journal, Court TV's Catherine Crier Live, Good Morning Jamaica, MSNBC, PBS's Evening Exchange and To the Contrary, NPR's Tavis Smiley Show and KLAS FM 89 (Jamaica). **Business Addr:** President, Chief Executive Officer, Independent Women, 1726 M St NW 10th Fl, Washington, DC 20036, **Business Phone:** (202)419-1820.

BERNARD, NESTA HYACINTH
College administrator. **Personal:** Daughter of Charles Reginald Grant and Edith Eliza Henry Grant; married Milton Desmond Bernard, Dec 22, 1962; children: Michelle, Nicole, Andrea & Desmond. **Educ:** Howard Univ, Wash, DC, BA, 1975; Univ Md, Col Park, MD, MS, 1977. **Career:** United Planning Orgn, chief new progs br; Howard Univ, Wash, DC, asst vpres; Howard Univ, Wash, assoc vpres univ advan, currently. **Orgs:** Nat Asn Fundraising Execs, 1983-; Alpha Kappa Alpha Sorority; Girlfriends; Links Inc. **Honors/Awds:** Distinguished Service Award, United Planning Org, 1977-79; Distinguished Service in the field of Development, Howard Univ, 1983; Distinguished Service Award, Nat Asn Blacks Higher Educ, 1990. **Business Addr:** Associate Vice President for University Advancement, Howard University, 2400 6th St NW, Washington, DC 20059, **Business Phone:** (202)238-2430.

BERNARD, NICOLE A.
Vice president (organization). **Educ:** Georgetown Univ, Law Ctr. **Career:** Pvt Prat, Law firm; Uptown& MCA Records, sr atty; Apollo Theater Found Inc, sr vpres, bus develop, currently. **Orgs:** Bd mem, Apollo Theater Found. **Business Addr:** Senior Vice President Business Development, Apollo Theater Found Inc, 253 West 125th St, 7th Ave & 8th Ave, New York, NY 10027, **Business Phone:** (212)531-5300.

BERNARD, PAUL
State government official. **Career:** City Detroit, dir planning & develop, 1998-02; State Mich, dir econ develop, currently. **Business Phone:** (313)224-6380.*

BERNARD, SHARON ELAINE
Banker, vice president (organization). **Personal:** Born Apr 19, 1943, Detroit, MI; daughter of John and Dorothea; children: Cylenthia, Sharon Gayle. **Educ:** Univ Ariz Sch Law, BSL, JD, 1969. **Career:** Banker (retired); Self-employed, attorney, 1970-74; Michigan Nat Bank, vice chair, exec vpres, 1975; Detroit Police Dept, police comnr, 1979-84. **Orgs:** Kappa Beta Pi Legal Sorority, 1968-, Women's Econ Club, 1975-; chairperson, C Trust Fund, 1982-88, Detroit Urban League Bd, 1984-89; dir, Nat Comt, Prev Child Abuse Bd, 1984-; pres, Neighborhood Serv Orgn Bd, 1987-; dir, vice chair, Ennis Ctr C Bd, 1987-; dir, United Way, SE Mich Bd, 1988-; dir, vice chair, United Community Serv Bd, 1989-; Mich Family Planning Adv Bd, 1990-. **Honors/Awds:** Minority Achiever Indust Award, YMCA, 1980; Spirit Detroit, City Coun Detroit 1984; Humanitarian of the Year, Optimist Youth Found, 1986; Outstanding Vol, Mich Nat Bank, 1987; Kool Achiever Award Nominee, Brown & Williamson, 1988; Mich 150 First Lady Award, State Mich, 1988; First Black Female Law Grad Award, Black Law Stud Asn, Univ Ark, 1989; Outstanding Leadership Award, Detroit Urban League, 1989; Vol Serv Award, Cent Region, Nat Urban League, 1990. *

BERNOUDY, MONIQUE ROCHELLE
Educator, athletic director. **Personal:** Born May 18, 1960, Detroit, MI; daughter of Benjamin Joseph and Cynthia. **Educ:** Univ Mich; Spel man Col, BA, 1983; Northern Ill Univ, MS, Educ, 1992, Ed-D,higher educ admin, currently. **Career:** Northern Ill Univ, asst dir, admin asst, 1984-86, Col Bus, acad counr, 1987-92, Student Athlete Support Serv, assoc athlete dir, currently; Valparaiso Univ, Student Affairs, dir multicultural prog. **Orgs:** Adv Coun Multiracial Concerns, 1992-; Campus Parking Comn, 1992-94; Coord Comn, Campus Diversity, 1992-; coord comn, Heritage Festival, 1992-; Intercultural Studies Comn, 1992-; adv comn, Knight Found, 1992-; planning comn, Martin Luther King Day Observance, 1992-; Porter County Comn Corrections Comn, 1992-; Town & Gown Comn, 1992-94; alumni bd, Valparaiso Univ, 1993-; Ind Coalition Blacks Higher Educ, 1993-; alumni bd-,Multiracial Sub-Comn, 1993-, guild, 1994-; co-chair, West Side High Sch Partnership Coord Comn; William Rand lph Hearst Scholar Comn, 1994-; co-chair, Campus Coord Comn, Sexual Harassment & Assault, 1994; develop comn, Diversity Plan, 1994; Judiciary Bd Hearing Panel, 1994; Racial Harassment Advocate, 1994-; stud senate, Intercultural Comn, 1994-; Week Challenge Coord Comn, 1994; evaluator, Goshen Col, Lilly Found Grant, 1994-95; Mid-Am Asn Educ Opportunity Prog Personnel, 1994-. **Special Achievements:** Given several presentations including: Physical Plant Employees Workshop, Racism in the Workplace, 1993; Athletic Directors Consortium Presentation, Achieving Diversity, 1994; Urban Sch Conf, Confronting Racist Attitudes, 1994. **Home Addr:** 3900 W 95th Suite 304, Evergreen Park, IL 60805-1917. **Business Addr:** Associate Athletic Director, Northern Illinois University, Students Athlets Sports Services, De-Kalb, IL 46383, **Business Phone:** (815)753-9182.

BERNSTEIN, MARGARET ESTHER
Newspaper editor. **Personal:** Born Nov 23, 1959, Los Angeles, CA; daughter of Morris and Alice Collum; married C Randolph Keller, Feb 16, 1991. **Educ:** Univ Southern Calif, BA, print jour, 1993. **Career:** Wave Newspapers, Los Angeles, CA, staff writer, 1981-84; Herald-Dispatch, Huntington, WV, feature writer, 1984-87; Tucson Citizen, AR, asst city ed, 1987-89; Plain Dealer, Cleveland, OH, feature writer/columnist, 1989-92, ed, women's sect, 1992-; feature writer, currently. **Orgs:** Delta Sigma Theta Sorority, 1981-; bd mem, Black Journalists Asn Southern Calif, 1982-84; founder/pres, Tri-State Black Media Asn, 1986-87; comt chair, Cleveland Chapter, Nat Asn Black Journalists, 1989-; Cath Big Sisters Cleveland, 1989-. **Honors/Awds:** Project Editor for "Tucson's Tapestry of Cultures," a 1988-89 newspaper series that received: Sweepstakes Award & 1st Place for In Depth News, Arizona Asniated Press, and 3rd Place, Staff Enterprise Award, Best of Gannett Competition; First Place, Ohio Excellence in Journalism Awards, Column-writing, 1992; Best in Media Award, Cleveland Services for Independent Living, 1992; Nat Big Sister of the Year, Big Brothers Big Sisters of Am, 2000. **Business Addr:** Feature Writer, The Plain Dealer, 1801 Super Ave, Cleveland, OH 44114-2198, **Business Phone:** (216)999-4876.

BERNSTINE, DR. DANIEL O.
President (organization), lawyer, educator. **Personal:** Born Sep 7, 1947, Berkeley, CA; son of Annias and Emma; married Nancy Jean Tyler, Jul 27, 1971 (divorced 1986); children: Quincy & Justin. **Educ:** Univ Calif, Berkeley, CA, BA, polit sci, 1969; Northwestern Univ Sch Law, JD, 1972; Univ Wis, Law Sch, L.L.M, 1975. **Career:** US Dept Labor, staff atty, 1972-73; Univ WI Law Sch, teaching fel, 1974-75; Howard Univ Law Sch, asst prof, 1975-78; Howard Univ, asst vpres,legal affairs, 1984-87, gen counsel, 1987-90, interim law sch dean, 1988-90; Univ WI Law Sch, prof, 1978-97, dean, 1990-97; Portland State Univ, pres, 1997-2007; Pres & CEO, Law Sch Admis Coun, currently. **Honors/Awds:** Sr ed, Clearinghouse Review, Northwestern Univ Sch Law, 1971-72; prof law,Fac Law Pontificial Catholic Univ Peru, Lima, Peru, 1996; fel, Wis Law Found, 2002; DHL, Nizhny Novgorod Linguistic Univ, Nizhny, Novgorod,Russia, 2004; Inter Nat Citizen Award, Oregon Consular Corps, 2004. **Special Achievements:** Various publications. **Business Addr:** President, Chief Executive Officer, Law School Admissions Council, PO Box 8512, Newtown, PA 18940.

BERNSTINE, RODERICK EARL
Football player. **Personal:** Born Feb 8, 1965, Fairfield, CA; married Stephanie Kay Smith, Feb 9, 1991; children: Payton Chaneln & Roderick Earl Jr. **Educ:** Tex A&M Univ. **Career:** Football player (retired); San Diego Chargers, tight end, 1987-92; Denver Broncos, 1993-95.

BERRY, ARCHIE PAUL
Executive. **Personal:** Born Nov 2, 1935, Akron, OH; married Sheila Yvonne Robinson; children: Troy Paul, Trent Anthony. **Educ:** Univ Akron, BSEE, 1963; Ky State Univ, MBA, 1979. **Career:** Akron Standard Mold, elec engr, 1963-64; IBM, systs engr, 1964-65, mkt rep, 1965-69, instr exec educ, 1969-71, instr mgr, 1971, mgr info serv, 1971-73, mgr comput serv, 1973-76, mgr, 1976-77, mgr castings & spl prods, 1977-79; Babcock & Wilcox, mgr prod educ. **Orgs:** Vpres bus & finance, Alpha Phi Alpha Homes; NAACP; Urban League; Alpha Phi Alpha; vis prof, Urban League BEEP Prog; trustee, Akron Regional Develop Bd. **Honors/Awds:** Four 100 Percent Sales Club Award, IBM, 1966-69; Golden Circle Sales Award, IBM, 1968; Man of Year, Alpha, 1976. **Military Serv:** USAF, 1954-57. **Business Addr:** Manager of Product Education & Training, Babcock & Wilcox, 20 S Van Buren Ave, Barberton, OH 44203.*

BERRY, BENJAMIN DONALDSON
School administrator, educator. **Personal:** Born Dec 22, 1939, Washington, DC; son of Benjamin D Berry Sr and Otis Holley Berry; married Linda Baker; children: Richard, Kathleen, Thena & Akuba. **Educ:** Morehouse Col, BA, 1962; Harvard Divinity Sch, STB, 1966; Case-Western Res Univ, PhD, 1977. **Career:** Educator (retired); Plymouth UCC, pastor, 1966-68; Tampa Inner City Parish, dir, 1968-70; Univ S Fla, Afro-Am Studies, dir, 1969-70; Heidelberg Col, Am Studies, asst prof, 1970-74; Col Wooster, Black Studies, dir, 1974-78; Skidmore Col, Minority Affairs, dir, 1978-84; Prairie View A&M Univ, Benjamin Banneker Honors Col, prof hist; Ball Dupont Vis Scholar Grant; Va Wesleyan community, prof, 1992-06, dir Am Studies. **Orgs:** Bd dir, Nat Am Studies Fac, 1974-78; Bd Educ, 1981; consult, Berry Assocs; pres, Am Asn Univ Prof; Gen Studies Rev Comt; chair & fac rep, Community Arbitration Bd. **Honors/Awds:** Merrill Scholar, Morehouse Col, 1961; Rockefeller Fel, Harvard Divinity, 1962-66; Danforth Assoc, Heidelberg Col, 1972; Mellon Vis Scholar, Skidmore Col, 1978; Morehouse Col, Phi Beta Kappa, 1987, Jesse Ball du Pont, Vis Scholar, 1992. **Home Addr:** Nashville, TN 37201. *

BERRY, BERTAND DEMOND
Football player. **Personal:** Born Aug 15, 1975, Houston, TX. **Educ:** Univ Notre Dame. **Career:** Indianapolis Colts, linebacker, 1997-99; Edmonton Eskimos, 2000; Denver Broncos, 2001-03, Ariz Cardinals, defensive end, 2004-. **Honors/Awds:** Pro Bowl, 2005. **Business Phone:** (602)379-0101.*

BERRY, BILL
Basketball coach. **Personal:** Married Clarice; children: Pam. **Educ:** Mich State Univ, BA, MA, phys educ, 1969. **Career:** Highlands High Sch, Sacramento, 1966-69; MI State Univ, asst coach, 1969, 1977-79; Cosumnes River Junior Col, head coach, 1970-72; Univ Calif, Berkeley, asst coach, 1972-77; San Jose State Univ, head coach, 1979-89; Sacramento Kings, asst coach, scout, 1989-91; Houston Rockets, scout, 1991-92, asst coach, 1994-95; Chicago Bulls, asst coach, 1998-01, coach, 2001-02, dir oper; Washington Wizards, asst coach, 2006-. **Honors/Awds:** Big Ten Champions, Michigan State Spartans, twice; NCAA Champions, MI State Spartans, 1979. **Special Achievements:** His 142 wins marked the second-highest win total for any coach in school history. **Business Phone:** (202)661-5000.*

BERRY, CHARLES EDWARD ANDERSON. **See BERRY, CHUCK.**

BERRY, CHARLES F, JR.
Auditor. **Personal:** Born May 15, 1964, Detroit, MI; son of Charles F Sr and Edna J Berry; married D Lynn, May 30, 1992. **Educ:** Univ Mich, Ann Arbor, bachelors, 1987. **Career:** Citizens Trust Bank & Trust, bank teller, 1986-87; Plante & Moran CPA's, auditor, beginning 1987; Dutch Ventures Ltd, auditor, currently.

Orgs: Toastmasters Int, pres, 1991-93; Volunteer Income Tax Assistance, tax preparer, 1987-92; Mich Asn Certified Pub Accts, 1987-; Nat Asn Black Accts, 1987-; Am Inst Certified Pub Accts, 1988-; United Way Health & Human Servs Allocation Comt, 1994-. **Honors/Awds:** Detroit Chamber Com, Leadership Detroit Grad, 1994. **Home Addr:** 17579 Ransgate Dr, Lathrup Village, MI 48076. **Business Phone:** (313)123-4567.

BERRY, CHUCK (CHARLES EDWARD ANDERSON BERRY)
Singer, composer, songwriter. **Personal:** Born Oct 18, 1926, St Louis, MO; son of Henry William and Martha Bell Banks; married Themetta (Toddy) Suggs, Oct 28, 1948; children: 4. **Career:** Sir Johns Trio, guitarist, 1952; solo rec artist, 1955-; Songs & Compositions: "Maybellene", 1955; "Roll Over Beethoven", 1956; "Too Much Monkey Bus/Brown Eyed Handsome Man", 1956; "Sch Day (Ring Ring Goes the Bell)", 1957; "Rock & Roll Music", composer, 1957; "Sweet Little Sixteen", composer, 1958; "Johnny B Goode/Around & Around", composer, 1958; Caraol, 1958; "Little Queenie/Almost Grown", 1959; "Nadine", 1964; "No Particular Place to Go", 1964; "Memphis/Back in the USA", composer, 1967; "My Ding-a-Ling", 1972; "Sweet Little Rock & Roller", composer, 1981; "My Ding A Ling", singer, 1982; Chuck Berry Hail! Hail! Rock n Roll, producer, 1987; "Run Rudoph Run", Home Alone, singer, 1990; "The Promised Land, writer, 1997; "You Never Can Tell", writer, 1998; "Surfin USA", writer, 1998; "No particular place to go", composer, 2002; Unaccompanied Minors, 2006; Elvis Presley: Love Me Tender, 2006; Aloha from Sweden, 2006; "The Sopranos", 2006; Camping, 2006; Cars, 2006; The Shaggy Dog, 2006; The Wendell Baker Story, 2005; Ganes, 2007; Yhden tahden hotelli, 2007; Albums: Rock Rock Rock, 1957; After School Session, 1958; Berry Is On Top, 1959; Rockin At The Hops, 1960; New Juke-Box Hits, 1961; Chuck Berry Twist, 1962; Chuck Berry On Stage, 1963; St. Louis To Liverpool, 1964; Fresh Berrys, 1965; Chuck Berry In London, 1965; Live At The Fillmore Auditorium, 1967; Chuck Berry In Memphis, 1967; Chuck Berrys Golden Hits, 1967; Chuck Berrys Golden Decade, 1967; From St. Louie To Frisco, 1968; Concerto In B. Goode, 1969; Back Home, 1970; San Francisco Dues, 1971; The London Chuck Berry Sessions, 1972; St. Louie To Frisco To Memphis, 1972; Johnny B. Goode, 1972; Sweet Little Rock And Roller, 1973; Wild Berrys, 1974; Flashback, 1974; Chuck And His Friends, 1974; Alive And Rockin, 1981; The Great Twenty-Eight, 1982; Hail Hail Rock N Roll, 1987; On The Blues Side, 1994; Roll Over Beethoven, 1996; Let It Rock, 1996; Guitar Legends, 1997; Blast From The Past, 2001. **Honors/Awds:** Triple Award, Billboard Mag, 1955; Best R & B Singer, Blues Unlimited, 1973; Nat Music Award, Am Music Conf, 1976; Grammy Award for Lifetime Achievement, 1984; Nashville Songwriters Asn Int Hall of Fame, 1982; Rock& Roll Hall of Fame, 1986; Guitar Player Mag, 1987; Hollywood Walk of Fame, 1987; Star, Hollywood Blvd Calif, 1987; Honored with a Star, Delmar Blvd, 1989; Icon Award, BMI, 2002. **Special Achievements:** First singer/songwriter of 1955; First guitarist/singer to get on Billboard charts; Released his autobiography in 1987. **Business Phone:** (212)586-5100.

BERRY, ERIC
Administrator. **Personal:** Born Nov 16, 1952, Salem, NJ; son of Daisy and Rev Adolphus (deceased); divorced; children: Erin. **Educ:** Cumberland County Col, AA; Glassboro State Col/Rowan Univ, BA, 1976; Rutgers Univ. **Career:** Boy Scout Am, paid prof scout, 1973-76; Asgrow Seed Com, Nat acct consult, 1976-88; Food Network Sears, regional mgr, 1988-90; Retebtion Syst/Workforce, radio vpres mkt, 1990-93; Shadow Broadcasting Serv, gen sales mgr, 1993-96; TBG, mkt, commun, contract consult, 1996-98; Tri-county Action Agency, dir fund develop, 1998-99; Township Fairfield, bus admin, currently. **Orgs:** Millennium Comn; Am Soc Pub Admin. **Business Addr:** Business Administrator, Fairfield Township, Fairton Gouldtown Rd, PO Box 240, Fairton, NJ 08320, **Business Phone:** (856)451-9284.*

BERRY, FREDRICK JOSEPH
Educator. **Personal:** Born May 29, 1940, Jacksonville, IL; married Quereda Ann Harris; children: Anthony & Frederick Jr. **Educ:** Roosevelt Univ, attended 1961; Southern Ill Univ, BMus, 1962, MMus, 1964; Stanford Univ, attended 1969. **Career:** Southern Ill Univ, Lab Sch, super music, 1964; Chicago Pub Sch Syst, instr, 1964-66; Stanford Univ, asst dir bands, 1966-69, Jazz Ensembles, dir, 1989-, Jazz Studies, lectr, currently; Col San Mateo, dir jazz ensembles, 1972-88, dir jazz prog; Nueva Learning Ctr, Hillsborough, CA, brass specialist, 1984-94. **Orgs:** Am Fed Musicians, 1956-; San Fran 49ers Band, 1970-; Am Fed Teachers, 1970-; vpres, Am Fed Music Local 6 Credit Union, 1973; Calif Teachers Asn, 1975-85; pres, Berry Enterprises & Music Serv, 1980-; Calif Music Educ Asn, 1980-. **Honors/Awds:** Black Filmmakers Hall of Fame, 1978-93; Golden Gate Theatre Orchestra, 1982-90; Musical Director Black Film Makers Hall of Fame, 1983; Outstanding Mentor to Black Students, Stanford Univ, 2000. **Business Addr:** Director, Stanford University, Department Music, 541 Lasuen Mall, Stanford, CA 94305-3076, **Business Phone:** (650)723-3811.

BERRY, GEMERAL E., JR.
Publisher, educator. **Personal:** Born Aug 9, 1948, San Antonio, TX; son of Leotha O Berry Sr and Gemeral E; married Elaine Berry, Dec 29, 1973; children: Gemeral III. **Educ:** Univ N Tex, BA, 1974. **Career:** Our Tex Mag, publ, 1990-; Univ North Tex, adj prof jour, 1996. **Orgs:** Dallas Black Chamber Com; Acres Home Citizens Chamber of Com; Ft Worth Metropolitan Chamber; Midland Black Chamber of Entreprenuers, Midland, DFW/ABC Journalists; Dallas Ft Worth/Asn Black Journalists. **Honors/Awds:** Press Club Dallas, Katie, Jour Excellence, 1993, Cert of Excellence, 1996; Outstanding Area Journalist, Univ N Tex, 1995; Torchbearer, Tex Nat Asn Advan Colored People, 1996; DFW/ABC Jour Excellence, 1996; Best Practs Award, NABJ, 2004; MA'AT Awards, NABJ, 2005. **Special Achievements:** Cert of Participation, Howard Univ, 1990. **Military Serv:** USAF, sergeant, 1966-70. **Business Addr:** Publisher, Our Texas Mag, 103 N Willomet Ave, PO Box 4463, Dallas, TX 75208, **Business Phone:** (214)946-5315.*

BERRY, DR. GORDON L
Educator, lecturer, writer. **Personal:** Son of Marcus and Gertrude; married G Juanita Berry; children: Gordon Jr, Steven & Cheryl. **Educ:** Central State Univ, BS, 1955; Univ Wis, MS, 1961; Marquette Univ, EdD, coun psychol, 1969. **Career:** Milwaukee Tech Col, coun psychologist; Marquette Univ, asst to acad vpres; Univ Calif, Los Angeles, asst dean, 1970-76, prof, prof emer, currently; TV progs: Captain Kangaroo Fraggle Rock, tech adv; Ghostwriter; Zoobilee Zoo, tech adv; Name your Adventure, tech adv; Barney & Friends, tech adv; Space Acad, tech adv; The Leopard Son, tech adv; Happily Ever After Fairy Tales for Every Child, tech adv; Fat Albert & The Cosby Kids, tech adv; Secrets of Isis, tech adv; Shazam, tech adv; NBC, KCET, Nickelodeon, consult; CBS network, sr tech adv, currrently. **Orgs:** Nat Asn Sch Psychologists, 1970-; Phi Delta Kappa; bd, Los Angeles Film Teachers Asn; Am Psychol Asn; Am Psychol Soc; Acad TV, Arts & Sci Found. **Honors/Awds:** Ralph Metcalfe Chair Lectr; cert hon, Acad TV, Arts & Sci. **Military Serv:** AUS, capt, 1955-57. **Business Addr:** Professor Emeritus, University California Los Angeles, 405 Hilgard Ave, Los Angeles, CA 90095-1538, **Business Phone:** (310)825-8316.

BERRY, HALLE M (HANNAH LITTLE)
Actor. **Personal:** Born Aug 14, 1966, Cleveland, OH; daughter of Jerome Berry and Judith Berry; married David Justice, Jan 1, 1993 (divorced 1996); married Eric Benet, Jan 1, 2001. **Educ:** Cleveland State Univ; Cuyahoga Community Col. **Career:** TV series: Living Dolls, lead, 1988-89; Knot's Landing, guest lead, 1991; tv miniseries: Queen, 1992; Episode No 1.18, 2004; Their Eyes Were Watching God, 2005; films: Jungle Fever, 1989; Strictly Business, 1990-91; The Last Boy Scout, 1991; Boomerang, 1992; Father Hood, 1993; Program, The, 1993; The Flintstones, 1994; Losing Isaiah, 1994; Solomon & Sheba, 1995; Executive Decision, 1996; Race the Sun, 1996; BAPS, 1997; Bullworth, 1998; The Wedding, 1998; Why Do Fools Fall in Love, 1998; Introducing Dorothy Dandridge, HBO, producer, 1999; X-Men, 2000; Swordfish, 2001; Monster's Ball, 2001; Die Another Day, 2002; X-Men 2, 2003; Gothika, 2003; Catwoman, 2004; Robots, 2005; Lackawanna Blues, producer, 2005; X-Men: The Last Stand, 2006; Perfect Stranger, 2006; Revlon, model. **Orgs:** Spokesperson, Juv Diabetes Asn; spokesperson, Children Outreach. **Honors/Awds:** Miss Teen Ohio; Miss Teen All America; Runner Up to Miss USA; Golden Globe Award; Best Actress in a Television Movie, 2000; Emmy Award; SAG Award, Best Actress, 2002; Best Actress, Berlinale Int Film Festival, 2002; Academy Award, Best Actress, 2002; Essence Award, 2002; Bambi Award, 2002; Black Reel for Theatrical Best Actress, 2002; Image Award, 2002; Image Award, 2002. **Business Phone:** (310)288-4545.

BERRY, JAY
Journalist, television news anchorperson. **Personal:** Born Aug 5, 1950, Tulsa, OK; married Claudia; children: Carla Michelle, Kristen Lynette & Kayla Renee. **Educ:** Univ WY, statist; Tulsa Univ; Bishop Col. **Career:** Gulf Oil Co, 1970-73; KTUL TV, news reporter sportscaster, 1973-74; KPRC TV Houston, news reporter, sportscaster, 1974-79; WLS-TV, sportscaster 1979-82; WXYZ-TV Detroit, sports reporter, 1982-, sports program: "Action News Weekend", currently, "UPN Detroit Action News Weekend", currently, Channel 7's, "Sunday Sports Update", currently. **Orgs:** NAACP; Black Communicators; co-chair, Black United Fund. **Honors/Awds:** Best Sportscaster in Texas Asn Press, 1977; Best Feature in Texas United Press Int, 1977; Outstanding Achievement "UPI" Sports Feature MI 1984; Emmy nominee "When the Cheering Stops," 1984. **Business Addr:** Sports Anchor, WXYZ-TV, 20777 W Ten Mile Rd, Southfield, MI 48037, **Business Phone:** (313)827-9420.

BERRY, LATIN
Football player. **Personal:** Born Jan 13, 1967, Lakeview Terrace, CA. **Educ:** Univ Ore, attended 1989. **Career:** Los Angeles Rams, corner back, 1990-92; Cleveland Browns, 1991-92; Green Bay Packers. **Orgs:** Kappa Alpha Psi Fraternity. **Honors/Awds:** Multicultural Leadership Award.

BERRY, LEE ROY
Educator, lawyer. **Personal:** Born Nov 5, 1943, Lake Placid, FL; married Elizabeth Ann Hostetler; children: Joseph Jonathan, Malinda Elizabeth & Anne Hostetler. **Educ:** Eastern Mennonite Col, BA, 1966; Univ Notre Dame, MA, 1969, PhD, 1976; Ind Univ, Bloomington, Sch Law, JD, 1984. **Career:** Cleveland Pub Schs, teacher, 1966-68; Goshen Col, prof, 1969-79, leader, study serv trimester, 1979-80, Dept Hist & Polit Sci, assoc prof polit sci, 1980-; Berkey Ave Mennonite, fel; atty, currently. **Orgs:** Gen bd, Mennonite Ch; chmn, High Aim Comt; Relief & Serv Comt; Mennonite Bd Missions; Peace Sect, Mennonite Central Comt. **Honors/Awds:** John Hay Whitney Fel, 1970-71; Nat Fellowships Fund Fel, 1975-76. **Home Addr:** 19736 Riverview Dr, Goshen, IN 46526, **Home Phone:** (574)533-5821. **Business Addr:** Associate Professor of Political Science, Goshen College, Department of Political Science, WY 309 1700 S Main St, Goshen, IN 46526-4795, **Business Phone:** (574)535-7000.

BERRY, LEROY
Educator. **Personal:** Born Oct 20, 1920, Birmingham, AL; son of Lester and Lubertha Foster (deceased); married Ruth Brothers Berry, Jul 28, 1949; children: Lorenzo Armstead. **Educ:** Western Res Univ, Ohio, 1946; UCLA-USC, Calif; UCLA, Calif, BA, Sociol, 1957; Calif State Univ, MA, Elem Teaching, 1961, state credential, Elem Admin, 1962, state credential, Coun, 1976. **Career:** Dept Water & Power, elec tester, 1948-54; Los Angeles Unified Sch Dist, teacher, 1957-77, substitute prin, 1969-72, coun, 1977-80, teacher adv, 1980-82; coordr, precinct community, Tom Bradley city coun & mayoral campaigns, 1980-88; Human Rels Community, comnr, mayor, 1983. **Orgs:** Kappa Alpha Psi Fraternity; life mem, Nat Advan Asn Colored People; Urban League S Christian Lead Corp, Crenshaw Neighbors; alumni life mem, Univ Calif, 1958-; pres, Leimert Dem Club, 1958-61; assembly dist rep, Calif Dem Coun, 1964-66; southern cred chmn, Calif Dem Coun, 1964-66; vpres region II, Calif Dem Coun, 1966-68; rep, Dem Co Comn, 1967-71; rep, State Dem Comn, 1967-73; Environl Qual Bd, 1976; Black Korean Alliance, 1984; AGENDA, 1992; Communuty Coalition, 1994; CRA & La Comm Adv Comn, 1995; Congressional Community Adv Comn, 2000. **Honors/Awds:** good conduct medal, AUS. **Military Serv:** AUS, 54th Coast Artill, corporal, 1941-44; US Air Corps, radio technician, 1944-45; marksman, sharpshooter. *

BERRY, MAJOR T., JR.
Police chief, manager. **Career:** Oklahoma City Police Dept, chief; Oklahoma Off Homeland Security, asst city mgr, currently. **Orgs:** Region 8 Coun. **Business Addr:** Assistant City Manager, Okla Office of Homeland Security, PO Box 11415, Oklahoma City, OK 73136, **Business Phone:** (405)425-7296.

BERRY, DR. MARY FRANCES
Educator. **Personal:** Born Feb 17, 1938, Nashville, TN; daughter of George F and Frances Southall. **Educ:** Howard Univ, BA, 1961, MA, 1962; Univ Mich, PhD, 1966, JD, 1970. **Career:** Howard Univ, teaching fel Am hist, 1962-63; Univ Mich, teaching asst, 1965-66, from asst prof hist to assoc prof hist, 1966-70; Univ Md, assoc prof, 1969-76; Univ Colo, Afro-Am Studies, acting dir, 1970-72, dir, 1972-74, Div Behavioral Social Sci, provost, 1974, chancellor, 1976-77, prof hist, 1976-80; US Dept HEW, asst secy educ, 1977-80; US Comn Civil Rights, mem, 1980-93, chair, 1993-2004; Howard Univ, Dept Hist & Law, prof, 1980-87; Univ Pa, Geraldine R Segal prof Am Soc Thought & prof hist, 1987-; auth, currently. **Orgs:** DC Bar Asn, 1972; consult to curator educ, Nat Portrait Gallery, Smithsonian Inst; consult, Off Policy Planning, HUD; bd mem, Afro-Am Bicentennial Corp; chmn, Md Comn Afro-Am/Indian Hist Cul, 1974; exec bd mem, Orgn Am Historians, 1974-77; exec bd, Asn Study Afro-Am Life Hist, 1973-76; Am Hist Asn; Orgn Am Historians; Am Bar Asn; Nat Bar Asn; nat panel adv, Univ Mid-Am; bd trustees, Tuskegee Inst; bd dirs, DC Chap, ARC. **Honors/Awds:** Civil War Round Table Fellowship Award, 1965-66; Honarary degree, Univ Akron, 1977; Honarary degree, Benedict Col, 1979; Honarary degree, Grambling State Univ, 1979; Honarary degree, Bethune-Cookman Col, 1980; Honarary degree, Clark Col, 1980; Honarary degree, Oberlin Col, 1983; Honarary degree, Langston Univ, 1983; Honarary degree, Haverford Col, 1984; Honarary degree, Colby Col, 1986; Honarary degree, DePaul Univ, 1987; Rosa Parks Award, Southern Christian Leadership Conf; Black Achievement Award, Ebony Magazine; Woman of the Year, Ms Mag, 1986; Lamplighter Award for Civil Rights, 2001; One of the women of the century, Women's Hall of Fame; NAACP's Roy Wilkins Award; Received 32 honorary doctoral degrees. **Special Achievements:** She is one of 75 women featured in I Dream A World: Portraits of Black Women Who Changed America. Sienna College Research Institute and the Women's Hall of Fame designated her one of "America's Women of the Century. Author of Black Resistance/White Law: A History of Constitutional Racism in America, 1971, Why ERA Failed: Women's Rights & the Amending Process of the Constitution, 1986. **Home Addr:** 2110 65th Ave, Philadelphia, PA 19138, **Home Phone:** (215)548-7925. **Business Addr:** Professor, University of Pennsylvania, Department of History, College Hall 216 E, Philadelphia, PA 19104-6379, **Business Phone:** (215)898-9587.

BERRY, ONDRA LAMON
Police officer. **Personal:** Born Oct 3, 1958, Evansville, IN; son of Charles and Ethel Gibson Kuykendall; married Margo Curry, Aug 14, 1980; children: Jarel. **Educ:** Univ Evansville, Evansville, IN,

BA, Educ, 1980; Univ Nev Reno, Reno, NV, MPA, 1996; Harvard Exec Leadership Develop prog. **Career:** Police Exec Res Forum, diversity trainer; Rapport Leadership Intl, cert asst instr; consult; Reno Police Dept, Reno, NV, lt, dep chief, currently. **Orgs:** Past pres, Northern Nevada Black Cultural Awareness Soc; vchair, United Way Nevada, 1991-97; State Job Training Coun, 1989-93. **Honors/Awds:** Outstanding Law Enforcement Officer, Reno Jaycees, 1989-90. **Military Serv:** Air Nat Guard, captain, major; Achievement Medal, 1989; Air Man of Year for Nevada, 1989; Outstanding Airman of Year for United States, 1989. **Business Addr:** Deputy Chief, Reno Police Department, PO Box 1900, Reno, NV 89505.*

BERRY, PAUL LAWRENCE
Journalist. **Personal:** Born Feb 15, 1944, Detroit, MI; married Marilyn; children: Karen. **Educ:** USAF Def Info Sch, Basic Med Sch, Basic Dent Sch. **Career:** WXYZ-TV, staff rep & co-anchor, 1969-72; WMAL-TV, anchor st rep & mod, 1972-75; WMAL-TV, st rep mod & co-anchor, 1975-; Am Black Forum, panelist; Paul Berry's WA, weekend anchor & host; Paul Berry Acad Scholar Found, dir, currently; Paul L Berry & Assocs, pres, 2002; AM570 WTNT, host, currently. **Orgs:** Wash DC Mayors Ad Hock Comm Criminal Justice; DC Fed 524 Coun Except Child; Sigma Delta Chi Prof Journ Soc; bd dir, Am Digest Disease Asn; Lion Club of Wash, DC; bd dir, The Neediest Kids; bd dir, Washington Jesuit Acad; comnr, Md Pub TV; bd mem, Nat Rehab Hosp. **Honors/ Awds:** Community Service Award, 1974; Dept Comm Service Award Am Amvets, DC, 1974; Nat Cap Area Health Association Award, 1974; Community Service Award, Unit Cit, 1975; Media Award, Cap Press Club, 1975; Outstanding City Award MMEOC Asn, 1976; Broadcasters Award, Chesapeake Assoc Press, 1976; Metro Wash Mass Media Award, Am Asn, Univ Women, 1976; Community Award, Mich Chap SCLC; Comm Service Award Rap, 1976; Humanitarian Award, Nat Martin Luther King Jr Stud Leadership Conf, 1986; Generous Heart Award, Olender Found, 1989; Washingtonian of the Year, Wash Mag, 1991; Silver Circle recognition, Nat Acad TV Arts & Scis. **Special Achievements:** In November 1982, Washington Mayor Marion Barry honored Berry by declaring November 12 "Paul Berry Day in the District". On February 15, 1994, D.C. Mayor Sharon Pratt Kelly repeated the honor. **Military Serv:** USAF, staff sgt, 1961-69. *

BERRY, PHILIP ALFONSO
Executive, manager, vice president (organization). **Personal:** Born Jan 28, 1950, New York, NY; married Karen Bryan; children: Kiel, Maya. **Educ:** Manhattan Community Col, AA, 1971; Queens Col City Univ New York, BA, 1973; Columbia Univ Sch Social Work, MS, 1975; Xavier Univ, Cincinnati, MBA, 1983. **Career:** Ford Found Fellowship; Urban League Westchester, NY, dir, 1975-78; Procter & Gamble, indust rels mgr, 1978-86; Digital Equip Corp, human resources consult, 1986-; Triboro Bridge & Tunnel Authority, NY, vpres human resources, 1988-90; Colgate-Palmolive, Human Resources Int, vpres, Europe HR, vpres, 1997-01; Colgate-Palmolive, Global Employ Rels, vpres, 2001-; City Univ New York, vpres, 2007-. **Orgs:** Chair, industrial social work, Nat Asn Social Workers, 1989-; memship comt, EDGES, 1990-; NY State Chmn Asn Black Social Workers, 1975-78; founder, pres, Housing & Neighborhood Develop Inst, 1976-78; pres, The Delta Group & Berry Asn Consult, 1983-; bd mem, Cincinnati Comt Action Agency, 1985-86; dean pledges, Alpha Phi Alpha Frat Alumni Chap, 1986; Am Soc Training & Develop; World Future Soc; pres, Black Student Union Queens Col; Black Student Caucus Columbia Univ; Nat Foreign Trade Coun; Columbia Univ Alumni Bd; chair, New York City Dept Educ Human Resources Adv Panel, 2004-; Bd Standing Comt Fiscal Affairs; Standing Comt Fac, Staff & Admin. **Honors/Awds:** Governor's Award for Community Distinction, 2004. **Special Achievements:** Mayor's Proclamation "Philip Berry Day" Mt Vernon NY 1978; one of New York's 100 most influential Black business executives, Crain's New York Business , 2003. **Business Addr:** Vice President, Colgate Palmolive Corporation, Global Employee Relations, 300 Park Ave, New York, NY 10022, **Business Phone:** (212)310-2947.*

BERRY, REGINALD FRANCIS
Government official. **Personal:** Born May 21, 1920, Washington, DC; son of John and Blanche; married Anna Pitts Berry, Apr 12, 1947. **Educ:** George Wash Univ, attended 1948; Howard Univ, attended 1952. **Career:** Government official (retired); Coast Guard, Dept Transp, sr investr; Civil Rights Act, 1964, Titles VI & VII, adminr; US Coast Guard, US Civil Rights officer, 1970-82. **Orgs:** Appointed Wash DC, Dioceasan Comn Racism, 1988-92; State MD, Prince George's County Central Comn, 1994-00. **Honors/ Awds:** Nominated to the Most Venerable Order of the Hospital of St John of Jerusalem, an Order of the British Crown under Warrant of Queen Elizabeth II, 1998; Twice cited by the Governor of MD for meritorious and political accomplishment to the State. **Special Achievements:** Citation from the Government of Haiti to direct and conduct a massed Am Choir in the Wash, Natl Cathedral in honor of the Consecration of Bishop James Theodore Holly; the first Episcopal african Bishop to serve the Diocese of Haiti from 1892-1911, 1975; Congratulatory message from Queen Elizabeth II in honor of our 50th wedding anniversary. **Military Serv:** AUS, sergeant, 1943-46, 10th Cavalry; 1 of 2 African Cavalry units. **Home Addr:** 912 Cox Ave, Hyattsville, MD 20783, **Home Phone:** (301)559-0830. *

BERRY, VENISE
Writer, journalist, educator. **Educ:** Univ Iowa, BA, 1977, MA, 1979; Univ Tex, PhD, 1989. **Career:** KFRD Radio, Tx, newscaster, 1979-80; Tex Southern Univ, instr, 1980-83; KCOH Radio, Tx, asst news dir, 1980-83; KTSU Radio, news dir, 1982-83; Tillotson Col, from asst prof to assoc prof, 1983-91, coun, 1986-91, dept head mass commun, 1989-91, spec asst to pres, 1990-91; KLBJ Radio, Tx, news reporter, 1983-84; KAZI Radio, news dir, 1983-86; Univ Tex, Sch Music, lectr, 1990-91; Univ Iowa, Sch Jour & Mass commun, asst prof, 1991-97, assoc prof, 1998-, int dir, 2001-02, assoc dir, 2004-, African Am Studies, assoc prof, 2006-; Auth: So Good, An African American Love Story, 1996; All of Me, A Voluptuous Tale, 2000; Colored Sugar Water, 2002; co-auth: The 50 Most Influential Black Films, Citadel, 2001; Mediated Messages & African-American Culture: Contemporary Issues, Sage, 1996; co-ed: Reflections on a Higher Power: Exceptional Writers Share Their Experience with Faith, Spirituality & Divine Intervention. **Orgs:** Asn Educ Jour & Mass Commun; Int Asn Study Popular Music; Nat Asn Black Journalists; Kappa Tau Alpha, Jour Hon Soc; Delta Sigma Theta, Pub Serv Sorority. **Honors/Awds:** Juneteenth Community Service Award, 1988; President's Outstanding Achievement Award, Huston-Tillotson Col, 1991; Meyers Center Award, Study Human Rights N Am, 1997; Honor Book Award, Black Caucus Am Libr Asn, 2001; Iowa Author Award, Pub Libr Found; Creative Contribution to Literature, Zora Neale Hurston Society, 2003. **Home Addr:** 3432 10th St, PO Box 5411, Coralville, IA 52241-1200, **Home Phone:** (319)377-7557. **Business Phone:** (319)335-3361.

BERRYMAN, MATILENE S.
Lawyer. **Personal:** Born in Prince Edward County, VA; divorced; children: D'Michele, Sherrill Diane Miller. **Educ:** Bluefield State Univ, WVa; Howard Univ, 1946; Pa State, Univ Calif Los Angeles, George Wash, 1965; Am Univ, Wash, DC, BMath, 1957; Howard Univ, Wash, DC, JD, 1973; Univ Rhode Island, MS, marine affairs, 1979. **Career:** US Naval Oceanographic Off, Suitland, phys oceanog, 1955-63, oceanog instr, 1963-68; Exec Off Pres & Defense Doc Ctr, Alexandria, VA, phys sci admin, 1968-70; Consortium DC, dir marine sci, 1973-76; Univ DC, prof marine sci, 1970; Wash Tech Inst, prof marine sci & oceanog; pvt prac, atty, currently. **Orgs:** Chmn, Environ Sci Dept, Univ DC, 1971-78; financial secy, Nat Asn Black Women Atty, 1975-; vis prof, Purdue Univ; Pa State Bar, 1974-; DC Bar, 1975-; trustee, Shiloh Baptist Church, Wash, DC; bd dir, DC Ment Health. **Honors/ Awds:** Nominated vice pres, Marine Tech Soc, 1978-79; Outstanding Service to Marine Science & Law, Nat Asn Black Women Atty, 1978. **Business Addr:** Professor of Marine Science & Oceanography, Washington Technical Institute, Washington, DC.*

BERTELSEN, PHIL
Writer, movie director, movie producer. **Personal:** Born in New Jersey. **Educ:** Rutgers Univ, BA, polit sci; NY Univ, MFA. **Career:** WYBE-TV, pub affairs TV, producer & dir; Films: Around the Time, 1997; The Sunshine, 2000; Outside Looking In: Transracial Adoption in America, 2001; Chisholm '72: Unbought & Unbossed, 2004; Rock the Paint, 2005; Beyond the Steps: Alvin Ailey American Dance, 2006. **Orgs:** Spike Lee Fel, NY Univ. **Honors/Awds:** Student Academy Award, NY Univ; Wasserman Award, NY Univ; Best Documentary; Best Short Documentary, Woodstock Film Festival; Jury Prize, Newport Int Film Festival; Roger Award, Avignon Film Festival; Director's Guild East Award; Creative Promise Award, Tribeca Film Festival, 2004. **Special Achievements:** The Sunshine, Best Doc, NY & Palm Springs Intl Short Film Festivals, Best Short Doc, Woodstock Film Festivals. **Business Addr:** Producer & Director, Writer, 160 W 106th St Apt 2c, New York, NY 10025.

BESHAH, GUENET
Lawyer. **Career:** Capital One, atty & assoc gen coun, currently. **Orgs:** Old Dominion Bar asn; Va State Bar. **Business Addr:** Attorney, Associate General Counsel, Capital One, Corporate Counsel Office, 15000 Capital One Dr, Richmond, VA 23238, **Business Phone:** (804)284-2721.

BESSENT, YVETTE E.
Gynecologist. **Educ:** Univ NC, Chapel Hill, MD; FACOG. **Career:** Univ Cincinnati, residency; Northcross Obstet & Gynec, Obstetrician & Gynecologist, 2001-. **Home Phone:** (704)948-9537. *

BESSON, PAUL SMITH
Lawyer. **Personal:** Born May 11, 1953, New York, NY; son of Frederick A and Patricia Smith. **Educ:** Cornell Univ, BS, labor rels, 1975, MBA, mkt/finance, 1976; Northwestern Univ, JD, 1980; Georgetown Univ Law Ctr, LLM, 1995. **Career:** Cummins Engine Co, mkt planning analyst, 1976-77; Jewel Companies, Inc, labor rels coun, 1980-82, mgr personnel & labor rels, 1982-83; NBC Inc, mgr labor rels, 1984-88, dir employee rels, 1988-98, Talent Negotiations & Labor Rels dir; Am Com Lines, LLC, sr vice pres human resources 1998, corp serv. **Orgs:** Ill, NY, & DC Bar Asn; bd dir, Cornell Club Asn 1982; pres, Cornell Black Alumni Asn Chicago, 1982-83; Am Arbitration Asn Panel Com Arbitrations; hearing officer, Civil Serv Commn IL; bd dir, ABE Credit Union; pres, Cornell Black Alumni Asn, Wash, DC, 1989-91; Capital Press Club; Wash Asn Black Journalists; mediator, US Dist Court, Dist Columbia; adv coun, GE African Am Forum; bd dir, Louisville Urban League; bd dir, March Dimes. **Honors/Awds:** Leadership Louisville, Class of 2000; Bingham Leadership Fel, 2001. **Special Achievements:** Contributing writer Black Enterprise Mag.

BEST, GLENN
Administrator. **Career:** Martin Luther King Jr Nat Mem Proj Found, proj coordr, 2001. **Business Addr:** Project Coordinator, Martin Luther King Jr National Memorial Project Foundation, 401 F St NW Suite 324, Washington, DC 20001, **Business Phone:** (202)737-5420.*

BEST, JENNINGS H
Lawyer. **Personal:** Born Aug 5, 1925, Jacksonville, FL; married Elizabeth Blake; children: Valorie. **Educ:** Lincoln Univ, Jefferson City, Mo, pre-law; Fla A&M Univ, Col Law, JD, 1956. **Career:** Pvt pract, lawyer. **Orgs:** DW Perkins Bar Asn; Nat Bar Asn; Phi Beta Sigma Fraternity; New Bethlehem Missionary Baptist Church; Phi Beta Sigma Fraternity; Fla Chap Nat Bar Asn; Grand Lodge. **Military Serv:** AUS, WW secound, 1944-46; Korean War, 1950-52. **Home Addr:** 2078 W 14th St, Jacksonville, FL 32209, **Home Phone:** (904)353-5017. *

BEST, JOHN T.
Counselor, federal government official, manager. **Personal:** Born Jan 24, 1936, Philadelphia, PA; son of John Thomas Best and Mary Elizabeth Armwood; married Mary Anna Grady; children: Toussaint, Johanna, Johnathan, Kevin, Deborah Stone-Patterson & LydiaTimmons. **Educ:** Henry George Sch Social Sci, New York, cert, 1972; La Salle Univ Inst,acct, certs, 1972; Community Col Philadelphia, AGS, 1972; Rutgers Univ, BA, 1974; Univ Pa, MCP, 1976; attended Philadelphia Govt Training Inst, 1972; Rutgers Univ, labor mgt, 1980; Am Mgt Asn, mgt studies, 1984; Franklin Inst, comput training, 1984; Morris Arboretum, landscape design cert, 1987; Rosemont Col, Holistic Health, cert, 1989. **Career:** City planner (retired); Best Assocs, urban planner begin, 1976; City Philadelphia, City Planner II, 1980-81; retired USPS, supvr, 1981; Radio, communicator, 1996. **Orgs:** Am Planning Asn, 1976-90; Soc Advan Mgt, 1981-90; Am Mgt Asn, 1981-91; comm mem, United Way, 1981-91; Dobbins Alumni Asn, 1990-; dist dir, Am Asn Retired Persons AARP, 1994-98; Am Legion Post 292; 101st Airborne Asn; Veteran Foreign Wars; NAACP; Fel Philaxis Soc; Prince Hall Affiliation, Lemuel Googins No 129 Philadelphia PA; Community Col Philadelphia Alumni Asn; Rutgers Univ, African Am Alumni Asn; Nat Caucus & Ctr Black Aged Inc; Philadelphia Sr Ctr; Nat Asn Retired Fed Employees. **Honors/ Awds:** Certificate of Award, USPO GPO Philadelphia PA, 1972-75; Certificate of Appreciation, Motivation Coun Philadelphia Prisons Philadelphia PA, 1976; Certificate of Recognition, Basic Reading Tutor Ctr Literacy Philadelphia, 1978; Certificate of Appreciation, Probation Counr Camden Co NJ, 1979; Certificate of Appreciation, United Way Southeastern Pennsylvania, 1988; Commendation, Sales Promotion & Merchandising Specialist, USPS, 1990; Certificate of Appreciation, AARP, 1988; Philadelphia Processing & Distribution Ctr, USPS, certificate of appreciation; Certificate of Appreciation, Willow Grove Air Station USAF, 1994; Cold War Recognition Certificate, Dept of Defense, 2000. **Military Serv:** AUS Airborne; Parachutists Badge, Nat Defense Medal 1954-57.

BEST, SHEILA DIANE
Physician. **Personal:** Born Feb 23, 1956, Sacramento, CA; daughter of Eddie Best and Elizabeth Best. **Educ:** Univ Calif, Riverside, BA, Biol, 1978; Howard Univ Col Med, MD, 1982. **Career:** Howard Univ Hosp, intern, 1982-83, resident, 1983-85; Independent Contractor, emergency med physician, 1985-; Extended Care Facil Morrow County Hosp, emergency med physician, currently; pvt pract, currently. **Orgs:** Emergency med physician, Med Residents Asn, 1984-85, Am Col Emergency, Physicians, 1985-, Action Alliance Black Managers, 1986-. **Business Addr:** Emergency medical physician, Extended Care Facility Morrow County Hospital, 200 Allen Memorial Dr, Bremen, GA 30110, **Business Phone:** (770)537-5851.

BEST, TRAVIS ERIC
Basketball player. **Personal:** Born Jul 12, 1972, Springfield, MA; son of Bobbie and Leo. **Educ:** Ga Inst Tech, BA, bus mgt, 1995. **Career:** Ind Pacers, guard, 1995-2000; Chicago Bulls, guard, 2001-02; Miami Heat, guard, 2002-03; Dallas Mavericks, guard, 2003-04; NJ Nets, guard, 2004-05; Italian League Virtus Bologna; Russian League, UNICS Kazan; Polish League, Prokom Trefl Sopot, 2007-. **Special Achievements:** Films: He Got Game; first three-time recipient of the John Lahovich Award. **Business Addr:** Guard, Prokom Trefl Sopot, Armii Krakowej 137-139, 81-824 Sopot, Poland, **Business Phone:** (485)8551-6570.

BEST, REV. WILLIAM ANDREW
Clergy. **Personal:** Born Sep 17, 1949, Newburgh, NY; married Sharon Gerald; children: Cleveland, Andrew, Stephany & Shawn. **Educ:** Revelation Bible Inst, AA, cert, 1973; Mt St Mary Col, BA, 1975; Western Conn State Col, MPS, 1981. **Career:** Middletown Minority Ministerial Alliance, pres, 1984-87; Church God Christ, regional pres, 1986-91; Inner Faith Coun, vpres, 1986-87; Church

God Christ, Nat Pastor's & Elder Coun, secy, 1993-; Catskill Dist Church God Christ, 2nd Ecclesiastical Jurisdiction, dist supt, 1994-; enlarged sch dist Middle town, educr, currently. **Orgs:** Pres, Middletown State Ctr, 1985-86; Mem Kiwanis, Nat Asn Advan Colored People, 1986-87; bd mem, YMCA, 1987-; mem bd educ, Enlarged City Sch Dist Middletown, 2001-. **Honors/Awds:** Cert Honor, City Middletown, 1983; Citation State of NY Assembly, 1985. **Home Addr:** 5 Hoover Dr, Middletown, NY 10940, **Home Phone:** (845)342-4773. **Business Addr:** Pastor, St James Church of God In Christ, 137-139 Linden Ave, Middletown, NY 10940, **Business Phone:** (914)342-4773.*

BEST-WHITAKER, VAUGHN (VON BEST WHITAKER)
College administrator. **Educ:** Columbia Union Col, RNC, BS; Univ Md, MS; Univ NC, Chapel Hill, MA, PhD. **Career:** NC A&T State Univ, asst dean & assoc prof, currently, clin asst prof, currently. **Orgs:** Bd dir, Wesley Long Community Health Found. **Business Addr:** Assistant Dean & Associate Professor, Clinical Assistant Professor, North Carolina Agricultural and Technical State University, School of Nursing, 1601 E Market St Noble Hall, Greensboro, NC 27411, **Business Phone:** (336)334-7751.

BEST WHITAKER, VON. See BEST-WHITAKER, VAUGHN.

BETHA, MASON DURRELL
Rap musician, clergy. **Personal:** Born Aug 27, 1974, Jacksonville, FL; married Twyla; children: 1. **Educ:** Clark Atlanta Univ, attended; St Paul's Bible Inst, New York, doctorate theol, 2002. **Career:** Rapper, pastor & songwriter; Albums: Harlem World, 1997; Double Up, 1999; Welcome Back, 2004; singles: Feel So Good, 1997; Lookin' at Me, 1998; What You Want, 1998; Breathe, Stretch, Shake, 2004; I Wanna Go, 2004; Appears on vocals with Puff Daddy, Notorious B.I.G, Tribe Called Quest, Tina Turner, One Twelve, Tasha Holiday, Mario Winans, Brian McKnight, Mariah Carey, Jermaine Dupri, South Park, DJ Clue, others; Harlem World, The Movement, producer, 1999; Mason Betha Ministries, Atlanta, founder & pastor, currently; Saving A Nation Endangered Church Int, founder & pastor, currently. **Honors/Awds:** Source Magazine Rapper of the Year, 1997; Honorary Doctorate of Theology, St Paul's Bible Inst, New York, 2002. **Business Addr:** Pastor, S.A.N.E. CHURCH INTERNATIONAL, 225 Ottley Dr, PO Box 53159, Atlanta, GA 30324, **Business Phone:** (404)320-3204.

BETHEA, EDWIN AYERS
School administrator. **Personal:** Born May 15, 1931, Birmingham, AL; son of Marzetta Bethea and Monroe Bethea; divorced. **Educ:** Knoxville Col, BA, 1953; Howard Univ, MSW, 1962. **Career:** United Planning Orgn, comm organizer, 1966-68; Youth Enterprises Inc, exec dir, 1968-70; Volunteers Int Tech Ctr, dir/regional dir, 1970-72; GA Tech Res Inst, sr res assoc & proj dir, 1972-86, assoc dir, Off Minority Bus Develop, 1987-88, dir, 1989-; Univ Ga, Small Bus Develop Ctr; Hudson Strategic Group, partner/assoc, currently. **Orgs:** Southern Indust Coun, 1974-, GA Indust Developers Asn, 1974-; GA Tech Centennial Comm, 1986. **Honors/Awds:** Outstanding Contribution White House Conf of Small Business, 1980; Certificate of Honor Mayor of Cleveland Contrib to Small Business 1984. **Military Serv:** AUS, pfc 1953-55; Korean Medal, Overseas Tour of Duty Medal. **Home Addr:** 50 Inwood Circle NE, Atlanta, GA 30309, **Home Phone:** (404)873-2303.

BETHEA, GREGORY AUSTIN
Government official. **Personal:** Born Sep 18, 1952, Hamlet, NC; son of Thomas J and Annie Austin; married Hope Stelter Bethea, Aug 21, 1983; children: Ryan Stelter, Austin Cox. **Educ:** NC Cent Univ, Durham, BA, 1974. **Career:** Forsyth Co, Forsyth Co NC, asst to mgr, sr asst to mgr, intergovernmental rels & budget analysis, 1975-84; United Way, Forsyth Co NC, dep dir, 1984-85; City Durham, asst city mgr, 1985, interim mgr, 2001. **Honors/Awds:** Edwin McGill Award, Univ NC Inst Govt, 1980. *

BETHEA-SHIELDS, KAREN LOUISE. See SHIELDS, KAREN BETHEA.

BETHEL, DR. AMIEL W.
Educator, neurosurgeon. **Educ:** Princeton Univ, BS, biol; Univ Pa Sch Med, MD, 1991; John hopkins hospital, fel, 1997. **Career:** Univ Md Med Systs, R Adam Cowley Schock Trauma Ctr, clin dir; Univ Md Sch Med, Dept Neuro surg, clinical asst prof, currently; Greater Baltimore MedCtr, physician, currently; Union Memorial Hosp, neurosurgery prog, chief, 2004-. **Orgs:** Greater Baltimore Neurosurg Assocs. **Honors/Awds:** Patients Choice Award, 2008.

BETHEL, KATHLEEN EVONNE
Librarian. **Personal:** Born Aug 4, 1953, Washington, DC; daughter of Frederick Errington and Helen Evonne Roy. **Educ:** Elmhurst Col, Elmhurst, Ill, BA, 1975; Rosary Col, River Forest, Ill, MALS, 1977; Northwestern Univ, Evanston, Ill, MA, African hist, 1989. **Career:** Newberry Libr, Chicago, Ill, receptionist, 1975-77; Maywood Pub Libr, Maywood, Ill, br librn, 1977-78; Johnson Publ Co, Chicago, Ill, asst libr, 1978-82; Northwestern Univ Libr, Evanston, Ill, African-Am studies, librn, 1982-. **Orgs:** Am Libr Asn, 1976-; Black Caucus Am Libr Asn, 1978-; Nat Asn Advan Colored People, 1983-; Asn Study Afro-Am Life & Hist, 1985-; bd trustees, DuSable Mus African Am Hist, 1994-; Toni Morrison Soc, 2000-; Asn Northwestern Univ Women; fel Alice Berline Kaplan Inst; Black Caucus Am Libr Asn; Asn Study African Am Life & Hist; DuSable Mus African Am Hist. **Honors/Awds:** Scholarship, Nat Bridge Asn, 1971; Fulbright Library Fel, Univ Durban-Westville, S Africa, 1996; Libr Fel, Alice Berline Kaplan Ctr Humanities, Northwestern Univ, 1999-00; Award Chicago Friends Amistad Res Ctr, Tulane Univ, 2003. **Special Achievements:** International non-gov observer, natl elections, Repub of S Africa, 1994; mem, research team, "Know Your Heritage" tv program, 1996-99. **Home Addr:** 1631 W Fargo Ave, Chicago, IL 60626-1720, **Home Phone:** (773)338-8722. **Business Addr:** African-Am Studies Librn, Northwestern University Library, 1970 Campus Dr, Evanston, IL 60208-2300, **Business Phone:** (847)491-2173.

BETHEL, DR. LEONARD LESLIE
Educator, administrator. **Personal:** Born Feb 5, 1939, Philadelphia, PA; married Veronica Bynum; children: Amiel Wren & Kama Lynn. **Educ:** Lincoln Univ, BA, 1961; Johnson C Smith Univ Sch Theol, MDiv, 1964; New Brunswick Theol Sem, MA, 1971; Rutgers Univ, DEd, 1975. **Career:** Raritan Valley Community Col, prof, Afro-Am Studies; Wash United Presbyterian Church, pastor, 1964-67; Lincoln Univ, asst chaplain, dir coun, 1967-79; Rutgers Univ, Dept African Studies, fac, staff, 1969-, chair, 1970-2003, assoc prof, 1980-; Woodrow Wilson fel, Princeton Univ, 1984; Bethel Presbyterian Church, pastor, 1982-92. **Orgs:** Bd Trustees Rutgers Prep Sch, 1971-84; Am Asn Univ Pres, Rutgers Univ, 1980-; bd dir, Plainfield Br, Union County Col, 1980-86; Frontiers Int, 1980-; Presbytery Elizabeth, 1982-; bd trustees, Bloomfield Col, 1980-86; bd trustees, Lincoln Univ, 1996-; bd dirs, UCC, 1980-87; Phi Delta Kappa. **Honors/Awds:** Paul Robeson Faculty Award, Rutgers Univ, 1978; NAFEO Pres Citation, Lincoln Univ, 1981; Rutgers Grad, Sch Education Distinguished Service Award, 2003; Warren I Susman Teaching Excellence Award, 2003; Oxford Round Table Inductee, Oxford Univ, Oxford, Eng; Omega Psi Phi Fraternity's Man of the Year. **Special Achievements:** Co-author: Advancement Through Service: A History of The Frontiers International, Lanham, University Press of America, 1991, Plainfield's African American: Northern Slavery to Church Freedom, University Press of America, 1997; author, Educating African Leaders: Missionism in America, Edwin Mellon Press, 1997; editor, Africana: An Introduction and Study, Kendall/Hunt Press, 1999; first Black fac mem Rutgers Coll; First Black faculty member at Rutgers College to be hired as assistant instructor to rise up through the tenure process. **Home Addr:** 146 Parkside Rd, Plainfield, NJ 07060, **Home Phone:** (908)756-2737. **Business Addr:** Associate Professor, Rutgers University, Department Africana Studies, 112 Beck Hall, Piscataway, NJ 08854-8040, **Business Phone:** (732)445-3334.

BETHEL, VERONICA B.
Educator. **Career:** Educator (retired); Raritan Valley Community Col, Dept Social Scis & Human Servs, prof. *

BETHEL-MURRAY, KIMBERLY
Physician. **Educ:** Howard Univ; Wright State Univ Sch Med. **Career:** Trotwood Physician Ctr, physician, 1990-. **Orgs:** Gem City Med, Dental & Pharmaceut Soc. **Special Achievements:** Become the first woman president of Gem City Medical, Dental and Pharmaceutical Society. **Business Addr:** Physician, Trotwood Physician Center, 3038 Olive Rd, Trotwood, OH 45426, **Business Phone:** (937)208-7050.*

BETTIE, DEMETRIUS ANTONIO. See BATTIE, TONY.

BETTIS, ANNE KATHERINE
Financial manager. **Personal:** Born Jun 16, 1949, Newark, NJ. **Educ:** Jersey City State Col, BA, 1972; Columbia Univ, MBA, 1979. **Career:** Avon Prod Inc, sr ed, 1973-77; AT&T, acct exec, 1979-82, nat acct mgr, 1983-85, staff mgr, 1985-. **Orgs:** Pres, 8th Irving Park Condominium Asn, 1984-; Calvary Baptist Church; Nat Black MBA Asn. **Honors/Awds:** Achiever's Club AT&T, 1982-84. **Home Addr:** 83 Boston St, Newark, NJ 07103. **Business Addr:** Marketing Staff Manager, AT&T Info Syst, 1 Speedwell Ave Suite 771E, Morristown, NJ 07960, **Business Phone:** (201)898-3967.

BETTIS, JEROME ABRAM
Football player, television broadcaster. **Personal:** Born Feb 16, 1972, Detroit, MI; son of Johnnie; children: Jerome Jr & Jada. **Educ:** Notre Dame Univ; Lawrence Tech Univ, PhD, 2006. **Career:** Football player (retired), co-host; Los Angeles Rams, running back, 1993-95; St Louis Rams, 1995; Pittsburgh Steelers, running back, 1996-05; NBC's new Football Night Am, studio commentator, 2006; KDKA TV sports prog, The Jerome Bettis Show, co-host. **Orgs:** Bus Stops Here Found, 1997. **Honors/Awds:** NFL Rookie of the Yr, 1993; Rookie of the Yr, Pro Football Writers Asn, 1993; Pro Bowl, 1993-94, 1996-97, 2001, 2004; Most Valuable Player, 1996-97; Offensive Player of the Month, 1996; Running Back of the Yr, NFL Alumni, 1996; Walter Payton NFL Man of the Yr, 2002. **Special Achievements:** Published Books: "Driving Home: My Unforgettable Super Bowl Run", September 2006, Triumph Books. *

BETTIS, LINDA
Administrator. **Career:** TAP Multimedia LLC, sr partner, 2001-. **Orgs:** Nat Tele Communs & Info Admin, US Dept Com. *

BETTY, LISA C.
Environmental scientist. **Personal:** Born Sep 9, 1961, Bronx, NY; daughter of Warren R Betty and Norma F Carter; married Rolf Demmerle, Apr 29, 2000. **Educ:** Polytechnic Univ, BSCF, 1992; City Col NY, MSCE, 2002. **Career:** NYC Govt Dept Environmental Protection, asst civil engineer, 1992-94,Newtown Creek Treatment Plant, process engr, 1994-98, Ward's IslandTreatment Plant, process engr, 1998-99, Red Hook Treatment Plant, process engr, 2000, Oakwood Beach Treatment Plant, process engr, 2000, mgt engr, 2001-. **Orgs:** Water Environment Federation, operator, 1994-; NY Water Environment Asn, operator, 1994-; United States Gymnastics Federation, gymnastics instructor, 1996-. **Honors/Awds:** NY Water Environment Agency, state operators challenge team, 2nd place,1998, 1st place, 1999, 1st place, 2000; Water Environment Federation, natloperators challenge, 5th place process control, 2000. **Business Addr:** Engineer, NY City Department Environ Engineering, 96-05 Horrace Harding Expy 2nd Fl, Corona, NY 11368, **Business Phone:** (718)595-5136.

BETTY, WARREN RANDALL
Physician, administrator. **Personal:** Born Apr 21, 1931, Chicago, IL; son of A L Lucas and E C Brewington; married Judy A Austermiller, Nov 25, 1988; children: Lisa C, Michael W. **Educ:** Ind Univ, BA, 1954; Ind Univ Sch Med, MD, 1959. **Career:** Physician (retired); Albert Einstein Col Med NY, asst clin prof pediat, 1965-95; Richmond Co Prof Standard Review Orgn, treas & bd dir, 1979-84; Health Ins Plan Greater NY, mem, bd dir, 1983-92, 1993-96; Group Coun Mutual Ins Co, mem, bd dir, 1983-96; Island Peer Review Orgn, treas & bd dir, 1984; Staten Island Med Group, medical dir, 1981-96; IPRO, treas. **Orgs:** Mem adv bd, Staten Island Urban League, 1982-90; Gov Comn Hosp Info Data, 1983; vpres Richmond County Med Soc, 1983-84; mem Reg Adv Coun, State Div Human Rights; bd dir, Prof Med Conduct, 1994-99; comnr, Cape May Culture & Heritage Comn; treas, Greater Cape May Hist soc; historian, Shoreline RR Hist Soc. **Honors/Awds:** Black Achiever Award, Harlem Br, YMCA, 1982. **Military Serv:** USAF, 1952-55. **Home Addr:** 4065 Bayshore Rd, Cape May, NJ 08204. *

BEVERLY, CREIGS C.
Educator, social worker, school administrator. **Personal:** Born Sep 5, 1942, Selma, AL; married Olivia D; children: Cheryl, Creigs Jr & Larry. **Educ:** Morehouse Col, BA, 1963; Atlanta Univ, MSSW, social work, 1965; Univ Wis, PhD, 1972. **Career:** Univ Ghana, prof, 1983-84, actg coordr, 1984; Atlanta Univ, Sch Social Work, prof, 1974-83, dean, 1984-86, vpres & provost, 1986-87, Social & Behavioral Sci, sr prof, 1987; Ctr African Life & Develop, post doctorate training, 1984; Wayne State Univ, Sch Social Work, vis prof, 1987, prof, 1988-04, prof emer, 2004-. **Orgs:** Special asst to the mayor, Carnegie Found Fel, 1976-77; bd dirs, Coun Intl Progs, 1985; Nat Asn Black Elected Officials; Nat Asn Social Workers; Nat Asn Black Social Workers; CSWE; ACSW; planning comn, City Detroit, 1988-; Nat Coun Black Alcoholism, 1980-82; Nat Asn Advan Colored People; Ga Coun Soc Welfare; Ga Chapter Social Workers; Nat Asn Community Developers; Asn Social Work Ed Africa; Nat Ctr Child Abuse; Mich Coun Child Abuse; Kellogg Found Youth Initiatives Prog; mem Intl comn, 2000-01; Detroit Planning Comn; bd pres, Detroit Youth Comn; Hartford Agape House. **Honors/Awds:** Achievement & Contribution Plaque, City of Atlanta, 1977; Fulbright Scholar, West Africa, 1983, 1984; Atlanta Univ, Distinguished Alumni Citation Award, Nat Asn Equal Opportunity, 1980; Distinguished Youth Service Award, State Okla, 1986; Martin L King Vis Scholar, Wayne State Univ, 1987-88; NASW Social Worker of the Year, 1992; NABSW Distinguished Service Award, 1992; Spirit of Detroit Award, 1991; NABSW Student Chapter, Distinguished Teaching Award, 1991; Social Worker of the Year, NASW S Eastern MI, 1992; Excellence in Teaching Award, Wayne State Univ, 1992-93; Distinguished Service Award, City of Detroit Youth Dept, 1996. **Special Achievements:** Author: Theory and Reality, 1986; Social Develop & African Develop, 1984;Black Men in Prison, 1990-92; Alcoholism in the Black Community, 1976, 1982, 1990, 1992; Beyond Survival, 1992; Characteristics of Progressive Social Workers, 1992; Of Utmost Good Faith, 1992; Schools as Communities in Communities, 1992; WSU Distinguished Faculty, 1993; Card for All Mothers, 1993; Card for All Fathers, 1994; Black on Black Crime:Compensation for Idomatic Purposelessness, 1997, 1998; Employment and Empowerment of People with Disabilities: A Social Develop Perspective, 2003; 1998; presentations social develop, South Africa, Turkey, Srilanka, India, Portugal, and Egypt, 1996-01. *

BEVERLY, ERIC
Football player. **Personal:** Born Mar 28, 1974, Cleveland, OH. **Educ:** Miami oh. **Career:** Football player(retired), Detroit Lions, ctr, 1997-03; Atlanta Falcons, tight end, 2004-06; Detroit Lions, tight end, 2007. *

BEVERLY, FRANKIE (HOWARD BEVERLY)
Singer, musician. **Personal:** Born Dec 6, 1946, Philadelphia, PA. **Career:** Frankie Beverly & Maze, founder & lead singer, 1977-; Albums: Maze Featuring Frankie Beverly, 1977, Golden Time of Day, 1978, Inspiration, 1979, Joy & Pain, 1980, Live in New Orleans, 1980, We Are One, 1983; Cant Stop the Love, 1985; Maze Featuring Frankie Beverly Live in Los Angeles, 1986; Silky Soul, 1989; Back to the Basic, 1993; Southern Girl, 1996; Rebel 4 Life, 1998; Whats the Worst That Could Happen, 2001; Cherish, 2002; Paid in Full, 2002; Bringing Down the House, 2003; Johnson Family Vacation, 2004; Get Rich or Die Tryin, 2005; ATL, 2006; Welcome Home, Roscoe Jenkins, 2008; Songs: "Running Away"; "Love Is The Key"; "Back In Stride"; "Too Many Games"; "Can't Get Over You"; "Silky Soul"; "Golden Time Of Day", writer, 1998; "Happy Feelins", writer, 2001; "Let Go", writer, 2003; "Before I Let You Go", writer, 2004; "Tavis Smiley", 2005. **Honors/Awds:** Eight gold recs. **Business Addr:** Singer, Capitol Records Inc, 1750 N Vine St, Hollywood, CA 90028, **Business Phone:** (213)462-6252.

BEVERLY, HOWARD. See BEVERLY, FRANKIE.

BEVERLY, MARIETTA
School principal. **Career:** Michele Clare Mid Sch, prin; Chicago Pub Sch, area instr officer, currently. **Business Phone:** (773)534-0709.*

BEVERLY, SHARON MANNING. See MANNING, SHARON.

BEVERLY, WILLIAM C
Lawyer, judge, president (organization). **Personal:** Born Jan 23, 1943, Los Angeles, CA; married Mona Birkelund. **Educ:** Pepperdine Univ, BA, 1965; Southwestern Univ Sch Law, JD, 1969. **Career:** Lawyer, Judge (retired), Executive; Los Angeles Super Ct, judge; Calif State Univ, Long Beach, instr bus law; DPSS, soc worker & supvr, 1965-70; pvt pract law, atty, 1970-2003, JAMS, arbitrator & mediator; Eighth & Wall Inc, founder, pres & dir, currently. **Orgs:** Co chmn, Mil Law Panel, 1971; Calif & Long Beach Bar Asn; Langston Law Club; Langston Bar Asn; vpres, La County Comn Human Rels; Hist Coun Calif African Am Mus; African Am Heritage Soc Long Beach. **Honors/Awds:** Outstanding Judicial Officer, Southwestern Univ Sch Law, 1996. **Special Achievements:** First African American employee of Security Pacific Bank. **Business Addr:** President, Director, Eighth & Wall Inc, 904 Silver Spur Rd, 317 Rolling Hills Estates, Los Angeles, CA 90274, **Business Phone:** (310)541-1690.

BEYER, TROY YVETTE
Actor, screenwriter, movie director. **Personal:** Born Nov 7, 1964, New York, NY; daughter of Jerrold and Hannan Wells Parks; married Mark Bug, Jan 1, 1994 (divorced); children: 1. **Educ:** City Univ New York, Sch Arts, actg & psycho biology; Univ Calif, LosAngeles, polit sci. **Career:** TV series: "Dynasty", 1986-87; "Murder One", 1995; TV movies: "Uncle Tom's Cabin", 1987; "Three Chains O' Gold", 1994; "Alien Avengers", 1996; Film appearances: Disorderlies, 1987; Rooftops, 1989; The White Girl, 1990; The Five Heartbeats, 1991; Weekend at Bernie's II, 1993; The Little Death, 1995; Eddie, 1996; BAPS, 1997; The Ginger bread Man, 1998; Let's Talk About Sex, 1998; Good Advice, 2001; John Q, 2002; A Light in the Darkness, 2002; Love Don't Cost a Thing, 2003. **Honors/Awds:** Newcomer of the Year Award, ShoWest; Nominated for BET Comedy Awars, 2004. **Business Addr:** Actress, c/o William Morris Agency, 151 El Camino Dr, Beverly Hills, CA 90212, **Business Phone:** (310)274-7451.*

BIAKABUTUKA, TIM (TSHIMANGA BIAKABUTUKA)
Football player. **Personal:** Born Jan 24, 1974, Kinshasa, Democratic Republic of the Congo. **Educ:** Univ Mich. **Career:** Foot ball player (retired); Carolina Panthers, running back, 1996-01; owner, Beya Jewelry store, currently. **Honors/Awds:** Ed Block Courage Award, Carolina Panthers, 1997. *

BIAKABUTUKA, TSHIMANGA. See BIAKABUTUKA, TIM.

BIASSEY, DR. EARLE LAMBERT. See Obituaries section.

BIBB, DR. T CLIFFORD
Educator. **Personal:** Born Oct 29, 1938, Montgomery, AL; son of Bennie Bibb and Alma Bibb; children: Tura Concetta. **Educ:** Ala State Univ, BS, 1960, MEd, 1961; Northwestern Univ, PhD, 1973. **Career:** Rust Col, chair, eng dept, 1961-65; Daniel Payne Col, chair eng dept, 1965-67; Miles Col, eng coordr, 1967-71; Northwestern Univ, eng supvr, 1971-72; Ala State Univ, chair advan studies & dir four year plus curriculum prog, chmn emer, currently. **Orgs:** Dir upward prog Northwestern Univ, 1972-73; comnr, composition NCTE, 1973-76; sec Peterson-Bibb Lodge 762, 1974-; fac adv, Alpha Phi Alpha, 1981-; exec comm, NCTE 1983-88; exec sec & bd mem, Cent Montgomery Optimists, 1984-86; desoto comn State Ala, 1986-95; Nat Coun Teachers Eng, 1991-93; newsletter ed, Ala Asn Develop Ed, 1992-95; Ala State Coun Arts, 1992-; Nat Coun Ed Opportunity Asn, 1992-; table leader (ETS), Ed Testing Serv APT/ENG, 1994-; Nat Asn Develop Educ (NADE), pres-elect, 1997-98, pres, 1998-99. **Honors/Awds:** Choir Dir/Singer in "The Long Walk Home", starring Whoopi Goldbert & Sissy Spacek. **Home Addr:** 5933 Provost Ave, Montgomery, AL 36116, **Home Phone:** (205)288-1554. **Business Addr:** Chairman Emeritus, Alabama State University, Department of Advancement Studies, 915 So Jackson St, Montgomery, AL 36101, **Business Phone:** (334)229-4479.

BIBBS, CHARLES
Business owner. **Personal:** Born in California. **Career:** B Graphics & Fine Arts, owner, 2004-; 626 Art Gallery Studio B, owner, currently. **Home Addr:** Moreno Valley, CA 92553-5235. **Business Addr:** Business owner, B Graphics & Fine Arts, 12625 Frederick Ave Suite 1 8, Moreno Valley, CA 92553-5235, **Business Phone:** (909)697-4752.*

BIBBS, PATRICIA
Basketball coach. **Personal:** Married Ezil; children: Sabrina and Satin. **Educ:** Grambling State Univ, BA, Health and Physical Educ, 1972, MA, Sports Admini, 1974. **Career:** Grambling State Univ, head womens basketball coach; Hampton Univ, basketball coach, 1997-04; NC A&T State Univ, head womens basketball coach, 2005-. **Orgs:** MEAC Basketball Tournament Comt, Women's Basketball Coaches Asn, mwm, Black Coaches Asn, NCAA Coun, 1987; Zeta Phi Beta Sorority; St. Rest Baptist Church. **Honors/Awds:** NAFEO Distinguished Alumni Award, Coach of the Year, Black Col Sports Inf Dires Asn. **Business Addr:** Head Coach of Womens Basketball, North Carliona A&T state University, 1601 E Mkt St, Greensboro, NC 27411, **Business Phone:** (336)334-7500.*

BIBBS-SANDERS, ANGELIA
Administrator. **Career:** Motown Records, dir artist rels; RCA Records, dir mkt oper; Nat Acad Rec Arts & Sci, Los Angeles Chapter, exec dir Los Angeles chap, vpres mem servs, currently. *

BIBBY, DEIRDRE L.
Museum director. **Personal:** Born Jun 9, 1951, Pittsburgh, PA. **Educ:** Mass Col Art, BFA, 1974; City Col NY, MA, 1983; Museum Mgt Inst. **Career:** Ile-Ife Mus, dir, curator 1974-76; ARO Hist & Cult Mus, curator, 1977-81; Mid-Atlantic Consortium, visual arts coordr; The Studio Mus Harlem, assoc curator, 1981-85; Schomburg Ctr Res Black Cult, Art & Artifacts Div, head, 1985-91; Mus African Am Art, exec dir; Amistad Found, exec dir; Wadsworth Atheneum, African Am Art, curator, currently. **Orgs:** African Am Mus Asn, 1978-; Nat Conf Artists ,1978-; co-chair, Women Caucus Art, 1985; The Links, Inc. 1999-. **Special Achievements:** First African-American to hold full-time curatorial post in a major New England museum. **Business Addr:** Executive Director, Wadsworth Atheneum, 600 Main St, Hartford, CT 06103.*

BIBBY, MICHAEL. See BIBBY, MIKE.

BIBBY, MIKE (MICHAEL BIBBY)
Basketball player. **Personal:** Born May 13, 1978, Cherry Hill, NJ; son of Henry Bibby and Virginia Bibby; children: Michael, Janae, Mia & Nylah. **Educ:** Univ Ariz. **Career:** Vancouver Grizzlies, guard, 1998-2001; Sacramento Kings, guard, 2001-08; Atlanta Hawks, guard, 2008-. **Honors/Awds:** Pac-10 Player of the Year, 1998; Freshman of the Yr; Conf Player of the Week, 2005. **Business Addr:** Professional Basketball Player, Atlanta Hawks, Centennial Tower, 101 Marietta St NW Suite 1900, Atlanta, GA 30303, **Business Phone:** (404)878-3800.

BIBLO, MARY
Librarian. **Personal:** Born Dec 31, 1927, East Chicago, IN; daughter of James Davidson and Flora Chandler Davidson; married Herbert D Biblo, Aug 27, 1950; children: Lisa, David. **Educ:** Roosevelt Univ, Chicago, IL, BS, 1966; Rosary Col, River Forest IL, MLS, 1970; Teachers Col, Columbia Univ, 1985. **Career:** S Chicago Community Hosp, Sch Nursing, Chicago, IL, med librn, 1966-67; Chicago Bd Educ, Chicago, IL, sch librn, 1967-70; Univ Chicago, Labr Schs, Chicago, IL, librn, 1970-98, Lincoln County Libr Dist, mem, currently. **Orgs:** Am Lib Asn; past pres, Children's Reading Round Table; Nat Caucus Black Librns; Nat Asn Independent Schs; vice chair, minority affairs comt, Ill State Bd Educ, 1988-90; Int Fedn Libr Asns, chair, Int Fedn Libr Asn's Round Table Women's Issues; Am Asn Sch Librn; intellectural freedom round table, social responsibility round table, Ill Libr Asn; Ill Asn Media Educ. **Honors/Awds:** Klingenstein fel, Columbia Univ, 1984-85; master teacher, Univ Chicago Lab Sch, 1985. *

BICKERSTAFF, BERNARD TYRONE, SR.
Basketball coach. **Personal:** Born Feb 11, 1944, Benham, KY; married Eugenia King, Jul 22, 1967; children: Tim, Robin, Cydni, Bernard & John Blair. **Educ:** Univ San Diego, BS, 1968. **Career:** Univ San Diego, ast basketball coach, 1967-70; Univ San Diego, head coach, 1970-73; Wash Bullets, ast coach & scout, 1974-85; Seattle SuperSonics, head coach & vpres, 1985-90; Denver Nuggets, gen mgr & vpres, 1990-95, head coach & pres, 1995-97; Washington Wizards, head coach, 1997; St Louis Swarm, head coach & gen mgr; Charlotte Bobcats, head gen mgr & vpres, 2003-. **Orgs:** Vpres, NBA Coaches Asn, 1980-90. **Honors/Awds:** Youngest Assistant Coach, Nat Basketball Asn; NBA Coach of the Year, Sporting News, 1987. **Special Achievements:** Named a street, Bernard Bickerstaff Boulevard; named a Kentucky Colonel. **Business Addr:** General manager, Vice President, Charlotte Bobcats, 129 W Trade St Suite 700, Charlotte, NC 28202, **Business Phone:** (704)424-4120.*

BICKERSTAFF, CYNDI L
Executive. **Personal:** Born in Columbia, MD; daughter of Bernie Bickerstaff. **Educ:** Hampton Univ, BS, acct; Fla A&M Univ, MBA. **Career:** ASCENT Sports; Denver Nuggets; Colo Avalanche & Host Communs; Bickerstaff Sports & Entertainment, ceo, 2001-. **Special Achievements:** Featured in various Magazine:Essence Magazine, 2003; Black Enterprise Magazine, 2004. **Business Addr:** Chief Executive Officer, Bickerstaff Sports & Entertainment, 2828 10th St NE, Washington, DC 20017, **Business Phone:** (202)832-8560.*

BICKHAM, DR. LUZINE B.
Educator. **Personal:** Born Mar 2, 1923, New Orleans, LA; married Dorothy B; children: Luzine Jr & Nedra E. **Educ:** Univ Mich, BBA, 1947, MBA, 1948; Univ Tex, PhD, mkt, 1965. **Career:** Dillard Univ, instr, 1949; Watchtower Life Ins Co, secy, 1950; Tex Southern Univ, instr, 1952; Tex Southern Univ Sch Bus, dean, 1970-78. **Orgs:** Am Mkt Asn; bd dirs, Std savs & Loan asn; Tex So Fin; St Eliz Hosp Found. **Military Serv:** Army Air Corps, 1943-45. *

BIDDLE, DR. STANTON F
Library administrator. **Personal:** Born Sep 16, 1943, Cuba, NY; son of Christopher F and Imogene M Peterson. **Educ:** Howard Univ, Wash, DC, BA, 1965; Atlanta Univ, Atlanta, GA, MS, libr sci, 1966; New York Univ, New York, NY, MS, pub admin, 1973; Univ Calif, Berkeley, CA, doctor libr & info studies, 1988. **Career:** The New York Pub Libr Schomburg Res Ctr, New York, NY, reference librn, archivist, 1967-73; Howard Univ Libr, Wash, DC, assoc dir, 1973-76; State Univ New York-Buffalo, assoc dir libr, 1979-84; Baruch Col, City Univ New York, chief librn, 1984-88; City Univ NY Cent Off, asst dean libr, 1988-89; Baruch Col, CUNY, admin serv librn, 1989-, prof, currently. **Orgs:** Black Caucus Am Libr Asn, 1976-82, 1989-91; pres, Schomburg Collection Black Lit, Hist & Art, 1988-90; corresp secy, City Univ African Am Network, 1990-93; treas, NY Black Librns Caucus, 1990-94; chair, Afro-Am Studies Librn Sect, Asn Col & Res Libr, 1991-92; pres, Libr Asn City Univ NY, 1992-94; pres, Black Caucus Am Libr Asn, 1994-96. **Honors/Awds:** William Wells Brown Award, Afro-Am Hist Asn, Buffalo, NY, 1984. **Business Addr:** Professor, Librarian, Baruch College, The City University of New York, 1 Bernard Baruch Way Bldg 151 E 25 Rm 424, PO Box H-0520, New York, NY 10010, **Business Phone:** (646)312-1653.

BIFFLE, CURTIS
Teacher. **Educ:** Ala A&M, attended. **Career:** Austin High Sch, adjust coordr, currently; Decatur City Schs, teacher, currently. **Special Achievements:** Credited by colleagues with keeping probable dropouts in school; coordinator, Southeastern Consortium for Minorities in Engineering; survived impoverished childhood in rural Alabama.

BIGBY YOUNG, DR. BETTY
Educator. **Personal:** Born in New York, NY; daughter of Dorothy Bigby and Lucius Bigby; married Haskell I; children: Haskell I II (Chato) & Jessica Melissa Bigby. **Educ:** CUNY, Brooklyn Col, BA, 1970, MS, 1972; Nova Univ, EdD, 1987. **Career:** Dept State Foreign Serv Corps, admin asst, foreign serv staff, 1959-67; Office Mayor, NYC, community rels specialist, 1968-71; CUNY, Brooklyn Col, dir, model city, TV training prog, 1972-73; Model City Prog, community rels specialist, 1974-77; Fla Int Univ, dir, univ rels & develop, 1977-83; dir, acad support prog, 1983-89; Fla Mem Col, dir, AIDS & drug abuse prevention prog, 1990-92, coordr, Dewitt Wallace, Reader's Digest Fund Pathways to Teaching Careers Prog, 1992-99; Lagos Christian Col, adjunct prof; Fla Mem Col, Div Humanities, adjunct prof speech, asst prof speech, 2002-. **Orgs:** Alpha Epsilon Rho Radio TV Frat; Am Asn Univ Women; Sigma Gamma Rho Sorority; Am Coun Educ; Southeast Dist Liaison for Minority Affairs, PRSA; YWCA Women's Network; Fla State Sickle Cell Found Inc, 1978-; White House Conf on Arts Testimony Congressional Hearing, 1978; Pub Rels Soc Am, Accredited Coun Advancement & Support Educ, 1978-80; FIU Black Stud Union Adv founder, 1978-89; Kappa Delta Pi Int Hon Soc Educ, 1980-; pres, Dade County Sickle Cell Found, 1980-82, 1992-94; founder, counr, Omicron Theta Chap KDP FIU, 1981-89; bd mem, Art Pub Places Trust; pres, Scott Lake Elem-Sch, PTA, Park view Elem, Greynolds Park Elem; Mental Health Asn, 1981-82;radio talk show host WMBM Miami, 1981-82; Congress Black Scholars Dade County, 1982; KDP Int Hon Soc constitution & bylaws chairperson, 1982-84;South Fla Ctr for the Fine Arts; nat mem, Smitnian Asn; Nat Asn Female Execs, 1984-89; Int Platform Asn; chief adv, Fla Black Stud Asn Inc,1988-89; Bd Mem, DCPS Magnet Adv Comt; Bd Mem, Ctr for Haitian Studies; Founder, counr, Phi Eta Chap KDP, FMC, 1995-; former

pres, FIUs Black Employees Asn. **Honors/Awds:** Community Service Award, Nat Congress Parents & Teachers, 1989; Dr B BYoung, Dr C McIntosh Scholar, Fla Sickle Cel Assn, currently; Outstanding Admin, FIU N Campus, 1985; Dr B B Young BSU Leadership Honor Roll, FIU NCampus, currently; Parkway Elem Sch, Outstanding Service Award; Scott LakeElem Sch, Outstanding Service Award, 1990; Florida African-Am Stud Asn, Exemplary Leadership, 1990; Fla Mem Col, Outstanding Service Award, 1996, 1997, 1998, 1999, 2000; KDP 25 yr. Service Award; Fla Int Univ, 10 yr service Award; Faculty Senate Awd, Fla Mem Col, 2003; Div Humanities Teacher of the Year, Fla Mem Col, 2005-06. **Business Addr:** Assistant Professor, Florida Memorial University, Division of Humanities, 15800 NW 42nd Ave, Miami Gardens, FL 33054, **Business Phone:** (305)626-3719.

BIGGERS, DR. SAMUEL LORING, JR.
Surgeon, president (organization). **Personal:** Born Nov 6, 1935, Crockett, TX; son of Samuel L Sr and Nelia J Martinez; married Florestine A Robinson; children: Samuel L III, Shaun Denise & Sanford Leon. **Educ:** Dillard Univ, AB, 1956; Univ Tex, MD, 1961; Am Bd Neurol Surg, Dipl, 1970. **Career:** Univ Tex Grad Sch, researcher & teaching asst, 1957-58; Orange County Gen Hosp, intern, 1961-62; Univ Southern Calif Med Ctr, instr clin, 1964-70; Los Angeles County Univ Southern Calif Med Ctr, asst prof clin, 1970-85; Calif Med Ctr, Los Angeles, chief surgeon, 1989-; Charles R Drew Med Sch, prof neuro science, 1993-; Charles R Drew Med Sch, Martin Luther King Jr Hosp, Dept Neurol Surg, vice chmn; Calif Med Ctr, vpres, med staff; Samuel L Bigger & John J Holly Inc Neurol Surg, pres. **Orgs:** Pres, Samuel L Biggers, John J Holly MD Inc, 1974-; bd dirs, CMCLA Found, 1990-; bd dirs, Unihealth Am Found, 1990-; Am Asn Neurol Surgeons; Kappa Alpha Psi; Alpha Kappa Mu; Alpha Omega Alpha; Sigma Pi Phi; bd trustees, Calif Hosp Med Ctr; bd mem, Cath Healthcare W. **Honors/Awds:** Alumnus of the Year, Dillard Univ, 1985; Humanitarian of the Year, Calif Med Ctr, 1992; Distinguished Physician Award, Minority Health Inst, 1994. **Military Serv:** USAF, Med Corp, capt, 1962-64. *

BIGGINS, J VERONICA
Executive, government official. **Personal:** Married Franklin; children: 2. **Educ:** Spelman Col, bachelor degree; Ga State Univ, masters degree educ; Duke Univ Fuqua Exec Mgt Prog. **Career:** Citizens & Southern Ga Corp, dir human resources; Nat Bank Corp, exec vprescorp community rels; The White House, asst to pres, dir pres personnel, US delegation UN Womens Conf Beijing, vice chmn; Heidrick & Struggles Int Inc, Atlanta, managing partner; HNCL Search, partner, currently. **Orgs:** Bd mem, Atlanta Life Ins Co; bd mem, Atlanta-Fulton County Recreation Authority; co-chairperson, Atlanta AIDS Walk, 1991; chmn, Czech Slovak Am Enterprise Fund; bd dirs, AirTran Airways; bd dirs, Avnet; bd dirs, Kaiser Permanente Georgia; trustee bd, Woodruff Arts Ctr; bd vis, Savannah Col Art & Design. **Honors/Awds:** Hall of Fame, Ga State Univ, 2003. **Business Phone:** (404)942-6305.

BIGGS, DR. SHIRLEY ANN
Educator. **Personal:** Born Mar 9, 1938, Richmond, VA; daughter of Richard B Hill and Jennie; married Charles F (deceased); children: Charles F Jr & Cheryl A. **Educ:** Duquesne Univ, BEd, elem educ, 1960; Univ Tenn, attended 1969; Univ SC, MEd, reading & psychol serv, 1972; Univ Pittsburgh, EdD, 1977. **Career:** Pittsburgh Pub Sch, teacher, 1961-68; Benedict Col, instr, 1968-72, reading specialist consult, 1972; Univ Pittsburgh, Sch Educ, instr & learning, assoc prof, asst dean student affairs, dir affirmative action, minority affairs, emer assoc prof, currently; Negro Educ Rev, executive ed and co-managing ed. **Orgs:** Pres, Gerald A Yoakam Reading Coun, 1978-79; chmn, Res Div, Pittsburgh Literacy Coalition, 1984-; Int Reading Asn, 1973-90; dir res, Coalition Advan Literacy Pittsburgh, 1985-; chair, Pittsburgh Peace Inst, 1997-; chair, Col Reading Improv Group; Imani Christian Acad Bd & Educ Chair, 2001-; Nat Conf Res Lang & Literacy, 2001-. **Honors/Awds:** Honored for Literacy Research Activities, Pittsburgh City Coun, 1986; Jean E. Wisand Distinguished Woman in Education Award, 2005. **Special Achievements:** Author, "The Plight of Black Males in American Schools: Separation May not be the Answer", "Building on Strengths: Closing the Literacy Gap", "African American Progress in the Face of Problems"; sr author, Administrators Reference Manual: Bridging Assessment and Instruction, 1998; "Minority Student Retention: A Framework for Discussion and Decision-making", 1998; College Reading Research and Practice (co-edit), 2003); Technology-Assisted College Skills (co-author) 2004; Reading Comprehension Instruction: Building on What We Have Learned, 2004-05; Book Review of The Bonds woman's Narrative, 2008. **Business Addr:** Emeritus Associate Professor, University of Pittsburgh, School of Education, Department Instruction & Learning, 5518 Wesley Posvar Hall, Pittsburgh, PA 15260, **Business Phone:** (412)648-7333.

BIGHAM, RITA LACY
Librarian, research scientist, executive director. **Personal:** Born Jan 7, 1949, Augusta, GA; daughter of Joseph Tolbertte and Ruth Jefferson; married Bruce W (divorced 1988). **Educ:** Morris Brown Col, Atlanta, GA, BS, 1969; Atlanta Univ, Atlanta, GA, MSLS, 1970. **Career:** Atlanta Univ, Sch Libr Sci, Ford Found fel, 1969-70; Morris Brown Col, Jordan-Thomas Libr, Atlanta, GA, cataloger, 1970-79; Mellon Asn Col & Res Librs, intern, 1976-77; Atlanta Univ, Trevor Arnett Libr, Atlanta, GA, head, tech servs, 1979-82; Atlanta Univ Ctr Inc, Robert W Woodruff Libr, Atlanta, GA, dir, tech servs, 1982-87; Interdenominational Theol Ctr, Atlanta, GA, res asst, 1987, Res & Eval, dir, currently. **Orgs:** Vpres & dean pledgees, Gamma Zeta Chap, Delta Sigma Theta Sorority, 1968-69; Am Libr Asn, 1970-; Beta Phi Mu, Int Libr Sci Honor Society, 1970-; Nat Coun Negro Women, 1990-. **Business Addr:** Director of Research & Evaluation, Interdenominational Theological Center, 671 Beckwith St SW, Atlanta, GA 30314, **Business Phone:** (404)527-7764.

BIGLOW, KEITH
Funeral director. **Educ:** Cent State Univ. **Career:** House Winn Funeral Home, Okmulgee; Keith D Biglow Funeral Dir Inc, owner, currently. **Business Phone:** (918)687-5510.*

BILAL, JAZZ. See OLIVER, BILAL SAYEED.

BILLINGS, CORA MARIE
Clergy. **Personal:** Born Feb 11, 1939, Philadelphia, PA; daughter of Ethel Lorraine Lee and Jesse Anthony. **Educ:** Gwynedd Mercy Col, Gwynedd, PA, 1963; Villanova Univ, Philadelphia, PA,BA, humanities, 1967; St Charles Borromed Sem, Philadelphia, PA, min relstudies, 1974. **Career:** WPCGHS, religion teacher, 1970-79; Nat Black Sisters' Conf, Philadelphia,PA, exec dir, 1977-79; Cardinal Krol, Philadelphia, PA, dir, 1979-80; Bishop Walter F Sullivan, Richmond, VA, VSU, campus minister, 1981-90; Off Black Catholics, dir, 1984-; St Elizabeth's Catholic Church, pastoral coordr, 1990-; Diocesan Off Black Catholics, dir. **Orgs:** Canon Law Soc Am, 1974-; pres, Nat Black Sisters Conf, 1975-77; Catholic Campus Ministry Asn, 1981-; chair, Black-Hispanic Caucus, 1986-; ed, Urban League, 1987-. **Honors/Awds:** Appreciation in Mayor-Bicentennial Celebration, Mayor Philadelphia, PA, 1976; Appreciation as President, Nat Black Sisters' Conf, 1985; Religious Service Award, St Martin De Porres Soc, 1987; Outstanding Woman Award, YWCA, Richmond, 1990; Bishop Walter F Sullivan Serra Award, 1990; Distinguished Catholic School Graduate Award, 1992; W Catholic Hall of Fame, 1994;Richmond Chapter Humanitarian Award, 2001. **Special Achievements:** First black woman in the nation to lead a parish Church. First African American woman to serve as Pastoral Coordinator in the diocese of Richmond. **Home Addr:** 1301 Victor St, Richmond, VA 23222-3997, **Home Phone:** (804)329-4599.

BILLINGS, EARL WILLIAM
Actor. **Personal:** Born Jul 4, 1945, Cleveland, OH; son of Willie Mae; divorced. **Educ:** Karamu House Theater, attended 1963; Cuyahoga Community Col, attended 1963. **Career:** Cleveland Summer Arts Festive, proj dir, 1967Cleveland Summer Arts Festive, proj dir, 1967; Karamu Theatre, dir performing arts, 1968-70; Ark Arts Ctr, dir performing arts, 1970-73; Free Southern Theater, artistic dir, 1973-76; New Orleans Pub Sch, artist-in-resident, 1976; actor, 1976-; Film appearances: Stakeout, 1988; Wired, 1989; One False Move, 1992; One False Move, 1992; Jimmy Hollywood,1994; Crimson Tide, 1995; Larger Than Life, 1996; The Fan, 1996; Con Air, 1997; Living in Peril, 1997; Antwone Fisher, 2002; Am Splendor, 2003; Mr Boats, 2003; Thank You for Smoking, 2005; Something New, 2006; Senior Skip Day, 2008; TV series: "What's Happening", 1976-79; "New Attitude", 1990; "South Central", 1993; "Without a Trace",2004; "Christmas at Waters Edge", 2004; "How I Met Your Mother", 2005; "Miss/Guided", 2008; "True Blood", 2008. ; Karamu Theatre, dir performing arts, 1968-70; Ark Arts Ctr, dir performing arts, 1970-73; Free Southern Theater, artistic dir, 1973-76; New Orleans Pub Sch, artist-in-resident, 1976; actor, 1976-; Film appearances: Stakeout, 1988; Wired, 1989; One False Move, 1992; One False Move, 1992; Jimmy Hollywood,1994; Crimson Tide, 1995; Larger Than Life, 1996; The Fan, 1996; Con Air, 1997; Living in Peril, 1997; Antwone Fisher, 2002; Am Splendor, 2003; Mr Boats, 2003; Thank You for Smoking, 2005; Something New, 2006; Senior Skip Day, 2008; TV series: "What's Happening", 1976-79; "New Attitude", 1990; "South Central", 1993; "Without a Trace",2004; "Christmas at Waters Edge", 2004; "How I Met Your Mother", 2005; "Miss/Guided", 2008; "True Blood", 2008. **Orgs:** Screen Actors Guild; Actors Equity Asn; Am Fedn TV & Radio Artists; Acad Motion Picture Arts & Sci. **Military Serv:** USN, 1965-67. **Business Addr:** Actor, 8271 Melrose Ave Suite 110, Los Angeles, CA 90046.*

BILLINGS, MAC
Administrator. **Career:** Atlanta City Govt, Fire Safety Educ Dept, fire chief, 2000. **Business Addr:** Fire Chief, Atlanta City Goverment, Fire Safety Education Department, 675 Ponce De Leon Ave NE, Atlanta, GA 30308-1807, **Business Phone:** (404)853-7000.*

BILLINGS-HARRIS, LENORA
Writer, educator. **Personal:** Born Aug 9, 1950, Newark, NJ; daughter of Wendell Kenneth and Lois Billings; married Charles Sommerville Harris, Aug 10, 1974. **Educ:** Hampton Univ, BS, 1972; Univ Mich, MA, 1977. **Career:** Ariz State Univ, adj prof; Gen Motors Corp, proj adminr; CIGNA Corp, dir human resources; Univ Mich, Exec Develop Ctr Grad Sch Bus, prog dir, 1970; Excel Develop Syst, founder, 1986-; Univ NC, adj fac, currently. **Orgs:** Bd dir, Nat Speakers Asn; bd mem, Win Win Resolutions, NC; past chmn, Phoenix Women's Comn; past pres, Nat Speakers Asn-Ariz Chap; past bd mem, Ariz Women's Educ & Employ; vpres, Nat Speakers Asn. **Honors/Awds:** Outstanding Marketing Awards, Carlson Learning Co; Named Certified Speaking Professional, Nat Speakers Asn. **Special Achievements:** Listed in International Who's Who of Professionals, Who's Who in the West and Outstanding Young Women of America; appeared on numerous radio talk shows and has been featured in various publications include: Adult Ed Today, Arizona Republic, Arizona Business Gazette, Learning 2001, The Black Perspective, Professional Speaker, Managing Diversity Newsletter, Micro Rave, News and Record, Vitality Magazine. first African American president in National Speaker Association 32-year history. **Business Phone:** (336)282-4443.

BILLINGSLEA, MONROE L.
Dentist. **Personal:** Born Aug 3, 1933, West Palm Beach, FL; divorced; children: Brent, Christa. **Educ:** Howard Univ Sch Dent, attended 1963. **Career:** Coney Island Hosp Brooklyn, intern oral surgery, 1963-64; Minot AFB ND, chief oral surgery, 1964-65; Self-employed, dentist, LA, 1965-. **Orgs:** Nat Asn Advan Colored People; Southern Christian Leadership Conf; Kendrin Mental Health. **Honors/Awds:** Educational Achievement Award, USAF, 1954. **Special Achievements:** author: Smoking & How to Stop, 1978; Better Health Through Preventive Dentistry & Nutrition, 1978. **Military Serv:** USAF, capt, 1965-67. **Business Addr:** Dentist, 8500 S Figueroa Suite 3, Los Angeles, CA 90003.

BILLINGSLEY, ANDREW
School administrator, educator. **Personal:** Born Mar 20, 1926, Marion, AL; son of Silas Billingsley and Lucy Billingsley; married Amy; children: Angela & Bonita. **Educ:** Hampton Univ, attended 1949; Grinnell Col, AB, political sci, 1951; Boston Univ, MS, social work, 1956; Univ Michigan, MA, sociol, 1960; Brandeis Univ, PhD, social welfare, 1964. **Career:** Wis Dept Pub Welfare, Mendota State Hosp, psychiatric social worker, 1956-58; Univ Mich, Ann Arbor, dir friends int student ctr, 1959-60; Res Asst Mass Soc Prevention Cruelty C, social worker, 1960-63; Univ Calif, asst dean stud, 1964-65, assoc prof social welfare, 1964-68, asst chancellor acad affairs, 1968-70; Howard Univ, vpres, 1970-75; Metro Applied Res Ctr, Nat Urban League NYC, fel, 1968; Morgan State Univ, pres,1975-84; Univ Md, prof Sociol & Afro-Am studies, 1985-87, Dept Family Studies, prof, chmn; J Negro Educ, J Family Issues, ed bd, 1987; Spelman Col, vis scholar residence, adj prof sociol, 1992-95; Univ SC, Bd Trustees, prof, prof emer, currently. **Orgs:** Bd mem, Shiloh Bapt Church, Wash DC; Joint Ctr Polit Studies DC, 1972-75; Asn Black Sociologists; Am Sociol Asn; Nat Asn Black Social Workers; chmn, Family Sect, Am Sociol Asn, 1972-73; chmn, Comt Mgt, Howard Univ Press, 1972-74; chmn adv bd, J Abstracts; chmn, Nat Asn Social Workers, 1973; Asn Black Sociologists; Nat Coun Family Rel, Groves Conf Marriage & Family. **Honors/Awds:** Bienneal Research Award, Nat Asn Social Workers, 1964; Michael Schwerner Memorial Award, 1969; Honorary DHL, Grinnell Col, 1971; Nat Leadership Award, Afro-Am Families & Community Serv, 1972; Appreciation Award, Howard Univ Sci Inst, 1974; Appreciation Award, Nat Coun Black Child Develop, 1974; Fros Award, Howard Inst Arts & Humanities, 1974; Outstanding Contribution to Excellence in Education Award, PUSH Nat Convention, 1975; Community Service and Promoting Racial Equality Excellence Award, India Forum, 1978; Honorary DHL, Mercy Col, 1982; Dubois Johnson Frazier Award, Am Sociol Asn, 1992; Distinguished Scholar Award, Asn Black Sociologist, 1991; Matie Peters Award, Nat Coun Family Rels, 1990. **Special Achievements:** Author of Books & Periodicals. **Military Serv:** AUS, Quartermaster Corps, personnel sgt, 1944-46. **Home Addr:** 501 Hawkesbury Lane, Silver Spring, MD 20904, **Home Phone:** (301)622-2203. **Business Phone:** (803)777-8760.

BILLINGSLEY, RAY C.
Cartoonist or animator, writer, artist. **Personal:** Born Jul 25, 1957, Wake Forest, NC; son of Henry and Laura Dunn. **Educ:** Sch Visual Arts, New York, NY, BFA, 1979. **Career:** Crazy Mag, New York, NY, humorous artist, writer, 1975-79; Ebony Mag, Chicago, IL, freelance cartoonist, 1979-87; Disney Prod, Orlando, FL, animator, 1979-80; United Feature Syndicate, syndicated cartoonist, 1980-82; freelance jobs (layouts, advertising, mag illustration, fashion), 1982-88; King Features Syndicate, New York, NY, syndicated cartoonist, 1988-. **Orgs:** Nat Cartoonists Soc; Int Mus Cartoon Art; African Am Lit Book Club; Am Lung Asn. **Honors/Awds:** Pioneer of Excellence, The World Inst Black Commun, 1988; Award of Recognition, Detroit City Coun, 1989; Arts & Entertainment Achievement Award, Nat Am Advan Colored People, New Rochelle Br, 1993; Humanitarian Award, Am Lung Asn, 1999; Presidents Award, Am Lung Asn, 2000. **Special Achievements:** Started Oct 1969, at age 12, with "KIDS Mag". Possibly first Black artist to become prof at such a young age. Creator of comic strip "Curtis," King Features, the most popular minority comic strip in history. First Black artist to have a second comic strip publications; Author of Curtis & Twist & Shout, Ballantine Books. **Business Addr:** Syndicated Cartoonist, King

Features Syndicate, 888 7th Ave 2nd Fl, New York, NY 10019, **Business Phone:** (212)455-4000.

BILLINGSLY, MARILYN MAXWELL
Physician, health services administrator, pediatrician. **Personal:** Born in St Louis, MO; daughter of Warren and Willie Mae; married Dwight, 1988. **Educ:** St Louis Univ, BA, Biol, 1977, MD, 1981. **Career:** St Louis Univ, asst prof, 1985-92, fac, 1997; People's Health Ctrs, med dir, 1992-97; St Louis Univ, Combined Internal Med Pediatric Residency Prog, Assoc Prog Dir, currently, Dept Pediat, assoc prof, currently. **Orgs:** Nat Med Asn, 1995-; Mound City Med Forum, local br, 1985-, pres, 1994-95; Am Acad Pediatrics, 1985-; Am Col Physicians, 1985-; Focus on the Family Physicians Resource Coun, 1994-; Christian Med & Dental Soc, 1995-; Med Inst for Sexual Health, adv bd, 1995-. **Honors/Awds:** Volunteer of the Year, Health Care for the Homeless Coalition, 1989; mem of the Yr, Salvation Army, Med Fel, 1993; Pub Health Serv Physician Award for Excellence, Natl Health Serv Corps, 1995; Sigma Gamma Rho George Washington Carver Distinguished Serv Award, 1996; Res & Status of Black Women Award, Miss Conf of the AME Church, 1996. **Special Achievements:** Provides a free clinic in a homeless shelter, 1986-; Postponing Sexual Involvement Prog for Teens, 1995-; Author, 'Complete Book of Baby and Child Care'. **Business Phone:** (314)977-8077.

BILLINGTON, CLYDE, JR.
State government official, chemical engineer. **Personal:** Born Aug 29, 1934, Hartford, CT; married Malora W; children: Mark, Christal, Courtney. **Educ:** Lincoln Univ, BA; Conn Univ; Md Univ. **Career:** Pratt & Whitney Aircraft, chem engr, 1961-65; State Conn, state rep, 1969-80; Clyde Billington Real Estate & Liquor Merchants Inc, CT, owner & operator, 1965-. **Orgs:** Area broker, US Dept HUD; Hartford Bd Realtors, 1967-74; pres, N Hartford Prop Owners Asn; pres, Oakland Civic Asn; bd dir, Businessmen's Asn; bd dir, Pioneer Budget Corp; Am Chem Soc; Nat Asn Advan Colored People; Urban League; dir, Gr Hartford Conv & Vis Bur; treas, Dem Town Comn. **Special Achievements:** Voted 1 of 1,000 Most Successful Black Businessmen, Ebony Mag. **Military Serv:** AUS, spp, 1959-61. **Business Addr:** Owner, Clyde Billington Real Estate & Liquor Merchants Inc, 1789 Albany Ave, Hartford, CT 06105.*

BILLOPS, CAMILLE J.
Artist, movie director, educator. **Personal:** Born Aug 12, 1933, Los Angeles, CA; daughter of Lucious and Alma Gilmore; married James Hatch. **Educ:** La City Col, AA, 1955; Calif State Col, BA, 1960; City Col, NY, MFA, 1973. **Career:** Huntington Hartford Found, fel, 1963; MacDowell Colony, fel, 1975; Hatch-Billops Col, co-founder; Afro-Am Bellwether Press, NY, ed, 1975-76; Rutgers Univ; City Col, artist, art educr & lectr; Rutgers Univ, Newark, instr art, 1975-87; Hatch-Billops Collection, pres & adminr, 1975-; Films: Older Women and Love; Suzanne, Suzanne; Finding Christa; KKK Boutique Ain't Just Rednecks; A String of Pearls. **Orgs:** Nat Conf Artists, 1972; Nat Conf Art Teachers; NY Women Film; NY State Coun Arts, 1987-88; NY Found Arts, 1989; Rockerfeller Found, 1991; Nat Endowment Arts, 1994. **Honors/Awds:** International Women's Year Award, 1975-76; Independent Focus Award, Mus Modern Art; New Dirs New Films Award, Mus Modern Art; Grand Jury Award, Sundance Film Festival, 1993; James Van Der Zee Award, Brandywine Graphic Workshop, 1994; Skowhegan Award, 2000. **Special Achievements:** Sculpture, drawings & prints have been exhibeted at The Studio Museum,Harlem; author of The Harlem Book of the Dead; art articles in NY Times, Amsterdam News, Newsweek; numerous exhibits US & abroad. **Business Addr:** President, Hatch-Billops Collection Inc, 491 Broadway Front, New York, NY 10012.*

BILLS, JOHNNY BERNARD
Physician. **Personal:** Born Oct 3, 1949, Hickory Valley, TN; married Hilda M; children: Jacqueline; Melissa; Johnny III. **Educ:** Memphis State Univ, adv chem courses, 1970; Rust Col, Holly Springs, BS, chem & math, 1971; Univ Miss Med Sch, Jackson, MD, 1977. **Career:** Ashland High Sch, math teacher, 1971-72; Rust Col, lab technician, 1972-73; Univ Hosp, intern, 1977-78; Jefferson County Hosp, staff physician, 1978-79; Madison, Yazoo, Leake Family Health Ctr, consult physician, 1979-80; Hosp Emergency Rm, physician, 1977-; Bills Med Clinic, med dir, 1980-. **Orgs:** Phi Beta Sigma Fraternity, 1968-; Am Med Asn, 1977-; Jackson Med Soc, 1977-; Southern Med Asn, 1980-; chmn infection control, Methodist Hosp, Lexington, MS, 1981-; Chamber Com, 1983-; secy, Miss Med & Surg Asn, 1983-85; Nat Asn Advan Colored People; Jackson YMCA; New Hope Baptist Church; Jackson Rust Col Club; Baptist Haiti mission, World Concern. **Honors/Awds:** Alpha Beta Mu Honor Society, 1967-71; Academic Achievement Award, Science Student of Year, Rust Col, 1971; Friend of Children Citation-World Concern, United League of Holmes C Citation, 1983. **Home Addr:** 324 Pratt Rd, Wiggins, MS 39577. **Business Addr:** Physician, 225 Community Dr, PO Box 248, Fayette, MS 39069.*

BILLUE, ZANA
Business owner. **Personal:** Born Feb 5, 1964, Brooklyn, NY; daughter of Windsor Rhoden and Erma. **Educ:** Temple Univ, BA, 1986; Culinary Inst Am, AOS, 1993. **Career:** Aramark corp, concept develop chef; Nestle USA, recipe develop specialist, 1996; Zana Cakes, owner, 1997-. **Orgs:** Retail Baker's Asn, 1998; comt mem, United Way Serv-Greater Cleveland, 1997-; comt mem, Harvest Hunger. **Honors/Awds:** feauted, Black Enterprise Mag. **Home Addr:** 7700 Stenton Ave Suite 214, Philadelphia, PA 19118-3102. **Business Addr:** Owner, Zana Cakes Inc, 12 W Willow Grove Ave Suite 153, Philadelphia, PA 19118, **Business Phone:** (215)248-1575.

BILLUPS, CHAUNCEY
Basketball player. **Personal:** Born Sep 25, 1976, Denver, CO; son of Ray and Faye. **Educ:** Univ Colo, 1999. **Career:** Boston Celtics, guard, 1997-98; Toronto Raptors, 1998-99; Denver Nuggets, 1999-00; Orlando Magic, 2000; Minn Timber wolves, 2000-02; Detroit Pistons, 2002-. **Honors/Awds:** Colorado Mr. Basketball, 1993, 1994, 1995; Big Eight Freshman, 1996; NBAFinals Most Valuable Player, 2004; All-Star, 2006, 2007; NBA Sportsmanship Award, 2008; All-NBA Third Team, 2009. **Special Achievements:** Ranks 10th in 3-pointers made; ranks 16th in 3-point field goal attempts. **Business Phone:** (248)377-0100.*

BILLUPS, MATTIE LOU
Government official. **Personal:** Born Mar 5, 1935, Bixby, OK; married Vernon S Billups Sr; children: Jacci Love, Jocelyn Palmer, Vernon Jr, Ricci Evans, Reginald Evans, Cheryl Lee, Robyn Evans, Murphy, Debi Cayasso, Beverly, Lesa Singleton. **Educ:** BTW High Sch, 1954. **Career:** Town Red Bird, OK, former mayor. **Orgs:** Church of Christ 1967-; treas, Red Bird Park Fund, 1977-80; treas, Branding Iron Saddle Club, 1972-85; Wagoner County Democratic Women, vpres, 1983-85. **Honors/Awds:** Most Outstanding Mayor for Black Mayors, Okla Conf Black Mayors, 1984. **Home Addr:** 679 S Market, Redbird, OK 74458. *

BILSON, CAROLE
Executive. **Educ:** Univ Michigan, BS, indust design, 1980; Amos Tuck Sch, Dartmouth, cert strategic mkt; Haas Sch Bus, Univ Calif Berkeley. **Career:** Eastman Kodak Co, prod develop & mkt mgt; PDU Consortium, founder; Pitney Bowes Inc, Prod Design & Usability, dir, currently. **Special Achievements:** First Black woman and one of three Black industrial designers in the U.S. holding executive positions with major corporations to lead a design and usability department. **Business Addr:** Director, Pitney Bowes Inc, Production Design & Usability, 1 Elmcroft Rd, Stamford, CT 06926-0700, **Business Phone:** (203)356-5000.

BINFORD, HENRY C.
Educator. **Personal:** Born May 2, 1944, Berea, OH; son of Dorothy Johnston and Henry F; married Janet Cyrwus; children: Charles & Evan. **Educ:** Harvard Univ, AB, 1966, PhD, 1973; Univ Sussex, Eng, MA, 1967. **Career:** Harvard Univ, teaching fel hist, 1969-73, asst head tutor hist, 1970-72; N western Univ, asst prof hist, 1973-79, Urban Studies Prog, dir, 1978-81, assoc prof hist & Urban Affairs, 1979-, Prog Am Cult, dir, 1982-85, MA Liberal Studies Prog, dir, 1997-. **Orgs:** Evanston Hist Soc; bd dir, Bus & Prof People Pub Interest, 1985-; Archit Alliance Chicago Hist Soc; Chicago Archit Found; Chicago Hist Soc; Pi Lambda Theta; Boy Scouts Am; Sigma Pi Phi. **Honors/Awds:** Outstanding Teaching Award, N western Univ, Col Arts & Sci, 1984; Alumni Asn Award, N western Univ, 1996; Nat Faculty Award, Asn Grad Liberal Studies Prog, 1998; Outstanding Faculty Member Award, N western Univ, 1999; Outstanding Affiilate Award, Northwestern Dept African Am Studies, 2005; Charles Deering McCormick Prof Teaching Excellence. **Special Achievements:** Auth: The First Suburbs, Univ of Chicago Press, 1985. **Business Addr:** Associate Professor of History, Director, Master of Arts in Liberal Studies Program, N western University, Department of History, 1800 Sherman 105, Evanston, IL 60208-2220, **Business Phone:** (847)491-7262.

BING, DAVE
Basketball player, mayor, executive. **Personal:** Born Nov 29, 1943, Washington, DC; married Yvette; children: Cassaundra, Bridgett & Aleisha. **Educ:** Syracuse Univ, BA, 1966. **Career:** Basketball player (retired), executive, politician; Detroit Pistons, 1966-74, WashBullets, 1975-77, Boston Celtics, 1977-78; National Paragon Steel, mgt trainee, 1978-80; The Bing Group, owner & pres, 1980-2009; Detroit City, mayor, 2009-. **Orgs:** Sigma Alpha Mu Frat, Syracuse; bd dir, Stand Fed Bank, 1997-. **Honors/Awds:** Rookie of the Year, NBA, 1967; All Am Career, Syracuse Univ; 7 time All Star; J Walter Kennedy Citizenship Award, 1977; inductee, Basketball Hall of Fame, 1980; Small Business Person of the Year, President Ronald Reagan, 1984; Schick Achievement Award, 1990; Naismith Memorial Basketball Hall of Fame, 1990; Business Newsmaker of the Year, Crains Detroit, 1994; Dr, Kettering Univ, 2000; Dr, Univ Mich, 2006; Humanitarian of the Year Award, Nat Conf Community & Justice Mich, 2006; Detroiter of the Year, Hour Magazine, 2007; Idealist in Action Award, City Year, 2008. **Special Achievements:** Named as one of the NBA's 50 Greatest Players of all time. One of the most successful black business owners in the United States. **Business Addr:** Mayor, City of Detroit, Coleman A Young Municipal Ctr, Two Woodward Ave Suite 1126, Detroit, MI 48226, **Business Phone:** (313)224-3400.

BING, RUBELL M.
Librarian. **Personal:** Born Jan 6, 1938, Rocky Mount, NC; daughter of Lonnie Moody and Alberta Green Moody; married Alex Bing Sr, Jan 7, 1961; children: Bonita, Tovoia, Yvonne, Alex J. **Career:** St Francis De Sales Sch, librn, 1977-; media specialist. **Orgs:** Lifetime mem, PTA, Wash, DC, 1975; supvr, Summer Youth Prog, Brentwood Sec, 1981; DC Bd Election & Ethics, 1984-; bd mem, Bettie Benjamin Scholar Funds, 1984-87; St. Anthony's Gospel Choir; Betty Benjamin Scholar Fund; treas, Cath Libr Asn. **Honors/Awds:** Girl Scout Council Award, 1974; William R Spaulding Award, 1981. *

BINGHAM, PORTER
Executive. **Educ:** Morehouse Col. **Career:** Malachi Group Inc, pres & chief exec officer, 1996-. **Business Phone:** (404)237-3031.*

BINGHAM, REBECCA JOSEPHINE
Educator, librarian, commissioner. **Personal:** Born Jul 14, 1928, Indianapolis, IN; married Walter D Bingham; children: Gail Elaine Simmons, Louis Edward Simmons. **Educ:** IN Univ, BS, 1950; Univ Tulsa, MA, 1961; IN Univ, MLS, 1969. **Career:** Alcorn A&M Col, asst librn, 1950-51; Tuskegee Inst, serials librn, 1952-55; Jarvis Christian Col, actg librn, 1955-57; Indianapolis Pub Libr, librn sch serv dept, 1957; Tulsa Jr High Sch, librn, 1960-62; Russell Jr High Sch, eng teacher, 1962-63; Jackson Jr High Sch, librarian, 1963-66; Louisville Pub Sch, supvr libr serv, 1966-70, dir media serv, 1970-75; KY Pub Schs, Jefferson Co, dir media serv (retired), 1975-00; US Nat Comn Libr & Info Sci, comnr, 1998-. **Orgs:** Alumni Bd Grad Libr Sch; chmn, Am Asn Sch Librns; Am Sch Coun Asn; Joint Media Com; pres, Ky Libr Asn, 1971; Ky Govs State Adv Coun on Libr, 1971-73; AA5L Nat Libr Week Com; Coun Am Libr Asn, 1972-; Ala Com Planning, 1973-; vpres, Alumni Asn Grad Libr Sch, 1973-74; Ky Lib Asn Legis Com, 1973-74; secy treas, S E Reg Libr Asn Resources & Tech Serv Div, 1973-75; exec bd, Am Libr Asn, 1974-78; pres, Alumni Bd Grad Libry Sch 1974-75; chmn, Am Asn Sch Libr, Ency Britannica Sch Lib Media Prog Yr Awards; com exec bd, Ky Asn Super & Curriculum Develop, 1976-77; KY Sch Supt Adv Coun Super, 1977-; adv com, Bro-Dart Elem Sch Lib Collection, 1975-77; Britannica Jr, 1975-76; World Book, 1977-79; White House Conf Libr & Info Serv, 1978-79; pres, Am Asn Sch Librn, 1979-80; Louisville Jefferson Co Health & Welfare Coun Bd Dirs; pres, Southeastern Libr Asn, 1984-86; sch adminr, Jefferson Co 1985-86. **Honors/Awds:** Tangley Oaks Fel, 1967; Beta Phi Lib Sci Hon; Outstanding Sch Librn KY Libr Trustees, 1969; Louise Maxwell Award Outstanding Achievement field Lib Sci Gra Lib Sch, Ind Univ; Woman of the Yr Louisville, YWCA, 1978. *

BINS, MILTON
Consultant. **Personal:** Born Dec 11, 1934, Hazlehurst, MS; son of John and Elizabeth Middleton; married Adrienne O King; children: Gregory Milton & Randall S Jackson. **Educ:** Univ Ill, BS, 1956, BS, 1960; Ill Inst Technol, attended 1959; Chicago State Univ, MS, 1966; Univ Pa, MS, 1972. **Career:** Chicago Brd Educ, high sch math teacher, 1960-66; Harcourt Brace Jovanovich, textbook salesman & urban educ consult, 1966-69; Coun The Grade City Sch, sr assoc, 1974-81; White House Initiative Historically Black Col & Univ, US Dept Educ, exec dir, 1981-82; Coun The Grade City Sch, dep exec dir, 1982-91; COT Vision Inc, vpres educ, 1994; GOP, Analyst 7 Activist, currently. **Orgs:** Corp dir, John F Small Advertising Agency, 1973-74; Alpha Phi Alpha Frat,1973-; Coun 100 Black Republican Leaders, 1974-; chmn, Coun 100, 1986-89,1991-; chmn & chief exec officer, Douglass Policy Inst; life mem, Nat Alliance Black Sch Educators, 1986-; life mem, Africare, 1984-; life mem, Am Israel Friendship League, 1987-; appointee, President George Bush's Adv Bd Historically Black Cols & Univs, 1990-93; Nat Adv Coun Elec Power Res inst, 1997-01. **Home Addr:** 1120 Columbia Rd NW, Washington, DC 20009, **Home Phone:** (202)462-0777. *

BIRCH, ADOLPHO A
Judge, educator, lawyer. **Personal:** Born Sep 22, 1932, Washington, DC. **Educ:** Lincoln Univ, attended 1952; Howard Univ, BA, 1956, JD, 1956. **Career:** Lawyer, Judge (retired), educator; pvt law pract, 1958-69; Meharry Med Col, adj prof legal med, 1959-69; Davidson Co, asst pub defender, 1964-66, asst dist atty gen, 1966-69; Davidson Co Part 1, Ct of Gen Sessions, judge, 1969-78; Fisk Univ, lectr law, 1970-72; Tenn State Univ, lectr law, 1970-72; Criminal Ct Davidson Co, Div III, judge, 1978-87; Tenn Ct Criminal Appeals, assoc judge, 1987-93; Nashville Sch Law, teaching fac law, 1991-2006, emeritus fac, 2006-; Supreme Ct Tenn, chief justice, 1996-97, justice. **Honors/Awds:** Justice AA Birch Bldg, named in hon; William H Hastie Award, Nat Bar Asn, 2005; Judicial Coun excellence in legal & judicial scholar & commitment to justice, NBA; Barbara Jordan Award, Phi Alpha Delta Law Fraternity. **Special Achievements:** First African American ever to serve as Chief Justice of the Tennessee Supreme Court. **Business Addr:** Emeritus Faculty, The Nashville School of Law, 2934 Sidco Dr Suite 1, Nashville, TN 37204, **Business Phone:** (615)256-3684.

BIRCH, WILLIE
Artist. **Personal:** Born Nov 26, 1942, New Orleans, LA; son of Wilson and Anna; children: Christopher, Postelle, Ama & Freedom. **Educ:** Southern Univ, attended 1961, BA, 1969; Md Inst, Col Art, MFA, 1973. **Career:** Bowie State Col, teacher, 1973;

Henry St Settlement, teacher, 1980; Guggenheim Museum, teacher, 1981; Hunter Col, teacher, 1988-96, artist, currently; Coun Arts, Nat Endowment Arts, NY, Visual Artist fel, 1989-90; Lila Wallace, Readers Digest, Int Artists fel, 1992; John Simon Guggenheim, Mem Found fel, 1993; Selected solo exhibitions: Smith-Mason Gallery, Wash, DC, 1973; Art Works Gallery, Baltimore, MD, 1975; The Studio Museum in Harlem, artist in residence, 1977-78; Miami-Dade Libr, Miami, FL, 1984; Philadelphia Art Alliance, Philadelphia, PA, 1990; Luise Ross Gallery, NY, 1996; Satori Fine Art, Chicago, IL, 1996; Gallery Joe, Philadelphia, PA, 1997-98; Witnessing New Orleans, Arthur Roger Gallery, New Orleans, LA; Del Ctr Contemp Arts, Wilmington, DE, 1998; Tamarind Inst, artist in residence, 2000; New Orleans Jazz & Heritage Found, artist in residence, 2002. **Orgs:** Luise Ross Gallery, New York; Arthur Roger Gallery, New Orleans; NYC Metro Transit Authority, Arts Transit, Philadelphia Int Airport, 1994; Munic Collab Proj, Downtown Winston-Salem, 1995. **Honors/Awds:** Artist in Residence, Henry Street Settlement, 1980-81; Visual Artist Fellowship Grant, sculpture, Nat Endowment Arts, 1984-85; Artist's Fellowship Award, painting, NY Found Arts, 1986; Minority Third World Fellowship Award, Printmaking Workshop, 1987; Mayor's Arts Award, New Orleans, 2002; Grant recipient, Joan Mitchell Found, 2006. **Military Serv:** USAF, airman first class, 1962-65. **Home Addr:** 2022 N Villerre St, New Orleans, LA 70116, **Home Phone:** (504)949-2365. **Business Addr:** Artist, Arthur Roger Gallery, 432 Julia St, New Orleans, LA 70130, **Business Phone:** (504)522-1999.

BIRCHETTE, DR. WILLIAM ASHBY, III
Educator. **Personal:** Born May 9, 1942, Newport News, VA; divorced; children: Stacy Olivia Edwards & William Ashby Birchette, IV. **Educ:** St Augustine's Col, BA, 1964; VA State Univ, MEd, 1973; Univ VA, EdD, 1982. **Career:** Eduactor (retired): Darden HS, teacher & coach; DE Tech & Community Col, teacher, Eng & Community; Johnson JHS, teacher; Banneker JHS, prin; Reservoir MS, prin; Magruder MS, prin; DC Pub Sch, asst to the reg supt; S Vance HS, prin; Isle Wight Cty Sch, asst supt; Spotsylvania County Sch, supvr, Eng Lang Arts; Twenty-Five Outstanding High Schs, NC Dept Educ, prin, 1991; Prince William County Pub Sch, assoc supt, 2004. **Orgs:** Omega Psi Phi; PDK; NABSE; ASCD; Optimist Club; NAACP; exec secy, ATA; NABSE; Achievable Dream, Exec Bd, Northern VA Workforce Investment Comm. **Honors/Awds:** Outstanding Leadership Award, Region V, DC Public Schools, 1978; Citizen Involvement in Education, 1980; Charles Stewart Mott Fellow, UVA, 1980; School of Education Fellow, UVA; Outstanding Small & Rural School Adminr, NSBA, 1995; Distinguished Graduate Award, Huntington HS Faculty, 1996; Coaches Hall of Fame, Wilson, NC, 2002. **Special Achievements:** NASSP, Middle School Principal of the Year, Finalist, 1987; Author, "Guidelines for Middle Schools in Virginia", VASSP Journal, 1988; USTA League Tennis - 4.5 National Champion, 1999; UNCF Feature Story, Spring 2003. **Home Addr:** 13010-106 Garden View Lane, Raleigh, NC 27614.

BIRCHETTE-PIERCE, CHERYL L.
Physician. **Personal:** Born Sep 25, 1945, New Orleans, LA; married Samuel H Pierce II; children: Samuel Howard. **Educ:** Spelman Col, AB, 1968; Meharry Med Col, MD, 1972; Harvard Univ, MPH, 1980. **Career:** Joslin Clin, patient mgt/instruction, 1972-75; Lahey Clin NE Deaconess Hosp, intern resident, 1972-75; Peter Bent Brigham Hosp, ambulatory care doctor, 1973-74; Harvard Univ Med Sch, instr med, 1973-80; NE Baptist Hosp, critical care cpr physician coord, 1975-78; Roxbury Dent Med Group, med dir, 1976-80; McLean Hosp, consult internal med, 1976-80; MIT-HMO Cambridge, MA, dir health screening physician provider, 1981-86; pvt pract, clinician. **Orgs:** Television/conference/health workshop appearances varied health issues, 1974-; attending physician, US Olympic Team Pan Am Games, 1975; sec house delegates 3rd vpres, Nat Med Asn, 1983-85, 1986-; work group participant Health Policy Agenda AMA, 1985-86; Amer Pub Health Asn. **Honors/Awds:** Merrill Scholarship Study & Travel Faculte de Medicine, Univ Geneva, Switzerland, 1966-67; Outstanding Young Women in America, 1973; US Dept of Health Human Serv Fel, 1980-81; Keynote/Founder's Day Speaker, Delta Sigma Theta, 1981. **Home Addr:** 2353 Manor Ave, East Point, GA 30344-1062. **Business Addr:** Physician, Private Practice, 91 Parker Hill Ave, Boston, MA 02120.

BIRDINE, STEVEN T
Administrator, president (organization). **Career:** Pres, Affirmations Action, currently. **Orgs:** Grand Polaris, Iota Phi Theta Fraternity Inc, nat pres. **Special Achievements:** Author: "A Common Sense Approach To Retaining Students of Color,? 1994; 100 Most Influential Blacks in US, Ebony Magazine, 2002-05.

BIRRU, MULUGETTA
Government official. **Personal:** Born Sep 30, 1946, Tig-Ray, Ethiopia; son of Mizan Berbe and Birru Sibhat; married Elizabeth Birru, 1974; children: Elizabeth, Meheret, Rahel. **Educ:** Addis Ababa Univ, BA, Mgt & acct, 1970; Syracuse Univ, MA, Econ, 1975, MBA, bus & Int finance, 1974; Univ Pittsburgh, PhD, pub & int affairs, 1991. **Career:** Agr & Ind develop Bank, Ethiopia, sr proj eval & res officer, 1970-75; Ethopian Beverage Corp, dir planning & bus develop, 1975-78; Nat Chem Corp, gen mgr & chief exec officer, 1978-80; Seminole Econ Develop Corp, vpres

& dir bus develop, 1980-83; Homewood-Brushton RDC, exec dir, 1983-92; Urban Redevelop Authority Pittsburgh, exec dir, 1992-04; Greater Wayne Co Econ Develop Corp, dir, currently. **Orgs:** Bd mem, Pittsburgh Downtown Partnership; bd mem, Pittsburgh Partnership Neighborhood Develop; bd mem, I Have A Dream Found, 1993; Carnegie Mellon Univ; adj prof, Heinz Sch Pub Policy & Mgt. **Honors/Awds:** Pittsburgh Man of the Yr, 1995; Best & Brightest Business and Professional Men, Dollars & Sense, 1993; Eastern Region Financial Servs of the Yr, Small Bus Asn, 1990; Financial Services Award, Pa Chamber, 1989. **Business Addr:** Director, Greater Wayne County Economic Development Corporation, 600 Randolph St, Detroit, MI 48226, **Business Phone:** (313)224-0410.*

BIRTHA, JESSIE M.
Librarian. **Personal:** Born Feb 5, 1920, Norfolk, VA; married Herbert M; children: Rachel Roxanne Eitches & Rebecca Lucille. **Educ:** Hampton Inst, BS, 1940; Drexel Univ, MLS, 1962. **Career:** Librarian (Retired); Pa Sch St Helena Island SC, sec sch teacher, 1941-42; Norfolk, elem sch teacher, 1942-46; Free Libr Philadelphia, br librn, 1959-80; Antioch Grad Sch, lit instr, adj fac Philadelphia Ctr, 1975-76. **Orgs:** Pub consult, McGraw Hill Lang Arts Prog Am Lang Today, 1974; Am Libr Asn; Pa Libr Asn. **Honors/Awds:** Free Library Citation as Supervisor of the Year, 1973; Josey & Shockley Handbook of Black Librarianship, 1977; Chapel of Four Chaplains Legion of Hon Award for Outstanding Work with Minority C, 1979; Jessie Carney Smith, Images Blacks Am Cult, 1987. **Special Achievements:** Articles published in PLA Bulletin, Top of News, McCann & Woodward-The Black American in Books for Children, 1972.

BISAMUNYU, JEANETTE
Marketing executive. **Personal:** Born in Kabale, Uganda; daughter of Eli Nathan and Irene Rosemary. **Educ:** Makerere Univ, Kampala, Bcom, 1981; Talladega Col, BA, 1983; Atlanta Univ, MBA, 1985. **Career:** Talladega Col, stud tutor, 1981-83; Equitable Life Assurance Soc, mgt intern, 1982; Atlanta Univ, grad asst, 1984-85; Citicorp Acceptance Co, mgt intern, 1984; US West, mgr, 1985-91; Environ Educ Solutions, gen mgr, 1991-; Golbal Insight, reg bus mgr, currently. **Orgs:** Toastmasters Int, vpres, 1985-90; Dale Carnegie Commun Course, grad asst, 1987; Nebraskans Peace, co-chair the bd, 1988-; Vision HOPE Prog, mentor, 1988-; Church Resurrection, organist & choir dir, 1991; Nat Asn Female Exec, 1991-; Am Asn Univ Women, 1991-; Omaha Womens Chamber Com, 1991-. **Honors/Awds:** Alpha Chi, 1983; Certificate of Honor for Student with Highest GPA Business, 1983; Beta Gamma Sigma, 1985; Nebr Music Olympics, piano performance, gold trophy, 1988, 1989, 1991, bronze medal, 1990. **Business Addr:** Regional Business Manager, Global Insight USA Inc, 530 5th Ave 7th Fl, New York, NY 10036, **Business Phone:** (212)884-9513.

BISHOP, DR. ALFRED A.
Consultant. **Personal:** Born May 10, 1923, Philadelphia, PA; son of Samuel and Rose; divorced; children: Janet L. **Educ:** Univ Pittsburgh, BS, chem, 1950; Univ Pittsburgh, MS, chem, 1965; Carnegie Mellon Univ, PhD, 1974. **Career:** Naval Res, engr, 1950-52; Fischer & Porter Co, engr, mgr, 1952-56; Westing house Corp, engr, 1956-65; Carnegie Mellon Univ, lectr, 1967-69; thermal & hydraul design & develop, mgr, reactor safety, 1965-70; Westinghouse Corp Nuclear Energy, consult engr, 1970-85; BB Nuclear Energy Consult, partner, 1974-; Univ Pittsburgh, res prof, 1970-74, assoc prof, chem engineering, dir, nuclear engineering prog, 1974-80, full prof, 1981-85, prof emer. **Orgs:** Am Indian Coun Architects & Engineers, 1960-; Am Soc Mech Engineers; Am Welding Soc; bd dir, United Fund, 1969-73; Am Soc Elec Engineers; bd dir, Pa Youth Ctr, 1973-; sr life master, Am Bridge Asn. **Honors/Awds:** Scholar Rutgers & Lincoln Univ, 1942; DuPont Research Award, 1971; NSF Award, 1975; Non-Newtonian Research, NSF, 1981-84. **Special Achievements:** Auth numerous publ field nuclear engineering heat transfer & fluid mechanics. **Military Serv:** AUS, T & 4, 92nd div, signal corps, 1943-46; three battle stars. **Home Addr:** 50 Belmont Ave, Bala Cynwyd, PA 19004. *

BISHOP, BLAINE ELWOOD
Football player. **Personal:** Born Jul 24, 1970, Indianapolis, IN; married Cella Butler, 1999. **Educ:** Ball State Univ, BS, ins. **Career:** Football Player (Retired); Houston Oilers, defensive back, 1993-96; Tenn Oilers, 1997-98; TennTitans, 1999-2001; Philadelphia Eagles, safety, 2002. **Honors/Awds:** Four Times Pro Bowler, 1995-97. 2000. *

BISHOP, CECIL
Clergy, bishop. **Personal:** Born May 12, 1930, Pittsburgh, PA; married Marlene, Mar 2, 1986; children: Jason, Dana. **Educ:** Knoxville Col, BA, 1954; Howard Univ, BD, 1958, MDiv; Wesley Theol Sem, STM, 1960; Livingstone Col, DDiv. **Career:** Bishop (retired) Ordained deacon, 1955; elder, 1957; Clinton AME Zion Ch, pastor, 1957-60; Trinity AME Zion Church, Greensboro, NC, 1960; AME Zion church, bishop, 2000, sr presiding prelate. **Orgs:** Dir, AME Zion Ch's Div of Preaching Ministries Dept of Evangelism; mem bd, Homes Missions; NC State Adv Com of US Commn on Civil Rights; chmn, Greensboro Housing Authority; pres, NC Coun Churches. *

BISHOP, CLARENCE
Manager. **Personal:** Born Feb 19, 1959, Selma, AL; married Caroly. **Educ:** Wayne Col, BA, 1980, MA, Spec Educ, 1985. **Career:** Lake Park Day Care Ctr, coun,1977-78; Mission Immaculate Virgin Group Home, sr counselor, 1978-79, child care worker, 1980-81; Wagner Col, asst lead teacher, 1980; NY State Div Youth, asst supvr; Baltimore City Mayor Martin O'Malley, Chief Staff; Maryland Dept Bus Econ Develop, dep secy, currently. **Orgs:** Organized Lake View Pk Basketball Leaguen teenagers; founder & regional dir & advisor, Sigma Phi Rho Frat; bus mgr, Nat Governors Coun, Sigma Phi Rho; Honorary Soc Art; Catholic Youth Orgn Basketball League; Rutgers Univ Pro-Basketball League; Sigma Phi Rho; Baltimore City Planning Comn; Baltimore Hotel Corp; Downtown Partnership Baltimore; Baltimore Develop Corp; E Baltimore Develop Inc; Nat Aquarium Baltimore; Reginald F Lewis Museum Maryland African American History & Culture. **Honors/Awds:** NY State Division for Youth's Regional Director Award, Academic Excellence & Career Develop; Founders Achievement Award, Sigma Phi Rho Frat. **Business Phone:** (410)767-6300.*

BISHOP, ERIC MARLON. See FOXX, JAMIE.

BISHOP, RON. See BISHOP, RONALD L.

BISHOP, RONALD L. (RON BISHOP)
Government official, executive director. **Personal:** Born Apr 24, 1949, Lewisburg, TN; son of David D and Erma L; married Sharon Wooten, Jul 7, 1973; children: Jennifer, Meredith. **Educ:** Fisk Univ, BS, health & phys educ, 1970; Tenn State Univ, attended 1971. **Career:** Tenn Dept Correction, assoc warden security, 1976-79, dir rehab servs, 1979-80, dir instnl progs, 1980-83, dir of spec progs, 1983, asst to the comnr, 1983, dep comnr, 1983-85; Tenn Bd Paroles, chmn parole bd, 1986-87, bd mem, 1988-90; Shelby Co Govt, Div Correction, dir, 1990-94, chief, 1995-98; Div Community Corrections, dir, currently. **Orgs:** Tenn Legis Comn, Tenn sentencing comn, 1987; bd dirs, Free the Cn, 1991-94; NACO, justice & pub safety steering comm, 1991-95; City Mayor WW Herenton, Transition Team, criminal justice comm, 1991; Leadership Memphis Class, 1992; chmn, United Way, Shelby Co Group, 1992; Mayor's Black-on-Black Crime Task Force, 1992. **Honors/Awds:** NABCJ, Jonathan Jasper Wright Award, 1992. **Special Achievements:** Auth: "Shelby Co Inmate Training Emphasizes Local Labor Market," Large Jail Network Bulletin, 1992. **Business Addr:** Director, Division of Community Corrections, 2020 Yonkers Rd MSC 4250, Raleigh, NC 27699-4250, **Business Phone:** (919)716-3100.*

BISHOP, SANFORD D
Lawyer, congressperson (u.s. federal government). **Personal:** Born Feb 4, 1947, Mobile, AL; son of Dr Sanford D Sr and Minnie S; married Vivian Creighton; children: Aayesha J Reese. **Educ:** Morehouse Col, BA, 1968; Emory Law Sch, JD, 1971. **Career:** Civil rights atty; Ga State House Reps, 1977-90; Ga State Senate, 1991-92; US House Reps, congressman, 1992-. **Orgs:** Eagle Scout; 32nd Degree Mason; Shriner; Sigma Pi Phi Fraternity; Kappa Alpha Psi Fraternity; Urban League; Cong Black Caucus; Blue Dog Dem Conservative Coalition in the House; State Bar Ga; Ala State Bar; Am Bar asn; Nat Bar Asn; Mt Zion Baptist Church; House Comt Appropriations. **Honors/Awds:** Spirit of Enterprise Award, US Chamber Com, 2000, 2004-05; Man of the Year Award, Columbus Men's Progressive Club. **Special Achievements:** 100 Most Influential Georgians, Georgia Trend Mag, 1997; One of the 100 most influential Georgians, 2005-06; Top 10 List of Georgia State Legislators, Southern Center for Studies in Pub Policy; 50 Most Influential Black Men in Georgia, Georgia Informer. **Business Addr:** Congressman, United States House of Representatives, 2429 Rayburn House Off Bldg, Washington, DC 20515-1002, **Business Phone:** (202)225-3631.

BISHOP, SHERRE WHITNEY (SHERRE MILLER)
Public relations executive, writer. **Personal:** Born Sep 2, 1958, Nashville, TN; daughter of Carrie Pillow and Christian Lytle; married Joseph Bishop, Apr 22, 1989; children: Joseph Bishop Jr. **Educ:** Tenn State Univ, BS, 1982, MA, 1994; Am Baptist Col, ThB, 2001. **Career:** WPTF-TV, news reporter, 1984-89; Meharry Med Col, media specialist, 1989-91; Black Entertainment TV, freelance reporter, 1989-94; Tenn State Univ, producer/public info officer, 1991-94, dir pub rels currently; WVOL Radio, producer/talk show host, 1992-94; WLAC-TV, talk show host, 1993-94; Nashville Airport Authority, pub affairs mgr; Tenn State Univ, dir pub rel, currently. **Orgs:** Bd mem, Int Asn Bus Communicators, 1994-; comt member, Nashville Area Chamber Com, 1994-; comt member, Mayor's Transp Workshop, 1994-; comt mem, Save Our Black Female Adolescents Proj, 1995-. **Honors/Awds:** Volunteer Service Award, Bethlehem Ctr, 1991; Scholarship Award, CASE District III, 1991; Raymond Black Service Award, Nashville Peace Officers Asn, 1993; Journalistic Achievement Award, Soc Prof Journalists, 1995. **Special Achievements:** Author: "Auntie's Grace," entered Essence Magazine writing contest, 1993; Playwright: How I Got Over, 1991; Supporting actress in Ossie Davis's, "Purlie," 1991; Just Like Me (A Black History Series), 1992; The Great Train Ride, 1978; From the Motherland to the

Promised Land, 2001 (an award-winning monologue chronicling the African American worship experience); Hands, 2003; and The Virtuous Woman, 2004.

BISHOP, VERISSA RENE
Law enforcement officer. **Personal:** Born Nov 22, 1954, Houston, TX; daughter of Julia Lee (deceased). **Educ:** Tex Southern Univ, BA, 1987. **Career:** Foley's Dept Store, Houston, TX, receptionist/beauty operator, 1973-75; Houston Police Dept, Houston, TX, clerk dispatchers div, 1975-78, police officer, 1978-90, juvenile div sgt, 1990-. **Orgs:** Bd mem & secy, Afro-Am Police Officers League; fin secy, secy & bd mem, Nat Black Police Asn; YWCA; Phi Beta Lambda; City Wide Beauticians; Christian Hope Baptist Church; Nat Asn Advan Colored People. **Honors/Awds:** Member of Year, Afro-American Police Officers League; Member of Year, National Black Police Asn, 1990; Outstanding Member of Southern Region, National Black Police Asn. **Business Addr:** Sergeant, Houston Police Department, 61 Riesner, Houston, TX 77001, **Business Phone:** (713)880-6000.*

BISHOP, WESLEY T
Lawyer. **Personal:** Born in New Orleans, LA. **Educ:** Southern Univ, BS, criminal justice; Univ Miss, MA, pub admin; Ohio State Univ Law Sch, JD. **Career:** Orleans Parish Dist Attys Off, law clerk; New Orleans Legal Assistance Corp, law clerk; New Orleans City Coun Res Off, legis intern; New Orleans Health Corp, chmn; Orleans Parish Dem Exec Comm, vchmn; La Dem State Cent Comt, House Dist 101, rep, 2004; Southern Univ New Orleans, asst prof criminal justice & assoc vice chancellor acad affairs, currently; B. Ray & Assocs Consult Group, atty & managing partner, currently; Spears & Spears, of coun, currently. **Orgs:** Bd dirs, Am Bar Asn; bd Dirs, N.O.J.A. Govs Adv Comn Equal Opportunities; bd dirs, La State Bar Asn; bd dirs, Nat Bar Asn; bd dirs, Louis A Martinet Legal Soc; bd dirs, Alpha Phi Alpha Fraternity; Beacon Light Baptist Church. **Honors/Awds:** Outstanding Alumnus, Southern Univ New Orleans, 1997; Outstanding Orator Award, Ohio State Univ. **Special Achievements:** One of the Top 30 Leaders under 30 nationwide, Ebony Magazine. **Business Addr:** Associate Vice Chancellor for Academic Affairs, Southern University at New Orleans, 6400 Press Dr Bldg 22B, New Orleans, LA 70126, **Business Phone:** (504)286-5232.

BISWAS, DR. PROSANTO K.
Educator. **Personal:** Born Mar 1, 1934, Calcutta, W. Bengal, India; married Joan; children: Shila. **Educ:** Univ Calcutta, BS, 1958; Univ Mo, MS, 1959, PhD, Plant Sci, 1962. **Career:** Univ Mo, res assoc, 1961; Tuskegee Realty, pres; Tuskegee Univ, Tuskegee Inst Campus, Dept Agr & Environ Sci, prof plant & soil sci, 1962-, head, currently. **Orgs:** Chmn, Macon County Bd Educ; Macon County Chamber Com. **Honors/Awds:** Faculty Achievement Award, Tuskgee Univ; Outstanding Faculty Performance Award, Tuskgee Univ; R D Morrison and F E Evans Outstanding Scientist Award, 1890 Asn Res Dir; R W Brown Distinguished Research Scientist Award. **Special Achievements:** Publ: 45 Refereed Journal Articles, 75 Technical Presentations & 5 Technical Reports. **Home Addr:** 608 S Main St, Tuskegee, AL 36083. **Business Addr:** Professor, Head, Tuskegee University, Department of Agricultural and Environmental Sciences, 201 Milbank Hall, Tuskegee Institute, AL 36088-1634, **Business Phone:** (334)727-8446.

BIVENS, SHELIA RENEEA
Nurse. **Personal:** Born Jul 10, 1954, Pine Bluff, AR; daughter of Leon J and Myrtle Jones Ervin; widowed; children: Cory, Ronnie & Ronniesha. **Educ:** Univ Ariz, Fayetteville, attended 1974; Univ AMS, Col Nursing, BSN, 1977, MNSC, 1982. **Career:** Dr C E Hyman, nurse practitioner, 1977-81; Jefferson Regional Med Ctr, charge nurse, 1981-83; Univ AMS, Univ Hosp, staff nurse, 1983-89, charge nurse, 1989-; Ark Cares, obstet gynec nurse & practr, currently. **Orgs:** Ark State Nurses Asn, 1977-; secy, Little Rock Br, Nat Asn Advan Colored People, 1983-84, state secy, 1984-; chap pianist, 19 Elect Chap 5 OES, 1984; Ariz Black Nurses Asn, 1987; Ark Perinatal Asn, 1987; Sigma Theta Tau Nursing Hon Soc, 1989-; Nat Perinatal Asn; Napare. **Honors/Awds:** Outstanding Youth Award, Livingstone Col Gen Educ African Methodist Episcopal Zion Church, 1970; Outstanding Service Award, OES Electa Chap 5, 1983; Five Year Service Award, Univ AMS, 1989; Outstanding Black Employee of the Month, Univ AMS, 1989. **Home Addr:** 54 Saxony Cir, Little Rock, AR 72209, **Home Phone:** (501)568-7642. **Business Addr:** Nurse, University Hospital, Medical Science Campus, 4301 W Markham Slot 711 A, Little Rock, AR 72205, **Business Phone:** (501)661-7987.

BIVINS, CYNTHIA GLASS
Lawyer. **Personal:** Born Dec 10, 1955, Houston, TX; daughter of Raymond and Mattye; married Demetrius K Bivins, Apr 16, 1983; children: Demetrius K II & Emily Jewel. **Educ:** Tufts Univ, BA, polit sci, 1978; Univ Tex, Law Sch, JD, 1981. **Career:** Harris County Dist Atty's Off, asst dist atty, 1981-83; William & Mary Col, asst vis prof, 1983; Bexar County Dist Atty Off, asst dist atty, 1984-88; Groce, Locke & Hebdon, PC, shareholder, 1988-96; Jenkens & Gilchrist, PC, shareholder, 1996-; Ogletree, Deakins, Nash, Smoak & Stewart, PC, shareholder, 2001-. **Orgs:** San Antonio Bar Asn, 1989-; San Antonio Black Lawyers Asn, 1989-; Bexar County Women's Bar Asn, former bd mem, 1989; Nat Bar Asn, 1989-; Am Bar Asn, 1989-; Fed Bar Asn, 1990-; Jack & Jill Am, prog chair for sandboxers, 1999-; Links Inc, 1999-; Defense Res Inst, bd mem former employment law comt chair, 2001-03. **Special Achievements:** Defense Research Organization's for the Defence, 1999, 2001. **Business Phone:** (210)354-1300.

BIVINS, DEMETRIUS
Lawyer. **Career:** Lawer (retired); City Pub Serv, atty. **Orgs:** Past chair, African-Am Lawyers Sect, State Bar Tex; adv, Comt Ct Security.

BIVINS, EDWARD BYRON
Executive. **Personal:** Born May 11, 1929, Birmingham, AL; married Sarah Felton; children: Cheryl Ann, Janet Yvette. **Educ:** Tuskegee Inst, BS, 1951; OH State Univ, MA, 1955; So IL Univ, Tuskegee Inst, attended 1963. **Career:** Secy, Greater KC Housing Inc; Savannah State Col, teacher, 1955-64; Oppors Indus Ctr, Philadelphia, 1964-68; OIC Nat Inst, training dir, branch dir, nat dir educ & training reg dir; Midwest Res Inst, sr staff, 1968-69; Urban Coalition Greater, KC, exec dir, 1969-70; Hallmark Cards Inc, dir urban & minority affairs, 1970-. **Orgs:** C of C Small Bus Affairs Comt, 1974-75; President's adv coun Minority Bus Enterprise; MO State Dept Educ Adv Comn; bdchmn, Bus Resources Ctr, 1974-75; KC MO Bd Police Commr, 1973-77; chmn, KC Region Manpower Coun; Downtown Kiwanis Club, KC; treasr, United Comn Serv; bd mem, C Mercy Hosp; bd mem, Family & C Serv. **Honors/Awds:** Kiwanian of the Year, 1972-73; Kappa Alpha Psi Achievement Award, Middlewestern Province, 1973; Kappa Man of the Year, KC Alumni Chap, 1973. **Special Achievements:** Author of several publs. **Military Serv:** AUS, 1952-54. **Business Addr:** Director of Urban and Minority Affairs, Hallmark Cards Inc, 25 Mc Gee Trafficway, Kansas City, MO 64141.

BIVINS, JIMMY
Boxer. **Personal:** Born Dec 6, 1919, Dry Branch, GA. **Career:** Boxer (retired); prof boxer, 1940-55. **Honors/Awds:** Int boxing hall of Fame inductee; interim heavyweight champion. **Military Serv:** AUS, hon.

BIVINS, SONJA F
Judge. **Educ:** Spring Hill Col, BS, 1985; Univ Ala, JD, 1988. **Career:** Minority Corp Coun Asn, magistrate judge; U.S. Dist Ct, Southern Dist Ala, magistrate judge, currently. **Orgs:** State Bar Ga. **Special Achievements:** First Black federal judge in the Southern District of Alabama. **Business Addr:** Magistrate Judge, U.S. District Court, Southern District of Alabama, 113 St Joseph St, Mobile, AL 36602, **Business Phone:** (251)694-4545.

BLACK, ALBERT, JR.
Administrator, president (organization), chief executive officer. **Personal:** Born Jan 1, 1959?. **Educ:** W W Samuel High Sch, Dallas, attended; Univ Tex, Dallas, attended 1982; Cox Sch Bus, Southern Methodist Univ, MBA, 1995. **Career:** On-Target Supplies & Logistics, pres, 1982-, chief exec officer, currently; JPMorgan Chase Tex; Rees Assocs; PrimeSource Food Equipment Co; Greater Dallas Chamber Com, chmn, 2000. **Orgs:** bd regents, Tex Southern Univ, Houston, 1977; bd dir, Cox Sch Bus; bd dir, Baylor Univ, Hankamer Sch Bus; advisory bd, Oncor Energy; bd gov, Dallas Found; trustee, Baylor Univ Med Ctr; advisory bd, Chase Bank; bd dir, Dallas-Tex; bd mem, Paul Quinn Col; Dallas Citizens Coun; Gov George Bush's Bus Coun; Omega Psi Phi; New Hope Baptist Church. **Honors/Awds:** Distinguished Alumni Award, Univ Tex, Dallas, 2003; 30th Cong Dist Award; Quest for Success Award, Dallas Black Chamber Com. **Business Addr:** President, Chief Executive Officer, On-Target Supplies & Logistics, 1133 S Madison Ave, Dallas, TX 75208, **Business Phone:** (214)941-4885.*

BLACK, BARRY C.
Military leader, chaplain. **Personal:** Born Nov 1, 1948, Baltimore, MD. **Educ:** Oakwood Col; Andrews Univ; NC Cent Univ; Eastern Baptist Sem; Salve Regina Col; US Int Univ, MA, coun, mgt & divinity, DMin & PhD, psychol. **Career:** US Senate, chaplain, 2003-. **Orgs:** Nat Asn Advan Colored People. **Honors/Awds:** Meritorious Service Medals (twice); Navy & Marine Corps Commendation Medals (twice); Renowned Service Award, Nat Asn Advan Colored People, 1995; Benjamin Elijah Mays Distinguished Leadership Award, Morehouse Sch Religion, 2002; Image Award, "Reaffirming the Dream — Realizing the Vision" for military excellence, Old Dominion Univ chap, Nat Asn Advan Colored People, 2004. **Special Achievements:** First African-American chaplain to the United States Senate; First Seventh-day Adventist to the United States Senate; First military chaplain to hold the office of chaplain to the United States Senate; first African American to serve as the U.S. Navy Chief of Chaplains; Author: "From the Hood to the Hill", 2006. **Military Serv:** USN, from chaplain, 1976, rear adm, chief navy chaplains, 2000-03 (retired). **Business Phone:** (202)224-3121.*

BLACK, DR. BILLY CHARLESTON
Educator. **Personal:** Born Feb 1, 1937, Beatrice, AL; married Helen Ruth Jeenings; children: James Edward & Marla Jeaninne. **Educ:** Tuskegee Inst, BS, 1960; Iowa State Univ, MS, 1962, PhD, 1964. **Career:** School administrator (retired); Tuskegee Inst, lab instr, 1959-60; Iowa State Univ, res asst, 1960-64; Albany State Col, prof chem, 1964, dept chem & physics, chmn, 1966-80, div sci & math, chmn, 1969-70, div arts& sci, chmn, 1970-80, acad affairs, interim asst dean, 1979-80, actg pres, 1980-81, pres 1981-96. **Orgs:** Consult, NSF, 1966; consult, NIH, 1966; AAAS; Gamma Sigma Delta; Soc Sigma Xi; Iowa Acad Sci; Phi Lambda Upsilon; Am Asn Clinical Chemists; Am Chem Soc; Am Oil Chemists Soc; Am Inst Chemists; Ga Acad Sci; Inst Food Technologists; basileus Omega Psi Phi Frat, 1980-; chmn bd, stewards Hines Memorial C Memorial Episcopal Church; chmn, Coun President SIAC, 1984-;Nat Serv Comn; Am Assoc State Cols & Univs, NCAA President's Comn, 1987-91. **Honors/Awds:** American Institute Chemists Award; Black Georgian of the Year Award, 1980. **Special Achievements:** Publications including "The Separation of Glycerides by Liquid-Liquid Column Partition Chromatography" J Am Oil Chemists Soc, 1963; "The Isolation of Phosphatides by Dielectrophoresis" J of the IA Acad Sci, 1964. *

BLACK, CHARLES E.
Pilot. **Personal:** Born Apr 2, 1943, Bainbridge, GA; divorced; children: Harriet & Michael. **Educ:** Purdue Univ, BS, 1964; GA State Univ, MS, 1976. **Career:** Ford fel, GA State Univ, 1971-73; Eastern Airlines Inc, pilot. **Orgs:** Nat Honor Soc, 1960; Alpha Phi Alpha Fraternity, 1961-65; Am Soc Pub Admin, 1971; coord, SW Atlanta Comprehensive Comt Planning Workshops,1974; Orgn Black Airline Pilots. **Honors/Awds:** Best All Around Student, Washington HS, 1960. **Military Serv:** USAF, capt pilot b-52, 1967-71; Air Medal with 2 Oak Leaf Clusters, 1970. **Business Addr:** Pilot, Eastern Airlines Inc, Flight Opers Hartsfield Int Airport, Atlanta, GA 30354.

BLACK, DANIEL L., JR.
Government official, chief financial officer. **Personal:** Born Sep 16, 1945, Sheldon, SC; son of Daniel and Susie; married Mary Lemmon; children: Carlita. **Educ:** SC State Col, bus admin, 1971; Univ SC, MBA, 1975. **Career:** Internal Revenue Serv, Jacksonville, exam group mgr, 1976-78, Atlanta, sr regional analyst, 1980-81, exam br chief, 1981-82, Oklahoma City, chief appeals officer, 1983-85, Greensboro Dist, asst dist dir; Laguna Niguel Dist, asst dist dir; Springfield, dist dir; Off Tax & Revenue, dep chief financial officer, 2004-. **Orgs:** Am Inst CPA's, 1977-86; Fla Inst CPA's, 1977-; Omega Psi Phi Fraternity, 1978-; Sr Execs Asn, 1985-; Beta Alpha Psi Acct Fraternity; Alpha Kappa Mu, Nat Hon Soc; Greater Wash Soc Cert Pub Accountants. **Honors/Awds:** Distinguished Alumni Award, 1985; Commissioner's Award, Internal Revenue Serv, 2002. **Military Serv:** AUS, specialist E-4, 1963-66; Good Conduct Medal; Vietnam Serv & Defense Medal. **Business Addr:** Deputy Chief Financial Officer, Office of Tax & Revenue, Off Chief Financial Officer, John A Wilson Bldg 1350 Pa Ave NW, Washington, DC 20004.*

BLACK, DAVID EUGENE, SR.
Educator, administrator. **Personal:** Born Nov 9, 1940, Columbus, OH; son of James E and Alberta L; married Marie Robinson, Oct 5, 1962; children: David E Jr, Monika L. **Educ:** Cent State Univ, BS, educ, 1964; Xavier Univ, educ admin, 1974. **Career:** Administrator (retired); Columbus Pub Sch, Columbus Alternative High Sch, asst prin. **Orgs:** Pres, Cent State Alumni Asn, Columbus Br, 1991-92; Nat Alliance Black Sch Educr, 1992; Ohio Asn f Sec Sch Adminr, 1992; Nat Asn Sec Sch Adminr, 1992; Columbus Admin Asn, 1992; Lenden Community Alliance, 1992; Columbus Pub Sch, Multi-Cultured Steering Comt, 1992; Vice Chmn Bd & chaired various committees. **Honors/Awds:** Upward Bound, Outstanding Adminr, 1980; Outstanding Educator Apple Award, Columbus Pub Sch, 1992.

BLACK, DON GENE
Public relations executive, administrator. **Personal:** Born Sep 6, 1945, Chicago, IL; son of Uster and Inez Franklin-Davidson; married Glenda Camp Black, Aug 14, 1966; children: Donerik, Shronda. **Educ:** Sinclair Community Col, attended 1967; Wright State Univ, BA, mass commun & mkt, 1970. **Career:** Dayton Express News, dir pub rels, 1967-68; Monsanto Res Corp, mkt, 1968-70; Don Black Assoc Photog & Pub Rel Inc, founder & pres, 1970-77; Multi-Western Pub Rel & Mkt Co Inc, pres, 1977-93; MWC Publ Inc, founder & pres, 1993-. **Orgs:** bd mem, Urban Youth Asn, 1976-81; pres, Ohio Assoc Black Pub Rel/Advert/Mkt Co, 1983-85; pres, Dayton Chap Nat Bus League, 1983-86; adv bd, Goodwill Industs. **Honors/Awds:** Achievement Award, Dayton Pub Sch, 1985; free lance writer; Community Service Award, USAF, 1987; Presidents Award, Nat Bus League, 1989; Martin Luther King Coordination Award, 1990; Success Guide Award; WROV Radio Award, 1995; Martin Luther King President's Award, 1995; WROU & WRNB Black Achiever Award; Journalist of the Year Award; Nat Bus League Community Service Award; Peace Bridge Award; Ohio Purchasing Council Hall of Fame Award. **Special Achievements:** Publisher: Dayton Weekly News; listed in Who's Who in Marketing, Who's Who Among African Americans, Who's Who in Business & Parity's Top Ten African American Males. **Business Addr:** President, Founder, MWC Publications Inc, Dayton Weekly News, 15 E 4th St Suite 601, Dayton, OH 45402, **Business Phone:** (937)223-8060.*

BLACK, FRANK S.
School administrator, educator. **Personal:** Born Feb 3, 1941, Detroit, MI; son of Frank Black and Zella Fisher Black; children: Piper L & Jason B. **Educ:** Cent State Univ, Wilberforce, OH, BS, 1967; Ohio State Univ, MA, 1969,PhD, 1972. **Career:** Columbus Ohio Pub Schs, eval asst, 1969-71; Ohio State Univ, proj dir & adj asst prof, 1972-73; Tex Southern Univ, assoc prof & dir institutional res, 1973-77, assoc prof educ, 1973-78; Murray State Univ, Col Human Develop & Learning, asst dean, 1978-84; Univ Southern Fla, Ft Myers, assoc dean acad affairs, 1984-85; Jackson State Univ, vpres acad affairs,1985-87; Univ Tenn, Martin, vice chancellor acad affairs, 1988-94, prof educ, 1994-2000, interim vice chancellor acad affairs, 2000-02; interim educ dean, 2002-. **Orgs:** Am Educ Res Asn, 1971-75; Phi Delta Kappa 1974-; mem exec comt, Asn Inst Res, 1977-79; Am Asn Col Teacher Educ, 1979; Murray KY Human Rights Comn, 1979-; adv bd, WKMS Univ Radio Sta, 1979-; adv bd, W Ky Regional Mental Health & Retarded Bd, 1979; Phi Kappa Phi, 1988-; Mid-South Educ Res Asn, 1995; Am Asn Schs, Cols & Univs, 1994. **Honors/Awds:** Grad Fel, Soc Ohio State Univ, 1967-69; Friend of Nursing Award, Tenn Nurses Asn, District 10, 1994; Alpha Kappa Alpha Award, AKA Sorority Inc, UTM Chap; Outstanding Achievement, 1994; Greek Man of the Year, Univ Tenn, 1997; Faculty Teaching Fall, 2005. **Military Serv:** AUS, sp4, 1958-61. **Home Addr:** 156 Baker Rd, Martin, TN 38237, **Home Phone:** (731)588-0741. **Business Addr:** Interim Dean of Education, The University of Tennessee at Martin, 237 Gooch Hall, Martin, TN 38238-5021.

BLACK, FREDERICK HARRISON
Executive. **Personal:** Born Nov 11, 1921, Des Moines, IA; son of F H Black; married Kay Browne; children: Joan Jackson, Lorna, Jai & Crystal. **Educ:** Fisk Univ, BS, engr physics, 1949; Univ S Calif, Los Angeles, MS, physics, 1952; Pepperdine Univ, MBA, 1972; Univ MA, DEd Personnel, 1975. **Career:** USN, consult chief naval personnel; pres Domestic Council, consult; General Electric Co, missile project engr, Wash DC; corp mgr EEO safety & security; Watts Indus Park, exec dir; FH Black & Assocs, mng partner; FH Black & Assocs, prin exec, currently. **Orgs:** Dipl, Am Personnel Soc; bd pres, TRY US; mem bd, ICBO; trustee, Fisk Univ; bd chmn, Myerhoff Fund, 1990-; vpres, Nat Minority Jr Golf Scholar Asn, 1988-; bd of dirs, Arts Coun Richmond, 1990-. **Honors/Awds:** Whitney Young Medal, Nat Urban League; Booker T Wash Award, Nat Bus League; Corp Pioneer Award, Bus Policy Rev Coun. **Special Achievements:** published several articles. **Military Serv:** AUS, second lt. **Business Addr:** Managing Partner, Principal Executive, FH Black & Assocs, 529 14th St Suite 1063, Washington, DC 20045.

BLACK, GAIL
Executive. **Personal:** Born Aug 29, 1950, Klamath Falls, OR; married Carl B Bowles; children: Amil Christopher Bowles, Teri Ruth Bowles. **Educ:** Portland State Univ, attended 1971; Portland OIC, cert legal sec, 1977. **Career:** Clairon Defender Newspaper, asst ed & pub, 1970-; Union Pac RR Co Law Dept, litigation specialist, 1977-. **Orgs:** Dir, Jimmy Bang-Bang Walker Youth Found, 1969-; chmn, Albina Rose Festival float com prize winning floats Portland Rose Festival Parade, 1969-71; asst, Albina area coord United Good Neighbors, 1970-73; bd mem, Knockout Indust, 1971-; exec bd mem, Tenth Ave Irregulars Chap Toastmasters Int, 1979-; United Way rep Union Pac RR Co, 1979-80; parent adv com mem, NE Christian Sch, 1980-. **Honors/ Awds:** Dean's List, Portland State Univ, 1970-71. **Business Addr:** Assistant Editor, Publisher, Clairon Defender Newspaper, 319 NE Wygant St, Portland, OR 97211.*

BLACK, HAROLD A.
Educator. **Personal:** Born Jul 3, 1945. **Educ:** Univ Ga, BBA, 1966; Ohio State Univ, MA, 1968, PhD, 1972. **Career:** HF Ahmanson & Co, Irwindale, Ca, dir; Nashville Br Fed Res Bank Atlanta, dir & chmn; Univ Fla, Dept Econ, Gainesville, FL, asst prof, 1971-75; Dept Econ Res & Anal, Off Comptroller Currency, dep dir, 1975-78; Univ NC Chapel Hill, Sch Bus Admin, NC, assoc prof finance, 1978-83; Howard Univ, Dept Finance & Ins, Sch Bus & Pub Admin, Wash, DC, prof & chmn, 1983-84; Am Univ, Dept Econ, Wash, DC, prof, 1985-87; Univ Tenn, Col Bus Admin, James F Smith Jr prof financial inst, 1987-, Dept Finance, head, 1987-95; pres, H A Black Co Inc, currently. **Orgs:** Bd mem, Nat Credit Union Admin; Savings Asn Ins Fund Adv Comt. **Honors/ Awds:** Special Achievement Award, Dept Treasury; Outstanding Service Award, Nat Urban League; Distinguished Alumnus Award, Univ Ga Col Bus Admin; Exceptional Service Award, Nat Credit Union Admin; Chancellor's Award for Research Excellence, Univ Tenn; John B Ross Teaching Award, 2001. **Business Addr:** Professor, University of Tennessee, College of Business Administration, 431 Stokely Mgt Ctr, Knoxville, TN 37996.

BLACK, DR. JAMES TILLMAN
Dentist. **Personal:** Born Feb 19, 1935, Guthrie, OK; married Joyce Toran; children: James Jr & Jeanine. **Educ:** Tenn State Univ, BS, 1955; Michael Reese Sch Med Tech, attended 1956; Cent State Univ, MA, 1960; Loyola Univ Sch Dent, attended 1964. **Career:** Crenshaw Prof Dent Ctr, founder & dentist, currently. **Orgs:** Officer Los Angeles Den Soc, 1977; Los Angels Co Pub Health Serv, 1964-71; NAACP; Am Dent Asn; Los Angels Dent Soc; Angel City Dent Soc; Kappa Alpha Psi Frat; Xi Psi Phi Dent Frat; sire archon, Xi Boule, 2005-07; nat chmn, Health & Wellness Comt. **Special Achievements:** Published: 'Dentistry in a Headstart Program', 1972; 'Changes in Dental Concepts', 1976. **Military Serv:** AUS, spec 3, 1956-58. **Home Addr:** 11920 Brentwood Grove Dr, Los Angeles, CA 90049. **Business Addr:** General Dentist, Crenshaw Professional Dental Center, 3015 Crenshaw Blvd, Los Angeles, CA 90016-4264, **Business Phone:** (323)731-0801.

BLACK, DR. KEITH
Physician. **Personal:** Born Sep 13, 1957, Tuskegee, AL; married Carol Bennett; children: 2. **Educ:** Univ Mich, degree, med training. **Career:** Univ Mich Med Ctr, Ann Arbor, internship gen surg & residency neurol surg; Univ Calif, Los Angeles, prof neurosurg, Dept Surg, Ruth & Raymond Stotter chair, 1992, Comprehensive Brain Tumor Prog, head; Cedars-Sinai Med Ctr, Maxine Dunitz Neurosurgeon Inst & Div Neurosurg, dir neurosurg, 1997-, Ruth & Lawrence Harvey chair neurosciences, 1997-, Dept Neurosurg, chmn, currently. **Orgs:** Joint Am Asn Neurol Surgeons; Cong Neurol Surgeons; Am Asn Neurol Surgeons; Neurosurg Soc Am; Acad Neurol Surg; founding mem, N Am Skull Base Soc; Nat Adv Neurol Disorders & Stroke Coun, Nat Inst Health, 2000-04; comt mem, Cali Inst Regenerative Med Independent Citizens Oversight Comt, 2004-06. **Honors/Awds:** Essence Awards, 2001. **Special Achievements:** Publ more than 100 sci articles. **Business Addr:** Director Neurosurgeon, Chairman, Cedars-Sinai Medical Center, Division of Neurosurgery, 8700 Beverly Blvd, Los Angeles, CA 90048, **Business Phone:** (310)423-0825.

BLACK, DR. LEE ROY
College teacher, administrator. **Personal:** Born Jul 29, 1937, Oakland, MS; married Christine Gray; children: Lori Lynette, Colette Marie, Angela Denise & Lee Roy Jr. **Educ:** Univ IL Navy Pier, 1958; Roosevelt Univ, BA, hist, 1962; Loyola Univ Sch Law, attended 1970; OH State Univ, NPEL, 1974; Union Grad Sch, PhD, admin criminal justice systems & correctional educ, 1976. **Career:** Tex Agr & Mech Univ, prof; Cook Cty Dept of Public Aid, caseworker, 1953-62; Juv Ct of Cook Cty, probation officer, 1963-67, suprv prob officer, 1966-67; Chicago Dept Human Resources, Div Correctional Serv, unit dir Lawndale-Garfield Corrections Unit, 1967-70, asst dir, 1967-70; UECU, dir Correctional Educ Prog, 1970-72; Teacher Corps Youth Adv Prog US Off Educ; field liaison rep, 1975-76; UECU, supvr, 1975-76; IN Univ Dept of Forensic St, vis asst prof, 1975-76; State IN, Dept Corr, Div Class & Treat, dir, 1976-77; State WI, Dept Health & Soc Serv, Div Correction, deputy admin, 1977-81; State Miss, Comnr Corrections; American Correctional Asn; State MO Dept Cor & Human Res, dir; Jackson State Univ, prof; Calif State Univ, Long Beach, prof; Calif Univ, Pa, assoc prof criminal just, 2001-. **Orgs:** Pres, Midwest Asn Corrections Admin; Am Corrections Asn; Nat Alliance for Shaping Safer Cities; NAACP; Nat Urban League; Alpha Phi Alpha; Nat Asn Blacks Criminal Justics; chmn, corrections subcommittee MO Governors Comm Crime; chmn & prog, coun ACA Nat Conf, 1986. **Honors/Awds:** Outstanding Achievers Awd, MO Black Leg Caucus; Great Guy Awd, WGRT Radio Station; Image Award, Outstanding Contrib to Youth Career Youth Devel; E R Cass Distinguished Achievement Award, American Criminal Justice Asn, 1989.

BLACK, LEONA R.
Lawyer, administrator. **Personal:** Born Jan 5, 1924, Galveston, TX. **Educ:** Prairie View Col; Roosevelt Univ; Chicago Univ; DePaul Univ. **Career:** Cook City Dept Public Aid, file clerk, finance clerk, head file clerk, office mgr, Chicago US Post Off, clerk supvr; Int Harvester Co, equipment expeditor; AA Rayner Alderman 6th Ward, alderman's sec, admin asst; AR Langford Alderman 16th Ward, alderman's sec, admin asst; Donald Page Moore, polit org; State's Atty Cook County, polit coordr Bernard Carrey; Fraud & Consumer Complaint Div Cook County, appt admin chief, 1972; Cook County States Atty Off, dir victim/witness asst proj, 1974-. **Orgs:** Ombudsman States Atty Off; polit activist, Nat Delegate, 1972; lobbyist, Local City State for Consumer Protection Judicial Reform; advocate, Criminal Justice, Consumerism, Judicial Reform, Child Abuse, Drug Abuse, Alcoholism; youth gr dir, founder, org SCAPY; bd dir, Nat Org Victim Asn, 1976. **Special Achievements:** Set up Consumer Fraud classes within City Col. **Business Addr:** Director of Victim, Witness Assistant, Cook Co States Atty Off, 2600 S California Ave, Chicago, IL 60608.*

BLACK, LUCIUS
State government official, educator. **Personal:** Born Oct 4, 1925; married Mildred; children: Urey Rufus, Lucius Jr & Don Keith. **Educ:** Ala State Univ, BS; Columbia Univ, MA. **Career:** Educator (retired), government official; Sumter County Sch Syst, teacher; York Citizens Fed Credit Union, mgr & treas; Ala House Representatives, Dist 67, rep, 1985-94, Dist 71, rep. **Orgs:** Nat Conf State Legis; SCLC; NBCSL; NAACP; Ala New S Coalition; Tuscaloosa County Legis. **Honors/Awds:** Appreciation Plaques & Awards from various organizations. **Home Addr:** 504 S Broad St, York, AL 36925-2507, **Home Phone:** (205)392-5713.

BLACK, DR. MALCOLM MAZIQUE (MIKE BLACK)
Educator, jazz musician. **Personal:** Born Nov 28, 1937, Vicksburg, MS; son of Henriette Grace Smith and Fred Bell; married Emma Kern; children: Varen Delois & Karen Barron. **Educ:** Jackson State Univ, BME, 1959; Univ Wis, MME, 1967; Nova Univ, EdD, 1975. **Career:** Fla & Miss HS, band dir, 1959-69; Fla Asn Collegiate Registrars & Admis Officers, vpres 1979; Broward Community Col, registrar, dir admis, 1969-79, dir Jazz Studies & Bands; Bronx Comm Col, dir; dirperformed with Patti Page, Sam Cooke, Marilyn McCoo, Billy Davis & others. **Orgs:** Placement Comn, Am Asn Collegiate Registrars & Admis Officers, 1975; Fla Veterans Adv Coun, 1975; Fla Sch Rels Comn, 1975; vpres, Fla Asn ColRegistrars & Admis Officers, 1977; bd mem, Broward County Housing Authority Adv Bd, 1978, Sunshine State Bank, Sistrunk Hist Festival Comt;Am Fedn Musicians; Music Educators Nat Conf; Nat Asn Jazz Educators; Kiwanis Club; S Fla Musicians Asn. **Honors/Awds:** Plaque, Fla Asn Col Registrars & Admis Officers, 1979; recognition as Broward County Black Pioneer, Links Inc, 1980; plaque, 47 Years Serv, Omega Psi Phi Frat, 1981; plaques, Sistrunk Hist Festival Comn, 1981-85;Outstanding Florida Citizen, Gov Fla, 1986; Good Neighbor Award, Miami Herald Newspaper, 1986; Sharps & Flats Freedom exhibit, Chicago, 1988. **Home Addr:** 2991 NW 24th Ave, Oakland Park, FL 33311, **Home Phone:** (954)731-7791.

BLACK, MIKE. **See BLACK, DR. MALCOLM MAZIQUE.**

BLACK, VERONICA CORRELL
Executive, vice president (organization). **Personal:** Born Oct 30, 1946, Winston-Salem, NC; daughter of Vance A and Beatrice Moore; married Isiah A Jr; children: Braswell & Sandra B. **Educ:** Livingstone Col, Salisbury, NC, BA, 1969; Am Bankers Assn, Wash DC, human resources cert, 1984; Univ NC, Chapel Hill, NC, young exec prog, 1987; Duke Univ, Sr Mgt Dev Prog, 1996. **Career:** Executive (retired); Wachovia Bank & Trust Co, Winston-Salem, NC, sr vpres, group exec, personnel, 1970-2001. **Orgs:** Personnel Comn, 1986, personnel comn chmn, YWCA, 1987-89, bd mem, 1985-89; regional vpres, Bankers Educ Soc, 1981-86; chmn, Career Serv Adv Comn,Winston-Salem State Univ, 1989; secy, Senior Servs, currently. **Honors/Awds:** Leadership Award, Winston-Salem State Co-op Off, 1986; Positive Image Award, Minority Recruiter Newspaper, 1992. **Home Addr:** 3400 Del Rio Ct, Winston-Salem, NC 27105, **Home Phone:** (336)725-5702.

BLACK, WALTER WELDON, JR.
Executive. **Personal:** Married Clairdean E Riley; children: Walter III. **Educ:** Morgan State Col, BS, 1958; Amer Univ Law Sch, 1962. **Career:** Prudential Ins Co Am, spec agent; Nat Assn Advan Colored People Spec Contrib Fund, urban prog dir, 1968-69; Pinkett-Brown-Black Assoc, chmn bd, 1969-72; Howard Univ, mkt res analyst, 1972-76; Alaska Assoc Inc, Flennaugh Reliable Serv, supt. **Orgs:** Pres, Md State Conf Br Nat Assn Advan Colored People; dir, Md State Conf Nat Assn Advan Colored People, 1965-68; vpres, DC Chap Morgan State Col Alumni Assoc, 1966-67; Alpha Phi Alpha. **Honors/Awds:** Meritorious Service Award, MD State Conf Br Nat Assn Advan Colored People, 1973. **Military Serv:** AUS, 1st lt, 1963-64.

BLACKBURN, ALPHA C.
Chief executive officer. **Educ:** Howard Univ, BA, 1961 MA, 1963. **Career:** Blackburn Architects Inc, pres & chief exec officer, currently. **Orgs:** Bd mem, Indianapolis Arts Coun; Am Pianists Asn; Indianapolis Symphony Soc; bd trustees, Indianapolis Mus Art; chairperson bd, Ind Mus African Am Hist; bd adv, Ind Univ-Purdue Univ Indianapolis. **Honors/Awds:** National award; Distinguished Alumna, Howard Univ. **Business Addr:** Chief Executive Officer, President, Blackburn Architects Inc, 3388 Founders Rd, Indianapolis, IN 46268, **Business Phone:** (317)875-5500.*

BLACKBURN, BENJAMIN ALLAN, II
Physician, dentist. **Personal:** Born Jun 10, 1940, Jackson, MS; married Sara Driver; children: Kellye, Benjamin III, Leigh. **Educ:** Morehouse Col, BS, 1961; Meharry Med Col, DDS, 1965; Sydenham Hosp, intern, 1966; NY Univ, cert prosthodontics, 1968. **Career:** pvt pract, prosthodontist, currently. **Orgs:** Fel Am Col Prosthdontist; Am Prosthodontist Soc; SE Acad Prosthodontist; Kappa Alpha Psi; Nat Asn Advan Colored People; Urban League; dipl Am Bd Prosthodontists. **Honors/Awds:** Hon fel GA Dent Asn. **Military Serv:** AUS, dent res maj. **Business Addr:** General Dentist, Private Practice, 75 Piedmont Ave NE Suite 400, Atlanta, GA 30303.*

BLACKBURN, CHARLES MILIGAN, II
Executive. **Personal:** Born Nov 4, 1937, Florence, AL; son of Charles M and Dovie E; married Jun 12, 1965; children: Mary L, Charles M. III, Mark E. **Educ:** Alabama A&M Univ, BS, Electrical Engg, 1960. **Career:** Com Bank, dir; Sigma Systs Inc, pres & chief exec officer; First Combined Community Federal Credit Union, Chmn, currently. **Orgs:** Packaging Machinery Manufacturers Inst; Prince Georges County Community Col; Queen Anne Sch Bd; Partnership Workforce Quality Adv bd, dept bus & econ develop, MD, 2002; chmn, bd dir First Combined Community. **Honors/Awds:** Outstanding Black Businessman, State Maryland. **Special Achievements:** PMMI, Bd Dirs. **Military Serv:** AUS, SP, 1960-64. **Business Phone:** (301)333-8442.*

BLACKMAN, ROLANDO ANTONIO
Basketball player, basketball coach. **Personal:** Born Feb 26, 1959, Panama City, Panama; married Laura; children: 4. **Educ:** Kans

State Col, BA, mkt & soc, 1981. **Career:** Basketball player (retired), basketball coach; Dallas Mavericks, 1981-92, defensive coordr, 2000, TV analyst, 2004-05, asst coach, dir player develop, 2006-; NY Knicks, 1992-94; AEK Athens BC, 1994-95; Olimpia Milano, Italy, 1995-96; German Nat Team, asst coach, 2001. **Orgs:** Dallas Independent Sch Dist; Big Bros & Big Sisters; Spec Olympics; Muscular Dystrophy Asn; C's Med Ctr Dallas; Just Say No Found; Summer Basketball Camp; dir, Assist Youth Found. **Honors/Awds:** Big Eight Conference Player of the Year, 1980; Pro Athlete of the Year, 1986-87. **Business Addr:** Director of Player Development, Dallas Mavericks, 2909 Taylor St, Dallas, TX 75226, **Business Phone:** (214)747-6287.

BLACKMON, ANTHONY WAYNE
Executive, lawyer. **Personal:** Born Feb 13, 1957, Newark, NJ; son of Bettye; married Pelicia; children: Terry & Johanna. **Educ:** Cornell Univ, NY SSILR, BS, 1979; LaSalle Law Sch, JD, 1996. **Career:** WTKO Ithaca NY, broadcaster, 1976-79; Meadow lands Sports Complex NJ, asst dir matrix opers, 1976-79; Hollywood Park Racetrack, dir matrix oper, 1979-; Blackmon Enterprises, pres, consult, 1981-. **Orgs:** Urban League, Nat Asn Advan Colored People, Black Bus Asn La, La Better Bus Arbitrator; BBB Am, arbitrator; cert assoc, Am Bar Asn; Maricopa County Sheriffs Exec Posse. **Honors/Awds:** Youngest & only black dir, Matrix Oper Hollywood Park Racetrack. **Business Addr:** President, TBE Office Business Service, 8405 W Sells Dr, Phoenix, AZ 85037, **Business Phone:** (623)849-6841.

BLACKMON, BARBARA MARTIN (BARBARA ANITA MARTIN)
Lawyer. **Personal:** Born Dec 7, 1955, Jackson, MS; daughter of Julious Martin Sr and Willie T Martin; married Edward Blackmon Jr, Sep 27, 1986; children: Madison Edward & Bradford Jerome. **Educ:** Jackson State Univ, BS, Bus Admin, 1975, MS, 1975; Univ Ala, MBA, 1976;Univ Santa Clara Law Sch, 1979; Univ Miss Law Sch, JD, 1981; New York Univ, LLM, taxation, 1982. **Career:** Hinds Jr Col, instr, 1976-78; Bristol-Myers Co, assoc tax atty, 1982-83; Banks & Nichols, assoc, 1983-84; Barbara Martin Blackmon, atty-at-law, 1984-87; Blackmon, Blackmon & Evans, partner, 1987-98; State Miss, Miss State Senate, sen, 1992-2003; Blackmon & Blackmon PLLC, partner, currently. **Orgs:** Nat Black Caucus States Inst, Pres; Nat Co-Chair, Campaign Jackson State Univ; Magnolia Bar Asn; Miss Bar Asn; Nat Bar Asn; New York State Bar Asn; JSU Develop Found. steering comt, B.B. King Museum, Indianola; bd dir, United Way Capital Area; bd dir, Boys & Girls Club Cent Miss; bd dir, Stewpot Canton; bd dir, Am Red Cross Cent Miss; bd dir, Chap & Found Educ & Econ Develop. **Honors/Awds:** Constance Baker Motley Award, 1981; Special Executive Business Partner Award, 1991; Medgar Evers Faces of Courage Award, 1992; Honary Degree, Doctor Humane Letters, Tougaloo Col, 2003. **Special Achievements:** Democratic Nominee for Lieutenant Governor, 2003 State of Mississippi. **Home Addr:** 907 W Peace St, Canton, MS 39046, **Home Phone:** (601)859-1567. **Business Addr:** Partner, Blackmon & Blackmon PLLC, 907 W Peace St, PO Box 105, Canton, MS 39046, **Business Phone:** (601)859-1567.

BLACKMON, BRENDA
Television news anchorperson. **Personal:** Born Aug 20, 1952, Columbus, GA; daughter of Melzetta and Lorenza Hinton; divorced; children: Kelly. **Educ:** Fairleigh Dickinson Univ, BA, commun, 2001. **Career:** WWOR-TV, news anchor, currently. **Orgs:** National Asn Black Narcotic Agents; active member in numerous serv Orgn. **Honors/Awds:** Recogition Award, March of Dimes; Recognition Award, US Navy; Rosa Parks Humanitarian Award; Public Serv Award, Alpha Phi Alpha, 1987; Citizen of the Yr, Zeta Phi Beta Soc, 1984; Martin Luther King Jr Award; Telling Our Story Award; Emmy Award, Best Single Newscast in the NY Area, 1995-98; Associated Press Award, Best New Series, 1995; Best Sport News, 1995; Best Sport News Coverage, 1996; Best Coverage of a Continuing Story, 1996; Best Newscast, 1998; Humanitarian Award, United Hosp Fund New Leadership Group, 2002. Won numerous awards & honors for her prof expertise & community serv. **Special Achievements:** Became the first African American anchor in the city's history. **Business Addr:** Anchor, WWOR-TV, 9 Broadcast Plz, Secaucus, NJ 07094-2913, **Business Phone:** (212)452-3962.*

BLACKMON, EDWARD
Lawyer, government official. **Personal:** Born Jul 21, 1947, Canton, MS; son of Edward Jr and Mollie; married Barbara Martin; children: Janessa, Madison, Bradford & Stephen. **Educ:** Tougaloo Col, BA, polit sci, 1970; George Wash Univ, JD, 1973. **Career:** N Miss Rural Legal Serv, staff atty, 1973-74; Blackmon & Smith, partner,1974-; Blackmon & Blackmon PLLC, sr partner, currently; Miss House Rep, chmn judiciary A comt, currently. **Orgs:** Cade Chapel Missionary Baptist Church; State rep, Miss House Rep, 1979,1984-; bd adv, George Wash Univ Sch Law, currently. **Honors/Awds:** Special award for outstanding leadership & service as president, Magnolia Bar Asn, 1984-85; R Jesse Brown Award, Magnolia Bar Asn, 1990-91;Outstanding Service Award, Canton Br Nat Asn Advan Colored People, 1991; Medgar Evers Medallion Award, Nat Asn Advan Colored People, 1992; Omega Psi Phi Man of the Year Award; numerous other honors and awards. **Business Addr:** Senior Partner, Blackmon & Blackmon Attorneys At Law PLLC, 907 W Peace St, PO Box 105, Canton, MS 39046-0105, **Business Phone:** (601)859-1567.

BLACKMON, JOYCE MCANULTY
Consultant, executive. **Personal:** Born Nov 25, 1937, Memphis, TN; daughter of Samuel McAnulty and Evelyn Simons; married Lawrence Burnett Blackmon Sr, Dec 21, 1956 (died 1985); children: Lawrence B Jr & David G. **Educ:** Memphis State Univ, Memphis, Tenn, BS, 1966, MS, educ, 1970. **Career:** Memphis City Sch, Memphis, Tenn, teacher, guidance co, 1959-79; Memphis Light, Gas & Water, Memphis, Tenn, sr vpres, admin & support, 1979-96; Pres, Memphis Chapter, The Links Inc, 1990-92; Blackmon & Assoc, pres, currently. **Orgs:** Alpha Kappa Alpha Sorority, 1956-; Bd trustees, Tougaloo Col, 1986-92; grad, former bd mem, Leadership Memphis; Memphis Rotary, 1988-; bd dir, Mid South Public Commun Found, WKN TV & FM, 1990-; pres, Memphis In May Int Festival Inc, 1993; Child Advocacy Bd, 1995. **Honors/Awds:** Distinguished Service Award, Nat Am Advan Colored People, Memphis Chap, 1982; Prominent Black Woman, Memphis State Chapter Alpha Kappa Alpha, 1990; Dedicated Service Award, Memphis in May Int Festival Inc, 1990; Dedicated Service Award, Lemoyne-Owen Col, UNCF Dr & Annual Fund Dr, 1990; Contempora, Coping with a Crisis Award, Contempora Mag, 1991. *

BLACKMON, MOSETTA WHITAKER
Executive. **Personal:** Born Jan 2, 1950, Homestead, PA; daughter of Garvis and Elgurtha Spruill; married Michael George Blackmon, Oct 19, 1975; children: Jason B, Jacqueline Renee, Jenelle Laraine. **Educ:** Univ Pittsburgh, Pittsburgh, PA, BA, 1970; Am Univ, Wash, DC, MS, 1986. **Career:** Comsat Corp, Wash, DC, job analyst, 1974-76, employ mgr, 1977-79; Marriott Corp, Bethesda, MD, sr compensation analyst, 1979-80; Mitre Corp, McLean, VA, employ mgr, 1980-96; Mitretek System Inc, dir human resources, 1996-. **Orgs:** Am Compensation Asn, 1975-89; Wash Tech Personnel Forum; Prince Georges Couty PTA, 1986-94; bd adv, US Black Eng Mag, 1988-90; Black Human Resources Prof, 1988-95; Alpha Kappa Alpha; CARE Adv Comn. **Honors/Awds:** Certified compensation prof, Am Compensation Asn, 1983; Outstanding Recruiter, Career Commun Group, 1988. **Business Phone:** (703)610-2002.*

BLACKMON, PATRICIA ANN
Judge. **Personal:** Born Aug 11, 1950, Oxford, MS; daughter of Willie James and Willie Mae. **Educ:** Tougaloo Col, BA, 1972; Cleveland Marshall Col Law, JD, 1975. **Career:** Advocate Victim Witness, counr, 1974-76; Asst City Prosecutor, lawyer, 1976-81; Johnson Keenon Blackmon Law Firm, partner, lawyer, 1980-83; UAW Legal Servs, staff atty, lawyer, 1983-86; Cleveland City Prosecutor, chief prosecutor, 1986-90; Ohio Turnpike, staff atty, lawyer, 1990-91; Cuyahoga County Ct Appeals, judge, 1991-; Dyke Col, prof, Victims/Witness Prog, asst dir. **Orgs:** Delta Sigma Theta Sorority, Inc, 1971-; founder, Black Women's Polit Action Comn, 1982-; Munic & Co Judges Law Enforcement & Nation's AIDS Crisis, 1986; Municipal & Co Judges Domestic Violence, Nat Crisis Am, 1987; Municipal & Co Judges Domestic Violence, Nat Crisis Am, 1987; bd dirs, Hitchcock House, 1991-; Nat Asn Women Judges, 1992-; ct master, Am Inns Ct; Am Judges Asn; Supreme Ct Ohio, Bd Comt Grievance & Discipline, 1993-96; consumer mem, Cent Ohio, Bd Health Systs Agency, 1996-; bd dirs, Downtown YMCA, 1996-; bd trustees, Ohio Judicial Col, 1999; Ohio Bar Asn; Cuyahoga Co Bar Asn; Olivet Inst Baptist Church; Woodruff Found. **Honors/Awds:** Ohio Women's Hall of Fame, 1996; Alumna of the Year, Cleveland Marshall Col Law, 1996; Distinguished Litigation Award, Nat Asn Advan Colored People, 1983; H Jones History Award, Tougaloo Col, 1971. **Special Achievements:** Raceway Video and Bookshop Inc, v Cleveland Bd of Zoning Appeals, 118 Ohio, App 3d 529, 1997; Cleveland Police Patrolman's Assn v City of Cleveland, 95 Ohio App 3d 645, 1994; Stephens v A-Able Rents Co, 101 Ohio App 3d 20, 1995; White v Fed Res Bank, 103 Ohio App 3d 534, 1995; City of Lakewood v Town, 106 Ohio App 3d 521, 1995; first African American Woman elected to Ohio court of appeals, 1991. **Home Addr:** 11432 Cedar Glen Pkwy Suite A-1, Cleveland, OH 44106, **Home Phone:** (216)791-4014. **Business Addr:** Judge, Court of Appeals of Ohio, Cuyahoga County Court of Appeals, Eighth Appellate District, 1 Lakeside Ave Suite 202, Cleveland, OH 44113-1056, **Business Phone:** (216)443-6358.

BLACKMON, ROOSEVELT, III
Football player. **Personal:** Born Sep 10, 1974, Pahokee, FL. **Educ:** Morris Brown Col, Atlanta, physical educ. **Career:** Green Bay Packers, 1988; Cincinnati Bengals, defensive back, 1998-99. *

BLACKSHEAR, JEFFERY LEON
Football player. **Personal:** Born Mar 29, 1969, Fort Pierce, FL. **Educ:** Northeast La Univ, Monroe. **Career:** Seattle Seahawks, guard, 1993-95; Cleveland Browns, 1995; Baltimore Ravens, guard, 1996-99; Kansas City Chiefs, 2000; Green Bay Packers, 2002.

BLACKSHEAR, WILLIAM
Businessperson. **Personal:** Born Jun 1, 1935, Marianna, FL; son of William Sr and Julia; married Betty Jean Booze; children: Bruce, Angelia, Edwina, Jeffery, Jacquline & Sylvia. **Educ:** State Fla, educ cert, 1963; Gen Elec Employ Educ, 1969. **Career:** Businessperson (retired); Gen Elec Co, 1958-70; Weekly Challenger News, 1968-2002; Black Gold Inc, mgr. **Orgs:** Consult, Black Media Inc; VAC; Black Gold Fla Inc; scout ldr, 1950-53; pres, PTA, 1960-63; pres & founder, Home Improv Comn, 1961-67; pres & founder, Lincoln Nursery Asn, 1961-67; pres, founder, HOPE, 1965-67; pres & founder, SE Black Pub Asn Inc, 1978; vice chmn, OIC Sun coast; adv bd,Youth Am, Nat Asn Advan Colored People; Urban League; Southern Poverty Asn; Dem Fla. **Honors/Awds:** Outstanding Community Service, Le Cercle Des Jeunes Femmes, 1965;Citation, Outstanding Efforts, Human Rights Ridg crest Improv Asn, 1966;Citation, Gen Elec Stud Guid Prog, 1970. **Special Achievements:** First African-American to run for office in Safety Harbor, and in Pinellas County; First Black person elected to public office in Florida since the end of Reconstruction in 1877, according to research by Gloria Gilghrest for the Pinellas County African History Museum. **Military Serv:** AUS, staff sgt, 1955-62. **Home Addr:** PO Box 12143, St Petersburg, FL 33733.

BLACKSHIRE-BELAY, CAROL AISHA
Educator. **Educ:** Princeton Univ, PhD. **Career:** Ohio State Univ, instr; Temple Univ, instr; Ind State Univ, Dept African &African Am Studies, chair, prof; Sonoma State Univ, vice provost acad affairs, 2005. **Special Achievements:** Booke published: Language and Literature in the African American Imagination; The African-German Experience; The Germanic Mosaic; Author, co-author, or editor of 14 books and 27 articles and book chapters.

BLACKWELL, ARTHUR BRENDHAL, II
County commissioner, government official. **Personal:** Born Jun 10, 1953, Detroit, MI; son of Robert Brendhal and Florrie Love Willis; married Zenobia Weaver, Oct 19, 1985; children: Mosii Mays Blackwell, Robert Brendhal Blackwell, II. **Educ:** NC A&T Univ, BA, polit sci, 1976. **Career:** Detroit Bank & Trust, Detroit, asst br mgr, 1978-79; 1980 Census, Detroit, dir field oper, 1980; Wayne Co Bd Comnr, comnr, 1980-82, chmn, 1989-94; Blackwell & Assoc, owner, 1983-86; Mayor Young's Re-election Campaign, hq coordr, 1985; Detroit Fire Dept, community admin coordr, 1986; Wayne Co Bd; Detroit-Wayne Co Port Authority, chmn, bd dir, 1999-01; DeWay Develop Corp, pres & chief exec officer, currently; Bd Police Comnrs, chmn, 2002-. **Orgs:** Chmn, Detroit/ Wayne Co Port Authority, 1988; Nat Orgn Black City Off; Mich Asn County Detroit Windsor Port Corp, 1988, first Cong Dist Dem Party; Mich Dem Party, City Resident Comn, Young Alliance; Nat League Co; Local Develop Finance Authority; Kids In Need Direction; Highland Park Caucus Club; New Detroit Inc, Govt Affairs Comn; Wayne Co Retirement Bd. **Honors/Awds:** Father/Son Outstanding Achievement Award, Northern Young Men's Christian Asn, 1981; Cert Appreciation, Wayne Co Bd Comnr, 1982; Outstanding Performance, Quarter State Music Competition, 1969. **Special Achievements:** Radio show: co-host, "Back to Back", WQBH. **Business Addr:** Chairman, Board of Police Commissioners, City Of Detroit Executive Office, 2 Woodward Ave, Detroit, MI 48226.*

BLACKWELL, BOBBI
Lawyer. **Career:** Atty, currently. *

BLACKWELL, DAVID HAROLD
Educator. **Personal:** Born Apr 24, 1919, Centralia, IL; son of Grover Blackwell and Mabel Blackwell; married Ann, Jan 1, 1944; children: 8. **Educ:** Univ Ill, AB, 1938, AM, 1939, PhD, 1941; Hon DSc, Univ Ill, 1965, Mich State Univ, attended 1968; Southern Ill Univ, attended 1970. **Career:** Inst Advan Study Princeton Univ, Post-doctoral Fel, 1941-42; Southern Univ, instr, 1942-43; Clark Col, instr, 1943-44; Howard Univ, asst prof, 1944-54, chmn, dept statistics, 1957-61; Univ Calif, Berkeley, Calif, prof statist, 1954-97, emer prof, 1997-. **Orgs:** Rosenwald Fel Inst Advan Study Princeton Univ, 1941-42; res fel Brown Univ, 1943; fel, Inst Math Statistics, 1947; pres, Inst Math Stat, 1955, AAAS, Am Math Soc; Nat Acad Sci, 1965; fac res lectr, Univ Calif, 1971. **Honors/Awds:** Neumann Prize, Oper Res Soc Am, 1986; Neumann Prize, Inst Mgt Sci, 1986; RA Fisher Award, Comt Presidents Statist Soc, 1986. **Special Achievements:** First African American to be inducted into the National Academy of Sciences. author: Large deviations for martingales. In Festschrift for Lucien Le Cam 89-91 Springer New York, 1997; The square-root game. In Game theory, optimal stopping, probability and statistics IMS, 2000; Large excesses for finite-state Markov chains. In System and Bayesian reliability, 2001; The prediction of sequences, 2002. **Business Addr:** Professor Emeritus, University of California, Department of Statistics, 367 Evans Hall, Berkeley, CA 94720-0001, **Business Phone:** (510)642-6446.

BLACKWELL, FAIGER MEGREA
Executive, president (organization), chief executive officer. **Personal:** Born Dec 14, 1955, Reidsville, NC; divorced; children: Alexdria. **Educ:** Winston-19Salem State, 1976; UNC Chapel Hill, BS. **Career:** Jones Cross Baptist Ch, chmn, trustee; NC Long Term Care Facilities, vpres; Caswell NAACP; Caswell Co Voters League, pres, 1976; Blackwell & Assocs; Carolina Pinnacle Studios, pres, ceo, owner, currently. **Orgs:** Founder, Blackwell

Bros Florist; pres, Blackwell Rest Home Inc; bd mem, Wiz 4-H Club; Caswell Co Planning Bd; bd mem, Caswell NAACP; pres, Dogwood Forest Rest Home Inc. **Honors/Awds:** Martin Luther King Jr Award Caswell Sportsman Club; Leader of the Yr NC Long Term Care; Outstanding Serv NC Long Term Care; Outstanding Serv Caswell Co Schl Bd. **Business Addr:** President, Chief Executing officer, Carolina Pinnacle Studios, 336 W Main St, PO Box 778, Yanceyville, NC 27379, **Business Phone:** (336)694-7785.*

BLACKWELL, FAYE BROWN
Educator, government official. **Personal:** Born May 10, 1942, Monroe, LA; married Fred. **Educ:** Southern Univ, BA, 1964. **Career:** Calcasiew Fed Teachers, 1978-82; Coalition Comm Prog, pres bd dir, 1983-85; Calcasiew Dem Asn, pres, 1984-85; Lake Charles City Council, vpres, 1984-85; Lake Charles City Coun, council mem dist B, currently; KZWA-FM radio sta, owner, mgr, currently. **Orgs:** Owner, oper Faye Brown Rental Inc, 1968-85; pres, Brown Enterprises PMonse LA, 1978-85; secy, Independent Invert Corp, 1980-85; Women League of Voters, Nat Asn Advan Colored People, Top Ladies of Distinction, Nat Asn Univ Women. **Honors/Awds:** Community Serv Zeta Sor; Ed Exal Nat Asn Univ Women; Woman of the Year, Martin L King Found, Los Angeles Municipal, Sch Los Angeles Municipal Asn. **Special Achievements:** The first African-American woman elected to the Lake Charles City Council, she is the first African-American to own and operate an FM urban radio station in Southwest Louisiana. **Business Addr:** Owner, General Manager, KZWA, 305 Enterprise Blvd, Lake Charles, LA 70601.*

BLACKWELL, DR. HARVEL E.
Educator, consultant. **Personal:** Born Sep 25, 1937, Hulbert, OK; son of Ruben and Lavada; married Sandra Sunday (divorced 1975); children: Carmella C & Howard E. **Educ:** Compton Col, AA, 1959; Calif State Univ, Los Angeles, BA, 1961; Univ Southern CA, MS, physics, 1963, PhD, physics, 1968. **Career:** Southern Assn Col & Sch, consult, 1970-; Tex Southern Univ, prof physics; Inst Serv Educ, consult, 1970-75; Natl Sci Found, proposal rev; Lovanium Univ, vis prof; JSC NASA, consult, 1975-85; K-RAM Corp, brd dir, 1980-84; BSA Serv, sci & eng consult & pres, 1997-. **Orgs:** Bd dir, United Cerebal Palsy Gulf Coast, 1978-80; Natl Tech Assn; Natl Soc Black Physicists. **Honors/Awds:** Grants, Nat Sci Found; grants, NASA. **Special Achievements:** Artist, Abstract Subj Realism & Portrait; co-author, Analysis of Flow From Arc-Jet Spectra, 1997. **Business Addr:** President, BSA Services, 4010 Tidewater, Houston, TX 77045, **Business Phone:** (713)433-3921.

BLACKWELL, JOEY
Entrepreneur, president (organization). **Career:** VDS Off Supply, pres & chief exec officer, currently. **Business Addr:** President, Chief Executive Officer, VDS Office Supply, 4810 fulton indust blvd, Atlanta, GA 30336, **Business Phone:** (404)691-9665.

BLACKWELL, JOHN KENNETH (KEN BLACKWELL)
Government official. **Personal:** Born Feb 28, 1948, Cincinnati, OH; son of George and Dana; married Rosa E, Aug 10, 1969; children: Kimberly A, Rahshann K & Kristin S. **Educ:** Xavier Univ, BS, Psycol, 1970, MEd, 1971, MBA; Harvard Univ, Prog Sr Execs State & Local Govts, 1981. **Career:** Cincinnati Bd Educ, teacher, coach, 1971; Model Cities Community Sch Assoc, educ & consult, 1973; Afro-Am Studies Univ Cincinnati, teacher; Xavier Univ, Univ & Urban Affairs, instr, dir; Cincinnati City Coun, mem,1977-; Community Rels, assoc vpres 1980-; City Cincinnati, vice mayor,1977-78, mayor, 1979-80, vice mayor, 1985-87; Cincinnati Employees Retirement Syst, vice chair, 1988; US Dept Housing & Urban Develop, depunder secy, 1989-91; UN Human Rights Comn, UNHRC, confirmed at the rank ambassador, US representative, 1991; State Ohio, treas, 1994-99; Certified Govt Financial Mgr, 1997; US Census Monitoring Bd, co-chair, 1998-2001; Ohio State, secy, 1999-; Republican Nat Comts Platform Comt & Vchmn, currently. **Orgs:** Chmn, Local Legislators Comm, 1978-79; vice chmn, Transp Comn 1979-80; Cable TV Task Force; Int Econ Develop Task Force; steering comn, CommCities in 1980; co-chmn, Labor Rels Adv Comn Nat League Cities; bd trustee, Pub Tech Inc; state & local govt bd adv, John F Kennedy Sch Govt Harvard Univ; adv comm, bd dirs, Am Coun Young Polit Leaders; Jerusalem Comm; bd mem, Nat Leg Conf Arson; Rotary Int, Cincinnati Fine Arts, Inst Bd, Cincinnati Opera; trustee, Birthright Cincinnati Inc; bd mem, Greater Cincinnati Coalition People with Disabilities; bd dir, Fifth Third Bancorp Cincinnati, 1993; bd dir, Fifth Third Bank Cincinnati, 1993; bd dir, Physicians Human Rights, 1993; bd dir, Greater Cincinnati Coun World Affairs, 1993; bd dir, Int Repuban Inst, 1993; bd dir, Congional Human Rights Found, 1993; Coun Foreign Rels, New York, NY, 1994; Nat AsnState Treasurers; Nat Asn State Auditors, Comptrollers & Treasurers; Nat Asn Securities Profs; Nat Comn Econ Growth & Tax Reform; Greater Cincinnati Urban Bankers Asn; bd trustees Xavier Univ; bd trustees, Wilmington Col; bd trustees, Wilberforce Univ; bd trustees, Cincinnati Tech Col; bd dirs, Grant/Riverside Hosp; bd mem, Nat Taxpayers Union Ohio; task force mem, Govt Accting Standards Bd; bd gov, Nat Coalition Black & Jewish Am; bd gov, Wash Legal Found; chmn, policy bd, Underground Railroad Found Inc; bd adv, John M. Ashbrook Ctr for Pub Affairs, Ashland Univ, mem, 1997; Pension & Pub Funds Comt; chmn, Nat Assoc State Auditors, Comptrollers & Treasurers, 1997; US Dept Labor Adv Coun on Employee Welfare & Pension Benefit Plans, 1997; bd dir, Nat Taxpayers Union; adv bd, Children's Eduuc Opp Am Found, 1999; Univ Findlay, Nat Bd Visitors, Mazza Collection, 1999; bd trustee, Int City Mgt Asn/ Retirement Corp,1999; adv panel, Fed Election Comn, 1999; bd mem, Black Alliance EducOptions, 2000; chair, Cincinnati Riverfront Classic Jamboree, 2000-03; pres, Nat Electronic Com Coord Coun, 2002; exec bd, Youth Voter Corps, 2001; vpres, Nat Asn Secretaries State, Midwest Region, 2001; chair, bd adv trustees, Govt Investment Found, 1999; Campaign Finance Inst, co-chair, 2003. **Honors/Awds:** Hon JD Wilberforce Univ 1980; Wilberforce Univ, Honorary Degrees, 1980; HUD Public Leadership Fellow Harvard Univ 1981; Gordon Chase Meml Fellow Harvard Univ 1981; The Aspen Institute, Fellow, 1984; Cincinnati Technical Col, Honorary Degree, 1987; Salzburg Seminar, Austria, Fellow, 1988; Republican candidate for congress, 1990; Franklin Pierce Col, Honorary Degree, 1992; Urban Morgan Institute for Human Rights, Univ of Cincinnati, Senior Fellow, 1992; Heritage Foundation, Washington DC, Senior Fellow & Domestic Policy Analyst, 1992; Recipient of Xavier Univ Distinguished Alumnus Award, 1992; School of Advanced Int Studies at Johns Hopkins University, Fellowship Award; US State Dept, Superior Honor Award, 1993; Family of the Year, Nat Council of Negro Women, 1994; Peace of the City Award, Cincinnati Jewish Comm Relations Council, 1994; US Small Business Administration Advocacy Award, 1995; Martin Luther King Dream Keeper Award,1996; NAACP Public Service Award, 1996; Ashbrook Center's Thomas A. Van Meter Scholarship Award for Outstanding Conservative Leadership, 1997; President's Award, Nat Asn of State Auditors, Comptrollers & Treasurers, 1996; Nat Government Finance Officers Assn, Excellence in Government Award, 1999; Meritorious recognition, Center for Digital Government, 2002; Government Technology magazine, recognition as one of top 25 public sector-leaders in information technology, 2002. **Special Achievements:** Co-editor: IRS vs The People: Time for Real Tax Reform, 1998. **Business Addr:** Secretary, State of Ohio, 180 E Broad St, Columbus, OH 43215, **Business Phone:** (614)466-2655.

BLACKWELL, KEN. See BLACKWELL, JOHN KENNETH.

BLACKWELL, PATRICIA A
Executive. **Personal:** Born in Metropolis, IL; daughter of Phinis N and Minnie Allen. **Educ:** Southern Ill Univ, Carbondale, attended 1965; Howard Univ, Small Bus Develop Ctr, 1984. **Career:** Nat Urban League, Wash Bur, admin asst, 1971-72; John Dingle Assocs Inc, Wash rep/lobbyist, 1972-73; E H White & Co Inc, dir E coast opers, 1973-74; Unified Industries Inc, prog mgr, 1974-84; Pa Blackwell & Assocs Inc, pres, 1984-. **Orgs:** Consult, DC Dem Comt, 1974; vpres, SIMBA Assocs Inc-Fund Raiser, 1978-80; bd mem, Reg Purchasing Coun Va, 1978-; Nat Conf Minority Transp Officials, 1983-; Nat Forum Black Pub Adminr, 1984-; Nat Asn Female Execs, 1984-; tutor oper, Rescue-Wash Urban League, 1984-; Women's Transp Seminar, 1987; Nat Coalition Black Meeting Planners. **Honors/Awds:** Certificate of Appreciation, Va State Off Minority Bus Enterprise, 1979. **Special Achievements:** Citation of Recognition, Governor's Office-State Va, 1978; Nominated Outstanding Young Women of America, 1984.

BLACKWELL, ROBERT, SR.
President (Organization), chief executive officer. **Personal:** Born Jul 28, 1937, Eastville, VA. **Educ:** Wichita State Univ, BA, psychol, 1966. **Career:** IBM, syst eng, 1966-70, salesman, 1970; IBM, Greater Chicago Consult Serv, dir; Blackwell Consult Serv, pres & ceo, 1992-. **Orgs:** Creative Arts Found. *

BLACKWELL, ROBERT B.
Consultant. **Personal:** Born Nov 4, 1924, Meridian, MS; son of Arthur B; married Florrie Love Willis; children: Brenda B Mims, June-Hatcher, Arthur & Bobbi. **Educ:** Howard Univ, BA, 1949; Detroit Col Law, attended 1968. **Career:** UAW, AFL-CIO, pres, local 889, 1955-62; City Highland Park, city police & fire comnr, 1958-63; Mich Labor Rels Bd, exec dir, 1962-67; City Highland-Park, city councilman, 1963-67, mayor, 1967-75; US Dept Labor, spl asst under secy, 1975-76; US Aid, Sen Dept, consult, 1976-78; City Highland Park, mayor, 1968-72, 1980-88; Wayne Co, comnr dist 3, 1995-04, vice chair Pro Tempore, 2003-04. **Orgs:** Life mem, Golden Heritage; Nat Asn Advan Colored People; Urban League; Kappa Alpha Psi Fraternity; guardsmen, Boys Club Am; bd dirs, Nat League Cities; chmn, labor comm, Mich Municipal League; trustee, US Conf Mayors; vice-chmn Comt Roads, Airports & Pub Serv. **Honors/Awds:** Alumni of the Year, Howard Univ; Man of the Year, Little Rock Baptist Church; founder & first sr chmn, Nat Black Caucus of Local Elected Officers. **Special Achievements:** First full-time elected African-American mayor in Michigan. **Military Serv:** AUS, master sgt, 1942-48; Purple Heart. **Home Addr:** 133 Mass, Highland Park, MI 48203. *

BLACKWELL, UNITA
Mayor, activist, politician. **Personal:** Born Mar 18, 1933, Lula, MS. **Educ:** Univ Mass-Amherst, regional planning. **Career:** Nat Coun Negro Women, community develop specist; City Mayersville, MS, mayor; Southern Inst C & Families, chmn & pres emer, currently. **Orgs:** Pres, Nat Conf Black Mayors. **Honors/Awds:** MacArthur Found Fel, 1992. **Special Achievements:** First African-American woman to be mayor of Mayersville; Instrumental in persuading federal govt to fund a 20-unit housing develop in Mayersville & give the town a new fire truck. **Business Addr:** Chairman, President Emeritus, Southern Institute on Children & Families, 500 Taylor St Suite 202, Columbia, SC 29201, **Business Phone:** (803)779-2607.

BLACKWELL, WILLIE
Food service manager, manager. **Personal:** Born Dec 1, 1954, St Louis, MO; son of Willie Blackwell Jr and Flora Lee Williams; married Kathy Loman Blackwell, 1981; children: Lamont Blackwell, Crystal Blackwell, April Blackwell. **Educ:** Morris Brown Col, Atlanta, GA, BS, 1977. **Career:** Dobbs Int Serv, Atlanta, GA, prod supvr, 1977-84, relief mgr, 1984-88, hot food mgr, 1988-, literacy coordr, currently. **Orgs:** Nat Restaurant Asn; Bd mem, Ga Literacy Coalition, currently; adv bd mem, Southside High Sch, Atlanta, GA, currently. **Honors/Awds:** Letter of Encouragement for Literacy, Mrs. Barbara Bush, 1990. **Business Addr:** Literacy Coordinator, Dobbs International Services, 1400 Aviation Blvd Suite 310, College Park, GA 30349-5463.*

BLACKWELL-HATCHER, JUNE E
Judge. **Personal:** Daughter of Robert Blackwell; married Jim Hatcher; children: two daughters. **Educ:** Syracuse Univ, BA, psychol, 1974; Am Univ, JD, 1979. **Career:** Wayne State Univ, admis counr, recruiter, 1974-76; legal intern, various agencies, 1977-79; Off Appeals & Review, Dept Employment Serv, hearing & appeals examr, 1979-80, chief dept, 1981-83; Midwest Legal Serv, dir opers, 1984-88; pvt pract, atty, 1988-92; Wayne County Probate Ct, Estates Div, judge, 1992-. **Orgs:** Nat Bar Asn; Mich Bar Asn; Wolverine Bar Asn; Women Lawyers Asn; vol, Meals on Wheels; pres, Asn Black Judges Mich; co-chair, Adopt-A-Sch Comt; Asn Black Judges Mich. **Honors/Awds:** Woman of the Year, Nat Polit Cong Black Women, 1995; Golden Gavel Award, Wayne County Probate Bar Asn, 1996. **Special Achievements:** Auth: "Law on Your Side", monthly column, appeared in over 250 labor publ throughout US. **Business Addr:** Judge, Wayne County Probate Court, 1307 Coleman A Young Munic Ctr, 2 Woodward Ave, Detroit, MI 48226, **Business Phone:** (313)224-5706.

BLACKWOOD, RONALD A.
Mayor, government official. **Personal:** Born Jan 19, 1926, Kingston, Jamaica; married Ann; children: Helen Marie. **Educ:** Kingston Tech Sch, attended 1944; Kingston Com Col, attended 1946; Westchester Comn Col; Elizabeth Seton Col; Iona Col, New Rochelle, NY, BBA, mgt. **Career:** Mayor (retired); Mount Vernon, NY, mayor, 1985-95; Westchester County Brd Supervisors; Mt Vernon City Coun. **Orgs:** Nat Assn Advan Colored People; brd dirs, Nat Conf Christians & Jews; Ment Health Assn Westchester Inc; United Way Westchester/Putnam; Boy Scouts Am-Westchester Putnam Coun; Rotary Club New Smyrna Beach, FL; Progressive Lodge No 64 AFM; All Islands Assn; Westchester 2000 Brd Dirs; Omega Psi Phi Fraternity; hon mem, Port Am Club; bd mem, Southeast Volusla Habitat Humanity; secy, Smyrna Yacht Club. **Special Achievements:** First African American to be elected mayor in NY state. *

BLACQUE, TAUREAN (HERBERT MIDDLETON, JR.)
Actor. **Personal:** Born May 10, 1941, Newark, NJ; divorced 1966; children: Shelby, Rodney & 11 adopted children. **Educ:** Am Musical & Dramatic Acad. **Career:** TV series: "What's Happening!!", 1976; "Sanford and Son", 1977; "Charlie's Angels", 1978; "Paris", 1979; Backstairs at the White House, 1979; Hill St Blues, 1981; The $520 an Hour Dream, 1980; Generations, 1989; She Stood Alone, 1991; Murder Without Motive; The Edmond Perry Story, 1992; "In the Heat of the Night", 1994; Soul Survivors, 1995; We Interrupt This Prog; The River Niger; Films: House Calls, 1978; Beyond Death's Door, 1978; Rocky II, 1979; The Hunter, 1980; Oliver & Co, 1988; Deep Star Six, 1989; Fled, 1996; Nowhere Road, 2002; The Kudzu Christmas, 2002; The Stick Up Kids, 2008. **Special Achievements:** Nominated for the Emmy. *

BLADES, BENNIE
Football player, school custodian. **Personal:** Born Sep 3, 1966, Fort Lauderdale, FL; children: Horatio Jr, Ashley, Amber, Jaylen & Bianca. **Educ:** Univ Miami, attended. **Career:** Football player (retired), school guard; Detroit Lions, cornerback & safety, 1988-96; Seattle Seahawks, cornerback & safety, 1997; Piper High Sch, security guard, currently. **Honors/Awds:** Pro Bowl, 1991; Jim Thorpe Award, 2006; College Football Hall of Fame, 2006.

BLADE-TIGGENS, DENISE PATRICIA
Lawyer. **Personal:** Born Dec 16, 1957, Chicago, IL; daughter of Marshall Blade and Mary Lucille; married Willie Jr, Apr 4, 1981. **Educ:** Southern Ill Univ, BS, 1978; Chicago State Univ, MS, 1979; John Marshall Law Sch, JD, 1989. **Career:** Volunteers Am, counsr, 1978-79; Dept Justice, correctional officer, 1979-81; Cook Co Juvenile Servs, caseworker, 1981-82; Chicago Police Dept, police officer, 1982-90; Hyatt Legal Serv, atty, 1990-91; Denise Blade-Tiggens & Assocs, partner, 1992-. **Orgs:** United Citizens Community Orgn, consult, 1980-; Am Bar Asn, 1986-; Ill State

Bar Asn, 1986-; Chicago Bar Asn, 1986-; Phi Delta Phi, 1987-. **Honors/Awds:** Scholastic Achievement Award, Int Legal Fraternity, Phi Delta Phi, 1987. **Business Addr:** Partner, Denise Blade-Tiggens & Associates PC, 17027 Meadowcrest Dr, Lockport, IL 60441, **Business Phone:** (815)462-1212.

BLAIR, CHARLES MICHAEL
Foundation executive, administrator, movie producer. **Personal:** Born Aug 5, 1947, Indianapolis, IN; married Margo Mills; children: Michael A & Tchad K. **Educ:** Oberlin Col, AB Commun, 1970; Kean Univ, MA, Personnel Admin, 1972. **Career:** Lilly Endowment Inc, prog evaluator, 1973, assoc prog officer, 1975, prog officer 1977, sr prog officer 1981; Grand Slam Inc & Interlace Mkt Inc, pres & owner 1986-91; Sports, entertainment & Mgt, Consults; Indianapolis Recorder Newspaper, co-owner, vpres & pres, 1990-97; Martin Univ, fac mem; Madame Walker Theatre Ctr, pres; Charles Blair Assoc, pres, 2003; Metrop Indianapolis Pub Broadcasting Inc, bd dirs, secy, 2004-; producer, writer, 5 Stage Plays; film: Facing the Facade, exec producer; Eyewitness Century, writer; Marion, script consult; Middle Passage, Songs Creator. **Orgs:** Chmn, Assoc Black Found Exec, 1980-83; founder, bd mem, Madame CJ Walker Bldg Restoration Proj; consult, Fund Raising Numerous Org; chmn bd, Blair Commun Indep Prod; bd dir, Big Bro Big Sisters Int; bd dir, founder, Youth Works Inc; bd dir, founder, Ind Black Expo Found; founder, BOS Community Develop Corp; bd sec, WFYI Channel 20; chair, Budget Comn IN State Mus Found. **Honors/Awds:** Honored Spec Advocate Girls, Girls Club Am, New York City, 1979; Martin Luther King Award, N Ward Ctr Newark, NJ, 1982; Community Service Award, Ctr Leadership Develop Indianapolis, 1984. **Business Addr:** Secretary, Board of Directors, Metropolitan Indianapolis Public Broadcasting Incorporation, WFYI TelePlex, 1401 N Merdian St, Indianapolis, IN 46202-2389, **Business Phone:** (317)636-2020.*

BLAIR, CHESTER LAUGHTON ELLISON
Lawyer, association executive. **Personal:** Born Jul 2, 1928, Corsicana, TX; married Judith K; children: Gregory, Bradford, Jefferson, Jan, Brent, Judy-Lee. **Educ:** Chicago Teachers Col, BEd, 1952; John Marshall Law Sch, JD, 1959. **Career:** Chicago Pub Sch, teacher, 1952-54, 1956-59; pvt pract atty, 1959-; 7th Congress dist of Ill, legal counr, 1974-78; Blair & Cole, founding partner, 1974-; Asn Trial Lawyers Am, lecturer & prof, currently. **Orgs:** pres, Chicago Bar Asn, 1989; pres, Cook County Bar Asn, 1978; Ill Trial Lawyers Asn; Asn Trial Lawyers Am; Am Bar Asn, Tort & Ins Pract Sect; rev bd, Atty Regist & Disciplinary Comn, 1978-84, chmn, 1984-89; Ill Supreme Ct Comt Prof Stand, 1977-84; bd managers, Chicago Bar Asn, 1985-87; bd dirs, Ill Inst Continuing Legal Educ, 1988-91; bd visitors, John Marshall How Sch, 1993-. **Honors/Awds:** Black Awareness Award, Col St Thomas Min Prog, 1977; Earl H Wright Award, Cook County Bar Asn, 1989; guest instr, Nat Col Advocacy, Advanced Trial Practice, 1991; guest speaker, Nat Asn Bar Exec Annual Meeting, 1990. **Special Achievements:** Author, Chapter 13, "Return of the Verdict," ICCLE Ill Civil Pract Series, 1988, 1992, 1999, 2002. **Military Serv:** AUS, 1954-56. **Business Addr:** Lawyer, Professor, Blair & Cole, 310 S Mich Ave, Chicago, IL 60604-4206.*

BLAIR, CURTIS
Basketball player. **Personal:** Born Sep 24, 1970, Roanoke, VA. **Educ:** Univ Richmond. **Career:** Houston Rockets, prof basketball player; Meysuspor, 1996-97.

BLAIR, GEORGE ELLIS, JR.
Executive, dean (education), chairperson. **Personal:** Born May 5, 1932, Braddock, PA; son of George E Sr and Edith Madden Cowans; married Eleanor Ann Blair, Sep 29, 1956; children: Cheryl Ann, Stephanie Rene Warner. **Educ:** Indiana Univ, BS, 1954; Adelphia Univ, Garden City, NY, MS, 1959; St John's Univ, Jamaica, NY, PhD, 1963. **Career:** Ind Pub Sch, teacher, 1953-54; Rockville Ctr Pub Sch, teacher, guid counr, adminr, 1956-66; Drug Prev, Treatment & Rehabil Prog, consult; Roslyn Pub Sch, asst supt spl prog, 1965-66; NY State Dept Educ, asst comnr innovations educ, 1966-70, assoc comnr urban educ, 1970-72; Long Island Univ, vpres planning & develop, 1972-75; US Steel Co Am, arbitrator; City Univ NY, Borough Manhattan Community Col, NY City Educ Opportunity Ctr, dean educ & dir, 1975-77; State Univ NY, asst vice chancellor spec progs, 1977-78, assoc chancellor spec progs, 1978-79, dep chancellor spec progs, 1979-82; exec asst chancellor, 1982-89; chmn, Ascent Publ Co; pres, Human Affairs Res Ctr; pres & chmn, Urban Ctr Res & Commun; chmn, Summit Transp; chmn, Summit Farms; chmn, Camp Pioneer; Black World Championship Rodeo, founder & pres, 1989-93; Ascent Found, pres, 1993-. **Orgs:** chmn, NY City Riding Acad; Community Adv Comt, NY City Rikers Island Correctional Facil. **Honors/Awds:** Light of the World Award, NY City Dept Parks & Recreation. **Special Achievements:** Editor, Indiana News; editor-in-chief, Ascent Magazine, Harlem Week Magazine, Tennis Classic Magazine, Metropolitan Profile Magazine and Black New Yorker Magazine. **Military Serv:** AUS, lt, 1954-61. **Home Addr:** RR 10, Summit, NY 12175. **Business Addr:** President, ASCENT Foundation, PO Box 148, Summit, NY 12175-0148.*

BLAIR, DR. LACY GORDON
Physician. **Personal:** Born Oct 10, 1937, Lynchburg, VA; son of Lacy and Sara Williams. **Educ:** Hampton Inst, BS, 1959; Meharry Med Col, MD, 1969. **Career:** Military Serv, lab technician, 1961-64; Pvt pract, physician, currently. **Orgs:** Writer, int traveler; stud Ethiopia's Hist & The Hebrews; Nat Med Asn; United African Movement. **Honors/Awds:** Bronx Club's, Man of the Year, 2000. **Home Addr:** PO Box 579, New York, NY 10023. **Business Addr:** Physician, 1731 Macombs Rd, Bronx, NY 10453-7047, **Business Phone:** (718)294-6800.

BLAISE, KERLIN
Football player. **Personal:** Born Dec 25, 1974, Orlando, FL. **Educ:** Miami Univ. **Career:** Detroit Lions, guard, 1998-04; Detroit Lions, free agent, 2004-. **Honors/Awds:** Top 100 players, Dallas Morning News. *

BLAIZE, MAVIS. See THOMPSON, DR. MAVIS SARAH.

BLAKE, B. DAVID
Administrator, physician. **Personal:** Born in Bronx, NY. **Educ:** Howard Univ, Wash, DC, BS, zoology; Morehouse Sch Med, Atlanta, Ga, MD; Morehouse Sch Med. **Career:** Morehouse Sch Med, Dept Family Med, Southwest Hosp & Med Ctr, residency; Legacy Med Ctr; Regency Hosp; Family First Healthcare PC, Mableton, Ga, med dir, currently. **Orgs:** Ringside physician, Ga State Boxing Comn; ringside physician, USA Boxing; numerous regional and national orgns. **Special Achievements:** Speaker's Bureau for Pfizer, Novartis, Astra Zeneca; Has written several publications. **Business Addr:** Medical Director, First Family Healthcare PC, 1221 Old Powder Springs Rd SW, Mableton, GA 31026, **Business Phone:** (770)739-1233.*

BLAKE, CARL LEROY
College teacher, pianist. **Personal:** Born Sep 25, 1951, Liberty, MO; son of William Louis and Hazel Roberson. **Educ:** Boston Univ, BS, music, 1973; San Jose State Univ, MA, music, 1976; Cornell Univ, Ithaca, NY, attended 1988. **Career:** City San Jose, Fine Arts Comn, music specialist, 1977-78; Bishop Col, Dallas, TX, chmn, music dept, asst prof music, 1978-79; Ohio Univ, Athens, OH, music lectr, 1980-84; Music & Arts Inst, San Francisco, CA, music instr, 1988-89; Pa St Univ, Univ Park, PA, asst dean, Inst Arts & Humanistic Studies, assoc dir & asst prof music, 1998. **Orgs:** Nat Music Honor Soc, Pi Kappa Lambda, 1973-; Am Matthay Asn, 1988-. **Honors/Awds:** Marian Anderson Young Artist Award, Today's Artists Concerts, Inc, San Francisco, CA, 1978; Carnegie Recital Hall debut presented by Today's Artists Concerts, Inc, 1986; Honors Award in Piano Performance, Boston University, 1972. **Business Addr:** Associate Director, Associate Professor Music, Institute for the Arts & Humanistic Studies, Ihlseng Cottage, University Park, PA 16802-1703, **Business Phone:** (814)865-0495.

BLAKE, CHARLES E
Clergy. **Personal:** Born Aug 15, 1940, Little Rock, AR; son of J A and Lula Champion; married Mae Lawrence, Jul 11, 1964; children: Kimberly Roxanne, Charles Edward II & Lawrence Champion. **Educ:** Calif Western Univ, BA, 1962; Interdenominational Theol Ctr, MDiv, 1965; Calif Grad Sch Theol, DD, 1982. **Career:** West Angeles COGIC, pastor, currently. **Orgs:** Jurisdictional prelate, First Jurisdiction Southern Calif, 1985-; gen bd, The COGIC, 1988-; founder, La Ecumenical Cong, co-chair, 1992-; presiding bd, The 12-mem Gen Bd COGIC; Pentecostal World Conf Adv Comn, 1999-; found & pres, Pan African C's Fund; exec comt bd dir, chair bd dir, C.H. Mason Theol Sem; bd mem, bd dir, Interdenominational Theol Sem; chair exec comt, dir bd mem, Oral Roberts Univ; mem bd dir, Int Charismatic Bible Ministries. **Honors/Awds:** William Booth Award, Salvation Army, 1997; Big Heart Award, Greenlining Inst, 1997; Whitney M Young Jr Award, LA Urban League, 2000. **Business Addr:** Bishop, West Angeles COGIC, 3045 Crenshaw Blvd, Los Angeles, CA 90016, **Business Phone:** (323)733-8300.*

BLAKE, GRACE
Foundation executive, movie producer, actor. **Career:** Film actor, Producer; Apollo Theatre Found, exec dir, 1995-; Actress: Mothers of Men, 1997; Beloved, 1998; Producer: The Wiz, prod off coordr, 1978; All That Jazz, prod coordr, 1979; Willie & Phil, prod coordr, 1980; Can't Stop the Music, prod secy, 1980; Eyewitness, prod coordr, 1981; Tempest, prod coordr, 1982; Still of the Night, prod coordr, 1982; The Cotton Club, prod supvr, 1984; Prizzi's Honor, prod coordr, 1985; Heaven Help Us, prod coordr, 1985; Something Wild, prod coordr, 1986; Power, prod coordr, 1986; School Daze, exec producer, 1988; Married to the Mob, financial rep, 1988; Lean on Me, prod coordr, 1989; The Silence of the Lambs, assoc producer & prod coordr, 1991; Boomerang, prod supvr 1992; Who's the Man?, line producer, 1993; Spirit Lost, line producer, 1996; Star 80, assoc producer, 1998. **Business Addr:** Executive Director, Apollo Theatre Foundation, 253 W 125th St, New York, NY 10027.*

BLAKE, DR. J. HERMAN
Educator. **Personal:** Born Mar 15, 1934, Mt Vernon, NY; son of J Henry and Lylace Michael; married Emily Moore; married Maria W Brown (divorced); children: Vanessa E, Lylace Y, Audrey RA, Denise L & L Sidney Nathaniel. **Educ:** NY Univ, BA, sociol, 1960; Univ Calif, Berkeley, MA, sociol, 1965, PhD, sociol, 1974. **Career:** Univ Calif, from asst prof to prof, 1966-84; Univ Calif Santa Cruz, Oakes Col founding provost, 1972-84; Tougaloo Col, pres, 1984-87; Iowa State Univ, African Am Studies Prog, dir, Educ Leadership & Policy Studies, prof social, 1998-2007; Med Univ SC, prof health prof & dent med, 2007-, humanities scholar residence; Univ SC, scholar in residence & dir sea islands inst; Ind Univ, v chancellor; Purdue Univ, v chancellor; Swarthone Col, Eugene M Lang vis prof social sci; Dillard Univ Louisiana, Provost & VPres Academic Affairs, currently. **Orgs:** Am Sociol Asn; Pop Asn Am; Pac Sociol Asn; bd trustee, Save the Children Fedn; bd trustee, Pa Comm Serv Fel Woodrow Wilson, 1960; fel John Hay Whitney, 1963; Pop Coun, 1964; fel Dan forth Found, 1964; fel Rockefeller Found, 1965; fel Ford Found, 1970. **Honors/Awds:** Iowa Professor of the Year, Carnegie Found Advan Teaching & Coun Advan & support Educ, 2002; Honorary doctorates, Ind Univ; Honorary doctorates, Univ Wis; Honorary doctorates, Purdue Univ; Honorary doctorates, Univ Mass; Honorary doctorates, Manchester Col Ind; Honorary doctorates, St Lawerence Univ New York; Honorary doctorates, Prof Sch Psycol Calif. **Special Achievements:** Co-author of "Revolutionary Suicide" 1973, named among Top 100 Emerging Young Leaders in Higher Education in the American Council of Education in 1978. **Business Addr:** Professor, Medical University South Carolina, 171 Ashley Ave Room 216, Charleston, SC 50011, **Business Phone:** (843)792-6138.

BLAKE, J PAUL
Educator, public relations executive. **Personal:** Born Mar 31, 1950, Neptune, NJ; son of Joseph E and Shirley T. **Educ:** Drake Univ, BA, 1972. **Career:** Univ Minn, asst dir univ rels, 1976-83, from asst to vpres stud develop, 1983-86; Pandamonium, pres, 1986-88; Seattle Univ, asst vpres, dir pub rels, Commun Dept, instr, 1989-98; Seattle Pub Utilities, commun dir, 1998-2004, community rels develop dir, 2004-. **Orgs:** Bd trustees, Coun Advancement & Support Educ, 1982-84, 1992-94; pres, MN Press Club, 1988; bd dir, US China Peoples Friendship Asn MN Chap; vice chair, Pub Affairs Coun; Am Water Works Asn; Water Utility Coun; vice chair, Evergreen State Chap, Am Soc Pub Admin; Pub Rels Adv Bd, Seattle YMCA; Pub Rels Adv Bd, Univ Wash Pub Rels Cert Prog; bd mem, Seattle Biomed Res Inst; Black Heritage Soc Wash State. **Honors/Awds:** Volunteer Service Award, Minneapolis Urban League, 1977; Good Neighbour Award, WCCO-AM Radio, 1982; Outstanding Service Award, Univ Minn, 1984; Positive Image Award, Minneapolis Urban League, 1984. **Home Addr:** 21121 SE 206th St, Renton, WA 98058-0246. **Business Addr:** Community Relations Development Director, Seattle Public Utilities, Seattle Munic Tower 700 5th Ave Suite 4900, PO Box 34018, Seattle, WA 98124-4018, **Business Phone:** (206)684-8180.

BLAKE, JAMES G.
Clergy, executive director. **Personal:** Born Dec 4, 1944, Charleston, SC. **Educ:** Morehouse Col, AB, 1965; Boston Univ Sch Theol, MTh, 1968. **Career:** Gov RI, spec asst, 1968; Interfaith City-Wide Coord Com NYC, exec dir, 1968-71; Union AME Church, Little Rock, pastor, 1971-72; Sen Hubert Humphrey, nat field coordr, 1972; SC Comm For Farm Workers Inc, exec dir; Morris Brown AME Church, pastor. **Orgs:** nat vpres, Nat Asn Advan Colored People; Selec Comn, US Youth Coun; del, World Assembly Youth Leige Belgium, 1970; del, The World Coun Churches, 1975; coordr, Del Black Religious Leaders Republic China, 1976; del, 1st Pan African Youth Festival Tunis, Tunisia, 1972.

BLAKE, JAMES RILEY
Tennis player. **Personal:** Born Dec 28, 1979, Yonkers, NY; son of Tommy Sr and Betty. **Career:** US Tennis Asn, 2000-. **Honors/Awds:** Rookie of the Yr, 2000; USTA Waikola Challenger, 2002; Pilot Pen Tennis; 2005; Shanghai, 2006; Indian Wells, 2006; Cincinnati, 2007. **Business Addr:** Professional Tennis Player, US Tennis Association, 70 W Red Oak Lane, White Plains, NY 10604-3602, **Business Phone:** (914)696-7000.*

BLAKE, JEFF (JEFF BERTRAND COLEMAN BLAKE)
Football player. **Personal:** Born Dec 4, 1970, Daytona Beach, FL; son of Emory; married Lewanna; children: Emory, Torre & Trey. **Educ:** E Carolina Univ. **Career:** Football player (retired); NY Jets, 1992-94; Cincinnati Bengals, 1994-99; New Orleans Saints, 2000-01; Baltimore Ravens, 2002; Ariz Cardinals, 2003; Philadelphia Eagles, 2004; Chicago Bears, quaterback, 2005. **Honors/Awds:** Pro Bowl, 1995. **Special Achievements:** One of nine African-American quarterbacks, largest number in NFL history, 1997.

BLAKE, JEFF BERTRAND COLEMAN. See BLAKE, JEFF.

BLAKE, JENNIFER LYNN
Activist, clergy. **Personal:** Born Mar 16, 1961, Fort Benning, GA; daughter of James K Wall and Fannie Bea; divorced; children: Lakisha, Leroy & London. **Educ:** Pittsburgh Beauty Acad, attended 1986. **Career:** White Umbrella Ministry, chief exec officer, currently; Cosmetologist, currently. **Orgs:** Children's Outreach Ministry; Action Christ Outreach Ministry; Prison Ministry.

Honors/Awds: One of the Best Dressed Women in America, nominated, 1998. **Special Achievements:** Teach abstinence classes; speaker; vocalist; songwriter; volunteer work; teach arts & crafts.

BLAKE, JOHN
Football coach, football player. **Personal:** Born Mar 6, 1961, Rockford, IL; married Freda; children: Jourdan. **Educ:** Univ Okla, BA, pub relations & recreation, 1986. **Career:** Univ Okla, player (Retired), 1979-82; Univ Okla, stud asst & defensive line, 1985; Univ Okla, grad asst, 1986, asst coach & defensive line coach, 1989, asst coach & linebackers, 1990-92, head coach, 1996-98; Univ Tulsa, asst coach & tight ends & wide receivers, 1987-88; Dallas Cowboys, asst coach & defensive line, 1993-95; Miss State Univ, asst coach & defensive line, 2003; Nebr Cornhuskers, asst-coach & defensive line, 2004-06; NC State Univ, defensive line coach & asst head coach, 2007-. **Business Addr:** Assistant Coach, Defensive Line Coach, University of North Carolina, Department of Athletics, Airport Rd Suite 114a, Chapel Hill, NC 27599, **Business Phone:** (919)962-2211.

BLAKE, MILTON JAMES
Labor activist, executive director, administrator. **Personal:** Born Nov 11, 1934, Chicago, IL; married Beverly Marlene Skyles; children: Milton J Jr (dec), Robin. **Educ:** Bradley Univ, Peoria, IL, BS, indust arts, 1957. **Career:** Chicago Police Dept , human rels officer, 1961-65; Continental Can Co, suprv indust rels, 1966-72; Whittaker Metals, div mgr indust rels, 1972-74; Gulf & Western Energy Prod Group, group mgr employee rels, 1974-78; Bunker Ramo Corp, corp mgr eeo & compliance mgt, 1979-; Gulf & Western, consult EEO, 1979; Amphenol Co, dir & salary admin, org planning & develelop, 1982-. **Orgs:** Youth adv comt, St James Luthern Church, 1961-66; indust rels adv comt, Univ Wis, 1971-; Oak Brook Asn Com & Indust, 1979-; bd dir, Chicago C Choir, 1980; Chicago Urban Affairs Coun, 1982; Alpha Phi Alpha; Alpha Phi Omega; Phi Mu Alpha. **Honors/Awds:** Hon Mention, Chicago Police Dept, 1961; vis instr, Affirm Action Prog, Univ Wis, 1977; Pub Affirm Action Prog, Bunker Ramo Corp, 1979. **Special Achievements:** Author "Supervisory Awareness Program", Continental Can Co, 1969. **Military Serv:** AUS, Active & Res, inf officer, 1955-; Good Conduct Medal, 1957; AUS, lt col, 30 yrs; Armed Forces Res Medal, 1976.

BLAKE, NEIL
Executive. **Personal:** Born Jan 1, 1962, Brooklyn, NY. **Educ:** Long Island Univ. **Career:** Long Island Univ, WLIU Radio, gen mgr; "A Current Affair," assoc dir & backup dir; Fox 5 TV, "Good Day New York," & "10 O'clock News," assoc dir; NBC, "Positively Black," assoc producer; BlakeRadio Network, founder, 2000-. **Orgs:** Dir Guild. **Business Addr:** Founder, BlakeRadio Network, PO Box 403, Massapequa Park, NY 11762, **Business Phone:** (516)557-5468.

BLAKE, PEGGY JONES
Librarian. **Personal:** Born Jan 26, 1946, Georgetown, GA; daughter of David and Carrie Griggs; married. **Educ:** Tuskegee Univ, Tuskegee, AL, BS, 1968; Univ Mich, Ann Arbor, MI, AMLS, 1974. **Career:** Nat Libr Med, Bethesda, MD, librn, 1974-87; Morehouse Sch Med, Libr, Atlanta, GA, AHEC librn, 1987-89; Nat Agr Libr, ARS coordr, 1989-96, spec asst to the dir, 1996-. **Orgs:** Am Libr Asn, 1974-76, 1989-; Med Libr Asn, 1974-87; United States Agr Info Network, 1989-; Black Caucus Am Libr Asn, 1990-; Assoc Nat Agr Libr; Tuskegee Univ Alumni Asn. **Honors/Awds:** Scholarship Award, Spec Libr Asn, 1972; Certification-Medical Librarian, Med Libr Asn, 1975-86; Post-Graduate Internship as Library Asniate, Nat Libr Med, 1980-81. **Business Addr:** Special Assistant to the Director, National Agricultural Library, Office of the Director, 10301 Baltimore Blvd Rm 205, Beltsville, MD 20705-2351, **Business Phone:** (301)504-6780.

BLAKE, WENDELL OWEN
Physician. **Personal:** Born Aug 9, 1940, Bartow, FL; married Mildred; children: Wendi, Michael. **Educ:** Howard Univ, BS, 1961; Meharry Med Col, Tenn, MD, 1967. **Career:** Good Samaritan Hosp, intern, 1967-68; George W. Hubbard Hosp, resident; Meharry Med Col, resident, 1968-72; Roswell Park Memorial Inst, fel surgical oncol, physician, 1974-75; Lakeland Regional Med Ctr, chief Gen Surgery, staff mem, 1984; family pract physician, currently. **Orgs:** Soc Abdominal Surgeons; FL Med Asn; Polk County Med Asn FL; Nat Med Asn; FL Med Dental & Pharmaceut Asn; Polemarch Lakeland Alumni Chapt; diplomate, Am Bd Surgery; Kappa Alpha Psi Frat; pres, Boys & Girls Club of Lakeland, Fla, 1993; fel Southeastern Surgical Cong. **Honors/Awds:** Award for Achievement in recognition of meritorious performance of duty, US Kenner Army Hosp, 1972-74. **Special Achievements:** Has published various articles in scientific journals. **Military Serv:** AUS mc major 1972-74. **Business Addr:** Family Practice Physician, 505 Martin L King Jr Ave Suite 2, Lakeland, FL 33815.*

BLAKE, REV. WILLIAM J
Educator, college administrator. **Personal:** Born in Akron, OH; son of William W Blake Jr and Maxine; married Vanessa A Drone; children: Jessyca, Janeil, William & Ashton. **Educ:** Ohio Univ, Athens, AB, polit sci, 1975; Atlanta Univ, MA, 1979; Capella Univ, PhD, currently. **Career:** Youngstown State Univ, dir stud activ, 1995-2004, dir stud diversity prog, 2004-. **Business Addr:** Director of Student Diversity Programs, Youngstown State University, Office of Student Diversity Programs, 1 Univ Plz Rm 2100 Kilcawley Ctr, Youngstown, OH 44555.

BLAKELY, ALLISON
Educator, writer. **Personal:** Born Mar 31, 1940, Clinton, AL; son of Ed Walton and Alice Blakely; married Shirley Ann Reynolds, Jul 5, 1968; children: Shantel Lynn & Andrei. **Educ:** Ore State Col, Corvallis, OR, attended 1960; Univ Ore, Eugene, OR, BA, 1962; Univ Calif, Berkeley, MA, 1964, PhD, 1971. **Career:** AUS, active duty, 1966-68; Stanford Univ, Stanford, CA, instr, 1970-71; Howard Univ, Wash, DC, from asst prof to prof, 1971-2001; Boston Univ, Boston, MA, prof, 2001-. **Orgs:** Chair, Scholarly Worth Comt, Howard Univ Press, 1989-; Comt Qualifications, Phi Beta Kappa Soc, 1991-97; Am Hist Asn; Asn Advan Slavic Studies; World Hist Asn; Gov Senate, Phi Beta Kappa, 1994-2012, pres, 2006-09. **Honors/Awds:** Woodrow Wilson fel, Woodrow Wilson Found, 1962-63; Andrew Mellon fel, Aspen Inst Humanities, 1976-77; Fulbright-Hays Res fel, 1985-86; American Book Award, 1988; George & Joyce Wein prof African Studies, 2003-. **Special Achievements:** Author, Russia & the Negro: Blacks in Russian History and Thought, 1986; Blacks in the Dutch World: the Evolution of Racial Imagery in a Modern Society, 1994. **Military Serv:** Mil Intelligence, capt, 1966-68; Bronze Star, Purple Heart, 1968. **Home Addr:** 42 Dalton Rd, Belmont, MA 02478-3725, **Home Phone:** (617)489-4932. **Business Addr:** Professor of European & Comparative History, Boston University, Department of History, Boston, MA 02215.

BLAKELY, CAROLYN
School administrator. **Personal:** Born Feb 13, 1936, Magnolia, AR; daughter of James D and Mary E; married Neal Nathanial Blakely; children: Karen Joy & Earl Kevin. **Educ:** Ark AM&N Col, BA, 1957; Atlanta Univ, MA, 1964; Okla State UNiv, PhD, 1984. **Career:** Teacher, 1957-62; Grambling State Univ, 1963-66; Univ Ark, Pine Bluff, asst prof Eng, 1968-86, asst to chancellor, 1986-90, interim vice chancellor acad affairs, 1990-91, interim chancellor, 1991; Hons Col, dean; Pinnacle Bus Solutions, bd dirs, currently. **Orgs:** Nat Colgiate Hons Coun, 1980-; Nat Coun Teachers Eng, 1980-; pres, 1991, Southern Regional Hons Coun; past pres, Nat Asn African-Am Hons Progs; bd dirs, Ark Blue Cross & Blue Shield. **Honors/Awds:** Top 100 Women in Ark; Distingushed Alumnus, Univ Ark, Pine Bluff. **Business Addr:** Board of Direstors, Pinnacle Business Solutions, 515 W Pershing Blvd, North Little Rock, AR 72114, **Business Phone:** (501)210-9000.

BLAKELY, CHARLES
School administrator. **Personal:** Born Jan 31, 1951, Batesville, MS; son of Willie and Edna; widowed. **Educ:** Coahoma Jr Col, AA, 1972; Jackson State Univ, BS, 1975; MS State Univ,attended 1973, Delta State Univ, attended 1982, Univ MS attended 1984. **Career:** Jackson State Univ, student admin clerk 1974-75; North Panola Vocational High Sch, substitute teacher 1975-78; Northwest Jr Coll Greenhill Elementary Sch, adult basic educ instructor 1981-88; Inst of Comm Serv, licensed social worker 1988-; North Panola Consolidated Sch Dist I, pres Sch bd, 1989-90, secretary, 1991; Panola Co, Sch attendance officer, counselor, 1989-; St Francis Behavior Ctr, counselor/consultant; Path Finder, youth counselor; North Panola High Sch, Continuing Educ Dept, site supervisor, 1992-98; Mississippi Dept EDU, Sch attendance officer, 1998-; Como Mid & Elem Sch, sch attendance officers, currently. **Orgs:** Pres, Sardis Panola County Voters League, 1980-88; part time Sunday sch teacher, mem choir, Miles Chapel CME Church, sch bd mem, 1980-92; selective serv bd mem, 1981-2000; asst supt Sunday sch, Miles Chapel CME Church, 1982-; MACE affiliate local bd continued educ, 1983-85; bd mem, Dem Exec Community Panola County, 1984-93; pres, N Panola Sch Bd Educ,1989-90; pres, Job Corps Community Rels Coun, 2002-04; Cavalette Social Club; chmn, Steward Bd. **Honors/Awds:** Certificate in recognition of noteworthy performance of service, MS United Progress Black Community, 1980-81; Certificate Award Outstanding Service in the Community, NAACP, 1982; Outstanding service, dedication & cooperation in the community Panola County Voter League Inc, 1982; Staff of the Year, Inst Community Serv Headstart Prog, 1989; Outstanding School Board Award for Service Rendered, 1990; Certified Master Addiction Counselor, 1996-; Certified Criminal Justice Specialist, 1996-. **Home Addr:** 19324 Hwy 51 S, Sardis, MS 38666, **Home Phone:** (662)487-3647. **Business Addr:** School Attendance Officer, Como Middle - Elementary School, 526 Compress Rd, Como, MS 38619-7302, **Business Phone:** (662)526-0333.

BLAKELY, DR. EDWARD JAMES
Educator. **Personal:** Born Apr 21, 1938, San Bernardino, CA; son of Edward and Josephine Carter; married Maaike van der Slessen; children: Pieta & Brette. **Educ:** San Bernardino Valley Col, AA, 1958; Univ Calif, BA, 1960, MA, 1964; Pasadena Col, MA, 1967; Univ Calif, PhD, 1971. **Career:** Univ Calif Los Angeles Ext, training dir, 1966-68; Western Community Action Training Inc, exec dir, 1968-70; US State Dept, spec asst to asst secy, 1970-71; Univ Pittsburgh, asst to chancellor, 1971-74; Univ Calif, Berkeley, dean, asst vpres, 1977-84, Sch Urban Planning & Develop, dean, 1994-98, Dept City & Regional Planning, prof, prof emer city & reg planning, currently; Univ Southern Calif, prof, 1994-99; New Sch Univ, Robert J Milano Grad Sch Mgt & Urban Policy, dean, 1999-2004. **Orgs:** Fel Colo Found, 1960; brd dir, YMCA, 1972-74; Natl Assn Advan Colored People, Pittsburgh, 1972-74; Community Develop Soc Am, 1976-; Int Soc Educ Planners 1977-; fel, Natl Acad Pub Admin, 2002; consult, US Agency Int Develop & UN-;leader, Civic Alliance for the Rebuilding of the City of New York since sept 11; Guggenheim fel; Fulbright fel. **Honors/Awds:** Young Man of the Year, San Bernardino, 1955, 1958; honorary mention, Small Col Coast Football, 1959; Scholar Athlete Award, Univ Calif, 1959; Most Inspirational Player, Univ Calif, 1959; Sergeant Shriver Rural Serv Award, 1968; Community Service Award, Natl Assn Advan Colored People, 1970;Civic Service Award, Richmond, CA, 1984; Hall of Fame Athlete, 1991; San Francisco Foundation Award, 1991; 125th Anniversary Professor Award, 1992. **Special Achievements:** Author of over 20 articles & 3 books on community planning & development. **Military Serv:** USAF, first lt, 1961-64; Outstanding Officer Training, 1961. **Home Addr:** 2709 Alida St, Oakland, CA 94602. **Business Addr:** Professor Emeritus of City & Regional Planning, University of California-Berkeley, Department City & Regional Planning, 228 Wurster Hall Suite 1850, Berkeley, CA 94720-1850, **Business Phone:** (510)642-3256.

BLAKEY, WILLIAM A.
Lawyer. **Personal:** Born Sep 1, 1943, Louisville, KY. **Educ:** Knoxville Col, BA, 1965; Howard Univ Sch Law, JD, 1968; Georgetown Law Ctr, pursuing LLM. **Career:** Sen Daniel Brewster, exec asst & spec asst, 1965-68; Dept HUD, atty adv, 1968-69; Nat Urban Coalition, exec asst to vpres for field opers, 1969-70; Transcentury Corp, vpres sr assoc, 1970-71; AL Nellum & Assoc, sr assoc, 1971-72; US Comn Civil Rights, spec asst to staff dir, 1972-74; KY Comn on Human Rights, legis specialist & atty, 1976-77; DHEW, dep asst sec for legis, 1977-80; US Comn Civil Rights, dir cong Liaison, 1974-; Jones, Tullar & Cooper, PC, atty, currently. **Orgs:** Consult, Neighborhood Consumer Info Ctr, 1968; instr, Common Legal Problems Ctl Data Corp, 1969-71; Cong Action Fund, 1970-72; KY, WA, Am Nat Bar Asns; Nat Bar Asn, 1975; Omega Psi Phi Frat; Phi Alpha Delta Law Frat; Sen Waeden St Stephen Incarnation Episcopal; bd mem, Louisville Br Nat Asn Advan Colored People Legal Aid Soc Louisville, 1976-77; The Inner Voices Inc; chmn, The Minority & Legis Educ Proj, 1979-80. **Honors/Awds:** Omega Psi Phi Dist Scholar, 1965; Alpha Kappa Mu & Phi Alpha Theta Hon Soc. **Business Phone:** (703)415-1500.

BLALOCK, MARION W.
School administrator. **Personal:** Born Dec 18, 1947, East Chicago, IN; married Roger; children: Erin Juliane. **Educ:** Purdue Univ, BS, Sociol 1969, MS, Coun & Personnel Servi 1973. **Career:** Parker Career Ctr, employment counr, 1970; Family Serv Metro Detroit, family caseworker 1970-71; Purdue Univ, grad teaching asst, 1971-73, asst dean studs, 1974-75, dir minority eng prog, 1975-2003, advs, asst to eng assoc dean undergrad prog, 2003-. **Orgs:** Fac adv & nat adv, hon mem, Nat Soc Black Engrs; Nat Asn Minority Eng Prog Adminrs, Am Soc Eng Educ, Black Col Develop Comm; vice chair, steering comm, Purdue Black Alumni Orgn; bd dirs, Tippecanoe Area Planned Parenthood Asn, 1985-88. **Honors/Awds:** Dean M Beverly Stone Award, 1982; Hon member Golden Key Nat Honor Soc;Vincent M Bendix Minorities in English Award, Am Soc Eng Educ, 1983;Reginald H Jones Distinguished Service Award, Nat Action Coun MinoritiesEng, 1984; President's Affirmative Action Award, Purdue Univ, 1985; BestTeacher Award, Dept Freshman Eng, Purdue Univ, 1985, 86; OutstandingAdvisor, Nat Adv Bd, Nat Soc of Black Engrs, 1986; Helen B Schleman Award,1986. **Business Addr:** Director, Purdue University, Minority Pre-Engineering, Rm 211 ENAD Bldg, CIVL G175F, West Lafayette, IN 47907.

BLANC, ERIC ANTHONY-HAWKINS
Manager. **Personal:** Born Jun 10, 1969, New Orleans, LA; son of Stephen and Rosa Hawkins; married Dori, Jun 13, 1992; children: Kendal. **Educ:** Fla State Univ, BS, Mkt, 1991. **Career:** Copitech Corp, mkt consult, 1991-92; Thunderdome, events coordr, 1992-93; Tampa Convention Ctr, sr events coordr, 1993-; Centennial Olympic Games, Atlanta, Ga, event coordr, 1996; Fla Classic Football Weekend, Tampa, Fla; Freeman Companies, Orlando, Fla, acct exec, currently. **Orgs:** Adv, NAACP Youth Coun, 1991-94; host comt chair, Fla Classic Asn, 1994-; Omega Psi Phi Fraternity Inc; Asn Convention opers Mgt. **Business Phone:** (407)857-1500.*

BLAND, ARTHUR HENRY. See Obituaries section.

BLAND, BOBBY BLUE (ROBERT CALVIN BLAND)
Singer. **Personal:** Born Jan 27, 1930, Rosemark, TN. **Career:** Miniatures Musical Group, 1949; BB King, chauffeur musical artist, 1950; Beale Streeters Musical Group, founder, 1951; Jr Parker, touring & rec, 1958; Joe Scott, touring & rec, 1958-68; Wayne Bennett, guitarist, 1958-68; Malaco Recs, 1985; Singles: "Farther on up the Rd", 1957; "I Pity the Fool", 1961; "That's the Way Love Is", 1963; "Stormy Mondy"; "Turn On Your Lovelight";

"Get Your Money Where You Spend Your Time"; "Ain't No Heart in the City"; Albums: Blues Consolidated, 1958; Two Steps From the Blues, 1961; Call On Me, 1963; The Soul of the Man, 1966; Touch of Blues, 1967; If Loving You Is Wrong, 1970; Calif Album, 1973; Woke Up Screaming, 1974; Reflections in Blues, 1977; Sweet Vibrations, 1980; Here We Go Again, 1982; Mems Only, 1985; After All, 1986; First Class Blues, 1987; Midnight Run, 1989; Portrait of the Blues, 1991; I Pity the Fool: The Duke Recs, 1992; Years of Tears, 1993; Live on Beale St, 1998; Memphis Monday Morning, 1998; Greatest Hits Vol 1, 1998; Greatest Hits Vol 2, 1998, Soulful Side of Bobby Bland, 2001; Blues at Midnight, 2003. **Honors/Awds:** Rock & Roll Hall of Fame, 1991. **Special Achievements:** Nominated for Grammy Award for "Get Your Money Where You Spend Your Time", 1989. **Military Serv:** AUS, 1952-55. **Business Addr:** Vocalist, c/o Rounder Records, 1 Camp St, Cambridge, MA 02140, **Business Phone:** (617)218-4495.

BLAND, EDWARD
Television producer, consultant. **Personal:** Born Jan 1, 1926?, Chicago, IL; divorced; children: Edward, Robert & Stefanie. **Educ:** Am Conserv Music, Chicago. **Career:** Mus Modern Art, mus consult, 1968-74; Mus Modern Arts Newsletter, 1968;Brooklyn Acad Music, mus consult, 1973-75; Vanguard Rec, exec producer & dir, currently; Welk Rec Group; TV series: A Soldier's Story, composer, 1984; A Raisin in the Sun, composer, 1989; 34th St. NYC, 2007; Film: Cry of Jazz, writer, dir & producer, 1959. **Special Achievements:** Innumerable music scores for documentary & educational films. **Military Serv:** USN, 18 months. **Business Phone:** (213)451-5727.

BLAND, ELLEN TAYLOR
Writer. **Personal:** Born Dec 31, 1944, Boston, MA; daughter of Leroy and Mildred; divorced; children: 2. **Educ:** Southern Ill Univ, BA, accounting & educ, 1981. **Career:** Abbot Labs, acct, 1981-99; Novels: Dead Time, 1992; Slow Burn, 1993; Gone Quiet, 1994; Done Wrong, 1995; Keep Still, 1996; See No Evil, 1998; Tell No Tales, 1999; Scream in Silence, 2000; Whispers in the Dark, 2001; Windy City Dying, 2002; Fatal Remains, 2003. **Orgs:** Mystery Writers of Am; Sisters Crime; co chair, Outreach Authors Color. **Honors/Awds:** nominee, Gold Pen Award, 2001; Pen Oakland Josephine Miles Award; Chester A Himes Mystery Fiction Award; Most Influential African American Artist of Lake County Award. **Business Addr:** Writer, c/o St Martin, 175 5th Ave Rm 1715, New York, NY 10010, **Business Phone:** (212)674-5151.*

BLAND, GLENN W
Activist. **Personal:** Born Jan 6, 1953, Augusta, GA; son of Allen and Felton; children: Terius Bland. **Career:** DuPoint, supvr, 1975-85; Laney-Walker Mus Inc, consult, 1976; Former Mayor Ed McIntyre, campaign coordr, 1982; Early Intervention Prog, consult, 1998. **Orgs:** Southern Christian Leadership Conf, 1975; Nat Asn Advan Colored People, 1980-. **Honors/Awds:** Man of the Year, Laney-Walker Mus, 1985. **Special Achievements:** Developed the first local Pilot Program to commemorate 9/11.

BLAND, HEYWARD. See Obituaries section.

BLAND, LARCINE
Executive. **Career:** Blockbuster Entertainment Corp OFC, mgr & dir intercultural & community affairs, 1998. **Orgs:** Nat Asn Advan Colored People. **Honors/Awds:** Corporate Citizen Award, PAFF. **Business Phone:** (214)854-3190.*

BLAND, DR. ROBERT ARTHUR
Government official. **Personal:** Born Jan 26, 1938, Petersburg, VA; married Shirley Thweatt; children: Angela Rene & Lael Gregory. **Educ:** Univ Va, BSEE 1959; CA State Univ, MA 1975; Nova Univ, Ed.D 1979. **Career:** Naval Weapons Ctr, proj engr 1959-71; Oxnard Comm Col, counr 1976-77,instr 1977-; Aquarius Portrait Photogr, photogr, 1983-; Naval Ship Weapons Syst Eng Sta, div head, currently. **Orgs:** Instr Oxnard Comn Col 1977-; Comn Ministry Episcopal Diocese Los Angeles,1980-; vice chmn Ventura Cty Affirmative Action Adv Comn, 1982-; photog, Aquarius Portrait Photog, 1983-; vestry St Patricks Episcopal Church, 1985-. **Honors/Awds:** First black undergrad to attend grad from Univ of VA 1959. **Home Addr:** 3915 Crownhaven Ct, Newbury Park, CA 91320, **Home Phone:** (805)498-5682.

BLAND, ROBERT CALVIN. See BLAND, BOBBY BLUE.

BLANDEN, LEE ERNEST
School administrator, dean (education). **Personal:** Born Sep 16, 1942, Arcadia, FL; divorced; children: Teresa, Toni, Yvonne & Curtis. **Educ:** Voorhees Jr Col, Denmark, SC, AA, 1962; Lane Col Jackson, TN, BA, elem educ, 1965; Univ Ill, Urbana, MEd, admin & suprv, 1970, Post Grad Study Ed Admin & Suprv; Eastern Ill Univ, Charleston, admin & sch law; Ill Asn Sch Bd, Negotiations & Sch Law. **Career:** Gen Develop Corp, 1958-60; Voorhees Jr Col, Gen Develop Corp, 1958-60; Voorhees Jr Col, Denmark, SC, maintenance, 1960-62; Wildwood Linen Supply, Wildwood, NJ, laborer summers, 1963-65; Lane Col Jackson TN, libr asst, asst varsity coach, 1965-70; Danville Dist 118, elem teacher, asst prin, 1965-70; Elem Bldg, prin, 1970-74; Danville Area Community Col, adult educ fac, 1970-74, dir personnel, 1974-80, asst to the pres, dean stud serv. **Orgs:** Alpha Phi Alpha Fraternity; Omicron Lambda Beta; Danville United Fund; Am Soc Personnel Admin; bd dir, chairperson, Laura Lee Fel House; trustee bd, sanctuary choir, Second Baptist Church; ed admin, Danville Rotary Int; personnel mgr, Danville Chamber Com; master & secy, Corinthian Lodge 31 F&AM; bd dir, Ctr C Serv; bd dir, treas, Vermilion City Opportunities Indust Ctr Inc; bell ringer, Salvation Army; sch bd mem, Danville Community Consol Sch Dist 118, Bd Policy Revisions; chief negotiator, Bd Educ; consult & speaker, Nat Sch Bd Annual Conv. **Honors/Awds:** Outstanding Educator Midwest; Cited, Cost Containment Related Personnel Absences. **Special Achievements:** Top 100 Administrators in North America, 1980. **Home Addr:** 4 W Bluff, Danville, IL 61832.

BLANDING, LARRY
Real estate agent, politician, association executive. **Personal:** Born Aug 29, 1953, Sumter, SC; son of Junius Blanding Sr and Rosa Lee Williams; married Peggy Ann Mack, Dec 24, 1977; children: Dreylan Dre. **Educ:** Claflin Col, BA, social sci, 1975; SC State Col, MEd, educ, 1977; SC Sch Real Estate, 1988. **Career:** United Way Jacksonville, campaign assoc, 1975; United Way Richland & Lexington Co, actg dir comm planning, 1976; SC State Col, head resident, 1976-77; SC Dem Party, vice chmn; SC House Rep, state rep, 1976-90; SC, state legislator; Univ SC, guest lectr, 1983; Realty World Colonial-Moses, sales assoc, 1987; Sumter, SC, councilman, 2006-; Santee Wateree Area Mental Health Center, asst exec dir, currently. **Orgs:** Nat Caucus Black Leg, 1976-; bd dir, Sumter Learning Develop Ctr, 1977-82; state dir, 1979-83, chmn, 1990-, Nat Real Estate Comt; Phi Beta Sigma; Sumter Pub Awareness Assoc, 1977-; NAACP, hon soc, Pi Gamma Mu Iota Chap, Orangesburg SC; chmn, SC Legis Black Caucus; St Paul Lodge 8, CC Johnson Consistory 136, Cario Temple 125; bd mem, Sumter Co Develop Bd, 1983-; Southern Legis Conf, 1986-; bd mem, Sumter Chamber Com, 1986-; Local, State & Nat Bd Realtors, 1987-; inspector gen, USCAAR 33rd degree Masons, 1986-; Claflin Univ Int Alumni Asn; Nat Honors Soc; pres, Student Gov Asn; pres, Walker Cemetery Asn; mme bd dirs, Jehovah Child Develop Ctr; vpres, B F Weston Educ Found. **Honors/Awds:** Sigma Man of the Year, Phi Beta Sigma Frat Inc, 1977; Man of the Year, Claflin Col, 1975; Citizen of the Year, Omega Psi Phi Frat Gamma Iota Chap, 1976; Alumni Award, Claflin Col, 1987; Family Pioneer, Williams Family Reunion Comt, 1989. **Special Achievements:** Listed as one of Fifty Future Leaders of America, EBONY Mag, 1978; First african american to hold the chairman position of SC Democratic party. **Business Addr:** Councilman, Summit, District 6, 13 E Canal St, Sumter, SC 29150, **Business Phone:** (803)436-2102.

BLANFORD, COLVIN
Clergy. **Personal:** Born Feb 6, 1938, Dallas, TX; son of John Hardee and Hattie Ellen; married Margaret Ann Tyrrell; children: Colvin II, Christopher. **Educ:** San Francisco State Col, BA, 1960; Berkeley Baptist Divinity Sch, BD, 1963; Southern Calif Sch Theol, RelD, 1969. **Career:** Third Baptist Church San Francisco, youth & asst minister, 1956-63; Cosmopolitan Baptist Church San Francisco, pastor, 1963-70; San Francisco Youth Guidance Ctr, prot chaplain, 1963-70; Brooks House Christian Serv Hammond IN, exec dir, 1970-73; First Baptist Church Gary IN, pastor, 1973-81; North Baptist Theol Sem, adj prof, 1974-; Christ Baptist Church, organizing pastor, 1981, pastor emer, 2004-. **Orgs:** Baptist Ministers Conf, 1973-; Interfaith Clergy Coun, 1973-; bd dir, Morehouse Sch Religion, 1976-; life mem, Nat Asn Advan Colored People, 1980-; bd mem, Gary Nat Asn Advan Colored People, 1986-. **Honors/Awds:** Youth of Yr, San Francisco Sun Reporter, 1958; sermon pub Outstanding Black Sermons Judson Press, 1976; represented Baptist denomination participant Baptist Lutheran dialogue meaning baptism, 1981; acclaimed Dollars & Sense Magazine one outstanding black ministers, Am, 1981; preaching missions Liberia, Malawi, Swaziland, Republic South Africa, 1985, 1987, 1989. *

BLANKENSHIP, GLENN RAYFORD
Government official. **Personal:** Born Aug 11, 1948, Memphis, TN; son of Geraldine Walton and Elbert; married Zita R Jackson; children: Maia & Rayford; married. **Educ:** Amer Univ, attended 1969; LeMoyne-Owen Col, attended 1970; Syracuse Univ, attended 1971; Univ Wis, attended 1973; Univ Colo, attended 1976. **Career:** Government official (retired); US Dept Housing & Urban Develop, Fed Energy Admin, 1974-77; US Dept Energy, 1977-79; USDA Forest Serv, 1979-97. **Orgs:** Life mem, Kappa Alpha Psi; life mem, Nat Asn Advan Colored People; Meals Wheels, St John AME Church, 1998-99; steward, St John AME Church, 2000-. **Honors/Awds:** USDA, Hon Awards, 1993-95. **Home Addr:** 409 Eaton Rd, Birmingham, AL 35242.

BLANKS, BILLY
Entrepreneur. **Personal:** Born Sep 1, 1955, Eerie, PA. **Career:** Billy Blacks World Training Ctr, pres & co-founder, currently; Films: Tango & Cash, 1989; Driving Force, 1990; Lionheart, 1990; The Last Boy Scout, 1991; Talons of the Eagle, 1992; TC 2000, 1993; Expect No Mercy, 1996. **Honors/Awds:** Karate Hall of Fame, 1982. **Special Achievements:** 7-time world karate champion; the first Amateur Athletic Union Champ in 1975; the 1984 Massachusetts Golden Gloves Boxing Champion; the Tri-State Golden Gloves Champion of Champions; He was the captain of the United States Karate Team and won over 30 gold medals in international competition; He was the number 1 or number 2 rated full-contact karate fighter in the United States for almost seven straight years; His epic battles with "Nasty" Anderson are legends among martial arts fans; He posted over 300 career victories. **Business Addr:** President, Co-Founder, Billy Blacks World Training Center, 14708 Ventura Blvd, Sherman Oaks, CA 91403, **Business Phone:** (818)325-0335.*

BLANKS, CECELIA (CECELIA OLIVER)
Counselor, administrator. **Personal:** Born in Galveston, TX; daughter of Ella L Oliver and Lovie L Oliver. **Educ:** San Diego State Univ, BA, social sci, MEd, coun; Calif State Univ, San Marcos, AS, bus admin & women studies. **Career:** Miramar Col San Diego, staff; Cuyamaca Col, Extended Opportunity Progs & Serv & Coop Agencies Resources Educ, counr; Calif State Univ, Educ Opportunity Prog, staff, 1990-, sch rel ambassador, coordr & acad counr, adminr, dir, currently. **Orgs:** Supportive Parents Info Network Bd. **Special Achievements:** "From Welfare to College Professor", Essence Mag; listed in Who's Who Among America's Teachers. **Business Addr:** Director Educational Opportunity Program, California State University, Education Opportunity Program, 333 S Twin Oaks Valley Rd, San Marcos, CA 92096-0001, **Business Phone:** (760)750-4861.

BLANKS, DELILAH BOWEN
Educator, college teacher. **Personal:** Born Apr 5, 1936, Acme, NC; married Eddie W; children: Sherri Ann & Rhonda Fay. **Educ:** Shaw Univ, AB, eng & social studies, 1957; E Carolina Univ, AB, libr sci,1965; Univ NC, MSW, 1972; Univ NV, PhD, 1984. **Career:** Income tax consult, 1957-; notary pub, 1957-; Whiteville City Sch, teacherebg, 1960-62; Wake Co Bd Educ, teacher & librn, 1963-67; Brunswick County Bd Educ, teacher & librn, 1963-67; Neighborhood Youth Corps, counr, 1967-68; Bladen County, Dept Social Serv, child welfare worker, 1968-71; NC State Dept Social Serv, community develop specialist I, 1971-72; Univ NC, asst prof sociol & social work, 1972; Bladen County, comnr, 1980-; NC Asn County Comnr, pres, currently; Univ NC, prof emer, currently. **Orgs:** Nat Asn Social Workers, 1974-; Nat Coun Social Work Educ, 1974-; bd mem, NC Comn Two Party Syst, 1974; Bladen County Bd Comnr, 1988-; vice chmn, Four County Community Serv; bd dir, Bladen Community Col Found; NC Asn Black Elected Officials; bd dir, Bladen County Partnership C; bd dir, NC Southeast Econ Develop Comn; Delta Sigma Theta; chair, Arcadia Bd Town Counmen; Nat Asn Adv Colored People; vice chair, Bladen County Dem Exec Comn; Bladen County Improv Asn Univ Prof; bd mem, Wilmington New Hanover Headstart Inc; NC Asn County Commissioners. **Honors/Awds:** NC Senclander of the Month, 1974; Bladen County Citizen of the Year, 1991. **Special Achievements:** One of the Most Distinguished Women in North Carolina in 1989; Cited as Who's Who Among Black Americans for outstanding achievement in Education & Community Services; The Delilah B Blanks Social Work Education Award was established in her name. **Business Addr:** Professor Emeritus, University North Carolina, Department Sociol Social Work, 5051 New Centre Dr, Wilmington, NC 28403.*

BLANKS, WILHELMINA E.
Government official. **Personal:** Born Nov 10, 1905, Decatur, AL; married Walter T; children: Wilhelmina Balla & Muriel Inniss. **Educ:** Atlanta Univ, AB 1927; attended Loyola Univ, N western Sch Journalism, Univ Chicago. **Career:** Prairie View State Col, teacher 1927-29; Cook Co Dept Pub Aid, 1936-74, asst dist off supvr, 1974-. **Orgs:** Organizer, Mich Ave Adult Educ Ctr; Tutoring Project Mothers Univ Chicago; Social Serv Guild St Edmund's Episcopal Church; bd mem, City Asn Women's Bd Art Inst Chicago; vpres, S Side Comn Art Ctr Chicago; Bravo Chap Lyric Opera Chicago; PUSH; Nat Asn Advan Colored People; Chicago Urban League; vpres Am Friends Liberia; Citizens Comn Du Sable Museum African Am Hist; freelance writer. **Honors/Awds:** Distinguish Service Award, Dedication Develop Art Black Comn S Side Community Art Ctr, 1970; Award for Achievement, Pub Welfare Int Travelers Asn, 1972. **Business Addr:** Assistant District Office Supervisor, Department Public Aid, 300 W Pershing Rd, Chicago, IL 60609.

BLANTON, DAIN
Athlete, volleyball player. **Personal:** Born Nov 28, 1971, Laguna Beach, CA. **Educ:** Pepperdine Univ, BA, Pub Rels. **Career:** Prof beach volleyball player, broadcaster, inspirational speaker, model;AVP, 1994-, USAV, 1999-2000; BVA, 2001. **Honors/Awds:** Blanton was named the Orange County Player of the Year, 1990; Miller Lite & AVP Hermosa Beach Grand Slam, 1997; AVP Special Achievement, 1997; bronze medal, Los Angeles, 1997; AVP Team of the Year, 2003; Olympic gold medal, beach volleyball, 2000; AVP, Offensive Player, 2003. **Special Achievements:** First & only African Am on the Association of Volleyball Profs Tour; first African American to win Pro Beach Volleyball tournament; became a pioneer in the sport of beach volleyball becoming the first African American pro player in the history of the sport to win a major title, 1997; TV appearance: ABC; speaker for various prog. **Business Addr:** Beach Volleyball Player, Laguna Beach, CA 92651.

BLANTON, JAMES B., III
Executive director. **Personal:** Born Feb 6, 1949, Knoxville, TN; son of James B Jr and Martha Luckey; married Emily DeVoi Besley, Dec 25, 1977; children: Joseph, Sidney, James IV. **Educ:** Knoxville Col, BS, com, 1971; Univ TN, MBA. **Career:** Executive director (retired); asst exec secy, Alpha Phi Alpha Frat Inc; TVA Knoxville, dir off serv, 1966-73; Our Voice Magazine, Knoxville, dir finances, 1970-72; TN Alpha Phi Alpha, asst state dir, 1970-73; US Postal Serv, Knoxville, asst chief acct, 1971-73; Alpha Phi Alpha Frat Inc, exec dir, 1977. **Orgs:** Am Accounting Asn; life mem, Alpha Phi Alpha; Pi Omega Pi; Phi Beta Lambda; Young Democrats Am; US Jaycees; Urban League; YMCA; Knoxville Col Nat Alumni Asn; Prince Hall Masons North Star Lodge; Prince Hall Shriner Arabic Temple; Order Eastern Stars; Western Consistory AASR Freemasonry; United Supreme Coun AASR Thirty Third Degree Mason; Imperial Coun AEAONMS; Holy Royal Arch Masons-Oriental; North Star F&AM; Am Biog Inst; Bldg Found; Nat Pan Hellenic Coun Exec Comt; Alpha Kappa Mu Nat Hon Soc. **Honors/Awds:** Brother of the Year Award, Alpha Mu Lambda Chap; Mary E Gilbert Scholarship Award for Grad Study,1972; MWPH Grand Lodge of IL-Grand Master's Award, 1982; Clarence Clinkscales Award, North Star Lodge, 1985; Outstanding Young Men of America, 1981 & 1985; Appreciation Award, Chicago Soc C & Families bd dir, 1985; Outstanding Service Award, Black Media Inc, 1986; Alpha Phi Alpha Presidential Award, 1988. *

BLANTON, RICKY WAYNE
Basketball player, basketball coach. **Personal:** Born Apr 21, 1966, Miami, FL. **Educ:** La State Univ. **Career:** Basketball player (retired), basketball coach; Pheonix Suns, 1990; Chicago Bulls, 1992-93; Nicholls State Univ, head coach.

BLAYLOCK, DARON OSHAY. See BLAYLOCK, MOOKIE.

BLAYLOCK, DR. ENID VERONICA. See Obituaries section.

BLAYLOCK, MOOKIE (DARON OSHAY BLAYLOCK)
Basketball player. **Personal:** Born Mar 20, 1967, Garland, TX; married Janelle; children: Zachary, Daron Jr & Domnick. **Educ:** Midland Col, attended 1987; Univ Okla, attended 1989. **Career:** Basketball player (retired); NJ Nets, guard, 1989-92, Atlanta Hawks, 1992-99; Golden St Warriors, res, 1999-2002.

BLAYLOCK, RONALD E.
Executive, executive director. **Educ:** Georgetown Univ, BS; NY Univ Stern Sch Bus, MBA. **Career:** Citibank, capital markets, 1986; PaineWebber Group, Inc, salesperson; Citicorp; Utendahl Capital Partners, exec vpres, 1992-; Blaylock & Partners LP, founder & chmn & chief exec officer, 1993-; WR Berkley Corp, dir, 2001-. **Orgs:** bd mem, Georgetown Univ; bd, Am Ballet Theatre; bd trustees, NY Univ; dir, Radio One Inc, 2001-. **Honors/Awds:** PaineWebber Group Inc, top salesperson, 1991; Black Enterprise mag, one of the 25 Hottest Blacks on Wall St, 1992; received numerous industry awards; frequent guest, CNBC's Squawk Box, Closing Bell & Bloomberg TV's Morning Call. **Special Achievements:** Company became the first minority firm to co-manage a Federal Home Loan Mortgage Corp deal; Georgetown's Final Four Basketball Team, 1982; Black Enterprise Top 100 Investment Banks List, Co ranked No 1, 2000; Blaylock & Company has also consistently ranked as the number 1 or 2 minority investment banking firm by Black Enterprise Magazine. **Business Addr:** Founder, Chairman & Chief Executive Officer, Blaylock & Company, 780 3rd Ave 44th Fl, New York, NY 10017, **Business Phone:** (212)715-6600.*

BLAYTON-TAYLOR, BETTY
Executive, artist, arts administrator. **Personal:** Born Jul 10, 1937, Newport News, VA; daughter of James Blain Blayton and Alleyne Houser; widowed. **Educ:** Syracuse Univ, BA, 1959; City Col; New Yok Art Student's League; Brooklyn Museum Sch. **Career:** Major exhibits 1959-; St Thomas, Virgin Island, art teacher, 1959-60; City New York, recreation leader, 1960-64; Haryou Art, Graphics & Plastics, art supvr, 1964-67; C Art Carnival, exec dir, 1969-98, artistic dir, bd mem, 1998-99, founder spec proj, bd mem, 2000-; City Coll, Elem Educ Dept, prof, 1974; consult, NYS Bd Educ, 1977-; New York City Bd Educ, consult, 1977-; C Art Carnival, Artist & Founder, currently. **Orgs:** mem bd, Major Exhibit, 1959-84; founding mem, Studio Museum, Harlem, 1965-77; bd mem, Printmakers Workshop, 1975-98, adv, 1998-; bd mem, Arts & Bus Coun, 1978-97; Comt Cultural Affairs, 1979-89; Natl Black Child Development Institute 1980-; David Rockefeller Jr, Art Educ Res Comt, 1984-85; founding mem Harlem Textile Works, 1992-; NY's Education's Art & Humanities Curriculm Div Comt, 1992-94. **Honors/Awds:** Empire State Woman of the Yr in the Arts NYS Governor's Award, 1984; Artist in Residence, Tougaloo Coll, 1982; Artist in Residence, Norfolk State Col, VA, 1980; Artist in Residence, Fisk Univ, TN, 1978; Black Women in the Arts Award, Governor of New York, 1988; CBS, Martin Luther King Jr "Fulfilling the Dream" Award, 1995. **Special Achievements:** Art included in following collections: The Metropolitan Museum, The Studio Museum, Philip Morris Corp, Chase Manhattan Bank. **Home Addr:** 2001 Creston Ave, Bronx, NY 10453. **Business Addr:** Founding Artistic Director Member of the Board, The Children's Art Carnival, 62 Hamilton Terr, New York, NY 10031, **Business Phone:** (212)234-4093.*

BLEDSOE, CAROLYN E. LEWIS
Government official. **Personal:** Born Jan 31, 1946, Richmond, VA; married Rev Earl L Bledsoe; children: Katrina L, Tanya N. **Educ:** Va State Univ, AB, 1968, MA. **Career:** King William Co Pub Schs, teacher, 1968-69; Richmond Pub Schs, teacher, 1969-71; Dept Develop Progs, res analyst, 1972-80; City Gov, sr planner, 1980-. **Orgs:** Vpres, bd dirs, Commonwealth Girl Scout Coun VA Inc, 1976-84, 1979-81; secy, treas, Northern VA Baptist Ministers' Wives, 1981-83; chair scholar, Comn VA State Asn Ministers' Wives, 1981-84. **Home Addr:** 711 Wadsworth Dr, Richmond, VA 23236. **Business Addr:** Senior Planner, Department Planning & Development, 900 E Broad St Rm 500, Richmond, VA 23219.

BLEDSOE, BR. JAMES L
Government official, administrator, chief financial officer. **Personal:** Born Dec 1, 1947, Tuskegee, AL; son of Willie James and Ada M Randle; married Clara A Fisher, Jun 14, 1975; children: Patrice Bledsoe. **Educ:** Univ West Florida, Pensacola, FL, BS, 1972, MPA, 1974. **Career:** Dept Budget, City Miami, chief mgmt analyst, 1978-86; Dept Solid Waste, City Miami, asst dir, 1986; Dept Solid Waste, City Miami, asst dir, 1987; Dept Budget, City Miami, asst dir, 1988; Sweet Home, Missionary Baptist church, chief financial officer, 1995-; church adminr, currently. **Orgs:** Am Soc Pub Admin, 1978-, Nat Forum Black Pub Admin, 1982-, Am Pub Works Asn, 1986-; bd mem, Selective Serv Syst, 1987-.

BLEDSOE, MELVIN
Executive, transportation consultant. **Personal:** Born Jun 5, 1955, Memphis, TN; son of Estell Bledsoe; married Linda Ann Bledsoe, Jun 20, 1976; children: Monica & Carlos. **Educ:** Milwaukee Area Tech Col, attended 1980. **Career:** Graceland Tours, supvr shuttle bus, 1982-83; Grayline Tours, oper mgr, 1983-87; Blues City Tours, pres & co-owner, currently. **Orgs:** Bd mem, Memphis Conv Visitor Ctr, 1992; Downtown Memphis Redevelopment Comn, 1993. **Honors/Awds:** Nominee, Best New Business Award, Black Bus Asn, 1989-90; Nominee, Most Outstanding Black Business in Memphis Award, 1992. **Special Achievements:** Recognized by the Local Jr Achievement of Greater Memphis for Applied Econ Proj Bus & Bus Basics; several local natl intl publs. **Business Addr:** President, Co-Owner, Blues City Tours, 325 Union Ave, Memphis, TN 38103, **Business Phone:** (901)522-9229.

BLEDSOE, TEMPESTT
Actor. **Personal:** Born Aug 1, 1973, Chicago, IL; daughter of Wilma; married Darryl M Bell. **Educ:** NY Univ, finance. **Career:** Actor, currently; TV: "The Cosby Show", 1984-92; "The Gift of Amazing Grace", 1986; "Dance Til Dawn", 1988; "Dream Date", 1989; "Santa & Pete", 1999; "The Expendables", 2000; ''Fire & Ice", 2001; "South of Nowhere", 2006; "That Is So Not Mom", 2006; films: Bachelor Man, 2003; Rock Me Baby, 2004; Strong Med, 2005; Fingers Walking, 2005; The View, 2006; VH-1s Celebrity Fit Club; Husband for Hire, 2008; South of Nowhere, 2008. **Honors/Awds:** Young Artist Award for Best Young Actor & Actress Ensemble in a TV Comedy, Drama Series or Spec, 1989; Nat Merit Scholar finalist; Clarence Muse Youth Award, 1992. **Business Phone:** (310)278-1310.

BLEDSOE, WILLIAM
Judge, school administrator. **Educ:** Olivet Col, attended 1952. **Career:** Attorney(retired); City Highland Pk, 30th Dist Ct, munic judge, 1985-2003. **Orgs:** Bd trustees, Olivet Col.

BLEVINS, TONY
Football player. **Personal:** Born Jan 29, 1975, Rockford, IL. **Educ:** Univ Kans. **Career:** Indianapolis Colts, defensive back, 1998, 1999-2000; San Francisco 49ers, 1998. *

BLIGE, MARY J. (MARY JANE BLIGE)
Singer, songwriter. **Personal:** Born Jan 11, 1971, Bronx, NY; daughter of Cora; married Kendu Isaacs, Dec 7, 2003. **Career:** Albums: What's the 411, 1994; My Life, 1994; Share My World, 1996; My Life, 1999; Mary, 2000; No More Drama, 2001; Dance for Me, 2002; Love &Life, 2003; The Breakthrough, 2006; Growning pains, 2007; Stronger, 2009. TV series: "The Jamie Foxx Show";"Divas Live", 1999, 2001, 2002; "Ghost Whisperer", 2007; film: Prison Song, 2000; I Can Do Bad All By Myself, 2009; 30 Rock, 2009. MCA records, vocalist, currently. **Honors/Awds:** Soul Train Music Award, 1993; New York Music Award; NAACP Image Award;double-platinum album award; Grammy award, 1996; Am Music Award, 1998;Soul Train Lady of Soul awards, 1997, 1998; celebrity spokeperson, MAC AIDS Fund, 2001, 2002; Grammy Award, 2003; Grammy Award, 2004, 2008, 2009; People magazine's 100 Most Beautiful People, 2008. **Special Achievements:** Grammy nomination for Best R&B Album, 1995, 1999, 2002; sold over 60million records around the world since her career began in 1991. **Business Phone:** (818)777-4000.*

BLOCK, CAROLYN B.
Psychologist, college teacher. **Personal:** Born Sep 7, 1942, New Orleans, LA. **Educ:** Xavier Univ, BS, 1963; Boston Univ, MS, 1965, MA, 1968, PhD, 1971. **Career:** Ctr Univ Calif, psychol couns, 1970-72; Wstsd Mental Health Ctr, psychol consult, 1972-; Family & Child Cross Serv, Mt Zion Hosp, San Francisco, dir, 1972-74; Pvt Pract, San Francisco, clincal psychol, 1973-; Univ Calif, Psychol Dept, lectr, 1973-93; C Youth Serv, Wstsd Community MentalHealth Ctr, dir, 1974-77; KQED-TV, content consult, 1977-80. **Orgs:** Nat Asn Black Psychol, 1970-; San Francisco Red Cross; Am Psychol Asn, 1972-75; bd mem, San Francisco Comt Children's TV, 1973-77; fel, Soc Psychol Study Ethnic Minority Issues, 2001. **Honors/Awds:** ABPP, 1998. **Business Addr:** Clinical Psychologist, Private Practice, 1947 Divisadero St Suite 2, San Francisco, CA 94115-2532.*

BLOCK, DR. LESLIE S.
Executive, consultant. **Educ:** Univ Pittsburgh, BA, polit sci, 1974, MPA, 1977, PhD, higher educ admin, 1982. **Career:** Nat-Louis Univ, adj grad fac; Spertus Col, vis grad fac; Northwestern Univ, vis scholar, 1986-93; Leslie S Block & Assocs, founder & pres, 1985-, owner, currently. **Orgs:** Bd dir, Citizens Info Serv, IL, 1990; mayoral appointee, Human Relations Comn, Youngstown, Ohio, 1974-76; exec bd, Evanston Township High Sch, Booster Club, 1993-2000, PTSA, chair, Legislation Comt, 1997-2000. **Honors/Awds:** Omicron Delta Kappa, 1973; 'Outstanding Young Man of America', 1988; Outstanding Entrepreneur Award, Dollar & Sense, 1991; Am's Best & Brightest Hall of Fame, 1994. **Home Addr:** 4255 Rosewood Lane N, Plymouth, MN 55442, **Home Phone:** (763)551-3640. **Business Addr:** Founder, President, Owner, Leslie S. Block and Associates, 4255 Rosewood Lane N, Plymouth, MN 55442-2611, **Business Phone:** (763)551-3640.

BLOCKER, TYREE C
Police officer, executive. **Career:** Police officer (retired), executive; Pa State Police, Bur Drug Law Enforcement, maj & dir, 2001; Silver Seals Consult, owner. **Orgs:** Pres, Police Futurists.

BLOCKSON, CHARLES LEROY
Educator, army officer. **Personal:** Born Dec 16, 1933, Norristown, PA; son of Charles E and Annie Parker; married Elizabeth Parker (divorced); children: Noelle. **Educ:** PA State Univ, attended 1956. **Career:** Norristown High Sch, adv, 1970; author, 1975-; Afro-Am Hist & Cultural Mus, Philadelphia, cofounder, 1976; Pa Black Hist Comt, dir, 1976-; Pa Afro-Am Hist Bd, dir, 1976-; Pa State Hist & Record Adv Bd & Black Hist Adv Bd, dir, 1980-; Black Writer's Conf Paris, France, moderator, 1992; lectr, US Inf Agency, 1990-; Valley Forge African-Am Revolutionary Soldier Monument, chmn, 1990-; Temple Univ Charles L Blockson Afro-Am Collection, cur, currently. **Orgs:** Nat Asn Advan Colored People, 1974-; bd mem, Hist Soc Pa, 1976-83; coun mem, PA State Univ Alumni Cncl 1982-; comt mem, Temple Univ Centennial Comt, 1983-; Urban League PA; Montgomery County PA Bicentennial Comt, 1982-83; Am Antiquarian Soc, 1996; Grolier Club, 1996; Underground Railroad Advisory Comt; Pa Abolition Soc. **Honors/Awds:** PA St Quarterback Award PA State Quarterback Club, 1984; PA Black Hist Book, 1975; Blk Genealogy Book, 1977; Alumni Fellow Award Penn State Univ, 1979; Underground Railroad in PA, 1980; Cover Story for Nat Geographic Mag "The Underground Railroad" 1984, "People of the Sea Island", 1987; The Underground Railroad First Person Narratives Book, 1987; Lifetime Achievement Award Before Columbus Found, 1987; Villanova Univ, Hon Degree Educ, 1979; Lincoln Univ, Hon Degree, 1987; Hon Degree, Holy Family Col, 1995; Storytellers, 1st Life Time Award, 1996; Founder's Award, Hist Soc Pa, 2002. **Special Achievements:** Publications: Philadelphia State Historical Marker Guide, 1992; Hippocrene Guide: The Underground Railroad, 1994; Chairperson: National Park Service; Underground Railroad Sites Study, 1990-1995; Damn Rare: Memoirs of an African-American Bibliophile, 1998; Book, African-Americans in Pennsylvania: Above Ground and Underground-An Illustrated Guice, 2001. **Military Serv:** AUS, 1957-58. **Business Addr:** Curator, Temple University, Charles L Blockson Afro-American Collection, 1st Fl Sullivan Hall, 12th and Berks Mall, Philadelphia, PA 19122, **Business Phone:** (215)204-6632.*

BLOOMFIELD, DR. RANDALL D.
Physician. **Personal:** Born in New York, NY; married; children: 2. **Educ:** CCNY, BS, 1949; Downstate Med Ctr, MD, 1953. **Career:** Kings City Hosp, intern, surgeon, 1953-54; Obs & Gyn, resident, 1954-58; Kings City Hosp, Pvt pract, physician, dir, dept Obstet & Gynec, currently, Med Soc County Kings, Assoc directing librn & cur, currently. **Orgs:** Brooklyn Cumberland Med Ctr; AMA; Kings City Med Soc; fellow, Am Col OB & GYN; Am Col Surg; Brooklyn Gyn Soc; NY Obs Soc; Nat Med Assoc; dipl Am Bd OB & GYN. **Honors/Awds:** Cert Gynecol Oncology; Frank Babbot Award. **Military Serv:** AUS, WWII, 1943. **Business Addr:** Associate Directing Librarian, Curator, The Medical Society of the County of Kings Inc, 480 77th st, Brooklyn, NY 11209.*

BLOUIN, ROSE LOUISE
Educator, photographer. **Personal:** Born Dec 13, 1948, Chicago, IL; daughter of Paul and Louise; children: Kimaada & Bakari. **Educ:** Univ Ill, Chicago, IL, BA, 1971; Chicago State Univ, MA, 1983. **Career:** Photogr, 1980-; Chicago State Univ, Ctr Women's Identity Studies, staff assoc, 1980-83, lectr, Eng Composition, 1983-87; Third World Press, assoc ed, 1983-89; City Harvey, IL

pub rels dir, 1984-86; Columbia Col, Chicago, prof eng dept, currently. **Orgs:** Pub rels consult, Inst Positive Educ, African-Am Book Ctr; Commun Ctr Inc, 1983-; freelance photography, Am Airlines, Mary Thompson Hosp, Citizen Newspapers, various artists & arts orgs. **Honors/Awds:** Best Photography Award, Milwaukee Inner City Art Fair, 1985; Purchase Award, Museum of Sci & Ind, Black Creativity Exhibit, 1986; Purchase Award, DuSable Museum Afro-Am Hist Art Fair, 1986; Art of Jazz, Chicago Jazz Festival, 1987-89; Rhythms, Axis Photo Gallery, 1987; Saphyre & Crystals: African Am Women Artists, S Side Community Art Ctr, 1987, 1990. **Special Achievements:** First Director, Columbia College Chicago Writing Center; Co-author, Experiencing Your Identity, Developmental Materials, 1982. **Home Addr:** 8236 S Michigan Ave, Chicago, IL 60619, **Home Phone:** (773)874-5896. **Business Addr:** Professor, Columbia College of Chicago, Department of English, 600 S Michigan Ave, 300-I 3rd fl 33 E Congress, Chicago, IL 60605, **Business Phone:** (312)344-8112.

BLOUNT, CHARLOTTE RENEE
Journalist. **Personal:** Born Mar 2, 1952, Washington, DC. **Educ:** Catholic Univ Scholastic Jour Inst; Ohio Univ, 1972; Am Univ, Wash, DC, BA, jour, 1974, grad courses, 1976. **Career:** WOUB-FM, Athens, OH, reporter & announcer, 1971-72; Wash DC Voice & Visions Prods, freelance talent, 1973-; WOOK-FM, Wash, reporter & announcer, 1973-74; WILD Boston, reporter & announcer, 1974; Securities & Exchange Comn, writer, 1974-75; George Wash Univ, assoc prof, 1978-; Mutual Black Network, White House & state dept corres. **Orgs:** Zeta Phi Beta Sor Beta Zeta Chap, Wash; nat pub rels dir, Zeta Phi Beta, 1976-78. **Honors/Awds:** Nominee, Most Outstanding Young Woman, 1976; News Woman of the Year, Nat Asn TV & Radio Artists, 1976; Young Career Woman DC, Nat Fedn Bus & Prof Women, 1976. **Business Addr:** Correspondent, Mutual Black Network, 1755 Jefferson Davis Hwy, Arlington, VA 22202.

BLOUNT, CORIE KASOUN
Basketball player, real estate executive. **Personal:** Born Jan 4, 1969, Monrovia, CA. **Educ:** Rancho Santiago Comm Coll, CA; Univ Cincinnati, attended 1993. **Career:** Basketball player (retired), coach, real estate exec; Chicago Bulls, forward, 1994-95; Los Angeles Lakers, 1996-99; Cleveland Cavaliers, 1999; Phoenix Suns, 1999-2001; Golden State Warriors, 2001; Philadelphia 76ers, 2002; Chicago Bulls, 2003-04; Toronto Raptors, forward, 2004; Univ Cincinnati, asst coach, 2005; real estate exec. **Honors/Awds:** JUCO Co-Player of the Year.

BLOUNT, HEIDI LYNNE
Banker. **Personal:** Born Apr 6, 1964, Cleveland, OH; daughter of Gilbert L and Sue H Johnson. **Educ:** Cleveland State Univ, BBA, 1996, MBA, 1997; paralegal cert, 2001. **Career:** Key Corp, dist security officer, 1981-98; Fifth Third Bank, asset recovery mgr, 1998-. **Orgs:** Am Asn Univ Women, educ meeting chair, 1996; Karamu House Inc, bd trustees, 1998-; Christmas in April, bd trustees, 1999-; Delta Sigma Theta Sorority Inc. **Honors/Awds:** Distinguished Service Award, Black Studies Prog, Cleveland State Univ, 1996. **Special Achievements:** Published: A Purpose for My Poetry, 1996. **Business Addr:** Asset Recovery Manager, Fifth Third Bank, 1404 E 9th St, Cleveland, OH 44114, **Business Phone:** (216)274-5302.

BLOUNT, MELVIN CORNELL
Activist. **Personal:** Born Apr 10, 1948, Vidalia, GA; son of James and Alice; married TiAnda Blount; children: Norris, Tanisia, Shuntel, Dedrick, Akil, Jibri, Khalid. **Educ:** Southern Univ, Baton Rouge, LA, BS, phys educ, 1970. **Career:** Pittsburgh Steelers, Nat Football League, prof football player, 1970-83; Nat Football League, dir player rels, 1983-90; Nat Football League, Comnr Player Adv Bd, consult & mem, 1990; Cobb Creek Farms, owner/oper; Mel Blount Cellular Phone Co, owner/oper; Mel Blount Youth Home Inc, founder, currently. **Orgs:** Bd dirs Pgh Cs Mus; mem, policy Coun Natl Ctr for Youth & their Families; mem, bd dir Am Red Cross; rep Red Cross on visit to Mauritania N Africa factfinding expedition; mem, Paint Horse Assn, Am Quarter Horse Assn, Natl Cutting Horse Assn. **Honors/Awds:** National Football League Leader in Interceptions, 1975; named Most Valuable Player, Pittsburgh Steelers, 1975; Player of the Year, Nat Football League, 1975; Most Valuable Player Pro Bowl, 1976; Pro Football Hall of Fame, 1989; Georgia Sports Hall of Fame, 1990; World Sports Humanitarian Hall of Fame, 1997. **Special Achievements:** Publ, 'The Cross Burns Brightly', 1993; ranked number 36 on The Sporting News' list of the 100 Greatest Football Players, 1999. **Business Addr:** Founder, Mel Blount Youth Home, 6 Mel Blount Dr, Claysville, PA 15323, **Business Phone:** (724)948-2311.*

BLOUNT, SHERRI N
Administrator, lawyer. **Personal:** Married Edward W Gray Jr. **Educ:** Univ NC, BA, 1977; Howard Univ Sch Law, JD, 1980. **Career:** Howard Univ, assoc ed Law J; Fed Trade Comnr, atty adv; Pub Broadcasting Serv, vpres, dep gen coun & corp secy; Morrison & Foerster LLP, partner, currently. **Orgs:** US Dist Ct; DC Ct Appeals; Supreme Ct US Am; DC Bar Asn; Canadian Retransmission Collective; Asn de Gestion Interationale Collective des Oeuvres Audiovisuelles. **Honors/Awds:** Wash Mag, top intellectual property lawyers, 2004; Wash Bus J, Top Intellectual Property Lawyer, 2006. **Business Addr:** Partner, Morrison & Foerster LLP, 2000 Pa Ave NW Suite 5500, Washington, DC 20006-1888, **Business Phone:** (202)887-8786.

BLOW, KURTIS (CURTIS WALKER)
Rap musician, musician. **Personal:** Born Aug 9, 1959, Harlem, NY; married; children: 3. **Educ:** City Col NY. **Career:** Break dancer; DJ; albums: Kurtis Blow, 1980; Deuce, 1981; Tough, 1982; Ego Trip, 1984; Rapper in Town, 1984; America, 1985; Kingdom Blow, 1986; The Breaks, 1986; Back by Popular Demand, 1988; films: Krush Groove, 1985; The Show, 1995; Rhyme & Reason, 1997; Allied Artists Entertainment Group, vpres, 2001; Disco: Spinning the Story, 2005; Breaking the Rules, 2006; Baisden After Dark, 2007. **Special Achievements:** First rap artist to cut records with major recording label. *

BLUDSON-FRANCIS, VERNETT MICHELLE
Banker. **Personal:** Born Feb 18, 1951, New York, NY; daughter of William Benjamin Bludson and Alfreda Peace; married Robert Francis Sr, Aug 15, 1981; children: Robert Jr. **Educ:** New York Univ, New York NY, BS, 1973, MPA, 1976. **Career:** Morgan Guaranty Trust, New York, NY, mgmt trainee, 1973-75; Citibank, NA, New York, NY, vice pres, 1975-; Nat Minority/Women's Vendor Prog, NY, dir, 1977-. **Orgs:** Nat Urban Affairs Coun, 1984-; Nat Minority Bus Coun, 1986-; Coalition of 100 Black Women; YW/YMCA Day Care Ctr Inc, 1986-; Nat Forum Black Pub Admins; Nat Asn Advan Colored People; UBC; Black Achievers Indust Alumni Asn; Images-Wall St Chap; Cornell Univ Coop Extension Prog; Nat Asn Women Bus Owners; NY State Dept Econ Develop/Minority & Women's Div. **Honors/Awds:** Black Achievers, Citibank/Harlem YMCA, 1984; Those Who Make A Difference, Nat Urban Affairs CNL, 1985; MNY Advocate of the Year, US Dept Com MBDA Regional Office, 1985; Mary McLeod Bethune Award, NCW, 1986; Public Private-Sector Award, US Dept Housing & Urban Develop, 1986; Banker of the Year, Urban Bankers Coalition, 1987; Woman of the Year, Harlem YMCA, 1987; Cecelia Cabiness Saunders Award, New Harlem YMCA, 1987. **Special Achievements:** Top 100 Black Business & Professional Women, Dollars & Sense Magazine, 1988; co-sponsor, Executive Banking programs with NMBC, 1983, 1984, 1985, Executive Banking Program with Westchester MNY Contractors Asn, 1986; Career Exploration summer internship program with Hunter Col & Coalition of 100 Black Women, 1986; co-host, First Annual BAI Alumni Fundraiser, 1986; chair, NUAC Student Develop Dinner, 1988; sponsor, Dept Defense Symposium for the Vendor Input Comn, 1988. **Business Addr:** Vice President, Citibank/Citicorp, 1 Ct Sq 10th Fl, Long Island City, NY 11101, **Business Phone:** (718)248-2096.

BLUE, DANIEL TERRY
State government official, lawyer, executive. **Personal:** Born Apr 18, 1949, Lumberton, NC; son of Daniel T Blue Sr and Allene Morris Blue; married Edna Earle Smith, Jan 26, 1972; children: Daniel Terry III, Kanika & Dhamian. **Educ:** NC Cent Univ, Durham, NC, BS, math, 1970; Duke Univ, Durham, NC, JD, 1973; Nat Inst Trial Advocacy, cert, 1997. **Career:** Sanford, Adams, McCullough & Beard, Attys at Law, Raleigh, NC, 1973-76; Nat Inst Trial Advocacy, fac, 1983, 1985-87; NC House of Reps, Dist 21 rep, speaker, 1991-95; Thigpen, Blue, Stephens & Fellers, Raleigh, NC, managing partner, currently; NC Gen Assembly, rep, 2007; state Senate, 2009. **Orgs:** Elder, Davie St Presbyterian Church; Alpha Phi Alpha Fraternity Inc; Wautauga Club, Kiwanis Club; bd dirs, First Union Nat Bank NC; trustee, Duke Univ; pres, Nat Conf State Legiss, 1998-99; chair, Clinton & Gore Campaign NC; bd visitors, Duke Law Sch; Am Bar Asn; NC Bar Asn; Wake County Bar Asn; NC Asn Black Lawyers, Asn Trial Lawyers Am; Bd Govs, NC Acad Trial Lawyers, 1982-86. **Honors/Awds:** Outstanding Legislator Award, NC Asn Trial Lawyers, 1985; Outstanding Legislature Award, NC Asn Black Lawyers, 1985; Martin Luther King Jr Serv Award, NC Gen Baptist State Conv, 1991; Citizen of the Year Award: Alpha Phi Alpha, Omega Psi Phi, Kappa Alpha Psi, Phi Beta Sigma, Alpha Kappa Alpha, Delta Sigma Theta, Zeta Phi Beta, Sigma Gamma Rho, 1977-91; Adam Clayton Powell Award; Robert F Kennedy-Jacob Javitz Award; Nat 4-H Alumni Award; Outstanding Black Men Award; recipient of eight honorary degrees; Outstanding Black Men Award. **Special Achievements:** First black state House speaker in the South, 1990. **Business Addr:** Managing Partner, Thigpen, Blue, Stephens & Fellers, 205 Fayetteville St Mall Suite 300, PO Box 1730, Raleigh, NC 27601, **Business Phone:** (919)833-1931.

BLUE, GENE C
Executive. **Educ:** MBA. **Career:** Ariz Opportunities Industrialization Ctr, pres & chief exec officer, currently. **Orgs:** Nat bd dirs, Ariz Fathers & Families Coalition, currently. **Business Addr:** President, Chief Executive Officer, Ariz Opportunities Industrialization Center, 39 E Jackson St, Phoenix, AZ 85004, **Business Phone:** (602)254-5081.

BLUE, OCTAVIA
Basketball player. **Personal:** Born Apr 18, 1976. **Educ:** Miami Univ, attended 1998. **Career:** Los Angeles Sparks; Minnesota Lynx; Houston Comets, forward, 2003-05; Bnei Yehuda, Israel, 2005; Villeneuve, France; Maccabi Tel Kabir, powerforward, Israel, 2006. **Honors/Awds:** Big E, All-Rookie Team, 1994-95; All-Big E, First Team, 1997-98. *

BLUE, VIDA ROCHELLE, JR.
Executive, actor, baseball player. **Personal:** Born Jul 28, 1949, Mansfield, LA; son of Vida Sr and Sallie A Henderson; married Peggy Shannon, Sep 24, 1989 (divorced 1996); children: 6. **Career:** Baseball player (retired), baseball coach; Oakland Athletics, pitcher, 1969-77; San Francisco Giants, 1978-81, 1985-86; Kans City Royals, pitcher, 1982-83; Vida Blue Baseball Camp, Pleasanton, CA, founder; Giants Fantasy Camp, NL pres; San Francisco Giants Baseball Camps, adult camp coach; Vida Blue Base Ball Clinics, Costa Rica, founder, currently. Film: Black Gunn, 1972. TV Series: "100 Years of the World Series", 2003; "Rebels of Oakland: The A's, the Raiders, the '70s",2003. **Honors/Awds:** American League Pitcher of the Year, The Sporting News, 1971; American League Most Valuable Player, Baseball Writers' Asn Am, 1971; American League City Young Memorial Award, 1971; Nat League Pitcher of the Year, The Sporting News, 1978. **Business Addr:** Founder, Vida Blue Baseball Clinic, C/o Paradigma Construction SA, Plaza Itskazu Local Suite 202, Escazu, San Jose, Cote d'Ivoire, **Business Phone:** (506)-2588-2400.

BLUFORD, GRADY L
Labor relations manager, president (organization). **Personal:** Born May 21, 1930, Flint, MI; son of William and Atha Smyers; married Harriet Trosper, Nov 14, 1959; children: Michelle & Derrick. **Educ:** Morningside Col, BS, 1958; Univ South Dakota, MA, guidance & coun, 1974; Covington Theol Sem, master's of bible ministry, master's of christian coun, doctor's of bible ministry; med technol training. **Career:** St Luke's Med Ctr, med tech; Goodwill Indust, med tach, 1967-, Wall St Mission, vpres personnel, bd dir; Westside Church of Christ, pastor. **Orgs:** Secy, Sioux & Youth Symphony; comt, Children's Miracle Network Telethon; NAACP; adv bd, Adult Basic Educ, state level; appointed by the governor, Comn Continuing Legal Educ Lawyers, state level; past pres, Iowa Rehabilitation, 1989-90; pres, Suburban Rotary Club. **Honors/Awds:** Outstanding Young Man Award Jr Chamber of Commerce, 1965. **Home Addr:** 2013 Grandview Blvd, Sioux City, IA 51104. **Business Addr:** Medical Technologist, Goodwill Industries, 3100 W 4th St, Sioux City, IA 51103.

BLUFORD, COL. GUION STEWART
Astronaut, president (organization), air force officer. **Personal:** Born Nov 22, 1942, Philadelphia, PA; son of Lolita and Guion; married Linda Tull; children: Guion Stewart III & James Trevor. **Educ:** Pa State Univ, BS, aerospace eng, 1964; Air Force Inst Technol, MS, aerospace eng, 1974, PhD, aerospace eng, 1978; Univ Houston, ClearLake, MBA, 1987. **Career:** Colonel, astronaut (retired), pres; Williams AFB, Ariz, pilot training, 1966; USAF F-4C pilot, Vietnam; Sheppard AFB, Texas, T-38A, instructor pilot, standardization/evaluation officer & asst flight commander, 1967; Squadron Officers Sch, Sch Secy Wing, 1971; Wright-Patterson AFB, staff devel engr, chief aerodynamics & airframe branch, Ohio, 1974-78; NASA, astronaut, 1979-93, mission specialist, STS-8 Orbiter Challenger, August, 1983; STS 61-A Orbiter Challenger, mission specialist, 1985; STS-39 Orbiter Discovery, point of contact, generic Spacelab systems & experiments, payload safety, orbitor systems & flight software issues, mission specialist, 1991; Orbiter Discovery, mission specialist STS-53, 1992; NYMA Inc, vpres & gen mgr eng serv div, 1993; Fed Data Corp, vpres, 1997; Micro gravity, vpres R&D Opers; Northrop Grumman, vpres, 2000-02; Aerospace Technol Group, pres, 2002-. **Orgs:** Assoc fel, Am Inst Aeronaut & Astronaut; Air Force Asn, Tau Beta Pi, Sigma Iota Epsilon, Nat Tech Asn & Tuskegee Airmen. **Honors/Awds:** Leadership Award, Phi Delta Kappa, 1962; Nat Defense Service Medal, 1965; Vietnam Campaign Medal, 1967; Vietnam Service Medal, 1967; 3 Air Force Outstanding Unit Awards, 1967, 1970, 1972; German Air Force Aviation Badge, Fed Repub W Ger, 1969; T-38 Instructor Pilot of the Month, 1970; Air Training Command Outstanding Flight Safety Award, 1970; Air Force Commendation Medal, 1972; Mervin E. Gross Award, Instit Technol, 1974; Air Force Meritorious Service Award, 1978; Distinguished Nat Scientist Award, Nat Soc of Black Engrs, 1979; 2 NASA Group Achievement Awards, 1980,1981; Distinguished Alumni Award, 1983, Alumni Fellow Award, 1986, Pennsylvania St Univ Alumni Asn; NASA Space Flight Medal, 1983, 1985, 1991, 1992; Ebony Black Achievement Award, 1983; Image Award, NAACP, 1983; Distinguished Service Medal, St of Pennsylvania, 1984; Whitney Young Memorial Award, New York City Urban League; Black Engineer of the Year Award, 1991; NASA Exceptional Service Medal, 1992; NASA Distinguished Serv Medal, 1994; inductee, Int Space Hall of Fame, 1997; numerous other awards. **Special Achievements:** First African American to fly in space, STS-8, the eighth flight of the Space Shuttle; first African American to return to space, STS-61A, the 22nd flight of the Space Shuttle, STS-39; the 40th flight of the Space Shuttle, and STS-53, the 52nd flight of the Space Shuttle; Who's Who Among Black Americans 1975-77; logged 688 hours in space, 1995. **Military Serv:** USAF, col, 1959-93. **Home Addr:** PO Box 549, North Olmsted, OH 44070. **Business Addr:** President, The Aerospace Technol Group, 2009 Corporate Dr, Boynton Beach, FL 33426, **Business Phone:** (561)735-3533.

BLUFORD, JAMES F
Insurance agent. **Personal:** Born Sep 6, 1943, Ontario;son of Francis J and Dorysse G; children: James Francis, Sherice S & Nataki Monique. **Educ:** Wayne County Community Col, arts, 1972. **Career:** Allstate Insurance Co, sr acct agt, currently. **Business Addr:** Senior Account Agent, Allstate Insurance Company, 5836 N Wayne Rd, Westland, MI 48185, **Business Phone:** (734)722-0700.

BLUITT, JULIANN STEPHANIE
Dentist, school administrator. **Personal:** Born Jun 14, 1938, Washington, DC; daughter of Stephen Bernard and Marion Eugene Hughes; married Roscoe C. Foster; children: Barbara, David. **Educ:** Howard Univ, BS, 1958, Dental Sch, DDS, 1962; Northwestern Univ, cert, personnel admin, 1984. **Career:** Louis Ball Scholar, 1955-59; Proj Headstart, dentist, 1964-66; Chicago Bd Health, dentist pub schs, 1964-67; Northwestern Univ Dental Sch, dir dent hygiene, 1967-70, asst dean auxiliary & community prog & patient rels, 1970-72, assoc dean, 1972-78, Dept Community Med, asst prof, Off Stud Affairs & Dent Admis, 1978-89, assoc dean stud affairs; Am Col Dentist, pres, 1994-95. **Orgs:** Omicron Kappa Upsilon hon dental fraternity; pres, Chicago Dental Soc, 1991-93; Am Col Dentists; Am Asn Dental Schs; Nat Dental Asn; Fed Dentaire Internationale; Am Soc Dentistry C; Am Asn Women Dentists; served as a mem of a variety of bds of dirs. **Honors/Awds:** Dentist of the Yr, Am Soc Dentistry C, Ill Chap, 1973; fel Am Col Dentists, 1974; Alumni Award for Distinguished Postgraduate Achievement, Howard Univ, 1974; Citation Award, Phi Delta Kappa, 1975; Outstanding Service Award, Am Dental Asn & Colgate-Palmolive Comp, 1983; fel LaVerne Noyes Found; Outstanding Serv Community & Prof Dentistry Award, Howard Univ, 1988. **Special Achievements:** Designed and wrote Hector and Timmy Coloring Book; contributed to The Profile of the Negro in American Dentistry, 1979.

BLUNT, MADELYNE BOWEN
Publisher. **Personal:** Born in Providence, RI; daughter of William Mansfield and Ora Jackson; married Leon Battle, Oct 19, 1981 (deceased); children: Rolanda Elizabeth. **Educ:** Numerous spec courses; Bryant Bus Col, RI; Case Western Res, Mgt. **Career:** Cleveland Call-Post, 1st full-time advert sales woman, 1959-60; Kaiser WKBF-TV, TV producer, 1968; Thomas J Davis Agency, admin asst; Hurray Black Women, prod, founder; US Dept Justice, traveling cons-media rels conf planner community rels dept; Clubdate magazine, pres, owner, publisher. **Orgs:** NAMD; NHFL; Nat Asn Advan Colored People; spec prog coord, Com Concern, United Pastors Asn; prog producer, Develop Consumer Conf, Hurray Black Women Founder; Leadership Cleveland. **Honors/Awds:** Recognition for Documentary Black Peace, 1968; Business Woman of the Year, Calif St Univ, 1975; Black Woman of the Year, City Coun, 1979; Award of Excellence, City Community, 1979; Government Business Award, 1980; Key Top Ladies of Distinction Award, Serv Comn, 1982; Business Award Black Media, 1983; Outstanding Business Contribution Media Award, United Way Sources, 1986; Award for Outstanding Contribution WJMO Bus, 1986; Rosa Parks Award, Pioneer Bus, 1989; Cleveland Roundtable, Congressman Louis Stokes 21st Congressional Caucus Award, Outstanding Business 1989; AKA Award. **Special Achievements:** Leadership Cleveland 1985 as one of cities Most Valuable Resources.

BLUNT, ROGER RECKLING
Executive. **Personal:** Born Oct 12, 1930, Providence, RI; son of Harry Weeden and Bertha Reckling; married DeRosette Yvonne Hendricks, Jun 9, 1956; children: Roger Jr, Jennifer Mari, Amy Elizabeth & Jonathan Hendricks. **Educ:** USMA West Point, NY, BS 1956; Mass Inst Tech, MS, 1962; Univ Md, Eastern Shore, MD, PhD, 2002. **Career:** Harbridge House Int, sr assoc, 1969-71; Tyroc Construction Corp, chief exec officer & chmn, 1971; Blunt Enterprises LLC, founder, 1979, exec vpres, pres, chmn & chief exec officer, currently; Blunt & Evans Consult engr, managing partner, 1979-84; Essex Construction Corp, chmn, pres & chief exec officer, 1985-; 97th Army Res Command, comdr, 1986; Potomac Elec Power Co & Ameritas-Acacia Mutual Holding Co, dir; Asn Gov Bds Univs & Cols, chmn bd, Univ Syst Md, Bd Regents, vice chmn, 1990-96; United Educ Ins Risk Retention Group Inc, dir, 1990-99; Md Chamber Com, dir, currently; Univ Md Found, Bd Dirs, chair; Greater Wash Res Ctr, dir; Acacia Group, dir. **Orgs:** Greater Wash Bd Trade, 1985-; Nat & DC Socs Prof Engrs; Am Soc Civil engrs; Univ Md Univ Col Leadership Circle; bd vis, Univ Md Univ Col. **Honors/Awds:** Bus Leadership Award, Greater Wash Bus Ctr, 1976,1978; Distinguished Service Award, Nat Asphalt Pavement Asn, 1984; Community Service Award, Jr Citizens Corps Inc, 1985; Whitney Young Award, Boys Scouts Am; Laureate Wash Bus Hall of Fame, 2001; Md Bus Hall Of Fame, 2005. **Military Serv:** AUS Corps, engr, officer, 1956-69; AUS Res, major gen, 1983; Distinguished Service Medal, 1986. **Business Addr:** Chairman, Chief Executive Officer, Blunt Enterprises LLC, 9440 Pa Ave Suite 200, Upper Marlboro, MD 20772, **Business Phone:** (240)492-2002.

BLY, DONALD ANDRE. See BLY, DRE'.

BLY, DRE' (DONALD ANDRE BLY)
Football player. **Personal:** Born May 22, 1977, Chesapeake, VA; married Kristyn; children: Trey, Jordan, Aaron & Peyton. **Educ:** Univ NC. **Career:** St. Louis Rams, defensive back, 1999-02; Detroit Lions, corner back, 2003-06, Denver Broncos, 2007-; corner back, San Francisco 49ers, 2009-. **Orgs:** Founder, Dre' Bly Found, 2003. **Honors/Awds:** Rookie, Super Bowl XXXIV; 2 time Pro Bowl selection, 2003, 2004. **Special Achievements:** First player in the history of the Atlantic Coast Conference to earn consensus All-America honors three time; First Lion since to lead the club or tie for its season high in interceptions during four consecutive years (2003-06). **Business Addr:** Professional Football Player, Denver Broncos Football Club, 13655 Broncos pkwy, Englewood, CO 80112, **Business Phone:** (303)649-9000.*

BLYE, CECIL A., SR.
Lawyer. **Personal:** Born Nov 10, 1927, Gainesville, FL; son of Richard Blye and Janie Blye; married Alice; children: Cecilia, Cecil Jr, Steven. **Educ:** Clark Col; Northwestern Univ; Univ Louisville. **Career:** The Louisville Defender, ed, 1958-68; Blye & Webb, sr partner, 1972-79; Blye, Blye & Blye, atty 1987. **Orgs:** Am Bar Asn; Ky Bar As;, Louisville Bar Asn; gen coun, KY Elks; Louisville-Jefferson Co Fedn Teachers & Am Postal Workers Union; Louisville Br; Alpha Phi Alpha Fraternity; chmn, Louisville Nat Asn Advan Colored People Legal Redress Com. **Military Serv:** AUS 1st lt 1952-54. **Business Addr:** Attorney.*

BOAFO, KWADWO I. See WILSON, REV. WILLIE FREDERICK.

BOARDLEY, CURTESTINE MAY
Government official. **Personal:** Born Dec 3, 1943, Sandersville, GA; daughter of William N and Zena Reaves; married James E, Jul 27, 1968; children: Angela B & Zena Y. **Educ:** Tuskegee Inst, BS, 1965, MEd, 1967. **Career:** Tuskegee Inst, admin asst dean women, 1966-67; Howard Univ, residence country, 1967-68; Pub Sch DC, counr, 1968; Voc Rehab Admin DC, voc rehab counr & acting co ordr counr, 1968-70; Fed Community Comn, employ counr, 1970-73, equal employ opportunity dir, 1973-76; Civil Serv Comn, Off Fed equal employ opportunity, 1976-79; US Off Personnel Mgt, equal employ opportunity specialist & mgr, Off Affirmative Employ Progs, 1979-83; Strayer Col, Wash, DC, instr, 1987, 1989, mgr, personnel mgt training div, 1983-95; US Dept Agr, prog mgt analyst. **Orgs:** Am CounAsn; Ebenezer African Methodist Episcopal Church; charter mem, vpres, Fort Wash Charter Chap; Am Bus Women's Asn; The Group, Wash DC Metrop Area, 1981-; Delta Sigma Theta, 1992-. **Honors/Awds:** Meritorious Performance Award, US Off Personnel Mgt, 1985; Directors Award, 1990; Special Act Award, 1991; Sustained Superior Performance, 1992. *

BOARDLEY-SUBER, DR. DIANNE
College president. **Personal:** Married; children: Nichole Reshan Lewis & Raegan LaTrese Thomas. **Educ:** Hampton Univ, BS, childhood educ; Univ Ill, MEd, curric develop; Va Polytech Inst & State Univ, PhD, educ admin. **Career:** Greensboro, NC, first grade teacher; Newport News, Va, lead kindergarten teacher; Hampton Univ, Hampton, Va, dean admin serv, asst provost, liaisongen assembly, Self Study Accreditation, dir, vpres admin serv; Saint Augustine's Col, pres, 1999-. **Orgs:** Pres Bush Bd Adv White House Initiative Hist Black Col & Univ; bd trustees, Triangle United Way; Cent Region bd dir, Wachovia Bank; bd dir,Cent Intercollegiate Athletic Asn; bd dir, United Negro Col Fund; bd dir,Bus & Technol Ctr; bd dir, NC Martin Luther King Jr Resource Ctr Founding; vpres & bd dir, Coop Raleigh Col; bd dir, Nat Asn Independent Col & Univ;Southeast Raleigh Improv Assembly; Livable St Comt; Triangle Family Serv; Asn Episcopal Cols. **Business Addr:** President, Saint Augustines College, 1315 Oakwood Ave, Raleigh, NC 27610-2298, **Business Phone:** (919)516-4200.

BOATMAN, MICHAEL PATRICK
Actor. **Personal:** Born Oct 25, 1964, Colorado Springs, CO; son of Daniel and Gwendolyn Pugh; married; children: Jordan. **Educ:** Western Ill Univ, BA, theatre prog, 1989. **Career:** TV series: "China Beach", 1988; "The Jackie Thomas Show", 1992; "Muscle", 1995; "Arli", 1996; "Spin City", 1996-2002; "Celebrity Dish", 2000; "Celebrity Mole Hawaii", 2003; Films: Hamburger Hill, 1987; Running On Empty, 1988; Unbecoming Age, 1992; Naked Gun 33 1/3 The Final Insult, 1994; The Glass Shield, 1994; The Peacemaker, 1997; Walking to the Waterline, 1998; Kalamazoo, 2005; TV films: "Donor", 1990; "Fourth Story", 1991; "In the Line of Duty: Street War", 1992; "House of Secrets", 1993; "Woman Thou Art Loosed", 2004; "Once Upon a Mattress", 2005; "Play Dates", 2005; Novels: The Red Wake; Revenant Road. **Honors/Awds:** Best Supporting Actor Award; Alumni Achievement Award, Western Ill Univ, 1997; GLAAD Award, Best Supporting Actor; Nominated for Image Award, 1998-2003. **Special Achievements:** Was also nominated for two NAACP IMAGE Awards; was nominated five timesfor the IMAGE Award for Best Supporting Actor in a comedy series. *

BOATWRIGHT, CYNTHIA
Executive. **Career:** WGFT Radio, prog dir, currently. *

BOATWRIGHT, JOSEPH WELDON, III
Physician. **Personal:** Born Jan 4, 1949, Richmond, VA; married Evelyn Donella Durham; children: Joseph Weldon IV. **Educ:** Davis & Elkins Col, BS, 1970; Univ Va, Sch Med, MD, 1974; Med Col Va, Grad Sch Med Educ, residency, 1978. **Career:** Pvt pract, pediatrician, currently; State Health Benefits Adv Coun, 2000-02. **Orgs:** Active staff, St Mary's Hosp; active staff, Richmond Memorial Hosp; clinical instr, Med Col Va; N Chamberlayne Civic Asn; fund raising comt, Florence Neal Cooper Smith Sickle Cell Initiative; Med Soc Va. **Honors/Awds:** Honourable Scholar, Davis & Elkins Col, 1966; Scholar, Univ Va, 1970. **Home Addr:** 8321 Futham Ct, Richmond, VA 23227. **Business Addr:** Pediatrician, Private Practice, 211 E Clay St, PO Box 26591, Richmond, VA 23261-6591.*

BOAZ, VALERIE A
Physician, health services administrator. **Educ:** MD. **Career:** Memorial Healthcare Syst Inc, Chattanooga, TN, physician; Hutcheson Med Ctr, Ft Oglethorpe, GA, physician; Grandview Med Ctr, Jasper, TN, Physician; Hamilton Med Ctr, Dalton, GA, physician; Chattanooga-Hamilton County Health Dept, health officer, currently.

BOBBITT, LEROY
Lawyer, manager. **Personal:** Born Nov 1, 1943, Jackson, MS; son of Leroy and Susie; married Andrea; children: Dawn, Antoinette. **Educ:** Mich State Univ, BA, 1966; Stanford Univ Sch Law, JD, 1969. **Career:** Paul, Weiss, Rifkind, Wharton & Garrison, atty, 1970-74; Loeb & Loeb, atty, 1974, partner; Street Smart Pictures Inc, co chmn, 2001. **Orgs:** State Bar Calif; Los Angeles Co Bar Asn; Am Bar Asn; Los Angeles Copyright Soc; Black Entertainment & Sports Lawyers Asn. *

BOBB-SEMPLE, CRYSTAL
Entrepreneur. **Personal:** Married Walston; children: 1. **Career:** Brownstone Books, founder & pres, 2000-08; The Parlor Floor Antiques, founder & owner, 2000-. **Orgs:** Am Booksellers Asn. **Business Addr:** Owner, Brownstone Books, 409 Lewis Ave, Brooklyn, NY 11233, **Business Phone:** (718)953-7328.

BOBINO, DR. RITA FLORENCIA
Consultant, psychologist. **Personal:** Born Jun 18, 1934, San Francisco, CA; daughter of Arthur E Cummings and Urania Prince Cummings; married Felix Joseph Bobino Jr (deceased); children: Sharelle Denice Hagg, Michael J, Mario K, Mauricio J & Malaika J. **Educ:** Laney Col, AA, 1973; Col Holy Names, BS, 1975; Calif State Univ, Hayward, MS, 1977; Wright Inst, PhD, 1985. **Career:** Oakland Poverty Prog, 1960-71; C Hosp Alameda Cty, dir women infants & children's prog WIC, 1973-76; Berkeley Mental Health Youth Prog, mental health worker, 1976-77; San Francisco Streetwork Prog, counr, 1977-80; Oakland Unified Schs Youth Diversion Prog High Sch, Cities Sch dir, 1980-84; Oakland Unified Sch Sr High, counr, family therapist; oncall-sexual assault therapist Highland Emergency Hosp Oakland; Oakland Unified Sch Farwest High Sch, prin TSA, 1987-88; Oakland Unified Sch, Elmhurst Middle Sch, admin asst prin, Elmhurst Middle Sch, prin, 1995; Contra Costa Col, instruct, Psychol African Am Women, 1994; Calif State Univ, Hayward, prof; Oakland, counr & family therapist, currently. **Orgs:** Co-founder, dir, BWAMU, 1976-, Relationship Strategy, 1978-; Bay Area Black Psychol, 1979; Nat Asn Advan Colored People, 1983-85, Juvenile Hall Diversion Prog Lucy King; Alpha Nu Omega Chap Alpha Kappa Alpha; Oakland Black Educators; mem, Oakland Educ Asn,1980-; licensed marriage family therapist, Calif, 1980-; Am Fed Sch Admin. **Honors/Awds:** Social Science Honor Soc Pi Gamma Mu, 1975; "Self-Concept of Black Students Who Have Failed" masters thesis; "African Amer Fathers & Daughters" doctoral dissertation completed; Alpha Kappa Alpha Sorority sixty third Far Western Regional, The Charlene V Carodine Unique Professional Achievement Award, 1992.

BOBO, ORLANDO. See Obituaries section.

BOBONIS, REGIS DARROW, JR.
Executive. **Personal:** Born Dec 8, 1960, Pittsburgh, PA; son of Regis and Hurley. **Educ:** Marquette Univ, BA, 1983. **Career:** Hearst Broadcasting, desk asst, 1983-85, night assignment ed, 1985-88, day assignment ed, 1988-89, assignment mgr, 1989-91, managing ed, 1991; WTAE-TV, managing ed, currently. **Orgs:** Chmn, Poise Found; chmn, Kiski Fund's trustee comt. **Honors/Awds:** Emmy Award. **Business Addr:** Managing Editor, WTAE-TV, 400 Ardmore Blvd, Pittsburgh, PA 15221, **Business Phone:** (412)244-4462.*

BOCAGE, RONALD J
Lawyer. **Personal:** Born Mar 18, 1946, New Orleans, LA; son of Charles L and Eva Charles; married Myrna DeGruy, Aug 16, 1969. **Educ:** Univ New Orleans, BA, 1968; Harvard Law Sch, JD, 1972. **Career:** Mintz, Levin, Cohn, Ferris, Glovsky & Popeo, Boston, MA, 1972-74; John Hancock Life Ins Co, Boston, MA, atty, 1974-79, asst counsel, 1979-83, assoc counsel, 1983-86, sr assoc counsel, 1986, second vpres & coun, 1986-88, vpres & coun, 1988-. **Orgs:** Am Bar Asn, 1972-; Mass Black Lawyers Asn, 1976-; Asn Life Insurance Coun, 1986-. **Military Serv:** AUS, E-7 staff sgt, 1969-75. **Business Addr:** Vice President, Counsel, John Hancock Life Insurance Co, John Hancock Pl, PO Box 111, Boston, MA 02117-0111, **Business Phone:** (617)572-6000.

BODDIE, ALGERNON OWENS
Contractor. **Personal:** Born Apr 3, 1933, Demopolis, AL; married Velma Fitzmon. **Educ:** Tuskegee Inst Ala, BS, indust educ, 1954.

Career: St Judes Educ Inst, Montgomery, AL, teacher, 1954-55; Boddie's Bldg Construct Inc, proprietor & estimator, 1963-70; FHA, Seattle, consult fee insp, 1969-71; Boddie's Bldg Construct Inc, pres, 1970-85; Tacoma Comn Develop, consult, 1976-77. **Orgs:** Tacoma Bldg & Fire Code Appeals Bd, 1969-76; Tacoma Chap Asn, Gen Contractors Am, 1974-85; pres, bd trustees, Tacoma Pub Libr, 1978-79. **Honors/Awds:** Comn Coop Award, Tacoma Pub Schs Div, Voc Rehab, 1971.

BODDIE, DR. ARTHUR WALKER. See Obituaries section.

BODDIE, DANIEL W.
Lawyer. **Personal:** Born Feb 10, 1922, New Rochelle, NY; married Annie Virginia Wise (deceased). **Educ:** Va Union Univ, AB, 1943; Cornell Law Sch, LLB, 1949. **Career:** Corp Coun, City New Rochelle, second asst; Law Secy; City Judge; pvt pract, atty, currently. **Orgs:** Bd mem, United Way New Rochelle; pres, New Rochelle Bar Asn, 1972; past chmn, New Rochelle Housing Authority; past legal & coun, New Rochelle Chap Nat Asn Advan Colored People; Omega Psi Phi; trustee, Bethesda Bapt Church. **Military Serv:** AUS, m/sgt, 1945. **Business Addr:** Attorney, Private Practice, 358 N Ave, New Rochelle, NY 10801.*

BODDIE, GWENDOLYN M
Educator. **Personal:** Born Aug 4, 1957, Columbus, GA. **Educ:** Mercer Univ, BA, 1979; Tuskegee Inst, MEd, 1981. **Career:** Tuskegee Area Health Educ Ctr, prog coordr, 1981-83; Booker Wash Comm Ctr, prog coordr, 1983; Atlanta Jr Col, counr, 1983-85; Southern Univ, dir stud recruitment, 1985-. **Orgs:** United Way. **Honors/Awds:** Kappa Delta Pi Lambda Delta, 1980. **Business Addr:** Director, Southern University, Stud Recruitment, PO Box 9399, Baton Rouge, LA 70813.

BODDIE, REV. JAMES R
Clergy. **Career:** St Pius V Catholic Church, pastor, 2000; St. Catherine Parish, pastor, currently. **Business Addr:** Pastor, St Catherine Parish, 1649 Kingsley Ave, Orange Park, FL 32073.

BODISON, WOLFGANG
Actor, manager. **Personal:** Born Nov 19, 1966, Washington, DC. **Educ:** Univ Va, attended 1988. **Career:** Columbia Pictures, file clerk; Castle Rock Productions, location mgr,mail room worker, prod asst, set asst, movies: A Few Good Men, 1992; The Big Gig, 1993; Little Big League, 1994; Criminal Passion, 1994; The Expert, 1995; Freeway, 1996; The M World, 1997; Goodbye America, 1997; Most Wanted, 1997; Blood Type, 1999; Joe Somebody, 2001; Where's Angelo,2003; Akeelah & the Bee, 2006; Now Here, currently; Not Another Not Another Moive, Currently. Tv series: "Murder She Wrote", 1993;"Sirens", 1994; "ER", 1995; "Highlander", 1995; "Silver Strand", 1995; "Dark Skies", 1997;"Nothing Sacred", 1997; "Between Brothers", 1997; "Nothing Sacred", 1998; "Family Law", 2000; "wedding Dress", 2001; "Charmed", 2003; "Skin Complex", 2003; "CSI: NY", 2006; "Cane", 2007. **Home Addr:** Los Angeles, CA 90048.

BODRICK, LEONARD EUGENE
Educator, counselor. **Personal:** Born May 17, 1953, Orangeburg, SC; married Sharon Trice; children: Jabari Talib, Nia Imani. **Educ:** Johnson C Smith Univ, BA (Cum Laude), 1976; Univ Pittsburgh, MPIA, pub admin, 1979; Univ NC-19Chapel Hill, PhD, prog, 1983. **Career:** Three Rivers Youth Inc, staff counsr, 1978-79; Southern Ctr Rural & Urban Devel, training dir, 1979-80; Educ Opportunity Ctr Roxboro NC, outreach coun, 1983-85; Johnson C Smith Univ, dir upward bound prog. **Orgs:** TransAfrica, 1977-; finance chair, 1985-87, conf chair, 1987, NC Southern Area rep, 1987-89; NC Coun Educ Opportunity Progs; Am Soc Pub Adminrs, Conf Minority Pub Adminrs; founding mem, UNCF Inter-Alumni Chap; founding mem, managing ed, GSPIA Jour; founding mem, Exec Coun Black Grad & Prof Stud Caucus; Charlotte Coun C; Nat Asn Advan Colored People; SCLC, Charlotte Drop-Out Prev Collaborative. **Honors/Awds:** Horne Scholarship, 1973; Babcock Scholarship, 1974; Pre-Doctoral Fel, 1976; Training Grant, 1977; founding mem & managing ed, Univ Pittsburgh GSPIA, 1979; Teaching Assistantship, Univ NC Chapel Hill, 1981-82; Outstanding Young Men of America, 1982. **Home Addr:** 3120 Airlie St, Charlotte, NC 28205. **Business Addr:** Director, Johnson C Smith University, Upward Bound Program, 100 Beatties Ford Rd, Charlotte, NC 28216.*

BOFILL, ANGELA
Singer. **Personal:** Born May 2, 1954, West Bronx, NY; daughter of Carmen. **Educ:** Hartt Col Music, 1973; Manhattan Sch Music, BMus, 1976. **Career:** New Yorks All City Voices; Dance Theater Harlem, lead soloist; Albums:This Time I'll be Sweater; Under the Moon & Over the Sky; Angie, 1978; Angel of the Night, 1979; Something About You, 1981; Too Tough, 1983; Teaser, 1983; Let Me Be the One, 1984; Tell Me Tomorrow, 1985; Intuition, 1988; Love Is In Your Eyes, 1991; I Wanna Love Somebody, 1993; Love in Slow Motion, 1996; Eternity, 2000; Something About You Expanded, 2002; Live from Manila, 2004; I Try. **Honors/Awds:** Most Promising New Female Vocalist, Latin New York Mag, 1979; No 1 Female Jazz Artist, Cash box, 1979; No 5 Female Vocalist, Cash box; Bammy Award; Black book Award. **Special Achievements:** American music award nominee. **Business Addr:** Singer, c/o Live at Night, PO Box 1140, Maplewood, NJ 07040.

BOGGAN, DANIEL, JR.
Executive, vice president (organization). **Personal:** Born Dec 9, 1945, Albion, MI; son of Daniel Boggan Sr and Ruthie Jean Crum Boggan; married Jacqueline Ann Beal Boggan, Oct 4, 1977; children: DeVone, Daniel III, Dhanthan, Alike. **Educ:** Albion Col, BA, 1967; Univ Mich, MSW, 1968. **Career:** Starr Commonwealth Boys, clinical supv, 1968-70; Jackson Mich, asst city mgr, 1970-72; Flint Mich, dep city mgr, 1972-74, city mgr, 1974-76; Portland, Oreg, dir mgt serv, 1976-78; San Diego Calif, asst Co admin, 1978-79; Essex Co, NJ, co admin, 1979-82; Berkeley Calif, city mgr, 1982-86; Univ Calif, Berkeley, assoc vice chancellor bus & admin serv, 1986, acting vice chancellor bus & admin serv, 1986-87, vice chancellor bus & admin serv, 1987-94; Nat Collegiate Athletic Asn, Educ Serv Div, head, 1994-96, sr vpres, 1996-03; Payless Shoesource Inc, dir, 1997-; Siebert Brandford Shank & Co LLC, dir bus develop, 2003-06. **Orgs:** Chmn, Alameda Cty Mgrs Assn, 1984-85; bd mem, Oakland Chap, 1985-94, pres, 1990-; chmn, comm on minorities & women League Calif Cities, 1985-; bd mem & dir, Clorox Corp, 1990-; bd mem, Coro Found, 1990; Nat Forum for Black Pub Adminrs; Nat Asn Adv Colored People; Carolina Freight Corp, 1995; bd mem, Payless Shoe Source; bd mem, Admin Fed, 1999; trustee, Calif Endowment, currently. **Honors/Awds:** Outstanding Public Administrator, 1975; Chapter Service Award, 1986; Marks of Excellence Award, 1987; Award, Nat Forum Black Pub Adminrs; Youth Leadership Award, 1965; Outstanding Alumnus Award, Albion Col, 1991; UC Berkeley Citation, 1994. **Business Phone:** (785)233-5171.*

BOGGER, DR. TOMMY (TOMMY L BOGGER)
Educator. **Personal:** Born May 7, 1944, Williamsburg, VA; son of Arthur Bogger Sr and Ethel Lee; married Nan H Bogger, Sep 19, 1969; children: Alexiss Nichole & Jared Edmund. **Educ:** VA State Col, Norfolk Div, BA, 1968; Carnegie-Mellon Univ, MA, 1969; Univ VA, PhD, 1976. **Career:** Norfolk State Col, hist instr, 1969-71; Norfolk State uiv, asst & assoc prof, 1974-85; prof hist, 1985-86, dir arch, 1986-93, dean, libr sci & spec col, 1993-97, Lyman B Brooks Libr, Harrison B Wilson Archives, dir, 1997-, records mgr, currently. **Orgs:** Mid-Atlantic Regional Arch Asn, 1978-80, 1997-; Rev bd, Va Hist Landmarks Comn, 1980-83; Southern Hist Asn, 1986-; Southern Hist Conf, local arrangements comt, 1988; Orgn Am Historians, 1990-; The VA Hist Soc, 1991-; Chrysler Mus Sub-Comt Hist Houses. **Honors/Awds:** Thomas Jefferson Foundation Fellowship, Univ VA, 1971-72; Fellowship, Nat Endowment for the Humanities, 1983-84; Distinguished Alumni Citation, NAFEO, 1985; Citation for Distinguished Contributions, Va Found Humanities, 1995. **Special Achievements:** Author of Books: A History of African-Americans in Middlesex County 1646-1992, 1994; Norfolk: The First Four Centuries, Parramore, Stewart and Bogger, 1994; Free Blacks in Norfolk, VA 1790-1860: The Darker Side of Freedom, 1997; Portsmouth Public Library, 1982; contributor: Dictionary of VA Biography, 1998.

BOGGER, TOMMY L. See BOGGER, DR. TOMMY.

BOGGS, DONALD W
Executive. **Educ:** Mich State Univ, BS, 1966; Univ Detroit, 1971. **Career:** Organ Sch Admin & Supvr, AFSA, AFL-CIO, 19939-99; Metrop Detroit AFL-CIO Coun, pres, currently. **Orgs:** Am Fed Schl Adminr; New Detroit Adv Brd; Am Red Cross Bd Dir; Nat Asn Advan Colored People; Coalition Black Trade Unionists; Indust Rel Res Asn; Nat Alliance Black Sch Educators. **Business Addr:** President, Metrop Detroit AFL-CIO Council, 600 W Lafayette Blvd Suite 200, Detroit, MI 48226, **Business Phone:** (313)961-0800.

BOGGS, DR. GRACE LEE
Writer, activist, public speaker. **Personal:** Born Jun 27, 1915, Providence, RI. **Educ:** Barnard Col, BA, 1935; Bryn Mawr Col, PhD, Philos, 1940. **Career:** Boggs Ctr, activist, writer & speaker, currently. **Orgs:** Founder, Detroit Summer, 1992-. **Honors/Awds:** Human Rights Day Award, Ctr Peace & Conflict Studies, 1993; Zenobia Paine Drake Award, Black Family Develop, 1998; Discipleship Award, Groundwork Just World, 2000; Distinguished Alumnae Award, Barnard Col, 2000; Chinese American Pioneers Award, Orgn Chinese Am, 2000; Women's Lifetime Achievement, Anti-Defamation League, 2001; Legacy Award, Mus Chinese Am, 2002; Grassroots Peacebuilder Award, Peace Action Mich, 2004; Interfaith Comittee on Worker Issues Award, 2004; Lifetime Commitment Award, Mich Coalition Human Rights, 2004; Lifetime Achievement Award, Mich Women's Fedn, 2005; Community Honoree Award, Women's Action New Directions, 2005; Urban Woman Writer Residence, Dept Interdisciplinary Studies, Wayne State University, 2005; Lifetime Achievement Award, Detroit City Coun, 2005; plaque made in honor; Doctor of Humane Letters degree, Kalamazoo Col, 2007. **Special Achievements:** Publisher: Revolution and Evolution in the Twentieth Century, 1974; Living for Change, 1998; Conversations in Main, 1978. **Business Addr:** Writer, Speaker, Boggs Ctr, 3061 Field St, Detroit, MI 48214.

BOGGS MCDONALD, LYNETTE MARIA
Government official. **Personal:** Born Jul 28, 1963, Washington, DC; daughter of Dr Nathaniel Boggs, Jr and Janice Costello Anderson; married Steve, May 27, 1995; children: Adam. **Educ:** Univ Notre Dame, 1985; Univ Nevada, MPA, 1998; Univ Oregon, Grad Sch Jour, attended 1990. **Career:** City Las Vegas, asst city mgr, 1994-97; Univ Nev Sch Med, dir mktg; Univ Nev, Las Vegas, dir Mktg & Community Relations, 1997-2000; City Las Vegas, councilwoman, 1999-2004; Las Vegas Valley Water Dist, gov bd mem; Univ Med Ctr, gov bd mem; McCarran Int Airport, gov bd mem; Clark County Govt Ctr, Bd County Comnrs, Comnr dist F, 2004-07. **Orgs:** Bd mem, Nat Conf Community & Justice, 1999; bd mem, S Nev Health Dist; Alpha Kappa Alpha Sorority, 2000; vpres, Nev League Cities & Municipalities, 2001; trustee, Catholic Charities Southern Nev, 2000; bd mem, Summerlin C's Forum, 2000; Nat Black Caucus Local Elected Officials, 2000; pres, Keep Memory Alive, found Lou Ruvo Alzheimer's Inst; Nat Comn Abraham Lincoln Study Abroad Fel Prog; bd mem, Miss Am Org. **Honors/Awds:** Top 40 Under 40, Las Vegas Business Press, 1997; Woman of Achievement, Notre Dame Alumni Asn, 1997; Distinguished Woman of Southern Nevada, Distinguished Publishing, 1997. **Special Achievements:** Miss Oregon, 1989; First councilwoman and African-American woman to take office in city of Las Vegas, 1999.

BOGLE, DONALD
Writer, educator, movie producer. **Personal:** Born Jul 13, 1944, Philadelphia, PA. **Educ:** Lincoln Univ, attended 1966. **Career:** Film historian; author; Rutgers Univ; Univ Pa; NY Univ's Tisch Sch Arts; Books: Eighty Years of America's Black Female Superstars, 1980; Blacks in American Film and Television: An Illustrated Encyclopedia, Simon & Schuster, 1989; Dorothy Dandridge: A Biography, Amistad Press, 1997; Primetime Blues: African Americans on Network TV, 2001; TV series: "Brown Sugar", dir, writer & producer, 1986; "Mo Funny: Black Comedy in America", 1993; "Intimate Portrait", 1998; "Inside TV Land: African Americans in Television", 2002; "It's Black Entertainment", 2002; "Jim Brown: All American", 2002; "Inside TV Land: Cops on Camera", 2004; "The N-Word", 2004; "Tavis Smiley", 2005; "20/20", 2005. **Honors/Awds:** Outstanding Contribution to Publishing Citation, BC Ala, 2002. **Special Achievements:** Appeared in the first experimental television broadcasts by NBC, 1939; The first African-American woman to be nominated for an Academy Award in the Best Actress in a Leading Role category; First time an African-American woman was portrayed on screen in a romantic lead as a beautiful, glamorous object of desire. **Business Addr:** Writer, Producer & Director, c/o Children's Marketing Department, Farrar, Straus & Giroux, 19 Union Sq W, New York, NY 10003, **Business Phone:** (212)741-6900.*

BOGLE, ROBERT W.
Newspaper executive. **Educ:** Cheyney State Col, BA, urban studies; Univ Penn Wharton Sch Bus & Finance, attended 1971; Temple Univ; Rochester Inst Technol. **Career:** Philadelphia Tribune, publ, advert dir, 1973-77, dir mkt, 1977-81, exec vpres & treas, 1981-89, pres, 1989-, chief exec officer, currently. **Orgs:** Pres, Nat Newspaper Publishers Asn, 1991-95; chair, Hosps & Higher Educ Facil Authority Philadelphia; comnr, Del River Port Authority; bd mem, Zool Soc Philadelphia; bd mem, Workforce Invest Bd; bd mem, African-American Chamber Com; coun trustees, Cheyney Univ; exec comt, Greater Philadelphia Chamber Com; bd mem, Kimmel Ctr Performing Arts; bd mem, Mann Music Ctr Performing Arts; bd govs, United Way Am; mem, National Museum of African American History and Culture Commission, 2002; life mem, Alpha Psi Fraternity Inc. **Honors/Awds:** Russwarm Award, NNPA, 1995, 1987, 1999; DHL, Drexel Univ, 2000. **Business Addr:** President, Chief Executive Officer, Philadelphia Tribune, 520 S 16th St, Philadelphia, PA 19146, **Business Phone:** (215)893-4050.*

BOGUES, MUGSSY. See BOGUES, TYRONE CURTIS.

BOGUES, TYRONE CURTIS (MUGSSY BOGUES)
Basketball player, basketball coach, business owner. **Personal:** Born Jan 9, 1965, Baltimore, MD; married Kimberly (divorced); children: Tyeisha, Brittney & Tyrone II. **Educ:** Wake Forest Univ, Winston Salem, NC, 1983-87. **Career:** Basketball player (retired), basketball coach; Wash Bullets, 1987-88; Charlotte Hornets, 1988-97; Golden State Warriors, guard,1997-99; Toronto raptors, 1999-2001; Bogues Enterprise LLC, owner; Charlotte Sting, head coach, 2005-07; Charlotte Bobcats, ambassadors & broadcasters, currently. **Honors/Awds:** Frances Pomeroy Naismith Award, 1986-87; Charlotte Hornets, Player of the Year, 1989-90. **Special Achievements:** Appeared in TV Shows: "Hang Time"; "Pros Vs Joes"; Also in the movie "Space Jam". **Business Addr:** Ambassadors & Broadcasters., Charlotte Bobcats, 333 E Trade Str, Charlotte, NC 28202, **Business Phone:** (704)688-8600.

BOGUS, DR. HOUSTON, JR.
Physician. **Personal:** Born Sep 10, 1951, Knoxville, TN; son of Houston and Louise; married Dorris Loretta Gray; children: Alisha Dione, Houston III, Alyson Gray. **Educ:** Univ TN, BA, 1973; Meharry Med Col, MD, 1979. **Career:** The Med Group Tex, gastroenterologist; Dallas Diag Assn, physician; Baylor Med Ctr Garland, gastroenterologist, currently; Med City Hosp, gastroenterologist, currently. **Orgs:** Omega Psi Phi Fraternity; Alpha Omega Alpha Hon Med Soc; Meharry Chap; Am Col

Gastroenterology. **Military Serv:** AUS, intern internal med, 1979-80, resident internal med, 1980-82, staff internist & chief emergency serv, 1982-83, fel gastroenterology, 1983-85, staff internist & gastroenterologist, 1985-90; Army Commendation Medal, 1983. **Business Addr:** Physician, Dallas Diag Asn, 601 Clara Barton, Garland, TX 75042, **Business Phone:** (972)494-6235.*

BOGUS, DR. S. DIANE ADAMZ
Educator, poet, publisher. **Personal:** Born Jan 22, 1946, Chicago, IL; married Frances J Huxie, Jun 11, 1976. **Educ:** Stillman Col, BA, 1968; Syracuse Univ, MA, 1969; Miami Univ, PhD, 1988; AmInt Univ, PhD, parapsychology, 1998. **Career:** LA Southwest Col, instr, 1976-81; Miami Univ, instr, 1981-84; WIM Publ,auth, 1971-, founder, 1979-, publ, currently; Calif State Univ, prof am lit, 1986-90; De Anza Col, Cupertino, CA, instr, 1990. **Orgs:** Delta Sigma Theta Sorority, 1965-; Nat Teachers Eng, 1981-; Feminist Writer's Guild, 1980-; Publ Triangle, 1992-; bd mem, Col Publisher's, 1989-92. **Honors/Awds:** Nominated, Pulitzer Prize, Sapphire's Sampler, 1982; Hon, Art & Music Dept, Trenton Pub Libr, 1983; Black Writer's Award, Peninsula Book Club, 1992; Woman Achievement Award, 1997; Nominated, Lambda Lit Award,Chant of the Women of Magdalena. **Special Achievements:** Works adapted into CA State Univ Archives 1982. *

BOHANNAN-SHEPPARD, BARBARA
Mayor, government official. **Personal:** Born Jun 15, 1950, Ornancock, VA; daughter of Robert Harry Lee (deceased) and Mary Sue Chandler. **Educ:** Delaware County Community Col. **Career:** City Chester, mayor, 1992-95; BB Educ Training & C's Servs, owner, currently. **Orgs:** Hon chairwoman, Nat Polit Cong Black Women; Conf Mayors; Nat Coun Negro Women; Nat Asn Advan Colored People. **Honors/Awds:** Peace & Justice Award, 1991. *

BOHANNON, ETDRICK
Basketball player. **Personal:** Born May 29, 1973, San Bernardino, CA. **Educ:** Auburn Univ, Montgomery, attended 1997; Univ Ariz; Univ Tenn. **Career:** Ind Pacers, forward, 1997-98; Wash Wizards, forward, 1998-99; New York Knickerbockers, forward, 2000; Los Angeles Clippers, forward, 2000-01; Cleveland Cavaliers, forward, 2001; Yakama Sun Kings, 2005-. **Business Addr:** Professional Basketball Player, Yakama Sun Kings, 1301 S Fair Ave Shattuck Bldg, Yakima, WA 98901, **Business Phone:** (509)248-1222.

BOI, BIG. See PATTON, ANTWAN ANDRE.

BOL, MANUTE
Basketball player, social worker. **Personal:** Born Oct 16, 1962, Gogrial, Sudan; son of Dinka and Okwok; married Atong; children: Abuk & Madut. **Educ:** Cleveland State Univ, attended 1984; Univ Bridgeport. **Career:** Basketball player (retired), social worker; Wash Bullets, ctr, 1985-88, 1994; Golden State Warriors, ctr, 1989-90, 1994; Philadelphia 76ers,ctr, 1990-93; Miami Heat, ctr, 1993-94; CBA, Fla Beach Dogs, 1995-96; social worker, currently. **Orgs:** Founder, Ring True Found, 2001-. **Honors/Awds:** Seventh overall pick in the 2004 NBA Draft; All-Rookie First Team, 2004-05. **Special Achievements:** Signed a one-day contract with the Indianapolis Ice of the Central Hockey League to raise money for the Sudanese; Only player in NBA history to block more shots than points scored.

BOLAND, D STEVEN
Banker, president (organization), chief executive officer. **Educ:** Northwestern Univ, BS, Orgn studies. **Career:** Landsafe Inc, pres & managing dir. **Honors/Awds:** 75 Most Powerful Blacks in Corporate America, Black Enterprise, 2005. **Business Addr:** Managing director, President & Chief Executive Officer, Landsafe Inc, 7105 Corporate Dr, Plano, TX 75024, **Business Phone:** (972)526-2302.*

BOLDEN, ALETHA SIMONE
Executive. **Personal:** Born in Bronx, NY; daughter of Althea and Cornelius Cherry; married Vernie Lee, Oct 8, 1994; children: Avery & Vaughn. **Educ:** Univ NC, Greensboro, BFA, 1989. **Career:** Harrison Mus African Am Cult, cur, 1993-95, exec dir, 1995-. **Orgs:** Adv bd mem, Burrell Nursing Ctr, 1998-; Dumas Music Ctr Bd Comners, 2000-; bd mem, Dumas Drama Guild, 2001-; bd mem, Am Cancer Soc, 2001-; Kiwanis Club Roanoke, 2001-; bd mem, Va Asn Mus, 2001-04. **Honors/Awds:** Outstanding Project, Am Cancer Soc, Prostate Cancer Detection, 2001. **Business Addr:** Executive Director, Harrison Museum African American Culture, 523 Harrison Ave NW, Ground Level, Roanoke, VA 24016, **Business Phone:** (540)345-4818.

BOLDEN, ALFRED, JR.
Executive. **Educ:** RN; BSN. **Career:** Transplantation Soc Mich, clin mgr; St John Detroit Riverview Hosp, admin dir emergency serv. **Orgs:** Bd dir, Tia Nedd Organ Donor Found, currently; Mich Proj dir, Minority Organ & Tissue Transplant Educ Prog. **Business Addr:** Board of Director, Tia Nedd Organ Donor Foundation, 48201 St, PO Box 20, Milan, MI 48160-0020, **Business Phone:** (313)842-6333.

BOLDEN, BARBARANETTE T.
Military leader. **Educ:** Arkansas State Univ, BA, hist, 1974, MA, hist, 1975; Howard Univ Sch Law, JD, 1978; AUS War Col, attended 1998. **Career:** 567th Engineer Battalion, Jonesboro, AK, 1975-78; 163rd Military Police Battalion, Wash, DC; 171st Military Police Battalion, Wash, DC, military police investigative officer, 1978-79; DC Army Nat Guard, Wash, DC, tactical officer, 1979-82, personnel mgt officer, 1990-94, dir personnel, 1996-97, dir plans, 1997-99, chief staff, 1999-04, comdr, 2006-; 163rd Military Police Battalion, Wash, DC, circulation control officer, 1982, detachment comdr, 1982-83; 163rd Military Police Battalion, Wash, DC, 1983-86; 260th Military Police Brigade, Wash, DC, 1986-88; 372nd Military Police Battalion, Wash, DC, 1990; 372nd Military Police Battalion, Wash, DC, 1994-96; US Northern Command, Colorado Springs, CO, oper dir, 2004; Armed Forces Inaugural Comt, Washington, DC, oper dir, 2004-05. **Honors/Awds:** Legion of Merit with 1 Bronze Oak Leaf Cluster; Defense Meritorious Service Medal; Meritorious Service Medal ; Army Commendation Medal; Army Achievement Medal; Army Reserve Components Achievement Medal; National Defense Service Medal; Global War On Terrorism Service Medal; Humanitarian Service Medal; Military Outstanding Volunteer Medal; Armed Forces Reserve Medal; Army Service Ribbon; Army Reserve Components Overseas Training Ribbon. *

BOLDEN, BETTY A.
Labor relations manager. **Personal:** Born Dec 24, 1944, St Louis, MO. **Educ:** Univ Illinois, BA, 1965; DePaul Univ, MA, 1969. **Career:** US Dept Labor, dep dir personal, exec asst, 1976-78, superior personal mgt spec, 1975-76; US Civil Serv Commn Wash, DC, personal mgt specialist, 1973-75; US Postal Serv Chicago/Wash DC, personal mgmt specialist, 1968-75; US Civil Serv Commun Chicago, career intern, 1967; Assoc Deputy Secretary Labor, 1993, Deputy Secretary; Dept Labor, career Federal employee ;Federal Serv Impasses Panel, exec dir, chmn, 1994-99. **Orgs:** personnel com Delta Sigma Theta, 1979-81. *

BOLDEN, CHARLES E.
Labor activist. **Personal:** Born Feb 12, 1941, Alabama; son of Charles H and Ernestine; married Diane Nation; children: Charles R, Marva L. **Educ:** Ala State Univ, BS, 1966; LaSalle Ext Univ, LLB, 1975; Univ Phoenix, Denver, MA, arts mgt, 1984. **Career:** Nat Educ Asn Chicago, fld rep, 1968-70; Nat Educ Asn Denver, org team coord, 1970-74; Nat Educ Asn, mgr shared staffing prog, 1974-76; Nat Educ Asn, Denver, orgn specialist, 1976-. **Orgs:** chmn, Ft & Madison IA Human Rel Comn, 1967-68; Orgn Pub Sch Teachers Collective Bargaining 1968-; Orgn Human Rights Ordinance Campaign; Sigma Rho Sigma, Omega Psi Phi Frat; bd dirs, Am Civil Libs Union PG Co MD, 1975; vpres, PTA Ft Wash Forest Elem Sch, 1975. **Honors/Awds:** Teacher Advocate Award Compton, CA, 1973; Outstanding Serv Award, United Fac Fla, 1984; Appreciation Serv Award, Okla Educ Asn, 1989; Friend Educ Award, Wyo Educ Asn, 1994. **Business Addr:** Organizational Specialist, National Education Association, 1401 17th St Suite 950, Denver, CO 80202-1398.*

BOLDEN, CINDY B.
Manager. **Educ:** MA. **Career:** Community Health Awareness Group, exec dir, 2003. *

BOLDEN, CLARENCE
Lawyer. **Career:** Conflict Resolution Skills Group, atty, currently. **Home Phone:** (947)279-3456. **Business Addr:** Attorney, Conflict Resolution Skills Group, PO Box 91804, Anchorage, AK 99509.*

BOLDEN, DOROTHY LEE
Executive. **Personal:** Born Oct 13, 1923, Atlanta, GA; daughter of Raymond and Georgia M Patterson; married Abram Thompson Sr; children: Frank, Avon Butts, Dorothy Ingram, Altenmiece Knight, Abram & Anthony. **Career:** Greyhound bus sta; Linen Supply Co; RR Express; Sears Roebuck; Nat Domestic Inc, pres, founder. **Orgs:** Vpres, Vine City NDP Housing, 1967; dir, Training Prog & Employment Agency, 1968; HEW Washington, 1975; contrib., Ms Magazine, Essence Magazine, Atlanta Magazine; Comn Status Women, 1975; vpres, Black Women Coalition Atlanta, 1973; mem, Fulton County Dem Party; vpres, City NDP; bd dir, NAACP; mem bd dir, WIGO Radio Station; mem exec bd, State Dem Party & Bd Gov; exec bd, Fulton County Dem legal aid; Citizens Trust Bank Adv Bd; Vine City Baptist Church; Adv Team Legal Aid Coun; OIC. **Honors/Awds:** Recip Atlanta Inquirer Mayors Award 1970; Wigo Advisory Council Community Action Award, 1971-72; Wigo Basic Community Award, 1973; Economic Opportunity Atlanta Neighbourhood, 1973; Omega Psi Phi Fraternity Outstanding Community Service Award 1973; Black Womens International Award, 1975; Concerned Citizens Award, 1975. **Business Addr:** Founder, Director, National Domestic Workers Union of America Inc, 52 Fairlee St NW, Atlanta, GA 30303.

BOLDEN, FRANK AUGUSTUS
Lawyer, executive. **Personal:** Born Aug 7, 1942, Albany, GA; son of Augustus and Geraldine; married Carol Penelope Parsons; children: Brian, Ian. **Educ:** Univ Vt, BA, 1963; Columbia Univ, Grad Sch Bus, MBA, 1972; Columbia Univ Sch Law, JD 1972. **Career:** Executive, Lawyer (retired); Woodrow Wilson Found, Martin Luther King Jr fel, 1969-72; Charles Evans Hughes fel, 1971-72; Columbia Univ, asst football coach, 1971; Inst Educ Develop, consult, 1972; Cahill Gordon & Reindel, assoc, 1972-75; Inst Mediation & Conflict Resolution, dir, 1972-90; Windsor Minerals Inc, dir, 1976-87; Western Sources Inc, dir, 1979-87; Healthcare Products Nigeria Ltd, dir, 1978-84; Chicopee, dir, 1980-84; Johnson & Johnson, atty, 1975, int atty, 1976-85, vpres corp staff, 1986, vpres serv, corp staff, 1994-01, vpres, diversity health giant, 2002-2007. **Orgs:** Dir, Raritan Credit Union, 1976-78; COGME Fel, 1970-72; adv Consortium Met Law Sch, 1972-73; dir, NJ Asn on Corrections, 1980-88; trustee Union County Col, 1983-98, vice chmn 1989-93, chmn 1993-95; vpres, NJ State Opera, 1984-; NJ Comn Pay Equity, 1984; Nat Bar Asn; bd trustee, Overlook Hosp, Summit, NJ, 1990-96, vice chmn, 1993-94, chmn, 1994-96; Black Leadership Coun, 1988-; bd trustees, City Market, New Brunswick, NJ, 1988-94; bd trustees, Crossroads Theatre, Inc, New Brunswick, NJ, 1989-94; adv comt, Fla A&M Sch Bus, 1986-90; adv comt, Univ Vt Bus Sch, 1992; bd trustees, Univ Vt, 1994-00, chair, Univ Vt, 1998-00; bd trustees, Nat Med Fel, 1995-; bd governers, Nat Conf Christians & Jews, 1991-, exec comt, Nat Conf Christians & Jews, 1992-; bd trustees, Atlantic Health Syst, 1996-; bd dir, NJ Chamber Com, 1999-, exec comt, NJ Chamber Com, 2001-. **Honors/Awds:** Distinguished Service Award, 1984; Outstanding Service Award, Nat Conf, 1984; Freedom Fund Award, Perth Amboy NAACP, 1995; Distinguished Service Award, NJ State Opera, 1996; City News 100 Most Influential, NJ, 1996; Athletic Hall of Fame, Univ VT, 2000. **Military Serv:** AUS, capt, 1963-69. *

BOLDEN, JAMES LEE
Executive. **Personal:** Born Jun 14, 1936, Quitman, MS; married Margaret P Hardaway; children: James Jr, Sherry, Margery & Jeffery. **Educ:** Topeka State Hosp, Cert 1959; LUCT Training Inst, Cert 1976; Washburn Univ, 1978. **Career:** Little Jim's Trucking Co, gen contractor, 1958-71; Bolden Radio & TV Repair, mgr, owner, 1958-66; Little Jim's Garage, mgr, owner, 1969-; Four M Develop Co Inc, pres, 1970-; Mid-Cent Ins Cons, owner, gen agt, 1974-; Mid-Am Aviation Inc, pres & owner, currently. **Orgs:** Treas, Mt Carmel Missionary Bapt Church, 1966-; bd mem, Household Tech, 1978-; bd treas, Black Econ Coun Topeka, 1979-; chmn supvry comn, The Capital City Credit Union, 1979-; Local Develop Corp, 1979-; chmn mem, comm., NAACP, 1979-; lectr, Enroute & Terminal ATC Procedures Oper Rain Check USA Dept Trans Fed Aviation Admin, 1980; Labor & Indust Chair, Nat Asn Adv Colored People Topeka Br, 2007-09. **Honors/Awds:** Certificate of Appreciation, Kans State Conf Br NAACP, 1979. **Home Addr:** 830 E 37th St, Topeka, KS 66605, **Home Phone:** (785)266-7916. **Business Addr:** President, Owner, Mid-America Aviation, Hangar 612, Forbes Field, Topeka, KS 66619, **Business Phone:** (785)862-2790.

BOLDEN, JURAN
Football player, executive. **Personal:** Born Jun 27, 1974, Tampa, FL; married Tina; children: Isiah. **Educ:** Miss Delta Community Col. **Career:** Football player (retired); Winnipeg Blue bombers, 1995; Atlanta Falcons, defensive back, 1996-97 & 2002-03; Carolina Panthers, 1998; Kansas City Chiefs, 1999; Winnipeg Blue bombers, 2000-01; Jacksonville Jaguars, corner back, 2004; Tampa Bay Buccaneers, corner back, 2005-07; Winnipeg Blue bombers, 2007-08; free agent & sr acct exec, currently. **Honors/Awds:** Defensive Player of the Yr; Miss Delta Defensive Player of the Yr; Outstanding Defensive. *

BOLDEN, RAYMOND A
Lawyer. **Personal:** Born Dec 17, 1933, Chicago, IL; married; children: Kathryn, Alan & Joseph. **Educ:** Univ Ill, BS, Bus, LLB 1981. **Career:** Intelligence Div US Treas Dept, agt, 1961-64; Will County, asst state atty, 1964-68; 12th Judicial Dist, assoc judge, 1986-2001; pvt practice, atty. **Orgs:** Nat & Will County Bar Asn; pres, Nat Black Lawyers Conf, Joliet Br, Nat Advan Asn Colored People, 1964-68; bd dirs, Joliet-Will County Comn Action Agency, 1967-73; Will County Legal Ast Prog; chmn, High Crime Red Ctr Comn, Joliet, 1975. **Honors/Awds:** Distinguished Citizens Service Award, Black Stud Union Lewis Univ, 1975; award, Nat Advan Asn Colored People, 1968. **Military Serv:** USAF, s/sgt, 1953-57. **Business Addr:** Lawyer, 54 N Ottawa St Suite 245, Joliet, IL 60432, **Business Phone:** (815)723-2895.

BOLDEN, STEPHANIE T
City council member. **Career:** Wilmington City Coun, coun mem 3rd dist, 2004-. **Special Achievements:** Initiated the Drug Mug prog, 2004. **Business Addr:** Council Member 3rd District, Wilmington City Council, 800 French St 9th Fl, Wilmington, DE 19801, **Business Phone:** (302)576-2140.*

BOLDEN, DR. THEODORE E.
Dentist. **Personal:** Born Apr 19, 1920, Middleburg, VA; son of Theodore Donald and Mary Elizabeth Jackson; married Dorothy M Forde (deceased). **Educ:** Lincoln Univ, AB, 1941, LLD, 1981; Meharry Med Col, DDS, 1947; Univ Ill, MS, 1951, PhD, 1958. **Career:** Dentist, educator (retired); Sch Dent, Meharry Med Col, instr, operative dent, periodontics, 1948-49, spec lectr, 1956, prof dent, chmn oral path, 1962-77, dir res, 1962-77, assoc dean, 1967-77, adj prof, 1988-; Univ Ill, Sch Dent, instr path, 1955-57, lectr post grad studies, 1956; Seton Hall Col Med & Dent, asst prof dent, 1957-60; Med Ctr, path, 1958-62, assoc prof oral diagnosis,

path, 1960-62; Colgate Polmolive Co Res Ctr, consult, 1962-; George W Hubbard Hosp Nashville, TN, med & dent staff, 1962-77; Univ Med & Dent NJ, dean, 1977-78, Univ Med & Dent NJ-NJDS, acting chmn gen & oral path, 1979-80, prof gen & oral path 1977-90. **Orgs:** Consult, VAH, Tuskegee, AL, 1958-90, Nashville, TN, 1965-77, Brooklyn, NY, 1977-90; secy, treas, George W Hubbard Hosp Med & Dent Staff, 1968-70; chmn standing comn, Alumni Asn Meharrry Med Col, 1970-73; counr-at-large, Am Asn Dent Sch, 1971; sub-comt, Curriculum Planning Comn Curric & Sched, Sch Dent, 1972; chmn, res comn, Acad Dent C Nat Dent Asn, 1974; chmn Dent, Am Asn Cancer Educ, 1976-77; exec comt, Am Asn Cancer Educ, 1977-78; ed, Quarterly Nat Dent Asn, 1977-82; trustee, Am Fund Dent Health, 1978-86; trustee & adv, Am Fund Dent Health, 1978-85; pres, Nashville Sect Am Asn Dent Res; res comn, 1980-81, 1983-84, admis comn minority sub-comt, 1980-82; Univ Med & Dent NJ; co-chmn, Montclair NJ Res Crusade Am Cancer Soc, 1980-82; vpres, Newark Unit NJ, Div Am Cancer Soc Inc, 1983; chmn bd, Newark Unit Am Cancer Soc, 1984-85; trustee, Neighborhood Coun, Montclair, NJ, 1988-. **Honors/Awds:** Capital City Dental Soc & Pan-TN Dent Asn Plaque, 1977; Dentist of the Year Award, Nat Dent Asn Inc, 1977; Boss of the Year, Plaque Sch Dent, Meharry Med Col, 1977; Service to Community as Dean Plaque, Nat Coun Negro Women, 1978; Plaque, Univ Conn, Carter G Woodson Collquim, 1979; Outstanding Contributions Plaque, Black Caucus Dentist 1979; Certificate of Appreciation for Service, 1979; PATCH Award of Excellence to Theodore E Bolden DDS, PhD, FICD for Excellence & Attainable Goal of CMD NJ-NJ DS, No 1 Patch, 1979; over 300 scientific publications including 14 books. **Military Serv:** AUS, sgt, lt, DC, 1943-44. **Home Addr:** 29 Montague Pl, Montclair, NJ 07042. *

BOLDEN, TONYA
Writer. **Personal:** Born Mar 1, 1959, New York, NY; daughter of Willie J and Georgia C; divorced 1990. **Educ:** Princeton Univ, BA, 1981; Columbia Univ, MA, 1985. **Career:** Westside Repertory Theatre Group, actor, stage mgr, asst dir; Charles Alan Inc, 1981-83; Raoulfilm Inc, 1985-87; res & ed asst, 1987-88; Malcolm-King Col, eng instr, 1988-89; Col New Rochelle Sch New Resources, eng instr, 1989-90, 1996-; HARKline, newsline ed, 1989-90; Quarterly Black Rev Books, ed, 1994-95; freelance writer & auth, 1990-; auth: Rock of Ages A Tribute to the Black Church, 2001; American Patriots: The Story of Blacks in the Military from the Revolution to Desert Storm, 2003; Portraits of African-American Heroes, 2003; CHAKA! Through The Fire, 2003; Wake Up Our Souls, 2004; The Champ, The Story of Muhammad Ali, 2004; Maritcha A Nineteenth-Century American Girl, 2005. **Orgs:** New York Coun Humanities Speakers Bur. **Honors/Awds:** Book for the Teenage Award, New York Pub Libr, 1992; Book for the Teenage Award, New York Pub Libr, 1998; Best Book for Young Adults, Am Libr Asn, 1998; Book for the Teenage, New York Pub Libr, 1999; Certificate for the Advance Study Soviet Union, Harriman Inst.

BOLDEN, VERONICA MARIE
Labor relations manager, government official. **Personal:** Born May 19, 1952, Brooklyn, NY; daughter of Arthur Greene and Ruth Mae Greene; married Fred A Bolden Jr, Jun 17, 1995; children: Jamal C & Jeron A. **Educ:** New York City Col, AAS, 1972; Univ Rochester, BA, 1975; Univ Cincinnati, MEd, 1976. **Career:** Ohio Valley Goodwill Rehab, prog mgr & voc evaluator, 1976-78; Citizen's COM Youth, intake assessment specialist, 1978-81; Univ Cincinnati, coordr stud employ, 1981-89; Hamilton County Bd Ment Retardation, assoc dir personnel servs, 1989-. **Orgs:** Black Career Women, 1981-; Ohio State Rep Stud Employ Adminrs, 1986-89; Stud Employ Adminrs Nominations Comt Chap, 1986-87; mem-at-large, Midwest Asn Stud Employ Adminrs, 1986-87 & 1987-88; Midwest Asn Stud Employ Adminrs, 1987-88; Minority Concerns Chapter, 1987-89; Ohio Asn Sch Personnel Adminrs, 1989-; Int Asn Personnel Women, 1989-; North Avondale Montessori Sch, PTA Mem Chap, 1989-90; Ohio Asn Female Execs, 1990-; Ohio Asn County Bd Ment Retardation, 1990-; Shroder JHS, 1991-92. **Honors/Awds:** Dedicated Serv Award, Univ Cincinnati, 1986; Leadership Recognition Award, Midwest Asn Stud Employ Adminrs, 1988; Outstanding Young Men/Women Am, Jaycees, 1988; YMCA Black Achiever, 1990. **Special Achievements:** Article written and published in response to the Campus Advisor, Black Collegian Magazine, Sept/Oct 1988. **Business Addr:** Associate Director of Personnel Services, Hamilton County Board Of Mental Retardation, 4370 Malsbary Rd Suite 200, Cincinnati, OH 45242, **Business Phone:** (513)794-3300.

BOLDEN, WILEY SPEIGHTS
Educator. **Personal:** Born Dec 18, 1918, Birmingham, AL; son of Wiley Lee Jr and Gertrude Mildred Speights; married Willie Creagh Miller, Aug 13, 1945; children: Millicent Ann, Lisa B Monette, Lelia E Bolden, Wiley Miller, Madeliene Ann. **Educ:** Ala State Univ, BS, 1939; Atlanta Univ, 1941; Columbia Univ, Teachers Col, New York NY, MA, psycol serv, 1947, EdD, psycol serv, 1957. **Career:** Educator (retired); Shelby County Bd Educ, Montevallo AL, prin Almont Junior High, 1939-42; Mobile County Bd Educ, Mobile AL, teacher, 1943-44; Clark Col, Atlanta GA, assoc prof psychol, 1948-57, prof psychol & chmn dept educ & psychol, 1957-63, dean fac & instr, 1963-67; licensed psychologist, State Ga, 1962; Southeastern Reg Educ Lab, Atlanta GA, assoc dir res, 1967-69; Ga State Univ, Atlanta GA, prof educ founds, 1970-87; Ga State Univ, prof emer educ found, 1987; Savannah State Col, Savannah GA, actg pres, 1988-89; Morris Brown Col, Atlanta GA, actg vpres acad affairs, 1993-94. **Orgs:** Coordr res, Phelps-Stakes Fund, Cooperative Pre-freshman Prog, Atlanta Univ Ctr & Dillard Univ, 1959-63; study dir, Tuskegee Univ Role & Scope Study, Acad Educ Develop, 1969-70; consult, 1971-76, bd dirs, 1978-82, United Bd Col Develop; bd dir, 1971-73, co-chmn educ comt, 1980-82, Atlanta chapter Nat Asn Advan Colored People; Educ Task Force, Atlanta Chamber Com, 1972-76; Fulton County Grand Jurors Asn, 1973-76; vpres spec proj & assoc dir Title III, Advan Inst Develop Proj, Univ Assoc, 1975-77, univ assoc, bd dirs, 1977-83; pres, 1978-82, bd, 1978-90, pres, 1983-85, Southern Educ Found; Ga State Bd Examiners Psychologists; Gov Adv Comt Ment Health & Ment Retardation, 1980-83; adv comt educ & career develop, Nat Urban League, 1982-91; Am Psychol Asn; Southeastern Psychol Asn; fel, Am Asn State Psychol Bd. **Honors/Awds:** Salutatorian of graduating class, Ala State Univ, 1939; Gen Educ Bd fel clinical psychol, Teachers Col, Columbia Univ, 1953-54; Phi Delta Kappa; Kappa Delta Pi; Nat Sci Found sci fac fel, 1963-64; Roger C Smith Service Award, Am Asn State Psychol Bd, 1988; Black Georgian of the Year Award, The State Comt Life & History Black Georgians, 1989. **Military Serv:** AUS, 1944-46; received Good Conduct Medal, 1945. **Home Addr:** 975 Veltre Cir, Atlanta, GA 30311. *

BOLDRIDGE, GEORGE
Executive, sales manager. **Personal:** Born Apr 15, 1947, Atchison, KS; son of Adrian Sr and Decima; married Cynthia Davis Boldridge, Jun 5, 1971; children: Eva, Tamara. **Educ:** Benedictine Col, BA. **Career:** Hallmark Cards Inc, dist sales mgr, currently. *

BOLEN, DAVID B
Consultant, athlete, ambassador. **Personal:** Born Dec 23, 1927, Heflin, LA; married Betty L Gayden; children: Cynthia, Myra White & David B Jr. **Educ:** Nat War Col; Univ Colo, BS, MS, 1950; Harvard Univ, MPA, 1960. **Career:** Am Embassy, Monrovia, Liberia, admin asst, 1950-52, Karachi, Pakistan, econ asst, 1952-55, Accra, Ghana, chief econ sect, 1960-62; staff asst asst Secy State Africa, 1962-64; officer in charge, Nigerian affairs, 1964-66, Bonn, W Ger, econ counr, 1967-72, Belgrade, Yugoslavia, econ/com counr, 1972-74, ambassador, Botswana, Lesotho, & Swaziland, 1974-76, dep asst, Secry State Africa, 1976-77, E Berlin, E Germany, ambassador to German Dem Repub, 1977-80; US Dept State, int economist Japan-Korea desk, 1955-56, Afghanistan Desk Officer, 1957-59; E I Du Pont de Nemours & Co Inc, Wilmington, Del, assoc dir int affairs, 1981-89; consult, 1989-. **Orgs:** Foreign Serv Asn, 1950-; Nat War Col Alumni Asn, 1967-; Am Coun Germany, 1980-; vpres/dir, Wilmington World Affairs Coun, 1981-; dir, Wilmington Trust Co, 1981-; Wilmington Club, 1982-; Rodney Sq Club, 1983-; trustee, Univ Del, 1983-; dir, Urban Fund, S Africa, 1987-; Del Coun Econ Educ, 1987-; trustee, Med Ctr Del, 1987-. **Honors/Awds:** Fourth place winner, 400 Meters, Olympic Games, 1948; Robert S Russell Memorial Awards, 1948; Dave Bolen Olympic Award, Univ Colo, 1948; Hall of Honor, Univ Colorado, 1969; Norlin Distinguished Alumni Award, Univ Colo, 1969; Superior Honor Award for Outstanding & Imaginative Performance, Dept State, 1972-73; Department Commercial Certificate of Sustained Superior Performance, 1974; Alumnus of the Century Award, Univ Colo, 1977; Distinguished Alumni Service Award, Univ Colo, 1983; Athletic Hall of Fame, Colo Univ, 2000.

BOLLES, A LYNN
Anthropologist, college teacher. **Personal:** Born Dec 4, 1949, Passaic, NJ; daughter of George and Augusta Beebe; married James Walsh, Feb 9, 1980; children: Shane Bolles Walsh & Robeson James Walsh. **Educ:** Syracuse Univ, Syracuse, NY, AB, 1971; Rutgers Univ, New Brunswick, NJ, MA, 1978, PhD, 1981. **Career:** Rutgers Univ, Livingston Col, New Brunswick, NJ, lectr & teaching asst, 1976-78, course coordr, women's studies prog, 1977; Bowdoin Col, Brunswick, ME, from asst prof to assoc prof anthrop, 1980-89, dir, Afro-Am studies prog, 1980-89; Univ Md, assoc prof women's studies, 1989-95, prof women's studies & affil fac, 1995-, acting chmn, Dept African Am Studies, currently. **Orgs:** Pres, Asn Black Anthropologist, 1983-84, secy-treas, 1988-91; prog chair, Asn Feminist Anthropologists, 1989-92, pres, 1999-2001, 2001-03; bd dirs, Asn for Women in Develop, 1984-86; exec coun, Caribbean Studies Asn, 1992-95, pres, 1997-98; Am Ethnological Soc, counr, 1993-96; Latin Am Studies Asn; Asn Black Women Historians; ed bd, Feminist Studies; ed & adv bd, Urban Anthrop; Alpha Kappa Alpha, Iota Lambda Omega; fel, Am Anthropological Asn. **Honors/Awds:** Race Unity Day Award for Bowdoin Afro-Am studies prog, Spiritual Assembly Baha'is, 1983; Black History Maker of Maine Award, Augusta Black Community, 1984; Martin Luther King Jr, Community Service Award, ME NAACP, 1988; numerous res grants; Syracuse Univ, chancellor's citation for excellence in educ, 1989; Soc Appl Anthrop, fel; Univ Md, Col Pk, 'Outstanding Minority Faculty Member of the Year', 1994. **Home Addr:** 3104 Bold Ruler Ct, Bowie, MD 20721-1281. **Business Addr:** Professor, University of Maryland, Department of African American Studies, 2101 Woods Hall, College Park, MD 20742, **Business Phone:** (301)405-6877.

BOLLING, BARBARA
President (Organization). **Educ:** Kettering Univ, Flint, BA; Valparaiso Univ Sch Law, 1989. **Career:** NAACP, atty & pres, 2003-. **Business Addr:** Attorney, president, National Association for the Advancement of Colored People, 575 Broadway Suite 1A Gary, Gary, IN 46402, **Business Phone:** (219)886-2227.*

BOLLING, BRUCE C.
Executive, contractor. **Career:** MA Alliance Small Contractors Inc, exec dir, currrently. **Home Addr:** 64 Harold St, Roxbury, MA 02119. **Business Addr:** Executive Director, Massachusetts Alliance Small Contractors Inc, 143 South St 4th Fl, Boston, MA 02111, **Business Phone:** (617)482-8010.*

BOLLING, CAROL NICHOLSON
Manager, executive. **Personal:** Born Jan 28, 1952, Jamaica, NY; daughter of Paris Nicholson Jr and Miriam Nicholson; married Bruce, Jan 27, 1980. **Educ:** State Univ NY, BS, liberal arts, 1974. **Career:** The Gillette Co, group leader collections, 1976-78, group leader customer serv, 1978, asst supvr sales admin, 1978-80, supvr records mgt, 1980-81, personnel recruiter, 1981-83, affirmative action adr, 1983-84, sr personnel rep, 1984-86, credit mgr employee rels, 1986-87; WCVB-TV, human resources mgr, 1987-; WCVB-TV, community serv & human resource dir, currently. **Orgs:** Black Achievers Asn, 1984-86; Big Sisters Asn, 1985-88; bd mem, Robert F Kennedy Action Corp, 1987-89; Roxbury Comprehensive Health Ctr, 1987-89; Greater Boston YMCA, 1988-89; MSPCC, 1988-89; Advert Club Boston Charitable Trust Fund, 1988-; Endowment C Crisis, 1990-; bd mem, Coalition of 100 Black Women, 1991-; Greater Boston Broadcasters Minority Search Group, 1991-; bd mem, Vis Nurses Asn, 1992-. **Honors/Awds:** Young Leaders Award, Boston Jaycees, 1986; Black Achiever Award, YMCA, 1980. **Business Addr:** Director Community Services, Human Resource Manager, WCVB-TV, 5 TV Place, Boston, MA 02494, **Business Phone:** (781)449-0400.

BOLLING, DEBORAH A
Movie director, executive. **Personal:** Born Jun 18, 1957, New York, NY; daughter of David and Daisy Alston. **Educ:** State Univ NY, Old Westbury, BA, 1979. **Career:** Freelancer, video/filmmaker, currently. **Orgs:** Black Filmmakers Found, 1989-; Women Makes Movies, 1990-. **Honors/Awds:** Best Documentary, "Two Dollars and a Dream," Nat Asn Black Journalists, 1988; Production of the Decade, "Two Dollars and a Dream," Black Filmmaker Found, 1989; Award of Excellence, "Portraits in Black," CEBA, 1990. **Home Addr:** 2241 92nd St, East Elmhurst, NY 11369-1116.

BOLT, USAIN
Athlete. **Personal:** Born Aug 21, 1986; son of Jennifer Bolt and Wellesley Bolt. **Educ:** William Knibb Memorial High School. **Honors/Awds:** Won his first annual high school championship medal, silver in the 200 meters, 2001; CARIFTA games, silver medal, 400 meters, 2001; IAAF Rising Star Award, 2002; World Youth Championship, gold medal, 2003. **Special Achievements:** Set championship records in the 200 meters and 400 meters, CARIFTA games, 2002; youngest world-junior gold medalist, 2002; first junior sprinter to run the 200 meter in under 20 seconds, CARIFTA games, 2004; Osaka World Championships, silver medal, 2007; World championships, 200 m race won by the biggest margion in World championship history, 2009; named the Laureus World Sportsman of the Year, 2009. **Business Addr:** Pace Sports Management, 6 The Causeway Teddington, **Business Phone:** (44)208 943 1072.*

BOLTON, ALICE RUTH. See BOLTON-HOLIFIELD, RUTHIE.

BOLTON, JULIAN TAYLOR
Executive, lawyer, city commissioner. **Personal:** Born Oct 28, 1949, Memphis, TN; married Joyce Walker; children: Julian II & Jared Walker. **Educ:** Rhodes Col, BA, commun, 1971; Memphis State Univ, MA, theater, 1973; Univ Memphis, Sch Law, JD, 1992. **Career:** New Theatre S Ensemble, producer, dir; S Cent Bell, tech designer commun syst; Bell Syst, systs design cons, telecommun; LeMoyne Owen Col, assoc prof theater; Shelby Co, bd comnrs, 1982-, chmn; Richardson Law Firm; Cochran Firm, managing partner. **Orgs:** Producer, New Theatre S Ensemble, 1977-80; Memphis Black Arts Coun, 1981-; bd dir, Shelby Co Community Serv Admin, 1982-; review comn, Memphis Arts Coun, 1985; Nat Asn Co Offices; treas, Memphis Black Arts Alliance; bd mem, Midtown Mental Health Ctr; Ben Jones Chap, Nat Bar Asn; Memphis Bar Asn; Ind Develop Bd evaluation comt. **Honors/Awds:** Producer, Dir over 40 theatrical prods, 1968-80; Fellow Recipient consortium, Grad Study Bus Blacks, 1971; Black Stud Asn. **Business Addr:** Managing Partner, Shelby County, 160 N Main St Suite 619, Memphis, TN 38103, **Business Phone:** (901)545-4301.

BOLTON, LINDA BURNES
Association executive. **Educ:** Ariz State Univ, BS; Univ Calif, MA, nursing, MA, pub health, PhD, pub health; RN; DrPH; FAAN. **Career:** pub mem govt adv bds, staff nurse, clinical nurse specialist, health care exec, comm & pub health nurse, univ faculty & consult; Univ Calif, Los Angeles, fac mem; Univ Calif, San Francisco, fac mem; Cedars-Sinai Health Syst & Res Inst, vpres & chief nursing officer, currently. **Orgs:** Past pre, Nat Black Nurses

Asn; Nat Black Nurses Asn; AWA; bd dirs, Nat Black Nurses Found; Am Orgn Nurse Execs. **Honors/Awds:** Fel, Am Acad Nursing. **Business Phone:** (310)423-6252.*

BOLTON, TERRELL D.
Police chief. **Personal:** Born Sep 12, 1958, Mississippi. **Educ:** Jackson State Univ, BA, criminal justice; Fed Bur Invest Nat Acad, Quantico, Va, grad. **Career:** Dallas Police Dept, police patrol officer, 1980, asst chief, 1991, chief, 2001-03. **Orgs:** Jackson State Alumni Asn; Phi Beta Sigma Fraternity; Southwest Law Enforcement Inst Adv Bd; bd trustees, Major Cities Chiefs. **Honors/Awds:** 10-Year Safe Driving Award; 10-Year Perfect Attendance Award; Marksmanship Award; Police Commend Award; various Community Awards. **Special Achievements:** First African-American chief of Dallas Police Dept; first African American to head the Dallas Police Dept. **Home Addr:** Dallas, TX. *

BOLTON-HOLIFIELD, RUTHIE (ALICE RUTH BOLTON)
Basketball player, basketball coach. **Personal:** Born May 25, 1967, Lucedale, MS; daughter of Linwood Bolton and Leola Bolton; married Mark, 1991. **Educ:** Auburn, BA, exercise physiol, 1989. **Career:** Basketball player (retired), basketball coach; Visby (Sweden), guard, 1989-90; Tungstrum (Hungary), 1991-92; Erreti Faenza (Italy), 1992-95; Galatsaray (Turkey), 1996-97; Sacramento Monarchs, guard, 1997-2004, fan rels, 2005-; William Jessup Univ, head coach, 2004-. **Honors/Awds:** USA Basketball Female Player of the Year, 1991; Gold Medal, US Olympic Basketball Team, 1996; All-WNBA First Team, 1997; Gold Medal, US Olympic Basketball Team, 2000. **Military Serv:** AUS Res, first lt. **Business Addr:** Head Coach, William Jessup University, 333 Sunset Blvd, Rocklin, CA 95765, **Business Phone:** (916)577-2366.

BOMMER, MINNIE L.
Activist, executive. **Personal:** Born Feb 3, 1940, Covington, TN; daughter of Malcolm Yarbrough and Eula Ray Maclin Burrell; married John Samuel Sr, Dec 24, 1957; children: Monica, Gina, John Jr. **Educ:** Univ Tenn, educ, 1976; Tenn State Univ, attended 1982; Spelman Col, attended 1983; Univ Calif, Davis, rural leadership develop inst, 1989; Memphis State Univ, BPS, 1991; Antioch Univ, MA, 1993. **Career:** Tipton Cty Hosp, LPN, 1968-73; Tipton City Human Serv, elig counr, 1974-82; City Covington, alderwoman, 1983; Douglas Health Clin, maternal infant health outreach worker, 1985; C & Family Serv, exec dir, founder, currently. **Orgs:** Chmn, Tipton County Libr Bd, 1983-85; chmn, Rural W TN African Am Affairs Coun, 1985-; bd mem, Community Resource Group, 1985-91; bd dirs, Tipton County Chamber Com 1986-96; delegate, Nat Dem Conv, 1988; bd dirs, Tenn Housing Develop Agency, 1988-91; life mem, Nat Asn Advan Colored People, 1990; Nat Black Women's Political Caucus, TN Women in Govt; Dyensbung State Adv Comm Tenn rep, Lower Miss Delta Ctr, 1990-; Eight Cong Rep State Bd Educ, 1990-97. **Honors/Awds:** Mother of Yr, Canaan Church Group, 1976; Delegate to White House Cont on Families State & Nat; served on Resolution Advance Drafting Comn, Nat Asn Advan Colored People, 1985; Tenn Women on the Move, Tenn Political Caucus, 1987; Distinguished Serv Award, Tenn Black Caucus State Legis, 1988; Nat Vol, Thousand Point of Light, 1989; AKA Award for Outstanding Community Serv, 1994; TN Advocates for Children Pioneer Award, 1995; Un-Sung Hero Award, Memphis Peace & Justice Ctr, 1996; Mentie Buckman Empowerment Award, 1999; Rural Health Worker of the Yr, 2000; vpres, TN State Nat Asn Advan Colored People. **Special Achievements:** First Black and First Female to serve city of Covington, 1983. **Business Addr:** Founder, Children & Family Service Inc, 412 Alston St Naifeh Bldg, PO Box 845, Covington, TN 38019, **Business Phone:** (901)476-2364.*

BONAPARTE, LOIS ANN
Social worker. **Personal:** Born Mar 17, 1941, New York, NY; daughter of Randolph Graves and Floree Wilson; married Charles Bonaparte Jr (died 1976); children: C Scott Bonaparte. **Educ:** Social Welfare, Garden City, BSW, 1980; Social Work, Garden City, MSW, 1988. **Career:** Family Serv Asn, Hempstead, NY, social worker, 1973-79; Holly Patterson Geriatric Ctr, Uniondale, NY, dir sr citizen ctr, 1979-92; Sch Social Worker, 1994; Hempstead Pub Sch Dist, social worker, currently. **Orgs:** Nat Asn Social Workers, 1979-; NY State Conf Aging Inc, 1979-92; chairperson, Comt Commemoration African-Am Hist, 1984-92; rec corresp secy, Long Island Sr Citizen Dirs Asn, 1987-88; Adv coun mem, Ministry Black Catholics, 1989-; adv coun mem, St Anthony's Guid Coun, 1990-. **Honors/Awds:** Nominee, Dr Martin Luther King Jr Award, Nassau County, 1991; Ebony Vanguard Enrichment Award, Comt Commendation African-Am Hist. **Special Achievements:** Certified Social Worker, 1989; originated, produced, an annual African-American history program, 8 years, county-wide. **Home Addr:** 254 Long Beach Rd, Hempstead, NY 11550. **Business Addr:** Social Worker, Hempstead Public School District, 185 Peninsula Blvd, Hempstead, NY 11550.*

BONAPARTE, NORTON NATHANIEL
Educator, city manager. **Personal:** Born Apr 10, 1953, New York, NY; son of Norton N Sr and Beryl Grant; children: Akia & Nathaniel. **Educ:** Worcester Polytech Inst, BS, 1975; Cornell Univ, Ithaca, NY, MPA, 1977; George Mason Univ, Fairfax, VA, PhD, pub admin, 1986. **Career:** City Grand Rapids, MI, asst city mgr, 1977-81; Am Soc Pub Admin, dir prog develop, 1981-83; Inst Govt Servs, govt consult, 1984-87; E Coast Migrant Head Start Proj, asst dir, 1987-88; Auto Cleaning Ser, gen mgr & owner, 1988; Chief Admin Officer, MD, municipal corp, 1988-94; City Glenarden, city mgr, 1988-94; Township Willingboro, township mgr, 1995-2000; Officer NJ Municipal Corp, Philadelphia Metrop Area, chief exec, 1995-2000; NJ Municipal Corp, Philadelphia Metrop Area, chief admin officer, 2000-03; NJ Municipal Corp, chief admin officer, 2003; Nat-Louis Univ, McLean, VA, sr adjunt instructor; New Jersey, city adminr plainfield; New Jersey, city adminr Camden; New Jersey, township mgr Willingboro; Glenarden, MD, city mgr; City Topeka, city mgr & chief exec officer, currently. **Orgs:** Pres, City & Town Adminr Dept, Md Municipal League, 1991; pres, Md City & Co Mgt Asn, 1992; chair, Prof Municipal Mgt Joint Insurance Fund, 1998-2000; chair, NJ Environ Joint Insurance Fund, 1999-2000; bd dir, United Way Burlington Co, 1999; mem, Int City Mgt Asn; Nat Forum Black Pub Admins; bd dir, Burlington Co Red Cross Chap; bd mem & pres, NJ Municipal Mgt Asn. **Business Addr:** City Manager, Chief Executing Officer, City of Topeka, Rm 352 215 SE 7th, Topeka, KS 66603-3914, **Business Phone:** (785)368-3725.

BONAPARTE, DR. TONY HILLARY
School administrator, educator. **Personal:** Born Jun 13, 1939, Grenada, West Indies; son of Norman and Myra; married Sueli Fugita; children: Yvette. **Educ:** St John's Univ, BBA, 1963, MBA, 1964; NY Univ, PhD, 1967. **Career:** St John's Univ, asst prof, 1964-68; Bus Intl Corp, res assoc, mgt syst, 1968-70; Rapan Res Corp, exec dir, 1970-73; Pace Univ, vpres, dean, prof intl bus, 1968-85; Bentley Col, vpres acad affairs & provost; St John's Univ, provost, 1993-99; Univ Strathdyde Univ Edinburgh, Visiting Prof, 1977; St Thomas Aquinas Col, vice chmn bd trustees; Peter J Tobin Col Bus, prof; St John's Univ, spec asst to pres, currently. **Orgs:** Dir, Robert Schalkenbach Found, 1975-, World Trade Inst Port Arthur, 1977-, Brazil-Interpart Cabaatia Brazil, 1979-; pres, Middle Atlantic Assoc Bus Admin, 1981-82, Fulbright Alumni Assoc, 1983-84; chmn, Intl Affairs Comn Am Assembly, 1983-; dir, Assoc Black Charities, 1983-. **Honors/Awds:** Fellow, Am Asn Adv Sci, 1969; Fulbright Sr Prof Col Liberia, 1973-74; Co-ed book Peter Drucker Contribs Bus Enterprise, 1978; Honor, DHL Southeastern Univ. **Business Phone:** (718)990-2000.*

BOND, ALAN D.
Consultant. **Personal:** Born Jul 16, 1945, Jefferson City, TN; son of Frederick D (deceased) and Edna Coleman; children: Melinda Bond Shreve & Clayton Alan. **Educ:** Cent State Univ, BS, bus admin, 1967; post degree studies law, bus & financial planning. **Career:** Detroit Pub Sch, instr, part time; Ford Motor Co, prod planning & invention control specialist, 1968-69; Control Data Corp, mat supr, 1969-70; Xerox Corp, 1970-71; City Detroit, police dept, 1971-73; Chrysler Corp, prod systems & mat control specialist, 1973-75; Equitable Life Assurance Soc US & other Co, ins broker, 1975-; Detroit Edison Co, corpins & real estate admin, 1978-86; Estate Enhancements, ins & real estate consult, owner 1986-. **Orgs:** Alpha Phi Alpha Frat, 1963-; trustee, Sanctuary Fel Baptist Church, 1970-; mem, Nat Asn Life Underwriters, 1975-; mem, ife mem, NAACP 1984. **Honors/Awds:** Elected delegate Wayne Co Convention of Precinct Delegates, 1972-; Honorary Graduation National Sales Development Program, Xerox Corp, 1970; Practical Electric Passenger Car Prom Prog, 1982-83; numerous Pub Serv Recog Awds; Men of Achievement Director, Cambridge University of English; Ford Motor Community Service Award; Spirit Detroit Awardee. **Home Addr:** 3500 S Liddesdale St, Detroit, MI 48217. **Business Phone:** (313)383-8956.

BOND, CECIL WALTON
Businessperson, transport worker. **Personal:** Born Dec 30, 1937, Chester, PA; son of Frinjela P and Cecil W Sr; married Linette H, Oct 10, 1986; children: Tracy, Cecil III, Devon & Denzel. **Educ:** Morgan State Univ, BS; Wharton Grad Sch, mgt prog. **Career:** Cent Pa Nat Bank, vpres, 1970-80; Southeastern Pa Transp Authority, dir civil rights, asst gen mgr, revenue opers, 1994-96, asst gen mgr, safety & security, currently; Strategic Bus Develop, asst gen mgr, currently. **Orgs:** Urban Bankers Coalition; bd mem, Comt Accts; bd mem, Greater Philadelphia Comn Develop Corp; Greater Philadelphia Venture Capital Corp; Nat Forum Black Pub Adminr; Philadelphia Orchestra's Cult Diversity Initiative;Philadelphia Young Men Chrisitian Assn, Adult Reading Prog; chmn, Am Pub Transp Assn, Minority Affairs Comt. **Honors/Awds:** Minority Business Advocate Award, Greater Philadelphia Chamber Com, 1989. **Military Serv:** AUS Mil Police, capt, 1961-70. **Home Addr:** 169 Carlton Ave, Marlton, NJ 08053, **Home Phone:** (856)596-4715. **Business Addr:** Assistant General Manager, Southeastern Pennsylvania Transportation Authority, 1234 Market St, Philadelphia, PA 19107, **Business Phone:** (215)580-7800.

BOND, ELROY
Insurance executive. **Personal:** Born Mar 28, 1934, Brownsville, TX; son of Alex T and Lucy Davis; married Sylvia A Bond, Jul 16, 1960; children: Michael Keith, Kelly Michelle. **Educ:** Fisk Univ, BA, 1957. **Career:** Golden State Mutual Life, sr vpres. **Orgs:** Pres, Los Angeles Fisk Univ Alumni Asn. **Honors/Awds:** Man of the Yr, Los Angeles Alumni Assn, 1982-83. **Military Serv:** AUS, Sp-4, 1957-59. *

BOND, GEORGE CLEMENT
School administrator, educator. **Personal:** Born Nov 16, 1936, Knoxville, TN; son of Ruth Clement and J Max Bond; married Murray; children: Matthew, Rebecca, Jonathan & Sarah. **Educ:** Boston Univ, BA, 1959; London Univ, London Sch Econ, MA, 1961, PhD, 1968. **Career:** Univ E Anglia Eng, asst lectr, 1966-68; Columbia Univ, asst prof, 1969-74; Teachers Col, Columbia Univ, prof, 1975-, William F Russell prof anthrop & Educ, 2001-; Bond African Christianity Acad Press, ed, 1979; Social Stratification & Educ in Africa, ed, 1981; Woodrow Wilson Ctr Inter Scholars DC, fel, 1981-82; Sch Int & Pub Affairs, Inst African Studies,Columbia Univ, dir, 1988-99; Social Construction of the Past, ed, 1994; AIDS in Africa & the Carribbean, ed, W view, 1997; Witchcraft Dialogues, OH Univ Press, co-ed, 2001; contested Terrains & Constructed Categories,co-ed, W view, 2002. **Orgs:** Fel Soc Applied Anthrop; fel Am Anthropol Asn; Social Anthropologists, Great Britain & Common wealth; Coun Foreign Rels; Inst Advan Studies,Princeton, 1983-84; pres, Asn Africanist Anthrop, Am Anthrop Asn, 1994-97; Int African Inst, London, Eng, 1995-. **Special Achievements:** Books: The Politics of Change in a Zambian Community, Univ Chicago, 1976. **Home Addr:** 229 Larch Ave, Teaneck, NJ 07666, **Home Phone:** (201)836-8346. **Business Addr:** Professor, International & Transcultural Studies, Columbia University, Teachers College, Rm 375B Grace Dodge Hall 525 W 120th St, New York, NY 10027, **Business Phone:** (212)678-3311.

BOND, HOWARD H.
Business owner, executive. **Personal:** Born Jan 24, 1938, Stanford, KY; son of Edna G Coleman Bond and Frederick D Bond; married Ruby L Thomas, Jan 24, 1970; children: Sherman, Howard Jr, Anita Warr, John, James, Edward & Alicia. **Educ:** Eastern Mich Univ, Ypsilanti MI, BS, Econ and Polit Sci, 1965; Pace Univ, New York NY, MBA, 1974. **Career:** US Govt, Detroit, MI, 1959-65; Ford Motor Co, Detroit, MI, labor supvr, 1965-68, mgr labour rels, 2003; Gen Electric Co, personnel mgr, 1968-69; Xerox Corp, personnel dir, 1969-75; Playboy Enterprises Inc, vpres, 1975-77; Phoenix Exec tech Group, pres, managing dir & prin, 1977-, chief exec officer, currently; Ariel Capital Mgt Inc, corp dir, 1983-98; Bond Promotions & Apparel Co, chmn & chief exec officer, currently. **Orgs:** Planning bd, United Way; Cincinnati Bd Educ, 1988-91; Salvation Army; Red Cross; Urban League Greater Cincinnati; Trans africa; Kappa Alpha Psi; Aleikum Temple; Alpha Delta Boule; founder, 100 Black Men of Am, Inc, Cincinnati Chapter; life mem, NAACP. **Honors/Awds:** Developed/implemented Xerox AA/EEO Strategies for Excellence, 1969; Special Recognition, Crusade Mercy, 1976; Board Member of the Year, Lake County Urban League, 1976; Role Model, Cincinnati Friends of Amistad Inc, 1987; Black Business & Professional Award, Quinn Chapel AME Church, 1987; Achievers Award, Robert A Taft High Sch, 1988. **Military Serv:** AUS, sgt, 1953-58; Soldier of the Month, three times. **Home Addr:** 3900 Rose Hill Ave, Cincinnati, OH 45229. **Business Addr:** Chairman, Cheif Executive Officer, Bond Promotions & Apparel Co, 111 E 13th St, Cincinnati, OH 45202, **Business Phone:** (513)381-3711.

BOND, JAMES G.
Politician. **Personal:** Born Nov 11, 1944, Fort Valley, GA. **Career:** City Hall of Atlanta, politician, currently. **Orgs:** Chmn, Pub Safety Comt, 1977; bd dir, Atlanta Legal Aid; Atlanta City Coun, 1973; chmn, Com Atlanta City Coun, 1975-76; chmn, Labor Educ Advan Proj, 1974; bd resources, Highlander Ctr; adv bd, Nat Conf Alternative State & Local Pub Policies; Voter Educ Proj Fel 1973; S Eastern dir, Youth Citizenshp Fund 1972. **Business Addr:** Politician, City Hall Atlanta, Atlanta, GA 30303.*

BOND, JAMES MAX
Architect. **Personal:** Born Jul 17, 1935, Louisville, KY; son of J Max Bond Sr and Ruth Elizabeth Clement; married Jean Davis Carey; children: Carey Julian & Ruth Marian. **Educ:** Harvard Col, BA (magna cum laude), Phi Beta Kappa, 1955; Harvard Grad, Sch Design, 1958. **Career:** Ghana Nat Construct Corp, architect, 1964-65; Univ Sci & Technol, Ghana, instr, 1965-67; Architect's Renewal Comn, Harlem, exec dir, 1967-68; Bond Ryder James Archit PC, partner, 1969-90; Grad Sch Archit & Planning, Columbia Univ, from asst prof to prof & chmn, 1970-85; City Col/Calif Univ NY, Sch Environ Studies, dean & prof, 1985-91; Davis, Brody, Bond LLP Architects, partner, currently. **Orgs:** Comnr, NY Planning Comn, 1980-87; bd mem, Studio Museum, Harlem, 1984-; Municip Arts Soc, 1986-88; Nat Org Minority Architects; fel, Am Inst Architects, 1995; fel, Am Acad Arts & Scis, 1996; chmn, Nat Asn Advan Colored People. **Honors/Awds:** Award of Excellence, Atlanta Urban Design Comn Martin Luther King, Jr Ctr & Mem, 1982; Harry B Rutkins Memorial Award, AIA 1983; Whitney M Young Jr Citation Award, AIA, 1987; DHL, New Jersey Inst Technol, 1994; Architectural Achievement Award, Ernest D Davis Scholar Fund, 2002. **Special Achievements:** Architect for: 'Schomburg Center for Research in Black Culture, Harlem', NY, 1980; 'Martin Luther King Jr Center and Memorial', Atlanta, GA, 1981; 'Birmingham Civil Rights Institute', Birmingham AL, 1993;

'Audubon Research Center', Columbia Univ, NY, 1996, Nat Univ Sci & Technol, 'Master Plan and Design', Zimbabwe, 1999; Harvard Club, New York, NY (completion 2003); Muntu Dance Theatre, Chicago, Ill, (completion 2004). **Home Addr:** 434 W 162nd St, New York, NY 10032, **Home Phone:** (212)568-3776. **Business Addr:** Partner, Davis Brody Bond LLP, 315 Hudson St 9th Fl, New York, NY 10013, **Business Phone:** (212)633-4700.

BOND, JULIAN
Government official, educator. **Personal:** Born Jan 14, 1940, Nashville, TN; son of Horace Mann Bond and Julia Louise Washington; married Pamela Sue Horowitz; married Alice Clopton, 1990 (divorced); children: Phyllis Jane, Horace Mann Jr, Michael Julian, Jeffrey Alvin & Julia Louise. **Educ:** Morehouse Col, BA, 1971. **Career:** GA House & Senate, 1965-86; The Am Univ, distinguished prof, 1991-; Univ VA, Dept Hist, prof, 1990-; Harvard Univ, Dept Afro-Am Studies, vis prof, 1989; Drexel Univ, prof History & Polits, 1988-89; Am's Black Forum, syndicated tv news show, host & commentator, 1980-; Stud Nonviolent Coordinating Comn, 1960-65; Atlanta Inquirer, managing ed, 1964; Am Univ Wash, distinguished adj prof; Univ Va, Hist Dept, prof Hist civil rights movement, 1990-. **Orgs:** Pres, Atlanta Nat Asn Advan Colored People, 1974-89; Southern Poverty Law Ctr Bd; chmn, Nat Asn Advan Colored People, 1998-. **Honors/Awds:** Nat Freedom Award, 2002; Hon LLD, Bates Col. **Special Achievements:** Commentator on America's Black Forum, the oldest black-owned show in television syndication; poetry and articles have appeared in numerous publications; narrated numerous documentaries, including the Academy Award winning "A Time For Justice" and the prize-winning and critically acclaimed series "Eyes On The Prize". **Home Addr:** 5435 41st Pl NW, Washington, DC 20015. **Business Addr:** Distinguished Adjunct Professor, American University, 4400 Massachusetts Ave NW, Washington, DC 20016, **Business Phone:** (202)885-6221.

BOND, LESLIE FEE
Physician. **Personal:** Born Feb 20, 1928, Louisville, KY; married Anita; children: Leslie Jr, Erik, Candace. **Educ:** Univ Ill, BA, 1948; Meharry Med Col, MD, 1952; Am Col Surgeons. **Career:** Metro Med & Health Serv Inc, pres; Wash Univ, GI Endoscopy; asst clin surg; Homer G Phillips Hosp, fel, resident, intern, 1951-58; Kingshighway & New Halls Ferry Med Servs, Physician, currently. **Orgs:** Fel, Am Col & Surgeons; Int Col Surgeons; Soc Abdominal Surgeons; Am Med Asn; Nat Med Asn; St Louis Surg Soc; Mo Surg Soc; pres, Mound City Med Soc; Mo-Pan Med Soc; Homer G Phillips Int Alumni Asn; St Louis Med Soc Coun; secy, cheif staff Christian Hosp; Kappa Alpha Psi; Chi Delta Mu; Sigma Pi Phi; Frontiers Int; founder bd mem, Gateway Nat Bank St Louis, MO; chair mem, Cent Bapt Ch; team physician, Country Day HS Football Team; Page Park Young Men's Christian Asn Bd. **Honors/Awds:** Over 20 med articles publ. **Business Addr:** Physician, Kingshighway & New Halls Ferry Medical Services, 3400 N Kingshighway, St Louis, MO 63115.*

BOND, DR. LLOYD
Educator, scientist. **Personal:** Born Nov 17, 1941, Brownsville, TN. **Educ:** Hillsdale Col, BS, 1964; Johns Hopkins Univ, MA, 1975, PhD, psychol, 1976. **Career:** Gen Motors, personnel rep, 1966-72; Univ Pittsburgh, Dept Psych, asst prof, 1976-82, Learning R & D Ctr, assoc prof, sr scientist, 1982; Univ NC Greensboro, Educ Res Methodology, prof, 1988-2002; Carnegie Found Advan Teaching, sr scholar, currently. **Orgs:** Phi Beta Kappa, 1977; fel Am Psych Asn, 1982, 1990; Spencer fel, Nat Acad Educ, 1980-83; bd trustees, Col Bd, 1984-88, 1997-2001; NAS Comt Math Assessment, 1990-; NAE Panel State, Nat Assessment Educ Progress, 1990-; Am Psychological Asn, and the Am Educational Res Asn; sradv, Nat Bd Prof Teaching Stand, 1997-2002. **Military Serv:** AUS, sgt, 1965-67. **Business Addr:** Senior Consulting Scholar, Carnegie Foundation for the Advancement of Teaching, Higher Education Programs, 51 Vista Lane, Stanford, CA 94305, **Business Phone:** (650)566-5175.

BOND, DR. LOUIS GRANT
Educator. **Personal:** Born Jan 6, 1947, Baltimore, MD; children: Jordan & Meredith. **Educ:** Boston Univ, BA, 1958; Harvard Univ, MTS, 1972; Boston Col, MEd, EdD, 1974; Western Univ, CA, PhD, 1977. **Career:** Boston Univ, lectr, instr, 1969-; Educ Develop Social Studies, dir, parent educ, teacher trainer, curriculum developer, 1972-74; St Andres United Meth Church, pastor, 1973-; J LU-ROB Enterprises Inc, pres; B&R Corrugated Container Corp & B&R World Oil, pres, chmn bd. **Orgs:** Black Meth Church Renewal; Nat Asn Black Sch Admins; Am Asn Jr & Community Cols; Asn Black Psychologist; Am Asn Gen Liberal Studies; Phi Beta Kappa, Harvard Univ Fac Club, NAACP; Comt Chairpersons; GDCA Nat Specialty, currently. **Honors/Awds:** Wm H Lemell Scholarship, 1964; Martin Luther King Jr Grant, 1970;Rockefeller Found Award, 1972; Fulbright Scholarship, 1973; Hatcher Scholarship, 1974. *

BOND, MAX, JR.
Business owner, architect. **Career:** Davis Brody Bond LLP, partner & owner, currently. **Business Addr:** Partner, Owner, Davis Brody Bond LLP, 315 Hudson St 3rd Fl, New York, NY 10013, **Business Phone:** (212)633-4700.*

BOND, MICHAEL JULIAN
Government official. **Personal:** Born 1966; son of Alice Clopton and Julian. **Educ:** Morehouse Col; Ga State Univ. **Career:** Atlanta City Council, councilman, pres, 1994-. **Orgs:** St James Lodge No 4, Prince Hall affiliate; Empowerment Bd; GABEO; Ga Municipal Asn, Atlanta NAACP; bd, Ollie St, SE & E Lake YMCAs, Atlanta Empowerment Zone; chm Bd, Laffapoolooza, youth mentoring orgn; Leadership Atlanta & Black-Jewish Coalition's Proj Understanding; Dep Dir & Chief Prog Off, Atlanta Nat Asn Advan Colored People; Am Fed State, County & Municipal Employees. **Special Achievements:** Fulfilled the City's 30 year old promise to rebuild the historic Washington Park Natatorium. **Business Phone:** (404)330-6046.

BOND, NORM. See BOND, NORMAN.

BOND, NORMAN (NORM BOND)
Business owner. **Educ:** Univ Pittsburgh, BD, bus & econs, 1986, MD, info sci. **Career:** Next Step Enterprises Inc, co-founder, publ, chief exec officer, 2000-. **Honors/Awds:** Numerous community service recognition form varoius organizations including Inroads, Black Women Publ, Granville Acad Nat & Lincoln Univ; quoted in Nat publications including Chicago Tribune, USA Today, Philadelphia Inquirer, Black Enterprise & Business Week. **Business Addr:** Chief Executive Officer, Next Step Enterprises Inc, 4548 Market St, Enterprise Ctr, Philadelphia, PA 19104, **Business Phone:** (215)387-2387.

BOND, RONALD A
Educator, manager. **Personal:** Born Nov 24, 1938, Chester, PA; son of Cecil W Bond and Frinjela Powell Bond; married Sonja, Oct 20, 1962; children: Ronald Jr & Lisa. **Educ:** Temple Univ, BS, 1963, MEd, 1970, ABD, 1994. **Career:** Philadelphia Pub Schs, teacher, 1964-70; Univ PA, Dept Recreation, dir, 1970-83; City Philadelphia, dep recreation comnr, stadium mgr, 1984-92; Temple Univ, guest lectr, 1987, 1989, 2000; CA State Univ-Fulleron, assoc athletic dir, sports & phys performance complex, dir, 1994-99, guest lectr, 1996, 1998; DE River Port Authority, proj mgr, 1999. **Orgs:** Life mem, Alpha Phi Alpha, 1960-; life mem, Nat Asn Advan Colored People; pres, Friars Sr Alumni Bd, Univ PA, 1984-86; Phys Ed, Recreation & Dance, Alumni Bd, Col Health, Temple Univ, 1990-94; pres, African-Am Fac Staff Asn, CA State Univ-Fullerton, 1994-99; USTA-Middle States Col Tennis Comt & multicultural participation comt, 1996-99; bd or dir, Am Heart Asn S CA, 1995-99; Hope Int Univ President's Forum, 1997-99, Nat Asn Black Pub Adminrs. **Honors/Awds:** Community Serv Award, W Philadelphia Chamber Com; Community Serv Award, Philadelphia Touch Football League; Community Service Award, Philadelphia Oldtimers Basketball League; Service Award, African-Am Fac Staff, CA State Univ-Fullerton, 1996, 1997. **Special Achievements:** Lobbied US Cong funding Nat Youth Sports Prog, 1978-79.

BOND, VERNON
Educator. **Personal:** Born Nov 15, 1951, Windsor, NC; son of Vernon and Sadie; married Johnetta Bond, Sep 7, 1978; children: Maya, Jennifer & Vernon III. **Educ:** St Augustine's Col, Raleigh, BS, 1974; NC Cent Univ, Durham, MS, 1976; Univ Tenn, Knoxville, EdD, 1979. **Career:** NC Cent Univ, assoc prof, 1979-80; Howard Univ, asst prof, 1980-85 & 1991-93, Dept Health Human Performance & Leisure Studies, prof exercise physiol, 1996-, Natural Scis Div, chair, 2001-02; Univ Tenn, assoc prof, 1989-90; La State Univ, assoc prof, 1993-94; Univ Md, assoc prof, 1993-96. **Orgs:** Fel Am Col & Sports Med, 1980-. **Special Achievements:** Co-Author: "Effects of small and moderate doses of alcohol on submaximal cardiorespiratory function, perceived exertion, and endurance performance in abstainers and moderate drinkers", Journals of Sports Medicine and Physical Fitness, vol 23 pgs 221-228, 1983; "Strength comparisons in untrained men and trained womeny body builders," Journals of Sports Medicine and Physical Fitness, vol 25: (3), pgs 131-134, 1985; "The effect of hand weights on the cardiorespiratory and metabolic response to treadmill running exercises," Australian Journal of Science and Medicine in Sports, vol 19, 23-25, 1987; "Effects of dietary fish oil or pectin on blood pressure and lipid metabolism in the DOCA-Salt hypertensice rat," Journal of Nutrition, vol 119: (5), pgs 813-817, 1989; "Exercise blood pressure and skeletal muscle vasodilator capacity in normotensives with a positive and negative family history of hypertension," Journal of Hypertension, col 12 pgs 285-290, 1994; written chapters "Muscular Strength and Endurance", "Exercise Prescription for Strength, Endurance, and Bone Density," in Health Fitness Instructor's Handbook, 3rd ed, Human Kinetics,Champaign, IL, 1997. **Home Addr:** 10905 Battersea Ct, Fort Washington, MD 20744. **Business Addr:** Professor of Exercise Physiology, Howard University, Department Health, Human Performance & Leisure Studies, Rm G-240 Burr Gymnasium 6th & Girard St NW, Washington, DC 20059, **Business Phone:** (202)806-6327.

BOND, WILBERT. See Obituaries section.

BONDS, BARRY LAMAR
Baseball player, baseball executive. **Personal:** Born Jul 24, 1964, Riverside, CA; son of Bobby and Patricia Howard; married Sun (divorced 1995); children: Nikolai & Shikari; married Liz Watson; children: Aisha. **Educ:** Ariz State Univ, Temple, BA, criminol, 1986. **Career:** Baseball Player (retired), baseball executive; Pittsburgh Pirates, outfielder, 1986-92; San Francisco Giants, 1993-2007; free agent, currently. **Honors/Awds:** Nat League Most Valuable Player, Baseball Writers Asn Am, 1990, 1992,1993, 2001, 2002, 2003, 2004; NL Gold Glove, 1990-94, 1996-98; NL All-Star Team, 1990, 1992-98, 2000-04, 2007; Silver Slugger Award, 1990-94, 1996-97, 2000-04; Jim Thorpe Pro Sports Award, 1993; AP Male Athlete of the Year, 2001; Hank Aaron Award, 2001-02, 2004. **Special Achievements:** First pro player to achieve 500 homers, 500 steals, 2003. **Business Addr:** Free Agent, Beverly Hills, CA 90212.

BONDS, KATHLEEN
College administrator. **Educ:** State Univ NY, Buffalo, BS, criminal justice; State Univ New York, Fredonia, MS, human resource mgt. **Career:** St Ann's Ctr, adminr; Community Action Orgn Erie County, adminr; State Univ New York Fredonia, Educ Develop Prog, counr, dir, 1992-2008. **Honors/Awds:** Exemplary Service Award, Fredonia Col, 2008.

BONDS, KEVIN GREGG
Executive. **Personal:** Born Mar 3, 1961, Lansing, MI; son of Solomon Jr and Anita Taylor. **Educ:** Community Col Air Force, AAS, 1990; Nat Univ, BBA, 1990. **Career:** USAF, personnel technician, 1981-90; Wis Physician's Serv, claims supvr, 1990-91; Wis Dept Develop, fiscal opers mgr. **Orgs:** Comnr, Affirmative Action Comn, 1992-, bd supvr, 1994-, Personnel/Finance Comt, supvr, 1994-, Housing Authority, comnr, 1994-; treas, So Madison Neighborhood Ctr, 1993-94; treas, African Am Ethnic Acad Inc, 1993-; treas, Wis Community Fund, 1994-; Dane Co Exec Off. **Honors/Awds:** America's Best & Brightest, Dollar's & Sense Mag, 1993; Outstanding African-American Role Model, Mother's Simpson St, 1994. **Special Achievements:** Depicting African-American History & Sites, 1995. **Military Serv:** USAF, staff sgt, 1981-90; Outstanding Airmen, 1983; Commendation Medal, 1985; Meritorious Medal, 1990. **Home Addr:** 1002 E Sunnyvale Lane, Madison, WI 53713.

BONDS STAPLES, GRACIE
Journalist. **Personal:** Born Oct 27, 1957, McComb, MS; daughter of Sula and Freddie Felder; married Jimmy, Dec 21, 1985; children: Jamila Felder & Asha Dianne. **Educ:** Southwest Miss Jr Col, Summit, MS, AA, 1977; Univ Southern Miss, Hattiesburg, MS, BA, 1979. **Career:** Enterprise-Jour, McComb, MS, 1979-80; Delta Democrat-Times, Greenville, MS, 1980-82; Raleigh Times, Raleigh, NC, reporter, 1983-84; Sacramento Bee, Sacramento, CA, reporter, 1984-90; Fort Worth Star-Telegram, Fort Worth, TX, reporter, 1990; Atlanta J-Const, reporter, currently. **Orgs:** Nat Asn Black Journalists, 1980-. **Honors/Awds:** Maggie Award, Planned Parenthood Sacramento Valley, 1986; Calif Educ Writers Asn Award, 1988; Cert Merit, Am Bar Asn, 1993; Black Image Award, Kappa Alpha Psi Fraternity, 1995; YMCA Minority Achiever, 1997; Frederick Douglas Award for Jour, Nat Asn Advan Colored People, 1997. **Special Achievements:** Award named in his honor: The Gracie Bonds Staples Community Organizer Award. **Business Addr:** Reporter, Atlanta Journal-Constitution, 72 Marietta St NW, PO Box 4689, Atlanta, GA 30303, **Business Phone:** (770)263-3621.

BONDY, KIM
Vice president (Organization), executive. **Educ:** Univ New Orleans, BA, 1988. **Career:** CNN, vpres, sr exec producer in-charge & gen mgr, 2004-. **Business Phone:** (404)827-1500.

BONE, WINSTON S.
Clergy. **Personal:** Born Apr 7, 1932, New Amsterdam, Guyana; married Faye Alma O'Bryan; children: Alma Lorraine Bone Constable, Brian Winston. **Educ:** InterAm Univ PR, BA, summa cum laude, 1958; Waterloo Luth Sem, grad, attended 1961. **Career:** Clergy (retired); Ebenezer Luth Church New Amsterdam Guyana, pastor, 1961-66; Luth Church Guyana, pres, 1966; Christ Luth Church Brooklyn, pastor, 1966-68; Incarnation Luth Church Queens, pastor, 1968-73; Met New York Synod Evangelical Luth Church Am, asst bishop, beginning 1973. **Orgs:** Chmn, Admin Coun Luth Church Guyana, 1965-66; bd trustees, Wagner Col Staten Island NY, 1969; bd dir, Luth Theol Sem Gettysburg, 1977-; chmn, S Queens Luth Parish, 1970-73; bd dir, Seamen & Int House NY, 1970-73; Mgt Com Div Prof Leadership, 1972-80. *

BONES, RICKY
Baseball player, athletic coach. **Personal:** Born Apr 7, 1969, Salinas, Puerto Rico. **Career:** Baseball player (retired), coach; San Diego Padres, 1991; Milwaukee Brewers, 1992-96; NY Yankees, 1996; Kans City Royals, 1997-98; Cincinnati Reds, 1997; Baltimore Orioles, 1999; Fla Marlins, 2000-01; Los Angeles Dodgers, 2001; Binghamton Mets, pitching coach, currently. **Honors/Awds:** Am League All-Star Team, 1994. **Business Addr:** Pitching Coach, Binghamton Mets, 211 Henry St, PO Box 598, Binghamton, NY 13901, **Business Phone:** (607)723-6387.

BONHAM, VENCE L
Lawyer, biotechnologist. **Educ:** Michigan State Univ, James Madison Col, E Lansing, MI, BA, honors), post graduate studies, 1979; Ohio State Univ, Columbus, OH, JD, 1982. **Career:** US Dist Ct Southern Dist Ohio, Columbus, OH, student judicial clerk,

1981-82; UAW Legal Serv Plan, Lansing, MI, staff atty, 1983-84; Eastern Mich Univ, Ypsilanti, MI, human resources assoc, 1984-85, univ atty, 1984-87; Mich State Univ, East Lansing, MI, asst gen coun, 1987-89, assoc gen coun, 1989-; Nat Human Genome Res Inst, chief, Educ & Community Involvement Br, assoc investr, Social & Behavioral Res Br, currently, NHGRI Edu & Community Involvement Branch, currently, sr advisor Dir on Societal Implications Genomics Nat Inst Health, currently. **Orgs:** Bd mem, Nat Asn Col & Univ Attys; The Mich Minority Health Adv Comt, 1990-92; Mich State Bar; Nat Health Lawyers Asn; Am Soc Law & Med; Am Bar Asn; Mich Soc Hosp Lawyers; Phi Delta Kappa Fraternity; Detroit Area Hosp Counsels Group; bd mem, Impressions 5 Mich Sci Mus; bd mem, Lansing Area Boys & Girls Club. **Special Achievements:** Author of: "Liability Issues Concerning Faculty and Staff: Academic Advising and Defamation in Context of Academic Evaluation," Am I Liable?: Faculty, Staff and Institutional Liability in the College and University Setting, 1989; "Health Law Update," Journal of the College of Human Medicine, 1990-. **Business Addr:** Chief, Associate Investigator, Senior Advisor, Director, National Human Genome Research Institute, Bldg 31 Rm B1B55, 31 Center Dr MSC 2070, Bethesda, MD 20892-2070, **Business Phone:** (301)594-3973.

BONILLA, BOBBY
Baseball player, baseball executive. **Personal:** Born Feb 23, 1963, Bronx, NY; son of Roberto and Regina; married Migdalia. **Career:** Baseball player (retired), baseball executive; Chicago White Sox, infielder, 1986; Pittsburgh Pirates, infielder & outfielder, 1986-91; NY Mets, 1992-95, 1999; Baltimore Orioles, 1995-96; Fla Marlins, 1997-98; Los Angeles Dodgers, 1998; Atlanta Braves, 2000; St Louis Cardinals, 2001; Maj League Baseball, union rep, MLB Players Asn, spec asst exec dir, currently. **Special Achievements:** Film appearance: Rookie of the Year, 1993; "New York Undercover," 1994. **Business Phone:** (212)826-0808.

BONNER, ALICE A.
Judge, lawyer. **Personal:** Born Apr 11, 1941, New Orleans, LA; married Al; children: Yvonne, Bernard, Lamont. **Educ:** Tex Southern Univ, BA, 1963, JD, 1966; Nat Col Judiciary; Am Acad Judiciary Educ. **Career:** Law Firm Bonner & Bonner, family law specialist, 1967-77; Munic Ct Houston, judge, 1974-77; Co Criminal Ct, Law 6, judge, 1977-78; 80th Civil Dist Ct, State Tex, judge, 1978-. **Orgs:** State Bd Specialization, 1975; State Dem Conv, 1974; mem bd govs, Nat Bar Asn, 1974-77; Founder & actg pres, Black Women Lawyers Asn, 1975; bd mem, Judicial Coun Nat Bar Asn, 1975-76; bd mem, Houston Lawyers Asn, 1978; Comt Indigent, State Bar, TX, 1980; life mem, Nat Asn Negro Bus & Prof Women Inc; Phi Alpha Delta Legal Fraternity; Baptist Sister head, TX; City Wide Beauticians Houston; Nat Coun Negro Women; Blue Triangle Br, YWCA; Women Achievemnets; Eta Phi Beta Bus & Prof Sorority; Nat Asn Advan Colored People; coordr, Nat Coun Negro Women; Nat Med Asn; Nat Immunization Prog. **Honors/Awds:** American Juris Prudence Award, Wills & Decedents Estates & Family Law, Tex Southern Univ, 1966; Attorney of the Year, Tom Kato Models, 1974; Bethune Achiever, Nat Coun Negro Women, 1975; Founders Award, Black Women Lawyers, 1978; Outstanding Service, Mainland Br, Nat Asn Advan Colored People, 1979; Black Women Lawyers Achievement Award, 1979. **Special Achievements:** First Black Woman Judge Houston & Harris Co, TX; First Black Civil Dist Ct, TX; First Black Woman to win a country-wide election Harris Co TX succeeded to Co Criminal Ct Dem Primary 1978; Cited Most Influential Black Woman in Houston Focus Mag, 1978. **Business Addr:** 80th Civil Dist Ct, 301 Fannin St Rm 212 A, Houston, TX 77002, **Business Phone:** (404)730-4166.

BONNER, ALICE CAROL
Journalist, foundation executive, educator. **Personal:** Born Dec 24, 1948, Dinwiddie, VA; daughter of James R and Doletha Edwards; married Leon Dash Jr (divorced 1982); children: Destiny Kloi. **Educ:** Howard Univ, Wash, DC, BA, 1971; Columbia Univ, New York, NY, cert, 1972; Harvard Univ, Cambridge, MA; Univ NC, Phd, sch jour mass commun, 1999. **Career:** Wash Post, DC, reporter, ed, 1970-85; Nieman fel, 1977-78; USA Today, Arlington, VA, ed, 1985-86; Gannett Co Inc, Arlington, VA, jour recruiter, 1986-89; Gannett Found, Arlington, VA, dir educ progs, 1990-; Univ Southern Calif, lectr, 2000-01; Freedom Forum, former dir, educ jour; Univ Md, Philip Merrill Col Jour, lectr, 2001-. **Orgs:** Nat Asn Black Jours, 1980-; bd mem, Community Hope, 1986-; Asn Educ Jour & Mass Commun, 1986-; summer prog dir, Inst Jour Educ, 1986; bd mem, Youth Commun, 1990-. **Home Addr:** 3800 Powell Lane, Falls Church, VA 22041. **Business Addr:** Lecturer, University of Maryland, Philip Merrill College of Journalism, 1117 Journ Bldg, College Park, MD 20742-7111, **Business Phone:** (301)405-7106.

BONNER, ANTHONY
Basketball player, basketball coach. **Personal:** Born Jun 8, 1968, St Louis, MO. **Educ:** St Louis Univ, attended 1990. **Career:** Basketball player (retired), coach; NBA, Sacramento Kings, 1990-93; NBA, NY Knicks, 1993-95; NBA, Orlando Magic, 1995-96; FIBA Europe, Paok Thessaloniki Bc, 1997; Unics, Kazan, Russia, 2001-02; NBA, Utah Jazz, 2002-03; PAOK BC, Greece; Virtus Bologna Italy; Vashon High Sch, St Louis, coach, currently. **Honors/Awds:** Mr. Show-Me Basketball, 1986.

BONNER, DELLA M.
Educator, college teacher. **Personal:** Born Nov 25, 1929, Red Oak, IA; married Arnett Jackson. **Educ:** Omaha Univ, BS, 1961; Univ NE, Omaha, MS, 1969. **Career:** Professor (retired); Omaha Pub Sch, teacher, 1962-68; Greater Omaha Comm Action Inc, dir, 1968-70; Creighton Univ, instr, 1970-73, asst prof educ,1973-90. **Orgs:** Bd dir, Urban League NE, 1964-72; secy, Scholar Comn; bd dir, Eastern NEMental Health Asn, 1969-74; exec comt, Vol Bur United Community Serv, 1969-71; charter pres, Omaha Chap Jack & Jill Am Inc, 1970-71; evaluator, Omaha Pub Sch, Self-Study Sr High Sch, 1970; fac adv, Col Arts & Sci,1970; coun & guid, Jr High Sch, 1971; spec adv comt mem, NE Educ TV Comn, 1971-72; chair, Human Rights Comn, NE Personnel & Guid Asn, 1972-74; Univ Comnunity Status Women, 1972-75; bd trustees, Joint Conf Comt, 1973-74; Task Force Resident Hall Life, 1973-75; vpres, Girls Club Omaha Bd,1973-77; Omaha Home Girls Study Comn, UCS, 1974; vice chair, US Dist Court, Judges 10-mem Interracial Comt, 1975-76; Phi Delta Kappa, 1976-90; educ rep, Boys Town Urban Prog Adv Bd, 1980-; chair, Nat Coun Accreditation Teacher Educ, 1984; chair, Educ Task Force; chair, Nat Trends & Serv Comn, Omaha Chap Links Inc. **Honors/Awds:** Nominee Woman of Year, Omaha Women's Polit Caucus Bus & Prof Category, 1974; Distinguished Fac Serv Award, Creighton Univ, 1991; Cand Outstanding Young Educator Award. *

BONNER, HARRY J
Administrator. **Career:** Minority Prog Servs, exec dir, currently.

BONNER, DR. MARY WINSTEAD
Educator, college teacher. **Personal:** Born Apr 20, 1924, Nash County, NC; daughter of Charles Edward Winstead and Mason Ann Whitted; married Thomas E, Aug 9, 1956. **Educ:** St Pauls Col, BS, 1946, LhD, 1979; VA State Univ, MS, 1952; NY Univ, attended 1967; Southern Univ, attended 1954; OK State Univ, EdD, 1968; Univ Calif, Berkeley, attended 1974; Instde Fililogia Satillo Mexico, attended 1984. **Career:** Greensville Co, VA, instr, 1946-52; Southern Univ, instr, 1952-57; StLouis Pub Schs, instr, 1957-64; Emporia State Univ, Dept Ed, Butcher CSch, 1964-86, prof emer, 1986-; OK St Univ, grad asst, 1965-66; Univ SC, vis prof, 1968; Norfolk St Col, vis prof, 1971-73. **Orgs:** Sigma Gamma Rho; Am Asn Univ Women; Nat Coun Negro Women; Nat Spanish HonSoc; Sigma Delta Pi, 1979; Int Platform Asn; Panel Am Women; KS Childrens Serv League; Retired Teachers Asn; asst dir, Dist coord, 1989-90; Ed State Newsletter, 1991- 92; Hosp Auxiliaries Kans; secy, Emporia Retired Teachers Asn, 1988-89; bd dirs, Societas Docta; Lycon co Bd Corrections,1990-91; Lyon Co Planning; Emporia State Univ Fac Senate, Kans Stand Comm; Emporia Human Rels Comm, vol mentor, 2001. **Honors/Awds:** Hall of Fame Sigma Gamma Rho; Certificate of Achievement in Spanish,Emporia State Univ, 1978; Outstanding Aluma, St Pauls Col, 1979, 1984; Unsung Heroine Award, Nat Asn Advan Coloured People, 1988; RuthSchillinger Faculty Award, 1998; Presidential Leadership in Diversity Award, Emporia State Univ, 2000. **Special Achievements:** Emporia State Univ second Afro Am Fac. **Home Addr:** 2314 Sunset lake Dr, Emporia, KS 66801-6636. **Business Addr:** Professor Emeritus, Emporia State University, 1200 Commercial St, Emporia, KS 66801, **Business Phone:** (620)341-1200.*

BONNER, ROBERT
Educator. **Career:** Hampton Univ, dean pure & appl sci, prof emer, 2002. **Business Phone:** (757)727-5328.*

BONTEMPS, JACQUELINE MARIE FONVIELLE
Educator, humanist. **Personal:** Born in Savannah, GA; daughter of William Earl and Mattie Louise Davis; married Arna Alexander, Jul 5, 1969; children: Traci, Arna & Fanon. **Educ:** Fisk Univ, BA, 1964, MA, 1971; Ill State Univ, EdD, 1976. **Career:** Lane Col, chairperson, 1966-68; Jackson Parks & Recreation, supvr, 1968; SSide Community Ctr, dir, 1969; Fisk Univ, Dept Art, admin asst, 1971; Tenn State Univ, Dept Art, instr, 1972-73; Univ Tenn, Dept Art, instr, 1972-73,lectr, 1973; Ill State Univ, Col Fine Arts, asst to dir, 1975-76, adminasst, 1976-77, asst prof art, 1976-78, assoc prof art, 1978-84; Hampton Univ, dept chairperson, Div Arts & Humanities, assoc prof, currently. **Orgs:** Trustee, Am Asn Mus; Am Asn Higher Educ; Am Coun Arts; Am Film Inst; Am Asn Univ Profs; Asn Teacher Educrs; comm mem, Int Coun Mus; Nat Coun Black Studies; Delta Sigma Theta; Phi Delta Kappa; nat arts res specialist,1978-86, dir arts, 1982-84, nat secy, 1988-90, Links; Coun Arts Adminrs VaHigher Educ, 1984-89; nat blue ribbon panel mem, Inaugural Nat Blacks Art Festival, 1987-88; bd dirs, Cult Alliance Greater Hampton Roads, 1987-91; Girl Scout Coun of Colonial Coast, 2009. **Honors/Awds:** Pacesetter Award, Ill Bd Educ, 1981; Certificate of Special Participation for community efforts, Ill State Univ, 1982; Honoree, Women in the Arts,Va Nat Orgn Women, 1986. **Special Achievements:** First African American female to receive a Doctorate of Education from Illinois State University, Normal, Illinois, curator and director of exhibit, Forever Free: Art by African-American Women, 1862-1980, 1981-82, selected as one of America's Top 100 Black Business & Professional Women, Dollars and Sense Mag, 1986, curator and director of exhibit, Choosing: An Exhibit of Changing Perspectives in Modern Art & Art Criticism by Black Americans, 1925-85, 1986-87. **Home Addr:** 1 Johnson Ct, Hampton, VA 23669. **Business Addr:** Associate Professor, Hampton University, Division of Art & Humanities, 533 E Queen St, Hampton, VA 23668-0101.

BOOKER, ANNE M
Public relations executive. **Personal:** Born in Spartanburg, SC; daughter of Claude C and Tallulah Jane Tanner. **Educ:** Mich State Univ, attended 1973, attended 1986. **Career:** Ford Motor Co, electronic media specialist, 1977-78, corp news rep, 1978-82, publ ed, 1982-84, sr producer, 1984-86, pub affairs assoc, 1986-88; asst mgr, 1988, regional commun mgr, currently. **Orgs:** Pub Rels Soc Am, 1978-; St Philip AME, Atlanta; Am Women Radio-TV; Press Club, 1978-; Women Commun, 1978-; Nat Black MBA Asn, 1983-; life mem, NAACP. **Honors/Awds:** Achiever in Industry, YMCA Detroit; Aftra Golden Mike Award; Kappa Tau Alpha Grad Journalism Honor Soc. **Home Phone:** (770)593-8597. **Business Addr:** Regional Communications Manager, Ford Motor Company, SE Region Public Affairs, 245 Peachtree Ctr Suite 2204, Atlanta, GA 30303, **Business Phone:** (404)577-2277.

BOOKER, CARL GRANGER, SR.
Government official, firefighter. **Personal:** Born Aug 16, 1928, Brooklyn, NY; married Jacqueline Mayo; children: Carl G Jr, Adele Williams, Wendy. **Educ:** Hampton Inst Univ, attended 1950; Springfield Community Col, MA, 1977; US Fire Acad, MD, 1979, 1980, 1982; Dartmouth, Yale, Quinsingamond Community Col. **Career:** City Hartford Conn Fire Dept, firefighter, 1958-66, driver-pump oper, 1966-67, fire prev inspector, 1967-68, fire prev lieutanant, 1969-79, fire prev capt/dep fire marshal, 1979-81, actg fire marshal, 1981-82, app fire marshal & fire prev chief, 1982-. **Orgs:** Bd dir & pres, Child Guid Clinic, 1972-74; pres, Phoenix Soc Firefighters, 1972-74; legis rep, Conn Fire Marshals Asn, 1982-84; bd dir, Capitol Reg Asn Fire Marshals, 1982-84; New England Asn Fire Marshals, 1983-85; bd dir Child & Family Serv, 1983-; bd dir, Friends Keney Park Golf Links, 1984-85. **Honors/Awds:** Front Page Weekly Reader, 1972; Firefighter of the Yr, Phoenix Soc Firefighters, 1972, 1976; Distinguished Serv Award, Radio WRCH, 1975; Community Award, Makalia Temple 172CT, 1983; Cert of Appreciation, US Consumer Prod Comn, Wash, DC, 1984. **Military Serv:** AUS, Inf s-4 rec spec, 2 yrs. **Business Addr:** Fire marshal, Fire prevention chief, Hartford Fire Department, 275 Pearl St, Hartford, CT 06103.*

BOOKER, CORLISS VONCILLE
Educator. **Personal:** Born Jun 22, 1954, Stuttgart, Germany; daughter of Curtis and Vera Wrenn; divorced; children: Andrea Voncille & Gorman Lasure. **Educ:** John Tyler Community Col, AAS, 1982; Va Commonwealth Univ, BSN, 1989, MPH, 1998, PhD, 2005; certif Clin Pastoral Educ, 2000. **Career:** Veteran's Admin, staff nurse, 1982-91; Va Commonwealth Univ, RN liaison, 1992-94, project dir, asst prof; Educ Resource, owner. **Orgs:** State Bd Social Servs, vice chair, 1994-; YWCA, secy, bd mem, 1994-98; Am Nurses Asn, 1982-; Oncol Nursing Soc, 1996-; Black Educ Asn, vpres, 1997-98, Outstanding Women of the Year, Nominations comt, 2001; Nat Black Nurses Asn, 1994-; chair, Health Social Servs Coun, Congress Nat Black Churches; admin coordr, 1998-00; Med Col Va, Issues Subcommittee, 1997-99; Susan G Komen Found, sci reviewer, 2001-04; VA Commonwealth Univ, Instnl Review Bd, 2001-02. **Honors/Awds:** Governor's Group Collaboration Award, Governor George Allen, 1997; Unsung Heroes Award, VA Health Care Found, 1996; Black Achievers Award, VA Commonwealth Univ, 1995; Minority Student Fellowship, Am Cancer Soc, 1989; Personality of the Week, Free Press Newspaper, 1997; Governor's Group Collaboration Award, 1997. **Special Achievements:** Has spoken before numerous groups and has published several articles. **Home Addr:** 3620 Mineola Dr, Chester, VA 23831. **Business Addr:** Assistant Professor, Virginia Commonwealth University, Dept Internal Med Div Quality Health Care, 1200 E Broad St, PO Box 843061, Richmond, VA 23284-3061, **Business Phone:** (804)828-4387.

BOOKER, JACKIE R
College teacher. **Personal:** Married Kathy; children: 2. **Educ:** Univ Calif, Irvine, PhD. **Career:** Claflin Univ, Dept Hist & Sociol, chmn & assoc prof, currently. **Business Addr:** Chairman, Associate Professor History and Sociology, Claflin University, Department of History & Sociology, 400 Magnolia St, Orangeburg, SC 29115, **Business Phone:** (803)535-5742.

BOOKER, JAMES E.
Executive. **Personal:** Born Jul 16, 1926, Riverhead, NY; married Jean Williams; children: James Jr. **Educ:** Hampton Inst, 1944; Howard Univ, AB, 1947; NY Univ; New Sch Social Res; Armed Forces Info Sch; AUS Psychol Warfare Sch. **Career:** NY Amsterdam News, columnist & political ed; Nat Adv Comn Civil Disorders, chief information consult; White House Conf Civil Rights, consult & dir info, 1966; Dem Pres Campaigns, consult, 1968 & 1972; consult, NY St Comn Human Rights; consult res specialist, NY St Joint Legislative Comn; James E Booker Consult, pres. *

BOOKER, JOHN, III
Executive. **Personal:** Born Dec 28, 1947, Augusta, GA. **Educ:** Paine Col, Hist major, 1969; NC Central Univ Law Sch, LLB, 1974; Univ RI, Cert Mgt, 1980. **Career:** Amperex Electronic Corp N Amer Philips Co, asst personal mgr, 1980-; Speidel Div of Textron, employ mgr & Urban affairs coordr, 1977-80; Center Savannah & River Area EOA Inc, equal opport ofc, 1976-77; Augusta Human Rel Commun, EEOC investigator & Field rep, 1975-76;

Atty John D Watkins, legal asst, 1974-75; Old Dominion Freight Line Inc, VPres & Controller & Chief Acct Officer, currently. **Orgs:** Woonsocket C of C, 1980; NAACP, 1980; Co rep, local minority & civil org, 1980. **Military Serv:** AUS, e-4, 1970-72. **Business Addr:** Vice President & Chief Accounting Officer, Controller, Old Dominion Freight Line Inc, 500 Old Dominion Way, Thomasville, NC 27360, **Business Phone:** (336)889-5000.

BOOKER, JOHNNIE B.
Executive. **Career:** Coca-Cola Co, dir supplier diversity, 2003. *

BOOKER, JOHNNIE BROOKS
Government official, executive director. **Personal:** Born Jul 31, 1941, Forsyth, GA; daughter of Willie F (deceased) and Lillian B Graves; divorced; children: Sylvester Courtney III. **Educ:** Hampton Inst, BS, 1961; Atlanta Univ Sch Social Work, MSW, 1969. **Career:** Los Angeles Comn Redevelop Agency, 1969-73; Western Regional Off Nat Urban League, asst regional dir, 1974-76; Nat Urban League-Wash Opers, asst dir, 1977-78; Fed Home Loan Bank Bd, dir consumer affairs, 1978-89; Dept Housing & Urban Develop, dep asst sec, 1989-91; Resolution Trust Corp, vpres, 1991; Fed Deposit Ins Corp, Dir Off Equal Opportunity; consult; Coca-Cola Co, Dir Supplier Diversity, 2001-. **Orgs:** Am Soc Pub Admin; Women Housing & Finance; Women Wash; Wash Urban League; Nat Asn Advan Colored People; Delta Sigma Theta Sorority; The Links, Inc, Capital City Chapter, chair, mem comt; Nat Black Child Devlop Inst; Metrop AME Church. **Honors/Awds:** Bd Resolution, Dryades Savings Bank, 1994; City Kans City, Mo Proclamation, 1994; Minority Asset Recovery Contractors Asn, 1994; Nat Bankers Asn, 1994; Nat Asn Black Accts, 1993; Dollar & Sense Mag, 1990. **Special Achievements:** Created unprecedented RTC contracting & investor opportunities for minorities and women; author and publisher of an informational booklet entitled, Fair Housing: It's Your Right; developed a system to detect discrimination in lending patterns and practices of regulated savings & loan asns. **Home Addr:** 1703 Leighton Wood Lane, Silver Spring, MD 20910, **Home Phone:** (301)565-5115. **Business Addr:** Director of Supplier Diversity, Coca-Cola Company, Washington, DC, **Business Phone:** (866)265-3638.*

BOOKER, KAREN
Basketball player. **Personal:** Born Apr 10, 1965, Franklin, TN. **Educ:** Vanderbilt Univ, bachelor's degree, economics. **Career:** Vanderbilt Univ, Volunteer Asst Coach, 1986-87,asst coach, 1991-92; Univ Kentucky, asst coach, 1989 - 91, assoc head coach, 1994-95; Univ Nevada, asst coach, 1993-94; Cal Poly, head coach, 1996-97; Colorado State Univ, asst coach, 1997-98; Utah Starzz, ctr, 1997; Action Fall tour, head coach Athletes, 1998; Sewanee, asst coach, 2000-01; Sewanee, head coach, 2001-03; WNBA Detroit Shock, volunteer asst coach, 2002; Colorado Chill,asst coach, 2006; Middle Tennessee Basketball Officials Asn, 2009. **Honors/Awds:** Dr. Jim Robbins Award, 1987; First woman win Dr. Jim Robbins Award. **Business Addr:** Assistant Coach, Colorado Chill, Triple Crown Sports, 3930 Automation Way, Fort Collins, CO 80525, **Business Phone:** (970)223-6644.*

BOOKER, LORETTA L. See HUFF, LORETTA LOVE.

BOOKER, MARILYN F
Executive. **Personal:** Born in Chicago, IL; married Walter; children: Walter Jr, Morgan & Maxwell. **Educ:** Harlan High Sch; Spelman Col, BS, IIT/Chicago Kent Sch Law, JD. **Career:** Morgan Stanley Pride Networking Group, Human Resources/Diversity, global head diversity currently, managing dir, 2004. **Orgs:** Bd dir, Michael J Found, 2001-05. **Honors/Awds:** Audrey P Berkeley Spirit Award, Michael J Berkeley Found, 2006. **Business Addr:** Managing Director, Global Head of Diversity Human Resources/Diversity, Morgan Stanley Pride Networking Group, 750 7th Ave, New York, NY 10019, **Business Phone:** (212)762-3412.

BOOKER, MICHAEL
Football player, newspaper editor. **Personal:** Born Apr 27, 1975, Oceanside, CA. **Educ:** Univ Nebr. **Career:** Football player (retired); Atlanta Falcons, defensive back, 1997-99; Tenn Titans, corner back, 2000-01; Daily Star Sunday, staff, 2002-07, dep ed, 2007-. **Honors/Awds:** Super Bowl XXXIII, 1997. **Business Phone:** (087)1520-7424.

BOOKER, ROBERT JOSEPH
Executive director. **Personal:** Born Apr 14, 1935, Knoxville, TN; son of Willie Edward (deceased) and Lillian Allen (deceased). **Educ:** Knoxville Col, BS, 1962. **Career:** Tenn Pub Sch, Chattanooga, teacher 1962-64; Tenn, elected mem legis, 1966-72; Mayor Knoxville, TN, admin asst, 1972-74; Stroh Brewery Co, Detroit, MI, mkt develop mgr, 1974-77; Beck Cultural Exchange Ctr, exec dir, 1978-84; City Knoxville, personnel dir, 1984-88; Knoxville Jourl, weekly columnist, 1987-92; Knoxville Col, historian, archivist, 1998-; Ctr Neighborhood Develop, community organizer, currently, interim exec dir, currently. **Orgs:** Phi Beta Sigma Frat; Nat Asn Advan Colored People; Veterans Foreign Wars; Am Legion; Martin Luther King Commemoration Comn; Knoxville Col Historian; Tabernacle Baptist Church. **Honors/Awds:** Bronze Man of the Year, 1990; Martin L King, Distinguished Service Award, 1994. **Special Achievements:** Author: 200 Years of Black Culture in Knoxville, Tennessee, 1791-1991; And There Was Light! The 120 Year History of Knoxville College 1875-1995; The Heat of a Red Summer: Race Rioting and Race Mixing in 1919 Knoxville. **Military Serv:** AUS, 1954-57. **Home Addr:** 2621 Parkview Ave, Knoxville, TN 37914. **Business Addr:** College Historian, Knoxville College, 901 Knoxville College Dr, Knoxville, TN 37915.*

BOOKER, SIMEON S.
Journalist, executive. **Personal:** Born Aug 27, 1918, Baltimore, MD; son of Simeon Sr and Roberta Warring; married Thelma Cunningham (divorced); children: Simeon Jr, James & Theresa; married Carol McCabe, Jan 1, 1973; children: Theresa, Simeon, Jr James (died 1992) & Theodore. **Educ:** Va Union Univ, BA, 1942; Cleveland Col, attended 1950; Harvard Univ, attended 1950. **Career:** Journalist, Executive (retired); Westinghouse Broadcasting Co, radio commentator; Wash Post, staff, 1952-54; Johnson Co Inc, bur chief, 1955-2006; Jet Mag, columnist, reporter, war cor resp, Wash bur chief, 1953-2006. **Honors/Awds:** Fourth Estate Award, Nat Press Club, 1982; Career Achievement Award, Wash Asn Black Journalists, 1993; Master Communicators Award, Nat Black Media Coalition, 1999; WABJ Lifetime Achievement Award, 2000; Newspaper Guild Award; Wilkie Award. **Special Achievements:** First full-time Black reporter on the Washington Post newspaper; First Black to win the National Press Club's Fourth Estate Award, 1982; Author, Man's King Taylor Black Mem, Wash's Speaker's Off.

BOOKER, VAUGHAN P L
Clergy. **Personal:** Born Sep 17, 1942, Philadelphia, PA; son of Lorenzo S and Mary E; married Portia A McClellan, Jun 30, 1979; children: Kimberly Nichole & Manuel B McClellan. **Educ:** Villanova Univ, BA, 1978; Va Theol Sem, MDiv, 1992. **Career:** Clergy (Retired); Xerox Corp, acct exec, 1981-87; Sprint Communs, major acct rep, 1987-89; Meade Memorial Episcopal Church, rector. **Orgs:** Protestant Correctional Chaplain's Asn, 1975-80; bd mem, Offender Aid & Restoration, 1980-87; bd mem,Va CURE; adv bd, George Wash Nat Bank; Omega Psi Phi. **Honors/Awds:** Alpha Sigma Lambda, 1977; Xerox Corp, Pres's Club, 1981. **Home Addr:** 7112 Lake Cove Dr, Alexandria, VA 22315, **Home Phone:** (703)971-5332. *

BOOKER, VAUGHN JAMEL
Football player. **Personal:** Born Feb 24, 1968, Cincinnati, OH; married Sheila; children: Vaughn Jr, Breana & DeVaughn. **Educ:** Univ Cincinnati. **Career:** Kansas City Chiefs, defensive end, 1994-97; Green Bay Packers, 1998-99; Cincinnati Bengals, defensive end, 2000-02. *

BOON, INA M.
Association executive. **Personal:** Born Jan 6, 1927, St Louis, MO; daughter of Lovie and Clarence; divorced. **Educ:** Oakwood Acad Huntsville, AL; Nat Bus Inst; Tucker's Bus Col; Wash Univ; Western Ill Univ. **Career:** St Louis Br NAACP, admin secy, 1962-68; AUS Transp Corp & AUS Dept Labor; NAACP, life mem field dir, 1968-73, dir, Region IV, 1973-. **Orgs:** St Louis Chap Nat Coun Negro Women; Nat Prof Women's Club; mem, MO Univ Adv Coun; bd mem, St Louis Minority Econ Develop Agency; secy, St Louis Mental Health Asn; second vpres, Top Ladies Distinction Inc; vpres, St Louis Chapter; vpres, Nat Financial Secy; chmn & bd dir, St Louis Comprehensive Health Ctr, 1983-87; organizer, cardinal chapter, Top Ladies Distinction, 1987; bd mem, St. Louis Black Leadership Roundtable; chair, Voter Awareness Comt, St. Louis Black Leadership Roundtable. **Honors/Awds:** Distinguished Serv Award, Top Ladies Distinction Inc; St Louis Argus Newspaper Cancer Soc, St Louis Black Firefighters Inst Racial Equality; Sigma Gamma Rho Sor; Kansas City KS Br NAACP; Kansas City MO Br NAACP & St Louis Globe Dem; Woman Achievers Social Welfare, 1970; Outstanding Leadership & Admin Abilities, 1973; Humanitarian Award; Human Dev Corp, 1976; Distinguished Serv Award, Union Memorial United Methodist Church, 1977; Director of the Year Award, Women Action Crusaders & Nat Resource Ctr, 1990. **Business Addr:** Director Region IV, NAACP, Legal Department, 4805 Mt Hope Dr, Baltimore, MD 21215.*

BOONE, ALEXANDRIA JOHNSON
Executive. **Personal:** Born May 15, 1947, Cleveland, OH; daughter of Alex Sr and Aria; children: Aria. **Educ:** Case Western Reserve Univ, MS, develop orgn develop & anal, attended 1981; Weatherheed Sch Mgt; Dartmouth Col, Amos Tuck Sch Bus Admin, attended 1991. **Career:** GAP Commun Group Inc, pres & chief exec officer, 1984-. **Orgs:** pres, Black Profs Charitable Found. **Honors/Awds:** Minority Entrepreneur of the Year, City Cleveland, 1988; Alexandria B Boone Day, Mayor Cleveland, 1988; Minority Business Advocate of the Year, State Ohio, 1989; CBS This Morning, Nat Network Prog; Business Woman of the Year, 1989. **Special Achievements:** MBE Profiles Mag, 1991, 1992; Reflections Mag, 1991, 1992. **Business Addr:** President, Chief Executive Officer, Gap Communications Group Inc, 1667 E 40th st, Cleveland, OH 44103, **Business Phone:** (216)391-4300.*

BOONE, DR. CAROL MARIE
Executive director, government official. **Personal:** Born Nov 22, 1945, Pensacola, FL; daughter of Benjamin J Butler and Clarice Thompson; married Robert L Boone, Sep 29, 1974; children: Carlotta & Robert Jr. **Educ:** Fisk Univ, BA, 1966; Univ Chicago, MA, 1968; Vanderbilt Univ, EdD, 1982. **Career:** Ill Children's Home & Aid Soc, adoption counr, 1968-69; Dede Wallace Ment Health Ctr, br dir, 1970-80; Tenn State, Dept Ment Health, State Employee Assistance Prog, dir, 1982-. **Orgs:** Alpha Kappa Alpha Sorority, 1965-; Nat Asn Social Workers, Nashville, 1969-; treas, Links Inc, Hendersonville Chap, 1976-; financial secy, Jack & Jill Am, Nashville Chap, 1982-; Nat Asn Employee Assistance Prof, 1982-; bd dirs, First Baptist Church, Capitol Hill Homes Inc. **Honors/Awds:** Social Worker of the Year Award, Middle Tenn Chap, NASW, 1977; Outstanding Prof Stud Award, Vanderbilt Univ, 1982; Outstanding Employee of the Year Award, Tenn Dept Ment Health, 1986; Outstanding Serv, Tenn Employee Assistance Prog, 1992, 1994, 1997. **Home Addr:** 320 Chicksaw Trail, Goodlettsville, TN 37072. **Business Addr:** Director Employee Assistance Program, Tennessee State Government, 312 8th Ave N Suite 1300, Nashville, TN 37243.

BOONE, CLARENCE DONALD
School administrator. **Personal:** Born Nov 23, 1939, Jackson, TN; married Louise May; children: Terrance A Beard & Torrance. **Educ:** Lane Col, BS, 1961; Memphis State Univ, MEd, 1977. **Career:** Nat Asn Advan Colored People, treas, 1957; United Teaching prof, mem, 1961; United Way, bd dir, 1980; West High Sch, prin, 2000. **Orgs:** Alpha Phi Alpha, 1959; Ambulance Authority, 1973, City Comn, 1977; YMCA, 1980; bd dir Headstart, 1980-83; JEA; bd dir, Lane Col Nat Youth Sports. **Honors/Awds:** Service Award Madison City Ambulance, 1973-77; Alumni Award, Lane Col, 1978; Service Award State Tenn, 1978; Educator of the Year, Phi Delta Kappa, 1984. **Home Addr:** 26 Brooks Dr, Jackson, TN 38301. *

BOONE, CLARENCE WAYNE
Physician. **Personal:** Born Aug 27, 1931, Bryan, TX; son of Elmo and Mae Frances Martin Marion; married Blanche Ollie Lane, Dec 18, 1954; children: Terrie, Clarence W Jr, Brian K. **Educ:** Ind Univ Sch Med, AB, anat & physiol, 1953, MD, 1956. **Career:** Physician (retired); Homer G Phillips Hosp, resident, 1957-61, intern, 1956-57; Planned Parenthood Asn, med dir; Gary Med Specialists Inc, pres, 1969-; pvt prac, physician, 1999. **Orgs:** Kappa Alpha Psi, 1950-; Am Col Obstet/Gynec, 1964-; Am Ferility Soc Dipl, Am Bd Obstet/gynec, 1964; Nat Med Asn, 1967-; pres, Gary Med Specl Inc, 1968-; Great Lakes Reg Med Adv Com Planned Parenthood Asn World Population, 1974-; staff phys, Meth Hosp Gary; St Mary Med Ctr; Homer G Phillips Alumni Asn; Asn Planned Parenthood Physician; bd mem, Neal-Marshall Comt, 1980-; rep, Exec Coun, 1983-; Asn Am Gynec Laparoscopists; trustee, Ind Univ Found, 1990-; Ind Univ Alumni Asn; Afr Am Doc Project. **Honors/Awds:** Chancellor's Medallion, In Univ Northwest, 1998; Distinguished Alumni Service Award; Gary Steel City Hall of Fame, 2000. **Military Serv:** USAF, capt, 1961-64. **Home Addr:** 2200 Grant St, Gary, IN 46404. **Business Addr:** Trustee, Indiana University Board of Trustees, African American Documentation Project, Ashton Aydelote 256, Gary, IN, **Business Phone:** (812)856-4830.*

BOONE, CLINTON CALDWELL
Government official, clergy. **Personal:** Born Feb 23, 1922, Monrovia, Liberia; son of Clinton C and Rachel; married Evelyn Rowland Boone; children: Evelyn & Clinton III. **Educ:** Houghton Col, BA, 1942; CW Post Ctr, MA, 1973; Va Union Univ. **Career:** Union Baptist Church, Hempstead NY, pastor, 1957-; Copiague Pub Sch Mem, teacher; former teacher, VA, NC, NY; Town Hempstead, Hempstead NY, comnr, 2005-. **Orgs:** Alpha Phi Alpha Fraternity, 1940; Va Union; bd dir, Nat Baptist Conv Inc, Hempstead Chamber Com; vpres, Park Lake Housing Develop, pres. **Honors/Awds:** CIAA Boxing Champion, 1940; Unispan Award, Hofstra Univ, 1974; Man of the Year, Hempstead Chamber Com, 1987. **Home Addr:** 41 Angevine Ave, Hempstead, NY 11550. **Business Addr:** Commissioner, Town of Hempstead, Department of Occupational Resources, 50 Clinton St Suite 400, Hempstead, NY 11550-4201, **Business Phone:** (516)485-5000.

BOONE, ELWOOD BERNARD, III
Chief executive officer. **Educ:** Morehouse Col, Atlanta, attended 1992; Univ Mich, Ann Arbor, attended 1995. **Career:** CJW Med Ctr, chief operating officer; HCA John Randolph Med Ctr, chief exec officer; Parkland Med Ctr, chief exec officer; John Randolph Med Ctr, bd trustees, currently. **Business Addr:** Board of Trustees, John Randolph Medical Center, 411 W Randolph Rd, PO Box 971, Hopewell, VA 23860, **Business Phone:** (804)541-1600.*

BOONE, DR. ELWOOD BERNARD
Physician. **Personal:** Born May 7, 1943, Petersburg, VA; son of Elwood B Boone Sr; married Carol Fraser; children: Elwood III & Melanie. **Educ:** Phillips Acad, 1961; Colgate Univ, AB 1965; Meharry Med Col, MD 1969; Med Col VA, internship 1970, surg resident, 1972, urol resident, 1975. **Career:** Med Col VA, clin instr, 1975-; Richmond Mem Hosp, staff physician, 1975-. **Orgs:** Am Bd Urol, 1977; Omega Psi Phi, 1967; Richmond Med Soc; Old Dominion Med Soc; Nat Med Soc; Richmond Urol Soc; Richmond Acad Med; Med Soc VA; Fellow Surg Am Cancer Soc, 1973-74; Nat pres Stud Nat Med Asn, 1968-69; VA Urol Soc; Am

Col Surgeons, 1979; pres, Old Dominion Medical Soc, 1981-82; Guardsmen Inc, 1983-; chief surg Richmond Memorial Hosp, 1985-86; Paradigm Communs, 1991-; Am Asn Clin Urologists; Alpha Beta Boule, Sigma Phi, 1992-. **Honors/Awds:** Certified American Board of Urology, 1977. **Military Serv:** USAR, capt, 1971-77. **Business Addr:** Physician, Richmond Memorial Hospital, 110 N Robinson St Suite 403, Richmond, VA 23220, **Business Phone:** (804)354-6202.

BOONE, EUNETTA
Screenwriter, television producer. **Career:** Films: Cuts, creator; TV shows: "Hip-Hop 101", creator & exec producer; "One On One", creator & exec producer; Daddy's Girl Productions, owner, currently; Paramount Network TV. **Business Addr:** Creator, Executive Producer, c/o United Paramount Network, 11800 Wilshire Blvd, Los Angeles, CA 90025, **Business Phone:** (310)575-7000.*

BOONE, FREDERICK OLIVER
Pilot. **Personal:** Born Jan 21, 1941, Baltimore, MD; married Penny Etienne; children: Vanessa, Frederick III, Kimberly, Sean, Shannon. **Educ:** Morgan State Col, BS, 1961. **Career:** Delta Airlines, flight engr, 1969-70, first officer, 1970-79, capt, 1980-86, capt, flight instr, evaluator, B727, 1986-91, chief instr, pilot, 1992. **Orgs:** Airline Pilots Asn; secy org, Black Airline Pilots, 1976-; Southern Christian Leadership Conf, 1977. **Honors/Awds:** Acheivement Award, Wall St Jour. **Military Serv:** USN, lt comdr, Vietnam; Air Medal USN.

BOONE, MELANIE LYNN
Dentist. **Personal:** Born Oct 21, 1973, Richmond, VA; daughter of Elwood B and Carol Ann Jr. **Educ:** Univ Va, BA, 1995; Howard Univ Dent, DDS, 1999. **Career:** Dr Jull Bussey Inc, dentist, 2002-. **Orgs:** Am Dent Asn, 2000-01; Nat Dental Asn, 2001-02; Peter B Ramsey Dent Soc, 2002-; Old Dominion Dent Soc, 2003-.

BOONE, RAYMOND HAROLD, SR.
Executive, editor, publisher. **Personal:** Born Feb 2, 1938, Suffolk, VA; married Jean Patterson; children: Regina, Raymond Jr. **Educ:** Norfolk St Col, attended 1957; Boston Univ, BS, 1960; Howard Univ, MA, 1985. **Career:** Suffolk, VA News-Herald, reporter, 1955-57; Boston Chronicle, city ed, 1958-60; Tuskegee Inst, dep dir, pub info, 1960-61; White House, Afro-American reporter, 1964-65; Richmond Afro-American, ed, 1965-81; Afro-American Co, ed & vpres, 1976-81; Howard Univ, visiting prof Jour, 1981-83, lecturer, 1983-88, assoc prof, 1988-91; Paradigm Commun Inc, founder, pres, CEO; Richmond Free Press, founder, ed & publ, 1991-; Imperial Bldg Property, LC, founder & pres, 2000. **Orgs:** Life mem, Nat Asn Advan Colored People; Kappa Alpha Psi; Sigma Delta Chi Professional Journalism Soc; Governor's Ethics Comn; Nat Assn Guardsmen Inc; bd dirs, Metropolitan Richmond Chamber Com, Metropolitan Richmond & Visitors Bureau. **Honors/Awds:** Carl Murphy Commission Service Award, NNPA; 1st Place Robt Abbott Editorial Writing Award, 1974, 1976; Distinguished Service Award, VA NAACP, 1974; Unity Award, Rpt Lincoln Univ, 1975; Humanitarian of the Year Award, Metro Richmond Bus League, 1976; VA State College Media Achievement Award, 1976; Pulitzer Prize Juror, 1978-79; Outstanding Suffolkian Morgan Memorial Library Suffolk, VA 1980; Metro Baltimore YMCA Outstanding Service Award, 1986-87; Poynter Institution for Media Studies Award, Outstanding Teaching in Journalism, 1988; Big Shoulders Award, 1992; Delver Woman's Club Award, 1992; Metropolitan Business Award, 1995; Commission Service Award, Nat Newspaper Publ Assn, 1996; Citizen of the Year Awd, Oliver W Hill, 1996; Economic Empowerment Award, Richmond NAACP, 1997; Richmond Magazine, 100 Power Players, 1998; Richmond's Movers & Shapers 20th Century, Valentine Museum, 1999; VA Commun Hall of Fame, 2000. **Business Phone:** (804)644-0496.*

BOONE, DR. ROBERT L
Executive, educator. **Educ:** Tenn State Univ, BS, 1970, MAEd, 1974; George Peabody Col, PhD, 1983. **Career:** Tenn State Univ, Dept Educ Admin, prof & assoc vpres acad affairs, currently. **Business Addr:** Professor, Associate Vice President of Academic Affairs, Tennessee State University, Department of Educational Administration, 3500 John A Merritt Blvd, Nashville, TN 37209, **Business Phone:** (615)963-5306.

BOONE, RONALD BRUCE
Television broadcaster, basketball player. **Personal:** Born Sep 6, 1946, Oklahoma City, OK. **Educ:** Iowa Western Community Col, Clarinda, IA; Idaho State Univ, Poacatello, ID. **Career:** Basketball player (retired), broadcaster; Kans City Kings, 1976-78; Los Angeles Lakers, 1978-79; Utah Jazz, 1980-81, color commentator, currently. **Business Phone:** (801)325-2500.

BOONE, DR. ZOLA ERNEST
School administrator. **Personal:** Born Oct 16, 1937, Wisner, LA; daughter of Zola Amond Ernest and Jesse Ernest Jr; married Arthur I Boone; children: Monica, Denise & Ivan. **Educ:** Mt St Mary's, BA, 1957; Mich State Univ, MS, 1970, PhD, 1972; Inst Educ Mgt Harvard Univ, cert, 1975. **Career:** Baltimore Pub Sch, teacher & dept chmn, 1962-69; Mich State Univ, 1970-71, Ford fel, 1971-72; Coppin State Col, honors prog adv, 1972-73, prof & dept chairperson, 1973-75, special asst vpres, 1975-76; Morgan St Univ, dir ctr curric improv, 1976-79; pres, Links Inc, 1977-78; Am Coun Educ, fel, 1978-79; SDIP Coord Morgan State Univ, special asst pres, 1979-80; US Dept Educ, Inst Educ Leadership, Wash, DC, policy fel, 1981-82; consult, 1982-84; Bowie State Found, Bowie, Md, exec dir, 1984-; Bowie State Univ, Bowie, Md, vpres planning & develop, 1984-88, vpres develop & univ rel, 1988-96, Inst Diversity & Multicultural Affairs, dir, 1996-; consult, Curric Develop. **Orgs:** Asn Supv & Curric Develop, 1972-77; Am Asn Higher Educ, 1976-77, 1984-; Soc Col & Univ Planners, 1984-; ACE NID Planning Coun, 1984-; Md Asn Higher Educ, 1984-; Coun Advan & Support Educ, 1984-; Mid-Atlantic Regional Coun, 1989-; Phi Kappa Phi; Delta Sigma Theta; Howard Co Dem Coalition; Prince Georges Coalition 100 Black Women; Nat Polit Cong Black Women; Prince Georges County, Delta Sigma Theta Sorority; comnr, Md Nat Capital Park & Planning Comn & Prince George's County Planning Bd. **Honors/Awds:** Outstanding Service Award, Adult Educ Coppin State Col, 1975; Legacy of Excellence Award, BSU Found, 1993; Case Comn Phil, 1996-97. **Home Addr:** 11124 Wood Elves Way, Columbia, MD 21044, **Home Phone:** (410)997-3661. **Business Addr:** Director, Bowie State University, Institute Diversity & Multicultural Affairs, 14000 Jericho Pk Rd, Bowie, MD 20715-9465, **Business Phone:** (301)860-4000.

BOONIEH, OBI ANTHONY
Executive. **Personal:** Born Jun 27, 1957, Onitsha, Nigeria; married Neka Carmenta White; children: Amechi. **Educ:** Morgan State Univ, BA 1983; Northeastern Univ Sch Law, JD, 1986. **Career:** Mangrover & Co Ltd, dir, 1979-; African Relief Fund, pres, 1982-84, dir, 1984-85; Culture Port Inc, consult & dir, 1986; Int Pollution Control Corp, dir, 1986-; First Writers Bureau Inc, managing ed, 1986-. **Orgs:** Big Brothers & Sisters Cent MD, 1980-83; NAACP; Phi Alpha Delta. **Honors/Awds:** Published article "Improving the Lot of Farmers," 1975; published book "A Stubborn Fate". **Business Addr:** Managing Editor, First Writers Bureau Inc, 819 E Fayette St, Baltimore, MD 21202, **Business Phone:** (410)625-2745.

BOOSE, DORIAN
Football player. **Personal:** Born Jan 29, 1974, Frankfurt, Germany. **Educ:** Walla Walla Comm Col; Wash State Univ. **Career:** New York Jets, def end, 1998-2000, Wash Redskins, def, 2001; Houston Texans, def end, 2002; Edmonton Eskimos, 2003-04. **Orgs:** Bd mem, Int Global Outreach. **Honors/Awds:** Defensive Lineman of the Year, Wash State Univ; Strength & Conditioning Award.

BOOTH, ANNA MARIA
Real estate executive, educator. **Personal:** Married; children: 2. **Career:** Atty; corp lobbyist; Nat Conf Community & Justice, exec dir; San Francisco Unified Sch Dist, vpres, 2002-03, substitute teacher, currently; real estate broker, currently. **Orgs:** Founder & vpres, Parent Teacher Stud Asn. **Business Addr:** Substitute Teacher, San Francisco Unified School District, 555 Franklin St, San Francisco, CA 94102, **Business Phone:** (415)241-6000.

BOOTH, CHARLES E.
Clergy, community college teacher. **Personal:** Born Feb 4, 1947, Baltimore, MD; son of William and Hazel (Deseased). **Educ:** Howard Univ, BA 1969; Eastern Bapt Theol Sem, MDiv 1973; VA Sem, DDiv, 1980; United Theol Sem, DMin, 1990. **Career:** Eastern Union Bible Col, lectr; Methodist Theol Sch, lectr; St Paul's Baptist Church W Chester PA, pastor, 1970-78; Mt Olivet Baptist Church, Columbus, OH, pastor, 1977-; United Theol Sem, prof preaching, 1987-94; Trinity, Affiliated Prof Homiletics, 1995-. **Orgs:** Progressive Nat Baptist Conv; Am Baptist Churches; Baptist Global Mission Bur; founder, Mt Olivet Christian Acad. **Honors/Awds:** Middler Scholar Award, Eastern Baptist Theol Sem, 1971; Dedicated Serv Award, W Chester State Col, 1977; Notable Am Bicentennial Era; Who's Who Among Black Am, 1974-75; Outstanding Young Men Am, 1980; Alpha Kappa Alpha Humanitarian Serv Award, 1981; delegate, Baptist World Youth Conf, 1984; morning preacher, Hampton Inst Ministers' Conf, 1984; Progressive Nat Baptist Preaching Team, Liberia, 1986; delegate, 15 mem Christian Apologetic Team, Russia, 1992; baccalaureate preacher, Howard Univ, 1992; Hon Roll Great Preachers, Ebony Mag, 1993; baccalaureate preacher, Morehouse Coll, 1994; conf preacher, 81st Hampton ministers' Conf, 1995; Keynote speaker, Columbus Conv Ctr, 1997. **Special Achievements:** Sermons: "When a Hunch Pays Off," Outstanding Black Sermons, vol III, published by Judson Press; "The Blessings of Unanswered Prayer and Spirituality," published by Judson Press; Meditation: "A Blessed Joy," From One Brother to Another: Voices of African-American Men, published by Judson Press. **Business Addr:** Sr Pastor, Mt Olivet Baptist Church, 428 E Main St, Columbus, OH 43215.*

BOOTH, GEORGE EDWIN
Administrator. **Career:** Comcast Cable, vpres & gen mgr, 2000, area vpres, currently. **Orgs:** CTAM Univ Midwest Chap. **Honors/Awds:** CTAM Univ Diversity Fel Winner, CTAM Univ Educ Found, 2005. *

BOOTH, KEITH
Basketball player. **Personal:** Born Oct 9, 1974, Baltimore, MD. **Educ:** Univ Md, BS, criminol & criminal justice, 2003. **Career:** Chicago Bulls, forward, 1997-99; Univ Md, Terrapins, asst coach, 2004-. **Honors/Awds:** NBA World Champion, 1998; Athletics Hall of Fame, Univ Md, 2008. **Business Addr:** Assistant Coach, University of Maryland, Terrapins, 3115 Chesapeake Bldg, College Park, MD 20742.

BOOTH, DR. LE-QUITA
Administrator. **Personal:** Born Oct 7, 1946, Columbus, GA; daughter of Joseph Reese and Hilda Reese; married Lester Booth; children: Joseph. **Educ:** Columbus Univ, BA, 1972, MBA 1977; Univ Ga, Athens, EdD, 1987. **Career:** Nat Bank & Trust, com officer, 1974-77; Small Bus Admin, disaster loan specialist, 1977-78; Small Bus Develop Ctr, Univ Ga, assoc dir, 1978-; Int Coun Small Bus, fel, 1986; Nat Sci Ctr Found, asst pres educ, 1988-; US Asn Small Bus & Entrepreneurship, fel; Fla A&M Univ, dir admin; Ala State Univ, Disadvantaged Bus Enterprises & Supportive Serv, dir, currently. **Orgs:** Bd dirs & regional vpres, Nat Bus League, 1983-85; Ga Asn Minority Entrepreneurs, 1981-85; vpres minority small bus, Int Coun Small Bus, 1984-86. **Honors/Awds:** Award for Achievement, Wall St Jour, 1972; Minority Advocate of the Year, Small Bus Admin, 1982; Public Service Extension Award, Univ Ga. **Home Addr:** 609 Zeron Dr, Columbus, GA 31907. **Business Addr:** Director Disadvantaged Business Enterprises Support Services, Alabama State University, Rm 430 600 S Ct St, Montgomery, AL 36101-0271, **Business Phone:** (334)229-4100 Ext 6007.

BOOZER, DARRYL
Founder (Originator), president (organization). **Career:** IBS Commun Inc, founder & pres, 2004-. **Orgs:** Minority Bus Enterprise Coun. **Business Addr:** Founder, President, IBS Communications Inc, 7500 Germantown Ave Elders Hall Suite 200-202, Philadelphia, PA 19119, **Business Phone:** (215)242-5934.

BOOZER, EMERSON
Administrator, sports manager. **Personal:** Born Jul 4, 1943, Augusta, GA; son of Emerson and Classie Mae; married Enez Yevette Bowins; children: Kiva. **Educ:** Univ Md Eastern Shore, BS, 1966. **Career:** Football player (retired), football analyst, dir (retired); CBS-TV, football analyst, 1976-77; New York Jets, football player, 1966-76; WLIB Radio, announcer, 1971-74; Long Island Cablevision, sports analyst col & hs football games; Town Huntington, NY, exec asst supvr, parks & recreation dir. **Orgs:** Police Athletic League; Nat Football League Players Asn. **Honors/Awds:** Rookie of the Year, Actors Guild Meth, Pittsburgh Courier, 1966; All-Am, 1964-65; Outstanding Small Col Athlete, Wash Pigskin Club, 1965; All-Star Team, Am Football League, 1966-68; AFC Scoring Touchdowns Champion, 1972; The Honors Court, Georgia Sports Hall of Fame, 1991; Suffolk Sports Hall of Fame, 1996. **Home Addr:** 25 Windham Dr, Huntington Station, NY 11746.

BORDEN, HAROLD F., JR.
Artist. **Personal:** Born Feb 3, 1942, New Orleans, LA; married Barbara Sullivan; children: Tony & Tina. **Educ:** La City Col, drawing; Trade Tech Col, LA, design; Otis Art Inst, LA, drawing. **Career:** Krasne Co, designer jewelry, 1969-71; Contemp Crafts, LA, exhibitor, 1972; H Borden Studios, master jeweler, sculptor, artist & owner. **Orgs:** Org Jua-Agr Ctr; design consult, Black Artists & Craftsman Guild; Am Guild Craftsman; bd mem, Jua. **Honors/Awds:** Special Achievement Award, Dept Recreation & Parks City, LA, 1972; Participation Award, City LA Day in the Park, 1974. **Business Addr:** 1255 12 S Cochran Ave, Los Angeles, CA 90019-2899.

BORDERS, FLORENCE EDWARDS
Historian, archivist. **Personal:** Born Feb 24, 1924, New Iberia, LA; daughter of Sylvanus and Julia Gray; married James Buchanan (died 1959); children: James Buchanan IV, Sylvanus Edwards Borders, Thais Borders Adams. **Educ:** Southern Univ, Baton Rouge, LA, BA, 1945; Rosary Col, Sch Libr Sci, River Forest, IL, BA, Library Sci, 1947, MA, Libr Sci, 1966; LA State Univ, Baton Rouge, LA, Post Master's fel, 1968. **Career:** Univ Chicago, Chicago, IL, libr asst, 1946; Bethune-Cookman Col, Daytona Beach, FL, asst librn, 1947-58; Tenn State Univ, Nashville, TN, cataloger, 1958-59; Grambling State Univ, Grambling, LA, head tech serv, 1959-70; Amistad Res Ctr, Tulane Univ, New Orleans, LA, sr & ref archivist, 1970-89; Southern Univ New Orleans, Ctr African & African Am Studies, New Orleans, LA, archivist, 1989-. **Orgs:** Founder, dir, Chicory Soc Afro-La Hist & Culture, 1986-; pres, Our Lady of Lourdes Parish Coun, 1986-87; pres, Greater New Orleans Archivists, 1987-88; vpres, Our Lady of Lourdes Parish Sch Bd, 1990-91; nominating comm, Acad of Certified Archivists, 1990-91; block capt, Mayoral Campaign, 1990; Soc Am Archivists; Soc Southwest Archivists; Coalition of 100 Black Women; Am Libr Asn; La Archives & Mss Asn; League Good Gov, Zeta Phi Beta Sorority; Archivists & Archives Color Roundtable. **Honors/Awds:** Cert of Merit, Phi Beta Sigma Fraternity, 1969; trophy, La World Exposition, Afro-American Pavilion, 1984; Cert of Recognition, Black Chorale, 1986; Cert of Appreciation, Equal Opportunity Adv Coun, 1986; Unsung Heroes Plaque, Crescent City Chapter of Links, 1987;Callaloo Award, Univ of Va, 1988; "Vital as a Heartbeat Award," Urban League, 1988; trophy, Calvary CME Church, 1988. **Business Addr:**

Archivist, Southern University New Orleans, Center African and American Studies, 6400 Press Dr, New Orleans, LA 70126.*

BORDERS, MICHAEL G.
Educator, artist. **Personal:** Born Oct 17, 1946, Hartford, CT; son of Thomas L and Marjorie Davis; married Sharon Armwood, Feb 4, 1984; children: Nicholas M A Borders. **Educ:** Fisk Univ, BA, 1968; Howard Univ, MFA, 1970. **Career:** Fisk Univ, instr, 1970-71; Fox Middle Sch, math teacher, 1971-72; S Arsenal Neighborhood Devel Sch, artist residence, 1974-78; Greater Hartford Community Col, art hist instr, 1978; freelance artist, 1978-. **Orgs:** Fisk Univ homecoming brochure covers, 1967-68; First Ann Fine Arts Exhib, 1968; First Annual Congreg Art Show, 1968; Stud Exhib, 1968; Stud Exhib, Skowhegan Sch Painting & Sculpture; One-Man Show Cent Mich Univ, 1970; Joint Fac Exhib Fisk, Vanderbilt, Peabody, 1971; display in lobby, Phoenix Mutual Life Ins Co, 1974; Unitarian Meetinghouse Hartford, 1974; artist in residence, Weaver, HS, 1973-74; lectr, Loomis-Chaffee Prep Sch, 1973; lectr, Trinity Col, 1973; portrait painter; works placed in local Washington galleries; billboard painter; CT Comn Culture & Tourism. **Honors/Awds:** Two-man Show Nat Ctr Afro-Amer Artists, 1975; mural displayed in Hartford titled "Genesis of Capital City" (largest mural in New England - first permanent monument by Black Amer in Hartford); 18-month trip to Africa, Asia & Europe 1976-77; CT State Panorama of Business & Indus 1980; two mural panels City Hall, Hartford (2nd permanent monument by Black Amer in Hartford) 1980-85; three murals AETNA Insurance Co, Hartford, 1989; four murals AI Prince Regional Vocational Tech School, Hartford 1989; many conceptual paintings and portraits. *

BORGES, LYNNE MACFARLANE
Executive. **Personal:** Born Oct 27, 1952, Middletown, OH; daughter of Victor MacFarlane Sr and Charma Jordan MacFarlane; married Francisco L, May 28, 1988; children: Ryan Elliot Jones. **Educ:** Wesleyan Univ, BA, Govt, 1975. **Career:** Aetna Life & Casuality, mgr, 1975-79; Conn Gen Life Ins, asst dir, 1979-82; CIGNA, dir, 1982-85; Heublein Inc, dir, 1985-. **Orgs:** Corp adv comn, Nat Asn Equal Oppourtinites Higher Educ, 1983-; bd dirs, Conn Black Women's Educ Res Found, 1985-; women's exec comm, Greater Hartford Chamber Com, 1986-; past chmn bd, Greater Hartford Urban League, 1989-; incorporator, Inst Living, 1990-; bd trustees, Mark Twain Mem; bd dirs, Child & Family Serv, 1991-; coun bd chairs, pres, Nat Urban League, 1992-. **Honors/Awds:** State of Conn Young Career Woman Bus/Prof Women's Fed, 1979; Mary McLeod Bethune Award, Nat Coun Negro Women, 1981; Outstanding Connecticut Women of the Decade, 1987. **Business Addr:** Director, Heublein Inc, Human Resources & Planning Department, 6 Landmark Sq Fl 9, Stamford, CT 06901-2704.

BORGES, SAUNDRA KEE
Government official, lawyer. **Personal:** Born Mar 21, 1959, Montclair, NJ; daughter of William Kee and Edith; divorced; children: Garrett, Julian, Adriana. **Educ:** Trinity Col, Hartford CT, BS, psychol, 1981; Univ Conn Sch Law, JD, 1984. **Career:** City Hartford, Off Corp Coun, lawyer, 1983-93, city mgr, 1993; bd trustees & secy, Conn Pub Broadcasting Inc; pvt pract atty, currently. **Orgs:** Alpha Kappa Alpha Sorority Inc, 1978-; corporator, St Francis Hosp, 1984-; corporator, Hartford Hosp, 1984-; bd mem, Univ Conn Law Sch Found, 1989-; Conn Town & City Managers Asn, 1993-; Int City Managers Assn, 1994-; bd mem, St Timothy Middle Sch, 1999-; bd trustees, Trinity Col, 1999-; bd mem, Nat Forum Blacks Pub Admin, 1999-; Conn Pub TV; bd mem, Conn Woman's Hall Fame. **Business Addr:** Attorney, 56 Harbor St, Hartford, CT 06106, **Business Phone:** (860)231-9664.*

BOROM, LAWRENCE H.
Social worker, executive. **Personal:** Born Feb 28, 1937, Youngstown, OH; son of Clarence H Russell and Cora Mildred Lewis; married Betty J Fontaine, Nov 29, 1963; children: Martin Antoine Borom. **Educ:** Youngstown State Univ, Youngstown, OH, BS, educ, 1958; Mankato State Col, Mankato, MN, MA, urban studies, 1970. **Career:** Executive (retired); Cleveland Pub Schs, Cleveland, OH, elem teacher, 1962-63; St Paul Urban League, St Paul, MN, employ & educ dir, 1963-66; MN Gov Human Rights Comn, exec dir, 1966-67; St Paul Urban League, comn, exec dir, 1967-74; Nat Urban League, New York City, NY, dir community develop, 1974-76; Urban League Metropolitan Denver, CO, pres & chief exec officer, 1976-98. **Orgs:** Kappa Alpha Psi Fraternity, 1956; Adv Comn, Denver Mayor's Black Adv Comt, 1985; pres, Colo Black Roundtable, 1988; Adv Comn, A World Differene Proj, 1988; bd dir, Colo African & Carribean Trade Off, 1989. **Honors/Awds:** Esquire Award, Esquire Club, 1984; Distinguished Service Award, UNCF, 1985; Distinguished Serv Award, Colo Civil Rights Comn, 1987. **Military Serv:** AUS, Sp4, 1959-62. *

BORUM, JENNIFER LYNN
Lawyer. **Personal:** Born Mar 15, 1965, Hampton, VA; daughter of Wilbert and Ethel Borum. **Educ:** Hampton Univ, BA, 1987; Harvard Univ Law Sch, JD, 1990. **Career:** US Ct Appeals 4th Circuit, law clerk, 1990-91; Cahill Gordon & Reindel, atty, 1991-93; Stillman, Friedman & Shaw, atty, 1993-96; Southern Dist NY, US Atty Off, asst US atty, 1996-2000; Hunton & Williams LLP, litigation atty, 2000-. **Orgs:** Alpha Kappa Alpha Sorority, 1985-; Shte Bar NY, 1991-; DC Bar Asn, 1993-; Commonwealth Va Bar, 2001-; Jr League Richmond, 2001-; newsletter ed, Rotary Club Richmond, 2001-; John Marshall Inn Ct, 2001-; bd dir, Big Bros Big Sisters, 2001-. **Honors/Awds:** Presidents Award, Hampton Univ, 1987; Outstanding Achievement Award, Alpha Kappa Alpha, 1997; Outstanding Achievement Award, Hunton & Williams, 2003. **Special Achievements:** Author: Note, And Forgive Them Their Trespasses, Harvard Law Rev, 1990. **Home Addr:** 3849 W Weyburn Rd, Richmond, VA 23235, **Home Phone:** (804)267-6532. **Business Addr:** Litigation Attorney, Hunton & Williams LLP, 951 E Byrd St Suite 1310, Richmond, VA 23219-4074, **Business Phone:** (804)788-8528.*

BOSCHULTE, ALFRED F
Executive, chairperson. **Personal:** Born Sep 18, 1942, St Thomas, Virgin Islands of the United States; married Kita. **Educ:** City Col New York, BME; City Univ, New York, MS, eng. **Career:** NY Telephone, staff, 1964-76; AT&T, dir cross indust, 1982; Pac Bell, vpres external affairs, 1983-87; NY NEX Serv Co, vpres carrier servs, 1987-90; NY NEX Corp, vpres mkt; Wireless One Corp, chmn, pres & chief exec officer; Detecon Inc, founder & chmn; AirTouch Communs, chmn & chief exec officer; NY NEX Mobile Communs, pres, 1990; TomCom LP, chmn & pres; SkyOptix Inc, chief exec officer; Advan Generation Telecom Group Inc, chmn & chief exec officer, currently; AFB Consult, pres, currently; Probe Financial Assocs Inc, chmn, currently. **Orgs:** Inst Elec & Electronic Engrs; chmn, INROADS, Westchester & Fairfield; bd dir, Jr Achievement; bd trustee, Clark Univ; bd trustee, Boys & Girls Clubs Am; vice chmn, Cellular Telecommunications Indust Asn; bd dir, United Way; TranSwitch & Symmetricom Corp; chmn, Wireless Access; bd mem, NE Utilities Corp. **Business Addr:** Chairman, Probe Financial Associates Inc, PO Box 286, Ironia, NJ 07845, **Business Phone:** (973)387-0443.

BOSCHULTE, JOSEPH CLEMENT
Physician. **Personal:** Born Feb 5, 1931, Tortola, British Virgin Islands; married Rubina; children: Cheryl, Jualenda, Joseph. **Educ:** City Col NY, BS, 1954; Howard Univ Col Med, 1958; Frdmn Hosp, Intern 1959, Res, 1967. **Career:** Pvt Prac, physician, 1972-; B Wash DC, chief inptnt serv area, 1969-72. **Orgs:** Chmn, Dept Psychiatry Ctr SE Community Hosp, 1972-; sr attending psychtrist WA Hosp Ctr, 1968-76; Prnc Grg's Hosp, 1968-75; Am Psychiat Asn; WA Psychiat Soc; AMA. **Honors/Awds:** DC Medical Society Fellowship, Grant Nat Inst Mental Health, 1964-67. **Military Serv:** AUS, MC gen med cr, capt, 1960.

BOSLEY, FREEMAN ROBERTSON, JR.
Mayor, lawyer. **Personal:** Born Jul 20, 1954, St Louis, MO; son of Freeman and Marjorie. **Educ:** Univ St Louis, BA, urban affairs & polit sci, 1976; Univ St Louis Sch Law, JD, 1979. **Career:** Legal Serv Eastern MO, staff atty, 1979-81; Bussey & Jordan, assoc, 1982-83; Circuit Ct St Louis, clerk, 1983-93; St Louis Dem Cent Comt, chmn, 1990-93; City of St Louis, mayor, 1993-97; Caldwell & Singleton LLC, atty, 1997-. **Orgs:** Mound City Bar Asn, 1980; Metro Bar Asn, 1980; Bd Jury Commissioners; Child Support Comn, comnr, 1985-; Black Stud Alliance; Black-American Law Stud Asn; bd dir, Cedric The Entertainer Charitable Found. **Special Achievements:** First African American mayor of St. Louis, Missouri; first African-American chairman of the Democratic party. **Home Addr:** 3508 Palm Pl, Saint Louis, MO 63107. *

BOSLEY, THAD
Baseball player, baseball manager. **Personal:** Born Sep 17, 1956, Oceanside, CA; married Cherry Sanders. **Educ:** Mira Costa Community Col, Oceanside, CA. **Career:** Baseball player, (retired), Basketball manager; Calif Angels, outfielder, 1977 & 1988; Chicago White Sox, 1978-80; Milwaukee Brewers, 1981; Seattle Mariners, 1982; Chicago Cubs, 1983-86; Kans City Royals, 1987-88; Tex Rangers, outfielder, 1989-90; Oakland Athletics, hitting coach, 1999-2002; Phoenix Devil Dogs, mgr, 2001; Bethany Univ, head coach, currently. **Honors/Awds:** Player of the Year, Calif League, 1976. **Special Achievements:** Recorded a Gospel Contemporary Album entitled "Pick Up the Pieces"; Working on Book of Poems for Children.

BOST, FRED M.
Government official. **Personal:** Born Mar 12, 1938, Monroe, NC; married Sara B; children: Sybil, Olantunji & Kimberly. **Educ:** Bloomfield Col, BS, 1976; Cook Col, environ-health/law 1979. **Career:** Elizabeth NJ Bd Educ, chmn title I, 1970-72; Dept Prop & Maint, asst mgr, 1976-79; Twp Irvington, comn drugs, 1977-79; Essex County, comn youth &rehab comn, 1977-80; ABC Irvington, comn chmn, 1982-84; Twp Irvington, councilman, 1980-04. **Orgs:** Pres, Fred Bost Civic Asn, 1975-81; rep, Bur Indian Affairs, 1976-78, pubrels rep, data processing, 1977-79; pres, E Ward Civic Asn, 1979-81. **Honors/Awds:** Concerned Citizen Award, PBA, Irvington, 1980. **Military Serv:** AUS, sgt, 2 yrs. *

BOSTIC, HARRIS, II
Executive. **Career:** Peace Corps, regional mgr, regional dir, currently. **Business Addr:** Regional Director, Peace Corps, 333 Market St Suite 600, San Francisco, CA 94105, **Business Phone:** (415)977-8800.*

BOSTIC, JAMES EDWARD, JR.
Administrator, scientist. **Personal:** Born Jun 24, 1947, Marlboro County, SC; married Edith A Howard; children: James E III, Scott H. **Educ:** Clemson Univ, BS, textile chem, 1969, PhD, 1972. **Career:** Clemson Univ, fel, 1969-72, grad resident counr, 1969-72; Am Enka & Res Corp, sr res sci, 1972; Dept Agri, spec asst sec agri, 1972-73, dep asst sec agri, 1973-77; Riegel Text Corp, corp regul dir tech analyst, 1977-81, convenience products div 1981-85; Ga Pacific Corp, gen mgr, 1989, exec vice Pres, 1991-2005; ACT Inc, bd dir, currently. **Orgs:** Asn Textile Chem & Color; Am Chem Soc; Phi Psi Fraternity; Blue Key Nat Hnr Frat; Nat Acad Engrs, 1975-76; bd trustees USDA Grad Sch, 1976-77; mem, pres Comn White House Fel Region Panel, 1975-78; FFA Hnr Am Farmer, 1976; coun mem, Clemson Univ Grad Sch, 1971-72; mem, US Dept of Commerce Mgmt Labor Textile Advisory Comn, 1978-85; vice chmn & chmn, SC Commn on Higher Educ, 1978-83; chmn & mem, Career Found Bd of Trustees, 1978-; mem, Pres Comn White House Fel, 1981-; mem, Clemson Univ, Bd Trustees, 1983-. **Honors/Awds:** Ford Found Doc Fel Black Students, 1969-70; White House Fel, 1972-73; Distinguished Serv Award Greenville Jaycees, 1979; Outstanding Pub Servant Year Award, 1983; SC Asn Minorities Pub Admin. **Special Achievements:** first African-American to earn a doctorate at Clemson University. **Military Serv:** USAR, secound lt, 1971-77. *

BOSTIC, LEE H.
Lawyer. **Personal:** Born Apr 17, 1935, Brooklyn, NY; married Gayle Spaulding; children: Lisa, Staci, Lee. **Educ:** Morgan State Col, BA, 1957; Boston Univ Law Sch, LLB, 1962. **Career:** Allstate Ins Co, claims adj, 1964; Solomon Z Ferziger NYC, assoc atty, 1964-65; Queens Co, asst dist atty, 1966; pvt pract atty, 1967-. **Orgs:** New York & Queens Co Bar Asn; Nat Asn Advan Colored People; male committeeman, 29 AD Reg Rep Club Queens Co; NY State Bar Asn; Macon B Allen Black Bar Asn; bd dirs, Jr Acad League Inc. **Military Serv:** AUS, lt, 1957-59.

BOSTIC, RAPHAEL W
Economist, educator. **Educ:** Stanford Univ, Ph.D, econ. **Career:** Fed Res Bd Wash, sr economist; Univ Southern Calif, Sch Policy Planning & Develop, assoc prof & dir master real estate develop prog, currently. **Business Addr:** Associate Professor, Director Master of Real Estate Development Program, University of Southern California, School of Policy Planning & Development (SPPD), Ralph & Goldy Lewis Hall 326, Los Angeles, CA 90089-0626, **Business Phone:** (213)740-1220.

BOSTIC, VIOLA W
Association executive, executive director. **Personal:** Born Oct 24, 1941, New York, NY; daughter of Peter Williams and Doris Andrews; married Raphael, Apr 24, 1965; children: Raphael William & Ebony Leigh. **Educ:** City Col NY, BA, 1963; City Univ NY, MA, 1965; Univ Pa, MS, 1992. **Career:** Morgan State Univ, instr, 1967-68; Burlington County Col, instr, 1969-70; Courier Post, reporter, 1973-74; Rohm & Haas Co, mgr mkt servs, 1974-93; Big Bros/Big Sisters Am, asst nat exec dir, 1994-; Nat Fedn Community Develop Credit Union, dep exec dir, 2003. **Orgs:** Adv chair, Philadelphia Salvation Army, 1976-; Nat Asn Media Women, Philadelphia, pres, 1982-85; Nat Asn Media Women, 1983; vice chair, Moorestown Vis Nurse Asn, 1984-; chair community relations, Contact 609, 1993-94; Soc Am, 1994-; Pub Rels Soc Am, 1995-; Male Advocacy Network, 1996-; chair emeritus, Philadelphia Urban Coalition, Educ Task Force; Nat Assembly Pub Rels. **Honors/Awds:** Salvation Army Advisory Council Award, 1985; BEEP Award, Nat Urban League, 1990; Board Member of the Year, MVNA, 1993; Bronze Anvil Award, Pub Rels Soc Am; Crystal Award, Communicator. **Business Addr:** Deputy Executive Director, National Federation of Community Development Credit Union Inc, 120 Wall St 10th Fl, New York, NY 10005-3902, **Business Phone:** (212)809-1850.

BOSTIC, WILLIAM C
Executive. **Personal:** Born Jun 19, 1943, Chattanooga, TN; son of William C Bostic Sr and Ruth L; married L Ann; children: 2. **Educ:** Tenn State Univ, BS, polit sci, 1968; Univ Pittsburgh, MS, 1979. **Career:** US Dept Educ, dep asst, 1978-90; Pa Dept Community Affairs, staff, 1980-87, secy, 1995-96; Urban Educ Found, chief exec officer, 1990-95; Pa Housing Finance Agency, exec dir, 1996-2003; Pa Higher Educ Facil Authority, exec dir, 2003-; State Pub Sch Bldg Authority, exec dir, 2003-. **Orgs:** Bd mem, United Way Lancaster Co, 1981-86; bd mem, Urban League Lancaster Co, 1981-86; bd mem, Nat Conf States Bldg Codes & Stand, 1986-87; bd mem, Lancaster Co Human Rels Community, 1992-95; bd mem, Am Red Cross-Susquehanna Valley; bd mem, Nat. Coun State Housing Agencies, 1997-2003; bd mem, Nat Housing Conf, 2000-03; assoc mem, Am Plan Asn. **Business Addr:** Executive Director, State Public School Building Authority, Pennsylvania Higher Educational Facilities Authority, PO Box 990, Harrisburg, PA 17001-0990, **Business Phone:** (717)975-2203.

BOSTON, ARCHIE, JR.
Arts administrator, college teacher. **Personal:** Born Jan 18, 1943, Clewiston, FL; married Juanita; children: Michael, Jennifer. **Educ:** Calif Inst Arts, BFA, 1965; Univ Southern Calif, MLA, 1977. **Career:** Hixon & Jorgensen Inc, art dir, 1965-66; Boston & Boston Design, partner, 1966-68; Cailf Inst Arts, 1966-68; Carson Roberts Inc, art dir, 1968; Botsford Ketchum Inc, sr art dir, 1968-

77; Cailf State Univ, instr, 1971, tenured prof & chmn, VC Design Prog, currently; Art Ctr Col Design, instr, 1976-77; Cailf State Univ, assoc prof, 1977; Design Concepts, pres, 1977-78. **Orgs:** pres, bd dir, Art Dir Club, LA, 1973; Mt Sinai Bapt Church; bd govs, Art Dir Club, LA 1974-; comt chmn, Graphic Arts Bicent Black Achivement Exhibit; New York Art Dir; San Francisco & La Art Dir Club Show; Type Dir & Aiga Show; Comun Arts & Art Dir Mag Show; Graphis Annual & Typomondus 20. **Honors/ Awds:** Intl Exp of "Best Graphics of the 20th Century". **Special Achievements:** Judge num award shows 1965-. **Military Serv:** AUSR, first lt, 1965-71. **Home Addr:** 5707 Aladdin St, Los Angeles, CA 90008. **Business Addr:** Professor, California State University, 401 Golden Shore, Long Beach, CA 90802-4210.*

BOSTON, DAVID BYRON
Football player. **Personal:** Born Aug 19, 1978, Humble, TX; son of Byron and Carolyn; married Renee Marisa Dota, Jan 1, 2004; children: Alaia Gianna Boston & Jaylen James. **Educ:** Ohio State Univ, sociol, 2000. **Career:** Ariz Cardinals, wide receiver, 1999-2002, San Diego Charger, 2003; Miami Dolphins, wide receiver, 2004-05; Tampa Bay Buccaneers, wide receiver, 2006; Toronto Argonauts, 2008. **Honors/Awds:** Pro Bowl Selection, 2001. **Special Achievements:** First-team All-Big Ten, 1997-98; First-team All-American, 1998. *

BOSTON, DENNIS H
Advertising executive. **Personal:** Born in Chicago, IL. **Educ:** S Jr Coll, Chicago; DePaul Univ. **Career:** Hertz Rent-A-Car, exec accounts mgr; Johnson Publ Co, advert sales rep, 1972-78, midwest advert dir, 1978-81, vpres & midwest advert dir, 1981-98; sr vpres, midwest advert dir, 1998-. **Orgs:** Mid-Am Comm; Usher Bd, St. Ailbe Church. **Business Addr:** Midwest Advertising Director, Senior Vice president, Johnson Publishing Company Inc, Ebony Fashion Fair, 820 S Michigan Ave, Chicago, IL 60605, **Business Phone:** (312)322-9200.

BOSTON, DR. GEORGE DAVID
Dentist, educator. **Personal:** Born Nov 1, 1923, Columbus, OH; son of Samuel David Boston and Iola Adelaide Benson; married Johanna Heidinger (deceased); children: George Jr (dec) & Donald Darryl (dec). **Educ:** Ohio State Univ, BA, 1949; DDS, 1952. **Career:** Dentist, educator (retired); Columbus State Hosp Dent Clinic, chief,1952-58; priv pract, 1953-87; Ohio State Univ, asst prof, 1957-84. **Orgs:** Columbus Dent Soc; Ohio Dental Assn; Am Dent Assn; Natl Dent Assn; Omega Psi Phi Frat; Sigma Pi Phi Frat; Cavaliers Inc; Nat Assn Advan Colored People;Nat Dent Honor Soc; Omicron Kappa Upsilon. **Special Achievements:** First Black Male Tenured Faculty Member in the Ohio State University in 1957. **Military Serv:** AUS, first lt, QMC, 1943-47. **Home Addr:** 1006 Wellington Blvd, Columbus, OH 43219-2121. *

BOSTON, GRETHA
Actor. **Personal:** Born Apr 18, 1959, Crossett, AR. **Career:** Stage performer: Show Boat, 1994-97; It Ain't Nothin' But the Blues,1999-; TV series: "Some Enchanted Evening: Celebrating Oscar HammersteinII", 1995; "Law & Order", 2001; "School Daze", 2001; "Hope & Faith", 2004; "Jury Duty", 2004; "D.A. W", 2004; "Law & Order: Criminal Intent", 2004. **Honors/Awds:** Tony Award, Featured actress in a musical, Showboat, 1995; Hayes Award,Best Actress, 2000; Theater World Award for Outstanding Debut Artist. **Business Addr:** Actress, c/o Ambrosio/ Mortimer & Associates Inc, 9150 Wilshire Blvd Suite 175, Beverly Hills, CA 90212, **Business Phone:** (310)274-4274.*

BOSTON, DR. HORACE OSCAR
Dentist. **Personal:** Born Jul 27, 1934, Clarksville, TX; married Iola. **Educ:** Southern Univ, BS, 1955; TX S Univ; Univ OK; Univ NM; Washingon Univ, DDS; Meharry Med Col, Sch Dent, 1973. **Career:** Wiley Col, former asst prof biol; former high sch sci teacher; Midwestern Univ, former asst prof; several nursing homes, cons; WF & Evening Lions Club; Pvt pract, dent, currently. **Orgs:** YMCA; past bd dir, Eastside Girls Club; former commr, Wichita Falls Housing Authority; former vpres, Wichita Dist Dent Soc; Gulf States Dent Assoc; former mem, TX Dent Asn; Kappa Alpha Psi Frat; former mem, City Coun, City Wichita Falls; Am Dent Asn. **Honors/Awds:** NSF, Grant. **Special Achievements:** Publications: "Prognathism: a Review of the Lit," 1972. **Military Serv:** USAR, capt, 1955-73. **Home Addr:** 4504 Barbados, Wichita Falls, TX 76308, **Home Phone:** (940)691-0190. **Business Addr:** Dentist, 1711 10th St, Wichita Falls, TX 76301, **Business Phone:** (940)723-7171.

BOSTON, MCKINLEY, JR.
School administrator, president (organization), chief executive officer. **Personal:** Born Nov 5, 1945, Elizabeth City, NC; son of McKinley and Lenora; married Magellia McIntyre, Jan 11, 1969; children: Lance & Kimberly. **Educ:** Univ Minn, 1968; Montclair State Col, BA, 1973, MA, 1973; NY Univ, EdD, 1988. **Career:** NY Giants, prof football player, 1968-71; B C Lions, Can football player, 1971-73; Monclair State Col, dir stud serv, 1974-85; Kean Col, dir athletics, 1985-88; Univ Rhode Island, dir athletics, 1988-91; Univ Minn, dir athletics, 1991-96, vpres stud develop & athletics, 1996; Harvard Univ, vis scholar, 1991-92; Mikael Blaisdell & Assocs Inc, pres & chief exec officer; NIRSA J, ed; New Mexico State Univ(NMSU), dir, athletics, 2004-. **Orgs:** Rhode Island Statewide Task Force Anti Drug Coalition, 1989; New Eng Asn Sch & Col Accreditation, 1989-; Eastern Col Athletic Asn Coun, 1990-91; Nat Ethic fel, 1990; Atlantic 10 Conf, 1991; bd trustees, Minneapolis Boy Scouts; bd trustees, Methodist Hosp Found; mem, NCAA Management Coun Leadership cabinet; mem, NCAA Certification Committee; bd mem, La Casa. **Honors/ Awds:** Watson Hon Award & Outstanding Alumni Award, Montclair State Col, 1991. **Special Achievements:** University of Mich, A Survey of Volunteerism in Low Income; Evolution of Intramural Program from Athletics to Physical Education to Student Activities, 1978; Institutional Racism: What is it?, 1980; Who's Boss Student Activities Program, 1981. **Business Addr:** Director of Atheletics, New Mexican State University, MSC 3HLS, PO Box 30001, Las Cruces, NM 88003.*

BOSTON, RALPH HAROLD
Executive, athlete. **Personal:** Born May 9, 1939, Laurel, MS; son of Peter and Eulalia Lott; divorced; children: Kenneth Todd & Stephen Keith. **Educ:** Tenn State Univ, BS. **Career:** Athlete (retired), executive; Nat Track & Field Team, long jumper & capt, 1960-69; Nat Track & Field, long jumper, 1960-69; Univ Tenn, Knoxville, asst dean, students, 1968-75; TV commentator, 1969; ESPN-TV, commentator, 1978-85; Integon Ins Corp, sales; S Cent Bell Adv Systs, acct exec; WKXT-TV, Knoxville, gen partner, 1988-92, limited partner, 1992-; Ericsson-General Electric Inc, major acct mgr, 1992-, dir customer rels; ServiceMaster Serv, pres & chief exec officer; The Forrest Investors Group LLC, vice chmn. **Orgs:** Field judge Special Olympics E Tenn; Gov Coun Phys Fitness & Health, TN;chmn & bd dir, Tenn Sport Fest. **Honors/ Awds:** Gold Medal, Rome Olympics, 1960; titlist, Nat Col Athletic Asn, 1960; Athlete of Year, N Am, 1961; Helms Hall of Fame, 1962; Silver Medal, Tokyo Olympics, 1964; Olympic Bronze Medal, Mex City, 1968; Tenn Sports Hall of Fame, 1970; Nat Track & Field Hall of Fame, 1974; US Track & Field Hall of-Fame, 1975; solo second Pl Team, Championship Nat Asn Intercollegiate Athletics Track Championship; Greatest Long Jumper of the Century, 1979; All Time All Star Indoor Track & Field Hall of Fame, 1982; KnoxvilleSports Hall of Fame, 1982; Mobile Oil Corp Track and Field Hall of Fame, 1983; Tenn State Univ Athletic Hall of Fame, 1983; Olympic Hall of Fame, 1985; Silver Anniversary Award, Nat Col Athletic Asn, 1985. **Special Achievements:** Broke Jesse Owens 25 Yearr Long Jump Record, 1960; First black inducted Mississippi Sports Hall of Fame in 1977; parks named in his honor, Laurel, MS in 1978; first man to jump 26 ft indoors, 27 ft outdoors. *

BOSTON, THOMAS DANNY
Educator. **Educ:** WVa State Univ, BS, 1968; Cornell Univ, MA, 1974, PhD, 1976. **Career:** Clark-Atlanta Univ, Atlanta, Ga, Dept Econ, from asst to assoc prof econ, 1976-78, chmn, 1978-85; Stanford Univ, Dept Econ, vis scholar, 1983-84; Shanghai Inst Finance & Econ, vis lectr, 1983; Ind Univ Pa, Benjamin E Mays Acad, distinguished vis scholar, 1984; Georgia Inst Technol, Ivan Allen Col, Sch Econs, assoc prof econ, 1985-95, prof econs, 1995-; Albany State Col, Sch Bus Admin, distinguished lectr bus, 1990-91; US Senate, Joint Econ Comt Cong, Wash, DC, sr economist, 1992; Boston Res Group Inc, pres & chief exec officer, 1994-2007; WVa State Univ Bd Gov, vpres, 2006-07; EuQuant, pres & chief exec officer, 2007?. **Orgs:** Consultant to numerous interNat & Nat organizations including ING Financial Serv; Inter-Am Develop Bank; UN Educ, Social & Cult Orgn; US Small Bus Admin; US Dept Com; pres, Nat Econ Asn; Black Enterprise Bd Economists; adv, Mayor Shirley Franklins Coun Econs; creator, Gazelle Index; Sigma Xi, Nat Sci Soc, 1989; Am Econ Asn, 2007; Asn Pub Policy Analysis & Mgt, 2007; Sigma Xi. **Honors/Awds:** Outstanding Undergraduate Professor Award, Clark-Atlanta Univ, 1981-82; George C Griffin Undergraduate Faculty of the Year Award, Stud Govt Asn, Ga Inst Technol, 1988-89; State of Georgia Economics Educator of the Year Award, Ga Coun Econ Educ, 1989-90; West Virginia State University ROTC Hall of Fame, 1993; Nat Black Col Alumni Hall of Fame, 2000; Ivan Allen Col Legacy Award, 2005-06. **Special Achievements:** Author or Editor of six books, The Inner City: Urban Poverty and Economic Development in the Next Century, 1997; Affirmative Action and Black Entrepreneurship, 1999; Leading Issues in Black Political Economy, 2002. **Military Serv:** Vietnam veteran, Purple Heart. **Business Addr:** Professor Economics, Georgia Institute of Technology, School of Economics, Rm 303 Habersham Bldg 781 Marietta St, Atlanta, GA 30332-0615, **Business Phone:** (404)894-5020.

BOSWELL, ANTHONY O
Secretary (Organization), executive, vice president (organization). **Educ:** Univ PA, law; Univ NC, Charlotte, MEd. **Career:** Laidlaw Bd Dir Health Care Comn, secy; Laidlaw Bd Dir Ethics & Compliance Comn, secy; AMEC, Ethics & Compliance, sr vpres; AMEC, US Govt Rels, sr vpres; Inst Corp Ethics & Governance, prin bus develop, 2004-. **Business Addr:** Principal, The Institute for Corporate Ethics and Governance, 6635 E 18 Ave Suite 310, Denver, CO 80220, **Business Phone:** (303)519-3296.*

BOSWELL, BENNIE
Banker, administrator. **Personal:** Born May 4, 1948, Danville, VA; son of Edith B Williams and Bennie Sr; married Helen Thomas. **Educ:** Williams Col MA, BA, cum laude, 1970. **Career:** Western Res Acad Hudson, Ohio, instr, 1970-73; Williams Col, asst dir admis, 1973-75; A Better Chance Inc, assoc dir stud affairs, 1975; Wachovia Corp, 1976, sr vpres & dir community affairs, currently. **Orgs:** Am Soc Personnel Admin; black Exec Exch Prog; former mem, ASTD; former pres, Nat Asn Bank Affirmative Action Dir; Nat Asn Advan Colored People; former bd, chmn, Fel Home Winston-Salem; former adv bd mem, Duke Univ LEAD Prog; former mem, exec comn, Williams Col Alumni Soc; consult, Atlanta Adopt-A-Student prog; bd mem, Atlanta Chap Am Inst Banking; alumni admis rep, Williams Col; bd mem, Ga Am Inst Banking; vpres, Bridge; chmn-elect, Atlanta C Shelter; bd mem, Ga Partnership Excellence Educn; asst treas, Atlanta Urban League; bd mem, Camp Best Friends; bd mem, Families First; bd mem, Res Atlanta; bd mem, Piedmont Park Conserv; bd mem, Proj READ; bd mem, Metro Atlanta Pvt Indust Coun; mem, Annual Fund Comt Northwest Ga Coun Girl Scouts; mem, United Way Found Comn; adv comt, Communities Sch Atlanta, 2006-07. **Honors/Awds:** Francis Session Mem Fel, Williams Col, 1970; Lehman Scholar, Williams Col, 1967; Nat Achieve Scholar, Nat Merit Found, 1966. **Business Addr:** Senior Vice President, Director of Community Affairs, Wachovia Bank of Georgia, 191 Peachtree St, Atlanta, GA 30303-8018, **Business Phone:** (404)332-6074.

BOUIE, JOSEPH, JR.
Educator, counselor. **Educ:** Southern Univ, New Orleans, bachelors degree, social work; Tulane Univ, masters degree, social work; Atlanta Univ, doctorate admin & planning. **Career:** Southern Univ New Orleans, chancellor, 2000-02, social work fac, currently. **Special Achievements:** Fifth chancellor & first alumnus of Southern University at New Orleans to hold the position. **Business Addr:** Faculty of Social Work, Southern University at New Orleans, 6400 Press Dr, New Orleans, LA 70126, **Business Phone:** (504)286-5311.*

BOUIE, DR. MERCELINE
Educator. **Personal:** Born Oct 18, 1929, St Louis, MO; daughter of Ray C Morris; married Harry J; children: Ray Anthony & Pamela Sue. **Educ:** Lincoln Univ, BA, behav sci phys educ health, 1953; Webster Univ, BA, social behav sci, 1972, MA, social & behav sci, 1973; Open Univ, PhD, educ social behav sci, 1976. **Career:** Educator (retired); St Louis Archdiocese Parochial Sch Syst, elem & high sch phys educ & health teacher, 1958-64; Venice, IL Sch Syst, dept chmn, phys educ & health teacher, 1964-68; Wheeler State Sch, dept head, young adults, 1968-74; St Louis Bd Educ, resource specialist, 1974-82; St Louis Pub Sch, conductor workshops, 1979-83; psychol examr, 1982-83, learning disabled specialist, 1985; independent speaker & consult, Spec C Learning Prob; Intership Prog, coordr; Right Proud Prog, coordr; Drug Free Sch(TREND) Cleveland NJROTC High Sch, coordr, 1992. **Orgs:** AAUW; except child specialist counr, Bouies Learning Ctr, 1978-85; secondvpres, Learning Disability Asn, 1976-79; adv, Mo Learning Disability Asn,1976-80; Int Platform Asn, 1976-; St Louis Asn Retarded C, 1979-;Grand-lady, Ladies Aux Peter Claver, 1979-82; Pro-life Comt, Our Lady GoodCoun Parish; adv bd, Human Rights Off Archdiocese; judge, Int Platform AsnConv, Wash, DC, 1987; adv, State Rep 56th Dist; pres, Mt Carmel Sch Bd,1989-93; vpres, chmn, Webster Univ Alumni Bd Dir, 1989-92; coordr, Soldan Parent's Orgn, 1989-93; charter mem, World Found Successful Women, 1991;ed bd, Tenn State Univ. **Honors/ Awds:** Parent Involvement, 1976; Committee Leadership, Am Asn Univ Women, 1977;Speaker's Award, Int Platform Asn, 1979; Fourth Degree Award, PeterClaver, 1981; Oryx Press, Dir Speakers, 1981, 1982; Special EducationAward, Civic Liberty Asn, 1982; Community Leadership Award, 27th Ward Alderman; American Association of Poetry Award, 1986; St Louis Symphony Ladies Association Award, 1986; Distinguished Alumni Award, Webster Univ Bd, 1991. **Special Achievements:** Article in North County Journal; published Poem of Life, 1989. **Home Addr:** 4602 Bircher Blvd, Saint Louis, MO 63115, **Home Phone:** (314)382-1079.

BOUIE, PRESTON L
Firefighter. **Personal:** Born Jan 22, 1926, St Louis, MO; son of Vennie Bouie and Emma Reed; married Stella M Mosby, Nov 3, 1946; children: Sylvia N Saddler & Sheila N Sledge. **Educ:** Vashon High Sch, 1944. **Career:** Firefighter (Retired); St Louis Fire Dept, pvt, 1952-63, fire capt, 1963-76, battalion fire chief, 1976-78, dep fire chief, 1978-83, asst fire chief,1983. **Orgs:** Trustee, Wash Metrop Am Zion Church, 1980-. **Honors/Awds:** Vashon High School Hall of Fame, Vashon Hall of Fame Community, 1989. **Special Achievements:** First African-Am to be promoted to Battalion Chief, 1976; first to be promoted to Dep Chief, 1978; the only African-Am Asst Fire Chief, 1983. **Military Serv:** USN, AMMC 3rd class 2 years. **Home Addr:** 1 Friese Dr, St Louis, MO 63132.

BOUIE, SIMON PINCKNEY
Clergy. **Personal:** Born Oct 3, 1939, Columbia, SC; married Willie Omia Jamison; children: Erich, Harold. **Educ:** Allen Univ, BA, 1962; Interdenomination Ctr, BD, 1966; SC State Hosp, clinical ct, 1968. **Career:** Metro AME Church, sr minister; Warwick Sch Boys, first Black Chaplain, 1972-74; Mother Bethel AME Church, sr minister; Emanuel Church, pastor, currently. **Orgs:** chair, Salute Schomburg Ctr Res Black Culture; Salute Harlem

Hosp; Bethel Day Cae Ctr; Ministerial Interfaith Asn Health Comn; The Harlem Civic Welfare Asn Comn Bd; NY AME Ministerial Alliance Social Action Comt; North Central Hosp Day; trustee bd NY Ann Conf AME Church; 100 Black Men Inc; Alpha Phi Alpha Frat; NY Chap NAACP; bd dirs NY City Coun Churches; NY Branch YMCA; Comn Soc Family Man Award; Bd NY State Coun Churches; pres Prince Hall Masons; pres, Harlem Coun; pres, Richard Allen Ctr Life. **Honors/Awds:** Outstanding Award, NY Conf, 1972; Lionel Hampton Award, 1975; Citizen of the Year Award, Bi Centennial, 1976; Suffolk Day Care Award, 1978; Metro AME Church Outstanding Award, 1980; Distinguished Health & Hospital Corporation Award, NY, 1980; first Disting Citizen Award, North Gen Hosp, 1982; DD Degree, Interdenominational Theol Ctr, 1982; DH Degree, Monrovia Col Monrovia W Africa, 1984;Outstanding Alumus Award, Turner Theol Sem, 2002. **Business Addr:** Pastor, Emanuel Church, 37 41 W 119th St, New York, NY 10029, **Business Phone:** (212)722-3969.*

BOUIE, TONY VANDERSON
Football player, chief executive officer. **Personal:** Born Aug 7, 1972, New Orleans, LA; married Allison; children: 2. **Educ:** Univ Ariz, BA, media arts, MA, lang, reading & cult. **Career:** Football player (retired); Tampa Bay Buccaneers, defensive back, 1995-98; Phoenix-based co, CEO, currently.

BOUKNIGHT, DR. REYNARD RONALD
Physician, educator. **Personal:** Born Dec 14, 1946, Washington, DC; son of Johnnie Bell DeWalt and Lue Dennis; married LaClaire Green, Mar 21, 1971; children: Tendai, Omari & Reynard II. **Educ:** Howard Univ, Wash, DC, BS, 1968; Mich State Univ, E Lansing, MI, PhD, 1974, MD, 1975. **Career:** Case Western Res Univ, Cleveland, OH, internal med residency, 1976-79; Hough-Norwood Clinic, Cleveland, OH, chief med, 1979-80; Mich State Univ, E Lansing, MI, asst prof, 1980-85, asst dean, 1983-; assoc prof med, 1985-. **Orgs:** Phi Beta Kappa, 1968; Mich State Med Soc, 1983-90; Am Pub Health Asn, 1987-92; vice-chairperson, Qual Intervention Comt, Mich Peer Rev Orgn, 1987-93. **Honors/Awds:** Fellowship, NSF, 1968; Young Investigator's Award, Nat Inst Allergy & Infectious Dis, 1978; Alpha Omega Alpha Honor Med Soc, 1988; Fellow, Am Col Physicians, 1990. **Home Addr:** 2557 Dustin Rd, Okemos, MI 48864. **Business Addr:** Associate Professor, Michigan State University, Division of General Internal Medicine, B431 Clin Ctr, East Lansing, MI 48824-1317, **Business Phone:** (517)355-9633.

BOULDES, CHARLENE
Accountant. **Personal:** Born May 5, 1945, Brooklyn, NY; children: Anthony, Christi, Minde. **Educ:** Univ Albuquerque, BA, acct, 1981, BA, pub admin, 1982; Univ NewMex, MA, 1983. **Career:** Grad Asst Univ NMex, researcher, 1983; City & Co Task Force, financial adv, 1984-85; Univ NMex, acct supvr; US Forest Serv, acct, 1988; Bernalillo County Treas Off, acct mgr. **Orgs:** Nat Asn Advan Colored People, 1951-, Nat Asn Advan Colored People Youth Sponsor, 1982-; Nat Asn Pub Acct, Univ Albuquerque, 1981; Am Soc Pub Admin, Univ NMex, 1982; grad asst, Univ NMex Pub Admin, 1982-84; pres, elect Civitan Int, 1984-85. **Honors/Awds:** Scholar Univ Albuquerque, 1981; Phi Alpha Alpha Nat Honor, Soc Univ NMex, 1984; Outstanding Grad Student, Univ NMex Pub Admin, 1984. *

BOULDES, RUTH IRVING
Automotive executive, manager. **Personal:** Born Nov 22, 1946, Bronx, NY; daughter of Charles Bouldes and Fannye Irving-Gibbs; divorced. **Educ:** Bernard Baruch, BBA, 1976; Fordham Univ, MBA, 1978. **Career:** Gen Motors, GM Overseas Group, 1965-78, GM Denmark, dist mgr, 1978-80, GM Continental, dealer orgn mgr, 1980-81, Mkt Res, asst mgr, 1981-82, Dealer Orgn & Planning, asst mgr, 1982-84; Chevrolet Motor Div, asst zone mgr (Detroit, MI), 1983-84, asst zone mgr (Minneapolis, MN), 1984-86, communs mgr, 1986-95, Total Customer Enthusiam & Orgna Learning, proj mgr, 1996-98; GM, market area mgr, 1999, zone mgr, currently. **Orgs:** Nat bd mem, Campfire Boys & Girls, 1993-96; immediate past pres, 1998-, pres, 1996-98, The Art Ctr. **Special Achievements:** First American female given a European sales assignment by GM, 1979-82; good command of German, Danish, 1979-82. **Business Addr:** Market Area Manager, General Motors Inc, 300 Renaissance Ctr, Detroit, MI 48265-4000, **Business Phone:** (313)556-5000.

BOULWARE, FAY D.
Educator. **Personal:** Daughter of Fay Hendley (deceased) and William R (deceased); children: William H. **Educ:** Hunter Col CUNY, BA; Teachers Col Columbia Univ, MA, prof dipl. **Career:** Educator (retired); Teachers Col Columbia Univ, assoc admis, 1960-64; Inst Dev Stds New York Med Col, adminr coord/inst, 1964-66; Inst Develop Studies New York Univ, dir admin & res scientist, 1966-71; Educ Studies Prog Wesleyan Univ, lectr, 1971-75; African Am Inst Wesleyan Univ, dir, 1971-75; Emmaline Prod, hist & literary researcher, 1982; Merrill Lynch, Pierce, Fenner & Smith, prof writer, 1983-92; Chuckles Prod, dir story develop & res, 1983-90. **Orgs:** Consult, St Croix VI, 1965, bd educ, Middletown, CT, 1972-73, Lansing, MI, 1971, Atlanta, GA 1971, Charlotte, NC, 1969-71, Model Cities, Pittsburgh, PA, 1969, Univ Hawaii, 1967, Virgin Isls Day Sch; consult, acad adv bd, Wesleyan Univ, 1971-75; consult, NY City Bd Educ, 1971-92. **Honors/Awds:** Wesleyan Master Teacher, 1972, 1973, 1974; Black Alumni Honoree, Wesleyan Univ, 1993.

BOULWARE, PETER NICHOLAS
Football player, politician. **Personal:** Born Dec 18, 1974, Columbia, SC; son of Raleigh and Melva; married Kensy; children: 3. **Educ:** Fla State Univ, BS, MIS. **Career:** Football player(retired), Politician; Baltimore Ravens, line back, 1997-2003, 2005; Tallahassee Toyota dealer, vpres, currently. **Orgs:** Peter Boulware Charitable Fund; UMM Children's Hosp Bd; founder, Peter Boulware Youth Tackle Football League. **Honors/Awds:** Nation's Top 50 Athletes, The Atlanta Jour-Constitution; Top 100 hons, The Dallas Morning News; Pro Bowl, first alternate, 1998; Good Guy Award, 1999; Ed Block Courage Award, 1999; Pro Bowls 2000, 2003, 2004; Ravens Ring of Honor. **Business Phone:** (850)668-5808.*

BOUQUETT, TAMARA TUNIE. See TUNIE, TAMARA.

BOURNE, DOUGLAS. See DOUG, DOUG E.

BOURNE, JUDITH LOUISE
Lawyer. **Personal:** Born Jul 2, 1945, New York City, NY; daughter of Gwendolyn Samuel and St Clair T. **Educ:** Cornell Univ, BA 1966; NY Univ Law Sch, JD, 1972, LLM Intl Law, 1974. **Career:** NY Univ Clin Learning, com asst, 1966-67; NYC Human Resources Admin, spec asst admin, 1967-68; NYC Neighborhood Youth Corps, spec consult dir, summer progs, 1968; Bd Fundament Educ, prog assoc admin liaison tech training, 1968-69; Nat Coun Crime & Deliquency, legal intern, 1970-71; NY State Spec Comn Attica, ed staff, 1972; NY Univ Sch Continuing Educ, instr, 1973; Emergency Land Fund, SC state, coord 1974; pvt pract, atty, 1974-77; Off Fed Pub Defender, asst fed pub defender, 1977-81; pvt pract, atty, St Thomas, US, VI, 1982-; lead defense coun, Intl Criminal Tribunal Rwanda, 1998-2000. **Orgs:** Nat Conf Black Lawyers, 1973-; Intl Affairs Task Force, SC State Dir, 1973-76; Jr fel NY Univ, Ctr Intl Studies, 1972-73; Nat co-chair, 1976-79; Intl Com Inquiry Crimes Racist & Apartheid Regimes Southern Africa, 1976-90;chairperson, Polit Affairs Task Force, 1979-80; VI Bar Asn, 1983, treas, 1984, sec, 1985, mem bd governers, 1987;VI Bar Asn; Almeric L Christian Lawyers, Asn; Caribbean Develop Coalition; chair, VI Anti-Apartheid Com, 1985-; sec, bd mem, United Way St Thomas & St John, 1987-91; bd dirs, Barbados Asn St Thomas-St John, 1995-97; pres, Interfaith Coalition St Thomas/St John, 1996-97; bd mem, UN Asn, VI, 1993-, vpres, 1995-97, pres, 1998-; Nat Conference Black Lawyers; Int Asn Dem Lawyers. **Honors/Awds:** Outstanding Young Women of America, 1976. **Business Addr:** Attorney, The Bourne Law Office PLLC, 19 Norre Gade, PO Box 6458, St Thomas, Virgin Islands of the United States 00804, **Business Phone:** (340)776-8487.

BOUTTE, ERNEST JOHN
Executive. **Personal:** Born Aug 18, 1943, Salinas, CA; son of Joseph Adbon and Rose Ann Broussard; married Eleanor Rojas, Feb 6, 1963; children: Mark Joseph & Marlo Shay. **Educ:** Hartnell Col, Salinas, CA, AS, elec eng, 1973; Fresno State Univ, Fresno, CA, ind tech, 1978-83; Univ San Francisco, San Francisco, CA, BS, bus mgt, 1983; Univ Idaho, Moscow, ID, Grad, exec degree prog, Mgt, econs, 1989. **Career:** Executive (retired): Pac Gas & Elec Co, gen mgr utility opers, 1965. **Orgs:** Pac Coast Employee Asn, 1965-; assoc mem, Pac Coast Elec Asn, 1978-; assoc mem, Am Mgt Asn, 1983-; life mem, Hispanic Employee Asn, 1985; assoc mem, Am Blacks Energy, 1988-; life mem, Black Employee Asn, 1991. **Military Serv:** USN, petty officer, 2nd class, 1962-65; Vietnam Service Award Medal.

BOUTTE, MARC ANTHONY
Football player. **Personal:** Born Jul 25, 1969, Lake Charles, LA; married Tananjalyn. **Educ:** La State Univ. **Career:** Football player (retired); Los Angeles Rams, defensive tackle, 1992-93; Wash Redskins, 1994-99.

BOUTTE, RHONDA
Artist, executive. **Career:** Undermain Theatre, mem; Kitchen Dog Theater, artistic assoc, currently. **Business Addr:** Artistic Associate, Kitchen Dog Theater, 3120 McKinney Ave, Dallas, TX 75204, **Business Phone:** (214)953-1055.*

BOWDEN, JOE. See BOWDEN, JOSEPH TARROD.

BOWDEN, JOSEPH TARROD (JOE BOWDEN)
Football player, football coach. **Personal:** Born Feb 25, 1970, Dallas, TX. **Educ:** Univ Okla, commun; Alcorn State univ. **Career:** Football player (retired), football coach; Houston Oilers, linebacker,1992-96; Tenn Oilers, linebacker, 1997-98; Tenn Titans, linebacker, 1999; Dallas Cowboys, linebacker, 2000; Scottish Claymores, intern coach, 2004;Buffalo Bills training camp, coach, 2004; Hamburg Sea Devils, defensiveasst, 2005; Alma Mater, Alcorn State Univ, Asst Football Coach, 2006. **Honors/Awds:** All-American.

BOWDEN, DR. REGINA GEORGE
Educator. **Personal:** Born Mar 14, 1947, Durham, NC; daughter of Reginald C; divorced; children: Merris. **Educ:** Tenn State Univ, BS, 1968; NC Central Univ, MA, 1972; NC A&T State Univ, MEd Ad, 1977; North Carolina State Univ, EdD, 1989. **Career:** Shaw Univ, prof sociol, educ, 1990-2000; NC C Univ, teacher educ liaison, 1997-2003; Holloway Neighborhood Achievement Sch, pres, owner, 2003-. **Orgs:** Southern Sociol Soc, 1972-; Nat Sch Bd Asn, 1995-; Urban Coun Bd Educ, 1995-; Delta Sigma Theta; The Girlfriends Inc; vice chair, Durham County Bd Comnrs; Durham Public Schs Bd Edu. **Honors/Awds:** Service Award, AIDS Found, 2000. **Special Achievements:** Author: "Passing on the Culture, Poverty, Immigration and the Affects of African-Caribbean Families in Limon Province, Costa Rica;" "Teen Mothers;" "Evaluation & Community Service Programs;" "Women in Costa Rica". **Home Addr:** 232 Monticello Ave, Durham, NC 27707, **Home Phone:** (919)490-1294.

BOWDOIN, ROBERT E.
Executive. **Personal:** Born May 4, 1929, Los Angeles, CA; married Joan; children: Kimberly J, Robert G & Wendy M. **Educ:** Univ Calif, LA, BS, 1951. **Career:** Pasadena Redevel Agy, dep adminstr tech serv redevel mgr; Bowdin Neal &Weathers, fedr; Fairway Escrow Co, LA, co-owner & mgr; Watts Savings &Loan, real estate appraiser, loan officer & escrow officer; Ginge Inc; Family Savings & Loan Assoc, pres & chief exec officer. **Orgs:** Bd mem, United Way; Nat Archit Engr Firm; Brotherhood Crusade; Altadna Lib Bd; bd mem, Calif Savings & Loan League; Am Savings & Loan League; US Savings & Loan League. **Business Addr:** President, Chief Executive Officer, Family Savings & Loan Associates, 3683 Crenshaw Blvd, Los Angeles, CA 90016.

BOWE, RIDDICK (RIDDICK LAMONT BOWE)
Boxer. **Personal:** Born Oct 8, 1967, Brooklyn, NY; son of Dorothy Bowe; married Judy, 1986; children: Riddick, Jr, Ridicia & Brenda. **Career:** Heavyweight boxer; US Marine Corps; boxer. **Honors/Awds:** heavyweight boxing champion, (WBA, IBF), 1992-93; heavyweight boxing champion, (WBC), 1992; WBO World heavyweight championship, 1995v1996; Seoul, Olympic medal record, Super heavyweight, 1998. **Special Achievements:** Guest appearance on The Fresh Prince of Bel Air; Giant Steps Award. *

BOWE, RIDDICK LAMONT. See BOWE, RIDDICK.

BOWEN, DR. BLANNIE
Educator. **Personal:** Born Apr 26, 1953, Wilmington, NC; son of Herman Thomas and Beulah Mae Bryant; married Cathy Faulcon, Jun 18, 1977; children: Marcus & Douglas. **Educ:** NC Agr & Tech State Univ, Greensboro, NC, BS, agr educ, 1974, MS, agr educ, 1976; Ohio State Univ, Columbus, OH, PhD, agr educ, 1980. **Career:** Miss State Univ, asst assoc prof, 1980-85; Ohio State Univ, Columbus, OH, assoc prof, 1985-88; Penn State Univ, Univ Park, PA, Graduate Sch, assoc dean & sr faculty mentor; Penn State Univ, Univ Park, PA, C Lee Rumberger chair Agr, 1988-2004, assoc dean, grad sch, 1996-98, dept agr & exten educ, head, 1998-2004, prof & vice provost acad affairs, 2004. **Orgs:** Ed, Ag Educ Mag, 1986-88; Univ Rep, Nat Coun Agr Educ, 1990-92; ed bd, Jour Appl Communications, 1990-92; ed bd, Jour Voc & Tech Educ, 1990-95; nat secy, Minorities in Agr & Related Sci, 1990-91. **Honors/Awds:** Outstanding Young Member, American Asn of Teacher Educrs in Agriculture, 1985; Service Award, Nat Agricultural Communicators Tomorrow Orgn, 1987-88; Distinguished Alumni of the Year, Nat Asn for Equal Opportunity in Higher Educ, 1990; Outstanding Service Award, Omicron Tau Theta Professional Society, Penn State Chapter, 1990; Outstanding Research Paper, Eastern Agricultural Education Research Conference, 1989; HO Sargent Award, Nat FFA Orgn, 1997. **Business Addr:** Vice Provost for Academic Affairs, The Pennsylvania State University, 201 Old Main, University Pk, PA 16802, **Business Phone:** (814)863-7494.

BOWEN, BRUCE
Basketball player. **Personal:** Born Jun 14, 1971, Merced, CA; married Yardley Barbon, Jan 1, 2004; children: Ojani & Ozmel. **Educ:** Fullerton Col, attended 1993, 2006. **Career:** Miami Heat, forward, 1996-97; Boston Celtics, 1997-98; Philadelphia 76ers, 1999-2001; San Antonio Spurs, forward, 2001-. **Orgs:** H-E-B; Spurs Found; founder & pres, Bruce Bowen Found, currently. **Honors/Awds:** All-Defensive hons; NBA Defensive Player of the Year, 2005, 2006. **Business Addr:** Professional Basketball Player, San Antonio Spurs, 1 AT&T Ctr, San Antonio, TX 78219, **Business Phone:** (210)444-5000.

BOWEN, DR. CLOTILDE DENT
Psychiatrist. **Personal:** Born Mar 20, 1923, Chicago, IL; daughter of William M Dent and Clotilde Tynes Dent; divorced. **Educ:** Ohio State Univ, BA, 1943; OH State Univ Med Sch, MD, 1947; Am Bd Psychiat & Neurol, dipl cert psychiat, 1966. **Career:** Psychiatrist (retired); Harlem Hosp, intern, 1947-48; NYC, residency in TB, 1948-49; NY State, fel in TB, 1950; pvt pract, Harlem, 1950-55; NY City Health Dept, TB clinic, chief, 1950-55; Valley Forge Gen Hosp, Army Captain, maj, 1955-59; Albany Vets Admin Hosp, residency, 1959-62; Active Reserve, 1959-67, VA Hosp, psych, 1962-67; Albany Med Curt Hosp, asst resident psychiat, 1961-62; Veterans Admin, Roseburg, OR, chief psychiat, 1964-67; AUS, Tripler Hosp, chief psychiat serv, 1967-68;

OCHAMPUS, chief patient serv div & psych consult, 1968-70; AUS, Vietnam, neuro psychconsult, 1970-71; Fitzsimons Army Med Ctr, chief dept psych, 1971; HSC Region V Area, consult, 1971-74; Univ Colo Sch Med, assoc clin prof psych,1971; US Probation Office Denver, psych consult, 1973-85; Tripler Army Med Ctr, chief dept psych, 1974-75; Univ HI, clin assoc prof, 1974-75; Dept Clinics Fitzsimons Army Med Ctr, liaison psych, 1976-77; AUS, Hawley Army Med Clinic, Ft Benjamin Harrison, IN, comdr, 1977-78; Fitzsimons Army Med Ctr, chief dept primary care, 1979-83; Joint Comn Accrediation of Health care Orgs, psychiat consult, 1985-92; Veterans Affairs Med Ctr, Cheyenne, WY, chief psychiat, 1987-90; Veterans Affairs Med Ctr, Denver, CO, staff psychiatrist, 1990-96; pvt pract & locum Tenens. **Orgs:** Fel, Am Psychiat Asn; Cent Neuropsychiat Asn; Alpha Epsilon Iota; Res Officers Asn; Colorado Psychiat Soc, 1971-90; Oregon Psychiat Asn; Historical Archives Colorado Med Soc; exec mem, Nat Endowment for the Humanities, 1971-75; APA Coun Emerging Issues, 1972-75; fel, Acad Psychosomatic Med; Intl Soc Electro therapy; Nat Med asn; fel, Menninger Found; Asn Mil Surgeons US; Joint Rev Comt Paramedic Stands, 1972-73; AMA; Nat Asn VA Chiefs Psychiat, 1989-90. **Honors/Awds:** Scholar, Achievement Delta Sigma Theta Sor, 1945; Certificate of Commendation, Veterans Admin, 1966; Nat Achievcment Award, Nat Asn Negro Bus & Prof Women's Clubs Inc, 1969; Woman of the Year, Denver Bus & Prof Women's Club, 1972; Ohio State Med Alumni Achievement Award, 1972; DeHaven-Hinkson Award, Nat Med Asn, 1972; Distinguished Award, OH State Univ, 1975; Hall of Champions, Champion Jr High Sch; fel, Acad Psychosomatic Med, 1978; Distinguished life fel, Am Psychiat Asn, 2001; President's 300 Commencement Award, OH State Univ, 1987; Distinguished Black Alumni Award, OH State Univ Stud Nat Med Asn, 1987; Ohio State Univ Professional Achievement Award, 1998; United Negro Col Fund Eminent Scholar, 1990; Peter Basso fel, Cent Neuro psychiat Asn, 2000; Award for Early Contributions in the Field, Am Asn Emergency Psychiatrists, 2002; Distinguished life fel, Am Psychiat Asn, 2003. **Special Achievements:** First Black woman to graduate from Ohio State University Medical School & residency in psychiatry at Albany VA & Albany Medical Center Hospitals; First Black Female Physician in the US Army and the first Black Female to attain the rank of Colonel; co-writer, Chapter on Military Psychiat, 1998; publs: "Black Ams in Military Psychiat," Black Psychiatrists & Am Psychiat, 1997; "My Pvt Vietnam: Men & Women Shadowed by a War They Can't Forget," Modern Maturity Mag, May-June 2000. **Military Serv:** AUS, capt-colonel, 30 yrs; first black female med officer, 1955; 1968; Bronze Star, 1971; Legion of Merit, for Serv in Vietnam, 1971; Meritorious Service Medal, 1974. **Home Addr:** 1020 Tari Dr, Colorado Springs, CO 80921.

BOWEN, ERVA J.
Sociologist. **Personal:** Born Oct 12, 1919, Winfield, KS; daughter of D W Walker; married John R; children: Randy, John H & Gary. **Educ:** Southwestern Col, Teacher's Cert, 1941; Univ Calif, Berkeley, Cert, social serv, 1961. **Career:** Sociologist (retired); Santa Cruz City Welfare Dept, social worker, 1958-72; Family Service Asn, sr outreach counr, 1989. **Orgs:** Del Assembly, Calif Sch bd Asn, 1979-81; pres, Santa Cruz City Sch, bd ed, 1976-77; Santa Cruz Housing Advisory comt, 1974-76; Citizen's Planning Advisory Comt, 1972; chmn, Santa Cruz Workable Program Comt, 1969-70; Santa Cruz City Comt on Status of Women, 1973-75; Calif Soc Workers Org; Calif Alphi Phi Sigma Alpha; bd dir, YWCA, 1960-64, 1974-75; Santa Cruz Br, NAACP, pres, 1962-66, 1968-70, secy, 1960-68, vpres, 1968-74; pres, Santa Cruz Church Women United, 1980-83; pres, District 28 Amer Legion Auxiliary Dept Calif, 1984-85; Salvation Army Advisory Bd, 1986-; secy & mem chmn, Senior's Coun (Area Agency on Aging) Santa Cruz & San Benito Counties SC County Affirmative Action Comm; Ch Intern affairs Sub Comm; Elected Santo Cruz City Sch Bd Educ, 1973, Reelected, 1979. **Honors/Awds:** NAACP Freedom Award, 1974; Women of Achievement, BPWC, 1974.

BOWEN, GEORGE WALTER
Educator. **Personal:** Born Dec 13, 1946, Council, NC; son of Estelle and Jesse W. **Educ:** Los Angeles Valley Col, AA, criminal justice, 1974; Calif State Univ, Los Angeles, BS, criminal justice, 1975, MS, pub admin, 1979. **Career:** Rochester City Sch Dist, dir, 1999-2001; Savannah-Chatham Co Pub Schs, dep supt, coodr, 2001-06, acting supt schs, 2004-06. **Orgs:** Air Force Asn, 1978-; Armed Froces Commun Electronics Asn, 1978-. **Honors/Awds:** Outstanding Graduate Student, Calif State Univ, LA, 1979; Outstanding Citizens Award, 2006. **Military Serv:** USAF, col, 1965-99; Meritorious Service Medal, 1995; Legion of Merit,1999.

BOWEN, DR. RAYMOND COBB
College administrator. **Personal:** Born Sep 19, 1934, New Haven, CT; son of Raymond Curtis and Lucille Cobb; married Joan; children: Raymond C III, Rebecca M, Ruth J & Rachel R. **Educ:** Univ Conn, BA, zool, 1956, PhD, 1966; Univ New Mex, MS, biol, 1962. **Career:** Col Administrator (retired); Ohio Wesleyan Univ & Univ Ill, post doctoral, 1966-67; Cleveland State Univ, prof biol, 1968, pres & dean develop progs, 1968-71; City Univ NY, LaGuardia Community Col, assoc prof nat scis, assoc dean fac, 1971, dean acad affairs, 1973, pres & prof natural & appl sci, 1989-99; Community Col, Baltimore, vpres acad affairs & stud affairs, 1975-82; Shelby State Community Col, pres, 1982-89; Morgan State Univ Grad Sch, vis prof, 1999. **Orgs:** ACE, AACC, 1981; bd dir, SACJC, 1985; bd trustee, Leadership Memphis, 1985; bd dir, United Way, 1985; vice chmn & bd dir, Bio-Med Res Zone, 1985. **Honors/Awds:** Outstanding Educator of Public Higher Education, Memphis Bd Educ, 1982. **Military Serv:** AUS, sgt, 1956-59.

BOWEN, RICHARD, JR.
Executive, educator. **Personal:** Born Apr 20, 1942, Colp, IL; son of Richard and Helen; married Cleatia B Rafe; children: Gerald & Chantel. **Educ:** VTI Southern IL Univ, AA, 1966; Southern IL Univ, BS, 1969; Purdue Univ, MS, 1971. **Career:** Restaurant Bar, owner, 1964-71; Purdue Univ, teaching asst, 1969-71; Lincoln Land Community Col, prof, 1971-78, div chmn, 1978-, bus, pub & human serv chair; Pillsbury Mills, mgt consult, 1973-75; real estate sales, mgr, 1985. **Orgs:** Secy, Chrysler Customer Satisfaction Bd, 1980-87; training officer, Small Bus Admin, 1982-85; suprv comn, 1984-85; vpres, Sangamon Sch Credit Union; prog chmn Breakfast Optimist Club, 1985; Frontiers Int Springfield Club; Chair, bd, Sangamon Schools Credit Union. **Military Serv:** AUS E-4, 2 yrs. **Home Addr:** 26 Vivian Ln, Springfield, IL 62707, **Home Phone:** (217)529-0767. *

BOWENS, GREGORY JOHN
Government official. **Personal:** Born Jan 7, 1965, Detroit, MI; son of Italee M; married Jeannine P, Jul 2, 1994; children: Langston & Zora. **Educ:** Morehouse Col, attended 1987; Wayne State Univ, 1992. **Career:** Automotive News, spec corresp, 1990-91; Detroit Free Press, reporter, 1991; Bus Week Mag, spec corresp, 1991-93; Cong Quarterly Mag, reporter, 1993-94; Flint Jour, reporter, 1994-95; Detroit News, reporter, 1995; Detroit Housing Comn, consult-media rels, 1996; Mayor's off, deputy press secy, 1996, dir media rels & pub affairs, 1998, press secy, 1999; Shaun Wilson & Assocs, vpres media rels & pub affairs. **Orgs:** Treas, Nat Asn Black Journalists, 1993-01, sgt at arms, 1997-. **Honors/Awds:** News Reporting Award, Detroit Press Club, 1991; Publishing Award, McGraw Hill, 1992; Best Story Award, 1994. **Special Achievements:** First reporter to publish article on Ford's return to #1 in family cars. **Military Serv:** USN, E-4, 1987-89, Sea Service Ribbon; Development Ribbon. **Business Addr:** Vice President of Media Relations & Public Affairs, Shaun Wilson & Associates, Troy, MI.

BOWENS, DR. JOHNNY WESLEY
Educator. **Personal:** Born Jun 2, 1946, Jacksonville, FL; married Monica Darlene Lewis; children: Torrence, Derick & Omari. **Educ:** Dillard Univ, BA, 1968; Univ Ariz, MEd, 1973; Union Inst, PhD, 1977. **Career:** Pima Community Col, dir student activities, 1970-86, coord financial aid, 1986-; Univ Ariz, Africana Studies Prog, adj lectr, currently. **Orgs:** Allocation chair, Tucson United Way, 1985-; First vpres, Tucson Br NAACP, 1985-87. **Business Addr:** Adjunct Lecturer, The University of Arizona, Africana Studies Program, 1512 E 1st St 223 LSB, Tucson, AZ 85721-0105, **Business Phone:** (520)621-5665.

BOWENS, TIM. **See BOWENS, TIMOTHY L.**

BOWENS, TIMOTHY L. (TIM BOWENS)
Football player. **Personal:** Born Feb 7, 1973, Okolona, MS; children: Camrin Deion. **Educ:** Miss State Univ. **Career:** Football player (retired); Miami Dolphins, defensive tackle, 1994-2004. **Honors/Awds:** NFL Defensive Rookie of the Yr, Associated Press & Pro Football Weekly,1994; Pro Bowl, 1998, 2002. *

BOWE-QUICK, MARIE
School principal. **Educ:** DC Teachers Col, BS, 1974; Univ Md, MA, 1975; George Wash Univ, ESOL cert, 1990; PhD, 1992. **Career:** Godwin Mid Sch, asst prin, 1974-90; Prince William County, Godwin Mid Sch,spec educ adminr, summer sch prin, 1997; Parkside Middle Sch, prin, 1998-. **Business Addr:** Principal, Parkside Middle School, 8602 Mathis Ave, Manassas, VA 20110, **Business Phone:** (703)361-3106.

BOWER, DR. BEVERLY L.
Educator. **Personal:** Born Sep 10, 1951, Washington, DC; daughter of James T Johnson and Bettylou C Johnson; married Jack R Jr. **Educ:** Univ Kans, BS, educ, 1973; Emporia State Univ, MLS, 1980; Fla State Univ, PhD, 1992. **Career:** Lansing Jr High Sch, reading teacher, 1973-74; Chillicothe High Sch, Fr &Eng teacher, 1974-75; Dept Defense Dependent Schs, Fr & Eng teacher, 1975-80; Pensacola Jr Col, librn, 1980-84, dir libr serv, 1985-92; Fla State Univ, fel, 1990-91; Univ SC, Col Educ, asst prof, 1993-96; Fla State Univ, Col Educ, asst prof, 1997-2002, assoc prof, 2002-08, Hardee Ctr Women Higher Educ, dir, 2002-04, assoc dept chair, 2003-04, prog coordr, 2005-07; Univ N Texas, Dir, 2008-. **Orgs:** Secy, W Fla Libr Asn, 1981-83; ALA-JMRT Minorities Recruitment Comn, 1982-83; community col caucus chair/chair-elect, Fla Libr Asn, 1986-88;regional dir, FL Asn Community Col, 1987; chap pres, Fla Asn Community Cols, 1988; bd dirs, YWCA Pensacola, 1989-91; founding chap pres, AAWCC, 1990-96; ASHE, 1991-; AERA, 1994-; bd govs, FSU Hardee Ctr, 1997-2002,exec dir, 2003-; bd, CSCC, 1998-; United Fac Fla, 2001-; FSU Fac Sen,2003-. **Honors/Awds:** Outstanding Teacher Award, USC Mortar Bd, 1994; Nat Achievement Scholar. **Business Addr:** Director, Bill J. Priest Center for Community College Education, University of North Texas, 1155 Union Circle 311277, Denton, TX 76203-5017, **Business Phone:** (940)565-2000.

BOWERS, GEORGE D
Executive director. **Career:** Fed Maritime Comn, Off Info Resources Mgt, head, dir, 2003. **Business Addr:** Director, Federal Maritime Commission, 800 N Capital St NW, Washington, DC 20573, **Business Phone:** (202)523-5835.

BOWERS, GWENDOLYN
Lawyer. **Career:** atty, currently. **Business Addr:** Attorney, Private Practitioner, 1712 W 3rd St, Dayton, OH 45407, **Business Phone:** (937)461-9297.*

BOWERS, MIRION PERRY
Physician. **Personal:** Born Aug 25, 1935, Bascom, FL; married Geraldine Janis Nixon; children: Jasmine Anusha, Mirion Perry Jr, Jarvis Andrew, Jeryl Anthony. **Educ:** Fla A&M Univ, Tallahassee, BA, 1957; Meharry Med Col, Nashville, MD, 1963. **Career:** Univ Calif Los Angeles, Sch Med, Dept Surg, asst prof, 1972-73; Martin Luther King Jr Gen Hosp, Div Otolaryngol, Charles R Drew Post Grad Med Sch, asst prof & chief, 1972-73; Univ Calif Los Angeles, Sch Med, Dept Head-Neck Surg, asst clin prof, 1973-; Good Samaritan Hosp, chmn otolaryngol, 1976-, secy/treas med staff, 1976-, secy operating rm comt, 1986-, bd trustees, 1989-, mem exec comt, 1989-, pres & chief exec officer, currently; USC Sch Med, Dept Otolaryngol, Head & Neck, clin profile; pvt pract, physician. **Orgs:** Taunus Med Soc Frankfurt, Ger, 1969-72; fel Am Acad Ophthalmol & Otolaryngol, 1970-; Am Col Surgeons, 1972-; Am Med Asn, 1972-; Nat Med Asn, 1973-; Charles R Drew Med Soc, 1973-; chmn, Otolaryngol Sect, Calif Med Ctr, 1982-85; bd dirs, Fla A&M Found, 1989-; bd dirs, City Nat Bank, Beverly Hills, CA, 1994-; bd dirs, Braille Inst, CA, 1995-; Am Coun Otolaryngol; bd dir, Los Angeles Chap, Am Cancer Soc; Los Angeles City Med Asn; Soc Upper Tenth, Meharry Med Col. **Special Achievements:** Numerous publications. **Military Serv:** AUS, Med Corps, lt col, 1963-72; AUS, Gen Hosp Frankfurt Ger, chief otolaryngol serv. **Business Addr:** Otolaryngologist, Good Samaritan Hospital, 1245 Wilshire Blvd Suite 514, Los Angeles, CA 90017.*

BOWIE, DR. JANICE
College teacher, educator. **Educ:** Shaw Univ, BS, 1974; Univ NC, Chapel Hill, MPH, 1986; Johns Hopkins Univ, PhD, 1997. **Career:** Virginia Dept Health, dir chronic disease control programs; Johns Hopkins Univ, Dept Health Policy & Mgt, asst prof, currently. **Honors/Awds:** Minority Student Scholarship, Johns Hopkins Sch Hyg & Pub Health, 1996. **Special Achievements:** Numerous publications including, "The Relationship Between Religious Coping Style and Anxiety Over Breast Cancer in African American Women", Jour Relig & Health, 2001; "Heart Disease: Implications for Patient Attitudes and Future Health Behavior", Phylon, 2003; "Spirituality and Care of Prostate Cancer Patients: A Pilot Study", JNMA, 2003. **Business Addr:** Assistant Professor, Johns Hopkins University, Department of Health Policy & Management, 624 N Broadway, Baltimore, MD 21205, **Business Phone:** (410)614-6119.

BOWIE, LARRY DARNELL, JR.
Football player. **Personal:** Born Mar 21, 1973, Anniston, AL. **Educ:** Northeastern Okla A&M Col; Univ Ga. **Career:** Football player (retired); Wash Redskins, running back, 1996-99.

BOWIE, OLIVER WENDELL
Certified public accountant. **Personal:** Born Jun 25, 1947, Detroit, MI; son of Ulvene Shaw; married Penelope Ann Jackson; children: Stephanie, Traci & Oliver II. **Educ:** Eastern Mich Univ, BBA, 1972; Elon Col, MBA, 1994. **Career:** Mich Dept Treas, revenue agt, 1970-73; Coopers & Lybrand, sr acct, 1973-75; Nat Bank Detroit, audit mgr, 1975-77; Wayne Co Community Col, dir acct, 1977-79; Garrett Sullivan Davenport Bowie & Grant, vpres, 1980-88; Bowie Oliver CPA, sole proprietor, 1988-94, pres, 1994-. **Orgs:** Am Inst CPA, 1975, Mich Asn CPA, 1975, NC Asn CPA, 1985, Greensboro W-S HP Airport Authority, 1985-; treas & pres, Triad Sickle Cell Found, 1985; pres, Trial Nat Asn Black Acct, 1986-; chmn, L Richardson Hosp, 1986; treas, Greensboro Br, Nat Asn Advan Colored People, 1993. **Honors/Awds:** Certificate of Apppreciation, Nat Asn Black Acct, 1977. **Home Addr:** 318 W Montcastle Dr, Greensboro, NC 27406. **Business Addr:** Owner, Bowie Oliver CPA, 1014 Homeland Ave Suite 102, Greensboro, NC 27420, **Business Phone:** (336)273-9461.

BOWIE, STAN L
Educator. **Educ:** Shippensburg Univ Pa, BA; Atlanta Univ, MSW; Barry Univ, PhD. **Career:** Univ Tenn, Col Social Work, assoc prof, currently. **Honors/Awds:** Hardy Liston Symbol of Hope Award. **Special Achievements:** Author of books and articles. **Business Addr:** Associate Professor, University Tennessee, College Social Work, 321 Henson Hall 1618 Cumberland Ave, Knoxville, TN 37996-3333.

BOWIE, DR. WALTER C.
Educator. **Personal:** Born Jun 29, 1925, Kansas City, KS; married Cornelia Morris; children: Carolyn Brown, Colleen Wells & Sybil

K. **Educ:** Kans State Univ, DVM, 1947; Cornell Univ, MS, 1955, PhD, 1960; Kansas State UNIV, Phd, Sci, 1984. **Career:** Vet Med Ti, instr 1947; Head Dept Physiol Sch Vet Med Tuskegee Inst,1960-71; Vet Admn Hosp Tuskegee, AL, res, 1965; Howard Univ, vis prof, 1965-90; Univ Al Med Ctr, vis prof, 1967-75; Sch Vet Med Tuskegee Inst, assoc dean, 1971-72; Cornell Univ, Dept Physiol, adj prof, 1972-73; Sch Vet Med Tuskegee Inst, dean,1972-90; Univ Al Med Ctr,vis head, Dept Physio Sch Vet Med Tuskegee Inst, assoc prof; Physio & Nicotine, consult; Tuskegee Univ, Dean Emer, currently. **Orgs:** Deans Adv Coun, Va Hosp, 1972-80; consult, Inst Med NAS, 1972-74; comn Human Resource Nat Res Coun, 1975-79; Comt Vet Med Sci Nat Res Coun, 1975-76; Bd dir, AL Heart Assoc, 1972-76; pres, Am Soc Vet Physio & Pharmacologists, 1966-67; sec World Soc Vet Physio & Pharm; chmn, Coun Deans AAVMC, 1977; consult, Health Prof Ed Sec DHEW; consult, Ford MotorCo S Africa, 1974; adv, screening com Coun Intl Exchange Scholar Wash,1976-79; delegate, Am Heart Asn, 1970-72; delegate, World Soc Vet Physio & Pharms Paris, 1968; res, Sec Off Am Vet Med Asn mem comt Am Physio Soc,1970-73; consult, NIH Arlington, 1968-70; Sigman Xi; Phi Kappa Phi; Am Vet Asn; AL Vet Med Asn; Primate Res Ctr Adv Comt NIH, 1972-76. **Honors/Awds:** Principal investigator following grants. **Special Achievements:** Pentose Metabolism Ruminant, 1956-57, Further Study Absorp & Util Pentose Sugar ruminants PHS, 1956-57,The Cerebrospinal Fluid Dogs, Its Physio Diag & Prognostic Eval Mark & L Morris Found, 1961-62, Mechanisms Infection & Immunity In Listeriosis NIH, 1961-64, Movement Mitral Valve NIH, 1964-72. **Military Serv:** AUS, 1st lt. **Business Addr:** Dean Emeritus, TUSKEGEE UNIVERSITY, COLLEGE OF VETERINARY MEDICINE, NURSING AND ALLIED HEALTH, Tuskegee, AL 36088, **Business Phone:** (334)727-8967.*

BOWIE, WILLETTE
Executive, executive director. **Personal:** Born Jul 24, 1949, Memphis, TN; daughter of John & Callie Jenkins. **Educ:** Alverno Col, BA, 1984; Cardinal Stritch Col, MS, 1996. **Career:** Northwestern Mutual, employee rels specialist, 1983-91, employee rels off, 1991-95, dir employee rels, 1995-. **Orgs:** NAACP Mem Comt, Milwaukee Branch, Leadership Forum, 1997-; Financial Servs Group, 1983-; Human Resources Mgt Asn, 1983-; Top Ladies Distinction, 1986-; Alpha Kappa Alpha Soc, 1986-; Zonta Club Milwaukee, 1991-; Eta Phi Beta Soc, 1986-. **Honors/Awds:** Women on the Move: Past, Present and Future, 2002; The Milwaukee Times Weekly Newspaper, Black Excellence Award, 1998; Girl Scouts of Milwaukee Area, Marion Chester Read Leadership Award, 1998. **Home Addr:** 10129 N Brookdale Dr, Mequon, WI 53092. **Business Addr:** Director, Northwestern Mutual Life Ins Co, Employee Rels, 720 E Wisconsin Ave, Milwaukee, WI 53202, **Business Phone:** (414)665-7120.*

BOWLES, BARBARA LANDERS
Executive. **Personal:** Born Sep 17, 1947, Nashville, TN; married Earl S Bowles; children: Terrence Earl. **Educ:** Fisk Univ, BA, math, 1968; Univ Chicago Grad Sch Bus, MBA, finance, 1971; CFA Designation, attended 1977. **Career:** Black & Decker Corp; bd dirs, Hyde Park Bank; First Nat Bank Chicago, trust officer, 1974-77, asst vpres, 1977-80, vpres, 1980-81; Beatrice Co, asst vpres, 1981-84; Dart & Kraft Foods Inc, vpres investr rels, 1984-; The Kenwood Group, founder, pres & chief exec officer, 1992-. **Orgs:** Pres, Chicago Fisk Alumni Asn, 1983-85; Alpha Kappa Alpha Sorority; bd mem, C Mem Hosp Chicago. **Special Achievements:** Top 100 Black Business & Professional Women, Black Book Delta Sigma, Jul-Aug 1985. **Business Addr:** President and Founder, Chief Executive Officer, The Kenwood Group, 10 S La-Salle St Suite 3610, Chicago, IL 60603-1002.*

BOWLES, HOWARD ROOSEVELT
City manager. **Personal:** Born Oct 14, 1932, Roselle, NJ. **Career:** Parson Inst; Seton Hall Univ City Home Delivery Wash Post, mgr; Baltimore News-Am, city mgr; Newark Evening News, dist mgr; Various Clg, auto salesman, sales mgr asst panel rep. **Orgs:** Interstate Circulation Mgrs Asn; bd dir, Wash Bus J, Jr Achievement, 2002-. **Honors/Awds:** Art award, 32nd Degree Mason Prince Hall F&AM; mgt & prod awards. **Military Serv:** AUS, sgt, 1952-55. **Business Addr:** 1150 15th St NW, Washington, DC 20017.

BOWLES, JAMES HAROLD, SR.
Physician. **Personal:** Born Jun 12, 1921, Goochland, VA; married Aretha Melton; children: Ruth Quarles, Jacqueline B Dandridge, James Jr. **Educ:** Va Union Univ, BS, 1948; Meharry Med Sch, MD, 1952. **Career:** Physician (retired); Wash Hosp Ctr, residency; pvt pract, family practr; teacher, Intermediate Sunday Sch Class. **Orgs:** Vpres & pres, Goochland Recreational Ctr, 1961-81; Recognition Negro Emancipation Orgn, Louisa & Adjacent Counties, 1979; vice chmn, Goodland City Bd Supervisors; Goochland NAACP; exec bd, Va Asn Counties; treas, Goochland Voters League; Goochland Dem Comt; vpres, bd dir, Citizen Develop Corp; Hazardous Waste Siting Comn Va; Am Legion; Goochland City Social Serv Bd; bd dir, Goochland Br Red Cross; Caledonia Lodge 240 F&AM PHA; Alpha Phi Alpha; pres, trustee bd, Emmaus Baptist Church; bd dir, Capital Area Agency Aging. **Honors/Awds:** Outstanding Leadership, Am Red Cross, 1969; Valuable Citizen, Goochland NAACP, 1978; Outstanding Serv, Goochland Recreational Ctr, 1979; Appreciation, Beulah Baptist Sunday Sch Conv, 1979; Appreciation, Am Heart Asn Va Affil, 1982. **Military Serv:** AUS, pvt, 1944-46. *

BOWLES, JOYCE GERMAINE
Educator, school administrator. **Personal:** Born May 16, 1942, Washington, DC; daughter of Harvey Johnson and Mary Gaines; married Robert L Bowles Jr, Jan 1982; children: Lee Robert. **Educ:** Univ Evansville, BSN, 1964; Univ Maryland, Baltimore, MSN, 1972, College Park,PhD, 1978. **Career:** Army Nurse Corps, progressive leadership nursing, 1962-84; Bowie State Univ, Dept Nursing, chairperson, 1985-94, prof nursing, dean, sch prof studies. **Orgs:** Nat League Nursing, 1974-; first vpres, MAR League Nursing, District 6, 1989-91; Chi Eta Phi Nursing Sorority, Alpha Chap, 1972-; pres, Top Ladies Distinction, Potomac Chap, 1988-92; Sigma ta Tau Nursing Soc, Pi Chap,1974-; Asn Black Nursing Fac, pres, 1996-98, nominating comt chair,souvenir prog book chair, 1993; FACE Fel, Kellog Found, 1992-; review bd, J ABNF, 1992-. **Honors/Awds:** Advanced certification, Am Nurses Asn, Nursing Admin, 1986-95. **Military Serv:** USY Nurse Corp, 1962-84; Army Commendation Medal, 1968, Bronze Star Medal, 1968, Meritorious Serv Medal w/ 2 Oak Leaf Clusters, Legion of Merit, 1984, Daughters Am Revolution, ANC of the Year, 1982.

BOWLING, LYSIA HUNTINGTON
Lawyer. **Personal:** Children: Malik, Belkis, Fabiola, Killian & Cullin. **Educ:** Yale Univ, BA, political sci, BA, latin am, 1976; Univ Va Law Sch, JD, 1979. **Career:** State Tex, atty; State Fla, atty; Corp Tax Policy, Comptroller Pub Accts, staff atty; Tex Gen Land Off, Energy Resources Div, staff atty; City Austin, Tex, chief prosecuting atty; Tex Dept Ins, Agent Licensing Div, staff atty; Tex Off Atty Gen, Criminal Prosecuting Div, asst atty gen; City Harlington Tex, city atty; City Temple Tex, city atty, chief prosecutor & legal police adv; City Miami, Miami Dade State Attorney's Off, asst state atty; Off City Atty, Miami Police Dept, police legal adv, 2008-; Miami-Dade Col, Sch Justice, law enforcement trainer & fac criminal justice prog. **Orgs:** Ebony Cultural Soc; State Bar Tex; Tex City Atty's Asn; Austin Black Lawyer's Asn; Tex Police Asn; Int Municipal Lawyers Asn; pres, March Dimes; pres, Optimist Club; chmn, Ebony Cultural Forum. **Honors/Awds:** Appreciation Award, Temple Police Dept, 1997; Optimist of the Year, 2000; Leader About Town, Miami Dade Col; Outstanding Black Women in the Legal Profession. **Business Addr:** Police Legal Advisor, City of Miami, Office of the City Attorney, 444 SW 2nd Av Suite 945, Miami, FL 33130, **Business Phone:** (305)416-1800.

BOWMAN, BUCK. See BOWMAN, DR. JANET WILSON.

BOWMAN, JACQUELYNNE JEANETTE (JACQUI BOWMAN)
Lawyer. **Personal:** Born Dec 4, 1955, Chicago, IL; married David Rentsch; children: Atticus David Bowman Rentsch. **Educ:** Univ Chicago, BA, 1976; Antioch Univ Sch Law, JD, 1979-2000. **Career:** West Tenn Legal Servs, staff atty, 1979-84; Greater Boston Legal Servs, sr atty, 1984-87, managing atty, 1987-92, assoc dir, 1997-2000, dep dir, 2000-; Mass Law Reform Inst, staff atty, 1992-97; Am Bar Asn, Comn Domestic Violence, comnr; Antioch Univ Sch Law, dep dir, 2000-. **Orgs:** Am Bar Asn, 1979-; Nat Conf Black Lawyers, 1980-; Battered Women's Working Group, 1984-93; vol, Proj Impact, 1984-93; Mass Bar Asn, 1986-; Gender Bias Community, task force dometic violence, 1992-94, juv justice community, 1992-94; Gov Community Domestic Violence, 1993-; Bd mem, Mass Advocacy Ctr, 1994-; Mass Black Lawyers, 1995-; Mass Black Women Lawyers Asn, 1997; bd mem, Mgt Info Exchange, 1997-, exec comt, 2000-; Dawe Sch PTO, bylaws chair, exec comn; bd mem, Mass Advocacy Ctr, Jane Doe Inc, 2000-. **Honors/Awds:** Silver Key Award, ABA-LSD, 1979; Certificate of Appreciation, EACH, 1982-84; George Edmund Haynes fel, Nat Urban League, 1982-83; Public Service Award, Proj Impact, 1985, 1986; Special Appreciation Award, Diversity Coalition, 1997; Special Recognition, Mass Legal Assistance Corp, 1997; Special Friend Award, Legis Foster C Caucus, 1998; Legislative Advocate Award, 1997; Legal Services Award, Mass Bar Asn, 1999-2000; Volunteer Recognition, Dawe Sch, 2000. **Home Addr:** 195 Glen Echo Blvd, Stoughton, MA 02072-1068, **Home Phone:** (781)344-9577. **Business Addr:** Deputy Director, Greater Boston Legal Services, 197 Friend St, Boston, MA 02114, **Business Phone:** (617)371-1234.

BOWMAN, JACQUI. See BOWMAN, JACQUELYNNE JEANETTE.

BOWMAN, DR. JAMES E.
Geneticist, educator, pathologist. **Personal:** Born Feb 5, 1923, Washington, DC; son of James and Dorothy; married Barbara Frances Taylor; children: Valerie June Jarrett. **Educ:** Howard Univ, BS, 1943; Howard Med Sch, MD, 1946. **Career:** Freed mens Hosp, intern, 1947; St Lukes Hosp, resident pathol, 1950; Provident Hosp, Chicago, chmn pathol, 1950-53; Nemezee Hosp, Shiraz, Iran, chmn pathol, 1955-61; Shiraz Med Sch, Shiraz, Iran, prof pathol, chair, 1959-61; Univ Chicago, asst prof, med dir blood bank, 1962-67, assoc prof, 1967-72; prof med & pathol, dir labs, 1971-81, comt genetics, 1972-; Comprehensive Sickle Cell Ctr, Univ Chicago, dir, 1973-84; Univ Chicago, Pritzker Sch Med, Dept Pathol, prof emer, currently; Ctr Clinic Med Ethics, Comt African & African Am Studies, sr scholar. **Orgs:** Galton Lab, Univ Col, London, Spec Res Fel, 1961-62; Hastings Ctr, NY, fel, 1979-; Kaiser Family Found Ctr Advance Study Behav Sci, Stanford, CA, fel, 1981-82; consult, Fed Gov Nigeria, 1985; consult, Med Corps Labs, Defense Forces, United Arab Emirates, 1987; Ministry Health, Islamic Repubic Iran, consult, 1992; Ethical, legal & social issues, working group; Nat Human Genome Prog, NIH; monitoring bd, NHLBI, NIH; Bone Marrow Transplentation Sickle Cell Disease & Thalassemia; Am Soc Human Genetics, AAAS; Col Am Pathologists, fel; Am Soc Clin Path, fel; Royal Soc Tropical Med & Hygiene, fel. **Honors/Awds:** Alpha Omega Alpha, Sigma Xi, Am Bd Pathol Anatol & Clinic Pathol. **Special Achievements:** Author 90 scientific publ in field of human genetics; edited book, "Dist & Evol of Hemoglobin and Globin Loci"; co-author with Robert F Murray,'Genetic Variation and Disorders in Peoples of African Origin', John Hopkins Univ Press, 1990; Biological Sciences Division's first tenured African-American Professor. **Military Serv:** AUS, pfc, 1943-46, capt, 1953-55. **Business Addr:** Professor Emeritus, University of Chicago, Pritzker School of Medicine, Department of Pathology, 924 E 57th St Suite 104, Chicago, IL 60637-5415.

BOWMAN, DR. JANET WILSON (BUCK BOWMAN)
School administrator, writer. **Personal:** Born in Charleston, WV; daughter of Earl and Roberta; married Richard; children: Karen McAfee, M Earl McAfee, Chris, Cheryl & Patricia. **Educ:** Tuskegee Inst, BS, MS; Univ Calif, Berkeley, PhD, 1973; Univ Oregon; CalifState Univ, San Diego. **Career:** Merritt Col, prof; Univ Calif, seismologist, 1960-73; Carnegie Found,consult, 1972-73; Diablo Valley Col, admin, 1973-85; Compton Col, adr,1986-94; Ashville YWCA, exec dir; author, currently. **Orgs:** Bd mem, Meridian Nat Bank, 1979; Tuskegee Alumni Asn; UNCF Inter AlumniCoun; United Way Prog Evaluator; Black Women's Leadership Group; MOSTE,Women Target; bd dirs, Memorial Mission Found; Kiwanis Int. **Honors/Awds:** George Washington Carver Fellowship; NSF Scholarship; Graduate StudentAssistantship, Univ Calif, Berkeley; Certificate of Appreciation, BusClub, 1988; Certificate of Commendation, Compton Col Bd Trustees, 1988. **Home Addr:** 24 Bevlyn Dr, Asheville, NC 28803. *

BOWMAN, JOSEPH E.
School administrator, technologist, educator. **Personal:** Born May 22, 1950, Brooklyn, NY; son of Joseph Sr and Violetta; married Etwin Mapp, Mar 27, 1987; children: Amber & Alicia. **Educ:** State Univ NY, BA, 1972; Nat Tchr Corp, MA, 1975, MLS, 1974; Teachers Col,Columbia Univ, New York, NY, MEd, 1984, MA, 1985, EdD, 1991. **Career:** Hamilton Hill Arts & Crafts Ctr, dir audio visual serv, 1974-75; WMHT Channel 17 Pub Afrs Div, asst prod, 1975-77; Educ Oppor Prog Stud Assn State Univ NY, tele Communs instr, 1975; WMHT TV, asst prod, dir, 1977-78;Hamilton Hill Arts & Craft Ctr Schenectady NY, instr, 1978-79; Siciliano Studio Schenectady, NY, photogr asst, 1978-79; Schenectady Access Cable Coun Channel 16 NY, location mgr, 1979; Olympic Village XIII Winter Games Lake Placid, fclty mgr, prod dir, supvr entertainment, 1979-80; Columbia Univ, Teachers Col, New York, NY, proj dir, 1982-, coordr, 1985-, instr,1985-; Univ State NY, Regent, 2001-; Ctr Urban Youth & Technol, dir, cur; State Univ New York, Albany, NY, serv assoc prof educ theory & pract, cur, Ctr Urban Youth & Technol, dir, currently. **Orgs:** Consult, Girl Scouts Am, 1990-; trainer, Boys Scouts Am, 1986-90. **Honors/Awds:** Outstanding Achievement Award, Schenectady Chpt, NAACP, 1975; Pride in Heritage Award Acad Achievement & Multi-Media Spclst; Theta Chap Nat Sor Phi Delta Kappa, 1978; award, Intl Nat Platform Soc, 1980; Outstanding Educational Achievement, Kappa Delta Pi, 1988. **Home Addr:** 1234 St John, PO Box 203, Brooklyn, NY 11213. **Business Addr:** Director, State University of New York, Center for Urban Youth & Technology, 1400 Washington Ave, Albany, NY 12222, **Business Phone:** (518)442-4987.

BOWMAN, PHILLIP JESS
Psychologist, educator. **Personal:** Born Feb 18, 1948, Kensett, AR; married Jacqueline E Creed; children: Phillip & Frederick Dubois. **Educ:** Northern Ariz Univ, BS, psychol/industrial technol, 1970; Univ Mich, MA/Ed.S (personal serv/coun), 1973, PhD/MA (soc psychol), 1977. **Career:** Univ Mich, Inst Social Res, res investr to study dir, Postdoctoral Training Prog Surv Res, dir, Dept Psychol/Afro-Am & African Studies, from lectr to asst prof, 1977-84, Ctr Study Higher & Postsecondary, prof, 2006-, Nat Ctr Inst Diversity, dir, 2006-, Inst Social Res/Nat Poverty Ctr, fac assoc, 2006-; Education; Northwestern Univ, Dept Human Develop & Social Policy/Dept African Am Studies, assoc prof, Inst Policy Res, fac assoc, 1991-2000; Univ Ill, Chicago, prof urban planning & policy/African Am Studies, Inst Res Race & Public Policy, dir, 2000-06. **Orgs:** Am Educ Res Asn; Am Pub Health Asn; Am Psychol Asn; Asn Pub Policy & Mgt; Nat Asn Black Psychol; Nat Coun Family Rel; Soc Res Child Develop; Soc Res Adolescence; Soc Psychol Study Social Issues. **Honors/Awds:** Exceptional Service Award, Ethnicity & Mental Health, 1979; Research Excellence Award, Urban League, 1987;

Academic Scholarship Award, Black Stud Psychol Asn, 1993; Charles & Shirley Thiomas Award, Am Psychol Asn, 2006. **Business Phone:** (734)764-6509.

BOWMAN, VIVIANE. See WINANS, VICKIE.

BOWMAN, WILLIAM ALTON
Military leader, government official. **Personal:** Born Dec 15, 1933, Fayetteville, NC; son of William H (deceased) and Rebecca L Johnson (deceased); married Sylvia I. (deceased); children: Carol, William A Jr (deceased), Arthur E, Susan Okediadi (deceased), Brenda Jones. **Educ:** Southeast Cot Col, assoc, human services, 2000. **Career:** Military leader (retired), Government official; Misle Imports Auto, serv writer, 1976-77; State Dept Rds, mech, 1977; Toms Car Care, mech, 1977-78; US Postal Serv, letter carrier, 1978-79, fleet mgr, 1979-90; Budget Rent A Car, shuttle driver, part time. **Orgs:** post comdr, Am Legion, 1995-96, dist 15 comdr, 1996-98; 40 & 8 Voiture 103, box car chr, star chr, 1994-; bd mem, Disabled Veterans, store, 1993-; Air Force Sergeants, 1976; Air Force Asn, 1963; Vietnam Veterans, 1995; Nat Asn Fed Ret, 1990; Va Hosp, volunteer-patient visitor, 1994; MAD DADS; detachment historian, Sons Am Legion, currently; comdr, Disabled Veterans Chap 7, 2000-. **Military Serv:** USAF, t & sgt, 1954-76; VSM 1968, RVCM, 1968, AFCM W/10LC, 1968, 1971, 1972. **Business Addr:** Detachment Historian, Sons of The American Legion, Department of Nebraska, PO Box 5205, Lincoln, NE 68505-0205, **Business Phone:** (402)464-6338.*

BOWNES, FABIEN ALFRANSO
Football player. **Personal:** Born Feb 29, 1972, Aurora, IL. **Educ:** Western Ill Univ. **Career:** Football player (retired); Chicago Bears, wide receiver, 1995-98, Seattle Seahawks, 1999-2001.

BOWRON, ELJAY B
Government official, vice president (organization). **Personal:** Born in Detroit, MI; married Sandy; children: one son. **Educ:** Mich State Univ, criminal justice. **Career:** Detroit Police Dept, officer, 1973; US Secret Serv, various positions, 1974, dir, 1993-97; Social Security Admin, sr exec, inspector gen; Vance Int Inc, exec vpres, chief operating officer, currently. **Orgs:** Int Asn Chiefs Police; Alpha Protective Serv. **Honors/Awds:** Numerous commendations and awards for outstanding service. **Business Addr:** Executive Vice President, Chief Operating Officer, Vance International Inc, 10467 White Granite Dr, Oakton, VA 22124-2700, **Business Phone:** (703)592-1400.

BOWSER, BENJAMIN PAUL
Educator. **Personal:** Born Aug 20, 1946, New York, NY; son of Benjamin J and Nathalia Earle; married K Deborah Whittle, Sep 19, 1992; children: Paul. **Educ:** Franklin & Marshall Col, Lancaster, Pa, BA, sociol, 1969; Cornell Univ, PhD, sociol, 1976. **Career:** State Univ NY, Binghampton, asst prof, social, 1972-75; Cornell Univ, asst dean grad sch, 1975-82; Western Interstate Commiss Higher Ed, dir minorityed, 1982-84; Univ Santa Clara, dir black stud resources, 1983-85; Stanford Univ, from asst dir, 1985-86; Evaluation & Training Network, res dir, 1985-; Bayview Hunter's Point Found, San Francisco, CA, res dir, 1990-91; Calif State Univ, E Bay, Dept Sociol & Social Serv, prof, 1987-; Calif State Univ Hayward, Dept Sociol & Social Serv, from asst prof to prof, 1987-94, dept chair, currently; Univ Paris, Sorbonne, vis prof, Spring, 2005. **Orgs:** Res assoc, Soc Study Contemporary Soc Problem 1980-82; consult, Western Interstate Comm Higher Ed 1981-83; Comt Appl Sociol Am Sociol Asn 1985-87; Comt, Am Sociol Asn, Washington, DC, 1985-87; bd mem, Dr. Martin Luther King, Jr. Ctr Social Change Santa Clara Valley, San Jose, Ca, 1986-89; bd mem, Peninsula Asn Black Personnel Adminr, Sunnyvale, Ca, 1987-88; alumni western adv comt, Franklin & Marshall Col, Lancaster, Pa, 1993-; bd mem, Glide Found Glide Mem Methodist Church, 1993-; rev panelist, Minority Grad Fel Prog, Nat Sci Found, Washington, DC, 1993-95; Am Social Health Asn, 1995-2002; planning comt, Nat Inst Health, Bestheda, MD, 1995-; bd chair, Am Social Health Asn, Durham, NC, 1996-2003; Asn Black Sociologists; bd dir, Glide Mem Methodist Church; pres, Asn Black Sociologists, 2004-05. **Honors/Awds:** Numerous research grants: Outstanding Professor, Calif State Univ Hayward, 1996; Choice Award Outstanding Acad Pub, 2003. **Special Achievements:** Co-Editor "Impacts of Racism on White Amers" 1981, 1995; "Census Data for Small Areas of NY City 1910-60" 1981; editor, Black Male Adolescents, 1991; Confronting Diversity Issues on Campus, 1993; Toward the Multicultural Univ, 1995; Racism & Anti-Racism in World Perspective, 1995; Impacts of Racism on White Americans, 1996; Against The Odds: Scholars Who Challenged Racism in the Twentieth Century, 2002. **Business Addr:** Department Chair, California State University East Bay, Department Sociol & Social Serv, 3103 Meiklejohn Hall, Hayward, CA 94542, **Business Phone:** (510)885-3173.

BOWSER, HAMILTON VICTOR
Executive, president (organization). **Personal:** Born Sep 20, 1928, East Orange, NJ; son of Edward T and Louise Pateman; married Merle Charlotte Moses; children: Hamilton V Jr, Rebecca Louise & Jennifer Lynn. **Educ:** NJ Inst Technol, BS, civil eng, 1952, MS, civil eng, 1956; Mass Inst Technol, Grad Sch Civil Eng, 1954; Licensed prof engr, NJ, NY, PA. **Career:** Porter Urguhart Eng, structural engr, 1954-55; Louis Berger Assocs, sr bridge engr, 1955-57; PARCO Inc, sr structural engr, 1957-59; Engrs Inc, vpres, 1959-69; Evanbow Construct Co Inc, exec, pres, 1969-; African Sci Inst, fel. **Orgs:** Mem, Men Essex NJ, 1959-, pres, 1969; pres, Nat Soc Prof Eng Essex Chap, 1966-68; fel Am Soc Civil Engrs, 1969; trustee & treas, Essex County Col, 1971-74; chmn bd, Assoc Minority Contractors Am, 1980-82; bd dir, treas, Reg Plan Assoc NY, NJ, CT, 1981-97; bd dir, Nat Asn Minority Contractors, pres, 1988-89, emer bd mem, currently; Am Arbitration Asn, Construction & Pub Works Panels, 1989-; bd chmn, Orange YMCA Community Mgmt; Prof Engrs, Construction Div Nat Soc Prof Engrs; Am Concrete Inst; NJ United Minority Bus Brain Trust; chmn, Mayor's Task Force Newark Econ Develop, NJ; rep, County Solid Waste Disposal Comn; rep, White House Conf Small Bus; Adv Coun Civil & Environ Eng, NJ Inst Technol, trustee bd, chair, Building Comn, 1989-; vchmn, New Jersey Govs Study Comn Discrimination Pub Procurement; vchair, Regional Alliance Small Contractors NY & New Jersey; chmn, NAMC Liaison Comn US Corp Surety Bond Ind; bd mem, Regional Plan Asn. **Honors/Awds:** Nat Advocate Award for minority & small bus develop, US Small Bus Admin, 1984; Outstanding Alumnus Award, NJ Inst Technol, 1985; NY Regional Contractor of the Year, US Dept Com, 1985; Outstanding Mem Awards, Nat Asn Minority Contractors & NJ United Minority Bus Brain Trust; NJIT Alumni Athletic Hall of Fame for Fencing; Bus included as one of Black Enterprise's Top 100 Service Firms, 1988; Contractors Hall of Fame, inducted, 1999. **Military Serv:** USMC, pfc 2 yrs; USAFR, capt, 14 yrs. **Business Addr:** President, Evanbow Construction Co Inc, 67 Sanford St, East Orange, NJ 07018, **Business Phone:** (973)674-1250.

BOWSER, KYLE D
Television producer, founder (originator). **Personal:** Married Yvette Lee. **Educ:** Ohio Univ, BS, 1980; Widener Univ Sch Law, JD, 1991. **Career:** Supreme Ct Pa, law clerk, 1989; NBC Bus Affairs, law clerk, 1990; Bowser, Weaver, & Cousounis, law clerk, 1991; Fox Inc, creative assoc, 1991-92; Fox Broadcasting Co, mgr current programing, 1992-93; Home Box Office Independent Productions, dir creative affairs, 1993-94; TV series: "Trial by Jury", exec producer, 1995; "Midnight Mac", exec producer; NAMIC Vision Awards ; The Thing About Family ; "Color TV"; Cult Heritage Comn, comnr, 2003-; Res Ipsa Media Inc, pres & founder, currently; Inspired By Media Group, exec partner, film & TV veteran, currently. **Orgs:** Black Entertainment & Sports Lawyers Asn; Black Filmmakers Asn; Nat Asn Minorities Commun; Hollyrod Found. **Business Phone:** (818)623-7600.*

BOWSER, LUCIUS A
Executive. **Career:** Genealogist & historian, currently. **Orgs:** Pres, Afro-Am Hist & Genealogical Soc. **Business Addr:** Genealogist, Historian, 758 Sterling Dr E, South Orange, NJ 07079-2425, **Business Phone:** (973)763-5892.

BOWSER, MCEVA R.
Educator, teacher. **Personal:** Born Nov 22, 1922, Elizabeth City, NC; daughter of Ivy Hillard Roach and Rosa Lillian Stewart; married Barrington H, Apr 12, 1952 (deceased); children: Angela & Barrington Jr. **Educ:** Elizabeth City State Univ, BS, 1944; Va Commonwealth Univ, MEd, 1970. **Career:** Educator (retired); Richmond Va Pub Schs, curric specialist, elem consult, teacher; Sussex County & Louisa County, teacher. **Orgs:** Pres, Richmond Med Aux, 1956-58; pres, Richmond Club, Chi Delta Mu Wives,1966-68; pres, Richmond Chap, Jack & Jill Am, 1964-66; pres, Women StPhilip's Episcopal Church, 1964-68; bd dir, Jack & Jill Am Found, 1968-70; Nat vpres, Chi Delta Mu Wives, 1970-72; treas, Richmond Chap, Links Inc, 1977-79; vice-chmn, Regional Reading Comn, 1977-; pres, Richmond ChapLinks, 1981-83; parliamentarian, Auxiliary Med Soc, 1980-90; Parliamentarian, Richmond Chap Links, 1985-87; Sch Bd, City Richmond, 1994; REA; YEA; NEA; ASCD; Alpha Kappa Alpha Maymont Civic League. **Honors/Awds:** Outstanding Serv Award, Jack & Jill Am Found, 1972. **Home Addr:** 1807 Hampton St, Richmond, VA 23220.

BOWSER, REGINALD
President (Organization). **Educ:** George Mason Univ, BS; Darden Grad Sch Bus, Univ Va, MBA. **Career:** Rollover Syst Inc, founder, pres & chief exec officer, 2007. **Business Addr:** Founder, Rollover Systems Inc, 4135 S Stream Blvd Suite 500, Charlotte, NC 28217, **Business Phone:** 888-600-7655.

BOWSER, REGINALD
Administrator. **Educ:** George Mason Univ, BS; Univ Va, The Darden Grad Sch Bus, MBA. **Career:** Eastman Kodak Co, sales & mkt mgr; LendingTree Inc, vpres mkt & advert; HorizonGuide Inc, mem exec mgt team & chief mkt officer; Rollover Systems Inc, owner, pres, chief exec officer, currently. **Business Addr:** Owner, Chief Executive Officer, Rollover Systems Inc, 2815 Coliseum Center Dr Suite 630, Charlotte, NC 28217, **Business Phone:** (704)295-1234.*

BOWSER, ROBERT LOUIS
Executive, mayor. **Personal:** Born Dec 13, 1935, East Orange, NJ; son of Edward T Sr. and Louise E Pateman; married Marilyn K Ward Bowser, Dec 30, 1989; children: David, Lisa K Ward, Leslie J Ward. **Educ:** Newark Col Engr, BSCE, 1958; Northwestern Univ, Cert, 1961; NY Univ, Cert, 1963. **Career:** City of Newark, city planner, 1958-60; Town of Montclair, traffic engr, 1960-65; structural engr, 1965-68; Bowser Engrs & Assoc, vpres, 1968-82; City of E Orange, NJ, dir of pub works, 1986-91; Robert L Bowser Assoc, owner, 1982-; Newark Bd of Educ, prin engr, 1991-97; City E Orange, NJ, elected mayor, currently. **Orgs:** Inst of Traffic Engr, 1959-65; Nat Soc of Prof Engrs, 1963; NJ Soc of Prof Engrs, 1963; Land Surveyors Functional Sect, NJ, 1969; Lic Prof Land Survr, NJ, 1969; Am Congress of Surv & Mapping, 1970; Lic Prof Planner, NJ, 1973; NJ Planners Asn, 1978-; vice chmn, E Orange Rent Level Bd, 1975-76; commr & fdr, Essex Co Touch Football League, 1975-; pres, Nat Asn Builders & Contractors NJ, 1976; Public Works Asn, 1986-; NJ Society of Professional Planners, 1976-; bd of dirs, Girl Scout Coun, 1989-93; adjunct prof, Essex Co Col, 1985-89; E Orange Planning Bd clerk, 1986-91; E Orange Kiwanis Club, 1990-98; E Orange Lions Club, 1989, pres, 1995; adv Bd, Rutgers Urban Gardening Prog, 1990-98, chmn, 1992-98; Citizens Adv Bd, Orange Hosp Ctr, 1994-; mem, US Conf of Mayor; bd of dirs, Conf of Black Mayors, 1999; bd mem, NJ Conf of Mayors, 2000; NJ Conf of Mayors, Legis comm; NJ Urban Mayors Asn, Urban Enterprize Zone Comm; bd mem, United Way; bd mem, E Orange Salvation Army. **Honors/Awds:** Black Heritage Award, City of E Orange, 1989; Dir of Pub Works Commendation, City Coun of E Orange, 1991; Man of the Year, NJ coun of Negro Bus Women, 1998; Eagle Flight Champion Award, 2000. **Special Achievements:** Holds the distinction of being the first African Am in the history of the City to have been elected to serve a third term. **Military Serv:** USCG, res, 1960-66. **Business Addr:** Mayor, City of E Orange, 44 City Hall Plz, East Orange, NJ 07017.*

BOWSER, YVETTE DENISE LEE
Executive, screenwriter. **Personal:** Born Jun 9, 1965; married Kyle D Bowser. **Educ:** Stanford Univ, attended 1987. **Career:** Screenwriter, executive; A Different World, producer, 1987, 1991-92; Living Single, writer, creator & exec producer, 1993; Lush Life, exec producer, 1996; For Your Love, exec producer, 1998; "Half & Half", exec producer, writer, 2003-05; "The Big My Little Pony Episode", writer, 2004; "The Big Fast Track Episode", writer, 2005; "The Big Training Day Episode", writer, 2005; "The Big Frozen Assets Episode", writer, 2005; "The Big My Funny Valentine Episode", writer, 2006; Sister Lee Productions, owner, currently. **Orgs:** Alpha Kappa Alpha. **Honors/Awds:** Image Award, Nat Asn Advan Colored People. **Special Achievements:** First African-American woman to develop her own prime-time series in TV. **Business Addr:** Onwer, Sister Lee Productions, 300 Television Plz bldg 136 Rm 147, Burbank, CA 91505, **Business Phone:** (818)954-7579.*

BOW WOW, LIL (SHAD GREGORY MOSS)
Rap musician, actor. **Personal:** Born Mar 9, 1987, Columbus, OH; son of Teresa Caldwell. **Career:** Albums: Beware of Dog, 2000; Doggy Bag, 2001; Unleashed, 2005; Wanted, 2005, The Price of Fame, 2006, Face Off, 2007; Films: Carmen: A Hip Hopera, MTV, 2001; All About the Benjamins, 2002; Like Mike, 2002; Johnson Family Vacation, 2004; Roll Bounce, 2005; The Fast & the Furious: Tokyo Drift, 2006; TV: "Smallville," 2006; Columbia Records, recording artist, currently. **Business Phone:** (212)833-8000.

BOX, CHARLES
Mayor, government official. **Personal:** Born Jan 1, 1951. **Educ:** Univ Mich Law Sch. **Career:** Rockford's municipal admin, City Adminr & Legal Dir; Rockford, IL, mayor, 1989-01; Ill Com Comn, chair, currently. **Orgs:** Chair, Community Develop Housing Comn; co-chair, Conf Mayors Liaison Comn, Nat Asn Realtors; co-chair, Community Develop Block Grant Task Force; chair, Subcomt Enterprise Zones; Ill Growth Enterprises; Rockford Col; Trustee & Adv Bd, US Conf Mayors. **Honors/Awds:** Dr Nathan Davis Award; Edward Potter Lathrop Medal, Winnebago County Bar Asn. **Business Addr:** Chair, Illinois Commerce Commission, 527 E Capitol Ave, Springfield, IL 62701, **Business Phone:** (217)782-7295.

BOXILL, JOHN HAMMOND
Association executive. **Personal:** Born Oct 22, 1961, Chillicothe, OH; son of John and Janice; divorced; children: Zuri F & Uele N. **Educ:** Ohio State Univ, BS, 1984; Methodist Theol Sch, OH, MA, 1998. **Career:** Columbus City, dist int specialist, 1987-88; ECCO Family Health Ctr, opers coordr, 1988-96; Arthur James Cancer Hosp, Community Develop, prog mgr, 1996-2000; Am Red Cross, Chap Servs, mgr, vol, currently; New Salem Baptist Missionary Church, chief operating officer, currently. **Orgs:** Deacon, New Salem Baptist Church, 1990-; United Way Franklin Cty, Vision Coun, Health, 1990-2000; minority involvement comt, Am Heart Asn, 1992-; educ chair, Alpha Phi Alpha Frat, 1995-; bd mem, Columbus Bd Health, currently. **Honors/Awds:** Jaycees, Ten Outstanding Young Citizens, 1997; Honorary Nurse, Columbus Black Nurses Asn, 1997; Outstanding Young Men of America, 1998; Circle of Friends, African American Cancer Support Group, 1999; President's Award, Alpha Phi Alpha Frat; President's Award, Alpha Rho Lambda, 1999. **Home Addr:** 1386 Aven Dr, Columbus, OH 43227. **Business Addr:** Chief Operating Officer,

New Salem Missionary Baptist Church, 2956 Cleveland Ave, Columbus, OH 43224, **Business Phone:** (614)267-2536 Ext 132.

BOYCE, CHARLES N
Executive. **Personal:** Born Jun 9, 1935, Detroit, MI; married Delma Cunningham; children: Terralyn, Tracy, Charles & LaShawn. **Educ:** Wayne State Univ, 1955-62, Univ Mich, Grad Sch Bus, 1981. **Career:** Mich Bell Tel, com oper asst, 1966-69, order unit mgr, 1969-71, dist com mgr, 1971-76, gen customer rels mgr, 1976-78, dir public affairs, 1979-83, asst vpres urban affairs, 1983-. **Orgs:** Bd trustees, New Detroit Inc, 1972-75, 1978-; bd dir, Asn Black Bus & Eng Studs, 1973-; comnr, Detroit Housing Comn, 1976-; bd dir, Nat Asn Advan Colored People, Detroit, 1978-, Million Dollar Club, 1978 & 1979, vpres, 1985-86; bd dir, Mich League Human Serv, 1979-; Soc Consumer Affairs Bus, 1979-; bd dir, Inner City Bus Improv Forum, 1987-89; African-Am Heritage Asn; Booker T Washington Bus Asn; Bus Policy Rev Coun; bd dir, Black Family Devel Inc; bd dir, Concerned Citizens Coun; bd dir, Jazz Devel Workshop; bd dir, March Dimes SE Mich Chap, Neighborhood Serv Orgn. **Honors/Awds:** Outstanding Service Award, Oakland Co Urban League, 1974; Service Award, Nat Asn Advan Colored People, Detroit, 1979; Outstanding Citizen Service Award, Detroit Housing Comn, 1979; Minority Achievers in Industry Award, YMCA, 1980; Excellence in Marketing Award, AT&T, 1982; Anthony Wayne Award for Leadership, Wayne State Univ 1983. **Business Addr:** Assistant Vice President, Michigan Bell Telephone Company, 444 Mich Ave, Detroit, MI 48226, **Business Phone:** (313)223-9900.

BOYCE, DR. JOHN G.
Gynecologist, educator. **Personal:** Born May 6, 1935; married Erma; children: Mindora & Jane. **Educ:** Univ British Columbia, MD, 1962; Columbia Univ, MSc, bio statist, 1971. **Career:** Kings County, chief gynec oncol, 1990-98, pres med bd, 1993-95; State Univ New York, prof Obstet & Gynec; State Univ New York, Health Sci Ctr Brooklyn, Dept Obstet & Gynec, chmn & distinguished service prof; Hosp San Rafael,Pres, chief infectious diseases & Hosp Epidemiol; Am Col obstetricians & Gynecologists, Chairperson, Dist II. **Orgs:** Kings County NY State Am; Nat Med Asn; Am Col Obstetricians & Gynecologists; Soc Gynec & Oncologists. **Honors/Awds:** Cert Spec Competence Gynec Oncol, 1974; pres, The New York Obstetrical Society. **Business Addr:** Chairperson District II, American College of Obstetricians and Gynecologists, 409 12th Str SW, PO Box 96920, Washington, DC 20090-6920.*

BOYCE, JOSEPH NELSON
Journalist. **Personal:** Born Apr 18, 1937, New Orleans, LA; son of John B and Sadie Nelson; married Carol Hill Boyce, Dec 21, 1968; children: Beverly, Leslie, Nelson, Joel. **Educ:** Roosevelt Univ, Chicago, IL, attended 1963; John Marshall Law Sch, Chicago, IL, attended 1965. **Career:** Journalist (retired); Chicago Police Dept, patrolman, 1961-66; Chicago Tribune, reporter, 1966-70; Time Mag, New York, NY, correspondent, bur chief, 1970-87; The Wall St Jour, NY, sr ed, 1987-98, consult; Stanford Univ, lectr; Univ Kans, lectr; SC State Univ, lectr; Univ Calif, Berkeley, lectr; San Francisco State Univ, lectr; Howard Univ, lectr; Bradley Univ, lectr; Columbia Univ, adj prof; Ind Univ, adj prof; Purdue Univ, adj prof; Maynard Inst Jour Educ, vis fac. **Orgs:** Am Fedn Musicians, 1955-; Nat Asn Black Journalists; life mem, Nat Asn Advan Colored People; CORE, 1967-70; vis fac, Summer Prog Minority Journalist, 1986-89. **Honors/Awds:** Lincoln University Award Educational Reporting, 1976; Black Achiever, Metropolitian YMCA New York, 1976; Time Inc Fel, Duke Univ, 1983; lectured at Poynter Inst, 1992. **Special Achievements:** First African American to join Chicago Tribune Magazine; First African American to Head bureau section of Times Magazine. **Military Serv:** USNR, 1954-62. **Business Addr:** Consultant, The Wall Street Journal, 200 Liberty St, New York, NY 10281, **Business Phone:** (212)416-2205.*

BOYCE, ROBERT
School administrator. **Career:** Detroit Bd Educ, pres. **Business Phone:** (313)494-1010.

BOYCE, WILLIAM M.
Labor relations manager. **Personal:** Born Jul 9, 1928, Brooklyn, NY; son of Darnley and Luddie; married Alice M Billingsley; children: David C & Lynne M. **Educ:** Brooklyn Col, AAS, 1957; City Col New York, AAS, 1962, BBA, 1965; Fairleigh Dickinson Univ, MBA, 1976. **Career:** Kings Co Hosp Ctr, dir of personnel, 1974-81; Muhlenberg Hosp, vpres human resources, 1981-85; Yonkers Gen Hosp, dir human resources, 1987-89; Boyce Consulting Group, pres, currently; Passaic County Community Col, dir, human resources & labor rels, 1990-. **Orgs:** Dir, Ft Greene Neighborhood Manpower Ctr, 1966-70; dir, Manpower Taskforce New Urban & Coalition, 1970-74; chmn, Brooklyn Health Manpower Consortium, 1975-77; Asn MBA Execs, 1975-; NY Asn Hosp Personnel Admin,1977-. **Honors/Awds:** Recipient of German Occupancy Medal AUS. **Military Serv:** AUS, pvt II, 1951-53. **Business Addr:** President, Boyce Consulting Group, 33 Elk Ave, New Rochelle, NY 10804, **Business Phone:** (914)235-5182.

BOYD, BARBARA JEAN
Librarian. **Personal:** Born Jul 14, 1954, Monroe, LA; daughter of Rube Robinson and Ora Lee Renfro Robinson (deceased); married Willian Boyd, Jun 25; children: Chaundra, Cameron & Chelsea. **Educ:** Univ Wis, Eau Claire, WI, Oshkosh, BS, 1979, Milwaukee, WI, MLIS, 1989. **Career:** Heritage Bank, Milwaukee, WI, clerk, 1979-80; City Milwaukee-Legis Ref Bur, Milwaukee, WI, LTA, 1980-89, librn, 1989-91; Houston Pub Libr, Johnson Br, mgr, Collier Reg, librn, 1991. **Orgs:** Am Libr Asn, 1987; Spec Librs Asn, 1987-89; Wis Black Librn Network, 1987-91; Spec Librs Asn, positive action prog minority groups stipend; Tex Libr Asn, 1995; Black Caucus Am Libr Asn, 1987. **Honors/Awds:** Libr Career Training Fel, UWM-Sch Libr & Info Sci, 1987-88. **Home Phone:** (281)261-2568. **Business Phone:** (832)393-1313.

BOYD, DELORES ROSETTA
Lawyer. **Personal:** Born Apr 24, 1950, Ramer, AL. **Educ:** Univ Ala, BA, 1972; Univ Va, JD, 1975. **Career:** Judge John C Godbold, law clerk Fed Judge, US Ct Appeals 5th Circuit; US Ct Appeals 11th Circuit, chief judge, 1975-76; Mandell & Boyd, partner, 1976-92, solo pract, 1992-2001; Montgomery Municipal Ct, presiding judge, 2000-01; US Dist Ct Middle Dist Ala, US magistrate judge, 2001-. **Orgs:** Ala State Bar Bd Bar Examiners, bar examiner, 1979-83; chairperson, Ala Bd Bar Examiners, 1995-98; fel Alabama State Bar; Am Bar asn, Federal Bar asn, Nat Bar asn; Alabama Lawyers asn. **Honors/Awds:** Constance Baker Motley Award, 1975; "The New Women in Court," Time Magazine, 1983; Outstanding Alumna Award Communication Studies, Univ Ala, 2000. **Special Achievements:** "best and brightest" women trial lawyers in the country. **Business Addr:** Magistrage Judge, United States District Court, Frank M Johnson Jr Federal Bldg, 1 Church St Suite B-100, Montgomery, AL 36104, **Business Phone:** (334)954-3740.

BOYD, EVELYN SHIPPS
Educator. **Personal:** Born in Birmingham, AL; daughter of Geneva White Shipps and Perry; married Gilbert M, Nov 28, 1948. **Educ:** Baldwin-Wallace Col, B MusEd (cum laude) 1959; Cleveland Inst Music, Master Music, hon grad, 1970. **Career:** Educator (retired); Cleveland Pub Schs, secy, 1942-55, teacher, 1959-71;Cuyahoga Comm Col, asst prof music, 1971-80; dept head performing arts,1977-81; Cleveland Inst Music, teacher, 1970-76. **Orgs:** OH Music Teachers Asn; Music Educ Nat Conf, 1961; organist, Western Res Psychiatric Hosp, 1981-88; tape recorder, Cleveland Soc Blind, 1984;organist, Miles Park Presbyterian Church, 1988-2000; chaplain staff, Univ Hosps Vol, 1992-; ombudsman off vol, Cleveland Clinic Found, 1993. **Honors/Awds:** Besse Award, Cuyahoga Com Col, 1980; Alumni Merit Award, Baldwin-Wallace Col, 1983; Award for 2000 Hours Volunteer, Univ Hosp SICU Unit, 1987; Phi Kappa Lambda Music Honorary, Soc Cleveland Inst Music; Baldwin-Walla Mu Phi Music Honorary, Sorority Dayton C Miller Hon Soc; Elizabeth Downes Award, Univ Hosps, 1989; ten Year Voluntary Service Award, Cleveland Clin.

BOYD, GEORGE ARTHUR
Scientist. **Personal:** Born Mar 7, 1928, Washington, NC. **Educ:** St Augustine Col, BS; Amer Univ, attended 1957; US Dept Agr Grad Sch, attended 1957; US Office Personnel Mgt Exec Inst, attended 1980, 1982. **Career:** US Naval Oceanog Off, phys scientist, 1958-79 (Retired); Phys sci tech, 1956-57; Mt Olivet Heights Citizens Asn, chmn; Defense Mapping Agency; Galloudet Univ, chmn, 1975-. **Orgs:** Sigma Xi, The Scientific Rsch Soc; pres, Mt Olivet Heights Citizens Asn; chmn, Gallaudet Univ Comm Rels Coun, 1977-; DC Fedn of Civil Asn Inc; former mem bd of trustees, St Augustine Col, 1982; former chmn, Adv Neighborhood Commission 5B, 1995; chmn, Metrop Police Dept Fifth Dist Citizens Adv Coun, Wash, DC;DC Consumer Utility Bd; Mt Olivet Height Citizens Asn. **Honors/Awds:** Award of Commendation, Pres of the US, 1970; Distinguished Alumni Award, Nat Assn for Equal Oppor of Higher Educ, 1985. **Military Serv:** AUS, AUS, pfc. **Home Addr:** 1264 Owen Pl NE, Washington, DC 20002. **Business Phone:** (202)651-5300.*

BOYD, GWENDOLYN ELIZABETH
Engineer. **Personal:** Born Dec 27, 1955, Montgomery, AL; daughter of Dora McClain. **Educ:** Ala State Univ, BS, math, 1977; Yale Univ, MS, mech eng, 1979; Howard Univ, attended 2007. **Career:** Johns Hopkins Univ Applied Physics Lab, submarine navigation systs analyst, 1980, exec asst chief of staff, 1998, asst develop prog, prin prof staff, chair, currently. **Orgs:** APL Fed Credit Union; Leadership Wash, 1996-; Children's Nat Med Ctr, 1996-; The Links Inc; Soc Women Engineers;Nat Pres, Delta Sigma Theta, 2000-04; Nat Coun Negro Women & Ebenezer AME Church, Ft Wash, ministerial staff; Diversity Leadership Coun. **Honors/Awds:** Maynard Jackson Leadership Award, Alpha Phi Alpha; United Way, Community Service Award, 1998; NAACP, Howard County, Outstanding Service Award, 1998; Special Congressional Recognition, presented by Hon Juanita Millender McDonald, 1999; Black Engineer of the Yr/Outstanding Alumnus Achievement, 2000; 20 Keys to the City; Chancellor's Award North Carolina Central Univ, 2006; Hon Doctorate, Bennett Col Women, 2007; Hon Doctorate, Lincoln Univ, 2007. **Special Achievements:** Black Engineer of the Year for Community Service, 1996. **Business Addr:** Assistant for Development Programs, Principal Professional Staff, Johns Hopkins University, Applied Physics Labratory, 11100 Johns Hopkins Rd Rm 1 S137, Laurel, MD 20723, **Business Phone:** (443)778-6031.

BOYD, GWENDOLYN VIOLA
Police chief, vice president (organization). **Personal:** Born Jun 4, 1954, Sneads, FL; daughter of Willie C Mathis and Vera Mae; children: Sherhonda & Lakeesha. **Educ:** Miami Dade Community Col, AA, 1974; Biscayne Col, BA, 1980; Fla Int Univ, MPA, 1982, EDd, 1997. **Career:** City Miami Police Dept, police major, 1974-97; City Prichard Police Dept, chief police, 1997; Fla, Miramar, chief police; Fla Int Univ, vpres admin & stud affairs, currently. **Orgs:** Ed, Nat Orgn Black Law Enforcement Execs; Intl Asn Women Police; Intl Asn Chiefs Police; Am Soc Training & Develop; AL Asn Chiefs Police; Nat Asn Negro Bus & Prof Women's Club; United Way Am; Mobile Co Chiefs Police Asn; Boys & Girls Club Mobile; Exec coun, Fla Intl Univ. **Honors/Awds:** Sojourner Truth, 1991; Women of the 90's Achievement Award; Outstanding Woman in Law Enforcement; Law Enforcement Community Service Award; gold medals, Fla Police Olympics; Who's Who in US Exec; Distinguished Serv Medallion, Fla Intl Univ, 1999. **Special Achievements:** Res on Male vs Female Police Officers' Job Performance, publ in fall issue of Women Police Mag; presenter, Human Resource Develop Conf, Atlanta, 1997; first female assistant chief in the Miami Police Department's 100-year history, and the first to retire and be selected to serve as a police chief in another city; first and only female police chief in Florida. **Business Addr:** Vice President Administration, Florida International University, 11200 SW Eigth St GC 219, Miami, FL 33199, **Business Phone:** (305)348-2797.

BOYD, REV. J. EDGAR
Clergy. **Career:** Bethel African Methodist Episcopal Church, treas, sr pastor, currently. **Orgs:** San Francisco Planning Comn. **Business Addr:** Senior Pastor, Bethel African Methodist Episcopal Church, 916 Laguna St, San Francisco, CA 94115, **Business Phone:** (415)921-4935.*

BOYD, JAMES
Executive. **Career:** AFC Enterprises, syst support Vpres, coo, 1999. **Business Phone:** (770)391-9500.*

BOYD, DR. JOHN W
Founder (Originator), president (organization). **Personal:** Born Sep 4, 1965, Queens, NY; son of John W Boyd Sr and Betty J; married Kim S Hardy (divorced 1994); children: 1. **Educ:** Southside Community Col, attended 1983; Clemson Univ, attended 1985. **Career:** Farmer, 1983-; Nat Black Farmers Asn, founder & pres, 1995-; John Boyd Agr & Technol Inst, founder, 2000-. **Orgs:** Nat Asn Advan Colored People. **Special Achievements:** Hundred Most Influential Black Americans, Ebony Magazine, 2006. **Business Phone:** (434)848-1865.

BOYD, DR. JOSEPH L.
School administrator. **Personal:** Born Dec 20, 1947, Columbia, SC; son of Frank Boyd; married Nellie Brown; children: Joseph Christopher, Michael Steven & Adrienne Kerise. **Educ:** Univ SC, BS, 1969, M.Acc, 1976, PhD, 1977. **Career:** Johnson C Smith Univ, instr, 1972-74; Univ SC, asst prof, 1976-77; Univ Ill, asst prof, 1977-78; NC A&T State Univ, assoc prof, 1978-83; Norfolk State Univ, sch bus, dean, 1983-98; Benedict Col, distinguished prof acct, 2000-; Tex Southern Univ, Jesse H Jones Sch Bus, dean, currently. **Orgs:** Beta Alpha Psi; Beta Gamma Sigma; Omicron Delta Kappa; Am Inst CPA; Am Acct Asn; NC Asn CPA; SC Asn CPA; Nat Asn Accts; Nat Asn Black Accts; Am Tax Asn; Ins Selling Practices Community; Curric Comn; Cluster Task Force; IRS Adv Group; Am Arbit Asn; Houston Urban League; mem, Initial Accreditation Comt (AACSB). **Honors/Awds:** Moderator of the Session on Tax Res, Am Acct Asn, Boston, MA, 1980. **Special Achievements:** Publications in Tax Adviser, Oil & Gas Tax Quarterly, Taxes-The Tax Magazine, Prentice-Hall Tax Ideas Service, 1978, 1979, 1983. **Business Phone:** (713)313-7215.

BOYD, JULIA A
Psychotherapist, writer. **Personal:** Born Apr 21, 1949, Camden, NJ; daughter of Joseph and Lavada Conyers; divorced; children: Michael Alan Boyd Jr. **Educ:** Antioch Univ, BA, psychol & coun, 1982; Pac Lutheran Univ, MEd, educ coun & guid, 1985; Seattle Univ, 1991; Univ Wash, ethnog interviewing & coun. **Career:** Pierce County Rape Relief, exec dir, 1985-86; Group Health Coop, psychotherapist, 1986-, Embracing Fire, Girlfriend Girlfriend, Co My Sisters, auth, currently; Essence, Ebony, Jet & Heart & Soul Mag; Black Women's Health Book; Seattle, pvt pract, psychotherapist. **Orgs:** Bd mem, Domestic Abuse Women's Network, 1983-85; Wash Sexual Assault Comn, Statewide Comt, 1984-86; Arts Comn, King County, 1986-89; AFA Women Forum, Western Wash State Univ, 1994. **Honors/Awds:** African American Women's Achievement Award, 100 Black Women, Jersey Chap, 1994; Distinguished Service Award, Wash State Univ. **Special Achievements:** Books: In the CPN of My Sisters; Black Women & Self-Esteem, Dutton, 1993; Girlfriend to Girlfriend; Everyday Wisdom & Affirmations from the Sister Circle, Dutton, 1995; Embracing the Fire: Sisters Talk About Sex and Relationships, Dutton, 1997; Documentary film: Secret Passages.

BOYD, KIMBERLY
Banker, executive. **Personal:** Born Jan 7, 1960, Georgetown, SC; daughter of Jack and Gertie Padgett; divorced; children: Curtis.

Educ: Purdue Univ, certif, Human Resource Mgt, 1998; Univ WI, Retail Banking Grad Prog, certif, 1999, 2000. **Career:** Anchor Bank, asst vpres training & develop, 1986-94; People's Bank, sr vpres Admin; Peoples Bancorp, sr vpres banking support, currently. **Orgs:** NC Cooperative Ext Minority Women, adv comt, 1999-. **Special Achievements:** Speaker, Minority Women's Conference, 1998-00; Chamber Womens Leadership Conference, Female Resilence, 2000; NAACP Key Note MLK Celebration, 2003; speaker, MLK Catawba Valley Community Col, 2003. **Home Addr:** 704 Carrick Ct NW, Conover, NC 28613, **Home Phone:** (828)465-0680. **Business Addr:** Senior Vice President Banking Support, Peoples Bancorp, Peoples Bancorp Ctr 518 W C St, Newton, NC 28658, **Business Phone:** (828)464-5620.

BOYD, LOUISE YVONNE
Software developer, manager. **Personal:** Born Jul 24, 1959, Newburgh, NY; daughter of Charles Carter and Louise Yvonne Lewis. **Educ:** Univ Fla, BS, math, 1981; Webster Univ, post grad, 1999. **Career:** NASA, Kennedy Space Ctr, software systs engr & workforce prog mgr, 1982-; Brevard Community Col, Cocoa, adj prof, 1984-88. **Orgs:** Pres, Nat Tech Asn, Space Coast Chap, 1987-89; region III dir, Nat Tech Asn, 1989-91; space coast div gov, Toastmasters Int, 1990-91; vpres, Space Coast Sect Soc Women Engrs, 1990-91; founder, chmn bd, Sweet Inc, 1990-; lt gov mkt, Toastmasters Int-Dist 47, 1991-92, treas, gov educ, 1992-93; treas, NASA Kennedy Mgt Asn, 1991-92. **Honors/Awds:** Hundred Black Sci Achievers, Chicago Mus Sci & Indust, 1989; 30 Leaders Future, Ebony Mg, 1989; Crystal Pyramid Award, Brevard Alumnae Chap Delta Sigma Theta Inc, 1990; Distinguished Toastmaster, Toastmasters Int, 1990; Distinguished Distrist Award, Toastmasters Int, 1992; Excellence Marketing Award, Toastmasters Int, 1992; NASA Points Light Award, 1992; NASA Exceptional Service Medal, 1998; Math Individual Tech Achiever Award, NTA Greater Houston Chap. **Business Addr:** Software Systems Engineeer, Workforce Program Manager, NASA, Kennedy Space Center, LPS Software Eng Div, TE-LPS-21, Orlando, FL 32899, **Business Phone:** (407)861-5020.

BOYD, MARSHA FOSTER
School administrator. **Personal:** Married Rev Kenneth; children: 1. **Educ:** Tufts Univ, BA; Interdenominational Theol Ctr, Atlanta, GA, MDiv; Grad Theol Union, Berkeley, PhD. **Career:** United Theol Sem, assoc prof pastoral care & coun; Payne Theol Sem, acad dean; Asn Theol Schs US & Can, Leadership Educ & Accreditation, dir, 1999, Ecumenical Theol Sem, pres, 2006-; Payne Theol Seminary, acad dean; United Theol Seminary, Pastoral Care & Coun, assoc prof. **Orgs:** AME Church, asst pastor; African Methodist Episcopal Church, itinerantelder. **Special Achievements:** First African American female academic dean in American Theological Schs. **Business Addr:** President, The Association of Theological Schools United States & Canada, Ecumenical Theological Seminary, 10 Summit Pk Dr, Pittsburgh, PA 15275, **Business Phone:** (412)788-6505.

BOYD, MARVIN
Banker. **Career:** Fed Res Bank, examiner, 1978-88; Security BancShares Inc, chief exec officer, 1999-; Gulf Fed Bank, pres & chief exec officer, currently. **Business Addr:** President, Chief Executive Officer, Gulf Federal Bank, 901 Springhill Ave, PO Box 40217, Mobile, AL 36640-0217, **Business Phone:** (251)433-2671.*

BOYD, MELBA JOYCE
Writer, educator. **Personal:** Born Apr 2, 1950, Detroit, MI; daughter of John Percy Boyd and Dorothy Wynn; divorced; children: John Percy III, Maya Wynn. **Educ:** Western Mich Univ, BA, eng, 1971, MA, eng, 1972; Univ Mich-Ann Arbor, Dr Arts, eng, 1979. **Career:** Cass Tech High Sch, teacher, 1972-73; Univ Mich, grad asst, 1978; Broadside Press, asst ed, 1972-77, 1980-82; Wayne County Community Col, instr, 1972-82; Univ Iowa, asst prof, 1982-88; Ohio State Univ, assoc prof, 1988-89; Univ Mich, dir African Am studies prog, 1989-, poet, cult activist, educr, currently. **Orgs:** Alpha Kappa Alpha Sorority Inc, 1968-71; African Am Studies Asn, 1982-; German Asn Am Studies, 1982-87. **Honors/Awds:** Individual Artists Award, Mich Coun Arts, 1980; Fulbright CMS, Senior Fulbright Lecturer-Germany, 1983-84; Research and Publication Award, Ohio State Univ, 1989; Culture Award, Soc Culturally Concerned, 1990; Faculty Research Grant, Univ Mich, 1991. **Special Achievements:** Cats Eyes and Dead Wood, Detroit, Fallen Angel Press, poetry, 1978; Song for Maya, Detroit, Broadside Press, 1983; Thirteen Frozen Flamingoes, Germany, Die Certel Press, poetry, 1984; Inventory of Black Roses, Detroit, Pasts Tents Press, poetry, 1989; Lied fur Maya/ Song for May, Germany, WURF Verlag Press, poetry, 1989. **Business Addr:** Poet, Director, University of Michigan, African-American Studies Program, 412 Maynard St, Ann Arbor, MI 48109-1399, **Business Phone:** (734)764-7260.*

BOYD, MURIEL ISABEL BELTON
School administrator. **Personal:** Born Feb 18, 1910, Haughton, LA; daughter of Lula Isabel Tyler (deceased) and Sank Beranger (deceased); married Charles Henry Boyd, Jun 24, 1940 (deceased); children: Dawud Abdus Salaam. **Educ:** Southern Univ Baton Rouge, BA, 1932; Columbia Univ Sch Libr Sci, MLS, 1950. **Career:** School administrator (retired); Lincoln Parish Sch, teacher, 1932-37; Caddo Parish Sch Bd, sch supvr & librn, 1937-70; staff, Lincoln Hosp. **Orgs:** Life mem, Nat Educ Asn; chmn, librn div, La Educ Asn; life mem, comt admin, YWCA Allendale Br; charter mem, Shreveport Nat Coun Negro Women; coordr, admin div, Nat Baptist Cong Educ; life mem, Southern Univ Alumni Asn. **Honors/Awds:** Woman of the Yr, Zeta Phi Beta, 1964; Shreveport Times Educator of the Yr, Caddo Educ Asn, 1970; featured in The Shreveport Sun, 1970; featured in The Shreveport J, 1988; featured in The Shreveport Times, 1989; featured on KEEL-Radio, 1990.

BOYD, PATRICIA M
Administrator. **Educ:** Brooklyn Col, BS; NY Univ, MS, taxation. **Career:** Arthur Andersen & Co, staff; M.R. Weiser & Co, staff; Benton & Bowles Inc., staff; Wachenheim Ltd Partners, staff; Texaco Int LLP, tax partner; Am Univ, staff; Guttenberg Found, staff; Kahn Boyd Levychin, tax partner. **Orgs:** Nat Asn Black Accts; Urban Bankers Coalition; bd chmn, Greater Harlem Chamber Com.

BOYD, ROZELLE
Educator. **Personal:** Born Apr 24, 1934, Indianapolis, IN. **Educ:** Butler Univ, BA, 1957; Ind Univ, MA, 1964. **Career:** Marion County, Dept Pub Welfare, caseworker, 1957; Indianapolis Pub Schs, teacher-counr, 1957-68; Indianapolis City councilman, 1966-; Ind Univ, asst dean, 1968-76, assoc dean, 1976-81, Groups Serv prog, dir; Marion Co, counr, 1970-2007. **Orgs:** Democratic Nat Committeeman; minority leader, Indianapolis City Coun; chmn, Indianapolis Black Polit Caucus. **Honors/Awds:** Lily Fel, 1957; Freedom's Found Award; Lifetime Achievement Award, Groups Student Support Serv Prog, Ind Univ, 2004; Annual Outstanding Achievement Award, Ind Christian Leadership Conf. **Special Achievements:** First African American man to serve as president of the city-county council. **Home Addr:** 2527 E 35th, Indianapolis, IN 46218. **Business Addr:** 2527 E 35th, Indianapolis, IN 46218, **Business Phone:** (317)327-4240.

BOYD, TERRY A.
Manager, executive. **Personal:** Born in Cleveland, OH. **Educ:** Defiance Col, BS, 1978; Ohio State Univ, attended 1981; PhD, 1993. **Career:** Human Resources Inc, asst dir, 1981-82; Franklin Co C Servs, child welfare worker III, 1982-84; City Columbus, adminr youth servs bur, 1984-87, exec asst dir human servs, 1987-89; adminr, community servs, 1989-90, adminr, OMB, 1990-91; US Health Corp, dir human resources, 1991-, Franklin Univ, course mgr & fac mem mba prog, currently. **Orgs:** Pres, Franklin Co C Serv Citizens Adv Coun, 1985-92; bd mem, Ohio's C Defense Fund, 1986-92; bd mem, Alliance for Coop Justice, 1985-89; COTA Transp Task Force, 1988-89; bd trustees, Franklin Co C Servs Bd, 1989-92; bd mem, Jobs for Columbus Grads, 1991-92; cabinet mem, United Way Campaign, 1992; bd trustee, treas, The Alcohol Drug & Mental Health Bd Franklin Co, 1992-; Columbus Metrop Libr Bd. **Honors/Awds:** Franklin Co Comnrs, Serv Merit, 1992; Distinguished Serv Award, Franklin Co C Serv, 1992. **Special Achievements:** Changing Attitudes: An Anti-Drug Abuse Policy, 1989. **Business Addr:** Faculty, Franklin University, 201 S Grant Ave, Columbus, OH 43215, **Business Phone:** (614)797-4700.*

BOYD, THEOPHILUS B., III
Executive. **Personal:** Born May 15, 1947, Nashville, TN; married Yvette Duke; children: LaDonna Yvette, Shalae Shantel, T B Boyd IV, Justin Marriell. **Educ:** Tenn State Univ, BBA, 1969; Shreveport Bible Col, DD, 1980; Easonian Baptist Sem, DHL, 1983. **Career:** Citizens Realty & Develop Co, pres, 1982; Citizens Sav & Develop Co, pres, 1982-; Meharry Med Col, vice chair, bd dir, 1982-; Nat Baptist Pub Bd, pres & chief exec officer; Citizens Bank, chmn bd dir; RH Boyd Publ Corp, pres & chief exec officer, currently. **Orgs:** Bd dirs, March Dimes Tenn Chapter; comnr human develop State, TN; bd dirs, Nashville Tech Inst; pres, 100 Black Men Middle Tenn Inc; past vpres finance & treas, 100 Black Men Am Inc; past Middle Tenn chmn, United Negro Col Fund Telethon; bd dirs, First Union Bank; mem bd gov, Nashville Area Chamber Com; vice chmn, Meharry Med Col Bd Trustees. **Honors/Awds:** March of Dimes, Man of the Year; life mem, Kappa Alpha Psi Fraternity Inc; mem, Chi Boule Sigma Pi Phi Frat; Best Dressed of Nashville. **Business Addr:** President, Chief Executive Officer, R H Boyd Publishing Corporation, 6717 Centennial Blvd, PO Box 91145, Nashville, TN 37209.*

BOYD, THOMAS
Manager. **Personal:** Born Apr 6, 1942, Philadelphia, PA; son of John and Thelma Archie; married Gwendolyn Lee, Dec 14, 1988. **Educ:** Temple Univ, BA, 1970. **Career:** Remington Rand Inc, mgr, 1979; Comput Sci Corp, mgr equal employ opportunity, 1979-81; Hahneman Univ, mgr employ, 1984-88; Syracuse Univ, dir, employ practices, 1988. **Orgs:** Consult, Navy Dept, 1981; consult, Nat Guard Bur, 1984.

BOYD, TOMMIE (TOMMIE LEESHAY BOYD)
Football player. **Personal:** Born Dec 21, 1971, Lansing, MI. **Educ:** Toledo Univ. **Career:** Detroit Lions, wide receiver, 1997-98; Rhein Fire; Detroit Fury, Arena Football League, 2001. *

BOYD, TOMMIE LEESHAY. See BOYD, TOMMIE.

BOYD, VALERIE
Writer, college teacher. **Educ:** Northwestern Univ, BS, 1985; Goucher Col, MS, 1999. **Career:** The Atlanta Jour-Constitution, copy ed, Int/Nat Desk, 1985-91, copy ed, features dept, 1988-92, reporter, 1991-92, asst arts ed & writer, 1992-95, asst ed, 1999-2000, arts ed, 2001-04; Univ SC, jour instr, 1987; Catalyst Mag, asst ed, 1989-95; Eight Rock Maga Book, founder, ed & publ, 1990-94; Health Quest Mag, co-founder & chief ed, 1992-97; Nat Black Arts Festival, lit cur, 1997-98; Optical Data, McGraw-Hill, writer & ed, 1998-99; Univ Ga, Grady Col, Dept Jour, asst prof, currently; Antioch Univ, assoc fac mentor, 2005-; Books: Spirits in the Dark: The Untold Story of Black Women in Hollywood; Wrapped in Rainbows: The Life of Zora Neale Hurston, 2003. Wrote numerous articles & chapters. **Orgs:** Nat Book Critics Circle; Nat Black Arts Festival; Alice Walker Literary Soc; Asn Writers & Writing Progs; Hurston/Wright Found. **Honors/Awds:** Pioneer Black Journalist Award, Atlanta Asn Black Journalists, 1993; Research Fellowship, Eliza Gardner Howard Found, Brown Univ, 1999; Southern Book Award, Southern Book Critics Circle, 2003; Notable Book Award, Am Libr Asn, 2004; Georgia Author of the Year Award, 2004. **Business Addr:** Assistant Professor, Grady College of Journalism and Mass Communication, University of Georgia, Rm 248, Athens, GA 30602-3018, **Business Phone:** (706)542-0887.

BOYD, DR. VIVIAN
Educator, administrator. **Educ:** Antioch Col, BA, 1961; Univ Colo, Boulder, MA, 1967; Univ Md, Okinawa, MA, 1969, Col Park, PhD, 1975. **Career:** Univ Md, Dept Coun & Personnel Serv, fac, 1966-, asst prof, 1976-89, actg asst dir, 1981-82, asst dir, 1982-88, actg dir, 1988, assoc prof educ & dir coun ctr, 1989-. **Orgs:** Int Asn Coun Serv; Governing Bd Comn Couns & Psychol Serv, Am Col Personnel Asn. **Honors/Awds:** Lifetime Achievement Award, Asn Col & Univ Coun Ctr Dirs Conf, 2003; Outstanding Woman of the Year, President's Comn Women, 2004. **Special Achievements:** Numerous publications including, "Sex-Fair interest measurements: Research and implications", Jour Voc Behavior, 1979; The university counseling center: An integrated service model, Am Col Personnel Asn, 1992; "Empirical sudy of Brozonski's Identity Styles Inventory based on Marcia's identity paradigm". **Business Addr:** Director of the Counseling Center & Associate Professor of Education, University of Maryland, Counseling Center, 1101 Shoemaker Bldg, College Park, MD 20742-8111, **Business Phone:** (301)314-7675.

BOYD, WILHEMINA Y.
Association executive. **Personal:** Born Sep 13, 1942, Baltimore, MD; daughter of William Woodley and Erma L Moore; married Raymond D, Apr 4, 1965; children: Adam & Jason. **Educ:** Morgan State Univ, Baltimore, BS, 1964; St Mary's Univ, San Antonio, MS, 1991. **Career:** Dept Defense/Heidelberg, Ger, preschool dir/ high sch teacher, 1978-80, Ft Hood Tex, youth activ, dir, 1981-83; City San Antonio, parks & rcrtn, spec activ supv, 1983-85, events coordr, 1985-87, conv facil, facil mgr, 1987-91; City Kans City, Mo, Conv & Entertainment Ctrs, exec dir, 1992-93; City Tampa, Conv Ctr, exec dir, 1993-98; Dallas Conv Ctr, dir, 1998-02; Roanoke Civic Ctr, dir, civic facilities, currently. **Orgs:** Nat Forum Black Pub Adminr, 1993-; bd dirs, Suncoast Girl Scout Coun Inc, 1994-98; bd trustees, Int Asn Assembly Mgr. **Special Achievements:** Cert facilities exec (CFE), 1998. **Business Addr:** Director, Roanoke Civic Center, 710 Williamson Rd, PO Box 13005, Roanoke, VA 24016, **Business Phone:** (540)853-2241.*

BOYD, WILLIAM. See COLLINS, BOOTSY.

BOYD, HON WILLIAM STEWART
Lawyer, accountant. **Personal:** Born Mar 29, 1952, Chicago, IL. **Educ:** Univ Ill, BS, Acct, 1974; Northern IL Univ Col Law, JD, 1981. **Career:** Legal Asst Found Chicago, clerk, 1979; Boyd & Grant, clerk, 1978-81; Arthur Anderson & Co, sr staff acct 1974-77, 1981-83; Boyd & Boyd Ltd, atty, 1983-86; Boyd & Crane, patrner, 1986-98; Traffic Ctr; Cook County, assoc judge, 1998; First Municl Dist, Domestic Rels Div, trial judge. **Orgs:** Bd dir, Grant Park Recreation Asn; Young Exec Politics; Nat Bus League, 1974; Am Bar Asn, 1981; Cook Co Bar Asn, 1981; bd dirs, NIA Comprehensive Ctr Inc, 1984; Northern Ill Univ Col Law Bd Visitors; Chicago & Cook County Bar Asn; Ill Judicial Coun; guest lect, John Marshall Law Sch. **Home Addr:** 436 W 100th Pl, Chicago, IL 60610.

BOYD-FOY, MARY LOUISE
Executive. **Personal:** Born Jun 30, 1936, Memphis, TN; daughter of Ivory (deceased) and Mamie E (deceased); married James Arthur Foy. **Educ:** Columbia Univ NY, BA, 1977; Boston Univ, Sch Soc Work, cert contract compliance adminr, 1989. **Career:** United Negro Col Fund Inc, pub info asst, 1956-60; Foreign Policy Asn, pub info asst, 1960-70; Columbia Univ Urban Ctr, off mgr, 1971-73, asst exec dean sch engineering, 1973-77, exec asst vpres & personnel admin, 1977-78; Int Paper Co, rep northeastern sales accts, 1978-80; Ebasco Serv Inc, coord legis affairs, 1980-86, corp mgr, subcontract compliance, 1986-; Ebasco Serv Inc, corp mgr. **Orgs:** Coalition 100 Black Women, 1980-; founding

mem, former vpres, Nat Asn Univ Women, Long Island, NY Br; past loyal lady, ruler Order Golden Circle, Long Island Assembly No 20, 1984, 1992; founder, past matron, Emerald Chap No 81 Order Eastern Star, Prince Hall Affil, 1986-; Daughters of Isis Abu-Bekr Ct No 74, Prince Hall Affil, 1986-; adv bd, United Negro Col Fund Inc, Queens, NY Br, 1986-; ad bd, United Negro Fund Inc, 1986-, Asn Minority Enterprises NY, 1986-; past natl chmn, bd dirs, Am Assn Blacks Energy, 1990-92. **Honors/Awds:** Woman of the Year, Nat Asn Univ Women, 1984; Outstanding Woman of NY State, NY Senate, 1984; Outstanding Service Certificate, United Negro Col Fund Inc, 1984; Distinguished Service Plaque, 1985-86; Recognition Award; Appreciation Award, Concerned Women Jersey City Inc, 1986; Outstanding Service Award, Asn Minority Enterprises NY, 1988; Inductee Registry of Distinguished Citizens, Queens, NY, 1989; Appreciation Award, US Dept Com, 1989; Hilda A Davis Award, Long Island Br, 1991; Nat Women Achievement Award, 1992. **Home Addr:** 117 20 232nd St, Cambria Heights, NY 11411. *

BOYER, CHARLES E.
Executive. **Career:** Blue Cross Blue Shield Mich, vpres human resources. **Orgs:** Bd mem, Am Soc Employers. *

BOYER, DR. HORACE CLARENCE
Educator. **Personal:** Born Jul 28, 1935, Winter Park, FL; married Gloria Bernice Blue. **Educ:** Bethune-Cookman Col, BA, 1957; Eastman Sch Music, Univ Rochester, MA, 1964, PhD, 1973. **Career:** Educator (retired); Monroe High Sch, instr 1957-58; Poinsett Elem Sch, instr, 1960-63; Albany State Col, asst prof, 1964-65; Univ Cent Fla, asst prof, 1972-73; Univ Mass Amherst, Dept Music, prof, prof emer, 1973-99,; Albany State Col, Ga, music theory & African-Am studies; Univ Cent Fla; Book: How Sweet the Sound: the Golden Age of Gospel. **Orgs:** A Better Chance, 1980-82; ed bd, Black Music Res J, 1980-83; vpres, Gospel Music Asn, 1983-84; cur musical instruments, Smithsonian Inst; cur, Nat Museum Am Hist, Smithsonian, 1985-86; Ford Found Fellow, Eastman Sch Music, 1969-72. **Honors/Awds:** Distinguished Scholar-at-Large, United Negro Col Fund, Fisk Univ, 1986-87; Outstanding Service, Univ Mass, 1990. **Special Achievements:** Horace Clarence Boyer Gospel Music Fund, 1999. **Military Serv:** AUS, sp-4, 1958-60. *

BOYER, JAMES B.
Educator. **Personal:** Born Apr 3, 1934, Winter Park, FL; married Edna Medlock. **Educ:** Bethune-Cookman Col, BS, 1956; Fla A&M Univ, MEd, 1964; Ohio State Univ, PhD, 1969. **Career:** Fla A&M Univ, teacher, admin vis prof, (retired), 1969; Univ Houston, asst prof, 1969-71; Kans State Univ, assoc prof, 1971, prof, Curric & Am Ethnic Studies, currently; George Mason Univ, Multicult Res & Resource Ctr, 2004-. **Orgs:** Dir, Inst Multi-Cult Studies; Asn Afro-Am Life & History; Asn Supr & Curric; Nat Alliance Black Edu; Coun Interracial Books C; Nat Asn Advan Colored People; Phi Delta Kappa; Nat Asn Multicultural Educ; Human Rel Bd; consult ed, publ articles field; founder, Nat Asn Multicult Educ. **Honors/Awds:** Kelsey Pharr Award, 1956; Teacher of the Year, 1957; Outstanding Churchman,1965, 1969. **Military Serv:** AUS, 1957-59. **Business Addr:** Professor, George Mason University, Multicultural Res & Resource Ctr, Stud Union Bldg I Room 225, 4400 Univ Dr MSN 2G6, Fairfax, VA 22030-4444.*

BOYER, MARCUS AURELIUS
Executive. **Personal:** Born Jul 10, 1945, Vado, NM; married Doris Ann Young; children: Malcolm. **Educ:** Univ NMex, BA, 1967; Wash Univ, MBA, 1972. **Career:** Small Bus Admin, trainee, 1967-68, econ dev asst, 1970, loan officer, 1971; Marine Midland Bank, asst officer, 1973-74, officer, 1974-76, asst vpres, 1976-77; Bank Am, vpres, sr acct officer, 1977-87; Resolution Trust Co, Atlanta, managing agent, oversight cluster mgr, 1990-; Nationsbank NA, sr vpres. **Orgs:** Consortium Grad Study Mgt, 1970; bd mem, Nat Black MBA Asn, 1973-76; pres, NY Chap Nat Black MBA Asn, 1975-76; Nat Asn Advan Colored People; Asn MBA Exec Fel. **Honors/Awds:** Black Achievers in Indiana Award, YMCA, 1975. **Military Serv:** AUS, sgt E-5. **Home Addr:** 26 Church St, South Orange, NJ 07079. *

BOYER, SPENCER H
Educator. **Personal:** Born Sep 23, 1938, West Chester, PA; married Prudence Bushnell; children: 6. **Educ:** Howard Univ, BS, 1960; George Wash Univ Law Sch, LLB, 1965; Harvard Law Sch, LLM, 1966. **Career:** US Com Dept, patenter, examiner, 1964-65; Fla Univ, Law Col, vis prof, 1968; Howard Univ, Sch Law, prof, currently, assoc dean, Howard Legal Intern Prog, dir; Fla Univ, vis prof; Iowa Univ, vis prof; Anitoch Sch Law, Wash, DC, vis prof; George Washington Univ, exec bd ed; Antioch Sch Law, Wa, vis prof; Trans Urban East Inc, consult; Univ Buffalo Sch Law, distinguished lectr taxation & urban econ; Univ DC, adj prof, currently. **Orgs:** Nat Bar Asn; DC Bar Asn; Am Coun Educ Comt; Nat Acad Sci Publishers; consult atty, CHANGE, 1967; com cit, Participation Model Cities, 1967-68; City Wide Nat Capitol Housing Authority, 1967-69; dir, Mid-Atlantic Legal Educ Opportunity Prog, 1970; dir, Atlanta Legal Educ Opportunity Prog, 1971, 1972; asst dev, HUMP; Asn Am Law Schs, Comt on Minority Studs; Am Trial Lawyers Asn; fac adv, Entertainment Law Stud Asn; fac adv, Stud Bar Assoc; fac adv, Barrister; fac adv, Howard Univ Law Sch Scroll & Howard Univ Law Jour; fac adv, Phi Delta Phi Fraternity; chmn, Admissions & Financial Aid Comt; fac adv, Comput & Technol Comt. **Honors/Awds:** Outstanding Professor Award, 1973-74; Paul L Diggs Award; Outstanding Professor, 1972-73; Student Bar Asnaition Award, Howard University Law School, 1970-71; Professor of the Year, Harvard Univ, 1998; Distinguished Faculty Author Award, Harvard Univ, 2000, 2002; Student Awards; Outstanding Alumni Award, Nat Howard Univ Sch Law Alumni Asn. **Special Achievements:** Contributed numerous publications. **Business Addr:** Professor, Howard University School of Law, 404 Houston Hall 2900 Van Ness St NW, Washington, DC 20008-1194, **Business Phone:** (202)806-8019.

BOYKIN, A. WADE, JR.
Educator. **Personal:** Born Feb 7, 1947, Detroit, MI; children: A Wade III & Curtis. **Educ:** Hampton Institute, BA, 1968; Univ Mich, MS, 1970, PhD, experimental psychol, 1972. **Career:** Hampton Inst, psychol lab student supvr, 1967-68; Cornell UNIV, asst toassoc prof, 1972-80; Rockefeller UNIV, adjunct assoc prof, 1976-77; JourBLACK Psych, assoc ed, 1978-81; Howard Univ, Dept Psychol, prof, DirDevelop Psychol Grad Prog, 1980-; Ctr Res Ed Students Placed At Risk,co-dir, 1994-; Capstone Inst, exec dir, currently. **Orgs:** Co-found, Conf Empirical Res BLACK Psych, Adv Comt, Am Psych Asn MNYFellowship Prog; Task Force Sci Persp Intelligence Test & Group Diff TestScores, APA, 1995; educ bds, Jour Ed Students Placed Risk, LearningEnviron Res, Am Ed Res Jour; Emergency Comt Urban Children; NEA, 1996-98;The Col bd Coun Inquiry & Praxis; Task Force Relevence Soc Sci BLACK Exp,Yale Univ, 1981-86; Nat Mathematics Adv Panel, currently. **Honors/Awds:** Third District Scholar of Year, Basileus of Year, Omega Psi Phi, 1967-68;fellow, Rockefeller Univ, 1976-; Alpha Kappa Mu; fellow, Ctr Advan Study-Behavioral Scis, 1978-79; Spencer Fellow, Nat Acad Educ, 1978-81;scholar-in-residence, Millersville Univ, 1985; co-editor, Res Dir BLACKPsychol, 1979; Disting Alumini Award, Hampton Univ. **Military Serv:** AUS, Med Serv Corps, 1st lt, 1971. **Business Addr:** Co-Director, Capstone Institute at Howard University, Holy Cross Hall, 2900 Van Ness St NW Suite 427, Washington, DC 20008, **Business Phone:** (202)806-8484.*

BOYKIN, JOEL S.
Dentist, teacher. **Personal:** Born Jul 23, 1926, Birmingham, AL; son of Joel Allen and Juliett Watson; divorced; children: Stephan, George, Joels, Jr, Lisa Boykin Bolden, Kristina, Joel Allen. **Educ:** Morehouse Col, BS, 1948; Atlanta Univ, MS, 1952; Meharry Med Col, DDS, 1956. **Career:** Birmingham Pub Sch Syst, 1948; Bullock Co Sch Syst, teacher, 1949-50; St Clair Co Sch Syst, 1949; pvt pratice dentist, currently. **Orgs:** Jefferson Co Dent Study Club; Nat Dent Asn; Ala Dent Asn; Am Dent Asn; pres, Ala Dent Soc; soc mem, Alpha Phi Alpha; deacon, 16th St Baptist Church. **Military Serv:** AUS, sgt, 1945-46. **Business Addr:** Dentist, 2723 29th Ave N, Birmingham, AL 35207-4635.*

BOYKIN, KEITH
Television show host, writer. **Personal:** Born Aug 28, 1965, St Louis, MO; son of William and Shirley Hayes. **Educ:** Dartmouth Col, BA, 1987; Harvard Univ, JD, 1992. **Career:** White House, spec asst, Pres US, 1993-95; NBGLLF, exec dir, 1995-98; Am Univ, adj prof gov, 1999-2000; BET J, TV host, My Two Cents, 2006-08; The Daily Voice, ed-in-chief, 2008-; Author: One More River To Cross, Doubleday, 1996; Respecting the Soul, 1999; Beyond The Down Low, Avalon, 2005. **Orgs:** Pres bd, Nat Black Justice Coalition. **Honors/Awds:** Dartmouth Freshman Prize, The Dartmouth Newspaper, 1983; Alpha Kappa Alpha Ivy Award, Nu Beta Omega Chapter, 1983; William S. Churchill Prize, Dartmouth Col, 1984; Track & Field Achievement Award, Dartmouth Col, 1984-85; The Barrett Cup, Dartmouth Col, 1987; Dartmouth Black Caucus Senior Honor Roll, Dartmouth Black Caucus, 1987; Muhammad Kenyatta Young Alumni Award, Harvard BLSA, 1994; Nat Services Award, The Brotherhood of the Gentleman, Inc., 1997; Recognition from Cambridge, MA City Coun, 1998; GMAD Angel Award, Gay Men African Descent, 1998; Audre Lorde-Joe Beam Literary Award, 1999; Lambda Literary Award, Lambda Lit, 1999; The Conscience of the Community Award, 1999; Solutions Award of Merit, Solutions DC, 1999; Nat Leadership Award, People of Color in Crisis, 2004. **Business Addr:** Author, PO Box 1229, New York, NY 10037.

BOYKINS, AMBER
Government official. **Personal:** Born Apr 4, 1969; daughter of Billie A Boykins and Amber; married Shaun. **Educ:** Columbia Col, Columbia; MBA, Juris Doctrate. **Career:** MO House Rep, state rep dist 60, 2003. **Honors/Awds:** Yes I Can Award, St. Louis Teachers and School Related Personnel Local 420; Dr. Joyce Thomas Leadership Award; oung Democrats Dedicated Leadership in Government Award; Making a Difference Award; 30 Women to Watch:Women at the Top of their Class. **Business Addr:** State Representative, MO House of Representatives, District 60, Rm 115A 201 W Capitol Ave, Jefferson City, MO 65102, **Business Phone:** (573)751-4415.

BOYKINS, EARL
Basketball player. **Personal:** Born Jun 2, 1976, Cleveland, OH. **Educ:** Eastern Mich Univ. **Career:** CBA, prof basketball player; NJ Nets, guard, 1999; Cleveland Cavaliers, 1999-00; Orlando Magic, 1999; Los Angeles Clippers, 2001-02; Golden State Warriors, 2002-03; Denver Nuggets, guard, 2003-07; Milwaukee Bucks, guard, 2007; Charlotte Bobcats, 2008; Virtus Bologna, 2008-09; Virtus Bologna, free agt, currently. **Honors/Awds:** All-Am hons; gold medal, World Univ Games, 1997; Frances Pomeroy Naismith Award, 1989; Sixth Man of the Year Award, Nat Basketball Asn, 2004, 2005. **Business Addr:** Free Agent.*

BOYKINS, ERNEST A.
Educator, college teacher. **Personal:** Born Oct 5, 1931, Vicksburg, MS; son of Ernest and Georgia; married Beverly Malveaux; children: Darryl, Rhea, Constance & Karen. **Educ:** Xavier Univ, BS, biol 1953; Tex Southern Univ, MS, biol, 1958; Cell Biol Univ,attended 1960; Mich State Univ, PhD, zool, 1964. **Career:** Educator (retired); Alcorn A & M Col, instr, 1959-61, Sci Dept, actg head,1958-59, instr, 1954-57; Mich State Univ, instr, 1964;Div Arts & Sci, 1970-71, prof, 1964-71; Miss Valley State Univ, pres, 1971-81; Univ Southern Miss, assoc prof, 1981-88; Pine Grove, Hattiesburg, MS, prog coordr, 1989-98. **Orgs:** Am Coun Educ, 1954-57; Miss Select Comn Higher Educ, 1973; exec bd, DeltaCoun BSA, 1973; Greenwood-Leflore Co C of C, 1974; Leflore Co UnitedGivers Inc, 1974; post secy, Educ Bd, 1974; Am Inst Biol Sci; AAAS; NatCoun Higher Educ; Miss Conserv Educ Adv Coun; Spec Health Career Opportunities Prog; Asn SE Biologist; Am Asn Higher Educ; Sigma Xi Sci Hon Soc; Nat Col Hon Coun; Phi Delta Kappa; Beta Kappa Chi; Omega Psi Phi; Alpha Kappa Mu. **Home Addr:** 9 Delond Pl, Hattiesburg, MS 39402. *

BOYLAND, DORIAN SCOTT
Automotive executive, baseball player. **Personal:** Born Jan 6, 1955, Chicago, IL; son of William and Alice Jones; married Denise A Wells Boyland, Apr 5, 1990; children: Shannon, Richard, Adriane. **Educ:** Univ Wis, Oshkosh, WI, BA, bus, 1976. **Career:** Pittsburgh Pirates, prof player, 1976-83; Ron Tonkin-Dodge, Gladstone, OR, owner & general mgr, 1985-86; Gresham Dodge Inc, Gresham, OR, pres, general mgr; Boyland properties, pres; Boyland Insurance Group, pres; Boyland Auto Group, Inc, pres, owner, 1996-. **Orgs:** chmn, Performance 20 Groups; bd mem, United Negro Col Fund; Portland Urban League; Oregon Arbitration Bd; APA Fraternity Inc, 1974; Dodge Denter Council. **Honors/Awds:** MLK Bus Leadership Award, State Ore, 1990; Urban League Award, Portland Urban League, 1990; Gold Medal Award, Special Olympics, 1989-90; Hall of Fame, Univ Wis, 1987; Top 100 Black Bus Award, Black Enterprise, 1988-92. **Business Addr:** Owner, Boyland Auto Group, 4301 Millenia Blvd, Orlando, FL 32839, **Business Phone:** (407)367-2700.*

BOYNTON, ASA TERRELL, SR.
School administrator, vice president (organization), executive director. **Personal:** Born May 20, 1945, Griffin, GA; son of Estell and Willie; married Evelyn Josephine Jordan; children: Asa Terrell Jr, Aaron Vernard, Antoine Debue. **Educ:** Fort Valley State Col, BS, bus admin 1967; Univ GA, MA, pub admin, 1973. **Career:** St Petersburg, Pub Safety Div, chief community rels, 1973; Univ Ga, Pub Safety Div, assoc dir, 1978, dir pub safety, assoc vpres security preparedness, currently; cert police instr. **Orgs:** Pres, Asn Campus Law Enforcement Admin, 1976; Eta Iota Lambda, 1977; Athens Rotary Club, 1983-; pres, Athens Breakfast Optimist Club, 1984; pres, fel Int Asn Campus Law Enforcement Adminr, 1987-88; adv bd, Northeast Ga Police Acad; pres, Alpha Phi Alpha Fraternity; FBI Nat Acad; chmn, Athens Regional Med Ctr. **Honors/Awds:** Seventh Army Soldier of the Month, AUS, 1968; Man of the Year, Alpha Phi Alpha, Eta Iota Lambda Chap, 1978; Mem of the Year, Ga Asn Campus Law Enforcement Admin, 1984; Jeanne Clery Campus Safety Award, Security Campus Inc, 2000; Nat Award. **Military Serv:** AUS, sgt, 2 yrs. **Home Addr:** 470 Millstone Cir, Athens, GA 30605. **Business Addr:** Associate Vice President, University of Georgia, 212 Terrell Hall Jackson St, Athens, GA 30602.*

BOZE, U LAWRENCE
Association executive, lawyer. **Personal:** Born Nov 1, 1949, Houston, TX; son of U L Boze and Iva Stewart Bozes. **Educ:** Univ Houston, BS, 1973; Tex Southern Univ, finance, JD, 1978. **Career:** Chevron USA & Gulf Oil Corp, bankruptcy coun, 1978-87; Allied Bankshares Inc, vpres & bankruptcy coun; Nat Bar Asn, pres, 1996; U Lawrence Boze & Assocs PC, atty, currently. **Orgs:** Nat Bar Asn, 1987-; pres, Houston Lawyers Asn, 1987; founder & pres, Tex Asn African Am Lawyers, 1991-. **Honors/Awds:** Distinguished Service to the Houston Community Award, Nat Asn Advan Colored People. **Special Achievements:** First black fee atty, Fidelity Nat Title, 1994. **Business Addr:** Attorney, U Lawrence Boze & Associates PC, 2212 Blodgett St, Houston, TX 77004, **Business Phone:** (713)520-0260.

BOZEMAN, BRUCE L
Lawyer. **Personal:** Born Jan 21, 1944, Philadelphia, PA; son of Hammie Winston and Herman H; married Patricia Johnson; children: Herman, Leslie, Patrick & Holly. **Educ:** Va Union Univ, BA, 1965; Howard Univ Sch Law, JD, 1968; NY Univ Sch Law, LLM, 1975. **Career:** Maxwell House Div GFC, asst counsel, 1969-71, Birds Eye div couns, 1971-73, beverage & breakfast foods div couns, 1973-78, dir, consumer affairs, asst gen couns,

1978-81; Norton Simon Inc, asst gen counsel, 1981-83; US Dist Ct Southern Dist NY; Bruce L Bozeman, PC, pres, currently; Westchester Financial Group Ltd, pres; pvt practice, atty, currently; Bozeman & Trott, LLP, atty; Bozeman Law Firm LLP, sr partner & prin, currently. **Orgs:** Nat Bar Asn; Am Bar Asn; NY Bar Asn; Westchester Cty Bar Asn; Asn Black Lawyers Westchester County Bar DC 1968, NY, 1969, US Ct Appeals, 1969, US Supreme Ct, 1978; Grievance Comm Westchester Cty Bar Asn; chmn, Black Dems Westchester County. **Business Addr:** Senior Partner, Principal, The Bozeman Law Firm LLP, 6 Gramatan Ave 5th Fl, Mount Vernon, NY 10550, **Business Phone:** (914)668-4600.

BRABSON, DR. HOWARD VICTOR
Educator. **Personal:** Born Sep 18, 1925, Knoxville, TN; son of Alfred L Jones Jr and Fannie R Burrough; married Rudiene Houston, Sep 13, 1952 (divorced). **Educ:** Col Ozarks, BS, 1956; Cath Univ, Nat Catholic Sch Social Serv, MSW, 1962, DSW, social work & helping services, 1975. **Career:** Cedar Knoll Sch, asst supt, 1958-62; Boys Indust Sch Lancaster, admin voced, 1962-63; Ohio Youth Comm, dep comnr, 1963-65; VISTA Training Ctr, Univ Md, asst proj dir, 1965-66; VISTA Eastern Region Wash DC, field supvr, 1966-67; Great Lakes Region VISTA, prog mgr, 1967-69; Univ Mich, assoc prof soc work, 1969-91, assoc prof emer social work, 1991-; Cath Univ DSW, fel, 1970-71. **Orgs:** Comt orgn consult, Neighborhood Groups, 1965-; chmn bd, Prog Mgt & Develop Inc, 1969-; Orgn Mich Asn BSW, 1970; consult, Control Syst Res, VISTA training, 1971-73; nat conf chmn, Nat Asn Black Social Workers, 1973-74, vpres, 1974-76, pres, 1978-82; vpres, OIC Bd Acad Cert Social Workers. **Honors/Awds:** Humanitarian Award, Willow Run Adversary Club, 1977; Certificate of Appreciation, NC ABSW, 1979; Outstanding Community Service Award, MI ABSW,1979; Community Service Award, KY ABSW, 1980; Distinguished Service Award, Albany NY ABSW, 1980; United Fund Special Award; Faculty Recognition Award, Univ Mich, 1981; Michigan Asn of Black Social Workers Tribute, 1999; Lifetime Achievement Award, Nat Asn Black Social Workers, 2002; Certificate of Appreciation, Univ Toledo; School of Social Work Alumni Society Award for Outstanding Teaching and Service to Social Work. **Special Achievements:** Author of Job Satisfaction, Job Stress & Coping Among African-American Human Service Workers, 1989; one of the consulting editor JOURNAL OF VOLUNTARY ACTION RESEARCH. **Military Serv:** AUS, capt, 1946-58; Commendation Ribbon. **Business Addr:** Associate Professor Emeritus of Social Work, University of Michigan, School of Social Work, Rm 2738 SSWB 1080 S Univ, Ann Arbor, MI 48109, **Business Phone:** (734)764-9484.

BRACEY, HENRY J.
Educator, counselor. **Personal:** Born Jan 31, 1949, Grand Rapids, MI; son of Joe and Sheba M Davis; married; children: Anton J, Candice G, Kwando A, Lisa K. **Educ:** Western MI Univ, BS, 1971; Univ SC, MEd, 1981. **Career:** SC Personnel & Guidance Asn, exec coun, 1982; SC Sch Counrs Asn, publicity comn, 1982; SC Asn Non-White Concerns, pres & bd mem, 1982; Southeastern Asn Educ Oppor Prog, personnel mgr, 1983; Midlands Tech Col, counr, 2003. **Orgs:** Public relations dir, Ms Black Columbia Pageant, 1980-82; bd mem, Columbia Youth Coun, 1982-84; bd mem, Brothers & Sisters, 1984-86; vpres, Col Place Comt, Coun, 1985-87; SC Tech Educ Asn, 1986-87; Southern Regional Coun, Black Am Affairs, 1986-87; Omega Psi Phi; pres, Heritage Comt Prods; stud involvement coord Southern Regional Coun Black Am Affairs Conf, 1986; pres, Kuumba Circle, 1988; pres, Eau Claire Comm Coun; Eau Claire Devel Corp; Ujamaa A Concern Group of Men; Nat Asn Advan Colored People; Ascac Asn study Classical African Civilizations; SC Conf, Shalom Zone Ministries; pres, mem, Francis Burns United Methodist Church; staff coun pres, Midlands Tech Col; adv bd, Columbia Citizens; PTA pres, Alcorn Middle Sch, CA Johnson HS. **Honors/Awds:** Published numerous articles on Cross-Cultural Couns, 1979-; Outstanding Young Men of America, 1980; Outstanding Service Award, Ms Black Columbia Pageant, 1980-82; designed & published, Cross-Cultural Couns Mode,l 1980; Citizen of the Week (WOIC) 1981; Recognition Award, SC Personnel & Guidance Asn; Columbia Citizens Adv Comt, Community Devel Appreciation Award. **Home Addr:** 5016 Colonial Dr, Columbia, SC 29203. **Business Addr:** Counselor, Midland Tech College, PO Box 2408, Columbia, SC 29202.*

BRACEY, JOHN HENRY, JR.
Educator. **Personal:** Born Jul 17, 1941, Chicago, IL; son of John H Sr and Helen Harris; married Ingrid Babb, Dec 19, 1975; children: Kali, Bryan & John Peter. **Educ:** Howard Univ, attended 1960; Roosevelt Univ, BA, 1964; Northwestern Univ, NDEA fel, 1969. **Career:** Northeastern Ill State Col, lectr, 1969; Northern Ill Univ, lectr, hist, 1969-71; Univ Rochester, asst prof hist, 1971-72; Univ Mass, W.E.B. Du Bois Dept Afro-American Studies, prof, 1972-, chm, 1974-79. **Orgs:** Asn Study African-Am Life & Hist; life mem, Org AM Historians, nominating comt, 1978-79; Phi Alpha Theta; Southern Historical Asn. **Special Achievements:** Published 14 books, numerous articles, reviews on various aspects of the history & culture of AROs. **Business Addr:** Professor, University of Massachusetts, W E B Du Bois Department of Afro-American Studies, 325 New Africa House, Amherst, MA 01003, **Business Phone:** (413)545-5160.*

BRACEY, WILLIE EARL
Lawyer, school administrator. **Personal:** Born Dec 21, 1950, Jackson, MS; son of Dudley and Alvaretta; married Dianne Fullenwilder, Aug 15, 1987. **Educ:** Wright Jr Col, AA, 1970; Mt Senario Col, BS, 1973; Eastern Ill Univ, MS, 1976; Southern Ill Univ, JD, 1979. **Career:** Southern Ill Univ, law clerk, 1978-79; Southern Ill Univ, Ctr Basic Skill, instr, 1977-78; Southern Ill Univ, Law Sch, res asst, 1977-78; Notre Dame Law Sch, teaching asst, 1977; Western Ill Univ, dir, stud legal serv, 1979-87, asst vpres, stud affairs support servs; adj prof, col stud personnel grad prog, 1987-, assoc vpres stud serv, 2002-. **Orgs:** Mem NAACP, 1979-, ATLA 1979-90, ABA 1979-90, IBA 1979-, McDonough City Bar Asn 1979-, Nat Asn Student Personnel Admin 1987-; faculty mem Blue Key Honor Soc; Housing Commissoner, McDonough County Housing Authority, appointment ends 1998; Illinois Attorney General Date Rape Drugs Steering Committee, 1999. **Business Addr:** Associate Vice President, Student Support Services, Western Illinois University, 1 Univ Cir, Macomb, IL 61455-1390, **Business Phone:** (309)298-1900.

BRACKEN, CHARLES O.
Management consultant, health services administrator. **Educ:** Wayne State Univ, Detroit, BS, Acct, MBA; Inst Cert Comput Prof, Cert Data Processing. **Career:** Multi-hosp corp, chief info officer; Healthcare Info & Mgt Systs Soc, exec vpres; Forum Healthcare Strategists, mem; Healthcare Strategy Inst, presenter; Harvard Sch of Pub Health Conf, ann presenter; Med Econ Soc of Fel, ann presenter; Superior Consult Co, exec vpres; ACS Healthcare Solutions, managing dir, currently. **Orgs:** Healthcare Info & Mgt Systs Soc; Nat Asn Health Serv Execs; Ctr for Health Info Mgt; bd mem, Ctr Health Info Mgt. **Business Addr:** Managing Director, Affiliated Computer Services Inc., 2828 North Haskell, Dallas, TX 75204, **Business Phone:** (214)841-6111.

BRACKENS, TONY LYNN, JR.
Football player, cattle breeder. **Personal:** Born Dec 26, 1974, Fairfield, TX; children: 3. **Educ:** Univ Tex. **Career:** Football player (retired); Jacksonville Jaguars, defensive end, 1996-03. *

BRACY, ADRIAN E. See BARR-BRACY, ADRIAN.

BRACY, DR. JAMES HARRISON
College teacher. **Educ:** Howard Univ, MS, 1971; Univ Mich, PhD, 1980. **Career:** Calif State Univ, Pan African Studies Dept, prof, currently.

BRADBERRY, DR. RICHARD PAUL
Librarian, library administrator. **Personal:** Born Dec 6, 1951, Florala, AL; son of Sam and Nettie Ruth Hightower. **Educ:** Ala State Univ, Montgomery, AL, BS, 1973; Atlanta Univ, Atlanta, GA, MSLS, 1974; Univ Mich, Ann Arbor, MI, PhD, 1988. **Career:** Auburn Univ, Auburn, AL, humanities librn, 1974-76; Langston Univ, Langston, OK, dir, librn chair librn sci dept, 1976-83; Lake Erie Col, Painesville, OH, dir libr, 1983-84; Univ Conn, W Hartford, CT, dir libr, 1984-89; Del State Col, Dover, DE, dir col libr, 1989-92; William Patterson Col, Sarah B Askew Libr, lib staff; Bowie State Univ, Thurgood Marshall Libr, dean, currently. **Orgs:** Am Libr Asn, 1984-; Asn Libr & Info Sci Educ, 1988-; treas, Land-Grant Libr Dir Asn, 1989-; Del Libr Asn, 1990-; Am Asn Higher Educ, 1990-. **Honors/Awds:** Education Professions Development Act Grant, US Govt, 1973; Oklahoma State Regents Doctoral Study Grant, State Okla 1980, 1981; Title II-B Fellowship, University of Michigan, 1980, 1981. **Home Addr:** 1300 S Farmview Dr H-31, Dover, DE 19901. **Business Addr:** Dean Library & Media Operations, Bowie State University, Thurgood Marshall Library, 14000 Jericho Pk Rd, Bowie, MD 19901.

BRADDOCK, CAROL T
Executive. **Personal:** Born Sep 7, 1942, Hamilton, OH; daughter of Rev Carlace A Tipton; married Robert L; children: Ryan Lawrence & Lauren Patricia-Tipton. **Educ:** Univ Cincinnati, BA, 1965, MA, 1976; Ind Univ, grad key, 1980. **Career:** McAlpins Dept Store, buyer 1969; Vogue Care Col, instr, 1971; Taft Broadcasting, prod coordr, 1972; Fed Home Bank Bd, urban prog coordr, 1973; Col Mt St Joseph, lectr, 1973; Neighborhood Reinvestment Corp, consult, 1974; Fed Home Loan Bank Cincinnati, exec asst, 1975, vpres com investment officer, 1978-85, asst vpres, 1978; Banking-financial consult. **Orgs:** Trustee, Nat Trust Historic Preservation; Jr League Sustainee; founder & past pres, Womens Alliance, 1966; exec comm mem, WCET-TV Pub TV, 1972-79; Queen City Beauty, Cincinnati Enquirer, 1973; pres, Minority Bus Devel Coalition, 1980. **Honors/Awds:** Outstanding Serv Award, Urban Reinvestment Task Force, 1975; Black Achievers Award, YMCA, 1978; Outstanding Career Woman, 1983.

BRADDOCK, DR. MARILYN EUGENIA
Educator, physician, dentist. **Personal:** Born Apr 25, 1955, Washington, DC; daughter of Ernest L and Rita H Glover. **Educ:** Marquette Univ, BS, 1977; Meharry Med Col, DDS, 1982; Univ NC, Chapel Hill, prosthetic dent & res fel, 1992, MS, Oral Biol Immunol, 1993. **Career:** Cook Co Hosp, GPR, 1982-83; US Navy Dent Corps, 1983-86, comdr, 2006-; US Navy Dent Corps, Periodontology fel, 1985-86; pvt pract, dent, 1986-89; Meharry Med Col, Sch Dent, Dept Prosthodontics, asst prof, 1992-95; COR US Navy Dent Corps, USS John F Kennedy, CV-67, 1995. **Orgs:** Delta Sigma Theta Sor Inc; Am Dent Asn; Fed Sers Asn; Am Col Prosthodontics; troop leader, Girl Scouts Am; Omicron Kappa Upsilon. **Honors/Awds:** National Serv Fel Award, NIH, 1991-92. **Military Serv:** USN, 1983-86, 1995-, Navy Recruiting Command, Campus Liason Officer, Nashville, TN. **Home Addr:** 9650 Santiago Rd, Columbia, MD 21045. **Business Phone:** (202)781-3634.

BRADEN, EVERETTE ARNOLD
Judge. **Personal:** Born Nov 3, 1932, Chicago, IL; son of Zedrick and Bernice; married Mary Jeanette Hemphill; children: Marilynne. **Educ:** Herzl Jr Col, 1952; Northwestern Univ, BS, 1954; John Marshall Law Sch, LLB, 1961, JD, 1969. **Career:** Cook Co Dept Pub Aid, caseworker, 1961-66; property & inst consult, 1966-69; Cook Co Pub Defender Off, trial atty, 1969-76, supv trial atty, 1976-77; Cook Co Circuit Ct, assoc judge, 1977-78, circuit judge, 1978-94; Ill Appellate Ct, justice, 1994-96, circuit judge, 1996-2002; pvt pract, 2002-; John Marshall Law Sch, Off Alumni Rels & Devel, bd visitors, currently. **Orgs:** Phi Alpha Delta Law; Nat Bar Asn; Ill State Bar Asn; Chicago Bar Asn; Meth Bar Asn; treas, Ill Judges Asn, 1980-81, bd dirs, 1985-91; Kappa Alpha Psi; secy, Ill Judicial Coun, 1982-84, chmn, 1985-86; pres, bd dir, John Marshall Law Sch Alumni Asn, vpres, 1988-90, pres, 1990-91; charter fel, Ill Bar Found; Am Trial Lawyers Asn; Cook Co Judicial Adv Coun. **Honors/Awds:** Golden Key Award, S Shore Valley Community Asn; We Can Inc Award; Black Gavel Award, Outstanding Judge Black Lawyers Network, 1984; Award Merit, Ill Judges Asn; Distinguished Service Award, John Marshall Law Sch Alumni Asn; Kenneth E Wilson Award, Ill Judicial Coun; Court Honor Award, Chicago Vol Legal Serv, 2000; MRT Scholar Community Service Award, 33 Degree Mason. **Military Serv:** AUS, sp-4, 1955-58. **Home Addr:** 8948 S Jeffery Blvd, Chicago, IL 60617. **Business Addr:** Board of Visitors, The John Marshall Law School, Office of Alumni Relations and Development, 315 S Plymouth Ct, Chicago, IL 60604, **Business Phone:** (312)427-2737.

BRADEN, HENRY E, IV
Lawyer. **Personal:** Born Aug 24, 1944, New Orleans, LA; married Michele Bordenave; children: Heidi E, Remi A & Henry E V. **Educ:** Le Moyne Col, BS, 1965; Loyola Univ Sch Law, JD, 1975. **Career:** LA Div Employment Security, coord Huricane Betsy Disaster Relief Proj, 1965; Neighborhood Youth Corps Out Sch Prog TCA Inc, dir, 1966; New Orleans Hometown Plan Urban League New Orleans, author & dir, 1974; Labor Educ & Advan Prog, Total Community Action Inc, dir On-the-Job Training & Prog; City New Orleans, dir, Ofc Manpower & Econ Develop, Murray, Murray, Ellis & Braden, atty pvt pract, currently; Braden, Gonzales & Assoc, atty, currently. **Orgs:** Dem Nat Committeeman St LA; exec comt, Dem Nat Com Mem Met Area Com; LA Manpower Adv Com; columnist, Op-ed; Page New Orleans States; exec vice pres, Community Orgn Urban Politics; New Orleans Indust Devel Bd, LA Dem State Cent Com; pres, St Augustines HS Alumni Asn; dir, Building Dr St Augustines HS; Asn La Lobbyists. **Home Addr:** 2453 Esplanade Ave, New Orleans, LA 70119, **Home Phone:** (504)947-1803. **Business Addr:** Attorney, Braden, Gonzales & Associates, 228 St Charles Ave Suite 1230, New Orleans, LA 70130, **Business Phone:** (504)581-2000.

BRADFORD, ANDREA
Executive. **Personal:** Born in Huntsville, AL. **Career:** Opera Co, singer; Opera Ebony, 1994; Right Mgt Consult, Client Serv, vpres, 2003-. **Special Achievements:** featured in "The Meetin", 2002. **Business Addr:** Vice President Client Services, Right Management Consultant, 1818 Market St 33rd Fl, Philadelphia, PA 19103-3614, **Business Phone:** (215)988-1588.*

BRADFORD, ARCHIE J.
Educator, army officer. **Personal:** Born Feb 6, 1931, Ripley, TN; son of Archie and Mildred; married Mariejo Harris; children: Kyle, Kevin. **Educ:** Southern Ill Univ, BA, 1960; Ball State Univ, MA, guidance & coun, 1965; Univ Notre Dame, attended 1974; St Marys Col, internship bus, 1966. **Career:** Educator (retired); Univ Notre Dame, dir Upward Bound; Hodges Pk Elem Sch, prin, 1959-60; S Bend Schs, elem sch counr, 1961-69; S Bend Community Schs, dir human resources, 1975-80, prin, 1980. **Orgs:** Am Personnel & Guidance Asn, 1962-; Am Sch Counrs Asn, 1962-61; Am Asn Non-white Concerns, 1971-; Mayors Comn Educ, 1972-74; St Joseph Co Urban Coalition Bd, 1972-; vpres, Urban Coalition, 1974-; chmn, Coalition Educ Task Force, 1972-; Eval & Allocation Div of United Way, 1974-; Rotary Club. **Honors/Awds:** Kappa Alpha Psi Fidelity Award; Outstanding Service Award, MAAEOPP; O C Carmichael Award, Boy's Club. **Military Serv:** AUS, corporal, 1950-53; USAC, A1c, 1953-57. *

BRADFORD, CHARLES EDWARD
Clergy, educator. **Personal:** Born Jul 12, 1925, Washington, DC; married Ethel Lee McKenzie; children: Sharon Louise Lewis, Charles Edward Jr & Dwight Lyman. **Educ:** Oakwood Col Huntsville AL, BA, 1946; Andrews Univ, Berrien Springs Mich, DD, 1978. **Career:** Pastor (retired), administrator (retired), preacher, teacher; Pastor, 1945-61; Lake Region Conf, Seventh-

day Adventists, pres, 1961-70; Seventh-day Adventist, North Am Div, pres, 1979-90; preacher & teacher, currently. **Orgs:** Trustee, Oakwood Col/Andrews Univ, 1961; trustee, Loma Linda Univ, 1979; bd trustees, Fla Hosp Col Health Sci. **Special Achievements:** First African-American president of the North American Division of Seventh-day Adventist; Book: Sabbath Roots: The African Connection, 1999. **Home Addr:** 10178 Sleepy Willow Ct, Spring Hill, FL 34608-4211, **Home Phone:** (352)688-5125. **Business Addr:** Preacher, 10178 Sleepy Willow Ct, Spring Hill, FL 34608-4211, **Business Phone:** (352)688-5125.*

BRADFORD, COREY LAMON
Football player. **Personal:** Born Dec 8, 1975, Baton Rouge, LA. **Educ:** Jackson State Univ. **Career:** Green Bay Packers, wide receiver, 1998-2001; Houston Texans, wide receiver, 2001-05; Detroit Lions, 2006; Redskins, 2007; free agent, currently. *

BRADFORD, EQUILLA FORREST
School administrator. **Personal:** Born Apr 11, 1931, Birmingham, AL; married William Lewis. **Educ:** Wayne State Univ, Detroit, BS, 1954, MS, 1963; Mich State Univ, E Lansing, PhD, 1972. **Career:** McNair & Daly Elem Sch, Westwood Sch Dist, teacher, 1955-66, art teacher, 1966-68; McNair Elem Sch, Westwood Sch Dist, prin, 1968-71; Mich Asn Individually Guided Educ, Consult, 1970-; Eastern Mich Univ, instr/lectr,1979-; Wayne State Univ Detroit, consult, 1979-; Westwood Community Sch Dist, asst supt personnel, 1971-74; exec asst supt, 1974-77, supt sch, 1979-. **Orgs:** Alpha Kappa Alpha Sorority Inc, 1954-; Am Asn Sch Adminr, 1968-; DetroitEcon Club; St Paul Am Church. **Honors/Awds:** Educr of Year, Delta Sigma Theta Sorority, 1979; Dist educr Nat Sor of PhiDelta Kappa Inc 1980, Woman of Year; Alpha Kappa Alpha Sor Inc Inc EtaIota Omega & Chap 1980. **Special Achievements:** First black hired to teach in Westwood in 1954 and also the first black female named to a superintendency in Michigan. **Business Addr:** 25913 Annapolis, Inkster, MI 48141.*

BRADFORD, GARY C.
Editor. **Personal:** Born May 4, 1956, Pittsburgh, PA; son of Frank M and Glenrose Beatrice Fields. **Educ:** Univ Pittsburgh, PA, BA, writing, 1979; Temple Univ, Philadelphia, PA, MA, jour, 1983. **Career:** WHCR-FM, New York, NY, vol host & producer, 1988-89; Pittsburgh Press, PA, reporter, 1979-81; Philadelphia Daily News, PA, copy editing intern, 1982; In Pittsburgh, PA, assoc ed, 1985; NY Times, copy ed, 1985-. **Orgs:** NY Asn Black Journalists, 1986-; Duke Ellington Soc, 1990-; 100 Black Men, 1991-. **Honors/Awds:** Publisher's Award Headline Writing, New York Times, 1987, 1988. **Business Addr:** Copy Editor Metropolitan News, New York Times, 229 W 43rd St 3rd Floor, New York, NY 10036.*

BRADFORD, JAMES EDWARD
Accountant, high school teacher. **Personal:** Born Jun 27, 1943, Jonesboro, LA; married Mae Lean Calahan; children: Roderick, Berkita, D'Andra. **Educ:** Grambling State Univ, BS, 1965; Wayne State Univ, attended 1966. **Career:** Sabine Parish Sch Bd, teacher, 1965-66; Bienville Parish Sch Bd, teacher, 1966-70; Continental Group, acct, 1970-76; Independent Consults Inc, pres, 1980-85; Bradco Sales, pres, 1984-85; Smurfit Stone Container Corp, super acct. **Orgs:** Bd chmn, Pine Belt CAA, 1979-85; bd chmn, Jackson Coun Aging, 1980-85; bd mem, N Delta Regional Planning Comt, 1983-85; Asn La Lobbyists. **Honors/Awds:** Outstanding Young Men of Am, 1975; Outstanding Blacks LA, 1982. **Home Addr:** 709 Leon Drive, Jonesboro, LA 71251. **Business Addr:** Superior Accountant, Smurfit Stone Container Corporation, Mill St, Hodge, LA 71247.

BRADFORD, MARTINA LEWIS
Executive, lawyer. **Personal:** Born Sep 14, 1952, Washington, DC; daughter of Martin Lewis and Alma Ashton; married William, Dec 24, 1982; children: Sydney. **Educ:** Am Univ, BA, 1973; Duke Univ, JD, 1975. **Career:** Southern Railways Inc, corporate legal intern; Interstate Com Div Finance Div, Wash, atty, 1976-78; Comn Appropriations, US House Rep, coun, 1978-81; Interstate Com Comn, Wash, DC, chief staff to vchmn, 1981-83; Am Univ Sch Law, adj prof, 1982; AT&T Corp, Legal Dept, NY, atty, 1983-85, atty, 1985-88, vpres; Akin Gump Strauss Hauer & Feld LLP, partner, currently. **Orgs:** Minority counsel, US House Representatives, 1978-79, minority counsel, US Sen, 1979-80; founding vpres, Women's Transportation Seminar, 1978; Dist Columbia Bar, 1976, Md Bar, 1983-, Women's Bar Asn, 1989; bd mem, INROADS Inc, 1989; Cadmus Communs Corp, dir, 2000-. **Honors/Awds:** Deans List, Am Univ, 1971-73; Scholastic Honary, Economics, Am Univ, 1973. **Business Phone:** (202)887-4000.

BRADFORD, PAUL
Football player. **Personal:** Born Apr 20, 1974, East Palo Alto, CA; married Margarita; children: Bella Mae & Antonio. **Educ:** Portland State, phys educ. **Career:** San Diego Chargers, corner back, 1997-00; Las Vegas Outlaws, corner back, 2000-01.

BRADFORD, RONNIE (RONNIE LEE BRADFORD)
Football player, football coach. **Personal:** Born Oct 1, 1970, Minot, ND; married Trish; children: Anthony & Kaylee. **Educ:** Univ Colo. **Career:** Football player(retired), football coach: Denver Broncos, defensive back, 1993-95; Ariz Cardinals, 1996; Atlanta Falcons, 1997-2001; Minn Vikings, safety (retired), 2002; Denver Broncos, spec teams asst coach, 2003-04, special-teams coach, 2004-07, asst defensive backs coach, 2007-08; Kansas City Cheif, 2008-. **Honors/Awds:** All-Am hon, USA Today. **Business Addr:** Special Teams Assistant Coach, Denver Broncos Football Club, 13655 Broncos Pkwy, Englewood, CO 80112, **Business Phone:** (303)649-9000.*

BRADFORD, RONNIE LEE. See BRADFORD, RONNIE.

BRADFORD, STEVEN C
Government official. **Educ:** San Diego State Univ, BA, Political sci; Calif State Univ, paralegal cert. **Career:** IBM, mkt rep, 1983-90; LA Conserv Corps, Prog dir, 1990-94; Congresswoman Juanita Millender-McDonald's Off, dist dir; Gardena City Coun, councilman, 1997, 2001, 2005, mayor pro team, currently. **Orgs:** Dr. Martin Luther King Jr. Cult Comt Gardena; chair, Black Hist Month celebration comt; PTA; past pres, Hollypark Homeowners Asn; nat dir, Phi Beta Sigma Fraternity; Boy Scouts; Hollypark Homeowners Asn. **Honors/Awds:** Gardena Black Hist Month Celebration Committee, Trailblazer Award, Southern Calif, Pub Servant of the Yr Award, 2003; named the 2003 Franklin and Eleanor Roosevelt "Democrat of the Year", Los Angeles County Democratic Party, 2003; Nat Leadership of Zeta Phi Beta Sorority Inc, Community Leadership Award, 2004; Man of the Year, Phi Beta Sigma Fraternity, 2005. **Special Achievements:** First African American Council member in Gardena, CA's history; Youngest Council member to serve in city's history. **Business Addr:** Mayor Pro Tem, Gardena City Council, 1700 W 162nd St, Gardena, CA 90247, **Business Phone:** (310)217-9500.

BRADFORD-EATON, ZEE
Advertising executive. **Personal:** Born Oct 10, 1953, Atlanta, GA; daughter of William Henry Davis and Betty Anthony Davis Harden; married Maynard, Dec 28, 1991; children: Quentin Eugene Bradford Jr & Qiana Yvonne Bradford. **Educ:** Morris Brown Col, 1975. **Career:** QZ Enterprises Inc, pub rels dir, 1979-83; First Class Inc, pub rels dir, 1983-84, exec vpres, 1984-. **Orgs:** Pres, Shaker Welcome Wagon, 1980-81; steering comt Mayor's Task Force Educ; bd mem, Am Diabetes Asn; steering comt, Black Pub Rels Soc; min affairs comt, Pub Rels Soc Am, 1985-86; pr comt, Atlanta Assoc Black Journalists, 1985-86; adv bd, Martin Luther King Jr Ctr Soc Chg, 1985-86; prog dir, Jack & Jill Am, 1985-86; activities chmn, Girl Scouts Am, 1985-87; youth activities chmn, Providence Baptist Ch; prog dir, Collier Heights Elem Sch; PTA; Grade Parent, 1985-89; publicity rel comt Am Heart Assoc, 1986-87; comn A Reginald Eaves Blue Ribbon Task Force Strenghthening Black Amer Family, 1986-87; econ develop task force, Nat Conf Black Mayors; United Negro Col Fund, Nat Forum pub Admins, 1986-87; United Way's Media Develop, 1987; chmn, SME, 1987; comn YWCA Salute Women of Achievement, 1987; Journalist, Jack & Jill Am, Atlantphoenix aza Chapter, 1990-92; vpres, Inman Middle Sch PTA, 1991-92; Fulton County Roundtable C, comnr, Nancy Boxill; Atlantic Historical Soc; Registered Lobbyist State Ga; exec bd mem, Leadership Atlanta, 1989-92; bd mem, Atlanta Chap Ronald McDonald C Charities; pub rels comt chmn, Coalition 100 Black Women Atlanta; bd mem, Charlee. **Honors/Awds:** Civic Award, United Way 1981; Cert Merit, Atlanta Asn Black Journalists, 1984; Girl Scouts of America, 1986; Leadership, Atlanta, 1986-87; NFL & AFL-CIO Community Service Award; Americans Best & Brightest Bus & Prof Men & Women, Dollars & Sense Magazine, 1991; One of Ten Outstanding Atlantans, Outstanding Atlantans Inc, 1989. **Business Phone:** (404)892-1434.*

BRADLEY, ANDREW THOMAS, SR.
Counselor. **Personal:** Born Jan 4, 1948, Johnstown, PA; married Annice Bernetta Edwards; children: Andrew T Jr, Elizabeth Lorine & James Christopher. **Educ:** Shaw Univ, Raleigh, BA, 1975; Univ DC, MA, 1982. **Career:** Seacap Inc, mainstream suprv, 1968-69; Neuse-Trent Manpower Devel Corp, instr, counr, 1970-72; Craven Comm Col, instr, counr, 1972-75; Neuse River Coun Govts, reg admin, 1975-77; Nat Ctr Black Aged Inc, dir, crises res, 1977-81; Bradley Assoc, consult, 1981-84; Family & C Serv, psychotherapist; Harrisburg Area Comm Col, counr acad found. **Orgs:** Trainer, Spec Training Abuse & Neglect C & Adults; consult, Mgt Awareness Training; presentor, Needs & Probs Minority Aged, Pract Approcahes Providing Soc & Health Serv Rural Elderly; pastoral coun, Faith Temple First Born Church; teaching suprv, Crisis Intervention Counseling; chairperson, Crime PrevTask Force; Nat Assoc Victim Witness Asst; Nat Assoc Black Soc Workers; Nat Ctr & Caucus Black Aged Inc; Nat Coun Aging; Am Mental Health Counselors Assoc; Am Assoc Counseling & Develop; Harrisburg Area Hospice; bonds comn, Harrisburg Human Rels Commn; WIZZ Calbe FM 1005 Radio. **Honors/Awds:** Outstanding Young Man, Am Nat Jaycees; Grad Scholarship Inst Geontology, Univ DC. **Military Serv:** USAR, sp4, 6 yrs. **Business Addr:** Counselor, Milton Hershey School, PO Box 830, Hershey, PA 17033-0830.

BRADLEY, DAVID HENRY, JR.
Educator, writer. **Personal:** Born Sep 7, 1950, Bedford, PA; son of Rev David (deceased) and Harriette Jackson (deceased). **Educ:** Univ Pa, BA, creative writing & eng, 1972; Univ London, King's Col, MA, US studies, 1974. **Career:** JB Lippincott Co, asst ed, 1974-76; Univ Pa, vis lectr, 1975-76; Temple Univ, vis lectr, 1976-77, asst prof, 1977-82, assoc prof, 1982-89, prof, 1989-96; Colgate Prof Humanities, 1988; Univ NC, Wilmington, Dist Found Prof Lit; Mich Inst Technol, vis prof, 1989; Guggenheim fel, 1989; Nat Endowment Arts, fel, 1991; William & Mary, vis prof, 1997; City Col NY, vis prof, 1998; Univ Tex, vis prof, 2000; Univ Ore, vis prof, 2000, 2002-03, dir creative writing prog, 2003-; Austin Peay State Univ, Roy Acuff chmn, 2001; Books: South Street, 1975; The Chaneysville Incident,1981; The Lodestar Project, 1986; From Text to Performance in the Elizabethan Theatre: Preparing the Play for the Stage, 1991; The Encyclopedia of Civil Rights in America, co-ed, 1998; Short Story: Our Roots Grow Deeper than We Know, 1985; Play: Sweet Sixteen, 1983. **Orgs:** Writers Guild Am E; Author's Guild; PEN. **Honors/Awds:** PEN/Faulkner Award, 1982; American Academic Award, Am Inst Arts & Letters, 1992. **Special Achievements:** Published articles in Esquire, New York Times, Redbook, The Southern Review, Transition, Los Angeles Times, Dissent; American Book Award nominee, 1982. **Business Addr:** Director of Creative Writing Program, University of Oregon, Eugene, OR 97403-5243, **Business Phone:** (541)346-3944.*

BRADLEY, HILBERT L.
Lawyer. **Personal:** Born Jan 18, 1920, Repton, AL. **Educ:** Valparaiso Univ Law Sch, JD, LLB, 1950. **Career:** Lake Co Prosecutor's Off, atty; Pvt Pract Atty; Div Air Pollution, dep prosecutor atty, corp coun atty; Super Ct, Lake Co, atty, currently. **Orgs:** Founder, Fair Share, 1957; founder, Ind Coalition Black Judicial Officials, 1987; Made Documentary Fed Gov Role Witness; involved, prepared, filed & litigated several landmark civil rights cases; Ind mem, Thur good Marshall Law Asn; Nat Black Bar Asn; life mem, NAACP; Ind Il Supreme Ct US Bars. **Honors/Awds:** Honorary degree, Ind Univ N w, 2006. **Special Achievements:** In 1947 he became the first African Am stud admitted to the Valparaiso Univ Sch Law; in 1950 he was the first African Am to grad. **Military Serv:** AUS, pvt, 1947. **Business Addr:** Attorney, State of Indiana, Supereme Court Lake County, 2293 N Main St, Crown Point, IN 46307, **Business Phone:** (219)398-7386.*

BRADLEY, JAMES GEORGE
Administrator. **Personal:** Born Sep 17, 1940, Cleveland, OH; married Lela; children: Wyette, James, Candace, Jason. **Educ:** Univ NMex, BEd, 1963; Univ Utah, MBA, 1973 PhD, 1977. **Career:** Human Resources, manpower dev spec, 1979; Clearfield Job Corps, dir, 1970; Detroit Manpower Center, dir, 1976-77; USDA, civil rights, 1986; Wheeling-Pittsburgh Steel Corp, pres, chmn & chief exec officer, currently. **Orgs:** Adv Bd Spec Ed, 1983; Nat Asn Adv Colored People, pres, 1985. **Honors/Awds:** Special Service Award, Ala Police Dept. **Home Addr:** 6013 Unitas Ct NW, Albuquerque, NM 87114. **Business Phone:** (304)234-2400.*

BRADLEY, JAMES MONROE, JR.
Clergy, minister (clergy). **Personal:** Born Aug 15, 1934, Mayesville, SC; married Nellie Chambers; children: James, III, Rosemary. **Educ:** Claflin Col, AB, 1956; Gammon Theol Sem, BD, 1959; Drew Theol Sem. **Career:** Aiken, minister, 1956-58; W Camden, minister, 1958-60; Cheraw, minister, 1960-61; Spartanburg, minister, 1962-63; Orangeburg Dist, dist supt, 1964-70; Emmanuel Church, Sumter, NC, 1970-74; Trinity United Methodist Church, Orangeburg, SC, minister, 1974-. **Orgs:** SC Conf, United Methodist Church On Trial, 1955; ordained, Deacon, 1957; Full Connecltion, 1958; Ordained Elder, 1959; deleg, World Methodist London, 1966; Sumter County Bd Educ, 1971-73; bd dirs, Sumter County Rehab Ctr; Nat Asn Advan Colored People; Phi Beta Sigma; vpres, Mason Past; Nat Asn Advan Colored People.

BRADLEY, JEFFREY
Educator, teacher, teacher. **Personal:** Born Jun 24, 1963, Bronx, NY; son of Harry (deceased) and Beatrice Stevens. **Educ:** Laguardia Community Col, AS, 1985; Hunter Col. **Career:** Merricats Nursery Sch, teacher, currently. **Orgs:** Asst staff mem other prog, Asn Benefit C, 1989-91; Aid, Variety House, 1990-91. **Honors/Awds:** Human Rights Award Winner, Reebok, 1990. **Business Addr:** Teacher, Merricats Nursery School, Asn Benefit C, 419 E 86 St, New York, NY 10128.*

BRADLEY, JENNETTE B.
Government official, politician. **Personal:** Born Jan 1, 1952?, columbus, OH; married Michael Taylor, 1990. **Educ:** Wittenberg Univ, BA, psycol, 1974. **Career:** Huntington Nat Bank, sr vpres, pub funds, 1989-2002; Columbus City Coun, mem, 1991-2002; State Ohio, lt gov, 2003-05, treas, 2005-07; Ohio Dept com, dir, 2003; Am politician of the Republican party. **Orgs:** Bd trustees, Wittenberg Univ. **Honors/Awds:** Columbia Public Schools Hall of Fame, 2000. **Special Achievements:** First African American woman to serve on the council; Ohio's First African-American Lieutenant Governor & First African-American woman to serve as Lt.Governor in the US. **Business Addr:** Treasurer, State Ohio, 30 E Broad St 9th Fl, Columbus, OH 43266-0421, **Business Phone:** (614)466-2160.

BRADLEY, LONDON M., JR.
Administrator. **Personal:** Born Mar 3, 1943, Chestnut, LA; son of London Bradley Sr. and Inez; married Olivia Woodfork; children:

London, Byron, Bradley. **Educ:** Southern Univ, BS, 1964. **Career:** Parks & Rcrtn Dept KC, MO, rcrtn dir, 1968-69; Bendix Corp, personnel interviewer, 1969-71. **Orgs:** Master mason MW Prince Hall Grand Lodge, 1963; NAACP, 1976; referee, Big Ten Basketball Conf, 1977; Sunday sch teacher, Second Baptist Church, 1984. **Military Serv:** USAF s & sgt, 4 yrs. **Business Addr:** Allstate Ins Co, 8501 W Higgins, Suite 120, Chicago, IL 60631.

BRADLEY, MELISSA LYNN
Association executive. **Personal:** Born Jan 14, 1968, Newark, NJ; daughter of Joan Bradley. **Educ:** Georgetown Univ, BS, 1989; Am Univ, MBA, 1993. **Career:** Sallie Mae, finance mkt specialist, 1989-91; Bradley Dev Inc, founder & pres, 1990-92; TEDI, founder & pres, 1991-; Reentry Strategies Inst, founder, 2005-; The Entrepreneurial Devlop Inst, founder, currently; New Capitalist, founder & pres, currently; US Treas, financial regulatory affairs fel. **Orgs:** Back Block Found, 1995-; bd mem, Mentors Inc, 1995-; bd mem, Who Cares, 1996-; bd dir, Tides Found. **Honors/Awds:** Do Something Brick Award Winner, 1996. **Business Phone:** (202)822-8334.*

BRADLEY, MELVIN LEROY
Consultant. **Personal:** Born Jan 6, 1938, Texarkana, TX; son of David Ella and S T; married Ruth A Terry; children: Cheryl, Eric, Jacquelyn & Tracey. **Educ:** La City Col, attended 1955; Compton Col, attended 1965; Pepperdine Univ, BS, 1973. **Career:** Real estate broker, 1960-63; La Co, dep sheriff, 1963-69; St Calif, staff asst gov's off, 1970-73; St Calif, asst to Gov Reagan mem gov'ssr staff, 1973-75; Charles R Drew Postgrad Med Sch LA, dir pub rel; United Airlines, asst to vpres, 1977-81; Pres US White House, sr policy advisor, 1981-82, spec asst to pres, 1982-89; Garth & Bradley Assocs, pres, 1989-. **Orgs:** Kiwanis Club; Toastmasters Am Inc; Nat Urban League; Nat Asn Advan Colored People. **Honors/Awds:** Award for Outstanding Contribution City Los Angeles; Awarded Mayor's Key to City, Riverside, CA; Award for Contribution in Field of Community Relations, Compton, CA; Community Service Award, Co Los Angeles; Honarary Doctor of Laws, Bishop Col, Shaw Univ; Distinguished Louisiana Award, Langston Univ.

BRADLEY, MILTON
Baseball player. **Personal:** Born Apr 15, 1978, Harbor City, CA. **Career:** Montreal Expos, 1999-2000; Cleveland Indians, 2001; Montreal Expos, 2001; Cleveland Indians, 2002-03; Los Angeles Dodgers, outfielder, 2004-05; Oakland Athletics, 2006-07; San Diego Padres, 2007; Texas Rangers, 2008; Chicago Cubs, 2009-. *

BRADLEY, PHILLIP POOLE
Baseball player, manager. **Personal:** Born Mar 11, 1959, Bloomington, IN; married Ramona; children: Megan & Curt. **Educ:** Univ Mo, BS, 1982. **Career:** Baseball player (retired), Manager; Seattle Mariners, outfielder, 1983-87; Philadelphia Phillies, outfielder, 1988; Baltimore Orioles, outfielder, 1989-90; Chicago White Sox, outfielder, 1990; Yomiuri Giants, 1991; Montreal Expos, outfielder, 1992; Major League Baseball Players Asn, special asst to gen mgr, curently. **Honors/Awds:** Mid-Season All-Star Team, 1985; Post-Season Sporting News All-Star Team, 1985; Am League All-Star Team, 1985. **Special Achievements:** Films: Senorita from the West, 1945; Operation Crossbow, 1965. Album: Rather Be Rockin, 1979; He was Selected by CA League managers as Best Defensive Outfielder. **Business Addr:** Special Assistant to the General Manager, Major League Baseball Players Asn, 24th Fl 12 E 49th St, New York, NY 10017, **Business Phone:** (212)826-0808.

BRADLEY, VANESA JONES
Judge. **Career:** State Mich, 36 Dist Ct, judge, currently. **Business Addr:** Judge, State Of Michigan, 36 District Court, 421 Madison Ave, Detroit, MI 48226, **Business Phone:** (313)965-8708.

BRADLEY, WAYNE W
Police officer, executive. **Personal:** Born Aug 20, 1948; married. **Educ:** Wayne State Univ, BA, 1972. **Career:** Detroit Police Dept, police officer; Cass Corridor Safety, Sr Proj, proj dir, 1974-75; Wayne County Community Col, instr, 1972-; Western Res Fin Serv Corp, sales rep, 1973-; Sears Roebuck & Co, security, 1973-74; Philco Ford Corp, acct receivable & payable, 1968-69; Mich Consol Gas Co, collection rep, 1969-70; Wellness Plan, dir govt & community affairs, 1980-2007; Detroit Community Health Connection Inc, bd mem, 1994-2006, pres & chief exec officer, 2007-. **Orgs:** Kappa Alpha Phi Frat; Trade Union Leadership Coun; vpres, Nat Pan Helenic Coun; Nat Asn Advan Colored People; 1st Precinct Comt Rel Asn; bd mem, ed bd, Community Reporter Newspaper; Detroit Police Officers Asn; Police Officers Asn Mich; Guardians Mich; Concerned Police Officers Equal Justice; chmn, Detroit Area Agency on Aging; bd mem, Greater Detroit Area Health Coun; Northeast Guidance Ctr, chmn bd; bd governer, Detroit Renaissance Club. **Honors/Awds:** Purple Heart Civilian Award, 1971; Detroit Police Dept Highest Award; Medal Valor, 1971; 12th Precinct Outstanding Service Award, 1972. **Special Achievements:** Listed in Leaders in Black Am; Detroit Police Dept Citation, 1972. **Business Addr:** President & Chief Executive Officer, Govt Community Affairs, Detorit Community Health Connection Inc, 13901 E Jefferson Ave, Detroit, MI 48201, **Business Phone:** (313)822-4188.

BRADLEY, WILLIAM B.
Educator, chairperson. **Personal:** Born Nov 28, 1926, Rushville, IN; married Pearle E Poole; children: William, Philip, Annette, Catherine. **Educ:** Ind Univ, BPE, 1949, MPE, 1955, PED, 1959. **Career:** Sumner High Sch, coach phys educ, 1955-58; Ind Univ, phys educ dir, 1957, Sch HPER, grad asst, 1958-59; Fayetteville State Univ, Dept Phys Educ, prof & chmn, 1959-60; Southern Univ, Dept Phys Educ, prof & chmn, 1960-64; Va State Univ, Dept Athletics & Phys Educ, dir, 1964-70; Western Ill Univ, Dept Phys educ, prof, coordr, sport mgt internship prog, 1970-. **Orgs:** Am Alliance Health, Phys Educ & Recreation; Ill Asn Health PE & Recreation; Va Asn Health, PE & Recreation; Am Asn Univ Profs; Phi Epsilon Kappa; Phi Delta Kappa; Ind Alumni Asn; "I" Mens Asn Indiana Univ; consult, Nat Youth Sports Prog Pres Coun Phys Fitness & Sports, 1970-79; bd mem, McDonough Co, YMCA, 1970-73; US Olympic Baseball Comn, 1972; US Olympic Weightlifting Comt, 1968. **Honors/Awds:** Cert of achievement, CIAA Baseball Coach of Yr, 1968; Va State Col, 1970; cert of appreciation, McDonough Co Am Legion, 1972; Quarter Century Club Award, Alpha Phi Alpha, Ill Asn Health, PE & Recreation, 1975. **Special Achievements:** Auth of article, "The Effects of Velocity & Repetition of Motion on the Develop of Isokinetic Strength of the Quadriceps Muscle Group". **Military Serv:** AUS, 1st lt, 1950-53. **Home Phone:** (309)837-9395. *

BRADSHAW, DORIS MARION
School administrator, educator. **Personal:** Born Sep 23, 1928, Freeman, WV; daughter of Fred and Roberta; married Virgil Alanda; children: Victoria Lee, Gary Dwayne, Eric Alanda & Barry Douglas. **Educ:** Concord Col, BS, 1976; WVa Col Grad Studies, MA, 1985. **Career:** Educator (retired); Raleigh County, vol head start, 1966; RCCAA Head Start Prog, head start teacher, 1967-69, head start teacher asst dir, 1969-70, head start dir. **Orgs:** Vpres, WVa Head Start Dirs Asn, 1970-; WVa Comn C & Youth, 1981-; consult, Head Start Rev Team Educ & Admin, Head Start Prog, 1983-; bd dirs, Region III Head Start Asn, 1984-. **Home Addr:** 121 Sour St, Beckley, WV 25801.

BRADSHAW, GERALD HAYWOOD
Executive. **Personal:** Born Dec 13, 1934, Larned, KS; married Wylma Louise Thompson; children: Kim Elaine, Gerri Lynn, Douglas Haywood. **Educ:** Kans State Teachers Col, attended 1956; Univ Colo, BS; Am Savings & Loan Inst, Denver. **Career:** Equity Savings & Loan Assoc, Denver, auditor, appraiser, 1958-67; Denver Urban Renew Authority, real estate dir, 1960-71; Colo Springs Urban Renew Effort, exec dir, 1971-76; GH Bradshaw & Assoc, pres, 1976-; BH Property Mgt Inc, owner, currently. **Orgs:** Past pres, Colo Chap Nat Asn Housing & Redevelop Officials; sr mem, Nat Asn Rev Appraisors; bd dir, Urban League Pikes Peak Region; Downtown Rotary Club Colo Springs; former mem, Site Selection Comt, El Paso Community Col; former sec Denver Oppurtunity; former chmn bd adv comt, Columbine Elem SchUS. **Honors/Awds:** Pres Cert of Awd Serving on Sel Serv Bd. **Business Addr:** President, B-H Property Mgt Inc, 315 N Weber St Fl 2, PO Box 9744, Colorado Springs, CO 80932.*

BRADSHAW, LAWRENCE A.
Educator. **Personal:** Born Sep 23, 1932, Philadelphia, PA; married Mary Ellen Osgood. **Educ:** Shippensburg St Col, BS, MEd; Bucknell Univ, grad studies; Univ Vt; Ball State Univ; The Am Univ, doctoral studies. **Career:** Educator (retired); Shippensburg Area Junior High Sch, teacher, 1961-62; Shippensburg Area Sr High Sch, teacher Eng & humanities, 1962-69; Shippensburg State Col, asst dean admis, 1970-72, Acad Affairs Off, asstvpres, 1972-73, asst pres, 1974-75, Dept English, assoc prof, 1999. **Orgs:** Phi Delta Kappa; Am Guild Organists; Nat Coun Teacher Eng; Col Eng Asn; Pennsylvania Coun English Teachers; Am Asn Univ Admin; Pennsylvania St Educ Asn; Nat Educ Asn; Kiwanis Club Chambersburg PA; bd dir, United Fund Chambersburg PA; bd dir, Franklin County Sunday Sch Asn; trustee, Chambersburg Hosp; 1st pres, Canterbury Club, Shippensburg State Col; 1stpres, Am Field Serv; Comn Concerts Asn, vestryman & organist, St Andrews Episcopal Church. **Honors/Awds:** Rockefeller Fellowship, Univ Admin, 1973-74; Outstanding Educator of America, 1974-75. **Military Serv:** AUS, sgt major, 1953-55. *

BRADSHAW, WAYNE-KENT
Executive, president (organization), president (organization). **Career:** Founders Savings & Loan Assocs, chief exec; Family Savings Bank, pres & chief exec officer; Wash Mutual Bank, regional pres community & external affairs, 2003-. **Orgs:** Bd dir, Calif Econ Develop Lending Initiative; Calif State Univ Northridge Community. **Honors/Awds:** Outstanding Performance Award, Community Econ Develop. *

BRADY, CHARLES A
Lawyer. **Personal:** Born May 1, 1945, Palestine, TX; son of Thomas F Sr and Leona V; married Ida A Powell; children: Kimberly & Charles A Jr. **Educ:** Coe Col, BA, 1967; Howard Univ, Sch Law, JD, 1970. **Career:** McDaniel Burton & Brady, atty, 1971-82; Charles A Brady & Assoc, atty, 1982-; Bus Law Fed City Col, sub instr; Fed Commun Comn, vpres opers, 2004-. **Orgs:** Treas, Inner-City & Investment Asn Inc; Forensic & Legal Fraternities & Asn. **Business Addr:** Vice President of Operations, Federal Communications Commission, 445 12th St SW, Washington, DC 20554, **Business Phone:** 888-225-5322.

BRADY, JULIO A.
Government official, judge. **Personal:** Born Aug 23, 1942, St Thomas, VI; married Maria de Freitas; children: Julie, Andrew. **Educ:** Cath Univ PR, BA, eng philos, 1964; NY Law Sch, JD, 1969. **Career:** NY Legal Aid Soc, pub defender, 1969-71; Dist VI, asst US atty, 1971-73, US atty, 1974-78; Fed Progs Off, coordr, 1979-82; Govt VI, lt gov, 1983; Dist VI, US atty, currently; Dist Ct VI, judge; Super Ct VI, judge, 2006-. **Orgs:** Pres, VI Bar Asn; co-chmn, United Way Campaign; state chmn, Dem Party VI. **Honors/Awds:** Am Juris Prudence Award, NY Law Sch, 1969; Ex Alumno Distinguido, Cath Univ PR, 1983; Certificates of Appreciation, Atlanta Univ, 1984, 1985. **Business Addr:** Judge, Superior Court of the Virgin Islands, Alexander A Farrelly Justice Ctr, 5400 Veterans Dr, St. Thomas, VI 00820.*

BRADY, WAYNE ALFONZO
Comedian, entertainer, actor. **Personal:** Born Jun 2, 1972, Orlando, FL; married Diana Lasso, Dec 31, 1993 (divorced 1995); married Mandie Taketa, Apr 3, 1999 (divorced 2008); children: Maile Masako. **Career:** Actor: Roll Bounce, 2005; Crossover, 2006; The List, 2007; Stage shows: A Chorus Line; Fences; A Raisin in the Sun; Jesus Christ Superstar; I'm Not Rappaport; The Only Game in Town; Wayne Brady & Friends; Brady Out-Crystaled Billy Crystal; TV series: "On Promised Land",1994; "Kwik Witz", 1996; "Vinyl Justice", 1998; "Hollywood Squares", 1998; "Whose Line Is It Anyway", 1998; "Survivor"; "The Sopranos"; "American Dreams", 2003; "Kevin Hill", 2005; "Girlfriends", 2006; "30 Rock", 2007; "How I Met Your Mother", 2006-07; "Everybody Hates Chris", 2006-08; VH-1 comedy series, host; Countdown to the American Music Awards, host; TV movie: Geppetto, 2000; The Electric Piper, 2003; writer & producer: "The Wayne Brady Show", 2001-02; host, "Don't forget the lyrics", 2008. **Honors/Awds:** Rookie of the Yr, Sak Theatre, 1992; Emmy Award, Outstanding Talk Show Host for The Wayne Brady Show, 2003; Daytime Emmy, 2003, 2004; Best Actor in a Musical for Cotton Patch Gospel. **Special Achievements:** Performed solo at the 52nd Annual Emmy Award, 2000; scored a 2nd Emmy Awd nomination, 2002; first African American to ever host the Miss America Competition; performed at the prestigious Mark Taper Forum in its production of Blade to the Heat. **Business Addr:** Actor, ABC Inc, C/o Riverside Production, 3727 W Magnolia Blvd, PO Box 525, Burbank, CA 91510-7711.*

BRAGG, JOSEPH L.
Journalist, baptist clergy. **Personal:** Born Jul 6, 1937, Jackson, NC; married Barbara Brandom. **Educ:** Georgetown Univ Sch Foreign Serv, Diplo & Consular Affairs; Career Acad Sch Famous Broadcasters, 1967; City Univ NY, BA, 1976. **Career:** WHN News City Hall Bureau Chief WHN Radio Storer Radio Inc, news reporter; McGovern & Nixon Pres Campaign, covered & pictures, 1972; Carter & Ford Pres Campaign, covered, 1976; Mutual Black Network, newsman; Mutual Broadcasting Sys, newscaster, 1971; Nat Acad TV Arts & Sci, journalist & mem, 1974; New York Press, former pres; Mt. Calvary Church, New York ,Assoc Pastor. **Orgs:** NY Chap Jonathan Davis Consistory 1 32 Deg AASR Free Masonry So Juris Wash, DC; Black Cits Fair Media, 1971; pres, Inner Circle; pres, NY Press Club. **Honors/Awds:** Top 100 Politics Writers, NY State. **Military Serv:** AUS, pvt, 1957. **Business Addr:** Pastor, Mount Calvary Baptist Church, 102 W 144th St, New York, NY 10017, **Business Phone:** (212)926-2848.*

BRAGG, ROBERT HENRY, II
Educator. **Personal:** Born Aug 11, 1919, Jacksonville, FL; son of Robert Henry and Lilly Camille McFarland; married Violette Mattie McDonald, 1947 (divorced 1990); children: Robert III & Pamela. **Educ:** Ill Inst Tech, Chicago, IL, BS, 1949, MS, 1951, PhD, physics, 1960. **Career:** Portland Cement Assn, Res Lab, asst physicist, 1951-54, assoc physicist, 1954-56; Ill Inst Tech, Res Inst, sr physicist, 1959-61; Lockheed Res Lab, mgr phys metallurgy, 1961-69; consult; Lockheed Missiles & Space Co; Palo Alto Res Lab, res scientist, 1961-63, sr staff scientist, 1963-69; Univ Calif, Lawrence Berkeley Lab, prin investr, Dept Material Sci, prof, 1969-87, dept chair, 1978-81, prof emer, 1987-; Fulbright Scholar, Nigeria, 1992-93; Robert H Bragg & Assocs, owner. **Orgs:** Fac sponsor, Black Engineering & Sci Studs Asn, 1969-87; NASA, Northern Calif Coun Black Prof Engrs, 1969-; Nat Tech Asn, 1978-2000; prog dir, Div Materials Scis, Office Energy Res, Dept Energy, 1981-82; adv comt, Div Materials Res, Nat Sci Found, 1982-88; evaluation panel, Res Assocs Prog, Nat Res Coun,1984-; evaluation panel, Fulbright CIES, Africa Prog, 1994-; NAACP; Am Phys Soc; Am Carbon Soc; Am Cryst Asn; AAUP; AAAS; Sigma Xi; Sigma Pi Sigma; Tau Beta Pi; Siemens-Allis, consult; Nat Sci Found, consult; Nat Res Coun, consult; mem, California Mus Of Afr Am Technology, 2006. **Honors/Awds:** Distinguished Service Award, AIME, 1972; Distinguished Service Award, ACS, 1982; Distinguished Service Award, NCCBPE; fel, Nat Soc Black Physicists, 1996; Am Man Sci, 1969; Berkeley Citation, Univ Calif, 1996. **Special Achievements:** Publ articles

in tech journs & books; developed an exhibit at the California's museum of African American technology titled "The Black Revolution in Science and Technology". **Military Serv:** AUS, second lt, 1942-46. **Business Addr:** Owner, Robert H Bragg & Associates, 2 Admiral Dr Suite 373, Emeryville, CA 94608-1502, **Business Phone:** (510)655-6283.

BRAILSFORD, MARVIN D.
Executive. **Personal:** Born Jan 31, 1939, Burkeville, TX; son of Geneva Vivian and Artie; married June Evelyn Samuel, Dec 23, 1960; children: Marvin D Jr, Keith A, Cynthia R. **Educ:** Prairie View A & M UNIV, BS, 1959; IOWA State UNIV, MS, 1966. **Career:** Retired: USY, 60th ordnance group, commanding officer, 1982-84, 59th ordnance brigade, commanding general, 1984-87, armament munitions & chem command, commanding general, 1987-90, materiel command, deputy commanding general, 1990-92; Metters Industries Inc, pres, 1992-95; Brailsford GRP, Chief Exec Officer & pres, 1995-96; Kaiser-Hill, sr vpres, 1996-02; Brailsford Group, chief exec officer, 2002. **Orgs:** chapter pres, ASN USY, 1984-87; exe comt, AMR Defense Preparedness ASN, 1978-; exec bd, United Way, 1989; bd adv, Geo Mason Univ, Bus Sch, 1993-96; bd dir, ILL Tool Works Inc, 1996-; bd dir, AGES Group Inc, 1997-; bd dir, Conn's Inc, 2003-; Southeast TX COT Develop, Corp, 2002. **Honors/Awds:** Boss of the Year, Chamber Com, 1969. **Military Serv:** USY, 1959-92; Defense Superior Service Award, Distinguished Service Medal; Legion Merit, Bronze Star, Army Commendation Medal, Parachute Badge, Army Staff ID Badge. *

BRAITHWAITE, GORDON L.
Executive. **Personal:** Born in Atlantic City, NJ. **Educ:** Hunter Col; UCLA; Herbert Berghof Acting Studios. **Career:** City NY Dept Cult Affairs, prog specialist; Nat Endowment arts, dir special proj. **Orgs:** adv com, comm Gallery Brooklyn Mus,1970-72; 100 Black Men Inc; nat assn advan colored poeple. *

BRAITHWAITE, MARK WINSTON
Dentist. **Personal:** Born Jul 15, 1954, New York, NY; son of David N and Grace C; married Carlene V; children: Mark II. **Educ:** Bowdoin Col, BA, biol, 1976; Columbia Univ, attended 1977; State Univ NY, Buffalo, Sch Dent Med, DDS, 1982; Columbia Univ, Sch Dent & Oral Surg, postgrad periodontics, 1993; Columbia Univ, Grad Sch Arts & Scis, MA, oral biol, 1995. **Career:** Pvt Pract, dent & gen pract, 1983-85; NY City Dept Health Bureau Dent, gen pract dent, 1984-87; Joint Dis N Gen Hosp, gen prac dent, 1985-90; Sydenham Hosp Neighborhood Family Care Ctr, attend dentist, 1987-90; Harlem Hosp Ctr, attend dent, 1987; Va Hosp, staff dent & periodontist, 1999; Loyola Univ Med Ctr, Dept Path, asst prof, 1999; clin coordr, currently. **Orgs:** License/certfication Northeast Regional Dental Boards, 1982; Nat Dent Bd, 1982; Nat Dent Asn; Nat Soc Dent Practitioners; Dent Health Serv Corp; Harlem Dent Soc; State Univ NY Buffalo Sch Dent Med Alumni Asn; Am Dent Asn. **Honors/Awds:** Spec Acad Achievement Periodontology, 1981-82; Attending of the Year, Harlem Hosp, 1988-89; Fellowship in Cell & Molecular Biology, Lab Tumor Biol & Connective Tissue Res, 1993; Melvin L Morris Research Fellowship. **Home Addr:** 159 Midwood St, Brooklyn, NY 11225. **Business Addr:** Clinical Coordinator, 159 Midwood St, Brooklyn, NY 11225, **Business Phone:** (718)287-6756.*

BRAMBLE, PETER W. D.
Clergy. **Personal:** Born Jul 24, 1945, Harris, Montserrat, West Indies; son of Charles William Bramble and Margaret B Bramble; married Jocelyn Cheryl Nanton, Dec 28, 1972; children: Jocelyn Cara, Peter David. **Educ:** Codrington College, Barbados, LTh, 1970; Yale Divinity School, MA, religion, 1972, STM, 1974; University Connecticut, Storrs, PhD, 1976. **Career:** School teacher, 1962-66; parish priest, 1972-73; University of Connecticut, teaching assistant and lecturer, 1974-76; St Katherine's Episcopal, rector, 1976-97; Morgan, St Mary's & Western Maryland univ, lecturer, 1978-. **Orgs:** Caribbean/African-American Dialogue, executive committee, 1992-; Governor's Commission on Homelessness, 1982-86; National Institute of Health, animal care committee, 1980-; Baltimore Public Schools, community outreach committee, 1988-, committee on Afro-Centric curriculum; Overcome Institute for Black Institution Development, founder. **Honors/Awds:** Junior Academy of Letters, Living Legend in Religion, 1990; Iota Phi Lambda Sorority, Living Maker of History Award, 1992; Congressional Service Award, 1986; Caribbean American InterCultural Organization, Values Award, 1991; Eco-Fun Project, Leadership and Commitment to Children, 1992. **Special Achievements:** The Overcome: A Black Passover, Fairfax, Baltimore, 1989; Baltimore Times, "Rites for Overcome," Baltimore, 1990. **Home Phone:** (410)728-4817. *

BRAMWELL, DR. FITZGERALD BURTON
Chemist. **Personal:** Born May 16, 1945, Brooklyn, NY; son of Fitzgerald and Lula Burton; married Charlott; children: Fitzgerald, Elizabeth, Jill & Christopher. **Educ:** Columbia Col, BA, 1966; Univ Mich, attended 1967, PhD, 1970. **Career:** Esso Res & Engineering, res chemist, 1970-71; Brooklyn Col, asst prof chem, 1971-72, dep chmn grad studies, 1981-84, actg dean grad studies & res, 1989-90, dean grad studies & res, 1990-95, prof emer, 1995-; CUNY Doctoral Fac, asst prof chem, 1972-74, assoc prof chem, 1975-79, prof chem, 1980-95; Univ Ky, prof biochem, 1995-, prof chem, 1995-, vpres res & grad studies, 1995-2001. **Orgs:** Col Bd Progs, Educ Testing Serv, Princeton, NJ; Bd Advisors Chem Innovation, 1985-2001; Col Chem Consults Serv, 1988-; Col Chem Consults Serv Advisory Bd, 1991-98, 2001-04; Test Develop Comt, 1994-98; chair, Consult LS-AMP Rev Comt La Bd Regents, 1995-; bd dirs, Ky Technol Serv, 1995-2001; bd dirs, Ky Sci & Technol Corp, 1995-2001; bd dirs, Oak Ridge Assoc Univs, 1995-2001; bd trustees, Southeastern Univs Res Asn, 1995-2001; chair, Alliances Minority Participation, 1998; Nat Sci Found Comt Visitors, 1998-2001; Adv Comt, NSF Dirate Edu & Human Resources, 1998-2000; Coun Res Policy & Grad Edu Exec Comt, 1999-2001; Nat Asn State Univs & Land Grant Cols; Am Chem Soc, Wash, DC; adv bd, Southern Univ HBCU-UP TEAMS, 1999-2008; sr consult, Qual Edu Minorities Network, 2000-; chair, Systemic Rural Initiatives, 2001; adv bd, Ky State Univ HBCU-UP TEAMS, 2001-06; Adv Bd CCNY Ctr Res Excellence Sci & Technol, 2002-; Panel, Site Visit, & Reverse Site Visit Rev Comts, Nat Sci Found, 2002-; AAAS Consult EPSCoR Infrastructure Grants, New Mexico, Idaho, 2003-05; Adv Bd San Francisco State Univ Res Minority Insts, 2003-; AAAS Consult INBRE Infrastructure Grants Delaware, 2004-05; chair, Am Inst Chemists, Inorganic Chem Ed Rev Bd, 2004-; Empire Sci Resources LLC Mgr Mem, 2005-. **Honors/Awds:** Prof of the Year Award, Nat Black Sci Studs Orgn, 1985; Professor of the Year Award, Nat Black Sci Studs Orgn, 1989; Distinguished Service Award, Nat Black Sci Studs Orgn, 1993, 1995; Distinguished Service Award, Brooklyn Col Grad Studs Orgn, 1994, 1995; Distinguished Service Award, Brooklyn Subsection Am Chem Soc, 1995; Distinguished Service Award, TRACC City Col New York, 1995; Citation in Distinguished African American Scientists of the 20th Century, Oryx Press, 1996; Dept of Chemistry Alumni Excellence Award, Univ Mich, 1996; Lyman T. Johnson Alumni Asn Award, Univ Ky, 1996; Claude Feuss Medal, Distinguished Public Service, Phillips Academy, Andover, MA, 2000; Outstanding Leadership Award, Ky Geol Surv, 2000; Founders Award, NYC LSAMP'CUNY, 2000; Citation in African Americans in Science, Mathematics, & Invention, Facts on File, 2003. **Special Achievements:** Co-author: Investigations in General Chemistry Quantitative Techniques and Basic Principles, 1977; Instructor's Guide for Basic Laboratory Principles in General Chemistry with Quantitative Techniques, 1990; Basic Laboratory Principles in General Chemistry with Quantitative Techniques, 1990; 6 books, 35 articles, 300 abstracts and presentations in the areas of physical chemistry and chemical education. **Business Addr:** Professor of Chemistry, University of Kentucky, Department of Chemistry, 313 Chem-Physics Bldg, Lexington, KY 40506-0055, **Business Phone:** (859)257-7058.

BRAMWELL, HENRY
Judge. **Personal:** Born Sep 3, 1919, Brooklyn, NY; son of Florence and Henry; married Ishbel W. **Educ:** Brooklyn Law Sch, LLB, 1948; Brooklyn Col, LLD, 1979. **Career:** Judge (retired); Borough Hall, Brooklyn, gen practr; Nat Alliance Postal Employees, legal coun; US Atty Office, asst atty, 1953-61, Criminal Div, prosecutor; NY State Rent Comm, assoc coun, 1961-63; spec hearing officer, 1965-66; Civil Ct City NY, judge, 1969-75; US Dist Ct, judge, 1974-87, sr judge. **Orgs:** Surface Line Operators Frat Orgn Inc; Higher Horizons Prog, Bd Educ City New York; Nat Fed NY, Am & Brooklyn Bar Asn; bd trustees, Brooklyn Law Sch, 1979; founding mem, Fed Judges Asn. **Special Achievements:** First African-American to be a prosecutor in the criminal division; first African-American appointed to the United States District Court for the Eastern District of New York. **Military Serv:** Sgt, 1941-45. **Home Addr:** 101B Clark St, Brooklyn, NY 11201.

BRAMWELL, PATRICIA ANN
Social worker. **Personal:** Born May 17, 1941, Brooklyn, NY; daughter of Arthur L and Miriam June Campbell. **Educ:** Cent State Univ, BA, 1965; Fordham Univ Sch Social Serv, MSW, 1969; Hofstra Univ, cert managerial studies & labor rels; Para Legal Cert; cert mediation arbitration. **Career:** Social worker (retired); Soc Seamen's C, Foster Home Care, 1966-70; City Col SEEK Prog, psychol couns, 1970-00, asst prof; E NY Ment Health Clin, grp therapy, 1977. **Orgs:** Cert State Soc Worker; vice chairperson, Comn Sch Bd Dist 16 1975-77; asst secy, Chama Day Care Ctr, 1974-76; life mem, Nat Coun Negro Women; bd dir, first vpres, Fordham Univ Sch Social Serv Alumni Asn; Brooklyn Community Planning Bd 3; Community Bd Kings County Hosp; vpres, bd dirs, New Horizons Adult Educ Prog, 1989; City Col Sexual Harassment Panel; vpres, City Col Chap Prof Staff Cong Union, Comnr; NY City Human Rights Comn. **Honors/Awds:** Numerous educ & community service awards. **Home Addr:** 458 MacDonough St, Brooklyn, NY 11233. *

BRANCH, ANDRE JOSE
Educator. **Personal:** Born May 12, 1959, Valhalla, NY; son of Virginia Ment Smith and Millard. **Educ:** Warnborough Col, Oxford, England, 1978; Inst Holy Land Studies, Jerusalem, Israel, 1979; The King's Col, Briarcliff, NY, BA, 1981; Fayetteville State Univ, Fayetteville, NC, teacher's cert, 1985; NC State Univ, Raleigh, NC, MEd, 1989. **Career:** CMML Sec Sch, Nigeria, W Africa, teacher, 1981-82; New Hanover County Sch, Wilmington, NC, teacher, 1983-84; City of Wilmington, Wilmington, NC, counr, 1986; Wake County Pub Schs, Raleigh, NC, teacher, 1987-89; NC State Univ, Raleigh, NC, counr intern, 1988-89; Northwest Asn AHANA Profs, founder, 1989; Whitworth Col, Spokane, WA, dir, multiethnic stud affairs, 1990-. **Orgs:** Am Asn Coun & Dev, 1989-; Am Col Personnel Asn, 1989-; Nat Asn Advan Colored People, 1989-; Black Educ Asn Spokane, 1989-; Wash Comt Minority Affairs, 1989-. **Special Achievements:** Designed & instituted the Nat Studs Color Symposium & Orientation, 1990; designed & provided Cross-Cultural Awareness for Action Seminar, 1990. **Business Addr:** Director, Whitworth College, 300 Hawthorne Rd, Spokane, WA 99251, **Business Phone:** (509)777-1000.

BRANCH, B. LAWRENCE
Labor relations manager. **Personal:** Born Sep 13, 1937, New York, NY; married Elva C; children: Erica Danielle, Gabrielle Angelique. **Educ:** Univ IL, 1959; Southern Ill Univ, BS 1961. **Career:** Traveler's Ins Co, underwriter, 1963-64; Chesebrough-Ponds Inc, wage & salary analyst, 1964-66; Merck & Co Inc, employment supvr, 1966-68, asst to vice pres personnel, 1968-72, dir equal employ affairs; EEO Cornell Univ Sch Ind & Labor Rel, prof; Nat Urban League BEEP Prog, vis prof, 1972; Ramapo Col, NJ, bd trustees, secy; Merck & Co Inc, dir, diversity/EEA, currently. **Orgs:** Bd mem Coun Concerned Black Exec, 1968-70; bd mem, Asn Integration Mgt 1970-74; bd & co-chmn Interracial Coun Bus Opportunity, NY 1973-78. *

BRANCH, CALVIN
Football player. **Personal:** Born May 8, 1974, Versailles, KY. **Educ:** Colo State; Iowa State. **Career:** Football player (retired), Oakland Raiders, defensive back, 1997-05. Oakland Raiders, currently. *

BRANCH, DR. GERALDINE BURTON
Physician. **Personal:** Born Oct 20, 1908, Savannah, GA; daughter of Joseph Burton and Agusta Freeman; married Robert Henry; children: Elizabeth Doggette & Robert Henry III. **Educ:** Hunter Col, BA, 1931; NY Med Col, MD, 1936; Univ Calif Los Angeles, MPH, 1961. **Career:** Pvt pract, physician, 1938-53; La Dept Health Serv, dist health officer,1964-71, reg dir health serv, 1971-74; Univ SC, assoc clinical prof commmed, 1966; Watts Health Found Inc, dir preventive health serv, 1976-78, med dir, med consult, 2001. **Orgs:** Walter Gray Crump Fel NY Med Col, 1932-36; Bd gov, La Co Med Asn, 1966-70; pres, Federated Kings Daughters Clubs, 1966-70; Nat Med Assn, 1968; bd dir, Am Lung Asn, 1970-76. **Honors/Awds:** Healing Hands Award, Univ Calif, Santa Barbara, 1992; Acad Boosters Award,King-Drew Med, 1992; Lifetime Achievement Award, Japanese Chamber Com, 2003; Lifetime Achievement Award, Drew Univ Med & Sci, 2003. **Special Achievements:** Author, "Study of Gonorrhea in Infants & Children," Pub Health Reports, 1964; "Study of Use of Neighborhood Aides in Control of a Diphtheria Outbreak," 1966; "Study of Use of Non-Physicians in HB Control, "Preventive Med, 1977; "Study of the Adult-Day-Health-Care Center of the Watts Health Foundation," paper presented to the ASA, 1990; "Study of the Problems Concerning the Care of the Alzheimer's patient," paper presentedto the Alzheimer's Society, 1992; Study of Generational gap-presented at Stanford Univ, 1996. *

BRANCH, PROF. HARRISON
Educator, artist. **Personal:** Born Jun 6, 1947, New York, NY; son of Harrison Branch Sr and Marguerite Williams; married Jacqueline Susan Hyde; children: Harrison III, Alexander Hyde & Olivia Marguerite Elizabeth. **Educ:** SF Art Inst, BFA, 1970; Yale Univ, Sch Art, MFA, 1972. **Career:** Univ Bridgeport, guest lectr & photogr, 1970-71; Yale Univ Sch Art, Alice Kimball Travelling fel, 1972; Ore State Univ, Dept Art, from asst prof to assoc prof art, 1972-84, prof art, currently, prof photog, currently, dir, External Rels Art Dept, currently; Owens Valley Photograph Workshop, 1978-86. **Honors/Awds:** Research Grant, Ore State Found, 1974; Research Grant, Ore State Univ Grad Sch, 1976-77. **Special Achievements:** Published photographs in Think Black, Bruce Publishing Co, NY, 1969, and An Illustrated Bio-Bibliography of Black Photographers, 1980-88, Garland Publishing Co, NY, photographs in collections of International Museum of Photography at George Eastman House, Rochester, NY, and Bibliotheque Nationale, Paris, France. **Home Addr:** 1104 NW 29th St, Corvallis, OR 97330. **Business Addr:** Professor of Art, Professor of Photography, Oregon State University, Department of Photography, 106 Fairbanks Hall, Corvallis, OR 97331, **Business Phone:** (541)737-5021.

BRANCH, JE
Accountant. **Educ:** Va State Univ. **Career:** LandAmerica Financial Group Inc, tax acct, currently. **Business Addr:** Tax Accountant, LandAmerica Financial Group Inc, 101 Gateway Centre Pkwy, Richmond, VA 23235-5136, **Business Phone:** (804)267-8000.

BRANCH, OTIS LINWOOD
School administrator. **Personal:** Born Sep 7, 1943, Norfolk, VA. **Educ:** Chicago Conserv Col, BMusEd, 1966; Roosevelt Univ, Chicago Mus Col, MMusEd, 1974. **Career:** School administrator

(retired); LaGrange Park Pub Sch, music dept, chmn, 1970; Bremen High Sch, Midlothian IL, choral music & humanities, dir, 1970; Chicago Conserv Col, admis & rec, dean 1979-82. **Orgs:** Curriculum writer, State Bd Educ Allied Arts Ill; evaluator, N Cent Asn & State Bd Educ Ill; Music Educr Nat Conf; Nat Educ Asn; Humanities Educrs Asn.

BRANCH, ROCHELLE
Manager. **Career:** Bowers Museum Cultural Art; Bronx Museum Arts; Museum Modern Art NY City; Craft & Folk Art Museum, dir public prog; City Pasadena, prog mgr cult affairs, currently. **Orgs:** LA Public Art Comm. **Business Addr:** Program Manager Cultural Affairs, City Pasadena, 175 N Garfield Ave, Pasadena, CA 91109-7215, **Business Phone:** (626)744-7062.

BRANCH, WILLIAM BLACKWELL
Playwright, television producer, college teacher. **Personal:** Born Sep 11, 1927, New Haven, CT; son of James Matthew and Iola Douglas; divorced; children: Rochelle Ellen. **Educ:** Northwestern Univ, BS, 1949; Columbia Univ, MFA, 1958; Columbia Univ,attended 1959; Yale Univ, res fel, 1966. **Career:** Actor, 1945-60; Ebony Mag, field rep, 1949-60; Theatre TV & MotionPictures, playwright, 1951-; The Jackie Robinson Column NY Post &Syndication, co-auth, 1958-60; John Simon Guggenhein fel, 1959-60; Channel13 Educ TV NYC, staff writer & producer, 1962-64; Am Broadcasting Co fel, Yale Univ, 1965-66; Columbia Sch Arts, assoc film, 1968-69; Universal Studios, screenwriter, 1968-69; NBC News, producer, 1972-73; William Branch Assocs, pres, 1973-; Univ Md, vis prof, 1979-82; Luce Fel Williams Col, 1983; Cornell Univ, prof, 1985-94; Univ Calif, regents lectr, 1985; William Paterson Col, vis distinguished prof, 1994-96; Cornell Univ, pro femer africana studies, 1994-; Editor & author: Black Thunder: An Anthology of Contemporary African-American Drama, 1992; Crosswinds: An Anthology of Black Dramatists in the Diaspora, 1993; Author: National Conference of Christians & Jews Citations for Light in the Southern Sky, 1958; FiftySteps Toward Freedom, 1959; A Letter from Booker T, 1988; Plays: A Medalfor Willie, 1951; In Splendid Error, 1954; Experiment in Black, 1955;Light in the Southern Sky, 1958; Fifty Steps Toward Freedom, 1959; A Wreath for Udomo, 1960; To Follow the Phoenix, 1960; The Man on Meeting Street, 1960; Baccalaureate, 1975; TV series: "This Way", 1955; "Light inthe Southern Sky", 1958; "Still a Brother: Inside the Negro Middle Class", 1968; "Afro-Amer Perspectives", 1973-74; "Black Perspectives on the News", 1978-79. **Orgs:** Consult, New York Bd Educ, 1975-77; consult, Ford Found Off Commun, 1976; nat adv bd, Ctr Book Libr Cong, 1979-83; treas, Nat Conf African Am Theatre, 1987-91; nat adv bd, WEB DuBois Found, 1987-. **Honors/Awds:** Hannah B Del Vecchio Award, 1958; Robert E Sherwood Television Award, 1958; Blue Ribbon Award, Am Film Festival, 1969; American Book Award, 1992; AUDELCO Black Theatre Award, 2001. **Military Serv:** AUS, 1951-53. **Home Addr:** 53 Cortlandt Ave, New Rochelle, NY 10801, **Home Phone:** (914)235-1809. **Business Addr:** President, William Branch Associates, 53 Cortlandt Ave, New Rochelle, NY 10801.*

BRANCH, WILLIAM MCKINLEY
Judge, clergy. **Personal:** Born May 10, 1918, Forkland, AL; married Alberta; children: William, Thaddeus, Patricia, Alberta, Malcolm, Vivian & Wanda. **Educ:** Selma Univ, BA, 1944; Ala State Univ, BS, 1956; Union Theol Sch Selma Univ, DD, LLD, 1976. **Career:** Greene County Courthouse, jugde; Eberneezer Baptist Church, pastor. **Orgs:** Probate judge & chmn, Greene Co Comn; co-chmn & pres, Greene Co Educ Asn; chmn, Greene Co Housing Authority; co-chmn, Greene Co Dem Exec Comm, 1976-77; bd dir, Greene Co Health Serv; Nat Asn Co Comnr; Ala Probate Judge's Asn; Asn Co Comn; Ment Health Asn AL; NACO Transp Steering Comm; chmn, Rural Transp Comm; Ala Law Enforcement Planning Agency State Supvry Bd; State-Wide Health Coun AL; Lt Gov Staff; Christian Valley Baptist Church. **Honors/Awds:** Certificate of Merit, Birmingham Urban League Guild; Certificate of Recognition. Fed Greene Co Employ; Leadership Award, Auburn Univ Exten Serv; Distinguished Serv Award, Greene Co Urban League; Award Outstanding Courage, S Polit Arena; Hon Lt Col, Aide de Camp; Certificate of Appreciation, Tenn Tombigee Waterway. **Home Addr:** Route 1 PO Box 1375, Forkland, AL 36740.

BRANCHE, GILBERT M.
Government official. **Personal:** Born Mar 16, 1932, Philadelphia, PA; son of Merwin E and Wilma M Brown; married Jean Overton; children: Andrea, Dolores & Kelle; married Joyce M Parks; children: Quincy & Nickkiiah. **Educ:** Univ Pa, BS, Polit Sci, 1968; Pa State Police Exec Develop Course, Cert, 1974; FBI Academy, Cert, 1975. **Career:** Philadelphia Police Dept, policeman, sgt, lt, capt, 1957-74; Philadelphia Dist Atty Off, dep chief co detective, 1970-74; Philadelphia Police Dept, inspector, 1974-78; Philadelphia Dist Atty Off, chief co detective, 1978; Deputy Sec Fraud & Abuse Invest & Recovery Commonwealth Penn; Nat Orgn Black Law Enforcement exec, asst exec dir. **Orgs:** Bd dir, vpres Safe St, 1968-80; police consult, Asn Consult Wash, DC1972-77; pres, Blacks in Blue, 1974-76; pres, Nat Orgn Black Law Enforce Exec, 1979-; comnr, Standard & Accred Police, 1979-; past pres, Circle NOBLE, 1983-; Free & Accepted Mason; Penn Comn Crime & Delinquency, 2003-. **Honors/Awds:** Meritorious Service Award, Philadelphia City Coun, 1968; Man of the Year Award, Voice Pub, 1978; Humanitarian Award, Chapel of Four Chaplains,1979; Distinguished Career Award, Co Detective Asn Penn, 1980;Humanitarian Award, Nat Orgn of Black Law Enforcement Exec, 1983; Trail Blazer in Law Enforcement Awards State Penn, 1985; James Reaves Man of the Year Award, 1986; inducted into PA Policeman Hall of Fame, Int Police, 1988. **Military Serv:** USAF, s/sgt, 1951-55; Good Conduct Medal; Korean Serv Medal. **Business Addr:** Board Member, Pennsylvania Commission on Crime and Delinquency, 3101 N Front St, PO Box 1167, Harrisburg, PA 17110.

BRANCHE, WILLIAM C., JR.
Scientist. **Personal:** Born Sep 5, 1934, Washington, DC; son of William C Sr and Frances; married Eloise; children: Christine, Michael, Marc. **Educ:** OH Wesleyan Univ, BA, 1956; George Washington Univ, MS, 1959; Cath Univ Am, PhD, bacteriology,1969. **Career:** Scientist (retired), board member: Walter Reed Army Med Ctr, dept bacterial diseases, virologist, 1958-61, Gastroenteritis Stud Sec, chief, 1961-68, Niesseria Meningitis Stud Sec, chief, 1968-72; Walter Reed Army Inst Res, safety officer div comm dis & immun, 1971-, safety officer dept bact dis, 1971-76; Inf Dis Serv Lab, chief, 1972-76; USAMRD Ad Hoc Comn Bact & Myopic Dis, asst proj dir, 1974-; Walter Reed Army Inst Res, health sci admin, 1976-78; NIH Bacteriology & Mycology SS Div Res Grant, health sci admin & scientific review admin, 1979-01; NIHAA Bd Dir, bd mem, currently. **Orgs:** Equal Employ Opportunity Coun Walter Reed Army Med Ctr, 1969-, Walter Reed Army Inst Res Inc Award Comt, 1969-73; Walter Reed Army Inst Res Ed Bd, 1969-; vpres, bd dir Pointer Ridge Swim & Rac Club, 1971-76; asst prof, Fed City Col & Nat Inst Res Camp, 1971-76; chmn, Walter Reed Army Inst Res Inc Award Comn, 1973-; bd dir South Bowie Boys & Girls Club, 1976-80; pres, bd dir Pointer Ridge Swim & Rac Club, 1976; Am Soc Microbiology; ASM Membership Comt, 1980-90; ASM Manpower Comt, 1989-; ASM Bd Ed, 1993; Sigma Xi, Am Wildlife Soc; Staff Training Extramural Programs Comn NIH, 1985-88. **Honors/Awds:** 1st black Teaching Assistant, George Wash Univ, 1956-58; Res Grant USN, George Washington Sch Med, 1956-58; Citizen Year Award, Kiwanas Club Bowie, 1980; NIH Merit Award, 1989. **Special Achievements:** Published numerous articles: Escherichia coli, Shigella flexneri, Neisseria gonorrhoeae & meningococcal infections. **Business Addr:** Board Member, National Institute of Health Alumni Association, 9000 Rockville Pk, Bethesda, MD 20892, **Business Phone:** (301)496-4000.*

BRANCH RICHARDS, DR. GERMAINE GAIL
Counselor, educator. **Personal:** Born in Philadelphia, PA; daughter of Germaine Lopez Jackson Branch and Earl Joseph Branch; children: Kwadjo. **Educ:** Interamerican Univ PR, attended; Bennett Col, BA, 1969; Montclair State Col, MA, 1971; Ohio State Univ, PhD, 1984. **Career:** NJ Bd Educ, Orange, teacher, 1969-71; Guilford Co NC Neighborhood Youth Corps, ed specialist, 1971-73; Ohio Dominican Col Upward Bound, assoc dir, 1973-77; Ohio State Univ, grad admin assoc, 1978-82; OH Bd Regents, res assoc, 1980; Ohio State Univ, Minority Assistance Prog, dir, 1982-89; Ohio State Univ, Medpath Col Med, dir, 1989-91; Palm Beach Community Col, adj prof; Lynn Univ, adj prof; Nova Southeastern Univ, adj prof, 1991-94; Palm Beach Co Sch, counr, 1994-. **Orgs:** Am Personnel & Guid Asn, 1978-; Nat Asn Women Deans & Counr, 1978-; adv bd, OSU Upward Bound, 1979-91; team sec, Mifflin Youth Asn, 1985-89; personnel admin, Nat Asn Stud, 1985-; consult, State OH, 1986; Northwest Col Placement Asn, 1986; Asn Study Class African Civilizations, 1986-; vpres, Asn Black Psychologists, 1988-89; Palm Beach Co Coun Asn. **Home Addr:** 177 Bobwhite Rd, Royal Palm Beach, FL 33411-1734. **Business Addr:** Counselor, Royal Palm Beach Community High School, 106000 Okeechobee Blvd, Royal Palm Beach, FL 33411.

BRAND, ADOLPH JOHANNES DOLLAR. See IBRAHIM, ABDULLAH.

BRAND, ELTON TYRON
Basketball player. **Personal:** Born Mar 11, 1979, Peekskill, NY; son of Daisy. **Educ:** Duke Univ, sociol. **Career:** Chicago Bulls, 1999-2000; Los Angeles Clippers, point forward, 2001-08;Philadelphia 76ers, currently; Film; Rescue Dawn, producer. **Orgs:** Founder, Elton Brand Found, 2000-;Home and Children's Institute InterNat. **Honors/Awds:** Male Athlete of the Year Award, 1998; ACC Player of the Year, 1999; Schick Rookie of the Yr Award, 1999-00; AP All-Am, 1999; co-NBA Rookie of the Yr, 2000; Schick Rookie of the Month,2000; Most Valuable Player, Schick Rookie Challenge, 2000; Western Conf Player of the Week, Natl Basketball Assn, 2001, 2004; Magic Johnson Award, 2002; Sportsmanship Award, Nat Basketball Assn, 2003-04;Sporting News Player of the Year. **Special Achievements:** First selection in 1999 NBA draft. **Business Addr:** Professional Basketball player, Wachovia Center 3601 South Broad Str, Philadelphia, PA 19148.*

BRANDEN, BARBARA. See BRANDON, BARBARA.

BRANDFORD, NAPOLEON
Executive. **Personal:** Born Feb 23, 1952, East Chicago, IN; son of Cora Lee Brandford; married Sharon Delores Bush. **Educ:** Purdue Univ, BA, 1974; Univ S Calif, MPA, 1978. **Career:** Union Carbide-Linde Air Div, summer intern, 1970; Standard Oil Ind, Summer intern, 1971-74; Pac Telephone, asst transp coordr, 1976-78; Dade County Finance Dept, asst finance dir, 1978-82; Shearson Lehman Bros Inc, vpres-pub finance; Grigsby, Brford Inc, dir, investment banking div, vicechmn; Siebert Brandford Shank & Co LLC, co-owner & chmn, currently, Southwestern & Western Regions, mgr, currently. **Orgs:** Nat Forum Black Pub Adminrs, 1983-; exec secy, Builders Mutual Surety Co, 1984-85; bd mem, Urban Econ Develop Corp, 1984-; comt mem, Mayor's Adv Comt Int Trade Foreign Investment Prog, 1985-; Nat Asn Securities Profs, 1987; Univ Southern Calif Alumni Asn, 1985; bd dirs, Alta Bates Med Ctr; trustee, San Jose Mus Modern Art; Nat Black MBAs; interim dep treas/chief financial officer, Calif Health Care Found; Southern California's Sch Policy; Nat Collegiate Athletic Asn; San Gabriel Boy Scouts Am. **Honors/Awds:** Basketball Hall of Fame, E Chicago Roosevelt, 1975; Employee Suggestion Award, Dade County Manager's Off, 1981; Recipient Leadership Miami Alumni Asn, 1982; Ebony Magazine, Young Tycoons, 1988; Men of Courage, Carnation, 1990. **Special Achievements:** Youngest African Am partner on Wall Street. **Business Addr:** Chairman, Partner, Siebert Brandford Shank & Company LLC, 1999 Harrison St Suite 2720, Oakland, CA 94612, **Business Phone:** (510)645-2245.

BRANDON, BARBARA (BARBARA BRANDEN)
Cartoonist or animator. **Personal:** Born Jan 1, 1960?, Long Island, NY; daughter of Brumsic Jr. **Educ:** Syracuse Univ, visual & performing arts, 1980. **Career:** Mag Essence, fashion & beauty writer, 1989; Universal Press Syndicate, cartoonist, 1991-. **Special Achievements:** First African-American woman to be syndicated in more than 50 newspapers nationwide for the 'Where I'm Coming From', comic strip. **Business Addr:** Cartoonist, Universal Press Syndicate, 10 Pk Ln, Providence, RI 02907, **Business Phone:** (401)944-2700.*

BRANDON, CARL RAY
Counselor. **Personal:** Born Nov 15, 1953, Port Gibson, MS; son of Alonzo and Marjorie Williams; divorced; children: Ashlea. **Educ:** Alcorn State Univ, BS, 1976, MS, 1984; Univ Southern Miss. **Career:** Thompson Funeral Home, Port Gibson, MS, funeral dir, 1971-; Claiborne City Pub Schs, counr, 1977-84; Southwest Mental Health Complex, case mgr II, 1984-88, therapist, 1988-. **Orgs:** Miss Asn Educ, 1977-; Miss Coun Asn, 1981-; Miss Dep Sheriffs Asn, 1982-; Miss Asn Constable, 1984-; bd dirs, Grand Gulf State Park, Port Gibson, MS, 1988. **Honors/Awds:** Citizenship Award, Charlie Griffin. **Home Addr:** 204 Mimosa St, Port Gibson, MS 39150. *

BRANDON, DR. IDA GILLARD
School administrator. **Personal:** Born Jun 27, 1936, Snow Hill, NC; daughter of Closton and Emily; married Dr Joseph, Feb 27, 1960 (deceased); children: Cynthia Michelle. **Educ:** NC A&T State Univ, BS, 1958; Va State Univ, masters, 1970; George WashUniv, educ specialist, 1975, EdD, 1976. **Career:** Teacher, 1958-69, adminr, 1969-70; Univ Va, NDEA fel, 1969; Bowie State Univ, Career Planning & Placement, dir, 1970-76, part-time fac mem, 1975-76, Continuing Educ, dir, 1976-82, Grad Sch & Cont Educ Ctr, dean, 1982-90, 1991-96, interim provost, vpres acad affairs, 1990-91, SCEES, asst provost & dean, 1996-; George Wash Univ, adj fac mem, 1978-81; Higher Educ Admin Inst, Harvard Univ. **Orgs:** Coun Historically Black Grad Schs, 1970-; Am Asn Cols Teacher Educ; Am Asn Higher Educ; Am Asn Higher Continuing Educ; Am Asn State Cols & Univs; Asn Career Devel Higher Educ; Adult Educ Asn USA; Am Asn Univ Profs; Leadership Inst Asn Cont Higher Educ, 1993. **Honors/Awds:** BSU SGA Award, Adminstrator of the Year, 1971; Distinguished Alumni, NCA &T State Univ, 1988; Presidential Citation, Bowie State Univ, 1991-92, Inst Found Legacy Excellence Award, 1992; Meritorious Civic Service Award, Seagram Am, 1997. **Special Achievements:** PG County Woman's Hall of Fame, inductee. **Business Addr:** Assistant Provost, Dean of Graduate School, Bowie State University, School of Graduate Studies and Continuing Education, Rm 0241 Henry Admin Bldg 14000 Jericho Pk Rd, Bowie, MD 20715-9465, **Business Phone:** (301)860-3413.

BRANDON, JEROME
Educator. **Educ:** Murray State Univ, BA, health, phy educ, 1969, MS, phys educ, 1971; Univ Ill, PhD, exercise physiol, 1983. **Career:** Murray High Sch, Murray, Ky, Teacher, 1969-71; Breckinridge Job Corps Ctr, counsr adv, 1977-78; Univ Ill Urbana Champaign, Phys Educ Dept, instr, 1978-79, res assoc, 1979-83; Ga State Univ, Dept Kinesiology & Health, Atlanta, from asst prof to assoc prof, 1983-2003, prof, 2003-; Dekalb Community Col, Dept Phys Educ, Clarkston, GA, adj instr, l984-86; Rehab Res & Develop Ctr, Vet Affairs Med Ctr, Decatur, GA, res health scientist, 1991-; Emory Univ Med Sch, Dept Rehab Med, Atlanta, GA, from clin instr to asst prof, 1992-; Ga State Univ,Gerontol Ctr, Atlanta, GA, fac & curriculum comm mem, 1997-. **Orgs:** Pres elect, Southeast Am Col Sports Med, 2006, pres, 2007, past pres, 2008; Am Alliance Health, Phys Educ, Recreation & Dance, AAHPERD. **Business Addr:** Professor, Georgia State University, Department of Kinesiology & Health, 125 Decatur St Suite 137, PO Box 3978, Atlanta, GA 30303-3087, **Business Phone:** (404)651-1120.

BRANDON, SYMRA D
Government official. **Personal:** Born Jan 20, 1947, New York, NY; daughter of Robert and Doris Thomas; married Turhan V Brandon Sr, Mar 1, 1970; children: Turhan Jr & Taniya. **Educ:** Morgan State Col, BA, 1969; Hunter Sch Social Work, CUNY, MSW, 1976; Pace Univ, MPA, 1982. **Career:** Iona Col, adjunt prof; Westchester County, Dept Social Services, staff devel specialist, 1981-87; Cornell Univ, Family Life Devel Ctr, consultant, trainer, 1982; Columbia Univ, adjunct prof, 1983-85; Westchester County Youth Bureau, prog adminr, 1992-95, UAW/GM Transition Ctr, staff development, 1996; Westchester Co Exec, special asst, 1998-; Yonkers City Coun, minority leader, 2000-. **Orgs:** NAACP, Yonkers branch, past 3rd vice pres; Alpha Kappa Alpha Sorority (AKA), Terrace City Chap, 1995-; bd mem, Inst for Responsible Fatherhood, 1997-; bd mem, Child Care Coun Westchester, 1998-; bd mem, Mt Vernon Health Care Ctr, 1998-; Cluster Adv chamn, Elejmal Ct 171, Voter Registration Comn, 1999; Bd, 1999; bd mem, Stardom Child Care Ctr, 1999. **Honors/Awds:** Westchester Distinguished Service Award, Nat Asn Social Workers; NY State NASW, Social Worker of the Year; Yonkers Guardians, Woman of the Year; Yonkers NAACP, Freedom Fighter Award; Mayors Community Relations Comt, Women's Equality Day Award, 1999. **Business Addr:** Assistant County Executive, Westchester County, Office of Economic Development, 148 Martine Ave Rm 906, White Plains, NY 10601, **Business Phone:** (914)995-2934.

BRANDON, TERRELL (THOMAS TERRELL BRANDON)
Basketball player, business owner. **Personal:** Born May 20, 1970, Portland, OR; son of Charlotte. **Educ:** Univ Ore, attended 1991. **Career:** Basketball player (retired), business owner; Cleveland Cavaliers, guard, 1991-97; Milwaukee Bucks, 1997-99; Minn Timberwolves, 1999-2002; Atlanta Hawks, 2004; Terrell Brandon's Barber Shop, owner, currently; Tee Bee Enterprises, owner, currently. **Honors/Awds:** Most Valuable Player, Univ Ore; NBA All-Rookie Second Team, 1992; NBA Sportsmanship Award, 1997. **Business Addr:** Owner, Tee Bee Enterprises, 1330 NE Alberta St, Portland, OR 97211.

BRANDON, THOMAS TERRELL. **See BRANDON, TERRELL.**

BRANDT, LILLIAN B.
Executive. **Personal:** Born Jul 4, 1919, New York, NY; married George W Sr. **Educ:** City Col NY. **Career:** James Daugherty Ltd, partner, vpres & secy; Teal Traing Inc; Sam Friedlander Inc; Capri Frocks Inc; Ben Reig Inc. **Orgs:** Fashion Sales Guild; Fashion Coun NY Inc.

BRANGMAN, H ALAN
Architect, executive director. **Personal:** Born Apr 20, 1952, Hamilton, Bermuda; son of Oliver G Jr and Carolyn I; married Patricia A, Sep 3, 1988; children: Jacob, Jessica & Alaina. **Educ:** Cornell Univ, BArch, 1976; Harvard GSD, Bus Sch, cert, 1984; Wharton Sch Bus, real estate primer cert, 1985; Georgetown Univ McDonough Sch Bus, EML, 2005. **Career:** RTKL Assocs, Inc, proj dir, mgr, 1977-83; Oliver Carr Co, dir DC develop, 1983-91; NEA-Design Arts Prog, dep dir, 1991-94; Georgetown Univ, dir facilities planning & proj mgt, 1994-96, univ architect, currently, Facilities Planning of Georgetown Univ, exec dir, currently; City Falls Church, mayor, 1996-98; State Md, lic architect. **Orgs:** Urban Land Inst, 1990-91; Am Inst Architects, 1992-; Planning Comn City Falls Church, 1992-94, Am Planning Asn, 1992-94; Lambda Alpha Int Real Estate Hon Soc; City Coun Falls Church, 1994-98. **Special Achievements:** Alternative Careers in Architecture, AIA Video, 1990. **Business Addr:** University Architect, Georgetown University, Office of University Architect, W Lobby New S Hall, 37th & O St NW, Washington, DC 20057, **Business Phone:** (202)687-3124.

BRANHAM, GEORGE, III
Bowler. **Personal:** Born Sep 21, 1962, Detroit, MI; son of George William Francis Branham II and Betty Ogletree; married Jacquelyne Phend, Sep 15, 1990. **Career:** Prof Bowlers Asn, bowler, 1984-02. **Orgs:** Prof Bowlers Asn, 1984-02. **Honors/Awds:** Southern Calif Jr Bowler of the Yr, 1983; Brunswick Memorial World Open, 1986, AC/Delco Classic, Professional Bowlers Assn Tournaments, 1987; Baltimore Open, 1993; Firestone Tournament of Champions, 1993; Cleveland Open, 1996. **Business Addr:** Professional Bowler, Professional Bowlers Association, 719 2nd Avenue Suite 701, Seattle, WA 98104, **Business Phone:** (206)332-9688.

BRANKER, JULIAN MICHAEL
Automotive executive. **Career:** Mike Branker Buick-Hyundai Nissan Inc, Lincoln, NE, chief exec officer, 1991-. **Business Addr:** Owner, Chief Executive Officer, Mike Branker Buick-Hyundai Nissan Inc, 421 N 48th St, PO Box 30184, Lincoln, NE 68504, **Business Phone:** (402)464-5976.*

BRANNEN, JAMES H., III
Pilot. **Personal:** Born Dec 25, 1940, Queens, NY; married; children: Keree, Myia, Christopher. **Educ:** Northrop Inst Tech, BS, aero engineering, 1964; Univ Baltimore Law Sch, JD, 1975. **Career:** Conn Legis, mem, 1972-74; US Patent Off, 1966-67; United Airlines, pilot flight mgr. **Orgs:** Rep Study Com, CT; Rep Town Com, 1972-; Jaycees, 1972-; bd dir, Colchester Montessori Children's House, 1973-; Can US Sen Rep Party, 1974.

BRANNON, DEBORAH DIANNE
Entrepreneur. **Personal:** Born Feb 1, 1956, Hempstead, TX; daughter of George L Smith Jr; married Roy; children: Jason, Jina, Christina. **Educ:** CA State Univ, Sacramento, BA, jour, 1984. **Career:** Pro line Corp, key acct mgr, regional sales mgr, currently. **Orgs:** Am Bus Women's Asn; Sigma Gamma Rho; Girls Inc, auxilary bd. **Special Achievements:** Launched Web site, www.greeklikeme.com, 1999. **Business Addr:** Reginonal Sales Manager, Pro-Line Corporation, 2121 Panoramic Cir, Dallas, TX 75212, **Business Phone:** (214)631-4247.*

BRANNON, JAMES K.
Chief executive officer, president (organization). **Career:** Orthop Sci Inc, founder, pres & ceo, 1999-. **Business Phone:** (562)799-5550.*

BRANNON, JAMES R.
Executive. **Personal:** Born Feb 26, 1943, Texarkana, TX; son of James and Ellen; married Dorothy Williams; children: Sherrilyn C, Deanna E. **Educ:** NC A&T State Univ, BS, bus admin, 1967; Harvard Univ, Grad Sch Bus Admin Prog Mgt Develop, cert, 1975. **Career:** Liberty Mutual Ins Co, bus lines underwriter, 1967-68, Roxbury Keypunch Training Ctr, mgr, 1968-69, com underwriter, 1969-71, coordr equal employment, 1971-78, asst vpres employ rels, 1978-, sales rep, currently. **Orgs:** Nat Asn Advan Colored People, 1967-; A&T State Univ Alumni Asn 1967-; Harvard Bus Sch Asn, Boston, 1976; Nat Urban League, Boston, 1980-; bd mem, Freedom House, Boston, 1984-; comt mem, Lexington Fair Housing, 1985-; Lena Pk Community Ctr; bd mem, Lexington Metco Scholar Comt. **Special Achievements:** Numerous articles written on career planning, preparation Black Collegian magazine. **Business Addr:** Sales Representative, Liberty Mutual Insurance Company, 173 Bedford St, Lexington, MA 02420, **Business Phone:** (617)861-8758.

BRANSFORD, PARIS
Surgeon. **Personal:** Born Jan 1, 1930, Huntsville, AL; married Gladys Toney; children: Paris, Toni, Traci. **Educ:** Tenn State Univ, BS, 1956; Meharry Med Col, MD, 1963. **Career:** Priv Prac, surgeon; NASA Huntsville, AL, res chem missile prog; Rvrsd Gen Hosp, chief emergency rm, 1972-; N Cent Gen Hosp, bd dirs chief staff, 1973-75; NC Med Bd, Physician, 2006-. **Orgs:** Vp secy, Hstn Med Firm, 1973-76; pres, Med Asn Almed Med Sq, 1973-; Alpha Phi Alpha Frat; Young Men's Christian Asn; Nat Asn Advan Colored People; Harris Co Med Asn; Am Med Asn; Tex Med Asn; Am Soc Abdominal Surg; lectr, Srs Am Cancer Soc. **Honors/Awds:** Recipient Of Service, Chap Comm Delta Theta Lambda Chaps, Alpha Phi Alpha Frat Inc, 1971; Appreciation, Kappa Psi Phramaceut Fraternity Serv Comn, 1975. **Military Serv:** USAF, 1950-53.

BRANTLEY, CLIFFORD
Baseball player. **Personal:** Born Apr 12, 1968, Staten Island, NY. **Career:** Baseball player (retired); Philadelphia Phillies, 1991-92.

BRANTON, LEO, JR.
Lawyer. **Personal:** Born Feb 17, 1922, Pine Bluff, AR; son of Branton, Sr and Pauline Wiley; married Geradine Pate. **Educ:** Tenn State Univ, BS, 1942; Northwestern Univ, JD, 1948. **Career:** Los Angeles, atty, 1949; Angela Davis, Hollywod Entertainers, represented atty; Communists, represented atty; Poor Blacks Rblnin Watts, atty, 1965; Black Panther Party; participated scsfl defense, 1972; Pvt practr, currently. **Orgs:** ACLU; Nat Asn Advan Colored People; St Bar Calif; Wilshire Bar Asn; J M Langston Law Club. **Honors/Awds:** Outstanding contrib to field of Criminal Litigation Award, 1972; Trial Lawyer of Yr, J M Langston Bar Asn, 1973; Lawyer of Yr, 1974; Several awards fom city of Los Angeles; Calif State Sen & the Nat Asn Advan Colored People, Legal Educ & Defense Fund. **Special Achievements:** Involvement in the civil rights movement; defended thirteen mem of the Los Angeles chapter of the Black Panther Party against an unlawful attack by the Los Angeles Police Dept; co 1st black juror. **Military Serv:** AUS, segregate unit. *

BRASEY, HENRY L.
Educator, college teacher. **Personal:** Born Nov 25, 1937, Cincinnati, OH; married Anna; children: Darrell & Jenifer. **Educ:** BS, 1972; IBM Corp, Cert. **Career:** Regional Comput, City Cincinnati, programming proj leader; Full House Inc,pres; Withrow HS Data Processing Prog, curric adv; Univ Cincinnati, asstdir comput serv & adj prof, asst prof eng anal, dir acad technol, adjctinstr info technol, currently. **Orgs:** Asn Comput Mach; Kennedy Heights Community Coun; Ken-Sil Athletic Club;Pleasant Ridge PTA; Cincinnati Youth Collaborative; dir, Community AccessTechnol. **Honors/Awds:** Senate President of the Year, 2003. *

BRASHEAR, DONALD
Hockey player. **Personal:** Born Jan 7, 1972, Bedford, IN; married; children: Jordan & Jackson. **Career:** Longueuil, 1989-91; Verdun, 1991-92; Fredericton, 1992-93; Montreal Canadians, 1993-97; Vancouver Canucks, left wing, 1997-01; Philadelphia Flyers, left wing, 2001-; Quebec RadioX, 2004-05; Philadelphia Flyers, 2005-06; Washington Capitals, 2006-07; New York Rangers, free agent, currently. **Honors/Awds:** Pelle Lindbergh Memorial, 2003. *

BRASS, REGINALD STEPHEN
Association executive. **Personal:** Born Sep 6, 1958, Los Angeles, CA; son of Ernest and Mildred Jackson; divorced; children: Stephen Reginald II. **Career:** Bodyguard; Saint Anne's Maternity House, teacher & coun; Mini House, teacher & counr. **Orgs:** Pregnant Minor Task Force of the Sex Equity Comn Los Angeles Unified Sch Dist; Maranatha Community Church; adv bd, Los Angeles Co; founder & pres, My Child Says Daddy, 1991-; adv bd, Am coalition Fathers & Children. **Honors/Awds:** Community Architect Award, Honorable Gwen Moore, 1994; Directors Award, Calif Dept Social Services, 1994; Yvonne Brathwaite Burke, Commendation, 1994; DHL, St Stephen's Edun Bible Col, 1996. **Business Addr:** Founder, President, My Child Says Daddy, 3856 Martin Luther King Blvd Suite 204, Los Angeles, CA 90008, **Business Phone:** (323)296-8816.*

BRASWELL, PALMIRA
Educator. **Personal:** Born Mar 23, 1928, Macon, GA. **Educ:** Fort Valley State Col, AB 1950; Teachers Col Columbia Univ, MA 1959; Univ Ga, EdS, 1969; Prin Ctr Harvard Univ, attended 1985. **Career:** Educator (retired); Bibb Co Bd Educ & NY Bd Educ, teacher 1950-64; Bibb Co Bd Educ, dir instrnl mat ctr, 1965-74, curriculum dir, 1977-83, dir staff develop, 1983-87. **Orgs:** Civil Serv Bd City Macon, 1976-79; basileus Epsilon Omega Omega-Alpha Kappa Alpha, 1979-83; Booker T Washington Community Ctr, 1979-83; curriculum coun, Mercer Univ Med Sch, 1979-80; Middle Ga Chap Am Red Cross, 1980-84; state sec Prof, Asn Ga Educr; pres, Mid Ga Chap Phi Delta Kappa, 1986; bd mem, state bd educ, Atlanta, Ga. **Honors/Awds:** Teacher of the Yr, BS Ingram Elem Sch, 1976; Distinguished Alumni Award; Presidential Citation, Nat Asn Higher Educ Equal Opportunity, 1986. **Special Achievements:** First Black female radio announcer City of Macon GA station WBML, 1956-58; 1 of 20 Most Influential Women in Middle GA NAACP Macon Chap, 1981. **Home Addr:** 3016 Paige Dr, Macon, GA 31211. *

BRAUGHER, ANDRE
Actor. **Personal:** Born Jul 1, 1962, Chicago, IL; married Amy Brabson; children: Michael. **Educ:** Stanford Univ, BA, theatre, 1984; Juilliard Sch, MFA, 1988. **Career:** TV series: "Homicide: Life on the Street", 1993-98; "The Tuskegee Airmen"; "Everybody Has To Shoot the Picture"; "Murder in Mississippi"; "The Court-Martial of Jackie Robinson"; "Passing Glory"; "Gideon's Crossing", 2000; "Hack", 2002; "Thief", 2006; "Men of a Certain Age", 2009; Films: Glory, 1998; Primal Fear, 1998; Get On The Bus, 1998; City of Angels, 1998; Thick as Thieves, 1999; All the Rage, 1999; Frequency, 2000; Duets, 2000; A Better Way to Die, 2000; Salem's Lot, 2004; Poseidon, 2006; The Mist, 2007; Live!, 2007; Fantastic Four: Rise of the Silver Surfer, 2007; Andromeda Strain, 2008; Passengers, 2008; Theatre: Henry V, King John, NY Shakespeare Festival; Othello; Folger Shakespeare Festival; The Way Of The World; Richard II; Measure for Measure; Twelfth Night; Coriolanus. **Honors/Awds:** Emmy Award for Outstanding Actor, Drama Series, 1998; TCA Award for Individual Achievement in Drama, 1998; Blockbuster Entertainment Award for Favorit eSupporting Actor Suspense, 2001. **Special Achievements:** One of the 50 Most Beautiful People in the World, 1997. **Business Addr:** Actor, c/o United Talent Agency, 9560 Wilshire Blvd F15, Beverly Hills, CA 90212.*

BRAXTON, DR. BRAD
Educator, clergy. **Educ:** Univ Va, BA, 1991; Univ Oxford, MPhil, 1993; Emory Univ, PhD, 1999. **Career:** Douglas Mem Community Church, Baltimore, MD, sr pastor, 1995-2000; Vanderbilt Divinity Sch, Jessie Ball duPont asst prof Homiletics & Biblical Studies, 2000-04, assoc prof homiletics & new testament, 2004-; Theologian-in-Residence, 2007-. **Honors/Awds:** Shannon Award, Univ Va, 1991; many other honors and awards. **Special Achievements:** Published The Tyranny of Resolutions: 1 Corinthians 7:17-24, 2000, Preaching Paul, 2004, numerous articles.

BRAXTON, EDWARD KENNETH
Priest, educator, bishop. **Personal:** Born Jun 28, 1944, Chicago, IL; son of Cullen L. Braxton Sr. **Educ:** BA, 1966; MA, 1968; M, Div, 1969; STB, 1968; PhD, 1975; STD, 1976; Univ Chicago, Postdoctoral Fellowship. **Career:** Harvard Univ, 1976-77; Notre Dame Univ, vis prof, 1977-78; Diocese Cleveland, chancellor theol affairs & personal theol; Archdiocese Wa, DC, chancellor theol affairs, 1978-81; Rome N Am Col, scholar residence, 1982-83; Univ Chicago, Catholic Stud Ctr, dir; William H Sadlier Inc, off theol consult, currently; 1988 winter sch lectr, South Africa; Auxiliary Bishop of Saint Louis, MO, 1995; Bishop of Lake Charles, LA, 2000; Bishop of Belleville, IL, 2005. **Orgs:** Am Acad Religion; Catholic Theol Soc Am; Black Catholic Clergy Caucus; Catholic Bishop's Comt Liturgy & Doctrine; bd dir, St Mary Lake Seminary, Chicago; keynote speaker, 43 Int Eucharistic Cong, Nairobi, Kenya; theol adv to bishops of Africa & Madagascan,

1984; del, writer & speaker for Hist Nat Black Catholic Cong, Wash, DC, 1987. **Special Achievements:** Published, The Wisdom Comn; numerous articles on Catholic Theol Religion; forthcoming book, One Holy Catholic and Apostolic: Essays for the Community of Faith. *

BRAXTON, HARRIET E.
Government official. **Personal:** Born Jul 18, 1926, Charlotte, NC; married Paul A Braxton; children: Paula E Arp, Rosemary L Smith, Harriet A Price, Regina B Mitchell, Julia L, Diana A, Paul M. **Educ:** William Pa HS, Cert Housing Inspectors, 1970, cert HAAC, 1972; Latestart Uptown Sr Citizens, cert, 1982. **Career:** Government official (retired); Mechanicsburg Naval Depot, clerk typist, 1945-49; PA Dept Revenue, addressograph op, 1961-63; City Harrisburg, housing inspector, 1968-71; Harrisburg Housing Authority, housing coun/res ad, 1972-73; City Harrisburg, councilwoman appointed, 1982, elected, 1983-; Capital Cty Ret Ctr Inc, by-laws comm mem. **Orgs:** Comm chair, Uptown Civic Asn, 1963-73; dir, Harrisburg Opportunity Bd, 1963-65; neighborhood aide, Harrisburg Opportunity Prog, 1965-67; bookmobile asst, Harrisburg Pub Libr, 1967; Mayor Adv Comm, 1966-68; bd mem, YMCA, 1968; inspector elections, Tenth Ward Sec Precinct, 1975-80; bd mem, YWCA, 1977; judge elect 10th ward 2nd precinct, 1980; Our Lady Blessed Sacrament Ch; OLBS Sch PTA. **Honors/Awds:** Capt, Soccer Team William Pa HS, 1943; 1st Nat Medal, Set Baseball throw Fager Field (235 ft) Harrisburg, PA; 2nd Place Winner AAU Basketball; Banneker Tennis Champion, 1940; Braxton Playground Uptown Civic Assoc & City, 1965; Merit of Honor, Sixth St Uptown Revit Eff, 1978-85; Am Red Cross, 1977; Faces & Places Harrisburg Historical Soc, 1984. **Home Addr:** 2142 N 7th St, Harrisburg, PA 17110. **Business Addr:** Councilwoman, Harrisburg City Council, City Govt Ctr, Harrisburg, PA 17101.

BRAXTON, JANICE LAWRENCE
Basketball player, basketball coach. **Personal:** Born Jun 7, 1962; married Steve. **Educ:** La Tech Univ, attended. **Career:** Basketball player (retired), basketball coach; Cleveland Rockers, 1997; Cleveland Rockers, asst coach, currently. **Honors/Awds:** Most Outstanding Player, 1982; Pan Am Games Basketball Team, Gold Medal,1983; World Championship Basketball Team, Silver Medal, 1983; US Olympic Basketball Team, Gold Medal, 1984; Women's Basketball Hall of Fame Class, 2006. **Business Addr:** Assistant Coach, Cleveland Rockers, 200 Huron Rd E, Cleveland, OH 44115, **Business Phone:** (216)420-2000.

BRAXTON, DR. JEAN BAILEY
Educator, dean (education). **Personal:** Born Jan 6, 1943, Hampton, VA; daughter of Christine and Linwood; married Wendell F Braxton, Aug 14, 1971; children: Michael & Traci. **Educ:** Bennett Col, BS, 1965; Hampton Univ, MA, 1972; Univ NC Greensboro, EdD, 1984. **Career:** Attucks High Sch, phys educ teacher, 1965-70; Hampton HS, phys educ teacher, 1970-71; Hampton Univ, PE Dept, asst prof, 1971-83, dept chair, 1984-88; Norfolk State Univ, PE Dept, assoc prof, 1988-93, dept chair, 1993-2000, Sch Educ, dean, 2000-. **Orgs:** Am Alliance Health; AACTE; accreditation team mem, Va Dept Educ; bd examr, Nat Coun Accreditation Teacher Educ. **Honors/Awds:** Outstanding Performance & Promotion of the Arts, Hampton Institute Alumni Award, 1984; Community Dance Award, Hampton Univ, 1984; Professional Award, Hampton Univ, 1985; EB Henderson Award, Am Alliance Health, Phys Educ, Recreation & Dance, 1998; CD Henry Award, Am Alliance Health, Phys Educ, Recreation & Dance, 1999; Eva Hamlin Outstanding Woman in the Arts, Bennett Col, 1999. **Home Addr:** 22 Pine Cone Dr, Hampton, VA 23669, **Home Phone:** (757)722-9252. **Business Addr:** Dean, Norfolk State University, School of Education, Rm 115 Bozeman Educ Bldg 700 Pk Ave Suite 340, Norfolk, VA 23504, **Business Phone:** (757)823-8701.

BRAXTON, JOHN LEDGER
Association executive, judge, educator. **Personal:** Born Feb 6, 1945, Philadelphia, PA; married Linda; children: 1. **Educ:** Pa State Univ, BS, 1966; Howard Univ Sch Law, JD, 1971. **Career:** Wolf, Block Schorr & Solis-Cohen, assoc, 1971-73; Braxton, Johnson & Kopanski, partner, 1973-76; Blue Cross Greater Philadelphia, assoc coun, 1976-78; Off Dist Atty Philadelphia, chief munic ct unit, 1978-81; Ct Common Pleas, judge, 1981-95; Phoenix Mgt Serv Inc, vpres; Temple Univ, Dept Law & Real Estate, adj prof, 1985-95; arbitrator & mediator currently. **Orgs:** Bd mem, Fel Comn, 1978-85; vpres, Child Psychiat Ctr St Christopher's, 1976-85; bd mem, Judicial Coun Nat Bar, 1984-85; bd mem, Philadelphia Citywide Devel Corp, 1981-85; pres, Homemaker Serv Metrop Area, 1995-99; vice chair, Cradle Liberty Coun BSA; chmn, Nat Bar Asn, Judical Coun,1992-93; Toll fel, Coun State Govt; alumni fel, Penn State Univ, 1996; bd gov, Am Red Cross; treas, Nat Bar Asn, currently; mem bd, Pa CASA; chmn bd, Philadelphia County, CASA, bd mem; mem bd, Cradle Liberty Coun Boy Scouts Am; mem bd, Juvenile Law Ctr, secy, currently; chmn bd, Bearean Bank, 1999-2003; chmn bd, Penn-Jersey Region, Am Red Cross Blood Servs. **Honors/Awds:** Outstanding Alumnus Award, Howard Univ; Silver Beaver Award, Boy Scouts Am, Phila Coun, 1989; Whitney M Young Service Award. **Military Serv:** AUS, lt, 1966-68; Bronze Star With First Oak Cluster, 1968. **Business Addr:** Secretary, Juvenile Law Center, Philadelphia Bldg 4th Fl, Philadelphia, PA 19107, **Business Phone:** (215)625-0551.

BRAXTON, STEVE
Executive, clergy, writer. **Personal:** Born Jan 30, 1941, Natchitoches, LA; son of Thomas (deceased) and Mary (deceased); divorced; children: Jason, Girard. **Educ:** Grambling State Univ, attended 1963; Wayne State Univ, attended 1973; Windsor Univ, BS, bus admin, 1975; McCormick Theol Sem, post-grad study, 1998; Loyola Univ, Inst Small Develop, Inst Pastoral Care & Study, cert, small group ministry, 1994. **Career:** Food Maker Inc, distrib supvr, 1970-73; Burger King, gen mgr, distib, 1973-76; McDonald's Corp, area supvr; Church's Fried Chicken, dist mgr, 1976-80; Inner City Foods, vpres, 1980-82, pres, 1982-86; Health Tech Inc, vpres, co-owner, 1986-94; BRME Enterprise, pres, 1994-00; Nat Progressive Inst, pres, 1996-00; United Church Hyde Park, youth pastor, 1999-00, interim sr pastor, 1999-01; Marketplace Consulting Inc, pres; Braxton Enterprise, Inc, pres; Health Tech Industries, pharmaceuticals, co-owner; BRME Enterprise, pres, currently. **Orgs:** Adv comm, Miss Black Chicago, 1980-85; bd mem, Chicago Opportunity Indust Ctr, 1980-84; bd mem, Black United Fund, IL, 1986-99; steering comt, Chicago Bus Develop Coun, 1990-99; deacon, 1990-96, ordained minister, 1997-, Progressive Community Church; bd mem, Inspired Partnerships, 1994-99; subcomt chair, State Ill, Access Capital, 1997-99; bd mem, trustee, Ecumenical Childcare Network, USA; coordr, United Church Hyde Park, Chicago, Youth Mentoring & Enrichment Progs; Am Clergy Leadership Coun; Inter-religious Int Coun World Peace; Nat Black Religious Coalition Reproductive Choice; bd mem, Children's Home & Aid Soc; chair bd dirs, Partnership Qual Child Care, 2003; pres, bd dirs, Ecumenical Childcare Network, 2003; co-convenor, United Way/ECCN Qual Partner Faith-based Child Develop Collaborative Cohort, 2003. **Honors/Awds:** Citation of Recognition, Chicago OIC, 1982; Role Model, Mentor, Bethune Cookman Col, 1984; Community Commitment, The League Black Women, 1992, 1993; Pinnacle Award, The Gillette Co, Harbor Publ, 1994; Layman of the Year, Int Coun Community Churches, 1996. **Special Achievements:** White Conf on Small Business, delegate, 1985-86, appointed moderator, 1994-97; delegate, World Forum Conference, Acapulco, Mexico, 2003; article published in Inclusive Pulpit, A Community Church Press; author, Agape. **Military Serv:** USN, petty officer first class, 1963-70; Good Conduct Medal, Vietnam Occupation Medal, Meritorious Service Medal. **Home Addr:** 7411 S Wabash Ave, Chicago, IL 60619. **Business Addr:** President, BRME Enterprise, 7411 S Wabash Ave, Chicago, IL 60619.*

BRAXTON, TONI
Actor, singer. **Personal:** Born Oct 7, 1967, Severn, MD; daughter of Michael and Evelyn; married Keri Lewis, Apr 21, 2001; children: Denim Kole Braxton Lewis & Diezel Ky Braxton Lewis. **Career:** Albums: Toni Braxton, 1993; Secrets, 1996; Heat, 2000; Snowflakes, 2001; More Than A Woman, 2002; Ultimate Toni Braxton, 2003; Libra, 2005; Love & Pain, 2008. Films: Kingdom Come, 2001; Broadway: Beauty & the Beast, 1998-99; Aida, 2003; "Kevin Hill", 2005; An Evening of Stars: Tribute to Stevie Wonder, 2006. **Honors/Awds:** American Music Awards, 1995, 1997; Favorite female R&B artist, 2001; F avorite soul album, 2001. **Business Addr:** Singer, c/o Laface Recs, 1 Capital City Plz 3350 Peachtree Rd Suite 1500, Atlanta, GA 30326.

BRAXTON, TYRONE SCOTT
Football player. **Personal:** Born Dec 17, 1964, Madison, WI; married Elizabeth. **Educ:** NDak State Univ. **Career:** Football player (retired); Denver Broncos, defensive back, 1987-93, 1995-99; Miami Dolphins, 1994; Arvada High Sch, Asst coach, currently. **Honors/Awds:** Unsung Hero, NFL Players Asn, 1996; Pro Bowl, 1996; Mackey Award, 1997; Nat Football League, True Value Man of the Yr, Denver Broncos, 1997. *

BRAY, LEROY, SR.
Engineer. **Personal:** Born Aug 1, 1950, Norwich, CT; son of Luther and Beatrice; married Patricia Baldwin, Dec 17, 1983; children: Anthony, Desiree, Marquita, Tiffany & Leroy Jr. **Educ:** Howard Univ, BSEE, 1973; Cent Mich Univ, MBM, 1980; Wayne State Univ, MS, 1995. **Career:** Owens Corning Fiberglass, process elec engr, 1973-76; Ford Motor Co, maintenance supvr, 1976-80, automotive safety prog mgr, 1987-; Gen Motors, mfg engr, 1980-87. **Orgs:** Sr mem, Am Soc for Quality Control, 1989-. **Honors/Awds:** Certified Quality Engineer, Am Soc Quality Control, 1989; Certified Quality Auditor, Am Soc Quality Control, 1990. **Business Addr:** Automotive Safety Program Manager, Ford Motor Company, 330 Town Ctr Dr Fairlane Plz S Suite 400, Dearborn, MI 48126, **Business Phone:** (313)594-9772.

BRAYNON, DR. EDWARD J
Dentist. **Personal:** Born Jan 15, 1928, Miami, FL; son of Edward J and May Dell Jackson; married Ann Carey; children: Edward III & Keith. **Educ:** Howard Univ, BS, 1949, DDS, 1954. **Career:** Dentist (retired); USAF, dental officer, 1954-56; pvt pract, dentist 1956-87; Family Health Ctr Inc, chief dental serv, 1981-87, vpres supplemental serv, 1987-96. **Orgs:** Past pres, Dade County Acad Med, 1962-63; past pres, Dade County Dent Soc, 1970-72; grand baseileus, Omega Psi Phi Frat, 1976-79. **Honors/Awds:** Key City Columbus, GA, 1973; Outstanding service to the community & profession, Howard Univ, Wash, DC, 1976; Key City Fayetville, NC, 1976; Key Dade County, FL, 1976; Key City Spartanberg, SC, 1977; One of the 100 Most Influential Black Americans, Ebony Mag, 1977-79; Honorary Citizen of Louisville, Louisville KY, 1977; Honorary Citizen of New Orleans, New Orleans, LA, 1977; Distinguished Service Award, Fla Dent Asn, 1990. **Special Achievements:** Dr E J Braynon, Jr Day City Miami, Florida 1976. **Military Serv:** USAF capt 1954-56. **Home Addr:** 2271 NE 191st St, Miami, FL 33180.

BRAZELTON, EDGAR
Executive, business owner. **Personal:** Born in Birmingham, AL; son of Edgar Brazelton and Rosa Mae; married Elizabeth. **Educ:** Univ Mich; Boston Sch Floral Cult, Mass. **Career:** Brazelton's Florist Inc, owner & pres, 1941-. **Orgs:** Vice chmn, Mich State Housing Develop Authority; Cotillion Club; pres, BTWBA, 1967-68; brd dir, Michigan Minority business development Coun. **Business Addr:** Owner, President, Brazelton, 2686 W Grand Blvd, PO Box 8006, Detroit, MI 48208-0006, **Business Phone:** (313)872-6900.

BRAZIL, ROBERT D.
Educator, administrator. **Personal:** Born Mar 19, 1939, Memphis, TN; divorced; children: Patrice & Alan. **Educ:** Chicago Teachers Col, BEd, 1960; DePaul Univ, MEd, 1965. **Career:** Chicago, teacher, 1960; Tesla Sch, prin, 1966; Headstart, prin, 1966-67;US Dept Jutice, Midwest educ, consult, 1967; Parkside Sch, prin, 1971;HEW Off Educ, non fed pnlst, 1974-75; Parker HS, prin, 1975; Sullivan High Sch, prin; Calumet & Manley high Schs, prin; Carver Elem Sch, prin; McGaw Grad Sch, adj prof educ; Nat Col Educ, instr; Univ Ill, asst prof; Paideia Inst Hyde Pk, dir, pres, currently. **Orgs:** Kappa Alpha Psi Frat; Nat Col Educ Past Vols Side Community Comt; Beatrice Caffrey Youth Serv; Betty Boys Found; Marillac Comn House. **Honors/Awds:** Outstanding Principal in District Two; Outstanding Secondary Principal in Chicago, Citizens Schools Committee; Outstanding Principal in Chicago, Whitman Foundation, 1992; Those Who Excel Award. **Business Phone:** (773)684-5118.

BRAZILE, DONNA L.
Political consultant, educator. **Personal:** Born Dec 15, 1959, New Orleans, LA; daughter of Jean and Lionel. **Educ:** La State Univ, BA, Psychol, 1981,. **Career:** Educator,author, syndicated columnist, Pol Strategist; US House Rep, del, Eleanor Holmes Norton, chief of staff, pres secy, 1991-2000; Univ MD-Col Park,guest lectr, 1996-99; Al Gore Pres Campaign, political dir, Dep Campaign,mgr, 1999-2000; Gore 2000, campaign Mgr; Harvard Univ, Inst Polit, fel,2001, fel; 2005 Senator Winona Lippman; Rutgers Univ Ctr Am Women Polit; Georgetown Univ, adj prof, currently; Brazile Assocs LLC, consult,currently, founder & managing dir, currently; Georgetown Univ, Women's Studies Prog, lectr. **Orgs:** Pres, Life Ins; Dem Nat Comt, mem-at-large; brd dirs, La Recovery Authority; chair, Dem Natl Comt's Voting Rights Inst; brd dir, Future PAC. **Honors/Awds:** Congressional Black Caucus Foundation's Award; Minority Woman of Excellence Award, Wash Univ Natl Assn Advan Colored People; Doctorate Humane Letters, 2005. **Special Achievements:** Radio One, "A View From the Hill," past host, producer; "Roll Call,"columnist; "Ms." magazine, contributing writer; CNN frequent guest commentator; ABC "This Week with George Stephanopoulos", frequent guest commentator; HBO's "K Street," guest appearance; Showtime's "American Candidate," premier guest appearance; author, Cooking with Grease; Stirring the Pots in American Politics, Simon & Schuster, 2004; Washingtonian magazine's 100 Most Powerful Women in Washington, DC; first African-American to direct a major presidential campaign. **Home Addr:** PO Box 15369, Washington, DC 20003. **Business Addr:** Founder, Managing Director, Brazile & Associates LLC, 1001 G St NW Suite 500E, PO Box 15369, Washington, DC 20003, **Business Phone:** (202)628-8081.

BRAZLEY, MICHAEL DUWAIN
Chief executive officer, architect, educator. **Personal:** Born Apr 6, 1951, Louisville, KY; son of William and Gwendolyn; married Vallejo Miller, Apr 24, 1982; children: Erin & Katelyn. **Educ:** Univ Kentucky, archit, attended 1973; Howard Univ, BA, archit, 1978; Univ Louisville, Sch Urban & Pub Affairs, PhD, urban infrastructure & environ anal, 2002. **Career:** Fed Railroad Admin, Dept Transp, MOM - PROVIDENCE, RI, project mgr, 1979; City Louisville, streetscape designer; Kentucky Air Nat Guard Airplane Hangar, architect; Eastern High Sch, renovator; Louisville & Jefferson County Metropolitan Sewer Dist, storm water drainage master plan implementation; Standiford Field Airport, Air Nat Guard civil engr, drainage, roadway & utility design; First Baptist Church, renovator; Mt Olive Missionary Baptist Church, designer; Greater Good Hope Baptist Church, designer; Southern Ill Univ, asst prof archit & interior design, 2003-; Brazley & Brazley Inc, pres & chief exec officer; Michael D Brazley & Assoc PLLC, pres, 1987-2001; Ctr for Sustainable Urban Neighborhoods Urban & Pub Affairs, grad res asst, 1996-2002. **Orgs:** Am Inst Archit; Kentucky Soc Archit; Construct Specif Inst; Urban Land Inst; Am Planning Asn; Kentuckiana Minority Supplier Devel Coun; Louisville Third Century; bd mem, Kentucky African Am Mus Coun; Kentuckiana Regional Planning & Devel Agency, mobility task force; YMCA; Louisville's Urban League; Nat Asn Advan Colored People; adv bd, Univ Louisville, Black Engrs & Technicians Asn; Howard Univ Alumni Asn; bd dirs, Wesley Community House. **Honors/Awds:** KMSDC Med Awards, Prof Service Firm

of the Year, 1992; Emerging Minority Enterprise Award, Louisville/Jefferson Co Office for Econ Devel, Minority Bus Devel, 1992; Minority Service Firm Year, Louisville Minority Bus Devel Ctr, 1992. **Business Phone:** (618)453-3734.

BRAZZELL, DR. JOHNETTA CROSS
College administrator, chancellor (education). **Educ:** Spelman Col, BA; Univ Chicago, MA; Univ Mich, PhD. **Career:** Spelman Col, fac; Univ Ariz, fac; Oakland Univ, fac; Univ Ark, vicechancellor stud affairs & adj assoc prof higher educ, currently. **Business Addr:** Vice Chancellor of Student Affairs, Adjunct Associate Professor of Higher Education, University of Arkansas, 325 Admin Bldg, Fayetteville, AR 72701, **Business Phone:** (479)575-5007.

BREAUX, TIMOTHY
Basketball player. **Personal:** Born Sep 19, 1970, Baton Rouge, LA. **Educ:** Univ Wyo. **Career:** Continental Basketball Asn, Sioux Falls Sky force; Nat Football League, Europe; Houston Rockets, 1994-95; Vancouver Grizzlies, 1996-97; Milwaukee Bucks, forward, 1997-98; Seattle Supersonics, 2000; Brand Hagen, Ger, 2000-01; Yakima Sun Kings, forward, 2003-05. *

BRECKENRIDGE, FRANKLIN E., SR.
Lawyer. **Personal:** Married Cora Smith, Jun 13, 1964; children: Lejene, Franklin Jr, Emma Estel. **Educ:** Ind Univ, BS, 1963, JD, 1968; Mennonite Bibl Sem, MDiv, 1999. **Career:** Lawyer (retired); Kokomo-Ctr Twp Consol Sch, teacher, 1963-65; Indianapolis Pre- Sch Inc, teacher, 1965-66; Ind Dept Revenue, admin supr corp income tax, 1966-68; pvt pract, 1968-73; Bayer corp, asst secy, assoc coun, 1973-96; St James AME Church, pastor, currently. **Orgs:** Elkhart City Bar Asn; Indiana Bar Asn, Am Bar Asn; Alpha Phi Alpha Social Fraternity; Phi Delta Phi Legal Fraternity; Nat Asn Advan Colored People; pres, Ind State Conf Brs Nat Asn Advan Colored People, 1978-00; Nat Bar Asn; Dem Precinct Com for Eklhart Co 1975. **Honors/Awds:** Numerous NAACP Awards. **Home Addr:** 1219 Briarwood Dr, Elkhart, IN 46514. *

BREDA, MALCOLM J
Educator. **Personal:** Born Aug 14, 1934, Alexandria, LA. **Educ:** Xavier Univ La, BS, 1956; Univ Ind, MMEd, 1962; Univ Southern Miss, PhD, 1975. **Career:** NO Archdiocesan Music Prog, lectr & cons; Ala A&M Univ, instr, asst prof, 1956-64; Boys Town NE, organist, pianist-in-residence, 1964-67; St John Preparatory Sch NO La, dir choral activities, 1967-73; Xavier Univ La, Dept Music, prof, currently. **Orgs:** Alpha Kappa Mu; Phi Mu Alpha, Sinfonia; Music Educrs Nat Conf; Nat Asn Sch Music. **Honors/Awds:** Sister M Cornelia Jubilee Award, 1952; Mother Agatha Ryan Award, 1956; ISSP Summer Fel, Harvard Univ, 1968; Nat Fel, 1973-75. **Military Serv:** AUS, sp-4, 1956-58. **Home Addr:** 5707 Prince Lane, New Orleans, LA 70126-1229, **Home Phone:** (504)246-3480. **Business Addr:** Professor, Xavier University, Department of Music, 1 Drexel Dr, New Orleans, LA 70125-1056, **Business Phone:** (504)486-7411.

BREEDING, CARL L.
Educator, government official. **Personal:** Born Aug 30, 1932, Indianapolis, IN; son of Otto E and Derotha Helen; divorced; children: Loveeta Louise Smith, Tara Lynne Mobley, Andre Lynn & Chad Lamont. **Educ:** Indianapolis Univ, BA, 1955; Mich State Univ, MA, 1970. **Career:** Jackson Mich Pub Sch, algebra teacher, 1960-88; City Jackson, vice mayor, 1999-01; Summer Youth Opportunities Prog, coord, 1971-72, 1974; Jackson City Coun, coun mem, 2006-. **Orgs:** Pres & vpres, Mich State Conf, Nat Asn Adv Colored People, 1969-70, 1971-; chmn, Region II Comn Action Agency, 1978; natl bd dir, Nat Asn Adv Colored People, 1983-96, 1998-; chmn, Jackson County Friend Ct Citizen Adv Comn,1997; Jackson Mich City Coun, 1997; adminr, Nat Asn Adv Colored People, 2004; Jackson Educ Asn Legis Comn; elected mem, Rep Assembly; Mich Educ Asn; Nat Educ Asn; mem, Jackson Br Exec Comn; bd dir, vice chmn, Jackson-Hillsdale Area EOC; mem exec comt, Summer Youth Opportunities Adv Coun; Mich Dem Black Caucus; bd mem, Jackson County Legal Aid Soc; Jackson Jaycees; Jackson Human Rels Comn; adv comt mem, Jackson Citizens Sch Bd; serv syst mem, Local Bd No 39 & McCulloch Sch PTA. **Honors/Awds:** Outstanding Young Educr, 1965; Resolution Tribute Mich Legis; Outstanding Nat Asn Adv Colored People State Conf Pres, 1989. **Special Achievements:** Named one of the Most Influential Citizens Jackson Century, Jackson Citizen Patriot Newspaper, 2000. **Military Serv:** AUS, 1956-57. **Home Addr:** 1124 S Milwaukee St, Jackson, MI 49203. **Business Addr:** Council Member, Jackson City Council, 161 W Mich Ave, Jackson, MI 49201-1324.*

BREMBY, RODERICK LEMAR
Secretary (Government), government official. **Personal:** Born Feb 4, 1960, Eufaula, AL; son of Johnny B and Margaret J Robinson-Johnson; married April Lynne Harris, Jun 19, 1982; children: Rachel & Arielle. **Educ:** Univ Kans, Lawrence KS, BA, 1982, MPA, 1984. **Career:** City Fort Worth, Fort Worth TX, mgt intern, 1983-84, admin analyst I, 1984-85, admin analyst II, 1985, admin analyst III, 1985-86, asst city mgr, 1986-90; City Lawrence, Lawrence, KS, asst city mgr, 1990-; Kans Depart of Health & Environ, secy, currently. **Orgs:** Assoc mem, Int City Mgt Asn, 1983-; Pi Sigma Alpha, 1984; pres, Urban Mgt Asn N Tex, 1986; City Fort Worth Juneteenth Planning Comn, 1986-; City Forth Worth MLK Planning Comn, 1986-; secy, Nat Forum Black Pub Admin, N Tex Chap, 1986-89, pres, 1989-; Leadership Fort Worth, 1987-; Forum Fort Worth, 1988-90; vpres, NFBPA Coun Pres, 1990-. **Honors/Awds:** Outstanding Young Man of Am, YMCA, 1983 & 1986; R Scott Brooks Memorial Award, Univ Kans, 1984. **Special Achievements:** Author, "Voice Processing Applications in the City of Fort Worth", Town & City Mag, 1988. **Business Addr:** Secretary, Kansas Department of Health & Environment, 1000 SW Jackson Suite 540, Topeka, KS 66612-1368, **Business Phone:** (785)296-0461.

BREMER, CHARLES E.
Educator, administrator. **Personal:** Born Sep 12, 1941, New Orleans, LA; married Jocelyn. **Educ:** Ohio Univ BS govt & hist, 1965; Kent State Univ, Certi voc guid & counr, 1965; Southern Ill & Rutgers Univ, grad labor internship, 1978. **Career:** Cleveland Pub Sch, teacher, 1965; OH State Dept Labor, voc guid coun, 1966; RTP Inc-Manpower Training & Develop, dept exec dir, 1968-74; Southern Ill Univ, teacher & counr, 1967; Contini & Riffs Retails Bus,pres, 1974-78; A Philip Randolph Educ Fund & YEP, nat dr, 1978-. **Orgs:** Bd mediation Inst Mediation & Conflict Resolution, 1971-; chmn, scholarcom WC Handy Scholar Club, 1975-; bd finance Workers Defense League, 1979-. **Honors/Awds:** Clg scholar, OH Univ, 1960-65; Meritorious Awrd, Cleveland Br RTP Inc, 1974; Serv Awrd, Minority Bus Ent Ctr Anchorage, AK, 1979. **Business Addr:** Assistant Director, Social Act Deparment, 1126 16th St NW, Washington, DC 20036.*

BRENT, CHARLES TYRONE
Lawyer. **Personal:** Born Jul 24, 1961, Savannah, GA; son of Johnny and Bernice Huff; married LaSean Z Brant, Nov 20, 1999. **Educ:** Morehouse Col, BA, 1984; Ga Inst Technol, BS, 1984; Mercer Univ, JD, 1990. **Career:** DC Pub Defender Off, intern, 1990-92; City Atlanta Pub Defendr Off, defender & investr, 1992-95; Law Off Charles Brant, pvt pract, 1995-; Ellenberg, Ogier & Rothschild, lawyer, currently. **Orgs:** Wash, DC Bar Asn, 1994-; Ga Bar Asn, 1994-. **Special Achievements:** 100 Black Men of Atlanta, 2001-. **Military Serv:** Navy Lt Comdr, Active Dep, 1984-86, Active Res, 1986-. **Business Addr:** Attorney, Ellenberg, Ogier & Rothschild, 170 Mitchell St SW, Atlanta, GA 30303-3424, **Business Phone:** (404)522-5900.

BREVARD, ANTHONY
Executive, banker. **Career:** Bank Am, banker, 1990; NC Nat Bank; BB & T Bank, VPres Emerging Markets; Prof African Am Market, nat develop officer. **Business Addr:** National Development Officer, Professional African American Market, Development Group - Nations Bank, 1901 Main St, SC3 240 01 02, Columbia, SC 29201, **Business Phone:** (803)255-7453.

BREWER, DR. ARTHELIA J
Executive. **Personal:** Born in South Carolina. **Educ:** Fisk Univ, BA; Vanderbilt Univ, MA; Meharry Med Col, MD, MSPH. **Career:** Gen Motors Corp, plant med dir, assoc div med dir; Gen Dynamics Land Systs, div med dir; Health Servs Int PC, pres, med dir, 1995-.

BREWER, GREGORY ALAN
Research scientist. **Personal:** Born Feb 3, 1968, Denver, CO; son of Riley and Aileen. **Educ:** Morehouse Col, BS, physics, 1990; Univ Calif, Los Angeles, 1990-. **Career:** Univ Calif, Los Angeles, GAAD Project 88 fel, 1990, researcher, 1991-. **Orgs:** NSBE, 1986-; IEEE, 1993-; Phi Beta Kappa, 1990-. **Home Addr:** 2568 Birch St, Denver, CO 80207-3133, **Home Phone:** (303)996-0044. **Business Addr:** Researcher, University Of California, Los Angeles, 405 Hilgard Ave, Los Angeles, CA 90024, **Business Phone:** (310)206-2573.

BREWER, JIM (JAMES TURNER BREWER)
Basketball player, basketball coach. **Personal:** Born Dec 3, 1951, Maywood, IL; married Patsy; children: Jim & Phera. **Educ:** Univ Minn, attended 1973. **Career:** Basketball player (retired), basketball coach: Cleveland Cavaliers, prof basketball player, 1974-79; Detroit Pistons, 1979; Portland Trail Blazers, 1980; Los Angeles Lakers, 1981-82; Cant, Italy, prof basketball player; Northwestern Univ, asst coach & recruit; Minn Timber wolves, recruit,dir player personnel role, asst coach, asst gen mgr; Los Angeles Clippers, lead asst coach, 1994-99; Orlando Magic, scout, 1999-00; Lenny Wilkens staff, asst coach, 2000-02; Boston Celtics, asst coach, 2004-06. **Special Achievements:** Played in the 1972 Olympics. *

BREWER, MOSES
Executive. **Personal:** Born Mar 12, 1947; married. **Educ:** Northeastern Jr Col, Sterling, CO, 1967; Univ Denver, BA, 1971, MA, 1975. **Career:** Baseball Prog Denver Boys, dir, 1969; St Anne's Elem Sch, teacher, 1970; City Auditors Off, coordr microfilm, 1969-71; Univ Denver, coordr recreational activities, 1971-72; Univ Denver, asst dean stud life, 1972-73; Denver Univ, univ consult at large, 1973-; Denver Pub Sch, consult, 1974-75; Adolph Coors Co, asst nat prog mgr, currently. **Orgs:** All-Regional 9 Basketball Team, 1966-67; Nat Asn Stud Personnel Adminr; Nat Speech Commun Asn; Pi Kappa Alpha Fraternity; United Negro Col Fund; Black Caucus; Black Alumni Asn Univ Denver; Western Regional Ombudsman Asn; Nat Scholarship Serv & Funds Negro Students. **Honors/Awds:** Outstanding Athlete Award, 1968; Outstanding Faculty Adminr Award, 1974; Outstanding Personality Award. **Business Addr:** Assistant National Program Manager, Adolph Coors Corporation, 311 10th St Suite NH420, PO Box 4030, Golden, CO 80401, **Business Phone:** (303)279-6565.

BREWER, DR. ROSE MARIE
Educator, sociologist. **Personal:** Born Oct 30, 1947, Tulsa, OK; daughter of Wilson and Cloviece; married Walter Griffin; children: Sundiata Brewer Griffin. **Educ:** Northeastern St Col, BA, 1969; Ind Univ, MA, 1971, PhD, 1976; Univ Chicago, PhD, 1983. **Career:** Ford Found fel, 1972-73; NIMH res fel, 1981-83; Rice Univ, vis lectr, 1976; Univ TX, asst prof, 1977-80, 1983-86; Univ Chicago, fel, 1981-83; Wiepking Distinguished vis prof, Miami Univ Ohio, 1996; Univ MN, asst prof; Univ Minn, Abrigail Quigley McCarty Ctr Women & Women's Studies, Col St Catherine, dir under grad studies, 1998-2001, Dept Afro-American & African Studies, interim chair, 1999-2001, assoc prof, dir, prof, currently; Souls J, contributing ed. **Orgs:** Bd dirs, vpres, Big Brothers & Big Sisters Austin, 1984-; bd dirs, vpres, Soc Study Social Problems, 1985-88; coun mem, Sect Racial & Ethnic Minorities, 1985-88; comt mem, Am Sociological Soc, 1986-87; chair, Comt Status Racial & Ethnic Minorities Asn, 1986-87; co-founder & core group mem, Freire Ctr, Minneapolis; bd dir, Midwest Sociol Soc, 1990-92; Comt Freedom Teaching & Res, ASA; Afro-Am & African Studies, chair, 1992-; CIC Leadership Fel, 1993-94; exec bd mem, Oakland Pvt Industry Coun, 1994; exec bd mem, Contra Costa Pvt Industrial Coun, 1995-; chair, Rhonda Williams Award Comt, Int Asn Feminist Economists. **Honors/Awds:** Bush Sabbitacal Award, Univ Minnesota, 1990-91; Multicultural Lectureship Award, Univ N Tex, 1990; Ctr Study Women & Soc Award, Univ Oregon, 1990; Morse Amoco/Alumni Teaching Award, Univ Minn, 1993. **Special Achievements:** Publications: A Special Issue on Gender, Color, Class, and Caste, 2002; Black Radical Theory and Practice: Gender, Race, and Class, 2003; Family Structure, Poverty & Race in United States, 2003; The Color Of Wealth, 2006. **Business Addr:** Professor, University of Minnesota, Department of Afro-American & African Studies, 267 19th Ave S, 810 Soc Sci Bldg, Minneapolis, MN 55455, **Business Phone:** (612)624-9305.

BREWER, WEBSTER L.
Judge. **Personal:** Born May 11, 1935, Clarksville, TN; son of Marvin and Margie Brodie; married Patricia Freeman; children: Elaine, Pamela, Webster Jr. **Educ:** Ind Univ, BS, 1957; Ind Univ Sch Law, JD. **Career:** Judge (retired); Marion County Welfare Dept, caseworker, 1957-58; Marion County Juv Ct, probation officer, 1958-60; US Bur Prisons, parole officer, 1960-64; United Dist Court Southern Dist Ind, probation officer, 1964-68; Indianapolis Lawyers Comn, exec dir, 1968-70; Ind Univ Sch of Law, seminar instr, 1970; Brewer Budnick & Sosin, lawyer pvt pract, 1970-75; Marion County Super Ct no 2, judge. **Orgs:** Am Bar Asn; Indianapolis Bar Asn; Ind St Bar Asn; Nat Bar Asn; nat officer, Phi Alpha Delta Legal Frat; Group Leader, Christamore Settlement House, 1958-60; Juv Ct Adv Comn, 1960-64; chmn bd, NAACP, 1963-64; chmn, Labor & Indust Comn, Indianapolis Chap, NAACP, 1964-66; bd mem, Forward Inc, 1968-70; bd mem, Indianapolis Legal Serv Orgn, 1970-75; bd mem, trustees & chmn, Ways & Means Comt, Bethel AME Church, 1973-; bd mem, Marion County Child Guidance Clin, 1973-; bd mem, Marion County Youth & Serv Bur, 1974-76; bd mem, Indianapolis Family Serv Agency, 1977-; spec proj dir, Ind Judicial Study Ctr; Kappa Alphsi Frat; Trinity Lodge 18; F&AM, PHA; Sigma Pi Phi Frat, 1971. **Business Addr:** Indianapolis, IN 46204.*

BREWINGTON, DONALD EUGENE
Clergy. **Personal:** Born Aug 29, 1954, San Antonio, TX; son of James B Bradley and Margie M. **Educ:** Sam Houston State Univ, BA, educ, 1977; Interdenominational Theol Ctr, MDiv, 1986. **Career:** Greater Corinth Baptist Church, minister youth/outreach, 1986-89; Ernest T Dixon United Methodist Church, pastor, 1989-92; Huston-Tillotson Col, col chaplain, campus minister, 1992-. **Orgs:** Tex Coun Churches, 1992-; Wesley Found Partnership Ministries, 1992-; bd higher educ, United Church Christ, 1992-; Southwest Tex Conf, 1992-; Church World Serv, Walk Hunger, 1992-; sponsor, Huston-Tillotson Col Gospel Choir, 1992-; Huston-Tillotson Col Concert Choir, 1992-. **Business Addr:** Campus Minister, Huston-Tillotson College, 900 Chicon St, Austin, TX 78702, **Business Phone:** (512)505-3054.*

BREWINGTON, RUDOLPH W
Journalist, association executive. **Personal:** Born Nov 2, 1946, New York, NY. **Educ:** Federal City Col, MA, cum laude, 1973. **Career:** WUST Radio, news reporter, 1969-70; Washington, DC, bus operator, 1969; WOOK Radio, news dir, 1970-71; WWDC Radio, news reporter, ed, 1971-75; WRC/NBC Radio News Wash DC, reporter, 1975-; Nat Syndctd TV Prog "America's Black Forum", res dir/pnlst 1978-79; Nat Syndctd Radio Prog "The Black Agenda Reprts", pres/exec prod, 1979-80; Asso Prsnl Inc, Washington DC, dir pub rels 1980; USNR, LIFELines Serv

Network, pub affairs officer & content mgr, currently. **Honors/Awds:** Recipient Robt F Kennedy Journalism Award Citation for "Diagnosis, Desperate, A Report on Minority Hlth Care" 1973; APHA Ray Bruner Sci Writing Fel, 1974. **Military Serv:** USMC corpl e-4, 1964-68. **Business Addr:** Public Affairs Officer, LIFE-Lines Services Network, DoD Information Technol Ctr, Washington, DC 20374-5046, **Business Phone:** (202)433-3865.

BREWINGTON, THOMAS E., JR.
Ophthalmologist. **Personal:** Born Oct 12, 1943, Dunn, NC; married Janice; children: Kathryne, Mitchelle, Tracy, Brea. **Educ:** Morehouse Col, BS, 1965; Meharry Med Col, MD, 1969; Homer G Phillips Hosp, intern, 1970, resident, 1973. **Career:** Eye, Ear, Nose & Throat Clinic, AUS, chief, 1973-75; Pvt Practice, opthalmologist, 1976-; Moses Cone Health Syst, med staff, currently. **Orgs:** Dipl, Am Bd Ophthal; fel, Am Acad Ophthal; Nat Med Asn; NC State Med Soc; Guilford Co Med Soc; Greensboro Acad Med; Greensboro Med Soc; Old N State Med Soc Exec bd Guilford Co Easter Seal Soc; Phi Beta Sigma Fraternity. **Military Serv:** AUS, maj 1973-75; Recipient Commendation Medal. **Business Addr:** Ophthalmologist, Moses Cone Health System, 807 Summit Ave, Greensboro, NC 27405, **Business Phone:** (336)272-5628.*

BREWSTER, LUTHER GEORGE
Executive, airline executive. **Personal:** Born Dec 16, 1942, Manhattan, NY; son of Alethia Samuels and Donald F; married Theresa Maria Smart, May 8, 1965; children: Maria, Luther Jr & Renee. **Educ:** Bronx Community Col, Bronx, NY, 1965-72; Col Aeronaut, Queens, NY, AAS, 1974; Lehman Col, Bronx, NY, 1980-87; N Cent Col, Naperville, Ill, 1988-; Olivet Nazarene Univ, Kankakee, Ill, BS, appl sci & mgt, 1995. **Career:** Pratt & Whitney Aircraft, Hartford, Conn, engine mechanic, 1964; Pan American, New York, NY, aircraft & engine mechanic, 1965-77; Seaboard World Airlines, Frankfurt, W Ger, maintenance rep, 1977; Am Airlines, Chicago, Ill, div mgr aircraft maintenance, 1977-95, managing dir, eastern div aircraft maintenance, 1995-2005; Air Jamaica Ltd, sr vpres maintenance & eng, 2005-. **Orgs:** Inst Cert Eng Tech; Aviation Maintenance Found; Am Mgt Asn; bd dirs, Mt Sinai Hosp. **Honors/Awds:** Honored by official resolution of Boston City Council, 1986; Certificate of Merit, Youth Motivation Prog, CACI, 1987-88. **Military Serv:** USAF, tech sgt, 1960-64; Good Conduct Medal, Expeditionary Medal, Outstanding Unit Award. **Business Addr:** Senior Vice President Maintenance and Engineering, Air Jamaica Ltd, 8300 NW 33rd St Suite 440, Miami, FL 33122, **Business Phone:** (305)670-3222.

BREWTON, DR. BUTLER E.
Educator, poet. **Personal:** Born Feb 7, 1935, Spartanburg, SC; son of J M Brewton and WO Brewton; married Blanca; children: Seneca, Monica & Catrina. **Educ:** Benedict Col, BA, 1956; Montclair State, MA, 1970; Rutgers Univ, PhD,1978. **Career:** SC State Col, NDEA fel, 1965; Montclair State Col, assoc prof eng, 1970, prof emer, 1996-; McGraw Hill Int Press, consult, 1972; Mod Century Encyclopedia, ed; Furman Univ, adj prof eng, currently; Books: South & Border States; Richard Wrights Thematic Treatment of Women; Poems: Tramp; Lady of the Evening; 5PM; Discovered; Pattern; Barren; Southbound; Idol; Yesterday Hangs; The Custodial Hour; Democracy; The Kiss; For A Reprieve; Peach Orchard; Full Measure; At the General Store; We Children, 1992; Grandpa's, 1992; Rafters, 1992; Indian Summer, 1997; Articles: "A Diploma Must Mean What It's Supposed to Mean," New York Times, 1986. **Orgs:** Poet-in-residence, NJ State Coun Arts, 1970-76; speaker, Nat Coun Teacher Educ, Kans City, 1978. **Honors/Awds:** First prize winner, Essence Mag poetry contest, 1993. **Special Achievements:** Has more than seventy-five poetry publications in literary journals and magazines, including Pulpsmith, Lips, Footwork, Midway Review, Nimrod & Essence. **Military Serv:** USAF, A/2. **Business Addr:** Adjunct Professor, Furman University, English Department, Furman Hall 100, Greenville, SC 29609, **Business Phone:** (864)294-2066.

BRICE, BARBARA
Educator. **Educ:** St Phillips Sch Nursing, Med Col VA, 1944; Clark Col, BS, 1975; Emory Univ, Cert, 1975; Central MI Univ, MA, 1978; GA State Univ, PhD, 1992. **Career:** Coligny Day Care Ctr, dir, 1966; St Joseph Hosp, staff nurse intensive care, 1968-72; Atlanta Job Corp, staff nurse & dir nursing serv, 1972-74; West End Med Ctr, dir med records & admiss, 1974-81; Clark Col, instr, 1977-81; Kean Col, assoc prof, 1981-83; Clark Col, asst prof, 1983-88; Clark Atlanta Univ, assoc prof, 1988, adj fac, currently. **Orgs:** Am & GA Information Mgt Asn, 1975-; GA Soc Allied Health Profs, 1977-80, 1990-93; Nat Sci Fac Atlanta Univ Ctr, 1978-79;Minority Women Sci, 1980-81; Kappa Delta Pi, Omicron Gamma Chapt Honor Soc Educ, 1988-; African Am Women Against Domestic Violence, 1989-01; Delta Sigma Theta Sorority Inc, 1992-; The Atlanta Proj Wa Cluster, 1992-; Nat Insts Health, NIDCD, CAU Student & Mentor, 1995-00; GA Nonpublic Post Sec Comn Accreditation Team, 1997; St John Catholic Church Hospitality Comt, 1999-01, AUC Catholic Ctr Adv Comt, 1997-01; Atlanta Area Tech Sch LPN, Adv Bd, 2000-02; Fulton County Juvenile Court Citizen Review Panel, 2000-. **Honors/Awds:** Teacher of the Year, Clark Col Allied Health, 1985; Health First FTD, Grand $222000, 1995-96. **Business Addr:** Associate Professor, Clark Atlanta University, Department Allied Health, Vivian Wilson Henderson Ctr Rm 121 VW, 223 James P Brawley Dr SW, Atlanta, GA 30314, **Business Phone:** (404)880-8000.*

BRICE, PERCY A., JR.
Musician, drummer. **Personal:** Born Mar 25, 1923, New York, NY; married Pearl Minott. **Educ:** Music Sch; Kingsborough Community Col, attended 1986. **Career:** Luis Russell Orchestra, 1944; Benny Carter Orchestra, 1945-46; Mercer Ellington, 1947; Eddie Vinson, 1947-51; Tiny Grimes Show Group, 1951-52; Billy Taylor Trio, 1954-56; George Shearing Quintet, 1956-58; Harry Belafonte Troupe, 1961-68; New Sound, leader; Albums: The Midnight Spec; The Many Moods Of Belafonte; Ballads, Blues & Boasters, 1964; An Evening With Belafonte/Mouskouri; An Evening With Belafonte/Makeba; Belafonte On Campus; Belafonte At The Greek Theatre; Musicals: Bubblin' Brown Sugar; Eubie; Ain't Misbehavin'; Ghost Cafe. **Orgs:** Masonic Order, 1949-; Famous Friendly 50 Club. **Honors/Awds:** Harlem District champion in table tennis; Award, The Grater Jamaica Develop Corp, 2000-03; African-Am Night Jazz Legends, Nassau Co, 2001. **Special Achievements:** Played at the Savoy with Tab Smith & Paul Williams. *

BRIDGEFORTH, ARTHUR MAC, JR.
Journalist. **Personal:** Born Sep 18, 1965, Pittsburgh, PA; son of Arthur Mac Bridgeforth Sr and Gwendolyn Holland. **Educ:** Mich State Univ, East Lansing, BA, jour, 1988. **Career:** Crain's Detroit Bus, Detroit, MI, ed asst, 1988-89; The Ann Arbor News, Ann Arbor, MI, bus reporter, 1989-; Wayne State Univ, media contact, currently. **Orgs:** Detroit Chapter, Nat Asn Black Journalists, 1988-; Nat Asn Black Journalist, 1989-; Mich State Univ Alumni Asn, 1988-. **Home Addr:** 19511 Greenfield Suite 3, Detroit, MI 48235, **Home Phone:** (313)837-8432. **Business Addr:** Media Contact, Wayne State University, 5700 Cass Ave 3100 Acad Admin Bldg, Detroit, MI 48202, **Business Phone:** (313)577-2150.

BRIDGEMAN, DEXTER ADRIAN
Executive. **Personal:** Born Jan 5, 1961, Grenada, West Indies; son of Donald E and Phylis Alexander; divorced. **Educ:** Hofstra Univ, BS, polit sci, 1984; State Univ New York, Stonybrook, 1984-85. **Career:** Ivac Corp, sales exec; GE Medical Syst, sales exec; Motorala sales exec; Velobind Inc, sales exec; Allnet Communications, sales exec; Mentor Mag, pres; Diversified Communications Group Inc, pres, currently. **Orgs:** Bd mem, Opportunities Industrialization Ctrs Am; creative adv coun, Nat Youth Develop Prog; adv bd, Nat Inner City Leadership Coun; adv bd, YACT; Alpha Phi Alpha Frat Inc; Concerned Black Men Am; Outstanding Young Men Am, 1996; Urban Bding Sch Fund; Nat Asn Black Minority Consultants. **Honors/Awds:** 40 UNDER 40 Achievement Award, The Network Journal, 2000. **Home Phone:** (917)507-8124. **Business Addr:** President, Chief Executive Officer, Diversified Communications Group Inc, 416 W 146th St Suite 2, Ardsley, NY 10031, **Business Phone:** (917)507-8124.

BRIDGEMAN, DONALD EARL
Banker, manager, government official. **Personal:** Born Mar 14, 1939, Grenville, Grenada; son of Julien Anthony and Madonna Theresa Hall; married Dr Rosemary Malcolm; children: Winston, Selwyn, Joie, Edelyne. **Educ:** Erdiston Teachers Col, AA Educ, 1960; Howard Univ, BSc, 1968; Northwestern Univ, Cert Mortage Banker, 1973; Southeastern Univ, MBPA, 1976. **Career:** Found for Coop Housing, dir Housing Spec Inst, 1969-72; Howard Univ, dir Ctr Housing & Real Estate, 1975-77; US Dept Housing & Urban Develop, employee develop spec, 1977-84; Prince George's County, dep personnel officer, 1984-91; SWAADA Imports, pres, 1988-, The MBA Group, pres, 1991-; Prince George's County, Off Human Resources, dir, 2004-. **Orgs:** United Way Health & Welfare Coun WA DC, 1965-76; co-founder, CHANGE Fed Credit Union Wash DC; co-founder, Nat Asn Housing Specialists, 1971; conf dir, Joint Annual Minority Housing Conf, 1974-80; consult, Winston-Salem State Univ, Southern Univ, Tex Southern Univ, Temple Univ, develop housing mgt curricula, 1975-77; pres, Housing Specialists Inst, 1977-81 & 1993-; pres, Local Govt Personnel Asn Baltimore-Wash Metro Area, 1986-91; pres, Caribbean Coun Prince George's County, 1989-; vpres, Coun Caribbean Org, WA, DC, 1991-93; Nat Forum Black Pub Adminrs, 1990-; Southern Md Bus League, 1991-. **Honors/Awds:** Samuel E Sessions Award, Nat Asn Housing Specialists Inst, 1975; Realist of the Yr Award, Wash Real Estate Brokers Asn, 1976; Personnelist of the Yr, Intl Personnel Mgt Asn, Eastern Region, 1989; Intl Exchange Fellow, Eng's SOCPO, Intl Personnel Mgt Asn-US, 1987; Special Achievement Award, Local Govt Personnel Asn Baltimore-Wash, 1991. **Business Addr:** Director, Office Of Human Resources Management, Prince George's County, 1400 McCormick Dr Suite 361, Largo, MD 20774, **Business Phone:** (301)883-6344.*

BRIDGEMAN, JUNIOR (ULYSSES LEE JUNIOR BRIDGEMAN)
Basketball player, businessperson. **Personal:** Born Sep 17, 1953, East Chicago, IL; married Doris; children: Justin & Ryan. **Educ:** Univ Louisville, BS, psychol, 1975. **Career:** Basketball player (retired), businessperson; Milwaukee Bucks, 1976-84, 1987-88; Los Angeles Clippers, 1985-86; Bridgeman Foods Inc, ceo & pres, currently. **Orgs:** Alpha Phi Alpha. **Honors/Awds:** All-Am honors, Univ LA; Most Valuable Player, Mo Valley Conf; Holds the team's record for most games played. **Business Addr:** Chief Executive Officer, President, Bridgeman Foods Inc., 2025 W S Branch Blvd, Oak Creek, WI 53154, **Business Phone:** (414)302-5650.

BRIDGEMAN, ULYSSES LEE JUNIOR. **See BRIDGEMAN, JUNIOR.**

BRIDGEMAN-VEAL, JUDY
Executive. **Educ:** Gen Motors Inst, BS, elec eng; Ga Tech Univ, MS, elec eng & biomed eng. **Career:** Ford Motor Co, spokeswoman. **Business Addr:** Spokeswoman, Ford Motor Company, 1 American Rd, Dearborn, MI 48126, **Business Phone:** (313)322-3000.

BRIDGES, BILL (WILLIAM C BRIDGES)
Basketball player. **Personal:** Born Apr 4, 1939, Hobbs, NM. **Educ:** Univ Kans, Lawrence, KS, attended. **Career:** Basketball player (retired); St Louis Hawks, 1962-68; Atlanta Hawks, 1968-71; Philadelphia Phillies, 1972-73; Los Angeles Lakers, 1973-75; Golden State Warriors, 1975. **Honors/Awds:** NBA All-Star Game, 1967, 1968, 1970; NBA Championship, 1975.

BRIDGES, CHRISTOPHER BRIAN. **See LUDACRIS.**

BRIDGES, DR. JAMES WILSON
Physician. **Personal:** Born Feb 16, 1935, Valdosta, GA; son of Leslie Bridges and Ora Lee Bridges; married Earnestine Bryant; children: Sabrina, Lloyd & Mark. **Educ:** Central State Coll, BS, 1956; Meharry Medical Coll, MD, 1960; Hmr G Phillips Hospital, intern, 1961, chief resident, 1966; Univ Miami, resident, 1967. **Career:** Pvt pract, physician, currently; Univ Miami, clin asst prof; Cedars Lebanon Health Care Ctr, chief; Christian Hosp, chief. **Orgs:** Diplomate, Am Bd Obstet & Gynec, 1969; bd trustees, Christian Hosp, 1973-76; bd dir, Fla Div Am Cancer Soc, 1972-77, Fla Physicians Ins Rec, 1985, Fla Physicians Ins Co, Fla Political Action Comn; chmn, Fla Div United Cancer Task Force, 1975-77; Beta Beta Lambda Chap, Alpha Phi Alpha, NAACP, Comm Minority Affairs Univ Miami Sch Med; Fla Bd Med, 1996-97; pres-elect, Dade County Med Asn, 1997; pres, Dade County Med Asn, 1998-99. **Honors/Awds:** scholar, Fla State Med Col, 1959-60; Fel, Am Col Obstet & Gynec, 1970. **Military Serv:** AUS, medical corps capt, 1961-63. **Home Addr:** 8340 NE 2nd Ave Suite 222, Miami, FL 33150-2064, **Home Phone:** (305)758-9215.

BRIDGES, LEON
Architect, executive. **Personal:** Born Aug 18, 1932, Los Angeles, CA; son of James Alonzo and Agnes Zenobia Johnson; married Eloise Avonne Jones; children: Vanessa Joy, Elise Gay, Leon Jr, Elliott Reynolds. **Educ:** Univ Wash, BArch, 1959; Urban Syst, post grad studies; Loyola Col MD, MBA, 1984. **Career:** Intern asst city, planner, 1956; Leon Bridges Arch, owner, 1963-66; Bridges/Burke Arch & Planners, partner, 1966-72; Hampton Inst, vis prof, 1971, 1973, 1975; Prairie View A&M, vis prof, 1972; The Archit Res Collabor Inc, partner, 1976-; Leon Bridges Co, owner, 1972-87; Morgan State Univ, assoc prof, 1985-88; TLBC Incorporated, pres, 1989-; The Leon Bridges Chartered, prs, cur; Obsidian Group, cfo, partner, 2001-. **Orgs:** KAP, 1954; Exec Comm Planned Parenthood/World Pop, 1968-74; particip, Tuskegee Inst Comm Arch Design Charette, Endowment, 1971; Guild Relig Archit; panelist, Mental Health Ctr Design, AIA and NIMH; Nat Urban League; MD State Arts Coun 1980-; bd dir, Lutheran Hosp, 1980-; bd dir, MD MNY Contractors Asn, 1981; chmn, Morgan State Univ Urban Dev Comm, 1981; bd dir, Roland Park Place, 1981; bd adv, Univ Knoxville TN, 1981-; bd dir Sch Deaf, 1981; bd dirs, Am Inst Architects, 1984-86; pres, Nat Org Minority Architects, 1979-80. **Honors/Awds:** Honor Award, Am Soc Landscape Architects, 1980; Black Pages Award, 1981; Merit Award, Am Inst Architects, Wash DC; Design Excellence Award, Nat Org Minority Architects,1983; Design Excellence Award, Am Inst Architects, 1985; Design Excellence Award, NOMA,1985; Grand Conceptor Award, Am Consult Engrs, 1986; Baltimore City Coun Presidential Citation, 1995; Baltimore City Mayor's Citation, 1995; Md State Legis Off Citation, 1995; State Md Gov Citation, 1995; Nat Citation Design Excellence Seattle Urban Design, 1971; Richard Upjohn Fel, Am Inst Architects, 1990; Valued Honors Award, Fullwood Found, 1995, 1999; Whitney M Young Junior Award, Am Inst Architects, 1998; Man of the Year, Nat Asn Negro Bus & Prof Women's Clubs, 1978; Dr Lillie Carroll Jackson Award, Baltimore City Br, NCP, 1991; Victor Frenkil Achievement Award, 1973; Conf MNY Transp Off's Annual FDR's Award, 1984; NCP Baltimore City Branch Hall of Fame Parren J Mitchell Award, 2001; Harlow Fullwood, Jr Serv Above Self Award, 2002. **Special Achievements:** First Registered African American Architect in Maryland; Founder of the second African American-owned firm in Seattle. **Military Serv:** USY Corpl 1952-54. **Business Addr:** President, TLBC Inc, 429 N Eutaw St, Baltimore, MD 21201, **Business Phone:** (410)659-0200.*

BRIDGES, RUBY
Association executive, activist. **Personal:** Born Jan 1, 1954?, Mississippi. **Career:** Ruby Bridges Found Inc, founder, currently. **Honors/Awds:** Made an honorary US Marshall, 2000. **Special Achievements:** Subject of Norman Rockwell painting, The Problem We All Live With, 1964. **Business Addr:** Founder, Ruby Bridges Found Inc, PO Box 127, Winnetka, IL 60093.*

BRIDGES, SHEILA
Interior designer. **Personal:** Born Jul 7, 1954, Philadelphia, PA. **Educ:** Brown Univ, 1986; Parsons Sch Design. **Career:** Bloom-

ingdale's; Shelton, Mindel, & Assoc, interior designer; Rebby B Salzman Interiors, interior designer; Sheila Bridges Design Inc, pres, chief exec officer, chmn, 1994-; www.thenestmaker.com, publ & creative dir, currently. **Special Achievements:** Author: Furnishing Forward: A Practical Guide to Furnishing for a Lifetime, 2002; host, Sheila Bridges Designer Living on the Fine Living, Network; Named "Ams Best Interior Designer" by CNN & Time Mag. **Business Addr:** President, Chief Executive Officer, Sheila Bridges Design Inc, 1925 7th Ave 8M, New York, NY 10026, **Business Phone:** (212)678-6872.

BRIDGES, TODD ANTHONY
Actor, writer, movie producer. **Personal:** Born May 27, 1965, San Francisco, CA; son of James Sr and Betty Bridges; married Dori Smith, May 25, 1998; children: Spencer Todd. **Career:** TV series: "Fish", 1977; "Different Strokes", 1978-86; "Son of the Beach", 2001; cinematographer, A Devil Disguised, 1997; producer, dir, actor, Building Bridges, 1999; films: Flossin, 2001; Inhumanity, 2001; Dumb Luck, 2001; Pacino Is Missing, 2002; The Beach House, 2002; The Climb, 2002; Welcome to Am, 2002; Scream at the Sound of the Beep, 2002; Baby of the Family, 2002; Black Ball, 2003; May Day, 2003; Alien Express, 2005; "Everybody Hates Chris", 2009; TV Films: After Different Strokes: When the Laughter Stopped, 2000; The Darkling, 2000; Ghost Dog: A Detective Tail, 2003; Hollywood Horror, 2004; Treasure in tha Hood, 2005;I Got Five on It, 2005; Alien Express, 2005; The Damned, 2006; Last Call,2006; Death Row, 2007; Big Ball'n, 2007; Foster Babies, 2007; Frankie D, 2007; Darkroom, 2008; Hollywood Horror, 2009; See Dick Run, 2009; I Got Five on It Too, 2009. **Orgs:** Founder, Todd Bridges Youth Found, 1992-. **Special Achievements:** Ranked No 40 in VH1's list of the "100 Greatest Kid Stars". *

BRIDGEWATER, ALBERT LOUIS
Government official. **Personal:** Born Nov 22, 1941, Houston, TX; son of Albert and Rita Narcisse; married Juanita Edington (divorced); children: Ramesi & Akin. **Educ:** Univ Calif, BA, 1963; Columbia Univ, MA, 1967, PhD, 1972. **Career:** Government Offical (retired); Univ Calif, post-doctoral fel, 1970-73; Elem Particle Physics, asst prof officer, 1973-74; Nat Sci Found, staff asst, 1973-76, special asst, 1976-86, acting asst dir, 1983-85, deputy asst dir, 1981-86, sr staff assoc, 1986-2001; Minority-Serving Institution Forum, pres, exec dir, 2001; recipient of an NSF grant, 2003-04. **Orgs:** Am Geophysical Union; AAAS; adv bd, LBL/SSU/AGMFF Sci Consortium, 1986-88; Indian Soc Tech Educ. **Honors/Awds:** Order of Golden Bear; Nat Sci Found grant to conduct major research instrumentation proposal writing workshops for Tribal Cols & Universities. **Military Serv:** AUS T4, 1943-46; 3 oversears serv Bars; Am Campaign Medal; Asiatic Pac Cmpgn Medal; Bronze Star; Good Conduct Medal; WWII Victory Medal. **Home Addr:** 3705 S George Mason Dr, Falls Church, VA 22041, **Home Phone:** (703)845-3646.

BRIDGEWATER, DEE DEE. See GARRETT, DENISE EILEEN.

BRIDGEWATER, DR. HERBERT JEREMIAH, JR.
Radio host, educator, journalist. **Personal:** Born Jul 3, 1942, Atlanta, GA; son of Herbert Bridgewater (deceased) and Mary Sallie Clark Hughes. **Educ:** Clark Col, BA, bus admin, 1968; Atlanta Univ, attended 1968; Univ Ga, Inst Govt & Ctr Continuing Educ, 1978; Atlanta Area Tech Sch, cert, 1980; Fed Law Enforcement Training Ctr, 1980; Spelman Col Inst Continuing Educ, 1984. **Career:** Atlanta Pub Sch Syst, teacher, bus & eng community, 1964-67; Atlanta Housing Authority, relocation & family serv consult, 1967-70; Fed Trade Comn, consumer protection specialist & dir pub affairs, 1970-83; Bridgewaters Personnel Serv, owner, 1971-75; Confrontation, host, 1974-;Atlanta Area Tech Sch, teacher, 1978-; Bridging Gap, host, 1981-; Clark Col, assoc prof, 1983-; Delta Airlines Inc, customer sales & serv, 1984-;Atlanta Daily World Newspaper, Unsung Heroes, Facts, Consumers, columnist,currently. **Orgs:** Bd mem, Ga Chap, Epilepsy Found Am; bd mem, Mid-Atlanta Unit Am Cancer Soc; bd chmn, Atlanta Dance Theatre; task force, Just Us Theater; foundingmem, Int Asn African Heritage & Black Identity; Atlanta Jr Chamber Comt;Big Brothers Coun Atlanta; Nat Urban League; United Negro Col Fund; CityAtlanta Water & Sewer Appeals Bd; Martin Luther King Ctr Non-Violent Social Change; Martin Luther King Ecumenical Holiday Comt. **Honors/Awds:** Outstanding Atlanta, 1977; Meritorious Service Award, Ga Chap, Epilepsy Found Am, 1981, 1985; Outstanding Service Award, Am Red Cross, 1981;Outstanding Service, Atlanta Fed Exec Bd Minority Bus Opportunity Comn,1981; Distinguished & Dedicated Service Award, Greater Travelers Rest Baptist Church, Decatur, GA, 1981; Outstanding Community Service Award, SW Career Coun; Dr Herbert J Bridgewater Jr Day, Atlanta, named in honor,1982; Best Talk Show Host on Radio, Atlanta Chap Nat Asn Black Journalists, 1983; Distinguished Supporter Top Star Award, Nat Asn Black journalists, 1983; Outstanding Service Award, Martin Luther King, Jr Ctr Social Change, 1984; Dr. Herbert J. Bridge water Jr Day, State Ga, 1985;Congressional Achievement Award, Congressman Wyche Fowler, 1985;Outstanding Communication Silver Voice Award, Bronner Brothers Int Beauty& Trade Show Conv, 1989. **Special Achievements:** Individually won the struggle to have Black College athletic scores airedon TV stations in GA 1966; assisted the City of Atlanta & Consumer Affairs Office in preparing proposed Consumer Protection Ordinance for the City of Atlanta, ordinance currently in existence; host/master of ceremonies of numerous pageants. **Business Addr:** Journalist, Atlanta Daily World, 145 Auburn Ave NE, Atlanta, GA 30303-2503.*

BRIDGFORTH, GLINDA
Financial manager. **Personal:** Born Jan 1, 1952?, Detroit, MI; daughter of Walter and Opal; married; (divorced 1988). **Educ:** Western Mich Univ, BS, 1974. **Career:** Calif Bank, asst vpres; Bridgforth Financial Mgt Group, founder, 1994-, Currently. **Special Achievements:** Author: Girl, Get Your Money Straight: A Sister's Guide to Healing Your Bank Account and Funding Your Dreams in Seven Simple Steps, 2000. **Business Addr:** Founder, Personal Financila Councellor, Bridgforth Financial Management Group, 1300 Lafayette E Suite 2302, Detroit, MI 48207, **Business Phone:** (313)566-0026.

BRIDGFORTH, WALTER, JR.
Entrepreneur, real estate developer. **Personal:** Born in Detroit, MI; married Anita Baker, Dec 31, 1988; children: Walter Baker & Edward Carlton. **Educ:** Western Mich Univ, degree finance, 1979. **Career:** IBM, salesman, 1979-89; self-employed mgr of residential properties; Brisson Develop, developer, currently; real estate developer, currently. **Business Phone:** (810)778-3038.

BRIEVE-MARTIN, ILA CORRINNA
Educator. **Personal:** Born Mar 20, 1939, Newark, NJ; married Robert H Dean. **Educ:** Bloomfield Col, BA, 1964; Rutgers Univ, Grad Sch Educ, EdM, 1972, EdD, 1975. **Career:** Cent High Sch, span teacher, 1964-67, title I coordr, 1967-70; US Dept Justice, Community Rels Dept, consult, 1968-70; Rutgers Univ Grad Sch Educ, asst prof, 1970-74; Va Commonwealth Univ Richmond, asst educ dean, 1975-80; Univ Ala, fel, 1979; Va St Univ, assoc prof, Dept Educ Leadership, 1984; Univ DC, dean educ. **Orgs:** Vpres, Bus & Prof Women, 1967-69; Phi Delta Kappa, 1973-; bd dir, Richmond Area Programs Minorities Engineering, 1977-; bd dir, Greater Richmond Transit Co, 1978-80. **Honors/Awds:** Outstanding Educator Award, Richmond Parent Teacher Asn. **Special Achievements:** Various publications in area of creative dynamics. *

BRIGANCE, O J
Football player, executive director. **Personal:** Born Sep 29, 1969, Houston, TX; married Chanda. **Educ:** Rice Univ, BA, managerial studies, 1992. **Career:** Football player (retired), Executive director; BC Lions, 1991-93; Baltimore Stallions, 1994-95; Miami Dolphins, linebacker, 1996-99; Blatimore Ravens, 1999-2000, dir player develop, 2003-; St Louis Rams, 2001-02. **Honors/Awds:** NFLPAs Unsung Hero Award, 1999; Winston & Shell Award, Nat Football League, 2005. **Business Phone:** (410)701-4000.

BRIGGINS, CHARLES E.
Educator. **Personal:** Born Nov 6, 1930, Helena, AL; married Mary Jones; children: Charles, Anthony & Tonya. **Educ:** Ala A&M Univ, BS, 1956, MS, 1961. **Career:** KY State Col, instr, 1956-68; Decatur City Schs, teacher coord, 1958-71; Huntsville City Schs, diversified occup coord; Huntsville Ala, vctnl T&I coord, 1971; SR Butler HS. **Orgs:** Ala Educ Asn; Ala Voc Asn; Am Voc Asn, 1958; Alpha Phi Alpha; RE Nelms Elks Lodge 977; Masn; VFW; Am Legion. **Military Serv:** AUS, sgt, 1951-54. *

BRIGGS, CAROL J.
School principal. **Career:** Dusable High Sch, prin; Alfred David Kohn Elem Sch, prin, currently. **Business Addr:** Principal, Alfred David Kohn Elementary School, 10414 S State St, Chicago, IL 60628, **Business Phone:** (773)535-5496.

BRIGGS, GREG
Football player. **Personal:** Born Oct 1, 1968, Meadville, MS. **Educ:** Tex Southern Univ. **Career:** Dallas Cowboys, 1995; Chicago Bears, 1996; Minn Vikings, 1997. **Orgs:** Men's Christian fel; Christian Athletes. **Honors/Awds:** Super Bowl Champions, 1992; Vince Lombardi Trophy, 1995. *

BRIGGS, DR. HAROLD E.
Educator. **Educ:** Morehouse Col, BA, sociol, 1977; Univ Pittsburgh, MA, sociol, 1978; Univ Chicago, MA, clinc social work, 1980, PhD, social develop, 1988. **Career:** Prog develop specialist, Found I Ctr Human Develop, 1979-81; coordr, Clin Serv & Psychotherapist Southwest Community Action Coalition Chicago, 1981-83; psychiat Social Worker, Wyman Gordon Pavilion Ingalls Mem Hosp, 1982-83; S Cent Community Serv, adminr, 1983-84; Habilitative Systs Inc, assoc exec dir, 1984-90; Portland State Univ, Grad Sch Social Work, from asst prof to assoc prof, 1990-2004, prof, 2004-. **Orgs:** Int Asn Psychosocial Rehab; Asn Behavioral Anal. **Business Phone:** (503)725-5026.

BRIGHAM, FREDDIE M
Banker. **Personal:** Born Mar 23, 1947, Minneapolis, MN; daughter of Fred W and Mary L Lewis; divorced; children: Matthew W, Michael F & Jaime M. **Educ:** Metropolitan Community Col, attended 1982; Nat Univ, attended 1988. **Career:** Pillsbury Co, exec sec to promotion dir, 1973-84; Bank Am Nev, exec secy to controller, 1988-93, mgr info processing, 1993-. **Orgs:** N Las Vegas Literacy Coun, 1990-92. **Special Achievements:** Volunteer tutor; aspiring fiction writer.

BRIGHT, ALFRED LEE
Artist, educator. **Personal:** Born Jan 9, 1940, Youngstown, OH; son of Henry and Elizabeth Lockhart Daniels; married Virginia Deanne Newell; children: Leslie, Alfred Jr, Nichole, Steven. **Educ:** Youngstown Univ, BS, 1964; Kent St Univ, MA, 1965. **Career:** Youngstown State Univ, distinguished prof artist, 1965-, dir black studies program, 1970-87, prof artist, fac emer, currently. **Orgs:** Alpha Phi Alpha Fraternity; St Dept Edn, Adv Com Arts; exec mem, Ohilo Arts Coun; Nat Humanities Fac; pres, Youngstown Area Arts Coun, 1979-80; exec bd, Ohilo Arts Coun, gov appointment, 1973-78; Phi Kappa Phi; Phi Beta Delta; The Golden Key Nat Honor Soc. **Honors/Awds:** Numerous solo exhibitions; pvt cols, perm cols dev, "Total Walk-In Environ Rooms", 1st & hon ment award Butler Art Inst, Youngstown 1967; best of show Haber-Gall 1966; 1st & 2nd awards, oils Village Ctr Fine Art Exhib, Niles OH, 1964-67; Outstanding Grad Achiever, Nat Junior Achievement Inc, 1975; consult, Nat Humanities Fac, 1977-; aid to individual artist, Ohio Arts Coun, 1980; painted with live jazz music: Art Blakey & Winton Marsalis, 1980, Jimmy Owens, 1985; Best of Show Butler Inst Am Art, 1984; Butler Inst Am Art, 1985; 1st place AAA Exhibit Butler Inst Am Art, 1985 & 1994; Distinguished Prof Award, Youngstown State Univ, 1980, 1985-96;Harmon-Meek Gallery, Naples, Fla, 1986, 1991; Roanoke Mus Fine Arts, 1986; Cleveland Playhouse Bolton Gallery, solo exhibitions, 1990; fellowship, Canton Mus Art, Ann Arundel Community Col, 1990; Malcolm Brown Gallery, 1990; Solo exhibitions: Cincinnati Art Mus, 1991; Beachwood Mus, 1992; Art Educr Year, The Ohio House Reps, 1992; The Harmon & Harriet Kelly Collection African Am Art (San Antonio, Tex). **Special Achievements:** Coauthor, An Interdisciplinary Introd Black Studies, Kendal-Hunt Publ, 1978. *

BRIGHT, DR. HERBERT L
Executive. **Personal:** Born Aug 20, 1941, Shelbyville, TN; son of Henry H and Alvirleen Buchanan; married Dzifa Killings, Jun 6, 1992; children: Troy, Sonja, Yolonda, Herbert Jr, Kristi & Kenji Horton. **Educ:** Thornton Jr Col, Harvey, IL; Seton Hall Univ, S Orange, NJ; Inst Bible Studies, Grad; Andersonville Bapt Sem, Camilla, GA, BA, Christian Educ, MA, ministry; Shiloh Theoll Sem, Stafford, VA, doctor divinity; Tabernacle Bible Col & Sem, doctor relig philos. **Career:** Nabisco Brands Inc, gen clerk, 1963-65, opers mgr, 1968-72, asst acct office mgr, 1972-73, personnel policies specialist, 1973-75, corp equal opportunity mgr, 1975-79, sr mgr personnel servs, 1979-83, dir personnel practices, 1983-87, dir personnel servs, 1987-89; dir minority affairs & bus develop, 1989-92; Faith Tabernacle Church, Faith Tabernacle Outreach Ministries Inc, sr pastor & founder, presiding bishop, currently; Bright Light Community Serv Inc, chair & chief exec officer; Charles Reid Bible Col & Sem, chancellor; Plainfield Police Dept, chaplain, currently; Plainfield Public Sch bd educ, elected official. **Orgs:** Pres, bd dirs, Nabisco Brands Employee Credit Union; US Chaplins Asn; Nat Asn Advan Colored People; Opportunities Industrialization Ctrs Am; Tom Skinner Assocs Ind & Labor Coun; Nat Urban League Com & Ind Coun; Am Soc Personnel Admin; Union County Urban League Bd; Va Union Univ Cluster; Howard Univ Cluster; Felician Col Bus Adv Bd; charter mem, Nat Urban League; 100 Black Men NJ; bd dirs, Carter Woodson Found; bd dirs, Nat Black United Fund; bd dirs, NJ Black United Fund; bd dirs, Plainfield Teen Parenting Prog; bd regents Tabernacle Bible Col & Semi. **Honors/Awds:** Whitney M Young Jr, Memorial Award, Morris County Urban League, 1985; Nat honoree, Afro-American History Award, 1987; Morris County Nat Asn for the Advancement of Colored People Community Service Award; Herbert H Wright Award, Nat Asn Mkt Developers; numerous others. **Military Serv:** AUS, 1960-63. **Business Addr:** Bishop, Senior Pastor, Faith Tabernacle Church, 1301 W Front St, PO Box 2779, Plainfield, NJ 07062-2779, **Business Phone:** (908)757-6358.

BRIGHT, JEAN MARIE
Educator, writer. **Personal:** Born Sep 13, 1915, Rutherfordton, NC; daughter of John W Bright Sr and Wollie Lynch. **Educ:** NC Agr & Tech State Univ, Greensboro, NC, BS, 1939; Columbia Univ, New York, NY, MA, 1953. **Career:** NC Agr & Tech State Univ, Greensboro, NC, prof Eng, 1951-78; NC Humanities Comt, lectr, 1977-79; Books: Images of the Negro in America, co-ed, 1965; Voices from the Black Experience, co-ed, 1972. **Orgs:** Am Red Cross, 1944-46; African Lit Asn; Col Lang Asn; pres, Bright Forest Enterprises Inc, 1980-89. **Home Addr:** 1008 S Benbow Rd, Greensboro, NC 27406. *

BRIGHT, KIRK
Executive. **Personal:** Born Jan 25, 1943, Louisville, KY; son of Lois S; married Shela, Oct 31, 1992; children: Greg, Yvette, Brett & Yvonne. **Educ:** Howard Univ. **Career:** IBM, customer engr, 1966-71; Bright's Dist Co, pres, 1971-89; Louisville Conv & Visitors Bur, conv sales mgr, 1990-2003; La Cent Develop Corp, dir, microbusiness develop Bus Plus, 2003-. **Honors/Awds:** Distinguished Sales Award, Sales Mkt Exec, 1992; Black Achiever, YMCA, 1995; Employee of the Yr, Conv Bur, 1997;

Doing My Job Award, Louisville Defender Newspaper & Anheuser-Busch, Inc, 1997. **Military Serv:** USAF, Staff Sgt, 1962-66. **Business Phone:** (502)583-8821.

BRIGHT, WILLIE S
Chief executive officer, consultant. **Personal:** Born Feb 7, 1934, Houston, TX; son of Willie S and Ovida Y Johnson; married Mildred Ball, Jun 4, 1960; children: Develous A & Nicole O. **Educ:** Tuskegee Inst, Tuskegee, AL, 1953; Tex Southern Univ, Houston, TX, BA, 1955, MEd, 1964. **Career:** Houston Independent Sch Dist, Houston, TX, teacher, 1959-66; Crescent Found, Houston, TX, counr, 1966-67; Concentrated Employ Prog, Houston, TX, training officer, 1967-68; Forera Southeastern Inc, Houston, TX, dir, 1968-71; Urban Placement Serv Inc, Houston, TX, owner & chief exec officer, 1971-. **Orgs:** Vice polemarch, bd mem, Kappa Alpha Psi, Houston Alumni 1954-; Nat Asn Personnel Consult, 1971-; vpres, dir, Houston Area Asn Personnel Consult, 1971-; life mem, Kappa Alpha Psi, 1974; bd dir, Ment Health Asn, Houston, Harris County, 1974-80; expert witness, Off Hearing & Appeal, Social Security Admin, 1975-80; bd mem, Citizens Good Sch, 1976-78; Nat Asn Mkt Developers, Houston Chap, 1978; Univ Oaks Civic Club, 1979-; Kiwanis Int, Houston Metrop Chap, 1985-; Houston Area Pan Hellenic Coun, 1986-; vchmn, PPR Comn, Mt Vernon United Methodist Church, 1989. **Honors/Awds:** Goodwill Ambassador Award, City Houston, 1975; Meritorious Service Award, City Houston, 1976; Certificate of Appreciation, Houston Area Pvt Employ Asn, 1977; Cert Pub Consult, 1978; Trailblazer Award, Kappa Alpha Psi, Houston Chap, 1983; Cert Appreciation, Ensemble Theatre, 1987; Cert Appreciation, Edison Middle Sch Career Awareness 1990; Cert Recognition, Houston Area Pan Hellenic Coun, 1990. **Military Serv:** AUS, E-4, 1956-58. **Business Addr:** Owner, Chief Executive Officer, The Urban Placement Serv, 602 Sawyer St Suite 460, Houston, TX 77007-7510, **Business Phone:** (713)880-2211.

BRIMM, DR. CHARLES EDWIN
Physician. **Personal:** Born May 22, 1924; married Edith Mapp; children: Charles Jr & Linda Jean. **Educ:** S Jersey Law Sch, 1947-48; Ottawa Univ, BS, 1951; Ottawa Univ Med Sch, MD, 1955. **Career:** Hahnemann Hosp, teaching, 1974-; Family Pract, specialist, 1975; Col Med & Dent NJ, teaching, 1977; Family Pract Hahnemann Hosp, instr, 1978-79; Gen Pract, physician, 1956-. **Orgs:** BPUM, 1978; founder, Concept House Drug Rehab Settlement, 1970; Camden Co Heart Assoc; bd trustees, Camden County Col; life mem, NAACP; booster club, Camden HS; Nat Med Asn; consult, Cooper Med Ctr, Dept Neurol & Psychiatrist, Dept Int Med, Dept Family Practice. **Honors/Awds:** 'Physician of the Year', Camden County Med Soc, 1971; Dipl Bd, 1974, Elected an affiliate, 1979, Royal Soc Med, Queen Eng, 1979; Postgrad Med Res Award, 1979. **Special Achievements:** Published, "Use of Fluplenazine Decanoate in Managing PCP Intoxication". **Military Serv:** AUS, chem warfare quartermaster, 1943-46.

BRIMMER, DR. ANDREW FELTON
Economist. **Personal:** Born Sep 13, 1926, Newellton, LA; son of Andrew and Vellar; married Doris Millicent Scott; children: Esther Diane. **Educ:** Univ Wash, BA, econ, 1950, MA, 1951; Univ Bombay; Harvard Univ, PhD, econ, 1957. **Career:** Fed Res Bank NYC, economist, 1955-58; Mich State Univ, asst prof, 1958-61;Wharton Sch Finance & Com Univ PA, asst prof, 1961-66; Dept Com Wash, dep asst secy, 1963-65, asst secy econ affairs, 1965-66; Fed Reserve Bd, 1966-74; Grad Sch Bus Admin Harvard Univ, Thomas Henry Carroll Ford Found, vis prof, 1974-76; Brimmer & Co Inc, pres, 1976-; Univ Mass, vice chmn Commodity Exchange & lects, 2003, Wilmer D Barrett, prof econs, currently. **Orgs:** Bd govs, vice chmn Commodity Exch Inc; dir, Bank Am; Am Security Bank; Int Harvester Col; United Air Lines; Du Pont Co; Gannett Co Inc; Fed Res Central Banking Mission to Sudan 1957; consult secy, 1962-63; Trilateral Commn; chmn bd trustees Tuskegee Univ Com Econ Devel; vis com NYU; co-chmn Interracial Coun Bus Oppurtunity; Am Econ Asn; Am Fin Asn; pres, Asn Study Afro-Am Life & Hist, 1970-73; Nat Economists Club, Coun Foreign Rels, Am Statis Asn; bd dirs, Mercedes-Benz N Am, 1990-. **Honors/Awds:** Govt Man of the Year, Nat Bus League, 1963; Arthur S Flemming Award, 1966; Russwurm Award, 1966; Capital Press Club Award, 1966; Golden Plate Award, Am Acad Achieve, 1967; Alumnus Summa Laude Dignatus Univ Wash Alumni Asn, 1972; Nat Honoree Beta Gamma Sigma, 1971; Horatio Alger Award, 1974; Equal Oppurtunity Award, Nat Urban League, 1974; One Hundred Black Men & NY Urban Coalition Award, 1975; Harvard Medal, 1997. **Special Achievements:** Author: "Survey of Mutual Funds Investors" 1963; "Life Insurance Companies in Capital Market" 1962; "Economic Development, International and African Perspectives" 1976; First African American governor of the Federal Reserve. **Military Serv:** AUS, staff sgt, 1945-46. **Home Addr:** 4910 32nd St NW, Washington, DC 20008. **Business Addr:** President, Brimmer & Company Inc, 4400 MacArthur Blvd NW Suite 302, Washington, DC 20007, **Business Phone:** (202)342-6255.

BRINKLEY, CHARLES H., SR.
Educator, president (organization). **Personal:** Born Nov 13, 1942, Gallatin, TN; son of Ellen and Hutch; married Gloria Johnson; children: Katrena, Angela & Charles II. **Educ:** Miss Vally State Univ, BS, MS; Tenn Tech Univ; Tenn State Univ, MA, educ, 1989. **Career:** Educator (retired); St Training Sch, Dept Corrections, teacher, 1967; NSF, fel grant, 1968; Taft Youth Ctr, prin, 1968-70; Sumner County Election Comn, 1983-89, chmn, 1985; TPSEA Unit, Tenn Prep Sch, pres. **Orgs:** Vice chmn, Gen Cent Comt, 1975-77; Dep Sheriff Command, 1975; C of C,1975; notary pub, State Tenn, 1975-78; NEA; MTEA; TEA; TPSEA; Deacon,1975-; chmn, Deacon's Bd, 1985-; pres, Nat Asn Adv Colored People GallatinBr, 1996; First Baptist Church; Local rep, TPS Educ Asn; Mid Tenn Coun Asn; Tenn Sheriff's Asn. **Honors/Awds:** Outstanding Serv Presidential Award, TPS Educ Asn, 1972; Outstanding ServAward, Nat Asn Adv Colored People, 1989, 1996. *

BRINKLEY, NORMAN, JR.
School administrator. **Personal:** Born Jul 7, 1931, Edenton, NC; son of Norman and Adell; married Pearl A Rozier; children: Franklin, Cassandra, Norman T, Carmellia & Christa A. **Educ:** NC Agr & Tech Col, BS, 1954, MS, 1974. **Career:** City Piladelphia, youth counr, 1959-61; State Pa, youth supvr, 1961-63; CServ Inc, Philadelphia, Pa, caseworker, 1963-64; Child Care Serv Media, Pa, social worker, 1965-69; Lincoln Univ, Lincoln, Pa, activ dir & community coordr, 1969-70; Miss Valley State Univ, dean studies, 1970-; Miss NASPA, state dir, 1979-80. **Orgs:** Voters League, 1970-80; Miss Stud Personnel Admin, 1970-80; officer, M WStringer Grand Lodge F & AM, 1976-80. **Honors/Awds:** Community Rels Award, Univ Miss, 1971; Develop Inst Award, Univ Wis, 1972-73; Supvr Leadership Skills Award, Southern Ill Univ, 1975. **Military Serv:** USAF, 2nd lt, 1955-58.

BRINN, CHAUNCEY J.
School administrator. **Personal:** Born Mar 21, 1932, Kalamazoo, MI; married Elizabeth L. **Educ:** BA, 1963; MA, 1975. **Career:** Asn Western Mich Univ, chem lab tech, res, past vpres, 1954-56; Indust chem lab tech, 1956-58; IBM Corp, admin, minority recruitment, 1963-65; Western Mich Univ, banking, br mgr, minority recruitment, 1965-68, spec prog office Stud Financial Aids, coord, 1968-71, dir acad affairs & minority student affairs, asst vpres, 1971, vpres. **Orgs:** Dir, Citizens Teen, 1960-62; exec bd nat asn, Finance Aid Admin, Kalamazoo Community Serv Coun, 1961-62; dir, Kalamazoo Jaycees, 1964-66; Kalamazoo Chap, NAACP, 1965; dir, Otsego-plainwell Jaycees, 1966-67; chmn, Mar Dime, 1966; chmn, Greater No Dist Explorer Scouts, 1967; consult, Civil Rights Commn Migrant Labour, 1969; dir, Region XI MI Stud Finance Aid Asn,1969-70; chmn, Minority Affairs Com, Mich Stud Finance Aid Asn, 1970-71;adv bd, Affirmative Action Bus & Indust, 1972-75; Mich Alliance BlackEduc, 1976; Minority caucus Midwest Asn Stud Finance Aid Admin, 1971; NatAsn African Am Educators; Kalamazoo County Personal & Gdnc Asn; MichPersonal & Gdnc Asn; mem, Midwest Asn Stud Finance Aid Admin. **Special Achievements:** Western Michigan University first Black Vice President; Author publ "Goingto College Costs Money". **Military Serv:** USN, secound cl petty off, 1950-54. **Business Addr:** Vice President, Western Michigan University, 1903 W Mich Ave, Kalamazoo, MI 49008-5200, **Business Phone:** (269)387-1000.

BRISBY, VINCENT COLE (VINCENT ULTIMATE BRISBY)
Football player. **Personal:** Born Jan 25, 1971, Houston, TX; children: Donovan Herbert. **Educ:** Univ Louisana, Monroe. **Career:** Football player (retired); New Eng Patriots, wide receiver, 1993-99; NewYork Jets, wide receiver, 2000. **Orgs:** Phi Beta Sigma. **Honors/Awds:** Miller Lite Player of the Game,1998.

BRISBY, VINCENT ULTIMATE. See BRISBY, VINCENT COLE.

BRISCO, GAYLE
Real estate agent. **Personal:** Born in Suffolk, VA; divorced; children: 1. **Educ:** Hampton Univ, bachelor's degree, psychol; Univ Md, master's degree, social work. **Career:** Greater Baltimore Bd Realtors, pres, 1 995; Otis Warren & Co, vpres, 1997; Coldwell Banker Residential Brokerage (CBRB), assoc broker, sales assoc, currently. **Orgs:** Life mem, Real Estate Million Dollar Asn. **Honors/Awds:** Outstanding African-American leader, The African Am Real Estate Prof (AAREP),2003; Maryland's Top 100 Women, Warfield's Magazine; Valued Hours Award, Wayland Baptist Church; Governor's Citation, Maryland's Gov. **Special Achievements:** First African Am woman to be elected pres for Greater Baltimore Bd of Realtors. "500 Most Powerful Women in Real Estate and Relocation" National Relocation and Real Estate Magazine; Named one of "Maryland's Top 100 Women," Warfield's Magazine. **Home Phone:** (410)788-8087. **Business Phone:** (410)480-1314.

BRISCOE, LEONARD E.
Executive. **Personal:** Born May 22, 1940, Ft Worth, TX; married Rosita; children: Edward, Rosanna. **Educ:** Pepperdine Univ, MBA, 1975; Univ TX, Currently Studying, PhD. **Career:** Expediters, pres; NAMCON, Briscoe-morrison, real est; Briscoe Consult Serv, Rolling Hills Bldg & Devel, Universal Financial Corp, Interntl Mortgage Corp, exec v p; Real & Est Broker, 1960-; Briscoe Construct Corp, owner, 2002-. **Orgs:** Local State & Natl Real Estate Brokers Assns; mem, Local State & Nat Home Builders Assns, Ft Worth City Coun, 1971-75; Nat League Cities; Ft Worth Comm Devel Coun; pres, Assn Mayors Cnclmn & Commrs. **Business Addr:** Owner, Briscoe Construct Corp, 2016 Evans Ave, Fort Worth, TX 76104, **Business Phone:** (817)926-5343.*

BRISCOE, MARLIN (MARLIN OLIVER BRISCOE)
Football player, teacher. **Personal:** Born Sep 10, 1945?, Oakland, CA. **Educ:** Univ NE-Omaha; teaching degree. **Career:** Football player (Retired), teacher; Director; Denver Broncos, 1968; BuffaloBills, wide receiver, 1969-71; Miami Dolphins, wide receiver, 1972-74; SanDiego Chargers and Detroit Lions, 1975; New England Patriots, 1976-77; Los Angeles area, teacher; Los Angeles Watts & Willowbrook Boys & Girls Club,asst proj mgr & fundraiser; Boys & Girls Club, Long Beach, California. **Honors/Awds:** Pro Bowler Selection Once, All Pro Selection, Once 1970; Super Bowler Champion Twice, VII, VIII. **Special Achievements:** First African-American starting quarterback in NFL; Book: The First BlackQuarterback: Marlin Briscoe's Journey to Break the Color Barrier and Startin the NFL, 2002. *

BRISCOE, MARLIN OLIVER. See BRISCOE, MARLIN.

BRISCO-HOOKS, VALERIE ANN
Track and field athlete, athletic coach. **Personal:** Born Jul 6, 1960, Greenwood, MS; married Alvin, Jan 1, 1981; children: Alvin. **Educ:** Long Beach Comm Col; Calif State Univ, Northridge. **Career:** Athletic player (retired); coach; Athletic Congress Natl Championships, 1984; Olympic Games, Los Angeles,1984, Seoul, Korea, 1988; UCLA Invitational, 1984; Bruce Jenner Meet, SanJose CA, 1984; Europ Track Circuit, 1984, 1985; Millrose Games, 1985; Sunkist Invitational, Los Angeles, 1985; Times-Herald Invitational,Dallas, Tex, 1985; LA Times-Kodak Games, Inglewood, CA, 1985; coach. **Honors/Awds:** Three Gold Medals,Olympics, 1984; Los Angeles; Silver Medal, 1988 Olympics,Seoul, Korea; Outstanding Mother's Award, Natl Mother's Day Comm, 1986;co-chairperson, Minnie Riperton Cancer Week, 1986, 1987; Bronze Medal,1987; USA Track & Field Hall of Fame, 1995. **Special Achievements:** First Olympian to win gold medals in both the 200- and 400-meter races at a single Olympics; First female asked to compete in Australia's Stalwell Gift Race, 1987. **Home Addr:** 1138 W 71st St, Los Angeles, CA 90044-2502. *

BRISKER, LAWRENCE
School administrator. **Personal:** Born Oct 5, 1934, St Louis, MO; married Flossie Richmond. **Educ:** Southern Ill Univ, BA, 1959; Univ NM, MA, 1966; Case-Western Res U, PhD, 1977. **Career:** Cleveland Pub Sch System, teacher, 1962-64; Ohio Bell Telephone Co Cleveland, employ supvr & traffic mgr, 1964-70; Cleveland Municipal Court,chief dep clerk, 1975-76; Cuyahoga Community Col, coord student assistance prog, 1976-77, spec asst to the chancellor, 1977-78, dean student life unit, 1978. **Orgs:** Bd trustees, Cleveland TB & Respiratory Fed, 1966; bd mem Glenwood Oak Pvt Sch Girls, 1968-; Urban League's Employ & Econs Comn, 1968; Citizen'sLeague, 1978-; bd dir, Cleveland Pub Radio, 1979-; United Area Citizens Agency, 1979-. **Honors/Awds:** Spinix award, Southern Ill Univ, 1958; Phi Delta Kappa, Univ NM 1960;Nat Defense Educ Act Fel, 1970, Fel award, Case-Western Res Univ 1972. **Military Serv:** AUS, e-4, 1958-60.

BRISKIE, DAVID
Chief executive officer. **Career:** Drew Pearson Mkt Inc, chief exec officer, 2004-. *

BRISTER, DARRYL SYLVESTER
Clergy. **Personal:** Born Sep 26, 1966, New Orleans, LA; son of Earlie Mae; married Dionne Flot, Oct 17, 1992; children: Darrylynn, Darryl Jr, Dariel & Trey Darius. **Educ:** McKienley Theol Sem, BA, theol, 1992; Friends Inst Christian Univ, MA, bible studies, 1995, DMin, 1998. **Career:** Greater St Stephen, Full Gospel Bapt Church, asst pastor, 1992-94; Beacon Light Bapt Church, sr pastor, 1993; Darryl S Brister Bible Col & Theol Sem, pres & founder, 1999-. **Orgs:** Pres, Beacon Light Christian Acad, 2002. **Honors/Awds:** Tribute to America's Most Outstanding Pastors, Upscale Magazine, 2000. **Special Achievements:** Bishop Brister is the author of five books that have ministered to thousands entitled, Exposing the Enemy, The Monster Within, Recovering From Ruptured Relationships, Don't Fight the Process and his most recent release, Talk To Me Afterwards. In March of 1999, Bishop Brister and the Beacon Light Mass Choir released their first CD entitled, "It's All About Him"; Top 50 Leaders of Tomorrow, Ebony Magazine, 1995. **Military Serv:** AUS, E-5, Sargent, 1986-90; Army Achievement; Good Conduct Medal; Overseas Medal. **Business Addr:** President, Founder, Darryl S Brister Bible College & Theological Seminary, 5134 Paris Ave, New Orleans, LA 70122, **Business Phone:** (504)283-8752.

BRISTOW, DR. LONNIE ROBERT
Physician. **Personal:** Born Apr 6, 1930, New York, NY; son of Lonnie H and Vivian W Bristow; married Marilyn, Oct 18, 1961; children: Robert E & Elizabeth E (divorced); children: Mary. **Educ:** Col City NY, BS, 1953; NY Univ, Col Med, MD, 1957. **Career:** San Francisco City & County Hosp, internship, 1958; USVA Hosp, San Francisco, Residency, Internal Med, 1960; Francis Delafield Hosp, Columbia Univ Serv, 1960; USVA Hosp,

Bronx, 1961; Univ Calif, San Francisco Sch Med, residency, occup med, 1981; pvt pract, internist; consult, currently. **Orgs:** Alameda-Contra Costa Med Asn, 1968-; E Bay Soc Internal Med, pres, 1969; Federated Coun Internal Med, 1976-78; pres, Calif Soc Internal Med, 1976; fel, master, Am Col Physicians, 1977, 1995; pres, Am Soc Internal Med, 1981-82; bd trustees, 1985-, chair, 1993-94, pres elect, 1994-95, pres, 1995-96, AMA; exec comm sect, Community Off Lab Assessment, 1989-91; comnr, Joint Community Accreditation Healthcare Orgn, 1990-92; Nat Med Veterans Soc; Calif Med Asn. **Honors/Awds:** Parket Health Memorial Lecturer, 1982; Contra Costa Humanitarian of the Year, Contra Costa Bd Supvr, 1989; California Most Distinguished Internist, CA Society IM, 1990; Honorary Degree, Morehouse Sch Med, 1994; Honorary Degree, Wayne State Univ Sch Med, 1995; Honorary Degree, City Col City Univ New York, 1995. **Special Achievements:** Board Certification, Am Bd Internal Med, 1969; Presidential appointment to serve as chair, board of regents, Uniformed Services University of the Health Sciences, 1996-; Contributing editor of The Internist; Emeritus Member Editorial Advisory Board of Medical World News; Publications: "The Myth of Sickle Cell Trait," medical opinion, The Western Journal of Med, p 77-82 & 121, July 1974; "Shared Sacrifice-The AMA Leadership Response to the Health Sec Act"JAMA, p 271 & 786, Mar 9, 1994; "Mine Eyes Have Seen," Journal of the AMA, p 261, 284-285, Jan 13, 1989. **Home Addr:** 3324 Ptarmigan Dr, Walnut Creek, CA 94595, **Home Phone:** (925)943-7326.

BRITT, DONNA
Journalist, columnist. **Personal:** Born Jan 1, 1954, Gary, IN; daughter of Thomas Britt and Geraldine Britt; married Kevin Merida; children: 3. **Educ:** Hampton Univ, BA; Univ Mich, MA. **Career:** Detroit Free Press, staff writer, 1978-85; USA Today, staff writer,1985-89; Wash Post, features writer, 1989, Metro section columnist, 1990-, columnist, 1991-. **Orgs:** The Trotter Group. **Honors/Awds:** Distinguished Writing Award, Am Soc of Newspaper Eds, 1994. **Special Achievements:** Nominee, Pulitzer Prize, 1990. **Business Addr:** Columnist, The Washington Post, 1150 15th St NW, Washington, DC 20071-0070, **Business Phone:** (202)334-6037.

BRITT, L. D.
Surgeon, college teacher, physician. **Personal:** Born Jun 28, 1951, Suffolk, VA; son of White Britt and Claretta. **Educ:** Univ Va, BA, 1972; Harvard Med Sch, MD, 1977; Harvard Sch Pub Health, MPH, 1977. **Career:** Univ Il, Dept Surg, clin instr, 1983-85; Bethany Hosp, active staff, asst dir emergency med, 1984-85; Md Inst Emergency Med Serv Systs, chief admin surg fel, 1985-86; Eastern Va Med Sch, asst prof surg, 1986-89, Div Trama & Critical Care, chief, 1987-97, assoc prof surg, 1989-93; Dept Surg, Henry Ford prof & vice chair, 1993-95; Edward Brickhouse, Dept Surg, chair, 1994-; Sentara Norfolk Gen Hosp, Dept Surg, chief, 1997-99; Shock Trauma Ctr, from asst med dir to med dir, 1986-97, Eastern Va Med Sch, Dept Surg, prof & chmn, 2004-; Howard Univ, VA, vis prof; St Louis Univ, vis prof; Current Surgery, ed bd; J Trauma, ed bd. **Orgs:** Senate Joint Subcommittee, EMS Personnel Training & Retention, 1988-91; adv bd, EMS, 1988-94; bd visitors, Norfolk State Univ, 1988-96; exec bd mem, Boy Scouts Am, 1989-; bd trustees, Sentara Health Syst, 1992-94; bd mgrs, Univ Va, 1993-; nat comt trauma, Am Col Surgeons, 1996-; bd dirs, Asn Prog Dirs Surg, 1996-; assoc examr, Am Bd Surg, 1997-; bd mgrs, Pan Am Trauma Soc; Sci Res Soc; Alpha Omega Alpha Hon Soc; bd regents, Am Col Surgeons; Am Asn Med Col; Am Surgeons Asn; ACGME, Residency Rev Comt; Halsted Soc; fel Royal Soc Med England; fel Am Asn Surg Trauma; fel Am Col Critical Care Med. **Honors/Awds:** Sir William Oster Award, Eastern VA Med Sch, 1988-89; Outstanding Attend Physician of the Year, 1992-97; Outstanding Fac Award, State Coun Higher Educ, 1994; Emmy Award, 1994; Man of the Year, NAACP, 1996; ML King Award, Outstanding Achievement & Community Serv, 1997. **Special Achievements:** Reviewer for Archives of Surgery and New Eng Jnl of Trauma. **Business Addr:** Brickhouse Professor, Chairman, Eastern Virgina Medical School, Dept Surg, 825 Fairfax Ave Hofheimer Hall Suite 610, Norfolk, VA 23507-1912, **Business Phone:** (757)446-8950.*

BRITT, PAUL D., JR.
School administrator. **Personal:** Born Feb 3, 1951, Franklin, VA; married Priscilla Harding; children: Pauleatha Clara & Taene Renita. **Educ:** Norfolk State Univ, BA, Social Serv, 1974; Va State Univ, MA, Educ Admin, 1984. **Career:** Southampton Co Schs, teacher & coach, 1975-79; Franklin City Schs, teacher, coach & social studies dept, chmn, 1979-84; Smithfield High Sch, asst prin; Roanoke City Pub Schs, exec for human resources; Vernon Johns Middle Sch, prin, currently. **Orgs:** Deacon First Baptist Ch, Franklin, 1979; coun mem, Franklin City Coun, 1982.

BRITT, SHARON FRIES. See FRIES, SHARON LAVONNE.

BRITTAIN, BRADLEY BERNARD, JR.
Engineer, editor. **Personal:** Born Mar 22, 1948, Arlington, VA; married Lenora C Robinson Freeman; children: Kandakai Freeman, Kini Freeman, Zina Freeman. **Educ:** Howard Univ. **Career:** ABC Inc, engr ed, newsfilm ed, apprentice film ed desk asst, 1972-; freelance photographer, 1976-77. **Orgs:** Life mem, Nat Asn Advan Colored People; Nat Rifle Asn; Nat Geog Soc; Radio & TV Corr Asn; Friends Nat Zoo; Smithsonian Resident Assocs, 1978-; Nat Capital Velo Club; Capitol Hill Correspondents Assoc, 1978-; Asn Corcoran; Nat Acad TV Arts & Sci, 1983-85; White House News Photographer Asn, 1983-85; public rels comn, Northern Va Gun Club, 1983-85. **Honors/Awds:** Achievement in TV Award, CEBA, 1982-83. **Home Addr:** 1314 S Poe St, Arlington, VA 22031. **Business Addr:** Engineer, American Broadcasting Co, 1717 DeSales St NW, Washington, DC 20036.

BRITTAIN, JOHN C.
College teacher, educator. **Educ:** Howard Univ, BA, 1966, JD, 1969. **Career:** N Miss Rural Legal Serv, Oxford, MS, regin ald Heber Smith fel & staff atty, 1969-71; Lawyers Comt Civil Rights Under Law, Jackson, MS, staff atty, 1971-73; pvt pract atty, San Francisco, CA, 1973-77; Univ Conn, Sch Law, Hartford, CT, prof law, 1977-99; Tex Southern Univ, Thur good Marshall Sch Law, Houston, TX, dean, 1999-2002, prof law, 2002-. **Orgs:** Chairperson, ACLU Acad Freedom Comt, 1985-88; Conn State Labor Rels Bd, 1990-95; Pres Nat Lawyers Guild, 1991-93; bd dir, Hartford Found Pub Giving, 1995-99; bd mem, Am Civil Liberties Union, 1998-99 & 2001-; sr felAm Leadership Forum, 2002; Soc Am Law Teachers; Nat Conf Black Lawyers; Int Asn Jurists; Int Asn Dem Lawyers; Nat Bar Asn; Charles Houston Bar Asn; George W Crawford Asn; Magnolia Bar Asn; Am Bar Asn; Houston Bar Asn; Houston Lawyers Asn. **Honors/Awds:** William Robert Ming Advocacy Award, 1996; Gavel Award, 2004. **Special Achievements:** Publications including Book Review, Paul Harris, Black Rage Confronts the Law, Guild Practitioner, Vol. 54, Num. 3, 1997; Remarks at Symposium: Brown V Board of Education at Fifty: Have We Achieved Its Goal? 78 St John's L Rev, 281, 2004. **Business Addr:** Professor of Law, Texas Southern University, Thurgood Marshall School of Law, Thurgood Marshall Law Sch Bldg 3100 Cleburne St, Houston, TX 77004, **Business Phone:** (713)313-1300.

BRITTON, BARBARA
Publishing executive, vice president (organization). **Career:** Essence Mag, vpres & assoc publ sales; Essence Mag, publ adv, currently. **Business Addr:** Publishing Advisor, Essence Magazine, 1500 Broadway Sixth Fl, New York, NY 10036, **Business Phone:** (212)642-0600.*

BRITTON, DR. CAROLYN B
Neurologist, educator. **Educ:** NY Univ, Sch Med, MD. **Career:** Harlem Hosp Med Ctr, resident internal med; Columbia Univ Med Ctr, Neurol Inst NY, NY Presby Hosp, resident & fel; Columbia Univ Med Ctr, Neurol Inst NY, assoc prof neurol, currently. **Orgs:** Pres, Nat Med Asn, 2008-; chair neurol/neurosurg sect, chair finance comt, chair bd trustees, pres-elect, Nat Med Asn; past chair, Doctor's Pvt Off Comt; chair, NY Presby Hosp. **Special Achievements:** First neurologist and the ninth woman to be named president of the National Medical Association, 2008. **Business Addr:** Associate Professor, Columbia University Medical Center, Neurological Institute of New York, 710 W 168th St, New York, NY 10032-2603, **Business Phone:** (212)305-5220.*

BRITTON, ELIZABETH
Nurse. **Personal:** Born Jul 18, 1930, Gary, IN; children: Darryl T Gillespie, Tamara A Gillespie, John G Gillespie, Lisa M Roach, Anthony L & Alycyn M. **Educ:** Mayfair-Chicago City Col, AA, 1969; Purdue Univ, BSN, 1974; Portland State Univ, MS, 1982. **Career:** Chicago Maternity Ctr, nursing serv admin, 1970-73; Beverly Learning Ctr, health educ instr, 1972-74; Univ Ore Health Scis Ctr Sch Nursing, instr, 1976-81; Ore Health Scis Univ of Minority Stud Affairs, asst prof, 1981-. **Orgs:** Pres, Willamette Valley Racial Minorities Consortium; Nat Asn Med Minority Educr; bd dirs, N Portland Nurse Practer Community Health Clinic; anti-basileus, Alpha Kappa Alpha Sor Zeta Sigma Omega; Ore Alliance Black Sch Educr; bd dirs, Ore Donor Prog; mem, The Link's Inc, Portland Chapter, 1988. **Honors/Awds:** Nat Honor Soc Nursing Sigma Theta Tau, 1976; Spec Contrib Indian Educ, 1981, 82, 83; Cert of Appreciation, Ctr Black Studies Portland State Univ, 1983; Outstanding AKA Woman, Zeta Sigma Omega Chapter 1986. **Business Addr:** Director International, Ethnic Affairs, Oregon Health Sciences University, 3181 SW Sam Jackson Pk Rd, Portland, OR 97201, **Business Phone:** (503)279-7574.*

BRITTON, JOHN HENRY
College administrator. **Personal:** Born Jul 21, 1937, Nashville, TN; son of Rev John Henry Sr and Martha Marie Parish; married Cherrie, Jan 1, 2002; married Betty (divorced 2002); children: John III. **Educ:** Drake Univ, BA, 1958; Syracuse Univ, MS, 1962. **Career:** Atlanta Daily World, reporter, 1958-62; Jet Mag, assoc ed, asst managinged, 1962-66; US Civil Rights Comn, asst info officer, 1966-67; Civil Rights Doc Proj Wash, assoc dir, 1967-68; Jet Mag, managing ed, 1968-71; Motown Rec Corp Detroit & La, pub rel mgr, 1971-73; Joint Ctr PolitStudies, pub affairs dir, 1973-76; Encore Mag, columnist, 1974-75; Wash Post, pub rel mgr, 1976-78; Univ DC, pub affairs dir, 1978-97; Bowie St Univ, pub rel dir, 1997-98; Meharry Med Col, assoc vpres mkt & commun, 1998-2002, spec asst to pres, 2002-. **Orgs:** Black Pub Rel Soc Wash; Nat Adv Comt, Nat Black Media Coalition; life mem, Nat Asn Advan Colored People; Nat Asn Black Journalists. **Honors/Awds:** Merit Award, Nat Newspaper Pub Asn, 1971. **Home Addr:** 1605 Harding Pl, Nashville, TN 37215, **Home Phone:** (615)665-5988. **Business Addr:** Special Assistant to the President, Meharry Medical College, 1005 Dr D B Todd Jr Blvd, Nashville, TN 37208-3599, **Business Phone:** (615)327-6282.

BRITTON, THEODORE R
Government official. **Personal:** Born Oct 17, 1925, North Augusta, SC; son of Theodore R Sr and Bessie B Cook; married Ruth B A Baker, Jun 17, 1950 (divorced 1979); children: Theodore (deceased), Renee, Warren, Sharon & Darwin; married Vernell Elizabeth Stewart, Feb 22, 1980. **Educ:** New York Univ, BS, 1952. **Career:** Government Official (retired); Carver Savings Bank, mortgage officer, 1955-64; Am Baptist Mgt Corp, pres, 1966-71; Res & Technol, HUD, dep asst secy, 1971-73; HUD, act asst sec for res & tech, 1973; Barbados & Grenada, ambassador, 1974-77; Assoc States Caribbean, spec rep, 1974-77; United Mutual Life Ins Co, NY, pres & chief exec officer, 1978-79; mgt consult, 1979-80; D Parke Gibson Int Ltd, sr consult, 1979; Logical Tech Serv Corp, exec vpres & secy; HUD, asst secy int affairs, 1981-89, NY, dep regional adminr, 1983-84, Newark, mgr, 1990-92; Nat Housing Ministries, vpres, 1994-99. **Orgs:** Chmn, New York City Urban Renewal mgt Corp, 1968-71; vice chmn, Sector Group Urban Environ Orgn Econ Coop & Develop, 1971-74, 1981-84, chmn, 1985-87; deacon, trustee, Riverside Church, NY, 1965-77; chair US/China Agreement Housing, 1981-89; vice chmn, 1982-84, chmn, 1985-87; OECD Group on Urban Affairs; dir, Riverside Broadcasting Corp; Inst Real Estate Mgmt; Nat Asn Realtors; Am Baptist Rep; bd dirs, Freedom Nat Bank, 1978; exec secy, US Agreement Housing & Urban Develop with Canada Mexico & USSR; Asn Former Intelligence Officers & Second Marine Div; former pres, Asn Black Am Ambassadors; mem, bd dir, Coun Am Ambassadors, 1983; comnr, vice chair chmn, Housing Authority County Dekalb, GA, 2002; mem, bd trustees, 2000, mem, bd dir, People to People Int, 2001. **Honors/Awds:** J Wallace Paletou Award, Institute of Real Estate Management, 1987; Distinguished Service Award, HUD, 1989; Thurgood Marshall Award, University Bridgeport Black Law School Student Assn, 1990. **Military Serv:** US Marine Corps Reserves, sgt, 1944-46, 1948-51; American Theater, Asiatic Pac Theater, WW II Victory Medal, Korean War Medal. **Home Addr:** 310 Somerlane Pl, Avondale Estates, GA 30002. **Business Addr:** Member, Council of American Ambassadors, 888 17th St NW Suite 901, Washington, DC 20006-3307, **Business Phone:** (202)296-3757.

BROACH, S. ELIZABETH JOHNSON
School administrator, consultant. **Personal:** Born in Little Rock, AR; daughter of Iris Addie and Nelvia; married Hughes M; children: Jacqueline Johnson Moore, David M Johnson & Anita M. **Educ:** Dunbar Jr Col, Teachers Cert, 1940; Philander Smith Col, BA, music educ, 1950; Univ Ark, MS, sec educ 1953; Calif State Univ, Hayward, Ed, psycho, 1974. **Career:** Little Rock & Pulaski County Public Sch, music instr, 1955-65; SFUSD, music specialist, 1967-69; Pelton Jr High Sch, dean women, 1969-70, asst prin, 1970-72; Ben Franklin Jr High Sch, asst prin, 1973-74; Wilson High Sch, asst prin, 1975-77; McAteer High Sch, asst prin, 1984-78; San Fran Unified Sch Dist, admin consult; Beebe Mem Cathedral. **Orgs:** Organist Beebe Meth Ch, 1967-85, 1998; organist European Tour Voices of Beebe, 1982; Nat Bus & Prof Women; dir instr, Creative Arts Ctr, San Fran; music dir, Mt Pleasant Baptist Church, Little Rock, AR; Nat Asn Negro Musicians, 1984-85; epistoleus, Sigma Gamma Rho Sor; Phi Delta Kappa Ed,1978; Nat Coun Negro Women; educ comt, Nat Asn Advan Colored People,1984-85; Oakland Symphony Guild; founding bd, Okla E Bay Symphony, 1988-; organist, Nat CME Women's Missionary Coun, 1987-. **Honors/Awds:** Diagnostic Counseling Learning Ctr SFUSD, 1973; Commendation Merit Letter Bay Area Rapid Transit; Certificate of Merit, Calif Conf 9th Episcopal Dist; organ performance Bristol England, Chippenham Methodist Church, Wesley Chapel, London England; Outstanding Bay Area Organist, Nat Asn Black Musicians, Golden Gate Branch. **Home Addr:** 7615 Hansom Dr, Oakland, CA 94605. *

BROADBENT, HYDEIA
Activist. **Personal:** Born Jun 14, 1984, Las Vegas, NV; daughter of Loren and Patricia. **Career:** AIDS activist, 1992-. **Honors/Awds:** A Time for Heroes Award, Pediatric AIDS Found; MLK Jr Drum Major Award; Humanitarian Spirit Award, Amer Red Cross; Grandma's House Award; CDC Award; Frederick Douglass Caring Award; AIDS Action Foundation Award; Millenium Dreamers Award, Disney; Pedro Zamora Award, Youth Advocacy; named one of Top Ten Female Role Models of the Year, Ms Fndn, 1999; honored Essence Award, 1999. **Special Achievements:** Co-author: You Can Get Past the Tears, 2000. **Business Addr:** Hydeia L Broadbent Found, 1425 N Sierra Bonita Ave Suite 411, Los Angeles, CA 90046-4198, **Business Phone:** (323)874-0883.

BROADNAX, MELVIN F.
Educator, mayor. **Personal:** Born Oct 21, 1929, Seaboard, NC; married Ruth Bracey. **Educ:** Shaw Univ, BA, 1963, LLD, 1972; A&T State Univ, MS, 1963. **Career:** Northampton Bd Educ, teacher; Seaboard NC, town comdr; Northampton County, Seaboard, mayor, currently. **Orgs:** Kappa Fraternity; deacon & trustee, Church; Nat Asn Adv Colored People; NEA. **Honors/Awds:** Personality S, NCTA, 1969; Kappa Man of Year, 1974.

Military Serv: AUS, sgt, Korean War. **Business Addr:** Mayor, Northampton County, PO Box 327, Seaboard, NC 27876.*

BROADNAX, WALTER DOYCE
Government official, president (organization). **Personal:** Born Oct 21, 1944, Star City, AR; son of Mary L; married Angel LaVerne Wheelock; children: Andrea Alyce. **Educ:** Washburn Univ, BA, 1967; Kans Univ, MPA, 1969; Syracuse Univ, Maxwell Sch Citizenship & Pub Affairs, PhD, 1975. **Career:** Fed Exec Inst, prof pub admin, 1976-79; State Kans, Serv C, Youth & Adults, dir, 1979-80; Dept Health, Educ & Welfare, Health & Human Serv, prin dep asst secy, 1980-81; Brookings Inst, Advan Study Prog, sr staff mem, 1981; Harvard Univ, JFK Sch Gov, Pub Mgt & Pub Policy, lectr, 1981-87; NYK State Civil Serv Comn, comnr, pres, 1987-90; Univ Tex, LBJ Sch Pub Affairs, vis lectr, 1989; Cleveland State Univ, Col Urban Affairs, eminent pub adv lectr, 1989; Ctr Goval Res Inc, pres, 1990-93; Pres-Elect Bill Clinton Transition Team, transition team leader, 1992; US Dept Health & Human Serv, chief oper officer, dep secy, 1993-; Clark Atlanta Univ, pres, 2002-. **Orgs:** Nat Comn Innovations State & Local Gov, Ford Found, Howard Univ, 1987-89; fel Nat Acad Pub Admin, 1988; Woodrow Wilson Nat Fel Found, Nat Adv Comn, 1989; S Africa Prog, Harvard Univ, 1992; bd dirs, Key Corp; bd dirs, Nat Civic League; adv comt mem, Ctr Study States, CASE Comn, Phase II; State Adv Coun; Nat Comn Am State & Local Pub Serv; NYK State Comn Cost Control; bd dirs, Rochester Gen Hosp. **Honors/Awds:** Rockefeller Col Medallion, 1989; Gordon Sherman Lect, Auburn Univ, 1991; John E Burton Lect, State Univ Albany, Rockefeller Col; John E Burton Award, Rockefeller Col. **Business Addr:** President, Clark Atlanta University, 223 James P Brawley Dr SW, Atlanta, GA 30314.*

BROADUS, CORDOZAR CALVIN, JR. See SNOOP DOGG, U.

BROADWATER, TOMMIE, JR.
Business owner, senator (u.s. federal government). **Personal:** Born Jun 9, 1942, Washington, DC; married Lillian; children: Tommie III, Tanya, Jackie & Anita. **Educ:** Southern Univ; Prince Georges Community Col. **Career:** MD State, sen, 1975-84; Broadwater Bonding Corp, owner; Ebony Inn, owner,1974-; Prince Georges Community Bank, vpres, 1976-77. **Orgs:** Counman, City of Glenarden, 1967-73; Prince Georges Chamber Com; tres, Md Legislators Black Caucus; bd dir, Prince George Community Bank; 25th Alliance Civic Group; NAACP; Sr Citizens Adv Coun; Subcomt Corrections & Transp, 1974-83; vice-chair, Rules Comt, 1974-83; mem, Comn Intergovernmental Coop, 1974-83; Joint Oversight Comn Corrections, 1974-83; Joint Oversight Comn Transp, 1974-83; Gov Juvenile Justice Adv Comt, 1974-83; Gov Housing Task Force, 1974-83; Gov Task Force Youth Employ, 1980-82; mem, Plough man & Fisherman Democratic Club; Boys & Girls Club, Glenarden; Bondsmen's Asn. **Honors/Awds:** Outstanding alumni award, Fairmont Heights Sch, 1976; outstanding leader, Prince Georges Co Civic Groups, 1977. **Special Achievements:** First black senator elected outside of Baltimore. **Home Addr:** 3309 Hayes St, Glenarden, MD 20706. **Business Addr:** Owner, Ebony Inn, Broaadwater Bonding Corporation, 5367 Sheriff Rd, Fairmont Heights, MD 20743.*

BROCK, ANNETTE
School administrator. **Educ:** Savannah State Col. **Career:** Sch administrator(retired); Savannah State Col, pres, 1991-93.

BROCK, GERALD
Judge. **Personal:** Born Aug 23, 1932, Hamtramack, MI; married Jacqueline B Holmes. **Educ:** Eastern Mich Univ, BS, 1953; Detroit Col Law, LLB, 1961. **Career:** Flint Pub Sch, teacher, 1953-57; Wayne County Training Sch, teacher, 1957-61; Pvt Pract, atty, 1961-81; 36th Dist Ct, judge, 1982-. **Business Phone:** (313)965-8716.

BROCK, LORRAINE
Vice president (government). **Career:** Nationwide Ins, vpres diverse & urban mkt develop, 2004. **Orgs:** Adv coun, eWomen-Network Inc; Key partnership with ASPIRA, Habitat for Humanity, L.I.S.C., NAACP, NFHA, Nat Hispanic Corp Coun, Nat Hispanic Scholar Fund, Nat Urban League, Neighborhood Reinvestment Corp, Urban Ins Partners Inst. **Honors/Awds:** Donald H Mc Gannon Award, Nat Urban League. **Business Addr:** Vice President, Nationwide Insurance, Urban Mkt Develop, 1 Nationwide Plz, Columbus, OH 43216, **Business Phone:** (614)249-8639.

BROCK, ROSLYN MCCALLISTER
Executive. **Educ:** Virginia Union Univ, BS; George Washington Univ, MHSA; Northwestern Univ, Kellogg School Mgt, MBA. *

BROCKETT, CHARLES A.
Educator. **Personal:** Born Jan 24, 1937, Princess Anne Co, VA; married Annette Lee; children: Troy Christopher. **Educ:** VA State Col, BS, 1961; Old Dominion Univ, MS, 1972; Univ VA, Norfolk State Col. **Career:** Booker T Wash High Sch, Norfolk, VA, asst prin, asst football coach, 1963-67, Biol teacher, 1963-70; Lake Taylor High Sch, Norfolk VA, 1979-86; Norview High Sch, asst prin, 1986-; Granby High Sch, asst prin, 2001. **Orgs:** Nat Asn Sec Prin; Sec Prin Asn Norfolk; VA Asn Sec Prin; vpres, Dist LPrin Asn; nat bd mem, Nat Black United Fund; pres, Black United Fund Tidewater; Kappa Alpha Psi; Chesapeake Men Progress; Chesapeake Forward; civic reg dir, Kappa Alpha Psi Guide Right Prog; Eastern Reg pres Kappa Alpha Psi; mem, planning comt, Alpha Phi Alumni Reunion. **Honors/Awds:** Outstanding Serv Award, Kappa Alpha Psi; Outstanding Community Service Award, 1973; Outstanding Community Service, 1986. **Military Serv:** AUS, sp 4, 1961-63. *

BROCKINGTON, DONELLA P
Executive. **Personal:** Born Nov 8, 1952, Washington, DC; daughter of Harriet Brown and Josiah Armstrong. **Educ:** Clark Univ, BA math & psychol, 1973; Howard Univ Sch Ed, MEd Guidance & Coun 1974, M Urban Sys Eng 1976. **Career:** Health Sys Agency N VA, sr health sys analyst, 1976-80; DC Govt Off City Admin, sr oper analyst, 1981-85; DC Govt Dept Admin Serv, dep real prop admin, 1985-87, assoc dir real property, 1987-88; Lockheed Datacom, vpres nat mkt, 1988-91; Lockheed Martin IMS, Wash, vpres mkt, 1991-96, regional vpres, 1996-99, vpres, operations, 2000-01; ACS State & Local Solutions, vpres, cooperations, 2001-04, vpres bus develop, 2004-. **Orgs:** Coord McKinley High Sch Alumni Orgn, 1980; secy, Capital Ballet Guild Inc, 1982; Nat Forum Black Pub Admin, 1984-; Nat Asn Female Exec, 1986-; secy, Girl Scout Coun Nation's Capital, 1993-96, first vpres, 1996-99, pres, 1999-; bd dir, Hoop Dreams Scholarship Fund. **Honors/Awds:** Distinguished Public Service Award, DC Govt, 1982; Salute to African-American Business & Professional Women, Dollars & Sense Mag, 1989; President's Award, Lockheed Martin IMS, 1998; Lifetime Achievement Award, Women Technol, 2001; Lifetime Achievement Award, ACS State & Local Solutions, 2003.

BROCKINGTON, EUGENE ALFONZO
Financial manager. **Personal:** Born Jun 21, 1931, Darien, GA; married Mable M; children: Eugene Jr & Karyn L. **Educ:** Comm Col Philadelphia, attended 1967-68. **Career:** DeMarco Printer Philadelphia, printing press oper, 1951; Am Fiber-Velop Co, Collingdale, Pa, printing press oper, 1954; Jones & Johnson Soft Ice Co, salesman, 1956; US Postal Serv Philadelphia, postal source data tech, 1958; Nat Alliance Postal & Fed Employees, treas, comptroller, data proc mgr, 1976-. **Orgs:** Fin secy, Nat Alliance Postal & Fed Employees, 1966; scout master, Boy Scouts Am Philadelphia Coun, 1968; lay leader, Sayre Meml United Meth Church, Philadelphia, 1969; football coach, Philadelphia Police Athleitc League, 1969; treas, bd dir, Nat Alliance Postal & Fed Employees, Fed Credit Union Wash DC, 1977; treas, bd dir, Nat Alliance Postal & Fed Employees, Housing Corp Wash DC, 1979. **Honors/Awds:** Legion of Merit, Chapel Four Chaplins Philadelphia, 1969; Merit Service Award, Dist Five Nat Alliance Postal & Fed Employees, 1973. **Military Serv:** AUS, corpl, 2 yrs. **Home Addr:** 593 Blue Heron Rd, Dover, DE 19904. **Business Addr:** Data Processing Manager, Data Systems, Natl Alliance of Post Federal Employee, 1628 11th St NW, Washington, DC 20001.

BRODERICK, JOHNSON
Movie producer, president (organization). **Career:** Alcon Entertainment LLC, co-pres & co-founder, 1997-; Films: Love Is All There Is, 1996; Lost & Found, 1999; My Dog Skip, 2000; Dude, Where's My Car?, 2000; The Affair of the Necklace, 2001; Insomnia, 2002; Love Don't Cost a Thing, 2003; Chasing Liberty, 2004; Racing Stripes, 2005; Sisterhood Traveling Pants, 2005; Whole Pemberton Thing, 2005; P S I Love You, 2007; One Missed Call, 2008; The Sisterhood of the Traveling Pants 2, 2008. **Business Addr:** Co-president, Co-founder, Alcon Entertainment LLC, 10390 Santa Monica Blvd Suite 250, Los Angeles, CA 90404, **Business Phone:** (310)789-3040.

BROGDEN, ROBERT, JR.
Automotive executive, president (organization). **Personal:** Born Feb 13, 1958, Roswell, NM; son of Robert Sr & Billie; married Kathy Brogden, Feb 1989; children: Robert III, Anna. **Career:** K-G Men's Store, salesperson; Auto Dealership, sales mgr, 1982-92; Gen Motors, 1992-93; Robert Brogden's Olathe Pontiac-Buick-GMC Inc, pres, owner & dealer, 1993-. **Orgs:** bd dirs, Olathe Chamber Com, 1995-. **Honors/Awds:** Minority-Owned Bus of the Yr award, Kans Dept Com & Housing; Mark of Excellence, 1999; Kans Med Week Award Recipient, 2000. **Special Achievements:** One of the top 100 auto dealers in the nation, Black Enterprise mag; ranks 24th on Top 25 Area Automobile/Truck Dealers, The Bus Jour, 1999. **Business Addr:** President Owner, Dealer, Robert Brogden Olathe Pontiac-Buick-GMC Inc, 1500 E Santa Fe St, Olathe, KS 66061, **Business Phone:** (913)782-1500.*

BROMELL, LORENZO
Football player. **Personal:** Born Sep 23, 1975, Georgetown, SC. **Educ:** Clemson Univ. BA, sociol; Georgia Mil Col, AA, General Studies. **Career:** Miami Dolphins, defensive end, 1998-2001; Minn Vikings, defensive end, 2002; Oakland Raiders, defensive end, 2003; NY Giants, defensive end, 2004; CEO and Chairman, Bromell & Associates, LLC, currently. **Orgs:** Chmn, Emergency Patient Care; vice chmn, The Nat Caucus & Ctr Black Aged, Inc. *

BROMERY, KEITH MARCEL
Television journalist, school administrator. **Personal:** Born Sep 19, 1948, Washington, DC; son of Cecile Trescott Bromery and Randolph Wilson Bromery; married Susan Stanger Bromery, May 7, 1983; children: Marc Russell. **Educ:** Washington Journalism Center, Washington, DC, certificate, 1972; Univ Massachusetts, Amherst, MA, BA, 1972. **Career:** Chicago Daily News, Chicago, IL, reporter, 1972-75; CBS News, New York, NY, writer, 1975-77; WBBM-AM Radio, Chicago, IL, anchor/reporter, 1977-83; WMAQ-TV, Chicago, IL, writer/reporter, 1983-84; WLS-TV, Chicago, IL, reporter, 1984-, Ameritech Comed Entergy & GPU, Dir & Mgr. **Orgs:** Member, National Association of Black Journalists, 1987-; mem, Chicago Association of Black Journalists, 1987-; mem, Society of Professional Journalists, 1983-; writer/mem, Chicago Headline Club, 1983-. **Business Addr:** Reporter, WLS-TV, 190 N State St Suite 1100, Chicago, IL 60601.*

BROMERY, RANDOLPH WILSON
Geophysicist, educator. **Personal:** Born Jan 18, 1926, Cumberland, MD; son of Lawrence R and Edith E; married Cecile Trescott; children: Keith M, Carol Ann Thompson, Dennis R, David T & Christopher J. **Educ:** Univ Mich, 1946; Howard Univ, BS, math, 1956; American Univ, DC, MS, geol & geophys, 1962; Johns Hopkins Univ, PhD, geology, 1968. **Career:** US Geological Survey, exploration geophysicist, 1948-67; Univ Mass, prof geophys & dept chmn, 1968-70, vice chancellor, 1970-71, chancellor, 1971-79, commonwealth prof geophys; Westfield State Col, acting pres, 1988-90; Weston Geophys Int Corp, pres, 1981-83; Geosci Eng Corp, pres, 1983-; Mass Bd Regents, interim chancellor, 1990-; Springfield Col, pres, 1992-98; pres emer, 1998-; commonwealth prof emer geosci, 1992-; Roxbury Community Col, interim pres, 2002; Springfield Col, pres emer. **Orgs:** Bd dirs, Exxon Corp, NYNEX Corp, Singer Co; Chem Bank; Chase Manhattan Bank; John Hancock Mutual Life Ins Co; trustee, Johns Hopkins Univ; bd trustees, Roxbury community col. **Honors/Awds:** Gillman Fel, Johns Hopkins Univ, 1965-67; Hon Doctor of Law Hokkaido Univ, Japan, 1976; Doctor of Sci, Frostburg State Col, MD, 1972; Doctor of Humane Letters, Univ Mass, 1979; Dr of Educ, Western New England Col, MA,1972; Doctor of Humane Letters, Bentley College, 1993; Doctor of Humanities, Springfield Col, 1993; Distinguished Alumni, Howard Univ & John Hopkins Univ; Hon Alumnus, Univ Mass; pres, Geol Soc Am, 1990; Doctor of Pub Serv, Westfield State Col; Doctor Publ Service, N Adams State Col. **Military Serv:** USAF, 3 medals. **Home Addr:** 75 Cherry Ln, Amherst, MA 01002. *

BROMFIELD, CASSANDRA
Executive, fashion designer. **Career:** Cassandra Bromfield's Co, pres, currently. *

BRONNER, BERNARD
Executive. **Personal:** Son of Nathaniel H Sr. **Educ:** GA State Univ, bus. **Career:** Bronner Bros, vpres mkt; Upscale Commun Inc, publ, 1989-; Bronner Bros, pres & chief exec officer, 1993-. **Special Achievements:** Listed in Black Enterprise's Top 100 indust serv co, 1996. *

BRONNER, SHEILA
Editor. **Personal:** Married Bernard Bronner; children: 5. **Career:** Upscale Mag, ed-in-chief, currently. **Business Addr:** Editor-in-Chief, Upscale Magazine, 2141 Powers Ferry Rd Suite 300, Marietta, GA 30067, **Business Phone:** (770)988-0015.

BRONSON, DR. FRED JAMES
Dentist, clergy. **Personal:** Born Jan 10, 1935, Cincinnati, OH; son of William; married Barbara Dobbins; children: Fred Jr, Mark, Stefanie, Shellie, Shawn & Sharon. **Educ:** Miami Univ, Oxford, OH, BA, 1958; Howard Univ, Wash, DC, DDS, 1962. **Career:** Ky Dent Col, instr, 1973-76; Cincinnati Dental Soc, chmn peer rev, 1979-81, vpres, 1980, pres elect, 1981, pres, 1982; Temple Church Christ Written in Heaven, pastor, sr paster, currently; pvt pract, dentist. **Orgs:** Alpha Phi Alpha, 1957; delegate & trustee, Nat Dent Asn, 1962; Delegate Ohio Dent Asn 1978-; chmn, Dentist Concerned Dentists, 1980; fel Int Col Dentists, 1978, Am Col Dentists, 1983; Pierre Fauchard Acad, 1988. **Honors/Awds:** Distinguished Service, Residents Lincoln Heights, OH, 1969. **Business Addr:** Pastor, Temple Church of Christ Written In Heaven, 9700 Wayne Ave, Lincoln Heights, OH 45215, **Business Phone:** (513)563-0624.

BRONSON, OSWALD P.
College president. **Personal:** Born Jul 19, 1927, Sanford, FL; son of Flora Hollingshed and Uriah Perry; married Helen Carolyn Williams, Jun 8, 1952; children: Josephine Suzette, Flora Helen & Oswald Perry Jr. **Educ:** Bethune-Cookman Col, BS, 1950; Gammon Theol Sem, BD, 1959; N western Univ, PhD, 1965; St Paul's Col, Lawrenceville, DD. **Career:** Pastor, 1950-66; Methodist Mission & Leadership Schs, lectr & teacher; Interdenominational Theol Ctr, Atlanta, GA, dir field educ, 1964-68, vpres, 1966-68, pres, 1968-75; Bethune-Cookman Col, pres, 1975-2004; Edward Waters Col, pres, 2004. **Orgs:** United Negro Col Fund; Am Asn Theol Schs; Fla Asn Cols & Univs; Nat Asn Advan Colored People; Sch Bd, Volusia Co; Fla Gov's Adv Coun Productivity; exec comt

mem, Southern Regional Educ Bd; adv comt mem, Fla Sickle Cell Found; bd, Inst Black World, Wesley Community Ctr; Martin Luther King Ctr Social Change; Am Red Cross; United Way; Nat Asn Equal Opportunity Higher Educ, United Methodist Comt Relief. **Honors/Awds:** Herbert M Davidson Community Service Award, 2004; The Shafts of Light & Distinguished Alumnus Awards, Gammon Theol Sem, Bethune-Cookman Col; Crusade Scholar; United Negro Col Fund Award; Keys to the Cities of Orlando, Ormond Beach, Lakeland, St. Petersburg, Jacksonville, Ft. Lauderdale, Florida; Appreciation Award, Nat Black Am Law Student Asn; Distinguished Service Award, United Beauty School Owners & Teachers Asn; Distinguished Asbury Award, The United Methodist Church; Dedicated Educational and Community Service Award, American Judges of the State of Florida, 2003; Lifetime Achievement Award, Alpha Phi Alpha, 2003; Citizen of the Year Award, March of Dimes of Volusia, 2003; Enterprise Award for Community Service, Halifax Area Chamber Commerce, 2004; J. Saxton Lloyd Distinguished Service Award, Civic League of Daytona and Halifax Area, 2004; Leadership and Accomplishment Award, St. Petersburg Chap B-CC Alumni Asn, 2004; Silas Tillman Award for Distinguished Service, 2004; State of Florida Congressional Resolution, 2004; ONYX Award in Education, Onyx Magazine Publishing Co, 2004; Herbert M. Davidson Memorial Award for Community Service, 2004; Education and Community Award for Service, Miami-Dade Chap B-CC Alumni Asn, 2004; Years of Service Award, Volusia County Police Chiefs & Sheriffs, 2004; DDiv, Saint Pauls Col; Doctor of Laws, Stetson Univ; Doctor of Laws, Albion Col.

BRONSON, ROBERT ZACK

Football player. **Personal:** Born Jan 28, 1974, Jasper, TX. **Educ:** McNeese State Univ. **Career:** Football player (retired); San Francisco 49ers, defensive back, 1997-03; St Louis Rams, defensive back, 2004. **Honors/Awds:** Rookie of the Year, 1997. *

BRONZ, LOIS GOUGIS TAPLIN

Government official, educator. **Personal:** Born Aug 20, 1927, New Orleans, LA; daughter of Alex Gougis and Elise Cousin; married Charles; children: Edgar, Francine Shorts & Shelly. **Educ:** Xavier Univ, BA, 1948; La State Univ, attended 1954; Wayne State Univ, MEd, 1961; Houston Tillotson Col, attended 1962; Col New Rochelle, attended 1974. **Career:** Orleans Parrish Sch Bd, classroom teacher, 1948-61; Xavier Univ, admr, 1960-66; Nat Merit Comm, consult, 1965-67; Civil Serv Comn, 1966; Manhattan ville Col, 1968-73; Greenburgh Cent 7 Sch Dist, teacher, 1968-82; Town Greenburgh, councilwoman, 1975-91; Westchester County Bd Legislators, legislator - dist 8 1993-, vice chair, 1996-2001, chmn, 2002-04. **Orgs:** Founder, League Good Gov, New Orleans, LA; League Women Voters, Greenburgh NY; Greenburgh Housing Coun; Community Facility Comn; Woodhill Neighborhood Asn; Xavier Univ Admis Comn; Inter-Alumni Coun United Negro Col Fund; Black Dems Westchester City; Afro-Am Found; co-chairperson, Westchester Womens Coun; bd dirs, United Way Westchester; Union Child Day Care Ctr, Westchester Coalition; pres, Westchester Community opportunity prog; White Plains-Greenburgh, Nat Asn Am Colored People; Westchester Cty Penitentary; treas, Greenburgh Teachers Assoc Ware Bd; charter & exec mem, Westchester Black Womens Political Caucus; Xavier Univ Nat Alumni Asn; Childrens Village Dobbs Ferry; Child Care Coun Westchester; Alpha Kappa Alpha; Pi Iota Omega. **Honors/Awds:** Woman of the Year Award, Westchester County, 1990; Lifetime Achievement Award, Westchester Music Am, 1999; Lifetime of Courage Award, Omega Psi Phi, 2002; Leadership Award, Union Child Day Care Ctr, 2002; Appreciation Award, Fairview Fire Dept, 2002; Woman of the Year, Stroke Persons Westchester, 2002; Old Guard of White Plains Award, 2003; Senator Clinton African American Heritage Award, 2003; Greensburgh Educational Foundation Award, 2003; Fathers & Children Together Award, 2003; Achievement Award, Kappa Alpha Psi, 2003; American Asn of University Women Award, 2003; Natational Asn of Negro Business & Professional Womens Club Awareness Award; Black Democrats of Westchester Political Awareness Award; Westchester Black Women's Political Caucus Award; Westchester Advocate Newspaper Achievement Award; New York State Women's Political Caucus Award; Community Service Award, Westchester Black Lawyers Asn; Public Official of the Year, Westchester Chapter Nat Asn Social Workers. **Special Achievements:** First Woman & the first person of African descent to lead the Board of Legislators. **Home Addr:** 282 Old Tarrytown Rd, White Plains, NY 10603.

BROOKE, EDWARD WILLIAM

Senator (u.s. federal government), businessperson, law enforcement officer. **Personal:** Born Oct 26, 1919, Washington, DC; son of Edward W and Helen Seldon; married Ann Fleming, 1979; children: 3. **Educ:** Howard Univ, BS, 1941; Boston Univ Law Sch, LLB, 1948, LLM, 1950. **Career:** Senator (retired), business person; law pract, 1948; Commonwealth Mass, atty gen, 1963-67; US Senate, sen, 1967-79; Csaplar & Bok, Boston, coun, 1979-90; O'Connor & Hannan, Wash, DC, partner, 1979-; Bear & Stearns, NY, ltd partner, 1979-; Meditrust Inc, Boston, bd dirs, currently. **Orgs:** Chmn, Boston Fin Comn, 1961-62; Nat Coun BSA; Nat Bd Boys Clubs Am; fel Am Bar Asn; Mass Bar Asn; Boston Bar Asn; AMVETS; chmn bd, Opera Co Boston Inc; chmn & bd dirs, Boston Bank Com; fel Am Acad Arts & Sci; Spingarn Medal Comn; pub mem, Admin Conf US; bd dirs, Wash Performing Arts Soc; chair, Nat Low-Income Housing Coalition, 1979-; chmn, World Policy Coun, Alpha Phi Alpha, 1996, chmn emer, currently. **Honors/Awds:** Distinguished Service Award, AMVETS, 1952; Spingarn Medal, Nat Asn Advan Colored People, 1967; Charles Evans Hughes Award, Nat Conf Christians & Jews, 1967; Mary Hudson Onley Achievement Award Recipient, 2001; Presidential Medal of Freedom, 2004; 33 hon deg from various col & univ. **Special Achievements:** The first African American popularly elected to the United States Senate to serve since Reconstruction and the first to be re-elected. **Military Serv:** AUS, capt, 1942-45; Bronze Star. **Business Addr:** Partner, O'Connor & Hannan, 1666 K St NW Suite 500, Washington, DC 20006-2803, **Business Phone:** (202)887-1400.

BROOKER, MOE ALBERT

Educator, artist. **Personal:** Born Sep 24, 1940, Philadelphia, PA; son of Mack Henry and Lumisher Campbell; married Cheryl McClenney Brooker, Sep 28, 1985; children: Musa & Misha. **Educ:** Pa Acad Fine Art, cert painting, 1963; Tyler Sch Fine Art, Temple Univ, BFA, 1970, MFA, 1972. **Career:** Cleveland Inst Art, assoc prof, 1976-85; Individual Artist fel, State Pa, 1989; Pa Acad Fine Arts, prof, 1985-91; Cleveland Arts fel, Womens Comm Cleveland, 1985; Parson Sch Design, chairperson found dept, 1991-93; Moore Col Art & Design, assoc prof, 1995-, chmn basics, 2004-, prof 2d fine arts & basics, currently; Millersville Univ, Conrad Nelson fel, 2004. **Orgs:** Bd mem, New Orgn Visual Arts, 1978-85; panelist, Ohio Coun Arts, 1980; Mayo's Comm Arts, City Philadelphia, 1985-; Pa Coun Arts, State Pa, 1985-87; artist adv bd, Fabric Workshop, 1985-; Fine Arts Comm Penn Conv Ctr, 1990-93; adv bd, Mainline Ctr Arts, 1990-; chair, Phil Art Comn, 2008-. **Honors/Awds:** First Prize, May Show, Cleveland Museum Art, 1978; Artist Giant to China, City Philadelphia, China, 1987; Van Der Zee Award, Brandywine Workshop; Van Der Zee Lifetime Achievement Award, 2003. **Special Achievements:** Commissioned by UNESCO, to produce two cards for world wide publishing, juror painting & drawing Scottsdale Center for the Arts AZ 1980. **Military Serv:** AUS, sp4, 1963-65. **Home Addr:** 6221 Greene St, Philadelphia, PA 19144.

BROOKS, AARON LAFETTE

Football player. **Personal:** Born Mar 24, 1976, Newport News, VA; married Tisa. **Educ:** Univ Va, anthropology, 1998. **Career:** Football player (retired); Green Bay Packers, 1999; New Orleans Saints, quarter back, 2000-05; Oakland Raiders, 2006. **Honors/ Awds:** NFC Offensive Player of the Week, 2000, 2002; NFL.com FedEx Air Player of the Week, 2004. **Special Achievements:** Named starting quarterback, New Orleans Saints, 2001. *

BROOKS, ALVIN LEE

Government official. **Personal:** Born May 3, 1932, North Little Rock, AR; married Carol Rich, Aug 23, 1950; children: Ronall, Estelle, Carrie, Diane, Rosalind & Tameisha. **Educ:** Univ Mo, Kansas City, BA, hist & govt, 1959, MA, sociol, 1973. **Career:** Kans City Police Dept, detective & police officer; Kans City Sch Dist,home sch coordr, 1964-66; Neighborhood Youth Corp, Cath Diocese, Kansas City, St Joseph, dir, out sch proj, 1966-67; Kans City, coordr pub info & com interpr, 1967-68; Human Rels Dept, Kans City, dir, 1968-73, 1980-; City Kans, MO, asst city mgr, 1973-80; Kans City, Mo, rep; Bd Mem, currently. **Orgs:** Past vpres, Bd Regents Ctr, Mo State Univ, 1975-82; chmn, Mo Comn Human Rights, 1975-82; chmn, Mo Black Leadership Asn, 1979-82; Nat Asn Human Rights Workers, 1968-; Int Asn Off Human Rights Agencies, 1969-; convenor, Ad Hoc Group Against Crime, 1977, pres, 1991-; vpres, Prime Heal Inc, 1987. **Honors/Awds:** Man of the Year, Ivanhoe Club, 1969; Outstanding Citizen of the Year, Beta Omega Chap, Omega Psi Phi, 1972; Outstanding Citizen of the Year, Young Progressives, 1973; Alumni Achievement Award, Univ Mo, Kans City, 1975; Kans City Tomorrow, 1988; Nat Conf Christians & Jews, 1989; Pres's Nat Drug Adv Coun, 1989-92; UMKC Alumnus of the Year, 2009. **Special Achievements:** Recognized by former Drug Czar, William Bennet, as being one of the nation's "el3frontline soldiers in our war against drugs;" honored by Pres George Bush in November, 1989, for his work with Ad Hoc. *

BROOKS, ARKLES CLARENCE, JR.

Salesperson. **Personal:** Born Aug 25, 1943, Detroit, MI; son of Arkles Clarence Sr; married Sarah L; children: Arkles III, Ira David, Alice Ruth & Sharon Louise. **Educ:** Southern Ill Univ, BA, 1967; Wayne State Univ, MA, 1976, educ specialist, gen admin, supv, 1999. **Career:** Nat Bank Detroit, asst br mgr, 1968-70; Aetna Life & Casualty, career agt, 1970-72; Detroit Bd Educ, math sci teacher, 1971-73; Upjohn Co, hosp sales specialist, 1973-; Allstate Ins, Southfield, Mich, sales assoc, 1987-; Dey L P Inc Distribr, Mich Dist, sales mgr, 1996-. **Orgs:** Wayne Co Notary Pub, 1968-; Nat Asn Life Underwriters, 1970-; pres, Varsity Club Inc, 1971-; corp treas, Gospel Chapel Detroit Inc, 1972-, assoc pastor, 1985-, exec vpres, 1989-, pastor, pres, 1999-; bd mem, Circle Y Christian Camp; bd mem, corp secy, Int Christian Ministries, pres, chief exec officer, Transplus Ministries. **Home Addr:** 30436 Embassy Dr, Beverly Hills, MI 48025, **Home Phone:** (313)642-6237. **Business Addr:** President, Pastor, Gospel Chapel, 16241 Harper Ave, Detroit, MI 48224, **Business Phone:** (313)885-7940.

BROOKS, AVERY FRANKLIN

Movie director, educator, actor. **Personal:** Born Oct 2, 1948, Evansville, IN; son of Samuel Leon and Eva Lydia Crawford; married Vicki Lenora; children: Ayana, Cabral & Asante. **Educ:** Indiana Univ; Oberlin Col; Rutgers Univ, New Brunswick NJ, BA, MFA. **Career:** Rutgers Univ, assoc prof theater, 1976-; Nat Black Arts Festival, artistic dir, 1993-96; Films: Solomon Northup's Odyssey, actor, 1984; Quest for Life, 2000; 15 Minutes, actor, 2001; Star Trek: Legacy, 2006; TV series: "Solomon Northup's Odyssey ", 1984; "Uncle Tom's Cabin ", 1987; "Roots: The Gift ", 1988; "A Man Called Hawk", 1989; "Track down", 1991; "The Ernest Green Story ", 1993; "Spenser: For Hire?; "A Man Called Hawk"; "X: The Life & Times of Malcolm X"; "Othello"; "Star Trek: Deep Space Nine", actor & dir; "Star Trek: Deep Space Nine", 1993-99; "Gargoyles", 1996; "Jesus: The Complete Story", 2001; "Ancient Evidence", 2003; "Russell Simmons Presents Def Poetry", 2005; Mason Gross Sch Arts, prof theater, currently. **Honors/Awds:** Hon Degrees, Oberlin Col, Tougaloo Univ, State Univ NY, Buffalo, Indiana Univ; Rutgers University Hall of Distinguished Alumni, 1993. **Special Achievements:** First African-American to receive an MFA in acting and directing from Rutgers University; ACE Award nomination. **Business Addr:** Professor of Theater, Mason Gross School of the Arts, 33 Livingston Ave, New Brunswick, NJ 08901-1959, **Business Phone:** (732)932-9360.

BROOKS, BARRETT

Football player. **Personal:** Born May 5, 1972, St Louis, MO; married Sonji, May 7, 1997; children: Romel, Jasmine Johnson, Asia Johnson, Izreal & Chyna. **Educ:** Kans State Univ. **Career:** Football player(retired); Philadelphia Eagles, tackle, 1995-98; Detroit Lions, 1999-2000; Green Bay Packers, 2002; New York Giants, 2002; Pittsburgh Steelers, tackles, 2003-06. *

BROOKS, BERNARD W.

Artist. **Personal:** Born Sep 6, 1939, Alexandria, VA; married. **Educ:** Univ Md, 1960; Philadelphia Music Col Art, attended 1961; Corcoran Gallery Sch Art, attended 1962; Howard Univ, attended 1965. **Career:** A&B Assoc, Washington, DC, assoc dir; Howard Univ, Col Dent, chief med illusr; Opus 2 Galleries, assoc dir; Just Lookin gallery, artist, currently; Van Heusen Shirt Co, asst art dir; Grand Union Food Co Inc, Landover, MD, asst advert mgr; Atlantic Res Corp, Alexandria, VA, tech illusr; Grand Union Food Co, Landover, MD, technician; Bernard W Brooks Studio, owner & dir; DC Art Asn, vpres; St. Croix, half time resident. **Orgs:** Publ artist, Am Chem Soc, Washington, DC; Wash Water Color Asn; pub rels dir, Nat Conf Artists. **Honors/Awds:** 1st prize, George F Muth Award, Howard Univ, 1962; 2nd prize, Howard Univ, 1963; 1st prize, D/C Rec Outdoor Art Show, 1971; 2nd prize, Montgomery Mall Outdoor Art Show, 1972. **Special Achievements:** Art exhibited in Georgetown Graphics Gallery; numerous professional exhibitions; collections; Radio-TV presentations; his art has been featured on national television on "Evening Magazine", Black Entertainment Television News Special, and the "Fresh Prince of Bel Air". **Military Serv:** USAR, pfc. **Business Addr:** Artist, Just Lookin Gallery, 40 Summit Ave, Hagerstown, MD 21740.

BROOKS, BRIAN A.

Executive, business owner. **Career:** EE Ward Moving & Storage Co LLC, pres & co-owner, currently. **Business Addr:** President, EE Ward Moving & Storage Company LLC, 1177 Joyce Ave Suite A, Columbus, OH 43219, **Business Phone:** (614)298-8414.

BROOKS, CARL

Executive. **Personal:** Born Aug 1, 1949, Philadelphia, PA; son of Nathaniel and Sarah Lee Williams; married Drena Hastings Brooks, Oct 6, 1973; children: Tarik, Karima. **Educ:** Hampton Univ, BS, 1971; Southern Ill Univ, MBA, 1976; Univ Iowa, exec develop prog, 1981; Dartmouth Col, Tuck exec prog, 1990. **Career:** Jersey Cent Power & Light Co, Morristown, NJ, corp mgr contracts, 1977-86; GPU Serv Corp, NJ, vpres, mats & serv, 1980-96; Allenhurst, NJ, shore div, div dir, 1986-90; GPU Generation Inc, vpres finance & admin; Howard Univ, Sch Bus Admin, hon chair; GPU Energy, Human & Tech Resources, vpres; Exec Leadership Found, chair, 1999-01; Exec Leadership Coun & Exec Leadership Found, pres & chief exec officer, 2001-. **Orgs:** Pres, Exec Leadership Coun & Found; exec bd dirs, Nat Minority Supplier Devel Coun; chmn, Advocacy Comn; chmn, corp fundraising, United Way, 1986-90; Leadership NJ; chmn, African Relief Fund; bd dirs, Red Cross; Red Bank Chamber Com, 1986-; YMCA; Franklin Little League; Am Soc Asn Exec; Nat Asn Corp Dir. **Honors/Awds:** Outstanding Scholar, Beta Gamma Sigma, 1978; Outstanding Alumni Award, Benjamin Franklin High Sch, 1989; Leadership Award, Leadership NJ, 1997; Nat Eagle Leadership Award, 1997; NAACP Leadership Award, 2001; Spirit of Partnership Award, EEOC, 2004; DHL, Richmond Va Seminary, 2005. *

BROOKS, CAROL LORRAINE

Government official, administrator. **Personal:** Born Nov 23, 1955, Brooklyn, NY. **Educ:** Univ Vt, BA, 1977; Rutgers Univ, attended 1979; Sch Int Training, attended 1975. **Career:** Walter Russell Scholar, 1977; CBS News Inc, proj coordr, 1978-81; NJ Off Gov, spec asst, 1981-85; NJ Dept Environ Protection, admin, 1985-, spec asst, 1982-90. **Orgs:** Bd dir, Family Serv Asn Trenton/ Hopewell Valley, 1983-; comt mem, NJ Martin Luther King Jr

Commemorative Comn, 1985-; Urban League Guild Metrop Trenton, 1986-. **Honors/Awds:** 100 Young Women of Promise, Good Housekeeping Mag, 1985; Outstanding Young Women of Am, 1986; Employ Serv Award, NJ State Govt, 1987. **Home Addr:** 15 Winthrop Rd, Lawrenceville, NJ 08648.

BROOKS, DR. CAROLYN BRANCH
Educator, college administrator. **Personal:** Born Jul 8, 1946, Richmond, VA; daughter of Charles W and Shirley Booker; married Henry M, Sep 28, 1965; children: Charles T, Marcellus L, Alexis J & Toni A. **Educ:** Tuskegee Univ, Tuskegee, Ala, BS, 1968, MS, 1971; Ohio State Univ, Columbus, OH, PhD, 1977. **Career:** Bullock County Bd Educ, Union Springs, Ala, science teacher, 1968-69; Macon County Bd Educ, Tuskegee, Ala, sci teacher, 1971-72; Va Hosp, Tuskegee, Ala, res technician, 1972-73; Ohio State Univ, Columbus, OH, grad teaching asst, 1975-77; Ky State Univ, Frankfort KY, prin investr & prog dir, 1978-81; Univ Md Eastern Shore, asst prof, 1981-87, assoc prof, 1987-96, prof, 1996-, dept chair, Sch Agr & Natl Sci, dean, currently, dir, Agr Exp Sta, currently. **Orgs:** Salvation Army Youth Club Coun; Nat Asn Advan Colored People; Nat Asn Univ Women; Minorities Agr, Natural Resources, Related Serv; Am Soc Microbiol, Multiple Sclerosis Coun, 1994-95. **Honors/Awds:** Outstanding Serv Award, Silhouettes of Kappa Alpha Psi, 1980; First Place Award, Competitive Paper Presentation, Seventh Biennial Research Symposium HBCU, 1987; Outstanding Faculty Award for Research, Sch Agricultural Sciences, 1987-88; Chancellor's Research Scholar Award, 1988; Woman of the Year Award, Maryland Eastern Shore Branch of the Nat Assn Univ Women, 1988; First Annual White House Initiative Faculty Award Excellence Sci & Technol, 1988; Outstanding Educator Award, Maryland Assn Higher Educ, 1990; Faculty Award Excellence & Achievement, UMES Alumni Assn. **Business Addr:** Dean & Director, Professor, University Maryland Eastern Shore, School Agriculture & Natural Science, Early Childhood Res Ctr, 3003 Hazel Hall, Princess Anne, MD 21853, **Business Phone:** (410)200-4566.

BROOKS, CLYDE HENRY
Labor relations manager, manager, executive director, abbot. **Personal:** Born Sep 5, 1941, Danville, IL; son of George and Venie. **Educ:** Western Ill Univ, BS, 1958, MS. **Career:** Harper Community Col, fac; Chicago Metro Chap S Christian Leadership Conf, pres, 1972-. **Orgs:** Coun, Marillac Settlement House, 1963-66; employ coun, Ill State Employ Serv Chicago, 1964; coun, Crane HS Chicago, 1964; neighborhood worker, Chicago Comn Youth Welfare, 1961-64; probation officer, Juv Ct Cook Co Chicago, 1959-61; teacher, Wendel Phillips Eve Sch, 1959-65; dir, Sears Roebuck Community Coop Proj Chicago, 1965-66; supvr, Dept Ed JOBS Proj Chicago 1964-65; area dir, Cook Co Off Equal Opport Inc Chicago, 1966-67; coun, Scott Foresman Pub Co, 1969-; coun, Ill Drug Abuse Prog, 1969-71; vis prof, Harper Col, 1970-77; pres & bd chmn, Behav Res Action Soc Sci BRASS, Chicago, 1969-71; chmn, Ed Labs IElk Grove Village, IL, 1969-71; teacher, St Mary Lake Sem Mundelein, IL, 1965; field work instr, Univ Chicago, 1972-; chmn & chief exec officer, Minority Econ Resourses Corp 1972-; assoc & exec dir & manpower dir, Cook Co Off Equal Opport Inc Chicago, 1968-73; dir, Nat Equal Employ Opport & Employee Rels Blue Cross & Blue Shield Asns, 1973-; Chicago C C & Indust, 1973-; Ill State C C, 1973-; Ill Parole Bd, 1993-; former mem, Ill Prisoner Review Bd; former mem, Ill Human Rights Comn; Mt Prospect Fire & Police Comn; retired chmn, Minority Econ Resources Corp; Interfaith Church Coun Mt Prospect; pres, Ill Comn Diversity & Human Rels or Suburban Human Rels Comn, currently. **Honors/Awds:** Publ, "Rockwell Garden Comm Appraisal Study"; Chicago authority publ, "Midwest Comm Teenage Study"; publ, "The Negro in Amer"; Hometown Award, 2005. **Special Achievements:** First African American to teach African American History at St Mary of the Lake Seminary. **Business Addr:** President, Suburban Human Relations Commission/Illinois Commission On Diversity & Human Relations, 1404 Apricot Suite A, Mount Prospect, IL 60056.

BROOKS, DR. DAISY M. ANDERSON
Child care worker, business owner, executive director. **Personal:** Children: Yolanda Denise, Wadell Jr & Cassandra Annette. **Educ:** Nat Inst Practical Nursing, Chicago, practical nurses training; Northwestern Med Sch, Chicago, training med tech; Pac Western Univ, MA, human resources develop; Faith Grant Col, EdD. **Career:** Tots & Toddlers Day Care Ctr Inc, Waukegan, IL, co-owner, gen contractor, 1975; Victory Mem Hosp, med tech, Phys & Surg Lab, Waukegan, IL, supvry med techl; Daisy's Nursery, co-owner & exec dir, Daisys Resource Ctr. **Orgs:** Worthy Matron Order Eastern Star, 1974; officer, Golden Circle 59; mem, Deaconess Shiloh Baptist Church; pres, Music Dept; N Chicago Br, NAACP; pres, Progressive Comt Organ N Chicago; secy, Cent Grade Sch PTA; treas, N Chicago Black Caucas; bd dir, Altrusa Int Clb/Day Care Crisis Coun State IL; Citizen Adv Comt, Lake Co Area Voc Ctr; N Chicago HS Voc Adv Comt; vpres, N Chicago Great Lakes VA C of C; vpres, Day Care Crisis Coun St IL/ Citizens Adv Comt, N Chicago Comn Block Develop; chairperson, Scholar Comn; Mt Sinai Baptist Church; pres, N Chicago Dist 64 Band Parents Asn. **Honors/Awds:** Bus Person of the Year; Citizen of the Year; Humanitarian of the Year. *

BROOKS, DR. DANA DEMARCO
Dean (education). **Personal:** Born Aug 1, 1951, Hagerstown, MD. **Educ:** Hagerstown Jr Col, Hagerstown, MD, AA, 1971; Towson State Col, Towson, MD, BS, 1973; WVA Univ, Morgantown, West VA, MS, 1976, EdD, 1979. **Career:** Wash County, teacher, 1974; W V Univ, grad teaching asst, 1974-78, from instr phys educ to assoc prof phys educ, 1978-88, provost off, minority recruitment, retention coordr, 1986-87, acting asst dean phys educ sch, 1986-87, acting chairperson, sport dept, 1987, Phys Educ Sch, prof, 1988-, acting dean, 1988, assoc dean, 1987-92, acting grad coordr, 1991, interm dean, 1992-93, dean, 1993-present. **Orgs:** Social justice chairperson, 1989-, W Va Asn Health, Phys Educ, Recreation, Dance, 1983-84; vpres, 1987-88, rep bd dirs, 1996-, Midwest Dist, Health, Phys Educ, Recreation, Dance; Phi Delta Kappa; N Am Soc Sport Sociol; pres, Am Alliance Health, Phys Educ, Recreation, Dance; Fellow, Am Acad Kinesiology & Physical Educ. **Honors/Awds:** Outstanding Teacher of the Year, W Va Univ, 1979-83, 1986-87; Honor Award, W Va Asn, Health, Physical Education, Recreation, Dance, 1985; Young Professional Award, Mid W Dist, Health, Physical Education, Recreation, Dance, 1982; Social Justice Award, W Va Univ, 1992; Ray O Duncan Award, W Va Asn Health, Physical Education, Recreation, Dance, 1991; Rev Dr Martin Luther King Jr, Achievement Award, 1997; Outstanding Alumnus Award, Hagerstown Jr Col, 50th Anniversary; Towson Univ Dean's Recognition Award, 1999; Midwest AAHPERD Honor Award, 2004-05; Hagerstown Community Col Sports Hall of Fame, 2003; Fellow of the North American Society of HPERSD Professionals, April 2008; E.B. Henderson Award, 2006. **Business Addr:** Dean, Professor, West Virginia University, College of Physical Activity and Sport Sciences, 258 Coliseum, PO Box 6116, Morgantown, WV 26506-6116, **Business Phone:** (304)293-0826.

BROOKS, DERRICK DEWAN
Football player. **Personal:** Born Apr 18, 1973, Pensacola, FL; son of Geraldine Mitchell; married Carol; children: Brianna Monai, Denice, Derrick Jr & Darius. **Educ:** Fla State Univ, BA, bus commun. **Career:** Tampa Bay Buccaneers, linebacker, 1995-2008; free agent, currently. **Orgs:** Brooks Bunch Found, founder; mem, Bd Trustees, Fla State Univ. **Honors/Awds:** Tampa Tribune People's Champion Award, 1998; Florida Sports Awards, 2000, 2001; Walter Payton Man of the Year Award, 2000; AP Defensive Player of the Year, 2002; EDDIE Award, Hillsborough Education Found, 2002; Bart Starr Award, 2003; Byron "Whizzer" White Award, 2004; Pro Bowl MVP, 2005. *

BROOKS, DIANE K
Executive director. **Educ:** Howard Univ, Wash, DC, BA, Psychol; Gallaudet Univ, MA. **Career:** Nat Tech Inst Deaf, assoc dir, 2003-, Northeast Tech Assistance Ctr, dir, assoc dean outreach & tech assistance, currently. **Orgs:** Postsecondary Educ Progs Network; Rochester Sch Deaf; Conf Educ Adminr Schs & Progs. **Business Addr:** Associate Dean for Outreach & Technical Assistance, Director, National Technical Institute for the Deaf, Northeast Technical Assistance Center, 52 Lomb Memorial Dr, Rochester, NY 14623, **Business Phone:** (585)475-6433.

BROOKS, DON LOCELLUS
Executive. **Personal:** Born in Galveston, TX; married Charlotte; children: Eric, Don Jr & Chris. **Educ:** Galveston Col, AA, mgt, 1975; Univ Houston, BS, mktg & mgt, 1977; Univ TX Austin, fin leadership, 1978. **Career:** Guaranty Fed Savings & Loans, mgt trainee, 1976-78, reg savings coordr, 1978-80, asst vpres, 1980-81, vpres savings, 1981. **Orgs:** Founder, Galveston Col Key Club, 1975; bd trustees, Galveston Park Bd, 1982-; bd dir, Family Serv Ctr, 1984-85; United Way Inc, Galveston, 1984-85, Legis Comt Galveston, 1984-; coun rep, City Galveston, 1984-; chairperson, Fiscal Auditing & Ins Comn, City Galveston Park Bd Trustees, 1984-85; Exec Comn, United Way Inc Galveston, 1985. **Honors/Awds:** Two President Award Certificate, Galveston Col, 1973; Two Deans Award Certificate, Galveston Col, 1974; Highest Vote, Getter Galveston City Coun, 1984-85.

BROOKS, DUNBAR
Executive. **Personal:** Born Oct 11, 1950, Baltimore, MD; son of Mable and Ernest Blackwell; married Edythe E Mason, Jun 8, 1977; children: Tracey Young, Gary Young & Cheryl. **Educ:** Community Col Baltimore, AA, urban develop, 1975; Morgan State Univ, BS, urban studies, 1976; Univ Baltimore, MPA, 1978; Johns Hopkins Univ, attended 1979. **Career:** US Dept Transp, mail & file clerk, 1973-74; Baltimore Regional Coun Govt, mgr, census & small area data, info systs planner, land use & housing planner, 1975-92; Baltimore Metrop Coun, mgr, census & small area data, sr demographer, 1992, mgr data develop, MetroResearch Div, dir, currently; Community Col Baltimore County, pres, Dundalk Campus adj fac mem. **Orgs:** Pres, Dundalk-Sparrows Point NAACP, 1978-; chmn bd, Turner Sta Develop Corp, 1980-; pres, Baltimore County Bd Educ, 1989-; fed rel network chairperson, Nat Sch Bd Asn; Md State Bd Educ Asn, 1992, vpres, currently; Selective Serv Syst, Local Draft Bd 36, Baltimore County, MD, 1994-; U.S. Selective Serv Bd; Visionary Panel Better Schs, Achievement Initiative Maryland's Minority Students Coun & Assoc Black Charities; Franklin Sq Hosp Bd Dirs, Southern Area dir, Nat Asn State Bds Educ, 2003-07; pres, Md State Bd Educ, 2007-. **Honors/Awds:** Distinguished Service Award, Human Resources Develop Agency Baltimore County, 1985; Distinguished Service Award, Baltimore County NAACP, 1987. **Military Serv:** AUS, sp 4c, 1971-72; Vietnam Meritorious Award, 2nd Oak Leaf Cluster. **Home Addr:** 102 E Ave, Dundalk, MD 21222, **Home Phone:** (410)282-6905. **Business Addr:** Director, Baltimore Metropolitan Council, 2700 Lighthouse Pt E Suite 310, Baltimore, MD 21224-4774, **Business Phone:** (410)732-0500.

BROOKS, FABIENNE
Law enforcement officer. **Educ:** FBI Acad, grad. **Career:** Commander (retired); King County Sheriffs Off, officer, sergeant, lt, capt, precinct comdr, chief; Atlantic fel pub policy, London, Eng, 1996; Wash Chap, FBI Nat Acad Assoc Inc. **Orgs:** Int Asn Women Police. **Special Achievements:** First African Am woman to be promoted to the ranks of sergeant, lt, capt, major and chief with the King County Sheriffs Off; First African Am officer with the King County Sheriffs Off to attend the FBI Academy; First female to head a major invests sect KCSO.

BROOKS, GOLDEN A.
Actor. **Personal:** Born Dec 1, 1970, San Francisco, CA. **Educ:** Univ Calif, Berkeley, BA, lit & sociol; Sarah Lawrence Col, MA. **Career:** TV series: "Linc's", 1998; "Girlfriends", 2000; Films: Drive by A Love Story, 1997; Hell's Kitchen, 1998; Timecode, 2000; Impostor, 2002; Motives, 2004; Beauty Shop, 2005; Something New, 2006; A Good man is hard to find, 2008. **Orgs:** Vol, Pediat AIDS Found; vol, AIDS Proj, Los Angeles. **Honors/Awds:** BET Comedy Award, Outstanding Supporting Actress in a Comedy Series, 2004; Nominee, Image Award, 2008. **Special Achievements:** Nominated for Outstanding Actress in a Comedy Series, Image Award, 2003;Black Reel Award for Best Actress, 2005. **Business Addr:** Actress, United Paramount Network (UPN), 11800 Wilshire Blvd, Los Angeles, CA 90025, **Business Phone:** (310)575-7000.*

BROOKS, HARRY W, JR.
Executive, army officer, chief executive officer. **Personal:** Born May 17, 1928, Indianapolis, IN; son of Harry W Sr and Nora E; married June Hezekiah, Nov 24, 1985; children: Harry W III, Wayne L & Craig E. **Educ:** Univ nebr, Omaha, BS, 1962; Univ Okla, MA, 1973; Univ Nebr, Omaha, BGE; AUS War Col, Carlysle, PA; Stanford Grad Sch Bus exec prog; Army Command & Gen Staff Col, Army War Col, attended. **Career:** Maj gen (retired), chmn: AUS, pvt maj gen, 1947-76, comndg gen, 25th Infantry Div, HI, 1974-76; USAR, 1962-65; Command & Gen Staff Col, stud officer, 1965-66; 72nd Field Artillery Group, comdr, 1970-72; 2nd Div, Korea, asst comdr, 1973-74; Amfac, Inc, sr vpres & pub affairs dir, 1978-82, exec vpres & chmn Horticulture group, 1982-84; Advan Consumer Mkt Corp, chmn & ceo, 1985-96; Gurney Seed & Nursery Corp, chmn & ceo, 1985-90; Gurney Wholesale Inc, chmn & ceo, 1985-90; Western Comput Group Inc, chmn & ceo, 1985-90; Brooks Intl, pres, 2004, chmn, currently. **Orgs:** Trustee, Freedom Forum, 1976-; dir, Occup Med Corp Am, 1985-96; trustee, San Mateo Easter Seals, 1988-89; dir, San Francisco Opera, 1988-92; Seven Air Medale, 1967. **Honors/Awds:** AUS, Distinguished Service Medal, 1976, Legion of Merit, 1970, Vietnamese Cross of Gallantry, 1967, Bronze Star, 1967; Leonard H Carter Award, Nat Asn Advan Colored People, Region I, 1988. **Military Serv:** AUS, major gen, 1947-76. **Home Addr:** 4679 Lomas Santa Fe St, Las Vegas, NV 89147-6028. **Business Addr:** President, Chairman, Brooks International, 4679 Lomas Sante Fe, Las Vegas, NV 89147, **Business Phone:** (702)871-1751.*

BROOKS, DR. HENRY MARCELLUS
School administrator. **Personal:** Born Oct 16, 1942, Tuskegee, AL; son of Ruth Jackson and Ewing Tipton; married Carolyn D Branch, Sep 28, 1965; children: Charles Tipton, Marcellus Leander, Alexis Janine & Toni Andrea. **Educ:** Tuskegee Univ, Tuskegee, Ala, BS, 1965, MEd, 1966; Ohio State Univ,Columbus, OH, PhD, 1975. **Career:** Auburn Univ, Union Spring, Ala, exten farm agent, 1967-73; Kentucky State Univ, Frankfort, KY, exten specialist, 1975-80; Univ Md Eastern Shore Exten, Princess Anne, exten admin, 1980-, assoc dir, assoc prof & coordr, currently, Agr Exp Sta, asst dir, currently. **Orgs:** Sigma Pi Phi; Kappa Alpha Psi. **Honors/Awds:** Eastern Shore President's Award, Univ Md, 1992; Pres Delegate Assembly, Mid-Eastern Athletic Conf, 1992, honored at an African American History Month ceremony, 2008. **Home Addr:** 30173 Stoneybrooke Dr, Salisbury, MD 21804-2486, **Home Phone:** (410)546-3414. **Business Addr:** Extension Administrator & Associate professor, Associate Director, University of Maryland Eastern Shore, Rm 2122 Richard A Henson Ctr, Princess Anne, MD 21853, **Business Phone:** (410)651-6206.

BROOKS, JAMES ROBERT
Football player. **Personal:** Born Dec 28, 1958, Warner Robins, GA; married Simone Renee; children: James Darnell & Tianna Renee. **Educ:** Auburn Univ, attended 1980. **Career:** Football player (retired); San Diego Chargers, running back, 1981-83; Cincinnati Bengals, running back, 1984-91; Cleveland Browns, running back,1992; Tampa Bay Buccaneers, running back, 1992. **Honors/Awds:** All-Am, Auburn Univ; High School All-American Nat Champion, Warner-Robins, Ga team; All Pro; played in Pro

Bowl, 1986, 1988-90. **Special Achievements:** Led the NFL in total yards, rushing, receiving, punt & kickoff returns, 1981-82.

BROOKS, JAMES TAYLOR
Military leader. **Personal:** Born Mar 3, 1945, Memphis, TN; son of Booker T and Elizabeth P; married Jacqueline D, Apr 11, 1969; children: Bryant O, Brandi C & Kamaroon A. **Educ:** Memphis Univ, BS, 1976. **Career:** Firestone Tire & Rubber Co, prod supvr, 1968-83; Albright Chemical Co, sales mgr, 1983-86; Mich Air Nat Guard, recruiting & retention supt, 1986-. **Orgs:** NCOA Grad Asn, 1983-; Nat Guard Asn Mich, 1986-; Cummings St Baptist Church, 1989-; Wade A McCree Jr Scholar Prog, 1990-; Big Brother & Big Sister, 1994-; Tuskegee Airmen, Detroit Chap, 1995-; Nat Asn Advan Colored People. **Honors/Awds:** Service Award, Wade A McCree Jr Scholarship Program, 1995. **Military Serv:** Mich Air Nat Guard, smsgt, 1986-; Airmen of the Year, TN, 1985. **Business Addr:** Recruiting, Retention Superintendant, Michigan Air National Guard, 25 S Washington, Lansing, MI 48913, **Business Phone:** (517)372-8767.

BROOKS, JOHN S.
Manager. **Personal:** Born Mar 4, 1951, Greenwood, MS; son of John J and Bernice; married Barbara E Brooks, Jul 27, 1973; children: Jason S. **Educ:** ITT Tech Inst Assocs, elec engineering technol, 1971; Ind Wesleyan Univ, BS, Bus Mgt, 1992; Anderson Univ, MBA, 1996. **Career:** JS Brooks Realty, owner; Delphi-E, prod worker, 1969-71, lab technician, 1972-83, supvr engineering labs, 1983-87, mgr prod engineering labs, 1987-88, supvr switch engineering, 1988-91, mgr, switch engineering, 1992, test & facil mgr, 1992-. **Orgs:** Anderson Zion Baptist Church, 1962-; past master, Peerless Lodge No 32 Masonic, 1980-; life mem, NAACP, 1983-; scholar comt, Prince Hall Grand Lodge Ind, 1984-; bd chmn, Wilson Boys & Girls Club, 1994-96; qual comt mem, St Johns Hosp, 1996-; coun pres, Ind Area Coun, Boys & Girls Clubs Am, 1997-; rep, IN & KY, Nat Area Coun; Boys & Girls Clubs Am, 1997. **Honors/Awds:** US Patent Off, US patent No 4,481,925, 1984; Worshipful Master of the Year, Prince Hall Grand Lodge Ind, 1984. **Home Addr:** 85 Royal Troon, Springboro, OH 45066. *

BROOKS, JOSEPH
City planner. **Career:** Emergency Land Fund, Atlanta, Ga, pres; Rev Black Polit Econ, New York, NY, ed; San Francisco Found, prog exec neighborhood & community develop; PolicyLink, vpres civic engagement, currently. **Orgs:** Nat co-chair, Neighborhood Funders Group; vice chair, Asn of Black Found Execs. **Business Addr:** Vice President for Civic Engagement, Policy Link, 1438 Webster St Suite 303, Oakland, CA 94612, **Business Phone:** (510)663-2333.*

BROOKS, JOYCE RENEE WARD
Systems analyst. **Personal:** Born Sep 9, 1952, Kansas City, MO; married John L; children: Carmen & Leah. **Educ:** Washington Univ, BS, bus admin, 1974. **Career:** Mobil Oil Corp, programmer & analyst, 1972-73; Southwestern Bell Tele Co, acct off supv 1974-78, acct mgr, 1978-80, asst staff mgr, 1980-85, systs analyst, 1985. **Home Addr:** 12844 Stoneridge, Florissant, MO 63033, **Home Phone:** (314)355-0377.

BROOKS, LEO AUSTIN, SR.
Military leader. **Personal:** Born Aug 9, 1932, Washington, DC; married Naomi Ethel Lewis; children: Leo Jr, Vincent Keith, Marquita Karen. **Educ:** Va State Univ, BS, instrumental mus educ, 1954; Cent St Univ, Wilbeforce, OH, bus admin addtinal study, 1962; George Wash Univ, Washington, DC, MS, finance mgt, 1966. **Career:** Military leader (retired); Headquarters Dept Army, Washington, DC, cong coordr, 1967-70; Joint Chiefs Staff, Washington, DC, Cambodian desk officer, 1972-74; Sacramento Army Depot, comndg officer, 1974-76; 13th Corps Sport Command, Ft Hood, TX, comndg officer, 1976-78; AUS, Troop Sport Agency, Ft Lee, VA, comndg gen, 1978, major gen. **Orgs:** master, Acacia Lodge #32 Prince Hall, F&A Masons, VA, 1967-; bd dir, United Urban League, Sacramento, CA, 1974-76; bd dir, Gr Sacramento United Way, 1974-76; chmn bd, Advis Jesuit High Sch, Sacramento, CA 1974-76; bd dir, United Serv Auto Asn, 1978-; pres, Fed Exec Asn 1979-. **Honors/Awds:** Fame of the Year, Freedom Found, Forge, PA, 1980; Recipient of Legion of Merit. **Military Serv:** AUS; Bronze Star, Meritorious Service Medal, Army Commendation Medal; Two Oakleaf Clusters.

BROOKS, LEROY
Government official. **Career:** Lowndes County, supvr dist 5, currently. **Orgs:** Nat Asn Counties. **Business Addr:** Supervisor, Lowndes County, County Courthouse, PO Box 1364, Columbus, MS 39703-1364, **Business Phone:** (662)329-5884.

BROOKS, MACEY
Football player. **Personal:** Born Feb 2, 1975, Hampton, VA. **Educ:** James Madison Univ. **Career:** Football player (retired); Dallas Cowboys, wide receiver, 1997; Chicago Bears, 1998-2000; Free agt, currently.

BROOKS, MARCELLUS
Educator, lecturer. **Personal:** Born Jun 24, 1941, Senatobia, MS; married Lula M; children: Marcellus Vaughn Brooks. **Educ:** Fisk Univ, BA, 1964; NY Univ & Univ Madrid, MA, 1965; Vanderbilt Univ, post grad work; Univ Ill; Univ Tenn. **Career:** Fisk Univ, Dept Foreign Langs, instr Span, 1965, dir study abroad, asst prof, currently, fulbright prog adv. **Orgs:** Sigma Delta Pi; Alpha Mu Gamma; Alpha Phi Alpha; Modern Language Asn; Tenn Lang Asn; Ford Foundation Grant, Univ Ill, 1968-69; Col Lang Asn. **Business Addr:** Assitant Professor, Fisk University, Department Foreign Langs, 1000 17th Ave N, Nashville, TN 37208-3051.

BROOKS, NORMAN LEON
School administrator. **Personal:** Born Feb 21, 1932, Port Chester, NY; son of William and Marion Harrell; married Barbara. **Educ:** State Univ NY, Potsdam Crane Sch Music, BS, 1954; Teachers Col, Columbia Univ, MA, 1961; NY Univ, A & Sup Cert, 1976. **Career:** Sch administrator (retired); Port Chester Pub Sch, gen music & instr, 1954-58; New Rochelle Pub Sch, vocal & gen mus instr, 1958-67; New Rochelle HS, choral instr, 1967-69; City Sch, Dist New Rochelle, supr mus educ, dir, 1969-97; Manhattanville Col, Music Educ, adj prof, 1997-2004; Sound Shore Chorale, artistic dir, 2003. **Orgs:** Choirmaster & organist, St Peter's Episcopal Ch, Port Chester, 1958-70; asst conductor, NY Collegiate Chorale, 1970-73; prog chmn, Keynote Fund Com, New Rochelle Libr, 1978-79; vestryman, St Peter's Episcopal Church Peekskill, 1987-; Phi Mu Alpha Sinfonia Hon Music Frat; pres, Westchester County, Sch Music Asn, 1990-92; vpres, New Rochelle Rotary Club, 1991-93, pres, 1993-94; chmn, Ministries Comt, St Peter's Episcopal Church, Peekskill, 1991-. **Honors/Awds:** Chairperson, Multi-Cultural Awareness Comn, NY Sch Music Asn, 1982-83; Leadership in Music Educ, Black Music Caucus Menc, 1989; Rotary Paul Harris fel, 1997. **Home Addr:** 1314 Edcris Rd, Yorktown Heights, NY 10598.

BROOKS, NORWARD J
Government official, college administrator. **Personal:** Born Sep 10, 1934, New Iberia, LA; son of Cleo Spencer and Ivory; married Violet Caldwell; children: Norward Jr, Cleoanna & David Eric Spencer. **Educ:** Southern Univ, BS, 1955; Seattle Univ, MBA, 1971; Univ WA, PhD, 1989. **Career:** Boeing Co Seattle, fac, 1959-69; United Inner City Develop Found, exec dir, 1969-70; King Co Govt Seattle, dir records & elections dept 1970-73; Wash State Employ Sec Dept, comnr, 1973-77; Univ Wash, dir admin data proc 1977-81; Model Capitol Corp, pres 1979-; Wash State Employ Security Dept, comnr, 1981-85; City Seattle, comptroller; Seattle Univ, adj prof, 1988-; Seattle Voc Inst, dir, 1995, exec dean, currently. **Orgs:** Past pres, Coun Minority Bus Enterprises Wash State, 1969-70; past pres, Seattle Econ Oppor Bd Inc, 1971-72; Govt Adv Coun Voc Educ; chmn, Wash Occupational Info Consortium; trustee, Wash State Asn Co Off, 1971-72; co-chmn, Wash State Co Auditors' Educ Comt, 1971-72; past pres, Int Thunderbird Little League Asn; past chmn, Minority Bus Develop Comn, Seattle Chamber Com; past mem, King Co Boys Club Bd Dir; past mem, United Way; mem bd dir, Nat Conf Christians & Jews; First African Methodist Episcopal Church; Alpha Phi Alpha; pres, Nat Black Caucus, Govern Financial Officers Asn, 1990-; pres, Black Elected & Appointed Offs, Region X, 1986-; regional pres, Blacks Govt, 1982-85; US Comn Civil Rights Western Region, 1992-. **Honors/Awds:** Magna Cum Laude Southern Univ, 1955; Golden Acorn Award, Newport Hills PTA 1971; Affirmative Action Award, Urban League, 1985; Employment Security Administrator of the Year 1985; One of 100 Outstanding Alumni, Seattle Univ, 1991. **Military Serv:** AUS first lt 1955-59; WA NG capt 1961-65. **Home Phone:** (206)361-8688. **Business Addr:** Executive Dean, Seattle Vocational Institute, 2120 S Jackson St, Seattle, WA 98144, **Business Phone:** (206)587-4940.

BROOKS, PATRICK, JR.
Educator. **Personal:** Born Jun 8, 1944, Newark, NJ; son of Patrick Sr and Ethel Fields; widowed; children: Lisa M. Ware, Chrisham, Patrick III. **Educ:** Lane Col, Jackson, TN, AB, 1967; Tex Southern Univ, Houston, MEd, 1970; Univ Minn, advan studies; NY Univ, advan studies; Jersey City State Univ, NJ, MA; Trenton State Univ, advan studies; Lydon State Univ, VT, advan studies. **Career:** Wildwood Consolidate Sch, Wildwood, NJ, crisis intervention counr; NY Housing Authority, NY, asst dist supvr; Essex County Col, Newark, NJ, instr sociol & counr; Kent State Univ, Frankfurt, KY, dir stud activities; Tex Southern Univ, Houston, asst resident hall dir & counr; Houston Urban League, Houston, TX, asst dir; coach: girls cross country, basketball, boys track, wrestling; Rutgers Univ, NJ, regional workshop dir & counr voc educ, 1982. **Orgs:** NJ Prof Counr Asn; NJ Career Counr Asn; NJ Counr Non-White Concerns; Cape May County; county adv, Stud Against Drunk Driving; trustee, NJ Youth Correctional Bd; County Mental Health Advocate Bd; County Prosecutors; Superintendent's Task Force Drug & Alcohol Abuse; South Jersey Coaches Asn; NJ Correctional Bd Trustees Penal Youth Prisons; County Mental Health, Drug & Alcohol Bd; County Prosecutor's County Supt Sch Alliance Drug Abuse; Mayor's Coun Drug Abuse; NJ Sch Counr Asn, middle sch adv coun; City Streets Road Improvement, Comnr, 1987; comnr, Wildwood Hist Soc, 1988; Stud Personal Servs, Alcohol Drug Counr.

BROOKS, PAULINE C
Executive. **Educ:** George Wash Univ, BA; Fiche Inst Data Processing, Computer Cert. **Career:** Natl Oceanic & Atmospheric Admin, prog mgr; Mgt Technol Inc, founder, pres & chief exec officer, 1985-. **Orgs:** Entrepreneur Year Inst; Nat Asn Female Exec; Comn Women Prince, George's Co, Md. **Honors/Awds:** MTI Entrepreneur Year, Ernst & Young, 1995; Distinguished Women's Leadership Award, Entrepreneurship, 2001; DC Chamber Com, 2002. **Special Achievements:** Named 9 of the Top 50 Woman Business Owners in the Washington, DC, 1997; Named one of the Top Black Business Women, 2001; Named one of the 25 Influential Black Women in Business, 2001. **Business Addr:** Chief Executive Officer, Management Technology Inc, 6710 Oxon Hill Rd Suite 400, Oxon Hill, MD 20745, **Business Phone:** (301)265-8900.

BROOKS, PHILLIP DANIEL
Executive. **Personal:** Born Mar 2, 1946, Charlottesville, VA. **Educ:** Norfolk State Col, BA, 1969; VA Commonwealth Univ, MA, 1971. **Career:** Norfolk Comm Hosp, admin, asst admins, 1971; Norfolk State Univ Athletics Found, treasurer, currently. **Orgs:** bd dir, Blue Cross Blue Shield, VA; Tidewater Hosp Coun; Am Hosp Asn; VA Hospital Asn, American Col Hospital Admin; Nat Asn Health Serv Execs; Tidewater Regional Political Asn; United Comn Fund Allocation Liaison Team, 1977; chmn, advisory com Hal Jackson's Miss US Talented Teen Pageant. **Honors/Awds:** Award of Recognition Norfolk Comm, 1976; Health Mgmt Achievement Award, Nat Asn of Health Serv Execs, 1976. **Business Addr:** Treasurer, Norfolk State University Athletics Foundation, 700 Pk Ave, Norfolk, VA 23504, **Business Phone:** (757)823-8600.*

BROOKS, ROBERT DARREN
Football player, president (organization). **Personal:** Born Jun 23, 1970, Greenwood, SC; married Diana, Nov 4, 1997; children: Robert, Elija & Austin. **Educ:** Univ SC, BSc, retailing. **Career:** Football player (retired), President; Green Bay Packers, wide receiver, 1992-98; Denver Broncos, 2000; Shoo-in four Life Rec Inc, pres, currently; Robert Brooks Football Camp, owner, currently. **Honors/Awds:** Comeback Player of the Year, Nat Football League, 1997; Super Bowl XXXI Champion. **Business Phone:** 800-807-8282.*

BROOKS, ROBIN C
Chief executive officer, chairperson. **Educ:** Smith Col, BA, econ; Northwestern Univ, JL Kellogg Grad Sch Mgt, MA, finance & econ. **Career:** Williamette Mgt Assocs; Deloitte & Touche; Arthur D Little Valuation Inc; Brooks Food Group Inc, chief operating officer & treas; Brooks Food Group Inc, chmn & ceo, currently. **Orgs:** Dir, United Enterprise Fund; Commonwealth Inst; tres, MultiCultural Foodservice & Hospitality Alliance, 2002-04; The Committee 200; Women's Foodservice Forum; treas, Commonwealth Inst S Fla. **Honors/Awds:** Virginia Entrepreneur of the Year, Ernst & Young, 2001; Entrepreneur of the Year, Women's Foodservice Forum, 2003. **Special Achievements:** Published several articles on the valuation of intangible assets and intellectual properties and has conducted seminars on her published materials. **Business Addr:** Chairman, Chief Executive Officer, Brooks Food Group Inc, 940 Orange St, Bedford, VA 24523, **Business Phone:** (540)586-8284.*

BROOKS, RODNEY ALAN
Journalist. **Personal:** Born May 29, 1953, Baltimore, MD; son of William F and Mattie Bell Crosson; married Sheila Smith, Aug 1, 1989; children: Rodney Alan Jr, Tahira & Andre. **Educ:** Cornell Univ, Ithaca, NY, BS, 1974. **Career:** Ithaca Jour, Ithaca, NY, reporter, 1974-77; Asheville, NC Citizen-Times, bus ed, 1977-80; The Bulletin, Philadelphia, PA, fin writer, 1980-81; Philadelphia Inquirer, Philadelphia, PA, asst bus ed, asst city ed, bus reporter, 1981-85; USA TODAY, McLean, VA, Money Sect, dep managing ed, 1985-; Northwestern Univ, McCormick-Tribune fel, 2008. **Orgs:** Co-founder/chmn, NABJ Bus Writers Task Force, 1989-93; City New Carrollton Adv Planning Comn, 1990-93; bd dir, Nat Asn Minority Media Execs, 1990-93, treas, 1991-93; bd govs, Soc Am Bus Ed & Writers, 1993-96; bd dirs, Nat Asn Black Journalists, Col Park, MD, treas, 1994-98, chair, finance comt, 2005-07; chmn, Strategic Planning Comn, 1994; bd dirs, Creative Writing Alliance, Hyattsville, MD, 2007-. **Honors/Awds:** Outstanding Contributions, Inroads Baltimore, 1994; Outstanding Contributions, Greater Ithaca Activ Ctr; President Award, NABJ, 2007. **Home Addr:** 201 Flannery Lane, Silver Spring, MD 20904.

BROOKS, RODNEY NORMAN
Executive. **Personal:** Born Jun 6, 1954, Asbury Park, NJ; married Mary Jane Carroll; children: Sheena Monique & Anneka LeChelle. **Educ:** Bowling Green State Univ, BS, secondary educ, 1976; Kent State Univ, attended 1981; Atlanta Univ, attended 1984. **Career:** Massillon Bd Educ, sub teacher, 1977-78; Supreme Life Ins Co, debit mgr, 1977-78; Canton Urban League Inc, proj dir, 1978-83; Planned Parenthood Stark Co, dir, 1984-; Massillon Urban League, pres & chief exec officer; Urban League Metro Harrisburg Inc, pres & chief exec officer; Hamilton Health Ctr, Capital Region Health Syst, Cares Proj, prog dir, currently. **Orgs:** Ddir, Westcare Ment Health Ctr, 1984-; dir, Social Planning Coun, United Way W Stark, 1984-; worshipful master, Simpson Lodge 1, IF & AMM, 1985. **Business Addr:** Program Director, Hamilton Health Center Inc, Capital Region Health System, 1821 Fulton St, Harrisburg, PA 17110, **Business Phone:** (717)232-9971.

BROOKS, ROSEMARIE
Educator. **Personal:** Born Aug 6, 1949, Detroit, MI; daughter of Leonard Richard Brooks and Bertha Corrine Brooks; children:

Wilbert O'Neil Barnes II & Sesmone Lanette Barnes-Cox. **Educ:** Univ Detroit, BA, 1980; Ferris State, Voc Ed cert, 1997; Univ Detroit, Teachers cert, 1997; Cambridge Col, MEd, 1997. **Career:** WXYZ-TV-7, producer & host, 1980-90; Sprint Communs, sales mgr, 1982-87; Detroit Bus Inst, placement dir, 1987-90; Brooks Right Price Convenience Plz, Chief exec officer, 1990-93; Detroit Pub Schs, Placement Specialist, 1993-; Shar Inc, assessment counr, 1995-97; Davenport Univ, fac, 1997-; Breithaupt Career & Tech Ctr, placement specialist, 1999-. **Orgs:** NAACP, 1977-; bd, Joint Apprenticeship Community, 1995-; Sex Equity & Diversity Proj, 1995-; Mich Ed Apprenticeship & Training Asn, 1997-; Detroit Workforce Develop, 1999-. **Honors/Awds:** Exemplary Leadership Award, Mich Asn Skills USA, 1999; McDonald's Corp, Portraits of the City, published 1999; Outstanding Achievement Award, Sex Equity & Diversity Project, 2000; Certificate of Recognition, Wayne County, 2000; Spirit of Detroit Award, Detroit City Coun, 2000; named one of Most Influential Black Women in Metro Detroit, 2000; Certificate of Achievement, City Detroit; Certificate of Recognition, WIN; Certificate of Appreciation, City Detroit; over 47 awards for outstanding sales, US Sprint; numerous other awards. **Business Addr:** Placement Specialist, Breithaupt Career & Tech Ctr, 9300 Hubbell, Detroit, MI 48228-2325, **Business Phone:** (313)866-9623.

BROOKS, ROSEMARY BITTINGS
Publisher, educator. **Personal:** Born Jan 2, 1951, East Orange, NJ; daughter of Patrick and Ethel Fields; divorced; children: Haven Michael, Ebony Mekia & Deja Renee. **Educ:** Claflin Univ, BA, 1971; Seton Hall Univ, MA, 1976; Kean Col, Commun Cert, 1978; Rutger's Union, MA, Phys Fitness Specialist, 1983. **Career:** East Orange Drug Ctr, substance abuse counr, 1975; Essex Valley Sch, The Bridge West, dir, 1981-82; Second Chance Coun Ctr, dir, 1982-83; NJ Black Caucus Legislators, lobbyist, 1984-87; Staying Fit Exercise Prog NJ Network, host, dir, 1984-86; Irvington Bd Educ, educr hist, 1984-; NJ Chapter Parents Joint Custody, lobbyist, 1985-87; Irvington High Sch NJ Law & Psychol, instr hist, 1985-87; Essex Co Fitness Prog, specialist, 1986-87; NJ Careers Coun, Irvington High, coordr, 1986-87; Person to Person Greeting Cards, pres, writer, 1988-, guidance counr, 1994-; Irvington Bd Educ, dir history & law. **Orgs:** Educ comn chmn, SOMAC Comn Coun, 1979-86; Governor's Coun Educ, 1982-87; NJ State Bd Lobbyists, 1982-87; NJ State Bd Fitness Specialist, 1984-87; project chmn, Maplewood PTA, 1985-86; dir, Afro-History Soc Irvington High Sch, 1983-87; treas, Irvington Awareness Coun, 1986-87; writer, consult, Sands Casino, Atlantic City NJ, 1988-89; writer, consult, Planned Parenthood NJ, 1988-89; NJ state deleg, Nat Conv, 2000-01; vice chair, Maplewood Democratic Party, 2001; Minority Comt chmn local & state NJ; State Instrnl Comt, NJEA; Guidance Counr Irvington Sch Dist; appointee govs comm, Adolescent Justice & Anti-Violence; State Bd Educ, State NJ, lobbyist. **Honors/Awds:** Award of Merit, Outstanding Educr, Nat Asn Advan Colored People, 1980-81; creator, dir first black fitness program on cable in NJ, NY, 1983-85; Citation for Excellence, NJ State Assembly, 1984; Career Coun Award Outstanding Participation, 1986-87. **Special Achievements:** TV & radio appearances; feature writer, Essence Magazine, 1982-87, Focus Magazine, 1984-87; choreographer "The Wiz", NJ Theatre Irvington, 1986-87; Person to Person Cards were recognized for its contributions to health, 1988-89; Author, NJ Legislation Anti-Violence Program for Adolescents; Feature Guest, A Kids TV Specials. **Home Addr:** 95 Parker Ave, Maplewood, NJ 07040. **Business Addr:** Director, Irvington Board of Education, Department of History & Law, 1034 Clinton Ave, Irvington, NJ 07111.

BROOKS, SHEILA DEAN
Entrepreneur, television journalist. **Personal:** Born Jun 24, 1956, Kansas City, MO; daughter of Stanley Benjamin Smith and Gussie Mae Dean Smith; married Rodney Alan Brooks Sr, Aug 1, 1988; children: Andre Timothy. **Educ:** Univ Wash, Seattle, WA, BA, broadcast jour, 1978; Seattle Univ, WA, 1980; Howard Univ, MA, 1998. **Career:** KCTS-TV, Seattle, WA, reporter & producer, 1978-81; KREM-TV, Spokane, WA, reporter & anchor, 1981-83; KAMU-TV/FM, Col Sta, TX, news dir & anchor, 1984-85; Dallas Morning News, Dallas, TX, exec mgt prog, 1985-88; Vanita Prods, Baltimore, MD, sr producer, 1988-89; SRB Prods Inc, Wash, DC, pres & chief exec officer, 1988-; WTTG-TV Channel 5, Wash, DC, exec producer, 1989-90; Crowe Chizek & Co LLC, corp adv bd, currently; adv bd, MassMutual Financial Group. **Orgs:** Exec bd officer & secy, 1986-91, chairwoman scholar comm, 1987-90, chairwoman internship comm, 1990-91, Nat Asn Black Journalists; bd dirs, Archbishop Carroll High Sch, 1990-95; bd dirs, New Carrollton Cablevision Inc, 1990-92; exec bd & pres, 1996-97, bd dirs, 1994-, pres, 1997, Nat Asn Women Bus Owners, Wash, DC; bd govs, Nat Acad TV Arts & Sci, NATAS-DC, 1996-; exec bd officer. Md Dist Columbia Minority Supplier Develop Coun, 1994-; bd dirs, 1994-96, adv bd, 1996-, Women Film & Video, Wash, DC Chap; The Presidents' Roundtable. **Honors/Awds:** Emmy Awards 1979, 1980; Texas Asn Broadcasters Radio Award, 1984; First Place CEBA Award of Excellence, Best Documentary in the Country, CEBA—World Inst Commun Inc, New York, 1990; Emmy Award Nomination, Best Local Documentary, 1990, Emmy Award Nomination, Best Local Information-Oriented Show, Nat Acad TV Arts & Sci, Wash, DC, 1990; First Place (RTNDA) Regional Award, Radio-TV News Dirs Asn, Wash, DC, 1990; Honorable Mention NABJ Award, Nat Asn Black Journalists, 1990; Supplier of the Year, Md Dist Columbia Minority Supplier Develop Coun, 1995; Telly Awards, 1995, 1996; Advocate of the year, Women Bus. **Military Serv:** USN Reserve, E-4, 1976-78. **Business Addr:** President, Chief Executive Officer, SRB Productions Inc, 1990 K St NW 2nd Fl, Washington, DC 20005, **Business Phone:** (202)775-7721.

BROOKS, SUZANNE R.
School administrator. **Personal:** Born Jan 20, 1941, Philadelphia, PA; daughter of Rayetta Ortiga and John Lemon. **Educ:** LaSalle Univ, Philadelphia, PA, BS, Educ/Eng, 1975; Wash State Univ, Pullman, WA, MA, Eng, 1979, adv lang studies, summers 1979, 1981; Univ Nev-Reno, grad courses, summers, 1982, 1983; Pa State Univ, Univ Park, PA, doct prog, 1985. **Career:** Philadelphia Police Dept, Philadelphia, PA, policewoman, 1968-72; Philadelphia High Sch Girls, Philadelphia, PA, teaching practicum, 1974; Pa Adv Sch, Philadelphia, PA, volunteer teacher, 1975; Wash State Univ, Pullman, WA, teaching apprentice, 1975-76, res asst, 1978-79, teaching asst, 1978-79, grad asst, 1978-79, GED instr, 1980, bi-lingual ESL instr, 1980-81, dir sci support servs, 1979-82; Andrew V. Kozak Fel, Pa State Univ Chap, Phi Delta Kappa; Univ Nevada Reno, affirmative action officer, 1982-84; Danforth Fel; Pa State Univ, Philadelphia, PA, affirmative action officer, 1984-89; Sign Lang Systs, co-owner & educ design/develop specialist, 1986-; Calif State Univ, Sacramento, CA, dir Multi-Cultural Ctr, 1990; Pa State Univ, affirmative action officer; Creative Concepts/Systs, owner, 1989, chief exec officer, currently. **Orgs:** Planning Comt, Ctr Women Policy Studies; Nat Asn Bus & Prof Women, State Col Chap; Nat Coun Negro Women; Nat Asn Women Deans, Adminrs & Counrs; Col & Univ Personnel Asn; bd mem, Nat Inst Women Color; chair, Founds Comt, State Col Bus & Prof Women's Asn; Affirmative Action Comt, Dem Party Ctr County; chief exec officer, pres & founder, Int Asn Women Color Day. **Honors/Awds:** McShain Award, LaSalle Col; Alpha Epsilon Honor Soc, LaSalle Col; Humbert Humphrey Scholar, Cheyney State Col; author/presentor, "Adult Education Programs: Addresssing Cross-Cultural Concerns," American Assn for Adult & Continuing Education Conference, 1987; author/presentor, "Image and Women of Color," American Imagery Conference, 1986; author with A. Hernandez, "Moving Mountains—Past, Present and Future: The Role of Women of Color in the American Political System," Natl Institute for Women of Color, 1984; author, "Life Through the Ivy," Essence, 1975; author and presentor of numerous other articles and publications; Awards include Who's Who Among Global Business Leaders, Who's Who Among American Women, Who's Who Among Students. **Business Addr:** Owner, Chief Executive Officer, Creative Concepts/Systems, 3325 Northrop Ave, Sacramento, CA 95864.*

BROOKS, TODD FREDERICK
Physician. **Personal:** Born Sep 1, 1954, New York, NY; son of Delaney and Effie C. **Educ:** Drew Univ, BA, 1976; Meharry Med Col, MD, 1980; Univ Tenn Health Sci, PhD, 1984. **Career:** Univ Tenn, clin instr, 1984-; Pvt Pract, obstet/gynec, 1984-; Memphis Health Ctr, consult, 1984-. **Orgs:** Bluff City Med Soc; chmn, Univ Tenn Obstet/Gynec Soc; fund raiser, Boy Scouts Am. **Special Achievements:** Publ "Perinatal Outcome," Journal of Ob/Gyn, 1984. **Business Addr:** Physician, 1211 Union Ave Suite 495, Memphis, TN 38104, **Business Phone:** (901)276-4895.*

BROOKS, TYRONE L
State government official. **Personal:** Born Oct 10, 1945, Warrenton, GA; son of Mose and Ruby Cody; married; children: Tyrone Jr & Nahede Teresa. **Career:** Tyrone Brooks & Assoc, nat pres, 1973-; Universal Humanities & Visions Literacy, founder & chmn, currently; African Am Bus Systs, pres; Ga State House Rep, Dist 54, state rep, 1980-. **Orgs:** Ga Legis Black Caucus; Southern Christian Leadership Conf; Nat Asn Advan Colored People; Am Civil Liberties Union; adv bd, Gate City Bar Asn; Ga Asn Black Elected Offs, pres, 1993. **Honors/Awds:** Roy Wilkins Award, Nat Asn Advan Colored People, 1984; Hall of Fame, 1986; Civil Rights Award, 1990; Inducted to NAACP Hall of Fame; Presidents Award, SCLC, 1990. **Home Addr:** 1315 Beecher St SW, Atlanta, GA 30310-0185, **Home Phone:** (404)753-3361. **Business Addr:** State Representative, Georgia House Representative, State Capitol, Legis Office Bldg 18 Capitol Sq Suite 511H, PO Box 11185, Atlanta, GA 30334, **Business Phone:** (404)656-6372.

BROOKS, WADELL, SR.
Labor relations manager. **Personal:** Born Jan 20, 1933, Lexington, MS; married Daisy Anderson; children: Yolanda, Wadell Jr, Cassandra. **Educ:** Ill State Normal Univ, BS, bus educ, 1957. **Career:** Labor relations manager (retired); VA Hosp, educ therapist, 1957-68; Naval Training Ctr, Great Lakes Naval Base, educ specialist, 1968-70; dir housing assignment & referral, 1970-79; master, Rufus Mitchell Lodge 107, 1972; Tots & Toddlers Day Care Ctr Inc, pres, 1974-;Pub Works Ctr Naval Base, Great Lakes, IL, dep equal employ opportunity officer, 1979-90; Daisy's Nursery Infant & Resource Develop Ctr, secy & treas, 1988; Gurnee Village Board, currently; Feed The C, volunteer, currently; Daisys Resource Ctr, bd dir, currently. **Orgs:** pres, Am Asn Rehab Ther, 1970; pres & life mem, NAACP, 1976-80; bd dir, Navy League; Lake Co Urban League; bd dir, Great Lakes Credit Union Naval Base Great Lakes, IL, 1980-90; Lake Co Race Unity Task Force, chmn, 1993-; First Midwest bank Community Reinvestment Coun, 1995-01; Natl Alumni Assn Faith Grant Coll, pres, 1996; pres, N Chicago Chamber Com, 1997-99. **Honors/Awds:** Super Performance Award, VA Hosp, 1967; Mason of the Year, Rufus Mitchell Lodge 107, 1987; Non-Fed Contribution Award, Pub Works Ctr, Great Lakes, IL, 1979; Super Achievement Award, We Do Care Orgn, Chicago, 1990; Faith Grant Col Aluminus of the Year, 1996; Past E. Burton Mercier Service Award, 1996; The Bahai Nat Spiritual Assembly Award, 2002. **Special Achievements:** The most influential African Americans in Lake County. **Military Serv:** AUS, spec/4, 1954-55. **Home Addr:** 1932 Sherman Ave, PO Box 468, North Chicago, IL 60064. **Business Addr:** Director, Daisy's Resource Center, 1010 Sherman Ave, North Chicago, IL.*

BROOKS, WILLIAM C
Chief executive officer, air force officer, businessperson. **Educ:** Long Island Univ, BA; Univ Okla, MBA; Harvard Bus Sch, advan mgt prog grad, 1985; Fla A&M Univ, DHL. **Career:** Gene Motors Corp, froup dir personnel, 1978-89, vpres, community & urban affairs, 1993-97; US Dept Labor, asst secy, 1989-90, Entech Human Resources, chmn, 1997-98; Brooks Group Int, chmn; United Am Healthcare Corp, chmn & pres & chief exec officer, currently; Caraco Pharmaceut Labs Ltd, dir, currently; Covansys Inc, bd dirs, currently; Off Mgt & Budget Exec Off, Pres, Dept Defense, Dept Labor, Dept Air Force. **Orgs:** Bd dir, La-Pac Corp; asst secy labor, Soc Security Adv Bd, 1996-98; chmn bd, Lason, Detroit, 2001; dir, United Am Healthcare Corp, 1997-2002; Gen Motors Dey Exec; Fla A&M Univ; Nat Inst Ed Adv Panel Employability; chmn & bd dir, 70001 Training & Employ; bd dir, Nat Coalition Black Voter Particitpation Inc; Ohio State Univ, Nat Center Res & Voc Ed; State Ohio Pub Employ Adv & Coun; dist chmn, Boy Scouts Am; chmn, adv bd, Detroit Pub Schs Bd Educ. **Honors/Awds:** Ombudsman Appreciation Award, Nat Asn Negro Bus & Prof Women, 1979; Bridge Builders Award, CETA, 1979; Outstanding MBA Year Award, Nat Black MBA Asn, 1980; Pathfinder Award, 70001 Ltd, 1981. **Special Achievements:** Numerous articles published in various journals including The National 1 Training Lab Journal for Social Change, The Black Collegian, etc. **Military Serv:** USAF, officer (retired). **Business Phone:** (313)393-4571.

BROOKS, WILLIAM P
Hospital administrator. **Personal:** Born Nov 19, 1934, Newkirk, OK; son of Carl F Sr; married Sue Jean Johnson; children: Barry P, Leslie J Lykes, Terryl D Abington, William R & Virgil A. **Educ:** Friends Univ, Wichita, KS, attended 1953; Wichita Univ, attended 1967. **Career:** Hosp administrator (retired); Winfield State Hosp Training Ctr, laundry worker, 1957, voc teacher, 1961, voc training supvr, 1966, unit b, 1970, unit dir, admin officer I, 1977-87, special asst to supt, 1987-95, supt, 1995-98. **Orgs:** Youth comt, Winfield Kiwanis Club, 1972-; pres, Winfield Quarterback Club, 1974; adv comt, Cowley City Community Col & Voc Tech Sch, 1975-; city planning comn, Winfield City, 1978-; Winfield Police Res, 1984-; bd dir, Eagle Nest. **Honors/Awds:** Distinguished Service Award, Winfield Jaycees, 1967; Outstanding Young Man, Kansas State Jaycees, 1967; Illustrious Potentate Emith Temple Wichita, 1975. **Business Addr:** Board of Director, Eagle Nest Inc, 112 E 9th Ave, PO Box 228, Winfield, KS 67156.

BROOME, SHARON WESTON. See WESTON, SHARON.

BROOMES, LLOYD RUDY
Psychiatrist. **Personal:** Born Feb 2, 1936; married Lauvenia Alleyne, Jun 2, 1963; children: Lloyda & Melissa. **Educ:** Shell Technol Sch, 1950-55; Oakwood Col, BA, 1961; Loma Linda Univ, MD, 1966. **Career:** Camarillo State Hosp, staff psychiatrist, 1969-71; Meharry Alcohol Drug Abuse Prog, asst prof, 1972-89; Meharry Community Mental Health Ctr, dir clinic serv; Nashville, pvt practice, 1973-86; Tenn Dept MH & MR, A & D Division, asst comnr, 1988-89; Alvin C York Va Med Ctr, Psychiatry Servs, chief, 1987-88; Madison Hosp, Dept Psychiatry, chief, 1978-80; Carl Vinson Va Med Ctr, psychiatry servs, chief, 1989-99. **Orgs:** Am Psychol Asn; Ga Psychiatric Physicians Asn; Gov Adv Comn Alcohol & Drugs, 1972-76; Black Adventist Med Dent Asn; exec vpres, Lupus Found Am, Nashville Chap, 1986-89; Am Col Physician Execs, 1991. **Honors/Awds:** Gold Medal Award, Shell Tech Sch, 1955; Fel, Am Psychiatric Asn, 1985; Am Bd Psychiatry & Neurol, Dipl Psychiatry, 1981. **Military Serv:** Civilian Work Prog, 1969-71. **Home Addr:** 6143 Loblolly Lane, Tuscaloosa, AL 35405. **Business Addr:** Physician, 3701 Loop Rd, Tuscaloosa, AL 35404.

BROSSETTE, ALVIN, JR.
Educator. **Personal:** Born May 16, 1942, Montgomery, LA; married Delores Gipson; children: Derrie, Alicia & Kathy. **Educ:** Grambling State Univ, BS, Elem Educ, 1962; N western State Univ, MEd, Admin, 1970; Western MI Univ, EdD Educ Learership, 1975. **Career:** Winn Parish Pub Schs, Winnfield LA, teacher, 1962-67; Grant Parish Pub Schs, Colfax LA, asst prin & teacher, 1967-73; Kalamazoo Pub Schs MI, program coordr & R&D, 1974-75; N western State Univ Los Angeles, asst prof Dept CI Col Educ, 1975-76; Prairie View A&M Univ TX, dept head Col Educ Curriculum & Instr, 1976-80; Wilmer-Hutchins Independent Sch Dist, gen supt; Dallas Pub Schs System, teacher, asst prin, prin,

prin planner, mgt sch, prin; Continuing Educ N western State Univ, acting dean, dir; Parks Elem, Prin, currently. **Orgs:** Nat Asn Curriculum Dev, 1976-; Teacher ctn adv bd Prairie View A&M Univ TX, 1979-; consult N Forest ISD Houston, 1979-; Phi Beta Sigma, 1968-; Phi Delta Kappa 1975-; Am Asn Sch Admin, 1980-; pres, Grant Parish Educ Asn, 1972-73. **Honors/Awds:** Fellowship-Grant, Western MI Univ, 1973-75. **Special Achievements:** First African American to become a professor at the North Louisiana school. **Business Addr:** Principal, Parks Elementary, 800 Koonce St, Natchitoches, LA 71457, **Business Phone:** (318)352-2764.

BROTHERS, AL
Secretary (office). **Career:** Raytheon, secy, prog mgr, currently.

BROTHERS, TONY
Basketball executive. **Personal:** Born Sep 14, 1964, Norfolk, VA. **Educ:** Old Dominion Univ, 1986. **Career:** TB Pro-Active Basketball Officiating Sch, refree & supervisor; Nat Basketball Asn, official, currently. **Orgs:** Founder, A Better Way; Hampton Rds Comt 200 Men Inc. **Business Addr:** NBA Official, National Basketball Association (NBA), 645 5th Ave 10th Fl, New York, NY 10022-5986, **Business Phone:** (212)407-8000.*

BROUGHTON, CHRISTOPHER LEON
Magician, actor. **Personal:** Born Mar 4, 1964, Detroit, MI; son of Theo Faye McCord and Ronald Leon. **Educ:** Mercy Col, Detroit, attended 1984. **Career:** Comedian, magician, actor, Los Angeles, 1976-; Films: Amazon Women on the Moon, 1987; Action Jackson, 1988; The New Adventures of Pippi Long stocking, 1988; Baby Geniuses, 1999; Playas Ball, 2003; Vegas Vampires, 2003; Tournament of Dreams, composer, producer & actor, 2007; Tvseries: "It's Show time at the Apollo", segment producer, 1987; "Hollywood Hounds", 1993; The 16th Annual Soul Train Music Awards, segment producer, 2002; The 30th Annual American Music Awards, segment producer, 2003; The Christopher Broughton Show, performer, currently. **Orgs:** Int Brotherhood Magicians, 1984-; Mystics, 1976-89; SAG, 1984-; AFTRA, 1984-; ICAP, 1988-. **Honors/Awds:** International Brotherhood of Magicians Award, 1989. **Home Addr:** 10458 Westover, Detroit, MI 48204. **Business Addr:** Magician, Comedian, The Christopher Broughton Show, c/o Venetian Hotel & Casino, 3355 Las Vegas Blvd S, Las Vegas, NV 89109, **Business Phone:** (702)414-9000.

BROUGHTON, LUTHER RASHARD (LUTHER RASHARD BROUGHTON, JR.)
Football player. **Personal:** Born Nov 30, 1974, Charleston, SC. **Educ:** Furman Univ. **Career:** Football player (retired);Carolina Panthers, tight end, 1998, 2001; Philadelphia Eagles, 1999-2000; Chicago Bears, free agent, 2002; Green Bay Packers, free agent, 2003. **Special Achievements:** Highest career receiving average with a minimum of five catches.

BROUGHTON, LUTHER RASHARD, JR. See BROUGHTON, LUTHER RASHARD.

BROUHARD, DEBORAH TALIAFERRO
Educator. **Personal:** Born Jul 7, 1949, Springfield, MA; daughter of Ernest Carter and Julia Beatrice Addison; married John Forrest, Jul 1, 1972; children: Benjamin Forrest & Rebecca Julia. **Educ:** McGill Univ, Montreal, Canada, 1970; Aurora Univ, Aurora, IL, BA, 1971; Ind Univ, Bloomington, IN, MSED, 1978. **Career:** Aurora E High Sch, East Aurora, IL, teacher, 1971-73; Miami Univ, Oxford, OH, coordr spec serv, 1981-83; Ariz State Univ, Mesa, AZ, counr, 1985-, stud recruitment & retention specialist, currently, Polytechnic campus Commission chair, 2009-. **Orgs:** Mid-Am Asn Educ Opportunity Progs, 1981-84; Black Caucus Ariz State Univ, 1985-; bd mem, Potentials Unlimited, 1991; Comn State Women, Ariz State Univ, 1996-97. **Honors/Awds:** Leadership Award, Phoenix Black Womens Task Force, 1990; Affirmative Action Award, 1990; Black African Coalition Outstanding Faculty Award, Ariz State Univ, 1998; Outstanding Service Award, Omega Psi Phi, 1998. **Special Achievements:** First African-American to serve as the chairperson of the Commission on the Status of Women at Arizona State University. **Business Addr:** Counselor, Faculty Associate & Student Recruitment, Arizona State University (East), College of Technology & Applied Sciences, 7001 E Williams Field Rd, Ctr 10 Bldg ctdo Room 121, Mesa, AZ 85287-0180, **Business Phone:** (480)727-1202.

BROUSSARD, ARNOLD ANTHONY
Administrator. **Personal:** Born Sep 26, 1947, New Orleans, LA; married Venita Lorraine Thomas; children: Danielle Lorraine & Darryl Anthony. **Educ:** Tulane Univ, BA, Sociol, 1969; Wharton Sch Univ, PA, MBA, acct oper res, 1971. **Career:** Arthur Andersen & Co, sr consult, 1971-75; J Ray McDermott & Co Inc, financial planning analyst, 1975-78; City New Orleans, exec asst to Mayor; Palm Beach Consult Group, consult, currently. **Orgs:** Co-coord Jr Achievement, 1975-77; bd dir, New Orleans Area Bayou River Health Sys Agency, 1975-78; mem, Nat Asn Black Acct, 1976-. **Business Addr:** Consultant, Palm Beach Consulting Group, 6406 Blue Bay Circle, Lake Worth, FL 33467-7397.

BROUSSARD, CHERYL DENISE
Writer, talk show host, chief executive officer. **Personal:** Born Sep 25, 1955, Phoenix, AZ; daughter of Theodore Douglas and Gwendolyn J Reid; married John B, Jun 27, 1981; children: J Hasan. **Educ:** Creighton Univ, 1973-75; Loyola Univ, BS, 1977. **Career:** Dean Witter Reynolds Inc, investment adv; CNN Financial Network & CNN &Co, financial adv; Broussard & Douglas Inc, prin & chief investment adv, currently; Sister CEO BootCamp, creator; Ms. Money Millionaire Financial Boot Camp, creator; Cheryl Broussard & Co, registered investment adv, money coach & ceo, currently; "Mind Your Money", producer & talk show host-,currently; "Ebony Money Power", co-host currently; Books: Sister CEO; The Black Woman's Guide To Starting Your Own Business; The Black Woman's Guide To Financial Independence; Smart Ways To Take Charge of Your Money, Build Wealth, & Achieve Financial Security.? Also "What's Money Got To Do WithIt?; co-author, The Ultimate Guide On How To Make Love & Money Work In Your Relationship"; Mind Your Money System with Cheryl Broussard. **Orgs:** Nat Asn Negro Bus & Prof Women; Econ Develop Comt. **Special Achievements:** Voted one of ten Woman Who Made a Difference, Minorities & Women in Business Magazine, 1992. **Business Addr:** Chief Executive Officer, Chief Investment Advisor, Cheryl Broussard & Co, PO Box 27287, Oakland, CA 94547, **Business Phone:** (510)245-7995.*

BROUSSARD, STEVEN (STEVEN NELSON BROUSSARD)
Football player, football coach. **Personal:** Born Feb 22, 1967, Los Angeles, CA; married Monique, Feb 22, 1991; children: Talin, Steve Jr & Kendra. **Educ:** Wash State Univ, attended 1990. **Career:** Football player (retired), football coach; Atlanta Falcons, running back, 1990-93; Cincinnati Bengals, running back, 1994; Seattle Sea hawks, running back, 1995-98; Don Lugo High Sch, Chino, CA, offensive cord; Diamond Ranch High Sch, offensive cord, 2001, head coach, 2002-03; Portland St vikings, wide receivers coach, 2004, offensive cord, 2005-07; Wash State Cougars, running backs coach, 2007-. **Business Phone:** 877-462-2684.

BROUSSARD, STEVEN NELSON. See BROUSSARD, STEVEN.

BROUSSARD, VERNON, SR.
Educator, college teacher. **Personal:** Born Jan 30, 1934, Shreveport, LA; son of Leon and Verdie Brannon; married Ida Mae Macias, Aug 8, 1982; children: Peggy Anne, Tona Collette, Vernon Jr, Gena Cecil, Steven Craig, Gayton, Ronald Wayne Gayton & Gina Marie Gayton. **Educ:** Southern Univ, Baton Rouge, BS, 1955; Calif State Univ, San Jose, MS, 1966; Mich State Univ, PhD, 1971. **Career:** Stockton Unified Sch Dist, teacher, 1958-66; planning consult, 1966-71; Unified Sch Dist, asst supt, 1968-71; Stockton Unified Sch Dist, math supvr, 1966-68; Calif State Dept Educ, chief bur prog develop, 1971-77; Univ Southern Calif, Sch Educ, assoc prof, 1977-00, assoc dean prog develop & opers, 1978; World Cong Comparative Educ, Soc London England/ Mexico City, Vancouver, BC, presenter & chmn, 1977; Univ Phoenix, instr math, 2000; Chicago Pub Sch, Lansing, MI; Calif Test Burs. **Orgs:** Alpha Kappa Mu, Southern Univ, Baton Rouge, 1955; pres, List Mich State Univ, 1977; Nat Asn Adv Colored People, 1978-; guest seminar lectr, Nat Inst Educ, 1978; presidential appointment, Nat Adv Coun Voc & Tech Educ, 1982-85; fel NSF, 1965-66. **Special Achievements:** Published various articles 1963-; State Kuwait Invitation, Lectr/Tour Educ Syst, 1987. **Military Serv:** AUS, major, 1955-63. *

BROUSSARD-SIMMONS, VANESSA
Museum director, administrator. **Personal:** Born Feb 17, 1959, Germany; daughter of Wilbert David and Verlee Bennett. **Educ:** Univ Md, BA, 1981; George Washington Univ, MA, 1987. **Career:** George Washington Univ & NMAH, Afro-American Communities Proj fel, 1983-84; Nat Mus Am Hist Smithsonian Inst, Archives Ctr, supvry archivist & curator, currently. **Orgs:** Bd trustee, Emma Willard Sch, 2005-07. **Honors/Awds:** Peer Recognition Award, NMAH, 1993, 2003. **Business Addr:** Supervisory Archivist, Curator, National Museum of American History Smithsonian Institution, 14th & Constitution Ave MRC 0601, Archives Center Suite 1100, Washington, DC 20560, **Business Phone:** (202)633-3719.

BROWDER, ANNE ELNA
Executive. **Personal:** Born Jun 13, 1944, Vernon, AL; daughter of Mary E and Eddie; divorced. **Educ:** LaSalle Exten, attended; Roosevelt Univ, attended. **Career:** NBC News, Chicago, Prod Talent Mgt, 1960-73; TV News Inc, Off Mgr, 1973-75; Tobacco Inst, asst pres; Tobacco Indust, nat spokesperson, 1976-86; Exec Tv Workshop, assoc, 1988-94; Inst Karmic Guid, admin asst, 1990-. **Orgs:** Nat Asn Advan Colored People.

BROWN, A. DAVID
Labor relations manager. **Personal:** Born Aug 4, 1942, Morristown, NJ; son of Arthur D Sr and Muriel Kyse; married Joan Currie, Jun 22, 1980. **Educ:** Monmouth Col, NJ, BS, 1965. **Career:** Bamberger NJ, Newark, NJ, personnel exec, 1968-71, admin, personnel, 1974, vpres, 1975; R H Macy & Co Inc, NY, vpres, personnel, 1981, sr vpres, personnel & labor rel, 1983-94, bd dir, 1987; bd, Zale Corp; bd, Selective Insurance Group, Inc; Korn Ferry Int, vpres, consult, 1994-97; Bridge Partners LLC, founder; Whitehead Mann Pendleton James, managing dir, 1997-03. **Orgs:** Black Retail Action Group. bd trustees, Morristown Memorial Hospital; bd trustees, Drew University and bd trustees, Jackie Robinson Foundation. **Military Serv:** AUS, Nat Guard, specialist fifth class, 1965-71. *

BROWN, A. SUE
Administrator. **Personal:** Born Jun 28, 1946, Lauderdale, MS. **Educ:** Bloomfield Col, BA, 1968; Rutgers Univ Grad Sch Social Work, MSW, 1969; Univ PA, cert mgmt, 1979; Harvard Univ Sch Pub Health, cert, 1980. **Career:** Urban League-Essex Co Newark, dir health, 1969-73; Col Med & Dent Newark, health planner, 1973-75; Newark Comprehensive Health Serv Plan, acting asst dir, 1973-75; Martland Hosp Col Med & Dent Newark, acting exec dir, 1975-77; Col Univ Hosp, Univ Med & Dent NJ, 1977-83; NJ Med Sch Newark, lectr, 1979-; Robert Wood Johnson Health Policy fel, Univ Med & Dent NJ, 1983-84; Inst Med Nat Acad Sci, fel, 1983-; DC Social Serv, dep comn, 1993-94; Comn Health Care Finance, acting comnr, 1994-96, dep dir, Dept Human Serv, 1996-97; Dept Health, Comn Social Serv, actg comnr; Dept Human Serv, Income Maintenance Admin, actg adminr, currently. **Orgs:** Comn Pub Gen Hosps, 1977; mem, acute care com Regional Health Planning Coun, 1980-82; mem, NJ Comprehensive Health Planning Council; mem adv com Region II Health Services Mental Health Admin Comprehensive Health Planning; mem, Am Pub Health Asn; founding mem, Nat Asn Pub Gen Hosps; mem, Asn C NJ; mem, NAACP; mem, Nat Coun Negro Women; mem, 100 Women Integrity Govt Baptist; Asn Am Med Cols; NIH; Am Col Hosp Adminr. **Honors/Awds:** Citizenship Award Bloomfield Col 1968; Community Serv Award, Nat Coun Negro Women, 1978; Leadership Health Serv Award Leaguers, 1978; Woman Achievement Essex County Col, 1979. **Home Phone:** (202)396-5908. **Business Addr:** Acting Administrator, Department of Human Services, Income Maintenance Administration, 645 St NE Suite 5000, Ste 302, Washington, DC 20002, **Business Phone:** (202)724-5506.*

BROWN, ABENA JOAN
President (Organization). **Educ:** Univ Chicago. **Career:** ETA Creative Arts Found, founder, 1971-, pres & producer, currently. **Special Achievements:** Only black theater company that owns its theater space. **Business Addr:** President, Founder, ETA Creative Arts Foundation, 7558 S Chicago Ave, Chicago, IL 60619-2644, **Business Phone:** (773)752-3955.*

BROWN, ABENA JOAN P. See BROWN, DR. JOAN P.

BROWN, ABNER BERTRAND
Insurance agent. **Personal:** Born Jan 20, 1942, De Quincy, LA; married Genevieve Mallet; children: Abner B Jr, Alvin D. **Educ:** Southern Univ, BA, 1964; TX Southern Univ, MEd, 1972, MA, 1974. **Career:** Family Serv Ctr, marriage & family counr, 1973-83; Tex Southern Univ, instr, 1975-77; State Farm Ins Co, ins agt, 1983-; Fire Honor Agent; Life Honor Agent. **Orgs:** past pres, Scenicwood Civic Club, 1975-77; Am Asn Marriage & Family Counrs, 1975-; pres, N Forest, ISD, 1983-85; Chamber Com; vol, Habitat Humanity; ambassador, Travel Qualifier. **Honors/Awds:** Bronze Tablet Qualifier. **Military Serv:** AUS, sp4, 2 yrs; Good Conduct Medal; Vietnam ERA. **Home Addr:** 10500 Caxton St, Houston, TX 77016. *

BROWN, ADRIAN DEMOND
Baseball player. **Personal:** Born Feb 27, 1974, McComb, MS; married Lynette; children: Adrian Jr & Quartez. **Career:** Pittsburgh Pirates, outfielder, 1997-2002; Boston Red Sox, 2003; Kansas City Royals, 2004; Texas Rangers, 2006; Free agent, currently. *

BROWN, AGNES MARIE
College administrator. **Personal:** Born Oct 13, 1933, North Holston, VA; daughter of Lonnie Johnson Broady and Frank Broady; married Robert, Aug 19, 1960; children: Agnes & Robin. **Educ:** Va Union Univ, Richmond, Va, BS, 1955; Bowie State Univ, Bowie, MD, MEd, 1977. **Career:** Educator (retired); Bowie State Univ, Bowie, Md, secy pres, 1955-67, prog coordr, asst dir fed prog, 1970-78, dir fed prog, 1978-92. **Orgs:** Bowie State Univ Women's Asn, 1985; Bowie State Univ Alumni Asn, 1978; Nat Asn Title III Admin, 1978-. **Home Addr:** 11422 Deepwood Dr, Bowie, MD 20720, **Home Phone:** (301)809-0292.

BROWN, ALBERT JOSEPH, III. See SURE, AL B.

BROWN, ALVER HAYNES
School administrator. **Career:** Black Educr Morris County, pres, currently. *

BROWN, ALVIN
Chairperson. **Educ:** Jacksonville Univ, MBA, 1989. **Career:** Nat Black MBA Asn Inc, nat chmn; The Staubach Co, partner, currently. **Business Addr:** Partner, The Staubach Company, 15601 Dallas Pkwy Suite 400, Addison, TX 75001, **Business Phone:** (972)361-5210.*

BROWN, ALVIN MONTERO
Physician. **Personal:** Born Jul 9, 1924, Prince George County, VA; son of Fitzhugh Lee and Lillian. **Educ:** Morgan State Col, BS,

1945; Columbia Univ, MA, 1947; NY Univ, attended 1954; Meharry Med Col, MD, 1960. **Career:** Physician (retired); Chester Co Hosp, intern, 1960-61; Phil Gen Hosp, 1962-63; NY Med Col, resident, 1963-65; Rehab Med VA Hosp, consult, 1969-; NY Med Col, asst prof, 1970-71; Emory Univ, 1969-70; Sinai Hosp Baltimore, staff psychiatrist, 1966-69; Va Hosp, asst chief, 1965-66; NY Med Col, resident physician, 1963-65; Mt Carmel Mercy Hosp, physician, 1972-85; MeHarry Med Col, consult physical med & rehab, 1987; Pvt Pract, physician, currently. **Orgs:** Staff mem, Meharry Med Col, 1965-69; Howard Univ, 1967-69; Univ MD, 1967-69; Emory Univ, 1969-70; NY Med Col, 1970-; bd dir, Mich Kenny Rehab Found, 1972-; Metro Soc Crippled C & Adults, 1972; Wayne State Univ, 1973-; bd trustees, Neuromuscular Inst, 1973-; adv bd, Comprehensive Health Ctr, 1974-; clin rep, Wayne State Univ, 1975-; sec/treas, Mich Acad Phys Med & Rehab, 1975-; bd dir, Met Home Health Care Serv, 1976-; Mich State Bd Phys Therapy Reg, 1977; pres, Mich Acad Phys Med & Rehab, 1979-80; Nat Med Asn; AMA; Am Cong Phys Med & Rehab; Am Acad Phys Med & Rehab; Am Col Sports Med; Mich Rheumatism Soc; Mich Rheumatism Soc. **Special Achievements:** Morgan State, coach. *

BROWN, DR. ALYCE DOSS
Educator. **Personal:** Born in Tuscaloosa, AL; daughter of John A and Julia; married Lelton C; children: Ouida & Kimberly. **Educ:** Tuskegee Inst, BS, 1956; Med Col GA, MSN, 1975; Nova Univ, EdD, 1993. **Career:** Mt Sinai Hosp, charge nurse, 1956-57; Colbert County Hosp, charge nurse, 1957-73; TVA, indust nurse, 1966-67; Univ N Ala, asst prof, 1973-93, assoc prof nursing, prof, currently. **Orgs:** Am Nurses Asn; Nat League Nurses; vice chairperson, Human Rights Comm Ala State Nurses Asn; pres, Muscle Shoals Chap Tuskegee Alumni Asn, 1985; dir,Christian educ N Cent Ala Conf CME Church; dir youth, WK Huntsville Dist CME Church; Univ N Ala Nursing Hon Soc; League Women Voters; bd trustees,Colbert County-NW Ala Health Care Authority; Chi Eta Phi Nursing Sorority; dir, Episcopal Dist, fifth Episcopal Dist CME Church, 1996; adv bd, Tri County Home Health Agency, 1999. **Honors/Awds:** Phi Kappa Phi Hon Soc Chap 132 UNA, 1977-; Lillian Holland Harvey Award,1986-87; Chi Eta Phi Nursing Sorority; Martin Luther King Jr Human Relations Award, Alpha Phi Alpha Fraternity, 1987; Shoals Area Woman of the Year, Shoals Coun Women's Orgn, 1988-89; Community Service Award, Ala Dem Conf (Colbert County Br), 1998. **Business Addr:** Professor of Nursing, University of North Alabama, 236 Stevens Hall, PO Box 5223, Florence, AL 35632-0001, **Business Phone:** (256)765-4579.

BROWN, DR. AMOS CLEOPHILUS
Clergy. **Personal:** Born Feb 20, 1941, Jackson, MS; son of Charlie Daniel Sr and Louetta Bell Robinson; married Jane Evangeline Smith; children: Amos Cleophilus Jr, David Josephus & Kizzie Maria. **Educ:** Morehouse Col, AB, 1964; Crozer Sem, MDiv, 1968; Va Sem & Col, DD, 1984; United Theol Sem; DMin, 1990. **Career:** St Paul Baptist Church, Westchester PA, pastor, 1965-70; Pilgrim Baptist church, St Paul, MN, pastor, 1970-76; Third Baptist San Francisco CA, pastor, sr pastor, currently. **Orgs:** Pres, MS Youth Coun, Nat Asn Advan Colored People, 1956-59, Hi-Y Clubs MS, 1958-59; nat chmn, Nat Asn Advan Colored People Youth Dept, 1960-62; chmn, Am Baptist Black Caucus, 1972-80, chmn, Nat Baptist Civil Rights Comn, 1982-; gov bd, Community Col, 1982-88; founding mem bd, Black Am Resp African Crisis, 1984; life mem, Nat Asn Advan Colored People; bd supervisors, San Francisco City County, 1996-2000; chmn bd, Community Housing Corp; St Paul Planning Comn; pres, Minnesota State Baptist Convention, 1971-74, nat bd dir; nat chmn, Black Caucus Am Baptist Churches; chmn, Midwestern Am Baptist Black Churchmen; nat co-chmn, Resolution Comt. **Honors/Awds:** Outstanding Young Man of America, Jr Chamber Commerce 1974-76; Martin Luther King Jr Ministerial Award, Colgate-Rochester Div School, 1984; Man of the Year, San Francisco Business & Professional Women Inc, 1985; Samuel D Proctor Award, Nat Rainbow & PUSH, 1997. **Home Addr:** 434 Bright St, San Francisco, CA 94132. **Business Addr:** Senior Pastor, Third Baptist Church, 1399 McAllister St, San Francisco, CA 94115, **Business Phone:** (415)346-4426 Ext 210.

BROWN, ANDREA
Executive. **Career:** Coca-Cola N Am, dir, Strategic Media Planning, currently. **Orgs:** Am Advert Fedn. **Business Addr:** Director, Coca-Cola North America, 1 Coca Cola Plaza, Atlanta, GA 30313-2499.

BROWN, ANGELA LAVERNE. See STONE, ANGIE.

BROWN, ANGELA YVETTE
Journalist. **Personal:** Born Jul 4, 1964, Sacramento, CA; daughter of Ernestine Rose Hatchette and Clinton Edward. **Educ:** Fla State Univ, Tallahassee, FL, BA, Commun, 1986. **Career:** WPEC-TV, West Palm Beach, FL, prod asst, 1987; WEVU-TV, Ft Myers, FL, TV news reporter, 1987-89; WCBD-TV, Charleston, SC, TV news reporter, 1989-. **Orgs:** Vpres, Broadcast SC Coastal Asn Black Journalists, 1989-; mem, Nat Asn Black Journalists, 1988-; mem, Alpha Kappa Alpha Sorority, 1985-. **Honors/Awds:** Emmy, Best Newscast, Natl Acad TV Arts & Sci, 1989; SCC Assn Black Journalists, founding mem, 1989; SCCAB Mentors Prog, Founder, 1989. **Home Addr:** 810-D Hideaway Dr, Mount Pleasant, SC 29464, **Home Phone:** (803)881-4034. **Business Addr:** Reporter, WCBD-TV, 210 W Coleman Blvd, Mount Pleasant, SC 29464, **Business Phone:** (803)884-2288.

BROWN, ANNIE CARNELIA
Financial manager, clergy. **Personal:** Born Jul 19, 1928, Switchback, WV; daughter of Rufus and Rozena Manns; married Samuel Leo Brown, Aug 2, 1947 (deceased); children: Samuel Jr, Carnelia Ann, Susan Leona, Reginald Lee. **Educ:** Wayne St Univ, BA, 1976, Theol, dipl, 1987; Wayne Co Community Col, AA, 1992. **Career:** Investor; Apostle Paul Missionary Baptist Church, co-pastor, currently. **Orgs:** Oper Get Down, 1969-72; Harambee House, 1969-72; Positive Images, 1989-. **Honors/Awds:** Ford Good Citizens Award, 1971; Recognition Award for Community Serv, Wayne Co Community Col, 1973; Hon DDiv, SJ Williams Sch of Rel, 1991; Distinguished Clergy Award, Urban Bible Col, 1995; Gov Honor Roll of Vols, 1996. *

BROWN, ANNIE GIBSON
Accountant. **Personal:** Born Aug 12, 1944, Lexington, MS; married Charles. **Educ:** S IL Univ; MS Valley St Univ, 1966. **Career:** pre-sch teacher, 1966; secy, 1966-69; bookkeeper, 1969-71; pub official dep, 1971-75; Holmes Co, tax assessor & collector. **Orgs:** PTSA Order E Star Daughter Elks; Assessor Collectors Asn State & Nat; vpres MS Health Serv Agency.

BROWN, ANTHONY MAURICE
Executive. **Personal:** Born Dec 19, 1962, Bronx, NY; son of Alfred and Annette; children: Nicole Gooden. **Educ:** Mercy Col. **Career:** Maternity Infant Care Serv, substance abuse teen counr, 1990-92; Northern Manhattan Perinatal Partnership, Substance Abuse Outreach, 1992-95; Christopher Columbus HS, sch air counr, coach, 1995-98; Pablo Casals Mid Sch, paraprofessional, conflict resolution, 1998-; Youthwise Inc, chief exec officer, 1999-. **Orgs:** Recreation leader & coach, Police Athletic League, 1999-00. **Honors/Awds:** Phat Friends Award, Allstars Talent Network, 2001. **Business Addr:** Chief Executive Officer, Youthwise Inc, The Mary Mitchell Family & Youth Center, 2007 Mapes Ave., Bronx, NY 10460, **Business Phone:** (718)583-1765.

BROWN, ARNOLD E.
Lawyer, president (organization). **Personal:** Born Apr 21, 1932, Englewood, NJ; son of John Scott Jr and Hortense Melle Stubbs; married Lydia Barbara White, Jun 25, 1955 (deceased); children: Crystal L Brown, Beverly M Brown-Fitzhugh, Dale E Brown-Davis, Arnold E Brown II; married Gwendolyn Wertby, Jul 21, 2001. **Educ:** Bowling Green State Univ, BA, 1954; Rutgers Univ Sch Law, JD, 1957. **Career:** Self-employed atty, Englewood NJ, 1957-86; Bergen County, assemblyman, 1966-67; pres, 1986; Dubois Book Ctr, owner & pres, currently. **Orgs:** Gen Assembly, NJ, 1965-66; pres, Bergen County Urban League; Nat Asn Advan Colored People Bergen County; bd mem, Adv Comt Salvation Army Bergen County; mem & pres, Kappa Theta Lambda Chap Alpha Phi Alpha Fraternity; forever pres, African Am Bus Enterprise Coun Northern NJ, 1986-; Bergen W Camp, Gideon Int; pres, Friends Libr; Coalition Preserv Teaneck's Indian Slave Cemetery. **Home Addr:** 383 Knickerbocker Rd, Englewood, NJ 07631. **Business Addr:** President, Dubois Book Center, PO Box 776, Englewood, NJ 07631-0776.*

BROWN, ATLANTA THOMAS
Librarian. **Personal:** Born Oct 30, 1931, Bennettsville, SC; daughter of Alice Reid Thomas and Julius A; married Samuel E Brown, Jan 30, 1965; children: Dale. **Educ:** SC State Univ, Orangeburg, BS, 1953; Univ Wis, Madison, MLS, 1963. **Career:** Librarian (retired); Columbia City Schs, librn, 1953-58; Richmond City Schs, librn, 1958-63; Wilmington City Schs, librn, 1963-82; Christina Sch Dist, librn, dist chair libr media, 1982-90. **Orgs:** New Castle County Libr Adv Bd, 1982-89; pres, Del Libr Asn, 1984-85; Am Libr Asn, nat libr week comt, 1984-88; charter mem, Am Asn Univ Women, Millcreek Hundred Br; Am Asn Sch Librn, legis comt, pub rels comts, 1984-86; founder, charter mem, Del Coalition Literacy, 1985-; bd dirs, Ingleside Homes; Chesapeake Ctr Bd: Speer Trust Comn; pres, Del Asn Supvrn &Curriculum Develop, 1988-89; pres, Nat Asn Univ Women, Wilmington Branch, 1994-; moderator, New Castle Presbytery, 1994-95; vol librn, Gander Hill Prison, 1994; Presbyterian Church, gen assembly coun, 1996-01; vol Against Adolescent Pregnancy; Delta Sigma Theta Sorority; charter mem, Nat Coun Negro Women, Wilmington Sect. **Honors/Awds:** Librn of the Yr, Wilmington City Schools, 1970; appointee, Del Gov, State Adv Coun Libr, 1971-75, 1983-89; Wilmington Br Membership Award, Nat Asn Advan Colored People, 1979; appointee, State's White House Conf Libr, 1990; Phi Delta Kappa Int. **Special Achievements:** Tech Trends, 1986; Delaware Library Association Bulletin, Winter 1986. **Home Addr:** 4502 Pickwick Dr, Wilmington, DE 19808, **Home Phone:** (302)998-0803. *

BROWN, BARBARA
Research administrator, engineer. **Educ:** Fla State Univ, BS, comput sci; Univ Cent Fla, MS, eng mgt. **Career:** NASA, Kennedy Space Ctr, Artificial Intelligence Lab, systs engr, Advan Software Lab, mgr, Future Launch Systs & Advan Progs Off, X-34 proj engr; Prof Develop Prog, chief engr, chief info officer, 1998-00, Ames Res Ctr liaison, currently; NASA, dep mgr intelligent syst human-centered comput, currently. **Honors/Awds:** NASA Exceptional Service Medal. **Business Addr:** Deputy Manager, Ames Research Center Liaison, Kennedy Space Center, NASA, Orlando, FL 32899-0001, **Business Phone:** (321)867-5000.*

BROWN, BARBARA ANN
Government official, photographer. **Personal:** Born Aug 17, 1949, Lynchburg, VA. **Educ:** Phillips Bus Col, AA, 1967; Cortez W Peters Bus Col, AA, 1971. **Career:** Bur Nat Affairs Inc, Data Entry Operator, 1971; NY Inst Photography, 1983. **Orgs:** Secy, Mayfair Mansions Res Coun, 1971; mem, 6th District Police-Citizens Adv Coun, 1979; corresponding secy, Marshall Highlights Community Develop Org Inc, 1983; mem, Citizens Adv Com DC Bar, 1984; mem, Prof Photographers Am Inc, 1985. **Honors/Awds:** Outstanding Community Serv ANC7A, Wash, DC, 1978-81. **Special Achievements:** For Women Only Moorland-Spingarn Res, 1983; For Black Women Photographers, Howard Univ, Wash, DC 1984.

BROWN, DR. BARBARA MAHONE
Poet, educator. **Personal:** Born Feb 27, 1944, Chicago, IL; daughter of Loniel Atticus and Anne Savage; married Rex Michael, Nov 24, 1978; children: Letta McBain, Aisha & Imani. **Educ:** Fisk Univ, Nashville, TN, 1965; Wash State Univ, Pullman, WA, BA, 1968; Univ Chicago, Chicago, IL, MBA, 1975; Stanford Univ, Stanford, CA, PhD,1988. **Career:** Educator (retired), poet; Burrell Advert, Chicago, IL, copy supvr, 1970-73; First Nat Bank, Chicago, IL, advert mgr, 1975; Nat Broadcasting Co, New York, NY, dir planning, 1975-77; Clark Col, Atlanta, GA, assoc prof bus admin, 1978-84; Univ Tex Austin, Austin, TX, assoc prof commun, 1988-90; San Jose State Univ, San Jose, CA, assoc prof mkt, prof; Fielding Inst, ODE Master's Degree Prog, founding fac. **Orgs:** Orgn Black Am Cult, OBAC, 1969-75; Steering Comt, U N Mid-Decade Women, SE Regional Conf, 1980; bd mem, Am Cancer Soc Austin, TX Chap, 1989-90; adv task force, Atlanta City Coun Finance Comt, 1981-82; Soc Res Child Develop, 1987-; Int Commun Asn, 1987-; trustee, Hillbrook Sch, Los Gatos, CA, 1995-; bd mem, Kids Common, San Jose, CA, 1997-. **Honors/Awds:** Teacher-Scholar, San Jose State Univ, 1993-94; Author, "Advertising Influences on Youth", Journal of Communication Inquiry, 1990.

BROWN, BARTRAM S.
Educator. **Educ:** Harvard Univ, BA; Columbia Univ, JD; Grad Inst Int Stud, Geneva, PhD. **Career:** Columbia Human Rights Law Review, managing editor; Law clerk, Int Criminal Tribunal; Ill Inst Technol, vis scholar, Cambridge Univ; Chicago-Kent Col Law, prof law, currently, Prog Int & Comparative Law, co-dir, currently. **Orgs:** Coun Foreign Rels; bd dirs, Amnesty Int USA; adv bd, Am Bar Asn Cent & Eastern European Law Initiative; legal adv, Rome Diplomatic Conf Establishment Int Criminal Ct, Repub Trinidad & Tobago, 1998; pub mem, US Deleg UN Comn Human Rights, Geneva, Switzerland, 2000. **Special Achievements:** Published a book on the law and politics of the World Bank, as well as articles on international human rights law, international humanitarian law, international criminal tribunals, and international trade law. **Business Addr:** Professor, Co-Director, Chicago-Kent College of Law, Illinois Institute of Technology, 565 W Adams St, Chicago, IL 60661-3691, **Business Phone:** (312)906-5000.

BROWN, BEATRICE S.
Educator. **Personal:** Born Jul 14, 1950, Louisville, KY; daughter of Thomas J Sr and Irene. **Educ:** Addis Ababa Univ, Ethiopia, psychol, 1990; Cornell Univ, Coop Nutrit Prog, PhD, cert, 1991; Postgraduate Ctr Mental Health, New York, cert, 1995. **Career:** Upper Manhattan Mental Health Ctr, c day treat unit dir, 1989-91; City Col, City Univ, NY, adj prof, 1990-; Jewish Bd Family & C Serv, residential treat facil girls unit, dir; Cent Brooklyn Coord Coun Inc, mental health unit psychol, 1997-; BSB holistic Consult Group Wellness Inc, founder, 1997-. **Orgs:** Am Psychol Asn; Am Asn Pastoral Counr; Nat Guild Hypnotists Inc; Ky Asn Hypnotherapists; Nat & Int Bd Missionaries; Sigma Gamma Rho. **Honors/Awds:** Letter of Award, Univ Louisville, 1970; Songwriter Award, St WLOU, Louisville, 1971; Certificate, Univ Louisville, 1974; Appreciation Award, African-Am Music Arts Festival Comn, 1984. **Business Addr:** Founder, Chief Executive Officer, BSB Wholistic Consulting Group of Wellness Inc, 687 Locust St, PO Box 172, Mount Vernon, NY 10552-2110, **Business Phone:** (914)699-1615.

BROWN, BERNICE BAYNES
School administrator, educator. **Personal:** Born Jun 19, 1935, Pittsburgh, PA; daughter of Howard and Henrietta Hodges; married James, May 4, 1963; children: Kiyeseni Anu. **Educ:** Carnegie Mellon Univ, BFA, 1957; Univ Pittsburgh, MEd, 1964. **Career:** School Administrator, educator (retired); Pittsburgh Pub Sch, art teacher, 1957-64; Carlow Col, lectr, 1964-67; Bay Area Urban League, educ specialist, 1967-68; San Fran Col Women, asst prof, 1968-733; Lone Mountain Col, dean stud, 1973-76; San Fran Found, prog exec, 1977-86; Clorox Co, found adminr, 1990-93; City Col San Francisco, dean fac & staff develop, 1991-93, educ

consult; City Col SF Campus, dean, SE Campus, City Col San Francisco, 1993-98; Cal Works Educ & Training, dean, Workforce Educ, 1998-2003. **Orgs:** Chairperson, Voc Educ Adv Comt Calif Sch & Col; bd, Asn Black Educ, Exec; Women & Found Corp Phil; trustee, San Fran Bar Asn Found; trustee, Sch Sacred Heart; bd mem, Found Community Serv CableTV; quarterly chairperson, bd mem, Commonwealth Club Calif; State Adv Comn Black Affairs; bd mem, High Scope Educ Res Found; bd mem, Urban Econ Develop Corp, Pediat Coun, Univ Calif, San Francisco; bd mem, Howard Thurman Educ Trust; bd mem, Presidio World Col; bd mem, Lorraine Hansberry Theatre. **Honors/Awds:** Vis Scholar, Stanford Univ Stanford Calif; Citizens Scholar Found Am,Milestone Award; YWCA, New Generation Leadership Award; Professional Womanof the Year, Nat Asn Negro Bus & Prof Women, San Francisco Chap, 1998;History Makers Award, 2002; Image Award, Delta Sigma Theta Sorority, 2003. **Home Addr:** 1271 23rd Ave, San Francisco, CA 94122.

BROWN, BERNICE H.
Podiatrist. **Personal:** Born Aug 23, 1907, Ronceverte, WV; widowed. **Educ:** Bluefield State Col; OH Col Podiatric Med. **Career:** Pvt Pract, podiatrist. **Orgs:** Act prof Negro Bus & Professional Women Assn; 4-H Club Extension Agr House wife; treas Altrusa Intl; mem Eta Phi Beta Sor; mem Civic Antioch Bapt Ch; NAACP; Urban League; Fifty-Plus Club. **Honors/Awds:** Appreciation Award Bus & Professional Club 1972.

BROWN, BERTRAND JAMES
School administrator. **Educ:** Parsons Jr Col, AA, 1953; Emporia State Univ, AB, 1957; Kans State Univ, MS, 1959; Univ Mass, EdD. **Career:** Sch administrator (retired); New York City, Youth & Adult Educ Ctr, teacher, sch prin, Dist prog, dir, Cult Enrichment Prog, dir, Spec Extended Sch Prog, dir, Community Sch Dist 5, supt schs. **Orgs:** Lifetime mem, NAACP. **Honors/Awds:** Educator of the Year, The City Tabernacle Church, 1978; Outstanding Educational Administrator Award, NY Community Sch Dist Five, 1982; Cardinal Citation, 1993.

BROWN, BETTYE JEAN (BETTYE JEAN CRAWLEY)
Manager. **Personal:** Born Jan 30, 1955, Hazlehurst, GA. **Educ:** FL State Univ, BS 1976; GA Southwestern Col, MEd, 1983. **Career:** Jeff Davis County Bd Educ, educr, 1977-85; Southern GA Col, instr, 1983; GA Assoc Educr, united serv dir 1985; Richmond County Asn educr, exec dir. **Orgs:** Founder & coordr, Stud Involvement Black Unity, 1978-85; coordr, Upward Bound Prog, 1981-85; pres, Jeff Davis Co Asn Educr, 1982-84; sec, Nat Asn Advan Colored People, 1984; pres, Jeff Davis County Clients Coun, 1984-88; coordr, Non-Urban Organizing Proj, 1986; vpres, Am Asn Univ Women; worthy matron Order Eastern Star; conf coordr, Nat Black Staff Network; Nat Educ Asn, Nat Coun Social Studies; vpres, Delta Sigma Theta; Negro Bus & Prof Women; Bulloch 2000 Comt; secy, State Human Rel Comt; monitor, GA Housing Coalition Comt Develop Block Grant Prog; designed & coordr progs, Am Educ Week; Miss Ebony Pageant; Jeff Davis Co Reapportionme Comn. **Honors/Awds:** Outstanding Serv Community Clients Coun, 1985; Outstanding Teacher, Y Clubs Model United Nat Club, 1985; Dedicated Serv, Nat Asn Advan Colored People, 1986; Outstanding Serv Wash Co Asn Educr, 1986; Friend Educ Award, Wash County Asn Educr, 1989.

BROWN, BEVERLY J.
Consultant, chief executive officer. **Personal:** Born Oct 8, 1958, Louisville, KY; daughter of Charles Jr and Beatrice (deceased). **Educ:** Tenn State Univ, BS, 1980; Univ Louisville, MEd, 1982. **Career:** State Ky Employ Serv, sr employ counr, 1982-87; Chestnut St YMCA, Louisville, black achievers dir, 1987-95; Johnston Mem YMCA, Charlotte, dir prog develop, 1995-96; YMCA USA, assoc dir, youth develop & nat black achievers dir, 1996-03; BJ Brown Enterprises, chief exec officer, 2003-. **Orgs:** Alpha Kappa Alpha Sorority, 1991-; YMCA Asn Prof Dirs, 1996-; Nat Black Child Develop Inst, 1999-00; Tavis Smiley Youth Leaders, 2000-; Nat Asn Advan Colored People, 2002-. **Honors/Awds:** Bethune Serv Award, Nat Coun Negro Women, Louisville Chap, 1992; Jefferson Cup Award, Louisville/Jefferson Co, KY, 1996; Merit Award, YMCA Greater Louisville, 1996; Hon Mayor, City Baton Rouge, 1997; Hall of Fame Inducted, YMCA USA Nat Black Achievers. **Special Achievements:** Served as Ambasador in Germany for the city of Lousiville, 1995; established YMCA Teen Achievement of the Year scholarship, 2002; established YMCA Natl Black Achievers Honarary Committee, 2002. **Business Addr:** Chief Executive Officer, BJ Brown Enterprises, 3318 Duvalle Dr, Louisville, KY 40211.*

BROWN, BOBBY (ROBERT BARISFORD)
Actor, songwriter, singer. **Personal:** Born Feb 5, 1969, Boston, MA; married Whitney Houston, Jul 18, 1992; children: Bobbi Kristina Houston. **Career:** New Edition, mem of the singing group, 1980-86; solo performer, 1986-; Albums: King of Stage, 1987, Don't Be Cruel, 1988, Bobby, 1992; Forever,1998; Ghost busters II Motion Picture Soundtrack, 1990; Films: Ghost bustersII, actor, 1989; Panther, actor, 1995; A Thin Line Between Love & Hate,actor, 1996; Two Can Play That Game, actor, 2001; Go For Broke, actor, 2002; Gang of Roses, actor, 2003; Nora's Hair Salon, actor, 2004.; TV progs: "Cedric the Entertainer Presents", 2003; "Jimmy Kimmel Live", 2005; "25 Strong: The BET Silver Anniversary Spec", 2005; "Cuts", 2005; "Gone Country", 2008; "What Perez Says", 2007; "Who Ate The Soul?", 2007; "Being Bobby Brown", exec producer, 2005. **Business Phone:** (818)777-4000.

BROWN, BOOKER T
Labor relations manager. **Personal:** Born Aug 10, 1950, Macon, MS. **Educ:** Forest Pk Community Col, 1971; Boise State Univ, BSEd, 1973. **Career:** Morrison-Knudsen Int Co, dir recreation; Idaho Nat Bank, loan cr. **Orgs:** Optimist Club; MCU Sports Softball Team; Boise State Univ Alumni Asn; Boise State Univ Found; bd mem, Idaho Womens Health & Fitness Educ Celebration Inc. **Honors/Awds:** Dean List Award, Boise State Univ, 1973; Todays Psychol, 1973; Outstanding Athlete of America Award, 1973.

BROWN, BRIAN A
Executive. **Personal:** Born Jul 7, 1952, Yonkers, NY; son of William T Brown Sr (deceased) and Demetra A; married Lorrie L Frost, 1994. **Educ:** Boston Univ, BA, sociol, 1976; SPC, mass commun, 1977. **Career:** Black Enterprise Mag, dir prom, 1977-81; AT&T, indust consult, 1980-84; Int Bus Mach ROLM, dist sales dir, 1984-86; Wang Labs Intecom, vpres sales, 1984-86; Prom Mng Am, pres, 1986. **Orgs:** A100 Black Men, 1991-; chmn, 100 Black C Inc, 1992; bd mem, Adv Comn, NY Urban League; 1992-; exec bd, Broadway Cares Equity Fights AIDS, 1994.

BROWN, BROADINE M.
Government official. **Career:** US Marshals Serv, sr budget analyst mgt chief, Mgt & Budget Div, asst dir, currently. **Special Achievements:** the first African-American to reach the executive level in the centuries-old law enforcement agency. **Business Phone:** (202)307-9032.*

BROWN, BYRON WILLIAM
Government official, mayor. **Personal:** Born Sep 24, 1958, New York, NY; son of Byron and Clarice Kirnon; married Michelle Austin Brown, May 25, 1990; children: Byron William II. **Educ:** State Univ NY, BA, journ & polit sci, 1983, MS, 1989. **Career:** City Buffalo, Coun Pres Off, exec secy coun pres, 1984-86; Erie County Legis Chmn Off, Buffalo, NY, news secy/exec asst, 1986-88; State NY Dep Speaker's Off, Buffalo, NY, dir pub rels, 1986-88; County of Erie, Div Equal Employ Opportunity, Buffalo, NY, dir, 1988; 60th Dist Erie & Niagara County, sen, 2001; NY State Dem Comt, citys chief exec, mayor, currently. **Orgs:** Rho Lambda Chap, Alpha Phi Alpha Fraternity, 1984-; vpres, bd dirs, St Augustine's Ctr, 1989-; judge, ACT-SO, Nat Asn Advan Colored People, 1989-; bd trustee, Western NY Pub Broadcasting, 1990-; asst scout leader, Boy Scouts Am, Troop 84, 1991-; mentor, Buffalo Pub Sch 38 Chamber Com, 1991-; St John Baptist Church. **Honors/Awds:** Jr Award, Martin Luther King, Alpha Phi Alpha Fraternity, 1984; Black Achiever in Indust, 1490 Enterprises Inc, 1988; 30 Leaders of the Future, Ebony Mag, 1989; Bus Study Exchange Cent Am, Rotary Int, 1990. **Special Achievements:** The City's First African-American Mayor. **Home Addr:** 613 E Ferry St, Buffalo, NY 14211, **Home Phone:** (716)897-4019. **Business Addr:** Mayor, New York State Democratic Committee, 60 Madison Ave, Buffalo, NY 10010, **Business Phone:** (212)725-8825.*

BROWN, CALVIN ANDERSON, JR.
Physician. **Personal:** Born Sep 13, 1931, Athens, GA; son of C A Sr and Ruth Haynes; married Joy San Walker; children: JoiSanne MD, SannaGai, MD. **Educ:** Morehouse Col, BBS, 1952; Meharry Med Col, MD, 1958. **Career:** Hubbard Hosp Nashville, intern, 1958-59; specialized family pract, 1959; Atlanta Southside Comprehensive Health Ctr, developer, dir, 1966-69; Pineview Convalescent Ctr Atlanta, med dir, 1968-76; Holy Family Hosp, Hughes Spalding Hosp Atlanta, staff; Atlanta Job Corp Ctr, physician, 1970-73; Henry Cty Health Access Station, developer, co-dir, 1971-73; Martin Luther King Jr Nursing Ctr, chief staff 1971-73; Fulton County Jails, chief physician 1971-83; Atlanta City Jail, chief physician, 1980-85; Peace Corp, regional med consult, 1982; Hughes Spalding Hosp Atlanta, developer, dir emergency room, 1984-86; Brown Med Assocs, founder, pres, 1989. **Orgs:** Pres, Nat Alumni Asn Morehouse Col, 1962-72; vchmn, bd trustees, Morehouse Col, 1975-89; asst prof, preventive med Emory Univ Med Sch, 1968-69; Task Force Cardiovascular Disease Hypertension & Diabetes GA Reg Med Prog, 1971; Atlanta Med Assoc; pres, Eta Lambda chap, Alpha Phi Alpha, 1966; vice chmn, bd trustees Morehouse Col, 1969-88; pres, Kappa Boule Sigma Pi Phi Frat, 1983-84. **Honors/Awds:** Honorary Doctor of Science, Morehouse Col, 1987; Doctor of Science, Morehouse Med Sch, 1998; Nash Carter Award, 2000. **Special Achievements:** First African American on the faculty of Emory Medical School, 1968. **Military Serv:** AUS, 1952-54. *

BROWN, CARLTON E.
Educator, president (organization). **Educ:** Univ Mass, BA, 1971. **Career:** Savannah State Univ, pres, 1997-. **Orgs:** Vchmn, 2002-04, chmn, Savannah Econ Devel Authority, 2004. *

BROWN, CAROL ANN
Educator. **Personal:** Born Jan 25, 1952, Ann Arbor, MI; married Marcellus B Brown; children: Brandon, Marc, Adam. **Educ:** Univ Mich, BS, 1974, MS, 1975. **Career:** Ann Arbor Pub Schs, instrumental music instr, 1974-75; Joliet Pub Schs, coordr music, 1975-82; Augustana Col, asst dean stud servs, 1982-. **Orgs:** Bd dirs, Vis Nurse Homemaker Assoc, 1985-; pres, Delta Sigma Theta Inc Moline Davenport Alumnae, 1985-, mem, 1972-; Sounds of Peace Ensemble, 1984-; Zonta Int, 1983-. **Honors/Awds:** Outstanding Service Award, Parent Teacher Asn, 1980; Joliet Band Parents Asn, 1982; Joliet Orch Parents Asn, 1982; Appreciation Award, Black Stud Union, Augustana Col, 1983-85; Honorary Membership, Ladies Vital Essence Club, 1984; Outstanding Service Award, Delta Sigma Theta Inc, 1985.

BROWN, CAROLYN M
Purchasing agent. **Personal:** Born Oct 12, 1948, Seattle, WA; married Jerome, Feb 13, 1951 (divorced 1985); children: Cesha, Channelle & Clifton. **Educ:** Anderson Col, BA, speech educ, sociol, minor educ, 1970; Baltimore State Univ, MA speech educ, Commun, 1976; Univ Berkeley, grad work educ; numerous educ & training seminars. **Career:** Purchasing Agent (retired); Indianapolis Publ Sch, teacher, 1970-71; Delco Remy, clerk,1971, secy, 1971-72, supvr, 1972-75, buyer, 1975-83, sr buyer, 1983-86, gen supvr central stores, 1986. **Orgs:** IN Reg Minority Purchasing Coun; Nat Minority Supplier Develop Coun; Channel 49; chairperson Telesale; TV personality; Women Church God; alumni dir, Anderson Col; Baltimore State Alumni Asso; capt, Telethon Night Dr; The Christian ctr, Alpha Kappa Alpha, Alpha Psi Omega; mayoral appoint educ comm Blue Ribbon; Madison County Fine Arts Coun, Urban League Madison County; bd dir, United Way, United Cerebral Palsy; NAACP; Nat Republican Comn; Career Guild Assoc; Am Bus Women Am; dir, Youth Choir; Sunday Sch teacher; Kodiakanal & Woodstock Found; Smithsonian Assoc; fel, sponsor Anderson Col; dr person Community Concert Series; IN Black Expo Inc; sponsor Theada Club Anderson Col; judge Black Baltimore State Pageant; Jr Miss Madison County. **Honors/Awds:** Sequentennial Queen; William B Harper Award Outstanding Community Serv Madison County; Outstanding Young Woman Am; Outstanding Black Am; Outstanding Elem Teacher Am; Pres Award Urban League of Madison County; Outstanding Conf Leader-NAACP Nat Convention Anderson IN; Outstanding Lady Day AME Church Anderson IN; nom Prof Achievers Award; IN Reg Minority Supplier Develop Coun Achievement Award; Nat Supplier Year Buyer Rec Award.

BROWN, CAROLYN THOMPSON
Library administrator. **Personal:** Born May 18, 1943, Brooklyn, NY; daughter of Frank and Martha Thompson; married Timothy E Eastman; children: 2; married; children: Christopher Leslie & Michael Arthur Brown. **Educ:** Cornell Univ, BA, 1965, MA, 1968; Am Univ, PhD, 1978. **Career:** Howard Univ, asst prof, dept eng, 1978-84, assoc prof, eng dept, 1984-91, Col Liberal Arts, assoc dean humanities, 1988-90; US Nat Comn on Libr & Info Sci, comnr; Libr Cong, dir educ serv, 1990-92, assoc librn cult affairs, 1992-95, asst librn libr serv, Area Studies Collections, actg dir, 1995-, heads Collections & Serv Directorate, 16th div, currently, comnr, currently. **Orgs:** Am Libr Asn, 1990-; Asn Asian Studies; bd mem, Contemplative Mind's Soc, 1997; bd trustees, Fetzer Inst, 2002-; adv bd, Nat Foreign Language Ctr; adv comt, Global Resources Prog, Asn Res Libraries; exec comt, John W Kluge Ctr Advan Res. **Honors/Awds:** Cornell Nat Fellowship, Cornell Univ, 1961-65; Nat Defence Foreign Lang, 1965-67; Graduate Honor Fellowship, Am Univ, 1975-78; Faculty Research Grant, Howard Univ, 1980, 1986. **Special Achievements:** Auth, Dramatic Prod "Goin' Home", 1981; produced numerous articles. **Business Addr:** Acting Director for Area Studies Collections, Assistant Librarian, Library of Congress, 101 Independence Ave SE, Washington, DC 20540-8000, **Business Phone:** (202)707-5000.

BROWN, CARROLL ELIZABETH
Government official, executive, vice president (organization). **Personal:** Born Aug 31, 1942, Ft Worth, TX; married Ralph Theodore Brown Sr; children: Ralph Jr, Erik & Shawn. **Educ:** Seattle Univ, attended 1963. **Career:** WADS Radio "Breakfast for Two," radio talk show hostess, 1976; TRW-Geometric Tool, personal asst, 1978-81; Capital Temporaries Inc, placement mgr, 1980-84; Shubert Theater, group sales assoc & community rels liaison, 1984-85; Conn Bus Inst, placement dir, 1985; Stone Acad, placement dir, 1986-90; New Haven Conv & Visitors Bur, dir visitors servs & admin, 1990-91; Legislative Asst to Labor Comt, 1992-93; Spokeswoman for Chief Quiet Hawk, Paugussett Indian Tribe, temporary/part-time, 1993-94. **Orgs:** Founder, pres, W Haven Black Coalition, Inc, 1986-; W Haven High Parents Club, 1987-88; YWCA Ballroom Restoration Comt, 1987-89; bd dir, YWCA, 1987-89; vpres, Conn State Nat Asn Advan Colored People, 1987-91; vpres, Greater New Haven NAACP, 1990-; adv bd, Inner-City Advertiser, 1990-; Yale-New Haven Hosp Annual Appeal Comt, 1990-; bd dir, Peabody Museum, 1990-91; adv bd, Am Nat Bank, 1991-; personnel comt, Citizens Television bd dirs, 1991-; vpres, Connecticut State Nat Asn Advan Colored People, 1991-; finance bd, West Haven, 1992-. **Honors/Awds:** Nominee Jefferson Award Community Servce, 1975; Outstanding Volunteer of the Year, Bridgeport Public School System, 1982-85; Mrs Connecticut Second Runner-Up, 1983; Black Family Achievement Award, West Haven High School, 1985; Nominated for Jefferson Awards, 1987; Civic/Community Service Award, Professional and Busi-

ness Assn of Greater New Haven, 1988; Outstanding Member Award, Dixwell United Church of Christ, 1990; District Citizen of the Year Award, 1994, Local Citizen of the Year Award, 1993, Omega Psi Phi Fraternity; Benjamin L Hooks Outstanding Leadership Award, Connecticut State Nat Asn Advan Colored People, 1992; Community Service Award, Elm City Business & Professional Women's Assn, 1993.

BROWN, CARRYE BURLEY
Government official. **Personal:** Born in Palestine, TX; daughter of WM Burley and Ecomet Sr; married Larry; children: Xavier & Xenia. **Educ:** Stephen F Austin State Univ, BS, home econs. **Career:** US Fire Admin, adminr, currently. **Orgs:** Nat Fire Acad Alumni Asn. **Special Achievements:** First woman and the first African American to head the US Fire Administration.

BROWN, CHAD EVERETT (CHADWICK EVERETT BROWN)
Football player. **Personal:** Born Jul 12, 1970, Pasadena, CA; married Kristin, Jun 11, 1994; children: Amani. **Educ:** Univ Colo, mkt. **Career:** Pittsburgh Steelers, linebacker, 1993-96, 2006; Seattle Seahawks, 1997-04; New England Patriots, 2005, 2007; Pro Exotics, owner. **Honors/Awds:** Three time Pro Bowler & Two time first-team All-Pro. **Business Addr:** Owner, Pro Exotics, 3911 Norwood Dr Suite C, Littleton, CO 80125, **Business Phone:** (303)347-0500.*

BROWN, CHADWICK EVERETT. See BROWN, CHAD EVERETT.

BROWN, CHARLES
Consultant, government official. **Personal:** Born Mar 8, 1938, Williston, SC; son of Charlie Jr and Ruth A Hickson. **Educ:** Cheyney State Col, BS, 1961; Ind Univ NW, MPA, 1980. **Career:** Gary Ind Pub Sch, teacher, 1961-68; Gary Youth Serv Bur, dir, 1983; Gen Assembly, state rep, 1983-95; City Gary, Gary, IN, affirmative action officer & risk mgr, 1988; Gary Comn Ment Health Ctr, chief exec officer, 1993; consult; Ind House Rep, state rep, currently. **Orgs:** Bd dir, Nat Civil Rights Mus & Hall Fame; Nat Alumni Asn Hall Fame, Cheyney Univ. **Home Addr:** 9439 Lake Shore Dr, Gary, IN 46403. **Business Addr:** State Representative, Indiana House of Representative, State House Room 4-2 200 W Washington St, Indianapolis, IN 46204, **Business Phone:** (317)232-9400.

BROWN, CHARLES EDWARD
Geologist. **Personal:** Born Sep 7, 1948, Buckingham, VA; son of Warren G H and Gretchen H Jackson; married Sadie Banks Brown, Dec 5, 1970; children: Karen Denise, Carla Denette. **Educ:** Va State Univ, Petersburg, VA, BS, geol, 1971; The Pa State Univ, State Col, PA, MS, geol, 1974, PhD, 1976. **Career:** US Geol Surv, Reston, VA, res hydrologist & geologist, 1969-88; Chevron Oil, USA, exploration geologist, 1976-78; Va State Univ, Petersburg, VA, asst prof, 1978-80; George Mason Univ, Visiting Common wealth Prof geological sci dept; Howard Univ, prof; US Dept Energy, int fossil energy specialist & sr geologist; US Geol Surv, Water Resources Div, res project chief; Chevron USA Inc, exploration geologist. **Orgs:** Soc Exploration Geophysicists; Geological Soc Am; Am Geophys Union; Nat Asn Black Geologists & Geophysicists; founder, dir, Int Geohydroscience & Energy Res Inst; Geological Soc Am; Nat Asn Black Geologists & Geophysicists; Asn Geoscientists Int Develop. **Honors/Awds:** Phi Kappa Phi Honor Society, Pa State Univ, 1974. *

BROWN, DR. CHARLES SUMNER
Clergy, educator. **Personal:** Born Sep 18, 1937, Plant City, FL; married Joan Marie Steed; children: Charles Jr, Gene Mitchell. **Educ:** Morehouse Col, AB, 1956; United Theol Seminary, MDiv, 1962; Boston Univ Sch Theol, ThD, 1973. **Career:** Wright-Patterson Air Force Base, mathematician fluid dynamics res br, 1956-59; Sheldon St Congregation Church Providence, pastor, 1964-66; Ebenezer Baptist Church Boston, interim pastor, 1966-67; United Theol Seminary, prof church & soc, 1968-79; Yale Univ Divinity Sch, assoc prof practical theol, 1979-83; Bethel Baptist Church, pastor, currently. **Orgs:** Secy, The Soc Study Black Religion; voluntary assoc prof, Dept Med Soc Wright State Univ Med Sch; bd mem, United Way Greater Dayton; Family Serv Asn; Dayton Coun World Affairs; Dayton Art Inst; pres, Metro Churches United; moderator Western Union Baptist Dist Asn; Kappa Alpha Psi Frat; Sigma Pi Phi Boule. **Honors/Awds:** Protestant Fellowship Award, Fund Theol Educ, 1961-62; Presbyterian Grad Fellowship, United Presby Church, USA, 1966-67. **Business Addr:** Pastor, Bethel Baptist Church, 401 S Paul Laurence Dunbar St, Dayton, OH 45402, **Business Phone:** (937)222-4373.*

BROWN, CHRISTINE JAMES
Executive. **Personal:** Born in Philadelphia, PA. **Educ:** Rutgers Univ, BA, 1974. **Career:** NY City Found Sr Citizens, 1977; Planning Consult Agency Opers, 1979; dep dir admin, 1982; Allocations & Agency Rels, 1985; Fund Distrib & Community Problem-Solving, dir, 1988; United Way Southeastern Pa, pres & chief exec officer, 2004; United Way Int, pres & chief exec officer, 2004-07; Child Welfare League Am, pres & chief exec officer, 2007-. **Orgs:** Chair, United Way America's Nat Prof Coun; Urban League Philadelphia; bd vice chair, Community Col Philadelphia; Greater Philadelphia Chamber Com; bd, Samuel S Fels Fund; Christopher Ludwick Found; Del Valley Grantmakers; Philadelphia Urban Affairs Coalition; Pa Bar Asn Judicial Eval Comn. **Honors/Awds:** United Negro College Fund Hobart C Johnson Award, 1995; Philadelphia Omega Psi Phi Citizen of the Year Award, 1997; Public Relations Society Leadership Award, 1997; Vicinity American Association of University Achievement Award, 1998; Center of Autistic Children Small Miracles Award, 1998; American Society for Public Excellence in Public Service, 1998; National Council of Negro Women Mary McLeod Bethune Award, 1999; B'nai B'rith Humanitarian Award, 1999; Operation Understanding Distinguished Community Leadership Award, 1999; Distinguished Daughter of Pennsylvania, Commonwealth of Pennsylvania, 2000; Unity Foundation Outstanding Leader Award, 2001; Outstanding Leader Award , Arthritis Found, 2001; Philadelphia Business Journal Woman of Distinction Award, 2003. **Business Addr:** President, Chief Executive Officer, Child Welfare League of America, 2345 Crystal Dr Suite 250, Arlington, VA 22202.*

BROWN, HON. CHRISTOPHER C
Judge. **Personal:** Born Nov 20, 1938, Pontiac, MI; son of Arthur Patrick and Ardelia Christopher; married Lillian Jean Twitty, Jun 19, 1966; children: Alesa Bailey & Tice Christopher Brown. **Educ:** Wayne State Univ, BA, 1962; Detroit Col Law, JD, 1966. **Career:** Pvt pract, atty 1966-73; 50th Dist Ct City Pontiac, judge, 1972-. **Orgs:** Nat Asn Advan Colored People; Urban League; Am Bar Asn; Mich Bar Asn; Wolverine Bar Asn; Oakland Bar Asn; Nat Bar Asn; D Augustus Straker Bar Asn. **Business Addr:** Judge, 50th Judicial District Court, 70 N Saginaw St, Pontiac, MI 48342, **Business Phone:** (248)758-3800.

BROWN, CHUCKY (CLARENCE BROWN)
Basketball coach, basketball player. **Personal:** Born Feb 29, 1968, New York City, NY. **Educ:** NC State Univ, attended 1989. **Career:** Basketball Player (retired), Coach; Cleveland Cavaliers, forward, 1989-91, 2001; Los Angeles Lakers, 1991-92; NJ Nets, 1992-93; Dallas Mavericks, 1993; Panna Firenze (Italy), 1992-93; Grand Rapid Hoops (CBA), 1993-94; Yakima Sun Kings (CBA), 1994-95; Houston Rockets, 1994-96; Phoenix Suns, 1997; Milwaukee Bucks, 1997; Atlanta Hawks, 1997-98; Charlotte Hornets, free agent, 1999-2000; San Antonio Spurs, free agent, 2000; Golden State Warriors, 2001; Cleveland Cavaliers, 2001; Sacramento Kings, 2002; Fayetteville Patriots, mentor; Raleigh Knights, head coach, 2004; Roanoke Dazzle, asst coach, 2004-. **Special Achievements:** Championship, NBA, 1995; All-League first team, CBA, 1995. **Business Phone:** (540)266-1000.

BROWN, CINDY (CYNTHIA LOUISE BROWN)
Basketball player. **Personal:** Born Mar 16, 1965, Portland, OR. **Educ:** Long Beach State, attended 1987. **Career:** Sidis Ancona, Italy, forward, 1987-88; Toshiba Yana Gi Cho, Japan, 1988-92; Faenza Errieti Club, Italy, 1992-94; Elitzur Holon, Israel, 1994-96; US Valenciennes Orchies, France; Detroit Shock, 1998-99. **Honors/Awds:** Gold Medal, Pan American Games, Indianapolis, Indiana, 1987; Gold Medal at the Olympics, Seoul, 1998. *

BROWN, CLARENCE. See BROWN, CHUCKY.

BROWN, CLARICE ERNESTINE
Accountant, president (organization). **Personal:** Born Jun 8, 1929, Toledo, OH; daughter of Robert Durham (deceased) and Margaret Durham (deceased); married Bud Luther; children: Gregory, Babette Jackson & Jocelyn. **Educ:** Roosevelt Univ, BS, Bus Admin, 1965; DePaul Univ; Cortez Bus Col. **Career:** Accountant (retired); US Treas IRS, internal revenue agent, 1960-84; Iota Phi Lambda Sorority Inc, nat pres, 1981-83. **Orgs:** Leader, first vpres bd, 1977-73, pres, 1977-81; Girl Scouts, 1964-81; pres, 1973-71, parliamentarian, 1985, Alpha Beta Chap Iota Phi Lambda; nat pres Iota Phi Lambda, 1981-83; nat finance secy, Top Ladies Distinction, 1985-88; NAACP, Oper PUSH, 1985; court 142 jr daughter counr, counr Cath girls, 7-18 Knights St Peter Claver Ladies Aux, 1985. **Honors/Awds:** Fed Employee of the Year, 1967; Outstanding Women, St Columbanus, 1972; St Anne's Medal, 1973; Mother of the Year, 1974; Volunteer of the Year; nominee Aldermans Awd, 1982; Cardinals Awd, Parish Awd, 1983; honoree, Alpha Gamma Pi; citations, WAIT & WBEE; Albert Gallatin Awd, Treas Dept US Govt; Pacesetter Award, Mary McCleod Bethune Nat Coun Negro Women, 1992. **Home Addr:** 9134 S Lowe Ave, Chicago, IL 60620.

BROWN, CLAUDELL, JR.
Association executive, educator, government official. **Personal:** Born Jun 8, 1949, Jackson, TN; married Linda Ruth Brogden. **Educ:** Lane Col, BA. **Career:** Bur Commun & Rels, teen counr, 1969-71; Tipton Co Sch Syst, teacher, 1974; Happy Children Multi-Serv Ctr, Happy Children Day-Care Inc, dir; Lane Col, Eng & French Black Lit, tutor; Jackson City Coun, Dist 5, comnr, currently. **Orgs:** Upward Bound Proj, 1969-70; Memphis Chap, Lane Col Alumni Asn, 1971; prog rep, US Dept Health, St Louis, 1971; bd dirs, Mid-South Med Centers Coun, 1973; Chelsea Community Coord Comt, 1972; Nat Social Workers of Am, 1972; bd dirs, Memphis-Shelby Co Legal Serv Asn, 1973; adv comt, Memphis-Shelby Co Legal Serv Asn 1973; basileus, Theta Iota Chap Omega Psi Phi Fraternity, 1973-74; social serv coordr, dep dir Memphis-Shelby Co Comm Action Agency; Nat Asn Advan Colored People; Concert Choir; Pre-Alumni Club; Student Christian Asn; French Club; Social Sci Club; Stud Tribune; Memphis Comm Singers, Inc; vpres, Shelby Co Dem Voters Coun. **Home Phone:** (731)424-9079. **Business Addr:** Commissioner, District 5, 100 E Main St Suite 301, Jackson, TN 38301, **Business Phone:** (731)988-3110.

BROWN, CLAUDINE K.
Lawyer, executive. **Educ:** Pratt Inst, BA; Bank Street Col, mus educ; Brooklyn Law Sch, JD. **Career:** New York City Pub Schs, art & drama teacher; Brooklyn Mus, staff, 1976, mus educr, mgr sch & community prog, 1984-85, asst dir govt & community rels, 1985-90; Smithsonian Institutions, dep asst secy mus, 1991; Nathan Cummings Found, atty, dir arts & cult prog, currently. **Orgs:** Am Asn Mus; Nat Pk Serv Fund; Asn Black Found Execs; pres bd, Grantmakers in the Arts; arts admin prog, NY Univ; Mus Leadership Prog, Bank Street Col. **Business Addr:** Director of the Arts and Culture Program, Attorney, Nathan Cummings Foundation, 475 10th Ave 14th Fl, New York, NY 10018-9715, **Business Phone:** (212)787-7300.*

BROWN, CLIFTON GEORGE
Journalist. **Personal:** Born Sep 3, 1959, Philadelphia, PA; son of George Alexander and Maurita Robinson; married Carolyn Martin (divorced 1987); children: Ashley Georgia, Alexander William; married Delores Jones. **Educ:** Howard Univ, Wash, DC, 1979; Temple Univ, Philadelphia, PA, 1981. **Career:** Boca Raton News, Boca Raton, FL, sportswriter, 1981-83; Detroit Free Press, Detroit, MI, sportswriter, 1983-88; NY Times, New York, NY, sportswriter, 1988-. **Orgs:** Nat Asn Black Journalists, 1983-. **Honors/Awds:** Second Place Feature Writing, Fla Sports Writer's Asn, 1983. **Business Addr:** Sports Writer, The New York Times, 229 W 43rd St 4th Fl, New York, NY 10036.*

BROWN, COLLIER. See BROWN, P J.

BROWN, CONELLA COULTER
Educator, school superintendent, college teacher. **Personal:** Born Sep 26, 1925, Kansas City, MO; daughter of Charles P and Carrie Davis; married Arnold A, Mar 25, 1956. **Educ:** Kans City Conservatory of Mus, 1949; Univ Mo, BA, 1953; Case W Reserve Univ, MA, 1961; Lincoln Univ; Ohio Univ; Cleveland State Univ; Bowling Green State Univ. **Career:** School Superintendent (retired), College Teacher(retired); Educator; Ford Fnd Proj, coordr area curric develop, 1963-64; Cleveland Pub Sch, Cleveland,OH, social studies teacher, 1954-63; Rawlings Jr. HS, asst principal,1964-65; Off Human Rel, asst supvr, 1965-66; Supt Off Hum Rel, admin asst, 1966-72, asst supt, 1972-80; Case W Reserve Univ, emer bd trustee, currently. **Orgs:** Adv Com Sch dent; Delta Kappa Gamma; Am Asn Sch Admin; Nat Asn Supv & Curric Develop; bd dir, Christian C Fund; bd trustee, Free Med Clin Greater Cleveland; Delta Sigma Theta Inc; Hon Life Mem, Cleveland Coun Parent Teacher Asn, 1974; Urban League Greater Cleveland; trustee, St. James AME Church, 1982-89; Phi Delta Kappa; adv bd, Accord Associates Inc, 1980-; chair, founding commt, bd dir, St James AME Churches Endowment fund,1993-; adv bd, Creative Writing Writing Workshop Proj, 2000-. **Honors/Awds:** Professional Award for Leadership in Education, Cleveland Bus & Prof women, 1973; Outstanding Achievement Award in Education, Cuyahoga Comm Col, 1973; Distinguished Educator Award, St. James AME Church; Conella Coulter Brown Day, City Cleveland, Tribute, US Rep Louis Stockes, 1989. **Special Achievements:** First President to Awd Urban League of Greater Cleveland. First Woman toattain the position of Asst Supt of major OH School Dist.

BROWN, CONSTANCE CHARLENE
Government official. **Personal:** Born Jun 12, 1939, Chicago, IL; daughter of Charles W Porter and Myrtle V Jones Porter-King; married Leon Paul, Nov 21, 1959 (died 1984); children: Paul Gerard, Donna Elise, Venita Charlene. **Educ:** Nat Louis Univ, Evanston, IL, BA, 1985. **Career:** Munic Tuberculosis (Sanitarium), Chicago, clerk, 1963-65; Dept Water, Chicago, prin clerk, 1965-70; Dept Housing, Chicago, asst comnr, 1970-. **Orgs:** Nat Asn Housing & Redevelop Officials, 1985; Nat Asn Females Exec, 1990; Altrusa Club Chicago Inc, 1990; pledgee, Iota Phi Lambda Sorority, Alpha Beta Chapter, 1991. **Business Addr:** Assistant Commissioner, City Chicago, Dept Housing, 318 S Michigan St 6th Fl, Chicago, IL 60604.

BROWN, CONSTANCE YOUNG
Educator, manager. **Personal:** Born Aug 4, 1933, Leonardtown, MD. **Educ:** Morgan State Col, BS, 1955; Univ Md, MEd, 1960, 1973. **Career:** Bd Educ, Baltimore County, bus educ teacher, 1955-69; distrib educ teacher & coordr, 1969-71, data processing instr, 1971-74; Western Placement ServBd Educ, Baltimore, mgr, 1974-; Morgan St Col, trustee & senatoral scholar. **Orgs:** Pres & treas, Anne Arundel Community Br, Nat Asn Adv Colored People, 1973-76, 1977-; corresp secy, Southgate Community Asn, 1973-; vpres, MdState Conf, Nat Asn Adv Colored People, 1974-; anti-

basileus, Delta PiOmega Chap, Alpha Kappa Alpha Sorority, 1974-76; basileus, Delta Pi OmegaChap, Alpha Kappa Alpha Sorority, 1977-80; Nat Asn Adv Colored People; Nat Nom Comt, Nat Asn Adv Colored People, 1980; TABCO; MSTA; NEA; MVA; secy & treas, MADECA. **Honors/Awds:** DAR Citizenship Award, 1950; Dr Carl Murphy Award, MD State Conf Br, NatAsn Adv Colored People, 1974; Nat Asn Adv Colored People Award, AnneArundel Community Br, 1977; Honoree, 1st Women's Conf, NY, Nat Asn Adv Colored People, 1980; cert, Gov Md, Mayor Annapolis/Anne Arundel Co Exec; Plaque Who's Who, Human Resources.

BROWN, CORNELL DESMOND
Football player, football coach. **Personal:** Born Mar 15, 1975, Englewood, NJ; son of Reuben Sr and Oglessa. **Educ:** Va Tech. **Career:** Football player(retired); football coach; Baltimore Ravens, linebacker, 1997-2000, 2002-04; Cologne Centurions, coach, 2005; Frankfurt Galaxy, defensive line coach, 2006; Virginia Tech Hokies, defensive line coach, 2007; stamps, defensive line coach, currently. **Honors/Awds:** Super Bowl ring, 2000. **Business Phone:** (496)99782-7910.*

BROWN, CORRINE
Congressperson (U.S. federal government). **Personal:** Born Nov 11, 1946, Jacksonville, FL; children: Shartrel Brown. **Educ:** Fla A&M Univ, BS, 1969, MS, 1971; Univ Fla, EdS, 1974. **Career:** Fla House of Reps, dist 17, state rep, 1983-92; US House Rep, Fla third dist rep, 1992-; Fla Community Col, Jacksonville, fac; Univ Fla, fac; Edward Waters Col, fac mem. **Orgs:** US House Reps Comms: Transp & Infrastructure, Veterans' Affairs; Sigma Gamma Rho; Phi Delta Kappa; Comt Transp & Infrastructure. **Honors/Awds:** LLD, Edward Waters Col. **Special Achievements:** Nat Dem Conv, delegate, 1988. **Business Addr:** Representative for 3rd District of Florida, US House Rep, 2444 Rayburn House Off Bldg, Washington, DC 20515-0903, **Business Phone:** (202)225-0123.

BROWN, CORWIN ALAN
Football player. **Personal:** Born Apr 25, 1970, Chicago, IL. **Educ:** Univ Mich, BA, Eng, 1994. **Career:** Football player (retired), football coach; New England Patriots, defensive back, 1993-96; Boston Univ, volunteer coach, 1996; NY Jets Patriots,1997-98; Detroit Lions, 1999-00; Univ Va, coach, 2001-04; NY Jets, asst defensive backs coach, 2004; Univ Notre Dame, asst coach, currently. **Honors/Awds:** Robert P Ufer Award, 1992. **Business Phone:** (574)631-7196.*

BROWN, COSTELLO L.
Educator. **Personal:** Born Oct 16, 1942, Mebane, NC; married Florida; children: Eric & Ninita. **Educ:** Hampton Inst, BS, 1963; Iowa State Univ, MS, 1966, PhD, 1968; Univ Ill,PhD, 1969. **Career:** Woodrow Wilson fel, 1963; NIH fel, 1969; Calif State Univ, from asst prof to assoc prof, 1969-77, prof chem, 1977-, assoc dean, grad studies & res,currently, actg dir fac affairs, currently, provost, currently; Univ Ga,vis prof, 1972-; Calif Inst Technol, visiting fac assoc, 1975; NIH Marcfel, 1975; Off Advan Sci, Eng & Math Educ, dir. **Orgs:** S Calif Sect Am Chem Soc; exec comm, Sigma Xi Hon Soc; Am Chem Soc. **Honors/Awds:** Career Development Award, 1975. **Home Addr:** 547 Cocopan Dr, Altadena, CA 91001, **Home Phone:** (626)791-5998. **Business Addr:** Associate Dean of Graduate Studies, Professor, California State University, 5151 State Univ Dr, Los Angeles, CA 90032, **Business Phone:** (323)343-3810.

BROWN, COURTNEY COLERIDGE
Administrator. **Personal:** Born Jul 29, 1924, New York, NY; married; children: Beverly, Courtney Jr. **Educ:** Shaw Univ, BA, 1954. **Career:** vpres, St Phillips Housing Corp; NY State Div Human Rights, dir, reg dir, 1968-76; Urban League, asst exec dir, 1965-66, coordr, 1966-68; Sarco Co, dept mgr, 1944-65; Graduate Sch Social Work, asst prof; NY Univ, instr; The Negro World, owner; Harlem Daily, owner; Brown Mag, ed; NY State Dept Educ, counr; Oral History, USA, dir; Columbia Univ Bus Sch, dean emer, currently. **Orgs:** Clerk St Phillips Prot Epis Chap; Interparish Coun; bd dir, Grace Episc Sch; C Study Well Met Inc; C Prepartory Entrepreneur Prog; Dunbar Tenants League. **Business Addr:** Dean, Emeritus Professor, Columbia University Graduate School Of Business, 3022 Broadway, New York, NY 10027, **Business Phone:** (212)854-5553.*

BROWN, CYNTHIA LOUISE. **See BROWN, CINDY.**

BROWN, CYRON
Football player. **Personal:** Born Jun 28, 1975, Chicago, IL. **Educ:** Univ Ill; Western Ill Univ. **Career:** Denver Broncos, def end, 1998-2002; Colo Crush, def end, 2003; Tampa Bay Storm, def end, 2004; Philadelphia Soul, defe end,2004-06; Kans City Brigade, 2006-07; Dallas Desperados, def end, 2008-. **Honors/Awds:** Bresee Award, Univ Ill, 1994.super Bowl Champ XXXIII, All Am Honors . **Business Phone:** (972)785-4900.

BROWN, D JOAN
Insurance executive. **Personal:** Daughter of Duplain W Rhodes III and Doris M Rhodes. **Career:** Rhodes Life Ins Co La, New Orleans, La, chief exec; Nat Serv Indust Life Ins Co, chief exec; Rhodes Mutual Life Ins Co, Mobile, Ala, chief exec, currently. **Honors/Awds:** Nat Serv Indust Life Ins Co; Black Enterprise, Rhodes Life Ins Co La; Rhodes Mutual Life Ins Co Ala, 1990. **Business Addr:** Chief Executive, Rhodes Mutual Life Insurance Co, 402 Dr Martin L King Jr Ave, Mobile, AL 36603, **Business Phone:** (251)432-3665.

BROWN, DALLAS C, JR.
Military leader. **Personal:** Born Aug 21, 1932, New Orleans, LA; son of Dallas C and Rita S Taylor; married Elizabeth T; children: Dallas C III, Leonard G, Jan B, Karen L & Barbara A. **Educ:** WVa State Col, BA, hist/polit sci, Distinguished Mil Grad, 1954; Defense Lang Inst, Distinguished Grad, 1965-66; Ind Univ, MA, 1967; AUS Command & Gen Staff Col, 1967-68; AUS Russian Inst, 1968-70; US Naval War Col, Distinguished Mil Grad, 1973-74. **Career:** Military leader (Retired); 519th Mil Intelligence Battallion, Vietnam, comdr, 1970-71; AUS Field Sta Berlin Ger, comdr 1977-78; USA FORSCOM Atlanta, GA, dep chief staff/ intelligence, 1978-80; Defense Intelligence Agency, Wash, DC, dep vice dir, 1979-80; AUS War Coll Carlisle, PA, dep commandant, 1980-84; WVa State Col, assoc prof hist, 1984-96. **Orgs:** Alpha Phi Alpha, 1951-; Nat Eagle Scout Asn, 1978-; Asn AUS, 1978-; chmn, Greater Atlanta Armed Forces Day, 1979; constituent, AUS War Col Found, 1981-; Am Asn Univ Prof, 1984-; Upsilon Boule Sigma Pi Phi, 1984-97; Pi Sigma Theta Nat Polit Sci Hon Soc, 1985-; Phi Alpha Theta Nat Hist Soc, 1985-; Rotary Club Int, 1987-97; Anvil Club, 1989-97; bd adv, WVa State Col, 1990-91; Wva Higher Educ Adv Bd, 1992; comdr, Sun City Veterans Asn, 1999-2000; Alpha Lambda Boule, 1998-. **Honors/Awds:** Alumnus of the Year, WVa State Col, 1978; ROTC Hall of Fame, WV State Col, 1980. **Special Achievements:** First African American general officer in the field of military intelligence; Contributing author, "Soviet Views on War and Peace," NDU, 1982. **Military Serv:** AUS, brig gen, 1954-84; DSSM; MSM 2 OLC; JSCM; ACM; master parachutist; air crewman. **Home Addr:** 17 Devant Dr E Sun City Hilton Head, Bluffton, SC 29910-4537, **Home Phone:** (843)705-5619.

BROWN, DALTON G
Marketing executive. **Career:** New Detroit Real Mgt LLC, managing partner & chief operating officer. **Business Addr:** Managing Partner, Chief Operating Officer, New Detroit Real Management LLC, 14648 Ohio St, Detroit, MI 48238.*

BROWN, DR. DARLENE MORGAN
Educator. **Personal:** Born in Crowley, TX. **Educ:** Univ La, BS 1983; Univ New Orleans, M Ed 1988, Ph D, 2005. **Career:** Uni New Orleans, Admin Staff; Dir, UNO Charter Network. **Business Addr:** Director, UNO Charter Schools, 2045 Lakeshore Dr, CERM Bldg Room 418, New Orleans, LA 70148.*

BROWN, DECOVAN KADELL. **See BROWN, DEE.**

BROWN, DEE (DECOVAN KADELL BROWN)
Basketball player, basketball coach. **Personal:** Born Nov 29, 1968, Jacksonville, FL; married Tammy; children: Alexis Kiah, Alyssa Milan, Alanni & Anakin. **Educ:** Jacksonville Univ, Jacksonville, FL, 1986. **Career:** Basketball player (retired), basketball coach; Boston Celtics, guard, 1990-98; Toronto Raptors, 1998-2000; Orlando Miracle, 2000-02, head coach, 2002-04; San Antonio Silver Stars, head coach, 2003-04; Springfield Armor, head coach, 2009-; Orlando Magic, community ambassador; ESPN, NBA Analyst; Sirius Satellite Radio, Full Court Press, cohost, currently; EDGE Basketball LLC, chief exec officer, pres & owner, currently; Deelightful Inc, chief exec officer & pres, currently. **Orgs:** Women's Nat Basketball Asn. **Honors/Awds:** NBA All-Rookie Team, 1991; won the NBA Slam-Dunk Competition during All-Star Weekend, 1991.

BROWN, DELORIS A
Lawyer. **Personal:** Born in Los Angeles, CA; children: Nitobi. **Educ:** Calif State Univ, BA, 1964; Univ So Calif, MA, 1970; Peoples Col Law, JD, 1978. **Career:** Peace Corps Brazil, vol, 1964; atty-at-law. **Orgs:** State Bar Calif. **Home Addr:** 655 E Fairview Blvd, Inglewood, CA 90302.

BROWN, DENISE J.
Executive, lawyer. **Educ:** New York Univ; Brooklyn Law School. **Career:** Lewis & Clarkson, assoc; Minter & Gaye, assoc, 1988-90; Mayer, Katz, Kaber, Leibowitz & Roberts, atty; Warner Brothers Rec, black music div, sr vpres; Denise J Brown law firm, atty, currently. **Orgs:** Bd Govs, Nat Acad Rec Arts & Sci; bd, Brooklyn Law Sch. *

BROWN, DENISE SHARON
Manager. **Personal:** Born Aug 2, 1957, Manhattan, NY; daughter of James (deceased) and Geraldine (deceased). **Educ:** NC A&T State Univ, Greensboro, NC, BS, 1982. **Career:** NY/ACS/DCA, New York, NY, supvr, 1988-. **Orgs:** Ministry Catholics African Ancestry, 1983-; Nat Black Child Develop Inst, 1990-; Parish Outreach, 1995-99; Prison ministry, 1994-96; Coalition Black Trade Unionists, 1999-; NAB Social Workers, 1999. **Home Addr:** 600 Fulton Ave, Hempstead, NY 11550-7310. **Business Addr:** Supervisor, ACS/DCA, 150 William St Fl 6, New York, NY 10038, **Business Phone:** (212)676-6774.

BROWN, DEREK DARNELL
Football player. **Personal:** Born Apr 15, 1971, Banning, CA. **Educ:** Univ Nebr, attended 1993. **Career:** Football player (retired); New Orleans Saints, running back, 1993-96. **Honors/Awds:** Glenn Davis Award, 1998.

BROWN, DEREK VERNON
Football player, executive. **Personal:** Born Mar 31, 1970, Fairfax, VA. **Educ:** Univ Notre Dame, BA, mkt, 1992. **Career:** Football player (retired), executive; New York Giants, tight end, 1992-94; Jacksonville Jaguars, 1996-97; Oakland Raiders, 1998-99; Ariz Cardinals, tight end, 1999-2000; SPD Sub Ventures IV LLC, partner, currently. **Honors/Awds:** Ed Block Courage Award, 1996. **Business Addr:** Partner, SPD Sub Ventures IV LLC, 1060 W Main St, Branford, CT 06405-3441, **Business Phone:** (203)481-0392.

BROWN, DERMAL
Baseball player. **Personal:** Born Mar 27, 1978, Bronx, NY. **Career:** Kans City Royals, outfielder, 1998-04; Tampa Bay Devil Rays, outfielder, 2004-05; Oakland Athletics; outfielder, 2007; Los Angeles Dodgers, outfielder, 2009-. *

BROWN, DERRICK LESLIE
Executive. **Personal:** Married Deborah; children: Linsey & Aaron. **Educ:** Eastern Mich Univ, BS, bus admin; Univ Mich, MBA. **Career:** Detroit Renaissance Ctr, off leasing vpres, 1983-94; Colliers Int; QC Network Int, co-owner, co-founder; Quorum Com Detroit, LLC, owner, pres & chief exec officer, 2000-; Alloy Real Estate Servs, owner/pres & chief exec officer, currently. **Orgs:** Detroit Bd Realtors, 1993; pres, Detroit Area Com Bd Realtors, 1995; dist dir, Mich Asn Realtors; Nat Asn Realtors; chmn, Realtors Polit Action comt, 2003. **Honors/Awds:** Realtor of the Year, 1995; 100% Club Award, 1999. **Business Phone:** (313)965-2255.

BROWN, DIANA JOHNSON
Police officer. **Personal:** Born Jan 25, 1951, Dania, FL; daughter of Walter Rolle and Enith Gloria Johnson Mulkey; married Sherman Leon Brown, Mar 28, 1987; children: Shantel Ramsey, Laquantas. **Educ:** Broward Community Col, assoc sci, 1983; Fla Atlantic Univ, attended 1984; Barry Univ, BS, 2002. **Career:** Broward Community Col, Davie, FL, clerk-typist, admis clerk, sect to registr, 1970-74; FAU-FIU Joint Ctr, Ft Lauderdale, FL, clerk-typist, 1974-77; Broward County Sheriff's Off, Ft Lauderdale, FL, corrections officer, 1977-79; City Pompano Beach, FL, police officer, 1979-88, sergeant, 1988-; Broward County Sheriff's Off, sergeant, 1999, lt, 2003-. **Orgs:** Fraternal Order Police, 1979-; pres, Broward County Law Enforcement Orgn, 1980-; secy, State Fla, 1983-85; Police Benevolent Asn, 1983-; financial secy, Southern Region, Nat Black Police Asn, 1986-; pres, Ely High Sch, Choral Parent's Asn, 1990-; steering comt mem, Preventing Crime Black Community, 4th Annual Conf; Bus & Prof Women's Asn, Pompano Beach, 1992-; pres, Nat Black Police Asn, Southern Region, 1993-99; pres, Broward County Crime Prev Asn, 1997-98; Nat Orgn Black Law Enforcement Execs. **Honors/Awds:** Officer of the Month, City Pompano Beach, 1982. **Military Serv:** AUS, res, Ssgt, 1976-, Sgt First Class, 1990; Humanitarian Award, 1980, Army Res Component Achievement Medal, 1981, 1992, 2001. **Business Addr:** Lieutenant, Broward County Sheriff's Office, 2601 W Broward Blvd, Fort Lauderdale, FL 33312, **Business Phone:** (954)831-8900.*

BROWN, DR. DIANE R
Administrator. **Personal:** Born Aug 11, 1944, Newark, NJ; daughter of Eugene and Mary Robinson; married George L Blair, Oct 25, 1997; children: Rochelle. **Educ:** Ind Univ, BA, 1966; Univ Mass, MA, 1968; Univ Md, PhD, 1984; Johns Hopkins Univ, attended 1986. **Career:** Wayne State Univ, Inst Geront, fac assoc, 1993-, Ctr Urban Studies, dir, 1995-97, CULMA Urban Health Prog, dir, 1997-2002; Karmanos Cancer Inst, Gender & Minorities, dir, 2000-02; Univ Med Dent NJ, Sch Pub Health, Inst Elimination Health Disparities, exec dir & prof, 2002-. **Orgs:** Am Sociol Asn, 1970-; Am Pub Health Asn; Asn Black Sociologists; Mich Pub Health Asn; DC Sociol Soc; N Cent Sociol Asn; Geront Soc Am; Soc Study Social Probs; Sociologists Women Soc; Southern Sociol Soc; Urban Affairs Asn; World Fedn Ment Health; Am Cancer Soc; Am Asn Cancer Res; bd mem, Am Cancer Soc Eastern Div 2003-; bd mem, Newark Community Health Ctrs, 2003-. **Honors/Awds:** President Award for Exceptional Service, Wayne State Univ, 1999; Recognition for Scholarly Accomplishments, Wayne State Univ, 2000; Recognition for Faculty Community Engagement, CULMA, 2001; fel GSA, 2002; Blackwell Service Award, Asn Black Sociologists, 2007. **Special Achievements:** Author of numerous articles, book chapters, & books. **Business Addr:** Executive Director, University of Medicine & Dentistry New Jersey, Institue for Elimination of Health Disparities School of Public Health, 65 Bergen St Suite 742, Newark, NJ 07107-3001, **Business Phone:** (973)972-4383.

BROWN, DONNA DAEL THERESA ORLANDER SMITH. **See ORLANDERSMITH, DAEL.**

BROWN, DORIS
Educator. **Career:** State Wage Deviation Bd, 1995-98; Brown's Restaurant Servers Acad, dir, currently. *

BROWN, DWAYNE MARC
State government official, lawyer. **Personal:** Born Mar 16, 1962, Indianapolis, IN; son of Jimmy Emitt Brown and Hattie Ligon Brown; married Autumn Brooks, Jul 7, 1984; children: James-Marc & Kristin. **Educ:** Morehouse Col, Atlanta, Ga, BA, cum laude, 1984; Columbia Univ, Sch Law, New York, NY, JD, 1987. **Career:** Bd Govs Fed Reserve Syst, Wash, DC, staff atty, 1987-89; Coun Secy State, Joe Hossett, Indianapolis, Ind, coun, 1985-90; Bingham, Summons, Welsh & Spilman, Indianapolis, Ind, assoc, 1990; Supreme, Appellate, & Tax Ct Ind, Indianapolis, Ind, clerk, 1991-94; Indianapolis, Indiana, atty gen Ind. **Orgs:** Nat Asn Advan Colored People, 1990. **Honors/Awds:** Cert Achievement, Negro Coun Women, Indianapolis, 1991; Cert Achievement, Van Buren Baptist Church, Gary, 1991; Trail Blazer Award, Fitzgerald's Bus Exchange, 1991; Community Player, Dr Mozel Sanders Award, Indianapolis, 1991.

BROWN, EDDIE C.
Financial manager. **Personal:** Born Nov 26, 1940, Apopka, FL; son of Annie M; married Sylvia Thurston; children: Tonya Yvonne & Jennifer Lynn. **Educ:** Howard Univ, BSEE, 1961; NY Univ, MSEE, 1968; Ind Univ, MBA, 1970; CFA,1979; CIC, 1979. **Career:** T Rowe Price Assoc Inc, investment counselor, 1973-83; Irwin Mgt Co,investment mgr, 1970-73; electrical engr; chartered financial analyst; chartered investment counr; IBM, engr, 1963-68; Brown Capital Mgt Inc, pres & portfolio mgr, chief exec officer, 1983-. **Orgs:** Baltimore Security Analysts Soc; Financial Analysts Fed; panelist Wall St Week; TR Baltimore Community Found; The Walters' Art Gallery; MAR Econ Develop cms; E Baltimore Develop; MUNIMAE. **Honors/Awds:** Fellowship Grant Consortium Grad Study Mgt, 1968; Hall of Fame, Wall Street Week, 1996. **Special Achievements:** Black Enterprise Top 100 Asset Managers List, company ranked #1, 2000. **Military Serv:** AUS, 1st lt, 1961-63. **Business Addr:** President, Chief Executing Officer, Brown Capital Management Inc, 1201 N Calvert St, Baltimore, MD 21202, **Business Phone:** (410)837-3234.*

BROWN, EDWARD LYNN
Clergy, bishop. **Personal:** Born Apr 2, 1936, Madison County, TN; married Gladys D Stephens; children: Alonzo, Cheronda. **Educ:** Lane Col, BS, 1960; Interdenominational Theol Ctr, MDiv, 1963; Miles Col, Honorary Doctoral Degree, 1979. **Career:** Christian Methodist Episcopal Church, Bishop, 1960-; Dept Evangelism & Mission , bd chmn, currently. **Orgs:** Gen secy, Bd Pub Serv, Gen Educ Bd, Christian Methodist Episcopal Church; Long Range & Planning Comn, Comn Pension; rep, World Methodist Conf Evangelism, 1974; bd dir, OIC; bd dir, Memphis Nat Asn Advan Colored People; exec bd, Nat OIC; bd dir, Memphis Urban League; Int Soc Theta Phi; bd mem, Orange Mound Community Action Agency; Orange Mound Consolidated Civic Club; dean, S Memphis Dist Leadership Training Sch; bd mem, Memphis Community Educ Proj; bd chmn, Orange Mound & Creative Involvement Prog; Memphis & Shelby Co Welfare Comn; pres, CME Min Alliance; vpres, Memphis Ministry Asn. **Honors/Awds:** Cert Appreciation, Community Action Agency, 1970; Cert Merit, Serv City Memphis, Mayor Wyeth Chandler, 1971; serv gen asst comn, Mayor Wyeth Chandler, 1971; Big "S" Citation, City Memphis Co Comn, 1972; Outstanding Religious Leader, Alpha Kappa Alpha, 1973; Outstand Community Serv, UMCAP; Outstanding Serv, Memphis Nat Asn Advan Colored People, 1973; Outstand Communtiy Serv, Memphis Urban League, 1973. **Business Addr:** Board Chairman, 1616 Illinois Ave, Dallas, TX 75216.

BROWN, ELLEN ROCHELLE
Executive, television broadcaster. **Personal:** Born Mar 10, 1949, Denton, TX; daughter of John Henry and Earlene Punch. **Educ:** Southern Methodist Univ, BFA, broadcast film arts, 1971. **Career:** Columbia Univ, fel; KERA-TV, Dallas, reporter, 1971-72; NBC News, NY, news researcher, 1973-75; WROC-TV, anchor & reporter, 1975-78; KDFW-TV, Dallas, educ community affairs dir, 1978-80, multicultural affairs dir; TV series: "Insights", producer & host, 1980-86. **Honors/Awds:** Alfred I DuPont-Columbia Award, KDFW-TV, 1979; Texas School Bell Award, Dallas, 1979; Dallas School Administartion Award, Dallas Sch Dist, 1979.KDFW-TV. **Home Addr:** 10905 Gable Dr, Dallas, TX 75229. **Business Phone:** (214)720-4444.

BROWN, EMERY N.
Physician, educator. **Educ:** Harvard Col, BA, appl math, 1978; Harvard Univ, MA, stat, 1984, PhD, stat,1988; Harvard Med Sch, MD, 1987. **Career:** Prof, Health Sciences & Technol & Prof Computational Neuro science, MassInst Technol, currently; Mass Gen Hosp Prof Anaesthesia, Harvard Med Sch,Dept Anaesthesia & Critical Care, Mass Gen Hosp, currently. **Orgs:** Asn Univ Anesthesiologists, 2002; fel Am Inst Med & Biol Eng, 2006; fel Am Stat Asn, 2006; fel AAAS, 2007; Inst Med Nat Academies, 2007; fel Inst Elec & Electronics Engrs, 2008. **Honors/Awds:** NIH Director's Pioneer Award, 2007. **Special Achievements:** First African American at Massachusetts General Hopsital to become achaired professor in the 196-year history of MGH; "onstruction of point process adaptive filter algorithms for neural systems using sequential Monte Carlo methods", IEEE, 2007, "Bayesian analysis of interleaved learning and response bias in behavioral experiments", 2007; "A mathematical model of network dynamics governing mouse sleep-wake behavior Journal of Neurophysiology", 2007; "General purpose filter design for neural prosthetic devices. Journal of Neurophysiology", 2007. **Business Addr:** Professor of Health Sciences & Technology, Professor of Computational Neuroscience, Massachusetts Institute of Technology, MIT-Harvard Division of Health Science & Technology, 77 Mass Ave 46-6079, Cambridge, MA 02139, **Business Phone:** (617)726-7487.*

BROWN, EMIL. See BROWN, EMIL QUINCY.

BROWN, EMIL QUINCY (EMIL BROWN)
Baseball player. **Personal:** Born Dec 29, 1974, Chicago, IL. **Educ:** Indian River Community Col. **Career:** Pittsburgh Pirates, outfielder, 1997-2001; San Diego Padres, outfielder, 2001; Kansas City Royals, outfielder, 2005-07; Oakland Athletics, 2008; New York Mets, 2009. **Business Addr:** Professional Baseball Player, New York Mets, Citi Field Roosevelt Ave, Flushing, NY 11368-1699.*

BROWN, EMMA JEAN MITCHELL
Educator. **Personal:** Born Jun 1, 1939, Marshall, TX; daughter of Elvia Washington Mitchell and Johnnie D Mitchell; divorced; children: Charles S Jr & Gene Mitchell. **Educ:** Bishop Col, BS, 1961; Univ Mass, MEd, 1966; Boston Univ, attended 1966; Howard Univ, attended 1984; Miami Univ, attended 1985; Univ Dayton, attended 1988; Bethany Seminary, PhD, theol, 1997. **Career:** Educator (retired); Kans City Schs, teacher, 1961-62; Boston/Needham Pub Schs, lang arts specialist, 1964-67; Sinclair Community Col, lectr, 1970-73; Wright State Univ, lectr, 1970-75; Univ Ibadan, Nigeria, W Africa, lectr, 1975-76; Dayton Pub Schs, teacher, 1978-86, supvr commun arts, 1986-88; int evangelist/ missionary, 1989; Prayer Fel Church, Dayton, Ohio, pastor. **Orgs:** Zeta Sorority Inc, 1958-; Miami Valley Affairs Orgn, 1975-90; Urban League Guild, 1975-85; Nat Coun Negro Women, 1975-90. **Honors/Awds:** City of Dayton Medallion, Miami Valley Affairs Orgnn; Teacher of the Month, Colonel White High Sch. **Special Achievements:** Author: Come Sit at My Table: An African Cookbook, 1985, Custodial Procedure Guide, 1978; Has God Said? Paul Affirms Women Ministers, 2003; writer: poetry, African Network, 1985; articles: ABC's of Education, 1980, Nigerian-English Studies Journal, 1980. **Home Addr:** 473 Marathon Ave, Dayton, OH 45406, **Home Phone:** (937)275-9133.

BROWN, EMMETT EARL
Manager. **Personal:** Born Jan 30, 1932, Chicago, IL; son of Joseph E and Julia H Knox; widowed; children: Paula Davis, Patricia E, Emmett E Jr, Cecilia B & Alan C. **Educ:** Pepperdine Univ, attended 1979; CA State Univ, BS, BA, Bus; Ottawa Univ, BA, BusEd. **Career:** SEIU AFL CIO Local 660, bus agent; Cent & West Basin Water Replenishment Dist, dir; Peoples Housing Rogers Park, dir community org; Emmett Brown &Assoc, labor consult; AFSCME Local 3190, bus agent, currently. **Orgs:** Am Federation State, County and Munipical Employees. **Military Serv:** USAF, A1 & C, 1950-53. *

BROWN, ERIC JON
Football player. **Personal:** Born Mar 20, 1975, San Antonio, TX; children: Taylor. **Educ:** Miss State, Bus Info; Blinn JC. **Career:** Denver Broncos, defensive back, 1998-2001; Houston Texans, strong safety, 2002-04. **Honors/Awds:** Super Bowl XXXIII. **Special Achievements:** Modeled in Texans Style Show to benefit Family Services of Greater Houston & Houston Texans Found. *

BROWN, ERNEST DOUGLAS
Educator. **Personal:** Born Jul 6, 1947, New Britain, CT; son of Ernest Brown and Alberta Coleman; married Susan Revotskie, Sep 25, 1973; children: Rafael, Kalafya, Maceo & Naima. **Educ:** Harvard Univ, BA, philosophy, 1969; Univ Calif Los Angeles, PhD, art hist, 1971; Univ Wash, PhD (music), ethno musicology prog, 1984. **Career:** Seattle Art Comn, Neighborhood Arts Prog, coordr, 1978-80; Cornish IST Allied Arts, fac mem, 1981-82; N eastern Univ, asst prof, 1984-87; Coun Int Exchange Scholars, Fulbright Prog, res fel, 1986; Harvard Univ, rew Mellon, fac fel, 1990-91; Williams Col, assoc prof music, prof, currently, Kusika, co-dir, Zambezi Marimba Band, dir. **Orgs:** Soc Ethno musicology, 1985-; African Studies Asn, 1986-. **Honors/Awds:** Andrew Mellon Teaching Fellowship, Andrew Mellon Found, Harvard Univ, 1990. **Special Achievements:** Co-director, Kusika and the Zambezi Marimba Band, 1989-; Nat Coun Negro Women, photography comn, Seattle, 1981; King County Arts Comn, photograph purchased, 1983; "Lozi", NY: Rosen Publishing Co, 1998; "Turn Up the Volume!" The Drama Review, Carnival Issue, 1998. **Business Addr:** Professor, Williams College, Department of Music, 54 Chapin Hall Dr, Williamstown, MA 01267-2687, **Business Phone:** (413)597-2415.

BROWN, ERROLL M.
Commander, military leader. **Educ:** US Coast Guard Acad, marine eng, 1972; Univ Mich, naval archit & marine eng; Rensselaer Polytech Inst, MBA, 1986; Naval War Col, nat security & strategic studies, 1994. **Career:** Military leader, commander (retired); Coast Guard Icebreaker Burton Island, damage control asst & asst engr officer, 11th Coast Guard Dist's Naval Engineering Br, type-desk mgr; USCG Cutter Jarvis, engr officer; Coast Guard Acad, Marine Eng Dept, instr; USCG Rush, exec officer; Off Chief Staff, Progs Div, prog reviewer, Budget Div, chief; Secy Transp, mil asst; Coast Guard Headquarters, supvr; USCG Integrated Support Command, Portsmouth, VA, commanding officer; Maintenance & Logistics Command Atlantic, Norfolk, VA, comdr; Thirteenth Coast Guard Dist, comdr, 2000-03; USCG, rear adm, Coast Guard Acad Task Force, dir, currently. **Orgs:** Soc Naval Engineers; Soc Naval Architects & Marine Engineers; Am Soc Eng Educators; prog evaluator, Accreditation Bd Eng & Technol. **Special Achievements:** Co-authored a University of Michigan text entitled "Ship Replacement and Prediction of Economic Life". **Military Serv:** USGC, rear adm; Legion of Merit, Meritorious Service Medal, Secretary's Award for Meritorious Achievement, US Coast Guard Commendation Medal, Unit Commendation, Meritorious Unit Commendation, National Defense Service Medal, Special Operations Ribbon, Bicentennial Unit Commendation Ribbon, Antarctica Service Medal, Arctic Service Medal, Sea Service Deployment Ribbon, Expert Rifleman Medal, Expert Pistol Shot Medal. **Business Addr:** Director, Coast Guard Academy Task Force, USCG, 15 Mohegan Ave, New London, CT 06320-8100, **Business Phone:** (860)444-8674.*

BROWN, EVELYN
Government official. **Personal:** Born May 15, 1930, Tifton, GA; married Macon (deceased). **Career:** Cafeteria aide; Evelyn Spiritual Hour Radio Sta WRMU FM, hostess; Alliance city, OH, councilwoman, 1984-85. **Orgs:** Gospel Announcer's Guild Am, 1975; Democratic Exec Comn, 1981; Christian Update TV, 1985; Mayor's Comn Aging, Alliance, OH. **Honors/Awds:** Nails Thounder Soc Club, 1984; Queen for a Day Comm Churches, 1976; gospel announcer, Gospel Music Workshop Am, 1978; Woman of the Year, Altrusic Club, 1980. **Special Achievements:** First Black Councilwoman. **Business Addr:** Radio Show Hostess, Mount Union College, 1972 Clark Ave, Alliance, OH 44601, **Business Phone:** (330)823-2414.

BROWN, EVELYN DREWERY
School administrator. **Personal:** Born Oct 29, 1935, Haddock, GA; daughter of Bennie Drewery and Ada Tatum Drewery; divorced; children: Clinton O & Toni A. **Educ:** Morris Brown Col, BS, 1957; Atlanta Univ, MA, 1969, attended 1975. **Career:** Columbia Co Bd Educ, teacher, 1957-62; Richmond Co Bd Educ, teacher, 1962-64; Atlanta Pub Sch, dept chairperson & teacher, 1964-70; Econ Opportunity Atlanta, head start dir, 1965-69; Mayor's Off Community Affairs, Youth Servs, adminr, currently; Zeta Phi Beta Sorority Inc, Nat Storks Nest, dir & coordr, currently; Econ Opportunity Atlanta, prog dir; Metro Atlanta Boys & Girls Club, coordr. **Orgs:** Nat vpres, Zeta Phi Beta Sor, 1978; pres, Better Infant Birth, March Dimes, 1978-80; secy orgns & comuns, Women's Missionary Coun, 1980-; Ga Asn Educators; Nat Asn C Under Six; consult & task force mem, Parent &Child Ctrs; dir & chmn, Overseas Mission, Joint Bd Finance; pres, Women's Missionary Soc, CME Church. **Honors/Awds:** Community Service Award, Zeta Phi Beta Sor Morris Brown; Outstanding Service Award; Zeta of Year Award; Outstanding Service, Holsey Temple CME Church, Atlanta. **Business Addr:** National Stork Nest Director, Storks Nest National Coordinator, Zeta Phi Beta Sorority Inc, 1349 Aniwaka Ave SW, Atlanta, GA 30311, **Business Phone:** (404)755-7170.

BROWN, DR. EWART F
Physician, politician. **Personal:** Born May 17, 1946; son of Ewart A and Helene A Darrell; married Wanda; children: Kevin, Maurice, Ewart III & Donovan. **Educ:** Howard Univ, Wash, DC, BSc, chem, 1968, MD, 1972; Univ Calif, Los Angeles, MPH, child health, maternal family pop control & int health, 1977. **Career:** Vermont-Century Med Clin, Los Angeles, CA, med dir, 1974-; Charles R Drew Univ Med & Sci, Dept Family Prac, asst prof; Marcus Garvey Sch, Los Angeles, CA, dir; Bermuda Health Care Servs Ltd, Paget, Bermuda, med dir; Western Pk Hosp, Calif, founder & chmn bd dir; Quality Assurance Los Angeles Doctor's Hosp, dir; Bermuda, Dep Premier, minister tourism & transport, 1998-, dep premier Bermuda, 2003-; Bermuda Progressive Labour Party, party leader & premier of Bermuda, currently. **Orgs:** Trustee, Charles R. Drew Univ Med & Sci, 1989-92; chmn bd, Bermuda Times, 1987-; trustee, Howard Univ, 1990-; vpres, Union Am Physicians & Dentists; mem ed bd, Feeling Good mag; bd dir, Marina Hills Hosp, Los Angeles, CA; Nat Med Asn; Am Col Utilization Rev Physicians; Golden State Med Asn; AMA, Am Acad Family Physicians; Am Pub Health Asn. **Honors/Awds:** Howard Univ Service Awards, 1968, 1972; Physician's Recognition Award, AMA, 1977; Grassroots Health Award, Sons of Watts, 1979; Community Leadership Award, DuBois Acad Inst, 1982; Pacesetter Award, Los Angeles Chap, Nat Asn Advan Colored People, 1984; Humanitarian of the Year Award, Marcus Garvey Sch Los Angeles, Calif, 1991; senator, House Parliament, Bermuda, 1993; Scroll Award, Union of Am Physicians & Dentists.

BROWN, FLOYD A.
Radio broadcaster. **Personal:** Born Nov 5, 1930, Dallas, TX; married Mary E Stephens; children: Floyd Keith, Diane Faye. **Educ:** Northwestern Sch Bus; Radio Inst Chicago, attended 1951. **Career:** WRMN, announcer, chief engr, prog dir & asst mgr, 1951-62; WYNR-WNUS Radio Chicago, 1962-65; NBC-WMAQ

Chicago, prog mgr & announcer, 1965-71; WGN TV, staff announcer & prog host, 1971-99; Floyd Brown Co, pres, currently; Selected Funds, dir, currently. **Orgs:** Bd dir, 1st Fed Savings & Loan; dir & bd dir, Selected Funds; co-owner, Pub Rels & Advertising Firm Rotary Int; bd dir, YMCA; bd dir, Fox Valley Coun; Boy Scouts Am; Nat Asn Advan Colored People; Urban League; Elgin C of C; bd dir, Larkin Home C Family Serv; chmn bd, deacons Elgin 1st Cong Chap; Elgin Citizens adv comm, Ment Health Asn; Chicago Sunday Evening TV WTTW; bd trustees, Adler Planetarium; comm man, US Golf Asn; bd gov, Chicago Dist Golf Asn. **Military Serv:** AUS, sergeant, 1953-55. *

BROWN, FOXY. See MARCHAND, INGA.

BROWN, FRANCHOT A
Lawyer. **Personal:** Born Jul 11, 1943, Columbia, SC; son of Sara D and Rupert A; children: Brian S Brown. **Educ:** Howard Univ, Wash DC, BA, 1965; Univ SC, Law Sch, Columbia SC, JD, 1969; Univ Pa, Reginald Heber Smith Comm Lawyer, 1969. **Career:** Legal Aid Serv Agency, Columbia, 1969-72; pvt law pract, 1972-73; Columbia SC Magistrate, 1973-76; Franchot A Brown & Assoc, lawyer, 1976-; Brown & Stanley, sr partner, 1976-90; Law Off Franchot A Brown, lawyer, 1990-. **Orgs:** SC Blue Cross-Blue Shield; Greater Columbia Chamber Comm; Victory Savings Bank; Drug Response Op; Vocational Rehab Midlands Ctr Retarded Children; chmn, Citizens Adv Comm Community Develop, Columbia, SC, 1975-; Mens Resource Ctr, Columbia, SC, 1990-; chair, Community Planning Group, SC Dept Health & Environ Control. **Business Addr:** Lawyer, Law Office of Franchot A Brown, 1324 Calhoun St, PO Box 543, Columbia, SC 29201, **Business Phone:** (803)779-7060.

BROWN, DR. FRANK
Educator. **Personal:** Born May 1, 1935, Gallion, AL; son of Thomas and Ora Lomax; married Joan Drake, Jul 6, 1963; children: Frank G & Monica J. **Educ:** Ala State Univ, BS, 1957; OR State Univ, MS, 1962; Univ Calif, Berkeley, MA, 1969, PhD, 1970. **Career:** OR State Univ, grad fel, 1961-62; Univ Calif, Berkeley, grad fel, 1968-70; NY State Comn Educ, assoc dir, 1970-72; Urban Inst CCNY, dir, 1971-72; State Univ New York, Buffalo, prof, 1972-83; Cora P Maloney Col, State Univ New York, Buffalo, dir, 1974-77; Buffalo Sch Desegregation Case, Federal District Western New York, consult & res, 1976-83; Univ NC, Chapel Hill, Sch Educ, dean, 1983-90; Inst Educ Mgt, Harvard Univ, fel, 1988; Inst Res Social Sci, Chapel Hill, NC, dir, educ res policy studies proj, 1990-; Univ NC, Cary C Boshamer prof educ, dean emer sch educ, 1990-; State of NC, judge for spec educ; Univ Calif, Berkeley, vis scholar, 1990-91. **Orgs:** Pres, Rho Lambda Chapt Alpha Phi Alpha Frat, Buffalo, NY, 1977-78; co-founder, Western New York Black Educators Asn & Nat Urban Educ Conf, 1975-83; co-founder, State Univ New York, Buffalo, Black Fac Asn, 1972; bd dir, Buffalo Urban League, 1978-81; bd dir, Langston Hughes Inst-Black Cultural Ctr Western New York & Buffalo, 1978-83; vpres, Div A Am Educ Res Asn, 1986-88; bd dir, Am Asn Col Teacher Educ, 1988-92; bd dir, Nat Org Legal Prob Educ, 1990-93; Nat Res Advisory Bd, US Dept Educ, 1994-2001; Univ Parking Comm, Univ NC, Chapel Hill, 1996-98; chair, Univ NC Fac Coun, 1997-99; Am Educ Res Asn; Planning Comm, Educ Law Asn, 1998-2001; Advisory Comm Minority Affairs, Am Educ Res Asn, 1998-2000; Dissertation Awards Comm, Educ Law Asn, 1999-2001; chair, Advisory Comm, Office Equal Opportunity, Univ NC, 2000-. **Honors/Awds:** Rockefeller Found Scholars Award, 1979-80; Langston Hughes Inst Award, Outstanding Serv & Leadership; State Univ New York, Buffalo, Spec Award, Achievement Res, Teaching & Serv; Tar Heel Week, Raleigh News & Observer; Am Educ Res Asn Award, Dedicated Serv & Leadership. **Special Achievements:** Pub: Assessment & Evaluation of Urban Sch; The Allocation of Educ Environ, 1976; Barriers to Excellence in Urban Sch, 1991; Am 2000 Education Strategy, 1991; Single-Sex Schs & the Law, 1999; Publ 5 books, monographs & 90 articles; Book Series Editor, Educational Excellence, Diversity, Equity. **Military Serv:** AUS, spec, 1958-60. **Home Phone:** (919)489-0757. **Business Addr:** Cary C. Boshamer Professor, University North Carolina, Sch Educ, 121 B Peabody Hall CB Suite 3500, Chapel Hill, NC 27599-3500, **Business Phone:** (919)962-2522.

BROWN, FRANK LEWIS
Police chief. **Personal:** Born Jul 30, 1945, Fayetteville, GA; son of Jeff and Annie; married Hazel Brown. **Career:** Police chief (retired); E Point Police dept, patrolman, 1967-74, sergeant, 1974-79, lt, 1979-84, capt, 1984-90, major, 1990-96, chief police, 1996-06. **Orgs:** Kiwans Club, pres, 1995; FBI Nat Acad, 1990; Ga Chiefs Asn, 1996; Nat Orgn Black Law Enforcement Execs, 1994; Int Asn Chiefs Police, 1996. **Honors/Awds:** Officer of the Year, 1975; Man of the Year Award, TRDC, 1990. **Special Achievements:** First African American chief of police in East Point, GA. **Military Serv:** USAF. *

BROWN, FREDDIEMAE EUGENIA
Library administrator. **Personal:** Born Oct 16, 1928, Racine, WI; daughter of Fred and Eunice Doss. **Educ:** Fisk Univ, Nashville, TN, BA, 1955; Univ Mich, Ann Arbor, MI, AMLS, 1959, PhD, 1973-79. **Career:** Library administrator (retired); Detroit Pub Libr, chief dept, 1956-70, asst dir, br serv, 1970-73, pre-prof, librn I, II, III, chief div; Wayne State Univ, Dept Libr Sci, asst prof, 1973-82; Houston Pub Libr, regional br librn, 1982-89, asst chief, br servs, beginning 1989, chief, br servs, 1992-98. **Orgs:** Univ Mich, Sch Libr Sci, Alumni Asn, 1979-; Am Libr Asn; Texas Lib Asn, 1982-; Fisk Univ, Alumni Asn; Wayne State Univ, Sch Lib Sci, Alumni Asn, 1982-; Pub Libr Asn, ALA, 1983-; Am Libr Asn, 1986-. **Honors/Awds:** Librarian-in-residence, Univ Iowa, 1974. **Home Addr:** 2823 Salt River Ct, Missouri City, TX 77459.

BROWN, FREDERICK L.
Judge, educator. **Educ:** Harvard Col, BA, 1954; Harvard Law Sch, LLB, 1967. **Career:** Mass Super ct, chief law clerk, 1967-69; Mass Comn Against Discrimination, legal consult, 1969-70; Owens, Dilday & Brown, pvt pract, 1969-70; State Health Facilities Appeals Bd, chmn, 1969-72; Boston Univ Law Sch, instr, 1969-72; US Dept Housing & Urban Develop, reg coun, 1970-73; Northeastern Univ Law Sch, assoc prof law, 1973-76; State Bd Higher Educ, legal consult, 1974-75; Mass Appeals Ct, judge, 1976-. **Orgs:** Lawyer's Comt Civil Rights Under Law, Boston chapt, 1969-72; dir, Boston Legal Aid Soc, 1970-75; Boston Bar Asn, 1973-76; NAACP; visiting comt, Harvard Law Sch, 1975-80; dir, Greater Boston Legal Serv, 1976; State Mass Comt Criminal Justice, 1976-82; bd trustees, Northeastern Univ Law Sch, 1977-; bd dir, Lena Park Community Develop Corp, 1981-95; pres, Mass Black Judges Conf, 1983-85, 1993-95; chmn bd, Lena Park Community Develop Corp, 1985-90; chmn bd hosing div, Lena Park Community Develop Corp, 1990-95; Dana-Farber Cancer Inst; Big Brother Asn Boston; United Way Corp. **Honors/Awds:** Army Commendation Medal; Alvin Brown Fel Aspen Inst, Colo, 1977; Honorary LLD, New Eng Sch Law, 1989. **Special Achievements:** First African American to serve on the Appeals Court. **Military Serv:** AUS, 1954-64. *

BROWN, FURNEY EDWARD, JR.
Educator. **Personal:** Born Nov 6, 1940; son of Edward (deceased) and Annie L; married Betty, Jun 4, 1966; children: Furney Alexander, Marcus Andrew, Sonya Renee. **Educ:** Livinsgstone Col, BS, 1963; NC Central Univ, MA, 1968; Univ Miami, PhD, 1975. **Career:** Educator (retired); Wake County Schs, math teacher, 1963-67; Alamance County, Media Servs, 1968-69; Durham High Sch, math teacher, 1969-71; NC Central Univ, dir media, 1971-72; St Augustines Col, assoc vres acad affairs, 1975-90, exec asst, prof educ, 1995-98. **Orgs:** Phi Beta Sigma. **Honors/Awds:** Sigma Man of the Year, Phi Beta Sigma; Chapter Educator Award, Phi Beta Sigma; Nat Alumni Asn, Livingstone Col. **Home Addr:** 3405 Middlebrook Dr, Durham, NC 27705, **Home Phone:** (919)489-0440. *

BROWN, GARY LEROY
Football player, football coach. **Personal:** Born Jul 1, 1969, Williamsport, PA; married Kim; children: Malena, Dorianna & Tre. **Educ:** Pa State Univ, rehab educ. **Career:** Football player (retired), Football coach; Houston Oilers, running back,1991-95; San Diego Chargers, 1997; New York Giants, 1998-99, coach, 2005; Williamsport Area High Sch, offensive coordr, 2000-02; Lycoming Col, asst coach, 2003-05; Green Bay Packers, coach, 2006; Susquehanna Univ, offensive coordr, 2006-07; Carolina Panthers, coach, 2007; Rutgers Football, running backs asst coach, 2008; Cleveland Browns, coach, 2009-. **Business Addr:** Coach, Cleveland Browns, 76 Lou Groza Blvd, Berea, OH 44017, **Business Phone:** (440)891-5000.

BROWN, GATES (WILLIAM JAMES BROWN)
Baseball player, athletic coach. **Personal:** Born May 2, 1939, Crestline, OH; married Norma; children: Pamela & Willima Jr. **Career:** Baseball player (retired), baseball coach; Detroit Tigers, outfielder, 1963-75; Detroit Tigers, coach, 1978-84; Orlando Juice, Sr Prof Baseball Asn, mgr, 1989. **Honors/Awds:** Played in World Series, 1968; played in AL Championship Series, 1972; Freedom Foundation Award, 1973; Batting Coach for the World Champion Detroit Tigers, 1984; African-Am Hall of Fame.

BROWN, GEOFF. See BROWN, GEOFFREY FRANKLIN.

BROWN, GEOFFREY FRANKLIN (GEOFF BROWN)
Journalist. **Personal:** Born Oct 30, 1952, Pittsburgh, PA; son of George F and Helen V; married Alice Clark Brown; children: Geoffrey F Jr & Christina. **Educ:** Bowdoin Col, BA, 1974. **Career:** Pittsburgh Press, gen assignment reporter, 1974-75, 1977-78; Jet Mag, asst ed, managing ed, features ed, 1975-77, 1978-80; Chicago Tribune, copy ed, nat-foreign news ed, suburban bur chief, entertainment ed, assoc managing ed, entertainment, assoc managing ed, lifestyle, 1980-. **Business Addr:** Associate Managing Editor, Chicago Tribune, 435 N Mich Ave, Chicago, IL 60611, **Business Phone:** (312)222-3482.

BROWN, GEORGE HENRY, JR.
Judge. **Personal:** Born Jul 16, 1939, Memphis, TN; married Margaret Solomon; children: Laurita, George III. **Educ:** Fla A&M Univ, BS, 1960; Howard Univ, Sch Law, JD, 1967. **Career:** Judge (retired); AA Latting, atty, 1967-70; Equal Employ Opport Comn, dep dir, 1969-70; Legal Serv Assoc, exec dir, 1970-73; Brown & Evans Law Firm, atty, 1973-; Shelby County Circuit Ct, judge, 1983-05. **Orgs:** Chmn, Memphis Bd Educ, 1974; Am Bar Asn; Nat Bar Asn; Memphis County Bar Asn; Shelby County Bar Asn; comnr, Memphis Bd Educ; vice-chmn, Steering Com, NSBA; trustee, Lane Col; trustee, memphis Acad Arts; bd dir, Memphis Chap, Nat Bus League; bd dir, Memphis Chap, Nat Asn Advan Colored People; vpres & bd mem, Beale St Hist Found; Vollentine & Evergreen Community Asn. **Military Serv:** USAR, Capt. *

BROWN, GEORGE HOUSTON
Clergy. **Personal:** Born Oct 15, 1916, Finchburg, AL; son of A D Brown and Annie D; married Amanda S; children: Marian Payne, LaVerne Bruce, Gwendolyn A Rothchild. **Educ:** Ala State Univ, BS, 1953, sch admin & supv, 1964, MEd, 1968; Inter-Baptist Theol Sem, DD, 1967; Selma Univ, LLD, 1982. **Career:** Free Mission Dist Cong, cong dean, 1955-75; Coneuch-Monroe Community Action, bd mem, 1950-77; Monroe County Ment Health, bd mem, 1972-80; Tom Bigbee Regional Comn, bd mem, 1973-89; E Star Dist Asn, moderator. **Orgs:** Independent Order Universal Brotherhood, 1936-; Blue Lodge Masons, 1940-; Order Eastern Star, 1941-; Enoch Consistory No 222, 1960-; Jericho Ala, 1961-; vice-moderator, Bethlehem No 2 Dist Asn, 1963-85; pres, Monroe County-Ministerial Asn, 1965-70; cong dean, Bethlehem No 2 Cong, 1970-85; Monroe County Bd Educ, 1980-; United Supreme Coun, 33 Degree A&ASR, 1988. **Honors/Awds:** Moderator's Award, E Star Dist, 1990; Dean Christian Educ Serv Award, Bethelhem 2 Dist Asn, 1988. **Special Achievements:** 1st black elected to high office in Monroe County, AL, 1980; Author of Tithing: God's Way of Financing His Church; God's Storehouse Robbers; The Ministries of Christ's Church. *

BROWN, DR. GEORGE PHILIP. See Obituaries section.

BROWN, GERALD
Basketball player. **Personal:** Born Jul 28, 1975, Los Angeles, CA. **Educ:** Pepperdine Univ. **Career:** Phoenix Suns, guard, 1998-99; Los Angeles Pro Am Summer League, 2000; Indiana Pacers, 2000-01; Los Angeles Pro Am Summer League, 2001. *

BROWN, GILBERT DAVID, III
Executive. **Personal:** Born Jul 22, 1949, Philadelphia, PA; son of Gilbert David Brown Jr and Rosalie Gaynor Allen; married Edythe MacFarlane, Jul 5, 1980; children: Gilbert David IV & Courtney Nicole. **Educ:** PA State Univ, BS, bus adm, 1973; Pepperdine Univ, MBA, 1983. **Career:** Gillette Co, territory sales rep, 1973-74; Inglewood Meat Co, sales mgr, 1974-79; Scott Paper Co, sr sales rep, 1979-84; Paxton Patterson, region mgr, 1984-87; McBee Looseleaf Binders Co, acct exe, 1987-88; AT&T, Gen Bus Systs, acct mgr, 1988-91, Commercial Markets, acct exe, 1991-92; Pacific Bell, Major BUS, acct exe, 1992-97; Consumer Mkt GRP, mgr, 1997-99; Pacific Bell Serv, sales support mgr, 1999-. **Orgs:** Life mem, Kappa Fraternity Inc, 1969-, life mem, Pepperdine Alumni Asn, 1983-; life mem, Penn State Alumni Asn, 1985-; mentor, Young Black Scholars Prog, 1986-; Epsilon Pi Tau Fraternity, 1986; alumni recruiter, PA State Univ, 1987-95; polemarch, Los Angeles Alumni Ch, 1990-93; chr, Alliance Black TeleCommun Employees, fundraising com, 1990-91, prof networking comt, 1991; Big Ten Club Southern Calif, 1991-; adv bd mem, MAARK, 1992-; Prof Community Asn, 1992-; pres, Kappa Achievement Fund Inc, 1994. **Home Addr:** 741 W 39th St Suite 3, San Pedro, CA 90731, **Home Phone:** (310)547-0105. **Business Addr:** Sales Support Manager, Pacific Bell Services, 1010 Wilshire Blvd Rm 305, Los Angeles, CA 90017.

BROWN, GILBERT JESSE
Football player, football coach, business owner. **Personal:** Born Feb 22, 1971, Detroit, MI; children: Jamal. **Educ:** Univ Kans. **Career:** Football player (retired), Football coach; Green Bay Packers, defensive tackle, 1993-99,2000-03; Milwaukee Mile, co owner, currently; Continental Indoor Football League, Milwaukee Bonecrushers, head coach, 2007-08. **Business Addr:** Co-owner, The Milwaukee Mile, 7722 W Greenfield Ave, West Allis, WI 53214, **Business Phone:** (414)453-5761.

BROWN, DR. GLENN ARTHUR
Executive, executive director. **Personal:** Born Jan 27, 1953, Fort Knox, KY. **Educ:** Harvard Univ, AB, 1975; Univ Pa, Wharton Sch, MBA, 1980; Univ Pa, Sch Dent Med, DMD, 1982; Temple Univ, Beasley Sch Law, JD, 2003. **Career:** Ambulatory Health Care, consult, managing partner, 1980-83; About Your Smile PC, pres & dent dir, 1983-. **Orgs:** Treas, Walnut Hill Community Develop Corp, 1986-90; vpres, W Philadelphia, Nat Asn Advan Colored People, 1989-91; vpres, Philadelphia Chap, Nat Black MBA Asn, 1989-90; bd mem, Lutheran C & Family Serv, 1989-96; bd mem, Greater Philadelphia Health Action, 1989-92; bd mem, Chess Pa Community Health Ctr, 1993-95; charter bd mem, African Am Chamber Com, Philadelphia, 1993-; adv comt, Philadelphia Burristers Asn, 1996-97; menon bd, A Better Chance Lowe, 1996-, treas, 1997-; Acad Gen Dent; Nat Dent Asn; New Era Dent Soc; Nat Dent Asn. **Honors/Awds:** Distinguished Alumni Award, Harvard Univ. **Home Addr:** 169 Palmers Mill Rd, Media, PA 19063, **Home Phone:** (610)891-9587. **Business Addr:** Dental Director, President, About Your Smile PC, 6772 Market St, Upper Darby, PA 19082-2432, **Business Phone:** (610)734-0666.

BROWN, REV. GREGGORY LEE
Clergy. **Personal:** Born Sep 14, 1953, Indianapolis, IN; son of Harold S Sr and Bettie J Palmer; married Beverly Whiteside, Sep

6, 1975. **Educ:** Indiana Univ, Bloomington, IN, BA, 1976; Union Theol Sem, New York, NY, MDiv, 1978-80. **Career:** Jarvis Christian Colege, Hawkins, TX, assoc prof, 1979-80; St. Albans Congregational Church, Queens, NY, assoc pastor, 1980-81; Springfield Garden Presby Church, Queens, NY, pastor, 1981-85; New Jersey Citizen Action, Hackensack, NJ, regional organizer, 1986-87; Black Tennis & Sports Found, New York, NY, exec dir, 1987-; Featherbed Lane Presby Church, Bronx, NY, interim pastor, 1988-90; Randall Memorial Presby Church, New York, NY, interim pastor, 1991. **Orgs:** Chmn, Youth March Jobs, 1977-79; pres, Black caucus, Union Theol Sem, 1978-79; chmn, St. Albans Resource Ctr, 1980-81; life mem, NAACP, 1983; vice-chmn, Queens Comt, United Negro Col Fund, 1984-86. **Honors/Awds:** Merit Award, NAACP, 1980; Coach of the Year, New York City Presbytery, 1983.

BROWN, HANNAH M
Airline executive. **Personal:** Born Jun 23, 1939, Stamps, AR; daughter of Joseph and Eliza Gardner Junior; divorced; children: Juanita LaKay. **Educ:** Univ Nev, Las Vegas, NV; San Mateo Col, San Mateo, CA. **Career:** Larry's Music Bar, Las Vegas, NV, salesperson & mgr; Delta Air Lines, mgr, 1968-89, regional mgr; Urban Chamber Com, pres. **Orgs:** Nat Asn Advan Colored People; YWCA; Nat Urban League; vpres, Caucus African-Am Nevadans; asst sunday sch supt, Holy Trinity AME Church; bd dir, Las Vegas / Clark Co. **Honors/Awds:** Black Women of Achievement Award, Nat Asn Advan Colored People, 1988; YWCA's Salute to Women of Achievement, 1990; 100 of the Most Promising Black Women in America, Ebony Mag, 1991; Kizzy Award; Dollars and Sense, 1991. **Business Phone:** (702)648-6222.

BROWN, HARDY
Publisher. **Personal:** Born Dec 8, 1942, Jones County, NC. **Educ:** Univ Redlands, Johnston Col. **Career:** Kaiser Permanente, personnel mgr; Black Voice News, chmn, co-publisher, currently; Brown Publishing Co, chmn, currently. **Orgs:** Pres, Calif Media Asn; Nat Newspaper Publishers Asn; Calif Newspaper Publishers Asn; New Calif Media; W Coast Black Publishers Asn; bd trustee, San Bernardino Unified Sch dist; past pres, San Bernardino Br, NAACP. **Honors/Awds:** Publisher of the Year, Nat Newspaper Publishers Asn, 2000.

BROWN, HAZEL EVELYN
Association executive. **Personal:** Born Sep 3, 1940, Eden, NC; daughter of Joseph (deceased) and Mary Sue Hairston. **Educ:** Russell's Bus Sch, Winston-19Salem, NC, cert sec, 1960; Winston-19Salem, NC, BA, bus admin, 1982; Babcock Ctr Wake Forest Univ, Winston-19Salem, NC, cert mgt develop, 1978; NC Central Univ, Durham, NC, cert coun & interviewing, 1982; A&T State Univ, Greensboro, NC, MS, adult educ, 1985. **Career:** Winston-Salem Urban League, Winston-Salem, NC, vpres, 1961. **Orgs:** NAACP, 1972; mem, Mt Zion Baptist Church, 1972; mem, Winston-Salem State Alumni Asn, 1982; mem, Up and Coming Invest, 1986; pres, Nat Women Achievement & Clemmons Chap, 1987; mem, Benton Convention Ctr Coliseum Comn, 1987; mem, Delta Sigma Theta Sorority, 1988; mem bd realtors, Housing Resource, 1988; mem, Urban Arts Arts Coun, 1988. **Honors/Awds:** Girl Friday, Urban League Guild, 1970; Service Award, NAACP, 1987; Leadership Award, Winston-Salem Urban League, 1988. *

BROWN, HEATHER M.
Entrepreneur, educator. **Educ:** Old Dominion Univ, BS, bus admin/mktg; George Mason Univ, MBA; Va Polytech Inst, PhD, adult educ/human resource devel. **Career:** Univ Md, adj fac; Northern Va Community Col, adj fac; Mt Vernon Col, asst prof bus admin; Prof Solutions Inc, owner, 2001. **Honors/Awds:** Alumnus of the 1999 Leadership Fairfax. *

BROWN, HELEN E.
Judge. **Personal:** Born in Detroit, MI. **Educ:** Wayne State Univ, BA, 1972, Sch Law, JD, 1979. **Career:** Wayne City Circuit Ct, judge; State Mich Circuit Ct, judge, currently. **Orgs:** Phi Alpha Delta; Am Bar Asn. **Business Addr:** Judge, State Mich Circuit Ct, 711 Coleman A Young Munic Ctr Suite 1107, Detroit, MI 48226.*

BROWN, HENRY H.
Chief executive officer, consultant, president (organization). **Personal:** Children: 4. **Educ:** Xavier Univ, New Orleans; Tex Southern Univ, Grad. **Career:** Consultant, Corporate Executive (retired). Howard Univ Sch Bus & Indust,adj prof; Anheuser-Busch Inc, vpres, sr vpres mkt develop & affairs,1964-94; HH Brown & Assocs, pres & chief exec officer, currently. **Orgs:** Develop Great Kings & Queens Africa, 1975; Anheuser-Busch's ambassador,major leading nat orgn; chmn, Nat Bus Policy Rev; past imperial, Potentate Prince Hall Shriners; Pub Rels Soc Am; Am Mgt Assoc; Amer Mkt Assoc; NAMD; St Louis Ambassador; Royal Vagabonds. **Honors/Awds:** Distinguished Award, World's Fair Knoxville, 1982; Omega Man of the Year1983, St Louis; Adolphus Award for Excellence, Anheuser-Busch;Distinguish ef American Award & 1985 Professional Business Leadership Award, Dollars & Sense Mag; Corporate Man of the Year, NAACP; Marketeer of the Year, NAMD; Par Excellence Award, Shielf Found; Daniel W Bowles Award, Alpha Phi Alpha; James Weldon Johnson Award, Phi Beta Sigma; Brotherhood Award, Chicago Conf Human Rels; Distinguished Pioneer Award, Am Black Artists; Corp Executor, Nat Assoc Univ Women; Golden Palm Award, Harris Stowe State; Distinguished Alumni Award, Tex Southern Univ; also various citations from the Links, Jack & Jill, and several munic for outstanding supportive serv.

BROWN, HERBERT R
Insurance executive. **Personal:** Born May 20, 1940, Ashville, NC; married Marcia; children: Cheryl, Adrian & Janice. **Educ:** Int Data Proc Inst, Cert, 1962; Univ Cincinnati, attended 1969. **Career:** Western & Southern Financial Group, comput systems mgt, 1964-78, personnel coordr/community affairs, 1978-87, vpres pub rels, 1987, sr vpres pub rels & corp commun, bd dir mem, currently. **Orgs:** Past pres, Cincinnati Bd Educ; Boy Scouts Am; St Johns Social Serv Ctr; C Protective Serv; Hoffman Elem Sch, chair LS-DMC; Asn Black Ins Professionals; bd mem, Cincinnati Br Key Bank; chair, bd governors, Greater Cincinnati Found. **Honors/Awds:** Jefferson Award for Public Service, Am Inst Pub Serv, 1979; Leadership Award, United Way, 1981; Ethelrie Harper Award, Cincinnati Human Rels Comn, 1990; Corporate Image Maker Award, Applause Mag, 1992; Key to the City of Cincinnati, 1993; hon doctorate, Cincinnati State & Tech Col, 1994; Silver Beaver Award, Boy Scouts Am, 1995; Joseph Hall Award, United Way & Community Chest, 1995; Reach for the Stars, Memorial Community Ctr, 1995; Bell Ringer Award, Cincinnati Union Bethel, 1995; Lifetime Achievement Award, 1996; Paul M Lund Public Service Award, 2004. **Military Serv:** AUS, sgt E-5, 1958-61. **Home Addr:** 6520 Greenfield Woods S, Cincinnati, OH 45224. **Business Addr:** Member of Board of directors, Western & Southern Financial Group, 400 Broadway, Cincinnati, OH 45202-3341, **Business Phone:** (513)629-1136.

BROWN, HEZEKIAH
Educator. **Personal:** Born Jul 29, 1923, Monticello, MS; married Rosa L S. **Educ:** Tuskegee Inst, BS, 1950; Tenn A & I State Univ, MS, 1958; Delta State Univ, educ spec or AAA cert, 1973. **Career:** Eutaula, teacher, 1950-51; Simmons High Sch, teacher, 1951-63, group guide instr, 1970-96; Carver Elem Sch, prin, 1963-70. **Orgs:** Past & treas, Sunflower Co Teachers Asn; Chaplain VFW Post 9732, 1955-75; Dept Chaplain, Dept MS, 1974-75; Adv Bd CHP; bd Alderman; vpres, Wash Teachers Asn, 1970-75; Wash Co Solid Waste Com; VFW; Miss Teachers Asn; Miss Voc Guid Asn; Alpha Phi Alpha; Miss Munic Asn; AVA; Mil Order Cooties SS No 13. **Honors/Awds:** Teacher Award, Miss State, 1975; President's Award for Outstanding Serv; Energy Award for Vol Serv, 1998. **Military Serv:** AUS, sgt, 1943-46. **Home Addr:** PO Box 294, Hollandale, MS 38748, **Home Phone:** (662)827-5366.

BROWN, INEZ M
Government official. **Career:** Off US Sen Don Riegle, various positions, 21 years, sr policy advr on urban affairs, 1989; US Small Bus Admin, regional advocate reg 5, currently. **Orgs:** Bd dir, Genessee County, Econ Develop Comn; Bishop Airport Authority; citizen adv bd, Univ Mich; adv, Genessee Econ Revitalization Agency; adv, Flint, MI, Mayor Woodrow Stanley, Urban Investment Plan. **Business Phone:** (202)224-3121.

BROWN, IRMA JEAN
Lawyer, superior court judge. **Personal:** Born May 17, 1948, Los Angeles, CA. **Educ:** Marymount Col, 1970. **Career:** LA Co Pub Defenders Off, law clerk, 1973; Calif Asn Black Lawyers; Greater Watts Justice Ctr Legal Aid Found, Los Angeles, law clerk, staff atty; Hudson Sndz & Brown, law firm partner; Los Angeles County Munic Ct, judge; State Calif Super Ct, Los Angeles County, judge, currently. **Orgs:** pres, Los Angeles Negro Bus & Prof Womens Club, 1965-66; vpres, So Chap Black Women Lawyers Asn, 1975-76, pres 1976-77; sgt arms, JM Langston Bar Asn, 1976-77; Los Angeles Co Bar Asn; CA Attys Criminal Justice; treas, Nat Conf Black Lawyers, 1976-77; Nat Bar Asn; Delta Sigma Theta Sorority; Urban League; Nat Asn Advan Colored People; Jordan H S Alumni Asn; Dem Club; trustee, First African Methodist Episcopal Church, Los Angeles; 100 Black Women Los Angeles, Nat Asn Women Judges; Calif Judges Asn. **Honors/Awds:** Grant Scholar Legal Educ Opportunity, 1970-73; Delta Sigma Theta Scholar, 1970; So Calif Gas Co Scholar, 1970; publ, The Minor & The Juv Ct Legal Aid Found Los Angeles, 1975; Cert of Recognition for Achievement US Congress, Calif Senate, City Compton, Carson-Lynwood, Los Agneles Co. **Business Phone:** (310)419-5275.*

BROWN, J. B.
Football player. **Personal:** Born Jan 5, 1967, Washington, DC; married Renee; children: Leia Paris Roberts, Michael & Janee Keanna. **Educ:** Univ Md. **Career:** Miami Dolphins, defensive back, 1989-96; Pittsburgh Steelers, 1997; Ariz Cardinals, 1998; Detroit Lions, 1999-2000.

BROWN, DR. J. THEODORE, JR.
Inventor, chief executive officer. **Educ:** State Univ NY, PhD, experimental clinical psychol, 1976. **Career:** Inventor; special consultant, Dept State NY; special consultant, Mayo Clinic; Personal health & Hygiene Inc, founder & chief exec officer; Virtual Health Systs Inc, pres, chief exec officer & prin, currently. **Orgs:** Am Psychol Asn. **Special Achievements:** Created an over-the-counter home drug test approved by the FDA; Author: Stop It Where It Starts; published many books & articles; founder and creator of the first acute PCP Treatment Unit in the United States; Appeared on many national and international talk shows, both on radio and television. **Business Phone:** (812)722-0523.

BROWN, JAMES. See BROWN, JIM.

BROWN, JAMES. See Obituaries section.

BROWN, JAMES G., JR.
Executive. **Career:** CBS NFL studio; ESPN, sr vpres, currently. *

BROWN, JAMES H. See Obituaries section.

BROWN, DR. JAMES HARVEY
Dentist, educator. **Personal:** Born Aug 30, 1924, Malcom, AL; son of Charlie Myles and Alice Woodyard Brown Ross; married Birdie Faulkner-Brown, Jun 1, 1946; children: Albert, Alice, Jacqueline, Renee & James Jr. **Educ:** Alabama A&M Univ, Normal, AL, BS, 1946; Meharry Med Col, Nashville, TN, DDS, 1952; Tenn State Univ, Nashville, TN, MS, zool, 1961, MEd, educ admin, 1964. **Career:** Meharry Med Col Sch Dent, Nashville, TN, assoc prof, 1952-; pvt pract, 1955-; Riverside Hosp, dent staff, 1958-78; Tenn State Univ Stud Health Serv, Nashville, TN, assist dir, 1958-64, dir, 1964-69; Clover Bottom Hosp & Sch, clinical supvry dent students, 1964-72; George W Hubbard Hosp Meharry Med Col, Nashville, TN, dent staff, 1952-, secy, treas, 1968-; Meharry-Hubbard Hosp, Dent Serv, Nashville, TN, dir, 1964-81; Veterans Admin hosp, Nashville, TN & Murfreesboro, TN, consult, 1968-81; pvt pract, dentist, currently. **Orgs:** Alpha Phi Alpha, 1949; charter mem, Am Asn Hosp Dentists; Capital City Dent Soc; Pan Tenn Dent Asn; Nat Dent Asn; Nashville Dent Soc; Tenn State Dent Asn; Am Dent Asn; Nashville Acad Med; Davidson County Medical Soc; Frontiers Inc; Tenn State Med Asn; Am Asn Dent Sch; fel, Am Acad General Dentistry, 1977; Am Acad Operative Dentistry; Am Asn Tension Control; diplomate, Nat Bd Dent Examiners, 1955. **Honors/Awds:** Omicron Kappa Upsilon Honor Dental Soc, 1959; President's Award, Meharry Med Col, 1977; Award for Excellence with Students, Pre Alumni Asn Meharry Col, 1982. **Special Achievements:** Author, "The Effect of Calcium Blood Levels in Strontum Fed Rats," "A Program for the Development of a Department of Hospital Dentistry," "The Predictive Value of the Manual Section of the Dental Aptitude Test on Clinical Performance of Third and Fourth Dental Students at Maharry Medical College"; subject of book, Educating Black Doctors - A History of Meharry Medical College by James Summerville, 1983; subject of article, "A Father and His Six Children Make Medicine Their Way of Life," Ebony Magazine, July, 1988. **Military Serv:** AUS, 11th Airborne Division, Dental Medical Corps, lt, 1953-55.

BROWN, JAMES LAMONT
Football player. **Personal:** Born Jan 30, 1970, Philadelphia, PA; children: Hasson & Semaj. **Educ:** Va State Univ. **Career:** Football player(retired), New York Jets, tackle, 1993-95; Miami Dolphins, 1996-99; Cleveland Browns, 2000.

BROWN, JAMES MARION
Government official. **Personal:** Born Jul 30, 1952, Holdenville, OK; son of Clearnce Jr and Carrie Mae Knox; married Clarice M (divorced); children: James Jr, Tiffany & Jamie. **Educ:** E Cent Univ, Ada, BS. **Career:** McAlester High Sch, psychol teacher, 1977-; City of McAlester, coun mem,1982; Okla Pardon & Parole Bd, chmn & gov. **Orgs:** Spec Serv Bd for State Okla Teachers, 1977-81; bd dirs, State Okla Teachers Convention Comt, 1977-81; trustee, McAlester Health Authority, 1982-86; trustee, McAlester Econ Develop Serv, 1982-86; Black Elected Offs, 1982-; Okla Munic League, 1982-86; McAlester Youth Shelter, 1984; State Atty Gen Adv Comn, 1985; Gov Comt Physical Fitness; bd, Pub Works Bd, McAlester, Okla; Appointed, Okla Human Rights Comn, 1984; bd, McAlester Boy's Club, 1984-86; First black vice mayor, City, 1990-92. **Honors/Awds:** Awarded Highest Grade Point Average of Alpha Phi Alpha, 1975; Nat Asn Advan Colored People Man of the Year Award, 1988-89. **Home Addr:** 1208 North G St, McAlester, OK 74501.

BROWN, JAMES MONROE
Executive. **Personal:** Born Jun 28, 1928, Pulaski, TN; son of John and Theola; married Ann McKissack. **Career:** Abraham McKissack Sr Citizens Homes Inc, chmn bd, pres; Tenn Voters Coun, gen chmn; Tenn Black Leadership Round Table, bd dir; Queen Ann Funeral Home, dir, currently. **Orgs:** Tenn Deleg Dem Nat Conv, 1968-72, 1976; Community S Bell Tel State Tenn, 1980-82; Elks Lodge 1489; trustee, State Coord Tenn Voters Coun; chmn, Giles Co Dem; Campbell AME Church. **Honors/Awds:** Man of the Year, Giles & Lawrence Cols, 1968; Man of the Year, Elks Lodge No 1489, 1973; Elks Man of the Year, Giles Co, 1985. **Military Serv:** USN, 1944-46, 1951-55. **Business Addr:** Director, Queen Ann Funeral Home, 410 N 1st St, Pulaski, TN 38478-2428, **Business Phone:** (931)363-1780.

BROWN, JAMES NATHANIEL. See BROWN, JIM.

BROWN, JAMES WILLIE, JR. See KOMUNYAKAA, YUSEF.

BROWN, JAMIE EARL S
Executive, lawyer. **Personal:** Son of Josephine and Jamie Brown Sr; married Daisy Gore, Aug 13, 1968; children: Michael, Mark &

Martin. **Educ:** Northern Mich Univ, BS, 1970; State Univ New York Buffalo, Sch Law, JD, 1973. **Career:** Kings County Dist Atty, law investr, asst dist atty, 1973-75; Dept Health Educ & Welfare, atty adv, 1975-83; J Earl Brown Realty Corp, pres, 1983-89; State Senator Andrew Jenkins, chief legis asst, 1989-92; J Earl Brown & Assocs, PC, law, real estate, 1992-. **Orgs:** Ancient Free & Accepted Masons, King Solomon Lodge no 5, 32nd Deg; Nat Bar Asn; Phi Alpha Delta Legal Frat; New York State Bar Asn; Omega Psi Phi Frat; NAACP; One Hundred Black Men New York; Am Bar Asn. **Honors/Awds:** Performance Outstanding Service Award, Dept Health & Human Servs, 1981; Outstanding Comm Citizen, Nat Asn, Each One Teach One, 1990. **Special Achievements:** Conference of Black Art Collectors, Panel Organizer; Fluent in language of Fante, Ghanian, mainly Western & Cent Africa. **Business Addr:** President, J Earl Brown Assocs Ltd, 431 W Chelten Ave, PO Box 48008, Philadelphia, PA 19144, **Business Phone:** 800-529-3275.

BROWN, JAMIE FOSTER
Writer, journalist. **Educ:** Univ Stockholm, Sweden. **Career:** Wash Theater Group, founder; Black Entertainment TV, "Video Soul", producer, "Video LP.", producer; Sister 2 Sister Mag, owner & publ, 1988-; Radio show "The Sister 2 Sister Celebrity Update", founder; Books: Betty Shabazz: A Sisterfriends' Tribute in Words and Pictures. **Orgs:** Keynote speaker, Inst Polit, Harvard Univ's John F. Kennedy Sch Govt; Midwest Radio & Music Asn. **Honors/Awds:** Jamie Foster Brown Day, mayor Washington, named in honor, 1998; Anheuser-Busch Eagle Award; Martin Luther King Jr. Scholarship Award for Outstanding African-American Women; IMPACT Super Summit Award. **Special Achievements:** Newsweek magazine, lauding Ms. Brown's influence, listed her among the nation's top "buzzmakers". **Business Addr:** Owner, Publisher, Sister 2 Sister Magazine, PO Box 41148, Washington, DC 20018, **Business Phone:** 800-223-2348.*

BROWN, JAMIE SHEPARD
Football player. **Personal:** Born Apr 24, 1972, Miami, FL; son of Jimmie and Jeannie Blunt. **Educ:** Fla A&M univ. **Career:** Football player (retired); Denver Broncos, tackle, 1995-97; San Francisco 49ers, 1998; Wash Redskins, tackle, 1999; Park View High Sch, offensive line coach, 2005-06.

BROWN, JANICE ROGERS
Judge. **Personal:** Born May 11, 1949, Greenville, AL; widowed; children (previous marriage): Nathan Allan; married Dewey Parker. **Educ:** Calif State Univ, BA, 1974; Univ Calif Los Angeles Sch Law, JD, 1977; Univ Va Sch Law, LLM, 2004. **Career:** Calif Dept Justice, dep atty gen, 1979-87; Calif Bus, Transp & Housing Agency, dep secy/gen coun, 1987-91; Gov Pete Wilson, legal affairs secy, 1991-94; Calif Ct Appeals, assoc justice, 1994-96; Calif Supreme Ct, assoc justice, 1996-2003; US Ct Appeals DC Circuit, fed judge, 2003-. **Honors/Awds:** Am Bar Asn; Calif State Bar Asn. **Special Achievements:** First African American woman to serve on the California Supreme Court. *

BROWN, JARVIS ARDEL
Baseball player, athletic coach. **Personal:** Born Mar 26, 1967, Waukegan, IL. **Career:** Baseball player (retired), baseball coach; Minn Twins, outfielder, 1991-92; San Diego Padres, 1993; Atlanta Braves, 1994; Cincinnati Reds, 1995; Baltimore Orioles, 1995-96; Milwaukee Brewers, 1997; Minn Orgn Class A Fort Myers, coach, 1999; Class AA New Britain, coach, 2000; Twins Gulf Coast League rookie team, coach, 2001; New Haven, Northeast League, mgr, 2004; Carthage Col, asst coach, 2003; Univ Wis-Parkside, head baseball Coach, 2006-. **Honors/Awds:** Am League Championship Series, 1991. **Business Addr:** Head Baseball Coach, University of Wisconsin Parkside, Athletic Department, 900 Wood Rd, PO Box 2000, Kenosha, WI 53141-2000, **Business Phone:** (262)595-2317.

BROWN, JASPER C., JR.
Lawyer. **Personal:** Born Mar 27, 1946, Columbia, SC; married Sandra Cox; children: Leslie, Douglass, Jasper David. **Educ:** Hampton Inst, BS, 1969; Cath Univ, Columbus Sch Law, JD, 1974. **Career:** Gen Electric Co, prod mgr, 1969-71; Nat Labor Rels Bd Div Adv, staff atty, 1974-77; Nat Labor Rels Bd, gen coun, currently. **Orgs:** Nat Bar Asn, 1974-; Pa Bar Asn, 1974-; NC Asn Black Lawyers, 1977-. **Business Addr:** General Counsel, National Labor Relations Board, 1099 14th St NW, Washington, DC 20570-0001, **Business Phone:** (866)667-6572.*

BROWN, JEAN MARIE
Editor. **Personal:** Born May 7, 1964, Gary, IN; daughter of Eugene and Patricia; married Tyrone Young, Aug 1, 1987; children: Lillian & Lucille. **Educ:** Northwestern Univ, BS, jour, 1986. **Career:** Wall Street Journal, reporter; Post-Tribune, Gary, IN, reporter; Charlotte Observer, city hall reporter, asst night city editor, night city editor, day city editor, deputy features editor; Star-Telegram, city editor, 2000-03, asst managing ed 2003-, managing ed & tarrant, currently. **Orgs:** Nat Asn Black Journalists; bd mem, Am Montessori Asn. **Business Addr:** Managing Editor, Star-Telegram, PO Box 915007, Fort Worth, TX 76115, **Business Phone:** (817)685-3823.

BROWN, REV. JEFFREY LEMONTE
Clergy. **Personal:** Born Dec 22, 1961, Anchorage, AK; son of Jesse L and Geraldine G; married Lesley A Mosley; children: Rayna Adair Brown. **Educ:** East Stroudsburg Univ, BA, 1982; Ind Univ, PA, Med, 1984; Andover Newton Theol Sch, MDiv, 1987. **Career:** Am Baptist Churches Inc, rep gen bd, 1987-91; Union Baptist Church, sr pastor, head, currently. **Orgs:** Racism/sexism task force, 1986-87; Andover Newton Theol Sch; secy, United Baptist Conv Ma, RI, & NH, 1988; bd mem, Dept Church & Soc; Am Baptist Churches, MA, 1988-90; bd mem, Bd Ministry, Harvard Univ, 1989-92; bd dirs, Cambridge Econ Opportunity Comn, 1990; pres, Cambridge Black Pastors Conf, 1991. **Honors/Awds:** Student Leadership Award, East Stroudsburg Univ, 1982; Outstanding Achievement Award, PA EEO-Act 101, 1986; Jonathan Edwards Hon, Soc Andover Newton Theol Sch, 1987. **Business Addr:** Pastor, Union Baptist Church, 874 Main St, Cambridge, MA 02139, **Business Phone:** (617)864-6885.*

BROWN, JENNIFER H.
Educator, administrator. **Personal:** Born Oct 10, 1934, Smithfield, VA; daughter of Charlie W and Caroline M Hill; married Oswald E, Dec 22, 1957; children: Shaun D. **Educ:** VA State Univ, BS, 1956; Hampton Univ, MA, 1975. **Career:** Educator, Administrator (retired); Newport News Pub Sch, GED Prog, part-time instr, supvr, Bus Edu; Thomas Nelson Comm Col, instr; JAS Int Sys, pres; Journey Global Develop Group, sec, tres; J Group, pres; Hampton Rods, educator. **Orgs:** NEA, 1957-91; Newport News Education Assn, 1957-91; Bus Educ Assn, 1957-91; Am Vocational Assn, 1980-91; Peninsula Assn Sickle Cell Anemia, brd chair 1998-; Delta Sigma Theta Sorority, Newport News Alumnae, pres, 1998-; Natl Assn Advan Colored People, 1998-. **Honors/Awds:** Volunteer of the Year, Peninsula Assn Sickle Anemia, 1996; Elizabeth Honors& Men at the Gate Award, Sister care Inl, 1997; Greek of the Year,Peninsula Pan Hellenic Coun, 1997; Certificate of Recognition, VA Governor's Mid-Atlantic Conf, 1997; Delta Sigma Theta, Delta Academy Award, Newport News Alumnae, 2000; Life Membership Award, Natl Assn Advan Colored People, 2001; Dream Maker of the Year, Delta Sigma Theta, 2001; SCLC, Recognition of Services Rendered, 2002. **Home Addr:** 1 Beatrice Dr, Hampton, VA 23666, **Home Phone:** (757)826-3319.

BROWN, JEROME
Educator. **Educ:** Lincoln Univ, BS, Comput Sci, 1996; Univ Md, MS, Comput Sci, 1998. **Career:** Harford Community Col, Comput & Technol Div, vis prof comput sci & math bus, currently. **Business Addr:** Visiting Professor, Harford Community College, Computing & Technology Division, 401 Thomas Run Rd, Bel Air Hall Room 126, Bel Air, MD 21015, **Business Phone:** (410)836-4125.

BROWN, JIM (JAMES BROWN)
Educator, manager. **Personal:** Married Pamela Barrett Brewer. **Career:** Henry Straus Productions Inc, from prod asst to prod mgr; Straus, dir,casting dir & ed; WNET Film Training Sch, tutor; Hartford Community Film Workshop Coun, dir; 1969; Howard Univ, WHUT-TV, sta mgr, 1996-98, John H Johnson Sch Commun, staff, multimedia mgr, currently. **Orgs:** VPres, Nat Acad TV Arts & Scis, 1998-2000. **Special Achievements:** Produced & hosted "Black Exposure" aired in Connecticut from 1970-72. **Business Addr:** Staff, The John H Johnson School of Communications, Howard University Deans Office, 525 Bryant St NW, Washington, DC 20059, **Business Phone:** (202)806-4074.

BROWN, JIM (JAMES NATHANIEL BROWN)
Actor, founder (originator), football player. **Personal:** Born Feb 17, 1936, St Simons Island, GA; married Sue, Jan 1, 1959 (divorced 1972); children: 3; married Monique, Jan 1, 1997; children: 1. **Educ:** Syracuse Univ, BA, econs, 1957. **Career:** Football player (retired), actor, founder; Cleveland Browns, fullback, 1957-65; Am-I-can, chmn & founder, 1988-; Films: Rio Conchos, 1964; The Dirty Dozen, 1967; Ice Station Zebra, 1968; Slaughter, 1972; Black Gunn, 1972; Three the Hard Way, 1974; Pacific Inferno, producer, 1979; Richard Pryor .Here & Now, exec producer, 1983; The Running Man, 1987; Mars Attacks!, 1996; On the Edge, 2002; She Hate Me, 2004; Dream Street, 2005; Animal, 2005; TV series: "The Magnificent Magical Magnet of Santa Mesa", producer, 1977; "Keeping the Music Alive", dir, 1999; "American Roots Music", dir, 2001;"Soul Food", 2004; "Sucker Free City", 2004; "Sideliners", 2006; numerous other films & TV series. **Honors/Awds:** Jim Thorpe Trophy, 1958, 1965; Player of the Year, 1958, 1963, 1965; Hickoc Belt Athlete of Year, 1964; Hall of Fame, 1971; named to every All-Star Team, 1963; second on all-time rushing list; greatest distance gained in one season; named best football player of the 20th Century, Sports Illustrated. **Special Achievements:** Author, Off My Chest, 1964 & recent autobiography; appointed by Calif Assembly Speaker, Willie L Brown Jr to the Comn on the Status of African American Males, 1994; In film director Spike Lee released the film Jim Brown: All-American; a retrospective on Brown's professional career and personal life, 2002. **Business Phone:** (310)652-7884.

BROWN, DR. JOAN P. (ABENA JOAN P BROWN)
Foundation executive, movie producer, businessperson. **Personal:** Born in Chicago, IL; daughter of Lueola Reed and Rufus Phillips; divorced. **Educ:** Roosevelt Univ, BA, 1950; Univ Chicago, MA, community orgn & mgt, 1963; Chicago State Univ, Hon Doctorate, Humane Letters, 1993. **Career:** YWCA Metrop Chicago, area dir, 1963-65, consult human rel, 1965-70, dir prog service, 1970-82; ETA Creative Arts Found, co-founder, pres & producer, currently. **Orgs:** Pres, Black Theatre Alliance Chicago, Ill, 1978-84; pres, Midwest Theatre Alliance 1982-86; chmn, City Arts Policy Comt, 1985-90; chmn, Subcomt Prog, Mayor's Dept Cult Affairs, 1985-; Women's Bd, Chicago Urban League; vice chair, Muntu Dance Theatre; chair adv bd, Chicago Dept Cultural Affairs, 1998-. **Honors/Awds:** Recipient of over 100 awards; Paul Robeson Award, Black Theatre Alliance Chicago, 1978; Governor's Award, 1981; Hazel Joan Bryant Award, Midwest African Am Theatre Alliance, 1988; Black Rose Award, League Black Women, 1988; Finalist Kool Achiever Award, 1988; Outstanding Achievement Award, Young Executive Politics, 1987; Outstanding Business Award, Iota Phi Lambda, Chicago, 1990; Award of Excellence, Arts & Theatre, Nat Hook Up Black Women, Chicago chap, 1990; Garvey, Muhammed, King Culture Award, Majestic Eagles, 1990; Women's Hall of Fame, City Chicago, 1992; Arts Entrepreneurial Award, Columbia Col Chicago, 1995; Black Theatre Alliance Award; Jeff Committee Lifetime Achievement Award, 1996. **Special Achievements:** Produced more than 175 theatrical productions; Director: "Shango Diaspora"; "Witness a Voice Anthology When the Wind Blows", 1981; "Passenger Past Midnight". **Home Addr:** 7637 S Bennett Ave, Chicago, IL 60649. **Business Addr:** President, Producer, ETA Creative Arts Foundation, 7558 S South Chicago Ave, Chicago, IL 60619-2644, **Business Phone:** (773)752-3955.

BROWN, JOE
Judge. **Personal:** Married Deborah Herron, Dec 1, 2001; children: 2. **Educ:** UCLA Law Sch, JD. **Career:** Pvt pract, 1978; pub serv, 1990; State Criminal Cts, Shelby Co, judge, 1990-2000; tv show, Judge Joe Brown, TV judge, 1998-; Judge Joe Inc, owner, currently. **Honors/Awds:** Olender Foundation's Advocate for Justice Award. **Special Achievements:** TV shows: "Entertainment Tonight,"Black Entertainment Television's "How I'm Living," Court TV's "Catherine Cryer Live," & CNN's "Crossfire". First African-American prosecutor, City of Memphis & director, City of Memphis Public Defender's Office. **Business Addr:** Television Judge, Judge Joe Inc, 5900 Wilshire Blvd Suite 2380, Los Angeles, CA 90036, **Business Phone:** 877-563-7529.

BROWN, JOE
Chef, entrepreneur, business owner. **Career:** Seafood Restaurant, dishwasher, line chef ; BYOB Cajun-Italian eatery, 1995; Melange Cafe, owner & exec chef, 1995-. **Special Achievements:** Book: Melange Cafe Cookbook. **Business Addr:** Owner, Chef, Melange Cafe, 1601 Chapel Ave, Cherry Hill, NJ 08002-2824, **Business Phone:** (856)663-7339.*

BROWN, JOHN, JR.
Automotive executive. **Career:** E Tulsa Dodge Inc, pres; Majestic Scholar Publ Co, pres, currently. **Orgs:** Kappa Alpha Psi Fraternity Inc; bd dir, Am Red Cross; bd dirs, Metrop Tulsa Chamber Com; bd dirs, Metrop Tulsa Urban League. **Honors/Awds:** Tulsa Chap National Association and Advancement for Colored People Freedom Fund Award, 1997. **Business Addr:** President, Majestic Scholar Publishing Company, PO Box 2892, Broken Arrow, OK 74013-2892, **Business Phone:** (918)355-4349.*

BROWN, JOHN ANDREW
Educator, school administrator. **Personal:** Born Jul 17, 1945, Birmingham, AL; son of Kalop Todd and Elmira Kelsey. **Educ:** Daniel Payne col, AA, 1965; Columbia univ, 1966; Dartmouth col, 1966; Miles col, BA, 1967; Yale univ Divinity Sch, MDiv, 1970, STM, 1972; completed PhD studies Union Theological Seminary, NYC, 1984, ABD. **Career:** Yale Univ Divinity Sch, assoc prof, 1970-73; Trinity Col Hartford, asst prof rel & dir ICS prog, 1973-76; CT Col New London, visiting prof rel, 1974-75;The Col New Rochelle NY, theol sem adj prof rel, 1980-; Audrey Cohen Col, prof & admin, 1979-93, adjunct prof bus ethics, 1988-93, spec asst to vpres & dir staff develop, 1991-93; Miles Col, adjunct prof hist, 1994-; Lawson State Community Col, adjunct prof hist, philosophy & religion, 1994-99; Univ Alabama Birmingham, consult, 1994. **Orgs:** Consult, Trinity Col, 1973, Manchester Community Col, 1976; educ admin, Bronx Extension Site Col Human Serv, 1986-; NY Urban League, Alpha Phi Alpha, NAACP, ASALH, Yale Alumni Assocs Afro-Americans, AAUP. **Honors/Awds:** Carnegie Fellowship, Columbia Univ, 1966; Richard Allen Award; Rockefeller Protestant Fellowship, Theological Educ, 1967-70; Oliver E Daggett Prize Yale Corp, 1969; Research Fellowship, Yale Univ, 1971-72; Pi Gamma Mu; Fellowship UTS Black Econ Develop Fund, 1976; Bio sketch Yale Univ, 1985 Alumni Directory; The Col New Rochelle, Ten Years of Outstanding Teaching & Contributions Col, 1989, Award Fourteen Years of Outstanding Teaching & Service Col, 1993; Crystal Award, Audrey Cohen Col, 1991; Award for Outstanding Service, Phi Theta Kappa Inc, Alpha Epsilon Gama Chapter, 1996. **Special Achievements:** Forthcoming biography of The Rev William Reuben Pettiford the father of African Amer Banking in the US, founded the fourth oldest bank establ in the US and the largest Afr Amer bank.

BROWN, JOHN C., JR.
Executive. **Personal:** Born Jun 9, 1939, Camden, NJ; married Gloria Brown; children: Jay, Ernie. **Educ:** Univ Syracuse, BA,

1962; Univ Pittsburgh, attended 1974; Stonier Grad Sch Banking, grad degree banking, 1980. **Career:** Pittsburgh Nat Bank Oakland, credit analyst, 1970-74, comn banking off, 1974, mgr Oakland off, 1977, asst vpres, 1978, vpres, 1979, dist mgr dist X, 1980; Cleveland Browns, prof football, 1962-66; Math & English, teacher & counselor, 1962-63; Firestone Tire & Rubber Co, franchise paul Warfield, 1964; Pittsburgh Steelers, prof football, 1966-72; NSD Bancorp Inc, bd dir, currently. **Orgs:** Bd dir United Way YMCA; treas, Nat Multiple Sclerosis Soc; NAACP; Rotary Oakland. **Business Addr:** Board of Directors, NSD Bancorp Inc, 5004 McKnight Rd, Pittsburgh, PA 15237, **Business Phone:** (412)231-6900.*

BROWN, JOHN E
Executive. **Personal:** Born Jul 2, 1948, Columbia, SC; son of John Jr and Naomi Burrell; married Jessie Gwendolyn Reardon, Jul 10, 1975; children: Michael, Roderick & Geoffrey. **Educ:** Palmer Junior Col, 1970-71; Columbia Bus Col, AA, bus admin & traffic mgt, 1979. **Career:** Richland County Sheriff's Dept, dep, 1971-72; SC Hwy Patrol, patrolman, 1972-85; Am-Pro Protective Agency, pres, chief exec officer, 1982-93, chmn, 1993-97; hazard waste bus. **Orgs:** Richland County's Bus Round Table Governor's Initiative Work Force Excellence; bd dirs, Am Legion; bd dirs, United Way Midlands; mem steering comt, Palmetto Boys State; bd dirs, Gillcreek Baptist Church; corp adv bd, Br Banking & Trust; bd dirs, SC State Mus; Columbia Urban League; Blue Ribbon Comn; United Black Fund; Community 100 Black Men; Columbia Bus Network Asn; Chamber Com Comn 100; SC Legis Black Caucus Corp Roundtable; adv comt, Palmetto Dockside Gaming Asn; bd governors, Entrepreneur Year Judging Comt, Capital City Club; SC Chat, Entrepreneur Year Inst. **Honors/Awds:** Gov SC, Order Palmetto, 1978; District One Highway patrolman of the Year, 1980; Minority Small Businessman of the Year Award, 1988; 8(a) Contractor of the Year, 1988; Nat Finalist Federal Sub-Contractor of the Year, 1988; Administrator's Award for Excellence, US Small Bus Admin, 1989; VC Summer Corporate Award, Columbia Urban League, 1992; Corp Award, SC Conf Branches NAACP, 1992 & 1994; Inducted to Entrepreneur of the Year Hall of Fame, 1993; SC Entrepreneur of the Year, Non-Financial Serv, 1993; Ruth Standish Baldwin, Eugene Kinckle Jones, Vol Serv Award, Nat Urban League, 1993; Outstanding Achievement Award, Hon SC Black Hall of Fame, 1994; Flour Daniel Contractor Recognition Award, 1994. **Special Achievements:** Listed 257 of the top 500 companies, 1990 & 1991; Listed 164 of top 500 companies, 1992. **Military Serv:** AUS, sgt, 1968-71; Bronze Star, National Defense Service, Expert Rifleman, Vietnam Service, Good Conduct Medal. **Home Addr:** 209 Meadow Creek Dr, Columbia, SC 29203.

BROWN, JOHN MITCHELL, SR.
Executive, historian, commander. **Personal:** Born Dec 11, 1929, Vicksburg, MS; son of Ernestine Foster and Joeddie Fred; married Louise Yvonne Dorsey, Dec 14, 1963; children: Ronald Quinton, Jan Michelle, John Mitchell, Jay Michael. **Educ:** W Point, US Mil Acad, BS, eng, 1955; Syracuse Univ, MBA, 1964; Univ Houston, attended 1978. **Career:** Executive (retired); US Army, 1955-88: Chief Staff Army, asst secy gen staff, 1970-71; 8th Infantry Div, battalion comdr, 1971-73; Comptroller Army, sr exec, 1973-77; 3rd Brigade, 2nd Div, Korea, comdr, 1976-77; 2nd Inf Div, Korea, asst comdr, 1979-80; Mat Plans, Progs & Budget; Off Army Res Develop & Procurement, dep chief staff, 1980-83; Comptroller, US Army Forces Command, 1983-85; III Corps & Ft Hood Tex, dep comdr; Repub S Vietnam, combat duty; Jarvis & Kive Realty, chmn, currently; Michael Brown Analytics, currently. **Orgs:** NAACP; Vet Foreign Wars; Am Legion; Coun 100; Chamber Com; Nat Urban League; Am Defense Preparedness Asn; Minority Develop Legal Fund; Nat Asn Minority Bus; Asn US Army; Masons. **Honors/Awds:** Three Army Commendations, 1955-; Published Defense Econ Anal Defense, Econ Anal Army, 1969; City Atlanta & State Ga Proclamation Designating June 19, "John M. Brown Day", 1985; Distinguished Serv Medal, Two Meritorious Serv Awards. **Military Serv:** AUS, 1955-88.

BROWN, JOSEPH CLIFTON
Museum director. **Personal:** Born Oct 15, 1908, Jackson, MS; married Rubye L Threlkeld; children: Velma, Thelma, Selma, Reuben M, Edwin & Edna. **Career:** Dusable Mus African Am, adminr; Taylor Voc Agr High Sch, prin, 1934-40; Picayune High Sch, prin, 1941; Oxford Training Sch, instr, 1943-45; WPA, instr, 1944; Processing Bur Employ Security & Sec State Ill, oper data Processing, 1945-75; Dusable Mus Afro-am Hist, admin staff mem, 1970-77. **Orgs:** Phi Beta Sigma Frat, 1932; contributor, Mich Black Educ Jour, 1941-42; chmn, Creative Writers Forum, 1946-48; lay leader, Christ UM, 1963-77. **Honors/Awds:** Humanitarian Award, Christ Chap, 1976. **Home Phone:** (773)775-9013.

BROWN, JOSEPH DAVIDSON, SR.
Government official. **Personal:** Born Dec 27, 1929, St Joseph, LA; son of Mitchell and Mary Deon; married Cleola Morris; children: Ann Marie Clayton, Mitchell George, Ollie Mae Neely, Joseph Davidson Jr,Joyce Lavel Davis & Claude Ernest. **Educ:** Eswege Germany Sch, mechanic, 1951; Tyler Barber Col, barber, 1954; Triton Col, supervision, 1978. **Career:** Government official (retired); Cent Area Park Dist, police officer, 1976-79, comm, 1979; Second Baptist Church, deacon, 1984; Maywood Village, pub works, 1962, dir, dep marshal, 1992-97; Maywood Park Dist, police officer, 1992-97. **Orgs:** Mason Pride of Tensas 99, 1954-. **Honors/Awds:** Maywood Village Code Enforcement Marshal; Natural Hazards Recovery Course Inland; Emergency Mgmt Inst Emmitsburg MD; Fundamentals Water Supply Operation, Illinois Environmental Protection Agency, 1977; Fred Hampton Scholarship Image Award, 1979; Police Law Enforcement Training, Central Area Park Dist Police Dept, 1981. **Military Serv:** AUS corp 1948-52. **Home Addr:** 223 S 12th Ave, Maywood, IL 60153. **Business Addr:** Director of Public Works, Public Works of Maywood, 1E Madison Plz, Maywood, IL 60153, **Business Phone:** (708)450-4482.

BROWN, JOSEPH N
Entrepreneur, lawyer. **Educ:** Hillsdale Col, BA, 1958; Univ Detroit Sch Law, LLB, 1961. **Career:** Law firm of Keith, Conyers, Brown, Wahls, & Baltimore, partner; Bodman, partner, currently. **Orgs:** City Detroit Civic Ctr Comn; life mem, Nat Asn Advan Colored People; bd trustee, Franklin wright Settlement; bd mem, Detorit Music Hall Ctr Performin arts; life mem, US Sixth Circuit Judicial Conf; State Bar Mich; Wolverine Bar Asn; Detroit Metropolitan Bar Asn. **Business Addr:** Partner, Bodman LLP, Bodman Longley & Dahling Law Firm, 6th Fl Ford Field 1901 St Antoine St, Detroit, MI 48226, **Business Phone:** (313)259-7777.

BROWN, JOSEPH SAMUEL
Government official. **Personal:** Born Dec 3, 1943, New York, NY; son of Austin Samuel and Ruby Reid; married Beverly, May 18, 1968 (divorced 1988); children: Jamal Hassan, Kareem Saladin & Paul Emmanuel. **Educ:** Elizabeth City State Univ, Elizabeth City, NC, BS, 1966; North Carolina Central Univ, Durham, NC, MS, 1968. **Career:** NY City Bd Educ Harlem High Sch, prin, 1975-77; NYC Dept Gen Serv, New York, NY, administrative staff analyst, 1977-79; NYC Dept Econ Dev Minority Bus Dev Office, New York, NY, dir, 1979-85; Darryl E Greene & Assoc, New York, NY, managing dir, 1985-88; Monroe Co, Dept Affirmative Action & HR, Rochester, NY, dir, 1988. **Orgs:** Omega Psi Phi Fraternity, 1965-; Baden St Ctr Adv Bd, 1988-; Montgomery Neighborhood Ctr, 1988-; ACLU Genesee Valley Chapter, 1988-; NYS Human Rights Comm Advi Coun, 1988-; East House Bd Dir, 1988; Austin Stewart Prof Soc, 1988-; Rochester/Monroe County Coun Disabled Persons, 1991-; Rochester/Monroe County Private Industry, 1991-; Am Asn Affirmative Action, 1991-; Urban League Rochester. **Honors/Awds:** Assemblyman Louis Nine Citizenship Award, NY State Assembly, 1971; Cert Recognition, Nat Alliance Businessmen, 1972, 1973; Certificate of Apppreciation, Jr. Achievement, 1973;Outstanding Young Men Am, US Jaycees, 1979; Certificate of Apppreciation NYC Bd Ed, Open Doors Prog, 1980-84.

BROWN, JOYCE
School administrator. **Personal:** Born Aug 2, 1937, La Grange, GA; daughter of Nellie Kate Harris Storey and Willis Storey; married Randolph F; children: Randette J, Randolph J, Ronda J & Randal J. **Educ:** Ohio State Univ, 1958; Sinclair Col, 1959. **Career:** Citibank NA, FISG Foreign Exchange, asst mgr, 1975-80, FMG Treas Serv mgr, 1980-83, NABG CSD Treas Serv Foreign Exchange, mgr, 1983-; Hempstead Pub Sch Brd pres; Citibank Citi corp, NY, asst vpres, 1983; 100 Black Women Inc, 1987-; NY State Sch, Sch Brd Assn, dir brd develop, NYC Community Sch Brd Improv Pro, 1989; JB Consult Serv, pres, currently, policy & governance consult, currently. **Orgs:** Chmn, Adv Com Minority Affairs NY; mem brd dir, Alliance Counr Drug &Alcohol Abuse; mem brd dir, Nat Bus & Prof Womens Clubs Inc; pres & mem, Hempstead Sch Bd, 1981-86; Nat Alliance Black Sch Educrs, 1984-; exec vpres, Nat Caucus Black Sch Bd Mems, 1986-87; chairperson, Govt Affairs,Natl Assn Black Bus & Prof Women's Clubs, 1987-; pres, Hempstead Civic Assn, 1987-88; chairperson, Hempstead Educ Comt, 1988-; life mem, Natl Assn Advan Colored People; co-chair, Nat Alliance Black Sch Educrs Policy Comn, 1991;supt search consult, NY Sch Brds Assn, 1992. **Honors/Awds:** Outstanding Service Award, 100 Black Men, 1984; Legislative Citation, Ohio State Assembly, 1984; Outstanding Service, Hempstead Sch Dist, 1986; Legislative Citation, NY State Assembly, 1989; Legislative Citation, Nassau County Elective, 1989. **Home Addr:** 254 Rhodes Ave, Hempstead, NY 11550.

BROWN, DR. JOYCE F.
Chief executive officer, psychologist, president (organization). **Personal:** Born Jul 7, 1946, New York, NY; daughter of Robert E and Joyce Cappie; married H Carl McCall, Aug 13, 1983. **Educ:** Marymount Col, BA, 1968; NY Univ, MA, 1970, PhD, 1980. **Career:** City Univ NY, Cent Off, univ dean, 1983-87, vice chancellor, 1987-90, prof clin psychol, 1994; City Univ NY, Baruch Col, actg pres, 1990; Fashion Inst Technol, pres, 1998-; Educ Found, Fashion Industs, chief exec officer, 1998-; Polo Ralph Lauren Corp, dir, 2001-; NY City, Pub & County Affairs, dep mayor, 1993. **Orgs:** Dir, Boys Harbor Inc, 1987-; Dir, NY City Outward Bound, Cent Park Conservancy; trustee, Marymont Col, 1994-2000; bd mem, Polo Ralph Lauren; bd mem, United States Enrichment Corporation (USEC); bd mem, Warm Up AmFoundation. **Honors/Awds:** Inst Educ Mgt, Harvard Univ, 1990; Current Crisis Recent Trends-Final Report, Task Force Black Family, 1987. **Special Achievements:** First African American president of Fashion Institute of Technology; first woman president of Fashion Institute of Technology. **Business Addr:** President, Chief Executive Officer, Fashion Institute of Technology, 27th St 7th Ave, New York, NY 10001-5992.*

BROWN, JULIUS J.
Real estate agent, educator, government official. **Personal:** Born Feb 17, 1907, Oak City, NC; married Roberta Lassiter; children: Robert D, Julia & Sherrian. **Educ:** A&T State Univ, BS, 1937. **Career:** Town Ayden, comnr, 1968-95, mayor pro-tem, 1974; Mitchell Co Training Sch, prin teacher agr; Pitt Co Training Sch, teacher agr; S Ayden Sch, teacher agr; Ayden-Grift Sch, teacher agr; Self employed Real Estate Salesman. **Orgs:** Mid E Exec Comt, 1970-74; Mideast Manpower & Finance Comt, 1974-; Finance & Exec Com; chmn, Pitt Co NC Precinct; Kappa Alpha Psi Fraternity; Knights Pythian; NACW; NEA. **Honors/Awds:** Cert of Appreciation, Mt Olive Baptist Church, 1970; Cert Meritorious Serv, Pitt Co United Fund, 1972; Achievement Award, Pitt Co Br NAACP, 1972; Cert of Merit, A & T St Univ, 1975; Cert of Merit, Pitt Co Schs; Cert of Appreciation, Occup Educ Ayden-Grifton HS; Cert of Appreciation, NC Voc Teachers Asn. *

BROWN, DR. JULIUS RAY
School administrator. **Personal:** Born Feb 18, 1940, Birmingham, AL; son of Sam and Clessie; married Betty Jean; children: Laura & Kenyen. **Educ:** Wayne State Univ, BA, 1963, MEd, 1971; Univ Mich, PhD, 1973. **Career:** School administrator (retired). Proj Equality Mich, exec dir, 1969-71; Univ Mich, regional dir, 1971-76; Wayne County Community Col, regional dean, 1976-83; Community Col Allegheny County, vpres exec dean, 1983-89; Wallace Community Col, Selma, pres, 1989-00, pres emer, 2001-. **Orgs:** Bd dirs, Northside Chamber Com, 1984-; bd dirs, Local Govt Acad, 1985-; bd dirs, St John's Hosp, 1985-; Am Asn Community Cols; Adv Technol Environ Educ Ctr.

BROWN, JURUTHA
Government official. **Personal:** Born Apr 11, 1950, San Diego, CA; daughter of Bertha Brown and Fred Brown. **Educ:** Occidental Col, BS, 1972; UCLA, Cert Exec Mgt Prog, 1988; Pepperdine Univ, MBA, 1991. **Career:** City Los Angeles, chief police & fire selection div, 1984-87, chief workers' compensation div, 1987-92, chief admin servs, 1992-95, personnel dir, 1996-97, dir pub safety employ, 1997-2001, EEO dir, 2001-; EEO & Employee Develop Div, chief, currently. **Orgs:** Treas & secy, Personnel Testing Coun So CA, 1982-84; Nat Forum Black Pub Admin, 1984-; chair, human rights comn, Int Personnel Mgt Asn, 1985; bd dirs, IPMA Assessment Coun, 1984-87, pres, vpres, treas, Western Regional Inter govt Personnel Assessment Coun, 1985-87; pres, Black Alumni Occident Col; frequent speaker on test devel & test rsch, police recruitment. **Business Addr:** Chief, Director, EEO & Employee Development Division, 700 E Temple St Room 380, Los Angeles, CA 90012, **Business Phone:** (213)473-9311.

BROWN, JUSTINE THOMAS
Mayor, educator. **Personal:** Born May 12, 1938, Guyton, GA; daughter of J W H Thomas Sr and Marie Easley-Gadson; married Willie Brown, Jul 27, 1961; children: Rahn Andre, Willie Antjuan, Jatavia Anreka. **Educ:** Savannah State Col, BS, 1959; Ga Southern Univ, attended 1989. **Career:** Screven County Bd Educ, teacher, 1959-; City Oliver GA, mayor, 1988-. **Orgs:** Nat Asn Educrs; Nat Conf Black Mayors; Alpha Kappa Alpha Sorority; Ga Asn Educrs; life mem, Ga Municipal Asn; dir, Econ Opportunity Authority. **Honors/Awds:** Educr of the Year Award, Screven County Rotary Club, 1988; First Black Mayor Award, City of Oliver GA, 1988; Outstanding Citizen, Screven County; Outstanding Serv, Sylvania-Screven County Recreation Bd Award; Black Renaissance Award, Ga Southern Univ, 1999. **Home Addr:** PO Box 82, Oliver, GA 30449. **Business Addr:** Mayor, City Oliver, Oliver City Coun, PO Box 221, Oliver, GA 30449.*

BROWN, KAY B.
Executive. **Personal:** Born Nov 1, 1932, New York, NY; children: Clifford, Clayton. **Educ:** The City Col, BFA, 1968; Howard Univ, MFA, 1986. **Career:** Medgar Evers Col, assoc prof humanities & coord art, 1972-89; Anne Arundel Community Col, asst prof, 1989-90; MLK Memorial Libr, workshop coordr, 1992-94, Wash lifelong learning ctr, creative writing instr, 1998; WritersCorps, Nat Serv Network, creative writing instr, 1994-96. **Orgs:** exec dir, Where We Black Women Artists, 1971-80; exec bd, Nat Conf Artists, 1974-78; sr writer's network, MLK Memorial Library, 1994-98. **Honors/Awds:** DC Comn on the Arts, Comprehensive Arts Development Grant, 1989; Prince George's Annual Writers Award, 1990; Certificate of Appreciation, Medgar Evers Col, 1972-89; Scholar Award, Wash Humanities Coun, 1994, Scholar's Award, Intergenerational Writing, 1999. **Special Achievements:** Artwork "The Black Soldier," & "The Devil And His Game" featured in Tradition and Conflict: Images of a Turbulent Decade 1963, 1973, by Mary Schmidt Campell, The Studio Museum in Harlem; Willy's Summer Dream, a novel for young adults, Harcourt Brace, 1989; Artwork "The Black Soldier" featured in A Different War: Vietnam In Art, by Lucy R. Lippard, Real Comet Press, 1990; Art of Love, a novel, CY Publishing Group, 1995; Profiled in the book Gumbo YaYa, Anthology of Contemporary

African American Women Artists, Midmarch Press, 1995; "The Emergence of Black Women Artists: 1970s, New York," International Review of African American Art, June 1998; Artwork "The Black Soldier" featured in, In the Spirit of Mortin, by Ctary Chassman, 2002. **Home Phone:** (202)243-3045. *

BROWN, KIMBERLY
College administrator, dean (education). **Career:** Va Tech, Univ Acad Advising Ctr, dir, 2003-, Univ Studies, dean. **Business Phone:** (540)231-8440.

BROWN, KWAME
Basketball player. **Personal:** Born Mar 10, 1982, Charleston, SC. **Career:** Wash Wizards, forward, 2001-05; Los Angeles Lakers, power forward & ctr, 2005-08; Memphis Grizzlies, 2008-. **Orgs:** Spokesman, Wash Chap, Nat Kidney Found. **Business Addr:** Professional Basketball Player, Memphis Grizzlies, 191 Beale St, Memphis, TN 38104, **Business Phone:** (901)888-4667.

BROWN, KWAME R
City council member, government official. **Personal:** Born Oct 13, 1970, Washington, DC; son of Marshall and Cammie Jeffress; married Marcia Brown, Jun 4, 1994; children: Lauren & Kwame II. **Educ:** Talladega Col, Morgan State Univ, BA, mkt, 1994; Dartmouth Col, Amos Tuck Bus Sch, MBEP, 1999. **Career:** MCI, asst sales mgr, 1991-93; Walmart Corp, financial mgr, 1994-96; Citigroup, personal banker, 1996-97; First Union Nat Bank, asst vpres, 1997-99; US Dept Com, polit appointee, sr advisor, 1999; Minority Supplier Develop Coun, MD, DC, pres & chief exec officer; Wash, DC, councilmember at-large, 2005-. **Orgs:** Asn Urban Bankers; founding mem, charter mem, Toastmasters Int; South Fairfax Bus Develop Ctr; Mt Vernon Chamber Com; Kappa Alpha Psi Frat Inc; Am Mkt Asn; vol, Good Samaritan Found; chair, Coun's Comt Econ Develop, 2007. **Honors/Awds:** MCI, 14 time Top Salesman, 1992-93, six time Presidents Club, 1991-93; Walmart, Net Profit Award, 1995; First Union, Presidents Club, Big Board, 1998-99. **Home Addr:** 2819 Hillcrest Dr SE, Washington, DC 20020, **Home Phone:** (202)584-7522. **Business Addr:** Councilmember At-Large, Office of Councilmember, 1350 Pa Ave NW Suite 506, Washington, DC 20004, **Business Phone:** (202)724-8174.

BROWN, L. DON
Executive, vice president (organization). **Personal:** Born Jul 15, 1945, Horatio, AR; son of Tommie and Snowie; married Inez Wyatt Brown, May 4, 1968; children: Daria Akilah, Ellynn Donisha, Dalila Jinelle. **Educ:** Univ Ark, Pine Bluff, BS, 1966; Univ Southwest Mo, attended 1972; Kutztown Univ, attended 1974; Univ Pa, attended 1987; Harvard Univ, attended 1987. **Career:** Howard C, instr, 1966-68; State Ark, job interviewer, 1968-69; Kraft Inc, food technologist, 1971-72; Lehigh Valley, PA, gen supt, 1972-79; Glenview, IL, plant mgr, 1979-85, Kraft USA, vpres prod, 1985-89; Kraft Gen Foods, White Plains, NY, vpres, mfg, 1989-91, vpres opers, Canada, 1991-94, exec vpres mfg; Coors Adolph Co, head & sr vpres opers & technol, 1996-, bd dir, currently. **Orgs:** Am Mgt Asn, 1972; Productivity Asn, 1975; NAACP, 1978-84; Urban League, 1978-84; head, Indust Div, United Way, Dallas, TX, 1984; Exec Leadership Coun, 1990-; Asn 100 Black Men, 1989-93; bd dir, Alumax Inc, 1994-; bd mem, Ariz Educ Trust. **Honors/Awds:** Outstanding Black Achievement, Chicago, YMCA, 1980; Kraft Achievement Award, Kraft Inc, 1982; hon doctorate, Univ Ariz. **Military Serv:** AUS, Spec 5, 1968-70; Commendation Medal-Vietnam Serv. **Business Phone:** (303)279-6565.*

BROWN, LARRY, JR.
Football player, radio broadcaster. **Personal:** Born Nov 30, 1969, Miami, FL; married; children: 1. **Educ:** Tex Christian Univ, BA, criminal justice. **Career:** Football player (retired), co-host; Dallas Cowboys, corner back, 1991-95 &1998; Oakland Raiders, cornerback, 1996-97; Sports Radio 1310 The Ticket, co-host, currently. **Honors/Awds:** Most Valuable Player, Super Bowl XXX, 1995. **Special Achievements:** TV SERIES: Actor, "Married with Children". **Business Phone:** (214)787-1310.

BROWN, LARRY T.
Automotive executive. **Personal:** Born Apr 21, 1947, Inkster, MI; son of Nander and Mattie Lewis; married Angelina Caldwell Brown, Aug 28, 1971. **Educ:** Wayne Co Comm Col, Detroit, MI, AA, 1971; Wayne State Univ, Detroit, MI, BA, 1973; Cent Mich Univ, Mt Pleasant, MI, MA, 1979. **Career:** Ford Motor Co, Dearborn, MI, mktg mgr, 1969-85; Landmark Ford, Niles, IL, pres, 1991; Ottawa Ford-Lincoln-Mercury Inc, Ottawa, IL, pres, currently. **Orgs:** Bd mem, Black Ford Lincoln & Mercury Dealers Asn, 1985-; Nat Auto Dealers Asn, 1985-; Ottawa Rotary, 1986-88; Ottawa Chamber of Commerce, 1985-90; Black Ford Lincoln & Mercury Dealers Asn, pres, 1992-93; Nat Automobile Minority Dealers Asn, pres, 1993-94, Vice-chmn Region III, currently. **Honors/Awds:** Push Capital Spirit Award, 1992. **Military Serv:** USAF, sergeant, 1965-69. **Business Addr:** President, Ottawa Ford Lincoln & Mercury Inc, Kia Ottawa, 1777 W US Hwy 30, Merrillville, IN 46410, **Business Phone:** (219)769-0350.*

BROWN, LAWRENCE E.
Executive. **Personal:** Born Jan 28, 1947. **Educ:** Bryant Col, BS, 1969; Bentley Col, MS, 1979. **Career:** Peat Mawrick Mitchell & Co, supv sr acct, 1970-75; Lawrence E Brown Cert Pub Acct, owner & prin; Omni Develop Corp, vpres finance & chief financial officer, currently. **Orgs:** Dir, Opportunity Indust Ctr RI, 1970-74; pres, chmn bd, dir, S Providence Fed Credit Union, 1971-; dir, Challenge House, 1971-74; adv bd, dir, Headstart, 1971-73; City coun, Providence, 1971-75; co-chmn, Nat Black Caucus Local Elected Officials, 1972-74; dir, Bryant Col Alumni Asn, 1974-; treas, dir, Accountants Pub Interest RI, 1975-; asst treas, Providence Dem Comn, 1975-; treas, Irreproachable Beneficial Asn, 1976-; bd dir, Bannister House, 1976-; RI Black Heritage Soc, 1976-; treas, dir, RI Minority Bus Asn, 1977-; RI Soc Cert Pub Accountants; Am Inst Cert Pub Accountants; Phi Beta Sigma; dir Comn, Workshops RI, 1974-76; Urban League RI; NAACP. **Honors/Awds:** South Providence Community Service Award, 1972. **Special Achievements:** First Black Certified Public Accountant in Rhodes Island in 1972; Second Black City Councilman in Providence. **Military Serv:** USMC, 1969-75. **Business Addr:** Vice President, Chief Financial Officer, Omni Development Corp, 150 Colfax St, Providence, RI 02905.*

BROWN, DR. LAWRENCE S
Physician. **Personal:** Born Dec 4, 1949, Brooklyn, NY; son of Lawrence and Mae Rose; divorced. **Educ:** Brooklyn Col, BA, 1976; Columbia Univ, Sch Pub Health, MPH, 1979; NY Univ, Sch Med, MD, 1979. **Career:** Addiction Res & Treat Corp, sr vpres, 1979-; Nat Football League, med adv, 1990-; Columbia Univ, asst clin prof med, 1986-; Cornell Univ, Weill Med Col, clin assoc prof, currently, sr vpres, Addiction Res & Treatment Corp, currently. **Orgs:** Am Pub Health asn, 1977-; Am Soc Internal Med, 1980-; Amer Coll Physicians, 1980-; Amer Diabetes asn, 1989-; Am Soc Addiction Med, pres, 1992-; Coll Probs Drug Dependency, fel, 1993-. **Special Achievements:** Over 30 peer-reviewed articles; Over 10 book chapters. **Military Serv:** AUS, spec-4; Bronze Star. **Home Addr:** 301 Hanna Rd, River Vale, NJ 07675. **Business Addr:** Clinical Associate Professor of Public Health, Cornell University, Division of Community and Public Health Programs, 1300 York Ave, PO Box 61, New York, NY 10021, **Business Phone:** (212)746-1067.

BROWN, LEANDER A
Media executive, president (organization). **Personal:** Born Jul 1, 1959, Chicago, IL; son of Leander A Jr and Joahn Weaver Nash; married Betty Catlett, Mar 11, 1989. **Educ:** Fisk Univ, Nashville, TN, BS, 1982. **Career:** City Harvey, Harvey, IL, employ coordr, 1983-85; Tri-Assoc, Chicago, IL, assoc, 1985-86; Payne Financial Serv, Chicago, IL, financial consult, 1986-88; B & H Radio Co, Harvey, IL, pres, 1988-. **Honors/Awds:** America's Best & Brightest, Dollars & Sense, 1989; Minority Business of the Month, Minority Entrepreneur, 1990; Business Profile, Chicago Defender, 1991. **Business Phone:** (708)596-7550.

BROWN, LEE PATRICK
Business owner, government official, chairperson. **Personal:** Born Oct 4, 1937, Wewoka, OK; son of Andrew and Zelma Edwards; married Yvonne C Streets, Jul 14, 1959; children: Patrick, Torri, Robyn & Jenna. **Educ:** Fresno State Univ, BS, criminol, 1960; San Jose State Univ, MS, sociol, 1964; Univ Calif, Berkeley, MS, criminol, 1968, PhD, criminol, 1970. **Career:** San Jose CA, police officer, 1960-68; Portland State Univ, prof, 1968-72; Howard Univ, prof, 1972-75; Multnomah Co, OR, sheriff, 1975-76, dirj ustice serv, 1976-78; Atlanta GA, pub safety comnr, 1978-82; Houston Police Dept, police chief, 1982-90; NY City Police Dept, police comnr,1990-92; Tex Southern Univ, instr, 1992; Off Nat Drug Control Policy, dir, cabinet mem, 1993-95; Rice Univ, sociol prof, 1996-97; City Houston, mayor, 1998-2004; Brown Group Int, chmn & chief exec officer, 2005-. **Orgs:** Chmn, Nat Minority Adv Coun Criminal Justice, 1976-81; founder, Nat Orgn Black Law Enforcement Exec, 1984-; Police Exec Res Forum, Harvard Univ Exec Session Police, 1985; pres, Int Asn Chiefs Police, 1990-91; dir, Houston Rotary Club; Nat Asn Advan Colored People; bd mem, Forum Club Houston; dir, Houston Boy Scouts Am; dir, Nat Black Child Develop Inst;dir, Houston Area Urban League; Nat Adv Comn Criminal Justice Stand &Goals, Wash, DC; Nat Comn Higher Educ Police; task force mem, Nat Ctr Missing & Exploited C; adv bd, Nat Inst Against Prejudice & Violence; Alpha Phi Alpha; Greek-letter fraternity; Sigma Pi Phi. **Honors/Awds:** Law Enforcement of the Year Award, Nat Black Police Officers Asn, 1982; Honorary Degree, Fla Int Univ, 1982; Criminal Justice Prof Award, Nat Asn Blacks Criminal Justice, 1984; Honorary Degree, John Jay Col Criminal Justice, 1985; Manager of the Year Award, Nat Mgt Asn, 1986; Communicator of the Year Award, Wash News Serv, 1986; Robert Lamb Jr Humanitarian Award, Nat Org Black Law Enforcement Execs, 1987; August Vollmer Award, Am Soc Criminol, 1988; Nat Public Service Award, Am Soc Pub Admin & the Nat Acad Pub Admin, 1989; Honorary Degree, Portland State Univ, 1990; Father of the Year, Nat Father's Day Comt, 1991; Cartier Pasha Award, Cartier Int, 1992; Gallup Hall of Fame, Gallup Inc, 1993; Politician of the Year, Libr Jour, 1999. **Special Achievements:** First African American mayor of Houston; co-auth of one book, ed of three books & auth of numerous articles & book chapters. **Business Phone:** (832)366-1584.

BROWN, REV. LEO C
Association executive, clergy. **Personal:** Born Jun 17, 1942, Washington, DC; son of Leo Charles Sr and Mildred Vera; married Barbara DeLespine; children: Debbie Jones, Fred Ross, Angela Ross, Wayne Brown, Charles Ross, Steve Ross, Renee Brown, Anthony Brown, Phillip Brown, Daniel Brown, Jimmy & Cindy. **Educ:** Seattle Community Col, Apprenticeship Cement Mason, 1969; Tacoma Community Col, Bus & Psychol, 1973; Evergreen State Col, BA, 1977; Am Baptist Sem W, MMA, 1981; Hardy Theol Inst, Seattle WA, DD, 1988. **Career:** Local 528 Cement Mason, cement mason, 1964-72; True Vine Comm COGIC, pastor 1975-; Progress House Assoc, exec dir, 1972. **Orgs:** Co-founder & dir, First Minority Christian Summer Camp, 1965-; founder & dir, Emmanuel Temple Prison Ministry McNeil Island, WA 1968; vpres, Metro Develop Coun, 1973-75; chaplain, Tacoma Fire Dept, 1975-79; vpres, United Brotherhood Fel, 1977-; founder & pres, True vine Multi-Serv Ctr, 1979-; bd mem, Tacoma Urban Policy, 1979; bd mem, Family Broadcasting Station, 1979-; founder & pres, True Vine Sr Citizen Ctr 1980-; pres, Tacoma Ministerial Alliance, 1982-; Int Halfway House Asn; Am Corrections Asn; Nat Asn Advan Colored People; Tacoma Urban League; Kiwanis Club; Prince Hall Masons; Acad Criminal Justice Soc; bd mem, United Way, Fel Reconciliation A; Am Correctional Asn; Govs Pub Safety Adv Group State Wash; comnr, State Wash Housing Finance Comn, 1985-. **Honors/Awds:** Service Manking Award, Sertoma Club 1978; Nominee & runner-up for Rockefeller Found Humanity Award, 1979; Distinguished Citizens Award, Tacoma Urban League, 1983; Newsmaker of Tomorrow Award, Time Mag, 1983; Distinguished Citizen Award, Wash State Senate & Office Lt Gov, 1984; Doctor of Divinity, Hardy Theological Institute of Seattle, 1988. **Military Serv:** AUS, sp4, 1961-64. **Business Addr:** Pastor, True Vine Community, 5715 N 33rd St, Tacoma, WA 98406, **Business Phone:** (253)759-9059.

BROWN, LEONARD
Educator. **Educ:** Wesleyan Univ, PhD; Univ Mass Amherst, MEd, art educ, 1977. **Career:** Boston's annual John Coltrane Memorial Concert, co-found & prod, 1997; Am Jazz Mus, Kansas City, MO, consult; Northeastern Univ, vice provost, assoc vice prof, currently. **Orgs:** Dir, Kansas City Inst Jazz Performance & Hist, develop & organizer, Charlie Parker Symp; Ctr Black Music Res, Int Asn Study Popular Music; Int Asn Jazz Educrs; Soc Ethnomusicology; Sonneck Soc Am Music. **Honors/Awds:** Distinguished Scholar Award, Univ Massachusetts & Boston; Distinguished Scholar Award, John D. O'Bryant African Am Inst, 1998. **Special Achievements:** Contributor to book: Kansas City.And All That's Jazz, 1999. **Business Addr:** Assistant Professor, Northeastern University, 360 Huntington Ave Ryder 361, Boston, MA 02115, **Business Phone:** (617)373-4128.

BROWN, LEONARD RAY, JR. See BROWN, RAY, JR.

BROWN, LEROY
School administrator. **Personal:** Born Dec 10, 1936, Buckner, AR; son of Odis Brown and Pearlie Brown; married Dorothy Jean Hughey; children: Johnny Otis, Cinini Yvette, Titian Valencia & Leviano Regatte. **Educ:** Univ Ariz, BS, Chem; E TX State Univ, MA. **Career:** School administrator (retired); Lewisville Sch Dist, middle sch, prin, 1978; City Buckner, mayor, 1975-78; Lewisville Sch Dist, asst prin & math, 1972-77; Lewisville Sch Dist, Foster HS, prin, 1970-71; Lewisville SchDist, Sci & Math teacher, 1960-69; City Buckner, mayor & judge, 1975-78; City Buckner, alderman, 1980-90; asst prin, math, Lewisville Sch Dist High Sch, 1983-90; Lafayette Co Ar, Govt Bill Clinton, 1990; Appointed Justice Peace, Dist IV; A O Smith Funeral Home, funeral dir, 1990; City Buckner, Alderman, 1994-96, 1996-98, 2000-02. **Orgs:** AR Educ Asn, 1960-80; Nat Educ Asn, 1970-80; vpres, Lafayette Co Alumni Asn, 1977-80; St John Bapt Church Buckner, 1948-80; NAACP Buckner Hpt, 1968-80; sr warden, Rose Sharon Lodge, 1978-80; justice peace, 1990, fairbd mem, 1990; quorum ct mem, Lafayette County, AR, 1990; bd mem, SW ArDevelop coun. **Honors/Awds:** Best School Award, Red River Vo-Tech Sch, 1981, 1982. *

BROWN, LEROY BRADFORD
Physician. **Personal:** Born Jun 5, 1929, Detroit, MI; married Ola Augusta Watkins; children: Leroy, Rene, Rita. **Educ:** SC State Col, BS, 1954; Howard Univ, MD, 1958. **Career:** Fresno Co Gen Hosp, intern, 1958-59; City Sacramento, city physician, 1958-71; Internal Med, resident, 1959-62; Prac Med, specializing internal med, 1962-; Mercy Hosp, staff mem, 1962-; Med Examr, aviation, 1966-; UC Davis Med Sch, clinic instr, 1977: pvt pract, currently. **Orgs:** Am Calif & Sacramento Co Med Asns; Am Calif & Sacramento Co Socs Internal Med; dir, Sacramento Co Heart Asn; Notomas Union Sch Bd, 1971-75; mem Ch God. **Business Addr:** Physician, Private Practice, 3031 G St, Sacramento, CA 95816.*

BROWN, LES
Chief executive officer, public speaker, writer. **Personal:** Born in Miami, FL; married Gladys Knight, Aug 29, 1995 (divorced 1997); children: 6. **Career:** Les Brown Unlimited, Detroit, MI, pres; "Les Brown Show", host, 1993; Les Brown Enterprises, chief exec officer, 1986-; prof speaker, currently; Books: Live Your Dreams; It's Not Over Until You Win!, 1997. **Honors/Awds:** DHL, Morris Brown Col; Council of Peers Award of Excellence, Nat Speakers Asn, 1989; Golden Gavel Award. **Special Achievements:** One of the World's Top Five Speakers for 1992 by Toastmasters International. **Business Phone:** 800-733-4226.

BROWN, LESTER J
Government official. **Personal:** Born Aug 24, 1942, New York, NY; son of James and Earlean Price; divorced; children: Natalie Milligan, Omar A & Lesondra E. **Educ:** Lincoln Univ, BA, 1966; Fel's Inst State & Local Govt, attended 1969; State Univ New York, Albany, 1973; Antioch Col New Eng Ctr, MEd Mgt & Orgn, 1978. **Career:** Philadelphia Model Cities Prog, manpower planner, 1967-68; Philadelphia Sch Dist, teacher, 1968-70; Schenectady County Community Col, sr counr, 1970-76; New York State Div Youth, resource & reimbursement agent, 1977-79, prog mgt specialist, 1979-89; New York State Div Youth, contract compliance specialist, 1989-. **Orgs:** Consumer panel mem, New York State Electric & Gas, 1991-; mem economic develop & employ comt, Broome Co Urban League; mem, allocation panel, Broome Co United Way; life mem, Omega Psi Phi Frat Inc; Lincoln Univ Alumni Asn; pres, Price Brown Family Reunion Org; vice chmn, New York Div Youth Affirmative Action Adv Comn; Broome County Nat Asn Advan Colored People; Prince Hall Masonic. **Honors/Awds:** District Service, Omega Psi Phi Frat, 1980-83. **Business Addr:** Program Management Specialist, New York State for Youth, 52 Washington St, Rensselaer, NY 12144, **Business Phone:** (518)486-5164.

BROWN, LEWIS FRANK
Lawyer. **Personal:** Born Aug 4, 1929, Cleveland, MS; son of Frank and Lula; married Dorothy Jean Fitzerald; children: Lewis Gene, Orville Frank. **Educ:** San Francisco State Univ, BA, 1957; Lincoln Univ Law Sch, DJ, 1964. **Career:** Vallejo Unified Sch Dist, educr, 1957-64; Calif Greenleigh Asn, asst dir, 1964-65, dir, 1965-66; Health Educ & Welfare, pvt consult, 1966-69; Am Arbit Asn, arbit; Brown & Bradley, atty, 1978-. **Orgs:** Committeeman, Solano County Demo Cent, 1959-66; Vallejo City Planning Comn 1963-65; Vallejo City Councilman, 1965-69; vmayor, Vallejo City, 1967-69; golden heritage life mem, Nat Advan Asn Colored People. **Honors/Awds:** First Jurisdiction Service Award, Church God Christ, NC, 1982; Distinguished Record, Calif State Senate & Assembly Resolution Commending Lewis F Brown, 1982; Civic Leader Award, 1982; Legal Commendation Award, Dist Atty Solano County, City Vallejo, 1982; Resolution Commendation, Jones County, Miss Bd Supvrs 1988; Resolution Commendation, City Coun Laurel, MS, 1988. **Special Achievements:** Vallejo City Council named street Lewis Brown Road, July 1995. **Military Serv:** AUS, pfc, 1951-53. **Business Addr:** Attorney, Brown & Bradley, 538 Georgia St, PO Box 432, Vallejo, CA 94590-0647, **Business Phone:** (707)643-4541.*

BROWN, LILLIE RICHARD
Nutritionist. **Personal:** Born Feb 25, 1946, Opelousas, LA; daughter of John Sr (deceased) and Hester De Jean; married Charles J Brown, Apr 20, 1968; children: Jeffrey Andre. **Educ:** Southern Univ, BS, 1968; Howard Univ, MS, 1972; Command & General Staff Col, dipl 1989; Early Childhood Educ, cert. **Career:** DC Pub Sch, nutritionist, 1972-96; DC Nat Guard, dietitian, 1977-96; Howard Univ, asst prof nutrit scis, 1997-; State Md, Dept Corrections, dietitian, 1998-99, dietary mgr; Baltimore City Public Sch Syst, dietitian, 1999-01. **Orgs:** Am Dietetic Asn, 1971-; Delta Sigma Theta, 1974-; Am Heart Asn, 1986-. **Honors/Awds:** Army Commendation Medal, 1990. **Special Achievements:** The Manual of Clinical Dietetics, assisted with writing, 1992. **Military Serv:** Army Nat Guard. **Home Addr:** 2006 Forest Dale Dr, Silver Spring, MD 20903. *

BROWN, LINDA JENKINS
Government official. **Personal:** Born Nov 8, 1946, Baltimore, MD; married Charles Edward II; children: Charles Edward III. **Educ:** Morgan State Univ, BS 1971; Univ Baltimore, MPA 1980. **Career:** Baltimore County Bd Educ, elem sch teacher 1971-73; Dept Defense, Ft Holabird, MD, equal employ opportunities specialist, 1973-75; Fed Hwy Admin, equal opportunities specialist, 1975-78, regional compliance Officer, 1978-80, dep, Chief Int EEO Div, 1980-84, chief, Int EEO Div, 1984, hist black cols & univs & univs coord, 1985, actg MUTCD Team Leader & proj mgr, currently. **Orgs:** Basileus Zeta Phi Beta Sor Inc; Alpha Zeta Chap, 1982-84; adv bd mem, Nat Festival Black Storytelling, 1983-86; charter mem, Asn Black Storytellers, 1983-; Nat Am Advan Colored People, 1983-; vpres, Howard Cornish Chap Morgan State Univ Alumni, 1984-; adv bd mem, US Off Personnel Mgt EEO Curric, 1984-; presidential adv coun mem, Morgan State Univ, 1985-; adv bd mem, Atlanta Univ Career Placement, 1986-; asst boule marshal, Zeta Phi Beta Sor Inc, 1986-88. **Honors/Awds:** Outstanding Women America, 1984; Outstanding Woman Award Fedly Employed Women, 1984; Zeta Year, Zeta Phi Beta Sor Inc Alpha Zeta Chap, 1985; Secretary's Award Merit Achievement, US Dept Transportation, 1985; Distinguished Alumni Award, Nat Asn EO Higher Educ, 1986. **Business Addr:** Acting MUTCD Team Leader, Project Manager, Federal Highway Administration, Off Transp Opers, 400 7th St SW, Washington, DC 20590, **Business Phone:** (202)366-2192.

BROWN, LLOYD
Social worker. **Personal:** Born Jul 5, 1938, St Louis, MO; son of Charles W Sr and Veldia B Sproling Brown Stinson; married Johnnie Mae Irvin; children: Marvin, Etoy, Rosalinda, Lloyd Jr, Donna & Tanya. **Educ:** Forest Park Col, AA, 1974; Northeast Miss State Univ, BS, 1976; Urban Develop & Black Community, Southern Ill Univ, cert, 1970; Community Organizing Parks Col, cert, 1970. **Career:** Tandy Area Coun, youth counr, 1974-76; Wellston Sch Dist, dep gen mgr, 1976-81; Int Revenue Serv, tax rep, 1982-83; Human Develop Corp, br mgr, 1983-91; Alpha Redevelopment Corp, exec mgr, 1991-94; The ABC Infants Inc & Child Care, co-owner; Lucas Heights Village, exec mgr, 1994-. **Orgs:** Community worker, Vols Serv Am, 1972-74; Nat Asn Housing & Redevelop, 1982-; Miss Asn Housing & Redevelop, 1982-; chmn, Wellston Housing Bd Comnr, 1982-; vpres, Wellston Bd Educ, 1983, 1986, 1989, 1992-; Miss State Sch Bd Asn, 1983; Nat Sch Bd Asn, 1983-; Welston City Coun. **Honors/Awds:** Special Service Award, Mathew Dicky Boys Club, 1968; Student Service Award, Forest Park Col, 1972, 1973, 1974; Community Service Award, Human Develop Corp, 1972; Resolution-Outstanding Sch Bd Mem, Miss State Legis, 1987; Youth Service Award, Providence Schs, St Louis, MO, 1985, 1986, 1987. **Military Serv:** USAF, airman 2nd class, 1957-61. **Home Addr:** 4313 Cranford Dr, St Louis, MO 63121. **Business Addr:** Executive Manager, Lucas Heights Village, 3114 Franklin Ave, St Louis, MO 63106, **Business Phone:** (314)534-1361.*

BROWN, LOMAS, JR.
Football player, radio host. **Personal:** Born Mar 30, 1963, Miami, FL; son of Lomas Brown Sr and Grace; married Dolores; children: Antoinette, Ashley & Adrienne. **Educ:** Univ Fla, 1996. **Career:** Football player (retired), radio host; Detroit Lions, offensive tackle, 1985-95; Ariz Cardinals, offensive tackle, 1996-98; Cleveland Browns, offensive tackle, 1999; New York Giants, offensive tackle, 2000-01; Tampa Bay Buccaneers, offensive tackle, 2002; NFL Network, analyst; ESPNEWS, analyst; WXYT, co-host sports radio show. **Orgs:** Phi Beta Sigma Fraternity; founder, Lomas Brown Found. **Honors/Awds:** NFL Extra Effort Award, 1991. **Business Addr:** Co-Host, WXYT, 26495 American Dr, Southfield, MI 48034, **Business Phone:** (248)455-7200.

BROWN, LOUIS SYLVESTER
Government official, association executive. **Personal:** Born Oct 11, 1930, Navassa, NC; son of Claus; married Ruby Moore; children: Yvonne, Yvette, Roderick, Valorie. **Educ:** Tyler Barber Col, Barber, 1959. **Career:** bd dir, Brunswick City Hosp, 1975-81; bd dir, Sencland, 1978-85; bd dir, Apri Inst, 1979-; Town Navassa, NC, mayor. **Orgs:** Masonic Pride Navassa Lodge, 1965-85; Noble Habid Temple, 1970-85; bd dir, Nat Asn Advan Colored People, 1970-; vice chmn, Recreation bd 1975-; Navassa Community Lion Club. **Special Achievements:** Organized the first Black Men's Lion Club in North Carolina, 1989; organized the first Black Women's Lion Club in North Carolina, 1990. **Military Serv:** AUS, corpl, 2 yrs. *

BROWN, DR. LUCILLE M.
School administrator. **Educ:** Va Union Univ, BA, 1950; Howard Univ, honors grad; Va State & Va Commonwealth Univ, Univ VA, addn grad studies. **Career:** Luther Jackson High Sch, teacher, 1954-57; Armstrong High Sch, teacher, 1957-74, prin, 1974-85; Richmond Pub Schs, VA, asst supt sec educ, 1985-89, asst supt inst, 1989-91, supt, 1991-95. **Orgs:** Va Union Univer Bd Trustees; Bd Heroes Found; Black Hist Mus & Cultural Ctr; James River Valley Chap Links Inc; bd dirs, Educ Advance Found; Alpha Kappa Alpha Sorority Inc. **Honors/Awds:** Lifetime Achievement Award, Urban League Greater Richmond; Flame Bearer Excellence Award, Negro Col Fund; Distinguished Alumna Award, Va Union Univ. **Special Achievements:** Lucille M Brown Middle Sch, accredited.

BROWN, MALCOLM MCCLEOD
Educator, artist. **Personal:** Born Aug 19, 1931, Crozet, VA; son of Franklin and Dorothy; married Ernestine Turner, 1964; children: Malcolm, Jeffrey & Rhonda. **Educ:** Va State Col, BS, 1964; Case Western Reserve Univ, MA, 1969. **Career:** OH, internationally exhibited & acclaimed watercolorist; Shaker Hts Schs, art teacher, 1969-2000; Malcolm Brown Gallery, Shaker Heights, OH, co-owner, 1980-. **Orgs:** Am Watercolor Soc; Shaker Heights bd educ Evening Faculty Clev Inst Art; Ohio Watercolor Soc; NAACP; Urban League; Friends Karama; Cleveland Museum Art; Nat Conf Artists; Calif Watercolor Soc; Omega Psi Am Watercolor Soc, 1973. **Honors/Awds:** Award Excellence, Mainstreams Int, 1970; First Prize Watercolor, Va Beach Boardwalk Show, 1971-74; Second Prize Watercolor, Canton Art Inst, 1971; Henry O Tanner & Award, Nat Exhib Black Artists, 1972; Purchase Award, Watercolor USA, 1974; Award in Rocky Mt Nat Watermedia Exhib Golden CO, 1975; Larry Quackenbush Award, 1980; Ohio Watercolor Soc Award, 1984, 1985; Board of Director's Award, Am Watercolor Soc; Distinguished Service to the Arts Award. **Special Achievements:** Work shown in museums & Colleges throughout US under auspices AWS, Watercolor USA & Mainstreams International traveling exhibitions & represented numerous private collections, work viewed internationally through CA Watercolor Soc & Am Embassy, Nat exhibitions, Am Watercolor Soc, Nat Acad Design, Butter Inst Am Art, Watercolor USA, CA Watercolor Soc, Mainstreams International, work featured Mag Art Review. **Military Serv:** First lt, 1956-59. **Business Addr:** Co-Owner, Malcolm Brown Gallery, 20100 Chagrin Blvd, Shaker Heights, OH 44122.

BROWN, DR. MALORE INGRID
Executive director, consultant. **Personal:** Born Sep 29, 1967, Half Way Tree, Jamaica; daughter of Esmie L and Mallothi. **Educ:** Marquette Univ, BA, Spanish, 1988; Univ Wis, Milwaukee, MLIS, 1991, MA,1991, PhD, 1996. **Career:** Milwaukee Pub Libr, community librn intern, 1990-91, librn I, 1991; Chicago Pub Libr, librn I, 1991-92, librn II, asst head, 1993; Univ Wis, Milwaukee, asst prof, 1996-2001; Rutgers Univ, vis asst prof, 2000-01; Am Libr Asn, exec dir, 2001-; US Dept Educ Title II-B Libr, career training doctoral fel; independent consult librn, currently. **Orgs:** Asn Libr Servo C, 1992-; Black Caucus Am Libr Asn, 1993-, exec bd, 1995-97; US Bd Books Young People, 1998-; Wis Black Librns Network, 1991-2000, pres, 1995-96; Am Soc Asn Execs, 2001-. **Honors/Awds:** Marquette Univ, Spanish Honor Soc, Sigma Delta Pi, 1988. **Special Achievements:** Author: "Issues In Selection & Evaluation of Multicultural Lit for Young People," Journal of Children's Lit, Spring, 1999; "An Offer He Can't Refuse' Is That Your Final Answer?" Library Jnl, Apr 1, 2000. **Business Addr:** Independent Consultant, 2801 S King Dr Suite 218, Chicago, IL 60616, **Business Phone:** (312)808-0565.

BROWN, MARGERY WHEELER
Writer, illustrator, educator. **Personal:** Born in Durham, NC; daughter of John Leonidas and Margaret Hervey; married Richard E Brown, Dec 22, 1936 (deceased); children: Janice Brown Carden. **Educ:** Spelman Col, Atlanta, GA, BA, 1932; Ohio State Univ, special art stud, 1934, 1935. **Career:** Educator (retired), writer, illustrator; Hillside High Sch, NC, art instr, 1934-35; Wash High, GA, art instr, 1935-37; Spelman Col, art instr, 1943-46; Newark Pub Sch Syst, art instr, 1948-74; Books: That Ruby, 1969; Animals Made by Me, 1970; The Second Stone, 1974; Yesterday I Climbed a Mountain, 1976; No Jon, No Jon, No!, 1981; Old Crackfoot, 1965; I'm Glad I'm Me, 1971; Book of Colors, Book of Shapes, 1991; Baby Jesus Like My Brother. *

BROWN, MARJORIE M
Government official, postmaster general. **Educ:** Edward Waters Col; Duke Univ; Emory Univ; Univ Va. **Career:** US Postal Serv, postmaster, Atlanta, GA, currently. **Orgs:** Leadership Atlanta 2001; Chairperson, Fed Exec Bd, Postal Customer Coun. **Honors/Awds:** Atlanta's Top 100 Women Influence. **Special Achievements:** Atlanta's first female postmaster. **Home Addr:** 381 Dollar Mill Ct SW, Atlanta, GA 30331, **Home Phone:** (404)696-4379. **Business Addr:** Postmaster, US Postal Service, Atlanta City Post Off, 3900 Crown Rd SW Rm 219, Atlanta, GA 30304-9998, **Business Phone:** (404)765-7300.

BROWN, MARSHA J.
Physician. **Personal:** Born Oct 27, 1949, Baltimore, MD; daughter of Elwood L and Bernice C; married Ray Brodie Jr MD (divorced); children: Bradley Ray, Sean Elwooa. **Educ:** Howard Univ, BS, 1971; Univ Md, MD, 1975. **Career:** Mercy Hosp, internal med residency; Baltimore City Police & Fire Dept, physician; dep chief physician; Pvt Pract, physician internal med; Mercy Health Serv, Internal Med, physician; Heartfelt Med Group Llc, physician, currently. **Orgs:** Adv bd, Cent Md Community Sickle Cell Anemia; bd dir, LM Carroll Home Aged; LM Carroll Nursing Home; Girl Scouts Am Teenage Pregnancy Task Force; med consult, Glass & Assocs Mental Health; Baltimore City Police Dept; Baltimore City Civil Serv Comn, 1982-; mem bd, Eligible Internal Med, Monumental City Med Assocs; Nat Med Asn; Baltimore City Chapter Links Inc; Alpha Kappa Alpha Sorority. **Honors/Awds:** Outstanding Young Women, Alpha Kappa Alpha Sorority, 1980; Citizens Service Recognition Award for Community Service, 1986; Nat Asn Negro Women Humanitarian Award, 1986. **Business Addr:** Physician, Heartfelt Medical Group Llc, 301 St Paul Pl Mercy POB, Baltimore, MD 21202, **Business Phone:** (410)837-2006.*

BROWN, MARVA Y
School administrator, social worker. **Personal:** Born Aug 25, 1936, Charleston, SC. **Educ:** SC State Col, BS, bus admin, 1958; Univ WA, MEd, rehab couns, 1970. **Career:** Berkley Training High Sch, Monks Corner SC, bus educ instr, 1958-59; Park City Hosp, Bridgeport CT, asst bookkeeper, 1959-62; State CT Welfare Dept & Health Dept, case worker & med & social worker, 1962-66; Poland Spring ME Job Corp Ctr, sr counr, 1966-68; Servs for Handicapped Studs, Edmonds Community Col, Lynwood, WA, counr, coordr, 1971-. **Orgs:** NEA, 1971; Wash State Human Rights Comn, 1977; Gov's Comn Employment Handicapped, 1977; Nat Asn Sex Educators & Couns, 1975; Snohomish Co Alcoholic Comn, 1978. **Honors/Awds:** Del The White House Conf on Handicapped Individuals WA DC, 1977. **Business Addr:** Coordinator, Edmonds Community College, 2000 68th Ave W, Lynnwood, WA 98036, **Business Phone:** (425)640-1459.

BROWN, MARY BOYKIN
Educator. **Personal:** Born Feb 1, 1942, Sampson County, NC; married Franklin Der; children: Franklin Jr & Franita Dawn. **Educ:** Winston-Salem State Univ, BS, Nursing, 1963; Long Island Univ, Community Ment Health, MS, 1978. **Career:** Long Island Jewish Med Ctr, instr inservice ed, 1966-70; Harlem Hosp Ctr NY, instr sch nursing, 1970-74; Midway Nursing Home, coord inservice ed, 1974-75; Mary Gran Nursing Ctr Clinton NC, dir inservice ed, 1975-76; Sampson community Col, Clinton, NC, instr, sch nursing, 1976, health progs, div chmn, 1988, nursing prog, chmn, currently. **Orgs:** Am Nurses Asn, 1964-, Nat League Nurs-

ing, 1964-, NC Nurses Asn Dist 14, 1976-; Coun Asn Degree Nursing, 1976-; teacher beginners class St Stephen Am Zion Church, 1976-84; chmn, sec Four Cty Med Ctr Bd Dirs, 1981-85; police comn, Garland Town Bd, 1983-; vpres, Browns Cleaners & Laundromat, 1985-; App Legis Comn Nursing, 1989; chmn, Sampson County Sch Bd, 1994. **Honors/Awds:** Outstanding Young Women of America, 1977; Most Outstanding 4-H Leader Sampson County, 4-H Clinton NC, 1977-78; Outstanding 4-H Volunteer NC, Gov Raleigh NC, 1980; Certificate of Appreciation Sampson County Voters League, 1981; Excellence in Teaching Award, finalist, Dept Comm Cols, 1993; Educator of the Year, Alpha Kappa Alpha Inc, Rho Omega Omega Chap, 1995. **Home Addr:** 98 E 3rd St, Garland, NC 28441, **Home Phone:** (910)529-1265. **Business Addr:** Chairman, Sampson Community College, 1801 Sunset Ave, PO Box 296, Garland, NC 28441, **Business Phone:** (910)592-8081.

BROWN, MARY KATHERINE
Administrator, association executive. **Personal:** Born Oct 14, 1948, Vicksburg, MS; daughter of Macie Little and Elijah. **Educ:** Tuskegee Inst, BS, social sci, 1971, MEd, stud personnel, 1972; Jackson State Univ, MPA, pub policy & admin, 1985. **Career:** MS Employ Servs, employ counr, 1972-73; Ala A&M Univ, dir new women's residence hall, 1973-74; Jackson State Univ, coordr special serv, 1974-82; Comn Housing Resources, dir 1982-84; Hinds Co Bd Supvrs, comn & econ develop specialist; Miss Bur Pollution Control, compliance officer, 1989; Miss democratic Party, chairs; founder, Mary Brown Environ Ctr, currently. **Orgs:** Treas, 1977-78, vpres, 1978-80 Jackson Urban League Guild; charter mem,Vicksburg Chap Delta Sigma Theta Sor, 1978; secy, MS Asn Educ Oppor Progs Personnel, 1979-80; pres, MS Caucus Conseumerism, 1979-81; treas, Asn Pub Policy & Admin, 1982-84; bd dirs, Jackson Urban League, 1984-87; comn chairperson, United Negro College Fund, 1986; chmn bd dirs, Jackson Community Housing & Resources Bd, 1987-89. **Honors/Awds:** Kappa Delta Pi & Phi Delta Kappa Honor Socs, 1972; Cert Appreciation Tampa Urban League, 1978; Outstanding Service Plaque Award, Jackson State Univ, Upward Bound Prog, 1980; Outstanding Service Plaque Award, Jackson State Univ Coronation Comn 1981; HUD Fel, Jackson State Univ, Dept Housing & Urban Develop, 1982-84. **Business Addr:** Founder, Mary Brown Environmental Center, 715 S Central Ave, Ely, MN 55731, **Business Phone:** (218)365-3364.*

BROWN, MAXINE J. CHILDRESS
Government official. **Personal:** Born Aug 13, 1943, Washington, DC; married James E; children: Scot, Nikki & Kimberly. **Educ:** Springfield Col, BS, 1971; Univ MA, MEd, 1973. **Career:** Rochester Inst Tech, asst prof, 1973-74; St Col Geneseo NY, asst prof, spec ed, dir learning disabilities, 1975-78; People Helping People, dir, 1978-80; City Rochester Dept Rec & Comn Servs, dir pub rel, 1980-83; City Rochester, councilwoman, 1999; Frederick Douglass Mus & Cult Ctr, pres, currently. **Orgs:** Nat cert interpreter for the deaf, Am Sign Lang, 1970-85; vpres, bd dir, Puerto Rican Youth Develop, 1982-; adv bd, chmn ed comn, NY St Div Human Rights, 1984; city coun rep, adv bd Monroe County Off Aging, 1984; adv bd Ctr, Ed Develop; vpres, bd visitors, St Ag & Indust Sch Indust; bd dir, Prog Rochester Interest Stud Sci & Math; pres, Metro Women's Network; chairperson, Arts Reach Arts Greater Rochester; bd dir, Rochester Area Multiple Sclerosis; Urban Ad Hoc Comn Home Econ Monroe County Coop Ext. **Honors/Awds:** Politician of the Yr, Eureka Lodge Award, 1984. **Special Achievements:** Nominated by Gov Carey & Approved by State Sen for Bd of Visitors State Ag & Indust School at Indust; 12 Publ including "About Time Mag", "Improving Police/Black Comm Relations", "A Not So Ordinary Man", "A Study Skills Program for the Hearing Impared Student" Volta Review Alexander Graham Bell Journal. **Home Addr:** 222 Chili Ave, Rochester, NY 14611. **Business Addr:** President, Frederick Douglass Museum & Cultural Center, 3200 Wayman Ave, Annapolis, MD 21403.*

BROWN, MICHAEL. **See EALY, MICHAEL.**

BROWN, MICHAEL (MIKE , BEAR)
Basketball player. **Personal:** Born Jul 19, 1963, Newark, NJ. **Educ:** George Wash Univ. **Career:** Basketball player (retired), basketball coach; Filanto Desio, 1985-86; Chicago Bulls, 1986-88, asst coach, 2008-; Utah Jazz, 1988-93; Minn Timberwolves, 1993-95; Philadelphia 76ers, ctr, 1995-96; Teamsystem Bologna, 1995; Phoenix Suns, ctr, 1996-97; Viola Reggio Calabria, 1996-98. **Business Addr:** Assistant Coach, Chicago Bulls, United Ctr 1901 W Madison St, Chicago, IL 60612-2459, **Business Phone:** (312)455-4000.

BROWN, MICHAEL DEWAYNE
Educator. **Personal:** Born Dec 18, 1954, Franklin, VA; son of Albert L and Lola B. **Educ:** Hampton Univ, Hampton, VA, BS, 1977; George Mason Univ, Fairfax, MS, 1991; Univ Va, Charlottesville. **Career:** Alexandria City Schs, teacher, 1977-93, lead teacher, 1993-94; Amideast, consult, asst prin, 1994-99; James K Polk Elem Sch, prin, 1999-. **Orgs:** Kappa Delta Pi, 1990-; Phi Delta Kappa, 1990-; Educ Tech Comm, 1990-; Strategic Planning Task Force, 1989; Supts Teacher Adv Coun, 1988-91; Mid Sch Steering Comm; Va Concerned Black Men Inc NOVA; Asn Supvn & Curric Develop. **Honors/Awds:** Washington Post Grants in Education, 1991-93; ARC Leadership Award, 1998; Mitsoff Award, 2001. **Special Achievements:** Educator's Book of Forms, copyrighted work, 1989. **Home Addr:** 272- S Arlington Mill Dr Suite 608, Arlington, VA 22206, **Home Phone:** (703)820-5848. **Business Addr:** Principal, James K Polk Elementary School, Alexandria City Public Schools, 5000 Polk Ave, Alexandria, VA 22304, **Business Phone:** (703)461-4180.

BROWN, MICHELE COURTON
Executive. **Educ:** Boston Univ, BA, Econ & Urban Studies. **Career:** FleetBoston Financial Found, dir, founding pres, 1999-02; Bank Am, sr vpres Charitable Mgt Servs, currently. **Orgs:** Nat Found Teaching Entrepreneurship; YouthBuild USA, The Partnershi; The Chestnut Hill Sch; Ctr Women & Enterprise; Museum Afro-Am Hist; Boston Symphony Orchestra Overseers; Wang Ctr Performing Arts; trustee, Roxbury Community Col, 2001. **Special Achievements:** Just Money: A Critique of Contemporary American Philanthropy, 2004. *

BROWN, MICHELLE LISTENBEE
Executive, television producer, television writer. **Career:** Photographers, prod coordr, 1999; "The Parkers", exec story ed, 2000-02, writer, 1999-04, producer, 2002-04; "Don't Believe the Hype", 2002; "Make a Joyful Noise", exec story ed, 2002; "It's Showtime", 2002; "Teach Me Tonight", exec story ed, 2002; "It's Showtime", exec story ed, 2002; "The Crush", exec story ed, 2002; " Road Trip", 2002; "Mother's Day Blues", exec story ed, 2002; " Kimmie Has Two Moms", 2003; "Judge Not a Book", 2004; "Who's Got Jokes?", 2006; "Second Time Around", 2004"; "At Last", 2004; "A Little Change Never Hurt Anybody", 2004; "Could It Be You", 2004; "Practice What You Preach", 2004; "Judge Not a Book", 2004; "Study Buddy", 2005; "One on One", 2005-06; "Fame and the Older Woman", 2006; United Paramount Network, co-exec producer, currently. *

BROWN, MIKE
Basketball coach, basketball player. **Personal:** Born Mar 5, 1970, Columbus, OH; married Carolyn; children: Elijah & Cameron. **Educ:** Univ San Diego, BA, bus finance, 1992. **Career:** Basketball player (retired), basketball coach; USD, 1990-92; Denver Nuggets, asst coach, 1992-97; Wash Wizards, 1997-2003; San Antonio Spurs, asst coach, 2000-03; Ind Pacers, asst coach; Cleveland Cavaliers, head coach, 2005-. **Honors/Awds:** Zable Athletic Award, Univ San Diego; Bugelli Leadership Award; Coach of the Month, Eastern Conf, 2008. **Special Achievements:** Sec Youngest Coach in the League. **Business Phone:** (216)420-2000.

BROWN, MILBERT ORLANDO
Photojournalist. **Personal:** Born Aug 12, 1956, Gary, IN; son of Milbert Sr and Mary Blanchard. **Educ:** Ball State Univ, Muncie, IN, BS, journ, 1978; Ohio Univ, Sch Visual Commun, Athens, OH, MA, photo commun, 1982. **Career:** Westside High Sch, Gary, IN, dir student publ, jour teacher, 1978-79; Dallas Times-Herald, photojournalist, 1980; Wash Post, Wash, DC, photojournalist, 1982; Veterans Admin, pub affairs writer, 1983; self-employed/freelance photographer, midwestern-based, 1983-86; Dept Army, Warren, MI, writer, ed, 1986; Wilberforce Univ, Wilberforce, OH, instr mass media, 1986-87; Patuxent Publ Newspapers, Columbia, MD, photojournalist, 1987-89; Boston Globe, Boston, MA, photojournalist, 1990-91; Chicago Tribune, photographer & picture ed, 1991-, photojournalist, 2001, staff photographer, currently; Open Shutters, instr, 1995, lectr. **Orgs:** Nat Press Photographers Asn, 1974-; Omega Psi Phi Fraternity, 1976-; Nat Asn Black Journalists, 1981-. **Honors/Awds:** Lect "Photography & Aesthetic Awareness," Morris Brown Col, 1987; Two Man Show & Lecture, Grambling State Col, 1987; Award of Excellence for essay "Pieces of Ebony," Chicago Asn Black Journalists, 1992; Visual Task Force "Photo Shoot-Out" Award, Nat Asn Black Journalists, 1992, 1993, 1998; US Photo "Shoot Out" winner, Nat Asn Black Journalists & Coca Cola, 1992, 1993, 1998; Journalism Award, Outstanding Coverage of the Black Condition Photography, Nat Asn Black Journalists, 1992, 1994, Award of Excellence, Nat Asn Black Journalists, 1998; First place winner, portrait/personality, Chicago Press Photographers Asn, 1993; Lect & Exhib, "Pieces of Ebony," Photo Exhibit, Dillard Univ, 1994, Morgan State Univ, 1995; Award of Excellence, Chicago Asn Black Journalists, 1995, 1998; Pulitzer Prize, Chicago Tribune, 1995, 1998; Photographer of the Year, Chicago Press Photographers Asn, 1995; Omega Man of the Year, Omega Psi Phi, 1997; Journalism Alumnus of the Year, Ball State Univ, Dept Journ, 1997; Lect "Photographers and writers working together," Nat Asn Black Jounalist Regional Conf, Minneapolis, 1998; Living Legends of the Negro League, Art Atrium II Gallery, Portsmouth, VA, 1999; Grand Prize Winner. **Special Achievements:** First Place Sports Picture, Boston Press Photographers Asn, 1991; "Pieces of Ebony," Morgan State Univ, Baltimore, MD, 1995; "The Million Man March," Milwaukee Hist Soc, Milwaukee, WI, 1996; Soul of a New Nation-Photographs the South African Elections, Univ of IL-Chicago, 1997; "Joy- A Celebration of the Black Experience," Univ of IL-Chicago, African American Cultural Ctr, 1997; Exhibition and lecture: "Photography & Aesthetic Awareness," Morris Brown College, Atlanta, GA, Grambling State College, Grambling, LA; First Place & Best of Show for Spot News, Maryland & Delaware/DC Press Asn, 1988. **Business Addr:** Photojournalist, Staff photographer, Chicago Tribune, 425 N Mich Ave, Chicago, IL 60611, **Business Phone:** (312)222-9100.

BROWN, DR. MILTON F
School administrator, educator. **Personal:** Born Apr 29, 1943, Rochester, NY; divorced; children: Damien. **Educ:** SUNY Oswego, BS, 1965; Columbia Univ Teachers Col, MA, 1973, PhD, 1983. **Career:** Nat Inst Ed, Educ Policy Fel, 1978-79; NY City Bd Ed, asst sup, 1979-80; NY State Educ Dept, dir 1980-82; NJ Dept Higher Ed, acad Affairs, dir, 1982-85; Malcolm X Col, Chicago, pres; Pasadena City Col, instr social sci. **Orgs:** Consult, Independent, 1975-83; sr res assoc, IUME Teachers Col, 1977-78; consult, US Dept Educ, 1975-83; vpres, Task Force Youth Employment, 1979-80; vpres, Mondale's Task Force Youth Employment, 1979-80. **Honors/Awds:** Heft Fel, Teachers Col Columbus Univ, 1972-73; Inst for Ed Leadership Ed Policy Fel, George Wash Univ, 1978-79. **Military Serv:** USMCR, L Corporal.

BROWN, MORSE L.
Government official, conservationist. **Personal:** Born Oct 10, 1943, Oakland, MS; son of Stephen and Fannie J Moore; married Arma George Brown, Aug 30, 1980; children: Khary Dia. **Educ:** Alcorn State Univ, Lorman, MS, BS, 1965. **Career:** Conservationist (retired); US Soil Conserv Serv, Claremont, NH, soil conservationist, 1965-67, soil conservationist, 1967-71, W Br, dist conservationist, 1971-73, Muskegon, dist conservationist, 1973-82, Ann Arbor, dist conservationist, 1982-85; Mich State Univ Exten Serv, Ann Arbor, co ext dir, 1985-88, co ext dir, 1988, agent. **Orgs:** Reg dir, Alpha Phi Alpha, Fraternity, 1975-82; reg dir, Soil Conserv Soc Am, 1983-84; chmn, Brown Chapel Bldg Comt, 1986-88; pres, Alpha Phi Alpha, Fraternity Theta Zeta Lambda, 1988-90. **Honors/Awds:** Appreciation for Serv, Soil Conserv Soc, 1985; Appreciation for Serv, Washtenaw County, 1988; Resolution of Appreciation Dept Heads, Washtenaw County, 1988; Resolution of Appreciation, Washtenaw County, Bd Comnrs Washtenaw County, 1988; Dairy Herd Imp Assoc Washtenaw County, 1988; Commendation Award, 1990; Alpha Man of Year, Theta Zeta Lambda Chapter, 1991; Presidential's Cit, Mich Assoc Ext Agents, 1992; Achievement Award, Nat Asn Ext Agents, 1994; Wayne County HSCB Recognition for Health & Comn Serv Prog, 1998-99; Mich State Univ Ext Team Award, 1998; SEMCOSH Environ Justice Award, 2000. **Military Serv:** AUS Res, sgt, 1966-72. *

BROWN, MORTIMER
Clinical psychologist. **Personal:** Born Feb 20, 1924, New York, NY; married Marilyn Green; children: Frank, Mark. **Educ:** Vanderbilt Univ, Nashville, PhD, 1961; City Col NY, BS, 1949. **Career:** Clinical psychologist (retired). Ill Dept Mental Health, Springfield, IL, asst dir, 1961-69; Fla State Univ, Tallahassee, prof, psychol, 1969-73; Fla Ment Health Inst, 1973-78; Independent Prac, 1978-96; St Leo Col, adj prof psychol, 1977; Univ Sarasota, adj prof psychol, Tampa Bay Campus, 1998; Nat Cancer Inst, Off Liaison Activ, currently. **Orgs:** Am Psychol Asn; Am Black Psychol Asn; Southeastern Psychol Asn; bd & comm mem, Fla Psychol Asn, pres, 1980, 1981; Am Cancer Soc. **Honors/Awds:** Distinguished Professor, Bedford Univ, 1960. **Military Serv:** USAF, 1942-46. **Home Addr:** 18825 Tracer Dr, Lutz, FL 33549, **Home Phone:** (813)949-3202. **Business Addr:** Member, National Cancer Institute, The Office of Liaison Activities, 6116 Exec Blvd Suite 3068 A, MSC 8324, MSC 8324, MD 20892-8324, **Business Phone:** (301)594-3194.*

BROWN, NA ORLANDO
Football player. **Personal:** Born Feb 22, 1977, Reidsville, NC; son of Nathan; married Erica Devon Featherstone, 2000. **Educ:** Univ NC. **Career:** Football Player (Retired); Philadelphia Eagles, wide receiver, 1999-2001.

BROWN, NANCY COFIELD
Administrator, executive director. **Personal:** Born Jul 25, 1932; married David; children: David, Stephen & Philip. **Educ:** Pratt Inst, attended 1954. **Career:** Trudy Rogers Co, asst designer, 1955-57; Family & Child Serv, coordr, 1974-77; Town of Greenwich, dir community develop block grant prog, 1978-. **Orgs:** Dir, Urban League SW Fairfield, CT, 1970-74; dir, CT Women's Book, 1974-78; grants consult, Town Greenwich, 1977; consult, Affirmative Act, Town Greenwich, 1977; YMCA, 1979; Links-Fairfield, CT, 1980; trustee, Stanford Found, 1980; Hartwick Col, trustee, 1990-; CT Housing Finance Authority. **Special Achievements:** 10 outstanding women BRAVO Award. **Business Addr:** Director, Town of Greenwich, Community Development Block Grant Program, 101 Field Pt Rd, Greenwich, CT 06830, **Business Phone:** (203)622-3791.

BROWN, NORMAN E.
Scientist, executive, government official. **Personal:** Born Feb 20, 1935, Cleveland, OH; married Mary Lee Tyus; children: Karen, Dianne, Pamela, David, Robert. **Educ:** Western Res Univ, Cleveland, OH, BA, biol, 1959; Univ MN, Minneapolis, MS, bio-

chem, 1970; Univ Mass, MS, labor rels. **Career:** Western Reserve Univ, res assoc, 1957-64; Univ Minn, res assoc; Hoffman-LaRoche Inc, asst sci II, 1969-71, assoc sci, 1971-73, mgr equal oppor, 1973-78, asst dir equal oppor, 1978-86; Tampa Bay Regional Planning Coun, assoc housing planner; NY State Coun Machinists, local chmn, gen chmn, legis dir, 2004-; Fairchild Repub Aircraft, Machinist; Berger Instrument Co, Machinist; Gen Mechatronics, Machinist; Macor Inc & Long Island Rail Rd, Machinist; Diesel Shop, LIRR, Machinist; Berger Instrument Co, apprenticeship. **Orgs:** Edges Inc, 1975-80; pres bd trustees, United Way Plainfield, 1978-; vpres bd trustees, United Way Union Co, 1978-; Plainfield NJ Sch Bd, 1982-85, pres, 1984-85; Long Island Railroad Labor Coun; Metro-North Labor Coun. **Honors/Awds:** Black Achievers in Ind Award; YMCA Harlem Br; New York City 1974.

BROWN, DR. O. GILBERT
School administrator, educator. **Personal:** Born Jun 12, 1954, Proctor, AR; son of Mable Brown and Zelner; children: Jacqueline & Jordan. **Educ:** Univ Kans, BS, 1976; Emporia State Univ, MS, 1984; Miami Univ-Oxford, Ohio, MS, 1986; Ind Univ-Bloomington, EdD, 1992. **Career:** Ind Univ-Bloomington, coordr, 1986-91; Earlham Col, assoc dean, 1992-93; Ind Univ, Indianapolis, dir residence life, 1993-95, asst dean educ student serv, dir stud serv, asst dean stud serv, 1999-2002, assoc dean; Purdue Univ, Sch Educ, asst dean, adj prof, 1999; Mo State Univ, assoc prof & dir student affairs prog, currently. **Orgs:** Nat Asn Stud Personnel Administrators, 1984-; Am Col Personnel Asn. **Special Achievements:** Helping African-American Students Attend College, 1997; Debunking the Myth: Stories About African-American College Students. **Business Addr:** Associate Professor, MS Student Affairs Program Director, Missouri State University, Siceluff Hall 166-B, 901 S Nat Ave, Springfield, MO 65897, **Business Phone:** (417)836-5287.

BROWN, DR. OLA M.
Educator. **Personal:** Born Apr 7, 1941, Albany, GA; daughter of Georgia Butler Johnson and Willie L Johnson. **Educ:** Albany State Col, BS, 1961; Univ GA, MEd, 1972, EdS, 1973, EdD, 1974. **Career:** Thomas County Schs, Thomasville GA, teacher, 1961-67; Dougherty County Schs, Albany GA, teacher, 1967-71; Univ GA Athens, grad asst, 1972-74; Valdosta State Col GA, prof educ, 1974-91; Dept Head, Early Childhood & Reading Educ, 1980-90; Valdosta State Univ, dept head, prof emer, currerntly. **Orgs:** Phi Delta Kappa Educ Frat, 1975-; recording sec GA Coun Intl Reading Asn,1977-79; treas, GA Asn Higher Educ, 1977-80; Am Asn Univ Prof, 1977-80; vpres, 1979-80, pres, 1980-81 GA Coun Intl Reading Asn; state coordr, Intl Reading Asn, 1988-91. **Honors/Awds:** Education Instructor of Year, Student GA Asn Educ, 1975; WH Dennis Memorial Award, Albany State Col, 1976; Ira E Aaron Reading Award, S Central GA Coun IRA, 1977. **Special Achievements:** Ola M Brown Scholarship, established in honor of Dr Ola M Brown. **Business Addr:** Professor Emeritus, Valdosta State University, 1500 N Patterson St, Valdosta, GA 31698, **Business Phone:** (229)333-5800.*

BROWN, OMAR
Football player. **Personal:** Born Mar 28, 1975, York, PA. **Educ:** NC State Univ. **Career:** Football player (retired), Atlanta Falcons, defensive back, 1998-99; Orlando Rage, safety, 2001.

BROWN, OTHA N
School administrator, commissioner, educator. **Personal:** Born Jul 19, 1931, De Queen, AR; son of Otha Sr and Elizabeth Gossitt; married Marjorie Gay, Jun 19, 1956 (divorced 1967); married Lela Evelyn Brown, Dec 30, 1975; children: Darrick O & Leland K. **Educ:** Cent State Univ, OH, BS, 1952; Ohio State Univ Law Sch, attended 1955; Univ Conn, MA, 1956; Univ Bridgeport, prof dipl admin, 1959; NY Univ, cert coun, 1965; Springfield Col, Mass, cert coun, 1966; Queens Col, cert coun, 1967; Boston Univ, cert coun, 1969. **Career:** Educator (retired), political official; Wooster Jr High Sch, Stratford, Conn, eng & soc studies, 1957-60; Rippowam High Sch, Stamford, Conn, counr, 1961-83; Stamford High Sch, 1983-90; City Norwalk, city councilman, 1963-69, 1977-81; Conn Gen Assembly, legis, 1966-72; Second Taxing Dist City Norwalk, comnr, 1981-, chairperson, 1982-; Fairfield Cablevision, vpres; Biebel Travel Agency, vpres; licensed notary, real estate broker; second Taxing Dist Water Dept, chair, 1982; Am Water Works Asn, Int Affairs Comt, 1992; State Conn, Dept Human Resources, coordr state prog, 1992-93; Sub-Comt Tech Info, chair, 1994; Univ Conn, Waterbury Campus, dir, 1994-98. **Orgs:** Regional dir, Alpha Phi Alpha, 1969-79; Am Personnel & Guidance Asn; Am Sch Couns Asn; Nat & State Educ Asn; Phi Alpha Theta; Kappa Delta Pi; Dem Town Comt, 1972-74; sec bd trustees, Univ CT, 1975-93; founder & pres, Norwalk Area Improvement League Inc, 1978-; founder & pres, Greater Norwalk Black Dem Club & Coalition, 1976-; pres & dep mayor, Norwalk Comt Coun, 1980; bd dir & vpres, Fairfield Cablevision; founder & pres, Southern CT United Black Fund, 1983-; co-chmn, Jesse Jackson Pres Norwalk, 1984; pres, Conn State Fedn Black Democratic Clubs Inc, 1972-76; State Task Force Justice & the Ct, 1987-89; Norwalk Dem Town Comt. **Honors/Awds:** Man of the Year Award, Alpha Phi Alpha, 1969; Distinguished Service Award, 1981; past pres, Award CT State Fed Black Democrats, 1979; Citizen of the Year, Omega Psi Phi, 1970; Young Man of the Year, Jaycees, 1967; NAACP Leadership Award, 1970; University Medal, Univ Conn, 1994; Polits & Service Award, Prince Hall Grand Chap, Order Eastern Star, State CT, 1987; Official Citation, City Hartford, 1989; Honorary Alumnus, Langston Univ, 1968; Achievement Hall of Fame, Cent State Univ, 1996. **Special Achievements:** Publications include: "Sch Counrs, A New Role & Image", Conn Teacher Mag, 1972; Remembering: A Book of Poetry 1977; "Polit Blackout", Conn Mag, 1979; "Fighting Apartheid UCONN Makes the Decision to Divest", The Stamford Advocate Viewpoint, 1986, "Thoughts on Educ" Sphinx Mag, Vol 74 No 4, Alpha Phi Alpha Fraternity, 1988. **Military Serv:** AUS, psychol warfare officer, 1952-54. **Home Addr:** 21 Shorefront Pk, Norwalk, CT 06854, **Home Phone:** (203)853-7739. **Business Addr:** Commissioner, Second Taxing District of the City of Norwalk Connecticut, 164 Water St, PO Box 468, South Norwalk, CT 06856-0468, **Business Phone:** (203)866-4446.

BROWN, OUIDA Y.
Lawyer. **Career:** Atty, currently. **Business Addr:** Attorney, 600 N Wash St, PO Box 587, Tuscumbia, AL 35674.*

BROWN, P J (COLLIER BROWN)
Basketball player. **Personal:** Born Oct 14, 1969, Detroit, MI; married Dee; children: Whitney, Briana, Kalani & Javani. **Educ:** La Tech, attended 1992. **Career:** Panionios (Greece), ctr, 1992-93; New Jersey Nets, 1993-96; Miami Heat, 1996-2000; Charlotte Hornets, 2000-02; New Orleans Hornets, 2002-06; NY Knicks, 2006; Chicago Bulls, 2006-07; Boston Celtics, 2007-. **Honors/Awds:** J Walter Kennedy Citizenship Award, 1996-97; NBA Nat Citizenship Award, Sports Alliance, 2005.

BROWN, PAUL, JR.
Manager. **Personal:** Born Oct 10, 1926, Chicago, IL; married Jean Pace. **Career:** Kicks & Co Chicago, mus lyrics & book writer, 1961; Brown Baby, 1960; WorkSong, 1960; Dat Der, composer, 1960; Village Vanguard, 1961; Apollo Theater, 1961; Carnegie Hall, 1962; Bule Angel, 1962; Hungry I, 1962; Crescendo, 1962; Berns Stockholm, 1963; The Sanke, 1963; Waldorf Asteria,1963; one-man shows Prince Charels Theater London, 1963; Mus Box Theater, Los Angeles, 1964; Gramercy Arts Tehater, NY City, 1965; Muffled Drums, 1965; Cool Elephand, London, Eng, 1965; Joy, prod dir, 1966, Happy Medium Theater; Summer in the City Harper Theater; Alley Theater; In de Beginin, 1977; series host 13 Prog Pub TV Series, From Jumpstreet A Story of Black Music, WETA Wash DC. **Orgs:** Author's League Am.

BROWN, PAUL E. X. See Obituaries section.

BROWN, PAUL L. See Obituaries section.

BROWN, PAULA EVIE
Educator. **Educ:** Loyola Univ, BS, 1973; Purdue Univ, MS, 1976; Harvard Univ, EdM, 1980; Northern Ill Univ, EdD, 1990. **Career:** Neighborhood Youth Corps, recruiter, 1973-74; Purdue Univ, instr, 1974-76; RR Donnelley & Sons, pricing estimator, 1976-79; Chicago & Northwestern Co, HRD adminr, 1981-82; Northern Ill Univ, instr, 1984-88, assoc prof, 1994-; F Webb Starks Inc, bus developer, 1989-90; Cent Mich Univ, prof, 1990. **Orgs:** Beta Gamma Sigma, 1973-; Phi Delta Kappa, 1980-; Black Alumni Coun, NIU, 1991-; Asn Bus Commun, 1991-; Nat Mich Bus Educ Asn, 1991-; Delta Pi Epsilon, 1991-; Nat Congress Black Fac, 1992-; Res Asn Minority Profs, 1992-. **Honors/Awds:** Doctoral Research Award, Delta Pi Epsilon, 1992; Woodson Fellowship, Awardee, Recipient for Minorities, 1984-87; Nominee 10 Outstanding Chicagoans, Chicago Junior Asn of C&I, 1982. **Special Achievements:** Publication based on award-winning dissertation, 1992; participant in a nationally recognized entrepreneurship program, 1987; first black to win doctoral research award from DPE, 1992. **Business Phone:** (815)753-6187.

BROWN, PHILIP LORENZO
Educator, historian. **Personal:** Born Jan 16, 1909, Annapolis, MD; son of William H and Julia Ann Dorsey; married Rachel Hall Brown, Sep 4, 1932; children: Philip Lorenzo, Jr, Errol Eugene, Sr. **Educ:** Bowie Normal Sch, elem sch teacher's cert, 1928; Morgan State Col, BS, 1947; NY Univ, MA, 1955. **Career:** Educator (retired); Anne Arundel County Bd Educ, MD, educr, elem sch teacher & prin, sec sch teacher & vice prin, 1928-70. **Orgs:** Treas, Anne Arundel County Colored Teachers Asn, 1930-52; treas, Anne Arundel County Colored Federation of PTA's, 1940-50; vpres, Arundel-on-the-Bay Property Owners Asn, 1975-76, treas, 1977-95; vol, life mem, Banneker-Douglass Mus, 1984-; bd dir, Red Cross; Mem Comm, Golden Heritage, life mem; bd dir, life mem, Brewer Hill Cemetery Asn; archivist, Mt Moriah African Methodist Episcopal Church. **Honors/Awds:** Man of the Year Award, Mt Moriah African Methodist Episcopal Church Annual Conf; Drum Major Award, Martin Luther King; Golden Heritage Award, Nat Asn Advan Colored People; Community Recognition Award, Historic Annapolis; Distinguished Citizen Award, City of Annapolis & State MAR. **Special Achievements:** Published "A Century of Separate But Equal Education in Anne Arundel County," a case study of educ for colored children during the school segregation years from 1866-1966; "The Other Annapolis," a review if the life and times of colored residents of Annapolis, MAR from 1900-50, illustrated by pictures; A History of Mt Moriah African Methodist Episcopal Church in Annapolis, work in progress. **Military Serv:** Harry S Truman Registration-World War II President's Cert, 1948. **Home Addr:** 3502 Narragansett Ave, Annapolis, MD 21403, **Home Phone:** (410)267-6677. *

BROWN, RALPH BENJAMIN
Clergy. **Personal:** Born Jul 28, 1924, Pittsburgh, PA; son of Harry H and Mary J; married Margaret L Brown, Jan 29, 1949; children: Ralph B Jr & Glenn B. **Educ:** Duquesne Univ, Pittsburgh, PA, BS, BA, 1949; Duquesne Univ Grad Sch; Howard Univ Grad Sch. **Career:** Pittsburgh Courier, asst prom mgr, res dir, 1947-54; Johnson Publ Co, field rep, 1954-56; Fodor's Modern Guides, Inc, rese writer, Sub Sahara Africa, 1957-59; Ethiopian Herald, Addis Ababa, city ed, 1958-59; US Info Agency, foreign serv officer, Ghana, Malawi, Somalia, 1960-69; Howard Univ, pub rels officer, 1970-73; RMA, dir commun, 1973-78; AT&T, mkt acct exec, 1978-85; Wisdom, Inc, pres, 1985-90; United Church of Christ, minister social outreach, currently. **Orgs:** Alpha Pi Alpha Fraternity, 1947-; sr vice commander, Veterans Foreign Wars, Post 2562, 1946-48; Montgomery County Criminal Justice Coordinating Comn, 1972-89; comn minister, United Church Christ, Social Outreach, 1989-; chair, M/C, Human Rel Comn, Real Estate Panel, 1989-97; parliamentar. **Honors/Awds:** Outstanding Service CJCC 17-years, Montgomery County MD, 1972-89; Inner Circle of Achievers, C&P Telephone Co, 1981; Award of Merit, Alpha Pi Alpha, 1987; Second annual M/C Human Relations Award, 1997; Distinguished Service, VFW Post 2562, 1998; Outstanding Contribution to Human Rights, United Nations Assn, 1999; Community Service Award, 2000, Humanitarian Award, 2001, M/C chap, Alpha Phi Alpha; inducted into M/C Human Rights Hall of Fame, 2002. **Special Achievements:** Helped convert weekly newspaper, Ethiopian Herald, into a daily publication, 1958-59; attended National Sales Conference, AT&T, Acapulco, MX, as one of Top 3% in Sales, 1981. **Military Serv:** AUS, T/5, 1943-46; including ASTP, Univ Nebr, Wilberforce Univ, 1943-44; 92nd Div Italy; 406 Port Co, Philippines, & Japan, 1944-46. **Home Addr:** 3805 Ralph Rd, Wheaton, MD 20906-5267, **Home Phone:** (301)946-5808. **Business Addr:** Minister of Social Outreach, Lincoln Congregational Temple, United Church of Christ, 1701 11th St NW, Washington, DC 20001, **Business Phone:** (202)332-2640.

BROWN, RANDY
Basketball player. **Personal:** Born May 22, 1968, Chicago, IL; son of Wille and Marie; married Katrina; children: Justin & Janel. **Educ:** NMex State, jour, 1991. **Career:** Basketball player (retired), coach; Sacramento Kings, guard, 1991-95, asst coach, currently; Chicago Bulls, 1995-2000; Boston Celtics, 2000-02; Phoenix Suns, guard, 2002-03.

BROWN, RAY, JR. (LEONARD RAY BROWN, JR.)
Football player, football coach. **Personal:** Born Dec 12, 1962, Marion, AR; married Ashley; children: Lentisha, Tyler, Andrea, Miriam & Leonard. **Educ:** Ark State Univ. **Career:** Football player (retired); Football, coach: St Louis Cardinals, guard, 1986-88; Wash Redskins, 1989-95; San Francisco 49ers, 1996-01; Detroit Lions, 2002-03;Wash Redskins, tackle, 2005: Buffalo Bills, asst off line coach, currently. **Honors/Awds:** All Pro Sel, 2001; Pro Bowl sel,2001, Co recipient of Detroit Lions' Joe Schmidt Leadership Award, 2003. *

BROWN, RAYMOND MADISON
Executive. **Personal:** Born Jan 12, 1949, Fort Worth, TX; son of Raymond E Brown and Lutiel V Houston; married Linda, May 17, 1974; children: Derek & Christopher. **Educ:** W Tex A&M, BA 1971. **Career:** Life GA, ins underwriter; Waldo Shirt Co, NY, sales rep; Atlanta Falcons, def ensive safety, 1971-77; New Orleans Saints, prof, 1977-; Real Estate Broker, 1980-; Brown Boy II Inc, pres, 1984-. **Orgs:** Omega Psi Phi Frat. **Special Achievements:** Author of one novel. **Business Addr:** President, Brown Boy II Inc, 4936 Lake Fjord Pass, Marietta, GA 30068, **Business Phone:** (770)642-1316.

BROWN, REGGIE
Football player. **Personal:** Born Jun 26, 1973, Highland Park, MI. **Educ:** Fresno State Univ. **Career:** Seattle Seahawks, running back, 1996-2000; Green Bay Packers, 2002.

BROWN, REGINALD DEWAYNE
Writer. **Personal:** Born Mar 14, 1952, Memphis, TN; son of Clarence and Nadolyn; married Robin Viva, Feb 16, 1980; children: Brian Alexander & Brittany Nicole. **Educ:** Univ Calif, Irvine, BA, drama, 1974; San Francisco State Univ, MA, film, 1979. **Career:** Reginald Brown Productions, writer, producer, dir, 1981-; Children's Defense Fund, Beat the Odds Celebration, producer, 1996-98; Cent City Productions Inc, writer, clip producer, 1991-94; Sam Riddle Productions, Inc, writer, assoc producer, segment dir, 1987-91; Dick Clark Productions Inc, asst producer, 1985-86; "Great Women of Color," dir, playwright, 1998; "An Alternative to Violence," co-exec producer, writer, dir, 2000. **Orgs:** Dir Guild Am, AASC, co-chair, 1997-98; Writers Guild Am, West, vchmn, black writers comt; AASC, dir & co-chair, currently. **Honors/**

Awds: TV Lab/WNET Thirteen Independent Filmmakers Grant, 1981; American Film Institute, Independent Filmmakers Grant, 1978; DGA George Schaffer Stage Directors Observership Program, 1999. **Home Addr:** 13691 Gavina Ave, Sylmar, CA 91342, **Home Phone:** (818)364-1983. *

BROWN, REGINALD L., JR.
Executive. **Career:** Xerox Corp; Oracle Corp, US Solutions Sales, vpres, currently. **Orgs:** Bd mem, Cyveillance Inc; Mem Bd Trustees, Community Academy PCS. **Business Addr:** Vice President, Oracle Corporation, US Solutions Sales, 1910 Oracle Way, Reston, VA 20190-4735, **Business Phone:** (703)478-9000.*

BROWN, REGINALD ROYCE
Administrator, law enforcement officer. **Personal:** Born Mar 18, 1946, Baton Rouge, LA; son of Theresa Mae Bell; children: Reginald Jr, Tashera Patrice, D'Laniger Royce & La Toya Renee. **Educ:** Southern Univ, BA, 1965. **Career:** Amendment Band 13, pub rel dir & mgr; Gov's Off Consumer Protection, prog supr, 1972-73; Southern Univ Baton Rouge LA, centex dir, 1972-75, asst to bus mgr, 1973; city councilman, Jospeh A Delpit, aide; Sheriffs Off, adminr asst, 1975-2000; Reginald Brown & Assocs Inc, pres, 1972-2000; city constable, City Baton Rouge, 2000-. **Orgs:** Bd mem, Baton Rouge YMCA; life mem, Nat Asn Advan Colored People; pres, Holiday Helpers Baton Rouge, 1987-; pres, Scotlandville Beautification Comt, 1989-; secy, Baton Rouge Detox Bd; Alcohol/Drug Detox Bd; La Bar Disciplinary Bd. **Honors/Awds:** Awards for Outstanding Service, Baranco Clark YMCA, 1972; Martin Luther King Award, Shady Grove Baptist Church, 1987; Award of Distinction, Alpha Kappaha, 1989; Distinguished Officer of the Year, Blacks Law Enforcement, 1990; Outstanding Black Achiever Award, YMCA; Outstanding Humanitarian Award, Baton Rouge Human Relations Council; Outstanding Law Enforcement Officer, 1990; Outstanding Law Enforcement Officer, Pres Clinton & Atty General Janet Reno, 1994; Golden Deeds Award, Baton Rouge, LA, 1997; Trailblazer Award, Southern Univ, 1998; FBI Leadership Award, 2001. **Business Addr:** Constable, Baton Rouge City Court, City Constable Office, 233 St Louis St Basement Rm 46, PO Box 881, Baton Rouge, LA 70802, **Business Phone:** (225)389-3004.

BROWN, RENEE
Sports manager. **Educ:** Univ Nev, 1978. **Career:** Univ Kans, asst coach; Stanford Univ, asst coach; San Jose State Univ, asst coach; USA Basketball Women's Nat Team, asst coach, 1995-96; USA Women's Olympic Team, staff, 1996; WNBA, from dir player personnel tosr dir, 1996-99, vpres, 2000, sr vpres player personnel, 2004-. **Business Addr:** Senior Vice President, WNBA, 645 5th Ave, New York, NY 10022, **Business Phone:** (212)688-9622.*

BROWN, REUBEN
Football player, fund raising consultant. **Personal:** Born Feb 13, 1972. **Educ:** Univ Pittsburgh. **Career:** Buffalo Bills, guard, 1995-2003; Chicago Bears, guard, 2004-07; Ruben Brown Motorcycle Run, founder, pres, chief exec officer.

BROWN, REUBEN D
Executive. **Personal:** Born Aug 11, 1948, Detroit, MI; son of Richard and Josephine; married Maria Yuzon; children: Rochelle, E Aminata & Reuben Brandon. **Educ:** Lawrence Technol Univ, BSIM, 1982; Univ Mich, MBA, 1984. **Career:** Gen Motors Corp, construct mgr, 1973-84; Rohm & Haas Co, financial anal mgr, 1984-91; Am Express Financial Advisors Inc, financial planner, sr financial advr, 1991-. **Orgs:** Black Bus Studs Orgn, corp rels chair, 1982-84; Univ Mich Steering Comt, 1982-84; A Better Chance, bd mem, 1989-91; bd mem, Int Child Resource Inst, 1996-. **Special Achievements:** Co-authored publication "Senior Counsel, Financial & Legal Strategies Age 50 & Beyond". **Home Addr:** 72 Jennings Ct, San Francisco, CA 94124, **Home Phone:** (415)467-2269. **Business Addr:** Financial Advisor, American Express Financial Advisory Inc, 255 Shoreline Dr Suite 500, Redwood City, CA 94065, **Business Phone:** (650)593-9170.

BROWN, RICHARD L
Executive. **Career:** Univ Tenn, Chattanooga, vice chancellor finance & operations, currently. **Business Addr:** Vice Chancellor of Finance & Operations, The University of Tennessee at Chattanooga, Department of Finance and Operations, 306 Fletcher 615 McCallie Ave, Chattanooga, TN 37403, **Business Phone:** (423)425-4393.

BROWN, RICHARD S., JR.
Clergy. **Career:** Payne Avenue Missionary Baptist Church, pastor, currently. *

BROWN, ROBERT
Consultant, government official. **Personal:** Born Mar 23, 1936, Lansing, MI; son of Robert Sr and Georgia L Dean; married Joy G Tunstall. **Educ:** Mich State Univ, BA, social work, 1958. **Career:** Mich Dept Corrections, prison counr, 1961-62, parole officer, 1962-67, dep warden, 1967-70, dep dir, 1970-84, dir, 1984-91; Fed Ct, consult; Bob Brown Enterprise, criminal justice consult, currently. **Orgs:** Alpha Phi Alpha 1955; exec bd mem, Youth Develop Corp, 1978-; pres & life mem, Mich Correctional Asn, 1984; vpres, Midwest Asn Correctional Admin, 1985-86, treas, 1986-89, pres, 1989-91; exec bd mem, Chief Okemos Coun Boy Scouts Am Exec Bd, 1986-91, vpres, 1989-91; exec comt mem, Am Correctional Asn, 1988-90; Sigma Pi Phi Frat, Alpha Chi Boule, 1988-; vpres, Asn State Correctional Adminr, 1989-91; Trinity AME Church; Nat Asn Advan Colored People. **Honors/Awds:** Black Achievers Award, Phi Beta Sigma 1986; Silver Beaver Award & Distinguished Eagle Scout Award, 1999; ER Cass Award, Am Correctional Asn; Distinguished Alumni Award, Lansing Educ Advan Found; Distinguished Alumni Award, Mich State Univ, Black Alumni Inc; Louie Wainwright Award, Asn State Correctional Adminr; Whitney Young Service Award, Boy Scouts Am. **Military Serv:** USAF, capt, 1958-60 & 1962. **Home Addr:** 1912 Kuerbitz Dr, Lansing, MI 48906, **Home Phone:** (517)323-1183. **Business Addr:** Criminal Justice Consultant, Bob Brown Enterprise, 1912 Kuerbitz Dr, Lansing, MI 48906, **Business Phone:** (517)323-1183.

BROWN, ROBERT CEPHAS, SR.
Jeweler. **Personal:** Born Dec 9, 1925, Meridian, MS; married Ranola Hubbard; children: Robert Cephas Jr, Ranola LaVohn, Michelle Lynette & Rochelle La Kaye. **Educ:** Van Slyke Sch Horology; Gemological Inst Am. **Career:** Brown's Jewelers, owner, inventor, master watchmaker, diamond appraiser, 1950-. **Orgs:** Downtown Merchant's Asn; vpres, Vallejo Revitilization Asn; Charter Review Com Vallejo; Nat Asn Advan Colored People. **Military Serv:** AUS, pfc, 1944-46. **Business Addr:** Brown jeweller's, 316 Georgia St, Vallejo, CA 94590.*

BROWN, ROBERT J., III
Educator, physician. **Personal:** Born May 31, 1919, Norfolk, VA; married Blanche Randall; children: Jeanne, Catherine & Marcia. **Educ:** Hampton Inst, BS, 1939; Howard Univ, MS, 1941, MS, MIT, MD, 1945. **Career:** Union Bay state Chem Corp, chemist, 1943-46; Howard Univ, Dept Med, asst prof, 1959-60, fel & psychiat, 1961-66, asst prof, 1966; Veterans Benefits Off, med officer, 1960-61; Clin Opers Area B, Community Mental Health Ctr, pres, asst dir, 1972; pvt pract, psychiat, currently. **Orgs:** Am Psychiat Asn, 1966-; Med Soc Dist Columbia, 1966-; AAAS; DC Civil Serv; CTMF Med Found. **Honors/Awds:** Res Steric, Hindrance & Enolization Acetylenic Precursors Vitamin A, 1939-45. **Military Serv:** USNR, Lt JG MC, 1955-56; Lt, 1956-57. **Business Addr:** Psychiatry, Private Practice, 2041 Georgia Ave NW, Washington, DC 20060.*

BROWN, ROBERT JOE
Administrator, chief executive officer. **Personal:** Born Feb 26, 1935, High Point, NC; married Sallie J Walker. **Educ:** Virginia Union Univ; NC A&T State Univ. **Career:** High Point Police Dept, law enforcement Officer, 1956-58; US Dept Treas, Fed Bur Narcotics, agt, 1958-60; B & C Assocs Inc, pres, 1960-68; White House, spec asst pres, 1968-73; B & C Assocs Inc, chmn & chief exec officer, 1973-. **Orgs:** Bd dirs, Oper PUSH Inc; bd dirs, MLK Ctr Social Change; bd dirs, First Union Corp; bd dir, Sonoco; bd dir, Duke Power; So Furniture Club; Nat Asn Advan Colored People; Wisemen; Arthur W Page Soc; United Nat Bank; vchmn, Am Cancer Soc. **Honors/Awds:** Outstanding Young Man in America, Jr Chamber Com Distinguished Serv; Achievement Award, Nat Med Asn; Nat Merit Award, Alpha Phi Alpha; Nat Exec Branch Govt Award, Alpha Phi Alpha; Honorary Chief, Sioux Indian Nat; Distinguished American Award, Horatio Alger Asn; Lifetime Achievement Award, Small Bus Admin; Drum Major for Justice Award, SCLC; Honorary Degrees: LHD, North Carolina A & T State Univ; LHD, Tarkio Col; LHD, Clark Col; LLD, High Point Col; LLD, Daniel Payne Col; LLD, Shaw Univ; LLD, Fla Mem Col; LLD, Malcolm X Col. **Business Addr:** Chairman, Chief Executive Officer, B & C Associates Inc, 808 Greensboro Rd, PO Box 2636, High Point, NC 27261-2636, **Business Phone:** (336)884-0744.

BROWN, HON. ROBERT LEE
Mayor, educator. **Personal:** Born Jul 31, 1947, Wetumpka, AL; son of Samuel Bernard and Annie Pearl Moore; married Donna Holland; children: Remington. **Educ:** Cent Conn State, Britain CT, BA Math, Rutgers Law Sch, Newark NJ, JD. **Career:** Wash DC, coun, 1973-76; Dept Pub Advocate, Newark NJ, asst dep pub defender; City E Orange, corp coun, 1980-81; Brown & Manns, Newark NJ, lawyer, 1981-83; Law Officers Robert L Brown, Newark NJ, lawyer, 1984-; City Orange NJ, mayor, 1984; Comm Judiciary, House Rep, US Cong; Rutgers Univ, Newark NJ, math instr. **Orgs:** NJ Trial Lawyers Asn; NJ Bar Asn; Nat Criminal Defense; Am Bar Asn; Criminal Trial Lawyers NJ; Essex Co Bar Asn; Roscoe Pound Found; NAACP; Omega Psi Phi Fraternity Inc. **Honors/Awds:** Outstanding Contribs Govt, Hillside Valley Presbyterian Church, 1988; Nat Tribute Black Heritage, Prince Hall Grand Lodge Masons; Congratulations Award, Alif Muhammad Prods, 1988; Resolution Congratulations, E Orange City Coun, 1988; featured Jet Mag, Newark Star-Ledger, Orange Transcript, Greater News Perspectus.

BROWN, RODGER L, JR.
Manager. **Personal:** Born Aug 15, 1955, Petersburg, VA. **Educ:** Boston Col, BA, 1977; MIT, 1982. **Career:** IBM, mkt rep, 1977-79; Sittler Assoc, consult, 1979-80; United S End & Lower Roxbury Develop Corp, proj mgr, 1980-83; Greater Boston Community Develop, proj mgr, 1983-86; Cruz Develop Co, develop proj mgr, 1986, vpres, currently; Mintz, Levin, Cohn, Rerries Glousky & Popeo, sr prof; Winn Develop Co, Inc, sr vpres, currently. **Orgs:** MA Minority Develop Assoc; Builder Assoc Greater Boston; Citizens Housing & Planning Assoc. **Honors/Awds:** US Dept of Housing & Urban Development Minority Fellowship, 1982. **Business Addr:** Sr Vice President, Winn Development, 6 Faneuil Hall Mkt pl, Boston, MA 02119, **Business Phone:** (617)742-4500.*

BROWN, RODNEY W
Executive. **Personal:** Son of Sidney and Elise. **Career:** Shelly's Delaware Inc, Wilmington, DE, chief exec. **Orgs:** Minority Contractors Asn; Delaware Minority Bus Asn; Nat Asn Advan Colored People; United Meth Men; New Castle City Chamber Com. **Business Addr:** Chief Executive, Shelly, 610 W 8th St, Wilmington, DE 19801, **Business Phone:** (302)656-3337.

BROWN, RONALD D.
Chief executive officer, president (organization). **Educ:** Morehouse Col; Columbia Univ. **Career:** Variant Group LLC; SYNAVANT; IMS Health Strategic Technologies; Atlanta Life Financial Group, pres & chief exec officer, 2004-. **Orgs:** Bd mem, Ga Power Co; bd mem, Metro Atlanta Chamber Com; African Amer Exp Fund; Emroy Hosp Visitors Comt; bd dir, Atlanta Bus League. **Honors/Awds:** Entrepreneur of the Year Award, Wall St Proj, 2005; Honorary Paramount Chief Title, Christian Fel Ministries, 2005. **Special Achievements:** Atlanta Business Chronicle selected as 100 Most Influential Atlantans in 2006. **Business Phone:** (404)659-2100.*

BROWN, RONALD EDWARD
Educator. **Personal:** Born May 5, 1952, Springfield, IL; son of Pearl Brown; married Lillie Sloan, Aug 24, 1974; children: Khari, Katura. **Educ:** Lincoln Land Community Col, Springfield, IL, AA, 1972; Southern Ill Univ, Carbondale, IL, BA, 1974; Univ Mich, Ann Arbor, MI, MA, 1976, PhD, 1984; attended 1985. **Career:** Eastern Michigan Univ, Ypsilanti, MI, assoc prof; Wayne State Univ, Col Libr Arts, assoc prof polit sci. **Orgs:** Am Polit Sci Asn, 1984-; Nat Asn Black Polit Scientists, 1984-; asst supt, Sunday Sch Bethel AME Church, 1987-. **Honors/Awds:** Research Grant, Social Sci Res Coun, 1991-92; Research Grant, Nat Sci Found, 1989-91; Research Grant, Nat Inst Aging, 1988-90. *

BROWN, DR. RONALD PAUL
Educator, school administrator, consultant. **Personal:** Born Mar 19, 1938, Ravenna, OH; son of Paul L and Agnes L Ervin; married Joyce Anita Jones; children: Todd Mason, Lisa Kay & Paula Marie. **Educ:** Univ Akron, BS, 1967, MS, 1969, PhD, 1974. **Career:** Univ Akron, coord develop serv & stud adv, 1969-74; Cuyahoga County Bd Mental Retardation, dir habilitation serv, 1974-80; Cuyahoga County Summit, admin asst, 1981-84; Kent State Univ, asst to dean for minority & women affairs, 1984-87; Kent State Univ Ashtabula Campus, asst dean & asst prof counr educ, 1987-92, asst prof Pan Africa studies & dir multi cultural affairs, 1992-98; Joparo Co, owner, currently. **Orgs:** Univ Akron Alumni Coun, 1978-81; bd trustee, Cuyahoga Valley Mental Health, 1982-84; Nat Cert Counr Nat Bd Cert Coun, 1984; bd trustee, St Paul Am Methodist Episcopal Church, 1978-; bd dir, Alpha Homes, 1982-; chap secy, Nat Old Timers, 1984-87; treas, Black Alumni Asn, 1987-; vpres, Community Action Coun, Ashtabula, OH; adv bd mem, Ashtabula Salvation Army; dir, Community Resource Econ Comm, Ashtabula; bd trustee, 1990, adv bd, 1992, Home Safe, 1990; adv bd, Pvt Indust Coun, 1990; bd dir, First Merit Bank, 1990-97; pres, Jobs for Ohio Graduates, 1992; bd adv, Goodwill Indust; consult & coordr, Brother to Brother Proj, 2002; E Akron Community House, 2000-; Area Aging Adv Bd, 2003; Bd Summit County, Am Cancer Control Unit; chair, Proj Blueprint Advisory Comt, 2009. **Honors/Awds:** Outstanding Service Award, Eta Tau Lambda, 1983; Key to the City of Ashtabula, Ohio, 1990; Developed African American Speaker Series, Ashtabula Campus, 1990; Man of the Year, Nat Asn Advan Colored People, 1991, 1995. **Military Serv:** AUS, 1961-63. **Business Addr:** Owner, Joparo Company, 951 Kickapoo Ave, PO Box 9301, Akron, OH 44305, **Business Phone:** (330)794-8942.

BROWN, RONALD WELLINGTON
Entrepreneur, lawyer, consultant. **Personal:** Born Oct 17, 1945, Elizabeth, NJ; son of Leroy and Mollie; married Geraldine Reed Brown, Aug 15, 1972; children: Kimberly & Michael. **Educ:** Rutgers Univ, BA, hist, 1967; Harvard Law Sch, JD, 1971; Harvard Grad Sch Bus Admin, MBA, 1973. **Career:** ITT World Headquarters, staff coun, 1973-85; Motion Picture Asn Am, N Am & Commonwealth Opers, dir, 1985-87; NJ Transit Corp, Real Estate Develop & Property Mgt, dir, 1988; Sammy Davis Jr Nat Liver Inst Inc, exec vpres, admin, chief oper officer, 1988-91; Reed-Brown Consult Group, exec vpres & managing dir, 1991-; BRS&W Prod, pres, chief oper officer, co-founder, 1992-94; Spooner & Burnett, Atty Law, coun, 1994-97; NorJean Entertainment Mgt, Bus Affairs, dir, 1996-; W Frye & Assocs PC, sr consult, spec projects mgr, 1998-; W F Golf Enterprises, chief oper officer, 1999-; Omega Golf Centers Inc, chief oper officer, 2001-.

Orgs: Am Arbitration Asn, Law Comn, Int Law Sect, 1981-; Prosperity NJ, Small Bus Comn, 1996-; chair, NJ United Minority Bus Brain Trust, 1997-; Township Montclair, Planning Bd, 1997-; bd educ rep trustee, Dr Martin Luther King Jr Scholar Comn; Omega Psi Phi Fraternity, Eta Pi Chap; Supplier Diversity Develop Comn, Bd Pub Utilities, State NJ. **Honors/Awds:** Advocate of the Year, United States Small Bus Admin, Minority Small Bus, 1999. **Special Achievements:** Author, "The New International Government Procurement Code Under GATT", NY State Bar Journal, 1981; Int Bar Asn, Int Law Symposium, Toronto Canada, speaker, 1983; Second OECD Symposium, Special Session of the Comt for Info, Computer & Communications Policy, one of four private sector reps on US delegation, London England, 1983; "Counseling Clients in Intl Business Transactions: Substance, Procedure, and Organization", principal organizer, 1984; Section of Int Law and Practice, annual meeting chair, 1984; publications include: "Economic and Trade Related Aspects of Transborder Data Flow: Elements of a Code for Transnational Commerce", The Northwestern Journal of International Law and Business, 1984; "Computers, Communications, and Information Exchange", Toward A Law of Global Networks, American Bar Assn Section of Science and Technology, 1985; "Protection of Intellectual Property and Promotion of International Trade: Piracy Effects and Policy Choices," Atwater International Conference, 1986; "Management Models Exist and Should be Adapted for Improving Environmental Equity Coordination at the Federal, State, and Local Levels", Symposium on Health Research and Needs to Ensure Environmental Justice, 1994; Sessions on Int Trade, The White House Conference on Small Business, NJ, moderator, 1995; NJ Public Policy Research Institute, Strategic Planning Session, facilitator, 1995; New Jersey Bus-Educ Summit, participant, 1996; Mayor's Administrative Retreat for Cabinet Heads, City of Trenton, NJ, facilitator, 1996. **Business Addr:** Executive Vice President, Managing Director, The Reed-Brown Consulting Group, 180 Union St, Montclair, NJ 07042-2125, **Business Phone:** (973)509-8243.

BROWN, ROOSEVELT LAWAYNE
Baseball player. **Personal:** Born Aug 3, 1975, Vicksburg, MS; married Ronita; children: Roosevelt Jr & Rosario. **Career:** Player (retired); Coach; GCL Braves, 1993; Idhao falls, 1994; Eugena, 1995; kane co, 1996-97; lowa, 1998-01; Chicago Cubs, outfielder, 1999-02, 2005; Orix, 2003-05; Atlanta Falcons, 2005; Mississippi Braves, hitting coach, currently. *

BROWN, DR. ROSCOE C.
College administrator, television show host, executive director. **Personal:** Born Mar 9, 1922, Washington, DC; divorced; children: Doris, Diane, Dennis & Donald. **Educ:** Springfield Col, MA, BS, 1943; NY Univ, MA, 1949, PhD, 1951. **Career:** West Va State Col, instr phys educ, 1947-48; NY Univ, prof educ, 1950-77; Bronx Community Col, pres, 1977-93; City Univ NY, Grad Sch & Univ Ctr, Ctr Urban Educ Policy, dir, currently; TV & Radio Prog: "Black Arts"; "Soul of Reason"; "Black Letters"; "A Black Perspective"; "African American Legends", host, currently. **Orgs:** Dir, Inst Afro-Am Affairs; pres, One Hundred Black Men; Boys & Girls Clubs Am; Jackie Robinson Found & Libraries Future; founding mem, Am Col Sports Med. **Honors/Awds:** Distinguished Alumni Award, Springfield Col, 1973; Distinguished Alumni Award, NY Univ, 1973; Emmy Award, 1973; Bronx Museums Education Award, 1990; Nat Asn for Sports & Physical Education Hall of Fame. **Special Achievements:** Co-ed, Negro Almanac, 1967; co-auth, Classical Studies Phys Activity, 1968; co-auth, New Perspectives Man Action, 1969; co-auth, Black Culture Quib, 1971, 1973; auth of more than 50 articles on educ, black studies,sports, & phys educ & phys fitness. **Military Serv:** US Air Force, 1943-45; Distinguished Flying Cross; Air Medal. **Business Phone:** (212)817-8280.

BROWN, ROSE DENISE
Banker. **Personal:** Born in Chicago, IL; daughter of Willie and Maggie Williams. **Educ:** Cornell Col, BS, 1979. **Career:** Continental Bank, acct adminr & sect mgr, documentation specialist, documentation supvr, loan documentation coordr, collateral analyst, job analyst, opers officer. **Orgs:** Nat Asn Urban Bankers; bd mem, Continental Bank Found; Com Finance Asn, Midwest Chap. **Special Achievements:** "Speaking of People," Ebony, 1992.

BROWN, DR. ROY HERSHEL
Educator, physician. **Personal:** Born Aug 2, 1924, Jamaica; married Lilly Berlinger; children: Geraldine, Lawrence, Christopher, Anthony & Andrew. **Educ:** Fordham Col, BS, 1945; Univ Zurich Med Sch, MD, 1956; NY Dip Med Lic,1960; Dip Phys Med & Rehab, 1971. **Career:** Pvt pract, 1960-66; PM&R, dipl, asst prof, 1968-; Off Voc Rehab, consult,1975-; Jamaica Hosp, dept rehab med, 1985; Total Health HMO, sr vpres, currently. **Orgs:** Bd trustee, Barlow Sch; Suffolk Co Med Soc; Nat Med Asn; Am Acad Phys Med & Rehab; AAAS; NY Soc PMYR; Am Geriat Soc. **Honors/Awds:** Publ "Innovative Aspect of Stroke Prgm In Ghetto" 1971, "The Role of MedSch in a Ghetto Population" 1971. **Business Addr:** Senior Vice President, Total Health HMO, 1010 Northern Blvd, Great Neck, NY 11021.*

BROWN, RUBEN PERNELL
Football player. **Personal:** Born Feb 13, 1972, Lynchburg, VA; married Kenia; children: Solomon and Benjamin & Isabelle. **Educ:** Pittsburgh Univ, phys educ. **Career:** Buffalo Bills, guard, 1995-03; Chicago Bears, guard, 2004-07. **Orgs:** Founder, Ruben Run Found., 2001. **Honors/Awds:** Pro Bowl, 1996, 1997, 1998, 1999, 2000, 2001, 2002, 2003, 2004, 2007; first-team All-American, American Football Coaches Association; Honorable Mention All-American, Football News; Virginia Male Athlete-of-the-Year, 1990. **Business Addr:** Founder, Ruben Brown Foundation, 712 Main St, Buffalo, NY 14202-1720.*

BROWN, DR. RUBY EDMONIA
Psychologist. **Personal:** Born Sep 5, 1943, Pittsburgh, PA; married Ephriam Wolfolk Jr; children: Kenneth, Kevin, Keith. **Educ:** Univ CO, BA, 1981; Univ OR, MS, 1982; Univ OR, PhD, 1987; Woodburn Comn Ment Health Ctr, Psych Intern, 1986. **Career:** Pikes Peak Ment Health Ctr, ment health therapist, 1976-81; Univ of OR, teaching asst, instr, 1981-85; Woodburn Comn Ment Health Ctr, intern, psych, 1985; Arlington Community Resilience Project, project dir, currently. **Orgs:** Alumni & Friend Stud Year Univ Colo, 1981; Phi Betta Kappa Hon Soc; Am Psych Assoc; assoc mem, Ctr Study Women; Minority Fed Am Psychol Assoc, 1981-84; Grad Teaching Fed Univ Ore, 1981-85; Res Grant Ctr Study Women Univ Ore, 1987; Jane Grant Dissertation Fed Univ Ore, 1987.

BROWN, RUBYE GOLSBY
Educator, elementary school teacher. **Personal:** Born Aug 20, 1923, Birmingham, AL; daughter of Clifford Golsby (deceased) and Augusta B Blalock Johnson (deceased); married Robert L, Jan 2, 1947; children: Harlean, Charles, Louis, Carson, Gloria, Robin & Debbie. **Educ:** Youngstown State Univ, BA, 1953, MD, 1981. **Career:** Ft Leonard-Wood, dept head, 1959-60, substitute teacher, 1960-61; Renanos' Jewelery, credit mgr, 1962-64; Mahoning Co Treas, dept treas, 1965-77; Princeton Sch, teacher, 1977; Youngstown Pub Sch, sch teacher, 1977-90; Round Rock Independent Sch Dist, Round Rock, TX, high sch teacher, 1991-. **Orgs:** Youngstown Bd Educ, 1977; comt mem, State Health Bd, 1979-88; bd mem,State Health, Dept Ohio, 1980; Am Univ Women, 1981-; Red Cross; bd mem,City Cedar Park, 1999; vpres, trustee, exec bd, Internal Mgt Proj Rev; bd trustee, Educ Opportunity Youngstown; vice-chmn, Consumer Protect Agency; Nat Asn Adv Colored People; vpres, Community Action Agency; Cavelle Club; bd dirs, Negro Bus & Prof Club; Planning & Develop State Health Dept;chair, CAC; trustee, Health Syst Agency, E Ohio Valley; Nat Coun Negro Women; exec comt mem, Dem party; pres, Mahoning County Court-Watch; PoliceTask Force. **Honors/Awds:** Cert, Community Involvement & Vol Work, Jr Civic League, 1986; Appointed by Gov, State Health Bd, Columbus, OH, 1986; Only Black 19th Dist, DelPres Carter; Community Serv, Cong Carney Award. **Home Addr:** 1700 Tracy Miller Ln, Cedar Park, TX 78613-3565. *

BROWN, RUSHIA (YERUSHIA BROWN)
Basketball player. **Personal:** Born May 5, 1972; daughter of Angie Brown. **Educ:** Furman, BA, sociol, 1994. **Career:** Player (retired); president; Cleveland Rockers, forward & ctr, 1997-02; Charlotte Sting, forward; Overtime Basketball Acad, pres, 2007-. **Honors/Awds:** Player of the Yr, Women's Natl Basketball Assn. **Special Achievements:** Conf Most Valuable Player. *

BROWN, SHARON MARJORIE REVELS
Media executive. **Personal:** Born Sep 26, 1938, Detroit, MI. **Educ:** Fisk Univ, 1953-57; Wayne State Univ, BA, 1957-60; Col Educ, post-degree work, 1960-61; Mich Bd Pub Instrn, Teaching Cert 1961; Wayne State Univ, 1966. **Career:** Detroit Pub Sch Hutchins Jr HS, instr 1961-70; Hutchins Jr HS, tchr coord, 1964-65; Univ MI, educ field consult, 1969-70; Univ Mich, resources Ctr Coord 1970-71; WKBD-TV, news & pub affairs sv, 1972-74; WXYZ-TV, comm rel dir, 1974. **Orgs:** Publicity com Freedom Fund Dinner NAACP, 1977; bd dir, Nat Coun Alcholism; Homes Black Children; Educ Comn New Detroit Inc; Urban Affairs Forum; Greater Detroit C of C; Keep Detroit Beautiful Community; Publicity Community United Negro Col Fund; Women's Advertising Club; Am Women Radio & TV; host "Ethnit-City"; chmn, Publicity Com Afro-Am Mus Detroit; Alpha Epsilon Rho; Mich Speech Asn. **Honors/Awds:** Frat sweetheart Kappa Alpha & Psi, 1958-59; 3rd pl winner scholarship contest Miss Marracci Beauty-Talent Pageant Shriners.

BROWN, SHEILA R.
Dentist. **Educ:** DDS. **Career:** Nat Dent Asn, treas, 2001; , pvt prac, gen dentist, currently. **Orgs:** Nat Dent Asn. *

BROWN, SHERMAN L.
Executive. **Personal:** Born Nov 18, 1943, Portland, OR; son of Bennie; married Mable J; children: Sherman Jr, Stephen, Stanton. **Educ:** BS, 1966; MSW, 1968. **Career:** St Elizabeth Hosp, psychiatric social worker, 1966-67; Comm Action Agency, urban planner, 1966-68; James Weldon Johnson Comm Ctr, prog dir, 1968-70; Chase Manhattan Bank, vice pres, 1970-80; MCAP Group Ltd, pres, currently. **Orgs:** Bd mem, United Neighborhood Houses; bd mem, Settlement Housing Fund; founder & bd mem, Queens Youth Fedn NY; Bankers Urban Affairs Com, Kappa Alpha Psi Frat; chmn bd dir, Neighborhood Housing Serv Jamaica Inc; bd mem, S Jamaica Restoration Devel Corp; vice pres bd, Bronx River Comm Ctr; bd mem, Nat Scholarship Serv Fund for Negro Students; Univ S Civ Rights Comm; chmn bd, Queens Urban League; bd mem, NAHRO Washington DC; bd mem, Nat Housing Conf Bd Washington DC; bd mem, United Black Men of Queens Co; Nat Asn of Redevelopment Officials; chmn bd, Queens Co Overall Econ Devel Corp; Instr, Urban Econ Amer Inst of Banking; lectr, Banks on Corporate Social Responsibility; lectr, Medgar Evers Col. **Honors/Awds:** Black Achiever in Industry Award, Harlem YMCA, 1973; Professional Serv Award, NY Chamber of Commerce, 1973. **Business Addr:** President, MCAP Group Ltd, 8950 164th St Suite 2B, Citibank Bldg, Jamaica, NY 11432.*

BROWN, SIMON F.
School administrator. **Personal:** Born Sep 17, 1952, Norristown, PA; son of Albert and Lessie Forbes; married LaVerne Ransom Brown, Mar 17, 1972; children: LaSia, Kevin. **Educ:** Goshen Col, BA, commun, 1974; Univ Houston, MA, higher educ admin, 1986. **Career:** Elkhart County Employment & Training Admin, Elkhart, coordr oper, 1974-77; St Joseph Hosp, mgr, AA/EEO employee rels, 1977-79; Univ Houston, asst pres affirmative action/EEO, 1979-89; Univ Med & Dent, Newark, NJ, assoc vpres, AA/EEO, 1989-95; Univ Va, Title IX coordr, Equal Opportunity Progs Officer, 1995-. **Orgs:** Am Asn Affirmative Action, 1975; Exec comt mem, secy, Ensemble Theatre Co, 1989; Newark Mus Coun, 1990. **Business Addr:** Title IX Coordinator, University Virginia, Equal Opportunity Progs Off, Washington Hall E Range, PO Box 400219, Charlottesville, VA 22904-4219, **Business Phone:** (434)924-3200.*

BROWN, STANLEY DONOVAN
Government official. **Personal:** Born Feb 4, 1933, Washington, DC; married Helen Hampton; children: Kevin, Kimberly & Karla. **Educ:** Southeastern Univ, BS, BA, 1962; Am Univ, attended 1968. **Career:** Dept Army, supr, comput specialist; Off Secy Defense, spec progs dir, 1984-; Town of Glenarden, mayor, 1983-85. **Orgs:** Councilman, Town Glenarden, 1967-73; chmn, Glenarden Housing Authority 1974-75; councilman, Town of Glenarden, 1975-78. **Honors/Awds:** Recognition Civic Involvement, MD House Deleg, 1978; Certificate of Apppreciation, Boys Scouts Am, 1980; Outstanding Loaned Exec, CFC Dept Army, 1984; Citizen of the Year, Omega Psi Phi Frat, 1984. **Military Serv:** USN quartermaster 2nd class, 4 years; Korean Conflict Medal, Good Conduct Medal, 1957. **Home Addr:** 7916 Grant Dr, Glenarden, MD 20706. **Business Addr:** Mayor, Town of Glenarden, 8600 Glenarden Pkwy, Glenarden, MD 20706.*

BROWN, TARRIK JUMAAN
Baseball player, baseball executive. **Personal:** Born Dec 25, 1973, Goleta, CA. **Educ:** Benetton Treviso. **Career:** Baseball player (retired), coach; Seattle Mariners, 1999; Chicago Cubs, out fielder, 2000; New York Mets, 2000; Los Angeles Dodgers, 2002-03; Ogden Raptors, coach, 2006. **Honors/Awds:** Northern League All-Star, 2001.

BROWN, THOMAS EDISON, JR.
Manager, police officer, sheriff. **Personal:** Born Aug 22, 1952, Atlanta, GA; son of Rosa B Branham and Thomas E Sr; married Yolanda Smith Brown, Sep 22, 1978; children: Brittany Joy, Justin Thomas. **Educ:** DeKalb Community Col, Clarkston, GA, emergency med serv, 1978, fire sci, 1980; Brenau Prof Col, BS, pub admin. **Career:** Atlanta Fire Bur, dep fire chief, 1972-85; DeKalb C Pub Safety, Decatur, GA, Countys Police, supv, Fire, supv, Emergency Med Servs, supv, 911 Communications Ctr, supv, Animal Control Div, supv, Emergency Mgt Homeland Security, supv, fire chief, 1985-90, dir pub safety, 1990-, sheriff, currently. **Orgs:** Int Asn Fire Chiefs, 1983-; Nat Fire Protection Asn, 1985-; Int Asn Black Prof Firefighters, 1986-; Nat Forum Black Pub Admin, 1986-; 100 Black Men Atlanta, 1988-; S Decatur Kiwanis, 1988-; Int Asn Chiefs Police, 1990-; Nat Orgn Black Law Enforcement Execs, 1990-; DeKalb Rape Crisis Bd; Decatur Rotary Club. **Honors/Awds:** Outstanding Alumnus, DeKalb Community Col, 1986; Outstanding Serv Award, Toney Gardens Civic Asn, 1986; Alumni of the Year, 2001. **Special Achievements:** 5th Fire Chief in the history of the DeKalb County. **Business Addr:** Sheriff, Director, DeKalb County Public Safety, Pub Safety Dept, 3630 Camp Cir, Atlanta, GA 30303.*

BROWN, TIMOTHY DONELL
Football player. **Personal:** Born Jul 22, 1966, Dallas, TX. **Educ:** Univ Notre Dame, sociol. **Career:** Football player (retired); Los Angeles Raiders, wide receiver, 1988-94; Oakland Raiders, wide receiver, 1995-2003; Tampa Bay Buccaneers, 2004; Drive for Diversity prog, Nat Asn Stock Car Auto Racing. **Honors/Awds:** First team All-Am, 1986-87; Heisman Trophy, 1986-87; Walter Camp Award, 1987; Pro Bowl, 1988, 1991, 1993-95, 1997, 2001.

BROWN, TODD
Administrator, executive. **Career:** kraft foods N Am, exec vpres, e Com div, pres; Food com, bd; Advo Inc, bd; Cleveland bank, chmn; Chicago & detroit bank, chmn; ShoreBank Corp, dir, 2000-03, vchmn, 2003-. **Orgs:** Kraft's African Am Coun; bd mem, Johnson Diversey Inc; bd mem, Colgate Univ; bd mem, Natl Charter Sch Inst; mem, Jessie Owens Found; ShoreBank Corp mgt comt. **Business Phone:** 800-669-7725.*

BROWN, TODD C.
Executive. **Personal:** Born Jun 12, 1949; married Sheryl; children: daughter. **Educ:** Colgate Univ, BA, sociol; Columbia Univ, MA,

higher educ admin; Wharton Grad Sch, MBA, mkg. **Career:** ALANA Cult Ctr, dir; Colgate Univ, asst dean students; Gen Foods, asst prod mgr; Wharton Grad Sch, Univ Pa, dir stud servs; Kraft Foods Inc, Desserts & Snacks Div, exec vpres & gen mgr, 1996-97, Beverages & Desserts Div, gen mgr, 1997-98, Food Servs Div, pres, 1998-00, e-Com Div, pres, 2001-03; ADVO Inc, dir, 2000-; JDI, dir, 2001-; Holdings Inc, dir, 2002-; ShoreBank Corp, vice chmn, 2003-; ShoreBank's Banking Opers, Chicago, chmn bd, currently; ShoreBank Cleveland, chmn bd. **Orgs:** Exec Leadership Coun; bd mem, JohnsonDiversey. *

BROWN, TOMMIE FLORENCE
Educator. **Personal:** Born Jun 25, 1934, Rome, GA. **Educ:** Dillard Univ, BA, 1957; Atlanta Univ, Sch Social Work, 1957; Wash Univ, MSW, St Louis, Mo,1964; Columbia Univ, DSW, 1984, PhD. **Career:** Educator(retired), Tenn House Representative; Tenn Dept Public Welfare, child welfare worker, 1957-64, case worker, supvr & dir training, 1954-71; Univ Tenn Chatanooga, asst prof sociol, 1971-73, dir human serv, 1977-82, SOCW & proj dir, dept head, 1977-82, assoc prof, 1982; Tenn House Representatives, Chatanooga, 1992-. **Orgs:** Nat Asn Social Workers, nat sec, 1972-74; bd mem, Chattanooga Psych Ctr, 1982-; Chattanooga Branch, NAACP, 1964-; bd mem, Chattanooga Model Cities Prog, 1969-73; elected comnr, Chattanooga/Hamilton Metro Charter; League Women Voters, 1968-70; steering commt, Urban Forum, 1980-81; mem, Joint Lottery Scholar Comt; mem, Joint Select Comt Pensions & Insurance; mem, House Domestic Relations Subcomt; co-founder, Chattanooga chap Nat Polit Cong Black Women; Hamilton County Dem Women's Club; Pi Omega Chap Alpha Kappa Alpha Sorority. **Honors/Awds:** Woman of the Year Award, Alpha Kappa Alpha, Pi Omega Chap, 1968-69; Social Worker of the Year, SE Tenn Chap, Nat Asn Social Workers, 1970; Nat Social Worker of the Year, Nat Asn Social Workers Inc, 1970; Tommie Brown Day, City of Chattanooga, 1970; Distinguished Alumni Award, Wash Univ, St Louis, 1971. **Home Addr:** 603 N Highland Pk, Chattanooga, TN 37404. **Business Addr:** Tenn House Representatives, 36 Legislative Plz, Nashville, TN 37243-0128, **Business Phone:** (615)741-4374.

BROWN, TONY
Executive. **Educ:** Am Int Col, Springfield, Mass, BA. **Career:** QMS Inc, exec dir; United Technologies Automotive, vpres supply mgt; Ford Motor Co, Ford Purchasing Global Strategic Planning & Process Leadership, dir, Mfg Procurement Opers, exec dir, vpres global purchasing, 2002-04, sr vpres global purchasing, 2004-. **Orgs:** Mem & co-chair, Procurement Coun, US Hispanic Chamber Com. **Honors/Awds:** Keeper of the Dream, Nat Action Network. **Business Addr:** Senior Vice president of Global Purchasing, Ford Motor Company, PO Box 1899, Dearborn, MI 48121, **Business Phone:** (313)322-3000.*

BROWN, TONY
Columnist, television producer, educator. **Personal:** Born Apr 11, 1933, Charleston, WV; son of Royal and Catherine; divorced; children: Byron Anthony. **Educ:** Wayne State Univ, BA, sociol, 1959; Wayne State Univ, MSW, 1961; Univ Mich, LLD, 1975. **Career:** Black J Nat Educ TV, exec producer; Detroit Courier, city ed; numerous mag, pub & ed; various TV shows, host & moderator; Howard Univ Sch Commun, first dean prof & founder; Howard Univ, commun Conf; Cent Wash State Univ, visiting prof; Tony Brown Prods, founder & pres, 1977-; Tony Brown's Jour, exec producer & host, 1978-; Tony Brown Prod, Inc, founder, currently. **Orgs:** Founder & pres, Video Duplication Ctr, 1986; Founder & chmn, Buy Freedom Comm, 1985; Nat Asn Black Media Producers; Nat Asn Black TV & Film Producers; bd govs, Nat Commun Coun; adv bd, Nat Coun Black Studies; chmn bd, WHUR-FM radio, 1971-74; bd mem, Nat Cent Afro-Am Artists; Nat Black United Fund; Commun Comm Nat Inst Ment Health; bd dirs, Asn Study Afro-Am Life & Hist; bd dirs, Nat Bus League; bd dirs, Harvard Found; Nat Newspaper Pub Asn. **Honors/Awds:** Living Legends In Black, 1976; Nat Urban League Pub Serv Award, 1977; Int Key Women Of America Award, 1977; Communicator for Freedom Award, Operation PUSH, 1973; Frederick Douglass Liberation Award; Solomon Fuller Award, Am Psychiatric Asn, 1989; Community Service Award, Black Psychologists, 1988; Special Image Award, Beverly Hills/ Hollywood NAACP; first recipient of the Nat Director's Legacy Award, US Dept Commerce Minority Bus Develop Agency. **Special Achievements:** First Dean and Professor of Scripps/ Howard School of Journalism and Communication at Hampton University, Top 50 Nat Black & Newsmakers of Yr 1974, bestselling author, Black Americans Reference Book, 1976, 100 Most Influential Black Am Ebony Mag, producer and director of The White Girl (motion picture), 1989; First recipient of the National Director's Legacy Award for Journalism. **Military Serv:** AUS, corporal, 1953-55. **Business Addr:** Founder, Tony Brown Productions Inc, 2214 Frederick Douglass Blvd Suite 124, New York, NY 10026, **Business Phone:** (718)264-2226.

BROWN, TONY (ANTHONY WILLIAM BROWN)
Basketball player, basketball coach. **Personal:** Born Jul 29, 1960, Chicago, IL; married Exquilynn. **Educ:** Univ Ark, attended 1982. **Career:** Basketball player (retired), basketball coach; Ind Pacers, 1984-85; Chicago Bulls, 1985-86; NJ Nets, 1986-87; Houston Rockets, 1988-89; Milwaukee Bucks, 1988-90; Los Angeles Lakers, 1990-91; Utah Jazz, 1990-91; Los Angeles Clippers, 1991-92; Seattle Supersonics, 1991-92; CBA, 1992-94; Milwaukee Bucks, scout, 1994-97; Portland Trailblazers, asst coach, 1997-2001; Detroit Pistons, asst coach, 2001-03; Toronto Raptors, asst coach, 2003-04; Detroit Pistons, asst coach, 2001-03; Boston Celtics, asst coach, 2004-07; Milwaukee Bucks, asst coach, 2007. **Orgs:** Invited to the Midwest Summer League. **Home Addr:** 5420 W Van Buren St, Chicago, IL 60644, **Home Phone:** (773)378-5193.

BROWN, TONY
Executive, president (organization). **Personal:** Born Mar 1, 1961, Phoenix, AZ; married Janet, Mar 1, 1990; children: 2. **Educ:** Ariz State Univ, attended 1979; Northern Ariz Univ, attended 1981. **Career:** Circles Rec, asst mgr, 1981-82; KUKQ AM Radio, Tempe, AZ, prom dir, 1982-85; Best Entertainment & Recreation, consult, 1982-92; Marshall Brown & Assocs, consult, 1982-92; Am Multi-Cinema Inc, mgr, 1985-88; Phoenix Suns Pro Basketball, community rels dir, 1990-91; Ariz Black Pages Inc, pres, 1992; Targeted Media Commun Inc, pres & creative dir, 1993-. **Orgs:** Bd mem, Volunteer Ctr Ariz, 1990-92; comt chair, Pub Rels Soc Am, 1991; bd mem, Black Theatre Troupe, 1991-96; bd mem, Am Heart Asn Ariz, 1991-93. **Honors/Awds:** Image Award, Maricopa C Nat Asn Advan Colored People, 1996. **Business Phone:** (602)230-8161.

BROWN, TROY (TROY FITZGERALD BROWN)
Football player. **Personal:** Born Jul 2, 1971, Barnwell, SC; married Kimberly; children: Sir'mon & SaanJay. **Educ:** Marshall Univ, comput Sci. **Career:** Football player (retired); New Eng Patriots, wide receiver, 1993-07. **Orgs:** Spokesperson, United Way. **Honors/Awds:** Staples Star of the Game, 1997; Miller Lite Player of the Game, 1997-01; All-Iron Award, 2002; Ron Burton Community Serv Award, 2004; Distinguished Alumni award, 2006. **Special Achievements:** Became the first Marshall University product to ever play for the Patriots.

BROWN, TROY FITZGERALD. **See BROWN, TROY.**

BROWN, TYRONE W.
Musician, composer, educator. **Personal:** Born Feb 1, 1940, Philadelphia, PA; son of Colbert and Rebecca. **Educ:** Berklee Sch Music, Boston, MA, cert arranging & compos, cert orchestration & mod harmony. **Career:** Pep's Show Bar, house bassist, 1964-69; Hist Jazz Lect & Concert Tours, staff bassist, 1968-71; Audi Prod TV Com Prod, staff bassist, 1970-72; Ill State Univ, instr jazz, 1971; Brigham Young Univ, instr jazz, 1972; Bellermine Col, instr jazz, 1975; Model Cities Cult Arts Prog, instr, 1972-74; Nat Endowment Arts, fel, 1983; 25th Anniversary Moers Ger Jazz Festival, Solo Bass Concert, 1996; Philadelphia Orchestra, guest artist, 1999; Pa Coun, Arts Artistic Excellence Jazz Compos, fel, 2001; Nirvana Music Co, owner & publ; PEW fel Arts, fel compos, 2003; Independence Found, fel compos, 2005; Moon of the Falling Leaves, 2008. **Orgs:** Dir, Music Dept, Model Cities Cult Arts Prog, 1974. **Honors/Awds:** First place, Fred Miles Publication Musicians Poll, 1974; "Best Acoustic Bass" honors, Jazz Philadelphia Mag Readers Choice Poll, 1993, 1994. **Special Achievements:** Thirty five recorded albums; 2 gold albums; performed 6 grant-sponsored concerts. **Home Addr:** 1510 St James Pl, Abington, PA 19001, **Home Phone:** (215)657-4585.

BROWN, DR. UZEE, JR.
Composer, educator, singer. **Personal:** Born 1950, Cowpens, SC. **Educ:** Morehouse Col, BA, 1972; Bowling Green State Univ, MMus, 1974; Univ Mich, MMus, 1978, DMA, 1980. **Career:** Clark Atlanta Univ, dept music chair, 1970-80; Opera singer, 1972-;Morehouse Col, Dept music, prof & chmn, 2002-; Ebenezer Baptist Church, pres, currently. **Orgs:** Co-founder, chair, bd dirs, Onyx Opera Atlanta, 1988-; Nat Asn Negro Musicians, pres, 1996-2002; pres, Nat Asn Negro Musicians. **Honors/Awds:** Outstanding Musical Dir & Arranger, Audelco Award in Black Theatre, Zion,1992; Award study at Graz Conservatory, Austria & Univ Siena in Italy. **Special Achievements:** Published composer and arranger, having written the musical prologue for Spike Lee's SCHOOL DAZE; Outstanding musical director and arranger; Audelco Award, 1992. **Business Addr:** Professor, Chairman, Morehouse College, Department of Music, Rm 306 Brawley Hall 830 Westview Dr SW, Atlanta, GA 30314, **Business Phone:** (404)215-2601.

BROWN, VENUS
Executive. **Career:** TBK V Enterprises LLC, owner, currently. **Business Addr:** Owner, TBK V Enterprises LLC, 20013 Roselawn Suite 1B, Detroit, MI 48221, **Business Phone:** (313)348-2848.*

BROWN, VIRGIL E
Judge. **Personal:** Son of Virgil E and Lurtissia; married JoAnn. **Educ:** Case Western Res Univ, BS, Physics, 1968; Cleveland State Univ, JD-cum laude, 1974. **Career:** Gen Elec, engr; Cleveland Growth Asn, consult; Cleveland Bus League, chmn; Shaker Heights Munic Ct, judge; Ohio Sch Dist, Dist 11, pvt pract, atty, currently. **Orgs:** Comner Ohio's Minority Financing Bd; Ohio Bus League. **Honors/Awds:** Negro Womens Bus & Prof Asn, Businessman of the Year Award, 1992. **Business Addr:** Attorney, State Board District 11, The Brown Bldg, 2136 Noble Rd, Cleveland Heights, OH 44112, **Business Phone:** (216)851-3304.

BROWN, VIVIAN
Television weathercaster, meteorologist. **Personal:** Born in Greenville, MA; daughter of William and ReJohnna. **Educ:** Jackson State Univ, BS, 1986. **Career:** The Weather Channel, meteorologist & prod specialist, 1986-88, broadcast apprentice, 1988-89, on-camera meteorologist, 1989-. **Orgs:** Am Meteorol Soc; Int Weather Asn; Alpha Kappa Alpha. **Honors/Awds:** 20th-Century Pioneer in Atmospheric Science, 1999. *

BROWN, DR. WALTER E
Executive. **Personal:** Born Mar 4, 1931, St Thomas, Virgin Islands of the United States; son of Arthur and Geraldine James; married Cheryl Ann Johnson, Dec 31, 1985; children: Walter E, Cheryl R & Jason Walter. **Educ:** City Col NY, BBA, 1958, MBA, 1961; NY Univ, MPA, 1972; Union Grad Sch, OH, PhD, 1978. **Career:** Shriro Inc NY, admin asst, 1956-58; Dept Health Govt VI St Croix, admin, 1962-71; NENA Comprehensive Health Serv Ctr, 1971-87; NY Univ HEOP, 1980-83; Hunter Col Sch Health Sci, City Univ NY, adj asst prof; Univ VI St Croix Campus, lectr, 1967-69; Univ Cincinnati Community Health Prog, 1973, Columbia Univ Sch Continuing Educ, 1973-75; Commercial Security Serv Ltd Inc, pres, currently. **Orgs:** Nat Asn Health Serv Exec; Am Pub Health Asn; Speaker House Del Nat Asn Neighborhood Health Ctrs, 1972-74; pres, Nat Asn Neighborhood Health Ctrs, 1974-75; pres, Nat Asn Neighborhood Health Ctr, 1975-76; pres, Pub Health Asn NY City, 1986-87; ed consult, J Pub Health Policy; Comt Ambulatory Care Am Hospital Asn, 1972-74; hon trustee, NY Infirmary Beekman Downtown Hosp NY, 1980-87. **Honors/ Awds:** 1st Morris De Castro Fellow, Govt VI St Thomas, 1970; Certificate of Appreciation for Outstanding Contribution to & Promotion of Community, Health Metro Boston Consumer Health Council Inc, 1975; Past President Award, Nat Asn Neighborhood Health Ctrs Inc, 1976; Past President Award, Pub Health Asn NY City, 1988. **Military Serv:** AUS, sgt e-5, 1956-58. **Business Addr:** President, Commercial Security Services Limited Inc, 70 Sub Base, St Croix, Virgin Islands of the United States 00820, **Business Phone:** (340)773-4100.

BROWN, WARREN ALOYSIUS
Journalist. **Personal:** Born Jan 17, 1948, New Orleans, LA; married Maryanne; children: Tony, Binta Niambi, Kafi Drexel. **Educ:** Xavier Univ La, BA, eng educ, 1969; Columbia Univ Grad Sch Journ, NY, MSJ, 1970. **Career:** New York Times, nat news desk aide, 1969-70; Garden City, LI, intern reporter, 1969; New Orleans States Item, city reporter, 1971; Johnson Publ Co Jet Mag, assoc ed, 1972; The Philadelphia Inquirer, gen assignment crime reporter, 1972-73; state correspondent, 1973-76; The Wash Post, fel, 1978; writer 3 books; African Am Wheels, sr ed; Automotive Rhythms, sr ed; The Wash Post, nat desktop writer, 1978-82, automotive writer, 1982-; Warton Sch Bus, fel, 1995. **Orgs:** Regular panelist, Am Black Forum, 1979; Xavier Univ Alumni Asn, 1969. **Honors/Awds:** Katharine Drexel Award, Xavier Univ, LA, 1969; New York Times Fellow, Ny Times, 1969-70; Award, MS Press Asn, 1971; Duke University Fellow, Wash Post 1978. **Business Addr:** Business Writer, Auto columnist, The Washington Post, 1150 15th St NW, Washington, DC 20071, **Business Phone:** (202)334-7685.*

BROWN, WESLEY ANTHONY
Naval officer, government official. **Personal:** Born Apr 3, 1927, Baltimore, MD; son of William and Rosetta Shepherd; married Crystal M; children: Willetta West, Carol Jackson, Wesley Jr, Gary. **Educ:** US Naval Acad, BSME, 1949; Rensselaer Polytechnic Inst, MCE, 1951. **Career:** Naval officer, government official (retired); Navy Civil Engr Corps Officer, pub works officer-in-charge construct, lt comdr, 1949-69; NY State Univ Construct Fund, proj mgr, 1969-74; NY State Dorm Authority, proj mgr, 1974-76; Howard Univ Office Univ Planning, facilities master planner, 1976-88; chmn/chief exec officer, Nat Bus Consult Inc, 1984-88. **Orgs:** alumni trustee, US Naval Acad, 1986-88; life mem, Alpha Phi Alpha Fraternity; Nat Naval Officers Asn; Naval Acad Alumni Asn; Asn Study Negro Life & Hist; Naval Inst; Navy League; Sigma Pi Phi Fraternity; delegate, US Serv Academies Nominations Bd, DC. **Honors/Awds:** The First Negro Graduate of Annapolis Tells His Story Saturday Evening Post 1949; article "Eleven Men of West Point" Negro History Bulletin. **Military Serv:** USN, lt comdr, 20 yrs; Antarctic Service, Korean Service World War II Victory, Navy Commendation for Achievement Medal, 1949-69. **Home Addr:** 6101 16th St NW Suite 805, Washington, DC 20011. *

BROWN, DR. WILLIAM, JR.
Physician, surgeon. **Personal:** Born Feb 5, 1935, New Haven, CT; son of William Sr and Viola P; married Sarah Robinson; children: Kirsten, Kecia, Kollette & Karlton. **Educ:** Univ CT, BA, 1957; Howard Univ Col Med, MD, 1961; Am Bd Family Pract, dipl, 1971-. **Career:** DC Gen Hosp, internship, 1961-62; Crownsville State Mental Hosp, resident psychiatrist, 1962-63; St Eliz Hosp, gen med officer, 1965; Howard Univ, Dept Family Pract, asst clin prof, 1972; pvt pract, physician. **Orgs:** Chi Delt Mu, 1960; nat bd mem, Nat Med Asn, 1965; DC Med Soc; Beta Sigma Gamma;

Med Chirurgical Soc DC; fel Am Acad Family Physicians. **Military Serv:** AUS, capt, 1963-65. **Business Addr:** Physician, Private Practice, 1210 Maple View Pl SE, Washington, DC 20020-5743.*

BROWN, WILLIAM H
Lawyer. **Personal:** Born Jan 19, 1928, Philadelphia, PA; son of William H Jr and Ethel L Washington; married D June Hairston, Jul 29, 1975; children: Michele Denise & Jeanne Marie. **Educ:** Temple Univ, BS, 1952; Univ Penn, Law Sch, JD, 1955. **Career:** Norris, Schmidt, Green, Harris & Higginbotham, assoc, 1956-62; Norris, Green, Harris & Brown, partner, 1962-64; Norris, Brown & Hall, partner, 1964-68; EEOC, comnr, 1968-69, chmn, 1969-73; Dep Dist Atty, chief frauds, 1968; Practicing Law Inst, fac mem, 1970-85; Schnader, Harrison, Segal & Lewis, partner, atty, 1974-; Nat Inst Trial Advocacy, fac mem, 1980-; Philadelphia Spec Invest Comn, chmn, 1985-86; Schnader Harrison Segal & Lewis LLP, sr coun, currently. **Orgs:** Regional Bd Dir, First Pa Banking & Trust Co, 1968-73; United Parcel Serv, 1983-; pres, mem, bd dir, Nat Black Child Develop Inst, 1986-; bd dir, Nat Sr Citizens Law Ctr, 1988-94; co-chair, mem exec comt, Lawyers Comt Civil Rights Under Law; founding mem, World Asn Lawyers; permanent mem, 3rd Cir Judicial Conf; mem, Alpha Phi Alpha; Am Fed & Pa Bar Asn; life mem Nat Bar Asn; Am Arbitration Asn; Am Law Inst; Inter-Am Bar Asn; Comn Higher Educ, Middle States Asn Col; Nat Sr Citizen's Law Ctr; mem, bd dir, Community Legal Servs; Nat Asn Advan Colored People Legal Defense & Educ Fund; fel, Am Bar Found; fel Int Acad Trial Lawyers; Philadelphia Diag & Rehab Ctr. **Honors/Awds:** Award of Recognition, Alpha Phi Alpha, 1969; Handbook Modern Personnel Admin, 1972; Fidelity Award, Philadelphia Bar Asn, 1990; Dr Edward S Cooper Award, Am Heart Asn, 1995; Whitney M Young Jr Leadership Award, Urban League Philadelphia, 1996; The Whitney North Seymoure Award, Lawyers Comt Civil Rights Under Law, 1996; William Schnader Pro bon Award, 1998; Philadelphia Nat Asn Advan Colored People Presidents Award. **Special Achievements:** Author of numerous articles. **Military Serv:** USAF, 1946-48; World War II Victory Medal. **Business Addr:** Senior Counsel, Schnader Harrison Segal & Lewis LLP, 1600 Mkt St Suite 3600, Philadelphia, PA 19103, **Business Phone:** (215)751-2000.

BROWN, WILLIAM J.
Association executive. **Personal:** Born May 17, 1917, Harrisburg, PA; widowed; children: Natalie Renee & Andrea Delores. **Educ:** WVa State Col, BA, 1942; Northwestern Univ, MA, 1947; George Williams Col, attended 1953. **Career:** Association executive (retired); Talladega Col, dean, 1947-51; Detroit Urban League, voc serv asst, 1956-61; S Bend Urban League, exec dir, 1961-64; Hartford & TTT Prog, dir, 1970; Urban League Greater Hartford, exec dir, 1964-69, 1971-83; NY City & 7 Boroughs Urban Leagues, interim pres, 1984; Urban League Eastern Mass, interim pres, 1988; SNET Corps Co, advisory bd; Hartford Neighborhood Ctr Inc, interim exec dir, 1993-. **Orgs:** Conn Comn Human Rights & Opportunities, comnr; Nat Exec Service Corps, consult; William A Hunton Br YMCA, exec sec, 1951-56; Free & Accepted Masons; Omega Psi Phi Fraternity; Metrop AME Zion Church; Bloomfield St Bank, bank dir; Later Security Bank-Then Union Trust Bank; Mental Health Asn Conn; Am Red Cross Conn; Greater Hartford Sr Citizens Coun; Mt Sinai Hosp, incorporator; Hartford Hosp, incorporator; Hartford Club; Salvation Army Bd mem Emeritus. **Honors/Awds:** Tau Iota Chapter, Omega Psi Phi Fraternity, Omega Man Yr; Greater Hartford Rotary, Rotarian Yr; Nat Coun Christians & Jews, Human Relations Award; Briarwood Coll, Honorary Doctorate Human Serv, 1983; Univ Hartford, Honorary Doctorate Laws; Nat Urban League Whitney M Young Jr, Commemorative Award, 1992; United Way Capital Area, Community Serv Award, 1993; Founding mem Bd High Noon Polit Award, 1993; Paul Harris Fell, Rotary Intl, 1998; Honoring Bill Brown Day, St CT, 1999; hon dep fire chief, city Hartford, 1999; Citizen yr, Bloomfield CT Town Coun, 1999. **Military Serv:** AUS, 1942-46; warrant officer jr. *

BROWN, WILLIAM JAMES. See BROWN, GATES.

BROWN, WILLIAM ROCKY, III
Government official, clergy. **Personal:** Born Oct 10, 1955, Chester, PA; son of Gwendolyn Carraway Brown and William Brown Jr (deceased); married Lorraine Baa Brown, Mar 23, 1991; children: Catrina J. **Educ:** Cheyney State Univ, BA, polit sci, 1977; Martin Luther King Jr Ctr, course non-19violence, 1980; Eastern Baptist Sem, MA, 1983; Jameson Christian Col, DDiv, 1986. **Career:** Chester-Upland Sch Dist, substitute teacher, 1978-81; Calvary Baptist Church, asst pastor, 1979-; State Pa, notary pub, 1980-; Pa Legis Dist 159, asst state rep, 1982-83; First Baptist Church Bernardtown, Coatesville, PA, pastor; City of Chester, city controller, Law Enforcement Planning Comn, St Thomas, VI, spec asst, currently. **Orgs:** Founder, pres, Chester Black Expo, 1979-; exec bd, Black Ministers Conf, 1979-; exec bd, Chester Br Nat Asn Advan Colored People, 1979-; vpres, Chester Community Improv Proj, 1981-; pres, Bill Dandridge Art Gallery, 1982-; exec bd, Kiwanis Club Chester, 1984-. **Honors/Awds:** Outstanding Young Man, US Jaycees, 1984; Johnson Freedom Award, Chester Branch Nat Asn Advan Colored People, 1984; Outstanding Alumni, Nat Asn Equal Opportunity Higher Educ, 1985. **Home Addr:** PO Box 642, St Thomas, Virgin Islands of the United States 00804. **Business Addr:** Special Assistant Drug & Crime Prevention Program, City of Chester, Law Enforcement Planning Commission, Off Gov, 116 164 Subbase, St Thomas, Virgin Islands of the United States 00801.

BROWN, WILLIAM T
Theater manager, educator. **Personal:** Born Mar 11, 1929, Washington, DC; son of William Brown and Henrietta Brown; married Frances Farmer; married Alfredine Parham; children: Camilla Parham, Darrell & Kevin. **Educ:** Howard Univ, BA, drama, 1951; Western Res Univ, MFA, darmatic arts, 1954. **Career:** Karamu Theatre Cleveland, tech dir, 1951-59; Howard Univ, assoc prof drama, 1959-70 & dept chmn, 1967-70; Theatre Univ of Ibadan Nigeria, sr lecturer & consultant 1963-65; Theatre Univ of Leeds, visiting prof 1975; Theatre Dept Univ of MD Baltimore Co, assoc prof & chmn 1970-75, 1982-94, assoc prof emer, 1997-. **Orgs:** E Cent Theatre Conf; Am Theatre Higher Educ; Md State Arts Coun, 1988-91; Howard County Artistic Review Panel, 1987-94; Shakespeare Theatre Asn Am, 1993-95; theatre review panel, Pa Coun Arts, 1993-94; bd dirs, Columba Candlelight Soc; set designer, dir, Columbia Comm Players; The Arena Players, Set Design, dir, 2000. **Honors/Awds:** Hines-Brooks Award of Excellence in Theatre, Howard Univ, 1961; Gold Medallion Award of Excellence in Theatre, Amoco Oil Co, 1971; Distinguished Program Award, Maryland Asn Higher Educ, 1988. **Home Addr:** 8499 Spring Showers Way, Ellicott City, MD 21043-6058.

BROWN, WILLIAM T.
Scientist. **Personal:** Born Jun 11, 1947, Columbus, MS; divorced; children: Kesha. **Educ:** Dillard Univ, BS, 1969; Univ NM, MS, PhD, 1984. **Career:** Los Alamos Sci Lab, tech staff physicist, 1969-73; Sandia Nat Lab, tech staff physicist, 1974-. **Orgs:** Pres, bd dir, Albuquerque Montessori Soc, 1975-77; NM Acad Sci, 1975-; bd dir, Nat Consortium Black Prof Develop, 1976-79; NAACP, 1976-; Am Phys Soc, 1977-; AAAS, 1978-; Soc Black Physicists, 1978-; Nat Tech Asn, 1979-; bd dir, Nat Tech Asn, 1983-; Nat Black Child Develop Inst. *

BROWN, WILLIE
Football player, football coach. **Personal:** Born Dec 2, 1940, Yazoo City, MS; married Yvonne; children: 3. **Educ:** Grambling Univ. **Career:** Football player (retired), football coach; Denver Broncos, defensive back, 1963-66; Oakland Raiders, defensive back, 1967-78, defensive backfield coach, 1979-88, dir squad develop & defensive backs asst, 1995-; Calif State Univ, Long Beach, head football coach, 1992; Los Angeles Jordan High Sch, coach, 1994. **Orgs:** La Sports; Grambling State Univ; Southwestern Athletic Conf; MS Sports Black Sports; Bay Area Sports Halls Fame. **Honors/Awds:** AFL All-Star, 1964-69; NFL Pro Bowl, 1970-73; Prof Football Hall of Fame, 1984; Louisiana Sports Hall of Fame, 1992; Mississippi Sports Hall of Fame, 1994. **Business Addr:** Director Squad Development, Defensive Backs Assistant, Oakland Raiders, 1220 Harbor Bay Pkwy, Alameda, CA 94502, **Business Phone:** (510)864-5000.

BROWN, WILLIE B. See Obituaries section.

BROWN, WILLIE LEWIS
Government official, politician. **Personal:** Born Mar 20, 1934, Mineola, TX; son of Willie Lewis Sr and Minnie Collins Boyd; married Blanche Vitero; children: Susan, Robin & Michael. **Educ:** Calif State Univ, San Francisco, BA, 1955; Hastings Col Law, JD, 1958. **Career:** Brown, Dearman & Smith, partner, 1959-; Calif St Assembly, St rep, 1964-95, speaker, 1981-95. City San Francisco, mayor, 1996-2004; San Francisco Air Am Radio, co-host, 2006; Dem Party, mem, currently. **Orgs:** Assembly Com Efficiency & Cost Control Elect & Reapportionment Govt Admin; Gov's Comn Aging; Joint Comt Master Plan Higher Educ; Legis Budget; Legis Space Needs Legis Audit; vice chmn, Select Comt Health Manpower; Select Com Deep Water Ports; co-chairperson, CA Delegation Nat Dem Conv, 1972; co-chmn, CA Del Nat Black Polit Conv, 1972; CA rep Credentials Com Dem Conv, 1968; bd mem, Nat Planned Parenthood Asn; fel Am Assembly; NAACP; League Women Voters; adv bd mem, CA & Tomorrow; honorary lifetime mem, ILWU Local No 10; San Francisco Planning & Urban Renewal Asn; Sunset Parkside Educ & Action Com; Fillmore Merchants Improvement Asn; Planning Asn Richmond; Hight Ashbury Neighborhood Coun; San Francisco Aid Retarded Children Chinese Affirmative Action. **Honors/Awds:** Outstanding Freshman Legislator Press Award, 1965; Man of the Year, Sun Reporter Newspaper, 1963; Children's Lobby Award for Outstanding Legis Efforts, 1974; Leader of the Future, Time Mag, 1974. **Special Achievements:** First African-American mayor of San Francisco; First African American speaker of the California assembly; appeared in film, The Godfather Part III, 1990; Just One Night, 2000; George of the Jungle; The Princess Diaries; Hulk, 2003. **Business Addr:** Member, Democratic Party, 430 S Capitol St SE, Washington, DC 20003.

BROWN, WINSTON D
Dean (Education). **Career:** Xavier Univ La, dean admis, currently. **Orgs:** Nat Asn Col Admis Coun; Am Asn Col Registrars & Admis Officers; Cath Col Admis Asn & Col Bd; New Orleans City Planning Comn; New Orleans chapter 100 Black Men Am; Kappa Alpha Psi Fraternity, Inc. **Business Addr:** Dean of Admissions, Xavier University of Louisiana, Office of Admissions, 1 Drexel Dr, New Orleans, LA 70125-1098, **Business Phone:** (504)483-7388.

BROWN, YERUSHIA. See BROWN, RUSHIA.

BROWN, YOLANDA B
Manager. **Career:** Dekalb County Sch Syst, coordr, currently.

BROWN, ZORA KRAMER
Association executive. **Personal:** Born Mar 20, 1949, Holdenville, OK; daughter of Willie and Helen Holden; divorced. **Educ:** Okla State Univ, BS, bus admin, 1969. **Career:** Pharmaceut Mfrs Asn, secy, 1969-70; Ford Motor Co, secy, 1970-76; The White House, admin asst, 1976-77; US House Majority Leader, staff asst, 1977; Fed Commun Comn, asst dir pub affairs, 1977-86; Broadcast Capital Fund Inc, pub affairs dir, 1989-91; Breast Cancer Resource Comt, founder & chairperson, currently; Broadcast Capital Fund, vice pres & chief operating officer, 1995-; Cancer Awareness Prog Serv, founder & chmn, currently. **Orgs:** Nat Cancer Adv Bd, 1991-98; President's Cancer Panel, Special Comn Breast Cancer, 1992-94; DC Cancer Consortium, 1989-, chairperson, 1993-; bd mem, Breast Health Inst, Philadelphia, PA, 1992; bd mem, Susan G Komen Breast Cancer Found, 1992. **Honors/Awds:** Marilyn Trish Robinson Community Service Award, Wash Asn Black Journalists, 1992; Community Service Award, Susan G Komen Found, 1992; Cancer Control Service Award, Natl Cancer Inst, 1991; Breast Awareness Award, Natl Women's Health Resource Ctr, 1991; Community Service Award, Auxiliary Veterans Foreign Wars, 1992; Gretchen Post Award, 1993; Citation US Senate, 1995. **Special Achievements:** First African-American woman appointed to the National Cancer Advisory Board. **Home Phone:** (202)328-1949. **Business Addr:** Chair, Breast Cancer Resource Committee, 2005 Belmont St NW, Washington, DC 20009, **Business Phone:** (202)463-8040.

BROWN BRYANT, JACQUELINE D.
Educator, dentist. **Personal:** Born Oct 27, 1957, Nashville, TN; daughter of James H and Birdie Faulkner. **Educ:** Brandeis Univ, Waltham, MA, BA, 1979; Meharry Med Col, Nashville, TN, DDS, 1983; Univ Mich, Ann Arbor, MI, MS, 1985. **Career:** Howard Univ, Dept Orthodontics, Wash, DC, asst prof, 1985-; pvt pract, Silver Springs, MD, 1986-; Howard Univ, Sch Dent, Adv Gen Dent Prog, consult, 1986-; Howard Univ, Sch Dent, Gen Pract Residency Prog, attend physician, 1986-. **Orgs:** Am Asn Orthodontists, 1983-; Int Asn Dent Res, 1983-; Middle Atlantic Soc Orthodontists, 1983-; Omicron Kappa Upsilon Dent Honor Soc, 1983-; Metrop Wash Study Club, 1983-; Am Asn Women Dentists, 1987-. **Honors/Awds:** Merit Fellowship, Univ Mich, 1983, 1984; Patterson Dental Supply Award, 1983; William H Allen Award, 1983; Certificate of Appreciation, Howard Univ, Col Dent, Adv Gen Dent Prog, 1988. **Special Achievements:** Author: abstract, "The Development of the Oxytalan Fiber System of the Mouse Periodontal Ligament," IADR meeting, 1986. *

BROWN-CHAPPELL, BETTY L.
Educator. **Personal:** Born Nov 25, 1946, San Francisco, CA; daughter of Benjamin F and Clara Lucille; married Micheal J Chappell, Oct 1975; children: Michael Jahi & Aisha Ebony. **Educ:** Univ Mich, BA, 1969, MSW, 1971; Univ Chicago, PhD, 1991. **Career:** City Detroit, admin, asst, 1973-77; Walter Reuther Sr Citizens Ctr, asst dir, 1977-79; Univ Ill, Chicago, vis instr, 1979-80; NE Ill Univ, assoc prof, 1980-84; Univ Chicago, asst dean, 1984-89; Univ Mich, fel, 1991-92, asst prof, 1992-96; Eastern Mich Univ, dir bachelor social work prog, assoc prof, 1996-, BSW Prog, dir, 2000-02. **Orgs:** Fel Delta Sigma Theta Sorority, 1988; Nat Asn Social Work, Mich Chap, 1997-; bd mem, 13th Congressional Dist, Sr Citizens Adv Coun, 1997-99; Coun Social Work Educ, Comn Racial, Ethnic, Cult Diversity, 1999-2001. **Honors/Awds:** Academic All American Citation, 1988; has received twelve academic & professional awards. **Special Achievements:** Black Politics, Redistributive Urban Policy & Homelessness, 1997; Community Organizations in Chicago, 1989; People to People, ambassador to Hungary, Poland, Czech Republic, 1998; The Social Security Act Amendments of 1974, position paper of Nat Assn Black Social Workers. **Business Addr:** Associate Professor, Eastern Michigan University, School of Social Work, Rm 351 351 Marshall, Ypsilanti, MI 48197, **Business Phone:** (734)487-9480.

BROWN-DICKERSON, TONIA
College administrator. **Career:** Savannah State Univ, interim dir comprehensive coun, asst to vpres student affairs; Southern Ill Univ, coordr. **Business Phone:** (912)356-2194.

BROWNE, ANUCHA CHIOGU. See SANDERS, ANUCHA BROWNE.

BROWNE, DR. CRAIG C.
Educator. **Personal:** Born Jan 29, 1947, Philadelphia, PA; son of Carter E and Juliette Browne; married Yvonne, May 30, 1970;

children: Craig Jr, Jeffrey & Christopher. **Educ:** Cheyney Univ, BS, 1969, sec educ admin cert, 1975; Temple Univ, EdM, 1973,Ed.D, 1981. **Career:** Philadelphia Sch Dist, math teacher, 1969-88, vice prin, 1988-90, prin,1990-95; Newark NJ Pub Sch, Harold Wilson Mid Sch, prin, 1995-. **Orgs:** Chair, Christian Stronghold Baptist Church, Deacon's Ministry, 1982-;Christian Stronghold Baptist Church, Church Bible Inst, 1985-87; sch bddir, Cheltenam Sch Dist, 1991-93; life mem, Alpha Phi Alpha Fraternity Inc; educ dir, Civil Air Patrol, Sayre Jr High Composite Sq; Orgn African Am Adminrs, 1996-. **Honors/Awds:** Grand Prize-Science Exposition, Cheyney Univ, 1966; Four Chaplains, 1978;Outstanding Young Men of America, OYM, 1981; Distinguished Service Award, Cheltenham Sch Bd, 1993; Mighty Man Award, Christian Stronghold Baptist Church, 2001. **Home Addr:** 7769 Green Valley Rd, Wyncote, PA 19095, **Home Phone:** (215)572-7865. **Business Addr:** Principal, Harold Wilson Middle School, 190-218 Muhammad Ali Ave, Newark, NJ 07108-2141, **Business Phone:** (973)733-6446.

BROWNE, JERRY
Baseball player, athletic coach. **Personal:** Born Feb 13, 1966, St Croix, Virgin Islands of the United States. **Career:** Baseball player (retired), coach; Tex Rangers, infielder, 1986-88; Cleveland Indians, infielder, 1989-91; Oakland Athletics, infielder,1992-93; Fla Marlins, infielder, 1994-95; Toronto Blue Jays, minor league infield instr, 2002; Augusta Green Jackets, coach, 2005; Savannah Sand Gnats, hitting coach, 2006; Hagers town Suns, hitting coach, currently. **Business Addr:** Hitting coach, Hagerstown Suns, Munic Stadium, 274 E Memorial Blvd, Hagerstown, MD 21740, **Business Phone:** (301)791-6266.

BROWNE, LEE F.
Educator, chemist. **Personal:** Born Dec 18, 1922, High Point, NC; son of Lula Winchester and Lee Browne; married Dorothy G; children: Gail, Daryl, Adriene, Scott (deceased). **Educ:** Storer Col, HS, 1940, AA, 1942; WVA State Col, BS, 1944; Univ PA, Navy V-197 Prog, 1947; UCLA, 1949; NYU, Doctoral Prog, 1955. **Career:** UCLA, teaching fel, 1946-49; Tuskegee Inst, instr, 1948-49; Knoxville Col, div chmn, 1950-51; Valley Jr Col, chem instr, 1952-56; Pasadena Schs, sci consult & chem instr, 1964-68; Calif Inst Technol, lect & dir, 1969-90, emer prof, 1990-; The African Sci Inst, sci educr & chemist, lectr emeritus, currently. **Orgs:** ACS, AAAS, AAUP, NSTA, NOBCCHE Natl Assoc of Curriculum Spec, CCTA, Kappa Alpha Psi, Phi Sigma Biol Soc, Phi Delta Kappa Ed Hon Soc; bd of dir Pasadena Hall of Sci, Sci Activities Mag, NACME Inc, 1980-, Pasadena Boys Club, 1981, NAMEPA Minority Eng Prog, 1980-; accred team WASA, 1970; vice chmn, chmn MESA, 1978. **Honors/Awds:** LA Co Sci & Eng Soc Teachers Award, 1968; ACS HS Chem Contest Teacher of No Team & No 1 Stud, 1968, 1969; Industry & Educ Coun Teacher of the Yr, 1968; Am Chem Soc Teacher of the Yr, 1970; Raymond Pitts Human Rel Award Pasadena Star News, 1970-76; CA Congress of Parent & Teachers Serv Award, 1970; Citizen of the Yr, 1980; Phi Delta Kappa Edu Honorary, 1971; Nominee to Pasadena Bd of Ed, 1971; founder & ed Pasadena Eagle newspaper, 1968-73; publ "Developing Skills for Coping", 1977, "Midpoint vs Endpoint", 1980; elected to Am Inst of Chemists, 1986. **Military Serv:** USN v-7 cadet, 1945-46. **Home Addr:** 871 W Ventura St, Altadena, CA 91001. **Business Addr:** Science Educator, Chemist, Lecturer Emeritus, The African Sci Inst, PO Box 12153, Oakland, CA 94604, **Business Phone:** (510)653-7027.*

BROWNE, ROSCOE LEE. See Obituaries section.

BROWN-ELLEN, KIMI
Businessperson. **Educ:** Univ Ill Urbana-Champaign, BS, accountancy. **Career:** Deloitte & Touche LLP, auditor; Ameritech Corp, staff; City Col Chicago, staff; Ace Hardware Corp, staff; Benford Brown & Associates LLC, managing partner, currently. **Orgs:** Am Inst Certified Pub Accts; Ill CPA Soc; Nat Asn Black Accts; Nat Asn Female Execs; Alpha Kappa Alpha Sorority Inc; Jack & Jill Am; bd dirs Game Time Inc; bd dirs, Imani Pearls Community Develop Found; treas, Bingham Human Servs Inc. **Business Addr:** Managing Partner, Benford Brown & Associates LLC, 2319 E 71st St, Chicago, IL 60649, **Business Phone:** (773)752-7078.*

BROWNER, JOEY MATTHEW
Football player, radio host. **Personal:** Born May 15, 1960, Warren, OH; married Valeria; children: 2. **Educ:** Univ Southern Calif, pub admin. **Career:** Football player (retired), radio host; Minn Vikings, 1983-91, Tampa Bay Buccaneers, 1992; Fox Sports, co-host; Nationwide Sports, host, currently. **Orgs:** NEL Boys & Girls Club AK Camp "87", camp confident Celebrity Tournament; Vikings Charity Basketball. **Honors/Awds:** Selected first team All PAC 10; UPI All Coast; Col Pro Football Newsweekly second-team All-Am; AP third-team All-Am; USC's MVP; captain of team in Japan Bowl, 1983; MVP on Defense Vikings, 1985; Pro Bowl teams, 1985-90; African-American hall of fame, 2004. **Special Achievements:** Five times NFL Hall of Fame Nominee; NFL Pro Bowl record with 3 fumble recoveries.

BROWNER, ROSS D
Chief executive officer, football player. **Personal:** Born Mar 22, 1954, Warren, OH; son of Jimmie Lee Browner Sr and Julia Geraldine Cook; married Shayla Simpson, Jun 14, 1986; children: Rylan Ross & Max Starks IV. **Educ:** Notre Dame, 1978. **Career:** Football player (retired), chief exec officer; Cincinnati Bengals, defensive lineman, 1978-86; Green Bay Packers, defensive lineman, 1987; Coldwell Banker, Cincinnati OH, realtor, 1989-91; Browner Productions Inc, chief exec officer, 1995-. **Orgs:** NFLPA; NFL Alumni; Notre Dame Alumni. **Honors/Awds:** Gator Bowl Hall of Fame, 1999; Warren Sports Hall of Fame, 1998; Nat Football Found Hall of Fame, 1999 . **Special Achievements:** Participated in Japan Bowl & Hula Bowl, 1978. **Home Phone:** (404)758-7900. **Business Addr:** Chief Executive Officer, Browner Productions Inc, PO Box 210585, Nashville, TN 37221, **Business Phone:** (615)646-7900.

BROWN-FRANCISCO, TERESA ELAINE
Activist, state government official. **Personal:** Born Feb 25, 1960, Oklahoma City, OK; daughter of Herman and Mary McMullen; married Andre Francisco, Nov 25, 1989; children: Aaron Geoffrey (deceased), Addam Michael. **Educ:** Phillips Univ, Enid, OK, 1980; Okla City Univ, Oklahoma City, OK, BA, 1983. **Career:** KOCO-TV, Oklahoma City, OK, assoc news producer, 1984-86; Bellmon Gov, Campaign, Oklahoma City, OK, asst press secy, 1986; Bellmon Gov, Inaugural Comn, Oklahoma City, OK, press secy, 1986-87; Off Gov, Oklahoma City, OK, asst gov soc servs & ethnic affairs, 1987-91; Total Concept Consults Inc, entrepreneur, 1992; Mkt & Visual Commun, pub rels. **Orgs:** Bd dir, Urban League Greater Oklahoma City, 1987-91; bd dirs, Metrop Fair Housing Coun, 1987-; Exec Leadership Inst, Nat Forum for Black Pub Adminrs, 1989-90; co-chmn, Adv Comt, Casey Family Prog, 1990-94; bd dirs, Inst Child Advocacy, 1988-91; bd dirs, Oklahoma City Univ Alumni Asn, 1991-95. **Honors/Awds:** US Delegate, World Youth Forum, Helsinki, Finland, Am Ctr Int Leadership, 1990; developer, Martin Luther King, Jr State of Excellence Scholar Award, 1988; developer, Oklahoma Youth Educ & Serv, 1990. **Special Achievements:** One of 50 Future Leaders in America, Featured Article by Ebony Mag, 1990. **Business Addr:** President, Total Concept Consults Inc, 1010 NE 14th St, Oklahoma City, OK 73117-1002, **Business Phone:** (405)272-9333.

BROWN-GUILLORY, ELIZABETH
Educator, playwright. **Personal:** Born Jun 20, 1954, Lake Charles, LA; daughter of Leo and Marjorie Savoie; married Lucius M Guillory, Aug 6, 1983; children: Lucia Elizabeth. **Educ:** Univ Southwestern La, BA, eng, 1975, MA, eng, 1977; Fla State Univ, PhD, eng, 1980. **Career:** Fla State Univ, res fel, 1979; Univ SC, Spartanburg, asst prof eng, 1980-82; Dillard Univ, asst prof eng, 1982-88; Univ Houston, assoc prof eng, prof eng, currently; Editor: Wines in the Wilderness: Plays by African-American Women from the Harlem Renaissance to the Present, 1990; Women of Color: Mother-Daughter Relationships in 20th Century Literature, 1996; Author: Their Place on the Stage: Black Women Playwrights in America, 1988; playwright: Somebody Almost Walked off With all of My Stuff, 1982; Bayou Relics, 1983; Marry Me Again, 1984; Mam Phyllis,Snapshots of Broken Dolls, 1990; Saving Grace, 1993; Just a Little Mark,1993; Missing Sister, 1996; La Bakair, 2001; When the Ancestors Call, 2003; The Break of Day, 2003; Plays; Bayou Relics; Snap shots of Broken Dolls; Mam phyllis; La Bakair; When the ancestors call; Break Of the Day. **Orgs:** Southern Conf Afro-Am Studies Inc; Col Lang Asn; S Cent Modern Lang Assn;Modern Lang Assn; Int Women's Writing Guild; Am Soc Theatre Res; Conf Col Teachers Eng Texas; Black Theater Network; Assn Theatre Higher Educ;founder, fac adv & mentor, Houston Suitcase Theater; Am Lit Assn; Assn Study Worldwide African Diaspora; mem, South Central Modern Language Assoc (SCLA); consultant, Natl endowment for Humanities,. **Honors/Awds:** Outstanding Professor, Sigma Tau Delta, 1991, 2000; Outstanding Professor, UH Council of Ethic Org, 1995; Cooper Teaching Excellence Award, Univ Houston, 1997; Young Black Achievers of Houston Award; First Place Playwriting Award, La state wide competition, 1985; The City of New Orleans Playwriting Award, 1983; numerous grants and other awards. **Business Addr:** Professor, University of Houston, Department of English, 4800 Calhoun Rd, 205 Roy Cullen Bldg, Houston, TX 77204-3013, **Business Phone:** (713)743-2976.

BROWN-HARRIS, ANN
Banker. **Personal:** Born Dec 5, 1955, Tallahassee, FL; daughter of Junilus A Brown (deceased) and Carrie M Ware; married Walter D Harris Jr, Jul 28, 1984; children: Geoffrey D Harris. **Educ:** Fla A&M Univ, BS, bus admin, 1977. **Career:** Human Resources Clearing House, fiscal officer, 1977-79; Suntrust Bank Central FL, vpres, 1979; Metro Savings Bank, pres & chief exec officer, 1996. **Orgs:** Exec officer, bd mem, Central Fla Urban bankers, 1983-; bd mem, City Orlando, munic planning bd, 1991; southern regional rep, Nat Asn Urban bankers, 1991-93; bd mem, City of Orlando Downtown Dev Bd, 1991-; mayors transition team, City Orlando, 1992; Off Gov, FL Comn African Am Affairs, comnr, 1993-. **Honors/Awds:** Outstanding Serv Award, Central Fla Urban Banker, 1985-86, 1988, 1990, 1994; Orlando Bus J, Up & domer Financial Serv, 1991; Outstanding Bus & Prof Award, Dollars & Sense Mag, 1992; Minority Retailer of the Yr, US Dept Com, 1993; Banker of the Yr award, Central Fla Urban Bankers Asn, 1966. **Special Achievements:** Banker of the Year, Cent Fla Urban Bankers Asn, 1996. *

BROWNING, JO ANN
Clergy. **Personal:** Born Sep 30, 1949, Nantucket Island, MA; daughter of James and Ruth Leonard; married Rev Dr Grainger Browning, Aug 4, 1979; children: Grainger III, Candace. **Educ:** Boston Univ, BA, Communs, 1976; Howard Univ, MDiv, 1986, DMin, 1991. **Career:** Howard Univ, grad admis counr, 1979-; Hemingway Mem AME Church, minister, 1982-86; Ebenezer African Methodist Episcopal Church, co-pastor, 1986-. **Orgs:** Founder, Journey of Faith, 2006. **Honors/Awds:** Benjamin E Mays Fellow, Howard Univ; Pew Fellow, Howard Univ & Whos Who Among Am Cols & Univs, 1989-90; honorable member, Delta Sigma Theta, 2002. **Special Achievements:** Released her first book "Our Savior, Our Sisters, Ourselves: Biblical Teachings & Reflections on Women's Relationships". **Business Addr:** Co-pastor, Ebenezer African Methodist Episcopal Church, 7707 Allentown Rd, Fort Washington, MD 20744, **Business Phone:** (301)248-8833.*

BROWNING, JOHN
Football player. **Personal:** Born Sep 30, 1973, Miami, FL. **Educ:** Univ WVa. **Career:** Kans City Chiefs, defensive end, 1996-06; free agent, currently. **Honors/Awds:** Rookie of the Year, 1996. *

BROWNLEE, DENNIS J.
Executive. **Educ:** George Washington Univ; Am Univ Grad Studies; Princeton Univ. **Career:** New Urban Entertainment TV Inc, founder & chief exec officer; ADVANCE Inc, founder & chief exec officer; US Satellite Broadcasting Co Inc, vpres; Clear Channel Mkg Partnerships, managing dir; Premiere Radio Networks, vpres & managing dir urban sales & mkt, 2005-. **Orgs:** Trustee, Princeton Univ. **Business Phone:** (818)377-5300.*

BROWNLEE, DENNIS J.
Executive. **Educ:** Princeton Univ; George Wash Univ; American Univ. **Career:** Clear Channel Mkt Partnerships, managing dir; New Urban Entertainment TV, founder & chief exec officer, 2000-02; Advance Inc, chief exec officer; United States Satellite Broadcasting Co Inc, vpres; Premiere Radio Networks, vpres & managing dir, currently. **Orgs:** trustee, american Univ. **Business Addr:** Vice persident, Managing Director, Premiere Radio Networks, Urban Sales and Market, 1270 Ave Am, New York, NY 10020, **Business Phone:** (212)445-3900.

BROWNLEE, DR. GERALDINE DANIELS
Educator. **Personal:** Born Apr 13, 1925, East Chicago, IN; daughter of Jerry Daniels and Nellie Cossey Daniels; married Brady, Aug 4, 1957. **Educ:** WVa State Col, BA, cum laude, 1947; Univ Ill, attended 1950; Univ Mic, attended 1950; Univ Chicago, MST, urban educ, 1967, PhD, 1975; IN Univ, post doctoral study; Am Coun Educ, fel, 1979. **Career:** Educator (Retired); Univ Mich, Lions fel, 1950; Cook County Dept Pub Welfare, caseworker, 1950-55; Chicago Pub Sch, teacher, 1955-66; Univ Chicago, staff assoc, asst dir teacher training, 1968-70; Univ ill Chicago, asst prof, asst dean, 1971-74; Park Forest ill Sch Dist, dirtitle VII proj, 1975-76; Univ Souther MS, vis prof, 1990; Univ Ill, assoc prof emer, 1990; DePaul Univ, consult, 1995-96. **Orgs:** Chairperson, Chicago Urban League Educ Adv Comm, 1983-90; bd dir, Chicago Urban League, 1984-90; bd dir, vpres, YWCA, 1991-97; comnr, Chicago United Way allocations, 1992-97; Am Educ Res Asn; Nat Soc Study Educ; Am AsnHigher Educ; Alpha Kappa Alpha; Am Asn Univ Women; Links Inc; Educ Network; Int vpres, Pi Lambda Theta Honor Asn Prof Educ; Asn Supervision & curriculum Develop; Asn Teacher Educ; Alpha Delta Sigma; Beta Kappa Chi. **Honors/Awds:** Beautiful People Award, Chicago Urban League, 1989; Fifteenth Annual Distinguished Res Award, Asn Teacher Educr; Outstanding Award, YWCA, 1990. **Special Achievements:** Publications: "Evaluating Nutrition Education Programs"; "Thresholds inEducation", 1978; "Parent-Teacher Contacts and Students Learning, A Research Report", The Journal of Educ Research, 1981; "Characteristics of Teacher Leaders" Educational Horizons, 1979; "Teachers Who Can, Lead", 1980; "The Indentification of Teacher Education Candidates", 1985; "Research & Evaluation of Alternative Programs for High School Truants", 1988, 1989; "Minorities in Education and Unfulfilled Responsibilities", 1989; "School Improvement: It All Begins With a Vision", Catalyst, 1990; Beautiful People Award, Chicago Urban League, 1989. **Home Addr:** 6937 S Crandon Ave, Chicago, IL 60649.

BROWNLEE, JACK M
Manager. **Personal:** Born Jul 24, 1940, St Louis, MO; son of Johnny and Clifford; married Martha Diaz, May 23, 1987; children: Bryan, Michael & Gabriel. **Educ:** San Diego City, grad; San Diego St Col, grad. **Career:** Manager (retired); KFMB TV, dir, 1972-73, TV oper mgr, 1973-75, prod supvr, 1975-95, prog coordr, 1995; Starburst Broadcasting, co-owner, vpres, 1990. **Orgs:** Bd gov, Nat Asn TV Arts & Sci, 1984-85. **Honors/Awds:** Upper Level Division Scholarship Award; Emmy Award, Nat Asn TV Arts & Sci, 1983. **Special Achievements:** First black dir & first black on KFMB TV managing staff. Auth: A Brand New Moon. **Military Serv:** USMC, 1959-64.

BROWNLEE, WYATT CHINA, III
Executive director. **Personal:** Born Mar 18, 1909, Hodges, SC; married Emma Roundtree (deceased); children: Wyatt Q. **Educ:**

Fenn Col, 1940; John Marshall Law Sch, LLB, 1944; Cleveland Marshall LawSch, doc law conferred, 1968. **Career:** Cleveland Eviction Ctr, referee, Small Claims Ctr, Traffic Ctr, 1977; pvt pract, probate, currently; Nat Ohio Minority Supplier Develop Coun, pres &chief exec officer, interim executive dir, currently. **Orgs:** Mem Judicial Coun NBA; asst atty & gen, OH, 1964-70; asst law dir, Cleveland, 1973-77; pres, Gamma Alpha Sigma Chap Phi Beta Sigma Frat Inc;pres, orgn Jr br NAACP; exalted ruler, King Tut Lodge 389; asst grandlegal adv IBPOE W; asst st legal adv; St Asn Elks; Mem various BarAsn; legal proffesion & commun, Cleveland Bar Asn. **Honors/Awds:** Saluted by TA-WA-SI Scholar Club; honours by Zeta Phi Beta Sor; Hall of Fame, NBA, 1986. **Home Addr:** 3019 Albion Rd, Cleveland, OH 44120. **Business Addr:** Interim Executive Director, Tower City Ctr 50 Pub Square Suite 200, Cleveland, OH 44113-2291, **Business Phone:** (212)621-3300.

BROWNRIDGE, J PAUL
Government official. **Personal:** Born Jun 10, 1945, Macon, MS; son of James and Arna M Moore; married Rose M; children: 4. **Educ:** Jackson State Univ, Jackson MS, 1966-68; Univ of Akron, BS 1970, JD 1974; Indiana Univ, master's degree 1980; Harvard Univ, sr execs prog 1987. **Career:** Goodyear Tire & Rubber Co, acct, 1971-73; Container Corp Am, tax atty, 1973-78; Clark Equip Co, tax atty, 1978-80; Phillips Petrol, sr tax atty, 1980-82; Ideal Basic Industs, tax coun, 1982-84; City & County Denver, dep mgr revenue, 1984-86; City Grand Rapids, treas, 1986-88; City Chicago, dir revenue, 1988; City Los Angeles, treas, 1999. **Orgs:** Bd mem, Jr Achievement, 1978-80; comnr, Denver's Comn Aging, 1984-86; chmn, Denver's Tuition Reimbursement Prog, 1984-86; mentor, Colo Alliance Bus, 1985-86; chmn, Cent Support Sub-Cabinet Mem, Exec Comn & Fin Policy Comn, City Chicago; exec bd, Govt Finance Officers Asn US & Canada. **Honors/Awds:** Proclamation Recipient Outstanding Serv, Mayor Denver, 1986; Leadership Cert, US Postal Serv, 1987. **Military Serv:** AUS, sp4, 3 yrs; various commendation medals, Vietnam Vet, 1963-66.

BROWN-WRIGHT, FLONZIE B
Executive. **Personal:** Born Aug 12, 1942, Farmhaven, MS; daughter of Frank Sr and Littie P Dawson; married William Russell, Dec 17, 1989; children: Cynthia Verneatta Goodloe-Palmer, Edward Goodloe Jr & Lloyd Darrell Goodloe. **Educ:** Tougaloo Col; Millsaps Col; Dr Humane Letters, LaMoyne Col, Syracuse, NY. **Career:** Fain Fel, Tougaloo Col; Nat Asn Advan Colored People, br dir, 1964-66; State Equal Employ Opport Officer & Training Coordr, recruiter, 1966-73; US Equal Employ Opport Comn, 1974-89; FBW & Assoc Inc, pres & chief exec officer; Miami Univ, stud affairs scholar residence, 2003-. **Orgs:** Nat Coun Negro Women; Nat Asn Advan Colored People; Southern Christian Leadership Conf; bd pres, Nat Caucus & Ctr Black Aged; founding mem & pres, Women Progress; charter mem, Bethune Day Care Ctr; founder, Vernon Dahmer Singers Freedom; pres, AFGE Local 3599 AFL-CIO. **Honors/Awds:** Wyche Fowler Congressional Citation; Salesperson of the Year, Hollingsworth Realty; Chairman's Special Commendation, EEOC; recipient of over 400 community awards and commendations. **Special Achievements:** The Songs That Brought Us Over; Martin, As I Knew Him; Author of, Looking Back To Move Ahead; established The Flonzie B Wright Scholarship Fund; Wrote 2nd Publication: "Its Prayer Time," for her senior friend, Mrs Mamie Clemons, 1997; published video, "And Before I'll Be Your Slave". **Home Addr:** 11942 Moses Rd, Germantown, OH 45327.

BROWN-WRIGHT, MARJORIE. **See Obituaries section.**

BRUCE, ADRIENE KAY
Executive. **Personal:** Born May 20, 1965, Detroit, MI; daughter of Rufus H and Rubye M. **Educ:** Howard Univ, BS, 1988. **Career:** Hecht Co, 1988-89; Dayton Hudson Corp, 1990-95; Kelly servs, Minority Owned Vendor Enterprise, prog specialist, 1996-98, prog mgr, 1998-2001; Bank One Corp, vpres, sr supplier & relationship mgr, 2001-05; Ameren Corp, managing exec, 2005-. **Orgs:** Nat Asn Advan Colored People; bd mem, Coun Supplier Diversity Profs, 1998-2005; co-chair, Mich Women's Bus Coun, 2000-01; bd mem, Mich Minority Bus Develop Coun, 2001-05; bd mem, Forte Found, 2005-; Wall St Diversity Recruiters Group Round Table, 2005-. **Honors/Awds:** Women's Informal Network, Metro Detroit's Most Influential Black Women, 2001. **Business Addr:** Managing Executive, Ameren Corporation, 1 Ameren Plz 1901 Chouteau Ave, PO Box 66149, St Louis, MO 63166-6149.

BRUCE, AUNDRAY
Football player. **Personal:** Born Apr 30, 1966, Montgomery, AL. **Educ:** Auburn Univ, educ, 1988. **Career:** Atlanta Falcons, defensive end, 1988-91; Los Angeles Raiders, 1992-94; Oakland Raiders, 1995-98. **Honors/Awds:** Citrus Bowl MVP, 1987. *

BRUCE, CAROL PITT
Government official. **Personal:** Born Dec 25, 1941, Elkton, MD; daughter of Ralph A Pitt and Elizabeth J Sawyer; married Don Franklin; children: Donna E Bowie, Keith, Kirk. **Educ:** Morgan State Univ, BA, 1964, MBA, 1979. **Career:** Hartford Co Dept Social Serv, asst dir income maint, 1975-77; AUS 8th Inf Div ADAPCP, clin supv, 1977-79; AUS Civilian Personnel Off Ft Polk, personnel staffing spec, 1981-84; AUS Civilian Personnel Ft Geo G Meade, chief tech serv, 1984-85; Chem Res Eng & Dev Ctr Aberdeen Proving Ground, chief alcohol drug control/ea off, 1985-. **Orgs:** Exec bd, Baltimore Urban League, 1976-79; Nat Assoc Female Execs; Youth Program Dir, St. James AME Church 1987-; Harford County Alumnae Chap, Delta Sigma Theta Inc, 1988-. **Home Addr:** 525 Oak St, Aberdeen, MD 21001. **Business Addr:** Chief Alcohol Drug Control Officer, Aberdeen Proving Ground, Aberdeen, MD 21001.*

BRUCE, ISAAC ISIDORE
Football player. **Personal:** Born Nov 10, 1972, Fort Lauderdale, FL. **Educ:** W Los Angeles Jr Col; Santa Monica Col; Memphis State Univ, Phys Educ, 1992. **Career:** St Louis Rams, wide receiver, 1994-2007; United Way, Rams spokesman, 1996; San Francisco 49ers, receiver, 2009-. **Orgs:** Bd dirs, Childhaven; Omega Psi Phi Fraternity, Inc. **Honors/Awds:** Rams ROY, 1994; Rams MVP, 1995, 1996; Rams True Value Man of the Year,1997; Rams Sprint Good Sport/Man of the Year, 1998; Super Bowl XXXIV, 1999; Sports Personality of the Year, Missouri Athletic Club, 2003; National Sportsmanship Award, 2006. *

BRUCE, JAMES C.
Educator. **Personal:** Born Jul 15, 1929, Washington, DC; divorced; children: James C Jr & Jason W. **Educ:** Howard Univ, AB, 1952, MA, 1956; Univ Chicago, PhD, 1963. **Career:** SC St Col, ger instr, 1956-57; Univ Chicago, ger instr, 1961-64, from asst prof ger, to assoc prof ger, 1964-89, assoc prof emer, 1989-; Soka Univ, Japan, prof engineering, 1989-2000, prof emer, currently. **Orgs:** Ill Comn Human Rel, 1971-73; secy, Am Asn Teachers German, 1974; Mod LangAsn Am; Midwest Mod Lang Asn; Literarische Gesellschaft Chicago; Sigma PiPhi; Kappa Alpha Psi. **Honors/Awds:** Fulbright Fel, Univ Frankfurt Am Main, Germany, 1960-61; Inland Steel FacFel, Univ Chicago, 1965. **Military Serv:** AUS, sp5, 1953-55. **Home Addr:** 1642 E 56th St, Chicago, IL 60637. **Business Addr:** Professor Emeritus, University of Chicago, Department of Germanic Studies, 1050 E 59th St, Chicago, IL 60637.

BRUCE, PRESTON, JR.
Government official. **Personal:** Born Sep 10, 1936, Washington, DC; married Kellene Margot Underdown; children: Preston III, Kellene Elaine. **Educ:** Lyndon State Col, BS, 1958; Univ Mass, EdD, 1972. **Career:** Readsboro Sch, prin, 1959-63; Off Econ Opport, admin asst dir, 1964-67; Head Start, dir exec asst, 1968-69; Off Child Develop, dir 4-c prog, 1969-71; Univ Mass, asst chancellor, 1971-74; Off Child Devel, dir daycare, 1974-83; ACYF-DHHS, dir NCCAN, 1983-84; USDHEW/ACYF-CB dep dir, Off Families; US Adv Bd, Dept Health & Human Servs, Child Abuse & Neglect, exe dir, currently; PKB & Assocs, consult. **Orgs:** Lion's Club, 1958-63; Jaycees, 1969-71; vestry mem, St Mark's Church, 1971-74; bd dir, Day Care Coun Am, 1975-83; bd dir, Capitol Ballet Guild, 1978-80; bd dir, Dist Columbia O/C, 1978-82; chmn, Howard Univ, Sch S/W Vis Comt, 1979-. **Honors/Awds:** Professional baseball pitcher Pittsburgh Pirates, 1958; horace mann lecturer, Univ Mass, 1971-72; distinguished alumnus, Lyndon State Col, 1973; Athlete's Hall of Fame, Lyndon State Col, 1985. **Home Addr:** 10341 Maypole Way, Columbia, MD 21044. *

BRUCE, RAYMOND L.
Judge. **Personal:** Born Jun 10, 1951, New York, NY; son of Lloyd and Jesuna; married Darlene, Nov 30, 1996; children: Precious. **Educ:** New York Univ, BA, 1973; Temple Law Sch, JD, 1976. **Career:** Carver Fed Savings Bank, gen counsel; NY State Atty Gen Off, asst atty gen; Bronx Criminal Ct, judge, 2002-. **Business Addr:** Judge, Bronx County Supreme Court, 215 E 161st St, Bronx, NY 10451.*

BRUMMER, CHAUNCEY EUGENE
Lawyer, educator. **Personal:** Born Nov 22, 1948, Louisville, KY; married Isabelle J Carpenter; children: Christopher & Craig. **Educ:** Howard Univ, BA; Univ KY, JD. **Career:** Louisville & Nashville RR Co, atty; Louisville Legal Aid, comm educ dir, 1973-74; Univ NC, Chapel Hill, fac, 1979-82; Univ Ark, dep chancellor, 1998-99, prof law, currently, spl asst to chancellor, interim assocv chancellor fac develop; Univ Mo-Kansas City, sr admin. **Orgs:** KY Bar Asn; Louisville Bar Asn; Nat Bar Asn Explorer advr; Law Explorer Post, 1974-; pres, Shawnee HS Alumni Asn; Alpha Phi Omega; Reginald Heber Smith fel, Louisville Legal Aid Soc; Am Bar Asn; bd dir, Ozark Guidance Mental Health Ctr; adv bd, Salvation Army, Northwest Arkansas. **Honors/Awds:** National Service Frat President Award, 1976; The Big E Award, 1976; Outstanding Alumnus Award, Shawnee HS, 1975. **Military Serv:** AUSR, 1970-76. **Business Addr:** Professor, University of Arkansas, 1045 W Maple St, Fayetteville, AR 72701, **Business Phone:** (479)575-2457.

BRUNER, VAN B., JR.
Architect, school administrator. **Personal:** Born May 22, 1931, Washington, DC; married Lillian E Almond; children: Scott V. **Educ:** Univ Mich, BS, design, 1957; Drexel Evening Col, BS, archit, 1965. **Career:** Pvt prac, archit, Pa, 1965; pvt prac, archit, NJ, 1968; Spring Garden Col, dept archit, dept chmn, 1965-72, 1979-81; Nat Org Minority Archit, charter mem, 1972-; Am Inst Archit, former nat vpres, 1972-74; Cornell Univ, vis lectr; Howard Univ, vis lectr; Honolulu Hawaii Univ, vis lectr; Harvard Univ, vis lectr; Bruner Firm, archit & owner, 1968-. **Orgs:** Former mem, NJ Hotel & Multiple Dwelling Health & Safety Bd, 1971-; elder Philadelphia Evangelistic Ctr; field rep, Full Gospel Bus Men's Fel Int; Sigma Pi Phi Fraternity-Delta Epsilon Boule; adv bd, Sch Archit, NJ Inst Technol. **Honors/Awds:** Hall of Fame (track) Woodbury HS, NJ; Whitney Young Award, Am Inst Archit, 1975; Fellow (FAIA), Am Inst Archit, 1979; NJ Sports Hall of Fame, Gloucester County; Architect of the Year, Nat Tech Asn, 1997. **Military Serv:** USAF, capt, 1954-57. **Business Addr:** Architect &, Owner, Bruner Firm, 506 W Park Blvd, Haddonfield, NJ 08033.*

BRUNSON, DAVID
Educator, manager. **Personal:** Born Aug 22, 1929, Ridgeway, SC; son of Avan Brunson and Rose Belton Peete. **Educ:** Univ Dis, AS, pub admin, corrections, 1976, BA, social rehab welfare, gerontology, 1978, MA, adult ed, gerontology, 1980. **Career:** Metropolitan Police Dept, Wash, DC, patrolman officer, 1962-89. **Orgs:** Mw grand master, MW Prince Hall Grand Lodge DC, Inc, 1989-90; Asn Retired Policeman, DC Inc; Am Asn Adult & Continuing Educ; Int Sr Citizens Asn; US Track & Field (USATF), Potomac Valley Asn, cert official track & field; Am Asn Retired Persons; Asn Retarded Citizens DC, Inc; life mem, Univ DC Alumni Asn; Univ DC, Inst Gerontology; Nat Caucus Ctr Black Aged. **Honors/Awds:** Nat Deans List, Univ DC, 1976-78; Golden Heritage, Life member, NAACP, 1989-; Hon Past Potentate, AEAONMS Inc (Shriners), 1980, Honorary Past Imperial Potentate, 1989; AASR, SJ USA, Grand Inspector Gen 33rd Deg United Supreme Coun, 1989. **Military Serv:** USY, E4, 1958-64; Expert Rifleman, Parachutist Sch, 1959; Parartrooper, 101st Airborne Div, 187th Infantry. *

BRUNSON, DEBORA BRADLEY
Educator. **Personal:** Born Apr 15, 1952, Orangeburg, SC; daughter of Louis and Blanche Williams; married John Edward Brunson II, Dec 18, 1971 (divorced 1987); children: Courtenay De'Von, Jon Emerson. **Educ:** SC State Col, Orangeburg, SC, BS, 1973, MEd, 1974, EdD, 1990. **Career:** Orangeburg City Schs, Orangeburg, SC, teacher, 1973-82, counr, 1982-86, prin apprentice, 1986-87, counr, 1987-; Elloree Elem Sch, prin. **Orgs:** SC Asn Coun/Develop; Nat Asn Advan Colored People; dep registr, Orangeburg County, secy, Orangeburg County Tourism Adv Bd; Delta Sigma Theta Sorority; SC Educ Asn; Nat Educ Asn; Phi Delta Kappa; Bd Higher Educ & Campus Ministry, United Methodist Church, vpres; Asn Supv & Curriculum Develop; SC Asn Sch Adminrs. **Home Addr:** 1229 Dunham St, Orangeburg, SC 29118. *

BRUNSON, DOROTHY EDWARDS
Executive, business owner, consultant. **Personal:** Born Mar 13, 1938, Glennville, GA; married; children: Edward Ross & Daniel James. **Educ:** State Univ NY, BS; Empire State Col; Clarke Atlanta Univ, doctorate. **Career:** Sonderling Broadcasting Corp, gen mgr, 1963-73; WWRL, NY, asst gen mgr,1969; Inner City Broadcasting Corp, vpres, gen mgr, 1973-79; WEBB RadioBaltimore, owner, 1979-; Brunson Commun Inc, gen mgr, pres & chief execofficer, 1995-; WGTW-TV, pres & chief exec officer; Amina Commun & Technol Inc, owner; Bright Light Inc, consult; Brunson Ross, part-owner; Capital Insurance Surety, part-owner. **Orgs:** Founding bd, Legal Mutual Liability Ins Soc Md Inc, 1988-89; Md Small BusFinance Develop Authority, 1988-; Md Venture Trust, 1990-; adv bd,Enterprise Found, 1992-; bd mem, Inst Mediation & Conflict Resolution,First Women's Bank; United Way NY, BEDCO; United Way Cent Md; John HopkinsMetro Ctr; Kennedy Inst Handicapped C; Greater Baltimore Comt, FoundationMinorities Media. **Honors/Awds:** Wilmington North Carolina Sickle Cell Asn Award, 1987; Nat Convention Distinguished Service Award, Blacks Govt, 1988; Small Business Media Advocate of the Year, United States Small Bus Admin, 1988; American Women Entrepreneur Development Recognition, 1988-90; Lifetime Membership Recognition Award, Nat Asn Advan Colored People, 1989; Women Hall of Fame Award, Baltimore City Comn, 1989; Business Woman of the Year, Bus & Prof Women's Club Baltimore. **Special Achievements:** First African-American female to co-own an advertising agency on Madison Avenue, New York City; First African-American woman to own a Television & radio station. **Business Phone:** (215)930-0482.

BRUNSON, FRANK
Electrical engineer. **Personal:** Born Jan 20, 1957, Cincinnati, OH; son of Robert Stokes and Arthur Lee; married Melony E White Brunson, Aug 24, 1985; children: Chanel D'Lynne, Frank Aaron, Jordan Tyler. **Educ:** Otterbein Col, 1976; Univ Dayton, BSEE, 1980. **Career:** Columbus Southern Power Co, elec engr, 1980-83, distrib engr, 1983-87, sr distrib engr, 1987-91, sr elec engr, 1991-. **Orgs:** Nat Soc Black Engrs, 1981-; Nat Soc Prof Engrs, 1982-; Young Men's Christian Asn, Black Achievers Prog, Steering Comt, 1992-. **Home Addr:** 3954 Sleaford Ave, Gahanna, OH 43230, **Home Phone:** (614)475-1029. **Business Addr:** Senior Electrical Engineer, Columbus Southern Power Company, 215 N Front St, Columbus, OH 43230, **Business Phone:** (614)464-7240.*

BRUNSON, RICK DANIEL
Basketball player, basketball coach. **Personal:** Born Jun 14, 1972, Syracuse, NY. **Educ:** Temple, attended 1995. **Career:** CBA, prof basketball player; Portland Trailblazers, guard, 1997-98; NY Knicks, 1999-2000; Chicago Bulls, guard, 2003-04; Los Angeles Clippers, guard, 2004-05; Seattle Supersonics, guard, 2005; houston rockets, 2006; Philadelphia 76ers, 2006; denver nuggets, player develop coach, 2007-09; Hawks, Univ Hartford, asst coach, 2009-. *

BRUNT, SAMUEL JAY
Financial manager. **Personal:** Born Jan 14, 1961, Baltimore, MD. **Educ:** Howard Univ, BA, 1979; Univ Baltimore, MPA, 1983. **Career:** Community Col Baltimore, admin asst, instr, 1983-84; Balitmore Fed Financial, new accts, invest clerk, 1984-85; MD State Legis, fiscal res, 1984, interim, 1985, leg session. **Orgs:** Nat Forum Black Pub Admin, 1984; adv, Youth Ministry Trinity Baptist Church, 1984; supt Trinity Baptist Church Sch, 1985. **Honors/Awds:** HUD Fel, Baltimore Reg Planning Coun, 1983; Contestant, 1983; Nat Pi Alpha Alpha Manuscript competition Pub Admin Lit; Delegate 4th Nat Model OAU, Howard Univ, 1983.

BRUTON, BERTRAM A
Architect. **Personal:** Born May 18, 1931, Jacksonville, FL; son of George W and Lula C; married Dorothy Garcia; children: Michelle Yvette & Sabra Lee. **Educ:** Howard Univ, BArch, 1953. **Career:** Paul Rader AIA, job capt, 1956-58; James H Johnson AIA, job capt, 1958-59; Donald R Roark Denver, assoc arch, 1959-61; Bertram A Bruton & Assoc, archit, 1961-, prin, currently. **Orgs:** Am Inst Architects, Nat Coun Archit Regist Bd; Nat Organ Black Arch; Mitchell Sixty-Six Assoc Develop; dir, Salvation Army; dir, Community Credit Union; CO State Bd Examiners Architects; Kappa Alpha Psi; Sigma Pi Phi. **Honors/Awds:** Award of Merit, AIA; Achievement Award, Kappa Alpha Psi; Denver Man of Year, 1974, 1984; Barney Ford Award. **Military Serv:** USAF, 1st lt, 1953-56. **Business Addr:** Principal, BAB Associates, PC/ Architects, 2001 York St, Denver, CO 80205, **Business Phone:** (303)388-4314.

BRUTUS, DR. DENNIS VINCENT
College teacher. **Personal:** Born Nov 28, 1924, Harare, Zimbabwe; son of Margaret Winifred Bloemetjie and Francis Henry; married May 14, 1950; children: Jacinta, Marc, Julian, Antony, Justina, Cornelia, Gregory & Paula. **Educ:** Fort Hare Univ, South Africa, BA, 1947; Witwatersrand Univ, Johannesburg, South Africa, 1963. **Career:** Univ Denver, Denver, Colo, vis prof eng, 1970; Northwestern Univ, Evanston IL, prof english, 1971-85; Univ Tex, Austin, Tex, vis prof english, African & African Am studies research, 1974-75; Amherst Col, Amherst, Mass, vis prof english 1982-83; Dartmouth Col, Hanover, NH, vis prof African & African Am studies 1983; Swarthmore Col, Swarthmore Pa, Cornell chair, 1985-86; Univ Pittsburgh, Pittsburgh, Pa, prof african literature & chmn dept black community educ res & devel, 1986; Univ Colo, Eng Dept, distinguished vis Humanist, currently; Univ Pittsburgh, prof emer africana studies, currently; ed brd, Africa Today; edn brd, Toward Freedom J; edn brd, Transition; ed brd, International Jazz Archives J. **Orgs:** Pres, South African Non-Racial Olympic Comm (San Roc), 1963-; founding mem, Troubadour Press, 1970-; vpres, Union Writers African Peoples,1974-75; founding chair, African Literature assn, 1975-; mem, Int Jury Books Abroad Award, 1976; chmn, Africa Network, 1984-; adv bd mem, African Arts Fund, 1985-; bd mem, Nicaragua Cultural Alliance, 1987-; adv bd mem,Am Poetry Ctr, 1988-; mem, Adv Comm, Nat Coalition to Abolish the Death Penalty, 1989; cord, Union Writers African Peoples, 1986-; prog dir, Program African Writers Africa & the Diaspora, 1988-. **Honors/ Awds:** Mbari Prize for Poetry in Africa, Mbari Press, 1963; Sirens, Knuckles,Boots, 1963; Thoughts Abroad, John Bruin (pseudonym), TX, 1970; A SimpleLust, 1972; Stubborn Hope, 1978; Doctor of Humane Letters, Worcester St Col, Worcester, Mass, 1985; Doctor of Humane Letters, Univ Mass, Amherst,MA, 1985; Langston Hughes Medallion, City Univ New York, 1986; Langston Hughes Award, 1987; Paul Robeson Award for Artistic Excellence, Political Consciousness and Integrity, 1989; Airs & Tributes, 1989; Doctor of Laws, Northeastern Univ,Boston, Mass, 1990; Mbari Poet Prize; South African Literary Award for Distinguished Lifetime Literary Achievement, 2008; honorary doc frm UKZN. **Special Achievements:** Twelve books of poetry including "Still the Sirens"; Published His autobiography "Poetry & Protest" in 2006. **Business Addr:** Professor Emeritus, University of Pittsburgh, Department of Africana Studies, 4C02 Wesley W Posvar Hall, 230 S Bouquet St, Pittsburgh, PA 15260, **Business Phone:** (412)648-7540.

BRYAN, ADELBERT M.
Government official. **Personal:** Born Aug 21, 1943, Frederiksted, Virgin Islands of the United States; son of Wilmot E and Anesta Samuel; married Jerilyn CO Ovesen; children: Lecia, Adelbert (deceased), Scheniqua, Lori, Andrea, Lyrhea & Mia. **Educ:** Col VI, AA Police Sci & Admin, 1975; Fed Bur Invest Acad, 1978; BS, 1988. **Career:** Retired (senator); St Croix Police Dept, police officer, 1966-72, sgt, 1972-74, capt, 1977-86; US VI, sen. **Orgs:** Chmn, Econ Develop & Affairs Comm 15th Legis; chmn, Educ Comn 16th Legis; Olympic Shooting Team; Delegate to Third & Fourth Const Conv. **Honors/Awds:** Medal of Honor Nat Police Award; Policeman of the Year. **Military Serv:** AUS, 1961-63.

BRYAN, ASHLEY F.
Writer. **Personal:** Born Jul 13, 1923, Harlem, NY. **Educ:** Cooper Union Sch; Columbia Univ. **Career:** Books: The Ox of the Wonderful Horns & Other African Folktales, 1971, 1993; The Adventures of Aku, or How It Came About That We Shall Always See Okra the Cat Lying on a Velvet Cushion While Okraman the Dog Sleeps Among the Ashes, 1976; The Dancing Granny, 1977; Beat the Story-Drum, Pum-Pum, 1985; Lion & Ostrich Chicks & Other African Folk Tales, 1986; Sh-Ko & His Eight Wicked Brothers, 1988; All Night, All Day, 1988; Turtle Knows Your Name, 1989; Sing to the Sun, 1992; The Story of Lightning & Thunder, 1993; Ashley Bryan's ABC of African Amer Poetry, 1997; Beautiful Blackbird, 2004; Queen's Col, painting & drawing teacher; Lafayette Col, Black Am poetry; Brooklyn Mus & Dalton Sch, teacher; Dartmouth Col, prof art & visual studies, prof emer; freelancer, currently. **Honors/Awds:** May Hill Arbuthnot Lecture, American Library Association, 1990; Parents' Choice Award; Coretta Scott King Award; Coretta Scott King honor book citations, 1983; Virginia Hamilton Literary Award. **Military Serv:** AUS, WWII. **Home Addr:** Hadlock St, PO Box 283, Islesford, ME 04646. *

BRYAN, DR. CURTIS E.
College president. **Personal:** Son of Alfred H and Betty L. **Educ:** Elizabeth City State Univ, BS, 1960; Temple Univ, MEd, 1968; NY Univ, PhD,1977. **Career:** Del State Col, asst acad dean; Fayetteville State Univ, head div ed &human develop, dir teacher educ; Va State Univ, exec vpres, vpres for admin, interim pres; Denmark Tech Col, pres. **Orgs:** Asn AUS; Nat Asn Higher Educ; AACJC Comn Small Cols; Bamberg Co Econ Develop Comn; Kappa Delta Pi Honor Soc; Phi Delta Kappa; Sigma Rho Sigma. **Special Achievements:** Author: "Quality Control in Higher Educ," 1973; "Fac Personnel, Perspectives on Acad Freedom, " 1976.

BRYAN, DAVID EVERETT, JR.
Lawyer. **Personal:** Born Sep 30, 1947, New York, NY; married Jacqueline Alice Weaver. **Educ:** St Johns Univ, BBA, 1970; St Johns Univ, Sch Law, JD, 1975. **Career:** Westvaco Corp, admin asst, 1970-71; SE Queens Community Corp, asst exec dir, 1971-72; US Securities & Exchange Comn, trial atty, 1975-77; NY Metro Coun, Nat Asn Advan Colored People, exec secy, 1978; Pvt Pract, atty, currently. **Orgs:** Past pres, Kappa Alpha Psi, 1966; past pres, Jamaica Br, Nat Asn Advan Colored People, 1970; pres, Jamaica Br, Nat Asn Advan Colored People Employ Develop Prog, 1975-76; Macon B Allen Black Bar Asn, 1975; bd dir, Carter Community Health Ctr, 1978. **Honors/Awds:** Martin Luther King Jr Scholar, St John's Univ Sch Law, 1972; Thurgood Marshall Award, NY State Trial Lawyers Asn, 1975; Merit Award, St Albans Chamber Com, 1978; Professional Award, Nat Asn Negro Bus & Prof Women's Clubs, Laureltono Club, 1979; Black & Puerto Rican, Caucus, NY State Legis, Outstanding Achievement Award, 1981; Freedom Fund Award, Jamaica Br, Nat Asn Advan Colored People, 1983. **Home Addr:** 11480 179th St, Jamaica, NY 11434. **Business Addr:** Attorney, Private Practice, 114 80 179th St, Jamaica, NY 11434.*

BRYAN, DR. FLIZE A
Physician. **Personal:** Daughter of H Bryan; children: Sylvia. **Educ:** Univ Wis, Nursing, 1956; Tuskegee Inst, BSC, 1967; Pomona Col, Dipl, 1968; Howard Univ Med Sch, MD, 1972. **Career:** Health Dept, nurse, 1956-58; Beth Israel Hosp New York City, nurse, 1958-60; Pvt Duty, RN, 1960-66; Sydenham Hosp NY, surgeon, beginning 1977; Met Hosp NY Med Col, clinical instr surg, 1979; Sydenham & Hosp NY, dir emergency room, 1980-99; SNFCC Harlem Hosp, surgeon, 1980; Brooklyn Hosp, staff. **Orgs:** Community Bd New York City, 1984-; deleg, Doctors Coun Union, 1980-; Susan McKinley Asn, 1983; Episcopal Women St Marks Church; St Luke's Guild. **Honors/Awds:** Mayoral Agency (AFL-CIO).

BRYAN, T.J.
Chancellor (Education), educator. **Educ:** Morgan State Univ,Masters Degree, eng; Univ Md Col Park, PHD, eng lang & lit. **Career:** Baltimore's Coppin State Col, eng fac, 1982, dept Chair, dean hons div & dean arts & sci, 1998; Univ Md Syst, vice chancellor, 1998-02; Pa State Syst, vice chancellor acad & stud affairs, 2002; Fayetteville State Univ, chancellor, 2003-. **Orgs:** Bd dirs, Wachovia Bank; vis bd, Cent Intelligence Agency; NC Defense & Security Technol Accelerator Adv Comt; Cumberland County Workforce Devel Bd; Fayetteville Mus Art Bd. **Honors/ Awds:** Nat Endowment Humanities Fel Col Teachers; Gov's Citation from the State of Md; Beta Chi Chap Omega Psi Phi Fraternity Citizen of the Year; Outstanding Contribution Award, Fayetteville Bus & Prof League; Trailblazer Award, Tau Epsilon Zeta Chapter of Zeta Phi Beta Sorority. **Special Achievements:** One of the nation's fourteen original Ronald McNair Post-Baccalaureate Achievement programs. *

BRYANT, ANDERSON B., JR.
Automotive executive. **Career:** Smokey Point Buick Pontiac GMC, chief exec officer, 2002-. **Orgs:** Smokey Point Chamber Com. **Business Phone:** (360)659-0886.*

BRYANT, ANDREA PAIR
Lawyer. **Personal:** Born Jul 19, 1942, Baltimore, MD; daughter of James M MD and Mamie Savoy(deceased); married Melvin W, Oct 19, 1968; children: James Burnett West & Michael David. **Educ:** Morgan State, BS, physics, 1965; Georgetown Univ, Law Ctr, JD, 1978. **Career:** Karlsruhe, Ger, fel, 1965-66; IBM Corp, programmer, 1967-73, programmer & instr, 1973-74, patent atty training, 1974-78, patent atty, 1978-92; Tex Resource Conservation Comm, deputy off public interest counsel, 1993-96; atty, pvt practice, 1996-. **Orgs:** Secy, Nat Bar Asn Bd, 1988-; bd, Legal Aid Soc Cent Tex, 1985-; Austin Black Lawyers Asn; bd mem, Paramount Theatre Performing Arts, 1989-; Travis County Bar Asn, 1994-; Austin Symphony Orchestra, 1993-; Am Bar Asn, State Bar Tex; chair, The Links Inc, Western Area Int Trends & Serv, 1993-95, pres, Round Rock Chap, 1994-96; Nat Consortium African Am C; NAACP, Delta Sigma Theta Sorority. **Honors/ Awds:** Leadership Austin Class, 1983-84; Leadership Texas, 1991; Leadership America, 1996; Austin Arts Commission, 1997-98; Outstanding Achievement, Travis City, Women Lawyers Asn, 1997. **Business Phone:** (512)345-5806.

BRYANT, ANTHONY
Electrical engineer, manager. **Personal:** Born Aug 27, 1963, San Francisco, CA; son of Soloman Jr and Mary A Newt. **Educ:** San Diego State Univ, BSEE, 1987. **Career:** Navy Pub Works Ctr, San Diego, CA, elec engr, 1984-87; NACME Scholar, NACME, 1986; Motorola GEG Inc, Phoenix, AZ, elec engr, 1987-89; Pac Gas & Elec, San Francisco, CA, elec engr, 1989-93; San Francisco Energy Co, AES Corp, elec engr, 1994-97; Munic Transp Agency, Dept Pub Transp, San Francisco, CA, energy analyst, 1997, Capital Planning & Construct Div, proj mgr, 2000-. **Orgs:** Vpres, treas, San Diego State Univ Nat Soc Black Engrs, 1984-86; San Diego Coun Black Engrs & Scientist, 1985-87; admin dir, Nat Soc Black Engrs, Region IV Alumni, 1991-; Ariz Coun Black Engrs & Scientist, prog dir, 1991-93. **Honors/Awds:** Serv Recognition, San Diego State NSBE, 1989. **Business Addr:** Project Manager, Municipal Transportation Agency, Dept Pub Transp Capital Planning Construct Div, 1 S Van Ness Ave 3rd Fl, San Francisco, CA 94103, **Business Phone:** (415)701-4309.*

BRYANT, ANXIOUS E.
Educator, broker. **Personal:** Born Jan 18, 1938, Nashville, TN; married Christie Tanner; children: Karen, Karl. **Educ:** State Univ Nashville, BS, 1959; Memphis State Univ, MS, 1970. **Career:** Carver High Sch, teacher, 1959-70; Jones & Thompson Archit, archit technician, 1973; Gassner Nathan Partners, archit technician, 1977; Thompson & Miller Architects, archit technician, 1978-79; State Tech Inst Memphis, assoc prof, 1979-; Memphis One Inc Realtors, affiliate broker, 1980-; Rust Col, part-time lectr, 1980-; SW Tenn Community Col, prof emer, currently. **Orgs:** Chmn exam bd, Shelby Co Plumbing Dept, 1977-. **Business Addr:** Professor Emeritus, Southwest Tenn Community College, 737 Union Ave, Memphis, TN 38103-3322.*

BRYANT, DR. BUNYAN I.
Educator. **Personal:** Born Mar 6, 1935, Little Rock, AR; son of Christalee; married Jean Carlberg, Jan 16, 1993. **Educ:** Eastern Mich Univ, BS, 1958; Univ Mich, Social Work, MSW, 1965, Univ manchester, PhD, 1973. **Career:** Univ Mich, Sch Nat Resources & Environ, asst prof, 1972- 95, UTEP, assoc prof, 1978-90, Ctr African-Am & African Studies, assoc prof, 1982- 95, Ctr African-Am & African Studies, adj prof, 1996-, prof natural resources, Sch Natural Resources & Environ, Arthur F Thurnau prof, 1996-, mem, Urban Technol & Environ Planning Prog. **Orgs:** Bd mem, League Conserv; adv comm, USEPA Clean Air Act. **Honors/Awds:** MLK Dreamkeeper Award, Distinguished Leadership Environ Justice Movement Award; Recognition Award, Environ Justice Adv Coun. **Special Achievements:** Author/editor, Environmental Justice: Race & the Indicence of Environmental Hazards, Westview Press, Baulder, 1992; Issues, Policies &Solutions, 1995. **Military Serv:** Nat Guard, specialist, 1960-66. **Home Addr:** 1902 Independence, Ann Arbor, MI 48104, **Home Phone:** (734)769-4493. **Business Addr:** Professor of Natural Resources, Arthur F Thurnau Professor, University Michigan, School of Natural Resources and Environment, Rm 1532 440 Church St Dana Bldg 505 S State St, Ann Arbor, MI 48109-1115, **Business Phone:** (734)763-2470.

BRYANT, CARL
Executive, educator. **Educ:** Univ Md Eastern Shore; Univ NDak; Univ Md Col Pk, PhD. **Career:** USAF Acad, assoc prof; Ctr Creative Leadership, vpres knowledge mgt & appl technol, 1998-05; Personnel Decisions Int Corp, gen mgr, 2005-. **Special Achievements:** First African American vice president of technolgy at Center for Creative Leadership. **Business Addr:** General Manager, Personnel Decisions International Corporation, 2000 Plaza VII Tower 45 S Seventh St, Minneapolis, MN 55402-1608, **Business Phone:** (920)997-6995.*

BRYANT, CASTELL VAUGHN
School administrator, president (organization). **Personal:** Born in Jasper, FL; daughter of Joseph and Bessie Mae; married Leonard Bryant Jr; children: Kathi Merdenia & Craig Leonard. **Educ:** Fla A&M Univ, BS, MS; Nova Univ, EdD. **Career:** Miami-Dade Community Col, dean stud servs, 1978, assoc dean acad support-,coordr curric/Job Placement STIP Grant, 1974-78; Dade Co Pub Sch Syst,teacher; Fla A&M Univ, 1964-74, sr interim pres. **Orgs:**

Coun Black Am Affairs; Family Christian Asn Am; Metro-Dade Art Pub Pl;Metro-Dade Addiction Bd; Delta Sigma Theta Sorority Inc. **Honors/Awds:** Unsung Heroines Award, City Miami Comn Status Women; Community Serv Award,Nat Asn Negro Bus & Prof Women; Golden Rule Award, JC Penney & United Way. **Special Achievements:** Miami Metro Mags 100 Women Watch. *

BRYANT, CLARENCE. See Obituaries section.

BRYANT, CLARENCE W.
Government official. **Personal:** Born May 22, 1931, Clarendon, AR; son of Clarence and Blonnell Guyden Bray; married Annie Laure Aldridge; children: Carolyn, Antonette, Sibyl & Johanna. **Educ:** City Col San Francisco, 1950, AS, elect, 1976; Calif State Univ, San Francisco, BA, design & indust, 1979, MA, 1981. **Career:** Government official (retired); Maintenance Eng Br, Los Angeles, CA, elect tech, installation, 1958-60; Western Reg, San Francisco, AF Sector Field Off, SFIA, elect tech, commun, 1960-68, Elect tech, radar, 1974, elect tech, 1974-78, elect tech regular relief, 1978-79; Fed Aviation Admin DOT, Wash, DC, supvr elect egr mgr, 1979-88, br mgr, 1988-90. **Orgs:** San Fran Black Catholic Caucus, 1972, Mayors Comn Crime, 1968-71, Arch-Bishops Campaign Human Develop, 1969-72, Black Leadership Forum San Francisco; exec bd, Catholic Social Serv; Top Flight Golf Club. **Honors/Awds:** Award of Achievement, Calif State Assembly, 1968; Award, OMICA, 1968; num tech award, FAA. **Military Serv:** USAF, a/1c, 1950-54. *

BRYANT, CONNIE L.
Labor activist. **Personal:** Born Dec 26, 1936, Brooklyn, NY; daughter of Charles (deceased) and Viola Barnes (deceased); married Alonzo Anderson (divorced); children: Bradley C Anderson. **Educ:** Empire State Labor Col, New York, NY; Cornell Univ, Extension, New York, NY. **Career:** Labor activist (retired). NY City Dept Transportation, New York, NY, various posts, 1963-83; Commun Workers Am, Wash, DC, int vpres, 1983-89, Cleveland, OH, staff rep, 1989-91. **Orgs:** Second vpres, Coalition Black Trade Unionist, 1986-; chair, Labor Ad Hoc Comt Nat Coun Negro Women; bd dirs, Indust Rels Coun Goals; exec bd, A Philip Randolph Inst, 1985-89. **Honors/Awds:** NY City, Dept Transportation Adminr & Trainer, 1981; Women Achievers, New York, NY, 1987; Special Women's Award, Nat Black Caucus State Legis Labor, Round Table, 1989; various other awards from local organizations. *

BRYANT, DAMON K
Manager. **Personal:** Son of Elmer and Dorothy. **Educ:** Univ Mo, BA, 1988. **Career:** KSMO TV 62; KCTV TV 5; WTVJ TV 6; WXYZ TV 7; WDAF TV FOX4, vpres mktg & creative servs, currently. **Honors/Awds:** Emmy Awards, Nat Asn Travel Agents Singapore, 1994, 1998; Golden Peacock, NBC Universal, 1995; Defying the Odd, Univ Mo-Kans City, 2005; Four Mich Asn Broadcasters Awards. **Business Phone:** (816)932-9133.

BRYANT, DONNIE L.
Financial manager. **Personal:** Born Dec 20, 1942, Detroit, MI. **Educ:** Walsh Inst Acct, attended 1963; Wayne State Univ, BA, 1970; Univ MI, MPub Policy, 1972. **Career:** Pub Admin Staff, staff assoc, 1973-77; Neighborhood Reinvest Corp, dirfinance & admin, 1977-83; Govt DC, dep city admin. **Orgs:** Intl City Mgt Asn 1972-; Nat Asn Black Pub Admins, 1984-. **Honors/Awds:** Graduate Fellowship, US Dept Housing & Intl City Mgt Asn, 1971-72. *

BRYANT, EDWARD ETHAN, JR. See BRYANT, JUNIOR.

BRYANT, EDWARD JOE, III
Manager. **Personal:** Born Sep 19, 1947, Shreveport, LA; son of Ester Lee Harper and Moses B; married Bettye Jeane Gordon, Nov 1981; children: Lorie, Khristopher & Elizabeth. **Educ:** Air Nat Guard & Air Res Acad, grad, 1972; Baptist Col, attended 1978; Propulison Br Mgt, Chanute Ill. **Career:** USAF, jet specialist, 1965-69; Sperry-Rand Corp, maintenance engr, 1969-72; Dept Defense, aircraft powerplant specialist, 1972-; Fed Civil Serv Employee, 1972-; Palmer Col, assoc, 1975; North Charleston SC, counr, 1978-89. **Orgs:** Air res tech, 1969-86; chmn legal, Nat Asn Advan Colored People, 1975-86, State Legal Redress Comt, 1988-89; Air Force Asn SC Personnel & Guidance Asn, 1978-80; counr, Guidance Sch Syst, 1978-79; legal staff, N Charleston Citizen Adv Coun, 1986-87; local chap, Air Force Asn; Partisan Defense Comt. **Honors/Awds:** Black Heritage Certificate, 1983-88; Sustained Superior Performance Award, 1983; Best Legal Activities & Staff, SC Nat Asn Advan Colored People, 1986-87; Superior Performance Award Civil Service, 1989. **Military Serv:** USAF, sgt, 4 yrs; Good Conduct Medal; Meritorious Serv Medal; Vietnam Ribbon Oversea Serv Medal. **Home Addr:** 5883 Mercia Lane, North Charleston, SC 29418, **Home Phone:** (803)744-2045.

BRYANT, FAYE B.
Educator. **Personal:** Born Mar 15, 1937, Houston, TX. **Educ:** Howard Univ, BA, 1958; Univ Houston, MEd, 1967. **Career:** Educator (retired); Houston Independent Sch Dist, teacher, 1960-67, TitleI counr, 1967-70; Houston Met YWCA, prog dir, 1968-69; Bellaire Sr HS, counr, 1970-75; QIE, HISD field inf co ordr, 1975; Supt Instr, prog admin, 1976; Off Supt Inst, assoc dir, 1977; Magnet Sch Prog, asst supt, 1978;Magnet Sch Prog & Alternate Educ, assoc supt, 1982, asst supt enrichment progs, 1987; Houston Independent Sch Dist, dep supt, personnel serv, 1988-89; dep supt, sch oper, 1989-92, dep supt, dist planning, accountability & technol. **Orgs:** Houston Professional Admins & Asn Supervision Curriculum Develop; pres,Houston Personnel & Guidance Asn, 1975-76; 1974 Task Force Human Concerns TX Personnel & Guidance Asn; chap senator, Houston Met YWCA, 1970-74; bd dirs, Comt Admin Blue Triangle Br; nat past pres, Top Ladies Distinct,1975; pres, Houston Chap, 1973-74; south central regional dir Alpha Kappa Alpha Sor, 1968-72; vpres, Alpha Kappa Alpha Sor, 1978; int nat pres, Alpha Kappa Alpha Sor, 1982-86; NAACP, 1982-86; Links Inc; NCNW Court Calanthe;Houston C C; bd mem, Nat Negro Col Fund; bd mem, nat chmn, Assault Illiteracy; Black Leadership Roundtable, Coalition 100 Black Women. **Honors/Awds:** Young Educator Award, Finalist, 1967; TX Personnel & Guidance Association Certificate of Appreciation, Recog Commitment & Serv Statewide Enchancement Counseling; TX Personnel & Guidance Asn Outstanding Counselor Award, 1975; 100 Most Influential Black Americans Ebony Magazine, 1983-86;Community Service Award, TX Southern Univ's Bd Regents; Outstanding Alumni Achievement Award, Howard Univ, 1987. *

BRYANT, FRANKLYN
Association executive. **Career:** Nat Alliance Black Salesmen & Saleswomen, pres, currently. **Business Addr:** President, National Alliance of Black Salesmen & Saleswomen, PO Box 2814, New York, NY 10027-8817, **Business Phone:** (718)409-4925.*

BRYANT, GREGORY
Educator, counselor, clergy. **Personal:** Born Dec 9, 1953, Atlanta, GA; son of Mildred and Silas Johnson; married Yvonne, Oct 26, 1996; children: Antoine, Shawana, Sheranda, Titus, Tiffany & Gregory Jr. **Educ:** Buelah Heights Bible Col; Atlanta Metrop Col; Christ Answer Univ, ThD; Jacksonville Theol Sem, BA, MA, 2001. **Career:** Fountain Praise Worship Ctr, pastor & founder, 1978-2004; More Than Conquerors Fel Int Inc, founder & chief exec officer, 1980-2004; G A Bryant Enrichment Ctr, founder & chief exec officer; G A Bryant Bible Inst, Atlanta, GA, founder & chief exec officer; Trumpet Zion Rivers Living Waters, Douglasville, GA, pastor & founder; Camp Praise Summer Camp Prog, Atlanta, GA, dir & founder; Shield Faith, founder; Fountain Praise, bishop & chief executive officer; bishop for more than 7 churches in Atlanta, GA, Winder, GA, Fayetteville, NC, Durham, NC. **Home Addr:** 255 Laureen Lane, Mableton, GA 30126. **Business Addr:** Bishop, Chief Executive Officer, Fountain Of Praise, 770 N Elizabeth Pl NW, Atlanta, GA 30318, **Business Phone:** (404)794-9514.

BRYANT, DR. HENRY C. See Obituaries section.

BRYANT, HOMER HANS
Choreographer, artistic director. **Personal:** Born in St Thomas, Virgin Islands of the United States; divorced; children: Alexandra Victoria. **Career:** Dance Theater Harlem, prin dancer; City Chicago's Gallery 37 prog, lead artist; Chicago Multi-Cultural Dance Ctr, founder & artistic dir, 1990-. **Orgs:** Bd mem, South Loop Neighbors Assoc. **Honors/Awds:** Monarch Award, AKA Sorority Inc, 1998; Cycle, Wizard Award, 1996; Welcome Home Award, Reichold Ctr Performing Arts, 1994. **Special Achievements:** "Rap Ballet" at the Symposium on "Emotional Intelligence, Education and the Brain," The Foundation for Human Potential. **Business Addr:** Founder, Artistic Director, Chicago Multi-Cultural Dance Center, 47 W Polk St, Chicago, IL 60605, **Business Phone:** (312)461-0030.

BRYANT, HUBERT HALE
Lawyer. **Personal:** Born Jan 4, 1931, Tulsa, OK; son of Roscoe Conkling and Curlie Beatrice Marshall; married Elnora Roberson, Oct 25, 1952; children: Cheryl Denise Bryant Hopkins & Tara Kay Bryant-Walker. **Educ:** Fisk Univ, BA, 1952; Howard Univ Law Sch, LLB, 1956. **Career:** Pvt law pract, 1956-61, 1986-; City Tulsa, OK, asst city prosecutor, 1961-63, city prosecutor, 1963-67; ND OK, asst US atty, 1967-77; ND OK Dept Justice, US atty, 1977-81; City Tulsa, OK, munic ct judge, 1984-86. **Orgs:** Tulsa Urban League bd, 1962-64; trustee, First Baptist Church N Tulsa, 1970-75, 1995-02; Sigma Pi Phi Alpha Theta Boule; exec bd, Tulsa Br, Nat Asn Advan Colored People; Alpha Kappa Alpha Sorority Inc; Nat Set Club. **Honors/Awds:** Mason of the Year, 1963; Outstanding Citizen Masons, 1978; Outstanding Alumni, Howard Univ Sch Law, 1981; Outstanding Citizen, Tulsa Br, Nat Asn Advan Colored People, 1981; Image Award Outstanding Community Service, Alpha Chi Omega Chap, 1988; Hall of Fame, Nat Bar Asn, 1997. **Home Addr:** 1818 N Boston Ave, Tulsa, OK 74106, **Home Phone:** (918)582-0484. **Business Addr:** Attorney, 2623 N Peoria Ave, PO Box 6281, Tulsa, OK 74148-0281, **Business Phone:** (918)428-6665.

BRYANT, JESSE A
Association executive. **Personal:** Born Aug 27, 1922, Supply, NC; married Eva Mae Fullwood; children: 4. **Career:** Int Longshoremans Asn, secy; Nat Asn Advan Colored People, Cedar Grove, pres. **Orgs:** Vpres, SENC Land Chap, A Phillips Randolph Inst; mem exec bd, Brunswick Co Cit Asn. **Honors/Awds:** Crowned as Mr NAACP of North Carolina. **Home Addr:** 1149 Morgan Rd SW, PO Box 338, Supply, NC 28462, **Home Phone:** (910)842-6670. *

BRYANT, JOHN
Association executive, entrepreneur. **Personal:** Born Feb 6, 1966, Compton, CA; son of Johnie Smith and Juanita; married Sheila Jenine Kennedy. **Educ:** Harvard Univ, John K Kennedy Sch Gov, exec educ prog. **Career:** Specly Lending Group, founder; Bryant Group African, staff; Oper Hope Inc, founder, chmn & chief exec officer, 1992-; President's Coun Financial Literacy, vice chmn, 2008-; Bryant Group Co Inc, chmn & chief exec officer, currently; Univ Calif, Los Angeles, Extension, bus mgt, instr, currently. **Orgs:** Bd dir, Audit Comt, Southern Pacific Bank; bd govs, Kravis Leadership Inst, Claremont McKenna Col; founder, New Leader; Banking on Future; Corporate Coun CEOs; bd dirs, Calif African-Am Mus Found; nat bd dirs, Teach Am; bd trustees, First Am Church; exec adv bd, Renaissance Prog. **Honors/Awds:** Public Counsel, Community Achievement, 1999; Housing Authority, Partners for Success, 1999; Trailblazer Award, 100 Black Men of Orange County; Life Enrichment Award, Charles R Drew Univ; CA's Top 100 Business Leaders, Calif Bus Mag; America's Top 100 Young Entrepreneurs, citation; Reginald F Lewis Entrepreneurship Award, Howard University Sch Bus; DHL, Paul Quinn Col, 2008. **Special Achievements:** Serving as US delegate to Japan, China, Korea and Africa; 19th JapaneseExternal Trade Organization, Export to Japan Prog, guest of Japanese govt,1994; White House Pacific Rim Economic Conf, panel participant, 1997; IVAfrican-American Summit, Johannesburg, South Africa and Hare, Zimbabwe; UNConf on Trade and Devel, Partners for Devel Summit, Tri-Partite Mtg onMicrofinance, delegate, speaker, Planning Group, 1998; US PresidentialMission, V African-American Summit, delegate, speaker, 1999; FamilyReunion 8: Family and Community Policy Conf, panel participant, 1999; UNConf on Trade and Devel, goodwill ambassador, special advisor; firstAfrican-American in history to be knighted by German Nobility and theHouse of Lippe. **Home Addr:** 7122 La Tisera, PO Box 205, Los Angeles, CA 90045. **Business Phone:** (213)891-2900.

BRYANT, JOHN RICHARD
Clergy, bishop. **Personal:** Born Jun 8, 1943, Baltimore, MD; son of Harrison James (deceased) and Edith Holland; married Cecelia Williams; children: Jamal, Thema. **Educ:** Morgan State Col, BA, 1965; Boston Univ Sch Theol, ThM, MDiv, 1970; Colgate Rochester Div Sch, DMin, 1975; Va Sem, Lynchburg; Paul Quinn Col; Payne Theol Sem. **Career:** Peace Corps, Liberia, vol, 1965-67, teacher; Various Cols & Univs, guest lectr, 1970-72; African Methodist Episcopal Church, 14th Episcopal Dist, Monrovia, Liberia, bishop, 1988-91, 10th Episcopal Dist, TX, bishop, 1991-00, 5th Episcopal Dist, bishop, 2000-; Boston Urban League, comt organizer; St Paul AME Church, pastor; Bethel AME Church, Baltimore, MD, pastor. **Orgs:** Bd mem, Nat Community Black Churchmen; Nat Coun Churches; Black Ecumenical Comn; World Methodist Coun Evangelism; bd mem, Ecumenical Inst; bd mem, CNBC; Interdenominational Theol Sem, Atlanta, GA; Nation Church Adv Coun, Am Bible Soc; vpres, N Am Sect, World Methodist Coun; Cong Nat Black Churches; S Dallas Accents. **Honors/Awds:** Springfield Outstanding Churchman Award, Outstanding Young Man's Award, Boston Jaycees; Outstanding Leader Award, Winkey Studios; Man of the Year Award; Outstanding Achievement Award, Delta Sorority; Theol Outstanding Alumni Award, Boston Univ Sch; Outstanding Alumnus Award, Morgan State Univ; Hall of Fame, High Sch, Baltimore City Col; Award, Prince Hall Masons. **Special Achievements:** Listed on Ebony Magazine's Honor Roll of Outstanding African American Preachers; Publ collection sermons entitled God Can: Sermons of encouragement from the Life of Elijah, 1997; contributed to Pastor's Manual and four other books; author, God Can: Sermons of Encouragement from the Life of Elijah. **Business Addr:** Bishop, African Methodist Episcopal Church, 5th Episcopal Dist, 1900 W 48th St, Los Angeles, CA 90062, **Business Phone:** (323)296-0877.*

BRYANT, JOY (KATE HUDSON)
Actor. **Personal:** Born Oct 19, 1976, Bronx, NY; married Dave Pope, Jun 28, 2008. **Educ:** Yale Univ. **Career:** Tommy Hilfiger, model; filmography: "Carmen: A Hip Hopera", 2001; Kite, 2002; Antwone Fisher, 2002; How to Get the Man's Foot Outta Your Ass, 2003; Honey, 2003; 3-Way, 2004; Spider-Man 2, 2004; Haven, 2004; Rhythm City Vol, Caught Up, 2005; The Skeleton Key, 2005; London, 2005; Get Rich or Die Tryin, 2005; Bobby, 2006; The Hunting Party, 2007; Welcome Home Roscoe Jenkins, 2008; Virtuality, 2009. **Orgs:** A Better Chance. **Honors/Awds:** Young Hollywood Award, 2003; Hollywood Film Award, 2006; Nominee, Black Reel Award, 2005, 2003; Screen Actors Guild Award, 2007. **Business Addr:** Actress, c/o Innovative Artists, 1505 10th St, Santa Monica, CA 90401.*

BRYANT, JUNIOR (EDWARD ETHAN BRYANT, JR.)
Football player. **Personal:** Born Jan 16, 1971, Omaha, NE. **Educ:** Univ Notre Dame. **Career:** San Francisco 49ers, defensive end, 1995-2000. **Orgs:** Founder, 90 Ways. **Honors/Awds:** Rookie of the Year, 1995. *

BRYANT, KATHRYN ANN
Banker, vice president (organization). **Personal:** Born Feb 25, 1949, Detroit, MI; daughter of Amos V and Mary Avery. **Educ:** Univ Mich, BA, polit sci, 1971; Wayne State Univ, MA, radio, tv & film, 1979. **Career:** City Detroit, 1972-77, City Coun, admin asst to Councilman Kenneth Cockrel, 1978-81, Cable Commission, dep dir, 1982-88, Bd Assessors, assessor, 1988; Warner Cable Commun Inc, dir gov & community relations, 1988-91; Comerica Inc, vpres, civic affairs, 1991-. **Orgs:** Bd mem, Mich Metro Girl Scout Coun, 1992-96; bd mem, Fair Housing Ctr Metro Detroit, 1991-; bd mem, Arab Am Ctr Econ Soc Servs, 1992-; treas/bd mem, Project Pride, 1991-93; Nat Asn Minorities in Cable, bd mem/membership chair, 1990-91; bd mem, Nat Asn Telecommunication Officers & Advisers, 1986-88. **Honors/Awds:** Fair Housing Center of Metro Detroit, Distinguished Services, 1992. **Business Addr:** Vice President, Comerica Inc, PO Box 75000, Detroit, MI 48275-3352, **Business Phone:** (313)222-7046.

BRYANT, KOBE B
Basketball player. **Personal:** Born Aug 23, 1978, Philadelphia, PA; son of Joe "Jelly Bean" Bryant and Pam Bryant; married Vanessa Laine, Apr 18, 2001; children: Natalia Diamante & Gianna Maria-Onore. **Career:** Los Angeles Lakers, guard, 1996-. **Orgs:** Nat basketball Asn; Make-a-Wish Found; St. Jude's Children's Hosp; The Lawyers? Comt Civil Rights; Plaza de la Raza; Vivo del Mondo. **Honors/Awds:** NBA All-Star, 1998-2008; NBA Champion: 2000-02; Most Valuable Player All-Star game, 2002, 2007; NBA Scoring Champion, 2006. **Special Achievements:** Youngest player to reach 20,000 career points; Youngest player to be named to the NBA All-Defensive Team; Youngest Slam Dunk champion (18 years, 175 days), after winning the contest at the 1997 NBA All-Star Weekend. **Business Phone:** (310)426-6000.

BRYANT, LEON SERLE
Counselor, educator. **Personal:** Born Jun 22, 1949, Akron, OH; son of Clyde H and Daisy; children: Cillicia N. **Educ:** Ariz State Univ, BA, 1974, MEd, 1991. **Career:** Dept Correction, State Ariz, correctional officer, 1974-75; Phoenix Urban League, manpower specialist, 1975-78; Ariz State Univ, career serv specialist sr, 1978-. **Orgs:** Omega Psi Phi, 1971-; bus adv comt, Phoenix Job Corp, 1988-; Nat Soc Experiental Educ, 1989-; Ariz Career Develop Asn, vpres progs, currently. **Home Phone:** (480)456-4292. **Business Addr:** Career Services Specialist Senior, Arizona State University, Career Service & Career Education Center, Student Services Bldg 329, PO Box 871312, Tempe, AZ 85287-1312, **Business Phone:** (480)965-2350.

BRYANT, PROF. LEROY
Educator. **Educ:** Northwestern Univ, MA, 1973. **Career:** Chicago State Univ, prof hist, currently. **Business Addr:** Professor of History, Chicago State University, 9501 S King Dr, Chicago, IL 60628-1598, **Business Phone:** (773)995-2000.*

BRYANT, DR. MARIAN L. See COMER, DR. MARIAN WILSON.

BRYANT, MARK
Basketball player, basketball coach. **Personal:** Born Apr 25, 1965, Glen Ridge, CA; married Shelley, Jan 1, 1989; children: Taige & Poe. **Educ:** Seton Hall Univ, psychol & communs. **Career:** Basketball player(retired), basketball coach; Portland TrailBlazers, forward-ctr, 1988-95; Houston Rockets, 1995-96; Phoenix Suns, 1996-98; Chicago Bulls, 1998-99; Cleveland Cavaliers, 1999-2000; Dallas Mavericks, 2000-01; Boston Celtics, 2002-03; Denver Nuggets, 2002-03; Philadelphia 76ers, 2002-03; Dallas Mavericks, asst coach, player develop staff, 2004-05; Orlando Magic, asst coach player develop, 2007-08; Seattle Supersonics, asst coach, 2008-. **Business Phone:** (206)281-5800.

BRYANT, MONA. See BRYANT-SHANKLIN, DR. MONA MAREE.

BRYANT, N Z, JR.
Insurance executive. **Personal:** Born Oct 25, 1949, Jackson, MS; son of N Z Sr and Christeen M. **Educ:** Western Mich Univ, BS, 1971, MA, 1972; Univ Mich, attended 1974. **Career:** Oakland Univ, instr, 1972-74; Detroit Col Bus, fac, acad coord, 1974-76; Pontiac Sch, teacher, 1976-79; Equitable Life Ins CPN, agt, 1979-93; Patterson Bryant Inc, pres & chief exec officer, 1982-. **Orgs:** Greater Detroit Area Life Underwriters Asn, 1980-93; pres, Positive People Pontiac, 1982-83; charter pres, Pontiac Optimist Club, 1983-84, vpres, 1984-85; trustee, Oakland Co Br, NCP, 1984-86, treas, 1989-90; qualifying mem, Million Dollar Round Table, 1989; finance comt, Pontiac Area Urban League, 1990-91. **Honors/Awds:** Young Man of the Year, City Pontiac, 1985; Sales Force Agent of the Year, Equitable Life Insurance CPN, 1988-89; Wall of Distinction, Western Mich Univ & Alumni Asn, 1992; Shooting Star Award. **Special Achievements:** Author: "Investing in the 90's," 1992. **Home Addr:** 4545 W Cherry Hill Dr, West Bloomfield, MI 48323, **Home Phone:** (248)681-3160. **Business Addr:** President, Chief Executive Officer, Patterson Bryant Inc, 30600 Telegraph Rd Suite 1160, Bingham Farms, MI 48025, **Business Phone:** (248)433-1902.

BRYANT, DR. NAPOLEON ADEBOLA, JR.
Educator. **Personal:** Born Feb 22, 1929, Cincinnati, OH; son of Napoleon and Katie Smith; married Ernestine C, Jul 15, 1950; children: Karen, Derek, Brian & David. **Educ:** Univ Cincinnati, BS, 1959; Ind Univ, MAT, 1967, EdD, 1970. **Career:** NDEA fel, 1968-70; Xavier Univ, sci resource teacher, prof educ, 1970-, dir sec educ, 1974-79, asst vpres stud develop, 1984-86; NSF, pre-col teacher develop proj, 1974-79, dir minority affairs, 1984-86; Danforth fel, 1983; Nat Sci Teachers Asn, dir multicultural sci educ, 1990-93; Cincinnati Pub Schs, teacher. **Orgs:** Basileus, Omega Psi Phi, Beta Iota Chap, 1965-; Rollman Psychist Hosp, 1976-78; co-organizer & partic, Caribbean Regional Orgn Asn Sci Educators Barbados, WI, 1979; hon life mem, Asn Sci Teachers Jamaica, 1979; ordained deacon Episcopal, 1984; Asn Supvn & Curric Develop, 1988-; charter mem, Asn Multicultural Sci Educ, 1990-; sci consult, Sci Adv Comm State Ohio; Ohio Coun Elem Sch Int; chmn, Comm Local Arrangements; life mem, Nat Asn Advan Colored People; Nat Sci Teachers Asn; consult, Elem & Sec Sci Educ Sch & Pub Firms; bd dir, Harriet Beecher Stowe Preserv Comm, William Procter Conf Ctr. **Honors/Awds:** Omega Man of the Year, Omega Psi Phi, 1973; Nation Builders Award, 1984; Faculty Support Award, Black Stud Asn, Xavier Univ, 1991. **Special Achievements:** Published numerous books; Author : African American Males : Soon Gone?. **Business Addr:** Professor, Xavier University, Department Educ, 3800 Victory Pkwy Dept 1, Cincinnati, OH 45207, **Business Phone:** (513)745-3000.

BRYANT, PAMELA BRADLEY
Public relations executive. **Personal:** Born Jun 11, 1970, Miami, FL; daughter of Matthew and Juanita; married Van K Bryant, Aug 13, 1993; children: Kavon & Quinn. **Educ:** Fla A&M Univ, BS, jour, 1991, MS, jour, 2000, cert pub mg, 2005. **Career:** Fla Dept Educ, asst dir commun; Images Design LLC, pres; Fla A&M Univ, Div Res, pub rels coordr & spec asst pres commun, currently. **Orgs:** Fla Pub Rels Asn; Nat Asn Female Execs; Fla A&M Nat Alumni Asn; Delta Sigma Theta Sorority Inc; Am Bus Women's Asn. **Honors/Awds:** Award of Appreciation, Fla A&M Univ Marching 100; Dean's Award, Fla A&M Univ Col Pharm; President's Award & Leadership Award, Fla A&M Univ Nat Alumni Asn, Leon County Chap. **Special Achievements:** consult, DH Community Housing & Pro Player Stadium Proj, Miami, FL, 1995. **Business Addr:** Public Relations Coordinator, Florida A&M University, Spec Asst Pres Commun, 682 Gamble St, Tallahassee, FL 32307, **Business Phone:** (850)412-7936.

BRYANT, PATRICK L.
Dentist. **Career:** Pvt Pract, dentist, currently. *

BRYANT, PRECIOUS
Singer, songwriter, guitarist. **Personal:** Born Jan 4, 1942; daughter of Lonnie James Bussey. **Career:** Terminus Rec Inc, rec artist, currently. **Business Addr:** Recording Artist, c/o Terminus Records Inc, PO Box 5701, Atlanta, GA 31107, **Business Phone:** (404)817-8155.*

BRYANT, PRESTON
Educator, high school teacher, high school principal. **Personal:** Born Aug 8, 1938, Chicago, IL; married Sandra; children: Carolyn & Beverly. **Educ:** Chicago Teachers Col, B Ed, 1961; Roosevelt Univ, MA, 1963; Nova Univ, Ed D, 1978. **Career:** Teacher, 1961-63; master teacher, 1963-67; Madison Sch, asst prin, acting prin, 1968-70; EF Dunne Elem Sch, prin, 1971-73; George Henry Corliss High Sch, prin, 1974-77; Chicago Bd Educ, supt, 1977-; Chicago Teachers Col, instr, 1975; Union Grad Sch, prof, 1979; Gov State Univ, instr, 1980; Dist ten, Chicago, IL, supt, 1977-; Shields Sch, Dept grants. **Orgs:** Samuel B Stratton Educ Asn; Ill Asn Supr & Curric Devel; Chicago Prins Asn; Nat Asn Sec Sch Prins; bd dir, George Howland Adminrs Asn, vpres; Roosevelt Univ Alumni Asn; bd mem, Roosevelt Univ Bd Govs; Roosevelt Educ Alumni Div; Citizens Schs Com; Nat Alliance Black Sch Educrs; adv coun, Olive Harvey Col Dept Nursing; Nat Asn Black Sch Educr; Nat Asn Advan Colored People; PUSH; Phi Delta Kappa; Zion Evangelical Luth Ch, mem, bd educ; Forum Civic Orgn. **Honors/Awds:** Sch & community award, 1974; outstanding service in educ, Edward F Dunne Sch Comn, 1974; Educators award, Operation PUSH, 1977; Outstanding Educators Award, Dr Roger's Belle Tone Ensemble, 1977. **Business Addr:** Department Of Grants, Shields Schools, 4250 S Rockwell St, Chicago, IL 60632.*

BRYANT, R. KELLY
Executive. **Personal:** Born Sep 22, 1917, Rocky Mount, NC; son of R Kelly and Maggie Poole; married Artelia Tennesse, Aug 26, 1945; children: Robert Kelly Bryant III & Sandra Artelia. **Educ:** Hampton Inst, BS, bus admin, 1940; NC Cent Univ, 1942. **Career:** Executive (retired); Peoples Bldg & Loan Asn, bookkeeper, 1940; Mutual Savings & Loan, bookkeeper, 1941-44; NC Mutual Life Ins Co, Ordinary Dept, chief clerk, 1944-56, mgr, 1956-60, asst secy, 1965-81. **Orgs:** Durham Chamber Com; pres, Chain Investment Corp; secy, AS Hunter Lodge No825 Free & Accepted Masons & First Worshipful Master, 1961-; registr,Burton Sch Voting Precinct No 3, 1951-; bd dir, Goodwill Indust Inc,1968-76; bd dir, Vol Serv Bur Inc; chmn, Sch Improv Comm-Burton Sch PTA,1968-70; chmn, Educ Comm-Durham Human Rels Comn, 1968-76; adv bd,Emergency Sch Assistance Act Prog-Oper Breakthrough Inc, 1972-77; grandsecy, Prince Hall Grand Lodge Masons, NC, 1981-98; educ comm, Durham CommNegro Affairs; Nat & Durham Chap Nat Hampton Alumni Asn; treas, NC Region;trustee, Auditing Comm, White Rock Baptist Church; leader, Friends GeerCemetery, currently; trustee, White Rock Baptist Church. **Honors/Awds:** NC Hamptonian of the Year, 1957; Man of the Year, Durham Housewives League, 1958; Silver Beaver Award; Alumni Merit Award, Nat Hampton Alumni Asn, 1969; Appreciation for Service Award, AS Hunter Lodge No 825 Free &Accepted Masons, 1974; Most Outstanding Secretary, AS Hunter Lodge No 825Free & Accepted Masons, 1976; Special Certificate, Durham Human Rels Comn,Durham City Coun, 1977; Appreciation for Service Award, Nat Hampton Alumni Asn, 1979; Plaque for 38 years of service, Durham Bus & Prof Chain, 1981; NAACP Freedom Fund Dinner Award, 1987. **Home Addr:** 618 Bernice St, Durham, NC 27703-5012.

BRYANT, REGINA LYNN
Educator. **Personal:** Born Dec 1, 1950, Memphis, TN; daughter of Al C and Dorothy Scruggs. **Educ:** Tenn State Univ, BA, Foreign Lang, 1974; Atlanta Univ, MBA, Finance, 1980; Clark Atlanta Univ, doctoral candidate. **Career:** IBM, mkg rep, 1976-77; Am Telephone & Telegraph, mgt develop prog, 1980-82; Comptroller Currency, asst nat bank examiner, 1983-84; Credit Bureau Inc & Equifax Inc, finan analyst, 1984-88; Gorby Reeves, Moraitakis & Whiteman, Atlanta, Ga, legal admin, 1988-92; Atlanta Public Schs, foreign lang instr, 1993-. **Orgs:** Alpha Kappa Alpha Sor Inc, 1971-; Nat Black MBA Assoc, second vpres acad, 1980-83; Jr Achievement Greater Atlanta, bus consult, 198-; Atlanta Univ, Sch Bus Admin Asn, pres, 1983-85; St Anthony's Catholic Church, chair finance comm, 1984-86; Animalife Inc, asst treas, 1984-86; Merit Employment Assoc, youth motivator, 1985-; St Anthony's Night Shelter Fund Raising Comn, 1986. **Honors/Awds:** Exxon Fel, 1979; Nat Black MBA Assoc, Outstanding Service Award, 1982; Outstanding Young Women Am, 1985. **Business Addr:** Instructor for Foreign Languages, Atlanta Public Schools, 765 Peeples St SW, Atlanta, GA 30310, **Business Phone:** (404)756-6414.

BRYANT, RUSSELL PHILIP
Executive, printer, business owner. **Personal:** Born Dec 11, 1949, Waterloo, IA; son of Russell Bryant Sr and Selena Bryant; married Linda Allen, Jan 16, 1982; children: Ian, Russell III & Julian. **Educ:** Ellsworth Jr Col, AA, mkt, 1969; Grand Valley State, BS, bus adminr, 1974;Colo Univ, currently attending. **Career:** Chrysler Financial Credit, sales rep, 1974-76; Petro Energy Int, pres, 1976-79; PB Steel Inc, prin, owner, 1979-82; John Phillips Printing, Inc,owner, 1982-. **Orgs:** Bd dir, Minority Enterprise Inc, Colo, 1992-93; bd dir, Mullen High Sch, 1992-93; Colo Asn Com & Indust, 1992-94; bd dir, Kid's Against Drugs, 1992-95; bd dir, Greater Denver Chamber of Com. **Honors/Awds:** Public Service, 1990; MBE/WBE Supplier of the Year, 1990; MEI, Service Company of the Year, 1992; Denver Post/Greater Denver Chamber, Minority Business, 1990-91; Rocky Mt Regional Minorty Purchasing, Minority Supplier, 1986; Southwest Business Development, 1989; Entrepreneur of the Year, Ernest & Young, 1996. **Special Achievements:** Part owner of largest black-owned printing company in the Western US. **Business Addr:** President, John-Phillips Printing Inc, 3840 Forest St, Denver, CO 80207-1121, **Business Phone:** (303)333-7989.

BRYANT, DR. T. J.
Physician. **Personal:** Born Dec 28, 1934, Wellston, OK; son of Minnie; married Rosie L; children: Daryl, Gregory & Cynthia. **Educ:** Ariz Univ, BS, 1957; Kans Univ Med Sch, MD, 1963; KUMC Menorah, Residency Training, 1967. **Career:** Jackson Co Med Soc, secy, 1973-75; UMKC Sch Med, assoc prof, 1977-; UMKC Sch Med, docent, 1974-79; Dept Med Bapt Med Ctr, chmn, 1980-82; Dept Med, Menorah Med Ctr, vchmn, 1980-; Menorah Med Ctr, bd dirs, 1989; Missouri Bd Healing Arts, 1989. **Orgs:** Mo State Med Asn, 1963-; Jackson Co Med Soc, 1963-; Am Col Gastroenterol, 1972-; Am Soc Internal Med, 1970-; Nat Asn Advan Colored People Urban League, 1980-81; Greater Kans City Chamber Com, 1978-; Am Med Asn; Metrop Med Soc Kans City, Mo; Greater Kans City SW Clin Soc; Kans City Med Soc; Assoc Clin Prof, UMKC Sch Med; App to the Mo State Bd of Healing Arts & Served, 1989, chmn, 1992-93; bd dirs, Menorah Med Ctr; chmn, Internal Med Dept, 1982-83; bd dirs, Baptist Med Ctr. **Military Serv:** USAF, a1c, 1959-65. **Business Addr:** Physician, 2525 E Meyer Blvd, Kansas City, MO 64132.

BRYANT, TERESENA WISE
Government official, school administrator. **Personal:** Born Jan 19, 1940, St Petersburg, FL; daughter of Mose Gardner (deceased) and Mattie Lee Cooksey; divorced; children: Donna Kaye Drayton. **Educ:** Fla A&M Univ, BS, 1962; Howard Univ, Cert Completion Prog Eval & Craftsmanship, 1976; NYU, MPA, 1977; Man Col, coun psych; Fordham Univ, Urban Educ Supv & Admin, post grad studies, 1989. **Career:** New York City, admin positions, 1974-81; State Senator, Bronx City NY, legis asst, comm liaison, 1978-83; Off of the Mayor, New York City Youth Bur, asst exec dir, 1981-83; NY State Tempy Comm to revise the SS Laws, contract mgr, sr prog analyst, 1983-; St Senator, Jos L Galiber, campaign mgr, 1978-; Off of the Mayor, New York City Youth Bur, dir planning; campaign mgr, Robert Johnson, dist atty, NY state, 1988; spec asst to Bronx City Central Bd, 1987-90; NY State Senator, Bronx, NY, legis stat & eval, 1990-92; City Affairs Liaison, admin mgr, 1992-.

Orgs: Alpha Kappa Alpha, Tau Omega, 1975-; coordr, Comm of Bronx Blacks, 1977-; under legis leadership of Sen Joseph L Galiber responsible for securing of additional minority councilman & black assembly seat in Bronx Co redistricting lines; chairperson & founder, Bronx Ctr Prog Serv Youth, 1981-; bd dir, PR Rep, Urban League Bronx Aux Chap, 1982-; Fla A&M Univ Alumni Asn; Am Asn Univ Women; NY City Managerial Employees Asn; Nat Asn Advan Colored People; Am Soc Pub Admin; Nat Forum Black Pub Admin; Nat Asn Female Exec; William Inst CME Church; Coun Concerned Black Exec; NY Univ Alumni NY Chap; Former women adv; New York City Youth Bur; Women Bus Owners of NY; Bronx Black Asn Educrs; Nat Coun Negro Women; Bronx Polit Women's Caucus. **Honors/Awds:** Cert Contrib, Time, New York City, Central Labor Rehab Coun, 1978-83; SAVE, Dept of Labor Serv Award, 1981-83; Outstanding Civic Leadership, Bronx Unity Democratic Club, 1981; Woman of the Yr, Morrisania Ed Coun, 1981; Serv Award, Bronx Ctr Prog Serv, 1982-84; Community Serv Award, Each One Teach One, 1983; Outstanding Serv & Dedication to the Youth of Our Community, Mid Brooklyn Health Soc, 1983; Distinguished Serv Award, NY State Asn Black & Pub Rel Legislators, 1989; Presidential Adv Award, Bronx Council Boy Scouts of Am, 1990; Community Serv Award, East Bronx Chap, Nat Asn Advan Colored People, 1989; Joseph L Galiber Award, 2004. **Special Achievements:** First black district attorney in NY state, 1988. *

BRYANT, VIVIAN
Administrator. **Career:** City Orlando, dir housing authority, currently. **Business Phone:** (407)894-0711.*

BRYANT, WAYNE R
Lawyer. **Personal:** Born Nov 7, 1947, Camden, NJ; son of Isaac R Sr and Anna Mae; married; children: Wayne Richard Jr. **Educ:** Howard Univ, BA, 1969; Rutgers Univ, Sch Law, JD, 1972. **Career:** Zeller & Bryant, gen partner, 1974-; Transp & Commun Comn, vice chmn, 1982-84, chmn, 1984-, majority leader, 1990-91; Independent Authorities & Commun Comn, staff, 1982-84, vice chmn, 1984-; State NJ, Dist Five, assemblyman, 1982-95; Camden Co Coun Econ Oppor, solicitor, 1982-; Borough Somerdale, spec solicitor, 1983-; Juv Resource Ctr, solicitor, 1983-; Borough Lawnside, bond coun, 1984-, solicitor, 1984-; Camden Co Housing Auth, solicitor, 1985-97; Borough Chesilhurst, spec solicitor, 1985-; NJ State Legis, sen, 1995-, asst dem leader, 2002-03, dep majority leader, 2004-; Twnp Deptford, Planning Bd, solicitor, 1996-. **Orgs:** Nat Black Caucus State Legislators; NJ Conf Minority Trans Offs; US Supreme Ct; US Ct Appeals Third Circuit Ct Appeals DC; Supreme Ct NJ; US Dist Ct Dist NJ; life mem Nat Asn Advan Colored People; adv bd, Educ Oppor Fund Comn Rutgers Univ; Lawnside Educ Asn; chmn, Co State & Local Govts United Way Campaign Camden Co; NJ State Democratic Platform Comn. **Honors/Awds:** Hon Doctorate Laws Deg, Howard Univ, 1991; Arthur Armitage Distinguished Alumni Award, Rutgers Univ Sch Law, 1992; Recognition Award, Nat Polit Cong Black Women; Distinguished Service Award, Camden Co Bd Chosen Freeholders; Distinguished Service Award, Camden Co Planning Bd; Award Merit, NJ Co Trans Asn; Legis Committment Award, Educ Improvement Ctr S Jersey Region; Outstanding Achievement Award, Lawnside Bd Educ; Award Merit, Asn Parking Authorities State NJ; Community Service Award, Gloucester Co Black Polit Caucus; Community Service Award, Grace Temple Baptist Church; Community Service Award, YMCA Camden Co; Mt Pisgah Man Year; Community Service Award, First Regular Democratic Club Lawnside; Outstanding Service to Community, Brotherhood Sheriff & Corrections Offrs; Outstanding Service Award, Good Neighbor Award, Juv Resource Ctr; Cert Appreciation, Camden City Skills Ctr; Outstanding Commitment to Human Service, Alternats Women Now Camden Co; Outstanding Service to Community Cert Appreciation Award, Camden Community Serv Ctr; Hairston Clan Community Service Award; Nat Bus League Award Distinguished Service Award, Haddon Heights HS Afro-Am Cult Club; Citizen of the Year, Alpha Phi Alpha Frat Inc Nu Iota Chap; NJ Asn Counties Achievement Award; Cooper Hosp Med Ctr Outstanding Legislator. **Business Addr:** Senator, Deputy Majority Leader, New Jersy State Legislation, Legislative District 5, 501 Cooper St, Camden, NJ 08102-1240, **Business Phone:** (856)757-0552.

BRYANT, WILLA COWARD
Educator, president (organization). **Personal:** Born Nov 21, 1919, Durham, NC; daughter of Owen Ward Coward Willa and Courtney King; married Harry Lee Bryant, Jun 6, 1942 (deceased); children: Dr Mona Maree Bryant-Shanklin. **Educ:** NC Cent Univ, AB, 1951; Temple Univ, MEd, 1961; Duke Univ, EdD, 1970. **Career:** Educator (retired). Durham City Schs, teacher, 1954-61; NC Cent Univ, asst prof educ, 1961-69, adj prof educ, 1990-94; Livingstone Col, chairperson, div educ & psychol, 1970-83. **Orgs:** Consult, Coop Sch Improvement Prog, 1964-66; pres, Alpha Tau Chap of Kappa Delta Pi at Duke Univ, 1969-70; Triangle Reading Asn, 1970-72; NC Asn Col Teacher Ed, 1980-81; Bd Educ Durham City Schs, 1984-92; Phi Delta Kappa Fraternity Carolina Chap, 1987. **Honors/Awds:** Southern Fel Found, 1968-70; "Two Divergent Approaches to Teaching Reading" Am Res Asn, 1970; "Crucial Issues in Reading" Views on Elementary Reading 1973; Phelps Stokes Scholar, 1975. **Home Addr:** 302 E Pilot St, Durham, NC 27707. *

BRYANT, WILLIAM ARNETT, JR.
Physician. **Personal:** Born Dec 31, 1942, Birmingham, AL; married Hidla R Timpson; children: Kristen, Lamont. **Educ:** Clark Col, Atlanta, BA, 1964; State Univ NY, Buffalo, Sch Med, MD, 1975. **Career:** Pvt Prac Pediatrics, physician, 1979-; Univ Md Hosp, Dept Pediatrics, intern/resident/chief resident, 1975-79; Buffao Med Sch, med stud & SUNY, 1971-75; Erie Cty Health Dept Buffalo, lab supvr, 1969-71; Erie Co Health Dept, Buffalo, vd epidemiologist, 1967-69; Provident Hosp Baltimore, MD, asst chief pediatrics, 1980-. **Orgs:** Peace Corps Vol US Govt, 1964-66; Nat Med Asn, 1975-; Chi Delta Mu Health Prof Fraternity, 1977-; pres, Baltimore Clark Col Club, 1979-; chairperson, J Archives Md. **Business Addr:** 1532 Havenwood Rd, Baltimore, MD 21218.

BRYANT, WILLIAM HENRY, JR.
Engineer, president (organization), chief executive officer. **Personal:** Born Feb 10, 1963, Garfield Heights, OH; son of William Henry Sr and Ruth Earle Bishop; married Myra Williams, Feb 10, 1990; children: Kyle J W. **Educ:** Kent State Univ, AAS, 1984; Pac-Western Univ, BS, 1987; ETI Tech Inst,prof dipl, eng design, 1989; Embry-Riddle Aeronaut Univ, master cert, corpaviation mgt, 1999. **Career:** AUS C Co 101 Aviation Battalion, 101st Abn Div, crew engr, 1986-88;Cleveland Rebar, cost estimator, 1989-; Veteran's Admin, Cleveland, OH,rec mgr, 1989-; Aquatech Inc, Cleveland, OH, design engr, 1989-90;Swagelok Toner Co, Solon, Ohio, comput aided design admin, 1990-94;Swagelok Co, tool design engr, 1994-00; Black Eagle Aviation, instr &charter pilot, 1996, pres & chief exec officer, currently; US AirwaysExpress, 2000-01. **Orgs:** Secy, Am Inst Aeronaut & Astronaut, 1982-86; Aircraft Owners & Pilots Asn,1982-; Epsilon, Epsilon Chap, 1984-85; Soc Mfg Engrs, 1984-; jr deacon,Starlight Baptist Church, 1984; Future Aviation Prof Am, 1986-88; pres,Phi Beta Sigma Fraternity, Gamma Alpha Sigma Chap, 1993; Tuskegee AirmenInc, N Coast Chap, 1993-; Asn Black Airline Pilots, 1995-; Nat Asn FlightInstrs, 1995-; F&AM Lodge Ecclesiastes, No 120, Prince Hall, Cleveland OH,1996-; Civil Air Patrol, 1996-; vpres, Phi Beta Sigma Fraternity. **Military Serv:** AUS, Warrant Officer, 1988-95; Ohio Nat Guard, OCS cadet, 1988; OverseasRibbon, 1988; Army Achievement Award, 3rd Armored Div, 1988; Letter ofCommendation, 101st Airborne, 1986; Letter of Commendation, 5th Group SpecForces, 1986; 101st Aviation Battalion Achievement Award, 1986; Letter ofCommendation, Task Force 16Oth, 1987; Good Conduct Ribbon, 1987; ArmyCommendation Award, 1987. **Home Addr:** 1195 Waldo Way, Twinsburg, OH 44087, **Home Phone:** (330)963-0419. **Business Addr:** President, Chief Executive Officer, Black Eagle Aviation Corporation, 1195 Waldo Way, Twinsburg, OH 44087, **Business Phone:** (330)592-6230.*

BRYANT, WILLIAM JESSE
Dentist, educator. **Personal:** Born Apr 8, 1935, Jacksonville, FL; son of Katie Brown; married Taunya Marie Golden Bryant, Feb 22, 1979; children: Kiwanis Linda, William, Deron, Vincent, Michael, Kimberly, Zachary, Jessica. **Educ:** Fla A&M Univ, BA, 1960; Ariz State Univ, attended 1962; Meharry Med Col, DDS, 1967; Boston Univ, cert orthod, 1970; Boston Univ, ScD, 1971. **Career:** Fla A&M, res asst, 1961-63; Boston Univ, instr, 1969-71; pvt pract, 1970; Whittier Dent Clin, orthodontist, 1970-72; Roxbury Comprehensive Community Health Ctr, dent dir, 1971-78; Boston Univ, asst prof, 1971-74; Boston Univ, chmn, assoc prof, 1972; Boston Univ, assoc prof, 1974; HEW Boston, dent consult, 1974; WPFL, Stuart, FL, pvt pract, 1986; pvt pract, dentist, currently. **Orgs:** Exec bd mem, Roxbury Med Tech Inst, 1972-74; exec bd mem, United Way, 1976; exec bd mem, NAACP, 1976; Am Acad Craniofacial Pain, 1998; Commonwealth Dent Soc Greater Boston; Am Asn Orthodontists; NE Soc Orthodontists; Int Asn Dent Res; Am Dent Asn; Nat Dent Asn; Mass Dent Asn; Capital City Dent Soc; Nashville TN FL TN MA GA State Dent Boards; Am Soc Dent C; Am Anesthesiol Asn; Soc Upper 10th; Alpha Phi Alpha; Guardsmen Inc; NAACP; exec bd mem, Health Planning Coun, Boston; Pub Health Coun; bd dir, United Way; bd mem, Big Brother Inc, Boston; bd mem, St Michael's Sch, FL; fel Int Col Craniomandibular Orthop; pres, Martin Co Chamber Com; bd mem, Martin Co & Palm Beach Comn Found. **Honors/Awds:** Numerous awards & publications. *

BRYANT-ELLIS, PAULA D.
Executive. **Personal:** Born Jan 20, 1962, Youngstown, OH; daughter of James F; married Wendell R Ellis, Aug 1, 1981; children: Wendell R Jr. **Educ:** Concordia Lutheran Col, BA, Acct & Bus Mgt, 1992. **Career:** KOTV-6, acct, 1991-92; Bank Okla, pvt banking officer, 1992-; BOK Financial Corp, Community Develop Banking Group, sr vpres, currently. **Orgs:** Nat Asn Black Accountants, 1992-93; chair, Nat Asn Black Accountants, Western Region, stud conf, 1993. **Business Addr:** Private Banking Officer, Bank Okla, 2021 S Lewis Suite 200, Tulsa, OK 74105, **Business Phone:** (918)748-7231.*

BRYANT-HOWROYD, JANICE
Chief executive officer, entrepreneur, founder (originator). **Educ:** Univ Md; NC A&T Univ. **Career:** ACT 1 Personnel Servs, founder, 1978, pres, chmn & chief exec officer, currently; Capital Campaign, NC A&T Univ, chair; Nat Acad Sci, ed; Billboard mag. **Orgs:** Econ Develop Corp C Los Angeles; Los Angeles Urban League; Loyola Marymount Univ, Northrop-Rice Aviation Inst Technol; bd, John F Kennedy Sch Govt, Harvard Univ; Int Womens Coun; Am Red Cross; Nat Acad Sci. **Honors/Awds:** Am Enterprise Award, 2005. **Special Achievements:** One of 50 Leading Woman Entrepreneurs of the World, Star Group. **Business Addr:** Founder, Chief Executice Officer, ACT 1 Personnel Services, 18520 Hawthorne Blvd, Torrance, CA 90504, **Business Phone:** (310)371-2151.*

BRYANT-REID, JOHANNE
Executive. **Personal:** Born Mar 11, 1949, Farmington, WV; daughter of Leslie and Jessie L Scruggs. **Educ:** W Va Univ, BS, 1971. **Career:** Executive (retired); Ran Assoc, gen mgr & recruiter, 1971-78; Merrill Lynch, exec recruitment mgr, 1978-81; corp human resources, vpres, 1981-89; dir human resources, 1989-95; Opers Serv, first vpres. **Orgs:** Am Soc Personnel Admin; Employ Mgrs Assoc; EDGES; mem adv bd, Nat Coun Negro Women; Black World Championship Rodeo; exec bd mem, Borough Manhattan; Commun Col; bd mem, James Robert Braxton Scholar Fund; bd dirs, W Va Univ Found Inc; bd mem, Funk City Records; Selection Comt, Jackie Robinson Found Scholars Prog; exec bd, Artist Space; fund raiser, United Negro Col Fund; bd dir, Romare Beardon Found. **Honors/Awds:** Black Achievers Award, YWCA, 1981; Hall of Fame Award, Nat Asn Negro Bus & Prof men's Club; United Negro College Fund Award. *

BRYANT-SHANKLIN, DR. MONA MAREE (MONA BRYANT)
Educator. **Personal:** Born Mar 26, 1954, Southern Pines, NC; daughter of Harry and Dr Willa Bryant; married Gerald Price, Dec 31, 1976; children: Gerald Kayin, Jamil Maree & Tai Miquel. **Educ:** NC Cent Univ, BA, 1976; Kans State Univ, MS, 1979; Univ NC, Chapel Hill, PhD, 1996. **Career:** Kans State Govt, voc rehabil counr, 1980-82; SC State Govt, Educ consult/MIS mgr, 1982-91; Univ NC, Chapel Hill, psychoeduc therapist, 1991-92; NC Cent Univ, adj prof, consult, 1994-96, educ res consult, 1996-97; Norfolk State Univ, Dept Early Childhood & Elem Educ, assoc prof, 1997-. **Orgs:** Alpha Kappa Alpha Sorority, 1981-; Jack & Jill Am 2003-; Nat Black Child Develop Asn, Columbia SC, pres, 1986-90; Nat Asn Educ Young C, 1986- Coun Exceptional C, 1992-; Int Reading Asn, 1997-2000; Asn Supervision & Curriculum Develop, 1996-2000; Am Educ Res Asn, 1997-. **Honors/Awds:** RJR res fel, Winston Salem Pub Schs/RJR, 1994-95. **Special Achievements:** Publisher: "A Comparsion of High and Low Achieving 4th Grade African-American Children," 1996; "Alcohol and Drug Abuse Prevention for Young Children on Measures of Nonverbal Communication," (dissertation), 1990; Pretty Special Children: A Curriculum Guide for Working with Abused & Neglected Children, 1988. **Home Addr:** 504 Wickwood Dr, Chesapeake, VA 23322-5853. **Business Addr:** Associate Professor, Norfolk State University, Department Early Childhood & Elementary Education, 700 Pk Ave, Norfolk, VA 23504-3989, **Business Phone:** (757)823-8280.

BRYCE, DR. HERRINGTON J
Economist, educator. **Personal:** Married Beverly J Gaustad; children: Marisa Jeanine, Shauna Celestina & Herrington Simon. **Educ:** Minn State Univ, BA, 1960; Syracuse Univ, PhD, 1966; Am Col, CLU, 1985, ChFC, 1985. **Career:** Nat Planning Assoc, economist, 1966-67; Clark Univ, fac, 1967-69; Urban Inst, sr economist, 1969-70; Brookings Inst, fel, 1970-71; MIT, fac, 1972-73; Joint Ctr Polit Studies, dir res, 1973-76; Harvard Univ, fel, 1978; Acad State & Local Govt, vpres, 1978-80; Carlogh Corp, pres; Nat Policy Inst, 1980-85; Col William & Mary, Life Va prof bus, 1986-. **Orgs:** Nat Asn Corp Dir; Am Soc CLU & CFC; Treasury Bd, State Va. **Honors/Awds:** Hon Citizen, City Atlanta, 1975; Minority Administrator of the Yr, Conf Minority Pub Admins, 1976; Hon Citizen, City New Orleans, 1976; Distinguished Alumnus, Mankato State Univ, 1982; Appointed Treas Bd, Commonwealth Va, 1990-94; Levine Prize, 2006. **Special Achievements:** Author of books on nonprofits and regional economics; Players in the Public Policy Process. **Business Addr:** Professor, The College of William & Mary, Mason School of Business, Tyler 226, PO Box 8795, Williamsburg, VA 23187-8795, **Business Phone:** (757)221-2856.

BRYCE-LAPORTE, ROY SIMON
Educator, sociologist. **Personal:** Born Sep 7, 1933; son of Simon J and Myra C; divorced; children: Camila, Robertino & Rene. **Educ:** Panama Canal Col, AA, 1954; Univ Nebraska-Lincoln, BS, educ, 1960, MA socio & educ; Univ Puerto Rico, Adv Cert, 1963; UCLA, PhD, socio, 1968; Yale Law Sch, MSL, 1985. **Career:** Hunter Col, City Univ New York, asst prof soc, 1968-69, org dir, 1986-89; Yale Univ, dir African-Am St prog, assoc prof socio, 1969-72; Nat Inst Ment Health, vis sci, 1971-72; Smithsonian Inst, dir, res sociologist, 1972-83; Univ Pa, vis prof, 1974-; Howard Univ, guest prof, 1975-; Cath Univ Am, dept anthrop; Res Inst Immigration Ethnics Studies Inc, dir & gen ed, 1972-83, dir & pres, 1983-86; adv bd, Cimarron Journal Carib Stud Assocs, City Univ New York, 1984; Schomburg Ctr Res Black Culture, guest Cur, 1985-86; City Univ New York, Col Staten Island, The Ctr Immigrant & Pop Studies, prof socio & dir, 1986-88; Colgate Univ, John D & Catherine T MacArthur prof sociol & anthrop & dir, Africana & Latin Am Studies, 1989-2000m, John D & Catherine T MacArthur prof emer sociol & anthrop, 2000-; DC Humanities Coun, lectr, 1990; Smith Col, vis Neilson prof, sociol, 1994.

Orgs: Bd dir, Caucus Black Sociologists, Am Acad Polit & Soc Scis; sec gen, I Cong Black Culture Am Cali Colombia, 1979; chmn, Frazier-Johnson-Dubois Awds Comm, Am Soc Asn, 1978-79; City Coun DC,1984; Alpha Kappa Delta; Pi Gamma Mu; Phi Delta Kappa; Mu Epsilon Nu; Phi Sigma Iota; Alpha Phi Alpha; adv bd, US Census Adv & Race Ancestry Minorities; Yale Law Schl Alumni Asn & Yale Club, Wash DC; bd mgr, Seamen's Children's Soc; adv bd, Schomburg's Afro-Am Sch Comt; col accreditation comm & dean's adv bds, Picker Gallery & Off Undergrad Studies, Colgate Univ; nominee, nomination comm, Am Sociol Asn; chair, acad adv bd, WADABAGI; ed bd, Caribbean Res Ctr, Medgar Evers Col, CUNY; adv bds res pub proj, Anacostia Mus; African Voices Proj, Museum Man & Nat Hist, Smithsonian Inst; adv bd, Caribbean Archival Res Proj, Schomburg Ctr; NAACP, Nat adv bd, 1998; charter fel Woodrow Wilson Intl Ctr. **Honors/Awds:** Mayor's Award, 1982; School Contribution Award, Caribbean Am Int Cult Org, 1981; Mayor's Award for Contrib to the Arts, Wash, 1981; Arturo Griffith Award, Afro Latino Inst Wash DC, 1983; Gelman Service Award, Eastern Sociol Soc; "Man of the Year Award," Panamanian Coun New York, 1986; Educational Award with Commendations from NY State Assembly and NY City Council, Panama Canal Int Alumni Asn, 1998; Distinguished Teaching Award, Colgate Univ Alumini, 2000. **Special Achievements:** Editor of "New Immigration Vols I & II," Transaction Books, 1980; "Inequality & the Black Experience, Some Int Dimensions" special issue"Journal of Black Studies; Who's Who listings and awards for distinguished service and contributions to Afro-Latino studies. **Business Addr:** Professor Emeritus, Colgate University, Department of Sociology & Anthropology, Alumni Hall 13 Oak Dr, Hamilton, NY 13346-1398, **Business Phone:** (315)228-7543.

BRYSON, CHERYL BLACKWELL
Lawyer. **Personal:** Born May 28, 1950, Baltimore, MD; daughter of Connie and Clarence D; married James; children: Bradley & Blake. **Educ:** Morgan State Univ, BS (magna cum laude), 1972; Ohio State Univ, Col Law, JD, 1977. **Career:** Ohio State Univ, Col Law, assoc ed law jour, 1976; Friedman & Koven, labor law assoc, 1976-80; Katten, Muchin & Zavis, partner/assoc, 1980-86; City Chicago, deputy corp coun, 1986-89; Bell, Boyd & Lloyd, partner, labor & employment law, 1989-92; Rivkin, Radler & Kremer, partner, 1992-95; Holleb & coff, partner, 1995-99; Duane Morris LLP, partner, 1999-. **Orgs:** Bd dir, Friends Prentiss Women's Hosp Northwestern Hosp, 1993; bd adv, Loyola Univ Chicago, Inst IDL Relations, 1986-94;; YWCA Metropolitan Chicago, 1994; IIT Chicago, Kent Col Law, bd adv, Public Sector Labor Law Conference Bd; The Neighborhood Inst Dev Corp; DuSable Mus African Am Hist; bd adv, Ctr Employment Dispute Resolution.; Am Bar Asn; Chicago Bar Asn; Asn Trial Lawyers Am; Cook County Bar Asn. **Honors/Awds:** Outstanding Achievement Award, Financial Independence Inst, 1987; Acad Olympics Appreciation, Chicago Pub Schools, 1989; Rising Sun Award, Chicago, IL, 2002. **Special Achievements:** Author: "Racial Prejudice," Ohio State Law Journal, 1976; "Unfair Labor Practices," ICLE Labor Law Handbook, 1984; "Sexual Harasssment," Employee Relations Law Journal, 1990; "Health Care Cost Containment," Illinois Public Employee Relations Report, 1990; "25 Influential Black Women in Business," New York , 2001;Today's Chicago Woman, "100 Women Making a Difference," Chicago, IL, 2001; Named to "Top 50 Leading Women Lawyers in Illinois" and "Top 50 Leading Women Business Lawyers in Illinois" by Leading Lawyers Network Magazine, 2006; Named an Illinois SuperLawyer for 2006. **Business Phone:** (312)499-6708.

BRYSON, PEABO (ROBERT PEABO BRYSON)
Singer. **Personal:** Born Apr 13, 1951, Greenville, SC. **Career:** Al Freeman and the Upsetters, singer, 1965; Moses Dillard and the Tex Town Display, 1968-73; Solo Albums: Peabo, 1976; Reaching for the Sky, 1978;Crosswinds, 1978; We're the Best of Friends, 1979; Paradise, 1980; Live &More, 1980; Turn the Hands of Time, 1981; I am Love, 1981; Don't Play with Fire, 1982; Born to Love, 1983; Straight from the Heart, 1984; Take No Prisoners, 1985; Quiet Storm, 1986; Positive, 1988; All My Love, 1989; Can You Stop the Rain, 1991; Through the Fire, 1994; Peace on Earth, 1997; Really Love, 1997; Family Christmas, 1998; Unconditional Love, 1999; The Essential, 2003; duet with Natalie Cole, "We're the Best of Friends;" due twith Roberta Flack, "Tonight I Celebrate My Love". **Honors/Awds:** Grammy Award, 1992, 1993. **Special Achievements:** Nine gold albums with songs reaching top ten lists in US and UK. **Business Phone:** (212)975-4321.*

BRYSON, DR. RALPH J.
Educator, president (organization). **Personal:** Born Sep 10, 1922, Cincinnati, OH; son of Ralph and Annie Davis. **Educ:** Univ Cincinnati, BS, 1947, MS, 1950; Ohio State Univ, PhD, 1953. **Career:** Southern Univ, instr Eng, 1949; Miles Col, instr Eng, 1949-50; Ala State Univ, assoc prof Eng, 1953-62; prof & dept head, 1962-75, 2001-, chmn div humanities 1975-77, prof Eng 1977-; Univ Ala, adj prof, 1987; Ala State Univ, actg chair & prof, currently. **Orgs:** Pres, Asn Col Eng Teachers AL; Ala Coun Teachers Eng Exec Bd; Nat Coun Teachers Eng; Modern Lang Asn; S Atlantic MLA; Col Lang Asn; Conf Col Composition & Community; Phi Delta Kappa; Lectr Auth & Consult; Kappa Alpha Psi; Ed Column Books & Such; chmn, Nat Achievement Comn; officer, Province Bd Dir; Am Bridge Asn; chmn exec bd & sectional vpres, Montgomery Seminar Arts; bd trustees, Mus Fine Arts Asn; bd dirs, Ala Writers' Forum; Herman Schneider Legacy Soc. **Honors/Awds:** Dexter Ave King Memorial Baptist Church; Outstanding Journalistic Contributions & Achievement Kappa Alpha Psi; Outstanding Men of Yr & Montgomery; Cited Outstanding OH State Univ Graduate in They Came & They Conquered; Bryson Endowed Scholarships Established at Univ Cinncinnati & Ohio State Univ, 1995; 56th Recipient of the Elder Watson Diggs Award, 72nd Grand Chapter elected grand historian, 73rd Grand Chapt, Kappa AlphaPsi, 1997. **Special Achievements:** Co-author, History of the Southern Province, Kappa Alpha Psi Fraternity, 1951-97, 1999. **Military Serv:** AUS, 1942-45; European Theater of Operations 1943-45. **Business Addr:** Professor, Alabama State University, Department of Languages and Literature, 314 McGhee Hall, Montgomery, AL 36101-0271.*

BRYSON, ROBERT PEABO. **See BRYSON, PEABO.**

BRYSON, SEYMOUR L.
School administrator, educator. **Personal:** Born Sep 8, 1937, Quincy, IL; son of Claudine Jackson; married Marjorie; children: Robin, Todd & Keri. **Educ:** Southern Ill Univ Carbondale, BA, sociol, 1959; MS, rehab coun, 1961, PhD,educ psychol, 1972. **Career:** St Louis State Hosp, rehab counr, 1961-65; Breckinridge Job Corps Ctr, admin, 1965-69; Develop Skills Prog, dir, 1969-72; Rehab Inst SIU, from asst prof to assoc prof, 1972-84, prof, 1984; Southern Ill Univ, Col Human Resources, assoc dean, 1977-78 & 1980-84, interim dean, 1978-80 & 1984,dean, 1984-88, asst pres, 1988-90, exec asst pres, 1990; Southern Ill Univ Carbondale, assoc chancellor diversity, currently. **Orgs:** Chmn, Racism Community Am Rehab Coun Asn, 1972-74; bd dir, Jackson County Community Ment Health Ctr, 1974-82; senate, Am Rehab Coun Asn Del Am Personnel & Guid Asn Personnel & Guid, 1976-78; bd dir Jackson County Community Ment Health Ctr, 1980-82; gov appointee, Dept Rehab Serv Adv Coun, 1980; State Use Comn 1983-; pres, Ill Asn Non-White Concerns,1984-85; chmn, Jackson County 708 Bd 1986-; bd dir, Res-Care, 1989-; Am Asn Univ Admin; Asn Non-White Concerns; Am Rehab Coun Asn. **Honors/Awds:** Phi Kappa Phi Nat Hon Soc, 1972-; Research Award, Asn Non-White Concerns,1976; Southern Illinois Univ Hall of Fame, 1977; Special Award for Distinguished Service, ICBC, 1985; Image Award for Education, Carbondale Br, Nat Asn Advan Colored People, 1988; Quincy High Hall of Fame, 1989; Illinois Hall of Fame. **Home Addr:** 905 S Valley Rd, Carbondale, IL 62901, **Home Phone:** (618)549-0290. **Business Addr:** Associate Chancellor, Southern Illinois University Carbondale, 110 Anthony Hall 1265 Lincoln Dr, PO Box 4341, Carbondale, IL 62901, **Business Phone:** (618)453-1186.

BUCHANAN, CALVIN D.
State government official. **Personal:** Married Donna C. **Educ:** Univ Miss, BA, JD. **Career:** US Army, judge advocate, 1983-90; Northern Dist MS, asst US atty, 1990-97, US atty, 1997-01. **Orgs:** MS State Bar; Magnolia Bar Asn; Second MB Church Univ. **Honors/Awds:** Hon Discharge, AUS. **Special Achievements:** First African American to serve as US attorney in the state of Mississippi. *

BUCHANAN, DARRYL E
City council member. **Career:** Flint City Coun, coun mem; Flint City Coun, coun pres, currently. **Business Addr:** Council President of Ward 1, Flint City Council, 1101 S Saginaw St, Flint, MI 48502, **Business Phone:** (810)766-7418.

BUCHANAN, RAYMOND LOUIS (BIG PLAY RAY)
Football player, musician, radio broadcaster. **Personal:** Born Sep 29, 1971, Chicago, IL; married Sheree; children: Destinee, Ray Jr & Baylen. **Educ:** Univ Louisville. **Career:** Indianapolis Colts, defensive back, 1993-96; Atlanta Falcons, defensive back, 1997-03; Oakland Raiders, 2004- rap artist, album: "Favor", 1998; "Roll With Me", 1999; Fox Sports, host. **Orgs:** Ray Buchanan Found, Make A Wish. **Honors/Awds:** Named to the NFL All-Rookie Team in 1993; American Football Conference Defensive Player of the Week, 1994; United Press International All AFC Second Team selection; Pro Bowl National Football Conference in 1998. **Special Achievements:** Starter in the Pro Bowl for the National Football Conference in 1998; NFL All-Rookie Team, 1993; Created Christian rap music album in 2002 . *

BUCHANAN, SAM H
Lawyer. **Educ:** Univ Iowa Sch Law, attended. **Career:** Miss Ctr Legal Serv, exec dir, currently. **Orgs:** Miss Bar Asn; Miss Volunteer Lawyers Proj. **Business Phone:** (601)545-2950.

BUCHANAN, SHAWN
Executive, baseball player. **Personal:** Born Feb 2, 1970, Gay, IN; married Kelli; children: 2. **Educ:** Nebr Univ. **Career:** Chicago White Sox, outfielder, 1991; Nebr Beef, 1995; All Am Meats Inc, pres & chief exec officer, 1996-. **Orgs:** Am Logistics Asn; Nat Minority Supplier; Better Bus Bur; Nat Meat Asn. **Honors/Awds:** Emerging Company of the Year Award, Black Enterprise, 2000. **Business Phone:** (402)453-0200.*

BUCHANAN, SHONDA T (NYESHA KHALFANI)
Editor, college teacher. **Personal:** Born Jan 1, 1968, Kalamazoo, MI. **Educ:** Loyola Marymount Univ, BA, MA. **Career:** Turning Pt, assoc ed; Marketplace Radio, commentator; Hampton Univ, prof eng, currently. **Orgs:** Sundance Inst Writing Fel. **Special Achievements:** Tales in Caffeine Mag, Venice Mag; Auth: Baring Cross, The Drumming Between Us, The Fire This Time. **Business Addr:** Professor, Hampton University, School of Liberal Arts & Education, Dept English, Hampton Univ, Hampton, VA 23668, **Business Phone:** (757)727-5506.

BUCK, IVORY M., JR.
School administrator. **Personal:** Born Dec 25, 1928, Woodbury, NJ; married Ernestine. **Educ:** William Paterson Bus Inst, Cert Bus Ad, 1954-56; Glassboro State Col, BA, 1960, MA, 1968. **Career:** School Administrator (retired); Pub Schs Deptford NJ, teacher, 1958-64; Johnstone Training Res Ctr, teacher, 1960-62; Jr High Sch Deptford, dirguid, 1964-68; Glassboro State Col, asst registr, 1968-71, Adv Ctr, asst dir; Gloucester Co Col, counr, 1969-72. **Orgs:** White House Conf Libr Serv, 1978; alumni treas, Glassboro State Col, 1979; Evaluation Team Sec Educ, 1980; secy gen, Prince Hall Scottish Rite Masons 33 Degrees, 1983; secy bd dirs, Fitzwater Housing Project, 1985; nat elected officer, Prince Hall Shriners, 1980-; bd dir, Camden Co YMCA; Berlin bd, Jr Chamber Com; chairperson Inclusion, Black Studies Monroe Twp Pub Schs; Nat Asn Advan Colroed People, Elks; Phi Delta Kappa Frat; co-chmn, Kappa Alpha Psi, Currently. **Honors/Awds:** Leadership Award, Marabash Museum New Egypt NJ, 1978; Legion of Honor Award for Leadership & Service Shriners, 1980; Distinguished Alumni Award, Glassboro State Col, 1981; The Chapel of Four Chaplains Award, Philadelphia PA, 1964, 1984; Honorary Police Captain, Capitol Heights Maryland, Commissioned Ky Colonel, Recipient Seagram Vanguard Award; Mayor City, Valdosta GA, proclaimed March 27, 1993, Ivory M Buck Jr Day. **Military Serv:** USAF sgt 4 yrs; Airman of the Month; Good Conduct Medal; Eastern Theatre & Korean Medals. **Business Addr:** Co-Chairman, Kappa Alpha Psi Fraternity Inc, 28 Harrell Ave, Williamstown, NJ 08094, **Business Phone:** (815)672-8075.

BUCK, DR. JUDITH BROOKS
Educator. **Personal:** Born Mar 3, 1949, Norfolk, VA; daughter of George A Sr; married Henry Jr; children: Kimberly & Michael Henry. **Educ:** Bennett Col, Greensboro NC, BA, Spec Educ & Psychol, 1971; Univ Va, M.Ed, Admin & Supv, 1986, PhD, Educational Policy Studies. **Career:** Coun Exceptional C, info spec, 1972; Fairfax County, bd educ, learning disabilities teacher, 1972-74; Harford County, bd educ, crisis resource teacher, 1974-76; Norfolk Pub Schs, child develop spec, 1976-77, learning disabilities teacher, 1980-81; USAF, child care ctr, pre sch dir, 1978-80, spec educ teacher, 1983-86; Huntsville Public Sch, alternative prog coord, 1981-83; Huntsville City Sch, spec educ area specialist, prin; Challenger Middle Sch, prin; Va State Univ, Grad Prof Educ Prog Educ Admin & Supv, assoc prof, currently. **Orgs:** Shiloh Baptist Church, 1959; Delta Sigma Theta, 1968; Nat Va Educ Assoc, 1976; Fed Women's Clubs Am, 1984-85; First Baptist Church, 1986; sec & bd dir, Huntsville & Madison County Daycare Asn, 1991-; Nat Asn Elem Sch Prin, 1988; Nat Asn Sec Sch Prin, 1986. **Honors/Awds:** Freedom Fund Award, Nat Asn Advan Colored People; Most Notable Women in America for the Year, 2003. **Business Addr:** Associate Professor, Virginia State University, Educational Administration and Supervision, 1 Hayden Dr, Petersburg, VA 23806, **Business Phone:** (804)524-5000.

BUCKHALTER, EMERSON R.
Physician. **Personal:** Born Nov 10, 1954, El Monte, CA; married Veretta Boyd; children: Monica. **Educ:** Univ Calif Los Angeles, BA, 1976; Howard Univ Col Med, MD, 1980. **Career:** Hawthorne Comm Med Group, physician, 1983-86; St Francis Care Med Group, physician, 1986-; Regal Med Group, sr physician, currently. **Orgs:** Am Med Asn. **Honors/Awds:** Alpha Omega Alpha Honor Med Soc, 1979; Nat Med Fel; Henry J Kaiser Found Merit Scholar, 1980. **Home Addr:** 5936 Croft Ave, Los Angeles, CA 90056. **Business Addr:** Physician, Regal Med Group, 3628 E Imperial Hwy Suite 202, Lynwood, CA 90262, **Business Phone:** (310)631-5000.*

BUCKHANAN, DOROTHY WILSON
Marketing executive. **Personal:** Born Jul 12, 1958, Sumter, SC; daughter of Ida Gregg; married Walt A Buckhanan, Aug 22, 1987. **Educ:** Benedict Col Columbia SC, BS, Bus, 1980; Atlanta Univ Grad School Bus, MBA, 1982. **Career:** Xerox Corp, mkt asst, 1982-84; SC Johnson & Son Inc, prod mgr; Top Ladies Distinction Inc, vpres. **Orgs:** Am Mkt Asn 1980; Toastmaster's Int, 1980-82; Nat Black MBA Asn 1984; vpres, fundraising chmn & corresp secy, Alpha Kappa Alpha, 1984-87; vpres, Top Ladies of Distinction Inc, 1985-88. **Honors/Awds:** Outstanding Undergrad Award, Alpha Kappa Alpha, 1979; Nat Deans List Atlanta Univ, 1980-82; Exec Scholar Fel, Atlanta Univ, 1982-84; Employee Recognition Award, Xerox Corp, 1983; Distinguished Alumni Award, Benedict Col, 1987; Serv Award, Alpha Kappa Alpha, 1988; Outstanding Speaker Award, Dale Carnegie Inst, 1989. **Special Achievements:** National 1st Vice President. *

BUCKHANAN, SHAWN L
Clergy, educator. **Personal:** Born Feb 22, 1962, Albuquerque, NM; son of George Kenneth and C Jacquelyn; married Rosalind G Chelf-Buckhanan, Aug 1, 1981; children: Shawn L Buckhanan

II & Solomon L Buckhanan. **Educ:** Phoenix Univ, BS, bus admin, 1996. **Career:** Chase Bank Ariz, asst br mgr, 1983-91; US W Commun, operator, 1991-93; Ctr Acad Success High Sch, prin, 1996-2002; Laymen's & Youth Dept, instr; St Paul Missionary Baptist Church, pastor, sr pastor, currently. **Orgs:** Omega Psi Phi, Baslieus, 1980-83; educr, Nat Baptist Conv, USA Inc, 1981-; Nat Asn Advan Colored People, Youth Servs Ministers Div, 1995-; pres, Phoenix Citywide Youth Ministerial Asn, 1998-2001; moderator, Southern Ariz Missionary Baptist Dist Asn, 1998?2006; pres, Sierra Vista Ministerial Asn, 1998-2001; Paradise Baptist State Conv, HMB liaison, 2000-; rep, Nat Baptist Convention Home Mission Bd; treas, Home Mission Bd. **Honors/Awds:** Chapter of the Year, Omega Psi Phi, 1981; Parent of the Year, Phoenix Pub Sch, 1991; Youth Division Image Award, Nat Asn Advan Colored People, 1992; numerous others. **Home Addr:** 5273 Highland Shadows Dr, Sierra Vista, AZ 85635. **Business Addr:** Senior Pastor, St Paul Missionary Baptist Church, 227 N Carmichael Ave, Sierra Vista, AZ 85635, **Business Phone:** (520)458-5809.

BUCKLEY, DOUGLAS TERELL. See BUCKLEY, TERRELL.

BUCKLEY, GAIL LUMET (GAIL HORNE JONES)
Writer. **Personal:** Born Dec 21, 1937, Pittsburgh, PA; daughter of Louis Jones and Lena Horne Hagton; married Kevin, Oct 1, 1983; married Sidney Lumet, Nov 24, 1963 (divorced); children: Amy & Jenny. **Educ:** Radcliff Col, BA, 1959. **Career:** Journalist, writer; Marie-Claire Mag, journalist, 1959-63; Nat Scholar Serv & Fund Negro Studs, stud counr, 1961-62; Life mag, journalist, 1962-63; contributor to periodicals, 1980; writer, currently; Books: The Hornes: An American Family, 1986; American Patriots: The Story of Blacks in the Military from the Revolutionto Desert Storm, 2001; Black American families for PBS, 2002. **Honors/Awds:** DHL, Univ Southern Ind, 1987. **Special Achievements:** Television Appearance: "American Masters", 1996. **Business Addr:** Author, c/o Lynn Nesbit, International Creative Management, 825 8th Ave, New York, NY 10019, **Business Phone:** (212)556-5600.

BUCKLEY, MARCUS WAYNE
Football player. **Personal:** Born Feb 3, 1971, Fort Worth, TX. **Educ:** Tex A&M Univ. **Career:** New York Giants, line backer, 1993-99; Atlanta Falcons, line backer, 2000.

BUCKLEY, TERRELL (DOUGLAS TERELL BUCKLEY)
Football player, football coach. **Personal:** Born Jun 7, 1971, Pascagoula, MS; married Denise; children: Sherrell, Brianna & 1 child. **Educ:** Fla State Univ, 2007. **Career:** Green Bay Packers, defensive back, 1992-94; Miami Dolphins, 1995-99, 2003; Denver Broncos, 2000; New England Patriots, 2001-02; NY Jets, 2004; NY Giants, 2005: FSU, asst strength coach, currently. **Honors/Awds:** Jim Thorpe Award winner, 1991; Consensus All-Am, 1991; AP All Am second team, 1990; fifth pick 1992 NFL Draft, Green Bay. *

BUCKNER, BRENTSON ANDRE
Football player. **Personal:** Born Sep 30, 1971, Columbus, GA; married Denise. **Educ:** Clemson Univ, English. **Career:** Football player (retired); Pittsburgh Steelers, defensive end, 1994-96; Cincinnati Bengals, 1997; San Francisco 49ers, 1998-2000; Carolina Panthers, defensive tackles, 2001-05. *

BUCKNER, FLOYD
Publisher, city council member. **Career:** Community Times Dispatch, publ, currently; Colleton County, councilman, currently. **Special Achievements:** First African-American descent to have a government building named after him in Colleton County. *

BUCKNER, DR. JAMES L
Dentist. **Personal:** Born Jul 29, 1934, Vicksburg, MS; son of Florice Williams and Clarence E; children: JaSaun & Justina Jordan. **Educ:** Univ Illinois, BSD, 1957, DDS, 1959. **Career:** Pvt pract, dentist. **Orgs:** Founder, bd dir, Seaway Nat Bank, 1965-86; pres, Lincoln Dent Soc, 1965-66; sec, bd dir, Nat Dent Asn, 1966-67; bd adv, Supreme Life Ins Co, 1970-; trustee, WTTW, Channel 11, 1970-74, City Col Chicago, 1971-76; chmn, Chicago Dent Soc Comn Pub Aid, 1971-80; vice chmn, Chicago Econ Develop Corp, 1972-75; pres, Coun Minority Bus Enterprise, 1972-75; Gov Walkers Pub Health Transition Task Force, 1972-73; bd adv, Midwest Sickle Cell Anaemia Inc, 1972-; trustee, Univ Ill Dent Alumni Asn, 1973-75; co-chmn, Chicago United, 1973-75; Ill Dent Soc; Am Dent Soc; Ill Dent Serv Corp; Ill Dept Pub Aid Dent Adv Comt; pres, Chicago Urban League, 1973-76; chmn, Chicago Fin Develop Corp, 1973-76; chmn, Coun Nat Urban League, 1975-76; pres, Trains & Boats & Planes Inc, 1978-92; The Foodbasket Inc, 1981, 1988-; Am Soc Travel Agents; vpres, Seaway Commun Inc, 1978-85; chmn, Seaway Commun Inc, 1985-; chmn, Push Found, 1987-; vice chmn, Ill Serv Fed Savings & Loan, 1988-. **Honors/Awds:** Ten Outstanding Young Men Award, South End Jaycees, 1965; Certificate Achievement, Am Inst Banking, 1965; Certificate Achievement, Nat Dent Asn, 1966; Certificate of Appreciation, Chicago Area Coun Boy Scouts, 1970; Community Service Award, Big Buddies Youth Serv Inc, 1971; Man of the Year Award, Chicago Urban League, 1972; Certificate of Appreciation, Commonwealth Church, 1972; Certificate of Recognition, Coun Nat Urban League Pres, 1977; Outstanding Achievement Award, Women's Div, Chicago Urban League, 1985. **Business Phone:** (207)945-6457.

BUCKNER, QUINN
Basketball player. **Personal:** Born Jan 1, 1954. **Educ:** Ind Univ, grad. **Career:** Basketball player (retired), basketball exec; Milwaukee Bucks, 1977-82; Boston Celtics, 1983-85; Indiana Pacers, 1986; NBC TV, NBA telecasts, analyst, 1993; Dallas Mavericks, head coach, 1993-94; Cleveland Cavaliers, analyst; Commun Pacers Sports & Entertainment, vpres, 2004-; FSN Midwest, Ind Pacers, color analyst, currently. **Orgs:** Pacers Found; Spec Olympics Ind; Community Health Found; Indianapolis Zool Soc; Ind Youth Inst; YMCA. **Special Achievements:** NBA Championship team, Boston Celtics, 1984. **Business Addr:** Color Analyst, FSN Midwest, The Annex Bldg, 700 St Louis Station Suite 300, St Louis, MO 63103, **Business Phone:** (314)206-7000.

BUCKNER, WILLIAM PAT
Educator. **Personal:** Born Oct 5, 1929, Brazil, IN; son of W P Buckner Sr and Mary E Patton; married Irene Smith, May 31, 1956; children: Lawrence & Douglas. **Educ:** DePauw Univ, AB, 1950; Ind Univ, MS, 1954, HSD, 1969. **Career:** Southern Univ, New Orleans, LA, Dept Health, Phys Educ Recreation, assoc prof & chair, 1959-70; Eastern Mich Univ, Ypsilanti, MI, Dept Health, Phys Educ & Recreation, assoc prof & health coordr, 1970-71; Prairie View A& M Univ, Prairie View, TX, Dept Health, Phys Educ & Recreation, prof & dept head, 1971-72; Univ Houston, Dept Health & Human Performance, prof & health coordr, 1972-; Baylor Col Med, Houston, TX, adj prof, 1987-. **Orgs:** Asn Adv Health Educ, 1955-; Family Life Coun, TX, 1977-; Nat Forum Death Educ & Coun, 1977-; grief coun Life Threatening & Illness Alliance,1972-; adv bd, ENCORE Gr Houston YWCA, 1978-; exec coun, constitution comn Nat Soc Allied Health Prof, Southern Dist; Am Alliance Adv Health Educ; Univ Houston Univ Park Fac Promo & Tenure Comm; Task Force Recruitment & Retention Minority Studs. **Honors/Awds:** Fel, Royal Health Soc, 1969; Scholar, Danforth Found, 1972; Faculty Excellence Award, Univ Houston, 1990; Presidential Citation Award, Asn Adv Health Educ, 1991. **Military Serv:** USMC, 1951-53. **Business Addr:** Professor of Health Science, Allied Health, University of Houston, Department of Health & Human Performance, Cent Campus 4800 Calhoun Rd, Houston, TX 77204, **Business Phone:** (713)743-9839.

BUCKSON, TONI YVONNE (TONI BYRD)
Transportation consultant. **Personal:** Born Jun 5, 1949, Baltimore, MD; married Robert Byrd Sr. **Educ:** Coppin State Col, BS, 1971; Univ Baltimore, MS, 1978; Northeastern Univ, cert, 1985; Atlanta Univ, cert, 1985. **Career:** Mayor & City Coun Baltimore, CATV task force mgr, 1979-81; Nat Aquarium Baltimore, group events coordr, 1981-82; Mass Transit Admin, ride sharing dir, 1982-86; Md Transp Authority, asst admin bridges, 1986; Wash Metrop Area Transit Authority, customer Serv Info Off, supvr, coordr, 1992-. **Orgs:** Curric adv, Goucher Col, 1975-78; bd mem, Jr League Md, 1978-80; trainer, Nat Info Ctr Vol, 1979-81; bd mem, Md Food Bank, 1979-81; bd mem, Future Homemakers Am, 1980-81; bd mem, Girl Scouts Cent Md, 1982-84. **Honors/Awds:** Service Award, Girl Scouts Cent Am, 1984; Affirmative Action Award, Md Dept Transp, 1984; Outstanding Young Women in America, 1985; presidential citation, Nat Asn Equal Opportunity Higher Educ, 1986. **Home Addr:** Six Tallow Ct, Baltimore, MD 21207. **Business Addr:** Coordinator, Washington Metropolitan Area Transit Authority, Customer Service Information Office, 600 5th St NW, Washington, DC 20001, **Business Phone:** (202)962-2765.

BUFFONG, ERIC ARNOLD
Physician. **Personal:** Born May 11, 1951, Oranjestad, Aruba, Netherlands; married Gail Helena LaBorde; children: Erica, Nicole, Alicia, Gabrielle. **Educ:** Manhattan Col, 1973; Howard Univ, MD, 1977; Harlem Hosp, PGY1, 1978; Albert Einstein, PGY2, 1983. **Career:** Harlem Hosp Ctr NY, resident & chief resident, Obstet-Gynecol, 1977-81, pres house staff 1980-81; Albert Einstein Col Med, fel reproductive endocrinol, 1981-83, assoc prof dept gynecol, 1983-84; pvt pract, Physician, 1984-99; Onslow Women's Health Ctr, sr partner; Columbus Obstet Gynec & Infertility, owner, currently. **Orgs:** Bd eligible Reproductive Endocrinol, 1983; Am Col Obstet-Gynecol, 1986-87; diplomate/bd cert FACOG; Nat Med Asn; Old North State Med Soc; chmn, region III Nat Med Asn, 1989-92; Trustee, Nat Med Asn, 1993-98. **Honors/Awds:** Bd dir, NCNB Jacksonville, NC 1986; Eastern Area Sickle Cell Asn, bd dir, 1986-; Doctor of the Year, Old N State Med Soc, 1989. **Special Achievements:** Performed the Vaginal Delivery of Quadruplets 1985; presented first eight cases of Laparoscopic Vaginal Hysterectomy in the world, First North American/South American Congress of Gynecologic Endoscopy Dallas, TX 1988. **Business Addr:** Owner, Columbus Obstet Gynec & Infertility, 951 Talbotton Rd Suite C, Columbus, GA 31904-8851.*

BUFORD, DAMON JACKSON
Baseball player. **Personal:** Born Jun 12, 1970, Baltimore, MD; son of Don. **Educ:** Univ Southern Calif. **Career:** Baltimore Orioles, outfielder, 1993-95; NY Mets, 1995; Texas Rangers, 1996-97; Boston Red Sox, 1998-99; Chicago Cubs, 2000-01; Wash Nat, outfielder, 2004. *

BUFORD, HOWARD
Chief executive officer. **Educ:** Harvard Colege; Harvard Business Sch. **Career:** Procter & Gamble brand management; Young & Rubicam advertising; Prime Access Inc, pres & chief exec officer, currently. **Honors/Awds:** Breaking Business Barriers award; ANA Advertising Award, 2008; ADCOLOR Innovator Award, Advertising Club of New York, 2008. **Business Addr:** President, Chief Executive Officer, Prime Access Inc, 345 7th Ave, New York, NY 10001, **Business Phone:** (212)868-6800.

BUFORD, JAMES A
Administrator. **Educ:** Tenn State Univ, BS, biol; William Jewell Col, nat sci found, 1959; Kans State Univ, nat sci found, 1960; Cent Mo State Univ, MS, educ admin, 1965; Univ Mich, MPH, med care orgn & admin, 1972; Harvard Univ, planning & regulation, 1977. **Career:** State Mo, former sci teacher; Kings Co Hosp, NY City, exec dir; Urban Community Serv Dept, Kans City, dir; DC Dept Human Serv, agency dir, proj mgr, dir, 1980-83; NY Health & Hosp Corp, 1986-92; Human Resources Admin, NY, mgt consult, 1992-94; Univ Res Corp, mgt consult, 1994-99; Dept Health & Welfare, Newark, dir; Detroit Health Dept, staff, 1999-2002, dir, 1999-; Govt DC, Dept Health, chief operating officer, 2002, interim dir, 2002, actg dir, 2002, dir, currently. **Orgs:** Am Pub Health Asn; Nat Asn Health Serv Exec; Am Magt Asn; Nat Pub Hosp Asn. **Business Phone:** (202)671-5000.

BUFORD, JAMES HENRY
Association executive. **Personal:** Born Jun 2, 1944, St Louis, MO; son of James and Myrtle Margaret Brown; married Helen Joyce Freeman, Jun 23, 1967; children: James H Jr, Jason. **Educ:** Forest Park Community Col, AA, bus admin; Elizabethtown Col, Elizabethtown, PA, BA human serv admin. **Career:** Smith, Kline & French, St Louis, MO, regional mkt rep, 1972-75; St Louis Community Col, St Louis, MO, prog coordr, 1975-76; Harris Stowe Community Col, emer staff; 70001 Ltd, St Louis, MO, vpres, 1976-80; Int Mgt & Develop Group LTD, Wash, DC, sr vpres, 1980-81, St Louis, MO, exec vpres, 1981-85; Urban League Metrop, St Louis, pres & cheif exec officer, 1985-. **Orgs:** Nat Asn Advancement Colored People; bd mem, Leadership St Louis, 1985-88; exec comt mem, Blue Cross/Blue Shield, 1986-; exec bd, Boy Scouts, 1986-; bd dir, St Louis Community Col Bldg Corp, 1986-; chmn, bd regents, Harris Stowe State Col, 1989; chair nominating comt, Sigma Pi Phi, 1988; Personnel Adv Comt Pres George Bush, 1989. **Honors/Awds:** Brotherhood & Sisterhood Award, Nat Conf Community & Justice; Humanitarian Award, Kappa Alpha Psi-St Louis, 1984; Professionalism Award, Kappa Alpha Psi-St Louis, 1986; Lamp Lighter Award, Pub Rels Soc Am, 1993; DHL, Harris Stowe Col, 1993; DHL, Univ Mo, 1995; Distinguished Alumni Award, St Louis Community Col, 1995; Lifetime Achievement Award, St Louis Gateway Classic,1997; Whitney M. Young Award, Boy Scouts,1999; DHL, Webdster Univ, 2000; Mentor St Louis Award, 2005; DHL, Eden Theol Sem, 2006. **Special Achievements:** Order of the 1st State, Governor of Delaware, 1981. **Business Addr:** President, Chief Executive Officer, Urban League Metropolitan St Louis, 3701 Grandel Sq, St Louis, MO 63108, **Business Phone:** (314)615-3600.*

BUFORD, WESLEY R.
Executive. **Personal:** Born Feb 17, 1949, Oakland, CA; divorced; children: Kyshanna Buford-Thompson. **Career:** Sarah Lee Corp, ProBall Food & Beverage Affiliate, pres & chief exec officer; Urban TV Network, chief exec officer & exec producer; The Montel Williams Show, co-creator, co-owner, co-exec producer; Freedom Card Inc, founder, chmn, pres & chief exec officer. **Orgs:** Co-developer, NFL Youth Edu Town; chair, State Ill, Minority & Small Bus Comt; founding co-chair, City of Los Angeles Task Force on African Am Affairs; bd dir, Boys Choir of Harlem; Operation Hope Banking Ctr, bd dir, Kappa Alpha Psi; dipl, Int Cir World Affairs Coun. **Honors/Awds:** Numerous awards & accommendations. **Special Achievements:** First African American member of CA Yacht Club. *

BUFORD, WILLIAM KEN M., III
Executive, president (government). **Career:** Reliant Indust Inc, chmn & chief exec officer. **Special Achievements:** Company is ranked #30 on Black Enterprise magazine's 1997 list of Top 100 Black businesses; Crains Chicago Business "40 under 40" 1994. *

BUGG, DR. GEORGE WENDELL
Physician, educator. **Personal:** Born Jun 17, 1935, Nashville, TN; children: George Jr, Michael Stanley, Kevin Gregory & Kisha Monique. **Educ:** Tenn State Univ, BS, 1958; Meharry Med Col, MD, 1962. **Career:** Pvt pract, gen surgeon; Dept Social Servs, med consult, 1989-; Grady Memorial Hosp, dir, currently; Emory Univ, asst prof, Pediatrics, med dir, Intermediate & Term Nurseries, Emory Univ Sch Med, Emory Reg Perinatal Ctr, Div Neonatal-Perinatal Med, currently. **Orgs:** Chmn, Cecil C Hinton Comm Ctr, 1969-72; chmn, W Fresno Fed Neighborhood Ctr, 1972; chmn, Comm Serv Am Heart asn, 1972; pres, Daniel H Williams Med Forum, 1974-77; mem, AMA, CMA, NMA, Surveyors,

JCAH, Alpha Phi Alpha Inc, Fresno-Madera Med Found; mem, Comm Cncl on Black Educ Affairs; treas, Ga Perinatal Asn; dist vrep, Georgia Chap Am Acad Pediatrics. **Honors/Awds:** AMA Physicians Recognition Award, 1969; ACE Award, 1993. **Military Serv:** AUS, med corps maj, 1967-69.

BUGG, MAYME CAROL
Lawyer, social worker. **Personal:** Born Apr 18, 1945, Portsmouth, VA; daughter of George W and Mayme P. **Educ:** Fisk Univ, BA, Sociol, 1966; George W Brown Sch Soc Work Wash Univ, MSW, 1968; Cleveland State Univ, JD, 1977. **Career:** Oberlin Col, educ prog dir, 1969-70; Cleveland City Hall, city planner, 1970-71; Cuyahoga Community Col, asst to dept head, 1971-74; Comt Action Against Addiction, ct liaison 1976-77; United Labor Agency, proj dir, 1977-79; Cuyahoga Co Juvenile Ct, referee, 1979. **Orgs:** League Park Neighborhood Ctr, 1979-84; bd mem, Citizens League Greater Cleveland, 1980-84; Nat Asn Advan Colored People; Drop-Out Prevention Comt, Cleveland Bd Educ, 1981-; vis comt, Case Western Reserve Univ Law Sch, 1986-; adv comt, Fenn Educ Fund, 1987-94; Serv Black Families, 1989-92; bd mem emer, Project Friendship Big Sister Prog, 1991; Harambee Serv Black Families; Fisk Univ Cleveland Alumni Club; Cuyahoga Co Bar Asn; Proj Friendship; Asn Blacks Juvenile Justice Syst; Leadership Cleveland; Alpha Kappa Alpha Sorority; United Way Serv Leadership Develop Prog; African-Am Family Cong; Norman S Minor Bar Asn; bd mem/first vpres, Harambee. **Honors/Awds:** Office of Economic Opportunity Scholar, Wash Univ, 1967; Tots & Teens leadership award, Cleveland Chap, 1986; Certificate of Recognition, Nat Asn Black Social Workers. **Home Addr:** 4421 Granada Blvd, Cleveland, OH 44128. *

BUGG, ROBERT
Government official, educator. **Personal:** Born Jun 3, 1941, Topeka, KS; son of Walter and Mattie; married Jacqueline Shope, May 28, 1970; children: Glen, Chris & Anton. **Educ:** Washburn Univ, Topeka, BA, corrections, 1974; Kans Univ, Lawrence, MPA, 1976. **Career:** Government official (retired), executive: State Kans, Topeka, correctional officer, 1962-66; City Topeka, Topeka, police officer, 1966-68; field rep human rels, 1968-69; E Topeka Methodist Church, Topeka, dir coun, 1969-70; Big Brothers & Big Sisters, Topeka, KS, dir vehicles, 1982-87; State Kans, Topeka, dir vehicles, 1982-87; City Topeka, Topeka, personnel dir & labor rels, 1987-; City Topeka, spec asst to the Mayor & chief admin officer, 1997-2000; Robert Bugg & Assocs, owner, currently. **Orgs:** Chmn, Black Democrats Caucus Kans, 1982-89; chair, founder, Martin Luther King Birthday Celebration, 1986-; exec bd mem, Nat Asn Advan Colored People; chair, Topeka Housing Authority; founder, Living in the Dream. **Military Serv:** AUS, SP 4, 1959-62; Good Conduct, Marksman. **Home Addr:** 3721 Evans Dr, Topeka, KS 66609. **Business Phone:** (785)232-4565.

BUGGAGE, CYNTHIA MARIE
Government official. **Personal:** Born Oct 26, 1958, Donaldsonville, LA; daughter of Wilfred Joseph Sr and Yvonne Stewart. **Educ:** Grambling State Univ, LA, BS, 1979; Tex Southern Univ, Houston, TX, MPA,1988. **Career:** Univ Houston, Houston, TX, adj prof, 1986-89; City Houston Parks & Rec,Houston, TX, grants adminr, 1980; US House Representatives Congresswoman Sheila Jackson Lee, dist dir & chief staff; Am Red Cross, sr assoc govtrels; Tex Southern Univ, Houston, TX, asst athletic dir & bus mgr; Southern Univ Law Ctr, Baton Rouge, LA, dir, Off Develop, currently. **Orgs:** Nat Asn Advan Colored People, 1979-; Grambling Univ Nat Alumni, 1980-; Nat Forum for Black Pub Adminrs, 1987-89; bd dir, Polit Activities League,1986-87; Nat Asn Female Exec, 1991; Alpha Kappa Alpha Sorority. **Honors/Awds:** Human Enrichment of Life Prog, Black Achiever Houston, TX Award, 1994. **Home Addr:** 745 Int Blvd Suite 745, Houston, TX 77024. **Business Phone:** (225)771-5044.

BUGGS, JAMES
Insurance executive, real estate executive. **Personal:** Born Apr 27, 1925, Summerfield, LA; son of Clifton and Lucille Franklin; married Johnye; children: James F & Bruce J. **Educ:** Spauling Bus Col. **Career:** Ins exec & real estate salesman, 1973-; Caddo Parish Shreveport, LA, dep tax assessor 1982-2003; Primerica Fin Serv, life ins exec. **Orgs:** Past pres, Shreveport Negro Chamber Com, 1972-73; deacon, Galilee Baptist Church; chmn trustees; Am Legion 525, 1973-78; past Worshipful Master, Fred D Lee Lodge Prince Hall affiliation. **Honors/Awds:** Prince Hall Masonic Lodge, Cert for 50 yrs membership, 1996. **Military Serv:** AUS, Corpl, 1943-46. **Home Addr:** 2839 Round Grove Lane, Shreveport, LA 71107. **Business Addr:** Life Insurance Executive, Independant/Individual Sales, 2839 Round Grove Lane, Shreveport, LA 71107, **Business Phone:** (318)425-1824.

BUIE, DR. SAMPSON, JR.
School administrator. **Personal:** Born Sep 18, 1929, Fairmont, NC; married Catherine O; children: Debra, Janice & Velma. **Educ:** NC A&T State Univ, BS, 1952; Univ NC, Greensboro, MEd, 1973, EdD, 1982. **Career:** School administrator (retired); Boy Scouts Am, asst scout exec, 1954-70; NC A&T State Univ, dir community relations, 1970-82; dir off alumni affairs, 1982-93; State NC, Dept Admin, dep secy progs. **Orgs:** Bd dir Greensboro Rotary Club 1969-; mem bd visitors, Shaw Univ Div Sch, 1981-;

NC Comn Develop Comn, 1982-; trustee, Gen Baptist State Conv NC, 1982-; Col & Grad Comt, Chamber Com, Greensboro United Fund; vpres, Gen Greene Coun BSA; NC A&T State Univ Nat Alumni Asn; Phi Beta Sigma; Greensboro Citizens Asn; Nat Univ Ext Asn; Guilford City Recreation Comn; Greensboro-Guilford City Pulpit Forum; Drug Action Coun Personnel Search Comn; NC State Adv Comn on Recruitment Minorities State Criminal Justice Syst; Nat Coun BSA; consult, Monitoring & Tech Asst Training USHUD; NC Comn Volunteerism & Community Serv, 2003; comnr, monitoring prm NC comn,2005-. **Honors/Awds:** Nathaniel Greene Award City of Greensboro, 1969; Achievement Award NC A&T State Univ Alumni Asn, 1969; United Negro Col Fund Award, Bennett Coll, 1972; Silver Beaver Award, BSA, 1978; Minister of the Year, Deep River Baptist Asn, 1983. **Special Achievements:** Numerous professional papers incl "Andragogy Pedagogy, Characteristics of Adults That Impact on Adult Learning & Dev" 1983; "Lifelong Learning, A Necessity & Not a Luxury" 1983. **Military Serv:** Infantry 1st lt 1952-54. *

BULGER, LUCILLE O. See Obituaries section.

BULLARD, EDWARD A., JR.
Educator, accountant, systems analyst. **Personal:** Born Apr 2, 1947, Syracuse, NY; married Terrlyon D; children: Lan R, Edward III, Terron D. **Educ:** Southern Univ, BS, 1969; Syracuse Univ, MBA, 1972; Univ Detroit Law Sch, JD, 1978. **Career:** Carrier Corp, analyst, 1969; Ernst & Young, acct, 1969-72; Univ MI, Flint, prof, 1972-93; GMI, assoc prof actg, 1972-93; Detroit Col Bus-Flint, prof; Tax Info Tech, consult. **Orgs:** Bd mem, Urban League Flint, 1984, Flint Comn Develop Corp, 1984; Am Actg Asn; adv, Flint City Schs Bus Prog, 1985; City Flint Cable TV Adv Panel; Small bus consult & urban analyst; Am Bus Law Asn; bd, Urban League Flint; bd, Flint Community Develop Coord; legal regress comn, exe comt, Nat Asn Advan Colored People, Flint; adv panel, Flint Cable TV; consult, Jr Achievement, Beecher High Sch; Cong Black Caucus-Flint; treas, ACLY Greater Flint; numerous others. **Honors/Awds:** CPA, NY, 1977-; Outstanding Prof, Univ MI, Flint, 1979; Univ Detroit Law Sch Moot Ct Tax Team, 1977. *

BULLARD, KEITH
Automotive executive. **Career:** Airport Lincoln Mercury, owner, currently; Keith Bullard Used Car Super Inc, owner, 2002-. **Special Achievements:** Company ranked No 96 on BE's Top 100 Auto Dealers list, 1992. **Business Addr:** Owner, Keith Bullard Used Car Super Inc, 1466 Beers Sch Rd, Coraopolis, PA 15108-2543, **Business Phone:** (412)299-0400.*

BULLETT, VICKY (VICTORIA BULLETT)
Basketball player. **Personal:** Born Oct 4, 1967. **Educ:** Univ Md, BA, gen studies, 2001. **Career:** Basketball player (retired): Bari, Italy, 1990-93; Cesena, Italy, 1993-97;Charlotte Sting, center, 1997-99; Washington Mystics, 1999-2002. **Honors/Awds:** US Olympic Basketball Team, Gold Medal, 1988, Bronze Medal, 1992; FIBA world championship, Gold, 1990; Maryland Athletics Walk of Fame, 2007; ACC Women's Basketball Legend, 2007; "Vicky Bullett Street", in honor. *

BULLETT, VICTORIA. See BULLETT, VICKY.

BULLINS, ED
Playwright, television producer, educator. **Personal:** Born Jul 2, 1935, Philadelphia, PA; son of Bertha Marie Queen Bullins. **Educ:** Los Angeles City Col, attended 1963; San Francisco State Col; New York School Visual Arts; New School Extension; Vista Col; William Penn Business Institute, gen business certificate; Antioch University, BA, 1989; San Francisco State University, MFA, 1994. **Career:** Black Arts/West, founder, producer, 1966-67; New Lafayette Theatre of Harlem, playwright, assoc director, 1967-73; Black Theatre Magazine, editor, 1968-73; New York Shakespeare Festival, writers unit coordinator/press assistant, 1975-82; New York Univ, School of Continuing Education, instructor, 1979, dramatic writing, instructor, 1981; Berkeley Black Repertory, public relations director, 1982; The Magic Theatre, promotion director pro tem, 1982-83; Julian Theatre, group sales coordinator, 1983; City Col of San Francisco, drama instructor, 1984-88; Antioch Univ, San Francisco, playwriting instructor, admin asst, public info & recruitment, 1986-87; Bullins Memorial Theatre, producer/playwright, 1988; lecturer, instructor, various universities and Cols throughout the US; Northeastern Univ, prof theater, distinguished artist in residence, 1995-00; playwriter, currently. **Orgs:** Dramatists Guild; mentor, Act Roxbury Playwrights Unit, 1999-03; mentor, Cherry Land Theatre, Playwrights, 2002-03. **Honors/Awds:** Vernon Rice Drama Award, The Electronic Nigger and Others, 1968; Village Voice, Obie Award, Distinguished Playwriting, In New England Winter, and The Fabulous Miss Marie, 1971; New York Drama Critics Circle Award, Obie Award for Distinguished Playwriting, The Taking of Miss Janie, 1975; American Place Theatre grant, 1967; Rockefeller Foundation, grants for playwriting, 1968, 1970, 1973; Guggenheim Fellowship grants, 1971, 1976; Creative Artists Program Service grant, 1973; Natl Endowment for the Arts, grant. **Special Achievements:** Plays: The Duplex, 1970; A Ritual to Raise the Dead and Foretell the Future, 1970; The Devil Catchers, 1970; In New England

Winter, 1971; The Fabulous Miss Marie, 1971; Ya Gonna Let Me Take You Out Tonight, Baby?, 1972; House Party, A Soulful Happening, book/lyrics, 1973; The Taking of Miss Janie, 1975; The Mystery of Phyllis Wheatley, 1976; Storyville, 1977; Michael, 1978; Leavings, 1980; Steve & Velma, 1980; The Hungered One, Short Pros II, 1971; The Reluctant Rapist, novel, 1973; wrote play, "Boy X Man," 1994. **Home Addr:** 37 Vine St Suite 1, Roxbury, MA 02119-3354. *

BULLOCK, ALICE GRESHAM
Lawyer, educator. **Educ:** Howard Univ, BA, 1972; Howard Univ Sch Law, JD, 1975. **Career:** Georgetown Law Ctr, fel; Off Chief Coun, IRS, trial atty, 1975-79; Howard Univ Sch Law, from asst prof to assoc prof, 1979-87, prof, 1987-, assoc dean, 1988-92, actg dean, 1990, interim dean, 1996-97, dean, 1997-2002; Hart Carroll & Chavers, coun, 1983-86; Asn Am Law Schs, dep dir, 1992-94. **Orgs:** Am Law Inst; ABA Comt Teaching Taxation; bd dirs, Coun Legal Educ Opportunity; bd visitors, Brigham Young Univ Law Sch; bd trustees, InstIndependent Educ; US Supreme Ct; Dist Columbia Bar; Soc Am Law Teachers; Am Asn Higher Educ Adv Comt; Am Bar Asn; Nat Bar Asn; Wash Bar Asn; fel, Am Bar Found. **Honors/Awds:** Outstanding Service Award, Nat Bar Asn, 1980; Meritorious Service Award, Howard Univ, 1996; President's Distinguished Service Award, Nat Asn Equal Opportunity, 1997; Outstanding Service Award, Student Bar Asn, 1997; NBA Gertrude B Rush Award, 2004; Hon Doctor of Laws, Suffolk Univ. **Business Addr:** Professor of Law, Howard University School of Law, 414 Houston Hall, 2900 Van Ness St NW, Washington, DC 20008, **Business Phone:** (202)806-8049.

BULLOCK, BYRON F
Special education teacher. **Career:** St Augustines Col, dean enrollment mgt; Univ Mass, Amhers, vice chancellor stud affairs, 2006-. **Business Addr:** Vice Chancellor, University of Massachusetts, Amherst, MA.

BULLOCK, J JEROME
Executive, legal consultant. **Personal:** Born Jan 3, 1948, Hogansville, GA; son of Vivian Baker and Jerry L. **Educ:** Tuskegee Univ, BS, Polit Sci, 1969; Howard Univ, Sch Law, JD, 1975. **Career:** US Marshals Serv, assoc legal coun, 1975-77, 1982-84, US Marshal, 1977-82, chief cong & pub affairs, 1984-85; Air Security Corp, vpres, 1983-85; Office Internal Security, chief, 1985-89; US Dept Justice, asst inspector gen Invest, 1989-94; Decision Strategies Inst, managing dir, 1994-97; Price Waterhouse, LLP, managing dir, 1997-; Bullock & Assocs Inc, pres, Currently. **Orgs:** Nat Asn Flight Instrs, 1984-; Iowa State Bar Asn; Phi Alpha Delta Law Fraternity; Int Asn Chiefs Police; Kappa Alpha Psi Am Region. **Honors/Awds:** Special Achievement Award, US Marshals Serv, 1976; Meritorious Service Award, US Marshals Serv, 1978; Tuskegee Alumni Award, Tuskegee Inst, 1979; Distinguished Service Award, US Marshals Serv, 1987. **Military Serv:** AUS, capt, 1969-72. **Business Addr:** President, Bullock & Associates Inc, 5335 Wisconsin Ave NW Suite 440, Washington, DC 20015-2034, **Business Phone:** (202)966-5006.

BULLOCK, JAMES
Educator, lawyer. **Personal:** Born Aug 22, 1926, Charleston, MS; married Lois; children: Joseph. **Educ:** Tex Southern Univ, BA, 1967; Thurgood Marshall Sch Law, JD, 1970. **Career:** US Postal Serv, supvr; Tex Southern Univ, assoc prof law, currently. **Orgs:** Justice Greener Chap Phi Alpha Delta Legal Frat; TX Black Caucus; Am BarAsn; Nat Bar Asn; St Bar TX; Houston Bar Asn; Houston Lawyers Asn; PhiAlpha Delta Legal Frat; S & Cent YMCA; NAACP; Harris Co Orgn; TX Asn Col Teachers. **Honors/Awds:** Phi Alpha Delta Outstanding Alumnus. **Military Serv:** USAF, s/surgent, 1947-56. **Home Addr:** 3704 S MacGregor Way, Houston, TX 77021, **Home Phone:** (713)748-1538. **Business Addr:** Associate Professor of Law, Texas Southern University, 3100 Cleburne St, Houston, TX 77004, **Business Phone:** (713)313-7395.

BULLOCK, THEODORE
Business owner. **Personal:** Born Aug 6, 1928, Pike Co, MS; son of Willie and Eugene; married Vivian Bridges (deceased); children: Brian Nichols, Reuben Nichols, Sherry Robinson & Cynthia. **Career:** Piggly Wiggly Stores, clerk, 1948-56; Railway Express Agency, materials handler, 1957-60; Veteran's Taxi, owner, 1970-73; US Post Office, mailclerk, 1961-70; Bullocks Washateria, owner, 1972-; Br & Recreation Inc,part owner, 1979; Bullock's Food Mart, owner; Bullock's Barber & Beauty Shop. **Orgs:** Bd mem, McComb C C, 1975; bd mem, Pike Co Bus League, 1976; bd mem, McCombCity Coun, 1979; supvr, Pike Co District 1, 1984. **Honors/Awds:** Certificate of Appreciation, 1975; First black selectman for McComb; C.C. Bryant Lifetime Achievement Award, NAACP, 2009. **Business Addr:** Owner, Bullock's Washeteria, 130 St Augustine St, McComb, MS 39648, **Business Phone:** (601)684-2332.

BULLOCK, THURMAN RUTHE
Municipal government official, association executive. **Personal:** Born Oct 6, 1947, Richmond, VA; son of Warren and Dorothy Hargrove; married Anne Leshner, Aug 31, 1976; children: Thurman Martin. **Educ:** Franklin & Marshall Col, Lancaster, PA, BA, 1970;

Temple Univ Philadelphia, PA, MS, 1979. **Career:** Comptroller Currency, Philadelphia, PA, asst nat bank examr, 1970-75; Deloitte Haskins & Sells, Philadelphia, PA, auditor, 1977-80; Bell Pa, Philadelphia, PA, internal auditor, 1980-82; City Pa Off Controller, PA, deputy city controller, 1982-; Philadelphia FIGHT, treas, currently. **Orgs:** Nat Asn Black Accountants, 1979; Am Inst Cert Pub Accountants, 1980-; past secy, Pa Inst Cert Pub Accountants, treas, 1980-89, pres elect, 1989-; Govt Finance Officers Asn, 1981; past pres, mem, Philadelphia Fedn Black Bus & Prof Orgn, 1981-; bd mem, Coun Int Progs, 1981-; Int Prof Exchange, 1981-; Opportunities Acad Mgt Training Inc, 1981-; bus adv bd, House Umoja, 1986-; Philadelphia Clearinghouse, 1989; past vpres, former adv bd mem, Community Accountants; Acct Res Asn, 1989; Am Soc Pub Admin, 1989; Asn Local Govt Auditors, 1989; fin adv, Lesbian & Gay Task Force, currently; Nat Jr Tennis League; Zion Nonprofit Trust; NGA Inc; East Mt Airy Neighbors; Fund Future Philadelphia; bd dirs, Philadelphia FIGHT, currently. **Honors/Awds:** CPA Cert, 1979; Distinguished Public Service Award, Pa Inst Cert Pub Accountants, 1986. **Special Achievements:** Appeared in Pennsylvania Institute of Certified Public Accountants career video, "Is an Accounting Career in Your Future?", 1987. **Business Addr:** Treasurer, Philadelphia FIGHT, 1233 Locust St 5th Fl, Philadelphia, PA 19107, **Business Phone:** (215)985-4448.

BULLS, HERMAN E.
Real estate executive, president (organization). **Personal:** Born Feb 4, 1956, Florence, AL; son of William George Bulls and Lucy Bulls Winchester; married Iris, Aug 30, 1980; children: Herman Jr, Nathaniel & Jonathan. **Educ:** US Mil Acad, Westpoint, BS, 1978; Harvard Univ, MBA, 1985. **Career:** Jones Lang La Salle, managing dir, 1989-2000; Green Park Financial, exec vpres& chief exec officer, 2000-01; Fannie Mae Delegated Underwriting & Servicing apartment lenders, chief operating officer, 2000-01; Bulls Advisory Group, pres & chief exec officer, 2001-; Bulls Capital Partners, pres & chief exec officer, 2004-. **Orgs:** Exec Leadership Coun, 1995-; bd mem, Kennedy Ctr Community & Friends, 1995-2003; bd trustees, West Point, 1996-; Adv bd Asset Mgt Sun Trust Bank(NYSE); bd dirs, Comfort Systs, USA NYSE, 2001-; Real Estate Exec Coun, 2003-; chair, Exec Leadership Found, 2005-; NY State Teachers' Retirement Syst Real Esate Adv Coun, 2003-; Lambda Alpha Int; Leadership Wash; Nat Black MBA Asn; Real Estate Group Wash, DC; founder, African-Am Real Estate Profs; Nat Asn Col & Univ Bus Officers; bd dir, Found Independent Higher Educ; bd dir, Comfort Systems, USA. **Honors/Awds:** Passing the Torch, honoree, African Am Real Estate Prof, 2003, honored by the Global Diversity Summit, 2008. **Military Serv:** Army, 1978-89 active duty, Depr Social Sci, asst prof; Army Reserves, col, 1989-. **Business Addr:** President, Bulls Advisory Group, 9610 Crosspointe Dr, Fairfax Station, VA 22039, **Business Phone:** (202)256-1814.

BULLY-CUMMINGS, ELLA
Police chief, lawyer. **Personal:** Born Jan 1, 1958; married William; married Warren C Evans (divorced). **Educ:** Madonna Univ, BA, pub admin, 1993; Mich state Uinv, detroit col law, JD, 1998. **Career:** Detroit Police Dept, police officer, 1977-87, sgt, 1987-93, lt, 1993-95, inspector, 1995-98; comdr, 1998-99, asst chief, 2002-03; Miller, Canfield, Paddock & Stone PLC, assoc atty, 1992-2002; Foley & Lardner, atty; Detroit Police Dept, chief police, 2003-. **Orgs:** State Bar Mich; Nat Bar Asn; Wolverine Bar Asn; Int Asn Chiefs Police; Nat Org Black Law Enforcement Execs; Mcih Asn Chiefs Police. **Special Achievements:** First female police chief of Detroit. **Business Addr:** Chief Police, Detroit Police Department, 1300 Beaubien, Detroit, MI 48226, **Business Phone:** (313)596-2200.

BUMPERS, KATRINA
Businessperson. **Career:** Benford Brown & Associates LLC, managing partner, currently. **Business Addr:** Managing Partner, Benford Brown & Associates LLC, 2319 E 71st St, Chicago, IL 60649, **Business Phone:** (773)752-7078.*

BUMPHUS, DR. WALTER GAYLE
Administrator, educator. **Personal:** Born Mar 19, 1948, Princeton, KY; married Aileen Thompson; children: Michael, Brian & Fran. **Educ:** Murray State Univ, BS (speech commun), 1971, MA (guid & coun), 1974; Univ Tex, Austin, PhD (higher educ admin), 1985. **Career:** Murray State Univ, counr & dormetry asst, 1970-72, dir minority affairs, 1972-74; E Ark Community Col, dean, 1974-78; Howard Community Col, dean stud, 1978-86, vpres; Univ Tex, Austin, Richardson fel, 1983; Regional Univ, admin; Brookhaven Col, Dallas County Community Col Dist, pres; Voyager Expanded Learning, Higher Educ Div, pres; Brookhaven Col, pres; Baton Rouge Community Col, chancellor, 2000-01; La Community & Tech Col Syst, pres, 2001-07, pres emer, 2007-; Univ Tex, Austin, prof & A M Aikin Regents Chair Community Col Leadership, 2007-. **Orgs:** Consult, Off Educ Title IV, 1986; chairperson, Middle Stated Accredited Asn Team, 1986; pres, Nat Asn Stud Develop; chmn, Am Asn Community Cols, 1996-; bd dir, Am Coun on Education. **Honors/Awds:** Key to City Award, Princeton, KY, 1984; Distinguished Service Award, Nat Council of Black American Affairs, 1991; Distinguished Alumnus, Murray Col Alumni Asn, 1992; Quality Organizational Leadership Award, 1995; Nat Initiative for Leadership and Institutional Effectiveness Lifetime Achievement Award, 1998. **Special Achievements:** Marie Y Martin CEO of the Year. **Business Addr:** President, Professor, College of Education University of Texas, Department of Educational Administration, SZB 348 1 Univ Sta D5400, Austin, TX 78712, **Business Phone:** (512)471-7551.

BUNCH, LONNIE G., III
Educator. **Educ:** Am Univ, Wash, DC, BS, 1974, MS, 1976. **Career:** Nat Air & Space Mus, educ specialist, 1978-79; Am Univ, Wash, DC, adj lectr, 1978-79; Univ Mass, Dartmouth, asst prof Am & Afro-Am hist, 1979-81; Packer Col Inst, Brooklyn, NY, teacher & historian, 1981-83; George Wash Univ, Wash, DC, adj prof mus studies, 1989-00; Calif African Am Mus, Los Angeles, curator hist & prog mgr, 1983-89; Am Hist mus, supvr curator, 1989-92, asst dir curator hist, 1992-94; Chicago Hist Soc, pres, 2001-05; Nat Mus African Am Hist & Culture, assoc dir, 1994-00, dir, 2005-. **Orgs:** Am Asn State & Local Hist; Orgn Am Historians. **Special Achievements:** First African American to head one of the city's major non-ethnic museums. ; Written several books, including Black Angelenos: The African American in Los Angeles, 1850-1950 and the exhibition catalog, The American Presidency: A Glorious Burden (2000); organized several award-winning exhibitions including, "The Black Olympians, 1904-1950" and "Black Angelenos: The Afro-American in Los Angeles, 1850-1950". *

BUNCHE, CURTIS J
Automotive executive, football player. **Personal:** Born Aug 4, 1955, Crystal River, FL; son of Ruth Bunche; married Melinda Bunche, Jan 1, 1982; children: Mykisha, Cetera & Malcolm. **Educ:** Albany State Col, 1979. **Career:** Philadelphia Eagles, defensive end, 1979-80; Tampa Bay Bandits, defensive end, 1983-84; C&C Assocs, pres, 1981-87; Mon-Valley Lincoln-Mercury, pres, 1987-93; Riverview Ford Lincoln Mercury, pres, 1994-. **Orgs:** Rotary, 1988-; premier mem, Nat Asn Minority Automobile Dealers. **Business Addr:** President, Owner, Riverview Ford Lincoln Mercury, 200 S Broadway, PO Box 306, Pennsville, NJ 08070, **Business Phone:** (856)678-3111.

BUNDLES, A'LELIA
Writer, executive. **Personal:** Born Jun 7, 1952, Chicago, IL; daughter of S Henry Bundles Jr and A Lelia Mae Perry Bundles. **Educ:** Harvard-Radcliffe Coll, AB (magna cum laude) 1974; Columbia Univ Grad Sch Jour, MSJ 1976. **Career:** TV news exec, author; Newsweek Chicago Bur, intern, 1973; Kennedy Inst Polit Harvard, summer res fel, 1973; WTLC-FM Indianapolis, anchor/reporter, 1974; Du Pont Co, Wilmington, DE, staff asst, 1974-75; Columbia Sch Jour, NBC/RCA fel, 1975-76; NBC News NY, Houston & Atlanta burs, field producer, 1976-85; NBC News Wash, DC, producer, 1985-89; ABC News Wash DC, World News Tonight, producer, 1989-96; ABC News Wash DC, dep bur chief, 1996-99; consult, 2000-01; ABC News, dir talent develop; freelance writer, Oprah Mag, New York Times Book Rev, Am Hist, Parade, Ms, Sage, Ebony, Jr, Essence, Radcliffe Quarterly, Seventeen, Indianapolis, Star, Indianapolis News, Crisis, Opportunity, AME Church Review, Inside Borders, Black Issues Book Review, Heart & Soul, Fortune Small Business; Links Inc. **Orgs:** Nat Asn Black Journalists, 1980-; trustee, Radcliffe Col, 1985-89; adv bd, Schlesinger Libr Hist Women, 1986-94; dir, Harvard Alumni Asn 1989-91; Alpha Kappa Alpha; bd, Harvard Club Wash, DC, 1995-99; Radcliffe Quarterly Adv Bd, 1996-; Madam Walker Theatre Ctr, 1997-; pres, Radcliffe Col Alumnae Asn, 1999-2001; co-chair, NABJ Authors Showcase, 2002-; vis fac, Hurtston/Wright Found Writers Workshop, 2003; dean's coun, Radcliffe Inst Advan Story, Harvard Univ, 2003-; Alpha Iota Chap, Phi Beta Kappa Harvard Col. **Honors/Awds:** First Place Features Award, Nat Asn Black Journalists, 1987; Emmy, Nat Acad TV Arts & Sci, 1990; Black Memorabilia Hall of Fame, 1991; American Book Award, 1992; First Place Feature Award, Am Women Radio & TV, 1992; North Carolina High School Hall of Fame, 1992; Letitia Woods Brown Book Prize, Black Women Historian, 2001; Borders/Hurston-Wright Legacy Award finalist for Nonfiction, 2002; Honor Book, Black Caucus Am Libr Asn, 2002; Award for Oustanding Service, Harvard Alumni Asn, 2002; Honorary Doctorate, Ind Univ, 2003. **Special Achievements:** Author: On Her Own Ground: The Life and times of Madam CJ Walker, Scribner, 2001; Madam C J Walker: entrepreneur.

BUNKLEY, ANITA RICHMOND
Writer. **Personal:** Born in Columbus, OH; married; married Crawford, 1997 (divorced); children: two daughters. **Educ:** Mt Union Col, BA. **Career:** Middle sch lang teacher; adult educ teacher; author, currently; Author: Emily: The Yellow Rose, 1989; Black Gold, 1994; Wild Embers, 1995; Starlight Passage, 1996; Balancing Act, 1997; Steppin' Out With Attitude: Sister, Sell Your Dream!, 1998; Mirrored Life, 2002; Silent Wager, 2006. **Orgs:** Tex Inst Letts. **Honors/Awds:** Excellence in Achievement Award, United Negro Col Fund; 10 best romances of the yr, Wild Embers Publishers Weekly, 1995; Woman of Excellence, River Oaks Bus Women's Exchange Club, 1996. **Special Achievements:** All of her novels have appeared on Blackboard: African American Bestseller List. **Home Addr:** 3554 Ashfield Dr, PO Box 821248, Houston, TX 77282-1248, **Home Phone:** (281)531-0566. **Business Addr:** Writer, Kensington Books, 850 3rd Ave, New York, NY 10022, **Business Phone:** 877-422-3665.

BUNKLEY, LONNIE R
Executive. **Personal:** Born Aug 12, 1932, Denison, TX; son of Ruth Smith Bunkley and C B Bunkley; married Charlene Marie Simpson, Jan 12, 1973; children: Karen Annette & Natalie Anitra. **Educ:** Prairie View Univ, BA 1952; CA State Univ LA, MS 1964; Univ So CA, grad studies 1965. **Career:** LA Neighborhood Youth Corps Econ & Youth Oppor Agency, dir, 1968; East LA Col & Compton Col, col instr, 1970-78; LA Co Probation Dept, div chief, 1982; Pac Properties, real estate develop & pres; broker; Com Devel Corp, pres; Bunkley Investment Mgt Co, owner, currently. **Orgs:** Mem exec comt, Southside LA Jr C C, 1966; SE Welfare Planning Coun, 1973; bd dir, Compton Sickle Cell Anemia Educ & Detection Ctr; CA Probation & Parole Asn; Black Probation Officers Asn; bd dir, Nat Black United Fund; bd trustees, Los Angeles Brotherhood Crusade; Omega Psi Phi Frat; ruling elder, St Paul's Presbyterian Church; bd dirs, Black Support Group, Calif State Univ; South Cent Diabeties Assoc; pres, Los Angeles Alumni, Prairie View Univ, 1960; founder, Burkley Found. **Honors/Awds:** Commendation Southside Jr Chamber Com, 1962; Cert, Prairie View Univ Alumni Award, 1970; Outstanding Serv Award, Brotherhood Crusade, 1972; Cert Ctr for Health Urban Educ & Res, 1982; Commendatory Resolution City of Compton, 1982; Compton Sickle Cell Educ & Detection Ctr, 1982; Cert of Appreciation, US Cong, 1983; Award, LA Co Bd Supvr, 1984; Commendation, State of Calif, 1990; Citizen of the Year, Omega Psi Phi, Lambda Omicrom Chap, 1997. **Military Serv:** AUS educ specl, 1953-55. **Home Addr:** 6711 Bedford Ave, Los Angeles, CA 90056.

BUNTE, DORIS
Administrator. **Personal:** Born Jul 2, 1933, New York, NY; divorced; children: Yvette, Harold & Allen. **Educ:** Boston Univ, Metro Col, Univ MA Amhurst/Suffolk Univ,1973; Harvard Univ, MA. **Career:** Seventh Suffolk Dist, state rep, 1972; Boston Housing Authority, bd comnr, 1969-75; Southern End Neighbourhood Action Prog Boston, dir personnel, 1970-72; Southern End Neighbourhood Action Prog & Boston, dir housing, 1969-70, Boston housing authority, chief exec officer, 1984-92; Northeastern Univ, Ctr Study Sport Soc, dir community rels & human resource coordr, currently; consult & mediator, housing & community develop issues, currently. **Orgs:** Dem Nat Conventions, 1972-76; Doris Bunte Day, named in honor, 1975; Loeb Fel, Harvard Grad Sch Design, 1975-76; MALEG Black Caucus; Third World Jobs Clearing Hse; Mass Asn Paraplegics; Combined Black Philanthropies; Mass Legis Women's Caucus; Nat Asn Advan Colored People; Nat Order Women Leglis; Black Polit Task Force; Mass Conf Human Rights; Citizen's Housing & Planning Asn; Solomon Carter Fuller Mental Health Ctr; Rosbury Multi-Serv Ctr Declaration; Urban Outreach Coun. **Honors/Awds:** Citizen Of Year, Omega Psi Frat Inc, Iota Chi Chap, 1978; Citizen Of Year Award, Nat Asn Social Workers, 1980; Notary Pub, Commonwealth Mass; appointee, Nat Rent Adv Bd Phase II Econ Stabilization Act; Award Black Housing Task Force; Award Roxbury Action Prog; Guest Lecturer to numerous Cols including Boston Col, Boston Univ, John F Kennedy Sch, Simmons Col, Suffolk Univ, Southern Univ & Univ Mass. **Special Achievements:** First African-American woman elected to the Massachusetts Legislature; Published, Address to City Missionary, 1973; "Child Advocacy" a dependency cycle is not a goal, 1977; "Our & Third World Comm Revitalization Through Access By Mandte Example & Monitoring". **Business Phone:** (617)373-4861.

BUNYON, RONALD S.
Executive, school administrator. **Personal:** Born Mar 13, 1935, Philadelphia, PA; son of Ulysses and Mamie; married Josephine; children: Ronald Jr, Judith, Joann, Joyce, Jodetta. **Educ:** Mitchell Col, ASE, 1965; Univ New Haven, CT, BS, 1969; Southern Conn State Univ, MS, urban studies; Researcher Polytech Inst, MS, urban environ, 1992. **Career:** Gen Dynamics Nuclear Ship Bldg, sr designer, 1958; Nat Prog asst Econ Devel, reg dir, 1972; Zion Investments Philadelphia, bus mgr, 1973; Opportunities Ind Ctr Int, mgt spec, 1976; Drexel Univ Philadelphia, asst vpres, 1979; Bus Ventures Int Inc, pres, 1979-. **Orgs:** Alpha Ki Alpha Hon Soc, 1967; Bd Educ, leadership comt, Philadelphia, 1978; US Dept Comn, Export Coun, 1979; World Trade Asn, Philadelphia, 1979; Nat Teachers Asn, 1986. **Special Achievements:** Author: Black Life Poetic Thinking, Vantage Inc, 1992; Family, short stories c, 1993; South Philly, novel, 1993; Black Bus, from experiences, 1993; excerpts Philosophic Thinking About Life. *

BURCHELL, CHARLES R.
Educational psychologist. **Personal:** Born Nov 24, 1946, New Orleans, LA; married Paulette Martinez. **Educ:** Tulane Univ, attended 1966; Southern Univ, attended 1968; La State Univ, BA, 1968, MA, 1971, PhD, 1977; Soc Police & Criminal Psychol, dipl. **Career:** WXOK Radio Baton Rouge, radio announcer, 1966-72; LA State Univ, Dept Psychol, instr 1971-; WRBT-TV, TV news & reporter, 1972-74, 1976; New Orleans Police Dept, psychologist, currently. **Orgs:** Psi Chi, 1968; AFTRA, 1970; Southern Psychol Asn, 1974-75; Int Asn Chiefs Police; Soc Police & Criminal Psychol. **Honors/Awds:** Welfare Rights Orgn Serv Award, 1973. **Business Addr:** Psychologist, New Orleans Police Department, 715 S Broad St, New Orleans, LA 70803, **Business Phone:** (504)658-5858.

BURD, STEVEN A
Executive. **Personal:** Born Jan 1, 1949?, Valley City, ND. **Educ:** Univ Wisc. **Career:** Safeway Inc, chmn, pres & ceo, currently. **Orgs:** Prostate Cancer Found. *

BURDEN, PENNIE L.
Community activist. **Personal:** Born Nov 26, 1910, Waynesboro, GA; daughter of John W and Sarah L Bell; married Sherman J Burden, Nov 4, 1959. **Educ:** Wayne State Univ; Detroit Inst Musical Art; Lewis Bus Col. **Career:** Detroit Gen Hosp, desk clerk regist patients clin, sec oral surg, 1969-70, technician radiol clin patients, sr clerk bus off. **Orgs:** Nat pres, Eta Phi Beta Sorority Inc, 1962-66; Campfire Girl Leader, 1970-80; Campfire Girl Leader, 1977-80; Historic Sites Comt, 1980-; UNCF MI Con Sr Prog, 1989; asst secy, St Stephen Am Church Bd Trustees; DABO bd dir; Nat Coun Negro Women; St Stephen Dir Sr Citizen; St Stephen pres Goodwill Club, 1989; dir, Sr Citizen Prog, St Stephen Am Church, 1980-89. **Honors/Awds:** Life mem, Nat Asn Advan Colored People; secy, Mortgage Fund; St Stephen Am Church; 1975; Golden Heritage, Nat Asn Advan Colored People, 1988; Town Hall Forum, St Stephen Am Church; Out Reach Prog, City Detroit Retirees, 1989. *

BURDEN, WILLIE JAMES
Administrator. **Personal:** Born Jul 21, 1951, Longwood, NC; son of John and Emily H; married Velma Stokes; children: Courtney, Willie James Jr & Freddie Hamilton. **Educ:** NC State Univ, BA, 1974; Ohio Univ, MA, sports admin, 1983; Tenn State Univ, EdD, 1990. **Career:** OH Univ, asst football coach, 1982-84; Calgary Stampeders CFL, prof athlete, 1974-81; NC State Univ, asst to athletics dir, 1976-82, asst football coach, 1974-76; Tenn Tech Univ, asst athletic dir, 1984-88; Ohio Univ, asst athletic dir, 1988-90; NC A&T Univ, athletics dir, 1998-98; Ga Southern Univ, assoc prof, 1999-. **Orgs:** Sr counr Am Legion Boys State Tenn, 1984, 1986; pres, Friends Distinction NC, 1969-; big bro counr, PHD Prevent High Sch Drop Outs Prog Raleigh, NC, 1973-74; Phi Delta Kappa, 1987-; Civitan Civic Org, 1988-90; Nat Greene Kiwanis, 1993-. **Honors/Awds:** Atlantic Coast Conf Football Player of the Year, 1973; all-star Can Football League, 1975-79; mvp Canadian Football League, 1975; Athletic endowment scholarship honoree Univ Calgary, Alberta, Can, 1983-; Calgary Stampeders, "Wall of Fame," 1992; Men of Valor Award, Ga Southern Univ, Nat Asn Advan Colored People; Canadian Football League Hall of Fame. **Business Addr:** Associate Professor, Georgia Southern University, Department Of Recreation And Sport Management, Hollis 1101C, PO Box 08034, Statesboro, GA 30460, **Business Phone:** (912)871-1927.

BURDETTE, LAVERE ELAINE
Clinical psychologist, executive. **Personal:** Born in Chicago, IL; daughter of Leonard Charles Dixon and Dorothy Earl. **Educ:** Kent State Univ, BA, 1969; Wayne State Univ, MSW, 1972; Union Grad Sch, MA, Psychol, 1982, PhD, 1985. **Career:** Cigna Ins Co, employee assistance specialist; Blue Cross & Blue Shield Mich, adv bd, 1990-; Burdette & Doss Training Inc, pres, Psychol Serv, prog dir, clin pract psychol, exec dir, currently. **Orgs:** Am Asn Black Psychologists; Mich Psychol Asn; Am Psychol Asn. **Special Achievements:** Author of: The Self in Search of Unity Through Confrontation, 1985, Stress Mgt Workbook, 1987, Handling Conflict: Fighting for Happiness, 1991. **Business Phone:** (248)559-0730.*

BURFORD, EFFIE LOIS
Educator. **Personal:** Born Feb 16, 1927, Learned, MS; married; children: Cecelia Adela Boler, Suzette Elaine & Maurice M. **Educ:** Butler Univ, AB, 1950; Christian Theol Sem, MA, 1955. **Career:** Indianapolis, teacher, 1957-65; Language Arts & Spanish, teacher, 1966; Language, Traveling Foreign teacher, 1970; Zeta Phi Beta Sor Inc, state dir, 1966, reg dir, 1968-74. **Orgs:** Bd mem & editor mem, Am Teachers Spanish & Portguese, 1974; IFT; bd mem, Second Christian Church; Comt Church Develop IN; life mem, NAACP; nat chmn, Reconciliation Christian Church; Publicity Comn. **Honors/Awds:** Black women's international conference award, journ Columbia Scholastic Press Asn, 1971; regional award, Zeta Phi Beta Sor, 1972; national regional director's award, 1974. *

BURGES, JOYCE
Association executive. **Personal:** Married Eric; children: Eric Jr, Lawrence, Candace, Candra & Victoria. **Career:** Lectr; adv; Nat Black Home Educators Resource Asn (NBHERA), co-founder, 2000-. **Special Achievements:** Guest on BET Tonight, national broadcast hosted by Queen Latifah on August 15, 2001; featured in several periodicals such as Newsweek Magazine, Essence Magazine Sept, 2002, Jet Magazine Sep, 2003. **Business Addr:** Co-founder, The National Black Home Educators Resource Association (NBHERA), 13434 Plank Rd, PO Box 110, Baker, GA 70714.*

BURGES, MELVIN E.
Executive. **Personal:** Born Oct 15, 1951, Chicago, IL; son of Ruth N. and Malcolm M. Sr.; children: Necco L McKinley. **Educ:** Loyola Univ, BA, accounting, 1982; DePaul Univ, MBA, 1984. **Career:** Ceco Corporation, regional controller, 1972-90; Winter Construction Co, corporate controller, 1990-92; Sanderson Industries, Inc, vp of finance & adm, 1992-93; System Software Assoc, finance application consul, 1994; Thomas Howell & McLarens Toplis Inc, nat finance mgr, 1995-97; Harcon, Inc, controller & chief financial officer, 1997-. **Orgs:** National Black MBA ASN, dr of corporate affairs, 1990-; NAT ASN of Black Accountants, 1990-; Ebenezer Baptist Church, trustee, chmn outside properties, 1992-; Construction Financial MGT ASN, 1989-, pres, 2000; IBT Capital Group Investment Club, 1991-; AMR IST of Certified Public Accountants, 1990-; Being Single Magazine Pinnacle Club, 1992. **Honors/Awds:** Being Single Magazine, The Pinnacle Award, 1991; YMCA, Motivator of Youth Award, 1980. **Business Addr:** Controller, chief financial officer, Harcon Inc, 905 Union Hill Rd, Alpharetta, GA 30004, **Business Phone:** (770)343-9998.*

BURGESS, CHAKA
Biotechnologist. **Educ:** Howard University. **Career:** Amegen, Inc., Director. **Orgs:** Member, Congressional Black Caucus Foundation, Inc. *

BURGESS, DWIGHT A.
Executive, teacher, government official. **Personal:** Born Dec 16, 1927, Bailey's Bay; married Delores L Caldwell; children: Daphne, Danita. **Educ:** Tuskegee Inst, BS 1952, MEd, 1953. **Career:** teacher, exec dir, government official (retired); Francis Patton Sch Bermuda, teacher, athletic coach, 1953-55; Hooper City High Sch, soc studies teacher, 1955; Summer Basic Skills Workshop Am Ethical Union, dir, 1964-66; New Castle High Sch, head soc & sci dept, oratorical coach, athletic bus mgr, 1966; Daniel Payne Col, dean acad affairs, 1968, interim pres, 1969; Birmingham Urban League, exec dir; Birmingham City Coun, comt asst; Birmingham Airport Authority. **Orgs:** Prof Rights & Responsibilities Comt, Ala State Teachers Asn , 1963; pres, Jefferson County Educ Asn, 1963-65, exec comt mem, Jefferson County Educ Asn, 1966; mem adv comt, Ala Ctr Higher Educ; chmn, Fac Sharing Emp Comt, Ala Ctr Higher Educ, 1968; Adv Bd, Curbar Asn Higher & Educ, 1968; secy, St John Fed Comt, 1969; consult educ, Group Res, 1969; chmn, Health Manpower Adv Comt, Health Planning Comn, Community Serv Coun Jefferson County, 1969; outreach supvr, Community Serv Coun, 1970; adv comt mem, Birmingham Police Dept, 1972; bd dirs, Crisis Ctr, 1972; coordr, Jeff County Drug Abuse Comt, 1973; Ala Comt Pub Progs Humanities, 1973; Birmingham Manpower Area Planning Coun, 1973; C C Manpower Voc Educ Comt, 1974; Birmingham Art Club, 1974; Birmingham Youth, 1974; Tuskegee Univ Alumni Asn; Sigma Pi Phi Fraternity; Alpha Phi Alpha Fraternity. **Honors/Awds:** Community Service Award, Delta Sigma Theta Sorority, 1973; Man of the Year, Alpha Phi & Alpha, 1974. *

BURGESS, JAMES (JAMES PAUL BURGESS)
Football player. **Personal:** Born Mar 31, 1974, Miami, FL. **Educ:** Miami Univ, Fla. **Career:** Kans City Chiefs, 1997; San Diego Chargers, linebacker, 1997-98; Oakland Raiders, line backer; Orlando Rage, 2001; Calgary Stampeders, line backer, 2002.

BURGESS, JAMES PAUL. See BURGESS, JAMES.

BURGESS, LINDA
Basketball player. **Personal:** Born Jul 27, 1969. **Educ:** Univ Ala, phys educ, attended. **Career:** Basketball player (retired); Belinzona, Switzerland, forward, 1992-93; Ramat HaSharon, Israel, 1993-94, 1996-97; Beni-Yeuda, Israel, 1994-95; SPO Rouen, France, 1995-96; Los Angeles Sparks, 1997; Sacramento Monarchs, 1998-2000.

BURGESS, LORD. See BURGIE, IRVING LOUIS.

BURGESS, MELVIN THOMAS, SR.
Government official, police officer. **Personal:** Born May 23, 1938, Memphis, TN; son of Eddie and Katherine S; married Johanna Sandridge, Feb 24, 1975; children: Melvin Thomas II, Pamela Camille. **Educ:** Memphis State Univ, BA, police admin, 1981; Grambling Col. **Career:** Police officer (retired); City Memphis, patrol officer, 1962-66, detective sergeant, 1966-79, lt, 1979-81, capt, 1981-85, inspector, 1985-86, chief inspector, 1986-88, dir police serv, 1991-94; Lin-Cris Inc. **Orgs:** NEI Major Cities Chief of Police, 1992; vpres, Kappa Alpha Psi; Nat Asn Advan Colored People; Int Asn Chiefs of Police. **Honors/Awds:** Man of the Yr Award, Kappa Alpha Psi, 1992. **Military Serv:** USAF, corporal, 1957-61; Overseas Good Conduct Medal. *

BURGESS, DR. NORMA J
Educator. **Personal:** Born May 24, 1954, Stanton, TN; daughter of John A and Athis M Bond; married Charlie, Sep 3, 1976; children: Wesley & Shenon. **Educ:** Univ Tenn Martin, BA, 1975; NC State Univ, MPA, 1980, PhD, 1986. **Career:** Miss State Univ, prof, 1986-93; Nat Sci Found, res fel, 1990-93; Syracuse Univ, Dept Child & Family Studies, prof, 1993-, chmn & sociologist, currently. **Orgs:** Southern Sociol Soc, 1985-; Southeastern Coun Family Rels, 1986-93; Nat Coun Family Rel, 1986-; chair, Am Asn Higher Educ, Women's Caucus, 2000-02. **Honors/Awds:** Paeidia Award, Miss State Univ, 1988; Outstanding Black Alumni, Univ Tenn, 1995; Marie Peters Award, NCFR, 2002. **Special Achievements:** Co-author, Afr Am Women: An Ecological Perspective, 2000; Author of numerous articles & book chapters. **Business Addr:** Professor, Sociologist, Chairman, Syracuse University, College of Human Services and Health Professions, 426 Ostrom Ave 202 Slocum Hall, Syracuse, NY 13244, **Business Phone:** (315)443-2757.

BURGESS, ROBERT E., SR.
Executive. **Personal:** Born Oct 13, 1937, Lake City, SC; married Mary Elizabeth, Nov 23, 1969; children: W Michael Tiagwad, Tamara Tiagwad Wagner, Robert E Jr. **Educ:** J M Wright Tech Sch, Electrical, 1957; Norwalk Comn Col Cert City Housing Planning & Develop, 1973; IBM Mgt Develop Prog Community Execs, 1983. **Career:** Self-employed, band leader 1958-63; Norden Aircraft, inspector, 1963-66; self-employed, restaurant owner, 1966-69; Comt Training & Employment, admin asst, 1966-71. **Orgs:** Chmn & organizer, Fairfield Cty Black Bus Assoc, 1969; organizer, Norwalk Conn Fed Credit Union, 1970; S Norwalk Comm Ctr Bd, 1970; Norwalk Econ Opportunity Now Inc, admin asst, 1970-72, exec dir, 1972-. State Manpower Training Coun Gov Meskill, 1972; bd dir, Springwood Health Unit, 1973; New England Comn Action Prog Dir Assoc, 1973; chmn & org dir Assoc, Nat Comn Action, 1973; chmn, Norwalk Comn Develop Citizens Partic Comn Mayor Irwin; State Employment Training Coun Gov Grasso, 1978; pres, CT Assoc Community Action, 1978-84; State Energy Adv Comm Gov Grasso, 1979; State Negotiated Invest Strategy Team Gov O'Neill, 1983; NAACP Exec Comm; legislative chmn, CT Assoc Comn Action; Dist Heating Comn, 1984; Review Team ACVS Headstart, 1984; mem Exec Comn, vpres, Action Housing 1989; Advisory Comn Housing Finance Authority, 1989; CT Employ & Training Comn, 1989; CT Comn Study Mgt State Govt, 1989; United Way Commnity Problem Solving Task Force; Gen Asst Task Force; UCONN Downstate Initiative Adv Comt; chmn, SW Region CT Housing Coalition Governor Weicker, 1991; Mayor's Blue Ribbon Comt Race Rel, 1993; Negotiating Team, Police Community Relations, 1993; bd dir, Norwalk Community Health Ctr, 1995; CT Employ & Training Commission, 1996; Work Force Develop Performance Measurement Comt, 1998; Welfare Reform Implementation Comt, 1998; sec, CT Employ & Training Commission, 1998; Norwalk Hosp Inst Review Bd, 1996; Citizens Fair Housing, 1997; Norwalk Tribal Coun, 1998; NAACP Negotiating Team Fair Housing Suit, 2002-03; chmn, Norwalk Br Capitol Region, 2003; Black Chamber Com; vchmn, Capitol Region Black Chamber Com, 2003. **Honors/Awds:** Roy Wilkins Civil Rights Award, CT State NAACP, 1984; Award for Outstanding Service to Norwalk Corinthian Lodge, 16 F&AM PHA, 1982; Citizen of the Year, Alpha Nu Chap Omega Psi Phi, 1981; recipient, Arthur L Green Human Rights Award, CT State NAACP, 2003; Roodner Court Tenants Award, 2003. **Military Serv:** AUS, Reserve, pfc. **Business Addr:** Executive Director, Norwalk Economic Opportunity Now Inc, 98 S Main St, South Norwalk, CT 06854-3126.*

BURGEST, REV. DR. DAVID RAYMOND
Educator, baptist clergy, consultant. **Personal:** Born Dec 10, 1943, Sylvania, GA; married Loretta Jean Black; children: Juanita Marie, Angela Lynore, David Raymond II & Paul Reginald. **Educ:** Paine Col, BA, 1965; Wayne State Univ, MSW, 1968; Syracuse Univ, PhD, 1974; Univ Chicago Sch Divinity, Postdoctoral studies 1984-85. **Career:** Clergy, consultant, prof (retired); Cent State Hosp, Milledgeville, GA, social work aide, 1965-66, chief social worker, 1968-69; Syracuse Univ, asst prof 1969-72; State Univ New York, Upstate Med Col, Syracuse, assoc prof psychol, 1971-72; Univ Nairobi, Kenya, vis prof sociol 1980-81; Atlanta Univ, Sch Social Work, social work consult, 1986-87; Governors State Univ, prof 1972-80, prof social work 1981-98; Roosevelt Univ, Chicago, IL, part-time prof, African-Amer studies, 1989-90; Univ W Indies, Vis Prof Social Work, 1993; Atlanta Univ, Sch Social Work,lectr; New Faith Baptist Church, ministry God; New Faith Baptist Church, Park Forest, Ill, co-founder & assoc minister; Greater Faith Baptist Church, assoc minister; St James AME Church, Chicago, Ill, assoc minister; Metropolitan AME Church, Trinidad, W Indies, assoc minister; Providence Missionary Baptist Church, Atlanta, Ga, assoc minister, currently. **Orgs:** Founder & pres, Cir Human Learning & Develop Specialists Inc, 1975-; licensed gospel minister 1976; ed bd, Black Caucus Jour Nat Asn Black Social Workers 1979-80; prison ministry, Stateville Prison Joliet Ill & other facilities in Ill 1982-; consult, Suburban Nat Asn Advan Colored People, 1984-; ed bd Jour Pan-Africans Studies, 1986-; Univ Park Library Bd, 1987-91; pres, Lower North Youth Centers/Chicago, 1989-91; WGCI-AM, ment health youth serv advr, 1988-90; pres, Abyssinia Repetory Theatre, 1990-; pres, Self Taught Publishers, 1989-; Consult, various local, nat & international social service organizations in Am, Europe, Canada & Africa such as Dept of Family Svcs, Alcoholism Couns, United Charities, & vocational Rehabilation. **Honors/Awds:** Social Worker of the Year Award, 1968; Everyday People Award, 1975; Man of the Year Award for Excellence, 1985; Appreciation Award, Far S Suburban Nat Asn Advan Colored People, 1983. **Special Achievements:** Presented various papers, workshops, & Institutes locally, nationally & internationally in Africa, America, Canada & Europe; published in such journals as Black Scholar, Social Work, Black Male/Female Relationships, Black Books Bulletin, Intl Social Work, Journal of Black Studies; author of Ebonics, Black Talk word game; Author, "Social Work Practice with Minorities," Scarecrow 1982, Proverbs for the

Young and Not So Young, Self Taught Publishers; "Social Casework Intervention with People of Color", Univ Press Am, 1985; Village of Univ Park proclaimed December "Dr David R Burgest Month" 1985; play, Harriet Tubman: One More River to Cross. **Business Addr:** Associate Minister, Providence Missionary Baptist Church, 2295 Benjamin E Mays Dr, Atlanta, GA 30311, **Business Phone:** (404)752-6869.

BURGETT, DR. PAUL JOSEPH
Executive, school administrator. **Personal:** Son of Arthur C and Ruth Garizio; married Catherine G Valentine, Jan 1, 1982. **Educ:** Univ Rochester, Eastman Sch Music, Rochester, NY, BM, 1968, MA, 1972, PhD, 1976. **Career:** Hochstein Mem Music Sch, exec dir, 1970-72; Nazareth Col, Rochester, NY, lectr, 1976-77, asst prof music, 1977-81; Univ Rochester, Eastman Sch Music, dean studies, 1981-88, vpres & dean studies, 1988-2001, vpres & gen secy, 2001-, adj prof music & sr adv pres, currently. **Orgs:** Chair, vice chair, Zoning Bd Appeals, 1981-86; dir, Governing Bd Hochstein Memorial Music Sch, 1982-88; dir, Corporate Bd YMCA Rochester & Monroe County, 1983-91; mem, Nat Adv Bd, Ctr Black Music Res, 1985-; dir, bd trustees, Margaret Woodbury Strong Museum, 1987-2000; dir bd dir, Urban League, Rochester, 1987-94; bd dir, Am Automobile Asn, Rochester, 1995; bd trustees, Genesee County Village & Museum, 2000-; bd governors, Hillside Family Agencies, 2001; Rotany Club, 2001. **Special Achievements:** Author: Vindication as a Thematic Principle in Alain Locke's Writings on the Music of Black Americans, 1989; Artistry in Student Affairs or Virtuosity in Practicing the Craft of Being Human, 1987; On the Tyranny of Talent: An Analysis of the Myth of Talent in the Art Music World, 1987; From Bach to Beethoven to Boulez and Very Few Women in Sight, 1987; On Creativity, 1982. **Military Serv:** AUS, sgt, 1969-75. **Business Addr:** Vice President, General Secretary, University of Rochester, Eastman School of Music, 236 Wallis Hall, Rochester, NY 14627, **Business Phone:** (585)273-2284.

BURGIE, IRVING LOUIS (LORD BURGESS)
Publisher, composer. **Personal:** Born Jul 28, 1924, Brooklyn, NY; married Page Turner (died 2003); children: Irving Jr & Andrew. **Educ:** Juilliard Sch Music, attended 1948; Univ Ariz, attended 1949; Univ SCalif, attended 1950. **Career:** Self-employed composer & lyricist; Harry Belafonte Albums, composer, 1955-60; Songs: "Jamaica Farewell"; "Island In the Sun"; "Day O"; Am Guild Authors & Composers, 1956; Ballad Bimshire, composer & writer, 1963; Barbados Nat Anthem, Barbados, composer, 1966. **Orgs:** Am Soc Composers, Authors & Publishers, 1956; Local no 802 Am Fedn Musicians; pres & publ, Caribe Music Corp; life mem, Nat Asn Advan Colored People; Harlem Writers Guild; United Black Men Queens; hon chmn, Camp Minisink; United Black Men Queens County Fedn. **Honors/Awds:** Numerous awards & citations including Silver Crown Merit, Barbados Govt, 1987; DHL, Univ Wis, 1989; Lord Burgess Caribbean Day, Assembly Prog Publ, named in honor. **Special Achievements:** Belafonte's Calypso Album, first album sold one million copies; Book: In Plenty & Time Need, 1966. **Military Serv:** AUS. **Home Addr:** 11215 177th St, Jamaica, NY 11433, **Home Phone:** (718)297-9080. **Business Addr:** Composer, Lyricist, 11215 177th St, Jamaica, NY 11433, **Business Phone:** (718)297-9080.

BURGIN, BRUCE L
Banker. **Personal:** Born Oct 22, 1947, Cincinnati, OH; married Ollie Keeton, Sep 20, 1980. **Educ:** NC Cent Univ, BS, com, 1970. **Career:** Freedom Savings Bank, br mgr, 1973-85; Empire Am Fed Savings Bank, br mgr, 1986-88; Life Savings Bank, br mgr, 1988-89; Fortune Bank, br mgr, 1989. **Orgs:** Tampa Alumni Chap, KAP, 1986-; Tampa Bay Urban Bankers, 1986-89. **Honors/Awds:** Polemarch Award, Tampa Alumni Chap, KAP, 1991. **Military Serv:** AUS, sgt, 1970-73. *

BURKE, BRIAN
Government official. **Career:** Domestic Policy Coun, sr policy analyst; State Wis, senate chmn, 2002, State Senate 3rd dist, 2002, joint comt finance, co-chmn, 2002. **Business Phone:** (608)266-8535.*

BURKE, DONNA M
Executive, vice president (organization). **Career:** SBC Ameritech Mich, vpres external affairs, 2003-. **Orgs:** Metrop Affairs Coalition. **Business Addr:** Vice President, External Affairs, SBC Ameritech Michigan, 444 Michigan Ave Suite 1700, Detroit, MI 48226, **Business Phone:** (313)223-6688.

BURKE, GARY LAMONT
Executive. **Personal:** Born Oct 4, 1955, Baltimore, MD; son of William A (deceased) and Gwendolyn I; married Nina J Abbott Burke, Aug 30, 1987; children: Brandon L, Christopher J, Jonathan D, Amanda J, Rachel N. **Educ:** Babson Col, BS, acct, 1977. **Career:** Coopers & Lybrand, staff acct, 1977-79, sr acct, 1979-81; Rouse CPN, internal auditor, 1981-82, sr auditor, 1982-83, acquisitions mgt, mgr, 1983-87; US F&G Realty Inc, investment officer, 1987-89, asst vip, 1989-90, US F&G Corp, chief staff, 1990-91, US F&G Financial Servs Corp, vip, 1991, US F&G Corp, vpres, admin, 1991-93; Fidelity & Guaranty Life Ins Co, vpres bus develop, 1994-95, vpres spec mkt, 1995-97; CMO Atlanta Life Ins Co, vpres, 1998; Structured Settlement Fidelity & Guaranty Life Ins Co, vpres, 1999-00, sr vpres, sales, 2000, TSA Sales, sr vpres, Brokerage & Agency Develop, 2000; Structured Financial Assoc Inc, pres & coo; Prudential Ins Co Am, agent, currently. **Orgs:** Past pres, Nat Asn Black Accts, 1982; Nat Tax Sheltered Accts Asn; Nat Structured Settlements Trade Asn. **Honors/Awds:** State Bd Pub Acct, CPA, 1983; Leadership Award for Confidence, US F&G, 1992. **Business Phone:** (206)436-0312.*

BURKE, KIRKLAND R.
Manager, basketball coach. **Personal:** Born Jan 4, 1948, Chicago, IL; son of Alonzo Waymond and Johnnie Irene. **Educ:** Chicago Tech Col, 1966; Chicago State Univ, BA, 1986. **Career:** Assistant M & M instructor, 1970; Holy Angels Roman Cath Sch, teacher, 1973-74; Reliable Prom, prom mgr, 1974-75; Warner, Elektra, Atlantic Corp, prom mgr, 1975-78; Warner Bros Records, midwest prom mgr; Whitney Young Magnet High Sch, Girl's Basketball, asst coach; American Coaching Effectiveness Prog, cert coach. **Orgs:** Speaker, Chicago Pub Sch Youth Motivation Prog; Nat Assoc TV & Radio Announcers, 1972-77; youth div asst chmn, Oper PUSH, 1972-75, Nat Choir, 1972-75; Black Music Assoc; asst coach, Near N High Sch Chicago, IL Girls Basketball, 1986-87; bd dirs, The RALD Inst, Chicago, 1994-97. **Honors/Awds:** Fifty four gold & platinum records, Warner Bros Records; Am Legion Nat Chmpnshp Chicago Cavaliers D & B Corps, 1969; VFW & Am Legion IL St Championship Chi Cavaliers, 1969; Cert Merit, Chicago Bd Educ, Special Arts Festival, 1980; Cert Merit, Mesetrey Sch, 1982; Cert Merit, James Madison Sch, 1985; Representative of the Year, Warner Bros Records Promotiom, 1994; Legacy Award, Warner-Elektra-Atlantic Corp, 1996. **Special Achievements:** Album: I Got a Feeling, Exec Prod, 1986. **Military Serv:** USN, 3rd class petty officer E-4, 1965-68; Nat Defense Serv Medal, 1965-68; Ancient Order Shellbacks, 1968. *

BURKE, LILLIAN W.
Judge. **Personal:** Born Aug 2, 1917, Thomaston, GA; married Ralph; children: Bruce. **Educ:** Ohio State Univ, BS, 1947; Cleveland State Univ, LLB, 1951; Cleveland Marshall Law Sch Cleveland State Univ, 1964; Nat Col St Judiciary Univ, 1974. **Career:** Judge (retired); Cleveland, gen pract law, 1952-62; sch teacher, bus educ & soc sci; St Ohio, asst atty gen, 1962-66; Ohio Indus Comn, vice chmn, 1966-69; Cleveland Community Col Western Campus, teacher const law; Cleveland Munic Ct, judge, 1969-87; Lectr, Heidelburg Coll Tiffin Ohio, 1971. **Orgs:** Pres, Cleveland Chap Nat Coun Negro Women, 1955-57; pres & former woman ward leader 24th Ward Rep Club, 1957-67; Cuyahoga Co Central Comt, 1958-68; secy E Dist Faily Serv Asn, 1959-60; Human Rel Cleveland Citizens League, 1959-; pres, Cleveland Chap Jack & Jill Am Inc, 1960-61; alternate delegate Nat Rep Conv Chicago, 1960; sec, Cuyahoga Co Exec Comm, 1962-63; Govs Comn Status Women, 1966-67; bd dirs, chmn minority div Nat Fed Rep Women, 1966-68; vpres, large Greater Cleveland Safety Coun, 1969-74; appointed serve four yr term Adv Comm Accreditation & Instnl Eligibility Bur Higher Educ, 1972; Am Asn Univ Women; past Grammateus Alpha Omega Chap Alpha Kappa Alpha Sor; Hon Adv mem, Women Lawyers Asn; Nat Asn Advan Colored People Cleveland Chap; Phyllis Wheatley Asn; trustee, Ohio Comm Status Women; Cleveland Landmark Comn, 1988-97; City Planning Comn, 1997-02; Cleveland Restoration Soc; African Am Outreach Comn, Cleveland Found; Cleveland City Club; Am Bridge Asn; Nat Asn Invstrs Clubs; Eastview United Church Chirst; Cleveland Restoration Soc & Preserv Resource Ctr Northeastern Ohio, currently. **Honors/Awds:** Achievement Award, Parkwood CME Church Cleveland, 1968; Career Woman Year, Cleveland Womens Career Clubs Inc, 1969; Martin Luther King Citizen Award, Recog Music & Arts Com Pgh, 1969; Award Recognizing Outstanding Achievement Field Law, Nat Sor Phi Delta Kappa, 1969; Award Nat Coun Negro Women, 1969; Outstanding Achievement Award, Te-Wa-Si Scholar Club Cleveland, 1969; Outstanding Service Award, Morning Star Grand Chap Cleve, 1970; Golden Jubilee Award, Zeta Phi Beta Sor, 1970; Outstanding Serv Award, Morning Star Grand Chap, 1970; Award Honor Cleveland Bus League, 1970; Serv Award St Paul AME Ch Lima Ohio, 1972; Woman Achievement Award, 1973; Inter-Club Coun, 1973; Leadership Award, Cleveland Found, 1997; Jewel Yr, Cleveland City Club, 2002. **Special Achievements:** Salute Am Woodmen First Elected Negro Female Judge Cleveland, 1970. **Business Addr:** Member, Cleveland Restoration Society, Preservation Resource Center of Northeastern Ohio, 3751 Prospect Ave Sarah Benedict House, Cleveland, OH 44115-2705, **Business Phone:** (216)426-1000.

BURKE, OLGA PICKERING
Executive. **Personal:** Born Jan 6, 1946, Charleston, SC; daughter of Dr L Irving and Esther Robinson; married Philip C Burke Sr; children: Philip C Jr, Brian. **Educ:** Johnson C Smith Univ, AB, Econ & Acct, 1968; Nat Rural Develop Leaders Sch, cert, 1976; Life Investors Inc Co, ins license, 1981. **Career:** HA Decosta Co, acct, 1969-70; Allied Chem Corp, lost acct, 1970-72; Charleston Area Minority Assoc, fiscal officer, 1972-75; Minority Develop & Mgt Assoc, exec dir, 1975-79; pres, Affiliated Mgt Serv Inc, owner, 1979-. **Orgs:** Martin Luther King Comm YWCA Charleston, 1977-79; organizer SC Rural Am, 1979; econ adv coun, Clemson Univ, 1978-81; vpres, Regional Minority Purchasing Coun, 1981; policy comm YWCA Charleston, 1981; Nat Assoc of Minority Contr; Charleston Bus & Prof Assn, 1980-83; treas, SC Sea Island Small Farmers Co-op, 1981-83; Columbia Adv, Coun US Small Bus Admin, 1981-83; MBE Governor's Comm State SC, 1982; Bus Develop, Sub-Committee City of Charleston, 1982; Am Soc Prof Consult, 1983; chmn bus comm, Charleston Trident Chamber Comm, 1984. *

BURKE, ROSETTA Y
Military leader. **Personal:** Divorced; children: Tirlon. **Educ:** Harlem Hosp Sch Nursing; Long Island Univ, CW Post Ctr, masters degree; Adelphi Univ. **Career:** Military leader (retired); USAR, Army Nurse Corps, lt gen duty nurse, 1962-66, captain & nurse instr, 1966-74, major, 1974-78, lt col, 1978-83, col, 1983-89, Nat Guard, col & chief nurse, 1993-94, adj asst gen, 1994-95, brig gen, 1995-97, major gen, 1997; 74th Field Hosp, Bronx, New York, chief nurse, 1974; 815th Sta Hosp, chief nurse, 1978-89; 365th Gen Hosp, chief nurse, 1978-89; NY State Dept Correctional Servs, coordr & dir nurses, 1983-89, Summit Shock Incarceration Correctional Facil, supt, 1989-92; St Joseph's Sch Nursing, nurse instr; Bronx State Hosp, nurse supvr; Develop Disabilities Prog, specialist & community res coordr; NY Selective Serv Syst, state dir, 2002. **Orgs:** Reserved Officers Asn; Asn Mil Surgeons US; Nat Black Nurses Asn; Harlem Hosp Sch Nursing Alumni; hon mem, Alpha Kappa Alpha Sorority; pres, Nat Asn Black Mil Women, 2002-. **Special Achievements:** First female General Officer in the 220 year history of the New York Army National Guard; first female Assistant Adjutant General in New York State and of the Army National Guard; first female to receive the brevet promotion to Major General in the history of the New York Army National Guard and in the Army National Guard; first female to be appointed as the State Director for Selective Service System for the State of New York. **Military Serv:** New York Army Nat Guard; Army Service Ribbon, Medjor Evers Courage Award, 1996, Conspicuous Service Medal, 1997, Carter G. Woodson Award, 1998. **Business Addr:** President, National Association of Black Military Women, 5695 Pine Meadows Ct, Morrow, GA 30261-1053, **Business Phone:** (404)675-0195.

BURKE, SOLOMON
Singer, songwriter. **Personal:** Born Mar 21, 1940, Philadelphia, PA. **Career:** Atlantic Recs 1960; Albums: You Can Run But You Cant Hide, 1958; Solomon Burke, 1962; I Wish I Knew, 1968; Electronic Magnetism, 1972; Sidewalks, Fences & Walls, 1979; Soul Alive, 1985; Homeland, 1990; Live at House Blues, 1994; We Need a Miracle, 1998; Hold On, 2002; Best Contemporary Blues, 2002; Don't Give Up on Me, 2002; Golden Slumbers; Zucherro; Not By Water But Fire This Time; Junkie XL; Radio JXL: A Broadcast From the Computer Hell Cabin, 2004; Make Do With What You Got, 2005; Radio JXL: A Broadcast From the Computer Hell Cabin, 2006; Nashville, 2006; Like a Fire, 2008; Film: Lightning in a Bottle, 2004. **Honors/Awds:** Rock & Roll Hall of Fame, 2001; Grammy Award, 2002. **Business Addr:** Artist, Singer, American Royalty Management, 9245 Reseda Blvd, Northridge, CA 91324, **Business Phone:** (818)349-2419.

BURKE, STERLING
Naval officer, administrator. **Educ:** Flight Sch, attended 1971. **Career:** Foster Group, sr partner, 2003; USN, aviation officer. **Special Achievements:** Bldg his own plane one that will fly faster. **Business Addr:** Senior Partner, The Foster Group Inc, 180 N Mich Ave Suite 2000, Chicago, IL 60611, **Business Phone:** (312)609-1009.*

BURKE, VIVIAN H.
Government official, educator. **Personal:** Born in Charlotte, NC; married Logan; children: Logan Todd. **Educ:** Elizabeth City State Univ, BS; NC A&T State Univ, MS. **Career:** Educator (retired), Government official: Forsyth County Sch Syst, Winston-Salem, sch guidance counr & Indust Educ Coord; NC Dept Environ & Natural Resources, field officer mgr; Winston-Salem State Univ, prog coord; City Winston-Salem, NC, NE Ward, coun mem, 1977-, alderman, 2004; Liberty St E Redevelopment Inc, adv; Guidance Counseling Admin & Curric Instrnl Specialist. **Orgs:** Bd dir, Piedmont Health Syst Agency; minority interest group, NC Sch Sci & math; Trans Adv Coun; chmn, Am's Four Hundredth Anniversary Comt; mem bd trustees, Elizabeth City State Univ; organizer, Flora Buffs Garden Club; Nat Women Achievement; past pres, PTA East Forsyth Sr High Sch; PTA Adv Coun; Forsyth Health Coun; admin coun Patterson Ave, YWCA; Recreation & Parks Comn; basileus Alpha Kappa Alpha Sorority; Nat memship chmn, Alpha Kappa Alpha Sorority; former chmn, Carver Precinct; co-chair, 5th Coun Dist elect Jimmy Carter; deleg, local State Dem Conv; NAACP; Meridian Chap Eastern Star; Alpha Kappa Alpha Sor; Forsyth Asn Classroom Teachers; NC Asn Educators; Top Ladies Distinction; 5th Dist Black Leadership Caucus; vice chair, Finance Admin Intergovt Rel Comt; League Women Voters; app State Dem Affirmative Action Comt, 1983; chmn, Mondale Pres Forsyth County, 1983; bd dir, 1983, mem-at-large 1984; League of Municipalities. **Honors/Awds:** Outstanding Political & Community Serv, NAACP; Outstanding Woman of the Year, Pres of the Year, Grad Leadership Award, Most Distinguished Political Award, AKA Soc; Outstanding Volunteer ESR; Outstanding Volunteer Heart Fund; Gen Alumni Outstanding Political Award, Elizabeth City State Univ; Gov's Order of

Long Leaf Pine; Outstanding Political & Community Serv Award, Black Polit Action League; Outstanding Serv Polit & Community Northeast Ward; Dedicated Serv Award, 5th Dist Black Leadership Caucus Banquet; Serv Award, Forsyth County Health Coun; Distinguished Citizen Award, Sophisticated Gents; Outstanding Women's Achievers Award, Prof Business League; DHL, Livingstone Col, 2002; DHL, Winston-Salem State Univ, 2004. **Special Achievements:** First woman and first black appointed to the public safety chairmanship City of Winson-Salem; one of first two women appointed to Public Works Commission. **Home Addr:** 3410 Cumberland Rd, Winston-Salem, NC 27105. *

BURKE, WILLIAM ARTHUR
Association executive, air force officer. **Personal:** Born May 13, 1939, Zanesville, OH; son of Leonard and Hazel Norris; married Yvonne Brathwaite Burke, Jun 14, 1972; children: Christine Burke, Autumn Burke. **Educ:** Miami Univ, BS, 1961; Boston Univ, attended 1964; Harvard Univ, attended 1964; Univ Mass, EdD, 1977; Lane Col, DCL, 1991. **Career:** S Coast Air Qual Mgt Dist, chmn; Tennis Commr XXIII Olympiad; Fish & Game Comn, State CA, pres; Wildlife Conserv Bd, pres, CA; Genesis Int, bd chmn; World Mining Devel Co Inc, pres; Los Angeles City Counman, dep, 1966-69; Radio & TV, CA State Legis, dir legis; Batik Wine & Spirits, pres; Gen Repub Mali, hon consult; City Los Angeles Marathon, pres, currently; S Coast Air Qual Mgt Dist, vchmn, currently. **Orgs:** Am Health Care Delivery Corp, pres; bd mem, State Calif Air Resources Bd, 2000; Fire Comn, Los Angeles, 2000; Calif Coastal Comn, 2002. **Honors/Awds:** Meritorious Serv Award, City of Los Angeles; Certificate AUS Citation of Honor, CA State Senate; Alpha Epsilon Rho; Nat Radio & Television Hon; First Annual Living Legends Award & Humanitarian Award, Mid-City Chamber Com; Man of the Year Award, Green Power Found's. **Military Serv:** US Air Force, major, 1961-65. **Business Addr:** President, Los Angeles Marathon Inc, 11110 W Ohio Ave Suite 100, Los Angeles, CA 90025.*

BURKE, YVONNE WATSON BRATHWAITE
Government official. **Personal:** Born Oct 5, 1932, Los Angeles, CA; daughter of James T Watson and Lola Moore Watson; married Jan 1, 1963 (divorced); married Dr William A, Jun 14, 1972; children: Autumn Roxanne & Christine Burke. **Educ:** Univ Calif, AA, 1951; Univ Calif, Los Angeles, BA, 1953; Univ Southern Calif Law Sch, JD, 1956. **Career:** CA State Assembly, mem, 1966-72; US House Rep 28th dist, mem, 1972-78; Los Angeles County 4th dist, supvr, 1979-80; Kutak Rock & Huie, partner, 1981-83; MGM/UA Home Entertainment, mem bd dir; Burke Robinson & Pearman, partner 1984-87; Jones, Day, Reavis & Pogue, Los Angeles & Cleveland, partner; Los Angeles Country 2nd dist, Supvr, 1992-. Chair, bd supvr, 1993-94, 1997-98, 2002-03. **Orgs:** The Trusteeship, Urban League, Women's Lawyer's asn; Nat Coalition 100 Black Women; former vice chmn, Univ CA Bd Regents; former bd mem, Educ Testing Svc; former dir & chair, Los Angeles Branch Federal Reserve Bank San Francisco; former mem, Ford Foundation Bd Trustee; chmn, Congressional Black Caucus, 1976; vice chmn, US Olympics Organizing Comt, 1984; former chm, Founders Savings & Loan. **Honors/Awds:** Loren Miller Award NAACP; fel, Inst Politics J F Kennedy School Gvt, Harvard 1971-71; Professional Achievement Award, UCLA, 1974, 1984; Future Leader of America, Time Magazine 1974; Outstanding Alumni Award, Univ Southern Calif, 1994; Alumni of the Year, Univ Calif, Los Angeles, 1996; Enterprise Person Of The Year, Metrop News, 2003. **Special Achievements:** First black woman from California to be elected to US House of Rep 1972. **Home Addr:** PO Box 25665, Los Angeles, CA 90025-0665. **Business Addr:** Supervisor, County of Los Angeles, Second Supervisorial District, 866 Kenneth Hahn Hall of Admin, 500 W Temple St, Los Angeles, CA 90012, **Business Phone:** (213)974-2222.

BURKEEN, ERNEST WISDOM
Government official. **Personal:** Born Aug 28, 1948, Chattanooga, TN; son of Mildred J and Ernest W; married Margaret, May 20, 1993 (divorced); children: Jeannee M & Ernest W III; married Margaret, May 20, 1993. **Educ:** Mich State Univ, BS, 1975, MA, 1976. **Career:** Mich State Univ, Grad asst, 1975-76; Univ Mich, asst dir, 1976-77; City Detroit, recreation instr, 1977-80; Huron-Clinton Metro Parks, from asst supt to supt, 1980-94; Detroit Parks & Recreation, dir, 1994; Family Life Ministry, Creighton Univ, 1990-; City Ft Lauderdale, Parks & Recreation Dept, dir, 2002; City Miami Parks & Recreation, dir, currently. **Orgs:** Prog comt, Nat Recreation Parks Asn; pres, Kiwanis Club; bd mem, EthnicMinority Soc; youth servs bd, Spectrum Human Servs; recreation adv comt,Eastern Mich Univ; pres Mich Recreation & Parks Asn; pres, Nat RecreationEthnic Minority Soc. **Honors/Awds:** Fellowship Award, Md Recreation & Parks Asn, 1988; Innovated ProgramAward, 1988; Appreciation Award, Detroit Metro Youth Fitness, 1993;Service Award, Nat Recreation & Park Ethnic Minority Soc, 1994; Am AcadPark & Recreation Admin. **Special Achievements:** Author: "Crossroads for Recreation," "Selective Law Enforcement," "WattNow," Michigan Leisure; "Handicapped Usage of Recreational Facilities,"NIRSA Journal; "Affirmative Action as Charades," NIRSA Newsletter. **Military Serv:** USN, e-4, 1969-73; Sailor of the Month, Navcomsta Morocco, 1971. **Business Addr:** Director, City of Miami Parks & Recreation, 444 SW 2 Ave 8th Fl, Miami, FL 33130.

BURKETT, GALE E.
Chairperson, chief executive officer. **Career:** Texas Aerospace Comn, commnr; GB Tech Inc, pres, chief exec officer & chmn, 1985-. **Orgs:** Bd mem, Houston Technol Ctr; Exec Comt, Bay Area Houston, 2007. **Honors/Awds:** NASA Public Service Medal, 2004. **Special Achievements:** Named to the list of "Fifty Influential Minorities in Business" by Minority Business & Professionals Network Inc. **Business Phone:** (281)333-3703.*

BURKETTE, DR. TYRONE L.
College president. **Career:** Col President (retired); Barber-Scotia Col, Concord, NH, pres, 1988-89.

BURKS, DARRELL
Executive, founder (originator). **Personal:** Born Sep 3, 1956, Indianapolis, IN; married Suzanne F Shank, Sep 5, 1992. **Educ:** Ind univ, BS, acct, 1978. **Career:** Coopers & Lybrand, IN, staff, 1978-86, Detroit, mgr, 1986-89; Detroit Pub Schs, dep supt, 1989-91; Price Waterhouse Coopers LLP, Detroit, dir, 1991-92, partner, 1992-. **Orgs:** New Detroit's Community Fund & Tech Asst Team; housing chmn,Kappa Alpha Psi; treasr; Urban Educ Alliance; bd dirs, treasr, Health Educ Advocacy League; bd dirs, treasr, Homes Black C; bd dirs, Easter Seals; bd dir, treasr, personnel & fin comt chmn, Mich Metro Girl Scouts; bd dirs, treas, Police Athletic League; bd dirs, treas, Am Inst Cert Pub Accts; Mich, Ohio, Connecticut & Ind Asn Cert Pub Accts; adv comt, Md Asn Cert Pub Accts; Greater Detroit Chamber Com - Bus Educ Alliance; Leadership Detroit; Adv Comn Mich Dept Treas Comn Govt Acct & Auditing; bd mem, Wilberforce Univ; Detroit African Am Museum; Coleman A. Young Found ; bd mem, Univ Detroit, Jesuit. **Honors/Awds:** Outstanding Achievers Award, Indianapolis Leadership Develop Bus Comm, 1984, 1985; Minority Achievers Award, YMCA, 1992; Honorary Educator, Detroit Bd Educ, 1991. **Special Achievements:** Crain's Detroit Bus, "Top Forty Under Forty" execs in Southeastern MI, 1991; featured in "Executive Style" supplement to Detroit Monthly & Crain's Detroit Bus, p 8, Sept 1992; City of Detroit, Detroit City Coun & Wayne Co, citations for outstanding serv. **Business Addr:** Partner, Price waterhouse Coopers LLP, 1900 Saint Antoine St, Detroit, MI 48226, **Business Phone:** (313)394-6000.*

BURKS, JAMES WILLIAM, JR.
Educator, manager. **Personal:** Born Feb 4, 1938, Roanoke, VA; married Janice A Kasey. **Educ:** Lincoln Univ, AB, 1959; Univ Va; Northwestern Uni; Roanoke Col; Lynchburg Col. **Career:** Manager, Educator (retired); Norfolk Southern Corp, marketing mgr; Addison High Sch, teacher. **Orgs:** Vice chmn, Roanoke City Sch; pres, bd dir, Gainsboro Elec Co, 1970-; Omega Psi Phi Frat; bd dir, Magic City Bldg & Loan Asn; City Planning Comn, 1973-76; Human Rel Comn; bd dir, Roanoke Neighbourhood Develop Proj; past dir, Roanoke Jaycees; Roanoke Valley Coun Community Service, 1974-77; Comn Study Relationship between Govt Entities & Elec Utilities; bd vis Norfolk State University Outstanding Service Award; bd commissioners, Roanoke Redevelopment & Housing Authority; bd commissioners, Roanoke Civic Ctr; bd mem, Mill Mountain Theatre; bd mem, Roanoke Valley Arts Coun; co-chair Norfolk State Univ Cluster Prog; Sigma Pi Phi Frat. **Honors/Awds:** Outstanding Service Award, City Planning Comn; Outstanding Service Award, Roanoke Jaycees. **Special Achievements:** First black on city planning commission. **Military Serv:** AUS, spec-4, 1960-63. **Home Addr:** 1836 Grayson Ave NW, Roanoke, VA 24017.

BURKS, JUANITA PAULINE
Executive. **Personal:** Born Jul 2, 1920, Marion, KY; daughter of Allen Farley and Donna Farley; married Ishmon C; children: Lt Col Ishmon F, Donna S, Rev Robert C. **Educ:** KY State Univ, attended 1942; Univ Louisville, 1971. **Career:** Park Duvalle Welfare, soc worker, 1968-71; Metro United Way, suprv, 1971-74; Burks Enterprises Inc, owner, pres & Chief Exec Officer, 1974-; JP Construct Co, chief exec officer, 1980-. **Orgs:** Louisville Urban League, 1975-, Nat Asn Christians & Jews, 1982-, Prof Bus Women's Asn, 1983-, Governor's Scholar Prog, 1983-; bd dir, Spaulding Univ, 1984-. **Honors/Awds:** Women in Business Game, 1980; Woman of Achievement, Pro Bus Women, 1983; Mayor's Citation, City Louisville, 1983; Black Enterprise Mag, 1983; Community Service, Eta Zeta, 1984; Equality Award, Louisville Urban League, 1984; Money Mag, 1984; Kentucky Entrepreneur of the Year, 1996. **Business Addr:** Chief Executive Officer, JP Construct Co, 332 W Broadway Suite 1602, Louisville, KY 40202, **Business Phone:** (502)581-1871.*

BURLESON, DR. HELEN L.
Real estate agent, poet, consultant. **Personal:** Born Dec 8, 1929, Chicago, IL; daughter of Blaine Major and Beatrice Hurley; divorced 1987; children: Earl Fredrick III & Erica Elyce Fredrick. **Educ:** Cent State Univ, BS, 1950; Northwestern Univ, MA, 1954; Nova South Eastern Univ, DPA, 1983. **Career:** High Sch Eng teacher, 1951-56, 1958-61; Bd Educ, Flossmoor, IL, 1972-75, 1975-78, re-elected 1978-81; Nurturing Experiences Enterprises, pres & founder 1987-; Century 21 Dabbs & Assocs, realtor, currently. **Orgs:** Alpha Kappa Alpha, 1948; Nat Asn Advan Colored People, 1950-; vpres & bd mem, SD 161, Flossmoor, IL 1972-81; proposal reader, Ill Humanities Coun, 1976-83; Ill St Bd Educ, 1981-83; Gov Task Force Study Med Malpractice, 1982; founder, Enhancement Orgn Olympia Fields, 1994. **Honors/Awds:** Alumni of the Year, Cent State Univ, 1973; Centurion Awards, Century 21 Int, 1991-95; Masters Hall of Fame, Century 21 Int, 1995; Centurion Hall of Fame, Century 21 Int, 1997; Humanitarian Awards, Dr Charles Gavin Found, St Matthews AME Church. **Home Addr:** 56 Graymoor Lane, Olympia Fields, IL 60461, **Home Phone:** (708)747-0919. **Business Addr:** Realtor, Century 21 Dabbs & Associates Inc, 905 W 175th St, Homewood, IL 60461, **Business Phone:** (708)957-7070.

BURLESON, JANE GENEVA
Government official. **Personal:** Born May 22, 1928, Fort Dodge, IA; daughter of William Kelly Jones and Octavia Bivens Jones Dukes; married Walter Burleson, Oct 22, 1954. **Career:** George A Hormel & Co, 1948-81; Ft Dodge Sch Syst, para prof, 1982-; Ft Dodge City Coun, councilwoman, 1984-, dean coun, currently. **Orgs:** Rec sec P-31 United Food & Comm Workers, 1974-75; League of Women Voters, Mayors Adv Comm, 1980; pres A Philip Randolph Inst Ft Dodge Chap; Superintendents Adv Comm, 1984; bd mem, Jazz Festival, 1984-85; Nat Camp Fire, 1985-86; IA Tomorrow Comm, 1985-;City Finance Comt, Govr Brandstad, 1986-94; nominating bd mem, Girl Scouts, 1990; bd mem, ICCC Illiteracy, 1989-; bd mem, County Magistrate, 1990-. **Honors/Awds:** Comm Status Women Cert State IA, 1979; Cert Apprec IA Devel Comm, 1983, 1984; First Black Woman Elected Ft Dodge City Coun. **Business Addr:** Dean, Councilwoman, Fort Dodge City Council, City Hall, 819 1st Ave S, Fort Dodge, IA 50501-4739.*

BURLEW, ANN KATHLEEN
Psychologist, educator. **Personal:** Born Dec 10, 1948, Cincinnati, OH; married John Howard. **Educ:** Univ Mich, BA, 1970, MA, 1972, PhD, social psychol, 1974. **Career:** Social Tech Syst, sr partner, 1974-80; Univ Cincinnati, Dept Criminal Justice, Dept Psychol, asst prof, 1972-78, Dept Psychol, prof, 1978-. **Orgs:** Chair, Evaluation Com & YWCA Shelter Battered Women, 1977-79; Cot Develop Adv Com, 1980; vip, Cincinnati Asn, Black Psychol, 1979-80; CETA Adv Com United Appeal, 1979-80; bd mem, United Appeal/Cot Chest Planning Bd, 1980; vip, United Black Asn Fac & Staff, 1980. **Honors/Awds:** Summer fac res grant, Univ Cincinnati, 1977, 1980. **Special Achievements:** Co-author, Minority Issues in Mental Health; co-author, Reflections on Black Psychol; Published numerous articles. **Business Addr:** Professor, University Cincinnati, Department Psychol, 2600 Clifton Ave, Cincinnati, OH 45221-0002.*

BURLEY, DALE S.
Engineer, journalist. **Personal:** Born Aug 6, 1961, New York, NY; son of Lloyd C. and Anne L. Thompson. **Educ:** Morgan State Univ, Baltimore, MD, BS, 1984. **Career:** WEAA-FM, Baltimore, MD, newswriter/reporter, 1982-84; WLIB-AM, New York, NY, newswriter/asst ed, 1983, 1984; WINS-AM, New York, NY, prod engr, 1984-86; WNYE-FM, Brooklyn, NY, prod engr, asst producer, 1986-; The Daily Challenge, Brooklyn, NY, reporter, 1993-. **Orgs:** Nat Asn Advan Colored People, 1980-; Omega Psi Phi Fraternity, 1985-; Abyssinian Baptist Church, 1988-; Nat Asn Black Journalists, 1988-. **Home Addr:** 100 LaSalle St, New York, NY 10027. *

BURLEY, JACK L
President (Organization), executive, chairperson. **Personal:** Born Apr 26, 1942, Pittsburgh, PA; son of Andrew C and Lynda Burley; married Joanne E, May 29, 1965; children: Diana Burley Gant & Jack L Jr. **Educ:** Penn State Univ, BS, 1965; Univ Pittsburgh, MBA, 1974. **Career:** Fed Power Comn, acct, 1965-66; Gen Foods, financial analyst, 1968-70; HJ Heinz, mgr financial planning, 1970-80; Heinz USA, controller, 1983-85, vpres finance & admin, 1985-89, vpres logistics & admin, 1989-91, vpres opers & logistics, 1991-93; Heinz Serv Co, pres, 1993; Manchester Bidwell Corp, bd vice chmn, currently. **Orgs:** Exec bd dir, Leadership Coun; bd dir, Urban League Pittsburgh; bd dir, Forbes Health Syst; Omega Psi Phi Fraternity; Sigma Pi Phi Fraternity; Bethesda Presbyterian Church. **Military Serv:** AUS, spec-4, 1966-68. **Business Phone:** (412)323-4000.

BURNETT, A. J. (ALLAN JAMES BURNETT)
Baseball player. **Personal:** Born Jan 3, 1977, North Little Rock, AR; married; children: 2. **Career:** Florida Marlins, pitcher, 1999-2005; Toronto Blue Jays, pitcher, 2006-08; New York Yankees, 2009-.

BURNETT, ARTHUR LOUIS
Judge. **Personal:** Born Mar 15, 1935, Spotsylvania County, VA; son of Robert Louis and Lena Bumbry; married Frisbieann Lloyd, May 14, 1960; children: Darnellena Christalyn, Arthur Louis II, Darryl Lawford & Darlisa Ann & Dionne. **Educ:** Howard Univ, BA (summa cum laude), 1957; NY Univ Sch Law, LLB, 1958. **Career:** Dept Justice, Adv Criminal Div, atty, 1958-65; asst US atty DC, 1965-68; Metrop Police Dept, legal advisor, 1968-69; US Magistrate, judge, 1969-75 & 1980-87; US Civil Serv Comn,

Legal Div, asst gen coun, 1975-78; Off Personnel Mgt, assoc gen counsel, 1979-80; Super Ct Dist Columbia, judge, 1987-98, sr judge, 1998; Catholic Univ Columbus Sch Law, adj prof, 1997; Howard Univ, adj prof, 1998-; Nat African Am Drug Policy Coalition, nat exec dir, currently. **Orgs:** Chmn, Conf Special Ct Judges, Am Bar Asn, 1974-75, chmn, Criminal Law & Juvenile Justice Comm, Admin Law & Regulatory Practice Sect, 1983-85, vice chair, Criminal Rules & Evidence Comt, Criminal Justice Sect, 1985-92, asst secy, Admin Law & Regulatory Pract Sect, 1990-93, chair, 1992-97, secy, 1993-95, Criminal Justice Mag Ed Bd, Criminal Justice Sect, chair, 1996-99, Steering Comt Unmet Needs C, 2003-04; chmn, Nat Com Utilization US Magistrates Fed Cts, Fed Bar Asn, 1980-, chmn, Fed Litigation Sect Admin Justice, 1983-85, pres, DC Chap, 1984-85; pres, Nat Coun US Magistrates, 1983-84; Coun Admin Law & Regulatory Pract Sect, Am Bar Asn, 1987-90; Juvenile Justice Comt, 1987-; admin conf US, 1990-94; chair, Audit Comt, Nat Fed Bar Asn, 1999-; counsel & spec asst to the pres, Nat Bar Asn, 2003-04; DC Bar Asn; Wash Bar Asn; Am Judges Asn; Am Judicature Soc; chmn, Nat Criminal Law Com. **Honors/Awds:** Attroney General's Sustained Superior Performance Award, 1963; Distinguished Service Award, US Civil Serv Comn, 1978; Office of Personnel Management Director Meritorious Service Award 1980; Flaschner Award Outstanding Special Court Judge in the United States, Nat Conf Spec Ct Judges, Am Bar Asn, 1985, Outstanding State Court Judge in the United States, Nat Conf State Ct Judges, 1999, Judicial Division & Litigation Award, 2002, Spirit of Excellence Award; President's Award, Fed Bar Asn, 1994, Earl Kinter Award, 2002, Distinguished Service Award,; President's Award, Nat Bar Asn, 1996; Ollie Mae Cooper Award, Wash Bar Asn, 1997; H Carl Moultrie Award for Judicial Excellence, Trial Lawyers Asn Metrop Wash, DC, 1999; ed-in-chief/auth FBA-BNA publ "Labor-Mgmt Relations Civil Serv Reform & EEO in the Fed Serv", 1980; author of numerous articles in law journals & reviews on role of US Magistrates in Fed Judiciary, on Federal Civil Practice, bail and search & seizure. **Special Achievements:** First African-American magistrate judge, 1969; first African-American chair of ABA Judges Conference, 1974-75. **Military Serv:** AUS, spec-4, 1958-60; AUS Reserves, 1960-63, first lt, Commendation Medal, 1960; E1-E4-drafted, 1958-60, second lt to first lt, 1960-63. **Business Addr:** Adjunt Professor, Howard University, School of Law, 2900 Van Ness St NW, Washington, DC 20008, **Business Phone:** (202)806-8000.

BURNETT, BESCYE P.
Librarian, educator. **Personal:** Born Apr 29, 1950, Roseboro, NC; daughter of Casey and Selena Boone; married Charles Burnett, Feb 24, 1983; children: Denise, Shawn. **Educ:** Winston-Salem State Univ, NC, 1972; Univ N Carolina, Greensboro, NC, MLS, 1977; Miami Univ, Oxford, OH, cert mgt, 1990. **Career:** Startown Elem Sch, Newton, NC, teacher, 1972-73; Winston-Salem & Forsyth Sch, Winston-Salem, NC, teacher & librn, 1973-79; State NC, Raleigh, NC, media consult, 1979-80; Univ Ill-Champ, Urbana, IL, vis prof, 1980-81; Fashion Inst, Los Angeles, CA, librn, 1981-82; County Los Angeles Pub Libr, Downey, CA, literacy librn, 1982-87; Johnson County Libr, Shawnee, KS, vol coordr adult servs, 1988-89; Cleveland Heights-Univ Heights, dep dir, beginning, 1989; Great River Regional Libr, dir, currently. **Orgs:** NAACP, 1980-; ALA, 1987-; PLA, 1987-; bd mem, Proj Learn, 1989-96. **Honors/Awds:** Veterans Four Yr Scholar, US Veterans Admin, 1968-72; RJ Reynolds Scholar, RJ Reynolds & Winston-Salem, Forsyth County, 1976; CH-UH Friends Scholar, Friends Lib, 1990. **Business Addr:** Director, Great River Regional Library, 405 W St Germain, St Cloud, MN 56301-3697, **Business Phone:** (320)251-7282.*

BURNETT, DR. CALVIN W.
School administrator. **Personal:** Born Mar 16, 1932, Brinkley, AR; son of Elmer Clay and Vera Rayford Payne; married Martha Alma Ware, Jul 21, 1956 (divorced 1976); children: Vera, Susan & David; married Gretta L Gordy, Sep 17, 1983; children: Tywana. **Educ:** St Louis Univ, BA, biol & polit sci, 1959, PhD, sociol psychol, 1963. **Career:** St Louis State Hosp, res social psychologist, 1961-63; Health & Welfare Coun Metro St Louis, res dir spec proj, 1963-66; Cath Univ Am, assoc prof, 1966-69; Upward Bound Prog, US Off Educ, consult, 1966-70; Nat Planning Orgn Wash, consult, 1967-68; Urban Syst Corp Wash, consult, 1967-69; Southern Ill Univ, assoc prof, 1969-70; Coppin State Col MD, pres, 1970;Md Higher Educ Comn, acting Secy higher educ, 2004, secy higher educ, 2004-. **Orgs:** Am Asn State Col & Univ, 1970-74; Correctional Training Comn, 1977-2003; chmn bd, YMCA Greater Baltimore, 1984-86; bd dirs, Nat Asn Equal Opportunity Higher Educ, 1985-; Empowerment Baltimore Mgt Corp, 1996-97; chair, State Planning Committee Higher Educ, 2004-; Maryland Educ Coun, 2005-; Statewide Comn Shortage Health Care Workforce, 2006-. **Honors/Awds:** Merit Award, St Louis Univ Alumni, 1973; Silver Beaver Award, Boy Scouts Am, 1983; Community Service Award, Alpha Phi Alpha, 1987; Distinguished Alumni Award, St. Louis Univ; Lifetime Achievement Award, Fullwood Found, 2001. **Special Achievements:** Recognized in Who's Who in Black America, Who's Who in American History, Outstanding Educator of America, and in Who's Who in America. **Military Serv:** AUS, 1953-55. **Business Addr:** Secretary of Higher Education, Maryland Higher Education Commission, 839 Bestgate Rd Suite 400, Annapolis, MD 21401, **Business Phone:** (410)260-4516.

BURNETT, CALVIN WALLER
Educator, college teacher, painter (artist). **Personal:** Born Jul 18, 1921, Cambridge, MA; son of Adelaide Waller and Nathan Lowe; married Torrey Milligan, Aug 20, 1960; children: Tobey Burnett Sparks. **Educ:** Mass Col Art, attended 1942, BS, 1951; Boston Univ, MFA, 1960, attended 1971. **Career:** freelance designer, illusr, 1943-83; Elma Lewis Sch, instr, 1951-53; Decordova Mus, instr, 1952-56; Mass Col Art, prof, 1956-87, prof emer, 1987; painter, currently. **Orgs:** co-founder & bd dirs, Boston African-Am Artists, 1961-; Northeastern Univ, African-Am Master, Artists in Residency Prog, 1977-; juror, Mus Nat Ctr African-Am Art, 1981-91. **Honors/Awds:** Printmaking Award, NY Asn Am Artists, 1959; Awards, Atlanta Univ, 1959-68; New Eng Print Award, 1960; Ger Book Award, Liepzig, 1965; Distinguished Serv Award, Mass Col Art, 1979; Drawing Award Finalist, Mass Artists Found, 1988; Hon BFA, Mass Sch Art, 1993. **Special Achievements:** Author, designer, illustrator, Objective Drawing Techniques, Reinhold Publisher NY, NY, 1966; Maidenhood, Print Portfolio, Woodcuts, Impressions Graphic Workshop, 1962; Portents & Omens, Serigraphs, Impressions Graphic Workshop, 1966. **Home Phone:** (508)533-2153. *

BURNETT, DAVID LAWRENCE
Journalist, television news anchorperson, consultant. **Personal:** Born Apr 6, 1956, Indianapolis, IN; son of Boyd Jr and Mary Ogburn; married Lauren Jefferson, Mar 6, 1987; children: David Jr & Janet Elaine. **Educ:** Ball State Univ, Muncie, IN, BS, commun, 1978. **Career:** WTLC-FM, Indianapolis, Ind, reporter & anchor, 1979; WTVW-TV, Evansville, Ind, reporter & anchor, 1979-81; WFIE-TV, Evansville, Ind, reporter, 1981-82; WHIO-TV, Dayton, Ohio, reporter & anchor, 1982-86; Hill & Knowlton Pub Rels, Wash, managing dir; WTTG-TV, Wash, DC, reporter-training prog, developer & coordr, reporter & anchor, 1986-99; The Pincus Group Inc, vpres & sr trainer, currently. **Orgs:** Alpha Phi Alpha Fraternity, 1975-; vpres, Dayton Asn Black Journalists, 1984-85; pres, Wash Asn Black Journalists, 1989-90; Alzheimer's Asn; Am Heart Asn; Concerned BlackMen; United Negro Col Fund; Ball State Univ Human Rels Comt; pres, Wash DC Chap Nat Asn Black Journalists. **Honors/Awds:** Numerous honors & awards including Spot Sports Radio, first place, "US Clay Courts Tourney", Assoc Press, 1980; prestigious Emmy award; Spot News Reporting, first place, "Washington Strike", Assoc Press, 1981; Best Series, first pl, "Evansville Housing Authority", Sigma Delta Chi, 1982; Best Spot News, first pl, "WIKY Fire", Sigma Delta Chi, 1982; Best General News Story, "County Council Fight", Sigma Delta Chi, 1982; Journalism Award, series first pl, "Collision Course", Nat Asn Black Journalists, 1987; Journalism Award, sports first pl, "Doug Williams Reflections" Nat Asn Black Journalists, 1988. **Business Addr:** Vice President, Senior Trainer, The Pincus Group Inc, 309 Reserve Gate Terr, Silverspring, MD 20016, **Business Phone:** (301)938-6990.

BURNETT, DR. MYRA N
College administrator, clinical psychologist, college teacher. **Educ:** Harvard Univ, BA; Stanford Univ, MA; Duke Univ, PhD. **Career:** Spelman Col, vice provost & assoc prof, 1985-; Peachtree Psychol Serv, psychologist, currently. **Orgs:** Fac Resource Network; Am Psychol Asn. **Business Addr:** Associate Professor, Vice Provost, Spelman College, Office of the Provost, 350 Spelman Lane SW Rockefeller Hall Rm 112, PO Box 249, Atlanta, GA 30314-4399, **Business Phone:** (404)270-5027.

BURNETT, ROB. See BURNETT, ROBERT BARRY.

BURNETT, ROBERT BARRY (ROB BURNETT)
Football player. **Personal:** Born Aug 27, 1967, East Orange, NJ. **Educ:** Syracuse Univ, econ, 1990. **Career:** Cleveland Browns, defensive end, 1990-95; Baltimore Ravens, 1996-2001; Miami Dolphins, 2002-03. **Orgs:** Toys for Tots; United Way; Police Athletic League; Make A Wish Found; founder, Facing Our C's Urban Situation. **Honors/Awds:** Pro Bowler, 1994; One Time Super Bowl Champion, XXXV.

BURNETT, ZARON WALTER, JR.
Writer, artist. **Personal:** Born Dec 16, 1950, Danville, VA; son of Zaron W Burnett Sr and Johnsie Broadway; married Pearl Cleage, Mar 23, 1994; children: Zaron W Burnett III, Deignan Cleage-Lomax, Meghan V Burnett. **Educ:** Hampton Inst, 1969; Pa State Univ, 1974; Ga State Univ, Atlanta, GA, BS, 1977. **Career:** Harrisburg Free Clin, dir pub outreach, 1972-74; CDC-VD Contrib Prog, health prog rep, 1978; N Cent Ga Health Systs Agency, proj review analyst, 1979-80; Atlanta Southside Community Health Ctr, dir res, 1980; Fulton County Gov, exec aide chair & bd commissioners, 1980-83; Just Us Theater Co, exec producer, 1989-, co-owner & dir, currently; Books: We Speak Your Names, 2006; The Carthaginian Honor Society. **Orgs:** Mayor's fel arts, Atlanta Mayor's Off, 1990. **Honors/Awds:** JAGE Grant, Rockefeller Found, 1988. **Special Achievements:** Performances at the National Black Arts Festival, National Black Theater Festivals, and the National Performance Festival. **Business Addr:** Director, Founder, Just Us Theater Company, 1665 Havilon Dr SW, Atlanta, GA 30311-0271, **Business Phone:** (404)753-2399.*

BURNETTE, DR. ADA PURYEAR
Educator. **Personal:** Born in Darlington, SC; married Paul Puryear Sr (divorced 1975); children: Paul Puryear Jr & Paula Puryear; married Thomas (divorced 2003). **Educ:** Talladega Col, BA, 1953; Univ Chicago, MA, 1958; Fla State Univ, PhD,1986; Tex Southern Univ; Chicago State Univ; Fla A&M Univ; Fla State Univ, cert pub supvr, 1989. **Career:** Winston Salem NC Pub Schs, high sch math teacher, 1953-54; Chicago Pub Schs, elem sch teacher, 1954-58; Norfolk State, adminr & teacher, 1958-61; Univ Chicago Reading Clinic, teacher, 1958; Tuskegee Inst, adminr &teacher, 1961-66; Fisk Univ, adminr & teacher, 1966-70; Fla DOE, adminr, 1973-88; Bethune-Cookman Col, adminr & teacher, 1988-90; Fla A&M Univ, Develop Res Sch Dist, supt & dir, 1990-93, dept chair, prof, & PhD dir, 1993-98, Robert H. Anderson Educ Leadership Libr, dir, fac senate pres, prof emer, 2003-, adj fac, 2007-; Col Ed Off-Campus coordr, 2005-07; Valdosta State Univ, assoc prof, 2005-07. **Orgs:** Secy & treas, Afro-Am Res Asn, 1968-73; bd dir, Christian Sch Performing Arts; deacon, Trinity Presbyterian Church; parliamentarian undergrad adv, treas & secy, Alpha Kappa Alpha; pres, historian, reporter & vpres, Drifters Tallahassee; pres, publicity chmn & initiation chmn, Phi KappaPhi, Fla State Univ; Phi Delta Kappa, Pi Lambda Theta; nat mem chmn, Drifters Inc; Fla Elem & Middle Schs; comnr, Southern Asn Col & Schs, 1978-88; Leon Dem Exec Bd, 1982-88; pres teen sponsor, Jack & Jill AmTallahassee, 1984-85; pres, Int Read Asn Affiliate Concerned Educ Black Students, 1984-86; Fla Coun Elem Educ; DOE liaison; secy & co-organizer, Societas Docta Inc, 1987-; Fla Asn Supv & Curriculum Develop Bd, 1988-;pres, Les Beau Monde, 1989-90; Fla Asn Sch-Adm; Am Asn Sch-Adm; Fla Elem &Middle Sch Principals; Nat Asn Elem Sch Principals; Nat Asn Sec Sch Prin; Links; pres, Ladies Art & Social Club; Nat Asn Female Execs; Friends theBlack Archives; SE Asn Prof Ed Lead; pres & nat financial secy, TheHolidays Tallahassee, 1993-97; Asn Supv & Curriculum Develop; Fla CounEduc Mgt, 1994-99; nat vpres, The Holidays Tallahassee, 1997-2001; pres, The Holidays Tallahassee, 2001-; bd mem, FSCPM; Societas Docta, Inc;secy, Links InterNat Trends. **Honors/Awds:** Nat Now Black Woman of the Year, Drifters Inc, 1984; Head Start Honoree of the Year for Florida, 1985; Humanitarian of the Year, 1987; NAACP Black Achiever, 1991; Key to Cocoa, FL, 1989; Martin Luther King Jr State Award; Distinguished Service Award, Fla A&M Univ; Meritorious Achievement Award, Fla A&M Univ; FAMU Gallery of Distinction. **Special Achievements:** First Black Admin in Fla Dept of Educ since Reconstruction period, 1973; co-author, member of early childhood panel, Four and Five Year Old Programs in Public Schools; delivered hundreds of speeches; wrote many articles and books. **Home Addr:** PO Box 38543, Tallahassee, FL 32315-8543, **Home Phone:** (850)575-8585. **Business Addr:** Professor, Department Chair, Florida A & M University, Tallahassee, FL 32307, **Business Phone:** (850)599-3000.

BURNEY, WILLIAM D
Government official. **Personal:** Born Apr 23, 1951, Augusta, ME; son of William D Sr and Helen Nicholas; married Lynne Godfrey Burney, Jun 16, 1990. **Educ:** Boston Univ, Boston, MA, BS, pub commun, 1973; Univ Maine Sch Law, Portland, ME, JD, 1977. **Career:** Maine State Housing Authority, Augusta, ME, asst develop dir, 1981; Augusta City Coun, mem, 1982-88; City Augusta, ME, mayor; Dept Housing & Urban Develop, field off dir, currently; Augusta Bd Educ, ME, chair, currently. **Orgs:** Transp & Commun Steering Comt, Nat League Cities, 1990; bd dirs, Holocaust Human Rights Ctr Maine; bd dirs, Am Baptist Churches Maine; nominating comt, Kennebec Girl Scout Coun Maine; bd dirs, Yankee Healthcare, Augusta, ME. **Special Achievements:** First African American mayor in Augusta, Maine. **Business Addr:** Field Office Director, US Department of Housing & Urban Development, 202 Harlow St Suite 101, Margaret Chase Smith Fed Bldg, Bangor, ME 04401-4919, **Business Phone:** (207)945-0468.

BURNHAM, MARGARET ANN
Judge, lawyer. **Personal:** Born Dec 28, 1944, Birmingham, AL. **Educ:** Tougaloo Col, BA, 1966; Univ Pa, Law Sch, LLB, 1969. **Career:** Mass Inst Technol, lectr polit sci; Boston Munic Ct, justice, Boston, 1977-82; Burnham & Hines, partner, 1989-; Northeastern Univ, Law Sch, prof law, currently; Harvard's DuBois Inst, fel; Radcliffe's Bunting Inst, fel. **Orgs:** Nat dir, Nat Conf Black Lawyers; fel, WEB DuBois Inst. **Honors/Awds:** Hon Degree, Lesley Col. **Business Addr:** Professor of Law, Northeastern University School of Law, 43 Cargill Hall 400 Huntington Ave, Boston, MA 02115, **Business Phone:** (617)373-8857.

BURNIM, MELLONEE VICTORIA
Educator. **Personal:** Born Sep 27, 1950, Teague, TX; married C Jason Dotson; children: Jamel Arzo. **Educ:** Northern Tex State Univ, BM, music educ, 1971; Univ Wisconsin Madison, MM, African music ethnomusicology, 1976; Ind Univ, PhD, ethnomusicology, 1980. **Career:** Delay Middle Sch, dir, choral music, 1971-73; Univ wisconsin, res asst, 1973; acad adv, 1973; Ind Univ, Bloomington, Afro-Am Choral Ensemble, dir, 1976-82; Opera Theater, choral dir, 1976-80; Dept Afro-Am Studies, assoc prof, Prof Folklore & Ethnomusicology, Adjunct Prof, currently; dir, archives african am music & cult. **Orgs:** Alpha Lambda Delta, 1968; Sigma Alpha Iota, NTSU, 1969; chapter vpres, Mortar Bd, NTSU, 1970-71; Pi Kappa Lambda, 1971; Musical dir, video tapes2-30 minutes, "The Life & Works Undine S Moore,"

Afro-Am Arts Inst, Ind Univ, 1979; musical dir, WTUI Bloomington, "Contemporary Black Gospel Music," 1979. **Honors/Awds:** Full Music Scholar, NTSU, 1969-71; Nat Defense Foreign Language Fellow,Arabic, Univ Wisconsin, 1973-74; fellow, Nat Fel Fund, Univ Wisconsin & Ind Univ, 1973-78; Eli Lilly Postdoctoral Teaching Fellow, 1984;alternate, National Research Council Postdoctoral Fellow, Wash, DC, 1984. **Business Addr:** Associate Professor, Indiana University, Department Afro American Studies, 400 E 7th St Kirkwood Hall 111, Bloomington, IN 47405-3085, **Business Phone:** (812)855-8853.*

BURNIM, DR. MICKEY L.
Educator. **Personal:** Born Jan 19, 1949, Teague, TX; son of A S and Ruby; married LaVera Levels; children: Cinnamon & Adrian. **Educ:** Univ N Tex, BA, econs, 1970, MA, econs, 1972; Univ Wis-19 Madison, PhD, econs, 1977; Brookings Inst, Wash, DC, post-19 grad work, 1981. **Career:** Fla State Univ, asst prof econs, 1976-82; Univ NC, Chapel Hill, asst vpres acad affairs, 1982-86; Univ Ga, asst vpres acad affairs, 1982-86; Univ NC-Chapel Hill, adj asst prof econs, 1983-85, adj assoc prof econs, 1985-86; NC Cent Univ, vice chancellor acad affairs, 1986-95, provost & vice chancellor, 1990-95; Elizabeth City State Univ, interim chancellor, 1995-96, chancellor, 1996-, chief exec officer, currently; Bowie State Univ, pres, 2006-. **Orgs:** Chmn, Educ Comn, Nat Asn Advan Colored People, 1979-80; mem & bd dirs, Tallahassee Urban League, 1979-80; Brookings Econ Policy fel, Brookings Inst, 1980-81; consult, Trans century Corp, 1986; Am Econs Asn; Nat Econs Asn; Durham Chamber Com; bd dirs, Bd Trustees, CAEL; Wachovia Adv Bd; Salvation Army; Elizabeth City Chamber Com; Southern Asn Col & Sch; Elizabeth City Rotary Club; Minority Adv Coun Wachovia Bank; N eastern NC School masters Club. **Special Achievements:** Publ:1.) "The Impact of the Brown Decision on Public HBCUs: A North Carolina Case Study" in Brown v. Board of Education: Its Impact on Public Education, 1954-2004; 2) "The Changing Status of Economic Minorities: 1948-77" (with David Rasmussen) in The Review of Black Political Economy; 3) "Benefits and Costs of a Public Service Employment Program: A Case Study in Florida" (with J.H. Cobbs) in Growth and Change; 4) "The Earnings Effect of Black Matriculation in Predominantly White Colleges" in Industrial and Labor Relations Review; 5) "Investments in College Education for Black Males" in Proceedings of the American Statistical Association; 6) A Survey of Minority Business in Florida; 7) An Evaluation of the Public Service Employment Projects in Florida Created Under Title VI of the Comprehensive Employment and Training Act of 1973; and 8) three invited presentations-"Equality in Education and Employment?" (Oliver Cromwell Cox Lecture Series of the Kennedy School of Government at Harvard University); "Black Employment, Unemployment, and Labor Force Participation During the 1980's" (Washington-Based Black Economists Organization); and "The Black Labor Force in the 1980's (Williams College, Williamstown, MA). **Home Addr:** 1304 Parkview Dr, Elizabeth City, NC 27909, **Home Phone:** (252)338-3075. **Business Addr:** Chancellor, Chief Executive Officer, Elizabeth City State University, 1704 Weeksville Rd, Elizabeth City, NC 27909, **Business Phone:** (252)335-3228.*

BURNLEY, KENNETH
School administrator. **Personal:** Married Eileen; children: Traci, Trevor, Tyler & Jonathan. **Educ:** Univ Mich, BS, MA, PhD. **Career:** Sch administrator (retired); Waverly Bd Educ, asst supt instr; Eastern Mich Univ, instr; Ypsilanti Bd Educ, dir, prin, asst prin, coordr, teacher; Univ Mich, asst track coach; Fairbanks N Star Borough Sch Dist, supt/chief exec officer; Colo Springs Sch Dist Eleven, supt sch, 1987; Detroit Pub Sch, chief exec officer. **Honors/Awds:** Nat Superintendent of the Year, Am Asn Sch Adminrs & Servicemaster Co, 1993; Distinguished Educator Award, Detroit Pub Sch. **Special Achievements:** First African American Superintendent of the Fairbanks, Alaska School System.

BURNLEY, LARRY. **See BURNLEY, REV. LAWRENCE A Q.**

BURNLEY, REV. LAWRENCE A Q (LARRY BURNLEY)
Clergy, administrator, educator. **Personal:** Married Naima Quarles; children: Rashad (deceased) & Thulani. **Educ:** Univ Cincinnati, BA, african am studies, 1979; Christian Theol Sem, MDiv, 1990; Univ Pa, PhD. **Career:** Ordained minister; Global Ministries Christian Church, Off Racial Ethnic Rels, exec; United Church Christ, exec; Messiah Col, assoc dean multicultural progs & special asst provost, currently. **Orgs:** Nat Campus Ministry Asn, 1990-96; Asn Christian Church Educr, 1990-; Asn United Christian Educr, 1997-; Nat Benevolent Asn. **Honors/Awds:** Community Involvement Award, Christian Theol Sem, 1990; Outstanding Community Service Award, African Am Asn, Univ PA, 1993. **Special Achievements:** Author: Pearls of Wisdom: Reflections of a Black Disciples Minister, 1996, The Education of African Americans in the U.S., 1865-1914: The Case of the Christian Church, 2008. **Home Addr:** 3499 Edison Rd, Cleveland, OH 44121-1525. **Business Addr:** Associate Dean of Multicultural Programs, Special Assistant to the Provost for Diversity Affairs, Messiah College, Office of Multicultural Programs, 1 College Ave, PO Box 3050, Grantham, PA 17027, **Business Phone:** (717)766-2511.

BURNS, BENJAMIN O.
Lawyer. **Career:** Atty, currently. **Business Addr:** 224 Saint Landry St Suite 3h, PO Box 3016, Lafayette, LA 70506, **Business Phone:** (337)232-7239.*

BURNS, CALVIN LOUIS
Clergy, journalist. **Personal:** Born Mar 16, 1952, Memphis, TN; son of Andrew and Freddie McClinton; married Regina Whiting, Nov 18, 1989. **Educ:** Memphis State Univ, Memphis, TN, BA, 1974, grad sch, 1983; Charles Harrison Mason Bible Col, assocs, 1979. **Career:** Memphis Press Scimitar, journalist, 1974-83; Interstate Transp, mgr comm, 1985-88; Church God Christ, Memphis, TN, assoc news dir; Tri-State Defender, Memphis, TN, managing ed, 1988-. **Orgs:** Exec dir, Bethesda Outreach, 1984-; commun dir, Memphis region, Nat Asn Black Journalists, 1990-; bd mem, Memphis State Univ Journalist Alumni, 1991. **Honors/Awds:** Outstanding citizen Award, Congressman Harold Ford, 1983; Citizen Achievement Award, Shelby County Sheriff's Dept, 1989; Ten Outstanding Achievement Award, Gov Tenn, 1990; Professional Achievement Award, Gospel Acad, Memphis, 1991. **Business Addr:** Managing Editor News/Editorial, Tri-State Defender Newspaper, 124 E Calhoun Ave, Memphis, TN 38101, **Business Phone:** (901)523-1818.

BURNS, DARGAN J.
Executive, consultant. **Personal:** Born Feb 26, 1925, Sumter, SC; son of Dargan J Sr and Julia; married Joyce Price; children: Dargan III & Cedric Charles. **Educ:** Hampton Inst, attended 1949; Boston Univ, MS, 1952. **Career:** Ala State Col, teacher & pub relations; Advert, Couyahoga Comm Col; Karamu House, Cleveland, OH, dir pub rel; Burns Pub Rels Serv, pres, 1960-90. **Orgs:** Pub Rels Soc Am; Lutheran Housing Corp; Cleveland Bus League; pres, Urban Counr; bd mem BSA; Omega Psi Phi; Co founder, Martin Luther King Jr Cleveland Chap SCLC. **Military Serv:** AUS 1942-46.

BURNS, DIANN
Journalist. **Educ:** Cleveland State Univ, polit & mass Commun; Columbia Univ NY Grad Sch Jour. **Career:** Cleveland Plain Dealer, gen assignment reporter; Cleveland Call & Post, ed, photogr & reporter; Independent Network News, field producer & reporter; WLS-TV, co-anchor, 1985-03; CBS2Chicago, co-anchor, 2003-. **Orgs:** Spokesperson, Pediatric AIDS Chicago; Ronald McDonald House; Northern Ill Chap Mult Sclerosis Soc, & Support Group; Nat Asn Black Journalists; Nat Asn TV Arts & Sci; active in several civic & charitable orgns. **Honors/Awds:** local Emmy Awards; Outstanding Individual Excellence. **Special Achievements:** The first African-American woman to serve as lead anchor of a 10:00 PM news broadcast in Chicago, and remains the only woman of color serving in that role today. **Business Addr:** Co Anchor, CBS 2 Chicago, 630 N McClurg Ct, Chicago, IL 60607, **Business Phone:** (312)202-2222.*

BURNS, FELTON
Educator, college teacher. **Personal:** Born Mar 12, 1936, Tillar, AR; married Verlene Dean; children: Gregory L & Pamele E. **Educ:** Fresno St, BA, 1962; Calif State Univ, Fresno, MA, 1972; Univ Southern Calif, EdD, 1977. **Career:** Calif, Fresno, social worker, 1962-65; Econ Opportunities Comn, asst dir,1965-68; Calif State Univ, Fresno, asst dean stud, 1968-71, staff coun, 1971, prof emer, 2000-; Foster Parent Training Proj, dir, 1994-99. **Orgs:** Pres, Spectrum Asn, 1977-85; dir, Advan Res Tech, 1978-83; Am Asn Coun & Develop, 1985; Calif Black Fac & Staff Asn. **Honors/Awds:** Troy Award, Educ Fresno Comt Serv, 1975; Albright Endowed Chair Excellence, Calif State Univ, Fresno, Stud Affairs Div, 1984-85; Rosa Parks Award, 1998; Fresno Foster Parents, 1999; Fresno State EOP Leadership Award, 1999. **Home Addr:** 6378 N Eigth, Fresno, CA 93710. **Business Addr:** Professor Emeritus, California State University, Univ Rels Off, 5241 N Maple Ave, Fresno, CA 93740.*

BURNS, JEFF
Executive. **Personal:** Born in Varnville, SC; son of Jeff Sr and Genevieve. **Educ:** Howard Univ, BBA 1972; Livingstone Col, DHL. **Career:** Howard Univ, MPA Mag publ Procedures Seminar, lectr; Johnson Publ Co, dir, vpres, 1984-93, sr vpres, 1993-, Ebony mag, assoc publ & sr vpres, 2001-. **Orgs:** PUSH Int; bd dirs Trade Bur; Caribbean Tourism Orgn; Howard Univ Alumni Asn NY; bd dirs, NY Urban League, African Am Mkt Asn; bd adv, Arthur Ashe Athletic Asn; Madison Ave Initiative; vice chmn, John H Johnson Sch Commun, Howard Univ; bd visitors, Howard Univ Sch Commun; bd visitors, Johnson C Smith Univ; Five Towns Community Ctr; Greater Harlem Chamber Com. **Honors/Awds:** Business Person of the Year, Nat Asn Negro Bus & Prof Women's Clubs 1989; Sylvia Lord Pioneer Excellence Award, Five Towns Community Ctr 1991; Award Recognition, Howard Univ Alumni Club New York, 1992; Award Recognition, Nat Coun Negro Women, Nassau County Section, 1993; NAFEO Award, 1994; Trey Whitfield Found Award, 2002; Alumni of the Year, Howard Univ Sch Communs 2002; judge CEBA Awards. **Special Achievements:** Created/founded EBONY presents "Hollywood In Harlem" film festival. **Business Addr:** Associate Publisher, Senior Vice President, Ebony Magazine, Johnson Publ Co, 1270 Ave Am, New York, NY 10020, **Business Phone:** (212)397-4500.

BURNS, JESSE L
School administrator, college president. **Educ:** Univ S Fla, DBA. **Career:** Edward Waters Col, interim pres, pres.

BURNS, KEITH BERNARD
Football player. **Personal:** Born May 16, 1972, Greeleyville, SC; married Michelle; children: Danielle & Rachel. **Educ:** Navarro Jr Col, AA; Okla State Univ, OK. **Career:** Football player (retired), football player coach; Denver Broncos, linebacker, 1994-98, 2000-03, 2005-07, asst coach, 2007-; Chicago Bears, 1999; Tampa Bay Buccaneers, linebacker, 2004. **Honors/Awds:** Super Bow Champion Twice XXXII, XXXIII. **Business Addr:** Professional Football Player, Denver Broncos, Dove Valley, 13655 Broncos Pkwy, Englewood, CO 80112, **Business Phone:** (303)649-9000.*

BURNS, KHEPHRA
Writer, editor. **Personal:** Born Oct 2, 1950, Los Angeles, CA; son of Isham A Rusty and Treneta C Burns; married Susan L Taylor, Aug 19, 1989; children: Shana-Nequai Taylor. **Educ:** MoorPark Community Col, AA, lib arts, 1970; Univ Calif, BA, Eng, 1972. **Career:** Golden State Mutual Life Ins, salesman, 1974-76; Various Bands, musician, 1976-78; WNET-13, writer, assoc producer, 1978-80; RTP Inc, speech writer, publicist, 1980-81; Self-Employed, freelance writer, ed, 1981-; co-producer & writer: Black Champions (WNET-13), 1986; Black Stars in Orbit (WNET-13), 1989; Images & Realities: African Am (NBC), 1992-94; Black Stars in Orbit, (Harcourt Brace), 1995; The Essence Awards (CBS, Fox), 1993-99; The Power of One (ABC), 1997; Books: Confirmation: The Spiritual Wisdom That Has Shaped Our Lives, 1997; Black Stars in Orbit; Mansa Musa; African Odyssey; Tall Horse. **Orgs:** Writers Guild Am, E Inc, beginning, 1993; The Auth Guild Am, beginning, 1995; One Hundred Black Men, beginning, 1995; Sigma Pi Phi Fraternity, Alpha Sigma Blvd, beginning, 1995. **Honors/Awds:** Award of Excellence, Communications Excellence to Black Audiences; Empire State Award. **Special Achievements:** Burns articles have appeared publ Essence, Swing Journal (Japan), Omni & Art & Auction. *

BURNS, LAMONT
Football player. **Personal:** Born Mar 16, 1974, Greensboro, NC; children: Dyion. **Educ:** E Carolina Univ, BA, communs. **Career:** Football player (retired); New York Jets, guard, 1997; Wash Redskins, guard, 1998; Xtreme Football League, Las Vegas Outlaws, offensive guard, 2000; Oakland Raiders, 2001. **Orgs:** Nat Hon Soc.

BURNS, LEONARD L
Manager, podiatrist. **Personal:** Born Jan 10, 1922, New Orleans, LA; son of George Burton Burns and Leona Galle Burns Gauff; married Phyllis Charbonnet; children: Debra E Barnes, Gary M Burns & Lenette P Plummer. **Educ:** Xavier Prep, Xavier Univ, pre-med, 1947; Temple Univ, Philadelphia, DPM, 1951; Tulane Univ, Leadership MPC, 1966. **Career:** Pvt med pract, New Orleans, LA, beginning, 1951; Four Corners Travel Agency, pres, currently. **Orgs:** Bd dirs, Nat Asn Advan Colored People, 1963-66; bd dirs trustee, Nat Asn Advan Colored People Spec Contrib Fund, 1966-; pres, LA Tourist Develop Comn, 1969; pres, InterAm Travel Agt Soc, 1974-78; bd mem, InterAm Travel Agt Soc, beginning, 1986; vpres, Cath Coun Human Rels. **Honors/Awds:** Man of the Year, Psi Chapter Alpha Phi Alpha Philadelphia, PA, 1950; Honorary Award, civic activities, New Orleans United Clubs, 1962; Small Business Coun Champion, New Orleans Chamber Com, 1985; Award of Merit, LA/New Orleans Host Comm, 1988; Lifetime Achiever Award, Dryades YMCA, 2001. **Special Achievements:** First African American appointed to the Louisiana State Tourism Comn; First African American to serve as president Nokia Suger Bowl; First African-American podiatrist in La & Miss; First African American to start a travel agency in La; founder of the Greater New Orleans Black Tourism Ctr. **Military Serv:** USMC, OCS/S-SGT, 1941-46; Bronz Star/First Black Vol 8 Dist. **Business Addr:** President, Four Corners Travel Agency, 1000 N Broad Ave, New Orleans, LA 70119-1403, **Business Phone:** (504)822-6244.

BURNS, REGINA LYNN
Publicist. **Personal:** Born Feb 19, 1961, Memphis, TN; daughter of Prince Whiting Jr and Rowena Hooks Whiting; married Calvin L Burns, Nov 18, 1989. **Educ:** Abilene Christian Univ, Abilene, TX, BA, 1983; State Tech Inst, Memphis, TN, attended 1989; Memphis State Univ, Memphis, TN, mag writing, 1990. **Career:** KRBC-TV, Abilene, TX, reporter & photogr, 1982-83; WSLI Radio, Jackson, MS, anchor & reporter, 1984; WMKW, Memphis, TN, anchor, 1984; WLOK-AM, Memphis, TN, news dir, 1984-85; WGKX-KIX 106, Memphis, TN, dir, news & pub affairs, 1985-; Tri-State Defender, Memphis, TN, freelance writer, 1986-; Univ Tex, Arlington, lectr, dept commun. Harvest Reapers Commun, owner, 2003-. **Orgs:** Pres, Tenn Assoc Broadcasters Asn, 1990-91; former pres, Memphis Asn Black Journalists, 1990-; Radio-Television News Dirs Asn; Nat Asn Black Journalists. **Honors/**

Awds: Journalist of the Year, Tenn Asn Press Broadcasters Asn, 1989; InterNat Radio Festival of New York Award, 1990; American Women in Radio and Television Award, 1991; Award, Radio-TV News Dir Asn, 1992; Nat Asn of Black Journalists Award; Ten Outstanding Young Americans, United States Jr Chamber Com, 1993. **Special Achievements:** First African American woman and the first Memphis journalist to win the Broadcaster of the Year award from the Tennessee Associated Press Broadcasters Association. **Home Phone:** (901)398-9334. **Business Addr:** Owner, Harvest Reapers Communications, PO Box 823551, Dallas, TX 75382-3551, **Business Phone:** (214)726-0978.

BURNS, RONALD MELVIN
Artist. **Personal:** Born Feb 2, 1942, New York, NY; married Edith Bergmann; children: Elizabeth & Alexi. **Educ:** Sch Visual Arts, New York, 1960. **Career:** Collections: Mus Modern Art, Stockholm, Sweden; Lincoln Ctr; Art Working Pl, Copenhaggen, Denmark; Kaptensgarden-Borstahusen-Landskrona-Sweden; Exhibs, Provinceton Gallery-Paul Kessler-USA, 1962; Gallery Sari Robinson, PA, 1964; Passepartout-Charlotteborg, 1966; Passepartout-Bergen, 1969; Landskrona Konsthall, 1969-70 & 1980; Galleri Heland-Stockholm, 1970; Galerie Migros-Lausanne, 1970; Teatergalleriet-Malmo, 1970; Graphikbienale-Wien, 1972; Corcoran Gallery Art, Wash, DC, 1975; Gallerie Unicorn, 1975; Fundacion Rodriquez-Acosta-Granada, 1977; Galleria II Traghetto-Venice, 1977-80; Galerie Schindler Bern, 1978; Hvidovre Bibliotek, 1980; numerous others in the USA, Denmark, Sweden, & Switzerland; Spelman Col, retrospective exhib, Dept Art, artist, 1994. **Orgs:** Artist's Exhib Group AZ-Venice Italy, Spain, Germany; Artist's Exhib Group-Gallery 2016 Switzerland; Artist's Exhib Group, Gronningen-Denmark-Gallery, Terry Dintenfass, NY; Peg Alston Fine Arts, NY, 2003; Galerie Eichenwand, Dusseldorf, Germany, 2003; Tempra Mus Contemp Arts, Mgarr, Malta; Wignacourt Mus, Rabat, Malta; Aghia Trias Permanent Collection, Greece. **Honors/Awds:** Hon mem, Danish Acad Art; First Prize Drawing & Fourth Prize Painting, Second Int Biennale, Malta, 1997. **Home Addr:** HC Orsteds Vej 71, 1879-V Copenhagen, Denmark. **Business Addr:** Painter, Gammel Kongvej 136, Copenhagen, Denmark.

BURNS, TOMMIE
Executive, president (organization). **Personal:** Born Jul 5, 1933. **Career:** Mercantile Bank, Louisville; Burns Packaging Inc, owner; Burns Rigging, owner; Burns Chem Co, owner; Bus Support Serv Inc; T&WA Inc, chmn & chief exec officer, 1995-; Burns Enterprises Inc, Ky, owner, chief exec officer & pres, currently; African-Am Venture Capital Fund, dir, currently. **Orgs:** Kentuckiana Minority Supplier Develop Coun; Boys Girls Clubs Am; Boy Scouts Am; March Dimes; Chestnut St YMCA; Third Christian Church; Big Brothers & Big Sisters Kentuckiana; Kentucky Ctr Arts. **Business Phone:** (502)585-4548.

BURNS, URSULA M
Executive. **Personal:** Born Sep 20, 1950, New York, NY. **Educ:** Polytech Inst New York, BS, 1980; Columbia Univ, MS, Mech Engineering, 1981. **Career:** Xerox Corp, mech engineering summer intern, 1980, prod develop & planning, exec asst chmn, 1991, ceo, 1991, sr vpres, Corp Strategic Serv, pres Doc Syst & Solutions Group, corp sr vpres, 2000-02, pres, Bus Group Oper, 2002-07, pres, 2007-. **Orgs:** Am Express Corp; Boston Sci Corp; Ctr Addiction & Substance Abuse Columbia Univ; Inspiration & Recognition Sci & Technol; Nat Asn Mfr, Univ Rochester; Rochester Bus Alliance; Nat Acad Found. **Business Addr:** President, Xerox Corporation, 800 Phillips Rd, PO Box 0212-06S, Webster, NY 14580, **Business Phone:** (585)265-5462.

BURNS-COOPER, ANN
Editor. **Personal:** Born in Charleston, SC; daughter of Walter Burns and Janie Williams Burns; married. **Educ:** SC State Col, BA, 1969; New York Univ, cert, 1978. **Career:** RR Bowker Co, booklister, 1970-73, ed asst, 1974-78, asst ed, 1979-81, ed coordr, 1982-87; Cahners Bus Info, staff ed, 1987-98; Reed Bus Info, Libr Jour, assoc ed, 1998-. **Honors/Awds:** Frederick Douglass Fellowship Journalism; Cahners Editorial Medal of Excellence, 1994. **Home Addr:** 1725 Purdy St Suite 6C, Bronx, NY 10462. **Business Addr:** Associate Editor, Reed Business Information, Library Journal, 360 Pk Ave S, New York, NY 10010, **Business Phone:** (646)746-6819.

BUROSE, RENEE
Television journalist. **Personal:** Born May 17, 1962, Memphis, TN; daughter of Aron and Beatrice Lewis. **Educ:** Memphis State Univ, Memphis, TN, BA, 1984. **Career:** WLOK-AM, Memphis, Tenn, anchor & producer, 1984-86; WHBQ-TV, Memphis, Tenn, prod asst & admin asst, 1986-88; WJTV-TV, Jackson, Miss, assoc producer, 1988-89; WJW-TV 8, Cleveland, Ohio, producer. **Orgs:** Nat Asn Black Journalists, 1989-. **Honors/Awds:** Best Newscast, Assoc Press, 1989. **Home Addr:** 3813 Faversham Rd, Cleveland, OH 44114.

BURRAS, ALISA (ALISA MARZATTE BURRAS)
Basketball player. **Personal:** Born Jun 23, 1975; daughter of Phil Burras and Nancy Burras. **Educ:** La Tech, BA, 1998. **Career:** Colo Xplosion, ctr, 1998; Cleveland Rockers, 1999; Portland Fire, ctr, 2000-02; Seattle Storm, ctr, 2003; Birmingham Power, 2004. **Honors/Awds:** La Player of the Yr; Kodak All-Am, 1996; Region II Most Outstanding Player, 1996; All-Am, second-team AP, 1998. All-Am, US Basketball Writers Asn, 1998. **Special Achievements:** Kodak hon mention All-Am, 1998. *

BURRAS, ALISA MARZATTE. **See BURRAS, ALISA.**

BURRELL, BARBARA
Advertising executive, business owner, real estate agent. **Personal:** Born Mar 19, 1941, Chicago, IL; daughter of Wiley Jones; children: Bonita, Aldridge, Alexandra & Jason. **Educ:** Northern Ill Univ, BS, 1963. **Career:** Chicago Brd Educ, teacher, 1963-65, 1966-67; Needham, Harper, Steers,Chicago, media estimator, 1965-66; Continental Bank, Chicago, personnel counr, 1973-74; Burrell Advert, Chicago, sr vpres, sec-treas, 1974, vchmn, currently; Hyde Park Fed Savings, Chicago, dir, 1979-82; South Shore Bank, Chicago, dir, 1982-; Burrell Commun Group, pres & managing broker; Burrell Realty, managing broker, pres & chief exec officer, currently; Ariel Capital Management, brd dir, currently. **Orgs:** Aux brd, Hyde Park Art Ctr, Chicago; Hyde Park-Kenwood Dev Corp, Chicago; SE Chicago Comn; adv comm, DuSable Mus African Am History, 1983-; educ fund, Inst Psychoanalysis, 1983-; Alpha Gamma Pi; gen chairperson, Blackbook's Natl Bus & Prof Awards, 1989; pres, Project Match Families In Transition; brd dir & vchmn, Chicago sisters Intl. **Business Addr:** President, Chief Executive Officer, Burrell Realty, 401 N Mich Ave Suite 1300, Chicago, IL 60611, **Business Phone:** (312)306-9984.

BURRELL, GARLAND, JR.
Judge. **Personal:** Born Jul 4, 1947, Los Angeles, CA. **Educ:** Calif State Univ, BA, sociol, 1972; George Warren Brown Sch Soc Work, Wash Univ, MSW, 1976; Calif Western Sch Law, JD, 1976. **Career:** Off Sacramento Dist Atty, Criminal Div, dep dist atty, 1976-78; Pvt bus litigation law firm, 1985-86; Off Sacramento City Atty, dep city atty, 1978-79, sr dep atty, 1986-90; Off US Atty, Civil Div Chief, Eastern Dist Calif, Sacramento, asst US Atty, 1979-85, 1990-92; US Dist Ct, Sacramento, CA, judge, 1992; US Dist Ct, Eastern Calif, chief dist judge, 2007-. **Orgs:** Calif Bar Asn, 1976. **Special Achievements:** Presided over the "Unabomber" trial, the first African American judge to hear a high-profile murder case; first African-American federal judge in Sacramento; publ: Mental Privacy: An International Safeguard to Governmental Intrusions Into the Mental Processes, 6 California Western Law Journal 613, 1975; Collective Bargaining Statutes And Their Effect On The Home Rule Of Municipalities, 39 National Institute of Municipal Law Officers Municipal Law Review No. 11, 1976. **Business Addr:** Chief District Judge, United States District Court, Eastern California, US Courthouse, 501 I St Suite 8 220, Sacramento, CA 95814-2322, **Business Phone:** (916)930-4115.*

BURRELL, GEORGE REED, JR.
Lawyer, government official. **Personal:** Born Jan 4, 1948, Camden, NJ; married Doris; children: Stephen & Leslie. **Educ:** Univ Pa, LLD, 1974; Wharton Sch, BS, 1969. **Career:** Goodis Greenfield, Henry & Edelstein, 1974-77; Wolf Block Schorr & Solis-Cohen, atty; Colonial Penn Ins Co, asst gen coun, 1978-80; Mayor Philadelphia, dep, 1980; City Philadelphia, secy external affairs, 2001-06; Exec VPres & General Counsel, PRWT Services, currently. **Orgs:** Empire Sports Inc, Denver Broncos, 1969; Nat Bar Asn; reg dir, bd dir, Philadelphia Baristers Asn; Am Judictre Soc; Am Bar Asn; Philadelphia Bar Asn; bd dir, World Affairs Coun; bd mgrs, Friends Hosp; mem bd dirs, Kimmel Ctr for Regional Performing Arts; bd mem, African-Am Museum; Philadelphia Theatre Co; Pennsylvania Convention Ctr. *

BURRELL, JOEL BRION
Physician. **Personal:** Born Nov 27, 1959, Orange, NJ; son of Robert and Barbara. **Educ:** Rutgers Univ, BS, 1982; Temple Univ, MD, 1987. **Career:** Abington Mem Hosp, internal med resident, 1987-88; Mt Sinai Med Ctr, neurology resident, 1988-91; Cleveland Clinic, neuroimmunology fel 1991-93; Med Col of OH, asst clinical prof of neurology, 1993-98; pvt pract, neurologist & neuroimmunologist, 1993-. **Orgs:** Am Acad Clinical Neurophysiology; Am Acad Neurol, 1990-98; Am Med Asn; 1990-00; Nat Ohio Med Asn, 1991-98; fel, Am Heart Asn, 1995-; life mem, Nat Asn Advan Colored People, 1995-. **Honors/Awds:** Names one of Top 8 Young Physicians, Ohio Med Assn, 1995; African American Business of the Year, Cleveland Black Pages, 1997. **Business Phone:** (440)365-2076.*

BURRELL, JUDITH ANN
Executive. **Personal:** Born Dec 28, 1952, Boston, MA; daughter of Bernice C and Wilbur C Burrell Sr; married Charles C Stephenson Jr, Sep 20, 1996; children: Zora Ayesha Burrell Stephenson. **Educ:** Brown Univ, BA, 1974; Columbia Univ, Grad Sch, jour, MSJ, 1976. **Career:** Muscular Dystrophy Asn, staff writer, 1976-77; Medgar Evers Col, CUNY, dir inst advan, 1977-80; US Dept Com, sr comn mgr, 1980-83; NYC Off Mayor, asst press sec, asst legislative rep, 1983-89; US Conference Mayors, asst exec dir, 1989-92; US Dept Transp, Off Sec, dir exec secretariat, 1992-96; Newspaper Asn Am, sr vpres commun, 1996-; Presstime, publisher, 1996-, Newspaper Assoc Am, sr vpres commun, 2003. **Orgs:** Women's Transp Seminar, 1987-96; YWCA DC, 1988-97; DC Taxicab Comn, 1995-97; Morris G Johnson Scholarsip Golf Classic, host, 1996-98. **Honors/Awds:** US Dept Transp Secretary's Award of Excellence, 1996. **Special Achievements:** Ready To Go, Volumes I & II, USCM Compilation & Public Works Projects, 1988-89; US Mayor, contributing ed, 1986-89. **Business Addr:** Publisher, Newspaper Association of America, Presstime, 1921 Gallows Rd Suite 600, Vienna, VA 22182-3900, **Business Phone:** (703)902-1650.

BURRELL, KENNETH EARL
Musician, educator. **Personal:** Born Jul 31, 1931, Detroit, MI. **Educ:** Wayne State Univ, MusB, 1955. **Career:** Oscar Peterson Trio, guitarist, 1955-57; Benny Goodman Orchestra, 1957-59; Jimmy Smith Trio, 1959; Kenny Burrell Trio, 1960; Kenny Burrell Quartet, 1963; Guitar Player Prods, exec dir; Jazz Heritage Found, pres, 1975-78; 50 Recs, rec artist; Univ Calif Los Angeles, fac, 1978-79, Jazz Studies Prog, prof & dir, currently. **Orgs:** Kappa Alpha Psi; Phi Mu Alpha. **Honors/Awds:** InterNat Jazz Critics Awards, 1957, 1960, 1965, 1969-73; Jazz Educator of the Year award, 2004; Jazz Master, Nat Endowment Arts, 2005. **Business Phone:** (310)206-3033.

BURRELL, LEROY
Athletic coach, athlete, entrepreneur. **Personal:** Born Feb 21, 1967; son of Leroy Brown and Delores; married Michelle Finn, Jan 1, 1994; children: Cameron & Joshua. **Educ:** Univ Houston, BA, commun. **Career:** Olympic athlete, 1992; Modern Men Inc, partner, currently; Univ Houston, head coach, track & field, currently. **Honors/Awds:** Winner, Grand Prix final & Goodwill games, 100 meters, 1990; two world rec, 60 meters, 1991; USA/Mobile Outdoor Track & Field Championships, world rec, 100 meters, 1991, 1994; Penn Relays, 4x200 meter relay team, world rec, 1992; Gold Medalist, Olympic Games, 4x100 relay, 1992; Jumbo Elliott Award; University Houston's Hall of Honor, 2000; NCAA Regional Coach of the Year, 2004; C-USA Coach of the Year, 2005. **Business Addr:** Head Coach, University of Houston, 3100 Cullen Blvd, Houston, TX 77204-6742, **Business Phone:** (713)743-9465.

BURRELL, SCOTT DAVID
Basketball player, basketball coach. **Personal:** Born Jan 12, 1971, New Haven, CT. **Educ:** Univ Conn, commun sci. **Career:** Charlotte Hornets, forward-guard, 1993-97; Golden State Warriors, 1996-97; Chicago Bulls, 1997-98; NJ Nets, 1999-2000; Charlotte Hornets, forward, 2000-01; Quinnipiac Univ, asst coach, 2007-. **Honors/Awds:** NBA Draft, First round pick, 1993; NBA Champion, Chicago Bulls, 1998; Most Improved Player award, Nat Basketball Asn; NBA Most Improved Player Award. **Special Achievements:** The first American athlete to be a first round draft-pick of two major sporting organizations (the NBA and MLB). **Business Addr:** Assistant Coach, Quinnipiac University, 275 Mt Carmel Ave, Hamden, CT 06518-1908, **Business Phone:** (203)582-8200.

BURRELL, STANLEY KIRK. **See HAMMER, M. C.**

BURRELL, THOMAS J., JR.
Executive, founder (originator). **Personal:** Born Mar 18, 1939, Chicago, IL; son of Thomas and Evelyn; married Joli; children: 3. **Educ:** Roosevelt Univ, Chicago, BA, eng, 1961. **Career:** Wade Advert Agency, mail room clerk, copy trainee, copywriter, 1960-64; Leo Burnett Co, Chicago, copywriter, 1964-67; Foote Cone & Belding London, 1967-68; Needham Harper & Steers, copy suprv, 1968-71; Burrell McBain Advert, co-owner 1971-74; Ad Coun Inc, dir-at-large; Burrell Commun Group, founder & chief exec officer, 1974-, chmn emer & consult, currently. **Orgs:** Exec Comt, Chicago United; Chicago Urban League; bd govs, Chicago Lighthouse Blind; Pres's Adv Coun Roosevelt Univ; Adv Coun Howard Univ Sch Commun; Exec's Club Chicago; Econ Club; Nat Advert Review Bd; chmn, Chicago Coun, Am Asn Advert Agencies. **Honors/Awds:** Clio Awards, Coca Cola, 1978; Adevertising Person of the Year Award, Chicago Advert Club, 1985; Lifetime Achievement Award, Publicity Club Chicago, 2007. **Special Achievements:** Profiled on the PBS show "Bridgebuilders," 1998; Advertising Hall of Fame, American Advertising Federation, 2005. **Business Addr:** Chairman Emeritus, Consultant, Burrell Communication Group, 233 N Mich Ave 29th Fl, Chicago, IL 60602, **Business Phone:** (312)297-9600.*

BURRIS, BERTRAM RAY
Entrepreneur, athletic coach, baseball player. **Personal:** Born Aug 22, 1950, Idabel, OK; son of Cornelius and Clara Mae; married Debra Marie Foots, Jan 24, 1986; children: Djemal Jermaine, Ramon Jerome, Damon Jevon, Deneen Janice & Bobby J. **Educ:** Southwestern Okla State Univ, BA, 1972. **Career:** Baseball player (retired), Athletic coach, Entrepreneur; Chicago Cubs, 1973-79; NY Yankees, 1979; NY Mets, 1979-80; Montreal Expos, 1981-83; Burris-Neiman & Assocs Inc, Canada, pres, 1983-; Oakland Athletics, 1984; Milwaukee Brewers, 1985, 1987; Burris-Neiman & Assocs Inc, US, bd dir, 1985, pres, 1985-; St. Louis Cardinals, 1986; Baseball Network, exec vpres, 1987-; Milwaukee Brewers,

admin asst, instr, 1987-; Circle Life Sports Agency, vpres, 1988; Burbrook Investments, founder, 1988; Sr Prof Baseball Asn, W Palm Beach Tropics, 1989; Oneonta Tigers, pitching coach, 2006; W Mich Whitecaps, pitching coach, 2006-07; Ray Burris Acad, owner & instr, currently; Detroit Tigers, Pitching Coach, currently. **Orgs:** Bd dir, Friendship Pentacostal Holiness Church; Citizen Adv Bd, United Cancer Coun; chmn, Athletic Adv Coun; bd dir, Baseball Network, BNA-Can; chmn, Fund Raising Comt, Baseball Network; bd dir, Mt Olive Baptist Church; adv bd, Child Abuse Prev Fund, 1990-. **Honors/Awds:** Player of the Month, Nat League, 1976; Athletic Hall of Fame, Southwestern Okla State Univ, 1985; Jackson County Oklahoma Hall of Fame, 1985; NAIA Hall of Fame, 1994. **Business Phone:** (248)258-4437.

BURRIS, CHARLES. See BURRIS, CHUCK.

BURRIS, CHUCK (CHARLES BURRIS)
Government official, executive, mayor. **Personal:** Born Mar 5, 1951, Franklinton, LA; son of Vermont and Seymour; married Marcia Baird; children: 5. **Educ:** Morehouse Col, BA, polit sci, 1971; John Marshall Law Sch, LLB, 1975; Marshall Law Sch, JD. **Career:** Crime Analyst Team, City Atlanta, res analyst, 1975-77; City Atlanta, supvr, Eval Div, budget officer police, fire, corrections, civil defense, municipal court & aviation, 1977-81; Finance Dept, Atlanta Housing Authority, acct serv supvr, 1981-82; Strategic Targeting & Res Comput Consult Firm, co-founder, 1981-86; Off Secy State, State Ga, consult comput proj, 1991-94; MountainWare, Ltd, pres, 1994-; Stone Mountain, GA, city councilman, 1991-96; Stone Mountain, GA, mayor, 1997-. **Honors/Awds:** Merrill Scholar, Morehouse Col. **Special Achievements:** First African American Mayor of Stone Mountain, GA. **Home Addr:** 003850.

BURRIS, JEFFREY LAMAR
Football player. **Personal:** Born Jun 7, 1972, Rock Hill, SC; married Lisa; children: Sienna & Jaden. **Educ:** Univ Notre Dame, bus mgt. **Career:** Football player (retired), coach; Buffalo Bills, defensive back, 1994-97; Indianapolis Colts, 1998-2001;Cincinnati Bengals, 2002-03; Sienna Amore, owner; Fishers High Sch, coach, currently. **Honors/Awds:** Most valuable Player, 1993; South Carolina Player of the Year . **Business Addr:** Coach, Fishers High School, 13000 Promise Rd, Fishers, IN 46038, **Business Phone:** (317)915-4290.

BURRIS, ROLAND W
Government official, legal consultant. **Personal:** Born Aug 3, 1937, Centralia, IL; married Berlean Miller; children: Rolanda Sue & Roland Wallace II. **Educ:** Southern Ill Univ, BA, polit sci, 1959; Univ Hamburg, Ger, attended 1960; Howard Univ, JD, 1963. **Career:** US Treasury Dept, comptroller & nat bank examr, 1963-64; Continental Ill Nat Bank & Trust, from tax acct to second vpres, 1964-71; State Ill Dept Gen Serv, cabinet appointee & dir, 1973-76; Oper PUSH, nat exec dir, 1977; State Ill, comptroller 1978-91, atty gen, 1991-94; Jones, Ware & Grenard, managing partner; Buford & Peters, coun, 1999-2002; Southern Ill Univ, adj prof, 1995-98; Burris & Lebed Consult LLC, prin & partner, 2002-. **Orgs:** Am Bar Asn; Cook County Bar Asn; Am Inst Banking; Independent Voters Ill; NAACP; Cosmopolitan Chamber Com; Nat Bus League; Chicago SoEnd Jaycees; Assembly Black State Execs; Alpha Phi Alpha; vice chair, Dem Nat Comt; Nat Asn State Auditors Comptrollers & Treasurers; past pres & chmn, Intergovermental Rels Comt; Nat Asn Attys Gen; bd dirs, Ill CPA Soc, 2000-02; life mem, Nat Asn Advan Colored People; life mem, Alpha Phi Alpha Fraternity; life mem, Southern Ill Alumni Asn; trustee, Financial Acct Found, 1991-94; bd mem, Nat Ctr Responsible Gaming, 1996-2005; Mental Health Asn Greater Chicago; US Jaycees; Southern Ill Univ Found; bd mem, Auditorium Theater Chicago, 2001-06. **Honors/Awds:** Distinguished Service Award, Chicago South End Jaycees, 1968; Jr Chamber Int Scholar, 1971; Cook County Bar Public Service Award, 1974-75; Outstanding Alumnus Award, Howard Univ Law Sch Alumni Asn, 1980; Award of Financial Reporting Achievement, Govt Finance Officers Asn US & Canada, 1985; President Award, Nat Asn; State Auditors, Comptrollers, & Treasurers Serv Award, Govt Finance Officers Asn, 1990; Alumnus of the Year Award, Howard Univ Alumni Asn, 1989; Distinguished Public Service Award, Anti-Defamation League B'nai B'rith, 1988; Peace & Justice Award, Kappa Alpha Psi, 1991. **Special Achievements:** First African American to examine banks in the US; One of 1000 Successful Blacks in America, 1973; One of 10 Outstanding Young Men of Chicago, 1970, 1972; One of 10 Outstanding Black Business People, Black Book Directory, 1974; One of the 100 Most Influential Black Americans, Ebony Mag, 1979-90; One of Top Three Government Financial Officers in the Nation, City & State Mag, 1989. **Business Phone:** (312)566-0202.

BURRIS-FLOYD, PEARL
County commissioner. **Educ:** Univ NC, Chapel Hill. **Career:** Cent Piedmont Community Col, adj fac, 1992-; UNC Sch, Cytotechnology, guest lectr, 2000-04; Gaston County Comn, Dallas Twp, comnr, 2001-. **Orgs:** Piedmont Chapter Links; Alpha Kappa Alpha Sorority; past vpres, pres, Carr Eleme Sch PTA; bd dir, Gaston County Health Dept; trustee, Schiele Mus, 2001-03; trustee, Gaston Mus Hist, 2004-. **Honors/Awds:** Distinguished Service Award, Outstanding Service NC Soc Cytology, 2000; Community Service Award, Community Spirit USA, 2002; Citizen of the Year Community Service Award, Gaston County Organization Community Concerns, 2002; Citizen of the Year, Epsilon Upsilon Chap, Omega Psi Phi Fraternity, 2004; Citizen of the Year, George Wash Carver Consistory #172 & George Wash Carver Assembly, 2005. **Business Addr:** County Commissioner, Gaston County, 518 E Main St, Dallas, NC 28034.

BURROUGHS, HUGH CHARLES
Executive. **Personal:** Born Feb 6, 1940, Trinidad and Tobago; son of Vernon and Evalina; married Linda D Kendrix; children: Kwame, Dawn; married Henrietta E Johnson (divorced). **Educ:** Columbia Univ, BA, econ, 1966, MA, econ, 1969; Harvard Univ, Non-profit Mgt, cert prog, attended 1973. **Career:** Columbia Univ, asst dean, 1966-69; Martin Luther King, Jr. Fel Prog Woodrow Wilson Nat Fel Found, assoc dir, 1969-71; John Hay Whitney Found, exec dir, 1971-77; William & Flora Hewlett Found, prog officer, 1977-87; Henry Kaiser Family Found, vpres, 1987-93; Packard Found, prog dir, 1993-01; David & Lucile Packard Found, dir ext affairs; part time mgt consult; The Berry Gordy Family Found, pres & chief exec officer, 2000-; Independent Philanthropic Advs, pres, currently. **Orgs:** Chmn, bd vis, Clark Col; bd overseers, Morehouse Sch Med; chmn, bd dir, Asn Black Found Exec, 1973-77; bd dir, Women Philanthropy, 1977-80; bd dirs, Coun Found, 1987-93; Northern Calif Grantmakers; Nat Charities Inform Bur; Peninsula Community Foundation; Hispanics Philanthropy; Grantmaking Sch Adv Bd; CIVICUS;bd trustees, The Found Ctr. **Honors/Awds:** James A. Joseph Lecture, 1999. **Military Serv:** AUS, civil servant, 1957-62. **Business Addr:** President and Chief Executive Officer, The Berry Gordy Family Foundation, 6255 W Sunset Blvd Suite 716, Los Angeles, CA 90028.*

BURROUGHS, JOAN
Educator. **Educ:** Tusgee Univ, BS; Ind Univ, MS; NY Univ, PhD, 2000. **Career:** NY Univ, adj prof Dance; Fla A&M Univ, Orchesis Contemp Dance Theatre, dir, 2004, dept Health, chair, vis asst prof, currently.

BURROUGHS, JOHN ANDREW
Government official, educator, football player. **Personal:** Born Jul 31, 1936, Washington, DC; son of John A and Yeasavale; married Audrey C Shields, Feb 25, 1966. **Educ:** Univ Iowa, BA, polit sci, 1959; George Wash Univ, post grad, 1962; Stanford Univ, attended 1974; Lincoln Univ, dipl-in-residence, 1992. **Career:** Football player, educator, government official (retired); Philadelphia Eagles, 1958; Dept State Wash, passport examr, 1960-63; Dept State Bur Econ Affairs, admin asst, 1963-66; Dept Navy Wash, employ rels spec, 1970-77; Dept Navy Wash, spec asst equal employ, 1970-77; Dept State Wash,asst sec equal employ oppor, 1977-81; Repub Malawi, US ambassador, 1981-84; Joint Ctr Polit Studies, sr res fel, 1985-; US State Dept, Cape Town, South Africa, Am consult gen, 1985-88; Repub Uganda, US ambassador, 1988-91; Lincoln Univ, teacher african polit; Sudan, spec coordr, 1993-94. **Orgs:** Pres & bd dir, Ridge crest Condominium, 1964-70; Kappa Alpha Psi; life mem, Univ Iowa Alumni Asn. **Honors/Awds:** Civilian Superior Service Award, Dept Navy Wash DC, 1977; Superior Honor Award, Dept State Wash DC, 1980. **Special Achievements:** First African-American assigned US Consul General in Cape Town, South Africa. **Military Serv:** AUS, PFC, 1961.

BURROUGHS, DR. MARGARET TAYLOR (MARGARET TAYLOR)
Educator, museum director, artist. **Personal:** Born Nov 1, 1917, St Rose, LA; daughter of Alexander and Octavia Pierre; married Bernard Goss, 1939 (divorced 1947); children: Paul Nexo & Gayle Goss Hutchinson; married Charles Gordon, Dec 23, 1949; children: Paul Nexo (adopted). **Educ:** Chicago Normal Col, Elem Teacher's Cert, 1937; Chicago Teachers Col, attended 1939; Art Inst Chicago, BA, art educ, 1946, MA, art educ, 1948; Esmerelda Art Sch, Mexico City, 1953; Teachers Col, Columbia Univ, summers, 1960; Field Mus Chicago, Intern under a grant Nat Endowment Humanities, 1968; Northwestern Univ, Courses Inst African Studies, 1968; Ill State Univ, Grad Sch, 1970; Art Inst Chicago, Courses Print making, 1987. **Career:** Chicago Bd Educ, substitute teacher, 1940-45, elem teacher, 1945-46; DuSable High Sch, teacher art, 1946-69; Elmhurst Col, African Am Art & Cult, prof, 1968; Barat Col, African Am Art, prof, 1969; Kennedy-King Community Col, prof humanities, 1969-79; instr, African & African-Am arthist, Chicago Inst Art, 1968; co-founder, officer, bd dirs, S Side Art Community Ctr, 1939-; co-founder, 1961, dir, 1961-85, dir emer, 1985-, DuSable Mus African-Am Hist; comnr, Chicago PK Dist, 1986-93; comnr, currently. **Orgs:** Nat Conf Negro Artists, founder, 1959-63; Phi Delta Kappa; Staff: Am Forum Africa Study Travel Africa, 1972-79; Staff African-Am Heritage Studies Prog travel & study Africa, dir, 1980-; bd, Chicago Coun Foreign Rels; bd, Hull House Asn; bd, Urban Getaways Adv; bd, Art Inst Alumni Asn; S Side Comn Art Ctr; bd, Am Forum Int Study; bd, African-Am Heritage Prog. **Honors/Awds:** Strategy for the New City Award, Better Boys Fed, 1969; Hon Dr, Lewis Univ, 1972; Distinguished Serv Award, Englewood Businessmen's Asn, 1972; Commended Resolution 183 in the 78th Gen Assembly Sen, Sen Richard Newhouse/State Ill, 1973; Nat Asn Col Women's Award, 1973; Urban Gateways Award Cult Contrib Arts, 1973; International Year Woman Award, Catalysts for Change, 1975; Am Fed Teachers, Cit Serv, 1976; Chicago Defender Survey, One Chicago's ten most influential women (Bettie Pullen Walker), 1977; Honorable Doctorate, Chicago State Univ. 1980; Pres's Humanitarian Award, Top Ladies Distinction, Inc, 1985; cited Outstanding Serv Arts & Humanities, Chicago DuSable Fort Dearborn Hist Comn Inc, 1986; Hon Dr, Art Inst Chicago, 1987; Lifetime Serv Award, Univ Dubuque, Iowa Black Presidium, 1989; Recognition Award, Phi Delta Kappa Sorority Mu Chap, 1989; Harold Wash Leadership Award, Frank Bennett Sch/Chicago, 1989; Friends Law Enforcement Humanitarian Award, 1989; Outstanding Religious Leader Award, Stateville New Era Jaycees, 1989; Chicago Woman of the Year, 1989; Numerous other awards. **Special Achievements:** Author, works include: Jaspar, the Drummin' Boy, 1947; Whip Me Whop Me Pudding and Other Stories of Riley Rabbit and His Fabulous Friends, Praga Press, 1966; What Shall I Tell My Children Who Are Black?, MAAH Press, 1968; Sketchbook, 1976; Editor, HOME, Broadside by Charles Burroughs, "I,Child of the Promise," by Gayle Goss Hutchinson, 1984; Editor, Home, poems by Charles Burroughs, 1985; Editor, Jazz Interlude, (12 poems) by Frank Marshall, 1987; Editor, Poems by Gayle Goss Hutchinson, 1987; selected 1of 16 women to tour China, 1977; 1 of 10 African-Amn artists honored by Pres & Mrs Carter at White House, 1980; exhibitions include: Two Centuries of African-Amn Art, Los Angeles Art Co Museum, 1976; Ten African-Amn Artists, Corcoran Art Galleries, Wash, 1980; Nicole Gallery, Chicago, 1992; High Museum, Atlanta; Studio Museum, New York; numerous others. **Home Addr:** 3806 S Mich Ave, Chicago, IL 60653, **Home Phone:** (773)373-0994. **Business Addr:** Commissioner, Chicago Park District, 541 N Fairbanks Ct, Chicago, IL 60611, **Business Phone:** (312)742-4737.*

BURROUGHS, ROBERT A
Lawyer. **Personal:** Born Mar 30, 1948, Durham, NC; son of Lottie Edwards and Leslie; married Laverne Davis; children: James, Christina & Whitney. **Educ:** NC Cent U, BA, 1971; Emory Univ, Atlanta, Ga, JD, 1978. **Career:** State NC, magistrate, 1970-71; USMC, defense coun; McCalla, Raymer, Padrick, Cobb, Nichols & Clark, partner, 1990; Burroughs & Keene, LLC, atty, currently. **Orgs:** Pres, De Kalb Lawyers Asn, 1985; Gate City Bar Asn; Gen Coun Nat Asn, Real Estate Brokers, 1985-. **Military Serv:** USMC, capt, 1971-75. **Business Addr:** Attorney, Burroughs & Keene, LLC, 6440 Hillandale Dr Suite 100, Decatur, GA 30035-1210, **Business Phone:** (770)484-4088.

BURROUGHS, SARAH G.
Advertising executive, president (government), executive. **Personal:** Born Oct 19, 1943, Nashville, TN; daughter of Herman Griffith and Celestine Long Wilson; divorced; children: Rachael Ann. **Educ:** Lincoln Univ, Jefferson City, MO, BA, 1964; Northwestern Univ, Chicago, IL, 1967. **Career:** Executive (retired); Foote, Cone & Belding, Chicago, IL, assoc res dir, vpres, 1964-74; Burrell Communications Group, Chicago, IL, Atlanta, GA, gen mgr, sr vpres, 1974-94; Burrell Communs Group, Chicago, IL, vice chmn, pres & chief operating officer, 1994, chief mkt & commun, 2001. **Orgs:** NAACP; Urban League; Bryn Mawr Community Church. **Honors/Awds:** Outstanding Women in Business, Dollars & Sense Mag, Kizzy Award, Kizzy Found. *

BURROUGHS, TIM
Basketball player. **Educ:** Jacksonville Univ. **Career:** Minn Timberwolves, 1992; Wash Bullets, 1994.

BURROUGHS, DR. TODD STEVEN
Journalist, writer. **Personal:** Born Feb 17, 1968, Newark, NJ; son of Doris Burroughs. **Educ:** Seton Hall Univ, South Orange, NJ, BA, 1989; Univ Md, MA, 1994, PhD, 2001. **Career:** The Star-Ledger, NJ, gen assignment reporter, 1989-93; Seton Hall Univ, South Orange, NJ, adj prof, 1990-93, 1997; Univ Md, Col Pk, MD, adj prof, 1998; Howard Univ, Wash, DC, adj prof, 2005-06; researcher & scholar, currently; journalist, The Newark, NJ Star-Ledger, The Source & The Crisis mags, The Black World Today, Nat Newspaper Publishers Asn News Serv, 1985-; Auth: Civil Rights Chronicle; Race & Resistance: African-Americans in the Twenty-First Century; Putting The Movement Back Into Civil Rights Teaching; Ethnic Media In America; Fifties Chronicle, Lincolnwood, Ill, Legacy Publ Int. **Honors/Awds:** Scholarship Recipient 1987; Internship Recipient, 1988; Nat Asn Black Journalists; Honorable Mention, American Journalism Historians Assn Doctoral Dissertation Prize Competition, 2002; Fel, Xerona Clayton Black Press, 2000; Fel, Knight-Ridder Minority Pub Affairs, 1992-93; Scholar, Martin Luther King, four-year renewable, 1985-89; Cand, Fulbright Sr Specialist Prog, 2002-. **Business Phone:** (301)405-6653.

BURROWS, CHELSYE J
Executive. **Career:** Film Life Inc, dir, currently; Starz Encore Group LLC, exec dir corp communs, vpres programming publicity, currently. **Business Addr:** Vice President Programming Publicity, Starz Encore Group LLC, Corp Communs, 8900 Liberty Circle, Englewood, CO 80112, **Business Phone:** (720)852-5838.

BURROWS, CLARE
Health services administrator. **Personal:** Born Sep 29, 1938, Kansas City, MO; married William L; children: James Michael

Pickens, Joye Nunn Hill, Carla Nunn, Anita Nunn Orme & Maurice Nunn. **Educ:** Col St Mary Omaha, BS, 1962; Univ Calif Los Angeles, MPH, 1972. **Career:** Stanford Univ Palo Alto, compliance auditor, 1975-78; Community Hosp Santa Rosa Calif, dir med records, 1978-80; Univ Calif San Francisco, dir patient serv, 1980-82; Calif Med Rev San Francisco, monitor, 1982-86; Beverly Enterprises Inc, dir bus admin. **Orgs:** Tutor Urban League 1980-82; consult Med Records Assoc, 1980-84. **Honors/Awds:** Outstanding Church Work Mt Hermon AME Church, 1984. **Military Serv:** USAR capt 6 yrs. **Business Addr:** Director, Beverly Enterprises Inc, 2900 E Ajo Way, Tucson, AZ 85713, **Business Phone:** (602)294-0005.

BURROWS, STEPHEN
Fashion designer. **Personal:** Born Jan 1, 1945?, Newark, NJ. **Educ:** Philadelphia Mus Col Art; Fashion Inst Technol, New York, attended 1966. **Career:** Fashion designer. **Honors/Awds:** Winnie Award, Community Am Fashion Critics, 1973, 1977; Critics Award, Coun Am Fashion, 1975; Crystal Ball Award, Knitted Textile Assocs, 1975. **Business Phone:** (212)921-7650.*

BURROWS DOST, JANICE H.
Manager, executive. **Personal:** Born Oct 24, 1944, Boston, MA; daughter of Bernice E Cross Howard and Lloyd F Howard; married Quentin C Burrows (divorced 1986); children: Matthew Howard, Christopher Lynch; married William A. Dost, 1995. **Educ:** Harvard Univ, Cambridge, MA, BA, 1966; Univ Calif, Berkeley, CA, MBA, 1987. **Career:** US Civil Serv Comn, Boston, MA, Wash, DC, personnel spec, 1966-68; US Gen Serv Admin, New York, NY, regional training officer, 1971-72; City Berkeley, Berkeley, CA, personnel spec, 1974-76; Alta Bates Hosp, Berkeley, CA, personnel dir, 1976-85; self-employed consult, human resource mgt, Berkeley, CA, 1985-; Univ Calif, Berkeley, CA, dir libr hum resources, 1988-. **Orgs:** Dir, Humanities West; Pres, Healthcare Human Resources Mgt Asn Calif, 1984-85; chair, Berkeley Unified Sch Dist Personnel Comn, 1978-79, 1987-91; vpres, Calif Sch Personnel Comnr Asn, 1991-92; pres, SF Chapter, Calif Hosp Personnel Mgrs Asn, 1980-81; Am Library Asn; Indust Rels Res Asn. **Special Achievements:** Author, Minority Recruitment and Retention in ARL Libraries, Association of Research Libraries, Office of Management Services, 1990; "Onward or Upward? Getting Ahead in an Unfair World," Proceedings of the Second National Conference of the Black Caucus of the American Library Association, 1994; "Training Student Workers in Academic Libraries, How and Why?," Journal of Library Administration, Volume 212, #3/4, 1994;" Minority Recruitment and Retention in ARL Libraries," Office of Management Services, Association of Research Libraries, 1990. **Business Addr:** Director Library Human Resources, University California, 110 Doe Libr, Berkeley, CA 94720-6000, **Business Phone:** (510)642-3778.*

BURRUS, CLARK
Banker. **Personal:** Born Nov 5, 1928, Chicago, IL; son of Lemuel and Mattie Hall; married Lucille Thomas; children: James. **Educ:** Roosevelt Univ, BSC, 1954, MPA, 1972. **Career:** Banker (retired); City Chicago, Dept Finance, asst & comptroller, dir acct & asst dir finance, 1954-73, chief fiscal officer city comptroller, 1973-79; First Nat Bank Chicago, sr vpres, Pub Banking Dept, co-head, 1979-81; First Chicago Capital Markets, vice chmn & co-chmn, 1991-98. **Orgs:** Govt Finance Officers Asn US & Can; bd trustees, Cosmopolitan Chamber Com; Chicago Planning Comn; Nat Asn Securities Prof; bd dirs, Evangelical Health Systs Found; bd dirs, Nat Urban Coalition; bd dirs, Chicago Coun Urban Affairs; bd dirs, Financial Res & Adv Comt; bd dir, Econ Develop Coun; bd dir, Nat Asn Securities Prof; chmn bd, Chicago Transit Authority; co chmn, Cook County Citizens Budget Rev Comt; Harold Wash Found; Regional Transp Authority; bd chmn, Chicago Transit Authority; bd dir, Isaac Ray Ctr. **Honors/Awds:** Executive of the Year, Exec Develop Alumni, 1974; Man of the Year, Sertoma Intl, 1975; one of 10 Outstanding Business & Professional People, Blackbook Bus & Ref Guide, 1979. **Special Achievements:** Author: Minorities in Public Finance, Government Magazine, 1972; Issues Concerning the Financing of Mortgages with Tax-exempt Bonds, City Chicago; First African American bond rating for conformance in accounting. **Business Addr:** Board of Director, Isaac Ray Center Inc, 1725 W Harrison Suite 110, Chicago, IL 60612, **Business Phone:** (312)829-1463.*

BURRUS, WILLIAM HENRY
Executive. **Personal:** Born Dec 13, 1936, Wheeling, WV; son of William Burrus and Gertude Burrus; married Ethelda I; children: Valerie, Doni, Kimberly & Kristy. **Educ:** WVa State Univ, attended 1957. **Career:** Ohio Postal Union, dir res & educ, 1971, pres, 1974-80; Am Postal Workers Union, dir, bus agent, 1978-80, exec vpres, 1980-2002, pres, 2002-. **Orgs:** Labor del, Cleveland Fed, AFL-CIO, 1977, vpres, Exec Coun, 2001, chmn, Civil & Human Rights Comt, 2005; vpres, Black Trade Labor Union, 1977; Ohio Adv Bd Civil Rights Comn, 1979-81; vpres, Philip Randolph Inst, 1982-. **Honors/Awds:** Ohio House of Representative, 1981; Frederick O'Neal Award, 1981; Philip Randolph Achievement Award, 1982; num union awards & recognition; Distinguished Service Award, Martin Luther King Ctr, 1989. **Special Achievements:** First African American to be directly elected president of a national union. **Military Serv:** AUS, sgt, 3 yrs. **Business Addr:** President, American Postal Workers Union, AFL-CIO, 1300 L St NW, Washington, DC 20005, **Business Phone:** (202)842-4250.

BURSE, DR. LUTHER
Association executive, educator. **Personal:** Born Jan 3, 1937, Hopkinsville, KY; son of Ernestine Perry; married Mamie Joyce Malbon; children: Luther Jr & Elizabeth N. **Educ:** Ky State Univ, BS, 1958; Univ IN, MEd, 1960; Univ MD, EdD, 1969. **Career:** Educator, association executive (retired); Chicago Pub Sch, teacher,1958-59; Elizabeth City State Univ, instr, 1960-66; Univ Md, res asst, 1966-69; Cheyney St Col, prof, 1969-81, actg pres, 1981-82; Chester Pub Sch, consult, Philadelphia Bd Exam; Fort Valley State Col, pres, 1983-89; US Forest Serv, spec asst to chief, staff dir civil rights; Nat Asn State Univ Land Grant Col, vpres spec proj, dir urban progs & diversity. **Orgs:** Am Coun Indust Techer Educ; Pa State Educ Asn; Am Asn State Cols & Univs; past pres, Indust Arts Asn Pa; past pres, Pa Asn Voc & Practical Arts Educ; Higher Educ Caucus; Black Caucus; Women's Caucus; Voc Caucus; NEA; Alpha Kappa Mu Honor Soc; Omega Psi Phi Frat; Iota Lamda Sigma Frat; life mem, NAACP; Am Coun Educ Leadership; bd dirs, Ga Asn Minority Entrepreneurs; Sigma Pi Phi Fraternity; Ga Asn Cols; Nat Asn State Univs; Land Grant Cols; Ky State Univ Nat Alumni Asn, sr pres, currently. **Honors/Awds:** Omega Man of the Yr, Nu Upsilon Chap; Leadership Award, Arts Asn; Service Award, Pa State Educ Asn; Centennial Alumni Award, Ky State Univ;Leadership Award, Nat Educ Asn. **Home Addr:** 2020 Brooks Dr Suite 729, Forestville, MD 20747.

BURSE, RAYMOND MALCOLM
Lawyer. **Personal:** Born Jun 8, 1951, Hopkinsville, KY; son of Joe and Lena Belle; married Kim M, May 17, 1980; children: Raymond M Jr, Justin Malcolm & Eric M. **Educ:** Centre Col Ky, AB, Chem & Math, 1973; Oxford Univ, Grad work, 1975; Harvard Law Sch, JD, 1978. **Career:** Ky State Univ, pres, 1982-89; Wyatt, Tarrant & Combs, assoc, 1978-82, partner, 1989-95; GE Appliances, sr coun, 1995-2002; GE Appliances, gen coun, 2002-04; GE Consumer & Indust, vpres & gen coun, 2004-. **Orgs:** Am Bar Asn; Ky Bar Asn; Nat Bar Asn; bd chmn, Louisville Fed Reserve, 1987, 1990; bd mem, State YMCA; Louisville Free Pub Libr Advy Comn; Greater Louisville Chestnut St YMCA; Louisville Community Found. **Honors/Awds:** Rhodes Scholar; Fred M Vinson Hon Grad, Centre Col; John W Davis Award, NAACP Legal Defense & Educ Fund. **Home Addr:** 7010 New Bern Ct, Prospect, KY 40059. **Business Addr:** Vice President, General Counsel, GE Consumer & Industrial, Appliance Pk AP2 226, Louisville, KY 40225, **Business Phone:** (502)452-3279.

BURT, CARL DOUGLAS
Government official. **Personal:** Born Mar 20, 1952, Newport News, VA; son of Will and Ella; married Helen Burt, May 8, 1976; children: Carl II & Michelle. **Educ:** Thomas Nelson Community Col, AAS, 1976; Christopher Newport Univ, BS, 1979; FBI Nat Acad, dipl, 1991; Sr Mgt Inst Police, dipl, 1997; Police Exec Leadership Inst, dipl, 1999. **Career:** Newport News Police Dept, sergeant, 1984-88, lt, 1988-95, capt, 1995-98, asst chief police, 1998, interim chief, 2004, dep chief police, 2005. **Orgs:** Fraternal Order Police, 1974-; Kappa Alpha Psi, 1986-; chair deacons, Zion Baptist Church, 1988-99; chap vpres, Nat Org Black Law Enforcement Execs; past pres, PTA, Moton Elem Sch; bd dir, vice chair, Peninsula Reads, 1996-99; bd trustee, vpres, Scott Ctr HOPE, 1999-00; bd mem, trustee, Newport City News Retirement Bd, 1999-; pres, Kiwanis Monitor Club, 2001-02; bd mem, Scott Ctr Hope, chmn; Am Red Cross, 2002; trustees, Zion Baptist Church, chmn, 2002. **Honors/Awds:** Outstanding Contribution to Law Enforcement, Newport News Police, 1985; Man of the Year, Zion Baptist Church, 1993; Star of Distinction in Law Enforcement Award, 100 Black Men of America, 1996; Unsung Hero Award, Zion Baptist Church, 1996; numerous letters of commendation from community & profession; COMPA Community Service Award, 2002. **Special Achievements:** Implemented first satellite community policing offices in the city, 1987; implemented police city schools training program, 1986; implemented mentorship program with local city high school, 1998. **Business Addr:** Deputy Chief Administration, Newport News Police Department, 2600 Wash Ave 9th Fl, Newport News, VA 23607, **Business Phone:** (757)926-8829.*

BURTON, BARBARA ANN
Executive. **Personal:** Born Dec 27, 1941, Houston, TX; daughter of Isiah and Alice; married James Henderson, Nov 4, 1980 (divorced). **Educ:** TEX Southern UNIV, BS, 1966, MS, 1972, MEd, 1974. **Career:** City Houston, cot develop mgr, 1966-70, City Coun, exec asst, 1980-83; Model Cities, prog mgr, TEX Southern UNIV, COT Develop, Soc Ins, dir, 1975-80; State TEX, prog mgr, cot develop, 1983-87; Austin Metropolitan BUS Resource CTR, pres, chief exec officer, 1987-, exec dir. **Orgs:** Capital Metro, chmn bd, 1987-; TEX Asn Minority BUS Enterprises, pres, 1991-; Capital Area Workforce Alliance, comt chair, 1990-; NCW, pres, 1986-; CNF MNY Transportation Officials, pres, 1991-; Women's COC, 1990-; Precinct 141, chair, 1991-; Tex Minority Bus Opportunity Comt, exec dir, 2001. **Honors/Awds:** MNY BUS News & USA, Women Who Mean BUS Award, 1993; Minorities & Women BUS, Women Who Make a Difference Award, 1992; Black Women Achievers, Black Woman's Hall Fame Inductee, 1992. **Special Achievements:** First African-American & first woman to be elected chair, Capital Metro Transit; responsible for first AFA McDonald's Franchise in Austin; televeision hostess: "MNY BUS Review," 1992-. *

BURTON, BRENT F.
Government official, president (organization). **Personal:** Born Nov 16, 1965, Los Angeles, CA; son of Adam and Marian; married Jeanetta S, May 15, 1987; children: Andre, Shani & Adam III. **Educ:** Dillard Univ, Exec Develop Inst, cert completion. **Career:** Los Angeles County Fire Dept, capt, 1985; Carl Holmes Exec Develop Inst, instr; The African American Fire Fighter Museum, pres, Currently. **Orgs:** Staff supv, primary inst, James Shern Fire Fighter Acad, 1994; exec vpres, Los Angeles County Black Fire Fighters Asn, 1997-; vpres, 1997, pres, African-Am Fire Fighter Musm, currently; asst regional dir, Southwest Region Int Asn Black Prof Fire Fighters, 1999-; pres, Stentorians LosAngeles County Inc, currently. **Honors/Awds:** Community Protector Award, Los Angeles County Bd Supvr, 1989; Outstanding Dedication, Stentorians, 1997; Outstanding Service Award, IABPFF, Southwest Region, 1998. **Business Addr:** President, The African American Fire Fighter Museum, 1401 S Central Ave, Los Angeles, CA 90021, **Business Phone:** (213)744-1730.

BURTON, CHARLES HOWARD, JR.
Army officer, gynecologist. **Personal:** Born Sep 21, 1945, Richmond, VA; married Adline Mildred Johnson; children: Stuart Howard, Stacee Michelle, Stephanie Brouke. **Educ:** VA State Col, BS, 1968; Meharry Med Col, MD, 1975. **Career:** US Army, chief obstet & gynec; Pvt Pract, currently. **Orgs:** Fellow Am Col Obstet & Gynec, 1983, Am Col Surgeons, 1984; Omega Psi Phi Frat; 32 Degree Mason, Shriner. **Military Serv:** AUS, col, 18 yrs; Army Commendation Medal, 1978. **Business Addr:** Chief Obstetrics & Gynecology, Private Practitoner, 2550 Windy Hill Rd Se Suite 312, Marietta, GA 30067, **Business Phone:** (770)994-6806.*

BURTON, CHERYL
Television news anchorperson. **Personal:** Born Jan 1, 1963?. **Educ:** Univ Ill, BS, psychol & biol. **Career:** WGN-TV, co-anchor; WMBD-TV, gen assignment reporter; KWCH-TV, Wichita, Kan, weeknight anchor; ABC 7 News, news anchor & reporter, 1992-. **Orgs:** Chicago Asn Black Journalists; Nat Asn Black Journalists; vol, Boys & Girls Club Am; motivational speaker, Chicago Pub Schs; bd mem, Life Lupus Guild; Soc Prof Journalists; Asn Black Journalists. **Honors/Awds:** Kizzy Image and Achievement Award, 1998; Russ Ewing Award, Chicago Asn Black Journalists, 1995, 2003, 2004; Phenomenal Woman Award, Today's Black Woman; Thurgood Marshall Award, 2004, 2005; Sisters in the Spirit Award, 2005. **Special Achievements:** Was the first recipient of the 2005 "Sisters in the Spirit" Award, given by Chicago area gospel singers to persons who exemplify a faith-based life. **Business Phone:** (212)456-7777.*

BURTON, DAVID LLOYD
Accountant. **Personal:** Born Aug 1, 1956, Detroit, MI; son of C Lutressie Johnson and Freddie George Sr; divorced 2002; children: David Malik. **Educ:** Wayne State Univ, BS, 1977, MBA, 1980. **Career:** Arthur Young & Co CPA, auditor, 1980-81; Barrow Aldridge & Co CPA, semi-sr auditor, 1981-84; Ford Motor Co, internal auditor, opers rep, 1985-88; Reeves & Assocs, Griffin, GA, controller, 1988-90; US Securities & Exchange Comn, Wash, DC, staff acct, 1991-. **Orgs:** Nat Asn Black Acct, 1979; Nat Black MBA Asn, 1981; Cascade United Methodist Church, 1986; Urban Round Table, 2001. **Home Addr:** 6197 Old Brentford Ct, Alexandria, VA 22310, **Home Phone:** (703)719-9312. **Business Addr:** Staff Accountant, United States Securities & Exchange Commission, 100 F St NE, Washington, DC 20549, **Business Phone:** (202)942-8088.

BURTON, DONALD C.
Law enforcement officer, consultant. **Personal:** Born Apr 21, 1938, Lawnside, NJ; son of William E Sr and Josephine B; married Marcia E Campbell; children: Donald Jr, Barry D, Jay S, Robert T, Christopher, Matthew. **Educ:** Camden County Col, AS, 1974; Rutger State Univ, BA, 1977. **Career:** Correction consult, pvt bus, 1973-; Cherry Hill Police Dept, Detective Sergeant, polygraph oper, 1973-, lt; Camden Co Sheriff's Dept, undersheriff, 1984-88; Bergen Co Sheriff's Dept, undersheriff, 1988-89; Mark Correctional Systems Inc, correctional consult, 1989-93; City Lawnside, dir pub safety, 1992-96; Donald C Burton & Assoc, consult; . **Orgs:** pres, Cherry Hill #176 PBA, 1969-71; delegate, NJ State PBA, 1970-72; pres, NJ Chap NOBLE, 1983-88; regional vpres, NOBLE, 1987-88; trustee, HOPE for Ex-Offenders. **Honors/Awds:** Valor Award Cherry Hill Twp, 1970; Comnr Citation US Customs, 1973; Alcohol Tobacco & Firearms Citation polygraph expert, 1974; numerous awds from law enforcement orgn munic & co, state, & nat groups. **Military Serv:** AUS, reserves, 1957-67. **Home Addr:** 22 Ashland Ave, Blackwood, NJ 08012. *

BURTON, IOLA BRANTLEY
Educator. **Personal:** Born in Ensley, AL; daughter of Willie Douglas Brantley and Cremonia D Watkins Brantley; married Herman L, Apr 1, 1945; children: Constance Parma Pulliam & Laura J Odem. **Educ:** Miles Col, Birmingham, AL, BA, 1941; Columbia Univ, New York, attended 1953; Univ Denver, 1955; Univ Southern Calif, Los Angeles, CA, attended 1964. **Career:** Limestone Co Bd Educ, Athens, AL, teacher, 1941-43; Jefferson Co Bd Educ, Birmingham, AL, teacher, 1943-45, 1948-56; Los Angeles Co Dept Soc Serv, case worker, 1957-60; Centinela Val-

ley Unified Sch Dist, teacher, 1963-83; Los Angeles City Dept Recreation & Parks, Los Angeles, CA, outreach consult, 1983-85; Centinela Valley Union High Sch Dist, Hawthorne, CA, substitute teacher, 1985. **Orgs:** Supreme Epistoleus, Nat Sorority Phi Delta Kappa Inc, 1987-; Supreme Grammateus, Nat Sorority Phi Delta Kappa Inc, 1967-71, Supreme Parliamentarian, 1985-86; Clerk Session, Westminster Presby Church, 1984-; corres sec bd dir, Nat Alumni Assoc Miles Col, 1988, pres, 1989-91. **Honors/Awds:** Serv, Los Angeles City, 1974; National Sojourner Truth Meritorious Serv, National Asn Negro Bus & Prof Women, 1977; Serv & Leadership, National Sorority Phi Delta Kappa Inc, 1980; Serv, Los Angeles City Dept Recreation & Parks, 1985; Serv 10 yrs, Our Auth's Study Club & African Festival, 1989; auth: The Way It Strikes Me, 1988, Yawl Come on Back Home Again, 1978. **Home Addr:** 3039 Wellington Rd, Los Angeles, CA 90016.

BURTON, KENDRICK
Football player. **Personal:** Born Sep 7, 1973, Decatur, AL. **Educ:** Univ Ala. **Career:** Houston Oilers, defensive end, 1996-97; Barcelona Dragons, NFLE, 1999.

BURTON, LANA DOREEN
Educator, school principal. **Personal:** Born Mar 25, 1953, Evansville, IN; daughter of William Dulin and Gloria Wickware Beckner; married Rickey Burton, Feb 8, 1977; children: Alexander Richard. **Educ:** Ind State Univ, Terre Haute, IN, BS, 1975; Univ Evansville, Evansville, IN, MA, elem educ, 1979, admin cert, 1990. **Career:** Breckinridge Job Corp Ctr, Morganfield, KY, teacher, 1975-76; Evansville-Vanderburgh Sch Corp, Evansville, IN, educr, 1976-92, adminr, 1992-; John M Culver Elem Sch, prin; Harper Elem Sch, prin, currently. **Orgs:** Jr League Evansville, 1986-; pres, Evansville Chap, 1985-90; Evansville Youth Coalition, 1989-93; vpres, Coalition African-Am Women, 1990-94; bd mem & pres, YWCA, 1990-; supt, Sunday Sch, Zion Baptist Church, 1991-94, 1998-. **Honors/Awds:** Black Women of the Year, Black Women's Task Force, 1985; Outstanding Young American, 1987. **Home Addr:** 1424 Brookside Dr, Evansville, IN 47714, **Home Phone:** (812)401-4449. **Business Addr:** Principal, Harper Elementary School, 21 S Alvord Blvd, Evansville, IN 47714-1291, **Business Phone:** (812)476-1308.

BURTON, LEVAR (LEVARDIS ROBERT MARTYN BURTON, JR.)
Television director, artistic director, actor. **Personal:** Born Feb 16, 1957, Landstuhl, Germany; son of Levardis Robert and Erma Christian; married Stephanie Cozart; children: Michaela & Eian. **Educ:** Univ Southern Calif. **Career:** Films: Looking for Mr Goodbar, 1977; The Hunter, 1980; The Supernaturals,1987; Star Trek Generations, 1994; Star Trek: First Contact, 1996;Yesterday's Target, 1996; Trekkies, 1997; The Tiger Woods Story, dir,1998; Star Trek: Insurrection, 1998; Our Friend, Martin, actor & dir,1999; Dancing in September, 2000; Ali, 2001; Star Trek: Nemesis, actor &dir, 2002; Blizzard, actor, 2003; Reach For Me, actor & dir, 2008; TVseries: "Boomtown", actor, 2003; "Family Guy", 2005; TV Episodes:"Charmed", dir, 2006; " The Torn Identity", dir, 2006; "Vaya Con Leos",dir, 2005; "Battle of the Hexes", dir, 2005; "Extreme Makeover WorldEdition" dir, 2005; "Enterprise", dir, 2005; Demons, dir, 2005; "TheAugments", dir, 2004; "The Forgotten", dir, 2004; "Similitude", dir, 2003;"Extinction", dir, 2003; "Miracle's Boys", dir, 2005; "JAG", dir, 2003;"Pulse Rate", dir, 2003; "Star Trek: Voyager", dir, 2001; "Homestead",dir, 2001; "Q2", dir, 2001; "Nightingale", dir, 2000; tv appearances:Roots, 1977; Reading Rainbow, series host, 1983-; Star Trek: The NextGeneration, 1987-88; Murder, She Wrote, 1987; Houston Knights, 1987;Captain Planet & the Planeteers, 1990-93; Christy, 1995; biographical TVmovies: A Spec Friendship, 1987; A Roots Gift, 1988. **Honors/Awds:** Peabody Award, 1993; Image Award for Outstanding Performance in aYouth/C's Series or Spec, 1995; Image Award for Outstanding Performance inYouth/C's Series or Spec, 1999; Daytime Emmy Award for Outstanding C'sSeries, 2001; Daytime Emmy Award for Outstanding C's Series, 2002; ImageAward for Outstanding Performance in a Youth/C's Series or Spec, 2002;Daytime Emmy Award for Outstanding C's Series, 2003; Image Award forOutstanding Performance in a Youth/C's Series or Spec, 2003. **Business Addr:** Actor, Marion Rosenberg Prods, 8428 Melrose Pl Suite B, PO Box 69826, Los Angeles, CA 90069-5308, **Business Phone:** (323)822-2793.

BURTON, RONALD J
Executive. **Personal:** Born Jun 12, 1947, Montclair, NJ; son of Joseph and Ruth Jackson; married Carolyn Ievers, Oct 1, 1975; children: Christopher & Alison. **Educ:** Colgate Univ, Hamilton, NY, BA, hist, econs, 1969; Wharton Sch, Philadelphia, PA, grad courses. **Career:** Dallas Cowboys, Dallas, TX, prof athlete, 1969; EI Dupont, Wilmington, mkt mgr, 1969-74; RH Donnelley, NY, mgr, 1975-87, vpres, 1987; Dun & Bradstreet Corp, vpres, exec dir, 2000-. **Orgs:** Bd mem & vpres, Colate Alumni Club, 1975-80; bd mem, George Jr Repub Asn, Ithaca, NY, 1979-85; Montclair Pub Schs, 1985-87; Mountainside Hosp, Montclair, NJ, 1987-; bd trustee, Colgate Univ; trustee, mem, Athletic, Develop, Admis & Stud Affairs comt. **Special Achievements:** First recipient of the Andy Kerr Trophy. **Business Addr:** Executive Director, Dun & Bradstreet Corporation, 103 JFK Pkwy, Short Hills, NJ 07078, **Business Phone:** (973)921-5500.

BURTON, VALORIE
Columnist, counselor. **Educ:** Fla State Univ; Fla A&M Univ, MA, jour; Coach Univ, prof coach training. **Career:** CPA firm, Dallas, mkt dir; Burton Agency, founder; Gov Comn Women, 2001-03; Inspire Inc, coach, colmnist & speaker, currently; Author: Listen to Your Life; What's Really Holding You Back?; Rich Minds, Rich Rewards & Why Not You?; 28 Days to Authentic Confidence; How Did I Get So Busy? The 28-Day Plan to Free Your Time, Reclaim Your Schedule, & Reconnect with What Matters Most. **Orgs:** Int Coach Fed; Nat Speakers Asn. **Honors/Awds:** Miss Black Tex USA; named one of the nations 30 rising stars in public relations, PR Week Magazine, 2000. **Business Addr:** Coach, Colmnist & Speaker, Inspire Inc, 1009 Bay Ridge Ave Suite 150, Annapolis, MD 20744, **Business Phone:** (410)561-6041.*

BURTON, WILLIAM A
President (Organization), chief executive officer. **Educ:** Loyola Univ, Chicago, bus mgt & Comput Sci. **Career:** Prof Systs Inc, pres & chief exec officer, currently. **Business Addr:** President, Chief Executive Officer, Professional Systems Inc, 14108 S Ind Ave, Riverdale, IL 60827, **Business Phone:** (708)849-7000.*

BURTON-LYLES, BLANCHE
Musician, educator. **Personal:** Born Mar 2, 1933, Philadelphia, PA; daughter of Anthony H (deceased) and Ida Blanche Taylor (deceased); children: Thedric (deceased). **Educ:** Curtis Inst Music, MusB, 1954; Temple Univ, Philadelphia, BMus Ed, 1971, MusM, 1975. **Career:** Educator (retired), Musician; Soc Orch LeRoy Bostic's Mellowaires, pianist; concert pianist, US, 1939; Philadelphia Bd Educ, teacher, 1960-93; Marian Anderson Hist Soc Inc, founder & pres, 1993-. **Orgs:** Delta Sigma Theta Sor, 1954; Pro Arts Soc; Music Ed Nat Conf, 1970-; Russell Johnson-Negro Asn Musicians, 1990-; founder, Marian Anderson Hist Soc. **Honors/ Awds:** Music Specialist, 25 Years, Women in Education, 1991; Shirley Chisholm Philadelphia Political Congress of Black Women Award for Achievement in Music, 1994; Black Music Caucus Award for Outstanding Woman in Music, 1995; Coalition Award of 100 Black Women; Mary McLeod Bethune Award, Nat-Coun Negro Women, 2000; All-Star Award, Philadelphia 76ers' Community Serv, 2004; Sadie T. Alexander Award, 2005; Edythe Ingram Award, Alpha Kappa Alpha Sorority, 2006; Martin Luther King Jr Drum Major Cultural Award, 2007; Unsung Hero Award, Nat Asn Negro Bus & Prof Women, 2007. **Special Achievements:** The first African American female pianist to play at Carnegie Hall with the New York Philharmonic Orchestra in 1947; First African-American woman pianist to graduate and receive a bachelors degree from Curtis Institute; first black woman pianist to graduate from Curtis Inst of Music Philadelphia 1953. **Business Phone:** (215)732-6723.*

BURTON-SHANNON, CLARINDA
Obstetrician, gynecologist. **Personal:** Born Jan 16, 1959, Philadelphia, PA; daughter of James and Gracie; married Charles Langford Shannon Sr, Jul 9, 1988; children: Michael Joshua Shannon. **Educ:** Cheyney State Col, BA, 1980; Meharry Med Col, MD, 1984. **Career:** Univ Med Ctr, physician, currently; Lebanon Womens Clin, obstetrician & gynecologist, currently. **Home Phone:** (615)758-5490. **Business Addr:** Obstetrician, Gynecologist, Lebanon Women's Clin, 437 Park Ave Suite A, Lebanon, TN 37087.*

BURTS, EZUNIAL
Government official. **Career:** Port Los Angeles, exec dir, 1997; Los Angeles Area Chamber Com, pres, 2001. *

BURWELL, BRYAN ELLIS
Broadcaster. **Personal:** Born Aug 4, 1955, Washington, DC; son of Harold H and Ursula Tomas; married Dawnn Turner, Jun 23, 1984; children: Victoria Renee. **Educ:** Va State Univ, Petersburg, VA, BA, eng lit, 1977. **Career:** Baltimore Sun, Baltimore, Md, sports reporter, 1977-79; Wash Star, Wash, DC, sports reporter, 1979-80; NY Newsday, New York, NBA writer, 1980-83; NY Daily News, New York, NY, NFL columnist, 1983-89; Detroit News, Detroit, Mich, sports columnist, 1989-; HBD Sports, New York, NY, Inside the NFL reporter; St Louis Post-Dispatch, sports columnist, currently. **Orgs:** Kappa Alpha Psi, 1975-; Pro Football Writers Am; Nat Asn Black Journalists. **Honors/Awds:** Number 5 Feature Writer in Country, APSE, 1988; Number 4 Columnist in Country, 1989; Michigan's Top Sports Columnist, UPI, 1989. **Business Addr:** Sports Columnist, St. Louis Post-Dispatch, 900 N Tucker Blvd, St Louis, MO 63101, **Business Phone:** (314)340-8000.

BUSBY, EVERETT C.
Educator, college teacher. **Personal:** Born in Muskogee, OK. **Educ:** Langston Univ, BA, sociol, 1950; Univ Norman, cert, social work, 1951; Univ Tex, Austin, MSW, 1953. **Career:** AUS, Med Serv Corps, psychiat social worker, 1953-55; Kings Col, Psychiat Hosp, NY, psychiat social worker, 1956-59; Seton Hall Col Med & Dent, Jersey City NJ, instr & dept psychiat, 1959-61; Fordham Univ, Grad Sch Social Serv, assoc prof, 1961, assoc prof emer, currently; NIAAA HEW, Wash DC, consult, 1970-72; Pvt Pract, supv psychotherapist, trianer & assoc, 1971-80. **Orgs:** Coun Soc Workers Educ, 1985; Am Asn Univ Prof, 1985; Nat Asn Black Soc Workers, 1985; Nat Conf Soc Welfare, 1985; Nat Conf Soc Welfare, 1985; Consult training ed, Bedford-Stuyvesant Youth Act, Brooklyn; consult training ed, Haryou-Act NYC; educ & training bd mem, Nat Coun Alcohol, NT; Am Civil Liberties Union; Alpha Phi Alpha Fraternity. **Honors/Awds:** Bene Merenti Award. **Military Serv:** AUS, spec II, 1951-53. **Business Addr:** Associate Professor Emeritus, Fordham University, Grad Sch Soc Serv Lincoln Ctr Campus, New York, NY 10023.

BUSBY, JHERYL. See Obituaries section.

BUSH, CHARLES VERNON
Executive, association executive, air force officer. **Personal:** Born Dec 17, 1939, Tallahassee, FL; son of Charles and Marie; married Bettina; children: 3. **Educ:** USAF Acad, BSE, 1963; Georgetown Univ, MA, int rels, 1964; Harvard Univ Grad Sch Bus Admin, MBA, finance, 1972. **Career:** Coprorate Executive (retired), Social Worker: USAF, intelligence officer 1963-70; White Weld & Co Inc, assoc corp finance 1972-74; Celanese Corp, asst treas 1974-78; Max Factor & Co, vpres, treas 1978-80, vpres, corp controller, 1980-83; ICN Pharmaceuticals Inc, vpres finance, chief financial officer, 1983-85; Greenberg, Glusker, Fields, Claman & Machtinger, exec dir, 1985-87; Unicel Inc, vpres, 1987-89; Marnel Investment Corp, pres, 1989-91; Nostalgia TV Network, pres & chief operating officer, 1991-92; GM Hughes Electronics Corp, vpres; Hughes Int, sr vpres; The Maecenas Fund, dir, currently. **Orgs:** Bd dirs, United Mutual Ins Co, 1976-78; Fin Exec Int, 1978-; exec coun, Harvard Bus Sch Alumni Asn, 1978-83; bd dir, Harvard Bus Sch, Southern Calif Alumni Asn, 1981-84; Harvard Bus Sch Black Alumni Asn; Am Montessori Soc. **Special Achievements:** First African-American Page on Capitol Hill. **Military Serv:** USAF capt; Bronze Star Medal, Joint Service Commendation Medal, Air Force Commendation Medal with Oak Leaf Cluster. **Business Addr:** Director, The Maecenas Fund Inc., 8119 Kloshe Court S, Salem, OR 97306, **Business Phone:** (503)566-7917.

BUSH, DEVIN M.
Football player. **Personal:** Born Jul 3, 1973, Miami, FL; married Kesha; children: Jazmin, Deja & Devin Jr. **Educ:** Fla State Univ. **Career:** Atlanta Falcons, defensive back, 1995-98; St Louis Rams, 1999-00;Cleveland Browns, defensive back, 2001-02. *

BUSH, ESTHER L
Association executive. **Personal:** Born Oct 26, 1951, Pittsburgh, PA; daughter of Willie C and Ola Mae. **Educ:** Morgan State Univ, BA; Johns Hopkins Univ, MS; Univ Hartford, JD, 1997; Carlow Col, PhD. **Career:** Baltimore Pub Sch, teacher, 1973-77; Coppin State Col, Career Planning & Placement Ctr, asst dir, 1977-80; Nat Urban League, Labor Educ Advan Prog, asst dir, 1980-81; Donchian Mgt Servs, assoc consult, 1982; Staten Island Urban League, dir, 1982-86; Manhattan Urban League, dir, 1986-89; Urban League Greater Hartford, pres & chief exec officer, 1989-94; WAMO AM 860, talk show host; Urban League Pittsburgh, pres & chief exec officer, 1994-. **Orgs:** State Bd Educ; Urban League Pittsburgh Charter Sch; August Wilson Ctr African Am Cult; Carnegie Mus Pittsburgh; trustee, Int Women's Forum Bd; Judicial Eval Comn; Pa Bar Asn; Pa Comn Crime & Delinquency; Pittsburgh Cult Trust; UPMC Health Syst. **Honors/Awds:** Women of Spirit Award, Carlow Col; Community Leadership of the Year Award, Jr Achievement S Western Penn; Distinguished Daughter of Pennsylvania, 2002; Whitney M Young Jr Award, Nat Urban League; YWCA Women of Distinctions Award; Distinguished Alumni Award, Pittsburgh Pub Sch; Pittsburgh Men & Women of the Year Award, Vectors, Pittsburgh. **Special Achievements:** Started the first Charter School in Pittsburgh; received several appointments by several governors to serve on Commissions & Boards. **Business Addr:** President, Chief Executive Officer, Urban League of Pittsburgh, 1 Smithfield St, Pittsburgh, PA 15222-2222, **Business Phone:** (412)227-4229.

BUSH, EVELYN
Police officer. **Personal:** Born Jan 8, 1953, Danbury, CT; daughter of Ruben and Annette; children: Maghan Kadijah. **Educ:** Univ Conn, Storrs, BA, 1975, MS. **Career:** Conn State Dept Corrections, affirmative action officer, 1976-77, personnel officer, 1977-79, dep warden, 1979-84, warden, 1984-92, 1995-; Correctional Servs Dir, dep comnr, 1992-94. **Orgs:** Bd mem, House Bread, 1982-83; vpres, bd Families Crisis, 1982-; vol counr, YWCA Sexual Assault Crisis, 1982-90; comnr, City Hartford Drug/ Alcohol, 1986-90; Manch Bd Educ, 1995-98; Tenn Mentor, 1996-; Conn Criminal Justice Asn; Am Correctional Asn; Mid Atlantic States Correctional Asn. **Honors/Awds:** Connecticut Zeta of the Year, Zeta Phi Beta Sorority, 1978; Community Service Award, Phoenix Soc Firefighters, 1985; Community Service Award, Hope SDA Church & Metro AME, 1985; Goverment Service Recognition, YWCA, 1985; Outstanding Working Women Glamour Magazine, 1985; Outstanding Connecticut Women, Conn United Nations Asn, 1987. **Special Achievements:** First African American woman warden. **Business Phone:** (860)487-2712.

BUSH, HOMER GILES
Baseball player. **Personal:** Born Nov 12, 1972, East St Louis, IL; married Monica. **Career:** Major League: New York Yankees,

infielder, 1997-98, 2004; Toronto Blue Jays, infielder, 1999-2002; Fla Marlins, 2002; Minor League: Pdres, 1991; Charleston Rainbows, 1992; Waterloo Diamonds, 1993; Ranca Cucamongo Quakes, 1994; Wichita Wrangles, 1994; Memphis chicks, 1995; Las Vegas Stars, 1996-97; Dunedin Blue Jays, 1999-2001; Syracuse Skychiefs, 2001; Columbus Clippers, 1997, 2004. **Honors/Awds:** James P. Dawson Award, 1999; Listed in "All Nice Guy" team for all of Major League Baseball by Ken Davidoff, 2008. *

BUSH, JAMES, III
Politician. **Personal:** Born Feb 13, 1955, Panama City, FL. **Educ:** Bethune-Cookman Col, BS, 1979; Nova Univ, MS, educ admin & supv, 1984. **Career:** Fla House Rep, dem exec committeeman, 1984-92; Fla House Rep, Dist 109, rep, 1992-. **Orgs:** Bd mem, Community Action Agency; bd mem, Opportunity Industrialization Ctr; United Teachers Dade; bd mem, Juv Justice Coun; assoc minister, Antioch Missionary Baptist Church Brownsville, 1990-92; chmn, Fla Martin Luther King Jr Inst Nonviolence Bd. **Business Addr:** Representative, Florida House of Representative, District 109, 513 The Capitol, 402 S Monroe St, Tallahassee, FL 32399-1300, **Business Phone:** (850)488-1157.

BUSH, LENORIS
Executive director. **Personal:** Born Jul 18, 1949, Colquitt, GA; married Helen. **Educ:** Para-Prof Inst, social serv aide, 1969; Univ UT, sociol, 1975; Westminster Col, BS behav sci, 1977; Univ Phoenix, MBA, 1984. **Career:** Probation Dept Juvenile Ct, caseworker, 1968-69; Granite Comn Ment Health Ctr, ment health aide, 1969-70; Second Dist Juvenile Ct, probation officer, 1970-74; Utah Opportunity Indust Ctr, job developer & indust relations dir, 1976, dir prog operation, 1977, dep dir, 1977-78, exec dir, 1978-; Univ Utah, Glendon Middle Sch, Bus Partnerships, vol coordr. **Orgs:** Cent City & Summer Sch Bd, 1974; Apprenticeship Outreach Bd, 1977-; Co-Op Exoffender Prog Bd, 1977-80; dir, Blacks Unlimited Bd, 1977-; Utah Adv Bd, 1978-; youth rep, Salt Lake County ETD Instit Task Force, 1978; asst chairperson, Support Serv Task Force ETD, 1978; asst chair, Salt Lake County Manpower Planning Coun, 1978; exec dir, Asn OIC's Am, 1978; Reg Plann Comn OIC's Am, 1978; Nat Alliance Businessmen, 1980; Nat Asn Advan Colored People, 1980-; Nat Asn Advan Colored People Scholarship Found, 1981; Minority Coalition, 1981; chmn, Black Educ Scholarship Found, 1982; reg adv bd, SBA, 1983; Voc Adv Bd Salt Lake Sch Dist, 1985; 1st vice pres, Salt Lake Nat Asn Advan Colored People, 1985; C C Indust Dev Comn; bd mem, Black Adv Coun; Black Adv Coun State Bd Educ; Governor's Voc Educ Adv Coun. **Home Addr:** 2528 Imperial St, Salt Lake City, UT 84109. **Business Addr:** Business Partnerships-Volunteer Coordinator, University of Utah, Glendon Middle School, 241 300 W, Salt Lake City, UT 84103, **Business Phone:** (801)578-8500.

BUSH, LEWIS FITZGERALD
Football player, radio broadcaster. **Personal:** Born Dec 2, 1969, Atlanta, GA. **Educ:** Wash State. **Career:** Football player (retired), Radio broadcaster; San Diego Chargers,linebacker, 1993-99; Kans City Chiefs, 2000-03; KIOZ, pre-game commentator, currently. **Business Addr:** Pre-game Commentator, KIOZ, 9660 Granite Ridge Dr Suite 100, San Diego, CA 92123, **Business Phone:** (858)292-2000.

BUSH, MARY K.
Banker. **Personal:** Born Apr 9, 1948, Birmingham, AL. **Educ:** Fisk Univ, BA, econ, 1969; Univ Chicago, MBA, fin, 1971. **Career:** Chase Manhattan Bank NA, credit analyst, 1971-73; Citibank NA, acct officer, 1973-76; Bankers Trust Co, vp, world corp dept, 1976-82; US Treasury Dept, exec asst dep secy 1982-85; Int Monetary Fund, us alternate ed, 1984; Bush Int, pres, 1991-; Reynolds Am Inc, dir, 1999-. **Orgs:** Vice chair, treas Women's World Banking, NY 1983-; Exec Women Gov, 1984-; Univ Chicago Bus Sch, 1979-; bd trustees, YMCA, Wash DC, 1985-; bd, Texaco; bd, Nat Bank Trust Co. **Honors/Awds:** Scott Paper Co Leadership Award; Who's Who in Finance & Indust; Outstanding Young Women Am; Who's Who Am Col & Univ. **Home Addr:** 4201 Cathedral Ave NW, Washington, DC 20016. **Business Addr:** Director, Reynolds Am Inc, 401 N Main St, Winston-Salem, NC 27102.*

BUSH, NATHANIEL
Lawyer. **Personal:** Born Jan 19, 1949, Washington, DC; son of Thelmen and Elouise Graves; married Marsha Diane Jackson; children: Traci, Nathan & Matthew. **Educ:** Ripon Col, BA 1973; Cleveland Marshall Col Law, JD, 1977; Wharton Sch Bus, cert, 1984. **Career:** Cambridge Univ, distinguished vis prof law, grad asst, 1976-77; Bur ATF Dept, treas, atty, 1979-81; Univ Dist Columbia, adj prof criminol, 1982-84; DC State Campaign Jesse Jackson, pres, gen coun 1983-84; DC Bd Educ, vpres; Ward VII rep; Pvt pract, lawyer, currently. **Orgs:** Bd dir, Southeast Neighbors Citizens Asn; bd dirs, Far East Comm Serv Inc; chmn, bd dirs, Concerned Citizens Alcohol & Drug Abuse; Bar State OH, 1977; State Bar Asn, 1979-; Moot Ct Bd Govs, Cleveland Marshall Col Law. **Honors/Awds:** First Place, Third Annual Douglas Moot Ct Competition, 1975; Outstanding Young Men America, 1984. **Business Phone:** (202)584-0007.

BUSH, PATRICIA
Executive. **Personal:** Born in Cambridge, MA. **Educ:** Mt Holyoke Col, BA, math; Univ Va, Darden Grad Sch Bus Admin, MBA. **Career:** Polaroid Corp, Channel Opers & Develop, dir; Balanced Scorecard Collab, vpres govt solution, currently; consult. **Orgs:** Co-chairperson, Polaroid Sr Black Mgrs; founder, Nat Coalition 100 Black Women, Boston Chap; bd dirs, Urban League Eastern Mass. **Business Phone:** (781)259-3737.

BUSH, T W
Law enforcement officer. **Personal:** Son of Thomas J and Wanda L. **Educ:** Morehouse Col, Atlanta Ga, 1964; Univ Ga, Mgt Develop, 19; US Dept Justice, Human Rel, 1982; Southern Police Inst Ga Police Acad, Admin Officers Training, 1984. **Career:** Dekalb Cty Dept Pub Safety, patrolman, 1974-79, master patrolman, 1979-80, sgt, 1980-82, lt, 1982-90, capt, 1990; DeKalb Co Police Dept, Comdr Spec Oper, currently. **Honors/Awds:** Numerous Commendations IntraDeptal; Police Officer of the Month, DEK Civic Orgn, 1980. **Business Addr:** Commander Special Operator, Dekalb County Government- Police & Fire Rescue Services, Center Precinct, 3630 Camp Circle, Decatur, GA 30032, **Business Phone:** (404)294-2693.

BUSIA, AKOSUA CYAMAMA
Actor, writer. **Personal:** Born Dec 30, 1966, Ghana; daughter of Kofi Abrefa Busia; married John Singleton, Oct 12, 1996 (divorced 1997); children: Hadar. **Educ:** Oxford Univ, Oxforshire, Eng, UK. **Career:** Films: Ashanti, 1979; The Final Terror, 1983; The Color Purple, 1985;Crossroads, 1986; Low Blow, 1986; Native Son, 1986; Saxo, 1987; The Seventh Sign, 1988; NewJack City, 1991; Rosewood, 1997; Mad City, 1997; Ill Gotten Gains, 1997; Beloved, writer, 1998; Tears of the Sun, 2003; A Collaboration of Spirits Casting and Acting The Color Purple, 2003; Ascension Day, 2007; Journey to Safety Making Tears of the Sun, 2003; TV appearances: "Warp speed", 1981; "Knight Rider", 1983; "Louisiana", 1984; "Late Starter",1985; "A.D.", 1985; "Badge of the Assassin", 1985; "Simon & Simon", 1985;"The George McKenna Story", 1986; "Babies Having Babies", 1986; "The Twilight Zone", 1986; "St. Elsewhere", 1986; "A Special Friendship", 1987; "Highway to Heaven", 1987; "A Different World", 1989; "Brother Future",1991;; "Dead Man's Walk", 1996; "ER", 1999; Book: The Seasons of Beento Blackbird: A Novel, 1997. **Orgs:** Royal Family Wenchi. **Honors/Awds:** Princess, Ghana, Africa; Best Actress, 2003. **Special Achievements:** Nominated for Oscar award in 1985; nominated for an Academy award, Golden Satellite Award and Black Film Award.

BUSKEY, JAMES E.
State government official. **Personal:** Born Apr 10, 1937; married Virgia. **Educ:** Ala State Univ, BS, sec educ; Univ NC, MAT, math; Univ CO, EdS. **Career:** Sch admin (retired), E.S. Chestang Middle Sch; Commonwealth Nat Bank, founder & dir; Franklin Primary Health Ctr, founder& dir; Community Convalescent Ctr, founder & dir; ES Chasting Middle Sch,sch adminr; Mobile Co House Legis Deleg, chmn; State AL, 99th Dist, rep,1976-. **Orgs:** Ala Democratic Conf; AL State Dem Exec Comt; Omega Psi Phi; SOMI; Aimwell Baptist Church. **Honors/Awds:** Citizen of the Year, Kappa Alpha Psi, 1976; Citizen of the Year, Omega Psi Phi, 1979; Outstanding Legislator, Omega Psi Phi, 1987; Aaron L Brown Award, Alumni Distinction, AL State Univ, 1999; Distinguished Service Award, Alpha Kappa Alpha, 2001. **Business Addr:** State Representative, House of Representatives of Alabama, 99th District, 104 S Lawrence St, Mobile, AL 36617, **Business Phone:** (251)463-0154.

BUSSEY, REUBEN T., JR.
Lawyer. **Personal:** Born Mar 7, 1943, Atlanta, GA. **Educ:** Morris Brown Col, BA, 1965; Tex Southern Univ, Law Sch, JD, 1969. **Career:** State Bar Tex, 1969; Legal Aid Soc, Atlanta, staff mem, 1969; Fed Trade Comn, Boston, atty, 1969-71; GA Bar, 1971; Kennedy Bussey & Sampson, partner, 1971-76; pvt pract atty, currently. **Orgs:** Housing Strategy Group Task Force; Atlanta C C; Gate City Bar Asn; Nat Bar Asn. **Business Addr:** Attorney, 5110 Kerry Dr SW, Atlanta, GA 30331.*

BUSTAMANTE, J W ANDRE
Publisher. **Personal:** Born Jun 18, 1961, Cleveland, OH; son of John Henry and Frances Joy Simmons; children: Auschayla Quinae Brown. **Educ:** Boston Univ, Boston, BS, 1986. **Career:** Wang Labs Inc, Lowell, MA, auditor, 1982; Trustees Health & Hosps City Boston, Inc, acct, budget controller, 1983; Commonwealth Massachusetts Dept Revenue, Boston, MA, tax examr, 1983-84, 1985-87; Harvard St Health Ctr, Boston, MA, bus mgr, 1985; First Bank Nat Asn, Cleveland, OH, exec asst chmn, 1987-88; Call & Post Newspapers, Cleveland, OH, pres/gen mgr, 1988-95; Bottom Line Productions Inc, vpres, 1987-; PW Publ Co Inc, pres & gen mgr, 1988-89; Augrid Corp, vpres, 1995-99, exec asst comnr; R.A.Energy Int Inc, vpres sales & mkt, 2002-. **Orgs:** Urban League, Cleveland Chap; Nat Asn Black Acct, Cleveland Chap; Am Entrepreneurs Asn; bd dirs, Job Corps Community Rels Comt; Cleveland Schs Summit CNL; bd & nominating comt, UNIV Circle Inc; Ohio Citizens; Adv Coun; Nat MNY Golf Asn Bd; Co-Chmn Ohio Bush-Quayle 92; Repub Nat Comt; Nat Rifle Asn; NCP, Cleveland Chap; adv, African Solar Village Proj; volunteer; Clergy United Juvenile Justice; volunteer, Peace in Hood; asst dir, Spirit a Rainbow; edial bd, SE J Ed, TN State Univ; chair, Youth Develop Coun; bd dir, WAS Nat Bank. **Honors/Awds:** Certificate of Appreciation, CARE, 1987; Certificate of Appreciation, Republican Nat Committee, 1988, 1989; Certificate of Appreciation, United Negro Col Fund, 1990; Certificate of Recognition, Republican Senatorial Inner Circle, 1990; Presidential Commission, 1992; Presidential Advisory Committee Commission, 1992; Senatorial Commission, 1991; Presidential Task Force Honor Roll, 1991; Order of Merit, 1991; Citation of Leadership, Republican Inner Circle, 1996; US Senatorial Commission, 1996; Outstanding Young Americans, 1997. **Home Addr:** PO Box 1892, Cleveland, OH 44106. **Business Phone:** (216)431-0200.

BUSTAMANTE, Z SONALI. See WILSON, SONALI BUSTAMANTE.

BUTCHER, ERNESTO L.
Executive, manager. **Educ:** Hunter Col, BA; Univ Pittsburgh. **Career:** Agencys Tunnels, Bridges & Terminals Dept, dir; George Wash Bridge, mgr; Port Authority Bus Terminal, mgr; Interstate Transp Dept, dep dir; Port Authority NY & NJ, trainee, 1971, cheif operating officer, 1999; Port Authority Trans & Hudson Corp, vpres & gen mgr, currently. **Honors/Awds:** New Jersey State Assembly for his Leadership, 2001. **Special Achievements:** One of seven African-Americans selected by the New Jersey Legislative Black, Latino and Asian Caucus for their leadership, outstanding achievements and contributions to the community. **Business Addr:** Vice President and General Manager, Port Authority NY & NJ, 225 Park Ave S, New York, NY 10003, **Business Phone:** (212)435-7000.*

BUTCHER, DR. PHILIP
Educator, writer. **Personal:** Born Sep 28, 1918, Washington, DC; son of James W and Jennie Jones; married Ruth B; children: 2. **Educ:** Howard Univ, AB, MA; Columbia Univ, PhD. **Career:** Opportunity, Journ Negro Life, 1947-48; Morgan State Col, eng teacher, 1947-49, asst prof, 1949-56, assoc prof, 1956-59; SC State Col, vis prof, 1958; Morgan State Univ, prof, 1959-79, dean grad sch, 1972-75, prof emer, 1979-. **Orgs:** Col Language Asn; Modern Language Asn; Soc Study So Literature; lectr. **Honors/Awds:** General Education Board & John Hay Whitney Fellowship; Creative Scholarship Award, Col Language Asn, 1964; many research grants; many citations, reference works; many books & articles published. **Military Serv:** AUS, T & Sgt, 1943-46. **Business Addr:** Professor Emeritus, Morgan State University, 1700 E Cold Spring Lane, Baltimore, MD 21251, **Business Phone:** (443)885-3333.*

BUTLER, ANNETTE GARNER
Lawyer. **Personal:** Born Jun 23, 1944, Cleveland, OH; daughter of Minnie Garner and Rudolph Garner; divorced; children: Christopher & Kimberley. **Educ:** Case Western Reserve Univ, BA, 1966; Cleveland State/Cleveland Marshall Law, JD, 1970. **Career:** Civil rights specist, D/HEW Off Civil Rights, 1970-74; assoc atty, Guren, Merritt, Sogg & Cohen, 1974-81; dir legal affairs, Off Sch Monitoring, 1981-82; US Atty Off ND, OH, asst US atty, lead trial atty; pvt prac, currently. **Orgs:** Trustee, vpres grievance comm, Cleveland Bar Asn; founder, past pres, Black Women Lawyers Asn; bar admiss OH 6th Circuit Court Appeals; Supreme Court US; trustee, treas, vice-chmn, Cleveland State Univ; past pres, Cleveland City Club; past pres, Cleveland Heights Univ Libr Bd; bd trustees, Shaker Heights Recreation Bd; pres, bd trustees, Shaker Heights Libr Bd; vpres, trustee, Citizens League Res Inst; past pres, Fed Bar Asn, Northern Dist OH Chap; Golden Key Nat Hon Soc. **Honors/Awds:** Distinguished Serv, Cleveland Jaycees; Outstanding Achievment Narrator, Cleveland Chap Nat Acad Arts & Scis; Woman Year, Negro Bus & Prof Club; Outstanding Achievement, Cuyahoga County Bar Asn; Distinguished Alumnus Award, Cleveland State Univ. **Business Addr:** Private Practice, 1057 E Blvd, Cleveland, OH 44108, **Business Phone:** (216)851-3259.

BUTLER, CHARLES H.
Physician. **Personal:** Born Feb 12, 1925, Wilmington, DE; children: Yvonne, Kathy, Charla, Leslie. **Educ:** Ind Univ; Univ Pa; Meharry Med Col, MD, 1953. **Career:** Pvt Pract, physician; Coatesville Hosp, staff. **Orgs:** Nat Med Asn; Am Acad Family Physicians; Pa Med Soc; med adv, Loacl Draft Bd Pres Pa State Conf Nat Asn Advan Colored People; pres, Coatesville Br Nat Asn Advan Colored People; vpres, Unite Polit Act Comt; Chester Co; past pres, Chester Co Rep Club; former exec comn, 32 deg Mason; Charles E Gordon Consistory no 65; IBPOE, Wilmington; treas, past pres, Pan-hellenic Assembly, Chester County Wilmington Alumni Chap Kappa Alpha Psi. **Honors/Awds:** Mason & Year, 1967; Citation Optimist Club Coatesville, 1972; Life member Humanitarian Award, Chester County Bus & Prof Women's Culb Inc, 1973; Community Achievement Award, Lily Valley Lodge no 59, 1973. **Military Serv:** USN, discharged as lt sr grade. *

BUTLER, CLARY KENT
Clergy, broadcaster. **Personal:** Born Jul 5, 1948, Charleston, SC; son of Carl Dallas and Mary Capers; married Patsy Swint Butler, Sep 20, 1970; children: Tammy R, Clary K Jr, Cora L. **Educ:** SC State Col, Orangeburg, SC, BA, 1970; Webster Univ, Charleston, AFB, 1986-87. **Career:** House of God Church, pastor, 1980-89;

Berkeley Broadcasting Corp, WMCJ Radio, Monicks Corner SC, pres, 1984-. **Orgs:** Omega Psi Phi;bd mem, Amer Cancer Soc, Charleston County Br, 1985; Berkeley County Chamber Com, 1989; dir large, SC Broadcasters Asn, 1989. **Business Phone:** (803)761-9625.*

BUTLER, DOUTHARD ROOSEVELT
Educator. **Personal:** Born Oct 7, 1934, Waxahachie, TX; son of Corine McKinney and Lonnie; married Jo Jewell Ray, Dec 11, 1954; children: Douthard Jr, Carolyn, Barbara & Katherine. **Educ:** Prairie View A&M Univ, BS, 1955; Cent Mich Univ, MA, 1976; George Mason Univ, Fairfax, VA, DPA, 1992. **Career:** George Mason Univ, Fairfax, VA, grad teaching asst, 1986-88, acad coordr,1990-95, assoc athletic dir, acad resources, 1995-2003, assoc athletic dir community rels, 2003-; Fairfax Co Pub Sch Syst, VA, math teacher, 1989-90; Pa State Univ, scholar-in-residence, 1989. **Orgs:** Pres, DC Metro Chap, Prairie View A&M Univ Alumni Asn, 1978-81; pres, Prairie View A&M Univ Nat Alumni Asn, 1981-83; pres, Mt Vernon VA Rotary Club, 1987-88, 2005-06; pres, Northern VA Chap, Nat Pan Hellenic Coun, 1989-91; gov, Rotary Dist, 1993-94. **Military Serv:** AUS, col, 1955-85; Army Commendation Medal, 1964; Air Medal, 1965-66; Bronze Star, 1966; Meritorious Service Medal, 1969, 1975; Master Aviator Badge, 1971; Legion Merit, 1981, 1985; Meritorious Service Award in Mil, Nat Asn Advan Colored People, 1982. **Business Addr:** Associate Athletic Director for Community Relations, George Mason University, Intercollegiate Athletic Department, 10515 Patriot Sq, Fairfax, VA 22030, **Business Phone:** (703)993-3251.

BUTLER, DUANE
Football player. **Personal:** Born Nov 9, 1973, Trotwood, OH. **Educ:** Ill State univ, 1996. **Career:** Minn Vikings, defensive back, 1997-98; London Monarchs, NFL Europe,1998-99; Cleveland Browns, 1999-2000; Berlin Thunder, NFL Europe, defensive back, 2000-01; Tiger-Cats, defensive back, 2001-03; Montreal alouettes, line back, 2003-07; Montreal Alouettes, Currently. *

BUTLER, EUGENE THADDEUS, JR.
Educator, vice president (organization). **Personal:** Born Dec 3, 1922, Washington, DC; married Dorothy Mary Dickson; children: Eugene T. **Educ:** Modesto Jr Col, AA, 1960; Stanislaus St Col, CA, BA, 1965; SD State Univ, MEd, 1969, PhD, 1980. **Career:** Handicapped, coordr; SD St Univ, Brookings, grad res & teaching asst, 1970-73, SD St Univ Brookings, EEO compliance of Title IX, 1975. **Orgs:** Vpres & past secy, Pi Gamma Mu Local Nat Soc Sci Hon Soc, 1973; AlphaKappa Delta Nat Sociol Hon Soc Gamma Sigma Delta No Pres; Nat Agr Hon SocPhi Kappa Phi. **Honors/Awds:** Human Rights Award, Brookings Human Rights Comt, 2006. **Military Serv:** USAF, lt col, Commendation Medal, Air Medal with Oak Leaf Cluster & Good Conduct Medal & 10 Yr Combat Crew Duty Cert, 1943-70. *

BUTLER, EULA M.
Educator. **Personal:** Born Oct 15, 1927, Houston, TX; married Henry C (deceased). **Educ:** TX So Univ, BS, 1954, MED, 1958; Univ TX, Grad Study; Prairie View Univ, Educ & Psychol, Coun & Guidance; TX Southern Univ, Spec Educ, Visting Teaching-,Coun; Mount Hope Bihle Col, DM, 1984. **Career:** Region IV Educ Serv Ctr, TX Educ Agency; classroom teacher; visiting teacher, counr, first teacher certified, Head Start Prog; writing demonstr; workshop presenter; TX Southern Univ, pub rels, community, 1985-87; Sch After Sch Inc, founder, dir & educ mgr. **Orgs:** First State Co ordr Rehab & Prog Fed Female Offenders; Delta Sigma Theta Sor; comn counr, Parents & Students; YWCA Nat Coun Negro Women Top Ladies Distin; Am Judicature Soc; bd dirs, ARC mem Harris Co Grand Jury, 1974-; Harris Co bd dirs; Girl Scout bd dirs; Task Force Quality Integrate Educ Houston Independent Sch Dist; dir, SW Region Delta Sigma Theta; past pres,Houston Chap Delta Sigma Theta; Am PGA NEA TSTA Guid & coun Asn; bd mem, Nat Delta Res & Educ Found Inc, 1985-88; Visiting Nurses Asn, The Light House Houston, Nat Housing & Properties, DeltaSigma Theta, Houston Network Family Life Edu; Houston Enrichment Life Prog Inc; bd mem, Metro Teache rEduc Ctr, Volunteers Pub Sch, Houston Independent Sch Dist; 15th Regional Dir, Houston Alumnae, currently. **Honors/Awds:** Teacher Year Award, 1969; Community Leadership Award; Delta Sigma Theta Cert Appreciation; Leadership Award, United Negro Col Fund; Golden Life Member, Delta Sigma Theta Sor; Christian Service Award, Beth Baptist Church, 1985; Community Serv Award, Mt Corinth Baptist Church, 1985; School After School Award, Sch After Sch Faculty & Staff, 1985; Recognition Excellence Achievement Award, Phillis Wheatley High Sch, 1985; Black History Making Award, 1986. *

BUTLER, FREDERICK DOUGLAS
Lawyer. **Personal:** Born Nov 5, 1942, Philadelphia, PA; married Sara Vitori; children: Frederick Douglas II. **Educ:** Rutgers Univ, BA, 1974; New York Univ, MA, 1977; Univ Calif Hastings Col Law, JD, 1986. **Career:** Newark Housing Authority, dir family & community serv, 1973-80; White Plains Housing Authority, exec dir, 1980-81; Govt Trinidad & Tobago Nat Housing Authority, consult, 1984-85; Carroll Burdick & McDonough, atty, 1986-88; Petitt & Martin, atty, 1988-89; State Calif, atty, 1989-2004; arbitrator, Mediator & Neutral, 1995-; Hastings Col Law, adj prof, 2003-. **Orgs:** World Affairs Coun; Am Soc Pub Admin; Inst Real Estate Mgt; Nat Asn Housing Officials; Afro-Am Hist Soc; former pres, United Community Corp, Newark NJ, Newark Citizen's Adv Bd; Soul-House Drug Abuse Prog; NJ Col Med & Dent. **Honors/Awds:** Community Service Awards, Newark Tenants Coun, Serv Employees Int Union, Newark Cent Ward Little League, Frontiers Int; American Jurisprudence Award. **Military Serv:** USAF, A2C 4 yrs; Good Conduct Medal. **Business Addr:** Mediator, Arbitrator, Fred D Butler Esq, 50 California St Suite 1500, San Francisco, CA 94111.

BUTLER, DR. GRACE L.
College teacher. **Educ:** Xavier Univ, BS; Northwestern Univ, MM; NY Univ, PhD. **Career:** Univ Houston, Educ Leadership & Cult Studies, prof emer, currently. **Orgs:** Pub mem, Exec Coun Physical Therapy & Occup Therapy Examiners. **Business Addr:** Professor Emeritus, Educational Leadership & Cultural Studies, University of Houston, 4800 Calhoun Rd, Houston, TX 77004.*

BUTLER, J. RAY
Clergy. **Personal:** Born Aug 5, 1923, Roseboro, NC; son of Amos Delonzo and Mary Francis Cooper; married Marion Lucas Butler, Dec 1943; children: Charles Ervin, Ellis Ray, Larry Davis, Vincent Recardo. **Educ:** Shaw Univ, BA, BD, Master Divinity, 1974, DD, 1973; Friendship Col, DD, 1966; Southeastern Theol Sem, 1967; McKinley Theol Sem, Doctor Laws, 1976; Southeastern Theol Sem DTh, 1969; Tri County Col & Sem, Maxton, NC, DMin, 1999. **Career:** Ebenezer Baptist Church Wilmington, pastor, 1954-70; First Baptist Church Creeddmoor, pastor; Mt Olive Baptist Church Fayeteville, pastor; New Christian Chapel Baptist Church RoseHill, pastor; Shiloh Baptist Church Winston Salem, pastor, 1970-90; United Cornerstone Baptist Church, founder, pastor. **Orgs:** Past pres, Interdenom Ministerial All; past pres, Interracieal Minister Asn; past pres, Wilmington Civic League; past pres, PTA; life mem, 1st vpres, NAACP; bd dir, ARC; Man Power Delvelop; Citizens Coalition Bd; presat large Gen Baptist State Conv; pres, Baptist Ministers Conf & Assoc; Forsyth Clergy Asn Chmn Gen Baptist St Conv NC Inc; extension teaching staff Shaw Univ; exec bd, Lott Carey Baptist Foreign Missions & Conv; appointed bd, licensed gen contractors Gov Jim Hunt NC; founder, Shilohian & St Peters Day Care; moderator, Rowan Baptist Missionary Asn, 1989-; life mem, Alpha Phi Alphi Fraternity. **Honors/Awds:** Various tours foreign countries; Pastor of Year Award, Midwestern Baptist Laymen's Fellowship Chicago, 1975, 1976; elected, Contbng Writer Nat Baptist Sunday Sch Pub Bd; author, The Christian Commun Related Jewish Passover & Monetary Commitment, 1985; From Playtime Pulpit Serv; The Chronicles Lifetime Achievers, 1998. *

BUTLER, JACK. See BUTLER, JOHN GORDON.

BUTLER, JEROME M.
Lawyer. **Personal:** Born Jul 15, 1944, Chicago, IL; married Jean Brothers. **Educ:** Fisk Univ, BA, 1966; Columbia Univ, JD, 1969. **Career:** Tucker Watson Butler & Todd, atty; Chicago Housing Auth Gen, Coun Off, atty, currently. **Orgs:** Cook County Chicago Bar Asns. **Business Addr:** Attorney, Chicago Housing Authority General, Counsel Office, 200 W Adams Suite 2100, Chicago, IL 60606-5230.

BUTLER, JERRY
County commissioner, singer. **Personal:** Born Dec 8, 1939, Sunflower County, MS; son of Jerry Sr and Arvelia Agnew; married Annette Smith, Jun 21, 1959; children: Randall Allen & Anthony Ali. **Educ:** Governors State Univ, BS, political sci, MA, criminal Justice studies. **Career:** Album: The Power of Love, Mercury, 1973; Sweet Sixteen, Mercury, 1974; Love's on the Menu, Motown, 1976; Suite for the Single Girl, Motown, 1977; Nothing Says I Love You Like I Love You, Philadelphia International, 1978; Best Love I Ever Had, Philadelphia Int, 1981; Ice 'n' Hot, Fountain, 1982; The Best of Jerry Butler, Rhino, 1987; Iceman: The Mercury Years, Mercury, 1992; Time & Faith, Ichiban, 1993; Jerry Butler Prod, Chicago, IL, owner, 1960-; Iceman Beverage Co, Chicago, IL, chief exec officer, 1984-89; Cook County, IL, comnr, 1985-; Chicago City, alderman. **Orgs:** Chicago Chap, Nat Asn Advan Colored People; N Star Lodge No 1 FAM PHA 33 degree; Groove Phi Groove Fel; bd dirs, Firman Comm Serv; vpres, Northern Ill Planning Comn, 1990; Alpha Phi Alpha; Rhythm & Blues Found; grand lectr, MWPHGL, State Ill & Jurisdiction, 1997; pres, Northeastern Ill Planning Comn, 1997. **Honors/Awds:** Musical Composition Citation Achievement, Broadcast Music, 1960, 1970; 3 Grammy Nominations; Song of the Yer, 1969; Clio Award Advert, 1972; Ceba Award Advert, 1983; Mason of the Year Award, Prince Hall Grand Lodge Ill, 1989; Valuable Research Award, Chicago Pub Schs; Elected Rock Hall of Fame, 1991. **Special Achievements:** more than 50 albums. **Business Addr:** City Commissioner, Cook County, 118 N Clark St Rm 567, Chicago, IL 60602, **Business Phone:** (312)603-6391.

BUTLER, JOHN GORDON (JACK BUTLER)
Management consultant, association executive. **Personal:** Born Apr 23, 1942, Pittsburgh, PA; son of John Donald and Marjorie Johnson; married Veronica Claypool, Sep 12, 2005; married Leslie Hansel, Sep 15, 1963 (divorced 1976); children: John Mason. **Educ:** Harvard Col, BA, econ, 1963; Harvard Grad Sch Bus Admin, MBA, 1966; Graduate Mgt Inst, Union Col, 1987. **Career:** Carver Fed Savings, admin asst, 1963-64; Mobil Intl Oil Co, fin analyst, 1966-68; Univ Nairobi, Kenya, lectr, 1968-69; Kaiser-Aetna Partnership, dir investment anal, 1970-71; Kiambere Ltd, Nairobi, Kenya, managing dir, 1971-83; consult, Bomas Kenya Cult Village, 1972-73; dir, Kiambere Bldg Soc, 1975-83; African Develop Group, assoc, 1979-82; State Univ NY, vis prof, 1983-85; NY African Am Inst, fel, 1986-88; John Butler Assoc, principal, 1987-; Partnership to Strengthen African Grassroots Org Inc, exec dir, secy & treas, 1998-. **Orgs:** Alpha Phi Alpha Fraternity, 1960; Village New Paltz Planning Bd, 1984-88; New Paltz Democratic Comm, 1987-88; treas, Harvard Bus Sch African-Am Alumni Asn, 1987-97, dir, 1997-; Muranderera Asn, 2005-. **Business Addr:** Executive Director, Secretary, Partnership to Strengthen African Grassroots Organizations Inc, 2 Old Mill Rd, New York, NY 12561, **Business Phone:** (845)255-1319.

BUTLER, JOHN O.
Executive. **Personal:** Born Nov 28, 1926, Bristol, TN; son of Pinkney and Olivia J; married Marjorie M Jackson; children: Deborah, David, Brian & Bruce. **Educ:** Howard Univ, BS, Mech Engineering, 1950. **Career:** GE Co, design engr, 1950-57; Raytheon Co, mgr indus engr, 1958-64; GTE Sylvania Inc, dir value engr, 1965-68; Deerfield Corp, founder & pres. **Orgs:** Registered prof engr MA; MA Bus Asn; Tau Beta Pi Engrg Hon Soc, 1952; cooperator, Framingham Union Hosp; Rotary Int; Twn Repub Com; Nat Soc Prof Engrs; comnr MA Gov's Exec Coun Value Analysis, 1966-72; comnr, Framingham Housing Auth; dir, Framingham Regional YMCA, 1971-75. **Military Serv:** AUS, tech fifth grade, 1944-46. *

BUTLER, DR. JOHN SIBLEY
Educator. **Personal:** Born Jul 19, 1947, New Orleans, LA; son of Johnnie Mae Sibley Butler and Thojest Jefferson Butler; married Rosemary Griffey, Oct 20, 1972; children: John Sibley. **Educ:** La State Univ, Baton Rouge, LA, BA, 1969; Northwestern Univ, Evanston, IL, MA, 1971, PhD, 1974. **Career:** Nat Ctr Neighborhood Enterprise, res fel, 1989-; Univ Tex, Dep Sociol, grad adv, 1978-81, African & Afro-American Res Ctr, interim dir, 1990-91, 1992, Centennial Prof Sociol, 1990-99, Arthur James Douglass Centennial Prof Entrepreneurship, 1991-, Sam Barshop Centennial Fel, 1992-, Dept Sociol, chair, 1992-96, Dept Mgt, chair, 1999-, Gale Chair Small Bus & Entrepreneurship, 1999-; State Farm Insurance, Southwest, mgt consult, 1990; Nissan N American Lectr, 1995; Aoyama Gakuin Univ, vis distinguished prof, 1996-99. **Orgs:** Pres, La St Univ, Alumni Asn, Austin, 1988-91; pres, Am Asn Black Sociologists, 1980-81; mem, Sigma Pi Phi (Boule); mem, Kappa Alpha Psi; mem, Omicron Nu; mem, Phi Delta Kappa; US Asn Small Bus & Entrepreneurship; Southwestern Sociol Asn; Inter Univ Seminar Armed Forces & Soc; Southern Sociol Asn. **Honors/Awds:** Alpha Kappa Delta Teaching Excellence Award, 1978; Teaching Excellence Award, A.K.D., Univ Texas Chapter, 1978; The Eyes of Texas Award, 1985;The Dallas TACA Centennial Professorship, Univ Texas, 1990; Distinguished Scholar Award, Am Asn Black Sociologists, 1992; WEB Dubois Excellence Research Award, Austin Independent School District. 1995. **Military Serv:** AUS, Enlisted Five, 1969-71; received: Bronze Star for Combat Valor, Vietnam, 1970. **Business Addr:** Director, University Texas, Herb Kelleher Center for Entrepreneurship & the IC2 Institute, 1 Univ Sta Stop B6300, Austin, TX 78712, **Business Phone:** (512)471-4788.

BUTLER, JOHNNELLA E.
Educator. **Personal:** Born Feb 28, 1947, Roanoke, VA. **Educ:** Col Our Lady Elms, BA, 1968; Johns Hopkins Univ, MA, 1969; Univ Mass Amherst, EdD, 1979. **Career:** Johns Hopkins Univ, Ford Found fel, 1968-69; Towson State Univ, instr,1970-84; Smith Col, instr, 1974-79, asst prof, 1979-81, assoc prof tenure,Dept Afro-Am Studies, instr, 1974-76, asst to dean, 1976-77, dept chair, 1977-79; Mt Holyoke Col, Womens Studies Dept, vis lectr, 1984; Univ Wash Seattle, Dept Afro-Am Studies, Grad Sch, prof, assoc dean & assoc vice provost am ethnic studies, 1988-2004; Spelman Col, provost & vpres acad affairs, currently. **Orgs:** Chair, 5 Col Black Studies Exec Comt, Towson State Univ, 1978-79; brd trustees, Col Our Lady Elms, 1984-89; consult, Womens Studies Prog, UnivIll Champagne-Urbana, 1984; Racism & Sexism, Patterson Col, 1984; Black Women Am Lit, Univ Ill, DeKalb, 1984; Black Studies & Womens Studies, Carleton Col, 1984; Wellesley Ctr Res Women, 1984; Drew Univ, Fac Develop Workshop, 1984. **Honors/Awds:** Award, Cazenovia Inst, 1971; Smithsonian Conference Scholarship, Black Scholars & Black Studies, 1983; Charles C Irby Distinguished Service Award, Natl Assn Ethnic Studies. **Special Achievements:** First Black woman to receive tenure at Smith College; author of "Studies &the Liberal Arts Tradition Through the Discipline of Afro-Amer Literature", University Press of America, 1981, "Toward a Pedagogy of Every woman's Studies", Minority Womens Studies, "Do We Want To Kill a Dream" Int Women Studies Quarterly, 1984. **Business Addr:** Provost, Vice President of Academic Affairs, Spelman College, Rm 112 Rockefeller Hall 350 Spelman Lane SW, Atlanta, GA 30314-4399, **Business Phone:** (404)681-3643.

BUTLER, JOYCE M
Marketing executive. **Personal:** Born Jun 12, 1941, Gary, IN; daughter of Robert W Porter and Dorothy Paige Porter; married

Mitchell, Jun 13, 1965; children: Stephanie Lynn & Adam Mitchell. **Educ:** Wright Col, Chicago, Ill, AA, 1963; DePaul Univ, Chicago, Ill, BA, urban planning, 1976, MS, mgt pub servs, 1980. **Career:** Loop Col, Chicago, Ill, admin asst, 1963-78; City Chicago, Dept Planning, Chicago, Ill, city planner, 1978-83, Mayor's Off Inquiry & Info, Chicago, Ill, prog mgr, 1983-88, dir prog serv, 1988-89; Michel Mkt, vpres, 1989-, City Col Chicago, Kennedy King Col, stud serv advisor, currently. **Orgs:** Operation PUSH, 1972-; Nat Forum Black Pub Adminr, 1985-; Soc Govt Meeting Planners, 1988-; Nat Asn Female Exec, 1989; Publicity Club Chicago, 1989. **Honors/Awds:** Paul Cornell Award, Hyde Pk Hist Soc, 1986. **Home Addr:** 11206 S Eggleston Ave, Chicago, IL 60628. **Business Phone:** (773)602-5037.

BUTLER, KATHLEEN JEAN
Librarian. **Personal:** Born Aug 8, 1967, Philadelphia, PA; daughter of William Deloatch and Elizabeth; married Tracey J Hunter Hayes, Jul 26, 1992; children: Jalaal A Hayes & Makkah I Hayes. **Educ:** Lincoln Univ, PA, BA, 1989; Cheyney Univ, PA, MEd, 1991; Univ Pittsburgh, MLS, 1992. **Career:** Sch Dist Philadelphia, teacher, 1989-91, sch librarian, 1996-; Ky State Univ, Curriculum Instructional Media Ctr, head, 1993-95; Southern IL Univ, educ/psychol librarian, 1995-. **Orgs:** Am Library Asn, 1991-; Black Caucus Am Library Asn, 1991-; Kappa Delta Pi Nat Honor Soc, 1991-; Ky Asn Blacks Higher Educ, 1994-97; chair, Bookfair Comt, 1996-; Asn Pub Sch Library, 1996-; Building Comt, Sch Dist Philadelphia, 1999-; pres, Parent Council, Sch Dist Philadelphia, 1999-. **Honors/Awds:** National Honor Society Award, Kappa Delta Pi, 1991. **Special Achievements:** Publication: "A View of the Academic Curriculum and Instructional Media Library Center in Educating Future Elementary School Teachers: An Analysis and Bibliography", Multicultural Review, 3 (4), Dec 1994; The Annual Fall Teachers Conference, workshop presenter, Oct 1994. **Home Phone:** (215)232-4262.

BUTLER, KEITH ANDRE
Government official, clergy. **Personal:** Born Nov 22, 1955, Detroit, MI; son of Robert L and Ida L Jackson; married Deborah Lorraine Bell, May 31, 1975; children: Keith Andre II, Michelle Andrea & Kristina Maria. **Educ:** Oakland Community Col, attended 1974; Eastern Mich Univ, Ypsilanti, MI, attended 1985; Univ Mich, Dearborn, MI, attended 1987; Univ London, NW, DDiv, 1988. **Career:** Word Faith Int christian ctr, Detroit, MI, founder & pastor, 1979-, bishop, currently; Word Faith Chrsitian Ctr, founder, 2008-. **Orgs:** Detroit Econ Develop Plan; adv bd, Henry Ford Hosp Care Prog, 1987; corp bd, Holy Cross Hosp; bd trustees, Metrop Youth Found; Alliance Against Casino Gambling Detroit; bd dirs, Mich Cancer Found, 1992; bd dirs, Teach Mich, 1992; Vision Faith Christian Acad; city coun mem, City Detroit, Detroit, MI. **Honors/Awds:** Five Outstanding Young People Mich, 1988; Ten Outstanding Americans Award, 1989. **Business Phone:** (248)353-3476.

BUTLER, LEROY
Football player. **Personal:** Born Jul 19, 1968, Jacksonville, FL; son of Eunice Butler; children: Sharon, L'Oreal & Gabrielle. **Educ:** Fla State Univ. **Career:** Football (retired); Green Bay Packers, defensive back, 1990-01. **Orgs:** Founder, LeRoy butler found. **Honors/Awds:** Prep All-America, 1985; All-Decade Team, 1990s; AP and UPI All-America, Florida St Univ, 1989; first team pro bowl All-Pro, 1993, 1996, 1997. *

BUTLER, MARJORIE JOHNSON
Educator. **Personal:** Born May 18, 1911, Oberlin, OH; daughter of Frank and Mary Jane Jones; divorced; children: Beverly Lavergneau, John G & Richard. **Educ:** Oberlin Col, AB, 1930; Ohio State Univ, MA, 1934; Univ Pittsburgh, PhD, 1965. **Career:** Educator (retired); WVa State Col, instr, 1930-31; Prairie View State Col, 1931-37; Sumner High Sch, teacher 1937-40; 5th Ave High Sch, 1955-58; Pittsburgh Pub Sch, psychologist, 1959-62; Univ Pittsburgh, instr, 1961-65; State Univ NY, asst prof, 1965-67, assoc prof, 1967-70, prof, 1970-85; Vasser Col, part-time prof, 1971. **Orgs:** Am Psychol Asn; NY State Psychol Asn; Asn Study Afro-Am Life & Hist; African Heritage Study Asn. **Honors/Awds:** Alpha Kappa Alpha Sorority; Psi Chi; Pi Lambda Theta; Delta Kappa Gamma Hon Sorority. **Special Achievements:** Author: "Criteria for creativity in counseling", 1965. **Home Addr:** 3 Field Sparrow Ct, Hilton Head Island, SC 29926.

BUTLER, MAX R.
Clergy, teacher. **Personal:** Born Jul 10, 1912, St Francisville, LA; married Leona Hickman; children: Angele B (Evans). **Educ:** New Orleans Univ, AB, BD, 1935; Inter-Baptist Theol Sem, DD, 1972. **Career:** Methodist Church, pastor, 1933-74; Adult Educ, teacher, supv & parish dir, 1937-41; US, letter carrier, 1941-70; chem mgf, 1946-74; Philips & Memi United Methodist Church, pastor. **Orgs:** Vpres, Dillard Univ Alumni Asn, 1956; asst secy, LA Annual Conf, United Methodist Church, 1968-71; mem adv coun, Hist & Cult Preserv Bd, 1973; Nat Asn Adv Colored People; Nat Urban League; 32 degrees Prince Hall Mason, New Orleans, LA. **Honors/Awds:** Hon Attorney Gen LA, 1973; New Orleans Second Most Popular Citizen, 1937; Boy Scout Leadership Award, 1973. *

BUTLER, MELBA
Executive. **Personal:** Born Apr 18, 1954, New York, NY; daughter of Martin and Juanita Jones; children: Thomas Martin, Sean David Hamilton. **Educ:** Northeastern Univ, Boston, MA, 1973; Long Island Univ, New York, NY, BA, psychol, 1975; Columbia Univ, New York, NY, MS, social work, 1979; Univ State New York, cert social worker. **Career:** St Joseph C Servs, caseworker, 1975; Queens Family Ct, Jamaica, NY, probation intern, 1977-78; Woodside Senior Asst Ctr, Woodside, NY, asst to dir, 1978-79; Madison Square Boys Club, New York, NY, asst to dir, 1978-79; Sr Counr State Communities & Aid, proj dir, 1979-82; New York City Bd Educ, New York, NY, sch social worker, 1983-84; Brooklyn Col Women's Ctr, Brooklyn, NY, volunteer supvr, 1983-84; Pub Mgt Systs Inc, New York, NY, consult & trainer, 1984-86; Harlem Dowling-Westside Ctr C & Family Servs, New York, NY, dep dir, 1984-90, LMSW, exec dir; Enter Inc, consult & supvr, 1989-90. **Orgs:** Vice chmn, Adv Comt, Urban Women's Shelter, 1986-88; Nat Asn Social Workers; Nat Black Child Develop Inst, 1986-; Black Agency Execs; bd dirs, Coun Family & Child Caring Agencies; bd pres, Harlem Community, Inc. *

BUTLER, MICHAEL E
Editor. **Personal:** Born Jul 14, 1950, New York, NY; son of Bernard E Butler Jr and Myrtle Martin; married Eileen Payne, Oct 10, 1982. **Educ:** Pace Univ, NYC, BBA, 1972; Univ CA, Berkeley, MPH, 1974. **Career:** NY City Health & Hosps Corp, asso exec dir, 1975-80; NYS Comt Health Educ & Illness Prvntn, exec dir, 1980-81; Comt Family Planning Coun, exec dir, 1981-82; NY State Div Youth, regional dir, NY City Health & Hosps Corp, asso exec dir, 1975-80; NYS Comt Health Educ & Illness Prvntn, exec dir, 1980-81; Comt Family Planning Coun, exec dir, 1981-82; NY State Div Youth, regional dir, NYC; Exec Health Group, vice pres; Lowe McAdams Healthcare, ed, 1991-97; Harrison & Star, mgr ed serv, 1997-2000; Falk Healthcare, dir ed serv, 2000-01. **Orgs:** Am Health Asn, Blue Cross Asn, 1974-75; 100 Black Men, 1977-85; bd dir, Pace Univ, Alumni Asn, 1983-86; Pace Univ, Bd Educ Plcs Comn, 1984-86. **Honors/Awds:** Outstanding Young Men of Am; US Jaycees, 1978; Trustees Award, Pace Univ, 1972. **Home Addr:** 624 E 20th Apt 4C, New York, NY 10009, **Home Phone:** (212)533-0197.

BUTLER, MICHAEL KEITH
Surgeon, college teacher, chief executive officer. **Personal:** Born Aug 29, 1955, Baton Rouge, LA; son of ildred Alexander and Felton Earl; married Marian Thompson Butler, Feb 10, 1990; children: Ebony Bolden, Yashica Bolden. **Educ:** Amherst Col, BA, 1976; Tulane Univ, Sch Med, MD, 1980, Sch Pub Health, MHA, 1990. **Career:** S La Med Assocs, gen surgeon, 1986-95; LSU Sch Med, chief admin officer, 1995-96; La Health Care Authority, med dir, 1996-; LSU Hosp, La Healt Care Serv Div, actg chief exec officer & prof surg, currently. **Orgs:** Fel Am Col Surgeons, 1989; Am Col Physician Exec, 1990; Am Bd Quality Assurance Utilization Rev Physicians, 1994; Am Bd Med Mgt; Am Soc Gen Surgeons; La Surg Asn; Nat Med Asn; Nat Asn Health Serv Exec. **Home Addr:** 1978 Indust Blvd, Houma, LA 70364, **Home Phone:** (985)873-1265. **Business Addr:** Professor, Acting Chief Executive Officer, LSU Hospital, Health Care Serv Div, 8550 United Plaza Blvd 4th Floor, Baton Rouge, LA 70809, **Business Phone:** (225)922-0488.*

BUTLER, MITCHELL LEON
Basketball player. **Personal:** Born Dec 15, 1970, Los Angeles, CA. **Educ:** Univ Calif, Los Angeles, commun, 1993. **Career:** Basketball player (retired); Wash Bullets, guard, 1993-96; Portland TrailBlazers, 1996-97, 2002; Cleveland Cavaliers, 1998-99; Wash Wizards, guard & forward, 2004; Denver Nuggets, guard. **Orgs:** Mitchell Butler Found; co chair, Fannie Mae Found. **Special Achievements:** Film appearances: Blue Chips, 1994; "Rebound: The Legend of Earl 'The Goat' Manigault," 1996.

BUTLER, OLIVER RICHARD
Executive, vice president (organization), executive director. **Personal:** Born Jul 3, 1941, New Orleans, LA; son of Richard M and Rose M Desvignes; married Naurine M Jackson; children: Janee, Eric & Shann. **Educ:** Xavier Univ LA, BS, Pharm, 1962; Univ IL Polk, St Campus, Grad Course Org Chem, 1968; Univ New Orleans, Grad Bus Courses, 1977. **Career:** Walgreen Co Chicago, store mgr & pharmacist, 1962-69; Bruxelles Pharm, store owner, 1970-73; Ayerst Labs, sales positions, 1974-78, dist mgr, 1978-83, asst field sales mgr, 1983-84, dir sales opers, 1984-88; Wyeth-Ayerst Labs (all divisions), sales admin, exec dir, 1988-91, asst vp, 1991-. **Orgs:** New Orleans Comm/Human Rels, 1970; exec comt, LA High Blood Pressure Prog, 1978; guest lectr, Xavier Univ Med Tech Dept, 1978-81; adv bd, Food/Drug Admin, 1979; vpres, Ursuline Acad, 1979-80; treas, Acro I Gymnastic Club, 1981-82; pharm dean search comt, Xavier Univ Col & Pharm, 1981-82; adv comt, Xavier Univ Col Pharm 1982-; Apothecary Bd Visitors, Fla A&M Col Pharm, 1990-93; Ad Hoc Comt Sampling, pharmaceut Mfr Asn, 1990-93; Philadelphia Credit Alliance Drug Educ, 1992. **Honors/Awds:** Achievement Award, Rexall Drug Co, 1962; Man of the Year, Chi Delta Mu Fraternity, 1969. **Business Addr:** Assistant Vice President, Wyeth-Ayerst Labs, 555 E Lancaster Ave, Radnor, PA 19087, **Business Phone:** (610)971-5552.

BUTLER, PATRICK HAMPTON
Lawyer, executive. **Personal:** Born Jul 24, 1933, Gonzales, TX; married Barbara; children: Daphne & Ann Marie. **Educ:** Colo Col, BA, 1956; Univ Colo Sch Law, JD, 1961. **Career:** Fed Trade & Comn, 1961-62; US Dept Justice, trial atty, 1962-65; US Dept Labor, spec asst, 1965-66; Ind Univ, asst prof, law, 1966-68; Eli Lilly & Co, asst coun. **Orgs:** Bd govs, Indianapolis Bar Asn, 1972-74. **Military Serv:** AUS, First lt, 1958.

BUTLER, PINKNEY L.
Government official, city manager, founder (originator). **Personal:** Born May 3, 1948, Greensboro, NC; son of James and Louise Alexander Thompson; married Mary Green Butler, Nov 4, 1972; children: Monecia, Patrick, Prentice. **Educ:** Southwestern Christian, Terrell, AA, 1969; Pepperdine Univ, Los Angeles, BA, 1971; Corpus Christi State Univ, MA, 1980. **Career:** Government official (retired), founder; City Victoria, TX, exec dir & dep community affairs, 1974-77; Nueces County Adult Probation, Corpus Christi, TX, adult probation officer, 1977-78; City Corpus Christi, TX, admin asst, 1978-83; City Tyler, TX, asst city mgr, 1983-97, city mgr, 1997; Better World Sounds, founder, 1992-. **Orgs:** Officer, E Tex City Mgr Asn, 1983-; Int City Mgr Asn, 1983-; Nat Forum Black Pub Admin, 1986; comt person, Tex City Mgr Asn, 1987-. **Business Addr:** Founder, Better World Sounds, PO Box 9903, Tyler, TX 75711, **Business Phone:** (903)372-1415.*

BUTLER, DR. REBECCA BATTS
Educator, founder (originator). **Personal:** Born in Norfolk, VA; daughter of William and Gussie Batts. **Educ:** Glassboro State Col, BS, 1942; Temple Univ, MEd, 1958. **Career:** Camden Pub Schs, elem teacher, 1937-51, supvr guidance, 1966-68; Adult-Voc-Community Progs Camden Schs, 1969-74; Camden Sec Eng Sch, teacher, 1951-59; NJ State Dept Educ, teacher, 1968-69; Glassboro State Col, adj prof; Sch Unwed Mothers, founder, currently; Spanish High Sch Equivalency Prog, founder; Adult Family Ctr Components Camden Pub Sch, founder. **Orgs:** Dir, Adult Cont Educ NANPW; asst chmn, Comn Teacher Educ Asn; nated-in-chief, KRINON Nat Sorority Phi Delta Kappa, 1972-76; bd mem,Trustees & Thomas A Edison Col, 1973-75; Nat Asn Negro Bus & Prof Women, 1974-98; Philadelphia Fel House; organizer & chmn, Comm Educ Chestnut StUAME Church; Civil Def Counc Camden City; exec bd, Camden County Red Cross; mem exec bd, Vis Nurses Asn; pres, Asn Negro Bus & Prof Women Camden & Vicinity; panel men, Unites Fund; mem bd dir, Mary H Thomas Nursery; chmn, Nat Adv Com Comm Servs Am Asn Retired Persons, 1978-80; natbd dir, AARP, 1980; particant, White House Briefing Women, 1980. **Honors/Awds:** Bishop Award, 1954; Mae S Moore Award, Nat Asn Bus & Prof Women Camden & Vicin, 1964; Chapel of the Four Chaplains, 1964; Outstanding Citizen Award, Awards Comm Ninth Annual Observ Tenth St Baptist Church, 1966; Outstanding Citizen of the Year, Goodwill Ind, 1972; Education of Year, Oppty Indn Cent, 1972; Cited as Adult Education of Year, Adult Educ NJ, 1973; Citation Spanish, Spkg Commun Camden, 1974; Citation Camden, Bd Educ, 1974; Volunteer of the Year, Elks Camden 1976; Outstanding Citizen Afro-American, Life & History Camden County, 1977; Nat Achievement Award & National Program Award, Adult Cont Educ NABPW Clubs Inc, 1977; Sojourner Truth Award, Camden B&P Club, 1977; Woman of the Year Award, Zeta Phi Beta1977; International Poetry Hall of Fame, 1998; Received over 50 plaques & citations. **Special Achievements:** Poem: "My Thoughts I Write", A Book of Poems, 1990. **Business Addr:** Director, Founder, School Unwed Mothers, 201 N Front St, Camden, NJ 08102, **Business Phone:** (856)966-2000.

BUTLER, REX L
Lawyer. **Personal:** Born Mar 24, 1951, New Brunswick, NJ. **Educ:** Fla Jr Col, AA, 1975; Univ N Fla, BA, 1977; Howard Univ Sch Law, Wash, DC, JD, 1983. **Career:** Howard Univ Sch Law, teaching asst, 1981-83; State Alaska, Atty Gen's Office, asst atty gen, 1984 -85; Anchorage Community Col, adj prof, 1985; Rex Lamont Butler & Assocs Inc, atty, 1985-; Univ Alaska Anchorage, adj prof, 1990-. **Orgs:** Anchorage Bar Asn, 1983-; Asn Trial Lawyers Am, 1984-; Am Bar Asn, 1985-; Nat Bar Asn, 1986-; Nat Asn Criminal Defense Lawyers, 1986-; Mt. KcKinley Lion's Int, 1989-; Eagle River Missionary Baptist Church, 1997-; life mem, Nat Asn Advan Colored People; Omega Psi Phi; Phi Alpha Delta; Phi Theta Kappa. **Honors/Awds:** Who's Who Among Students in American Cols and Universities, 1978; Outstanding Young Men of America, 1984; Featured in Black Enterprise Mag, 1984; Certificate of Appreciation, Anchorage Equal Rights Comn, 1987; Public Service Award, Major Tony Knowles, 1987; Martin Luther King, Jr. Community Service Award, 1987. **Business Addr:** Attorney, Rex Lamont Butler & Associates Inc., 745 W 4th Ave Suite 300, Anchorage, AK 99501-2136, **Business Phone:** (907)272-1497.

BUTLER, ROSALIND MARIE
School administrator. **Personal:** Born Feb 19, 1955, Detroit, MI; daughter of Booker Dennis and Marion Riddick; married Rev Charles W Butler, Apr 2; children: Keith M Curry. **Educ:** Eastern Mich Univ, BS, 1976; Wayne State Univ, MEd, 1993. **Career:** Detroit Pub Schs, teacher, 1976-86, Title 1 Reading Support, 1986-97, staff coordr, 1997, ast prin; Rose Elem Sch, prin, currently. **Orgs:** Asn Supv & Curriculum Develop; Int Reading Asn; Metrop Reading Asn; Black Female Adminr Network, 1997; Detroit Orgn Sch Adminr & Supv. **Honors/Awds:** Educator's Achievement Award, Booker T Wash Bus Asn, 1997. **Business**

Addr: Principal, Detroit Public School, Rose Elemenatry, 5830 Field St, Detroit, MI 48213, **Business Phone:** (313)852-3400.*

BUTLER, ROY
Manager. **Personal:** Born Jun 24, 1949, Tyler, TX; son of Roy and Gertha McClendon; married May 15, 1976 (divorced 1989); children: Stephen & Shannon. **Educ:** Univ Colo, Boulder, CO, BSCE, 1975. **Career:** Western Slope Gas Co, Denver, CO, eng tech, 1970-74, spec proj engr, 1974-76; Sun Pipe Line Co, Tulsa, OK, sr pipeline engr, 1976-78, Seminole, OK, mgr field eng, 1978-80, gen foreman maintenance & opers, 1980-83, Drumright, OK, gen foreman maintenance & opers, 1980-83, Tulsa, OK, mgr bus opers, 1987-. **Home Addr:** 1909 N 24th W Ave, Tulsa, OK 74127-2252, **Home Phone:** (918)582-2846. **Business Addr:** Manager, Sun Pipe Line Co, Rm 1119 907 S Detroit St, Tulsa, OK 74120, **Business Phone:** (918)586-6943.*

BUTLER, TONIA PAULETTE
Educator, nurse. **Personal:** Born Jun 5, 1970, Florence, AL; daughter of Paul Hamilton and Madgie Hill; married James Spencer, Jan 6, 1996; children: Kesley & Kayla. **Educ:** Northwest Shoals Community Col, LPN, 1991, AAS, 1993, ADN, 1995; Univ N Ala, BSN, 1995; Univ Ala, MSN, nursing admin, 1998, post MSN nurse practitioner, 1999. **Career:** Glenwood Nursing Home, 1992-97; EMC Hosp, intensive care unit, regist nurse, 1997-98; Sunrise Muscle Shoals, asst dir nursing, 1998, dir nursing, 1998-99; Huntsville Hosp, regist nurse, critical care, 1999-2000, nurse practitioner, 2000-; Calhoun Community Col, nursing instr, 2000-. **Honors/Awds:** First place, poster presentation, "Laser Eye Oximetry", Ala State Nursing Asn, 1999. **Business Addr:** Nursing Instructor, Calhoun Community College, PO Box 2216, Decatur, AL 35609, **Business Phone:** (256)306-2500.

BUTLER, WASHINGTON ROOSEVELT, JR.
Manager, activist, educator. **Personal:** Born Jan 5, 1933, New Orleans, LA; son of Washington R Sr (deceased) and Althea Landry (deceased); divorced; children: Landry, Luthuli & Leiah. **Educ:** Clark Col, BS, 1953; Univ Tenn Knoxville, MA, 1964; ABD, 1965; Trevecca Nazarene Univ, orgn mgt, MAOM, 2001. **Career:** Urban & Fed Affairs State Tenn, comnr, 1975-79; Riverside Hosp Nashville, Tenn, vpres, 1981-83; self-empl Madison, Tenn, develop consult; Advan Innovative Technol Inc, pres, 1987-94; Vol State Community Col, adj instr, 1990-91; Hunan Col Finance & Econ, Changsha, Hunan, People's Republic China, eng instr, 1993-94; Olsten Staffing Serv, temp data processor, 1994; Participant Serv Rep, BT Serv Tenn Inc, 1994-96; Technical Writer, Bankers Trust Co, 1996-97; MetLife Co, oper rep, 1998-99; Robert J Young Co, 1999-2001; State Tenn, disabilities claims examr, 2001-; Yancheng Teacher?s Col, prof, currently. **Orgs:** Bd dir, Oakwood Col Huntsville, Ala, 1977-82; bd dir Riverside Hosp Nashville, Tenn, 1975-81; former secy, treas, bd mem, Nat Asn Comm Develop; former bd mem, Southeastern Reg Asn Comm Action Agencies; electd two four-yr terms City Coun Oak Ridge, Tenn; served Oak Ridge Reg Planning Comn; Oak Ridge Beer Bd; Anderson Co Citizens Welfare Adv Bd; former mem, Agricultural Ext Comn; bd dir, Memphis Opport Indust Ctr; Nat Bus League Memphis Chap; former pres, Memphis Inter-Alumni Coun United Negro Col Fund; AARP; Am Legion; candidate, nom Gov Dem Primary, 1974; Former First Elder Riverside Chapel Seventh-day Adventist Ch Nashville, Tenn; Former chmn, Bldg Comm FH Jenkins Elem Sch; candidate, Tenn Pub Serv Comn, 1985; candidate, Metro Coun Large, 1986. **Honors/Awds:** Beta Kappa Chi Nat Hon Sci Soc. **Special Achievements:** First black man to run for governor of Tenn. **Military Serv:** AUS, USAREUR Command spec e-4, 1953-56; USAR, 5 yrs. **Home Addr:** 1017 S Graycroft Ave, Madison, TN 37115. *

BUTLER-BUSH, TONIA
Government official. **Career:** White House, Off Commun, Stud Correspondence, dep dir, staff asst dir. **Business Phone:** (202)456-1414.

BUTTERFIELD, G.K.
Congressperson (U.S. federal government). **Personal:** Born in; children: Valeisha, Lenai. **Educ:** North Carolina Central University, Political Science and Sociology; North Carolina Central University, JD, 1974. **Career:** Lawyer; Resident Superior Court Judge, 1988; North Carolina Supreme Court Member, 2001-2002; Member of the US House of Representatives, 2004. **Orgs:** Energy and Commerce Committee. **Special Achievements:** Chief Deputy Whip. **Military Serv:** US Army, personnel specialist. **Business Addr:** 413 Cannon House Office Building, Washington, DC 20515, **Business Phone:** (202)225-3101.*

BUTTERFIELD, TORRIS JERREL
Lawyer. **Personal:** Born Nov 14, 1971, Miami, FL; son of Thomas and Margaret Cason; married Kimley Butterfield, Jun 24, 1995; children: Nadia & Jared. **Educ:** Fort Valley State Col, BA, eng, 1993; Mercer Univ, Walter F George Sch Law, JD, 1997. **Career:** Fulton County Public Defender's Off, sr staff atty, 1997-; Torris J Butterfield & Assoc; TJB Recovery Syst LLC, pres & chief exec officer, currently. **Orgs:** Ga Asn Criminal Defense Lawyers, 1998-; juvenile law comt, 1999-, criminal law comt, 2000-, State Bar Ga. **Honors/Awds:** Young Positive Men, Certificate of Appreciation, 2001. **Business Addr:** President, Chief Executive Officer, TJB Recovery Systems LLC, The Grant Bldg, 44 Broad St NW Suite 501, Atlanta, GA 30303, **Business Phone:** (404)522-5056.

BUTTS, CALVIN OTIS
Clergy, educator. **Personal:** Born Jul 19, 1949, Bridgeport, CT; married Patricia; children: 3. **Educ:** Morehouse Col, BA, philos, 1972; Union Theol Sem, MDiv, 1975; Drew Theol Sch, DMin, 1982. **Career:** City Col New York, adjunct prof African Studies dept; Fordham Univ, Black Church Hist; Abyssinian Baptist Church, asst minister, pastor, 1972-77, exec minister, 1977-89, head pastor, 1989-; NY Col, Old Westbury, pres, 1999-. **Orgs:** Pres, Coun Churches City NY; vchmn bd dirs, United Way New York, 1999; mem bd dir, The September 11th Fund; chmn, Nat Affil Develop Initiative Nat Black Leadership Comn AIDS, 1999; bd trustees, N Gen Hosp Harlem; mem bd, Am Baptist Col, Nashville, TN; pres, Africare; chmn bd, The Harlem YMCA; Kappa Alpha Psi Fraternity; Prince Hall Masons. **Honors/Awds:** Man of the Year, Morehouse Col Alumni Asn; Louise Fisher Morris Humanitarian Award, Utility Club New York; Community Against Social Injustice Award, Am Corp; Candle Award, Morehouse Col; William M Moss Distinguished Brotherhood Award; honorary degree, The City Col New York; honorary degree, Tuskegee Univ, Alabama; honorary degree, Claflin Col, Orangeburg, SC; honorary degree, Dillard Univ, New Orleans; honorary degree, Muhlenberg Col, Allentown, PA; honorary degree, Trinity Col, Hartford, CT; Recognized as Living Treasure, New York Chamber Com & Indust. **Business Addr:** Pastor, The Abyssinian Baptist Church, 132 Odell Clark Pl, New York, NY 10030, **Business Phone:** (212)862-7474.

BUTTS, CARLYLE A.
Executive. **Personal:** Born Nov 10, 1935, Richmond, VA; son of Thomas A and Coral P; married Omeria A Roberts, Jun 11, 1966; children: Brian, Gregory. **Educ:** Howard Univ, BSEE, 1963; USC, MBA, 1969; UCLA, Exec Mgt Prog, 1988. **Career:** exec (retired); Howard Univ, electronic lab instr asst, 1958-63; Hughes Aircraft Co, electronics test engr 1963-64, various positions material dept, 1964-69, head prod control, 1969-70, head facilities planning, 1972-76, proj mgr 1970-72, proj mgr, 1977, dept mgr radar systems group, 1978, prod operations mgr, 1987, asst div mgr, ground systems group, 1988-90, quality dir, electro-optical & data systems group, 1990-92, aerospace & defense sector, 1992-94, quality dir, staff vp quality, 1994-96; Ladera Career Paths, chmn, bd dir, 1993-97. **Orgs:** Am Mkg Asn; Nat Contracts Mgt Asn; Intercollegiate Coun Black Col; Bus Mgt Consult; Hughes Mgt Club; past pres, bd trustees, Crenshaw Ch Religious Sci, 1974-77; den leader Webelos Pack 162c Holman Meth Chl, 1978; pres, Howard Univ Alumni Club So CA, 1971-73, 1980; Basileus Omega Psi Phi Fraternity, LA chapter, 1993-94, 1996-98; Founding mem, The Mended Hearts Inc; vpres, 1998-00, Pres, bd of dir, American Diabetes Asn, afa Chap LA CA. **Honors/Awds:** Howard Hughes Fellowship, 1967; Los Angeles City Resolution for Service to Youth & Community, 1983; Omega Man of the Year, Lambda Omicron, 1992, 1994, 1998; Omega Psi Phi Fraternity; BLK Engineer of the Year, Hughes Aircraft Co, 1989; Distinguished Alumni and Mentor Award Recipient, Howard Univ, 1998; Alumni Asn Southern CA, 1998. **Military Serv:** USAF, A1/c, 1954-57. *

BUTTS, DR. HUGH F
Psychiatrist, psychoanalyst, physician. **Personal:** Born Dec 2, 1926, New York, NY; son of Lucius C and Edith Eliza Higgins; married June Dobbs, Jun 9, 1953 (divorced 1971); children: Lucia Irene, Florence & Eric Hugh; married Clementine, Dec 11, 1971; children: Sydney Clementine, Samantha Florenz & Heather Marguerita. **Educ:** City Col NY, BS, 1949; Meharry Med Col, MD, 1953; Morrisania City Hosp, intern cert 1955; Bronx VA Hosp, resd, 1958; Columbia Univ Psychoanalytic Clinic, Cert Psychoanalytic Med 1962. **Career:** St Lukes Hosp, staff physician, 1958-74; Hillcrest Ctr C, staff psych, 1959-61; pvt prac, psych, 1959-74; Wiltwyck Sch Boys, clinical dir, 1961-63, chief, in-patient psych serv, 1962-69; Gracie Sq Hosp, staff physician, 1961-66; Montefiore Hosp, staff physician, 1961-65; Beth-Israel Hosp, staff physician, 1962-63; Harlem Hosp Ctr, assoc prof & dir psych, 1962-69; Vanderbilt Clin Presbyterian Hosp, staff physician, 1963-65; New York Dept Voc Rehab, staff physician, 1963-69; pvt prac, psychoanalyist, 1962-74; Columbia Univ Col Phys & Surgeons, asst clin prof psych, 1967-74; NY St Dept Mental Hygiene, staff physician, 1974-76; Bronx State Hosp, dir, staff physician, 1974-79; Albert Einstein Col Med, prof psychiat, 1974-81; New Hope Guild, Brooklyn NY, psychiat consult, 1980-96; Literary Mind Asn, pres 1986-; Clementine Publ Co, Leeds NY, pres & founder, 1989-; Episcopal Diocese NY, psychiat consult, 1989-; Columbia Law Sch-Fair Housing Clin, psychiat consult, 1993; Open Housing Ctr, psychiat consult, 1996-; St. Vincent's Mental Health Serv, psychiat, 1996-; New York Col Podiatric Med, Dept Primary Podiatric Med Sci, adj prof, 1995-. **Orgs:** Consult, Neuropsychiatric Ctr, NY, 1957; psych consult, Jewish Bd Guardians, 1962; NY Psych Inst 1962-74; supvr training analyst, Columbia Univ Psychoanalytic Clinic Training & Res, 1968-81; Assoc Psychoanalytic Med, 1968-71; Am Psych Assoc, 1970, Am Orthopsychiatric Assoc, 1970-73; psych consult, Fieldston-Ethical Culture Sch, 1970-74; US Fed Ct, 1970-75; staff psych, Manida Juv Detention Ctr, 1972-74; supvr psych, Bronx State Hosp, 1973-79; NY City Police Dept Psychol Clinic, 1974-76; psych consult, Allegheny City Mental Health & Mental Retardation Asn, 1974-75; training analy, supvr analyst Post-Grad Ctr Mental Health, 1975-; actg dir residence training, Bronx State Hosp, 1977-79; Nat Med Asn, AMA, NY Med Soc, Alumni Asn Psychoan Clin Training & Res; fel, NY Acad; Med Adv Bd; chmn, Med Herald, 1990-. **Honors/Awds:** Spec Merit Award, Asn Psychoanalytic Med, 1967; Nat Med Asn Award, 2005; Annual Dr Eugene F Williams Sr Scholar of Distinction Award, Nat Med Asn, 2006. **Special Achievements:** New York State Department of Mental Hygiene, first deputy commissioner, 1975. **Military Serv:** USAF, private 1st class 1944-45, Good Conduct Medal. **Home Addr:** 350 Central Pk W, New York, NY 10025, **Home Phone:** (212)864-6191. **Business Addr:** Adjunct Professor, New York College of Podiatric Medicine, Department of Primary Podiatric Medical Sciences, 1800 Pk Ave, New York, NY 10035, **Business Phone:** (212)410-8000.

BUTTS, JANIE PRESSLEY
Educator. **Personal:** Born Aug 25, 1936, Nesmith, SC; daughter of Ollie Epps and Lillie D; married Thomas A Butts Jr, Oct 1, 1960; children: Derrick, Steven & Karlton. **Educ:** SCA State Col, BBA, 1958; Eastern Conn State Col, elem cert, 1973. **Career:** Educator (retired); Groton Bd Educ, sixth grade teacher, 1968-69; East Lyme Bd Educ, fifth grade teacher, 1969. **Orgs:** Nat Edu Asn; NCW Inc; NCP; Shiloh Baptist Church; Conn Coop Mentor Teaching Prog. **Honors/Awds:** Woman of the Year, NCW Inc, 1985; Conn Celebration Excellence Award, 1986; Exemplary TCR Citation, 1987; Nat Educr Award, 1990; Distinguished Alumni Citation Year Award, Nat Asn Equal Opportunity Higher Educ, 1992.

BUTTS, MARION STEVENSON, JR.
Football player. **Personal:** Born Aug 1, 1966, Sylvester, GA. **Educ:** Neastern Okla A&M Univ; Fla State Univ. **Career:** Football player (retired); San Diego Chargers, running back, 1989-93; New England Patriots, 1994; Houston Oilers, 1995. **Honors/Awds:** Pro Bowl, 1990, 1991.

BUTTS, SAMANTHA F.
Educator, physician. **Educ:** Harvard Univ. **Career:** Asn Reproductive Health Prof, fac; Univ Penn, Asst Prof Obstet & Gynec, currently; Penn Fertility Care, physician, currently. **Business Addr:** Physician, Penn Fertility Care, 8th fl, 3701 Market St, Philadelphia, PA 19104, **Business Phone:** 800-789-7366.*

BYARS, KEITH ALLAN
Football player, television sportscaster. **Personal:** Born Oct 14, 1963, Dayton, OH; married Margaret; children: Taylor Renae & Keith Allan II. **Educ:** Ohio State Univ, attended 1985. **Career:** Football player (retired), coach, TV sportscaster; Philadelphia Eagles, runningback, 1986-92; Miami Dolphins, 1993-96; New Eng Patriots, 1996-97; NYJets, 1998; OH State Univ, pre & post-game radio analyst; YES Network,"New York Football Weekly" & "This Week in Football", tv analyst, currently; Boca Raton High Sch, coach, currently. **Orgs:** Founder, Keith Byars PRO Found. **Honors/Awds:** Humanitarian of the Year, Philadelphia Sports Writers Asn, 1991; Community Service Award, Big Bros Big Sisters Philadelphia, 1991; Pro Bowl, 1993. **Business Addr:** TV Analyst, Yankees Entertainment And Sports Network LLC, New York Football Weekly, The Chrysler Bldg, 405 Lexington Ave 36th Fl, New York, NY 10174-3699, **Business Phone:** (646)487-3600.

BYARS, DR. LAURETTA F
College administrator. **Personal:** Born Jan 1, 1949. **Educ:** Morehead State Univ, BA; Univ Ky, MSW, social work, 1972, EdD, educ, 1982. **Career:** Univ Ky, vice chancellor minority affairs; Social Servs Coun, chair; Prairie View A&M Univ, vpres instnl rels & pub servs, currently, asst dean stud affairs, currently. **Orgs:** Ky Hist Soc. **Honors/Awds:** Alumni Hall of Fame, Univ KY, 1998.

BYAS, DR. ULYSSES S.
Educator. **Personal:** Born Jun 23, 1924, Macon, GA; son of Marie Sharpe; married Annamozel Boyd, Jul 5, 1953; children: 4. **Educ:** Fort Valley State Col, BS, 1950; Columbia Univ, MA, 1952; Univ Mass, EdD,1976; Atlanta Univ; NC Col; Bennington Col; Colo Col. **Career:** Educator (retired); Elberton, teacher, 1951-53; Hutchison Elem & HS, supt prin; Butler High Sch, EE, 1957-68; Ga Teachers & Educ Asn, asst exec secy, 1968; Ga Asn Educ, dir, 1970; Macon County Bd Educ, Tuskegee, Alasupt schs, 1970-77; Roosevelt Union Free Sch Dist, NY, supt schs, 1977-87; Hempstead Union Free Sch Dist, NY, interim supt schs, 1990-91; educ consult. **Orgs:** Am Asn Sch Adminr; Nat Alliance Black Sch Educ; Nassau Co Chief Sch Asn; NY Asn Sch Adminr; Nat Asn Sec Sch Prins; Phi Delta Kappa; exec comn hon chmn, United Negro Scholar; life mem, Kappa Alpha Psi Fraternity; vpres, Long Island Cancer Coun; partic, 23rd Annual Air War Col, Nat Security Forum; life mem, Fort Valley State Col Alumni Asn; former chmn, CME; past pres, Ga Coun Sec Sch Prins; past pres, Ga Teachers & Educrs Asn; past pres, Nat Alliance Black Sch Supts; past pres, Nat Alliance Black Sch Educrs; past mem, NY State Examina-

tions Bd, Nat Asn Adv Colored People, Comn Bd; consult, Univ Mass; adj prof, Long Island Univ; past pres-elect, Nassau County, NY Supt; Macon, Ga Area Habitat Humanity; Cent Ga Alzheimers Asn. **Honors/Awds:** Ulysses Byas Elem Sch, named by Roosevelt, NY Bd Educ, 1987; Education Hall of Fame, Fort Valley State Col, GA, 1988. **Military Serv:** USNR, 1943-46. **Home Addr:** 5675 Kesteven Lane, Macon, GA 31210. *

BYAS, WILLIAM HERBERT
School administrator. **Personal:** Born Nov 26, 1932, Macon, GA; married Carolyn Kelsey; children: Yolanda E & William H. **Educ:** Tenn State Univ, BS, 1957; The Ft Valley St Col, MS, 1957; The Univ TN, EdD, 1971. **Career:** Univ Tenn, dean stud servs, 1979; Memphis St Univ, assoc prof res,1978-79; Saginaw Valley St Col, dir acad & support serv & assoc prof educ psychol, 1973-78, dir stud pers servs, 1971-73; New Careers Inst Knoxville Col, dir, 1970; The Ft Valley St Col, dir Col educ achievement proj, 1966-70. **Orgs:** Am Psychol Asn, 1972; Nat Asn Stud Pers Admin, 1978; comtman, BSA, 1966-69; bd dirs, Big Bros Am, 1971; rotarian, Rotary Int, 1971; Phi Delta Kappa, 1971. **Honors/Awds:** Recipient National defense award, USN; doctoral fellowship Univ Tenn, 1970-71; cert for outstanding serv So Asn Cols & Schs, 1973; couns studs with spec needs Saginaw Valley St Col, 1974; consult, US Office of Educ, 1975. **Military Serv:** USN, seaman 1950-52. **Business Addr:** Executive, University of Tennessee, 3113 Cir Pk Dr, Knoxville, TN 37916.*

BYEARS, LATASHA (LATASHA NASHAY BYEARS)
Basketball player. **Personal:** Born Aug 12, 1973, Memphis, TN. **Educ:** DePaul Univ, physical educ, attended 1996. **Career:** Sacramento Monarchs, guard, 1997-00; Los Angeles Sparks, forward, 2001-03;Wash Mystics, 2006; CSKA Sofia, Bulgareia, 2006; Houston comets, Guard-Forward, 2007-. **Orgs:** Meals on Wheels. **Business Addr:** Professional Basketball Player, Houston Comets, Toyota Ctr 1510 Polk St, Houston, TX 77002, **Business Phone:** (713)758-7200.

BYEARS, LATASHA NASHAY. See BYEARS, LATASHA.

BYERS, SUSAN M
Executive director. **Career:** Seattle Pub Sch, dir spec proj, currently. **Orgs:** Steering comt, Eliminating Achievement Gap Action Comt, Seattle Pub Sch. **Business Addr:** Director, Seattle Public Schools, Special Project, PO Box 34165, Seattle, WA 98124-1165, **Business Phone:** (206)252-0199.

BYNAM, SAWYER LEE, III
Construction worker, founder (originator). **Personal:** Born Sep 15, 1933, Houston, TX; married Betty Ann; children: Keith Wayne. **Educ:** Tex S Univ, BS, Cert, Construct Planning & Estimating. **Career:** Gen & Sub-Contractors Asn, contract develop; co-founder, Africa AIDS Fund.

BYNER, EARNEST ALEXANDER
Football coach, football player. **Personal:** Born Sep 15, 1962, Milledgeville, GA; married Tina; children: Semeria, Adrian Monique, Brandi & Kyara. **Educ:** E Carolina Univ, phys educ. **Career:** Cleveland Browns, running back, 1984-88, 1994-95; Wash Redskins, running back, 1989-93, coach, 2004-07; Baltimore Ravens, running back, 1996-97, dir player develop, 1998-2003; Tenn Titans, running backs coach, 2008-. **Orgs:** Kappa Alpha Psi Fraternity. **Honors/Awds:** AFC Championship Game, 1986 & 1987; Pro Bowl, 1990 & 1991; Ed Block Courage Award, 1986; NFL Extra Effort Award, 1986; NFL PA Unsung Hero Award, 1997; True Value NFL Man of the Year Award, 1997; Sports Hall of Fame at his alma mater, E Carolina Univ. **Business Addr:** Runningbacks Coach, Tennessee Titans, 460 Great Circle Rd, Nashville, TN 37228, **Business Phone:** (615)565-4000.

BYNES, FRANK HOWARD, JR.
Physician. **Personal:** Born Dec 3, 1950, Savannah, GA; son of Frank and Frenchye Mason; married Janice Ann Ratta, Jul 24, 1987; children: Patricia F Bynes, Frenchye D Bynes. **Educ:** Savanna State Col, BS, 1972; Meharry Med Col, MD, 1977. **Career:** USAF, internist, 1986-87; self-employed, internist, 1987-. **Orgs:** Alpha Phi Alpha Fraternity, 1969-; Am Med Asn, 1973-; NY Acad Scis, 1983-; AAAS, 1984-; Am Col Physicians, 1985-; Air Force Asn, 1987-; Asn Military Surgeons US, 1987-. **Military Serv:** USAF, maj, 1986-87. **Home Addr:** 703 Noble Oaks Dr, Savannah, GA 31406. **Business Addr:** Physician, 703 Noble Oaks Dr, Savannah, GA 31406, **Business Phone:** (912)354-0899.*

BYNES, GLENN KENNETH
Auditor. **Personal:** Born Jan 17, 1946, Orlando, FL; son of Arthur; married Norma, Jul 31, 1971; children: Glenn K III & Ingrid N. **Educ:** Hampton Jr Col, AS, 1966; Tenn State Univ, BS, 1971. **Career:** McDonnell Douglas, aircraft maintenance engr, 1971-73; EI DuPont deNemours, prod supvr, 1973-74; Martin Marietta Info group, mgr, auditor operations, 1974-. **Orgs:** Registr, Accreditation Bd; regist lead auditor, 1993-. **Special Achievements:** Plan, develop, implement & manage group audit activities. **Business Addr:** Manager, Martin Marietta Information Group, 12506 Lake Underhill Rd, Orlando, FL 32825, **Business Phone:** (407)826-1707.

BYNOE, JOHN GARVEY
Government official. **Personal:** Born Oct 25, 1926, Boston, MA; son of John Leo and Edna V; married Louise V Granville; children: Sandra M, John L, James G & Jonathan K. **Educ:** Boston Univ, New Eng Sch Law, JD, 1957. **Career:** Government official (retired); Fed Security Agency, Boston, regional off, 1948-50; Social Security Admin dist off, Mass, claims rep, 1950-54, asst dist mgr, Salem, 1954-55; mgr, Norwood, 1956-66; Roxbury Comn Coun, pres, 1964-69; HEW, prog cord, 1966-67; Unity Bank & Trust Co, founder, dir,1968-76; Office Civil Rights, Dept Health Ed & Welfare Reg I Boston, dir, 1967-82; Exec Serv Corps, New Eng, brd mem, clerk, 1994-96; attny, real estate broker; Real Estate Developer. **Orgs:** Chmn, Veterans commt NAACP,Boston, 1947; Chmn brd, Urban League, Eastern MA, 1979-82; bd mem, Freedom House, Boston; brd dir & legal asst, Boston Legal Aid Soc; Alpha Phi Alpha; pres adv comt, Mus Nat Ctr Afro-Am Artists; bd mem, MA Pre-Engineering Prog Minority Students; legal coun, Nat Bus League Boston Chap, 1974-80; chmn brd, Prof &Bus Club Boston Mass; bd mem, Nat Ctr Afro-Am Artists; brd dir, Resthaven; Big Brother Assn Boston, 1963-86; Boy Scouts Am Boston Metro Chap, 1983; Boston Branch NAACP, 1987-88; past worshipful master, Widow Son Lodge 28,1990-; legal adv most worshipful grand master, Most Worshipful Prince Hall Grand Lodge Mass; dep grand master, 1997-98, sr grand warden, Prince Hall Grand Lodge, jurisdiction Mass, 1995-96; Chmn, adv comn, Roxbury Heritage State Park; bd mem, Roxbury Hist Soc. **Honors/Awds:** Honorary Doctor of Laws, New Eng Sch Law, 1987; 33 Degree, United Supreme Coun, Prince Hall Masons, 1989; Martin Luther King Jr Community Service Award. **Special Achievements:** Founder and director of Boston's first Black-owned bank, Unity Bank and Trust. **Military Serv:** AUS sgt, 1945-46; comdr, Post 953, Boston, 1947. **Home Addr:** 82 Harold St, Roxbury, MA 02119. *

BYNOE, PETER CB
Lawyer. **Personal:** Born Mar 20, 1951, Boston, MA; son of Victor C and Ethel M Stewart; married Linda Walker Bynoe, Nov 1987. **Educ:** Harvard Col, Cambridge, Mass, BA, cum laude, 1972; Harvard Bus Sch, Boston, Mass, MBA, finance & mkt, 1976; Harvard Law Sch, Cambridge, Mass, JD, 1976. **Career:** Citibank, exec intern, 1976-77; James H Lowry & Assocs, exec vpres, 1977-82; Telemat Ltd, chmn, 1982-; Ill Sports Facilities Authority, exec dir, 1988-92; Denver Nuggets, gen partner, 1989-92; DLA Piper Rudnick Gray Cary US LLP, sr coun, 1995-. **Orgs:** Chmn, Chicago Landmarks Comn, 1986-97; dir, chmn, Goodman Theatre, 1987-; trustee, Rush-Univ Med Ctr; dir, Uniroyal Technol Corp; overseer, Harvard Univ, 1992-2001; dir, Ill Sports Facilities Authority, 1993-2002; dir, Dine Rewards Network, Inc; pres, United Ctr Community Econ Develop Fund; dir, Covanta Holding Corp; trustee, CORE Ctr; consult, Atlanta Fulton County Recreation Authority; consult, Atlanta Comt Organize Olympic Games, 1996; Ill State Bar Asn; Chicago Bar Asn; Ill Sports Facil Authority; Chicago Art Inst Alliance; Harvard Club Chicago. **Business Addr:** Senior Counsel, DLA Piper, 203 N LaSalle St Suite 1900, Chicago, IL 60601-1293, **Business Phone:** (312)368-4090.

BYNUM, HORACE CHARLES, SR.
Pharmacist. **Personal:** Born Nov 2, 1916, New Orleans, LA; son of Henry Bynum Jr and Amanda Medlock; married Ethel Frinkle, Feb 14, 1975; children: Adolph F, Horace C Jr. **Educ:** Xavier Univ, New Orleans, LA, BS, Pharm, 1936. **Career:** US Post Office, New Orleans, LA, carrier, 1936-46; Bynum's Pharm, pharmacist, currently. **Orgs:** Secy, New Orleans Br Nat Asn Advan Colored People, 1955-66;Alpha Phi Alpha Fraternity; pres, Nat Asn Advan Colored People, New Orleans Br, 1966-69; treas, Nat Asn Advan Colored People, State Br, 1969-75; treas, Lafon Home Bd Dir, 1969-89; pres, Nat Pharmaceut Asn, 1970-71. **Honors/Awds:** Pharmacist of Yr, New Orleans, Progressive Asn; Man of the Yr, Chi Delta Mu Fraternity. **Business Addr:** Pharmacist, Owner, Bynum's Pharmacy, Bynum & Son Inc, 3840 St Bernard Ave, New Orleans, LA 70122, **Business Phone:** (504)288-4829.*

BYNUM, DR. JUANITA
Writer, public speaker. **Personal:** Born Jan 16, 1959; married Bishop Thomas Weeks III, Jan 1, 2003; (divorced 1985). **Career:** Recorded videos include: No More Sheets; Are You Planted for the Kingdom; I'm Too Fat For the Yoke; Limp of the Lord; Now That's Dominion; The Refiner's Fire; My Delivery; The Spirit of Isaac; The Umpire of my Soul; Tied to the Altar; auth: The Threshing Floor; The Matters of the Heart; Juanita Bynum Ministries, founder & pres, currently; Juanita Bynum enterprises, founder & pres, current;y. **Business Addr:** President, Founder, Juanita Bynum Ministries, 415 N Crawford St, Waycross, GA 31503.

BYNUM, KENNETH BERNARD
Football player. **Personal:** Born May 29, 1974, Gainesville, FL. **Educ:** SC State Univ, bus admin. **Career:** Football player (retired); San Diego Chargers, running back, 1997-2000.

BYNUM, DR. RALEIGH WESLEY
Optometrist. **Personal:** Born May 27, 1936, Jacksonville, FL; son of John T and Corene Brown; married Thelmetia Argrett; children: Raleigh, Monjya & Zerrick. **Educ:** Fla A&M Univ, attended 1956; Ill Col Optom, BS & OD, 1960; Univ SC, MPH, 1975; Command & Gen Staff Col AUS, cert, 1976. **Career:** Am Opt Asn Retirement Fund, trustee, various comt, 1978; Optometrist (retired); Nat Optom Asn, pres, bd chmn, 1979; Am Acad Optom, vpres, NC chap, 1980-85; Nat Optom Found, chmn bd, 1980-88; RMZ assoc, pres; Pvt Pratice, Optometrist, currently. **Orgs:** Regional dir, NOA Minority Recruitment Proj, 1971-77; past pres, bd dirs, Charlotte Bethlehem Ctr, 1973; Nat HBP Coordinating Comt, 1976-84; gen partner, Westside Prof Assoc, 1972-; pilot-instr, Rated Single Engine Land Airplane, 1975-; vice chmn, bd dirs, McCrorey Br YMCA, 1983-91; vice chmn, bd dirs, Charlotte Mint Mus, 1983-87. **Honors/Awds:** Optometrist of the Year, Nat Opt Asn, 1980; Deacon, Friendship Baptist Church, 1978-; Pres Medal Hon, Ill Col Optom, 1999. **Military Serv:** AUS, Col, 32 yrs; serv-Reserves, Active & Nat Guard. **Home Addr:** 6426 Heatherbrook Ave, Charlotte, NC 28213, **Home Phone:** (704)596-6270. **Business Addr:** Optometrist, 401 S Independence Blvd Mid Town Square Mall, Charlotte, NC 28204, **Business Phone:** (704)375-9001.

BYNUM, VALERIE COLLYMORE
Musician. **Personal:** Born Mar 9, 1942, Bronx, NY; married Louis Jr; children: Adam & Tanisha. **Educ:** Ithaca Col Sch Music, BS, 1963; Sch Arts, NY. **Career:** Freelance musician, 1965; Jr High Sch, teacher, 1965-67. **Orgs:** Radio City Music Hall Symphony, 1963-66; Symphony New World, 1965-72. *

BYRD, ALBERT ALEXANDER
Educator. **Personal:** Born Nov 6, 1927, Baltimore, MD; married Alice Muriel Poe; children: Karen Leslie Forgy-Hicks. **Educ:** Howard Univ, BA, 1949; Temple Univ, MFA, 1959; Universidad Naciona lAutonoma de Mexico, 1959; Instituto Statele D'Arte Per La Porcellana SestoFlorentino, Italy, 1962; Instituto Statale D'Arte Porto Romano Florence, Italy, 1962. **Career:** Educator (retired); Baltimore Pub Sch Dist, art teacher, 1949-63; Sacramento City Col, Humanitites & Fine Arts, prof, 1963-91. **Orgs:** Am Fed Teachers; Fac, Asn Calif Community Col; Kappa Alpha Psi; Howard Univ Alumni Asn. **Honors/Awds:** United Nations Service Medal, Nat Defense Serv; Nat Endowment for the Humanitites, Wash, DC, 1972-73; Grant, Am Forum Int Study, Cleveland OH,1975. **Military Serv:** AUS, pvt first class, 1951-53; Korean Serv Medal 2 Battle Stars.

BYRD, ALICE TURNER
Administrator. **Career:** CIGNA Corp; Turning Training Inst, owner & pres, 2003-. **Business Phone:** (860)243-3900.*

BYRD, ARTHUR W
Social worker. **Personal:** Born Dec 24, 1943, Washington, DC; son of Arthur W and Doris Littlejohn; married Inez Marie Coleman, Nov 26, 1967; children: Arthur III William, Ashley Wendall & Allyn Winthrop. **Educ:** Livingstone Col, BS, 1965; Univ NC, MSW, 1972; Univ Ky, postgrad; Univ Chicago. **Career:** Clinch Valley Col, Univ VA, fac, 1972; Longwood Col, Farmville, VA, fac, 1972; Livingstone Col, Salisbury, 1974; Va Asn Community Serv Bd, community contracting adminr, currently. **Orgs:** Rowan Co, Civic League, 1973; NC Neighborhood Workers Asn, 1969; NASW 1970; CSWE 1970; S Asn Undergrad SW Educ, 1973; NAACP, 1964; dir Neighborhood Corps, 1965-68; Salisbury & Statesville, NC; dir, Neighborhood Youth Sch & out Sch Progs, Salisbury, NC, 1968-70; dir, Outreach to Teenage Fathers, Durham, NC, 1970; comm contact Rep, Youth Serv Bur, Winston Salem, NC, 1971; state dir, Res Facil Mently Retarded; Adj J Sargent, Reynolds Comm Col, 1975. **Honors/Awds:** Babcock Fel, 1970-72; Distinguished Serv Award, Salisbury Rowan Com Serv Coun; POP Award, Coop Sch Girls Durham, NC; estab Social Work Action Group, SWAG Livingstone Col, 1973-74. **Special Achievements:** Estab first Afro-Am Student Org Longwood Col, 1972-73. **Home Addr:** 6801 W Rd, Chesterfield, VA 23832.

BYRD, BUTCH. See BYRD, GEORGE EDWARD.

BYRD, CAMOLIA ALCORN
Educator. **Personal:** Born in Baton Rouge, LA; married Lionel Patrick Byrd; children: Cheryl P, Lionel P Jr, Judith I, Roderick J & Janell M. **Educ:** Southern Univ Baton Rouge, BA, 1944; Cent State Univ, MA, 1964. **Career:** Okla City Pub Schs, teacher, 1959-70, consult, 1970-76, asst coordr, 1976-80, coordr, 1980-86; "I Can" Reading & Math Ctr, dir, 1987-. **Orgs:** Assault on Illiteracy, NTU Art Asn, 1986; campaign mgr, Senator Vicki Lynn Miles LaGrange, Okla City, 1986; Asn Supv & Curric Develop; Int Reading Asn & Okal Reading Asn; Teachers Eng Speaker Other Lang & Okla TESOL; Nat & Local Black Educrs Asn; Nat Coun Negro Women; Fed Col Womens Club; Phi Delta Kappa Inc; African Art Mus; Jack & Jill Inc; Okla ESide Culture Club; Alpha Kappa Alpha Sor. **Honors/Awds:** Eminent Women, Phi Delta Kappa Inc Gamma Epsilon Chap, 1985. **Business Addr:** Director, 2613 NE 22nd St, Oklahoma City, OK 73111, **Business Phone:** (405)424-0651.*

BYRD, DORIS M.
Police officer. **Educ:** Chicago State Univ. **Career:** Chicago Police Dept, sergeant, 1977-. **Orgs:** Coalition Law Enforcement Officers, 1985-98; regional pres, Nat Black Police Asn, 1998-00; chairperson, Nat Black Police Asn, 2000-02. **Honors/Awds:** Chicago Police Dept, Dept Commendation, 1980, Unit Meritorious Award, 1983; Community Serv, NBPA Midwest Region, 1997.

Business Addr: Sergeant, Chicago Police Department, 300 East 29th St, Chicago, IL 60616, **Business Phone:** (773)747-8340.*

BYRD, EDWIN R.
Educator. **Personal:** Born Feb 23, 1920, Kansas City, KS; married Dorothy Wordlow; children: Terri E. **Educ:** Kans State Teachers Col, BS; Univ KS, ME, 1950. **Career:** Educator (retired); Mo Sch Dist, 1946-81, elem sch teacher, 1946-55, jr high sch teacher, 1955-56, counr jr & sr high Schs, 1956-60; Yates Elem Sch, prin, 1960-61; Dunbar Sch, prin, 1961-63; Richardson Sch, prin,1963-68; Martin Luther King Jr High Sch, prin, 1968-75; Nowlin Jr High Sch, prin. **Orgs:** KC Sch Admin Assoc; NEA; Mo State Teachers Assoc; prin, Mo Assoc Sch; prin, Nat Assoc Sch Prin; Phi Delta Kappa; PTA; Am Legion 149; Nat Advan Asn Colored People; YMCA; Kiwanis Club; inst rep Boy Scouts; elder Swope Pkwy United Christian Ch; Alpha Phi Alpha; Res Acad KC, Selective Serv Bd49; adv comn, Jr Red Cross; pres, Inter-City Kiwanis Club, 1983-84; Am Assoc Retired Persons. **Honors/Awds:** Outstanding Sec Educator Am, Sigma Pi Phi, 1974; Athletic Service Award, 1973; PTA Service Award, 1968; YMCA Service Award, 1962; Kin Community Service Award, 1975; Outstanding Member Award, Beta Lambda Chap Alpha Phi Alpha, 1979; YMCA Super Quota Buster Award, 1984. **Military Serv:** USAF, sgt, 1942-46. **Business Addr:** Independence, MO 64052.*

BYRD, GEORGE EDWARD (BUTCH BYRD)
Loan officer, football player. **Personal:** Born Sep 20, 1941, Troy, NY; son of George Byrd Sr and Louise Collins-Byrd; married Alice Hill, Jul 8, 1967; children: Sharon Collins, George III, Michael & Christopher. **Educ:** Boston Univ, Boston MA, BS 1964; Univ Mich, Ann Arbor, Exec Mgt Prog, 1980. **Career:** Buffalo Bills, 1964-70; Denver Broncos, 1970-72; Chrysler/Plymouth Corp,Atlanta, GA, sales mgr, New Haven, CT, opers mgr, 1973-81; Polariod Corp, Oakbrook IL, regional mkt mgr/regional oper mgr, 1981-86, mkt mgr, 1986-87, gen mgr; Primary Residential Mortgage Co, sr loan officer. **Honors/Awds:** Thomas Gastall Award, 1963; All-Pro, NFL, Buffalo Bills, 1965, 1966, 1968, 1969; Am Football League All-Star; Man of the yr, African Meeting Houses, 1989; Boston Univ Hall of Fame, 1980; Greater Buffalo Sports Hall of Fame, 2008. **Business Addr:** Senior Loan Officer, Primary Residential Mortgage Co, Westboro, MA 01581.*

BYRD, HARRIETT ELIZABETH
Politician, government official, teacher. **Personal:** Born Apr 20, 1926, Cheyenne, WY; daughter of Robert C Rhone and Sudie E Smith; married James W, Aug 8, 1947 (died 2005); children: Robert C, James W II & Linda C. **Educ:** WVa State Col, BS, educ, 1949; Univ WY, MA, elem educ, 1976. **Career:** Dept Admin Training & Supply, Ft Francis E Warren, civilian instr, 1949; Cheyenne's Sch Dist, elementary teacher, 1959; WY Educ Asn, WY TEPS Comt, 1970-73; Marshall Scholar Comt, comt mem, 1972-79; WY State Adv Coun, comt mem, 1973-80; NEA Albuquerque, inserv training ctrsl, 1979; WY State Legis, House Reps, state rep, 1980-89; Dept Education's Int Youth Year Awards comt, staff, 1985; WY State Senate, sen, 1989-93. **Orgs:** Life mem, Kappa Delta Pi; Delta Kappa Gamma; Kappa Kappa Iota; Laramie Co Coll Booster Club; adv bd, Laramie Co Sr Citizens; vpres, pres, 1992-95, Laramie Co Dem Women's Club; United Med Ctr Cheyne; Univ WY Alumni; St Mary's Catholic Church; League Women Voters; WY State Mus; state contact, State WY Dr Martin Luther King Jr State & City King Holiday Fed Comt; Love & Charity Club. **Honors/Awds:** Instructor Excellence in Teaching Award, Instr mag, 1967; Distinguished Citizen Award by the Boy Scouts of America, Cheyenne, 1990; Wash, DC, forher efforts toward peace, justice, freedom and dignity for all people,YWCA, 1990; Volunteer Award, Churchill-Corlett Elementary Sch, 1990; Special Recognition Award, Colorado Black Women for Political Action, 1990. **Special Achievements:** First African American legislator in Wyoming; First African American woman to serve in the Wyoming State Legislature; First African American to serve in the Wyoming State Senate.

BYRD, DR. HELEN P BESSENT
Educator. **Personal:** Born Feb 27, 1943, Waynesboro, GA; daughter of Oscar S Bessent and Josie C Bessent; married Shedrick, Jun 15, 1979; children: Shedrick Tyrone. **Educ:** Warren Wilson Col, AA 1961; Berea Col, BA, 1963; Temple Univ, MEd, 1965; Univ Conn, PhD, 1972; Columbia Univ Teachers Col, Postdoctoral Study, 1973, 1976; Long Island Post Campus, Columbia Univ, attended 1987; Univ Ga, attended. **Career:** Educator (retired); Sch Dist Philadelphia, teacher, 1963-65; Atlanta Pub Sch System, teacher, 1966-68; Atlanta State Univ, vis prof, 1968; Savannah GA State Col, vis prof, 1971; Norfolk State Univ, spec educ dept, prof, head, 1977-80, coordr, Spec Educ Grad Progs. **Orgs:** Fel BEH-USOE Ment Retardation, 1965-66; fel Soc Fellowship Fund, 1970-72; Comn Minority Groups; bd trustees, Boggs Acad, 1976-83; prog agency bd, United Presbyterian Church USA, 1977-83, bd mem, 1976-79, vchmn, 1979-80; bd mem, Norfolk Comm Improvement Educ; bd mem, Hope House Found, 1977-83; Presbyterian Comn Minority Educ, 1982-88, sec, 1985, mem, 1983-88, vchmn, 1988; Norfolk Comm Serv Bd; bd mem, Cultural Experiences Unlimited; bd, Norflolk Pub Libr, 1992-97; Va Interagency Coordinating Coun, 1987-2003; Coun Presbytery Eastern Va, 1998-2002. **Honors/Awds:** Scholar Wm H Hess Memorial Scholarship Fund, 1961; Grant Recipient BEPDU-SOE Proj, 1972-76; Grant Recipient BEH USOE Proj, 1977-80; Education Award Aurora 60 Order of Eastern Star, 1983; Sigma Woman of the Year, Delta Beta Sigma Chap, 1988; Distinguished Scholar, 1988; Special Olympics Award, 1986; Woods Teacher of the Year, Univ RA, 1997; Grant Recipient, Dept Educ, Rehab Serv Admin, 1998-03. **Home Addr:** 7112 Hunters Chase, Norfolk, VA 23518, **Home Phone:** (757)853-6553.

BYRD, HERBERT LAWRENCE
Electrical engineer. **Personal:** Born Oct 12, 1943, Hampton, VA; son of Pearline Singleton and Henry Singleton; children: David H II. **Educ:** Am Inst Engineering & Technol, BSEE, 1966; Syracuse Univ, MSEE, 1975. **Career:** IBM Corp, proj mgr, 1966-78; Sycom Inc, pres & chief exec officer, 1978-; MOJA, Inc, chmn, gen mgr, prog mgr & chief exec officer, currently. **Military Serv:** AUS, a1c, 1962-65. **Business Addr:** Program Manager, General Manager, Chief Executive Officer, MOJA Inc, 7010 Infantry Ridge Rd, Manassas, VA 20109, **Business Phone:** (703)369-4339.

BYRD, ISAAC
Football player. **Personal:** Born Nov 16, 1974, St. Louis, MO. **Educ:** Kans Univ. **Career:** Football player(retired), Tennessee Oilers, wide receiver, 1997-99; Tennessee Titans, wide receiver,1999; Carolina Panthers, wide receiver, 2000-02.

BYRD, ISAAC, JR.
Judge. **Personal:** Born Jan 1, 1952. **Educ:** Tougaloo Col, 1973; Northwestern Univ Law Sch, Chicago, 1976. **Career:** Miss Bd Corrections, vice chmn; chancery judge state Miss, 1989; Byrd & Assoc, Managing Partner, currently. **Orgs:** Presidential Club mem, Asn Trial Lawyers Am; Miss Trial Lawyers Asn. **Honors/Awds:** Vernon Dahmer Award, Nat Asn Advan Colored People; Goodman Chaney Schwerner Award; Stanford Young Lifetime Achievement Award, 2006; Trial Lawyer of the Year Award. **Special Achievements:** In 2003 Black Enterprise Magazine recognized him as one of the top black lawyers in the country. **Business Addr:** Managing Partner, Byrd & Associates PLLC, 427 Fortification St, Jackson, MS 39201, **Business Phone:** (601)354-1210.*

BYRD, JERRY STEWART
Lawyer. **Personal:** Born Dec 11, 1935, Greenville, SC; son of Elliott and Ethel; married Paula Deborah Aughtry; children: Jerry Stewart Jr. **Educ:** Fisk Univ, BA, 1961; Howard Univ, JD, 1964; Southeastern Univ, AS, bus admin, 1975. **Career:** Nat Labor Rels Bd, Regional Adv Br, atty, 1964-65; Neighborhood Legal Serv, managing atty, 1965-69 & 1974-81, dep dir, 1970-71; Howard Univ, polit sci instr, 1971-72; Thompson, Evans & Dolphin, pvt pract, lawyer, 1971; United Planning Orgn Model Cities Consumer Protection Prog, supervising atty, 1972-73; Super Ct, DC, hearing comnr, 1981-97; Soc Security Admin Super Ct, magistrate Judge, 1998-02; DC Super Ct Judges (51), Dept Justice, assoc judge, 2003-. **Orgs:** Fed Admin Law Judges Conf; Spec Judges Div, Am Bar Asn; Wash Bar Asn; Nat Bar Asn; gen secy & vpres, Wash Buddhist Vihara Soc Inc; bd dir, Hospitality Comn, Fed Credit Union; DC Consumer Goods Repair Bd, 1974-77; Hearing Comn, Bd Prof Responsibility, 1982-85. **Honors/Awds:** Black Belt, Jhoon Rhee Inst Tae Kwon Do, 1982; Federal Adminstrative Law Judge Certificate, 1997. **Special Achievements:** Publ: Parental Immunity in Negligence Actions Abolished, 9 How L J 183, 1963; Courts, Slums and Feasibility of Adopting the Warranty of Fitness The DC Housing Research Comm Report, 1967; Important Cases, Thompson v Mazo 421 F 2d 1156, 137 US App DC 221, 1970; rev 245 A2d 122 (DC App 1968); Durmu v Gill 227 A2d 104 (DC App 1970); Coleman v District of Columbia 250 A2d 555 (DC App 1968); Nix vs Watson, RS-650-80R; 18 Family Law Reporter (Nov 12, 1991). **Military Serv:** AUS, gunner, 1954; Fort Carson Colorado Army Band. **Home Addr:** 2110 T St SE, Washington, DC 20020, **Home Phone:** (202)889-1392. **Business Addr:** Associate Judge, DC Superior Court Judges (51) Department of Justice, 500 Indiana Ave NW, Washington, DC 20001, **Business Phone:** (202)879-4797.*

BYRD, JOAN EDA (JOAN EDA)
Librarian. **Personal:** Born May 12, 1942, Washington, DC; daughter of Robert and Edna; married Leonard, Oct 5, 1986; children: Kai-Mariama. **Educ:** Howard Univ, BFA, 1965; Cath Univ Am, MLS, 1976; New Sch Social Res, Media Studies Dept, MA, 1978. **Career:** DC Pub Libr, ref librn, 1965-76; John Jay Col, mgr, librn, 1979-81; Brooklyn Publ Libr, ref librn, 1983-86, asst div chief, 1986-88; Donnell Media Ctr, NY Pub Libr, supv librn film/audio, 1996-2001, asst librn, librn, currently. **Orgs:** NY Film/Video Coun, 1988-; pres & bd trustees, Black Maria Film/Video Festival. **Honors/Awds:** Purchase Award for Photography, Perkins Ctr Arts, 1988. **Special Achievements:** Cover art for 10th anniversary publication of The Color Purple (Alice Walker), 1992; photography-in-performance piece: Friends and Friends II, by Blondell Cummings, 1980; numerous photography exhibitions. **Business Addr:** Librarian, Donnell Media Center, Donnell Libr Ctr Lower Level 20 W 53rd St, New York, NY 10019-6185, **Business Phone:** (212)621-0609.

BYRD, JOSEPH KEYS
School administrator. **Personal:** Born Oct 3, 1953, Meadville, MS. **Educ:** William Carey Col, BS 1975, MEd, 1980. **Career:** William Carey Col, counr & instr, 1980-82; Univ New Orleans, develop specialist counr, 1981-82; Xavier Univ LA, gen counr, 1982-83; Univ New Orleans, asst dir dev ed, 1983-86; Xavier Univ, asst dean stud serv, 1986-, Stud Serv, vpres, currently. **Orgs:** Counr, tutor & coordr, William Carey Col, 1975-80; exec secy, Sigma Lambda Chap Alpha Phi Alpha Frat, 1982-; adv, Omicron Delta Kappa, 1978, Chi Beta Phi 1980; NAACP New Orleans LA, 1984; pres, Greater New Orleans Chap Nat Pan-Hellenic Coun Inc, 1989; pres, La Conf - Alpha Phi Alpha Fraternity Inc; steering comm, Greater New Orleans Found; bd dirs, Human Serv Cable. **Honors/Awds:** Outstanding Young Educator, William Carey Col, 1981; Distinguished Service Award, Alpha Phi Alpha Fraternity Inc, 1989; Advisor of the Year - Stud govt, Xavier Univ.

BYRD, KATIE W.
Manager. **Personal:** Born in Mobile, AL; children: Marcus Dalton, Taynetta Joi. **Educ:** Ala A & M Univ, BS, MS; Pa State Univ, PhD. **Career:** Teacher educ specialist; counr; equal opportunity officer; supvry mgt analyst; Univ Ala A & M, Prof. **Orgs:** Womens Equity Action League; Nat Asn Black Psychologists; Nat Asn Adminr Counrs & Deans; Pi Lambda Theta; Nat Asn Advan Colored People; Phi Beta Kappa; Md Asn Univ Women; chairperson, Social Action-Delta Sigma Theta Sorority Inc; Womens Polit Caucus; state recorder, vpres, Huntsville Chap AL New S Coalition; chair, bd, Harris Home C & Community Action Agency; pres, DeltaSigma Theta Sorority, 2005-07. **Honors/Awds:** Equal Employment Opportunity Award; Outstanding Young Women Am; Outstanding Black Human Service; Good Govt Award, Huntsville Jaycees; Outstanding Leadership Award; Outstanding Committee Service Award; Class Achievement Award. **Military Serv:** AUS, Missile Command. *

BYRD, LANIER
College administrator, educator. **Educ:** Prairie View A&M Univ, BA, MA, DSc, 1995. **Career:** Col admin (retired), educator (retired); St Phillips Col, prof & vpres acad affairs.

BYRD, LEWIS E.
Entrepreneur. **Educ:** Harvard Col, undergraduate, Econ; Harvard Bus Sch, MBA, gen mgt. **Career:** opportunity capital partners; Meridian Point Partners, managing dir, currently; Opportunity Capital Partners, gen partner, currently. **Orgs:** Dir, Harvard Bus Sch Alumni Asn; Chair, Bd Trustees SFJAZZ. **Business Addr:** General Partner, Opportunity Capital Partners, 2201 Walnut Ave Suite 210, Fremont, CA 94538, **Business Phone:** (510)795-7000.*

BYRD, LUMUS, JR.
Executive. **Personal:** Born Apr 25, 1942, Clinton, SC; son of Lumus Sr. and Mary J. **Educ:** SC State Col, BS, Bio, 1965, MS, Bio, 1969. **Career:** Charleston, SC Sch Dist 20, educ, 1965-70; Jos Schlitz Brewing Co, dist mgr, 1970-74; Greyhound Lines, Inc, dir Sales, 1974-78; The Greyhound Corp, mgr mkt develop, 1978-82; T & T Iron Works, pres, 1989; Byrd Enterprises Inc, pres, chmn, ceo; sc state univ, Acad Affairs & Faculty Liaison Comt, vice chair, currently. **Orgs:** Vpres Nat Asn Mkt Develop, 1980; treas, Am Mkt Asn, 1982; vpres, Phoenix Advert Club 1984; dir, bd Valley Leadership Inc, 1984; vpres, Alpha Hi Alpha Frat, 1985; adv bd, YMCA, 1985. **Honors/Awds:** Distinguished Alumni, SC State Col, 1984; Man of the Year, Alpha Phi Alpha Frat, 1983; Outstanding Toastmasters, 1984. **Business Addr:** Vice Chair, South Carolina State University, Academic Affairs & Faculty Liaison Committee, 300 College St NE, Orangeburg, SC 29117, **Business Phone:** (803)536-7000.*

BYRD, MANFORD, JR.
School administrator. **Personal:** Born May 29, 1928, Brewton, AL; son of Manford and Evelyn Patton; married Cheri; children: Carl, Bradley & Donald. **Educ:** Iowa Cent Col, BA, 1949; Atlanta Univ, MA, 1954; Northwestern Univ, PhD,1978. **Career:** School administrator (retired). Quincy, Il, teacher, 1949-54; Chicago Pub-Schs, teacher & prin, asst gen supt, dep supt, gen supt, 1954-90. **Orgs:** Bd dir, Chicago State Univ; Joint Negro Appeal; Chicago State Univ Found, Mid-Am Chap; Am Red Cross; Sigma Pi Phi, Beta Boule; Nat Treas, Sigma Phi Fraternity, 1980; Nat Alliance Black Sch Educrs; chmn, Christian Educ, Trinity United Church; Large Unit Dist Asn; bd dir, Coun Great City Schs; Found Excellence Teaching. **Honors/Awds:** Recipient of more than 100 awards and commendations for excellence in teaching and academic administration, including honorary doctorates from Central College, Hope College and the National College of Education. *

BYRD, DR. MARQUITA L.
Educator. **Personal:** Born Mar 24, 1950, Atlanta, GA; daughter of Robert Byrd and Wilhelmina; married Henry Neal Wilbanks III (divorced); children: Marquis Lawrence. **Educ:** Cent Mo State Univ, BS, 1972; Southern Ill Univ, Edwardsville, MA, 1975; Univ Mo, Columbia, PhD, 1979. **Career:** Univ Southern MS, asst prof, 1977-81; Univ Houston-Downtown, asst prof, 1981-83; Southeast MO St Univ, asst prof, 1983-87; Central MO St Univ, asst prof, 1987-91; San Jose St Univ, assoc prof, 1991-. **Orgs:** Nat Commun Asn, 1977-; Am Acad Religion, 1999; Phi Beta Kappa, 1989. **Honors/Awds:** Service Award, NASA Ames Res Ctr, 1999;

Women's Resource Center, Unsung Heroine, 1997; "10 Most Influential African Americans in the Bay Area", City Flight Media Network, 2005. **Special Achievements:** Written: The Intracultural Communication Book, 1993; Multicultural Communication and Popular Culture: Racial and Ethnic Images in Star Trek,1998; "Black Characters on TV", Encore, 1997; "Black Screen Images-,"Journal of Communication and Minority Issues, 1998. **Business Addr:** Associate Professor, Department of Communication, San Jose State University, 1 Washington Sq, HGH 206, San Jose, CA 95192-0112.

BYRD, BRIGADIER GEN. MELVIN L.
Military leader. **Personal:** Born Nov 1, 1935, Suffolk, VA; son of Harry A and Lenora Pergram; married Diane Diggs, Dec 27, 1968; children: Donna, Melanie, Rosslyn & Melvin Jr. **Educ:** Howard Univ, BA, 1958; Babson Inst, MBA, 1974; Army War Col, 1980; Harvard Univ, attended 1989. **Career:** Military leader (retired); AUS, Hq Dept Army, Wash, DC, inspector gen, 1977-79; dep dir joint actions, DCSLOG, 1980-81; 82nd Airborne Div, Ft Bragg, NC, div support command, comdr, 1981-83; Vint Hill Farms Stations, Warrenton, Va, electronics material readiness activity, comdr, 1983-86; Heidelberg, Ger, army materiel command, comdr, 1986-88, Ft Monmouth, NJ, commun electronics command, dep commanding gen, 1988. **Orgs:** Armed Forces Commun & Electronics Asn; Am Soc Mil Comptrollers; Asn AUS, Ft Monmouth Chap; Soc Logistics Engrs. **Military Serv:** AUS, brigadier gen, 1959-; two Legion of Merit awards, three Bronze Stars, Air Medal, Army Commendation Medal, three Meritorious Serv Medals, Distinguished Serv Medal. **Home Addr:** 4561 La Salle Ave, PO Box 9068, Alexandria, VA 22304-0068.

BYRD, SHERMAN CLIFTON
Clergy, police officer, president (organization). **Personal:** Born Dec 6, 1928, Mesquite, TX; married Dorothy Barksdale; children: Duane Edward, Dorothy Eleanor, James, Henry, Thomas, Nancy Ellen, Sandra Kay, Johnathan Earl, Joyce Jean. **Educ:** St Philip's Col, attended 1956, 1966; Guadalupe Col, BDiv, DD, 1962; Bible World Christian Univ, ATh. **Career:** San Antonio Police Dept, 1953-62; Bexar County DA's Off, criminal invest, 1963-78; cert law enforcement instr; Holy Land Mus Am, bd chmn, chief exec officer, founder & pres; Guadalupe Baptist Theol Sem; First Providence Baptist Church, pastor. **Orgs:** Community Workers Coun, 1955; coord & vpres, San Antonio Child Care Asn, 1963; Bexar County Fed Credit Union, 1964; Tex Baptist Ministry Union; founder, Emancipation Day Comn, 1980; founder, Non Profit 501C3 Corp, Holy Land Am Inc, 1987; Providence Baptist Church; pres & founder, United Coun Civic Action; Christian Action Prog. **Special Achievements:** Author "The Transplant," "God's Plan To Heal Our Land;" est min wage law first city in TX. **Military Serv:** USN, 1948-50. **Business Addr:** Pastor, 1st Providence Baptist Church, 1015 Clark Ave, San Antonio, TX 78210-2612.*

BYRD, DR. TAYLOR
Educator, college teacher. **Personal:** Born Nov 2, 1940, Greene County, AL; married Katie W; children: Marcus Dalton & Taynetta Joy. **Educ:** Ala A&M Univ, BS, 1963; Tuskegee Inst, MEd, 1969; PA State Univ, PhD, 1972. **Career:** TN Valley High Sch, instr, 1963-64; AL Agr & Mech Univ, NASA tech, Agr Bus Educ Dept, chmn, 1972-, dir & prof agr bus educ, currently; Woodson High Sch, Andalusia, AL, instr, asst coach, 1964-66; TN Valley High Sch, instr, asst prin, 1966-70; PA State Univ, grad res asst, 1970-72. **Orgs:** Proj dir, Cross-Cultural Skills & Interpersonal Effect Urban Environ, 1972; Evaluator, So Reg Agr Educ Conf Mobile, Al, 1973; chmn, Greater Huntsville 100 Black Men Am; Nat Educ Asn; Am Evaluation Asn. **Honors/Awds:** Student Council Avd Award, TN Valley HS, 1968; Teacher of the Year, TN Valley HS, 1969; Outstanding Achievement, Ed Phi Beta Sigma, 1973; Class Achievement Award, Nat Alumni-normalite Asn, 1973; Citation for Outstanding Contributions to Research Devel, Reg Adaptive Tech Ctr, Honolulu, 1975. **Business Addr:** Professor, Agricultural & Mechanical University, Department Agr Bus Educ, 225 Dawson Bldg Meridian St, Normal, AL 35762.

BYRD, TONI. See BUCKSON, TONI YVONNE.

C

CABBELL, EDWARD JOSEPH
Educator. **Personal:** Born Jun 26, 1946, Eckman, WV; son of John Marshall and Cassie Haley King; married Madeline Harrell (divorced); children: Melissa Yvette & Winnia Denise. **Educ:** Concord Col, BS Ed, 1970; Appalachian State Univ, MA, 1983. **Career:** Upward Bound & Spec Serv Disadvantaged Stud, dir, 1969-75; Creativity Appalachian Minorities Prog, coordr, 1975; John Henry Folk Fest, dir, 1975-; John Henry Records, producer, 1978-; Black Diamonds Mag, ed, 1978-; John Henry Mem Found Inc, founder, dir; John Henry Blues Society, coord, 1988-; Appalachian documentary, dir; Appalachian St Univ, financial aid asst, 1993, John Henry Ctr Cult & History Exchange, curator, currently, John Henry Festival & Conf, dir, currently. **Orgs:** Photog Proj, 1977-; adv comm, Folklife Festival, 1982; Worlds Fair, 1982; bd Coun, the Southern Mountains, 1984; gov appointee bd mem, WV Martin Luther King Jr State Holiday Comm, 1986-97; Birthplace Country Music Alliance/Smithsonian Cult Comt, 2001. **Honors/Awds:** Writer's Scholarship Breadloaf Writers Conf, 1970; Black Studies Fellowship, Univ Louisville, 1971; Appalachian Studies Fellowship Berea Col, 1980-81; James Still Fellow in Appalachian Studies Univ Ky, 1981; WEB DuBois Fellow, WVa Univ, 1987-89; Edward J. Cabbell Endowment for Appalachian studies, Appalachian State Unv, 1999-. **Special Achievements:** Co-editor: Black in Appalachia Univ Press Ky, 1985; Edited Blacks in Appalachia with William H Turner, University Press of Kentucky, 1985; Contemporary Authors, 1987. **Home Addr:** 352 Demain Ave, Morgantown, WV 26501. **Business Addr:** Curator, Appalachian University, John Henry Center for Culture & History Exchange, 247 Beechurst Ave Suite 1-A, PO Box 1172, Morgantown, WV 26507, **Business Phone:** (304)292-0767.

CABBIL, LILA
Manager, president (organization). **Personal:** Born in Detroit, MI. **Educ:** Wayne State Univ, BS, MS, human develop & resources. **Career:** Univ Mich Hosp, Occup therapist; Asn Educ & Rehab, Rehab teacher; Upshaw Inst Blind, Detroit, MI, supvr occup info & children's servs, 2003; LMC Diversified Consult, pres; Multicultural Experience Leadership Develop Prog, dir, 2003-; Rosa & Raymond Parks Inst, pres, pres emer; Wayne State Univ, Ctr Peace Conflict Studies, prog dir. **Orgs:** Proj dir, High Vision Games; Multicultural Curric Develop Master Teachers Visually Impaired, Univ Colo; bd mem, Am Found Blind; Vis Nurse Asn; Mr Bus & Youth Club; Child Care Coord Coun; Ethnic Coun; Detroit Asn Black Orgns, & Mich Coalition Human Rights.

CABELL, ENOS M
Baseball manager, executive, baseball player. **Personal:** Born Oct 8, 1949, Fort Riley, KS; widowed; children: Marcus, Stephen & Cordell. **Career:** Baseball player (retired), baseball manager, executive; Baltimore Orioles, third baseman, first baseman & outfielder, 1972-74; Houston Astros, 1975-80; San Francisco Giants, 1981; Detroit Tigers, 1982-83; Houston Astros, 1984-85, consult baseball opers, spec asst gen mgr, 2004-; Los Angeles Dodgers, 1985-86; HSE Telecasts, analyst, 1991-94; KCOH Radio, host weekly call-in show, 1991-96; Enos Cabell Chevrolet & Buick, car dealership owner, 1992-95; Cabell Motors Inc, chief exec officer, 1999; Tex Southern Univ, interim athletic dir, 2000. **Orgs:** Tex Southern Univ Bd Regents, 1995-2001; bd dir, Joe Niekro Found. **Business Phone:** (713)259-8000.

CADDELL, PHYLLIS
Entrepreneur. **Personal:** Born in Los Angeles, CA. **Educ:** MA, organizational communs. **Career:** Pc Pub Rels & Mgt Inc, Chief Exec Officer, 1996-; PC2 Media, Chief Exec Officer, 2003-. **Special Achievements:** Author, Put Your Best Foot Forward; featured in the July 2001 issue of Essence Magazine. **Business Addr:** Chief Executive Officer, Pc Public Relations & Management, 1680 N Vine St Suite 716, Los Angeles, CA 90028, **Business Phone:** (323)993-0773.*

CADE, ALFRED JACKAL
Military leader. **Personal:** Born Feb 4, 1931, Fayetteville, NC; married Florence; children: five. **Educ:** Va State Col, BS, Gen Psychol; Syracuse Univ, MBA, 1965; Artillery Sch; Quartermaster Sch; AUS Field Artillery Sch; AUS Command & Gen Staff Col; Indust Col Armed Forces. **Career:** Retired, US Army, 2nd Lt, 1952-54, brig gen, 1954-78; asst sector adv, 1966-67; Phu Yen Prov Vietnam, sector adv, 1967; US Milit Command Vietnam, dep sr prov adv, 1967; Pac-Vietnam, comdr 1st Battalion 92nd Arty, 1967-68; budget opers officer, 1968-69; Dir Army Budget Wash, exec officer, 1970-72; Mat Command Wash, DC, asst comptroller budget 1972; 210th Field Arty Group Europe, comdr, 1973-74; Caesars Atlantic City, sr vpres, govt rels, 1979-96; Fleet Bank NJ, Off Chmn, spec adv. **Orgs:** chair, NJ Comn Higher Educ, 1999; bd trustees, Rowan Univ & Atlantic Cape Community Col; pres, Vietnam Veterans Memorial Found; chmn emer, Atlantic County Conf Community & Justice; chmn, NJ State Chamber Com; Syracuse Univ, Sch Mgt, Corp Adv Bd. **Honors/Awds:** Hon degree, St. Peter's Col. **Military Serv:** AUS Brig Gen; Recipient Legion of Merit (with 2 Oak Leaf Clusters); Bronze Star Medal (with 3 Oak Leaf Clusters); Meritorious Serv Medal; Air Medal; Army Commend Medal; Combat Infantryman Badge; Parachutist Badge. *

CADE, HAROLD EDWARD
School administrator. **Personal:** Born Aug 25, 1929, Bon Ami, LA; married Josephine Lockhart; children: Deryl Vernon. **Educ:** Prairie View A&M Univ, BA, 1955, BS, 1958; Univ Colo, MA, 1960; North Tex State Univ, M.Ed, 1967. **Career:** VISD Gross HS, football coach, 1960; VISD Victoria/Stroman HS, counr, 1965-; TSTA Dist 3, pres, 1975; VISD Patti Welder Jr High, prin, 1975-85. **Orgs:** Football coach, Lockhart Pub Schs, 1953; football coach, FW Gross, 1955-66; counr, Victoria HS, 1965-67; asst prin, Stroman HS, 1967; pres, Victoria Kiwanis Club, 1975; lt govr, Div 25 Tex/Okla Dist, 1977; pres, Victoria TSTA, 1978. **Honors/Awds:** Tex State Teacher Asn, 1967; bd dir, Victoria Chamber Com, 1978; supt, Palestine Baptist Church SS, 1979-85; Young Men's Christian Asn Victoria, 1980-85. **Military Serv:** USMC, lt, 1954-57. **Business Addr:** Victoria, TX 77901.*

CADE, WALTER, III
Artist, actor, musician. **Personal:** Born Jan 1, 1936?, New York, NY; son of Walter and Helen Henderson Brehon; married. **Educ:** Inst Modern Art NY; Lee Strasberg Sch Dramatic Arts; Muse Drama Workshop. **Career:** Movies: Cotton Comes to Harlem; Education Sonny Carson; The Wiz; Claudine; F/X, Angel Heart; TV series: "Joe Franklin Show"; "Positively Black", "Soul"; "Sammy Davis Telethon"; "Musical Chairs"; "Big Blue Marble". **Honors/Awds:** Best Show, Whitney Mus, NY, 1978; Best Show, Mus Modern Art, NY, 1979; Award of Distinction, Nat Endowment Arts Mus Prog, 1979; Best Show, Metro Mus Art, NY, 1980; Best Show, Nat Gallery Art, Washington, DC, 1980; Award of Distinction, Guggenbeim Mus, NY, 1981; Best Show, Smithsonian Inst, Washington, DC, 1981; Best Show, Bruce Mus, CT, 1994; Award of Merit, Mus Modern Art, NY, 1986. **Special Achievements:** Numerous exhibitions. *

CADET, RON
Executive. **Educ:** Rensselaer Polytechnic Inst, BS, comput & syst eng, 1986. **Career:** Systs Programming Analyst, Westinghouse; Wild 107 & KSOL-FM, San Francisco, CA, prog dir; XHRM-FM, San Diego, CA, prog dir; KBLX-FM, San Francisco, CA, music dir; BayView Systs, co-founder, pres, & chmn, 1999-2002; comput & systs eng; radio prog dir; MusicNet, NT City, dir tech partnerships; Imhotech Inc, co-founder, chmn, pres & chief technol officer; Sawyer Law Group, tech specialist digital media, currently. **Honors/Awds:** Nominated three times as Nat Smooth Jazz Director of the Year. **Military Serv:** Patents pending in the areas of Digital Rights Management, Encoding Processes, and Business Methods relating to the distribution and sale of digital media. **Business Addr:** Technology Specialist Digital Media, Sawyer Law Group, Embarcadero Corporate Center, 1275 Fairfax Ave Suite 203, 2465 E Bayshore Rd Suite 406, Palo Alto, CA 94303, **Business Phone:** (650)493-4540.

CADOGAN, MARJORIE A.
Lawyer. **Personal:** Born Dec 11, 1960, New York, NY; daughter of George and Doreen Leacock. **Educ:** Fordham Univ, BA, 1982, JD, 1985. **Career:** NY City Law Dept, asst corp coun, 1985-90; NY City Loft Bd, coun, 1990-91; NY City Dept Parks & Recreation, gen coun, 1991-95; Primary Care Dev Corp, dir external affairs; City NY, Mayor's Off Health Insurance Access, exec dir, exec deputy comnr, currently. **Orgs:** Am Bar Asn, 1985-; Asn Black Women Attys, treasr, 1991-93, vpres, 1993-. **Honors/Awds:** Robert B McKay Advocacy Award, 1985; Outstanding Asst Corp Coun, NY City Bar Asn, 1990; Fordham Univ Sch Law. **Business Addr:** Executive Deputy Commissioner, City of New York, Mayor Off Health Insurance Access, 291 Broadway Bsmt, New York, NY 10007, **Business Phone:** (212)693-1850.*

CADORIA, SHERIAN GRACE
Military leader. **Personal:** Born Jan 26, 1940, Marksville, LA; daughter of Joseph and Bernice McGlory. **Educ:** Southern Univ, BS, bus educ, 1961; AUS, Command & Gen Staff Col, dipl, 1971; Univ Okla, MA, human rels, 1974; AUS, War Col, dipl, 1979; Nat Defense Univ, Inst Higher Defense Studies, 1985. **Career:** Military (retired), Consultant; Women's Army Corps Sch & Ctr, instr, human rels officer, 1971-73; Women's Army Corps Br, AUS Military Personnel Ctr, exec officer/personnel officer, 1973-75; Law Enforcement Div Officer, deputy chief staff, Personnel Hq Dept Army, personnel staff officer, 1975-76; Military Police Stud Battalion, battalion comdr, 1977-78; Phys Security Div AUS Europe & 7th Army, div chief, 1979-82; 1st Region Criminal Invest Command, brigade comdr, 1982-84; Dept Army, chief, Office Army Law Enforcement, 1984-85; Pentagon Orgn Joint Chiefs Staff, dir manpower & personnel, 1985-87; US Total Army Personnel Command, deputy comdr, dir mobilization & oper, 1987-90; Cadoria Speaker & Consult Serv, pres, 1990-; CLECO, Compensation Comn, 1993-. **Orgs:** Hon mem, La Asn Develop Educ; WAC Vet Asn, 1980-; Vet Foreign Wars, 2000; Order of the Holy Sepulchre of Jerusalem, 2000; Horatio Alger Asn, 2003; volunteer prin, Marksville Cath Sch. **Honors/Awds:** George Olmstead Scholar, Freedom Found, Valley Forge, PA, 1972; Social Aide to the Pres USS, 1975-76; Distinguished Alumni Award, Southern Univ, 1984; Distinguished Serv Medal, Hofstra Univ 1986; Int Black Woman of the Year, Los Angeles Sentinel 1987; Roy Wilkens Meritorious Serv Award, NAACP, 1989; Hall of Fame, LA Black Hist, 1992; DHL, OHI Dominican Univ, 1992, Benedictine Univ, 1993; YMCA Spirit of Giving, 1999; Strong Men & Women Excellence in Leadership, 1999; Regional Hall of Fame, AUS Military Police, 2000; LA Vet Hall of Honor, 2002; Horatio Alger Distinguished Am, 2003. **Special Achievements:** First woman to command an all-male battalion; first woman to lead a criminal investigation brigade; First African-American woman to be admitted to Command and General Staff College and the US Army War College; First African-American woman director for the Joint Chiefs of Staff. One of Ams Top 100 Black Bus & Professional Women 1985; One of 75 Black Women who helped change history in the I Dream A World photo exhibit in Corcoran Gallery, USA West/Life Mag, 1989. **Military Serv:** AUS, Brigadier Gen, 29 yrs; Legion of Merit, 3 Bronze Stars, 2 Meritorious Serv Medals, Air Medal, 4 Army Commendation Medals;

Distinguished Service Medal; Defense Superior Serv Medal. **Home Addr:** 107 Lancelot Dr, Mansura, LA 71350-3900. **Business Addr:** President, Cadoria Speaker Service, 107 Lancelot Dr, Mansura, LA 71350-3900.*

CADWELL, HAROLD H., JR.
Clergy. **Career:** Mt. Olive Baptist Church, Detroit, MI, admin asst, pastor, 1999-. *

CAESAR, DR. LAEL O.
Educator. **Personal:** Born in Guyana; son of Riley Caesar and Lucy Caesar; married Lena; children: Lloyd & La Vonne. **Educ:** Caribbean Union Col, BTh, 1973; Andrews Univ, MA Religion, 1986; Univ Wis-Madison, Hebrew & Semitic Studies, MA, 1988, PhD, 1991. **Career:** Univ Montemorelos, Montemorelos, NL, Mexico, assoc prof, 1993-96; adj prof OT, Andrews Univ MA Religion exten prog Montemorelos Univ, Universite Adventiste dHaiti, Zaokski Theol Sem, Russia, Cernica, Ilfov, Romania, 1994-; Solusi Univ, Zimbabwe, vis prof, 1999; Andrews Univ, assoc prof, religion, 1996-2003, prof, 2003-, Currently. **Honors/Awds:** Jewish Learning Mansoor Award, Wis Soc, 1990; Teacher of the Year Award, Sch Theol, Montemorelos Univ, 1994; Teacher of the Year Award, Col Arts & Sci, Andrews Univ, 1998-99, 2000-01, 2003-04.

CAESAR, LOIS
Musician, educator. **Personal:** Born Apr 4, 1922, Texarkana, AR; married Richard C. **Educ:** Wiley Col, AB; State Univ Iowa, MA; State Univ Iowa, MFA. **Career:** Fisk Univ, asst prof, 1943-49; Europe & Am, concert pianist, 1949-66; Paris, France debut Salle Gaveau, 1950; Town Hall, NY Debut, 1950; Monsieru & Ciampi, Paris repetitrice, 1951-53; Tenn State Univ, artist in residence, 1955-56. **Orgs:** Bd dir, San Francisco Symphony Found, 1965-75; San Francisco Symphony Asn, 1969-; exec bd, San Francisco Spring Opera, 1969-; San Francisco Grand Jurists, 1972; exec bd, Mayor's Criminal Justice Coun, 1974-; minority chmn, Juvenile Justice Comn, 1976-78; pres, San Francisco WATF; pres, San Francisco Women's Auxiliary Dental Soc, 1977; San Francisco Links; life mem, Nat Asn Advan Colored People; Auxiliary Am Dent Asn, 1979; exec bd, San Francisco Bay Area United Way; Honoree, WAVE Luncheon. **Honors/Awds:** Thomas Jefferson Award, Am Inst, 1978; 6 Best Dressed Awards; 4 Outstanding Community Service Awards. **Special Achievements:** First Black Recipient of Thomas Jefferson Award for Public Service, Am Inst, 1978.

CAESAR, SHIRLEY
Singer, evangelist. **Personal:** Born in Durham, NC; married Bishop Harold I Williams. **Educ:** Shaw Univ, BS, 1984. **Career:** Song: "I'd rather have Jesus", 1951; Caravan Singers, singer, 1958; The Caesar Singers, singer; The Caravans, singer; Mt Calvary Holy Church Winston-Salem, pastor, 1990-; The Shirley Caesar Outreach Ministries Inc, pres, currently; Albums: Albums: I Remember Mama, 1992; Live.He Will Come, 1996; You're Next in Line, 1997; He Will Come to You , 2002; The Passion of Jesus, 2004; I Know the Truth, 2005; Church Is in Mourning, 2006; This Is Gospel: King & Queen, 2007. **Orgs:** Shirley Caesar Outreach Ministries, NC; bd dirs, Divinity Sch Shaw Univ, 1984; spokeswoman, McDonald's Salute to Gospel Music, 1987. **Honors/Awds:** Grammy Award, 1972; Best Female Gospel Singer, Ebony Magazine 1975; performed at the White House for Jimmy Carter, 1979; Dr Martin Luther King Jr Drum Major Award; Top Female Gospel Singer in the Country Ebony Mag Music Poll, 1977; Stellar Award, Gospel Music Industry, 1987; 11-time Grammy Award-winning artist ; 3 Gold Albums; seven Dove Awards; Stellar Award, 2002; hon doctorates, Shaw Univ; hon doctorates, Southeastern Univ. **Special Achievements:** Author: Shirley Caesar: The Lady, The Melody and the Word, 1998; several songs that sold over a million copies including "No Charge", "Don't Drive Your Mother Away"; named proclamation Oct and Nov as Shirley Caesar's Months in Durham NC 1978. **Business Addr:** President, The Shirley Caesar Outreach Ministries Inc, PO Box 3336, Durham, NC 27702.*

CAFFEY, JASON ANDRE
Basketball player. **Personal:** Born Jun 12, 1973, Mobile, AL; son of Thomas and Rose. **Educ:** Univ Ala, attended 1995. **Career:** Basketball player(retired); Chicago Bulls, forward, 1995-98; Golden State Warriors, 1998-2000; Milwaukee Bucks, forward, 2000-03. **Honors/Awds:** NBA Championship, 1996, 1997.

CAFRITZ, PEGGY COOPER
Executive, school administrator, founder (originator). **Personal:** Born Apr 7, 1947, Mobile, AL; daughter of Gladys Mouton Cooper and Algernon Johnson Cooper; married Conrad Cafritz, Dec 21, 1981; children: Zachary & Cooper. **Educ:** George Wash Univ, BA, 1968; Nat Law Ctr George Washington Univ, JD, 1971. **Career:** Executive (retired); Post-Newsweek Stations Inc, spec asst pres, 1970; Duke Ellington High Sch Fine & Performing Arts, Wash, DC, founder & developer; DC Arts Comn, exec comt chmn, 1969-74; St People Study Plan Redevelopment Pub Spaces Downtown Wash, Wash proj dir; Trustee Am Film Inst, independent consult, 1970-73; Woodrow Wilson Int Ctr Scholars, fel, 1972; Minority Cult Proj, exec dir, 1977-79; WETA, Channel 26, Wash, DC, arts critic, 1986-; Wash DC Bd Educ, pres, 2001-04. **Orgs:** DC Bar, 1972; exec comt, DC Bd Higher Educ, 1973; Arts Educ & Am Nat Panel, 1975-; Nat Assembly State Art Agencies, 1979-, exec bd, 1980-86, planning comt 1986-; chair, DC Comn Arts & Humanities, 1979-87; bd trustees, Atlanta Univ, 1983-86; Wash Performing Arts Soc, 1983; bd dirs, PEN/Faulkner Found, 1985-88; Nat Jazz Serv Orgn, 1985-; bd trustees, Kennedy Ctr Performing Arts, 1987; bd mem, Women's Campaign Fund, 1987; co-chair, Smithsonian Cult Equity Subcomt, 1988-; chair, Smithsonian Cult Educ Comt, 1989-; co-founder, Duke Ellington Sch Arts; pres Clinton's Comt Arts & Humanities, 1994. **Honors/Awds:** John D Rockefeller InterNat Youth Award, 1972; Presidents Medal, Catholic Univ Outstanding Comn Serv, 1974; New York Black Film Festival Award 1976; George Foster Peabody Award for Excellence in Television, 1976; 27th Annual Broadcast Media Award, Alvin Brown fel, Aspen Inst, 1977; finalist Nat Emmy Award, 1977; Washingtonian of the Year; Woman of the Year, Mademoiselle Mag; Emmy Award; Peabody Award; Mayor's Art Award for Arts Advocacy, 1991. **Home Addr:** 3030 Chain Bridge Rd NW, Washington, DC 20016.

CAGE, ATHENA
Singer. **Personal:** Born in Russellville, KY. **Educ:** Western Ky Univ. **Career:** Country star Amy Grant; R&B giants; Isley Brothers; Sweat's Elektra; KutKlose; chorus accolades police & fire personnel; Wash Redskins; Priority Rec, solo recording artist. **Orgs:** The Athena Cage Scholarship Fund, Western Kentucky Univ. **Honors/Awds:** Pop Song of the Year, BMI; Screaming Eagles Award. **Special Achievements:** Hey Hey, premiered in Billboard Rhythmic Top 40. **Home Addr:** 304 Pk Ave S Suite 3, New York, NY 10010-4301. **Business Phone:** (212)627-8000.*

CAGE, MICHAEL JEROME
Basketball player, television broadcaster. **Personal:** Born Jan 28, 1962, West Memphis, AR; married Jodi; children: Alexis, Michael Jr & Sydney. **Educ:** San Diego State Univ, attended 1984. **Career:** Basketball player (retired), business man; Television analyst; Pan Am Games, United State Men's Basketball Team, 1983; Los Angeles Clippers, 1984-88; Seattle Supersonics, 1988-94; Cleveland Cavaliers, 1994-96; Philadelphia 76ers, 1996-97; NJ Nets, 1999-2000; Memphis Grizzlies, TV analyst, commentator; Michael Cage Found, founder, currently. **Orgs:** Pres, Fel Christian Athletes. **Honors/Awds:** Western Athl Conf Player of the Year; UPI West Coast Player of the Year; Sports Illustrated's Collegiate Player of the Week, 1984; US Olympic Teamtryouts; Ark Sports Hall of Fame. **Special Achievements:** NBA Draft, First round pick, No 14, 1984.

CAGE, PATRICK B
Lawyer. **Personal:** Born Aug 11, 1958, Chicago, IL; son of Thomas and Gwendolyn Monroe. **Educ:** Ill State Univ, BS, psychol & criminal justice; Ohio Northern Univ, JD, 1984. **Career:** Lima State Hosp, patient advocate; State Farm Ins Cos, arbitrator; Cook County Ct Annexed, Arbitration Prog; City Chicago, sr atty, corp coun, 1985-88; French, Kezelis & Kominiarek, sr assoc, 1988-; O'Hagan Smith & Amundsen LLC, atty & partner, currently. **Orgs:** Alpha Phi Alpha, 1978-; Cook County Bar Asn, 1984-; Am Bar Asn, 1984-; Ill State Bar Asn, 1984-; Chicago Bar Asn, 1984-. **Honors/Awds:** Broker of Year Award, Alpha Phi Alpha, 1979. **Home Addr:** 345 W Fullerton Pkwy, Chicago, IL 60614, **Home Phone:** (773)883-3489. **Business Addr:** Attorney, Partner, O'Hagan Smith & Amundsen LLC, 150 N Mich Ave Suite 3300, Chicago, IL 60601, **Business Phone:** (312)894-3200.*

CAGGINS, DR. RUTH PORTER
Educator. **Personal:** Born Jul 11, 1945, Natchez, MS; daughter of Corinne Baines Porter and Henry Chapelle Porter; married Don Randolph, Jul 1, 1978; children: Elva Rene, Don Randolph Jr & Myles Chapelle. **Educ:** Dillard Univ, BSN, 1967; NY Univ, MA, 1973; Tex Woman's U, PhD, 1992. **Career:** Montefiore Hosp & Medical Center, staff & head nurse, 1968-71; Lincoln Comm Mental HTH Center, staff nurse & therapist, 1972-73; Metropolitan Hosp & Med Center, nurse clin & clin adm sup, 1973-76; Univ Southwestern LOU, asst prof, 1976-78; Prairie View A&M Univ, assoc prof, tenured, 1978-, flc dir, 2001. **Orgs:** Prairie View A&M Univ College Nursing, LIFT Center project dir, 1994; A K Rice IST, assoc mem, Central States Center, 1992-93, gen mem, Texas Center, 1992-93; Asn Black Nursing Faculty, program chair, 1993 Spring Regional; Nat Black Nurses Asn; Sigma Theta Tau, 1973-93; AMR Nurses Asn; Nat League for Nursing; Houston Asn Psychiatric Nurses. **Honors/Awds:** Prairie View A&M Univ, New Achievers Award, 1992; Asn of Black Nursing Faculty, Dissertation Award, 1990; Prairie View A&M Col of Nursing, Distinguished Faculty Award, 1990; AMR Nurses Asn, Minority Fellowship, 1989-92. **Special Achievements:** Author of: The Caggins Synergy Nursing Model, ABNF Journal, 2(1), pp 15-18, 1991, Professional Cohesiveness Among Registered Nurses (dissertation sent to Dissertations Abstracts Intern), 1992; Violence prevention Grant, US Dept HTH & Human Services, Office of Minority HTH, 1997-2000; Urban Family Life Ctr, Prairie View A&M Univ, col Nursing, dir of clinical research, 1997-2000. **Home Addr:** 5602 Goettee Circle, Houston, TX 77091, **Home Phone:** (713)682-1264. **Business Addr:** Associate Professor, Prairie View A&M University, Col Nursing, 6436 Fannin St 9th Fl, Houston, TX 77030, **Business Phone:** (713)797-7058.

CAILLIER, JAMES ALLEN
School administrator, executive, vice president (organization). **Personal:** Born Sep 24, 1940, Lafayette, LA; married Geraldiner Elizabeth Raphael; children: Jennifer, Gerard & Sylvia. **Educ:** Univ Southwestern La, BS, 1964; Southern Univ, MS, 1968; La State Univ, EdD, 1978. **Career:** Pub Schs, Lafayette, LA, supvr, 1967-69, teacher, 1964-67; Univ Southwestern La, dean & prof jr div, 1975, dir & prof, 1970, vpres admin affairs, 1984; US Off Educ, nat field reader, 1972-77, Nat consult, 1974; Comnr Lafayette Harbor Term & Indust, 1975; Delgado & Nunez Community Col, pres; Univ La Syst, pres, pres emer, currently; Taylor Energy Co LLC, bd dirs & vpres external affairs, 1997-; Patrick Taylor Found, exec dir, currently. **Orgs:** Bd dir, Lafayette Chamber Com, 1975-. **Honors/Awds:** Outstanding Young Businessmen of America; American Legion Honor Award; Pacesetter Award; Nat Sci Found Grant, 1966-68. **Special Achievements:** First dean of the College of General Studies in University of Southwestern Louisiana. **Home Addr:** 140 Nickerson Pkwy, Lafayette, LA 70501, **Home Phone:** (337)261-5965. **Business Addr:** Vice President of External Affairs, Taylor Energy Company LLC, 1615 Poydras St Suite 1100, New Orleans, LA 70112, **Business Phone:** (504)581-5491.

CAIN, FRANK
Government official. **Personal:** Born Sep 30, 1930, Mocksville, NC; son of Arthur Reece and Ella Florence Eaton; divorced; children: DiShon Franklin. **Educ:** A&T State Univ, BS, 1956, MS, 1967; NC State Univ; Univ Okla. **Career:** Government official (retired); NC Agr Ext Serv, asst co-agt, 1957-62; USDA-FmHA, asst co-supvr, 1962-66, co supvr, 1966-85. **Orgs:** Black & Minority Employee Orgn; NC Asn Co Supvr; chmn, trustee bd, Bldg Fund Chinquepin Grove Baptist Church; Prince Hall Grand Lodge F&A Masons NC; pres, Alamance County Chap, A&T State Univ Alumni. **Honors/Awds:** Cert Merit, USDA-FmHA, 1977, 1982; Cert Appreciation, Human Rights Comn, 1981. **Special Achievements:** First black FmHA supvr in State of NC. **Military Serv:** AUS, spec E-4, 1953-55; Nat Defense Serv Medal, Good Conduct Medal, Letter of Commendation. **Home Addr:** 857 Dewitt Dr, Mebane, NC 27302. *

CAIN, FRANK EDWARD, JR.
Lawyer. **Personal:** Born Feb 1, 1924, Blenheim, SC; married Dollie M Covington; children: Cherryetta, Anthony. **Educ:** SC State Col, BA; SC State Col, LlB, 1951. **Career:** Kollock Elem Sch Wallace SC, teacher, 1653-55; Bennettsville, SC, atty pvt practice, currently. **Orgs:** SC Bar Asn; SC State Bar; SC Black Lawyers Caucus; Marlboro Co Bar; past & Polemarch Cheraw Alumni Chapt; Kappa Alpha Psi Fraternity; Sr Warden Sawmill Masonic Lodge 375; vpres, Marlboro Co Br, Nat Advan Asn Colored People; past comn, Am Legion Post 213; US Dist Ct Dist SC; US Ct Appeals; pres, W Bennettsvl Precinct Dem Party, Marlboro Co. **Honors/Awds:** Cert Dist Educ, SC Dept Educ, 1966; Cert Achievement, Kappa Alpha Psi Fraternity, 1966. **Military Serv:** AUS, Signal Corps corpl, 1943-46. *

CAIN, HERMAN
Executive, speaker of the house of representatives (u.s. federal government). **Personal:** Born Dec 13, 1945, Memphis, TN; son of Luther and Lenora; married Gloria Cain; children: Melanie & Vincent. **Educ:** Morehouse Col, BS, Maths, 1967; Purdue Univ, MS, comput sci, 1971. **Career:** Pillsbury Co, vpres & corp, syst & servs, 1977-82; Burger King Corp, regional vpres, 1982-86; Godfather's Pizza Inc, pres, 1986-96, chief exec officer, 1988-96, chmn bd, 1996; Nat Restaurant Asn, chief exec officer & pres, 1996-99; The New Voice Inc, pres & chief exec officer, currently. **Orgs:** Bd mem, Creighton Univ, 1989-95; bd mem, Super Valu Inc, 1990-99; bd mem, Utilicorp United Inc, 1992; bd mem, Whirlpool Corp, 1992; bd mem, Fed Res Bank Kans City, 1992-96; pres & chmn bd, Nat Restaurant Asn, 1994-95; bd mem, Nabisco Inc, 1995-2000; bd mem, Hallmark Cards, 2001; bd mem, Reader's Dig, 2001; founder, New Voice Found; former chmn & pres, Tax Leadership Coun, pub educ component Am Fair Taxation; bd dir, AGCO Inc; bd dir, Aquila Inc; bd dir, Ga Chamber Com; bd dir, Morehouse Col, Atlanta, Ga. **Honors/Awds:** Hon Doctorate, Morehouse Col, 1988; Top 25 Black Executive, Black Enterprise, 1988; Hon Doctorate, Tougaloo Col, 1989; Hon Doctorate, Univ Nebr, 1990; Entrepreneur of the Year, Univ Nebr, 1990; Operator of the Year & Gold Plate Award, Int Foodserv Mfr Asn, 1991; Hon Doctorate, NY Tech Col, 1995; Hon Doctorate, Johnson & Wales Univ, 1996; Horatio Alger Award, 1996; Hon Doctorate, Creighton Univ, 1997; Hon Doctorate, Suffolk Univ, 1999. **Special Achievements:** Radio: The Herman Cain Show; TV Appearences: Pizza and Politics , Herman Cain on the Economics; The Cost of Freedom; Author: Leadership Is Common Sense 1997, Speak As A Leader, 1999, CEO of SELF, 2001, They Think You're Stupid, 2005. **Business Addr:** President, Chief Executive Officer, THE New Voice Inc, 825 Fairways Ct Suite 303, Stockbridge, GA 30281, **Business Phone:** (678)565-5335.

CAIN, JOSEPH HARRISON, JR.
Football player. **Personal:** Born Jun 11, 1965, Los Angeles, CA; married; children: Ayana & Joseph III. **Educ:** Ore Tech, Stanford univ, attended. **Career:** Football player (retired); Seattle Seahawks, linebacker, 1989-92, 1997; Chicago Bears, 1993-96.

CAIN, NATHANIEL Z, JR.
Automotive executive. **Personal:** Born Feb 1, 1946, Gary, IN; son of Nathaniel Sr and Evelyn Carr (deceased); married Jacqueline

Weaver, May 26, 1970; children: Fredrick, Jeffrey & Natalie. **Educ:** Purdue Northwest, attended, 1969-70. **Career:** Mad Hatter Rest & Show Lounge, owner, 1976-81; Bart Allen Buick, gen mgr, 1982-85; Chuck White Buick, gen mgr, 1985-86; Tyson Motor Corp, vpres, 1986-; Tyson Lincoln Mercury, pres & gen mgr, 1989-, chief exec officer, 1996-; Melrose Lincoln Mercury Inc, co-owner & vpres, 1997-; Highland Lincoln Mercury Inc, chief exec officer, currently. **Orgs:** Chrysler Minority Dealers Asn, 1986; Nat Automobile Dealers Asn, 1986; Ind COC, 1989; Highland COC, 1989; Northwest Ind Auto Dealers Asn, 1989; Ford Lincoln Mercury Minority Dealers Asn, 1989; Nat Asn Minority Auto Dealers, 1990; bd dirs, Boys & Girls Clubs Am; bd trustees, Gary YWCA; bd dirs, NW Ind Urban League; bd dirs, Gary Men Health Asn. **Honors/Awds:** 100 Champions Award, Tyson Motor Corp, 1996; received numerous awards at the Tyson Motor Corp. **Military Serv:** USMC, cpl, 1963-67, National Defense Service medal, two Vietnam service medals, and Vietnam campaign medal, Good Conduct Medal. **Home Phone:** (219)985-9621. **Business Addr:** President, Chief Executive Officer, Highland Lincoln Mercury Inc, 2440 45th St, Highland, IN 46322, **Business Phone:** (219)924-5500.

CAIN, ROBERT R, JR.
President (Organization). **Personal:** Born Mar 2, 1944, Chicago, IL; married Azucena Becerril; children: Azucena II, Lisa, Carla & Paula. **Educ:** Univ Nebraska, BS, 1977; Northern Colo, MA, 1978; Nat Univ, MBA, 1986, JD, 1995, PhD, 1999. **Career:** US Govt Serv, 1962-82; Super Care Inc, clinic dir, 1982-86; Northeast Clin Care Serv, chief exec officer, 1986-88. **Orgs:** Scottish Rite Mason Shriner 32 degree Mason, 1976-86; Alpha Phi Alpha, 1982. **Military Serv:** USN, W-3, 20 yrs; Vietnam Service Medal. *

CAIN, RUBY
Administrator, executive. **Educ:** Wayne State Univ, BA, sociol; Univ Phoenix, MA, orgn mgt; Ball State Univ, EdD. **Career:** United Way Allen Co, adminr diversity & inclusivness; Creative Training Excellence Inc, pres & chief exec officer, currently; NE Ind Area Health Educ Ctr, dir, currently. **Orgs:** Fort Wayne African Am Cancer Alliance; founding mem, Health Disparity Coalition; pres, Pi Lambda Theta; publicity chair, The Links Inc, Fort Wayne Chapter; diversity chair, Am Asn Univ Women; bd mem, YWCA. **Honors/Awds:** Urban League Outstanding Service, 1997-2000; United Way Outstanding Service, 2003; Chapter of Honor, Pi Lambda Theta, 2004; Faith in Action Volunteer Recognition, 2003, 2004; Great Men & Women of Diversity, 2005; TV21 Indiana NewsCenter Women in Leadership Award, 2006; American Asn of University Women's Eleanor Roosevelt Award, 2006. **Special Achievements:** INK Newspaper One of 7 to Watch and One of 50 Most Influential African Americans in Northeast Indiana, 2004.

CAIN, RUDOLPH ALEXANDER
College administrator, educator. **Personal:** Born Sep 13, 1940, Richmond, VA; son of William and Mary Cain. **Educ:** Hampton Inst, BA, 1962; NY Univ, MA, 1968; Columbia Univ Teachers Col, MA, 1976, EdD, 1977. **Career:** Catholic Home Bur Dependent C, case aide, 1962-65; City Courts of NY, probation officer, 1965-68; Manpower Develop Training Prog, New York City bd educ & supv counr, 1968-69; Pace Univ, Mgt Career Prog Disadvantaged Stud, asst dir, 1969-73; City Univ New York, Medgar Evers Col, SEEK acad counr, 1973-74; State Univ NY, Empire State Col, prof & dir, 1974, Bedford-Stuyvesant Unit, mentor & coordr. **Orgs:** Omega Psi Phi Fraternity; Health Task Force, NY African Am Inst, 1984; chair, Educ Taks Force, Bedford-Stuyvesant Community Conf, 1986-91; trustee, Soc Preserv Weeksville & Bedford-Stuyvesant Hist, 1988-90; community bd, Parks & Recreation Comt, 1994-96. **Honors/Awds:** Dept Health, Educ & Welfare fel, 1966-68; Kings county Club, Professional Award, Nat Asn Bus & Prof Women's Clubs, 1993; Dr Rudy Cain Scholar Fund established, 1999. **Special Achievements:** Author, Alain Leroy Locke: Race, Culture, and the Education of African American Adults, Rodopi Press 2002; Visual artwork selected for group showings, 1999, 2000. *

CAIN, SIMON LAWRENCE
Lawyer. **Personal:** Born Dec 19, 1927, Augusta, GA; married Ada Spence. **Educ:** Howard Univ, BA 1949, LLB 1956. **Career:** pvt pract, atty, currently. **Orgs:** Wash Bar Asn; Am Bar Asn; Nat Bar Asn; DC Bar Asn; pres, Lamond-Riggs Citizen Asn 1968-70; pres DC Fedn Civic Asn, 1969-71; chmn, highways & transp Palisades Citizens Asn, 1974. **Honors/Awds:** Recipient Korean/UN 3 Battle Stars, USAF, 1950. **Military Serv:** USAF, Lt col, 26 yrs. **Home Addr:** 4901 Kingle St NW, Washington, DC 20016-2651, **Home Phone:** (202)362-3093. *

CAIN, WALDO
Surgeon. **Personal:** Born Sep 29, 1921, East Gadsden, AL; son of James L and Evelyn Croft; married Natalia; children: Sheila, Anita. **Educ:** Meharry Med Col, MD, 1945. **Career:** SW Detroit Hosp, chief surg; Meharry Med Col, clinical asst prof surg, 1946-52; Grace & Harper Hosps, physician, 1968- ; Wayne State Univ Sch Med, assoc prof, currently. **Orgs:** State Mich Judicial Tenure Commn Physician Yr Detroit Med Soc, 1969; founder, First Independence Nat Bank Detroit; life mem, Nat Asn Advan Colored People; Am Col Surgeons; Soc Mil Surgeons; Detroit Acad Surgery; pres, Cain-Tanner Asn; pres, Cain-Wood Surg Asn; Sigma Pi Phi Boule honor fraternity; Alpha Omega Alpha honor soc; Nat Med Asn; Detroit Med Soc; Mich State Med Soc; Wayne County Med Soc; Soc Mil Surgeons; Am Soc Abdominal Surgeons; Am Col Surgeons. **Military Serv:** AUS, MC capt, 1953-55. **Business Addr:** Associate Professor of Surgery, Wayne State University, 4201 St Antoine, Detroit, MI 48201, **Business Phone:** (313)577-3587.*

CAINES, BRUCE STUART
Photographer. **Personal:** Born Jan 7, 1959, Jamaica, NY; son of David Caines and Inez; married Lisa Bernad, May 1994. **Educ:** Sch Visual Arts, NY, BFA, photog, 1981. **Career:** Nickelodeon's Blue's Clues, dir; Bruce Caines Photog, photogr & dir, currently. **Orgs:** NY Cares, vol, 1990-94; Black Women in Publ, 1994-96; Film Video Arts, NY; Asn Independent Video & Filmmakers. **Special Achievements:** Our Common Ground, Portraits of Blacks Changing the Face of America, Crown Publ, 1994; Our Common Ground, Nat Photography Exhibit, Art Inst Chicago, 1994-95; Contributing Photogr For Jazziz Mag, La Style, Essence, Emerge, Newsweek, Philadelphia Inquirer, Sunday Mag; Dir, Music Videos; Producer & Dir, Short Film, "Breaking Up", 2001; Contributing Ed, Archetype Mag; Emmy nomination for Outstanding Directing in a Children's Series, 2003. **Business Addr:** Photographer, Director, Bruce Caines Photography, Wacky Dog Imageworks, Inc., 2 Adrian Ave Suite 2A, New York, NY 10463, **Business Phone:** (718)295-0950.

CAISON, THELMA JANN
Physician. **Personal:** Born Apr 26, 1950, Brooklyn, NY. **Educ:** Winston Salem State Univ, BS, 1972; State Univ NY, Buffalo Sch Med, MD, 1977. **Career:** Bd Educ New York City, biol teacher, 1972-73; Harlem Hosp Med Ctr, med externship trauma surg & surg ICU, NY, 1974, med externship obstet & gyn, 1975; Downstate Med Ctr Kings Co Hosp Ctr, summer med externship internal med, NY,1976; Montefiore Hosp Med Ctr & N Central Bronx Hosp, physician, 1977-83; Henry Ford Hosp Dept Pediat & Div Adolescent Med, div head, 1983; pvt prat, currently. **Orgs:** AMA, 1970-80; Nat Med Asn, 1979-80; Comt Residents & Interns, 1979-80; State Univ NY Buffalo & Sch Med Alumni Asn; Delta Sigma Theta Nat Sor; Winston Salem Univ Alumni Asn. **Honors/Awds:** Medical Scholastic Honor, State Univ NY Buffalo Sch Med, 1973-77; Pride in Heritage Award, field med Phi Delta Kappa Nat Sor, 1978; guest speaker, seminar hypertension & nutrition Phi Delta Kappa Sor, 1979; accomplished pianist. *

CALBERT, ROOSEVELT
Government official. **Personal:** Born Nov 13, 1931, Philadelphia, MS; son of Jim and Ann; married Thelma Nichols; children: Debra C Brown, Jacquelyn C Smith, Rosalyn C Groce, Lori A. **Educ:** Jackson State Univ, BS, 1954; Univ Mich, MA, 1960; Univ Kans, MS & PhD, plasma physics , 1971. **Career:** Alcorn State Univ, physics prof, 1960-63; AL State Univ, math & physics coordr, 1963-68; Univ Kans, res asst, 1969-71; Inst Servs Educ, dir cooperating acad planning, 1971-75; Nat Sci Found, prog dir, div dir, currently. **Orgs:** Phi Beta Sigma Frat, 1951-; Alpha Kappa Mu Nat Honorary Soc, 1952-; founder, Heritage Fellowship Church, 1978; bd chmn, Community Investors Corp, 1982-; AAAS, 1984-. **Honors/Awds:** Distinguished Alumnus Award, Jackson State Univ, 1986. *

CALBERT, REV. WILLIAM EDWARD, SR.
Clergy. **Personal:** Born Jun 11, 1918, Lemoore, CA; son of William Riley (deceased) and Sadie Emma Hackett (deceased); married Katie Rose Baker (divorced 1961); children: William E (deceased), Rose M Findley, Muriel L, Katherine E Jackson &Yvonne A DeSena; married Madlyn G Williams, Jun 15, 1963; children: William E Jr. **Educ:** SF State Col, CA, AB 1949; Am Baptist Sem W, Berkeley, M Div, 1952; Teachers Col, Columbia Univ, MA 1963; Am Univ, Wash DC, Post Grad Study, 1970-71. **Career:** AUS, enlisted & warrant Officer serv, 1942-46, Comned first Lt, chaplain, AUS, 1952; US, Far East, Ger, unit & org chaplain, 1952-62; AUS Chaplain Sch, Brooklyn, NY, staff & fac, 1963-67; Concord Baptist Church Brooklyn, NY, Pastoral Assoc & dir christian educ part-time, 1964-67; AUS, Vietnam, staff chaplain, dep Staff, 1967-68; Hq first AUS, Ft Meade MD, asst army chaplain, Lt Col, 1968-69; Far East Comm Serv Anti-Poverty Agency, DC, asst dir/exec dir 1970-73; St Elizabeths Hosp, DC, staff chaplain,1973-81; Shiloh Baptist Church, Minister educ Wash, DC, 1981-85; Chaplaincy & Pastoral Coun Serv, Am Baptist Churches, USA, Valley Forge, PA, interim dir, 1986-87; Shiloh Baptist Church, Wash, DC, pulpit assoc,1987-. **Orgs:** Phi Delta Kappa; NAACP; Urban League; Asn study Afro-Am Life & Hist; Afro-Am Hist & Genealogical Soc; Alpha Phi Alpha; past pres, DC Grad chp; Retired Officer Asn; Nat Genealogical Soc; Asn Prof Chaplains; Nineth & Tenth Calvary Asn; Wash DC Vote Coalition; bd mem, Housing Develop Corp, DC, 1972-76; DC Mayor's Health Planning Adv Comt, 1972-77; pres, Am Baptist Sem W, 1989-93, int pres, 1990-92, sem trustee, 1990-92; memship comt, Asn Mental Health Clergy, 1988-90; State Adv Coun Adult Educ, Wash, DC, 1990-93; past pres, Wash DC Chap; Nat Trustee Bd, 1996-99; adv bd, Comm Ment Health Ctr, No 2 Wash, DC; Wash, DC Hist Records Adv Bd, 2002-05; Hist Comn, DC Baptist Conv; past trustee & exec comt mem, Nat Military Chaplains Asn. **Honors/Awds:** Certificate of Apppreciation, DC Govt, 1973; Superior Performance Award, St Elizabeth's Hosp, Wash, DC, 1981; Cert Commendation, Am Baptist Churches, 1987; Am Baptist Seminary of the West, Alumnus of the Year, 1996; Mary McCleod Bethune Award, Asn Study Afro-Am Life & History, 2002. **Military Serv:** AUS, Lt Col, WW II 1942-46, 1952-69; 15 military awards & decorations including the Meritorious Service Medal 1969, Bronze Star with Oak Leaf Cluster, Letter of Appreciation, AUS Chief of Chaplains, 1969. **Home Addr:** 1261 Kearney St NE, Washington, DC 20017-4022. *

CALDWELL, ADRIAN BERNARD
Basketball player. **Personal:** Born Jul 4, 1966, Falls County, TX. **Educ:** Navarro Col, Corsicana, TX, attended 1984; Southern Methodist Univ, Dallas, TX, attended 1986; Lamar Univ, Beaumont, TX, attended 1987. **Career:** Basketball Player (retired); Houston Rockets, 1989-91; Shamp Clear Cantu (Italy), 1991-93; Sioux Falls Sky force (CBA), 1993-95; Houston Rockets, 1994; Indiana Pacers, 1995-96; NJ Nets, 1997; Philadelphia 76ers, 1997; Dallas Mavericks, 1998.

CALDWELL, ARDIS
Executive. **Personal:** Born Jun 14, 1953, Ypsilanti, MI; children: Jason & Lyndsi. **Educ:** Wayne State Univ, BS, 1977; Leading Strategic Change, cert, 2002. **Career:** Bank One, teller, 1976-78, mgt trainee, 1978-79, sr asst mgr, 1980-85, br mgr, 1985-92, call ctr site mgr, 1993-. **Orgs:** Vpres, Justice Unity Generosity & Serv; steering comm, African Am Network; African Am Museum. **Honors/Awds:** Lead Award Diversity, 1996, Committment to Excellence, Bank One, 2000-01. **Special Achievements:** Team Captain in UNCF Walkathon, 2002. **Business Addr:** Senior Vice President, Bank One, Oakland Office of Commons, 1235 E Big Beaver Rd, Troy, MI 48083, **Business Phone:** (248)680-2750.

CALDWELL, BARRY H
Vice president (Government), executive. **Educ:** Dartmouth Col, BA; Georgetown Univ Law Ctr, JD. **Career:** US Senator Arlen Specter, chief staff; CIGNA Corp, vpres govt rels, 2000-02; Waste Mgt Inc, Govt Affairs & Corp Communs, sr vpres, 2002-. **Orgs:** Vpres, Fed Affairs Pharmaceut Res & Manufacturers Am, 1996-2002; Nat Solid Wastes Mgt Asn; bd dirs, Keep Am Beautiful. **Business Phone:** (713)512-6200.

CALDWELL, BENJAMIN
Playwright. **Personal:** Born Sep 24, 1937, New York, NY. **Career:** Guggenheim fel playwriting, 1970; Plays: Four plays, 1968; Prayer Meeting or The First Militant Minister, 1968; Hypnotism, Afro-Arts Anthology, 1969; The King of Soul, Family Portrait, New plays From the Black Theatre: An Anthology, 1969; The Job, Black Identity, 1970; All White Caste, Black Drama Anthology, 1970; An Obscene Play, 1971; The Wall, 1972; What Is Going On, 1973; The World of Ben Caldwell, 1982; The Solutions to All the World's Problems: An Evening of Short Works for the stage. **Orgs:** Black Arts Movement, 1960-. **Business Addr:** PO Box 656 Morningside Sta, New York, NY 10026.

CALDWELL, DR. CLEO HOWARD (CLEOPATRA CALDWELL)
Educator. **Educ:** NC A&T State Univ, BS, 1973; Human Develop Wayne State Univ, MA,1975; Univ Mich, AM, 1983; PhD (social psychol), 1986. **Career:** Univ Mich Sch Pub Health, Dept Psychol, Health Behav & Health Ed, fac, Inst social Res, staff, Res Ctr Group Dyn, staff, Sch Pub Health, staff, Health Behav & Health Ed, assoc prof, currently, Prog Res Black Am, Co Assoc dir, currently. **Orgs:** Am Pub Health Asn; Soc Res Adolescents; Soc Res Child Develop. **Business Phone:** (734)647-3176.

CALDWELL, ELETA J.
School principal. **Career:** Art High Sch, Newark, prin. *

CALDWELL, DR. ESLY SAMUEL
Physician. **Personal:** Born Sep 25, 1938, Lancaster, SC; married Judith Mary Slining; children: Esly III, Christina C & Robert S. **Educ:** Howard Univ, Col Liberal Arts, BS, 1960, Col Med, MD, 1964; Univ Mich Sch Pub Health, MPH, 1979. **Career:** Daugherty Med Group, physician; intern physician, pvt pract, currently. **Orgs:** Phi Beta Kappa; pres, Cincinnati Med Asn. **Honors/Awds:** Fel Royal Col Physician Canada; fel Am Acad Family Physicians; fel Am Col Physicians. **Military Serv:** AUS, medl group capt, 2 yrs. **Business Addr:** Physician, 629 Oak St, Cincinnati, OH 45206.

CALDWELL, GEORGE THERON, SR.
Government official. **Personal:** Born Jun 5, 1939, Mississippi County, AR; son of Harry Larnell and Mary Alice Warren; married Jacqueline Romaine Hinch; children: Darri Alice, Jacqueline Michelle, George T II, Robert L, Richard D, Marilynn Kitt, Felecia, Terry, Delores S, Pammela, Shelly Murphy. **Educ:** Gen Col, Univ MN, AA, 1972; Col Liberal Arts, Honors Div, Univ MN, BA, 1976. **Career:** Affirmative Action Dept, County Hennepin, res analyst, 1973-76, asst dir, 1976-80; Dept Civil Rights, City Minneapolis, exec dir, 1980-84; Minnesota Valley Transportation Co Inc SW, owner, 1984-86; Univ Minnesota, asst dir EO & AA, 1986-91, human resources adr, 1991-97; Dept Civil Rights, City

Minneapolis, Minneapolis Pub Schs, deputy dir, 1997-03; City Minneapolis, Human Resources, Dir Employ Servs, 2004-. **Orgs:** Bd dirs, Minneapolis Branch NAACP, 1976-77; bd dirs, Benjamin E Mays Fundamental Sch, 1977-81; trustee, Mt Olivet Baptist Church, 1978-80; chmn, Intergovt Compliance Inst, 1978-81; pres, MN State Affirmative Action Assoc, 1979-80; founder & directorate, MN Soc Open Community, 1983. **Honors/Awds:** NACo New County Achievement Award, Nat Asn Counties, 1977; Outstanding Leadership Award, MN Affirmative Action Asn, 1982; Proclamation GTC Day, City Minneapolis, 1984; Citation Honor, Hennepin County Bd Comnrs. 1984; co owner, one first black owned railroads US hist, Minnesota Valley Transportation Co Inc, Southwest; featured Ebony mag, 1984, Black Enterprise, June 1984, The Top 100 Black Businesses. **Military Serv:** AUS, spec 5 & E-5, 1958-64; Good Conduct Medal, 1st 2nd award; Seventh Army Citation Outstanding Soldier, 1962. **Business Addr:** Director Employment Services, City of Minneapolis, Human Resources, Public Service Center, 250 S 4th St Rm 100, Minneapolis, MN 55415, **Business Phone:** (612)673-2282.*

CALDWELL, JAMES E.
Lawyer. **Personal:** Born May 22, 1930, Louisville, KY; son of George and Emmie Lou; married Dolores Robinson; children: Janelle, James, Randall. **Educ:** Univ Pittsburgh, BA, 1952; ROTC Univ Pittsburgh, grad, 1952; Howard Univ, Sch Law, JD 1958; Univ Chicago, MBA, 1973. **Career:** Stand Oil Co, sr tax atty, 1971-84; Amoco Oil Co, tax atty, 1970-71; Chief Coun Off & IRS, sr trial atty, 1959-70; Gen Coun, US Treas Dept, Honor Law Grad Prog, 1959; James E Caldwell & Assocs, managing partner, 1984-; Chicago Bd Appeals, vice chmn, 2006-. **Orgs:** Joint bd trustees, bd pres, St Anne's & St Elizabeth Hosp; pres, Roseland Econ Develop Corp; mem bd, mgrs treas, Chicago Bar Asn, 1973-75; Chicago Bar Asn, 1975-77; Cook County Bar Asn; Nat Bar Asn; Ill Bar Asn; Supreme Ct; US Bar Asn; bd dirs, Univ Chicago Club XP Prog, MBA; alumni, Grad Sch Busi, Univ Chicago; bd trustees, CBA Pension Fund; bd dirs, CAM Health Trust; Comnr, Supreme Ct, Ill; Coun Legal Edu Opport, pres. **Military Serv:** AUS, Col, 1952-81; Commendation Medal, UN Medal, Korean Serv Medal. *

CALDWELL, JAMES L
Football coach. **Personal:** Born Jan 16, 1955, Beloit, WI; son of Willie and Mary Evelyn; married Cheryl Lynn Johnson, Mar 19, 1977; children: Jimmy, Jermaine, Jared & Natalie. **Educ:** Univ Iowa, BA, Eng, 1977. **Career:** Univ Iowa, grad asst; Southern Ill Univ, football coach, defensive backs, defensive coordr, 1978-81; Northwestern Univ, football coach, defensive backs, 1981-82; Univ Colo, football coach, outside linebackers, quarterbacks, 1982-85; Univ Louisville, football coach, defensive backs, 1985; PA State, football coach, quarterbacks, passing game, 1986-92; Wake Forest Univ, head football coach, 1993-2000; Tampa Bay Buccaneers, quarterback coach, 2001; Indianapolis Colts, asst head coach & quaterback coach, 2002-. **Orgs:** Kappa Alpha Psi Fraternity Inc; Omicron Delta Kappa. **Business Addr:** Assistant Head Coach, Quaterback Coach, Indianapolis Colts, 7001 W 56th St, Indianapolis, IN 46254, **Business Phone:** (317)297-2658.

CALDWELL, JOHN EDWARD
Insurance executive, chief executive officer. **Personal:** Born Feb 10, 1937, Newberry, SC; son of George and Elmira; married Patricia Henderson; children: Sean. **Educ:** Benedict Col, BS, Chemistry & Mathematics, 1965. **Career:** Insurance executive (retired), chief executing officer; Independent Life & Accident Ins Co, staff sales mgr, 1965-96; JE Caldwell Properties, owner & chief exec officer, currently. **Orgs:** Trustee 1970-80, chmn trustee bd, 1980-82, Newberry Co Mem Hosp; bd mem, Newberry Co Task Force Educ, 1982-87; bd mem, United Way Midlands, 1983-86; bd mem, Cent Midlands Human Resources, 1983-87; Newberry Co Coord United Negro Col Fund, 1983-87; bd mem, Newberry Co Voc Educ, 1984-87; bd mem, Piedmont Area Occup Training; State Community Block Grant Bd; mem bd comnr, GLEAMNS Human Resources Comn; Overall Econ Develop Bd; Bethlehem Baptist Ch; chmn & treas, Deacon Bd; chmn, Newberry Co Coun, 1997-2002; bd mem, Nat Asn Counties, 2000; Newberry Co Coun, Counman; bd dir, SC Asn Counties, 2004-08; shriner; 32nd degree Mason; mem, Bethlehem Baptist Church. **Honors/Awds:** Civic Award Outstanding Services, 1984; Outstanding Alumni, Newberry Co Alumni Club, 1985; recognized in Who's Who Among Black Leaders, 1988; National Sales Award, Independent Life & Accident Co Inc. **Special Achievements:** First black Staff Sales Manager in the State of South Carolina; First Black elected to Newberry Co Coun, 1983; First & only black staff mgr for Independent Life & Accident Ins Co; First blacks elected to Newberry County Memorial Hospital Board of Trustees . **Military Serv:** AUS, sp/4 1960-62; Redstone Arsenal AUS Missile Command, missile mech; Outstanding Trainee. *

CALDWELL, LISA JEFFRIES
Lawyer. **Personal:** Born Jan 14, 1961, Burlington, NC; daughter of Roy and Pauline; married Alan Lorenzo Caldwell, Jun 23, 1984; children: Tyler Alan, Lauren Brianna. **Educ:** Univ NC, Chapel Hill, BS, bus admin, 1983; Wake Forest Univ, Sch Law, JD, 1900. **Career:** Womble Carlyle Sandridge & Rice, atty, 1986-90; West & Banks, atty, 1990-91; RJ Reynolds Tobacco Co, mgr, employ practs, 1991-93, personnel mgr, Manuf Opers, 1993-94, personnel mgr, Eng Environ/Support, Distribution/Logistics, 1994-96, dir Human Resources eng, distribution & logistics & leaf opers, 1996-00, dir, Human Resources Strategic Planning, 2000-02, vpres, human resources, 2002-06; sr vpres human resources, 2006-. **Orgs:** Delta Sigma Theta Sorority, 1988-; const comt co-chair, corresponding secy, Moles Inc, 1991-93, recording secy, 1996-98, vpres, 1998-00; bd mem, Univ NC Gen Alumni Asn, 1990-93; Forsyth Co Morehead Scholar Selection Comt, 1988-93; bd mem, Goodwill Inc, 1995-; bd mem, Reynolds Fed Credit Union, 1995-; W Cent Region, Morehead selection comt, 1994-; bd dirs, Safe Passage Group, 1997-; bd dirs, Hospice, 1998-00; bd dirs, CERTL, 1997-00; bd dirs, Piedmont Triad Partnership Found, 2000. **Honors/Awds:** Morehead Scholarship, Morehead Found, 1979-83; National Achievement Scholarship, 1979-83; Wake Forest Law Scholarship, Wake Forest Univ, 1983-86. **Business Addr:** Senior Vice President of Human Resources, RJ Reynolds Tobacco Company, 401 N Main St, PO Box 2959, Winston-Salem, NC 27101, **Business Phone:** (910)741-5000.*

CALDWELL, MARION MILFORD, JR.
Educator. **Personal:** Born Mar 11, 1952, San Antonio, TX; son of Marion Milford (deceased) and Mazie Hammond (deceased); married Priscilla Robertson; children: Priscilla, Marina. **Educ:** Delaware State Col, BS, 1978; Univ DC, MBA 1983; Howard Univ, Doctoral Stud. **Career:** Delaware Tech Community Col, instr bus, 1984; Delaware State Col, prof mkt, 1984-91. **Orgs:** Omega Psi Phi; Prince Hall Mason Prudence Lodge No 6; Am Mkt Assoc; Nat Black MBA Assoc; MBA Exec; Nat Advan Asn Colored People; rep, Fac Senate; Int Platform Asn; Prudence Lodge No6 F & AM, PHA; Nat Community Asn, 1995. **Honors/Awds:** Scholar Award, Del State Col State, 1971; Psi Epsilon Chap Serv Award, Omega Psi Phi, 1980; Cert Recognition Serv, Del State Col, 1989, 1990; Cert Appreciation, 18th Ann Off Educ Leadership Conf, Del State Col, 1986; Outstanding Young Man Am, 1983, 1986. **Business Addr:** Doctoral Student, Howard University, School Communication, C P Powell Bldg, Washington, DC 20059.*

CALDWELL, MIKE ISAIAH
Football player, football coach. **Personal:** Born Aug 31, 1971, Oak Ridge, TN; son of Bobbie; married Sue; children: Sydnei, Saniah & Simeon. **Educ:** Mid Tenn State Univ, BS, bus admin, 1996. **Career:** Football player (retired), Football coach; Cleveland Browns, line backer, 1993-95; Baltimore Ravens, 1996; Ariz Cardinals, 1997; Philadelphia Eagles, 1998-2001; Chicago Bears, 2002; Carolina Panthers, 2003; intern coach, 2004, defensive quality control coach, 2008-. **Business Phone:** (215)463-2500.

CALDWELL, DR. SANDRA ISHMAEL
Dentist. **Personal:** Born Aug 23, 1948, Fort Knox, KY; children: Rhonda. **Educ:** Howard Univ, BS, 1971; Howard Univ Col Dent, DDS, 1981. **Career:** Food & Drug Admin, microbiologist, 1971-77; Ton Ron Productions, vice pres; Pvt practice, dentist, 1991-; Full Circle Dent, owner. **Orgs:** Nat Dent Assoc; Acad Gen Dent; Beta Kappa Chi Honor Soc; Prince George's Soc Health Profls, Sigma Xi Scientific Res Soc; co-chmn, secy, Robert T Freeman Dent Soc; co-chmn Delta Sigma Theta Sor Inc; dent alumni recruiter Howard Univ; Minority Women Sci. **Honors/Awds:** Outstanding Young Women of America, 1980; Who's Who Among Stud, Am Univ & Cols, 1981. **Business Addr:** General Dentist, Full Circle Dentistry, 5505 5th St NW Suite 302, Washington, DC 20011, **Business Phone:** (202)726-3600.*

CALHOUN, CECELIA C.
Educator, nurse. **Personal:** Born Sep 22, 1922, New Roads, LA; daughter of Elie Christopher and Celesea Christopher; married Noah R; children: Stephen, Marc & Cecelia N C Wells. **Educ:** Southern Univ, BS, 1944; Cath Univ, BS, NEd, 1950; Univ Chicago, MS, 1953. **Career:** Vet Admin Med Ctr, staff nurse, head nurse, supr, res nurse, skin integrity, nursing instr. **Orgs:** Consult, Life Styles Wellness; partic, Cath Renewal Prog; pres, Alpha Wives DC; Alpha Kappa Alpha Sorority; Sigma Theta Tau Nurses Hon Soc. *

CALHOUN, DOROTHY EUNICE
Administrator. **Personal:** Born Jul 16, 1936, Salitpa, AL; daughter of Joshua and Maggie Cunningham; married Roosevelt, Apr 11, 1969; children: Michael W Moore & Daryl T Moore. **Educ:** Ala State Univ, BS, 1957; Atlanta Univ, MLS, 1972; Auburn Univ, attended 1973. **Career:** Administrator (retired); Clarke Co Bd Educ, teacher, 1957-59; Montgomery Co Bd Educ, teacher & librn, 1959-70; Maxwell AFB, AL, librn, 1970-94. **Orgs:** NEA, 1959-70; Am Libr Asn, 1970-85; Ala Libr Asn, 1979-83; Delta Sigma Theta Sor; Spec Libr Asn, 1986. **Honors/Awds:** Teacher of the Year, Clarke Co Bd Educ, 1958; Twenty Years Cert Serv, 1970-90; Theses, A Study of the Jr High Sch Libr Fac & Serv, Atlanta Univ 1972; Librarian of the Year, ATC Comdr, 1980. **Military Serv:** USAF; 2 Sustained Superior Award; Ten Year, Cert Serv, 1980; Outstanding serv Award 1989. **Home Addr:** 9006 Brixham Ct, Montgomery, AL 36117, **Home Phone:** (334)215-9973. *

CALHOUN, ERIC A
Government official, real estate agent. **Personal:** Born Nov 20, 1950, Gary, IN; son of Lillian B and William; married Delores Brown, Apr 22, 1983; children: Asha D Calhoun. **Educ:** Wilberforce Univ, Wilberforce, OH, BS, acct, 1974; Ky State Univ, Frankfort, KY, MPA, 1982; Miles Law Sch, Fairfield, AL, Juris Doctorate (cum laude), 1989. **Career:** Cent State Univ, Wilberforce, OH, adminr, 1972-78; Wendy's Int, Dayton, OH, store co-mgr, 1978-79; Ky State Univ, Frankfort, KY, adminr, 1979-83; Miles Coll, Fairfield, AL, adminr, 1983-85; City Birmingham, Birmingham, AL, admin analyst, 1985-87; Mayor's Off, Birmingham, AL, admin asst, 1987-98; Birmingham Parking Authority, asst dir, 1998-; White & Assocs Realty, realtor, 1996-. **Orgs:** Drug Abuse Task Force, Bethel Baptist Church, 1989-; UAB Special Studies Adv Comt Black Professionals, 1989-. **Honors/Awds:** Deans List, 1987. **Business Addr:** Realtor, White & Associates Realty, 813 3rd Ave N, Birmingham, AL 35203, **Business Phone:** (205)326-3000.

CALHOUN, ESSIE LEE
Executive, executive director. **Educ:** Univ Toledo, BEd, social sci; Bowie State Univ, MS, admin & supv. **Career:** Eastman Kodak Co, Copy Prod Div, sales rep, 1982, mkt specialist, sales mgr, Community & Pub Affairs Div, dir pub affairs planning, 1988, dir community rels, 1989, dir community rels & contributions, 1994, vpres, 1999-00, corp vpres, 2000, dir multicultural mkt, 2002-, chief diversity officer & dir, 2003-, vpres community affairs, currently; Rochester Inst Technol, Minett prof, 2001-02. **Orgs:** vice chair, Greater Rochester Health Found; bd mem, Roberts Wesleyan Col; bd mem, Rochester Inst Technol; mem, Muhammad Ali Ctr; chair, Urban League Rochester; bd mem, United Way Greater Rochester; founder of various organization including: United Way Rochester's African Am Leadership Develop Prog; African Am Leadership Roundtable; Kodak Youth Leadership Acad. **Honors/Awds:** Hon Doctorate, Roberts Wesleyan Col; Volunteer of the Year Award, Nat Urban League Northeast Region; Women's History Month Award; Network N Star's Annual Leadership Award; Outstanding Leader Award, NAACP; About Time Magazine's Exemplar Award; Martin Luther King Commission's Individual Award. **Business Addr:** Chief Diversity Officer, Director, Eastman Kodak Co, 343 State St, Rochester, NY 14650-0517, **Business Phone:** (716)724-1980.*

CALHOUN, FRED STEVERSON
Educator. **Personal:** Born Mar 20, 1947, McDonough, GA; son of Mattie W and Willie M (deceased); married M Janice Wright. **Educ:** Fullerton Col, 1966; Cypress Col, AA, 1971; Univ Calif, Irvine, BA, social ecol, 1973; California State Univ, Long Beach, MA, psychol, 1977; Nova Univ, EdD, 1989. **Career:** Educator (retired); Cypress Col, Stud Educ Devel Ctr, work study jobs & recruitment coord, 1968-71; UC Irvine, Social Ecol Dept, res asst, 1971-73; Corbin Ctr, asst coord, 1973; Cypress Col, Stud Educ Devel Ctr, asst dir, 1973-79, dir 1979. **Orgs:** Bd trustees, N Orange County Community Col, 1988; N Orange County Community Col Affirmative Action Task Force; Cypress Col Affirmative Action Comn, N Orange County Community Col Dist; Mgt Group, N Orange County Community Col Dist; EOPS Adv Comn, Cypress Col; Extended Opportunities Prog & Serv Asn. **Honors/Awds:** Ford Foundation Upper Division Scholarship for Outstanding Minority Students, 1971; voted co-captain, Cypress Col football team, 1968; Certificate of Merit, Mentoring Prog, 1991; Developed Summer Readiness Program for pre-college students, 1980, scholarship program, 1980, English as a second language conversational groups, 1981, Adult Literacy Program, 1987. **Special Achievements:** Developed and implemented a Cooperative Agencies Resources for Education, CARE, Program, designed for single parent college students, 1992. **Military Serv:** AUS, sgt, 1966-68; Good Conduct Medal, Old Guard.

CALHOUN, GREGORY BERNARD
Entrepreneur, president (organization). **Personal:** Born Sep 10, 1952, Detroit, MI; son of Thomas and Coretta; married Verlyn Pressley; children: Malcolm, Shakenya, Gregory. **Educ:** Trenholm Jr Col, 1973; Cornell Univ, attended 1979. **Career:** Hudson & Thompson Supermarkets, package clerk, 1970-71, stock clerk, 1972-73, asst mgr, 1973-75, co-mgr, 1975-79, mgr, 1979-82, pub rels dir, 1982-84; Calhoun Enterprises Inc, pres & chief exec officer, currently; Calhoun & Assocs Network, consult & owner, currently. **Orgs:** bd mem, Food Mkt Inst, 1994-; bd mem, Sterling Bank, 1990-; bd mem, Montgomery Area Chamber Com; bd mem, Tuskegee Savings & Loan; Montgomery Area Lions Club; bd mem, Hot 105 Radio; exec roundtable, IGA Inc; pres & bd dirs, Sickle Cell Anemia Found; bd mem, Montgomery Area Comt 100; Young Men's Christian Asn. **Honors/Awds:** National Minority Retailer of the Year, US Dept Com, 1990, Regional Minority Retailer of the Year, 1990; Progressive Junior Collegian, SCLC, 1989, Annual Leadership Award, 1987; Entrepreneur Dreamer Award, MLK Found, 1988; Governor of Alabama, Mar 24, "Greg Calhoun Day", Honoree, 1992. **Special Achievements:** Black Enterprise's Top 100 Industrial/Service companies, ranked No 28, 1999, No 23, 2000. **Military Serv:** AUS, sgt, 1971-72. **Business Addr:** President, Chief Executive Officer, Calhoun Enterprises Inc, 4155 Lomac St Suite G, Montgomery, AL 36106-2864, **Business Phone:** (334)272-4400.*

CALHOUN, JACK JOHNSON, JR.
Law enforcement officer. **Personal:** Born Sep 5, 1938, Canton, OH; son of Jack Johnson Sr and Jessie Mae; married Constance

Butler, Jun 2, 1979; children: Jack III, Leslie A, Lisa J & Rayetta J. **Educ:** Central State, Wilberforce, OH, 1958; Kent State, Kent, OH, 1988. **Career:** Law Enforcement Officer (retired); Republic Steel, Canton, OH, security guard, 1966-69; Canton Police Dept, Canton, OH, patrolman, 1969-79; Stark County Sheriff, Canton, OH, dep sheriff, 1979-81; sergeant, 1981-85; Lt, 1985-90, capt, 1990-2000; maj, 2000-06; Stark County Bd Mental Retardation & Develop Disabilities, bd dir, 2006-. **Orgs:** Fraternal Order Police, 1969-; Buckeye Sheriff, 1979-; pres, Ebony Police Asn Stark County, 1983-89; Nat Black Police Asn, 1983-; Am Jail Asn, 1986-; Ohio Correctional Ct Serv Asn 1986-; Am Corrections Asn, 1986-95; consult, TANO, State Ohio, 1987-; Nat Org Black Law Enforcement Executives, 1990-. **Honors/Awds:** Stark County Amateur Baseball Hall of Fame, 1989. **Military Serv:** AUS, sp 4, 1961-65. **Home Phone:** (330)454-6722. **Business Addr:** Board of Director, Stark County Board of Mental Retardation and Developmental Disabilities, 2950 Whipple Ave NW, Canton, OH 44708, **Business Phone:** (330)477-5200.

CALHOUN, JOSHUA WESLEY
Psychiatrist. **Personal:** Born Mar 21, 1956, Macon, GA; son of E M (deceased) and Harriett Hixon Williams; married Deloris Davis, Dec 12, 1981; children: Joshua W II, Amanda Joy, Adrianna Jade, Austin Judge. **Educ:** Yale Univ, BA, 1978; Univ Cincinnati, MD, 1982. **Career:** Cincinnati Gen Hosp, med internship, 1982-83; MA Ment Health Ctr, resident psychiatry, 1983-87, chief resident child psychiatry, 1986-87; Harvard Med Sch, clinical fellow psychiatry; St Louis Univ Med Sch, asst clinic prof; pvt practice, 1990-; Our Lady Residential Home C, med dir, 1997-. **Orgs:** Adolescent Task Force, 1986-87; consult, Annie Malone C Home, 1988-90; consult, C Ctr Behavioral Develop, 1987-90; Am Psychiatric Asn; Am Academy Child Psychiatry; Black Psychiatrists Am; Am Med Asn; bd mem, Nat Alliance Mentally Ill, St Louis, 1998; bd mem, Gateway Adv Bd Develop Disabilities, 1998; adv bd, HealthLink Inc, 1996; Fellow, Am Psychiatric Assoc; Nat Inst Ment Health, 1983-86; ed bd, Jefferson J Psychiatry, 1985-87. **Honors/Awds:** . **Business Addr:** Assistant Clinical Professor, St Louis University, 221 N Grand Blvd, Saint Louis, MO 63103, **Business Phone:** (314)977-2500.*

CALHOUN, KEVIN
Engineer, administrator. **Career:** Corning Cable Systs, dir & mgr global qual, moderator, currently; Qyest Forum, proj dir. **Business Addr:** Moderator, Corning Cable Systems, 9275 Denton Hwy, Keller, TX 76248, **Business Phone:** (817)431-1521.

CALHOUN, MONICA
Actor. **Personal:** Born Jul 29, 1971, Atlanta, GA. **Educ:** Los Angeles County High Sch Arts. **Career:** Films: Sister Act 2: Back in the Habit, 1993; Jack the Bear, 1993; What About Your Friends, 1995; Sprung, 1997; The Players Club, 1998; Park Day, 1998; The Best Man, 1999; Love & Basketball, 2000; Faux Pas, 2001; Final Breakdown, 2002; Civil Brand, 2002; Pandora's Box, 2002; Guns & Roses, 2003; Gang of Roses, 2003; Love Chronicles, 2003; From the Outside Looking In, 2003; Justice, 2004; TV movies: She Stood Alone, 1991; Jacksons: An American Dream, 1992; The Ernest Green Story, 1993; Rebound, 1996; The Ditchdigger's Daughters, 1997; Intimate Betrayal, 1999; Nature Boy, 2000; tv Guest Appearances: A Different World, 1987; The Wayans Brothers, 1996; The Jamie Foxx Show, 1998; Malcolm & Eddie, 2000; NYPD Blue, 2003; Coming Clean, 2003; Strong Medicine, 2003; Break on Through, 2006; Everybody Hates Chris, 2006; Everybody Hates Funerals, 2006; Dirt, 2007; Pilot, 2007. **Honors/Awds:** Best Performance by an Actress, Am Black Film Festival, 2002. **Business Addr:** Actress, Abrams Artists & Associates, 9200 Sunset Blvd Suite 1130, Los Angeles, CA 90069, **Business Phone:** (310)859-0625.

CALHOUN, DR. NOAH ROBERT
Oral surgeon. **Personal:** Born Mar 23, 1921, Clarendon, AR; son of Noah and Della Calhoun; married Cecelia C, Oct 19, 1950; children: Stephen M & Cecelia N. **Educ:** Dental Sch Howard Univ, DDS, 1948; Tufts Med & Dent Col, MSD, 1955. **Career:** Med Ctr Va, asst oral surg, 1964-72, asst chief dent, 1972-75, chief dent surg, 1975-82, coordr, Dent Res; Dent Sch Howard Univ, prof, oral maxillofacial surg, 1982-92, prof emer, 1992-. **Orgs:** Oral surgeon, Med Ctr, Tuskegee, AL, VA, 1950-64; prof, lectr, Georgetown Dent, 1970-; consult, Va & Atena Ins Co, 1982-; dir, Red Cross, Tuskegee Inst, 1962-64; dir, vpres, Credit Union, Va, 1982; adv comn, Am Bd Oral Surg, 8 yrs. Inst Med, selection ed & ed bd, Int Oral & Maxillofacial Surg; St Michael's Church Fin Comt; Inst Med (Acad Sci); pres, Bridge Masters, ABC Bridge Asn. **Honors/Awds:** Fel, Am Col Dentistry; Fel, Int Col Dentistry; Inst Med, 1982; Dental Alumni Award, Howard Univ, 1972. **Military Serv:** USAF, cap, 2 yrs. **Home Addr:** 1413 Leegate Rd NW, Washington, DC 20012-1211. **Business Addr:** Professor Emeritus, Howard University, College of Dentistry, 600 W St NW, Washington, DC 20059, **Business Phone:** (202)806-0440.

CALHOUN, DR. THOMAS
Educator. **Personal:** Born Oct 6, 1932, Marianna, FL; son of Thomas Pittman and Sylvia Barnes Thompson; married Shirley Kathryn Jones; children: Thomas Jr, Christine, Kathy & Maria. **Educ:** Fla A&M Univ, BS, 1954; Fisk Univ, grad sch, attended; Meharry Med Col,MD, 1963; Am Bd Surg, dipl, 1971. **Career:** Fisk Univ, instr, 1957-58; Tennis Circuit, amateur traveller, 1958; US Postal WA, employee, 1958-59; Howard Univ, clin assoc prof surg; Delmarva Med Found, assoc med dir, 2002; DC Med Res Corp, med dir, 2004-. **Orgs:** Life mem, Am Tennis Asn; Am Med Tennis Asn; life mem, US Tennis Asn; District Columbia Med Soc; Bd Surgeons Police Fire Dept; St Thomas Apostle Catholic Church; fel Am Col Surgeons, 1972; fel Am Asn Abdominal Surgeons,1977; med adv, Care-Plus, Delmarva reg med dir; fel Am Col Nutrit; pres, Med-Dent Staff, Providence Hosp, Wash DC; Am Col Physician Execs. **Military Serv:** AUS, 2nd lt, 1954-56. **Home Addr:** 4010 Argyle Ter NW, Washington, DC 20011, **Home Phone:** (202)291-2327. **Business Addr:** Medical Director, DC Medical Reserve Corporation, 16020 L St NW Suite 1275, Washington, DC 20036.

CALHOUN, THOMAS C
Educator, school administrator. **Personal:** Born Aug 31, 1946, Crystal Springs, MS; son of Walter Calhoun and Ernestine Abney. **Educ:** Tex Wesleyan Col, BA, 1970; Tex Tech Univ, MA, 1971; Univ Ky, PhD, 1988. **Career:** Western Ky Univ, instr, 1984-88; Ohio Univ, asst prof, sociol, 1988-96; Univ NE Lincoln, from asst to assoc prof sociol, African Am studies, 1996-2001, Inst Ethnic Studies, dir, 1998-2000, interim assoc vice chancellor academic affairs, 2000-01; Southern Ill Univ, prof sociol, 2001-, chair social dept, 2003-, assoc provost acad affairs, currently. **Orgs:** Vpres, N Cent Sociol Asn, 1997, pres; vpres, Mid-South Sociol Asn, 1997, pres; chair, Asn Black Sociologist, 1998-2000; pres, Asn Social & Behav Scientists, 2000-; pres elect, N Cent Sociol Asn. **Honors/Awds:** Outstanding Teacher, Ohio Univ, 1994, Outstanding Teacher, Col Arts & Sci, 1995; A Wade Smith Award for Outstanding Teaching, Mentoring, & Service, Asn Black Sociologists; Aida Tomeh Distinguished Service Award, N Cent Sociol Asn & Pres of the Mid-S Sociol Asn. **Special Achievements:** Co-ed, Sociological Spectum, 1996-98; Dep Sociol Ed, J of Contemporary Ethnography, 1999. **Military Serv:** USAF, AIC, 1963-67; Meritorious Award. **Business Addr:** Professor, Associate Provost for Academic Affairs, Southern Illinois University, Department Sociology, Mail Code 4524, Carbondale, IL 62901, **Business Phone:** (618)453-7629.

CALLAWAY, DWIGHT W
Automotive executive, executive. **Personal:** Born May 22, 1932, Cincinnati, OH; son of H C and Virginia Moody Gordon; married Roberta F Leahr, Aug 6, 1955; children: Denise Reistad, Gordon C & Dwight W II. **Educ:** Morehouse Col, Atlanta, Ga, BS, 1953; Univ Cincinnati, Cincinnati, Ohio, MS, 1956; Pa State Univ, eight week exec mgt, 1979. **Career:** Executive, Automotive executive (retired); D H Baldwin Co, Cincinnati, Ohio, sr engr, 1955-62; Electra Mfg Co, Independence, Kans, mgr res & develop, 1962-64; Delco Electronic Div, GMC, Kokomo, Ind, chief engr, 1964-81; Youngwood Electronic Metals, Murraysville, Pa, chief exec officer, exec vpres, 1981-82; A C Rochester Div, GMC, Flint, Mich, dir int operations, 1982; Bumex Corp, Mexico City, Mexico, bd dirs, 1986; GM Luexenbourg, staff, 1987; AG Australia, Melbourne, staff, 1986. **Orgs:** Alpha Phi Alpha Frat, 1952-; pres, Int Soc Hybrid Microelectronics, 1970-72, bd dir, 1972-; Sigma Pi Phi Frat, 1984-; Air Port Authority, Flint, Mich, 1986-; bd dir, Flint Sch System Pre Engineering Prog; bd dir, Howard Community Hosp, Kokomo, Ind; United Way, Kokomo, Ind; YMCA, Carver Community Ctr, Kokomo, Ind; pres bd, Kokomo OIC. **Honors/Awds:** Engineer of the Year, Nat Electronic Prod Conf, 1970; Daniel M Hughes Award, Int Soc Hybrid Microelectronics, 1972; Fel, Int Microelectronics & Packaging Soc, 1972.

CALLAWAY, LOUIS MARSHALL, JR.
Manager. **Personal:** Born Jan 22, 1939, Chicago, IL; married Duryea Dickson. **Educ:** Drake Univ, BA, 1961. **Career:** Ford Motor Co, from asst plant mgr to plant mgr; Ford Truck plant, asst plant mgr, qual control mgr; Adv Mat Processing Corp, exec vpres & chief operating officer. **Orgs:** Chicago S C of C; dir, Chicago Asn Com & Indust; corp mem, Blue Cross Blue Shield; trustee, New Help Source.

CALLENDER, CARL O.
Commissioner, lawyer. **Personal:** Born Nov 16, 1936, New York, NY; married Leola Rhames. **Educ:** Brooklyn Community Col, Brooklyn NY, AB, BA, econ, political econ, 1961; Hunter Col, Bronx NY, AB, 1964; Howard Univ Sch Law, Wash DC, JD. **Career:** Hunter Col, New York, asst libr aide, 1966; Palystreet New York, dir, 1967; Harlem Assertion of Rights Inc, staff atty, 1968-70; Prentice-Hall's Federal Tax Serv Bulletins NJ, legal edit, 1968; Regin Ald Heber Smith fell Harlem Assertion Rights, 1969-70; CALS Reginald Heber Smith Fell Prog, New York, coordr, 1970-71; US Dist Ct Southern Dist New York, 1970; Comn Law Offices, dep dir, 1971-72; US Ct Appeals 2nd Circuit, 1972; benezer Gospel Tabernacle, ordained minister, 1972; Comn Law Off Prog, dir, 1972-75; Housing Litigation Bureau, New York, dir, 1975-76; New York Civil Ct Kings County, judge, currently. **Orgs:** Chmn & pres, Nat Young People's Christian Asn; chmn & pres, Christian Leaders United; elec comn, Stud Bar, Asn admin asst; Housing Res Com; Phi Alpha Delta Legal Fraternity. **Honors/Awds:** American Jurisprudence Award, 1967. **Military Serv:** USAF, airman, 1st class, 1951-55. **Business Phone:** (347)401-9870.

CALLENDER, DR. CLIVE ORVILLE
Educator, physician. **Personal:** Born Nov 16, 1936, New York, NY; son of Joseph and Ida; married Fern Irene Marshall; children: Joseph, Ealena & Arianne. **Educ:** Hunter Col, AB, 1959; Meharry Med Col, MD, 1963. **Career:** Univ Cincinnati, internship, 1963-64; Harlem Hosp, asst resident, 1964-65; Howard Univ & Freedmen's Hosp, asst resident, 1965-66, chief resident, 1967-69, instr, 1969-70; Hosp Cancer & Allied Dis, asst resident, 1966-67; DC Gen Hosp, med officer, 1970-71; Port Harcourt Gen Hosp Nigeria,consult, 1970-71; Univ Minnesota, spec post-doctoral res & clin transplant fel, 1971-73; Howard Univ Med Col, asst prof, 1973-76, assoc prof, 1976-80, prof, 1980-; Howard Univ, prof, vice chmn dept surg, 1982-95, transplant ctr, dir, 1973-, Howard Univ Col, LaSalle D Leffall Jr Prof Surg, prof surg & chmn, Dept Surg, HUH, 1996-. **Orgs:** Pres, Alpha Phi Omega Frat, 1959; fel Am Cancer Soc, 1965-66; DC Med Soc;Soc Acad Surg; Transplant Soc; Am Soc Transplant Surg; ed adv bd, New Directions; bd dir, Kidney Found Nat Capital Area; dip, Am Bd Surg, 1970; fel Am Col Surg, 1975; pres, Nat Kidney Found Nat Capital Area, 1979-; chmn & mem comt, Am Soc Transplant Surgeons; pres, Med Dent Staff Howard Univ Hosp, 1980; pres, Alpha Omega Alpha; Alpha Phi Alpha; liver transplant fel, Univ Pittsburgh, 1987-88; adv comt secy health, End Stage Renal Dis Data, 1990-; founder & prin investr, MOTTEP- Nat Minority Orgn, tissue transplant educ prog; bd gov, NMA Gov ACS, 1991; Am Surg Asn, 1991; Southern Surg Asn, 1996; bd trustees, Hunter Col Found, 1999; vpres, pres,Soc Black Acad Surgeons, 1999-. **Honors/Awds:** Hoffman LaRoche Award, 1961; Nat Med Asn Aux Scholar, 1961; Joseph Colins Scholar Award, 1961-63; Charles Nelson Gold Medal, Meharry Med Col, 1963; Hudson Meadows Award, Meharry Med Col, 1963; Scholar Award, Nat Med Asn, 1963; Charles R Drew Research Award, Howard Univ & Freedmen's Hosp, 1968; Daniel Hale Williams Award, Howard Univ & Freedmen's Hosp, 1969; res fel,Spec Post-doctoral NIH, 1971-73; clin transp fel, Univ Minn, 1971-72; vistrans plant fel, Univ Pittsburgh, liver, 1987-88; Hall Fame, Hunter Col Alumni, 1989; Physician Year Award, Nat Med Asn, 1989; Distinguished Surgeon Award, Howard Univ, Dept Surg, 1989; Distinguished Service Award,Nat Med Asn, Surg Sect, 1990; Medal Excellence, AAKP, Am Asn KidneyPatients, 1997; Jr Award, Am Col Surgeons, DC Chapt, LaSalle D Leffall,1998; Honorary Doctorate, Hunter Col, 1998; Scroll Merit, Nat Am Med Asn,1998; Bethune Legacy Award, 2000; Role Model Awardee, Minority Access, Inc, 2006; Honorary Doctorate, Meharry Med Col, 2008. **Special Achievements:** Numerous presentations, publications & abstracts. **Business Addr:** Founder, Chairman, National MOTTEP, Ambulatory Care Ctr, 2041 Ga Ave NW Suite 3100, Washington, DC 20060, **Business Phone:** (202)865-4888.

CALLENDER, LEROY R.
Engineer. **Personal:** Born Feb 29, 1932, New York, NY; divorced; children: Eric. **Educ:** City Col City NY, BCE 1958. **Career:** LeRoy Callender PC Consult Engrs, founder & struct ngr, 1969-. **Orgs:** Distinguished jury, Pier 40 Design Competition, 1998. **Honors/Awds:** Black Engr of the Year Award, 1992. **Business Addr:** Founder, LeRoy Callender PC, Callender ConsuLT Engrs, 236 W 26 St, New York, NY 10001-5926.*

CALLENDER, LUCINDA R.
Educator. **Personal:** Born Oct 26, 1957, Xenia, OH; daughter of Richard E Sr and Isabel Long. **Educ:** The Ohio State Univ, Columbus, OH, BA, 1979, MA, 1980, PhD, 1985. **Career:** Ohio Wesleyan Univ Upward Bound Project, Delaware, OH, teacher & acting assoc dir, 1977-84; The Ohio State Univ, Columbus, OH, grad teaching assoc, 1980-85; Univ Missouri-Columbia, Columbia, MO, asst prof, 1985-88; San Diego State Univ, San Diego, CA, asst prof polit sci. **Orgs:** Western Polit Sci Asn, 1990-; Midwest Polit Sci Asn, 1983-89; Southern Polit Sci Asn, 1989-90; Am Polit Sci Asn, 1985-90; Nat Conference Black Polit Scientists. **Honors/Awds:** Outstanding Faculty Award, San Diego State Univ, 1990; Honorary Coach University Missouri-Columbia Male Basketball Team, Univ Missouri-Columbia, 1987-88; Summer Research Fellowship, Univ Missouri-Columbia, 1986; Commendation for excellence many pursuits, Ohio House Reps, 1985; William Jennings Bryan Prize, dissertation award manuscript judged outstanding, The Ohio State Univ, 1984; Summer Research Fellowship, San Diego State Univ, 1991, Research, Scholarship and Creative Activity Award, 1991, Outstanding Faculty Award, 1993. *

CALLENDER, WILFRED A.
Educator, lawyer. **Personal:** Born Mar 23, 1929, Colon, Panama; son of Newton N (deceased) and Isaline Brathwaite (deceased); married Beth Robinson; children: Neil & Melissa. **Educ:** Brooklyn Col, BA, 1954, MA 1963; Brooklyn Law Sch, JD, 1969. **Career:** Boys High Sch Brooklyn, educr, 1957-69; Dept Real Estate Com Labor Indust Corp Kings, asst dir, 1969-70; Wade & Callender, atty, 1972-; Hostos County Col, prof, 1970-91; Wade & Callender ESQS Pract Law. **Orgs:** Brooklyn Bar Asn; Bedford Stuyvesant Lawyers Asn; Nat Conf Black Lawyers; bd Trustees, Encampment Citizenship, 1971-; pres, Black Caucus Hostos, 1972-; bd trustees, Social Serv; bd, NY Soc Ethical Culture. **Military Serv:** AUS, pvt 2, 1954-56. **Business Addr:** 1501 No Strand Ave, Brooklyn, NY 11226.*

CALLOWAY, CHRISTOPHER FITZPATRICK
Football player. **Personal:** Born Mar 29, 1968, Chicago, IL. **Educ:** Univ Mich, commun & film. **Career:** Football player

(retired); Pittsburgh Steelers, wide receiver, 1990-91; NY Giants, 1992-98; production asst, MTV Live; 1998. Atlanta Falcons, 1999-99; New England Patriots, wide receiver, 2000. *

CALLOWAY, LAVERNE FANT
Librarian. **Personal:** Born Mar 6, 1950, Byhalia, MS; daughter of Ralph and Alanza Saulsberry; married Otis, Jan 8, 1988; children: D. **Educ:** Wayne State Univ, BS, 1993, MLIS, 1996. **Career:** Schroeder Info Servs Gen Motors Media Archives, indexer, 1996-98; McGregor Pub Libr, dir, 1998-2001; Univ Detroit Mercy, Outer Dr Campus Libr, dir, 2001-. **Orgs:** Mich Libr Asn, 1998-; Wayne State Univ, Alumni Asn, 1996-; Lions Club Highland Park, 2000-; McGregor Pub Libr Comn, 2002-. **Honors/Awds:** Beta Phi Mu. **Home Addr:** 99 McLean, Highland Park, MI 48203. **Business Addr:** Director, University of Detroit Mercy, Outer Drive Campus Library, 8200 W Outer Dr, PO Box 19900, Detroit, MI 48219-0900, **Business Phone:** (313)993-6228.

CALLOWAY, VANESSA BELL
Actor. **Personal:** Born Mar 20, 1957, Cleveland, OH; married Dr Anthony, Sep 1988; children: Ashley & Alexandra. **Educ:** Ohio Univ, BA. **Career:** Broadway Prodn drem girls, dancer: TV : "All My Children",1985; "Days of Our Lives", 1985; "The Colbys"; Simon & simon", 1986; "227", 1987; "In The Heat Of the Night",1989; "Polly", 1989; "Piece of Cake", 1990; "Memphis", 1992; "Stompin' at the Savoy", 1990; "Rhythm & Blues", 1992;'Under One Roof", Orleans; "Oh Drama!"; "Black in the 80s", 2005; "Stompin", 2007; "VANESSA BELL CALLOWY: IN THE COMPANY OF FRIENDS", TV ONE, 2007; Films: Coming to Am, 1988; Bebe's Kids,1992; What's Love Got to Do With It, 1993; The Inkwell, 1994; Crimson Tide, 1995; Daylight, 1996; Archibald the Rain bow Painter, 1998; When It Clicks, 1998; The Brothers, 2001; All About You, 2001; Biker Boyz, 2003; If You Were My Girl, 2003; Cheaper by the Dozen, 2003; Love Don't Cost a Thing, 2003; 10-8: Officers on Duty, 2004; Speed Kills, 2004; Shadows & Light, 2005; Killing Of wendy, 2008; "Aussie & Ted", 2009; Stage: "Louie & Ophelia", 2000. **Orgs:** Alpha Kappa Alpha Sorority Inc. **Honors/Awds:** Image Award, Nat Assn Advan Coloured People; Greek Alumni Hall of Fame, Ohio Univ. **Business Phone:** (310)289-1088.*

CALLOWAY-MOORE, DORIS
Administrator, scout. **Career:** Franklin County C Serv, spokeswoman, assoc dir community rels, recruitment dir, currently. **Business Addr:** Recruitment Director, Franklin County Children Services, 855 W Mound St, Columbus, OH 43223, **Business Phone:** (614)275-2571.*

CALLUM, AGNES KANE
Genealogist, historian, writer. **Personal:** Born Feb 24, 1925, Baltimore, MD; daughter of Philip Moten and Mary Priscilla Gough; married Solomon Melvin Callum, Jul 7, 1944 (deceased); children: Paul A Foster, Agnes H Lightfoot, Arthur M Callum, Martin J Callum, Martina P Callum. **Educ:** Morgan State Univ, BA, 1973; Univ Ghana, W Africa, 1973; Morgan State Univ, MS, 1975. **Career:** Baltimore City Evening Sch, teacher; Beauty Queen Co, sales mgr, 1954-58; NC Mutual Life Ins Co, 1958-62; Rosewood State Hosp, Ownings MD, practical nurse, 1962-66; US Postal Serv, review clk, 1966-86; Douglass High Eve Sch, teacher 1977-80; Coppin State Col, teacher 1978; Forest Black Geneal Journ, Founder & ed, 1982-; Author: Kane-Butler Family Genealogical History of a Black Family, 1978; founder & editor, Kane Family News Notes, 1979; founder, ed, publisher, Flower of the Forest Black Genealogical Journal, 1982-; author, Inscriptions From The Tomb Stones at Mt Calvary Cemetery 1926-82, 1985; Colored Volunteers of Maryland, 7th Regiment United States Colored Troops, 1990; Black Marriages of St Mary's County, 1991; Black Marriages of Anne Arundel County, Maryland 1950-86, 1994. **Orgs:** Nat Asn Advan Colored People; Asn Study Afro-Am Life & Hist; Baltimore City Hosp; Md Geneal Soc; Afro-Am Hist & Geneal Soc; historian, Nat Alliance Postal & Fed Employees Local; historian, St Francis Xavier Cath Church, 1988; Adv Comt Md State Archives 1989; Archive Comt Md Comn Afro-Am Life & Cult; trustee, Satterly Plantation Mansion, Hollywood, MD, 1991; comnr, Md Civil War Heritage Comn, 1993-95; trustee, Sotterley Found. **Honors/Awds:** City Baltimore Mayor's Citation, Citizenship, 1967; Senate of Maryland Award Outstanding Community Worker, 1986; City Coun Baltimore Retirement, 1986; Citizen Citation of Baltimore Leadership 1986; US Postal Service 20 year Service Award, 1986; Nat Coun Negro Women Historian Award, 1988. **Business Phone:** (301)373-2280.*

CALVERT, DR. WILMA JEAN
Educator. **Personal:** Born Nov 25, 1997, St Louis, MO; daughter of John Phillip and Amanda Bond. **Educ:** Oral Roberts Univ, BSN, 1981; Univ Okla, MS, 1986; Univ Mo, St Louis, MO, PhD, 2002; Wash Univ, MPE. **Career:** Deaconess Hosp, staff nurse, 1981-82; St John Med Ctr, staff nurse, 1982-84; City Faith, Tulsa, OK, staff nurse, 1984-87; Oral Roberts Univ, instr, 1987-82; Hillcrest Med Ctr, staff nurse, 1989-91; St John Med Ctr, staff nurse, 1991-92; Barnes Col, asst prof, 1992-; Univ Mo, St Louis, MO, Barnes Col Nursing & Health Studies, clinical asst prof, currently. **Orgs:** Asn Black Nursing Faculty, 1990-; Mu Iota Chap, Sigma Theta Tau, NAACOG, 1989-; Soc Sci Study Relig; Res Soc Alcoholism. **Special Achievements:** Medical mission trip to Guatemala, 1992; completing research on adolescent health compromising and promotive behaviors, and the role of religion and spirituality in these behaviors. **Business Addr:** Assistant Professor, College of Nursing, University of Missouri, One University Blvd, Saint Louis, MO 63121-4400, **Business Phone:** (314)516-7073.

CALVIN, MICHAEL BYRON
Judge, lawyer. **Personal:** Born in Nashville, TN; married Vanessa; children: Michael Langston, Justin Kinnard, Patrice. **Educ:** Govt Monmouth Col, BA, hist, 1972; St Louis Univ Sch Law, JD, 1975. **Career:** City St Louis, circuit judge; Black Am Law Stud Asn BALSA Reports, former ed; 22nd Judicial Circuit, presiding judge, 1990-00; Mo Circuit Ct, judge, 2001-. **Orgs:** Mound City Bar Asn. **Honors/Awds:** Outstanding Young Alumnus, Monmouth Col, Ill 1979; BALSA Alumnus Award, Black Am Law Stud St Louis Univ, 1979. **Business Addr:** Circuit Judge, Circuit Court 22nd Circuit, State of Missouri, Civil Ct Bldg, 10 N Tucker Blvd, St Louis, MO 63101-2097, **Business Phone:** (314)622-4929.*

CALVIN, DR. VIRGINIA BROWN
School administrator. **Personal:** Born Jun 16, 1945, Lake Providence, LA; daughter of Arthur Brown and Vera Brown; married Richmond E Calvin; children: Brent Tremayne & Shannon D. **Educ:** Alcorn State Univ, BS, 1966; NMex Highlands Univ, MA, 1970; Tex Womens Univ, EdD, 1973; North Tex State Univ, attended 1970; Ind Univ, South Bend, attended 1979. **Career:** Teacher, 1967-71; South Bend Community Sch Corp, counr, 1972-76, adminr, 1977-2000, Muessel Elem Sch, prin, actg exec dir, div instruct & curric, 1991-93, supt sch, 1993-2000; Ivy Tech State Col, chancellor, 2000-. **Orgs:** Chairperson, Validation-Head Start, 1979; secy, Delta Kappa Gamma Honor Society, 1984; bd mem, Leadership Chamber Com, 1985-93; bd dir, Jr League S Bend, 1984, Art Ctr 1985; bd mem, Broadway Theatre League, 1986-; bd mem, St Joseph County Parks Bd, 1990-; pres, Alpha Kappa Alpha Sorority, 1991-93; bd mem, United Way St Joseph County, 1991-92; bd mem, St Joseph County Children's Ctr, 1992-; bd mem, Firefly Festival, 1992-; bd mem, Healthy Comm Initiative, 1992-; bd mem, Jr Achievement; bd dir, Am Red Cross; bd dir, Michiana Inc; S Bend Community Revitalization Dist; St Joseph County Minority Health Coalition; St Joseph Parks; Urban League, St Joseph County; bd, Festival & Broadway Theatre League; India Comn Women; Nat Adv Comt, New Venture Philanthrophy; Workforce Invest Bd; S Bend Rotary Club. **Honors/Awds:** Women of Year, Plano, TX, 1971; Women of Year, SBCSC YWCA, 1984; Educator of the Year, Executive Journal, 1991; Bond Award, AKA, 1976, 1991; Nat Blue Ribbon School Award, Muessel Elem Sch, 1992; Redbook Magazine's America's Best Elementary School Award, Muessel Elem Sch, 1993; Educator of the Year, Comm Educ Roundtable, 1991; Indiana State Superintendent of the Year, 1996; Lifetime Achievement Award, Fest Inc, 1996; Distinguished Service Award, S Bend Asn Pub Sch Adminr, 1999; Outstanding Science, Technology or Engineering Educator in Indiana, Hi Tech Inc, 2002; Distinguished Alumna, Alcorn State Univ, 2003; Age of Excellence Honoree, REAL Services Inc; Vision Award, St Joseph County Health Initiatives; Community Service Visionary Award, Urban League South Bend. **Special Achievements:** First African-American and the first female chief executive South Bend School Corporation in 1993. **Home Addr:** 17530 Bending Oaks, Granger, IN 46530. **Business Addr:** Chancellor, Ivy Tech Community College, 220 Dean Johnson Blvd, South Bend, IN 46601, **Business Phone:** (574)289-7001.

CAMBOSOS, BRUCE MICHAEL
Educator. **Personal:** Born Jul 20, 1941, New Haven, CT; married Syleatha Hughes; children: Shanay. **Educ:** George Washington Univ, 1961; Howard Univ, BS, 1964; Howard Univ, MD, 1969. **Career:** Va Hosp, staff pyschiatrist, 1973-75; Ugast Treat Ctr, WA, staff psychiatrist, 1976-. **Orgs:** Am Psychiat Asn; Wash Psychiat Asn; St George Soc; Capital Med Soc Trustee. **Honors/Awds:** Scholarship, George Wash Univ, 1959; Tutorial Scholarship, Howard Univ, 1965; Williams Award, Howard Univ, 1969. **Business Addr:** 2041 Georgia Ave, Washington, DC 20060.*

CAMBRIDGE, DEXTER
Basketball player. **Personal:** Born Jan 29, 1970, Eleuthra, Bahamas. **Educ:** Univ Tex, Austin. **Career:** Dallas Mavericks, forward, 1992-93.

CAMBY, MARCUS D
Basketball player. **Personal:** Born Mar 22, 1974, Hartford, CT. **Educ:** Univ Mass, Amherst, educ, 1997. **Career:** Toronto Raptors, forward-ctr, 1996-98; NY Knicks, 1998-2002; Denver Nuggets, ctr, 2002-. **Orgs:** Cambyland Found. **Honors/Awds:** Atlantic 10 Freshman of the Year, 1993-94; NCAA East Regional Most Outstanding Player, 1995-96; The Sporting News Col Player of the Year; Oscar Robertson Trophy, 1995-96; Naismith Col Player of the Year Award, 1995-96; John R. Wooden Award, 1995-96; Athlete of the Year, NY Mag, 1999; Metlife Community Assist of the Month Award, 2001; Chopper Travaglini Award, 2004; NBA Defensive Player of the Year Award, 2006-07. **Business Addr:** Professional Basketball Player, Denver Nuggets, 1000 Chopper Cir, Denver, CO 80204, **Business Phone:** (303)405-1100.

CAMERON, JOHN E., SR.
Clergy. **Personal:** Born Jun 11, 1932, Hattiesburg, MS; son of Courtney and A.C. Cameron; married Lenora Woods; children: Jonetta, John Earl Jr. **Educ:** Alcorn A & M Col; Am Bapt Theo Sem, BTh, 1956; Rust Col, BS, 1957. **Career:** First Baptist Church, Oxford; Mt Calvary Bapt Church, Minister; Mt Calvary Community Develop Agency Inc, coord, 1974; Div Youth Affairs Gov's Jackson, coordr, 1972; Star Inc Jackson, coach, 1968-71; Star Inc Natchez, ctr dir, 1966-68; Hattiesburg Ministers' Proj, dir, 1954-65; Greater Mt Calvary Baptist Church, pastor, 1970-. **Orgs:** Cand, US Cong fifth Cong Dist MS, 1964; ambassador, Cent Am, 1954; pres, Nat Bapt Stud Union, 1954; job Develop Specialist Star Inc, 1969-71; sponsor, Boy Scouts; Mason; historian Progressive Nat Bapt Conv; comnr, Criminal Justice Syst State, MS; Comnr, LEAA; bd dir, pearl River Valley Redevelop Basin Hinds Co. **Home Addr:** 311 Overlook Cir, Jackson, MS 39213. **Business Addr:** Pastor, Greater Mount Calvary Baptist Church, 1400 Robinson St, Jackson, MS 39203.*

CAMERON, JOSEPH A.
Educator. **Personal:** Born Apr 25, 1942, Fairfield, AL; son of Arthur and Searcie; married Mary E Stiles; children: Joseph Jr, Jozetta, Cecelia & Juanita. **Educ:** Tenn State Univ, BS, 1963; Tex So Univ, MS, 1965; Mich State Univ, PhD,1973. **Career:** Tex Southern Univ, grad teaching asst, 1965; Dept Biol Sci, Grambling State Univ, instr 1965-66, asst prof, 1967-69; high sch sci teacher, consult, 1967-69; Equal Opportunity Prog, Mich State Univ, ulty tutor, 1969-71; Nat Sci Lab Manual, Mich State Univ, contributing author, 1971; Dept Natural Sci, Mich State Univ, instr, 1969-73; Dept Natural Sci, Mich State Univ, asst prof, 1973-74; Dept Biol, Jackson State Univ, asst prof,1974-78, coordr, grad progs, 1976-85; prof, 1978-; dir, biomed sci prog, 1980-84; acting dean, Sch Sci & Technol, 1984; dir minority instnl restraining prog, 1986; Bridges Baccalaureate Degree Prog, dir, 1993-95; Univ Miss Med Ctr/Jackson State Univ, health careers opportunity prog, fac, 1985; Nat Sci Found, consult & reviewer, 1978-91; Nat Inst Health, consult & proposal reviewer, 1978-95; Ind Univ, Coordr, Bridges Doctorate Degree Prog, currently; Purdue Univ Indianapolis, currently; Jackson State Univ; dir, Baccalaureate Degree Prog, currently. **Orgs:** Tri Beta Biol Honor Soc; Am Soc Zool; Am Asn Univ Prof; Tissue Culture Asn; Soc Sigma XI; AAAS; Miss Acad Sci, Alpha Phi Alpha Frat Inc; Am Heart Asn; Endocrine Soc; Phi Delta Kappa; pres, Phi Kappa Phi, 1990; Outstanding Contributions to Sci in Mississippi Award, Miss Acad Sci, 2004. **Honors/Awds:** Academic Tuition Scholarship, Univ Iowa, 1966-67; Soc Sigma XI Award, Meritorious Res, Mich State Univ, 1973; apptd Fair field Ind HS Hall Fame, 1973; King/Chavez/Parks Vis Prof, Mich State Univ, 1992. **Special Achievements:** Published numerous journal articles. **Business Addr:** Professor, Jackson State University, Department of Biology, 1400 Lynch St, PO Box 18540, Jackson, MS 39217.*

CAMERON, KRYSTOL
Executive. **Personal:** Born Mar 14, 1967, Brooklyn, NY; son of John and Jean Clark; married Deidre DeRiggs, Aug 15, 1987. **Educ:** Mass Inst Tech, comput eng, 1980. **Career:** Int Bus Mach, sr design engr, 1984-85; ComputerLand; BusinessLand; Computer Factory; Entre Computer; Cameron Systems Inc, pres, 1987-; Chase Records Inc, vpres, prod, 1990-; Facile Mgt, vpres, commun, 1990-; ATC Music, pres, publ, 1992-; Hudson Delta Group, founder; Digital Frames Inc, founder; Ashton Film Inc, pres, 1992-; SimplyTV Inc, chief exec officer & pres, currently; World Lock Records, chief exec officer, currently. **Orgs:** Patron, Black Filmmaker Found, 1988-; Nat Technical Asn; Nat Christina Found; Nat Asn Market Developers; Caribbean-Am Chamber Com; USA Chamber Com; Orgn Black Designers Comput Technol; Industry Asn; Hollywood E Found; Nat Asn Television Arts & Scis; UN / IMSCO; Lotus Develop Asn; Video Software Dealers; Asn Website Adv Coun; Visionary Network Asn; Who's Who in Entertainment; Internet Developers Asn; Black Data Processing Asn; CMP Channel Adv Coun; Who's Who of Info Technol; Int Soc Internet Prof; Asn Interactive Media. **Honors/Awds:** Ernst & Young, Entrepreneur of the Yr, 1987; Local Area Network Degree, Comput Land, 1986; IBM, Authorized Dealer, 1990; Shell Oil Entrepreneur of the Yr; nominee, Emmy telepic Miracle Cures, 1994; Pre-Grammy for Excellence Music Prodn, 1996. **Special Achievements:** Develop two ROM Chips for the IBM XT-286, 1985; re-vamped, Billboard, Essence, Class, & Carib News through comput, 1988-; automated the Black Filmmaker Found bus NY & CA.

CAMERON, MARY EVELYN
Educator, college teacher. **Personal:** Born Sep 8, 1944, Memphis, TN; married Dr Joseph Alexander; children: Jozetta Louise, Joseph Alexander Jr, Cecelia Denise & Juanita Evette. **Educ:** Marian Col, Indianapolis, IN, BA, 1966; Univ Iowa, Med Ctr, ADA cert, 1967; Jackson State Univ, MS, 1979. **Career:** State Miss, nutritionist, mem surv team, 1967-68; Grambling State Univ; admin dietitian, 1968-69; Sparrow Hosp, clin dietitian, 1969-74; Hinds Gen Hosp, clin dietitian, 1974-79; Va Med Ctr, clin dietitian, 1979; Univ Miss Med Ctr, asst prof, 1979-, res nutrition-

ist, Univ Med Ctr, 1980-84; Belhaven Col, adj prof biol, currently. **Orgs:** Pre Cent Dist Dietetic Asn, 1978-79; Tri Beta Biol Hon Soc, 1979-; pres, Nutritionists Nursing Educ, 1981-82; Miss Heart Asn, Prof Educ Comn, 1982-84; chmn, Nutrit Subcomt, Prof Educ Comn, 1982-85; Diocesan Sch Bd, 1982-86; nutrit consult, Oper Head start Prog, 1982-; Miss Heart Asn Nutrit Comn, 1983-; pres, Miss Dietetic Asn, 1983-84; bd dirs, Miss Dietetic Asn, 1985-; pres, Health Adv Comn Hinds County Proj Head start, 1987; Am Cancer Soc, 1987-; Am Heart Asn, 1991-; PTSA pres, Forest Hill HS, 1991-; Bd CUP, Univ S Miss; Phi Delta Kappa Hon Soc. **Special Achievements:** Reviewed several articles for professional journal, 1982-84; Presented res abstract at Reg Hypertension Mtg, 1983; Reviewed a major nutrition text Mosby Publ, 1984; Publ article in professional refereed journal, 1985. *

CAMERON, MICHAEL TERRANCE
Baseball player. **Personal:** Born Jan 8, 1973, La Grange, GA; married JaBreka; children: Taja, Dazmon & Mekhi. **Career:** Chicago White Sox, outfielder, 1995-98; Cincinnati Reds, 1999; Seattle Mariners, 2000-03; NY Mets, 2004-05; San Diego Padres, center fielder, 2006-07; Milwaukee Brewers, 2008-. **Orgs:** Make-A-Wish Foundation; Starlight Foundation; Cam4Kids Foundaton. **Honors/Awds:** Rawlings Gold Gloves, 1998, 1999, 2001, 2003, 2006; 7th among all NL outfielders, All Star Game votes. **Business Addr:** Professional Baseball Player, Milwaukee Brewers, Miller Pk, One Brewers Way, Milwaukee, WI 53214.*

CAMERON, RANDOLPH W
Marketing executive. **Personal:** Born in Jersey City, NJ; son of Randolph W Cameron; married Martha; children: Randolph Jr & Michele. **Educ:** Delaware State Col, BS, bus admin, 1958; New Sch Social Res, MA, commun, 1985. **Career:** D Parke Gibson Assoc Inc, vpres, 1962-72; Avon Prod Inc, div sales mgr, 1972-73, dir field sales support, dir corp commun, 1978-85; Cameron Enterprises, founder, pres, currently. **Orgs:** Bd mem, Am Cancer Soc; Econ Adv Comn; New York City Bus Soc; adv comt, New York Jobs Youth. **Honors/Awds:** Athletic Hall of Fame, Delaware State Univ, 1989. **Special Achievements:** The Minority Executives' Handbook, revised, Amistad Press, 1998; Black Achievers Indust; Author: "The Minority Executives' Handbook," Warner Books, 1989. **Military Serv:** AUS, PFC. **Home Addr:** 100 W 94th St, New York, NY 10025, **Home Phone:** (212)662-7177. **Business Addr:** President, Cameron Enterprises, 11877 Goldring Rd, Arcadia, CA 91006, **Business Phone:** (626)358-6130.

CAMERON, ULYSSES
Librarian. **Personal:** Born Dec 4, 1930, Sanford Heights, NC; son of Archie and Pearlie Judd; married Ida R Womack; children: Sylvia Mortensen, Byron, Cynthia Moorman, Myrna Maunuksela. **Educ:** Howard Univ, BMusEd, 1952; Atlanta Univ, MSLS, 1965; Federal City Col, MA, 1974; VA Polytech Inst & State Univ, CAGS, 1977, EdD, 1984. **Career:** Retired: Enoch Pratt Free Lib, librn, 1965-68; Federal City Col Media Ctr, assoc dir, 1968-74, deputy dir, 1974-77; Univ DC, assoc dir univ lib, 1977-82, head librn, bus lib, 1982-84, head librn, educ lib, 1984-86, librn & spec proj dir, serials librn, 1986-94. **Orgs:** Phi Delta Kappa. **Honors/Awds:** What's Wrong with our Library Schools, Cameron et al, 1966. **Military Serv:** USAF, capt, 1953-62. *

CAMERON, WILBURN MACIO, JR.
Dentist. **Personal:** Born in Richmond, VA; married Jacqueline Amelia; children: Wilburn Macin III, Charles Anderson. **Educ:** Va State Col, BS, 1950; Howard Univ Grad Sch; Meharry Med Col, attended 1956. **Career:** Pvt Pract, dent, curently. **Orgs:** Peter B Ramsey Dent Soc; Old Dominion Dent Soc; Va Acad Gen Dent; Chi Delta Mu Frat; YMCA; Kappa Alpha Psi Fraternity; Va Acad Gen Dent, fel, Int Acad Gen Dent. **Honors/Awds:** President Award, Old Dominion Dentist Soc, 1977, 1978; Meharry's President Award. **Military Serv:** AUS, capt, 1946-48, 1956-58. **Business Addr:** Dentist, 12 W Marshall St, Richmond, VA 23220.*

CAMMACK, CHARLES LEE, JR.
Manager, vice president (organization), journalist. **Personal:** Born Oct 8, 1954, Fort Wayne, IN; son of Charles Lee Sr and Sarah Elizabeth Jackson; married Michelle Lynn Duncan Cammack, Aug 10, 1986. **Educ:** Purdue Univ, BA, 1977; Univ Wis, Madison, MA, 1978. **Career:** WKJG-TV, Ft Wayne, broadcast journalist, 1978-89; Ft Wayne Newspapers, mgt trainee, 1987-89, benefits & systs mgr, 1989-, mgr employ safety & security, 1992-; PNI, dir, 1998; Philadelphia Daily News, vpres human resources, currently. **Orgs:** Youth Resources, 1988-; Bd diversity comt, Newspaper Asn Am; chairman, Workplace Issues Comt Newspaper Asn Am; co-chairman, Youth Leadership, Ft Wayne; bd mem, Leadership Ft Wayne; fel McCormick Tribune, 1998; Pa Newspaper Asn. **Honors/Awds:** First Place News Documentary, Ind Assoc Press, 1980; First Place News Feature, Ind Assoc Press, 1981; Community Service Award, Union Baptist Church, 1982; Second Place News Documentary, Ind Press Photographers Asn, 1982. **Business Addr:** Vice President, Philadelphia Daily News, 400 N Broad St, Philadelphia, PA 19101-4099, **Business Phone:** (215)854-2000.*

CAMP, KIMBERLY
Artist, arts administrator. **Personal:** Born Sep 11, 1956, Camden, NJ; daughter of Hubert E and Marie Dimery; divorced 2004. **Educ:** Am Univ, Wash, DC, 1974; Univ Pittsburgh, Pittsburgh, PA, BA, studio arts & art hist, 1978; Drexel Univ, Philadelphia, PA, MS, arts admin, 1986. **Career:** Kellogg Nat Leadership Prog fel XVI; City Camden, NJ, visual arts dir, 1983-86; Nat Endowment F/T Arts, arts mgt fel, 1986; Commonwealth Pa, Coun Arts Harrisburg, PA, dir, artist educ & minority arts serv, 1986-89, prog dir; Smithsonian Inst, Wash, DC, Experiment Gallery, dir, 1989-94; Charles H Wright Mus African Am Hist, exec dir & pres, 1989-94; Barnes Found, chief exec officer & exec dir, 1998-. **Orgs:** Detroit Chap, 1994-98, Arlington Va Chap, Links Inc, 1990-94; vice chairperson, Asn Am Cult, 1984-89; bd mem, Intercult Advancement Inst Gettysburg Col, 1988-89; bd mem, Arlington Art Ctr, 1990-94; nat adv comm mem, Nat Asn Artists Orgns, 1989-90; bd mem, Bus Vols Arts, 1994-97; adv bd, Jr League, 1994-97; bd mem, Empowerment Zone Develop Corp, 1996-97; bd mem, Am Asn Mus, 1995-97. **Honors/Awds:** NJ Senate Citation, 1986; Arts Achievement Award, City Camden, 1986; Purchase Award, JB Speed Museum, KY, 1988; Roger L. Stevens Award for Nat Contributions to the Arts, H. John Heinz Sch Carnegie Mellon Univ, 1999; Nat Endowment Arts Fellowship; Kellogg Nat Leadership Prog Fellowship; Visiting Scholar, Tokyo Gedai Univ; Visiting Scholar, Spirit Detro. **Special Achievements:** Exhibitions at over 50 museums, galleries and organizations in the USA, 1988-. **Business Addr:** Executive Director, Chief Executive Officer, The Barnes Foundation, 300 N Latch, Merion, PA 19066-1729, **Business Phone:** (610)667-0290.

CAMP, MARVA JO
Lawyer, businessperson. **Personal:** Born Sep 17, 1961, Washington, DC; daughter of Fab Jr and Ernestine Alford. **Educ:** Univ Va, Charlottesville, BA, 1983; Univ Va, Sch Law, Charlottesville, JD, 1986. **Career:** Gartrell & Alexander Law Firm, Silver Spring, MD, atty, assoc, 1986-87; Congressman Harold E Ford, Wash, DC, legislative dir, tax coun, 1987-88; Congressional Task Force Minority Bus, Wash, DC, dir, legal counsel, 1987-; Congressman Mervyn M Dymally, Wash, DC, adv, 1988-; Crenshaw Int Corp, Wash, DC, pres, chief exec officer; Md State Bar Asn, comt mem, currently. **Orgs:** Vpres & bd dir, Edward C Mazique Parent Child Ctr, 1986; legal coun, Inst Sci, Space & Technol, 1987-; consult, Minority & Small Bus, 1987; adv, Dem Nat Comn, 1988; legal coun, Carribean Am Res Inst, 1988; pres, bd dir, Young Black Prof, 1988-; co-chair, treas, African-Am Polit Fund, 1988; bd dir, 14th & U Coalition, 1988; adv pres, Congressional Black Asn, 1988; Soc Outstanding Young Am. **Honors/Awds:** Congressional Certificate of Recognition. **Special Achievements:** Author, Federal Compliance with Minority Set-Asides, 1988, Future of African-Amer, 1988. **Business Addr:** Committee Member, Maryland State Bar Association, 520 W Fayette St, Baltimore, MD 21201, **Business Phone:** (410)685-7878.

CAMPBELL, ALMA PORTER
Educator. **Personal:** Born Jan 5, 1948, Savannah, GA; daughter of Gladys B Porter and William Porter; divorced 1978. **Educ:** Savannah State, BS, 1969; State Univ New York Col Brockport, NY, MS, 1971, CAS, 1988. **Career:** Educator (retired); Rochester City Sch, Rochester, NY, third grade teacher, 1974-87, chp one reading teacher, 1987, basic skills cadre, 1988-90, lead teacher mentor, 1991-92; Theodore Roosevelt Sch no 43, vice prin, 1993-94, prin, 1992-2003. **Orgs:** Chmn, Nominating Comt, Alpha Kappa Alpha, 1988-90; Phi Delta Kappa Hon Fraternity Educ, 1989-; bd dir, Hamm House, 1990-91; bd dir, Jefferson Ave Early Childhood Ctr, 1990-91; bd Christian Ed, Memorial AME Zion Church, 1986-; Alpha Kappa Alpha, Ivy Leaf reporter; African-Am Leadership Develop Prog, steering-comt; chairperson, Climate Comt, No forty three Sch, Introduced twenty four staff mems Peer-Mediation Training Module; chairperson, Artist in Residence Progs; teacher trainer, Coop Learning; Leadership Group, Local Statewide Systemic Initiative, R&D Schs; LARC-Lyell Ave Revitalization Comt; RCEL, Rochester Coun Elem Adm; Internal Reading Leadership Asn; Rochester Teaching Ctr & Steering Comn; treas, Phi Delta Kappa Hon Educ Fraternity; speaker, African Am Critical Issues Network, 1998; Rochester Teachers Policy Bd. **Honors/Awds:** Phi Delta Kappa Hon Educ Fraternity; appointed to focus group, Prof Develop Acad; vis practr, Harvard Principals Ctr, ASAR rep; inductee, Hall of Fame First Church Award, Educ Achievement. **Special Achievements:** Co-author: Quick Reference Manual for Teachers, RCSD, 1990-; Super Teaching Tips, 1992; Submitted two curriculum guides to the New York State Education Department to be included in the New York Academy for Excellence in Teaching and Learning; appointed to Career In Teaching Panel (CIT) by Supt Clifford Janey; appointed to Supt Instructional Cabinet, 2001-02; one of 40 sch prin worldwide to participate in the Oxford Univ Round Table in Eng. **Home Phone:** (716)256-1679.

CAMPBELL, DR. ARTHUR REE
Nurse, educator. **Personal:** Born Feb 20, 1943, Bessemer, AL; daughter of Levi Williams Sr and Menyarn Miller Williams; married Shadrach Campbell, Jun 25, 1966; children: Korey Lanier, Kareem Damohn, Kheela Delores. **Educ:** Tuskegee Univ, Tuskegee, AL, BSN, 1965; Univ Md, Baltimore, MD, MSN, 1967; Univ Ala, Tuscaloosa, AL, EdD, 1984. **Career:** Univ Ala Hosp, Birmingham, AL, charge nurse, 1965; Jefferson County Dept Health, Birmingham, AL, psyciatric nurse, 1967-75; Univ Ala, Sch Nursing, Birmingham, AL, assoc prof, 1975-. **Orgs:** Pres, Ment Health Asn Cent Ala; treasurer & vpres, Family & Child Serv; YWCA; Am Red Cross. **Honors/Awds:** Outstanding Volunteer, Am Red Cross, 1980; Distinguished Service Award, Ala State Nurses Asn, 1981; Craig Award, Volunteer of the Year, Family Ct Jefferson County, 1984; Volunteer of the Year Award, Ment Health Asn Cent Ala, 1987. **Business Addr:** Associate Professor, University of Alabama, School of Nursing, 1530 3rd Ave S, Birmingham, AL 35294-1210, **Business Phone:** (205)934-3485.*

CAMPBELL, BILL. See CAMPBELL, WILLIAM.

CAMPBELL, BLANCH
Executive. **Personal:** Born Dec 4, 1941, Biscoe, AR; daughter of Oscar Louderdale and Louella Calbert Louderdale; divorced; children: Tanja Marie Smith. **Educ:** Webster Col, St Louis, MO, BA, 1981. **Career:** Retired: Southwestern Bell Telephone, St Louis, MO, serv asst, 1966-68, group chief operator, 1968-72, supvr bus serv, 1972-74, supvr course develop, 1974-75, staff mgr training, 1975-78, district mgr, 1978-91; Trip With Me Travelers Inc, founder, chief exec officer, pres. **Orgs:** Pres, Junior Kindergarten Bd, 1981-87; pres, Project Energy Care Bd, 1984; loan exec, United Way, 1984-85; pres elect, 1985-86, pres, 1986-88, City North Y's Men Club; Monsanto YMCA Bd Dir, 1989; chairperson, placement educ info comt, Greater Mount Carmel Baptist Church; Women Leadership, 1984-; consult, Emprise Designs, 1988-89; regional dir elect, 1990-91, regional dir, 1991-92, Y's Men Intl; pres, Continental Soc Inc, St Louis Chap, 1989-97, 1999-; admin coun, 1993-97; Phyllis Wheatley YWCA, 1991; regional dir Continental Soc Inc Midwest-Western Region, 1997-99; bd mem, new Mid-Co Chamber. **Honors/Awds:** Volunteer Service Award, United Way Greater St Louis, 1984; Outstanding Leadership, The Junior Kindergarten, 1984, 1985; Continental Society Volunteer Award, Educ Div, 1986; Y's Men of the Year, City North Y's Men, 1987-90; Youth Serv Award, Monsanto YMCA, 1989; Finalist, Missouri Mother & Daughter Pageant, 1989; Outstanding New Member, Continental Societies Inc, 1993-; Volunteer Award, Top Ladies Distinction, 1991; Division Leader, Monsanto YMCA Partner Youth Campaign, 1992; Y's Men International, Golden Book Endowment Award, 1996. *

CAMPBELL, BOBBY LAMAR
Government official, businessperson, manager. **Personal:** Born Sep 30, 1949, Fairmont, NC. **Educ:** Brooklyn Col, BA, 1979; Howard Univ, MCP, 1982; Nat Inst Power Engrs, attended 1984. **Career:** US HUD, prog analyst, 1980-81; Howard Univ, researcher, 1981-82; Polinger Mgt Co, resident mgr, 1983-85; DC Mutual Housing Asn Inc, property mgr,1985-. **Orgs:** Vet counr, Brooklyn Col, 1975-79; ANC comt, 4D Adv Neighborhood Comn,1980-84; stud rep, Am Planning Asn, 1981-82; site coordr, Nat Capitol Health Fair Proj, 1982; steering comt mem, DC Off Planning, 1983-84; pres,Upper Northwest Civic Group, 1984. **Honors/Awds:** Outstanding Community Serv, DC Recreation Dept, 1983; Contrib Auth, Wash Foot NCAC APA/Smithsonian Press, 1983; Outstanding Community Serv, 4D Adv Neighborhood Comn, 1984. **Military Serv:** USAF, SS6T, 4 yrs; Air Force Accomendation Award, 1970-71.

CAMPBELL, CALVIN C.
Judge. **Personal:** Born Aug 20, 1924, Roanoke, VA; children: Cathleen. **Educ:** Howard Univ, AB, 1948; Univ Chicago Law Sch, JD, 1951. **Career:** US Supreme Ct, pract, 1966; Ill Supreme Ct, Circuit Ct, 1977; Appellate Ct Ill, justice, 1978-; Circuit Ct, judge, 1977-78; Ill, asst atty gen, 1957-77; Ill Appellate Ct, Revenue Litigation, chief; First Appellate Dist, fifth div, presiding judge, 1978, fourth div, appellate judge, currently. **Orgs:** Cook County Bar Asn, present; Ill State Bar Asn; Forty Club Chicago. **Honors/Awds:** Outstanding alumni, Chicago Howard Univ Alumni Asn, 1965; outstanding Attorney General, State Ill Employee Off, 1976. **Military Serv:** AUS, pfc, 1943-45; Recipient bronze Star, AUS, 1945. *

CAMPBELL, CARLOS, SR.
Manager, president (organization). **Personal:** Born Dec 23, 1946, Warrenton, VA; son of Albert and Martha; married Ethel Douglas; children: Carlos II. **Educ:** AUS, Air Defense Sch, Cert Completion Opers & Intelligence Specialist, 1967; North AL Col Com, Cert Completion Bus Admin & Acct, 1972; Alabama A&M Univ, BS 1975; Alabama A&M Univ, MBA. **Career:** AL A&M Univ, univ recruiter, 1975-76, dir veterans affairs, 1975-76; Chesebrough Ponds Inc Prince Matchabelli Div, prod scheduler, 1976-78, sr prod planner, 1978-80, supvr warehousing & inventory control, 1980-86, senior prod supvr, 1986-87; Consolidated Industries, prod control mgr, 1989-. **Orgs:** Mem Madison Co Dem Exec Comn, Exec Bd, Madison Co Nat Asn Advan Colored People; vice chmn, AL Dem Conf Exec Bd; chmn, Univ and Indust Cluster AL A&M Univ; chmn bd mgr, N W YMCA; chmn, athletic exec bd, AL A&M Univ; prof, Black Exec Exchange Prog Nat Urban League; Youth Motivation Task Force Nat Alliance Bus;Alpha Phi Alpha Frat, Govt Rel Comn AL A&M Univ; Bd Dir, N Ala Regional Hosp; life mem 1814 Color Guard US Army Air Defense Command; exec bd, Police Athletic Asn; pres, JD Johnson High Sch PTA, pres, Sch Bd Parents Asn. **Honors/Awds:** Presidential Citation, Nat Asn Equal Opportunity Higher Educ; Outstanding Leadership Award; National Alliance Business

Washington DC; Alumni of the Year, Sch Bus Ala A&M Univ; Distinguished Service Award, Outstanding Service Award, Ala A&M Univ; Citation the National Urban League, National Alliance of Business, AL Veteran Affairs Assoc of AL; Distinguished Servcie Awardd; Phi Beta Lambda Professional Business Frat; Outstanding Young Man of America, US Jaycees. **Military Serv:** Vietnam Vet, 1970; AUS Air Defense, Comdr, 1966-72. **Home Phone:** (205)852-8876. **Business Addr:** Production Control Manager, Consolidated Industries, 4015 Pulaski Pike NW, Huntsville, AL 35810, **Business Phone:** (205)859-6890.

CAMPBELL, CARLOS CARDOZO
Banker, association executive. **Personal:** Born Jul 19, 1937, New York, NY; married Sammie Marye Day (divorced 1988); children: Kimberly, Scott. **Educ:** MI State Univ, BS, 1959; US Naval Post Grad Sch, Diploma Engr Sci, 1965; Catholic Univ Am, MA City & Regional Planning, 1968. **Career:** VA Polytech Inst & State Univ, adj prof summer, 1974; Am Revolution Bicentennial Admin, dep asst admin, 1974-76; Carlos C Campbell & Assoc, principal & owner, 1976-81; US Dept Comt, asst secy econ develop, 1981-84; Inter Am Develop Bank, alternate exec dir designee; CC Campbell & Co, mgt, consult, 1985-; Cataray, Inc, bd dirs, 1985-89; Graphic Scanning Inc, 1987-89; Dominion Bank, Tysons, 1988-92; Comput Dynamics Inc, 1992-96; Resource Am Inc, 1992-; Fidelity Leasing Inc, 1996-; NetWolves Corp, dir, 2003-; Resource Am Inc, dir, currently; Pico Holdings Inc, dir, currently; Resource Am Inc, dir; Herley Industries Inc, dir. **Orgs:** Sr systems analyst Ctrl Data Corp, 1968-69; spec asst, US Dept Housing & Urban Develop, 1969-72; Screen Actors Guild, 1972-; vpres, Corp Comt Develop, 1973-74; bd dir, Am Soc Planning Officials, 1973-74; bd dir, McLean Savings & Loan Assoc, 1975-77; vpres, Am Coun Intl Sports, 1978-81; comnr, Northern VA Reg Planing Dist Comt, 1980-82. **Honors/Awds:** Grant Nat Endowment Arts, 1972, Ford Found, 1973; Author New Towns, Another Way Live, 1976; Book Month Club Alternate Selection, 1976. **Military Serv:** USN, lt comdr, 1959-68; Naval Flight Officer, Navy Achievement Medal, National Defense Medal. **Business Addr:** Director, NetWolves Corporation, 4805 Independence Pkwy Suite 101, Tampa, FL 33634-7527, **Business Phone:** (813)286-8644.*

CAMPBELL, DR. CHARLES EVERETT
Dentist. **Personal:** Born Aug 13, 1933, Statesboro, GA; son of Fred and Ernestine; married Phyllis; children: Charles, Jacqueline & Andrea. **Educ:** Oakwood Col, 1959; Meharry Med Col, 1968; Univ NC, attended 1974. **Career:** Dentist (retired); Mt Sinai Hosp, 1959-60; Va Hosp, med tech, 1960-64; Hubbard Hosp & Va Hosp, dental intern, 1968-69; Neighborhood Health Ctr, staff dentist, 1969-73; Orange Chatham Comprehensive Health Serv Inc, Carrboro, NC, dental dir, 1974-94. **Orgs:** Old N State Dent Soc; Durham Acad Med; Nat Dent Asn; Black Adventist Med Dent Asn; treas, Oakwood Col Nat Alumni Asn; Meharry Med Col Alumni Asn; Immanuel Temple Seventh-day Adventist Church, Durham, NC. **Honors/Awds:** Nashville Dental Prize; John Bluford Award; Cumberland Chap Oakwood Col Alumni Asn Award, 1973; Oakwood Col Natl Alumni Award, 1993; Meharry Med Col Alumni Award, 1993; Outstanding Alumanus Oakwood Col, 2001. **Military Serv:** AUS, mc, 1956-58. **Home Addr:** 343 Warren way, Chapel Hill, NC 27516. *

CAMPBELL, CHRISTOPHER LUNDY
Lawyer, athlete. **Personal:** Born Sep 9, 1954, Westfield, NJ; son of Howard Thomas and Marjorie Lee; married Laura Sue Beving, Mar 11, 1979; children: Christopher Lundy, Auasa Ebony & Jonathan Edward. **Educ:** Univ Iowa, BS, sociol, 1979; Iowa State Univ, 1983; Cornell Law Sch, JD, 1987. **Career:** Iowa State Univ, asst wrestling coach, 1979-83; Iowa Univ, asst wrestling coach, 1983-84; Cornell Univ, asst wrestling coach, 1985-87; United Technologies CRP, staff atty, 1987-88; Carrier CRP, atty, 1988; Carlton Di Sante & Freudenberger, atty; Pvt Pract, currently. **Orgs:** Mem exec comt, USA Wrestling, 1992; chair educ comt, Black Law Student Asn, 1986; Athletes Adv Bd, US Olympic Comt, 1992; bd dirs, US Olympic Comt, 1993; bd dirs, Vegetarian Times, 1993. **Honors/Awds:** Bronze medal winner, US Olympic Team, Barcelona, 1992; Olympic Trials Champion, 1980, 1992; world champion, selected as the "world's most technically prepared wrestler," first Am receive award, 1981; world silver medalist, 1990; World Cup champion, 1981, 1983-84, 1991; Tbilisi champion, 1991; Sullivan Award, 1981; National Freestyle Champion, 1980, 1983,1990-91; Distinguished Member, Nat Wrestling Hall Fame. **Business Addr:** Attorney, Private Practitioner, 515 Oak Manor Dr, Fairfax, CA 94930.*

CAMPBELL, DIANE
College administrator. **Educ:** Morgan State Univ, Baltimore, Md, BS; Trenton State Col, MEd; Col NJ; Rutgers Univ, EdD. **Career:** Inner workings Inst, consult; Mercer County Community Col, exec dean stud affairs, dean enrollment & stud serv, currently; Kellogg fel. **Orgs:** Vice chairperson, Virtual Community Col Consortium; liaison, Distance Learning Adv Bd JEdge Steering Comt. **Business Addr:** Dean for Enrollment & Student Services, Mercer County Community College, 1200 Old Trenton Rd, PO Box B, West Windsor, NJ 08550, **Business Phone:** (609)586-4800.

CAMPBELL, E ALEXANDER
Clergy. **Personal:** Born Jan 31, 1927, Montego Bay, Jamaica; married Estelle Jones; children: Alexis, Paula, Edwin & Susan. **Educ:** Cornwall Col, Jamaica, 1944; Va Union Univ, BA, 1952; Va Union Theol Sem, MDiv, 1955; Hartford Sem Found, MA, 1957; McCormick Theol Sem, DMin, 1975. **Career:** Clergy (retired); Churches-in-Transition, Proj dir, prog devel; Urban Church Strategy IN-KY Conf UCC, cons; Ind-Kentucky Conf United Church Christ, pastor. **Orgs:** Dorm dir, counr men, Va Union Univ, 1954-55; assoc conf minister, RI Conf United Church Christ, 1962-72; area chmn, NE Comn Church Leadersn 1971-72; dir, host Church & Comm TV Prog RI; chairperson, Oak River Forest HS Human Rels Comn; past pres, Christian Educ Coun United Church Christ; past vpres, Greater Hartford Coun Church; past vpres, NE Comm United Ministry Higherr Educ; bd dir, United Church Bd World Ministries; dir, Black Church Empowerment Prog; past vpres, Barrington Prog Action; past bd mem, RI People Against Poverty; bd mem Ed Comm RI Childrens Ctr; bd dir, Oak Park Housing Ctr; Negro Hist & Cult; Apha Phi Alpha, Urban League; pres, Louisville InterdenomiNat Ministerial Alliance; bd mem, Nat Asn Advan Colored People. **Honors/Awds:** Citation United Church Christ Churches in Chicago; Citation for Outstanding Leadership RI United Church of Christ Conf; Citation for Achievement in Bringing Understanding of Church & Comm through TV RI Council of Church.

CAMPBELL, EDNA
Basketball player. **Personal:** Born Nov 26, 1968, Philadelphia, PA. **Educ:** Univ Md, College Park; Univ Tex, attended 1991. **Career:** Basketball player (retired), 2006; Hungary, 1995-96; Colo Xplosion, guard, 1996-98; Phoenix mercury, guard, 1999; Seattle Storm, guard, 2000; Sacramento monarchs, guard, 2001-04; San Antonio Silver Stars, guard, 2005-06; TV commentator, WNBA, 2006; realtor & loan consultant, currently. **Orgs:** Nat spokesperson, Breast Cancer Found. **Honors/Awds:** New comer of the Year, SWC, 1989-90; Jones Cup, MVP, 1986; World Championship, gold medal, 1998. *

CAMPBELL, ELDEN
Basketball player. **Personal:** Born Jul 23, 1968, Los Angeles, CA. **Educ:** Clemson Univ, attended 1990. **Career:** Basketball player (retired); Los Angeles Lakers, forward-center, 1990-99; Charlotte Hornets, 1999-2002; Seattle Supersonics, 2003; NJ Nets, 2005; Detroit Pistons, 2004-05; Oklahoma City Hornets, head coach.

CAMPBELL, EMMETT EARLE
Educator, physician. **Personal:** Born Dec 22, 1927, Dayton, OH; married Geneva Sydney; children: Michael, Heather, Kimberly & Laura. **Educ:** Univ Dayton, Pre-med, 1948; Univ Cinn, MD, 1953. **Career:** Am Acad Opthalmology & Otolaryngology, fel; Am Bd Otolaryngology, diplomat, 1966; Mercy Med Ctr, Rockville Ctr, New York, staff, chief otology; State Univ NY, Brooklyn, Temporal Bone Lab, NY Eye & Ear Infirmary, asst dir; Long Island Jewish Hosp, staff; Nassau County Med Ctr, staff; Cleft Palate Clin, N Shore Univ Hosp, consult; Otolaryngologist, 2000; Winthrop Univ Hosp, staff; New York Med Col, prof Otolaryngology; State Univ New York Health Sci Ctr, Brooklyn, prof; Temporal Bone Lab, NY Eye & Ear Infirmary, dir; NY Eye & Ear Infirmary, physician. **Orgs:** Fel Am Col Surgeons; Am Bd Otolaryngology; fel Nassau Acad Med; pres, coun mem, chmn, Nassau Surgical Soc; AMA; Nassau Otolaryngol Soc; NY St Soc Surgeons; Empire Med Polit Action Comt; Nassau Physicians Guild; Am Coun Otolaryngology; Nassau County Peer Review Comt; Continuing Med Educ Comt; Nassau Acad Med. **Honors/ Awds:** Asn phy recognition award, 1977; paper "Tympanoplasty Using Homograft Tympanic Membranes & Ossicles" Nat Med Asn, 1976. **Special Achievements:** Established the first "ear bank" at Mercy Medical Center in 1975, which was the only one in the New York Metropolitan Area; headed the first Cochlear Implant Center on Long Island circa 1991. **Military Serv:** USAF base flight surgeon 1954-57, aviation med examiner, otology consult.

CAMPBELL, EMORY SHAW
Health services administrator. **Personal:** Born Oct 11, 1941, Hilton Head Island, SC; son of Reginald and Sarah; married Emma Joffrion; children: Ochieng, Ayaka. **Educ:** Savannah State Col, BS, biol, 1965; Tufts Univ, MS, 1971. **Career:** Harvard Sch Pub Health, Boston, MA, res asst, 1965-68; Process Res Cambridge, Boston MA, biologist, 1968-70; Bramley Health Comm Ctr, Boston MA, asst dir, 1971; Beaufort Jasper Comprehensive Health, dir comm serv, 1971-80; Pa Ctr, exec dir, exec emer, 2004; Gullah Heritage Consult Servs, pres, currently. **Orgs:** Hilton Head Rural Water, 1980; bd dir, Beaufort Jasper Water Admin, 1978-82; Planning comm, Beaufort Co Planning Comm, 1982. **Honors/ Awds:** South Carolina Black Hall of Fame, 1999; DHL, Bank Street Col, 2000; Carter G. Woodson Memorial Award, 2005. **Special Achievements:** Author: Gullah Cultural Legacies, 2003. *

CAMPBELL, ERICA. **See ATKINS, ERICA.**

CAMPBELL, DR. EVERETT O.
Physician. **Personal:** Born Nov 15, 1934, Chicago, IL; married Anne Big Ford. **Educ:** Univ Mich, Med Sch, MD, 1958; UCLA, Chas Drew Post, Grad Med Sch. **Career:** UCLA, asst clinical prof; Chas Drew Post Grad Med Sch, asst prof; Martin Luther King Hosp; Pvt Pract, currently. **Orgs:** AMA; Calif Med Asn; Los Angeles Co Med Asn; Applied Health Res. **Honors/Awds:** Organizing dept of Sexual studies at Martin Luther King Hosp. **Special Achievements:** Author of paper on cancer. **Military Serv:** AUS, chf dept obstet-gynec, 1962-64. **Business Addr:** Physician, 1141 W Redondo Beach Blvd Ste 40, Gardena, CA 90247.

CAMPBELL, FRANKLYN D.
Airplane pilot. **Personal:** Born Feb 11, 1947, Washington, DC. **Educ:** Embry-Riddle Aeronaut Univ, pilot training; BS, 1971. **Career:** Flying Tiger Line Inc, Airline Pilot, 1974; Garrett Air Res Aviation Co, test pilot, 1974; Saturn Airways Inc, aircraft planner, 1971-72; Embry Riddle Aero Univ, stud flight dispatcher, teacher, 1970-71; Page Airways Inc, lineman, 1970; Dept Recreation, neighborhood youth corps, coordr, 1969. **Orgs:** Nat Col Flight Safety Coun; Nat Asn Advan Colored People; Brotherhood Crusade; Airline Pilot Asn; Negro Airman Int Inc. **Honors/Awds:** Outstanding Flight Student, 1970. *

CAMPBELL, GARY LLOYD
Educator, football coach. **Personal:** Born Feb 15, 1951, Ennis, TX; married Alola McKinney; children: Phyllis, Traci & Bryan. **Educ:** Univ Calif Los Angeles, BA, sociol, 1973. **Career:** Univ Calif Los Angeles, grad asst, 1976-78; Southern Univ, asst coach, running backs football, 1978-80; Howard Univ, running backs football asst coach, 1981; Pacific Univ, running backs football asst coach, 1982; Univ OR, running backs football asst coach, running back football coach, currently. **Orgs:** Am Football Coaches Assoc, 1978-; Am Cong on Real Estate, 1984-. **Business Addr:** Football Coach, University of Oregon, 1098 E 13th Ave 5210 Univ Oregon, Eugene, OR 97401-8833, **Business Phone:** (541)346-1000.

CAMPBELL, GEORGE, JR.
Association executive, president (organization). **Personal:** Born Dec 2, 1945, Richmond, VA; son of George and Lillian Britt (deceased); married Mary Schmidt, Aug 24, 1968; children: Garikai, Sekou & Britt. **Educ:** Drexel Univ, Philadelphia, PA, BS, 1968; Syracuse Univ, NY, PhD, 1977; Yale Univ, New Haven, CT, Exec Mgt Prog, 1988. **Career:** Nkumbi Col, Kabwe, Zambia, sr fac, 1969-71; AT&T Bell Lab, Holmdel, NJ, tech staff mem, 1977-83, third level mgr, 1983-88; NACME Inc, New York, NY, pres, 1989-00; Cooper Union Advan Sci & Art, pres, 2000-; bd dirs, Edison Inc, currently. **Orgs:** Emer mem, Secy of Energy Adv Bd, 1989-; AAAS Comt on Sci Eng & Pub Policy, 1990-; Am Phys Soc, 1968-; pres, Coun NY Acad Sci, 1984-; Nat Soc Black Physicists, 1977-; chmn, Nat Adv Comt, NSF Comprehensive Regional Ctr Minorities, 1989-91; bd trustees, Rensselaer Polytech Inst, 1992-; bd trustees, Crossroads Theater Co, 1991-; adv Coun NY State Off Sci, Technol & Acad Res. **Honors/Awds:** Simon Guggenheim Scholar, Drexel Univ, 1963-67; Sigma Pi Sigma, 1967; AT&T Bell Lab Excep Contrib Award, AT&T, 1985, 1986, 1987; Black Achiever in Indust, Harlem YMCA, 1988; Outstanding Black Am Scientist, Brooklyn Sci Skills Ctr, 1990; Synthesis Medallion, Nat Eng Educ Coalition, 1992; Centennial Medal, Drexel Univ, 1992; George Arents Pioneer Medal in Sci, 1993; EPIC Award, US Dept of Labor's; Presidential Award for Excellence, NACME. **Special Achievements:** First African Am pres of Cooper Union for the Advan of Sci and Art. **Business Addr:** President, The Cooper Union, 30 Cooper Sq eigth Floor, New York, NY 10003-7120.*

CAMPBELL, GERTRUDE M.
Association executive. **Personal:** Born Aug 3, 1923, Dallas, TX; married Quintell O; children: Patricia. **Educ:** Prairie View Col, BS, 1943; USC, attended 1968. **Career:** US Energy Res & Dev Adminstrn, dir officer mgt serv, 1975;US employ disadv Adults, Oakland Adult Minor Proj, br mgr; Berkeley Human Resource Develop Ctr, ctr mgr. **Orgs:** Life mem, Past Western Dist Govern; E Bay Area Nat Asn Negro Bus & Prof Women's Clubs; life mem Nat Coun Negro Women; Zeta Phi Beta; Past Matron Order Eastern Star; secy El Cerrito Br NAACP; Golden State Bus League; Prairie View Alumnae Asn; Bay Area Personnel Women; N CA Ind rel coun Who's Who Am Women 1971; comn mem, Govern Comm Status Women. **Honors/Awds:** Service Awards, Zeta Phi Beta; Community Service Award, Order Eastern Star; Employer Awards, Nat Assn Negro Bus & Prof Women. **Special Achievements:** First female To serve in US Energy Research and development adminstration; First female centre manager in Berkeley Human Resource Development Center; First president in Past Western District Government. **Military Serv:** USAF, capt; Mary T. Klinker Award, 1971.

CAMPBELL, GERTRUDE SIMS
Government official, postmaster general. **Personal:** Born May 13, 1942, Greenville, MS; daughter of Eugene Sims and Beatrice Parker Smith; married Willie James, Jul 1, 1960 (deceased); children: Kimberly Jamille. **Educ:** Wm F Bolger Acad, Supvr Skills Training, Memphis, TN, 1990. **Career:** US Postal Serv, clerk positions, 1966-90, supvr customer serv, 1990, postmaster, 1997-. **Orgs:** Afro Am United Success Postal Serv, 1990-93; League Postmasters, 1992; Nat Asn Postal Supvr, 1993; Nat Asn Postmasters United States, 1997. **Honors/Awds:** Special Achievement Award, US Postal Service, 1973, 1987; Diversity Peacesetters Award, 1996. **Business Addr:** Postmaster, US Postal Service, 822 Hwy 12 W, Starkville, MS 39759, **Business Phone:** (662)323-4752.

CAMPBELL, GILBERT GODFREY
Clergy, dean (education). **Personal:** Born Jan 16, 1920, Plainfield, NJ; son of Daniel Young (deceased) and Lulu Conover (deceased); married Bertha Vernice Morgan; children: Gilbert G Jr, Rosalind V Taylor. **Educ:** Union Univ, Richmond, VA, AB, 1941, MDiv, 1944, DD, 1967. **Career:** Clergy (retired); 1st Baptist Church, Cape Charles, VA, pastor, 1946-49; Theol Dept, VA Sem & Col, dean, 1947-50; Grove Baptist Church, Portsmouth, VA, pastor, 1949-64; Chesapeake Pub Sch, prin & teacher, 1950-64; Gethsemane Baptist Church, Suffolk, VA, pastor, 1950-64; 1st Gravel Hill Baptist Church, Rushmore & VA, pastor, 1953-64; Va Union Univ, pastor, 1971-88; Moore St Baptist Church, pastor, 1994, pastor emer, currently. **Orgs:** Dir, Christian Educ, Baptist Gen Conv Va, 1944-46; bd mem, Richmond OIC, 1965; pres, Baptist Gen Conv Va, 1970-73; bd mem, Richmond Nat Asn Adv Colored People/Sickle Cell Anemia, 1977-. **Honors/Awds:** Outstanding Leadership Award, Va Union Univ, 1977; Pres Award, Baptist Gen Conv Va, 1979; Gold Key Award, OIC, 1980. *

CAMPBELL, DR. HELEN
Educator. **Educ:** Ala State Univ, BS; Univ Ala, MA, PhD. **Career:** Bishop State Community Col, instr & directress choir, currently. **Home Phone:** (251)438-1922. **Business Addr:** Instructor & Directress of Choir, Bishop State Community College, Music, 351 N Broad St, Gymnasium Bldg Main Campus, Mobile, AL 36603, **Business Phone:** (251)690-6838.

CAMPBELL, JAMES W.
Clergy. **Personal:** Born Mar 17, 1945, Chicago, IL; married Anne; children: James, Jesse, Jared, Bridgett. **Educ:** Wilson Jr Col; Moody Bible Inst. **Career:** St James Church God Christ, ministry, 1966, supt State, 1977; dist supt, 1972; 5th Jurisdiction Il, secy, 1973; pastorate, currently. **Orgs:** Resolution Comn Nat & Elders Coun, 1975-77; Westside br NAACP; Nat Petrolmans Asn; NACD; Intl bd Minister's; Intl Asn Pastor's; Nat Elder's Coun. **Honors/Awds:** COGIC special citation, City Chicago; pastor of the year Award, Christian Guild Soc, 1979; Award for Dedicated & Faithful Services, State Sunday Sch supt Sunday Sch Dept Ill, 1980. **Business Addr:** Pastor, St James Church Of God In Christ, 10920 S Princeton Ave, P O Box 219, Chicago, IL 60623, **Business Phone:** (773)468-4600.*

CAMPBELL, LAMAR
Football player. **Personal:** Born Aug 29, 1976, Chester, PA. **Educ:** Univ Wis. **Career:** Football player(retired); Detroit Lions, defensive back, 1998-2002. **Honors/Awds:** Rookie of the Year, 1998.

CAMPBELL, LLOYD E
Executive. **Educ:** Georgetown Univ, BS, bus admin; Univ Pa, Wharton Sch, MBA. **Career:** Teachers Insurance, staff; Credit Suisse First Boston, Pvt Finance Group, managing dir & head; Rothschild Inc, head global pvt placement group, managing dir, 2002-. **Orgs:** Bd mem, Spartech Corp; Rothschild, Inc firms Investment Banking Comm; bd dir, Alderwoods Group; bd trustees, Georgetown Univ; chmn & founder, Pride First Corp; bd dirs, Spartech Corp; dir & chair nominating & governance comt, Argyle Security Inc. **Business Addr:** Managing Director, Head, Rothschild Inc, Global Private Placement Group, 1251 Ave of the Americas 51st Fl, New York, NY 10020, **Business Phone:** (212)403-3500.

CAMPBELL, MAIA
Actor, chairperson. **Personal:** Born Nov 26, 1976, Takoma Park, MD; daughter of Tiko and Bebe Moore. **Educ:** Spelman Col, Atlanta, GA, theatre. **Career:** TV series: "Thea", 1993; "South Central", 1994; "In The House", 1995-98; "Moesha", 1997; Films: Poetic Justice, 1993; Kinfolks, 1998; Trippin', 1999; The Luau, 2001; The Trial, 2002; With or Without You, 2003; Sweet Potato Pie, 2004; Envy, 2005; Sorority Sister Slaughter, 2007; MCC Inc, owner, producer, writer, head chmn & chief exec officer, 1994-. **Special Achievements:** Nominee, Young Artist Award, 1996. **Business Addr:** Owner, Chief Executive Officer, MCC Inc, 3607 S Main St, Blacksburg, VA 24060, **Business Phone:** (540)951-8202.*

CAMPBELL, MARGIE
Educator. **Personal:** Born Jun 17, 1954, Musella, GA; daughter of Margret Smith; children: MeQuanta. **Educ:** Gordon Col, AS, 1991; Mercer Univ, BS, 1995. **Career:** Monroe Co Bd Educ, sch secy, 1978-; Mary Persons High Sch, teacher, currently. **Orgs:** Parker Chapel AME Church; GA Munic Asn, 1984; Gov Proj Steering Comt, 1984; vol Fire Fighter, 1977-; vpres, Band Booster, 1990-; vpres, Basketball Tip-Off Club, 1991. **Honors/Awds:** Comm Leader Award, Gov's Project Competition Atlanta, 1982; Teacher of the Year, Monroe Achievement Ctr. **Special Achievements:** Selected as one of the 50 most influential Black women in GA-GA Informer 1983. **Home Addr:** PO Box 13, Culloden, GA 31016. **Business Addr:** Teacher, Mary Persons High School, Monroe Crossroads Academy, 25-A Brooklyn Ave, PO Box 1308, Forsyth, GA 31029, **Business Phone:** (478)994-7072.

CAMPBELL, MARY ALLISON
Educator, city council member. **Personal:** Born Feb 18, 1937, Shelby, NC; daughter of A C Allison; married Fred N Campbell Sr; children: Alison Winifred & Fred N Jr. **Educ:** Benedict Col, BS, 1960; Winthrop Col, attended 1973. **Career:** Educator (retired); Harold Fagges Assoc, NY, clerk, 1963-68; Clover Town County, coun mem; Clover Sch Dist, teacher, 1968-98. **Orgs:** Pres, The Progressive Women's Club, 1970-75; assoc matron. Magnolia Chap OES #144, 1982-84; pres, YCEA, 1988-89. **Honors/Awds:** School Yearbook Dedication, Roosevelt Sch, 1970; Appreciation Award, United Men's Club 1980; Outstanding Black Citizen of Clover Community, 1989; Citizen of the Year, Clover County, 1993. **Home Addr:** 104 Wilson St, Clover, SC 29710. *

CAMPBELL, MARY DELOIS
Administrator. **Personal:** Born Jul 21, 1940, Greenville, TX; married David; children: Keith Devlin. **Educ:** Jarvis Christian Col Hawkins, Tex, BS, bus admin, 1962; Bishop Col Dallas,1963. **Career:** Bishop Col Dallas Co Community Action, clerical, 1962-68; Dallas Co Comn Action Inc, Neighborhood Ctr coordr, 1968-69; City Dallas, asst youth coordr, 1969-71; N Central TX Coun T, manpower planner, 1971-76, human serv & planner, 1976-77; Housing Auth City Dallas, asst dir Soc Serv, 1979-80; Housing Auth City Dallas, asst dir res selection, 1980. **Orgs:** Bd dir, Dallas Urban League, 1974-77; Dallas Comn C & Youth, 1975; pres bd dir, Dallas Urban League, 1977-78; bd dir, Goals Dallas, 1977-79. *

CAMPBELL, DR. MARY SCHMIDT
Dean (education), college administrator. **Personal:** Born Oct 21, 1947, Philadelphia, PA; daughter of Harvey N Schmidt and Elaine Harris Schmidt; married George Campbell Jr, Aug 24, 1968; children: Garikai, Sekou & Britt Jackson. **Educ:** Swarthmore Col, BA, eng lit, 1969; Syracuse Univ, MA, art hist, 1973, PhD, 1982. **Career:** Syracuse Univ, Syracuse, NY, lectr; Nkumbi Int Col, Kabwe, Zambia, instr, 1969-71; Syracuse New Times, writer, art ed, 1973-77; Ford Found, fel, 1973-77; Everson Mus, curator, guest curator, 1974-76; Studio Mus Harlem, exec dir, 1977-87; Rockefeller Found, fel, 1985; NY City Dept Cult Affairs, NY, comnr, 1987-91; NY Univ, Inst Humanities, fel, 1989-; Tisch Sch Arts, dean, 1991-, Dept Art & Pub Policy, chair, 2000-, assoc provost, 2004-07; NY Coun Arts, staff, 2007-09. **Orgs:** Chair, Adv Comt African Am Instnl Study, Smithsonian Inst, 1989-91; Barnes Found, 1991-; chair, Stud Life Comt, Swarthmore Col Bd Mgrs, 1991-; VisCom Fine Arts, Harvard Col Bd Overseers, 1991-93; Am Acad Arts & Sci; Hon degrees, Col New Rochelle, Colgate Univ, City Univ NY, Pace Univ & Md Inst Col Art. **Honors/Awds:** Candace Award, 100 Black Women, 1986; Honorary Degree, City Col NY, 1992. **Special Achievements:** Author, Black Am Art & Harlem Renaissance, 1987; Author of numerous articles on Black American Art. **Business Addr:** Associate Provost for the Arts, Dean, Tisch School of the Arts, 721 Broadway Fl 12, New York, NY 10003, **Business Phone:** (212)998-1800.

CAMPBELL, MELANIE L
Chief executive officer, association executive, executive director. **Personal:** Born in Titusville, FL; daughter of Isaac Campell Sr and Janet; divorced. **Educ:** Clark Atlanta Univ, BA, bus & finance, 1983. **Career:** City Atlanta, Off Educ, asst dir, 1990-92; Mayor's Off Youth Servs, dir, 1992-94; self-employed polit strategist, 1994-95; Nat Coalition Black Civic Participation, dep dir, 1995-97, int dir, 1997-98, exec dir & chief exec officer, 1998-. **Orgs:** Delta Sigma Theta; Nat Coun Negro Women; Nat Asn Advan Colored People; Rainbow/PUSH Coalition; Nat Asn Female Exec; Nat Polit Cong Black Women; SCLC Women. **Honors/Awds:** Distinguished Leader Award, Emerging Leadership Inst, 1998. **Special Achievements:** Washington DC Top 40 Under 40, 2000. **Business Addr:** Executive Director, Chief Executive Officer, National Coalition Black Civic Participation Inc, 1900 L St NW Suite 700, Washington, DC 20036, **Business Phone:** (202)659-4929.

CAMPBELL, MICHELE
Basketball player. **Personal:** Born Feb 20, 1974. **Educ:** Univ Southern Calif, attended. **Career:** Basketball player (retired); Philadelphia Rage, ctr, 1997.

CAMPBELL, DR. MILTON GRAY
Athlete, public speaker, football player. **Personal:** Born Dec 9, 1933, Plainfield, NJ; married; children: Grant & 2 children. **Educ:** Ind Univ, attended 1957. **Career:** Football player (retired), athlete, speaker; US Olympic Team, decathlete,1952, 1956; Georgia State Univ, asst coach; Natl Football League, Cleveland Browns, player; Can Football League, player; motivational speaker,currently. **Orgs:** Black Athletes' Hall of Fame; US Olympic Hall of Fame. **Honors/Awds:** AAU Decathlon Winner, 1953; first place, AAU & NCAA high hurdles, 1955; World Rec, 120 yard hurdles; Intl Swimming Hall Fame, 1995; NJ Sports Hall Fame; Natl Track & Field, Hall Fame; Ind Univ Hall Fame; NJ Interscholastic Hall Fame; US Olympic Hall Fame; NFL Cleveland Browns; NJ Athlete Century, 2000; Awarded Doctor of Public Service, honoris causa by Mon Mouth Univ, 2008. **Special Achievements:** Olmpics: Silver Medal, Decathlon, 1952; Gold Medal,Decathlon, 1956. **Military Serv:** USN, 1955-56. **Home Addr:** 1132 St Marks Pl, Plainfield, NJ 07062-1410. *

CAMPBELL, DR. OTIS, JR.
Physician, educator. **Personal:** Born Sep 9, 1951, Tampa, FL; son of Otis Campbell, Sr and Georgia Mae Campbell; married Carol Y Clarke; children: Davin, Desmond, Donovon & Danyel. **Educ:** Fla A&M Univ, BS, biol, 1973; Meharry Med Col, PhD, pharmacol, 1982; Meharry Med Col, MD, 1986; Am Bd Internal Med, dipl. **Career:** Spec Med Prog Meharry Med Col, instr, 1982-84; Biomed Sci Prog Meharry Med Col, instr, 1982-84; UNCF Fisk Univ Pre-Med Inst, 1982-84; Vanderbilt Univ, summers, post doctoral res fel, 1982-85; Tenn State Univ Weekend Col, prof, 1982-86; Meharry Med Col, Dept Pharmacol, Nashville, TN, prof,1986-; pvt pract, internal med, McMinnville, TN, 1990-. **Orgs:** Middle Tenn Neuroscience Soc; Am Med Asn. **Honors/Awds:** Alpha Omega Alpha Medical Honor Soc, 1986; Hall of Natural Scientists, Fla A&M Univ, 1987. **Home Addr:** 3723 Stevens Lane, Nashville, TN 37218. **Business Addr:** Physician, 1499 R W Moore Memorial Hwy, Only, TN 37140, **Business Phone:** (931)729-5161.

CAMPBELL, OTIS LEVY
Business owner, chancellor (education). **Personal:** Born Jan 9, 1935, Slidell, LA; married Lois Ziegler; children: Cherry Ann, Barry, Maynard & Lajuana. **Educ:** Worsham Col Mortuary, Sci, 1962; Christian Bible Col Kenner La, BA, theol,1980, doctorate, theol, 1984. **Career:** Campbell's Funeral Home, mgr & owner, 1952; O L Campbell Agy, broker &mgr, 1952; St Tammany & Progressive Civic League, 1952-62; Christian BibleCol Southeast La, chancellor, 1995-. **Orgs:** Secy, Nat Asn Advan Colored People Local Chap, 1952-62; vpres, CBC Citizens Better Community, 1974. **Special Achievements:** First Black Mem Sch bd Saint Tammany Parish La, 1978. **Home Addr:** 711 Daney St, Slidell, LA 70458. **Business Addr:** Owner, Manager, Campbells Funeral Home, 2522 4th St, Slidell, LA 70458, **Business Phone:** (504)643-5452.

CAMPBELL, ROGERS EDWARD, III
Executive. **Personal:** Born Jul 14, 1951, Jersey City, NJ; son of Rogers E Jr. and Anne Mae Powell. **Educ:** Saint Peter's Col, BS, 1973; Rutgers Univ, MBA, 1974. **Career:** General Mills Inc, asst product mgr 1978-81; Mattel Electronics, product mgr, 1982-83; Schering-Plough Corp, dir of marketing, 1983-88; Marketcare Consumer HTH, svp, managing dir, 1988-. **Orgs:** Admissions liaison officer, US Military Acad; chmn, public relations comm Rutgers Grad Sch of Business; IOTA Phi Theta Fraternity; Clinton Hill Develop Corp. **Honors/Awds:** Distinguished Military Graduate. **Military Serv:** USY, 1st lt, 1974-77; Army Commendation Medal Meritorious Servs. **Business Addr:** 500 W Putnan Ave, Greenwich, CT 06830.*

CAMPBELL, SANDRA
Library administrator. **Career:** Univ Ark Monticello Libr, dir, currently. **Business Addr:** Director, University of Arkansas, Monticello Library, 514 Univ Dr, PO Box 3599, Monticello, AK 71656, **Business Phone:** (870)460-1780.

CAMPBELL, SANDRA DUPREE. **See DUPREE, SANDRA KAY.**

CAMPBELL, SANDRA PACE
Government official, consultant. **Personal:** Born Aug 24, 1955, Detroit, MI; daughter of Willie and Laura Pace; married John F Campbell Jr, Jun 1976 (divorced); children: Domonique, John III, Scott & Clarissa. **Educ:** Wayne State Univ, BBA, 1985; Univ Detroit, MBA, 1991. **Career:** Alan C Young & Assoc, sr acct, 1985-87, acct supvr, 1987-93; Eastern Mich Univ, asst controller, 1993-95; City Detroit, mgr rev collections, 1995-2002; Pacemaker acct, chief exec officer, 2002-. **Orgs:** Dir, Univ Mich Credit Union, 1993-; dir, secy, Booker T Wash Bus, 1992-96; audit chair, Elliotorians Bus women, 1991-; vpres, Nat Assoc Black Acct, 1984-85; membership co-chair, Nat Assoc Black MBAs, 1996-97; Junior Achievement, bus trainer volunteer, 1982-96; mentor, WADE McCree Incentive Scholarship Prog, 1988-97; dir, Detroit Black Chamber Com, 2001; dir, Black United Fund 2002-; dir, Travelers AID Soc, 2003-; treas, Delta Sigma Theta Sorority Inc, Detroit Alumnae Chap, 2003-05; bd dirs, Black United Fund MI. **Honors/Awds:** Women's Informal Network, Most Influential African Am Women in Metropolitan Detroit, 1998. **Home Addr:** 18314 Warrington Dr, Detroit, MI 48221.

CAMPBELL, DR. SYLVAN LLOYD
Physician. **Personal:** Born Oct 8, 1931, Boston, MA; son of Vera and Silvanis; children: Steven. **Educ:** Boston Col, AB, 1953; Howard Univ, MD, 1961. **Career:** Philadelphia Gen Hosp, intern, 1961-62, res, 1962-65; Boston, Practice med, specializing ob & gynecol, 1965-2000; Beth Israel Hosp, Boston, Mass, obstetgynecol, 1965-2000; Harvard Univ, obstet asst clinical prof emeritus, 1975. **Orgs:** Hon Staff Beth Israel Hosp; Am Bd Obstet-Gynecol Boston Obstetrical Soc; Mass Med Soc, 1966-; Am Col Obstetricians-Gynecologists, 1969-2000. **Military Serv:** USNR, lt jg, 1953-57.

CAMPBELL, TEVIN JERMOD
Singer, actor. **Personal:** Born Nov 12, 1976, Dallas, TX; son of Rhonda Byrd. **Career:** Albums: TEVIN, 1991; I'm Ready, 1993; Back To The World, 1996; Tevin Campbell, 1999; The Best of Tevin Campell, 2001; Qwest & Warner Bros, singer, currently; Films: Graffiti Bridge, 1990; A Goofy Movie, 1995; TVseries:

Wally & the Valentines, 1989; "Saturday Night Live", 1990; "The Fresh Prince of Bel-Air", 1991; "Moesha", 1999; "Tomorrow (A Better You, ABetter Me) With Quincy Jones", 1989; "Round & Round", 1990; "Just Ask Me To", 1991; "Tell Me What You Want Me to Do", 1991; "Goodbye", 1992;"Strawberry Letter 23", 1992; "Alone With You", 1992; "Confused", 1993;"One Song", 1993; "Can We Talk", 1993; "I'm Ready", 1994; "Always In My Heart", 1994; "Don't Say Goodbye Girl", 1995; "Back To The World", 1996;"I Got It Bad", 1996; "You Don't Have to Worry", 1997; "Could You Learn To Love", 1997; "Another Way", 1998; "For Your Love", 1999; "Losing All Control", 1999. **Honors/Awds:** Young Artist Award, 1990; Soul Train Music Award, 1994. **Special Achievements:** Nominated for many Grammy awards & Am Music Awards, 1992-98. **Business Addr:** Singer, Qwest & Warner Brothers, 3300 Warner Blvd, Burbank, CA 91505, **Business Phone:** (818)846-9090.*

CAMPBELL, THOMAS W.
Musician. **Personal:** Born Feb 14, 1957, Norristown, PA. **Educ:** Berklee Col Music. **Career:** Webster Lewis, drummer, 1978; Mar-Lena Shaw/Gap Mangione, drummer, 1979; Berklee Performance Ctr, concert, 1979; Baird Hersey & Year of the Ear, drummer; Own Group "TCB", Boston, drummer; Dizzy Gillespie Band, prof jazz drummer, 1985; First Music Group; The Mandells. **Orgs:** Big Brother Activities. **Business Addr:** Musician, Sutton Artists Corporation, 119 W 57 Suite 818, New York, NY 10019.

CAMPBELL, TONY
Athletic director, basketball player, basketball coach. **Personal:** Born May 7, 1962, Teaneck, NJ. **Educ:** Ohio State Univ, Columbus, OH, 1984. **Career:** Basketball player (retired), basketball coach, athletic dir; Detroit Pistons, 1984-87; Albany Patroons, 1987-88; Los Angeles Lakers, 1987-89;Minn Timber wolves, 1989-92;New York Knicks, 1992-94; Dallas Mavericks,1993-94; New York Knicks, 1993-94; Cleveland Cavaliers, 1994-95; Paramus Catholic High Sch, athletic dir & boy's basketball head coach, 2006-07,Bay Ridge Preparatory Sch, athletic dir. currently. **Honors/Awds:** NBA Championship Team, 1988; CBA All-Star First Team, 1988; Newcomer of the Year, Continental Basketball Asn, 1988. **Business Addr:** Athletic Director, Bay Ridge Preparatory School, 421 78th St Suite B, Brooklyn, NY 11209, **Business Phone:** (718)833-8650.

CAMPBELL, TRECINA EVETTE. See ATKINS, TINA.

CAMPBELL, WENDELL J.
Executive, architect. **Personal:** Born Apr 27, 1927, East Chicago, IN; son of Herman and Selma; married June Bernice Crusor, Nov 6, 1955; children: Susan Maria & Leslie Jean. **Educ:** Ill Inst Technol, BA, arch & city planning, 1956. **Career:** Purdue Calumet Devel Found, staff architect & dir rehab, 1956-66; Campbell & Mascai, pres; Wendell Campbell Assocs Inc, chief exec officer; Campbell & Tiu Campbell Inc, chief exec officer, currently; Yale Univ, pres lectr; Mass Inst Technol, pres lectr; Univ Ill, pres lectr. **Orgs:** Urban Planning & Design Comt, Am Inst Architects; bd dir, Chicago Am Inst Architects; founder & pres, Nat Orgn Minority Architects, 1971; Chicago Asn Com & Ind; Nat Asn Advan Colored People; Nat Urban League Develop Found; fel Am Inst Arch, 1979, bd mem, Chicago Chap; bd mem, Cosmopolitan Chamber Com; bd mem, Mercy Hosp & Med Ctr; bd mem, Black Ensemble Theater; Chicago Architect Assistance Ctr; S Side YMCA. **Honors/Awds:** Distinguished Building Award, 1973; Construction Man of the Year, 1973; Whitney M Young Junior Medal, Am Inst Architects, 1976; Design Excellence Award, 2005. **Military Serv:** AUS, sgt major. **Business Addr:** President, Campbell Tiu Campbell Inc, 1326 S Mich Ave Suite 200, Chicago, IL 60605, **Business Phone:** (312)922-4244.

CAMPBELL, WILLIAM (BILL CAMPBELL)
Government official, politician. **Personal:** Born Jan 1, 1953, Raleigh, NC; married Sharon; children: Billy & Christina. **Educ:** Vanderbilt Univ; Duke Univ, law. **Career:** Dem Party, mem; Atlanta City Coun, 12 yrs; City Atlanta, mayor, 1994-2002; pvt pract, atty. **Orgs:** Omega Psi Phi Fraternity. **Special Achievements:** first black student to attend an all-white school in Raleigh, NC.

CAMPBELL, WILLIAM EARL
Government official. **Personal:** Born Aug 26, 1965, Dermott, AR; son of Eddie Sr and Alice Allen. **Educ:** Univ Ark-Monticello. **Career:** City Reed, Ark, mayor, 1990-98; Ariz Employment Security Dept, prog supvr, 1992-. **Orgs:** Gen secy, bd dirs, New Hope Baptist Church, 1985-91; Southeast Ark Literacy Coun; past mem, bd dir, Nat Conf Black Mayors; past pres, Ariz Conf Black Mayors; TEA Coalition; Monticello Econ Develop Comn; adv bd, Workforce Training Ctr; School bd, McGehee Spec Sch Dist. **Honors/Awds:** Valedictorian, Tillar High Sch, 1983; Mr Boss, Black Org Spec Servs, Univ Ark-Monticello, 1990; Andrew Gregory Man of the Year Award, Southeastern Ark Charity Org, 1991. **Business Addr:** Program Service Advisor, Arkansas Employment Security Department, 477 S Main St, PO Box 30, Monticello, AR 71655, **Business Phone:** (870)367-2476.

CAMPBELL, ZERRIE D
Educator, school administrator. **Personal:** Born Feb 9, 1951, Chicago, IL; daughter of Robert Rice and Lorraince Rice; children: Sydney Adams. **Educ:** Northern Ill Univ, BA, 1972, MS, 1974; Chicago State Univ, MA, 1978. **Career:** Northern Illinois Univ, graduate asst, 1972-73, asst dormitory dir, 1973-74; Malcolm X Col, dir, student supportive services, 1974-77, instr, 1977-82, vpres, acad affairs, 1989-92, pres, 1992-; Harold Wash Col, ast prof, 1983-87; City Col Chicago, acting assoc, vice chancellor, liberal arts & scis, 1987-89. **Orgs:** Past pres, Alpha Kappa Alpha, Xi Nu Omega Chap; past pres, Monarch Awards Found; Langston Hughes Lit Asn; NIU Black Alumni Coun; Modern Lang Asn; Ill Comt Black Concerns Higher Educ; Nat Coun Instrnl Administrators; Am Coun Educ/Nat ID Prog AWHE; Am Asn Women Community Cols; Am Asn Univ Women; Nat Asn Female Execs; bd mem, Am Asn Community Col; adv coun, Nat Inst Leadership Develop; Chicago Network; N Cent Asn Cols & Schs/Consult-Evaluator Corps; Economic Club Chicago; bd dirs, Habilitative Systems Inc; bd dirs, Chicago Multi-Cult Dance Ctr; bd mem, United Ctr Community Econ Develop Fund, bd mem; Ill Comt Black Concerns Higher Educ; Networking Group Minority Exec; adv bd, Community Bank Lawndale, adv bd. **Honors/Awds:** Administrator Appreciation Award, Malcolm X Col, 1990; Fred Hampton Image Award, 1990; 2000 Notable American Award, 1990; Work Force 2000: Women's Day, Chancellor's Award, 1991; Spirit Award, Malcolm X Col, 1991; Distinguished Service in Education Award, Midwest Community Col, 1992; Distinctive Imprint Award, Nat Assn Univ Women, Chicago Br, 1993; Woman of the Year, Proviso Leyden Coun Community Action Inc, 1993; Woman of the year, Eta Phi Beta Sorority Inc, 1994; Kathy Osterman Award Outstanding Exec Employee (finalist), 1994; Kizzy Award, Black Women's Hall of Fame Found, 1995; MLK Jr Legacy Award, Boys & Girls Club Chicago, 1997; named one of 100 Women Making a Difference, Today's Chicago Women Mag, 1997; Executive of the Month, Chicago Bus Women, 1998; Outstanding Educator Award, 7th Cong Dist, 1998; Salute to Black President Award, 1999; Outstanding Women Awaed, Harold Wash Col, 1999; Phenomenal Woman Award, Expo Today's Black Woman, 2000; Community Achievement Award, African-Am Contractors Asn, 2001; Faith in Action Award, Westside Holistic Family Serv, 2001; Profile Col Organ Develop, Consortium Community Col Develop, 2001; Trailblazers Award, Pathfinders Prev Educ Fund, 2001; Legends of the West Award; Distinguished Leadership Award, God First Ministries; Outstanding and Dedicated Community Service Award, Nat Asn Univ Women. **Special Achievements:** The first woman appointed to the permanent position. **Home Addr:** 1220C S Fed, Chicago, IL 60605. **Business Addr:** President, Malcolm X College, 1900 W Van Buren Rm 1100, Chicago, IL 60612-3197, **Business Phone:** (312)850-7037.

CAMPBELL-MARTIN, TISHA
Actor, movie director, television comedy writer. **Personal:** Born Oct 13, 1968, Oklahoma City, OK; daughter of Clifton Campbell and Mona; married Duane Martin, Aug 17, 1996; children: Xen Martin. **Career:** Films: Little Shop of Horrors, 1986; Sch Daze, 1988; Rooftops, 1989; House Party, 1990; Another 48 Hours, 1990; House Party 2, 1991; House Party 3,1994; Boomerang, 1992; Snitch, 1996; Homeward Bound II: Lost in San Francisco, 1996; Sprung, 1997; Get Up Stand Up Comedy, dir, 2001; The Last Place On Earth, 2002; The Seat Filler, writer, 2004; Angels Can't Help But Laugh, 2007; TV series: "Gina on Martin", 1992-97; "Linc's", 1998; "TheSweetest Gift", 1998; "Sabrina, the Teenage Witch", 2000; "The HalloweenScene", 2000; "The Victoria's Secret Fashion Show", 2001; "My Wife &Kids", dir, 2001-05; "The Last Place On Earth", 2002; "Calvin Goes to Work", 2004; "A Family Affair", 2004; "The Proposal", 2004; "The Maid", 2004; "All of Us", 2004-06; "The 'V' Story", 2005; "Silence Is Golden", 2005; "My Wife & Kids", dir, 2005; "My Two Dads", 2006; "The Courtship of Robert's Father", 2006; "Carmen's Karma", 2006; "Trying to Love Two", 2006; "All of Us", 2006-07. **Orgs:** Am Film Inst. **Honors/Awds:** Image Award for Outstanding Actress in a Comedy Series, Nat Asn Advan Colored People, 2003; BET Comedy Award, 2004. **Special Achievements:** Nominated 5 times for Image Awards. **Business Addr:** Actress, c/o ABC Inc, 500 S Buena Vista St, Burbank, CA 91521-4551, **Business Phone:** (818)460-7477.

CAMPER, DIANE G
Journalist, editor. **Personal:** Born Feb 27, 1948, New York, NY; daughter of Roosevelt P and Clinice Coleman. **Educ:** Syracuse Univ, Syracuse, NY, BA, 1968; Yale Univ, New Haven, CT, MSt, law, 1977. **Career:** Newsweek, ed asst, 1968-72; Washington Bur corresp, 1972-83; The New York Times, ed writer, 1983-97; Annie E Casey Found, pub affairs mgr, 1997-2004; The Baltimore Sun Ed Bd, asst editorial page ed, 2004-. **Orgs:** Women in Commun Inc, 1968-; Delta Sigma Theta Sorority, 1974-; Nat Assoc Black Journalists, 1985. **Honors/Awds:** Page One Award, New York Newspaper Guild, 1977; Chancellor's Citation, 1986, Syracuse Univ; Publisher's Awards, New York Times, 1988, 1990; George Arents Pioneer Medal, 1990. **Business Addr:** Editorial Writer, The Batlimore Sun Co, 501 N Calvert St, PO Box 1377, Batlimore, MD 21278, **Business Phone:** (410)332-6000.

CAMPHOR, MICHAEL GERARD
Health services administrator. **Personal:** Son of James and Lillie. **Educ:** Morgan State Univ, BA, 1978; Univ Baltimore, MPA, health serv admin 1984; Naval Health Sci Educ & Training Command, cert financial & supply mgt, 1986. **Career:** Columbia Res Syst, res asst, 1976-77; N Cent Baltimore Health Corp, ctr adminr, 1980-84; Dept Housing & Community Develop, proj mgr, 1983-84; Cent Md Health Systs Agency, health implementor & liaison, 1984-85; US Naval Hosp, Philadelphia, PA, comptroller/hosp adminr, 1985-; US Naval Hosp, Mat Mgt & Contracting, Yokosuku, Japan, head officer; Dept Housing & Urban Develop, Grad Studies fel. **Orgs:** E Baltimore Community Orgn, 1978-83, Waverly Human Serv Coord Coun, 1980-83; site coord, Nat Health Screening Coun Vol Orgn, 1980-83; Dallas F Nicholas Elem Sch Adv Bd, 1981-84; Johns Hopkins Hosp Community Develop Adv Bd, 1983-84; Nat Naval Officers Asn. **Honors/Awds:** MJ Naylor Award, Highest Dept Average Morgan State Univ, 1978; Admin of the Year, N Cent Baltimore Health Corp, 1981; Outstanding Young Men of America Jaycees, 1983. **Military Serv:** USN, Med Officers Corp, 1992; Navy Achievement Medal, 1988, 1990, Overseas Service Ribbon, Armed Forces Service Medal, 1991.

CANADA, ARTHUR
Presbyterian clergy. **Career:** Grandale Presbyterian Church Master, presbyter; 212th General Assembly, Detroit, vice moderator, comnr currently. **Business Phone:** (313)836-8411.*

CANADA, BENJAMIN OLEANDER
School administrator. **Personal:** Born Nov 22, 1944, Tallulah, LA; son of Archie and Thelma Victoria Harrison; married Doris Malinda Colbert, Aug 17, 1968; children: Julie Malinda & Christina Malinda. **Educ:** Southern Univ, BA, 1967; Univ Wash, MEd, 1971; Univ Tex, PhD, 1989. **Career:** Las Vegas Sch Dist, elem teacher, 1967-68; Seattle Sch Dist, sec teacher, middle sch asst prin, elem sch prin, jr high sch prin, sr high sch prin,1968-83; Tucson Unified Sch Dist, regional asst supt, 1983-86, asst supt,1987-88, dep supt, 1988-90; Univ Wash, fel, 1970-71; Tex Asn Sch Bds, consult & trainer, 1986-87, Dist Serv, assoc exec dir, 2002-.; Jackson Pub Schs, supt, 1990-94; Atlanta Pub Sch, supt, 1994-98; Portland Pub Schs, supt, 1998-2001; educ consult, 2001-. **Orgs:** Univ Tex Supt's Prog, 1986-87; Phi Kappa Phi; Kappa Delta Phi; Urban Supts; nat adv bd, Active Citizenship Today, 1992; pres, Am Asn Sch Adminrs; Am Arts; Asn Supv & Curric Develop; nat adv bd, Ctr Res Eval, Stand & Stud Testing, 1996; CEO's Portland Bus Community; adv bd, Forum Am Sch Supt Dan forth Found; adv bd, Harvard USP; pres, Horace Mann League; supt, Large City Sch; Nat Alliance Black Sch Educrs; Nat Bd Prof Teachers Stand; Nat Endowment Arts; Nat Fedn Urban-Suburban Sch Dists; OR Asn Sch Execs, Legis Comt; pres, Coun Arts; pres, Arts Educ Adv Group; Portland Progress bd; Rose Festival; Finance Proj; Nat Asn Supt Searchers. **Honors/Awds:** Outstanding Achievement, Mayor Tucson, AZ, Copper letter; Meritorious Service Award, Seattle Prins Asn; First African-American Award, Urban League Jackson; Medgar Evers Statue Fund Award; Achievement in Education Award, NW Jackson Optimist Club; Appreciation & Commendation Award; Executive Committee Award, AASA; The Executive Educator 100, 1993; Golden Lamp Award, MS Asn Sch Adminrs; Atlantans on the Move Award, 100 Black Men; Religs Liberty Award, Am United Separation Church & State; hon degree, Lewis & Clark Col. **Special Achievements:** Sang theme song, "CBS This Morning," CBS-TV; first African-American president of AASA. **Business Addr:** Associate Executive Director, Texas Association of School Boards Inc, 12007 Research Blvd, PO Box 400, Austin, TX 78767-0400, **Business Phone:** (512)467-0222.

CANADA, GEOFFREY
Chief executive officer. **Personal:** Born Jan 1, 1954?, South Bronx, NY; son of McAlister and Mary. **Educ:** Bowdoin Col, Brunswick, ME, BA, psychol & sociol, 1974; Harvard Grad Sch Educ, MA, 1975. **Career:** Camp Freedom Ctr Ossipe, New Hampshire, supvr; Robert White Sch, fac, dir, 1977-83; Marion Wright Edelman & C's Defense Fund, partner; Rheedlen Ctrs C & Families, pres & chief exec officer, 1990-; Black Community Crusade c, E Coast reg coordr, 1991. **Orgs:** Bd trustees, Black Child Develop Inst, 1992-; bd dirs, Fund City NY & Found Ctr, 1995. **Honors/Awds:** Heroes of the Year Award, Robin Hood Found, 1992; Common Good Award, Bowdoin Col, 1993; Heinz Family Found Award, 1995; Children's Champion Awards, Child Mag, 2004; Liberty Medals, NY Post, 2005; Heinz Award, 2006; hon degree, Brown Univ, Sch Med, 2006. **Special Achievements:** Books: Fist Stick Knife Gun, A Personal History of Violence in America, Beacon Press, 1995; Reaching up for Manhood: Transforming the Lives of Boys in America, Beacon Press, 1997; The Culture of Violence, 2002; New York Magazine names Canada as one of New Yorkers who are affecting real change in education; 'Individuals dedicated to improving education in the United States', McGraw-Hill Cos, 2004; America's Best Black Leaders, J Blacks Higher Educ, 2005; America's Best Leaders, NY Times, 2005. *

CANADY, DR. ALEXA IRENE
Physician, educator. **Personal:** Born Nov 7, 1950, Lansing, MI; daughter of Clinton Jr and Hortense Golden; married George Davis, Jun 18, 1988. **Educ:** Univ Mich, Ann Arbor MI, BS, zool, 1971, MD, (cum laude), 1975. **Career:** Chief Pediatric Neurosurgery (Retired); Univ Pa, instr neurosurg, 1981-82; Henry Ford Hosp, Detroit, Mich, instr neurosurg, 1982-83; Wayne St Univ, Sch Med, Detroit, Mich, clin instr, 1985, clin assoc prof, 1987-90,

assoc prof neurosurg, 1990-97, prof neuosurg, 1997-; vice chmn neurosurg, 1991-; Children's Hosp Mich, Detroit, Mich, asst dir, neurosurg, 1986-87, chief pediat neurosurg, 1993-, neuro surgeon. **Orgs:** Am Col Surgeons; Am Asn Neurol Surgeons; Cong Neurol Surgeons; AMA; Nat Med Asn; Am Soc Pediat Neurosurg; Mich St Med Soc. **Honors/Awds:** Womens Med Asn citation, 1975; Teacher of the Year, C Hosp Mich, 1984; Woman of the Year Award, Detroit Club Nat Asn Negro Bus & Prof Women's Club, 1986; Candace Award, Nat Coalition of 100 Black Women, 1986; Michigan Womans Hall of Fame; Woman of the Year, Am Women's Med Asn, 1993; hon degree, Marygrove Col, 1994; Athena Award, Univ Mich Alumnae Coun, 1995. **Special Achievements:** First African American to become a Neurosurgeon. **Home Addr:** 6064 Forest Green Rd, Pensacola, FL 32505.

CANADY, BLANTON THANDREUS
Executive. **Personal:** Born Nov 25, 1948, West Point, GA; son of William Jr and Grace Warrick; married Mae Newbern; children: Andre Reynolds & Blanton T II. **Educ:** Univ Ill, BA, 1970; Univ Chicago, MBA, 1975. **Career:** Ill Bell Tel, Chicago, commun consult, 1970-73; Xerox Corp, telecomm mgr, 1973-76; Am Hosp Supply, fin mgr, 1976-80; Nat Black McDonalds Owners Asn, Great Lakes Div, pres, 1981; McDonald's Corp, exec vpres & chief oper, currently. **Orgs:** Pres, Black McDonald's Owners Asn, Chicago, 1986-88; pres, McDonald's Owners Chicagoland & NW, IN, 1990-92, vpres, 1988-90; exec comn, S Side Planning Bd, 1990-; bd mem, Midwest Asn Sickle Cell Anemia, 1990-; New S Planning Bd. **Honors/Awds:** Business & Professional Awards, Donald C Walker Publ; Empire Salute Award, Black McDonald's Owners Asn, 1990; Monarch Award, Alpha Kappa Alpha, 1990. **Special Achievements:** First black McDonald's licensee. **Military Serv:** Ill Nat Guard, E4, 1970-76. **Home Addr:** 4901 S Greenwood, Chicago, IL 60615, **Home Phone:** (312)624-1544. **Business Addr:** President, McDonald Corporation, 2111 Mcdonalds Dr, Oak Brook, IL 60521, **Business Phone:** (630)623-3000.

CANADY, HERMAN G., JR.
Judge. **Career:** Circuit Court, Charleston, WV, judge.

CANADY, HORTENSE GOLDEN
School administrator, educator. **Personal:** Born Aug 18, 1927, Chicago, IL; daughter of Alexander H and Essie Atwater; married Clinton Canady Jr; children: Clinton III, Alexa I, Alan L & Mark H. **Educ:** Fisk Univ, BA, 1947; Mich State Univ, MA, 1977. **Career:** Educator (retired); Community Nursery Sch, dir, 1947-48; Lansing Bd Educ,elected bd mem, 1969-72; Women's Comn State Mich, establishing comn, 1967-71; Auxiliary NDA, nat pres, 1976-77; Lansing Community Col, Lansing Community Col Found, dir; Les Meres, founder. **Orgs:** Nat bd, YWCA, 1976-82; bd dirs, First Am Cent Bank, 1977-92; nat pres,Delta Sigma Theta Sorority Inc, 1983-88; First Am Corp Bd, 1985-92; pres,Delta Res & Educ Found; charter mem, Lansing-East Lansing Chap Links; Am Asn Univ Women; Nat Asn Advan Colored People; League Women Voters;advisory bd, Wheaton Ctr Performing Arts; nat pres, Delta Sigma Theta Nat Serv Sorority. **Honors/Awds:** DIANA Award, YWCA, 1977; Frederick D Patterson Founder's Medallion, Mich United Negro Col Fund, 1979; Citizen of the Year, Nat Asn Advan Colored People, 1980; Black Book Award, 1984; Mich Women's Hall Fame, 2002; Hugo Lundberg Award, Lansing Human Rels Community; Athena Award, Lansing Regional Chamber Com; Sojourner Truth Award, Negro Bus & Prof Women; Mary Church Terrell Award; Women of Achievement and Courage Award, Mich Womens Found. **Special Achievements:** First African American Elected to the Lansing Board of Education; 100 Top Black Business & Professional Women, 1985; 100 Most Influential Americans. **Home Addr:** 3808 W Holmes Rd, Lansing, MI 48911.

CANADY-LASTER, RENA DELORIS
Executive. **Personal:** Born Jul 29, 1953, Effingham County, GA; daughter of Rev JB and Rena Elizabeth; married Willie L Laster; children: Hawa Shahlette, Sherri Latrice, Elizabeth Renae, Omega Lynn. **Educ:** GA Southwestern Col, BS Psycol, 1976; Augusta Col, MS Clinical Psycol, 1977. **Career:** Sumter Cty Taylor Cty Mental Retard Ctr, behavior spec, 1977-78; Taylor Cty Mental Retard Ctr, acting dir, 1978; Middle Flint Behavioral Healthcare, equal employment oppty rep, dir child & adolescent outpatient servs, 1978-, part time employment area PhD Psychol; behavior spec child & adolescent prog, 1978-88; Child & Adolescent Program Dir, 1988-97; Child & Adolescent Intake worker, counr, supvr; 1997-02. **Orgs:** City Zoning Appeals Bd, 1996-; Habitat Humanity, family selection comt; life mem, Delta Sigma Theta, 1973-; sch bd mem, Am City Bd Ed, 1980-93; provider area workshops, Child Sexual Abuse & Child Abuse, other children's issues; sec Early Bird Civitan Club 1983-84; jr hs group facilitator Taylor Cty Pregnancy Prevention Prog, 1984-; pres, Sumter Cty Mental Health Asn, 1984-85; bd dir, GA Mental Health Asn, 1984-85; group facilitator, Arrive Alive GA, 1985; pres, elect Early Bird Civitan Club, 1985, pres, 1986-; District 8 Infant Mortality Task Force, 1986-; Sumter 2000 Comt; consult area agencies & sch; vice chmn, Americus City Bd Ed, 1980-93; pres, Visions Sumter, 1995-96, bd mem, 1984-; pres, Visions Sumter, 2002. **Honors/Awds:** Blue Key Nat Honor Frat GA Southwestern Col, 1981; Outstanding Serv Award, Sumter Cty Mental Health Assoc, 1982; Employee of the Year, C&A Program, 1997; Outstanding Service, AFA Drum Majors, Americus Sumter Cty, 1997; author children's coloring books & stories; Outstanding COT Service, 1998. **Business Addr:** Consultant & Speaker & Trainer, Behavior Specialist Senior, 110 Buckskin Dr, Warner Robins, GA 31088, **Business Phone:** (478)929-8585.*

CANE, RUDOLPH C
Engineer, government official, executive. **Personal:** Born May 23, 1934, Somerset County, MD; married; children: Rudolph C Jr & Renee A. **Educ:** Md State Col, attended 1957; Coppin State Col, attended 1968. **Career:** Cane's Rentals, vpres, 1955-; State Hwy Admin, Bur Mat & Res, eval engr, 1957-68; Eastern Regional Lab, dir admin, 1968-84; Shore Up Inc, bd dirs, 1978-83, adminr community & housing develop, 1984-; Housing & Community Develop, adminr; Md House Delegates, Dist 37A, delegate, currently. **Orgs:** Md Asn Engineers, 1963-84; vpres, Nat Asn Advan Colored People, 1969, Md State Conf Branches, co-ordr spec projects, 1968; vpres, Westside Schs, 1970-71; Coop Area Manpower Planning Syst, 1975-77; chair, New Directions Polit & Social Change, 1977; pres, Mardela Middle & High Schs, 1977-78; Wicomico County Zoning Bd Appeals, 1980-90; chairperson, Md legis Black Caucus, 2005-06. **Honors/Awds:** Award for Outstanding Work in Wicomico County, Nat Asn Advan Colored People, 1974; Outstanding Citizen Award for Community Service, Kappa Alpha Psi, Salisbury State Univ, 1977; Outstanding Rural Legislator Award, Rural Md Coun, 2004; Legislative Leadership Award, Community Action Partnership, 2005. **Military Serv:** AUS, radar sgt, 1955-55. **Business Addr:** Delegate District 37A, Lowe House Off Bldg Rm 364, 6 Bladen St, Annapolis, MD 21401.

CANEDY, DANA
Writer, journalist. **Career:** Times, reporter; NY Times, reporter, currently. **Honors/Awds:** Pulitzer Prize. **Business Addr:** Reporter, New York Times, 229 W 43rd St, New York, NY 10036, **Business Phone:** (212)556-1234.*

CANNADY, ALONZO JAMES. See MUWAKKIL, SALIM.

CANNIDA, JAMES THOMAS, II
Football player. **Personal:** Born Jan 3, 1975, Savannah, GA; married Ieesha; children: Jameson. **Educ:** Univ Nev, Reno, broadcast jour. **Career:** Football player(retired); Tampa Bay Buccaneers, defensive tackle, 1998-01; Indianapolis Colts, 2002; Wash Redskins, 2003; Dallas Desperado, 2004. *

CANNON, DR. BARBARA E M
School administrator. **Personal:** Born Jan 17, 1936, Big Sandy, TX; daughter of Jimmie Jones and Archie; married Rev Dr Booker T Anderson Jr (deceased). **Educ:** San Francisco State Univ, BA, 1957, MA, 1965; Sorbonne Univ Paris, Cert Pedagogiques, 1967; Alliance Francaise, Paris, Cert Pedagogiques, 1967; Univ Calif, Berkeley, Attended 1973; Stanford Univ, MA, 1975, EdD, 1977. **Career:** Berkeley Pub Schs, teacher, staff develop, assoc admin, 1958-74; Univ Calif, govt fel, 1968; Univ Ghana, govt fel, 1968; Stanford Univ, teaching fel, res assoc, 1974-75; Natl Teacher Corp, US Off Educ, Wash, DC, educ policy fel, 1975-76; Stanford Univ, res asst, 1976-77, res assoc, 1977-78; Col Alameda, asst dean, 1978-85; Merritt Col, asst dean, 1985-95, Math & sci Div, dean, 1995-96, dean emer, 1996-; Educ TV consult; African Am Mus Coalition, founding vpres; "Oakland Is" Show, co-host; Family/Parent Educ TV, host & producer. **Orgs:** Educ policy fel, Inst Educ Leadership, Wash, DC, 1975-76; Urban Educ Inst,1982-83; exec bd mem, East Bay Consortium Educ Inst, 1982-84; Soroptimist Int Alameda, 1984-86; Bus & Prof Women Alameda, 1984-; Black Women OrgnPolit Action, 1968; Jones United Methodist Church; Assn Calif Community Col Admin; Pi Lambda Theta; Phi Delta Kappa; adv brd, Today's Women Inc; adv brd chairperson, Today's Women Inc, 1994; steering comm, Mayor's Literacy;Mayor's Church City Coalition; Oakland Sharing The Vision: Educ & Lifelong Learning Task Force; New Oakland Comm Race Rels Round table; Black Women's Roundtable; Black Women Organized Polit Action; Black Women Stirring the Waters; adv chairperson, Jr Achievement the Bay Ares Inc, 1998-99; codir,2000-02, Natl dir, 2002-04, consortium doctors Ltd; brd dir & vpres, African-Am museum coalition, 2001-03; natl dir, Consortium Doctors Ltd,2002-04; trustee, Found, San Francisco Community Col Dist; brd dirs, C'sAdvocate Newspaper; chairperson adv coun, Jones Mem United Methodist Church Preparatory Sch; brd dirs, Successful Black/Minority Sch Proj; chair, dir, 2003-04, Alameda County Juvenile Justice/Delinquency Prevention Comn. **Honors/Awds:** Outstanding Senior of the Year, Mu Phi Epsilon, San Francisco State Univ, 1957; Inductee, Consortium Doctors Ltd, 1993; Honoree: Outstanding Bay Area Educator, Iota Phi Lambda, 1994; Outstanding Educator Award, Black Bus Prof Women, 1996; Inductee, Int Educator Hall of Fame, 2000. **Home Addr:** 2101 Shoreline Dr Suite 458, Alameda, CA 94501.

CANNON, CALVIN CURTIS
Manager. **Personal:** Born Mar 2, 1952, Lenoir, NC; married Anna Laura Copney; children: Calvin IV. **Educ:** Univ Mich Grad Sch Bus, BBA, 1974; Wayne State Univ Sch Engineering; Howard Univ Sch Divinity. **Career:** Proctor & Gamble Co, client rep, 1974-76; Vitro Labs, sect leader, 1977-79; Planning Res Corp, unit mgr, 1979-81; General Elec Info Serv Co, proj coordr, 1981-83; Comp-U-Staff, staff mgr, 1983-84; Exec Off Pres, Wash, DC, mgr info serv, 1984-. **Orgs:** African Methodist Episcopal Zion Church. **Home Addr:** 10606 Wheatley St, Kensington, MD 20895. *

CANNON, CHAPMAN ROOSEVELT, JR.
Executive. **Personal:** Born Nov 14, 1934, St Louis, MO; son of Chapman Roosevelt Sr and Geneva Gaines; married Donnie Easter Cannon, Oct 10, 1954; children: Donald Chatman, Emily Easter. **Educ:** Mich State Univ, BS, bus admin, 1964. **Career:** Am Beauty Mfg Inc, chief exec officer. **Orgs:** Nat Asn Advan Colored People, 1965-; Metrop Baptist Church; United Church Sci Living Inst; Metrop Tulsa Chamber Com, 1975-; Greenwood Chamber Com, 1980-; bd dirs, Am Health & Beauty Aids Inst, 1981-. **Honors/Awds:** Outstanding Achievement Award, Black Hair Olympics, 1982, Manufacturer of the Year Award, 1983; Top Businessman of the Year, 1984; Outstanding Achievement Award, Tulsa Urban League, 1984; Small Businessman of the Year, Tulsa Metro Chamber Com, 1985; Black Enterprise 100 listing of America's Most Successful Black Owned Companies; 1985, 1986, 1987. **Special Achievements:** Co-author, autobiography, How We Made Millions & Never Left the Ghetto, 1983; co-publisher, Beauty Classic Magazine, 1984-87; co-founder, NY Beauty Classic Rolls Royce Competition; composer/singer, Rejuvenation, record, 1984; artist, painting, New York skyline, 1961. **Military Serv:** USAF, capt, 1952-68; served in USA, SE Asia, Japan, Vietnam, Republic of China, Dominican Republic. *

CANNON, DR. CHARLES EARL
Educator. **Personal:** Born Jan 30, 1946, Sylacauga, AL; son of Eugene and Carrie. **Educ:** Ala A&M Univ, BS, 1968; Univ Wis-Milwaukee, PhD, 1975. **Career:** Amoco Corp, res scientist, 1974-85; W Aurora Sch Dist, educr 1985-86;Elmhurst Col, adj fac, 1984-87; Ill Math & Sci Acad, prof chem, 1986-92; Columbia Col, chair, sci & math dept, distinguished prof, currently. **Orgs:** Am Chem Soc Chicago, 1974-; Nat Asn Negro Musicians, dir, 1975-; Am Inst Chemists, fel, 1979-92; Exec Interested Polit, 1982-88; Nat Alumni Asn Ala A & M Univ, pres, 1984-86, 2000-04; Apostolic Church God, Chicago; Great Lakes Regional ACS Meeting Planning Comm, 1986-87, at-large, 1987-88; Nat Asn Advan Black Chemists & Chem Eng; Ill Asn Chem Teachers, pres, 1998-99. **Honors/Awds:** Merit Award Public Service Cultural Citizen Foundation; J Org Chem 41,1191 1976; Grignard Reagents Rearrangements ACS Natl Mtg Fall 1985; paper Semi-Automated Sep of Oils Resins Asphalcenes; Greenhouse Effect and Other Environmental Issues, ISTA, Fall 1990; Alumnus of the Year, Ala A&M Univ, 1992; Distinguished Service Award, Nat Asn Negro Musicians Inc, 1992; Lilly Multicultural Award, Columbia Col, 1994; Host Col Grant, Spectroscopy Soc Pittsburgh, 1996; Service Award, Ala A&M Univ Alumni Asn Presidential Citation & Achievement Award, Reunion Class, 1968, 1998; Chicago Asn Tech Societies Award of Merit, 1998; Alumni Hall of Fame,2000; Mamie Labon Foster Award, 2000. **Home Addr:** 8120-B Prairie Pk Pl, Chicago, IL 60619-4800, **Home Phone:** (773)651-4588. **Business Addr:** Distinguished Professor, Columbia College, Department of Science & Mathematics, 600 S Michigan Ave, Chicago, IL 60605, **Business Phone:** (312)344-7396.

CANNON, DAVITA LOUISE BURGESS
Editor. **Personal:** Born Mar 17, 1949, Jersey City, NJ; daughter of James (deceased) and Bernice. **Educ:** St Peters Col, BS, mkt mgt, 1967-73; New York Univ Grad Sch Bus, advan mgt prog, 1979-83; Am Computa, 1988. **Career:** JM Fields, dicta sec, 1978-79; Off Force Inc, exec secy & admin asst, 1979-83; NJ Afro Am, columnist, 1980; Cannon Clues, publ, chmn, 1981-, owner, 1988-. **Orgs:** Bd dir, Bayonne Youth Ctr, 1974-92; pres chair, New York Metro Area Chap Am Asn Blacks Energy, 1983-84; chmn, US Rep Parren J Mitchell Brain Trust, 1984; Nat Bd Adv, Am Biol Inst, 1985; NJ Coalition 100 Black Women, prin officer, 1986-91; Concerned Comn Women JC Inc, pres chair, 1986-92; Governor's Planning Comn, 1986-87; comnr, NJ Develop Authority Small Minority & Women's Bus, 1987-92; Gov Adv Coun Minority Bus Develop, reappointed coun mem, 1987-92; chair, charter mem, Republican Presidential Task Force, 1989-; Chandeliers United Nations, 1992-; comnr, Presidential Comn Am Agenda; 100 African Peoples Nation, 1998; chair bd, Ford Found, 2000-; vchmn, Coun HOS. **Honors/Awds:** Distinguished Serv Award, Pavonia Girl Scout Coun, 1981; Mary McLeod Bethune Award, Com-Bin-Nations, Jersey City, 1984; VIP Award, Concerned Comn Women Jersey City Inc, 1984; Small Business Award, Roselle Br Nat Asn Advan Colored People, 1984; Woman of Achievement, 1986; Black Leadership Reception 100 Black Men NJ, 1988; Outstanding Am Award, Outstanding Young Am. **Home Addr:** 528 Ave A-5, Bayonne, NJ 07002. **Business Addr:** Principal Owner, Cannon Clues, 528 Ave A5, Bayonne, NJ 07002-1627.

CANNON, DR. DONNIE E.
Business owner. **Personal:** Born in Magnolia, AR; married Chapman R Jr; children: Donald Chatman. **Educ:** MME C J Walker Beauty Col, Grad; Eugene Hairstyling Acad, Paris, France-;Myriam Carriages Inst De Beaute, Paris, France; The Ophelia De

Voores Modeling & Charm Sch, Grad; Bethune-Cookman Col, doctorate. **Career:** Am Beauty Prod Co Inc, co-owner & treas 1966-; Johnson Prods, natl rep; LaRoberts & Gray's Beauty Sch, NY. **Orgs:** Alpha-Chi Pi Omega organized First chap, Hempstead; Tulsa Urban League Guild; Greenwood C C; Tulsa Community Develop Ctr; Okla Beauty Culturist League; Tulsa Urban League Inc; hon mem, YWCA; Nat Beauty Culturist League; bd trustees, Bethune-Cookman Col; Tulsa C C; NAACP. **Honors/Awds:** Bus & Indust Award, 1973; Service Awd, Greenwood C C, 1974; Basilleus Tulsa Chap Alpha Chi Pi Omega; Top 100 Black Bus & Professional Women in America, 1985; Hon Deg Dr Law, 1984; Outstanding Women Indust, YWCA, 1977;Outstanding Achievement Award, Nat Beauty Culturists League, 1982; Outstanding Achievement Award, Black Hair Olympics, 1982; Mfr of the Year Award, Black Hair Olympics, 1983; Hon Alumnus Award, Langston Univ. **Special Achievements:** Co-author, autobiography, How We MAde Millions and Never Left the Ghetto,1983; co-publisher, Beauty Classic Magazine, 1984-87; co-founder New York Beauty Classic Rolls Royce Competition. **Business Addr:** Co-Owner, American Beauty Manufacturing Inc, 1623 E Apache St, Tulsa, OK 74106, **Business Phone:** (918)425-4241.

CANNON, EDITH H
Educator. **Personal:** Born Aug 8, 1940, Tougaloo, MS; married Dan Cannon Jr; children: Audra Charmaine & Portia Camille. **Educ:** Tougaloo Col, BS, 1961; Boston State Col, grad studies, 1976; Bridgewater State Col, grad studies, 1983; Eastern nazarene Col, MEd, 1984. **Career:** Greenville MS Pub Schs, elem teacher, 1961-65; Boston Head Start, educ dir, 1969-73; Randolph Pub Schs, elem teach, 1973-81; North Jr High Sch, diagnostic prescriptive teacher reading, 1981-. **Orgs:** Past vice chmn, Randolph Fair Practices, 1980-81; conf presenter, Mass Teachers Asn, 1982-84; mem, Gov's Task Force Educ Reform, 1983-84; bd mem, S Shore Coun C, 1983-85; Randolph Fair Practices, 1973-; chair, minority affairs comn, Mass Teachers Asn, 1982-; bd dir, Norfolk County Teachers Asn, 1983-; commun, Mass Teachers Asn, 1984-. **Honors/Awds:** Outstanding Service, Randolph Teachers Asn, 1980-82; Citation for Service, Gov Michael Dukakis, 1983; Delta Kappa Gamma Soc, Int Honor Soc Women Educrs, 1985. **Home Addr:** 38 Sunset Dr, Randolph, MA 02368. **Business Addr:** Principal, North Jr High School, High St, Randolph, MA 02368.

CANNON, DR. JOSEPH NEVEL
Chemical engineer, educator. **Personal:** Born May 2, 1942, Weldon, AR; son of Joseph Henry and Elmer Lewis; married Carmen Bianchi, 1978; children: Devi, Arville, Bianca, Changa & Erin. **Educ:** Univ Wis, Madison, WI, BS, 1964; Univ Colo, Boulder, CO, MS, 1966, PhD, chem eng, 1971. **Career:** Dow Chem Co, Midland, MI, process engr, 1964; Procter & Gamble, Cincinnati, OH, res chem engr, 1965-68; Howard Univ, Wash, DC, Sch Engineering & Comput Sci, Dept Cham Engineering, prof, 1971-, acad consult, HUSEM prog, currently; Nat Insts Health, Bethesda, MD, res chem engr, 1972-78. **Orgs:** Am Inst Chem Engrs, 1970-; Sigma Xi Scientific Res Soc, 1980-; Am Asn Advancement Sci, 1978-; Tau Beta Pi Nat Hon Soc, 1980-; Nat Org Black Chemists & Chem Engrs; Kappa Alpha Psi. **Honors/Awds:** Outstanding Fac, Chem Engr Stud Soc, 1977, 1979, 1981, 1986; Outstanding Prof, Nat Org Black Chemists & Chem Engrs, 1983; Distinguished Engr Alumnus, Univ Colo, Sch Engineering, 1989; Centennial Medal, Univ Colo, Col Engineering & Appl Sci, 1994. **Business Addr:** Professor, Academic Consultant, HUSEM program, Howard University, School of Engineering & Computer Science, 2300 6th St NW Rm 1016, Washington, DC 20059, **Business Phone:** (202)806-6669.*

CANNON, REV. DR. KATIE GENEVA
Theologian, educator. **Personal:** Born Jan 3, 1950, Concord, NC; daughter of Esau Lytle and Corine Lytle. **Educ:** Barber-Scotia Col, BS, Elem Educ, magna cum laude, 1971; Johnson C Smith Sem, Atlanta, MDiv, 1974; Union Theol Sem, New York, NY, MPhil, 1983, PhD, christian ethics, 1983. **Career:** Rockfeller Protestant Fel Fund Theol Educ, 1972-76; Episcopal Divinity Sch, asst prof; New York Theol Sem, admin fac, 1977-80; Ascension Presby Church, pastor, 1975-77; Roothbert Fel, 1981-83; Yale Divinity Sch, vis lectr, 1987; Harvard Divinity Sch, vis scholar & woman res assoc, 1983-84; Wellesley Col, vis prof, 1991; Temple Univ, Dept Relig, from assoc prof ethics to prof ethics & theol, 1993-2001; Union Theol Sem & Presby Sch Christian Educ, Annie Scales Rogers prof christian ethics, 2001-. **Orgs:** Ecumenical dialogue, Third World theologians, 1976-80; Middle E travel guide, NY Theol Seminary, 1978-80; Am Acad Relig, 1983-; Asn Black Women Higher Educ, 1984-; bd dir, Women's Theol Ctr, 1984-; mem bd dir, Soc Christian Ethics, 1986-90; from mem to pres, Soc Study Black Relig, 1986-; World Alliance Reformed Churches Presby & Congregational, 1986-91. **Honors/Awds:** Isaac R Clark Preaching Award, InterdenomiNat Theol Ctr, 1973; Episcopal Church's Conant Grant, 1987-88; Asn of Theological School Young Scholar Award, 1987-88. **Special Achievements:** The first African-American woman ordained in the United Presbyterian Church USA; Author, Black Womanist Ethics, Scholars Press, 1988; co-ed, God's Fierce Whimsy, 1985; Inheriting Our Mothers' Garden, Westminster Press, 1988; Interpretation for Liberation,1989; Katie's Canon: Womanism and the Soul of the Black Community, 1995.

CANNON, NICHOLAS SCOTT. See CANNON, NICK.

CANNON, NICK (NICHOLAS SCOTT CANNON)
Actor, writer, rap musician. **Personal:** Born Oct 8, 1980, San Diego, CA; son of James and Beth Hackett. **Career:** TV series: "Kenan & Kel", 1996; "Cousin Skeeter", 1998; "All That", 1998-00; "The Nick Cannon Show", producer, 2002; Films: Whatever It Takes, 2000; Men In Black II, 2002; Drumline, 2002; Love Don't Cost a Thing, 2003; Garfield, 2004; Shall We Dance, 2004; Underclassman, 2005; Roll Bounce, 2005; Even Money, 2006; The Adventures of Brer Rabbit, 2006; Weapons, 2006; Monster House, 2006; Bobby, 2006; Goal II: Living the Dream, 2007; American Son, 2008; Day of the Dead, 2008; Ball Don't Lie, 2008; The Killing Room, 2009; Mr. Renaissance, owner, currently. **Honors/Awds:** Nickelodeon Kids Choice Awards, Favorite Television Actor, 2002; Hollywood Film Festival, Ensemble of the Year, 2006; Cannes Film Festival, Male Revelation, 2007. **Business Addr:** Actor, c/o Nickelodeon, 231 W Olive St, Burbank, CA 91502.*

CANNON, PAUL L
Chemist. **Personal:** Born Nov 21, 1934, Harrisburg, PA; son of Paul L and Mildred A Mercer. **Educ:** Lincoln Univ, BA, 1956. **Career:** Harrisburg Hosp, clin chem, 1956-58; PA Dept Highways, chemist, 1958; Dept Army, res chem, 1958, AUS Edgewood Res Dev Eng Command, res chemist, currently. **Orgs:** Omega Psi Phi Frat; Sigma Xi. **Honors/Awds:** Electrochemistry Patents US. **Special Achievements:** Published articles on electrochemistry and analytical chemistry. **Military Serv:** AUS, PFC, 1958-60. **Home Addr:** 21 N 15th St, Harrisburg, PA 17103, **Home Phone:** (717)238-7639. **Business Addr:** Research Chemist, US Army, Edgewood Chemical and Biological Center, AMSRD-EBC-RT-AE, Aberdeen Proving Ground, MD 21010-5424, **Business Phone:** (410)436-7639.

CANNON, REUBEN
Executive, television producer. **Personal:** Born Feb 11, 1946, Chicago, IL; married Linda Elsenhout; children: Tonya, Reuben Jr, Christopher & Sydney. **Educ:** SE City Col. **Career:** Univ Studios, mail room clerk, sec casting dept, casting dir, 1970-77; Warner Bros, head TV casting, 1977-78; cast: The Rockford Files; Roots II; The Next Generation; A Soldier's Story; The Color Purple; The A-Team; Hunter; Riptide; Moonlighting; Amen; Amerika; Ironside; Under One Roof, Touched By An Angel; Eddie What's Love Got to Do With It; American Heart; Who Framed Roger Rabbitt; The Women of Brewster Place, producer; Reuben Cannon & Assoc, owner & pres, 1979-; Get On The Bus, producer, 1996; TV series: "Hunter: The Princess & the Marine", 2001; "Hunter: Return to Justice", 2002; "Johnson Family Vacation", 2004; "30 Days Until I'm Famous", 2004; "Night of Terror", 2005; "Bernie Mac Show", 2005-06; "Fumes of Detente", 2006; "Bernie's Angels", 2006; "Tom, Sarah & Usher", 2007; "Thank You for Not Snitching", 2007; "Stinkmeaner Strikes Back?", 2007; "The Story of Thugnificent", 2007; "Attack of the Killer Kung-Fu Wolf Bitch", 2007; "The Boondocks", 2007; "Conditional Love", 2008. **Orgs:** Bd dir, Los Angeles Urban League. **Honors/Awds:** Emmy Roots II TV Academy, 1979; Behind the Lens Award, DCX, 2002. **Special Achievements:** Has been credited with launching the careers of many of today's major film and television stars, including Oprah Winfrey, Danny Glover, Bruce Willis, Michael J. Fox and Whoopi Goldberg. **Business Addr:** President, Reuben Cannon & Associates, 5225 Wilshire Blvd Suite 526, Los Angeles, CA 90036, **Business Phone:** (323)939-3190.

CANNON, TYRONE HEATH
Dean (education), library administrator. **Personal:** Born Jan 16, 1949, Hartford, CT; son of Laura R Cohens and Jesse Heath. **Educ:** Univ Conn, BS, 1973, MSW, 1975; Univ Pittsburgh, MLS, 1981. **Career:** Hartford Pub Schs, sch soc worker, 1975-77; Child & Family Serv Inc, clin soc worker, 1977-80; Univ Tex, Arlington, soc sci librn, 1981-83; Columbia Univ, soc work librn, 1984-88; Okla St Univ, Soc Sci Div, head, 1988-89; Boston Col, head res, 1989-91, sr assoc univ librn, 1991-95; Univ San Francisco, dean univ libr, 1995-, Currently. **Orgs:** Title IIB Fel Univ Pittsburgh, 1980; counr, ACRL Div, Am Libr Asn; Asn Col & Res Libr; Black Caucus Am Libr Asn; Am Asn Higher Educ. **Business Addr:** Dean, University San Francisco, University Libraries, 2130 Fulton St, San Francisco, CA 94117, **Business Phone:** (415)422-5555.

CANSON, FANNIE JOANNA
Educator, marriage counselor. **Personal:** Born Apr 26, 1926, Bainbridge, GA; married Robert L. **Educ:** Spelman Col Tuskegee Inst, BS, 1945; Univ Ore, MS, 1967, PhD, 1967. **Career:** Calif St Univ, Sacramento, assoc prof; former high sch teacher; univ admin dir, teacher corps, Corrections Proj; Nat Coun Chap, teacher; licensed marriage & family counr. **Business Addr:** Educator, California State University, 6000 J St, Sacremento, CA 95819.

CANTARELLA, MARCIA Y
Educator. **Personal:** Born Oct 31, 1946, Minneapolis, MN; daughter of Whitney M Young Jr and Margaret Buckner Young; married Francesco Cantarella, May 24, 1980; children: Mark Boles, Michele Cantarella & Maratea Cantarella. **Educ:** Bryn Mawr Col, Pa, BA, 1968; Univ Iowa Law Sch, attended 1968; Simmons Col, Boston, Mass, middle mgt prog; NY Univ, Mass, Am studies, 1992, PhD, 1996. **Career:** Medicare Health Care Quality Improv, dir; Sen Robert F Kennedy's Wash Off, summer intern, 1967; Rabat Am Sch, Rabat Morocco, social studies teacher grades 6-8, 1970-71; Zebra Assoc, NY, advert, 1971-72; Avon Prod Inc, NY, dir sales develop, dir, 1972-85; Mom's Amazing, NY, pres, 1985-88; Nat Coalition Women's Enterprise, NY, exec dir; NY Univ Stern Sch Bus, mgt consult, 1988-90; Acad Enhancement, NY Univ Col Arts & Sci, dir, 1991-99; NY Univ Gallatin Sch Individualized Study, fac, 1995-2000; Princeton Univ, asst dean/lectr; Metrop Col NY, vpres stud affairs; Hunter Col, Sch Arts & Sci, actg assoc dean, assoc dean stud opportunities, currently. **Orgs:** Dir, Children's Mus Manhattan, 1986-91; Vaseline Baby Care Coun, 1987-88; bd dir, New York Police Found, 1988-91; Equity Inst, 1990-92; planning comt, Support Ctr NY, 1992-; Fedn Protestant Welfare Agencies; Blue Cross-Blue Shield Greater New York; trustee, Trickle-Up Prog. **Honors/Awds:** Woman of the Year, Nat Coun Negro Women, 1976. **Special Achievements:** Published articles in Working Mother, McCalls, Essence, Working Parent, Boardroom Reports, Lears. **Business Addr:** Associate Dean for Student Opportunities, Hunter College, School of Arts and Sciences, Rm 803 E 695 Pk Ave, New York, NY 10021.

CANTRELL, BLU (TIFFANY COBB)
Singer. **Personal:** Born Oct 1, 1976, Providence, RI. **Career:** Albums: So Blu, 2001; Bittersweet, 2002; Songs: "Hit 'em Up Style(Oops!)", 2001; "Round Up", 2002; "Breathe", 2003; "Make Me Wanna Scream", 2004; Film: Drumline, 2002; TV : "Soul Food", 2001; "Soul Train", 2002-03; "Celebrity Circus", 2008. **Special Achievements:** Included in top ten of Billboard 200 and Billboard Top R&B/Hip-Hop Albums Charts for So Blu, 2001; "Hit 'Em Up Style (Oops!)" #1 song on Billboard's Top 40 Mainstream and Top 40 Tracks Charts, 2001. **Business Addr:** Recording Artist, c/o Arista Records, 6 W 57th St, New York, NY 10019, **Business Phone:** (212)489-7400.*

CANTRELL, FORREST DANIEL
Executive. **Personal:** Born Dec 30, 1938, Atlanta, GA; married Cheryl Francis; children: John Daniel. **Educ:** San Francisco State Univ, BA, 1968; Univ CA, MBA, 1970; Harvard Bus Sch, AMP, 1977. **Career:** Mile Sq Health Ctr Inc, pres, proj dir, adminr; San Francisco Police Dept, police & Officer; Vallejo Police Dept, patrolman; Dept Corrections, corr officer. **Orgs:** Pres, Nat Asn Neighborhood Health Ctr Inc; pres bd dir, Miles Sq Serv Corp; commr, Chicago Health Planning & Resources Develop Comn; bd dir, Chica United Black Appeal Fund. **Military Serv:** USN, airman, 1955-58.

CANTY, CHRIS
Football player. **Personal:** Born Mar 30, 1976, Long Beach, CA. **Educ:** Kans State Univ. **Career:** New Eng Patriots, defensive back, 1997-98; Seattle Seahawks, 1999-2000; New Orleans Saints, 2000; Las Vegas Gladiators, 2005; Rio Grande Valley Dorados, defensive back, 2006-. **Special Achievements:** First round pick, No 29, NFL Draft, 1997. **Business Addr:** Defensive Back, Grande Valley Dorados, 2600 N 10th St, Hidalgo, TX 78557, **Business Phone:** (956)843-7825.

CANTY, GEORGE
Executive. **Personal:** Born Dec 7, 1931, Manning, SC; married Mabel Lucille Scott; children: Andria G & Alison D. **Educ:** Univ Pittsburgh, BS, Chem, 1954; Am Univ, MS, Physics & Chem, 1966. **Career:** NIH Bethesda MD, chemist, 1958-63; Nat Bur Stand, Wash DC, chemist, 1961-63; Gillete & Res Inst, Wash DC, res & develp, 1965-67; Celanese Res Co, Summit NJ, sr res chemist, 1967-73; 3m Ctr, St Paul, MN, supr prod devel, 1973. **Orgs:** Mem & past basileus, NJ Chap Omega Psi Phi Fraterity, 1953-; Am Chem Soc, 1960-; MN Chem Soc, 1973-; guest lectr, Black Exec Exchange Prog, Nat Urban League, 1974. **Honors/Awds:** Catalyst Club Award, 3m Co Film & Allied Prod Div, 1977; patented Photosensitive Composite Sheet Material, 1979. Publisher of articles and books. **Military Serv:** USN, seaman recruit, 1952.

CANTY, OTIS ANDREW
Administrator. **Personal:** Born May 12, 1934, Troy, AL; son of Candus McGhee and Roscoe; married Flora (divorced 1990); children: Virginia, Elezibeth, Barbara, Sandra, Marian, Sheila; married Gloria J Fuller Canty, Aug 17, 1990. **Career:** Administrator (retired); The Detroit Lions Inc, Pontiac, MI, dir player rels. **Honors/Awds:** First African American to serve on a National Football League team video crew. *

CANTY, RALPH WALDO
Clergy, executive. **Personal:** Born Oct 9, 1945, Sumter, SC; married Jacqueline Wright; children: Ralph Jr, Serena. **Educ:** Morris Col, AB, 1967, BD, 1970, DD, 1978. **Career:** Morris Col, pub rel dir, 1970-75; BF Goodrich, asst personnel dir, 1975-78; Progressive Nat Baptist Convention, pres; Savannah Grove Baptist Church, pastor, currently. **Orgs:** Pres & chmn, bd Job's Mortuary,

1970-; pres, Brenca, 1976-; bd mem, Nat Coun Churches, 1980; bd mem, Baptist World Alliance, 1980; bd mem, Morris Col, 1982. **Honors/Awds:** Citizen of the Year, Gamma Iota Chapter, 1979; Citizen of the Year, Key Pub, 1980; Omega Man of the Year, Gamma Iota Chapter, 1985. **Business Addr:** Pastor, Savannah Grove Baptist Church, 2620 Alligator Rd, Rte 3 PO Box 475, Effingham, SC 29541, **Business Phone:** (843)662-7851.*

CAPEL, FELTON JEFF
Basketball coach. **Personal:** Born Jan 6, 1953; son of Felton Jeffrey and Jean; married Jerry; children: Jeff III & Jason. **Educ:** Univ Hampton Inst, Hampton. **Career:** Wake Forest Univ, asst coach; Fayetteville State Univ, coach, 1989-93; Old Dominion, NC A&T State Univ, head coach, 1993. *

CAPEL, FELTON JEFFREY
Executive. **Personal:** Born Feb 26, 1927, Ellerbe, NC; son of Acie and Elnora Leak; married Jean Walden, Jul 12, 1951; children: Jeff, Mitch & Ken. **Educ:** Hampton Univ, BS, 1951. **Career:** Century Metal Craft Corp, salesman, 1958-61, sales mgr, 1958-61, reg sales mgr, 1965-77; Century Asn NC, pres, chief exec officer, 1977-; First Savings Bank, Moore County, dir, 1990-98; First Bank, Troy NC, dir, 1999-; Century Asn NC, pres & chmn, currently. **Orgs:** City Counman, Southern Pines, 1959-68; dir, Carolina P & L Co, 1972-, Southern Nat Bank, 1974-85, First Fed Savings & Loan, 1978-85, NC Asn Minority Bus; Durham Corp, 1988-; Durham Life Ins, 1988-; NC Citizens Bus & Ind, Raleigh, NC, 1988-; Wachovia Corp, Winston-Salem, NC, 1989; Wachovia Bank & Trust Co, NA Winston-Salem, NC, 1989; city treas & chmn, Moore County, Bd Elections, 1980-86; dist gov, Rotary Int; chmn, Moore Co United Way; chmn, Moore County Chap Am Red Cross; NC Comn for Educ, 1989; chmn, bd trustees, Fayetteville State Univ; Dist 7690 Rotary Int, gov; bd dir, NC Found; bd dir, GTP; bd dir, Boys & Girls Club Sandhills; bd dir, First Tee Sandhills. **Honors/Awds:** Int Mgr Sales Award Century Metalcrft, 1962; Bd Mem of Year, NC Dept Conservation & Devel, 1971; chmn of the year, Sandhills Area Chamber Com, 1977; Delta Mu Delta Nat Hon Bus, FSU; Fayetteville State Univ, Basketball Arena Named Felton J Capel Arena; Rotary Int, Distinguished Service Award, 1981-82; Meritoriuos Service Award, 1984-87; Inducted into the NC Bus Hall of Fame, 1998; University Award, Bd Govs, Univ NC, 2000. **Military Serv:** AUS, staff sgt, two yrs. **Business Addr:** Chairman & Cheif Executive Officer, President, Century Associates of North Carolina, 800 Hwy 1 S, PO Box 37, Pinebluff, NC 28373-0037, **Business Phone:** (910)281-3194.

CAPEL, WALLACE
Physician. **Personal:** Born Nov 12, 1915, Andalusia, AL; son of Henry and Callie; married Carrie Ford; children: Carolyn Capel Harrison, Jacqueline D, Denise L, Wallace Capel Jr. **Educ:** Howard Univ, BS, 1940, MD, 1944; Baylor Univ, MHA, 1970. **Career:** Physician (retired). Va Med Ctr, chief staff. **Orgs:** Am & Nat Med Asn, 1970; Macon County Med Soc, 1973. **Honors/Awds:** Exec of the Year, Prof Secretaries Int, 1979. **Military Serv:** AUS, col; Legion of Merit w/Oak Leaf Cluster. **Home Addr:** Franklin Rd, PO Box 2608, Tuskegee, AL 36083, **Home Phone:** (334)727-5270. *

CAPERS, JAMES, JR.
Basketball executive. **Personal:** Born Nov 8, 1961, Chicago, IL; son of James Capers Sr. **Career:** Nat Basketball Asn, referee, currently. **Business Addr:** Referree, National Basketball Association, 645 5th Ave 10th Fl, New York, NY 10022-5986, **Business Phone:** (212)407-8000.*

CAPTAIN, MYRTLE L
Army officer. **Personal:** Born Nov 26, 1939, Temple, TX; daughter of Mack and Ruby; divorced; children: Charmin LT Truesdale, Brian Flakes & Garland Flakes. **Educ:** Temple Col, AA; Calif Coast Univ, attended; Prairie View A&M Univ, attended; wide variety of govt training. **Career:** Army officer (retired); FHTX, various positions, supply mgr, 1964-76, MER specialist, 1976-86, EEO officer, 1986-95. **Orgs:** Local chap, pres, life mem, Nat Asn Advan Colored People, 1973-86, state sec, 1982-97, region III sec; Int Training in Commun, 1973-; numerous city & sch dist comns, 1964. **Honors/Awds:** Army Civilian, Decoration of Exceptional Civilian Service, 1994; NAACP, Unsung Heroine, 1984; Jefferson Memorial Award, KCEN-TV; various 150 trophies, plaques, awards, 1972-99. **Special Achievements:** Authored The Warden and His Brother; From Their Mother's Point of View, 1999; Twisted Fate; keynote speaker and workshop leader for many important civic, social and spiritual functions. *

CARADINE, TRACY
Executive. **Career:** Jarvis Christian Col, dir libr serv, 2003. **Business Addr:** Director, Jarvis Christian College, Library Services, 1470 Hwy 80, PO Box 1470, Hawkins, TX 75765, **Business Phone:** (903)769-5820.

CARAWAY, YOLANDA H
Public relations executive, manager. **Personal:** Born Sep 1, 1950, Rochester, NY; daughter of Earl and Cecile Carr; divorced; children: Theron Tucker Jr. **Career:** State Rep Wendell Phillips, admin asst, 1976-80; Congresswoman Barbara Mikulski, legis aide, 1980-81; Dem Nat Comn, dir educ & training, 1981-85, spec asst chmn & staff dir, Fairness Comn, 1985, Chmn Paul G Kirk, Jr, dep chair, 1988-89; Mondale & Ferraro Gen Election Campaign, dep asst polit dir, 1984; Nat Rainbow Coalition, chief staff, 1985-86; Citizenship Educ Fund, exec dir, 1986-87; Jesse Jackson Pre, chief staff, 1987-88; Pres Inaugural Comn, off chmn, dir, 1992-93; 2000 Site Adv Comt, vice chmn, 1998; Democracy Live! 2000, exec producer, 2000; Caraway Group Inc, pres & chief exec officer, currently. **Orgs:** At-large mem, Democratic Nat Comt; bd dirs, Am Univ Campaign Mgt Inst; mem bd dirs, Am Democratic Action Educ Fund; Am Coun Young Polit Leaders; steering comt, Ronald H Brown Found; vice chair, Democratic Nat Conv, Site Adv Comn, 2000; bd dirs, Ellington Fund; bd dirs, Naval. **Business Addr:** President, Chief Executive Officer, The Caraway Group Inc, 1010 Wisconsin Ave NW Suite 550, Washington, DC 20007, **Business Phone:** (202)965-2810.

CARBY, HAZEL V.
Educator. **Personal:** Born Jan 15, 1948, Oakhampton, Devon, England; daughter of Carl Colin and Iris Muriel; married Michael Denning, May 29, 1982; children: Nicholas Carby-Denning. **Educ:** Portsmouth Polytechnic, BA, 1970; London Univ, Inst Educ, PGCE, 1972; Birmingham Univ, Ctr Contemporary Cult Studies, MA, 1979, PhD, 1984. **Career:** High school teacher, London, 1972-79; Yale Univ, Eng Dept, lectr, 1981-82, Am & African Am studies, prof eng, 1989-94, Am studies & African Am studies, prof, 1994-, African Am studies, chair, 1996-, Charles C & Dorothea S Dilley prof african am studies, currently, dir initiative race gender & globalization, currently; Wesleyan Univ, English Dept, instr, 1982-84, asst prof, 1985-88, assoc prof, 1988-89. **Orgs:** Ed Bd, Yale J Criticism; Ed Bd, Callaloo & Diaspora. **Special Achievements:** Author, Reconstructing Womanhood; The Emergence of the Afro-American Woman Novelist, Oxford Univ Press, 1989; Race Men: The Body and Soul of Race, Nation and Masculinity, 1998; Cultures in Babylon: Black Britain and African America, 1999; Child of Empire, currently. **Business Addr:** Charles C & Dorathea S Dilley Professor African American Studies, Chair, Yale University, Department of African American Studies, 493 College St, New Haven, CT 06511, **Business Phone:** (203)432-9059.

CARD, LARRY D
Judge. **Personal:** Born Oct 23, 1947, Liberal, KS; married Mini E; children: Larry II, Krista & Kenneth. **Educ:** Wichita State Univ, BA, polit sci, 1969; Kans Univ Law, JD, 1976. **Career:** Judge (retired); pvt & public law pract, 1976-93; asst US atty, 1989-91; State Alaska, Super Ct, 3rd Judicial Dist, judge, 1993-2005; Univ Alaska, adj prof. **Orgs:** Inns Ct; Am Bar Asn; Alaska Bar Asn; Anchorage Bar Asn; Am Trial Lawyers Asn; bd mem, Boys & Girls Club Alaska. **Special Achievements:** First African American judge in Alaska, 1993. **Military Serv:** USAF, 8 yrs; USAF Res, 12 yrs, maj; USAF Commendation Medal; National Defense Service Medal.

CAREY, ADDISON, JR.
Educator, president (organization). **Personal:** Born Mar 10, 1933, Crescent City, FL; son of Addison Carey Sr and Laura Dowdell; married Clara Lee Parker; children: Leon, Alphonso, Pamela, Katrenia, Addison III, Michael, Douglas. **Educ:** Fla A&M Univ, BS, 1958; The Ohio State Univ, MA, 1960; Tulane Univ, PhD, 1971. **Career:** Southern Univ, New Orleans, prof polit sci, 1960; dir vis scholars lect series, 1972-78, admin asst to chancellor, 1983-85. **Orgs:** Bd mem, YMCA, 1978-; pres, Retired Military Asn New Orleans, 1980-89; pres, Econ Devel Unit, 1984-94; Civil Serv Comn, City of New Orleans, LA, 1987-93; pres, LA Polit Sci Asn; Nat Conf Black Polit Scientists; Pi Sigma Alpha Hon Soc; African Am Heritage Asn. **Honors/Awds:** Ford Found fel; Southern Fel Found Fel; Outstanding Professor, Southern Univ New Orleans, 1965,74; Citations for work in voter registration drives YMCA & stud orgns. **Military Serv:** AUS, pvt first class, 3 yrs; Purple Heart, Korean Service Medal, Syngman Rhee Unit Citation, National Defense Medal, 1950-53; Army of Occupation Medal (Japan), 1950. **Home Addr:** 4844 Mendez St, New Orleans, LA 70126, **Home Phone:** (504)288-5400. **Business Addr:** New Orleans, LA 70126, **Business Phone:** (504)286-5368.*

CAREY, AUDREY L.
Government official, nurse. **Personal:** Born Nov 28, 1937, Newburgh, NY; widowed; children: Davina Henry, Dana & David C Jr. **Educ:** St Luke's Hosp Sch Nursing, Reg Prof Nurse, 1961; NY State Dept Educ, cert sch nurse teacher, 1971; NY Univ Grad Sch Educ, advan deg admin & super, 1976; Up State Med Col SUNY, pediat nurse practitioner cert, 1980; State Univ Col, One onta, BS, Educ Nursing. **Career:** St Luke's Hosp, asst head nurse, 1963-69; Head start & N Jr HS, sch nurse teacher, 1966-69; Newburgh Sch Dist, drug educ coord, 1969-74; Newburgh Free Acad, sch nurse teacher, 1975-80; Newburgh Free Acad HS, pediat nurse practitioner, 1980-; City Newburgh, Newburgh, councilwoman & mayor, 1991-96; Newburgh Enlarged City Sch Dist, health serv coordr, dir Nursing & Health, 2009. **Orgs:** Bd dirs, Orange Co Dept Ment Health, 1971-73; Inst Black Studies Mt St Mary's Col, 1973-74; assoc coord, Non-Credit Progs St Mary's Col, 1973-74; panelist, NYS Bd Regents Conf, 1973-74; bd trustees Orange Co Comn Col, 1973-82; bd dirs, YWCA, 1975-76; Newburgh City Counwoman, 1977-; panelist, Robert Wood Johnson Found Sch Health Conf, 1980-81; chmn, Newburgh Comn Action Head Start Policy Adv Coun, 1983-84; bd dirs, Newburgh Performing Arts Acad. **Honors/Awds:** Prof Achievement Award, Omega Psi Phi Frat Upsilon Tau Chap, 1961; Distinguished Serv Award, Jaycees, 1973; Outstanding Comm Serv Award, Nimrod Lodge 82 AF & AM, 1977; Continuous Serv Award, Black Commonwealth of Newburgh, 1979; Distinguished Serv Award, NAACP, 1981; Outstanding Comn Serv HVOIC Mary C Christian Award, 1982; Achievement Award Newburgh Comn Action Head Start, 1984; Comn Achievement Award, Black History Month,1985; Recognition Award, Newburgh Optimist Club, 1985. **Special Achievements:** First African-Am woman ever elected mayor in the State of NY, Publication "Adolescence, Feeling Good, Looking Fine, Acting Fit" Natl Sch Health Digest, 1981. **Business Addr:** Director, Newburgh Enlarged City School District, 124 Grand St, Newburgh, NY 12550.*

CAREY, CARNICE
Government official. **Personal:** Born Dec 17, 1945, Chicago, IL; daughter of Joe Stephen and Ora Gardner Stephen; married Lloyd L Carey, Oct 29, 1966; children: Patrice Carey-Houston, Leslie Carey. **Educ:** Loop Jr Col, Chicago, Ill; Northeastern Ill Univ, Chicago, Ill. **Career:** City Chicago, Ill, contract compliance coord, 1972-75; Regional Transportation Authority, Chicago, Ill, eeo officer, 1975-84; City Chicago, Ill, contract compliance coord, 1985-94, dir contact monitoring & compliance, 1994-02, City Chicago, Dept Procurement Serv, dep procurement officer, 2002-. **Orgs:** Administrative bd, Redeemer Methodist Church, 1970; Wesley Methodist Church, 1980-; Seventh Ward Democratic Org, 1988-; exec dir, Cosmopolitan Chamber Com; adv comt, Consumers Organized Reliable Electricity. **Honors/Awds:** Contract Compliance Admin of the Yr, Bulk Contractors United, 2002; Cert Appreciation, Friends of Cook County & the City; 30-Yr Commemoration Appreciation Award, Asn Contractors; Kathy Osterman Award. **Home Addr:** 9017 S Crandon Ave, Chicago, IL 60617. *

CAREY, CLAIRE LAMAR
Manager. **Personal:** Born Aug 11, 1943, Augusta, GA; daughter of Peter W and Serena James; married Harmon Roderick; children: Roderick Lamar. **Educ:** Fisk Univ, BS, chem, 1964; Ohio Univ, attended 1965; Univ Del, mgt cert, 1975. **Career:** Hercules Inc, dir workforce diversity, col rel & regulatory compliance, dir corp pub rels, currently. **Orgs:** Pres, Alpha Kappa Alpha Sorority Zeta Omega, 1962-; Sigma Xi Sci Honor Soc, 1969-; Am Chem Soc Educ Comn, 1974-; adv bd, Del Tech Comn Col, 1974-76; secy, Govt Comn Magistrates Screening; vpres & bd dir, YWCA; bd dir, NCCJ; pres & bd dir, YWCA, 1987-89; bd dir, Boy Scouts Am; bd dir, Nat YWCA, 1990. **Honors/Awds:** Committee Service Award, United Way Del, 1975; Minority Achiever in Industry Award, Wilmington Br, YMCA, 1976; Leadership Award, Alpha Kappa Alpha, N Atlantic Region, 1979; Outstanding Achiever in Industry, Brandywine Prof Asn, 1985; inducted into Del Womens Hall of Fame, 1992; NCCJ Award, 1996; Girls Inc Award, 1996. **Business Addr:** Director Workforce Diversity, Hercules Inc, Hercules Plz, 1313 Market St, Wilmington, DE 19894-0001.

CAREY, HARMON RODERICK
Executive, businessperson. **Personal:** Born Jul 7, 1936, Wilmington, DE; married Claire D Lamar; children: Roderick. **Educ:** Cent State Univ, BA, 1957; Univ PA, MSW, 1962, post grad; Temple Univ Law Sch, 1965; Univ DE, MA, 1977; Univ DE, doc candidate, 1996. **Career:** Dept Pub Welfare Wilmington, caseworker, 1958-60; YMCA, dir youth lounge, 1959-64; Family Ct, supr, 1960-65; Peoples Settlement Asn, prog dir exec dir, 1965-70; Asn Greater Wilmington Neighborhood Ctrs, exec dir, 1970-74; Pine Beverage Inc, pres; Bar-B-Que Pit Windsor Market & Deli, owner & operator; Haral Realty, pres; Human Resources Consult, founder & pres; Afro-Am Hist Soc DE, founder, pres, exec dir. **Orgs:** Bd dir, Equity Farm Trust; instr, Univ DE Extension Div; founder, King Collection; vpres, Commun graphics Inc; conf coord, Nat Fed Settlements, 1971; Nat Asn Soc Workers, Acad Cert Soc Workers; NAACP; Black Alliance; Kappa Alpha Psi; Alpha Kappa Mu; Equity DE Monday Club; numerous publ; founder, Minority Bus Asn DE; pres, Carey Enterprises Unlimited; founder & pres, African-Am Heritage Coalition; founder, African-Am Family Reunion Festival; founder, African-Am Heritage Day DE; co-founder, Slave Ship Replica Project; pres, African-Am Heritage Tours DE; exec asst, African-Am Heritage, Dep Historical & Cult Affairs, State DE. **Special Achievements:** First African-American art gallery in Delaware. **Military Serv:** AUS, secound lt, 1957-58. **Business Addr:** President, Afro-American Historical Society of Delaware, 512 East 4Th St, Wilmington, DE 19801.*

CAREY, JENNIFER DAVIS
Educator, secretary general. **Personal:** Born Oct 2, 1956, Brooklyn, NY; daughter of Phillippa Stoute and Reuben K; married Robert J Carey Jr; children: Michael, Christopher & Helena. **Educ:** Harvard & Radcliffe Col, AB, 1978; Harvard Grad Sch Educ, EdM, 1979. **Career:** Ohio Univ, asst dir stud prog, 1979-81; Harvard & Radcliffe Col, srad missions & financial aid officer, dir minority recruitment prog, 1982-92; Vista Group, partner,

1986; Bancroft Sch, Worcester, dir colcouns, 1992-98; spec asst to Governor Cellucci; Mass Exec Off Elder Affairs, state aging disaster officer, secy, currently. **Orgs:** Bd dir, Albert Oliver Prog, 1983-; Asn Afro-Am Mus, 1986; Visions Found, 1986; Nat Asn Advan Colored People. **Business Addr:** Secretary, Massachusetts Executive Office of Elder Affairs, Rm 501 1 Ashburton Pl, Boston, MA 02108, **Business Phone:** (617)222-7470.

CAREY, MARIAH
Actor, singer. **Personal:** Born Mar 27, 1970, Huntington, NY; daughter of Alfred Roy and Patricia; married Tommy Mottola, Jun 1993 (divorced 1998). **Career:** Vocalist, songwriter, rec producer, 1987-; albums include: Mariah Carey, 1990; Emotions, 1991; Daydream, 1995; Butterfly, 1997; Rainbow, 1999; Glitter, 2001; Charmbracelet, 2002; Songs: "All I Want For Christmas Is You", 2003; "I Know What You Want", 2004; "Fly Like a Bird", 2005; We Belong Together/Fly Like a Bird", 2006; actress, 1999-; films include: The Bachelor, 1999; Glitter, 2001; Wisegirls, 2002; Death of a Dynasty, 2003; State Property two, 2005; The Sweet Sci, 2005, State Property 2, 2005; Tennessee, 2008; producer: Lovers & Haters, 2007. **Honors/Awds:** Grammy nominations for Best Album, Song of the Year, Rec of the Year, 1990, won Grammy Awards for Best New Artist, Best Pop Vocal Performance by Female, 1990; People mag, named one of Twenty-Five Most Most Intriguing People, 1991; World Music Award, Best-Selling Female Artist of the Millenium, 2000; Billboard Music Award, Artist of the Decade, 2000; World Music Award, Diamond Award, 2003. **Special Achievements:** First recording artist to have her first five singles top the U.S. Billboard Hot 100 chart. **Business Addr:** Actress, Singer, Tommy Mottola, Sony Music Entertainment Inc, 550 Madison Ave 32nd Fl, New York, NY 10022, **Business Phone:** (212)833-8000.

CAREY, PATRICIA M
School administrator. **Personal:** Born in Chicago, IL; daughter of Mildred Fowler Morris and Ezekiel J Morris, Jr; married Robert B Carey, Aug 28, 1965; children: Meredith Brooke & Jason Morris. **Educ:** Mich State Univ, BA, Psychol, 1962, MA, Psychol, 1963; New York Univ, New York, NY, PhD, Educ Psychol, 1982. **Career:** Mkt Res, New York, NY, psychologist, 1968-69; New York Univ, New York, NY, counr, 1970-76, dir, coun servs, 1976-79, dean stud affairs, 1979, asst provost & assoc dean stud servs & pub affairs, currently. **Orgs:** NY City Comn Status Women, 1986-; Am Asn Univ Women, Am Psychol Asn, Asn Black Women Higher Educ Inc; trustee, Bennett Col, 1987-; Nat Asn Women Higher Educ; Arts Connection Bd, 1989-; Manhattan Country Sch Bd, 1991-. Cathedral Saint John Divine, currently; United Neighborhood Houses. **Honors/Awds:** Distinguished Service Award, Grad Sch Orgn, New York Univ, 1987; Distinguished Alumnus Award, New York Univ Black Alumni Asn; Outstanding Leadership Award, Higher Educ Opportunities Prog, New York Univ, 1987; Named One of America's top 100 Black Business & Professional Women, Dollar & Sense Mag, 1988; Fac Resource Network Achievement Award, New York Univ, 1991; Martin Luther King Jr, Scholars Prog Leadership Award, 1992. **Business Addr:** Assistant Chancellor, Associate Dean, New York University, The Steinhardt School of Education, Pless Hall 82 Wash Sq E 2nd Fl, New York, NY 10003-6680, **Business Phone:** (212)998-5025.

CAREY, PEARL M.
Beautician. **Personal:** Married. **Educ:** Chatman Col, AA. **Career:** Monterey Peninsula Unified Sch Dist, CETA coordr; EDD, manpower specialist; Child Care Ctr, owner; Naval Postgrad Cafeteria, supvr; Youth Corps/Job Corps, employ interviewer; NYC, employ clerk; Historical Comn Seaside Calif; Bayonet & Black Horse Golf Courses. **Orgs:** Western States Golf Asn; Dem Womens Club; Nat Asn Advan Colored People; Bus & Prof Womens Club; YMCA; United Fund; Welfare Rights; Nat Coun Negro Women; CA Elected Womens Asn; Eskaton Aux Vol; woman Heart Fund & Infant Care Ctr; Nat Dem Com Woman; Monterey Area Dir; Pac Women's Golf Asn; Pac Womens Golf Asn; US Golf Asn. **Honors/Awds:** Monterey County Comn Status Women, Outstanding Woman Monterey County, 1988. **Special Achievements:** 5 most activist women Monterey Peninsula Herald, 1977; California Woman of Achievement, Beverly Park Wesleyan Church. **Home Addr:** 1231 Olympia Ave, Seaside, CA 93955. *

CAREY, DR. PHILLIP
Educator. **Personal:** Born Mar 3, 1942, Andros, Bahamas; son of Gerald and Edna Smith Lewis; married Jean Harvey, May 27, 1973; children: Phillipa, Phillip Jr & Peter. **Educ:** Okla State Univ, Stillwater, Okla, BS, 1969, MS, 1970, PhD, 1975. **Career:** Am Sociol Asn, Wash, DC, dir, fel prog, 1975-76; Ark State, Jonesboro,chair, arts & sci, 1976-77; Univ Minn, Minneapolis, MN, dir, minority affairs, 1977-79; Morgan State Univ, Baltimore, MD, dir, urban research, 1979-81; Bahamas Govt, Nassau, dir, nat ins bd, 1981-84; Austin Peay State, Clarksville, MD, asst pres, 1989-90; Langston Univ, Langston, Okla,assoc vpres, acad affairs, 1990-91; NC Agri & Tech State Univ, Col Arts & Sci, dean & prof sociol, dir, undergrad social work prog, currently. **Orgs:** Am Sociol Asn, Wash, DC, 1975-; Chair, Academic Policies & Curric Comt,Langston Univ, 1990-; chair, Acad Retention Task Force Comt, Langston Univ, 1990; chair, Presidential Special Comt, Langston Univ, 1990-; Okla Acad State Goals, State Okla, 1990-; Asn Higher Educ, 1990-. **Honors/Awds:** Graduate Excellence Award, Oklahoma State Univ, 1973; Outstanding Counseling Award, Alpha Phi Alpha, Oklahoma State Univ, 1974; Recognitionin Profiles of Service, Caucus of Black SDA Admin, 1990; Community Service Award, Okla Community Services, 1991. **Business Addr:** Dean, Professor, North Carolina Agri & Tech State University, 201 Gibbs Hall, Greensboro, NC 27411, **Business Phone:** (336)285-2295.

CAREY, TANISHA MONET. See MONET, JERZEE.

CAREY, VINCE
Broker. **Educ:** BS, Physics; MS, Elec Engineering; MBA, currently. **Career:** IBM Corp, engr; Howard Perry & Walston, broker, currently. **Orgs:** Pres, Int Focus Inc; Pres election, Raleigh Regional Asn; Cary & Garner Chambers Com. **Business Phone:** (919)388-4810.

CAREY, WAYNE E
Executive. **Personal:** Born Feb 8, 1945, Norwalk, CT; son of Edward E and Etta J; married Olivia Thompson, Jun 19, 1986. **Educ:** Howard Univ, Col Liberal Arts, BA, 1968, Sch Law, JD, 1971. **Career:** Bendix Corp, contracts mgr, prog develop mgr, Affirmative Action Affairs, creative dir, social responsibility; Mich Nat Corp, creative dir, staffing-staff rels; Abbott Laboratories, dir, corp staffing. **Orgs:** Soc Human Resources Mgt; Employ Mgt Asn; SPP Fraternity. **Honors/Awds:** Man of the Year, Key Women's Club of America, 1981.

CARGILE, C. B., JR. See Obituaries section.

CARGILE, WILLIAM, III
Founder (Originator), president (organization). **Career:** William Cargile Contractor Inc, Cincinnati, OH, founder, chief exec & pres; William Cargile Construct II Inc, pres, currently; AlCargile Construct Servs Ltd, managing dir, currently. **Business Phone:** (513)381-2442.*

CARGILL, SANDRA MORRIS
Executive. **Personal:** Born May 8, 1953, Boston, MA; daughter of Richard B Morris and Ida R Morris; married Ronald Glanville. **Educ:** Univ bedlands, BS, bus admin, 1984. **Career:** Am Acquisitions Inc, admin asst, 1976-77; Mode O' Day Co, asst buyer, secy, 1977-78; Loral Xerox Electro Optical Syst, sr contract admin, 1978-85; Calif Inst Tech Jet Propulsion Lab, contract specialist, 1985-91; Cargill Planning & Predevelopment Serv, pres, 1990-. **Orgs:** Pres, Prin Developer Xerox Electro Optical Systs Tutorial Prog, 1980-83; Black Women's Forum, 1980-83; Youth Motivation Task Force, 1981-83; Loral EOS Mgt Club, 1983-85; gen mem, Jr Achievement Prog, 1983-85, bd dir logistics, 1986-87, exec adv, 1984-85; Nat Contract Mgt Asn, San Gabriel Valley, 1983-; Caltech Mgt Club, Calif Inst Tech, 1985-. **Honors/Awds:** Outstanding Achievement in Contract, Admin Xerox Electro Optical Systs, 1981;Group Achievement Award, NASA, 1989; Outstanding Achievement Award, General W Harmon, 1990; Outstanding Achievement Award, NCMA, 1990; Clinton's National Service Prog Award, Los Angeles Pilot, 1993. **Home Phone:** (818)780-9510. **Business Addr:** President, Cargill Planning & Predevelopment Services, 6442 Coldwater Canyon, Panorama City, CA 91606, **Business Phone:** (818)760-0289.

CARLISLE, JAMES EDWARD, JR.
Educator, lawyer. **Personal:** Born May 30, 1944, Acmar, AL; son of James E Carlisle Sr and Juanita; married Deborah Ann Carter, Jun 19, 1976; children: Constance Isabelle & Phillip Joseph. **Educ:** Youngstown State Univ, BA, 1967; Bowling Green State Univ, MEd, 1978; Univ Toledo Col Law, JD, 1985. **Career:** Perkins Bd Educ, staff, 1967-69; Toledo Bd Educ, staff, 1969-; Waite High Sch, educr; atty, currently. **Orgs:** Pres, Youngstown Univ Chap, Nat Asn Advan Colored People, 1966-67; Am Fed Teachers, 1969-; Big Brothers Am, 1970-73; Homeless Awareness Proj, 1988-; Nat Bar Asn, Ren Daniels Pres, campaign organizer, 1992; reading coordr, Nubia; Toledo Alliance Black Educr; Toledo Bar Asn; Am Bar Asn; Ohio Bar Asn; Wood Co Bar Asn. **Honors/Awds:** Am Jurisprudence Award, 1985. **Home Addr:** 110 Harmony Lane, Toledo, OH 43615. **Business Addr:** Educator, Waite High School, 301 Morrison Dr, Toledo, OH 43605, **Business Phone:** (419)691-4687.*

CARLO, NELSON
Executive. **Personal:** Born Jan 1, 1938?, Boqueron, PR. **Educ:** Career Automotive Trade Sch, voc course, 1961. **Career:** Abbott Prod Inc, Chicago, IL, chief exec officer; Carlo Steel Corp, owner & pres 1991-. **Military Serv:** AUS 4yrs. **Business Phone:** (773)375-9600.*

CARLTON, BARBARA
Librarian. **Career:** George Hall Elem Sch, librn, currently. *

CARLTON, PAMELA GEAN
Banker. **Personal:** Born Oct 17, 1954, Cleveland, OH; daughter of Mildred Myers and Alphonso A; married Charles Jordan Hamilton Jr; children: Charles III, Samuel Aaron Hamilton. **Educ:** Williams Col, BA, Polit Econ, 1976; Yale Sch Mgt, MPPM Bus, 1980; Yale Law Sch, JD, 1980. **Career:** Cleary Gottlieb Stein & Hamilton, assoc counsel, 1980-82; Morgan Stanley Co Inc, assoc investment banking, 1982-85, vpres investment banking, 1985, principal, finance dept; JPMorgan Chase, managing dir; Springboard Partners, pres & co-founder, currently. **Orgs:** NY State Bar; bd mem, Studio Mus in Harlem, 1982-87; Westchester Bd Planned Parenthood; Grad Sch City Univ NY; bd mem, World Resources Inst, 1991-94; JPMorganChase Corp Diversity Coun; adv bd, Yale Sch Mgt. **Business Addr:** Principal, Morgan Stanley & Co Inc, Finance Dept, 1251 Ave of the Am, New York, NY 10020.*

CARMAN, EDWIN G.
Government official. **Personal:** Born Feb 13, 1951, New Brunswick, NJ; married Pamela M Vaughan. **Educ:** Rutgers Univ, BA, journalism & political sci, 1974. **Career:** Middle sex County Col Found, bd mem, 1980-; Middlesex County Econ Opportuniy Corp, bd mem, 1975-, chmn, 1981-84; City NB, coun mem, 1975, coun pres, 1987; NJ Sch Bd Asn, Govt Rels Dept, sr lobbyist; NJ Dept Community Affairs, chief staff, 2007-. **Orgs:** Am Coun Young Political Leaders; bd mem, NJ Foster Grandparents, 1986; mem, Transportation Task Force, 2006. **Honors/Awds:** Political Action Award, New Brunswick Area, NAACP, 1983. **Business Addr:** Chief of Staff, New Jersey Department of Community Affairs, 101 S Broad St, PO Box 800, Trenton, NJ 08625-0800, **Business Phone:** (609)292-6055.

CARMICHAEL, BENJAMIN G.
Educator. **Personal:** Born Jul 7, 1938, Atlanta, GA; married Dorothy; children: Christopher & Jennifer. **Educ:** San Francisco St Col, BA, 1963; Univ CA, MA, 1972. **Career:** US Comm Porno, prin invest; Transit Robby Study, Univ CA, asst proj dir, 1968-70; Univ San Francisco, lectr, 1968-69; Hunters Pt Comm Devel Proj, proj dir, 1966-68; CA State Univ, prof, 1969-, chmn, dept criminal justice admin, 2004. **Orgs:** Dir Crim Just Admin Prog Calif State Univ; consult Law Enforce Asst Admin; adv bd mem, Admin Just Prog, Ohlone Jr Col, Alpha Phi Alpha; Nat Urban League; Nat Coun Cr & Delinq Youth Cr Urban Comm, St Hustlers & Their Crimes, Crime & Delinq Vol 21, 1975; The Hunters Pt Riot, Pol the Frust,Issues in Crime, Vol 4 1969. **Honors/Awds:** Fel, Nat Inst Ment Health Univ Calif, 1966-68. **Military Serv:** AUS, 1957. **Business Addr:** Chairman, California State University, Department Criminal Justice Admin, 25800 Carlos Bee Blvd E Bay, Hayward, CA 94542-3095, **Business Phone:** (510)885-3590.

CARMICHAEL, CAROLE A
Journalist, editor. **Personal:** Born Jul 9, 1950, Brooklyn, NY. **Educ:** NY Univ, BA, 1972; Roosevelt Univ, MS, mgt & human resources. **Career:** Chicago Tribune, former careers ed; Clmb Col Chicago, instr journalism 1978-79; Fairchild Publ Inc, NY, news reporter 1976; UPI Omaha & NY, news reporter 1973-76; Stephen Decatur Jr High Sch, English teacher 1972-73; Philadelphia Daily News, news reporter; Seattle Times, asst news managing ed, currently; Chicago Tribune, Business Reporter, currently; Daily News, exec asst, currently. **Orgs:** Contrib writer Working Women Mag 1977-; pres, Chicago Asn Black Journalists, 1978-80; bd dir, YWCA Metro Chicago, 1978-79. contrib writer Essence Mag, 1979. **Honors/Awds:** Advan Study Fel Econ for Journalists Brkngs Inst, WA, 1978; selected as one of 50 ftr leaders of Am Ebony Mag 1978; Sojrnr Truth Award, Nat Asn Negro Bus & Prof Women, NY 1980; Comm Serv Award, Nat Asn Negro Bus & Prof Women, Chicago 1980. **Business Addr:** Assistant News Managing Editor, Seattle Times, 1120 John St, PO Box 70, Seattle, WA 98111, **Business Phone:** (206)464-3116.

CARMICHAEL, RICHARD O.
Executive. **Career:** Summit Bank, Capital Markets & Treasury Servs Div, sr managing dir; FleetBoston Financial Corp, Global Servs Div, exec vpres global serv, head cash mgt.

CARNELL, LOUGENIA LITTLEJOHN
Manager. **Personal:** Born Mar 12, 1947, Memphis, TN; children: Gizele Montrece. **Educ:** Dept Agr Grad Sch; Catholic Univ; Univ DC Chester. **Career:** MEECN Systs Eng Off Def Commun Agency, Wash, DC, div sec steno, 1971-73; Staff Chaplain Mil Dist, Wash, DC, admin sec steno, 1973-75; Inter agency Coun Minority Bus Enterprise Dept Com, personal asst exec dir, 1975-76. **Orgs:** Med asst, vol ARC Alexandria Chap, 1973-76; Fed Women's Prof; chmn, Dept Energy Task Force Concerns Minority Women, 1979-80; Nat Coun Career Women; Nat mem, Smithsonian Assos. **Honors/Awds:** Key to City, New Orleans, 1975; recital WTOP-TV Wash DC 1975; cert pin ARC Alexandria Chap, 1976; People on the Move, Black Enterprise Mag, 1979; Women in Energy, Newsletter, 1979; cert participation, IL Off Minority Bus Enterprise Statewide Annual Conf, 1979; observance black history month Prog Adv Dept Energy. **Special Achievements:** First female in 108 yrs to be mem of bd of trustees, Mt Olive Bapt Ch Arlington, 1977; first chmn, Dept Energy Task Force, Minority Women Wash DC, 1979.

CARNEY, LLOYD
President (Organization), chief executive officer. **Educ:** Wentworth Inst, BS, elec eng technol; Leslie Col, MS. **Career:** Well-

fleet Commun, dir tech opers, 1990, vpres, 1993; Bay Networks; Nortel Networks, pres; Juniper Networks, chief operating officer & exec vpres; Micromuse, chmn & chief exec officer, 2003; Int Bus Mach, NetCool Div, gen mgr; BigBand Networks, bd dir, currently; Cypress Semiconductor Corp, dir, 2005-; Carney Global Ventures, chmn & chief executive officer, currently. **Orgs:** pres, Adv Coun; dir, Boys & Girls Club Peninsula. **Business Phone:** (408)943-2600.*

CARO, RALPH M
Executive. **Personal:** Born Jun 8, 1948, Kansas City, MO; son of Ralph and Lena Caro; married Carolyn W Cameron, Dec 17, 1990. **Educ:** Univ Kans, BA, 1969; Univ Miss, Kans City, MBA, 1998. **Career:** Xerox Corp, high volume mkt exec, 1978-97; Swope Pkwy Health Ctr, adminr & chief exec officer, 1997-, pres & chief exec officer, 2002. **Orgs:** Pres, Spoilers Golf Club, 1994-; alumni bd, Univ Miss, Kans City, 1998; adv bd, Capper Found, 1999-; pres, Beta Lambda Educ Inst, 1998-; chapt pres, Alpha Phi Alphi Fraternity, 1994-97; Nat job fair chair, Alpha Phi Alpha Fraternity, 1996-99; bd mem, Full Employment Coun, 1998-; bd adv, Kans Univ Mini-Med Sch, 1999-2000. **Honors/Awds:** Man of Year in Medicine, Blacks Govt, 1994. **Business Addr:** President, Swope Health Serv, 3801 Blue Pkwy, Kansas City, MO 64130, **Business Phone:** (816)923-5800.

CAROL DENISE, ENSLEY. **See NASH, NIECY.**

CAROLINE, J. C.
Football coach, football player. **Personal:** Born Jan 17, 1933, Warrenton, GA; married Laverne Dillon; children: Jayna & Jolynn. **Educ:** Ill Univ, BS, 1967. **Career:** Football player, Football coach (retired); Montreal Allouetts, 1955-56; Chicago Bears, defensive back, 1956-65; Univ Ill Athletics Asn, asst football coach, 1967-76. **Orgs:** Bd dir, Don Moyers Boys Club. **Honors/Awds:** All-am Football, 1953; All Prof, 1956; Inducted into the College Football Hall of Fame, 1980.

CARPENTER, ANN M.
Chiropractor, educator. **Personal:** Born Jul 1, 1934, New York, NY; daughter of James Gowdy and Charity Gowdy; divorced; children: Karen, Marie. **Educ:** City Col NY, BS, educ, 1960, MA; NY Chiropractic Col, DC 1978; Univ Bridgeport CT, MS, Nutrit, 1980. **Career:** Haaren High Sch NY, teacher eng, 1957-67, chmn eng dept, 1967-68; Harlem Prep Sch, asst prin teacher educ & curric, 1968-75, prin, 1975; pvt pract, 2004-. **Orgs:** Am Chiropractic Asn 1975-; NY Asn Black Educators II, 1978-; Bergen Co NJ Urban League of Bergen Co, 1978; Nat Asn Sec Sch Admin, 1979; NY State Chiropractic Asn, 1979-; Am Black Chiropractors Asn, 1985-; NY State Bd Chiropractic Asn, 1985; pres, NYSCA Dist Nine, 1985-86, 1986-87; chair, NY State Bd Chiropractic Asn, 1988-89 . **Honors/Awds:** Youth Guid Award, Bergen Co Negro Bus & Prof Women 1974; Community serv award, Harlem Prep Sch, 1976; Citizen of the Yr, Awards in Black; Serv prof, NY State Chiropractic Asn, 1988; Fel Am Col Chiropractors, 1992. **Business Addr:** Doctor, Private Practice, 125 S Chestnut St, Beacon, NY 12508, **Business Phone:** (845)831-2222.*

CARPENTER, BARBARA WEST
Association executive, educator. **Personal:** Born in Baton Rouge, LA. **Educ:** Southern Univ-Baton Rouge, BS, voc educ & sec sci, MEd, sec educ; Kans State Univ, PhD, adult & occupational educ. **Career:** Colo Col, Ohio Univ, post-doctoral fel; Southern Univ, from prof to admin, 1980; Ctr Int Educ, Southern Univ, dir Continuing Educ & Ctr for Serv Learning, dean Int Educ, currently. **Orgs:** Pres, Zeta Phi Beta Sorority Inc, 1996-2002; March Dimes; Phi Delta Kappa Educ Fraternity; Rotary Int Baton Rouge; Phi Upsilon Omicron Honor Soc; bd comnr, Baton Rouge Housing Authority. **Special Achievements:** Authored numerous articles. **Business Addr:** Dean of International Education, Southern University, Center for International Education, 1100 Harris Hall, PO Box 9772, Baton Rouge, LA 70813, **Business Phone:** (225)771-2613.

CARPENTER, CARL ANTHONY
School administrator, dean (education), vice president (organization). **Personal:** Born Feb 29, 1944, Gaffney, SC; son of John H and Teacora; married Parthelia Davis Carpenter, Aug 6, 1967; children: Carla P Adams, Carl A II. **Educ:** SC State Univ, BS, 1966, MEd, 1970; Univ SC, PhD, 1973. **Career:** Sumter, SC Sch Dist 17, teacher, 1966-70; Sc State Dept Educ, 1972; SC State Univ, from asst prof to assoc prof, 1972-75, asst vpres acad affairs, 1975-80, vpres acad affairs, 1980-86, prof, 1986-92, interim pres, 1992-93, prof educ, 1993-94, Div Acad Affairs, interim vpres, 2007-; Consol Consultative Serv, pres, 1994-96; Voohees Col, exec vpres & acad dean, 1996; Claflin Univ, prof. **Orgs:** NAFEO; MEAC Coun Presidents; Nat Asn Adv Colored People; Omega Psi Phi Fraternity Inc; Phi Delta Kappa Educ Fraternity; Alpha Kappa Mu; bd trustees, Presbyterian Col & Rabun Gap Nacoochee Sch; bd dirs, Presbyterian Church Found; bd dirs, Heritage Corridor Partnership. **Honors/Awds:** Outstanding Educrs Am, 1974; Citizen of the Year, Omega Psi Phi Fraternity Inc, 1981; Honoree Distinguished Alumni, SC State Univ, 1984; Man of the Year, Omega Psi Phi Fraternity Inc, Epsilon Omega Chap, 1992. **Special Achievements:** Institutional Effectiveness Measures for Adult and Continuing Educ, 1992; Factors Influencing Access & Equality in Higher Education, 1991; Review, Analysis & Projections of Academic Programs, 1978; Performance Based Teacher Education Specifications, 1973. **Home Phone:** (803)536-1793. **Business Phone:** 800-260-5956.*

CARPENTER, CLARENCE E., JR.
Executive, manager. **Personal:** Born Feb 5, 1941, Nashville, TN; son of Clarence E Carpenter Sr and Mary Carney; married Faye Powell Carpenter, Apr 7, 1990; children: Brenda Thomas, Yvonne Campbell, Gail, Clarence E III, Tiffany, Bryanna. **Educ:** Southwestern Christian Col, Terrell, TX, AA, 1961; Northeastern Ill Univ, Chicago, Ill, BA, 1988. **Career:** Mother of Savior Seminar, Blackwood, NJ, mgr, admin, 1962-65; Chem Co, Pavisboro, NJ, shipping mgr, 1965-68; Kraft, Philadelphia, PA, acct exec, 1968-71; Kraft, NY, WA, DC, supvr, zone mgr, 1971-76; Kraft, Albany, NY, Rochester, NY, dist mgr, area mgr, 1976-82; Kraft, Chicago, IL, region grocery mgr, region vpres, 1982-89; Kraft Gen Foods, Glenview, IL, vpres retail opers, 1989, vpres E sales, region mgr, Charlotte, NC. **Orgs:** Vis prof, exec, Urban League, 1988-. **Honors/Awds:** Chicago YMCA Black Achievers Award, YMCA Metropolitan Chicago, 1988; Food Mktg Inst Award, Food Market Inst, 1990; Martin Luther King Award, Minority Econ Coun, 1989. **Home Addr:** 3734 Providence Manor Rd, Charlotte, NC 28270. *

CARPENTER, LEWIS
Government official. **Personal:** Born Feb 1, 1928, Brantley, AL; son of H D Carpenter and Bessie; married Myrtice Bryant Carpenter, Nov 18, 1950. **Educ:** Covington Cty Training Sch, AA, 1956; LBW Jr Col, acct, 1982. **Career:** Government official (retired); Covington County Bank, custodian, 1959; City Andalusia, councilman, 1984; Covington County Bank, banker. **Orgs:** Masonic Rose Sharon Lodge, 1965-, Adv Comm LBW Jr Col, 1970-; Covington County Sheriff Res, 1970-; adv, Local Draft Bd, 1980-; adv, OCAP Comm, 1982-. **Honors/Awds:** First black City Councilman Andalusia City Coun, 1984. **Military Serv:** AUS, corporal, 1952-54, 18 mos Korea. **Home Addr:** 210 Lowe Ave, Andalusia, AL 36420. *

CARPENTER, RAYMOND PRINCE
Lawyer. **Personal:** Born Apr 2, 1944, Little Rock, AR; son of Reuben and Ellen; married Barbara Pearson, Sep 2, 1971; children: Raymond Prince Jr. **Educ:** Philander Smith Col, 1963; Univ AR, BA, 1966; Emory Univ Sch Law, JD, 1975. **Career:** Lockheed Ga Co, assoc atty, 1975-76; City Atlanta-Solicitor's Off, asst solicitor, 1976-78; Sears Roebuck & Co, sr atty, 1978-86; Price Waterhouse LLP, managing dir, 1986-92; Huey, Guilday & Tucker, managing partner, 1992-94; Holland & Knight, partner, 1994-, dir's comn, 1999-2002. **Orgs:** Chair-elect taxation sect, State Bar Ga, 1995-97; secy-treas, Atlanta Bar Asn, 1996-; bd mem, Nat Inst State Taxation, 1990-; state tax section bd, Am Bar Asn, 1990-; bd pres, Child Welfare League Am Inc; Nat Asn State Bar Asn. **Honors/Awds:** Outstanding Public Achievement, Fulton County Ga, 1990. **Special Achievements:** Keynote Speaker, ML King Holiday Celebration, 1992, Tax Executive Institute, National Mtg, 1989; Journal of State Taxation, Florida Svc Taxes, 1986; Georgia Bar Journal, State Tax Issues, 1989. **Military Serv:** US Marine Corps, cpl, 1969-70. **Business Addr:** Attorney, Holland & Knight LLP, 1201 W Peachtree St NE Suite 2000, 1 Atlantic Ctr, Atlanta, GA 30309, **Business Phone:** (404)817-8532.

CARPENTER, RONALD
Football player. **Personal:** Born Jan 20, 1970, Cincinnati, OH; married Sheri; children: Kamron. **Educ:** Miami Univ, Ohio, urban & regional Plng. **Career:** Cincinnati Bengals, def back, 1993; Minn Vikings, 1993; New York Jets, 1995-96; Amsterdam Admirals, World League, 1995, 1997; St Louis Rams, 1998-99; New York City Hawks, 1998; Las Vegas Outlaws, 2000; Los Angeles Xtreme, 2000; Nashville Kats, 2000-01; Ga Force, 2002; Detroit Fury, 2003-04; Las Vegas Outlaws, currently. **Business Phone:** (702)242-5489.

CARPENTER, VIVIAN L. (VIVIAN CARPENTER STRATHER)
Educator. **Personal:** Born Nov 3, 1952, Detroit, MI; daughter of Doyal Wilson Thomas (deceased) and Jennie Pettway; married Herbert J Strather; married Aldan J Carpenter (died 1978); children: Andrea Nicole Strather & Carmen Lavern Strather. **Educ:** Univ Mich, Ann Arbor, BSE, 1973, MBA, 1975, PhD, 1985. **Career:** Ford Motor Co, Dearborn, MI, res engr, 1972-73; Arthur Andersen & Co, Detroit, MI, sr consult, 1975-77; Mich Dept of Treas, Lansing, dep state treas, 1979-81; Univ Mich, Ann Arbor, vis prof indust & opers eng, 1990-91; Wayne State Univ, Detroit, MI, asst prof acct, 1984-92; Fla A&M Univ, assoc prof, dir acad progs, 1992-95; Sch Bus & Indust, asst dean, 1995-; Atwater Entertainment Assocs, LLC, pres & founder, 2002-05; Comt MotorCity Casino, chair mgt & audit, , Detroit, MI, currently. **Orgs:** Am Inst CPA's, 1979-; Mich Asn CPA's, 1979-; Govt Finance Officers Asn, 1978-84, 1990-93; Nat Asn Black Accts, 1979-90, 1994-; Am Acct Asn, 1984-; dir, Atwater Entertainment Assocs; dir, Detroit Com Bank; dir, Motor City Casino; dir, Atwater Found; dir, Detroit Inst Arts; chairperson bd, Detroit Black Chamber Com; bd mem, Mich Front Page newspaper; bd mem, Univ Mich Sch Bus Alumni Asn. **Honors/Awds:** Nat Award, Nat Asn Black Accts, 1991; Nat Sci Found, 1987, 1990; fel Ford Found, 1985; Asn Govt Accts Author's Award, 1991; Best Interdisciplinary Paper Award, Decision Sci Inst, 1991; Nissan Int Fel, 1993. **Business Addr:** Chair, MotorCity Casino, 2901 Grand River Ave, Detroit, MI 48201.*

CARPENTER, WILLIAM ARTHUR
Writer, editor. **Personal:** Born in Fayettesville, NC; son of William A Carpenter Sr and Via Maria Randall. **Educ:** Univ Dijon, France, Certif, 1985; Am Univ, BA, 1990. **Career:** Smithsonian-Nat Mus Am History, exhibit writer, 1987; Vietnam Veterans Am, Wash, DC, press asst, 1987; Gospel Highlights Newsletter, ed, 1987-89; Bush/Quayle Campaign, Wash, DC, campaign worker, 1988-89, 1992; J Gospel Music, Mitchellville, MD, ed, 1990-92; Wash New Observer, staff writer, 1990-93; Carp Shank Entertainment, sr publicist, 1992-95; All-Music Guide, Miller-Freeman, gospel ed, 1992; Capital Entertainment, co-founder, 1996-; radio host, Music Jam, currently; Freelance articles: American Gospel, Destiny, Goldmine, Living Blues, YSB, Players, People Magazine, Rejoice, The Washington Post. **Orgs:** Nat Asn Black Journalists; Gospel Music Prof Network. **Business Addr:** Co-Founder, Capital Entertainment, 217 Seaton Pl NE, Washington, DC 20002, **Business Phone:** (202)636-7028.

CARPER, GLORIA G.
Educator, social worker. **Personal:** Born Aug 10, 1930, Montclair, NJ; widowed; children: Gladyce & Terri. **Educ:** Morgan State Col, BS, 1950; WVa Univ, MA, 1971. **Career:** Educator, social worker (retired); WVa Dept Welfare, social worker, 1961-64; WVa Dept Ment Health, welfare supvr, 1964-67; WVa DeptMent Health, admin asst med div, 1967-72; Day Care Ctr, Ment Retarded C, Dept Ment Health, dir, 1972-73; WVa State Col, acting dir guid & placement, foreign stud adv & counr devel serv, 1982-98. **Orgs:** Nat Asn Retarded C Inc; Kanawha Asn Retarded C Inc; pres, Charleston Inst; Delta Sigma Theta, bd mem, Charleston Oppty Indust Ctr Inc; organist, First Baptist Church. **Honors/Awds:** Mother of the Year, First Baptist Church, 1972.

CARR, CHRIS DEAN
Basketball player. **Personal:** Born Mar 12, 1974, Ironton, MO. **Educ:** Southern Illinois Univ. **Career:** Basketball player (retired), basketball coach, speaker; Phoenix Suns,guard, 1995-96; Minn Timberwolves, 1996-98; New Jersey Nets, 1999; Golden State Warriors, 2000; Chicago Bulls, 2000; Boston Celtics, 2001; Cleveland Cavaliers; 43 Hoops Basketball Acad, founder, owner & coach, currently. **Honors/Awds:** Mo Valley Conf MVP; Mo Conf Tournament MVP. **Business Addr:** Owner, Coach, 43 Hoops Basketball Academy, 1002 Second St NE, PO Box 157, Hopkins, MN 55343, **Business Phone:** (952)294-4667.

CARR, COREY JERMAINE
Basketball player. **Personal:** Born Dec 5, 1975, Fordyce, AR. **Educ:** Tex Tech Univ, attended 1998. **Career:** Texas Tech Raiders, 1994-98; Atlanta Hawk, 1998; Chicago Bulls; 1998-99; Ironi Nahariya, 2006; Elitzur Ashkelon, 2007-08; Maccabi Givat Shmuel, currently. *

CARR, GWEN L.
Executive. **Career:** Eastern Dist Mich, asst atty; MetLife Inc, vpres & secy, currently. *

CARR, KENNETH ALAN
Basketball player. **Personal:** Born Aug 15, 1955, Washington, DC; married Adrianna; children: Cameron & Devon Roberts. **Educ:** NC State Univ, 1978. **Career:** Baskeball player (retired); Los Angeles Lakers, forward, 1977-80; Cleveland Cavaliers, forward, 1979-82; Detroit Pistons, forward, 1981-82; Portland Trail Blazers, forward, 1982-87. **Honors/Awds:** All Am squad; Gold Medal, Montreal, US Olympic team, 1976.

CARR, KURT
Gospel singer, music director. **Educ:** Univ Conn, BA, fine arts. **Career:** Worked as pianist and musical dir for James Cleveland, late 1980-91; Toured with Andrae Crouch as musical dir, 1991-94; The Kurt Carr Singers, founder, 1991, recording artist, 1991-, producer, 2003-; West Angeles Church of God In Christ, musical dir, minister of music, 1990-01, creative dir, currently; Albums: Together, Serious About it, 1994; No One Else, 1997; Awesome Wonder, 2000; One Church, 2004; Come Let us Worship, 2005; Just the Beginning, 2008. **Honors/Awds:** Stellar Award Song of the Year, for "In The Sanctuary," 2002; Stellar Award Song of the Year, for "The Presence of the Lord Is Here", 2005. *

CARR, LENFORD
Government official, business owner. **Personal:** Born Sep 21, 1938, Haywood Co Bural, TN; married Ella R Porter; children: Vincent Louis & Bridgett Genese. **Educ:** Knoxville Col, 1958. **Career:** Milan Arsenal; Humboldt City Park Comn Bd, mem, 1977-85; Humbol dt City Sch Bd, mem & secy, 1979-88, bd mem, currently; Carr's Catering Serv, owner, currently; Humbol dt Dist 4, County Comnr, 2005-. **Orgs:** City Schs-Transp-Building & Calendar Comn; Morning Star Baptist Church; NAACP Humboldt Chap; pres, Humbol dt Dem Concerned Citizens Club; Gibson County Dem Exec; Comt mem, Stigall Ethnic Libr Hist

Museum. **Honors/Awds:** Plant Manager Award, Martin Marietta Aluminum Sales, 1970; culinary serv, Morning Star Baptist Church 1977; community serv, NAACP-, IBPOWELK, 1980-83; educ boardsmanship, Humbol dt City Schs Bd, 1983; Outstanding Citizen Polit Involvement AKA Sorority, 1983. **Military Serv:** AUS, Sp4 1961-64. **Home Addr:** 94 Maple St, Humboldt, TN 38343.

CARR, M L (MICHAEL LEON CARR)
President (Organization), basketball player. **Personal:** Born Jan 9, 1951, Wallace, NC; married Sylvia. **Educ:** Guilford Col, BA, hist. **Career:** Basketball player (retired), pres; Detroit Pistons, 1976-79; Boston Celtics, forward, 1979-85, scout, 1985-91, dir community rels, 1991-94, sr exec vpres & dir of basketball group, 1994-97, head coach, 1995-97; M L Carr Enterprises, pres; WARM2Kids Inc, pres & chief executive officer, currently. **Orgs:** Founder, ML Carr Scholarship Found, Guilford Col, 1987; founder, John Henry Carr Alzheimer & Aging Found. **Honors/Awds:** Martin Luther King Jr Image Award; Toastmaster's Communication Award; Camille Cosby's Citizenship Award; Good Scout Award. **Special Achievements:** Authored three books, Don't Be Denied, Enough is Enough, and Winning Through Persistence. **Business Addr:** President, Chief Executive Officer, WARM2kids Inc., 61 N Beacon St, Boston, MA 02134, **Business Phone:** (617)254-9276.

CARR, MICHAEL LEON. See CARR, M L.

CARR, PERCY L.
Basketball coach. **Personal:** Born Nov 19, 1941, Longview, TX; married Helen; children: Kacy. **Educ:** Calif State Univ, BS, Phys Educ 1968, MA, Phys Educ 1972. **Career:** Tulare Union High Sch, teacher & coach, 1968-70, basketball camps & clins, 1971-74; Stanford Univ, asst basketball coach, 1974-75; Edison High Sch,teacher, asst vice prin & dean of boys, coach, 1970-74; San Jose City Col, Jaguars, head basketball coach, currently. **Orgs:** Masonic Lodge; Alpha Phi Alpha. **Honors/Awds:** All metro coach of the Year, 1971; Coach of the Year, Central CA Basketball Coaches Asn, 1974; All metro coach of the year Fresno Bee,1974; Coach of the Year, 1976; Outstanding Teacher-Coach Award, 1988; Inductee of the CA Community Col Basketball Hall of Fame, 1998; Coast Conference Coach of the Year, 1996-97; Northern Calif Coach of the Year, 1994; Educator of the Year, 100 Black Men of the Silicon Valley Organization, 2000. **Special Achievements:** An academic program that involves all the student athletes Creative Athletic Retention Response(C.A.R.R). **Business Addr:** Basketball Coach, San Jose City College, Athletic Department, Rm 301 2100 Moorpark Ave, San Jose, CA 95128, **Business Phone:** (408)288-3739.

CARR, RODERICH MARION
Investment banker, executive. **Personal:** Born Nov 5, 1956, Birmingham, AL; son of Edgar A Carr; married Charlotte Bland; children: Hamilton Taylor & Chesleigh Marie. **Educ:** Johns Hopkins Univ, BSEE, 1978; Univ Chicago, Grad Sch Bus, MBA, Fin & Mkt, 1980. **Career:** Salomon Smith Barney, dir; Johns Hopkins Univ, Whiting Sch Engineering, adv mem & trustee; Salomon Brothers Inc, vpres; Citigroup, Global Transaction Serv, dir & sales mgr, prod mgr asset mgt; Wachovia Securities, managing dir & exec search consult, 2005-. **Orgs:** Vpres, 1978-80, Nat Black MBA Asn, 1978-; bd dirs, Jobs for Youth, 1986-. **Business Addr:** Managing Director, Executive Search Consultant, Wachovia Securities, 301 S College St One Wachovia Ctr Suite 4000, Charlotte, NC 28288, **Business Phone:** (704)342-9000.

CARR, SANDRA JEAN IRONS
Labor activist, educator, executive. **Personal:** Born Jul 17, 1940, Middlesboro, KY; divorced. **Educ:** Ky State Col, BS, math & chem, 1960; Purdue Univ, MA, 1965; Ind Univ, MA, 1980. **Career:** Labor Activist (retired): State Ohio Div Aid Aged, caseworker, 1960-61; Gary Community Sch, IN, teacher, math, 1961-71; Northwest Ind Fed Labor, vpres; Gary Teachers Union, IN, pres. **Orgs:** Vpres, Ind Fed Teachers, 1971-; vpres, Am Fed Teachers, 1974-; trustee,1976-79, treas, 1986, Lake Area United Way; co-chairperson & mem comt, Nat Asn Advan Colored People, 1977; Gamma Psi Omega Chap; Alpha Kappa Alpha; Gary Comn Status Women; co-dir, Christian Educ New Revelation Baptist Church Gary, 1980-; Citizens Task Force St Gangs & Sch Discipline, 1983-; secy, Gary Educ Develop Found, 1984-; pres, Mental Health Asn Lake Co; Ind Fed Teachers; vpres, pres, NW Indiana Federation of Labor, 1995. **Honors/Awds:** Viola Briley Service Award, Gary Teachers Union; Adam Benjamin, Jr., Advocacy Award, Mental Heath Association; Labor Leader of the Year Award, Calumet Project; Joseph A. Beirne Community Service Award, United Way of America. **Home Addr:** 2058 Vermont St, Gary, IN 46407, **Home Phone:** (219)885-5927.

CARR, WILLIAM
Football player. **Personal:** Born Jan 13, 1975, Dallas, TX. **Educ:** Univ Mich. **Career:** Carolina Panthers, defensive tackle, beginning, 1997; Orlando Predators, defensive back, beginning, 1999; Ga force, defensive back, 2003-04; Orlando Predators, defensive back, 2004.

CARREATHERS, KEVIN R
Educator. **Personal:** Born Feb 26, 1957, Denison, TX; son of Raymond E and Ernestine T. **Educ:** N Tex State Univ, BS, 1979; Prairie View Agri & Mech Univ, MEd, 1980. **Career:** Depauw Univ, asst dean students, 1980-82; E Tex State Univ, head resident advisor, 1982-83; Tex Agri & Mech Univ, stud develop specialist, 1983-88, multicultural servs coordr, 1988-, dept multicultural servs, dir, 1989-, asst pres, 1994; Univ Memphis, assoc dean students, 1998; Salisbury Univ, asst to provost, dir instnl diversity, currently. **Orgs:** Life mem, Alpha Phi Alpha, 1976-; personnel admin, Tex Asn Univ & Col Stud, 1982-; Tex Asn Black Personnel Higher Educ, 1982-; coord bd, Minority recruitment & retention comn, Texas Col & Univ Syst, 1985-88; adv bd, TAMU Nat Youth Sports Prog; adv bd, Minority Leadership Develop; Statewide Retention Comm. **Honors/Awds:** Certificate of Appreciation, Tex Asn Col & Univ Personnel Adminr, 1985; Certificate of Appreciation, Prairie View A&M Univ, 1985; Certificate of Recognition Delta Sigma Pi, 1986; Certificate of Appreciation, Delta Sigma Theta Sor Inc, 1987; Houston Young Black Achiever, Human Enrichment Prog, 1988; John J Koldus Faculty/Staff Award, Texas A&M University, 1989; Fac Distinguished Serv Award. **Business Addr:** Assistant to the Provost, Director of Institutional Diversity, Salisbury University, Holloway Hall 134, 1101 Camden Ave, Salisbury, MD 21801, **Business Phone:** (410)543-6426.

CARREKER, WILLIAM, JR.
Educator. **Personal:** Born Oct 17, 1936, Detroit, MI. **Educ:** City Col San Francisco, AA, 1964; Univ Calif, AB, 1966, MSW, 1968, MPH,1971; Univ Calif, Berkeley. **Career:** Columbia Univ Sch Social Work, asst dir admis, financial aid off; Alameda County Welfare Dept, child welfare worker, 1968-70; Tufts-Delta Health Ctr, intern, 1971; Univ Calif Med Ctr, staff assoc, 1971-72; Golden State Med Asn, proj dir, 1972-73. **Orgs:** Vol coun Jr Leadership Prog, 1968; Calif State Sch Deaf & Blind, 1971; Offenders Aid & Restoration, 1974-75; Nat Asn Black Soc Workers, 1974-77. **Special Achievements:** Publ article Comm Health Agency Partic in Planning; Univ Ambulatory Care Prog; conf bd papers Am Pub Health Asn, 1972. **Military Serv:** Attended, 1955-59. **Business Addr:** 622 W 113th St, New York, NY 10025.*

CARRIER, CLARA L DEGAY
Educator. **Personal:** Born Jan 15, 1939, Weeks Island, LA; daughter of Georgianne Henry DeRoven and Clarence DeGay; divorced; children: Glenda, Melvin T, Marcus W, Robby Bethel, Clarence (deceased), Patrick R &Dawn Nicole. **Educ:** Dillard Univ, attended 1956-57; Southwestern Univ, attended 1976-80. **Career:** JHH Sch Stud Body, pres, 1955-56; JB Livingston Elem PTC, secy, 1961-67; Les Aimu Civic & Social Club, secy, 1974-; Iberia Parish Sch Bd, exec mem, 1979-82, vpres, 1985-, sch bd vice mem, pres; Smile, CAA, teacher; City New Iberia Parks & Recreations, supvr. **Orgs:** Nat Asn Advan Colored People, 1963-65; teacher's aide Acadiana Nursery Head Start, 1965; teacher's aide SMILE CAA Head Start, 1970-76; social worker, SMILE CAA, 1976-79; La Caucus Black Sch Bd Mem, 1980-85; bd dir,Bayou Girls Scout Coun, 1983-84; La Sch Bd Asn, Nat Sch Bd Asn (LSBA); bd dir, La Sch Bd Asn, 1993; bed mem, Iberia Parish Sch Bd. **Honors/Awds:** USL Honor Soc, Psi Beta Honr Soc, 1978; Service Youth Award, Park Elem, 1982-84; The President's Award, Park Elem, 1982-84; Cert Recognition Contrib, Comm Zeta Phi Beta Sor, 1983; Omega's Citizen of the Year, Omega Rho Omicron Chap, 1983; Martin Luther King Jr Award, 1995. **Special Achievements:** First African amercian woman to be elected president in the Iberia Parish School System, 1992. **Home Addr:** 717 Elizabeth St, New Iberia, LA 70560, **Home Phone:** (318)364-2049. **Business Addr:** Board Member, Iberia Parish School Board, 1500 Jane St, New Iberia, LA 70560, **Business Phone:** (337)365-2341.

CARRIER, MARK ANTHONY
Football player, football coach. **Personal:** Born Apr 28, 1968, Lake Charles, LA; married Andrea; children: Mark Anthony III & Lexi. **Educ:** Univ Southern Calif, BA, commun, 1993. **Career:** Player (retired), coach; Chicago Bears, defensive back, 1990-96; Detroit Lions, 1997-99; Wash Redskins, 2000; WGN, Chicago, sports commentator; ESPN XTRA 910, sports commentator; Brophy Prep, Phoenix, sec coach, 2003; Sun Devils, Ariz State Univ, sec coach, 2004-05; Baltimore ravens, sec coach, defensive backs coach, 2006-. **Orgs:** MacKids Found, founder. **Honors/Awds:** Pro Bowl, 1990, 1991, 1993; Defensive Rookie of the Year, Associated Press, 1990; Defensive Rookie of the Year, Football News, 1990; Joe Schmidt Leadership Award winner, 1998, 1999. **Business Addr:** Secondary Coach Football, Baltimore Ravens, 1 Winning Dr, Owings Mills, MD 21117, **Business Phone:** (410)701-4000.*

CARRINGTON, CHRISTINE H.
Psychologist. **Personal:** Born Jun 7, 1941, Palatka, FL; divorced; children: Michael, David, Lisa. **Educ:** Howard Univ, BS, 1962, MS, 1965; Univ MD, PhD Psychol, 1979. **Career:** DC Public Schs, sch psychol, 1966-70, consult sch psychol, 1971-72; Bowie State Col, instr, 1970-74; Fed City Col, asst prof, 1972; Bowie State Col, res consult, 1974-75; Howard Univ Hosp, Psychiatric Inst Wash, Psychiatric Inst Mont Co, consult psychol privileges; Dept Human Res Wash DC, consult psychol; Howard Univ, Couns Serv, couns psychol, asst prof psychiat, chief psychol, Nat Depression Screening Day site dir, currently. **Orgs:** Couns therapist Family Life Ctr Columbia MD; psychol Res Team Howard Univ Med Sch; Am Psychol Asn; Am Asn Psychol Pvt Pract; Asn Counseling Ctr Training Dirs, 1981-; Nat Asn Sch Psychol, 1970-79; Am Asn Univ Profs, 1972-; Nat Asn Black Psychol, 1970-; DC Psychol Asn, 1969; bd dirs, Asn Psychol Internship Ctrs; liaison bd APA; DC Asn Black Psychol 1972-. **Business Addr:** Assistant professor, Pychologist, Howard University, Department of Psychiatry, 2041 Georgia Ave, NW Suite 5B01, Washington, DC 20060, **Business Phone:** (202)865-6100.*

CARRINGTON, LEON T., JR.
Athletic coach. **Career:** St Augustine's Col, assoc athletic dir & coach, currently. **Business Addr:** Head Coach, Associate Athletic director, St Augustine College, 1315 Oakwood Ave, Raleigh, NC 27610-2298, **Business Phone:** (919)516-4236.

CARRINGTON, MARIAN
Business owner. **Career:** Carrington & Carrington Ltd, prin & co-owner, currently. **Orgs:** Fel Leadership Greater Chicago. **Business Phone:** (312)606-0015.*

CARRINGTON, TERRI LYNE
Musician, songwriter, singer. **Personal:** Born Aug 4, 1965, Medford, MA; daughter of Solomon Mathew and Judith Ann Sherwood. **Educ:** Berklee Col Music, Boston, MA, 1983, hon doctorate, 2003. **Career:** Clark Terry, New York, NY, drummer, 1984; David Sanborn, New York, NY, drummer, 1986-; Wayne Shorter, Los Angeles, CA, drummer, 1986-; Stan Getz, Los Angeles, CA, drummer, 1988, 1990; Arsenio Hall Show, Los Angeles, CA, drummer, 1989; Polygram Recs, New York, NY, rec artist, singer, songwriter & drummer, 1988-; Al Jarreau, Los Angeles, CA, drummer, 1991-94; Herbie Hancock, LA, drummer, 1994; Dianne Reeves, Los Angeles, CA, drummer, 1996-97, producer, 1997; Vibe TV show, house drummer, 1997; Jazz Is A Spirit, 2002; Structure, 2004; Univ Southern Calif, prof, currently. **Orgs:** NARAS. **Honors/Awds:** Youth Achiever Award, NAJE, 1981; Boston Music Awards, 1988, 1989; Nominee, Grammy, NARAS, 1990; Nominee, NAACP Image Award, NAACP, 1990; Dr Martin Luther King Music Achiever Award, City Boston, 1991. **Home Addr:** 10524 Arnwood Dr, Lake View Terrace, CA 91342-6801. **Business Phone:** (213)740-2311.

CARROLL, BEVERLY A
Clergy. **Personal:** Born Oct 23, 1946, Baltimore, MD; daughter of James E and Lillian N Mercer; children: Rudolph Weeks II. **Educ:** Univ Md, Col Park, MD, BA, 1981; Towson State Univ, Towson, MD, MA, 1987. **Career:** Archdiocese Baltimore, Baltimore, MD, exec dir, assoc dir, clerk typist, 1967-87; Baltimore's Urban Affairs Off, dir; US Conf Catholic Bishops, Secretariat African Am Catholics, Wash, DC, exec dir, 1988-, founding dir, currently. **Orgs:** Pres, Fr Charles A Hall Sch Bd, 1970-75; secy, Nat Asn Black Cath Adminr, 1985-87; Mayor's Comt Alt Use Firehouses, 1988-; adv comt, Inst Black Cath Studies; bd mem, Secours Health Syst, MD; trustee, Siena Col; bd mem, Nat Black Cath Congress; Holy Name Province Franciscans' African Am Comt; bd mem, Bon Secours Health Syst Md; trustee, Siena Col. **Honors/Awds:** Woman of the Year Award, Zeta Phi Beta Sorority Inc, 1998; Martin Luther King Award; Honorary Doctorate of Human Letters, Siena Col, 1999. **Business Addr:** Executive Director, US Conference of Catholic Bishops' Secretariat, 3211 4th St NE, Washington, DC 20017-1194, **Business Phone:** (202)541-3177.

CARROLL, CHARLENE O.
Executive. **Personal:** Born Apr 17, 1950, Boston, MA; married Ronald Carroll; children: Kiet, Robyn, Ronald. **Educ:** La Newton Beauty Rama, dipl, 1971. **Career:** Charlene's Hair Salon, pres & owner, currently. **Orgs:** Mass Cosmetologists; Nat Cosmetologists; Hair Am; Black Hair Olympics, pres, 1984. **Special Achievements:** Featured in numerous publications including: Black Hair; Shoptalk; Black Enterprise; Essence; Milany Standard Text Book, co-author with Floyd Kenyatta, 1998; consulted for major companies including Revlon, American Beauty Products, Soft Sheen. **Business Addr:** Owner, President, Charlenes Hair Salon Inc, 53 Humboldt Ave, PO Box 365016, Roxbury, MA 02119, **Business Phone:** (617)427-7718.*

CARROLL, DR. CONSTANCE MARIE
School administrator. **Personal:** Born Sep 12, 1945, Baltimore, MD. **Educ:** Duquesne Univ, BA, 1966; Knubly Univ Athens Greece, cert, 1967; Univ Pittsburg, MA, 1969, PhD. **Career:** John Hay Whitney Scholarship Marshall fel Classics, 1968; Univ Pittsburgh, Col Arts & Sci Advising Ctr, asst dir, 1970-71, dir freshman advising, 1971-72; Univ Maine, Portand-Gorham, Col Arts & Sci, from asst dean to assoc dean, from asst prof classics to assoc prof classics, 1972-77; Marin Community Col District, interim chancellor, 1979-80; Indian Valley Col,pres, 1977-83; Saddle back Col, pres, 1983-93; San Diego Mesa Col, pres, 1993-2004; San Diego Community Col District, chancellor, 2004-. **Orgs:** Calif Coun Humanities; adv bd, Inst Leadership Develop; adv bd, Policy Analysis Calif Educ; Nat Humanities Fac; Calif Post secondary Educ Community Task Force Women & Minorities; evaluator, Western Asn Schs & Cols; Am Philol Asn; Class Asn New England; Vergilian Soc Am; Nat Asn Black Prof Women Higher Educ; Coun Cols Arts & Sci; Community Concerns Women New England Cols & Univ; bd mem, Film Study Ctr Portland; Commonwealth Club Calif; Community Concerns

Women CA Cols & Univ; Coun Black Am Affairs Western Region; Asn Calif Community Col Adminr; Nat Adv Coun Continuing Educ, 1980-81; bd dir, Nat Inst Leadership Develop, 1985-,chair, 1987-89; mem, Calif Coun Humanities, 1985-89, chair, 1987-89; Delta Sigma Theta Sorority, Inc., 1988-; bd dir, Community Col Humanities Asn, 1989-; mem & founding chair, Community Col Leadership Develop Initiatives & Found, 1999-; Am Asn Community Col; Coun Higher Educ, 1999-2001; Calif Joint Legislative Comt, 2000-02; Calif Dept Educ Prof Develop Task Force, 2000-02. **Honors/Awds:** Col of Arts & Sciences Distinguished Teaching Award, Univ Pittsburgh, 1971; Outstanding Educators of America, 1975; Excellence in Education Award, YWCA, S Orange County, 1984; Woman of Distinction Award, San Diego Chapter Nat Coun Negro Women, Inc., 1993; President of the Year Award, Am Asn Women Community Cols, 1992; Distinguished Humanities Educator Award, Community Col Humanities Asn, 1993; Harry Buttimer Distinguished Administrator Award, Asn Calif Community Col Adminr, 1996; Pioneering Women of Achievement Award, Catfish Club, 2003; Local Heroes Award, KPBS/Union Bank Calif, 2003; Visionaries Award, Econ Opportunity, 2004. **Special Achievements:** Author of numerous publishers; Article :"Shaking the Leadership Blues", 2002. **Business Addr:** Chancellor, San Diego Community College, 10440 Black Mountain Rd, San Diego, CA 92108, **Business Phone:** (858)536-7800.

CARROLL, DIAHANN (CAROL DIAHANN JOHNSON)
Actor. **Personal:** Born Jul 17, 1935, Bronx, NY; daughter of John Johnson and Mabel Faulk; married Vic Damone, Jan 1, 1987 (divorced 1996); children: Suzanne Ottilie; married Robert DeLeon (died 1977); married Fred Glusman, Jan 1, 1973 (divorced). **Educ:** NY Univ; Manhattan's Sch Performing Arts. **Career:** Films: Carmen Jones, 1954; Porgy & Bess, 1959; Goodbye Again, 1961; Paris Blues, 1961; Hurry Sundown, 1967; The split, 1968; Claudine, 1974; The Five Heartbeats, 1991; Eve's Bayou, 1997; TV Series: "The Man in the Moon", 1960; "Death Scream", 1975; "I Know Why the Caged Bird Sings", 1979; "Julia", 1984-87; The Sweetest Gift, 1998; "Having Our Say: The Delany Sisters First 100 Years", 1999; "The Courage to Love", 2000; "Sally Hemings: An American Scandal", 2000; "The Natalie Cole Story", 2000; "The Ct", 2002; "Half & Half", 2002; "Strong Med", 2003; "Whoopi", 2003; "Soul Food", 2004; "Grey's Anatomy", 2006; "Hug & Tell", 2008; "Back To You", 2008; "White Collar", 2009. **Orgs:** AEA; AFTRA; SAG; hon mem, Alpha Kappa Alpha Sorority Inc. **Honors/Awds:** Tony Award, 1962; Golden Globe, 1969; Oscar Nomination for "Claudine", 1974; Recipient Nat Asn Advan Colored People eighth Image Award (Best Actress), Black Filmmaker's Hall of Fame, 1976; Crystal Award, Women in Film, 1993; Lucy Award, 1998; Ten Int Best Dressed List; Patron Performer John F Kennedy Ctr; Two Emmy Nominations; Entertainer of the Year, Cue Mag; Won first prize on TV's "Chance Of A Lifetime"; Groundbreaking Show, 2003. **Special Achievements:** Author, Diahann: An Autobiography, 1986; Own Designer Label of clothes, 1998; First African American actress to star in her own television series. **Home Addr:** PO Box 57593, Sherman Oaks, CA 91403. **Business Addr:** Actress, Jeffrey Lane & Associates Inc, 6363 Wilshire Blvd, Los Angeles, CA 90048, **Business Phone:** (323)852-0492.

CARROLL, GEORGE D
Judge. **Personal:** Born Jan 6, 1923, Brooklyn, NY; married Janie. **Educ:** Brooklyn Col, BA, cum laude, 1943; Brooklyn Law Sch, JD, cum laude, 1950. **Career:** Judge (retired); Richmond City Coun, coun mem, 1961; City Ricmond, mayor, 1964; Gov Edmund E Brown, judge, 1965; Bay Munic Ct, judge, 1970, 1976, 1982, 1985. **Orgs:** CA Bar Asn, 1953; NY Bar Asn, 1950; Judicial Coun, Nat Bar Asn; CA Judge Asn; Jud Admin Sect, Am Bar Asn; pres, Richmond Bar Asn; life mem, Nat Asn Advan Colored People. **Honors/Awds:** John Russwurm Award, 1965; Man of the Year, San Francisco Sun Reporter, 1964; Hall of Fame, Nat Bar Asn, 2002. **Military Serv:** AUS, sgt, 1943-45. **Home Addr:** 280 Washington Ct, Richmond, CA 94801.

CARROLL, JAMES S
Lawyer. **Personal:** Born Sep 17, 1945, Brooklyn, NY; son of James S and Mabel G Duncan; married Celia Antonia, Mar 14, 1981; children: Jason Sean, Jamaal Samuel, Khadijah & Jameson. **Educ:** NY Univ, BA, 1966; Howard Law Sch, JD, 1970. **Career:** Nat Conf Black Lawyers, atty, 1970-72; Com Develop Harlem Assertion Rights, dir, 1972-73; Pvt Pract, atty, 1973-79; VI, asst US atty, 1979-92, sr litigation coun, 1992-95, civil chief, 1995-98, 2001-; US Atty's Off, Chief Civil Div, first asst US atty, 1998-2001, civil chief, currently. **Orgs:** Nat Bar Asn; Am Bar Asn; Nat Asn Asst US Attys; Nat Black Prosecutors Asn. **Honors/Awds:** Root-Tilden Scholarship; Reginald Heber Smith Fel, 1970-72; Directors Award, Atty Gen US, 1990; Special Achievement Award, US Dept Justice, 1992, Spec Commendation, 1995. **Business Addr:** Civil Chief, US Attorney Office, Rm 260 5500 Veterans Dr, St Thomas, Virgin Islands of the United States 00802-6424, **Business Phone:** (340)774-5757.

CARROLL, JOE BARRY
Basketball player, businessperson. **Personal:** Born Jul 24, 1958, Pine Bluff, AK. **Educ:** Purdue Univ, BA, 1980. **Career:** Basketball player (retired), businessperson; Golden State Warriors, ctr, 1980-87; Houston Rockets, 1987-88; NJ Nets, 1988-90; Denver Nuggets,1990-91; Phoenix Suns, 1991; businessperson, currently. **Honors/Awds:** Rookie-of-the-Year, Basketball Digest, 1980-81; All-Rookie Team, 1980-81; First-Team All-Big Ten, 1980; First Team All-American, 1980; NBA All-Star Team, 1987. *

CARROLL, LAWRENCE WILLIAM, III
Television journalist. **Personal:** Born Dec 11, 1950, Chicago, IL; son of Lawrence William Carroll Jr and Annie Lee Goode; married Roman Abebe Wolder-Selassie, Apr 19, 1986; children: Yenea Lucille & Lawrence William IV. **Educ:** Pomona Col, Claremont, Calif, BA, 1973. **Career:** KABC-TV, Los Angeles, Calif, reporter & anchor, 1973-89; KCAL-TV, Los Angeles, Calif, news anchor, 1989-; KFWB News 980, news anchor, 2001-; KSPC-FM, news dir & prog dir; KHJ-TV Channel 9, asst producer. **Orgs:** Acad TV Arts & Sci, 1989-; Radio TV News Asn, 1989-. **Honors/Awds:** Numerous honors including an Emmy award, Image Award nomination, 6 Emmy nominations, 7 Golden Mike Awards, an Associated Press Award and Grand award. **Business Addr:** News Anchor, KFWB News 980, 5670 Wilshire Blvd Suite 200, Los Angeles, CA 90036, **Business Phone:** (323)525-0980.

CARROLL, DR. NATALIE L
Physician, president (organization). **Personal:** Born Jan 26, 1950, Nashville, TN. **Educ:** Lake Forest Col, BA; Meharry Med Col, MD, 1974. **Career:** Wash Hosp Ctr, Wash, DC, surgery intern, 1974-75, ob gyn resident, 1975-78; Darnell Army Hosp, chair, 1978-81; Hermann Memorial Hosp, assoc clinical instr, 1980-, staff physician, 1980-, quality assurance sub-committee, 1980-;Howard Univ Col Med, externship; Baylor Col Med, externship; pvt pract, obstetrician & gynecologist, currently. **Orgs:** Alpha Kappa Alpha Sorority Inc; Meharry Alumni Asn; pres, Nat Med Asn, 2002-. **Honors/Awds:** March of Dimes' Outstanding Service Award; Crusade InterNat Scholarship Award, 1974; Outstanding Service Award, March Dimes; NMA Award, 2000. **Special Achievements:** First African American female to complete an internship in obstetrics & gynecology and the first female to complete an internship in surgery at Washington Hospital Center in Washington, DC; 100 most influential black Americans, Ebony Mag, 2003. **Business Addr:** President, National Medical Association, 1012 10th St NW, Washington, DC 20001.

CARROLL, RAOUL LORD
Lawyer, administrator. **Personal:** Born Mar 16, 1950, Washington, DC; son of John Thomas and Gertrude B Jenkins; married Elizabeth Jane Coleman, Mar 22, 1979; children: Alexandria Nicole & Christina Elizabeth. **Educ:** Morgan State Col, BS, 1972; St John's Univ, Sch Law, JD, 1975; Georgetown Univ Law Ctr, attended 1981. **Career:** Attorney (retired): Dept Justice, asst US atty, 1979-80; US Bd Veterans Appeals, assoc mem, 1980-81; Hart Carroll & Chavers, partner, 1981-86; Bishop Cook Purcell & Reynolds, partner, 1986-89; US Dept Veterans Affairs, Wash, DC, gen coun, 1989-91; US Dept Housing & Urban Develop, pres, Govt Nat Mortgage Asn, 1991-92; chief operating officer, MR Beal & Co, New York, NY, 1992-95; Christalex Partners, partner, chmn, 1997-. **Orgs:** Wash Bar Asn, 1976-, DC Bar, 1979-; New York Bar Asn, Los Angeles, CA, 1976-2003; Nat Bar Asn, 1977-; pres, Black Asst US Atty Asn, 1981-83; chmn, Christian Brothers Investment Servs Inc; chmn, Am Ctr Int Leadership, 1985; former trustee, The Enterprise Found. **Special Achievements:** "After the Dust Settles, Other Modes of Relief," The Advocate Vol 10 No 6, 1978. **Military Serv:** AUS, capt, 1975-79; Joint Serv Commendation Medal, Army Commendation Medal. **Home Addr:** 585 M Rosemore Ave, Los Angeles, CA 90004. **Business Addr:** Partner, Christalex Partners, 6101 16th St NW Apt 312, Washington, DC 20011, **Business Phone:** (202)726-0776.

CARROLL, ROBERT F
Executive. **Personal:** Born Jun 18, 1931, Bartow, FL; son of Robert F Carroll Sr (deceased) and Emma H Carroll (deceased); married Gwendolyn Jackson; children: Tosca, Denise & Robert III. **Educ:** Fla A&M Univ, BA, 1960; Univ Conn, attended 1961; Columbia Univ, MA, 1963; Yale Univ, attended 1964. **Career:** NY City Dept Social Serv, dep comt, 1967-71; NY City Human Resources Admin, dep admin, 1971-74; City Col NY, vpres, 1974-78; Cong Chas B Rangel, chief staff, 1978-81; R F Carroll & Co, chmn & chief exec officer. **Orgs:** Am Asn Pub Admin, 1973-; Bd mem, WNET TV, 1982-85; Pub Rels Soc Am; Am Asn Polit Sci; Alpha Phi Alpha Fraternity; bd gov, Mill River Country Club; bd mem, exec comt, Metrop Golf Asn. **Honors/Awds:** Educator of Year, Asn Black Educrs, 1975; Distinguished Service Award, Univ Taiwan, 1979; Public Service Award, US Dept HEW, 1970. **Military Serv:** USAF, sgt; Service medal, 1955. **Home Addr:** 37 Reynolds Rd, Glen Cove, NY 11542.

CARROLL, ROCKY
Actor. **Personal:** Born Jul 8, 1963, Cincinnati, OH. **Educ:** Attended Sch Creative & Performing Arts. **Career:** Films: Born on the Fourth of July, 1989; Prelude to a Kiss, 1992; Fathers & Sons, 1992; The Chase, 1994; Crimson Tide, 1995; The Great White Hype, 1996; Best Laid Plans, 1999; The Ladies Man, 2000; Spider-Man 2, 2004; tv series: Roc, 1991-94; Chicago Hope, 1996-2000; The Agency, 2001; tv movie: Five Desperate Hours, 1997; TV guest appearances: Law & Order, 1990; Gargoyles, 1994-96; Early Edition, 1998; Welcome to New York, 2000; The West Wing, 2001; Family Law, 2001; "The Agency", 2002; "Boston Legal", 2004; "Am Dreams", 2005; "Invasion", 2006; "The Game", 2006; "Haunt You Every Day", 2007; "Grey's Anatomy", 2007; "Yes Man", 2008. **Business Addr:** Actor, Starstruck Films, c/o Shelley Browning, 100 Universal City Plz Bldg 1320 Suite 3D, Universal City, CA 91608, **Business Phone:** (818)777-2868.

CARROLL, RODNEY
Association executive, executive. **Personal:** Born in Philadelphia, PA. **Career:** UPS, part-time unloader, 1978, hub mgr, Willow Grove Facil, 1983, opers div mgr, Phila Air Hub; Business Interface (formerly Welfare Work Partnership), vpres bus outreach, 1998-2000, pres & chief exec officer, 2000-. **Honors/Awds:** Mickey Leland Humanitarian Award, Cong Black Caucus, 2000; Martin Luther King Jr Humanitarian Award, Univ Ga Perimeter Col, 2003. **Special Achievements:** Author: No Free Lunch, 2002. **Business Addr:** Chief Executive Officer, President, Business Interface, 1150 Conn Ave NW Suite 525, Washington, DC 20036, **Business Phone:** (202)955-3005.

CARROLL, SALLY G.
Association executive. **Personal:** Born in Roanoke, VA. **Educ:** Essex Jr Col. **Career:** retired: Newark Police Dept, 1949-51; Essex Co Sheriff's Office, ct attend, 1951. **Orgs:** trustee, Bd Gr Newark Urban Coalition; Newark Museum; Milt Campbell Youth Ctr; chmn, Newark NAACP Day Care Bd; pres, Batons Inc; mem, Nat Asn Negro Bus & Prof Women's Club; adv bd, Proj, COED; Hich Impact Anti-Crime Bd; Affirmative Action Review Coun; Citizens Adv Bd Mayor's Policy & Develop Office; life mem, 1970-, former secy, treas, pres, Newark Br NAACP. **Honors/Awds:** Woman of the Year Award, Frontiers Internat; Sojourner Truth Award, Bus & Prof Women; Outstanding Negro Woman, Imperial Ct Isis PHA; 1st woman NJ appointed, NJ St Parole Bd six yr term. *

CARROLL, DR. WILLIAM
Writer, chief executive officer, educator. **Personal:** Born Jan 4, 1936, Brooklyn, NY; son of Willie Ann and Grover Cleveland Chatman; married Thelma Ellen Young, Nov 26, 1966; children: William Stewart & Valinda Sue. **Educ:** Harvard Univ, Cambridge Mass, 1964; Norfolk State Col, Norfolk Va, BA, 1965; Temple Univ, Philadelphia Pa, MA, 1967; Univ NC, Chapel Hill NC, PhD, 1978; NC Cent Univ, attended 1969. **Career:** Educator (retired), chief executive officer, writer; Norfolk State Univ, Norfolk, Va, instr, 1967-73, asst prof, 1974-77, assoc prof, 1978-95, prof, 1995-99, prof emer, 1999; William & Thelma Carroll Co, chief executive officer & publisher, currently; Co-author: Rhetoric & Readings for Writing, 1981, Variations on Humankind: An Introduction to World Literature, 1990; author: "George Moses Horton," Dictionary of Literary Biography, 1986; Songs, Scenes, & Sentiments: Lyrical Works of Dr. Bill (poetry), 2003; THE UNTIED SATS ON AMERICCAN: & Other Computer Assisted Writing Errors (humorous reference book), 2005; A GROWN-UP'S GARDEN OF VIRTUES: Inspirational Poems by Dr. Bill (poetry) 2007; contributor, Fifty More Southern Writers; Dunbar's We Wear the Mask in Masterplots II Revised, 2002; Norfolk Virginian-Pilot, guest columnist, 2003. **Orgs:** Alpha Kappa Mu Nat Hon Soc, 1963-; Norfolk State Univ Alumni Asn, 1965-; Col Lang Asn, 1967-70, 1984-; Am Asn Univ Prof, 1969-; vpres, Tidewater Fair Housing Inc, 1969-70; Nat Coun Teachers Eng, 1975-86, 1988-; Sigma Tau Delta Int Hon Soc, 1979-; NAACP, 1982-; publicity dir, Voter Regist, 1982-84; United Coun Citizens & Civic Leagues, 1982-; adv bd, Planned Parenthood Southeastern Va, 1993; bd mem, George Moses Horton Soc; lifemem, Middle Atlantic Writer's Asn, 1987-, vpres, 1992-94; chair, NSU Retirees Asn, 2002-. **Honors/Awds:** Summer Sch Coop Scholar, Harvard Univ, 1964; Teaching Fel, Univ NC, 1971. **Special Achievements:** Weekly poetry column in New Jour & Guide newspaper, 2003-04. **Military Serv:** AUS, specialist E4, 1959-62. **Home Addr:** 5903 Clear Springs Rd, Virginia Beach, VA 23464, **Home Phone:** (757)420-5055. **Business Addr:** Chief Executive Officer, Publisher, William & Thelma Carroll Co, PO Box 13752, Chesapeake, VA 23325, **Business Phone:** (757)823-9167.

CARRUTHERS, DR. GEORGE ROBERT
Physicist. **Personal:** Born Oct 1, 1939, Cincinnati, OH; son of George and Sophia. **Educ:** Univ Ill, BS, aeronaut eng, 1961, MS, nuclear eng, 1962, PhD, aeronaut & astron eng, 1964. **Career:** US Naval Res Lab, res physicist, 1964-82, head ultraviolet measurements br, 1980-82, Ultraviolet Measurements Group, Space Sci Div, sr astrophysicist head, 1982-. **Orgs:** AAAS; Am Astron Soc; Am Geophys Union; Am Inst Aeronaut & Astronaut; chmn edit & rev comt, edit j, Nat Tech Asn, 1983-; Soc Photo-optical Instrumentation Engrs. **Honors/Awds:** Arthur S Flemming Award, Wash Jaycees, 1970; Exceptional Achievement Scientific Award Medal, NASA, 1972; Samuel Cheevers Award, Nat Tech Asn, 1977; Black Engineer of the Year, 1987; Warner Prize, Am Astron Soc; NSF fel; Honorary Doctor of Engineering, Mich Technol Univ; First Recipient of NIS Outstanding Scientist Award, 2000. **Business Addr:** Astrophysicist, US Naval Research Laboratory, Space Science Division, 4555 Overlook Ave SW, PO Box 7645, Washington, DC 20375-5320.

CARRY, REV. HELEN WARD
School administrator. **Personal:** Born in Chicago, IL; daughter of Anderson and Minnie; widowed; children: Ronald & Julius J III. **Educ:** Xavier Univ New Orleans, La, BA, 1946; Loyola Univ Chicago, MEd, 1963; Calif Coastal Univ, EdD, 2000. **Career:** Chicago Pub Schs, teacher 1952, adjust counr 1962; Chicago Pub Schs Head Start, coord, 1965-69; Webster Sch, Chicago Pub Schs, asst prin 1965, prin, 1970; Johnnie Colemon Inst, dir; Christ Universal Temple, Chicago, IL, asst minister, 1990, exec minister, dir, currently; Johnnie Colemon Acad, dir & prin, 1999. **Orgs:** Consult, David Cook Publishing; Delta Sigma Theta Sor. **Honors/Awds:** Outstanding Prin, Dist 8 Chicago Pub Schs; Black Rose Award, League BlackWomen, 1987; Lifetime Career Achievement Award, Nat Pub, 1990; Positive Image Award, Westside Ctr Truth, 1990; Tubman & Truth Woman of the Yr Award, 1992. **Business Addr:** Assistant to the Minister, Christ Universal Temple, 11901 S Ashland Ave, Chicago, IL 60643-5434, **Business Phone:** (773)568-2282.*

CARRY, JULIUS J
Actor. **Personal:** Born Mar 12, 1952, Chicago, IL; son of Julius J Jr and Helen W. **Educ:** Quincy Col, attended 1972; Loyola-19Marymount Univ, BA, 1977, MA, 1978. **Career:** TV Series: "Dribble", 1980; "Goldie & the Bears", 1985; "Independence", 1987; "Why on Earth", 1988; "Perry Mason: The Case of the All-Star Assassin", 1989; "Jake Spanner, Private Eye", 1989; "Doctor, Doctor", 1989; "Murphy Brown", 1992-93; "The Adventures of Briscoe Country Jr", 1993; "Misery Loves Co", 1995; "Cosby", 1997; "Two Guys, a Girl & a Pizza Place", 1998; TV Movies: Goldie & the Bears, 1984; Police Story: Monster Manor, 1988; Jake Spanner, Private Eye, 1989; Perry Mason: The Case of the All-Star Assassin, 1989; Columbo: Columbo Likes the Nightlife, 2003; "Half & Half", 2003; JAG, 2004; "The 12th Man", 2006; "The Unit", 2006; "Films: The Fish That Saved Pittsburgh", 1979; The Last Dragon, 1985; The Man With One Red Shoe, 1985; World Gone Wild, 1988; The New Guy, 2002; actor, currently. **Special Achievements:** childrens book The Alphabet Calendar Fun Book. **Business Addr:** Actor, Innovative Artists Talent & Literary Agency, 1999 Ave Stars Suite 2850, Beverly Hills, CA 90210, **Business Phone:** (310)553-5200.

CARSLEY, ELAINE O. See DAVIS, DR. ELAINE CARSLEY.

CARSON, ANDRE
Congressperson (U.S. federal government). **Personal:** Born in Indianapolis, IN; married Mariama Carson; children: Salimah. **Educ:** Concordia University-Wisconsin, Bachelors Degree in Criminal Justice Management; Indiana Wesleyan University, Masters Degree, Business Management. **Career:** Indiana State Excise Police Department, Investigative Officer; Department of Homeland Security's Intelligence Fusion Center, 2006; Indianapolis City-County Council Member; Member of the U.S. House of Representatives, 2008. **Orgs:** Indy Parks Kennedy-King Park Advisory Board; Citizens Neighborhood Coalition; Financial Services Committee. **Business Addr:** 2455 Rayburn House Office Building, Washington, DC 20515, **Business Phone:** (202)225-4011.*

CARSON, DR. BENJAMIN SOLOMON
Physician, neurosurgeon. **Personal:** Born Sep 18, 1951, Detroit, MI; son of Robert Solomon and Sonya Copeland; married Candy, Jul 6, 1975; children: Murray Nedlands, Benjamin Jr & Rhoeyce Harrington. **Educ:** Yale Univ, New Haven, CT, BA, 1973; Univ Mich, Ann Arbor MI, MD, 1977; Gettysburg Col, Hon Doctor Sci, 1988. **Career:** Johns Hopkins Univ, Baltimore MD, chief resident neuro surg, 1982-83; asst prof, neuro surg, 1984, asst prof, oncol, 1984, asst prof, pediat, 1987,dir pediat neuro surg, 1984-91; assoc prof, 1991-99; prof, 1999-; Queen Elizabeth II Med Ctr, Perth, Australia, sr registr neuro surg, 1983-84. **Orgs:** AAAS, 1982-; Nat Pediat Oncol Group, 1985-; Nat Med Asn, 1986-; honorary chmn, Regional Red Cross Cabinet, 1987-; med adv bd, C Cancer Found, 1987-; life mem, Maryland Cong Parents & Teachers, 1988-; Am Asn Neurol Surgeons, 1989-; Cong Neurol Surgeons, 1989-; dir: Kellogg Co, Costco Whole sale Corp; trustee, Yale Univ; pres co-founder, Carson Scholars Fund. **Honors/Awds:** Citations for Excellence, Detroit City Coun, 1987, Philadelphia City Coun, 1987, Mich State Senate, 1987, PA House of Representatives, 1989, Detroit Medical Society, 1987; American Black Achievement Award, Bus & Prof, Ebony & Johnson Publs, 1988; Clinical Practitioner of the Year, Nat Med Asn Region II, 1988; Certificate of Honor for Outstanding Achievement in the Field of Medicine, Nat Medical Fellowship Inc, 1988; Candle Award for Science and Technology, Morehouse Col, 1989; Black book Humanitarian Award, Black book Publ, 1991; Excellence in Leadership Award, Center for New Black Leadership, 2000; Spingarn Medal, NAACP, 2006; Presidential Medal of Freedom, 2008. **Special Achievements:** Numerous scientific publications (books and journals 1982-); numerous natl network television appearances (med & social issues), 1985-; performed first intrauterine shunting procedure for a hydrocephalic twin, 1986, first successful separation of occipital craniopagus Siamese twins, 1987; author: Gifted Hands (autobiographic sketch), 1990; Think Big; Big Picture. **Home Addr:** 15117 Old Hanover Rd, Upperco, MD 21155, **Home Phone:** (410)955-7888. **Business Addr:** Director of Pediatric Neurosurgery, Johns Hopkins Medical Institute, 600 N Wolfe St Harvey 811, Baltimore, MD 21287-8811, **Business Phone:** (410)955-7888.

CARSON, CURTIS C., JR.
Judge. **Personal:** Born Feb 5, 1920, Cowpens, SC; married Vida Timbers; children: Curtis III, Gregory, MD, Carol & Esq. **Educ:** Va State Col, AB; Univ Pa Law Sch, LLB; Nat Judicial Col, Reno, NV, 1975. **Career:** Judge (retired); Law Off Raymond Alexander, pvt practice, 1946-49, sole practitioner, 1946-52; Trial Asst Dist Atty, 1952-57; pvt practice, 1957-71; Philadelphia Community Pleas Ctr, 1972-90; sr judge, 1993. **Orgs:** Philadelphia Bar Asn; charter mem, Barristers Asn; Judicial Section Nat Bar Asn; Phila Anti-Poverty Comn; Phila Bar Rep, Bd Community Legal Serv; Phila Law Examiners, 1966-69; Am Arbit Asn, 1966-71; bd & chmn, Parkside YMCA, 1950-71; Philadelphia Nat Advan Asn Coloed People, 1946-80, chmn, Legal Redress Comt, 1962-69; John M Langston Law Asn, 1945-50; pres, Const Philadelphia Barrister Asn; Pa Sentencing Comn, 1980-86; elder, German town Community Presbyterian Church. **Special Achievements:** Appointed by the Judicial College as Faculty Advisor, 1979, 1983; Appointed by the Judicial College to serve on its Committee to critique apposed course to be inserted in the College Curriculum. *

CARSON, EMMETT D.
Association executive. **Personal:** Born Oct 6, 1959, Chicago, IL; son of Emmett and Mary. **Educ:** Morehouse Col, BA, econs, 1980; Princeton Univ, MPA, pub & int affairs, 1983, PhD, pub & int affairs, 1985. **Career:** Libr Cong, social legislation anal, 1985-86; Joint Ctr Political & Econ Studies, proj dir, 1986-89; Univ Md, Col Park, adj lectr, 1987-89;Ford Found, Rights & Social Justice Prog, prog officer, 1989-92; Governance & Pub Policy Prog, prog officer, 1989-92; Minneapolis Found, pres & chief exec officer, 1994-06; Silicon Valley Community Found, pres & chief exec officer, 2006-. **Orgs:** chair, bd dirs, Asn Black Found Exec, 1994-95; bd dirs, Nat Econs Asn, 1993-95; bd chair, Coun Found, Blue Cross Blue Shield Minn, Southern Educ Found, Univ Minn Humphrey Inst Pub Policy. **Honors/Awds:** Phi Beta Kappa, 1981; Grad Fel, Princeton Univ, 1981-85; Dissertation Award, Nat Econ Asn, 1985; Super Performance Award, Joint Ctr Polit & Econ Studies, 1988; E B Williams Econs & Bus Award, Morehouse Col, 1981. **Special Achievements:** Designed and directed the first Nat comparative study of the charitable giving and volunteer behavior of Black and White Am; internationally recognized as a catalyst for progressive social change. **Business Addr:** President, Chief Executive Officer, Silicon Valley Community Foundation, 1700 S El Camino Real Suite 300, San Mateo, CA 94402-3049.*

CARSON, IRMA
Counselor, executive director. **Personal:** Born Jun 24, 1935, Monroe, LA; children: Sharon, Karen, Camille. **Educ:** Bakersfield Col, AA; Calif State Col, BA; Kern Co Law Enforcement Acad, Grad; Univ Santa Barbara, Cert Criminal Justice; Univ CA, Cert Instruction; CA Teaching Credential. **Career:** Bakersfield City Sch Dist; bd mem; Bakersfield City Police, police sergeant; Bakersfield City Schools, pres bd educ; Ebony Coun Ctr, dir, exec dir, currently; Bakersfield City Coun, vice mayor, 1998-00; City of Bakersfield, coun mem, currently. **Orgs:** Am Bus Women's Asn; Kern Co Child Sex Abuse Treatment Comt; Black Hist Comn; BAPAC; Nat Asn Advan Colored People; CFBL; Cain Mem AME Church; co-auth "The Handbook for Battered Women"; Rape Prevention Workshop; Parent's Rights & Responsibilities Workshop; Nat Polit Inst Workshop, 1984; NSBA Urban Bd Educ Coun; State Supt, Ethic Adv Coun; Dem Nominee State Assembly, 1992. **Honors/Awds:** Officer of the Yr, 1974; Nat Asn Advan Colored People Comm Serv Award, 1979; People's Baptist Church Community Serv Award, 1980; Black Hist Parade Grant Marshal, 1980; The Golden West Leadership Award, 1981; Elks Lodge Community Serv Award, 1981; CA Alliance of Black Educators Distinguish Serv Award, 1982; Comm Appreciation Reception, 1982; Black Hist Parade Grand Marshal, 1983. **Business Addr:** Council member, Ward 1, City of Bakersfield, 1501 Truxtun Ave, Bakersfield, CA 93301.*

CARSON, JOHN H., JR.
Lawyer. **Career:** Pvt Prac, atty. **Business Addr:** Attorney, Private Practice, Rockefeller Bldg Suite 800, 614 Superior Ave NW, Cleveland, OH 44113-1306, **Business Phone:** (216)795-1515.*

CARSON, JOHNNIE
Diplomat, ambassador, government official. **Personal:** Born Apr 7, 1943, Chicago, IL; son of Dupree and Aretha Rhodes; married Anne Diemer Carson, Feb 9, 1969; children: Elizabeth Diemer, Michael Dupree & Katherine Anne. **Educ:** Drake Univ, BA, 1965; Univ London, Sch Oriental & Afr Studies, MA, 1975. **Career:** Am Embassy in Lagos, Nigeria, Consular & Polit Officer, 1969-71; Namibia Bur Intelligence & Res, 1971-74; Am Embassy, Maputo, Mozambique, dep chief, 1975-78; US House Rep, staff dir, Africa Subcommittee, 1979-82; Dept State, desk officer, Angola, Mozambique; Am Embassy in Gaborone, Botswana, dep chief, 1986-90; Republic Uganda, US Ambassador, 1991-94; Republic Zimbabwe, US Ambassador, 1995-97; Am Embassy, Harare, Zimbabwe, ambassador, 1995-99; US Dept State, Africa Bur, prin dept asst secy, 1997-99; Am Embassy, Nairobi, Kenya, ambassador, 1999-2003; Nat Defense Univ, sr vpres, 2003-. **Honors/Awds:** Superior Honor Award, Dept State, 1997; Presidential Service Award, White House, 1998; Doctor of Public Affairs, Drake Univ, 1998; Champion of Prevention Award, Ctrs for Disease Control, 2003. **Business Addr:** Senior Vice President, National Defense University, Ft Lesley J McNair, 300 5th Ave Bldg 62, Washington, DC 20319-5066, **Business Phone:** (202)685-4700.

CARSON, LISA. See CARSON, LISA NICOLE.

CARSON, LISA NICOLE (LISA CARSON)
Actor. **Personal:** Born Jul 12, 1969, Brooklyn, NY; daughter of Lester Carson and Fannie Carson. **Career:** TV: "ER", recurring role, 1996-2001; "Ally McBeal", 1997-2002; tv movie, Aftershock: Earthquake in NY, 1999; Film roles: Jason's Lyric, 1994; Devil in a Blue Dress, 1995; Love Jones, 1997; Eve's Bayou, 1997; Life, 1999; Ally, 1999. **Honors/Awds:** Actor Guild Award for Outstanding Performance, 1999. **Special Achievements:** Voted to "10 Sexiest Women of the Year", Black Men Mag, 2000.

CARSON, LOIS MONTGOMERY
Administrator. **Personal:** Born Jul 3, 1931, Memphis, TN; married Harry L; children: Harry Jr, William, Patricia, John, Brian & Felicia. **Educ:** Wilberforce Univ; Calif State Col, BA, 1967; Univ Calif, MA, 1974; Calif State, Secondary Teaching Credential, 1970. **Career:** Freewalk Gazette, 1963-64; San Bernardino County Probation Dept, counr, 1964-68; precinct reporter, 1964-69; San Bernardino County Sch, teacher, 1968-72; Am News, staff, 1969; Univ Calif, dir proj Upward Bound, 1973-76; Calif State Univ, prof eng & educ, 1977-78; Comm Serv Dept, dep dir, 1978-80; Community Action Partnership Riverside Co, exec dir, currently. **Orgs:** Calif Teachers Asn, 1968-73; Calif Conf Black Elected officials, 1973-74; Mil Acad Bd 38th Cong Dist, 1973-74; past pres bd, San Bernardino Comm Col Dist, 1973; state vice chairperson, Calif Adv Health Coun, 1976-; Nat Bd Asn Comm Col Trustees, 1978; Delta Kappa Gamma Int Soc; Alpha Kappa Alpha Sorority; Calif OEO Adv Bd; secy, Nat Bd Nat Coun Negro Women; bd dir, Nat Asn Clean Air Agencies. **Honors/Awds:** Distinguished Achievement Award, 1969; Calif State Assembly Public Service Award, 1973; Woman of Yr, Inland Empire Sect NCNW, 1973; Black Woman of Yr, San Bernardino 1974; Women of Achievement, San Bernardino, 1975; Good Citizenship Award, Alpha Kappa Alpha, 1976; Outstanding Achievement Award, Far Western Region, 1979 & 84; Public Administrator of the Year, 1980; Calif State Distinguished Alumnus, 1980. **Business Addr:** Executive Director, Community Action Partnership, Riverside County, 2038 Iowa Ave Suite B102, Riverside, CA 92507, **Business Phone:** (909)955-4900.

CARSON, REGINA M. E.
Educator. **Personal:** Born in Washington, DC. **Educ:** Howard Univ Col Pharm, BS, 1973; Loyola Col, Baltimore, MD, MBA, mkt, 1987, health servs admin, 1987. **Career:** Provident Hosp, Baltimore, MD, dir, pharm servs, 1979-86; Ridgeway Manor, Catonsville, MD, mgr, pharm servs, 1986-87; Univ MD, Sch Pharm, asst prof, 1987-88; Howard Univ, Col Pharm & Pharmaceut Scis, coordr prof pract prog, asst prof, 1988-95; Off Educ, consult, 1990-; Marrell Consult, consult, 1995-; Sunrise Towson, MD, Assisted Living Residence, exec dir, 1997-. **Orgs:** Chair, Bus & Econ Develop Comn, 1991-92; Nat Black MBAs, DC Chap; bd mem, Auxiliary, Northwest Hosp Ctr; steering comt, Home Health Care Comn, 1990-92; NARD; life mem, Nat Pharmacist Asn; Nat Asn Health Serv Exec; fel, Am Soc Consult Pharmacists; bd trustees, Community Col Baltimore Co; bd dir, Alzheimers Asn. **Honors/Awds:** Women Pharmacists of the Year, MD Pharm Soc, 1984; Outstanding Women in Pharm, Stud Nat Pharmacist Asn, 1984; Outstanding Alumni, HU Copps, 1992; Leadership, Baltimore Co Chamber, 1999; work recipient Greghor T. Poue Pedal, UMF-Iasi, Romania, 2000. **Business Addr:** Executive Director, Sunrise of Towson, 7925 York Rd, Randallstown, MD 21133, **Business Phone:** (410)296-8900.*

CARSON, WARREN JASON
Educator. **Personal:** Born Feb 12, 1953, Tryon, NC; son of Warren J and Esther Maybrey. **Educ:** Univ NC, AB, 1974; Atlanta Univ, MA, 1975; Univ SC, Columbia, SC, PhD, 1990. **Career:** Isothermal Community Col, instr, 1975-76; Piedmont OIC, head career prep div, 1975-80; Rutledge Col, dean acad affairs, 1980-84; Univ SC, Spartanburg, prog dir, prof dept eng, 1984-, chmn, currently, asst dean, Col Arts & Sci, currently; Roseland Community Ctr, pres, currently. **Orgs:** Pres Polk County, NAACP, 1976-96; chmn, Mayor's Adv Task Force, 1980-83; pres, Tryon Schs, PTA, 1980-81; Polk Co (NC), Bd County Comners, 1986-88; Polk Co, Dept Soc Serv, 1986-94; City Coun, Tryon, NC, 1989-; Polk County Child Protection Team, 1993-; trustee Isothermal Comm Col, 1997-. **Honors/Awds:** Outstanding Teacher Award, Piedmont OIC, 1980; Outstanding Teacher Award, Rutledge Col, 1982-83; Church & Comm Award,1984; Teacher of the Year, Univ SC, Spartanburg, 1989; Amoco Outstanding Teacher Award, Univ SC, 1989; Governor's Distinguished Professor award, SC Comn Higher Educ, Governor's Office, 1989, 2002, 2003; Carson Scholarship Program established, 1998. **Home**

Addr: 631 E Howard St, PO Box 595, Tryon, NC 28782, **Home Phone:** (828)859-6793. **Business Addr:** Professor, Chairman, University South Carolina Upstate, Department of Languages, Literature & Composition, Smith 215C 800 Univ Way, Spartanburg, SC 29303, **Business Phone:** (864)503-5634.

CARSWELL, DWAYNE
Football player. **Personal:** Born Jan 18, 1972, Jacksonville, FL; married Tamara; children: Ashley & Aaron. **Educ:** Liberty Univ. **Career:** Denver Broncos, guard, 1994-2005. **Honors/Awds:** Top 100 Athletes of Jacksonville list, 1999; Broncos' Ed Block Courage Award nomination, 2005. *

CARSWELL, GLORIA NADINE SHERMAN
Certified public accountant. **Personal:** Born Dec 27, 1951, Cairo, GA; daughter of Eugene Martin and Mary Martin; married Willie F Carswell Jr; children: Mercedes Elaine & John Garfield. **Educ:** Mercer Univ Macon Ga, BS, magna cum laude, 1972; Fla State Univ, MA, 1976. **Career:** Grady Cty Bd Ed, math instr, 1972-74; Deloitte Haskins & Sells, sr acct, 1976-81; Charter Oil Co, plng analyst, 1981-82; Charter Co, sr internal auditor, 1982-83, mgr internal finance reporting, 1983-86; AT & T Am Transtech, mgr ESOP record keeping, 1986-94; JEA, mgr, 1994-. **Orgs:** Fla Inst CPA's, Am Inst CPA's; Jacksonville Women Network; Jr League Jacksonville; Community Connectors Inc; Nat Coun Negro Women. **Home Addr:** 1634 Dunsford Rd, Jacksonville, FL 32207, **Home Phone:** (904)399-1523. **Business Addr:** Manager, Accounts Payable, JEA, 21 W Church St, Jacksonville, FL 32202, **Business Phone:** (904)632-6257.

CARTER, ALLEN C.
Clinical psychologist. **Educ:** Morehouse Col, BA; Columbia Univ, PhD, clin psychol; Univ Calif Sch Med, San Francisco, Calif, intern. **Career:** Morehouse Col, Wellness Resource Ctr, clin psychologist, dir, 2004; pvt pract, Atlanta, Ga, currently; WSB-TV, Channel 2, consult; WAGA, Channel 5, consult; Jet Mag, consult; Atlanta Tribune & The Atlanta Daily World, writer. **Orgs:** Comt Advan Prof Pract Am Psychol Asn; pres, Ga State Bd Examiners Psychologists; pres, Ga Psychol Asn; Bd Prof Affairs; Comt Urban Initiative; Comt Recruitment, Training & Retention Minority Psychologists; CAPP Liaison State Leadership Organizing Comt; Bd Dirs; CAPP Coordr Comt; Subcomt Implementations Integration Diverse Pract Agenda; Consult, Govt Rels Pract Directorate; Personnel Subcomt Pract Directorate; Bd Conven Affairs. **Honors/Awds:** Karl F Heiser Presidential Award, 2000. **Special Achievements:** The first African American elected President of state leaders for the American Psychological Association. **Business Addr:** Clinical Psychologist, Private Practice, Wellness Resource Ctr, 830 Westview Dr SW, Atlanta, GA 30314, **Business Phone:** (404)681-2800.*

CARTER, ALLEN D.
Artist, educator. **Personal:** Born Jun 29, 1947, Arlington, VA; married Mae Ira; children: Flora Ophelia & Cecilia. **Educ:** Columbus Col Art & Design Ohio, BFA, 1972; Am Univ, grad study. **Career:** Adult Educ Prog, art instr; artist. **Orgs:** Arlington Independence Day Celebration Community, 1974; Children's Day Smithsonian Inst, 1974; Nat Portrait Gallery, 1975. **Honors/Awds:** Distinguished Merit Award, Fifth Annual Juried Athenaeum Show, 1974;Kansas City key to the city, 1986; Fellowship Award, Va Mus Fine Arts, 1987; Contemporary Modes of Expression, Marsh Gallery Richmond Va, 1987; One Man Show, Va Mus Fine Arts, 1993. **Special Achievements:** Solo exhibitions: Anton Gallery Shows, Washington, DC, 1982, 1986; group exhibitions: Next Generations, Southeastern Center for Contemporary Art, Winston-Salem, NC 1990-92, 23 works at Madeira School/ Big Al Carter Drawing & Prints. **Business Addr:** Art Instructor, Artist, Adult Educ Prog.

CARTER, ALPHONSE H.
School administrator. **Personal:** Born Oct 3, 1928, Baton Rouge, LA; son of Elvinna Pritchard Yarborough (deceased) and Haley (deceased); married Carolyn McCraw; children: Cynthia Susan. **Educ:** Albany St Col, 1956-57; Duquesne Univ, BS, 1961; Univ Cincinnati, PhD, 1975. **Career:** School Administrator (retired); R Housing Authority City Pittsburgh, interviewer, 1961-62, asst mgr, 1962; Kroger Co, mgt trainee, 1962-63, store mgt, 1963-65, div indust engineering, 1965-66, div personnel mgt, 1966-68, corp personnel coord, 1968-72; Carter Carter & Assoc Inc, mgt consult pres; 1972-76, dir, human resources, 1976-81; Westinghouse Elec Corp, Pittsburgh, PA, mgr, Corp Quality training, 1981-86; Grambling St Univ, Grambling, LA, assoc prof, mgt, 1986-88; Hampton Univ, Hampton, VA,dean, sch bus, 1988-99. **Orgs:** Nat Asn Advan Colored People, 1946-; Soc Advancement Mgt, 1958-; Urban League, 1958-; BOAZF & AM, 1960-; Personnel Asn, 1966-; bd mem, Cit Com Youth, 1969; Nat Alliance Businessmen Col Cluster, 1969-72; bd mem, Opportunities Industrialization Ctr, 1969-72; block club pres, Homewood-Brushton Improvement Asn, 1958-61; bd mem, Victory Neighborhood Serv Agency, 1969-72; Community Chest, 1970-72; Nat Urban League, 1970-71; met dir, Nat Alliance Businessmen, 1971; trustee, Funds Self Enterprise,1972-; Task Force Com Univ Cincinnati Sch Educ, 1972; adv com, Retired Sr Vol Prog, 1972-73; Alpha Mu Sigma Prof Fraternity Mgt Devel 1974; pres, Churchill Area Kiwanis, 1978-79; lt gov Kiwanis Div 6-A, 1980-81; bd mem, Allegheny Trails Boy Scout Coun, 1979; bd mem, Hampt Parking Authority,1990-; bd mem, Va Peninsula Chamber Com, 1991-; bd mem, Penninsula Chapter, Nat Conf Christians & Jews, 1990; Delta Beta Lambda Chapter; Alpha Phi Alpha Fraternity, 1995. **Honors/Awds:** Alpha Mu Sigma Award for Excellence in Scholarship Achievement in Management, 1975. **Home Addr:** 15 Pine Ridge Rd, Arlington, MA 02476-7501.

CARTER, ANTHONY JEROME
Programmer analyst. **Personal:** Born Jun 28, 1956, Tuscaloosa, AL; son of George Carter Jr and Hazel Carter; married Anna, Aug 7, 1977; children: Anthony Jerrard. **Educ:** Barry Univ, BS, comput sci, 1988. **Career:** SystemOne, sr syst analyst/team leader, 1978-89; Burger King Corp, sr programmer analyst, 1989-. **Orgs:** Cub master, Boy Scouts Am, 1991-; Leadership Miami, 1992-; Burger King Reach Adv Comt; Cre Acad Cities Schs/Burger King Acad Prog; Kids Power Work Prog; adv, Jr Achievement. **Special Achievements:** Americas Best and Brightest, Dollars and Sense Magazine, Sept 1992. **Business Addr:** Senior Programmer Analyst, Burger King Corp, 17777 Old Cutler Road, Miami, FL 33157, **Business Phone:** (305)378-3112.

CARTER, ARLINGTON W., JR.
Executive. **Personal:** Born Mar 13, 1933, Chicago, IL; son of Arlington Sr and Martha; married Constance E Hardiman. **Educ:** IL Inst Tech, BSEE, 1961. **Career:** Retired: Seattle Housing Develop, exec dir, 1971-73; The Boeing Co, prog mgr, 1973-77, gen mgr, 1977-81, prog mgr, 1981-85, gen mgr space syst, 1985-88, Defense Syst Div, vpres, 1988-89, Missile Syst Div, vpres & gen mgr, 1989-90, CQ 1, vp, 1990-93, Facilities & CQ 1, vpres, 1993. **Orgs:** Pres, Boeing Mgt Asn, 1982-84; Nat Space Club, 1981-85; exec bd mem, Seattle Comt Col Found, 1982-85; chmn, King County Personnel Bd, 1970-77; chmn, Western Region NAACP, 1966; exec bd mem, United Way, 1978-82; Am Defense Prepared Assoc; exec bd mem, Metropolitan YMCA; Seattle Urban League; exec bd mem, Seattle Hearing & Speech Ctr; secy & treas, Northwest Chapter Ill Inst Alumni Asn; NC A&T Bd Visitors; Am Inst Aeronautics & Astronautics; Ill Inst Tech Pres's Coun; Nat Adv Comt Nat Engg Educ Coaltion; bd dir, Seattle Alliance Educ; bd dir, Seattle Pub Library Found; bd dirs, Sand Point Country Club; co-chmn, exec adv comt, Advan Minority Interest Engg. **Honors/Awds:** Black Engineer of the Year, 1990; Professional Achievement Award, Ill Inst Tech, 1991. **Military Serv:** USAF, S & Sgt. *

CARTER, DR. ARTHUR MICHAEL
Government official. **Personal:** Born Apr 27, 1940, Detroit, MI; son of Arthur and Alberta. **Educ:** Wayne State Univ, Detroit, MI, BA, 1962, MA, 1964, ED, 1971. **Career:** Detroit Pub Sch, Detroit, MI, teacher; Wayne County Community Col, Detroit, dean; Wayne County Gov chmn; Governmental Relations & Community Serv, dep supt, currently; exec producer, host, Showcase Detroit, Barden Channel 6, Cable TV Prog; Wayne County Dept C Family Serv, dir, currently. **Orgs:** Delinquency Pre Subcomt; Detroit Sci Ctr; Detroit Pub Tv. **Honors/Awds:** Film: I Am Somebody, 1969; contributor, Career & Voc Develop, 1972. **Special Achievements:** Author, Black Family Role in Political Educ, 1987.

CARTER, DR. BARBARA LILLIAN
Educator. **Personal:** Born Jun 20, 1942, Mexia, TX. **Educ:** Fisk Univ, AB 1963; Brandeis Univ, MA 1967, PhD 1972; Harvard Univ Inst Educ Mgt, attended 1984. **Career:** Federal City Col, asst prof 1969-72, from assoc provost to assoc prof, 1972-77; Univ District Columbia, assoc vpres, prof, 1977-80, vpres acad affairs 1980-81; Spelman Col, vpres acad affairs, dean 1981-, acting pres, 1986-87, prof sociol & Anthrop, currently. **Orgs:** Am Sociol Asn, 1969-; bd dirs YWCA Atlanta, 1982-; bd dirs, United WayAtlanta 1985-, Pub Broadcast Asn, 1985-; bd trustees, Atlanta Col Art,1986-; bd trustees Chatham Col. **Honors/Awds:** Woodrow Wilson Fellow, 1963; Phi Beta Kappa 1963; Fellow Nat Inst Ment Health 1964-67; Aspen Inst Humanistic Studies Fellowship 1981. **Special Achievements:** Co-author: "Protest, Politics and Prosperity", 1978. **Business Addr:** Professor, Spelman College, Department Sociology & Anthropology, 350 Spelman Lane SW, PO Box 325, Atlanta, GA 30314-4399, **Business Phone:** (404)270-6054.

CARTER, BILLY L.
Lawyer. **Personal:** Born in Montgomery, AL; married Brenda T. **Educ:** Tuskegee Inst, BS, 1967; Howard Univ Law Sch, JD, 1970; Univ Va, attended 1971. **Career:** Gray Seay & Langford, atty, 1970-71; AUS, Ft Meade, MD, chief defence coun; Gray Seay & Langford, assoc atty, 1974-; Recorder's Ct City Tuskegee, prosecutor atty, 1974-; Carter & Knight Law Offices, atty, currently. **Orgs:** Am Bar Asn; Nat Bar Asn; Am Trial Lawyers Asn; Ala Bar Asn; Ala Black Lawyers Asn; DC Bar Asn; Kappa Alpha Psi. **Honors/Awds:** Distinguished Military Graduate, 1967. **Military Serv:** AUS, capt, 1971-74; Army Commendation Medal, 1974. **Business Addr:** Attorney, Carter & Knight Law Offices, 1120 S Court St, Montgomery, AL 36104.*

CARTER, BUTCH (CLARENCE EUGENE CARTER)
Basketball coach, basketball player. **Personal:** Born Jun 11, 1958, Springfield, OH; married Jill; children: Brandon, Blake & Baron. **Educ:** Ind Univ. **Career:** Basketball player, basketball coach (retired); Los Angeles Lakers, 1981; Ind Pacers, 1982-84; NY Knicks, 1985; Philadelphia 76ers, 1986; Middletown Ohio High Sch, coach, 1986-88; Long Beach State Univ, asst basketball coach, 1989; Univ Dayton, asst coach, 1990-91; Milwaukee Bucks, asst coach, 1991-96; Toronto Raptors, asst coach, 1997-98, head coach, 1998-2000. **Honors/Awds:** Ohio Coach of the Year, AP, 1988.

CARTER, CECILIA K.
Association executive. **Career:** Rhythym & Blues Found, exec dir, 2003-. **Business Phone:** (212)491-7700.*

CARTER, CHARLES MICHAEL
Lawyer, executive. **Personal:** Born Apr 18, 1943, Boston, MA; son of Charles and Florence; children: Brandon H, Chad F, Courtney C & Candice A. **Educ:** Univ Calif, Berkley, BS, 1967; George Wash Univ Sch Law, JD, 1973. **Career:** Lawyer, Executive(retired); Winthrop, Stimson, Putnam, & Roberts, assoc, 1973-81; The Singer Comp, div coun & finance staff & investment coun, 1981-83; RJR Nabisco Inc, sr corp coun, 1983-87; Concurrent Comput Corp, vpres, gen coun & secy Corp Develop, 1987-. **Orgs:** Am Bar Asn; Nat Bar Asn. **Business Addr:** Vice President, General Counsel, Secretary, Concurrent Comput Corp, Corp Develop, 3535 State Rte 66 Suite 3, Neptune, NJ 07753-2624, **Business Phone:** (908)870-4226.

CARTER, CHESTER C.
Executive. **Personal:** Born Feb 14, 1921, Emporia, KS; married Claudia; children: Chester Jr, Marise, Carol. **Educ:** Univ SC, AB, 1944, MA, 1952; Loyola Law Sch, JD, 1958. **Career:** Capitol City Liquor Co Wholesale, pres chmn bd; US State Dept, Peace Corps, ambassador, 1962-68; Sup Ct LA Co, juvenile traffic hearing officer, 1956-62. **Military Serv:** AUS, first lt, 1942-46, major 1950-52. **Business Addr:** 645 Taylor St NE, Washington, DC 20017-2063.

CARTER, CHRIS (CHRISTOPHER GARY CARTER)
Football player. **Personal:** Born Sep 27, 1974, Tyler, TX. **Educ:** Univ Tex. **Career:** New England Patriots, defensive back, 1997-99; Cincinnati Bengals,defensive back, 2000-01; Houston Texans, defensive back, 2002.

CARTER, CHRISTOPHER ANTHONY
Police officer. **Personal:** Born Jul 23, 1963, Columbus, GA; son of Jeff Fred and Artha Dean; married Gwendolyn Denise Martin, Dec 27, 1987; children: Precious Gwendolyn. **Educ:** Columbus Col, 1983; Columbus Area Voc Sch, 1983-84. **Career:** Blue Cross/ Blue Shield, electronic data processor, 1980-81; Manpower Temp Serv, data entry operator, 1983-84; Columbus Police Dept, patrolman, 1984; Georgia State Patrol, trooper, currently. **Orgs:** Family Law Bar Asn, 1981; Voice Tibet, 1981; YMCA, 1984; master guide, Pathfinders, 1990; Prof Bowlers Asn; FOP. **Honors/Awds:** Officer of the Year, Columbus Exchange Club, 1992; Officer of the Year, Optimist Club, 1992; Officer of the Year, Am Legion No 35, 1992; Officer of the Year, Columbus Police Dept, 1992; GEO's Officer of the Year, Am Legion 40/8, 1992. **Special Achievements:** Poems published by the Columbus Times, Columbus Ledger/ Enquirer, and various other sources, 1987-; Most commendated officer in the history of the Columbus Police DPT, 1992; third place winner for Officer of the Year for the United States, 1992; first black officer to be Officer of the Year for Columbus, 1992; Published: From My Heart To You. **Home Addr:** 120 Cosby Rd, Junction City, GA 31812-4202, **Home Phone:** (706)269-2707. **Business Addr:** Trooper, GA State Patrol, 7800 Scenic Heights, Manchester, GA 31816, **Business Phone:** (706)846-3106.

CARTER, CHRISTOPHER GARY. **See CARTER, CHRIS.**

CARTER, CLARENCE EUGENE. **See CARTER, BUTCH.**

CARTER, CRIS
Football player, television show host. **Personal:** Born Nov 25, 1965, Troy, OH; married Melanie; children: Duron Christopher & Monterae. **Educ:** Ohio State Univ. **Career:** Football player (retired); Philadelphia Eagles, wide receiver, 1987-89; Minnesota Vikings, 1990-2001; Miami Dolphins, 2002; HBO, Inside the NFL host, currently; Yahoo Sports, NFL Analyst, currently. **Honors/ Awds:** Pro Bowl, 1993-2000; NFL Extra Effort Award, 1994; Bart Starr Award, Athletes in Action, 1995; Citizen Athlete Award, Midwest Sports Channel, 1995; Byron "Whizzer" White Award, NFL Players Asn, 1999; Walter Payton Man of the Year, 1999. **Special Achievements:** Associated Press First-team All-Pro selection, 1994 & 1999; Associated Press Second-team All-Pro selection, 1995; NFL 1990s All-Decade Team. *

CARTER, DAISY
Government official. **Personal:** Born Oct 17, 1931, Stuart, FL; daughter of Robert C Carter and Lottie Thompson Simmons; children: Marilyn D Jewett. **Educ:** St Joseph's Col, Social Work, 1972; Temple Univ, BS, Recreation Admin, 1980. **Career:** Government Offical (retired); Philadelphia Dept Recreation, ctr

recreation leader, asst day camp dir, drama specialist, dist coordr retarded prog, 1968-71; Zion Church, ctr supvr, 1969-70, sr citizen's community worker, 1971-72; E German town Recreation Ctr, day camp dir, 1972-78, sr citizen's prog supvr, 1972-81; Penrose Playground, ctr supvr, 1981-88; Juniata Park Older Adult Ctr, prog dir, 1989-91, therapeutic recreation prog dir, 1989-91; City Philadelphia, Dept Recreation, ctr supvr, 1991-99, grant coordr, 1996-99. **Orgs:** Penn Park & Recreation Soc; Penn Therapeutic Recreation Soc; Black Social Workers Asn; Nat Park & Recreation Asn; Nat Therapeutic Recreation Asn; Nat Recreation & Parks Asn Ethnic Minority Soc; Philadelphia Young Women Christian Asn; Nat Asn Advan Colored People; Philadelphia People Fund; West Mt Airy Neighbors; chairperson, PA Park & Recreation Soc Minority & Women Comm; comm chairperson, State Rep David P Richardson Jr, Sr Citizens & Recreation Progs; pres & bd dir, Temple Univ Health, Physical Educ, Recreation, & Dance Alumni Comm Chmn; bd dir, HPERD Alumni Temple's Gen Alumni Bd; vpres, Temple Alumni Bd Dir; bd mem, Pennsylvania Chap; Nat Coalition 100 Black Women, 1986; life mem, Nat Coun Negro Women, Philadelphia Coun, 1986-; bd mem, Quantum Leap Publisher I, 1990-; Temple Univ Alumni Athletic Comt, 1987-99; pres, Temple Univ Col HPERD Alumni Asn; bd mem, historian, Ethnic Minority Soc, Nat Recreation & Parks; adv comm, Intercolgiate Athletics, Temple Univ, 1998, steering comm; bd dir, Hist Lyric Theater, 1999-; Recreation Adivsory Bd, City Stuart, 2000-; exec comm, Martin County Democratic Party, 2001-. **Honors/Awds:** East Germantown Sr Citizens Service Award, 1976; Commonwealth of PA House of Rep Citation, Sr Citizens & Comm Prog, 1976; finalist, Nat Recreation & Pk Asn, West Francis Audio Visual Contest, 1976; Citation Award, Nat Recreation & Pk Ethnic Minority Soc, 1977, 1979; Appreciation Award, Lincoln Univ, 1981; Admiration & Appreciation Award, East Germantown Sr Citizens, 1981; Certificate of Appreciation, Recreation Dept, Lincoln Univ, 1982; Nat Recreation & Pk Asn Ethnic Minority Soc Recognition Award, 1982; President's Certificate, EMS, 1983; Youth Award, N Philadelphia Br, Nat Asn Advan Colored People, 1986; Service Award, Philadelphia Child-Parent Asn, 1988; Ernest T At well Award, 1993; Woman of Distinction Award, Philadelphia Soroptimist Int 5 Points Magenta, 1995; President's Award, Temple Univ Col HPERD Alumni Asn, 1998; Legends Award, Nat Black Women Sports Found, 1998. **Home Addr:** 1352 SE Madison Ave Sarita Hts, Stuart, FL 34996.

CARTER, DALE LAVELLE
Football player. **Personal:** Born Nov 28, 1969, Covington, GA. **Educ:** Univ Tenn. **Career:** Kans City Chiefs, defensive back & corner back, 1992-98; Denver Broncos, defensive back & corner back, 1999; Minn Vikings, defensive back & corner back, 2001; New Orleans Saints, defensive back & corner back, 2002-03; Baltimore Ravens, corner back, 2005. **Honors/Awds:** NFL Rookie of the Yr, Pro Football Writers, 1992; Bert Bell Trophy, 1992; Rookie of the Yr, UPI AFL-AFC, 1992; Four Times Pro Bowler, 1992-97.

CARTER, DARLINE LOURETHA
Library administrator. **Personal:** Born Dec 7, 1933, Pinola, MS; daughter of Cora Lee and Gennie. **Educ:** Tougaloo Col, Miss, BS, elem educ, 1955; Syracuse Univ, NY, MLS, 1960. **Career:** Cleveland Miss, sch librn, 1955-59; Syracuse Univ, asst librn, 1959-60; Tougaloo Col Miss, circulation librn, 1960-62; West Islip Public Libr, NY, children's librn, 1962-66, asst dir, 1966-69, libr dir, 1969-. **Orgs:** Exhibits Comn, Membership Comn NY Library Asn, 1962-85; Am Library Week Comn, HW Wilson Awards Jury, Membership Comn Am Libr Asn, 1969-85; vpres recording sect & chmn, Pub Libr Dir Asn, 1969-85; 6th Annual Libr Admin Devel Prog, Univ Md, 1972; hon life mem, West Islip PTA, 1971; exec bd, Suffolk Co Libr Asn, 1973-85; reaccreditation comn, Palmer Sch Libr & Info Sci, Long Island Univ, CW Post Ctr 1983; pres, Suffolk Library Consortium Inc, 1986-92; pres, Spring Inst. **Business Phone:** (631)661-7080.

CARTER, DR. DAVID G.
School administrator, educator, scholar. **Personal:** Born Oct 25, 1942, Dayton, OH; son of Richard and Esther Dunn; children: Ehrika Carter Gladden, David Holley, David George Jr & Jessica. **Educ:** Cent State Univ, BS, 1965; Miami Univ, MEd, 1968; Ohio State Univ, PhD, 1971. **Career:** Dayton City Schs, 6th grade teacher, 1965-68, asst prin, 1968-69, elem prin, 1969-70, unit facilitator, 1970-71; Dayton Pub Sch, serv unit dir, 1971-73; Wright State Univ, adj prof, 1972; Booz-Allen & Hamilton Inc, consult, 1972-73; Pa Dept Educ, consult, 1973-77; So Ea Delco Sch Dist,consult, 1973-83; Penn State Univ, Dept Educ Admin, from asst prof to assoc prof, 1973-77; Syracuse Univ Res Corp, consult, 1976; Univ Conn,Dept Educ Admin, assoc prof, 1977-79, prof, 1980-, Sch Educ, assoc dean, 1977-82, assoc vpres acad affairs, 1982-; Pressional Develop Assoc, consult, 1979-80; Jour Eduquity & Leadership, ed bd, 1980; Milwaukee Pub Sch, consult, 1980; Windham l Comm Hosp, corporator, 1982, trustee, 1984; Univ Conn, Storrs, CT, assoc vpres acad affairs, 1982-88; Windham Healthcare Sys Inc, dir, 1984; Eastern Conn State Univ, Willimantic, pres, 1988-2006; Conn State Univ Syst, chancellor, 2006-. **Orgs:** Good Samaritan Ment Health Adv, 1968-73; bd trustees, Dayton Mus Nat Hist, 1973; Ctr County Ment Health & Ment Retardation Adv Bd, 1974-76; Adv Coun Bd Ment Health Prog Dev, 1977-80; Governor's Task Force Jail & Prison Overcrowding, 1980; bd dir, Nat Organiz Legal Prob Educ, 1980-83; bd dir, New Eng Reg Exchange, 1981-; Conn State chmn, 1990-94; Urban League Greater Hartford, bd dirs, 1994-97; Millennium Leadership Initiative Founding, 1996, co chair, 1996-99; IAUP/UN Comm Disarmament Educ, Conflict Resolution & Peace, 1997-; Marine Corps Univ, 1998-; Am Coun Educ, 1999-2001; bd visitors, 2001, chair, 2003-; Comm Div III NCAA, chair, Am Asn State Col & Univ, 2003-; Phi Delta Kappa; Am Educ Res Asn; Nat Asn Advan Colored People; Pi Lambda Theta; Phi Kappa Phi; Int Union Univ Pres. **Honors/Awds:** Selected Young Man of the Year Dayton Jr C of C, 1973; Inducted into the Donald K Anthony Achievement Hall of Fame, 1993; Roy Wilkins Civil Rights Award, Nat Asn Advan Colored People, 1994; 39th Americanism Award, Conn Am Legion Dept, 1994; Excellence Award, 1997; Man of the Yr, Afro Am Affairs Comm, 2000; Man of the Year, African-Am AFF Comm, 2000; Greater Hartford Nat Asn Advan Colored People Award of Honor, Nat Asn Advan Colored People, 2001; Good Citizen Award, Conn Lodge Order Sons Italy Am, 2001; Educator of the Yr, Greater Hartford Nat Asn Negro Business & Pro Women's Club, 2001; Tapestry Award, Hartford Courant, 2002; Whitney M. Young Jr. Service Award, (The Urban Scouting Comt, 2003; Hon Doctorate Laws Degree, Briarwood Col; Hon Doctorate Humane Letters, Goodwin Col. **Special Achievements:** First African American president of a four-year institution of higher education in Connecticut. **Military Serv:** Published over 70 articles and chapters in books. **Business Addr:** Chancellor, Connecticut State University System, 39 Woodland St, Hartford, CT 06105.

CARTER, EDWARD EARL
Executive, mayor. **Personal:** Born Oct 9, 1939, Havelock, NC; son of Nettie Morris and Leander; married Evelyn Jean Carter, Jan 17, 1966; children: Regina Yvette, Tonya Denise, Jacquelyn. **Educ:** Va State Univ, Petersburg, VA, BS, 1963; Pitt Community Col, Greenville, NC, AAS, 1979. **Career:** Columbia Univ, Hudson Labs, NY, res asst, 1962-63; Burroughs Wellcome Co, Greenville, NC, Admin Servs Dept, head, 1971-95; City Greenville, NC, mayor, 1987-89. **Orgs:** Life mem, Alpha Phi Alpha Fraternity, 1960-; Transp Policy Commun Safety Comn, N Carolina League Cities, 1988-89; Pitt County Mayors Asn, 1987-89; Black Nat Conf Mayors, 1987-89, Black Mayors Conf, 1987-89; bd dir, Govs Crime Comn NC, 1988-; bd dir, Pitt-Greenville Chamber Com, 1988-89; bd dir, Proj Parenting, 1988-; charter mem & bd dir, Milennia Community Bank, 2001-. **Honors/Awds:** Gus Witherspoon Leadership Award, NC Asn Alpha Men, 1975; Community Service Award, Omega Psi Pi, 1975; TAR-Heel-of-the-Week, Raleigh News & Observer, 1979; Citizen of the Year, Mid Atlantic Region Alpha Kappa Alpha Sorority, 1989. **Special Achievements:** Appeared in army air defense movie, Nike-In-the-Attack, 1965; appeared in New York Times and New York Times Magazine army promotional, 1965. **Military Serv:** AUS capt, 1963-71; two Bronze Stars, 1971, three Army Commendation Medals, 1964, 1966 & 1971; Vietnam Cross of Gallantry. **Home Addr:** 104 Fireside, Greenville, NC 27834. *

CARTER, ESTHER YOUNG
Educator. **Personal:** Born Feb 8, 1930, North Carolina; daughter of Johnny Argro Young and Bertha Perry; married Robert, Jun 25, 1950; children: Gwendolyn C Adamson, Johnny Jerome & Robert Gilbert. **Educ:** NC Central Univ, BS, 1953; Johnson C Smith Univ, elem edu cert; NC A&T State Univ, MS, 1975. **Career:** Carver Col, secy & teacher, 1954-59; Douglas Aircraft Co, secy, 1959-66; Greensboro Pub Schs, teacher, 1966-92. **Orgs:** Nat Educ Asn, 1966-92; Greensboro Alumnae Chap, 1976; corresp secy, 1986-90, pres, 1990-94, Delta Sigma Theta Sorority Inc,; life mem, NC Cent Alumni Asn; Black Child Develop Inst, 1988-; Metrop Coun Negro Women, 1989-; Pinochle Bugs Social & Civic Club Inc, Greensboro Chap, pres, 1991-; NEA-R, 1993-. **Honors/ Awds:** Teacher of the Yr, W M Hampton Elem Sch, 1988.

CARTER, ETTA F
Educator. **Personal:** Born in Warren, AR; daughter of Edward and Mamie Wilborn; married William T Carter, Dec 2, 1963; children: Carla F & William T Jr. **Career:** Chicago Bd Edu, elementary teacher & reading spec, 1966-79; NYC Bd Ed, coordr student serv, 1986-88; Public Sch 220, interim prin, 1987-89; Public Sch 80, asst prin, 1989-93; Public Sch 50, prin, 1993-96; Dis 16, dep supt, 1996-98; Bd Educ City NY, dep supt, 1998-. **Orgs:** Pres, Beta Omicron Chap, 1989-; bd dir, Beta Omicron Early Childhood Ctr, 1991-; ASCD, 1993-; bd dir, Big Sister Ctr, 1996-; Phi Delta Kappa, 1998-; eastern regional dir, Nat Sorority Phi Delta Kappa Inc, 1999-. **Honors/Awds:** Service Award, NSPDK Inc, 1991; Community Award, Antioch Baptist Church, 1993; Achievement Award, NSPDK Inc, Eastern Region, 1995; Educator Award, Crossover Baptist Church, 1998; Achievement Award, NSPDK Inc, 1999; Service Award, IS 347, 2001. **Business Addr:** Deputy Superintendent, Board of Education City New York, District 28, 109-59 Inwood St, Jamaica, NY 11435, **Business Phone:** (718)526-5523.

CARTER, FREDRICK CARTER
Basketball player, basketball coach, business owner. **Personal:** Born Feb 14, 1945, Philadelphia, PA; married Jacqueline; children: Stephanie, Mia, Christopher, Amee, Jason & Aaron. **Educ:** Mt St Mary's Col, Emmitsburg, MD, 1969. **Career:** Basketball player, basketball coach (retired); Baltimore Bullets, 1969-72; Philadelphia76ers, 1972-77; Wash Bullets, 1974; Milwaukee Bucks, 1977; Atlanta Hawks, asst coach, 1981-83; Chicago Bulls, asst coach, 1984-85; Wash Bullets,asst coach, asst coach, 1986-87; Philadelphia 76ers, asst coach, 1988-89, head coach, 1992-93; Philadelphia 76ers, PRISM, analyst; TNT, studio analyst; ESPN, Nat Basketball Asn, analyst; SAMJAC Indust Inc, owner,currently. **Orgs:** Instrumental in the devt & instr of Mayor Wash's inner-city basketball clinics; involved with Little City Found. **Business Addr:** Owner, President, SAMJAC INDUSTRIES INC, 5070 Parkside Ave, PHILADELPHIA, PA 19131, **Business Phone:** (215)877-9513.*

CARTER, DR. GENE RAYMOND
School administrator. **Personal:** Born Apr 10, 1939, Staunton, VA; married Lillian Young; children: Gene Raymond Jr & Scott Robert. **Educ:** Va State Univ Petersburg, BA, 1960; Boston Univ, ME, 1967; Teachers Col Columbia Univ, NY, EdD, 1973. **Career:** St Emma Mil Acad & Norfolk Pub Sch, teacher, 1960-69; Campostella Jr High Sch, educ develop spec, intern prin, 1969-70; Maury High Sch, Norfolk VA, asst prin instr, 1970-71; Englewood Pub Sch NJ, admin asst res & planning, 1972-73; Norfolk Pub Sch, supvr curriculum resources, 1973-74; Sch Educ Old Dominion Univ, Norfolk VA, adj assoc prof 1974; Norfolk Pub Schs, reg asst supt, 1979-83, supt sch 1983; Asn Supvr & Curriculam Develop, exec dir & chief exec officer, 1992-. **Orgs:** Bd mem, Tidewater Juvenile Detention Home Adv Bd, 1978-80; bd mem, Comm Mgt Serv YMCA Norfolk, 1978-80; pres, exec bd mem Sunrise, Optimist Club Norfolk, Va, 1979-80; pres, Gene R Carter & Assoc, Chesapeake VA, 1979; bd mem, St Marys Infant Home Norfolk, 1980; bd trustees, Va Wesleyan Col,Educ Comt States Adv Bd; Norfolk Southern Corp Bd Dir. **Honors/Awds:** Nat Grad Fel Training, Teachers Col, Columbia Univ, 1971-72; Minority Stud Scholarship, Teachers Col, Columbia Univ NY, 1972; Minority Affairs Adv Comt, Talent Bank Consult Am Asn Sch Admin, 1979; Optimist of the Year, Sunrise Optimist Club, Norfolk VA, 1979-80; Nat Supt Yr, Am Asn Sch Adminr, 1988; Distinguished Alumni Award Recipient, Teachers Col, Columbia, 1991. **Business Addr:** Executive Director, Chief Executive Officer, Assn Supv & Curric Develop, 1703 N Beauregard St, Alexandria, VA 22311-1714.*

CARTER, GEOFFREY NORTON
Commissioner. **Personal:** Born Jan 28, 1944, St Louis, MO; son of Robert and Daphne Louise Tyus. **Educ:** St Louis Univ Sch Arts & Sci, AB cum laude, 1966; St Louis Univ Law Sch, JD 1969. **Career:** Legal Aid Soc St Louis, staff atty, 1969-70; USAF, judge advocate, 1970-74; atty pvt pract, 1975-88; Oakland Munic Ct, Oakland, CA, comnr, 1988-98; Alameda City Superior Ct, comnr, 1998-. **Orgs:** Treasr, Calif Asn Black Lawyers 1978 & 1979; vpres, Charles Houston Bar Asn, 1980; cmnr, City Oakland Citizens' Complaint Bd, 1980; mem, bd, Heritage Trails Fund, 1987-97; mem, bd dir, Bay Area Ridge Trail Coun, 1994-; bd dir, Metrop Equestrian Preservation Soc. **Honors/Awds:** Full tuition Scholar, St Louis Univ Sch Law, 1966. **Military Serv:** USAF, capt, 1970-74; Commendation Medal, USAF, 1974. **Business Addr:** Commissioner, Alameda County Superior Court, Allen E Broussard Justice Ctr 661 Washington St, Oakland, CA 94607, **Business Phone:** (510)268-7606.

CARTER, GILBERT LINO
Government official, administrator. **Personal:** Born Jul 6, 1945, Richmond, VA; married Joyce Jones; children: Jana, Gilbert Jr & Ridgely. **Educ:** Morgan State Univ, AB, 1967; Howard Univ, JD, 1970. **Career:** Va Commonwealth Univ, asst dean stud life, 1971-73; Commonwealth Va, asst dir, 1973-75; Va Union Univ, asst vpres financial affairs, athletic dir, dir annual Fund & planned giving, currently. **Orgs:** Exec dir, Model Cities/City Richmond, 1975-77; vice-chair Assistants Int City Mgt Asn, 1983-. **Business Addr:** Director, Annual Fund, Planned Giving, Virginia Union University, Office of Institutional Advancement, C D King Hall Rm 214, Richmond, VA 23220, **Business Phone:** (804)354-5934.

CARTER, GWENDOLYN BURNS
Educator. **Personal:** Born Nov 21, 1932, Lufkin, TX; daughter of Robert and Tressie Stokes; married Purvis Melvin Carter, Jun 2, 1957; children: Purvis Melvin III, Frederick Earl, Burnest Denise. **Educ:** Univ Denver, Univ Colo, Univ Southern Ill, Univ Tex; Huston Tilloston Col, BS, 1954; Prairie View A&M Univ, MEd, 1960. **Career:** Hempstead Elem Sch, resource teacher. **Orgs:** Pres, Jack & Jill Am Inc, 1980-82; pres, Waller Co Teachers Assoc, 1983-84; Delta Sigma Theta Sorority; career treas, Top Ladies Distinction Inc, 1985-87; Coun Exceptional C; Nat Educ Asn; adv coun, Exceptional C, 1986-; youth develop comn, Mount Corinth Baptist Church, 1986-; pres, Top Ladies Distinction, 1988-; vpres, Delta Sigma Theta Sorority, 1988-. **Honors/Awds:** Outstanding Leadership Award Girl Scouts, 1984; San Jacinto Council Appreciation Award ,1984; Distinguished Service, Prairie View Local Alumni Asn, 1984; Certificate of Recognition, Mt Corinth Baptist Church, 1985; Human Relations Award, Waller County Teachers Asn, 1986; Outstanding Service Award, Top Teens Am Inc, 1986; Certificate of Recognition, Prairie View Local Alumni Asn, 1986; Top Lady of The Year, Top Ladies Distinction, 1989. **Home Addr:** 319 Pine St, PO Box 2243, Prairie View, TX 77446. **Business Addr:** Resource Teacher, Hempstead Elementary School, Hempstead, TX 77445.*

CARTER, HARRIET LASHUN
Executive, executive director. **Personal:** Born Feb 16, 1963, Muskegon, MI; daughter of John Edward and LuLa Fae Williams. **Educ:** Mich State Univ, East Lansing, BA, 1985. **Career:** Muskegon Harbour Hilton, Muskegon, MI, supvr, night auditor, 1986-88; Radisson Resort Hotel, Ypsilanti, MI, sales mgr, 1988-89; Metro Detroit Conv & Visitors Bur, Detroit, MI, acct exec, 1989, dir bur serv, currently. **Orgs:** Alpha Kappa Alpha Sorority Inc; Nat Coalition Black Meeting Planners. **Home Addr:** 200 Riverfront Dr, Detroit, MI 48226, **Home Phone:** (313)877-9771. **Business Phone:** (313)202-1981.

CARTER, DR. HAZO WILLIAM
School administrator. **Personal:** Born in Nashville, TN; son of Hazo William Sr and Elizabeth Forbes; married Phyllis Harden; children: Angela. **Educ:** Tenn State Univ, BS, Eng, 1968; Univ Ill, MS, jour, 1969; Vanderbilt Univ,EdD, 1975. **Career:** Southwestern Bell, Chicago, IL, supr servs, 1969-71; Norfolk State Univ, asst to pres, 1975-76, asst vpresstud affairs, 1976-77, vpresstudent affairs, 1977-83; Philander Smith Col, Little Rock, AR, pres, 1983-87; WVa State Univ, WV, pres, 1987-, Board of Directors, Am Asn State Cols, 2001; President's Board of Advisors, Historically Black Coll and Uni, 2002. **Orgs:** NACCP; Civic League; Phi Delta Kappa; Alpha Kappa Mu; Psi Chi; bd dir, Am Asn State Cols & Univs; Pres's Coun for the W Va Higher Educ Policy Comn; Nat Inst Chem Studies; pres, Asn Col Univ; mem, Pres Bush's Bd Adv, HBCUs; bd mem, Chem Alliance Zone W Va; Simpson Memorial United Methodist Church, Charleston; Kanawha Scholars Fund; Pres Coun Nat Col Athletic Asn; W VaState Col Found Inc. **Honors/Awds:** Outstanding Serv Award, KWTD-FM, 1985; Man of the Year, Simpson Memorial United Methodist Church, 1997; President of the Century Award, W Va State Col Nat Alumni Asn, 2000. **Business Addr:** President, West Virginia State University, President Office, Ferrell Hall 103, PO Box 1000, Institute, WV 25112-1000.

CARTER, HERBERT E.
Educator. **Personal:** Born Sep 27, 1919, Amory, MS; son of George and Willie Sykes; married Mildred L Hemmons; children: Herbert E Jr, Gene Kay, Kurt Vincent. **Educ:** Tuskegee Univ, BSc, 1955, MEd, 1969. **Career:** Educator (retired); USAF, fighter pilot, 1943-44, group maintenance officer, 1945-48, flight test maintenance officer, 1948-50, prof air sci, 1950-55, dep dir military adv group German Air Force, 1955-59, chief maintenance, 1959-63, 1963-65; Tuskegee Inst, prof aerospace studies, 1965-69, assoc dean stud serv, 1970-75, assoc dean admis & recruiting, 1975-84. **Orgs:** Presidential Scholars Review Comt; Coll Bd Educ Testing Serv; Am Asn Col Registr & Admis Officers; Sigma Pi Phi; Kappa Delta Pi; Nat Asn Col Admis Counr; Tuskegee Chap Tuskegee Airmen Inc; numerous speaking engagements over the past ten years on "Professionalism, Commitment & Performance of Blacks in Aerospace Careers". **Honors/Awds:** Air Medal w/4 Clusters; Air Force Commendation Medal; Distingushed Unit Citation; European Theater Medal w/5 Bronze Stars; Nat Defense Medal w/1 Bronze Star; Air Force Longevity Award w/5 Oak Leaf Clusters; Tuskegee Univ, Alumni Merit Award, 1994; Tuskegee Airmen BG Noel F Parris Gold Medallion Medal, 1993. **Military Serv:** USAF Lt col (retired). **Home Addr:** 2704 Bulls Ave, Tuskegee Institute, AL 36088. *

CARTER, J B
Manager. **Personal:** Born Oct 5, 1937, Pascagoula, MS; married Mary Mallard; children: J B III, Joy Bonita & Janelle Betrice. **Educ:** Tougaloo Col, BA, 1960. **Career:** Manager (retired); Pub Sch Miss, teacher coordr; Litton Industs, labr rels, rep EEO coor mgr; Keesler AFB, mgt specialist; Miss State Employ Security Comn, employ interviewer; Jackson Co Neighborhood Youth Corps, dir; Jackson Co Justice Ct, ct admin, 1994-2003; Gulf Coast Safety Soc, secy, 1975-2005. **Orgs:** Jackson Co Civic Action Com, 1969; decon, First Christian Church; Omega Psi Phi Frat;chmn Pas-point Handicap Comt, 1972; co-chmn, Bi-racial Com, Moss Point Sch Syst, 1972; pres, Jackson Co Task Force; secy & bd trustees, Moss Point Munic Separate Sch Dist, 1975; adv bd, Jackson Co Salvation Armys Bldg Fund Dr, 1975; adv bd, Asbury 25 Chapel African Methodist Episcopal Zion Church. **Honors/Awds:** Omega Man of Year, 1967; Distinguished Service Award, Pas Point Jaycees, 1972; Outstanding Citizen, Jackson County Non-partisan Voters League, 1974. **Special Achievements:** First Black Employment Interviewer in Mississippi Employment Security Commission Office 1966. **Home Addr:** 2744 Briarwood Circle, Moss Point, MS 39563, **Home Phone:** (228)475-5698.

CARTER, JAMES
Educator, mayor, businessperson. **Personal:** Born Jul 6, 1944, Woodland, PA; son of Jimmie L and Mae Bell. **Educ:** Albany St Col, Albany, Ga, BS, Bus, minor Math, PE; Ga State Univ, Atlanta, Ga; Univ Ga, Athens, Ga, Finance. **Career:** City Woodland, Woodland, Ga, mayor, 1982-; Self-employed, small bus mgr; Home S, Greenville, Ga, contract writer, 1988. **Orgs:** Baptist Stud Union; Nat Conf Black Mayors; Joint Ctr Political Studies-SBCC; Nat Towns & Townships-GRWA; Small Towns; Ga Conf Black Mayors; Master Mason; Ga Asn Black Elected Officials; bd mem, Rural Develop Ctr; chair, Mayor's Motorcade; GMA, Municipal & Finance Comt. **Honors/Awds:** Teacher of the Year, Cent High Sch, 1979; Man of the Century Award, Concerned Citizens, 1988; Special Alumni Award, Albany St Col, Albany, Ga, 1989; GMA Community Leadership Award, 1993; Community Leader Award, Nat Advan Asn Colored People, 1993; Man of the Year Award, Nat Advan Asn Colored People, 1994; Montel Williams Award, 1994; Outstanding Service award, Rural Develp Ctr, 1997; Outstanding Citizen Award, Farm City, 1997; Children Research Award, St Judge Cancer, 1997; Community Service Award, St Judge C Hosp, 2000; Community Service Award, Delta Sigma Soroity, 2000; Outstanding Community Service Award, Nat Advan Asn Colored People, 2000. **Special Achievements:** First African American mayor and judge of Woodland, GA. **Business Addr:** Mayor, City of Woodland, Woodland City Hall, 220 W South Ave, PO Box 148, Woodland, GA 31863, **Business Phone:** (706)674-2700.*

CARTER, JAMES EARL, JR.
Physician. **Personal:** Born Oct 13, 1943, Kansas City, KS; son of James E Sr and Anna Sneed; married Nina Sharon Escoe; children: Chisty, Kimberly. **Educ:** Univ Mo Kansas City, BS, 1965; Univ Mo, MD, 1969. **Career:** Walter Reed Hosp, internal med, 1969-70; Ventura County Hosp, residency, 1972-73; Wayne Miner Health Ctr, family physician, 1973-75; Family practitioner, 1975; James E Carter, MD, PC Kansas City, MO, family physician & pres, 1975-. **Orgs:** Am Heart Asn, Kansas City Chap; life mem, Nat Asn Advan Colored People; life mem, Africare; Metrop Med Soc. **Honors/Awds:** Fellowship Award, Am Acad Family Pract, 1975. **Military Serv:** AUS, med corp capt, 1969-72. **Business Addr:** Physician, 7800 Paseo Blvd, Kansas City, MO 64131.*

CARTER, DR. JAMES EDWARD, III
School administrator. **Personal:** Born Sep 3, 1938, Columbia, SC; son of James E Carter Jr and Lakesha Hudgens; married Judy Luchey; children: James E IV & Mason Johnson III. **Educ:** Howard Univ, 1958; Paine Col, BS, 1958-60; SC State Col, MEd, 1971-73; Faith Col, LHD, 1978. **Career:** School Administrator (Retired); Richmond County Bd Educ, teacher, counr,prin, 1960-73; AUS, AUSR, instr med corps, 1963-67; Franklin LifeInsurance Co, agent, financial consult, 1969-72; Med Col Ga, recruiter-,counr, assoc dean, stud affairs, 1973-97, Dept Pediatrics, prof emer. **Orgs:** Pres, Belair Hills Asn, 1973-75; vice dist rep, 7th Dist, Omega Psi Phi,1974-77; chair, Black Heritage Community, 1975-; pres, Alpha Mu Boule;Sigma Pi Phi, 1979-81; appointee, Governor's Adv Coun Energy, 1980-82;pres, Nat Asn Med Minority Educ, 1983-85; pres, Nat Asn Stud AffairsProfessionals, 1987-88; bd dirs, Health Cent, 1988-91; appointee,Govenor's Intercultural Speakers Bur, Human Rels Comn, State Ga, 1990;appointee, Richmond County Comn Hist Preser, 1990; exec bd, Boy Scouts Am,1993-; exec bd, Augusta Housing Authority, 1994-99; trustee, Hist Augusta;1997-; Augusta African Am Hist Community, 1999-; comnr, Downtown DevelopAuthority, 1999-; chair, 1-cent sales tax community, 1999-2000; trustee,Augusta Mus Hist, 2002-. **Honors/Awds:** Distinguished Achievement Awards, United Negro Col Found, 1977-83;President Alumni Award, Paine Col, 1979 & 1997; Distinguished AlumniAward, Lucy C Laney High Sch, 1983; Arkansas Governor's Award, 1984;Presidential Award, Nat Asn Personnel Workers, 1985, 1989, 1991 & 1996;Presidential Citation, Nat Asn Med Minority Educr, 1982, 1984, 1985, 1987,1990 & 1996; Nat Humanitarian Award, Chi Eta Phi, 1997. **Special Achievements:** Article, "The Need for Minorities in the Health Professions in the 80's:The National Crisis and the Plan for Action," 1986. **Military Serv:** AUS, Good Conduct Medal, 1963; Honorable Discharge, 1969. **Home Addr:** 1-7th St Suite 1001, Augusta, GA 30901-1364.

CARTER, CDR JAMES HARVEY, JR. (JAY CARTER)
Physician, educator. **Personal:** Born Jan 17, 1960, Raleigh, NC; son of James Harvey Carter Sr and Jettie Lucille Strayhorn; married Brigit Maria, Sep 11, 1993. **Educ:** Morehouse Col, BA, 1981; Duke Univ, BHS, 1986, MHS, 1994. **Career:** Southeastern Emergency Med Serv, emergency med technician, dispatcher, 1980-81; Fulton County Alcoholism Treatment Ctr, emergency med technician, 1980-81; Tom Higgs Serv, emergency med technician, 1981-82; NES Govt Serv Inc, physician asst, 1995-98; Duke Univ Med Ctr, physician asst, 1986-88, Div Neurosurg, Dept Surg, 1986-, sr physician asst, 1988-96, clin assoc, 1996-2002, asst clin prof, 2002-. **Orgs:** Am Acad Physician Asst, 1984-; Duke Univ Phys Asst Soc, 1986-; Triangle Area Phys Assts, 1988-, vpres, 1988-91, pres, 1991-96; Asn Mil Surgeons US; Am Asn Surg Phys Asst; Naval Asn Phys Asst; Res Officers Asn US; US Naval Inst; Asn Neurol Phys Asst; Asn Med Serv Corps Officers USN; NC Med Soc; Nat Asn Emer Med Technician; Am Asn Neurol Surgeons; Southern Med Asn; NAACP, 1990-; Compassionate Tabernacle Faith Missionary Baptist Church, 1992-, Finance Comt, 1994-97; trustee, NCAPA Endowment, 1992-98, bd dirs, 1993-96, Conf Planning Comt, 1993-96; Am Legion, Post No 1981, 1995-. **Honors/Awds:** Cert Merit, 1993; Cert Appreciation, Am Heart Asn, 1994; Cert Appreciation, Am Acad Phys Assts, 1994; Cert Appreciation, NC Acad Physician Assts, 1994; Cert Recognition, Church God Propey Youth Dept, 1995. **Special Achievements:** Co-published articles including: "Dorsal Root Entry Zone Lesions for the Treatment of Post Brachial Plexus Avulsion Injury Pain," Periphal Nerve Lesion, pgs 416-421, 1990; "Central Nervous System Melanoma in Children", Can J Neurol Sci, 20, 1993; "Demographics, Prognosis, and Therapy in 702 Patients With Brain Metastases from Malignant Melanoma," Journal of Neurosurgery, pgs 11-20, 1998; published "African-American Health Care: Crisis of Inequality," Journal of Am Academy of Phys Assts, pgs 738-743, 1994. **Military Serv:** USNR, cdr, 1989-; Navy & Marine Corps Achievement Medal; Armed Forces Reserve Medal; Expert Rifle Medal; cert appreciation; 2 letters of appreciation; Cert Commendation; letter commendation; Sharpshooter Pistol Ribbon; Nat Defense Serv Medal. **Business Addr:** Assistant Professor, Duke University Medical Center, Department of Surgery Division of Neurosurgery, 4520 Busse Bldg, PO Box 3807, Durham, NC 27710, **Business Phone:** (919)681-6421.

CARTER, JAMES L.
Social worker. **Personal:** Born May 20, 1933, Camden, NJ. **Educ:** Howard Univ, BA; NY Univ, MSW. **Career:** Inst Black Cult Univ FL, founder acting dir, 1971-72; Student Devel Univ FL, asst dean, 1971-72; Black Cult Ctr Penn State Univ, dir, 1972-73; Univ FL, clin soc worker, 1975. **Orgs:** Nat Asn Soc Workers; Asn Black Soc Workers; Acad & Cert Soc Workers; citizen adv comn, Alachua Co Div Corrections. **Honors/Awds:** Radio station WRUF Salute dist comn serv, 1972. *

CARTER, DR. JAMES P.
Educator. **Personal:** Born in Chicago, IL. **Educ:** Northwestern Univ, BS; Columbia Univ Sch Pub Health, MS, PhD. **Career:** Tulane Univ Sch Pub Health, Dept Nutrition & Nursing, prof, head & chmn; Ibadan Univ, chmn; Egypt, staff pediatrician. **Honors/Awds:** Numerous publ. **Business Addr:** Professor, head & chairman, Tulane University, Department of Nutrition, Sch Pub Hlth and Trop Med, 1430 Tulane Ave, New Orleans, LA 70112.

CARTER, JANDRA D.
Government official. **Personal:** Born May 11, 1948, St Louis, MO; daughter of Larry Spinks and Mamie France Spinks; married Alvin Carter, Jul 24, 1971; children: Brian, Traci Carter-Evans, Chaun. **Educ:** Univ Mo, Columbia, MO, BS, 1979; Central Mo State Univ, Warrensburg, MO, MS, 1984. **Career:** Mo Div Youth Serv, Jefferson City, MO, training officer, delinquency prev spec, facility mgr, group leader, youth spec, 1971-81; Mo Dept Mental Health, Jefferson City, staff develop, 1981-84; Mo Dept Corrections, Jefferson City, dir training, 1984; Mo Dept Mental Health, Jefferson City, dir invest, 1989-92, prog coordr, 1992-95, dir caring communities, 1995; Mo Dept Corrections, Bd Probation & Parole, Western Zone, asst div dir. **Orgs:** Nat Asn Blacks Criminal Justice, 1979-; State Training Adv Bd State Mo, 1984-89; pres, Mo Chapter NABCJ, 1985-87; Self Eval Task Force Girl Scouts, 1990-; Chair, adv bd, William Woods Col Sch Social Work, 1991-92. **Honors/Awds:** Phi Kappa Phi Honor Society; Governor's Diversity Award, 1995. *

CARTER, JAY. See CARTER, CDR JAMES HARVEY, JR.

CARTER, JIMMY
Government official. **Personal:** Born Jun 12, 1947, Memphis, TN; married Sharon Singleton; children: Sherrie, Torrie, Denise. **Educ:** Univ Louisville, BS, 1974, MS, 1978. **Career:** Jefferson Co Police Dept, 1972-80; US Dept of Justice, FBI asst dir, sr exec serv, 1995. **Orgs:** Chief exec officer, Nat Orgn Black Law Enforcement; Int Asn Chiefs Police; FBI Nat Acad asn; Blacks Govt; Nat Exec Inst, 1999-. **Honors/Awds:** Presidential Rank Award, 2000. *

CARTER, JOANNE WILLIAMS
Educator, artist, community activist. **Personal:** Born Mar 19, 1935, Brooklyn, NY; daughter of Edgar T and Elnora Bing Morris; married Robert L Carter, Sep 17, 1960; children: Anthony Tyrone, Tiffany Lucille, Janine Lynn Carter-Chevalier. **Educ:** Brooklyn Col, City Univ NY, Brooklyn, NY, BA, 1976, MA, 1986. **Career:** New York City, bd educ, 1974-94; prof artist, 1980-. **Orgs:** Patron, Studio Mus Harlem; adv coun, Brooklyn Mus Art; former pres, Soc Preservation Weeksville & Bedford/Stuyvesant Hist (an African Am Mus); charter mem, Schomberg Soc Schomberg Libr NY; charter mem, Nat Mus Women Arts; mem/patron, panelist, Nat Endowment Arts, Wash, DC, 1994; Delta Rho Chap, Alpha Kappa Alpha Sorority; former mem, Brooklyn Chap, LINKS Inc; founding mem, Emily Pickens Club; pres, Eastville Hist Soc Sag Harbor; Artists Alliance E Hampton, NY; trustee, Sag Harbor, Whaling & Historical Mus; Warden, Vestry Christ Episcopal Church, Sag Harbor. **Honors/Awds:** Prize winning painting, Kingsboro Community Art Gallery, 1988; participant, Sag Harbor Initiative, an annual gathering of artists, philosophers & writers, 1987-89. **Home Addr:** 153 Hampton St, Sag Harbor, NY 11963. *

CARTER, JOHN E. See Obituaries section.

CARTER, DR. JOHN H
Executive. **Personal:** Born Sep 26, 1948, Thomaston, GA; son of Augustus Carter Jr and Rosa Mathews; married Susan Gibson, Aug 20, 1970; children: Gregory L & Candace M. **Educ:** Robert E Lee Inst, dipl, 1966; Morris Brown Col, BA, social studies, 1970; Univ Utah, MS, human resources mgt, 1977; Univ Southern Calif, MS, mgt, 1989; Calif Coast Univ, DBM, 2001. **Career:**

Cambridge Sch System, instr, 1970; Southern Bell Tel & Tel Co, Atlanta, mgt asst, 1972-73, bus off mgr, 1973-74, 1976-77, personnel supr, 1974-76; dist mgr personnel admin, 1979-80, dist mgr copr plg, 1982-87, opers mgr supplier rels, dir purchasing, 1987-88, gen mgr, property & serv, 1989-91, asst vpres, procurement, property & serv mgt, 1991-92; Am Tel & Tel Co, Basking Ridge, NJ, dist mgr eeo goals/anal, 1977-79; Am Tel & Tel Co, Atlanta, GA, dist mgr assessment, 1980-81; BellSouth Fel, Univ Southern Calif, 1988-89; City Atlanta, Mayor's Off, loan exec, 1992; Fleet & Serv, asst vpres, 1992-93; BellSouth, Operator Serv, pres, 1993-95, Corp Resources, pres, 1995-99; Carter & Carter LLC, exec coach & owner, 2001-; Strayer Univ, adj prof, 2005-. **Orgs:** Pres, Alpha Phi Alpha Fraternity, 1969-70; pres, Mt Olive Jaycees NJ, 1977-78; chmn admin bd, SuccaSunna United Meth Chap, 1978-79; bd dirs, Atlanta Met Fair Housing 1983-84; loan exec, Fulton Co Comn, GA, 1981-82; pres, Huntington Comt Asn Atlanta, 1981-82; vpres, Clark Col Allied Health Comn Atlanta, 1981-; vpres, Fulton Co Zoning Orgin Review Comt, 1982-; vpres, Seaborn Lee Sch PTA Atlanta, 1983-84; Econ Develop Adv Bd, 1985-; chmn, Douglas HS Bus Adv Coun, 1985-92; BellSouth Fel, Columbia Univ, 1986; Adult Sch Super Ben Hill United Meth Church, 1986-87; bd dirs, Renaisssance Capital Corp, 1987; bd dirs, Opportunities Industrialization Ctr, 1989-92; bd dirs, Bobby Dodd Ctr, 1989-92; bd dirs, Am Lung Asn, 1990-94; dir educ, Alpha Phi Alpha Fraternity, Ga Dis, 1991-98; bd dirs, Am Red Cross, 1992-97; proj mgr, MLK Memorial Proj; Worldwide Asn Bus Coaches; Int Asn Facilitators; Bd Ctr African-Am Male Res, Success & Leadership, Univ W Ga; adv, Strayer Univ Cobb Campus Bus Club. **Honors/Awds:** New Jersey Jaycee of Year, 1978; Outstanding Young Man in America, 1978; AT&T Community Achievement Award, 1978; Who's Who in Black America, 1981; Loaned Executive, Fulton County Comn, 1981; Who's Who in the South and Southeast, 1984; Businessman of Year, Douglass High Sch, 1987; Leadership South Fulton, 1987; Alumni of Year, Morris Brown Col, 1988; Who's Who in America, 1988; Nat Black Col Hall of Fame, 1989; Leadership Atlanta, 1990/91; Success Guide, 1991; Metro Atlanta, 1991; Nat Alpha Phi Alpha "Man of the Year", 1992; Loaned Executive, Mayor of Atlanta, 1992; BellSouth Quality Champion of the Year, 1994; Certification of Appreciation, Alpha Kappa Alpha Sorority, Inc; Distinguished Leadership Award, United Negro Col Fund, 1999; President's Distinguished Alumnus Award, Morris Brown Col, 1999; Executive Sponsor Award, Morris Brown Col Advan Degree Prog, 1999; Executive Sponsor Award, BellSouth Network African-Am Telecommunications Prof, 1999. **Special Achievements:** Initial Project Manager for the Washington D. C. Martin Luther King, Jr. Memorial Project Foundation, Inc. **Military Serv:** AUS, sp/5, 1970-72; Good Conduct Medal. **Home Addr:** 3465 Somerset Trail SW, Atlanta, GA 30331, **Home Phone:** (404)349-4333. **Business Addr:** Executive Coach, Owner, Carter & Carter LLC, 3465 Somerset Trail, Atlanta, GA 30331, **Business Phone:** (404)349-4332.

CARTER, JOHN R.
Mayor. **Personal:** Born Sep 2, 1941, Laurens County, SC; married Carrie (deceased); children: Anthony, Wadis & Kris. **Career:** Laborer, 1960-69; Laurens Co Dept Soc Serv, human serv specialist; TownGray Ct, mayor, currently. **Orgs:** Pres, SC Conf Black Mayors; pres, Laurens Chap, St Employees Asn; Deacon Pleasant View Baptist Church; Opportunity Off & Assocs; past-pres, Laurens County Chap Nat Asn Advan Colored People; worship fel minister, Red Cross Masonic Lodge FMPHA; pres, SC Equal Opportunity Assocs; former mem, Laurens County Select Serv Bd Town Coun Gray Ct SC; Nat Conf Black Mayors Inc. **Special Achievements:** Numerous achievements including First African-American to serve on Gray Court Council. **Business Addr:** Mayor, Town of Gray Court, 329 Main St, PO Box 438, Gray Court, SC 29645, **Business Phone:** (864)876-2581.

CARTER, JOSEPH CHRIS
Baseball player, broadcaster. **Personal:** Born Mar 7, 1960, Oklahoma City, OK; son of Joseph and Athelene Carter; married Diana; children: Kia Kionne, Ebony Shante & Jordan Alexander. **Career:** Baseball player (retired), broadcaster; Chicago Cubs, outfielder, 1981-83; Cleveland Indians, right fielder, 1984-89; San Diego Padres, right fielder, 1990; Toronto Blue Jays, right fielder, 1991-97; Baltimore Orioles, 1998; San Francisco Giants, 1998; CTV Sports net, Toronto Blue Jays, announcer, 1999-2000; WGN-TV, Chicago Cubs, color commentator, 2001-02. **Honors/Awds:** American League Player of the Month, 1991, 1994; Canadian Baseball Hall of Fame; Major League Baseball Hometown Heroes Award, 2006; Kansas Baseball Hall of Fame, 2008.

CARTER, DR. JOYE MAUREEN
Consultant, pathologist, writer. **Personal:** Born Jun 3, 1957, Wellsville, OH; daughter of Russell and Marjorie Hart. **Educ:** Wittenberg Univ, Springfield, BA, 1979; Howard Univ, MD, 1983. **Career:** Booth Memorial Hosp, NY City, NY, intern, 1983-84; Howard Univ, resident, 1984-88, chief resident pathol, 1988-89; Dade County, forensic pathol fel, 1988-89; George Washington Univ, assoc prof, 1989, Armed Forces Intitution Pathol, dir forensic sci master's prog, 1989-92, dep chief med examr, 1991-92, asst clin prof, 1991; Wash, DC, chief med examr, 1992-96; Harris County, TX, chief med examr, 1996-2002; J&M Forensic Consult, independent forensic consult, 2002; Biblical Dogs Inc, owner, currently. **Orgs:** DC Med Soc, 1992-96; secy pathol sect, NMA, 1992-94; Nat Asn Advan ColoredPeople; Nat Asn Med Examiners; Am Acad Forensic Sci; Aerospace Med Asn; founder, Save Our Kids, 2000-; Healthy People 2000 Anti-Violence Campaign; Chair, sci adv comt, Bd Life; pres, Houston Med Forum; Asn St & Territorial Health Officials. **Honors/Awds:** Honoree, Metro's Annual Black History Month Celebration, 2002; Contemporary Black History Maker, Houston Community Col, 2002; Lou Holtz Upper OH Valley Hall of Fame, 2002. **Special Achievements:** First African American chief medical examiner in Houston (Harris County); first woman chief medical examiner in Houston, first woman chief medical examiner in Washington, DC; Author: My Strength Comes From Within, 2001; ISpeak for the Dead, 2003; first female & first African American to be appointed Chief Forensic Pathologist in the history of the State of Indiana. **Military Serv:** USAF Med Corps, maj, 1979-00. **Business Addr:** Owner, Biblical Dogs Inc, 303 High St, Petersburg, VA 23803, **Business Phone:** (804)722-8267.

CARTER, DR. JUDY L.
Educator. **Personal:** Born Jun 7, 1942, McCormick, SC; married James III, Feb 10, 1968; children: Mason III. **Educ:** Paine Col, Augusta, GA, BA, 1967; Augusta Col, Augusta, GA, MEd, 1976;Univ SC, Columbia, SC, Ed.D, 1981. **Career:** Richmond County, Bd Educ, Augusta, GA, teacher, 1967-76; Paine Col,Augusta, GA, instr, 1976-80; Univ SC, Aiken, SC, dir stud teaching,1980-84; Paine Col, Augusta, GA, chmn div educ, 1984; Dillard Univ, New Orleans, LA, chmn dept educ, 1993-98; Voorhees Col, Denmark, SC, assoc vpres acad affairs, Livingstone Col, asst pres instnl & educ improv;Benedict Col, Columbia, SC, prof educ, chmn educ, dept educ, child & family studies, consult, currently; Fort Valley State Educ, Col Educ,dean, 2006-; Preparation Academic Advisory Committee. **Orgs:** Vpres, Alpha Kappa Alpha Sorority Inc, 1985-87; pres, The Augusta Chap Links Inc, 1986-89; chairperson, Ga Adv Coun, 1988-89; dir, Bush Fac Develop Prog, 1988-; site coordr, Ford Teacher-Scholar Prog, 1990-; Ga Asn Col Teacher Educ, 1985-; bd dir, Child Enrichment; health care bd, Univ Hosp; bd dir, Girls Club; mem, Preparation Academic Advisory Committee. **Honors/Awds:** Teacher of the Year, Paine Col, 1979-80; Graduate Advisor of the Year,Alpha Kappa Alpha Sorority Inc, 1988; Minority Teacher Recruitment Project, Consortium Advan Pvt Higher Educ, 1988-90; Outstanding Community Leader, Wrights Enterprise, 1990; Distinguished Teacher of the Year, Paine Col, 1992-93; Woman of the Year, Nat Sports Found, 1996; Achiever 96, Women Bus Owners Asn. **Business Addr:** Dean, Fort Valley State University, College of Education, 1005 State Univ Dr, Fort Valley, GA 31030, **Business Phone:** (478)825-6365.

CARTER, JUDY SHARON
Labor relations manager. **Personal:** Born Dec 22, 1951, Miami, FL; daughter of James and Ola. **Educ:** Fisk Univ, BS, 1973; Univ MI, MA, 1974, Col Financial Planning, AFP. **Career:** Dade Cty Sch Miami FL, teacher, 1974-75; City Miami FL, admin asst, 1975-77, personnel officer, 1977-78, sr personnel officer, 1978-79, exec dir, civil serv bd, 1979; Assoc Financial Planning. **Orgs:** 1st black trustee, Bd Trustees City Miami Pension Bd, 1980; pres, Nat Assoc Civil Serv Comn, 1983; Leadership Miami Alumni Assoc; nat Forum Black Pub Admin, Intl Personnel Mgt Assoc, FL Pub Personnel Assoc, Federal Selective Serv Syst Be, Nat Assoc Female Exec; Delta Sigma Theta Inc; secy, Miami-Fisk Alumni Club; Young Adult Choir & New Way Fellowship Baptist; Nat Assoc Negro & Prof Womens Club, Credit Union Loan Comt, Carver Young Mens Christian Assoc, Greater Miami Urban League, Am Assoc Individual Investors, Intl Assoc Financial Planners; YWCA; Coordr, Women's Growth Inst, New Way Fellowship Baptist; NAACP; Inst Certified Financial Planners. **Honors/Awds:** Grad Class Leadership in Miami, Greater Miami Chamber Com, 1980; article & pub, Carter, Judy S & Timmons, Wm M "Conflicting Roles in Personal Bds, Adjudications vs Policy Making "Public Personnel Mgt, Vol 14, 2, 1985. *

CARTER, KEITH
Educator, ophthalmologist. **Personal:** Born Apr 19, 1955, Indianapolis, IN; son of James O and Pearlie G Carter; married Cheryl, Apr 6, 1985; children: Evan & Erin. **Educ:** Purdue Univ, BS; Indiana Univ, MD, 1983. **Career:** Methodist Hosp, In, intern, 1983-84; Univ Mich, W K Kellogg Eye Ctr, resident, 1984-87; Univ IA, Dept Opthamology, Oculoplastics & Orbital Surg, fel, 1987-88; Univ Iowa Hosps & Clinics, Col Med, Dept Ophthal, from asst prof to assoc prof, 1988-2001, clin med dir; currently, prof ophthal, 2001-; Lillian C O'Brien and Dr. C. S. O'Brien Chair & head 2006-; Veterans Admin Hosp, Iowa City, IA, Oculoplastics Surg Serv, staff physician, 1998-. **Orgs:** Resident selection comm, prog dir resident educ, 1990-2006; Univ Iowa Col Med, Dept Ophthal, 1989-; fel, CIC Acad Leadership Prog, 1995; treas, Am Soc Ophthal Plastic & Reconstructive Surg (ASOPRS), 1998-2000; off provost, Univ Iowa; Am Acad Ophthamol; Am Col Surgeons; AMA; fel, Am Acad Facial Plastic & Reconstructive Surg; Asn Res Vision & Ophthalmology; Iowa Eye asn; Am Eye Study Club (2002-06: Recording Secy, pres Elect, President); Am Acad Ophthalmol Bd Trustees (at-large member) 2006-. **Honors/Awds:** Walter R Parker Resident Teaching Award, Univ Mich, 1986; The George Slocum Resident Research Award, 1987; American Academy Ophthalmology Honor Award, American Society Ophthalmic Plastic & Reconstructive Surgery Research Award, (ASOPRS); American Academy of Ophthalmology Senior Achievement Award, 2006; Lillian C. O'Brien and Dr. C. S. O'Brien Chair in Ophthalmology, Univ of Iowa, 2006-. **Special Achievements:** ProVision: Preferred Responses in Ophthal, series 2, Am Acad Ophthal, 1996 Awards in Excellence in Education, Am Soc Asn, Exec (ASAE); co-authored: "Size Variation of the Lacrimal Punctum in Adults," Opthalmic Plastic and Reconstructive Surgery, 4(4):231-233, 1988; "Magnetic Resonance Imaging of Intraorbital Wood," Opthalmology 97(5):608-611, 1990; "A System for Measurement of Prosthetic Eye Movement Using a Magnetic Search Coil Technique," Opthalmic Plastic Reconstructive Surgery 7(1):31-40, 1991; "The Long Term Efficacy of Orbital Decompression for Compressive Optic Neuropathy of Graves' Eye Disease," Opthalmology 98:1435-1442, 1991; "Clinical Factors Influencing Periocular Surgical Defects After Mohs Micrographic Surgery," Opthalmic Plastic and Reconstructive Surgery, 1999; Blepharoplasty Course Director, American Academy of Ophthalmology, 1998-. **Business Addr:** Professor, Head, University Iowa, Department Ophthalmology, 11136F-PFP, Iowa City, IA 52242, **Business Phone:** (319)356-2867.

CARTER, KELLY ELIZABETH
Writer. **Personal:** Born Nov 27, 1962, Los Angeles, CA; daughter of Lucille Turner Carter and Ernest Carter. **Educ:** Univ Southern Calif, Los Angeles, CA, AB, Journalism, 1985. **Career:** Iowa City Press-Citizen, Iowa City, IA, sportswriter, 1986-87; Pittsburgh Press, Pittsburgh, PA, sportswriter, 1987-89; Dallas Morning News, Dallas, TX, sportswriter, 1990-; American, writer, currently. **Orgs:** Member, Delta Sigma Theta Sorority, Inc, 1982-; regional coordinator, Association for Women in Sports Media, 1986-; mem, National Assn of Black Journalists, 1986-; mem, Dallas-Fort Worth Assn of Black Communicators, Currently. **Honors/Awds:** Golden Quill Award, Pittsburgh Press Club, 1989. *

CARTER, KENNETH GREGORY
Executive. **Personal:** Born Aug 12, 1959, Louisville, KY; son of Garland K and Laura L Grant; married Ellen Melissa Pullen Carter, Feb 14, 1987; children: Kenneth Jr, Brandon G. **Educ:** Univ Louisville, BSC, 1981; Ohio State Univ, MBA, 1983. **Career:** Int Bus Mach, KY, sales, 1980-90; D&D Consult Serv Inc, adv coun; Brown-Forman Beverage Co, KY, nat sr brand mgr, 1990, vpres, dir ethnic mkt, currently. **Orgs:** Bd dirs, Urban league, 1990; Nat Asn Advan Colored People; Advisory Council. **Honors/Awds:** Black Achiever, YMCA, 1987; Am Best & Brightest, Dollars & Sense Mag, 1988; Ky Col, Jaycees, 1989. **Special Achievements:** Key to the City, New Orleans City Govt, 1990. **Business Addr:** Vice President, Brown-Forman Beverages Corporation, 850 Dixie Hwy, Louisville, KY 40210.*

CARTER, KENNETH LEONARD. See CARTER, KI-JANA.

CARTER, KENNETH WAYNE
Advertising executive. **Personal:** Born Sep 8, 1954, Muskogee, OK; son of Ira Carter McCoy and Doris; divorced; children: Burch Merrick. **Educ:** Southern Univ, BA, 1976. **Career:** KALO Radio, sports dir, 1976-77; Am Heart Asn, dir pub rel, 1977-81; Focus Commun Inc, exec vpres, 1981-87, pres & ceo, 1988-. **Orgs:** PRSA, Multicultural Affairs Comt, 1982-; bd mem, Dallas Ft Worth Minority Bus Develop Div Coun, 1983-86; City Dallas, Pub Info Task Force, 1990; Dallas Citizens Coun, 1994-95; bd mem, Dallas Urban League, 1994-98; bd mem, Dallas Conv & Vis Bur, 1996-98; bd dir, DFW Regional Sports Comn, currently. **Honors/Awds:** Target Impact Award Tex, Affiliate Am Heart Asn, 1980; Man of the Year, Nat Asn Negro Bus & Prof Women, 1986; Dallas Black Coc, Quest Success, 1987. **Special Achievements:** First Black mem, bd dir, Pub Rel Soc Am, North Tex Chap, serv two terms, one as scy; only Black mem, Pub Info Task Force, City Dallas, also serv Steering Comt. **Home Addr:** 4909 Haverwood Lane Suite 2106, Dallas, TX 75287, **Home Phone:** (972)447-9298. **Business Addr:** President, Chief Executive Officer, Focus Commun Inc, 1401 Elm St Suite 1900, Dallas, TX 75202, **Business Phone:** (214)744-1428.

CARTER, KEVIN ANTONY
Executive, executive director. **Personal:** Born May 23, 1960, Cleveland, OH; son of John and Lavenia; divorced. **Educ:** Vanderbilt Univ, BA, philos, 1982; Weatherhead Sch Mgt, Case Western Res Univ, MBA, finance, 1987. **Career:** Ernst & Young, sr consult strategic planning, 1986-89; LTV Steel Co, sr analyst strategic planning, 1989-93; McDonald & Co Investment, Diversity & Bus Develop, vpres & dir , 1993-06; Nat City Corp, Work Force Diversity, dir, 2006-. **Orgs:** exec comt mem, NAACP, Cleveland Br, 1992-94; chairperson, African Am Bus Consortium, 1992-; telethon chairperson, United Negro Col Fund, Cleveland/Canton/Akron, 1993-; advisory bd chairperson, Kaleidoscope Mag, 1994-; bd chair, City Cleveland Community Rels, Youth Subcommittee, 1994-; City Cleveland Investment Oversight Comt, 1994-; nat bd mem, Nat Black MBA Asn, 1994-; bd mem, Securities Indust Asn. **Honors/Awds:** H Naylor Fitzhugh Award of Excellence, Nat Black MBA Asn, 1993; Man of the Year, Kaleidoscope Mag, 1994. **Special Achievements:** Cleveland Success Guide, Top Ten to Watch, 1991; Cleveland Crains' Business, 40 under 40 Club, 1993; Columnist, Call & Post Newspaper, Minority Investor

Forum, weekly column, Feb 1993-; Leadership Cleveland, Class of 1993-94; Kaleidoscope Mag, Forty-Forty Club, 1994; Series 7 & 63, Investment Securities Licenses. **Business Phone:** (216)222-2000.*

CARTER, KEVIN LOUIS
Football player. **Personal:** Born Sep 21, 1973, Miami, FL; married Shima. **Educ:** Univ Fla. **Career:** St Louis Rams, defensive end, 1995-2000; Tennessee Titans, defensive tackle, 2001-04; Miami Dolphins, 2005-06; Tampa Bay Buccaneers, 2007-. **Orgs:** Kevin Carter Found, 2002;, exec comm mem, NFL Players assn. **Honors/Awds:** Carroll Rosenbloom Memorial Award as the team's rookie of the yr, 1995; Tennessee Titans Community Man of the Yr, 2002. **Business Phone:** (813)870-2700.*

CARTER, KI-JANA (KENNETH LEONARD CARTER)
Football player. **Personal:** Born Sep 12, 1973, Westerville, OH. **Educ:** Pa State Univ, bus mkt. **Career:** Cincinnati Bengals, running back, 1996-99; Wash Redskins, 2001; New Orleans Saints, running back, 2003-04. **Orgs:** Big Bros Big Sisters. **Honors/Awds:** Ed Block Courage Award, 1998. **Special Achievements:** Film: Jerry Maguire. *

CARTER, LAMORE JOSEPH
School administrator, psychologist. **Personal:** Born Apr 18, 1925, Carthage, TX; married Lena Mae Jones; children: Greta Lisa, Kris-Lana. **Educ:** Wiley Col, 1947; Fisk Univ, AB, 1950; Univ Wis, MS, 1952; Univ Chicago, postgrad, 1954; State Univ Iowa, PhD, 1958; Univ Tex, 1966; Univ Columbia, 1967; Emory Univ, 1970; Harvard Univ, 1976. **Career:** Grambling Col, LA, instr, 1952-54, asst, 1961-66; State Univ Iowa, res asst, 1956-58; Inst Res, admin, 1966-68; Southern Asn Cols & Schs, res fel postdoctoral, 1969-70; Morehouse Col, vis distinguished prof Psychol, 1970; Tex Southern Univ Houston, dean faculties, 1970-71; Grambling State Univ, assoc dean admin, 1971-76; consult, Peace Corps W Africa, 1971-76; Southern Asn Cols & Schs, consult, 1971-82; Am Coun Educ, fel acad admin, 1976-77; Grambling State Univ, provost & vpres acad affairs, 1977; Wiley Col, pres, 1993-. **Orgs:** Am Educ Res Asn; dipl, Am Bd Prof Psychol; chap pres, Am Asn Univ Profs, 1960-63; consult, Headstart Prog, 1968-76; Am Southwestern; La Psychol Asn; Am Asn Higher Educ; Am Asn Ment Deficiency; Nat Soc Study Educ; La Asn Ment Health; Nat Educ Asn; Phi Delta Kappa; Phi Beta Sigma; Dem; Meth; Am Psychol Asn; founder & pres, Lions Club Int, 1981-84; bd dirs, United Campus Ministry; Am Coun Fel, La State Univ. **Honors/Awds:** Mason 33rd degree; Fellow, Am Asn Ment Deficiency; Dipl, Am Bd Prof Psychol; Licensed School Psychologist, La Bd Examiners Psychologists. **Special Achievements:** Contributed articles to professional journals, books and monographs. **Military Serv:** AUS; Bronze Star. **Business Addr:** President, Wiley College, 711 Wiley Ave, Marshall, TX 75670, **Business Phone:** (903)927-3200.*

CARTER, LAVONYA QUINTELLE. See CARTER, QUINCY.

CARTER, DR. LAWRENCE
College administrator, educator. **Personal:** Born Oct 4, 1942, Valdosta, GA; son of Isabell Beady; married Mrs Marva L Moore, Jan 28, 1968; children: Mauri D Carter & Laurent L Carter. **Educ:** Ft Valley State Col, GA, BS, agr educ, 1968; Tuskegee Inst, AL, MS, agr educ, 1969; Fla State Univ, Tallahassee, FL, EdS, 1973, PhD, adult educ, 1976. **Career:** Goldkist Indust, Atlanta GA, mgr trainee, 1969-71; Tuskegee Inst, Tuskegee, AL, asst prof adult educ, 1973-74; Fla A&M Univ, Tallahassee, FL, exten rural develop specialist, 1974-80, actg dir agr res, 1980-87, dir coop exten, 1980, assoc dean, dir & prof, currently. **Orgs:** Ft Valley State Col Alumni Asn, 1968; Tuskegee Alumni Asn, 1969; Adult Educ Asn Am, 1973, Fla A&M Univ Alumni Asn, 1974; consult, Univ Fla Int Prog, 1980; dir, Steering Comt, Bethel Baptist Church, 1982-84; mem bd dir, Southern Rural Develop Ctr, 1987; pres, Phi Beta Sigma, Local Chap, 1987; consult, Kellog Proj, NC A&T Univ, 1988; Policy Comm, Exten Serv, USDA, 1989; Rural Am Virtual Community Ctr; Nat 4 H Agents Asn; Phi Delta Kappa; Southern Asn Horticulture Scientists; Am Asn Agr Engrs; Asn 1890 Agr Administrs Asn. **Honors/Awds:** Leadership Award, Phi Beta Sigma Fraternity, 1977; Man of the Year, Fort Valley State Col Alumni, 1978; Leadership Award, Florida A&M Univ, 1978; Certificate of Appreciation, Govs Off, State Fla, 1981; Certificate of Appreciation, 1984, 1987, Service Award, 1988, Fla A&M Univ; Meritorious Achievement Award, Univ Fla, 1986; State Mid-Career Award, 1994. **Special Achievements:** Author of Thesis, "Adult Educ," 1969, The Effect of Readability on Comprehensive of Consumer Laws, 1976, A Package Approach for Rural Clientele, 1979, Small Farm Development in Florida's Vegetable Industry, 1979, Strategic Planning for Cooperative Extension Involvement in International Programs, 1985. **Military Serv:** AUS, Spec 4, 1961-65; Good Conduct Medal, 1964. **Business Addr:** Professor, Director, Florida A&M University, CESTA Cooperative Extension & Outreach Programs, Perry-Paige Bldg Rm 215 S, Tallahassee, FL 32307, **Business Phone:** (850)599-3546.

CARTER, LAWRENCE EDWARD, SR.
Clergy, dean (education), college teacher. **Personal:** Born Sep 23, 1941, Dawson, GA; son of John Henry III; married Marva Lois Griffin; children: Lawrence Edward Jr. **Educ:** Va Univ, Lynchburg, BA, soc studies, 1964; Boston Univ, MDiv, theol, 1968, STM Pastoral Care, attended 1970, PhD, pastoral care & coun, 1978; Andover Newton Theol Sch; Ohio State Univ; NY Univ; Harvard Univ; Ga State Univ; Univ Wis; George Wash Univ; Lewis Univ. **Career:** Roxbury United Presbyterian Church, minister youth, 1965-67; Boston Pub Schs, sub teacher, 1966-77; Twelfth Baptists Church, minister coun, 1968-71; Boston Univ Warren Residence Hall, resident coun & asst dir, 1968-71; Boston Univ MLK Jr African-Am Cult Ctr, dir, 1971-73; People's Baptist Church, assoc minister, 1971-78; Harvard Univ, Div Sch, clergy teaching adv, 1976-77; Marsh Chapel Boston Univ, assoc dean, 1978-79; Morehouse Col, prof philol & relig, 1979-, Martin Luther King Jr Int Chapel, dean, 1979-, col cur, 1979-; archivist & cur, 1982-97; Fulbright Scholar, Brazil, 1994. **Orgs:** Coordr, Afro-Am Studies Prog, Simmons Col, 1977-78; Am Acad Relig, 1979; bd dirs, Nat Coun Churches Christ, 1983-90; Soc Study Black Relig, Class Leadership Atlanta, 1986; bd visitors, Mercer Univ Sch Theol, 2001-03;Nat Asn Col & Univ Chaplains; ACLU; Am Acad Relig; Asn Black Prof Relig; Ministries Blacks Higher Ed; Nat Asn Adv Colored People; Atlanta UN Asn; fel Nat Endowment Humanities; bd trustees, Soka Univ Am. **Honors/Awds:** Citizenship Medal of the Yr, Va Col, 1964; Recognition of Outstanding Achievement Relig & Humanitarianism, Omega Scroll Hon, Morehouse Col, 1979; Distinguished Alumnus Award, 2002; Nat Black Christian Stud Leadership Consult Award; Fac Mem of the Yr, Morehouse Col Stud Newspaper. **Special Achievements:** Has made over sixty radio and television appearances, including nationwide in England, Canada, Japan, New Zealand, Australia, South Africa, continent wide in Africa, Singapore and ten countries in Malaysia. **Business Addr:** Dean, Professor, Morehouse College, Martin Luther King Jr Int Chapel, 830 Westview Dr SW PO Box 24, Atlanta, GA 30314.*

CARTER, DR. LAWRENCE ROBERT
Educator. **Personal:** Born Nov 24, 1936, Washington, DC; son of John Harold Sr and Mary Magdalene King; married Maile Louise Crooker; children: Elizabeth Miriam & Christopher. **Educ:** Howard Univ, Wash, DC, BS, 1958; Univ Ore, Eugene, OR, MA, 1970, PhD, 1973. **Career:** Lane County Youth Proj, community organizer, 1965-67; Univ Oregon, res asst & instr, 1967-71; US Off Educ, pre-doctoral fel, 1969; Nat Sci Found, NSF fel, 1971; Univ Pac, asst prof, 1971-73; Univ Ore, asst prof, assoc prof, prof head, 1973-; Social Sci Res Coun, staff assoc, 1975-76; Int J Forecasting, assoc ed, currently; Univ Ore, dept sociol, prof emer, currently. **Orgs:** Eugene Human Rights Comn, comnr, 1967-71; Pop Asn Am, 1970-; Danforth assoc, Danforth Found, 1973; Ore Health Coun, vice chairperson, 1988-91, comnr, 1988-; Am Statist Asn, 1989-; City Club Eugene, 1990-. **Honors/Awds:** Citation for Service, City Eugene, 1970-71. **Military Serv:** USAF, capt, 1959-65. **Home Addr:** 2112 Agate St, Eugene, OR 97403. **Business Addr:** Professor Emeritus, University of Oregon, Department of Sociology, 804 PLC, Eugene, OR 97403, **Business Phone:** (503)346-5169.

CARTER, LEMORIE, JR.
Businessperson, business owner. **Personal:** Born Dec 9, 1944, Birmingham, AL; son of Lemorie and Gloria; children: Kristie, Ronnie & Lemorie III. **Educ:** Morehouse Col, 1963-65; Miles Col, BA, Soc Sci, 1967; Life UnderwriterTrain Coun, 1972. **Career:** Firestone Tire & Rubber Co, sales mgr, 1968-70; Met Life Ins Co, sales rep, 1977; Lemorie Carter Ins Agency, Midland Nat Life Ins Co, ins broker, gen agent, 1977-; AL Williams Fin Serv Org, sr vpres, 1983-; Carter-CarterIns Agency, owner; Mayor Richard Arrington Jr Birmingham AL, admin asst,1977; sr vpres First Am Nat Securities & The A L Williams Corp; Primerica Financial Serv, nat sales dir, 1989. **Orgs:** Treas, Birmingham Urban League, 1973; Initiated voter reg Birmingham, 1973; adv bd, Sickle Cell Anemia Screening Found, 1979, Birmingham Creative Dance Co, 1980; instr, inst seminars Miles Col, Daniel Payne Col, Lawson St Comm Col; pub rel dir Alpha Phi Alpha Omicron Lambda Chapt; budget comm Six Ave Bapt Church; bd dirs Positive Maturity, United Way Agency. **Honors/Awds:** Numeours institute organisation awards; frat award; Outstanding Young Men Am, 1972-77; Outstanding Bd Mem Award, Outstanding Serv Pin Birmingham Urban League 1975, 1978; several Financial Services Industry Awards.

CARTER, LENORA
Publisher. **Personal:** Born Mar 12, 1941, Corrigan, TX; married Julius Carter (died 1971); children: Constance Yvette, Karen Yvonne. **Educ:** Ariz State univ, bus Admin. **Career:** Forward Times Newspaper, gen mgr & adv dir, 1960-71, chief exec officer & publ, 1971-; Amalgamated Publ Inc, bd of dir, currently. **Orgs:** Riverside Hosp; Eliza Johnson Home for Aged; 20th Century Fund; Nat Asn Mkt Developers; Nat Newspaper Publ Asn; Am Red Cross; United Fund; United Negro Col Fund; Eta Phi Beta Sorority; Gamma Phi Delta; Riverside Nat Bank; Riverside Gen Hosp; Eliza Johnson Home Aged; Independent State Bank, United Negro Col Fund; YMCA; St. Luke's First Missionary Baptist Church; Nat Asn Media Women. **Honors/Awds:** Mickey Leland Humanitarian Award, Nat Asn Advan Colored People; Pioneer Award; Alma Newsom Vision Award; Nat Emphasis Award, Nat Alliance Mkt Developers; Fred D Patterson Leadership Award; Nat Asn Media Women; Houston Med Forum Recognition Award; Robert S. Abbott Award; Anheuser Busch Women Sci, Eng & Construct Award; Illustrious Potentate's Distinguished Service Award; St. Joseph Volunteer Service Award; Tex State Teachers Asn Dedicated Service Award; San Jacinto Girl Scout Merit Award; TSU Tennis Club Leadership Award; Toombs-Brown Award, Prof Black Women's Enterprise Inc; "Pace Setter" Award, Sigma Gamma Rho Sorority Inc; Nat Coun Negro Women Pacesetters Award, 2002. **Special Achievements:** Outstanding Citizen, State of Mich; Publisher of the Year, Nat Newspaper Publishing Asn , 2004. **Business Addr:** Publisher, Chief Executive Officer, Forward Times, PO Box 2962, Houston, TX 77004.*

CARTER, MARGARET LOUISE
Educator, senator (u.s. federal government), government official. **Personal:** Born Dec 29, 1935, Shreveport, LA; daughter of Emma. **Educ:** Portland State Univ, BS, educ; Wash State Univ, post-grad studies; Ore State Univ, MEd, psychol. **Career:** Albina Youth Opportunity Sch, instr, 1971-73; Portland Community Col, counr, 1973; bus woman, 1975-; House Educ Comt, mem, 1985-; Conf Comt Martin Luther King Jr State Holiday, co-chair, 1985; Ore House, 1984; Joint House-Senate Comt Trade & Econ Develop, 1985-; Spec Joint Comt Health Care, mem, 1986; Ore House Human Resources Comt, vice chair, 1987-; Ore State, Dist 22, senator, 2000-, senate pres pro tempore, 2005-. **Orgs:** Ore Alliance Black Sch Educ; Portland Teachers Asn; Ore Assembly Black Affairs; Am Fedn Teachers; Spec Comn Parole Bd Matrix Syst; NAACP; Ore Polit Women's Caucus; Alpha Kappa Alpha Sorority; co-founder Black Leadership Conf, 1986; gov appointee, Ore Task Force Drug Abuse, 1986-; Gen Adv Comt Victims Rights, 1986-. **Honors/Awds:** Zeta Phi Beta Sorority Award; Musical Director of the Joyful Sound, Piedmont Church Christ, Portland; Jeanette Rankin First Woman Award, Ore Women's Polit Caucus, 1985; Jefferson Image Award, 1985; Elliott Human Rights Award; Legislator of the Year Award, Nat Black Caucus State Legislators. **Special Achievements:** First black woman in history to be elected to Oregon Legislative Assembly. **Business Addr:** Senator, President Pro Tempore, Oregon State Senate, District 22, 900 Court St NE S-311, Salem, OR 97301, **Business Phone:** (503)986-1722.

CARTER, DR. MARION ELIZABETH
Educator. **Personal:** Born in Washington, DC; daughter of James Martin and Marion Jackson. **Educ:** Wellesley Col; Howard Univ, MA; Middlebury Col, MA; Georgetown Univ, MS; Cath Univ, PhD; Georgetown Univ, PhD. **Career:** World Univ, trustee; Wellesley Col, vis prof; Gordon Col, prof; Teachers Col, prof; Howard Univ, instr; Barber Scotia Col, assoc prof; Wiley Col,assoc prof; Univ La Gaguna, lectr; Univ Andes, Meridan, Venezuela, lectr;Am Lang Inst Georgetown Univ, teacher; St Mary Univ, Nova Scotia, lectr. **Orgs:** Nat Asn Foreign Stud Affairs; Le Droit Park Civic Asn; Smithsonian Inst;past sec, Am Asn Teachers Spanish & Portuguese; Am Asn Univ Professors; Am Asn Univ Women; trustee, World Univ; elected mem, Order Int Fel. **Honors/Awds:** Buena Aires Conv Award; Agnes Meyer Award; American Association of Teachers of Spanish and Portuguese Award, Spain; Directory of Am Scholars; Fulbright Award, Spain; plaque, Lifetime Bd Gov, Am Biog Inst; Int Hall of Leaders, Great Minds of the 21st Century; IBC Book of Dedications; ABI Int Peace Prize. **Home Addr:** 402 U St NW, Washington, DC 20001-2333. *

CARTER, MARTIN JOSEPH
Clergy. **Personal:** Born Jul 31, 1930, High Point, NC. **Educ:** Emersin Col, BA, 1956; Cornell Univ, BA, 1956, MEd, 1960. **Career:** Harvard Univ, consult, 1970-74; St Joseph Comm Parochial Sch, teacher coordr facilitator, 1970-75; Dissemination Prog, participant, 1971-72; Univ Ill Curric Studies Math, model teacher; St Francis De Sales Church, 1975-76; Archdiocese Kingston, Jamaica, pastor, 1976-. **Orgs:** Nat Black Catholic Clergy Caucus, 1968-77; Caribbean Ecumenical Const for Devel, 1976-77; exec, Jamaica Coun Churches, 1976-77. **Honors/Awds:** Published "Teen-Age Marriage", 1974; "Homiletic & Pastoral Rev - Diocesan Policy on Teenage Marriages", 1975; "Dignitatis Humanae Declaration on Religious Freedom"; The New Catholic Encyclopedia, 1979. **Business Addr:** Church of Reconciliation, Kenton Ave, Bridge Port, Jamaica.

CARTER, MARTY LAVINCENT
Football player. **Personal:** Born Dec 17, 1969, La Grange, GA. **Educ:** Middle Tenn State Univ. **Career:** Football player (retired); Tampa Bay Buccaneers, defensive back, 1991-94; Chicago Bears, 1995-98; Atlanta Falcons, 1999-01; Detroit Lions, safety, 2001-02. *

CARTER, MARVA GRIFFIN
Educator. **Personal:** Born Jun 4, 1947, Cleveland, OH; daughter of Marvin C; married Dr Lawrence E Carter Sr, Jun 22, 1969; children: Lawrence E Jr. **Educ:** Boston Conservatory Music, BM, 1968; New England Conservatory Music, MM, 1970; Boston Univ, MA, 1975; Univ Illinois, PhD, 1988. **Career:** Boston Univ, administrative asst, Afro-Am Studies Prog, 1970-71, coordr freshman & sophomore seminars, 1972-73; Simmons Col, coordr Afro-Am studies prog, 1973-77; Clark Atlanta Univ, adjunct assoc prof music, 1988-89; Ebenezer Baptist Church, organist & music

coordr, 1982-92; Morris Brown Col, coordr music, 1988-93; Georgia State Univ, asst dir, Sch Music, 1993-95, asst prof music hist & lit, assoc prof music hist & lit, currently. **Orgs:** Am Musicological Soc, cultural diversity & comt publication American music, 1973-77, 1993-; Sonneck Soc Am Music, nominating comt, educ comt & cultural diversity comt, 1973-77, 1993-; Ctr Black Music Res, assoc mem, 1993-; Soc Ethnomusicology, 1973-77, 1993-; Young Audiences Atlanta, bd mem, ed comn, 1992-94; Atlanta Symphony Action Comt Black Audience Develop, 1992-94. **Honors/Awds:** Miss Texas High, poise, 1964; Winner piano award, 1964; Smithsonian Institution Research Fellow, 1983. **Special Achievements:** First African American to receive the PhD in musicology from the Univ of Illinois, 1988; Roland Hayes, Expresser of the Soul in Song, Black Perspective in Music, pp 189-220, Fall, 1977; Articles published in Black Women in the US and Notable Black American Women; musical biography on Will Marion Cook, forthcoming. **Business Addr:** Associate Professor, Georgia State University, School Music Department Music History & Literature, 712 Haas Howell, PO Box 4097, Atlanta, GA 30302-4097, **Business Phone:** (404)413-5932.*

CARTER, MARY LOUISE
Government official, mayor. **Personal:** Born Jun 27, 1937, Clarksdale, MS; daughter of Mrs Julia M Turner; married Everett L; children: Danny C & Eric L. **Educ:** Coahoma Jr Col, AA, 1959; Alcorn Col, 1960; Fontbonne Col, attended 1977. **Career:** Sears Credit Cent, credit analyst, 1969; City Pagedale, alderperson,1981-92, actg mayor, 1984-85, mayor, 1992-; Mo Div Families Servs, caseworker, 1995; City Pagedale, Mayor, 2008-. **Orgs:** Bd mem, Normandy Munic Coun, 1981-88; bd mem, Adult Basic Educ, 1981-86;actg pres bd, City Pagedale, 1984-86; chair, Pub Awareness Adult BasicEduc, 1984-85; Black Elected Offs St Louis Co, 1990; Nat Conf Black Mayors. **Honors/Awds:** Positive Imate; Award for Services, Scout Troop, 1995. **Special Achievements:** Outstanding Contrib in Adult Literarcy, 1994. **Home Addr:** 1284 Kingsland Ave, Pagedale, MO 63133. **Business Addr:** Mayor, City Pagedale, 1420 Ferguson Ave, Pagedale, MO 63133-1720, **Business Phone:** (314)726-1200.*

CARTER, NANETTE CAROLYN
Artist, educator. **Personal:** Born Jan 30, 1954, Columbus, OH; daughter of Matthew G and Frances Hill. **Educ:** L'Accademia di Belle Arti, Perugia Italy, 1975; Oberlin Col, OH, BA, 1976; Pratt Inst Art, Brooklyn, NY, MFA, 1978. **Career:** Dwight-Englewood Sch, Englewood NJ, teacher of printmaking & drawing, 1978-87; self-employed artist & painter, 1987-; City Col New York, adj prof, 1992-93; Pratt Inst Art, vis asst prof fine arts, 2001-. **Orgs:** Bd mem, Harlem Sch Arts. **Honors/Awds:** Jerome Found Grant, 1981; Nat Endowment for the Arts Grant, 1981; Artist in Residence Grant, New York State Coun Arts, 1984; New Jersey State Coun Grant, New Jersey State Coun Arts, 1985; fel, Bob Blackburn's Printmaking Workshop, 1989; N'Namdi Gallery, Birmingham, MI, 1989; New York Found for the Arts Grant, 1990; Pollock-Krasner Found Inc Grant, 1994-; The Wheeler Found Grant, 1996; Brandywine Workshop fel, Phila, PA; fel, Lower Eastside Printshop, 1997; fel, Brandywine Workshop, 1999. **Special Achievements:** Yale Gallery of Art, New Haven CT; Mus of Art, Rhode Island Sch of Design, RI; ARCO, Philadelphia, PA; Studio Mus in Harlem, NY; Merck Pharmaceut Co, PA; Motown Corp., CA; MCI Telecommunication IL; IBM, CT; Pepsi-Cola, NY; Gen Electric, Fairfied, CT; Salomon Bros, NY; Schomburg Libr, NY; Reader's Digest, Pleasantville, NY; Morgan Guaranty, NY; The Libr of Cong, WA, DC; Planned Parenthood, NY; Bristol-Meyers Squibble Co, Princeton, NJ; Merch Pharmaceut Co, Phildelphia, PA; Nextel Corp; Los Angeles, CA; Magic Johnson Enterprises, Los Angeles, CA; AT&T, NJ; Collections: Mudd Libr, Oberlin Coll; Rutgers Grad Sch of Mgt; Cochran Found, Am Express, Minneapolis, MN; Solo Groups: June Kelly Gallery, NYC, NY, 2000; Sante Webster Gallery, Philadelphia, PA, 2001; Conkling Gallery, MN State Univ, MN, 2001; GR N-Nanti Gallery, Chicago, IL, 2002; GR N'Nanti Gallery, Detroit, MI, 2002; O.G.T. Gallery, NYC, NY, 2002; Sante Webster Gallery, Philadelphia, PA, 2003; Group Shows: Rhode Island Sch of Design, Providence, RI, 2000; Jack Tilton/Anna Kustera Gallery, NYC, NY, 2000; Pratt Inst of Art, Brooklyn, NY, 2000; Pa Acad of the Fine Arts, Philadelphia, PA, 2000; Cover for "The Intl Review of African-Am Art," Hampton Univ, VA, Vol 18 No 4, 2003; Collections: Columbus Mus of Art, Ohio; Newark Mus, NJ; The Pa Acad of the Arts, PA; Schomburg Ctr for Res, Black Culture, NY; AT&T, NJ; Nat Steel Corp, Pittsburg, PA. **Business Addr:** Visiting Assistant Professor, Pratt Institute of Art, Rm 1 S Hall 144 W 14th St, New York, NY 10011, **Business Phone:** (718)636-3634.

CARTER, NIGEA
Football player. **Personal:** Born Sep 1, 1974, Coconut Creek, FL. **Educ:** Mich State Univ, attended 1996. **Career:** Tampa Bay Buccaneers, wide receiver, 1997. **Honors/Awds:** Player of the Year, 1996.

CARTER, NORMAN L
Executive, manager. **Personal:** Born Jun 16, 1949, Pittsburgh, PA; married Zelia, Jul 19, 1986; children: Norman IV. **Educ:** Ind Univ, Pa, BA, 1971; Johns Hopkins Univ, MS, Mkt, 1997. **Career:** Brown & Root Inc, Houston, Tex, sr auditor; Ernst & Young, sr auditor; Westinghouse Elec Corp, internal auditor; Ft Wash Hosp, mem & bd dir; Potomac Elec Power Co, sr auditor, mgr Minority Bus Develop, div mgr; mgr econ develop, 1981-. **Orgs:** Am Inst Cert Pub Acct; founder & past pres, Nat Asn Black Acct; bd dir & treas, Prince Georges Chamber Com; past chmn, Utility Network Community Based Develop; bd dir, Wash Cathedral Choral Soc; vpres, Md & DC Minority Supplier Develop Coun; bd dir, Downtown Bus Improv Dist; Maryland Indust Develop Asn; Int Develop Res Coun; Am Econ Develop Corp; Coun Urban Econ Develop; Fort Wash Hosp; Int Develop Res Coun; Gateway Ga Ave Revitalization Corp. **Business Addr:** Manager of Economic Development, Potomac Electric Power Co, 1900 Pennsylvania Ave NW, Washington, DC 20068, **Business Phone:** (202)872-3357.

CARTER, ORA WILLIAMS
Educator, artist. **Personal:** Born Aug 25, 1925, Ferndale, MI; daughter of Samuel and Emma Kinney; married Walter H Carter (deceased). **Educ:** Clark Col, AB, 1947; Wayne State Univ, MEd, 1963. **Career:** Black Mountain Col, Rosenwald fel, 1946; Detroit Bd Educ, teacher, 1953-67; Harvard Univ, Rosenwald fel, 1965; Commun Skills Ctr, instr & diagnostician, 1967-72; Bow Elem Sch, instr, 1972-76; Roosevelt Elem Sch, precision teacher, 1976-81; Ora's Studio, artist, 1978-. **Orgs:** Mich Asn Calligraphers; Nat Conf Artists, Metrop Detroit Reading Coun, 1965-81; bd dirs, Delta Home Girls, 1968-78; Detroit Fedn Teachers; charter mem, Fred Hart Williams Geneal Soc; Founders Soc & Friends African Art; life mem, Nat Asn Advan Colored People; Charles H. Wright Mus African Am Hist; bd mgt, YWCA, 1972-79, 1980-84; pres, Detroit Alumnae Chap Delta Sigma Theta Sorority, 1973-75; bd dirs, Fedn Girls homes, 1975-78; chairperson bd mission, Educ & Social Action, 1976-80; Detroit Arts Comt, 1982-89; vpres, Top Ladies Distinction, 1987-88; vice moderator, Church Coun, 1991-92; Mayflower Congregational United Church Christ; Div Mission Detroit Metro Asn United Church Christ; Clark Atlanta Univ Alumni Asn. **Honors/Awds:** Artist of the Month, Afro-Am Mus Detroit, 1975; Community Service Award, 1993. **Special Achievements:** Exhibited and juried calligraphy shows; first vice president, Top Ladies of Distinction, 1987-88. **Home Addr:** 19501 Hubbell St, Detroit, MI 48235. *

CARTER, OSCAR EARL, JR.
Physician. **Personal:** Born Aug 2, 1922, Chesterbrook, VA; married Edna; children: Oscar III, Don, Donna, Kim. **Educ:** Meharry Med Col, MD, 1952; Dillard Univ, BA, 1948. **Career:** Lower 9 Methadone Clinic Inc, med dir sponsor; physician family pract, 1959-76; Well Baby Clinics Eastside Health Dist, dir, 1954-59; gen pract, 1953-59; Lower 9 Methadone Clinic Inc, dir, 1970-76; Desire Narcotics Rehab Ctr, med dir, 1971-72; Com Alcoholism & Drug Abuse, med coordr, 1971-72, Dr Oscar Carter Jr Mem Rehab Ctr, physician, 2001. **Orgs:** Sanity Comn Sect I Criminal Dist Ct, 1971-72; Drug Abuse Rehab Team; consult, SUNO'S Dept Drug Abuse; Dist I Adv Bd La; adv bd bur Drug Affairs New Orleans; New Orleans Med Soc; Nat Med Asn Cert Drug Abuse; Univ Miami Dept Urban Studies, 1972; LSU Med Sch Dept Continuing Med Educ, 1975. **Business Addr:** Doctor, Memorial Rehabilitation Center, 5500 N Johnson St, New Orleans, LA 70117, **Business Phone:** (504)949-2767.*

CARTER, PAMELA LYNN
State government official, vice president (organization). **Personal:** Born Aug 20, 1949, South Haven, MI; daughter of Dorothy Elizabeth Hadley Fanning and Roscoe Hollis Fanning; married Michael Anthony, Aug 21, 1971; children: Michael Anthony Jr & Marcya Alicia. **Educ:** Univ Detroit, BA (cum laude), 1971; Univ Mich, MSW, 1973; Ind Univ, JD, 1984. **Career:** Univ Mich, Sch Pub Health, res analyst, treatment dir, UAW, Detroit, 1973-75; Ment Health Ctr for Women 7 C, exec dir, 1975-77; UAW-Gen Motors Legal Servs, Indpolis, consumer litigation atty, 1983-87; Secy State, Ind, securities atty, 1987-89; Gov Ind, exec asst for health & human servs, starting 1989; State IN, atty gen, 1993-97; Cummins Inc, vpres, gen coun & corp secy, 1998-2005; Fleetguard Inc, pres, 2005-06; Cummins Filtration, pres, 2006-. **Orgs:** Ind Bar Asn, 1984-; Catholic Social Servs; Jr League; Nat Bar Asn; Coalition 100 Black Women. **Special Achievements:** First African Am female to become a State's Atty Gen; first female President of a major filtration and exhaust company. **Business Addr:** President, Cummins Filtration, 500 Jackson St, PO Box 3005, Columbus, IN 47202-3005, **Business Phone:** (812)377-5000.

CARTER, PAT. See CARTER, PATRICK HENRY.

CARTER, PAT
Football player, football coach. **Personal:** Born Aug 1, 1966, Sarasota, FL; married Charlene; children: Jamelle & Alec. **Educ:** Fla State univ. **Career:** Football player (retired), football coach; Detroit Lions, tight end, 1988; Los Angeles Rams, 1989-93; Houston Oilers, 1994; St Louis Rams, 1995; Ariz Cardinals, 1996-97; St Louis rams, offensive asst, coaching intern, 2004-05; Detroit Lions, asst coach, tight ends coach, 2006-. **Business Addr:** Tight ends coach, Detroit Lions, 222 Republic Dr, Allen Park, MI 48101, **Business Phone:** (313)216-4056.*

CARTER, PATRICK HENRY (PAT CARTER)
Executive. **Personal:** Born Jan 8, 1939, Memphis, TN; son of Patrick Carter and Annie Carter; married Mattie Pearl Bland; children: Kimberly & Patrick H III. **Educ:** Miss Valley State Univ; LeMoyne Col; Gen Motors Inst. **Career:** Exxon USA, instr, 1972; Pat Carter Pontiac Inc, pres; Superior Serv, partner, 1990-; Memphis Rockets Basketball Team, owner; Olympic Staffing Inc, owner & pres, 1993-. **Orgs:** Deacon, Mid Baptist Church, 1970-; exec bd, Liberty Bowl, 1982-; bd mem, Boy Scouts Am, 1986; bd mem, Pub Bldg Authority, 1988-94; bd mem, Sr Citizens, 1990-95; Chamber Com, 1992-94; pres, Whitehaven Community Develop Corp, 1994-97; mem, Memphis Sports Authority. **Honors/Awds:** Achiever, Pontiac Motor Div, 1984-86; Top 100 Black Businesses, Black Enterprise Mag, 1984, 1985, 1986 & 1987; Small Business of the Year, Memphis Business Jour, 1988. **Military Serv:** USN, petty officer second class, 4 yrs. **Business Addr:** Owner, President, Olympic Staffing Inc, 1230 Southbrook Mall, Memphis, TN 38116, **Business Phone:** (901)344-9664.

CARTER, PERRY LYNN
Football player. **Personal:** Born Aug 15, 1971, McComb, MS; married; children: 1. **Educ:** Southern Miss Univ. **Career:** Kans City Chiefs, defensive back, 1995-96; Oakland Raiders, 1997-98; Detroit Lions; Houston Texans, defensive asst, currently. *

CARTER, PHILIP W.
School administrator, educator. **Personal:** Born Feb 1, 1941, Widen, WV; married Beverly Thomas; children: Philippa, Stacey & Frederick. **Educ:** Marshall Univ, BA, polit sci, 1964; Univ Pittsburgh, MSW, 1970. **Career:** Cong Racial Equality, Cleveland, dir, 1967-68; Univ Pittsburgh, Grad Sch Pub Int Affairs, instr, 1970-78; Comn Action Reg Training, dir, 1972-73;Univ Pittsburgh, asst provost, 1979; DIGIT Inc, pres, 1967-; Ford Found, fel, 1968; Univ Pittsburgh, Intercultural House, consult, 1969-70; ClarionUniv Pa, consult, 1973, 1976, 1980-81 & 1983-85; Marshall Univ, dir social work prog, prof & chmn soc work, currently. **Orgs:** Chmn, Western Pa Black Polit Assembly, 1974-; campaign mgr, Mel King Mayor Boston, 1979; bd mem, Schuman Juvenile Ctr, 1979-81; bd mem, Human Rels Comn, 1982-; bd mem, Barnett Day Care Ctr, Huntington, WVa, 1982-84; campaign mgr, Doris Smith Judge Spring, 1985. **Honors/Awds:** Outstanding Man of the Year, Talk Mag, 1974; Outstanding Contribution in Politics, Black Republicans, 1978; Outstanding Black Alumni, Marshall Univ, 1978. **Business Addr:** Professor, Chairman of Social Work, Marshall University, Department of Social Work, Rm 307 Old Main 1 John Marshall Dr, Huntington, WV 25755, **Business Phone:** (304)696-2790.

CARTER, PHYLLIS HARDEN
State government official. **Personal:** Born Oct 28, 1948, Norfolk, VA; daughter of Wilbur and Mable; married Hazo W Carter Jr, Aug 8, 1981; children: Angela Mable Elizabeth. **Educ:** Inst European Studies, Paris, France, 1969-70; L'Alliance Francaise, Paris, France, 1970; St Augustine's Col, BA, hist & french, 1971; Col William & Mary, Marshall-Wythe Sch Law, JD, 1975. **Career:** Little Rock, Ark, asst city atty; Charleston, WV, asst atty gen; WVa Human Rights Comn, dir; Dept Human Serv, comnr; State-Fed Rels, Off Gov, Charleston, WV, dir, currently. **Orgs:** Methodist Charities WVa, 1989-93; Black Diamond Girl Scouts, 1989-93; Charleston-Inst Alumnae Chap, 1990-92; WVa Literacy Coun, 1991-94; pres, Dist Sorority Inc; Appalachian Educ Lab, 1991-93; Social Action Comn, 1992-94; Am Red Cross, Cent WVa, 1992-95. **Honors/Awds:** Outstanding Personalities of the South, 1984; Commendation, City Council of Little Rock Ark, 1987; Merit Award, Gov Bill Clinton, 1987; Outstanding African Am Women in the Kanawna Valley, Nat Orgn Women, WVa Chap, 1991. **Special Achievements:** Author: "Judge George Howard", 1987, "Scholars, Balancing Out the Under Representation", 1987, "Has the Color Barrier Fallen", 1988, Ark Lawyer. **Home Addr:** PO Box 622, Institute, WV 25112. **Business Addr:** Director of State and Federal Relations, State of West Virginia Officer of the Governor, 1900 Kanawha Blvd E Bldg 1, Charleston, WV 25305-0009, **Business Phone:** (304)558-3829.

CARTER, QUINCY (LAVONYA QUINTELLE CARTER)
Football player. **Personal:** Born Oct 13, 1977, Decatur, GA. **Educ:** Univ Ga. **Career:** Dallas Cowboys, quater back, 2001-04; New York Jets, quater back, 2004-05, Bossier-Shreveport Battle Wings, quarter back, 2007. Kansas City Brigade, 2008, Abilene Ruff Riders, quater back, 2009-. *

CARTER, DR. RAYMOND GENE, SR.
Educator. **Personal:** Born Nov 12, 1936, Youngstown, OH; married Virginia Averhart; children: Raymond Gene, John Amos & Dewayne Dwight. **Educ:** Youngstown State Univ, BA, 1959, M.Ed, 1975; Univ Pittsburgh, PhD. **Career:** McGuffey Ctr Inc, admin dir, 1976-86; Youngstown State Univ, ltd serv faculty, 1976-; Model City, dep dir; Curbstone Coaches, bd dir; Youngstown State Univ, limited serv fac polit & social dept; Park view Coun Ctr, sr therapist, currently. **Orgs:** Minority rep Stub Canal pvt Sector; chmn, Welf Adv Bd; Social Serv; bd dir Assoc Neighborhood Ctr; vpres, bd dir, Meth Comn Ctr; Eval Com Area Health; bd dir, C C; Kiwanis Club; Big Brothers; bd dir, Eastern Ment Health High Sch; Selective Svc; foreman Mahoning County Jury, 1981. **Honors/Awds:** Leadership & Citizenship Award; Col Most Valuable Athlete; Curbstone Coaches Hall of Fame Youngstown; Athletic Achievement Award, Service Award,

Youngstown City Mayor; Community Service Award, Black Knight Police Assoc; Choffin Career Center Award, 1988; Youngstown State Univ Football Hall of Fame, 1997. **Military Serv:** AUS, 1960-62. **Business Addr:** Senior Therapist, Parkview Coun Ctr, 611 Belmont Ave, Youngstown, OH 44502.*

CARTER, REGINA
Jazz musician. **Personal:** Daughter of Grace. **Educ:** Oakland Univ, Rochester, BA; New Eng Conservatory Music, Boston. **Career:** Berklee Col Music, instr; Albums: I'll Be Seeing You: A Sentimental Journey, 2006; Paganini: After a Dream, 2003; Free fall, 2001; Motor City Moments, 2000; Rhythms of the Heart, 1998; Something For Grace, 1997; Regina Carter, 1995; MacArthur fel, 2006. **Honors/Awds:** LHD, Albion Col, MI, 2006; MacArthur Fellows Program grant, award, 2006. **Special Achievements:** Nominated for Grammy Award, 2002; Distinguished Artist Award, Int Soc for Performing Artists, 2007. *

CARTER, RICARDO
Physician. **Career:** Pvt Prac, physician, currently. **Home Addr:** 310 Electric Ave Suite 231, Lewistown, PA 17044. **Business Addr:** Physician, 310 Electric Ave Suite 231, Lewistown, PA 17044.*

CARTER, ROBERT HENRY
Insurance executive. **Personal:** Born Aug 2, 1941, Chicago, IL; married; married Marlene Y Hunt; children: Robert H IV, Kimberly & Brandon Robert. **Educ:** Chicago City Col, attended 1962; Worshams Col Mortuary Sci, attended 1963; Ill Inst Technol, attended 1964. **Career:** Lawndale Packaging Corp, sales mgr, 1971-72; Chicago Minority Purchasing Council, purchasing specialist, 1972-75; Robert H Carter, III & Assocs, Inc, pres, 1975-; Group Ins Admin Ga Inc, pres, 1982-. **Orgs:** Cosmopolitan Chamber Com, 1972-, Chicago Urban League, 1975-, Chicago Asn Com & Indust, 1979-; Self Ins Inst Am, 1983; Soc Prof Benefit Adminr; 1984-; Prof Ins Mkt Asn, 1986-. **Honors/Awds:** Ten Outstanding Young Men of Chicago Jaycees, 1974. **Business Addr:** President, Group Insurance Administration GA Inc, 200 W Adams St, Chicago, IL 60606, **Business Phone:** (312)795-0932.

CARTER, ROBERT LEE
Judge. **Personal:** Born Mar 11, 1917, Caryville, FL; widowed; children: John & David. **Educ:** Lincoln Univ, AB, pol sci, 1937; Howard Univ, Sch law, LLB (Magna CumLaude), 1940; Columbia Univ, law sch, LLM, 1941; Lincoln Univ, DCL, 1964. **Career:** NAACP Legal Defense & Educ Fund, asst coun, 1945-56, gen coun, 1956-68; Poletti, Freiden, Prashker, Feldman & Gartner, mem firm, 1969-72; US Dist Ct, S Dist NY, judge, 1972-. **Orgs:** NY Bar Asn, 1941-; NY Mayor's Jucic Comn, 1968-72; educ bd, NY Law J, 1969-72; pres, Nat Comn Against Descrimination in Housing, 1966-72; NY St Spl Comn on Attica, NY Ct Reform, 1970-72; Nat Conf Black Lawyers. **Honors/Awds:** Distinguishing Alumni Award, Howard Univ, 1980; Fel, Columbia Urban Ctr, 1968-69; Resenwald Fel, 1940-41; Lincoln Univ, Hon Doctor Laws, 1965; NorthEastern Univ, Hon Doctor Laws, 1985; Holy Cross, Hon Doctor Laws, 1990; Howard Univ, Hon Doctor Laws, 1994; New Sch, Hon Doctor Humane Letters, 1998; Honorary Juris Doctor Degree, Fordham Univ Sch Law, 2004. **Special Achievements:** Wrote numerous law review articles and essays on civil rights; published awell-received memoir of his struges as a civil rights advocate, 'A Matterof Law'. **Military Serv:** USAF, 2nd Lt, 1941-44. **Home Addr:** 65 Central Pk W, New York, NY 10023. **Business Addr:** Judge, U.S. District Court for the Southern District of New York, 225 Cadman Plz E 640, Brooklyn, NY 11201-1832.

CARTER, ROBERT LOUIS, JR.
Educator, school administrator. **Personal:** Born Nov 11, 1937, Loganville, GA; son of Robert Louis and Elizabeth; married Cathleen Jane Cole, Jun 4, 1974; children: Robert Louis, William Stephen, Joyce Elizabeth, Valerie Denise. **Educ:** Beloit Col, BA, classics, 1962; Northwestern Univ, MA, 1964, PhD, 1980. **Career:** Northwestern Univ Fel, 1962-65; Univ Ill, classics instr; Beloit Col, classics instr, dir High Potential Progr, exec dir, Beloit Improv Coalition, 1971-73, spl asst provost, 1969-73; Assoc Col Midwest, dir, Educ Develop Prog, 1973-83; exec bd, Wis Higher Educ Aids Bd, 1982-84; Wayne State Univ, dir, Univ Studies, Weekend Col Prog, 1984-86, assoc dean, Adult Degree Progs, 1986-87, dean, Col Lifelong Learning, 1988-; Univ Pittsburgh, Pitts Col Gen Studies, dean, 1996. **Orgs:** bd dirs, Nat Coun Educ Opportunity Asns, 1980-82; Mid-Am Asn of Educ Opportunity Prog Personnel, pres, 1981, pres-elect, 1980, pres 1982, exec secy, 1984; Nat Univ Continuing Educ Asn, 1987-; Asn Continuing Higher Educ; chair, Coordinating Coun Continuing Higher Educ, 1991-. **Honors/Awds:** Outstanding Service & Leadership, MAEOPP, 1981. **Special Achievements:** Systematic Thinking Curriculum, Kendall/Hunt Publishing Co, 1980; "The Role of Formal Syntax in Critical Thinking," MAEOPP Journal of Educ Opportunity, 1986; "Uncle Tom and the Pedestal," Chicago Defender, 1968. *

CARTER, ROBERT T.
Executive. **Personal:** Born Mar 21, 1938, Cleveland, OH; married Virginia; children: Robert John. **Educ:** Baldwin Wallace Col, BA, 1959; Pepperdine Grad Sch Bus. **Career:** Cleveland, teacher, 1959-64; Shell Oil Co Long Beach, sales rep, 1964-66; Hoffman LaRoche, sales & hosp rep, 1966-68; KFI Radio Inc, acct exec, 1968-. **Orgs:** Nat Asn Market Develop; Radio Salesman LA; Southern Calif Broadcasters; LA Brotherhood Crusade; New Frontier Dem Club; United Crusade Fund Raising Comt, 1974-75; Leukemia Soc Am; Southern Calif Striders Track Club. **Honors/Awds:** Martha Jennings Teaching Award, 1963; Pharmaceuticals Sales Award, LaRoche, 1968; California delegate Democratic Convention, 1968; Calif Democratic Coun, 1968; Democratic State Central Comn, 1968.

CARTER, ROBERT THOMPSON
School administrator, executive director. **Personal:** Born Mar 16, 1937, Cleveland, OH; son of Robert (deceased) and Evelyn (deceased); married Tessa Rosemary Felton; children: Robert & Jacqueline. **Educ:** Dartmouth Col, BA, 1959. **Career:** Joseph T Ryerson & Son Inc, supvr personnel admin, 1967-68, mgr, comm relations 1968-70; N Lawndale Econ Develop Corp, asst gen mgr, 1970-72; Inland Steel Develop Corp, asst reg mgr & proj mgr, 1972-77; Inland Steel-Ryerson Found, exec dir, sec, 1981-86; Dearborn Park Corp, vpres, corp commun & corp sec, 1977-81; Nat Merit Scholar Corp, exec dir, 1987-88, vpres, 1988-; Chicago Bridges Work demonstration, project dir; Music Theatre Workshop, dir; Suburban Job-Link Corp, dir, currently, Public/Private Ventures, dir, currently. **Orgs:** Co-founder Black Contractors United, 1979; bd chairperson, Just Jobs Inc, 1982-86; dir, Performance Comm, 1982-86; vpres, Asn Black Found Execs, 1984-86; founding mem, dir, Indiana Donors Alliance, 1984-86; corp adv bd, Independent Col Funds Am,1984-86; vpres, Music Theatre Workshop, 1986-; dir, Brass Found Inc, 1987; dir, Blacks Develop, 1987-; trustee, Gaylord & Dorothy Donnelley Found, 1988-; Horizon Hospice, dir, 1992-; Garfield Counseling Ctr. **Honors/Awds:** Leadership Award, Black Contractors United, 1979; Beautiful People Award, Chicago, Urban League, 1980. **Military Serv:** USAF, capt, 1959-66; Air Force Commendation Medal, 1964. **Business Phone:** (215)557-4400.

CARTER, RODA WARD
Executive. **Educ:** Fashion Inst Technol, NY, fashion design. **Career:** Beauty Enterprises; Naomi Sims Cosmetics, vpres prod develop; Universal Colors Cosmetics, pres & chief exec officer, 1999-. **Orgs:** NAFE; Boys & Girls Club; contribr, United Way. **Honors/Awds:** The Pillar Award Up & Coming Entrepreneur of the Year, 2001. **Special Achievements:** Featured in the August 2001 issue of the Pittsburgh Mag; WPIX, Channel Eleven talk show, guest. *

CARTER, ROLAND
Composer, educator. **Career:** Univ Tenn, Chattanooga, UC Found, distinguished composer-arranger & conductor, prof music, currently, Cadek Dept Music, Ruth S Holmberg Prof music; MARVEL, founder & chief exec office; "The Choral Music of Roland M. Carter, Volume I", 2009. **Orgs:** Nat Asn Negro Musicians; life mem, Nat Asn Negro Musicians, bd dir, chair comt Choral Standards; life mem, Am Choral Dir Asn; Music Educrs Nat Conf; Music Teachers Nat Asn; Phi Mu Alpha Sinfonia; Kappa Alpha Psi Fraternity; co-chair, NEA; Chattanooga African Am Mus; Chattanooga Symphony & Opera Asn; dir, Choral Soc Preservation African Am Songs. **Business Addr:** Professor, University of Tennessee, Department of Music, 308 Fine Arts Dept 1451 615 McCallie Ave, Chattanooga, TN 37403, **Business Phone:** (423)425-4601.

CARTER, RUBIN
Boxer, association executive. **Personal:** Born May 6, 1937, Delwanna, NJ; married Lisa Peters; children: Theodora & Raheem; married Lisa Peters. **Career:** Boxer, 1954-66; Asn Defence Wrongly Convicted, founder & exec dir. **Orgs:** Bd dir, Southern Ctr Human Rights; bd dir, Alliance for Prison Justice; trustee, Friends Griffith Univ, US Inc. **Honors/Awds:** European Lightweight Champion, 1956; Middleweight Championship Belts of the World, World Boxing Coun & World Boxing Assn; inducted, Int Boxing Hall of Fame, 1994; hon doctorate of laws, Griffith Univ, Australia, 2003. **Special Achievements:** Published autobiography, The Sixteenth Round: From Number One Contender to Number 45472, 1974; subject of Bob Dylan song, "Hurricane"; Film, The Hurricane, based on his life, 1999.

CARTER, RUTH E. (RUTHE CARTER)
Costume designer. **Personal:** Born in Massachusetts. **Educ:** Hampton Univ, Fine & Performing Arts. **Career:** assoc prod, The Family Man, 1979; costume designer: School Daze, 1988; I'm Gonna Git You Sucka, 1988; Do the Right Thing, 1989; Mo' Better Blues, 1990; The Five Heartbeats, 1991; Jungle Fever, 1991; House Party 2, 1991; Malcolm X, 1992; What's Love Got to Do with It, 1993; The Meteor Man, 1993; Surviving the Game, 1994; Crooklyn, 1994; Cobb, 1994; Money Train, 1995; Clockers, 1995; Rosewood, 1996; The Great White Hype, 1996; How Stella Got Her Groove Back; Sunchaser, 1996; Amistad, 1997; B*a*p*s, 1997; Rosewood, 1997; Bamboozled, 2000; Price of Glory, 2000; Shaft, 2000; Love & Basketball, 2000; Dr. Dolittle 2, 2001; Baby Boy, 2001; Dr. Dolittle 2, 2001; I Spy, 2002; Daddy Day Care, 2003; Against the Ropes, 2004; Four Brothers, 2005; Serenity, 2005. **Honors/Awds:** Am Black Film Festival Career Achievement Award for Women, 2002. **Home Addr:** 003450.

CARTER, RUTHE. See CARTER, RUTH E.

CARTER, SHAWN COREY
Rap musician, actor, entrepreneur. **Personal:** Born Dec 4, 1969, Brooklyn, NY; son of Adnis Reeves and Gloria Carter; married Beyonce Knowles, Apr 4, 2008. **Career:** Roc-A-Fella Records, co-founder, vocalist, 1997; Albums: Reasonable Doubt, 1996; In My Lifetime, 1997; Hard Knock Life, 1998; (with various artists) Streets Is Watching, 1998; The Life & Times of Shawn Carter, 1999; TheDynasty: Roc la Familia, 2000; The Blueprint, 2001; Jay-Z: Unplugged, 2001; Chapter One: Greatest Hits, 2002; (with R. Kelly) The Best of Both Worlds, 2002; The Blueprint 2: The Gift & the Curse, 2002; Bring It On:The Best of Jay-Z, 2003; The Blueprint 2.1, 2003; The Black album, 2003; (with R. Kelly) Unfinished Business, 2004; (with Linkin Park) Collision Course, 2004; Greatest Hits, 2006; Kingdom Come, 2006; American Gangster, 2007; The Blueprint 3, 2008; "Criminal Minds", 2008; "Dancing on Ice", 2009; The Taking of Pelham 1 2 3, 2009; Films: Streets Is Watching, 1998; Hard Knock Life, 2000; State Property, 2002; Paper Soldiers, 2002; Fade to Black, 2004; I Will Not Lose, 2004; Diary of Jay-Z: Water for Life, 2006; Def Jam Recordings, pres & ceo; The 40/40 Club, co-owner, currently; New Jersey Nets, co-owner, currently. **Orgs:** Shawn Carter Scholarship Fund. **Honors/Awds:** Numerous honors & awards including multiple Grammy, American Music, MTV Music Video, Soul Train and Billboard Awards. **Special Achievements:** First Hip-Hop artist to be featured on the news program; First non-athleteto have a signature sneaker line; The S. Carter is the fastest selling sneaker in Reebok history; One Of The 10 Most Fascinating People of 2006. **Business Addr:** Owner, The 40/40 Club, Six W 25th St, New York, NY 10010, **Business Phone:** (212)832-4040.*

CARTER, STEPHEN L
Educator, novelist. **Personal:** Born Oct 26, 1954; married; children: 2. **Educ:** Stanford Univ, BA, 1976; Yale Univ Law Sch, JD, 1979. **Career:** US Supreme Ct Justice Thurgood Marshall, clerk; Yale Law Sch, from asst prof to prof, 1982-91, William Nelson Cromwell prof law, 1991-; Novels: The Emperor of Ocean Park, 2002, New England White, 2007. **Honors/Awds:** LLD, Bates Col, 2003. **Special Achievements:** author: Reflections of an Affirmative Action Baby; God's Name in Vain; The Emperor of Ocean Park. **Business Addr:** William Nelson Cromwell Professor of Law, Yale Law School, 127 Wall St, PO Box 208215, New Haven, CT 06520, **Business Phone:** (203)432-4992.

CARTER, THOMAS
Dean (Education). **Educ:** Henderson State Univ, BS. **Career:** Univ Ark, Dept Chem Eng, asst dean, currently. **Business Addr:** Assistant Dean, University Arkansas, Department of Chemical Engineering, 3189 Bell Eng Ctr, Fayetteville, AR 72701, **Business Phone:** (479)575-5009.

CARTER, THOMAS, II
Lawyer. **Personal:** Born Feb 27, 1953, St Louis, MO; son of Thomas and Everline; married Dorothy L, Sep 25, 1972; children: LaDon D. **Educ:** Univ Md, BS, 1980; St Louis Univ Sch Law, JD, 1983. **Career:** Law Officers Bussey & Jordan, law clerk, 1981-93, assoc, 1993-94; Off Atty Gen, asst atty gen, 1984-85; Moser & Marsalek, PC assoc, 1985-92, shareholder, 1992-95; Collier, Dorsey, Carter, Williams, partner, 1995; Pvt pract, atty, currently. **Orgs:** Am Bar Asn; MO Bar Asn; Bar Asn Metrop, St Louis; MO Orgn Defense Lawyers; Asn Defense Coun St Louis; Nat Bar Asn; Ill State Bar Asn; Mound City Bar Asn, pres, 1991-92. **Honors/Awds:** State MO, License, 1984; US Dist Ct Eastern MO, Admis, 1985; US Dist Ct Western MO, Admis, 1985; State Ill, License, 1986; US Ct Appeals, 8th Circuit, Admis, 1987. **Special Achievements:** Lawyers Role Polit Empowerment: the Struggle Continues Minorities & Women, St Louis Daily Records, May 1, 1990. **Military Serv:** USAF, sgt, 1972-80; Two Air Force Commendation Medals. *

CARTER, THOMAS, III
Football player. **Personal:** Born Sep 5, 1972, St Petersburg, FL; married Renee; children: Cameron, Peyton, Madison & Alex. **Educ:** Notre Dame Univ. **Career:** Football player (retired); Washington Redskins, defensive back, 1993-96; Chicago Bears, 1997-99; Cincinnati Bengals, 1999-2001.

CARTER, THOMAS ALLEN
Consultant. **Personal:** Born Jul 12, 1935, Cincinnati, OH; son of Fernando Albert and Mary Gladys Gover; married Janet Tucker, Oct 14, 1956; children: Barry E, Duane A & Sarita A. **Educ:** Jones Col, AB, 1980, BBA, 1982. **Career:** Consultant (retired); Red Lobster Restaurant Const Dept, contract adminr, 1976-78; Harcar Inc, pres, 1978-80; Blacando Develop Corp, exec secy, 1980-84; Solomon A Williams Inc, proj engr, 1984-2002, chief engr, 2002. **Orgs:** Consult cost estimating, JH Dunlap Roofing Co, 1978-84, Robinson's Custom Homes, 1980-84; Bluejackets Choir USN, Bluejackets Octet USN, Fleet Reserve Asn; Rafman Club Inc. **Honors/Awds:** Sailor of the Year, 9th Naval Dist, 1960; SeaBee of the Month Argentia Newfoundland Canada, 1965. **Military**

Serv: USN, master chief constructionman, 22yrs; Navy Commendation; Naval Unit Citation; Vietnam Expo; Good Conduct Medals (5); Presidential Unit Citation; Expert Rifleman. **Home Addr:** 4128 Arajo Ct, Orlando, FL 32812, **Home Phone:** (407)859-9948. *

CARTER, TONY A. (ANTONIO MARCUS)
Football player. **Personal:** Born Aug 23, 1972, Columbus, OH. **Educ:** Univ Minn. **Career:** Chicago Bears, running back, 1994-97; New England Patriots, 1998-2000; Denver Broncos, 2001; Green Bay Packers, right back, 2002.

CARTER, TRACY L
Health services administrator. **Personal:** Born Oct 9, 1970, Akron, OH; daughter of Bennie and Tanya; married Stanley Johnson, Jun 28, 2003; children: Jaylen. **Educ:** Ohio Univ Col Bus, BBA, 1993; Univ Mich Sch Pub, masters, health admin, 1995. **Career:** Ohio Univ, stud ctr mgr, 1992-93; Henry Ford Health Syst, mkt & outreach intern, 1994; WK Kellog Found, community based pub health liaison, 1994-95; Summa Health Syst, admis fel, 1995-96, dir, corp projs, 1996-99, dir, corp projs, community serv, 1999-. **Orgs:** Bd chair, Healthy Connections Network, 1996-; Leadership Akron, 1998-; vpres, YWCA bd, 1999-; personnel chair, Summa Cty C Servs Bd, 2000-; personnel chair, Caring Communities Summit Community, 2001-; EJ Thomas Hall/ Akron Civic Theatre, multicultural prog comn, 2002-; adv comn, United Way, Proj Blueprint, 2002-; Area Helath Educ Ctr Bd, 2002-. **Honors/ Awds:** Alumna of Year Award, INROADS, 1997; Community Service Award, Delta Sigma Theta, 1998; Caring Manager of Year, Summa Health Syst, 2000; 100 Women Award, YWCA, 2001; Distinguished Service Nominee, Akron Jaycees, 2002. **Special Achievements:** Co-author of Afro-American Health Resource Guide for State of Michigan, 1994-95. **Business Phone:** (330)375-7566.

CARTER, TROY A
Government official, educator, vice president (organization). **Personal:** Born Oct 26, 1963, New Orleans, LA; son of Theodore R and Eartha F; married Melanie Sanders. **Educ:** Xavier Univ, BA, polit sci & bus admin, 1986; Carnegie-Mellon Sch Urban & Pub Affairs, MPA. **Career:** New Orleans, exec aide to mayor Sidney J Barthelemy, 1988-91; La State, rep, 1992, City Council, rep Dist C, 1994; WD Scott Group Inc, Environ Eng Consult, vpres; Xavier Univ, polit sci instr, currently. **Orgs:** Bd dirs, Big Brothers & Big Sisters; bd dirs, Nat Youth Sport Found; chmn dict C, Orleans Parish Dem Exec Comt; charter mem, 100 Black Men New Orleans; Nat Asn Advan Colored People; Nat Orgn Black Pub Admin; Kappa Alpha Psi Fraternity Inc; chmn, Opers Comt, Controversial Opers Comt, Sewerage & Water Bd. **Special Achievements:** First African-American Elected District 102; First African American to be elected to New Orleans City County District. **Home Addr:** 92 Eng Turn Dr, New Orleans, LA 70131, **Home Phone:** (504)392-6213. **Business Addr:** Political Science Instructor, Xavier University, 3800 Victory Pkwy, Cincinnati, OH 45207, **Business Phone:** (513)745-3718.

CARTER, VINCE (VINCENT LAMAR CARTER)
Basketball player. **Personal:** Born Jan 26, 1977, Daytona Beach, FL. **Educ:** Univ NC. **Career:** Toronto Raptors, forward, 1998-2005; Olympics, Sydney, Australia, US men's basketball team, 2000-04; NJ Nets, guard & forward, 2004-; Visions InFlight Inc, pres. **Orgs:** Founder, Embassy of Hope; goodwill ambassador, Big Bros Big Sisters Am. **Honors/Awds:** John Wooden Award. Rookie of the Yr, Schick, 1999; Rookie of the Month, March, April, NBA, 1999; Rookie of the Yr, NBA, 1999; Slam Dunk Champ, 2000; Gold Meda, US Olympic Team, 2000; Child Advocate of the Yr, Children's Home Soc, 2000; Community Assist Award, NBA, 2005; 8-timeAll-Star; INDUCTED, FHSA HALL OF FAME. **Business Phone:** (201)935-8888.*

CARTER, VINCENT G
Manager, interior designer. **Personal:** Born Feb 22, 1956, Milwaukee, WI; son of Walter A Carter Sr and Lessie M; married Jun 30, 1979 (divorced 1981). **Educ:** Univ Wisconsin-Milwaukee, BA, 1977; Univ Wisconsin-Madison, MS, 1983. **Career:** Visual Graphics Created, designer, 1980-95; World Bank, client rep, 1983-95; Howard Univ, asst prof, 1984-2000; Vincent G. Carter Assocs Inc, vice chair, prin, 1994-; Karn Charuhas Chapman Twohey Architects, sr interior designer, 1997-99; McKissack & McKissack, sr interior designer, 1999-2003. **Orgs:** Am Soc Interior Designers, 1980-; Facil Mgt Asn, 1988-; Interior Design Educr Coun, 1990-; Int Interior Design Asn, 1991-; Nat Coun Interior Design Qualifications, 1991-; Nat Legis Coalition Interior Design, 1992-; Int chair, Wash DC Bd Interior Designers, 1993-97; Woodlawn Plantation/Pope-Leighey House Coun, 1997-2000; vice chair, Int Codes Coun, 2001-. **Honors/Awds:** America's Best & Brightest Young Bus Professionals, 1990; Howard Univ Teaching Award, 1994; Wash Metro ASID Design Humanity, 1998; ASID Medalist Award, 2000; Fasid Community Ser Award, Sheri K Lake, 2002. **Home Addr:** 2243 Eutaw Pl, Baltimore, MD 21217-3903, **Home Phone:** (410)728-0587. **Business Addr:** Principal, Vincent G. Carter Associates Inc., Washington, DC.

CARTER, DR. WARRICK L.
Educator, composer. **Personal:** Born May 6, 1942, Charlottesville, VA; son of Charles M and Evelyn; married Laurel (Latta), Apr 17, 1993; children: Keisha. **Educ:** Tenn State Univ, BS; Blair Acad Music, Advan Percussion, 1965; Mich State Univ, MM 1966, PhD, 1970; Univ Chicago, Cert Fund Raising, 1978. **Career:** Univ Md, asst prof dept Music, 1966, 1971; Mich State Univ, dir dept urbanmusic, 1970, 1971; Governors State Univ, coordr, fine & performing div, 1971-76, coord music prog, 1976-79; Northwestern Univ, guest prof Afro-Am Studies, 1977-84; Governors State Univ, chmn div Fine & Performing Arts, 1979-84; Univ Santa Cantarina Floriano polis Brazil, guest lectr dept music, 1980; Berklee Col Music, dean fac, 1984-95; Calif State Univ LA, vis prof, Music Dept; Sch Music Univ Sao Paulo Brazil, guest lectr, 1976; Berklee Col Music, provost/vip academic affairs, 1995-96; Walt Disney Attractions, dir academic arts, 1996-00; Columbia Col, pres, 2000-. **Orgs:** Past pres NAJE, 1982-84; chmn, Jazz Panel Nat Endow Arts, 1982-85; co-chair Music Policy Panel Nat Endowment, 1983-84; nat sec, Black MusicCaucus, 1974-78; ASCAP; bd mem Nat Jazz Cable Network, 1982-84; bd mem Found Advan Music, 1982; adv bds, Music Fest USA & EPCOT Inst Entertainment Arts; bd dirs, Int House Blues Found, 1993-; IAJE, 1982-. **Honors/Awds:** Distinguished Teacher Award, Gov's State Univ, 1974; Best Drummer Award Collegiante Jazz Festival Notre Dame Univ, 1970; Fac Mem of the Yr, Univ Md, 1967-68; Grad Fel Ctr Urban Affairs Mich State Univ, 1969-70; named as one of ten Outstanding Music Educr Sch Musician, 1983; "The Whistle" comn Nat Endowment Arts, 1982-83; IAJE, Hall of Fame, 1997. **Special Achievements:** First African American pres of Columbia Col Chicago. **Business Addr:** President, Columbia College Chicago, 600 S Mich Ave Room 505, Chicago, IL 60605.*

CARTER, WESLEY BYRD
Psychiatrist, physician. **Personal:** Born Apr 22, 1942, Richmond, VA; son of Wesley T; married Norma Archer. **Educ:** Va Union Univ, BS, 1964; Med Col Va, attended 1968; Med Col Va, pediat internship, 1969; Gen Psychiat Residency, MCV, 1971. **Career:** Va Treat Ctr C, child psychiat fel, 1973; Child Psychiat Ltd, child psychiat, 1975-83; Psychiat Inst Richmond C Unit, med chief, 1983-87; Horizons Inc, pres, 1986-93; Psychiat Inst Richmond, actg med dir, 1986; Charter Westbrook Hosp, clin dir adult serv, 1987, clin dir RTP, 1989-92, actg med dir, 1990; Host Radio Show Whats on Your Mind, WANI Richmond, Mem Child Guid Clin, psychiatist, 2004; Richmond Pub Schs, psychiat consult; Caroline County Pub Schs, psychiat consult; Friends Asn Richmond, psychiat consult; Psychiat Med Col Va, asst clin prof; Real Sch Richmond Pub Schs, spec consult; St Mary's Hosp, hosp appts; Richmond Mem, Richmond Community Hosp, hosp appts; Richmond Metro Hosp, hosp appts; Westbrook Hosp, hosp appts; Psychiat Inst Richmond, hosp appts; Med Col Va, hosp appts; Chippenham Hosp, hosp appts. **Orgs:** Bd dirs, Mental Health Asn Va, 1991; Youth Serv Comn Richmond; Spec Educ Adv Comt; Richmond Pub Schs; Med Col Va Med Curric Comt; Richmond Acad Med; pres, Richmond Med Soc; pres, Va Coun Child Psychiat; pres-psychiat, Soc Va; Va Soc Adolescent Psychiat; Med Soc Va; fel Am Psychiat Asn; Am Acad Child Psychiat; Black Psychiat Am; Asn Air Force Psychiat; Chi Delta Mu; fel Alpha Phi Alpha; Thebans Richmond; Old Dominion Med Soc; Nat Med Asn; Am Med Asn; State Human Rights Comt Va, Dept Mental Health, Mental Retardation & Substance Abuse Serv; Am Acad Child & Adolescent Psychiat; fel Beta Kappa Chi; Cent Tex Med Found. **Military Serv:** USAF, 1973-75; Commendation Medal. **Home Phone:** (804)353-8006. *

CARTER, WILL J.
Executive. **Career:** Carter Indust Serv Inc & Carter Express Inc, Anderson, IN, chief exec officer. **Orgs:** GAAFU Pres, NY Fisk Alumni Asn. **Business Phone:** (317)644-6601.*

CARTER, WILLIAM BEVERLY
Executive. **Personal:** Born Feb 22, 1947, Philadelphia, PA; son of W Beverly Carter Jr and Rosalie A Terry; married Kay Sebekos; children: Terence S. **Educ:** Univ Col Nairobi, Kenya, attended 1966; Univ de Paris Sorbonne, attended 1966; Howard Univ, BA, 1971; Johns Hopkins Univ Sch Adv Int Studies, MA, 1973. **Career:** Executive (retired); Rockefeller-Luce Fel, 1971-73; US Community Orgn Govt Conduct Foreign Policy, staff mem, 1972-75; US Dept State, escort interpreter, 1972-75; Brookings Inst, res asst, 1974-75; US Dept Energy, sr foreign affairs officer, 1976-81; Inst Int Educ, Prof Exchange Progs, assoc dir, interim dir, 1984-2005. **Orgs:** Nat Geneal Soc, 1974-; bd dir, Lupus Found Greater Wash DC, 1984-93; adv bd, Lupus Found Greater Wash, 1993-; chmn, Nat Adv Comt Diversity, NCIV, 1993-96; bd dir, Nat Coun Int Visitors, NCIV, 1994-2000; bd dir, Int Asn Black Prof Int Affairs, 1999-2002. **Honors/Awds:** William C Foster Award, JH Univ Sch Advan Int Studies, 1972-73. **Military Serv:** AUS, sgt; Bronze Star, 1967-70.

CARTER, WILLIAM THOMAS, JR.
Physician. **Personal:** Born Apr 27, 1944, Norfolk, VA; married Juatina M Redd; children: William III, Dominique Michelle, Tiasha Malitha. **Educ:** Fisk Univ, AB, 1967; Tenn A&I State Univ, MS, 1969; Meharry Med Col, MD, 1973. **Career:** USN, dir emergency med. **Orgs:** Kappa Alpha Psi Frat, 1963-; dir emergency med, Nat Naval Med Ctr, 1980-82; Assoc Mil Surgeons US, 1981-; ATLS instr, Am Col Surgeons, 1982-; Pigskin Club Inc, 1984-, Nat Asn Advan Colored People, 1987-, Nat Med Asn, 1987-, Am Col Emergency Physicians, 1987-. **Honors/Awds:** Publication: "Gunshot Wounds to the Penis", NY Acad Urol, 1979. **Military Serv:** USN, commander; Navy Commendation Medal, Meritorious Achievement, 1984. **Home Addr:** 4411 Marquis Pl, Woodbridge, VA 22192. **Business Addr:** Director of Emergency Medicine, US Navy, Naval Medical Clinic, Quantico, VA 22134.*

CARTER, DR. WILMOTH ANNETTE
School administrator, writer, educator. **Personal:** Born in Reidsville, NC; daughter of William Percy (deceased) and Margaret Lee Milner (deceased). **Educ:** Shaw Univ, BA, 1937; Atlanta Univ, MA, 1941; Univ Chicago, PhD, 1959; Shaw Univ, LHD, 1986. **Career:** School administrator, educator (retired), writer; Atlanta Univ, Dept Sociol, grad asst, 1943-47; Univ Chicago, Rosenwald fel study, 1947-49, Danforth fel, 1957-59; Shaw Univ, Raleigh, Sociol Dept, chmn, 1959-63, socsci div, chmn, 1966-69, educ develop officer, 1972-73, dir res, 1969-72, vpres inst res, 1973-76, vpres acad app acad affairs & res, 1978-86; Univ Mich, res assoc, 1964-65; Tuskegee Inst, res assoc, 1965-66. **Orgs:** Delta Sigma Theta Sor, 1935-; Delta Kappa Gamma, 1974-; Nat Coun Alpha ChiScholar Soc, 1977-89; Alpha Kappa Delta. **Honors/Awds:** Honor Soc Alpha Omicron, Shaw Univ, 1936-37. **Special Achievements:** Author of The Urban Negro in the South, published 1961, The New Negro ofthe South, published 1967, Shaw's Universe, published 1973. **Home Addr:** 1400 E Davie St, Raleigh, NC 27610.

CARTER, YVONNE P.
Educator, artist. **Personal:** Born Feb 6, 1939, Washington, DC; daughter of Lorenzo Irving Pickering and Esther Robinson Pickering; married Joseph Payne (divorced); children: Cornelia Malisia. **Educ:** Traphagen Sch Design, NY, cert interior design, 1959; Howard Univ, BA, 1962, MFA, 1968. **Career:** Dist Display Wash, DC, display coordr, 1962-63; Howard Univ, libr asst, 1963-68, asst librn, 1968-71; Fed City Col, asst prof art; Univ DC, Art Dept, prof art; Dept Mass Media Visual & Performing Arts, chairperson, 2004-. **Orgs:** Col Art Asn, 1971-; Nat Asn Study Negro Life & Hist, 1971-72; Am Asn Univ Prof, 1974-; DC Registery, 1973-74; Am Soc African Cult, 1966; Artists Equity, 1987-89; Women's Caucus Art, 1976-; Col Art Assoc, 1976-; WOCA, 1996-97; MOCA, 1996-97. **Honors/Awds:** Visual Artist Grant, DC Commission of the Arts & Humanities, 1981, 1982, 1995; Corrine Matchell Award (WCA/DC); Commonwealth George Mason U. 1990-92; Mobile Oil Grant, Artisisin Kazakstan; Exhibitor, Howard Univ JA Porter Gallery, one-woman show 1973; Paintings WA Gallery Wash DC, two-woman show; Smith-Mason Gallery Nat Exhbn Black Artist Wash DC; selected group shows & performances: NJ State Museum black artist show; Howard Univ Art Gallery; Franz Bader Gallery Wash DC; Corcoran Gallery of Art; Miami-Dade Public Library; Los Angeles African-Amer Museum; Kenkelaba House, New York, NY; Baltimore Museum; Fendrick Gallery; Walters Art Gallery, MD; CA Afro-American Museum; Anacostia Museum Kenkeleba Gallery; NY, Bronx Museum of Arts; Natl Museum of Women in the Arts; Publ imprints by American Negro artists, 1962, 1965; Gumbo Yayya: Anthology of Contemporary African American Women Artists, 1989. **Business Addr:** Chairperson, University of Disctrict Columbia, Depp of Mass Media Visual & Performing Arts, 4200 Conn Ave NW, Washington, DC 20008.*

CARTER, ZACHARY WARREN
Lawyer. **Personal:** Born Mar 19, 1950, Washington, DC; son of Joseph W and Margaret G; married Rosalind Clay, Apr 4, 1992; children: Chandler Clay Carter. **Educ:** Cornell Univ, BA, 1972; NY Univ Sch Law, JD, 1975. **Career:** EDNY Deputy Chief, Crim Div, asst US atty, 1975-80; Patterson, Belknap, Webb & Tyler, gen litigation, 1980-81; DA Kings County DA's Off, exec asst, 1982-87; NYC Courts, from asst to the dep chief admin, 1987; Criminal Ct, City NY-Queens, County, judge, 1987-91; EDNY, US magistrate judge, 1991-93; US Dept Justice, US atty - EDNY, 1993-99; Cablevision NY Group Inc, dir, 1999-; Dorsey & Whitney LLP, partner, currently, co-chair, currently. **Orgs:** Exec comt mem, Criminal Law Sect, NY State Bar Asn; assoc bar, Comn Encourage Judicial Serv; bd trustees, Fed Bar Coun; bd trustees, NYU Law Found; past vice chair, bd dirs, Community Action Legal Serv; past vpres, Nat Black Prosecutors Asn. **Business Addr:** Partner, Co-Chair, Dorsey & Whitney LLP, 250 Pk Ave, New York, NY 10177, **Business Phone:** (212)415-9345.

CARTHAN, EDDIE JAMES
Government official. **Personal:** Born Oct 18, 1949, Tchula, MS; married Shirley Unger; children: Cissye, Neketa & Jowina. **Educ:** Miss Valley State Univ, BS, 1971; Jackson State Univ, MS, 1977; Univ Miss. **Career:** St Col, instr, 1972; US Dept Comn Off Minority Bus Enterprise, bus develop; Lexington Bus Serv Inc, bus specislist, 1973; Holmes Co Bd & Educ, pres, 1973; Sch Durant Attendance Ctr, teacher; Saints Col Lexington, Miss, teacher; Carthan's Convenience Store, owner mgr; Carthan's Pkg Store; Crystal Resturant; Tchula, mayor, 1979. **Orgs:** Bd dir, Delta Found; Gov Midas Comn; King David Mason Lodge 112; Holmes CoBd Educ; Holmes Co Elks. **Honors/Awds:** The Sacco-Vanzetti Memorial Award, 1983. **Special Achievements:** Book: The Last Hired & First Fired; Success & Hard Work; If Things CouldTalk, ed; We've Come A Long Way Baby; Bus Ruralite. *

CARTHEN, JOHN, JR.
Automotive executive. **Career:** River View Ford Mercury Inc, owner, currently; Lakeland Ford Lincoln Mercury Inc, owner, currently. **Special Achievements:** Listed 42 of 100 top auto dealers, Black Enterprise, 1992. **Business Phone:** (618)457-0247.*

CARTLIDGE, ARTHUR J.
Educator, school superintendent. **Personal:** Born Jun 28, 1942, Rolling Fork, MS; married Helen Rose King; children: Byron Darnell, Arthur J Jr & Kirsten Jamille. **Educ:** Miss Valley State Univ, BS, 1965; Delta State Univ, MS, 1972; Spec Degree Admin, attended 1977. **Career:** T L Weston High Sch, teacher 1965-70; H W Solomon Jr High Sch, 1970-72, asst prin, 1973; Greenville Pub Schs, supt, 1999-. **Orgs:** Bd mem, Miss Valley State Univ, 1964-65; Math Teacher Asn; Greenville Teacher Asn; Dist Teacher Asn; Miss Teacher Asn; Nat Educ Asn; Nat Coun Sect Prin; Uniserve Bd; Jr Warden Lake Vista Masonic Lodge; Mt Horeb Bapt Church; Southern Asn Col & Schs Coun Accreditation & Sch Improvement. **Honors/Awds:** Outstanding Teacher of the Year, Weston High Sch, 1969-70; Outstanding Teacher of the Year, Solomon Jr High Sch, 1970-71. **Business Addr:** Superintendant, Greenville Public Schools District, PO Box 1619, Greenville, MS 38702-1619.

CARTWRIGHT, BILL (JAMES WILLIAM CARTWRIGHT)
Basketball player, basketball coach. **Personal:** Born Jul 30, 1957, Lodi, CA; married Sheri Johnson; children: Justin William, Jason James Allen & Kristen. **Educ:** Univ San Francisco, BA. **Career:** Basketball player (retired); basketball coach; NY Knicks, 1980-84, 1986-88, Chicago Bulls, 1989-94, asst coach,beginning, 1996-01; Seattle Supersonics, 1994; West Coast consult; chicago, 2002-03; Nets staff, head coach, 2004-08; asst coach, Phoenix Suns, 2008-. **Orgs:** Charity work Easter Seals; Boys Hope, Chicago. **Honors/Awds:** All-Rookie Team, 1980; East All-Star Team, 1980; Starting center, World Champion Chicago Bulls, 1991-92. *

CARTWRIGHT, BRENDA YVONNE
Educator. **Personal:** Born Aug 30, 1950, Richmond, VA; daughter of Louise Haynie. **Educ:** Western Md Col, BA, 1972; Univ Mich, MA, 1979; George Wash Univ, EdD, 1996. **Career:** Mich Sch Deaf, spec educ teacher, 1972-76; Bur Rehab, voc rehab counr, 1976-79; Rehab Serv Admin, voc rehab spec, 1979-98; George Wash Univ, vis prof, 1997-98; Coppin State Col, asst prof, 1998-2001; Univ Hawaii, Manoa, HI, asst prof counr educ, 2001, assoc prof counr educ, currently, dept chair, currently. **Orgs:** Ed rev bd, J Coun & Develop, 1995-2005; chair, 1999-, bd mem, 2000-, Nat Asn Multicultural Rehab Concerns; Am Coun Asn; secy, Rehab Asn Hawaii, 2002-; scholar chair, Delta Sigma Theta Inc, Hawaii Alumnae Chap, 2002-; bd mem, Hawaii Rehab Coun Asn, 2003-; mem comt, Nat Rehab Asn, 2003-; lanakila pacific, bd dirs. **Honors/Awds:** Andrew Woods Advocate of the Year Award, DC Rehab Asn, 1983; Humanitarian Award, NRA, Mid-Atlantic Region, 1984; USN Good Conduct Award, 1989; President Award, 2003, Sylvia Walker Education Award, Bobbie Atkins Award, Nat Asn Multicultural Rehab Concerns; Excellence in Teaching Award, Univ Hawaii col educ, 2005. **Special Achievements:** Authored & co-authored 7 publications in referred journals; authored 1 book chapter, and a training videotape; proficient in Spanish; proficient in Amer Sign Language. **Military Serv:** USN, E-6, 1985-89; Sr Communicator of the Quarter, 1989; USN Security Group Activity Letter of Commendation, 1988. **Business Addr:** Associate Professor, Department Chair, University of Hawaii at Manoa, Department of Counselor Education, 1337 Lower Campus Rd PE/A 217, Honolulu, HI 96822, **Business Phone:** (808)956-4386.

CARTWRIGHT, JAMES WILLIAM. See CARTWRIGHT, BILL.

CARTWRIGHT, JOAN S.
Judge. **Personal:** Married Lawrence R Neblett. **Educ:** Mich State Univ, BA, 1965; Univ Iowa, Col Law, JD, 1976. **Career:** State Calif, Munic Ct Judge, 1991-96, Alameda County Super Ct, judge, 1996-. **Orgs:** Calif Bar Asn, 1979-. **Business Addr:** Judge, Alameda County Superior Court, Rene C Davidson Courthouse, 1225 Fallon St Rm 209, Oakland, CA 94612-4293.*

CARTWRIGHT, JONATHAN
Executive. **Career:** Wayne Co Community Col, exec dist dir govt rels, currently. **Business Addr:** Director, Wayne County Community College, 801 W Fort St, Detroit, MI 48226, **Business Phone:** (313)496-2731.

CARUTHERS, DR. PATRICIA WAYNE
School administrator. **Personal:** Born Aug 28, 1939, Kansas City, KS; daughter of Bertram Caruthers Sr and Evelyn W. **Educ:** Emporia State Univ, BS, 1962; Univ Mo, Kansas City, MA, 1965, PhD, 1975. **Career:** US Dist No 500, teacher, 1962-69; Kansas City Community Col, teacher, 1969-72, asst dean cont educ, 1972-76, asst to pres, 1978-92, Instnl & Stud Serv, vpres, 1992-94; Donnelly Col, part-time instr, 1997; PennValley Comn Col, part-time instr, 1997; Kansas City Bd Pub Utilities, Ethics Comn, comn mem, 2006-. **Orgs:** Comn Kansas City Kans Planning & Zoning Bd, 1975-; govt intern, Off Educ HEW, 1976-78; chmn, Kansas City Kans Econ Devel Comn, 1980-; past pres, Alpha Kappa Alpha Sorority Inc, 1981-83; regent, KS Bd Regents, 1982-86; treas, Links Inc, 1984-86; Kansas City Zoning Appeals Bd; Kansas City Consensus, 1990-94; Youth Empowerment Task Force, 1994; Empowerment Zone Comn, 1994; comnr, Kansas City Area Transp Authority, 1994-; bd dirs, Friends Union Sta, 1994; bd mem, Cancer Action Inc; chair, Wyandotte Co Overall Econ Develop/SIA Bd. **Honors/Awds:** Top Girl Winner Gr KC Science Fair 4th Place Tokyo 1957; Most Outstanding Young Woman in America, 1976; Mary McLeod Bethune Alpha Phi Alpha Fraternity, 1982; Alumni Achievement Award, Univ, Mo, Kansas City, 1994; Alumni Achievement Award, Univ Mo, Kansas City, 1994; Missionaries Higher Education Award, Asn Mfg Excellence, 1995; Education Hall of Fame, Kansas City Kans Community Col, 2005. **Business Addr:** Member, Kansas City Board of Public Utilities, Ethics Commission, 540 Minn Ave, Kansas City, KS 66101-2930, **Business Phone:** (913)573-9000.

CARVER, DR. JOANNE
College administrator, administrator. **Career:** Hampton Univ, Sch Libr Arts & Educ, asst dean, currently; Va Dept Educ, dir teacher educ, currently. **Business Addr:** Director of Teacher Education, Virginia Department of Education, PO Box 2120, Richmond, VA 23218, **Business Phone:** (805)225-2540.

CARVER, SHANTE
Football player. **Personal:** Born Feb 12, 1971, Stockton, CA. **Educ:** Ariz State Univ, Law. **Career:** Football player (retired); Dallas Cowboys, defensive end, 1994-97; Dallas Desperados, defense, 2000-05; Defensive line coach, scottsdale Community col, currently. **Honors/Awds:** Two time All-America selection, 1992, 1993; Super Bowl champion XXX. *

CARWELL, HATTIE V
Physicist. **Personal:** Born Jul 17, 1948, Brooklyn, NY; daughter of George and Fannie Tunstall. **Educ:** Bennett Col, BS, chem & biol, 1970; Rutgers Univ, MS, 1971; UC Berkeley, post grad work, PhD. **Career:** US Dept Energy, San Francisco Oper Office, health physicist, 1973-80, sr health physicist, 1985-90, high energy & nuclear sci prog mgr, 1990-92, Berkeley Site Off, sr fac ops mgr, 1992, Lawrence Berkeley Nat Lab, opers lead, 1994-; Atomic Energy Agency, Vienna, nuclear safeguards inspector & group leader, 1980-85; Thomas Jefferson Univ, res asst. **Orgs:** Nat Health Physicist Soc, 1971-; Nat Soc Black Physicists, 1975-; Nat Technical Asn, 1975-80; Western Reg Coun Engrs & Scientists, 1977-79; Nat Asn Advan Colored People, 1986-; pres, 1986-87, 1994-95, 2000-02, Northern Calif, Coun Black Prof Engr; chairperson, 1983-, int comm chair, 1990-, Develop Fund Black Students Sci & Technol; Nat Coun Black Engrs & Scientists, 1994-. **Honors/Awds:** Special Mgr's Recognition, US Dept Energy, 1977-; Fed Community Service Award, 1977; North Calif Coun Black Prof Engrs, Prof Service Award, 1981; Elijal McCoy Award, 1989; Nat Black Col Hall of Fame, 1991; Bennett Col, hon doctorate, 1993; James C Jones Humanitarian Award, 2000; Inspiring Scientist Award, Oakland Junior Arts & Science Ctr, 2002. **Special Achievements:** Published numerous articles in tech publications, 1974-; book, Blacks in Science: Astrophysicist to Zoologist, 1977; booklet, In Pursuit of Excellence (Dr Warren Henry: World Class Scientist), 1998; co-founded the Develop Fund Black Students Sci & Technol, 1983; co-founded Museum African Am TechSci Village, 2000. **Business Addr:** Operations Lead, US Department of Energy, Lawrence Berkeley National Laboratory, 1 Cyclotron Road Mail Stop 90R1023, Berkeley, CA 94720, **Business Phone:** (510)486-4296.

CARY, LORENE
Writer. **Personal:** Born Nov 29, 1956, Philadelphia, PA; daughter of John W Cary and Carole J Cary; married R C Smith, Aug 27, 1983; children: Geoffrey Smith (stepson), Laura & Zoe Smith. **Educ:** Univ Pa, BA, MA, 1978; Sussex Univ, MA, 1980. **Career:** Time, intern writer, 1980; TV Guide, assoc ed, 1980-82; St Paul's Sch, teacher, 1982-83; Antioch Univ, Phila campus, lectr, 1983-84; Phila Univ Arts, lectr, 1984-86; Essence, AMR Visions, Philadelphia Inquirer Sunday Mag, Philadelphia TV Guide, freelance writer, 1985-88; Newsweek, contributing ed, 1991-93; Univ Pa, eng, lectr, 1995-, sr lectr creative writing, cur. Author: Black Ice, 1981, 1991, Price A Child, 1995, Pride, 1998; The Price of A Child; Pride; Free! Great Escapes from Slavery on the Underground Railroad; Art Sanctuary's, founder & exec dir, currently. **Orgs:** Author's Guild, 1991-. **Honors/Awds:** Hon Doctorate, Letters, Colby Col, 1992; Notable Books Citation, Black Ice, Am Library Asn, 1992; Bronze Star Award, Nat Hook-up Black Women, 1992; Hon Doctorate, Keene State Col, 1997; Hon Doctorate, Chestnut Hill Col, 1997; Rising Star Award, American Red Cross, 2000; Women's Way Agent of Change Award, 2002; Price of A Child Named "One Book, One Philadelphia," Choice, 2002. **Business Addr:** Author, Senior Lecturer, University Pennsylvania, English Department, 3451 Walnut St, Philadelphia, PA 19121.

CARY, REBY
Legislator, city council member. **Personal:** Born Sep 9, 1920, Cary, TX; married Nadine S; children: Faith Annette. **Educ:** Prairie View A&M Univ, BA, MS, 1948; Tex Christian Univ, attended 1953; N Tex State Univ, attended 1971. **Career:** McDonald Col Indust Arts, dir/teacher, 1946-49; Tarrant Co/Johnson Co Voc Sch, lead teacher, 1954-64; Dunbar High Sch, counr, 1953-64, asst prof, 1964-67; Tarrant Co Jr Col, asst prof, 1966-69; Univ Tex Arlington, assoc dean stud life, asst prof hist, 1969-78; Tex House Rep, Dist 32-B State Legis, state rep, 1978-82; Real Estate Broker, Cary's Real Estate, 1980; Tex State Rep, Dist 95, 1979-85; state legislator; Fort Worth city coun, bd dir, currently. **Orgs:** Nat Educ Found Bd; Alpha Phi Frat, 1974-75; reg educ dir, 1972-75; sec Ft Worth Independent Sch Bd, 1974-75; trustee, choir dir New Rising Star Baptist Church; bd dirs, Boy Scouts Am; Am Legion; bd, Tarrant Co United Way; community dev bd, City Ft Worth; Tex Coun Black Republicans. **Honors/Awds:** Man of year, Omega Psi Phi, 1974; Outstanding Citizen Award, St James AME, 1975. **Special Achievements:** First African-American elected at-large to the Fort Worth independent School District School Board; author:A Magnified Princes Shall Come Out of Egypt, Texas, & Fort Worth; Intercultural History: The Negro. **Military Serv:** USCG, 1942-45. **Business Addr:** Real Estate Broker, Cary's Real Estate, 1804 Bunche Dr, Fort Worth, TX 76112.*

CARY, REV. WILLIAM STERLING
Clergy. **Personal:** Born Aug 10, 1927, Plainfield, NJ; son of Andrew and Sadie; married Marie B Phillips; children: Yvonne, Denise, Sterling & Patricia. **Educ:** Morehouse Col, BA, 1949; Union Theol Sem, MDiv, 1952. **Career:** Butler Mem Presby Church, pastor, 1953-55; Int Church Open Door, Brooklyn, NY, pastor, 1955-58; Grace Congregation Church, New York, pastor, 1958-68; Metro & Suffolk Asss NY Conf United Church Christ, area minister, 1968-75; Ill Conf United Church Christ, conf minister, 1975-94, emer minister, 2001-. **Orgs:** Pres, Nat Coun Churches, 1972-75; UCC Coun Ecumenism, 1977; chair, Comn Racial Justice; mem gov bodies, Coun Christian Soc Action & Off Commun; Task Force Vietnamese Refugee Relocation; UCC rep, Church Union; Nat Ministerial Adv Coun; Chicago Theol Sem Bd; Comt Denominational Exec Ill Conf Churches; Exec Coun United Church Christ; Church World Serv Comn; chair, Coun Religious Leaders Metrop Chicago; chmn, Coun Religious Leaders, Chicago. **Honors/Awds:** LLD, Bishop Col, Dallas, Tex, 1973; DD, Elmhurst Col, Ill, 1973; DD, Morehouse Col, 1973; honorary doctorate, Alen Univ, Columbia, SC, 1975; DHL, Ill Col, 1988. **Special Achievements:** First African American President of the National Council of Churches in 1972. **Business Addr:** Emeritus Minister, Illinois Conference United Church of Christ., 1840 Wchester Blvd Suite 200, Westchester, IL 60154, **Business Phone:** (708)344-4470.

CASANOVA, DR. GISELE M (GISELE CASANOVA OATES)
Clinical psychologist, educator. **Personal:** Born Apr 27, 1960, Chicago, IL; daughter of Isidro and Marguerite Boudreaux; children: Tatiyana Noelle. **Educ:** Ill Wesleyan Univ, BA, 1982; Northern Ill Univ, MA, 1986, PhD, 1989. **Career:** Inst Stress Mgt, clinal assoc, 1989-90, consult, 1990-95; Purdue Univ, Calumet, asst prof psychol, 1990-94, Ethnic Studies Prog, coordr, 1994-2000, assoc prof psychol, 1995-. **Orgs:** Alpha Kappa Alpha, Xi Nu Omega Chapter, 1981-, pres, 1995-96. **Honors/Awds:** Calumet, Scholarly Research Award, Purdue Univ, 1992, 1993, 2001, 2002; TRIO Dir's Award, Purdue Univ Calumet, 1997; Outstanding Teaching Award, Purdue Univ Calumet, 2002-03. **Special Achievements:** Co-author, Effects of Impaired Hearing and Favorable vs Unfavorable Personal Feedback on Negative Emotional Reactions, Journal of Clinical Psychology, p 982-987, 1988; Co-author, Physiological Responses to Non-Child-Related Stressors in Mothers at Risk of Child Abuse, Child Abuse and Neglect, p 31-44, 1992; Co-author, Physiological Repsonses to Child Stimuli in Mothers with/without a childhood history of physical abuse, XXV International Congress of Psychology Abstracts, p 15, 1992; Child Abuse & Neglect, p 995-1004, 1994; co-editor, Violence in the Intimate Relationships, 1998; author, Cultural Perspectives on Intimate Violence, 1998. **Business Addr:** Associate Professor of Psychology, Purdue University Calumet, Department of Behavioral Sciences, 2200 169th St PORT 218A, Hammond, IN 46323-2094, **Business Phone:** (219)989-2781.

CASE, ARTHUR M.
Dentist. **Personal:** Born May 18, 1950, Philadelphia, PA. **Educ:** Temple Univ, DDS, 1979. **Career:** Pvt Pract, dentist; JFK Mem Hosp, staff. **Orgs:** Alpha Omega Fraternity, New Era Dent Soc. **Honors/Awds:** Mem Oral Surg Hon Soc, Peridontal Hon Soc. **Business Addr:** 5555 Wissahickon Ave, Philadelphia, PA 19144.*

CASEY, CAREY
Association executive, president (organization), chief executive officer. **Educ:** Univ NC, Chapel Hill. **Career:** Nat Ctr Fathering, Kans City, chief exec officer, 2006-; Inner-City Church, Ill Community, pastor; Fel Christian Athletes, found pres; Lawndale Community Church, co-pastor; World Cong Sports & Sr Bowl, lectr. **Orgs:** chaplain, Dallas Cowboys, 1983-88; chaplain, Summer Olympic Games, Seoul, 1988; chaplain, NFL Team. **Honors/Awds:** Juanita Craft Award, Dallas Nat Asn Advan Colored People; Alumni Hall of Fame, Salem, VA; Alumnus of the Yr, Northeastern Oklahoma A&M. **Special Achievements:** Lead football team, Atlantic Coast Conference Championship, 1977;

Featured in many local and national publications, including The New York Times, Atlanta Constitution, Los Angeles Times, The Kansas City Star, Chicago Tribune, Ebony, Christianity Today, ESPN.com and Leadership Magazine; an authentic athletic in the award-winning movie, Remember the Titans. **Business Addr:** Chief Executive Officer, National Center for Fathering, PO Box 413888, Kansas City, MO 64141.*

CASEY, REV. CAREY WALDEN, SR.
Clergy. **Personal:** Born Oct 12, 1955, Radford, VA; son of Ralph Waldo Jr and Sarah Adline Coles; married Melanie Little, May 15, 1977; children: Christie, Patrice & Marcellus. **Educ:** Northeastern Oklahoma, Miami, OK, phys educ, 1976; Univ NC, Chapel Hill, BA, relig, 1979; Gordon-Conwell Theol Sem, S Hamilton MA, MDiv, 1981; Sch Theol Va Union Univ, Richmond, VA, MDiv, 1984. **Career:** Northeastern Univ, Boston, MA, student athletes counr, 1980-81; Total Action Against Poverty, Roanoke, VA, youth employment coordr, 1981; First Baptist Church, Petersburg, VA, residence minister, 1982-83; Christian Athletes Fel, Dallas, TX, urban dir, 1983-88; Mount Hebron Baptist Church, Garland, TX, interim pastor, 1984-85; Dallas Cowboys Football Club Training Camp, counr, 1986-87; Christian Athletes Fel, Kansas City, MO, nat urban dir, 1988-92; Olympic Protestant Chaplain, Seoul, Korea, 1988; Lawndale Community Church, Chicago, IL, pastor, 1992; Nat Ctr Fathering, chief exec officer, 2006-; Miss Univ, Kans City, MO, Guest lectr. **Orgs:** Martin Luther King Ctr, Dallas, TX, 1984-88; speaker, Athletes Action, 1984-; Boys & Girls Clubs Am, 1986-; Nat Asn Advan Colored People, 1986-; nat consult, Salvation Army, 1988-; bd consult, Int Sports Coalition, 1988-; steering comt, Kansas City Star-Times, 1989-; bd mem, Mich Asn Leadership Develop Inc, 1989-; bd mem, sports Outreach USA, 1990-; bd mem, Urban Life Outreach, Kansas City, MO, 1990-. **Honors/Awds:** Outstanding Young Men Am, US Jaycees, 1980; NFL, Major League Baseball Chapel Speaker USA, 1980; Juanita Craft Contribution to Sports in Community, Nat Asn Advan Colored People, 1984; Alumni of the Year, Northeastern Oklahoma A&M, 1991. **Special Achievements:** Proclamation Carey Casey Day, Louisville City, KY, December 5, 1988. **Business Addr:** Executive Director, The National Center for Fathering, 10200 W 75th St Suite 267, PO Box 413888, Kansas City, MT 66204, **Business Phone:** (913)384-4661.

CASEY, FRANK LESLIE
Journalist, television journalist. **Personal:** Born Jan 29, 1935, Stotesbury, WV; son of Conston and Mary; married Lenore Thompson, Apr 16, 1988; children: Zauditu, Tamarat, Bakaffa & Charles Arnold. **Educ:** WVa State Col, BS, 1962. **Career:** Repub Aviation, tech illusr, 1963; New York Dept Welfare, social worker, 1969; WPIX-TV, New York City, tv reporter. **Orgs:** Nat Asn Advan Colored People. **Honors/Awds:** Good Conduct Medal; New York Area Television Academy Award, Nat Acad TV Arts & Sci, 1976-77; Uniformed Firefighters Association Award for excellence in T.V. coverage for fire fighting, 1971; Humorous Writing Award, Soc Silurians, New York, 1986; Honorary Membership for Fair & Impartial Reporting for Police Stories, Retired Detectives Police Dept city New York Inc, 1984. **Military Serv:** AUS, sp2, 1954-57.

CASH, BETTYE JOYCE
Executive, nurse. **Personal:** Born Feb 19, 1936, Fort Worth, TX; divorced; children: Ardranae, James Jr, Anthony, Lisa & Janine. **Educ:** Contra Costa Col, attended 1963, AA, 1975. **Career:** Nurse, executive (retired); W Contra Costa Healthcare Dist, dist hosp dir, bd dir & treas, 2002-06. **Orgs:** Nat Womens Polit Caucus; Black Bus & Prof Asn; Church Missionary; Cailf Hosp Asn; med Staff, Asn Women Hosp; Am Hosp Asn; Asn Dist Hosps; Robinson Weeks Robinson Found. **Special Achievements:** First & only black elected female West Contra Costa City. **Home Addr:** 2732 Groom Dr, Richmond, CA 94806. *

CASH, DR. JAMES IRELAND
Educator. **Personal:** Born Oct 25, 1947, Fort Worth, TX; married Clemmie; children: Tari & Derek. **Educ:** Tex Christian Univ, BS, mathematics & comput sci, 1969; Purdue Univ, MS, comput sci, 1974, PhD, mgt info syst & acct, 1976. **Career:** Tex Christian Univ Comput Ctr, syst programmer, 1969; Langston Univ, dir comput ctr, 1969-72, instr & asst prof vo-tech prog, 1969-72; Arth Drug Stores, Inc, syst analyst & programmer consult, 1973-76; Inst of Educational Mgt, exec educ course, MIS instr, 1977-79; Harvard Grad Sch Bus Admin, asst prof, 1976-81, instr exec educ course, James E. Robisonprof Bus Admin; James E. Robison prof Bus Admin Emer currently; IBM Syst Res Inst, adj prof, 1980; Harvard Grad Sch Bus Admin, assoc prof bus admin, 1981-85, prof bus admin, 1985. **Orgs:** Bd adv, Am Acct Asn; Asn r Comput Mach; Qual Assurance Inst; adv bd, Soc Info Mgt; Strategic Mgt Soc; US Dept State Adv Comn Trans Nat Enterprises, 1976-83; Index Syst Inc, 1978-; bd trustees, Park Sch, 1983-; adv bd, BOSCOM, 1983-; ed bd, Harvard Bus Rev, 1983-; MA Gov's Adv Comn Info Processing, 1983-88. **Honors/Awds:** Outstanding Instructor Award, Vo-Tech Dept, Langston Univ, 1971; Purdue Univ fel, 1972; Phi Kappa Phi, 1974; Hall of Fame, Tex Christian Univ,1982. **Special Achievements:** Three books & three papers published; All Am Acad Basketball team, 1968; First Century Disting Alumni Ft Worth Independent Sch Dist, 1983. **Business Addr:** James E. Robison Professor of Business Administration Emeritus, Harvard Business School, Soldiers Field, Boston, MA 02163, **Business Phone:** (617)495-6471.

CASH, LISA
Executive. **Educ:** Howard Univ, commun; French Culinary Inst. **Career:** Sheraton Hotel Restaurant; B Smith's Restaurant, 1988; Shark Bar, fl mgr, 1989, vpres opers, 1999; Soul Food Concepts, vpres opers, 2003. *

CASH, PAMELA J.
Librarian. **Personal:** Born Oct 26, 1948, Cleburne, TX; daughter of James and Juanita Beatty; married Gervis A Menzies Sr, Sep 17, 1983; children: Gervis A Menzies Jr. **Educ:** Univ Okla, BA, 1970; Univ Ill, MLS, 1972. **Career:** Univ Ill, asst Afro-Am bibliographer, 1970-71, librarian Afro-Am studies, 1971-72; Univ Tex, humanities librarian, 1972-73; Johnson Publ Co, libr, 2003. **Orgs:** Black Caucus Am Libr Asn; Spec Libr Asn; Asn Black Librarians Chicago. **Business Addr:** Librarian, Johnson Public Company, 820 S Michigan Ave, Chicago, IL 60605.*

CASH, SWINTAYLA MARIE
Basketball player. **Personal:** Born Sep 22, 1979, Pittsburgh, PA; daughter of Cynthia. **Educ:** Univ Conn, Commun Science, 2002. **Career:** Detroit Shock, forward, 2002-08; Seattle Storm, 2008-; founder, swincash enterprises, 2002. **Orgs:** Cash for Kids, 2005. **Honors/Awds:** NCAA Women's Division I Basketball Championship, 2000, 2002; WNBA All-Star, 2003,2005,2009; gold medal,US Olympics games, 2004; Dapper Dan Sportswoman of the Yr award, 2007; Sidney Crosby & Dan Rooney. **Special Achievements:** Movie:Bring It On: All or Nothing. **Business Addr:** Professional Basketball Player, Seattle Storm, 3421 Thorndyke Ave W, Palace Auburn Hills, Seattle, WA 98119.*

CASHIN, JOHN
Dentist, government official. **Educ:** DDS. **Career:** Nat Democratic Party Ala cand, 1970, nominee; Tuskegee atty; Pvt Pract, dentist, 2001. **Orgs:** Nat Asn Advan Colored People. *

CASHIN, SHERYLL D.
Government official, educator. **Personal:** Born in Huntsville, AL; son of John and Joan; married Marque Chambliss; children: Logan & Langston. **Educ:** Vanderbilt Univ, BE, elec eng, 1984; Oxford Univ, MA, Eng law, 1986; Harvard Univ, JD, 1989. **Career:** Off Vpres, Community Empowerment Bd, staff dir; US Ct Appeals, Dist Columbia Circuit, law clerk; Supreme Ct Justice Thurgood Marshall, law clerk; Clinton White House, adv urban & econ policy; Georgetown Univ Law Ctr, prof law, currently. **Orgs:** Harvard Law Rev. **Honors/Awds:** Walter R. Murray Jr. Distinguished Alumnus Award, Asn Vanderbilt Black Alumni, 2000. **Special Achievements:** Author: The Failures of Integration: How Race & Class are Undermining the Am Dream, 2004, The Agitator's Daughter: A Memoir of Four Generations of One Extraordinary African-American Family, 2008; appeared on NPR All Things Considered, The Diane Rehm Show, The Tavis Smiley Show, The Newshour With Jim Leher. **Business Phone:** (202)662-9401.

CASH-RHODES, WINIFRED E.
Educator. **Personal:** Born in Savannah, GA; daughter of Clifford Brown Cash and Rev William L Cash Sr; married Augustus H Rhodes; children: Eva Carol, Lydia Ann & Victoria Elizabeth. **Educ:** Fisk Univ, AB, 1934; Univ Southern Calif, MS, 1959. **Career:** Educator (retired); Teacher Sec Math, 1935-40, 1945-52; Dept Chairperson, Math, 1957-65; Univ Calif, Berkley, fel, 1960; Los Angeles Unified Sch, supvr sec Math teachers, 1966-68, specialist res & develop, 1968-78; NY Univ, fel, 1970. **Orgs:** Sec Baldwin Hills Home owners Assoc, 1976-82; dir, Far Western Regional Dir Alpha Kappa Alpha Sorority Inc, 1970-74; Exec Coun United Church Christrepresenting So, CA & NV, 1981-87; chmn, Nominating Comn, Southern Calif Ecumenical Coun, 1987-92; Southern Calif Interfaith Coalition Aging Bd, 1989-94; Am Asn Univ Women, 1989-; Calif Retired Teachers Asn, 1992-. **Special Achievements:** Article "What Jesus Means to Me", United Church of Christ, New York, 1982.

CASON, DAVID, JR.
City planner. **Personal:** Born Jun 20, 1923, Selma, AL; son of David Sr and Mattie Clark; married Armene B. **Educ:** BA, 1950; MA, 1959; Wayne State Univ, MUP, 1966; Univ Manchester Eng, 1972; Univ Mich, PhD, 1976. **Career:** Univ Mich, adj prof, 1977-; CRW Assoc Consult Plng Detroit, pres, 1977; Univ Mich, lectr urban planning; Res Asn Environ Res Inst Mich, 1972-73; Univ Mich, instr, Dept Urban Planning, 1970-; Mich Dept Corrections Prog Bur, asst bur chief, 1985-89, dir prog, 1989-95; Detroit City Planning Comn, comnr, 1995. **Orgs:** Dir, Model Neighborhood Agency Detroit, 1967-70; teacher, Merrill-Palmer Inst, 1975; proj mgr, Neighborhood Conservation Housing Comn, 1962-65; dir, Urban Renewal Ypsilanti, 1961-62; pub aide worker, Receiving Hosp Detroit, 1956-61; part-time work, studies field Wayne State Univ, 1966-67; past mem, Nat Asn Redevelop & Housing Officials; MI Soc Planning Officials, Am Inst Planners; written several articles; Met Fund Detroit; co-vice chairperson, Southeastern MI Regional Citizens; bd mem, vpres, 1987. MI Coun Girl Scouts, Detroit Area Agency Aging, Ctr Humanistic Studies; Alpha Phi Alpha; vpres, The Prometheas, 1988-. **Military Serv:** AUS, inf, 92nd div, PFC, 1944-45. **Business Addr:** Planning Commissioner, Detroit City Planning Commission, 202 CAYMC, Detroit, MI 48226, **Business Phone:** (313)224-6225.*

CASON, JOSEPH L.
School administrator, construction manager. **Personal:** Born Mar 24, 1939, Anderson County, SC; son of William and Conyers Williams; married Margaret Johnson; children: Ajena Lynette, Kenneth Todd, Shawn Douglas, Valerie Kay. **Educ:** Hampton Inst, BS. **Career:** Roanoke Valley Bus League, exec dir, 1973-81; Cason Enterprises, owner, 1970-; Eli Lily Corp, indust engr tech, 1968-70; City Roanoke, proj engr, 1967-68; Better Housing Inc, mgr, 1965-67; Roanke City Sch Bd, Roanke, Va, coordr maintenance & construction systems, 1988, supvr, currently. **Orgs:** Charter mem, pres, Roanoke Vly Contractors Asn, 1970; dir, Roanoke Valley Bus League; charter mem, vpres, Afro-Am Builders Va, 1973; bd mem, SW Va Community Develop Fund, 1971-75; Roanoke C C; Hunton YMCA; group chmn, United Fund, 1977; Minority Bus Opportunity Comn; Kappa Alpha Psi; Comm Orgn Res & Develop; Nat Bus League; dir, Nethel Am Ment Educ Ch; Hampton Inst Alumni Asn; US Army Res; originator & administrator, Off Minority Bus Enterprise Prog SW Va. **Special Achievements:** 1st black prof hired by City Roanoke, 1967; 1st State Registerd Gen Contractor SW Va. **Military Serv:** AUS, capt, 1963-65. **Business Addr:** Supervisor, Roanoke City Public Schools, Maintenance and Operations Department, PO Box 13145, Roanoke, VA 24031-4699, **Business Phone:** (540)981-2851.*

CASON, MARILYNN JEAN
Executive. **Personal:** Born May 18, 1943, Denver, CO; daughter of Evelyn L Clark and Eugene M; married P Wesley Kriebel, Dec 12, 1987. **Educ:** Stanford Univ, BA, polit sci, 1965; Univ Mich Law Sch, JD, 1969; Roosevelt Univ, MBA, 1977. **Career:** Executive (retired); Dawson Nagel Sherman & Howard, assoc atty, 1969-73; Kraft Inc, atty, 1973-76; Johnson Prods Co Inc, vpres, managing dir, 1980-83, vpres & corp coun, 1976-86, vpres int, 1986-88; DeVry Inc, vpres & gen coun, 1989-96, sr vpres, secy & gen coun. **Orgs:** Dir, Arthritis Found, Ill Chap, 1979-; Ill Humanities Coun, 1987-96.

CASON, UDELL
School administrator, educator. **Personal:** Born Jul 30, 1940, Glasgow, MO; married Emma R Bothwell; children: Carmen Q & Udell Q. **Educ:** Drake Univ, BS, 1965; Drake Univ, MS, 1970. **Career:** Educator, school administrator (retired); City Des Moines, admin asst, 1965-68; Des Moines Pub Sch, teacher, 1968-70, prin, 1972-, coordr, 1970-72; Moore Elem Sch, prin. **Orgs:** Chmn & vchmn & trustee bd, Union Bapt Chap, 1965-; pres, United Black Fedn, 1967-69; sec chmn prin, Des Moines Pub Sch; pres, Kappa Alpha Psi Fraternity, 1980-81; bd dirs, Des Moines Young Men's Christian Asn, 1982-89; chmn, bd dirs, Iowa C & Family Serv, 1984-89; metro bd dirs, Young Men's Christian Asn, 1993-97; bd dirs, Cent Iowa AIDS, 1997-99; amp bd, Young Men's Christian Asn, 1998-. **Honors/Awds:** Task Force Award State Of Iowa, 1968; Mayor Task Force Award, City Des Moines, 1968; Outstanding Achievement, Kappa Alpha Psi, 1975; Double D Award, Drake Univ, 1979; Service to Youth Award, YMCA, 1988; Tae Kwon Do Instructor, Young Men Christian Asn, 1979-; One of Des Moines Finest Citizens, 1999.

CASSELBERRY, JAMES ARTHUR
Executive, consultant. **Educ:** Univ Ill, BS, economics; Univ Chicago, MBA. **Career:** Wedgewood Capital Mgmt, chief operating officer; Millennium Income Trust, chmn, chief exec officer & portfolio mgr; Trias Capital Mgt Inc, ceo & chmn; prin, Ennis Knupp Assoc; consult. *

CASSELL, SAMUEL JAMES
Basketball player, entrepreneur. **Personal:** Born Nov 18, 1969, Baltimore, MD; son of Donna. **Educ:** San Jacinto Col; Fla State. **Career:** Houston Rockets, guard, 1993-96; Dallas Mavericks, 1996-97; Phoenix Suns, 1996; New Jersey Nets, 1997-99; Milwaukee Bucks, 1999-2003; Minn Timberwolves, 2003-05; Los Angeles Clippers, guard, 2005-08; Boston Celtics, currently; We R One, co-founder, currently. **Honors/Awds:** High school player of the year, 1988-89. **Special Achievements:** NBA, Championship, 1994, 1995. **Business Addr:** Professional Basketball Player, Boston Celtics, 226 Causeway St 4th Fl, Boston, MA 02114, **Business Phone:** (866)423-5849.

CASSIS, GLENN ALBERT
School administrator, executive director. **Personal:** Born Nov 11, 1951, Jamaica, NY; married Glynis R; children: Glenn Jr. **Educ:** Univ Con, BA polit sci, 1973, MFA arts admin, 1974. **Career:** N Adams State Col, dir campus ctr, 1978; Oakland Ctr, Oakland Univ, Rochester, asst dir 1976-78, asst dir stud acct, 1974-76; Jorgensen Auditorium, Univ Conn, Storrs, admin asst, 1973-74; Assoc Col Union-Int, region I comp coord, 1979-; Conn Pre-Engineering Prog, exec dir, currently. **Orgs:** Bd dir, Nat Entertainment & Campus Act Asn, 1972-74; co-founder, minority affairs, comm Nat Entertainment & Campus Act Asn, 1973; adv bd, Salvation Army, 1980-; Min Coun Comm Concerns, 1980-;

Conn TRAC currently; Nat Soc Black Engr. **Honors/Awds:** Founders award, Nat Entertainment & Campus Act Asn, 1974; Black Faculty & Admin Service Award, Oakland Univ Rochester, 1977. **Business Addr:** Executive Director, Connecticut Pre Engineering Program, 45 Wintonbury Ave, Bloomfield, CT 06002, **Business Phone:** (860)769-5283.

CASTENELL, DR. LOUIS ANTHONY
School administrator, educator. **Personal:** Born Oct 20, 1947, New York, NY; son of Louis and Marguerite; married Mae E Beckett; children: Louis C & Elizabeth M. **Educ:** Xavier Univ LA, BA, educ, 1968; Univ Wis, Milwaukee, MS, educ psychol, 1973; Univ Ill, PhD (educ psychol), 1980. **Career:** Univ Wis-Milwaukee, coordr, acad adv & bus mgr, 1971-74; Xavier Univ, dir alumni affairs, 1974-77, from asst prof to assoc prof, 1980-88, dean grad sch, 1981-89; Univ Ill, fel, 1977-78; Nat Inst Ment Health, fel, 1978-80; Univ Cincinnati, dean, col educ, 1990-99; Univ Ga, Col Educ, dean, 1999-. **Orgs:** Editorial Bds, J Curriculum Theorizing, 1990-95; reviewer, J Teacher Educ; reviewer, J Educ Founds, Educ Task Force Urban League, 1984; chair, Human Rights & Acad Freedom AERA, 1985-86; consult Sch Educ, 1980-; bd mem, Ronald McDonald House La, 1987; bd mem, NAACP; bd mem, C Mus Cincinnati; Nat Bd Professional Teaching Standards; chair, Am Asn Cols Teacher Educ; Kappa Delta Epilson; Am Educ Studies Asn; Asn Multicultural Counseling & Develop; Am Educ Res Asn; Am Asn Col Teachers Educ; Nat Honor Soc Psychol. **Honors/Awds:** Craig Rice Scholarship, Xavier Univ, 1968; over 15 published works on aspects of educ; Critic's Choice Awards, Am Educational Studies Asn, 1993; Presidential Award, Networking Together Inc, 1996. **Military Serv:** AUS, sgt. **Business Addr:** Dean, Professor, University Of Georgia, College Of Education, G-3 Aderhold Hall, Athens, GA 30602, **Business Phone:** (706)542-6446.

CASTLE, KEITH L
Executive. **Career:** Phase One Off Prods Inc, Cambridge, MA, pres, currently. **Orgs:** New Eng Minority Purchasing Coun; Cambridge Chamber Com. **Honors/Awds:** Vendor of the Yr, New Eng Minority Purchasing Coun, 1981, 1991; Award for Excellence, SBA; Black Enterprise Top 100, 1989, 1991; Outstanding Serv & Qual Award, Gillette Co, 1991. **Business Addr:** President, Phase One Off Prod Inc, 89 Fulkerson St, Cambridge, MA 02141-2093, **Business Phone:** (617)547-0700.

CASTLEBERRY, EDWARD J.
Television news anchorperson. **Personal:** Born Jul 28, 1928, Birmingham, AL; son of Edward and Lillian; married Frances Bassett (deceased); children: Terrie Wade, Sharon Bryant, Susan, Bradley. **Educ:** Miles Col Birmingham, AL, 1951. **Career:** WEDR, WJLD, Birmingham, AL, disc jockey, 1950-55; WMBM, Miami, FL, prog dir & disc jockey, 1955-58; WCIN, Cincinnati, OH, disc jockey & newsman, 1958-61; WABQ, Cleveland, OH, disc jockey & newsman, 1961-64; WVKO, Columbus, OH, prog dir & disc jockey, 1964-67; WHAT, Philadelphia, PA, disc jockey, 1967-68; WEBB, Baltimore, MD, disc jockey & newsman; Mutual & Nat Black Networks, anchorman & entertainment ed. **Honors/Awds:** Newsman of the Year, Coalition Black Media Women, NY, 1980; Newsman of the Year, Jack the Rapper Family Affair, Atlanta, 1980; Outstanding Citizen Award, Ala House Rep, Montgomery, 1983; Honoree, Smithsonian Inst, Washington, 1985. **Special Achievements:** Part of the first black news team to broadcast a presidential election, 1972. **Military Serv:** USN, Yeoman 3rd Class, 3 yrs; WWII Victory Medal, 1945-47. *

CASTLEMAN, ELISE MARIE
Social worker. **Personal:** Born May 30, 1925, Duquesne, PA; daughter of Guy L Tucker (deceased) and Fannie M Ridley (deceased); divorced; children: John II. **Educ:** Howard Univ, BA, 1947; Univ Pittsburgh, attended 1949. **Career:** Fel grad study social work, Family Serv Asn, 1947-49; Family & Childrens Agency, social worker, 1949-53; DC Gen Hosp, social worker, 1953-58; Wayne County Gen Hosp & Consult Ctr, social worker, 1958-59; United Cerebral Palsy, social worker, 1960-66; Mental Hygiene Clinic Veterans Admin, social worker, 1967-; Defense Construction Supply Ctr, mgt analyst, 1982-85. **Orgs:** Columbus Bd Educ, 1971-79; exec adv comn, Office of Minority Affairs, Ohio State Univ, 1972-73; bd mem, Martin Luther King Serv Ctr, 1963-67; Howard Univ Womens Club, 1953-58; exec comn, Ohio Sch Bds Asn; bd mem, Young Women's Christian Asn, 1974-76; bd mem, Columbus Civil Rights Coun, 1973-, Ohio Sch Bd Asn, 1972-, Nat Asn Advan Colored People, Black Womens Leadership, 1973-76. **Honors/Awds:** Public Service Award, 1979; Public Service Award, Inner City Sertoma Club, 1978; Public Service Award, Nat Asn Advan Colored People, Columbus Chap, 1980; Certificate of Appreciation for Service & Leadership in the Field of Public Education, Ky State Univ, 1980; Award for Distinguished Community Service, Ohio House Rep, 1981.

CASTRO, GEORGE A
State government official, association executive. **Personal:** Born Dec 27, 1936, Providence, RI; married Avis L; children: Regina, Terri & Brian Dave. **Educ:** Duke Univ, Providence Col. **Career:** Rhode Island Gen Assembly, state rep, dist 20; Vol Ctr RI, Blacks Interested Commun, pres & dir, currently. **Orgs:** Chmn, Martin Luther King Jr State Holiday Comn; bd mem, RI Black Heritage Soc; Int Inst; bd mem, Cranston Gen Hosp Corp; Nat Asn Advan Colored People, Newport Chap; chmn, Comn Boxing & Wrestling RI; Gov Adv Comn Sr Citizens; Urban Educ Ctr; adv comn mem, Radio & TV; Minority Adv Comn; Pep Mgt Adv Comn, Boxing, Wrestling, Kickboxing. **Home Addr:** 57 Carolina Ave, Providence, RI 02905. **Business Phone:** (401)941-9370.

CASTRO, OCTAVIO ANTONIO. See FERNANDEZ, TONY.

CASWELL, ROSELL R
Executive, counselor. **Educ:** Fla A&M Univ, BA, bus educ, MA. **Career:** Fla A&M Univ, Ctr Human Develop, coordr stud affairs, dir stud affairs, Coun Serv, res coordr, currently. **Orgs:** Nat Asn Stud Personnel Administr. **Honors/Awds:** Sadie M Yancey Professional Service Award, Nat Asn Stud Affairs Profs, 2001. **Business Phone:** (850)599-3145.

CATCHING-KYLES, SHARRON FAYE
Police officer. **Personal:** Born Jan 3, 1950, Jackson, MS; daughter of Willie Lee and Bennie Lee Lewis; married James Tyrone, Aug 9, 1978 (divorced); children: Darrell Augustues & La Keista Renee. **Educ:** Jackson State Col, Jackson, Miss, 1968-69; Jackson Police Training Acad, Jackson, Miss, 1975. **Career:** Jackson Police Dept, patrol sgt, 1978-95, lt, 1995-98, dep chief police, 1998-; Juvenile Detention Ctr, dir. **Orgs:** Pres, Smith Chapel Freewill Baptist Church Choir, 1975-85; pres, Jackson Concerned Officers Progress, 1980-88; Community Admin, YWCA, 1984-94; Nat Black Police Asn, 1986-92; New Mt Zion Inspirational Choir; Nat Asn Advan Colored People; Miss Mass Choir Live Gospel Rec, 1988; Anderson United Methodist Church; Nat Orgn Black Law Enforcement Exec. **Honors/Awds:** Outstanding Heroic Performance Award, Lanier Class, 1965 & 1985; Outstanding Bravery, N Jackson Kiwanis Club, 1983; Lawman of the Year, La & Miss & W Tenn Dist Kiwanis, 1983-84; Distinguished Service Award, Jackson Police Dept, 1984; Police Officer of the Month, Jackson Asn Life Underwriters, 1984; J-Cop Silver Shield for Community Service, Jackson Concerned Officers Progress, 1985. **Home Addr:** 486 Hanging Moss Circle, Jackson, MS 39206, **Home Phone:** (601)366-5060. **Business Addr:** Deputy Chief, Jackson Police Department, 327 E Pascagoula St, Jackson, MS 39205, **Business Phone:** (601)960-1365.

CATCHINGS, HOWARD DOUGLAS
Insurance agent. **Personal:** Born Jun 19, 1939, Copiah County, MS; son of Corean and H D Catchings; married Danella Brownridge; children: Sebrena, Douglas, James & Daniel. **Educ:** Jackson State Univ, BEd, 1963, MEd, 1973. **Career:** Jackson Pub Sch, teacher, 1963-80; United Founders Ins Co, rep, 1967-68; Trans-Am Life, gen agt; Transamerica Life/Catchings Ins Agency, gen agt, 2003-. **Orgs:** Vpres, 1098-88, pres, 1993-94, Jackson State Univ; pres, Miss Asn Life, 1985-89 & 1993-94; comt mem, Million Dollar Round Table; pres, Jackson GAMA, 1986-87; bd dirs, Jr Achievement; State Job Training Coord Coun; coun mem, Bus, Indust, Educ Regional Coun; past chmn bd, Jackson Chamber Com; regional officer, GAMC; nat bd mem, Pub Educ Forum; past pres, Miss Asn Life Underwriters; chmn, Jr Achievement Miss; bd mem, past pres, Rotary Club Jackson; Metrop Crime Comn; First Am Bank; St Dominic Health Serv; Hancock Group Incl Jackson Gen Agents Mgr AsnCourt the Table; adv bd, Top the Table; adv bd, TransAm Life Ins Co; adv bd, Standard & Poor's Rating Co; First Am Bank; Miss Econ coun; pres, Jackson State Univ Nat Alumni Asn; Jackson State Univ Develop Found; St Dominic Health Serv; Universities Ctr; Metropolitan Crime Comn. **Honors/Awds:** one of top ten agents, Nat Old Line Ins Co, 1971-94; Outstanding Teacher in Human Relations, Jackson Pub Schs, 1972; Outstanding Achievement Award, Jackson State Univ Nat Alumni Asn; No 1 Salesman (Natly) 1986 & 1993-94; Citizen of the Year, March Dimes; Hall of Fame, Jackson Asn Life Underwriters; Hall of Fame, Miss Asn Life Underwriters; Nat Sales Rep, 1993-97. **Home Addr:** 6027 Woodlea Rd, Jackson, MS 39206. **Business Addr:** General Agent, Transamerica Life/Catchings Insurance Agency, 945 N State St, PO Box 2509, Jackson, MS 39202, **Business Phone:** (601)355-7489.

CATCHINGS, DR. YVONNE PARKS
Educator. **Personal:** Born in Atlanta, GA; daughter of Andrew Walter Parks and Hattie Marie Brookins Parks; married James Albert A (deceased); children: Andrea Hunt Warner, Wanda Hunt McLean & James A A Jr. **Educ:** Spelman Col, AB, 1955; Teachers Col Columbia, MA, 1958; Univ Mich, MMP, 1971, PhD, 1981. **Career:** Spelman Col, instr, 1956-57; Marygrove Col, instr, 1970-72; Specialist; Detroit Bd Educ, instr, 1959-; Valdosta State Col, asst prof art, 1987-88; Detroit Bd Educ, specialist, 1988-. **Orgs:** Nat Art Educ Asn, 1956-; prog chr bd, Detroit Soc Genelogical Res, 1965-; nat treas, The Smart Set, 1976-78; archivist pub rel, Mich Art Therapy Asn, 1981-; reg art therapist, Am Art Therapy, 1981-; chmn, Heritage Archives Delta Sigma Theta Sor, 1983-; bd chr, peace Am Asn Univ Women, 1981-; art chr, The Links, 1981-. **Honors/Awds:** Exhibited Atlanta Univ Negro Art Show, 1953-63; One Woman Art Show, Through the Year, Nat Dent Asn, 1973; President Special Award, Nat Dental Asn, 1973; First Award Art & Letters, Delta Sigma Theta Sorority, 1978; Mayor's Award, Merit Mayor Coleman Young, 1978; Won Honorable Mention four times, Clark Atlanta Univ; James D Parks Award, Nat Conf Artist, 1979; Fulbright Hayes Award, Study in Zimbabwe, 1982; Service Award, Afro Am Mus, 1983; Outstanding Black Woman in Michigan, 1785-85, Detroit Hist Mus, 1985. **Home Addr:** 1306 Joliet Pl, Detroit, MI 48207. *

CATES, HON. SIDNEY HAYWARD, IV
Judge. **Personal:** Born Mar 10, 1931, New Orleans, LA; married Betty; children: Sidney IV & Kim. **Educ:** Loyola Univ, BA, 1968, JD, 1976. **Career:** Government official, attorney; Housing Authority New Orleans,exec dir; La Dept Justice, atty gen; GSS Inc, vpres gen mgr; Hibernia Nat Bank, mkg officer; Law Enforce Asn Admin, consult; City New Orleans, asst chief admin off; New Orleans Police Dept, Judge; Division "C" New Orleans City, currently. **Orgs:** Bd dir, Loyola Univ; Red Cross; Boy Scouts Am; United Way; Goodwill; St.Claude Gen Hosp; Mid Winter Sports Asn; Knights St Peter Claver;Equestrian Knights Holy Sepulchre; pres, Studs Club; Chamber Com; vice chmn, Bicentennial Comt, City New Orleans; C Bur City New Orleans; New Orleans Bar Asn, 1976-; Alpha Sigma Nu; Nat Jesuit Honor Soc; Delta Epsilon Sigma; New Orleans Alcoholic Beverage Control Bd; New Orleans City Coun; bd gov, La Trial Lawyer's Asn; Louis A Martinet Legal Soc; Law Vis Comt, Loyola Univ. **Honors/Awds:** Alfred E Clay Award; Honour, Charles E Dunbar; Career Civil Service Award;Papal Honor, Knights of the Holy Sepulcher. **Military Serv:** Sgt, 1951-53. *

CATHEY, LEON DENNISON
Lecturer. **Personal:** Born Oct 11, 1932, San Diego, CA; son of Joseph Cathey and Barbara Cathey Dennison. **Educ:** San Francisco State Col, BA, geog, 1958, MA, biol, 1972; Stockholm Univ, grad dipl, social studies, 1979; San Francisco State Univ, MA, ethnic studies, 1990. **Career:** San Francisco Unified Sch Dist, sci instr, 1960-88; San Francisco State Univ, lectr ethnic studies, 1994-. **Special Achievements:** Man and Land: One Man, Whose Land, 1983; Philippine News SF, LA, NY, Dec 7-13, 1983. **Military Serv:** California Nat Guard, sgt, 1955-57. **Business Phone:** (415)338-1111.

CATLETT, ELIZABETH
Sculptor. **Personal:** Born Apr 15, 1915, Washington, DC; daughter of John H and Mary Carson; married Francisco Mora, Oct 31, 1946; children: Francisco, Juan & David. **Educ:** Howard Univ, Sch Art, DC, BS, cum laude, 1935; State Univ Iowa, Iowa City, IA, MFA, 1940. **Career:** Teacher Tex, La, Va & New York City; Nat Sch Fine Arts; Nat Autonomous Univ Mexico, prof, sculpture, dept head, 1959-73; freelance sculptor, printmaker. **Orgs:** Delta Sigma Theta, 1932-. **Honors/Awds:** First prize in sculpture, Golden Jubilee Nation Exposition, 1941; Tlatilco Prize, First Sculpture Biannual, 1962; Xipe Totec Prize, Second Sculpture Biannual, 1964; first prize in sculpture, Atlanta Univ Annual, 1965; first purchase prize, Nat Print Salon, 1969; Alumni Award, Howard Univ, 1979; Award from Women's Caucus for Art, National Congress, 1981; Brandywine Workshop Award, Philadelphia Mus Art, 1982; purchase prize, Salon de la Plastica Mexicana, Drawing Salon, 1985; Art Award, AMISTAD Res Ctr, 1990; DHL, Morgan State Univ, 1993; DFA, New Sch Social Res, Parsons, 1995; DHL, Tulane Univ, 1995; DFA, Spelman Col, 1995; DHL, Howard Univ, 1996; DFA, Cornell Col, 1996; DFA, Col Art, Maryland Inst, 1999; DFA, New Jersey Univ, 2002. **Home Addr:** PO Box AP694, 62000 Cuernavaca, Mexico.

CATO, KELVIN T.
Basketball player. **Personal:** Born Aug 26, 1974; son of Donald Cato and Carolyn Cato. **Educ:** Iowa State univ, attended 1997. **Career:** Portland TrailBlazers, ctr, 1997-99; Houston Rockets, ctr, 1999-04; Orlando Magic, ctr, 2004-05; Detroit Pistons, ctr, 2006; New YorkKnicker bockers, 2006-07. Free agent, currently. *

CATOR, JOHNNY
Executive. **Career:** Microsoft Inc, sr acct exec; Vietnam Express, founder, 1990-; Network Plus; Compu-Tel, founder; City Soft, sr vpres opers; WebcTel Inc, founder, pres & chief exec officer, 2000-. **Orgs:** Haitian Am Health Asn. **Business Addr:** Founder & President, Chief Executive Officer, WebcTel Inc, 162 2nd St, Cambridge, MA 02142, **Business Phone:** (617)573-5225.*

CAUDLE, ANTHONY, SR.
Banker, vice president (organization). **Personal:** Born May 20, 1965, Indianapolis, IN; son of Harvey and Ann; married Nina Simone Caudle, Oct 27, 1964; children: Anthony L II, Krysten Simone. **Educ:** Purdue Univ, BS, 1987; Univ Chicago, MBA, 1994; Howard Univ Sch Divinty. **Career:** Merrill Lynch, assoc, investment banking, 1994-95; Ford Motor Co, sr financial analyst, treas, 1996-99; Delphi Automotive, mgr capital markets treas, 1999-01; Comerica Securities Inc, vpres investment banking, 2001-. **Orgs:** Alpha Phi Alpha, 1985-; assoc minister, Tabernacle Missionary Baptist Church, 1996-; 100 Black Men Detroit, 2003-; trustee, Henry Ford Health Systs, 2003-; bd mem, Detroit Rescue Mission Ministries. **Special Achievements:** Started Comerica Bank's Cooperate Investment Banking Pract. **Business Addr:** Vice President, Comerica Securities Inc, 25 Mich Ave W, Battle Creek, MI 49017-3610, **Business Phone:** (313)964-5068.*

CAULKER, FERNE YANGYEITIE
Dance director. **Personal:** Born Aug 9, 1947, Sierra Leone; divorced; children: Yetunde Bronson. **Educ:** Univ Ghana, Am

Forum African Studies, cert, 1969; Univ Wis, BS, 1972. **Career:** Ko-Thi Dance Co, founder & artistic exec dir, 1969-, prog asst, tutor, 1971-72; Creative Dance Workshop, dir, 1975-77; Univ Wis-Milwaukee, lectr, 1971-77, asst prof, 1977-88, dept dance, prof, 1989-. **Orgs:** Wis Arts Bd, 1974; Wis Acad Sci, Fel, 1990; Fulbright Res Fel, 1994-95. **Honors/Awds:** Governor's Special Award, Wis Gov, 1984; Woman of the Year, Woman Woman Conf, 1989; Outstanding Contribution in Arts, Black Women's Network, 1994; Women's History Month Award, US Postal Serv, 1999; Outstanding Artist Award, City Milwaukee, Milwaukee Arts Bd, 2000; Distinguished Alumna Award in the Field of Arts & Humanities, Univ Wis Milwaukee, 2006. **Special Achievements:** Presentation, "Religious Dance In the Black American Experience," WI Dance Coun Conf, 1977; "Benito Cerno," guest choreographer, Milwaukee Repertory Theater, 1996; author, "Saving Children Through the Arts," WI Sch News, 2000. **Business Addr:** Founder, Executive Director, Ko-Thi Dance Co, 342 N Water St 7th Fl, PO Box 1093, Milwaukee, WI 53202, **Business Phone:** (414)273-0676.

CAUSEY-KONATE', TAMMIE
Educator. **Educ:** Univ New Orleans, BA 1986, MEd 1996, PhD 2000. **Career:** Assoc Prof,Grad Coord K-12 Educational Leadership. **Business Addr:** Associate Professor and Graduate Coord,K-12 EL, Univ New Orleans, 2000 Lakeshore Dr., Education Bldg. 348, New Orleans, LA 70148.*

CAUSWELL, DUANE
Basketball player. **Personal:** Born May 31, 1968, Queens Village, NY; married Leslie; children: Kaelyn Alana, Dylan & Jalen. **Educ:** Temple Univ, attended 1990. **Career:** Basketball player (retired); Sacramento Kings, ctr, 1990-97; Miami Heat, 1998-2001; San Antonio Spurs, 2000, free agent, currently. **Business Addr:** Basketball Player, San Antonio Spurs, 1 AT&T Ctr, San Antonio, TX 78219, **Business Phone:** (210)444-5000.

CAUTHEN-BOND, CHERYL G.
Ophthalmologist. **Personal:** Born Nov 13, 1957, Flint, MI; daughter of Joseph Jr. **Educ:** Howard Univ, attended 1977; Howard Univ Col Med, MD, 1981. **Career:** DC Gen Hosp, intern-med, 1981-82; Howard Univ Hosp, resident ophthal, 1982-85; Howard Univ Col Med, instr dept surg ophthal div, 1985-86; Norfolk Eye Physicians & Surgeons, physician, 1986-; Eastern Va Med Sch, asst prof ophthal, currently. **Orgs:** Am Acad Ophthal; Nat Med Asn; Am Med Asn; Norfolk Med Soc; Norfolk Acad Med; Old Dominion Med Soc; Med Soc Va. **Business Addr:** Assistant Professor of Ophthalmology, Eastern Virginia Medical School, 880 Kempsville Rd Suite 2500, Norfolk, VA 23502.*

CAVE, DR. ALFRED EARL
Physician. **Personal:** Born Jan 23, 1940, Brooklyn, NY; son of Alfred Cave Sr and Theodora; married Jeanne Byrnes; children: Christine. **Educ:** Columbia Col, BA, 1961; Downstate Med Ctr, MD, 1965. **Career:** Downstate Med Ctr, instr, 1971, asst prof surg, 1971-77; Kings County Hosp Brooklyn, attending physician, 1971-77; Long Beach Mem Hosp, attending surgeon, 1976-79; Lydia Hall Hosp, attending surgeon, 1977-78; Nassau Co Med Ctr, attending surgeon, 1978-2002; Syosset Community Hosp, attending surgeon, 1978-2002; pvt pract, currently. **Orgs:** Sigma Pi Phi Frat. **Honors/Awds:** 'National Medical Fellowship Award', 1961; 'New York State Medical Scholarship', 1961. **Military Serv:** AUS Reserve, capt, 6 yrs; Hon Discharge, 1972. **Home Addr:** 1 Hutch Ct, Dix Hills, NY 11746, **Home Phone:** (516)462-6050. **Business Addr:** Physician, 1 Hutch Ct, Dix Hills, NY 11746, **Business Phone:** (631)499-3997.

CAVE, PERSTEIN RONALD
School administrator, government official. **Personal:** Born Sep 24, 1947, Brooklyn, NY; son of Perstein and Dorothy; divorced; children: Christopher, Joscelyn & Jeralyn. **Educ:** Kingsborough Comm Col, AA, 1967; City Col NY, BA, 1970; Univ Hartford, MBA, 1981; CGFM. **Career:** The Aetna Life & Casualty Ins Co, expense coordr, 1977-80; ESPN & ABC TV, spec proj consult, 1980-85; Asnuntuck Comm Col, bus mgr & assoc dean, 1985; Twins Community Col, bus mgr, 1988-89; State CT, asst financial dir, 1989, fiscal admin mgr, currently. **Orgs:** Ministerial servant, Windsor CT Congregation Jehovah's Witnesses, 1980-; Nat Asn Acct, 1980-; Nat Black MBA Asn, 1982-; Asnuntuck Community Col; Affirmative Action Comt, 1985-; Asn Govt Accts; Inst Internal Auditors; AGA Boston Chapter. **Honors/Awds:** Citation for Outstanding Community Service. **Business Addr:** Fiscal Administrative Manager, State of Connecticut, Department of Banking, 250 Constitution Plz, Hartford, CT 06103, **Business Phone:** (860)240-8121.

CAVIN, DR. ALONZO C.
School administrator. **Personal:** Born Jul 17, 1939, Savannah, GA; son of Willie Cavin Dale; married Gwendolyn Mary Wells; children: Alonzo & William. **Educ:** Cheyney State Col, PA, BS, 1961; West Chester State Col, PA, MA, 1969; Temple Univ, EdD, 1979. **Career:** Bayard Middle Sch, eng teacher, 1965-69; PMC Col, dir proj; Widener Univ, assoc prof educ & dir state fed prog, assoc prof emer, currently. **Orgs:** Assn for Supv & Curriculum Develop, 1972-, PA Assn Supv & Curriculum Develop, 1972-, Mid-Eastern Assn Educ, Opportunity Prog Personnel, 1972-; pres, Chester PA Rotary Inc, 1985; bd mem, DE Gov Coun Exceptional Citizens, 1979-, Walling ford Chester Am Red Cross, 1985. **Honors/Awds:** Legion Honor Chapel Four Chaplains, 1980; publ Cognitive Dissonance affective Domain ERIC, 1979, Affective Variable Indicating Acad Success ERIC, 1978, Pre Col Exp, An Opportunity Assessment, PA Dept Educ, 1974; C Service Award, Omega Psi Phi Fraternity Inc, Epsilon Pi Chap 1987; Chmn, Chester-Wallingford Am Red Cross, 1989-90; Outstanding Service Award, Act101 Dirs Assn, 1990; Award of Advocate, Nat Coun Educ Opportunity Assn, 1990; Rotarian of the Year Award, Chester Rotary Club, 1991; Lucy G Hathaway Memorial Award, Am Red Cross, Chester Wallingford Chap, 1992. **Special Achievements:** Testimony: "The Philadelphia Higher Education Equal Opportunity Act (Act101), " Pennsylvania Legislative Black Caucus Public Hearing, Pittsburgh,1991; Discussions/interviews: "Legislation and Higher Education, " Edie Huggins, WCAU-TV, Philadelphia, 1992; "Higher Education and Black America, " Rica Duffus, WPHL-TV, Philadelphia, 1992. **Military Serv:** USN, lt jg, 1961-65.

CAVINESS, E. THEOPHILUS
Clergy, president (organization). **Personal:** Born May 23, 1928, Marshall, TX; married Jimmie; children: Theophilus James, Theodosia Jacqueline. **Educ:** Bishop Col, BA; Eden Theol Sem, BD; VA Seminary & Col, DD. **Career:** Greater Abyssinia Bapt Church Fed Credit Union, pres; Greater Abyssinia Bapt Ch, pastor, currently. **Orgs:** Historian & mem bd dir, Nat Bapt Conv USA Inc; pres, OH Bapt State Conv; pres, Bapt Min Conf; exec asst, Mayor of Cleveland Off; bd dirs, Blacktie Cleaveland, currently. **Business Addr:** Pastor, Greater Abyssinia Baptist Church, 1161 E 105 St, Cleveland, OH 44108.*

CAVINESS, LORRAINE F.
Educator. **Personal:** Born Apr 8, 1914, Atlanta, GA; married Clyde E; children: Muriel E. **Educ:** Spelman Col, BA, 1936; Atlanta Univ, attended 1948; Am Univ, attended 1952; DC Teachers Col, attended 1960. **Career:** Winston-Salem Teachers Col, asst teacher, 1936-37; Voc High Sch, teacher, 1937-38; US Govt Dept Labor, res asst, 1942-44; Dept Army, 1947-51; Wash DC Pub Sch, 1946, 1963-64. **Orgs:** Spelman Col Alumnae Asn; Century Club Spelman Col, 1977; DC Nat Retired Teachers Asn; Wash Urban League; Brightwood Community Asn, treas, 1968-70; chmn, Educ Comt, 1969; Fedn Civic Asn; Adv Neighborhood Coun. **Honors/Awds:** Hon Service Award, US Dept Labor, 1958; Grass Roots Honoree Award DC Fedn Civic Asn, 1969; Wash Real Estate Brokers Award, 1970.

CAYOU, NONTSIZI KIRTON
Educator. **Personal:** Born May 19, 1937, New Orleans, LA; married William. **Educ:** San Francisco State Univ, AB, 1962, MA, 1973. **Career:** Educator (retired). San Francisco Unified Sch Dist & Woodrow Wilson HS, 1955; San Francisco State Univ, coordr dance prog; Stanford Univ, 1976-77; San Francisco State Univ, teacher dance prog, 1963, 1965, 1967; San Francisco Unified Sch Dist & Woodrow Wilson High Sch, 1963; Univ San Francisco, 1972-73, teacher guest artist, 1969-70; San Francisco State Univ, chair, 1995. **Orgs:** Dir founder, Wajumbe Cultural Ensemble, 1969; chmn, Oakland Dance Asn, 1966-68; chmn, Comn Black Dance, 1969; Calif Dance Educrs Asn; Nat Dance Asn; Host Chair, Fifth world Congress, Int Cong Orisa Tradition & Culture, 1997, Dep Secy, 97-99. **Special Achievements:** Griot Soc Publ, "The Dance is People", New African article, 1965; article, "Origins of Jazz Dance", Black Scholar, 1970; book, "Modern Jazz Dance",1973.

CAZENAVE, DR. NOEL ANTHONY
Educator. **Personal:** Born Oct 25, 1948, Washington, DC; son of Herman Joseph and Mildred Depland; married Anita Washington, Jun 20, 1971 (divorced 2009); children: Anika Tene. **Educ:** Dillard Univ, BA, psychol magna cum laude, 1970; Univ Mich, MA, psychol, 1971; Tulane Univ, PhD, sociol, 1977; Univ NH, attended 1978; Univ Pa, attended 1989. **Career:** Temple Univ, asst, 1978-84, assoc prof, 1984-91; Univ Conn, assoc prof sociol, currently. **Orgs:** Am Sociol Asn; Asn Black Sociologists, Urban Affairs Asn. **Honors/Awds:** Conn Bloomer Award, NE Mag, 1999; Five awards for co-edited Welfare Racism book. **Special Achievements:** Numerous journal articles; Books: Impossible Democracy: The Unlikely Success of the War on Poverty Community Action Programs; Co-author of Welfare Racism: Playing the Race Card Against America's Poor. **Business Addr:** Associate Professor of Sociology, University of Connecticut, 344 Mansfield Rd U-Box 68, 123 Manchester Hall, Storrs, CT 06269-2068, **Business Phone:** (860)486-4190.

CEBALLOS, CEDRIC Z.
Basketball player, basketball coach. **Personal:** Born Aug 2, 1969, Maui, HI. **Educ:** Ventura Col, Ventura, CA, 1988; Calif State Univ, Fullerton, CA, 1990. **Career:** Basketball player (retired), basketball coach; Phoenix Suns, forward, 1990-94, 1997-98; Los Angeles Lakers, 1994-97; Dallas Mavericks, 1997-2000; Detroit Pistons, 2000-01; Miami Heat, 2000-01; HYB (Handle Your Bus), founder, 2000; Hapoel Tel Aviv, 2002-03; Phoenix Flame, 2007; Phoenix Mercury, spec asst coach, 2004; Alik Entertainment, owner, currently; Phoenix Suns, emcee, currently; Nothing but Net, host, currently; Phoenix Flame, coach, currently. **Orgs:** Cystic Fibrosis Found. **Honors/Awds:** NBA All-Star, 1995; NBA Player of the Week, 1995; NBA Slam Dunk Champion. **Special Achievements:** Released album in the summer of 2000 titled "Nuff Ced"; Writes music and lyrics, and his single "Flow On" was included on Immortal Records "Basketball's Best Kept Secret" release; bit roles in movies like Space Jam and Eddie. **Business Addr:** Assistant Coach, Phoenix Flame, 111 W Monroe, Phoenix, AZ 85003, **Business Phone:** (602)258-0175.

CEDENO, CESAR
Baseball player, baseball executive. **Personal:** Born Aug 18, 1951, Santo Domingo, Dominican Republic; married Cora Lefevre; children: Cesar Jr, Cesar Roberto & Cesar Richard. **Career:** Baseball player (retired), Baseball Executive; Houston Astros, outfielder1970-81; Cincinnati Reds, outfielder 1982-85; St Louis Cardinals, outfielder, 1985; Los Angeles Dodgers, outfielder, 1986; Dominican & Venezuelan Winter Leagues, fielding & hitting coach; Washington Nationals, coach, currently. **Honors/Awds:** All-Star, nat league, 1972-74, 1976; National League Player of the Month, 1972 & 1977; Gold Glove Award, nat League, 1972-76; named to the post-season NL All-Star team by Sporting News three times.

CELESTINE, VON C
Association executive, vice president (organization). **Career:** United Healthcare, finance mgr; Prudential Health Care, compliance mgr; Smith, Graham & Co Investment Advisors LP, sr vpres & dir finance & admin, currently. **Business Addr:** Senior Vice President, Director Of Finance, Administration, Smith, Graham & Co Investment Advisors LP, 6900 JPMorgan Chase Tower 600 Travis St, Houston, TX 77002, **Business Phone:** (713)227-1100.*

CENTERS, LARRY EUGENE
Football player. **Personal:** Born Jun 1, 1968, Tatum, TX; son of Don and Margie; married Vanessa Lampkin; children: Larry II, Sydni & Kennedi. **Educ:** Stephen F Austin State Univ. **Career:** Football player (retired); Phoenix Cardinals, running back, 1990-93; Ariz Cardinals, 1994-98; Wash Redskins, 1999-00; Buffalo Bills, 2001-02; New England Patriots, 2003. **Honors/Awds:** Pro Bowl, 1995-96, 2001; Pro Bowl alternate, 1998; Super Bowl champion (XXXVIII). *

CHAFFERS, JAMES ALVIN
Educator. **Personal:** Born Nov 30, 1941, Ruston, LA; married Geraldine; children: Pedra & Michael. **Educ:** Southern Univ Baton Rouge, BArch (cum laude) 1964; Univ MI, MArch, 1969, DArch, 1971. **Career:** La State Univ, Dept Psychol, educ prog consult, 1970; Southern Univ, Col Eng, assoc prof archit, 1971; State La, Off Gov, environ design consult, 1971; Wastenaw Co, comnr, 1970-71; Stanford Univ, fel, 1980-81; Nathan Johnson & Assoc, arch; Univ Mich, Alfred Taubman Col Archit & Urban Planning, from asst prof to assoc prof, 1973-75, prof, 1979-, chair doctoral prog, 1991-94; Villa Corsi-Salviati Design Studio, Italy, dir,1995; Taubman Col W African Studio, dir; J Chaffers Archit, pres & design prin; Woodrow Wilson fel. **Orgs:** Chmn, Southern Univ Dept Archit; dir, Community based Design Workshops N Cent Ann Arbor & SW Detroit; Am Inst Architects; Mich Soc Architects; Asn Col Sch Archit; Mich Acad Sci, Arts & Letters. **Honors/Awds:** Outstanding teacher award, Southern Univ, 1989, 2005; Grand Prize Award, 1992; Distinguished Faculty Award, Univ Mich, 1999; Educator Of the Year, Archit Studies Found, 1995. **Military Serv:** AUS, CEngr capt, 1964-68. **Home Addr:** 1415 Normandy Rd, Ann Arbor, MI 48103, **Home Phone:** (734)769-9016. **Business Addr:** Professor, University of Michigan, Alfred Taubman College Architecture & Urban Planning, 2000 Bonisteel Blvd, 3138 Art & Arch, Ann Arbor, MI 48109-2069, **Business Phone:** (734)936-0213.

CHALLENOR, HERSCHELLE
School administrator. **Personal:** Born Oct 5, 1938, Atlanta, GA; divorced. **Educ:** Spelman Col, BA; Univ Grenoble; Sorbonne Univ; Johns Hopkins, MA; Columbia Univ, PhD. **Career:** Polit Sci Dept Brooklyn Col, asst prof, 1969-72; Am Polit Sci Assoc, cong fel, 1972-73; Div Ed & Res Ford Found, prog officer, 1973-75; UN Ed Sci & Cult Org Wash Liaison Off, dir, 1978-93; Clark Atlanta Univ, Sch Pub & Int Affairs, dean, 1993-2002, prof int rels & african affairs, 2002; Asst Adminr Bur Africa, sr adv & consult, currently; USAID AAAS diplomacy fellow AA/AFR. **Orgs:** Consult, Sub-com Africa; UN Assn Coun Foreign Rel, Am Polit Sci Assn, Natl Conf Black Polit Sci, Brd Oper Crossroads Africa; Intl Block United Fund; Spelman 1 Scholar; chair, brd dir, Natl Summit Africa. **Honors/Awds:** Charles Merill Study Travel Award; Woodrow Wilson Fel; John Hay Whitney Fel; NY State Merit Fel; Am Assn Univ Women Fields Res Grant; Fel Adlai Stevenson Inst Int Affairs Chicago; Ford Found Travel & Study Award. **Business Addr:** Senior Advisor, Consultant, USAID, Bureau for African Affairs, Ronald Reagan Bldg, 1300 Pennsylvania Ave NW, Washington, GA 20523, **Business Phone:** (202)712-1562.

CHALMERS, THELMA FAYE
Executive director. **Personal:** Born Feb 21, 1947, Shreveport, LA; daughter of Leonard Hampton and Ivy Williams Hampton; mar-

ried Jimmy Chalmers; children: Troy, Douglas & Celeste. **Educ:** Chandler Col, assoc degree, 1966; Southern Ill Univ, Edwardsville Sch Bus, assertive mgt cert, 1985; Bus Women's Training Inst, image & commun skills cert, 1986. **Career:** St Clair Co Intergovernmental Grants Dept, prog monitor, 1979-81, prog planner, 1981-83, equal employ opportunity officer, 1982-, spec assignment supvr, 1983-86, div mgr, 1988-90, exec dir, 1990-. **Orgs:** Staff liaison, Serv Delivery Area 24 Pvt Indust Coun, 1984-; Ill Employ & Training Asn, 1985; Ill Employ & Training Partnership, 1988-91; bd mem, Ill Employ & Training Asn, 1989-90; IETP Prof Develop Comt, 1989-90; vice chair, Adv Coun Prog Serv Older Persons. **Honors/Awds:** Staff Award, Annual Job Training Partnership Act, 1989. **Home Addr:** 1517 Oak Meadow Dr, O Fallon, IL 62269. **Business Addr:** Executive Director, St Clair County Intergovernmental Grants Department, 19 Public Sq Suite 200 1220 Centreville Ave, Belleville, IL 62220, **Business Phone:** (618)277-6790.

CHAMBERLAIN, BYRON DANIEL
Football player. **Personal:** Born Oct 17, 1971, Honolulu, HI; married Robyn. **Educ:** Univ Mo; Wayne State Univ, commun. **Career:** Football player (retired); Denver Broncos, tight end, 1995-2000, 2004; Minn Vikings, tight end, 2001-02; Wash Redskins, tight end, 2003. **Honors/Awds:** Harlon Hill Trophy finalist; Pro bowl, 2001. *

CHAMBERLAIN, WESLEY POLK
Baseball player. **Personal:** Born Apr 13, 1966, Chicago, IL; son of Bettie L; children: Wesley Polk II. **Educ:** Simeon Career Acad, attended 1984. **Career:** Pittsburgh Pirates, 1987-90, free agent, 1997; Philadelphia Phillies, outfielder, 1990-94; Boston Red Sox, 1994-95; Winnipeg Goldeyes, 2000; Schaumburg Flyers, 2001-02; Newark Bears, 2002; Northern League, Gary SouthShore RailCats, 2003; Japan Chiba Lotte Marines, 2006. **Orgs:** SAA. **Honors/Awds:** MVP, Eastern League, 1989; Minor League Player of the Year, 1989; Topps All-Star, 1989; Eastern League All-Star, 1989; Player of the Month, 1989; Topps Player of the Month, 1989; NL Player of the Week, 1991.

CHAMBERS, CAROLINE E.
Executive, president (organization). **Personal:** Born Mar 30, 1964, Detroit, MI; daughter of DeMarr and Blanche Solomon; married Anthony Chambers, 1997; children: Eve. **Educ:** Univ Ga, BA, journ & mass commun, 1986; Univ Mich, MA, pub admin, 1994. **Career:** ICMA Retirement Corp, midwest mkt mgr, 1987-92; Mich Metro Girl Scout Coun, develop dir, 1992-94; Mich Health Care Corp, pub affairs dir, 1994-97; Comerica Charitable Found, Comerica Bank, corp contributions mgr, 1997-, vpres corp contributions & secy, pres, currently. **Orgs:** Bd chair, Core City Neighborhoods Non Profit Housing Corp, 1998-00; bd treasurer, Elder Law Mich, 1999-; bd mem, Communities Schs, 2000-; bd mem, Detroit Discovery Mus, 2001-. **Special Achievements:** Article on Corporate Philanthropy published in Michigan Forward, 1999. **Business Addr:** President, Comerica Bank, Comerica Charitable Found, 500 Woodward Ave, Detroit, MI 48226-3390, **Business Phone:** (313)222-7356.*

CHAMBERS, CHRIS
Executive. **Educ:** NY Univ, BA, jour. **Career:** Acct exec, 1990-92; Mercury Rec, mgr, dept dir, 1992-95; EMI Rec, sr dir publicity, 1995-97; Interscope Rec, sr dir publicity, 1997-2000; Arista Rec, vpres publicity, 2000-04; SONY BMG Music Entertainment, sr vpres publicity & artist develop; The Chamber Group, founder & pres, currently.

CHAMBERS, CHRISTOPHER J.
Football player. **Personal:** Born Aug 12, 1978, Cleveland, OH; son of Linda; married; children: Chaz. **Educ:** Wis, sociol & law. **Career:** Miami Dolphins, wide receiver, 2001-07; San Diego Chargers, wide receiver, 2007-. **Orgs:** Founder, C.A.T.C.H. 84 Foundation. **Honors/Awds:** AFC Offensive Player of the Week; Man of the Year, 2006; Pro Bowl, 2007; named the Dolphin team MVP. **Business Addr:** Professional Football Player, San Diego Chargers, PO Box 609609, San Diego, CA 92160-9609.*

CHAMBERS, CLARICE LORRAINE
Government official, clergy. **Personal:** Born Oct 7, 1938, Ossining, NY; daughter of Willie Cross (deceased) and Louise McDonald Cross (deceased); married Albert W, Jun 9, 1962; children: Albert W Jr, Cheryl L Fultz. **Educ:** Manna Bible Inst, teachers cert, 1965; Trinity Col Bible, B Biblical Studies, 1983; Int Bible Col & Seminary, MTh, biblical theol, 1986. **Career:** Naval Supply Depot, master data spec, 1957-65; dir training Tri-Cty OIC, 1970-72; PA State Dept Revenue, asst pub info dir, 1972-79; Antioch Tabernacle UHC A, pastor, 1979-; pres, Harrisburg Sch Bd, 1975-01. **Orgs:** Sec Tri-Cty OIC Bd, 1980-; Tri-Cty United Way Bd, 1983-89; S Cent PA Food Bank Bd, 1983-89; bd mem, YMCA 1989-93; bd mem, Delta Dental 1989-95; coun trustees, Shippenburg Univ, 1989-96; bod, Pa, 2000, 1992-96; Pa Stand & Practices CMS 1992-96; pres, PA Sch Bds Asn, 1992; Nat Sch Bd Asn, 1993-02, pres, 2000-01. **Honors/Awds:** Volunteer Comm Serv Tri-Cty OIC, 1977; Community Serv Award, Nat Asn Black Accts, 1984; Cert Recog Christian Churches United, 1984; African-Am Comn Serv Award, Harrisburg Chap Black United Fund Pa, 1989. **Special Achievements:** First African American woman president Nat School Bds Assn. **Home Addr:** 140 Sylvan Terr, Harrisburg, PA 17104. **Business Addr:** Pastor, Antioch Tabernacle UHC, 1920 N St, Harrisburg, PA 17103.*

CHAMBERS, DONALD C.
Physician. **Personal:** Born May 17, 1936; married Jacqueline; children: Christopher, Kimberly, Bradley. **Educ:** NY Univ, BA 1957; Howard Univ, Col Med, MD, 1961. **Career:** Kings Co Hosp Ctr, res training, 1961-66; St Univ NY, asst prof, 1964-66; Baltimore Pvt Prac, 1968-; Sinai Hosp, physician; Provident Hosp, physician; Lutheran Hosp, physician; Northwest Hosp, physician gynec, currently. **Orgs:** Pan Am Med Soc; Am Soc Abdominal Surgeons; Nat Asn Advan Colored People; Monumental City Med Soc; Health Care Standards Comt; Md Found Health Care; Wash Policy & Asn Mgt. **Honors/Awds:** Contributing author for Urban Health Magazine; fel, Am Col Obstet & Gynec, 1969; fel, Am Col Surgeons, 1973; fel, Royal Soc Health. **Military Serv:** USAF, capt, 1966-68. **Business Addr:** Physician, Northwest Hospital, 2300 Garrison Blvd Suite 200, Baltimore, MD 21216.*

CHAMBERS, FREDRICK. **See Obituaries section.**

CHAMBERS, HARRY
Educator, consultant. **Personal:** Born Jul 4, 1956, Birmingham, AL; son of Harry A Chambers Sr and Bessie L Chambers; married Linda Giles; children: Hali Alexandria, Harry Alonso III & Kayla Melissa. **Educ:** Ala State Univ, BS, 1979; Samford Univ, MBA, 1985; Dale Carnegie, Human Rel & Leadership Training. **Career:** US Gen Acct Off, co-op stud, 1976-77; Bank Am NT & SA, int auditor Europe, 1979-80; Amsouth Bank NA, div acct officer opers, 1980-86; US Treas, IRS agent, 1987-88; Chambers Consult Ltd, financial partner, 1985-; Chambers Consult Ltd, managing partner, 1986-; Birmingham Southern Col, adj prof, 1988-; Drake Beam Morin, consult, 1996-; Alternative Bd-Tab, Facilitator, 1999; Osborne Enterprises, Inc, managing partner, currently; vpres, Samford Univ, MADD, 2001. **Orgs:** Life mem, Kappa Alpha Psi 1980-; life mem, Nat Black MBA Asn Birmingham Chap, 1985-; Sunday sch teacher, Sixth Ave Baptist Church, 1985-; deacon, Sixth Ave Bapt Church, 1986-; treas, bd mem, Acad Fine Arts Inc, Birmingham Ala, 1988-. **Honors/Awds:** Consult, Magic City Boys choir, 1998. **Home Addr:** 1040 50th St, Birmingham, AL 35208. **Business Addr:** Managing Partner, Chambers Consulting Ltd, 800 25th St Ensley, Birmingham, AL 35218-1936, **Business Phone:** (205)780-7903.

CHAMBERS, JOHN CURRY, JR.
Lawyer, manager. **Personal:** Born May 22, 1956, Newark, NJ; son of John and Naomi McGriff; married Georgette Sims-Chambers, Nov 28, 1981; children: John Curry III, Candace Dane. **Educ:** Univ Pa, BA; The Washington Col Law, Am Univ, JD. **Career:** American Petroleum Institute, principal RCRA atty, 1981-84; CONOCO, in-house coun, 1985; McKenna & Cuneo, partner, 1986-97; Arent Fox, partner. **Orgs:** DC Bar; Am Bar Asn; Nat Bar Asn; Environmental Law Ed Inst; adv bd, J Environmental Permitting; adv comt, Am Bar Asn; Conf Minority Partners; comt, Nat Inst Environment; vchair, Am Bar Asn Teleconference & Video Prog Sonreel; vchair, Am Bar Asn Sonreel Diversity Comt; guest commentator, Nat Pub Radio; founder, Brownfields Bus Info Network; co chair, Am Bar Asn Video Teleconferences Comt; EPA NACEPT Title VI Fed Adv Comn Implementation Environmental Justice. **Special Achievements:** first African American equity partner in its history; Book: Of Color and Love, 1997. *

CHAMBERS, DR. JULIUS LEVONNE
Lawyer. **Personal:** Born Oct 6, 1936, Mount Gilead, NC; son of William and Matilda; married Vivian Verdell Giles; children: Derrick & Judy. **Educ:** NC Cent Univ Durham, BA, History (summa cum laude), 1958; Univ Mich, MA, 1959; Univ NC Sch Law, JD, 1962; Columbia Univ Sch Law, ML, 1963. **Career:** Lawyer (retired), attorney; Columbia Univ Sch Law, assoc law, 1962-63; NAACP Legal Def & Educ Fund Inc, legal intern, 1963-64; Chambers Stein Ferguson & Becton PA, founder & pres, 1964-84, atty, 2001-; Harvard Univ Law Sch, lectr, 1965; Univ Va Law Sch, guest lectr, 1971-72, adj prof, 1975-78; Univ Pa Sch Law, lectr, 1972-90; Columbia Univ Sch Law, adjunct, 1978-91; NAACP Legal & Educ Fund Inc, dir coun, 1984-92; Univ Mich Law Sch, adjunct, 1989-92; NC Cent Univ, chancellor, 1993-2001. **Orgs:** Am, Nat, 26th Judicial Dist NC Bar Asn; NC Asn Black Lawyers; Am Bar Asn Section Indiv Rights & Responsibilities; adv com Nat Bar Asn Equal Employment Oppor; NC Bar Asn Comt Rules Appellate Procedure; NC State Bar Asn Const Study Com; bd dirs, Epilepsy Asn NC; various Univ bd; various alumni asns; various frats; Friendship Baptist Church Charlotte. **Honors/Awds:** WEB DuBois Award, Scotland Co, 1973; Hall of Fame Award, NAACP, 1975; numerous hon LLD degrees; various distinguished serv awards, frats & Assns; Adam Clayton Powell Award for Legis & Legal Perfection, Cong Black Caucus. **Military Serv:** USNR, 1960-63; AUSR, 1963-66. **Home Addr:** 18 Appleton Pl, Durham, NC 27705. **Business Phone:** (704)375-8461.

CHAMBERS, MADRITH BENNETT
Government official. **Personal:** Born Oct 23, 1935, Beckley, WV; married Robert E Chambers; children: Stephanie M Rosario, Gregory B, Patrick M, Jennifer E, Sharri L. **Educ:** Bluefield State Col, AS, law enforcement, BS, criminal justice admin, 1985. **Career:** Social Security Admin, contact rep. **Orgs:** Councilwoman City Pax, 1972-74; vpres, Am Legion Women's Aux, 1982-84; chairperson, City Beckley Human Rights Comn, 1978-; pres, Beckley Chap Bluefield St Col Alumni Asn, 1983-; Alpha Kappa Alpha; bd dir, Community Health Syst; Heart god Ministries; NAACP Raleigh. **Honors/Awds:** DHHS Special Award, Social Sec Admin, 1980; Outstanding Serv Award, Bluefield St Col Alumni Asn, 1984; Mountain State Bar Asn Cit, Mt State Bar Asn, 1984. **Business Addr:** Contact Representative, Social Security Administration, 214 N Kanawna St, Beckley, WV 25801.

CHAMBERS, OLIVIA MARIE
Government official. **Personal:** Born Sep 27, 1942, Denver, CO; married Bill D; children: Maria. **Educ:** Dale Carnegie Ctrs Human Rel, cert, 1977; Univ Denver, Mgt Cert Prog, 1983; Colo Univ Ext Ctr & Community Col. **Career:** State Colo, Interstate Dept Employ & Training Unit, mgr, 1976-77, chief benefits, 1977-84, Dept Labor & Employ, Tax Dept, chief, 1984-. **Orgs:** IAPES; bd mem, Community Homemaker Suc, 1981-83. **Honors/Awds:** Distinguished State Service Award, Denver Fed Exec Bd, 1981. **Special Achievements:** Speaking of People, Ebony Mag, 1979. **Business Addr:** Chief, Colorado Department of Labor and Employment, Tax Department, 1515 Arapahoe Tower 2 Suite 400, Denver, CO 80202-2117, **Business Phone:** (303)603-8235.

CHAMBERS, PAMELA S
Police officer. **Personal:** Born Nov 5, 1961, Gasden, AL; daughter of Hurley S and Mildred L Douglas. **Educ:** Ferris State Col, Big Rapids, MI, AA, pre-law, 1982. **Career:** Not Just Nails, a nail salon, owner & pres, 1989; City Pontiac MI, police cadet, 1982, police officer, 1982, police sergeant, 1988, police capt, currently, Admin Serv Div, div comdr, currently. **Orgs:** Secy, Soc Afro-Am Police; bd mem, Nat Black Police Asn; assoc mem, Nat Org Black Law Exec (NOBLE), officer leader. **Honors/Awds:** Distinction of being the first black woman promoted to police sergeant in the history of the city of Pontiac; also the youngest person ever to be promoted to sergeant in the city of Pontiac. **Special Achievements:** First Black Fmale Lt of the Pontiac Police Dept, 1998; First Black Female Captain of the Pontiac Police Dept, 1999; First Female Black Dir for City of Pontiac Homeland Security, 2003. **Business Addr:** Police Captain, Division Commander, City of Pontiac, Pontiac Police Department, 110 E Pike St, Pontiac, MI 48342, **Business Phone:** (248)758-3400.

CHAMBERS, VAN B.
Educator, artist. **Personal:** Born Mar 23, 1940, Lyon, MS; children: three. **Educ:** Xavier Univ, BA, 1961; Notre Dame Univ, MFA, 1963. **Career:** Practicing artist, 1963-; Southern Univ, instr, fine arts, 1963-69, asst prof, 1969-74, assoc prof, 1974-. **Orgs:** Baton Rouge Gallery, 1971-. *

CHAMBLISS, ALVIN ODELL, JR.
Lawyer. **Personal:** Born Jan 22, 1944, Vicksburg, MS; son of Alvin O Sr and Ledorsha A; married Josephine Johnson Chambliss, Dec 31, 1973; children: Sadarie, Alvin O III, Alvenia. **Educ:** Jackson State Univ, BA, 1967; Howard Univ, JD, 1970; Univ Calif, Masters Law, 1972. **Career:** Nat Conf Black Mayors; Oper PUSH; Legal Aid Soc Alameda County; New Orleans Legal Assistance; Cohon, Jones & Fazande Law Firm, 1972-74; North Miss Rural Legal Serv, lawyer; Atty Law WW Wright Educ 4260, atty, currently; Ind Univ, fac, currently. **Orgs:** Vice chair, Nat Black Media Coalition; gen coun, Black Mississippian Coun Higher Educ; pres, Oxford-Lafayette County Br NAACP; chmn, Nat Conf Black Mayors; court watch chair, Magnolia Bar Asn; affiliate adv, Mississippi Asn Educators; community liaison, Methodist Men Burns. **Honors/Awds:** Ming Award Lawyer of the Year, Nat Asn Advan Coloured People, 1992; SCLC Chauncy Estridge Distinguished Barrister of Law, 1992; Lawyer of the Year, Miss Educ Asn, 1993; Lawyer of the Year, Miss Legislative Black Caucus, 1993; Man of the Year, Masonic Orders, PHA North Miss, 1993. **Special Achievements:** Nat NAACP 8th Lawyers CLE Seminar: Honoring Our Past, Fulfilling Our Present, Preparing for Our Future; Voting Rights & Citizen Participation Manual, 1986; Ayers Brown III The New Frontier in Higher Education, 1989; Trends in the Eighties, Mississippi State Practice, 1989; Natl NAACP Summit on Higher Education, Higher Education Desegregation Advancing African-Americans Towards Equality, 1992; Ayers v Fordice, "Where Do We Go From Here in Higher Education Desegration," 1993; Ayers v Fordice, Reversing the Trend in Higher Education Desegration From Closure to Parity for HBCUs, 1993; "Black Colleges Under Fire," Emerge, 1993. **Business Addr:** Attorney, Attorney at Law WW Wright Education 4260, 201 N Rose Ave, Bloomington, IN 47405, **Business Phone:** (812)856-8587.*

CHAMBLISS, PRINCE C
Lawyer. **Personal:** Born Oct 3, 1948, Birmingham, AL; son of Rev Prince C Chambliss Sr; married Patricia Toney Chambliss, Dec 26, 1971; children: Patience Bradyn. **Educ:** Wesleyan Univ, attended 1967; Univ Ala, Birmingham, BA, 1971; Harvard Univ, Sch Law, JD, 1974. **Career:** Univ Ala, Birmingham, spec asst to

pres, 1974-75; Judge Sam C Pointer Jr, law clerk, 1975-76; Armstrong Allen, et al, atty, 1976-2001; Stokes Bartholomew, Evens & Petree PC, partner & atty, 2001-. **Orgs:** Bd dirs, Memphis Mid-South Chap; bd dirs, Am Red Cross, 1987-; Tenn Bd Law Examiners, vpres, 1988-; Tenn Bar Asn, secy, 1994-97; Memphis Bar Asn, bd dirs, 1994-, pres, 1997-98; Ben F Jones Chap Nat Bar Asn, chmn, judicial recommendations comt; Grant Info Ctr Inc; AC-CTM, 1999-. **Honors/Awds:** Judicial Conference Community Service Award, Nat Bar Asn, 1986; Boss of the Year, Memphis Legal Secretaries Asn, 1983; Named one of America's leading lawyers, Black Enterprise Mag, 2003; Best Lawyers in America for Commercial Litigation, listed, 2006. **Special Achievements:** Legal Ethics for Trial Lawyers, The Litigator; "Inconsistent Verdicts: How to Recognize & Cope With," The Litigator; listed in the 2006 ed, The Best Lawyers in America for Commercial Litigation. **Business Addr:** Partner, Evans & Petree PC, 1000 Ridgeway Loop Rd Suite 200, Memphis, TN 38120, **Business Phone:** (901)521-4590.

CHAMPION, JAMES A
President (Organization), executive. **Personal:** Born May 9, 1947, Bronx, NY; son of James William and Jean Simmons; married Victoria Lindsey, May 25, 1985; children: Nicole, Jayson, Christopher & Lindsey. **Educ:** Al A & M Univ, Huntsville, BS, 1970; Rutgers Uni, NB, credits labor rels & human resource mgt, 1976. **Career:** Chase Manhattan Bank, asst mgr, 1970-72; US Dept Labor Recruitment & Training Prog, exec dir, 1972-79; Merrill Lynch & Co, asst vpres, human resource, 1979-85; Ryder Truck Rental Inc, div dir employee rels, 1985-89, dir human resource, 1989-93, corp dir diversity & employee affairs, 1993-95; Champion Serv Group Inc, pres & chief exec officer, 1995-. **Orgs:** Kappa Alpha Psi Fraternity; pres, Asn Affirmative Action Prof, Miami; chmn adv group, The Focal Pt Elderly; bd mem, Miami & Dade Chamber Com; bd mem, Jobs Progress, Miami; bd mem, The Epilepsy Found Miami; bd mem, Jackson Mem Found; bd mem, Fla Regional Minority Bus Coun; bd mem, Exec Comn, Greater Miami Chamber Com; bd mem, Exec Comn, Greater Miami Tennis Found; bd mem, Black Exec Forum; bd mem, New World Sch Arts; S Fal Indust - Off Fed Contract Compliance Prog Liaison Group; Black Human Resources Network; Soc Human Resources Mgt; United Way Dade Co Ctr Excellence; One Hundred Black Men NY; former bd mem, Mus Sci; former bd mem, Vis Indust Coun; former bd mem, Urban League Greater Miami; former bd mem, Miami Cares Kids; founder & former nat pres, Ryder Black Employees Network; Miami Dade Chamber Com. **Honors/Awds:** Black Achiever, Harlem YMCA, 1982; Black Achiever, Family Christian Asn Am, 1986; Prof Achiever, Dollars & Sense Publ, 1987; Community Achiever, NC A&T Alumni, 1990; Community Achiever, Comn Total Employ, 1990; Humanitarian Award, 1990; Service Award, 1990; Community Achiever, Alpha Kappa Alpha, 1991; Achiever, Nat Asn Equal Opportunity Higher Educ, 1993; Small Business of the Year, Miami-Dade Chamber Com, 1998; Emerging Black Business of the Year, Greater Miami Chamber Com, 1998; Minority Business Year Runner Up, Small Bus Admin, 2000; President Award, Fl Regional Minority Bus Coun, 2002. **Business Addr:** President, Chief Executive Officer, The Champion Services Group Inc, 6501 NW 36 St Suite 300, Miami, FL 33166, **Business Phone:** (305)871-4866.

CHANCE, DR. KENNETH BERNARD
Dentist, educator, administrator. **Personal:** Born Dec 8, 1953, New York, NY; son of George Edward and Janie Bolles; married Sharon L Lewis (divorced); children: Kenneth B II, Dana Marie, Christopher Weldon & Jacquelyne Lee. **Educ:** Fordham Univ, BS, 1975; Case Western Reserve Univ Dent Sch, DDS, 1979; Jamaica Hosp GP Residency Prog, cert, 1980; NJ Dent Sch, cert Endodontics, 1982; PEW Nat Dent Educ Prog, cert, 1986. **Career:** Harlem Hosp, attending 1981-90; N Cent Bronx Med Ctr, asst attending, 1982-92; Jamaica Hosp, asst attending, 1982-86; Kings Co Med Ctr, chief endodontics, 1983-91; Kingsbrook Jewish Med Ctr, asst attending, 1985-89; NJ Dent Sch, dir external affairs 1985-89; assoc prof endodontics, 1987-97; Univ Med & Dent New Jersey, asst dean external affairs & urban resource develop, 1989-97; Comnr health, Dept Health, consult, NJ, 1991-97; Health Policy Prog, The Joint Ctr Polit & Econs Studies, dir, 1992-93; US Senator Frank Lautenberg (D-NJ), health policy advr, 1992-94; Meharry Med Col, Sch Dent, dean, prof, 1997-2000, Univ Ky Col, Dent, chief, prof endodontics, 2000-. **Orgs:** Am Asn Endodontists, 1980-86, Nat Dent Asn, 1980-; minister, music & sr organist Sharon Bapt Ch, 1983-94; Int Asn Dent Res, 1984-86-; pres, elect Greater Metro Dent Soc NY, 1985-86; consult, Commonwealth Dent Soc, NJ 1985-97; Am Asn Dent Schs, 1990-; Am Dent Asn, 1993-; Am Polit Sci Asn, 1992-99; Ky Asn Endodontists, 2000-; Bluegrass Dent Soc, 2000-; bd trustees, Case Western Reserve Univ, 2005-. **Honors/Awds:** Dr Paul P Sherwood Award, Case Western Reserve Dent Sch, 1979; Award for Excellent Service, Jamaica Hosp, 1981; Research Award, The Foundation of the UMDNJ 1985; Exceptional Merit Award, NJ Dent Sch, 1986; Nom Excellence Teaching Award, NJ Dent Sch, 1985; Univ Med & Dent NJ Award Educ, 1990; Fellowship Award, Robert Wood Johnson Health Policy, 1991; Fellowship Award, Pew Nat Dent Leadership Develop, 1991; Fellow, Omicron Kappa Upsilon Honor Dent Soc, Omega Omega Chapter, 1992; Int Col Dentists, Am Col Dents, 1993; Pierre Fauchard Acad Int Honor Orgn, 1994; Fellow, Acad Polit Sci, 1995; Community Service Award, Univ Med & Dent NJ, 1997; Tennessee's Outstanding Achievement Award, Governor Don Sundquist, 1998; Outstanding Academician Award, Univ Med & Dent NJ, 1999; Elected, Distinguished Practitioner, Nat Acad Practice Dent, 2001; elected in "The Best Dentists in America", 2004; Distinguished Alumnus of the Year, Case Western Reserve Univ Sch Dent Med, 2004; Excellence Award in Education, Univ Med & Dent NJ; New Jersey Community Service Award, Univ Med & Dent. **Special Achievements:** Delivered Commencement Address, Case Western Reserve University, School of Dental Medicine, 2005. **Home Addr:** 2140 Mangrove Dr, Lexington, KY 40513.

CHANCELLOR, CARL EUGENE
Lawyer. **Personal:** Born Mar 1, 1929, Cleveland, OH; son of James H (stepfather) and Helen L Leonard; married Joyce Marshall; children: Carl C, Bruce E, Steven E & Yvette. **Educ:** Ohio State Univ, BA, 1951; Case Western Res Univ, Sch Law, JD, 1954; Univ Mich, Grad Sch Bus Admin, Pub Utility Exec Prog Cert, 1973. **Career:** Cleveland Electric Illuminating Co, assoc atty, atty, sr atty, gen suprv atty claims, 1954-72, mgr legal serv dept, 1972-82, asst gen coun, 1982-, secy & gen coun, 1986-90. **Orgs:** Spec coun, Atty Gen Ohio, 1953-69; sec bd dir, Raymilton Land Co Coal Mining, 1956-64; labor adv comn, Ohio C C, 1977-; pres, Self Insurers Group Ohio, 1965-70; chmn, Edison Elec Inst Claims Comn, 1985-86, Frankfort Pol Action Comn, 1977-84; exec bd, life mem, Cleveland Br, Nat Asn Advan Colored People; Alpha Phi Alpha. **Honors/Awds:** 'Certificate of Appreciation', VPres Humphreys Plans for Prog Comn, 1969; Meritorious Service Award, Cleveland Bar Asn, 1972; Legal Study Scholar, Rainey Found, 1951-54. **Home Addr:** 1 Bratenahl Pl, Bratenahl, OH 44108, **Home Phone:** (216)451-0112.

CHANCEY, ROBERT DEWAYNE
Football player. **Personal:** Born Sep 7, 1972, Macon, AL; children: Ja Myra Jackson. **Career:** Football player (retired); San Diego Chargers, running back, 1997, 2000; Chicago Bears, 1998; Dallas Cowboys, 1999. *

CHANDLER, ALLEN EUGENE
Physician, military leader. **Personal:** Born Sep 16, 1935, Hagerstown, MD; married Barbara Hardiman Chandler; children: Allen (deceased), Rodney, Roderick. **Educ:** Morgan State Col, Baltimore, MD, BS, chem, 1957; Jefferson Med Col, Philadelphia, PA, MD, 1961. **Career:** Gen Leonard Wood Army Hosp, Fort Leonard Wood, MS, chief pediat dept, 1964-66; Pa Army Nat Guard, 108th Combat Support Hosp, chief med servs, 1976-83, state surgeon, Hq State Area Command, 1983, advr Nat Guard Bur Surgeon, 1984, asst adj gen, State Area Command, 1987-; pvt med pract, Philadelphia, PA, currently; Philadelphia Health Dept, sr pediatrician, currently. **Orgs:** Nat Med Asn; Am Acad Pediat; US Mil Acad Selection Comt Cong man & House Majority Whip William H Gray; Nat Guard Asn Pa; Nat Guard Asn US; Asn Mil Surgeons. **Military Serv:** Pennsylvania Army Nat Guard, Brigadier Gen, 1976-; Meritorious Service Medal, Army Commendation Medal, Army Reserve Components Achievement Medal with one Oak Leaf Cluster, Armed Forces Reserve Medal, National Defense Service Medal, Army Service Ribbon, Pennsylvania Twenty-year Service Medal, General Thomas R White Ribbon, General Thomas J Stewart Medal, Adjutant General's Staff Identification Badge. **Business Addr:** Physician, Private Practice, 901 W Mt Airy Ave, Philadelphia, PA 19119.*

CHANDLER, ALTON H
Publisher. **Personal:** Born Oct 4, 1942, Philadelphia, PA; son of Herman A and Frances Houston-Chandler Leysath. **Educ:** Pa State Univ, Univ Pk, PA, attended 1964; Cooper Sch Art, Cleveland, OH, attended 1965; Philadelphia Col Textiles & Sci, attended 1967; Philadelphia Col Art, attended 1969. **Career:** AT&T, Wayne, PA, Newark, NJ, art dir, 1964-70; Am Baptist Churches, Valley Forge, PA, art dir, 1975-76; Perkasie Industs Corp, Perkasie, PA, advert & mkt dir, 1976-80; Magnatite Inc, Boston, MA, advert & mkt dir, 1980-84; Black Family Mag, Chicago, IL, creative dir, 1984-85; Chandler White Publ Co Inc, Chicago, IL, founder & pres, 1985-. **Business Addr:** President, Chandler White Publishing Company Inc, 30 E Huron St Suite 4403, Chicago, IL 60611.

CHANDLER, DEBORAH
Executive. **Career:** Mortuary Transp Serv, owner.

CHANDLER, EFFIE L.
Executive. **Personal:** Born Aug 13, 1927, Houston, TX; divorced; children: Donald C. **Educ:** Franklin Beauty Col, Cosmetology TX License, 1945; Tex State Univ, BA, 1966, MEd, 1975; Massey Bus Col, 1968. **Career:** US Postal Serv, distrib clerk, 1959-63, job instr, 1963-65, scheme instr, 1963-65; Personnel Sect, clerk steno, 1965-68; actg & employ asst, 1968-74; asst learning coun, 1971-73; dist EEO specialist, assoc employee develop adv, 1973. **Orgs:** Secy, Cambridge Civic Club, 1967; secy & treas, 1968-69; pres, Cambridge Village Civic Club, 1973-74; ed, Houston's Oldest Black Weekly Newspaper, Effie's Excerpts, 1973-74; Nat Coun Negro Women; YWCA; Nat Asn Postal Supr Br 122; Fed Minority Bus Opportunity Comt; instr EEO Div, So Region Headquarters chap; Cit Against Drug Abuse Comt; chmn exec adv bd, Anti-Basileus Gamma Phi Sigma Chap; Sigma Gamma Rho Sorority; campus adv Alpha Lambda Chap; Sigma Gama Rho Sorority. **Honors/Awds:** Cert & cash award for adopted suggestion, US Postal, 1967; Superior Accomplishment Award with cash award, US Postal, 1968; Quality Step Increase, 1968; Fed Women's Award, 1975; Outstanding Serv Community, Cambridge Village Civic Club, 1977; The Lt Col Cleveland Roy Petit Merit Award; Certificate of Appreciation recognition performance interest improved Postal Serv, US Postal Serv, So Region.

CHANDLER, EVERETT A.
Lawyer. **Personal:** Born Sep 21, 1926, Columbus, OH; son of Everett P and Mary Turner; divorced; children: Wayne B, Brian E, V Rhette, Mae Evette. **Educ:** Ohio State Univ, BSc, educ, 1955; Howard Univ Law Sch, JD, 1958. **Career:** Juvenile Ct Cuyahoga County, referee, 1959; City Cleveland, OH, housing inspector, 1960; Cuyahoga County Welfare Dept, legal investr, 1960-64; Cuyahoga County, OH, asst city prosecutor, 1968-71; City Cleveland, OH, chief police prosecutor, 1971-75; pvt pract atty, 1975-. **Orgs:** Mt Olive Missionary Baptist Church, 1958-; bd mem, Cedar Br, YMCA, 1965; Comt Action Against Addiction, 1975-80, bd chmn, 1980-87; polemarch & bd chmn, Cleveland Alumni Chap, Kappa Alpha Psi Inc, 1976, 1980-83; bd mem, Legal Aid Soc Cleveland, 1980; Nat Asn Advan Colored People; Urban League; bd mem & bd pres, CIT Mental Health; Excelsior Lodge 11 F&AM. **Honors/Awds:** Meritorious Service Award, Cleveland Bar Asn, 1972. **Special Achievements:** Book review, Vol 21 #2 Cleveland State Law School Law Review 1972; main speaker banquet Frontiers Intl Columbus OH 1972. **Military Serv:** USN, qmq2. **Business Addr:** Attorney, PO Box 28459, Cleveland, OH 44128-0459, **Business Phone:** (216)283-1677.*

CHANDLER, JAMES PHILLIP
Educator, lawyer. **Personal:** Born Aug 15, 1938, Bakersfield, CA; children: Elizabeth Lynne, James Phillip Jr, Isaac, Dennis Augustine, Ruth Rebekah,Aaron Daniel Pushkin & David Martin Thompson. **Educ:** Univ Calif, Berkeley, AB; Univ Calif, Davis, JD; Harvard Univ, LLM. **Career:** Harvard Univ, grad fel, 1970; Nat Acad Scis, Acad Engineering, fel, 1971; Stanford Univ Engineering Dept, fac fel, 1972-75; Univ Miss Sch Law, distinguished vis prof law, 1975-77; Harvard Univ, vis scholar, 1984; George Wash Univ, Nat Law Ctr, Law Sch, prof law, 1977-94, prof emer, 1994-; Chandler Law Firm Chartered, chmn, currently; Nat Intellectual Property Law Inst, pres, currently. **Orgs:** Alpha Phi Alpha Frat, 1961-; DC Bar; Pa Bar, Am Soc Int Law, 1969-; Am Asn Univ Profs, 1971-; Fel Acad Engineering Nat Acad Scis, 1971; Am Soc Law Profs, 1974-; Comput Law Asn, 1974-84; sect coun mem, Am Bar Asn, 1974-98; bd dir, Ch God Evening Light Saints, 1992-97. **Honors/Awds:** Presidential Appointment, Nat Infrastructure Assurance Coun, 1999; Int Legal Scholar. **Business Addr:** President, National Intellectual Property Law Institute, 1815 Pa Ave NW Suite 300, PO Box 27457, Washington, DC 20006, **Business Phone:** (202)789-0234.

CHANDLER, DR. MITTIE OLION
Educator, consultant, research scientist. **Personal:** Born Jul 25, 1949, Detroit, MI; daughter of Lurie Mae and Johnson Davis; children: Mae Evette. **Educ:** Mich State Univ, Lansing, Mich, BA, 1971; Wayne State Univ, Detroit, Mich, MUP, 1979, PhD, polit sci, 1985. **Career:** Detroit Housing Dept, public housing mgr, 1972-77; Detroit Community & Economic Develop Dept, city planner, 1977-81; New Detroit Inc, Detroit, Mich, dir, neighborhood stabilization & housing div, 1981-85; Cleveland State Univ, Cleveland, OH, asst prof, 1985-91; assoc prof, 1991-; Master Urban Planning, Design & Dev Prog, dir, 1993-99; Master Science Urban Studies Prog, dir, 1995-99; asst dean student serv, 1999-2001; Cleveland State Univ, Maxine Goodman Levin Col Urban Affairs, Urban Child Res Ctr, dir, 2002-. **Orgs:** Renaissance Develop Corp, 2002-; Help Found, 1999-2001; North Coast Community Homes, 1997-2001; The Empowerment Ctr Greater Cleveland, 1997-; vpres, The Empowerment Ctr Greater Cleveland, 2000-; Living in Cleveland Ctr, 1986-92; pres, Living In Cleveland Ctr, 1990-92; Garden Valley Neighborhood House, 1987-93; pres, Garden Valley Neighborhood House, 1991-93; bd trustees, Professional Housing Services, 1990-92; Alpha Kappa Alpha Sorority, 1969-; Nat Conference Black Political Scientists, 1990-; Nat Asn Advancement Colored People; trustee, Policy Bridge, 2005-; trustee, Kids Health 2020, 2005-. **Honors/Awds:** Urban Homesteading: Programs & Policies, Greenwood Press Inc, 1988; Clifford Kaufman Memorial Award in Urban Politics, Wayne State Univ, 1986; Pi Alpha Alpha, Nat Honor Soc Pub Affairs & Admin, 1982; Minority Fel Award, Urban Inst, 1984; Outstanding Young Woman of Am, 1979. **Business Addr:** Director Urban Child Research Ctr, Associate Professor, Maxine Goodman Levin College of Urban Affairs, Cleveland State University, 2121 Euclid Ave UR 208, Cleveland, OH 44115, **Business Phone:** (216)687-2135.

CHANDLER, TYSON
Basketball player. **Personal:** Born Oct 2, 1982, Hanford, CA; married Kimberly; children: Sacha Marie & Tyson Chandler II. **Career:** Chicago Bulls, power forward, 2001-06; New Orleans Hornets, center, 2007; Oklahoma City Thunder, 2009; Charlotte Bobcats, 2009-. **Orgs:** Bulls All-Star Reading Team, NBA's All-Star Reading Team. **Honors/Awds:** FIBA Americas Championship, 2007; California State Player of the Year. *

CHANDLER-STAGGERS, ROBIN. See STAGGERS, ROBIN L.

CHANEY, ALPHONSE (AL CHANEY)
Manager, insurance agent. **Personal:** Born Jul 24, 1944, Detroit, MI; son of Norman and Gussie; married Clara Hinton, Feb 14, 1981; children: Kristina, Stacy Sanders, Jason. **Educ:** Western Mich Univ, BS, 1967; Univ Mich, attended 1970. **Career:** DC Heath & Co, sales rep, 1973-87; State Farm Ins Co, agent, 1987-, agency mgr. **Orgs:** Nat Asn Life Underwriters. **Honors/Awds:** Nat Sales Achievement Award, DC Heath & Co, 1985; Mich Life Hall of Fame, State Farm Ins, Charter Member Health Hall of Fame, 1987; Mich Life Hall of Fame, 1988-91; Mich Life Hall of Fame, 1987, 1993. **Business Phone:** (248)652-6636.

CHANEY, DONALD RAY
Basketball coach, basketball player. **Personal:** Born Mar 22, 1946, Baton Rouge, LA; married Jackie; children: Michael, Donna & Kara. **Educ:** Univ Houston, attended 1968. **Career:** Basketball player (retired), basketball coach; NBA, Boston Celtics, prof basketball player, 1968-75, 1978-80; ABA, St Louis Spirits, 1975-76; NBA, Los Angeles Lakers, 1976-78; San Diego Clippers, asst coach, 1983-85; Los Angeles Clippers, head coach, 1985-87; Atlanta Hawks, asst coach, 1987-88; Houston Rockets, head coach, 1988-92; Detroit Pistons, asst coach, 1980-83, 1992-93, head coach, 1993-95; NY Knicks, asst coach, 1995-2002, head coach, 2002-04. **Honors/Awds:** La Sports Hall of Fame, 1991; NBA Coach of the Year, 1991; Two NBA Championships; gold medal, World Championship Games, 1994.

CHANEY, JOHN
Basketball coach. **Personal:** Born Jan 21, 1932, Jacksonville, FL. **Educ:** Bethune-Cookman Col Univ, BS, educ, 1955; Antioch Univ. **Career:** Basketball coach (retired); Cheyney State univ, basketball head coach, 1972-82; Temple Univ, basketball coach, 1982-06. **Honors/Awds:** Philadelphia Public League's Most Valuable Player, 1951; Division II National Coach of the Year, 1978; named to Basketball Hall of Fame, 2001. *

CHANEY, MATTHEW
School administrator. **Educ:** Ferris State Univ, BS. **Career:** Ferris State Univ, interim dir, asst dir minority stud affairs, interim dir; Multicultural Student Services, dir, currently. **Business Phone:** (231)591-2783.

CHANEY, REGMON A
Association executive. **Educ:** La State Univ, BS, Political Sci, 1966. **Career:** La State Univ, minority recruitment, asst dir, currently. **Orgs:** Pres, Black Fac & Staff Caucus, La State Univ. **Business Addr:** Assistant Dir for Minority Recruitment, La State University, Office of Recruiting Services, 2106 Pleasant Hall, Baton Rouge, LA 70803, **Business Phone:** (225)578-6652.*

CHANNELL, EULA L.
Secretary (office). **Personal:** Born Jan 29, 1928, Greenville, SC; daughter of Caesar and Ruby Davenport. **Educ:** Benedict Col; Greenville Tech Col, AA, 1974. **Career:** Allen Music Co, sheet music dept, mgr; SC Comt Aging Greenville, office worker, 1972; Phillis Wheatley Asn Greenville, girls worker, 1965-69; Recreation Dept City Greenville, supvr, 1955-65. **Orgs:** Greenville Urban League; NAACP; ARC; Bethel Church God; Blue Triangle Garden Club; Lend-A-Hand Federated Club; Greenville Dem Women; SC Literacy Asn; YWCA; Adv Housing Comn; Girl Scout Leader; Greenville Chap Human Servs; SC Fed Women & Girls Club; pres, Lend-A-Hand Fed Club; PTA; deleg state conv Guille County Dems; charter mem, secy, Greenville Chap Top Ladies Distinction; Camp for Pregnant Girls; Girl Scouts; Boy Scouts; Cancer Soc; Arthritis Found; March Dimes; United Fund. **Honors/Awds:** Honored, serv rendered Family Planning Asn; Citizen of week, Focus Newspaper; letter of congratulations, US Senator James R Mann; First runner up, Woman of Yr Greenville Chap NAACP; hon, Mayor of City vol Serv creation; record of award vol services, exec dir Phyllis Wheatley Asn; part in City wide voter registration project, Political Action Comn. **Home Addr:** 144 Catlin Cir Hyde Pk, Greenville, SC 29607. **Business Addr:** Para Professional, School District of Greenville County, Camperdown Way, Greenville, SC 29602, **Business Phone:** (803)235-2959.

CHANNER, COLIN
Writer, educator, journalist. **Personal:** Born Oct 13, 1963, Kingston, Jamaica; son of Charles and Phyllis; married; children: Addis & Makonnen. **Educ:** CUNY Hunter Col, City Univ NY, BA, Media Commun. **Career:** Essence, asst ed; freelance writer & copy ed; Eziba, co-creative dir,2001; Calabash Int Lit Festival Trust, founder & artistic dir, 2001-; Medgar Evans Col, NY, asst prof eng, currently; contributor: Soul fires:Young Black Men on Love & Violence, 1996; Got to Be Real: Four Original Love Stories, 2000; novels: Waiting In Vain, 1998; Satisfy My Soul, 2002; Passing Through, One World Ballantine, 2004; The Girl With the Golden Shoes; Lovers Rock, 2008. **Orgs:** Pres, Jamaican Ctr Int PEN; mem int steering comt, World Festival Black Arts; bd mem, Brooklyn Literary Coun; bd mem, Up South Int Book Festival; founder, Calabash InterNatLiterary Festival Trust, 2001. **Honors/Awds:** Critic's Choice Award, Wash Post for Waiting in Vain, 1998. **Special Achievements:** Bass player in the reggae band Pipecock Jaxxon. **Home Addr:** 158 S Oxford St, Brooklyn, NY 11217, **Home Phone:** (718)399-6305. **Business Addr:** Author, c/o One World/Ballantine Books, 1745 Broadway, New York, NY 10019.

CHAPMAN, AUDREY BRIDGEFORTH
Physician. **Personal:** Born Aug 30, 1941, Yonkers, NY; daughter of Leon Charles and Alice Lee Bridgeforth. **Educ:** Goddard Col, Plainfield, VT, BA, 1974; Univ Bridgeport, Bridgeport, CT, MA, 1976; The Fielding Insti, Santa Barbara, CA, pre-doctorate psychology candidate, currently. **Career:** Hamden Mental Health Serv, mental health therapist, 1976-78; Ctr Syst & Prog Develop, staff develop, trainer, 1979-80; Howard Univ, Inst Urban Affairs & Develop, dir community action prog, 1980-81, Coun Serv, family marriage counr & trainer, 1981-; A B Chapman Assocs, pres human rels training & staff mgt, 1988-, family therapist, currently; author trainer & relationship expert, currently. **Orgs:** Nat Bd Cert Counselors, 1983-; Counselors Asn, 1983-. **Honors/Awds:** APA Minority Fel Social Res, 1983; Certification of Appreciation, Howard Univy, Div Student Affairs, 1988. **Special Achievements:** Author: Mansharing: Black Men and Women: Battle For Love and Power; "Black Men Do Feel About Love," article; WHUR-FM, "All About Love," hostess, 1981-; Entitled to Good Loving: Black Men and Women and the Battle for Love and Power, Henry Holt, 1994. *

CHAPMAN, CLEVELAND M.
Executive. **Career:** Englewood Construct Co, Chicago, IL, chief exec, currently.

CHAPMAN, DAVID ANTHONY
Lawyer. **Personal:** Born Nov 6, 1949, Akron, OH; married Sharon Gail McGee; children: Brandon. **Educ:** Univ Akron, BA, 1972; Univ Cincinnati, Col Law, JD, 1975. **Career:** City Cincinnati Law Dept, asst city solicitor, 1975-82; Civil Pract Cincinnati, atty gen, 1975; City Atlanta, GA, dep chief procurement officer, currently; pvt pract atty, currently. **Orgs:** Mayor's Task Force Minority Bus Enterprise, 1978; OH State Bar Asn, 1975; Cincinnati Bar Asn, 1975; Black Lawyers Asn Cincinnati, 1975. **Home Addr:** 1110 Cheyenne Dr, Cincinnati, OH 45216, **Home Phone:** (513)641-1500. **Business Addr:** Deputy Chief Procurement Officer, City of Atlanta, General Fund/Procurement Division, 55 Trinity Ave Suite 1790, Atlanta, GA 30303, **Business Phone:** (404)330-6204.

CHAPMAN, DIANA CECELIA
Detective. **Personal:** Born Sep 3, 1954, Mobile, AL; daughter of John Williams and Cleo Miller Williams; married Nathan (divorced 1985); children: Miquel. **Educ:** Jarvis Christian Col, Hawkins, TX, BS, 1977. **Career:** Mobile County Youth Ctr, Mobile, AL, house-parent, 1982-83; Mobile Police Dept, Mobile, AL, detective, 1983. **Orgs:** Vpres, Mobile Police Benevolent Asn, 1990; secy, South Region Nat Black Police Asn, 1990-94; Semper Fidelis Federated Club, 1990; vpres, Mobile Police Benevolent Asn, 1990-93; Zeta Phi Beta Sorority, 1973; organist, Azalza City Elks, 1992-93; treas, Mobile Police Benevelent Asn, 1993; bd, Nat Black Police Asn, 1996. **Honors/Awds:** Wille "WD" Camron Leadership Award, 1991.

CHAPMAN, DR. GEORGE WALLACE, JR.
Educator. **Personal:** Born May 14, 1940, Somerville, TX; son of George W and Angelona Goin; divorced; children: Craig, Kevin & Jennifer. **Educ:** Prairie View A&M Univ, BS, 1957; Howard Univ, MD, 1966. **Career:** Univ Iowa, asst prof, 1981-83; Boston Univ, asst prof, 1983-85; La State Univ, asst prof, 1985-89; Univ Calif-Irvine, asst prof, 1988; New Jersey Med Sch, assoc prof, 1989-92; Howard Univ Hosp, assoc prof; staff, Brooke Army Med Ctr; staff, Kaiser Permanente Med Ctr. **Military Serv:** AUS, Med Corp, capt, 1966-67.

CHAPMAN, DR. GILBERT BRYANT
Automotive executive. **Personal:** Born Jul 8, 1935, Uniontown, AL; son of Gilbert Bryant and Annie Lillie Stallworth; married Loretta Woodard Chapman, Jun 5, 1960 (deceased); children: Annie L, Bernice M, Gilbert B III, Cedric N, David O, Ernest P & Frances Q H; married Betty J Ellis Carithers, Jun 27, 1999. **Educ:** Baldwin Wallace Col, BS 1968; Cleveland State Univ, MS 1973; Mich State Univ, MBA, 1990. **Career:** NACA Lewis Res Ctr, propulsion test tech, 1953-58; NASA Lewis Res Ctr, mat characterization engr, 1961-77; Ford Motor Co Res, proj engr leader, 1977-86; DaimlerChrysler Corp Eng, advan mat testing specialist, 1986-89, advan mats specialist, 1989-91, advan prod specialist, 1991-94, advan mats consult, 1994-98, Advan mats, sr mgr, currently, Advan Transp Tech, dir, 2003-; Wayne State Univ, MLK prof physics, 2001. **Orgs:** Vice chair & prog chair Cleveland Sect, Special Air Serv, 1977; lay leader, SDA Church Southfield, 1983-95; chmn, Detroit Sect Am Soc Nondestructive Testing, 1985-86; bd mem, Mt Vernon Acad; adv bd, chair, Soc Mfg Engineers & CMA, 1996; Int Symposium on Automotive Technol & Automation, matls conf, 1996; Automotive Composites Consortium, 1996, 1999; AAAS; Am Chem Soc; Asn Psychol Sci; Am Soc Cinematographers; Am Soc Microbiol; Am Soc Nondestructive Testing; ASTM; Energy Sustainable Develop; Nat Treatment Agency; SAE; Inst Elec & Electronics Engineers; SPIE, Sigma Pi Sigma; Nat Physics Honor Soc; Am Soc Nondestructive Testing; indust adv bd mem, Iowa State Univ, 1990; Univ Tex Pan Am; Cent State Univ, Wayne State Univ; Lay Leader, Farmington SDA Church. **Honors/Awds:** Apollo Achievement Award, NASA, 1969; Group Achievement Award, Outstanding Employees Actively Participating, NASA-Lewis, 1970; Excellence in Oral Presentation Award, SAE 1982; Henry Ford Tech Award, Ford Motor Co, 1981, 1982; Spirit Detroit Award, Sci & Serv Youth; Black Engineer Year Award, Career Achievement, 1999. **Special Achievements:** He led and coordinated support for advanced materials and other technology applications to advanced concept vehicle development in the Liberty and Technical Affairs activity. He is also responsible for locating and arranging for the transfer of advanced technology from universities, R&D laboratories and other sources into corporate applications for product and process improvements. **Military Serv:** USAF, aviation cadet, 1959-61. **Home Addr:** 38671 Greenbrook Ct, Farmington Hills, MI 48331-2979, **Home Phone:** (248)324-5037. **Business Addr:** Senior Manager of Advanced Materials, DaimlerChrysler Corp, Liberty and Technical Affairs, 800 Chrysler Dr E, Auburn Hills, MI 48326-2757, **Business Phone:** (248)324-5037.

CHAPMAN, JOSEPH CONRAD, JR.
Physician. **Personal:** Born Nov 18, 1937, Poplar Bluff, MO; son of Joseph and Louise; married Myrna Loy; children: Joseph, Christopher. **Educ:** Howard Univ, BS, 1959, MD, 1953; Georgetown Univ Hosp, residency, 1968. **Career:** pvt pract, otolaryngologist, 2004. **Orgs:** Medico Churgical Soc DC, Med Soc DC, Nat Med Asn, Am Acad Otolaryngology, Am Coun Otolaryngology; asst clinical prof, Howard Univ; Alpha Phi Alpha; fellow, Am Bd Otolaryngology, 1970. **Military Serv:** USN, lt cmdr, 1968-70. **Business Phone:** (202)529-2626.*

CHAPMAN, LEE MANUEL
Insurance executive. **Personal:** Born Aug 4, 1932, Chesterfield, SC; son of Jesse and Marie M; married Emily Bernice, Jun 16, 1957; children: Victoria Lenice & Leander M. **Educ:** SC State Col, Orangeburg, BA, 1954; Biblical Sch Theol, Hatfield, attended 1958; Temple Univ, Philadelphia, attended 1958. **Career:** NC Mutual, spec ordinary agent, 1957-60; Equitable Life Assurance Soc, agency mgr, 1960-81; Lee Chapman & Assocs, financial planner, 1981-. **Orgs:** Christian Bus Men Int, 1982-; camp pres & reg dir, Gideon Int, 1986-; pres, Int Asn Stewardship, 1990-. **Honors/Awds:** Young Man of the Year, Jaycees Awards, 1967; Developers Award, Nat Asn Mkt, 1967; National Citation Award, Equitable Life Assurance Soc, 1967, 1968 & 1980. **Military Serv:** AUS, 1st Lt, 1954-56; Platoon leader awards. **Home Phone:** (215)844-3054. **Business Addr:** Financial Planner, Lee Chapman & Associates, 6850 Anderson St, Philadelphia, PA 19119, **Business Phone:** (215)844-2264.

CHAPMAN, MELVIN
Association executive. **Personal:** Born Mar 16, 1928, Detroit, MI; married Elizabeth Patton; children: Carolyn & Melvin. **Educ:** Wayne State Univ, BA, 1949, MEd, 1953, EdSpec, 1965, EdD, 1973. **Career:** Detroit, teacher, 1949; Northwestern High Sch, counr, 1962; Wayne State Univ, High Educ Opportunity Comn, dir, 1964; Cent High Sch, asst prin, 1966; Northwestern High Sch, prin, 1967; Detroit Pub Schs, asst supt, 1970-; Diversified Educ Serv Inc, pres, 2002-, Nonprofit Welfare-To-Work Prog, dir, currently. **Orgs:** Corp Body Mich Blue Shield; Trio Adv Comn; Nat Alliance Black Sch Educ; Mich Asn C Learning Disabilities; Met Detroit Soc Black Educ Adminr; Am Asn Sch Adminr; Nat Asn Advan Colored People; Kappa Alpha Psi USC C. **Honors/Awds:** Leadership Award, Chrysler Corp & NW HS, 1968. **Business Addr:** President, Director, Diversified Educational Services Inc, 1505 Woodward Ave, Detroit, MI 48226.

CHAPMAN, NATHAN A
Banker. **Personal:** Married Valerie; children: three daughters. **Career:** The Chapman Co, chief exec officer, 1986, pres & chmn bd dir; Univ Syst Md Bd Regents, chmn, 1999; eChapman Inc, founder; Chapman Capital Mgt Inc, founder. **Special Achievements:** Black Enterprise, Top Investment Banks list, co ranked No 13, 1999, No 9, 2000.

CHAPMAN, ROSLYN C.
Executive. **Personal:** Born Mar 10, 1956, Richmond, VA; daughter of Howard and Bertha. **Educ:** Hampton Inst, BA 1978. **Career:** Johnson Products Co, sales rep 1979-80, key acct mgr 1980-81, dist mgr 1981-83, regional mgr 1983-84, natl accts mgr 1984-85; Alberto Culver Co, natl accts mgr 1985-90; Alberto Culver Co, national sales manager, 1990-94, dir retail sales, 1994-. **Orgs:** Cabrini Green Tutorial Bd; Midwest Women's Center Bd; Delta Sigma Theta Sor, Nat Black MBA. **Home Addr:** 4170 N Marine Dr Suite 21K, Chicago, IL 60613. *

CHAPMAN, SAMUEL OTHA, JR.
Chief executive officer. **Personal:** Son of Samuel O Chapman Sr; married Carolyn, Sep 4, 1965. **Career:** Shop Rite of West Haven, chief exec officer, 1998. **Business Addr:** Chief Executive Officer, Shop Rite of West Haven, 1131 Campbell Ave, West Haven, CT 06516, **Business Phone:** (203)934-5660.*

CHAPMAN, SHARON JEANETTE
Marketing executive. **Personal:** Born Oct 25, 1949, St Louis, MO; children: Leslie Michelle Lee. **Educ:** Southern Ill Univ, BS, 1970;

Col St Thomas, MBA, 1981. **Career:** Famous Barr Dept Store, asst buyer, 1971-72; Donaldson's Dept Store, dept mgr, 1972-75; IBM, systs engr, 1976-83, mkt rep, 1983-86; Job Trak Systs Inc, dir mkt & sales, 1986-. **Orgs:** Second vpres, 1983-85, pres, bd mem, 1985-87, Twin Cities Chap Black MBA's; trustee, Pilgrim Bapt Church, 1984-87; bd dirs, Survival Skills Inst, 1985-; chap pres, Delta Sigma Theta, 1987-; Minneapolis Urban League, St Paul Nat Asn Adv Colored People. **Home Addr:** 1435 Hampshire Ave S Apt 215, St Louis Park, MN 55426-2165. **Business Addr:** Director Marketing, Operations, Jobtrack Systems Inc, 7269 Flying Cloud Dr, Eden Prairie, MN 55344, **Business Phone:** (612)829-0337.*

CHAPMAN, SUSAN
Administrator, Businessperson. **Educ:** Vanderbilt Univ, BS; Univ of Massachusetts at Amherst, MS. **Career:** Dir of global Real Estate and Global Procurement for Level 3 Communications; Global Head of Operations for Citi Realty Services. **Orgs:** Board member the Brotherhood Sister Sol, the largest youth services organization in West Harlem; the Executive Leadership Foundation; member of CoreNet Global, the New York Univ Adv bd, the Urban Land Institute; Wisconsin Real Estate Alumni Assoc; serves on the Dean's Adv Bd ath the Univ of Wisconsin School of Business and The Center for Urban Land Economics Research Board. **Special Achievements:** Distinguished Young Alumni, Univ of Wisconsin Foundation, 2007; named on the "Hot List: Best and Brightest Under 40", by Black Enterprises in 2003, 2005, and 2007;. **Business Addr:** Citigroup Center, 153 E. 53rd Street, 16 Fl, Zone 19, New York, NY 10022, **Business Phone:** (212)559-9124.*

CHAPMAN, TRACY
Singer, songwriter. **Personal:** Born Mar 30, 1964, Cleveland, OH; daughter of George and Hazel Winters. **Educ:** Tufts Univ, BA (cum laude), anthrop, 1986; Am Conserv Theater, MA, fine arts, 2009. **Career:** Singer-songwriter; Elektra rec; Song: "Fast Car"; "Baby Can I Hold You"; "Talkin' about Revolution", 1988; "Telling Stories", 2000; "It's OK", 2000; "Wedding Song", 2000; "Baby Can I Hold You", 201; "You're The One", 2002; "Another Sun", 2003; "Change", 2005; "America", 2006; Albums: Crossroads, 1989; Matters of the Heart, 1992; New, 1995; Telling Stories, 2000; Collections, 2001; Let It Rain, 2002; Where You Live, 2005. **Honors/Awds:** Numerous Grammy Awards; Best New Artist; Best Contemporary Folk Recording; Best Female Pop Vocal Performance, 1988; Best Selling Album by a New Artist; Best Selling Album by a Female Artist, Nat Asn Rec Merchandisers, 1988; Best Int Newcomer; Best Int Female Artist, The Brits, 1989; Favorite New Artist Pop & Rock, Am Music Awards, 1989. **Special Achievements:** Plays the ukulele, organ, clarinet, & guitar; played at Wembley Stadium, Eng, Nelson Mandela Birthday Tribute. **Home Phone:** (213)394-2944. **Business Addr:** Recording Artist, Elektra Entertainment, 16th Fl 75 Rockefeller Plz, New York, NY 10019-6908, **Business Phone:** (212)275-4490.

CHAPMAN, DR. WILLIAM TALBERT
Neurologist. **Personal:** Born Oct 15, 1944, Camden, NJ; married Ingrid; children: William Jr, Marcus, Blaire & Leigh. **Educ:** Rutgers Univ, BA, 1966; Howard Univ, Col Med, MD, 1971. **Career:** Ninty Seventh Gen Hosp, asst chief neurol, 1976-78; Silas B Hayes Hosp, chief neurol, 1978-79; Pvt Pract, neurologist, 1979-. **Orgs:** Nat Med Asn, 1971, Am Bd Neurol, 1977, Am Bd EEG, 1985, AMA, 1987; Epilepsy Found San Diego County. **Honors/Awds:** Alpha Omega Alpha Med Hon Soc. **Military Serv:** AUS, major, 1976-79; Army Commendation Medal, 1979. **Home Addr:** 3951 The Hill Rd, Bonita, CA 91902. **Business Addr:** Neurologist, Private Practice, 2340 E 8th St Suite G, National City, CA 91950.

CHAPMAN, WILLIE R
Research scientist. **Personal:** Born Sep 2, 1942, Memphis, TN; married Marion N Evans; children: William Eric & Lamont Everett. **Educ:** LeMoyne Owen Col, BS, chem, (Cum Laude), 1964; Memphis State Univ, MAT, chem, 1975. **Career:** Schering/Plough Inc, sr res chemist, 1965-77; Chattem Inc, mgr/res & develop, 1977-87; Chattanooga State Tech Community Col, instr chem. **Orgs:** Soc Cosmetic Chemists; conduct & ethics comn, chap affairs comn, 1982, chmn prof rels & status, 1983, area dir, 1984-86, chmn educ comn, 1986-; Alpha Phi Alpha founder/minority leadership conf, 1985-87, social chmn, 1985-86, chair educ comn, 1986-87; Phi Delta Kappa, 1987; Sigma Phi Fraternity; Nat Asn Advan Colored People; Explorer Prog/BSA; Alpha Phi Alpha Fraternity; Urban League. **Special Achievements:** Author: "Cosmetic Creams and Lotions for Dark Tone Skins," 1980; Cosmetics and Toiletries; "The Development of Skin Lighteners", 1983 Cosmetics and Toiletries.

CHAPMAN-MINUTELLO, ALICE MARIAH
Executive, executive director. **Personal:** Born Dec 31, 1947, New York, NY; daughter of Elijah Sr and Elizabeth Brooks; divorced. **Educ:** City Univ NY, lib arts, 1969; NY Univ, bus admin, 1974. **Career:** RKO Gen Inc, corp equal employ compliance mgr, 1976-78, corp dir equal employ opportunity, 1983-87; WOR Radio, dir pub serv & community affairs, 1978-80; Waxy Radio, dir pub affairs & community rels, 1980-83; City NY, dep city personnel dir-equal employment opportunity, 1987-89; NY Health & Hosp Corp, Affirmative Action, actg vpres, 1989-92; Darryl E Greene & Assocs, chief exec officer, 1992-94; NY Unified Ct Syst, Workforce Diversity Off, Div Human Resources, adminr, dir, currently. **Orgs:** Bd dir, Raritan Valley Chap, Links Inc; Jr League Greater Princeton. **Honors/Awds:** Black Achievers in Industries Award, Harlem YMCA, 1979; Cecelia Cabiness Saunders Award, New Harlem YWCA, 1985; Corporate Recognition Award, Metrop Coun Nat Asn Advan Colored People Br, 1987. **Home Addr:** PO Box 956, Far Hills, NJ 07931. **Business Addr:** Deputy Director, New York State Unified Court System, Workforce Diversity Office, Div Human Resources, Rm 1009 25 Beaver St, New York, NY 10004, **Business Phone:** (212)428-2540.

CHAPPELL, EMMA CAROLYN
Banker. **Personal:** Born Feb 18, 1941, Philadelphia, PA; daughter of George Bayton Sr and Emma Lewis (deceased); married Verdayne (deceased); children: Tracey & Verdaynea. **Educ:** Berean Bus Inst, Temple Univ, 1967; Am Inst Banking, Stonier Grad Sch Banking, Rutgers Univ, attended. **Career:** Continental Bank Philadelphia, clerk-photogr, vpres, community bus loan & develop dep, 1959-2001; United Bank Philadelphia, chair, chief executive officer & pres, 1992-2000, bd mem. **Orgs:** Am Bankers Asn; Nat Bankers Asn; Robert Morris Asn; Nat bd mem, PUSH; adv bd dir, Girl Scouts Greater Philadelphia Inc; vpres, admin & treas, Nat Rainbow Coalition; founder & chair, Women's Network Good Govt; bd mem, Temple Univ, Col Arts & Scis; Chestnut Hill Col Pres Coun, Cheyney Univ Found, United Way Southeastern Pa; United Negro Col Fund, Philadelphia Chap, PA; Econ Develop Partnership; bd, March Dimes, Delaware Valley Chap; vchmn, African Develop Found. **Honors/Awds:** Motivational Speaking Exec Leadership & Professional Salesmanship Achievement Award, Dale Carnegie Inst; Achievement Award, Philadelphia Police Dept; Certificate of Appreciation, Soc Advan Mgt; Counseling Selling Achievement Award, Larry & Willson; Achievement Award, N Philadelphia Action Br NAACP; President Award, Nat Asn Colored Women's Clubs Inc; Recognition Award, PA Contractors Coalition Inc; Achievement Award, Club VIP; Honored as One of America's Top 100 Black Business & Professional Women by Dollars and Sense Magazine, 1986; Business & Professional Award, Blackbook Mag, 1987; Bishop R R Wright Humanitarian Award, Ward AME Church, 1987; Achievement Award, W Philadelphia Econ Develop Corp, 1988; Outstanding Businesswoman the Year, Tex Asn Minority Enterprises, 1993. **Special Achievements:** First vpres admin Nat Rainbow Coalition; first black woman to establish a bank since Maggie Lena Walker founded Richmond's St. Luke Penny Savings Bank in 1903. **Home Addr:** PO Box 43581, Philadelphia, PA 19106.

CHAPPELL, KEVIN
Editor. **Career:** Ebony Mag, sr ed, currently. **Business Addr:** Senior Editor, Ebony Magazine, 820 S Mich Ave, Chicago, IL 60605.

CHAPPELL, MICHAEL JAMES
Government official, educator. **Personal:** Born Dec 27, 1946, Ann Arbor, MI; son of Willie and Dorothy Freemen; married Betty Brown-Chappell, Oct 1, 1975; children: Michael Jahi & Aisha Ebony. **Educ:** Eastern Mich Univ, BS, 1970; Keller Graduate Sch Mgt, MBA, 1982. **Career:** Government official (retired), educator; Northeastern Ill Univ, part-time instr, 1983; Social Security Admin, dist mgr, 1971; Davenport Univ, part-time instr, 1995-. **Orgs:** Adv & mentor, Black Affairs Adv Coun; past pres, Chicago Social Security Mgt; past chair, adv coun alternate bd member, Sr Alliance, Area Agency Aging; vice chmn bd dirs, Wayne Metropolitan Community Serv Agency; Local Fed Coord Comt mem, Combined Fed Campaign Local Fed Coord Comm, Detroit Fed Exec Bd. **Honors/Awds:** Regional Dirs Citation, Dept Health & Human Serv, 1988; vpres, Chicago Region Social Security Mgt Asn, 1988-90; Charles E Lawrence Award, Social Security Administration Black Caucus, 1992; Honor Award, The Govt Col Rels Coun, 1992; The Senior Alliance Meritorious Service Award, 1996; Certificate of Appreciation, Detroit Fed Exec Bd, 1997; Edward H McNamara Award; Inducted into the Greater Lansing Area Sports Hall Fame, 1998; Robert P Fleminger Award, Chicago Social Security Mgt Asn, 1998; Outstanding Performance Award, Detroit Fed Exec Bd, 2000; Dedicated Service Award, Metro Detroit Black Affairs Adv Coun Social Security. **Home Addr:** 44999 Claymore Dr, Canton, MI 48187, **Home Phone:** (734)451-0063. **Business Addr:** Local Federal Coordinating Committee Member, Combined Federal Campaign, 44999 Claymore Dr, Canton, MI 48124.

CHAPPELL, RUTH RAX
Management consultant, manager. **Personal:** Born Apr 20, 1932, Los Angeles, CA; daughter of George and Helen Finley; married Joseph Chappell; children: Valinda, Patricia, Jerome, Kevin, Michael, Michelle, Sakeenah. **Educ:** CA State Univ, BS, 1977, MA, 1986. **Career:** State Personnel Bd, training officer, 1976-79, mgr admin serv, 1979-81, asst mgr statewide women's prog, 1981-82, mgr appeals div, 1982-83; pvt consult, 1983-87. **Orgs:** Nat League Women Polit Caucus; chair, Human Right Comn, CA State Employees Asn, 1987-; Nat Asn Advan Colored People. **Honors/Awds:** Cert Merit, CA State Govt. **Business Addr:** Communications Consultant, California State Personnel Board, 2551 5th Ave, Sacramento, CA 95818.*

CHAPPELLE, DAVE (DAVID KHARI WEBBER CHAPPELLE)
Comedian, television producer. **Personal:** Born Aug 23, 1973, Washington, DC; son of William David III and Yvonne K. Reed; married. **Educ:** Washington's Duke Ellington Sch Arts, theatre arts, 1991. **Career:** Films: Robin Hood: Men in Tights, 1993; The Nutty Professor, 1996; Damn Whitey, 1997; Half Baked, 1998; Woo, 1998; You've Got Mail, 1998; 200 Cigarettes, 1998; Blue Streak, 1999; Screwed, 2000; Undercover Brother, 2002; Dave Chappelle's Block Party, 2005; TV Series: "Buddies", 1995; "Dave Chappelle: Killin' Them Softly", 2000; "Dave Chappelle: For What It's Worth", 2004; "Chappelle's Show", 2003-06; "All Star Def Comedy Jam", host. **Special Achievements:** Is Number 43 on Comedy Central's 100 Greatest Standups of All Time and is the youngest person to make the list; Nominated for Emmy Awards and Image Awards. *

CHAPPELLE, DAVID KHARI WEBBER. See CHAPPELLE, DAVE.

CHAPPELLE, EDWARD H
Dentist. **Personal:** Born Sep 15, 1954, Washington, DC; son of Edward Sr and Nelli Mitchell Chappelle; married Sherra H, Jul 4, 1982; children: Edward H III & April Nicole. **Educ:** Rutgers Col, Rutgers Univ, BA, 1975; Meharry Med Col, DDS, 1979; Eastman Dent Ctr, GPR cert, 1980; The Gennessee Hosp, GPR cert, 1981. **Career:** Family Dent Care, dentist, 1981-83; pvt pract, 1983-; Aesthetic Dental Care Inc, owner & pres, 1983-. **Orgs:** Pres, Robert T Freeman Dent Soc, 1999; treasr, Nat Dent Asn; Acad Gen Dent; fel Groove Phi Groove Social; Omega Psi Phi Frat; Holmehurst S Civic Asn; Am Acad Cosmetic Dent; adv panel, Am Dent Asn. **Honors/Awds:** Fel Acad Gen Dent, 1996. **Business Addr:** President, Owner, Aesthetic Dental Care Inc, 3060 Mitchellville Rd Suite 107, Bowie, MD 20716, **Business Phone:** (301)390-9185.

CHAPPELLE, JOSEPH C
Executive. **Personal:** Born Nov 24, 1969, Jacksonville, FL; son of Dennis and Juanita; married Nicole; children: Jade & Joseph II. **Educ:** Florida State Univ, attended. **Career:** Premier Holdings Group Inc, chmn, founder & chief exec officer, currently. **Orgs:** Chmn, Eastside Historical Community Found. **Business Addr:** Chairman, Chief Excutive Officer, Premier Holdings Group, 112 W Adam St Suite 816, Jacksonville, FL 32202, **Business Phone:** (904)355-8381.

CHARBONNET, LOUIS, III
Funeral director. **Personal:** Born Mar 12, 1939, New Orleans, LA; son of Louis Jr (deceased) and Myrtle Labat (deceased); married Simone Monette; children: Kim Marie. **Educ:** Commonwealth Col Sci, BS, 1957. **Career:** State La, state rep; Total Community Action Agency, pres, 1973-; Cresent City Funeral Home, dir; Cooper-Glapion Funeral Home, owner; Charbonnet Labat Funeral Home, owner, currently. **Orgs:** Cresent City Funeral Dir Asn; bd dir, Treme Child & Enrichment Ctr; bd mem, Criminal Justice State La; vice chmn, Bd Appropriations State LA; bd dir, La State Mus Bd. **Military Serv:** AUS, SP-4. **Business Addr:** Owner, Charbonnet Labat Funeral Home, 1615 St Phillip St, New Orleans, LA 70116.*

CHARGOIS, JAMES M
Automotive executive. **Personal:** Born in Houston, TX. **Career:** Pavillion Lincoln Mercury, owner, 1988; Northwood Lincoln Mercury, owner & pres, 1996-; San Marcos Toyota, owner & pres, 2000-; JMC Auto Group LLC, owner, currently; Triangle Restaurant Group, head, currently. **Orgs:** United Negro Col Fund; Boys & Girls Club Austin. **Honors/Awds:** Quality Dealer Award, Time Mag, 2005. **Business Addr:** Owner, President, Northwood Lincoln-Mercury Inc, 20440 I 45 N, Spring, TX 77373, **Business Phone:** (284)539-4900.

CHARIS (SHARON DIANA JONES)
Clergy. **Personal:** Born Nov 14, 1948, Fort Riley, KS; daughter of Theodore D and Agnes D Burrus. **Educ:** Mo Valley Col, Marshall, MO, BA (magna cum laude), 1970; Ga State Univ, Atlanta, GA, MA (cum laude), 1974; Univ Calif, Santa Barbara, Santa Barbara, CA, 1988. **Career:** Muscogee County Sch Dist, Colubmus, GA, math teacher, 1970-78; Sisterhood Holy Nativity, Fond Du Lac, WI, religious sister, 1978-. **Orgs:** Gamma Sigma Sigma Sorority, 1968-70; Union Black Episcopalians, 1988-. **Honors/Awds:** Numerous religious awards, 1979-. **Business Addr:** Religious Sister, Church of the Advent, 338 Academy St, Madison, GA 30650, **Business Phone:** (706)342-4787.

CHARITY, LAWRENCE EVERETT
Executive. **Personal:** Born Jun 21, 1935, Washington, DC; married Suzanne G Leach; children: Alexander PL & Danika EN. **Educ:** Rhode Island Sch Design, BFA & Int Arch Des, 1957; Cranbrook Academy Art, MFA & Design, 1958. **Career:** Skidmore Owings & Merrill, designer, 1958-68; Sewell & Charity Ltd Designers, prin, 1968-74; RI Sch Design, adj asst prof & design, 1972-73; Interior Concepts Inc, prin, 1974-86; Lawrence Charity Design, prin & designer, 1986-. **Orgs:** Indust Designers Soc Am, 1974-. **Honors/Awds:** Best of Competition Award for design,

1992; Retail Design Award for design, Am Soc Interior Designers, 1992. **Military Serv:** AUS, sp4, 1959-62. **Business Addr:** Principal, Designer, Lawrence Charity Design, 8 Gracie Sq, New York, NY 10028, **Business Phone:** (212)737-9793.*

CHARLES, BERNARD L.
Educator. **Personal:** Born Feb 27, 1927, New York, NY; married Eleanor; children: Bernard II, Dominique & Bridgette. **Educ:** Fisk Univ, BS, 1952; Yeshiva Univ, MS, 1965; Rutgers Univ Grad Sch Educ. **Career:** Livingston Col Rutgers Univ, dept urban educ, prof & chmn, 1970-; TownRamapo, county man & dep supvr, 1966-74; Rockland County Legis, vice chmn, 1975-77; Dem Nat Comn, NY State Voter Reg Drive, dir, 1976; NY St Coun Black Elected Democrats, treas, 1965-77; Off Master Plan Bd Higher Educ City, Univ NY, coordr, 1968-70; Qual Educ Minorities, sr vpres; McKenzieGroup, sr exec; Carnegie Corp, sr programmer, NY; Univ Cape Town, SAfrica; Univ Cape Coast, Ghana. **Orgs:** Dir spec proj, Human Resources Admin, 1968; dep dir, Office Civil Rights Region II, NY, 1966-68; dir, Life Skills Educ Training Resources Youth, 1965-66; asst dir, Jr Guidance Classed Prog, NY City Bd Educ, 1962-66; teacher, Pub Sch 613, Brooklin Pub Sch 614, Bronx, 1955-62; street clubworker, NY City Youth Bd, 1954-55; co-dir, Univ Summer workshop teachers, Emotionally & socially maladjusted childred; guest lectr, mem, Asn Teacher Educ; Am Asn Higher Educ; Am Asn Univ Profs; Am Asn Sch Adminr; Nat Adv Coun; Nat Adv Health Coun; treas, Inst Mediation & Conflict Resolution; pres, Broadjump Inc; dir, Action Priorities Inc; Rockland Community ActionCoun; bd dir, World Rehab Fund; Bulova Watchmaking Sch, St Cordr, GovSamuels paign, 1974; chmn, NY St Govr's Adv Comn Black Affairs; nat advbd, res & training ctr, Howard Univ. **Home Addr:** 109 Old Nyack Tpke, Spring Valley, NY 10977. *

CHARLES, DAEDRA
Basketball player, basketball coach. **Personal:** Born Nov 22, 1968; daughter of Helen Charles; married Anthony Furlow; children: Anthonee. **Educ:** Tenn State Univ, BS, child & family studies, 1991. **Career:** Basketball player (retired), basketball coach; USA Natl Teams, 1989, 1992, 1994; City Detroit, Don Bosco Hall, supvr; Como, Italy, ctr, 1991-92; DKB, Japan, 1992-93; US Women's Olympic Basketball team, 1992; Sireg, Italy, 1993-94; Tarbes, France, 1994-95; Galatasaray, Turkey, 1995-96; Sopron, Hungary, 1996-97; Los Angeles Sparks, 1997; DePorres High Sch, coaching staff, 2001-02; Detroit Titan, grad asst coach, 2003-04, asst coach, 2004-08; Auburn Tigers, asst coach, currently. **Honors/Awds:** Wade Trophy, Natl Assn Girls & Women in Sports, 1991; Southeastern Conf Woman Athlete of the Yearr, 1991; Player of the Week, Sports Illustrated,1991; Bronze Medal, 1992, Gold Medal, 1996, Olympic Games; Bronze Medal, World Championship Team, 1994; Tenn Lady Vol Athletic Hall of Fame; Women's Basketball Hall of Fame, 2007. **Special Achievements:** Two-time KODAK All American & two-time NCAA Champion at Tennesse. **Business Addr:** Assistant Coach, Lady Vols, Univ Tenn, Knoxville, TN 37996, **Business Phone:** (865)974-4275.

CHARLES, DOREEN ALICIA. See LATIF, NAIMAH.

CHARLES, JOSEPH C.
Law enforcement officer. **Personal:** Born Jan 12, 1941, Lake Charles, LA; married Doris J; children: Caron Scott. **Educ:** BA, AA, 1969. **Career:** Mitchell Pacific Devel Corp, pres; San Diego Co Probation Dept, dep probation officer II; Webchar Construction Corp, pres. **Orgs:** Black Bus Asn; Black Investors; secy, Reserve Officers Asn; charter mem, Black Stud Union San Diego St Col; San Diego Co Employ Asn; Calif St Corrections Asn. **Military Serv:** USAR, capt.

CHARLES, LEWIS
Welder. **Personal:** Born Aug 24, 1945, Jackins Co, GA; married Rosetta W; children: Tracy C. **Educ:** Atlana Univ. **Career:** Fulghum Indust Mgt Co, demonstr; Hudson Mortuary Wadley, GA, asst mgr;city-councilman, 1970. **Orgs:** GA State Fireman Wadley, GA No 2217; Dem Party GA, 1972; Free & Accepted Mason; Brinson Hill Baptist Church; life mem, Ga Munic Asn; Wadley & Borlow City League; Nat Pilots Asn. **Honors/Awds:** Award Wadley & Borlow City League, 1972; Spec Award, Brinson Hill Baptist Church, 1973. **Business Addr:** Demonstrator, Fulghum Indust Mgt Co, Wadley, GA 30477.

CHARLES, DR. RODERICK EDWARD
Psychiatrist. **Personal:** Born Sep 4, 1927, Baltimore, MD; married Mamie Rose Debnam; children: Kimberly Anne & Roderick Todd. **Educ:** Howard Univ, BS 1951; Univ MD, MD, 1955. **Career:** Mil City Gen Hosp, internship 1955-56; Meyer Memorial Hosp, psychiatrist resident, 1956-59; NYS, 1959-60; Erie County Med Ctr, att psychiatry, 1960-66; State Univ NY, Brooklyn Sch Med, asst clin prof, 1966-96; pvt practice, psychiatry 1966-; Univ Buffalo, fac, currently. **Orgs:** Build Acad H Prog, 1971-75; state coun Met H Plan, 1977-81; pres, WNY Psych Asn, 1967-68; Fedn Citizens Coun Human Rel, 1964; Am Psych Asn; Black Psychiatrists Am; Nat Med Asn; adv SMNA Univ Buffalo, 1975; consult, Gowando State Hosp, 1982-87. **Special Achievements:** First black medical student at the University of Maryland. **Military Serv:** USN, 1944-46. **Business Addr:** President, NMA Buffalo Chapter, 142 N Pearl St, Buffalo, NY 14202-1108.

CHARLES, RUPAUL ANDRE (RUPAUL)
Entertainer. **Personal:** Born Nov 17, 1960, San Diego, CA; son of Irving and Ernestine. **Career:** Entertainer (actor, singer, talk-show host, dancer), 1981-; Album: Sex Freak, 1985; RuPaul is Starbooty, soundtrack, 1986; Supermodel of the World, 1993; Foxy Lady, 1996; Ho, Ho, Ho, 1997; Arrested Soul, 2002; The Lizzie McGuire Movie, writer, 2003; Party Monster, writer, 2003; Red Hot, 2004; Beauty Shop, writer, 2005; Whitepaddy, 2006; Zombie Prom, 2006; Bachelor Party Vegas, soundtrack, 2006; Starrbooty, 2007; TV: "The Truth About Jane", 2000; "V.I.P.", 2001; "The Groovenians", voice, 2002. **Orgs:** Co-chair, MAC AIDS Fund, 1995-; spokesmodel, MAC cosmetics, 1995-; spokesmodel, Bailey's Irish Cream, 1995. **Honors/Awds:** Vito Russo Award, 1999. **Special Achievements:** Letting It All Hang Out, autobiography, 1994. **Home Addr:** c/o Randy Barbato, 1157 N Highland Ave 1st Fl, Los Angeles, CA 90038. **Business Addr:** Entertainer, c/o Tommy Boy Entertainment, 32 W 18th St, New York, NY 10011-4612.

CHARLESTON, GOMEZ, JR.
Cardiologist. **Personal:** Born Mar 19, 1950, Chicago, IL; son of Gomez and Margie Williams; married Robin Prince, Jun 21, 1975. **Educ:** Univ Chicago, BA, 1971, MD, 1975. **Career:** Stony Island Med Assoc, Chicago IL, partner, 1980-; Michael Reese Hosp, Chicago, attend physician cardiol, 1980-, dir cardiac catheterization lab, 1987-88, Pritzker Sch Med, Univ Chicago, asst clinical prof med, 1980-. **Orgs:** Am Med Asn; Ill Med Soc; Chicago Cardiol Group. **Honors/Awds:** Sigmund E. Edelstone fel cardiol, Michael Reese Hosp & Med Ctr, 1980; fel, Am Col Cardiol, 1982. **Business Addr:** Partner, Stony Island Medical Association, 9000 S Stony Island, Chicago, IL 60617.*

CHARLTON, REV. CHARLES HAYES
Educator, clergy. **Personal:** Born Dec 22, 1940, Radford, VA; son of Lawrence and Ollie; married Janet Lee Lewis; children: Charles. **Educ:** Christiansburg Inst, attended 1959; Va Sem; E Tenn State Univ, BS, 1982, MEd, 1984; Emmaus Bible Inst Sem, Elizabeth, TN, ThD, 1986; Cornerstone Univ, PhD, temperament ther, 1995. **Career:** Radford City Sch Bd, staff, 1972-74; Radford City, VA, mayor, 1974-76; Friendship Bapt Church, pastor; Emmaus Bible Inst & Sem, Elizabethton, TN, dean educ, 1984-89; CASA Northeast, Johnson City, TN, coordr, 1987-; CASA, staff, 1987-92; ETSU, Johnson City, TN, career counr, 1991-92; Johnson City, planning comn, 1990-; Northeast State Tech Community Col, instr, 1992, counr & advisor, 1994, asst prof study skills, assoc prof reading & learning strat, currently; Johnson City, bd dirs. **Orgs:** Moderator Schaetter Mem Asn SW Va, 1974-77; moderator, Bethel Dist Asn Tenn, 1982-; dean ed, Emmaus Bible Inst & Sem, Elizabethton, TN, 1984-; dir, Pastors Conf TN BM&E Conv, 1984-; pres, Black Ministers Alliance, 1990-91; zone chmn, Wash Co Democratic Party, 1994-, bd educ, 1996-, elected comn, 2001-; treas, Bethel Dist Asn; vpres, Radford Jaycees. **Honors/Awds:** Radfords Outstanding Young Men, Radford Jaycees, 1973; Honors for Contributions to the State of Virginia, Va Hist Soc. **Special Achievements:** Published "Agony & Ecstasy of the Ministry, Making The Fundamentals Fun", 1993; "Love is the Key, To Love And Be Loved, How To Really Love Your Pastor, This We Believe, Meditations on Love", 1994; Author of Religious Columns Published in Radford News Journal and Johnson City Press. **Home Addr:** 511 Rose Ave, Johnson City, TN 37601. **Business Addr:** Associate Professor, Northeast State Technical Community College, PO Box 246, Blountville, TN 37617-0246, **Business Phone:** (423)354-2560.

CHARLTON, GEORGE N., JR.
Executive director. **Personal:** Born Apr 12, 1923, Pittsburgh, PA; son of George N Sr and Mildred F Woods; married H Nadine Branch, Jun 1964; children: George N III, Diana C Jones, Susan C Harrison, Ronald, Lena Coleman. **Educ:** Univ Pittsburgh, BBA, 1955. **Career:** Executive director (retired). AUS, clerk-typist, 1943-45, transfer unit asst supvr, analyst admin div, 1945-48; Va Pittsburgh, regis clerk, 1948, collection officer, collection div, 1948-51; US Treas Dept IRS Intell Div Pittsburgh, spec agent, 1953-63; Pittsburgh Pvt prac, spec investr, 1964-65; Commonwealth Pa Dept Revenue Bur Sales & Use Tax Harrisburg, spec audit staff, 1965-67; Opps Indust Ctr Inc Pittsburgh, dir admin serv, 1967-68; Homewood-Brushton Neighborhood Health-Ctr Inc Pittsburgh, bus mgr, 1968-71; Pittsburgh Model Cities, asst exec dir, 1971-73, exec dir 1973-76; Pub Parking Authority Pittsburgh, exec dir, 1976-88; self-employed real estate property mgr, 1988. **Orgs:** Treas, bd dir, Housing Auth Pittsburgh, 1973-78; Mayors Econ Manpower Adv Comn, 1974-83; treas, Community Action Pittsburgh Bd, 1975-78; Reg Personnel Serv Ctr SW Pa, 1974-78; life mem, Kappa Alpha Psi, 1969-; life mem, Reserve Officers Asn; first vice chmn, Bd Mgt Homewood-Brushton, Young Men's Christian Asn Prog Ctr, 1970-77; Province Polemarch, E Cent Province, Kappa Alpha Psi Frat Inc, 1971-84; Grand Bd Dirs Kappa Alpha Psi Frat Inc, 1985-88; bd govrs, co-vice chmn, Nat Parking Asn, 1983-88; United Way Pittsburgh, 1986-89; exec mem, Urban League Pittsburgh Inc, 1986-89; St Cyprian-Alpha Lodge No 13 F & A M 1970-; life mem, Nat Asn Advan Colored People, 1981; life mem, 1965-, commander 2001-02; Angell-Bolen VFW Post No 4040; chmn, trustee bd, Grace Memorial PresbyterianChurch; Chadwick Civic League, 1975-; pres, Chap 4542 Am Asn Retired Persons Inc, 1996-99. **Honors/Awds:** Man of the Year Achievement Award, Pittsburgh Alumni Chap, 1971; Meritorious Service, Opp Indus Ctr Inc, Pittsburgh, 1972; Achievement Award, Delta & Delta Zeta, 1973; Service to Youth Black Achievers Award, Young Men's Christian Asn, Pittsburgh, 1973; Outstanding Achievement, E Control Province, 1974; Leadership Dayton Kappa League 1974; Meritorious Service Medal, 1976; Honor Black Cath Ministers & Laymen's Coun, 1976; Community Leader Award, 1977; Citation 26 years of service, AUS, 1976; Elder Watson Diggs Achievement Award, Kappa Alpha Psi Frat Inc, 1986; Certificate of Achievement, Nat Parking Asn, 1987. **Special Achievements:** Selected as 1 of 25 most influential blacks in Metro, Pittsburgh Talk Mag, 1975. **Military Serv:** AUS lt col retired WWII Vet 23 yrs; received Army Meritorious Service Medal, 1976; Society for the Preservation & Encouragement of Barber Shop Quartet Singing in Am, (SPEBQSA), 1991. **Home Addr:** 1714 Lincoln Ave, Pittsburgh, PA 15206. *

CHARNA, DANIEL A.
Entrepreneur, executive. **Career:** Glory Foods Inc, co founder & vpres opers, 1992-, chief operating officer. **Business Addr:** Co Founder, Glory Foods Inc, 901 Oak St, Columbus, OH 43205-1204, **Business Phone:** (614)252-2042.*

CHASE, ANTHONY R. See CHASE, TONY.

CHASE, ANTHONY R
Executive, founder (originator), educator. **Educ:** Harvard Col, BA, 1977; Harvard Bus Sch, MBA, 1981; Harvard Law Sch, JD, 1981. **Career:** Telecom Oppurtunity Inst, co-founder, 1998; ChaseCom L.P., chmn & cheif exec officer, currently; SBC Commun Inc, co founder & chmn, currently; Fed Reserve Bank Dallas, dir, currently; Leap Wireless Int Inc, dir, currently; Cornell Co Inc, dir, currently; Chase Radio Partners, chmn & chief exec officer, currently; Faith Broadcasting, L.P, pres & chief exec officer, currently; Univ Houston Law Ctr, assoc prof, currently. **Orgs:** Chmn, Houston Zoo Develop Bd; Coun Foreign Rels; bd dir, United Way Tex Gulf Coast & Houston Parks. **Honors/Awds:** Edith Baker Faculty Award, Univ Houston Law Sch, 1994; Businessman of the Year, Bus & Prof Mens Clubs, 2000; Ernst & Young Entrepreneur of the Year, 2001; Lamont Godwin Nat Achievement Award, Rainbow Push Coalition; Outstanding Young Businessman Award, Tex Bus Mag; Endicott Saltonstall Award, Harvard Univ; Williston Prize, Harvard Law Sch. **Special Achievements:** Published many books. **Business Addr:** Associate Professor of Law, University of Houston Law Center, 100 Law Ctr 222 BLB, Houston, TX 77204, **Business Phone:** (713)743-2162.

CHASE, ARNETT C
Executive. **Personal:** Born Apr 5, 1940, Green Cove Springs, FL; married Dianne J Thomas; children: Avis Chiquita & Arnett Cameron. **Educ:** Am Acad Funeral Serv, 1963; Univ FL, Cert Ophthalmology, 1972. **Career:** Apprentice embalmer & funeral dir, 1965, mgr, 1970; Leo C Chase & Son Funeral Home, funeral dir, currently. **Orgs:** Nat Funeral Dir & Morticians Asn; State Auditor Fla Morticians Asn; chmn, 4th Regional & Dist Morticians Asn; USO Coun; Coun Aged; Ancient City Charity Club; lifetime mem, Nat Asn Advan Colored People. **Honors/Awds:** Certificate of Apppreciation, St Paul AME Church, 1973; Fla Morticians Service Award, 1974. **Military Serv:** AUS sp/5 1963-65. **Business Addr:** Funeral Director, Leo C Chase & Son Funeral Home, 262 W King St, St Augustine, FL 32095, **Business Phone:** (904)824-2865.

CHASE, DOOKY, JR. (EDGAR DOOKY CHASE, JR)
Entrepreneur, chef. **Personal:** Married Leah Lange; children: 4. **Career:** Dooky Chase Restaurant, owner, currently. **Business Addr:** Owner, Dooky Chase Restaurant, 2301 Orleans Ave, New Orleans, LA 70119, **Business Phone:** (504)821-0535.

CHASE, EDGAR DOOKY, JR. See CHASE, DOOKY, JR.

CHASE, JOHN SAUNDERS
Architect. **Personal:** Born Jan 23, 1925, Annapolis, MD; son of John S Sr and Viola Hall; married Drucie Rucker; children: John Jr, Anthony & Saundria. **Educ:** Hampton Inst, BS, 1948; Univ Tex, Austin Sch Archit, MArch, 1952. **Career:** Tex Southern Univ, asst prof; John S Chase FAIA Architect Inc, pres & chmn bd, currently. **Orgs:** AIA; Tex Soc Architects; notable contr advcmt archt Col Fellows AIA, 1977; pres, Nat Orgn & Minority Architects; consult, architect Tex So Univ Bd Regents; bd mem, Huston-Tillotson Col; mem bd, Standard Savings & Loan Asn; Houston Engring & Sci Soc; Univ Tex Adv Coun; secy, Greater Houston Conv & Visitors Coun; mem bd, Houston Visitors & Conv Coun; bd trustees, Herman Hosp, Hampton Univ; US Comn Fine Arts; bd trustees, Antioch Bapt Ch; bd trustees, Univ Houston Found; Tex Southern Univ; Univ Tex Presial Search Comt; bd dirs, Golden State Mutual Life Ins Co; bd dir, Tex Southern Univ Found; Asn Black Consult Engrs & Architects. **Honors/Awds:** Nu Phi Chap Omega Si; trustee, Antioch Bapt Ch; Whitney M Young Citation; NOMA Design Excellence Award; John S Chase Scholar Archit; McGraw Hill Publ Co Golden 100 Fleet Award. **Special Achievements:** First African-American licensed to practice architecture in the state of Texas; First African American admitted to the Texas Society of Architects and the Houston Chapter of the American Institute of Architects. **Military Serv:** AUS. **Business**

Addr: President, Chairman, John S Chase FAIA Architect Inc, 1201 Southmore Blvd, Houston, TX 77004, **Business Phone:** (713)524-8413.*

CHASE, SONIA
Basketball player. **Personal:** Born Mar 9, 1976. **Educ:** Univ Md, College Park, attended 1998. **Career:** Charlotte Sting, forward, beginning, 1998-99; Minn Lynx, guard, 2003; Birmingham Power, guard; Lady Eagles Girls Basketball Team. asst coach, currently. **Honors/Awds:** All-ACC, Honorable Mention; NWBL All-Star, 2005. *

CHASE, TONY (ANTHONY R CHASE)
Educator, chairperson, chief executive officer. **Educ:** Harvard Col, BA, 1977; Harvard Bus Sch, MBA; Harvard Law Sch, JD, 1981. **Career:** Univ Houston, Bauer Col Bus, assoc prof law, 1990-; SBC Communs Inc, Telecom Opportunity Inst, chmn & co-founder, 1998-; Fed Reserve Bank, Dallas, chmn pro tem, currently; Leap Wireless Int Inc & Cornell Cos Inc, bd dirs; ChaseCom LP & Chase Radio Partners, chmn & chief exec officer, currently. **Orgs:** Vchmn, Fed Res Bank; chmn, Houston Zoo Develop Bd; chmn, Technol Opportunity Inst; bd mem, Fisk Univ; United Way; Greater Houston Partnership; Coun Foreign Rels; Am Bar Asn; State Bar Tex. **Honors/Awds:** Ernst & Young Entrepreneur of the Year, US Black Engr & Info Technol Mag, 2005; Rainbow Push Coalitions Lamont Godwin Nat Award; Endicott Saltonstall Award, Harvard Univ; Williston Prize, Harvard Law Sch; Edith Baker Faculty Award, Univ Houston, 1994; Bank Am Pinnacle Award; Lamont Godwin Nat Achievement Award, Rainbow Push Coalition; Outstanding Young Businessman Award, Tex Bus Mag; Businessman of the Year Award, Bus & Prof Men's Club. **Special Achievements:** Author, Race, Culture & Contract Law, 1995; Author, Telecommunications Law in the United States, Comparative Law Yearbook of International Business, Volume 21, 1999. **Business Addr:** Chairman, Chief Executive Officer, ChaseCom LP, Chase Radio Partners, 3311 W Alabama St, Houston, TX 77098, **Business Phone:** (713)874-5800.*

CHASE-RIBOUD, DR. BARBARA DEWAYNE
Sculptor, writer. **Personal:** Born Jun 26, 1939, Philadelphia, PA; daughter of Charles Edward and Vivian May Braithwaite West; married Marc Eugene, Dec 25, 1961 (divorced 1981); children: David & Alexis; married Sergio G Tosi, Jul 4, 1981. **Educ:** Temple Univ, BFA, 1957; Yale Univ, MFA, 1960. **Career:** One-woman shows: The Univ Mus, Berkeley, CA; The Mus Modern Art, Paris, France; The Kunstmuseum, Dusseldorf, Germany; The Detroit Art Inst, Detroit, MI; The Indianapolis Art Museum, Ind, IN; The Mus Modern Art, New York, NY; From Memphis & Peking: poetry, Random House, 1974; The Kunstmuseum, Freilburg, West Germany, 1976; The Musee Reattu, Arles, France, 1976; European Drawings, Berlin, West Germany, 1980; five-museum tour, Australia, 1980-81; Studio Mus, 1996; Milwaukee Art Mus, 1997; Chicago Cult Ctr, 1997; Mus SC, 1997; Mint Mus, 1997; Los Angeles Mus Contemporary Art, 1997; Smithsonian, 1998; Metrop Mus Art, NY; The Studio Mus, NY 2000; The Metropolitan Mus Art, NY, 1999; The Walters Mus Art, Baltimore, 2000; The British Mus, London, 2001; The Philadelphia Mus, 2002-03; selected group exhibitions include "Documenta 77" Kessel, West Germany, 1977; Mus Contemporary Crafts, NY, 1977; Smithsonian Inst Renwick Gallery, 1977; Sally Hemings: A Novel, 1979; The Whitney Museum Noeuds et Ligatures Fond Nationale des Arts, 1983; Calif Mus Afro-Amer Art, 1985; "Celopatra," The British Mus London, 2001; selected public collections, Mus Art New Orleans; The Philadelphia Art Mus; The Philadelphia Art Alliance; The Scnburg Collection New York; NY State Coun on the Arts; St John's Univ, Harlem State Off Bldg, The Metrop Mus Art, NY; The Nat Collections, France; Mus Modern Art, Berkley Mus, Los Angeles; The British Mus, London; Monuments: "Africa Rising" Foley Square, NY. Author: Sally Hemings, Viking, 1979; Albin Michel, 1981; Valide: A Novel of the Harem, 1986; Portrait of a Nude Woman as Cleopatra, William Morrow, 1987; Echo of Lions, William Morrow, 1989; The President's Daughter, Crown Publishers, 1994; Egypt's Nights, Editions Felln, Paris, 1994; monograph: Barbara Chase-Riboud, Sculptor, A Jansen & P Selz, 1999; By Herself: Collected poems; under press, Sally Hemings, New Revision, Little Brown, UK, 2001; Hottentot Venus: novel, Doubleday, 2003; Hottentot Venus, Doubleday, NY, 2004; Book: Black Writers, first edition, 1989; St. James Guide to Black Artists, 1997; Barbara Chose-Riboud: Sculptor. Harry N. Abrams, 1999. **Orgs:** PEN; PEN Am Ctr; Century Asn; Yale Alumni Asn; Alpha Kappa Alpha; John Hay Whitney Found Fel, 1957-58. **Honors/Awds:** Nat Fel Arts; Carl Sandburg Poetry Award as Best American Poet, 1988; Janet Kafka Award for Best Novel by an American Woman, 1979; Honarary Doctorate of Arts & Humanities, Temple Univ, 1981; Muhlenberg Col, Honarary LHD, 1993; Van der Zee Achievement Award, 1995; Conn State Univ, Honarary Doctorate, 1996; Knighthood for Contributions to Arts & Letters, France, 1996; one of the best historical novelists in America. **Business Addr:** Author, Palazzo Ricci, Piazza Ricci, 00186 Rome, Italy.

CHASTANG, MARK J.
Hospital administrator, executive director, vice president (organization). **Educ:** Fisk Univ, attended 1974; Univ Kans, MPA, 1976; Ga State Univ, MBA, 1984. **Career:** DC Gen Hosp, exec dir, chief exec, 1989-95; E Orange NJ Gen Hosp, pres & chief exec officer, 1995-04, admin; Med Col Ohio Hosp, vpres & exec dir, 2004-; Essex Valley Healthcare Inc, pres; Emory Univ Hosp, asst dir; Cathedral Healthcare Syst Inc, vpres. **Orgs:** Hosp Coun Nortwest Ohio. **Business Addr:** Vice President, Executive Director, Medical College of Ohio Hospitals, 3000 Arlington Ave, Toledo, OH 43614-5805, **Business Phone:** (419)383-4000.*

CHASTINE, ROBERT
President (organization). **Career:** Mgt Technol Assoc, chief exec officer & pres, currently. **Orgs:** Soc Am Military Engineers(S.A. M.E).

CHATMAN, ALEX
Educator, magistrate, county commissioner. **Personal:** Born Oct 6, 1943, Greeleyville, SC; son of Alex Oscar (deceased) and Alma Montgomery; married Mariah Williams Chatman, Sep 26, 1986. **Educ:** Williamsburg County Training Sch, attended 1962; Benedict Col, dipl, 1965; SC State Col, BS, 1973; Univ RI, ME, 1966; Univ SC, attended 1970. **Career:** Greeleyville, teacher, 1965-; magistrate, 1973-81; Williamsburg Co Coun, supvr, chmn, 1996. **Orgs:** pres, Greeleyville Br Nat Bus Leauge, 1970-; Credential Com State Dem Conv, 1971 & 1974; pres, Williamsburg County Educ Asn, 1974-75; chmn, sixth Cong Dist Polit Action Com Educ, 1974; Nat Asn Advan Colored People; United Teaching Prof; Nat Bus League; mem off, Black Caucus Nat Educ Asn; SC Magistrate's Asn; SC Assn Co, 1982-; Governor's Coun Rural Devel, 1982-86; SC Pvt Indus Co, 1984-87. **Honors/Awds:** Award Phi Beta Sigma Frat, 1973; Award, SC Educ Assn, 1975; Presidential Citation, Natl Assn Equal Opportunity Higher Educ, 1985; Citizen of the Year, Outstanding Pub Serv, Delta Rho Chapter Omega Psi Phi Frat, 1982; Distinguished Service Award, Williamsburg Branch NAACP, 1985; Certificate Appreciation, Kingstree Kiwanis Club, 1988. **Special Achievements:** First black to be elected a county administrator in South Carolina. *

CHATMAN, DONALD LEVERITT
Physician. **Personal:** Born Dec 27, 1934, New Orleans, LA; married Eleanor; children: Lynn Ann, Eleanor Louise, Eric Leveritt. **Educ:** Harvard Univ, AB 1956; Meharry Med Col, MD 1960. **Career:** Cooper Hosp NJ, rotating intrnshp 1960-61; Lake Charles LA, gen Practice, 1961-63; Chicago, ob gyn, 1969-; Dept Obstetrics & Gynec, Michael Reese Hosp & Med Ctr, asst Attending, 1969-74; Dept Obstetrics & Gynec Univ Chicago-Pritzker Sch Diamine Oxidase Pregenancy, clin instr; Northwestern Univ Feinberg Sch Med, assoc prof; Pvt pract, Physician, currently. **Orgs:** Chicago Med Soc; pres Chicago Med Soc S Chicago Br 1969-70; Am Asn Gynec Laparoscopists; Ill State Med Soc; Am Med Soc; Nat Med Asn; Am Col Obstetrics & Gynec; Am Bd of Obstetrics & Gynec, 1972. **Military Serv:** USAF capt 1963-65. **Business Addr:** Physician, 111 N Wabash Ave Suite 1017, Chicago, IL 60602, **Business Phone:** (312)220-9255.*

CHATMAN, JACOB L.
Clergy. **Personal:** Born Aug 5, 1938, Patterson, GA; married Etty; children: Mario. **Educ:** FL Memorial, BS, 1963; Eastern Theol Sem, MDiv, 1968; Univ Ma, DEd, 1974. **Career:** Sec Baptist Church Coatesville PA, pastor; organized coordinated tutorial progs socially deprived children; written training current employabel disadvantaged Chester; counseling drop-outs, drugs, planned parenthood, family counseling, organizer Day Care, chmn comn support; Pinn Memorial Baptist Church, pastor, currently. **Orgs:** Dir, Pinn; Ctr PA Chmn Title I Coatesville Sch Dist; Am Asn Univ Profs; Coatesville Area Clergy; Kappa Alpha Psi Frat; trustee, Cheyney State Teachers Col; pres, Comn Disadvantaged Eastern Sem; bd mgrs, exec bd PA DE Churchs Am Baptist Conv; Task Force Foreign Mission; Black Churchmen Am Baptist Conv; vpres, Coatesville Opportuinity Coun; chmn, Non profit Housing Corp Sec Baptist Church; chmn, Comn Support Day Care; Coatesville vice chmn Task Force World Hunger; Am Baptist Conv; rotary mem. **Honors/Awds:** Recipient, citizenship YMCA, 1955; Eagle Scout, 1955; Chapel Four Chaplains Award, 1969; censtitation award, Mt Labanon HRAM PA, 1972; outsanding service award, FL memorial col, 1972; Humanitarian Award, 1973; outstanding youth man of America, 1972; cited, Coatesville Record Outstanding Service, 1970-74. **Business Phone:** (215)878-2742.*

CHATMAN, MELVIN E.
Educator. **Personal:** Born Feb 9, 1933, Springfield, TN; married Velma R; children: Vera, Melvin Jr, Carol, Bobby, Jeff & Karl. **Educ:** Lane Col, BS, 1955; Fisk Univ, MA, 1963; Univ Tenn, EdS, 1975; Am Baptist Col, ThB, 1996. **Career:** R Bransford High Sch, teacher, coach, 1957-68; Springfield High Sch, teacher, 1968-70, asst prin, 1970-73, supvr spec educ, 1973-95. **Orgs:** Nat Educ Asn; Robertson City Teacher Asn; Coun Exceptional C; Tenn Asn Suprv & Curriculum Develop; former mem, Mid-Cumberland Coun Gov; Mental Health Harriett City; Tenn Voter Coun, City Ctr, 1972-74; Alpha Phi Alpha; Beard Chapel Baptist Church. **Military Serv:** AUS, 1955-57. **Home Addr:** 4940 Hwy 41 N, Springfield, TN 37172. *

CHATMAN, RONALD DEAN
School administrator, college administrator. **Personal:** Born Nov 28, 1946, Mobile, AL; son of John A and Bessie Mae Gholston; divorced; children: Ronald Dean Chatman II. **Educ:** Ala State Univ, BA, 1965; Calif State Univ, Los Angeles, MA, 1972. **Career:** Compton Community Col, dean develop & continuing edu, 1979-81, dean spec proj, 1981-82, dir develop, 1982-85, exec dir instnl develop, 1985-96, vpres instnl develop & external affairs, 1996-98, dep supt & exec vpres. **Orgs:** Nat Asn Advan Colored People, 1971-; Vestry Bd, St Timothy's Episcopal Church, 1990-; Fac Asn Calif Community Col, 1993-; Asn Calif Community Col Adminrs, 1983-; 100 Black Men of Los Angeles, 1992-; bd dir, Inner City Theater, 2001-; Los Angeles County Beach Comn, 2001-. **Honors/Awds:** Man of the Yr, 100 Black Men of Los Angeles Inc, 1993. **Special Achievements:** Oxford Roundtable on Edu Issues, participant, Oxford, England, 2001.

CHATMAN, TYRONE
Association executive, executive director. **Personal:** Born Jan 1, 1952. **Educ:** Highland Park Community Col. **Career:** Salesman; Mich Automobile Indust, staff, 1972-72; Mich Veteran's Found, Detroit Vet Ctr, Detroit, MI, assoc exec dir, currently. **Orgs:** Intern, advocate serv, Neighborhood Serv Orgn; Detroit City Coun President's Shelter Ordinance & Lic Task Force; State Mich Target Cities Adv Comt. **Honors/Awds:** Robert Wood Johnson Community Health Leadership Award, 1999; Spirit of Detroit Award; John J Gunther HUD Best Practices Award. **Military Serv:** AUS, 1970-71; mil adv, vietnam. **Business Addr:** Associate Executive Director, Michigan Veterans Foundation, Detroit Veteran Center, 2770 Pk Ave, Detroit, MI 48201, **Business Phone:** (313)831-5500.

CHATMAN-DRIVER, PATRICIA ANN (PAT DRIVER)
Software developer. **Personal:** Born Jul 19, 1956; daughter of Mamie Chatman; married Allen Jerome, Aug 9, 1985; children: Khaalid, Allen Jr & Amanda. **Educ:** SC State Col, BS Math, 1979. **Career:** Vitro Labs, mathematician, 1979-82; Sperry & UNISYS, mem eng staff, 1982-87; self-employed, 1987-88; Mystech Assocs Inc, sr software Engr, 1988-. **Business Addr:** Senior Software Engineer, Mystech Associates Inc, 5205 Leesburg Pike Suite 1200, Falls Church, VA 22041, **Business Phone:** (703)671-8680.

CHATMON, LINDA CAROL
Educator, consultant. **Personal:** Born Nov 13, 1951, Louisville, KY; daughter of L C Fox and Betty A Savage; children: Dana Marie. **Educ:** Univ Louisville, BA, 1980, MSSW, 1982; Univ Louisville, PHD, Social Work, . **Career:** Creative Employment Project, counr, 1982-84; Univ Louisville, coord cooperative educ, 1984, instr & counr 1984-89; GYSG Corp, consult, 1986-88; Univ Louisville, Kent Sch Social Work, dir admis & stud serv, adj asst prof. **Orgs:** Community chair, Urban League, 1982-88, Youth Performing Arts Sch, 1983-87; secy bd, Seven Counties Ment Health Serv. **Honors/Awds:** Outstanding Young Women Am, 1984. *

CHATTERJEE, LOIS JORDAN
Banker. **Personal:** Born Aug 4, 1940, Nashville, TN; married Suchindran S. **Educ:** Tenn State Univ, BS, 1962; Univ Tenn, attended 1963. **Career:** Com Union Bank, bank officer bus develop, 1972-; Model Cities Prog, evaluator, 1971; St Dept Corrections, counselor youthful offenders, 1966-70; Juvenile City Davidson Co, legal secy, 1962-66; Essence Mag, Publ, 1974. **Orgs:** Metrop Coun, 1971-; Negro Bus & Prof Womens League; Middle Tenn Bus Asn; Nat Bus League; secy, SE Nashville Civic League; charter mem, Dudley Park Day Care Ctr; bd dirs, Goodwill Indust; House Between; Nashville County C; League Women Voters; YWCA; Nat Coun Crime & Delinquency; Nat League Citizens. **Business Addr:** Educator, Metropolitan School System, 2601 Bradford Ave, Nashville, TN 37204.

CHAUNCEY, MINION KENNETH. See MORRISON, DR. K C.

CHAVIS, BENJAMIN FRANKLIN, JR. See MUHAMMAD, BENJAMIN CHAVIS.

CHAVIS, OMEGA ROCHELLE
Banker. **Personal:** Born in Tennessee; daughter of Eddie H and Estella M. **Educ:** Wayne State Univ, bachelors degree, 1970. **Career:** Security Pacific Nat Bank, asst vpres, 1973-86; Fox Film Corp, assoc dir, 1986-87; Glendale Fed Bank, sr vpres, 1987-. **Orgs:** Bd dirs, Savings Asn Mortgage Co Inc; exec bd, Los Angeles Home Loan Coun Ctr; United Negro Col Fund; Nat Asn Female Execs; Los Angeles Urban Bankers; C's Defense Fund; Alpha Kappa Alpha Sorority Inc; First AME Church; Co-founder, Calif State EDD Adv Coun. **Honors/Awds:** State of California Health & Welfare Agency Public Serv Award. **Special Achievements:** LDF Black Woman of Achievement.

CHAVIS, THEODORE R.
Educator. **Personal:** Born Jun 14, 1922, Asheville, NC; son of Theodore and Anna; married Montios; children: Carolyn & Lisa. **Educ:** Talladega Col, BA, 1942; Atlanta Univ, MSW, 1951; Smith Col Sch Soc Work, grad studies; Univ MI Sch Soc Work. **Career:** NC Employ Security Comn, interviewer, 1947-49; Vet Admin Guid Ctr Atlanta, GA, trainee, 1949; Bur Ment Hygiene, Wash, DC, 1950-51; Percy Jones Army Hosp, social worker, 1951-53;

Vet Admin Hosp, Battle Creek, Mich, asst chief, social worker, 1953-65; Mich State Univ, Sch Social Work, prof & past coord, practr cum instr, 1965-88, prof emer, 1988-2006, prof emer, 2006-. **Orgs:** Mich Chap Prof Stand Comn; Nat Asn Social Workers; Coun Social Work Educ; Budget Panel United Way; bd mem, chmn serv comn, Big Brothers & Big Sisters; bd mem, Capitol Area Child & Family Serv; chap chmn, treas, Nat Assembly Delegate NASW; past mem, Legis Task Force, Mich Chap Am Asn Retired Persons; coordr, Capitol City Task Force; Mich State Legis Comt; AARP 1987-; past bd mem, Capital Area Interfaith Respite; State Mich Adv Coun Aging, 1994-. **Honors/Awds:** Outstanding Performance Award, Vet Admin Hosp, Battle Creek, Mich, 1957. **Military Serv:** AUS, 1942-46. **Home Addr:** 1950 Mendota Dr, East Lansing, MI 48823, **Home Phone:** (517)351-6687. **Business Addr:** Professor Emeritus, Michigan State University, School of School Work, 254 Baker Hall, East Lansing, MI 48824, **Business Phone:** (517)353-8616.*

CHAVOUS, BARNEY LEWIS
Executive, football player. **Personal:** Born Mar 22, 1951, Aiken, SC; married Odessa; children: Shedric, Jasmine, Nikeya Monique. **Educ:** SC State Univ, Phys Ed. **Career:** Football player (retired), executive; Denver Broncos, defensive end, 1973-85; Minority Arts & Educ Found, chmn; TW Josey High Sch, Augusta, GA, football coach. **Honors/Awds:** Defensive Rookie Year Hon, NFLPA, 1973; Defensive Lineman Year, Pittsburgh Courier's NFL, 1978; All-Conf & defensive MVP at SC State; All-Am by AP; collegiate Defensive Lineman Year; North-South Game; The Senior Bowl; Coaches' All-Am Game.

CHAVOUS, COREY
Football player. **Personal:** Born Jan 5, 1976, Aiken, SC. **Educ:** Vanderbilt Univ, human & orgn develop. **Career:** Ariz Cardinals, defensive back, 1998-01; Minn Vikings, defensive back,2002-05; st louis rams, safety side, 2006-08. Free agent currently. **Orgs:** Vol, Minneapolis Pub Sch; vol, Shriners Hosp & United Negro Col Fund. **Honors/Awds:** Defensive Player of the Week, Natl Football League, 2003; Ed Block Courage Award. **Special Achievements:** Analyst, Super Bowl XXXVIII, ESPN. *

CHAVOUS, MILDRED L.
School administrator, executive director, counselor. **Personal:** Born in Columbia, AL; daughter of William H Lynn and Juanita Jackson; married Jarret C Chavous, Oct 2, 1951. **Educ:** Franklin Univ, BS, 1946. **Career:** Ohio State Univ Grad Sch, counr, 1964-77, acad counr, 1977-84, acad counr & staff asst, 1984-86, assoc, 1986-90, dir grad serv, 1990-97. **Orgs:** Bd dirs, chairperson, League Women Voters, Educ Comn, 1965-; CMS Pub Sch Personnel Policies Ohio, 1971-73; exec comt mem, Ohio Humanities Coun, 1974-80; trustee, Franklin County Bd Ment Retardation & Develop Disabilities, 1974-77; founding mem, Metrop Human Serv Comn, 1977-90; State Libr Ohio, Adv Comn, Fed Libr Prog, 1984-87; trustee & chairperson, Players Theatre Columbus, Outreach Comt, 1989-95; European Womens Mgt Network, 1992-; Coun Acad Excellence Women, 1994-; trustee, Thurber House, Thurber Nat Award Am Humor Comn, 1995-; trustee, Scioto Valley Health Systs Agency, 1996-; bd gov, Ohio State Univ Critical Difference Women, Int Coun, 1996-; adv bd, Jefferson Fel, 1996; nat pres, Circle-Lets Inc, 1997-; Links Inc; Asn Fac & Prof Women; treas, Crichton Club. **Honors/Awds:** Commendation, Ohio House Rep 110th Gen Assembly, 1971; Distinguished Serv Award, United Negro Col Fund, 1981; Mayors Cert Recognition, City Columbus, 1982; Commendation, Ohio House Rep 116th Gen Assembly, 1983; Commendation, Ohio Sen 116th Gen Assembly, 1983; Distinguished Staff Award, Ohio State Univ, 1986; Cert of Appreciation, Health Plan Rev, 1988-95; Coalition, 100 Black Women Honoree, 1992; Black Women Courage Honoree, 1995; Commendation, Coun City Columbus, 1996; Commendation, Recognition of Accomplishments, Ohio House Rep, 121 Gen Assembly, 1995; Distinguished Vol Serv, Columbus Cancer Clinic, 2001. **Special Achievements:** 1st African American and woman co-chair, Ohio State Univerisity, United Way Annual Campaign, 1981; 1st woman general chair, United Negro College Fund Annual Telethon, Central Ohio, 1982; co-editor, "Graduate School News," The Ohio State University, 1990-97; women's editor, Columbus Call and Post, 1970-1985; 1st African American President, board of directors, Columbus Cancer Clinic, 1993-01; 1st African American president Promusica Sustaining Board. *

CHEADLE, DON (DONALD FRANK CHEADLE)
Actor. **Personal:** Born Nov 29, 1964, Kansas City, MO; son of Donald Cheadle and Betty. **Educ:** Calif Inst Arts, BA, fine arts. **Career:** TV series: "Fame", 1986; "L.A. Law", 1986; "Hill Street Blues", 1987; "The Bronx Zoo", 1987; "Night Court", 1988; "Hooper man", 1988; "Booker", 1989; "China Beach", 1990; "The Fresh Prince of Bel-Air", 1990; "Hang in' With Mr. Cooper", 1992; "The Golden Palace", 1992-93; "Picket Fences", 1993-95; "The Colbert Report", 2006; "The Henry Rollins Show", 2007;Films: Moving Violations, 1985; Hamburger Hill, 1987; Colors, 1988; Roadside Prophets, 1992; The Meteor Man, 1993; Lush Life, 1993; Things to Do in Denver When You're Dead, 1995; Devil in a Blue Dress, 1995; Volcano,1997; Rosewood, 1997; Boogie Nights, 1997; Out of Sight, 1998; The Rat Pack, 1998; Bulworth, 1998; Traffic, 2000; Mission to Mars, 2000; The Family Man, 2000; Things Behind the Sun, 2001; Manic, 2001; Swordfish, 2001; Abby Singer, 2003; The United States of Leland, 2003; Ocean's Twelve, 2004; The Cookout, 2004; After the Sunset, 2004; The Assassination of Richard Nixon, 2004; Hotel Rwanda, 2004; Crash, 2005; Reign Over Me,2007; Talk to Me, 2007; Ocean's Thirteen, 2007; "Darfur Now", 2007; "Traitor", Producer, 2008; "Hotel for Dogs", 2009; "Brooklyn's Finest", 2009. **Honors/Awds:** LAFCA Award for Best Supporting Actor, 1995; NSFC Award for Best Supporting Actor, 1996; Golden Globe Award for Best Performance by an Actor in a Supporting Role in a Series, 1999; Black Reel Award for Network/Cable, Best Actor, 2000; Black Reel Award for Theatrical, Best Supporting Actor, 2001; Screen Actors Guild Award for Outstanding Performance by the Cast of a Theatrical Motion Picture, 2001. **Special Achievements:** Co-author of the book Not On Our Watch: The Mission to End Genocide in Darfur and Beyond, 2007; Nominated for Oscar and 18 other awards. *

CHEANEY, CALBERT N
Basketball player. **Personal:** Born Jul 17, 1971, Evansville, IN. **Educ:** Ind Univ, attended 1993. **Career:** Wash Wizards, guard-forward, 1993; Wash Bullets, 1994-99; Boston Celtics, 2000; Denver Nuggets, 2001-02; Utah Jazz, 2003; Golden State Warriors, guard-forward, 2004-06; free agent, currently. **Honors/Awds:** All-Am, 1991-93; All-Big Ten, 1991-93; Big Ten Conf MVP, 1993; USBWA Col Player of the Year, 2003; Big Ten's All Time Scoring Leader; Ind Univ's All-Time leading scorer; Four time IU team MVP; Selected to Ind Univy's All-Century First Team. **Special Achievements:** NBA Draft, first round, sixth pick, 1993. **Business Phone:** (510)986-2200.

CHEATHAM, BETTY L.
Government official, manager. **Personal:** Born Dec 5, 1940, South Carolina. **Educ:** Benedict Col, BS, bus admin, 1962. **Career:** Int City Mgt Asn, prog mgr, 1974-80, minority prog dir, 1980-83; DC Water & Sewer Authority, chief, asst gen mgr, currently. **Orgs:** Coalition, Black Pub Admins, 1982-85; Int City Mgt Asn, 1983-85; Black Pub Admins Forum, 1984-85. **Honors/Awds:** Award Coalition, Black Pub Admins, 1982. **Home Addr:** 859 Venable Pl NW, Washington, DC 20012. **Business Addr:** Assitant General Manager, DC Water & Sewer Authority, 810 1st St NE, Washington, DC 20002-4227.*

CHEATHAM, HENRY BOLES
Television director, educator. **Personal:** Born Oct 5, 1943, Bentonia, MS; son of Thomas and Maude; married Helen M Hughes, Nov 23, 1966; children: Tonita R & Jomo K. **Educ:** Columbia Col, BA, radio & tv, 1973; Univ Ill, Chicago, MA, mass commun, 1980. **Career:** Ford Motor Co, utility man, 1965-73; WISH-TV Indianapolis, producer, 1973; WSNS-TV, Chicago, producer, dir, writer & cameraman, 1973-; Yoton Commun Inc, pres, founder & owner, 1980-; Richard J Daley City Col, Chicago, instr, 1997-. **Orgs:** Exec bd, Union steward NABET, 1980-; Chicago Area Broadcast Pub Affairs Asn, 1980-83; Nat Black United Front, 1983-; Oper PUSH, 1983-; vpres & bd dirs, Order Kush, currently. **Honors/Awds:** Image Award, Fred Hampton Found, 1983. **Special Achievements:** Articles published in NABET-NEWS, Beverly Review, Chicago Defender. **Military Serv:** AUS, E-4, 2 yrs; Honorable Discharge, 1965. **Business Addr:** Instructor, Richard J Daley City College, 7500 S Pulaski, Chicago, IL 60652, **Business Phone:** (773)838-7500.

CHEATHAM, LINDA MOYE
Government official, executive. **Personal:** Born Nov 2, 1948, Richmond, VA; married Harold D Cheatham Jr; children: Michelle, Maxanne, Harold,III. **Educ:** Wheaton Col, BA, 1970; Va Commonwealth Univ. **Career:** City Norfolk, planner, 1970-72; City Richmond, planner, 1972-75, opers mgr, 1975-79, sr budget analyst, 1979-84, dir gen serv, 1984-87, budget dir, 1987-91; US Dept Comn, Int Trade Admin, chief financial officer & dir admin, 1999-. **Orgs:** Int City Mgt Asn, 1980-; bd govs, William Byrd Community House, 1983-; Conf Minority Pub Admin, 1983-; bd dirs, City Richmond, Fed Credit Union, 1984; chap coun, VA Chap Am Soc Pub Admin, 1984-; treas, John B Cary PTA, 1985-88. **Honors/Awds:** Outstanding Woman of 1984; N Richmond YMCA Black Achiever, 1985; Presidential Award, US Off Personnel Mgt, 2004. **Business Addr:** Chief Financial Officer, Director, US Dept Comm, Intl Trade Admin, 1401 Const Ave NW Suite 2810, HCH Bldg Rm 3827, Washington, DC 20230-0002.*

CHEATHAM, DR. ROY E.
Educator. **Personal:** Born Sep 14, 1941, Memphis, TN; married Gertie Brenell Wilson; children: Roy III & Gina Rochele. **Educ:** Lincoln Univ, BA, 1965; St Louis Univ, MA, 1969, PhD, 1975. **Career:** Human Dev Corp, adult & educ cord, 1966-67; adult educ curriculum specialist, 1969; Metropolitan Col, dean; St Louis Univ, Col Arts & Sci,asst dean, 1969-70, dir spec acad prog, dir col asst prog & upward bound, 1970-73, Educ leadership & higher educ, asst prof. **Orgs:** Educ Enrichment Prog, 1972-75; Basic Educ Opportunity Grant Planning Comn,1972; Am Col Pesonnel Assn Comn XIV, 1973-76; pres, Roy Cheatham & Assoc; Financial Aid Panel, 1973; vchmn brd dir, Inroads Inc, 1973-76; brd educ, Univ City Pub Sch Dist, 1974-77; Reg VII off Higher Educ pres, 1976-77; comnr, Mark Twain Boy Scout Dist; brd dir, Comm Learning Ctr; brd dir, Sophia House. **Honors/Awds:** Comm Service Award, Org Black Entrepreneurs, 1972; meritorious serv award, Lincoln Univ Alumni Assn, 1973; Outstanding Serv Award, Black Students St Louis Univ, 1973. **Home Addr:** 12173 Royal Valley Dr, St Louis, MO 63141, **Home Phone:** (314)576-6059.

CHECKER, CHUBBY. See EVANS, ERNEST.

CHECOLE, KASSAHUN
Publisher. **Personal:** Born Jan 22, 1947, Asmara, Ethiopia; married Nevolia E Ogletree; children: MuluBirhan, Senait. **Educ:** SUNY Binghamton, BA Hons, 1974, MA, 1976. **Career:** Rutgers Univ, instr, 1979-85; Af Res & Publishing Proj, dir, 1979-; El Colegio De Mexico, res prof, 1982-; The Red Sea Press, pres & publ, 1982-; Wash Sch Inst Policy Studies, lect; Af World Press, pres & publ, currently. **Orgs:** Vice chmn, Eritrean Relief Comn Inc, 1983-85; editorial bd Saga Race Rels Abstracts, Horn Africa; editor RSP current issues series. **Business Addr:** President, Publisher, Africa World Press Inc, The Red Sea Press Inc, 541 W Ingham Ave Suite B, Trenton, NJ 08607, **Business Phone:** (609)695-3200.*

CHEEK, DONALD KATO
Educator. **Personal:** Born Mar 24, 1930, New York, NY; married Calista Patricia Duff (deceased); children: Don Jr, Gary, Alan, Stephan & Donna; married Patti Dorothy Walker. **Educ:** Seton Hall Univ, BS, 1953; Fordham Sch Soc Serv, MSW, 1955; Univ Southern Calif, doctoral curric, 1959; Temple Univ, PhD, 1971. **Career:** National Inst Mental Health, grad fel, 1965-69; Lincoln Univ PA, vpres stud affairs, dean, lectr, 1967-69; Claremont Col, dir black studies, 1969-73; Calif Polytech St Univ, prof, 1973-99, prof emer, currently; rehabilitation counr, 1984-; ordained minister, 1987-; Nat Bd Officer, Prison fel, 1989; Calif St Univ, Col Soc Sci, Fresno, part-time lectr, 2003-. **Orgs:** Presenter, Int Consult Coun& Ethnic Minorities, Univ Utrecht Netherlands, 1985; consult speaker & workshop facilitator, Milwaukee; Ment Health Ctr, Orangeburg, SC; Annual Guid Conf, NY Salomon Brothers, Las Vegas, NV; Am Personnel & Guid Asn Conv, New Orleans; La Asn Black Soc Works; Drug Educ Prev & Treatment, Daytona Beach, FL; Bethune Cookman Col; Emporia Kans St Univ; Omaha NE Crighton Univ; Sanford Fl Seminole Comm Col; Xenia Ohio Co Ment Health; Evansville Ind Human Rel Comn; Univ CinnCol Nursing; Cleveland Urban Minority Alcoholism Outreach Proj, SC Sch Alcohol & Drug Studies, City Portland, OR; Univ ND, LA Black Prof Engrs. **Special Achievements:** Named One of the Pioneers of Cognitive Behavior Therapy, 1992; published 5 books. **Business Addr:** Part-Time Lecturer, California State University, College of Social Sciences, 2225 E San Ramon, PO Box MF100, Fresno, CA 93740-8029.

CHEEK, DONNA MARIE
Athlete. **Personal:** Born Dec 5, 1963, Philadelphia, PA. **Career:** Equestrian; Exhib Equestrian, coordr; Seven Star Farms, Hunter & Jumper Training Facil Horses & Riders, owner & operator. **Orgs:** Corp sponsorship Univox CA Inc, Pro-Line Corp, Quincy Jones Prod, Ed Laras Westside Distr; spokesperson Involvement for Young Achievers Inc, 1982; Avon Found NY, 1983. **Honors/Awds:** Financial Grant Black Equestrian Sports Talent, 1980-. **Special Achievements:** Pub "Going for the Gold-The Story of Black Women in Sports," 1983; NAACP Image Award for "One More Hurdle-The Donna Cheek Story," 1984; "One More Hurdle" Autobiography NBC TV, starred in one hour drama 1984; "Profiles in Pride" NBC TV, starred 1985; first equestrienne inductee, Womens Sports Hall of Fame, 1990; first black on US Equestrian Team.

CHEEK, DR. JAMES EDWARD
College administrator, college president. **Personal:** Born Dec 4, 1932, Roanoke Rapids, NC; son of Lee Ella Williams and King Virgil; married Celestine Juanita Williams, Jun 14, 1953; children: James Edward & Janet Elizabeth. **Educ:** Shaw Univ, BA, sociol & hist, 1955; Colgate-Rochester Div Sch, MDiv, 1958; Drew Univ, PhD, 1962. **Career:** Drew Theol Sch, teaching asst, 1959-60; Union Jr Col, instr western hist, 1959-61; Va Union Univ, asst prof NT hist theol, 1961-63; Shaw Univ, pres, 1963-69; Tenn Wesleyan Col, pres; Howard Univ, pres, 1969-89, pres emer, currently. **Orgs:** Alpha Theta Nu; Alpha Phi Alpha; Sigma Pi Sigma; Am Soc Church Hist; Am Asn Univ Profs; Am Acad Relig. **Honors/Awds:** Recipient of hundreds of awards and nineteen honorary degrees including L'Universite d'Etat d'Haiti, 1972, Deleware State Col, 1972, Univ MD, 1975, Bucknell Univ, 1975, New York Inst Tech, 1980, Univ NC, 1980, Duke Univ, 1982, Fisk Univ, 1984, Cent State Univ, 1988, Tuskegee Univ, 1989, Adelphi Univ, 1989, Rider Col, 1989. **Special Achievements:** Awarded the nation's highest civilian Honor, Presidential Medal of Freedom by President Ronald Reagan. **Military Serv:** USAF, 1950-51. **Home Phone:** (336)273-5550. **Business Addr:** President Emeritus, Howard University, 2400 6th St NW, Washington, DC 20059, **Business Phone:** (202)806-6100.

CHEEK, KING VIRGIL, JR.
Educator, vice president (organization), writer. **Personal:** Born May 26, 1937, Weldon, NC; married Annette Walker, Aug 10, 1968; children: King Virgil III, Kahlil, Antoinette & Antoine.

Educ: Bates Col, Lewiston, Maine, BA, econ, 1959; Univ Chicago, MA, 1967; Univ Chicago, JD, 1969. **Career:** Shaw Univ, dean & vpres, 1964-69, pres, 1970-71. Morgan Univ, Baltimore, MD, 1971-74; Union Experimenting Col & Univ, Pres, 1976-78; New York Inst Tech, ctr leadership & career develop, exec dir, 1975-85, vpres, 1985-89; Inst Advan, vpres, 1989-91; New York Col health, prof, 2001-03; Col Integrated Med, founder, 2005-. **Orgs:** Bd dir, Baltimore Contractors, 1974; bd dir, Inst Econ Develop, 1978; Martin Ctr Col; bd trustees, Shaw Col, Detroit; bd visitors, Univ Chicago Law Sch; bd trustees, Warnborough col, Oxford, Eng. **Honors/Awds:** Grand Commander Order of Star Africa, 1971; Hon Doctoratre, Bates Col,Univ MD 1972. **Special Achievements:** American Academy change magazine awarded as Top young leader award in 1978; author, 'The Quadrasoul', four novels that explore four dimensions of the human spirit. **Military Serv:** Disting Civilian Award, AUS, 1973.

CHEEK, ROBERT BENJAMIN, III
Dentist. **Personal:** Born Sep 12, 1931, New York, NY; married Geraldine M Manley; children: Albert, Sonseeahray. **Educ:** NC Col, BS, 1954; Howard Univ, DDS, 1962. **Career:** Underwood Corp, sales rep, 1954; Robert B Cheek DDS PC, pres, 1956-; Am Airlines, sales rep, 1956; pvt prac, currently. **Orgs:** Nat Dental Asn; Acad Gen Dent; Bridgeport Dent Asn; Guardsmen; NAACP. **Military Serv:** USAF, Fighter Wings, 1956; USAF, 2nd lt, 2 yrs. *

CHEEKS, CARL L.
Dentist. **Personal:** Born Jul 7, 1937, Poplar Bluff, MO; married Shirley K Magness; children: Darryl, Shalonda. **Educ:** Fisk Univ Nashville, BA, 1960; Meharry Med Sch, DDS, 1965. **Career:** Pvt pract, dentist, 1967-. **Orgs:** Am Dent Asn; Nat Dent Asn; Northshore Dent Asn; Lincoln Dentl Soc; Am Acad Gen Dent; Relative Analgesia Seminars; Chicago Dent Soc; Nat Asn Advan Colored People; Kappa Alpha Psi Frat; United Community Serv Evanston; Martin Luther King Lab Sch PTA; Black Bus & Prof Asn; Evanston Sch Bd; Fisk Jubilee Singers; Black male stud Naval Acad. **Honors/Awds:** Cert merit, Minority Youth Motivation, 1968-74; Chessman Club Award, Aiding civic prog. **Military Serv:** USN dental & lt 1965-67. **Business Addr:** Dentist, 1626 Darrow Ave, Evanston, IL 60201-3418.*

CHEEKS, DARRYL LAMONT
Auditor, executive. **Personal:** Born Apr 7, 1968, Evanston, IL; son of Carl and Beaulah Brittain. **Educ:** Univ Ill, Champaign, BS, acct, 1990; Harvard Summer Venture Mgt Prog. **Career:** Dent asst, 1978-86; Golden Touch Cleaners, Evanson, IL, owner & mgr, 1987-88; Krispy Kits Karmel Korn, Evanston, IL, owner & mgr, 1988; Arthur Andersen, Chicago, IL, auditor, 1989-93; Abbott Labs, North Chicago, IL, financial & oper consult, 1993-95; Soul Food Prison Ministries, founder & exec dir, 1993-; Hoyt Fastener Co, Niles, IL, controller, 1995-; Chicagoland Barbecue Inc, founder, 1996-; Black Rhino Financial Group, ceo & managing partner, 2006-; Monroe St Church Christ, asst pastor; AXS Solutions, chief financial Officer; Taylor Cheeks & Assoc, co-managing partner. **Orgs:** Dir educ, asst minister, jail ministry dir, trustee, Monroe St Church Christ, 1989-; Nat Asn Black Accountants, 1991-; Ill CPA Soc, 1992-; bd dirs, treas, Reba Place Day Nursery, 1992-; bd dirs, treas, Jan Erkert & Dancers, 1994-. **Honors/Awds:** President's Scholarship Award, Univ Ill, 1986-90; Fred G Carpenter Award, Business, Evanston Township, MS, 1986; Outstanding College Students of America, 1987-90; Mom's Day Scholastic Award, Univ Ill, 1987, 1988, 1990; High Honor Roll, Dean's List, Univ Ill, 1987; Ebony Mag, 1990. **Business Addr:** Managing Partner, Black Rhino Financial Group Inc, 1480 Renaissance Dr Suite 410, Park Ridge, IL 60068, **Business Phone:** (847)268-8440.*

CHEEKS, MAURICE EDWARD
Basketball player, basketball coach. **Personal:** Born Sep 8, 1956, Chicago, IL; married; children: 2. **Educ:** W Tex State Univ, 1978. **Career:** Basketball player (retired), head coach; Philadelphia 76er's, guard, 1978-89; San Antonio Spurs, guard, 1990; NY Knicks, guard, 1990-91; Atlanta Hawks, guard, 1991-93, NJ Nets, guard, 1993; CBA, Quad City Thunder, asst coach; Portland Trail Blazers, head coach, 2001-05; Philadelphia 76ers, head coach, currently. **Honors/Awds:** NBA Championship Award, 1983; NBA, All-Star Game, four times; NBA,All-Defensive, First Team, four times. **Business Addr:** Head Coach, Philadelphia 76ers, 3601 S Broad St, Philadelphia, PA 19148, **Business Phone:** (215)339-7600.

CHENAULT, JOHN
Playwright, poet, labor activist. **Personal:** Born Jan 3, 1952, Cincinnati, OH; married Gwendline Harper, 1976. **Educ:** Union Inst, BFA, 1977; Univ Louisville, grad studies. **Career:** Librettist; poet; playwright; theatrical producer; Poetry: Blue Blackness, 1969; The Invisible Man, 1992; Plays: Blood Ritual, 1971; Warren is Back in the World, 1993; The Buckwheat Book of the Dead, 1995; The X-periment, 1996; Stolen Moments, 1997; Librettos: Ode to A Giant, 1993; Ghost in Machine, 1995; The Buckwheat Book of the Dead, 1995; The X-periment, 1996; Stolen Moments, 1997; Mingus—Live in the Underworld, 1997; More Than Miles, 1997; Yesterday's News, 1999; The Fools of Time, 2000; My Name is Citizen Soldier, 2000; New Theatre/Free Theatre Cincinnati, actor, playwright, producer, stage tech & playwright, 1967-; Black Arts Ensemble, performer, 1968-70; author, 1969-; Univ Cincinnati, instr African & African-Am studies, 1972; Sunship percussion group, founder & performer, 1973; Zamani Band, Wash, DC, founder & performer, 1977; Beacon Col, instr African & African-Am studies, 1977; Wash Int Col, exec dean, 1978-82; Sickle Cell Awareness Group, exec dir, 1986-94; Applause, columnist, 1991-93; Artrage, columnist, 1992-93; WAIF Radio, writer & co-producer, 1993; liberettist, 1993-; TV series: "Young Men Grow Older"; Trane: Beyond the Blues, music designer, 2002; Univ Louisville Libr, staff mem, currently. **Honors/Awds:** Brotherhood Award, Nat Conf Christians & Jews, 1972; nominee, Emmy Award, 1972. **Home Addr:** 1370 S Sixth St Suite 1, Louisville, KY 40208. **Business Addr:** Librettist, 1370 S Sixth St Suite 1, Louisville, KY 40208.*

CHENAULT, KENNETH I.
Chief executive officer, lawyer, consultant. **Personal:** Born Jun 2, 1951, Long Island, NY; son of Hortenius and Anne; married Kathryn; children: 2. **Educ:** Bowdoin Col, BA, hist, 1973; Harvard Law Sch, JD, 1976. **Career:** Firm Rogers & Wells, atty, 1977-79; Bain & Co, mgt consult, 1979-81; Am Express, div head green cards, 1981-89; Consumer Card Group US, pres, 1989; Travel Related Serv, US Div, pres, 1993-95, vice chairman, 1995-97, pres & chief operating officer, 1997-2001; Am Express Co, chief exec officer & chmn, 2001-. **Orgs:** Bd mem, Int Bus Mach. **Honors/Awds:** Robie Award for Achievement in Industry, Jackie Robinson Fed, 1996; Corporate Executive of the Year, Black Enterprise, 1999; Catalyst Award, Am Express, 2001. **Special Achievements:** One of 50 Most Powerful African American Executives in America, Fortune, 2001. **Business Addr:** Chief Executive Officer, Chairman, American Express Company, World Financial Center, 200 Vesey St, New York, NY 10285-5104, **Business Phone:** (212)640-2000.

CHENEVERT, DR. PHILLIP JOSEPH
Physician. **Personal:** Born Feb 15, 1948, Detroit, MI; son of Wendell Sr and Mary Pembroke; married Judith Grandy; children: Belen & Amber. **Educ:** Highland Park Community Col, AA, 1970; NC Central Univ, BS (Cum Laude), 1974; Meharry Med Col, MD, 1978; Children's Hosp Mich, Residency, 1981. **Career:** Pvt Practice, physician, 1981-86; Cigna Health Plan Tex, pediatrics, 1986-; Univ Tex Southwestern Med Ctr, Dallas Fel Develop & Ambulatory Pediatrics, 1988-91; New Bern Develop Eval Ctr, Develop Pediatrician, currently. **Orgs:** Bd dirs AYD Youth Job, 1982-83; chief pediatrics, L Richardson Mem Hosp, 1982-86; med dir, United Way Greensboro NC, 1983-84; bd dirs, Am Diabetes Asn, Greensboro, NC, 1985-86; volunteer Med Instr, Pa Prog, Bowman Gray Sch Med, 1985-86; bd dirs, Arlington Charities, 1986-. **Honors/Awds:** Fel, Nat Inst Health. **Special Achievements:** Outstanding Young Men of America, 1986. **Business Addr:** Developmental Pediatrician, New Bern Developmental Evaluation Center, 1405 S Glenburnie Rd, New Bern, NC 28562, **Business Phone:** (252)514-4770.

CHENEVERT-BRAGG, IRMA J.
Judge. **Personal:** Born Nov 17, 1951, Detroit, MI; daughter of Arthur and Ruth Green; married Sidney Bragg, Sr, Mar 7, 1992; children: Arica Chenevert, Arianna Powers. **Educ:** Eastern Mich Univ, BS, 1973; Detroit Col Law, JD, 1982. **Career:** US Dist Ct, Eastern Dist MI, law clerk, 1982-84; Wayne County Prosecutor's Off, asst prosecuting atty, 1984-85; Joselyn Rowe Etal, atty, 1985-86; Detroit Bd Police,spec proj asst, 1986-87; self-employed, atty, 1986-89; State Mich, law judge, 1986-89; 36th Dist Ct, magistrate, 1989-. **Orgs:** State Bar Mich, 1985-. **Honors/Awds:** Handgun Intervention Prog, HIP Award, 1996; Wolverine Student Bar Asn, Special Alumni Award, 1985. **Business Phone:** (313)965-5220.*

CHENNAULT, DR. MADELYN
Educator. **Personal:** Born Jul 15, 1934, Atlanta, GA; daughter of Benjamin Q and Othello Ann Jones; married Thomas Mark, Jul 14, 1982 (deceased). **Educ:** Morris Brown Col, BS, 1957; Univ Mich, MA, 1961; Ind Univ, PhD; Univ Ga, Post Doctoral Study Clin Psychol; Univ Miss Med Ctr, Post Doctoral Internship. **Career:** Pub Schs Ga CA, Mich, educr, 1957-62; Albany State Col, asst prof Psychol, 1962-64; Ind Univ, res asst, 1964-66; Atlanta Univ, asst prof educ, 1966-67; Ft Valley State Col, assoc prof educ, 1967-70, prof educ,1970-72, prof educ & clinical dir Community Hypertension Intervention Prog, 1972-89; Chennault Enterprise, pres 1974-. **Orgs:** Counsult, Coun Exceptional C Regional Meeting; consul, Atlanta, Ga, 1967; spl educ consult, Grambling Col, 1968; educ psych consult, Univ of Conn,1969; elementary educ consult, Ala A & M Univ, 1969; ment retardation consul, Ga State Dept Educ, 1969-71; sch integration consul, Americus Ga Pub Schs, 1970; spec educ, vis scholar NC Cent Univ, 1971; Nat Sci Found Visit Scientist Ala State Univ, 1971; Head Start consul, Heart Ga Project, 1970-71; spec serv proj consult, Ft Valley State Col, 1971-72; Nat Sci Found Vis Scientist Talledega Col, 1972; main speaker, Alpha Kappa Alpha Sor Founders Day Prog, 1972; spec educ consult & psychometrist, Peach Co Pub Sch, 1972; So Regional Rep Asn Black Psychologists, 1972-74; exec adv comn, Comn-Clinical Psych Project So Reg Educ Bd Atlanta, 1972-75; cont psych, Jackson Hinds Comn Ment Health Ctr, 1973; psych consult, Miss State Univ, 1973; Asn Adv, Behav Therapy; Am Asn Ment Def; Am Asn Univ Profs; Am Psych Asn; Am Res Asn; Ga Psych Asn; Nat Educ Asn; Alpha Kappa Alpha Sor Links Inc. **Special Achievements:** Published numerous articles. *

CHEROT, NICHOLAS MAURICE
Lawyer. **Personal:** Born Jun 30, 1947, Ann Arbor, MI; son of Romeo Augustus and Flora L. **Educ:** Univ MI, BA, 1969; NY Univ Sch Law, JD, 1972. **Career:** Autumn Indust Inc, secy, treas, 1977-; Autumn-Everseal Mfg Co Inc, secy, treas, 1979-; Powell Blvd Holdin Co Inc, dir & partner; Cherot & Michael PC, atty, currently. **Orgs:** Powell Blvd Asn, 1979-; Harlem Lawyers Asn, NY; New York County Lawyers Asn; Nat Bar Asn; Black Allied Law Students Asn. **Business Addr:** Cherot & Michael PC, 305 Broadway Suite 600, New York, NY 10007-1109.

CHERRY, DR. CASSANDRA BRABBLE
School administrator. **Personal:** Born May 29, 1947, Norfolk, VA; married Capt Maurice L (deceased). **Educ:** Bennett Col, BA, 1969; VA State Univ, MEd, 1974; Richard Bland Col, the Col Wilson & Mary, Mgt diploma, 1975; Nova Univ, EdD, 1980. **Career:** School administrator(retired): US Army Quartermaster Sch, educ specialist, 1974; US Army Logistics Ctr, educ specialist, 1974-78; US Army Training Support Ctr, educ specialist, 1978-79; Naval Supply Ctr, employee develop specialist, 1979; Defense Activ Non-Traditional Educ Support, mgr instrnl delivery prog, 1980-03. **Orgs:** Phi Delta Kappa; bd dirs, Minorities in Media, 1982-83; Federally Employed Women; publicity chmn Equal Employ Opportunity Coun Pensacola Naval Complex, 1985, 86; Am Inst Mortgage Brokers; Nat Asn Advan Colored People. **Honors/Awds:** One Woman Art Exhibit, Bennett Col 1969. *

CHERRY, DERON
Football player. **Personal:** Born Sep 12, 1959, Palmyra, NJ; son of George and Lillian; children: 2. **Educ:** Rutgers Univ, BS, 1980. **Career:** Football player (retired), exec; Kans City Chiefs, safety, 1981-91; United Beverage, owner, 1992-;Deron Cherry's All Pro Ford, owner, 1990s; Jacksonville Jaguars, partner, 1993; bd mem, Jackson County Sports Complex Authority, 2006-. **Orgs:** Bd dirs, Kans City Sports Comn. **Honors/Awds:** AFC Defensive Player of the Year, 101 Committee, 1986; Byron White Humanitarian Award, NFL Players Asn, 1988; Sports Hall of Fame of New Jersey, 1996; Missouri Sports Hall of Fame, 2002. **Special Achievements:** Tied NFL record for most interceptions in a game (4) against Seattle Seahawks, 1985; played in Pro-Bowl, 1983-88 seasons; second African Am to attain part ownership in an NFL franchise, 1993. **Business Addr:** Board Member, Jackson County Sports Complex Authority, No 4 Arrowhead Dr, 8501 Stadium Dr, Kansas City, MT 64129, **Business Phone:** (816)921-3600.

CHERRY, EDWARD EARL
Executive. **Personal:** Born Dec 4, 1926, Greenville, NC; son of Jasper and Velma Smith; married Tarah Stanton; married Mary Jean Jordan, May 31, 1987 (deceased); children: Edward Jr & Todd J (deceased). **Educ:** Howard Univ, BArch, 1953. **Career:** Edward Cherry Architect, pres, 1963; Yale Univ Sch Archit, asst prof, 1971, vis critic, 1972-81; Edward E Cherry & Assocs, pres, currently. **Orgs:** Basileus, Chi Omicron Chap, Omega Psi Phi Fraternity, 1957-; corp mem, Conn Soc Architects, AIA, 1960-; founder, bd dir, pres, Greater New Haven Bus Prof Asn, 1964-; worshipful master, Oriental Lodge No 6, F&AM PHA, 1966-68; New Haven Consistory No 7, AASR PHA, 1968-; pres, Heritage Hall Develop Corp, 1980; State Hist Preserv Rev Bd, Conn Hist Comt, 1980-; grand inspector gen, AASR, PHA, Northern Jurisdiction, 1986; archon, Beta Tau Boule, Sigma Pi Phi, 1986; bd dir, Found New Haven Green, 1986-89. **Honors/Awds:** Man of the Year, New Eng States, First Dist, Omega Psi Phi Fraternity, 1979; Grand Basileus Service Award, Omega Psi Phi, 1979; AIA Design Award, Conn Soc Archit, AIA. **Military Serv:** AUS, pvt, 1945-46; Occup Medal, 1946; Victory Medal. **Home Addr:** 22 Pine Ridge Rd, Woodbridge, CT 06525. **Business Addr:** President, Edward E Cherry & Associates, 60 Connolly Pkwy Bldg 15A, Hamden, CT 06514, **Business Phone:** (203)281-1300.

CHERRY, JE'ROD L.
Football player. **Personal:** Born May 30, 1973, Charlotte, NC; married Lisa; children: Jay Martin. **Educ:** Univ Calif, polit sci, 1995, MEd, 2000. **Career:** Football player(retired), New Orleans Saints, defensive back, 1996-99, Philadelphia Eagles, 2000;New Eng Patriots, defensive back, 2001-04. *

CHERRY, LEE OTIS
Executive, research scientist. **Personal:** Born Nov 20, 1944, Oakland, CA; son of Knorvel and Lucy; married Lauran Michelle Waters, Aug 30, 1980; children: Aminah L & Jamilah L. **Educ:** Merritt Comm Col, AA, 1965; San Jose State Univ, BSEE, electronic engineering, 1968; Hazardous Mat Mgt, Univ Calif, cert, 1995; Site Assessment & Remediation, registered environ assessor, CA, 1997. **Career:** African Sci Inst, pres & chief exec officer, 1967-; Int Bus Machines, systems analyst, 1968-69; Pacific Gas & Electric Co, elec engineer, 1969-79, Dept Defense, project mgr, 1979-92, Dept Defense, environmental mgr, 1992-2000; US Trade Rep, Indonesia Country, currently; landmine clearing, tech adv, currently; Int Inst Engineering, exec dir; Northern Calif Coun

Black Prof Engr, co-founder, pres, 2006. **Orgs:** Proprietor, L&L & Assocs Network Marketing, 1980-; Linkages Int, 1993-; Hollywood, Our Town Inc, co-founder, bd dir, 2001-. **Honors/Awds:** Co-founder & vpres, Ghanaian-Am Chamber Comn. **Special Achievements:** Published "Technology Transfer," a monthly magazine 1979-83; co-founder/vp, the Ghanaian-American Chamber of Commerce; Developer of Blacks in Science Calendar annually 1986-97; produced general and technical conferences; performed public speaking; made numerous TV appearances and radio shows; written articles for various newspapers and magazines; Publisher, Sci Tech 1986-1993, nationally distributed newspaper about developments in science and technology; currently enhancing an international network of great achievers in science and technology (ASI Fellows). **Business Addr:** President, Chief Executive Officer, African Science Institute, 527 32nd St, PO Box 12161, Oakland, CA 94609, **Business Phone:** (510)653-7027.

CHERRY, ROBERT LEE
School administrator. **Personal:** Born Feb 17, 1941, Barrackville, WV; married Anna Luckett; children: Mary Elizabeth, Robert Lee & Ebon Michael. **Educ:** Wittenberg Univ, EdB, 1964; Wright State Univ, EdM, 1973. **Career:** Educator (retired); Int Harvester Co, supvr, 1964; Wittenberg Univ, Upward Bound Prog, prog dir, 1968; Clark Tech Col, admis officer, 1973; Springfield Ohio, city commnr, 1974; DMVC-EDNL Opportunity Ctr, exec dir, 1975; Clark Tech Col, dir student serv, 1975. **Orgs:** Past mem & pres, Ohio Asn Upward Bound Dir, 1970; bd mem, OpportunitiesIndustrialization Ctr, 1974; cert com mem, Ohio Asn Student Financial AidAdminstr, 1974; Ohio Asn Student Serv Dir, 1977; chmn, Clark Co 648 MentalHealth & Retardation Bd, 1975; bd mem, Clark State Community Col,2007-08. **Honors/Awds:** Community Merit Award, Springfield Frontiers Int, 1962; Outstanding Young-Men, Am OYMA, 1970; Community Service Award, St John Baptist Church, 1980. **Home Addr:** 303 W Perrin Ave, Springfield, OH 45506. *

CHESS, EVA
Executive. **Personal:** Born Feb 6, 1960, High Point, NC; daughter of Hon and Sammie Jr. **Educ:** Univ NC, Chapel Hill, BA, 1982; Univ Va, JD, 1985. **Career:** JP Morgan & Co, Inc, private banker, 1985-91; Sara Lee Corp, sr mgr, pub responsibility; RR Donnelley Found, vpres external affairs, currently. **Orgs:** Bd dirs, United Way of Stamford, CT; officer, bd dirs, Coalition 100 Black Women Lower Fairfield County; Bus Policy Rev Coun; Urban Bankers Coalition; Am & Va Bar Asns; bd dirs, Chicago Cosmopolitan Chamber Com; Deacon, Chicago United; corp adv comt., Ctr Women Policy Studies; corp adv coun, League of Women Voters; bd dirs, Am Asn of Univ Women Educ Found; bd dirs, Midwest Women's Center. **Honors/Awds:** America's Best & Brightest, Dollars & Sense Mag, 1993. **Business Phone:** (312)326-7129.

CHESTANG, DR. LEON WILBERT
Educator. **Personal:** Born May 16, 1937, Mobile, AL; married Aurelia C Taylor; children: Nicole & Yvette. **Educ:** Blackburn Col, BA 1959; Wash Univ, MSW 1961; Univ Chicago, PhD 1977. **Career:** Ill Dept C & Family Serv, supvr 1961-65; Ill Dept Pub Aid, social casework instr, 1967-68; Family Care Chicago, dir casework serv, 1968-71; Univ Chicago, asst prof, 1971-78; Univ Ala, prof, 1978-81; Wayne State Univ, dean prof, 1981, distinguished prof, 2000-04, distinguished prof emer, 2005-; VA Univ Commonwealth, distinguished commonwealth prof, 1984-86; Smith Col, distinguished Lydia Rapport prof, 1985. **Orgs:** Bd mem, Childrens Aid Soc Detroit, 1984-; bd mem, Detroit Urban League, 1985-; bd mem, Nat Asn Social Workers, 1985-88. **Honors/Awds:** ACE Fellow 1979; Distinguished Service Award, Mich Asn Sch Social Workers, 1986; Silver Antelope Award, Boy Scouts Am, 1996; Black Achievers Award, YMCA, 1997; William H Cosby Jr & Camille 0 Hanks Cosby Visiting Scholar, Howard Univ. **Home Addr:** 682 Pallister St, Detroit, MI 48202. **Business Addr:** Distinguished Professor Emeritus, Wayne State University, School of Social Work, 5050 Anthony Wayne Dr, Detroit, MI 48202.

CHESTER, LARRY
Football player. **Personal:** Born Oct 17, 1975, Hammond, LA. **Educ:** Temple univ. **Career:** Football player (retired), Indianapolis Colts, defensive tackle, 1998-00; Carolina Panthers, 2001; Miami Dolphins, defensive tackle, 2002-04. **Honors/Awds:** Second-team All-Big East, 1997. *

CHESTNUT, DR. DENNIS EARL
Educator, psychologist. **Personal:** Born May 17, 1947, Green Sea, SC. **Educ:** E Carolina Univ, BA, Psychol & Soc, 1969, MA, Clin Psychol, 1971; Univ Utah, Doc Prog Clin Psychol, 1974; NY Univ, PhD (comm psychol), 1982. **Career:** NIMH fel, Univ Utah, 1971-74; Camden Co MH Ctr, psychol consult, 1974-75; Neuse Ment Health Ctr, qual assurance consult, 1975-77; NIMH fel, NY Univ, 1978; Medgar Evers Col City Univ NY, instr psychol, 1979-81; E Carolina Univ, asst prof psychol, 1974, prof, currently. **Orgs:** Pres, Young People's Holiness Asn, United Pentecostal Holiness Churches AmInc; Alpha Phi Alpha Frat; Nat treas, Asn Black Psychologists, 1983-84; original liaison, Asn Humanistic Psychol, 1983-84; s regional rep, Asn Black Psychologists, 1984-85; mem at large bd dirs, Asn Humanistic Psychol, 1984-85; reg rep, NC Group Behavior Soc, 1981-; vice bishop, United Pentecostal Holiness Churches Am, 1981-; pastor, Mt Olive Holiness Church Tabor City NC, 1984-; treas, NC Asn Black Psychologists; Pitt Ment Health Asn; pres, NC Chap Asn Black Psychologists, 1986-87; dir, Minority Affairs Asn Humanistic Psychol, 1986-; co-chmn, Nat Black Family Task Force Asn Black Psychologists; Lifelong resident of Ward 7; mem, Neighborhood/ Environmental activist. **Honors/Awds:** Outstanding Sr Dept Sociol, E Carolina Univ, 1969; NEH Summer Stipend study Southern Black Cult, 1982. **Home Addr:** 1801 E 5th St, Greenville, NC 27858. **Business Addr:** Professor, East Carolina University, Department of Psychology, Rawl 239, Greenville, NC 27858-4353, **Business Phone:** (252)328-6308.

CHESTNUT, MORRIS L.
Actor. **Personal:** Born Jan 1, 1969, Cerritos, CA; married Pam Byse (divorced). **Educ:** Univ Calif, Northridge, finance & drama. **Career:** Films : Boyz 'N the Hood, 1991; Under Seige 2, 1995; GI Jane, 1997; The Best Man, 1999; The Brothers, 2001; Two Can Play That Game, 2001; Scenes of a Crime, 2001; Like Mike, 2002; Half Past Dead, 2002; Confidence, 2003; Ladder 49, 2004; Breakin' All the Rules, 2004; Anacondas: The Hunt for the Blood Orchid, 2004; The Cave, 2005; The Game Plan, 2007; The Perfect Holiday, 2007; Prince of Pistols, 2008; Not Easily Broken, 2009; TV credits: In the Line of Duty: Street War, 1992, The Ernest Green Story, 1992; Out All Night, 1992; Firehouse, 1997; The Killing Yard, 2001; "Black stage", Exec producer, 2007. **Honors/Awds:** Annual Madden Bowl, 1998; NAACP Image Award nomination. **Business Phone:** (310)288-4545.*

CHEW, BETTYE L.
College administrator. **Personal:** Born Dec 10, 1940; children: Gordon W, Cheryl L & Donna V. **Educ:** Rosenwald Community Jr Col, attended 1959; Cortez W Peters Bus Sch, attended 1964; Bowie St Col. **Career:** Annapolis Urban Renewal & Program, secy, 1967-69; Univ Md Cooperative Extension Serv, Annapolis MD, secy, 1969-72; Bowie St Col, Bowie Md, Office Dean, secy, 1972-. **Orgs:** Nat Asn Advan Colored People; reg rep, Annapolis Sr HS Citizens Adv Comt, 1974-; sunday sch teacher, First Baptist Church, 1964-; Offender Aid & Restoration Counr, Anne Arundel Co Detention Ctr; chmn, Citizen Adv Comt, Annapolis Sr HS, 1976-77; mem, Human Rel Comt Annapolis Sr HS, 1977; proj coordr, Am Issues Forum Prog, Bowie St Col, 1976; leader Girl Scout Troop 43, 1974-. **Honors/Awds:** Certificate for serv Nat Asn Advan Colored People, 1974; employee of month Award, Bowie St Col, 1974; 5 yr serv Award, Bowie St Col, 1975. **Business Addr:** College Administrator, Bowie State College, Office Of Dean, 14000 Jerico Park Rd, Bowie, MD 20715-6943.

CHEW, CHERYL
Executive. **Career:** Nat Black MBA Asn Inc, dir, currently. **Business Addr:** Director, National Black MBA Association Inc, Corp Partner Develop, 180 N Mich Ave Suite 1515, Chicago, IL 60601, **Business Phone:** (312)236-2622.

CHEW, VIVIAN SCOTT
Executive, founder (originator). **Personal:** Married Ray Chew; children: Loren, Bianca. **Career:** Kashif, personal asst; Louise C W Esq, exec asst; Polygram Records, dir artist & repertoire, 1987-89; Sony Music Entertainment, dir artist & repertoire, Epic Rec, 1990; Epic Records, vpres artist & repertoire, 1992; Urban Music Dept, Epic Records, vpres, 1993; Urban Music Dept, head, 550 Music & Sony, Epic Records, head artist repertoire & urban music, 1996-97; Time Zone Intl, prin & founder, 1997-. **Orgs:** founder, Juvenile Diabetes Found Music Indust Dinner; Am Soc Composers, Auth & Publs; bd mem, Black Rock Coalition; bd mem, Winston Prepatory Sch; co-founder, Chew Entertainment. **Business Addr:** Founder, Principal, Time Zone International, P O box 412 teaneck, **Business Phone:** (201)928-1999.*

CHICAGO, DENOVIOUS ADOLPHUS (D ADOLPHUS RIVERS)
Judge. **Personal:** Born Feb 2, 1928, Chicago, IL; son of Irene and Denovious; married Loretta Faulkner (deceased); children: Donald Adolphus. **Educ:** Wilson Jr Col, cert, 1948; John Marshall Law Sch, JD 1951. **Career:** Judge (retired); Ill Supreme Ct, admitted Ill Bar, 1951; US Dist Ct, Northern Dist Ill, admitted, 1958; US Dist Ct, Northern Dist Ind, admitted, 1960; State Ill, licensed real estate broker, 1971-; Circuit Ct Cook Co, assoc judge, 1983-85; US Supreme Ct, admitted, 1991; Parentage Courts, supv judge, 1991-94; Forciable Entry & Detainer Courts, supv judge, 1994-96; Circuit Ct, Cook Co, judge, 1983-95. **Orgs:** Cook County Bar Asn, 1951-; Nat Bar Asn, 1954-; Chicago Bar Asn, 1968-; Ill State Bar Asn, 1982-; Ill Judges Asn, 1983-; Ill Judicial Coun, 1983-; asst sec 1984, secy, 1985, chair-elect, 1991-92, chairperson, 1992-93, exec comt, 1993-95; trustee, Abraham Lincoln Ctr, secy & chmn By-Laws, 1968-84; treas, St Bartholomew Episcopal Church, 1970-76; Messiah-St Bartholomew Episcopal Church, 1976-; treas, Omega Psi Phi Frat, Iota Chap 1948-; gov bd, treas, vpres, pres: The Chicago Assembly, 1959-; Chicago Steering Comt, Nat Asn Advan Colored People Legal Def & Ed Fund 1967-84; The Druids Club 1984-; bd mem, Harvard St George Sch 1971-80. **Honors/Awds:** FBI Commendation, 1971; Meritorious Service Award, Big Buddies Youth Serv Inc, 1972; Hall of Fame, Nat Bar Asn, 1991; Judicial Award Cook Co Bar Asn, 1984; Outstanding Service Award, Phoenix Park Dist, 1984; Distinguished Service Award, Ill Judicial Coun, 1993, Kenneth E Wilson Memorial Award, 1996, Judicial Career Service Award, 1997. **Military Serv:** Ill Nat Guard, Infantry 1st lt 20 yrs. **Home Addr:** 6947 Cregier Ave, Chicago, IL 60649.

CHICOYE, ETZER
Research administrator. **Personal:** Born Nov 4, 1926, Jacmel, Haiti; son of Appoline Briffault and Rigaud; married Dolores Bruce; children: Lorena & Rigaud. **Educ:** Univ Haiti Port Au Prince, BS, 1948; Univ Wis Madison, MS, 1954, PhD 1968. **Career:** Research administrator (retired); Chicago Pharmacol, chemist qual control, 1955-57; Julian Labs, prod chemist, 1957-62, chemist res & develop, 1962-64; Miller Brewing Co, chem res supvr, 1968-72, mgr res, 1972-77, dir res & develop, 1977-92. **Orgs:** YMCA; Am Chem Soc; Am Soc Brewing Chemists. **Honors/Awds:** Black Achiever Harlem, YMCA, 1979; Philip Morris Silver Ring; Local Section Award, Am Chem Soc; Milwaukee Section Award, Am Chem Soc, 1993. **Special Achievements:** Several technical publications and 18 patents dealing with steroid chemistry, food and brewing tech. **Home Addr:** 1259 SW 172nd Terr, Pembroke Pines, FL 33029.

CHIDEYA, FARAI
Writer, journalist. **Personal:** Born in Baltimore, MD; daughter of Lucas and Cynthia. **Educ:** Harvard Univ, BA, magna cum laude, 1990. **Career:** Newsweek, researcher & reporter, 1990-93; Wash bur, reporter, 1993-94; MTV News, assignment ed, 1994-96; Freedom Forum Media Studies Ctr, fel, 1996; CNN, polit analyst, 1996-97; ABC News, corresp, 1997-99; "Pure Oxygen," Oxygen Media, host, 1999-; Los Angeles Times Syndicate, syndicated columnist, 2000-; Knight Fel Stanford Univ, 2001-02; PopandPolitics.com, founder; NPR's News & Notes, currently; Author: Don't Believe the Hype, Plume/Penguin, 1995; The Color of Our Future, William Morrow, 1999; Trust, Soft Skull Press, 2004. **Orgs:** Nat Asn Black Journalists, 1992-; bd mem, Pop & Politics, currently; Jour Adv Comn, Knight Found, currently. **Honors/Awds:** Nat Education Reporting Award, 1992; Ed Press Award, 1992; NABJ Unity Award, 1994; Glaad Media Award, GLAAD, 1994; WIN Young Women of Achievement Award; named as Dream Team, 1996; named to Newsweek's Century Club, 1997; MOBE IT Innovator Award; Young Lion Award, Black Entertainment & Telecommunications Asn, 2004. **Special Achievements:** Named one of Alternet's New Media Heroes; ranked in PoliticsOnline.com's worldwide survey of 25 Who Are Changing the World of Internet and Politics; Published articles in newspapers and magazines including The New York Times, The Los Angeles Times Magazine, Time, Spin, Vibe, O, The California Journal, Mademoiselle, and Essence.

CHIGBU, GIBSON CHUKS
President (Organization), executive. **Personal:** Born Sep 21, 1956, Aba, Nigeria; son of Jason N and Rhoda N Amadi; married Florence Ihekwoaba Chigbu, Sep 13, 1986; children: Gibson Jr, Krystal, Jasmine & Michael. **Educ:** Southern Univ, Baton Rouge, LA, BS, archit, 1981, MS, arts, 1982. **Career:** Hunt-Thurman & Assocs, Baton Rouge, LA, draftman, 1979-81; Barber & Johnson Engrs, Baton Rouge, LA, designer, 1981-82; Hewitt-Wash Archits, New Orleans, LA, project archit, 1982-85; Gee Cee Group Inc, New Orleans, LA, owner & pres, 1985-. **Orgs:** Pres, Asn Nigerians New Orleans, 1985, 1986; provost, Orgn Nigerian Profs-USA, 1986-87; chmn, Construct Comt, Black Econ Develop Coun, 1991; nat pres, Orgn Nigerian Profs, USA Inc, 1992-; nat bd dirs, Nat Bus League, 1996-; nat pres, Nkwerre Aborigine's Union, USA, elected Dallas, TX, 1996; bd mem, Urban League Greater New Orleans; pres, La Contractors Asn; bd mem, Specialty Bus & Indust Develop Corp; pres bd, New Orleans Tech Initiative Contractor Emergence. **Honors/Awds:** Certificate of Recognition, US Dept Com, 1989-90. **Business Addr:** President, Owner, Gee Cee Group Inc, 13020 Carrere Ct Suite 109, PO Box 29544, New Orleans, LA 70189-0544, **Business Phone:** (504)254-1212.

CHILDRESS, RANDOLPH
Basketball player. **Personal:** Born Sep 21, 1972, Washington, DC; married Jenai; children: Brandon & Devin. **Educ:** Wake Forest Univ. **Career:** Portland Trailblazers, 1995-96; Detroit Pistons, 1996-97; Tofas Bursa, Turquie, 1997-98; Kombassan Konya, Turquie, 1998-99; Cholet Basket, France, 1999-2000; Record Naples, Italy, 2000-01; Sydney Kings, Australia, 2000-01; Rida Scafati, Italy, 2001-03; SLUC Nancy, France, 2003-04; Premiata Montegranaro, Italy, 2004; Pallacanestro Varese, Italy, currently. **Honors/Awds:** ACC Male Athlete of the Year, 1995.Portland Trailblazers, 1995-96; Detroit Pistons, 1996-97; Tofas Bursa, Turquie, 1997-98; Kombassan Konya, Turquie, 1998-99; Cholet Basket, France, 1999-2000; Record Naples, Italy, 2000-01; Sydney Kings, Australia, 2000-01; Rida Scafati, Italy, 2001-03; SLUC Nancy, France, 2003-04; Premiata Montegranaro, Italy, 2004; Pallacanestro Varese, Italy, currently. **Business Addr:** Basketball Player, Pallacanestro Varese, Viale Sanvito Silvestro 80, 21100 Varese, Italy, **Business Phone:** (390)33224-0990.*

CHILDS, CHRIS
Basketball player. **Personal:** Born Nov 20, 1967, Bakersfield, CA; son of James Childs; married Maisha McGee; children: 1; married

Karla (divorced); children: Jesse, Jenne & Jade. **Educ:** Boise State Univ, attended 1989. **Career:** CBA: Columbus Horizon, 1989-90, 1990-91; Rapid City Thrillers, 1989-90; La Crosse Catbirds, 1990-91; Rockford Lightning, 1990-91, 1991-92; Bakersfield Jammers, 1991-92; Quad City Thunder, 1992-93, 1993-94; US Basketball League: Miami Tropics, 1993, 1994; NBA: NJ Nets, guard, 1994-96, 2002-03; NY Knicks, 1996-2001; Toronto Raptors, 2000-02. **Honors/Awds:** Most Valuable Player, CBA, 1994; MetLife Community Assist Award, 1998, 2000; Good Guy Award, NY Press Photographers Assn, 2000. **Special Achievements:** CBA, Championship, 1994.

CHILDS, DR. FRANCINE C.
Educator. **Personal:** Born in Wellington, TX; children: Jimmy Fenley. **Educ:** Paul Quinn Col, BS, 1962; E Tex State Univ, MEd, 1970, EdD, 1975;Jacksonville Theological Seminary, PhD, 1996. **Career:** Wiley Col, dean studs, 1970-72; E Tex State Univ, proj dir spec servs, 1972-74; Ohio Univ, prof afro-am studies, 1974-85, chmn, afro-am studies, 1984-89, prof afro-am studies, 1985-2007, prof emer afro-am studies, 2007-. **Orgs:** Local pres & adv, Ohio Univ Chap NAACP, 1971-; League Women Voters, 1977-; educ chair, Ohio Conf Br NAACP, 1978-; nat coord, Booker T Wash Alumni Asn, 1982-; prayer coord, Athens Christian Women Club, 1984-86; workshop leader, Ohio Bapt Women Auxillary Conv, 1985-; local conf host & prog comm, Nat Coun Black Studies, 1987; Nat Alliance Black Sch Educ; assoc pastor, Mt Zion Baptist Ch, currently. **Honors/Awds:** Outstanding Alumni, Paul Quin Col, 1982; Individual Witness for Peace & Justice Award, 1985; OU Higher Education Management Development Prog, 1985-86; Outstanding Black Alumni Award, 1986; Peace Corp Black Educator of Year, 1988-89; Anna Cooper Presidential Award, 1992; Phenomenal Woman Award, 1996; Marcus Foster Distinguished Educators Award, 1996; Ohio University Honorary Alumni Award, 1997. **Special Achievements:** Author: A National Analysis of Problems Encountered by the Socially Disadvantaged in the Family, An Educational Sociology? Monogram of East Texas State University Commerce, TX; "Quality Education Can It Be Achieved? Journal of Ethnic and Special Studies; "Black Women's Role in Bringing About Educational Change? Journal of Confrontation; and "Americaat the Crossroads? the Ohio University Post. **Business Addr:** Professor, Ohio University, 314 Lindley hall, Athens, OH 45701, **Business Phone:** (740)593-1307.

CHILDS, JOSIE L.
Government official. **Personal:** Born in Clarksdale, MS; married James M Childs Sr, May 24, 1969 (deceased). **Career:** City Chicago, dir planning, 1989-, Dept Cult Affairs, currently. **Orgs:** Bd mem, Friend Chicago Pub Libr; bd mem, Know Your Chicago; Univ Chicago; Vivian Harsh Soc, 2003. **Honors/Awds:** Pride Award, outstanding contributions to Image & Pride Black Womanhood, 1985; Unsung Hero Award, Congional Black Caucus, 2002; Vivian Harsh Society Award, Outstanding contributions to African-Amn Music, 2003. **Home Addr:** 6935 S Crandon Ave Apt 2D, Chicago, IL 60649. **Business Phone:** (312)744-6630.

CHILDS, JOY
Lawyer. **Personal:** Born Apr 10, 1951, Wilmington, NC; daughter of Joseph and Mable. **Educ:** Univ Calif, Los Angeles, BA, 1973, MA, 1975; Georgetown Univ Law Ctr, JD, 1981. **Career:** Screen Actors Guild, contract admin, 1981-83; Atlantic Richfield Co Legal Dept, paralegal, 1983-84; Peace Officers Res Asn CA, labor rels rep, 1984-86; CA State Univ, employee rels admin, 1986-90; Hughes Aircraft Co, sr labor rels consult, 1990-94; Warner Bros, Employee Rels, mgr; Dunn-Edwards Corp, dir human resources, currently. **Orgs:** KCET Comm Adv Bd, 1984-, Univ Calif, Los Angeles, Black Alumni Asn 1985-, Black Labor Attys LA, 1985-, Black Entertainment & Sports Lawyers Asn, 1986-; Women Color, 1987-; chair, Donor Recruitment Devel Comt, Dunn-Edwards Corp; Am Red Cross Serv. **Home Addr:** 620 W Hyde Pk Blvd Suite 121, Inglewood, CA 90302. **Business Phone:** (323)771-3330.

CHILDS, OLIVER BERNARD
Association executive, educator. **Personal:** Born Jan 15, 1933, Philadelphia, PA; son of Edmond A Childs Sr and Ogetta Faust Childs; married Dorothy Collins, Feb 7, 1953; children: Renee Olivia, Oliver Jr & Sean Vincent. **Educ:** Cheyney State Teachers Col, Cheyney, PA, BS, 1958; Univ Utah, Salt Lake City, UT, MS, 1980. **Career:** Philadelphia Bd Educ, Philadelphia, PA, teacher, 1958-65; Opportunities Industrialization Ctrs, Philadelphia, PA, dir training, 1965-66, Los Angeles, CA, exec dir, 1966-68; OIC Inst, Philadelphia, PA, asst dir ext serv, 1968-71; OIC Am, Dallas TX, regional dir, 1971-74, dir fund develop, 1974-83; OIC Int, Philadelphia, PA, dir resource develop, 1984-; Univ Md, Eastern Shore, asst prof, 1990-94, Hotel & Restaurant Mgt, asst prof & actg chmn, currently; Richard A Henson Conf Ctr, dir, currently. **Orgs:** Kappa Alpha Psi Fraternity, 1956-, Nat Soc Fund Raising Exec, 1976-; Nat Asn Advan Colored People, 1978-; chmn, Troop Comt, Boy Scouts Am, 1980-; bd mem, Independent Charities Am, 1989-; Minority Adv Comt, Philadelphia Visitors & Convention Bur, 1989-; pres, bd dirs, Nat Coalition Black Mgt Planners, 1989. **Honors/Awds:** Mayoralty Awards, Los Angeles, CA, 1968, New Orleans, LA, 1972, Lubbock, TX, 1972; Professional Pioneer Award, Nat Coalition Black Mgt Planners, 2000. **Military Serv:** AUS, corporal, 1952-54. **Business Addr:** Assistant Professor, Acting Chair, University Maryland Eastern Shore, Department of Hotel & Restaurant Management, 1 Backbone Rd, Princess Anne, MD 21853, **Business Phone:** (410)651-6563.

CHILDS, WINSTON
Lawyer, executive, chief executive officer. **Personal:** Born Feb 14, 1931, Savannah, GA; son of Inez Childs Scoggins; children: Evan, Julie & Stephanie. **Educ:** Am Univ, BA, 1957, JD, 1959. **Career:** Booker T Washington Found, spec coun; Minority Consult & Urbanologists, nat asn; GEOC, CIO Labor Union, pres; stock broker; pvt law pract; DC Republican Cent Comn, gen coun; Nat Bus League, gen coun; Graham Bldg Assocs, Real Estate Develop Co, pres; Am Univ Law Sch, adj prof; MSI Serv Inc, syst engr & mgt consult, Wash DC, founder, chmn, Chief Exec Officer. **Orgs:** DC Bar Asn; Am Mgt Asn; Armed Forces Commun & Electronics Asn; Republican Senatorial Inner Circle; DC Metrop Boys Girls Club; bd mem, Georgetown Symphony Orchestra; John Sherman Myers Soc.

CHISHOLM, JOSEPH CARREL, JR.
Physician. **Personal:** Born May 16, 1935, Detroit, MI; son of Joseph and Maizie Jones; married Maurita, Nov 6, 1965; children: John, Lynn, Kim, Kelly. **Educ:** Univ Chicago, BS, 1958, MS, 1960; Meharry Med Col, MD, 1962. **Career:** Va Hosp, Wash DC, consult, 1968-77; US Dept State, consult, 1970-; DC Soc Internal Med, mem exec bd, 1972-80; DC VNA, mem exec bd, 1982-; Am Col Physicians, Wash DC, governor's bd, 1984-; physician. **Orgs:** Alpha Phi Alpha, 1957; Alpha Omega Alpha Honor Soc, 1960-; Am Lung Asn, 1970-; Am Heart Asn, 1970; DC Soc Internal Med, 1970; NY Acad Sci, 1975-; Nat Asn Advan Colored People, 1978-; Southern Med Soc, 1980-; Nat Med Asn; DC Thoracic Soc; DC Heart Asn; DC Med Soc; Sigma Pi Phi Frat, 1986-; Viceroys, 1990-. **Honors/Awds:** Order of the C Univ Chicago 1954-; Rockefeller Research School Allergy Immunology, 1959-61; Pulmonary Research School, NIH, 1965-66; Fel Am Col Physicians, 1970-; Pigskinners of Washington DC 1980-. **Military Serv:** USN, comdr, 1962-68; Korean Service Medal; Vietnam Service Medal, 1966-68. **Business Addr:** Physician, 106 Irving St NW Suite 2000, Washington, DC 20010.*

CHISHOLM, JUNE FAYE
Clinical psychologist, educator. **Personal:** Born Apr 29, 1949, New York, NY; daughter of Wallace and Luretta Brawley. **Educ:** Syracuse Univ, BA, Psych, 1971; Univ Mass, MS, psychol, 1974, PhD, psychol, 1978. **Career:** NY Univ Med Ctr, intern psychol, 1975-77, dept Psychiat, adj prof, 1984-; pvt pract, Manhattan, 1980; Harlem Hosp, sr psychologist, 1982-; Pace Univ, asst prof, 1986-. **Orgs:** NY Asn Black Psychol, 1977-; Am Psychol Asn, 1979-; NY Soc Clinical Psychologists, 1980-; NY State Psycholl Asn, 1980; EPA 1988-. **Honors/Awds:** Teaching fellow, NY Univ Med Ctr, 1976-77. **Business Addr:** Professor, Pace University, Psychology Department, 13th fl 41 Park Row, New York, NY 10038.*

CHISHOLM, DR. REGINALD CONSTANTINE
Educator, physician. **Personal:** Born Oct 13, 1934, Jamaica, WI; married Cecilin Coy. **Educ:** Howard Univ, BS, 1962, MD, 1966. **Career:** Freedmens Hosp, intern, 1966-67, residency internal med, 1967-70; Shaw Comm Health clin, internist, 1970-71; Howard Univ, chief med oncol; Nat Cancer Inst-Va, oncol Serv, WA, fel clin assoc, 1971-73; Cancer Screening & Detection clin, chief, 1977; Howard Univ, assoc dir, 1977; Howard Univ Cancer Ctr, physician, currently. **Orgs:** Post-grad fel, 1971-73; DC Med Soc; Wash Soc Oncol; Nat Cancer Inst, Nat Med Asn. **Honors/Awds:** Recommended for Student Teaching Award, 1990; H.U Oncology Fellows Teaching Award, 2005. **Special Achievements:** Publ, "Hypercalcitonemig Cancer of the Breast", Nat Med Asn, 1975. **Business Addr:** Physician, Howard University Cancer Center, 2041 Georgia Ave NW Suite 5100, Washington, DC 20060.*

CHISHOLM, SAMUEL JACKSON
Advertising executive. **Personal:** Born May 15, 1942, Philadelphia, PA; son of Thomas J and May L Jackson; married Thelester McGinns, May 13, 1979; children: Heather & Jason. **Educ:** Va State Univ, Petersburg, VA, BS, bus admin & acct, 1965, NY Univ, grad studies. **Career:** Corn Products Corp, New York, NY, claims adjuster, 1965-66; Phelps Dodge, NY, jr acct, 1967; Benton & Bowles, NY, media planner, 1967-69; Jack Tinker & Partner, NY, asst media dir, 1969; Continental Can Co, NY, adv dir, 1969-74; Malk Co & Uniworld Group Inc, NY, acct supv, 1974-80, Chisholm-Mingo Group, NY, vpres & mgt supvr, 1980-84, sr vpres & dir clients, 1984-86, exec vpres & gen mgr, 1986-88, pres, 1988-90, chief exec officer, 1990-, chmn, currently. **Orgs:** Advert Coun, Kappa Alpha Psi Fraternity; bd mem, Conn Comn Regional Planning Asn; Traffic Audit Bur; NY Bd Govs 4/a's; Worldwide Partners; Ad Hall Fame Coun Judges; Urban League 4/a's SW Conn. **Honors/Awds:** Nat Bus & Prof Men & Women, Dollars & Sense, 1990; Kappa Alpha Psi Community Award, 1990; Outstanding Minority Bus Award, Nat Minority Bus Coun Inc, 2000; Entrepreneur of the Year, Ernst & Young, 2001. **Military Serv:** AUS, spc 4, 1966-75; National Guard. **Business Addr:** Chief Executive Officer, Chairman, The Chisholm-Mingo Group Inc, 228 E 45th St, New York, NY 10017, **Business Phone:** (212)697-4515.

CHISM, HAROLYN B.
Financial manager. **Personal:** Born Jan 4, 1941, Columbia, SC; divorced; children: John Patrick & Sharon Elizabeth. **Educ:** Benedict Col, BS, 1967. **Career:** Gen Accounting Office, clk typist, 1962-63; Fed Power Comn, clk typist, 1963-64; IRS, sec, 1964-65; USDA-Off Mgt Serv, budget analyst, 1967-72; USDA-Animal & Plant Health Insptn Serv & Food Safety & Quality Serv, supr budget analyst, 1972-78; US Dept Commerce Minority Bus Develop Agency, budget officer, 1978. **Orgs:** Am Asn Budget & Prog Analyst, 1980; secy, Boy Scouts Am T351, 1973-75; EEO counr, USDA APHIS & FSQS, 1974-78; bd mem, USDA Credit Union, 1977-78. **Honors/Awds:** Incentive award, Fed Power Comn, 1964; cert of merit USDA & APHIS, 1975; cert merit USDA & FSQS, 1978.

CHISUM, GLORIA TWINE
Psychologist. **Personal:** Born May 17, 1930, Muskogee, OK; daughter of Chauncey Depew (deceased) and Nadine (deceased); married Melvin Jackson. **Educ:** Howard Univ, BS, 1951, MS, 1953; Univ Pa, PhD, 1960. **Career:** Univ Pa, lectr psychol, 1958-68; Naval Air Develop Ctr, res psychol, 1960-65, head vision lab, 1965-80, head environ physiol res team, 1980-90; Free Lib Philadelphia, emer, currently. **Orgs:** Trustee, 1974-00, vice chair, 1990-00, Univ PA; trustee, Philadelphia Saving Fund Soc, 1977-85; dir, Fischer & Porter Co, 1978-94; bd mem, Arthritis Found of E PA, 1972-80; bd mem, World Affairs Coun Philadelphia, 1977-80, Philadelphia Orchestra Asn, 1979-85; dir, Meritor Fin Group, 1985-92; bd mem, 1979-93, chmn, bd trustees, 1990-93. **Honors/Awds:** Raymond F Longacre Award, Aerospace Med Asn, 1979; Distinguished Daughter Pa, 1983; Okla Hall of Fame, 1984. **Special Achievements:** First black chairman, bd trustees, Free Libr Philadelphia. **Business Addr:** Emeriti, Free Library of Philadelphia, 1901 Vine St, Philadelphia, PA 19103, **Business Phone:** (215)686-5322.

CHIVERS, GWENDOLYN ANN
Pharmacist, educator. **Personal:** Born Jun 30, 1946, Sturgis, KY; daughter of Herman and Lillian McGee; married Richard, Oct 10, 1972. **Educ:** Kellogg Community Col, assoc degree, 1968; Univ MI, BS, 1972; Century Univ, MBA, health care mgt, 1993. **Career:** Catherine McAuley Hosp, pharmacist, 1983-85; Perry Drugs, pharmacist, 1988-89; Univ Mich, pharmacist, 1972-76, asst chief pharmacist, 1976-83, chief pharmacist & adj clin instr, 1983-, INterium admin Lead PT, x-ray, lab, 2001-02. **Orgs:** Univ MI Health Serv, administration comn, 1994-; bd dirs, Am Soc Pharmacy Law, 1994-96; State MI Health Occupations Coun, 1991-93; Univ MI Pharmacy Alumni Bd Governors, 1992-94; Am Pharmaceutical Asn, 1985-; MI Pharmacists Asn, 1993-; Am Col Health Asn; Am Soc Pharm Law Bd Dirs. **Honors/Awds:** Ten Leaders in Pharmacy Award, Univ M Col Pharmacy. **Special Achievements:** Appointed by Governor of MI to State Health Occupations Council; Selected to represent US Pharmacists at a Women in Pharmacy Leadership Symposium in Europe. **Business Addr:** Adjunct Clinical Instructor, chief pharmacist, University Michigan, College Pharmacy, 428 Church St, Ann Arbor, MI 48109-1065, **Business Phone:** (734)764-7312.*

CHIVIS, MARTIN LEWIS
Banker, financial manager. **Personal:** Born Oct 5, 1952, Washington, DC; son of Samuel Lewis and Odesa Penn. **Educ:** Drexel Univ, BS, 1976; Am Inst Banking, graduated, 1983; Stonier Grad Sch Banking, attended 1988. **Career:** NASA, aide, 1969-70; Comptroller of the Currency, fel, 1971-72; KPMG pre pro intern 1973-74; Covington & Burling, Col co-op, 1975-76; continental Bank, exec trainee, 1976-89; Industrial Bank, funds mgr, 1977-97; consult, currently. **Orgs:** NABA, NBMBA, BDPA; bd mem, Urban Bankers; Concerned Black Men, 21st Century PAC; jr deacon, 12th St Christian Church; BPRS; NAMB; WABJ; PGBOT; PGCC; DCCC; HR-57; Savoy Thursday Club; NBCC. **Honors/Awds:** Most Outstanding Employee, OCC, 1971; Outstanding Prof Bus Exchange Network Inc, 1987; Outstanding Prof, Urban Bankers Asn, 1990; Loyalty Award, BHRN, 2000. **Business Addr:** Financial Consultant, 328 36th St NE, Washington, DC 20019-1416.*

CHONG, RAE DAWN
Actor. **Personal:** Born Feb 28, 1961, Alberta;daughter of Tommy Chong; married Owen Baylis; children: Morgan. **Career:** Cursed Part 3, dir, writer & producer, 2000; Films: Stony Island, 1978; Quest for Fire, 1982; Beat Street, 1984; The Corsican Brothers, 1984; Choose Me, 1984; Fear City, 1984; American Flyers, 1985; City Limits, 1985; The Color Purple, 1985; Commando, 1985; Running Out of Luck, 1986; Soul Man, 1986; The Squeeze, 1987; The Principal, 1987; Walking After Midnight, 1988; Far Out, Man!, 1990; Tales from the Dark side: the Movie, 1990; Denial: the Dark Side of Passion,1991; Loon; Chaindance; In Exile; The Borrower, 1991; Amazon, 1992; When the Party's Over, 1992; Time Runner, 1993; Boca, 1994; Boulevard, 1994; Crying Freedom, 1994; Power of Attorney, 1995; The Break, 1995; Mask of Death, 1996; Starlight, 1996; Goodbye America, 1997; Highball, 1997; Small Time, 1998; Dangerous Attraction, 2000; The Visit, 2000; Constellation, 2005; Solitaire, 2006; Max Havoc: Ring of Fire, 2006; tv movies: The Whiz Kid and the Mystery at Riverton, 1974; Top of the Hill, 1980; Badge of the Assassian, 1985; Curiosity Kills, 1990; Prison Stories: Women on the Inside,

1991; Broadway credits: Oh Kay!, 1991; Father & Son: Dangerous Relations, 1993; For Hope, 1996; Valentine's Day, 1998; tv series: "Disneyland", 1974; "Lou Grant", 1980; "St. Elsewhere", 1983-85; "Tall Tales and Legends", 1986; "The Hitchhiker", 1991; "Nitecap", 1992; "Melrose Place", 1992-93; "Lonesome Dove: The Series", 1994; "Crazy Love", 1995; "The Outer Limits", 1995; "Highlander", 1996; "Poltergeist: The Legacy", 1997; "Mysterious Ways", 2000-02; "Judging Amy", 2002; "Wild Card", 2003-04; Greasy Rider, 2006; "That's So Raven", 2007. **Orgs:** Screen Actors Guild; Am Fed TV Recreation Arts & Radio Artists. **Honors/Awds:** Clarence Muse Award, Black Filmmakers Hall of Fame, 1986. **Special Achievements:** Sex, Drugs & AIDS, educ documentary, narrator, book, contributor, 1987. **Business Addr:** Actor, Metropolitan Talent Agency, 4526 Wilshire Blvd, Los Angeles, CA 90010.*

CHOWNING, FRANK EDMOND
Dentist. **Personal:** Married Edith Mae Jenkins. **Career:** Morgan Health Ctr, dentist. **Orgs:** Kappa Alpha Psi Frat; Sigma Pi Phi Frat; past pres, Ethical Culture Soc; past pres, Nat Dent Asn; past trustee, Nat Dent Asn; trustee & past asst supvr, Allen Chapel AME Ch; bd dir, Alpha Home; bd Dir, Citizens Forum; past bd mem, YMCA Exec Bd; Nat Dent Asn; Ind State Dent Asn; past, Polemarch Kappa Alpha Psi; Sigma Pi Phi; life mem, NAACP; past pres, Ind State Med Dent & Pharm Asn; past pres, Indianapolis Frontiers Serv Club; past mem, Peer Review Comt. **Honors/Awds:** Dentist of the Year, Nat Dent Asn; fel, Am Col Dentists; fel, Int Col Dentists; Am Dent Asn; Am Prosthodontic Soc. **Home Addr:** 5011 Kessler Blvd E Dr Suite 208, Indianapolis, IN 46220-6328. *

CHRETIEN, GLADYS M.
Executive. **Personal:** Born in Texas; divorced; children: Joseph P, III & Perry Duncan. **Educ:** Prairie View Col; Wiley Col. **Career:** Salesman, 1961; broker, 1962; Gladys M Chretien Realty Co, real estate broker, realtor & realtist; Consolidated Realty Bd, pres; Multiple Listing, chmn; Wash Escrow Co, part owner & vpres; Wall St Enterprises & Wash Reconveyance Corp, part owner & stock holder; Century 21 Chretien Realty, owner. **Orgs:** Church Christ; La County Tax Appeals Bd Found. **Honors/Awds:** La County Tax Appeals Bd Founders Achievement Award, Consolidated Realty Bd, 1969-70; Top Ten Contributers, Consolidated Realty; many sales awards. *

CHRICHLOW, LIVINGSTON L
Administrator. **Personal:** Born May 13, 1925, Brooklyn, NY; son of Alfred and Viola; married Mary Atkinson; children: Gordon H. **Educ:** Queens Col City Univ NY, BA, 1975; Baruch Col City Univ NY, MPA, 1979. **Career:** Administrator (retired); Dept Defense, contract admin, 1951-80; Lutheran Immigration & Refugee Serv, coordr 1980-82; Lutheran Church Am, dir urban ministry, 1982-87. **Orgs:** Better Comt Civil Asn, 1955-57; vpres, Comn Sch Bd, 1965-70; chmn, Finance Comt New Hope Church, 1975-89; Sec Asn Black Lutherans, 1979-88; mem chmn, Minority Concerns Comt, NY Synod, 1979-87; dir, Proj Equality, NY, 1980-87; secy, Boy Scouts Am Alumni, 1980-; pres, Parkhurst Civic Asn, 1984-96; vol, Income Tax asst, 1989-2003; treas, New Hope Church, 1990-93; stewardship comt, Metro NY Synod, Lutheran Church Am, 1990-93; vpres, New Hope Church, 1994-97. **Honors/Awds:** Distinguished discipleship, Metro NY Synod, Lutheran Church Am, 1970; Distinguished Citizen, Springfield Gardens Sr Citizens, 1980; Community Service Award, Elmont Youth Outreach, 1994; Black History Month Award, ECAP, 2005. **Military Serv:** USN; Good Conduct Am Theatre, USN, 1944. **Home Addr:** 2232 Leighton Rd, Elmont, NY 11003-3515.

CHRISS, HENRY THOMAS
Sports manager. **Personal:** Born Nov 24, 1964, Cleveland, OH; son of Frank James and Mary Glynn; married Sandra Renee, Aug 10, 1985; children: Henry II, Jasmine & Tiffany. **Educ:** Bowling Green State Univ, bus admin, 1984-86; Akron Univ, polymer sci, 1985-86; Kent State Univ, bus mgt, 1990. **Career:** Polychem Dispersions, prod & lab mgr, 1985-87; Duramax Johnson Rubber, prod supvr, 1987-88, prod technician, 1988-89, qual control chem lab supvr, 1989-91; NIKE Inc, chem lab mgr, 1991-93, environ affairs dir, 1993-94, dir acct logistics, 1994-96, gen mgr, 1997-2000; Aramark, vpres, 2000-03; Clariante Growth Solutions Inc, pres & founder, 2003. **Orgs:** Am Chem Soc, 1991-; Am Black Sporting Goods Prof, 1992-. **Honors/Awds:** State Qualifier Wrestling, Ohio High Sch Athletic Asn, 1983; 2nd Team All Nation, US Semi-Pro Football League, 1987. **Special Achievements:** Congressional nomination to West Point, 1982; US Patent, Recycling Polymer Technology, 1994.

CHRISTBURG, SHEYANN WEBB
School administrator. **Personal:** Born Feb 17, 1956, Selma, AL; daughter of John Webb and Betty; married Andre Christburg, Aug 19, 1999. **Educ:** Tuskegee Inst, BS, social work, 1979; Ala State Univ. **Career:** Ala State Univ, Stud Activities Ctr, coordr, currently; author; KEEP Prod Youth Develop Prog, dir, owner & pres, currently. **Orgs:** Chair, Martin Luther King B'Day Celebration, 1993-; bd mem, State SCLC, 1996-; chair, Lyceum Committee, 1997-98. **Honors/Awds:** Ladies of Distinction, Woman of Distinction, 1999; Community Serv Award, First Congregational Church, 2000; Drum Major for Justice Award, SCLC, 2000; nominated, Presidential Award, Ariz State Univ, 1999. **Special Achievements:** Authored: Selma Lord, Selma, 1997; Selma Lord Selma, Disney movie made from book, 1999; nominated, Nat Asn Advan Colored People Image Award, 2000. **Business Addr:** President, Owner, KEEP Productions Youth Development & Modeling Program, 2847 Jan Dr, PO Box 4121, Montgomery, AL 36104.*

CHRISTIAN, CORA LEETHEL
Physician. **Personal:** Born Sep 11, 1947, St Thomas, Virgin Islands of the United States; daughter of Ruth and Alphonso; married Simon B Jones-Hendrikson; children: Marcus Benjamin, Nesha Rosita. **Educ:** Marquette Univ, Milwaukee WICS, BS, 1967; Jefferson Med Col Phila, PA, MD, 1971; Johns Hopkins Univ Baltimore, MD, MPH, 1975. **Career:** Howard Univ Family Pract, admin chief resident, 1973-74, instr, 1974-75; Ingeborg Nesbitt Clinic Dept Health, physician charge, 1975-77; VI Med Inst, exec dir & med dir, 1977-94; VI Dept Health, asst comnr, 1977-81, asst comnr, ambulatory care serv, 1981-87; asst comnr, prevention, health promotion & protection, 1987-92; Hovensa, med dir, 1992-; Thomas Jeffer Univ, lect, 1990-; Virgin Islands Med Inst, med dir, 1994-. **Orgs:** Dir, family planning VI Dept Health, 1979-, proj dir, Frederiksted Health Ctr, 1978-80, act dir, MCH, 1982-, chief staff, 1983; delegate Am Pub Health Asn; League Women Voters VI, 1979; pres, Charles Harwood Meml Hosp Med Staff, 1978-79, vpres, 1977-78; secy, VI Med Soc, 1976-77, treas, 1980-81 & 1983-84, pres, 1985-; pres, Am Acad Family Pract, 1978-; vice territory chief, Caribbean Terrtory Soka Gakkau Intl; exec secy & treas, Virgin Islands Med Soc, 1997-02; VI Olympic Comt physician, 1998-; pres, Caribbean Shedus Asn, 2001; exec secy & treas, VI Med Soc, 1997-02; AARP Nat Bd. **Honors/Awds:** Wilmont Blyden Scholarship VI, 1963; John Hay Whitney Fellowship John Hay Whitney Found, 1969; Nat Urban Coalition Fellowship Nat Urban Coalition Found, 1974; Outstanding Woman, AKA, 1997; Paul Harris Fellow, 1997; VIMS, 1997; Best Doctors America, 1999; Physician Award, Community Serv; Physician of the Year, 2003. **Business Addr:** Medical Director, Virgin Islands Medical Institute Inc, 1AD Diamond Ruby Sunny Isle, PO Box 5989, Christiansted, Virgin Islands of the United States 00823-5989, **Business Phone:** (340)712-2400.*

CHRISTIAN, DOLLY LEWIS
Executive, manager, vice president (organization). **Personal:** Born in New York, NY; daughter of Daniel and Adeline Walton; divorced. **Educ:** Manhattan Comm Col, attended. **Career:** Vice president, Executive, Manager (retired); IBM Corp, program mgr affirmative action program (Retired); The Sperry & Hutchison Co, personnel mgr, supvr, spec proj & rec, employ specialist, dir civic affairs, currently. **Orgs:** Chmn, bd NY Urban League, 1977-85; Panel Arbitrators Am Arbitration Asn, 1978; commissioner, New York, Comn Human Rights, 1987-90; bd mem, Coalition 100 Black Women, 1979; past vpres, The Edges Group Inc; Coun Concerned Black Exec; Nat Urban Affairs Coun Office; Mgt Assistance Comm Greater NY Fund. **Honors/Awds:** Scroll Honor, Nat Coun Negro Bus & Prof Women's Clubs; Community Service Award; Ambudswoman Award; Youth Salute Black Corp Exec Award, Nat Youth Movement; Corp Recp Mary McCleod Bethune Award; Nat Coun Negro Women; Spec Corp Recognition Award; Metro Coun Brances; Nat Asn Advan Colored People; Woman Achiever, YWCA NY; Black Achiever, Harlem YMCA.

CHRISTIAN, ERIC OLIVER, JR.
Consultant. **Personal:** Born Jan 1, 1951, Tortola, British Virgin Islands; son of Eric O Sr and Ethel Trotman Thomas; married Shelia, Dec 23, 1973; children: Eric O III & Cosine. **Educ:** Tenn State Univ, BSed, 1973. **Career:** Gov Virgin Islands, teacher, 1973-85; Am Bankers Life, mgr, 1975-89; Black Bus Coun, pres, 1988-; Gov St Kitts, West Indies, consult, 1989-90; Caribbean Small Bus Asn, consult, 1989-; Gov Virgin Islands, consult, 1990-. **Orgs:** Exec coun, Am Fed Teachers, 1973-85; Tony Browns Buy Freedom Movement, 1989-; exec mem, Nat Asn Black Chambers; Status CMS, VI, 1989-; Black Meeting Planners, 1990-. **Honors/Awds:** Manager of the Year, Am Bankers Life, 1990; Musician & Choral DRR of the Year, AT&T, 1991. **Business Addr:** President, Black Business Chamber of Commerce, PO Box 8033, St Thomas, Virgin Islands of the United States 00801, **Business Phone:** (809)774-8784.

CHRISTIAN, JOHN L.
Executive. **Personal:** Born Jan 27, 1940, Winton, NC; son of John Albert and Addie Beatrice Weaver; married Lesley Evans Christian; children: Andrea Lenore, John A II. **Educ:** Hampton Univ, Hampton, VA, BS, 1961; Wharton Sch, Philadelphia, PA, cert, 1978; Harvard Sch Pub Health, Boston, MA, cert, 1988. **Career:** Leasco Systs & Res Corp, Bethesda, MD, div mgr, 1964-69; Polaroid Corp, Cambridge, MA, div mgr, 1969-74; Trustees of Health & Hosps, Boston, MA, vpres, 1974-92; Enterprise Group Ltd, exec vpres, treas, pres & cheif exec officer, currently. **Orgs:** Pres, Int Soc Res Adminr, 1988-89; pres, Nat Guardsmen Inc, 1978-79; bd chmn, Crispus Attucks Children's Ctr, 1972-; pres, Sigma Pi Phi-Beta Beta, 1981-82; bd, Brookline Community Fund, 1988-; allocations rev comt, United Way Mass Bay, 1980-91. **Honors/Awds:** Outstanding Citizen, Nat Asn Advan Colored People, 1982; Hartford-Nicholson Service Award, Soc Res Adminr, 1985. **Business Addr:** Executive Vice President, Treasurer, Enterprise Group Ltd, PO Box 925, Brookline, MA 02446-0007, **Business Phone:** (617)232-9790.*

CHRISTIAN, MARY T
State government official. **Personal:** Born Jul 9, 1924, Hampton, VA; married Wilbur B; children: Benita D Toler & Carolyn D Taylor. **Educ:** Hampton Inst, BS, 1955; Columbia Univ, MA, speech & drama, 1960; Mich State Univ, PhD, 1967. **Career:** State government official (retired); Hampton Univ, Sch Educ, prof emer, dean; Va House Reps, state rep. **Orgs:** First Baptist Church Auxiliary; bd mem, Peninsula Asn Sickle Cell Anemia; Am Asn Univ Women; NAACP; chmn, Groups Representing Org United Progress; Hampton Crusade Voters; Coalition 100 Black Women; Am Lung Asn; Jr League Hampton Rds; VA Adv Bd on Gifted Educ; chair, Va Legis Black Caucus; bd mem, Nat Patient Advocate Found. **Honors/Awds:** Hall Fame, Hampton-Newport News Serv Bds; Delegate Yr Award (House Bill 1330) Peninsula Attention Deficit Disorder Asn Social Justice Award, Tidewater Social Justice League; William H. Butts Memorial Award, Peninsula Ctr for Independent Living Outstanding Service Award, NAACP, Va State Conf. **Special Achievements:** First African-American woman to serve on the Hampton School Board; First African American since Reconstruction to represent the City of Hampton in the Virginia House of Delegates.

CHRISTIAN, SPENCER
Meteorologist, television show host. **Personal:** Born Jul 23, 1947, Newport News, VA; son of Spencer and Lucy Greene; married Diane Chambers Christian, Jun 20, 1970; children: Jason & Jessica. **Educ:** Hampton Univ, Hampton, VA, BA, eng, 1970. **Career:** Stony Brook Prep Sch, Long Island, NY, teacher, 1970; WWBT-TV, Richmond, VA, news reporter, 1971, weatherman, 1972-75; WBAL-TV, Baltimore, MD, weatherman, 1975-77; WABC-TV, New York, NY, weatherman, 1977-86; Good Morning Am, weatherman, co-host, & interviewer, 1986-98; BET, "Triple Threat" Game Show, host, 1993-; ABC7 News team, KGO-TV, weather forecaster, 1999-. **Orgs:** March Dimes, Spec Olympics, Cystic Fibrosis Found, Am Cancer Soc, Big Brothers, Boy Scouts & Girl Scouts Am, Tomorrow's C, United Negro Col Fund; Up With People; Daytop Village; Make-A-Wish Found. **Honors/Awds:** Better Life Award; Emmy Award; Whitney M Young Jr Service Award, Greater New York Coun, Boy Scouts Am, 1990; Honorary Chairman, NJ Chap, March Dimes, 1979; Virginia Communications Hall of Fame, 1993; Virginian of the Year, Va Press Asn, 1993. **Special Achievements:** Author of Spencer Christian's Weather Book, Spencer Christian "s Geography Book, and Electing Our Government. **Military Serv:** AUS Reserves. **Business Phone:** (415)954-7263.

CHRISTIAN, WILLIAM LEONARD
Actor. **Personal:** Born Sep 30, 1955, Washington, DC; son of William L and Evelyn M Shaw; married Gail, Jan 1, 2002; children: 1. **Educ:** Cath Univ, AME, BA, 1976; Am Univ, MA, 1980. **Career:** Films: The January Man, 1989; Love & Orgasms, 2003; Nine Lives, 2004; Contradictions of the Heart, 2009; Three Takes, 2009; TV Series: Another World, 1964; "The Cosby Show", 1985; All My Children, 1990-2005; "Law & Order", 1997-2001; Spin City", 1999; "Malcolm in the Middle", 2003; "Without a Trace", 2003; "All My Children", 2005; ER, 2008; Moonlight, 2008; "Prison Break", 2008; "Hannah Montana", 2008; "Desperate Housewives", 2008; "Monk", 2009. **Honors/Awds:** Nominee, Daytime Emmy Award for Best Supporting Actor in Drama " All My Children"(1970), 1991. **Home Addr:** 1499 La Loma Rd, Pasadena, CA 91105-2194. **Business Addr:** Actor, c/o William Morris Agency, 151 El Camino Dr, Beverly Hills, CA 90212, **Business Phone:** (310)859-4000.*

CHRISTIAN-CHRISTENSEN, DONNA-MARIE
Congressperson (U.S. federal government). **Personal:** Born Sep 19, 1945, Teaneck, NJ; daughter of Almeric Leander and Virginia Sterling; married Christian Christensen, Dec 31, 1998; children: Rabiah Layla Green, Karida Yasmeen Green. **Educ:** St Mary's Col, Notre Dame, IN, BA, 1966; George Wash Univ, Wash, DC, MD, 1970. **Career:** Family Physician; Virgin Islands Dept Health, St Croix, Virgin Islands, various positions, 1975-80; F'sted Health Ctr, St Croix, Virgin Islands, med dir, 1980-85; Dir Mch & Family Planning, St Croix, Virgin Islands, med dir, 1985-87; St Croix Hosp, St Croix, Virgin Islands, med dir, 1987-88; Virgin Islands Dept Health, St Croix, Virgin Islands, asst comnr, 1988-92; US House Reps, congresswoman, 1997-. **Orgs:** Democratic Nat Women Comt, 1984-; Democratic Territorial Comt, 1980-; Virgin Islands Bd Educ, 1984-86; pres, Virgin Islands Med Soc, 1990-91; Christiansted chair, Friedenstal Moravian Church, 1988-; chair, Congressional Black Caucus Health Braintrust. **Business Addr:** Congresswoman, United States House Representatives, 1510 Longworth House Off Bldg, Washington, DC 20515-5501, **Business Phone:** (202)225-1790.*

CHRISTIE, ANGELLA
Saxophonist, gospel musician. **Personal:** Born in Los Angeles, CA; daughter of Girvin and Catherine. **Educ:** Houston Baptist Univ, BSW, BA, music, 1984. **Career:** Saxophonist; Angella Christie Sound Ministries, founder & ceo, 1985-;Sisters In The Spirit Tour, artist, 2000; Albums: Because He Lives, 1985;

Rejoice, 1986; It Is Well, 1987; Eternity, 1996; Hymn & I, 1998; Draw the Line, 2003; The Breathe of Life, 2008. **Orgs:** Dir, Angella Christie Found. **Honors/Awds:** Award of Excellence, Gospel Music Workshop Am, 1999; Instrumental Gospel of the Year, Nat Black Progammers Coalition, 1999; Stellar Award, Instrumental CD of the Year-The Breath of Life, 2009. **Special Achievements:** Stellar Award Nominee, 1997, 1999, 2006; performed for former US President Bill Clinton, Bishop T D Jakes's Woman Thou Art Loosed Conference, NBAAll-Star Weekend & National Association of Black Journalists. **Business Addr:** Founder, Chief Executive Officer, Angella Christie Sound Ministries, PO Box 361888, Decatur, GA 30036, **Business Phone:** (770)498-0404.*

CHRISTIE, DOUGLAS DALE
Basketball player. **Personal:** Born May 9, 1970, Seattle, WA; son of John and Norma; children: Chantell. **Educ:** Pepperdine Univ, attended 1992. **Career:** Basketball player (retired); Seattle Supersonics, guard-forward, 1992-93; Los Angeles Lakers, 1993-94; New York Knicks, 1994-96; Toronto Raptors, 1996-2000; Sacramento Kings, 2001-05; Orlando Magic, 2005; Dallas Mavericks, 2005-06; Los Angeles Clippers, 2007; free agent, currently. **Special Achievements:** NBA Draft, First round pick, 1992.

CHRISTIE, JAMES ALBERT
Veterinarian, commissioner, government official. **Personal:** Born Nov 2, 1939, Stuart, FL; son of James Sr and Minnie Christie; married Helen L Christie, Oct 13, 1957; children: Gary, Donald, Tracy Christie, Lanier & James A III. **Educ:** Stuart Training Sch. **Career:** Stuart Animal Hosp, sr head tech, 1977; City of Stuart, mayor, 1986, 1992; Stuart City Comn, Stuart Community Redevelop Agency, bd mem, city comnr, currently. **Orgs:** Fla Black Caucus Asn Elected Off, 1984-94; second vpres, Martin County Black Heritage Asn, 1985; Martin County Dem Asn; Martin County Nat Asn Advan Colored People; Fla League Cities; pres, Concerned Citizens E Stuart/Martin County Inc, 2001. **Honors/Awds:** Martin County Black Image Award; Martin County Politician of the Year; Achievement Award, E Stuart Civil Asn. **Home Addr:** 915 SE Hall St, Stuart, FL 34994. **Business Addr:** City Commissioner, City of Stuart, 121 SW Flagler Ave, Stuart, FL 34994.

CHRISTOPHE, CLEVELAND A
Capitalist or financier. **Personal:** Born Jan 1, 1946, Savannah, GA; son of Cleveland and Lucy; married Cheryl S Chistophe, Dec 28, 1966; children: Jean-Paul & Kimberly D. **Educ:** Howard Univ, BA, 1966; Univ Mich, Grad Sch Bus, MBA, 1967. **Career:** First Nat City Bank, securities analyst, 1967-69, venture capital analyst, 1971-72, investment analyst team head, 1972-75, Paris, county opers head, 1975-79, San Francisco, corp banking team head, 1980-83, Jamaica, country head, 1983-85, Columbia, country head, 1985-87; Kenton Corp, asst to chmn, 1969; Soul Stop Inc, pres, 1970; TLC Group, sr vpres, 1987-88; Christophe Corp, pres, 1988-89; Equico Capital Corp, vpres, 1990-92; TSG Ventures, prin, 1992-95, TSG Capital Group, LLC, managing partner, 1995-. **Orgs:** Bd dir, Nat Conf Comm & Justice; RF Toigo Found; Stamford Health Syst SACIA; Nat Asn Investment Co. **Honors/ Awds:** Chartered Financial Analyst, Inst Chartered Financial Analysts, 1975; Walter H. Wheeler Jr Leadership Award, 2004. **Special Achievements:** Author of Competition in Financial Services, Citicorp, 1973. **Business Addr:** Managing Partner, TSG Capital Group, LLC, 177 Broad St Suite 12, Stamford, CT 06903, **Business Phone:** (203)541-1500.

CHRISTOPHER, JOHN A.
Microbiologist, immunologist, college teacher. **Personal:** Born Aug 19, 1941, Shreveport, LA. **Educ:** Tex State Univ, attended 1963; Bishop Col, BS, 1964; Baylor Univ, MS, 1967; Iowa State Univ, PhD, 1971. **Career:** Univ Tex S western Med Ctr, res tech, 1964-65; Inst Baylor Univ, grad res fel, 1965-67; Iowa State Univ, grad res/teaching asst, 1967-71; Univ Minn Med Sch, post doctoral res fel, 1971-73; Southern Univ, prof dept chem. **Orgs:** AAAS; Soc Sigma Xi; S Cent Br Am Soc Microbiol; YWCA; Nat Asn Advan Colored People; Community Coun Inc; Nat Fund March Dimes. **Business Addr:** Professor, Southern University, 3050 Cooper Rd, Shreveport, LA 71107.

CHUKS-ORJI, AUSTIN (AUSTIN OGONNA CHUKS-ORJI)
Automotive executive. **Personal:** Born May 29, 1943, Anambra, Nigeria; son of Arum Okosisi and Maria Nneze; divorced 1978; children (previous marriage): Loretta & Leslie Austin Jr; married Gloria; children: Nancy, Brenda, Michael & Robert. **Educ:** Col Marin, AA, 1965; San Francisco State Univ, BA, 1968; Univ San Francisco, MBA, 1970; Oxford Univ, PhD, 1976. **Career:** McDonald's, Oakland, Calif, franchise owner, 1971-85; Martins Fast Foods, Lagos, Nigeria, founder, 1979-84; Macon's, Lagos, Nigeria, chmn, 1979-86; Real Co Ltd, San Francisco, pres, 1973; Am Investrade, Oakland, Calif, chmn, 1984; Mission Blvd Lincoln-Mercury Inc, ceo, currently. **Orgs:** Black Automobile Dealers Asn; Nat Automobile Dealers Asn; Lincoln-Mercury Dealers Asn; Ford Dealers Asn; Nat Asn Advan Colored People. **Special Achievements:** Listed 69 of 100 top auto dealers, Black Enterprise, 1992. **Business Addr:** Chief Executive Officer, Mission Boulevard Lincoln-Mercury Inc, 24644 Mission Blvd, Hayward, CA 94544, **Business Phone:** (415)886-5052.*

CHUKS-ORJI, AUSTIN OGONNA. See CHUKS-ORJI, AUSTIN.

CHUNN, DR. JAY CARRINGTON
Research scientist, educator. **Personal:** Born Dec 26, 1938; son of Jay C and Carrie M (Reed) Chunn; children: Tracey & Jay Carrington III. **Educ:** Ohio Univ, BSc, 1957 & BS, bus admin, 1961; Case Western Res Univ, MS, social work, 1965; Univ MD, PhD, human develop, 1978. **Career:** Community Coordinated Child Care, staff coordr, 1970; Coun Econ Opportunity Greater Cleveland, child develop coordr, 1970; Nat Child Develop Day Care & Child Develop Am, pres, 1970-71; Day Care & Child Develop Coun Am, Wash, assoc dir & dir Early Childhood Develop, 1970-71;Nat Child Develop & Day Care Consult Inc, pres, 1971-73; Howard Univ, prof, 1972-84, dean social work, 1974-84; City Univ New York, Medgar Evers Col, pres, 1984-87; City Univ New York Hunter Col, Sch Health Sci, dir res & develop & prof, 1988-89; Ala A&M Univ, vpres acad affairs & res, 1989-91, univ prof & MSW planning dir, 1991-92; George Washington Univ, adj prof, 1995-96; Union Grad Sch, Cini, adj fac, prof, 1997-99; Nat Ctr Health Behav Change, dir, prin investr, 2003-. **Orgs:** Nat Asn Social Workers; pres, Nat Asn Black Social Workers, Calif, 1972-74, nat pres, 1974-78, re-elected Baltimore, MD term ending, 1978; mem exec bd, Nat Coun Black Child Develop, 1976-78, pres, 1978-81; chmn, 100 Black Men Int Affairs Comm, 1985-; 100 Black Men Inc, 1986-; Gov Adv Comm Black Affairs, 1986; Am Psychol Asn; Am Pub Health Asn; Acad Cert Social Workers; mem house deleg, Coun Social Work Educ; Psychiat & Behav Scis Sect, Nat Med Asn; nat adv bd, Pub Health Progm Morgan State Univ. **Honors/Awds:** Ohio Univ Alumni Medal of Merit for Outstanding Contributions in Human Development; Highest Alumni Award, Ohio Univ, 1980; Graduate of Year Award, 1981, Black Alumni Asn, Ohio Univ, 1981; Mayor's Citation for Outstanding Leadership Award, Mid-Brooklyn Polit Asn, 1984; Man of the Year Award, Black Women's Polit Leadership Caucus NY, 1984; Outstanding Faculty Member, Howard Univ; Dr Benjamin E Mays Award, Bessie Smith Democratic Club NY, 1985; Dr Martin Luther King Award, Baptist Pastors & Churches Union Brooklyn Long Island, 1987; The Dictionary of Int Biography, Volume XVII, 1989-91; Who's Who Internationality, 1991-92; Who's Whoin Medicine & Health Care, 2003. **Special Achievements:** Author of: "The Black Aged and Social Policy" in Aging, 1978, "Mental Health & People of Color, Curriculum Development & Change", Univ Press, 1983; "Stress Mgt & the Black Female in Corporate Environment", 1983. **Military Serv:** Marine Reserves 6 months.

CHURCH, ROBERT T., SR. See Obituaries section.

CHURCHWELL, CAESAR ALFRED
Dentist. **Personal:** Born Nov 26, 1932, Newton, GA; married Ruth; children: Caesar Jr, Gabrielle, Eric, Jonathan. **Educ:** Mt Union Col, BS, 1956; Howard Univ Col Den, DDS, 1967. **Career:** Self-Employed, dent. **Orgs:** Nat Advan Asn Colored People; personnel comn mem, Bd Dir, Nat Advan Asn Colored People Urban League, 1971-72; adv bd, Fulcrum Saving & Loan, 1973; Black Leadership Forum; Men Tomorrow; Black Unity Coun; past pres, W Twin Peaks Lions Club, 1973; activity chmn, BSA, 1974; vpres, San Francisco Black Chamber Com; pres, San Francisco Black Leadership Forum; adv bd, SE Community Col; SF Dental Forum; Acad Gen Dent; No Chap Med; Dent & Pharm Asn; past pres, NCNDA, 1974; ADA; SFDS; CDS; Western Peridontal Soc; SF Dental Found, 1975; Bicentennial Comn So SF, 1975-76; Co San Mateo, 1975-76. **Military Serv:** AUS, pvt, 1955-56. **Home Addr:** 2309 Wexford Ave, South San Francisco, CA 94080. *

CHURCHWELL, CHARLES DARRETT
School administrator, educator. **Personal:** Born Nov 7, 1926, Dunnellon, FL; son of John Dozier and Lee Annah De Laughter; married Yvonne Ransom, Aug 25, 1957; children: Linda & Cynthia. **Educ:** Morehouse Col, BS, 1952; Atlanta Univ, MS, 1953; Univ, Ill, PhD, libr sci, 1966; City Col attended; Hunter Col attended; NY Univ, 1959-61. **Career:** Educator, school administrator (retired); Prairie View A & M Col, instr, 1954-57; Univ Houston, assoc dir libr, 1966; Miami Univ, prof, dir libr, 1970-72, prof, assoc provost acad serv, 1972-74; Univ Mich, vis lectr,1972, 1976; Brown Univ, libr, 1974-78; Wash Univ, dean libr serv, 1978-87; Wayne State Univ, vis prof, libr sci, 1987, prof, 1988-90; Clark Atlanta Univ, Sch Libr & Info Studies, dean, 1990-99, interim provost, vpres acad affairs, 1990-91; Atlanta Univ Ctr, Robert W Woodruff Libr, dir, 1991-; New York City Pub Libr, reference librn; Univ Ill, librn. **Orgs:** Life mem, Am Libr Asn, 1968-; life mem, Nat Asn Advan Colored People; Ga Libr Asn; vice chmn, bd dirs, Coun Libr Resources. **Honors/Awds:** Acad Admin Fel, Am Coun Educ, 1971-72; Outstanding Alumni Award, Atlanta Univ, Sch Libr & Info Studies, 1986. **Special Achievements:** First African American male to earn a Ph.D. from the Univ of Illinois. **Military Serv:** USAF. **Home Addr:** 5621 Waterman Blvd Suite 1, St Louis, MO 63112.

CICCOLO, ANGELA
Lawyer. **Personal:** Born in Indianapolis, IN; married Christopher; children: Christopher, Nicholas, Danielle. **Educ:** Georgetown University, Bachelor's Degree in Foreign Service; Georgetown University's Law Center. **Career:** Ashcraft and Gerel, Attorney. **Orgs:** National Association for the Advancement of Colored People (NAACP), Interim General Counsel/Secretary. **Honors/ Awds:** NAACP Staff Lawyer of the Year, 2003; Medgar W. Evers Award for Excellence for Executive Staff, 2006. **Home Addr:** 004850. *

CISSOKO, ALIOUNE BADARA
School administrator, psychotherapist, artist. **Personal:** Born Jun 15, 1952, Kolda Casamance, Senegal; son of Fatoumata Mara and Moussa Balla; married Sonia H; children: Moussa Balla, Fatoumata, Djibril Kalif. **Educ:** Univ Dakar Inst Arts, BA, 1975; RI Schl Design, MFA, 1979; Univ RI, Arts Mgt Cert, 1982; Northeastern Univ, MA, 1984, PhD; cert case mgr. **Career:** Intl House RI, prog asst, 1978-80; Soc Cons, arts consult, 1979-; Am Sociological Asn, mem, 1983-; Am Anthropological Asn, mem, 1983-; Northern RI Community Mental Health Ctr Psychiatric Counr Crisis Beds, psychol social counr & therapist; Southeastern MA Univ, publ rel prof arts, 1985-; Brown Univ, Dept Police & Security, mgr spec servs, 1993, counr, mem bd dir, dir training, currently. **Orgs:** Fine artist Performing Arts RI, 1977-; folk artist artist educ RI State Coun Arts, 1980-; listed Talent Bank NEA Wash DC, 1983-; RI Black Heritage Soc, 1979-, Intl House RI, 1979-; Nat Coun Creative Educ Therapy; co-founder, Black Artists RI. **Honors/Awds:** Citation, State RI & Providence Plantations, 1984; founder, Dougouto Ngnagnya Af Drums & Dance Ensemble, 1982-; RI State Council Award, Creative Educ Therapy. **Business Addr:** Counselor & Director of Training, Member Board of Director, Brown University Police Department, 54 Doyle Ave, PO Box 603227, Providence, RI 02906-0227, **Business Phone:** (401)863-2542.*

CLACK, FLOYD
State government official, educator. **Personal:** Born Dec 21, 1940, Houston, TX; married Brenda J Jones; children: Michael & Mia. **Educ:** Tex Southern Univ, BS, 1965; Tex Southern Univ Sch Law, 1966; Eastern Mich Univ, MA, 1972, educ leadership, 1985. **Career:** Old Fisher Body Plant, factory worker; Houston Pub Sch, teacher; Fed Govt Job Corps Ctr, teacher, 1967-68; Flint Community Sch Syst, teacher, 1968-82; Mich House Reps, state rep, 1982-96; Genesee Co Metrop Planning Comn, bd comnr, comnr, 1997; Genesee County Bd of Commrs Dist2, councilman, 1996-2004; Eastern Mich Univ, Flint Community Sch, bd of regents, 2005, 2007-. **Orgs:** Kappa Alpha Psi Fraternity; Nat Conf State Legiss; Nat Conf Black Legis; Mich Alternative Educ Asn; Nat Alternative Educ Asn; Urban League Flint; bd dir, Genesee Co Boy Scouts Am; Coun State Govts; The Acad Criminal Justice; Am Corrections Asn; Mich Corrections Asn; Flint Inner City Lions Club; Kentucky Colonels; Genesee Co Community Action Agency; Metrop Chamber Com; Mich Polit Hist Soc; Nat Dem Party; Dem Leadership Conf; Dem Black Caucus; Mich State Alumni Asn; Eastern Mich Alumni Asn; Buckham Alley Theater; Nat Civic League; Am Legis Exchange Coun; CARE Adv Bd; founder, Youth Leadership Inst Flint; founder, Floyd Clack Thanks giving Dinner Citizens, 1983; Floyd Clack Comt Proj; charter mem, Flint Inner City Lions Club; pres Flint Nat Asn Advan Colored People. **Honors/Awds:** David McMahon Award, Mich Educ Asn, 1988; Boy Scouts Am Appreciation, City of Flint, 1989; Supportive Service Award, Metrop Chamber Com, 1989, Harry L Redds Award, 1991; Equal Opportunity Award, Urban League, 1990; Appreciation Award, Genesee Co Community Action Agency, 1990; Leadership Award, Flint NAACP, 1990, Service Award, 1990; Outstanding Service to Mankind Award, Alpha Kappa Alpha Sorority, 1990; Outstanding Service Award, Concerned Pastors Social Action, 1990; Martin Luther King Memorial Award, Genesee Co Tribute Comt, 1990; Appreciation Award, The Forum Mag,1991; Good Old Kappa Spirit Award, Kappa Alpha Psi, 1991; Outstanding Service Award, Greater Flint Jaycees, 1991; Floyd J McCree Leadership, Panhellic Coun, 1991; Man of the Year, Flint Inner City Lions Club, 1991;Certificate of Appreciation, Genesee Fedn Blind Inc, 1992; Gift of Life Award, Am Red Cross, 1994; Foss Ave Baptist Church Award, 1994; Person of the Week Award, WJRT TV Channel 12, 1994; Black History Month Award, Univ Mich-Flint, 1996.

CLAIBORNE, CHRIS (CHRISTOPHER ASHONE CLAIBORNE)
Football player. **Personal:** Born Jul 26, 1978, San Diego, CA. **Educ:** Univ Southern Calif, pub policy & mgt. **Career:** Detroit Lions, linebacker, 1999-02; Minn Vikings, linebacker, 2003-04; St Louis Rams, 2005-06; new york giants, 2006; Jacksonville Jaguars. 2007. Free Agent, Currently. **Honors/Awds:** Nat Defensive Player of the Yr, The Sports Network & Football News; Pac -10Defensive Player of the Yr; Dick Butkus Award, 1998; Lions Mel Farr Rookie of the Yr, 1999; Lions Lem Barney Devensive Most Valuable Player, 2002. *

CLAIBORNE, LLOYD R.
Government official. **Personal:** Born Feb 15, 1936, Newport News, VA; son of John and Alma E Dennis; married Dorma J Robinson; children: Renee, Cheryl, Denise & Lloyd II. **Educ:** City Col NY, BS, 1958. **Career:** Government official (retired); FDA NY, food & drug insp, 1958-67, supvr food & drug insp, 1967; DHEW/ PHS/FDA Bur Compliance Wash, FDA exec develop prog, prog

analyst, 1968-71; DHEW/PHS/FDA Kansas City, dep & reg food & drug dir, 1971-77; US Food & Drug Admin: Chicago, Ill, regional food & drug dir, 1977-81, San Francisco, CA, regional food & drug dir, 1981-90, Kans City, MO, asst assoc comnr regulatory affairs, 1990-91. **Orgs:** Nat Asn Advan Colored People; Assoc Food & Drug Off; DHEW; PHS; Food & Drug Admin; Adv Comt, Field Med Device, 1978-83. **Honors/Awds:** Commendable Service Award, US Food & Drug Administration, 1985; Commissioner Special Citation, US Food & Drug Administration, 1985. **Home Addr:** 12900 Mastin St, Overland Park, KS 66213. *

CLAIBORNE, LORETTA
Athlete, public speaker. **Personal:** Born Jan 1, 1953?, York, PA; daughter of Rita. **Career:** Spec Olympics athlete. **Orgs:** Bd dir, PA Spec Olympics, 1982; Spec Olympics Int, 1991; Proj GOLD Comm, US Olympics, 1996. **Honors/Awds:** Spirit of Spec Olympics Awd, 1981; Female Athlete of the Yr, PA Spec Olympics, 1988; Int Athlete of the Yr, Spec Olympics, 1990; Athlete of the Quarter Century, Runner's World mag Special Olympics, 1991; USA Sports Hall of Fame, 1992; Hall of Fame, William Penn High Sch Alumni, 1992; Honorary Doctorate Degree Humane Letters, Quinnipiac Coll, 1995; Arthur Ashe Awd for Courage, 1996; Heroes Award for State of PA, Sporting Goods Manufacturers Assc (SGMA), 1996; Gold Medal half-marathon, Spec OlympicsWorld Summer Games, 1999; Gold Medal, 3K Run, Bronze Medal, Mile Run, 2003; Silver Medal, 2005. **Special Achievements:** Subj of the Disney Movie "The Loretta Claiborne Story"; Guest Appearance son Oprah Winfrey Show thrice; carried the torch in the Int Spec Olympics. *

CLANCY, MAGALENE ALDOSHIA. See Obituaries section.

CLANCY, SAM, JR.
Basketball player. **Personal:** Born May 4, 1980, Pittsburgh, PA. **Educ:** Univ Southern Calif. **Career:** Philadelphia 76ers, forward, beginning 2002; Forum Filatelico Valladolid Spain, Continental Basketball Assn, basketball player; Idaho Stampede, Continental Basketball Asn; Portland Trail Blazers, 2005; Vive Menorca, Spanish pro basketball league, 2006; Inchon ET L and Black slamer, South Korea, currently, 2006-07; Krasnie Krilya Samara, Russia, 2007-08; Free agent, currently. **Honors/Awds:** Pac-10 Player of the Yr, 2002; CBA's Defensive Player of the Year, 2004-05. *

CLANSY, CHERYL D.
Educator. **Personal:** Born Oct 8, 1961, Los Angeles, CA; daughter of Sidney D and Beverly Jones. **Educ:** Univ La, Monroe, BS, 1984; Midwestern State Univ, MS, 1986; Grambling State Univ, DEd, 1997. **Career:** Southern Univ, chmn vocal music & dir choral activities, 1987-89; Grambling State Univ, coordr vocal music, 1989-98; Wiley Col, dean enrollment mgt, 1998-00; Jarvis Christian Col, assoc vpres academic affairs & choir dir, 2000-. **Orgs:** Tex Music Educators Asn; Delta Sigma Theta Sorority Inc; life mem, Delta Omicron; Top Ladies of Distinction, Inc; Phi Delta Gamma; Phi Kappa Lambda. **Honors/Awds:** Grady Harlan Award for Professional Promise, 1985; Teacher of the Year, Grambling State Univ, College of Liberal Arts, 1991; Appointed to State of Lousiana Governor's Pan American Commission, 1994; Recipent of the J.K. Haynes Award, 1992, Biographical listing in Outstanding Young Women of America, 1985, 1988. **Special Achievements:** Studied in Austria, 1985; Fulbright-Hayes Scholarship for Summer research in Egypt, 1992; participated in research exchange with Cuba, 1994-96; dissertion: The Effects of Cognitive and Non-Cognitive Factors on the Academic Achievement of Music Students, 1997. *

CLANTON, LEMUEL JACQUE
Physician. **Personal:** Born Mar 11, 1931, New Orleans, LA; married Barbara Guy; children: Mark, Lynn, Justine, Lemuel J, Leslie. **Educ:** Howard Univ, BS, 1952; Meharry Med Col, MD, 1956. **Career:** Med Asn, physician; pvt pract, physician, currently. **Orgs:** Bd Cert Surgeon; Am Bd Surg; AMA; Natl Med Asn; bd mem, Lafon Home Aged, 1975. *

CLARDY, WILLIAM J.
Manager. **Personal:** Born May 1, 1935, Newalla, OK; married Patricia Ann Lomax; children: D Vincent, Terri Lynette & William Gerald. **Educ:** Okla State Univ, 1960; USN Community Tech Class A Sch; Iowa State Univ, 1972. **Career:** Lennox Ind Inc Pacific Div, terr mgr htg & air cond equip, instr; LA Unified Sch Dist, instr; Lincoln Job Corp Ctr Northern Sys Co, sr instr htg & air cond; Utah Sheet Metal Con Asn, 1971; Cal-Poly Workshop, 1972; Annual Ed Con CARSES, 1974. **Orgs:** Bd dir, Marshall town Chap Jaycees; bd dir, Marshall town Chap Am Field Serv; bd dir, YMCA Omaha; Marshall town, IA Optimist Club Int. **Military Serv:** USN, tech 3 class, 1952-56.

CLARK, ANTHONY CHRISTOPHER. See CLARK, TONY.

CLARK, AUGUSTA ALEXANDER
Lawyer, government official. **Personal:** Born Mar 5, 1932, Uniontown, AL; married Leroy W Clark; children: Mark, Adrienne. **Educ:** WVa State Col, BSBA, 1954; Drexel Univ, MLS, 1958; Temple Univ, Sch Law, JD, 1976. **Career:** Fed Defense Installations & Free Libr Philadelphia, librn, 1958-66; Gen Elect Co RESD, mkt res analyst, 1967-69; Auerbach Corp, consult, 1970-71; Philadelphia Model Cities Prog, admin, 1971-73; Gen Elect Co, affirm action requirement mgr, 1973-75; Majority Whip City Coun Philadelphia, councilwoman-at-large, atty; Mayor's Bus Action Team, vice chmn, retired in 2000; Mayor John Street's cabinet, Secy Agencies, Authorities, Bds & Comns. **Orgs:** Bd dir, Friends Free Libr Philadelphia; New Horizons Res Inst; Horizon House; Shalom Inc; N Cent Br Young Women's Christian Asn; Orgn Women & Girls Offenders, PILCPO; bd trustees, Philadelphia Col Arts; advy bd, Pa Women's Campaign Fund; law comn, Am Baptist Churches USA Inc; founder & co-chair, Bright Hope Survival Prog; sponsor, Month Woman, 1983; delegate, Nat Women's Conf, Houston; co-chair, Pa Int Women's Year Coord Comn; Barristers, Pa Bar Asn; Alpha Kappa Alpha Sorority; W Broad St Coalition; WVa State Alumni; Steering Comt Chessfest; Black Women's Network; organizer, Jefferson Manor Tenant Asn; coun, Minority Contractors Adv Comn. **Honors/Awds:** Outstanding Service in the Community, Nu Sigma Nat Sorority, 1980; Alumnus of the Year & Outstanding Citizen & Humanitarian, WVa State Col, Theta Chap Theta, 1981; Support to Delta, Iota Chap, Alpha Kappa Alpha Sorority Inc, 1983; Sponsored a number of Bills & Resolutions to assist in improving the quality of life; Honorary Doctorates Degree, Drexel Univ, 1985. *

CLARK, DR. BERTHA SMITH
Educator. **Personal:** Born Sep 26, 1943, Nashville, TN; daughter of James Robert and Louise; married Phillip Hickman, Apr 21, 1973; children: Phillipa Jayne, Margaret Ann & Sheryll Clark Nelson. **Educ:** Tenn State Univ, BS, speech correction, 1964; George Peabody Col Teachers, MA, deaf educ emphasis, 1965; Nat Inst Ment Health, Pre Doctoral Fel, 1980; Vanderbilt Univ, PhD, early childhood educ, 1982. **Career:** Bill Wilkerson Hearing & Speech Ctr (BWHSC), head teacher OE 1 proj, 1965-70, speech pathologist, 1965-78, 1980-87; Tenn State Univ, Area Speech Language path, Instr, 1969-78, asst Prof, 1982-87; Mama Lere Parent Infant Home, Bill Wilkerson Hearing & Speech Ctr, parent-infant trainer, 1982-87; Vanderbilt Univ, Div Hearing & Speech Scis, from instr to asst prof, 1970-87, supvr aural rehab, adj asst prof, 1987-98; Middle Tenn State Univ, Dept Speech & Theatre, asst prof, 1987-90, assoc prof, 1990-96, prof commun dis, 1996-. **Orgs:** Delta Sigma Theta Sorority Inc, 1962-; bd dir, League Hearing Impaired, 1973-87; Childrens House, 1984-86; adv Comt, Early Develop & Assistance Proj Kennedy Ctr, 1984-88; co-chair person, YWCA, 1985; admin comm, vice pres for educ TN Speech & Hearing Asn, 1985-87; chairperson, Cochlear Implant Scholar Comm, 1985-86; Compton Scholar Community Vanderbilt Univ, 1985-86; bd dirs, Peabody Alumni, 1986-89; bd dirs, Bill Wilkerson Ctr, 1990-95; bd dirs, Effective Advocacy Citizens Handicaps, 1991-92; bd dirs, CFAW, Mid Tenn State Univ, 1991-95; Founding Chair, Tenn Asn Audiologists & Speech Language Pathologists, 2001-02; bd dirs, TAASLP, 2002-06; pres, Nat Asn Pre professional Progs, 2006-07. **Honors/Awds:** Honors grad Haynes HS, 1960, Tenn State Univ, 1964; Honors Tenn Speech Lang Hearing Asn, In Speech, Language Hearing Asn, 1988; Public Service Award, 1995; Outstanding Teacher Award, Mid Tenn State Univ, 1995; Recipient, John Pleas Faculty Recognition Award, 2003. **Special Achievements:** National Student Speech, Language Hearing Association for 17 years of service as MTSU Chapter Advisor, 2004. **Business Addr:** Professor, Middle Tennessee State University, Department Speech & Theatre, 1301 E Main St, Murfreesboro, TN 37132-0001.

CLARK, BEVERLY GAIL
Writer. **Personal:** Born Jul 23, 1947, Oklahoma City, OK; daughter of James and Isabella; married Alvin, Oct 1, 1966; children: Catana Clark-Hughes, Alvin Jr, Dayna, Ericca & Gloria. **Educ:** Lawrence Technological Univ, genre fiction writing, attended. **Career:** Book Nook, bookseller, 1992-; Walden Books, bookseller, 1996-98; Book Stop, bookseller, 1998-; Novels: Yesterday Is Gone, 1997; A Love to Cherish, 1998; The Price of Love, 1999; Bound by Love, 2000; Cherish the Flame, 2002; A Twist of Fate, 2003; Echoes of Yesterday, 2005; Beyond the Rapture, 2005; A Perfect Frame, 2007; The Fires Within, 2007. **Orgs:** Friends Lib, 1991-; Romance Writer Am, 1990-. **Honors/ Awds:** Publ Writer-Fiction, Romance Writer Am, 1996.

CLARK, CAESAR A. W. See Obituaries section.

CLARK, DR. CHARLES WARFIELD. See Obituaries section.

CLARK, CLAUDE LOCKHART
Artist, educator, businessperson. **Personal:** Born Mar 28, 1945, Philadelphia, PA; son of Claude and Daima Mary Lockhart. **Educ:** Calif Col Arts & Crafts, BA, 1968; Univ Calif, Berkeley, MA, 1972. **Career:** Oakland High Sch, instr, 1969-70; Calif Col Arts & Crafts, instr, 1970-; Alameda Col, instr, 1971-72; San Jose State Univ Afro-Am Studies Dept, instr crafts course, 1974-; Univ Calif, Berkeley, Afro-Am Studies Dept, 1974, 1977, SOS upward bound prog, 1974-80; House Vai African Imports, owner, 1977-; craftsman; photographer; painter; Calif Acad Scis, consult, 1982-92; African Metropolis, co founder, 1997-; African Metropolis Profiles, founder, 1998-; Frick Middle Sch, staff, 1997-2000. **Orgs:** Music Publications Am, 1947; Acts art gallery, NY, 1973; A third world painting, sculpture exhib, San Francisco Mus Art, 1974; W Coast 1974 the Black Image, Eb Crocker Art Gallery, 1974-75; Amistad catalogue exhibits Emanuel Walter & Atholl Mcbean Galleries, San Francisco Art Inst, 1976; II Afro-Am art, Dept Art, Fisk Univ, 1975-76; Am Fedn Arts, 1976; Tuesday Club Picture Rental Serv Sacramento, 1972; catalogue exhibits Black Artist, Huntsville, AL, 1979; participant, Nat African-Am Crafts World Print Coun, 1979; Conf & Jubilee, Memphis, 1979; Smithsonian Inst,1980; Contemporary African-Am Crafts Exhib Brooks Memorial Art Gallery, Memphis, 1979; mosaic exhibit Meml Union-Art Gallery Univ Calif, Davis CA. **Honors/Awds:** Included Numerous Private Collections, 1971-; recipient 3rd prize Nat Ford Indus Arts Contest; 1st prize Oakland Art Museum's Exhibit for Public Schools; elected citizen of the day KABL Radio San Francisco; scholarship CA Col of Arts & Crafts 1963. **Special Achievements:** Co-Auth: A Black Art Perspective: A Black Teacher's Guide To A Black Art Curriculum, 1970; Auth: The Complete Annotated Resource Guide to Black America Art, 1978. **Business Addr:** Owner, House Vai, PO Box 8172, Oakland, CA 94662.

CLARK, DAVE. See CLARK, DAVID EARL.

CLARK, DAVID EARL (DAVE CLARK)
Baseball player, manager. **Personal:** Born Sep 3, 1962, Tupelo, MS; married Vivian; children: Meki & Kiki. **Educ:** Jackson State Univ. **Career:** Baseball player, Manager (retired); Cleveland Indians, outfielder, 1986-89; Chicago Cubs, 1990 & 1997; Kans City Royals, 1991; Pittsburgh Pirates, 1992-96; Los Angeles Dodgers, 1996; Chicago Cubs, 1997; Houston Astros, 1998; Round Rock Express, mgr. **Special Achievements:** National League Division Series, 1996 & 1998.

CLARK, DELLA L
Executive. **Personal:** Born Jul 20, 1953, Tyler, TX; married Alfonso; children: Alorie & Allee. **Educ:** Am Univ, BS, 1975. **Career:** Martin Marietta Aluminum, acct; Delark Indust, Inc, owner; W Philadelphia Enterprise Ctr, pres, 1992-. **Orgs:** Bd mem, United Way Southeastern Pa; small bus adv bd, Fed Reserve Bank Pa; bd mem, Univ Pa Museum Archael & Anthrop; bd Philadelphia Conv & Visitors Bur; bd mem, Forum Exec Women; bd mem, Nat Bus Incubation Asn; sr policy fel, George V Voinovich Ctr Leadership & Pub Affairs, Ohio Univ, 1998-2000; bd mem, St Christopher Found. **Honors/Awds:** Minority Business Advocate Award, Greater Philadelphia Chamber Com, 1995; Supporter of Entrepreneurship Award, Ernest & Young LLP, 1996; New Horizons Award, Minority Bus Enterprise Coun, 1997; Whitney Young Service Award, Urban League Philadelphia, 1999; Take the Lead Award, Girl Scouts of Southern PA, 2001; Honorary Citizen, City Coun Austin, TX, 2002; Beyond the Glass Ceiling Award, Am Red Cross, 2002; Community Service All-Star Award, Philadelphia Tribune, 2002; Local Hero Award, Bank of America, 2005; Entrepreneur Role Model Award, Nat Asn Minority Contractors, 2006. **Special Achievements:** Named one of 25 Most Influential Black Women in Business, Network Jour, 2000. **Business Addr:** President, The Enterprise Center, 4548 Market St, Philadelphia, PA 19139, **Business Phone:** (215)895-4005.

CLARK, DORINDA GRACE. See COLE, DORINDA CLARK.

CLARK, DOUGLAS L.
Educator. **Personal:** Born May 2, 1935, Swedesboro, NJ; married Ellen; children: Douglas Jr & Dana Lynn. **Educ:** Glassboro State Teachers Col, BS 1956, MA, 1970; Laurence Univ, PhD, 1975. **Career:** Glassboro State Col, dir educ opportunity prog, 1970-, asst dir, 1968-70; NJ Rural Manpower Prog, educ specialist, 1967-68; jr high sch NJ, inst, 1956-67; Real Estate, licensed salesman, 1963-. **Orgs:** Mt Calvary Baptist Church; Businessman Asn, 1975; NJ Dirs Asn EOF; Nat Asn Advan Colored People; bd dirs, UYA. **Business Addr:** Director of Education Programme, Glassboro State College, La Spata House, Glassboro, NJ 08028.

CLARK, EDWARD
Artist. **Personal:** Born May 6, 1926, New Orleans, LA; son of Edward and Merion. **Educ:** Art Inst Chicago, attended 1951; L'Academie de la Grande Paris, attended 1952. **Career:** Univ Del, vis artist, 1969-78; Univ Ore, vis artist, 1969-78; Art Inst Chicago, vis artist, 1969-78; Showkegan Sch Painting & Sculpture, vis artist, 1969-78; Ohio State Univ, vis artist, 1969-78; La State Univ, vis artist, 1969-78; Syracuse Univ, 1985; artist, currently. **Orgs:** Bd dir, Orgn Independent Artists, NY; adv bd, Cinque Gallery NY; charter mem, Brata Gallery NY. **Honors/Awds:** Adolph Gottlieb Award, 1981; National Endowment Grant, 1982; Congressional Achievement Award, 1994; Joan Mitchell Awards, 1998; "art for life"Honored Artist, Rush Philanthropic Arts Found, 2000. **Special Achievements:** Numerous exhibits & one-man shows at Cont Arts Center New Orleans, NC A & T Univ, Randall Gallery NYC, Museum of Solidarity Titograd Yugoslavia, Art Salon NYC, LA State Univ, "Contemp Black Art" FL Intl Univ, Sullivant Gallery OH State Univ, James Yu Gallery NYC, Acad of Arts & Letters NYC,Whitney Mus NYC, Lehman College NYC, Afro-Amer

Exhib Mus of Fine Arts Boston, Morgan State Coll, Mod Mus Tokyo, Stockholm, Nova Gall Boston,Amer Ctr Artists, Amer Embassy Paris, Gall Creuze Paris, Salon d'Automne Paris, and numerous others, 1952-.

CLARK, DR. EDWARD DEPRIEST, SR.
Educator. **Personal:** Born May 24, 1930, Wilmington, NC; son of Ethel Exum Clay and Junius Clark; married Evangeline Merritt (divorced 1961); children: Edward D Jr. **Educ:** NC A&T State Univ, Greensboro, NC, BS, 1948; NY Univ, NY, NY, MA, 1955; Syracuse Univ, Syracuse, NY, PhD, 1971. **Career:** Union Point High Sch, Union Point, GA, Eng dept head, 1948-51; Greensboro High Sch, Greensboro, GA, Eng dept head, 1953-54; Emanuel County High Sch, Swainsboro, GA, Eng dept head, 1954-57; Albany State Col, Albany, GA, asst prof, Eng, 1957-59; Southern Univ, Baton Rouge, LA, asst prof, Eng, 1960-61; Fayetteville State Univ, Fayetteville, NC, assoc prof, chmn, 1961-66, chmn, prof, Eng, 1971-75; NC State Univ, Raleigh, NC, assoc prof, Eng, 1975-. **Orgs:** Col Lang Asn, 1961-; Modern Lang Asn, 1961-; South Atlanta Mod Lang Asn, 1975-. **Honors/Awds:** Outstanding Teacher Award, 1989, elected to Academy of Outstanding Teachers, 1989, NC State Univ; Alumni Outstanding Teacher Award, NC State Univ, 1989. **Military Serv:** AUS, Sgt, 1951-53; Outstanding Teaching Award, 1952, 1953. **Business Addr:** Professor, NC State University, English Department, Raleigh, NC 27602, **Business Phone:** (919)737-3863.

CLARK, ELIGAH DANE, JR.
Government official. **Personal:** Born Apr 20, 1943, Aliceville, AL; son of Elijah and Lula Clark. **Educ:** Stillman Col, Tuscaloosa, Ala, BS, 1963; Emporia State Univ, Kans, MS, 1968; Univ MS, JD, 1977. **Career:** Alcorn State Univ, French instr, 1972-74; Navy-Marine Corps, judge advocate, 1974-87, Trial Judiciary, judge, 1987-94, Ct Criminal Appeals, judge, 1994-98; Dept Vet Affairs, chmn bd vet appeals, 1998-2004; US Bankruptcy Ct, 2005-. **Orgs:** Omega Psi Phi; MS State Bar; Nat Naval Officers Asn; Ct Appeals Armed Forces Bar; Fed Bar Asn; US Supreme Ct Bar; Nat Bar Asn; Am Judges Asn. **Honors/Awds:** Distinguished Alumni, NAFEO, 1989; Outstanding Young Am, US Chamber Com, 1978; Exceptional Service Award, Dept Veterans Affairs, 2000. **Military Serv:** USMC, Radiotech, inf officer, 1968-99. **Home Addr:** 9403 Caldran Dr, Clinton, MD 20735, **Home Phone:** (301)856-0544. **Business Addr:** Washington, DC 20420.*

CLARK, FRANK M
Executive. **Personal:** Born Sep 3, 1945, Chicago, IL; married Vera; children: Frank III & Steve. **Educ:** Chicago's DePaul Univ, law, bus admin. **Career:** Exelon Corp, sr vpres, 2001-; Exelon Energy Deliver, sr vpres, currently; Waste Mgt Inc, dir, 2002-, Commonwealth Edison, IL, exec vpres, pres, chmn & chief exec officer, currently; Harris Financial Corp, bd dir; Aetna Inc, bd dir. **Orgs:** Bd trustees, DePaul Univ; Adler Planetarium & Astronomy Mus; Univ Chicago Hosps & Health Syst; Peggy Notebaert Nature Mus; bd dirs, Metrop Family Serv; bd dirs, Gov State Univ Found; bd dirs, Ill Mfrs Asn; bd dirs, Ill Coalition, Big Shoulders Fund; bd dirs, United Way Metrop Chicago; gov bd, Ill Coun Econ Educ; Chicago Bar Asn; Econ Club Chicago; Exec Club Chicago. **Honors/Awds:** HistoryMakers Award, 2002; DHL, DePaul Univ, 2004; DHL, Gov State Univ, 2005; National Humanitarian Award, Nat Conf Community & Justice; Man of the Year Award, Rich Township Bus Asn; Rerum Novarum Award, St Joseph's Sem, Loyola Univ. **Special Achievements:** Fifty Most Powerful Black Execs in Am, Fortune mag, 2002. **Military Serv:** AUS, 1967. **Business Addr:** Chairman, Chief Executive Officer, Exelon Corporation, Commonwealth Edison, 440 S Lasalle St, Chicago, IL 60603, **Business Phone:** (312)394-4321.

CLARK, DR. FRED ALLEN
Psychologist. **Personal:** Born Jul 8, 1929, Toledo, OH; son of Idus and Rose; divorced; children: Kevin & Kim. **Educ:** San Francisco State Col, BA, 1967, MA, 1968; Wright Inst, PhD, social-clin psychol, 1971. **Career:** Coun Clins Inc, exec dir, 1972-81; Calif Youth Authority, staff psychologist, 1982-89; pvt pract, psychologist, 1989-; Nat Univ, instr; Clarco Enterprises, owner & chief exec officer, currently. **Orgs:** Am Psychol Asn; Calif Asn Marriage Counrs. **Special Achievements:** Author: All for Nothing, 1989; Teenage Gangs, 1993; articles: "Series on Teenage Gangs", Ebony Magazine, Sep 1992; Observer Newspaper, 1992; lecturer, "Teenage Gangs," Sierra Vista Hospital, 1991-92; Author, Teenage Street Gangs, 1996. **Business Addr:** Psychologist, Clarco Enterprises, Teenage St Gangs, PO Box 162550, Sacramento, CA 95816, **Business Phone:** (916)488-8068.

CLARK, GARY C.
Football player, restaurateur. **Personal:** Born May 1, 1962, Radford, VA. **Educ:** James Madison Univ. **Career:** Football player (retired), Restaurateur; USFL, Jacksonville Bulls; Wash Redskins, wide receiver, 1985-92; Phoenix Cardinals, 1993; Ariz Cardinals, wide receiver, 1994; Miami Dolphins, wide receiver, 1995; Am Mortgage Bank, financial serv provider; South Beach Restaurant & Martini Bar,owner, currently. **Orgs:** Rep, Host Comt, James Brown Awards, Nat Football League Players Asn. **Honors/Awds:** College Offensive Player of the Year, James Madison Univ, 1983; Redskins Offensive Player of the Game, 1985; Virginia Sports Hall of Fame, 2007. **Special Achievements:** Guest, The Darrell Green Show. **Business Phone:** (301)718-9737.

CLARK, GRANVILLE E., SR.
Physician. **Personal:** Born Jun 14, 1927, Santiago, Chile; married Mary; children: Granville Jr, Robert, Joseph, James. **Educ:** Inst DeSegunda Ensenanta De, Santiago, BS, 1947; Univ Havana, MD, 1954. **Career:** Provident Hosp, intern, 1954-55; Norfolk Community Hosp, physician, 1955-57; Resd Gen Hosp, physician, 1957-59; Pvt Pract, physician, 1959; KCMC DayCare Ctr, pediatrician consult; Truman Med Ctr-West, pediatrics; pvt prac, currently. **Orgs:** SW Pediatric & Soc; KC Med Soc; Pan-MO State Med Soc; NMA; Jackson Co Med Soc; Mo Med Asn; Coun Selection Med Sch; bd mem, Lead Poison Prog; KC Sickle Cell Anemia; Mid-Am Comprehensive Health Planning Agency; chmn, Med Exec Comt, Martin Luther King Hosp; adv bd, Douglas State Bank; pres, Metro-Metic Clin; NAACP; YMCA; Greater Ky Boys Club; Cent Tex Med Found. **Honors/Awds:** Numerous awards & recognitions. *

CLARK, HARRY W.
Physician, educator. **Personal:** Born Sep 6, 1946, Detroit, MI. **Educ:** Wayne State Univ, BA, 1969; Univ Mich, Med Sch, MD, 1973; Univ Mich, Sch Pub Health, MPH, 1974. **Career:** Exec asst, Nat Inst Ment Health; pvt pract, Psychiatrist, currently.

CLARK, IRMA (IRMA CLARK-COLEMAN)
School administrator, government official. **Personal:** Born in Georgia. **Educ:** Wayne State Univ, detroit, MI. **Career:** Wayne County Rd Comn, 1967; Wayne County Human Rels Div, dir; Detroit Sch Bd, pres, 1998; Mich Senate Dem Caucus, Dist Three, sen, 2004-. **Orgs:** Nat Asn Advan Colored People; vpres bd dirs, God Land Unity Church; Mich Dem Party; Travelers Aid Soc; March Dimes; Detroit Goodfellows; Civic Ctr Optimist Club; TULC; United Way Community Servs; vice cochair, Detroit Pub Schs.Nat Sch Bd Asn; Bd Dirs; Mich Asn Sch Bds, Bd Dirs; Nat Alliance Black Sch Educrs. **Honors/Awds:** Adelita Award, MANA de Mich; Spirit Detroit Award, City Detroit; Distinguished Serv Award, Wayne Co Clerk; Exec Declaration Award, State Mich; Tomorrow Power, Mich Girl Scouts; Am Bus Womens Asn Award; Headliner Award, Women Wayne State Univ Alumni Asn, 1997; List of 150 Most Influential Black Women in Metro Detroit, Women Informal Network, 1997. **Special Achievements:** One of the first African-American women to hold a management position at the Wayne County Road Commission. **Business Phone:** (517)373-7370.*

CLARK, DR. IRVIN R.
College administrator, executive, football coach. **Educ:** Fla A&M Univ, BS, Polit sci, 1990; Savannah State Univ, MS, Public Admin, 1999; Ed.D, 2003. **Career:** Football player (retired); Tampa Bay Buccaneers, DL, 1991; Savannah State Univ, football asst coach & residence hall dir, 1993-97,Ctr Residential Serv & Progs, dir, interim athletics dir, Off Stud Affairs, asst vpres, vpres, currently. **Orgs:** Chair, self study steering comt, Savannah State Univ; NCAA Athletics Cert Steering Comt. **Military Serv:** USN, 1983-87. **Business Addr:** Vice President, Savannah State University, Office of Student Affairs, King-Frazier Complex Suite 247, PO Box 20521, Savannah, GA 31404, **Business Phone:** (912)356-2194.

CLARK, JAMES IRVING, JR.
Manager, clergy. **Personal:** Born Apr 18, 1936, Paterson, NJ; married Shirley Lorraine Matthews; children: James I III, Renee Therese, Rhonda Ellise. **Educ:** Am Divinity Sch, BTH, 1966; Baruch Col, attended 1968; Columbia Univ, MBA, 1973. **Career:** Slant/Fin Corp, asst rels mgr, 1962-69; New Era Learning Corp, exec vpres, 1969 -71; Christ Temple Church, pastor, 1969; Church Christ Bible Inst, actg dean, 1971; Columbia Univ, COGME fel, 1971; Pfizer Diagnostics, personnel rels mgr, 1973-75, mgr prof placement, 1975-78, mgr training & develop, 1978. **Orgs:** Pres, Columbia Univ, Grad Sch Bus, 1971-73. **Honors/Awds:** Serv Award, Columbia Univ, Grad Sch Bus, 1973; Black Achiever Award, Pfizer Inc & YMCA, NY, 1974. **Military Serv:** USAF, a/2c, 3 1/2 yrs.

CLARK, DR. JAMES N.
Dentist, consultant. **Personal:** Born Sep 16, 1934, Brooklyn, NY; son of Luther and Augusta Neale; married Patricia; children: Melissa, Holly & James II. **Educ:** City Col NY, BS, 1956; Columbia Univ, Col Dent Med, DDS, 1964; Acad Gen Dent, FAGD (Hon), 1974; Am Col Dentists, FACD (Hon), 1980-. **Career:** ITT, dent dir, 1965-69; Pvt Prac, dent; World Wide ITT, dent consult, 1969-90. **Orgs:** Nat Asn Advan Colored People, Omega Psi Phi, 1955-; secy, Commonwealth Dent Asn, 1969; Newark Beth Israel Hosp Attendant, 1969; Civil Defense, 1972-79; pres, Am Asn Indust Dentists, 1973; co-chmn, United Way, 1973; secy, Cent Pkwy Asn, 1974; 100 Black Men, 1975; Life mem, Omega Psi Phi, 1976; pres, Ad Hoc Community Orange Cent Young Men's Christian Asn, 1976-80; secy, 100 Black Men, 1980; fel, Am Col Dentists, 1980-; bd trustees, Rampo Col, 1982-93; pres, Univ Med & Dent NJ, Dent Assisting Adv Bd, 1986-90; chmn, bd trustees, Ramapo Col, 1988-; vpres, external affair, 100 Black Men, 1988-94; treasurer, Columbia Univ Alumni Asn, 1986-92; bdgovrs, Ramapo Col, 1993-; Essex County Vincinage Comt, Minority Concerns Judicial, 1994-; consulting staff, Newark Beth Israel, 1969-; adv coun, NJ Corrections Dept, 1994; Dent asn attendant, Hosp Ctr Orange, 1988-96. **Honors/Awds:** John Hay Whitney Fel, 1963; Smith & Noyes Scholar, 1960, 1964; Gold Foil Award First Prize, Dent Stud Exhibit; Superstar Award, Young Men's Christian Asn, 1979; Centennial Community of Orange Award, 1989; Minority Achievement Award, Ramapo Col, 1990. **Military Serv:** AUS, pvt. **Business Addr:** Dentist, 185 Cent Ave Suite 301, East Orange, NJ 07018-3318, **Business Phone:** (973)672-1717.*

CLARK, JESSE B., III
Administrator. **Personal:** Born Feb 12, 1925, Philadelphia, PA; married Lucille Field; children: Bruce, Kevin, Blair & Cynthia. **Educ:** Pa State Univ, BA, 1950; Grad Work Univ, PA, 1952. **Career:** Urban League, dir vocaliors, 1954-59; Campbell Soct Co, personnel spec, 1959-62; Abbotts Dairies, dir pub rels, 1962-64. **Orgs:** Pres & bd chmn, St Edmonds Home Children, 1983-; trustee, St Charles Seminary Archdiocece Philadelphia, 1984, Mercy Catholic Medical Ctr, 1974-; past pres, Serra Club Philadelphia, 1972; treas, Catholic Soc Serv Bd, 1974-; trustee, Villanora Univ Villanora PA, 1974-84; comnr, Charter Revision Comn Philadelphia, 1976; bd mem, Nat Catholic Stwrdshp Coun,1983-; bd mem Inst Mentally Retarded, 1985-; sec Nat Adv Comt US Conference Bishops, 1987. **Honors/Awds:** Knight of the Order Saint Gregory the Great, 1977; Commandor Knight of the Order Saint Gregory the Great, 1986. **Military Serv:** USNA, s & sgt.

CLARK, JOE LOUIS
School administrator, educator, public speaker. **Personal:** Born May 8, 1939, Rochelle, GA; son of Maggie Majors Clark and Rhomie Clark; children: Joetta, Joe Jr & Hazel. **Educ:** William Paterson Col, BA, 1960; Seton Hall Univ, MA, 1974. **Career:** Educator (retired), speaker; Bd Educ, Paterson NJ, teacher, 1960-74, coordr lang arts, 1976-79, elem sch prin, 1979-82, sec sch prin, 1983-90; Keppler Assoc, lectr; ed reformer; motivational speaker, currently; Essex Co Juv Detention Newark, NJ, dir, div youth serv, currently. **Orgs:** Nat Asn Sec Sch Prin; NAACP; NJ Prins & Adminrs Asn; Paterson Prins Asn. **Honors/Awds:** Community Service Award, NAACP Paterson Chap, 1983; New Jerseyan of the Year, Newark Star Ledger, 1983; Outstanding Educator, NJ Monthly mag,1984; Distinguished Alumnus Award, Seton Hall Univ, 1985; Distinguished Service Award, Fairleigh Dickinson Univ, 1985; honored at presidential conf on acad & displinary excllence at White House, 1985; Principal of Leadership Award, Nat Sch Safety Ctr, 1986; Humanitarian Award, Nat Black Policemen's Asn, 1988; 60 Minute Profile; Presidential Citations. **Special Achievements:** Dramatized version of his struggle in ridding Eastside High Sch of violence & drugs depicted in major motion picture, Lean On Me, 1989; Book: Laying Down The Law; Time Cover, Feb 1988. **Military Serv:** USAR, e5, 1958-66.

CLARK, JOHN JOSEPH
Executive. **Personal:** Born Jun 26, 1954, Pittsburgh, PA; son of John L and Anna Bluett; married C Lynne Clark, Jun 24, 1989. **Educ:** Northeastern Univ Boston, BS, BA, 1977; Univ Chicago, MBA, 1985. **Career:** Boston Celtics, basktball player, 1976; Arthur Andersen & Co, auditor, 1977-80; Bell & Howell, sr auditor, 1980-81; Baxter Travenol Labs, mkt mgr, 1981-86; Community Col Allegheny Co, prof, 1992-97; Clark & Assocs, pres, 1986-. **Orgs:** Sch coordr, Chicago Asn Com & Ind Youth Motivation Prog, 1977-; Nat Asn Black Accts, 1978-86, treas, 1980; Nat Black MBA Asn, 1985-96; bd mem, Hollywood Tower Condo Asn, 1986-88; Greater Pittsburgh Chamber Com, 1987, Pittsburgh Regional Minority Purchasing Coun, 1996; Alumni Assocs, Chicago Coun Foreign Rels; comn mem, PACE, 1990-93; co-chair, Allegheny County MBE Adv Comt, 1990-92, bd dirs, Garfield Jubilee Asn, 1991-95, bd dirs, E Liberty Develop Inc, 1993-95; vpres communs, Am Mkt Asn, Pittsburgh Chap. **Honors/Awds:** Outstanding Young Men of America, 1985; Certificate of Appreciation, Chicago Asn Com, 1986; Northeastern Univ Athletic Hall of Fame, 1987. **Business Addr:** President, Clark & Associates, 5933 Baum Blvd, PO Box 17126, Pittsburgh, PA 15206, **Business Phone:** (412)361-3200.

CLARK, KAREN VALENCIA. See CLARK-SHEARD, KAREN.

CLARK, KEON ARIAN
Basketball player. **Personal:** Born Apr 16, 1975, Danville, IL. **Educ:** Univ Nev, Las Vegas, criminal justice, 1998. **Career:** Denver Nuggets, ctr, 1998-2001; Toronto Raptors, ctr, 2000-02; Sacremento Kings, 2002-03; Utah Jazz, ctr forward, 2003-04; Phoenix Suns, 2004.

CLARK, LARON JEFFERSON
School administrator, librarian. **Personal:** Born Dec 6, 1938, Atlanta, GA; son of Laron Jefferson Clark Sr and Doshia Mary Alice Blasingame Clark; married Mary Ellen Smith; children: Laron III, Jeremy & Allison. **Educ:** Morehouse Col, BA, 1961; Atlanta Univ, MS, 1965; Univ Tulsa, attended 1968. **Career:** Brooklyn Pub Libr, Adult serv librarian, 1961-63; Queensborough Pub Libr,

suprv, branch librarian, 1963-66; Langston Univ, chief librarian, Libr Sci Dept chmn, assoc prof, 1966-68; Langton Univ, dir develop, 1968-71; Atlanta Univ, exec dir, univ relations & develop, 1971-75; Hampton Univ, vpres develop, 1975-; Morehouse Col, vpres inst advan, res & planning, 1998. **Orgs:** Trustees, Hampton Rd Acad, 1978-; Kiwanis Club, 1979-, Tidewater Longshoremen Scholarship Comt, 1982-, Soc Fund Raisers, 1980-; mem bd dirs, Cultural Alliance Greater Hampton Roads, 1985-; secy/bd dirs, Cultural Alliance Greater Hampton Roads; Fund Raising Comt, Va Air Space Ctr Mus; treas, Cultural Alliance Greater Hampton Roads, 1990-; bd dirs, Yorktown Found. **Honors/Awds:** Academic Scholarship, Morehouse Col, 1956. **Home Addr:** 1733 Golfcrest Ct, Stone Mountain, GA 30088. **Business Addr:** Vice President for Development, Hampton University, Office of the Vice President for Development, PO Box 6174, Hampton, VA 23668, **Business Phone:** (757)727-5356.

CLARK, DR. LAWRENCE M
Educator, school administrator. **Personal:** Born Apr 4, 1934, Danville, VA; son of Lawrence U and Ida Bell; married Irene Reynolds, Aug 20, 1960; children: Deborah, Linda, Lawrence Jr & Shelia. **Educ:** Va State Univ, Petersburg, VA, BS, 1960; Univ Va, Charlottesville, VA, MS, 1964, EdD, 1967. **Career:** Norfolk State Univ, Norfolk, VA, assoc prof math, 1969-70; Fla State Univ, Tallahassee, Fl, assoc prof math, 1970-74; Va State Col, fac; NC State Univ, Raleigh, NC, assoc provost, prof math ed, 1974-94, consult, currently. **Orgs:** Co-founder, African Am Cultural Ctr. **Honors/Awds:** Kappa Mu Epsilon Math Hon Soc, 1959; Phi Delta Kappa, 1965; Admin fel, Am Coun Educ, 1976-77; Phi Kappa Phi, NC State Univ, 1977; Alpha Phi Alpha Fraternity; Benjamin E Mays Award, 2007; L M Clark Lect, NC State Univ, named in honor. **Special Achievements:** NC State's second African American to serve as a University Administrator; named Lawrence M. Clark Rm, The Friday Inst. **Military Serv:** Army, Corporal, 1954-56.

CLARK, LEON STANLEY
Educator, government official. **Personal:** Born Mar 31, 1913, Bunkie, LA; son of Daniel and Leola Dodson; married Ernestine Mack, Nov 11, 1933; children: Mary D, Leon S Clark Jr. **Educ:** Southern Univ, Baton Rouge, BS, 1959, MEd 1966, Cert Supv & Admin, 1970. **Career:** Avoyelles Parish Sch, Marksville, teacher, 1959-69; Avoyelles Parish Sch, Alexendria, LA, teacher, 1969-70; Saginaw Schs, Saginaw, teacher, 1970-83; Saginaw County Juven, Sagniaw, unit supvr, 1970-74; Buena Vista Charter Twp, supvr, currently. **Orgs:** Bethel AME Ch; Kappa Alpha Fraternity. **Honors/Awds:** Outstanding Award Serv, Cub Scout master, 1976; Outstanding Serv Award, Buena Vista Men's Club, 1984; Booker T Wash Cert Outstanding Serv, 1987; Appreciation Continued Serv, Buena Vista Parks & Rec, 1990. **Military Serv:** Army, Pfc, 1950-54; KSM, UN, SM, NDSM, GCM Awards. **Business Addr:** Supervisor, Buena Vista Charter Township, 1160 S Outer Dr, Saginaw, MI 48601.*

CLARK, LINDA DAY
Artist, educator. **Educ:** Howard Community Col, AA; Md Inst Col Art, BFA; Univ Del, MFA. **Career:** Baltimore Mus Art, educr; Coppin State Univ, assoc prof, 1998, prof, currently; visual artist, currently. **Special Achievements:** Photographs included in books Reflections in Black: A History of African American Photography 1840-99, Committed to the Image, and Spirit of Family, media appearances include a feature as a "Woman of Triumph" by Maryland Public Television and "Winners: Linda Day Clark" by WJZ Channel 13. **Business Phone:** (410)951-3365.

CLARK, MARIO SEAN
Executive, football coach, football player. **Personal:** Born Mar 29, 1954, Pasadena, CA; son of Oscar Clark and Lois Prince Clark; married Lisa Clark Adkins; children: Taylor Alexander Clark. **Educ:** Univ Ore, interior design, 1972-76. **Career:** Football player, football coach (Retired), executive; Buffalo Bills, defensive back, 1976-83; San Francisco 49ers, Defensive Back, 1983- 1984; John Muir High Sch, Sec Coach, C.I.F. Go-Champions, 1988-89; Pasadena City Col, Sec Coach, Pony Bowl Champions, 1989-90; Elegant Pillow Upholstery, owner; Rose Bowl Operating Co, community outreach coord, community outreach dir, currently. **Orgs:** Bd mem, George Steuart Memory Football Camp, 1985; consult, Boys Club Pasadena 1985. **Honors/Awds:** Super Bowl Winner, San Francisco 49ers, 1985; Pasadena High School Hall of Fame, 1996; Certificate of Apppreciation, Pasadena Police Dept. **Special Achievements:** All-rookie team Buffalo Bills, 1976. **Business Addr:** Community Outreach Director, Rose Bowl Operating Company, 1001 Rosebowl Dr, Pasadena, CA 91103, **Business Phone:** (626)577-3100.

CLARK, MILDRED E.
Educator. **Personal:** Born Dec 16, 1936, Columbus, GA; married Henry L; children: Henry L & Kenneth. **Educ:** Jesup W Scott High Sch, 1954; Lane Col, Jackson, Tenn, Liberal Arts, 1957; Elsa Cooper Sch, Detroit, Mich, Ct Reporting, 1960; Wayne State Univ, Detroit, Mich, Adult Educ Training, 1958; Davis Bus Col, Comput Prog,1981; Univ Toledo, BA, 1963, MA, 1982. **Career:** Toledo, legal secy, 1958-59; Realty Co, secy, 1960-61; Rossford Ordinance, clerk typist, 1961-63; Eli B Williams Sch, educr, 1963-65; Anna Pickett Elem Sch, educ; Toledo Pub Sch Syst, 1963-93, adult educ classes, 1982, grad assist, 1965-67, adult night classes, instr; Martin Luther King JrElem Sch, 1983; WNGT-TV, channel 48, co-owner; Ghana's Academies & Cul Arts Acad, Founder & Admin, 1997; Ghanashia Bed & Breakfast Haven, owner, currently. **Orgs:** Founder, Ghanited Neighborhood Orgn 1970-; Toledo Fed Teachers, 1973; The Black Caucus Toledo Teachers; Frederick Douglass Community Asn Nat Adv Asn Colored People; Toledo Educ Asn, 1965-72; Black African Peoples Asn; Black Historical Soc; Secy, PTA; chmn, Human Rels Bd, Toledo Educ Asn, 1966-67, 1973; founder, Ghanaian Foundation, 1981; building rep, Toledo Fedn Teachers, 1983; founder, Honor Soc honor Dr Martin Luther King Jr. **Honors/Awds:** Outstanding service Doer's Award, Toledo Educ Assoc; Media Achievement Award, 2002. **Special Achievements:** Developed career unit for students' enrichment; produced and directed TV program for elem students, "The Beat Goes On," channel 30, WGTE-TV, 1970; initiated, produced, First Annual Black History Quiz Bowl for elem students, Toledo, channel 13, WTVG-TV, 1977; Off Minority Affairs, organized, prepared job opportunity announcements Collegiate newspaper, Univ Toledo, 1982; organized city-wide "King's Oratorical" contest: a celebration of Dr King's birthday and holiday, 1984-; Ex Producer & Dir:Step Up Toledo, tv program, 1996; appointed by governor to serve as MLK Jr Ohio Comnr. **Business Addr:** Owner, Ghanashia Bed & Breakfast Haven, 11 S Centennial Rd, Holland, OH 43528-9702, **Business Phone:** (419)868-8396.*

CLARK, DR. MORRIS SHANDELL
Surgeon. **Personal:** Born Nov 27, 1945, Princeton, WV; son of Willie R Sr and Clarie; married; children: Gregory Morris & Angela Maureen. **Educ:** WVa State Col, BS, 1967; Univ Calif, San Francisco, BDS, 1973, DDS, 1973. **Career:** Columbia Univ, internship residency oral & maillofacial surg, 1976; Univ Med & Dent NJ, asst prof oral & maillofacial surg, 1976-81; Univ Colo Sch Dent, Sch Med, prof surg dent, currently, dir anesthesia, 1982-; Nationwide Parking, owner, currently. **Orgs:** Am Asn Oral & Maxillofacial Surgeons; bd dirs, Am Dent Soc Anesthesia; Coun Sci Affairs; Am Dent Soc; bd dirs, Make-A-Wish Found; fel Am Col Dent. **Honors/Awds:** Excellence Teaching Award, 1981; Chancellor's Diversity Award, Univ Colo Denver & Health Sci Ctr, 2003. **Special Achievements:** Over 50 publications in medical & dental literature; 2 books; 15 major research projects; spoken & lectured throughout the world. **Business Addr:** Professor, Director, University Colorado Health Science Center, Department of Surgical Dentistry, 4200 E 9th Ave, PO Box 6508, Aurora, CO 80045, **Business Phone:** (303)724-6975.

CLARK, PATRICIA ANN
Research librarian. **Personal:** Born May 12, 1951, Philadelphia, PA; daughter of George Clark and Rosalie Maynor Clark. **Educ:** Barnard Col, BA, 1972; Columbia Univ, Sch Libr Serv, MLS, 1974. **Career:** Columbia Univ, ref librn, 1974-76; Time Warner Inc, res librn, 1976-92, The Res Ctr, Time Inc, mgr cent res group, 1992-. **Orgs:** Special Libraries Asn, 1990-. **Business Phone:** (212)522-1212.

CLARK, RALPH H
Executive. **Educ:** Univ Pacific, BS, econs; Harvard Bus Sch, MBA. **Career:** IBM, investment banker; Goldman Sachs, investment banker; Merrill Lynch, investment banker; Blue Makoi, founder & chief exec officer; Adaptec, vpres, fin; Snap Appliance, chief financial officer; Ascend Venture Group LLC, venture partner; GuardianEdge Technologies Inc, chief operating officer, currently. **Orgs:** Bd dir, Oakland Boys & Girls Club; Silicon Valley Community Ventures; Mus Childrens Art. **Business Addr:** Chief Operating Officer, GuardianEdge Technologies Inc, 475 Brannan St Suite 400, San Francisco, CA 94107-5421, **Business Phone:** (415)683-2200.

CLARK, RANDOLPH A.
Architect. **Personal:** Born Nov 25, 1939, Marshall, TX; married Mae A Wesley; children: Dawn & Randalyn. **Educ:** Prairie View A&M Univ, BS, 1961. **Career:** Gen Serv Admin, archit, 1963-73; Randolph A Clark & Assoc Archit, owner, 1973-; Hex Learning Ctr Urban Six Partnership, owner. **Orgs:** Am Inst Archit; Nat Orgn Minority Archit; Rotary Int; Alpha Phi Alpha; bd dir, Hex Learning Ctr. **Military Serv:** AUS, capt, 1963. *

CLARK, ROBERT G.
State government official, executive. **Personal:** Born Oct 3, 1929, Ebenezer, MS; son of Robert Fletcher and Julian Williams; married Essie B Austin, 1970 (deceased); children: Robert George III & Bryant Wandrick. **Educ:** Jackson St Col, BS, 1953; Miss Valley St; Mich State Univ, MA, 1959; Fla A&M Univ, attended 1960; Western Mich Univ attended 1965. **Career:** Lexington High Sch, teacher & coach; St Miss, Holmes & Vazoo Counties, Dist 49, rep, 1968; House Clark Furniture Store, owner, currently. **Orgs:** Founder & bd mem, Cent MS Inc Comt Action Progs; Int Bd Basketball Officials; past pres, Cent MS Bd Athletic Officials; pres, Holmes CoTeachers Asn, 1969; fel Inst Polit John F Kennedy Sch Govt Harvard Univ, 1979; dem party nominee, Cong Seat, 1982, 1984; past pres, Fine Housing Enterprises; chmn, Ed Comt House Reps; appropriations comm., House Reps; sec rules comm, House Reps; pres & bd trustees, C Ctr Lexington; Nat Coalition Advocates Studs; Dem Nat Comt Voter Participation Task Force; co-chmn, MS Del So Reg Coun. **Honors/Awds:** Alumnus of the Year, Jackson St Col, 1968; Outstanding Service & Inspiration to Humanity Award; Distinguished Alumni, Nat Asn Equal Opportunity Higher Educ, 1982. **Special Achievements:** First African-American to be elected to a Mississippi House of Representatives; first African American to have a Mississippi state building named after him; his biography was published in a book named, Robert G Clark's Journey To The House: A Black Politician's Story, 2003.

CLARK, ROSALIND K.
Singer, actor. **Personal:** Born Nov 16, 1943, Dallas, TX. **Educ:** Tex Southern Univ, BMus, 1965. **Career:** Las Vegas Hilton, nightclub performer; Playboy Club, nightclub performer; Jackson's Penthouse, nightclub performer; After Dark, nightclub performer; Studio One, nightclub Performer; The Tonight Show, guest; Merv Griffin, guest; Dinah, guest. **Orgs:** Vpres, Celebration Soc, 1970-74; Alpha Kappa Alpha Sor. **Honors/Awds:** Entertainment Hall of Fame Awards. **Business Addr:** Actor, c/o Actors Equity, 165 W 46th St, New York, NY 10036.

CLARK, DR. SANZA BARBARA
Educator. **Personal:** Born Jul 3, 1940, Cleveland, OH; daughter of Dewell Davis and Gladys Sanders Davis; divorced; children: Msia. **Educ:** Ky State Univ, BA, 1967; Duquesne Univ, MA, 1970; Howard Univ, CAS, 1980; Univ Ill, PhD, 1985. **Career:** Univ Pittsburgh, Swahili instr, 1969-72; Tanzanian Min Nat Educ, educ officer, IIA, 1972-78; Univ Ill, statistical consult, 1980-83; Ohio State Univ, Swahili instr, 1983-84; Cleveland State Univ, assoc prof educ & res, 1985-, Dept Curric & Found, Social Founds Search Comt, chmn, currently. **Orgs:** Pres, Orchard Family Housing Coun, 1981-83; Guide-Formulas-Hypothesis Testing Univ Ill, 1982; pres, Parents Qual Educ, 1986-87; chmn, Mali Yetu Alternative Educ Sch, 1988-; trustee, Ctr Human Servs, 1989-91; Phi Delta Kappa Prof Soc; Phi Kappa Phi Honor Soc. **Honors/Awds:** Effects-Parental Educ & Sch Ach, Univ Ill, 1985; Honoree, Outstanding African-Am Women, 1996; Queen Mother Award, Excellence in Service & Conn, 1996. **Special Achievements:** Publ: "State of Black Cleveland", 1989; "Persistence Patterns of African American College Students," Readings on the State of Education in Urban America, 1991; "An Analysis of African American First Year College Student Attitudes & Attrition Rates," Journal of Urban Education, 1992; "The Great Migration," Mali Yetu, 1993; "The Schooling of Cultural and Ethnic Subordinate Groups," Comparative Education Review, 1993; "Rediscovering Our Roots in Ghana, Africa," Mali Yetu, 1995. **Business Addr:** Associate Professor, Chairman, Cleveland State University, Department of Curriculum & Foundations, 2121 Euclid Ave RT 1349, Cleveland, OH 44115.

CLARK, SAVANNA M. VAUGHN
Educator, lecturer. **Personal:** Born in Hutchinson, KS; daughter of Charles Theola and Helen Vermal Grice; married Charles Warfield Clark. **Educ:** Prairie View A&M Univ, TX, BS, 1949; Univ Okla, Norman, MEd; Okla State Univ, Stillwater, postgrad & doctoral studies. **Career:** Southern Univ, Baton Rouge LA, instr; Ponca City Pub Schs, Ponca City OK, instr; NC Cent Univ, Durham, NC, instr; Langston Univ, OK, asst prof; Univ DC, asst prof, 1974-. **Orgs:** Am Public HTH Asn; Am Alliance Health, Phys Educ, Recreation & Dance; Nat Educ Asn; Am Med Auxiliary Asn Inc; founding mem, Phi Delta Kappa, Univ DC Chap; Delta Sigma Theta Sorority; founding mem, Friends of the Kennedy Ctr; vpres, Women's Comm, Wash Ballet; patron, Mus African Art; donor, Mus Women Arts, WA DC; exec bd mem, YWCA, WA DC area, 1974; founder, 1979, pres, 1981, Capital City Links Inc, WA DC; chairperson, Northwest Quadrant, Am Cancer Soc, 1984; chairperson, Fund-Raiser Arts, C's Mus, 1988; bd mem, Peoples Bank & Trust Co Inc; comnr, Southern Asn Cols & Schls; President's Roundtable; bd mem, The Innovation Cte. **Honors/Awds:** Award of Appreciation, Prairie View Univ Stud Body; alumnus of Prairie View A&M Univ, Nafes Award; Award of Contribution & Presidents Club, Prairie View Univ; fund-raiser chairperson, raised $100,000 for Gems Prog Minority Med Studs, Georgetown Univ Med Sch; hon, Georgetown Univ Med Sch, 1988, 1989; Tex Hall of Fame; James Wells $1000,000 Art donated to Prairie View Univ Tex of Black Am; Richard Dempey-Samuel Gilliam & Africa sculpture from Kenya, W Africa; 3 Citations, Best Dressed Woman; Exhibition of my Couture wardrobe at Neiman Marcus, 1996, a selection from 1960-80; Women's Inner Circle of Achievements, 1997; Phi Theta Kappa, Shirley B Gordon Award; Univ Montevallo, Kent Matheson Award; appointed to serve on the Mayor's Int Protocol Comt, DC, 1999-00; DC Med Bd appointed, 1999-03; vol, White House, 2003. **Home Addr:** 2922 Ellicott Terr NW, Washington, DC 20008. *

CLARK, SHEILA WHEATLEY
Executive. **Personal:** Born Sep 4, 1948, Houston, TX; daughter of Reuben and Helen; divorced. **Educ:** Univ North Tex, BBA, Accounting, 1969, MBA, Accounting, 1972. **Career:** Shell Oil Co, gas accountant, 1969-70; Peat Marwick Main & Co, audit partner, 1972-. **Orgs:** Am Inst Certified Pub Accountants; Nat Asn Black Accountants; Am Women's Soc CPA; Comn Tech Standards TX State Bd pub Accountancy; TX Soc CPA; TASBO; N TX State Univ Dept Accouting; Delta Sigma Theta Sor Inc; Houston Bus

Forum; BOLD Black Organ Leadership Develop; NAACP; Houston Chamber Com; United Way Houston; YWCA; Prof Christian Women Asn; Nat Coalition 100 Black Women; INROADS; acct instr, TX Southern Univ, 1977-78; teaching fellow, N TX State Univ; instr, TX Soc of CPA Continuing Prof Educ seminars; auditing instr, Miller CPA Review Courses, 1980-82; guest lecturer, AICPA summer seminar, 1978 & 1983; bd regents, TX State Univ System; Chmn Bd, Inroads Houston. **Honors/Awds:** National Accounting Achievement Award, NABA; Accountingtg Achievement Award, NABA Houston Chapt; Cert appreciation, NABA Annual Convention, 1981; Alumni of the Year, Phillis Wheatley Sr HS, 1982; NABA Achievement Award, NY Chap, 1982; Outstanding Alumni Award, N TX State Univ, 1987; Women on the Move Houston Post, Texas Exec Women, 1986; Eagle within Award, Inroads, 1986. *

CLARK, SHIRLEY LORRAINE
Executive. **Personal:** Born Oct 26, 1936, Boston, MA; married James I Jr; children: James I III, Renee T, Rhonda E. **Educ:** Am Bible Col, BRE, 1961; CPCU Col Ins, 1978; Am Inst Prop & Liability Underwriters, 1978. **Career:** E G Bowman Co Inc, supr, 1974, mgr, 1975, asst vpres, 1978, vpres, 1980. **Orgs:** Dir, Christian educ Christ Temple Apostolic Faith, 1975-80; NY Chap Soc Chartered Pro & Casualty Underwriters, 1979-80; Notary Public, 1980. **Special Achievements:** First black woman in US to receive CPCU Designation 1978. *

CLARK, TAMA MYERS
Judge. **Educ:** Univ Pa Law Sch, JD, 1972; Univ Pa Grad Sch, MA, City Planning, 1972; Morgan State Univ, BS, 1968. **Career:** Off Dist Atty for the City & City Philadelphia, asst dist atty, 1973-80; Human Serv Div City Philadelphia Law Dept, dep city solicitor, 1980-83; Ct Common Please Criminal Trial Div, judge, 1984-. **Orgs:** Pa State Conf of Trial Judges; bd dir, Community Serv Planning Coun; Family Welfare Asn; The Links Inc; Coalition of 100 Black Women; Women & Girl Offenders Task Force; Mayor's Comn Women. **Honors/Awds:** Woman of the Yr, Nat Sports Found, 1984; Distinguished Alumni Yr, Morgan State Univ; Nat Asn Equal Opportunity Higher Educ, 1984; Outstanding Woman, Community Bright Hope Baptist Church Women's Comn, 1984; Distinguished Alumnus, Philadelphia Chap Morgan State Univ Alumni Asn, 1984.

CLARK, THEOTIS
Scientist, scholar, educator. **Personal:** Born Sep 15, 1961, Akron, OH; son of Theotis Sr and Alberta June Norman. **Educ:** Marion Tech Col, AS, mech eng technol, 1983, AS, indust engineering technol, 1985, AS, elec & electronics engineering, 1987; Wright State Univ, BS, chem, 1990; Iowa State Univ, MS, chem, 1995; Univ Wyoming, PhD, chem, 1998. **Career:** Quaker Oats Comp, chem clerk, 1982-87; Los Alamos Nat Lab, res scientist; Truman State Univ, Div Sci, asst prof, currently. **Orgs:** Am Chem Soc, 1990-; Electro Chem Soc, 1990-; Div Anal Chem, 1991-; Younger Chemist Comt, 1992-; Microscope Soc Am, 1996-; Mat Res Soc, 1999-. **Honors/Awds:** Excellence Award, Iowa State Univ, 1995; Outstanding Merit & Accomplishment, Who's Who ASAUC, 1997; Grad Fellowship Award, Univ Wyoming, 1997; President's Post Doc fellow, Univ Calif, 1998; Univ Calif-Berkley, post doctorate scholar, 1998-99. **Special Achievements:** Los Alamos National Laboratory, speaker, "Optical Microscopy of Giant Vesicles of Synthetic Surfactant," 1999; Pittsburgh Conference, speaker, "Voltammetric Repsonse of dissolved Oxygen and Hydrogen Peroxide at Titanium Electrodes in Alkaline Media," 1994; Univ of Nebraska, Minority Graduate Research Symposium, speaker, "The Chemistry of Characterization of Fisher-Tropsch Iron Nitrided Surfaces," 1991; co-author, "Simultaneous Decontamination and signaling of Chemical Agents," Proceedings of the 1996 Scientific Conference on Chemical and Biological Defense Research, 1996; numerous other speaking engagements and publications. *

CLARK, TONY (ANTHONY CHRISTOPHER CLARK)
Baseball player. **Personal:** Born Jun 15, 1972, Newton, KS. **Educ:** San Diego State Univ. **Career:** Detroit Tigers, infielder, 1995-2001; Boston Red Sox, 2002; NY Mets, 2003; NY Yankees, 2004; San Diego Padres, 2008; Ariz Diamondbacks, first baseman, 2005-09; Free agent, Currently. **Honors/Awds:** Iron Man Award, Honey Baked Ham, 1997; All-Am & Acad All-Am hons; Tony Clark Negro League Scholar; All-Star, 2001. *

CLARK, VINCENT W.
Government official, vice president (organization). **Personal:** Born Apr 11, 1950, Bronx, NY; son of Vincent and Gladys Young; married LaVerne McBride; children: Derrick, Noelle. **Educ:** LaGuardia Communtiy Col, AS, 1979; York Col, BA, 1983; NY Univ, MPA, 1987. **Career:** NY City Bd Educ, 1980-90; NY Univ, mayor's scholar, 1985-86; NY City Emergency Med Serv, assoc exec dir, 1990; NY City Health & Hosp Corp, sr asst vpres, currently; NY City Bd Educ, asst dir, mgt analyst, bus mgr, budget dir. **Orgs:** Am Soc Pub Admin, 1982-; Asn Sch Bus Officials. **Special Achievements:** Top 40 Prog NY City, 1986-87. **Home Addr:** 120 Maryton Rd, White Plains, NY 10603. *

CLARK, WALTER H.
Consultant. **Personal:** Born Jun 5, 1928, Athens, GA; son of John and Beulah; married Juanita E Dillard; children: Hilton P & Jaunine C. **Educ:** Southern Ill Univ, BBA, 1951; DePaul Univ, MBA, 1958; Harvard Univ, Postgrad, 1971. **Career:** Ill Fed Savings & Loan Asn, acct, 1952, 1954-55; First Fed Savings & Loan Assoc Chicago, exec vpres, astron & mem bd dir, 1955-; Citicorp, 1983-86; Chicago Transit Authority, chmn, 1986-88; Bear Stearns Co Inc, vpres, 1986-91; financial consult, 1991; Wheat First Securities Inc, sr financial analyst & broker; Clark Consult Co, 1991; Harold Washington's Finance Comt, 1983; Chicago Bd Education, finance authourity; Peer Group, chrmn. **Orgs:** Travelers Aid Soc Serv League, 1967; Invest Comt, YMCA Metro Chicago; bd dirs, Better Govt Asn; adv coun, Col Bus Admin; Univ Ill; Univ Southern Ill, bd dirs; Nat Soc Controllers & Fin Officers; Fin Exec Inst Econ Club; Alpha Phi Alpha; Union League Club; bd dir, Harvard Bus Sch, Snakes Soc Club; trustee, Park Manor Congregational Church. **Honors/Awds:** Black Achievers of Industry Recognition Award, YMCA 1974; Business School Hall of Fame, Southern Ill Univ, 1986. **Military Serv:** AUS, sargent, 1952-54.

CLARK, WALTER L
Executive. **Personal:** Born Dec 5, 1963, Baltimore, MD; married Mikki Clark; children: Aaron. **Educ:** RETS Electronic Eng, AA, 1985; Howard Co Community Col, AA, 1995; Johns Hopkins Univ, BS, finance, 1996. **Career:** Wheat First Securities, investment officer, 1988-92, vpres & investment officer, 1992-95; Gruntal & Co LLC, vpres investment, 1995-96, pres, 1996-; Clark Capital Financial LLC, pres & chief executive officer, 1999-. **Orgs:** Wheat First's Exec Club, 1990-95; visiting Nurse Asn Found; Howard County Pension Oversight Commn; BE's Million Dollar Round Table; adv, Wash Women's Investment Club. **Business Phone:** (410)381-9500.

CLARK, WILLIAM
State government official, school administrator. **Personal:** Born May 16, 1937, Meridian, MS; married Hattie Giles; children: William H & Reginald A. **Educ:** Dillard Univ, BA, 1961; Tuskegee Inst, MEd, 1967; AL State Univ, EdS, 1978; Univ Ala. **Career:** Mobile Co Training Sch, teacher/coach, 1961-70; Vigor HS, asst prin, 1972-73; Property Real Estate Co Inc, pres, 1974; Citronelle Middle Sch, asst prin, 1977-86, prin, 1986; State AL, state rep. **Orgs:** Elks Lodge No 361, 1980-; Mobile United, 1982-85; Phi Delta Kappa,1982-85; Holmes St Baptist Church; Omega Psi Phi Fraternity; Citronelle Kiwanis Club; Whistler Civic Club; Gulf City Golfers' Asn; Ala Dem Conf; Ala Dem Exec Comt; Ala Legis Black Caucus; Nat Educ Asn; Nat AsnSec Prins; Dillard Univ Alumni Asn. **Home Addr:** 711 S Atmore Ave, Prichard, AL 36612, **Home Phone:** (334)242-7756. **Business Addr:** Member, Omega Psi Phi Fraternity Inc, 3951 Snapfinger Pkwy, Decatur, GA 30035, **Business Phone:** (404)284-5533.

CLARK, WILLIE CALVIN, JR.
Football player. **Personal:** Born Jan 6, 1972, New Haven, CT. **Educ:** Univ Notre Dame. **Career:** Football player (retired), San Diego Chargers, defensive back, 1994-96, 1998; Philadelphia Eagles, 1997. *

CLARK DIGGS, JOETTA
Track and field athlete, president (organization). **Personal:** Born Aug 1, 1962, East Orange, NJ; daughter of Joe Clark and Jetta; married Ronald Diggs, Sep 24, 1999. **Educ:** Univ Tenn, attended 1984. **Career:** Track & field athlete; Fitkidz, host & producer; Joetta Sports & Beyond LLC, pres, currently; NJ Attorney Genl's Off, Drug Diversion Sect, spec investr. **Orgs:** Comnr sports, NJ Sports & Exposition Authority. **Honors/Awds:** Pan American Gold Medalist, 1980; USA Junior Champion, 1980; Olympic Festival Champion, 1986; US Indoor Champion, 1988, 1989, 1990, 1996, 1997, 1998; US Champion, 1988, 1989, 1992, 1993, 1994; NCAA Champion; Bronze Medalist, World Indoors, 1993, 1997; Visa Humanitarian Award; Univ Tenn Hall of Fame, 2001; Millrose Games Hall of Fame, 2002; Penn Relays Hall of Fame, 2004; NJ's Women Athlete of the Century; Sports Illustrated Hometown Hero, Sports Illustrated; NJ Pioneer Woman of the 90's Award; Women of Achievement Award, Rolling Hills Girl Scouts. **Special Achievements:** Featured on MSNBC News Broadcast, CNN, Jet Magazine & Women's Sports & Fitness. **Business Phone:** (908)371-1865.

CLARKE, ALYCE GRIFFIN
State government official, educator. **Personal:** Born Jul 3, 1939, Yazoo City, MS; daughter of Henry Griffin and Fannie Merriweather Griffin; married L W Clarke Jr, Jun 24, 1972; children: DeMarquis. **Educ:** Alcorn State Univ, Lorman MS, BS, 1961; Tuskegee Univ, Tuskegee, AL, MS, 1965; Miss Col, Clinton, MS, 1979; Jackson State, Jackson, MS, 1982. **Career:** Wash County Pub Schs, Leland, Miss, teacher, 1961-68; Miss Action Progress, Jackson MS, nutritionist, 1969-71; Jackson Hinds Health Ctr, Jackson MS, nutritionist, 1971-87; Nutritionist, currently; Miss State House Representatives, state rep, 1985-. **Orgs:** Alcorn State Univ Alumni, 1961-89; Miss Asn Community Health Centers, 1971-89, Nat Soc Nutrit, 1980-89, Mayor's Adv Comn, 1980-89; bd mem, Miss Multiple Sclerosis Nat Soc, 1984-89; Miss Food Network, 1985-89; NatWomen's Polit Caucus, 1985-89; bd mem, United Way, 1986-89, Southeastern Educ Improv Lab, 1986-89; chmn, Jackson Crime Prev Comn, 1988; Alpha Kappa Alpha; Jack & Jill Am; Miss Pub Health Asn; Regional Asn Drug Free Schs &Communities; State Parent Teacher Asn; chair, House Committee on Ethics. **Honors/Awds:** WIC Coordinator of the Year, Miss Bd Health, 1984; Employee of the Year, Jackson Hind Health Center, 1984; Outstanding Service to Education, Int Alumni Coun, 1984; Mississippi Woman of the Year, Hind County Fedn Dem Women, 1985; Alcornite of the Year, Alcorn State Alumni, 1987; Leadership & Service Award, Alpha Kappa Alpha Sorority, 1987. **Special Achievements:** First black woman legislator in Mississippi, 1985. **Home Addr:** 1053 Arbor Vista Blvd, Jackson, MS 39209, **Home Phone:** (662)354-5453. **Business Addr:** State Representative, Mississippi State House of Representatives, District 69, 400 High St Room 119A-NC, PO Box 1018, Jackson, MS 39215-1018, **Business Phone:** (601)359-3096.

CLARKE, DR. ANGELA
Physician. **Personal:** Born Nov 4, 1932, Baltimore, MD; daughter of Luke E Webb and Cora Webb; divorced; children: Wuan, Indranee & Tarita. **Educ:** Univ Md, Sch Med, MD, 1961; Am Bd Family Pract, dipl, 1972. **Career:** Physician (retired); Univ Calif, Los Angeles, Dept Community Med, assoc prof, 1970-76; Univ Nev, Med Sch, assoc prof, 1978; pvt pract, 1962-87. **Orgs:** Links Inc, 1983-92; pres, CI W Chap NMA, 1984; pres, Clark Co Med Soc, 1985; Phi Beta Kappa; founder, Sun City Summerlin Ebony & Ivory Club, 2000; life mem, Nat Asn Advan Colored People; VFW, Am Legion, TROA. **Military Serv:** WAF, 1951-53; AUS, lt col, 1985-87. **Home Addr:** 2505 Desert Butte Dr, Las Vegas, NV 89134-8869, **Home Phone:** (702)228-4028.

CLARKE, ANNE-MARIE
Lawyer. **Personal:** Born in St Louis, MO; daughter of Thomas P and Mary Ann; married Richard K Gaines, Apr 3, 1979. **Educ:** Forest Park Community Col, 1968; Northwest Mo State Univ, BA, 1970; St Louis Univ Sch Law, JD, 1973. **Career:** Arthur D Little Inc, researcher, 1974-94; Northeast Utilities, asst corp sec, 1974-77; Bi-State Develop Agency, staff coun, 1977-79; Self Employed, pvt pract law, 1980-92; City St Louis, hearing off family ct, 1986-, 30 Div, comnr family ct, Domestic Rels div, 2005. **Orgs:** Nat Bar Asn; Exec Coun NBA Judicial Coun; bd govs, Mo Bar, 1986-90, 1991-95; pres, Mound City Bar Asn, 1981-83; chair prevention juv crime task force, Confluence St Louis, 1993; diamond life member, Delta Sigma Theta Sorority Inc; dir, Bar Plan Mutual Ins CPN, 1986-; pres, St Louis Bd Police Comnrs, 1993-98. **Honors/Awds:** Achievement Award, Nat Coun Negro Women Bertha Black Rhoda Sect, 1990; Achievement Award, Nat Orgn Blacks Law Enforcement, 1993; Jordan-McNeal Award, Mo Legis Black Caucus, 1994. **Special Achievements:** "The History of the Black Bar", St Louis bar J, spring 1984; first Black woman to serve on the St. Louis Board of Police Commissioners; first Black member of the Board of Governors of The Missouri Bar. **Business Phone:** (314)552-2030.*

CLARKE, BENJAMIN LOUIS
Labor relations manager. **Personal:** Born Mar 5, 1944, Springfield, OH; married Janet; children: Bryan & Darryl. **Educ:** Lincoln Univ, BS, soc sci, 1966; Xavier Univ, Med Coun, 1972; Univ Cincinnati, MA, indust rels, 1984. **Career:** Ford Motor Co, supvr personnel, mgr personnel serv, currently. **Orgs:** Just Us Individual Investment Club, 1985-; unit comt, Detroit Boy Scout Leader, 1985-; Hartford Optimist Club; bd mem, Lincoln Univ Found; Xavier Univ Alumni Asn; Univ Cincinnati Alumni Asn; NACIREMA Club, 1998; Ford African-Am Network; pres, Detroit Chap, Lincoln Univ Alumni. **Military Serv:** AUS, capt, 2 1/2 yrs; Army Commendation Medal, 1967. **Business Addr:** Manager Personnel Service, Ford Motor Co., Hourly Personnel & Personnel Serv, 3001 Miller Rd, Dearborn, MI 48120-1496, **Business Phone:** (313)322-3000.

CLARKE, BRYAN CHRISTOPHER
Engineer. **Personal:** Born May 23, 1971, Cincinnati, OH; son of Benjamin L and Janet E. **Educ:** Mich State Univ, BS, elec eng, 1998. **Career:** Ford Motor Co, assembly technician, 1996; Dept Com & Indust, Financial Inst Bur, info systs analyst, 1997-98; Silicon Graphics Inc, syst support engr, 1998-. **Orgs:** Nat Soc Black Engrs, 1990-. **Honors/Awds:** NSBE, Pepsi-Cola Scholar Award. *

CLARKE, CHARLOTTE
Engineer, golfer. **Educ:** Eastern Mich Univ, BS, 1987; Purdue Univ. **Career:** Digital Equip, mfg engr, 1988-92; Pitney Bowes, mfg engr, 1992-96, staff engr; Golf player, currently. **Orgs:** Nat Soc Black Engrs; Nat Black MBA Asn. *

CLARKE, CHERYL
College administrator, poet, executive director. **Personal:** Born May 16, 1947, Washington, DC; daughter of James and Edna. **Educ:** Howard Univ, BA, 1969; Rutgers Univ, MA, 1974, MSW, 1980, PhD. **Career:** Conditions, ed, 1981-90; Ctr Gay & Lesbian Studies, City Univ New York Grad Ctr, co-chair brd, 1990-92; Rutgers Univ, Off Diverse Community Affairs & Lesbian Gay Concerns, dir, 1992-; Film Appearance: TheWater melon Woman, 1997; Corridors of Nostalgia, 2006; Poetry collection:Living As a Lesbian, 1986; Gay Community News; The Advocate; Blue Stones &Salt Hay: An Anthology Of New Jersey Poets; Radical

America; Callaloo;Dangerous Liaisons: Blacks & Gays Fighting Oppression; Black Like Us: A Century of Black Gay, Lesbian, Bisexual Fiction; Bloom: A Journal of Writing by Lesbian & Gay Writers. **Orgs:** NY Women Against Rape, 1985-88; grad fac, Women & Gender Studies; steering comt mem, NJ Women & Aids Network. **Business Addr:** Director of Diverse Community Affairs & LGBT Concerns, Rutgers University, 3 Bartlett St, New Brunswick, NJ 08901, **Business Phone:** (732)932-1711.

CLARKE, DR. DONALD DUDLEY
Scientist, educator. **Personal:** Born Mar 20, 1930, Kingston, Jamaica; son of I Dudley and Ivy Burrowes; married Marie B Burrowes; children: Carol, Stephen, Paula, David, Ian, Sylvia & Peter. **Educ:** Fordham Col, BS (cum laude) 1950; Fordham Univ, MS, 1955, PhD 1955. **Career:** NY Psychiat Inst, res assoc, 1957-62; Columbia Univ Med Sch, sr res scientist, 1960-62; Fordham Univ, assoc prof, 1962-70, prof 1970-, Currently. **Orgs:** Consult Nat Inst Ment Health, 1972-76, Nat Inst Health, 1981-85; chmn, chem dept Fordham Univ, 1978-84; chmn, Counlor NY secy Am Chem Soc, 1976-; co-chmn Kingsbridge Manor Neighborhood Asn, 1980-84. **Military Serv:** Research Publications in Professional Journals. **Home Addr:** 2528 Grand Ave, Bronx, NY 10468, **Home Phone:** (718)733-3638. **Business Addr:** Professor, Fordham University, Department of Chemistry, 441 E Fordham Rd, John Mulcahy Hall Room 532, Bronx, NY 10458, **Business Phone:** (718)817-4444.

CLARKE, EVEREE JIMERSON
Educator. **Personal:** Born Jul 6, 1926, Merritt Island, FL; divorced; children: Frances Yvette. **Educ:** Lincoln Univ, 1948; Juilliard Sch Music, 1954; Nova Univ, 1982. **Career:** Everee Clarke Sch Charm & Dance Inc, pres, 1960-; Nat Bus League, nat sec, 1972-76; asst regional, vpres, 1986-, pres & ceo; Tri Co Chap NBL, pres; Elegante Int. **Orgs:** Frances Bright Women's Club Debutante Cotillion, The C Hour early childhood develop prog, Palm Beach Co Cities Schs prog, 1985-86; Broward Co Republican Exec Comm, 1985-88; Serv Tri-Co Chapter, Nat Bus League, founder, 1986; City West Palm Beach HCD Educ Comm, 1987; Broward Co Coun Black Economic Develop; Pleasant City Family Reunion Comm, Inc & Heritage Gallery, founder & pres; consult, Prof Beauty & talent pageant; Urban League; Nat Asn Advan Colored People; Voters League. **Honors/Awds:** Service Award, Nat Bus League, Wash, DC, 1977. **Special Achievements:** Author of Pleasant City, West Palm Beach, 2005. **Business Addr:** Founder, President, Pleasant City Family Reunion Committee Inc, 2117 N Dixie Hwy, West Palm Beach, FL 33407-0816, **Business Phone:** (561)832-9799.

CLARKE, GRETA FIELDS
Physician, dermatologist. **Personal:** Born in Detroit, MI; daughter of Willa Fields and George Fields; divorced; children: Richard. **Educ:** Univ Mich, BS 1962; Howard Univ, MD 1967. **Career:** Harlem Hosp NY, internship 1967-68, residency internal med, 1968-69; NY Univ Med Ctr, residency dermat, 1969-72; Pvt Pract, dermatologist, 1979-. **Orgs:** Am Acad Dermat; Nat Med Asn; Calif Med Asn; San Francisco Dermat Soc; The Links Inc; Reg VI Nat Med Asn, 1986-90; Comt Women Med, Calif Med Asn, 1986-90; Oakland Chapter Carrousels Inc; Women's Dermat Asn; Soc Cosmetic Chemists. **Special Achievements:** Established the Fields Dermatologic Group, Inc, Parent company of The Clarke Collection, 1992. **Business Addr:** Dermatologist, 2500 Milvia St Suite 124, Berkeley, CA 94704-2636, **Business Phone:** (510)843-2384.*

CLARKE, HUGH BARRINGTON
Lawyer. **Personal:** Born Jul 14, 1954, Detroit, MI; son of Hugh B and Gwendolyn; married Judith, Jun 1, 2000; children: Hugh B Clarke IV. **Educ:** Oakland Community Col, assoc arts, 1973; Wayne State univ, BS, 1975; Thomas M Cooley Law Sch, JD, 1979. **Career:** Mich state senate, senate judiciary comt, senate spec consult, 1977-79; State Mich/State Senate, assoc gen coun, 1979-81; self-employed, atty, 1981-. **Orgs:** State Bar Mich, equality justice comt, 1999-2001, standard criminal jury instructions comt, 2000-; Ingham County Bar Asn; past pres, Lansing Black Lawyers Asn. **Honors/Awds:** Alumni of the Year, TM Cooley Black Law Student Asn, 2000. **Business Addr:** Attorney, Hugh B Clarke Jr & Associates, 215 S Washington Sq Suite 210, Lansing, MI 48933-1888, **Business Phone:** (517)487-1401.

CLARKE, JOSEPH LANCE
Executive. **Personal:** Born Apr 6, 1941, New York, NY; married Marion Joyce Herron; children: Bernadette, Leslie & Lancelot. **Educ:** Southern Ill Univ, Carbondale, IL, attended 1963; City Col NY, BA, 1967; NY Univ, attended 1968. **Career:** Livingston Inst, mgr, 1966-67; Supreme Beauty Prod, dir sales, 1971-73; Fashion Fair Cosmetics, dir sales, 1973-74, exec vpres, 1974-. **Orgs:** Vpres, Alpha Phi Alpha Frat Beta Eta Chap, 1962-63; vpres, Young Dem MtVernon, NY, 1966-68. **Honors/Awds:** Business Award, Supreme Beauty Prod, 1970. **Military Serv:** AUS, spec/e5, 1963-66; Plaque for Exemplary Serv, 1963-66; Letter of Accommodation, 1963-66. **Business Addr:** 820 S Michigan Ave, Chicago, IL 60605.

CLARKE, JOY ADELE LONG
Writer, elementary school teacher. **Personal:** Married Ronald Eugene, Nov 19, 1960; children: Dylan Terence, Kelcey Lamar & Darcy Marie. **Educ:** Cent State Univ, Wilberforce, Ohio, BS, elem educ, 1960; Univ Northern Colo, Greeley, Colo, MA, 1978. **Career:** Boulder Valley Schs, Boulder, Colo, teacher, 1972-83; libr media specialist, Lngmnt, Co, St Vrain Valley Schs, libr media specialist, 1992-93; Aims Community Col, Greeley Colo, teacher multicultural diversity; Springfield Pub Schs, Springfield, Ohio, teacher, 1960-62; Denver Pub Schs, Denver, Colo, 1985-92; Creekside Elem Sch, pe, currently; Pershing Elem Sch, Fort Leonard Wood, Mo, 1962-63; Tucson Pub Schs, Tucson, AZ, libr media specialist, 1978-81; Books: African Am Activities, 1997, 2002; Spiritual Nourishment Selected Bible Verses Arranged from A to Z, 2002. **Orgs:** Am Sch Librns; Alpha Kappa Alpha Sorority; Alpha Delta Kappa Teacher's Sorority; NAACP; Am Libr Asn; Asn Black Caucus Am Libr Asn. **Honors/Awds:** Miss Ohio Campus Queen, Cent State Univ, Wilberforce, OH; publ devotional bk: Spiritual Nourishment; two Booklets Conflict Mgt; Oratorical contest winner, Nat Sunday Sch, BTU Cong; Black Hist Activities Book K-12.

CLARKE, KENTON
Executive, president (organization), chief executive officer. **Personal:** Born Nov 17, 1951, Bridgeport, CT; son of Haywood and Ruth. **Educ:** Norwalk State Tech Col, AS, comput sci, 1972; Univ New Haven, BS, 1979; Northwestern Univ, JL Kellogg exec mgt prog. **Career:** Comput Consult Assocs Int Inc, pres, chief exec officer & founder, 1980-. **Orgs:** Dir, Nortech Found, 1989-; bd dirs, Conn Minority Purchasing Coun; bd dirs, Norwalk Community Tech Col; United Fund; Gov's Coun on Econ Competitiveness & Technol; bd mem, Univ New Haven; adv bd, Grad Sch Mgt Sacred Heart Univ. **Honors/Awds:** Supplier of the Year, Conn Minority Purchasing Coun, 1990; Shining Star, CMPC, 1996; Small Bus Person of the Year Award, Small Bus Asn, 1998; Southwestern Connecticut Entrepreneur of the Year Award, Ernst & Young Mag, 2000; Regional Minority Small Bus Person of the Year Award, US Small Bus Admin, 2001; Nation's Top Diversity Owned Bus Award, US Small Bus Admin, 2001. **Special Achievements:** Black Enterprise's Top 100 Industs/Serv Co, ranked 96, 2000; frequently quoted in local & natl publ on diversity bus develop & technol issues including Fortune & Black Enterprise mag; TV & Radio appearnces: PBS; CNBC; CBS News Radio. **Business Addr:** Chief Executive Officer & Founder, President, Computer Consultant Associates International Inc, 200 Pequot Ave, Southport, CT 06890, **Business Phone:** (203)255-8966.*

CLARKE, LEON EDISON
Health services administrator, consultant, surgeon. **Personal:** Born Nov 17, 1949, Monrovia, CA; married Fatu; children: Tanya, Nina & Lee Ann. **Educ:** George Wash Univ, MD, 1975; Hosp Univ PA, Surg Residency, 1977; Med Col PA, 1977-80; Surg Oncol, Med Col PA, 1980. **Career:** Veterans Admin Hosp, Philadelphia PA, consult, 1981-; Med Col PA, attending surgeon, beginning 1981-, instr surg, 1982-, med dir surg procedure unit, 1985-; Mercy Catholic Med Ctr, dir surg, 1988-; Thomas Jefferson Univ Hosp, clin assoc prof surg currently; Misericordia Hosp, dir surg, currently. **Orgs:** Am Cancer Soc; Am Col Physician Execs; Soc Black Acad Surgeons. **Honors/Awds:** two consective academic yars Senior Medical Students Selection of the Best Teacher The Medical College of PA; Summer Research 1973; Golden Apple Award, 1978-79; Valedictoria (Dux) High Sch; Phi Sigma Biol Hon Soc Wash & Jefferson Col Graduatation Cum Laude; Student Representative on the Committee for New Chairman, Dept Anatomy, George Wash Univ Sch Med; Histamine Release from Mast Cells: The Possible Effect of Papain on Bee Venom George Washington Univ School of Medicine. **Business Addr:** Director of Surgery, Misericordia Hospital, 53rd & Cedar Ave 5th Fl, Philadelphia, PA 19143, **Business Phone:** (215)748-9343.

CLARKE, LEROY P
Artist, poet, painter (artist). **Personal:** Born Nov 7, 1938, Port-of-Spain, Trinidad and Tobago; divorced; children: Kappel & Rankosane. **Career:** John John, teacher, 1959-67; prof painter, 1969-; Studio Mus, prog coordr & artist-in-residence, 1971-74; Portfolios drawings: In a Quiet Way, 1971; Fragments of a Spiritual, 1972; Douens, 1976; poems: Taste of Endless Fruit, 1974. **Orgs:** Art Soc Trinidad & Tobago. **Special Achievements:** First artist-in-residence, Studio Museum, 1969-75; Numerous exhibits, 1969-.

CLARKE, PRISCILLA
Photographer, publicist, business owner. **Personal:** Born Aug 3, 1960, Swindon, England; daughter of Gilbert Lee and Dorothy Sharples; children: Huda, Ilyas & Qasim. **Educ:** NY Inst Photog; Columbia Union, BA, bus admin; Western New Eng Col, BA, acct. **Career:** Channel 10 Fairfax County TV, producer; Eat To Live Health Food Store, owner, 1988-; NEB Security, pres & owner, 1992-97; NEB Entertainment, pres, 1995-, publicist, currently; Black Belt Chinese Kenpo Karate, martial arts instr; N Am Sch Firearms, PA, gun prof; Rouse Sch Spec Detective Training, pvt invest; Clarke & Associates. **Orgs:** Nat Asn Female Execs, 1986-; officer, Nat Asn Exec Bodyguards, Inc, 1990-; MAR state rep, US Karate Asn, 1990-93; Rouse Detective Asn; Nat Coun Negro Women; Parent Teachers Asn; Nat Asn Advan Colored People; Better Bus Bur; vol, Conn State Black Caucus. **Honors/Awds:** Presidential Sports Award for Karate. **Special Achievements:** Black Enterprise Magazine Articles, 1990, 1991, featured on Channel 13, WJZ Baltimore, MD, 1991; Held Top Female Black Belt titles: Number One female champion on the east coast for serveral years, ranked No: Two in the United States, also held AAU Female Black Belt Championship title, held No1 Canadian Championship in Karate for 3 years, worked security/bodyguardpositions for celebrities, conducted rape prevention/self defense seminarson television, colleges, Production and PR contracts include: Johnnie Cochran, Russell Simmons DEF Comedy Jam, 1996 Essence Awards, "The First Kid," movie with Sinbad, Telly Awards, the "Comedy Tonight" Show, Women in Film & Video, Photography published in Jet, Vibe, Sister 2 Sister, Afro-American Newspaper and many others. **Business Addr:** Publicist, NEB Entertainment, 2020 Pa Ave NW Suite 271, Washington, DC 20006, **Business Phone:** (202)723-2200.

CLARKE, RAYMOND
President (Organization). **Personal:** Born Aug 2, 1950, Cincinnati, OH; son of William Clarke and Genie Johnson Clarke; married Debra, Dec 29, 1984; children: Terri & Paul. **Educ:** Univ Ariz, Tucson, AZ, BS 1973, MS, 1978. **Career:** Univ Ariz, counr youth, 1971, 1972; Pima County Juv Ct Ctr, dep dir probation, 1973-84; Univ Ariz, consults stud athletes, 1980-81; Governor Bruce Babbitt, exec dir health coun, 1984-86; Tucson Urban League Inc, pres & chief exec officer, 1986-2006; Las Vegas Clark County Urban League, pres & chief exec officer, currently. **Orgs:** Pi Lambda Theta, 1977-; pres, Tucson Chapter Nat Asn Black Social Workers, 1978-79; Ariz Small Bus Asn, 1979; Mayor's Task Force, Econ Develop, 1988-89; Governor's Task Force Welfare Reform, 1988-89; Regents Ad-Hoc Comt, Minority Access & Retention, 1988-; State Supreme Ct Taskforce, 1989; Tucson Community Found Grants Comt, 1988-; US Selective Serv Syst, 1981-; Citizens-Police Adv Comt, City Tucson, 1984; vpres, western regional coun exec, Nat Urban League, 1991; Tucson Local Develop Corp, City Tuscson, 1987; Tucson Civil Rights Coalition, Tucson Community, 1990. **Honors/Awds:** Co-Founder, Tucson Chapter Natl Asn Black Soc, 1978; Meritorious Recognition & Nat Juvenile Delinquency Prevention, 1980; State Image Award, NAACP, 1980; Service to Youth, Foundation, Pima County, 1983; Service to Community, Optimist Club, Tucson, 1983; UA Black Alumni Award, 1988; Panelist, Documented Forum Civil Rights AZ, 1989; Certificate of Dedication, Southern Az Chapter, A Philip Randolph Institute, 1990; Mayor's Copper Letter of Appreciation, Mayor Tucson, 1984, 1989; Corporate Solicitor-Professional, United Way, 1987;Certificate of Appreciation, Tucson Human Relations Commission, 1990; Community Service Award, NAACP-Tucson, 1990. **Special Achievements:** Outstanding Young Men, OYM Am, 1980, 1982. **Business Addr:** President, Chief Executive Officer, Las Vegas Clark County Urban League, 930 W Owens, Las Vegas, NV 89106, **Business Phone:** (702)636-3949.

CLARKE, RICHARD V.
Executive, president (organization). **Personal:** Born Jun 11, 1927, New York, NY; divorced; children: Tracy, Chip. **Educ:** City Col NY. **Career:** Hallmark Employ Agency, fdr, 1957; State & Pvt Agencies, consult fed; Richard Clarke Assos Inc, pres, currently. **Orgs:** NY State Econ Develop Bd; NY State Bd Tourism; bd dirs, NY State Coun Arts; bd dir, Legal Aid Soc; bd dir, Tri-State United Way; bd dir, NAACP, NY; bd dir, New Lincoln Sch; bd dir, 100 Black Men; chmn, bd trustees, The Studio Mus Harlem; Jaybees; NY Bd Trade; consult, Fed Equal Opportunity Comn; Dept Justice, Comn Rels Serv; Manhattan Adv sub-comt, Urban League; Com & Indust Asb NY; Interracial Coun Bus Opportunity; Nat Coun Christians & Jews. **Business Addr:** President, Richard Clarke Associates Inc, 9 W 95th St Suite C, New York, NY 10025-6779, **Business Phone:** (212)222-5600.*

CLARKE, SHIRLEY. **See FRANKLIN, SHIRLEY CLARKE.**

CLARKE, STANLEY MARVIN
Composer, musician. **Personal:** Born Jun 31, 1951, Philadelphia, PA; son of Marvin and Blanche Bundy; married Carolyn Helene Reese, Nov 29, 1974; children: Christopher Ivanhoe. **Educ:** Philadelphia Music Acad, 1971. **Career:** Mem: Horace Silver Band, 1970; Joe Henderson Band, 1971; Stan Getz Band, 1971-72; Return to Forever, 1972-76; New Barbarians tour group (with Rolling Stones mems Keith Richard, Ron Wood), 1979; Clarke/Duke Proj, 1980-; Stanley Clarke Group, leader, 1976-; Composer, Life is Just a Game, Stanley Clarke Songbook, 1977; I Wanna Play for You Songbook, 1979; albums: Find Out, 1985; Modern Man, 1985; If This Bass Could Only Talk, 1988; Midnight Magic; Hideaway, 1986; Clarke Duke Proj II, 1983; song: "Sweet Baby", 1981. **Orgs:** Musicians Local 802 Union; Nat Acad Rec Arts & Sci; AFTRA; Screen Actors Guild; Hubbard Asn Scientologists Int. **Honors/Awds:** Bassist of the Year award, 1973; Acoustic Bassist of the Year award, 1974; Electric Bassist of the Year award, 1974-76; Grammy award nominee, 1976, 1978, 1981; Bassist Year, 1973, Electric Bassist Year; Bassist Year, Playboy Readers' Poll, 1976, 1977, 1978, 1979, 1980; Jazz Artist Year, Rolling Stone Music Critics' Poll, 1977; named to Guitar Gallery Greats, 1980. **Special Achievements:** First bassist in history to headline tours, selling out shows worldwide, and have his albums certified gold, first bassist in history to double on acoustic and electric bass with

equal virtuosity, power, and fire, had also invented two new instruments: the piccolo bass and the tenor bass. **Business Phone:** (310)235-4700.

CLARKE, YVETTE DIANE
City council member. **Personal:** Born Nov 21, 1964, Brookyln, NY. **Educ:** Oberlin Col; Medgar Evers Col. **Career:** Bronx Overall Econ Develop Corp, dir Bus Develop; New York, Coun, Dist 40, coun mem, NY 11 Dist, congresswomen, currently. **Business Addr:** Congresswoman, New York City Council, 123 Linden Blvd, Brooklyn, NY 11226, **Business Phone:** (718)287-1142.

CLARK-HUDSON, VERONICA L
Administrator, educator, executive director. **Personal:** Born Aug 22, 1946, Baltimore, MA; daughter of Harold A Clark and Flozella R; married Arturio M; children: Kristin Jordan. **Educ:** Albright Col, attended 1963; Howard Univ, BA, 1967; Univ Pa Sch Law, attended 1972; Gemological Inst Am, GG, CG, 1985. **Career:** Int Bus Mach Corp, instr, analyst, 1967-70; Sperry Rand Corp, Univac Div, instr, mkt, 1971-72; Hong Kong Int Sch, instr upper div, 1974-78; Summer Olympics, microcomputer analyst, 1981-84; ABC TV, staff, 1984; Hospity Lane Flowers, owner, 1984-87; Best Jewelry, asst store mgr, 1987-89; Gemological Inst Am, instr, 1989-92, sales mgr, 1992-97, dir Los Angeles educ, 1997-. **Orgs:** GIA Alumni Asn, 1986-; Am Gem Soc, 1990-; prog chmn, Women's Jewelry Asn, 1997-. **Honors/Awds:** Personal Achievement, Nat Asn Trade & Tech Schs, 1990; Staff Mem of the Year, 1993. **Special Achievements:** First African American woman director of education at institute. **Business Addr:** Director of Los Angeles Education, Gemological Institute of America, 550 S Hill St Suite 901, Los Angeles, CA 90013-2407, **Business Phone:** (310)670-2100.

CLARK-SHEARD, KAREN (KAREN VALENCIA CLARK)
Gospel singer. **Personal:** Born Nov 1, 1960?, Detroit, MI; daughter of Elbert and Mattie Moss; married Rev John Drew Sheard; children: Keirra & John Drew Sheard II. **Career:** Gospel vocalist; The Clark Sisters; Island Inspirational All Stars, vocalist, 1996; Island Black Records, solo artist, 1997-; Broadway play, Mr. Right Now, vocalist, 1999. IInd Chance, vocalist, currently; Albums: Finally Karen, 1992; 2nd Chance, 2002; The Heavens Are Telling, 2003; It's Not Over, 2006. **Orgs:** Found & chief exec officer, KCS Ministries. **Honors/Awds:** Stellar Awards, Female Vocalist of the Year, 1999; Music Video of the Year; Contemporary Female Vocalist of the Year; nominated, Grammy Award; Lady Of Soul award. **Special Achievements:** Member of the Clark Sisters; has appeared on the albums of several other artists. **Business Addr:** Gospel Vocalist, Care of Elektra records, 75 rockefeller plz, New York, NY 10019, **Business Phone:** (212)275-4000.*

CLARK-TAYLOR, KRISTIN
Executive, poet laureate, columnist. **Personal:** Born Jan 1, 1959?, Detroit, MI; daughter of James Clark and Elizabeth Clark; married Lonnie; children: Lonnie Paul & Mary Elizabeth. **Educ:** Mich State Univ, BA 1982. **Career:** Author, lectr & consult, currently; USA Today, ed bd, 1982-87; White House, sr adv, corp pub rels exec & journalist, dir media rels, 1987-90; Bell South Corp, dir commun, 1990; Sallie Mae, vpres external affairs; Author: The First to Speak: A Woman of Color Inside the White House; Black Mothers. **Business Phone:** (212)572-6066.

CLARK-THOMAS, ELEANOR M. (ELEANOR M THOMAS)
Educator. **Personal:** Born Sep 18, 1938, Houston, TX; daughter of George Jr (deceased) and Alberta Palmer Henderson; married Bob Thomas; children: Natalie, Brandon & Shannon. **Educ:** Kent State Univ, BS, 1960; Calif State Univ, MA, 1973; ASHA, Cert Clin Competence Speech Path, Cert Clin Competence Audiol; Univ Southern Calif, EdD. **Career:** Educator (retired); Stockton Unified Sch Dist, speech & hearing therapist, 1960-61; Ella Sch Dist & Olive hurst, speech & hearing therapist, 1961-63; Sacramento City Unified Sch Dist, speech & hearing specialist, 1963-76; St Dept Educ, consult, educ communicable handicapped, 1976; Calif St Univ N ridge, assoc prof, 1985; Folsom Cordova Sch Dist, speech therapist; Sacramento Co Schs, speech therapist C, admin asst special educ, Calif Dept educ, compliance unit mgr. **Orgs:** Delta Kappa Gamma, 1977; Calif Speech & Hearing Asn, 1986-87; bd dir, Sacramento Hearing Soc; Am Speech & Hearing Asn; treas, coordr, coun, Sacramento Area Speech & Hearing Asn; NAUW, NBLSHA, NASDSE; pres, La S Bay Alumnae Chap, Delta Sigma Theta, 1989-91. **Honors/Awds:** Sustained Superior Accomplishment Award, State Dept Educ, 1983-85. *

CLASH, KEVIN
Actor, television producer, movie producer. **Personal:** Born Sep 17, 1960, Baltimore, MD; son of George and Gladys; married Genia; children: Shannon Elise. **Career:** Films:Muppet Monster Adventure, 2000; Elmo's Letter Adventure, 2001; Elmo's World: The Wild Wild West, 2001; Sesame Street: Computer Caper, 2002; Elmo Visits the Fire House, 2002; Zoe's Dance Moves, 2003; Sesame Street: 4-D Movie Magic, 2003; Muppets Party Cruise, 2003; Sesame Street: Happy Healthy Monsters, 2004; What's the Name of That Song, 2004; Sesame Street: Friends to the Rescue, 2005; Sesame Street: All-Star Alphabet, 2005; Elmo Visits the Doctor, 2005; Elmo's World: Reach for the Sky, 2006; Guess That Shape & Color, 2006; Sesame Beginnings: Beginning Together, 2006; Sesame Beginnings: Make Music Together, 2006; Elmo's World: Pets!, 2006; Elmo's Potty Time, 2006; A Sesame Street Christmas Carol, 2006; Sesame Beginnings: Exploring Together, 2006; Kids Favorite Country Songs, 2007; Sesame Beginnings: Moving Together, 2007; Elmo's World: What Makes You Happy?, 2007; Ready for school, 2007; TV Series: "Elmo's Musical Adventure", 2000; "Deadline", 2001; "Oobi", 2003; "The West Wing", 2004; Sesame Street Presents: The Street We Live On, 2004; The Muppets' Wizard of Oz, 2005; A Capitol Fourth, 2006; "Rove Live", 2007; Elmo's Christmas Countdown, 2007; "Sesame Street", 2008; Macy's Thanks giving Day Parade, 2008; "Scrubs", 2009; "The Game", 2009; "Late Night with Jimmy Fallon"; 2009. **Honors/Awds:** Emmy award, Nat Acad Tv Arts & Sci, 1990, 2000, 2005, 2006. **Home Addr:** The Muppets, PO Box 20726, New York, NY 10023. **Business Addr:** Principal Muppeteer, Jim Henson Productions, 117 E 69th St, New York, NY 10021, **Business Phone:** (212)794-2400.

CLAXTON, MELVIN L
Journalist. **Personal:** Born in Antigua-Barbuda. **Career:** The Daily News, part time reporter & writer, 1983-85, reporter, 1985, frelancer, reporter, 1994-97; The Detroit News, reporter, 1998, sr investigative reporter; The Tennessean Nashville, sr investigative reporter, currently. **Honors/Awds:** Pulitzer Prize, 1995; Outstanding Achievement by an Individual; Nat Headliner Awards, 2006, 2007. **Business Addr:** Senior Investigative Reporter, The Tennessean Nashville, 1100 Broadway, Nashville, TN 37203, **Business Phone:** (615)259-8278.

CLAY, DR. CAMILLE ALFREDA
School administrator, mental health counselor. **Personal:** Born Aug 21, 1946, Washington, DC; daughter of James and Doris Coates. **Educ:** Hampton Inst, BA, 1968; Univ DC, MA, 1974; Psychiatric Inst Ctr Group Studies, cert, 1974; George Wash Univ, EdD, 1984. **Career:** DC Comn Mental Health Dept, mental health specialist, 1971-72; SW Interagency Training Ctr, manpower develop specialist, 1972-74; pvt practice, group therapist 1973-79; City Bowie Md Youth Serv Bureau, asst dir, 1974-76; private practice, mental health & career counr, 1983-; Towson State Univ, sr counr, 1977-85, asst vpres diversity, 1986-. **Orgs:** Nat Advan Asn Colored People; Phi Delta Kappa; Alpha Kappa Alpha; bd dirs, Alfred Adler Inst DC; past pres, DC Mental Health Counr Asn; Am Coun Asn, DCCA; Asn Multi-Cultural Counseling & Develop; Am Mental Health Counrs Asn; Asn Black Psychologists; past pres, DC Mental Health Counr Asn; Omicron Delta Kappa Honor Leadership Society, 1988; chair Bd prof Counr; chmn, Licensure DCACD; Am Asn Health Educ, NAWDAC. **Honors/Awds:** TSU Outstanding Black Faculty & Staff Award, TSU Black Alumni, 1989; McCully Award, DCCA, 1997. **Business Addr:** Assistant Vice President, Towson University, 8000 York Rd Univ Union Rm 232, Towson, MD 21252-0001, **Business Phone:** (410)704-2000.*

CLAY, CASSIUS MARCELLUS, JR. See ALI, MUHAMMAD.

CLAY, CLIFF
Artist. **Personal:** Born in Greenwood, MS. **Educ:** Cleveland Inst Art; Cooper Art Sch. **Career:** Self employed painter. **Orgs:** The Karamu House; Nat Asn Advan Colored People; Urban League Hon Am Indian PowWow, 1969; hon mem, 101 Ranch Ponca & City OK; bd mem, 101 Ranch Restoration Found, Ponca City, OK; bd mem Afro Am Hist & Cult Mus, Cleveland, OH; scout, Red Carpet County. **Honors/Awds:** Honorary Official deputy sheriff, Kay Co, OK. **Special Achievements:** Has had various exhibits & one man shows. **Business Addr:** 10605 Chester Ave, Cleveland, OH 44106.*

CLAY, ERIC LEE
Lawyer. **Personal:** Born Jan 18, 1948, Durham, NC; son of Austin Burnett and Betty Allen (deceased). **Educ:** Univ NC, BA, 1969; Yale Univ Law Sch, JD, 1972. **Career:** US Dist Ct Eastern Dist Mich, law clerk, 1972-73; Lewis White & Clay PC, dir, atty, 1973-97; State Mich, special asst atty gen, 1974-75; Ct Appeals US 6th Circuit Judges, circuit judge, 2001-. **Orgs:** Arbitrator Am Arbit Asn, 1976-; Mich Soc Hosp Atty, 1978-; 6th Circuit Judge Conf, 1979; State Bar Mich, 1972-; Wolverine Bar Asn, 1973-; Am Bar Asn, 1973-; Detroit Bar Asn, 1973-; special asst atty gen, State Mich, 1974-75; Nat Asn Railroad Trial Coun, 1978-77; Phi Beta Kappa; Nat Bar Asn; life mem, Nat Advan Asn Colored People; State Bar Mich Ins Law Comn, 1984-88; trustee, Detroit Bar Asn Found, 1985-88; Hearing Panelist, Atty Discipline Bd State Mich, 1985-97; Merit Selection Panel Bankruptcy Judgeships, 1986-87; 6th Circuit Comt Bicentennial Const, 1986-; Exec Comt, Yale Law Sch Asn, 1989-; Merit Selection Panel US Magistrates, 1980-81; mem bd dirs, Detroit Bar Asn, 1990-; co-chmn, Pub Adv Comt Detroit Bar Asn, 1988-90; Mediator, Mediation Tribunal Asn, The Third Judicial Circuit Mich, 1993-97; DC Bar Asn, 1994-; Bar Dist Columbia Ct Appeals, 1997-. **Honors/Awds:** John Hay Whitney Opportunity Fellow, Yale Univ. **Business Addr:** Judge, US Court of Appeals, 231 W Lafayette Blvd 5th Fl, Detroit, MI 48226.*

CLAY, ERNEST H., III.
Architect, college teacher, chief executive officer. **Personal:** Born Feb 17, 1972, Chicago, IL; son of Ernest and Beatrice. **Educ:** Univ Ill, Urbana, BAr, 1969, MAr, 1970; State Ill, lic pract archit, 1973. **Career:** Nat Aeronaut & Space Admin, res fel, 1978-79; Univ Ill, Sch Archit, prof emer, 1991-; Hardwick & Clay Architects, partner; Hardwick, Clay, Voelker & Petterson Architects, owner/partner; Univ Ill, Sch Archit, Urbana, IL, assoc prof; E H Edric Clay & Assocs, chief exec officer, currently. **Orgs:** Exam rev mem, Nat Coun Archit Regist Bd, 1979; AIA; founding mem, Nat Orgn Minority Architects, Ill Chap. **Honors/Awds:** Execellence in Architecture, Soc Gargoyle, 1971; Ill Pub Serv Award, Excellence Design, City Champaign, 1979-82; Cert Recognition Archit, Ill House Representatives, 1991. **Special Achievements:** Appointed a NASA Res Fel in 1978, 1979 to begin preliminary design work on Space Station Freedom. **Business Addr:** Professor Emeritus, University Illinois, 117 Temple Hoyne Buell Hal, 611 Lorado Taft Dr MC 621, Champaign, IL 61820, **Business Phone:** (217)333-1330.*

CLAY, HENRY CARROLL, JR.
Clergy. **Personal:** Born Jun 8, 1928, Yazoo City, MS; married Effie Husbands; children: Henry III. **Educ:** Rust Col, BA, MS, 1952, DD, 1969; Gammom Theol Sem, BD, 1956. **Career:** Clergy (retired); Pub Sch, teacher, 1952-53; UMC, deacon, 1954, elder, 1956; MS Ann Conf, trail, 1954, full connection, 1956; St Mark UMC, pastor, 1956-61; Christian Educ MS Conf, exec secy, 1959-67; St Paul UMC, pastor, 1961-67; Jackson Dist & United Methodist Church, dist supt, 1967-73; Central United Methodist Church Jackson MS, minister. **Honors/Awds:** Citizen year award, Omega Psi Phi Frat; outstanding religious leader award, MS Religious Leadership Conf. *

CLAY, REV. JULIUS C.
Clergy. **Personal:** Married Denise M Cummings-Clay; children: Kimberly. **Educ:** Lane Col, BS; Univ Mo, MEd; Eden Theol Seminary, MDiv; United Theol Seminary, ThM. **Career:** Greater Cleaves Christian Methodist Episcopal Church, paster. **Orgs:** Del, World Methodist Coun, Nairobi, Kenya, 1986; vpres, pres, Interfaith Clergy Coun, 1992-94; vpres, Police Chaplaincy; vpres, Nat Advan Asn Colored People, Milwaukee Chap; nat chmn, Friends Phillips Sch Theol; dean, Gary Dist Leadership Sch, CME Church; Omega Psi Phi Faternity. **Honors/Awds:** Distinguished Man of the Milwaukee, Top Ladies Distinction Inc; Student Christian Association Award, Lane Col. *

CLAY, LACY. See CLAY, WILLIAM LACY.

CLAY, REUBEN ANDERSON, JR.
Physician. **Personal:** Born Feb 8, 1938, Richmond, VA; son of Reuben A and Sue Clarke; married Ardelia Brown, Jun 17, 1967; children: Raymond Alan, Adrienne Beth. **Educ:** Amherst Col, BA, 1960; Univ Rochester, MD, Obstet & Gynec, 1964. **Career:** San Francisco Gen Hosp, internship, 1964-65; Cornell Univ Med Ctr, resident, 1967-68; Univ Calif, resd obstet-gynec, 1968-71; pvt prac, physician; Univ Calif San Francisco, assoc clin prof, 1981; Ralph K Davies Med Ctr, chief gynec, 1982-86; Pac Gynec Ctr, gynec, 2004-; Nat Med, Fel; Pvt Prac, gynec, currently. **Orgs:** San Francisco City Med Soc, 1971-; Nat Med Asn; Am Med Asn; Am Fert Soc; dipl, Am Bd Obstet Gynec, 1973; fel, Am Col Obstet Gynec, 1974; asst clin prof, Univ Calif San Francisco, 1974-; San Francisco Gynec Soc; pres, Parnassus Hosps Obstet Gynec Med Group Inc, 1979-89; secy, Dist IX Am Col Obstet Gynec, 1981-88. **Military Serv:** USAF, capt, 1965-67. **Home Addr:** 2100 Webster St Suite 319, San Franciso, CA 94115-2377, **Home Phone:** (415)923-3123. *

CLAY, ROSS COLLINS
Educator. **Personal:** Born Dec 15, 1908, Conehatta, MS; married Ollie Dolores Billingslea; children: Ross Jr. **Educ:** Jackson State Univ, Attended 1934; Fisk Univ, MA 1940; N western Univ, MUSM, Educ, 1953; Ind Univ, Study 1962; Miss Southern Univ, Workshop, 1970. **Career:** Dir Music Educ Tutorial Teacher, composer ch music, piano, organ, instruments, voices; Corinth High Sch, dir music, 1934-35; Humphries Co Tr Sch, music educ, 1935-36; AR Baptist Col, music educ, 1936-38; Geeter High Sch, music educ, 1940-43; Friendship Jr Col, dir music defense worker, 1943-46; Philander Smith Col, dir music, 1946-48; Lane Col, dir music, 1948-53; Jackson State Univ, dir music educ, tutorial teacher, 1953-74. **Orgs:** Music Educators Nat Con; Ind Educ Asn; MTA; Am Asn Univ Profs; Nat Coun Sr Cits; AARP. **Honors/Awds:** NART Cert Merit, JSU, 1974; Honorary Doctorate of Divinity, Mc Kinley Theological Seminary, 1981. *

CLAY, RUDOLPH
Government official. **Personal:** Born Jul 16, 1935, Gary, IN; son of Willie; married Christine Swan Clay; children: Rudolph Jr. **Educ:** Ind Univ, 1956. **Career:** State Ind, state senator, 1972-76; Lake County, Ind, county councilman, 1978-85, recorder, 1985-, co comnr, comnr, currently; City Gary, mayor, currently. **Honors/Awds:** 50 Outstanding Service Awards, 1994; 50 awards last 15 years from various organizations. **Military Serv:** AUS, SP4, 1960; Good Conduct Medal. **Home Addr:** 2293 N Main St Bldg A 3rd Fl, Crown Point, IN 46307. **Business Addr:** Mayor, City of Gary, 401 Broadway St, Gary, IN 46402, **Business Phone:** (219)881-1301.

CLAY, STANLEY BENNETT

Actor, writer, television producer. **Personal:** Born Mar 18, 1950, Chicago, IL; son of Raymond Leon Fleming and Bertha Florence Fleming. **Career:** Argo Reportory Co, artistic dir, 1971-74; One Flight Up Theatre Co, resident dir playwright, 1974-80; Preceptor Commun, producer, dir, playwright; Sepia mag, entertainment ed, 1981; London's Blues & Soul mag, am corresp, 1984-87; Los Angeles Theatre Review, theatre critic, 1989-91; Why Do Fools Fall In Love, music dir; SBC Mag, auth, ed, currently; TV Series: Room 222, 1970; Sanford and Son, 1972; Marcus Welby, M.D., 1973; Police Story, 1974; Good Times, 1975; Harry O, 1976; Serpico, 1977; Police Woman, 1978; Annihilator, 1986; Cheers, 1991; Ritual, writer & dir, 2000; In Search of Pretty Young Black Men, auth, 2001; Novels: Diva, In Search Of Pretty Young Men; Looker, 2007. **Orgs:** Exec comt, NAACP, Beverly Hills, 1977-80; bd dirs, Int Friendship Network; vpres, bd dirs, The Los Angeles Black Theatre, 1989-92; Los Angeles Black Playwrights, 1988-; vpres, bd dir, Minority AIDS Proj, 1990-97. **Honors/Awds:** Three Drama Logue Awards; NAACP Image Award; 2 NAACP Theatre Awards; Outstanding Cultural Achievement Award, African Am Gay & Lesbian Cultural Alliance, 1990; 2 Drama-Logue Awards, Jonin, Drama-Logue Mag, 1989; Lifeguard/Role Model Award, Genre Magazine, 1993; Pan African Film Festival Jury Award; Int Edna Crutch field Founders Literary Achievement Award, Black Writers & Artists, 1997. *

CLAY, TIMOTHY BYRON

Manager. **Personal:** Born Sep 22, 1955, Louisville, KY; son of Bernard H and Louise Middleton; married Phyllis Wells Clay, May 11, 1978; children: Jacqueline Simone Clay & Arielle Christine Clay. **Educ:** Oakwood Col, Huntsville AL, BS, 1976-78; Univ Ala, Birmingham, AL, MBA, 1978-82. **Career:** Bell South Servs, staff analyst, 1978-86; Protective Indust Ins Co, Birmingham AL, comptroller, 1986-87; Porter White Yardley Capital Inc, Birmingham, AL, proj dir, 1987. **Orgs:** Writer Birmingham Times; Big Brothers/Big Sisters; Birmingham Asn of Urban Bankers, 1988-; bd dir, Nat Alliance Tax Bus Owners, 2003-. **Honors/Awds:** Leadership Award, Birmingham, AL, 1989. **Business Phone:** 800-984-1040.

CLAY, WILLIAM L.

Congressperson (u.s. federal government), social worker. **Personal:** Born Apr 30, 1931, St Louis, MO; son of Irving C and Luella Hyatt; married Carol Ann Johnson, 1953; children: Vicki Flynn, William Jr & Michelle Katherine. **Educ:** St Louis Univ, BS, hist & polit sci, 1953. **Career:** Congressperson (reitred); Real estate broker, St Louis, Mo, 1955-59; Indust Life Ins Co, mgr, 1959-61; 26th Ward, St Louis, Mo, dem alderman, 1959-64; St Co & Munic Employees Union, bus rep, 1961-64; 26th Ward, dem-committeeman, 1964-85; US House Rep, Dist one, congressman, 1969-2000; Comt Post Office & Civil Serv, chmn. **Orgs:** NAACP; CORE; St Louis Jr Chamber Com; founder, William L Clay Scholarship & Res Fund, 1983-; hon bd adv, Nat Stud Leadership Conf. **Honors/Awds:** Distinguished Citizens Award, Alpha Kappa Alpha, 1969; Argus Award, St. Louis Argus Newspaper, 1969; LLD, Lincoln Univ. **Special Achievements:** Book: Just Permanent Interests: Black Americans in Congress, 1870-1991, 1992. **Military Serv:** AUS, 1953-55. **Business Addr:** Founder, William L Clay Scholarship and Research Fund, PO Box 4693, Saint Louis, MO 20515, **Business Phone:** (314)721-0091.

CLAY, WILLIAM LACY (LACY CLAY)

Government official. **Personal:** Born Jul 27, 1956, St Louis, MO; son of William L and Carol A; married Ivie Lewellen; children: Carol & William III. **Educ:** Univ Md, BS, polit sci, 1983, Cert Paralegal Studies, 1982; Harvard Univ, John F Kennedy Sch Govt, attended 1991; Lincoln Univ, Harris-Stowe State Univ, Hon Doctorate Laws. **Career:** US House Rep, asst door keeper, 1976-83; paralegal; Mo Gen Assembly, senator; US House Reps, mem, 2000, first dist, MO, rep, 2004-. **Orgs:** Bd dirs, Cong Black Caucus Found & William L Clay Scholar & Research Fund 1989-; Missouri Legis Black Caucus; Dem Nat Comt; Cong Black Caucus; Cong Progressive Caucus. **Honors/Awds:** Legislator of the Year, Mo Asn Social Welfare; Political Leadership Award, Young Democrats City St Louis. **Home Addr:** 6023 Waterman, St Louis, MO 63112. **Business Addr:** Representative, United States House of Representatives, First District Missouri, 625 N Euclid St Suite 326, St Louis, MO 63108, **Business Phone:** (314)367-1970.

CLAY, WILLIE JAMES

Football player. **Personal:** Born Sep 5, 1970, Pittsburgh, PA; son of Marsha. **Educ:** Ga Tech Technol. **Career:** Football Player(Re-tired); Detroit Lions, defensive back, 1992-95; New Eng Patriots, 1996-98; New Orleans Saints, 1999. *

CLAYBORN, RAY DEWAYNE

Football player. **Personal:** Born Jan 2, 1955, Fort Worth, TX; son of Jessie Wilson Clayborn and Adell Clayborn; married Cindy Cavazos, Nov 12, 1984; children: Lindsey Marie. **Educ:** Univ Tex, Austin, BS, Communications, 1977. **Career:** Football player (retired); New England Patriots, corner back, 1977-89; Cleveland Browns, corner back, 1990-91. **Orgs:** Pro Bowl teams, 1984, 1986 & 1987; Nat Found & Hall of Fame. **Special Achievements:** Pro Football Weeklys All-AFC & All-Pro squads as a kick of fre-turner; set 5 Patriot kick off return records as a rookie; Second

Team All-AFC by UPI; Second Team All-Pro by Col & Pro Football News weekly; Second Team All-NFL by NEA; Three Pro Bowl selection, 1983, 1985 & 1986.

CLAYBORNE, ONEAL

Government official. **Personal:** Born Dec 17, 1940, De Kalb, MS; married Deborah Roberts; children: Michelle & Shaneal. **Career:** Pct no 48 E St Louis, pct committeeman, 1979-87; City E St Louis, alderman, 1979-89; Aldermanic Pub Safety Comn, chmn, 1981-85; St Clair Co, spec dep sheriff, 1989-. **Orgs:** Chmn, Proj ONEAL Citizen Patrol Neighborhood Watch, 1982-85. **Honors/Awds:** Special Achievement Award, Nat Coalition Ban Handguns, 1982. **Home Addr:** 840 N 79th St, East St Louis, IL 62203. **Business Addr:** Special Deputy Sheriff, St Clair County, Alderman Ward 1 7 Collinsville Ave, East St Louis, IL 62201.

CLAYBROOKS, JOHN, JR.

Executive, vice president (organization). **Personal:** Born Jan 21, 1968, Nashville, TN; son of John Sr and Gwendolyn; married Yolanda, Dec 29, 1990; children: Morgan Isabella. **Educ:** Univ Tenn, Knoxville, BS, 1990; Emory Univ, JD, 1995; Vanderbilt Univ, MBA, 1997. **Career:** Proctor & Gamble, sales rep, 1988-92; Gen Electric, MBA intern, 1996; IBM, global client exec, 1997-99, e-business mktg mgr, 1999-00; Lease Plan, vp bus integration, 2000-01, sr vpres sales & chief mkg officer, 2001-. **Orgs:** Alpha Phi Alpha, 1987-. **Home Addr:** 713 Peteywood Dr, Austell, GA 30106, **Home Phone:** (770)434-9957. **Business Addr:** Vice President, Chief Marketing Officer, LeasePlan USA, 1165 Sanctuary Pkwy, Alpharetta, GA 30004.*

CLAY CHAMBERS, JUANITA

Executive. **Educ:** Wayne State Univ, BS, sci educ, MS, Sci Educ, doctorate, Educ Admin. **Career:** Detroit Pub Sch, chief acad officer, Div Educ Serv, assoc supt, currently; Dwight D. Eisenhower Prog, proj dir, currently; Detroit Urban Syst Initiative, proj dir, currently; Ctr Learning Technol Urban Sch, proj dir, currently; Math & Sci Ctr Prog, proj dir, currently. **Business Addr:** Associate Superintendent Educational Services, Detroit Public Schools, Sch Ctr Bldg 5057 Woodward Ave, Detroit, MI 48202, **Business Phone:** (313)494-1092.

CLAYE, CHARLENE MARETTE

Art historian. **Personal:** Born Apr 6, 1945, Chicago, IL; daughter of Anne and Clifton; divorced. **Educ:** Univ Bridgeport, BA, 1966; Univ Paris, cert, 1968; Howard Univ, MA, 1970. **Career:** Univ DC, instr, 1970, 1973; Howard Univ Wash, instr, 1970, 1973; Spelman Col, Atlanta, instr, 1971-72; Clayton Jr Col, instr, 1972-; New Muse, exec dir, 1974-78; Calif African Am Museum, exec dir, 1982-83; Claye Inst, exec dir, currently. **Orgs:** Assoc dir, African Cult Serv, 1970; pres, Nat Conf Artists, 1976-78; Am Soc Aesthetics; Nat Educ Asn. **Honors/Awds:** Pubished curator "The Black Artist in the WPA" 1933-43, article on symbolism of African Textiles Contemporary Weavers Asn of Texas, cover design for Logic for Black Undergrad, Curator permanent exhibit on "The Black Contrib to Devel of Brooklyn 1660-1960", grants, Travel for Museum Professional Nat Museum Act, 1976, Aid to Special Exhibitions Nat Endowment of the Art, 1976, 1977, Planning Grant Nat Endowment for the Humanities, 1976. **Home Addr:** 3209 Ewing St, Houston, TX 77004.

CLAYTON, DR. CONSTANCE ELAINE

School administrator, educator. **Personal:** Born Jan 1, 1937?, Philadelphia, PA; daughter of Levi and Willabell Harris. **Educ:** Temple Univ, BA, elem educ, MA, elem sch admin, 1955; Univ Pa, PhD, 1974. **Career:** Philadelphia Pub Sch Syst, Harrison Elem Sch, fourth grade teacher,1955-64, social studies curric designer, 1964-69, African & Afro-Am studies prog, head, 1969-71, US Dept Labor, Women's Bureau, dir, Middle Atlantic States, 1971-72, Early Childhood Develop Prog, dir, 1973-83;assoc supt, supt, 1982-93; Harvard Grad Sch Educ, first supt-in-residence,1994; MCP Hahnemann Sch Med, Sch Pub Health, assoc dean, 1995; Drexel Univ, Ctr Community Health & Prev, prof & assoc dean community affairs. **Orgs:** NAACP; Delta Sigma Theta; St Paul's Baptist Church; NAACP; Delta Sigma Theta; fel Rockefeller Found; Asn Schs Pub Health. **Honors/Awds:** Outstanding Alumnae, Univ Pa Grad Sch Educ, 2005. **Special Achievements:** Philadelphia's first African-American woman superintendent.

CLAYTON, EVA

Congressperson (U.S. federal government), consultant, politician. **Personal:** Born Sep 16, 1934; married Theaoseus; children: Joanne, Theaoseus Jr, Martin & Reuben. **Educ:** Johnson C Smith Univ, BS, 1955; NC Cent Univ, MS, 1962. **Career:** NC State Dept Natural Resources & Community Develop, asst secy, 1977-81; Warren County Comn, chairperson, 1982-90, comnr, 1990-92; US House Rep, congresswoman, 1993-2003; UN Food & Agr Orgn, Rome, Italy, spec adv asst dir gen; Int Alliance against Hunger, secy; World Food Summit, spec adv. **Honors/Awds:** Outstanding County Commissioner, NC Asn County Comnrs, 1990;Women of Faith Award, 2003; Most Influential Newcomer, 103rd Congress. **Special Achievements:** One of the first two African Ams voted into Cong from NC in the 20th Century.

CLAYTON, JANET THERESA

Journalist, editor. **Personal:** Born May 10, 1955, Los Angeles, CA; daughter of Pronzell B and Pinkie B Hodges; married

Michael D Johnson, Jul 27, 1985; children: Jocelyn Michelle & Aaron Clayton. **Educ:** Univ Southern Calif, Los Angeles, CA, BA, jour, 1977; Cambridge Univ, study prog. **Career:** Los Angeles Times, staff writer, 1977-87, ed writer, 1990, asst ed, ed page, 1990-95, ed, ed pages, 1995-2004, vpres, 1997-, asst managing ed, 2004-07. **Orgs:** Black Journalists Asn Southern Calif, 1980-; Nat Asn Black Journalists, reporting team, 1986-; Am Soc Newspaper Eds; Phi Beta Kappa; fel, British-Am Conf; fel, Williamsburg Conf, Hong Kong. **Honors/Awds:** Reporting Team Award, Nat Asn Black Journalists, 1983; Black Woman of Achievement, Nat Asn Advan Colored People Legal Defense Fund.

CLAYTON, LLOYD E

Association executive, businessperson. **Personal:** Born Jul 8, 1921, Mobile, AL; son of William H and Ruby Roberts; married Lela Maxwell, Aug 4, 1947; children: Kenneth R, Robert L & Carole M. **Educ:** Howard Univ, BS, 1955. **Career:** Walter Reed Army Inst Res, res chemist, 1951-68; Task Force Health Care Disadvantaged, dep chmn, 1968-71; Status Health Black Community, proj officer, 1971; Status Dent Health Black Community, proj officer, 1972; Minority Physician Recruitment Nat Health Serv Corps, proj officer, 1973; Sickle Cell Disease Prog, proj officer, 1976; Black Cong Health & Law, proj officer, 1980, staff consult, 1980-88; Health Pact Inc, pres & chief exec officer, currently. **Orgs:** Asn Sports Int Track Club, 1967; off timer, Nat Invitational Track Meet, 1967-68. **Honors/Awds:** Appreciation and Gratitude Award for Outstanding Leadership in the Field of Sickle Cell Anemia San Juan PR, 1978; Superior Service Award, Nat Black Health Planners Asn Wintergreen VA, 1986; Meeting Planner of the Year, Nat Coalition Black Meeting Planners, 1989; Community Service Award, Am Diabetes Asn, 2000. **Military Serv:** AUS, tech sgt, 1944-46. **Home Addr:** 4821 Blagden Ave NW, Washington, DC 20011. **Business Addr:** President, Chief Executive Officer, Health Pact Inc, 4821 Blagden Ave NW, Washington, DC 20011, **Business Phone:** (202)726-7510.

CLAYTON, MATTHEW D.

Lawyer. **Personal:** Born Mar 5, 1941, Philadelphia, PA; married Ramona Carter; children: Rebecca, Janice, Matthew D III. **Educ:** Univ Md, attended 1961; Univ Minn, attended 1963; PA State Univ, BA, 1966; Howard Univ Sch Law, JD, 1969. **Career:** Philadelphia Prisons Syst, correctional officer, 1963; Philadelphia Crime Presention Asn, staff, 1966; Small Bus Admin, legal asst, 1968; US Dept Labor, regional trial atty, 1969-72; Counsel Corp Law, 1972-74; Smith Kline Corp, corp employee relations & litigation coun, 1974-; Pvt Pract, atty; Clayton & Assoc, atty, currently. **Orgs:** Nat Bar Asn; Am Bar Asn; Fed Bar Asn; PA Bar Asn; Philadelphia Bar Asn; Indust Rel Res Asn; sect labor study young prof, US Dept Labor, 1970-72; coord, US Dept Labor; Nat Urban League; Nat Panel Arbitrators; Am Arbitration Asn; Am Mgt Asn; Am Trial Lawyers Asn; Barristers Club; fund mem, World Lawyers Asn. **Honors/Awds:** Outstanding Academic Achievement Am Jurisprudence Award; Outstanding Legal Service Small Business Admin. **Military Serv:** USAF, 1959-63. **Business Addr:** Attorney, Clayton & Assoc, 865 Belmont Ave Suite 1, Philadelphia, PA 19104.*

CLAYTON, MINNIE H.

Librarian. **Personal:** Married Robert L; children: Robert J III, Myrna A. **Educ:** Ala State Univ, BS, 1954; Atlanta Univ, MLS, 1970. **Career:** Dev & Book Col Porton, all ages, consult; Martin Luther King Ctr Social Change, libr archivist, 1969-78; Atlanta Univ Ctr, Southern Regional Coun Archives Proj, Dept Arch & Rec Mgt, proj archivist, 1978-80; RW Woodruff Libr, Div Arch & Spec Collections, dir, 1982-88, processing archivist, 1988-. **Orgs:** Am Libr Asn; Ga Library Asn; Metro-Atlanta Libr Asn; Nat Hist Soc; Soc Am Archivists; Am Asn Univ Professors; African Am Family Hist Asn; Ga Archivists; adv bd, State Hist Record Ga. **Honors/Awds:** Coretta King Award Comt; League of Women Voters; Nat Asn Advan Colored People, Jessie S Noyes Foundation Grant, 1966-68; certificate Archival Adm, Emory University, 1973; Danforth Foundation Assn, 1966-67. **Special Achievements:** Author: Black History & Bibliography of Civil Rights, 1954; Lectures & Life of Martin Luther King Jr. *

CLAYTON, ROBERT L

Labor relations manager. **Personal:** Born Dec 6, 1938, Morris Station, GA; son of Henry and Willie Mae Mercer; married Sharon Cage, Mar 25, 1976; children: Robert & Angela. **Educ:** Cent State Univ, Wilberforce, BS, bus admin, 1962; Akron Univ, Akron, post-19Grad studies, 1966. **Career:** Co-op Supermarkets, Akron, comptroller, 1965-73; Fiberbd, San Francisco, CA, sr financial analyst, 1973-79; CH2M Hill, vpres diversity, 1979; BOBBY C's Lounge & Grille, owner, currently. **Orgs:** Soc Human Resources, 1980-; Nat Asn Minority Eng Prog Admin, 1983-; Nat Forum Black Pub Admin, 1984-; adv bd, Univ Calif, Los Angeles, 1986-93, indust tech adv bd, Statewide MESA, 1986-93, minority eng bd, Univ Calif Fullerton, 1988-93; Kappa Alpha Psi Fraternity; 32nd Degree, Mason Shrine; Owl Club Denver, 1994-. **Military Serv:** AUS, 1st lt, 1962-65. **Business Addr:** Owner, Bobby C's Lounge and Grille, 1140 E Wash St, Phoenix, AZ 80111, **Business Phone:** (602)252-2273.

CLAYTON, ROYCE SPENCER

Baseball player. **Personal:** Born Jan 2, 1970, Burbank, CA. **Career:** Baseball player (retired), San Francisco Giants, shortstop,

1991-95; St Louis Cardinals, 1996-98; TexRangers, 1998-00; Chicago White Sox, 2001-02; Milwaukee Brewers, 2003; Colo Rockies, 2004; Ariz Diamondbacks, 2005; Washington Nationals, 2006; Cincinnati Reds, 2006; Toronto Blue Jays, 2007. **Orgs:** Founder, Royce Clayton Family Foundation, 1997; vice pres for external affairs, Nat Alliance of African Am Athletes. **Honors/Awds:** All-Star selection, 1997. *

CLAYTON, THEAOSEUS T.
Lawyer. **Personal:** Born Oct 2, 1930, Roxboro, NC; married Eva McPherson; children: Joanne , Theaoseus T, Jr , Martin & Reuben. **Educ:** Johnson C Smith Univ, AB, 1955; Cent Univ, Sch Law, JS, JD, 1958. **Career:** McKissick & Berry Durham, NC, atty, 1961; Gilliland & Clayton, jr partner, 1961-66; Theaoseus T Clayton PA Inc, sole propietorship, 1963-66, pres, atty law, 1979-; Clayton & Ballance, sr partner, 1966-78; District Ct, law pract; Superior Ct, law pract; Ct Appeals, law pract; NC Supreme Ct, law pract; Fed Dist Ct, law pract; US Supreme Ct, law pract. **Orgs:** Nat Bar Asn; Am Bar Asn; NC State Bar; NC Bar Asn; NC Trial Lawyers Asn; NC Asn Black Lawyers; Nat Conf Black Lawyers; past secy & treas, ninth Jud Dist Bar Asn; pres, Charles Williamson Bar Asn; chief coun, Floyd B McKissick & Floyd B McKissick Enterprises Inc; life mem & past state vpres, Nat Asn Advan Colored People; Warren County Dem Party; Warren County Polit Action Coun; second Cong Dist Black Caucus; past vice chmn, NC Bd Youth Develop. **Special Achievements:** First black lawyer to practice in Warren County. **Military Serv:** AUS, corpl, 1952-54. *

CLAYTON, XERNONA
Executive. **Personal:** Born Aug 30, 1930, Muskogee, OK; daughter of James Brewster; married Paul Brady. **Educ:** TN State Univ, BS, 1952; Ru-Jac Sch Modeling, Chicago. **Career:** WAGA-TV, hostess; Atlanta Voice, newspaper columnist; Chicago & LA, teacher pub schs; photog & fashion modeling; Turner Broadcasting Syst Inc, consult, corp vpres, 1988; Pres & Chief Exec Officer, TRUMPET AWARDS FOUNDATION INC, currently. **Orgs:** Atlanta Women's C C; State & Manpower Adv Comt GA Dept Labor; Nat Asn Market Develop; Arts Alliance Guild; Am Women Radio & TV; Nat Asn Media Women; Nat Asn Press Women; Atlanta Chap Sigma Delta Chi; Atlanta Broadcast Exec Club; founder, Atlanta Chap Media Women; Nat Acad TV Arts & Sci; Ebenezer Bapt Ch; Alpha Kappa Alpha Sorority; bd dir, Greater Atlanta Multiple Sclerosis Soc; honorary assoc, So Ballet; founder, Trumpet Awards. **Honors/Awds:** Outstanding Leadership Award; winner, Nat Asn Mkt Develop, 1968; Bronze Woman of Yr; Human Relations Award, Phi Delta Kappa Sorority, 1969; Press Award, GA Assoc, 1969-71; Excellence in TV Programming Award, LA Chap Negro Bus & Prof Women, 1970; Mother of Yr, Future Homemakers Am Douglas HS, 1969; Flying Orchid Award, Delta Airline; named Atlanta's Five Best Dressed Brentwood Models, 1971; named Atlanta's Ten Best Dressed Women Women's C C, 1972; Corp Award, NAFEO, 2003; Local Community Service Award, 2004; Leadership & Dedication in Civil Rights Award, 2004. **Special Achievements:** south 1st Black person to have her own tv show; appointed by Gov of GA to Motion Picture & TV Commn for4-yr term, 1972-76. **Business Addr:** President, Chief Executive Officer, TRUMPET AWARDS FOUNDATION INC, CENTENNIAL TOWER, 101 Marietta St Suite 1010, ATLANTA, GA 30303, **Business Phone:** (404)878-6738.*

CLAYTOR, CHARLES E.
Association executive. **Personal:** Born Jun 2, 1936, Hotcoal, WV; son of Fairy Hickman and Harvey; married Annette Broadnax; children: Dreama, Charles Jr, Brien. **Educ:** NY City Col. **Career:** United Brotherhood Carpenters, pres, 1967-. **Business Addr:** president, United Brotherhood Carpenters Joiners Am, 87 80 153 St, Jamaica, NY 11432.*

CLEAGE, PEARL MICHELLE (PEARL LOMAX)
Writer, novelist. **Personal:** Born Dec 7, 1948, Springfield, MA; daughter of Albert B Jr and Doris Graham; married Zaron W Burnett, Jr, Mar 23, 1994; married Michael Lomax (divorced 1979); children: Deignan. **Educ:** Howard Univ, attended 1969; Spelman Col, BA, 1971. **Career:** Just Us Theater Co, playwright-in-residence, 1981-86, artistic dir, 1987-94; Just Us Theater Co, NEA grant, 1983-87; CATALYST Mag, founding ed, 1986-96; Atlanta Tribune, columnist, 1988-; Spelman Col, playwright-in-residence, instr drama, 1991-93; Smith Col, playwright-in-residence, 1994; Univ Mass, Amherst, Bateman scholar-in-residence, 1996; Agnes Scott Col, Laney prof-in-residence, 1997; writer, currently; plays: Flyin' West, 1992; Blues for An Alabama Sky, 1995; Bourbon at the Border; essays: Mad at Miles: A Black Woman's Guide to Truth, 1990; Good Brother Blues; Deals with the Devil; novels: What Looks Like Crazy on An Ordinary Day, Avon Books, 1997; I Wish I Had a Red Dress, Morrow/Avon, 2001; Some Things I Never Thought I'd Do, 2003; poems: Broadside Press, 1971; We Don't Need No Music. **Honors/Awds:** Bronze Jubilee Award, 1983; Outstanding Columnist Award, Atlanta Asn Black Journalists, 1991; Onstage Award, Outstanding New Play, AT&T, 1992; Outstanding Columnist Award, Atlanta Asn Media Women, 1993; Award, Asn Southern Writers, 1994; 2 Audellco Awards, Hon off Broadway Achievements, Best Play & Best Playwright.

CLEAMONS, JAMES MITCHELL (JIM CLEAMONS)
Basketball coach, basketball player. **Personal:** Born Sep 13, 1949, Lincolnton, NC. **Educ:** Ohio State Univ. **Career:** Basketball player (retired), basketball coach; Los Angeles Lakers, 1971-72; Cleveland Cavaliers, 1972-77; New York Knicks, 1977-79; Washington Bullets, 1980; Furman Univ, asst coach, 1982-83; Ohio State Univ, asst coach, 1983-87, coach, 1987-89; Chicago Bulls, asst coach, 1989-96; Dallas Mavericks, head coach, 1996-97; Oklahoma City Hornets, 2006; Los Angeles Lakers, asst coach, 2006-. **Business Addr:** Assistant Coach, Los Angeles Lakers, 555 N Nash St, El Segundo, CA 90245, **Business Phone:** (310)426-6100.

CLEAVER, EMANUEL, II
Government official, mayor, clergy. **Personal:** Born Oct 26, 1944, Waxahachie, TX; married Dianne; children: Evan Donaldson, Emanuel III, Emiel Davenport & Marissa Dianne. **Educ:** Prairie View A&M Col, BS; St Paul Sch Theol Kans City, MDiv; St Paul Sch Theol, DSE. **Career:** St James-Paseo United Methodist Church, pastor, 1972-2009; Kansas City, City Coun, councilman, 1979-91; City Kans City, mayor, 1991-93; KCUR-FM, host; US House Rep, Mo 5th Cong Dist, 2005-. **Orgs:** Bd dir, De La Salle Ed Ctr; mid-cent reg vpres, Southern Christian Leadership Conf; pres, bd trustees, Leon Jordan Scholarship Fund; bd trustees, St Paul Sch Theol; coun finance, United Methodist Conf; bd dir, chmn bd, Freedom; Alpha Phi Alpha; Nat Asn Advan Colored People. **Honors/Awds:** Achievements & honors, 41; Man of the Year, Alpha Phi Alpha, 1968;Community Leaders Am, 1971; Builder of Boys Award, Boys Club Am, 1976; White House Guest, Pres Jimmy Carter, 1977; Recognition of Thanks, Woodland Elem Sch, 1983; Apprec Award, NAACP, 1984; Black History Award, Univ MO-Kans City, 1984; Distint Service Award, Exceptional Leadership & Devoted Serv Civil Rights, Alpha Phi Alpha, 1984; Award for Outstanding Service, Freedom Inc, 1984; Citizen of the Year, Omega Psi Phi; Harold L Holliday Sr Civil Rights Award, NAACP, 1992; Distinguished Graduate Award, St Paul Sch Theol, 1993; Kansas City Anti-Apartheid Award, 1993; James C. Kirkpatrick Excellence for Government Award, 1993; Distinguished Citizen of the Midwest Award, Nat Conf Christians & Jews, 1993; Highest Distinction Award, Alpha Alpha Chapter, 1999; LLD, Ottawa Univ, 1999; Conspicuous Service Medal, Mo Governor Mel Carnahan, 1999; Fannie Lu Hamer Award, Nat Conf Black Mayors, 2001. **Special Achievements:** First African American elected to Kansas City office. **Home Addr:** 8217 E Gregory Blvd, Kansas City, MO 64133. **Business Addr:** Representative, US House Representatives, Missouri 5th Congressional District, 400 E 9th St Suite 9350, Kansas City, MO 64106, **Business Phone:** (816)842-4545.

CLEGG, LEGRAND H
Lawyer. **Personal:** Born Jun 29, 1944, Los Angeles, CA. **Educ:** Univ Calif Los Angeles, BA, 1966; Howard Univ, Sch Law, JD, 1969; Compton Community Col, AA. **Career:** Compton Community Col, instr; Robert Edelen Law Offices, atty, 1975-; La legal aid found, 1972-74; Compton Calif, admin asst, 1970-72; Dept Justice Wash, legal intern, 1968-69; pvt law practr, 1974-; Compton Unified Sch Dist, co-coun, 1976-77; City Compton, Calif, chief deputy city atty, 1981-93, city atty, currently. **Orgs:** La Bar asn; Calif Lawyers Criminal Justice; Langston Law Club; Nat Conf Black Lawyers; Compton Cultural Commn; Asn Black Psychol; Pilgrim Missionary Bapt Ch. **Honors/Awds:** Pubs La Times, 1974; current bibliography on African Affairs, 1969, 1972; guest lecturer Vassar Coll, UCLA Sothern Calif, 1978-79. **Business Addr:** Attorney, The City Compton, 205 S Willowbrook Ave, Compton, CA 90220, **Business Phone:** (310)605-5500.

CLEMENDOR, DR. ANTHONY ARNOLD
Physician, educator, dean (education). **Personal:** Born Nov 8, 1933; son of Anthony and Beatrice Stewart Thompson; married Elaine C Browne (died 1991); children: Anthony A & David A; married Janat Jenkins, Sep 23, 1993. **Educ:** NY Univ, BA, 1959; Howard Univ Col Med, MD, 1963. **Career:** NY Med Col, clin prof, OB-GYN, dir off minority affairs, assoc dean; pvt pract gynec, currently. **Orgs:** Pres, Stud Am Med Asn Chap, Howard Univ, 1961-62; dir, Off Minority Affairs, NY Med Col, 1974-97; pres, NY Gynec Soc, 1988; bd dirs, Caribbean Am Ctr, 1988; pres, NY County Med Soc, 1992; Nat Urban League; NAACP; 100 Black Men; NY Urban League; bd mem, Elmcor; fel Am Col OB-Gyn; Am Pub Health Asn; co-chair, Med Soc State NY, Health Care Disparity. **Honors/Awds:** SNMA Award, Univ Buffalo Chap, 1984; T & T Alliance Award, Trinidad & Tobago Alliance NA, 1984; Trinidad & Tobago Nurses Asn Am Inc Award, 1988; Nat Award, Nat Asn Med Minority Educr, 1989; Physician of the Year Award, Manhattan Cent Med Soc, 1989. **Special Achievements:** Publ: Achalasia & Nutritional Deficiency During Pregnancy, 1969; Transient Asymptomatic Hydrothorax in Pregnancy, 1976. **Business Addr:** Physician, Private Practice, 125 E 80 St, New York, NY 10021.*

CLEMENT, ANTHONY
Football player. **Personal:** Born Apr 10, 1976, Lafayette, LA; married Fatima; children: Ebony, Langhsten, Anthony Jr & Caleb. **Educ:** Southwestern La Univ. **Career:** Ariz Cardinals, tackle, 1998-04; San Francisco 49ers, 2005; New York Jets, tackle, 2006-07; New England Patriots, 2008-. **Special Achievements:** Only Cardinals Offensive Liner to start all 16 games. **Business Addr:** Professional Football Player, New York Jets, 1000 Fulton Ave, Hempstead, NY 11550-1099, **Business Phone:** (516)560-8100.*

CLEMENT, WILLIAM A., JR.
Computer executive. **Personal:** Born Jan 22, 1943, Atlanta, GA; married Ressie Guy; children: Anika P, Leanetta Spencer. **Educ:** Morehouse Col, BA; Wharton Sch Finance & Com Univ, PA, MBA; Am Col Life Underwriters, CLU. **Career:** NC Mutual Life Ins Co, life ins agent; Robinson Humphrey & Am Express Inc, stockbroker; Prudential-Bache Securities Inc, stockbroker; NC Nat Bank, credit analyst & com loan officer; Citizens Trust Bank, vpres & sr loan officer; US Small Bus Admin, assoc adminr; Dobbs Corp, pres & chief exec officer; Robinson-Humphrey Co; chmn bd dirs, USEP Inc; The Dobbs Corp, Nat Bank Wash, Natl Consumer Coop Bank; Citizens Trust Bank Atlanta, vpres & loan officer; Dobbs Ram & Co, chmn & chief exec officer, currently. **Orgs:** Bd dir, Bus League, Atlanta Urban League; bd dir, Big Bros Atlanta; bd chm, chief vol officer, Atlanta Bus League; bd dirs, Atlanta Chamber Com; bd dirs, The Metrop Atlanta Community Found; bd dirs, Leadership Atlanta; bd dirs, Atlanta Conv & Visitors Bur; bd mem, Res Atlanta, The Atlanta Exchange, The Alliance Theatre Co; Atlanta Coalition 100 Black Men; Soc Int Bus Fels; Int Bus fel London Bus Sch. **Honors/Awds:** Entrepreneur of the Year, NABMBA, 1990; Small Bus Person of the Year, Atlanta Chamber Com, 1990; Entrepreneur of the Year, Crim High Sch, 1992; Bus Owner of the Year, Atlanta Tribune, 1992; Entrepreneur of the Year, SuccessGuide, 1992. **Business Addr:** Chairman, Chief Executive Officer, Dobbs Ram & Co, Two Midtown Plz, 1349 W Peachtree St NE Suite 1550, Atlanta, GA 30308.*

CLEMENTS, FR. GEORGE H.
Priest, founder (originator). **Personal:** Born Jan 26, 1932, Chicago, IL. **Educ:** St Mary Lake Sem, BA, MA, philos, 1957. **Career:** Pastor (retired), Executive; Quigley Sem, first black grad ordained, 1957; Holy Angels Roman Catholic Church, pastor, 1969-85; One Church-One Addict, founder, currently; One Church-One Inmate Initiatives, founder, currently; One Church-One Child, founder, currently. **Orgs:** Chaplain, Afro-Am Patrolmen's League; Afro-Am Firemen's League; Postal Workers' League; bd, SCLC's Oper Breadbasket; Nat Asn Advan Colored People; Urban League; Better Boys Found; Black Panther Party Malcolm XCol; organizer, Black Clergy Caucus. **Honors/Awds:** Family Spirit Award, 1998; Trumpet Awards; Has been honored by numerous organizations, including the Kentucky State Senate, which issued are solution praising his deeds. **Special Achievements:** First black pastor of Holy Angels Catholic Church on the South Side of Chicago; A film starring Lou Gossett, Jr., The Father Clements Story, was produced and broadcast by NBC.

CLEMENTS, WALTER H.
Lawyer. **Personal:** Born Oct 28, 1928, Atlanta, GA; son of Emanuel and Lucile; divorced; children: Kevin M, Alisa C. **Educ:** Morehouse Col, BA, 1949; Univ Mich Law Sch, JD, 1952. **Career:** Pvt pract, atty, 1953-59, 1991-; Vet Admin, adjudicator, 1962-65; Small Bus Admin, asst area coun, 1966-69; State Mich, asst atty gen, 1969-73; Southeastern Mich Transp Auth, gen coun, 1973-88; Wayne Co Community Col, gen coun, 1988-91; NASD, arbitrator, mediator. **Orgs:** State Bar Mich; Wolverine Bar Asn; Nat Bar Asn; Am Arbitration Asn; referee, Mich Civil Rights Community. **Business Addr:** 20070 Lichfield Rd, Detroit, MI 48221, **Business Phone:** (313)862-6638.*

CLEMMONS, CLIFFORD R.
Law enforcement officer. **Personal:** Born in Kansas City, KS; son of H B Clemmons and Constance Alice Sargent; married Jimmie E Hill (deceased); children: Jennifer M Johnson-Barnett, C Robert Jr. **Educ:** Oakwood Jr Col, Huntsville, AL, dipl, 1939; Cent State Univ, Wilberforce, OH, BS, social work, 1948; Ohio State Univ, MS, social admin, 1950; NY Univ; Columbia Univ, criminal justice. **Career:** Law enforcement officer (retired); Greenpoint Hosp, med social worker, 1950; Probation Dept NY, probation officer, 1951-66, supvr probation officer, 1966-82; City NY, Dept Probation, br chief, 1982-87. **Orgs:** Pres, Counrs, Probation & Parole Officers, 1964-68; pres, bd dir, United Veterans Mutual Housing Co, 1967-70; chmn, bd dir, Fedn Negro Serv Orgn Inc, 1968-77; vpres, bd dir, Munic Credit Union, 1971-77; state dir, Alpha Phi Alpha Fraternity Inc, 1971-87; chmn emer, bd dir, Sickle Cell Disease Found, Greater NY, 1972-87; pres, Consumer Groups Greater NY, 1973-75. **Honors/Awds:** Community Serv Award, Leadership Bell Park Manor Terr Community Coun Inc, 1964; Middleton Spike Harris Award, Counseliers Inc, NY, 1978; Comnr Probation Merit Award, Probation Dept, NY, 1980; Alpha Award of Merit, Alpha Phi Alpha Fraternity Inc, Queens Chap, 1972; Over 35 awards & citations. **Military Serv:** AUS, first sgt. **Home Addr:** 4345 Senna Dr, Las Cruces, NM 88011-7636. *

CLEMMONS, PROF. JACKSON JOSHUA WALTER
Pathologist, educator. **Personal:** Born Mar 24, 1923, Beloit, WI; son of Ora Bell and Henry; married Lydia Monroe, Dec 27, 1952; children: Jackson, Lydia, Laura, Jocelyn & Naomi. **Educ:** Univ Wis, BS, biochem, 1947, MS, Biochem, 1949, PhD, biochem & exper path,1955; Western Res Univ, MD, 1959. **Career:** Univ Wis Madison, res asst, Biochem, 1942-43, res assoc, biochem & experpath, 1947-52; Karolinska Inst biophys & Cell Res Stockholm, Sweden, resfel, 1950; Sloan Kettering Inst Cancer Res NY, special res fel, 1953; Univ Wis Madison, Wis, proj assoc exper path, 1953-55; Am Cancer Soc Inst Path,Western Res Univ, Cleveland Ohio, postdoctoral fel, 1956-57, fel path,1957-61, Helen Hay Whitney

fel, 1961-64; Univ Vt Col Med, Burlington Vt, asst prof, 1962-64, prof emer path, currently. **Orgs:** Am Bd Path Anatomic Path, 1964; Univ VT Radioisotope Comn, 1968-; exec comt, Grad Sch Fac, 1969-71; deleg, VT White House Conf C & Youth, 1971;path trainicomm Nat Inst Gen Med Sci, 1971-73; vpres, Univ Vt Chap Sigma Xi, 1971-72, pres, 1971-72; Univ Vt Admin Policy Comt, 1971-76; admiss comt, Univ Vt Col Med, stud affairs comt, 1974-; Nat Adv Coun Health Prof Educ, 1975-78; admiss comn, Univ Vt, 1977-, exec comt, 1977-; sch dir, Champlaign Vlly Union HS, 1967-74, vice chmn, Gov Adv Comm Coun Aging,1970-72; AMA; Am Asn Path & Bacteriologists; VT State Med Soc; Chittenden Co Med Soc; New Eng Rheumatism Soc; Sigma Xi; Phi Lambda Upsilon; Gamma Alpha; Am Soc Exp Path; Int Acad Path; Am Soc Clinal Chem; NY Acad Sci; AmSoc Clin Pathologists. **Special Achievements:** Author of "Influence in Estrogen on Nuclear Volumes & Chemical Composition", 1955; "Thermoluminescence & Fluorescence in Alkai Halide Crystals Induced by Soft X-Ray", 1955; "Occurrence Multiple Fractures in suckling Rats Injured with B-Aminopropionitrile", 1957; "Quantitative Historadiography", 1957; "Inhibition Cytochrome Oxidase by Aminoacetonitrile", 1962; "Proline Metabolism Colagen Formation & Lathyrism", 1966; "Effect Lathyrogenic Compounds on Oxygen ConsumptionDevel Chick Embroys", 1966; Radiorespirometer for Study C14-Labeled Substance Administered to Chick Embryos, 1971; "Ornithine as a Precursor Colagen Proline & Hydroxyproline in Chick Embryo", 1973; "Embryonic Renal Injury-A Possible Factor in Fetal Malnutrition", 1977; "Electrolytic Radio respirometer for Continuouonitoring Chick Embryo Devel", 1979;"Fetal-Maternal Hemorrhage, A Spectrum Disease", 1980. **Home Addr:** 2190 Greenbush Rd, Charlotte, VT 05445. **Business Addr:** Professor Emeritus, University of Vermont, College of Medicine, Department of Pathology, 89 Beaumont Ave, Burlington, VT 05405-0068, **Business Phone:** (802)656-2156.

CLEMMONS, REGINALD C
Educator, military leader. **Personal:** Born in Wilmington, NC; married Sylvia; children: Regina & Adrienne. **Educ:** NC A&T, BS, math, 1960; SC State Col, ME, educ, 1970; Field Officer Basic & Advanced courses, 1972; Armed Forces Staff Col, attended 1984; US Army War Col, attended 1990. **Career:** Military leader (retired), educator; AUS, commissioned field artillary 2nd lt, 1968, forward observer, 1968-69; served Vietnam, 1968-69; Fort Carson, 5th battalion, commander, 1969-70, 4th infantry battalion, commander, 1970-71; served Germany, 1972-75; AUS Europe & Seventh Army, commander, 1972-74, Liaison Officer, 1974-75; SC State Univ, AUS Reserve Officers Training Corps Instr Group, asst prof military scI, 1975-79; served Korea, 1979-80; AUS Logistics Ctr, logistics assessment officer, 1980-84; Fort Bragg, 18th Airborne Corps & 82nd Airborn Div, exec officer & battalion commander, 1984-89, 1992-94, commander officer, 1991-92; Schofield Barracks, 25th Infantry Div, commander, 1992-94; Fort Sill, Fire Support & Combined Ops Directorate, dir, 1994-95; Allied Land Forces Cent Europe, asst chief staff ops, 1995-96; AUS Europe & Seventh Army & Task Force Able Sentry, commander, 1996-97; Allied Land Forces SE Europe, dep commanding gen, 1997-99; AUS Europe & Seventh Army, dep commanding gen, 1999-2000; Nat War Col, commandant, 2000-03; Grantham Univ, Acad Adv Bd, bd mem, currently. **Honors/Awds:** Defense Distinguished Service Medal with Oak Leaf Cluster; Legion Merit with Oak Leaf Cluster; Bronze Star Medal; Meritorious Service Medal with five Oak Leaf Clusters; Army Commendation Medal with two Oak Leaf Clusters; Master Parachutist Badge; the Distinguished Service Medal. **Business Addr:** Board Member, Grantham University, Academic Advisory Board, 7200 NW 86th St, Kansas City, MO 64153, **Business Phone:** (816)595-5759.*

CLEMMONS, DR. SONYA SUMMEROUR
Executive. **Personal:** Born Aug 10, 1971, Gainesville, GA; daughter of Leroy and Alice M. **Educ:** Spelman Col, BS, physics, 1993; Ga Tech, BS, mech engineering, 1994; Univ Calif, San Diego, MS, 1996, PhD, 1999. **Career:** Univ Pa Sch Med, postdoctoral res fel, 2000; SSC Enterprises, pres & chief exec officer, 2000-; VitaGen Inc, prin res bioengineer, 2000-02; MediVas, dir bus develop, 2004-06; Biotech Vendor Serv Inc, vpres strategic mkt & corp develop, 2006-. **Honors/Awds:** Women Who Mean Business, San Diego Bus Jour, 2006. **Special Achievements:** Featured in Black Enterprise Magazine (May & Dec 2003); Featured in book commissioned by the White House entitled "Extraordinary Female Engineers"; First African American to earn a Ph.D. in Bioengineering from the University of CA, San Diego; First Group of UNCF-Merck Fellowship recipients. **Business Addr:** President, Chief Executive Officer, SSC Enterprises, 5068 Hartford Pl, Flowery Branch, GA 30542, **Business Phone:** (619)823-7418.

CLEMON, U. W.
Judge. **Personal:** Born Apr 9, 1943, Fairfield, AL; son of Mose and Addie Bush; married Barbara Lang Clemon; children: Herman Isaac, Addine Michelle. **Educ:** Morehouse Col, Atlanta, GA, 1961; Miles Col, Birmingham, AL, BA, 1965; Columbia Univ Sch Law, NY, JD, 1968. **Career:** Nat Asn Advan Colored People, Legal Defense Fund, New York, NY, law clerk, 1966-69; Adams, Burg & Baker, Birmingham, AL, assoc, 1969-70; Adams, Baker & Clemon, Birmingham, AL, partner, 1970-77; Adams & Clemon, Birmingham, AL, partner, 1977-80; State AL, Montgomery, AL, senator, 1974-80; US Courts, Birmingham, AL, dist judge, 1980; US Dist Court Northern Dist Ala, chief judge, 1999-. **Orgs:** Pres, AL Black Lawyers Asn, 1976-78; coun mem, Section Individual Rights, 1976-79; legal coun, AL Chap, Southern Christian Leadership Conf, 1974-80. **Honors/Awds:** Drum Major Award, Southern Christian Leadership Conf, 1980; C Francis Stradford Award, Nat Bar Asn, 1986; William H Hastie Award, Judicial Coun, Nat Bar Asn, 1987. **Business Addr:** Chief Judge, United States District Court, Northern District of Alabama, 519 US Courthouse, 1729 5th Ave N, Birmingham, AL 35203, **Business Phone:** (205)278-1700.*

CLEMONS, ALOIS RICARDO
Public relations executive, president (organization), executive director. **Personal:** Born Jan 19, 1956, Durham, NC; son of Theodore Quick and Mary Alice; married Gail Melinda Shaw, Feb 4, 1983; children: Jason Alois & Perry Ricardo. **Educ:** Univ Mar, BS, journalism, 1977, pursuing MA, journalism. **Career:** Howard Univ, from asst sports info dir to sports info dir, 1980-85, asst athletic dir, 1989-91; Miller Brewing Co, mkt commun, 1985-88; ARC & Assoc, pres, 1988-91; Major League Baseball, mgr, pub rels, 1991; Nat League Prof Baseball Clubs, exec dir pub rels, 1994-. **Orgs:** Pres, Kappa Alpha Psi Fraternity, Theta Theta Chapter, 1977-78; NABJ, 1989. **Honors/Awds:** Tough-Minded Businessman, Salesmanship Award, The Southwestern Co, 1979; Outstanding Alumni Award, 1988; Journalism Grant, 1989. **Special Achievements:** Produced more than 50 media guides for Howard Univ Athletic Dept, 1980-85; venue press chief for Olympics, 1984; Facilities for Journalists, Vol 1 & 2, Los Angeles Olympic Comt, 1984; press liasion, USOC, 1985; Howard Univ Spring Media Guides, second place, Col & Sports Info, dir am, 1985; The Olympian, US Olympic Comt, 1985; track & field interview room mgr, Olympics, 1996.

CLEMONS, CHARLIE FITZGERALD
Football player. **Personal:** Born Jul 4, 1972, Griffin, GA; married Wanda; children: Briana, Joshua & Colton. **Educ:** Ga, BA, recreation & leisure studies. **Career:** Football player(retired); St Louis Rams, linebacker, 1997-99; New Orleans Saints, linebacker, 2000-02; Houston Texans, linebacker, 2003-04. **Honors/Awds:** St Louis Rams Super Bowl XXXIV Champions. *

CLEMONS, CLARENCE
Musician, actor. **Personal:** Born Jan 11, 1942, Norfolk, VA. **Career:** Saxophonist, 1971-; Bruce Springsteen's E Street Band, performer, 1979-89, 1999-; Red Bank Rockers, performer, 1980; Temple Soul, performer, 1990-; Albums: Rescue, 1983; Hero, 1985; A Night With Mr. C, 1989; Live in Asbury Park, 2002; Live in Asbury Park Vol. II, 2004; "Swing"; Actor: "All In theFamily"; "Thats Life"; "Nash Bridges"; "The Sentinel"; "Viper"; Films-;"Fatal Instinct"; "Blues Brothers 2000". Live in Barcelona, 2003; Hammer smith Odeon, London '75, 2005; TV: Diff'rent Strokes, 1985; Jake and the Fatman, 1989; "Honor Among Thieves", 1990; "Mining Accident", 1997; "The Getaway", 1998; Grift of the Magi, 1999; "Micheal's Band", 2004. **Special Achievements:** He has performed & recorded with the European Super Star Zuchero. **Business Addr:** Musician, Long Distance Entertainment, 562 E Woolbright Rd Suite 234, Boynton Beach, FL 33435.*

CLEMONS, DUANE
Football player, business owner. **Personal:** Born May 23, 1974, Riverside, CA; married Rana; children: Brea. **Educ:** Univ Calif, ethnic studies. **Career:** Minnesota Vikings, defensive end, 1996-99; Kansas City Chiefs, defensive end, 2000-02; Cincinnati Bengals, defensive end, 2003-05; Unicept, co-owner, currently. *

CLEMONS, EARLIE, JR.
Clergy. **Personal:** Born Oct 9, 1946, Austin, TX; son of Earlie Sr and Velma Piper; married Carolyn Hickman, Jul 7, 1967; children: Rodney L & Roland E. **Educ:** Tex Southern Univ, BS, 1969; Episcopal Theol Sem, MDiv, 1982. **Career:** Walgreen's Drugs, chief pharmacist, 1971-76; Medi Save Pharmacy, pharmacist, mgr, 1976-79; Paul Quinn Col, asst prof, 1983-85; St James Church, vicar, 1987-90; Chaplain Prairie View, chaplain, 1990-; St Francis Church, rector, vicar, 1990; Upper Manhattan Day Care & Child Develop Ctr Inc, dir, 2003-. **Orgs:** Chi Delta Mu Prof Fraternity, 1968; Alpha Phi Alpha Fraternity, 1972; Episcopal Coalition Human Needs, 1990; Prairie View-Waller Ministerial Alliance, 1990; bd mem, Waller Closet & Pantry, 1990; vice chmn, Episcopal Comn Black Ministry, 1990; chmn, Diocesan Comn Black Ministry, 1991; steering comt, Episcopal Soc for Ministry Higher Educ, 1991. **Honors/Awds:** Merit Award, Black Cult Workshop, 1985. **Business Addr:** Director, Upper Manhattan Day Care & Child Develop Ctr Inc, 207 W 133rd St, New York, NY 10030, **Business Phone:** (212)368-3500.

CLEMONS, JAMES ALBERT, III
Journalist. **Personal:** Born Nov 10, 1953, Lake Charles, LA; son of James A Jr and Rupert Florence Richardson; married Linda E Lewis, Nov 24, 1990; children: Anitra Jornell, Jasmine Angelle & James A IV. **Educ:** Univ Southwestern La, attended 1973; McNeese State Univ, 1982; Georgia State Univ, currently; Master's Divinity Sch, 2001. **Career:** Hughes Tool Co, assembly line worker, 1975-76; LA Dept Corrections, prison guard, 1977; Cities Servs Oil Co, operating engr, 1977-83; Lake Charles LA, Am Press, sports writer, 1979-81; Lake Charles LA, Recorder, owner & publisher, 1980-82; Monroe, LA, News Star World, sports writer, 1983-84; Louisville KY, Courier-Jour, sports writer, 1984-89; Atlanta Jour Consitution, night sports editor, 1989-97; Montgomery Advertiser, sports editor, 1997-99; Atlanta Jour-Constitution, sports editor & columnist, 1999. **Orgs:** Nat Asn Black Journalists, 1984-; Atlanta Asn Black Journalists, 1996-; Assoc Press Sports Editors, 1996-; Soc Prof Journalists, 1996-; Atlanta Press Club, 1996-; Nat Asn Advan Colored People; Laborers Intl Union North Am, Local 706. **Honors/Awds:** Column writing, 2nd place, AL Sports Writers Asn, 1998; Man of the Year, Gumbeaux Magazine, 1996; First Place Editing, Georgia Sports Writers Asn, 1991; Salute, Nat Asn Women's Basketball Coaches, 1996; Second Place, LA Sportswriters Asn Contest, 1984. **Business Addr:** Assistant Sports Editor, Columnist, Atlanta Journal Constitution, 72 Marietta St 8th Fl, Atlanta, GA 30302, **Business Phone:** (404)526-5334.*

CLEMONS, JOHN GREGORY
Public relations executive. **Personal:** Born Mar 24, 1954, Newark, NJ; son of John and Laura Christine Adams; married Corine Kendrick Clemons, Aug 31, 1981; children: Diarra Joi. **Educ:** Seton Hall Univ, S Orange, NJ, 1973; Syracuse Univ, Syracuse, NY, BS, News Journ, 1976. **Career:** Star-Ledger, Newark, NJ, reporter, 1976-79; Black Enterprise Mag, New York, NY, assoc ed, 1979-81; AT&T, Basking Ridge, NJ, & Atlanta, GA, pub rels spec, 1981-87; Contel Corp, Atlanta, GA, mgr-internal communications, 1987-88; GTE, Tampa, FL, pub affairs dir, 1989-93; Joint Ctr Polit & Econ Studies, vp commun, beginning 1992; Nextel Commun Inc, vpres internal commun, 2001-. **Orgs:** Pub Rels Soc Am, 1987; Tampa Chamber Com, 1989-92; Tampa Bay Male Club, 1990-92; dir, exec bd, Int Asn Bus Communicators, 1990-92; bd dirs, PRSA Nat Capital Chap, 1994; Capital Press Club; Black Pub Rels Soc; chmn, Int Asn Bus Communicators, 2001. **Honors/Awds:** Newsletter Award-First Place, Int Asn Bus Communicators/Atlanta, 1987; Golden Flame, Int Asn Bus Communicators/Atlanta, 1988. **Special Achievements:** Hearst vis Prof, Univ Fla, Col Journ & Commun, 1995. **Business Phone:** (703)433-4000.*

CLEMONS, LINDA K
Association executive. **Personal:** Born Dec 26, 1957, Cleveland, OH; divorced. **Educ:** Ball State Univ, BA. **Career:** Christ In My Life Found, founder; Living Legends Black, founder; Women Rainbow, Award of Excelience, nat founder; Sisterpreneur Inc, founder, pres, chief exec officer, currently; Nat Asn African Am Entrepreneurs, founder. **Honors/Awds:** Minorities & Women Bus, Role Model of Year, 1992; listed in the Congressional Record of United States, 1992, proclamation from governor of Ind, 1992; Sagamore Of The Wabash Award, Ind State. **Special Achievements:** Artistic director/writer, two plays: When God Calls A Woman, Lord I Wanna Dance. **Business Addr:** Chief Executive Officer, Founder, Sisterpreneur Inc, PO Box 1191, Indianapolis, IN 46206, **Business Phone:** (317)466-9556.

CLEMONS, DR. MICHAEL L
College teacher, school administrator. **Personal:** Born Jul 18, 1955, Worth, WV; son of Delores S and Lawrence D; married Sharon D Brown Clemons, Aug 14, 1982; children: Miisha Michelle, Nyasha Denise & Nia Sabree. **Educ:** Univ Md, Col Park, Md, BA, 1976, MA, 1979; Atlanta Univ, Atlanta, Ga, PhD, 1987. **Career:** Honeywell Info Syst, McLean, Va, assoc syst analyst, 1977-79; Gen Electric Info Serv, Atlanta, Ga, programmer, analyst, 1979-80; Atlanta Jr Col, Atlanta, Ga, res assoc syst analyst, 1981-84; State Univ New York, Oswego, NY, dir, instnl res & MIS, 1984-87; Old Dominion Univ, Norfolk, Va, Univ Planning & Instnl Res, dir, 1987-, assoc prof polit sci, currently. **Orgs:** Nat Conf Black Polit Scientists, 1982-; Am Polit Sci Assoc, 1986-; Soc Col & Univ Planners, 1986-; Asn Instnl Res; Va Asn Mgt & Planning, 1987-; Southern Asn Instnl Res, 1987-. **Honors/Awds:** Grad Fel, Univ Md Urban Studies, 1977-78; Omicron Delta Kappa Nat Hon & Leadership Soc, 1977; Nat Sci Found Fel, Dept Polit Sci, Atlanta Univ, 1979-82; Va Mgt Inst, 1989. **Business Addr:** Director, Associate Professor of Political Science, Old Dominion University, University Planning & Institutional Research, 350 W 21st St, Norfolk, VA 23517, **Business Phone:** (757)683-2355.

CLEMONS, SANDRA L.
Government official. **Personal:** Born Dec 12, 1945, Detroit, MI; daughter of George Rodgers and Inez Rodgers; married Lloyd F Clemons; children: Theresa Calhoun, Karen A Russell. **Educ:** Madonna Univ, BS, 1987; Univ Mich, MPA, 1989. **Career:** Detroit Police Dept, Police Communs asst, 1966-79; Detroit Election Comn, Ballot Tabulation supvr, 1979-84; Focus Hope, admin asst, 1987-89; City Detroit, Water & Sewage Dept, gov analyst, 1989-92, Recreation Dept, human resources officer, 1992-95, Human Resources, training dir, 1995-97; Detroit Pub Libr, assoc dir, 1997-99, dep dir, 1999-. **Orgs:** Bd mem, Int Personnel Mgt Asn, 1997-98; bd mem, League Women Voters-Detroit, 1995-98; chair, Pub TV WTVS Comt Adv Panel, 1999; Univ Miami Alumni Asn, 1992-; Asn Qual & Participation, 1995-; Am Libr Asn, 1997-; Nat Asn Advan Colored People, 1980-; Mich Libr Asn, 1997-. **Honors/Awds:** Systems Approach To Quality, Asn Qual & Parti-

ciaption, 1996; Customer Satisfaction Award, Mayor-City Detroit, 1996; Letter of Commendation, Detroit Police Dept, 1999; Distinguished Panel of Leaders, Franklin Covey Comp, 1997; Distinguished Panel of Leaders Covey Leadership Symposium, panel mem, 1997. **Special Achievements:** Participated in the Society of Chief Personnel Officers (SOCPO) Conference in Brighton, England, 1999. **Business Addr:** Deputy Director, Detroit Public Library, 5201 Woodward Ave, Detroit, MI 48202, **Business Phone:** (313)833-1000.*

CLEMONS, THOMASINA
College administrator. **Personal:** Born Nov 23, 1938, Charleston, WV; daughter of Charles Henry and Fannie Estelle Hairston Coles; married Otis William Wade (divorced 1972). **Educ:** Howard Univ, Wash, DC, 1956-58; Univ Hartford, W Hartford, CT, BA (cum laude), 1964; Univ Conn, Storrs, CT, MBA, 1982. **Career:** CT Comn Human Rights & Opportunities, New London, CT, investr, regional mgr, 1967-75; Univ Conn, Storrs, CT, dir, affirmative action, 1975; Employment Task Force, Conn Dept Higher Educ, chair, 1983-85; Harvard Univ, Mgt Develop Prog, fac, 1990. **Orgs:** Past state coordr, Community Coun, Am Asn Affirmative Action, 1978-; Nat Coalition 100 Black Women, Vernon Democratic Town Comt, 1980-83, 1986; bd dirs, Hockanum Valley, 1990; pres, Northeastern Conn Chap, 1990. **Honors/Awds:** Certificate of Apppreciation, Nat Coalition 100 Black Women, 1990.

CLERMONT, VOLNA
Health services administrator, physician. **Personal:** Born Sep 15, 1924, Jeremie, Haiti; married Hazel Baggett; children: Karen, Kimberly, Christopher. **Educ:** Lycee Petion Port-au-Prince Haiti, BA, 1943; Ecole Nationale de Medecine et de Pharmacie Univ d'Haiti Port-au-Prince Haiti, MD, 1949. **Career:** Childrens Hosp Mich, pathologist, 1960-69; Comprehensive Neighborhood Health Ctr, chief pediatrics, 1969-72; SW Detroit Hosp, chief staff; DMIC-PLRESCAD, med dir, 1972-; pvt pract pediat, currently. **Orgs:** Detroit Med Soc; life mem, Nat Asn Advan Colored People; Nat Med Asn; Detroit Pediatric Soc; Dipl Bd Pediatrics, Wayne County Med Soc; Mich State Med Soc; Medical staff Hutzel Hosp Children's Hosp; Grace Hosp; Urban League; Founders Soc, MI; African Art Gallery; Int African Mus Soc; Alpha Phi Alpha Frat. **Business Addr:** 2814 Oakman Blvd, Detroit, MI 48238.*

CLEVELAND, CLYDE. See Obituaries section.

CLEVELAND, GRANVILLE E.
Librarian. **Personal:** Born Nov 25, 1937, Springfield, OH; married Juanita; children: Granville, Tivonnia. **Educ:** Tougaloo Col, attended 1957; Central State Col, BS, 1960; Wittenberg Univ, attended 1963. **Career:** Univ Notre Dame Law Sch, asst law lib & fac mem, 1969; Springfield Bar & Law Libr Asn, lib & exec sec, 1963-68; basketball referee; Univ Notre Dame Law Sch, emer asst law librn, currently. **Orgs:** Am Asn Law Libr; Ohio Reg Asn Law Libr; Univ Notre Dame; Community Welfare Coun; Housing & Jobs Human Rels Comt; adult adv Springfield Youth Club; Legal Aid Soc; United Appeal Fund; City Rec Dept; Planned Parenthood; YMCA; Univ Notre Dame; Black Student Affairs Comt; asst dir Civil Rights Ctr. **Honors/Awds:** Black Am Law Studies Asn Award; Univ Notre Dame Law Sch. **Military Serv:** Air Nat Guard sgt 1956-60. **Business Addr:** Assistant Law Librarian, Notre Dame Law Sch, Notre Dame, IN 46556.

CLEVELAND, HATTYE M. See Obituaries section.

CLEVERT, HON. CHARLES N.
Judge. **Personal:** Born Oct 11, 1947, Richmond, VA. **Educ:** Davis & Elkins Col, Elkins, BA, 1969; Georgetown Univ Law Ctr, WA, JD, 1972. **Career:** Milwaukee Co Dist Atty's Off, asst dist atty, 1972-75; US Atty's Off, Eastern Dist WI, asst US atty, 1975-77; US Att Northern Dist Ill, special asst, 1977; US Bankruptcy, judge 1977-86; US Bankruptcy Crt, Eastern Dist WI, US bankruptcy judge, 1977-96, chief judge, 1986-96; Univ Wis Law Sch, lectr, 1989-90; US Dist Crt, Eastern Dist Wis, Judge, 1996-. **Orgs:** WI Bar Assn; Milwaukee Bar Assn; WI Assn Minority Attys; 7th Circuit Bar Assn; Alpha Phi Alpha; Judicial Coun NBA; African Methodist Episcopal Church; vice chair, Natl Conf Fed Trial Judges; bd mem, Am Bankruptcy Inst; bd mem, Am Judicature Society; immediate past pres, Thomas Fairchild Am Inn Ct; bd mem, Men Tomorrow; bd mem, Anvil Housing Corp; comt on the budget, Judicial Conf US; Sigma Pi Phi; Fed Judicial Ctr Dist Judges Educ Comt, 2001-; Am Jury Proj Adv Comt. **Honors/Awds:** Fel, Am Col Bankruptcy; Federal Employee of the Year, Milwaukee Fed Executives Assn, 1991; Administrative Excellence Award, Natl Conf Bankruptcy Clerks; Milwaukee Times Black Excellence Award, 1993. **Business Addr:** Judge, The United States District Court, Eastern District of Wisconsin, Room 208 US Courthouse, 517 E Wisconsin Ave, Milwaukee, WI 53202, **Business Phone:** (414)297-1585.

CLIFF, MICHELLE
Writer. **Personal:** Born Nov 2, 1946, Kingston, Jamaica. **Educ:** Wagner Col, AB, 1969; Warburg Inst, London, MPhil, 1974. **Career:** Life, reporter & researcher, 1969-70; WW Nortont & Co, production supervisor of Norton Library, 1970-71, copyeditor, 1974-75, manuscript & production editor, 1975-79; Sinister Wisdom, co-publisher & editor, 1981-83; Norwich Univ, cycle faculty, adult degree prog, 1983-84; Martin Luther King Jr Pub Libr, teacher, creative writing & hist; Author: Claiming the Identity They Taught Me to Despise, 1980; Abeng, 1984; The Land of Look Behind: Prose & Poetry, 1985; No Telephone to Heaven, 1987; Bodies of Water, 1990; Free Enterprise, 1993; The Store of a Million Items: Stories, 1998; Free Enterprise: A Novel of Mary Ellen Pleasant, 2004. **Honors/Awds:** Fel, McDowell Col, 1982; Fel, NEA, 1982; Fel, MA Artists Found, 1984; Eli Kantor Fel, Yaddo, 1984; Fullbright Fel, New Zealand, 1988; Fel Fiction, NEA, 1989. *

CLIFFORD, CHARLES H.
Consultant. **Personal:** Born Sep 8, 1933, Sacramento, CA; married Claudean Akers; children: Carla, Carolyn & Caren. **Educ:** Sacramento Jr Col, AA, 1958; Sacramento St Col, BA, 1965. **Career:** Dept Corr St CA, human rel consult, 1964. **Orgs:** Area pres, Black Corr Coalition; pres, Calif corrections officers, 1969-72; Urban League, Black Caucus, Nat Asn Advan Colored People; Calif Young Dems. **Honors/Awds:** Co-author, Dept Corrs Affirmative Action Plan; first black corrections sgt Folsom Prison; first black Lt Folsom, 1970. **Special Achievements:** First state black dep sheriff Sacramento Co, 1960. **Military Serv:** USN, 1951-55.

CLIFFORD, THOMAS E.
Military leader, business owner. **Personal:** Born Mar 9, 1929, Washington, DC; married Edith Sanders; children: Maria, Edwin, Larry & Mark. **Educ:** Howard Univ, BA, cum laude, 1949; George Wash Univ, MBA, 1963. **Career:** Military leader, Business owner (retired); USAF, jet fighter pilot &officer, 1949-79; Gen Motors Corp, plant mgr, 1979-86; Clifford Motors, owner, 1987-93. **Orgs:** VFW; Am Legion; AFA; Nat Asn Advan Colored People; Daedalians; comt mem, SCOPED. **Honors/Awds:** Legion of Merit with two oak leaf clusters, Distinguished Flying Cross, Air Medal with four oak leaf clusters, the Air Force Commendation Medal with oak leaf cluster, the Air Force Outstanding Unit Award ribbon and the Republic of Vietnam Gallantry Cross with palm. **Military Serv:** USAF, major gen, 30 yrs; Distinguished Flying Cross; Rotary; TROA; MOWW; Tuskegee Airmen; numerous others. **Home Addr:** 11940 W 14th Ave, Blythe, CA 92225. **Business Addr:** Committee Member, SCOPED, 2 N Franklin St, Watkins Glen, NY 14891, **Business Phone:** (607)535-4341.

CLIFT, JOSEPH WILLIAM
Physician. **Personal:** Born Apr 24, 1938, Patoka, IN; son of Mary Esther Lucas and Cecil William; married Ulyssine Gibson Clift, Aug 10, 1963 (died 1998); children: Kory Grant & Nathalie Louise; married Earlyne Rand Manigault-Clift, May 29, 1999. **Educ:** Tex Sothern Univ, BS, 1959; Univ Tex Med Br, MD, 1965. **Career:** Physician(retired); Physician, self employed, 2003. **Orgs:** Pres, Delta Theta Chap Alpha Phi Alpha Fraternity, 1959; pres, Alameda Contra Costa Co Diabetes asn, 1975; mem, bd dir, Samuel Merritt Hosp, 1976-79; diplomate, Am Bd Internal Med, 1978; pres med staff, Highland General Hosp, 1983-84; pres, East Bay Soc Internal Med, 1984-; mem, Nat Med asn; AMA; Calif Med asn; mem, counselor, pres Alameda-Contra-Costa Med asn, 1992-; Calif Soc Internal Med, 1991-92; Sigma Pi Phi Fraternity, Alpha Gamma Boule, Oakland-Berkeley, Calif, 1987. **Honors/Awds:** Resident of the Year, Highland General Hosp, 1971. **Military Serv:** USAF, capt, 1967-69; Commendation Medal USAF, 1969.

CLIFTON, DR. IVERY DWIGHT
Educator. **Personal:** Born Apr 6, 1943, Statesboro, GA; son of B J and Rosetta B; married Patricia A Davis, May 28, 1967; children: Kalisa & Kelli. **Educ:** Tuskegee Inst, BS, 1965, MS, 1967; Univ Ill, PhD, 1976. **Career:** Educator (retired); Univ GA, prof & vpres, Acad Affairs, Col Agr & Environ Sci, 1988-, assoc dean, 1988, sr assoc dean, int head dept; US Dept Agr, DC, agr econ, 1970-76; TVA AL, agr econ 1967. **Orgs:** Secy, Alpha Phi Alpha, 1975; Chi Gamma Iota Univ Ill Chapter Urbana, 1975; spec asst to vpres acad affairs, Univ GA, 1977-78; Phi Kappa Phi Univ GA, Chapter Athens, 1979; consult, Resources Future, 1979; Gamma Sigma Delta, Univ GA Chapter Athens, 1980; pres, Steward Bd First Am Church, 1979-80. **Honors/Awds:** Achievement Award, USDA, 1971; Faculty Service Award, Univ Ga Alumni Asn, 2005; Outstanding Minority in Agricultural Economics Award, Am Agr Econ Asn; Lee Arrendale Voc Award; John Madden Creative Leadership Award. **Military Serv:** AUS qm ltc(p) reserves 20 yrs; AUS VA & Vietnam, officer advr, 1967-70; commendation Bronze Star. **Home Addr:** 162 Doubles Bridges Xing, Winterville, GA 30683-9674.

CLIFTON, LUCILLE (THELMA LUCILLE CLIFTON)
Writer, poet, educator. **Personal:** Born Jun 27, 1936, Depew, NY; daughter of Samuel Sayles Sr and Thelma Moore Sayles; married Fred J Clifton, May 10, 1958 (deceased); children: Sidney, Fredrica (deceased), Channing, Gillian, Graham & Alexia. **Educ:** Howard Univ, Wash, DC, drama, 1955. **Career:** Educator, writer, poet; Fredonia State Teachers Col, actress, 1955; New York State Div Employ, Buffalo, NY, claims clerk, 1958-60; US Off Educ, Cent Atlantic Regional Educ Laboratory, lit asst, 1969-71; Coppin State Col, Baltimore, MD, poet residence, 1974-79; Columbia Univ Sch Arts, vis writer; George Wash Univ, Jerry Moore vis writer, 1982-83; Univ Calif, Santa Cruz, prof lit & creative writing, 1985-89; St Mary's Col, St Mary's, MD, distinguished prof humanities, 1989-91; Columbia Univ, prof writing, 1995-99; Duke Univ, Durham, NC, prof creative writing, 1998; St. Mary's Col, Hilda C Landers Endowed chair, 2005, prof emer, currently; writer, currently; Books: The Black BCs, 1970; All Us Come Cross the Water, 1973; Don't You Remember?, 1973; The Boy Who Didn't Believe in Spring, 1973; The Times They Used to Be, 1974; My Brother Fine with Me, 1975; Three Wishes, 1976; Generations: A Memoir, 1976; Amifika, 1977; The Lucky Stone, 1979; My Friend Jacob, 1980; Sonora Beautiful, 1981; Ten Oxherding Pictures, 1988; Poetry: Good Times, 1969; Some of the Days of Everett Anderson, 1970; Everett Anderson's Christmas Coming, 1971; Good News about the Earth, 1972; Good, Says Jerome, 1973; An Ordinary Woman, 1974; Everett Anderson's Year, 1974; Everett Anderson's Friend, 1976; Everett Anderson's 1—2—3, 1977; Everett Anderson's Nine Month Long, 1978; Two-Headed Woman, 1980; Everett Anderson's Goodbye, 1983; Good Woman: Poems & a Memoir, 1969-80, 1987; Next: New Poems, 1987; Quilting: Poems 1987-90, 1991; The Book of Light. Port Townsend, 1993; The Terrible Stories: Poems, 1996; Dear Creator: A Week of Poems for Young People & Their Teachers, 1997; Blessing the Boats: New & Selected Poems 1988-2000, 2000; One of the Problems of Everett Anderson, 2001. **Orgs:** Int PEN; Authors Guild; Authors League Am; fel Am Acad Arts & Sci; Bd Chancellors, Acad Am Poets. **Honors/Awds:** Discovery Award, New York YW-YMHA Poetry Ctr, 1969; Nat Endowment for the Arts Fellows, 1970 & 1972; Honorary Degree, Univ Md, Towson State Univ, Colby Col & Alma Col; Poet Laureate of the State of MD, 1979-84; Juniper Prize, Univ Mass, 1980; Coretta Scott King Award, Am Libr Asn, 1984; Nominated for Pulitzer Prize for poetry, 1980 & 1988; Nat Book Award for Poetry, 2000; Shelley Memorial Prize; Charity Randall Prize; Shestack Prize; Am Poetry Review; Emmy Award, Am Acad Tv Arts & Sci; Lannan Literary Award; Ruth Lilly Prize, 2007. **Home Addr:** 7441 Swan Point Way, Columbia, MD 21045, **Home Phone:** (410)381-2847. **Business Addr:** Writer, Curtis Brown Limited, 10 Astor Pl, New York, NY 10003, **Business Phone:** (212)473-5400.

CLIFTON, ROSALIND MARIA
Health services administrator, president (organization), chief executive officer. **Personal:** Born Oct 23, 1950, St Louis, MO; son of Houston Gant and Lois; married Pierce T, 1987. **Career:** Internal Revenue Serv, agt; Claims Overload Syst, bus mgr, 1986-89; Blacklog Ltd, owner, pres, ceo, 1989-. **Business Phone:** (312)554-8800.

CLIFTON, THELMA LUCILLE. See CLIFTON, LUCILLE.

CLINE, DR. EILEEN TATE
School administrator. **Personal:** Born Jun 25, 1935, Chicago, IL; daughter of Herman and Inez Duke; married William P (deceased); children: Jon Christopher & Joy Michele. **Educ:** Geneva C Robinson Chicago Musical Col, priv piano study, 1952; Univ Chicago, liberal arts, 1952; Helen; Curtis Chicago Musical Col, class piano course, 1950; Rudolph Ganz scholar stud, priv piano study, 1958; Oberlin Conserv Music, B Mus Educ, 1956, B Mus piano perf, 1956; Univ Colo, Boulder, M Mus piano perf, 1960; independent piano studio, 1975; Ind Univ Sch Music, Doctor Mus Educ, 1985; Harvard Inst Educ Mgt, 1986. **Career:** School administrator(retired); Univ Colo, co ordr cont educ piano, 1965-75; Neighbourhood Mus Sch, New Haven, CT, exec dir, 1980-82; Peabody Conserv Mus, Johns Hopkins Univ, assoc dean, 1982-83, dean, 1983-95; Inst Policy Studies, Johns Hopkins Univ, sr fel, 1998, Peabody Conserv, dean emer, currently. **Orgs:** Founder/dir, Boulder C's Choir, 1972-75; stud activities chmn, Colo State Music Teachers' Asn, stud activities chmn, exec bd; prog chmn, Boulder Area Music Teachers' Asn; Music Prog Prof Training Panel, Nat Endowment Arts, 1980-; pres, Young Musicians Boulder; alumni-elected trustee,Oberlin Col, 1981-88; bd trustees, Hopkins Sch, 1981-82; bd mem, Nat Guild Community Schs Arts, 1982-88; nat Keyboard Community Music Educs; Nat Conf; adv bd, Young Women's Christian Asn, Univ Colo; Music Community Colo Coun Arts & Humanities; Col Bd, Theory AP Test Develop Comn, ETS, 1983-; Eval Team Middle States Accredit Asn, 1983-; MTNA, MENC, Col Music Soc, Nat Guild Piano Teachers, Soc Values Higher Educ, bd mem, Am Symphony Orchestra League, 1989-; Baltimore Symphony Orchestra Community Outreach Comt, Educ Outreach, 1989-95, music comn, 1993-; bd mem, Nat Guild Community Schs Arts, 1982-88; bd mem, Kenan Inst Arts; advy bd mem,Harvard Univ Kennedy Sch Prog Non-Profit Leadership; Md State Dept Educ, arts advy panel, 1995-; bd mem, Marlboro Music; advy bd, El Paso Pro Musica; advy bd, Van Cliburn Int Piano Competition; advy bd, Am Bach Soc. **Honors/Awds:** Research grants, Ind Univ Found, Ind Univ Office Res & Grad Develop; Oberlin Col Alumni Res Grant; acad scholars & hons, Univ Colo, 1958-60, Oberlin Col, 1953-56; Danforth Found Fel, 1975-; lectures, performance competitions; Outstanding Woman Awd Natl Exec Club 1984; Outstanding Alumni Awd Univ of Colorado College of Music 19 Peabody Faculty and Administration Award for Outstanding Contribution to the Peabody Community, 1986; Article of the Year Award for "Anyone

Can Winel3," at wo-part article in American Music Teachers, 1990; Keynote speaker ASOL/Unv of Chicago/Chicago Symphony Orchestra 100th Anniversary Symposium: "The Training of Orchestral Musicians"; Torch Bearer Award for distinguished service, Coalition of 100 Black Women, 1991; Panelist: NJ State Arts Council; Massachusetts Cultural Council; Keynote Speaker, Coll Music Society Annual Mtg, 1995; My Father Never Told Me., or, A View From this Bridge; NASM Task Force Report: Minority Access to Music Study, Nov 1994. **Special Achievements:** Published, "Reflections of Cultural Synthesis and Social Reality as Seenin George Walker's Sonata No 2" Soc for Values in Higher Education Conf Dickinson Col, 1979; "The Competition Explosion, Impact on Higher Education" MTNA Natl Convention 1980; "Education Relationships to Professional Training and Career Entry" NASM Conv Dallas, TX 1981; "The Competition Explosion, Impact on Education" The American Music Teacher Parts I-III Jan-March, 1982. **Business Addr:** Dean Emeritus, Johns Hopkins University, Peabody Conserv, 1 E Mount Vernon Pl, Baltimore, MD 21202.*

CLINGMAN, KEVIN LOREN
Executive. **Personal:** Born Oct 9, 1961, Detroit, MI; son of Simeon and Gloria; married Sherry Bryant, Jul 2, 1988; children: Kameron. **Educ:** Morehouse Col, AB, econ, 1985. **Career:** Owens Corning Fiberglass, supvr, materials & logistics, 1985-86; Union Pacific Railroad, prod mgr, 1988-92; Omaha Small Bus Network, pres, 1993-96; N Omaha Bus Develop Corp, 1993-96; LCBD Enterprise Group, pres, 1996; Republic Bank, Ohio, commercial loan officer, 2003. **Orgs:** Finance comn, Salem Baptist Church, 1989-96; bd dir, Ctr Stage Theatre, 1989-94; bd dir, Omaha Small Bus Network, 1992-96; bd dir, Nat Business Incubation asn, 1996; bd dir, North Omaha Bus Developt Corp, 1992-96; pres, Black Employee Network Union Pacific Railroad, 1992. **Honors/Awds:** Union Pacific Railroad, Special Commendation, 1989. Microenterprise Incubator of the Year, National Business Incubation Asn, 1996.

CLINKSCALES, JERRY A.
Educator. **Personal:** Born Sep 25, 1933, Abbeville, SC; married Jerrolyn Holtzclaw; children: Mary, Jerry, David & Stephen. **Educ:** SC State Col, BSA, 1956; Tuskegee Inst, DVM, 1960; Univ Ill, advanced training, 1972; Univ Tex, advanced training, 1981. **Career:** Tuskegee Inst, instr, 1960, 1967; USDA, poultry insp div, 1966; small animal clinic, 1968;, Tuskegee Univ, asst prof, dir vet admis, 1994. **Orgs:** Am Vet Med Asn; Am Asn Vet Clinicans; Am Animal Hosp Asn; Tuskegee Area CC; Omega Psi Phi Frat; Phi Zeta Hon Vet Frat; adv, City Recreation Dept;City Canine Control Ctr. **Honors/Awds:** Outstanding Teacher of the Year Award Norden's 1972-73. **Military Serv:** AUSR, 1956-90. *

CLINKSCALES, KEITH
Executive. **Educ:** Fla A&M Univ, BA; Harvard Bus Sch, MBA. **Career:** Vanguarde Media Inc, chmn & chief exec officer, 2001-; ESPN Publ, sr vpres & gen mgr, 2005-; VIBE mag, pres & chief exec officer; KTC Ventures, pres, currently. **Orgs:** Tres, Apollo Theater Found Board Trustees; mem, Pepsico's Multicultural Adv Bd. **Special Achievements:** American Advertising Federation (AAF) Advertising Hall of Achievement. **Business Phone:** (646)654-4200.*

CLINKSCALES, REV. DR. MARCIA J
College teacher. **Educ:** Univ Northern Colo, BA; Emory Univ, Mdiv; Univ Denver, PhD, 1975. **Career:** Facilitator, Nat Commun Asn Organ Commun Pre-Conference, 2002; Howard Univ, Dept Human Commun Studies, asst prof, 2003-. **Orgs:** Founder & pres, Ctr Is you; itinerant elder, African Methodist Episcopal Church; ministerial team, Payne Memorial A.M.E. Church, Baltimore, MD. **Honors/Awds:** Presented a paper & book Understanding Organization through Culture and Structure. **Business Addr:** Assistant Professor, Howard University, Department of Human Communication Studies, 2400 6th St NW, Washington, DC 20059, **Business Phone:** (202)806-6100.

CLIPPER, MILTON CLIFTON, JR.
Executive. **Personal:** Born Feb 3, 1948, Washington, DC; son of Milton Clipper Sr and Gladys Robertson; divorced; children: Faith Ann Clipper, Jaime Marie Clipper. **Educ:** Montgomery Col; Corcoran Sch Art. **Career:** Wash Post, graphic designer; Corcoran Sch Art, art teacher; WTOP-TV, artist, 1970-73; WJXT-TV, art dir, 1974-76; WDVM TV 9 Wash, DC, asst prom mgr, 1985; Atlanta Educ Telecommunications Collaborative Inc, pres & chief exec officer, currently. **Orgs:** Ed bd, WJXT-TV, 1975-76; Metro Art Dirs & Club WA; guest lectr, TV & Newspaper Graphics; Black Ski; Wash Urban League; Am Film Inst; adv bd mem, Big Brothers of the Nat Capital area. **Honors/Awds:** 2nd place Metro Art Dirs Club, 1972; Exhib Abstract Art, 1973; Gold Award, Broadcast Designers Asn, 1984; Finalist Inst Film Fest, 1984. **Business Phone:** (678)686-0321.*

CLOSE, BILLY RAY
Educator. **Personal:** Born Jan 1, 1965, Donalsonville, GA; son of Frank Close Sr and Daisy; married Fran T, May 7, 1994; children: Nia SeKayi, Nataki Adia & Nyla Imani. **Educ:** Fla State Univ, BS, criminol & psychol, 1988, MS, criminol, 1992, D Phil, criminol & criminal justice, 1997. **Career:** Governor's Coun Phys Fitness & Sports, admin asst, 1988; Lincoln High Sch, head men's track & field coach, 1988-89; Supreme Court State Fla Racial & Ethnic Bias Study Comn, res consult, 1989-91; Fla Agr & Mech Univ, adj prof, 2004; Fla State Univ, Black Studies Prog, grad res, 1988-94, Summer Black Grad Orientation Prog, prog dir, 1989-2004, Black Studies Prog, asst dir, 1994-98, African- American Studies Prog, fac assoc, 1994-, acting dir, 1995-96, Brother Pride, dir, 1992-, Sch Criminol & Criminal Justice, asst prof, 1997-, Ctr Acad Retention & Enhancement, summer fac mem, 2003-; Paradigm Consult & Assocs Inc, pres, 2001-; Beyond The Athlete Inc, pres & founder, 2005-. **Orgs:** Founder & exec dir, Beyond The Athlete Inc; pres, Paradigm Consultants & Assoc Inc; Fla State Univ Athletic Bd Comt, 1986-88, 2009-; McKnight Achievers Soc, 1990-; The Acad Criminal Justice Sci, 1997-; Nat Asn Blacks Criminal Justice,1997-; vpres & bd dir, Lincoln High Sch Alumni Asn, 2002-; The Am Soc Criminol; community consult, Steele-Brooks Inst, Tallahassee, Florida, 2003-; bd mem, life mem, Fla State Univ Varsity Club, 2003-; bd mem, Tallahassee Marine Inst Inc, 2004-; mem, Leon County Sch Found Inc, 2007-; Nat Orgn Black Law Enforcement Exec. **Honors/Awds:** Track & Field Hall of Fame- Golden South Classic, Lincoln High School Hall of Fame; Track & Field Scholarship, 1983; McKnight Doctoral Program, Fla Educ Fund, 1989; Russel V Ewald Award for Academic Excellence and Human Service, 1991; University Teaching Award, Fla State Univ, 2000, 2007; Martin Luther King Distinguished Service Award, The Fla State Univ, 2001; Distinguished Teacher Award, Fla State Univ, 2005-06; Faculty of the Year Award, Nat Soc Collegiate Scholars, 2006; Advising Award, Fla State Univ, 2005, 2006. **Special Achievements:** Published numerous articles & research papers. **Business Addr:** Assistant Professor, The Florida State University, School of Criminology & Criminal Justice, 319 Hecht House, Tallahassee, FL 32306-1127, **Business Phone:** (850)644-5344.

CLOSE, FRAN
Educator. **Educ:** Fla State Univ, BS, Biol Sci; Fla A&M Univ, PhD, Pharmacol & Toxicol. **Career:** Fla A&M Univ, Col Pharm & Pharmaceut Studies, asst prof, 2003-, interim asst dean stud serv. **Orgs:** Pres & bd dir, Capital Area Healthy Start Coalition; Ctr Healthy Options & Innovative Community Empowerment. **Business Addr:** Assistant Professor, Interim Dean, Florida A&M University, Inst Pub Health, Rm 110 311 New Pharm Bldg Sunshine MNR, Tallahassee, FL 32307-3800, **Business Phone:** (850)599-3053.

CLOSS, KEITH MITCHELL, JR.
Basketball player. **Personal:** Born Apr 3, 1976, Hartford, CT. **Educ:** Cent Conn State Univ. **Career:** Los Angeles Clippers, 1997-2000; Rockford Lightning, forward; Pennsylvania Valley Dawgs, 2003; Buffalo Silverbacks, center, 2007-08; Yunnan Bulls, 2008-. *

CLOUD, W. ERIC
Lawyer. **Personal:** Born Feb 26, 1946, Cleveland, OH; son of William Walter and Alfreda Ruth; married Carole Anne Henderson; children: Andre Deron, Sharrief. **Educ:** Morris Brown Col, BA, 1973; Dag Hammarskjold Col, fellowship, 1974; Antioch Sch Law, JD, 1977; George Wash Law Sch, LLM, Int & Comparative Law, 1980. **Career:** Pvt Practice Int Law, atty; US Dept Treasury, consult, 1979-80; US Dept Labor, special asst int tax counsel, 1976-78; atty, 1982-; Wash Afro-Am Newspaper, corresp; Morris Brown Col, lecturer. **Orgs:** Am Bar Asn, 1977; Nat Bar Asn; Morris Brown Col Alumni Asn. **Honors/Awds:** Good Samaritan of the Year, Mayor Carl Stokes, 1968; Award for Best Article, 1990. **Special Achievements:** Book: Tax Treaties the need for the us to extend its treaty network to developing countries in light of the new Intl Economic and Polit Realities; Four Walls/Eight Window, 1990. **Business Addr:** Lawyer, 1003 K St NW, Washington, DC 20001, **Business Phone:** (202)347-5724.*

CLOUDEN, LAVERNE C.
Music director, educator. **Personal:** Born Dec 6, 1933, Cleveland, OH; married Aubrey B; children: Norman, Karen & Nathan. **Educ:** Case Western Res Univ, BS, 1966, MA, 1970. **Career:** Buckeye State Band, dir, 1958-; F D Roosevelt Jr High Sch, instr & dir, 1966-72; Music Dept Nathan Hale Jr High Sch, chmn, 1972-74; John F Kennedy High Sch, music dir, 1974-85; E High Sch, fine arts dept chmn & instr, dir & vocal dir, 1985-. **Orgs:** Mt Pleasant Symphony Orchestra Parma Symphony; Cleveland Women's Symphony; Buckeye State Band; Mt Pleasant Musician's Guild; dir, Musicians Union 4; Music Educrs Nat Conf Ohio Music Educrs Asn; Women Band Dirs Nat Asn; Nat Band Asn; Int Platform Asn; Nat Asn Music Ther; Mu Phi Epsilon; Nat Bd Am Youth Symphony & Chorus. **Honors/Awds:** Congrats resolution Mayor & City Cleveland, 1975. **Special Achievements:** First female marching band director at Cleveland High School; featured in newspapers & Magazines. **Business Addr:** Chairman, East High School, Department of Fine Arts, 1349 E 79th St, Cleveland, OH 44103.

CLOWNEY, AUDREY E
Manager. **Personal:** Born Aug 29, 1961, Pittsburgh, PA; daughter of Gordon W and Helen A. **Educ:** Univ Mich, Ann Arbor, BSE, 1983; Columbia Univ, New York, MBA, 1985. **Career:** Quaker Oats Co, Chicago, brand mgr, 1985-. **Orgs:** Youth Guidance, 1988-89; Nat Black MBA Asn-Chicago Chapter, 1990-; Arts Forum, 1990-. **Honors/Awds:** One of "The 100 Most Promising Black Women in Corporate America," Ebony Magazine, 1991. **Business Phone:** (312)821-1000.

CLYBURN, JAMES EMOS
Congressperson (u.s. federal government). **Personal:** Born Jul 21, 1940, Sumter, SC; son of Enos Lloyd and Almeta; married Emily; children: Mignon, Jennifer & Angela. **Educ:** SC State Col, BS, hist, 1962; USC Law Sch, 1974. **Career:** High sch, hist teacher, 1962-65; SC Employee Sec Commn, couns, 1965-68; Neighborhood Youth Corps, dir, 1966-68; SC Commn for Farm Workers Inc, exec dir, 1968-71; Gov John C West SC, spec asst human resource develop, 1971-74; SC Human Affairs Comn, comnr, 1974-92; CBC, head, 1998-2000; US House Rep, 6th Dist SC, congressman, 1993-; House Democrat's Faith Working Group, leader. **Orgs:** Pres, Nat Asn Advan Colored People; US House Rep; numerous political & civic orgns; Omega Psi Phi fraternity. **Honors/Awds:** Recipient of 36 citations & awards. **Special Achievements:** First black pres SC Young Democrats; first minority advisor to a South Carolina Governor in 1971. **Home Addr:** 501 Juniper St, Columbia, SC 29203, **Home Phone:** (803)786-1402. **Business Addr:** Congressman, US House Representative, 6th Dist SC, 2135 Rayburn House Off Buldg, Washington, DC 20515-4006, **Business Phone:** (202)225-3315.

CLYBURN, JOHN B
Executive. **Personal:** Born Oct 22, 1942, Sumter, SC; married Vivian Hilton; children: Jeffrey, Erica & Kimberly. **Educ:** SC State Col, BS, 1964; Northeastern Univ, MEd, 1968; Univ WI, PhD, Urban Ed. **Career:** Wiltwyck Sch Boys Inc, sr counr; New Eng Home, weekend supvr; Hayden Goodwill Inn Sch Boys, exec asst; SC Voc Rehab Dept, voc rehab counr; ESC, nat coord, 1969-70, proj dir, 1970-71, vpres, 1971-72, exec vpres, 1972-73; Decision Info Systs Corp, chmn; Precise Solutions Inc, chmn & chief exec officer; Repub Sq Ltd, staff. **Orgs:** Nat Asn Mkt Develops; Am Mgt Asn; Child Care Proj Adv Comn; Nat Rehab Asn; Day Care & Child Develop Corp Am; Nat Asn Educ Young C; Delta Psi Omega; lectr, Nat Head Start Conf; Nat Asn Black Soc Workers; Nat Conf Inst Serv. **Business Addr:** Staff, Republic Square Limited, 1280 Maryland Ave SW Suite 280, Washington, DC 20024.*

CLYNE, JOHN RENNEL
Lawyer, consultant. **Personal:** Born Feb 25, 1926, New York, NY; son of Reginald and Urielle Linard; married Jessie MacFarlane, Dec 28, 1954; children: Diana, Reginald & Robert. **Educ:** St Johns Univ Sch Law, LLB, 1958; St Johns Univ Sch Law, JD, 1968. **Career:** US & W Indies, engr, 1958; pvt practice lawyer, NY, 1958-62; Govt (retired);New York City Transit Auth, atty, 1963-65; US Agency Intl Develop Nigeria, Brazil,Nicaragua, Honduras, regional legal adv, 1965-83; US Agency Intl Develop, asst gen coun, 1983-85; self-employ, econ develop consult, currently. **Honors/Awds:** Nominated, Fed Exec Sr Sem, 1977; Senior Foreign Service Award, 1984; Secy State's Tribute Appreciation Distinguished Serv Foreign Disaster Asst, 1985. **Military Serv:** USN, 1944-46. *

COAKLEY, HM
Entrepreneur, executive, movie producer, movie producer. **Personal:** Born in Saint Thomas, VI. **Educ:** Howard Univ, BS, physics, Columbia Univ, Master's Degree; Univ Calif Lod Angeles, PhD, physics. **Career:** producer; adj prof, Columbia Col Hollywood, Cal State Univ-Fullerton; Rockstone Pictures Inc, chmn, chief exec officer, co founder & exec dir, currently. **Special Achievements:** produced: Ten Benny & Restaurant. *

COAKLEY, WILLIAM DEXTER
Football player. **Personal:** Born Oct 20, 1972, Charleston, SC. **Educ:** Appalachian State Univ, Physical Educ, 1998. **Career:** Football player (retired); Dallas Cowboys, linebacker, 1997-04; St Louis Rams, linebacker, 2005-06; free agent currently. **Honors/Awds:** Buck Buchanan Award; Southern Conference Freshman of the Year, 1993; Southern Conference Defensive Player of the Year, 1994, 1995, 1996; Southern Conference Male Athlete of the Year, 1995, 1996; All-Iron Award, 1999; Pro Bowl, 1999, 2001& 2003. *

COAR, DAVID H.
Federal court judge. **Personal:** Born Aug 11, 1943, Birmingham, AL. **Educ:** Syracuse Univ, BA, 1964; Loyola Univ Chicago Law Sch, JD, 1969; Harvard Univ, LLM, 1970. **Career:** Nat Asn Advan Colored People Legal Defense & Educ Fund, NY, atty, 1970; Pvt pract, Ala; Crawford & Cooper, Mobile, AL, atty, 1971; Adams, Baker & Clemon, Birmingham, AL, atty, 1972-74; DePaul Univ, instr, 1974-79; Dept Justice, trustee, 1979-82; DePaul Univ, prof law, 1982-86; US Dist Ct, Northern Dist Ill, bankruptcy judge, 1984-94, district ct judge, 1994-. **Orgs:** Fed Bar Asn; Nat Conf Bankruptcy Judges; Ala Bar Asn; Chicago Bar Asn; bd dirs, Boys & Girls Clubs Chicago; Am Bankruptcy Inst; Nat Bankruptcy Conf; Bankruptcy Judges Educ Comt, Fed Judicial Ctr; Bur Nat Affairs; Am Bar Asn; Legal Club Chicago; Chicago Inn Ct; Chicago Bar Asn. **Business Phone:** (312)435-5648.*

COASTON, SHIRLEY ANN DUMAS
Educator, president (organization). **Personal:** Born Nov 27, 1939, New Orleans, LA; daughter of Cornelius and Pearl Bailey; mar-

ried George Ellis Sr, Jul 21, 1962; children: Debra Coaston Ford, George E Jr & Angela R. **Educ:** Dillard Univ, New Orleans, LA, BA, 1962; Univ Calif, Berkeley, CA, MLS, 1970. **Career:** Univ Calif, San Francisco, CA, libr asst, 1966-69; Peralta Community Col Dist, Oakland, CA, evening ref librn & head librn, dir, 1970-87, head librn, 1988-; Contra Costa Community Col Dist, Richmond, CA, ref librn, 1987-88; Laney Col, head librn & fac sen pres, currently. **Orgs:** Treas, Calif Librns Black Caucus, N, 1980-; secy & bd dirs, Salem Lutheran Home, 1986-91; chairperson, Prof Develop Comt, Laney Col, 1989-91; Aid Asn Lutherans, 1989-; secy, BayNet, 1990-92; vpres, Peralta Fed Teachers, 1991-; asst secy, San Francisco Bay Area Panhellenic Coun, 1992-; annual conv planning comt mem, Calif Libr Asn, 1993; Am Libr Asn; ALA Black Caucus; Delta Sigma Theta Sorority; Nat Asn Advan Colored People. **Special Achievements:** Author: Books by & about Blacks Laney Col Libr, Laney Col, 1973. **Home Addr:** 3226 Hood St, Oakland, CA 94605, **Home Phone:** (510)632-0702. **Business Addr:** Head Librarian, Faculty Senate President, Laney College, 900 Fallon St, Oakland, CA 94607, **Business Phone:** (510)986-6947.

COATES, BEN TERRENCE
Football player, football coach. **Personal:** Born Aug 16, 1969, Greenwood, SC; married Yvette; children: Lauren, Brianna & Destiny. **Educ:** Univ Livingstone, sports mgt. **Career:** Football player (retired), Football coach; New England Patriots, tight end, 1991-99; Baltimore Ravens, 2000; Livingstone Col, head coach; Carolina Sharks Atlantic Indoor Football League, coach & gen mgr, 2004;Cleveland Browns, football coach, 2005. **Honors/Awds:** Livingstone's Most Valuable Player Award, 1987, 1988 & 1990; Won Baxter Holman Mem Award freshman; S W Lancaster Award; Offensive Player of the Year, 1993; Baltimore Ravens Super Bowl XXXV Champions; New England Patriots Hall of Fame, 2008. **Special Achievements:** Ranked seventh among the Patriots' all-time leading scorers with 290 career points; Owns franchise records for most receptions in a season (96).

COATES, JANICE E.
Optometrist. **Personal:** Born Aug 27, 1942, Zanesville, OH; daughter of Bessie Kennedy Mayle and Urschel Mayle; children: Stephanie, Stephlynn, Melissa, Tischa. **Educ:** Marion Col, attended 1962; Wright State Univ, BS, comprehensive sci & BS, sec educ, 1974; Ind Univ, Dr Optometry, 1979. **Career:** Dr Frederick Grigsby, urologist asst, 1963-65; Sanders Stone Ins Agency, ins rater, 1965-66; Montgomery Co Welfare Dept, welfare worker, 1967-69; Dayton Bd Educ, substitute teacher, 1969-74, sci teacher, 1974-75; Capital Univ, educ, 1980-82; Pvt Pract, optom, 1980-. **Orgs:** Prog coordr, 1982-83, treas, 1983-84, Am Bus Womens Asn; minority recuirt Am Optometric Asn, Ohio Optometric Asn, 1980-; liasion, state rep Miami Valley Soc Optometrists, 1981-; Gem City Med Soc, 1982-; trustee, Nat Optometric Asn, 1983-, exec bd, 1983-89, secy, 1985-87; Nat Asn Advan Colored People, 1983-; exec bd, Youth Engaged Success, 1985-97. **Honors/Awds:** One of Dayton's Top Ten African Am Women. *

COATIE, ROBERT MASON
Educator. **Personal:** Born May 19, 1945, Mound City, IL; son of Rev Dixon C Coatie and Georgia B Mason Coatie; married Birdeen Golden, Jun 29, 1968; children: Dionne & Robert M II. **Educ:** Ball State Univ, BS, 1968, MA, 1972. **Career:** Muncie Comm Sch Corp, teacher, 1967-68; Ind Civil Rights Comn, proj dir, 1968-69; Ball State Univ, asst dir minority student develop, 1969-84; Univ Louisville, dir Ctr Acad Achievement, 1984-92; Fla Int Univ, Multicultural Progs & Servs, dir, sr dir, 2002-. **Orgs:** Kappa Alpha Psi Fraternity, 1964-; past chmn, treas, Area VI Coun Aging, 1974-84; four bd mem, Hoosiers Excellence, 1983-85; Nat Asn Develop Educ, 1985-; vpres, Cent High Sch Parent Teachers Asn, 1985-89; Southeastern Asn Educ Prog Personnel, 1986-90; YMCA Black Achiever's Parent Adv Comt, 1986-89; Am Asn Counseling & Develop, 1987-90, Nat Asn Student Personnel Admin, 1987-; Asn Supervision & Curriculum Develop, 1987-90; secy, Brown School Parent Teachers Asn, 1986-89; Am Asn Univ Administrators, 1989-92; Am Asn Higher Educ. **Honors/Awds:** Observer White House Conference on Aging, 1981; Black Achiever, Muncie, Indiana, 1988; Athletic Hall of Fame, Delaware County (Indiana), 1988; Retention Excellence Award, Noel & Levitz, 1991; Outstanding Black Alumni, Ball State Univ Alumni Asn, 1998. **Home Addr:** 8360 NW 166th Terr, Hialeah, FL 33016, **Home Phone:** (305)826-3100. **Business Addr:** Senior Director, Florida International University, Multicultural Progs & Servs, 11200 SW 8th St, Miami, FL 33199, **Business Phone:** (305)348-2436.

COAXUM, HARRY LEE
Executive, vice president (organization), manager. **Personal:** Born Sep 25, 1953, Awendaw, SC; son of Henry Sr and Myrtle W; married Donna Bunch; children: Todriq, Nia & Maya. **Educ:** Talladega Col, BA, econs, 1975. **Career:** McDonald's Corp, Philadelphia Region, multi dept head, 1986-89, dir field training, 1989-90, dir minority opers, 1990-94, dept dir western zone, 1994-96, asst vpres, franchising, 1996; McDonalds Corp, vpres worldwide store opers & gen mgr, currently. **Orgs:** Omega Psi Phi Fraternity, 1972; Urban League Leadership Inst Philadelphia charter, 1988; Trinity United Church Christ, 1993; 100 Black Men Am, Chicago, 1996; Nat Asn Guardsmen, 2002; Sigma Pi Phi, 2002. **Honors/Awds:** Restaurant Security Award, 1978; Corporate Award, Nat Black McDonald's Operator Asn, 1991, 1993; Presenters Award, Nat Alumni Coun UNCF, 1993; Am Best & Brightest Award, Dollar & Sense Mag, 1993; Outstanding Contributor, McDonalds Corp, 1985. **Special Achievements:** Author, Economic Development: Capacity Building Community Development, 1988. **Business Addr:** Vice President Worldwide Store Operations, General Manager, McDonald Corporation, 2111 McDonald, Oak Brook, IL 60523, **Business Phone:** (630)623-3000.

COAXUM, HENRY L
Executive. **Personal:** Born Jan 27, 1951, Charleston, SC; son of Henry Coaxum Sr and Myrtle Weston. **Educ:** Talladega Col, BA, hist & polit sci, 1973. **Career:** City Chicago, planning analyst, 1975-79; DuSable Mus African-Am Hist, develop officer, 1979-81; Southtown Planning Assoc, exec dir, 1981-83; Amistad Res Ctr, dir develop, 1983-84; McDonalds Corp, staff, 1984-2001; Coaxum Enterprises Inc, pres, 2002-. **Orgs:** Pres, Chicago Talladega Col Alumni Club, 1977-81; dir, United Bank & Trust New Orleans, 1995-; 100 Black Men Metro New Orleans, 1995-; dir, Grambling State Univ Athletic Found, 2000-; dir, United Way Greater New Orleans, 2002-; dir, New Orleans E Businessmens Asn, 2004. **Honors/Awds:** Successful Setting Restaurant Award, Nation Restaurant News, 2003; Success Guide's Minority Achievers Award, City Bus Mag, 2003; McDonald's Great Southern Region Rookie of the Year, 2003; Howie Technology Award, 2003; Nat Black McDonald's Operator Asn Award, 2003; C Ray Nagin Minority Entrepreneurship Award, 2004; Nation's Restaurant News Franchisee Star Award, 2007; Nat Black Chamber of Commerce Entrepreneur of the Year Award, 2007. **Special Achievements:** Honorary Ambassador, La Dept Econ Develop, 2004. **Business Addr:** President, Coaxum Enterprises Inc, 1215 Prytania St Suite 109, New Orleans, LA 70130, **Business Phone:** (504)569-0120.

COBB, CYNTHIA JOAN
Manager. **Personal:** Born Sep 22, 1959, Indianapolis, IN; daughter of Marcella Jean Collins Taylor and Henry Marshall Taylor; married Arthur Cobb Jr, Aug 31, 1985. **Educ:** Purdue Univ, West Lafayette, BSE, 1981; Ind Univ, Bloomington, MBA, 1985. **Career:** Corning Med, Medfield, MA, process eng, 1981-83; Eli Lilly, Indianapolis, summer intern, 1984; Baxter Healthcare Corp, Deerfield, compensation analyst, 1985, sr compensation analyst, 1986, assoc, col rels, 1986-88, supvr, col rels, 1988, staffing mgr, 1988-91; hr mgr, 1991-92, dir, staffing & develop, 1992-95, dir, strategic staffing, 1995-96, dir, Human Resource, 1996-. **Orgs:** Chair, pharmaceut, HC employers, Midwest Col Placement Asn, 1987-89, vpres-employer, 1990-91, vice chair, ed adv bd, 1989-90, assembly, 1989-90; bd dir, YWCA Lake County, 1994-95, secy, 1998, pres, 1999-2002. **Honors/Awds:** YMCA of Metro Chicago Leadership Award, 1989; 100 Most Promising Black Women in Corporate Am, Ebony/Johnson Publishing 1991; Eagle Award, Most Influential AFA Lake County, 2001. **Business Addr:** Director, Baxter Healthcare Corporation, Transfusion Therapies Division, 1 Baxter Pkwy, Deerfield, IL 60015-4625, **Business Phone:** (847)948-2000.

COBB, DELMARIE L.
Consultant, journalist, president (organization). **Personal:** Born in Chicago, IL; daughter of James A Wells and Johnnie Mae. **Educ:** Univ Cincinnati; Northwestern Univ. **Career:** WSBT-TV, CBS, gen assignment reporter, 1981-83; WVEC-TV, ABC, gen assignment reporter, 1983-85; WTHR-TV, NBC, gen assignment reporter, 1985-87; Jackson Pres, nat traveling press secy, 1988; WVON-AM, talk show host, 1988-89; Dem Nat Conv Comt, press secy, 1996-; Publicity Works, pres, 2002-; Deleco Commun Inc, owner, currently. **Orgs:** Women & media proj adv bd, Fairness & Accuracy Reporting, 1995-; bd mem, Chicago Asn Black Journalist, 1996-97; pres, Dem Nat Conv Comt, 1996; vice chmn, Gamaliel Found Bd. **Honors/Awds:** Black Rose Award, League Black Women, 1992; Unity Awards, Lincoln Univ, 1993; Echoes of Excellence, Delta Sigma Theta, 1995; Achievement Award, Oper Push, 1996; N'Voice, N'Digo Fedn, 1997; Phenomenal Afa Women Award, 2003. **Special Achievements:** Street Life, TV newsmagazine program (PBS-TV), 1990, 1991; Congressman Bobby Rush Camp, dir of communications, 1992; Congressman Jesse Jackson Jr Camp, dir of communications, 1995; First Afa to serve as Press Secretary to the Democratic National Convention Committe. **Business Phone:** (773)373-3860.*

COBB, ETHEL WASHINGTON
Government official. **Personal:** Born Jun 10, 1925, Ravenel, SC; married Shedrick Cobb; children: 7. **Career:** City Ravenel, bd execs, 1970-; mem & exec comt mem, Dem Party; poll mgr, Primary & Pres Elections, Dem Party; Charleston County Sch Dist, St Paul's Constituent Dist 23, vice chairperson, currently. **Orgs:** recording secy & pres pulpit aid bd, St John Baptist Church; founder/chmn, St John Day Care Ctr; Yonges Island Headstart Bd; Daycare Ctr Bd; Rural Mission Coun; Biracial Comt Charleston Co Community Develop Bd; vol firefighter, Sea Island Prog; Clemson Univ Ext Community Develop Progs; chmn, Polit Action Comt Dist 116; Dem Coun, 1984; Budget Proposal Comt; rep Ravenel, Charleston Berkley & Dorchester Comt; rep Ravenel, Firemen Asn; Eastern Star. **Honors/Awds:** Civil Defense Award; 5 Year Recognition Award, Clemson Univ Ext Prog; Outstanding Assistance Award, Who's Who Among Southern Am; Outstanding Assistance Award, Baptist Hill High Sch Athletic Dept; Outstanding Democratic Female; Certificate, Gov's Rural Sch. **Special Achievements:** First Black Woman to be elected to the Bd of Execs in Ravenel.

COBB, REV. HAROLD
Clergy, government official, business owner. **Personal:** Born Jul 20, 1941, Covington, GA; son of Toy Quintella and Mary Alice; married Reta Jean Davis; children: Sheila, Shermekia & Harrell. **Educ:** Atlanta Area Tech Sch, attended 1970; Marsh-Drangron Bus Col, attended 1972; Oxford Col, Emory Univ, attended 1978; DeKalb Community Col, attended 1981; Emory Univ, ministerial course, 1989. **Career:** Cobb's Printing, founder & owner, 1971-80; Cousins Mid Sch PTO, pres, 1973-75; City Covington, lab analyst water treat, 1974-78; Newton City Ment Health, bd dir, 1974-76; Ford Motor Co, lab analyst water treat, 1978-; C&C Rental, founder & owner, 1984-; City Covington, comnr; E FlatRock United Methodist Church, minister. **Orgs:** Masonic Lodge Friendship No 20 F&AM, 1969-; pres & founder, Newton City Voter League, 1970-77; Wash State Community Ctr, 1980-83; bd mem, Newton City Pub Defenders, 1980-; co-founder, Newton Co King Scholar Prog, Emory Univ, Oxford Col, 1986-. **Honors/Awds:** Inkind Contrib Headstart, 1977; Outstanding Progress, Newton City, 1978; Appreciation Awards, Recreation Dept Supporter, 1981-84; Outstanding Serv,1981; Gaithers Chapel United Methodist Church Appreciation, 1983; Support Indust Growth, Newton City Chamber Com, 1984; I Have A Dream Award, Martin Luther King Scholar Fund, 1988; Outstanding Serv, Toney Gardens Civic Asn, 1989; Appreciation Award, Union Grove Church, 1990. **Military Serv:** USAF, E-3, 4 yrs. **Home Addr:** 5224 Avery St SW, Covington, GA 30014. *

COBB, REV. HAROLD JAMES, JR.
Clergy. **Personal:** Born Jun 10, 1958, Burlington, NC; son of Harold James Sr and Armadia Goodson; married Sheliah Jeffries Cobb, Jun 29, 1991. **Educ:** Univ NC, Chapel Hill, BA, 1982; Episcopal Theol Sem, MDiv, 1990. **Career:** Good Samaritan Church, pastor & founder, 1980-87; Saint Stephen's Church, rector, 1990; Grace Church, rector, currently. **Orgs:** Comnr, NC Governor's Comn Family, 1985-88; alumni exec comt, Episcopal Sem, 1990-91; bd higher educ, Diocese NC, 1990-; Youth Comn, 1990-; NC Episcopal Clergy Asn, 1990-; Alpha Pi Alpha; The Order Cross; The Royal Order Soc, Saint George. **Honors/Awds:** Harold J Cobb Jr Day, 1989. **Special Achievements:** Author, The Organization of Black Episcopal Seminarians, Seminary Jour, 1987. **Business Addr:** Rector, Grace Church, 1400 E Brambleton Ave, Norfolk, VA 23504, **Business Phone:** (757)625-2888.

COBB, DR. JEWEL PLUMMER
Cancer researcher, college administrator, educator. **Personal:** Born Jan 17, 1924, Chicago, IL; daughter of Frank V and Carriebel Cole; married Roy Cobb, Jul 4, 1954 (divorced); children: Jonathan Cobb. **Educ:** Talladega Col, Talladega, AL, BA, 1944; NY Univ, New York, NY, MS, 1947, PhD, 1950. **Career:** New York Univ, NY City, instr, 1955-56, asst prof, 1956-60; Hunter Col, vis lect, 1956-57; Sarah Lawrence Col, Bronxville, NY, biol prof, 1960-69; Conn Col, New London, CT, zool prof, dean, 1969-76; Rutgers Univ, Douglass Col, New Brunswick, NJ, biol prof, dean, 1976-81; Calif State Univ, Fullerton, CA, pres, 1981-90, pres emer, 1990-, Fullerton & Trustee Prof, Los Angeles, currently; Access Ctr, princ dir, 1991-, princ investr, currently; Ascend Proj, Sci Eng Prog Up Youth, 2001-. **Orgs:** Bd trustees, Inst Educ Mgt, 1973-; developer & dir, Fifth Yr Post Bacc Pre-Med Prog; bd dir, Am Coun Educ, 1973-76; bd dir, Educ Policy Ctr, NY City; Nat Acad Scis, Human Resources Comn, 1974-; Nat Sci Found, 1974-; bd dir, Travelers Ins Co, 1974-; bd dir, 21st Century Found; trustee, Nat Fund Minority Eng Studs, 1978-; bd dir, Califs Prev Violence, 1983-; bd dir, First Interstate Bancorp, 1985-; bd dir, Am Assembly Barbard Col, 1986-; bd mem, Newport Harbor Mus. **Honors/Awds:** Res grant, Am Cancer Soc, 1969-74, 1971-73, 1974-77; hon doctorates from Wheaton Col, 1971, Lowell Tech Inst, 1972, Pa Med Col, 1975, City Col City, Univ NY, St Lawrence Univ, Col New Rochelle, Tuskegee Univ, Fairleigh Dickinson Univ. **Special Achievements:** Author, "Filters for Women in Science", 1979, Breaking Down Barriers to Women Entering Science, 1979, Issues and Problems: A Debate, 1979. **Business Addr:** President and Professor of Biological Science Emerita, California State University Fullerton, 800 N State Col Blvd, PO Box 34080, Fullerton, CA 92834-9480.*

COBB, KEITH HAMILTON (TYR ANASAZI)
Actor. **Personal:** Born Jan 28, 1962, North Tarrytown, NY; son of James and Mary Lane. **Educ:** Westchester Community Col; NY Univ, Tisch Sch Arts, attended 1987. **Career:** Youth Theatre Interactions Inc, theatrical consult; TV appearances: "All My Children", 1994-96; "Beastmaster", 1999; "Gene Roddenberry's Andromeda", 2000; "The Young and the Restless", 2003-05; "Noah's Arc", 2006; Films: Eyes Beyond Seeing, 1995; Astonished, 1988. **Honors/Awds:** Award for Outstanding Male Newcomer, Soap Opera Digest, 1995; Soap Opera Dig Awards for Hottest Romance, 1996; Nominated for Image Award, 2005. **Special Achievements:** Emmy nominee, Award for Outstanding Younger Actor in a Drama Series, 1995; nominated four times for Image Award; named one of 50 Most BeautifulPeople in the

World, People mag, 1996. **Business Addr:** Actor, The Young & the Restless, Bell-Phillip TV, 7800 Beverly Blvd, Los Angeles, CA 90036.*

COBB, REGINALD JOHN
Football player. **Personal:** Born Jul 7, 1968, Knoxville, TN; married Stephanie; children: DeMarcus. **Educ:** Univ Tenn. **Career:** Football player (retired); Tampa Bay Buccaneers, running back, 1990-93; scouting interns; Green Bay Packers, running back, 1994; Jacksonville Jaguars, running back, 1995; New York Jets, running back, 1996. **Honors/Awds:** MVP, Peach Bowl, 1987.

COBB, DR. THELMA M.
Educator. **Personal:** Born in Portsmouth, VA; married Henry E (deceased). **Educ:** Hampton Inst, BS, 1941, MA, 1946; Univ Houston, EdD, 1976; Temple Univ; Univ Conn; Columbia Univ; Indiana Univ. **Career:** Tuskege Inst, instr, 1948-52; Fla A & M Univ, asst prof, 1952-55; Southern Univ, prof, 1958-89, prof emer, 1989-; Consult Black Lit, Multicultural Studies, Women's Lit. **Orgs:** Reg dir, Delta Sigma Theta; CLA; Delta Sigma Theta; Young Women's Christian Asn; Phi Delta Kappa; Pi Gamma Mu; Nat Coun Teacher Educ; admin bd, Camphor Memorial United Methodist Church; Links Inc. **Honors/Awds:** Gen Educ Bd Fel; Outstanding Woman in Education, Baton Rouge Delta Sigma Theta; Teacher of the Year, Southern Univ & Alumni Fed. **Home Addr:** 2145 78th Ave, Baton Rouge, LA 70807. *

COBB, TIFFANY. See CANTRELL, BLU.

COBBIN, W. FRANK, JR.
Executive. **Personal:** Born Jul 2, 1947, Youngstown, OH; married Deborah Walk; children: Kevin, Kimberly. **Educ:** Cleveland State Univ, BA Psychol, Eng, 1971; IN Univ Exec Pgm, Prof Mgr & Bus Functions, 1981. **Career:** OH Bell Telephone Co, mgr bus office, 1973-77, mgr installation, 1977-78, dist mgr installation, 1978-79, mkt mgr, 1979, dist mgr, 1979-82; AT&T Am Transtech, dir telephone response ctr, 1982-83, exec dir mkt serv, vpres direct mkt serv, 1987-. **Orgs:** Direct Mkt Assoc, Telemarketing Assoc, Mayor's Econ Develop Coun, Jax Urban League Bd; Basileus Omega Psi Phi Frat Inc; United Way, Univ North FL Bus Adv Coun, Jacksonville Univ Career Beginnings Prog. **Military Serv:** Reserves staff, sgt 6 yrs; 1 in class NCO Acad. **Business Addr:** Vice President, AT&T American Transtech, 8000 Baymeadows Way, Jacksonville, FL 32216, **Business Phone:** (904)636-1000.*

COBBINS, LYRON DURYEA
Football player. **Personal:** Born Sep 17, 1974. **Educ:** Univ Notre Dame. **Career:** Ariz Cardinals, linebacker, 1997; Barcelona Dragons, linebacker, 1999.

COBBS, DAVID E.
Educator. **Personal:** Born May 26, 1940, Nashville, TN; married Margaret; children: Amy Elizabeth. **Educ:** Tenn State Univ, BS, 1961; Mich Univ, MMus, 1961; Univ Mass, MMus, 1968; Northern Tex State Univ, attended 1965; Univ Southern Calif, Grad Study, 1973. **Career:** Compton Community Col, prof, dir, 1970, prof emer, currently; Prairie View Col, 1963-70; Edward Waters Col, Jacksonville FL, fac, 1962-63; Prairie View Univ, Prairie View, fac, 1963-67; Univ Mass, teaching asst, 1967-68; Univ Southern Calif, teaching asst, 1971-73. **Orgs:** Bd dir, Compton & Comm Symphony; western rep Black Music Caucus Mu Sic Educ Nat Conf; Kappa Alpha Psi Fraternity; Music Asn Calif Community Col; Col Band Dir Nat Asn; Int Asnal Jazz Educ. **Honors/Awds:** Award instrumental music; Award asst dir of marching bands. **Business Addr:** Professor Emeritus, Compton Community College, 1111 E Artesia Blvd, Compton, CA 90221, **Business Phone:** (310)900-1600.

COBBS, HARVEY, JR.
Counselor. **Personal:** Born Mar 19, 1952, Twist, AR; son of Harvey and Paralee Jackson; married Willie Mae Lewis, Apr 27, 1973; children: Harvey III, Carolyn, Davina & Yvonne. **Educ:** Bakersfield COL, AA, 1976; CA State UNIV, Bakersfield, BA, 1980. **Career:** Counselor (retired); USY, military policeman, sentry dog handler, 1972; CA DEPT Corrections, correctional officer, 1979-82, Junipero Serra-Work Furlough, inmate supvr, counr, 1987. **Orgs:** NCP, life & golden heritage, 1990; AM Correctional officers ASN, 1989; life mem, NAT ASN Black Veterans; Nat Asn Blacks Criminal Justice, 1998; life mem, Col Allensworth Historic Black Park; life mem, Ninth-Tenth Cavalry Asn. **Honors/Awds:** Golden Heritage Award, NCP, 1990; Certificate & Badge, CA Corrections Officers ASN, 1987; Recognition Plaque, AM Criminal Justice ASN, 1990; INTL ASN Correctional Officers, Certificate; Nat Asn Black Veterans, 1971; CA State Senator. **Military Serv:** USY, spec-4, 1972-73; Good Conduct Medal, 1973, NAT Defense Medal, 1973. *

COBBS, DR. PRICE MASHAW
Executive, psychiatrist. **Personal:** Born Nov 2, 1928, Los Angeles, CA; son of Peter Price and Rose Mashaw; married Evadne Priester, May 30, 1957 (died 1973); children: Price Priester & Marion Renata; married Frederica Maxwell, May 26, 1985. **Educ:** Univ Calif, Berkeley, BA, 1954; Meharry Med Col, MD, psychiat med, 1958. **Career:** San Francisco Gen Hosp, intern, 1958-59; Mendocino State Hosp, psychiatric res, 1959-61; Langley Porter Neuropsychiatric Inst, psychol resident, 1961-62; psychiat pvt pract, 1962-; Univ Calif, San Francisco, asst clin prof psychiat, 1963-; Pac Mgt Syst, founder, pres, 1967-, chief exec officer, currently; Cobbs Inc, chief exec officer. **Orgs:** Nat Med Asn; Nat Asn Advan Colored People; consult many Fortune 500 companies, govt agencies & community groups; charter mem, Nat Urban League; chair, First Nat Diversity Conf; co-founder/pres, Renaissance Books; adv bd, Black Scholar; bd dirs, Found Nat Progress; fel, Am Psychiatric Asn; Nat Acad Sci; Inst Med Nat Acad Sci; Black Behav Scientists; Univ Cali Black Caucus. **Honors/Awds:** Outstanding Psychiatrist, Black Enterprise, 1988; Pathfinder Award, Asn Humanistic Psychol, 1993. **Military Serv:** AUS, corporal, 1951-53. **Business Addr:** President, Chief Executive Officer, Pacific Management Systems, 3528 Sacramento St, San Francisco, CA 94118-1847, **Business Phone:** (415)922-1017.

COBBS, DR. WINSTON H B
Physician. **Personal:** Born May 7, 1955, Flushing, NY; married Valerie Crouch; children: Noelle Bianca & Paige Alfreda. **Educ:** Boston Univ, BA, biol, 1976; Meharry Med Col, MD, 1980. **Career:** Long Island Jewish Med Ctr, internship internal med, 1980-81; Nassau Co Med Ctr, residence internal med, 1983-85; Franklin Hosp & Med Ctr, secy med staff; Booth Memorial Med Ctr, pulmonary med, 1986-88; pvt pract, 1988-. **Orgs:** Am Soc Int Med; Am Thoracic Soc; assoc mem, Am Col Physicians, Am Col Chest Physicians; fel, Am Col Chest Physicians. **Honors/Awds:** Martin Luther King Scholarship Award. **Special Achievements:** Publications, "The Effects of Phospho-Diesterase on Insulin Metabolism," A Research Study The Diabetes and Endocrinology Ctr Nashville 1972; "The Spirometric Standards for Healthy Black Adults," A Research Study Meharry Medical Coll Nashville, The Journal of the Natl Medical Assoc 1981. **Business Addr:** 1800 Dutch Broadway, Elmont, NY 11003.

COCHRAN, DANIEL CHESTER
Executive. **Personal:** Born Nov 14, 1946, Chicago, IL; son of Jacqueline and Conrad. **Educ:** Amherst Col, BA, 1968; Princeton Univ, MPA, 1974. **Career:** US State Dept, foreign serv officer, 1969-73; Exxon Corp, asst treas-USA, 1974-89; Merrill Lynch & Co, chief fin officer, Global Markets & Invet Banking, chief acct officer, Global Private Client, sr vpres, 1989-, dir, 2000-05, head admin, office pres, currently; ML LGBT Professional Network, sr advr, 2002-; ML Bank & Trust Cayman, dir, 2006. **Orgs:** Trustee, Winthrop H Smith Mem Found, 2001-; ML Diversity Employee Adv Coun, 2003-06; dir, Human Rights Campaign 2007-; dir, Lambda Legal 2007-. **Honors/Awds:** Black Achievers Award, YMCA, 1992. **Business Addr:** Senior Vice President & Head of Administration, Office of the President, Merrill Lynch & Co Inc, 4 World Fin Ctr 34th Fl, 250 Vesey St, New York, NY 10080, **Business Phone:** (212)449-1000.

COCHRAN, EDWARD G.
Manager. **Personal:** Born Jun 16, 1953, Chicago, IL; married Barbara Porter; children: Rashida, Marcus. **Educ:** Lake Forest Col, BA, 1975; DePaul Univ, MBA, 1985. **Career:** Continental Bank, opers analyst, 1975-77; IBM, systs engr, 1977-81; Sears Commun, telecomm mgr; Consult Telecommun; Mundelein Col, undegrad, adj fac; DePaul Univ, grad, adj fac. **Honors/Awds:** Forester Athletic Hall of Fame, 1990; Several articles and papers published on Telecommunications.

COCHRAN, DR. JAMES DAVID, JR.
Pediatrician. **Personal:** Born Oct 24, 1951, Muskegon, MI. **Educ:** Univ MI, BS, 1973; Howard Univ, MD, 1977. **Career:** Howard Univ Hosp, pediatric resident, 1977-80; Nat Health Serv Corps, med officer, 1980-83; Collier Health Servs, staff physician, 1983-84, med dir. **Orgs:** local vpolemarch, Kappa Alpha Psi Frat; Am Nat Med Assocs; Collier County Med Soc; counr, Collier County Youth Guidance; Big Bros Collier County. **Special Achievements:** Publication "Study of Sickle Cell in an Animal Model," J of NMA, 1980. **Business Addr:** 4048 Evans Ave Suite 209, Fort Myers, FL 33901, **Business Phone:** (239)278-9983.

COCKBURN, ALDEN GEORGE, JR.
Surgeon. **Personal:** Born Mar 8, 1947, Ancon, Panama; son of Alden G Sr and Edith E Gittens; divorced; children: Alexis, Justin. **Educ:** City Col NY; Tufts Univ, Boston, MA, 1974. **Career:** Tufts New Eng Med Ctr Hosp, Boston, surgical intern, 1974-75, surgical asst resident, 1975-76; Lahey Clinic Found Hosp, Burlington, MA, urol resident, 1976-79; Lahey Clinic, Boston, MA, asst attendant urologist, 1979-80; Memorial-Sloan Kettering Cancer Ctr, NY, NY, urol-oncol fel 1980-81; Harlem Hosp Med Ctr, NY, dir, div urol, 1981-85; Columbia Univ Sch Med, NY, asst prof urol, 1981-85; self-employed surgeon, Tampa, FL, 1986-; Vasectomy Reversal Ctr, surgeon; Tampa Gen Hosp, vice chief surg. **Orgs:** Pres, Bay Area Med Asn; Sigma Pi Phi; bd trustee, Tampa Gen Hosp. **Business Addr:** Vice Chief of Surgery, Vasectomy Reversal Center, 4700 N Habana Ave Suite 500, Tampa, FL 33614.*

COCKERHAM, HAVEN EARL
Manager. **Personal:** Born Aug 13, 1947, Winston-Salem, NC; married Terry Ward; children: Haven Earl Jr, Audra. **Educ:** NC A&T Univ, BS Econ, 1969; MI State Univ, MBA, 1979. **Career:** GMC, personnel admin exec comp, 1978-79, admin personnel, 1979-80; Fisher Body, gen off gen admin, 1980-82;Pgh plant, dir personnel, 1982-83; Gen Motors, world hq dir personnel, 1983-84, gen dir personnel; McCain & Assocs, pres, 1991-94; Detroit Edison, vpres human res, 1994-98; R R Donnelley & Sons Co, sr vpres human resources, 1998. **Orgs:** Pres, Detroit Chap Nat Black MBA Asn, 1981; bd mem, Nat Black MBA Asn, 1981; Mon Yough Chamber Com Pgh, 1982-83; leadership mem, Leadership Detroit Chamber Comt; bd mem, Detroit South Macomb Hosp; chmn, ea cent sec Detroit Area Coun Boy Scouts Am; Leadership Detroit VI; Hope United Methodist Church. **Honors/Awds:** Outstanding Leadership award, Detroit Chap Nat Black MBA Assoc, 1982; Outstanding Service award, Detroit Area Boy Scouts. *

COCKERHAM, PEGGY
Automotive executive, business owner. **Personal:** Married John Ali; children: Pam, Anwar. **Career:** Southlake Buick & Imports, pres & owner, 1992-. **Orgs:** Nat Asn Minority Automobile Dealers. **Special Achievements:** Company is ranked 94 on Black Enterprise magazine's 1997 list of Top 100 Black businesses. **Business Addr:** Owner, President, Southlake Buick Volvo Subaru, 1345 Southlake Pkwy, Morrow, GA 30260.*

COCKRELL, MECHERA ANN
Insurance agent. **Personal:** Born Jul 8, 1953, Brookshire, TX; married Thomas; children: Twanna Nicole Randle. **Educ:** TX Southern Univ, BS, 1975, MA, 1978; Espanola's Beauty Col, Licensed Cosmetologist, 1978; Leonard's Sch Ins, Group II license, 1986. **Career:** Cockrell Ins, gen agent. **Orgs:** Teachers Educ Assoc; adv, Jack & Jill Am; teacher, 4H Prairie View Chap; Home Econ Educrs Amer. **Business Addr:** General Agent, Cockrell Insurance, 33405 Reynolds Rd, Simonton, TX 77476, **Business Phone:** (713)346-1302.

CODY, WILLIAM L.
Clergy. **Personal:** Born Jun 9, 1934, Philadelphia, PA. **Educ:** Univ PA, AB, 1955; Temple Univ, STB, 1958; Monrovia Col, DD; St Davis Sem, DD. **Career:** St Paul AME Ch Ben Salem, 1955-56; St Paul AME Ch Malvern, 1956-58; Union AME Ch, 1958-60; Vernon Temple AME Church, 1960-64; Fisk Chaplian AME Church, 1964-66; Grant AME Church, 1966-72; St James AME Church, pastor, 1972-. **Orgs:** Past pres, Greater Boston Inter Denominational & Inter Racial Ministers Alliance; past bd dir, Boston Br NAACP; Cooper Community Ctr; Conv Coun Black Ecumenical Comn; past trustee, Boston Univ Without Walls; past pres, bd dir Grant Manor Apts; past mem, Black Studies Comn Boston Theol Inst; Steering Comt Metro Boston Comn Black Chmn Act; presiding elder, Atlantic City Dist African Methodist Episcopal Church; 1st vpres, Atlantic City NAACP; pres, Atlantic City Chap Frontiers Internat; trustee, Atlantic Community Col; mgr Bright's Villa N & Bright's Villa S; chmn, NAACP Atlantic City Housing Corp. **Business Addr:** Pastor, St James AME Church, James 3 Merrywood Dr, West Orange, NJ 07052, **Business Phone:** (973)325-8267.*

COFER, JAMES HENRY. See Obituaries section.

COFER, MICHAEL LYNN
Football player. **Personal:** Born Apr 7, 1960, Knoxville, TN. **Educ:** Univ Tenn. **Career:** Football player (retired) Detroit Lions, linebacker, 1983-92. **Honors/Awds:** Pro Bowl, 1988.

COFFEE, LAWRENCE WINSTON
Dentist. **Personal:** Born Apr 29, 1929, Detroit, MI; married Drexell R; children: Lawrence Jr, Roderic, LaJuan. **Educ:** Wayne State Univ, BS, 1957; Meharry Med Col, DDS, 1961. **Career:** Dentist (retired); Chrysler Corp, mach oper, 1949-51; Detroit First Aid Co, drug shipper, 1953-55; Pvt practice, dent surgeon; Children's Hosp Mich, med tech, 1955-57. **Orgs:** Mich Dent Asn; Am Dent Asn; Nat Dent Asn; Wolverine Dent Soc; Detroit Dist Dent Soc; trustee, St Stephen AME Church; BSA; dist comnr, Chi Health & Safety, 1968-77; bd mgt, Meharry Med Col Alumni Asn; pres, Meharry Med Col Alumni Asn. **Honors/Awds:** Trophies BSA, 1966-67; Dentist of the Yr, Meharry Detroit Chap, 1972. **Military Serv:** AUS, mc corpl, 1951-53.

COFFEY, DR. BARBARA JORDAN
Educator. **Personal:** Born Nov 24, 1931, Omaha, NE; daughter of Earl L Waldron Sr and Eva Williams Waldron-Cooper; divorced; children: William Jai III. **Educ:** Univ Nebr, BA, 1951, PhD, 1976; Fisk Univ, MA, 1953. **Career:** Educator (retired); US Dept Comn, Chicago Regional Off, survey statist, 1963-65; United Comn Serv Omaha, planning assoc, 1965-67; Greater Omaha Comn Action Inc, dep dir, 1967-70; Univ Nebr, Omaha, assoc dean stud & instr sociol, 1970-71; US Dept HEW, consult region VII, 1971; Univ Nebr Syst, from asst to pres, equal opportunity coord, 1971-78; Northwestern Bell Telephone Co, supvr mgt training, 1978-81; Metro Community Col, scampus mgr, 1981-84, dir mkt, 1984-95, Barbara M Angelillo, exec dir. **Orgs:** Bd dir, United Comn Serv, 1972-74; bd dir, United Way Midlands, 1988-96; vpres & founding dir, NE Civil Liberties Union; Omaha Metro Nat Asn Advan Colored People Hon Soc; Nat Asn Women Deans Admin & Couns; chairperson, NE Equal Opportunity Comt; Alpha Kappa Delta; Alpha Lambda Delta; Phi Delta Kappa; pres, Omaha Chapter

Links Inc; charter, Omaha Chapter Jack & JillInc; Delta Sigma Theta Sorority; United Methodist Comn Ctr; All Saints Episcopal Church; bd dir, Omaha Head Start Child Develop Corp; mem, Conference Inclusive Commun, 2008. **Honors/Awds:** Nat Leadership Honor, Omicron Delta Kappa, 1986; Outstanding NE Women of Color, 1990; Dr Geil M Browning Award, ICAN, 1992; Outstanding Woman of Distinction-Educ, Omaha YWCA, 1994; Nat Prominence Award, Urban League of NE, 1995. **Special Achievements:** One of Outstanding Black Women of Omaha Quinn Chapel AME Church, 1975. **Home Addr:** 6940 Burt St, Omaha, NE 68132.

COFFEY, DR. GILBERT HAVEN, JR.
Government official, physician. **Personal:** Born Nov 27, 1926, Lackawanna, NY; married Madelyn Elizabeth Brewer; children: Denise E. **Educ:** Univ Buffalo, BA, 1952; cert physio therapy, 1955; Meharry Med Col, MD, 1963. **Career:** Wayne Co Gen Hosp Eloise MI, physio therapist, 1956-59; Am Acad Phs Med & Rehab Comnr Parks & Recreation Instr, MI, 1958-59; intern, 1963; Va Hosp Buffalo, resident, 1964-67; asst chief phys med & Rehab serv, 1967-69; chief phys med & rehab serv, 1969-70; Cent Off, VA, Wash, prog develop policy, chief phys med & rehab, 1970; Univ Buffalo Med Sch, prof, 1968-70; Howard Univ Med Sch, Wash, 1971; George Wash, Univ Med Sch, asst dir prof, 1971-; dipl, Am Bd Phys Med & Rehab; Nat Med Asn; Am Cong Rehab. **Orgs:** Alpha Phi Alpha; Montgomery County Stroke Asn; Mason 32nd degree; contributed articles for professional journals. **Military Serv:** AUS, 1946-47. **Business Addr:** Physician, Howard University Hospital, Medical School, 2041 Georgia Ave NW, Washington, DC 20060.*

COFFEY, RICHARD LEE
Basketball player, basketball coach. **Personal:** Born Sep 2, 1965, Aurora, NC; married; children: 3. **Educ:** Univ Minn. **Career:** Basketball player (retired), coach; Minn Timber wolves, 1990-91; Reel Experts, host & exec producer; Minneapolis Select, coach, currently.

COFIELD, DR. ELIZABETH BIAS
Government official, educator. **Personal:** Born Jan 21, 1920, Raleigh, NC; married James; children: James Edward & Juan Medford. **Educ:** Hampton Inst, BS; Columbia Univ, MA; dipl, admin & supvr. **Career:** Educator (retired); Wade Co Bd Comnr; Juan Medford Co, comnr, 1972; Shaw Univ, prof educ. **Orgs:** Bd, Raleigh Sch, 1969-72. *

COFIELD, JAMES E
Executive. **Personal:** Born May 16, 1945, Norfolk, VA; son of James E and Elizabeth B; married Carolyn W; children: Nicole. **Educ:** Univ NC, BS, 1967; Stanford Univ, Grad Sch Bus, MBA, 1970; Howard Univ, Law Sch. **Career:** Roxse Homes Inc, chair, 1971-92; Babson Col, mem bd overseer; Cofield Properties Inc, Brookline, MA, pres, currently. **Orgs:** MAS Black Legislative Caucus. **Honors/Awds:** Outstanding Committee Service Annual Award, Comt Boston, 1979; Bus Award, 1991. **Special Achievements:** Ten Outstanding Young Leaders Boston Jaycees 1980. **Business Addr:** President, Cofield Properties Inc, 10 Malcolm Rd, PO Box 470827, Boston, MA 02130, **Business Phone:** (617)524-9090.

COFIELD, MARVIS
Chief executive officer. **Career:** County Wayne, MI, Dept C & Family Serv, pres; Alkebu-Lan Ctr, chief exec officer, currently. **Orgs:** Detroit Pub Sch; Nat Asn Advan Colored People; chmn, African Centered Ed Sub Comt, currently. **Honors/Awds:** Community Leader of the Year, Detroit Col Law, 1999. **Business Addr:** Cheif Executive Officer, Alkebu-Lan Village, 7701 Harper Ave, Detroit, MI 48213, **Business Phone:** (313)921-1616.

COGDELL, D PARTHENIA
School administrator. **Personal:** Born Sep 12, 1938, Wayne County, NC; daughter of Nathaniel and Geneva Herring; divorced; children: Samuel George Sanders III. **Educ:** Fayetteville State NC, BS, 1959; Trenton State, NJ, MA, 1971; Glassboro State, NJ, 1974; Hunter Col, NY, 1982. **Career:** Sch administrator (retired);. Burlington Co Spec Serv, prin, 1974-76, prog dir, 1976-79; NJ Dept Educ, admin asst, 1979-81, bur dir, 1981-92; Camden City Schs, Off Personnel Serv, 1992-98; Rowan Univ, adj prof. **Orgs:** Reader, US Dept Educ & Spec Educ Off, 1974-79; chairperson, NJ State Adv Coun Handicap, 1974-76; pres, Int Coun Except C, 1978-79; proj dir, Low Incidence Handicap Proj, 1979-80; Phi Delta Kappa; pres, Rancocas Valley, Delta Sigma Theta Sor, 1988-92; pres, Found Except C, 1989-91; pres, NJ State Coun Delta Sigma Theta Sor, 1999-2002, corresp secy, currently. **Honors/Awds:** Dan Ringeheim Award of Excellence, NJ State Fedn; Outstanding Special Educator, Int Coun Except C, 1998; Woman of the Year, Zeta Phi Beta Sorority. **Home Addr:** 117 Harrington Circle, Willingboro, NJ 08046, **Home Phone:** (609)877-9516. **Business Addr:** Corresponding Secretary, Delta Sigma Theta Sorority, Inc., Rancocas Valley Alumnae Chapter, PO Box 262, Rancocas, NJ 08073-262.

COGGS, GRANVILLE COLERIDGE
Physician. **Personal:** Born Jul 30, 1925, Pine Bluff, AR; son of Tandy and Nannie; married Maud; children: Anita, Carolyn. **Educ:** Univ Nebraska, BS, 1949; Harvard Med Sch, MD, 1953. **Career:** Univ Texas Health Sci Ctr, prof radiology dept, 1975-89; Univ Calif Sch Med, assoc clinical prof, 1971-75; asst chief, 1969-71; Kaiser Hosp, staff radiologist, 1959-71; Univ Calif, resident, 1955-58; Letterman Gen Hosp, intern, 1954; Murphy Army Hosp, 1953-54; Gonzaba Med Group, staff radiol, 1998-; Otto Kaiser Mem Hosp, radiol, 1994. **Orgs:** Phi Beta Kappa, 1949; Am Col Radiology, 1959-; Harvard Med Sch Alumni Survey Comn, 1973-78; assoc mem, Sigma Xi; fellow, ACR, 1972; Am Inst Ultrasound Med, 1972-82; Am Thermographic Soc, 1972-80; Permanente Med Group Northern Calif. **Military Serv:** USAAC, 1943-46; USAF, 1953-55; USAFR, lt Colnel, 1956-85. *

COGHILL, GEORGE
Football player. **Personal:** Born Mar 30, 1970, Fredericksburg, VA; married Belisa Davidson. **Educ:** Wake Forest Univ, BA, sociol, 1993. **Career:** Football player (retired); Scottish Claymores, 1995-97; Denver Broncos, defensive back, 1998-2001. **Honors/Awds:** Claymores Hall of Fame, 1999. *

COGSVILLE, DONALD J.
Executive. **Personal:** Born May 16, 1937, New York, NY; son of Johnny and Frances; married Carol Atherton Cogsville (deceased); children: Rachel, Donald Paul. **Educ:** Mt Union Col, BA, 1963. **Career:** Off Econ Opportunity, dep dir, 1968-71; Clark-Phipps-Clark & Harris Consults Firm, affirmative action advisor; NY State Urban Develop Corp, affirmative action officer; Harlem Urban Devel Corp, gen mgr, pres & chief exec officer. **Orgs:** Nat Task Force Educ & Training Minority Bus; pres, NY Urban League Trenton, NJ. **Military Serv:** AUS, spec 4th class, 1958-60. *

COHEA, FR. VICTOR (VICTOR H COHEA)
Clergy. **Educ:** John Carroll Univ, BA, sociol; Notre Dame Sem, MDiv, Old Test; Xavier Univ, MTh, Hist Theol; Union, PhD. **Career:** St. John Prep Sem, teacher, 1982-85; Community Faith Econ Empowerment, vice chair, currently; St Francis De Sales Church, Pan African Roman Cath Clergy Conf, pres; St Francis De Sales Church, pastor, currently. **Business Phone:** (504)895-7749.

COHEA, VICTOR H. **See COHEA, FR. VICTOR.**

COHEN, GWEN A
Executive. **Personal:** Born in Eufaula, AL; daughter of Johnie and Clementine Morris Gilbert; married Paul M, Feb 3, 1990. **Educ:** Tuskegee Univ, BS; Northwestern Univ, Kellogg Grad Sch Mgt, MBA, 1982. **Career:** BM, mkt, mfg, 1974-80; Quaker Oats, brand mgt, 1982-84; Morgan Stanley Dean Witter, acct exec, assoc vpres, vpres invest, 1986-. **Orgs:** Chair, Children's Hosp, child life, 1976-80; exec comt, Nat Black MBA, Chicago, 1984-89; exec comt, 1990-, pres, Leadership IL, 1992-94; judge, Hugh O'Brian Youth Found, 1993-; co-chair, ETA Cult Arts, Gala, 1994-; judge, Am Jr Miss, IL, judge, 1994-; judge, Miss Am, Chicago, 1995-; Leadership Am, 2004; bd mem, Chicago Col Performing Arts; bd mem, Chicago Found Women; bd mem, Leadership Ill; Womens Networking Community. **Honors/Awds:** Childrens Memorial Hosp Humanitarian Award, 1979; Outstanding Young Women of America, 1986; Achievement Award, Leadership IL, 1993; Achievement Award, Urban Potential IA, 1994. **Special Achievements:** Chicago Sun Times Supplement, "Municipal Bonds," Aug 1990; Keynote speaker for HOBY, General Federations of Women's Clubs, etc, 1992-; N'Digo Magazine, Charitable Givings, Retirement Planning, etc, 1994; Afrique, "Global Investing," Tax Deferral Strategies, 1994; Black Enterprise, "Money Moves for 1995," 1995; Writer of quarterly newsletter; Judge, Miss Illinois Scholarship Competition, 1996; Ebony, "Retirement Nestegg," Sept 1996. **Business Addr:** Vice President Investments, Morgan Stanley Dean Witter, 1585 Broadway, New York, NY 10036, **Business Phone:** (212)761-4000.

COHEN, VINCENT H
Lawyer. **Personal:** Born Apr 7, 1936, Brooklyn, NY; son of Victor and Marion; married Diane Hasbrouck; children: Robyn, Traci & Vincent Jr. **Educ:** Syracuse Univ, BA, 1957, LLB, 1960. **Career:** Consol Edison Co, NY, 1960-62; US Dept Justice, 1962-67; EEOC, staff, 1967-69; Hogan & Hartson, partner & atty, 1969-; Off US atty, fed prosecutor; US Dist Ct, trial coun; pvt pract law. **Orgs:** Admis NY Bar, 1960; US Supreme, CT, 1966, OH, 1967, DC, 1968; Nat Jud Conf DC Circuit, 1972, 1975; Am Nat NY State Bar Asn; Justinian Law Soc; secy, Comn Med Malpract; bd visitors, Syracuse Univ Col Law; bd gov's, DC Bar; bd dirs, ACLU; Young Lawyers Sect Bar Asn DC; Neighborhood Legal Serv Prog; Justinian Law Soc. **Military Serv:** AUS, first lt, 1957-65. **Business Addr:** Attorney, Partner, Hogan & Hartson, 555 13th St NW Suite 13W202, Washington, DC 20004-1109, **Business Phone:** (202)637-6586.

COKER, ADENIYI ADETOKUNBO
Educator. **Personal:** Born Sep 27, 1962, Nigeria; son of Modupe and Adeniyi; married Angela Denise Johnson, Jan 2, 1987; children: Kikelomo, Morenike & Modupeola. **Educ:** Univ Ife, Nigeria, BA, 1983; City Univ NY, Brooklyn Col, MFA, 1987; Temple Univ, PhD, 1991. **Career:** William Paterson Col, NJ, asst prof, 1987-91; Univ Colo, assoc prof, 1991-92; Univ WY, dir & assoc prof; Eastern Ill Univ, dir & assoc prof, currently; Univ Ala, dir & assoc prof, Dept Theatre, currently. **Orgs:** Ed bd, Jour Black Studies, 1993-; exec bd mem, Nat Coun Black Studies Inc, 1994-. **Special Achievements:** Emmy Award Nomination. Sizwe Bansi Is Dead, Fringe Theater Festival Canada, 1990; Woza Albert, Eulipions Theater, Denver, 1991; Ouray, A Historical Drama on Southern Ute Indians of Colorado, 1992. **Business Addr:** Associate Professor, Director African American Studies, University of Alabama, Department Theatre, 1530 3rd Ave S 1055 Bldg, Birmingham, AL 35294-2060, **Business Phone:** (205)975-9652.

COLBERT, BENJAMIN JAMES
Educator. **Personal:** Born Jun 2, 1942, Savannah, GA; son of Jack B and Anna Chaplin; married Deborah Raikes, Dec 1982; children: Edwin, Kenneth & Jonathan. **Educ:** Savannah State Col, BS, 1963; Univ Ga, MFA, 1971. **Career:** Metro Atlanta Talent Search Prog, dir; Nat Scholar Serv & Fund Negro Studs; Univ Ga, admissions counr, instr; Savannah Bd Educ, teacher, assoc prog dir admissions testing prog; HHS fel, 1980-81; Educ Testing Serv, assoc dir, 1981. **Orgs:** Consult, Col Entrance Exam Bd & US Office Educ Trio Prog; adv bd, Southern Educ Found; Human Rels Comn; Nat Asn Col Admissions Counrs; Nat Scholar Serv & Fund Negro Studs; Nat Asn Advan Colored People; APGA; Alpha Phi Alpha; Elder, Witherspoon Presbyterian Church. **Honors/Awds:** Callaway Foundation Award for Painting, 1970.

COLBERT, GEORGE CLIFFORD
School administrator. **Personal:** Born Mar 22, 1949, Cedar Rapids, IA; married Marion Patricia Clark; children: Bridget Lynette Clark & Donta Kami. **Educ:** Kirkwood Community Col, AA, 1972; Mt Mercy Col, BA, 1974; Northern Ariz Univ, M.ED, 1993. **Career:** IA State Men's Reformatory, correctional officer II, 1975-76; Rock wellInt, security guard, 1976-78; Kirkwood Community Col, outreach worker & employer, sch prog, 1978-89; Cent Ariz Col, dir, community educ & stud serv, 1989-. **Orgs:** Chmn, Gen Mills, FMC Minority Scholarship Prog, 1978; vpres, Nat Advan Asn Colored People, 1978; founder & chmn, Higher Educ Minority Scholarship Prog, 1979; Nat Coun Instr Adminr; Nat Coun Community Serv & Continuing Educ; lifetime mem, AMVETS Post 15. **Honors/Awds:** Certificate Volume Service Award, Jane Boyd Comn House, 1974; Humanities Award, Nat Advan Asn Colored People Freedom Fund Banquet, 1979; Appreciation Recog Serv Stud Affairs, Kirkwood Community Coll, 1979; several awards serv, Apache Junction Community Sch System. **Military Serv:** USMC, E-3, 1967-69; Nat Defense Serv Medal; Purple Heart; Pres Citation; Vietnam Campaign; Vietnam Serv Medal. **Business Addr:** Student Service Associate, Central Arizona College, 8740 N Overfield Rd, Coolidge, AZ 85228.*

COLBERT, VIRGIS W.
Executive, vice president (organization). **Personal:** Born Oct 13, 1939, Mississippi; son of Quillie and Eddie Mae; married Angela Johnson; children: Jillian, Alyssa & V William II. **Educ:** Cent Mich Univ, BS; Earlham Col Exec Inst. **Career:** Chrysler Corp, gen mfg supt, 1977-79; Miller Brewing Co, asst to plant mgr, 1979-80, prod mgr, 1980-81, plant mgr, 1981-87, asst dir can mfg,1987-88, dir can mfg, 1988-89, vpresmaterials mfg, 1989-90, vpresplan toper, 1990-93, sr vpres opers, 1993-95, sr vpres worldwide opers, 1995-97, exec vpres worldwide opers, 1997-2005, bd dirs, currently; Stanley Works,dir, 2003-; Manitowoc Co, bd mem, 2001-; Delphi Corp, bd dir, 1999-2006; Sara Lee Corp, dir, 2006-. **Orgs:** RBDM, OIC, Fisk Univ; Omega Psi Phi; Prince Hall Masons; Shriners; Nat Asn Advan Colored People; NUL Black Exec Exchange Prog; Exec Adv Coun, Sigma Pi Phi; Wey co Group Inc; Delphi Automotive Syst; bd mem, Fisk Univ; chmn-,Thurgood Marshall Scholar Fund. **Honors/Awds:** Black Achiever Milwaukee YMCA; Role Model Nat Alliance Bus; Silver Ring Merit Award, Philip Morris Co Inc; Role Model, Several Black Cols; Trumpet Award, Turner Broadcasting. **Special Achievements:** One of the Top 40 Black Exec in Am, Ebony Mag; One of the Top 24 Black Exec in Am, Black Enterprise Mag; Top 50 African-Am in Corp Am Fortune Mag.

COLE, ANDREA M
Executive director, chief executive officer. **Career:** Skillman Found, staff, 1987-2007; asst vpres & controller, treas, dir finance, chief financial officer; Ethel & James Flinn Found, exec dir & chief exec officer, 2008-. **Business Addr:** Executive Director, Chief Executive Officer, Ethel and James Flinn Foundation, 500 Woodward Ave Suite 3500, Detroit, MI 48226-3485, **Business Phone:** (313)965-8580.

COLE, DR. ARTHUR
Educator. **Personal:** Born Nov 6, 1942, Buffalo, NY; married Alice Bailey; children: Arthur & Brandon. **Educ:** State Univ NY, Buffalo, BS, 1964, MS, rehab coun, 1968, PhD, found educ, 1974. **Career:** State Univ Col Buffalo, counr, 1967-68, res asst, 1968-70, personnel dir libr, 1973-75; Dept HEW, fel, 1975; US Off Educ, educ prog specialist, 1975-79; White House, asst to dep asst to pres, 1979-80; Earmark Inc, vpres, 1979-; US Dept Educ, dep dir Horace Mann Learning Ctr, Sch Improv Off, dir sch improv progs, 2000; Univ Okla, Pub Serv Inst, exec prog adv, sr advisor, 2003-; analyst, Teachers Corp; analyst, Off Civil Rights; analyst, White House, Off Hispanic Affairs. **Orgs:** Chap secy, Omega Psi

Phi, 1967-69; Phi delta Kappa, 1967-; Am Lib Asn, 1973-. **Honors/Awds:** Graduate School Education Distinguished Alumni Award, State Univ NY, Buffalo, 2007. **Business Addr:** Senior Advisor, University of Oklahoma, Public Service Institute, 1156 15th St NW Suite 1005, Washington, DC 20005.

COLE, BARBARA DOWE
Writer, association executive. **Personal:** Born Jun 1, 1943, Washington, DC; daughter of Roy and Edith Dowe; divorced; children: Maurice E. **Educ:** Roosevelt Univ, BSBA, 1979. **Career:** United Planning Org, vol coordr, 1964-70; Johnson Publ, bookkeeper, 1978-79; Continental Bank, auditor, 1979-80; Lucent Technol, tech writer & instrnl designer. **Orgs:** Bd mem, Proniso Area United Way, 1983-, pres, 1987-97; Soc Tech Commun, 1988-; Maywood Better Gov Commun, 1989-90; comnr, Maywood Civic Ctr Authority, 1989-; Loyola Healthy Teens Proj, 1994-; Girl Scouts, Strategic Planning Comn, 1996-97; pres, Proviso Area United Way, 1997-00; Maywood Alliance for Better Gov, 1999-; secy, Maywood Alliance for Better Govt, 2000-; adv, Univ Ill 4-H Leadership Club, 2000-. **Honors/Awds:** Community Serv Award, Maywood ChamberCom, 1992; I Care Award, Girl Scouts, 1995; Community Spirit Award, Maywood Park Dist, 1997; Community Service Award, Jeptha Lodge 90, 1997. **Special Achievements:** Published: Just-In-Time, AT&T APEX Conference Proceedings, 1995. *

COLE, CHARLES ZHIVAGA
Association executive. **Personal:** Born Oct 7, 1957, Birmingham, AL; son of Howard Hover and Louise. **Educ:** Mc Neese State Univ, law major. **Career:** CBC Organ & Mc Neese, mr calendar, 1978; John G Lewis Consistory, Thirty Second degree, mason nat, 1981-85; S Bapt Conv, travels local state & nat ambassador goodwill, speaks lectr & teaches, nat vol consult. **Orgs:** ROTC, 1976-78; N Lake Charles Kiwanis, 1977; Mc Neese State Lions Club, 1978; assoc secy, Nat Asn Advan Colored People, 1978-85, nat youth ambassador, 1980-84, civil rights activist, 1984-; nat ambassador speaker, Christian Educ Spec Sci Olympic, 1984-; musician dir, Music Ministry,Tarsus Bible Baptist Church & Curry Chapel CME, Local State & Nat 1985; Star Bethlehem Baptist Ctr; Macedonia Baptist, Cameron, LA. **Honors/Awds:** All Star Drum Major, 1973-74; Mr Calendar, Mc Neese State, 1978; Louisiana State Senatorial Award, Hon State Sen Clifford L Newman, 1986; Distinguished American Citizens, Emory Univ, 1993-94; Governors Award; Outstanding Leadership Award for Service to Community. **Special Achievements:** Author of books and articles. **Home Addr:** 2817 1/2 Fitz/M L King, Lake Charles, LA 70615.

COLE, DEBORAH A.
President (Organization). **Educ:** Tennessee State Univ, MBA; DDiv; La State Univ, Grad Sch Banking S; Univ Notre Dame, Cannon Financial Inst; Gemological Inst Am. **Career:** Citizens Savings Bank & Trust Co, pres & ceo, currently. **Orgs:** Gov Rels Comt, Tenn Bankers Asn, 2005-06. **Business Phone:** (615)327-9787.*

COLE, DORINDA CLARK (DORINDA GRACE CLARK)
Singer. **Personal:** Born Oct 19, 1957, Detroit, MI; daughter of Mattie Moss. **Career:** Clark Conserv Music, Detroit, adminr & instr, currently; Greater EmmanuelInstnl Church God Christ, adminr, currently; Lifeline Prod Inc, founder &chief exec officer, 1999-; Albums: Dorinda Clark-Cole, 2002; Live From Houston: The Rose of Gospel, 2005; Take It Back, 2008; Songs: "No Not One", 2002; "Great IsThe Lord", 2005; "So Many Times", 2005; "Take It Back", 2008. **Orgs:** Pres, First Ecclesiastical Southwest Jurisdictional No. 1, Church GodChrist; vpres, Church God Christ Int Music Dept. **Honors/Awds:** Honorary "Doctorate of Divinity", Mt. Carmel Theol Sem Fresno, CA. **Business Addr:** Singer, Cole Enterprises, Haith Johnson & Cymantha Channey, PO Box 3936, Southfield, MI 48034.*

COLE, EDYTH BRYANT
School administrator. **Personal:** Born in Detroit, MI; children: Charles R, Constance A & Leslie B. **Educ:** Eastern Mich Univ, BA, 1945, MA, 1952; Univ Mich, EdD, 1972; Univ Toledo, OH; Ypsilanti Mich Pub Sch, social studies. **Career:** Ypsilanti Mich Pub Sch, teacher, 1945-66; Wayne Co Mich Intermediate Sch Dist, educ consult rede segregation, 1966-69; Wayne Co Intermediate Sch Dist, shared learning experiences prog, 1967-69; Highland Pk Mich Pub Sch, admin ast curriculum, 1969-71; Nat Resolutions Comn, asn supervision & curriculum develop, 1971-74; NC St Univ; Elizabeth City, chmn dept educ & psychol, 1972-, dir summer sessions, 1973-80. **Orgs:** Nat Defense Educ Act Grant Univ Toledo, 1965; chmn teacher educ, Elizabeth City St Univ, 1972-78; chap basileus, Alpha Kappa Alpha Sorority, 1976-78; pres, L'Esprit Club; bd dir, Mus Albermarle, 1977-79. **Special Achievements:** Pub article re curriculum changes "Curriculum Trends" Croft Pub Co, 1974. **Business Addr:** Director, Elizabeth City State University, Campus Box 982, Elizabeth City, NC 27909, **Business Phone:** (919)335-3400.

COLE, HARRIETTE
President (organization), writer. **Personal:** Born Mar 14, 1961, Baltimore, MD; daughter of Harry A and Doris Freeland; married George Chinsee; children: 1. **Educ:** Howard Univ, attended 1983.

Career: Essence Mag, lifestyle ed & fashion dir; Harriette Cole Prods (formerly Profundities, Inc.), pres & creative dir, 1995-; Uptown, ed dir; Ebony mag, creative dir. Books: Vows; Coming Together; Choosing Truth: Living an Authentic Life; Jumping the Broom: The African-American Wedding Planner; Jumping the Broom Wedding Workbook; Sense and Sensitivity; How to Be: Contemporary Etiquette for African Americans; Entitled Vows(simon&schuster), 2004. **Orgs:** Adv bd mem, The Knot. com; Nat Comn Arts & Letters; Delta Sigma Theta Sorority; Phi Beta Kappa. **Special Achievements:** Has appeared on numerous TV shows such as "Perfect Match New York" "The Oprah Winfrey Show", "The View"; has appeared in mag such as O, In Style, Brides & more. **Business Addr:** President, Creative Director, Harriette Cole Productions, 10 W 15th St Suite 526, New York, NY 10011, **Business Phone:** (212)645-3005.

COLE, JAMES O
Lawyer. **Personal:** Born Feb 6, 1941, Florence, AL; married Ada; children: Barry. **Educ:** Talladega Col, BA, 1962; Harvard Univ, Law Sch, JD, 1971. **Career:** Clorox Co, assoc gen coun, 1973-93, vpres, corp affairs, 1993-97; Kirkland & Ellis Chicago, 1971-73; AutoNation Inc, sr vpres, gen coun & corp secy; Ruden McClosky Smith Schuster & Russell PA, corp, mem real estate & land use pract groups, currently. **Orgs:** Ill Bar Asn; Calif Bar Asn; Am Bar Asn; Alpha Phi Alpha; Urban League; past pres, Nat Bar Asn; Calif Asn Black Lawyers; Charles Houston Bar Asn; past chair, State Bar's Judicial Nominations Evaluations Comn; bd dirs, Black Filmmakers Hall Fame; Nat Asn Advan Colored People; Legal Defense & Educ Fund; African Am Experience Fund; Calif Asn Black Lawyers; Charles Houston Bar Asn; Joe Dimaggio & Memorial Hosp Found. **Honors/Awds:** Program Award for Volunteer Legal Service; Hall of Fame, Charles Houston Bar Asn.

COLE, DR. JOHNNETTA BETSCH
School administrator, educator. **Personal:** Born Oct 19, 1936, Jacksonville, FL; daughter of John Sr and Mary Frances; married Robert (divorced 1982); children: David, Aaron & Che; married Arthur J Robinson Jr, Jan 1, 1988. **Educ:** Oberlin Col, BA, sociology, 1957; Northwestern Univ, MA, 1959, PhD, anthrop, 1967. **Career:** WA State Univ, asst prof & instr anthrop, dir black studies, 1964-70; Univ MA, fac anthrop, Afro-Am studies, 1970-84; Hunter Col, Russell Sage vis prof anthrop, 1983-84, prof anthrop, 1984; Spelman Col, Atlanta, pres, 1987-97, pres emer, currently; Emory Univ, prof emer anthrop, Womens Studies, & African Am studies, currently; Bennett Col Women, pres, 2002-. **Orgs:** Fel Am Anthrop Asn, 1970-; Coalition 100 Black Women; contrib & adv ed, The Black Scholar, 1979-; pres, Asn Black Anthropologists, 1980-; bd chair, United Way Am, Tampa, FL, 2004-; bd trustee, Bennett Col Women. **Honors/Awds:** Elizabeth Boyer Award, 1988; Essence Award in Education, 1989; Hon Doctorate, Bates College, 1989; Hall of Fame; Jessie Bernard Wise Woman Award, 1990 American Woman Award, 1990; Sara Lee's Front runner Award, 1992; Presidential Distinguished Prof of Anthrop Woman's Studies & African Am Studies, Emory Univ, 1998-01; Hon Doctorate, Mount Holyoke College, 1998; Honorary Doctor of Humane Letters, Spelman Col, 1999; McGovern Behavioral Sci Award, Smithsonian Inst, 1999. Hon Doctorate, Howard University, 2009. **Special Achievements:** Profiled on the PBS show "Bridge builders," 1998; co-auth, Gender Talk: The Sruggle for Women's Equality, 2003; First African American female president of Spelman College. **Business Phone:** (336)273-4431.

COLE, JOYCE BOWMAN
Educator. **Personal:** Born Sep 18, 1936, Racine, WI; daughter of Fred and Eunice; divorced; children: Michelle Lynn Lusk, Michael Timothy Bland & Monique Tori Roberson/Davis. **Educ:** Del Mar Col, Assoc, 1969; Tex A & I, BA, 1975; A & M Univ, master, 1976. **Career:** Crossroads Bus Training Sch; Clear Creek Independent Sch Dist; Corpus Christie Independent Sch Dist; El Paso Pub Libr. **Orgs:** Coordr & dir, ASPIRE, 1987-88; coordr & dir, COLORS, 1989-93; counr & teammate, Bill Glass Prison Ministries, 1997-. **Honors/Awds:** Outstanding Teacher Statewide, 1994; Medal presented by Superintendent of CCISD for excellence, 1997. **Home Addr:** 2823 Salt River Court, Missouri City, TX 77459. **Business Addr:** Educator - English Teacher, Clear Creek Independent School District, PO Box 799, League City, TX 77574, **Business Phone:** (281)488-3255.

COLE, LYDIA
Executive. **Personal:** Married Dr. Reginald Cole; children: Iman, Maya. **Educ:** Howard Univ. **Career:** Black Entertainment Television, dir music & prog mgt, 1987-96; BET Cable Network & BET Jazz, vpres prog, 1997-. **Special Achievements:** Created cable shows such as "Unreal", "The Hit List". **Business Phone:** (202)608-2901.*

COLE, MARK
Administrator, business owner. **Career:** Inner City Fishing Inst, founder & chief exec officer, 2003-. **Orgs:** Human Dimensions Recreational Fisheries AFS Comt. **Business Addr:** Founder, Chief Executive Officer, Inner City Fishing Institute, 1715 Live Oak Ln, PO Box 832917, Allen, TX 75002, **Business Phone:** (214)910-3795.

COLE, NATALIE (STEPHANIE NATALI COLE)
Singer, actor. **Personal:** Born Feb 6, 1950, Los Angeles, CA; daughter of Nathaniel Adam and Maria Hawkins; married Marvin

J Yancy, Jul 31, 1976 (divorced 1980); children: Robert Adam; married Andre Fischer, Jan 1, 1989 (divorced 1995); married Bishop Kenneth H Dupree, Jan 1, 2001 (divorced 2004). **Career:** Capitol Recs, rec artist, 1975-; Big Break, tv show, host & performer, 1990-; Films: "De-Lovely", 2004; TV series: "Lily in Winter", 1994; "Abducted; A Father's Love", 1997; "Concert of Hope", 1997; Always Outnumbered, 1998; "Livin For Love: The Natalie Cole Story", exec producer, 2000; "Natalie: A Woman Who Knows", exec producer, 2002; "Great Performances", exec producer, 2002; "Law & Order: Special Victims Unit", 2006; "Greys Anatomy", 2006; "Frosted Pink", 2007; Albums: Inseparable, 1975; Good To Be Back, 1989; Unforgettable With Love, 1991; Everlasting, 1991; I'm Ready, 1992; Take a Look, 1993; Holly & Ivy, 1994; I've Got Love On My Mind, 1995; Stardust, 1996; Snowfall On the Sahara, 1999; Sing Like Natalie Cole, 2000; Livin' For Love, 2001; Ask A Woman Who Knows, 2002; The Easter Egg Adventure, composer, 2004; Eclectic Soul, 2005; Leavin', 2006; Love Songs, 2007. **Honors/Awds:** Gold Rec, "Inseparable"; Eight Grammy Awards; four gold albums; two platinum albums; Image Award, 1976, 1977, NAACP Image Award, 2000 & 2002; Am Music Award, 1977, 1978 & 1991; Cowboy Award, 2004. **Business Addr:** Singer, Actress, c/o Capitol Recs Inc, 1750 N Vine St, Hollywood, CA 90028, **Business Phone:** (323)462-6252.

COLE, OLEN, JR.
College administrator, educator. **Educ:** Calif State Univ, Fresno, BA, MA; Univ NC, Chapel Hill, PhD. **Career:** NC Agr & Tech Univ, prof & chairperson hist, currently. **Special Achievements:** Published an article in Steven A. Reich s Encyclopedia of the Great Black Migration book. **Business Addr:** Professor, Chairperson of the History Department, North Carolina Agricultural & Technical State University, History Department, 1601 E Market St, Greensboro, NC 27411, **Business Phone:** (336)334-7831.

COLE, PATRICIA A
Consultant, executive. **Personal:** Born Oct 25, 1940, Detroit, MI; daughter of Thomas Aaron Allen and C Marie Johnson Wilson; married Jun 1, 1965 (divorced); children: B Derek & Jason A. **Educ:** Univ Detroit, MI, BA, bus admin, 1980. **Career:** Cole Financial Serv, Detroit, MI, pres & founder, 1983-. **Orgs:** Gen chairperson, Am Asn Prof Consults, SE Conf, 1987-; nat adv bd, Black Career Women, Exec circle, 1989-; Nat Asn Woman Consults, 1990-; counr, presentor, Score, SBA Chap 48, 1990-; co-chairperson, Metro Atlanta Coalition 100 Black Women, 1990-; Women's Informal Network; Vols Am; Civic Searchlight. **Honors/Awds:** Outstanding Volunteerism, Optimist Club NW Detroit, 1987; Black Career Women, Nat Adv Bd, 1989; Certified Professional Manager, Prof Servs Mgt Inst, 1990; Registered Professional Consultant, Am Asn Prof Consults; Women Who Make a Difference, Minorities & Women Bus; Sojourner Truth Award, NANBPWC; Best Business Entrepreneur, Black Women Contracting Asn, 2005.

COLE, RANSEY GUY, JR.
Lawyer, judge. **Personal:** Born May 23, 1951, Birmingham, AL; son of Ransey G Sr and Sarah Coker; married Kathleine Kelley, Nov 26, 1983; children: Justin, Jordan, Alexandra. **Educ:** Tufts Univ, BA, 1972; Yale Law Sch, JD, 1975. **Career:** Varys, Sater, Seymour, & Pease Law Firm, assoc, 1975-78, 1980-82, partner, 1983-86, 1993-95; Civil Div Com Litigation Br, Dept Justice, trial atty, 1978-80; Civil Serv Comn, comnr, 1986; US Bankruptcy Ct, judge, 1987-92; US Ct Appeals Sixth Circuit, judge, 1996-. **Orgs:** Bd trustees, Nationwide Investing Found, 1984-86; trustee, C Hosp, 1990-; bd govs, Columbus Bar Asn, 1990-94; trustee, Univ Club, 1992-; Am Bankruptcy Inst, 1993-95; dir, Am Bankruptcy Bd Cert, 1993-; dir, Bankrupty Arbit & Mediation Servs; trustee, US Health Corp, Community Health & Wellness; trustee, I Know I Can; Ohio Bar Asn; Nat Bar Asn; Sigma Phi Fraternity; Alpha Phi Alpha Fraternity. **Honors/Awds:** Founders Day Award, Alpha Phi Alpha Fraternity; Professionalism Award, Alpha Phi Alpha Fraternity, 1994. **Special Achievements:** Second African-American to work, law firm of Vorys, Sater, Senour and Pease, Columbus, OH, 1975; first African-American partner at the firm, 1983; One of Ten, Emerging Leaders for Columbus, The Columbus Dispatch, 1985. **Business Phone:** (513)564-7000.*

COLE, STEPHANIE NATALI. See COLE, NATALIE.

COLE, DR. THOMAS WINSTON
Educator, president (organization), school administrator. **Personal:** Born Jan 11, 1941, Vernon, TX; son of Thomas and Eva Sharp; married Brenda S Hill, Jun 14, 1964; children: Kelley ,Susan & Thomas Winston III. **Educ:** Wiley Col, Marshall, TX, BS, 1961; Univ Chicago, PhD, 1966. **Career:** Woodrow Wilson, fel, 1961-62; Atlanta Univ, asst prof, 1966-82, Fuller EC allaway prof, 1969-79, chmn dept chem, 1970-79, proj dir resource ctr sci& eng, 1978-82, univ provost, vpres acad affairs, 1979-82; Miami Valley Lab, Procter & Gamble Co, summer chemist, 1967; Univ Ill, vis prof, 1972;Mass Inst Technol, vis prof, 1973-74; Celanese Corp, Charlotte, NC,chemist, 1974; UNCF, lectr, 1975-84; WVa State Col Inst, pres, 1982-86; WVa Bd Regents, chancellor, 1986-88; Clark Col, pres, 1988-89; Clark Atlanta Univ,

Atlanta, GA, pres, 1989-2002, pres emer, currently. **Orgs:** Allied Chem fel, 1963; bd mem, Fernbank Mus, 1989-; Am Chem Soc; AAAS; NatInst Sci; Nat Orgn Prof Advan Black Chemists & Chem Engrs; Sigma Xi; Sigma Pi Phi; Alpha Phi Alpha; bd mem, Qual Educ Minorities. **Honors/Awds:** Honorus Causa DLL, W Va State Col, 1987; Honorus Causa DHL, Univ Charleston, 1988. **Special Achievements:** The First President of Clark Atlanta Univ. **Business Addr:** President Emeritus, Clark Atlanta University, 223 James P Brawley Dr SW, Atlanta, GA 30314, **Business Phone:** (404)880-8000.

COLE CAREY, WILHEMINA
Consultant, business owner. **Personal:** Daughter of Estell Swinton Nesmith; children: Gilbert Flemin Jr & Tyrone Sr. **Educ:** Univ Md, AA, BS, MBA, PhD; St Elizabeths Hosp, Wash, DC, post-grad course psychiat, 1960; exec housekeeper cert, 1967. **Career:** Exec housekeeper, 1951-58; St Elizabeths Hosp, lpn, supvr, 1960-65, asst hosp housekeeping officer, 1965-78, hosp housekeeping off, 1978-89; fed govt employee, 1960-87; city govt employee, 1987-91; Logistics Mgt Br, dep chief, 1984-91; Carey & Hester Inc, consult, owner, 1991-; St Elizabeths hosp Mus, founder, cur mgr; Arlington Pub Sch, teacher, mkt, currently. **Orgs:** Coordr, Upper Rm Baptist Church, 1991; bd mem, Int Exec Housekeepers Asn; life mem, Veterans Foreign Wars. **Honors/Awds:** The Wilhemina C. Carey Retirement Resolution, named in honor for 30 years of Outstanding Public & Dedicated Service, St Elizabeths Hosp, DC Govt, 1992. **Special Achievements:** Author: The Housekeeping Manual, 1979; "Hospital Housekeeping Education and Training, A Case Study", 1971; Designed and established a library which is affiliated with the DC Library; developed and implemented a nine month Housekeeping Training Prog for two Liberian students under the auspices of the Agency for International Development, US Dept State; First woman to be Supreme Master of the National Ideal Benefit Society; Developed and implemented programs of lesser training for others under similar housekeeping programs for US Dept State. **Business Addr:** Consultant, Owner, Carey & Hester Inc, 33 54th St SE, Washington, DC 20019-6560, **Business Phone:** (202)584-7010.*

COLEMAN, ANDREW LEE
Public relations executive, parole officer, photographer. **Personal:** Born Jan 30, 1960, Humboldt, TN; son of Lonnie Lee(deceased) and Mae Doris Scott Lovelady. **Educ:** Vanderbilt Univ, BS Polit Sci, Sociol 1982; Dyersburg Community Col, 1990; Jackson State Community Col, Jackson, TN, parole training, 1987. **Career:** Humboldt City Parks, asst supvr summer, 1977; Jones Mfg Co, laborer, 1978-79; Foster & Creighton Const Co, laborer, 1981; Denver Broncos, prof football player, 1982; New Orleans Saints, prof football player 1982; Classic I Kitchenware Inc, sales distribr, 1983; Humboldt Sch, sub teacher, 1983; City Humboldt, alderman, 1983; Gibson City Vote Coordr, coordr Albert Gore Jr, 1984; Jesse Jackson Pres, coordr, 1984; The Drew Enterprise, pres, 1985; Jonah, Inc, organizer/off mgr, 1985; Al Williams, Inc, sales rep, 1986; TN Bd Paroles, parole officer/counselor, 1986; Morgan & Assocs Realtors, affiliate broker 1987; co-chmn Humboldt Strawberry Patch, 1988; Jackson State Community Col, 1993. **Orgs:** TN Black Elected Officials; TN Voters Coun; Gibson City Voters Coun; Nat Asn Advan Colored People; Am Probation & Paroles; Decatur County Community Corrections; patron Order Eastern Star; Gibson County Fraternal Order of Police; Brownstown Alumni Club Memphis, 1990; Lane Col Alumni Asn, 1989; TN State Troopers Asn; TN Correctional Asn; Am Correctional Asn; Just Organized Neighborhood Area Hq; Steward, Lane Chapel CME Church; TN Sheriff Asn; Nat Asn Advan Colored People; Golden Heritage; 100 Black Men W Tenn; Beta Upsilon Lambda Chapter; Alpha Phi Alpha; Vanderbilt Alumni Asn; Miracle Develop Acad Lane Chapel CME Church; Nat Asn Blacks Criminal Justice; TN Sch Bd Asn; TN Legislative Network. **Honors/Awds:** Most Valuable Player, Vanderbilt Football, 1980; voted Most Athletic Class of 1982; All Am Mid Linebacker, Vanderbilt Univ, 1982; Am Outstanding Names & Faces Nat Org, 1982; Community Serv Award, Humboldt Nat Asn Advan Colored People, 1988; Community Service Award, Phi Delta Kappa, 1992; Community Service Award, Phi Delta Kappa, 2001; Community Serv Award, Comm Action Dream Keepers, 2003. **Special Achievements:** Outstanding Young Men of America, National Nominating Comt. **Home Addr:** 1610 Osborne, Humboldt, TN 38343. **Business Addr:** President, The Drew Enterprise, 1610 Osborne St, Humboldt, TN 38343, **Business Phone:** (731)784-5774.

COLEMAN, APRIL HOWARD
School administrator, lawyer. **Personal:** Married Donald; children: Rebekah & Donald. **Educ:** Univ Mich; Tex Southern Univ, Thurgood Marshall Sch Law. **Career:** Univ Detroit Mercy, adj prof; Wayne State Univ, adj prof; Swanson, Torgow & Lyons, PC, atty; Detroit Bd Educ, past pres; pvt prac atty, currently. **Orgs:** Founder, Detroit Teen Anti-Violence Prog; charter mem, Detroit City Coun's Youth Adv Comt; chair, Youth Task Force Citizens Comt, Wayne County; founder, Detroit St Law Proj; chair, Community Confidence Comt, Detroit Sch Bd, 1989, 1991 & 1992. **Military Serv:** AUS, first lt. **Business Phone:** (313)494-1270.

COLEMAN, ASHLEY
Fashion model. **Personal:** Born Jan 1, 1981?, Camden, DE. **Educ:** Del State Univ, degree, educ. **Career:** Fashion model, currently. **Honors/Awds:** Miss Delaware Teen USA, 1998; Miss Teen USA, 1999.; Third Runner-up, Miss California USA 2006 pageant. **Special Achievements:** First delegate from Delaware to win the national title.

COLEMAN, AUDREY RACHELLE
School administrator. **Personal:** Born Aug 26, 1934, Duquesne, PA; daughter of Dave and Ola Dixon; married William Franklin Coleman Sr; children: William Franklin Jr. **Educ:** Youngstown Univ, BMus; Boston St Col, MEd, Advanced Admin. **Career:** Youngstown Ohio Pub Schs, teacher; Boston Pub Schs, teacher, asst prin, admin, dir comprehensive sch planning, currently. **Orgs:** Nat First Anti-Basileus Lambda Kappa Mu; conductor Nat Workshops Lambda Kappa Mu; conductor City wide Workshops Boston Pub Schs; Mass St Review Team Chap I Prog, 1978; grand basileus Lambda Kappa Mu, 1981-85; bd dir, Nat Coalition-Black Meeting Planners, 1984-86; nat bd mem, Lambda Kappa Mu(past nat pres); nat vpres, Am Fed Sch Admin; bd mem, Boston Convention and Visitor's Bureau; pres Middlesex County Chap Links Inc; Nat nominating committee, 1992, Nat protocol committee, found bdm-at-large, Links Inc. **Honors/Awds:** Certificate of Achievement & Leadership Urban League, 1979; 'Mary MBethune Award', Nat Coun Negro Women, 1982; Distinguished Serv Key Award Lambda Kappa Mu, 1983; featured on front cover of Black Monitor Magazine, 1984; Dollars & Sense Magazine Award to Outstanding Afro-American Women, 1989; Mayor of Boston Award for Leadership, 1988; Humanitarian Award, South Shore United Methodist Church, Chicago, Ill, 1987; Nat Freedom's Found Award; Bd mem, Mass Lodging Asn Educ Found; Links Inc. Assembly, General chmn, 1998. **Business Addr:** Director, The Boston Public Schools, 26 Court St, Boston, MA 02108, **Business Phone:** (617)635-9000.

COLEMAN, AVANT PATRICK
Educator, government official. **Personal:** Born Jun 16, 1936, Rocky Mount, NC; son of Edward William and Bessie D Phillips; married Willa Jean Monroe, Apr 28, 1960; children: Jacqueline, Elliotte & Wanda. **Educ:** Agr & Tech State Univ, BS, 1960; NC State Univ, MS, 1978. **Career:** Lenoir City Bd Ed, teacher, voc agr, 1960-61; Greene City Bd Ed, teacher, voc agr 1961-62; NC Agr Exten Svc, exten agt 4-H, 1962-; Coun Dist 1, NC, coun mem; Wilosn City Coun, Council mem, currently. **Orgs:** Distinguished Service Award, State Nat Assoc 4-H Agents, 1975; Certificate Appreciation Mid-Atlantic Reg, MD-NC 4-H Caravan Six Weeks, 1977; Distinguished Service Award, Alpha Kappa Alpha Sorority, 1982; Distinguished Humanitarian Award, Gamma Beta Omega Chap Alpha Kappa Alpha Sorority, 1982; Recipient the Outstanding Leadership Award, NC Ag Exten Serv, 1989. **Business Addr:** Councilmember, Wilosn City Council, 112 N Goldsboro St, PO Box 4185, Wilson, NC 27893, **Business Phone:** (252)243-5656.

COLEMAN, BARBARA SIMS
Social worker. **Personal:** Born Mar 5, 1932, Wichita, KS; daughter of Hugh Napoleon and Rossa Velma Whitehead; married Julian D Coleman Jr, Aug 8, 1953; children: Julian, Hugh, Mark. **Educ:** Howard Univ, BS, 1953; Univ WI, MS, 1956. **Career:** Social worker (retired); Larue Carter Memorial Hosp, asst dir soc work, 1957-73, supvr, 1957-73, psychiatric soc worker, 1957-73; Ind Univ Med Ctr, asst dir soc work & psychiatry Riley Child Psychiatry Clinic, 1973-93. **Orgs:** Mem bd pres, Raines Couns Central, 1968-84; consult supvr, Christian Theological Seminary Pastoral Couns Prog, 1972-; mem bd, Planned Parenthood Central IN, 1980-89; Nat Asn Social Workers & Acad Cert Social Workers; bd, C Bur Indianpolis Inc, 1993-00; adv coun, Buchanan Coun Ctr, 1994-00; Greater Indianapolis Literary League, 1995-99. **Honors/Awds:** Social Worker of the Yr, Region 7, Ind, Nat Asn Social Workers, 1989. **Home Addr:** 4370 Knollton Rd, Indianapolis, IN 46228, **Home Phone:** (317)299-2900. *

COLEMAN, BEN. See COLEMAN, BENJAMIN LEON.

COLEMAN, BENJAMIN LEON (BEN COLEMAN)
Football player. **Personal:** Born May 18, 1971, South Hill, VA; married Krista; children: Haley, Tori & Ben. **Educ:** Wake Forest Univ. **Career:** Phoenix Cardinals, 1993; Arizona Cardinals, guard, 1994-95; Jacksonville Jaguars, linemen, 1995-99; San Diego Chargers, 2000; Washington Redskins, 2001; Carolina Panthers, defensive linemen, 2002. **Honors/Awds:** All-District Lineman of the Yr; Jacobs Blocking Trophy, 1992.

COLEMAN, CECIL R.
Executive, association executive. **Personal:** Born May 15, 1934, Centralia, IL; married Betti Thomas; children: Karla M, Mark C. **Educ:** Northwestern Univ, Kellogg Grad Sch Mgt, BBA, 1970. **Career:** Mammoth Life Ins Co, sales rep asst mgr & mgr, 1954-65; Harris Trust & Savings Bank, asst mgr, 1965, vpres, 1978-80; dir; C Home & Aid Soc Ill, chmn bd trustees, Community Leader, currently. **Orgs:** Chicago Chap AIB Bd Regents; TAP Cons; Alpha Delta Sigma; Chicago Student Symp; Sci & Math Conf, 1973; bd dir, Chatham YMCA; Community Fund Rev Panel; Old Town Boys Club; chmn, CHASI. **Honors/Awds:** Chicago merit Employee week, 1967; jaycee month Chicago Chap, 1969; WGRT Radio Great Guy Award, 1973; Chicago black achiever, 1974; numerous Nat Inst Asn awards and sales achievements. **Special Achievements:** The first African American named as chairman of the board of trustees at Children's Home & Aid Society of Illinois in the 115-year history of the organization. **Military Serv:** AUS, sp/4, 1956-58. **Business Addr:** Community Leader, Children's Home & Aid Society of Illinois, 125 S Wacker Dr 14th Fl, Chicago, IL 60606, **Business Phone:** (312)424-0200.*

COLEMAN, CHRISENA ANNE
Journalist, writer. **Personal:** Born Mar 20, 1963, Hackensack, NJ; daughter of Wilbert and Dorothy. **Educ:** Northeastern Univ, BA, 1968; Emerson Col, attended 1982. **Career:** Hackensack Bd Educ, counr family literacy prog; Record, staff writer, journalist, currently. **Orgs:** vice pres, Garden State Asn Black Journalists; Nat Asn Black Journalists; Aka Sorority. **Honors/Awds:** Black Woman of Inspiration, Aka, Bergen Chap, 1992; Black Hist Honoree, NAACP, Passaic Chap. **Business Addr:** Journalist, The Record, 150 River St, Hackensack, NJ 07601-7172, **Business Phone:** (201)646-4100.*

COLEMAN, CLAUDE M
Executive, judge. **Personal:** Born Oct 26, 1940, Newberry, SC; son of Willie and Roberta Spearman; married Barbara Saunders, Apr 16, 1983 (divorced); married Barbara Bell, May 6, 1994. **Educ:** Rutgers Univ, Newark, NJ, BS, 1971-74; Rutgers Law Sch, Newark, NJ, JD, 1974-77; Fed Bur Invest Nat Acad, Va 1978; Nat Fire Acad, MD, 1987. **Career:** City Newark, NJ, police officer, 1964-80, police legal adv, 1980-86, fire dir, 1986-88; police dir, munic judge; State NJ Superior Court, judge, currently. **Orgs:** Former pres, Bronze Shields Inc, chmn, 1964-; 100 Black Men NJ; Nat Orgn Black Law Enforcement Execs; IACP; chmn, Law Enforcement Exec Forum. **Military Serv:** USAF, Sgt 1st class, 1959-63; Good Conduct. **Home Addr:** 649 Lake St Suite 653, Newark, NJ 07104. **Business Addr:** Judge, State of New Jersey Superior Court, 50 W Mkt St Rm 514 NCB, Newark, NJ 07102, **Business Phone:** (973)693-5800.

COLEMAN, DR. COLLIE. See Obituaries section.

COLEMAN, COLUMBUS E., JR.
Executive. **Personal:** Born Jul 13, 1948, Wharton, TX. **Educ:** Univ Tex, BS, 1970; Univ NC, MBA, 1975; Univ San Francisco, Law Courses, 1979. **Career:** Gulf & Oil Co, elec engr, 1970-71; First Nat Bank Dallas, corp banking officer, 1975-77; Wells Fargo Bank, asst vpres, 1977-79; Wells Fargo Securities Clearance Corp, exec vpres & gen mgr, 1979-. **Orgs:** Pres, Alpha Phi Alpha Epsilon Iota Chap, 1970-71; Adv capt Am Cancer Asn Dr, 1977; Small Bus Asn; adv, Jr Achievement, 1978; partic Big Bros Asn; NAACP. **Military Serv:** AUS, spec-5, 1971-72; Soldier of Year, 1972. *

COLEMAN, DEEDEE M.
Clergy. **Personal:** Born in New Orleans, LA. **Educ:** William Tyndale Col, BA, Bus Admin; Marygrove Col, MA, Pastoral Ministry. **Career:** Russell St Missionary Baptist Church, pastor, currently. **Business Addr:** Pastor, Russell St Missionary Baptist Church, 8700 Chrysler Dr, Detroit, MI 48211-1249, **Business Phone:** (313)875-1615.*

COLEMAN, DENNIS
Entrepreneur. **Personal:** Born Dec 31, 1951, North Chicago, IL; son of J C Sr and Eupha Lee; married Cheryl Diane Jarnigan, Aug 31, 1974; children: Dennis II, Felicia Marie, Steven Anton. **Educ:** Knoxville Col, BS, bus, 1974. **Career:** Burger King Corp, crew supvr, 1970-74, restaurant mgr, 1974-77, dist mgr, 1977-81; Coleman Enterprises, pres, 1981-90; Five Star Inc, DBA Rally's Hamburgers, pres. **Orgs:** Phi Beta Sigma, 1971-; Big Fellas Asn; Minority Franchise Asn. **Honors/Awds:** Minority Franchisee of the Year, Michigan Dept Com, 1992. **Special Achievements:** First minority to own a Rally's Franchise in the country, 1992; highest award received at Whopper College, 1974; Top Ten Graduates at Burger King University. *

COLEMAN, DERRICK D.
Basketball player, business owner. **Personal:** Born Jun 21, 1967, Mobile, AL; married Gina Cook, Jul 30, 2000. **Educ:** Syracuse Univ, Syracuse, NY, 1990. **Career:** Basketball player (retired), business owner; NJ Nets, forward, 1990-95; Philadelphia 76ers, 1995-98, 2001-04; Charlotte Hornets, 1998-2001; Detroit Pistons, forward, 2004-05; SNYX Sneaker Studio, owner, currently. **Honors/Awds:** NBA Rookie of the Year, 1991; Gold Medal, World Championships, 1994.

COLEMAN, DON
Administrator, chief executive officer. **Educ:** Univ Mich; Hofstra Univ, MBA. **Career:** Campbell-Ewald Advert, vpres; Don Coleman Advert, 1988; New Am Strategies Group, ceo; GlobalHue, chmn & ceo, currently. **Orgs:** Bd Control, Univ Mich Athletic Dept ; NFL Players Asn; bd, C's Ctr Mich; bd dir, Ad Coun; chmn, Am Advert Fedn Found; Multicultural Task Force, Am Advert Fedn Found; Adcraft Club Detroit. **Business Phone:** (248)223-8900.*

COLEMAN, DR. DON EDWIN
Educator. **Personal:** Born May 4, 1928, Ponca City, OK; son of George and Nancy; married Geraldine J Johnson; children:

Stephanie Lynn. **Educ:** Mich State Univ, BS, 1952, MS, 1956, MA, 1958, PhD, 1971. **Career:** Educator (retired); Flint Mich Sch, teacher, 1954-67; Doyle Community Sch, prin, 1966-68; Mich State Univ, teacher, coach, 1968-69; asst dean, gradsch, Col Osteop Med, prof community health sci, 1978-92, prof emer. **Orgs:** Pres, Mich Health Coun, 1980; Am Pub Health Asn; Am Col Pers Asn; Nat Asn Stud Pers Admin; Nat Comm Sch Dir Asn, 1963-67; Mich Elem Prin Asn, 1967-68; Phi Delta Kappa; Alpha Phi Alpha Frat; Epsilon Upsilon Lambda; Kappa Delta Lambda; Red Feather United Fund 1964-68; BS Am; Prince Hall Masonic Order; Elks Genesee Temple; Nat Asn Advan Colored People; Urban League; exec comt, Planned Parenthood, 1952-60; Flint Jr Chamber Comm; bd mem, Listening Ear, 1970-73; Air Pollution Bd; Tri-Co Plannig Comt; Mich State Univ Athletic Coun; Alpha Phi Alpha Frat; exec dir, Black Child & Family Inst, 1986; chmn Ingham County, Bd Health, 1987; bd trustees, Mich Capital Med Ctr, 1988. **Honors/Awds:** The 10 Year Award Big Brothers Am, 1955-68; Blue Key Nat Scholastic Honor; Unanimous All-Am Tackle 1950-51; Outstanding Lineman, 1951 1952; Col All Star game, 1952; Outstanding Lineman Hula Bowl Silver Anniversary, 1971;Nat Football Found & Hall Fame, 1975; Nat Col Athletic Asn Silver Anniversary Award, 1976; Greater Flint Area Sports Hall Fame, 1980; Greater Flint African-American Hall of Fame, 1988; Mich State Univ (MSU) Athletic Hall of Fame, 1992; Michigan Sports Hall of Fame, 1997. **Special Achievements:** First Spartan football player ever to have his jersey retired, 1952. **Military Serv:** AUS, 2nd Lt, 1952-54. *

COLEMAN, DONALD
Police officer. **Personal:** Born Aug 18, 1953, Marion, AL; son of Elijah (deceased) and Alma; married Constance Lin, Jan 6, 1979; children: Benjamin Ashley & Christopher Andrew. **Educ:** New Hampshire Col, BS, bus mgt, 1976. **Career:** City Detroit, police sgt, police officer, 1987-; Flowers Miss Marion, co-owner, currently. **Orgs:** Kappa Sigma Int Fraternity, 1974; Barney McCosky Baseball League, little league coach, 1986-93. **Honors/Awds:** Fraternity Brother of the Year, 1975; 8th Precinct, Police Officer of the Year, 1993; Police Officer of the Month, 3 times; Performance Award, 6 times. **Business Addr:** Police Officer, City of Detroit, Police Department, 14655 Dexter Ave, Detroit, MI 48238, **Business Phone:** (313)596-2660.

COLEMAN, DONALD ALVIN
Advertising executive. **Personal:** Born Jan 11, 1952, Toledo, OH; son of Augustus and Dorothy Bowers; married Jo Moore Coleman, Oct 5, 1976; children: Kelli. **Educ:** Univ Mich, BA, journalism, 1974; Hofstra Univ, Hempstead, NY, MBA, 1976. **Career:** Lintas Campbell-Ewald Advert, Warren, MI, vpres, 1977-85; Burrell Advert, Chicago, IL, sr vpres, 1985-87; Don Coleman & Assocs, Southfield, MI, pres & chief exec officer, 1988-. **Orgs:** Am Asn Advert Agencies; Nat Football League Players Asn; adv comt, Reggie McKenzie Found, 1988; Nat Asn Advan Colored People; Nat Asn Mkt Developers; bd dir, C's Ctr Mich; bd dir, Charles H. Wright Mus African Am Hist; Adcraft Club Detroit. **Special Achievements:** Black Enterprise's list of Top Advertising Agencies, ranked #3, 1999, #2, 2000. **Business Addr:** President, Chief Executive Officer, Don Coleman & Assocs, 26555 Evergreen Rd, 18th Fl, Southfield, MI 48076-4206.*

COLEMAN, REV. DONALD LEROY, SR.
Association executive, executive. **Personal:** Born Oct 25, 1937, Greenfield, OH; son of Charles and Susie (Jackson); married Ann, May 31, 1959; children: Donna Coker, Robin Jackson, Donald Jr, John, Timothy. **Educ:** Doane Col, Lincoln, NE, BA, 1995. **Career:** Lincoln Pub Schs, security, 1992-94; Lincoln Police Dept, youth aid, 1992-01; MAD Dads Lincoln Inc, pres, 1993-. **Orgs:** Assoc pastor, Gospel Tabernacle; chaplain, past sr chaplain, Lincoln Police & Fire Chaplain Corps, 1987, 1993-96; chaplain, Vietnam Veterans Am, 1990-; Kiwanis Int, 1997-; vpres, Optimist Int, 1998-01; Lincoln Rotary 14 Int, 1998-; Urban League, Lincoln, 1998-; Nat Asn Advan Colored People, Lincoln Chap, 1999-; life mem, Disabled Am Vet; Parent's Day Coun. **Honors/Awds:** Gospel Announcer of the Yr, Savoy Record Co, 1978; Volunteer of the Yr, United Way, 1993; received gold key, City of Lincoln, 1993-94, 2000; Senior Award, Doane Col Alumni, 1995; Serv to Mankind Award, Sertoma Int, 1995; Community Hero Torch Bearer, 1996; hon asst applied sci, Lincoln Sch Com, 1996; Lincoln Interfaith Leadership Award, 1997; Forensic Speaker of the Yr, Univ Nebr, 1997; Friend of Youth Award, Optimist Int, 1999; Nebr Parents of the Yr, 1999; Nat Parents of the Yr, 2000; Steven G Gilbaugh Vietnam VFW Post 10617 Award, 2001; hon asst bus admin, Lincoln Sch Com, 2001; Bus Resource Award, Lincoln Independent Bus Asn, 2001. **Special Achievements:** Iowa Army Nat Guard, state career counr, 1980-84; Radio KOJC, sta mgr, 1981-84; KBMT-FM, gospel announcer, 1994; KLIN-AM, talk show host, 1997; KZUM-FM, talk show host, 1998-. **Military Serv:** AUS, SFC-E-7, 1955-58, 1961-67, 1978-93; Vietnam Serv Medal, 1967; Three Meritorious Units Citations w/Oakleaf Clusters, 1967; Vietnam, supvr teletype maintainance, 1967, Europe, supvsr teletype maintenance, 1961-66; Reserve Component Achievement Medal, 1981; Career Counselor Badge, 1982; Army Commendation Medal, 1985; Recruiting Badge, 1987; Individual Meritorious Service Awards, 1992. **Business Addr:** President, MAD Dads Lincoln Inc, 555 Stockton St, Jacksonville, FL 32204, **Business Phone:** (904)388-8171.*

COLEMAN, DR. EDWIN LEON, II
Educator. **Personal:** Born Mar 17, 1932, El Dorado, AR; son of Mae Otis and Edwin; married Charmaine Joyce Thompson; children: Edwin III & Callan. **Educ:** City Col San Francisco, AA, Bus Admin, 1955; San Francisco State Univ, BA, Theatre Arts, 1960, MA, Theatre Arts, 1962; Univ OR, PhD, 1971. **Career:** Educator (retired); Melodyland Theatre, technician, 1960; Chico State Univ, Speech Dept, asst prof, 1963-66; Speech Dept, Instr, 1966-69; Off Acad Advising, instr, 1969-70; Univ OR Dept Eng, dir, Folklore 1 Ethnic Prog; prof musician. **Orgs:** Bd Campus Interfaith Ministry, 1975-; bd Sponsors Inc, 1980-; bd Clergy & Laity Concerned, 1980-; bd OR Arts Found, 1981-84; pres, OR Folklore Soc, 1983-84; consult, Nat Endowment Arts, 1983-; Nat Humanities, faculty; Am Folklore Soc; NAACP; Kappa Alpha Psi; Oregon Track Club; bd, Western States Arts Found. **Honors/Awds:** Ford Fellow, Educ Grant, 1970; Danforth Assoc, 1977-; Distinguished Black Faculty, 1978; Outstanding Faculty, Nat Mgt OR Art Comn, 1982; Frederick Douglass Scholarship Award, Nat Coun Black Studies, 1986; Charles S.Johnson Service Award, UNIV Oregon; Lifetime Achievement Award, NAACP; Dr.Edwin Coleman Speaker Series Award, Univ Oregon, 1998; Achievement Award Racial Justice, Ba-ha Faith, Lane County, 1991. **Military Serv:** USAF, Staff Sgt, 1951-56. *

COLEMAN, ELIZABETH SHEPPARD
Manager. **Personal:** Children: Nedra, Andre, Jalinda, Angela & Aretha. **Educ:** Muskegon Comm Col, Assc, 1973; Grand Valley State Col, BS, 1975, Masters Gen & Urban Educ, 1979. **Career:** Adv Coun Muskegon Heights Police, 1975-77; Muskegon Heights Bd Educ, trustee, secy, 1975-81; Muskegon County Repertory Ctr, dir, 1976-85. **Orgs:** Muskegon County Coun Black Org, 1975-77; Muskegon County Human Res Comt, 1977-79; secy, Muskegon Co Black Org, 1977-79; Muskegon Co Human Resource, 1979; Muskegon Co Nat Asn Advan Colored People.

COLEMAN, ERIC DEAN
Lawyer, government official. **Personal:** Born May 26, 1951, New Haven, CT; son of Julius and Rebecca Ann Simmons; married Pamela Lynette Greene, May 19, 1979; children: Trevonn Rakeim, Lamar Ericson & Erica Lynette. **Educ:** Columbia Univ, BA, 1973; Univ Conn, JD, 1977. **Career:** Hartford Neighborhood Legal Serv, staff atty, 1977-78; Conn Div Pub Defense Serv, asst pub defender, 1978-81; Aetna Life & Casualty, consult, 1981-86; Conn Gen Assembly, state rep, 1983-95, state sen, 1995-; pres, Bloomfield Black Democratic Club, 1998-; chair judiciary community, 2001. **Orgs:** Greater Hartford Urban League, 1974-; Greater Hartford NAACP, 1974-; AmBar Asn, 1978; Conn Bar Asn, 1978-; George Crawford Law Asn, 1978; Action Plan Infant Health, 1984-2000; Charter Oak Lodge Elks, 1982-; Omega Psi Phi; Bloomfield Dem Town Community, 1984-; Metro AME Zion Church; mem bddirs, Greater Hartford Legal Assistance Asn Inc, Ciritan Club, 2000-. **Honors/Awds:** Citizen of the Year, Omega Psi Phi Fraternity Tau Iota, Conn, 1982; Citizen of the Year, Omega Psi Phi Frat Delta Lambda, Conn, 1983; First Report (Weekly Neighborhood Newspaper Column), 1983-88; Marital Deduction Planning under ERTA 1981; Legislator of the Year, African-Am Affairs Comn, 2001; Clarence Daniels Advocacy Award, Conn AIDS Residence Coalition; Achievement Award, Conn Chap Men & Women for Justice. **Special Achievements:** First African-American to serve as Chair of the Judiciary Community. **Home Addr:** 77 Wintonbury Ave, Bloomfield, CT 06002, **Home Phone:** (203)243-8118. **Business Addr:** State Senator, Connecticut General Assembly, Legislative Office Bldg Room 2100, Hartford, CT 06106-1591, **Business Phone:** (860)240-5302.

COLEMAN, FAYE
Administrator. **Educ:** Simmons Col, sociol; Univ MA, MA; Univ Md, EdD. **Career:** Tech & mgt consult firms, WA, prog mgr & proj dir; Southeastern Univ, bd dirs; USAF, contracted proj; Westover Consults Inc, Silver Spring, MD, pres & chief exec officer, currently. **Orgs:** Bd dirs, Wash C Develop Coun; bd dir, Leadership Wash. **Honors/Awds:** Distinguished Award of Excellence, Small Bus Admin, 1994. **Business Phone:** (301)657-5800.*

COLEMAN, FRANKIE LYNN
Manager. **Personal:** Born Aug 21, 1950, Columbus, OH; daughter of Franklin L R Young and Mary A Young; married Micheal Bennett, Aug 31, 1983; children: Kimberly, Justin & John-David. **Educ:** Mount Union Col, BA, 1972; Cent Mich Univ, MA, 1974. **Career:** City Columbus, lead planner, 1974-83; State Ohio Bur Employment Serv, Job Training Partnership, dir, 1983-88; Pvt Indust Coun Columbus & Franklin Co Inc, exe dir & chief exec officer; Ohio state community affairs, dir, 2001, asst mgr work force affairs, 2006-07. **Orgs:** Employ comt chair, Governors Black Male Comn, 1990; exec bd, Ohio Job Training Partnership, 1992; fundraising co-chair, Jack & Jill, Columbus Chapt, 1993-94; Links Inc, Columbus Chapter; Nat Asn Pvt Indust; chair, Commun Comt,; Columbus Rotary Club; bd mem, Columbus One-Step Governace. **Honors/Awds:** Excellence in Community Service Award, WCKX, 1990; Woman of the Year, YMCA, 1991; Mayor's Excellence in Business Award, 1991; EEO Award, Columbus Urban League, 1992; YWCA Woman of Achievement, 1994. **Special Achievements:** Co-Author, The State of Black Males in Ohio, 1991; Induction into the Columbus Public Schools' Hall of Fame.

COLEMAN, GARY WAYNE
Business owner, actor. **Personal:** Born Feb 8, 1968, Zion, IL; son of W G and Edmonia Sue; married Shannon Price, Aug 28, 2007. **Career:** Video Game Arcade, Santa Monica, CA, owner, currently; TV Series: "The Jeffersons", 1978; "Different Strokes," 1978-84; "Good Time," 1979; "The Kid from Left Field," 1979; "The Big Show", host, 1980; "Scout's Honor", 1980; "The Gary Coleman Show", 1982; "The Jamie Foxx Show," 2000; "The-Drew Carey Show," 2001; "The Rerun Show", 2002; "A Carol Christmas", 2003; Videos: A Christmas Too Many, 2005; Films: Jimmy the Kid, 1982; Church Ball, 2006; All Comedy Radio, commentator, currently; Simmons Media Group, Salt Lake City, Utah, secy controller. **Orgs:** Honorary Gift Life Chmn Nat Kidney Found. **Honors/Awds:** Young Artist Special Award, 1980; Young Artist Award for Best Young Comedian, 1981; Young Artist Award for Best Young Actor in a Comedy Series, 1983; Young Artist Award for Best Young Actor in a Movie Made for TV, 1984. **Special Achievements:** Ranked #10 in E's cutest child stars all grown-up, 2005; Biography "Gary Coleman-Med Miracle"; Ranked 1 in VH1's list of the "100 Greatest Kid Stars". **Business Addr:** Comedian, The Artists Group, 10100 Santa Monica Blvd Suite 2490, Los Angeles, CA 90067, **Business Phone:** (310)552-1100.

COLEMAN, GEORGE EDWARD
Bandleader, saxophonist. **Personal:** Born Mar 8, 1935, Memphis, TN; son of George and Indiana Lyle; married Gloria Bell (divorced); children: George & Gloria; married Carol Hollister, Sep 7, 1985. **Career:** BB King Band, mem, 1952 & 1955; Walter Perkins' group, saxophonist, 1956-58; music shows, writer & arranger; Lenox MA Jazz Sch Music, consult, 1958; Max Roach Quintet, 1958-59; Miles Davis Quartet, 1963-64; Lionel Hampton Orchestra, 1965-66; Lee Morgan Quintet, 1969; Elvin Jones Quartet, 1970; George Coleman Quartet & George Coleman Octet, 1974-; Film appearances: Sweet Love Bitter, 1967, Freejack, 1992; Preacher's Wife, 1996; Albums: Four Generations of Miles, 2002; Danger High Voltage, 2003; private teaching jazz educ; New Sch Univ, consult & teacher; New Sch Soc Res, consult & teacher; Long Island Univ, consult & teacher; New York Univ, Mannes Sch Music, consult & teacher; Tenor alto & soprano saxophonist, currently; Albums: Revival, 1976; Dynamic Duo, 1977; Manhattan Panorama, 1989; My Horns of Plenty, 1991; At Yoshi's (Live), 1992; I Could Write a Book: The Music of Richard Rodgers, 1998; Danger High Voltage, 2000; Four Generations of Miles: A Live Tribute to Miles, 2002. **Honors/Awds:** Numerous honors & awards including International Jazz Critics Polls, 1958; Artist of the Year, Rec World Mag, 1969; Knight of Mark Twain, 1971; Grantee National Endowment of the Arts, 1975 & 1985; Beale St Musical Festival Award, 1977; Tip of the Derby Award, 1979 & 1980; New York Jazz Award, 1979; Gold Note Jazz Award, 1982; Key to the City of Memphis, 1992; Life Achievement Award, Jazz Found Am, 1997; Concertband Jazz Award, Netherlands, 2002. **Home Addr:** 63 E 9th St, New York, NY 10003, **Home Phone:** (212)982-4154. **Business Addr:** Musician, c/o Maurice Montoya Music Agency, 1133 Broadway Suite No 1605, New York, NY 10010, **Business Phone:** (212)229-9160.

COLEMAN, GILBERT IRVING
Educator. **Personal:** Born Jan 20, 1940, Fredericksburg, VA; married Pearlie Ball; children: Darryl Langston. **Educ:** Educator(retired); Va Union Univ, BS, 1960; Howard Univ, MS, 1962; Univ Va, EdD, 1980. **Career:** Microbiol Assoc, res assoc, 1962-63; Nat Inst Health, res asst, 1963-64; Smithsonian Inst, jr res analyst, 1964-68; Spotsylvania Sr HS, biol teacher, 1968-70; Germanna Community Col, instr, 1970-73, asst prof, 1973-76, assoc prof, 1976- 92, prof, 1992; div chmn, arts scis & nursing, George Mason Univ, assoc dir, 2000-. **Orgs:** Shiloh Baptist Church, 1949-; mem, Personnel Bd Mary Washington Hosp, 1984-; mem, of the bd Rappahannock Serv Corp, 1984-; Germanna Community Col Educ Found Bd. **Honors/Awds:** Man of the Year Veterans of Foreign Wars, 1984; Man of the Year Fraternal Order of Police, 1984. *

COLEMAN, HARRY THEODORE
Dentist. **Personal:** Born Jul 6, 1943, Somerville, TN; married Olivia Jackson; children: Brian, Chandra. **Educ:** Johnson C Smith Univ, BS, 1965; Meharry Med Col, DDS, 1970. **Career:** Hubbard Hosp, intership, 1970-71; bd dir, Boys Club; dentist, currently. **Orgs:** Nat Dent Asn; Shelby Co Dent Soc; Pan Tenn Dent Asn; Am Dent Asn; Memphis Jr C C; Kappa Alpha & Psifrat; Nat Asn Advan Colored people; YMCA. **Military Serv:** USN, lt, 1971-73. **Business Addr:** Dentist, 3087 Park Ave, Memphis, TN 38111-3019, **Business Phone:** (901)327-4200.*

COLEMAN, HURLEY J., JR.
Government official, executive director, commissioner. **Personal:** Born Apr 14, 1953, Saginaw, MI; son of Hurley J Jr and Martha Chatman; married Sandra Morris, Jul 18, 1981; children: Natoya Dinise, Hurley J III, Tasha Noel. **Educ:** Eastern Mich Univ, BA, com recreation admin, 1977. **Career:** Washtenaw County Parks & Recreation Comn, Ann Arbor, MI, prog specialist, 1977-78; Saginaw County Parks & Recreation Comn, Saginaw, MI, recreation prog coordr, 1979-85; City Saginaw Recreation Div, Saginaw, MI, recreation admin, 1985-89; Wayne County parks, dir, 1989, strategic planning & prog develop, asst co exec, 2001; MRPA fel, 1994; Dept Natural Resources, comnr, currently. **Orgs:** Mich State

Univ, Natural Resources/Pub Policy, 1986-88; pres, Ethnic Minority Soc, Nat Rec & Park Asn, 1987-96; exec bd mem, Saginaw County Leadership Saginaw Prog, 1987-88; chmn, Governor's Recreation Adv Comn, 1988-; pres, Mich Recreation & Park Asn, 1988; Mich State Univ, Mich Outdoor Recreation Task Force, 1988; comt mem, Nat Recreation & Park Asn; Nat Forum Black Pub Admin, United Way Saginaw County, Kappa Alpha Psi Fraternity; mem, Saginaw Human Rels Comn; Optimist Club; Lions Club; Exec mem, Michigan Recreation & Park Asn. **Honors/Awds:** Ten Outstanding Young People in Mich, Jaycees, 1986; Distinguished Alumni, Eastern Mich Univ, 1988; Community Serv Award, Phillip Randolph Inst, 1988; Serv Award, Nat Parks & Recreation Asn, 1991; Presidential Award, Nat Parks & Recreation Asn, 1995; NRPA EMS Young Prof Award, 1993; Employee of the Year, 1996. **Business Addr:** Commissioner, Department of Natural Resources, 2405 Bay Rd, Saginaw, MI 48602.*

COLEMAN, JAMES WILLIAM
Construction worker. **Personal:** Born Mar 29, 1935, Mound Bayou, MS; son of Harriet B and Gus C Sr; married Lois Bradley, Sep 12, 1964; children: Bradley C. **Educ:** Tougaloo Col, BS, 1957; Tuskegee Univ, MS, 1965; Univ Louisville, PhD, 1972. **Career:** Joseph E Seagram & Sons Inc, sr res scientist, 1969-85; Univ Louisville, Sch Med, assoc prof, 1974-79; Coleman Builders, builder, currently; Cancer Res Ctr Am, pres, chief exec officer, 1999-. **Orgs:** Beta Kappa Chi Sci Soc, 1958-; Am Soc Microbiol, 1958-85; first vpres, Louisville Br, NCP, 1972-74, 1990-92. **Military Serv:** USF, a1c, 1958-62. **Home Addr:** 8622 Blackpool Dr, Louisville, KY 40222, **Home Phone:** (502)426-5815. **Business Addr:** President, Chief Executive Officer, Cancer Research Center of America Inc, 8622 Blackpool Dr, Louisville, KY 40222, **Business Phone:** (502)339-1282.

COLEMAN, JOHN H.
Government official, building inspector. **Personal:** Born Jul 29, 1928, Memphis, TN; married Willa Nicholson; children: Patrice, Sylvia, John jr, Elissia & Tracey. **Educ:** Ind Univ, BS, phys educ, 1951; Ill Univ. **Career:** Steel mills post off, 1955-59; caseworker, 1959; off mgr, 1969; admin asst, 1972; Quad Co IL Dept Pub Aid, bldg oper supvr, 1974-. **Orgs:** Planning comn, Ill Welfare Asn; bd mem, Strong Ctr; Maple Pk United Methodist Church; prog chmn, Maple Pk Methodist Men's Club; vpres, 116 Ada St Block Club; Maple Pk Home owners Asn. **Military Serv:** USAF, 1951-55.

COLEMAN, KENNETH L.
Computer executive, founder (originator), chief executive officer. **Personal:** Born Dec 1, 1942, Centralia, IL; married Caretha; children: Kennetha, Karen, Kimberly, Kristen & Kenneth. **Educ:** Ohio State Univ, BS, indust mgt, 1965, MBA, 1972. **Career:** Hewlett-Packard Co, corp staffing mgr div personnel, mgr northern European personnel, mgr, 1972-82; Activision Inc, Product Develop, vpres human resources, vpres; Silicon Graphics Inc, Global Sales, Serv & Mkt, execvpres, sr vpres global serv, sr vpres admin & bus develop; ITM Software, founder, chmn & chief exec officer, 2001-06; Accelrys Inc, leadindependent dir, dir, 2003-, chmn, currently. **Orgs:** Bd dirs, City Nat Bank; bd dirs, MIPS Technologies; bd dirs, United Online; past pres, Peninsula Assoc Black Person Admin, 1975-; State Calif, MESA Bd, 1984-85; bd mem, Bay Area Black United Fund, 1984-85; Univ Santa Clara, Indus Adv Comn, 1984-85; Ohio State Bus Adv Bd, 1984-85; industadv, Bay Area Black MBA Asn; bd mem, San Francisco Exploratorium; Ohio State Univ Col Bus Dean's Adv Coun; bd mem, C Health Coun; bd mem, The Community Found Santa Clara County; bd mem, Univ Calif, San Francisco. **Honors/Awds:** Award for Excellence, Community Serv, San Jose, CA, 1981; Mkt Opportunities in Bus & Entertaiment award, 2001; The Ohio State Univ Distinguished Service Award; Living Legend Award, Nat Alliance Black Sch Educr; The American Leadership Forum of Silicon Valley Exemplary Leader Award; The One Hundred Black Men of Silicon Valley Lifetime Achievement Award; The Silicon Valley Jr Achievement Bus Hall of Fame. **Military Serv:** USAF, capt, 1968-72. **Business Addr:** Chairman, Accelrys Inc, 10188 Telesis Court Suite 100, San Diego, CA 92121, **Business Phone:** (858)799-5000.

COLEMAN, LEMON, JR.
School administrator. **Personal:** Born Jan 14, 1935, Pineville, LA; son of Lemon Sr and Bessie; married Dorothy Ruth Wilson; children: Valerie. **Educ:** Grambling State Univ, BS, 1957; Southern Univ, EdM, 1968. **Career:** School administrator (retired). Pinecrest St Sch Mentally Retarded, teacher, recreation worker, 1957; CC Raymond High Sch Lecompte, coach, teacher, 1960-69; Lincoln St Hosp, rec sup therapist, 1964; Boyce High Sch, coach, teacher, 1969-71; Rapides High Sch, asst prin, 1971-72; Slocum High Sch, asst prin, 1972-73; Pineville High Sch, asst prin, 1973-80, prin, 1980; Pineville Jr High Sch, prin. **Orgs:** Nat Ed Asn, 1957; La Educ Asn, 1957; Rapides Parish Educ Asn, 1957; asst exec dir, Rapides Parish Poverty Agency, 1965; Cent La Hosp Bd, 1970-, Goals La Community, 1970, Priorities La Conv, 1979; mayor pro-tem, 1979, 83; del, 8th Cong Dist Dem Party Nat Conv, 1980; Nat Asn Advan Colored People; bd dir, Family Serv Agency; Reg VI ment Health Bd; Omega Psi Phi; Bros & Sisters Solidarity; Pineville Neighborhood Coun; N Rapides Civic & Polit Orgn; Nat Black Caucus; bd dir, Boys Club Alexandria-Pineville; secy & treas, La Pub Facilities Authority. **Special Achievements:** First Negro Member in the City of Pineville Recreation Board; first Negro City Councilman in the History of Pineville; first Negro Member in the Central Louisiana Hospital Baord of Directors. **Military Serv:** USAR, E-3. *

COLEMAN, LEONARD
Baseball executive, executive. **Personal:** Born Feb 17, 1949, Newark, NJ. **Educ:** Princeton Univ, BA, 1971; Harvard Univ, MA, pub admin & MA, educ & social policy. **Career:** Protestant Episcopal Church US, consult, 1976-80; NJ Dept Community Affairs, Dept Energy, comnr, 1982; State Comn Ethical Stand, vice chmn; NJ Housing & Mortgage Finance Agency, chmn; Hackensack Meadowlands Develop Comn, chmn; Kidder, Peabody & Co, munic finance banker; Major League Baseball, Mkt Develop, dir, 1992, pres, 1994-99; H J Heinz Co, bd dirs, currently. **Orgs:** Urban Enterprise Zone Authority; Econ Develop Authority; Urban Develop Authority; pres, State Planning Comn; pres, NJ Pub Tv Comn; dir, Children's Defense Fund; dir, Metrop Opera; dir, Schumann Fund; dir, Little League Baseball; chmn, Jackie Robinson Found; pres, Nat League Prof Baseball Clubs; US chmn, Bishop Tutu Scholarship Fund; pres, Greater Newark Urban Coalition. **Special Achievements:** One of the highest ranking African-American executives in the sports world; Only the second African-American to assume the role of president of the National League. **Business Phone:** (412)456-5700.

COLEMAN, MARCO DARNELL
Football player. **Personal:** Born Dec 18, 1969, Dayton, OH; married Katrina; children: children, Kabrione & Kennedy. **Educ:** Ga Tech univ, mgt. **Career:** Football player (retired); Miami Dolphins, defensive end, 1992-95; San Diego Chargers, 1996-98; Washington Redskins, 1999-01; Jackson ville Jaguars, 2002; Philadelphia Eagles, 2003; Denver Broncos, defensive end, 2004-05; Alpha Phi Alpha. **Honors/Awds:** NFL Rookie of the Yr, Sports Illustrated, 1992; Defensive Rookie of the Yr, Football News, 1992; Pro Bowls, 2000. **Special Achievements:** Acted in movie: Ace Ventura; Pet Detective, 1994. *

COLEMAN, MARCUS
Football player. **Personal:** Born May 24, 1974, Dallas, TX. **Educ:** Tex Tech Univ, communs. **Career:** NY Jets, defensive back, 1996-2001; Houston Texans, free safety, 2002-05; Dallas Cowboys, 2006. **Orgs:** Spokesperson, Texans Blood Dr. **Honors/Awds:** All-conf hons; AFC Defensive Player of the Week, 1999; NFL Play of the Week, Direc TV, 2000; AFC Defensive Player of the Month, 2003. *

COLEMAN, MARIAN M.
Educator. **Personal:** Born Aug 7, 1948, Laurens, SC. **Educ:** Friendship Jr Col, AA, 1967; Claflin Col, BS, 1969. **Career:** Palmetto High Sch, instr, 1969-70; Benning Terrace Recreation Ctr, recreational specialist, 1970; Pamplico Middle Sch, instr, 1970-72; Laurens Community Action Inc, social worker, 1973-74; Comprehensive Employ Training Act, couns; Gleams Community Action Inc, counr, 1974-. **Orgs:** SC Educ Asn, 1969-73; asst secy, Usher Bd White Plain Baptist Church, 1973-75; adv, Youth Chap Nat Asn Advan Colored People, 1974; asst secy, April Shower Chap 184 OES, 1974-75; SC Head Start Asn, 1975. **Business Addr:** PO Box 1001, Laurens, SC 29360-1001.

COLEMAN, MELISSA SCOTT
Manager. **Career:** Detroit Advantage Acad, prin; A new Day in Detroit, campaign mgr. **Business Addr:** Campaign Manager, A new Day in Detroit, Detroit, MI 48204, **Business Phone:** (313)850-8893.

COLEMAN, MELVIN D.
Psychologist, commissioner. **Personal:** Born Oct 9, 1948, Cleveland, OH; son of James and Neda. **Educ:** Univ Wis, BS, 1969, MS, 1974; Univ Minn, cert, behavioral anal, 1978. **Career:** Youth Employ Orgn, youth counr summers, 1967-68; Cuyahoga County Welfare, social worker, 1969-70; Ohio Youth Comn, parole officer, 1970; Univ Wis, Stout, teaching asst, 1970-71; State Minn, med disability adj, 1971-72, voc rehab, 1972-79; Harley Clin, MN, psychologist, 1978-92; Inst Black Chem Abuse, consult, 1990-91; pvt pract, psychologist; MN, comnr health, currently. **Orgs:** Minn Behavioral Anal Asn, 1978-87; consult, Pilgrim Baptist Church, 1984-90, Bryn Mawr & Queen Nursing Homes, 1985-90; Gestalt Family Preserv Consult Serv, 1990; State Bd Psychol. **Honors/Awds:** Basketball Hall of Fame, Univ Wis, Stout, 1978; Black Gestalt, 1987; Reclaiming Black Child, 1989; Parenting Skills Training Cert, Prog Mothers Attempting Reunite Infant C, 1996-; BC & Phoenicia, 1998. **Special Achievements:** 1st Team Nat Asn Inter Col Athelete, Basketball All Am, 1969; 3rd Round Draft Choice, Carolina Cougars Basketball ABA, 1969; 6th Round Draft Choice, Cincinnati Royals Basketball NBA, 1969; Florence Meets Africa: A Jazz Concerto, 1988; auth: Parenting Fundamentals 101, 2000; Black Fatherhood: A Call From the Heart, 2002; established Gestalt Publications as distribution outlet for positive black literature. **Business Addr:** Commisioner, Commisioner of Health Minnesota, 625 N Robert St, St Paul, MN 55155-2538, **Business Phone:** (651)201-5810.*

COLEMAN, MICHAEL BENNETT
Government official, lawyer, mayor. **Personal:** Born Nov 18, 1954, Indianapolis, IN; son of John and Joan; married Frankie L; children: Kimberly, Justin & John David. **Educ:** Univ Cincinnati, BS, polit sci, 1977; Univ Dayton Sch Law, JD, 1980. **Career:** City Columbus, councilman, 1992-99, Columbus City Coun, pres, 1997-99; City Coun's Finance & Zoning Comt, chair; Coun Utilities's Safety & Judiciary, develop, rules & reference comt; Schottenstein, Zox & Dunn, partner; City Columbus, mayor, 2000-. **Orgs:** Nat Conf Black Lawyers, 1980-; Columbus Conv Ctr Citizens Adv Group, 1986; Downtown Develop Corp's Retailer's Task Force, 1987; vpres, Robert B Elliot Law Club, 1989; Union Grove Baptist Church; OH State Bar Asn, 1990-; Am Bar Asn, Minority Coun Demonstration Prog, 1990-; Comt Housing Network Inc; CMACAO; Columbus Youth Corps Inc; Rosemont Ctr; Veterans Memorial Conv Ctr; Black Family Adoption; Cent OH Transit Authority. **Honors/Awds:** Community Serv Award, Columbus Bar Asn; Citizen's Leadership Award; WCKX Citizen of the Week. **Special Achievements:** Accomplishments since becoming city councilman: Urban Recovery Fair to repair & rebuild the inner-city; Boys to Men Volunteers Fair (mentor prog); Bikeway Adv Comm, which designed & constructed bikeways, bikepaths, & bike routes; Neighborhood Partnership Fund; Cent City Develop Corp; Summer Urban Repair & Fix-Up Prog; "Constituency Days"; First African American mayor of Ohio's capital. **Business Addr:** Mayor, City of Columbus, City Hall 2nd Fl 90 W Broad St, Columbus, OH 43215, **Business Phone:** (614)645-7671.

COLEMAN, MICHAEL VICTOR
Government official, lawyer. **Personal:** Born Oct 12, 1953, Detroit, MI; son of Mary Elizabeth and Osborn V; married Andrea Arceneaux; children: Lauren, Ashley, Christopher, Jonathan, Justin & Jordan. **Educ:** Univ Evansville, BS, 1976; Vanderbilt Univ, Sch Law, JD, 1979. **Career:** Manson, Jackson & Assoc, law clerk, 1977-78; Tenn State Atty Gen Office, law clerk, 1978-79; Securities Divi, Tenn Dept Ins, staff atty, 1979-80; Hon Horace T Ward, law clerk, 1981-82; Wildman, Harrold, Allen, Dixon & Branch, assoc, 1982-84; Trotter, Smith & Jacobs, assoc, 1984-88, shareholder, 1988-90; City Atlanta, city atty, 1990-94; Troutman Sanders LLP, partner, 1994; Lord Bissell & Brook LLP, partner & atty, currently. **Orgs:** Grady Hospl Bd Visitors, 1983-; chmn, Gate City Bar Asson, CLE committee, 1984, exec comt, 1984-88; Butler Street YMCA, 1986; Am Civil Liberties Union Ga, 1986-88; Nat Asn Securities Prof, 1989-; Am Bar Asn; Gate City Bar Asn; Atlanta Bar Asn; bd dir, Atlanta Comt Olympic Games, 1994-99; bd mem, Metrop YMCA, 1996-98; Nat Bar Asn; bd mem, Res Atlanta, 1997-2000; trustee, Univ Ga Found, 1995-98; Vanderbilt Law Sch Alumni Bd, 1993-96. **Honors/Awds:** Outstanding Bus & Prof Award, Dollars & Sense Magazine, 1991. **Special Achievements:** Co-author, Regulatory Evolution of Limited Offerings Georgia, 1984; author, A Review of the Business Judgment Rule, 1990; panelist, The Purchase & Sale of a Going Concern, NBA Convention, 1990. **Business Addr:** Partner, Attorney, Lord Bissell & Brook LLP, Proscenium Suite 1900, 1170 Peachtree St NE, Atlanta, GA 30309, **Business Phone:** (404)870-4612.

COLEMAN, MONTE
Football player, football coach. **Personal:** Born Nov 4, 1957, Pine Bluff, AR. **Educ:** Cent Ark Univ, attended. **Career:** Football player (retired), football coach; Wash Redskins, linebacker, 1979-95; Data Distribution Serv, vpres pub rels & sales; Univ Ark, Pine Bluff, linebacker coach & team chaplain, head football coach, 2007-. **Orgs:** Co-chair, Majors City Character Bd. **Honors/Awds:** Post-season play: NFC Championship Game, 1982-83, 1986-87, NFL Championship Game, 1982-83, 1987; Redskin Ring Stars; All Madden Team, 1993; Washingtonian of the Year Award, 1996; Arkansas Hall of Fame, 1998; Redskins 70th Greatest Players, Univ Central Ark, 2003; Elijah Pitts Award, 2007. **Special Achievements:** Co-hosted his own weekly TV show on Home Team Sports "National Defense", a celebrity guest on ESPN-Talk2, BET, PSA Commercials & numerous featured guest spots on television and radio; played more games & years than any other Redskin in history, 216; helped Redskins win three Super Bowls. **Business Phone:** (870)575-8000.

COLEMAN, QUINCY
Football player. **Personal:** Born May 23, 1975, Macon, MS. **Educ:** Jackson State Univ. **Career:** Chicago Bears, defensive back; Can Football League, Edmonton Eskimos, 2001-05; Can Football League, Ottawa Renegades, free agt, 2005-. *

COLEMAN, ROBERT A
Government official, activist. **Personal:** Born Feb 8, 1932, Hopkinsville, KY; married; children: Dominic Joseph. **Educ:** Paducah Community Col. **Career:** US Postal Serv, postal carrier; Paducah, Ky, city comnr, mayor pro tem; ed, Masonic Herald. **Orgs:** Pres, Nat Asn Letter Carriers, Paducah Br 383, 1971, 73; chmn exec bd, Ky State, 1974; bd dir, Paducah McCracken County Red Cross Chap; bd dir, Boys Club Paducah; adv bd, Paducah Community Col; bd dir, Opportunity Industrialization Ctr; bd dir, Family "Y" Paducah mem, Ky Crime Comn. **Honors/Awds:** 32 Degree Mason; post masterStone Sq Lodge #5; Hall of Fame, Ky Comn Human Rights. **Military Serv:** USAF, sgt, 1950-54. **Home Addr:** 639 N 23rd St, Paducah, KY 42001, **Home Phone:** (270)442-1502.

COLEMAN, ROBERT EARL, JR.
Journalist. **Personal:** Born Jan 27, 1961, St Louis, MO; son of Robert E Coleman Sr and Fredonia West. **Educ:** St Louis Univ, St

Louis, MO, BA, 1987. **Career:** KMOX-AM, St Louis, MO, writer, ed, 1982-83; Church God Christ, St Louis, MO, dir pub rels, 1984-90; KTVI-TV, St Louis, MO, video tape ed, 1983-. **Orgs:** Nat Asn Black Journalists, 1987-; Greater St Louis Asn Black Journalists, 1987-; Nat Acad TV Arts & Scis, 1987-; Nat Asn Advan Colored People, 1988-. **Honors/Awds:** Delegate Elect to Inter Radio & TV Soc Workshop, 1984; Best Bus & Prof Speech, St Louis Univ, 1985; Best Video Content Award, United Press Int, 1987-88; Emmy Nominee, St Louis Chap, 1988, 1992; Double Black Excellence Award Winner, St Louis Asn Black Journalists, 1989; Grad Poynter Inst for Media Studies, 1990. **Business Addr:** Editor, KCAL-TV, 5515 Melrose St, Los Angeles, CA 90039, **Business Phone:** (213)960-3840.

COLEMAN, ROBERT L
Executive. **Personal:** Married Carolyn; children: 1. **Educ:** Univ Mo-Rolla, BSC; Stanford Univ, MBA. **Career:** Composite Holdings LLC, chair; Booz, Allen & Hamilton, consult; Prepac Inc, pres, ceo, gen mgr; Minority Bus Develop Ctr, exec dir, 1985; Seven-Up Bottling Co, pres, chmn, chief exec officer; Wittnauer Int, chmn, ceo; Alert Staffing, chief restructuring officer; Composite Resources LLC, managing mem, currently. **Business Addr:** Managing Member, Composite Resources LLC, PO Box 640, Bridgeton, MO 63044-0640, **Business Phone:** (314)533-4228.*

COLEMAN, RODNEY ALBERT
Executive. **Personal:** Born Oct 12, 1938, Newburgh, NY; son of Samuel C and Reba Belden; divorced; children: Terri Lynne & Stephen A. **Educ:** Howard Univ, Wash, DC, BArch, 1963; Univ Mich, Ann Arbor, MI, Exec Mgt Prog, 1988. **Career:** USAF, captain & proj architect, 1963-73; White House, White House Fel, 1970-71; Dist Columbia City Coun, exec asst chmn, 1973-78; Pa Ave Develop Corp, design consult, 1978-80; Gen Motors Corp, dir Govt rels, 1980-85, dir munic govt affairs, 1985-90, exec dir urban & Munic affairs, 1990-94; USAF, asst secy, dept Air Force, 1994-98; ICF Kaiser Int, exec vpres, 1998-99; Alcalde E Fay, partner, 1999-; bd adv, i2Telecom, 2006-; Govt Mkt & Procurement, sr adv, currently. **Orgs:** White House Fellows Asn, 1971-; bd dir, Nat Coun Urban Econ Develop, 1986-93; corporate rep, Nat League Cities, 1986-94, US Conf Mayors, 1986-94; Gen Motors rep bd, New Detroit Inc, 1986-94, Detroit Econ Growth Corp, 1986-94; Urban Affairs Comm, Greater Detroit, Chamber Com, 1986-94; corp rep, Nat Forum Black Pub Admin, 1987-94; Exec Leadership Coun, 1991-; chmn, bd adv, Mus Aviation, 1999-; trustee, Air Force Aid Soc, 1998-2004; bd dir, Wash Hosp Ctr, 2003-05. **Honors/Awds:** Pony Baseball Man of the Year, Pony League, Newburgh, NY, 1960; The Air Force Commendation Medal, 1965; The Air Force Meritorious Service Medal, 1968; Republic of Vietnam Honor Medal, 1st Class, 1972; The Bronze Star Medal, 1972; Distinguished Alumus Award, Newburgh Free Acad, 1994; Distinguished Alumni Award for Postgraduate Achievement in Corporate and Government Service, Howard Univ, 1996; Distinguished Achievement Award, The Tuskegee Airmen, 1996; The Black Engineer of the Year Dean's Award, 1996; Execptional Civilian Service Award, USAF, 1997. **Military Serv:** USAF, Capt, proj architect, 1963-73. **Business Addr:** Partner, Alcalde & Fay, 2111 Wilson Blvd 8th Fl, Arlington, VA 22030.

COLEMAN, DR. RONALD GERALD
Educator, association executive. **Personal:** Born Apr 3, 1944, San Francisco, CA; son of Gertrude Coleman Hughes and Jesse Coleman; children: Danielle D, Joron S & Cori D. **Educ:** Univ Utah, BS, sociol, 1966, PhD, hist, 1980; Calif State Univ, Sacramento, CA, teaching cert sec, 1968, MA, soc sci, 1973. **Career:** Gen Mills Inc, grocery sales rep, 1966-67; San Francisco Unified Sch Dist, fac teacher social studies phys ed, 1968-70; Sacramento City Col, fac instr social sci, 1970-73; Univ Utah, Afro-Am Studies, dir, 1981-, coordr ethnic studies, 1984-, assoc prof hist, Diversity & Fac Develop, assoc vpres, prof hist, currently, Honors Col, affiliated fac, currently, African Am Studies, coordr, currently; Calif State Univ, Haywood, vis prof Afro-Am studies, 1981. **Orgs:** Consult, Utah State Cultural Awareness Training Prog, 1974-76; Phi Kappa Phi 1979; consult, Utah State Hist Soc, 1981; consult, Utah State Bd Educ, 1981; Utah Endowment Humanities, 1982-88; commnr, Salt Lake City Civ Serv Comn, 1983-; chairperson, Salt Lake City Br, Nat Asn Advan Colored People Educ Comn, 1984-85; Utah Chap, Am Civil Liberties Union, 1989-; Salt Lake Sports Adv Bd, 1990-. **Honors/Awds:** Merit Society for Distinguished Alumni George Washington High School; Hatch Price Award for Distinguished Teaching, Univ Utah, 1990. **Business Addr:** Professor of History, Coordinator of African American Studies, University of Utah, Department of History, Rm 00211 Carlson Hall 380 S 1400 E, Salt Lake City, UT 84112, **Business Phone:** (801)581-6990.

COLEMAN, RONNALD DEAN
Bodybuilder, police officer. **Personal:** Born May 13, 1964, Monroe, LA; son of Jessie Benton; children: Jamilleah & Valencia Daniel. **Educ:** Grambling State Univ, BS, acct, 1986. **Career:** Bodybuilder (etired), Police Officer; Arlington Police Dept, res police officer, 1989-; professional bodybuilder. **Honors/Awds:** Mr. Texas, 1990; World Amateur Championships, 1991; Mr. Olympia, 1998-06; Admiral in the Texas Navy Certificate Award, 2001. **Special Achievements:** featured in various magazines. **Home Phone:** (817)465-3676. **Business Addr:** Reserve Police Officer, Arlington Police Dept, 620 W Division St, Arlington, TX 76011, **Business Phone:** (817)459-5600.*

COLEMAN, RUDY B.
Judge. **Personal:** Born Jan 1, 1947?, Tams, WV; married Marguerite; children: Matthew. **Educ:** Marshall Univ, BA, 1968; State Univ NJ, Sch Law, JD, 1974. **Career:** Carpenter, Bennett & Morissey law firm, atty; US Dist Ct Dist NJ, 1974; US Ct Appeals 3rd Circuit, 1976; US Ct Federal Claims, 1978; Richard J. Hughes Am Inn of Ct, Master & treas, 1991-; Super Ct, NJ, judge, 1995-03, Appellate Div, 2002-. **Orgs:** Comn Rules Prof Conduct, Supreme Ct, NJ; Comn on Prof Law, Supreme Ct, NJ; Vicinage Adv Comt Minority Concerns; NJ Bar Asn; Am Arbitration Asn; co-chair, Comt Prods Liability, Am Bar Assn; subcomt, Automobile Prod Liability; Kappa Alpha Psi; Kappa Delta Pi; mem bd trustees, Essex County Bar Asn, 1987-90; secy, Essex County Bar Asn, 1990-91; treas, Essex County Bar Asn, 1991-92; pres, Essex County Bar Asn, 1992-94. **Business Addr:** Judge, State of NJ Super Court Appellate Div, 155 Morris Avenue, Springfield, NJ 07081-1216, **Business Phone:** (973)921-9181.*

COLEMAN, DR. SINCLAIR B
Economist, statistician. **Personal:** Born Feb 17, 1946, Halifax, VA; son of N Wyatt and Bessie Bowman. **Educ:** Hampton Inst, BA, 1967; Univ Chicago, MS, 1970; Rand Grad Sch, PhD, 1975. **Career:** US Cong Budget Off, analytic staff, 1976-78; The Rand Corp, res staff, consult, 1968-76, 1978-. **Honors/Awds:** Woodrow Wilson Fel, Univ Chicago, 1967-68. **Special Achievements:** Published numerous articles, reports & reviews; sem & briefings univs, rsch inst, govt agencies, confs, & prof meetings. **Home Addr:** 112 19th Pl, Manhattan Beach, CA 90266-4517.

COLEMAN, TREVOR W
Journalist. **Personal:** Born Jan 12, 1960, Hudson, NY; son of Leonard Gresham and Mary C; married Karl Elaine Coleman, Sep 3, 1988; children: Sydnie Lianne & Trevor W II. **Educ:** Ohio State Univ, BA, 1986. **Career:** Author: Cover Story Emerge Mag : Clarence Thomas, 1993; Cover Story Emerge Mag: Clarence Thomas, 1996; "Friend of a Friend", 1996; Affirm Action Wars, 1998; Satin Mag, reporter, 1985-86; The Times-Leader, reporter, 1987; The Hartford Courant, reporter, 1987-90; The Detroit News, reporter, 1990-93; The Cincinnati Enquirer, ed writer, 1993-94; The Hartford Courant, columnist & reporter, 1994-96; Knight Ctr Specialized Jour, Univ Md, fel, 1996; The Detroit Free Press, ed writer, 1996-97; Free Press, replacement worker, 1997-, ed writer, currently, chief writer to Governor, 2003-. **Orgs:** The Nat Asn Black Journalist, 1987-; vice chair, The Nat Conf Ed Writers, Mny Concerns Com, 1994-; The Detroit Press Club, 1992-; Alpha Phi Alpha Fraternity Inc, 1982-; Detroit Chap Nat Asn Black Journalist, 1990-; The Ohio State Univ Black Alumni Soc, 1990-. **Honors/Awds:** Distinguished Alumni Award, Kappa Chap & Alpha Phi Alpha, 1992; Award News Reporting, Detroit Press Club, 1992; Unity Award, Lincoln Univ, 1st Place Coverage Minority Affairs & Soc Issues, 1992; Best Gannet Award, Pub Serv Reporting, 1992; Award for Distinguished Jour, Columbia County, Nat Asn Advan Colored People, 1992; Pulitzer Prize, Pub Serv Reporting, 1992; Detroit Press Club, 1998; Pulitzer Prize for Ed Writing, 1999; MI Press Asn Award for column writing, 1999; Lincoln University Award for Magazine writing, 2000; Nat Asn of Black Journalists Award for commentary, 2000; American Diabetes Asn Award, 2000. **Special Achievements:** Hudson NY High School, Commencement Speaker, 1994. **Business Addr:** Editorial Writer, Free Press, 100 Main St, PO Box 28, Northampton, MA 01061.

COLEMAN, VERONICA F
Government official, advocate. **Personal:** Daughter of Robert and Mary Freeman. **Educ:** Howard Univ; Memphis State Univ, JD. **Career:** Fed Express Corp, sr atty; Memphis State Univ, legal coun, pres; dist atty; gen pub defender; Western Dist Tenn, US atty, 1993-2001; Nat Inst Law & Equity, NILE, pres & chief exec officer, currently. **Orgs:** Asst Tenn Comn Criminal Rules Procedures; Law bd examiners; adv bd, Univ Tenn Health Sci Ctr; bd dir, Bank Bartlett. **Special Achievements:** Third African-Am female US Atty in the country. **Business Phone:** (901)448-1298.

COLEMAN, WANDA (WANDA EVANS)
Lecturer, entertainer, writer. **Personal:** Born Nov 13, 1946, Los Angeles, CA; married Austin Straus, May 1, 1984; children: Anthony, Tunisia & Ian Wayne Grant. **Career:** Writer; poet & performer; NBC-TV, Days Our Lives, staff writer, 1975-76; Loyola Mary mount, Dept English, Fletcher Jones Chair, 1994; Books: Art In The Court of The Blue Fag (chapbook), 1977; Mad Dog Black Lady, 1979; Heavy Daughter Blues: Poems & Stories 1968-86, 1987; A War of Eyes & Other Stories, 1988; Dicksboro Hotel & Other Travels, 1989; African Sleeping Sickness: Stories & Poems, 1990; Breaking Ice-Contemporary African-American Fiction, 1991; Hand Dance, 1993; American Sonnets(chapbook), 1994; Native in a Strange Land: Trails & Tremors, 1996; Norton Anthology of African American Literature, 1997; Bathwater Wine, 1998; Mambo Hips & Make Believe, novel, 1999; Mercurochrome New Poems, 2001; Ostinato Vamps, Pitt Poetry Series, 2003; The Riot Inside Me, 2005, Jazz and Twelve O' Clock Tales, 2008; Anthologies: African American Writers in The West, 2001; Off the Cuffs: Poetry By & About The Police, 2002; A Stranger Among Us, 2007; Letters to Younger Poets, 2008. Recorded on: Twin Sisters, 1985; Black Angeles, 1988; On Nation of Poets, 1990; High Priestess of Word, 1990; Black & Blue News, 1990; Berserk On Hollywood Blvd, 1992. **Orgs:** Authors Guild, Writers Guild Am, W, 1969-; PEN Ctr, USA, W, honorary mem 1983-. **Honors/Awds:** Emmy Award, Academy TV Arts & Sci, 1976; NEA fel, 1981; Guggenheim fel, 1984; Writing Woman's Building, LA, 1988, poetry, 1989, fiction, 2002, Calif Arts Council fel; Harriette Arnow Simpson Prize for Fiction, Am Voice, 1990; Lenore Marshall Poetry Prize, 1999; National Book Awards, bronze-medal finalist, poetry, 2001;Vesta Award, 2002; COLA-Los Angeles Dept Cultural Affairs, 1st literary fellow, 2003-04. **Business Addr:** Author, c/o David R Godine Publishers Inc, Black Sparrow Books, 9 Hamilton Place 3rd Fl, Boston, MA 02108-4715, **Business Phone:** (617)451-9600.

COLEMAN, WARREN B.
Educator. **Personal:** Born Aug 8, 1932, Swarthmore, PA; married Carole Berry; children: Warren, Kim, Fawn & Carole. **Educ:** Hampton Inst, BS, 1956; Pa State Univ, MED, 1974. **Career:** Pa State Univ, asst prof, phys educ, 1968-; Carver High Sch, Newport News. head football & track, coach, 1956-68; Heritage Realty Group Inc,owner. **Orgs:** Real Estate Asn; bd dir, Pa State Univ, Black Christian Fel; originator,Black Cultural Ctr, Pa State Univ. **Military Serv:** AUS, 2d, lt.

COLEMAN, WILLIAM T., JR.
Lawyer, executive. **Personal:** Born Jul 7, 1920, Germantown, PA; married Lovida Hardin; children: William T III, Louida Jr & Hardin L. **Educ:** Univ Pa, AB, 1941; Harvard Bus Sch; Harvard Law Sch, LLB, 1946. **Career:** Harvard Law Review, ed; Judge Herbert F Goodrich US Ct Appeals 3rd Circuit, law secy, 1947-48; Justice Felix Frankfurter Assoc, Judge Supreme Ct, law secy, 1948-49; Paul Weiss Rif kind Wharton & Garrison NY, assoc, 1949-52; City Philadelphia, spec coun transit matters, 1952-63; Dilworth Paxson Kalish Levy & Coleman, partner law firm, 1956-75; South Eastern Pa Transp Authority, spec coun, 1968-; US Dept Transp, secy, 1975-77; dir, Pan Am World Airways Inc; dir, IBM; dir, Pepsi Co; dir, Chase Manhattan Corp; dir, Amax Inc; dir, CIGNA Corp; O'Melveny & Meyer, sr partner & sr counr, 1977-. **Orgs:** Vpres, Philadelphia Mus Art; chmn bd, Nat Asn Advan Colored People Legal Defense & Educ Fund; trustee, Rand Corp; trustee, Brookings Inst; fel Am Col Trial Lawyers; fel, Am Col of Appellate Lawyers; Trilateral Commun Coun Foreign Rels; officer, Fr Legion Honor; coun, Am Law Inst; Am Bar Asn; Am Bar Asn Task Force Judicial Admin; Philadelphia Bar Asn; DC Bar Asn; Am Arbitration Asn; Bd Trustees, Carnegie Institution of Washington; Brookings Institution; Philadelphia Museum of Art (Vice President); New York City Ballet, Inc.; Bd Dir, Nat Symphony Orchestra; Trustee Coun, Nat Gallery of Art. **Honors/Awds:** Pres Medal Freedom; Thurgood Marshall Lifetime Achievement Award, Nat Asn Advan Colored People Legal Defense & Educ Fund. **Special Achievements:** Author, co-author contributor numerous legal writings. **Business Addr:** Senior Partner, Senior Counselor, O'Melveny & Myers LLP, 1625 Eye St NW, Washington, DC 20006, **Business Phone:** (202)383-5300.*

COLEMAN, WISDOM F
Dentist, educator, administrator. **Personal:** Born Jun 20, 1944, Batesville, MS; married Veronica Freemon; children: Wisdom III, Daivd & Anthony. **Educ:** Howard Univ, BS, 1965, DDS, 1969; MPHA. **Career:** Emory Col Dent, instr; VA Hosp, St Louis, internship, 1969-70; VA Hosp, Atlanta GA, dentist, 1970-71; Univ Tenn Health Sci Ctr, assoc prof, currently, assoc dean, admis & stud affairs, currently. **Orgs:** Dental dir, Memphis & Shelby Co Head Start, 1974-77; exec secy, Pan Tenn Dental Soc; pres, Shelby County Dent Soc, 1974-77. **Honors/Awds:** Dean's honor society, Univ Tenn, 1976. **Business Addr:** Associate Dean, Associate Professor, University of Tennessee Health Science Center, College of Dentistry, 875 Union Ave, Memphis, TN 38163.

COLEMAN-BURNS, DR. PATRICIA WENDOLYN
Educator. **Personal:** Born Nov 23, 1947, Detroit, MI; daughter of Jessie Mae Ray and Dandie; married John II, Jul 29, 1977; children: Robert Burns. **Educ:** Wayne State Univ, Detroit, Mich, BA, 1969, MA, 1978, PhD, commun & rhet criticism, 1987. **Career:** Motown Rec, Detroit, Mich, admin asst, 1969-72; Inst Labor Studies, Detroit, Mich, part time fac, 1972-87; Wayne State Univ Detroit, Mich, speech comt, grad asst, 1972-76, Africana studies, grad asst, 1976-78, part-time fac, Africana studies, lectr, 1978-91; Univ Mich, Off Multicultural Affairs, asst prof & dir, 1991-. **Orgs:** Chairperson, WSU Pres Comn Status Women, 1985-89; Pres Coun Non-Discrimination, Affirmative Action, 1986-90; pres, bd dirs, Women's Justice Ctr, 1990-. **Honors/Awds:** Faculty Research Award, WSU, 1987-88; Woman of the Year, Dorcas Soc, 1988; Participant, Summer Inst Women Higher Educ, 1990; Fel, Nat Coun Black Studies, 1990; Faculty Research Award, Univ Mich, 1992-93. **Business Addr:** Assistant Professor, Director-Office of Multicultural Affairs, University of Michigan School of Nursing, 400 N Ingalls Bldg Rm 1179, Ann Arbor, MI 48109-0482, **Business Phone:** (734)936-1615.

COLEMAN JAMES, PATRICIA REA
Lawyer. **Personal:** Born Jun 22, 1959, Tachikawa, Japan; married. **Educ:** Univ Calif, Los Angeles, CA, BS, 1982; George Wash

Univ, JD, 1990. **Career:** Fliesler Dubb Meyer & Lovejoy, 1990-94; Limbach & Limbach LLP, assoc, 1994-98; Limbach & Limbach, LLP, partner, 1998-2000; McCutchen Doyle Porown & Enersen LLP, partner, 2001-02; Abbott Labs, patent coun, 2002-, corp liaison. **Orgs:** Mem pro pono comt, Abbott Labs; mem exec comt, Nat Bar Asn. **Business Addr:** Patent Counsel, Abbott Laboratories, Counsel, Patents and Trademarks, Dept 377 Bldg Apt 6a-1 100 Abbott Pk Rd, Abbott Park, IL 60064-6008, **Business Phone:** (847)937-4558.

COLEMAN MORRIS, VALERIE DICKERSON
Journalist. **Personal:** Born Nov 25, 1946, Philadelphia, PA; son of William O and Vivien A; married Robert Lee Morris Jr, Dec 31, 1993; children: Michon Allyce & Ciara Ashley. **Educ:** San Jose State Col, BS, 1968; Columbia Univ, Grad Sch Jour, MA, broadcast jour, 1969. **Career:** KRON-TV, production asst & res, 1969-73; KGO-TV, reporter, 1974-79; KRON-TV, news anchor/reporter, 1979-82; KGO-TV, news anchor/reporter, 1982-85; KCBS-Radio, news anchor, 1985-87; KCBS-TV, news anchor/reporter, 1987-89; KCBS-Radio, news anchor, 1989; WPIX-TV, reporter, 1996; CNN, fin, reporter, 1996-07; narrator, currently. **Orgs:** Delta Sigma Theta Sorority, 1968-; Oakland Bay Area Links, 1989-; Hearing Soc Bay Area, vpres, 1983-; Chronic Fatigue Fund, adv bd, 1984-; Children's Hosp, bd dir, 1990-92; Alumnae Resources, vpres, 1990-. **Honors/Awds:** Received three Emmy Awards between 1975 & 1988; RTNDA Best Live Coverage News Story, Class A Division, "Earthquake", 1987; Soulbeat Civic Award, 1990; Natl Org Women, Los Angeles Chapter, Award of Courage, 1987. **Home Addr:** 3794 W Placita Del Correca, Tucson, AZ 85745.

COLE-MCFADDEN, CORA. See MCFADDEN, CORA.

COLEMON, REV. DR. JOHNNIE (JOHNNIE COLEMON NEDD)
Clergy. **Personal:** Born in Columbus, MS; daughter of John Haley and Lula Haley; married Don Nedd. **Educ:** Wiley Col, BA, 1943, DD, 1977, DHL; Monrovia Col, DDiv; GMOR, PhD, 2003. **Career:** Chicago Mkt Ctr, price analyst; Chicago Pub Schs, teacher; Christ Univ Temple, founder, minister, pres emer, currently; Christ Univ Temple Better Living, pastor, founder & minister, 1974-; Johnnie Colemon Inst, founder & pres, 1974-. **Orgs:** Pres, Exec Bd Unity Sch Christianity; Univ Found Better Living; guest speaker, Festival Mind & Body, London, Eng; Int Thought Alliance; dist pres, bd dir & chair, 60th Anniversary INTA Cong; New Thought Church World; guest speaker, AKA Boule 1986; guest speaker, Prayer BreakfastAtlanta, Ga; dir, Chicago Port Authority; comnr, Chicago Transit AuthorityOversight Comt. **Honors/Awds:** Tremendous Ten Years, Unity Chicagoland Asn, 1966; Deep Appreciation,Unity Asn Unity Churches, 1969-70; major contributions, Asn Unity Churches, 1970; Golden Anniversary Award, Alpha Kappa Alpha Sor, 1972; Recognition Award, First CP Church, 1972; Service to Youth Award, YMCA, 1973; Outstanding Achievement in Gospel Ministry Youth for Christ, 1974; Love with Sincere Appreciation Award, Hillside Chapel & Truth Ctr, 1974;Outstanding Christian Service, Civic Liberty League Ill, 1974; Women's Day Ann Black Excell Operation, PUSH, 1974; The Year of the Woman Award, PUSH Found, 1975; Certificate of Appreciation, Chicago Coun, BSA, 1975;Certificate of Appreciation, Comt Civic & Cult Affairs, 1975; Outstanding& Dedicated Service as chairperson 60th Anniversary, INTA Cong, 1975; Blackbook's Humanitarian Award, Blackbook Bus & Ref Guide 1; Excellence in Religion, PUSH Found, 1977; 100 Outstanding Black Women Dallas, 1985; Blackbook's Par Excellence 1986; Dr Martin L King Drum Major Award, 1987;Candace Award, 1987; Appreciation Award for Service Thompson Company Singers, 1989; Stellar Award For Inspiration Central City Productions, 1991; Minister of the Century, Int New Thought Alliance; African American History Maker, DuSable Mus; Ministry of the Century Award, International New Thought Alliance (INTA), 2000; Turner Broadcasting Systems Tower of Power Award, 2002. **Special Achievements:** Author, Open Your Mind and Be Heard, 1997; First Black woman of executiveboard of Unity School of Christianity; guest speaker & consult, seen onradio & TV shows; "A Woman Called Johnnie" TV Channel 2. **Business Addr:** President Emeritus, Christ Universal Temple, 11901 S Ashland Ave, Chicago, IL 60643, **Business Phone:** (773)568-2282.

COLES, DR. ANNA BAILEY
School administrator, nursing home administrator. **Personal:** Born Jan 16, 1925, Kansas City, KS; daughter of Gordon Alonzo and Lillie Mai Buchanan Thomas; married Herbert R Coles, May 19, 1953 (divorced); children: Margot, Michelle, Gina. **Educ:** Avila Col, Kansas City, Mo, BS, nursing, 1958; Catholic Univ Am, Wash, DC, MS, nursing, 1960, PhD, 1967. **Career:** School administrator (retired); Va Hosp, Topeka, KS, supvr, 1950-58; Freedmen's Hosp, Wash, DC, dir nursing, 1961-68; Howard Univ Col Nursing, Wash, DC, dean, 1968-86. **Orgs:** Inst Med; Nat League Nursing; Alpha Kappa Alpha Sorority; pres, Societas Docta Inc; dir, Minority Develop Univ Kansas Sch Nursing, Kansas City, Kansas, 1991-95. **Honors/Awds:** Sustained Superior Performance, Dept Health, Educ & Welfare, 1965; Avila Medal Honor, Avila Col, 1967; Distinguished Alumni Award, Howard Univ, 1990; Alumni Award in Nursing, Avila Col, 2006. *

COLES, BIMBO
Basketball player, radio host, basketball executive. **Personal:** Born Apr 22, 1968, Covington, VA. **Educ:** Va Polytech Inst & State Univ, Blacksburg, VA, 1990. **Career:** Basketball player (retired), basketball executive; Miami Heat, guard, 1990-96, 2003-04, asst coach & advan scout, 2005-; Golden State Warriors, 1996-99; US Olympic team, 1998; Atlanta Hawks, 1999-2000; Cleveland Cavaliers, 2000-03; Boston Celtics, 2002-03; 560 WQAM Sports Radio, "Opening Tip with Bimbo Coles," host, 2006-. **Honors/Awds:** Bronze Medal, Olympics, Seoul, 1988; Virginia Tech Sports Hall of Fame. **Business Addr:** Assistant Coach, Advance Scout, Miami HEAT, AmericanAirlines Arena, 601 Biscayne Blvd, Miami, FL 33132.

COLES, DARNELL
Baseball player, sports manager. **Personal:** Born Jun 2, 1962, San Bernardino, CA; married Shari; children: Deanna. **Educ:** Orange Coast Col, Costa Mesa, CA. **Career:** Seattle Mariners, infielder 1983-85; Detroit Tigers, infielder, 1986-87; Pittsburgh Pirates, infielder & outfielder, 1987-88; Seattle Mariners,infielder & outfielder, 1988-90; Detroit Tigers, infielder & outfielder,1990; Toronto Blue Jays, 1992-94; St Louis Cardinals, 1995; colorado rockies, 1997; Countryside High Sch, coach; Vermont Lake Monsters, manager. Syracuse Chiefs, Batting Coach, currently. **Business Phone:** (315)474-7833.*

COLES, JOHN EDWARD
Chief executive officer. **Personal:** Born Jul 18, 1951, Roanoke, VA; married Jerelena Perdue; children: Caron N, Jonlyn E, John E Jr & Christin N. **Educ:** Tenn State Univ, attended 1970; Hampton Univ, BS, bus mgt, 1973. **Career:** Citizens Budget Adv Comt, mem, 1980-81; Consumer Credit Counsling Peninsula, mem, 1982; Bd Educ, City Hampton, Va, mem, 1982-83; A Builders Va, dir, 1983; People Savings & Loan Asn, former exec secy & chief managing officer, former pres. **Orgs:** Keeper fin, Omega Psi Phi Frat Zeta Omicron, 1977-80; Va Peninsula Econ Develop Coun, 1982-; treas, Peninsula Asn Ment Retardation, 1982-84; pres, Citizen's Boys Club, Hampton, 1982-84; life mem, Nat Asn Advan Colored People; Omega Psi Phi Fraternity. **Honors/Awds:** Outstanding Young Men of America Award, 1981; Distnguished Leadership Award, United Negro Col Fund, 1982; Omega Man of Year, Omega Psi Phi Frat Zeta Omicron Chap, Hampton, Va, 1982.

COLES, KIMBERLEY
Actor, writer, television producer. **Personal:** Born Jan 11, 1966, Brooklyn, NY; divorced. **Career:** Lane Bryant clothing stores, spokesperson; The Single Life According to Kim Coles, 1997; Kids in America, 2005; Wig, 2009; TV series: "Bigger Brother", 1990; "Deandra and Them", 1996; "Forgive Us Our Trespasses", 1997; "Mary Christmas", 2000; "Follow That Car", 2004; Real Gay, 2005; Hell on Earth, 2007; Living Single: The Reunion Show, 2008; "10 Items or Less", 2009. **Orgs:** Delta Sigma Theta Sorority. **Honors/Awds:** Nominated for 3 NAACP Image Awards as Best Actress in a Comedy for herwork on "Living Single," 1996-98; nominated as Best Supporting Actress for a guest appearance on "Frasier," 2001. **Special Achievements:** Appeared in commercials for BurgerKing and Sears; performed "Homework", HERE Theater in NYC; Book: I'm Free, But It'll Cost You. **Business Phone:** (213)965-7327.*

COLES, ROBERT TRAYNHAM
Architect. **Personal:** Born Aug 24, 1929, Buffalo, NY; son of George Edward and Helena Vesta; married Sylvia Rose Meyn, Mar 28, 1953; children: Marion B & Darcy E. **Educ:** Univ Minn, BA, 1951, BArch, 1953; MIT, MArch 1955; Hampton Inst, attended. **Career:** Perry Shaw Hepburn & Dean, 1955-57; Shepley Bulfinch Richardson & Abbot, 1957-58; Carl Koch & Assoc, designer, 1958-59; Boston Architectural Ctr, 1957-59; NY State Univ Col, 1967, Hampton Inst, 1968-70, Univ Kans, teacher, 1969; Adv Planning Assoc, assoc, 1959-60; Techbuilt Inc, design mgr, 1959-60; Deleuw Cather & Brill Engrs, coord architect, 1960-63; Robert Traynham Coles Architect PC, pres, 1963-; Am Inst Architects, dep vice pres minority affairs, 1974-75; Univ Kans, pro architecture & urban studies; Carnegie Mellon Univ, Pittsburgh, PA, assoc prof, 1990-95. **Orgs:** Consult, Union Carbide Corp, 1963; treas, 1975-77, vpres, 1977-79, Nat Org Minority Architects; secy, bd dir, Preserv League NY State Inc, 1976-; AIA, Comt Planning Assistance Ctr; Assoc Comn Design Develop Ctr; NY State Assoc Architects; mayors adv comn, Buffalo Urban Caucus, BANC; Cit Adv Coun; Goals Met Buffalo; comt, Urban Univ; E Side Comn Org; Ellicott Talbert Study Comt; NY State Sub-Comn US Comt Civil Rights; Comt Community Improvement; Friendship House Study Comt; vpres, Buffalo Arch Guidebook Corp, 1979-82; pres, Am Arch Mus & Resource Ctr, 1980-82; trustee, Western NY Pub Broadcasting Assoc, 1981-; Fel AIA, 1981, exec comt, 1990-95, chancellor, 1995; NY State Bd Archit, 1984-; comnr, Erie County Horizons Waterfront Comt, 1989-94; chair, NY State Bd Archi, 1990-91. **Honors/Awds:** Outstanding Professor Achievement, Urban League, 1961; Centennial Medal, Honorary Doctor of Letter, Medaille Col, 1975; Whitney E Young Award, AIA, 1981; Langston Hughes Distinguished Professor of Architecture & Urban Design, Univ Kans, 1989; Sam Gibbons Chair Nominee, Univ S Fla, Tampa, FL, 1990; Citizen of Distinction, City Buffalo, 1997; Alumni Achievement Award, Univ Minn Col Archit & Landscape Archit, 1997. **Business Addr:** President, Robert Traynham Coles Architect PC, 295 Main St Suite 730, Buffalo, NY 14203, **Business Phone:** (716)842-2280.*

COLIN, GEORGE H.
Educator, funeral director. **Personal:** Born in Cleveland, OH. **Educ:** Col conserv Music Cincinnati, Mus B; Temple Bible Col, BA; Miami Univ, MA; Temple Bible Col & Sem, SMD. **Career:** Cincinnati, teacher music; Geo H Colin Mortuary, owner, currently. **Orgs:** Pres, Buckeye State Funeral Dirs & Embalmers Asn; bd dirs, Nat Asn Advan Colored People Cincinnati Br; trustee, Temple Bible Col; bd mem, Small Bus Found Cincinnati; Phi Mu Alpha Fraternity; Hamilton Co Black Caucus; Am Guild Organists; Nat Funeral Dirs Asn. **Honors/Awds:** Hon Dr Music, 1962. **Military Serv:** AUS, sp4. **Business Addr:** Owner, Geo H Colin Mortuary, 1309 Calif Ave, Cincinnati, OH 45237.*

COLIN, KATHLEEN
Executive. **Career:** Prudential Securities Inc, vpres, 1998-; Intercapital Securities Harbourside Financial, NJ, rep, currently. **Orgs:** Pres Detroit Chap, Nat Asn Securities Professionals, first vpres, 2008.

COLLETON, KATRINA (KATRINA YVETTE COLLETON)
Basketball player, basketball coach. **Personal:** Born Mar 17, 1971; daughter of Pamela. **Educ:** Univ Md, criminal justice, 1993; Barry Univ. **Career:** Rananna, Israel, pro basketball player, 1995-96; Los Angeles Sparks, forward, 1997-98; Miami, forward, 2000-01; Barry Univ, asst coach, 2001-02. *

COLLETON, KATRINA YVETTE. See COLLETON, KATRINA.

COLLEY, NATHANIEL S.
Playwright. **Personal:** Born Jun 8, 1956, Sacramento, CA; son of Nathaniel S Colley Sr and Jerlean J; married Toni Denise Conner (divorced); children: Jasmine Nicole, Aishah Simone, Mazuri Francis. **Educ:** Univ Mich, BA, 1977, Law Sch, JD, 1979; Univ Calif, Davis, grad study, anthropol. **Career:** Colley-Lindsey & Colley, partner, 1980; Sextus Prod, partner, 1974-; WCBN-FM Radio Sta, gen mgr, 1979, prog dir, 1978, talk show host, 1976-78, disc jockey, 1974-76; Nat Colley Law Off, atty, currently; Sacramento law firm Colley, Lindsey & Colley, partner; McGeorge Law Sch, adj prof; Playwright: The Shoebox; A Sensitive Man; The Doctor of Rome; Moving Arts; Films: The Abortion of Mary Williams. **Orgs:** Nat bd dirs, Nat Asn Advan Colored People, 1972-75; Am Legion Boy's State, CA, 1973; Calif Youth Senate, 1973; Univ Mich Asn Black Communicators, 1974; vpres, Sacramento Nat Asn Advan Colored People Youth Coun, 1973-74; Black Music Asn, 1979-; Calif Bar Asn, 1980. **Honors/Awds:** National Merit Scholarship Finalist, 1974; Finalist, Showtime's Black Filmmaker Prog, premiered on Showtime, 1998. **Business Addr:** Attorney, The Law Office of National Colley, PO Box 741825, Los Angeles, CA 90004, **Business Phone:** (323)769-5753.*

COLLIE, KELSEY E
Educator, administrator, talent agent. **Personal:** Born Feb 21, 1935, Miami, FL; son of James George and Elizabeth Malinda Moxey; married; married Joyce Jenkins Brown, Dec 28, 1995 (divorced); children: Kim Denyse & Vaughn Hayse. **Educ:** Hampton Inst, AB, 1957; George Wash Univ, MFA, 1970; Howard Univ, PhD, 1979. **Career:** Libr Cong, accessioner & doc librn, 1960-70; Col Fine Arts Drama Dept, prof & asst dean, 1976-79; Kelsey E Collie Playmakers Repertory Co, artistic dir, 1976-; Diva Productions, artistic dir, 1986-87; Howard Univ, C's Theatre, 1973-91; playwright; Kelsey E Collie Talent Assoc, talent mgr; Howard Univ, prof drama, 1973-95, consult, currently; Color Me Human Players Inc, currently; Kelsey E Collie C Theatre Experience, artistic dir & owner, currently. **Orgs:** Bd dir, Pierce Warwick Adoption Serv, 1973-89; Am Community Theatre Asn, 1977-87; Theatre Arts Prods Inc, 1980-87; Artist-in-Educ Panel DC Comn Arts, 1983-85; Am Coun Arts, 1985-86; Black Theatre Network, 1986-; artistic dir, Color Me Human Players, 1986-; pres, OPM Prods, 1991-93; exec dir, Nat African Am C's Theatre, currently; founder, Howard Univ C's Theater; moderator, Helen Hayes Theatre Legacy Proj. **Honors/Awds:** President's Award, 1977, Premiere Award, 1979, Dundalk Int Maytime Festival, Ireland; Community Service Award, Salisbury Cult Arts Comm, 1978; Distinguished Service Award, Univ Without Walls, 1980; Coalition of Prof Youth on the Move Award, 1981; Appreciation Award, Syphax Sch, Wash DC, 1989; dir, Night of the Divas: Tribute to Marian Anderson, J F Kennedy Ctr, 1985; Mainline to Stardom Award, 1996. **Special Achievements:** Plays: Black Images! Black Reflections, 1977, Brother, Brother, Brother Mine, 1979, directed productions at Howard Univ, Kennedy Ctr, Lincoln Ctr, Loyola Univ, Uriah McPhee Sch & Caribana Festival, conducted workshops in the former Czecho- slovakia, Finland, Bahamas, Canada & across US; authored several articles, contributed to Nellie McCaslin's Theatre for Young Audiences. **Military Serv:** AUS, sp4, 1958-60. **Home Addr:** 1924 Shepherd St NE, Washington, DC 20018-3230.

COLLIER, DR. BARBARA
Manager, federal government official. **Personal:** Born Dec 18, 1943, Athens, AL; daughter of John Robert and Eunice Louise.

Educ: Ala A&M Univ, BS 1965; Am Univ Biblical Studies, MA, 1996, PhD, 1998. **Career:** Federal government official (retired); Dept Energy, compliance Officer, 1973-78; Dept Labor, prog analyst, 1978-79, supvr, 1979-80, area Off dir, 1980-84, dir opers, 1984-88, asst dist dir, 1989-91, sr compliance Officer, 1991-98; Colier & Assocs Counseling Servs, 1998. **Orgs:** Black Pilots Asn; Biblical CounFound; Zeta Phi Beta Sor; Am Cancer Asn, volunteer fundraiser; Black Cowboy Asn; Kiwanas, Atlanta; Toastmasters. **Honors/Awds:** BACS 1982, VEVA 1984; Spec Achievement Dept Energy 1976, Dept Labor 1984; Outstanding Young Women Women's Suffrage Award, 1984; Outstanding Young Women Am 1986; Community EEO/AA Action Award, Top Ladies Distinction, 1989; Distinguished Career Service Award, 1994. **Home Addr:** 144 Big Springs Rd, Lawrenceburg, TN 38464-6823.

COLLIER, CLARENCE MARIE
Educator. **Personal:** Born in St Francisville, LA. **Educ:** Southern Univ, BS; Tuskegee Inst, MS; La State Univ, MS; Grambling State Univ; New York Univ System. **Career:** Southern Univ, vpres; Teacher Corps Prog, admin; Parish Sch Syst, elemprin, supvr educ. **Orgs:** Asn Supvr & Curric Develop; Phi Delta Kappa; Na Educ Asn; La Educ Asn; Nat Alliance Black Sch Educr; Am Coun Educ; Nat Asn Women Deans, Adminr, & Counselors; SW Asn Stud Personnel; admin co-chmn, La Comn Observance Int Women's Year; Delta Sigma Theta; State & Nat Women's Polit Caucus; Leauge Women Voters; Women Politics; Nat Coun Negro Women; Comn Asn Welfare Schc; bd dir, YWCA. **Honors/Awds:** Operation Upgrade Advancement of Women Award, Nat Orgn for Women; Arts &Letters Award, Delta Sigma Theta Inc; Certificate of Merit, Gov La; Certificate of Recognition, E Baton Rouge City Parish Coun; Citation of outstanding contribution to educ Prince Hall Masons.

COLLIER, DR. EUGENIA W.
Educator. **Personal:** Born Apr 6, 1928, Baltimore, MD; daughter of Harry Maceo and Eugenia Jackson; married Charles S, Jul 23, 1948 (divorced); children: Charles Maceo, Robert Nelson & Philip Gilles. **Educ:** Howard Univ, BA, 1948; Columbia Univ, MA, 1950; Univ MD, PhD, 1976. **Career:** Educator (retired); Balt Dept Pub Welfare, case worker, 1950-55; Morgan State Univ, from asst instr to asst prof, 1955-66, Dept Eng, chair; Comm Col Baltimore, from asst prof to prof, 1966-74; Workshop Ctr African &Afro-Am Studies, consult, 1969; Pine Manor Jr Col, fac, 1970; S Ill Univ, vis prof, 1970; Atlanta Univ, vis prof, 1974; Univ MD, assoc prof, 1974-77; Howard Univ, assoc prof, 1977-87; Coppin State Col, prof, 1987-92; Morgan State Univ, prof eng, 1992-96; Author: Impressions in Asphalt: Images of Urban America, 1969; A Bridge to Saying It Well, 1970; Langston Hughes: Black Genius, 1971; Afro-American Writing: An Anthology of Prose & Poetry, 1972; Modern Black Poets: A Collection of Critical Essays, 1973; Ricky, 1976; Spread My Wings, 1992; Breeder & Other Stories,1993. **Orgs:** Nat Conf African-Am Theater; Nat Coun Teachers Eng; Middle Alantic Writers Asn; Col Language Asn; African-Am Writers Guild; Arena Players; Col Language Asn; Asn Study Negro Life & History; Middle Atlantic Writers Asn; African Am Writers Guild. **Honors/Awds:** Gwendolyn Brooks Award for Marigold :Fiction, 1969; MAW, Creative Writing Award, 1984. **Special Achievements:** Author: Breeder and Other Stories, 1994; co-editor, Afro-American Writing, w/Richard A Long; co-author :Political Corruption In The Caribbean Basin: Constructing A Theory To Combat Corruption, 2007. **Home Addr:** 2608 Chelsea Terr, Baltimore, MD 21216, **Home Phone:** (410)664-5228.

COLLIER, JULIA MARIE
School administrator. **Personal:** Born Aug 23, 1949, Athens, AL; daughter of John Robert Sr and Louise Benford. **Educ:** Berea Col, BA, 1971; Temple Univ, MEd, 1973; Eastern Kent Univ, MA, 1979. **Career:** Ministry Educ, Nassau, Bahamas, fac, 1973-76; Manchester Col, fac, 1978-79; Franklin Wright Settlement, admin coordr, 1979-80; Aldine Independent Sch Dist, counr, 1980-83; Kenne saw Assoc, assoc dir admis; National Expansion Leader, Independent Rep, Am Comm Network, currently; Carter, Reddy & Associates Inc, regional dir, currently. **Orgs:** Comt mem, Southern Assoc Collegiate Register & Admis Offices 1985; conf presenter Southern Assoc Collegiate Register & Admis Offices 1986-87; workshop presenter, ELS Language Ctr, 1986; comt mem, Ga Educ Articulation Comt, 1987-89; exec comt, Ga Asn Colegiate Registrars & Admissions Officers, 1988-95; chmn, Ga Asn Foreign Stud Affairs, 1989-90; bd mem, ELS Language Ctr; Nat Adv Bd Comt, ELS, Language Ctrs. **Honors/Awds:** Fulbright Scholar, Germany, 1987; Outstanding New Professional, Ga Asn Collegiate Registrs & Admis Officers, 1988; Humanitarian of the Year, Omega Psi Phi Fraternity, 1990. **Business Addr:** Regional Director, Carter,Reddy & Associates Inc., 3902 Brentmoor Ct, Kennesaw, GA 30144, **Business Phone:** (404)667-0145.

COLLIER, LOUIS KEITH
Baseball player. **Personal:** Born Aug 21, 1973, Chicago, IL. **Educ:** Triton Community Col. **Career:** Baseball player (retired); Pittsburgh Pirates, infielder, 1997-98; Milwaukee Brewers, 1999-01; Montreal Expos, 2002; Boston Red Sox, beginning 2003; Philadelphia Phillies, left fielder, 2004; Korean Baseball Org, Lucky Goldstar Twins, 2005-06; Ottawa Lynx, 2007. *

COLLIER, DR. MILLARD JAMES, JR.
Physician. **Personal:** Born Nov 8, 1957, Atlanta, GA; son of Millard James Collier Sr and Catherine Walker; married Dolores Maire Perez; children: Millard J Collier III. **Educ:** Morehouse Col, BS; Georgia's Health Scs Univ, Med Col Ga, MD, 1984. **Career:** Atlanta W Health Care Primary Care Asns, med dir, 1990-; pvt pract, currently. **Orgs:** Am Med Asn; Atlanta Med Asn; Nat Med Asn; Am Acad Family Physicians; vpres, Ga Acad Family Physicians; Ga State Med Asn; pres, 100 Black Men Am, S Metro chap; Alpha Phi Alpha Fraternity Inc. **Honors/Awds:** Young Physician of the Year, Atlanta Med Asn, 1996; 100 Black Men, Member of the Year, 1996; AAFP, Teaching Recognition Award, 1996. **Special Achievements:** Radio Talk Show Host "Your Health is Important", WYZE 1480 AM. **Business Addr:** Physician, 939 Thornton Rd, Lithia Springs, GA 30122-2676, **Business Phone:** (770)948-5400.

COLLIER, TROY
Educator. **Personal:** Born Apr 19, 1941, Nacogdoches, TX; married Claudette Liggns. **Educ:** Phoenix Col, AA, Bus Admin, 1962; UT State Univ, BS, social work, 1964; S Meth Univ, MLA, 1971; Nova Univ, PhD. **Career:** Harlem Globetrotters Basketball Team, prof basketball player 1964-67; City Phoenix AZ, youth progs coordr & neighborhood organizer, supvr, 1967-68; Youth Progs Coordr & Neighborhood, organizer supvr, 1968-69; Univ Southern Fla, asst vpres, sudent affairs; Clearfield Job Corps Ctr, res life counr 1969-71; Univ South Fla, Off Adult & Transfer Student Servs, assoc dean, dean, currently. **Orgs:** Bd dir, DACCO; Citizens Adv Com, Hillsborough Co Sch Bd; Am Civil Liberties Union, State Bd & Tampa Chap; bd mem, Nat Asn Human Rights Workers; Soc Asn Black Adminr; Am Asn Affirmative Action; Tampa Urban League; Nat Asn Advan Colored People; Tampa-Hillsborough Manpower Coun; Phi Theta Kappa Hon Soc Zeta Fla Alumni Asn. **Home Addr:** 6101 E 112th Ave, Tampa, FL 33617-3131, **Home Phone:** (813)987-2063. **Business Addr:** Dean of Student Affairs, University of South Florida, 4202 E Fowler Ave, Tampa, FL 33620, **Business Phone:** (813)974-6444.

COLLIER, WILLYE
Educator. **Personal:** Born Sep 26, 1922, Hattiesburg, MS; married Cisero. **Educ:** Tuskegee Inst, BS, 1943; Univ Wis, MS, 1946. **Career:** SC Public Schs, home econs teacher, 1946-49; Southern Univ, dir dietetics, 1949-56; Los Angeles Paso Robles & San Luis Obispo, consult diet, 1956-57; San Luis Obispo City Schs, teacher, 1960-64; Bakersfield Col, prof Food & Nutrition, 1964. **Orgs:** Chmn, Home Econ Dept Benedict Col; Liasion Rep, Home Con Asn Calif Teachers Asn & NEA; Am Dietetic Asn; Am Pub Health Asn; Am Home Econ Asn; Basileus, Gamma Alpha Sigma Chap Sigma Gamma Rho Inc, 1976-78; Int Fed Home Econ; chmn, bd Kern County Health Asn; chmn, Nut Comn KC Heart Asn, 1970-76; mem bd, Kern Co Ment Health Asn, 1974-80, organizer, pres, 1977-79; chmn bd, Kem Co Ment Health Asn, 1980-81; Links Bakersfield, 1977; Nat Advan Asn Colored People. **Honors/ Awds:** Outstanding Contrib, Kern County Heart Asn, 1974; Sigma of the Year, Sigma Gamma Rho Sor, 1975; Who Award. Calif Higher Educ, 1976. **Business Addr:** Professor, Bakersfield College, 1801 Panorama Dr, Bakersfield, CA 93305.

COLLIER-MILLS, CHERYL
Educator. **Career:** Univ Md Eastern Shore, Princess Anne, MD, dir admis, regist & recruitment, asst vpres, enrollment mgt, currently, Div Stud Affairs, chair & asst vpres. **Business Addr:** Assistant Vice President, Chair, University of Maryland Eastern Shore, 1 Backbone Rd, Princess Anne, MD 21853-1299, **Business Phone:** (410)651-8466.

COLLIER-THOMAS, DR. BETTYE
Educator, administrator. **Personal:** Born in Macon, GA; married Charles John. **Educ:** Allen Univ, BA, magna cum laude, 1963; Atlanta Univ, MA, 1966; George Wash Univ, PhD, 1974. **Career:** WA Perry Jr High Sch, Columbia, SC, instr 1963-65; Howard Univ, instr,1966-69, Col Lib Arts, dir honors prog, 1969-71, prof, 1969-76; Wash Tech Inst, asst prof, 1969-71; William & Mary Col, assoc prof, 1969-70; Univ Md, lectr, hist, 1971; Nat Endowment for the Humanities, consult, 1977-81; Bethune Mus-Archives Inc, exec dir, 1977-89; Temple Univ, assoc hist prof,Ctr African-Am Hist & Cult, dir, 1989-, prof hist, 1997-. **Orgs:** Am Asn Univ Profs; Nat Educ Asn; Asn Study Afro-Am Life & Hist; Alpha Kappa Alpha; Orgn Am Historians; Am Historical Asn. **Honors/ Awds:** Scholarship Award, Delta Sigma Theta, 1960; Mark Schaefer History Award, 1963; Nat Asn Col Women's Award, 1963; Presidential Scholarship, Atlanta Univ, 1965-66; America's Top 100 Black Business & Professional Women, Dollars & Sense, 1986; Conservation Services Award, Dept of the Interior, 1994; Conservation Service Award; fellowship, Woodrow Wilson Center International Scholars, 2008-09. **Special Achievements:** Co-editor, Vindicating the Race: Contributions to African-American Intellectual History, 1996; Co-editor, African-American Women & the Vote,1997; author, Daughters of Thunder: Black Women Preachers & Their Sermons,1850-1979, 1998; co-author: My Soul is a Witness: A Chronology of the Civil Rights Era, 2000; author, Sisters in the Struggle: African-American Women in the Civil Rights-Black Power Movement, 2001. **Business Addr:** Professor of History, Director of Center for African-American History & Culture, Temple University, 1115 W Berks St 810 Gladfelter Hall, Philadelphia, PA 19122, **Business Phone:** (215)204-8491.

COLLIER-WILSON, WANDA
President (Organization), chief executive officer. **Career:** Jackson Conv & Visitors Bur, pres & chief exec officer, 1998-. **Orgs:** Missi Tourism Asn; Destination Mkt Asn Int; Metro Jackson Attractions Asn; Travel & Tourism Res Asn; Southeast Tourism Soc; adv bd, Downtown Jackson Partners. **Honors/Awds:** Tourism Hall of Fame, Miss Develop Authority-Division Tourism, 2006; 2005 Mississippi CVB of the Year, 2005; Dr. Jessie Bryant Mosley Award of Excellence. **Special Achievements:** Fifty Leading Business Women, Mississippi Bus Jour, 2006. **Business Addr:** President, Chief Executive Officer, Jackson Convenion & Visitors Bureau, 921 N Pres St, PO Box 1450, Jackson, MS 39215, **Business Phone:** (601)960-1891.

COLLINET, GEORGES ANDRE (MAXI VOOM VOOM)
Television producer. **Personal:** Born Dec 16, 1940, Sangmelima, Cameroon; son of Raymond Maurice and Myriam Nyangono K'Pwan; married Louise Wilma Lutkefedder, Sep 21, 1980; children: Georges-Alexandre William Zuom. **Educ:** Univ de Caen, France, BA. **Career:** Voice Am, producer, 1964-; Soul Music Mag, founder, ed, 1975-79; USIA TV, talent coordr, 1976-; GC Prods, pres, 1979-; Afropop Worldwide, host, currently. **Orgs:** Marracas d'Or, founding mem, 1975-78; Prix de la Jeune Chanson Francaise, 1976-78; Sharon Pratt Kelly, art steering community. **Honors/Awds:** Gold Award for Best Series, Silver Award for Best Prog, Corp for Pub Broadcasting. **Business Addr:** Host, Afropop Worldwide, 688 Union St storefront, Brooklyn, NY 11215, **Business Phone:** (718)398-2733.*

COLLINS, ANDRE PIERRE
Football player, football executive. **Personal:** Born May 4, 1968, Riverside, NJ. **Educ:** Pa State Univ, BS, Health Policy & Admin, 1991. **Career:** Football player (retired), Asn dir; Wash Redskins, linebacker, 1990-94; Cincinnati Bengals, linebacker, 1995-98; Chicago Bears, linebacker, 1998; Detroit Lions, linebacker, 1999; NFL Players Asn, dir retired players, currently. **Honors/Awds:** First-team All-Am selection, Football Writers Asn, 1989. **Special Achievements:** A Butkus Award finalist. **Business Phone:** (202)463-2200.

COLLINS, ANNAZETTE
Government official. **Personal:** Born Apr 28, 1962, Chicago, IL; married Keith Langston; children: Angelique Nicole & Taylor Kourtnie. **Educ:** Northern Ill Univ, BA, sociol; Chicago State Univ, MS, criminal Justice. **Career:** Chicago Bd Educ, adminr; Ill Dept C & Family Serv, pub serv adminr; Cook County Social Serv, Probation Dept; Bur Prisons, correctional officer; 10th Dist, rep, 2001-. **Orgs:** Alpha Kappa Alpha Sorority Inc. **Business Addr:** State Representative, 10th District, 259 N Pulaski Rd, Chicago, IL 60624.

COLLINS, BARBARA-ROSE
Congressperson (u.s. federal government). **Personal:** Born Apr 13, 1939, Detroit, MI; daughter of Lamar Richardson and Versa Richardson; married Bruce Simpson Sr; children: Cynthia, Christopher, Bruce Jr, Amber Rose & Shaina Marie. **Educ:** Wayne State Univ, Anthrop & Polit Sci. **Career:** Wayne State Univ, bus mgr, physics dept, 9 yrs, off asst equal opportunity off, neighbhorhood rels; Detroit Sch Region I, bd mem, 1970-73; Mich House Rep, 21st Dist Detroit, state rep, 1974-82; Detroit City Coun, coun mem, 1982-91, 2001-; US House Rep, congress woman, 1991-92; US House Rep, 13th Dist Mich, state rep, 1991-97. **Orgs:** Regional co ord Mich, Ohio Nat Black Caucus Local Elected Officials, 1985; trustee, Mich Munic League, 1985; bd mem, Comprehensive Health Planning Coun S eastern Mich, 1985; trustee, Int Afro-Am Mus; chair, Region I Polit Action Comm; City-Wide Citizens Action Coun, Dem Party, ACLU, League Women Voters, Am Dem Action, Kenyatta Home owners & Tenants asn; Black Teachers Caucus; Black Parents Qual Educ; Inner-City Parents Coun; Nat Order Women Legislators; bd mem, Detroit Black United Fund; Spec Comm Affirmative Action; Shrine Black Madonna Church; I WY State Coord Comm Nat Int Women's Year Comm; Mich Deleg to IWY Conv; chair, Const Rev & Women's Rights Comm; prin sponsor bills which were later passed, including The Food Dating Bill, The Sex Educ Bill, The Pregnancy Ins Bill; past mem, Detroit Human Rights Comm; regional dir, Nat Black Caucus Local Elected Officials. **Honors/ Awds:** Feminist of the Year Award, 1977; featured in How Mich Women Make It Happen, Red book Mag, 1978; Woman of the Year Award, Eta Phi Beta Sor Inc, Eta Lambda Zeta Chap, 1979; Distinguished Service, Shrine Black Madonna Pan African Orthodox Christian Church, 1981; Devoted Service, Metro Boy Scouts of Am, 1984; Valuable Serv, Inter Nat Freedom Festival, 1983; Invaluable Service, Pershing High Sch, Detroit Pub Schs, 1985. **Business Addr:** Council Member, US House Representative, Detroit City Council, Coleman A Young Munic Ctr, 2 Woodward Ave Suite 1340, Detroit, MI 48226.

COLLINS, BERNICE ELAINE
Manager. **Personal:** Born Oct 24, 1957, Kansas City, KS; daughter of William H and Wanda J Coby. **Educ:** Ringling Brothers Barnum Bailey Clown Col, Diploma, 1977; Transworld Travel Col, Kansas City, KS, Diploma, 1985. **Career:** Doctor Off, receptionist, 1975-77; Ringling Bros Barnum Bailey Circus, clown, 1978-79, dancer & showgirl, 1980-84, apprentice tiger trainer, 1983; Trans World Airlines, int flight attend, 1985-86; Kansas City Riverboat, entertainer & asst mgr, 1986-87; Ringling

Bros Barnum & Bailey Circus, dancer & showgirl, 1988-90, horse act, 1992-93, admin asst, 1994-96; Big Apple Circus, co mgr, 1996-00; Alvin Ailey Am Dance Theater, co mgr, beginning 2000. **Honors/Awds:** HS Art Award; Gold Key Awards, 1974-75. **Special Achievements:** 1st African-Am woman clown Ringling Bros Barnum & Bailey Circus, 1978; 1st African-Am woman tiger trainer, 1983. **Business Addr:** Manager, Alvin Ailey American Dance Theater, The Joan Weill Center for Dance, 405 W 55th St 9th Ave, New York, NY 10019, **Business Phone:** (212)405-9000.*

COLLINS, BERT
Insurance executive. **Personal:** Born Nov 9, 1934, Austin, TX; son of James K (deceased) and Marie (deceased); married Carolyn Porter; children: Suane, Brandy Collins Suggs, Bert E. **Educ:** Hoston-Tillotson Col, BBA, 1955; Univ Detroit, MBA, 1959; NC Cent Univ Law Sch, JD, 1970; Univ NC-Chapel Hill, Young Exec Prog. **Career:** Sidney A Sumby Memorial Hosp, chief acct, 1956-61; Austin Wash & Davenport CPA's, sr staff acct, 1962-67; NC Mutual Life Ins Co, admin asst, 1967, asst vpres, off staff, 1970, vp, controller 1974, bd dir, exec comt, 1978, finance comt, 1979, sr vpres, controller, 1982, sr vpres, admin, 1983, chmn securities comt, 1983, chmn field comn, 1986, exec vpres, chief operating officer, 1987-90, pres & chief exec officer, 1990-. **Orgs:** Kappa Alpha Psi; Sigma Pi Phi Boule'; First Church Christ Scientist; Mich Asn CPA's; NC Asn CPA's; Am Inst CPA's; Am Bar Asn; NC State Bar; George White Bar Asn; bd visitors, NC A&T State Univ; Durham Comn Affairs Black People; Durham Bus & Prof Chain; Durham Chamber Com; bd dir, treas, former pres, State Easter Seal Soc; vice chair, exec comn, bd, Mutual Savings Bank; coun mgt, bd dir, NC Amateur Sportsmem, Africa News; appointed Bd Arts & Humanities (NC); Nat Bd Boys & Girls Clubs Am; NC Bus Coun Mgt & Develop; bd gov, Univ NC, Chapel Hill, 1998-99. **Honors/Awds:** Doctor of Humane Letters, Barber Scotia Col; CC Spaulding Award, Nat Bus League. **Special Achievements:** Black Enterprise's list of Top Insurance Companies, ranked No. 1, 1999, 2000. **Business Addr:** President, Chief Executive Officer, NC Mutual Life Insurance Company, 411 W Chapel Hill St, Durham, NC 27701, **Business Phone:** (919)682-9201.*

COLLINS, BOBBY L
Dentist. **Educ:** Univ Iowa, Col Dent, grad, 1975. **Career:** Pvt pract, dentist, currently; SmartPract Dent Consult LLC, founder, 2004-; fac mem, Univ Tenn Sch Dent. **Orgs:** Pres, Tenn Bd Dent, 1988, 1993; Am Dent Asn; Acad Gen Dent; Tenn Dent Asn. **Honors/Awds:** Fel Award for Distinguished Service, Tenn Dent Asn. **Special Achievements:** First African-American president, second African-American appointed mem, Tennessee Board of Dentistry. **Business Phone:** (901)322-4430.

COLLINS, BOOTSY (WILLIAM BOYD)
Singer, songwriter, bass guitarist. **Personal:** Born Oct 26, 1951, Cincinnati, OH. **Career:** Solo Albums: Stretchin Out, 1976; Ahh The Name is Bootsy, Baby, 1977; Bootsy? Player of the Yr, 1978; Ultra Wave, 1980; The One Giveth & the Count Taketh Away, 1982; What's Bootsy Doin?, 1988; Jungle Bass, 1990; Back in the Day: The Best of Bootsy, 1994; Fresh Outta "P" Univ, 1997; Glory B da Funks on Me, 2001; Play With Bootsy - A Tribute To The Funk, 2002; Live In Concert 1998, 2006; Christmas Is 4 ever, 2006; Bootzilla Productions Inc, owner, currently. **Special Achievements:** Performed & recorded with James Brown, Parliament, & Funkadelic.

COLLINS, CALVIN LEWIS
Software developer, football player. **Personal:** Born Jan 5, 1974, Beaumont, TX. **Educ:** Tex A&M Univ, BA, bus admin; SetFocus LLC, C Masters Prog Cert. **Career:** Football player (retired), Software developer; Atlanta Falcons, guard, 1997-2000; Minn Vikings, 2001; Houston Texans, 2002; Pittsburgh Steelers, 2003; Denver Broncos, guard, 2004; CFC Capital Group LLC, owner & pres, 2001-05; Set Focus LLC, software developer, currently. **Honors/Awds:** NFL All-Rookie Team, 1997. **Special Achievements:** Dot NET Developer - Masters Programmer in Set Focus LLC. **Business Phone:** (973)889-0211.*

COLLINS, CARDISS H. (CARDISS ROBERTSON)
Congressperson (u.s. federal government). **Personal:** Born Sep 24, 1931, St Louis, MO; daughter of Finley Robertson and Rosia Mae; married George (died 1972); children: Kevin. **Educ:** Northwestern Univ, attended 1967. **Career:** Ill Dept Revenue, revenue auditor; US House Rep, mem, 7th Ill Dist, 1973-97; Nielsen Media Res, head African Am TV, 2004; Dem Party, mem at-large, currently. **Orgs:** Chair comn, consumer protection & competitiveness, S Comn Govt Ops, Subcomt Oversight and Investigations, Energy & Com Comt; House Select Comt Drug Abuse & Control; chairwoman, Mem Cong Peace through Law Subcomt Africa; secy, vice chair & chair, Cong Black Caucus; dem comt woman, 24thWard Chicago, Nat Asn Advan Colored People; Chicago Urban League; Northern Va Urban League; Nat Coun Negro Women; Nat Womens Polit Caucus; Alpha Kappa Alpha; Alpha Kappa Psi; Black Women's Agenda; Links; Dem Nat Comt. **Honors/Awds:** Hon Degree, Spelman Col; Hon Degree, Winston-Salem St Univ; Hon Degree, Barber-Scotia Col. **Special Achievements:** First African American woman to represent the Midwest in Congress; USPS processing & distribution center named in honor. **Home Addr:** 1110 Roundhouse Lane, Alexandria, VA 22314, **Home Phone:** (703)684-6337. **Business Phone:** (202)863-8000.

COLLINS, CARL
Executive. **Career:** Charity Motors, pres & cheif exec officer, currently. **Business Addr:** President, Chief Executive Officer, Charity Motors, 21501 W 8 Mile Rd, Detroit, MI 48219, **Business Phone:** (313)255-1000.*

COLLINS, CHARLES MILLER
Real estate executive. **Personal:** Born Nov 22, 1947, San Francisco, CA; son of Dr Daniel A; married Paula Robinson; children: Sara & Julia. **Educ:** Williams Col, BA (hons), 1969; Athens Ctr Ekistics, Athens, Greece, Cert, 1971; Mass Inst Technol, MCP, 1973; Harvard Law Sch, JD, 1976. **Career:** Pvt law pract, atty, 1976-79; State Calif, Dep Sec Bus, Transp & Housing, 1980-82; WDG Ventures Ltd, managing gen partner, 1987-; Western Develop Group Inc, prin, 1982-87; WDG Ventures Inc, chmn & pres, 1987-; Venture Philanthropy Partners Inc, patner, currently. **Orgs:** Trustee, Howard Thurman Educ Trust, 1976-97; Alpha Phi Alpha; Sigma Pi Phi; trustee, Nat Urban League, 1989-; trustee, San Francisco Mus Modern Art; chmn, Spec Awards Comn, San Francisco Found; dir, San Francisco Jazz Orgn; pres, chief exec officer, YMCA San Francisco; sr vchmn, Bd Trustees, Nat Urban League, 2003. **Honors/Awds:** fel, Thomas J Watson Found, 1969-71. **Special Achievements:** Editor, "The African Americans A Celebration of Achievement", Viking Studio Books, 1993. **Business Addr:** Chairman, President, WDG Ventures Inc, 735 Market St, San Francisco, CA 94103.

COLLINS, CLIFFORD JACOB
Association executive. **Personal:** Born Mar 6, 1947, Jamaica, NY; son of Clifford Collins Jr and Mamie Hale; married Electra Bazemore Collins, Jan 13, 1973; children: Makina & Ahmed. **Educ:** Roger Williams Col, AA, 1970; Shaw Univ, BA, 1975; Ga State Univ, MEd, 1977. **Career:** Goodwill Industries, Atlanta, GA, dir, industrial serv, 1983-84; Atlanta Regional Comm, Atlanta, GA, chief planner, 1985-86, prin planner, 1986-87; NAACP Baltimore, MD, asst dir, back-to-sch/stay-in sch, 1987-88, promotion dir, back-to-sch/stay-in sch, 1988, 1992; dir, voter educ, 1989; Second Congressional Dist, delegate; Job Opportunities Task Force, exec dir. **Orgs:** Bd dirs, Nat Coalition Black Voter Participation, 1990-; Minority Educ Coordinating Coun Baltimore County Pub Schs, 1990-; Citizens Adv Comm Gifted & Talented Prog, Baltimore Co Pub Schs, 1990-; Nat Comn Renewal Am Democracy; Nat Asn Secretaries State; 2000 Census Adv Comn, US Census Bureau; NW Adv Coun, 2003; Decennial Census Adv Comn; Nat Asn Advan Colored People. **Honors/Awds:** Award Outstanding Coop Advancing Pub Understanding, Census, 1990; US Dept Com Bureau Census, 1991; Co-auth, Nat Asn Advan Colored People Redistricting Proj Handbook, Nat Asn Advan Colored People, 1991; Cert Recognition Outstanding Volunteer Serv, Old Court Middle Sch; Pub: Personal Care Homes: A Local Govt Perspective, res study personal care homes Atlanta, GA, Atlanta Regional Comn. **Business Phone:** (410)234-8040.

COLLINS, CONSTANCE RENEE WILSON
President (organization). **Personal:** Born Nov 25, 1932, New York, NY; married Alphonzo S; children: Michael Alan & Tonilyn. **Educ:** Skidmore Univ, 1975; Harvard Univ, Med, 1979. **Career:** United & Elec Workers Am Local 207, pres, 1965-69; Arsenal Develop Corp, assoc dir, 1969- 72; Poor People's Fedn Inc, exec dir, 1972-80; Silver Strands System Inc Consult Firm, dir Admin, 1976-80; Conn United Labor Agency New Britain, exec dir, 1982-99; United Labor Agency Inc, pres. **Orgs:** Alderman City New Brit, 1969-75; bd advs, Burrit Bank New Brit Ct, 1975-80; dir, City Plan Comn, 1978-80; grand dist dep, IBPO Elks World, 1961-80; nat bd mem, Opportunities Indust Ctrs Am, 1972-80; organizer bdchmn, OIC New Brit, CT, 1976-80; alderman, City New Brit, 1985-; Nat chair, Opportunities Industrialization Ctrs Am, 2001; Capital Work force Partners, currently; Substance Abuse Action Coun; Cent Conn Inc; New Britain Chamber Com. **Honors/Awds:** Recipient Dedication Award for Service Bd & Staff, Poor People's Fedn Inc, 1974; Torch Bearer Award OIC's Am 1976; Martin Luther King Comm Serv Award MLK Monument Com, 1977; Elk of the Year Award, 1999; New Eng Sts & Eastern Canada Asn IBPOE of W 1979; Outstanding Woman of the Year Award, State Conn Gov Ella Grasso, 1979; Leader of the Month of Greater Hartford CT, Mutual Ins Co, 1979; One of CT Outstanding Woman in Labor CT, Historial Cos, 1984. **Home Addr:** 242 Belden St, PO Box 2201, New Britain, CT 06050, **Home Phone:** (860)223-8042.

COLLINS, CORENE
Government official, administrator. **Personal:** Born Apr 20, 1948; married Tony; children: Craig & Kisten. **Educ:** Fla A&M Univ, BA, sociol & criminol, 1970; Rutgers Univ, MA, criminal justice admin. **Career:** Youth Serv Bur, E Orange, NJ, dir, 1974-78; United Way Community Planning & Develop, Newark NJ, dir, 1978-80; Black Spectrum TV Show, producer & host volunteer, 1978-79; Div Community Serv, Tampa FL, dep dir, 1981-85; Div Cult Serv, Hillsborough County, dir; Univ S Fla, Sch Social Work, asst dir, Fl Kinship Ctr, currently. **Orgs:** Exec dir & volunteer, Oper PUSH, 1977-79; pub rels coordr & newsletter co-ed, Tampa Orgn Black Affairs, 1980-84; pres, Tampa Bay Investment Club, 1982-85; Nat Forum Black Pub Admin; Tampa Chamber Com, Govt Comn; bd mem, Am Cancer Soc; N Am Coun Adoptable C. **Honors/Awds:** Award for Outstanding Chapter Development, Nat PUSH, 1978; Outstanding Young Woman of America, 1979; Selected 1 of 33 Women Achievers, Tampa Tribune Newspaper, 1982; Selected Minority Woman of the Year, Zeta Phi Beta Sorority, 1984; Up & Comers Award, price waterhouse. **Home Addr:** 5209 Gorham Ct, Tampa, FL 33624.

COLLINS, CORNELL
Fashion designer. **Personal:** Born Nov 2, 1974, Trenton, NC. **Educ:** Brooks Col, grad; Los Angeles Fashion Inst Design & Merchandising. **Career:** Fashion designer, currently. **Special Achievements:** Collections featured in numerous magazines & fashion shows.

COLLINS, DAISY G.
Judge. **Personal:** Born Feb 5, 1937, Butler, AL; daughter of Booker T Sr (deceased) and Luevinia Mitchell; divorced. **Educ:** Ohio State Univ, Acct major, 1958, BS, Bus Admin, 1958; Howard Univ Sch Law, JD, 1970. **Career:** Judge (retired); Commonwealth Edison Co, Chicago, Mgt trainee, 1958-60; City Detroit, acct, 1960-64; Gen Foods Corp, White Plains, cost & budget analyst, 1964-66; Stud asst asst legal adv, US State Dept, African Affairs, 1969; N MS Rural Legal Serv Greenwood, staff atty, 1970-71; OH Turnpike Comn, asst gen coun & staff lawyer, 1973-74; Northern Dist Ohio, asst us atty, 1975-77; Capital Univ Law Sch, vis assoc prof law, 1981-82; Equal Opportunity Comn, Cleveland Dist Off, admin judge, 1986-90; Off Hearings & Appeals, admin law judge, Social Security Admin, 1990-94; Business Law & Acct, Cleveland State Univ & Cuy CC, part-time instr. **Orgs:** exec secy, Cleveland Br, Nat Advan Asn Colored People, 1979-80; Alpha Kappa Alpha Sor; life mem, Nat Advan Asn Colored People. **Honors/Awds:** Hon Mention, Cleveland Fed Exec Bd Community Serv, 1976; Meritorious Serv Awards, Cleveland Bar Asn, 1972-73; Six American Jurisprudence Awards; Appreciation Award, Law J Notes Ed, 1970; Most Outstanding Grad Woman Col C & Admin, Phi Chi Theta Scholarship Key; inducted, Berea High School Distinguished Alumni Hall of Fame, 2002. **Special Achievements:** articles published in Howard Law J & Crnt Bibliography African Affairs; HLJ Notes Ed. *

COLLINS, DAMON JAMAL MO. **See COLLINS, MO.**

COLLINS, DOROTHY
College administrator, basketball coach, basketball player. **Personal:** Married David; children: Doriyon & David. **Educ:** Youngstown State Univ, BS, educ, 1990, MS, educ, 1994. **Career:** Penguins, basketball player, 1984-88; Calvary Christian Acad, asst coach, 1996-98; Pro-Star Basketball Camp, camp coach, 1996-98; Youngstown YMCA, vol head coach, 1997-; Youngstown State Univ, campus supvr, 1999-2002, coordr multicultural stud serv, 2000-02, asst women's basketball coach; Mahoning & Columbiana Training Asn, career consult; Jefferson Community Col, TRiO stud support servs, dir, currently. **Honors/Awds:** Ohio Valley Conference Player of the Year, 1998.

COLLINS, DOROTHY LEE
Educator. **Personal:** Born Jan 19, 1932, Nacogdoches, TX; married Samuel M Prin. **Educ:** Tex Southern Univ, attended 1952; Our Lady Lake Univ, MEd, 1973; Trinity Univ, MA, 1977. **Career:** Las Palmas Elem Sch San Antonio; Edgewood Independent Sch Dist, elem teacher, 1957-71, prin, 1973; jr high sch, counr, 1971-73. **Orgs:** Bd dir, Young & Women Christian Asn, 1966-69; Tex Congress Parents &Teachers, 1969; Ella Austine Community Ctr, 1969-77; pres, Edgewood Classroom Teachers Asn, 1969-71; ambassador, Good Will State Tex, 1970; exec comn, United Negro Col Fund Inc; adv bd, Edgewood ISD, 1970-75; exec comn, Tex State Teachers Asn, 1971-77; Tex State Teachers Asn & Nat Educ Asn; Tex Elem Prins Asn; vpres, San Antonio Leag Bus & Prof Women Inc, 1971-76; Nat Educ Asn Task Force Testing, 1972-75; rep, proj area comn San Antonio Develop Agency, 1973-78; State Bd Exam Teacher Educ, 1975-77; adv bd, educ dept Our Lady Lake Univ, 1976-77; pres, Edgewood Admin & ServsPersonnel Asn, 1976-77; life mem, Nat Coun Negro Women Inc, 1979; vpres,San Antonio Chap Our Lady Lake Univ Alumni Asn, 1979-80; chmn, Tex Educ Agency Teacher Educ Evaluation Team Visit, 1979; treas, Dist XX Tex ElemPrin & Supr Asn, 1980-81; bd dir, Bexar Co Opportunity Indst Ctr; lifemem, Nat Advan Asn Colored People; spec state mem, comn Tex State Teachers Asn. **Honors/Awds:** Hon roll cert Tex, Southern Univ, 1951; Citation-Historical Achievement Among Negroes San Antonio Smart Set Club, 1965; citation, Woman's Pavilion Hemisfair 68 Vol Guide, 1968; past pres award, Edgewood Classroom Teachers Asn, 1971; distinguished education service award, Prince & Princess Soc &Civic Club Inc, 1971; Outstanding education award, Zeta Phi Beta Sorority, 1973; Tex Classroom Teachers Association Service Award, 1973; distinguished service award, Task Force Testing Nat Educ Asn, 1976; miss black san antonio board of director model community leadership award, 1976; service

award, Tex State Teachers Asn, 1977; cert apprec, Tex State Teachers Asn, 1977; boss of the year, Mission City Chap Am Bus Women's Asn, 1978; educ adminstrator of the year, Delta Rho Lambda Ch Alpha Phi Alpha Frat, 1978; cert apprec, Edgewood Inde Sch Dist, 1978. **Special Achievements:** Firsst black to Integrate Teaching Profession, Edgewood ISD, 1963; First black pres, Tex State Teachers Assn Affiliate, 1969-71; First black mem, Tex Classroom Teachers Asn Bd Dirs Rep Dist, 1973-73. *

COLLINS, DR. ELLIOTT
Educator. **Personal:** Born Mar 18, 1943, Eastman, GA; son of Johnnie C and Elvin W; married Carol Jones, Sep 9, 1967; children: Kimberly L. **Educ:** Univ Del, BA, 1966; NY Univ, MPA, 1971; Drew Univ, Madison, NJ, MA, polit sci, 1983; NY Univ, PhD, am studies, 2000. **Career:** City E Orange NJ, asst city planner 1969; Drew Univ, Upsala Col, Educ Opportunity Fund Prog, dir & coordr, 1970-76, lectr polit sci, 1974-79, affirmative action off, 1974-77, coordr sci enrichment prog, 1976-77, asst dean acad coun, 1976-77; Passic Co Community Col, Paterson, NJ, Dept Hist, dean students, 1979-86, dean acad servs, 1986-89, vpres, 1989-90, prof hist, 1990-, interim pres, 1990-91, pres, 1991-96. **Orgs:** Vpres, United Way & Community Serv Coun, 1971-75; vpres & bd dir, Rotary Club E Orange, NJ, 1971-72; bd trustees, Family Servs & Child Guid Ctr,1975-76; bd dirs, Paterson YMCA, 1983-87; bd dirs, Opportunities Industrialization Ctr, 1987-95; bd trustees, Passaic-Clifton YMCA, 1989-93; NJ Regional Chamber Comm, 1991-95; secy, bd trustees, Passaic Co Community Col, 1991-96; bd dirs, United Way Passaic Valley, 1992-95; bd trustees, Inner City Christian Action Housing Inc, 1992-96; exec bd mem-,Passaic Valley Coun Boy Scouts Am, 1992-95; bd trustees, Passaic County Hist Soc, 1993-98. **Honors/Awds:** Alpha Phi Alpha Scholarship, 1962-64; Young Man of the Year, Unity Club, Wilmington, DE, 1965; Martin Luther King Scholarship, NY Univ, 1968-70. **Business Addr:** Professor, Passaic County Community College, History Department, 1 Col Blvd, Paterson, NJ 07505, **Business Phone:** (973)684-6868.

COLLINS, ELSIE
Educator, teacher. **Personal:** Born in Durham, NC; divorced; children: Leslie Jean & Kimberly Ruth. **Educ:** Del State Col, BA, 1945; Columbia Univ, MA, 1952; Union Grad Sch, PhD, 1977. **Career:** Dover DE Jr & Sr High Schs, teacher, 1945-59; Beth Jacob Jewish High Sch, New York City, teacher, 1960-61; Core Curr Jr High Sch, Trenton NJ, teacher, 1961-62, 1964-68, demonstration teacher, 1965-68; Consult Serv & In-serv Workshops, Trenton; NJ State Dept Higher Educ, Teacher Educ, 1967-72; Nat Teachers Corp, Trenton NJ, team leader, 1968-71; Afro-AmStudies, 1969-76; Urban Educ Curric Spec, 1972-; Trenton State Col, NJ, supvr summer semester teachers, 1965-75, asst prof & asst dir Corp; emer educ, currently. **Orgs:** Am Asn Univ Women, 1954-60; Community Leaders & Noteworthy Am, 1979; Doctorate Asn NY Educrs, 1980; NJ Hist Soc Am Asn Negro Mus; Nat Asn Adv Colored People; Urban League Coun Soc Studies Nat Educ Asn; New Jersey Educ Asn; Poverty Law Ctr AKA Asn; Supvr & Curric Develop. **Honors/Awds:** Scholar student of music, Teachers Col Columbia Univ, 1950-57; contributed to Develop Urban Educ Series Prob Am Soc, 1966-68; soloist, St Paul United Meth Church, Trenton, 1967-; Special award, World Who's Who of Women in Educ,1977-78; Int Artists & Fellows of Distinction, 1980. **Business Addr:** Emeritus of Education, Trenton State College, 2000 Pennington Rd, Ewing, NJ 08628-0718, **Business Phone:** (609)771-1855.*

COLLINS, JAMES (JAMES EDGAR COLLINS)
Basketball player. **Personal:** Born Nov 5, 1973, Jacksonville, FL. **Educ:** Fla State Univ. **Career:** Los Angeles Clippers, guard, 1997-98; Air Avellino, 2002-03; Eurorida Scafati, 2003-04; Cimberio Novara, 2004-06; Vertical Vision Cantu, 2006; Indesit Fabriano, 2006-07.

COLLINS, JAMES DOUGLAS
Educator, radiologist. **Personal:** Born Dec 11, 1931, Los Angeles, CA; son of James and Edna Alice O'Bryant; married Cecila Edith Lyons, Feb 7, 1954; children: Keith, Jelana Carnes & Jenine. **Educ:** Univ Calif, BA, 1957, MA, 1959; Meharry Med Col, Nashville, MD, 1963. **Career:** Los Angeles City Gen Hosp intern, 1963-64; Univ Calif, LA, resident radiol, 1964-68; Martin Luther King Jr Hosp, attend physician, 1969-; Vet Admin (Wadworth/Spelveda), attend radiologist, 1972-; Martin Luther King Jr Gen Hosp Los Angeles, attend radiologist, 1973-; Olive View Mid-Valley Hosp Van Nuys, attend radiologist, 1976-; Univ Calif, Los Angeles, assoc prof radiol, 1976-96, prof, 1996-. **Orgs:** Search Comt Chmn, Radiol Dept, Martin Luther King Jr Gen Hosp, 1969-70; vol, Venice Community Health Ctr; Los Angeles County Radiol Soc; Nat Med Asn; Radiol Soc N Am, 1969-; Asn Univ Radiologist, 1971-; Am Asn Clin Anatomists, 1993-; Am Asn Anatomists, 1996-; Brit Asn Clin Anatomists; Alpha Omega Alpha Hon Med Soc. **Honors/Awds:** Josiah Macey Fellow, 1959-63; William Allan Jr, MD, Memorial Lectr, Ninety eighth NMA, 1993. **Military Serv:** AUS, medic, corpl, actg first sergent, 1954-56. **Business Addr:** Professor, University of California Los Angeles, Department of Radiological Sciences, 10833 Le Conte Ave CHS Bldg, PO Box 951721, Los Angeles, CA 90095-1721.*

COLLINS, JAMES EDGAR. See COLLINS, JAMES.

COLLINS, JAMES H.
Executive director. **Personal:** Born Feb 1, 1946, Moline, IL; son of Alphonso and Mattie Pennington; married Karen J Raebel; children: James Jr, Kimberly, Candace, Anthony, Kevin. **Educ:** St Ambrose Col, BA, Sociol, 1969. **Career:** Proj Now Comt Action Agency, exec dir, 1968-71; John Deere, indust rels rep, 1971-74, EEO, coordr, 1974-75, mgr prsnl, 1975-83; Deere & Co, dir community rels, currently; John Deere Found, pres, currently. **Orgs:** Quad Cities Merit Employ Coun; Iowa Human Rights Comn; Quad Cities United Way; Quad Cities Coun Crime & Delinq; Human Rights & Employ Practices Comm; Bus Adv Coun, Ill Dept Rehab Serv; Iowa Civil Rights Com; John Deere Found; St Ambrose Univ. **Honors/Awds:** Athletic Hall of Fame, St Ambrose Col, 1984; Citizen Community Rehab Service Award, Ill Rehab Asn, 1989. **Business Addr:** Director, St Ambrose University, 518 W Locust St, Davenport, IA 52803.*

COLLINS, JEFFREY G
Judge. **Educ:** Howard Univ Sch Law; Northwestern Univ. **Career:** Detroit Recorder's Ct, judge; Eastern Dist MI, US atty; Foley & Lardner LLP, partner, currently. **Orgs:** Pres-elect, Asn Black Judges Mich; mentor, Man to Man; deacon, Plymouth United Church Christ; chmn, Wayne Co Criminal Advocacy Prog. **Honors/Awds:** Founder's Award Outstanding Achievement, Nat Black Prosecutors Asn, 2004; Mich Lawyer of the Year, Mich Lawyers Weekly, 2003; Damon J Keith Community Spirit Award, Wolverine Bar Found, 2003; Named a Michigan "Super Lawyer," Law & Politics Media Inc, 2006; D Augstus Straker Bar Asn Trailblazer Award, 2006. **Special Achievements:** One of the nation's top African-Am attys, Black Enterprise Mag, 2003; Published, Congress Passes Internet Gambling Legislation Aimed at the Banks; Coordination is Essential. **Business Phone:** (313)234-7104.

COLLINS, DR. JOANN RUTH
School administrator. **Personal:** Born in Nashville, TN; married John H; children: John K & Guy R. **Educ:** Mich State Univ, BS, 1971, MA, 1973, PhD. **Career:** Dept Civil Serv, State Mich, women's training officer; Mich State Univ, coord col work study prog; Breckinridge Job Corps Ctr KY, dir, family servs, dir & nursery & kindergarten. **Orgs:** Nat Task Force Stud Aid Problems; Black Fac & Admin, Mich State Univ,1973; women's steering com, Mich State Univ, 1973; bd dir, Lansing Sr Citizens Inc, 1974-76; adv com bus & office Educ Clubs, Mich HS, 1974-; pres, Nat Asn Fin Assistance Minority Stud, 1974-.

COLLINS, JOANNE MARCELLA
Banker, activist. **Personal:** Born Aug 29, 1935, Kansas City, MO; daughter of William and Mary Frances Porter; married Gerald A Spence (divorced 1961); children: Jerri Ann, Francis Damont; married Robert Lawrence Collins, Jun 10, 1962. **Educ:** Kansas Univ, attended 1955; Stephens Col, BA, 1988; Baker Univ, MS, 1990; St Louis Univ, cert; Weaver Sch Real Estate, sales & property mgt. **Career:** Univ Kans Med Ctr, Clendenning Med Libr, libr clerk, 1955-58; Robert Hughes & Co Real Estate, agt, 1958-62; US Post Office, postal clerk, 1960-63; Wheatley Provident Hosp, The Greater Kansas City Baptist & Community Hospital Asn, admin asst, 1964-72; US Dept Com, Metrop Kans City, supvr dicennial census, 1970-71; Kansas City, MO, city councilwoman, 1974; Halls Crown Ctr, Retail Sales Div, 1973-75; Conn Mutual Life Ins Co, assoc, 1977-79; United Mo Bank Kans, NA, asst vpres; US Dept Housing & Urban Develop, community builder fel. **Orgs:** Salvation Army, Greater Kansas City Chapter, Adult Rehabilitation Ctr; life mem, Nat Asn Advan Colored People; Delta Sigma Theta; Urban League Greater Kansas City; St Paul AME Zion Church; Women's Pub Serv Network; Emily Taylor's Women Resource; bd dirs, Liberty Memorial Asn; Miss Capital Punishment Resource Ctr; adv bd, United Minority Media Asn; Urban Youth Corps; Women's Leadership Fountain Comt; Women's Public Serv Network; Fifth Cong Dist Republican Club; Soroptimist Int Inc; Financial Women Int; Ethnic Enrichment Comn; Avila Col Sch Nursing; Stephens Col Alumnae Asn; United Way Wyandotte County Inc. **Honors/Awds:** Distinguished Service Award, Eleventh Episcopal District, AME Zion Church; Award of Appreciation for Community Service, Women's Political Caucus; Builder of Boys Award, Boys Club; Honoree, Greater Kansas City Comn Status Women; YWCA Volunteer Award; AT&T Margit Lasker Award; Women's Hall of Fame, Univ Kans; Zonta International Award; Women of Achievement Award, Girl Scouts Am, Kansas City Chapter; Junior Achievement Recognition Award; Hawk Award, Black Economic Union; Citizen of the Year, Omega Psi Phi; Leadership Award, Kansas City Council of Youth Develop, 1991; Distinguished Service Award, Miss Munic League, 1991; Black Women Portraits Award, AME, 1992; Leadership Award, YouthNet, 1992. **Home Phone:** (816)861-6604. **Business Addr:** Immediate Past Chair, United Way of Wyandotte County Inc, 434 Minnesota Ave, PO Box 17 1042, Kansas City, MO 66117.*

COLLINS, KENNETH L.
Lawyer. **Personal:** Born Aug 23, 1933, El Centro, CA; married Beverly Jean Sherman; children: Kevin, Leslie. **Educ:** Univ Calif, Los Angeles, BA 1959; Univ Calif, Los Angeles, JD, 1971. **Career:** Fed Pub Defenders Off, pub defender, 1972-75; San Fernando Valley Juvenile Hall, acting dir; La Co, probation officer, 1957-68; RK Law Group, currently. **Orgs:** Langston Law Club; Calif Attys Criminal Justice; Calif State Bar; chmn bd dir, Black Law J; past pres, Kappa Alpha Psi Upsion, 1957-58; co-founder Black Law J. **Honors/Awds:** Chancelors Award, Univ Calif, Los Angeles, 1971. **Military Serv:** AUS, corpl, 1953-55. **Business Addr:** Lawyer, RK Law Group, 555 W 5th St 31 Fl, Los Angeles, CA 90013.

COLLINS, LAVERNE VINES
Government official. **Personal:** Born Feb 3, 1947, Livorno, Italy; daughter of Myrtle Elizabeth Coy Vines (deceased) and Thomas Fulton Vines (deceased); married Alfred Collins, Jun 21, 1969 (divorced 1985); children: Alfred (deceased), Anthony, McAllister. **Educ:** Univ Michigan, Ann Arbor, MI, 1966; Western Michigan Univ, Kalamazoo, MI, BA, 1968, MA, 1971. **Career:** Western Michigan Univ, Kalamazoo, MI, dean of students staff, 1969-71; US Census Bureau, Suitland, MD, statistician, 1971-72; Office of Management and Budget, Washington, DC, statistician, 1972-82; US Census Bureau, Atlanta, GA, survey statistician, 1982-83; US Census Bureau, Los Angeles, CA, assistant regional director, 1983-85; US Census Bureau, Philadelphia, PA, regional director, 1985-91, Washington, DC, supervisory social science analyst, 1992-94; Chief, Public Information Office 1994-99; US Census Bur, asst to the assoc dir commun, 1999-. **Orgs:** Member, Alpha Kappa Alpha Sorority, 1965-; board of directors, Budget Federal Credit Union, 1980-82; mem, American Statistical Association, 1973-83; mem, American Population Association, 1985-86; board of directors, United Way of Southeastern PA, 1987-90; mem, Coalition of 100 Black Women of Southern New Jersey, 1989-90. **Honors/Awds:** US Census Bureau, Equal Employment Opportunity Award, 1991. **Business Addr:** Assistant to the Associate Director, US Census Bureau, 4700 Silver Hill Rd, Rm 2085-3, Washington, DC 20233-0001, **Business Phone:** (301)763-8469.*

COLLINS, LENORA W.
Consultant, special education teacher. **Personal:** Born Feb 25, 1925, Fayette, MS; married Joe H. **Educ:** Xavier Univ, BS, 1946; Governors State Univ, MA, 1974; Univ Sarasota, EdD, 1977; DePaul Univ, advan study. **Career:** Chicago Bd Educ, home econs teacher, 1948-54; supvr caseworker 1959-61; supvr home econs 1962-63; Bur Home Econs Cook County Dept Public Aid, asst chief, 1964-73; Dept Pub Aid St Ill, econs consult; Lorman Community Develop Orgn, Lorman, Miss, exec dir. **Orgs:** Chmn, Health & Welfare Sect Ill Home Econ Asn, 1968-69; pres, Chicago Home Econ Asn, 1970-71; secy, Jefferson Co Hosp, 1979-80; life mem, Am Home Econs Asn; life mem, Ill Home Econs Asn; vice chmn, Human Serv Sect; Chicago Nutrit Asn; Am Pub Welfare Asn; bd mem, Chicago Met Housing Coun Tenant Proj; trustee, Jefferson Co Hosp; Nat Negro Bus & Prof Women's Club; Delta Sigma Theta; Wacker Neighborhood Asn Chicago Urban League; Nat Asn Advan Colored People. **Honors/Awds:** Recipient Finer Womanhood Award, Zeta Phi Beta 1967; Silver Jubilee & Alumnus Award, Xavier Univ 1971; listed in Chicago Almanac & Ref Book, 1973.

COLLINS, LEROY ANTHONY, JR.
Government official, president (organization). **Personal:** Born Jan 13, 1950, Norfolk, VA; son of Leroy and Thelma Taylor; married; children: Kisten Collins & Lyndsey Collins. **Educ:** Howard Univ, attended 1970; Rutgers Univ, BS, 1973; Temple Univ Sch Bus, attended 1981. **Career:** City Newark, NJ, asst budget dir, 1974-78; City Miami, FL, asst city mgr, 1978-80; Pa Mutual Life Ins Co, sr investment analyst, 1980-83; City Tampa, FL, mgr econ develop, 1983-86; City St Petersburg, FL, dir econ develop, currently; Promethens Innovations Inc, pres. **Orgs:** Chmn, Black Bus Investment Bd, 1988-; bd mem, Oper PAR; bd mem, Suncoasters; Fla Export Finance Authority; Tampa Bay Defense Transition Task Force; Tampa Bay Partnership; Enterprise Fla Capital Devt Bd; bd dirs, Bennett Bank Pinellas County; Enterprise Fla Int Trade & Econ Develop Bd; bd mem, vice chair mkt comn, Tampa Bay Partnership. **Honors/Awds:** Focus Develop, Penn Mutual Life, 1982; Leadership Tampa, Tampa Chamber Com, 1985; Service Award, City Tampa, 1986. **Military Serv:** USMC, E-4, 1970-73; American Spirit of Honor Award, 1971.

COLLINS, MARK ANTHONY
Football player. **Personal:** Born Jan 16, 1964, Louis, MO. **Educ:** Fullerton State Univ. **Career:** Football player (retired); NY Giants, defensive back, 1986-93; Kansas City Chiefs, 1994-96; Green Bay Packers, 1997; Seattle Seahawks, 1998. **Honors/Awds:** Defensive Player of the Year, 1985; All-NFL Team, Sports Illustrated, 1993. *

COLLINS, MARVA DELORES NETTLES
Educator. **Personal:** Born Aug 31, 1936, Monroeville, AL; daughter of Alex L Nettles and Bessie Maye Knight Nettles; married Clarence, Sep 4, 1960; children: Cynthia Beth, Eric & Patrick. **Educ:** Clark Col, BA, 1957; Northwestern Univ. **Career:** Monroe Co Training Sch Monroeville, AL, tchr 1958-59; Delano Elem Sch, tchr 1960-75; Westside Prep Sch, founder/dir 1975-; Delano Sch, teacher 13yrs; Marva Collins Seminars Inc, owner, currently;

Marva Collins Preparatory Sch, dir, currently. **Orgs:** Dir, Right Read Found 1978; Sunday sch tchr, Morning Star Bapt Ch 1978-79;President's Comn White House Fellowships 1981-; Alpha Kappa Alpha, NAACP; President's Citizens' Group 1989-. **Honors/Awds:** Fred Hampton Image Award Fred Hampton Found 1979; Watson Wash burne Award Reading Reform Found 1979; Educator of the Year Award Phi Delta Kappa1980; Endow a Dream Awd 1980; Jefferson Natl Awd 1981; The Humanitarian Award for Excellence; Legendary Women of the World Award; Amer Public Serv Awd Amer Inst for Public Serv 1981; featured on TV's "60 Minutes"; subject of a made-for-TV movie "The Marva Collins Story" 1981; publs including Marva Collins' Way 1982; Honorary Degrees from: Washington Univ, Amherst,Dartmouth, Chicago State Univ, Howard Univ, Central State Univ, St Louis Univ; The prestigious Natl Humanities Medal, Pres Bush, 2004. **Special Achievements:** Several schools follow her methodology; teaches seminars all over the world; speaking engagements all over the world; Featured on Good Morning, Am, 20/20, Fox News. **Business Addr:** Director, Marva Collins Preparatory School, 8035 S Honore St, Chicago, IL 60620.

COLLINS, MO (DAMON JAMAL MO COLLINS)
Football player. **Personal:** Born Sep 22, 1976, Charlotte, NC. **Educ:** Univ Fla. **Career:** Football player (retired); Oakland Raiders, tackle, 1998-2003.

COLLINS, DR. PATRICIA HILL
Educator. **Personal:** Born May 1, 1948, Philadelphia, PA; married Roger L Collins; children: Valerie Lisa. **Educ:** Brandeis Univ, AB 1969, PhD 1984; Harvard Univ, MAT 1970. **Career:** Harvard U TTT Prog, teacher, curriculum spec, 1970-73; Harvard Univ, Teacher, 1970-72; Design Programs, Inc, Educ Consult, 1972-73; St Joseph Community Sch, curriculum specialist 1973-76; Tufts Univ, dir African Am Ctr 1976-80; Univ Cincinnati, from asst prof to assoc prof African-Am Studies, 1982-94, prof, 1994-2005, assoc prof social, 1988, Taft prof social, 2003, Dept African Am Stud, chmn, 2003, Charles Phelps Taft Distinguished prof, 1996-2005; Charles Phelps Taft Distinguished Emer, 2005-; PHC Educational Services, Inc, pres, 2002-; Univ Md, Col Park, Wilson Elkins prof, sociol, 2005-. **Orgs:** Chair Minority Fellowship Program Comm, 1986-89; Am Sociol Asn; vpres, Great Rivers Girl Scouts Coun, 1992-94. **Honors/Awds:** Black Arts Festival Award, Univ Cincinnati, 1983; Emphasis on Diversity Award, Univ Cincinnati, 1989; Faculty of the Year Award, Univ Cincinnati, 1991; Letitia Woods Brown Memorial Book Prize, Asn Black Women Historians, 1991; Distinguished Publication Award, Asn Women Psychol, 1991; C Wright Mills Award, Soc Study Social Problems, 1991; Career Woman of Achievement Award, YWCA of Cincinnati, 1993; Jessie Bernard Award, Am Sociol Asn, 1993. **Special Achievements:** C Wright Mills Award for "Black Feminist Thought," 1990. **Business Addr:** Distinguished University Professor, University of Maryland, Department of Sociology, 4105 Art Sociol Bldg, Cincinnati, OH 45221, **Business Phone:** (301)405-7707.

COLLINS, PAUL
Artist. **Personal:** Born Dec 11, 1936, Muskegon, MI. **Career:** Paintings C Harlem, 1976-78; Joseph P Kennedy Found, spec olympics drawings & paintings, 1976-79; paintings & book Great Beautiful Black Women, 1976-78; Famous Moments Black Am Hist, mural, 1978-80; paintings Working Americans, 1980-83; mural & book Gerald R Ford, A Man in Perspective 1976; paintings-Voices of Israel, 1986-89; paintings, drawings & book-Black Portrait African Journey, 1969-71; Collins Fine Art, artist & painter, currently. **Orgs:** Bd trustees, Robeson Players, 1972-80; Am Indian Movement, 1972-84; adv bd, John F Kennedy Ctr Performance Arts, 1976-80; co-chmn, Western Mich United Negro Col Fund, 1989-90. **Honors/Awds:** Mead Book Award, 1972; People's Choice Award, Am Painters Paris, 1976; Arts Council Award, Grand Rapids Arts Coun, 1979; Designer Martin Luther King Jr Non-Violent Peace Prize Medal, 1979-80; Black Achievement Award, 1979; Tadlow Fine Art Award. **Special Achievements:** 20 Outstanding Figure Painters & How They Work, 1979, first artist from the United States invited to participate in the International Arts Festival in Sarajevo in 1998. **Business Addr:** Artist, Figure & Cultural Painter, Paul Collins Fine Art, 220 Lyon NW Suite 101 Amway Grand Plz, Grand Rapids, MI 49503, **Business Phone:** (616)742-2000.

COLLINS, PAUL L.
Clergy, executive director. **Personal:** Born Apr 19, 1931, Shreveport, LA; son of Paul (deceased) and Willie Mae Adams (deceased); married Shirley Alexander; children: Paula, Darryl. **Educ:** Southern Univ, BA & MEd, 1958; George Washington Univ, EdD, 1976. **Career:** Carver Jr High School, 1958-59; BTW High School, prof military Sci, 1959-62; Wash Jr High Sch, teacher, 1962-65; Roosevelt High Sch, dir guidance, 1965-68; Off Human Rights, asso exec int rels, govt res policy & analysis-registered lobbyist Prof Devel Prog; Non White Concerns, dir; Wash Tech Inst, asso prof, 1968-71; Am Asn Coun & Devel, assoc exec, 1970-83; prof counr, 1978-; Nazarene Outpost Ministries, exec dir, 1990-. **Orgs:** Pres, Asn Specialists in Group Work, 1985-86; pres, Capitol Hill Kiwanis Club, 1981-82; chmn bd, Prepare Our Youth, 1987-; dean, Mt Bethel Baptist Educnl Cong, Nat Baptist Conv, 1984-92; assoc pastor, New Order Christian Fel, 1987-90; community adv bd dirs, Wash CTR for Aging Servs, 1988-; pres, DC Ment Health Counsrs Asn, 1992-93; asst to chief prot chaplin, DC Gen Hosp, 1989-92; certified crisis intervener, ABECI, 1990; Am Evangelistic Asn, 1992-; Mt Bethel Baptist Asn, field missionary, 1994-. **Honors/Awds:** Outstanding teacher award, 1960; outstanding leadership award, 1962; outstanding leadership voc guidance, 1970; Christian Leadership, 1967; United Nations USA Award, 1971-72; Nat Counr Cert, Nat Bd Cert Counr, 1983-88; Cert Excellence Spiritual Aims, 1988, Outstanding Club Leadership Award, 1982, Capitol Hill Kiwanis Club; Clin Pastoral Edu Cert, 1990. **Military Serv:** AUS, first lt, 1954-56. **Business Addr:** Executive Director, Nazarene Outpost Ministries, 111 Rhode Island Ave NW, Washington, DC 20018.*

COLLINS, DR. PAUL V.
Educator, basketball coach. **Personal:** Born Sep 7, 1918, Philadelphia, PA; married Margaret Anne Chambers; children: Paula L, Pamela E, Richard Paul & Margaret Nicole. **Educ:** Livingstone Col, Salisbury, NC, BA, 1941; NY Univ, New York, MA, Sociol, 1948; TN State Univ, Nashville, MS Health & PE, 1958; NY Univ, New York, Doctoral Studies, 1968-69. **Career:** Educator, Basketball coach (retired); SA Owen Jr Col, Memphis, TN, head basketball coach, 1955-57; Miss Valley State Col, Etta Bena, MS, head basketball coach, asst football coach, scout, assoc prof sociol, 1957-60; Lane Col, Jackson, TN, head basketball coach, assoc prof health & physical educ 1960-61; Wiley Col, Marshall, TX, head basketball coach & asst prof Sociol, 1961-65; JHS 139 Manhattan, New York Bd Educ, dean boys, 1965-67; IS 201 Manhattan, New York Bd Educ, master teacher, 1966-68; New York Univ, instr educ, 1968-69; US Off Educ, Wash, DC, educ prog specialist, 1969-70; Weaver High Sch, Hartford, CT, Bd Educ, prin 1970-73; Calif State Univ, Hayward, assoc prof educ & coordr multi cult educ, 1973-93. **Orgs:** Dir, Pac Ctr Educ Res & Develop, Castro Valley, PA, 1974; multi cult educ adv comt, Calif State Dept Educ, 1977-78; ad hoc com Racial Isolation Sch, Calif State Dept Educ, 1977-78. **Honors/Awds:** Superior Service Award & HEW Office Educ, 1972. **Military Serv:** USN, amm 3/c 2 years served.

COLLINS, ROBERT FREDERICK
Judge. **Personal:** Born Jan 27, 1931, New Orleans, LA; son of Frederick and Irma Anderson; married Aloha M, Dec 27, 1957; children: Francesca McManus, Lisa Ann, Nanette C & Robert A. **Educ:** Dillard Univ, BA (cum laude), 1951; La State Univ, JD; Univ NV Nat Judge Col, 1973. **Career:** Augustine Collins Smith & Warren New Orleans, partner, 1956-59; Southern Univ Law Sch, Baton Rouge LA, instr, 1959-61, 1981-90; Collins Douglas & Elie New Orleans, sr partner, 1960-72; New Orleans Police Dept, asst city atty, legal adv, 1967-69; Traffic Ct New Orleans, judge ad-hoc, 1969-72; State LA, asst bar examr, 1970-78; Housing Authority New Orleans, atty, 1971-72; Criminal Dist Ct Orleans Parish LA, judge magistrate sect, 1972-78; US Dist Ct, Eastern Dist LA, judge, currently. **Orgs:** Trustee, Loyola Univ, 1977-83; La Bar Asn; Am Bar Asn; Alpha Phi Alpha; Sigma Pi Phi; Phi Alpha Delta; pres, Louis A Martinet Legal Soc, 1959-60; regional dir, Nat Bar Asn, 1964-65; Am Judicature Soc; 5th Circuit Dist Judges Asn. **Honors/Awds:** Honor Soc, Alpha Kappa Mu, 1950; Passed Bar, LA, 1954; LLD, Dillard Univ, 1979. **Military Serv:** AUS, 1954-56. **Home Addr:** 4840 St Bernard Ave, New Orleans, LA 70122, **Home Phone:** (504)283-9601. **Business Phone:** (504)589-7600.

COLLINS, RODNEY
Manager. **Career:** J & W Seligman & Co Inc, co-portfolio mgr, 2001. *

COLLINS, ROSECRAIN
Dentist. **Personal:** Born Feb 14, 1929, Nashville, TN; married Elizabeth; children: Michelle, Adrienne. **Educ:** TN State Univ, BS, 1952; Meharry Med Col, DDS, 1958. **Career:** Martin Luther King Health Ctr, dentist, 1971-74; Kennedy Ryan & Monigal Realtors Asn, 1973-; Chicago Child Care Soc, dentist, 1976-; Chicago Dept Pub Aid, dental consult, 1977-; pvt pract, currently. **Orgs:** Treas, Great Western Investment Ltd, 1969-; dir, Intl Sporting Club, 1974; partner, Forestry Recycling Mill, 1975-; Dental Health Screening Chicago Pub Sch, 1961-63; Lincoln Dental Soc, 1959-; chicago Dental Soc treas, 1970-74; IL Dental Soc, 1959-; Am Dental Soc, 1959-; Nat Dental Soc, 1959-; Acad Gen Dent, 1974-. **Honors/Awds:** Citation, pub serv City Chicago, 1962-63. **Military Serv:** AUS, sgt, 1952-54. **Business Addr:** Dentist, Private Practitioner, 1525 E 53rd St No 904, Chicago, IL 60615-4572, **Business Phone:** (773)536-0753.*

COLLINS, TESSIL JOHN
Manager, television producer. **Personal:** Born Aug 29, 1952, Boston, MA; son of Tessil A and Evelyn A Gill; children: Dionna Collins. **Educ:** Boston Latin Sch, 1971; Tufts Univ, BA, Eng, 1975; Boston Univ, Exec Prog Cert Small Bus Develop Prog, 1985. **Career:** Boston Pub Sch, Madison Park Tech Vocational High Sch, instr, Commun Arts & Television Prod, 1984-; Beantown Music, nat sales & promotions; RCA & A&M & Arista Records, field merchandiser, 1981-83; WILD Radio, Boston, acct exec, 1975, 1980-81; Rep Melvin H King, campaign mgr, 1978-79; WBCN Radio, acct exec, 1978-80; WBZ Radio, producer, 1973-78; Spectrum Broadcasting Corp, owner, 1984-, pres & chief exec officer, currently. **Orgs:** Prince Hall Grand Lodge F & AM; bd mem, Dimock COT HTH CTR, Proj Africa; bd mem, Berklee Col Music Community Adv Comt; bd mem, ford hall forum; trustee, Roxbury Crossing Historical Trust. **Honors/Awds:** Certificate Media Technology, MA Dept Educ Div Occup Educ, 1985; position at Beantown, Black Enterp May & Feb, 1984; producer video stud diversity "I'm Different, You're Different, We're All Okay" Tufts Univ, 1985; producer video, Mrs Black Boston Pageant, 1986; Grand Prize, Fl Citrus Comn Music Video Competition, 1987; Writer & Producer, "It's Christmastime Again," recorded by TSOC, 1994; Producer, "The Beat," A Street Smarts Collaborative Video Proj, Boston Police Dept, 1995; producer, "The Voice," WBPS-AM, Boston; one of six Greater Boston "Unsung Heroes", Tribune Broadcasting, WB56 Boston & BlackVoices.com, 2002. **Business Addr:** President, Chief Executive Officer, Spectrum Broadcasting Corporation, PO Box 201045 Mission Hill Sta, Boston, MA 02120, **Business Phone:** (617)287-8770.*

COLLINS, WILLIAM, JR.
Clergy. **Personal:** Born Jul 3, 1924, St Louis, MO; married Margaret Elizabeth Brown; children: Sylvia, Deirdre, William & III. **Educ:** St Louis Univ, BS, 1956; Colgate Rochester Div Sch, BD, 1960; Univ Rochester, MEd, 1960; Colgate Rochester Div Sch, MDiv, 1972; E NE Christian Col, DD, 1972; St Louis Univ, PhD, 1973. **Career:** MO Dept Welfare St Louis, caseworker, 1948-51; US Postal, employee, 1951-56; Second Baptist Church Leroy NY, student pastor, 1959-60; Antioch Baptist Church St Louis, minister christian educ, 1960-61; Blue field State Col, dir pub rel & asst registrar, 1961; Antioch Baptist Church, St Louis, pastor, 1961-. **Orgs:** Eagle Scout, 1939; Alpha Phi Alpha Frat, 1947; Preaching Mission Am Baptist El Salvador & Nicaragua Latin Am, 1966; bd, Health & Hosp St Louis, 1968-; Landmark & Urban Design Comn St Louis, 1968- 72; bd mem, Annie Malone C Home St Louis, 1970-; bd, St Louis Munic Nurses, 1970-; Adult Welfare Comns St Louis, 1970-; Am Baptist Conv; Task Force; Intl Ministries Africa, 1971-; Missionary Involvement Tour; Am Baptist W Africa, 1972; bd trustees, St Louis Jr Col Dist elected six yr term, 1975. **Military Serv:** AUS, sgt, 1943-46. **Business Addr:** Pastor, Antioch Baptist Church, 4213 West North Market, St Louis, MO 63113, **Business Phone:** (314)535-1110.*

COLLINS-EAGLIN, DR. JAN THERESA
Counselor, psychologist. **Personal:** Born Dec 2, 1950, New York, NY; daughter of John E and Naomi Fraser; married Fulton Eaglin; children: Christopher, Jennifer & Jessica. **Educ:** Calif State Univ, Dominguez Hills, BA, 1977; Univ Mich, Ann Arbor, MA, MS, 1980, EdS, 1980, PhD, 1983. **Career:** Univ Mich, Ann Arbor, Mich, lectr, 1983-85; Eastern Mich Univ, Ypsilanti, Mich, psychologist, 1985-87, coordr, 1987-90, prof, 1990-; Wayne State Univ, dir coun servs, dir stud affairs; Mich State Univ, Dept Multi Ethnic Coun Ctr Alliance, dir, currently. **Orgs:** Alpha Kappa Alpha Sorority, 1975-; Am Psychol Asn, 1983-; Mich Col Personnel Asn, 1987-; Links, 1988-; regional found Offr, Jack & Jill Am, 1988-. **Honors/Awds:** Am Psychol Asn Fel, 1978-82; Nat Inst Ment Health Fel, 1977-81; Res & grants col retention black studs: Select Stud Support Servs, State Mich, 1987-90; Summer Incentive Prog, Dept Labor, 1987-90. **Business Addr:** Director, Michigan State University, Multi Ethnic Counseling Center Alliance, 27 Stud Serv, East Lansing, MI 48824, **Business Phone:** (517)355-8270.

COLLINS-GRANT, EARLEAN
State government official. **Personal:** Born in Rollingfork, MS; married John; children: Dwarrye. **Educ:** Univ Ill, BS, soc, Ed. **Career:** Collins Realty & Ins Agency, self employed, 1969-72; State IL, Dept C & Family Servs, soc serv admin, 1972-76; State IL, sen; Cook Co, Dist I, comnr, currently. **Orgs:** Westside Bus Asn; Nat Asn Soc Workers; Nat Conf State Leg; Conf Women Leg; Intergovernmental Coop Coun; comt chair, Bus & Econ Develop; Pub Health; Family Ct & Juv Detention Ctr; bd mem, Forest Preserve Dist. **Honors/Awds:** Best Legislator Award, Independent Voters IL; IL Business & Professional Women's Award; IL Ed Asn Award; Am vet's Award; Beautiful People Award, Chicago Urban League. **Special Achievements:** First African-American woman elected to the Illinois Senate. **Business Addr:** Commissioner, Cook County, 118 N Clark St Room 567, Chicago, IL 60602, **Business Phone:** (312)603-4566.

COLLONS, FERRIC JASON
Football player. **Personal:** Born Dec 4, 1969, Bellville, IL. **Educ:** Univ Calif, criminal justice. **Career:** Football player (Retird); New Eng Patriots, defensive end, 1995-99. *

COLLYMORE, DR. EDWARD L.
Educator. **Personal:** Born Jan 5, 1938, Cambridge, MA; son of Eulah M Johnson and Percival E; married Marcia L Burnett; children: Sandra Coleman & Edward Jr. **Educ:** Villanova Univ, BS, econ, 1959, MA, counseling, 1971; Univ PA, EdD, admin, 1984. **Career:** Educator (retired); Cambridge Pub Sch, substitute teacher, 1963; Liberty Mutual Ins Co, casualty underwriter, 1963-66; Third Dist Ct Cambridge; juv probation officer, 1966-69; Villanova Univ, Off Soc Action Prog, staff, 1960, Off Multicultural Affairs, exec dir, 2005. **Orgs:** Bd Rosemont Optimist; bd vpres,

Comt Action Agency Delaware, CO. **Honors/Awds:** Co-holder, World Record, 60-yd dash, AAU Track, 1957; All-Am 220 yard dash, NCAA Track, 1957-59; rep, US Track Europe, Russia AAU, 1957-58; Society Action Award, Villanova Univ, 1978; Hall of Fame, Villanova Univ Alumni Asn, 1980; Distinguished Alumnus Black Cultural Soc, 1982; Rosemont Optimist Man of the Year, 1985; Wall of Fame, Villanova Univ, 1996; Wall of Fame, Univ Pa, 2000; WEB Dubois Award, Black Cult Soc, 2000; Man of the Year, Bethel AME Church, 2003; Mass State Coaches Asn, Athletic Hall of Fame, 2008; Alumni Medal for 1959 alumna, Alumni Asn Villinova Univ, 2009. **Military Serv:** USMCR, Col. **Home Addr:** 715 Polo Rd, Bryn Mawr, PA 19010, **Home Phone:** (610)525-7577.

COLON, HARRY
Football player, football coach. **Personal:** Born Feb 14, 1969, Kansas City, KS. **Educ:** Univ Mo. **Career:** Football player (retired); New England Patriots, defensive back, 1991; Detroit Lions, 1992-94, 1997; Jacksonville Jaguars, 1995; John H. Reagan High Sch, coord.

COLSON, LEWIS ARNOLD
Educator, community activist. **Personal:** Born Aug 3, 1947, Miami, FL; son of Arthur Mae Ross and Booker T (deceased); married Glendoria Saine, May 14, 1982; children: Doria Arne, Lewis Arnold Jr, Roviere Jordan, Charles, Lewis Armand & Michelle. **Educ:** Wayne State Univ, polit sci, 1973-75; Mercy Col, criminal justice, 1976. **Career:** Detroit Police Dept, 1972-82; Tru-Vue Restaurant, co-owner, 1982-86; Guardian Police Asn, exec dir, 1986-89; Nat Black Police Asn, asst, 1986-88; Upward Entrepreneurial Consult Servs, Inc, sr partner, 1986-; Southern Corner Caterers, co-owner, 1986-; Detroit Underground Restaurant, Inc, 1988-90; Doty Multiservice Ctr Inc, founder & exec dir, 1990-92. **Orgs:** Chairperson, Nat Black Police Asn, 1973-91; exec dir & founder, Guardian Police Asn, Peoplemakers Project, 1978-89; econ comm, NCP, 1991-; Urban League, Our Own Hands, 1991; regional chairperson, lead agency head, Youth Comn, 1991-; volunteer & trainer, SOSAD; youth instr, UAW & Univ Detroit, 1991; chairperson, Youth Comn, Black Men Inc, 1992-; chairperson, New Detroit Anti-Violence Prog, 1992; founder & dir, Detroiters Organized Train Youth, Inc, 1992-. **Honors/Awds:** Certificate of Achievement, Nat Crime Preven Coun, 1989; Mayor of City of Detroit, Anti-Crime Week, 1991; Certificate of Appreciation, REACH Comm Orgn, 1991; Spirit of Detroit, Detroit City Coun, 1992. **Special Achievements:** Establishment of First Police Dept Drug Educ-Prevention Program in Nation, 1976, Solutions to the Detroit Drug Problem, 1978, Creation of Detroit/Peoplemakers Project, 1979, First Crime Prevention Consultant Firm in Michigan, 1990, first African Centered Management Program, 1991. **Military Serv:** USY, 1966-69; Honor Guard/Military Police-European Headquarters. **Home Phone:** (313)863-9190. **Business Addr:** Founder, Director, Detroiters Organized To Train Youth Inc, 1600 Lawrence Ave, Detroit, MI 48206, **Business Phone:** (313)863-9190.

COLSTON, DR. FREDDIE C.
Educator. **Personal:** Born Mar 28, 1936, Gretna, FL; married Doris Marie; children: Deirdre & Charisse. **Educ:** More house Col, BA, 1959; Atlanta Univ, MA, 1966; OH State Univ, PhD (polit sci), 1972. **Career:** Educator (retired); OH State Univ, Dept Polit Sci, teaching assoc, 1968-71; Southern Univ, Baton Rouge, LA, fel, 1971-72, assoc prof, polit sci, 1972-73; Univ Detroit, MI, assoc prof, polit sci, 1973-76; Dillard Univ, New Orleans, LA, chmn, div soc sci, 1976-78; Delta Col, Univ Cent Mich, asst prof, polit sci, 1978-80; Exec Sem Ctr, US Off Personal Mgt, assoc dir, 1980-87; TN State Univ, prof & cood grad studies, 1987-88; NC-Cent Univ, prof & cood grad studies, 1988-89; NC Cent Univ, dir public admin prog, 1989-91; Ga Southwestern State Univ, Dept Hist & Polit Sci, GA, prof, 1992-97. **Orgs:** Pi Sigma Alpha Nat Pol Sci Hon Soc, 1958-; Alpha Phi Gamma Nat Hon Soc,1958-; Am Polit Sci Asn, 1968-, Ctr Study Presidency, 1976-; Am Soc Publ Admin, 1983-, Omega Psi Phi Frat, 1956; bd mgmt, YMCA Metrop, Detroit,1976; Govt Subcmt Task Force 2000, Midland, MI, 1979; Nat Forum Black Publ Admin, 1984-; Am Asn Higher Educ, 1987-; Am Mgt Asn, 1988; Oak Ridge Conv & Visitors Bur bd. **Honors/Awds:** Mr. Psi, Psi Chap, Omega Psi Phi, 1959; hon fel, John F. Kennedy Presidential Library, 1986; Outstanding Fac Award, Kappa Delta Sor, 1995;Outstanding Fac Award, South western State Univ, 1997; Superior Serv Award, 1996, 1997. **Home Addr:** 126 Hazleton Ln, Oak Ridge, TN 37830. *

COLSTON, MONROE JAMES
Executive, consultant, association executive. **Personal:** Born Sep 5, 1933, Richland, TX; married Frances V Brown; children: Rhonda Wardlow, Marietta. **Educ:** Univ Minn, AA; Nat Exec Inst; Univ Colo, cert US Chamber Com Orgn Mgt Sch; Tex Col, Tyler; Grand View Col, hon doc law. **Career:** Executive (retired), consultant; Urban Affairs Greater Des Moines C, mgr; Boy Scouts Am, exec dir, 1968-71; Blacks Mgt Inc, founder; Greater Des Moines Community Found, pres, 1992-98, consult, currently. **Orgs:** Real estate comnr State IA; bd dir, IA Soc Mgt Nat; mem & Metro Assistance Team; Nat Alliance Businessmen; Brain Trust Congressional Balck Caucus; chmn & co-founder, Blacks Mgt; coun mem, Boy Scouts Am; Kappa Alpha Psi; comt person, IA Career Educ; Civilian Serv Club; Am Cham Com; bd mem, Drake Univ, 1991-; NAACP; Mercy Med Ctr Bd, Bankers Trust Bd; Fed Home Loan Bank Des Moines; Iowa Lottery Bd; Human Serv Co-ord Bd, Rotary Club Des Moines; Nat Alliance Bus; and also served on many boards and councils. **Honors/Awds:** Dist scouter yr; IA All Am Family, 1970; presidential citations, White House, pres Jimmy Carter, 1979; presidential citations, pres Ronald Reagan, 1994; Medal of Serv, Drake Univ, 2000; Frederick D Patterson Award; Mary Louise Smith Human Rights Award, Des Moines Human Rights Comn; cert recognition Amnesty Int. **Special Achievements:** Becoming the first African-American to join Des Moines' exclusive Wakonda Club; the first African-American to be elected in Bankers Trust Board. **Military Serv:** AUS, corp, 1954-56; outstanding serviceman, 1954. **Business Addr:** Consultant, Greater Des Moines Community Foundation, Finkbine Mansion, 1915 Grand Ave, Des Moines, IA 50309, **Business Phone:** (515)883-2626.*

COLSTON, DR. WANDA M
Administrator, executive. **Educ:** Shaw Univ, attended; Univ DC, attended; Howard Univ, attended. **Career:** Norfolk State Univ, assoc vpres acad affairs; Univ Md Eastern Shore, Off Pres, exec vpres, currently. **Orgs:** Chair, Univ Strategic Planning Comt, Univ Md Eastern Shore. **Business Addr:** Executive Vice President, University Of Maryland Eastern Shore, 1 Backbone Rd, Princess Anne, MD 21853, **Business Phone:** (410)651-6101.

COLSTON BARGE, GAYLE S
Executive. **Personal:** Born Jun 9, 1951, Columbus, OH; daughter of Geneva Laws Colston and Ervin M Colston; married Carlos H, Jul 24, 1971; children: Darron Barge & Mario Barge. **Educ:** Ohio Univ, attended 1971; Wright State Univ, attended 1972; Minot State Univ, BA, 1981. **Career:** City Columbus, pub educ spec, 1976-78; KBLE Ohio, admin mgr, 1978; JC Penney Ins Co, customer serv rep, 1978-80, from underwriter to sr underwriter, 1980-82; JC Penney Co, syst proj coordr, 1982-83, mkt pub affairs coordr, 1983-88, field pub affairs coord dir, 1988-90, field pub affairs mgr, 1990; The Barge Group, pres, 1995-98; Landsafe, vpres, 1998; Pepperdine Univ, Grad Sch Edu & Psychol, staff, currently; Winston-Salem State Univ, asst vice chancellor & chief mkt & commun officer, currently. **Orgs:** Bd dirs, M L King Performing Arts Ctr, 1986-88; comnr, State Ohio Job Training Partnership Act Comn, 1987-88; comm chair, The 500 Inc montage & auction, 1988; co-chair, Dallas Black Dance Theatre Gala Comm, 1990; class mem, Leadership Dallas, 1992-93; mem nat comt, Delta Sigma Theta Sorority, 1993-97; exec comm, The Links Inc, Plano Chap, 1995; bd mem, Bryan's House, 1995; bd mem, Dallas Women's Found, 1998. **Honors/Awds:** Outstanding Black Woman Alumnus, Ohio Univ, 1980; Ten Outstanding Citizens Award, Columbus Jaycees, 1984; Bellringer Award of Excellence, Community Relations Report, 1992; One of Ten Most Influential Women in Dallas, 1993; She Knows Where She's Going Award, 1997. **Special Achievements:** Co-ed, Focus 2000, JC Penney's diversity publ, 1993; named one among top African Am by PR Week, 1999. **Business Addr:** Assistant Vice Chancellor, Chief Marketing & Communications Officer, Winston-Salem State University, 601 S Martin Luther King Jr Dr, Winston-Salem, NC 27110, **Business Phone:** (336)750-2000.

COLVIN, ALEX, II
Educator. **Personal:** Born Nov 17, 1946, Birmingham, AL; son of Alex and Novella; divorced; children: Atiba, Jawanza, Kimba, Alex III, Marc & Taylor. **Educ:** Univ Calif Los Angeles, 1974; Univ DC, 1978. **Career:** DC Gov, chief boiler inspector, 1972-. **Orgs:** Instr, Nat Asn Power Engrs, 1974-; Am Soc Mech Engrs, 1981-; rec secy, Nat Asn Black Scuba Divers, 1993-; nat bd, Boiler & Pressure Vessel Inspectors, 1993-. **Honors/Awds:** Educator of the Year, Nat Asn Power Engrs, 1997; Outstanding Service, Nat Asn Black Scuba Divers, 1997. **Special Achievements:** Author of book of poetry, "To the People," 1978. **Military Serv:** USN, 1963-66; US Marine Corps, 1967-71, E-5, Purple Heart, 1968. **Home Addr:** 1183 Neal St NE, Washington, DC 20002. **Business Addr:** Chief Boiler Inspector, District of Columbia Government, 941 N Capitol St NE, Washington, DC 20002, **Business Phone:** (202)442-4695.

COLVIN, ALONZA JAMES
Government official. **Personal:** Born Jul 8, 1931, Union Springs, AL; married Charlene A Bacon; children: Judy Webb, James E, Jimmie, Chris, Mark & Elizabeth. **Educ:** GED only. **Career:** Gen Motors, gen labor, 1950-75; Saginaw Model Cities Inc, chmn, 1967-71; Valley Star News, ed-publ, 1967-73; Buena Vista Charter Township, trustee, 1980. **Orgs:** Nat Newspaper Publ Asn, 1967-73; producer & dir, Autumn Leaves Pageant, 1967-73; bd dirs, Police-Comn Rels Comn, 1970-83; vpres, Miss Saginaw County Pageant, 1970-; bd dirs, Saginaw Econ Develop Corp, 1971-72; bd dirs, Big Brothers Saginaw, 1972-76. **Business Addr:** Trustee, Buena Vista Charter Township, 160 S Outer Dr, Saginaw, MI 48601.*

COLVIN, CEDRIC B
Government official, lawyer. **Personal:** Born Dec 1, 1962, Tuscaloosa, AL; son of Isaac and Mary Colvin; married. **Educ:** Univ Akron, BS/AAS, 1990; Univ Ala, JD, 1993. **Career:** Summit Co Presecutor's Off, atty, 1991; Ala Atty Gen Off, asst atty gen, 1993. **Orgs:** Proj Plus Adult Reading Prog, 1992-93; Partner's in Educ, 1993-94; Boy Scouts, 1993; AL Bar Asn, Access to Legal Servs Comt, 1996-98, Taskforce on Minority Participation, 1997-00. **Home Addr:** 4001 Pickfair St, Montgomery, AL 36116, **Home Phone:** (334)288-6279.

COLVIN, ERNEST J.
Dentist. **Personal:** Born Jan 20, 1935, Chester, SC; son of Alex and Alberta Moffett; married Shirley Beard (divorced); children: Ernest J II. **Educ:** Morgan State Col, BS, 1956; Howard Univ Sch Dent, DDS, 1968. **Career:** Howard Univ Sch Dent, adj fac, 1968-71; Colvin Ernest J Dr & Assocs, pvt pract, currently. **Orgs:** Bd dir, Horseman's Benevolent Protective Asn, WV; Chi Delta Mu Frat; Am Dent Asn; financial secy, Md State Dent Asn; Baltimore City Dent Soc; Am Indodontic Soc; Am Dent Soc Anesthesiol; Am Soc Gen Dent; Kappa Alpha Psi Frat; Columbia Chap Jack & Jill Am Inc; Columbia Nat Asn Advab Colored People; Am Cancer Soc; Com Health Coun Baltimroe City; bd dir, NW Baltimore Community Health Care; St Johns Evangelist Roman Cath Church; comn chmn, Md Racing Comn. **Military Serv:** AUS, pfc, 1956-58. **Business Addr:** Dentist, Colvin Ernest J Dr & Assocs, 4413 Pk Heights Ave, PO Box 39308, Baltimore, MD 21215, **Business Phone:** (410)664-1900.*

COLVIN, DR. WILLIAM E
Educator, school administrator. **Personal:** Born May 27, 1930, Birmingham, AL; son of Lucius Will and Lucille White; married Regina A Bahner, Jun 9, 1956; children: Felicia Imre & Gracita Dawn. **Educ:** Ala State Univ, BA, 1951; Ind Univ, MA, 1960; Ill State Univ, PhD, 1971. **Career:** Stillman Col, Dept Art, chair, 1958-69, chair, 2003-; Ill State Univ, dir ethnic studies, 1974-78, prof art, 1971-91; Eastern Ill Univ, prof art, 1987-, chair afro studies, 1991-. **Orgs:** Elected rep, US/Brazilian Mod Art Soc, 1981-; dir career prog, Ill Comn Black Concerns Higher Educ, 1983-; Nat Conf Artists; Nat Art Educ Asn; Phi Delta Kappa Hon Soc Educ. **Honors/Awds:** Rockefeller Fel, 1973-74; Phelps-Stokes Fund Grant, 1973; Martin Luther King BLM Normal Human Relations Award, 1983; Outstanding Artist in the Field, Ala State Univ, 1985; Outstanding Service Award, Ill Comt Black Concerns Higher Educ, 1985; Fulbright Lectr/Res Fulbright, Brazil, 1981-85; univ grant, Belize res, 1989. **Home Addr:** 507 N Grove St, Normal, IL 61761. **Business Addr:** Chairman, Stillman College, PO Box 1430, Tuscaloosa, AL 35403, **Business Phone:** (205)366-8814.

COLYER, DR. SHERYL LYNN
Labor relations manager, athletic coach, labor activist. **Personal:** Born Dec 20, 1959, Portsmouth, VA; daughter of Joshua and Lubertha Alexander. **Educ:** Howard Univ, WA, DC, 1981; Columbia Univ, NY, MA, 1983; George Wash Univ,WA, DC, PhD, 1996. **Career:** Internal Revenue, WA, DC, pers psychologist, 1983-84; Technol Appls Inc, Falls Church, VA, consult, 1984-85; Gen Motors, Fort Wayne, IN, 1985-88, human resource specialist; Fed Home Loan Mortgage Corp, training & devel consult, 1988-90; Pepsico, KFC, Hanover, MD, div mgr, 1990-92; Hechinger Co, dir, 1992-95; Independent mgt consult, 1995-97; US Retail & HNW; Citigroup Global Markets, managing dir & head admin, 1997; Citi group Asset Mgt, dir global human resources, 2006-. **Orgs:** Pres, Alpha Chap, Delta Sigma Theta, 1980-81; Am Psychol Asn; Am Soc Training & Devel; Soc Indust & Orgn Psychol Inc; Am Soc for Personnel Admin; Nat Assn Securities Dealers. **Honors/Awds:** Outstanding Young Women of Am, Ebony Magazine. **Special Achievements:** Listed among 100 Most Promising Black Women in Corp America, 1991. **Home Addr:** 135 W 70th St Suite 8H, New York, NY 10023. *

COMBS, DR. JULIUS V
Executive. **Personal:** Born Aug 6, 1931, Detroit, MI; son of Everlee Dennis and Julius; married Alice Ann Gaston, Dec 27, 1956; children: Kimberly A & Julius G. **Educ:** Wayne State Univ, BS, 1953, MD 1958; Wayne State Univ, Affilated Hosp, 1964; Am Bd Ob-Gyn, dipl, 1967. **Career:** Vincent & Combs Bldg Corp, pres; Wayne State Univ, Sch Med, clin asst, 1976; Omni Care Health Plan, dir, 1973; chmn bd, 1980-92, exec comt; Assoc Med Develop Corp, vpres, 1979-81; United Am Health Corp, chmn, chief exec officer; Nat Healthcare Scholars Found, chmn & pres, currently; AGOG, fel. **Orgs:** Kappa Alpha Psi Frat; House Del NMA, 1967-; Detroit Med Soc; chmn, Region IV NMA, 1975-77; Am Fertility Soc; NMA; Detroit Med Soc; Mich State Med Soc; Wayne Co Med Soc; Am Asn Gyn Laparoscopists; Am Col Obstet-Gynec; Detroit Inst Arts comnr; Nat Asn Advan Colored People; bd mem, Music Hall Ctr Performing Arts; bd mem, Oakland Univ; bd mem, United Way Southeastern Mich. **Honors/Awds:** Michiganian of the Year, The Detroit News, 1994. **Business Phone:** (313)393-4549.

COMBS, SAMUEL, III
Executive. **Personal:** Married Rita. **Educ:** Okla State Univ, BS, indust eng; Univ Michs Bus Sch, exec Prog, 1999; Harvard Univ. **Career:** Okla Nat Gas Co, vpres, Co Okla City Dist, 1996, vpres Western Reg, 1998, pres & chief operating officer; ONEOK Distrib Co, pres, 2005-; First Fidelity Bank i2E inc, Southern Gas Asn & SSM Health Care Okla, dir. **Orgs:** Govs Coun Workforce, Econ Develop & bds Okla State Univ Found; Urban League Greater

Oklahoma City; Okla Judicial Nominating Comn; Nat Asn Corp Dir. **Honors/Awds:** Distinguished Alumni Award, Okla State Univ. **Special Achievements:** Oklahoma Star by Oklahoma Governor Brad Henry and the Department of Commerce; 75 most powerful African Americans corp Am, Black Enterprise mag. **Business Addr:** President, ONEOK Distribution Companies, 100 W 5th St, PO Box 871, Tulsa, OK 74103, **Business Phone:** (918)588-7000.*

COMBS, SEAN J
Executive, rap musician. **Personal:** Born Nov 4, 1969, New York, NY; son of Melvin Earl and Janice; children: Justin Dior & Christian Casey. **Educ:** Howard Univ, bus admin, attended 1990. **Career:** Directed & Produced: Jodeci, Mary J Blige, Craig Mack, the Notorious BIG, Faith Evan; Albums: Puff Daddy & The Family, No Way Out, 1997; Forever, 1999; The Saga Continues, 2001; Press Play, 2006; Songs: "I'll Be Missing You"; "with Faith Evans & group 112, 1997"; Films: Monster's Ball, 2001; Death of a Dynasty, 2003; Broadway: A Raisin in the Sun, 2004; Uptown Records, intern; Uptown Entertainment, vpres A&R, 1990-91; Justin's Bar & Restaurant, Manhattan, owner, 1997; Daddy's House Rec Studios; Notorious Mag, founder; Sean John clothing line, owner; Bad Boy Entertainment, chief exec officer, founder, currently. **Orgs:** Am Fedn Musicians, 1993-; Am Fedn Tv & Radio Artists, 1994-; Daddy's House Progs; founder, Sean "Puffy" Combs & Janice Combs Endowed Scholar Fund. **Honors/Awds:** Gavin, Rap Indie Year, 1995; Visionary Award for Producing, 3M, 1994; Award Merit for Creative Excellence, Impace, 1994; Rhythm & Soul Award "Juicy", ASCAP, 1995; Grammy Award, Best Rap Performance By a Duo or Group, with Faith Evans & 112, 1998; Alumni Award for Distinguished Postgrad Achievement, Howard Univ, 1999. **Business Addr:** Founder, Bad Boy Entertainment Inc, 8-10 W 19th St 9th Fl, New York, NY 10011.

COMEGYS, DAPHNE D. See HARRISON, DR. DAPHNE DUVAL.

COMER, DR. JAMES PIERPONT
Psychiatrist, educator, school administrator. **Personal:** Born Sep 25, 1934, East Chicago, IN; son of Hugh and Maggie Nichols; married Shirley Ann Arnold (deceased); children: Brian Jay & Dawn Renee. **Educ:** Ind Univ, AB, 1956; Howard Univ Col Med, MD, 1960; Univ MI Sch Pub Health, MPH, 1964. **Career:** St Catherine Hosp, E Chicago, intern, 1960-61; US Pub Health Serv DC, intern, 1961-63; Yale Univ Sch Med, psychiat residency, 1964-74, assoc dean, 1969-, Child Study Ctr, asst prof, 1968-70, co-dir, Baldwin-King Prog, 1968-73, assoc prof, 1970-75, dir, Sch Develop Prog, 1973-, prof psychiat, 1975-, Maurice Falk Prof of Child Psychiat, 1976-; Nat Inst Ment Health, staff mem, 1967-68; Parent's Mag, columnist, 1978-; Sch Develop Prog, Yale Univ Sch Med Child Study Ctr, founder & chmn, currently. **Orgs:** Dir, Conn Energy Corp, 1976-; trustee, Conn Savings Bank, 1971-91; dir, Field Found, 1981-88; trustee, Hazen Found, 1974-78; trustee, Wesleyan Univ, 1978-84; trustee, Albertus Magnus Col, 1989-; trustee, Carnegie Corp NY, 1990-; trustee, Conn State Univ, 1991-94; co-founder, 1968, vpres, 1969-72, pres, Black Psychiats Am, 1973-75; Am Psych Asn, 1970-; Ad Hoc Com Black Psychiatrists APA, 1970-71; Nat Med Asn, 1967-; Am Ortho psychiat Asn, 1968-; chmn, Coun Problems Minority Group Youth, 1969-71; chmn, Adolescent Comt, 1973-77; Inst Med Nat Acad Sci, 1993; Nat Acad Educ, 1993; Laureate Chap, Kappa Delta Pi, 1993; bd mem, Nellie Mae Education Foundation, 2003-. **Honors/Awds:** Distinguished Alumni Award, Howard Univ, 1976; Outstanding Service to Mankind Award, Alpha Phi Alpha E Region, 1972; Rockefeller Public Service Award, 1980; John & Mary Markle Scholar in Academy Medicine, 1969-74; Vera Paster Award, Am Ortho psychiat Asn, 1990; Solomon Carter Fuller Award, Am Psychiat Asn, 1990; Harold W McGraw Jr Prize in Education, 1990; Dana Prize in Education, 1991; John P McGovern Behavioral Sciences Award, Smithsonian Inst, 2004; University of Louisville Grawemeyer Award, 2007. **Special Achievements:** Auth: Beyond Black & White, 1972; Sch Power, 1980; co-auth: Black Child Care, 1975; Maggie's Am Dream, 1988; developed Comer Process, a sch improvement prog now used in numerous schs in eight states, Yale Child Study Ctr; Waiting For a Miracle: Why Schs Can't Solve Our Problems And How We Can, 1997. **Military Serv:** USPHS, lt col, 1968. **Business Addr:** Maurice Falk Professor of Child Psychiatry, Associate Dean for Student Affairs School of Medicine, Yale University Child Study Center, Comer School Development Program, 230 S Frontage Rd NIHB 102, PO Box 207900, New Haven, CT 06520-7900, **Business Phone:** (203)785-2548.

COMER, JONATHAN
Government official. **Personal:** Born Mar 21, 1921, Eufaula, AL; son of Jesse and Beatrice Sanders; married Emma Mount Comer, Jul 28, 1942; children: William, Joseph, Kathy. **Career:** LTV Steel, East Chicago, IN, first helper, 1948-69; Local Union 1011, USWA, E Chicago, IN, pres, 1967-68; United Steelworkers Am, Pittsburgh, PA, asst dir, civil rights dept, 1969-83; Gary Human Rels Comn, Gary, exec dir, comnr, 1989-. **Orgs:** Steering comt/ chairperson, A Philip Randolph Inst, 1977-79; chmn labor & industry, 1965-70, exec secy, Ind conf br, 1983-89, State Nat Asn Advan Colored People. **Honors/Awds:** Distinguished Service Award, District 31, USWA, 1972; Labor Man of the Year, State/ Nat Asn Advan Colored People, 1981; Labor Man of the Year, E Chicago Branch, Nat Asn Advan Colored People, 1984; Distinguished Service Award, Labor Union/Virgin Islands, 1985; Ovington Award, Nat Asn Advan Colored People, 1987. **Military Serv:** AUS, T-5, 1942-45; Good Conduct Medal, Sharpshooters Medal. **Home Addr:** 2575 W 19th Ave, Gary, IN 46404. *

COMER, DR. MARIAN WILSON (DR. MARIAN L BRYANT)
Executive director, school administrator. **Personal:** Born Nov 26, 1938, Gary, IN; daughter of Mary Shuler Bryant Hess and Ernest T Bryant; married Richard Comer; children: Lezlie Jo Thompson, Samuel Grady Wilson, Denise Dillard & Michael. **Educ:** Roosevelt Univ Chicago, BS, 1966; Ind Univ Bloomington, MAT, 1969; Univ Ill Urbana, PhD, bot, 1975; Nat Inst Health, postdoctoral study; Purdue Univ, master gardner, 1991. **Career:** St Margaret Hosp Hammond, clin chem med tech, 1964-66; Pub Sch Syst Gary, teacher, 1966-68; Univ Ill Cir Campus, teaching asst, 1970-74; Ind Univ NW, assoc fac, 1972-74; Am Coun Educ, Chicago State Univ, post doctoral fellow, 1974-84; NIH, extramural assoc, 1978; Chicago State Univ, from asst to vpres, res & develop, 1978-79, acting dean stud develop, 1979-81, assoc vpres acad affairs, 1981-84, prof boil, 1984-, Inst Transition Gary, pres, 1984-94, Chicago Alliance Minority Participation, exec dir, 1994-, Dept Biol Sci, chmn. **Orgs:** Am Inst Biol Scientist; Bot Soc Am; Nat Asn Biol Teachers; Alpha Kappa Alpha; Horticult Soc; Save the Dunes Coun; Gary Pub Libr; Rotary Int, 1991-92; Sickle Cell Found; Trade Winds. **Honors/Awds:** Distinguished Minority Speaker, Univ Calif Berkeley Develop Prog Grad Level; Dr Marian Wilson Scholar, Chicago State Univ, Biol Soc; Acad Excellence Award, Ind Univ. **Business Addr:** Professor of Biological Sciences, Executive Director, Chicago State University, Illinois Louis Stokes Alliance for Minority Participation, 9501 King Drive Sci Rm 101 A, Chicago, IL 60628, **Business Phone:** (773)995-3296.

COMER, DR. NORMAN DAVID
School administrator, educator. **Personal:** Born Dec 8, 1935, East Chicago, IN; married Marilyn Gaines; children: Norman & Karen. **Educ:** Northwestern Univ, BS, 1958; IN Univ, MS, 1965; Loyola Univ, EdD, 1974. **Career:** Educator, School Administrator (retired); Loyola Univ, adj fac; E Chicago Pub Sch, eng teacher, 1960-66, asst prin, 1966-70, asst supt, 1970-93; Ivy Tech Community Col Ind, exec dean, 1996-06. **Orgs:** Evaluator, Princeton Desegregation Plan, Jackson MI Bd Educ, 1973; chmn, N Cent Asn Evaluations, Gage Park & Hirsch High Sch, Chicago, 1973-74; consult, Chicago Pub Sch, Yr Round Sch Study, 1974; Alpha Phi Alpha, 1958; Phi Delta Kappa, 1972; Asn Supervision & Curriculum Develop, 1972; Rockefeller Eval Task Force, E Chicago Pub Sch. **Special Achievements:** First black teacher at Roosevelt High School & First black superintendent in East Chicago History. **Military Serv:** AUS, m sgt E-8, 1960-65.

COMPTON, CHARLETTA ROGERS
Administrator. **Educ:** Mountain View Col, AA; Dallas Baptist Univ, BBA. **Career:** Dallas County Community Col Dist, bd audit comt, 2000-01, chmn, 2004, bd trustee, currently, audit comt, 2004-; Rogers & Assocs, Creative Productions, pres, 2004. **Orgs:** Mgt rev comt, Intel Corp; bd mem, N Cent Tex Regional Cert Agency; Dallas Conv & Visitors Bur; Dallas Together Forum; DFW Minority Bus Develop Coun; bd dirs, Arts Dist Friends; bd dir, Partnership Art Cult & Educ; Dallas County Hist Comn; Dallas County Col Fac Asn; Conv & Tourism adv comt mem, Dallas Black Chamber Com; pres, Kimball United Neighborhood Association; parliamentarian, Southwest Dallas Neighborhood Asn; bd dir, Dallas County Heritage Soc; diversity comt, Asn Community Col Trustees. **Honors/Awds:** Heritage Award, Dallas County Heritage Society; Helping Hands Award, DFW Minority Business Development Council & Minority Business News, 1997; Women Who Mean Business 2000 Award, Minority Business News, 2000. *

COMPTON, JAMES W.
Executive director, association executive. **Personal:** Born Apr 7, 1939, Aurora, IL; married; children: Janice H & James Jr. **Educ:** Morehouse Col, AB, 1961; Univ Grenoble, Grenoble, France. **Career:** Chicago Urban League, on-the-job training rep, 1965-67; W Side Off Employment Guid Dept Chicago Urban League, pecialist-in-charge, 1967-69; WSide Project Urban League, dir, 1968-69; Comt Serv Dept Chicago Urban League, dir, 1968-69; Broome Co Urban League Binghamton NY, exec dir, 1969-70; Opportunities Broome Broome Co Urban League & Bingham, NY, interim exec dir, 1970; Urban League, pres & chief exec officer, 1978-2005; Chicago Urban League Develop Corp, pres & chief exec officer,1983-2005; Seaway Nat Bank Chicago, bd dir, currently. **Orgs:** Teacher, Upper Grade Social Studies, Chicago Bd Educ; dir, Chicago Com Urban Opportunities; dir, Chicago Regional Purchasing Coun; dir, Comt Fund Chicago; dir, Leadership Coun Metro Open Comt; dir, Roosevelt Univ Col Educ; dir, Union Nat Bank Chicago Chicago & Alliance Collaborative Effort,Steering Comt; Chicago Manpower Area Planning Coun; adv bd, WNUS AM/FM;dean, adv bd, Col Educ Roosevelt Univ; Chicago Press Club; Chicago Forum; Citizens Com Employment; Citizens Com Greater Chicago Inc; Com Foreign & Domestic Affairs; Mayor's Comn Sch Bd Nominations; Concerned Citizens Police Reform; Cong Blue Ribbon Panel; Nat Conf Social Welfare; NE IL Planning Comn; WBEE Radio Comt Needs Comt; WGN Cinental Broadcasting Co; DePaul Univ; bd trustees, Ariel Mutual Funds; Com Ed; Field Mus Natural Hist; Northwestern Univ Bd Community Assocs. **Honors/Awds:** Merrill Scholar, 1959-61; S End Jaycees Certificate of Appreciation, 1972. **Special Achievements:** Ten Outstanding Young Men Award, Chicago Jr Asn Com & Indust, 1972; Ten Outstanding Young Men Award, S End Jaycees Chicago. **Military Serv:** US & USSR, 1959. **Business Addr:** Board of Director, Seaway National Bank Chicago, 645 E 87th St, Chicago, IL 60619, **Business Phone:** (773)487-4800.

COMVALIUS, NADIA HORTENSE
Obstetrician. **Personal:** Born Jan 21, 1926; daughter of Rudolf B W and Martha James. **Educ:** Univ Utrecht, MD, 1949; Bd Certified Obstet Gynec, 1970. **Career:** Retired: Jewish Meml Hosp, dir Gynec; Lenox Hills Hosp NYC & Beth Israel Hosp NYC, attending Obstet-Gynec; Hahnemann Med Col, cancer res, 1959-61; Planned Parenthood Westchester, med dir, 1970-72; Pvt Pract, USA; Petromin Med Ctr Yeddah K Saudi Arabia, consult Obstet & Gynec; White Mountain Community Hosp, dir obstet & gynec, 1994. **Orgs:** Mt Sinai Alumni ASN. *

CONAWAY, MARY WARD PINDLE
Government official. **Personal:** Born Jan 26, 1943, Wilson, NC; married Frank M; children: Frank M Jr, Belinda & Monica. **Educ:** NC Cent Univ, BA, 1964, 1970; Juilliard Sch Music, 1966; Coppin State Col,MEd, 1975; Univ Md, College Park, attended 1978; Wesley Theol Sem, MDiv. **Career:** Yonkers Bd Ed, music teacher, 1970-71; Martin Luther King Jr Parent & Child Ctr, cord, 1971-72; Baltimore City Schs, music teacher, 1972-74,spec teacher, 1974-81; prof singer: John Wesley Waterbury United Meth Church, pastor; Baltimore City, register wills, 1982-. **Orgs:** Women of the Month, Ebeneezer Baptist Church Wilson, NC; Afro Am Cert of Appreciation; Special Achiev Award, Baltimore City Coun; Award of Merit; Award for Demonstrating Outstanding Courage, HUB Inc; Honoree, Natl United Affiliated Beverage Assn Convention Baltimore City; Delegate, Dem Party Natl Convention, 1988, 1992; Baltimore City Dem Cent Comt, 1990-94; Humanitarian Service Award, United Cerebral Palsy; Recognition, Negro Nat Col Fund; Stalwarts & Achievers, Nat Assn Advan Colored People. **Honors/Awds:** Baltimore City Mayor's Citation of Merit & Appreciation; Dem Natl Convention Citations. **Home Addr:** 3210 Liberty Heights Ave, Baltimore, MD 21215. **Business Addr:** Register of Wills, Baltimore City, 111 N Calvert St Suite 311, Baltimore, MD 21202, **Business Phone:** (410)752-5131.*

CONAWAY, SAMUEL L
Executive. **Career:** Cardiovasc technologist; Mallinckrodt Med, sales exec; Guidant, Device Vascular Invention, staff, 1990, Cardiac Heart Pacemaker Div, staff, 1995, Guidant Cardiac Rhythm Mgt Div, dir sales, 2000-. **Business Addr:** Director of Sales, Guidant Cardiac Rhythm Management Division, 10500 Little Patuxent Pkwy Suite 500, Columbia, MD 21044.*

CONCHOLAR, DAN
Executive director. **Career:** Art Info Ctr Inc, exec dir, currently. **Orgs:** Panelist, The Gallery Syst, 1994. **Business Addr:** Executive Director, Art Information Center, 280 Broadway Suite 412, New York, NY 10012, **Business Phone:** (212)966-3443.*

CONDE, SANTOS ALOMAR, SR. See ALOMAR, SANDY.

CONE, DR. CECIL WAYNE
School administrator. **Personal:** Born May 21, 1937, Bearden, AR; married Juanita Fletcher; children: Cecil Wayne, Leslie Anita & Charleston Alan. **Educ:** Shorter Col, AA, 1955; Philander Smith, BA, 1957; Garrett Theol Sem, M Div, 1961; Emory Univ, PHD, 1974. **Career:** Union AME Little Rock, pastor, 1964-69; OIC Little Rock, exec dir, 1964-69; Turner Theol Sem, dean, 1969-85; Edward Waters Col, pres, Jacksonville, FL, 1977-2007. **Orgs:** Soc Study Black Rel; Black Theol Proj Theol Am; Nat Asn Advan Colored People; Alpha Phi Alpha Fraternity; Nat Urban League; bd govr, Cof C Jacksonville, FL, 1978-81; St Ethics Comn, State Fla, 1979-81; bd dir, Jacksonville Symphony Asn, 1984-85, Mayor's Comn High Tech, 1984-85; Gamma Beta Boule. **Honors/Awds:** Distinguished Service Award, United Negro Col Fund, 1984; Outstanding Educator of the Year, Jacksonville Jaycees, 1985; hon doctorates, Temple Bible Col, Sem; hon doctorates, Philander Smith Col. **Special Achievements:** Author, "Identity Crisis Black Theleogy", 1975.

CONE, DR. JAMES H.
Educator. **Personal:** Born Aug 5, 1938, Fordyce, AR; son of Charlie and Lucille Cone; widowed. **Educ:** Philander Smith Col, BA, 1958, LHD, 1981; Garrett Theol Seminary, MDiv, 1961; Northwestern Univ, MA, 1963, PhD, 1965. **Career:** Philander Smith Col, asst prof, 1964-66; Adrian Col, asst prof, 1966-69; Union Theol Sem, Dept Theol, from asst prof to prof, 1973-77, Charles A Briggs prof, 1977-87, Charles A Briggs distinguished prof, 1987-. **Orgs:** The Journal of the InterdenomiNatTheological

Ctr; Sojourners; The Journal Religious Thought; mem, Soc for the Study Black Religion; Am Acad Religion; Ecumenical Asn Third World Theologians. **Honors/Awds:** LLD, Edward Waters Col, 1981; LHD, Philander Smith Col, 1981; American Black Achievement Award, in the category of Religion, 1992; Theological Scholarship & Research Award, Assn Theological Sch, 1994; Fund for Theological Education Award, Am Acad Religion, 1999; Arkansas Balack Hall Of Fame,2003; Paul Robeson Award, 2006; Julius C. Hope Champion of Social Justice Award, Natl Assn Advan Colored People, 2006; Samuel DeWitt Proctor Conference Award, 2007; Honorary Degree, Denison Univ; Honorary Degree, Payne Theol Seminary; Honorary Degree, Hamilton Col; Honorary Degree, Colby Col; Honorary Degree, Shorter Col; Honorary Degree, Garrett-Evangelical Theol Seminary Adrian Col. **Special Achievements:** First African-American professor, Union Theological Seminary; 11 book publications including, "Black Theology & Black Power" 1969; "Martin & Malcolm & America: A Dream or a Nightmare?" 1991; "Risks Of Faith", 1996. **Home Addr:** 99 Claremont Ave Apt 302, New York, NY 10027, **Home Phone:** (212)662-9402. **Business Addr:** Charles A Briggs Distinguished Professor, Union Theological Seminary in the City of New York, Deptartment of Systematic Theology, 3041 Broadway 121st St, New York, NY 10027, **Business Phone:** (212)280-1369.

CONE, DR. JUANITA FLETCHER
Physician. **Personal:** Born Nov 13, 1947, Jacksonville, FL; married Cecil Wayne Cone. **Educ:** Howard Univ, BS, 1968, MD, 1974; Morehouse Sch Medicine, Master Pub Health & Prev Med Residency, 2003. **Career:** Pvt Pract, med doctor; Crescent Med Ctr, Kaiser Permanente facil, The Southeast Permanente Med Group Inc, adult internist, currently. **Orgs:** Am Col Physicians; Jacksonville Med Dent & Phar Asn; Nat Med Asn; Jacksonville Chamber Com; Nat Coun Negro Women; Jacksonville Chap Links Inc. **Honors/Awds:** Dipl, Am Bd Internal Med, 1979. **Home Addr:** 580 W Eigth St Suite 610, Jacksonville, FL 32209-6553. **Business Addr:** Internist, Kaiser Permanente Crescent Medical Centre, 3495 Piedmont Rd NE Bldg 9, Atlanta, GA 30305, **Business Phone:** 800-877-0409.

CONEY, LORAINE CHAPELL
Educator. **Personal:** Born Feb 8, 1935, Eustis, FL; son of Francis (deceased) and Julia M Graham; married Bettye Jean Stevens; children: Gessner & Melodi. **Educ:** Fla A&M Univ, BS, 1958. **Career:** Streep Music Co, sales rep, 1964-69; Omega Psi Phi, bas Gamma Tau, 1965-67; Sumter Co Music Teachers, chmn, 1973-77; Sumter Co Bd Pub Instr, band & choral dir. **Orgs:** Chmn, FL Band Dirs, 1963-67; chmn, Music Educ Nat Conf, 1958-77; Sumter Co Educ Asn Nat Asn Advan Colored People; Omega Psi Phi; Masonic Lodge; guest woodwind tutor, LCIE Univ Fla, 1971, 1974. **Honors/Awds:** Sch Band Man Sumter Co, 1959-77; Organized Band & Prod Super Performers; Fla Bandmasters Asn Adjudicator, 1986. **Special Achievements:** First Award Winning Co Band Dir, 1959; First Black Instrument Salesman, Fla, 1964-69. **Business Addr:** PO Box 67, Bushnell, FL 33513.*

CONGLETON, WILLIAM C.
Counselor. **Personal:** Born Feb 13, 1935, Mt Sterling, KY; married Norma Peterson. **Educ:** Marshall Univ. **Career:** Counselor (retired); Huntington Post Office, equal employment off, counr; Parish Coun, St Peter Claver Cath Church, pres, 1972-73, adv, 1974; Cabell Co Parks & Recreation Comn, vpres, 1974; Community Col, adv, 1975; Marshall Univ, 1975, speaker, 1976 & 79; Huntington High Sch, speaker, 1977-78; loan officer, Nat Alliance Businessmen. **Orgs:** Pres, vpres, chmn, labor com, Nat Asn Advan Colored People; Huntington Human Rights Comn, 1979; commodore Ship State WV, 1979; bd dirs, Action;Region II Planning & Develop Coun, six Co Area; voice Black Hist WGNT Radio four yrs; speaker & chmn, Hal Greer Blvd Dedication; chmn, Huntington Human Rights Comn, 1980. **Military Serv:** AUS, corpl, 1953-56. *

CONGREAVES, ANDREA
Basketball player. **Personal:** Born Jun 3, 1970. **Educ:** Mercer Univ, BS, human serv, 1993. **Career:** Viterbo, Italy, 1993-94; Vivo Vicenza, Italy, 1994-95; Dorna Codella, Spain, 1995-96; Como, Italy, 1996-97; Charlotte Sting, forward-center, 1997-98; Orlando Miracle, 1998-99; Barcelona, 2002-03; Alessandria, 2004-05; Rhondda Rebels, 2005. **Honors/Awds:** Kodak All-America Team, 1993; Eng Natl Team, 1991, 1993, 1995, 1997; England Basketball senior Player of the Year Award, 2006; Bronze medal, Melbourne Commonwealth Games, 2006.

CONLEY, CHARLES S.
Lawyer. **Personal:** Born Dec 8, 1921, Montgomery, AL; son of Prince E and Fannie T; married Ellen M Johnson, Aug 8, 1987. **Educ:** Ala State Univ, BS, 1942; Univ Mich, AM, educ, 1947, AM, hist, 1948; NY Univ, JD, 1955. **Career:** Fla A&M Col Law, prof, 1956-60; Ala State Univ, 1962-64; Dr Martin Luther King SCLC, coun; Recorder's Ct, judge, 1968-73; Macon County Ct Common Pleas, 1972-, Macon County atty, 1986; Ala Dist Court, judge, 1976 (retired), atty,1992; Charles S Conley, atty, currently. **Orgs:** Am Nat Ala Bar Asn. **Business Addr:** Attorney, 3321 Rosa L Parks Ave, Montgomery, AL 36105.*

CONLEY, JAMES SYLVESTER
Executive. **Personal:** Born Jun 7, 1942, Tacoma, WA; son of James S and Vera F Dixon; married Eileen Louise Marrinan, Jun 30, 1990; children: Kimberly, Kelli, James III, Ward James W Martin Jr, Erin & Matthew. **Educ:** Univ Puget Sound, Tacoma, WA, 1961; US Military Acad W Point, NY, BS, engineering, 1965; NY Univ, GBA, MBA, finance, 1982. **Career:** Capital Formation, NY, exec dir, 1970-72; CEDC Inc, Hempstead, NY, vpres, 1972-74; Avon Products, NY, dir sales coord, 1981-82; Delco Moraine, Dayton, OH, plant mgr, 1985-88, dir tech serv, 1988-89, dir mkt & planning, 1989-90; Gen Motors Corp, Detroit, MI, n am truck planning dept, 1990-92, automotive components group, technol & planning, 1992, dir, minority supplier develop, 1992-95, dir, raw mat group, worldwide purchasing, 1995-98. Main CHB Inc, pres & chief exec officer, 1998-. **Orgs:** Bd dir, Nat Devel Coun, 1973-80; trustee, bd dir, emer, Asn Graduates, US Military Acad, 1975-; lifetime mem, W Point Soc NY; Soc Automotive Engrs, 1986-. **Military Serv:** AUS, capt, 1965-70; Bronze Star Valor, 1966; Bronze Star Meritorious, 1967; Army Commendation Medal, 1970; Presidential Unit Citation, 1967, Airborne & Ranger, 1965. **Business Addr:** President, Chief Executive Officer, Main ChB Inc, 4924 Contec Dr, Lansing, MI 48910.

CONLEY, JOHN A.
Lawyer, educator. **Personal:** Born Mar 10, 1928, Springfield, IL; married Beverly J. **Educ:** Univ Pittsburgh, BS, 1952, JD, 1955, MSW, 1961. **Career:** Univ Pittsburgh, prof, 1969-; housing developer. **Orgs:** Hill House Asn, 1955-69; Neighborhood Ctrs Asn, 1963-65; Allegheny Co; Pa Bar Asns; bd dirs, Pittsburgh Pub Schs; Freedom House Enterprise; chmn bd, Neighborhood Rehab. **Business Addr:** Professor, University Pittsburgh, Department Social Work, 2201 C1, Pittsburgh, PA 15260.

CONLEY, MARTHA RICHARDS
Executive, lawyer. **Personal:** Born Jan 12, 1947, Pittsburgh, PA; married Charles D; children: David & Daniel. **Educ:** Waynesburg Col, BA, 1968; Univ Pittsburgh Sch law, JD, 1971. **Career:** Sch Dist Pittsburgh, asst solicitor, 1972-73; Brown & Cotton, atty, 1973-74; US Steel Corp, asst mgr labor rel, arbitration, asst mgr compliance, 1984-85, compliance mgr, 1985-87, atty, 1987-93, gen atty, 1993-. **Orgs:** Admitted pract, Bar Supreme Ct Pa, 1972; bd dir, Louise Child Care Ctr, 1973-77; comn, Prog Aid Citizen Enterprise, 1973-78; admitted pract, Supreme Ct US, 1977; bd dir, Health & Welfare Planning Assoc, 1978-84; former mem, Int Toastmistress Club inc; pres, Aurora Reading Club Pittsburgh, 1984-85; Nat Asn Advan Colored Peopel, 2005-; Homer S Brown Law Assoc; Allegheny City Bar Assoc; life mem, NBA; Am Bar Assoc; Alpha Kappa Alpha. **Honors/Awds:** Consortium Doctors Award, 1993. **Special Achievements:** First Black Woman Graduate from Pennsylvania Graduate School of Law. **Home Addr:** 6439 Navarro St, Pittsburgh, PA 15206. **Business Addr:** General Attorney, USX Corporation, US Steel Group 600 Grant St Rm 1580, Pittsburgh, PA 15219-2749, **Business Phone:** (412)433-5391.

CONLEY, MIKE
Athlete, executive. **Personal:** Born Oct 5, 1962, Chicago, IL; married Rene; children: Mike Conley Jr, Jordan, Sydney & Jon. **Educ:** Univ Ark, attended 1985; Ind Wesleyan, BS, bus admin, 2004. **Career:** Olympic athlete triple jump, 1984, 1992; USA Track & Field, Elite Athlete Progs, exec dir; World Sport Chicago, exec dir, currently; NBA, agent, currently. **Honors/Awds:** Third Place Long Jump & Fourth Place Triple Jump, World Championships, 1983; Triple Jump Second Place, World Univ Games, 1983; Silver Medal Triple Jump, Olympic Games, 1984; USA Indoor Championships, 1985, 1986, 1987 & 1992; Gold Medal Triple Jump, Olympic Games, 1992. **Business Addr:** Executive Director, World Sport Chicago, 180 N Stetson Suite 1500, Chicago, IL 60601, **Business Phone:** (312)616-5450.

CONNALLY, C ELLEN (CECELIA ELLEN CONNALLY)
Judge. **Personal:** Born Jan 26, 1945, Cleveland, OH; daughter of George L and Gwendolyn J; widowed; children: Seth George. **Educ:** Bowling Green State Univ, BS, 1967; Cleveland State Univ, JD, 1970; Cleveland State Univ, MA, 1997. **Career:** Judge (retired); 8th District Ct Appeal, law clerk, OH, 1971-72; Cuyahoga County Probate Ct, trial referee, 1972-80; Cleveland Municipal Ct, judge, 1980-2003. **Orgs:** Northern OH Municipal Judges Asn, past pres, sec, treas; Task Force Violent Crime, Youth Violence Comm, chair; Mayor's Adv Comm Gang Violence, chair; Bowling Green State Univ Black Alumni Asn, founding mem, pres; Greater Cleveland Safety, CNL, Traffic Safety, vice pres; Cleveland Public Theater, bd trustees; Amer Judges Asn; Cuyahoga County Ct Col, Women's Ctr/Women's Studies Adv Comm; Cleveland Catholic Diocese, Church City Proj; Ch Savior UMC.

CONNALLY, CECELIA ELLEN. See CONNALLY, C ELLEN.

CONNELL, ALBERT GENE ANTHONY
Football player. **Personal:** Born May 13, 1974, Fort Lauderdale, FL. **Educ:** Tex A&M Univ. **Career:** Football Player (retired); Washington Redskins, wide receiver, 1997-00; New Orleans Saints, 2001; Calgary Stampeders, CFL, 2003. *

CONNER, GAIL PATRICIA
Law enforcement officer. **Personal:** Born Mar 20, 1948, Detroit, MI; daughter of George and Alice. **Educ:** Exchange stud Bates Col, 1967; Wilberforce Univ, BA, 1969; Antioch Col, MA, 1970. **Career:** Detroit Pub Schs, teacher, 1971-73; State Mich, state probation/parole officer, 1973-77; US Courts-Detroit, sr US probation/parole officer, 1977-. **Orgs:** Greater Quinn AME Church, 1948-; NAACP, 1971-; Fed Probation Officers Asn, 1977-; Erma Henderson re-election steering comt, 1978; vpres, Wilber force Alumni Asn, 1978-82; bd mem, YWCA Detroit, 1983-; nat dir educ, 1983-87, nat dir memship, 1987-92, Nat Asn Negro Bus & Prof Womens Club Inc, 1983-; Nat Asn Black Alumni Steering Comt; parliamentarian, Alpha Kappa Alpha Sorority Inc, 1990-. **Honors/Awds:** Spirit Detroit City Detroit, 1981; Scroll Distinction Negro Bus & Prof, 1982; Appreciation Detroit Pub Schs Award Jr Achievement, 1982; NANBPW Yellow Rose Award Nat, 1982; Appreciation Award Mott Community Col, 1983; Nat Black Monitor Hall of Fame, 1985; Mich Women Resource Guide, 1785-1985; Wilberforce Univ Dist Alumni Serv Award, 1985; NANBPW Club Woman of the Year, 1982; AOIP Hall of Fame, 1985; Outstanding Alumni of Wis Univ, 1985. **Home Addr:** 2082 Hyde Pk Dr, Detroit, MI 48207. **Business Addr:** Probation/Parole Officer, US Justice Department, 415 Federal Bldg, Detroit, MI 48226, **Business Phone:** (313)234-5436.

CONNER, DR. LABAN CALVIN
Librarian. **Personal:** Born Feb 18, 1936, Ocala, FL; son of Dorothy Helen Todd and Laban Calvin. **Educ:** Univ Nebr-Omaha, Omaha, Nebr, B Gen Ed, 1959; Emporia State Univ, Emporia, Kans, MSLS, 1964; Nova Univ, Ft Lauderdale, Fla, EdS, 1979; Pacific Western Univ, Los Angeles, Calif, PhD, 1980. **Career:** Librarian (retired); Dade County Public Schs, Miami, Fla, teacher, librn, 1959-68, cord libr services, 1968-70, teacher, librn, 1973-81; Miami Dade Community Col, Miami, Fla, asst prof, libr sci, 1970-73; Fla Memorial Col, Miami, Fla, libr dir, 1981-98. **Orgs:** Am Library asn, 1965-; Fla Libr asn, 1963-; Dade County Library asn, 1963-; African Methodist Episcopal Ch, 1936-. **Honors/Awds:** Kappa Delta Phi (Phi Eta Chapter), 1995. **Military Serv:** USAF, A/2C, 1956-59.

CONNER, LESTER ALLEN
Basketball player, basketball coach. **Personal:** Born Sep 17, 1959, Memphis, TN; married Stacy; children: Simone & Alana. **Educ:** Los Medanos Col, Antioch, CA, 1979; Chabot Col, Hayward, CA, 1980; Ore State Univ, Corvallis, OR, 1982. **Career:** Basketball player (retired), basketball coach; Golden State Warriors, 1982-86; Houston Rockets, 1987-88; NJ Nets, 1988-93; Los Angeles Clippers, 1993-94; Ind Pacers, 1994, asst coach, currently; Philadelphia 76ers, assoc head coach, 2004-05; Milwaukee Bucks, asst coach. **Business Addr:** Assistant Coach, Indiana Pacers, 125 S Pennsylvania St, Indianapolis, IN 46204, **Business Phone:** (317)917-2500.

CONNER, MARCIA LYNNE
City manager. **Personal:** Born Feb 26, 1958, Columbia, SC; daughter of Edward Eugene and Joan Delly. **Educ:** Talladega Col, Talladega, Al, BA, 1980; Univ Cincinnati, Cincinnati, Ohio, MCP, 1982. **Career:** Metropolitan Dade County Miami, FL, mgt intern, 1982-83, budget analayst, 1983-85; City Opa-Locka, Opa-Locka, FL, asst city mgr, 1985-87, city mgr, 1987; City Durham, city mgr, 2004. **Orgs:** Am Soc Pub Adminrs, 1982-; Int City Mgr's Asn, 1982-; Leadership Miami, 1986-; secy, Greater Miami YWCA, 1987-; Big Brothers & Sisters Miami, 1987-; bd mem, Nat Forum Black Pub Adminrs, 1987-. **Honors/Awds:** Outstanding Young Professional, S Fla Am Soc Pub Admin, 1982; Up & Comers Award, S Fla Bus Jour, 1989. **Special Achievements:** One to Watch in '88, S Fla Mag, 1988.

CONNER, STEVE
Career: Steve Agency, founder; Burrell Commun Group LLC, chief creative officer, managing partner, currently. **Honors/Awds:** Judge, Nat ADDY Awards, 2005; Judge, Multicultural Advert. **Special Achievements:** Director and part of the creative team that brought forth the award-winning "Whassup!" campaign for Budweiser in 2000. **Business Addr:** Managing Partner, Chief Creative Officer, Burrell Communications Group LLC, 233 N Michigan Ave, Chicago, IL 60601, **Business Phone:** (312)297-9600.*

CONNOR, DOLORES LILLIE
Entrepreneur. **Personal:** Born Sep 15, 1950, Mineral Wells, TX; daughter of Walter Malone and Alpearl Sadberry. **Educ:** Univ Tex, Arlington, Tex, BS, 1975; Amber Univ, Garland, Tex, MS, 1989. **Career:** Vought Systems Div LTV, Dallas, Tex, material control analyst, 1969-76; Recognition Equipment, Irving, Tex, buyer, 175-77; Tex Instruments, Dallas, Tex, buyer, 1977-78, small & minority bus liaison officer, 1978-87, int officer, 1978-80, small bus prog, mgr, 1987-89, small bus prog mgr, 1985-89, mgr, corporate minority procurement, 1989-91; A Piece Mine Corp, pres, currently. **Orgs:** Zeta Phi Eta Honor Fraternity & Commun, 1975; Ft Worth Negro Bus & Prof Women's Club 1975-77; bd mem, Dallas Urban League, 1979-80; Richardson Bus & Prof Women's Club, 1979-86; Leadership Dallas; Leadership Tex Alumni, 1991-92; bd chmn, D & FW Minority Purchasing Coun, 1980-83; Tex Governor's Comt Employ Disabled, 1981; bd mem, Mayor's Comt Employ Disabled, 1981-85; exec dir, Loan-D & FW Minority Purchasing Coun, 1983; capt, Neighborhood Watch, Richard-

son, Tex, 1983-87; Delta Sigma Theta Sorority Inc. **Honors/Awds:** Young Careerest, Richardson Bus & Prof Women's Club, 1980; Youth Motivator, Nat Alliance Bus, 1983; Supporter Entrepreneurs, Venture Magazine & Arthur Young, 1987; Entrepreneurs Hall of Fame, 1988; Outstanding Business woman of the Year, Iota Phi Lambda Sorority, 1995; Quest for Success Winner, Dallas Black C C, 1996-97; Busines of the Year, St Luke COT United Methodist Ch, 1997. **Special Achievements:** Published article "Winning Ways for Women Managers" in Hispanic Engineer and US Black Enterprise, Fall 1990. **Business Addr:** President, A Piece of Mine Corp, Ethnic Greeting Cards & Gifts, PO Box 201338, Arlington, TX 76006-1338.*

CONNOR, HERMAN P
Executive. **Personal:** Born Aug 27, 1932, Garfield, GA; son of George and Melvina; divorced; children: Sharon, Gregory, Stephanie, Leigh & Donna. **Career:** Consoar Corp, vpres, currently. **Business Addr:** Vice President, Consoar Corp, 18 Central Ave, PO Box 132, West Orange, NJ 07052, **Business Phone:** (201)678-1408.*

CONNOR, DR. ULYSSES J., JR. See Obituaries section.

CONRAD, CECILIA ANN
Educator. **Personal:** Born Jan 4, 1955, St Louis, MO; daughter of Emmett J Conrad and Eleanor N; married Llewellyn Miller, May 26, 1984; children: Conrad Jr. **Educ:** Wellesley Col, BA, 1976; Stanford Univ, MA, 1978, PhD, 1982. **Career:** Bell Laboratories Cooperative, res fel, 1976-81; Federal Trade Comn,economist, 1978-79; Duke Univ, asst prof, 1981-85; Hunter Col, vis asst prof, 1984-85; Barnard Col, assoc prof, 1985; Black Enterprise Mag, bd economists, 1993-; Pfizer Inc, consult, 1992-, Review Black Political Econ, ed; former pres, Nat Econ Asn; Pomona Col, Dept Econ, fac, 1997-, assoc dean, 2004-07, Stedman-Sumner prof, currently. **Orgs:** Chair, Nat Econ Asn, Col Bd; Test Develop Comt, advanced placement exam econ; pat bd mem, Comn Status Women Econ Prof, Phi Beta Kappa, 1976. **Honors/Awds:** Gladys Brooks Junior Fac Excellence Teaching Award, 1990; California Professor of the Year, Carnegie Found Advan Teaching, 2002; Women of Achievement Award of Distinction, San Gabriel Valley YWCA, 2007. **Special Achievements:** Publications: "The Economic Costs of Affirmative Action: A Review of the Evidence," The Economics of Affirmative Action, 1995; "Why Black Economists?", Review of Black Political Economy, 1994; "Pay Now or Later", Black Enterprise Magazine, Sept 1994; numerous others; Speeches and Public Addresses: "The Role of Government in Dependent Care", Barnard Coll, 1994; "Where's My Forty Cents?", Barnard Business and Professional Women, 1994; numerous others. **Business Addr:** Professor, Associate Dean, Pomona College, 550 N Col Ave, Claremont, NY 91711, **Business Phone:** (909)621-8328.

CONRAD, JOSEPH M., JR.
Executive. **Personal:** Born Jan 16, 1936, New Orleans, LA; married Bernadine Barard; children: 3. **Educ:** Xavier Univ, BS, 1962. **Career:** Off Prog Planning & Control, US Small Bus Admin, 1968-; St Luke Parish, deacon; NCCIJ, Exec Dir, currently. **Orgs:** mem & bd dir, Black Sec Catholic Archdiocese of Wash Bdc; permanent deacon, Catholic Archdiocese, 1971. **Honors/Awds:** William A & Jump Mem Award 1973; SBA Medal for Meritorious Serv 1970. **Military Serv:** AUS, 1955-58. **Business Addr:** Executive Director, NATIONAL CATHOLIC CONFERENCE FOR INTERRACIAL JUSTICE, 1200 Varnum St NE, Washington, DC 20017, **Business Phone:** (202)529-6480.*

CONTEE, DR. CAROLYN ANN (CAROLYN CONTEE-LASSITER)
Dentist. **Personal:** Born Feb 14, 1945, Washington, DC; married Dr James E Lassiter Jr; children: Lisa C Butler. **Educ:** Howard Univ, BA, 1969, MEd, 1973, DDS, 1981; MPH. **Career:** DC Pub Schs, elem teacher, 1969-77; pvt dent pract, dentist, 1981-86; Upper Cardozo Community Health Ctr, staff dentist 1982-86; Shaw Community Health Ctr, staff dentist 1982-86; Fairleigh Dickenson Col Dent, asst prof, 1987; Airport Dental Ctr, asst dir, 1986-; Eric B. Chandler Health Ctr, dent dir, currently; pvt pract, dentist, currently. **Orgs:** Dir continuing educ exec bd, Robert Freeman Dent Soc, 1982-84; house delegates, 1982-86, exec comt, 1986, asst treas, 1986, Nat Dent Asn; bd trustees, Nat Dent Asn Found, 1983-; Potomac Chap Links, 1984-. **Honors/Awds:** Outstanding Service, Robert T Freeman Dent Soc, 1984; Outstanding Service Capital Headstart Certificate, 1985.

CONTEE-LASSITER, CAROLYN. See CONTEE, DR. CAROLYN ANN.

CONWAY, CURTIS LAMONT
Football player, television actor. **Personal:** Born Mar 13, 1971, Los Angeles, CA; married Laila Ali, Jul 23, 2007; children: Curtis Mohammad Conway Jr; married Leoria (divorced); children: Cameron, Kelton & Leilani. **Educ:** Univ Southern Calif, pub admin. **Career:** Football,television actor; Chicago Bears, wide receiver, 1993-99; San Diego Chargers, wide receiver, 2001-02; New York Jets, wide receiver, 2003; San Fransisco 49ers, 2004. TV: "DAmn Bundys, 1997; "Married with children",1997; "ESPN's Sunday Night Football", 1993-2000; "NFL's Monday Night Football", 1994-2003; "Rome is Burning", 2005-06; "Dancing with the Stars", 2007; "Entertainment Tonight", 2007; "11-04-04: The Day of Change", 2009. **Honors/Awds:** Trojans Offensive Player-of-the-Year,1992 First Team All American. **Business Addr:** Televison Actor, Starz Entertainment LLc, 8900 Liberty Circle, Eaglewood, CO 80112, **Business Phone:** (720)852-7700.*

CONWAY, WALLACE XAVIER, SR.
Museum curator. **Personal:** Born Jun 11, 1920, Washington, DC; son of Jessie Taylor and Ewell Lucas Jr; married Jessie Elizabeth Dedeaux (deceased) (died 2001); children: Dianne Pettie, Wallace X Jr (deceased) & Stephanie Victorian. **Educ:** Miner Teacher Col, BS, 1941; Cooper Union Sch Arts & Sci, attended 1942; US Dept Agr Grad Sch, attended 1953; Trenton St Col, attended 1953; Mercer Community Col, attended 1979; Paris-Am Acad, Univ Paris, attended 1977; NY Univ, MA, attended 1987; Venice, Italy, painting, 1988; Chicago Univ Art Inst, painting, 1989. **Career:** Museum Curator (retired); Co-Art Studios, Visual Commun, owner/dir, 1950-64; Dept Educ, NJ, consult, 1962-82; US Weather Bur, graphic artist, 1964-65; Smithsonian Inst, graphic supvr, 1965-69; NJ St Mus, cur, chmn exhibits, 1969-88; Trenton St Col, NY, adj fac, 1978-80; Afro-Am Mus Asn, Wash, DC, advisor, 1980; Afro Am Mus, Philadelphia, PA, consult, 1981-83; NJ Civil Serv Comn, consult, 1981-84; Afro-Am Mus Asn, consult, 1981-85; Martin Luther King Nat Holiday Mem Mural, Martin Luther King Libr, Washington, DC, tech consult, 1986; Rouse Assocs, consult, 1987-88; fel Kellogg Found, Field Mus, Chicago, 1987; Merrill Lynch, consult, 1987-88; Church & Dwight, consult, 1988-89; Bedford-Stynt Hist Asn Brooklyn, NY, consult; self-employed artist, mus consult, educr, lectr. **Orgs:** Chmn cult comt, Cable TV Network, NJ 1983-85; Beta Kappa Chap KAU, 1945-85; Rotary Int, 1975-; Trenton Artists Workshop Asn, 1980-91; bd dir, Trent YMCA, 1988-; adv bd, Minority Arts Assembly, 1988-; Dist Colo Art Asn, 1970-90; Nat Conf Artists, 1970-91; bd mem, chair, memship comm, Art Stud League, Colo Springs, 1994; validating comt, Presbytery New Brunswick, NJ; YWCA Comt Cult Enrichment Prog Trenton; adv bd, ColoSprings Mus. **Honors/Awds:** Major Art Retrospective Exhib, City Trenton Mus, 1989; 19 Black Artists ofMercer City Exhibit, Mercer County Col, 1989; One Man Exhibit, Black Dimensions Art, Schenectady Mus, NY, 1990; Best of Show Award, 2 Hon Mentions, First Place, Print Category, Art Stud League. **Special Achievements:** Artist, Don Miller making of mural traveling exhibit, 1986-87. **Military Serv:** USCG, seaman 1/c; Hon Discharge. **Home Addr:** 2119 Olympic Dr, Colorado Springs, CO 80910. *

CONWILL, GILES
Educator. **Personal:** Born Dec 17, 1944, Louisville, KY. **Educ:** Univ San Diego, BA, philos, 1967; Athenaeum OH, MDiv, 1973; Emory Univ, PhD, cult studies, 1986. **Career:** Barona & Santa Ysabel Missions, religious educ instr, 1965-67; Miramar Naval Air Sta, chaplains asst, 1966-67; St Henrys Sch, elem sch teacher, 1967-68; Verona Fathers Sem, choir dir, asst organist, 1968-69; St Rita's Church, assoc pastor, 1973-76; San Diego Religious Vocations Off, diocesan coordr, pre-marriage instr, 1975; Nat Off Black Catholics, Dept Church Vocations, dir, 1976-80; St Anthony's Church, Atlanta, assoc pastor, 1980-85; St Joseph's Cathedral, San Diego, assoc pastor, 1985-86; Morehouse Col, Dept Hist, assoc prof hist, 1987-, chmn, currently; Xavier Univ, Inst Black Cath Studies, New Orleans, assoc prof, 1990; Emory Col, assoc prof, currently; Upper Room Publ Co. **Orgs:** Vpres, Southeast San Diego Interdenomi Nat Ministerial Alliance, 1975; Black Cath Clergy Caucus, 1975; Asn Study African Am Life & Hist, 1987-; Southern Conf African Am Studies Inc, 1987-; Black Cath Theol Symp, 1990; Asn Southern Historians, 1992-; Ga Asn Historians, 1992; Am Anthrop Asn, 1994. **Honors/Awds:** Key to the City, City Selma, AL; Interdenomi Nat Sermon Contest Winner; numerous other awards. **Special Achievements:** Author of Tell It Like It Is: A Black Catholic Perspective on ChristianEduc, Natl Black Sisters Conference, 1983, Black Music: The Spirit Will Not Descend Without Song, Pastoral Life, Vol XXXII, June 1983, Blackology vs Ecology, Leadership Council of the Laity; Liturgical Sensitivity to the Black Aesthetic, in The Critic, Summer, 1986, "The Word Becomes Black Flesh: A Program for Reaching the American Black," What Christians Can Learn from One Another, Tyndale House Publishers, 1988, workshop presenter: "Understanding Transitions: How to Relate to Candidates from Various Backgrounds," Seventh Annual Formation Workshops, Bergamo Center, July 8-10, 1988, African-American history lecture, Shrine of Immaculate Conception, Jan 1991, "Blackology vs Ecology," Leadership Council of the Laity Conference, Feb 1991. **Business Addr:** Professor of History, Administrative Assistant, Chairman, Morehouse College, Department of History, Rm 202 Brawley Hall 830 Westview Dr SW, Atlanta, GA 30314, **Business Phone:** (404)215-2620.

CONWILL, HOUSTON EUGENE
Sculptor. **Personal:** Born Apr 2, 1947, Louisville, KY; married Kinshasha Holman Conwill, Dec 18, 1971. **Educ:** Howard Univ, attended 1973; Univ Southern Calif, 1976. **Career:** Self-employed artist, 1987-. **Honors/Awds:** John Simon Guggenheim Fellowship, 1983; Fellowship, Prix De Rome, 1984; Louis Comfort Tiffany Foundation Award, 1987; Niagara Univ, Hon Doctorate, 1991. **Special Achievements:** Public Art Monuments in cities throughout the nation and some international. **Military Serv:** USAF, 1966-70. **Business Addr:** Ted Weiss Fed Bldg, 290 Broadway, PO Box 230719, New York, NY 10023.*

CONWILL, KINSHASHA
Museum director. **Career:** Studio Mus Harlem, dir, exec dir, 1988, dir emer, currently. **Business Phone:** (212)864-4500.*

CONWILL, WILLIAM LOUIS
Psychologist, educator, consultant. **Personal:** Born Jan 5, 1946, Louisville, KY; son of Adolph Giles (deceased) and Mary Luella Herndon; married Faye Venetia Harrison, May 17, 1980; children: Giles Burgess, Leonart Mondlane & Justin Neal. **Educ:** Univ San Diego, BA, philos, 1968; St Patrick's Sch Grad Theol, attended 1969; Calif State Univ, San Jose, MA, experimental psychol, 1973; Stanford Univ, PhD, coun psychol, 1980. **Career:** Santa Clara County, Juvenile Probation Dept, group counr I, group counr II, sr training counr, 1969-72; Cities Richmond & San Francisco, Police Dept, trainer, res asst, 1972-73; Univ Calif, Santa Cruz, coun psychologist II, 1974-77; Mental Health Dept, County San Mateo, CA, coordr, chief consult & educ, 1980-82; Univ Louisville, dept Psychiatry, dir pain prog, 1983-88; City Louisville, Dept Human Servs, community status res asn, 1988-90; Family Stress Inst Inc, pres & founder, 1988-97; State Tenn, Dept Mental Health, Mental Retardation, psychologist, chief psychol, Children & Youth Servs, 1990-97; Univ Tenn, Coun, fac; Family Stress Inst, pres, founder, 1997; Minority Male Consortium, prevention specialist; Am Psychological Asn, trainer; HIV Office for Psychol Ed (HOPE) Prog; Univ Tenn, asst prof; Univ Fla, Counr Educ & African Am Studies, Affiliate fac, Ctr African Studies, asst prof, Col Educ, currently. **Orgs:** Am Psychol Asn; Am Pain Soc; Asn Black Psychologists; Tenn Psychol Asn; Ky Soc Psychologists; NCP; Behav Med Soc; Knoxville Area Psychol Asn; Asn Behavioral Sci & Med Educ. **Honors/Awds:** Grad Fellowship, Stanford Univ, 1973-79; Univ Louisville, Sch Med Grant, 1984; numerous other grants. **Special Achievements:** Actor: Learning to CARE, behavioral therapy movie, 1978; "The Inheritance of IQ and Scholastic Achievement: Further Comments on the Jensen Article," Journal of Negro Education, 1980; pre-post filming of rheumatoid arthritic group as co-therapist, 1983; 16-Session videotaping of chronic pain group as therapist, 1984; dissertation: A Conceptual Analysis of Black Family Instability, 1980; Chronic Pain Conceptualization & Religious Interpretation, Journal of Religion & Health, 1986; "Training Parents in Child Behavior-management Skills: A Group Approach," Journal of Negro Education, 1986. **Home Addr:** 1709 Dunraven Dr, Knoxville, TN 37922-6237. **Business Addr:** Assistant Professor, Affiliate Faculty, University of Florida, College of Education, Center for African Studies, 1215 Norman Hall, PO Box 117046, Gainesville, FL 32611-7046, **Business Phone:** (352)392-0731.*

CONYERS, CHARLES L.
School administrator. **Personal:** Born Sep 8, 1927, Cyrene, GA; son of Luther H Sr and Ella Brown; married Mary Foster, Jun 11, 1952; children: Charles C, Andrei B & Brian K. **Educ:** Savannah State Col, BS, 1949; Va State Col, BS, MS, 1958; Univ Ill, Grad Study; Univ Va. **Career:** School adminis (retired); G W Carver High Sch, Culpeper, VA, teacher, 1949-51; Mary N Smith High Sch, VA, 1952; AG Richardson High Sch, Louisa, VA, teacher, 1952-61; Cent Acad Sch, Fincastle, VA, prin, 1961-63; John J Wright Sch, Snell, VA, prin, 1963-66; State Dept Educ, Richmond, VA, asst super title one, 1966, supvr, title I & migrant educ,1972, assoc dir, title one, 1979, dir, div compensatory educ, 1981, dir, div spec & compensatory progs, 1987, educ lead specialist, grants admin, 1992. **Orgs:** Nat Educ Asn; Va Educ Asn; life mem, Iota Sigma Chapter; Phi Delta Kappa; first pres, Nat Asn State Dirs Migrant Educ; pres, Nat Asn State Dirs Chapter one; Nat Adv Coun Neglected or Delinquent Progs; Phi Beta Sigma Fraternity. **Honors/Awds:** Outstanding Educator Award, Phi Delta Kappa, 1976; State Superintendent's Award, 1989; Literacy Award, International Reading Asn, 1989; Distinguished Alumni Award, Nat Asn Equal Opportunity Higher Educ, 1990. **Home Addr:** 3213 Griffin Ave, Richmond, VA 23222. *

CONYERS, DR. JAMES ERNEST
Educator. **Personal:** Born Mar 6, 1932, Sumter, SC; son of Crenella Conyers and Emmett Conyers; married Jean Farris, Jun 4, 1956 (divorced); children: Judy, Jimmy & Jennifer. **Educ:** Morehouse Col, BA, 1954; Atlanta Univ, MA 1956; WA State Univ, PhD 1962. **Career:** Lemoyne Col, teacher, 1955-56; Wash State Univ, teaching asst, 1958-61; Atlanta Univ, assoc prof, 1964-68; Ind State Univ, from asst prof to prof, 1962-96, prof emer, 1996-. **Orgs:** Young Men Civic Club, Terre Haute, 1970-; pres, Asn Social & Behav Scientists, 1970-71; comn chmn, Participation & Status of Racial & Ethnic Minorities; prof, Amer Sociol Asn, 1971-72; chmn, Caucus Black Sociologists Am, 1973-74; Selection Comt Nat Fel Fund Grad Fel Black Am, 1973-78; Adv Panel Sociol, NSF, 1975-77; Coun N Cent Sociol Asn, 1991-93; life mem, Nat Asn Advan Colored People. **Honors/Awds:** WEB Dubois Award, Asn Social & Behav Scientists, 1981; Distinguished Scholar Award, Asn Black Sociologists, 1994. **Special Achievements:** Various articles published in Sociology & Social Research; Co-editor, Sociology for the Seventies, 1972; Co-author, Black Elected Officials, 1976; First African American professor at Indiana State Teachers College. **Military Serv:** AUS,

E-3, 1956-58. **Business Addr:** Professor Emeritus, Indiana State University, 200 N 7th St, Terre Haute, IN 47809-9989, **Business Phone:** (812)237-4114.

CONYERS, JEAN L.
Association executive. **Personal:** Born Nov 10, 1932, Memphis, TN; daughter of Marshall D and Jeffie Ledbetter Farris; married Dr James E Conyers, Jun 4, 1956 (divorced); children: Judith, James Jr, Jennifer. **Educ:** Lemoyne Owen Col, BA, 1956; Univ Tenn Sch Social Work, attended 1959; Atlanta Univ, Sch Bus, MBA, 1967. **Career:** Vigo County Community Action, planner, 1968-78, dir, 1978-79; United Way Genessee & Lapeer Counties, sr assoc exec, 1980-82; GFOTC, prog coordr, 1982-86; Metrop Chamber, pres & chief exec officer, 1980-; USDOT LOSP Small Bus Off, regional dir. **Orgs:** Alpha Kappa Alpha Basileus, 1992-; pres, Opportunity Network, 1997. **Honors/Awds:** Meritorious Service Award, Nat Asn Negro Bus & Prof Women, 1994; Partner in Community Service, Black Caucus Found Mich, 1994; Community Activist Award, Community Coalition, 1996; Community Service Award, Boy Scouts Am, 1996. **Special Achievements:** Designed Special Entrepreneurial Curriculum and had it licensed by the Michigan Department of Education; Developed Kidpreneur Training Prog for 5th & 6th Graders; Initiated Community Business Partnership Project. **Business Addr:** President, Chief Executive Officer, Metropolitan Chamber of Commerce, 400 N Saginaw St Suite 101A, Flint, MI 48502.*

CONYERS, JOHN
Congressperson (U.S. federal government). **Personal:** Born May 16, 1929, Detroit, MI; son of John and Lucille; married Monica Ann Esters, Jun 1990; children: John III & Carl. **Educ:** Wayne State Univ, BA, 1957, JD, 1958; Wilberforce Univ, Hon LLD, 1969. **Career:** Congressman John Dingell, legis asst, 1958-61; Conyers Bell, Carl Edward & Townsend, sr partner, 1959-61; Mich Workman's Compensation Dept, referee, 1961-63; US House Representatives, rep, 1964-, Mich 14th Dist, rep, 1964-. **Orgs:** Nat Bd Am Dem Action; Nat Adv Bd Am Civil Liberties Union; exec bd mem, Detroit br NAACP; Wolverine Bar Asn; Tabernacle Baptist Church; Kappa Alpha Psi Frat; Pub Field; chmn, House Comn Govt Operations, 1988-94; ranking mem, House Comn Judiciary, 1994-; orginal co-founder, Cong Black Caucus; chmn, House Judiciary Comt. **Honors/Awds:** Numerous honors & awards including Rosa Parks Award, 1967; Southern Christian Leadership Conference Award. **Military Serv:** AUS, 1950-54. **Business Addr:** Representative, Congressman, US House of Representatives, Michigan 14th District, 2426 Rayburn Bldg, Washington, DC 20515, **Business Phone:** (202)225-5126.

CONYERS, NATHAN
Publisher. **Career:** Milwaukee Times, publ & pres, currently. **Business Addr:** President, Publisher, Milwaukee Times Printing & Publishing Co, 1938 N Martin Luther King Dr, Milwaukee, WI 53212, **Business Phone:** (414)263-5088.

CONYERS, NATHAN G.
Automotive executive, president (organization). **Personal:** Born Jul 3, 1932, Detroit, MI; son of John Sr. and Lucille Simpson; married Diana Callie Howze, 1956; children: Nancy, Steven, Susan, Ellen, Peter. **Educ:** Wayne State Univ, Detroit, MI, LLB, 1959. **Career:** Attorney pvt practice, 1959-69; Small Bus Admin, closing attorney, 1963; Veteran's Admin, closing attorney, 1964-65; State Mich, Attorney Gen Office, spec asst, 1967-70; Keith Conyers Anderson Brown & Wahls, sr partner, 1969; Conyers Riverside Ford Inc, Detroit, MI & Supreme Ford Inc, Mason, MI, pres, 1970-; Jaguar of Novi, pres, 2001-. **Orgs:** Life mem, NAACP; ACL; YMCA; bd mem, Greater Detroit COC; bd mem, Blue Cross & Blue Shield MIC; bd mem, tre, Diversitech; Wolverine Bar Asn; NAT Lawyers Guild; Detroit Bd Police CMSers, 1987-89; bd mem, Black Ford Lincoln & Mercury Dealers Asn, 1979-; bd dirs, PUSH Intl Trade Bureau; Rivertown Auto Dealers Asn; Greater Detroit Area Hosp CNL, 1972-73; UNF, 1972-75; United FND Adv Bd, 1973-75; State Canvassers, bd mem, 1968-74; State MICH, Com DEPT, minority BUS Advi Coun, 1986-. **Honors/Awds:** North American Customer Excellence Award, FMCE Partners Quality, 1997-98; Time Magazine Quality Dealer Award, 1999. **Special Achievements:** Dealership recognized for commitment to excellence by: Howard Univ School of Business, former President Jimmy Carter, former Atlanta Mayor Andrew Young with the Key to the City. **Military Serv:** AUS, 1953-55. **Business Addr:** President, Jaguar of Novi, 24295 Haggerty Rd, Novi, MI 48375, **Business Phone:** (248)478-1111.*

COOK, ANTHONY ANDREW
Football player. **Personal:** Born May 30, 1972, Bennettsville, SC. **Educ:** S Carolina State Univ, attended.1995-99. **Career:** Houston Oilers, defensive end, 1995-96; Tenn Oilers, 1997-98; Wash Redskins, 1999; NY jets, defensive end. *

COOK, CHARLES A
Physician, executive. **Personal:** Born Jun 19, 1946, Biloxi, MS; son of Norman Cook Sr and Eleanor Posey Shelby; married Shirley A Bridges Cook, Oct 23, 1967; children: Timothy, Tamotha & Torryhe. **Educ:** Tougaloo Col, Tougaloo, BA, MS, 1971; Tufts Univ, Sch Med, Boston, MA, MD, 1975; Harvard Univ, Sch Pub Health, Boston, MA, MPH, 1975; Univ NC, Chapel Hill NC, Cert, 1982. **Career:** State MA, Boston, spec asst, mental health, 1974-75; State Miss, Jackson, asst chief, disease control, 1979-80; Univ Miss Med Ctr, asst prof med, 1979-80; State NC, Raleigh NC, chief adult health, 1980-85; Univ NC, Chapel Hill, Sch Public Health, adj assoc prof, 1987-; Assoc Resources Consult Group, pres, currently. **Orgs:** Bd mem, Am Heart Asn, NC, 1980-89; bd mem, Am Cancer Soc, NC, 1980-85; NC Ins Comn, 1988-89. **Honors/Awds:** Airman of the Month, US Air Force, 1965; Doctor of the Year, Hinds County Med Soc, 1979; Tarheel of the Week, Raleigh News & Observer 1983; Honored Volunteer, NC Diabetes Asn 1983; Volunteer of the Year, State Baptist Convention, 1984. **Special Achievements:** Has Published various articles. **Military Serv:** USAF, sgt, Airman of the Month (April 1967), 1964-68. **Business Addr:** President, Assoc Resources Consult Group, 3414 6 Forks Rd Pk Pl, Raleigh, NC 27609, **Business Phone:** (919)783-0200.*

COOK, ELIZABETH G
Newspaper editor. **Personal:** Born Jun 30, 1960, Lexington, KY; daughter of Roy L Lillard and Betty L Lillard; married Robert B, Jun 6, 1986; children: Casey A. **Educ:** Univ NC, attended 1977; Ohio State Univ, Columbus, OH, BA, 1983. **Career:** Columbus Call & Post Newspaper, Columbus, OH, sports writer, 1986-88; State Ohio, Columbus, OH, pub info officer, 1983-88; Ohio State Univ, asst dir sports info, 1988; Salisbury Post, ed, currently. **Orgs:** Col Sports Info Dirs Am, 1988-; Am Soc Newspaper Ed. **Honors/Awds:** State Career Women of the Year, 1995. **Business Addr:** Editor, Salisbury Post, 131 W Innes St, PO Box 4639, Salisbury, NC 28144.

COOK, FRANK ROBERT, JR.
Lawyer, accountant. **Personal:** Born Aug 19, 1923. **Educ:** BS, 1945, JD, 1949, LLM, 1955, BCS, 1963, MCS, 1964, PhD, 1951, DD, 1967. **Career:** Frank R Cook Jr, atty pub acct & mgt cnsult, real property appraiser, 1950; C Church Christ, minister, 1966-; RE Broker, bus chance broker, 1945-; Integrity Adjustment Co, owner, 1944-49. **Orgs:** Wash Bar Asn; Nat Soc Pub Acct Adm Planned Parenthood & Sex/Marriage Coun Prog, 1967.

COOK, FREDERICK NORMAN
Banker. **Personal:** Born Feb 19, 1968, Tupelo, MS; son of Richard Cook Jr; married Gwendolyn Woodard Cook, Aug 2, 1997; children: Jamie Mariah & Reagan Michelle. **Educ:** MO Valley Coll, BS, 1992; MS Sch Banking, 1999; TN Consumer Lending Sch, 2001. **Career:** Fleet Finance, asst mgr, 1993-94; Money Tree Finance, asst mgr, 1995-97; Peoples Bank & Trust Com, lending officer, 1997-. **Orgs:** St Joseph Masonic Lodge #131 Verona, MS, past sr warden, 1993; Traveling Consistory #20 Tupelo, MS 32, 1997; Neighborhood asn, president, 2000-; Boys and Girls Club North MS, bd mem, 2000-; Black Business asn, dir, 2001-; Family First, bd mem, 2001-. **Home Addr:** 3093 Monterey Dr, Tupelo, MS 38801. **Business Addr:** Loan Officer, Peoples Bank & Trust Co, 209 Troy St, PO Box 709, Tupelo, MS 38802, **Business Phone:** (662)680-1221.

COOK, DR. HENRY LEE, SR.
Dentist. **Personal:** Born Sep 7, 1939, Macon, GA; married Mamie R Richmond; children: Cathy L & Henry L II. **Educ:** Tuskegee Univ, BS, 1962; Meharry Medical Col, DDS, 1969. **Career:** Pvt pract, dentist, currently. **Orgs:** Chmn, Minority Asst Corp, 1977-87; mem Col Bd Health, 1976-87; pres, Alpha Phi Sigma, Phi Beta Sigma, 1980-87, L & L Sports Unlimited, 1980-87; vicechmn bd, YMCA, 1982-87; treas, Ga Dental Soc, 1983-87; nat vice pres, Tuskegee Nat Alumni, 1985-87; nat trustee Nat Dental Assoc, 1986-87. **Honors/Awds:** Outstanding Young Man of America; Civil Rights Award, Natl Dental Assoc; Governor, Statewide Health Coord Coun. **Military Serv:** USAF 1st lt, 1962-65. **Home Addr:** 5409 Chatham Woods Ct, Columbus, GA 31907, **Home Phone:** (706)568-9010. **Business Addr:** Physician, 1190 Martin Luther King Jr Bl, Columbus, GA 31906, **Business Phone:** (706)322-3218.

COOK, JEFFREY
Artist, manager. **Personal:** Born Feb 1, 1961, New Orleans, LA; son of Margaret and Harold Wellington Cook. **Educ:** Xavier Univ, attended 1983; San Francisco Art Inst, attended 1984. **Career:** New Orleans Mus Art, preparator, 1997-98; Amistad Research Ctr, preparator, 1999; Black Arts Nat Diaspora, preparator, 2000; Ashe Cult Ctr, preparator, 2000; Stella Jones Gallery, preparator, 2000; New Orleans Charter Middle Sch, teacher, 2000; Roger Houston Ogden Collection, New Orleans, La; ASHE Cult Arts Ctr, artist, currently. **Orgs:** Illusr, The Josephite Org, 1983; juror, The Arts Coun New Orleans,1997; speaker, Humanities Fest The Arts, 1997; curator, Xavier Univ Art Alumni Asn, 1998; speaker, The Nana Kwandwo Adu II Found Guana Inc, 1998. **Honors/Awds:** Essence Festival, Essence Mag, 1997; First Place Award, Perspectives In African Am Art, 1998; Fellowship Award, La Division of The Arts, 1998. **Special Achievements:** Amistad Research Center Collection; New Orleans Museum of Art Collection; The Roger Ogden Collection; Virlane Foundation K and B Collection; WEB DuBuois Center Collection. **Business Addr:** Artist, Ashe Cultural Arts Center, 1712 Oretha Castle Haley Blvd, New Orleans, LA 70113, **Business Phone:** (504)569-9070.*

COOK, JOYCE MITCHELL
Educator, writer. **Personal:** Born Oct 28, 1933, Sharon, PA; daughter of Isaac William (deceased) and Mary Bell Christman (deceased); divorced. **Educ:** Bryn Mawr Col, AB, 1955; Oxford Univ, BA, 1957, MA, 1961; Yale Univ, PhD, 1965. **Career:** Educator, Writer (retired); White House Staff, staff asst 1977-81; Howard Univ, spec asst commun, 1981-89, dir honors prog, mem dept philos, 1966-68, 1970-76; CT Col, dept philos, 1968-70; Off Econ Opportunity, publ Head, 1965-66; US Dept State, foreign serv res officer, 1964-65; Wellesley Col, dept philos, 1961-62; Yale Univ, dept philos, 1959-61. **Orgs:** Managing ed Rev, Metaphysics 1959-61; consult, Inst Serv Educ, 1972-76; Am Philos Asn; Com Blacks Philos, 1970-76; prog com Eastern Div, 1974-76. **Special Achievements:** First African American woman with a Ph.D. in philosophy; At Yale University she was the first woman graduate student to be appointed as a teaching assistant; Interviewed in George Yancy, Ed. African-American Philosophers: 17 Conversations (New York: Routledge, 1998), pages 263-286. **Home Addr:** 429 N St SW, Washington, DC 20024. *

COOK, JULIAN ABELE
Judge. **Personal:** Born Jun 22, 1930, Washington, DC; son of Julian Abele Cook Sr and Ruth Elizabeth McNeill; married Carol Annette Dibble, Dec 22, 1957; children: Julian Abele III, Peter Dibble & Susan Annette. **Educ:** Pa State Univ, BA, 1952; Georgetown Univ, JD, 1957; Univ Va, LLM, 1988. **Career:** Judge Arthur E Moore, law clerk, 1957-58; pvt pract atty, 1958-78; State MI, special asst & atty gen, 1968-78; Univ Detroit-Mercy, adjunct prof law, 1970-74; Eastern Dist MI, US Courthouse, Detroit, US Dist judge, 1978-89, chief judge, 1989-96, sr judge, 1996-; Harvardn Univ, Trial Advocacy Workshop, instr, 1988-; US Dept Justice's Trial Advocacy Prog, instr, 1989-. **Orgs:** Am Bar Asn; Nat Bar Asn; State Bar Mi; Wolverine Bar Asn Am Bar Found; co-chmn, Prof Develop Task Force, MI Bar Asn; MI Asn Black Judges; Fed Bar Asn; chair & bd dir, Oakland Univ Proj Twenty Comt, 1966-68; pres, Pontiac Area Urban League, 1967-68; chair, MI Civil Rights Comt, 1968-71; bd dir,Todd Phillips C's Home, 1968-78; bd dir, Am Civil Liberties Union,1976-78; pres, master bench, chap XI, Am Inn Ct, 1994-96; Cont Legal Educ Comt, Oakland County Bar Asn, 1968-69, judicial liaison, Dist Ct Comt, vice chair, 1977; Cont Legal Educ Comt, 1977; Unauthorized Prac Law, 1977;MI Supreme Ct Defense Serv Comt, 1977; exec bd dir, 1968-89, pres, 1975-76, Child & Family Serv MI; chmn, Sixth Circuit Comt Stand Jury Instr, 1986-; bd dir, Am Heart Asn MI; fel, Am Bar Asn, 1981-; bd dir, Detroit Urban League, 1983-85; Brighton Health Srev Corp, 1985-92; Georgetown Univ Alumni Asn; chmn, Comt Financial Disclosure, Judicial Conf US, 1990-93; Harvard Univ, trial advocacy workshop, instr, 1988-; lifemem, NAACP; Pa State Univ Alumni Asn, alumni coun, 1986-92; bd dir, Hutzel Hosp, 1984-95; bd visitor, Georgetown Univ, 1992-; NY Univ Root Tilden Snow Scholar Prog, screening panel, 1991-99; Mediation Tribunal Asn; bd dir, Third Judicial Circuit MI, 1992-; Am Law Inst, 1996-; Judicial Coun Sixth Circuit, sr judge personnel comt, 1996-97; fel, MI Bar Found, 1987-, chair, 1993-; co-chair, Nat Exec Comm, Archives Labor & Urban Affairs Wayne State Univ, 1988-. **Honors/Awds:** Distinguished Citizen of the Year, NAACP, 1970; Citation of Merit, Pontiac, MI Area Urban League, 1971; chmn, Civil Rights Commn, achieved resolution, State of MI, House of Representatives, 1971; Boss of the Year, Legal Secretary Asn, 1973-74; Pathfinders Award, Oakland Univ, 1977; Serv Award, Todd-Phillips Home Inc, 1978; Focus & Impact Award Oakland Univ,1985; Distinguished Alumnus Award, Pa State Univ, 1985; Distinguished Alumnus Award & John Carroll Award, Georgetown Univ, 1989; Augustus Straker Award, 1988; Absalom Jones Award, Union Black Episcopalians, Detroit Chap, 1988; Bench-Bar Award, Wolverine, Detroit Bar Asn, 1987; Presidential Award, North Oakland Co, NAACP, 1987; Honor Soc, Univ Detroit Sch Law, 1981; B nai B rith Barrister, 1980; Fed Bar Asn, 1978; Doctor of Law, Honoris Causa, Georgetown Univ, 1992; Brotherhood Award, Jewish Law Veterans of the US, 1994; Champion of Justice Award, MI State Bar, 1994; Doctor of Laws, Honoris Causa, Univ Detroit-Mercy, 1996; Wayne State Univ, Doctor of Laws, Honoris Causa, 1997; Paul R Dean Award, Georgetown Univ, 1997; Humanitarian Award, City Wide Choir Union; named one of the Most Respected Judges in Michigan. **Special Achievements:** Published: Jurisprudence of Original Intention, co-author, 1986; A Quest for Justice, 1983; Some Current Problems of Human Administration, co-author, 1971; The Changing Role of the Probation Officer in the Federal Court, article, Federal Sentencing Reporter, vol 4, no 2, p 112, 1991; An Overview of the US District Court for the Eastern District of Michigan, article, Inter Alia, vol 28, no 1, winter 1990; Rule 11: A Judicial Approach to an Effective Administration of Justice in the US Courts, 15Ohio N U L 397, 1988; ADR in the United States District Court for Eastern District of Michigan, Michigan Pleading and Practice ADR, Section62A-405-62A-415, 1994; Thur good Marshall and Clarence Thomas: A Glance at Their Philosophies, Michigan Bar Journal, March 1994, Vol 73, No 3, p298; George A Googasian-58th President of the State Bar of Michigan, Michigan Bar Journal, Oct 1992, vol 71, No 10; "Family Responsibility, Federal Sentencing Reporter," 1995; Federal Civil Procedure Before Trial: Sixth Circuit, 1996; "Dream Makers: Black Judges on Justice," Univ of MI Law Review, 1996; "Death Penalty," co-author Cooley Law Review, 1996; "Closing Their Eyes to the Constitution: The Declining Role of the Supreme Court in the Protection of Civil Rights," co-author, Detroit Col of Law, 1996;"Professionalism: An Order of the Court," Michigan Bar Journal, August1998, No 8, p 848; voted one of the "Most Respected Judges in Michigan" by the subscribers to Michigan

Lawyers Weekly, 5 Michigan Law Weekly, 666, April 29, 1991; MI Lawyers Weekly, voted 1 of 25 Most Respected Judges in MI, 1990, 1991; Detroit Monthly, voted 1 of the best Judges in the Metro Detroit area, 1991. **Military Serv:** AUS, Signal Corps, first lt, 1952-54. **Business Addr:** Senior Judge, United States District Court, Eastern District of Michigan, 231 W Lafayette Blvd Fl 5, Detroit, MI 48226, **Business Phone:** (313)234-5100.

COOK, KEITH LYNN
Banker. **Personal:** Born May 24, 1963, Chicago, IL; married Tia Cook, Feb 1, 1996. **Educ:** Roosevelt Univ, 1989-92. **Career:** Citibank ISB, mortgage acct exec, 1986-92; Harris Trust & Savings Bank, residential mortgage specialist, 1992-95, asst mgr, 1995-, mgr, bus developt, currently. **Orgs:** Nat Asn Black Accts, 1990; S & Southwest Bd Realtors, affil mem, 1992; Dearborn Real Estate Bd, 1994; Chicago Real Estate Fund, 1994; Urban Bankers Chicago, 1996-;Network Black Real Estate Profs, 1993; Cosmopolitan Coun, 1996-. **Honors/Awds:** Reinvestment Act Award, Harris Bank, 1992, 1993. **Home Addr:** 901 E 47th St, Chicago, IL 60615. **Business Addr:** Manager Business Development, Harris Trust & Savings Bank, 111 W Monroe, Chicago, IL 60603.

COOK, LADDA BANKS
Executive, president (organization), manager. **Personal:** Born Aug 22, 1935, Lancaster, SC; married Jessie Lee Oliver; children: Anita & Deborah. **Educ:** Johnson C Smith Univ, BS, 1957; Am Col Life Underwriters, CLU, 1972, CHFC, 1986. **Career:** Executive, President, Manager (retired); NY Dept Hosp & Health, asst chemist, 1960-65; Gen Agents & Mgrs Asn Brooklyn Chap, pres, 1976; NY Life Ins Co, gen mgr, 1965-93, managing partner, 1994. **Orgs:** Pres, Johnson C Smith Univ Alumni Asn, 1969; dir, Reg I 1969; Kiwanis Club, 1971; Am Soc Chartered Life Underwriters, 1972-93; bd dirs, Nat Asn Life Underwriters, 1977; Hundred Black Men, 1977; second vpres, Nat Alumni Asn, 1977; elder Siloam Presby Church, 1977-97; Nat Asn Advan Colored People, 1979; bd disting vis, Johnson C Smith Univ, 1979; basileus, Omega Psi Phi, Alpha Upsilon Chap, 1984; bd trustees, Claflin Col, 1984; bd dirs, NY Chap Gen Agents & Mgrs Asn. **Honors/Awds:** Robert Brown Member Scholar Award, 1957; Black Achievers Indus Award, YMCA of Gr NY, 1971; NY Lifes Pres Trophy, 1972. **Military Serv:** AUS, 1958-60. **Home Addr:** 228-03 139th Ave, Jamaica, NY 11413.

COOK, LEVI
Executive, president (organization), chief executive officer. **Career:** Advantage Enterprises Inc, pres & chief exec officer, 1980-. **Business Phone:** (419)727-0027.

COOK, DR. NATHAN HOWARD
Educator. **Personal:** Born Apr 26, 1939, Winston-Salem, NC; married Thelma Vernelle Upperman; children: Carlene Y & Erika Y. **Educ:** NC Cent Univ, BS 1961, MA 1963; Univ NC Greensboro, 1964; NC State Univ, Grad Credit, 1965; Okla State Univ, PhD 1972. **Career:** Barber-Scotia Col, asst prof biol, 1962-68; Wica Chem Inc, fac intern, 1968; Okla State Univ, grad teaching asst, 1968-69; Lincoln Univ, Dept Biol, vpres acad affairs, prof emer, head, currently. **Orgs:** Fel Ford Found, 1969-71; chmn, Sickle Cell Adv Comm Mo Div Health, 1972-79; eval, panelist Nat Sci Found, 1976; bd dirs, Am Cancer Soc Cole Unit 1981-85; consult, rev panelist, Nat Inst Health/div Res Resources, 1982; Environ Quality Comm, 1981-; pres elect, Mo Acad Sci, 1984-85; pres, Sunrise Optimist Club Jefferson City, 1984-85. **Honors/Awds:** Blue Tiger Award, AUS ROTC Unit Lincoln Univ, 1982. **Home Addr:** 2908 Sue Dr, Jefferson City, MO 65101.

COOK, RALPH D
Judge. **Personal:** Born Apr 29, 1944, Birmingham, AL. **Educ:** Howard Univ Sch Law; Univ Nashville. **Career:** Legal Asst Found, 1971-72; City Berkeley, Calif, 1972-73; Miles Col, prof; Bessemer, asst dist atty, 1974-76; Miles Law Sch, dean, 1975-90; Miles Law Sch, prof law, 1975-99; San Jose State, prof, 1975-99; Cabrillo Col, prof; Frequent CLE speaker; Family Ct Jefferson County, dist judge, 1977-81; 10th Circuit, Circuit Judge, 1981-93; Supreme Ct Ala, assoc justice, 1993-2000; Supreme Ct Ala, justice; Hare, Wynn, Newell & Newton LLP, atty, currently. **Orgs:** Birmingham Bar; Calif State Bar; Ala State Bar; Am Bar Asn; Ala Trial Lawyers Asn; Bessemer Bar Asn; Am Law Inst; Nat Bar Asn; pres, Ala Law Asn, 1992-93; charter mem, W Jefferson Kiwanis Club; former chmn, bd trustees, Bethel African Methodist Episcopal Zion Church. **Honors/Awds:** Recipient Judicial Award Merit, Ala State Bar, 1996; Outstanding Alabama Alumnus, 1999, Howard Univ Alumni Club Ala; Distinguished Service Award, Tenn State Univ, 1999; Resolution Honing Justice Ralph D Cook, Ala State Bar, 2000; Awards by Churches, Orgns, & Community Groups from around State Ala Classes/Seminars Taught. **Business Addr:** Attorney, Hare, Wynn, Newell & Newton LLP, 2025 3rd Ave N Suite 800, Birmingham, AL 35203-3378, **Business Phone:** (205)328-5330.

COOK, RASHARD
Football player, real estate executive. **Personal:** Born Apr 18, 1977, San Diego, CA. **Educ:** Univ Southern Calif, BA, sociol, 1998. **Career:** Football player (retired); Philadelphia Eagles, defensive back, 1999-2002; Home team Mortgage & Realty/ Intero Real Estate Serv, owner, currently. *

COOK, ROBERT
Administrator, executive. **Educ:** Delaware State Univ, BS, mkt bus admin. **Career:** Augusta Neighborhood Improv Corp, pres & chief exec officer, currently. **Business Addr:** President, Chief Executive Officer, Augusta Neighborhood Improvement Corporation, 953 Laney Walker Blvd Suite 300, Augusta, GA 30901, **Business Phone:** (706)724-5565.

COOK, RONALD R
Association executive. **Career:** Health Alliance Plan, Detroit, dir legis affairs & vpres, currently. **Orgs:** Assoc coun & chair, Legis Comt, Mich Asn Health Plans; Detroit Regional Chamber. **Special Achievements:** Named in 100 Emerging Business Leaders by Detroit Regional Chamber. **Business Addr:** Director of Legislative Affairs, Vice President, Health Alliance Plan, 2850 W Grand Blvd, Detroit, MI 48202, **Business Phone:** (313)872-8100.

COOK, RUFUS
Lawyer, executive. **Personal:** Born Nov 22, 1936, Birmingham, AL; divorced; children: Bruce. **Educ:** Talladega Col, BA, 1956; Univ Chicago, Phd, 1959. **Career:** Judge Luther M Swygert US Dist CT, law clerk, 1959-60; pvt pract lawyer, 1963; Cook & Revak Ltd, pres, currently. **Orgs:** Pres & bd chmn, Continental Inst Tech Inc; pres, Phoenix Realty Inc; partner, Cook Apts Assocs; pres, Pinnacle & Graphics Corp; Nat Moot Ct Team Univ Chicago, 1958-59; chmn bd, Hyde Park -Kenwood Community Conf, 1966-68; bd mem, Chicago Fedn Settlements, 1967-69; Daniel Hale Williams Univ. **Honors/Awds:** Prize, Univ Chicago, 1958. **Military Serv:** USAF, capt, 1963-66; Commendation Medal, 1963. **Business Addr:** President, Cook & Revak Ltd, 1625 E 74th St, Chicago, IL 60649, **Business Phone:** (773)752-6972.

COOK, DR. SAMUEL DUBOIS
College administrator, college president. **Personal:** Born Nov 21, 1928, Griffin, GA; son of Manuel and Mary Beatrice Daniel; married Sylvia Merelene Fields, Mar 18, 1960; children: Samuel Jr & Karen Jarcelyn. **Educ:** Morehouse Col, AB, 1948; Ohio State Univ, MA, 1950, PhD, 1954. **Career:** Educator (retired); Southern Univ, prof, 1955-56; Atlanta Univ, chmn, 1956-66; Univ Ill, vis prof, 1962-63; Duke Univ, prof, 1966-74; Ford Found, prog officer, 1969-71; Dillard Univ, pres, 1975-97. **Orgs:** Bd trustees, Martin Luther King Ctr Soc Change, 1969-; ed bd, Am Polit Sci Rev; ed bd, Jour Polit; ed bd, Jour Negro Hist; bd dir, Southern Christian Leadership Conf; bd dir, Am Coun Libr Resources; bd trustee, Coun Relig Int Affairs; pres, Southern Polit Sci Asn; Mayor's Charter Revision Comt; bd dir, Inst Serv Educ; Exec Coun, Am Polit Sci Asn; past vpres, Am Polit Asn; Phi Beta Kappa; Pi Sigma Alpha; Nat Coun Humanities, Omicron Delta Phi; Omega Psi Phi; Sigma Pi Phi; trustee emer, Duke Univ. **Honors/Awds:** Hon Degree, Morehouse Col, 1972; Hon Degree, Ohio St Univ, 1977; Hon Degree, Duke Univ, 1979; Hon Degree, Ill Col, 1979; Hon Degree, Chicago Theol Sem, 1988; Hon Degree, Univ New Orleans, 1989; Samuel DuBois Cook Society, named in honor, 1997; Outstanding Professor Award, Duke Univ; Distinguished Acheivment Award, St Augustine's Col; Citation Achievement Award, Ohio St; Torch of Liberty Award, Anti-Defamation League. **Special Achievements:** First African American professor at Duke University; Published numerous articles. **Military Serv:** AUS, 1953-55.

COOK, TOI FITZGERALD
Football player. **Personal:** Born Dec 3, 1964, Chicago, IL. **Educ:** Univ Stanford, commun. **Career:** New Orleans Saints, defensive back, 1987-93; San Francisco 49ers, 1994-95; Carolina Panthers, 1996-97; Stanford Athletic Bd of Dir, currently.

COOK, TONYA DENISE
School administrator. **Personal:** Born Feb 4, 1968, Atlanta, GA; daughter of Robert Stinson, Jr and Mary Cook. **Educ:** Ga State Univ, BA, mkt, 1994; Andrew Young Sch Policy Studies, MS, human resource develop, 2006. **Career:** Ga State Univ, Off African Am Stud Serv & Prog, spec events coordr, 1996-99, Off Diversity Educ Prog, admin coordr, 1999, Off Stud Life & Leadership Intercultural Rels, prog specialist, currently. **Orgs:** Zeta Phi Beta Sorority Inc, 1989-; vol, Atlanta Convention & Visitor's Bur, 1994-; chair, African Am Heritage Awards, 1994, 1997, 1998 & 1999; World Union African People, 1998-; Atlanta Asn Black Journalists, 1999-; Nat Asn Exec Secretaries & Admin Assts, 1999-; adv bd, Event Planning Mag, 1999-; Vol Steering Comt, Jomandi Prod, 1999-; Enlighten Cir, 2000-. **Honors/Awds:** Phyllis Weatley Heritage Award, Off Multicultural Progs, Ga State Univ, 1990, Senior Award, 1994, Nat Asn Advan Colored People Meritorious Service Award, 2006. **Special Achievements:** Women Hold Up Half the Sky Total Dance Company, dancer/actress, 1989-1998; National Black Arts Festival, Dance With Total Dance Company, 1994 & 1996. **Home Addr:** 270 Martin St Suite 91, Atlanta, GA 30312, **Home Phone:** (404)584-7706. **Business Addr:** Program Specialist, Georgia State University, 44 Courtland St, Atlanta, GA 30302-3965, **Business Phone:** (404)413-1586.

COOK, VICTOR TRENT
Singer, actor. **Personal:** Born Aug 19, 1967, Brooklyn, NY. **Career:** TV Series: "The Days & Nights of Molly Dodd", 1991; "Smokey Joe's Cafe: The Songs of Leiber & Stoller", 2000; "My Favorite Broadway: The Love Songs", 2001; "Three Mo' Tenors", 2001; "Cook, Dixon & Young: In Concert", 2005; "Tavis Smiley", 2006. **Honors/Awds:** Nominee, Tony Award, 1995; $100,000 Male Vocal Champion!, Star Search, 1998. **Business Phone:** (212)581-6181.*

COOK, WALLACE JEFFERY
Clergy, dentist. **Personal:** Born Jul 14, 1932, El Reno, OK; married Martha; children: Cheryl, Jeffery, Jeryl. **Educ:** AZ State Univ, BA, 1954; Howard Univ, DDS Col, Dent, 1957; Crozer Theol Sem, MDiv 1964; VA Union Univ, DDiv, 1973; Union Theol Sem Richmond VA, D Ministry, 1978. **Career:** Clergy (retired); USAF, Dentist, 1957-61; First Baptist Church Yardley PA, pastor, 1963-64; Ebenezer Baptist Church Providence RI, pastor, 1964-94; Joseph Samuels Dent Clin, dentist, 1969; Providence Pub Sch, dentist dept health, 1970. **Orgs:** Urban League, 1970; Urban Coalition 1970; Richmond Comm Sr Ctr, 1975; Richmond Oppty Indus Ctrs, 1976. **Military Serv:** USAF, capt, 1957-61. *

COOK, WILLIAM WILBURT
Educator. **Personal:** Born Aug 4, 1933, Trenton, NJ; son of Frances Carter and Cleve. **Educ:** Trenton State Col, BS, valedictorian, 1954; Univ Chicago, MA, 1976. **Career:** Trenton Pub Sch, teacher Eng & social studies, 1954-61; Princeton Regional Sch, Eng Dept, teacher Eng, chair, 1961-73; Dartmouth Col, dir African & Afro-Am studies, 1977-84, 1985-90, assoc prof Eng, prof Eng, 1973; Dartmouth Col, Israel Evans Prof Oratory & Belles Lettres, 1991-, Dept Eng, chair, 1994, prof Eng & African Am studies, currently. **Orgs:** Humanities consult, Nat Fac Arts & Sci, 1976-; Danforth Asn, 1979-85; bd dirs, Am Folk Theater, 1982-; patron & dir, N Country Theater, 1983-; chair & adv comn minority affairs, Conf Col Comp & Commun, 1983-85; c media consult, Nat Endowment Humanities, 1984-; adv bd, Nat Civil Rights Mus, 1986-88; asst chair, Conv Col Comp & Commun, 1990, assoc chair, 1991, prog chair, 1991, chair, 1992. **Honors/Awds:** Distinguished Alumni Citation, Trenton State Col, 1977; Dartmouth Distinguished Teaching Award, 1989; Professor of the Year, Coun Advan & Support Educ, New Hampshire, 1993; DHL, Rivier Col, 1994. **Special Achievements:** Published poetry, literary criticism; ed 3 books; author, Hudson Hornet & other Poems, 1989. **Military Serv:** AUS, sp-4, 1957-59. **Business Addr:** Professor of English & African American Studies, Israel Evans Professor of Oratory and Belles Lettres, Dartmouth College, English Department, 210 Sanborn House, PO Box 6032, Hanover, NH 03755, **Business Phone:** (603)646-2316.

COOK, YVONNE MACON. See POWELL, YVONNE MACON.

COOKE, ANNA L
Librarian. **Personal:** Born in Jackson, TN; daughter of Thurston Lee and Effie Cage Lee; married James A; children: Elsie Cooke Holmes. **Educ:** Lane Col, BA, 1944; Atlanta Univ, MLS, 1955, Honorary Degree, Doctor Humane Letters, 1993. **Career:** Librarian (retired); Douglas Jr High Sch Haywood County, TN, prin, 1944-46; Jackson City Sch, teacher, 1947-51, librn, 1951-63; Lane Col, catalog librn, 1963-67, PR & Alumni dir, 1966-69, head librn, 1967-88; Metro Forum, Jackson Sun, freelance writer, 1990-. **Orgs:** Am Libr Asn, 1964-; bd dir, Am Cancer Soc, 1967-73; sec bd dir, Jackson Arts Coun, 1974-76; bd dir, Reelfoot Girl Scout Coun, 1974-86, First vpres, 1983-86; bd trustees, Jackson Madison Co Libr, 1984-93; Tenn Libr Asn; W Tenn Libr Asn; Am Libr Asn; Delta Sigma Theta Sorority Inc; Links Inc; NAACP; bd dirs, Jackson Volunteer Ctr, 1988-90; chmn, women's adv bd, HCA Regional Hosp Jackson, 1990-96; Jackson/Madison County Historic Zoning Comm, 1993-96. **Honors/Awds:** Library Sci Lane Col, 1966; Hon Fellow Philosophical Soc Eng, 1969; Alumni Plaque Lane Col, 1975; Action Award, Radio Station WJAK, 1982; Serv Plaque City of Jackson 1972; Girl Scout Friendmaker Award, 1985; Serv Plaque Delta Sigma Theta Sor; Distinguished Service Award, State Tenn, 1988; Diamond Jubilee Service Award, Delta Sigma Theta Sorority, 1988; Certificate of Merit, Lane Col, 1988; Presidential Citation, National Asn Equal Opportunity Higher Educ, 1989; Distinguished Service Award, City of Jackson, 1992; Metro Forum Service Award, 1991-97; Distinguished Service Plaques, Delta Sigma Theta Sorority, 1994-95; Jackson/ Madison County Library Board Service Award, 1993; Hall of Fame, Alpha Kappa Alpha Community Affairs, 1995; Service Award, Delta Sigma Theta, 1995; Service Award, Housing Historic Zoning CMS, 1996; Treasure Award, Jackson City Community, 1997; Metro Forum Publisher's Award, 1997; Recognition Award, City of Jackson, 2001; Meritorious Sevice Award, NAACP, Jackson-Madison Cty Branch, 2002; Griat Literary Award, 2003. **Special Achievements:** Author "History of Lane College," 1987; Published poem God's Love in Dark Side of the Moon: The Natl Library of Poetry, 1994.

COOKE, LEONARD
Law enforcement officer. **Personal:** Born in Weldon, NC. **Career:** City Wash, DC, police officer, 1970-92; City Eugene, Ore, chief police, 1992-98; City Portsmouth, Va, chief police, 1998; Commonwealth Va, Dept Criminal Justice Serv, dir, currently. **Orgs:** FBI Nat Acad; nat pres, Nat Orgn Black Law Enforcement Exec; Off Comnr Pub Appointments; Int Asn Chiefs Police, Civil Rights

Comn; Va Asn Chiefs Police; Nat Asn Advan Colored People. **Honors/Awds:** Fellowship, Int Asn Chiefs Police, 1988; Humanitarian Award, Jewish Fedn Lane Country, Ore, 1998. **Business Addr:** Director, Commonwealth of Virginia, Department of Criminal Justice Services, 5th Fl 202 N 9th St, Richmond, VA 23219-1926, **Business Phone:** (804)786-8718.

COOKE, NELLIE
Educator. **Personal:** Born Dec 17, 1948, Brighton, AL; daughter of Loudelia Freed Cooke and Prentis Cooke; married Robert Jefferson, Oct 18, 1990; children: Derek Vincent. **Educ:** Bethune-Cookman Col, Daytona Beach, Fla, 1965-67; DC Teachers Col, Wash, DC, BA, 1973; VPI-Va Tech, Blacksburg, Va, Masters, 1988. **Career:** Shaw Jr High Sch, Wash, DC, teacher & dean stud, 1974; Bertie Backus Mid Sch, asst prin. **Orgs:** Chmn, Nat Jr Red Cross; adv comn, WHMM-TV, Wash, DC, currently; adv bd, Young Writers Contest Found. **Honors/Awds:** Woman of the Year, Shiloh Baptist Church, 1989; Torchlighter Award, Potomac LINKS, Wash, DC, 1989; cover story, Wash Post Mag, 1989; educ consult, Nightwatch, CBS. **Home Addr:** 10835 Lockwood Dr, Silver Spring, MD 20901. **Business Addr:** Assistant Principal, Bertie Backus Mid Sch, 5171 S Dakota Ave NE, Washington, DC 20017, **Business Phone:** (202)576-6110.

COOKE, DR. PAUL PHILLIPS
Educator, lecturer. **Personal:** Born Jun 29, 1917, New York, NY; son of Louis and Mamie K (deceased); married Rose Clifford, Aug 22, 1940; children: Kelsey C (deceased), Paul C, Anne & Katherine. **Educ:** Miner Teachers Col, BS, 1937; NY Univ, MA, 1941; Catholic Univ Am, MA, eng lang & lit, 1943; Columbia Univ, EdD, 1947. **Career:** Miner Teachers Col & DCTC, prof eng, 1944-74; DC Teachers Col, prof, 1954-66, pres, 1966-74; Am Asn State Cols & Univ, dir int progs, 1974-75; Sch Edu, consult, 1979, 1988; Howard Univ, Dept Physics, spec consult, 1976-81; Beacon Col, vpres acad affairs, 1984-85; AASCU, 1974-90; Goethe Ins Wash, Panel discussion, 2005. **Orgs:** Consult, World Peace through Law Ctr, 1974-78; consult, Am Bar Asn Standing Comm World Order under Law, 1975-77; consult, Anacostia Neighborhood Mus 4 exhibits, 1979-92; spec asst, pres, Univ DC Hist Res, 1982-83; World Veterans Fedn; life mem, Nat Asn Advan Colored People; life mem, Kappa Alpha Psi Fraternity; Cath Interracial Coun. **Honors/Awds:** Am Vet Com Bessie Levine Award, 1960; Nat Sor Phi Delta Kappa Award, 1975; Thomas Wyatt Turner Award, Office of Black Catholics, Wash, DC; His Holiness Pope John Paul II Pro Ecclesia Et Pontifice, 1984; Doctor of Laws Degree, Honoris Causa, Univ DC, 1986; DC Hall of Fame, 2001. **Special Achievements:** More than Publications & papers, numerous publications including, The Centennial Drama, A History of Miner Teachers College, Civil Rights in the United States, The Cooke Lecture Series; Educ of the Disadvantage in the Model Sch Div 1965; 22 articles in the Journal of Negro Education, 1949-82 & other articles in the Negro History Bulletin 1958-82, Negro Educational Review, Mid-West Journal. **Military Serv:** USAF, corp, 1945-46. **Home Addr:** 2480 16th St NW, Washington, DC 20009, **Home Phone:** (202)232-7684. *

COOKE, THOMAS H, JR.
Executive. **Personal:** Born Oct 13, 1929, Camden, SC; married Audrey E Wilson; children: Bonnye A Jefferson, Julie L & Michael W Thomas III. **Educ:** New York Univ, BS, 1954; Montclair State Col, MA, 1974. **Career:** US Veterans Admin Hosp, corrective therapist, 1957-58; Newark Bd Educ, Victoria plan coordr, 1958-77; City E Orange, mayor, 1978-85; McLaughlin PivenVogel Inc, sr govt bond specialist, 1986-87; Maintenance Mgt Specialists Inc, pres. **Orgs:** Bd dir, vice pres, Nat Conf Black Mayors, 1978-85; govt relations comn, Nat United Way, 1979-; bd dirs, exec comt, US Conf Mayors, 1981-85; bd dirs, finance comt, Nat League Cities, 1981-85; comnr, NJ Martin L King Commemorative Comn, 1983-; comnr, NJ Drug Adv Comn, 1983-; bd dirs, NJ Multi Housing Indust, 1987-; life mem, Nat Asn Advan Colored People; Nat Coun Negro Women; Nat Coun Jewish Women. **Military Serv:** USN Reserves, asst psychologist, 1954-56; Honor Man Grad Co, 1954. **Home Addr:** 74 Hawthorne Ave, East Orange, NJ 07018.

COOKE, WILCE L.
Government official. **Personal:** Born Jun 18, 1939, Benton Harbor, MI; son of Elizabeth Walker; married Beverly. **Educ:** Oakland Community Col Sch, prac nursing, 1968; Inst Adult Educ, 1970; Lake Mich Col, AA, 1975; Western Mich Univ, BS, 1976, MA, 1985. **Career:** City Benton Harbor, mayor, currently. **Orgs:** Adv brd, Tri-Can; former suprv comn, Ppl Comm Fed Credit Union; former brd dir, org Self Help Co-Op; former charter revision comn, Benton Harbor Charter Comn; treas, mercy Hosp Staff Coun, 1977-82; Phi Theta Kappa; Benton Two Black Coalition; brd dir, Berrien County Heart Unit, Mich Heart Assn; trustee brd, asst sunday school supt, Bethlehem Temple Pentecostal Church; Alpha Kappa Delta. **Honors/Awds:** Scholarship Compet, Natl Upper Div, 1976; Outstanding Serv Award, Benton Harbor Concerned Citizens; Spearheading drive in retaining Open Heart Surgical Unit at Mercy Hosp in Southwestern Michigan, Berrien County Med Soc, 1978. **Home Addr:** 1130 Salem, Benton Harbor, MI 49022. **Business Addr:** Mayor, City Benton Harbor, 200 E Wall St, Benton Harbor, MI 49022.*

COOLEY, KEITH WINSTON
Consultant, executive, government official. **Personal:** Born Oct 7, 1945, Ann Arbor, MI; son of Roy Van and Hyacinth Holmes; married Yvonne A Smiley, May 21, 1977; children: Brett Winston, Todd Lloyd, Ross Allyn, Erin Blair. **Educ:** Univ Mich, BS, engineering physics, 1967, MS, nuclear engineering , 1972. **Career:** Gen Elec Corp, Knolls Atomic Power Lab, exp physicist, 1968-69, res engr, 1972-73, Environ Activ Staff, staff proj engr, 1973-78, Cadilac Motor Car, staff proj engr, 1978-83, prog mgr, future car line, 1983-86, engineering dept head, 1986-94, dir strategic planning & issues mgr, 1994-96; Principia Inc, bus consult, pres, 1997-; Motorola Corp, dir; Telematics Int Sales, GM acct, 2001; Focus: HOPE, chief operating officer, 2002-06, chief exec officer, 2006-; Dept Labor & Econ Growth, MI, dir, 2007-. **Orgs:** Engineering Soc Detroit, 1980-; Detroit Inst Ophthal; Workforce Innovation Regional Econ Develop; Nat Black MBA Asn; Tau Beta Pi Engineering Hon Soc; Tenn Squire Asn; Univ Mich Alumni Soc; bd dirs, Univ Mich Engineering Alumni Asn, 1991-93. **Honors/Awds:** Best of the Best, Gen Motors, 1995; Tau Beta Pi Eminent Engineer, 1989; General Motors President's Council Honors; Silver & Bronze Award, Mich Occup Safety & Health Asn, 2005, 2007. **Special Achievements:** Gymnast - the first African-American to compete in that sport at U-M - and was a member of a U-M Big Ten Championship team. *

COOLEY, WENDY
Television show host, judge, television producer. **Personal:** Born Jan 1, 1952, Birmingham, AL; daughter of Louise Cargill and Bessie Crenshaw; divorced. **Educ:** Eastern Mich Univ, educ, 1968; Univ Mich, higher educ, 1972; Univ Detroit, JD, 1980. **Career:** Judge (retired), host, producer; 36th Dist Ct, judge, 1984; "Winning Ways", TV & Radio show, host & producer, 1990. **Orgs:** Mich Dist Judges Asn; Asn Black Judges; Mich State Bar Asn; Nat Bar Asn; Nat Asn Negro Bus & Prof Women's Club Inc; Coalition 100 Black Women; Delta Sigma Theta; Gamma Phi Delta; Mich Martin Luther King Jr Holiday Comn; Nat Speakers Asn. **Honors/Awds:** Michigan Outstanding Volunteer; Nat Leadership Prog Am; Golden Heritage Award, Little Rock Baptist Church; Judical Excellence Award, Top Ladies Distinction; Foremost Woman 20th Century; Gov Jim Blanchard, Mich Correctional Officer Training Coun. **Special Achievements:** founder & pres, Women Who Win.

COOL J, L L. See SMITH, JAMES TODD.

COOMBS, FLETCHER
Executive. **Personal:** Born Jul 8, 1924, Altanta, GA; son of Fletcher and Pearl Magnolia Floyd; married Helen Grimes, May 21, 1955; children: Toni, Kei. **Educ:** Morehouse Col, AB; Atlanta Univ Sch Bus Admin, MBA; Ind Univ Bloomington, Ind, Grad Sch Savings & Loan, Cert, 1971. **Career:** Mutual Fed Savings & Loan Assn, various positions 1953-73, pres 1973-90, vice chmn, bd of dirs, 1990-97 (retired). **Orgs:** GA AAA Adv Bd, AAA S; fin chmn, bd mem, Sadie G Mays Nursing Home. **Honors/Awds:** Boss of the Year, Golden Dome Chap Am Bus Women Assn; Butler St YMCA. **Military Serv:** 2nd lt reserves, t/sgt active duty.

COOMBS, HARRY JAMES
Executive, manager. **Personal:** Born Sep 19, 1935, Washington, DC; married Barbara Ann Parrish. **Career:** Schwartz Bros Whis Rec Dist, local prom mgr, 1965-67; Ramsel Prods, dir, 1968-68; CBS Recs Inc, E coast regional prom rep, 1969-69; Capitol Rec Dist Corp, E coast regional prom rep, 1969-70; Tangerine Recs Corp, nat field rep, 1970-71; Philadelphia Int Rec, exec vpres, 1971, mgr, currently. **Orgs:** Mem exec coun, Black Music Asn, 1978. **Military Serv:** AUS, spec 4, 1954-56. **Business Addr:** Manager, Philadelphia International Records, 309 S Broad St, Philadelphia, PA 19107, **Business Phone:** (215)877-6753.

COOPER, ALBERT, SR.
Executive. **Personal:** Born Sep 22, 1934, Americus, GA; son of Anderson; married Josephine Wiggins; children: Albert Jr, Booker Alphonse, Jerel Boyd. **Educ:** GA Southwestern Col, Americus, GA, 1987. **Career:** Cooper's Groc & Mkt, 1979-83; Cooper's Const Co, owner, 1970-85. **Orgs:** Councilman, Americus GA, 1979-91; elected mayor, protem, 1982, 1985; Early Bird Ctr, 1980; bd governors, Chamber Com, 1981; zoning bd, City Americus, 1978-85. **Honors/Awds:** Excellence in Business Award, Ed Bryant, 1978; Disting Service Male Award, Oscar Marwell, 1979; Men Business League Award, 1984; Volunteer work providing housing for the poor, 1984; Community Service Award, Black Business Achievement Award, 1988; Certificate of Appreciation, Chamber Com, 1989; Thurgood Marshall Award, United Holiness Church, 1991. *

COOPER, ALMETA E
Lawyer. **Personal:** Born Dec 27, 1950, Durham, NC; daughter of Patricia Carter and Horton; children: Elise Adele Nelson. **Educ:** Wells Col, BA, 1972; Northwestern Univ, Sch Law, JD, 1975. **Career:** Vedder Price Kaufman & Kammholz, assoc, 1975-77; Am Med Asn, asst dir health law div, 1977-82; Tuggle Hasbrouck & Robinson, partner, 1980-82; Meharry, Medical Col, corp secy & gen coun, 1982-88; St Thomas Hosp, Nashville, TN, gen coun; Col St Francis, Nashville, TN, adj fac; Sr coun, MCP-Habemann Univ; Ohio State Med Asn, gen coun, 1999-. **Orgs:** Lectr, Joint Community on Accreditation Hosps; lectr, Am Col Hosp Adminrs; lectr, New England Hosp Assembly; Am Soc Hosp Attys; bd dir, Minority Legal Educ Resources; alternate mem, Hines Veterans Admin Cooperative Studies Prog Human Rights Comn; pres, bd dir, Ill Family Planning Coun; Renaissance Women; appointed mem, Nashville Pvt Ind Coun; fin comn, League Women Voters Nashville; Leadership Nashville, 1986-87; Music City Chap Links; Tenn Bar Asn; Napier-Looby Bar Asn; Am Acad Hosp Attys; pres-elect, Am Health Lawyers Asn, 2002-03. **Honors/Awds:** Outstanding Alumna Spelman Colegel; Outstanding Volunteer Chicago Urban League; Nat Finalist White House Fellowship, 1982. **Special Achievements:** Publs, J Am Med Asn & St Louis Univ Law J. **Home Addr:** PO Box 1212, Hillard, OH 43026. **Business Addr:** General Counsel, Ohio State Medical Association, 3401 Mill Run Dr, Hillard, OH 43026, **Business Phone:** (614)527-6762.

COOPER, BARBARA J
Federal government official, security guard. **Personal:** Born in North Carolina; daughter of Ezola Cooper Britt and Jasper Cooper. **Educ:** Hampton Univ, BS; Mich State Univ, MBA; Stanford Univ, Grad Cert. **Career:** Federal government official, Security guard (retired); Portsmouth VA Sch Syst, teacher; Cent Intelligence Agency, spec asst dep dir, dep dir personnel; dep inspector gen invests, dep dir financial mgt, dir financial mgt; security officer III. **Orgs:** Alpha Kappa Alpha Sorority; Nat Hampton Alumni Asn; vpres, Northern VA Chap, Nat Hampton Alumni Asn, 1984-86; adv coun, Howard Univ Sch Bus; adv bd, Omniplex World Servs Corp. **Honors/Awds:** Pub Affairs fel, Stanford Univ; Distinguished Intelligence Medal. **Home Addr:** 1641 Morrill Ct, McLean, VA 22101.

COOPER, BARRY
Entrepreneur, editor. **Personal:** Born Jan 1, 1956. **Career:** Orlando Sentinal Online, mgr, ed; Blackvoices.com, founder, creator, chief exec officer. **Orgs:** Nat Asn Black Journalists; YMCA Black Achievers; Boy Scouts of Am; Nat Asn Advan Colored People. **Honors/Awds:** Pulitzer Prize nomination, 1983; MOBE IT Award, 1999-00. *

COOPER, BARRY MICHAEL
Screenwriter, journalist. **Career:** Journalist; William Morris Agency LLC, screenwriter, currently; Films: New Jack City, screenplay, 1991; Above the Rim, screenplay, 1994; Sugar Hill, writer, 1994. **Business Addr:** Screenwriter, c/o William Morris Agency LLC, 151 El Camino Dr, Beverly Hills, CA 90212, **Business Phone:** (310)274-7451.

COOPER, BOBBY G.
Educator. **Personal:** Born Nov 3, 1938, Bolton, MS; married Della M Larkin; children: Christopher, Demetria & LaCarole. **Educ:** Tougaloo Col Touglaoo, BS, 1961; Univ Ill, Urbana, MS, 1970; Univ COBoulder, EdS, 1971, EdD, 1977. **Career:** E T Hawkins High Sch, Forest MS, music tech, 1961-68; Camp Tree Tops, Lake Placid NY, counr, 1968-69; Special Educ Opportunity Univ Ill Urbana, counr, 1969-70; Utica Community Col, chmn, 1972-, Humanities Div chair,music instr, currently, opera S, chorus master, 1980-81; Jubilee Singers, dir, currently. **Orgs:** Am Choral Dir Asn; Music Comt Meth Church, 1976; Phi Delta Kappa; organist Asbury United Meth Church, Bolton, 1961-; trustee, Asbury United Meth Church Bolton, 1975-. **Honors/Awds:** Music scholarship Tougaloo Coll, 1958; leadership develop grant, Ford-Found, 1968; inducted into Tougaloo Col Nat Alumni Hall of Fame. *

COOPER, BRIDGETT LOUISE
Opera singer. **Personal:** Born Jan 24, 1968, Washington, DC; daughter of Clement; children: Darby. **Educ:** E Carolina Univ, BM, 1990; Am Inst Musical Studies, attended 1993. **Career:** Wa Opera; Lyric Opera Chicago; Livent, Showboat; Living Arts Intl Tour;Aspen Opera Theater; Isreal Music Festival; Diaspera Opera Co; opera singer, currently. **Orgs:** Alpha Kappa Alpha Sorority; Am Guild Musical Artists; Music Educators; Opera Am. **Honors/Awds:** Bel Canto Competition Chicago, Semi Finalist, 1998; Voices of the New Millenium, Carnegie Hall, 2000; Black Archives of Southern Florida, 2001;Marjorie Lawrence Intl Vocal Comp, Semi Finalist, 2001; 1st place, Paul Robeson Nat Vocal Competition, 2001; Ms. American Achievement of Washington DC. **Special Achievements:** AIMS, Graz Austria, 1993; Washington Opera, 1999; Bicentenial Celebration Recital, Christ Episcapal Church, 2002.

COOPER, HON. CANDACE D
Judge, lawyer. **Personal:** Born Nov 23, 1948, Los Angeles, CA; daughter of Eunice and Cornelius. **Educ:** Univ Southern Calif, BA, 1970, JD, 1973. **Career:** Gibson Dunn & Crutcher, atty, 1973-80; Los Angeles Munic Ct, judge, 1980-88; Los Angeles Superior Ct, judge, 1987-99; Calif Ct Appeal, second Appellate Dist, Div two, assoc justice, 1999-2001, Div eight, presiding justice, 2001-. **Orgs:** Calif Asn Black Lawyers, 1975-87, Black Woman Lawyers Los Angeles, 1975-87; Nat Asn Women Judges, 1980-87; life mem, Nat Bar Asn; Nat Asn Advan Colored People; bd dir, Watts/Willowbrook Boys & Girls Club, 1982-87; Exceptional C Found, 1982-87; pres, Calif Judges Asn, 1988-89. **Honors/Awds:** Outstanding Alumni Ebonics, Univ S Calif, 1982; Woman of Achievement, Bus & Prof Women Los Angeles Sunset

Chap, 1985; Bernard S Jefferson Judge Of the year Award, 1986; Beta Pi Sigma Sor Inc Alpha Chap Outstanding Black Achievement Award, 1986; A Los Angeles Ernestine Stalhut Award, Women lawyers, 1990; Judge Of the year, Los Angeles County Bar Asn, Criminal Justice Section, 1990, 1992; Criminal Judge Of the year, Century City Bar Asn, 1992; Silver Achievement Award, Los Angeles YWCA, 1991; Jurist Of the year Award, Los Angeles County Bar Asn; Achievement Award, YWCA, 1991; Alumni Merit Award, Univ Southern Calif Gen Alumni Asn, 1994; Outstanding Achievement in the Legal Profession Award, Univ Southern Calif Asn Black Law Alumni, 1996; Justice Joan Dempsey Klein Distinguished Judge Award, Calif Women Lawyers, 1997; Power of One" Award, Black Women Lawyers Asn Los Angeles Found, 2006. **Business Addr:** Presiding Justice, California Court of Appeal, Ronald Reagan State Bldg, 300 S Spring St 2nd Floor, Los Angeles, CA 90013, **Business Phone:** (213)830-7000.

COOPER, CARDELL
Government official. **Personal:** Married. **Educ:** Montclair State Univ, BS, polit sci, 1974; Rutgers Univ, MA, pub admin, 1978. **Career:** City E Orange, NJ, mayor, 1989-95; Essex, NJ, county adminr, 1989-90; US Dept Housing & Urban Develop, asst secy community planning & develop, 1998-; Cooper Assocs, , pres, 2001-; Nat Community Develop Asn, Wash, exec dir, 2006-. **Orgs:** Advy bd, Conf Mayors; chair, Health & Human Servs Comt & Task Force Immigration. **Honors/Awds:** National Community Development Leadership Award. **Special Achievements:** Youngest mayor in the East Orange city's history; traveled to Taiwan in 1995; to Jerusalem in 1994; and to Japan in 1993. These visits focused on issues such as economic development and international trade opportunities. **Business Addr:** Executive Director, National Community Development Association, 522 21st St NW Suite 120, Washington, DC 20006, **Business Phone:** (202)293-7587.*

COOPER, CECIL CELESTER
Baseball player. **Personal:** Born Dec 20, 1949, Brenham, TX; married Octavia; children: Kelly, Brittany & Tori Camille. **Educ:** Prairie View A&M Col. **Career:** Baseball player (retired); Boston Red Sox, infielder, 1971-76; Milwaukee Brewers, infielder, 1977-87, drr of player dev, 1996-99; special asst, 1999; Coordinated Sports MGT Co Inc, vp, sports operations/owner; Houston Astros, mgr, currently. **Orgs:** Milwaukee Brewers Baseball Club. **Honors/Awds:** Golden Glove Awards, 1979, 1980; MVP and Wisconsin Sports Personality of Year,1980; named AL Player of the Month, 1980; Silver Slugger Award, 1980, 1981, 1982; Distinguished Athlete Award, 1982; Roberto Clemente Award, 1983; earned team MVP & HR Award, 1983; named AL Player of the Week & Player of the Month, 1983; Silver Bat Awards, from Sporting News; winner Harvey Kuenn Award; club's MVP 1985; Athlete for Youth's "Good Guy" Award, 1985. **Business Addr:** Manager, Houston Astros, Minute Maid Pk, 501 Crawford Street, Houston, TX 77002.*

COOPER, CHARLES W.
Physician. **Personal:** Born Jun 13, 1929, Hayti, MO; son of Roy Sr and Louise Black; married Bobbye Jean Hollins; children: Terri Lyn, Janis Kaye, Karyl Jean, Daryl Dean, Alan Jeffrey. **Educ:** Lincoln Univ, MO, BS, 1951; Univ Wichita, attended 1956; Meharry Med Col, MD, 1964. **Career:** Physician, Currently. **Orgs:** Trustee, Quinn Chapel Am Methodist Episcopal Church, 1967-; Pres, Lincoln Univ Found, 1972-73; Am Hereford Asn. **Honors/Awds:** Nat Methodist Scholar, Meth Church, 1962-63; Mead Johnson Award, Mead Johnson Pharm Co, 1966; dipl, 1973, fellow, Am Acad Family Phys. **Military Serv:** USAF, sgt, 1951-55; Good Conduct Medal, 1954. *

COOPER, CLARENCE
Lawyer, judge. **Personal:** Born May 5, 1942, Decatur, GA; married Shirley; children: Jennae & Corey. **Educ:** Howard Univ Sch law; Clark Col, BA, 1964; Emory Univ Sch Law, JD, 1967; MIT Comm Flws Prog, fel, 1977; Harvard Univ, John F Kennedy Sch Govt Pub Admin, MPA, 1978. **Career:** Atlanta Legal Serv Prog, atty, 1967-68; Fulton Co Ga, asst dist atty, 1968-76; City Atlanta Municipal Ct, judge, 1975-80; Atlant Munic Ct, assoc judge, 1976; Fulton Co Super Ct, judge; Ga Ct Appeals, 1990-94; US Dist Ct, Northern Dist Ga, judge, 1994, fed judge, currently. **Orgs:** Nat Bar asn, Gate City Bar asn; Nat Conf Black Lawyers, State Bar Ga, Atlanta Bar asn; Atlanta Br NAACP; Nat Urban League; bd dir, Amistrad Prod, EOA's Drug Prog; Atlanta Judicial Comn. **Honors/Awds:** Scholar Clark Col, 1960-64; publ "The Judiciary & It's Budget an adminstrvhassle". **Special Achievements:** First African-American appointed to a full-time judgeship on the AtlantaMunicipal Court; first African-American ever elected to a county-wide judgeship on the Fulton Superior Court, 1968. **Military Serv:** AUS, E-6, 1968-70; Bronze Star, Cert of Commendation. **Business Addr:** Federal Judge, US District Court, Northern Dist Georgia, 1721 US Dist Ct 75 Spring St, Atlanta, GA 30303-3309, **Business Phone:** (404)215-1390.

COOPER, CONSTANCE M.
Educator. **Personal:** Born in Lorain, OH; married Hewitt J; children: Candace, Adrienne & Hewitt Jr. **Educ:** Univ Mich, BBA, 1975, MBA, 1977. **Career:** Univ Cincinnati, Dept Bus & Com assoc prof & head, currently. **Orgs:** Treas, SUMA, 1999; secy & bd dir, Coun Aging, 2001; treas, Victory Neighborhood Serv Agency, 2003. **Honors/Awds:** CPA Ohio, 1984. **Business Addr:** Associate Professor, Department Head, University of Cincinnati, Business & Commerce Department, 2220 Victory Pkwy, Cincinnati, OH 45206-2839, **Business Phone:** (513)556-0871.

COOPER, CYNTHIA
Basketball player, basketball coach. **Personal:** Born Apr 14, 1963, Chicago, IL; daughter of Mary Cobbs. **Educ:** Univ SC, attended 1986. **Career:** Basketball player (retired), basketball coach; Valencia team, Spain, 1986-87; Parma team, Italy, 1987-94, 1996-97; Alcamo team, Italy, 1994-96; Houston Comets, WNBA, guard, 1997-2000, 2003; Phoenix Mercury, head coach, 2000-02; Houston Rockets, analyst & halftime reporter; Prairie View A&M Univ, head women's basketball coach, currenlty. **Honors/Awds:** Nat Collegiate Athletic Asn, Championship, 1983, 1984; Most Valuable Player, Europ League, All-Star Game, 1987; Gold medal, 1988, Bronze Medal, 1992, US Olympics Women's Basketball; Player of the Week, WNBA, 1997; All-WNBA First Team, 1997; Most Valuable Player, 1997; Championship Most Valuable Player, 1997, 1998, 1999.Won city championship, 300 Hurdles. **Special Achievements:** General Motors, spokeswoman, 1997; author, autobiography, She Got Game: My Personal Odyssey, 2000. **Business Addr:** Head Women, Prairie View A&M University, PO Box 519, Prairie View, TX 77446-0519, **Business Phone:** (936)857-3311.

COOPER, DANEEN RAVENELL
Engineer, manager. **Personal:** Born Oct 27, 1958, St Albans, NY; daughter of James Ravenell and Carrie; married Maurice N Cooper; children: Elana Simone, Kellen Marsalis. **Educ:** Columbia Univ Sch Engineering & Appl Sci, BSEE, 1980. **Career:** Bell Labs, sr tech assoc, 1976-79; NJ Bell, engr, 1980-86; United Parcel Serv, Wireless Date Dept, mgr, 1986-. **Orgs:** Bell Labs Engineering Scholar Prog, 1976-80; counr, Sponsors Educ Opportunity, 1982-84; pres, Coun Action Minority Prof, 1983-87; pres, Coun Action Minority Prof, 1984-85; Consortium Telecommunications Execs, 1985-86; 100 Black Women, 1985-; Black Data Processing Asn, 1989-; Inst Elec & Electronics Engrs, 1989-; Maplewood/So Orange, Parents Adv Coun, 1993-; pres, YMCA, Jaguar Track Club Parents Asn. **Home Addr:** 25 Highland Ave, Maplewood, NJ 07040. *

COOPER, DRUCILLA HAWKINS
Police officer. **Personal:** Born Dec 27, 1950, Riverside, CA; daughter of Alton and Thelma Anthony Williams; married Aubery J (divorced 1976); children: Alton C Strickland & Crusetta A. **Educ:** City Col, San Francisco, 1969-70; Los Med Amos Col, Pittsburg, basic law cert, 1970; Contra Costa Col, San Pablo, AA (with honors), 1982. **Career:** Police Officer (retired); Plaza Hotel, San Francisco, maid, 1966; Sutter Hotel, San Francisco, maid, 1969-70; Blue Shield Ins Co, San Francisco, claims examr, 1973-78; Contra Costa County, Martinez, dep sheriff, 1978; Dr C Stephens, Richmond, billing clerk, 1979-80; City Berkeley, police officer. **Orgs:** Berkeley Black Police Officers Asn, 1981-; nat deleg, Nat Black Police Officers Asn, 1984-; Women's Peace Officers Asn, 1989-; star point, Order Eastern Star, 1990-. **Honors/Awds:** Basic Intermediate & Advance Certificate, State CA Dept Justice, 1981, 1985, 1989; Three Certificate of Completion, Juvenile Law & Procedures, Univ Southern CA, 1985-86; Certificate of Training, Sexual Assaults Warrants, Dom Viol, Leandro Police Dept, 1985-85; Six Certificates, Criminal Justice Admin, NBPA, 1985-90. **Home Addr:** 5067 Hartnett Ave, Richmond, CA 94804, **Home Phone:** (510)233-9914.

COOPER, DUANE (SAMUEL DUANE COOPER)
Basketball player. **Personal:** Born Jun 25, 1969, Benton Harbor, MI. **Educ:** Univ Southern Calif. **Career:** Basketball player (retired); Los Angeles Lakers, guard, 1992-93; Phoenix Suns, guard, 1994; Charlotte Hornets, 1995; Toronto Raptors, 1996.

COOPER, EARL
Management consultant. **Personal:** Born Feb 4, 1944, Oakland, CA; son of Martha and Earl. **Educ:** Merritt Col Oakland, AA, 1968; Golden Gate Col, San Francisco, BA, 1970; Univ Southern Calif, MBA, 1973. **Career:** IMPAC, bus anal, 1972-74; Jim Dandy Fast Foods Inc, mkt rep, 1974; Los Angeles Econ Develop Corp, exec dep dir, 1974-83; EC II & Assocs, pres, 1979-; White House Conf Small Bus, deleg, 1980; Counman Gilbert W Lindsay, Los Angeles, spec consult, 1983-86. **Orgs:** Nat Black MBA Asn, LA Chap, 1974-; US Small Bus Admin, Region Adv Comm, 1978-; pres, Black Bus Asn, Los Angeles, 1979-; Los Angeles Co Pvt Indust Coun, 1979-84; Mayor's Off Small Bus Assistance, 1980-; comnr Housing Auth Los Angeles, 1984-86; vpres, Nat Asn Advan Colored People, Los Angeles Br, 1986-88; pres, African Am Develop Consortium; nat bd mem, Minority Bus Enterprise Legal Defense & Educ Fund Inc; bd advisors, Oper HOPE Inc; Bd Advocates Consumer Equity Inc; adv comt mem, African Am Tobacco Educ Network. **Honors/Awds:** Nat Education for Business Development Award, 1983; Nat Award Excellence, SBA, 1983; Minority Business Advocate Year for State CA, US Small Bus Admin, 1985. **Military Serv:** AUS, spl 4, 1965-67; Nat Defense Serv, Vietnam Service Medal, Combat Med Badge, Marksman Rifle, 10/S bar, 1965-67. **Business Addr:** President, EC II & Associates, Los Angeles, CA 90036-4305.

COOPER, DR. EDWARD SAWYER
Educator. **Personal:** Born Dec 11, 1926, Columbia, SC; son of Dr H H Cooper Sr and Ada Sawyer Cooper; married Jean Marie Wilder, 1951; children: Lisa Cooper Hudgins, Edward S Jr (deceased), Jan Cooper Jones & Charles W. **Educ:** Lincoln Univ PA, AB, 1946; Meharry Med Col, MD, 1949; Univ PA, MA, 1973. **Career:** Philadelphia Gen Hosp, internship med res, 1949-54, staff physician, fel cardiol, 1956-57, co dir, 1968-74, pres med staff, 1969-71, chief med serv, 1972-76; Nat Heart Inst, fel, 1956-57; Univ Pa, prof med, 1973-95;prof emer med, 1996-. **Orgs:** Cert & recertified Am Bd Internal Med, 1957-74; chmn talent recruitment coun & mem ed bd, J Nat Med Asn, 1959-77; Master Am Col Physicians, 1960;co-dir Stroke Res Ctr Philadelphia Gen Hosp, 1968-74; mem coun, Col Physicians Philadelphia, 1970-84, 1994-98; bd dir, Blue Cross Greater Philadelphia, 1975-; mem bd dir, Am Found Negro Affairs, 1977-; chmn & mem exec comt, Stroke Coun Am Heart Asn, 1982-84; pres, Am Heart Asn, 1992-93;Am Col Physicians. **Honors/Awds:** Hartley Gold Medal, highest hons, Meharry Med Col, 1949; Distinguished Alumnus Award, Lincoln Univ, PA, 1959; Distinguished Alumnus Award,Meharry Med Col, 1971; Alpha Omega Alpha, Hon Med Soc, 1962; Charles Drew Award Distinguished Contributions Med Educ 1979; award merit, Am Heart Asn, 1986; Gold Heart Award, 1997; Strittmatter Award, Phila, Co Med Soc; Edna Kynett Memorial Award, 2003. **Special Achievements:** First African American president of the American Heart Association. **Military Serv:** USAF, capt, 1954-56; 6208 USAF Hosp, chief med serv. **Home Addr:** 6710 Lincoln Dr, Philadelphia, PA 19119, **Home Phone:** (215)662-2650. **Business Addr:** Professor Emeritus, University of Pennsylvania, Univ Penn Hosp, 3600 Market St Suite 240, Philadelphia, PA 19104-2646, **Business Phone:** (215)662-2560.

COOPER, ERNEST, JR.
City planner, educator. **Personal:** Born Jun 19, 1941, Toone, TN; son of Ernest and Pauline Anderson; married Marva Harper; children: Jeanine, Ernest III, Keita. **Educ:** Lincoln Univ, BS 1963; Howard Univ, MA, 1970; Univ PA, ABD. **Career:** Nia Group, pres; Adult & Vocational Sch Cairo IL, math instr, 1965-68; Wash Tech Inst, asst prof, math, 1968-70; ML King Jr Study Grant Woodrow Wilson Found 1969-70, 1971-72; Wash Tech Inst Conceptualized Urban Plnng Tech Prog, train para-prof; Urban Inst, consult eval staff, 1971; Univ DC, Dept Urban & Reg Planning, chmn. **Orgs:** Am Planning Asn; Nat Asn Planners; Am Asn Univ Prof; Metrop Wash Planning & Housing Asn. **Business Addr:** Chairman, University DC, Dept Urban & Regional Planning, 4200 Conn Ave NW, Bldg 52 Rm 7920, Washington, DC 20008.*

COOPER, EVELYN KAYE
Judge. **Personal:** Born Jun 23, 1941, Detroit, MI. **Educ:** Univ Detroit, BBA, 1968; Wayne State Univ, postgrad Math; Wayne State Univ Law Sch, JD, 1973. **Career:** Detroit Jr High Sch, bd educ, 1966-70; Self-employed, atty law off, 1974-77; Detroit Traffic Ct, traffic ct referee, 1977-78; Recorder's Ct, judge, 1978-. **Orgs:** Nat Asn Women Judges; Mich State Bar Asn; Mich Judges Asn; Womens Lawyers Asn; Women's Conf Concerns; Nat Asn Advan Colored People; March of Dimes; Delta Sigma Theta Sorority; Nat Bar Asn; Wolverine Bar Asn. **Business Addr:** Judge, Recorders Ct, 1441 St Antoine, Detroit, MI 48226.

COOPER, GARY T.
Physician. **Educ:** Marquette Univ, BS, 1970; Howard Univ Col Med, MD, 1975; Loyola Col Md, MBA, 1996. **Career:** Planned Parenthood Wash, med dir, 1979-80; Pvt Pract, physician Ob & Gyn, 1979-92; Howard Univ Hosp, resident coordr, 1980-87; instr, 1980-86; asst prof, 1986-87; Prudential HealthCare Mid Atlantic Region, med dir. **Orgs:** Am Col Ob & Gyn, 1978; Med Soc of the Dist Columbia, 1979; Diplomate, Am Bd Ob & Gyn, 1983; Wash Gynecological Soc 1981; Kappa Alpha Psi Fraternity; Southern Med Asn. *

COOPER, GORDON R., II
Lawyer. **Personal:** Born Mar 22, 1941, Wallisville, TX; married Barbara Ellison; children: Gordon R III. **Educ:** Tex Southern Univ, BA, 1965; JD, 1970. **Career:** Humble Oil Co, labor rels dept; Inst Underwriter, pvt pract; Cooper & Cooper, lawyer, currently. **Orgs:** Tex Am Houston Jr Bar Asn; regional dir, Nat Bar Asn; Alpha Phi Alpha Fraternity; Phi Alpha Delta Legal Fraternity; Harris County Criminal Lawyers Asn. **Business Addr:** Lawyer, Cooper & Cooper, 3003 S Loop W Suite 108, Houston, TX 77054-2641.*

COOPER, IRIS N.
Educator. **Personal:** Born Oct 30, 1942, Ahoskie, NC. **Educ:** NC Cent Univ, BA, 1964. **Career:** Portsmouth Sch System, instr; Norfolk State Evening Coll, instr, 1968-69;Palmer Memorial Inst, instr, 1964; Proj Upward Bound, Norfolk St Col, instr, 1968-71; Church land High Sch, Dept foreign lang, head. **Orgs:** NEA; VA Educ Assn; Portsmouth Educ Assn; VA Assn Classroom Teacher-s;Portsmouth Assn Classroom Teachers; Am Assn Women; Tidewater Alliance Black Sch Educs; Am Assn Teachers Spanish

& Portuguese; Ebenezer Bapt Chap; NCCU Alumni Assn; Norfolk Players Guild; Portsmouth Chap Delicados Inc; Gamma Delta Omega Chap; Alpha Kappa Alpha. **Honors/Awds:** Outstanding young woman of America, 1974. **Home Addr:** 5033 Reese Dr N, Portsmouth, VA 23703, **Home Phone:** (757)483-4424.

COOPER, IRMGARD M
Executive. **Personal:** Born Jun 29, 1946, Teisendorf, Germany; daughter of Senator Richard A and Ruth St Ville. **Educ:** DePaul Univ, Chicago, IL, BS, 1968; Northern Ill Univ, DeKalb, IL, MS, 1976. **Career:** Grad fel, Northern Ill Univ, DeKalb, IL; Jones Metrop High Sch, Chicago, IL, teacher/coordr, 1970-82; IMC Automation Inc, Chicago, IL, pres, 1985-90; IMC Products Inc, Muskegon, MI, founder & pres, 1990-. **Orgs:** Bd dirs, Streeterville Chamber Com, Chicago, 1991, pres, 1996-98; exec club, 1998-, edu comt; Panelist, W Mich Supplier Diversity Conf, 2001; Luncheon Co-Chair, W Mich Supplier Diversity Conf, 2002; bd mem, MMBDC W Mich Roundtable, 2003-; W Mich Alliance Women Entrepreneurs, 2004-; Panelist, Muskegon Community Col, "Growing Entrepreneurship Mich", 2005; Entrepreneurship Video Contributor, Muskegon Career Technol Ctr, 2005; Panelist, Alliance Women Entrepreneurs Women Business Owners, 2005; Panel Facilitator, Muskegon Chamber Com Bus Diversity Showcase, 2005; Presenter, Muskegon Community Col, "Secrets to Success" Noon Hour Col Series Working Women, 2005; bd mem, Muskegon Area Chamber Com, 2002-06. **Honors/Awds:** Medical Minority Supplier/Distributor of the year, 1997; nominee, Mercedes Mentor Awards, 2001; Minority Business Owners Salute, Grand Rapids Bus J, 2002. **Business Addr:** President, IMC Products Inc, 2653 Olthoff Dr, Muskegon, MI 49444, **Business Phone:** (231)777-4777.

COOPER, J. CALIFORNIA
Playwright. **Personal:** Born in Berkeley, CA; daughter of Joseph C Cooper and Maxine Rosemary Cooper; children: Paris A Williams. **Educ:** Attended various cols. **Career:** Plays: A Piece of Mine, 1984; Homemade Love, 1986; A Piece of Mine: A New Short Story Collection, 1984; Some Soul to Keep, 1987; Family, 1991; The Matter is Life, 1991; In Search of Satisfaction, Doubleday, 1994; Some Love, Some Pain, Some Time, Doubleday, 1996; Wake of the Wind, 1998; The Future Has a Past, 2001; Some People, Some Other Place, 2004; Wild Stars Seeking Midnight Suns: Stories, 2006. **Honors/Awds:** Black Playwright of the Yr, 1978; American Book Award, 1986, James Baldwin Award, 1988; American Library Asns Literary Lion Award, 1988; Notable Book Award. **Business Addr:** Author, Doubleday Publishing, 1540 Broadway, New York, NY 10036, **Business Phone:** (212)354-6500.

COOPER, JEROME GARY
Marine Corps officer. **Personal:** Born Oct 2, 1936, Lafayette, LA; son of Algernon Johnson (deceased) and Gladys Catherine Morton (deceased); married Beverly; children: Patrick C, Joli & Gladys Shawn. **Educ:** Univ Notre Dame, BS, 1958; George Wash Univ, grad study; Harvard Sch Bus, attended 1979; Troy State Univ, Hon LLD, 1990. **Career:** Army Official (retired), business executive; State Ala Dept Human Resources, Montgomery, AL, comnr, 1974-78; David Volkert & Assocs, Mobile, AL, vpres, 1981-89, sr vpres, 1992-94; USMC, Wash, DC, dir personnel procurement, 1988; US Dept Defense, Wash, DC, asst secy air force, 1989; Commonwealth Nat Bank, chmn & chief exec officer, currently. **Orgs:** AFCOMAP, 1990-; Air Force Asn, 1990-; Nat Image, 1991-; life mem, Res Officers Asn; life mem, Montford Point Marine Asn; Marine Corps Res Asn. **Honors/Awds:** Man of Year, Nonpartisan Voters League, 1977; Highest Award, 1978; MO Beale Scroll of Merit for Good Citizenship, Mobile Asn, 1979; John J Cavanaugh Award, Alumni Asn Univ Notre Dame, 1987; Roy Wilkins Meritorious Service Award, Nat Asn Advan Colored People, 1989; Benjamin Hooks Meritorious Service Award, 1990; Distinguished Service Medal, 1991. **Special Achievements:** First Black to lead infantry into combat USMC, 1967; Second African-American General in the Marine Corps. **Military Serv:** USMC, maj gen, active 1958-69; USMCR, 1969-91; Silver Star; Legion of Merit; Bronze Star with Combat V; Purple Heart (2); Vietnam Cross of Gallantry with palm & two stars; numerous others. **Business Addr:** Chairman, Chief Executive Officer, Commonwealth National Bank, 2214 St Stephens Rd, PO Box B, Mobile, AL 36601, **Business Phone:** (334)476-5938.

COOPER, JOSEPH
Lawyer, educator. **Personal:** Born Dec 20, 1937, Hemingway, SC; son of Harmon and Mary; children: Kenneth. **Educ:** Calif State Univ, Sacramento City Col, BA, 1965; Univ Pac, McGeorge Law-Sch, JD, 1969. **Career:** First Capital Real Estate, pres; atty gen pract, 1969-; Northwestern Calif Univ, prof law & dean acad affairs, currently; Joseph Cooper Law Corp, pres & atty, currently; Sacramento Super Ct, Settlement Conf, judge proterm, currently. **Orgs:** Bd dirs, Calif Trial Lawyers Asn; Am Trial Lawyers Asn; founder & pres, Success Inst Am Inc; Am Back Soc; Sacramento Consumer Atty Asn; Calif St Bar; Am Bar Asn; bd reagents mem, Northwestern Calif Univ. **Honors/Awds:** Distinguished Service Award, City of Sacramento. **Military Serv:** AUS, 1960-62. **Business Addr:** Attorney, Joseph Cooper Law Corporation, 1310 H St, Sacramento, CA 95814, **Business Phone:** (916)441-5300.*

COOPER, JOSEPHINE H.
Educator. **Personal:** Born Apr 7, 1936, Salinas, CA; married. **Educ:** Houston- Tillotson Col, BA; San Francisco State Univ, MA. **Career:** Educ Serv Inst, asst dir; Progs Mentally Handicapped, head teacher; Meritt Col, GED prog, 1968; Low Income Housing Prog Voc Coun; Laney Col, counr, currently. **Orgs:** Calif Teachers Asn; Nat Asn Advan Colored People; United Taxpayers & Voter's Union Calif; Alameda Co Contra Costa Co Community Equal Opportunity Apprenticeship Training; Berkeley Dem Club; Nat Coun Negro Women Inc; Peralta Col Dist, bd trustees, currently. **Honors/Awds:** Numerous scholars grants for further study; mem CA Comm & Jr Coll Asn "Minorities & the Voc Disadv Occup Prog Calif Comm Col Trade Tech Schs". **Business Addr:** Counselor, Laney Coll, 900 Fallon St, Oakland, CA 94607.

COOPER, JULIUS
Law enforcement officer. **Personal:** Born Jan 8, 1944, Sarasota, FL; son of Julius Cooper Sr and Johnnie Mae Jones Ramey; married Barbara Irene Campbell; children: Julius, Julian, Adrienne, Tara, Taheim & Wanda. **Educ:** Essex Co Col, attended 1977; Nat Crime Prevention Inst, attended 1983;Security Mgt & Admin Inst, attended 1984; Rutgers Univ, BS, 1985; Seton Hall Univ, MS, 1990. **Career:** Law enforcement officer (retired); Essex Co Police Dept, breathaly zeroper, affirmative action officer, supvr, 1983-84, instr 1983-85, crime prev coordr, 1983-86, sgt; Newark, NJ Bd Educ, substitute teacher, 1991; Rutgers Univ, guest prof, 1991; Essex Co Col, prof, 1992; Zion Missionary Baptist Church, deacon, 1996-97; Zion Bapt Church, deacon, 1997, minister, 2001, assoc minister, 2002. **Orgs:** Vpres, Ebony Six Coop; life mem, Nat Asn Advan Colored People; PBA. **Honors/Awds:** Certificate Award, US Dept Health & Human Serv, 1985; Achievement Award, Essex Co PBA Conf, 1985; Achievement Award, 1986; Valor Award, 1987; Essex Co Bd Freeholders.

COOPER, KENNETH JOSEPH
Writer, journalist. **Personal:** Born Dec 11, 1955, Denver, CO; son of George Howard Jr and Maxine Marie; married Lucilda Loretta Dassardo, Jun 10, 1985. **Educ:** Wash Univ, BA, 1977. **Career:** St Louis Am, assoc ed, 1977; St Louis Post Dispatch, staff writer, 1977-80; Boston Globe, staff writer, 1980-86; Knight Ridder Inc, nat reporter, 1986-89; Wash Post, nat reporter, 1989-95, S Asia bur chief, 1996-99, nat reporter, 1999-2000; Boston Globe, nat ed; freelance writer, currently. **Orgs:** Nat Asn Black Journalists, 1978-; Omega Psi Phi Fraternity, 1983-. **Honors/Awds:** Public Service Award, 1984; Pulitzer Prize, Spec Local Reporting, Columbia Univ, 1984; Distinguished Alumni, Wash Univ, 1989; SAJA Journalism Award, 1998. **Business Addr:** Freelance Writer, 14814 Reddington, Maple Heights, OH 44137, **Business Phone:** (216)663-9984.

COOPER, DR. LAMOYNE MASON
Educator. **Personal:** Born Aug 8, 1931, Emporia, VA; son of Edgar and Theresa; married William Franklin, Nov 26, 1988; children: Derrick Matthews, Yvette Matthews & Kevin Matthews. **Educ:** Morgan State Univ, AB, 1951; Howard Univ, MSW, 1961; Univ Md, PhD, 1976. **Career:** Educator (retired). Morgan State Univ, prof social work, 1969-82; Foreign Serv, US Dept State, 1987-91. **Orgs:** Life mem, Delta Sigma Theta 1950-; Baltimore Mus Art; Baltimore Zoo; Chesapeake Audubon Soc; Tucson Desert Mus. **Honors/Awds:** Education to Africa Study Grant, 1974; 100 Outstanding Baltimore Women,Delta Sigma Theta, 1974; Award, Baltimore County Bd Educ, 1979-84. **Home Addr:** 2150 N Sarnoff Dr, Tucson, AZ 85715. *

COOPER, LARRY B
Manager. **Personal:** Born Jul 25, 1946, Fordyce, AR; son of Charles and Brucella; children: Sherri Jean. **Educ:** Univ Ark, Pine Bluff, BS, 1969; Southern Methodist Univ, MBA, 1996. **Career:** Kans City Sch Dist, teacher & coach, 1969-72; Southwestern Bell Tele Co, mgt trainee, 1972-73, engr, 1973-74, sr engr, 1974-77, mgt dev supvr, 1977-79, dist staff mgr-pers/budgets, 1979-81, staff mgr mgt develop, 1981-83, dist staff mgr res serv, 1983-85, dist mgr res serv, 1985-87, dist mg bus serv, 1987-89, div mgr educ & econ develop, St Louis, MO, gen mgr, operator servs, dir, Local Provider Acct Team, 2002, sr vpres. **Orgs:** Kappa Alpha Psi Alumni Asn, 1972-; pres, Tall Timber Home Owners, 1978-79; United Way Planning & Allocation Comt, 1982-84; bd dirs, Southwest City Civitan, 1985-; exec bd dirs, Boy Scouts Am, 1985-; comnr, Tall Timber Imp Dist, 1986; adv bd, Voc Tech Educ, 1989-92; chmn, Ark Regional Minority Purchasing Coun, 1986-92; Ark Advocate Family & Children, 1990-; Ark State Coun Econ Educ, 1991-92; Dallas Downtown Improv Dist. **Honors/Awds:** Distinguished Achievement Award, Kappa Alpha Psi, 1985; Distinguished Alumni Award, NAFEO, 1986; Bernard De La Harde Award for Community Leadership, Little Rock Chamber Com, 1989-91; Black Corporate Executives Award, Nat Am Advan Colored People, 1991.

COOPER, LINDA G
Entrepreneur, president (organization). **Personal:** Born Jun 1, 1954, Jacksonville, FL; daughter of Benjamin H Groomes and Freddie Lang Groomes. **Educ:** FL State Univ, BS, 1974; Ind Univ, MBA, 1977. **Career:** Hallmark Cards Inc, budget analyst, 1977-81, mktg budget mgr, 1981-85, dir minority affairs, 1985-92; LGC & Assocs Inc, pres & owner, 1992-. **Orgs:** Alpha Kappa Alpha Sorority, 1972-; Defense Adv Comn Women Serv, 1984-87; pres & bd trustees, Greater KC Black Econ Union, 1984-92; Nat Asn Market Developers, 1985-91; bd mem, YMCA, 1987-90; Greater KC Chamber Com; pres, Cent Exchange; Nat Black MBA Asn; bd gov, Urban League GKC. **Honors/Awds:** Black Achiever in Business & Industry, SCLC, 1984; President's Award, Black Chamber Com Kans City, 1988; YWCA Hearts of Gold Award, 1993; Up & Comers Award, 1996. **Special Achievements:** 100 Most Promising Black Women in Corporate America, Ebony Mag, 1991; 100 Most Influential African-American in KC, KC Globe Newspaper, 1997. **Business Addr:** Owner, President, LGC & Associates Inc, 600 Broadway Suite 230, Kansas City, MO 64108, **Business Phone:** (816)842-0542.

COOPER, LOIS LOUISE
Civil engineer. **Personal:** Born Nov 25, 1931, Vicksburg, MS; widowed; children: Wyatt E, Christopher. **Educ:** Tougaloo Col, MS, 1949; Calif State Univ, Los Angles, BA, Math, 1954; Calif State Univ, civil eng, 1975. **Career:** Civil engineer (retired); Div Hwys, Caltrans, eng aid, 1953-58, jr civil engr, 1958-61; Caltrans, asst transp engr, 1961-84, assoc transp engr, 1984-88, sr transp engr, 1988-91. **Orgs:** Past Bd dir, sec Los Angeles Coun Engr Sci; adv bd, Minority Engr Prog Calif State Univ, Los Angles; past co-chair, career guid Soc Women Engrs, 1985; pres, vpres, sec & treas, La Coun Black Prof Engrs, 1975-76; Am Soc Civil Engrs; Nat Soc Prof Engrs. **Honors/Awds:** Trail Blazer, Nat Asn Negro Bus & Prof Womens Inc, 1964; fel Inst for the Adv Engr, 1982; fel Soc of Women Engrs, 1989. **Special Achievements:** First Black Woman to attain a Profl Engrs Lic in Civil Engineering in Califorina, 1978; First Black Woman to achieve all positions at Caltrans, 1983. **Home Addr:** 14324 S Clymar Ave, Compton, CA 90220, **Home Phone:** (310)639-0293. *

COOPER, MARGARET J
Administrator. **Personal:** Born in Wadesboro, NC; married Aubrey; children: 1. **Educ:** Federal City Col, BA, 1972; Bowie State Univ, MA, 1997; Bowie State Univ, post-master cert, 1997. **Career:** Nat Asn Colored Women's Clubs, Wash, DC, secy; Dept Veterans Affairs, Wash DC, personnel mgt, 1976-89; Family Intervention Ctr, Wash DC, site coordr, 1992-97; United Planning Orgn, Wash DC, case mgr, 1997-2000; Dept Veterans Affairs, Wash DC, human resource specialist, 2000-. **Orgs:** Vpres, 1996-2002, pres, Nat Asn Colored Women's Clubs. **Business Addr:** Human Resource Specialist, Department of Veterans Affairs, 50 Irving St NW, Washington, DC 20422, **Business Phone:** (202)745-8000 Ext 6899.

COOPER, DR. MARVA W
Educator. **Career:** Univ DC, Dept Mass Media, Visual & Performing Arts, prof, currently.

COOPER, MAUDINE R
Association executive, chief executive officer. **Personal:** Born Sep 30, 1941, Benoit, MS; divorced; children: Maria Teresa. **Educ:** Howard Univ, BA, bus admin, 1964, Sch Law, JD, 1971. **Career:** Nat Urban League, asst dir, 1973-76, dep dir, 1976-79, asst vpres pub policy, 1979, vpres Wash Oper, 1980-83; DC Off Human Rights, dir, 1983-89; DC OHR & Minority Bus Opportunity Comn, exec dir & head, 1987-89; staff dir, Off Mayor, 1989-90; Greater Wash Urban League, chief exec officer & pres, 1990-; Emergency Transition Ed Bd, Wash DC, chair. **Orgs:** Bd dirs, Nat Bar Asn, 1979-80; mem, bd dirs, Centennial One Inc, 1982-87; vpres legis affairs Black Women's Agenda, 1983-; legal adv, MCAC & Delta Sigma Theta Sor, 1985-88; treas, Wash Chap Nat Asn Human Rights Workers, 1986-87; mem, several bar Asns; mem, bd dirs, Doug Williams Found; bd dir, DC Pvt Indus Coun, 1993; bd dir, Bell Atlantic, Wash, DC, 1994; DC Bar Asn; Nat Asn Advan Colored People; life mem, Greater Wash Urban League; bd dir, Women Wash. **Honors/Awds:** Alumni of the Yr, Howard Univ Law Alumni Asn, 1984; Woman of the Year, Capitol Hill Kiwanis Club, 1985; chair, DC Govt's 32nd One Fund Drive, 1986; Nat Asn Minority Polit Women's Diamond award, 1988. She was named McDonald's Black History Maker of Today in the Washington, DC area in 1998; DC Captain's Award, DC Col Access Prog, 2003; Generous Heart Award, Olender Found, 2004; Sam Lacy Community Service Award, Washington Afro; Isaiah Award, Am Jewish Comt, Wash DC. **Special Achievements:** One of the Women to Watch in the 80's Ebony Mag, 1982; Am's Top 100 Black Bus & Prof Women, Dollars & Sense Mag, 1986; Judge for the first Ms Black USA Scholar Pagent, 1987. **Business Addr:** President, Chief Executive Officer, Greater Wash Urban League, Headquarters Bldg, 2901 14th NW, Washington, DC 20009.

COOPER, MERRILL PITTMAN
Executive. **Personal:** Born Feb 9, 1921, Charlestown, WV. **Educ:** Storer Col, attended 1938. **Career:** Transp Workers Union, int exec bd, 1965-68, int vpres, Local 234, secy, treas & vpres, 1968-77, pres. **Orgs:** Vpres, Philadelphia AFL CIO, 1977-; int vpres, Transp Workers Union, 1977-; Urban League; Negro Trade Union Leadership Coun; Nat Asn Advan Colored People.

COOPER, MICHAEL GARY
State government official. **Personal:** Born Jan 11, 1954, Cleveland, OH; son of Fletcher Lee Bailey Cooper and Clifford Cooper Sr; married Corrinne Crockett, May 26, 1984; children:

Stacy, Michael Fletcher & Malik. **Educ:** Univ Pittsburgh, BA, 1975; Atlanta Univ, MA, hist, 1979, MSW, 1979. **Career:** Young Men's Christian Asn, asst dir, 1975-76; City Atlanta, field coordr, 1979; DeKalb Co Comn Off, affirmative action officer, 1979-88; Fulton Co Govt, dir contract compliance & eeo, 1988-98; GA Dept Transp, div dir contract compliance & eeo, 1998-; dir equal opportunity, GA Dept Transp, currently. **Orgs:** Am Asn Affirmative Action, 1982-; Southern Civil Rights Transp Asn, 1998-; Am Asn State & Hwy Transp Officials, Sub-Comt Civil Rights, 1999-; vpres, Stone Mountain Youth Soccer Asn; Boy Scouts Am. **Honors/Awds:** Gov Intern Program 1978; Distinguished Service Award, Univ GA Extension Serv, 1985; Community Involvement Award, Black Pages Mag, 1990; President's Award, AAAA; Community Advocate of the Year, Atlanta Black Pages Mag. **Business Addr:** Division Director, Georgia Department of Transportation, 2 Capitol Sq Suite 142, Atlanta, GA 30334, **Business Phone:** (404)656-5323.

COOPER, MICHAEL JEROME
Basketball player, administrator, athletic coach. **Personal:** Born Apr 15, 1956, Los Angeles, CA; married Wanda; children: Michael Jr, Simone, Miles. **Educ:** Pasadena City Col; Univ NM, 1978. **Career:** basketball player (retired), basketball coach; Los Angeles Lakers, professional basketball player, 1979-90; Los Angeles Lakers, asst coach, 1994-98; Los Angeles Sparks, head coach, 1999-. **Orgs:** Jr Blind Founf; state spokesperson, NM Red Ribbon Campaign Nationwide; Hollywood Senior Citizen Center. **Honors/Awds:** Walter J Kennedy Award; Defensive Player of the Year, NBA, 1987. **Business Addr:** Head Coach, Los Angeles Sparks, 888 S Figueroa St Suite 2010, Los Angeles, CA 90017, **Business Phone:** (213)929-1300.*

COOPER, ROBERT N.
Executive. **Personal:** Married Marcia; children: Robin, David. **Educ:** Oakland Univ, BA; Mich State Univ, MBA. **Career:** Mich Bell, technician, 1973-89; Ameritech, MI, sr dir distrib serv, 1989-93, pres; Ameritech Cellular, vpres human resources, 1993-96; SBC, MI, pres; Amcor N Am, mgr controls engineering, currently. **Honors/Awds:** ACC Award Recipients. **Business Addr:** Manager of Controls Engineering, Amcor Limited, 935 Technology Dr Suite 100, Ann Arbor, MI 48108-8919, **Business Phone:** (734)428-9741.*

COOPER, RONALD
Football coach. **Personal:** Born Feb 11, 1962, Huntsville, AL; son of Wilbert H Cooper and Martha B; married Kim, Jun 3, 1989. **Educ:** Jacksonville State Univ, BS, edu, 1983; Appalachian State Univ, MA, 1984. **Career:** UNV of MIN, asst coach, NG; Austin Peay St Univ, asst coach, recruiting crd, linebackers; Murray St Univ, defensive crd, defensive backs; East Carolina Univ, asst coach, linebackers; Univ Nevada at Las Vegas, defensive crd, linebackers; Univ Notre Dame, asst head coach, defensive backs; Eastern Mic Univ, head football coach, beginning, 1992; Univ La, head football coach, 1995-97; Univ SC, asst Head Coach, currently. **Orgs:** Fellowship of Christian Athletes, 1980-; KAP Fraternity Inc, 1982-; AMR Football Coaches asn, 1983-; Black Coaches, 1989-; Masonic Order, 1983-. **Honors/Awds:** Sugar Bowl, Notre Dame vs FLA, 1992; Cotton Bowl, Notre Dame vs TEX A&M, 1993. **Special Achievements:** Teaching films: Deep Coverage, 2 vols; Coverage, 3 vols; Punt-Block; drill film: UNLV Defensive Team and Position Drills; manual: Techniques of Defensive Backs. **Business Addr:** Head Football Coach, University South Carolina, Roost Bldg B 1322 1322 Heyward St, Columbia, FL 29208, **Business Phone:** (803)777-5204.*

COOPER, SAMUEL DUANE. See COOPER, DUANE.

COOPER, SAMUEL H
Government official. **Personal:** Born Feb 2, 1955, Nassawadox, VA; son of Samuel H Cooper Sr and Margaret C; married Sandra; children: Cedrick & Shenae. **Educ:** Norfolk State Col, attended 1975; John Tyler Col, AAS, 1977. **Career:** Cooper & Humbles Funeral Co Inc, owner; Accomack Circuit Ct, clerk, currently. **Orgs:** Macedonia AME Church; Macedonia Lodge; Va Ct Clerks Asn; bd mem, Tidewater AAA; Va Hist Soc. **Home Addr:** PO Box 35, Accomac, VA 23301. **Business Addr:** Clerk, Accomac Circuit Court, Courthouse Rd, PO Box 126, Accomac, VA 23301-0126, **Business Phone:** (757)787-5776.

COOPER, WALTER
Research scientist, chemist. **Personal:** Born Jul 18, 1928, Clairton, PA; son of Alonzo and Lula; married Helen E Claytor; children: Robert B, Brian P. **Educ:** Wash & Jefferson Col, BA, 1950; Univ Rochester, PhD, phys chem, 1956; Wash & Jefferson Col, ScD, 1987. **Career:** Research scientist, chemist (retired); Eastman Kodak Co, res chemist, 1956, sr res chemist, 1964, res assoc, 1965; Action Better Community, assoc dir, 1964-65; res assoc, 1966; NY State Adv Comn, US Civil Rights Commn 1966; US Small Bus & Admin, spec consult admin, 1968-69; Eastman Kodak Co, res assoc, 1969; Eastman Kodak Co, mgr, Off Tech Comun, 1984-86. **Orgs:** Celanese Corp Am Fel, 1952-54; NSF Fel, 1955-56; Sigma Xi, 1956; Am Chem Soc, 1959; AAAS, 1960; Am Phys soc; Nat Asn Advan Colored People, 1960-65; Urban League Rochester, 1965-71; bd Govs, Genesee Hosp,1966; Urban Suburban Pupil Transfer Prog, 1973; Genesee Regional Health Planning Coun, 1974; bd trustees, Wash & Jefferson Col, 1975; bd dir, Rochester Area Found, 1975; NY State Bd Regents, 1988-97. **Honors/Awds:** Leroy E Snyder Award, Rochester Jr Chamber Com, 1966; Outstanding Achievement Award & Rochester Club Nat Negro Prof & Bus Women Inc, 1966; Rochester Chamber of Commerce Development Award, 1966; Distinguished Alumni Award, Washington & Jefferson Col, 1968; Achievement Award, Int Org Eastern Stars, 1974; Knight Nat Order Repub Mali, 1982; International Relations Award, Rochester Chamber Com; Hutchinson Medal, Univ Rochester, 1994; hon degree, Doctor of Humane Letters, State Univ NY. **Special Achievements:** First African American to earn the PhD in Physical Chemistry from the University of Rochester; 3 patents in Photographic Science & Technology; 25 scientific & technical publications. *

COOPER, WARREN
Executive, founder (originator), president (organization). **Career:** Fed Aviation Admin, Air Traffic Control Specialist, 1980-93; Merrill C Meigs Field; Midway & O'Hare Int Airports; Chicago City Cols, 1988; Cook Co Sheriff's Dept, solicitor; Gen of the US; Johnson & Johnson Corp; Methadone clins, bd dir; Accu-Lab Med Testing Inc, founder & pres, 1991-. **Orgs:** Am Ass Clin Chemist; Regional Purchasing Coun Chicago Urban League; Cosmopolitan Chamber Com. **Special Achievements:** First African-Am to work in that capacity assigned to O'Hare Intl Airport in Chicago; ACCU-Lab Med Testing is the only African Am-owned forensic lab in the country. **Business Addr:** Owner, President, AccuLab Medical Testing Inc, 1300 S Wabash Ave, Chicago, IL 60605, **Business Phone:** (312)939-3535.*

COOPER, WILLIAM B.
Executive. **Personal:** Born Sep 5, 1956, Washington, DC; married Sandra F Burrus. **Educ:** Control Data Inst, 1976; Univ Md, 1980. **Career:** Control Data Corp, systs analyst, 1974-79; TYMSHARE Inc, applications consult, 1979-80; CGA Computer Assoc Inc, 1980-84; Cray Res Inc, analyst-in-charge, 1984. **Orgs:** Chmn, Montgomery County Republican Party, 1979-80; Assoc Comput Machinery, 1979; Nat Panel of Consumer Arbitrators, 1980-; Deacon Plymouth Congregational UCC, 1981-; cub master, Cub Scout Pack 340, 1981; pres, Cooper & Assocs, 1982. **Honors/ Awds:** Comnr Adv Neighborhood Comn, 1982-85; delegate DC Statehood Const Conv, 1982-85; Outstanding Young Men Am, 1983.

COOPER, WINSTON LAWRENCE
Advertising executive. **Personal:** Born Oct 27, 1946, Port-of-Spain, Trinidad and Tobago; married Jeanne A Cox; children: Zara. **Educ:** Trinity Col WI, GCE, 1963; Univ West Indies, BA, 1967. **Career:** Ogilvy & Mather Inc, acct suprv, 1970-77; Case & McGroth Adv Inc, mgt suprv, 1977-79; Uniworld Group Inc, vice pres mgt suprv, 1982-85.

COOPER-FARROW, VALERIE
Executive. **Personal:** Born Oct 18, 1961, Stamford, CT. **Educ:** Morgan State Univ, BS, 1983; Columbia Univ Grad Sch Bus, MBA, 1987. **Career:** Travelers Co, comput programmer, 1983-85; Goldman Sachs & Co, vpres. **Orgs:** Alpha Kappa Alpha Sor Inc, 1980-; Nat Black MBA Asn, 1985-; Network Inc, 1986-; life mem, Morgan State Univ Alumni Asn. **Honors/Awds:** COGME Fellowship 1985.

COOPER-GILSTRAP, JOCELYN ANDREA
Executive. **Personal:** Born Jun 29, 1964; daughter of Andrew and Jocelyn Cooper. **Educ:** Hampton Univ, BA, commun, 1986. **Career:** Polygram Rec, tracking airplay for new releases & promoting the co urban music; Warner Chappell Music Inc, creative mgr; Mercury Rec, 1992; Midnight Songs, co-founder & pres, currently; Universal Music Group, sr vice pres & special asst to chmn, currently. **Orgs:** Bd mem, RUSH Philanthropic Arts Found; bd mem, City Sun Publishing; Nat Asn Recording Arts and Sciences Inc, 1991-, bd governors, 1999-; bd mem, Prospect Park Alliance. **Business Addr:** Senior Vice President, Special Assistant to the Chairman, Universal Music Group, 1755 Broadway 7th Fl, New York, NY 10019, **Business Phone:** (212)373-0731.

COOPER-LEWTER, REV. DR. NICHOLAS CHARLES
Clergy, writer, educator. **Personal:** Born Jun 25, 1948, Washington, DC. **Educ:** Ashland Col, BA, 1970; Ecumenical Ctr, African-Am church studies, adv studies, DMin prog, 1978; Univ Minn, MSW, 1978; Calif Coast Univ, PhD, psychol, 1988. **Career:** Auth, Motivational Speaker, 1972-; Univ Minn, Ctr Youth Develop Res, res specialist, 1972-73, teaching asst, 1974-75, Sch Social Work, deans grad fel, 1974; Sports Performance consult, Personal Success Coach, 1976-; Pastoral Care & Coun, clergy consult, Soul Therapy, 1976-; Greater Bethel Missionary Baptist Church, San Bernardino, Calif, ordained clergyman, 1977; Cooper Lewter Hypnosis Ctr, NB CA, dir owner, 1978-83; New Garden Gethsemane, sr pastor, 1985-90; Bethel Col & Sem, prof social work, Cross Cultural Coun, vis instr, 1990-95; Cooper-Lewter Rites Passage Inc, founder, 1995-; Metrop State Univ, psychol & social work fac, 1997-2000; Benedict Col, prof, chair social work, 2000-02; Univ SC, vis prof social work, 2002-03, lectr social work, 2005-. **Orgs:** Chap founder, First basileus, Xi Theta Chap, Omega Psi Phi Fraternity, Ashland Univ, 1966-70; bd dir, Am Acad Med Hypnoanalysts, 1977-83; Nat Asn Social Workers; ACSW; Nat Asn Black Social Workers; Minn Bus Prof Am; TDVP; bd mem & dir, Hmong Golden Village Cult Ctr, 1997-2000; Nat Asn Advan Colored People; Nat Urban League; Big Brothers & Big Sisters Greater Columbia, 2002-04; Nat African Am Drug Policy Coalition; VI Basketball Fedn, 2004-; bd mem, TURN Leadership Found; Minn Black Psychologists Asn; Baccalaureate Prog Dirs? Asn; adv bd mem, Salvation Army, St Paul, Minn; bd mem, Adoptive Families Am Inc; bd mem, Minn Coun Social Work Educ; charter mem, Rotary Int, Fountain Valley. **Honors/Awds:** Presidential Grant/Award for Student Leadership, Ashland Col, Ashland, Ohio, 1969-70; Journal of the SMH Outstanding Contributing Author Award, 1976; Distinguished Faculty Service Award, Bethel Col Seminary, 1992; SE Hall Community Service Award, St Paul Urban League, 1992; Nominee Excellence in Teaching Award, Metropolitan State Univ, Minn, 1999. **Special Achievements:** US Junior Olympic Team NRA, 1983-90; California State Fullerton Football Program, 1983-84; UCLA Basketball Program, 1984-85; "My Jesus was Jim Crowed!" Colors Magazine Vol 3 Issue 3 May/June 1994; co-author: Soul Theology: The Heart of American Black Culture, 1986, 1991; Black Grief and Soul Therapy, Univ of Richmond, Tubman Press, 1999 (4th Printing); "Keep On Rollin' Along: The Temptations and Soul Therapy," The Journal of Black Sacred Music, vol 6, num 1, Spring 1992; "Soul Therapy: A Call to Resilience" in Mental Health in the African American Community, In Press; "The Initial Environmental Experience: A Powerful Took for Psychotherapy & Hypnotherapy," Journal of Medical Hypnoanalysts, 1981, "Sports Hypnotherapy: Contenderosis & Self Hate," Jrnl of Med Hypnoanalysts, 1980; "Concerns of Working Youth," People Human Svs MN, 1974, "Working Youth: Selected Findings from Exploratory Study," Journal Youth & Adolescence, 1974; Los Angeles Olympic Committee, Judge, 1984. **Business Addr:** Lecturer in Social Work, University of California, College of Social Work, 301 DeSaussure, Columbia, SC 29208, **Business Phone:** (803)777-1382.

COOPER TAYLOR, JEANINE Y.
Chief executive officer, public relations executive, president (organization). **Personal:** Born in Washington, DC; married. **Educ:** Hampton Univ, BA, mass media, 1991; Univ DC, MBA, mkt, 1994; North western Univ, IAMC. **Career:** Jeanine Cooper Entertainment & Commun, pres & chief exec officer pub rels,currently. **Orgs:** Pub Rels Soc Am. **Honors/Awds:** Best Bus Award, Atlanta Bus League, 1999; Power-broker 2000, Upscale Mag, 2000; Blue Print Award of Excellence, 2002. **Special Achievements:** Women Looking Ahead Millenium Trendsetters; Named One of GA's 100 Most Influential, 2000. **Business Phone:** (213)739-5009.

COOPER WALTON, LINDA G. See KEE, LINDA COOPER.

COPAGE, MARC DIEGO
Entertainer, actor, singer. **Personal:** Born Jun 21, 1962, Los Angeles, CA. **Career:** Actor, singer & comedian; Metro media Rec, rec artist; Avco Rec & Sussex Rec, rec artist, currently; Films: Twisted Nightmare, 1987; The Kid, 2000;TV series: "Julia", 1968-71; Honeymoon Game?, 1971; "Young Dr. Kildare", 1972; "Temperatures Rising", 1973; "Sanford & Son", 1975; Best of Times,1981; "CBS Afternoon Playhouse", 1981; "ABC After school Specials", 1981;The Wave, 1981; "Diff'rent Strokes", 1985; "CBS Summer Playhouse", 1987;"Cop Rock", 1990; "TV Land Confidential", 2005; Changing Times and Trends (2005, 2005. **Orgs:** Screen Actors Guild; Am Fedn Tv & Radio Artists. **Honors/Awds:** Numerous honors & awards including Human Rights Award, NEA, 1970; Nominee Best Actor, Nat Asn Advan Colored People Image Awards, 1971; Community Award, Calif Teachers Asn. **Business Addr:** Actor, c/o William Morris Agency, 151 El Camino Dr, Beverly Hills, CA 90212, **Business Phone:** (310)859-4000.

COPE, DONALD LLOYD
Government official. **Personal:** Born May 16, 1936, Kansas City, KS; married Eddie L. **Educ:** Weber St Col, BS, 1973. **Career:** Govt Scott M Mattheson, ombudsman, pres; Ogden City Police Dept, community rel officer, 1971-72; consult & lectr race rel, Cont Educ Dept, Weber St Col, 1973. **Orgs:** Govt intern prog, Brigham Young Univ; Univ Utah Soc Dept; Weber St Col Black Std Union; Nat Advan Assn Colored People; Ogden Breakfast Exchange Club; pres, League Utah Consumers, 1974-75; mem adv, News Brd KTUX, Chan 4,1974; Govt Policy Std & Goals Task Force; brd dir, St Girl Scout Coun Comn. **Honors/Awds:** Service Award, Nat Advan Assn Colored People, 1975; Community Achievement Award, Ogden Community Action Agency, 1977.

COPELAND, BARRY B
Manager. **Personal:** Born Aug 1, 1957, Paterson, NJ; son of Albert and Levonia; married Canary Gasaway; children: Eric, Antoine, Elise, Timothy & Malcolm. **Educ:** Prairie View Agr & Mech Univ, BBA, 1979. **Career:** Internal Revenue Serv, IRS agt, 1979; AUS, acct, 1980-82; Corpus Christi Army Depot, auditor, 1982-85; Beeco Acct Serv, owner & acct, 1985-; Defense Contract Audit

Agency, supvr auditor, 1985-2002; Barry B Copeland, cert pub acct, 1988-; NASA Johnson Space Ctr, prog analyst, 2002-. **Orgs:** Alpha Phi Omega, 1977-, Nat Asn Advan Colored People, 1986-; Asn Govt Acct, 1988. **Honors/Awds:** Exceptional Performance Award, Corpus Christi Army Depot, 1985; Exceptional Performance Awards, Defense Contract Audit Agency, 1988, 1990, 1994, 1996, 1999, 2000; Exceptional Performance Award, NASA, 2003, Group Achievement Award, 2007. **Military Serv:** AUS SP/4 E-4 2 yrs; Army Commendation Medal. **Home Addr:** 26803 Cascade Woods Lane, Cypress, TX 77433-3539. **Business Addr:** Program Analyst, NASA Johnson Space Ctr, 2101 NASA Pkwy MC AF2 Bldg 45 Rm 441A, Houston, TX 77058, **Business Phone:** (281)244-5361.

COPELAND, BETTY MARABLE
Consultant. **Personal:** Born Aug 31, 1946, Durham, NC; divorced; children: Abosede O. **Educ:** NC Cent Univ, BA, psychiat, 1975; NCCU, MA, psychiat, 1980. **Career:** Durham Tech Inst, instr, 1978-80; Mental Retardation & Substance Abuse Durham County, forensic screening examr, 1980-; Rural Day Care Assn North eastern NC Div Mental Health, training consult, 1982-; Durham County Community Mental Health Ctr, psychotherapist, 1969-96; Durham Pub Schs, family specialist, 1996-. **Orgs:** Chairperson, NC Assn Black Psychiat, 1980-; mental health consult, various organizations, 1982-; NC Test Study Comn, 1982-; NC Black Leadership Caucus, 1982-, Nat Black Child Develop Inst Durham Affil, 1982-; co-chair health comn, Durham Comn Affairs Black People, 1983; Durham NC City Brd Educ, 1983-; adv bd mem, Creative Arts Pub Schs, 1984-; NCNW Durham Affil, 1984-; state treas, Nat Coun Negro Women NC, 1984-; adv bd mem, Creative Arts Pub Schs, 1984-90; serv unit mgr, Cent Unit, Durham Cty Pines Carolina Girls Scouts, 1984-; founder & coord, Coalition Prev Adolescent Pregnancy, 1984-; Nat Orgn Legal Problems Educ, 1984-, Nat Assn Female Execs, 1985-; Nat Orgn Legal Problems Educ, 1985-90; Greater DurhamChamber Com Human Rels Ed Comt, 1985-87; brd nominating comt, YWCA, Durham,1987; vice chmn, Durham City Brd Educ, 1987-; brd dirs, Child & Parent Support Serv, 1987. **Honors/Awds:** Advocate of the Year, Admin Category NC Sch Counselors Assn, 1984; Woman in Leadership, Durham Comn Affairs Black People, Nat Coun Negro Women 3rd Annual Bethune Recognition Luncheon, 1984; Serv Award, Durham Comn Affairs Black People, 1987; Cert Adv Achievement, NC Sch Bd Acad, 1987;Outstanding Leadership & Serv Black Elected Off, NC Leadership Conf, 1986; Serv Award, Interdenomination Health & Human Serv, 1988; Cert Appreciation, Dedication & Serv Rendered, Durham Child Advocacy Comn, 1986. **Home Addr:** 6710 Mt Hermon Church Rd Lot 63, Durham, NC 27705-7911. *

COPELAND, DR. ELAINE JOHNSON
Educator, administrator. **Personal:** Born Mar 11, 1943, Catawba, SC; daughter of Aaron J Johnson and Lucille Hawkins Johnson; married Robert M; children: Robert M Jr. **Educ:** Livingstone Col, BS, biol, 1964; Winthrop Col, MAT, psychol, 1971; Oregon State Univ, PhD, counr ed, 1974; Univ Ill, Urbana-Champaign, MBA, 1987. **Career:** Wilson Jr High Sch, biol teacher, 1964-65; Jefferson High Sch, biol teacher, 1966-70; Oregon State Univ, counr/ instr, 1970-74; Univ Ill, assoc dean/assoc prof emer, 1975-, assoc vice chancellor acad affairs; Harvard Univ, instr educ mgt, 2001; Clinton Jr Col, pres, 2001-. **Orgs:** Pres, Girls Club Champaign County, 1977; pres, Univ Ill YWCA, 1979; pres, Univ Ill Chap Honor Soc, Phi Kappa Phi, 1982; pres, Champaign-Urbana Alumnae Chap, Kappa Phi Delta Sigma Theta Sorority, 1984-86; affirmative action rep, Div E coun & Develop, Am Educ Res Assoc, 1984-86; vpres, Assoc Rels Nat Assoc Women Deans Adminrs & Counr, 1985-87; pres, Nat Asn Women Deans, Adminr & Counr, 1988-89; Rock Hill Rotar, 2004-06; Chamber Com Bd, 2004-05; Am Asn Univ Women; Am Psychol Asn; Am Educ & Res Asn; life mem, Delta Sigma Theta Inc; Am Coun Educ; Comn Advan Racial & Ethic Equity. **Honors/Awds:** Distinguished Service Award, Col Agr, 1979; Distinguished Alumni Presidential Award, Nat Asn Educ Opportunities Higher Educ, 1986; Outstanding Leadership & Service, Univ Ill Mother's Association Medallian Honor, 1993; Students Colon Award for Breaking Down Barriers & Daring to Dream, Univ Ill MBA, 1994 & 1997; Leadership award, Transnational Asn Christian Cols and Schs. **Special Achievements:** Numerous publications including "Cross-Cultural Counseling and Psychotherapy, An Historical Perspective, Implications for Research and Training", Personnel and Guidance Journal, 1983; co-authored The Production of Black Doctoral Recipients, A Description of Five States Title IV Regulation, Problem and Progress, Teachers College Press, 1988; African American President for the National Association of Women in Education, 1989. **Business Addr:** President, Clinton Junior College, 1029 Crawford Rd, Rock Hill, SC 29732, **Business Phone:** (803)327-7402.

COPELAND, HORACE NATHANIEL
Football player. **Personal:** Born Jan 2, 1971, Orlando, FL; married Tangela; children: Christopher Alan & 3 children. **Educ:** Univ Miami. **Career:** Tampa Bay Buccaneers, wide receiver, 1993-97, 1998; Miami dolphins, 1998; Oakland Raiders, 1999-2000. *

COPELAND, JOHN
Football player. **Personal:** Born Sep 20, 1970, Lanett, AL. **Educ:** Univ Ala. **Career:** Football player (retired), Cincinnati Bengals, defensive end, 1993-00. *

COPELAND, KEVON
Financial manager. **Personal:** Born Mar 29, 1953, Pittsburgh, PA; son of Edward S Copeland Jr and Mary Jo Boxley; married Valire Renaye Carr, Aug 18, 1990 (divorced). **Educ:** Conn Col, BA 1976; Univ Pittsburgh Sch Bus, MBA Finance 1980. **Career:** PNC Bank, Asia, acct officer, 1981-90, asst vpres, foreign direct investment, 1987-91, vpres, credit policy div, 1991-93, asst vpres, Affil Nat Banking, 1993-; Urban Redevelop Authority Pittsburgh, sr bus develop specialist, currently. **Orgs:** Pres, vpres & secy, Nat Black MBA Asn Pittsburgh Chap; Founding mem 100Black Men Western PA; Alumni Comt Conn Coll, 1987-96; exec bd mem, Alumni Asn Conn Coll 1987-96; bd trustees, Sewickley Acad, 1991-95; bd trustees,Conn Col, 1991-96; pres Bd, Fund Advan Minorities Through Educ, 1992-97;adv bd & founding mem, Summer bridge Pittsburgh, 1992-96. **Honors/Awds:** Robert L Hampton Award, Unity Alumni Council Conn Col. **Home Addr:** 5700 Callowhill St, PO Box 23031, Pittsburgh, PA 15206. *

COPELAND, LEON L
Educator. **Personal:** Born Sep 14, 1945, Portsmouth, VA; married Mary B; children: Leon Jr. **Educ:** Norfolk St Col, BS, 1968; VA St Col, MEd, 1974; VA Tech, EdD, 1977. **Career:** Smith High Sch, Chesapeake, Va, teacher 1968-75; Univ Md, asst prof; VZ Tech, co-op counr, 1975-77; Univ Md Eastern Shore, Dept Technol, asst prof, 1977-89, assoc prof & chmn, 1990?99, prof & chair, 1999-, dir, currently; Technol Educ Regional Prof Develop Md State Dept Educ, proj dir, 1998-2000; Enterpreneuiral Develop Inst, co-proj coordr; proj investr,Technol Educ Leadership Proj, Nat Sci Found. **Orgs:** Kappa Alpha Psi Fraternity, 1968-; Ind Arts Asn, 1973-; Phi Delta Kappa, 1977-79; Am Vocational Asn, 1977-; Emergency Sch Aid Adv Comn, 1978-79; Salisbury Housing Rehab Com, 1980; Am Coun Construction Educ; Int Technol Educ Asn; Md Technol Educ Asn; Am Soc Eng Educ. **Honors/Awds:** Recipient Outstanding Young Men of America Award; US Jaycees, 1979; Dept Instructor of the Year, Univ Md, 1979; One of Ten Nat Leaders, Ind Arts Va Tech, 1979; Board of Faculty Regents Award, Univ Syst Md, 1998; Leadership Award, Technol Educ Asn Md, 1998; Distinguished Service Award, Nat Asn State Dir Career Technol Educ, 2001. **Business Addr:** Director of Technology, Professor and Chairman, University of Maryland Eastern Shore, Technology Department, MD-21853, Princess Anne, MD 21853-1299, **Business Phone:** (410)651-6468.

COPELAND, MISTY
Ballet dancer. **Personal:** Born in Kansas City, MO. **Educ:** San Pedro Dance Ctr, ballet studies; Lauridsen Ballet Ctr; San Francisco Ballet Sch. **Career:** ABT's Studio Co; Am Ballet Theatre, mem corps de ballet, 2001-; Dance Performances: Don Quixote; Sugar Plum Fairy; The Nutcracker; La Bayadre; Swan Lake; Sechs Tnze; Within You Without You: A Tribute to George Harrison; Amazed in Burning Dreams; Gong & HereAfter. **Honors/Awds:** Music Center Spotlight Awards. **Business Phone:** (212)477-3030.*

COPELAND, RICHARD ALLEN
Executive, chief executive officer. **Personal:** Born Aug 5, 1955, Minneapolis, MN; son of John and Laura; divorced; children: Leo, Laura & Derick. **Educ:** Univ Minn, BS. **Career:** Mr Rib, mgr; Lincoln Deli, cook; Flyers Bar & Deli, owner; Copeland Cartage, vpres; Thor Construct, founder, pres & chief exec officer, 1983-; Copeland Truc-King Inc, chief exec officer, 1985-; Milestone Growth Fund, dir. **Orgs:** Pacesetters, 1985-90; pres, Nat Asn Minority Contractors, 1990-92; Minneapolis Minority Purchasing Coun; Minority Bus Enterprises Input Comm; Rotary, 1992; bd mem & co-founder, African-Am Chamber Com. **Honors/Awds:** MMPC Supplier of the Year, Insight, 1990; Adminr Minority Bus Enterprise Award, US DOT, 1990; Minority Supplier of the Year, MMPC, 1990; Charles W Poe Entrepreneur of the Yr, MEDA, 1992; Supplier of the Year, Natl Minority Supplier Development Coun Conf, 1992; Local Suppliers Receive Awards, Insight, 1992; Entrepreneurial Hall of Fame Award, Metrop Econ Develop Asn. **Special Achievements:** Making Do in '92, Star Tribune, 1991. **Business Addr:** Chief Executive Officer, Copeland Truc-King Inc, 5400 Main St Suite 201, Minneapolis, MN 55421-1132, **Business Phone:** (763)572-0505.

COPELAND, ROBERT S
Secretary (Office), college administrator. **Educ:** Walsh Univ, BA. **Career:** Wilberforce Univ, dir develop; Univ Dayton, asst vpres; Wright State Univ, Sch Med, sr develop officer, assoc vpres develop & dir advan, currently. **Business Addr:** Associate Vice President of Advancement, Director of Development, Wright State University, 108 Allyn Hall 3640 Col Glenn Hwy, Fairborn, OH 45324, **Business Phone:** (937)775-3232.

COPELAND, DR. RONALD LOUIS
Physician, surgeon. **Personal:** Born Jul 5, 1951, Rochester, NY; son of Claude and Sarah; married Vicki, Aug 25, 1973; children: Airrion, Jamon & Nia. **Educ:** Dartmouth Col, BA, 1973; Univ Cincinnati Med Col, MD, 1977. **Career:** Ohio Permanente Med Group, chief surg, 1989-91, regional dir, surgical servs, 1991-93, assoc med dir, 1993-96, vpres & assoc med dir, 1996-97, pres & med dir, 1998-. **Orgs:** Co-chair, Health & Safety Servs, Am Red Cross, 1995-; Liaison Coun Cert Surg Tech 1995-; Cleveland Acad Med, 1998-; Adv Bd,UNCF, 1998; adv bd, Minority Organ Tissue Transplant Ed Prog, 1999-; Kaiser Permanente Nat Diversity Coun; Kaiser Permanente Care Experience Coun, 1999-; bd dirs, Kaiser Permanente Care Mgt Inst, 1999-; Kaiser Permanente Partnership Group, 2000-; Permanente Fed Exec Comn, 2000-; adv bd, Cuyahoga Comn Col Surg Tech, 2001-. **Honors/Awds:** Upstate Medical Center Outstanding Teaching, State Univ NY, Dept Surg, 1982; Mayor's Certificate of Recognition, 1986; Physician Recognition Award, Am Med Asn, 1986-89; Outstanding Physician Award, Asn Surg Technologist, 1995-97; Alumni of the Year Award, James Madison High, 2000. **Special Achievements:** Author of numerous articles. **Military Serv:** United States Air Force, 1982-88; Commendation Medal, 1984; Meritorious Service Medal, 1986; Oak Leaf Cluster, 1988. **Business Addr:** President, Medical Director, Ohio Permanente Medical Group, 1001 Lakeside Ave Suite 1200, Cleveland, OH 44114, **Business Phone:** 800-837-6764.

COPELAND, RUSSELL SAMOAN
Football player. **Personal:** Born Nov 4, 1971, Tupelo, MS. **Educ:** Univ Memphis. **Career:** Football player (retired); Buffalo Bills, wide receiver, 1993-96; Philadelphia Eagles, 1998; Green Bay Packers, 1998; Philadelphia Eagles, 1998. **Home Addr:** 100 Bradley Rd, Tupelo, MS 38801-9370.

COPELAND, TERRILYN DENISE
Pathologist. **Personal:** Born in Toledo, OH. **Educ:** Kent State Univ, BS; Bowling Green State Univ, MA; Univ Toledo, MS, 1999. **Career:** Lucas Co Bd Ment Retardation, instr & speech pathologist, 1978-81; contract home health speech pathologist, 1981-86; St Francis Rehab Hosp, staff speech pathologist, 1986-88; Flower Mem Healthplex, staff speech pathologist, 1988-89; St Francis Rehab Hosp, dir speech pathology & audiology, 1989-94; Rehab Am, rehab coordr, 1994-95; St Charles-Mercy Hosp, inpatient coordr, 1995-02; The Med Col OH, speech pathologist; Sylvania Pub Schs, speech pathologist, 2002-04, curently. **Orgs:** Delta Sigma Theta Sor; Am Speech & Hearing Asn; area rep, legis rep, Aphasiology Asn OH, 1987-92; Am Asn Univ Women, 1986-89, 2002; League Women Voters, 1986-01; bd dirs, 1986-94; OH Speech & Hearing Asn, 1980-93; Am Bus Womens Asn, 1989-93; The Nat Head Injury Found, 1986-90; The Jr League; bd dirs, Toledo Hearing & Speech Ctr, 2000-02. **Business Addr:** Speech Pathologist, 6850 monroe st, Sylvania, OH 43560, **Business Phone:** (419)824-8500.*

COPELIN, SHERMAN NATHANIEL
Businessperson, legislator. **Personal:** Born Sep 21, 1943, New Orleans, LA; son of Sherman N Sr and Marie Armant; married Donna Sorapuru, Sep 21, 1990; children: Sherman Nathaniel III, Michon Jarel, Shane Nathan & Courtney Marie. **Educ:** Dillard Univ, BA, 1965; Loyola Univ, New Orleans, advanced study in psychol, 1966, advan study real estate investment, 1978. **Career:** Pro Tempore, speaker, 1992-96; Superdome Serv Inc, pres & chief exec officer, 1973-; Mkt Serv Inc, pres & chief exec officer, 1978-; State La, state rep; Health Corporation of the South, chmn, 1989-; 107 Group Inc, pres, currently; EST Inc, chair bd, currently; Gateway South Travel Agency, sec & trea, currently. **Orgs:** Nat Bus League, 1977-; Vice chmn bd, 1984-92, pres, 1992-; cochmn, La Coun Policy Rev, 1985-; chair, La Bus League; chair, Nat Coun Policy Rev; treas, chair, La Legis Black Caucus; exec comt, Nat Black Caucus State Legislators; exec comn, Southern Legis Conf; Nat Democratic Committeeman; State Cent Committeeman; US Chamber Com, Small Bus Coun; pres, New Orleans E Bus Asn. **Special Achievements:** Author: How Can the US & Local Chamber Encourage and Support the Emerging Minority-Owned Business?; US Chamber of Commerce Small Bus Council Task Force on Emerging Business, 1992. **Business Addr:** President, National Bussiness League, New Orleans Office, 107 Harbor Cir, PO Box 26306, New Orleans, LA 70186.

COPES, RONALD ADRIAN
Insurance executive, executive director. **Personal:** Born Dec 1, 1941, Hartford, CT; son of Aelix and Mamie Weaver Bailey; married Melva Washington Copes, Jun 12, 1964; children: Ronald A II, Rodney A. **Educ:** Lincoln Univ, BS, 1963; Atlanta Univ, MBA, 1973. **Career:** Mass Mutual Life Ins Co, vpres disability income, 1990, vpres community rels; exec dir MassMutual Found, currently. **Orgs:** Vice Basileus, Omega Psi Phi Fraternity, 1989-90. **Honors/Awds:** Hon Soc, Delta Mu Delta, 1971-73. **Military Serv:** AUS, Coll, 1963-90; AUS Vietnam; dis sr adv, 1970-71; AUS, Fort Leavenworth, KS, auth/instr, 1973-77; AUS, 1st armored div, squadron exec officer, squadron comdr, 1977-82; AUS, Baltimore, MD, prof mil sci, 1982-85; AUS, St Louis, MO, dir info mgt, 1985-90; Silver Star, Bronze Star, Air Medal, Parachute Badge. **Home Addr:** 54 Blueberry Ridge, Westfield, MA 01085. **Business Addr:** Vice President, Massachusetts Mutual Life Insurance Co, Corp Commun Div, 1295 State St F 084, Springfield, MA 01111-0002.*

COPPEDGE, ARTHUR L
Artist, lecturer. **Personal:** Born Apr 21, 1938. **Educ:** Brooklyn Col; Brooklyn Museum Art Sch; Pratt Graphic Art Ctr; Art Stud League. **Career:** Am Beautiful Fund, artist residence; teacher art classes, pvt studio; Brooklyn Museum Art Sch, teacher; Walden Sch NYC, teacher; NY Soc Ethical Culture, teacher adult educ;

Brooklyn Col, Cornell Univ, Nat Conf Artists, Am Asn Mus Waldoft Astoria Hotel, lectr; Inst Jamaica, painting & drawing teacher. **Orgs:** Founder & pres, Brooklyn Consortium Artists & Arts; founder, estab Brooklyn Artists Coalition; 1st dir exhib ept New Mus Comm Mus; art consult, Gallery NYC; hon chmn, Com Honor Judge Bruce Wright; estab art dept NY Soc Ethical Culture; art consult, African-Am Caribbean Cult Ctr, Brooklyn, NY; bd mem, Brooklyn Downtown Develop Corp.

CORAM, WILLIE MAE
School administrator. **Personal:** Born Apr 20, 1934, Fayetteville, NC; daughter of Willie Clayton and Mary Helen Council; divorced; children: Lynn D Coram-Allen & Bruce Allan Coram Sr. **Educ:** Boston Univ, BA, 1955; Univ Med & Dent NJ, PhD, 1983. **Career:** Sch administrator (retired); Grassland Hosp, res technician, lab supvr, 1955-63; Montefiore Hosp, lab supvr, 1963-64; GEIGY Chem Corp, res scientist, supvr autonomic pharmacol group, 1964-71; CIBA-GEIGY Corp, numerous positions, 1971-89; Univ Med & Dentistry New Jersey, asst dean stud & alumni affairs, 1989-2000. **Orgs:** Nat Asn Grad Admis Professionals; Sigma Xi; AAAS; NY Acad Scis; MSACRAO;AACRAO; bd dir, Carlisle Commonwealth Community Asn. **Honors/Awds:** Achievement Award, Nat Asn Negro Bus & Prof Women's Clubs Inc, 1985;Certificate of Recognition, Nat Urban League, 1986; CIBA-GEIGY TWIN Award,1986; Outstanding Leaders in Business, Education & Industry, Jersey City State Col, 1988. **Special Achievements:** Restoration of Normal Tissue K Levels in Heart, Aorta and Skeletal Muscleof Furosemide-Treated Rats on Mg-Deficient Diet, 1988; Effects of CGS10078B on Catecholamine Content of Brain, Heart, Uterus and Plasma in Conscious Rats, 1986; numerous others. **Home Addr:** 4074 Armswood Pl, Stone Mountain, GA 30083.

CORBETT, DR. ALEXANDER E., III
Administrator. **Personal:** Born Feb 13, 1944, Portsmouth, VA; son of Alexander Corbett Jr (deceased); married Barbara W, Jun 28, 1969; children: AC Corbett. **Educ:** Kennedy-Western Univ, BS, bus admin, 1989; Saint Paul's Col, LHD, 2001. **Career:** Joslyn MFG & Supply Co, clerk & expeditor, 1971-74; AMF-World Tobacco Group, buyer, 1974-76; Dominion Va Power, sr supply chain specialist, 1976-00; The Town of Belmont, clerk. **Orgs:** Am Asn Blacks in Energy, 1993-95; Va Mus Fine Arts Multicultural Coun, 1994; bd trustees, comt co-chair, Saint Pauls Col, 1996-00, 2001; Asn Governing Bds, colleges & universities, 1996-00; Jamestown-Yorktown Found Partnership Group, 1999-; Acute Care Bd Dirs, Bon Secours Health Syst, 2003. **Honors/Awds:** Commonwealth of Virginia, Certificate of Recognition, 1981-83. **Special Achievements:** Published essays: Univ of Virginia Minority Career Day Guide, 1995; Saint Paul's College Career Guides, 1995-97. **Military Serv:** AUS, specialist E-4, 1963-66. *

CORBETT, DR. DORIS R
Educator, chairperson. **Personal:** Born Jun 9, 1947, Elizabethtown, NC; daughter of Henry Edward and Isadora Beatty White; married William Johnson, Oct 20, 1982. **Educ:** NC Col, Durham, NC, BS, 1969; NC Cent Univ, Durham, NC, MS, 1972; Univ Md, Col Park, MD, PhD, 1981. **Career:** Camp Curtin Jr High Sch, Harrisburg, PA, high sch teacher, 1969-70; John Harris Sr High Sch, Harrisburg, PA, high sch teacher, 1970-71; Howard Univ, WA, DC, Dept Phys Educ & Recreation, assoc prof, 1972-, dir grad studies, prof sport sociol, currently, Dept Health, Human Performance & Leisure Studies, chairperson, currently; US Capitol Hist Soc, fel; US Mil Acad, vis prof. **Orgs:** Pres, Nat Asn Girls & Women Sports, 1980-81; pres, Eastern Dist Asn, 1987-88; pres, Am Alliance Health, Phys Educ, Recreation & Dance, 1990-91, chmn bd gov, 1990-91; int pres, Int Coun Health, Phys Educ & Recreation, 1991-99. **Honors/Awds:** Honor Award, DC Asn Health, Phys Educ, Recreation & Dance, 1979; Honor Award, Eastern Dist Asn, Health, Phys Educ, Recreation & Dance, 1984; R Tait McKenzie Award, Am Alliance Health, Phys Educ, Recreation & Dance, 1989; Mabel C Robinson Lecturer Award, Ala State Asn Health, Phys Educ, Recreation & Dance, 1990; Ethics Scholar, Univ RI Inst Int Sport, 1990-91; Luther Halsey Gulick Medal, Am Alliance Health, Phys Educ, Recreation & Dance. **Special Achievements:** Publication: "Outstanding Athletes of Congress," US Capitol Historical Society Washington, DC, 1997. **Business Addr:** Professor of Sport Sociology, Chairperson, Howard University, College of Arts and Sciences, Dept Health Human Performance & Leisure Studies, 6th Girard St NW, Washington, DC 20059, **Business Phone:** (202)806-7142.

CORBETT, MERLISA EVELYN LAWRENCE. See LAWRENCE, MERLISA EVELYN.

CORBI, LANA E.
Executive. **Personal:** Born Jan 1, 1955?, Los Angeles, CA; daughter of Carl King and Elizabeth; married Al; children: two. **Educ:** Univ So CA, BA, journalism, 1979; CA State Univ, grad studies, tv & film, 1980. **Career:** Fox Broadcasting, vp, 1991-94, sr vp, 1994-95, exec vp, 1996-97, pres, 1997-99; Blackstar, pres & COO, 1995-96; Odyssey Holdings, COO, 1999-00; Crown Media Holdings, exec vpres & COO, 2000-01; Crown Media US, pres, ceo, 2001-02; Corbico, pres, ceo, 2002-. **Orgs:** Monte Carlo Festival Honorary Comt; Entertainment Industries Coun; Int Academy TV, Arts & Sci; Nat Asn Minorities Commun; Women Cable Telecommun; American Women Radio & TV. **Honors/Awds:** Congressional Award, Adoption Advocacy, 2002; Publisher's AwARd, Minorities Bus Mag, 2002; Ebony, 2002. **Business Phone:** (760)519-5761.*

CORBIE, DR. LEO A. See Obituaries section.

CORBIN, ANGELA LENORE
Physician. **Personal:** Born Nov 19, 1958, Washington, DC; daughter of Maurice C and Ruby. **Educ:** Howard Univ, BS, 1980; Meharry Med Col, MD, 1984; Univ Md, Internship & Hosp resident, 1987; Univ Md, Hosp nephrology, 1989. **Career:** Univ Md Hosp, resident, 1984-; Univ Md Med Syst, fel, 1989; Med Syst, pvt pract, physician, currently. **Orgs:** Am Col Physicians; Am Med Asn; Alpha Omega Alpha Med Honor Soc, 1984; Nat Med Asn. **Home Addr:** 11304 Class Lane, Silver Spring, MD 20901. *

CORBIN, SEAN
Manager. **Personal:** Born Jan 1, 1920?. **Career:** Nat Basketball Asn, Utah Jazz, San Antonio Spurs, currently. **Honors/Awds:** City Community Service Award, Baltimore Mayor's Off, 1997 & 1998. **Business Addr:** Official, National Basketball Association, 645 5th Ave 10th Fl, New York, NY 10022-5986.*

CORBIN, STAMPP W
Chief executive officer, executive. **Educ:** Stanford Univ, BA, econ, 1982; Harvard Univ, MBA, 1986. **Career:** Resource One Comput Systs Inc, pres, 2002, owner, currently; RetroBox LLC, founder & chief exec officer; Intechra LLC, chief strategic officer, currently; Nat Recycling Coalition, bd dirs, currently. **Orgs:** Asn Ohio Recyclers; pledging mem, Basel Action Network. **Business Addr:** Owner, Resource One Computer Systems Inc, 1159 Dublin Rd, Columbus, OH 43215, **Business Phone:** (614)485-4800.

CORBIN, TYRONE KENNEDY
Basketball player, basketball coach. **Personal:** Born Dec 31, 1962, Columbia, SC; married Dante; children: Tyjha & Tyrell. **Educ:** DePaul Univ, BS, comput sci, 1985. **Career:** Basketball player (retired), basketball coach; San Antonio Spurs, forward, 1985-87, Cleveland Cavaliers, 1987-88, Phoenix Suns, 1988-89, Minn Timber wolves, 1989-91; Utah Jazz, 1991-94, asst coach, 2005-; Atlanta Hawks, 1994-95, 1996-99; Sacramento Kings, 1995-96, 1999-2000; Miami Heat, 1995; Toronto Raptors, 2000-01; Charleston Lowgators, mentor; NY Knicks, mgr player develop, 2003-04. **Business Phone:** (801)325-2500.

CORBITT, DR. JOHN H
Clergy. **Personal:** Born Aug 24, 1941, Salley, SC; son of John and Thelma; married Betty Starks; children: Bruce & Terry. **Educ:** SC State Univ, BA, 1962; Interdenominational Theol Ctr, MDiv, 1966; Vanderbilt Univ Div Sch; Yale Div Univ; McCormick Theol Sem, DMin, 1979; Morris Col, DDiv, 2001. **Career:** Bells Chapel Baptist Church, pastor, 1966-67; Owen Col, col minister & prof bible & relig, 1966-67; Ark Baptist Career, interim dean relig; Philander Smith Col, col chaplain & prof relig & philos, 1970-74; Mt Pleasant Baptist Church, Little Rock, pastor, 1967-74; Springfield Baptist Church, pastor, 1974-, minister,currently; Nat Baptist Student Union Retreat, nat dir, 1973-96; Nat Baptist Congress Christian Educ, dean, 1984-99; SC Baptist Congress Christian Educ, pres, 1986-90. **Orgs:** Foreign Mission Bd Nat Baptist Conv USA Inc, 1968-74; consult, Nat Student Ministries So Bapt Conv, 1969-87; Gov's Comn First Offenders State Ark, 1969; Nat Asn Col & Univ Chaplains; Ministries Blacks Higher Educ; pres, InterdenomiNat Ministerial Alliance, Greater Little Rock; appointed by Gov Dale Bumpers Bd Pardons & Parole, State Ark, 1971; nat dir, Nat Baptist Student Union Retreat 1973-96; nat dir, NH Baptist Student Union Retreat, 1973-96; Nat Asn Advan Colored People; pres, Enoree River Congress Christian Educ, 1975-79; pres, Greater Greenville Ministerial Asn, 1980-81; dean, Nat Baptist Congress Christian Educ, 1984-99; bd adv, Little Rock Urban League; appointed by Gov James B Edwards to Greenville Area Bd Mental Health; pres, SC State Congress Christian Educ, 1986-90; Preaching Teams, Africa, 1979, Soviet Union, 1988; former pres, Greater Greenville Ministerial Asn; former chap pres, Phi Beta Sigma Fraternity Inc; Comn Evangelism & Educ, Baptist World Alliance; Religions Educ Asn US & Canada; bd trustee, SC State Univ, 2001-. **Honors/Awds:** The Order of the Palmetto, 1988; Alumnus of the Year, McCormick Theological Seminary, 1991; Order of the Palmetto, Governor of SC, 1988; Honored by Morehouse Col, 1992; Arkansas Traveler Award, 1992; Named to Martin Luther King, Morehouse Col, 1992. **Special Achievements:** Author, Black Churches Reaching Coll Students, 1995. **Business Addr:** Pastor, Springfield Baptist Church, 600 E McBee Ave, Greenville, SC 29601, **Business Phone:** (864)271-3494.

CORDELL, LADORIS HAZZARD
Judge. **Personal:** Born Nov 19, 1949, Bryn Mawr, PA; divorced; children: Cheran & Starr. **Educ:** Antioch Col, BA, 1971; Stanford Law Sch, JD, 1974. **Career:** NAACP Legal Defense & Educ Fund, staff atty, 1974-75; atty, pvt pract, 1975-82; Stanford Law Sch, asst dean, 1978-82; State Court Appeal Sixth Dist, justice pro tem, 1986-87; Munic Ct Santa Clara Co, judge, 1982-88; Supr Ct Santa Clara Co, judge, 1988-2001; Stanford Univ, vp & spec counr, pres, campus rels, 2001-. **Orgs:** Nat Bar Asn; Am Bar Asn; NAACP; Calif Judges Asn; Calif Women Lawyers; chairperson, bd dirs, Manhattan Playhouse, E Palo Alto, 1980; bd dirs & steering comt, Nat Conf Women & Law, 1980, 1984-85; policy bd, Ctr Res Women Stanford Univ, 1980-82; chairperson, bd dirs, E Palo Alto Community Law Project, 1984-87; bd trustees, United Way Santa Clara County, 1987-; bd dir, Police Activities League (PAL), San Jose Chap, 1987-89, Nat Conf Christians & Jews Inc, Santa Clara County, 1988-; bd trustees, Mills Col, Oakland, CA, 1996-; bd dir, Lucile Packard Found Children, Stanford, CA, 1997-; Silicon Valley Forum Coun, Commonwealth Club Calif, 1997-; bd dir, Asian Law Alliance, San Jose, CA, 1997, Adv bd, Healthy Alternatives African Am Babies, San Jose, CA, 1994-; Am Law Inst, 1996-. **Honors/Awds:** Black History Award, Tulip Jones Womens Club 1977; nominated for Black Enterprise Mag Annual Achievement Award in under 30 category, 1977, 1978; Community Involvement Award, E Palo Alto Chamber Com, 1982, 1983; Public Service Award, Delta Sigma Theta, 1982; Public Service Awards, Nat Coun Negro Women, 1982; Outstanding Mid-Peninsula Black Woman Award, Mid-Peninsula, YWCA, 1983; Political Achievement Award, Calif Black Women's Coalition & the Black Concerns Asn, 1982; Featured in Ebony Mag, 1980, 1984; Implemented a minority recruitment prog, Stanford Law School asst dean; elected presiding judge Municipal Court, 1985-86 term; Achievement Award, Western Ctr Domestic Violence, 1986; Santa Clara County Woman of Achievement Award, 1985; Recipient of first Juliette Gordon Lowe Award for Community Serv, 1987; Distinguished Citizen Award, Exchange Club, 1989; Don Peters Outstanding Volunteer Award, United Way Santa Clara County, 1991; Baha'i Community Service Award, 1992; Special Recognition Award, Human Relations Comn, Santa Clara County, 1994; Youth Service Award, Legal Advocates Children & Youth, 1996; Unsung Heroes Award, Minority Access Comt, Santa Clara County Bar Asn, 1996; Social Justice award, San Franscisco Women's Ctr, 1996; Legal Impact Award, Asian Law Alliance, 1996, Advocate for Justice Award, Legal Aid Soc, Santa Clara County, 1996; Martin Luther King, Junior Award, The San Jose Peace Ctr, 1998; Josephine and Frank Dulveneck Humanitarian Award, 1998; Jacqueline Kennedy Award, John F Kennedy Univ, 1999; Rosa Parks Ordinary People Award, San Jose, NAACP, 1999; Women's Equality Award, Comn Status Women, 2000. **Special Achievements:** First Black Woman Judge in Northern Calif; first black woman on Superior Court in Northern California 1988-; first lawyer to open a private law practice in East Palo Alto, CA; author, "Before Brown v Bd of Educ—Was It All Worth It?", Howard Law J Vol 23 No 1 1980; co-author, "The Appearance of Justice: Judges' Verbal and Nonverbal Behavior in Criminal Jury Trials", Stanford Law Review Vol 38, No 1, 1985; "Black Immigration, Disavowing the Stereotype of the Shiftless Negro", Judges' J Spring 1986; Co-author, "Musings of a Trial Court Judge," Indiana Law J, vol 68, No 4, 1993. **Business Addr:** Special Counselor to the President, Vice Provost for Campus Relations, Stanford University, Bldg 310 Main Quad, Stanford, CA 94305-2100, **Business Phone:** (650)723-3484.

CORLETTE, EDITH
Lawyer. **Personal:** Born Oct 19, 1942, Oklahoma City, OK; daughter of Stephen Parker and Gwendolyn Parker. **Educ:** Hampton Inst, BS, 1964; Northwestern Sch Law, JD, 1974; Univ Calif, MS, 1975. **Career:** Woodrow Wilson fel, 1964; NW Urban fel, 1973-74; Self-employed, atty. **Orgs:** Delta Sigma Theta Sorority, 1962; Alpha Kappa Mu Hon Soc, 1963-64; Langston Law Club, 1974; SW Bar Asn, 1974; La Co Bar Asn, 1975; Nat Conf Black Lawyers, 1975; Calif State Bar Asn, 1975-; pres, Womens Div NBA; sec, CA Asn Black Lawerys; Nat Bar Asn; secy, Black Women Lawyer S CA, 1975; Nat Bus Asn, 1976; Beverly Hills Law Asn, 1977; bd dir, Nat Asn Advan Colored People, Hollywood Br; bd dirs, Proj heavy. **Honors/Awds:** Outstanding Young Women America, 1966. **Business Addr:** Attorney, PO Box 8692, Los Angeles, CA 90008-0692, **Business Phone:** (323)298-7223.

CORLEY, DR. CHARLES J.
Educator. **Educ:** Hampton Inst, BA, sociol/social work, 1981; Bowling Green State Univ, MA, criminol, 1984, PhD, social psychol family, 1986. **Career:** Less Secure Detention Facil, Hampton, Juvenile supv, 1980-81; Bowling Green State Univ, grad asst, 1981-83, teaching fel, 1983-86; Lucas County Ct Intake officer, Toledo, 1982-84; Lucas County Criminal Justice Training Acad, Toledo, tech asst, 1982; Winthrop Col, asst prof sociol, 1986-89; Mich State Univ, Sch Criminal Justice, asst prof, assoc prof, Lilly Endowment teaching fel, 1992, prof, currently. **Honors/Awds:** Nat and Inter Nat Curriculum Diversity Development Grant, Mich State Univ, 1991. **Special Achievements:** Publisher: "Correlates of the Failure of Police Officers to Report Pursuits", Delinquents on Delinquency by Arnold P. Goldstein, Socio economic, Socio demographic and Attitudinal Correlates of the Tempo of Divorce". Author: The Consequences of Divorce: Economic and Custodial Impact on Children and Adults; The Consequences of Divorce: Economic and Custodial Impact on Children and Adults. **Business**

Addr: Professor, Michigan State University, School of Criminal Justice, 522 Baker Hall, East Lansing, MI 48824-1118, **Business Phone:** (517)353-5225.

CORLEY, EDDIE B., SR.
Automotive executive. **Educ:** Prairieview Col. **Career:** Humble Oil Serv Sta; Clothing Store, owner; Grocery Store, owner; Fast Food Restaurant, owner; Ed Corley Automotive Group, Ed Corley Ford Lincoln Mercury Inc, chief exec officer, 1982; Ed Corley Nissan, 1996; Ed Corley Chrysler Jeep Dodge, NM, 1997. **Special Achievements:** CPN is ranked 100th on Black Enterprise magazine's list of top 100 auto dealers, 1992. **Business Addr:** Chief Executive Officer, Ed Corley Chrysler Dodge Jeep, Ed Corley Automotive Group, 1870 W Santa Fe Ave, PO Box 908, Grants, NM 87020, **Business Phone:** (505)863-6823.*

CORLEY, LESLIE M
Investment banker, chief executive officer. **Personal:** Born May 1946, Chicago, IL; son of Lorena Turner and Leslie T. **Educ:** Univ Ill, BS with high honors, Aeronaut & Astronaut Engineering, 1969; Harvard Grad Sch Bus Admin, MBA, 1971. **Career:** Exxon Inc, fin analyst, 1969-71; Fidelity Investments, sr securities analyst, 1972-77; Norton Simon Inc, mgr acquisitions strategic planning, 1977-81; Kelso & Co, gen partner, 1981-88; LM Capital Corp, Pres & chief exec officer, 1988-; Convenience Corp Am Inc, chmn, 1995-96. **Orgs:** Urban League Palm Beach County, dir, 1996-97; d'essence Designer Fragrances, LLC, dir, 1996-97; Tri-West, Inc, dir, 1986-88; Am Sterilizer Inc, dir, 1984-86; Manhattan Community Bd 9, treas, 1991-92; Aaron Davis Hall, treas/dir, 1986-95; Personal Luxury Products Int Inc, dir, 1998-; bd dirs, Enterprise Fla; Fla Atlantic Univ Found; Bus Develop Brd Palm Beach County; Economic Coun Palm Beach County. **Honors/Awds:** Phi Eta Sigma, Freshman Collegiate Honorary Society, 1965; Sigma Gamma Tau, Engineering Honorary Society, 1967; Edmund J James Honors Program, Univ Ill, 1965-69; Tabernacle Missionary Bapt Church, Businessman of the Year, 1997; Urban League Palm Beach County Endowment Award, 1998. **Special Achievements:** Formed largest minority owned convenience store operator, 1995; Company was ranked eigthh on Black Enterprise's 1997 list of Top 100 Black businesses. **Business Phone:** (561)981-8410.

CORLEY, TODD L.
Vice president (Organization). **Personal:** Born Jan 20, 1969, Glen Cove, NY; son of Luther Corley and Lillian Mitchell. **Educ:** Le Moyne Col, BA, finance; Georgetown Univ, MBA, 1997. **Career:** Towers Perrin's Global Diversity & Change Mgmt Pract, sr consult & area leader, 1997-03; Starwood Hotels & Resorts-Worldwide, sr mgr, diversity & inclusion, 2003-04; Abercrombie & Fitch, diversity & inclusion, vpres, 2004-. **Orgs:** Nat INROADS Alumni Asn, 1991-; Alhpa Phi Alpha, dir, 1992-; Nat Black MBA Asn, lifetime mem, 1997-; 100 Black Men, 1999-; mem adv bd, LeMoyne Coll, 1999-; mem bd, UNCF Columbus; bd mem, Cornell Univ, Chief Diversity Officer Roundtable. **Special Achievements:** Published article in National Assn of Colleges and Employees, 1999; Cited by Black Meetings and Tourism magazine as one of the top African-Americans in the lodging industry. **Business Addr:** Vice President, Abercrombie & Fitch, 6301 Fitch Path, New Albany, OH 43054, **Business Phone:** (614)283-6500.*

CORLEY-BLANEY, JANICE
Broker. **Career:** Remax Exclusive Properties, broker & owner, currently. **Business Addr:** Broker, Owner, Remax Exclusive Properties, 1618 N Wells St, Chicago, IL 60614, **Business Phone:** (312)337-3629.*

CORLEY-SAUNDERS, ANGELA ROSE
Government official. **Personal:** Born Jun 9, 1947, Washington, DC; divorced. **Educ:** Howard Univ, BA, 1975; Sch Divinty, attended. **Career:** White House, spec asst, 1977-77; US Dept Agri Off, Asst Secy Rural Develop, spec asst, 1977-79; US Dept Agri Farmers Home Admin, mgt analyst, 1979-; Equal Opportunity Specialists, 1986-; US Dept Agri Rural Econ &Community Develop, civil rights staff & equal employ specialist, 1987-. **Orgs:** Nat Coun Negro Women, 1978-; bd mem, Unity Wash, DC, 1983-; lic unity teacher, Asn Unity Churches, 1996-. **Business Addr:** Equal Employment Specialist, United States Department of Agriculture, 1400 Independence Ave SW Suite 2077, PO Box 0703, Washington, DC 20250, **Business Phone:** (202)720-6633.

CORMIER, LAWRENCE J.
Executive. **Personal:** Born Sep 26, 1927, San Benito, TX; married Helen Jones; children: Patricia Watkins, Janet, Lawrence. **Educ:** Pace Univ, attended 1972. **Career:** US Merchant Marine, third officer, 1950-55; Ebony Oil Corp, bd chmn, chief exec officer, 1955-87; Cormier & Ebony Trucking Inc, bd chmn & chief exec officer, 1964-87; The Inner-City Mgt Co, chief exec officer & bd chmn, 1977-85; Cormier Group Ltd, Jamaica, NY, chief exec officer & bd chmn, 1990-. **Orgs:** Charter mem, bd mem, Assoc Minority Bus Enterprise NY; bd mem, past vpres, Gr Jamaica Chamber Com; past pres, Int Kiwanis, Jamaica Club; past pres, bd mem, charter mem, United Black Men Queens City; br pres, Jamaica NAACP, St Albans, NY; past pres & dir emer, Greater Jamaica Develop Corp. **Honors/Awds:** Business & Commerce Service Award, Omega Psi Phi, 1965; NY State Small Businessman of the Year, US Small Bus Admin, 1967; Special Recognition Award, NAACP, 1968; Outstanding Service Award, Jamaica Chamber Com, 1970; Businessman of the Year, Jamaica Chamber Com, 1974; Delta Sigma Theta Outstanding Community Service Award, 1974; Asn Minority Enterprise Service Award, 1979; NY Urban League community Service Award, 1981; Outstanding Leadership Award, NY State Dept Com, 1982; Outstanding Leadership Award, Queens Fed Churches, 1983; Outstanding Community Service Award, Nat Cancer Soc, 1984; Businessman of the Year, St Albans Chamber Com, 1985; Benjamin S Rosenthal Humanitarian Award, B'nai B'rith, 1985; Regional Minority Manufacturer of the Year Award, US Dept Com, 1986; National Minority Manufacturer of the Year Award, US Dept Com, 1986; Outstanding Business Achievement Award, US Small Bus Admin, 1986. **Military Serv:** US Merchant Marines. **Business Addr:** Chief Executive Officer, Chairman of Board, Cormier Group Ltd, 90 25 161st St Suite 510, Jamaica, NY 11431, **Business Phone:** (718)298-9010.*

CORMIER, RUFUS
Lawyer. **Personal:** Born Mar 2, 1948, Beaumont, TX; married Yvonne Clement; children: Michelle, Geoffrey & Claire. **Educ:** Southern Methodist Univ, BA, anthrop, 1970; Yale Univ, JD, 1973. **Career:** Paul Weiss Rifkind Wharton & Garrison, atty, 1973-74; US House Reps Judiciary Comm, spec asst counsel, 1974; Baker & Botts, atty & partner, currently. **Orgs:** Am Bar Asn; Am Bar Found; Houston Bar Asn; Houston Lawyers Asn; Houston Bar Found; State Bar Tex; Tex Bar Found. **Honors/Awds:** Avella Winn Hay Achievement Award, 1970; Karen H Susman Jurisprudence Award, 2004. **Special Achievements:** Selected by Texas Jaycees as one of Five Outstanding Young Texans, 1981; Listed in The Best Lawyers in America since 1983; Recognized by Texas Monthly and Law & Politics as a "Texas Super Lawyer" since 2003. **Business Addr:** Partner, Baker & Botts LLP, 1 Shell Plz 910 Louisiana St, Houston, TX 77002-4995, **Business Phone:** (713)229-1544.

CORNELIUS, CHARLES HENRY
Insurance executive, president (organization). **Personal:** Born Nov 13, 1955, Bronx, NY; son of Melvin and Dolores; married Sheila Harris, May 12, 1984; children: Charles Jr & Michael. **Educ:** Univ Hartford, BA, 1977; Univ Va, Exec Prog, attended. **Career:** Allstate Ins Co, mgr, 1977-84; Chubb Group Ins Co, br mgr & vice pres, 1984-96; Atlanta Life Financial Group Inc, pres & ceo, 1996-2005; Inroads Inc, pres & chief exec officer, 2005-. **Orgs:** Atlanta Action Forum, 1996-; dir, mem, Nat Ins Asn, 1997-; 100 Black Men Atlanta, 1996-; Nat Asn Advan Colored People, 1997-; dir, Albany Inst Art & History, 1993-96; dir, Urban League NE NY, 1994-96; bd visitors, Metrop Atlanta Chamber Com, 1998-; dir, Atlanta Asn Ins Profs, 1998-2000; dir, Butler St YMCA, 1998-2002; dir, Zoo Atlanta, 1998-2002; dir, High Mus Art, 1998-2000; bd visitors, Emory Univ, 1998-01; bd visitors, Grady Health Syst, 1998-; dir, Altanta Comn Pub Educ, 1998-; Aid Atlanta, 1998-; dir, Atlanta Urban League, 1999-2001; bd trustees, Leadership Atlanta, 1999-2001; adv coun, Cool Girls Ins; adv coun, Rotary Club Atlanta; bd couns, Carter Ctr, 2002-. **Honors/Awds:** Black Achievers Industries, YMCA Harlem Br, 1991; Honoree, Nat Ins Ind Asn, 1996. **Special Achievements:** Black Enterprise's list of Top Insurance Companies, ranked 2, 1999, 2000. **Business Addr:** President, Chief Executive Officer, Inroads Inc, 10 S Broadway Suite 300, St Louis, MO 63102, **Business Phone:** (314)241-7488.*

CORNELIUS, DONALD CORTEZ
Television show host, actor. **Personal:** Born Sep 27, 1936, Chicago, IL; married Delores Harrison, 1956; children: Anthony & Raymond. **Career:** Golden State Mutual Life, ins salesman, 1956-66; WVON, announcer, 1966; WCIU-TV, sports anchor, 1968; Soul Train, writer, exec producer & creator, 1971-; Soul Train Recs, founder, 1975, creator & exec producer, 1987-2005, Soul Train Comedy Awards, creator, 1993; Films: Roadie, 1980; Tape heads, 1988; Album: The Soul Train Gang; "The 8th Annual Soul Train Christmas Starfest", writer, 2005; Don Cornelius Prod, owner, currently. **Military Serv:** USM, 1954-55. **Business Addr:** Executive Producer, Writer, Soul Train, c/o Don Cornelius Productions Inc, 9255 Sunset Blvd Suite 420, Los Angeles, CA 90069, **Business Phone:** (310)858-8232.

CORNELIUS, ULYSSES S., SR.
Clergy. **Personal:** Born Dec 12, 1913, Waskom, TX; married Willie Hicks; children: Ulysses Sidney Jr. **Educ:** Bishop Col, BA, 1947, MEd, 1952, DD, 1975; Miami Univ; Va Univ. **Career:** Mt Sinai Baptist Church, Dallas, pastor; TX, pastor; LA, pastor; Waskom, TX, instr pub schs; Interracial Baptist Inst, Dallas, instr; Bishop Col, instr. **Orgs:** Vpres, Nat Baptist SS & Baptist Training Union-Cong Inc; pres, BM & E St SS & BTU Cong TX; secy & treas, LK Williams Ministers Inst; Inter dnmntnl Ministerial All Dallas; trustee bd, BM & E Conv TX; bd dir, Interracial Baptist Inst Dallas; 32 Deg Prince Hall Masons; bd trustees, Bishop Col; bd dir, Black C of C, Dallas; bd dir, Tex Fed Garden Clubs. **Honors/Awds:** Alumni Citation Award, Bishop Col, 1968; Cert of Appreciation, Advan Bishop Col, 1969-75; Serv Award, Bethlehem Baptist Church, Bonham, TX, 1971; Serv Award, Mt Sinai Baptist Church, Dallas, 1973; Serv Award, NW Dist Baptist Asn, 1974; Big Boss Leadership Award, YMCA. **Military Serv:** AUS, t/sgt, 1943-46.

CORNELL, BOB
Executive. **Personal:** Born in Jersey City, NJ; son of Frank and Sylvia; children: Patricia, Valerie, Robert, Andrew & David. **Educ:** Arapahoe Community Col, AAS, 1975; Metrop State Col, 1979; Colo Sales Training Inst, cert. **Career:** Colo Sales Training Inst, consult; US Fed Protective Serv, training officer; Littleton Police Dept, police officer; People Skills Inst, pres, chief exec officer & founder, 1978-. **Orgs:** Bd mem, Colo Chap, Inst Mgt Consults. **Honors/Awds:** Colorado Black Leaders Profile, 1990, 2001; E E Van Stee Scholarship, Univ Wis, Bus Mgt Sem; Rocky Mountain & Nat Small Business Supplier of the Year, 1993; President's Award, Motel 6. **Special Achievements:** Certfied MasterStream Instructor, Certified Management Consultant, Certified Professional Development Trainer, Certified Sales Professional, Certified Vocational Instructor, State of Colorado. **Military Serv:** USAF, Vietnam Veteran; recipient, two Air Force Commendation Medals. **Home Addr:** PO Box 101148, Denver, CO 80250-1148, **Home Phone:** (303)756-6771. **Business Addr:** Founder, President & Chief Executive Officer, People Skills Institute, Rocky Mountain MasterStream, 4225 E Mex Ave Apt 508, PO Box 101148, Denver, CO 80250-1148, **Business Phone:** (303)756-6771.

CORNISH, BETTY W.
School administrator. **Personal:** Born Jul 10, 1936, New York City, NY; daughter of John A Williams and Edna Charles Williams; married Edward H (deceased). **Educ:** Boston Univ, BFA, 1958; Univ Hartford, MEd, 1962, MAEd, 1980. **Career:** Hartford Neighborhood Ctrs, youth group leader, 1959-63; Bloomfield Pub Schs, teacher, 1958-68; Cent Conn State Col, asst prof, art ed, 1966-83; Gemini User Group Inc, exec dir, 1983-91, educ consult, 1991-92; St Joseph Col, dir, inter cultural affairs, 1992-01. **Orgs:** Conn Educ Assoc, 1960-74; coord, Afro-Am Studies Prog, 1969-73; pres & exec bd, Conn Art Educ Asn, 1975; Am Asn Univ Profs, 1976-; exec bd, New Eng Art Educ Conf, 1977-79; pres, affirm action comn, Cent Conn State Univ, 1978-80; co-chair, Cent Conn State Univ, Pres Comn Race Rels; Soc Conn Craftsmen, Hartford Reading Is Fundamental Comn; presentations civic sch & adult groups; Afro-Am Studies Prog, CCSC, chmn stud fac comn; Coun Unitarian Soc Hartford; Literacy Vols Am; Conn Col Personnel Asn. **Honors/Awds:** Delta Sigma Theta Scholarship Award, 1954-55; Boston Univ Full-Tuition Scholarship Award, 1954-58; Outstanding Art Education in Connecticut Award, 1979; Black Alumni CCSU Service Award. *

CORNISH, JEANNETTE CARTER
Lawyer. **Personal:** Born Sep 17, 1946, Steelton, PA; daughter of Ellis Pollard and Anna Elizabeth Stannard; married Harry L Cornish, Dec 24, 1970; children: Lee Jason, Geoffrey Charles. **Educ:** Howard Univ, BA, 1968; Howard Univ Law Sch, JD, 1971. **Career:** Off Gen Coun USDA, law clerk 1968-71; Newark-Essex Jt Law Reform Proj, atty, 1971-72; Equal Employment Opportunity Comn, atty, 1972-73; BASF Corp, sr atty, 1974. **Orgs:** Am Bar Asn; Nat Bar Asn; Am Corp Coun Asn; bd mem, Paterson YWCA; bd mem, Lenni-Lenape Girl Scout Coun; trustee, Barnert Hosp, Paterson, NJ. **Business Addr:** Senior Attorney, BASF Corp, 1255 Broard St, Clifton, NJ 07015-6001, **Business Phone:** (973)426-3241.*

CORNISH, MAE GOLDER
Educator. **Personal:** Born Mar 19, 1918, Baltimore, MD; daughter of Enoch and Virginia; married Emile B Cornish (deceased); children: Zenobia C Dupree. **Educ:** Coppin Normal Sch, attended 1938; Morgan State Univ, BS, 1949; New York Univ, MA, 1954. **Career:** Educator (retired); Baltimore City, elem sch teacher, 1938-41, demonstration teacher, 1941-45, pract teacher, 1945-54, elem specialist, 1954-56, asst prin, 1956-61, elem supvr, 1961-64, elem sch prin, 1964-74; Morgan State, State Md, instr, 1954-55. **Orgs:** Educ consult, Charles E Merrill Book Co, 1975-85; bd mem, League for the Handicapped, 1975-85; chairperson, Church Comt Social Concerns, 1976-80; chairperson, Church Family Ministries, 1980-90. **Honors/Awds:** The Point of Excellence Award, Kappa Delta Pi, 1995; Distinguished Alumni Award, Nat Asn Equal Opportunity; Outstanding Teacher, City Coun Baltimore, 1994; Dedicated Service, PTA, 1974; Outstanding Service, Govr Md, 1995; Mayor of Baltimore, Citation for the Quality of Public Service Rendered, 1995; Lifetime Achievement Award, Former Sixth Graders, 1994. **Special Achievements:** The Diary of an Educator, 1992; Like a Rose, Friendship is a Beautiful Thing, 1996. **Home Addr:** 2036 Braddish Ave, Baltimore, MD 21216. *

CORNWALL, DR. SHIRLEY M.
Dentist. **Personal:** Born Dec 8, 1918, Panama City, Panama; married Jerlene; children: Howard, Caral, Cedric, Rupert, Vicount & Francis. **Educ:** BS, 1946; MS, 1947; DDS, 1952; NC Col, Durham, MA. **Career:** Charlotte NC, intern & residency, 1952; DDS, pvt pract, 1955; real estate bus, 1960. **Orgs:** N MS Med Dental Pharm & Nurses Soc; Kappa Alpha Psi Fraternity; St &Francis Cath Church. **Special Achievements:** First black to receive MA from NC Col Durham NC.

CORNWELL, DR. JOANNE
Educator. **Personal:** Born Dec 17, 1948, Detroit, MI; daughter of Joseph and Dora Lee Smith Jenkins; divorced. **Educ:** Univ Calif, Irvine, PhD, French African lit, 1981. **Career:** San Diego St Univ, asst prof, 1984-92, assoc prof, French/AfricanStudies, 1992-; Sisterlocks, founder & owner, 1993-. **Orgs:** African Studies Asn, 1990-; founder & co-dir, African Ctr Cult Literacy &Res, SDSU, 2000; hq dir, African Literature Asn, 2000-; founding mem,African Am Alumni Chap, SDSU, 2001; Am Hairbraiders & Natural Haircare Asn. **Special Achievements:** Author: That Hair Thang, 1997; The Sisterlocks Book, 2002. **Business Addr:** Founder, Owner, Sisterlocks, 5663 Balboa Ave Suite 355, San Diego, CA 92111, **Business Phone:** (619)291-5116.

CORNWELL, W. DON
Executive. **Personal:** Born Jan 17, 1948, Cushing, OK; son of Felton and Lelia; married Saundra Williams; children: Don, Samantha. **Educ:** Occidental Col, AB, 1969; Harvard Univ, MBA, 1971. **Career:** Corp Finance, vpres; Goldman, Sachs & Co, vpres; Hartford Comn Capital Corp, Hartford Nat Corp, mgr, 1970; Goldman Sachs, Invest Banking Div, vpres, 1976-88, Finance Dept, chief exec officer, 1980-88; bd dirs, Avon Prod; bd dirs, CVS Corp; bd dirs, Pfizer Inc; Granite Broadcasting Corp, co foundr, chmn & chief exec officer, 1988-. **Orgs:** Bd trustee, Nat Urban League; bd trustee, Big Brothers Big Sisters NY; Zeta Boule; chmn bd, Telecommun Develop Fund; bd dirs, Hershey Trust; bd dirs, Milton Hershey Sch. **Honors/Awds:** National Merit Achivement Scholar, 1965. **Special Achievements:** Listesd eleventh largest Black-owned co US. **Business Addr:** Chairman and Chief Executive Officer, Granite Broadcasting Corp, 767 3rd Ave 34th Flr, New York, NY 10017.*

CORPREW, CHARLES SUMNER, JR.
Educator. **Personal:** Born Feb 14, 1929, Norfolk, VA; married Bertha Delois Bryant; children: Jovandra Stacey Sanderlin & Charles Sumner III. **Educ:** WVa State Col Inst, AB, 1951; NY Univ, MA, 1963; Kent State Univ; Old Dominion Univ. **Career:** Educator (retired); Norfolk City Sch bd, adv coun vice chmn, 1965, elemprin, 1967-69; Educ Asn Norfolk, pres, 1969-70; Norfolk City Sch, asst prin admin, 1969-71, prin sec 1971-93, personnel coordr, 1993-94; Norfilk teachers asn, chmn. **Orgs:** Keeper recs & seals, Omega Psi Phi Fraternity, 1954-55; Classroom teacher sstate pres, Norfolk City Sch, 1960; eastern reg dir, Nat Coun Urban Educ Asn, Nat Educ Asn, 1964-67; educ com chmn, Chamber Com, Norfolk, 1969; Phi Delta Kappa Educ Fraternity, 1970; pres, Norfolk Teachers Asn, Fed Credit Union, 1978-; music dept chmn, First Baptist Church, Norfolk, 1978-80; trustee, finance comm, First Baptist Church, Norfolk, 1990-; Optimist Club, Norfolk Chap, 1992; Retired Teachers Asn-Dist L; life mem, Nat Ed Asn; life mem, Omega Psi Phi Fraternity. **Honors/Awds:** Outstanding Contribution Field Educ Award, Omega Psi Phi Frat Norfolk, VALambda Omega Chap, 1971; Outstanding Contrib Field Education Award, VA Educ Asn Minority Caucus, 1977; NAACP, Thurgood Marshall Serv Award, partic "In The Trenches" Civil Rights Struggle, 1994. **Military Serv:** AUS, maj, 1951-69; Medal of Honor. **Home Addr:** 1204 Gladiola Cres, Virginia Beach, VA 23453, **Home Phone:** (757)427-3407. **Business Addr:** Chairman, Norfolk Teachers Association, 2539 Corprew Ave, Norfolk, VA 23501, **Business Phone:** (757)627-0845.*

CORPREW, WILBERT E.
Teacher. **Personal:** Married. **Educ:** Va Union Univ, BA, 1964; Crozier Theological Seminary, attended 1965; Rutgers Univ, attended 1972; State Univ NY, Binghamton, MA, 1990. **Career:** J J Newberry, asst mgr, 1965-68; Rutgers Univ, asst registr, 1968-73; State Univ NY, Binghamton, assoc registr, 1974-94; Broome Community Col, registr, 1994-2004; State Univ NY, NY, vpres regist & record mgt; Broome Community College, adj hist prof, currently. **Orgs:** Am Asn Registr & Admis Officers, 1968-; Am Fed Teachers, 1974-; NY United Teachers, 1974-; pres, United Univ Prof, 1974-94; from vice pres to pres, State Univ NY Registrars Asn; vpres, 1992-94, pres elect, 1996-97, pres, 1997-98, Mid States Asn, Col Registrars & Officers Admis; Alpha Phi Alpha Fraternity; vpres prof develop & publ, Am Asn Col Registrars & Admis Officers, 2000-03; bd dir, Boys & Girls Club Western Broome. **Honors/Awds:** Award for Excellence in Professional Services, State Univ NY, Binghamton, 1985. **Business Addr:** Adjunct Faculty, Broome Community College, PO Box 1017, Binghamton, NY 13902, **Business Phone:** (607)778-5000.

CORROTHERS, GARRY JAMES
Lawyer. **Personal:** Born May 4, 1956, Warren, AR; son of Charles and Billie; married Donna, Jul 28, 1984; children: Garry Jr. **Educ:** Univ Cent Ark, BMusEd, 1979, MmusEd, 1981; Univ Ark Little Rock, JD, 1988. **Career:** State Ark, admin hearing officer, 1998-90; Cross, Kearney & McKissic, atty, 1990-91; Corrothers Law Off, atty, 1991-; sole practitioner, currently. **Orgs:** Ark Bar Asn, 1989-; W Harold Flowers Law Soc, 1989-. **Military Serv:** AUS, Capt, 1979-95; SW Asia Service Medal, 1991; Kuwaiti Liberation Medal, 1991; National Defense Service Medal, 1991. **Home Addr:** 9801 Grapevine Dr, Little Rock, AR 72210, **Home Phone:** (501)455-5306. **Business Addr:** Attorney, Corrothers Law Office, 111 Ctr St Suite 1200, Little Rock, AR 72201, **Business Phone:** (501)376-0812.*

CORTADA, DR. RAFAEL LEON
School administrator. **Personal:** Born Feb 12, 1934, New York, NY; son of Rafael and Yvonne; married Selonie Head, Jun 24, 1961; children: Celia, Natalia & Rafael. **Educ:** Fordham Col, AB, 1955, PhD, 1967; Columbia Univ, MA, 1958; Harvard Grad Sch Bus, cert, 1974. **Career:** New Rochelle High Sch, New York, teacher, hist, 1964-66; Univ Dayton,Ohio, asst prof, 1964-66; State Dept, foreign serv off, 1966-69; Federal City Col, Wash DC, Smith Col, Mass; Howard Univ; Medgar Evers Col; Hostos Community Col, New York; Metrop Community Col, Minneapolis, MN, pres, 1974-77; Community Col, Baltimore, 1977-82; El Camino Col, Torrance,Calif, 1982-87; Univ DC, pres, 1987-90; Wayne County Community Col, Detroit, MI, 1987-90; Central Ohio Tech Col, Newark, OH, pres 1994-99; Ohio State Univ, Newark, hist, dean & dir, 1999-2001, assoc proff emer,2001-. **Orgs:** Vpres, Wash Task Force On African Affrs, 1969; Overseas Liaison Comt, 1970; bd gov, Univ Guyana, 1971-; Nat Adv Comm Danforth Found; E Harlem Experimental Col, 1971-75; consult, Media Sys Corp, 1976; adv, KTCA TV Minneapolis, 1976; visitor, Middle States Asn; ed bd "Current Biblio on African Affrs" 1973; Am Coun Educ Comn Minorities Higher Educ, 1982-. **Honors/Awds:** Pub 88 articles & reviews In Caribbean, Afro-Amer, Latin Amer; history publ "Black Studies, An Urban & Comparative Curriculum", 1974. **Military Serv:** AUS, Lt, 1955-57. **Home Addr:** 2912 Constellation Way, Finksburg, MD 21048, **Home Phone:** (410)857-7696. **Business Addr:** Associate Professor Emeritus, Ohio State University, School of Educational Policy & Leadership, Ramseyer Hall Bldg 090 29 W Woodruff Ave, Columbus, OH 43210, **Business Phone:** (614)688-4007.

CORTEZ, JAYNE
Poet, business owner. **Personal:** Born May 10, 1936, Ft Huachuca, AZ; married Melvin Edwards, 1975; children: Denardo Coleman. **Career:** Author: Pissstained Stairs & the Monkey Man's Wares, 1967; Scarifications, 1973; Celebrations & Solitudes, 1974; Mouth on Paper, 1977; Taking The Blues Back Home, 1996; Somewhere In Advance of Nowhere, 1996; Jazz Fan Looks Back, 2002; Borders of Disorderly Time, 2003; The Beautiful Book; Jazz Fan Looks Back; Watts Repertory Co founder; Bola Press, founder, 1972-. **Orgs:** Orgn Women Writers Africa; Pen Am Ctr; Acad Am Poets. **Honors/Awds:** Inter Nat African Festival Award; Langston Hughes Award; American Book Award; Rockefeller Found Grant, 1970; Creative Artists Public Service Poetry Award, New York State Coun Arts, 1973 & 1981; Nat Endowment for the Arts fellowship in Creative Writing, 1979-80, 1986; New York Foundation for the Arts award, 1987; American Book Award, 1980; Arts Inter Nat Award, 1996; Langston Hughes Award, 2001; Thelma McAndless Distinguished Professorship Award. **Business Addr:** Poet, c/o Bola Press, Village Sta, PO Box 96, New York, NY 10014, **Business Phone:** (212)831-7738.

CORTOR, ELDZIER
Artist, printmaker. **Personal:** Born Jan 10, 1916, Richmond, VA; son of John Cortor and Ophelia Twisdale; married Sophia Schmidt, Aug 20, 1951; children: Michael, Mercedes, Stephen & Miriam. **Educ:** Art Inst Chicago, attended 1941; Inst Design, Columbia Univ, attended. **Career:** Rosenwald Fel, 1944-45; Guggenheim Fel, 1949; Ctr D'Art, Port-au-Prince, Haiti, teacher, 1949-51; Kenkeleba Gallery, exhibitor, NY, 1988; Fed Art Proj; Southern Gate, exhibitor, 2002; Studio Mus Harlem, Mus Nat Ctr Afro-American Artist, currently. **Orgs:** Soc Am Graphic Artists; Asn Am Artists; Founding mem, South side Community Art ctr, Chicago; Asn Am Artists. **Honors/Awds:** Carnegie Award; Bertha Aberle Florsheim Award; William H Bartels Award; Am Negro Expos Award. **Special Achievements:** One of the first African-American artists to make Black women his major theme. *

CORYATT, QUENTIN JOHN
Football player. **Personal:** Born Aug 1, 1970, St Croix, Virgin Islands of the United States. **Educ:** Tex A&M Univ. **Career:** Football player (retired); Indianapolis Colts, line back, 1992-98; Dallas cowboy, line back, 1999. *

COSBY, BILL. See COSBY, DR. WILLIAM HENRY.

COSBY, CAMILLE OLIVIA HANKS (CAMILLE HANKS)
Philanthropist, actor, television producer. **Personal:** Born Jan 1, 1945?, Washington, DC; daughter of Guy Hanks and Catherine; married William Henry, Jan 1, 1964; children: Erika, Erinn, Ennis (deceased), Ensa & Evin. **Educ:** Univ Md, psychol; Univ Mass, Amherst, MA, 1980, EdD, educ, 1992. **Career:** Speaker, educator; Plays: "Bill Cosby: Mr Sapolsky, with Love", 1996; Ennis Gift, 2000; Fat Albert, 2004; TV Programmes: "The Cosby Show", actress, 1986; "No Dreams Deferred", 1994; "Having Our Say: The Delany Sisters First 100 Years", actress & producer, 1999; "Sylvia's Path", 2002. **Orgs:** Commencement speaker, Howard Univ, 1987; commencement speaker, Spelman Col, 1989; hon mem, Delta Sigma Theta Sorority. **Honors/Awds:** Candace Award, Nat Coalition 100 Black Women, 1992; Tony Award Nomination, Having Our Say: The Delany Sisters' First 100 Years; hon degree, Spellmen Col, 1989. **Special Achievements:** Camille Olivia Hanks Cosby Academy Center Constructed in Honor; appeared on PBS-TV's MacNeil-Lehrer News Hour.

COSBY, DR. WILLIAM HENRY (BILL COSBY)
Entertainer, comedian, actor. **Personal:** Born Jul 12, 1937, Germantown, PA; son of William Henry Cosby Sr and Anna C; married Camille Hanks, Jan 25, 1964; children: Erika, Erinn, Ennis (deceased), Ensa & Evin. **Educ:** Temple Univ, BA, 1971; Univ MA, MA, EdD, PhD, 1977. **Career:** Comedian, appearing in numerous night clubs; guest appearances on TV shows: "The Electric Co", 1972; "Capt Kangaroo"', "I Spy", 1965-68; "The Bill Cosby Show", 1969, 1972-73; recs: Revenge, To Russell, My Brother, With Whom I Slept, Top Secret, 200 MPH, Why Is There Air?, Wonderfulness, It's True, Bill Cosby Is a Very Funny Fel, Right, I Started Out as a Child, & numerous others; has appeared on several TV commercials; Film: Hickey & Boggs, Man & Boy, 1972, Uptown Saturday Night, 1974, Let's Do It Again, 1975, Mother Jugs & Speed, 1976, Aesop's Fables, A Piece of the Action, 1977, Calif Suite, 1978, Devil & Max Devlin, 1979, Leonard Part VI, 1987, Ghost Dad, 1990; star & producer, The Cosby Show, 1984-92; You Bet Your Life, 1992; The Cosby Mysteries, 1995; Cosby 90, 1996-; Kids Say The Darnedest Things, 1997; NJ Nets, part-owner; Fat Albert, 2004, 500 Years Later, 2005, The Pact, 2006, A Table in Heaven, 2007; TV Movies: "The Oprah Winfrey Show", 1989-2008, "Late Show with David Letterman", 1995-2008, "Larry King Live", 2003-07, "Hey Hey Hey: Behind the Scenes of Fat Albert", 2004, "An Evening of Stars: Tribute to Quincy Jones", 2004, "The Tonight Show with Jay Leno", 2004-07, "Dr. Phil", 2005, "The Harlem Globe trotters: The Team That Changed the World", 2005, "ABC News Nightline", 2005, "The Electric Company's Greatest Hits & Bits", 2006,"Buffy Sainte-Marie: A Multimedia Life", 2006, "Good Morning America", 2007. **Orgs:** Pres, Rhythm & Blues Hall Fame, 1968-; bd dirs & nat chmn, Sickle Cell Found; United Negro Col Fund; life mem, NAACP; Oper PUSH; Omega Psi Phi Fraternity. **Honors/Awds:** Golden Apple Awards, 1966, 1985; Daytime Emmy Awards, 1981, 2002, 2004; Afton bladet TV Prize, 1986-90; BMI Film & TV Awards, 1987-98; Vision Awards, TV's Man of the Year, 1999; Presidential Medal of Freedom, 2002; Emmy, Bob Hope Humanitarian Award, 2003; Ford Freedom Award, 2004; Hollywood Walk of Fame; Eight Grammy Awards; Four Emmy Awards; NAACP Image Award; Mark Twain Award, Am Humor, 2009. **Special Achievements:** Auth: The Wit & the Wisdom of Fat Albert, 1973, Fatherhood, 1986, Time Flies, 1987, Love & Marriage, 1989, Childhood, 1991, Acad of TV, Arts & Scis, Hall of Fame, 1992, Little Bill Books for Beginning Readers, 1997; Friends of a Feather: One of Life's Little Fables, illus by daughter, Erika, 2003; I Am What I Ate And I'm Frightened, 2004; Bill Cosby's Personal Guide to Power Tennis. **Military Serv:** USNR, 1956-61. **Business Addr:** Comedian, Richard De La Font Agency Inc, 4845 S Sheridan Rd, Tulsa, OK 74145, **Business Phone:** (918)665-6200.

COSE, ELLIS
Writer, journalist, columnist. **Personal:** Born Feb 20, 1951, Chicago, IL; married Lee Llambelis; children: Elisa Maria. **Educ:** Univ Ill, Chicago, BA, psychol, 1972; George Washington Univ, MA, sci, technol & pub policy, 1978. **Career:** Chicago Sun-Times, columnist & reporter & ed, 1970-77; Joint Ctr Polit Studies, sr fel & dir energy policy studies, 1977-79; Detroit Free Press, ed, writer & columnist, 1979-81; Nat Acad Sci, res fel, 1981-82; USA Today, spec writer, 1982-83; Inst Journalism Educ, pres, 1983-86; Columbia Univ, Ctr Media Studies, 1987; Gannett Time Mag, contrib ed, essayist, 1989-90; New York Daily News, edit bd chmn, 1991-93; Newsweek Mag, author, contrib & columnist, 1993-; Books: Energy & Equity, Some Social Concerns, 1978; Energy & the Urban Crises, 1978; The Rebirth of Community Power, 1983; The Press, 1988; A Nation of Strangers, 1992; Decentralizing Energy Decisions: The Rage of a Privileged Class, 1993; The Rage of a Privileged Class, 1994; A Man's World, 1995; Color-Blind: Seeing Beyond Race in a Race-Obsessed World, 1997; The Best Defense, 1999; The Envy of the World, 2002; Bone to Pick: On Forgiveness, Reconciliation, Reparation & Revenge, 2004; Beyond Brown v. Board: The Final Battle for Excellence in American Education, 2004. **Orgs:** Nat Asn Black Journalists; Env Adv Comn, Dept Energy, 1978-79; Nat Urban League Energy Proj, 1979-80. **Honors/Awds:** Named Outstanding Young Citizen of Chicago Jaycees, 1977; News Writing Award, United Press Int, 1973; Stick-o-Type Award, Chicago Newspaper, Guild, 1975; Best Polit Reporting, Lincoln Univ Nat Unity Award, 1975, 1977; Fellowship, The Ford Found; Fellowship, Andrew Mellon Found; Fellowship, Rockefeller Foundation Grant; Fellowship, Aspen Inst Humanistic Studies; Myers Center Award, Human Rights N Am; numerous others; Vision Award, Maynard Inst Jour Educ. **Business Addr:** Contributing Editor, Essayist, Newsweek Mag, 251 W 57th St, New York, NY 10019, **Business Phone:** (212)445-4000.

COSHBURN, HENRY S., JR.
Executive. **Personal:** Born Mar 15, 1936, New York, NY; son of Henry and Dorothy; married Veanna G Ferguson; children: Williams S Coshburn. **Educ:** Univ PA, BS, 1957; Columbia Univ, MS, 1964. **Career:** US Army Signal Corps, chem engr, 1958-60; Yardney Elec Corp, sales engr, 1960-63; Mobil Oil, sr engr, 1964-68; Esso Eastern, mkt analyst, 1968-71; Exxon Intl Co, acct exec, 1973-82; First Nat Crude Oil, vpres. **Orgs:** Alpha Phi Alpha, Alpha Chi Sigma, Am Inst Engrs, Am Electrochem Soc, ACS, Am Soc Lub Engrs, Princeton Club; NY Admission Rep Univ PA; visiting prof mkt, Southern Univ Bethune Cookman Col, Wilberforce Univ, Miles Col, Norfolk St Col; instr, ICBO Mkt mem Harlem Hosp Bd; pres, Harlem Civ Imp Coun; vpres Penn & Princeton Club NYC; bd dirs, Univ PA Alumni Asn; patents hardware

greases. **Honors/Awds:** Certificate of Recognition, Am Inst Chem Engr NY Sect, 1970; Certificate of Appreciation, Urban League, 1971-74; Volunteer Service Award, ICBO, 1971-74; Citation, Univ PA, 1974; Alumni Award Merit, Univ PA. *

COSTA, ANNIE BELL HARRIS
Journalist. **Personal:** Born Oct 24, 1943, New Madrid, MO; married Ernest Antone, Mar 4, 1972; children: Kara Ann & Todd Bernard. **Educ:** Mich State Univ, BA, Jour, 1978; Univ Calif, Berkeley & Inst Jour Educ Minority Reporting Prog, 1985; MA, Christian Educ, Union Theol Sem & Presby Sch Christian Educ, Richmond, Va, 2003. **Career:** Mich Dept Corrections, pub info specialist, 1978-80; Mich Employ Security Comn, ed, 1980-85, 1987-91; Lansing State J, staff writer & reporter, 1985-87; Mich Off Community Corrections, pub info officer, 1991; pub rels consult & freelance writer. **Orgs:** Inst Jour Educ Alumni Asn; Detroit Black Writers Guild. **Honors/Awds:** Award of Merit for Spec Publ, Torch Dr United Fund, 1981; Selected for the Univ Calif, Jour Educ Minority Reporting Prog, Berkeley, 1985; hon mention Ninth Annual Paul Lawrence Dunbar Poetry Contest, Detroit Black Writers Guild, 1995; hon mention Thumb Area Writers Conf, Winter Writing Contest, 1995; hon mention External Newslettter, Intl Assn of Bus Communicators, Detroit Chap, 1990; Mich Woman Courage Cert Recognition, Women of Color Health Conf, 1997. **Special Achievements:** Torch Dr United Fund, Award of Merit Spec Publ, 1981; Univ Calif, Berkeley, Summer Prog Minority Journalists, 1985; Intl Assn of Bus Communicators, Detroit chap, External Newsletter, Hon Mention, 1990. **Home Addr:** 3438 Capland Ave, Clermont, FL 34711, **Home Phone:** (352)241-9255.

COSTEN, DR. MELVA WILSON
Theologian. **Personal:** Born May 29, 1933, Due West, SC; daughter of John Theodore Wilson Sr and Azzie Lee Ellis Wilson; children: James Jr, Craig Lamont & Cheryl Costen Clay. **Educ:** Harbison Jr Col, Irmo SC, 1950; Johnson C Smith Univ, Charlotte NC, BA, educ 1952; Univ NC, Chapel Hill, NC, MA, music, 1964; Ga State Univ, Atlanta GA, PhD, curric & instr music, 1978. **Career:** Mecklenburg County Sch, Charlotte NC, elem teacher, 1952-55; Edgecombe Co, Rocky Mount, Nashville, NC, elem teacher, 1956-57; Nash Co, Nashville, NC, elem & music teacher, 1959-65; Atlanta Pub Schs, Atlanta, Ga, itinerant music teacher, 1965-73; Interdenominational Theological Ctr, Dept Music, Atlanta Ga, Helmar Emil Nielsen prof worship & music (retired), 2005; Yale Divinity Sch, vis prof liturgical studies, currently. **Orgs:** Regional dir, Nat Asn Negro Musicians, 1973-75; co-chair, Choral Div, Dist V Ga Music Educr Asn, 1981-82; bd mem, Presby Asn Musicians, 1982-86; chairperson, Presbyn Church Hymnal Comt, 1984-90; bd mem, Liturgical Conf, 1985-91; bd mem, Mid-Atlanta Unit, Cancer Soc Am, 1985-87; chairperson, Presbyterian Hymnal Comt, 1985-90; artistic dir, Atlanta Olympics, 1996-99; Atlanta Univ Ctr Choruses, 1996; Adv Comt, African Am Heritage Hymnal. **Honors/Awds:** Teacher of the Year, Slater Sch, Atlanta Ga, 1973; Teacher of the Year, InterdenomiNat Theological Ctr, 1975; Golden Dove Award, Kappa Omega Chap, Alpha Kappa Alpha Sorority, 1981; conducted 800-voice adult choir, Reuniting Assembly of Presbyterian Church, 1983; Two Doctor of Humane Letters, Erskine Col, Due West SC, 1987; Two Doctor of Humane Letters, Wilson Col, Chambersburg, Pa. **Special Achievements:** Published book African-American Christian Worship, Nashville, Abingdon press, 1993. **Home Addr:** 225 East Ct Dr SW, Atlanta, GA 30331. **Business Addr:** Visiting Professor of Liturgical Studies, Yale Institute of Sacred Music, Yale Divinity School, 409 Prospect St, New Haven, CT 06511, **Business Phone:** (203)432-5180.

COTHORN, JOHN A
Lawyer. **Personal:** Born Dec 12, 1939, Des Moines, IA; son of John L and Marguerite E; married Connie, Aug 6, 1996; children: Jeffrey A & Judith A. **Educ:** Univ Mich, BS, maths, BS, aeronaut engineering, 1961, JD, 1980. **Career:** US Govt, exec Officer, 1966-88; Washtenaw County, MI Prosecutor's Off, asst prosecutor, 1981-83; Kitch, Drutchas, Wagner & Kenney, PC, partner, 1983-93; Meganck & Cothorn, PC, partner, 1994-96; Meganck, Cothorn & Stanczyk PC, managing partner, 1996-98; Cothorn & Stanczyk PC, managing partner, 1998-; Cothorn & Assocs PC, managing partner, 2000-. **Orgs:** NAACP; Am Bar Asn; Nat Bar Asn; State Bar MI; Detroit Bar Asn; Soc Automotive Engrs; Kappa Alpha Psi Fraternity; Phi Alpha Delta Law Fraternity, 1982; contributor, Inst Continuing Legal Educ. **Special Achievements:** Proficient in Korean & French languages. **Military Serv:** AUS, capt, 1961-66. **Business Addr:** Managing Partner, Cothorn & Associates PC, 535 Griswold Suite 1525, Detroit, MI 48226-3602, **Business Phone:** (313)964-7600.

COTMAN, HENRY EARL
Physician. **Personal:** Born Apr 13, 1943, Archer, FL; married Jacqueline Nickson. **Educ:** Fla A&M Univ, BA, 1965; Univ FL; Harvard Peter Bent Brigham Hosp, externships; MD, 1970. **Career:** Union Mem Hosp, med internship, 1970-71; Univ Minn, resident, 1971-74; Univ Ariz Health Div Sci Ctr Div Radiation Oncol, asst prof, 1975-77; Women Beaumont Army Hosp Med Ctr Div Radiation Oncol, chief, 1975; Mich State Univ, asso clin prof; Bayfront Med Ctr, Radiation Oncologist, 2004; Gulf Coast Oncol Ctr, pvt prac, currently; Union Memorial Hosp, Vet Affairs Med Ctr, Fairview-Univ Med Ctr, resident. **Orgs:** Am Col Radiol; Am Soc Therapeut Radiol; Nat Med Asn; Ingham Co Med Soc; Alpha Phi Alpha Frat Inc; clin fel Am Cancer Soc, 1971-74; cheif resident, Radiation Oncology 1974. **Honors/Awds:** "The Usage The Bipedal Lymphogram As A Guide During Laparotomy in Hodgkin's & Non-Hodgkin's Lymphomas" ACTA Radiol; "Combination Radiotherapy & Surger in the Mgmt of Squamous Carcinoma of the Head & Neck" Radiology Soc meeting 1976. **Special Achievements:** first Black graduates College of Medicine, 1970. **Military Serv:** Med Corp maj, 1975. **Business Addr:** Physician, Gulfcoast Oncology Center, 701 6th St S, PO Box 383, St Petersburg, FL 33731, **Business Phone:** (727)893-6103.*

COTMAN, DR. IVAN LOUIS
State government official. **Personal:** Born Apr 4, 1940, Detroit, MI; son of Louis Richard and Marguerite Kaine; married Jeanetta Hawkins; children: Ivan Louis Jr, Arthur Robert & Amir Charles. **Educ:** Ky State Univ, BA Engl, Soc Sci 1962; Atlanta Univ, MA Social Work 1964;Univ Mich, Sch Pub Health Med Care Orgn, 1970; Univ Manchester (England),Cert New Town Planning, 1972; Wayne State Univ, Ed.D Curriculum & Admin1975; Univ Okla, Advan Studies, 1983; Harvard Univ JFK Sch Govt. **Career:** Detroit Bd Educ, sch social worker, 1964-69; United Co Serv Detroit, agcyprog consul/assist budget dir, 1969-72; Detroit Bd Educ, electee, 1971-73;New Detroit Inc, dir employ, 1972-73; Mich Dept Ed Disability Deter Serv, area admin, 1973-79; Mich Dept Educ, assoc supt, 1979-, intern, regtlobbyist, 1989-, direct servs, dep supt, 1992-97; Davenport Univ, dir,1992-97; Cotman & Assocs, chief exec officer, 1997-. **Orgs:** Bd, Mountain Retreat & Learning Ctr, 1999-2002; bd, Davenport Ed Found,2000-; Acad Certif Social Workers; Nat Assoc Disability Exams; Nat Asn Social Workers; Nat Rehab Asn; Mich Civil Serv Oral Appraisal Bd; Mich Occup Info Statutory Comm; past nat vpres, Alpha Phi Alpha Frat Inc; past bd mem, United Neighborhood Ctr Am; NAACP; adj prof, Mich State Univ;State Credit Union Supvr Comt; Past bd Govs, Univ Chicago,Meadville/Lombard Theol Sch. **Honors/Awds:** Resolution of Tribute MI Senate, 1973; Distinguished Alumni, KY State Univ, 1975; Dist Citizen MI House of Rep, 1977-80; Regional Commissioner's Citation Social Sec Administration, 1979; Order of KY Colonels; board of directors, United Community Service, 32 Degree Prince Hall Mason; Disting Alumni Awd KY State Univ, Nat Asn for Equal Oppor in Higher Educ; citedfor Leadership by US Sec of Educ; 6 week exec placement in Washington based Commn on Excellence, US Dept of Education; articles on Leadership published in MI Sch Bd Journal, Waterloo (Ontario) Press, Detroit News,Michigan Chronicle, Congressional Record; Board of Governors, Meadville Lombard Theology School (Univ of Chicago); Resolution of Merit, MI House,1989; Israel Study Mission, 1994; Davenport University Education Foundation, 2000; US Taxpayers Advocacy Panel, 2002-. **Business Addr:** Chief Executive Officer, Cotman & Associates, 4605 Cass Ave, Detroit, MI 48201, **Business Phone:** (313)833-1181.

COTTLE, CHRISTOPHER
Educator. **Career:** Essex Co Col, Clara E Dasher Ctr, asst dean stud life & activ, currently. **Honors/Awds:** Joseph H Benedict Outstanding Service Award, 2003.

COTTON, GARNER
Civil engineer. **Personal:** Born Nov 10, 1923, Chicago, IL; son of Deleon (deceased) and Pearl Little; children: Garner T, Atry S. **Educ:** Lincoln Univ, BS, bldg eng, 1943; Drexel Univ, civil eng, 1951; Edison Tech Sch, basic electronics, 1960; Temple Univ, naval archit & metall, 1961. **Career:** Gen Indust Eng, struct designer & checker, 1947-54; City Philadelphia, Water Dept, struct designer & checker, 1954-56; United Eng & Construct Co, 1956-58; Frederick Massiah Concrete Contractor, asst construct supt, 1958-59; Boeing Aircraft Co, facil & struct engr, 1959-60; United Engrs & Construct Co, 1960-62; NY Shipbuilding Corp, Sci Group, struct engr, 1962-65; Allstate Engr & Develop Co, struct engr, 1965-67; Sch Dist Philadelphia, staff construct engr & struct designer, 1967-88; G Cotton Eng Assocs Inc, founder & partner, 1976-. **Orgs:** Am Soc Civil Engrs; Nat Soc Prof Engrs; Asn Sch Adminrs; Am Arbit Asn; Lincoln Univ Found. **Honors/Awds:** Citizen Award of the Year, NJ Soc Prof Engrs, 1977; Citizen Award, Lawnside Democratic Club, 1970; Registered Prof Civil Engr NJ; Registered Prof Planner NJ; Fel, Am Soc Civil Engrs; Prof Civil Engr; DHL, Lincoln Univ, 1997; Distinguished Engr, Am Soc Civil Engrs, 2000; Specialty Award, Drexel Univ Evening Col Alumni Asn, 2000. **Home Addr:** 505 N Warwick Rd, Lawnside, NJ 08045. *

COTTON, JAMES (JAMES WESLEY COTTON)
Basketball player. **Personal:** Born Dec 14, 1975, Los Angeles, CA. **Educ:** Calif State Univ. **Career:** Player (retired); Long Beach State, shooting guard; Denver Nuggets, 1997; Seattle Super Sonics, guard, 1997-99; Chicago Bulls, 1999; West Sydney Razorbacks, ANBL. *

COTTON, JAMES WESLEY. See COTTON, JAMES.

COTTON, JOSEPH CRAIG
Executive, administrator. **Personal:** Born Nov 3, 1954, Greensboro, NC; son of Harold C and Mary B. **Educ:** NC A&T State Univ, BA, 1980; Temple Univ, MEd, 1994. **Career:** Md Eastern Shore, sports info dir, 1981-88; Temple Univ, assoc sports info dir, 1988-92; Delaware State Univ, sports info dir, 1992-97, pub rels dir, 1997; Olympic Festival, St Louis, MO, press officer, 1993; Pan America Games, US media rep, 1994; Summer Olympics, press operations mgr, 1996; Norfolk State Univ, assoc athletics dir external affairs, 2001-, Athletics Found, asst to exec dir, currently. **Orgs:** Col Sports Info Dirs Asn, 1981-; Kappa Alpha Psi Fraternity, 1985-; Nat Asn Black Journalist; Pub Rels Soc Am, 1998-. **Home Addr:** 804 Woodcrest Dr, Dover, DE 19904, **Home Phone:** (302)677-0218. **Business Addr:** Associate Athletics Director, Assistant to Executive Director, Athletics Foundation, Norfolk State University, 331 Harrison B Wilson Hall 700 Pk Ave, Norfolk, VA 23504, **Business Phone:** (757)823-2667.

COTTON, THOMASENIA
Executive. **Educ:** NC Cent Univ, BA, sociol; Univ Utah, MS. **Career:** IBM Community Exec Prog, Tarrytown, NY; Philadelphia Employ Develop Corp, supvr; Opportunities Industrialization Centers Am, proj officer, supvr, chief protocol & mgr, field specialist, dir off field serv coordn, pres & chief operating officer, 2003-. **Orgs:** Prog dir, YWCA, SW Belmont. **Military Serv:** AUS, civilian employee. **Business Addr:** President, COO, OIC of America Inc, 1444 N Broad St, Philadelphia, PA 19122.*

COTTRELL, COMER J.
Executive. **Personal:** Born Dec 7, 1931, Mobile, AL; married Felisha Starks; children: Renee, Comer III, Aaron. **Educ:** Univ Detroit, 1952. **Career:** Sears Roebuck, sales mgr, 1964-69; African Heritage Network, partner; Texas Rangers, 1989; Bishop Col Dallas, 1990; Universal Packaging Co, co-owner; Pro-Line Hair Prods, founder, pres, chief exec officer, 1970-. **Orgs:** bd dir, Dir Republic Bank; Sw Dallas Hosp Corp; Western Pacific Indust; Dallas Financial Corp; Pro-Ball Inc; Sigma Pi Phi Boule; partner, Texas Rangers Baseball Inc. **Honors/Awds:** Bishop col, Doctor Laws; Northwood univ, Doctor Laws; City univ Los Angeles, Doctor Laws. **Military Serv:** USAF. **Business Addr:** Founder, Pro-Line International Consumer Relations, 2121 Panoramic Cir, Dallas, TX 75212, **Business Phone:** (866)730-9101.*

COTTROL, ROBERT JAMES
Educator. **Personal:** Born Jan 18, 1949, New York, NY; son of Robert W and Jewel Gassaway; married Susan Lemmerbrock, Jun 20, 1987; children: John Marshall II. **Educ:** Yale Univ, BA, 1971, AM, hist, 1973, PhD, american studies, 1978; Georgetown Univ Law Ctr, JD, 1984. **Career:** Conn Col, instr, 1974-77; Emory Univ, asst prof, 1977-79; Georgetown Univ, lectr, 1979-84; Boston Col Law Sch, from asst prof to assoc prof law, 1984-90; Rutgers Sch Law, Camden, NJ, assoc prof, 1990; George Wash Univ Law Sch, prof law, hist & Sociol, 1995-, Harold Paul Green res prof law, currently. **Orgs:** Consult, GA Commn Humanities 1978-79; Am Hist Assn, 1974-, Am Soc Legal Hist, 1982-, Am Bar Assn, 1985-; Law & Soc Assn, 1985-. **Honors/Awds:** Outstanding Academic Book, Choice, 1983. **Special Achievements:** Author: The Afro Yankees, Providence's Black Community in the Antebellum Era publ by Greenwood Press 1982; Numerous publications. **Military Serv:** AUS, (Reserve) capt, 1971-81; USAFR, capt, 1981-87, major, 1987-; Air Force Commendation Medal, Joint Service Commendation Medal. **Business Addr:** Professor, George Washington University Law School, 2000 H St NW, Washington, DC 20052, **Business Phone:** (202)994-5023.

COUCH, JAMES W
Executive, executive director. **Personal:** Born Oct 15, 1934, Ingram Branch, WV; son of Richard Couch and Daisy Hall; married Eileen, Aug 22, 1981; children: Kevin Turney, Jamir & Sasha. **Educ:** State Univ New York, Stoneybrook, MA. **Career:** Florence High Sch Dept, chair, teacher social studies, 1963-69; Patterson Task Force, exec dir, 1969-70; Nassau Economic Opportunity Comn, exec dir, 1970-74; Long Island Sickle Cell Corp, exec dir, 1974-88; Suffolk County, asst dep exec, 1988-92; Ga Dept Community Health, dep comnr, chief, Health Improvement Prog, currently. **Orgs:** Suffolk County Caucus Black Democrats, chmn, 1974-92; Black Health Advocates Network, chmn, 1978-88; Suffolk County Gov, founder/organizer, 1988-92; Vision 2020, mem, 1992-; The Atlanta Project, 1992-;NACHC, chmn bd, 1996-97; chmn legislative comn, 1997-; GAPHC, pres-elect, 1998-99. **Honors/Awds:** Rev MLK Jr Holiday Commission, Humanitarian Award, 1989; People of Colour, Achievement Award, 1994; State of Georgia, Comm Svc Award, 1996; NACHC, Chmn Achievement Award, 1997; Quality of Life Health Svcs, CHC Programs Award, 1997. **Special Achievements:** Publ, Atlanta Bus Chronicle, 1995; CNN Talk Back Live, 1995, 1996; gave keynote addresss in Montgomery, AL, 1996; appeared before Congressional Black Caucus, 1997; keynote address at Martin Luther King Jr Anniversary, 1997. **Military Serv:** Air Force, airman first class, 1953-57. **Business Addr:** Chief, Health Improvement Programs, Georgia Department of Community Health, 2 Peachtree St NW, Atlanta, GA 30303, **Business Phone:** (404)463-4078.

COULON, BURNEL ELTON
Educator. **Personal:** Born Jul 6, 1929, New Orleans, LA; married Sylvia; children: Michele, Angela, Burnel II & Sylvia II. **Educ:** Tuskegee Inst, BS, 1953; NC A&T State Univ, MS, 1960. **Career:**

Educator (Retired); MS Valley State Univ, dir pub rels, 1953-60; Louisville Pub Schs, instr graphic arts, 1961-64; Shortridge Press & Indianapolis Pub Schs, instr & mgr, 1964-76; Paramount Graphics, pres, 1970; chmn indust arts 1976-79; Indianapolis Pub Schs, dean stud. **Orgs:** Vpres, Iota Omicron; bd dirs, MS State Negro Fair, 1957-59; secy, Marion Co Graphic Arts Asn,1968-70; pres, Indianapolis Fedn Teachers, 1973-76; secy, Indianapolis Chap Phi Delta Kappa, 1978-79; vpres grand basileus, Omega Psi Phi Fraternity, 1978-79; grand basileus, Omega Psi Phi Fraternity, 1979-82; Grand Marshal, Omega's Nat Conv, 2000; bd dir, Omega Life Mem Found, 2001-04. **Honors/Awds:** Outstanding Graduate Alumnus, NC A&T, 1975; Certificate of Merit, Mayor New Orleans, 1980. **Special Achievements:** Omega Man of the year, 10th Dist Omega Psi Phi Fraternity, 1976.

COULTER, PHYLLIS A
Association executive. **Personal:** Born May 5, 1962, Newark, NJ; daughter of Arthur and Maxine; married Craig, May 27, 1989. **Educ:** Purdue Univ, BS, acct, 1984; Univ Minn, MBA, 1990. **Career:** Pillsbury Co, supvr, 1984-86; Am Express Financial Advisors, mgr, 1986-93; St Davids Sch, controller, 1993-96; Metro Detroit Conv & Visitors Bur, finance & admin, vpres, 1996-, dir. **Orgs:** Alpha Kappa Alpha Sorority; Black MBA Asn; consult, Jr Achievement; Int Asn Convention & Visitor Bureaus. **Business Addr:** Direcotr, Metropolitan Detroit Convention & Visitors Bureau, 211 W Fort St Suite 1000, Detroit, MI 48226, **Business Phone:** (313)202-1800.

COUNTEE, THOMAS HILAIRE
Lawyer, executive, consultant. **Personal:** Born Aug 7, 1939, Washington, DC; son of Thomas H Countee Sr and Arrieanna C T Countee; divorced; children: Mekela I J. **Educ:** Amer Univ, Wash, DC, BA, 1963; Georgetown Univ, Law Ctr, JD, 1967; Harvard Bus Sch, MBA, 1971. **Career:** Attorny (retired), executive, consultant; Securities & Exchange Commn, Wash, DC, atty, 1969; Roxbury Small Bus Develop Ctr, Boston, consult, 1970; Poloroid Corp, Cambridge MA, asst general counsel, 1971; MODEDCO Inv Co, pres, 1971-75; Fed City Coll, prof, 1973; Howard Univ, Wash, DC, prof, 1973; Off of Mat & Budget, legislative counsel; exec offce of pres, 1975-76; Nat Capital Park & Planning Comn, gen counsel, 1977-78; Countee, Countee & Assoc, Inc, chmn, ceo, 1988-. **Orgs:** DC Bar Asn; Harvard Bus Sch, 1971; bd dir, New Life, Inc 1972-; alumni recruiter, Phillip's Acad, 1979; Nat Coun Therapeutic Riding, 1980-; Kappa Alpha Psi. **Honors/Awds:** Harvard Univ Scholarship, 1956-58; Harvard Business School Fellowship,1969-71; Georgetown Law School, Lawyers Co-op Publishing Co Prizes; Published History of Black-Owned & Operated Finance Institutes, 1968; State of Maryland Disabled Person of the Year, 1980.

COUNTS, ALLEN W
Executive, chairperson. **Educ:** Howard Univ, BS, JD; Wharton Sch, Univ Pa, MBA. **Career:** Lic atty; Citibank World Corp, head shipping group, 1973-80; Pryor, McClendon, Counts & Co, cofounder & pres; Citibank NA, vpres; Doley Securities, chmn, currently. **Orgs:** Gen Securities Prin, Financial & Oper Prin, Regist Rep, NASD. **Business Phone:** (504)561-1128.

COUNTS, DR. GEORGE W.
Physician, educator. **Personal:** Born Jun 14, 1935, Idabel, OK; children: George IV, David & Philip. **Educ:** Univ Okla, BS, 1957, MS, 1960; Ohio State Univ, MD, 1965. **Career:** Educator (retired), physician; Leopold Schepp Found Scholar, 1961-65; Ohio State Univ Hosp, internal residence, 1965-68; Univ Wash, fel, Infectious Diseases, 1968-70, from assoc prof to prof, 1975-89; Univ Miami, asst prof med, 1970-75; Univ Miami Sch Med, asst prof pathol, 1972-75; Jackson Mem Hosp, dir clin microbiol secy, 1972-75, dir infection control dept, 1972-75; Harbor view Med Ctr, chief div infectious diseases, 1975-84; CRMB, Div AIDS, chief, 1989-94; NIH, assoc dir Clin Res Activities, Div Microbiol & Infectious Disease, dir, Off Res Minority & Women's Health, Nat Inst Allergy & Infectious Diseases, 1994-04; Pub Health Seattle & King County, bd mem, currently. **Orgs:** Nat Med Fel, 1961-65; Soc Hosp Epidemiol Am; Am Fed Clin Res; fel, Am Col Physicians, 1971; fel, Infectious Diseases Soc Am, 1974; Bd dir, Asn Practitioners Infection Control, 1977-85; fel, Am Acad Microbiol, 1996. **Honors/Awds:** Leinfelder Award, Univ Iowa, 1965; diplomate Am Bd Internal Med, 1970; Alpha Omega Alpha, 1965; Service Award, 1992; Distinguished Service Award, Am Soc Microbiol, 2006. **Special Achievements:** Co-authored an article on "Provision of treatment in HIV-1 vaccine trials in developing countries", 2003; Co-authored ten other articles. **Business Addr:** Board Member, Public Health Seattle & King County, 401 5th Ave Suite 1300, Seattle, WA 98104, **Business Phone:** (206)296-4600.*

COURSEY, DR. LEON N
Educator. **Educ:** Queens Col, BS, MS; Ohio State Univ, PhD. **Career:** Univ Md Eastern Shore, Dept Phys Educ, asst prof, assoc prof, prof & actg chmn & phys educr fac, currently. **Business Addr:** Physical Educator Faculty, Professor & Acting Chair, University of Maryland Eastern Shore, Department of Physical Education, 1 Backbone Rd Tawes Gym & Pool 108, Princess Anne, MD 21853-1299, **Business Phone:** (410)651-6494.

COURTNEY, DR. CASSANDRA HILL
School administrator, educator. **Personal:** Born Feb 8, 1949, Newport News, VA; daughter of Marion Alton and Mary S; married Vernon Stanley, Sep 28, 1974; children: Aliya Diane. **Educ:** Wilson Col, AB, 1971; Pa State Univ, MS, 1974, PhD, psychol, 1980. **Career:** Middlesex Co Sch Bd Saluda Va, dir fed projects, 1974-76; Pa St Univ, acad counr, 1979-81; Wilberforce Univ, social sci div chmn & asst prof psychol, 1982-83, vpres acad affairs, 1983-88, exec asst pres, 1989-91, vpres adult & continuing educ, 1991-94; Fund Improvement Post sec Educ, staff, 1994-, US Dept Educ, prog officer, dep dir, coordr & officer comprehensive prog. **Orgs:** Acad Dean's Task Force Coun Independent Cols, 1983-85; Adv Communtiy Campus Trends, Am Coun Educ, 1985-91; Am Educ Res Asn; Phi Delta Kappa; Am Asn Higher Educ; Cooperative Educ Asn; Nat Asn Women Educ; Alpha Kappa Alpha; Reston, Va Chap Links; Am Asn Univ Women; Accreditation Review CounN Cent Asn. **Business Addr:** Coordinator, Higher Education of the Disaster Releif, FIPSE-Fund for the Improvement of Postsecondary Education, 1990 K St 6th Fl, Washington, DC 20006-8544, **Business Phone:** (202)502-7506.

COUSIN, ERTHARIN
Executive, vice president (organization). **Personal:** Born May 12, 1957, Chicago, IL; daughter of Julius and Annie; divorced; children: Maurice. **Educ:** Univ IL, Chicago, BA, 1979; Univ GA, JD, 1982. **Career:** AT&T; Chicago Ethics Bd; Ill Atty Gen off; Dem Nat Comt; US Dept of State, white house liaison; Albertson's Inc, sr vpres pub affairs; Am Second Harvest, exec vpres & chief operating officer, currently. *

COUSIN, REV. PHILIP R
Clergy. **Personal:** Born Mar 26, 1933, Pittston, PA; married Joan; children: Philip Jr, Steven, David, Michael & Joseph. **Educ:** Cent State Univ; BA; Boston Univ, Master deg, divinity; ThM; Colgate Rochester Divin Sch, PhD, Ministry. **Career:** Pastored churches NC/VA/FL; Kittrell Coll, pres, 1960-65; AME Church, bishop, AL; Edward Waters Col, pres; African Methodist Episcopal Church, bishop 11th episcopal dist, bishop, 4th episcopal dist, sr bishop, currently; Philip R Cousin African Methodist Episcopal Church, owner & pastor. **Orgs:** Pres, bd govs, Nat Coun Churches Christ; chmn bd, Edward Waters Col; nat bd, SCLC; trustee Lincoln Hosp, Durham, 1966-72; chmn, Polit Comm Durham Comm Affairs Black People, 1966-; chmn, Human Rels Comn, Durham, 1968-69; chmn, NC Voter Educ Proj, 1968-; Durham County Bd Soc Serv, 1970-; trustee, Fayetteville State Univ, 1972-; Durham County Bd Educ, 1972-. **Honors/Awds:** Kellogg fel, 1965; Martin Luther King Fel Black Ch Studies, 1972; conducted Days Dialogue Ger AUS Europ, 1973; 1985 Honoree The Relig Award achievements; Leadership bishop, pres, Nat Coun churches, AME Church. **Military Serv:** AUS, second Lt, 1953. **Business Addr:** Paster, Philip R Cousin African Methodist Episcopal Church, 110 S Wash St, Naperville, IL 60540, **Business Phone:** (630)742-1102.

COUSINS, ALTHEA L.
Educator. **Personal:** Born Nov 5, 1932, New York, NY; married Carl M; children: Kimberly & Karen. **Educ:** Fisk Univ, BA, 1953; Columbia Univ, MA, 1955; Temple Univ, MA, 1957;Walden Univ, doctoral prog, 1976. **Career:** Barratt Jr High Sch, teacher, 1953-54; Sartain Elem Sch, teacher, 1954-57, coun teacher, 1957-66; Friends Neighborhood Day Camp, supvr, 1958 -59;Gideon Summer Sch, teacher, 1960; Wagner Jr High Sch, asst prin, 1966-67;Miller Sch, outreach counr, 1966, head start coun summer, 1966, elem sch prin, admin asst dist supt, 1967-70; Compers Elem Sch, prin, 1970-71 & 1972-73; Sch Dist Philadelphia, Div Pupil Personnel & Coun, dir. **Orgs:** Exec bd, Ithan Elem Sch, 1969-71; Golden Circle Women 32 degree Masons,1975; Nat Asn Pupil Personnel Adminr; Nat Educ Asn; Am Personnel & Guidance Asn; Am Sch Counselors Asn; Pa Sch Counselors Asn; Nat Asn Col Admiss Counselors; Philadelphia Asn Sch Adminr; Women Educ; bd dir, MainLine Day Care Ctr; Rotary Ann's Group; Mt Hebron Friends & Neighbors Comn Group; Women's Aux; Am Vet Med Asn; Links Inc; Delta Sigma Theta Sor; Zion Baptist Church; Women's Aux; Alpha Phi Alpha Fraternity; League Women Voters. **Honors/Awds:** Recognition Award, Philadelphia Sch Adminr Asn; Chapel of the Four Chaplins Award; Philadelphia Home & School & Council Award; Dist Two Superintendent Recognition Award. *

COUSINS, FRANK, JR.
Law enforcement officer. **Educ:** MS, criminal justice. **Career:** Newburyport City coun; MA State Legis, state rep, 1993-96; Essex Co, sheriff, 1996-. **Honors/Awds:** Fleming Fellowship Award, 1995. **Special Achievements:** First elected African American sheriff in Massachusetts. **Business Addr:** Sheriff, Essex Co, Correctional Facility & Sheriff's Headquarters, 20 Manning Ave, PO Box 807, Middleton, MA 01949-2807, **Business Phone:** (978)750-1900.*

COUSINS, WILLIAM
Government official, lawyer. **Personal:** Born Oct 6, 1927, Swiftown, MS; son of William and Drusilla Harris; married Hiroko Ogawa, May 12, 1953 (died 2005); children: Cheryl, Noel, Yul & Gail. **Educ:** Univ Ill, BA, polit sci, 1948; Harvard Univ, LLB, 1951. **Career:** Lawyer (retired), government official; Chicago Title & Trust Co, atty, 1953-57; Cook Co, asst state's atty, 1957-61; Turner, Cousins, Gavin &Watt firm, pvt pract law, 1961-76; 8th Ward Chicago, alderman 1967-76; DePaul Law Sch, lectr, 1981-84; Circuit Ct Cook Co, judge, 1976-92; Ill Appellate Ct, justice, 1992-2002. **Orgs:** Asst moderator, United Church Christ 1981; US Dist, Fed Ct Appeals & US Supreme Ct; exec comt, IL Supreme Ct; Ill Judicial Conf, 1984-2002; Am Bar Asn; Chicago Bar Asn; Ill Bar Asn; Nat Bar Asn; Cook Co Bar Asn; Delta Sigma Rho; Kappa Alpha Psi; Sigma Pi Phi; bd mem & chair, Nat Ctr State Courts, 1996-2002; Judicial Coun, Nat Bar Asn, 1995-96; bd mem, Judicial Coun NBA, 1997-2002; former trustee, Lincoln Memorial United Church Christ; former pres, Chatham Avalon Pk Comm Coun; former vpres, Independent Voters IL; former bd mem, PUSH; former bd mem, Chicago Chap, Nat Asn Advan Colored People; former bd mem, Planned Parenthood Asn; Parkway Comm House; Am Dem Action; chmn, Ill Judicial Coun, 1987-88; chmn, Ill Judicial Conf, 1989-90. **Honors/Awds:** Edward N Wright Award, Cook Co Bar Asn, 1968; William R Ming Jr Civil Rights Award, 1974; Kenneth E Wilson Award, Ill Judicial Coun, 1992; Nat Bar Asn Hall of Fame, 1994; Outstanding Judge of Year Award, John Marshall Chap Black Law Students Am, 1980; del, Dem Natl Conv, 1972; Outstanding Layman of Year, Lincoln Mem Church, 1958; Thur good Marshall Award, IIT Chicago-Kent, 1985; Outstanding Jurist Award, John Marshall Law Sch, 1989; Hall of Fame, Cook Co Bar Asn, 1997; Earl B Dickerson Award, Chicago Bar Assn, 1998; Raymond Pace Alexander Award, Judicial Coun, Nat Bar Asn,1999; Mary Herrick Lifetime Achievement Award; C Francis Stratford Award, Cook Co State's Atty, 2001; Access to Justice Award, Ill State Bar Asn, 2002. **Special Achievements:** Author, A Judges View of Judicial Selection Plans, Ill Bar Jour, 1987. **Military Serv:** AUS, lt, 1951-53; JAG, army reservist, lt col, 1975. **Home Addr:** 1745 E 83 Pl, Chicago, IL 60617.

COVIN, DR. DAVID L.
Educator. **Personal:** Born Oct 3, 1940, Chicago, IL; son of David and Lela Jane Clements; married Judy Bentinck Smith; children: Wendy & Holly. **Educ:** Univ Ill, BA, 1962; Colo Univ, MA, 1966; Wash State Univ, PhD, 1970. **Career:** Calif State Univ, Sacramento, Govt & Ethnic Studies, asst prof, 1970-74, assoc dean gen studies, 1972-74, from assoc prof govt & ethnic studies to prof govt & ethnic studies, 1975-2005; Union Grad Sch, adj prof, 1979-; Pan African Studies, Ethnic Studies Dept, dir, prof, 1990-2004, emer prof govt & pan African studies, currently; Sate CA, consult, 1979; Race & Dem Am, founding proj, co-dir, 1998-2005. **Orgs:** Sacramento Citizens Comn Police Practices, 1972-73; contrib ed, Rumble,1973-80; comnr, CA Educ Eval & Mgt Comn, 1977-81; Cong Black Caucus Criminal Justice Brain Trust, 1977-90; vice-chmn, Sacramento Area Black Caucus, 1978-83; consult, Sacramento City United Sch Dist, 1980; pres, Party for the New Black Polit, 1980-81; The Natl Fac, 1988-; Calif Co-convener, NBIPP, 1980-81; actg chair, Natl Ed Rev Brd, NBIPP, 1982-84; co-chair, Sacramento local organizing Comt NBIPP, 1981-85; Sacramento Chap, Nat Rainbow Coalition Org Comt; deleg, Natl Party Cong, Natl Black Independent Polit Party, Natl Party Cong, 1981; pres, World Peace Assn, 1985-86; educ co-chair, Black Community Activist Comt, 1985-86; act chair, Save Our Children Task Force Against Drugs & Gangs, 1987-88; act chair, Black Sci Resource Ctr, 1987-2005; exec brd, Women's Civic Improvement Club, 1987; Sacramento City Police Dept Task Force Black Youth Gangs & Drugs, 1987-92; steering comt, Cooper-Woodson Col, 1988-; chair, SABC, 1988-90, 1995-96; participant, The Am Assembly, 1990; ed, SABC Newsletter, 1990-96, chair, SABC Polit Comt, 1997-2006; co-chair, Man March Comt, Sacramento, 1995-96; Calif State Supt Educ African Am Adv Comt, 1998-2000; Ed Brd, 1999-2005, exec coun, 2001, pres, 2003-05, organizer, Natl Conf Black Polit Scientists; Sacramento Cong African Peoples, 2002-; Natl Black Conv Planning Comt, Natl Black Conv, 2004; second vpres, WCIC, 2005-; founder, The Black Group, 2005; mem, Sacramento Black Parallel School Board Exec Coun, 2006-. **Honors/Awds:** Community Service Award, Sacramento Area Black Caucus, 1976; grant, CA Coun Humanities Pub Policy, 1977; Sacramento Community Service Award, Sacramento Kwanzaa Community, 1978; Man of the Year, Omega Psi Phi, 1982; Community Serv Award, All African People, 1986; Meritorious Performance Award, Calif State Univ, 1988; John C Livingston distinguished faculty lect, Calif State Univ, 1992; The Black Scholar; Am Philos Soc Grant,1992; NSF Grant, 1993, 1999; Howard Bremen Community Service Award, Sacramento Black United Fund, 1999; Cooper Woodson Col Medal, 1999; Ford Found Grant, 2000, 2003; Dr David Covin Community Libr, 2003; Sacramento Observer Medallion, 2003; Community Service Award, Col Social Sci &Interdisciplinary Studies, 2004; Peace Education Award, Ctr African Peace& Conflict Resolution, 2005; NCOBPS Presidential Award, 2002, 2006, Women of Color Diversity Award, 2008; Life Time Contributions Award, Cooper-Woodson College, 2009. **Special Achievements:** Publications in The Western Jour Black Studies; Ethnic Studies Jour; The Jour Third World Studies; Nat Polit Sci Rev; The Black Lit Forum; Chap Dilemmas Black Polit, Impuruzu; novel, Brown Sky, 1987; monographs: The Unified Black Movement in Brazil, 1978-2002, Mc Farland Press, 2006; Black Politics After the Civil Rights Movement, McFarland Press, 2009; articles in the Black Scholar, 2001, 2004, 2009; articles in SOULS; Short Story, The Walk, 1988; Short Story, Home for the Holidays, in Drum Voices, 2004; Article, "Towards A Pan African Vision of the Caribbean," 1988; "Afrocentricity in O Movimento Negro Unificado," The Journal of Black Studies, 1990. **Business Addr:**

Emeritus Professor, Pan African Studies, Ethnic Studies Department, 6000 J St, Sacramento, CA 95819-6013, **Business Phone:** (916)278-5363.

COVINGTON, DR. H. DOUGLAS
College president. **Personal:** Born Mar 7, 1935, Winston-Salem, NC; son of Henry and Fannie; married Beatrice Mitchell, Jun 14, 1958; children: Anthony Douglas & Jeffrey Steven. **Educ:** Cent State Univ, BS, 1957; Ohio State Univ, MA, 1958, PhD, 1966. **Career:** Col President (retired); Montclair NJ Pub Schs, dep supt schs, 1972-74; Tuskegee Univ, vpres develop affairs, 1974-77; Winston-Salem State Univ, chancellor, 1977-84; Ala A&M Univ, pres, 1984; Radford Univ, pres, 1995-2005, pres emer, 2005-; Emory & Henry Col, interim pres, 2006. **Orgs:** Bd dirs Coun, Advan & Support Educ; Am Asn State Cols & Univs; bd trustee, Faulkner Univ; chmn, HBCU Adv Comn, US Dept Interior; bd dir, Am Heart Asn, Huntsville Chamber Com; state chmn, Africa town Comn. **Honors/Awds:** Distinguished Alumnus Award, Ohio State Univ; Distinguished Alumnus Award, Cent State Univ; Academic Scholar, Jessie Smith Noyes Found; Douglas & Beatrice Covington Fine Arts Ctr, named in honor, 2005; various other awards. **Special Achievements:** Presidency of Radford University, becoming the first African-American to head a predominantly white university in the Commonwealth of Virginia. **Business Addr:** President Emeritus, Radford University, E Main St, Radford, VA 24142, **Business Phone:** (540)831-5000.

COVINGTON, KIM ANN
Journalist. **Personal:** Born Mar 30, 1964, Centreville, IL; daughter of Wendell Sr and Delores Collins; married Derrick Grant; children: Jordan & Camille. **Educ:** Univ Mo, Columbia, MO, broadcast journalism, 1986. **Career:** KYTV, Springfield, MO, news reporter, 1986-88; KPLR-TV, St Louis, MO, dir pub affairs, 1988-89, news reporter, 1989-, WZZM 13 TV, co anchor, 1998-2005; KPNX 12 News, anchor, 2005-. **Orgs:** Delta Sigma Theta Sorority Inc, 1984-; Nat Asn Black Journalists, 1986-; Commun comt, Urban League Greater St Louis, 1987-90; Multiracial Asn Professionals. **Honors/Awds:** Unity Award, Lincoln Univ, 1988; Arkansas Asniated Press Award, Investigative Reporting, 1988; Investigative Reporting, Mo Asniated Press Award, 1988; Investigative Reporting, Nat Asn Press Honorable Mention; Distinguished Service Award, Sigma Delta Chi, Reporting, 1988; Horace Mann Award, PSA, 1989; Won Local Emmy, for Spot News Coverage; Rocky Mountain Southwest Chapter Emmy Award, 2007. **Business Phone:** (602)257-1212.

COVINGTON, TARRIEL
Executive. **Personal:** Married; children: 4. **Educ:** Univ Mo, attended 1980; Bachelors degree jour, radio/TV prod. **Career:** Emory Univ, Atlanta, GA, media specialist & prod coordr; Proj Video, owner & exec producer, 1999-. **Orgs:** Independent Nat Producers Asn; Image Film & Video; GA Lawyers for the Arts; Actg pres, Avondale Bus Asn; bd chmn, Youth VIBE Inc. **Honors/Awds:** Outstanding Radio Reporting Award, United Press Int, 1984; Nat Communicator's Award, 2002. **Business Addr:** Owner, Executive Producer, Project Video, 120 N Avondale Rd, Avondale Estates, GA 30002, **Business Phone:** (404)299-0299.

COWAN, DR. JAMES R. See Obituaries section.

COWAN, LARINE YVONNE
Administrator. **Personal:** Born Mar 25, 1949, Kensett, AR; daughter of William and Ola Mae; children: Alexander Milton Omar & Christopher Alvin Lamar. **Educ:** Univ AR, Pine Bluff, BA, 1971; Univ Ark, Little Rock, MSW, 1973. **Career:** City Champaign, Community Rels Dept, dir, 1974-79; Univ Ill, Urbana-Champaign, Affirmative Action Nonacad Off, equal opportunity Officer, 1982-85, dir, 1984-91, Off Vice Chancellor, affirmative action dir, asst vice chancellor, 1991-92, asst chancellor, assoc dir, 1992-94, asst to chancellor & dir, 1994-. **Orgs:** State coord, Ill State Coun Opportunities Industrialization Ctrs Am, Inc (OIC), 1983-87; campus coord, Nat Coalition Building Inst (NCBI), Prejudice Reduction Team, 1987-93; Conf Comm, co-chair, 1989-90; Savoy Rotary Club, 1990-92; Univ Ill Black Fac & Prof Staff Caucus & Adv Comn, 1991-93; Nat Asn Female Execs, 1993; Am Asn Affirmative Action; Am Asn Higher Educ; Am Asn Univ Women, Champaign-Urbana Chap; bd dirs, Champaign County Urban League; Exec Women's Club-Champaign County; co-chair, Ill Affirmative Action Officers Asn, Educal Initiative Comm, Ill Comm for Black Concerns Higher Educ; NAACP; Pvt Indust Coun-Champaign, Ford, Iroquois & Piatt Counties, Prog Servs Comm; State Ill Job Serv, Employ Comm; Southern Poverty Law Ctr & Klanwatch Proj. **Honors/Awds:** Boss of the Year Award, Champaign-Urbana Jaycees, 1978; Outstanding Contributions in the Field of Human Rights, City of Urbana Mayor Jeffrey Markland and the Urbana Human Relations Commission, 1979; Outstanding Services in Human and Civil Rights, Champaign Human Rels comn, 1979; Proclamation-Special Achievements in Human Rights, presented by Mayor Joan Severns, City Champaign, 1979; "The Very Best Campaign at Any State University" Award, United Way of Champaign Cty, 1988; Chancellor Morton W. Weir's Award of Appreciation for Outstanding Service as Chair of Campus Charitable Fund Dr, 1988; United Way Gold Award, United Way Champaign County, 1989; Special Award, Martin Luther King, Jr, presentation, presented by Major General Lawrence Day, Ctr Comdr, Chanute Air Force Base, 1990; Outstanding Achievement in Volunteerism, United Way Champaign County, 1992. **Special Achievements:** Co-author: The Human Rights Ordinance for the City of Champaign, IL; "Police Community Relations: A Process, Not a Product," The Police Chief's Magazine, 1976. **Business Addr:** Assistant Chancellor, Director, University of Illinois at Urbana-Champaign, 100 Swanlund Admin Bldg, Champaign, IL 61820, **Business Phone:** (217)333-0885.

COWANS, ALVIN JEFFREY
Executive. **Personal:** Born Jun 15, 1955, Alexandria, VA; son of Willie L and Jessie M; married Shirley Mae Smith, Dec 18, 1976; children: Alvin Jeffrey II, Marcus Adrian. **Educ:** Univ Fla, BS, 1977; Inst Financial Educ, supvry training cert, 1979; Fla Credit Union Mgt Inst, attended 1988. **Career:** Pittsburgh Steelers, draft choice, 1977; US Pipe & Foundry, sales rep, 1977-78; Pioneer Fed Savings & Loan, asst vpres, off mgr, admin asst, 1978-83; McCoy Fed Credit Union, sr vpres, 1983-85, pres & chief exec officer, 1986-. **Orgs:** bd mem, Univ FL Found; Credit Union Exec Soc; past pres, Univ Fla Lettermens Asn; dir, Gator Booster Bd; former bd mem, Cent Fla Kidney Found; Nat Asn Fed Credit Unions, regional dir; Fed Reserve's Consumer Adv Coun; former dir, Southeast Fed Credit Union; Cent Fla Amateur Athletic Union; Orange Co Schs Partners Educ; mem bd govs, African Am Chamber Com Cent Fla. **Honors/Awds:** Graduate of the Chamber of Commerce Leadership Orlando Program, 1980; Outstanding Young Men in Ameria, 1981; Citizen of the Year, Chi Tau Chap, Omega Psi Phi Fraternity. **Business Addr:** President, Chief Executive Officer, McCoy Federal Credit Union, PO Box 593806, Orlando, FL 32859-3806, **Business Phone:** (407)855-5452.*

COWARD, ONIDA LAVONEIA (ONIDA COWARD MAYERS)
Educator. **Personal:** Born Sep 26, 1964, Panama City, Panama; daughter of Ricardo E and Marcia E Pitter. **Educ:** Buffalo State Col, NY, BA, 1986; Zicklin Sch Bus Baruch Col, MBA. **Career:** Paragon Cable Manhattan, NY, pub & leased mgr, 1987-89; Brooklyn Community Access TV, Brooklyn, NY, founding dir, 1989-; New York City Voter Assistance Comn, exec dir & coordr, 2004-. **Orgs:** Nat Asn Minorities Cable, 1987; Nat Asn Black Jour, 1988; One Hundred Black Women, 1988; bd mem, Am Cancer Soc, Harlem Unit, 1991; bd mem, Harlem YMCA 100 Years Basketball, 1991. **Honors/Awds:** Community Service Award, Community Bd No. 11, Manhattan, 1989; Creator/Exec Producer PAL Awards, Paragon Cable Manhattan, 1988-89; Open Doors Award, Bd Educ, 1988; Jewell Ryan-White Award, 2002. **Home Addr:** 5810 Beverly Rd, Brooklyn, NY 11203.

COWART, SAM (SAMUEL COWART, III)
Football player. **Personal:** Born Feb 26, 1975, Jacksonville, FL. **Educ:** Fla State Univ, bus; Harvard Bus Sch, exec educ prog, 2005. **Career:** Buffalo Bills, linebacker, 1998-2001, NY Jets, 2002-04; Minn Vikings, 2005; Off Season Player, Houston Texans, 2006. **Orgs:** Ronald McDonald House; United Way. **Honors/Awds:** All-ACC hons; ACC's Brian Piccolo Award; named to All-Rookie teams by Col & Pro Football Weekly, Pro Football Weekly & Football Digest, 1998; ProBowl, 2000. *

COWART, SAMUEL, III. See COWART, SAM.

COWDEN, MICHAEL E.
Educator, actor, poet. **Personal:** Born Jul 17, 1951, Louisville, KY. **Educ:** Shoreline Commun Col, AA, 1971; Univ Wash, BA, Am, ethnic studies. **Career:** Louisville Pub Sch, martial arts instr, chinese boxing, 1975-; poet; playwright; Film: Abby, 1974. **Honors/Awds:** US Achievement Academy's All Am Scholar, 1993-94. *

COWELL, CATHERINE
Nutritionist. **Personal:** Born Nov 13, 1921, Norfolk, VA. **Educ:** Hampton Inst, BS, 1945; Univ CT, MS, 1947; New York Univ, PhD, 1983. **Career:** Univ CT, grad asst nutrition, 1945-47; Metabolism Clinic Mt Sinai Hosp, NYC, lab tech, 1947-49, pub health nutrionalist, 1969; Bur Nutrit, acting dir, 1971; NY Med Col Flower Fifth Ave Hosp, asst clin instr preventave med pub health indust & hygiene, 1953-55; Albert Einstein Sch Med Yeshiva Univ, instr nutrit environ med, 1962-69; NY Univ, vis lectr; Montclair State Tchr; Col Rep NY Nutrit Coun 1963; Nutrit Bur Dept Health, NY, dir, 2002; Mailman Sch Pub Health, clin prof pop & family health, currently. **Orgs:** Manhattan Br; Nat Coun Negro Women; fel Am Pub Health Asn; Am Home Econ Asn; NY State Home Econ Asn; chmn, Health & Welfare Sect, 1961-62, pres, 1971-; St George Asn New York Health Dept; Royal Soc Health; Hampton Alumni Asn; nat pres, Lambda Kappa Kappa Mu, 1961-65; White House Conf Food Nutrit & Health, 1969; adv coun, Ch Human Ecol, Cornell Univ, 1970-72; Order Eastern Star Club. **Honors/Awds:** Recipient Nutritional Award, New York Pub Health Asn, 1960; JF Goodwin Scholarship, Reading PA. **Special Achievements:** Author: Nutrit Assessment A Comprehensive Guide for Planning Intervention; contrib articles to professional jours. **Business Addr:** Clinical Professor, Columbia University, Mailman School of Public Health, Allan Rosenfield Bldg 722 W 168th St Suite 14, New York, NY 10032, **Business Phone:** (212)305-4797.

COX, DR. ARTHUR JAMES, SR.
Educator. **Personal:** Born Jun 15, 1943, Avon Park, FL; married Deloris Murray; children: Arthur Jr, Travis J & David I. **Educ:** Howard Univ, AB, 1965, MSW, 1970; Columbia Univ, DSW, 1978. **Career:** NIMH fel; doctoral study, 1973-74; Fla State Univ, asst prof, 1975-78; E Tenn State Univ, chmn & assoc prof, 1978-83; Southern Ill Univ, dir & assoc prof, 1983-86; Salem State Col, dean & prof, 1986-. **Orgs:** Fel ACE, 1979; chmn, Human Serv Goals Directions 2000 Prog, 1980-83; secy & treas, Inst C Resources, 1980-82; steering comn mem, Southeast Child Welfare Training Resource Ctr, Univ Tenn Sch Social Work, 1981-82; treas, Asn Baccalaureate Prog Dirs, 1981-83; pres, Tenn Chap, Nat Asn Social Workers, 1981-82; Publ Comn Coun Social Work Educ, 1981-84; Alcohol Treatment Serv Adv Bd Jackson Co Comn Ment Health Ctr, Carbondale, IL, 1984-; mem ed rev bd, Jour Social Serv Res GWB Sch Social Work, Wash Univ, St Louis, 1985-88; Nat Asn Black Social Workers; Nat Asn Social Workers; Coun Social Work Educ; Nat Conf Social Welfare; elected deleg, Tenn Gov's State Conf Families, White House Conf Famili Minneapolis; pres & chief exec officer, Mid Fla Ctr Ment Health & Substance Abuse Serv Inc, currently. **Honors/Awds:** Teacher of the Year, City Univ NY, Lehman Col, 1973, Teacher of the Year, Sch Social Work, Fla State Univ, 1977; Jaycees Man of the Year, 1979; Social Worker of the Year, Tenn Chap, NASW, 1980. **Special Achievements:** Has presented numerous papers, workshops, special lectures,TV appearances, chapters in books and has published articles. **Home Addr:** 1282 Lake Lotela Dr, Avon Park, FL 33825-9737. **Business Phone:** (863)533-2321.

COX, BRYAN KEITH
Football player. **Personal:** Born Feb 17, 1968, St Louis, MO; married LaTonia; children: Lavonda, Brittani, Chiquita & Bryan Jr. **Educ:** Western Ill Univ, mass communications. **Career:** Football player (retired); Miami Dolphins, linebacker, 1991-95; Chicago Bears, 1996-97; New York Jets, asst Defensive Line, 1998-2000; New England Patriots, 2001; New Orleans Saints, 2002; TVG Network, analyst, 2004-05; Cleveland Browns, defensive line coach, currently. **Honors/Awds:** Pro Bowl, 1992, 1994, 1995; Extra Effort Award, Nat Football League, 1994; All-Pro selection, 1992, 1994 & 1995. **Business Addr:** Defensive Line Coach, Cleveland Browns, 76 Lou Groza Blvd, Berea, OH 44017, **Business Phone:** (440)891-5000.*

COX, CORINE
Editor. **Personal:** Born May 31, 1944, Mansfield, LA; married Doyl; children: Dwayne E. **Educ:** Tex Southern Univ, attended 1963; Univ Bus Col, cert sec training, 1964. **Career:** Soc & Women's Ed Forward Times Pub Co, compositer, supvr, news writer soc ed, 1964-. **Orgs:** Adv bd, Ct Calanthe; Eta Phi Beta; Mt Rose Missionary Baptist Church; secy, Prairie View A&M Univ. **Honors/Awds:** Award media coverage, 1974; Outstanding Neophyte Award, 1974-75; Woman of the Year Award. **Business Addr:** Editor, 4411 Almeda Rd, Houston, TX 77004.

COX, COURTLAND
Federal government official. **Career:** City Wash, DC, Minority Opport Comn, dir, 1980-83, Off Int Bus, dir, 1983-85, spec asst to mayor; US Dept Com, Off Civil Rights, dir, MinorityBus Develop Agency, dep secy, dir; pvt bus advisor & consult; Off Civil Rights, agency dir & Int Trade Admin, spec asst; DC Sports & Entertainment Comn, bus enterprise develop, LSDBE Develop, dir, currently. **Orgs:** Stud Non-Violent Coordinating Comt; Emergency Fund S Africa; Ctr Nat Security Studies; Sixth Pan-African Cong. **Special Achievements:** Developed in-depth expertise on Africa, and promoted awareness of economic development, technology advancement, advanced cultural and racial issues to increase cooperation and communication between US and foreign nations. **Business Phone:** (202)547-9077.

COX, DR. GEORGETTA MANNING
Educator. **Personal:** Born Sep 16, 1947, Washington, DC; married Walter Bishop Cox Jr; children: Malakia Iman. **Educ:** Hampton Inst, BA, 1970; Howard Univ Col Dent, DDS, 1976; Johns Hopkins Univ, MPH, 1979. **Career:** Howard Univ, Sch Dent, prog coordr, 1977-78, asst prof, 1979-86, chmn & assoc prof, currently. **Orgs:** Consult, United Planning Org Health Adv Comt, 1982-; managing ed, NDAJ Nat Dent Asn, 1983-, vpres, 1984, pres, 1985; vpres, Howard Univ Dent Alumna Asn, 1985; presentor & mem, Int Asn Dent Res; Sigma Xi Res Soc, Am Pub Health Asn; Omicron Kappa Upsilon Nat Dent Honor Soc. **Honors/Awds:** Presidents Award, Nat Dent Asn, 1984; Outstanding Service Award, Nat Dent Asn, 1986. **Special Achievements:** Articles published "Pathological Effects of Sickle Cell Anemia on the Pulp," Journal of Dent for Children, 1984, "Oral Pain Experience in Sickle Cell Patients," Oral Surgery, Oral Medicine, Oral Pathology, 1985; "The Psycho Social Aspects of Pregnant Adolescents, A Dental Perspective, "Journal of Dentistry for Children, 1986. **Business Addr:** Associate Professor, Chairman, Howard University, School of Dentistry, 600 W St NE, Washington, DC 20059, **Business Phone:** (202)806-0084.

COX, J. LINLOY
Accountant. **Educ:** Howard University, Bachelors of Business Administration, 1987; University of Maryland at College Park, Masters of Business Administration, 1992. **Career:** Deloitte and Touche. **Orgs:** NAACP, Chief Financial Officer. **Honors/Awds:** Summa Cum Laude, Howard University, 1987. *

COX, FR. JESSE
Church historian, preacher. **Educ:** Loyola Univ, BA, theol & Eng; Dominican Novitiate, 1981; Aquinas Inst Theol, MDiv, 1987;

Xavier Univ, ThM. **Career:** Hales Franciscan High Sch, teacher, 1987-91; Dominican Fathers, 1987; Dominican Friars, voc dir, 1991-97; Archdiocese Detroit, dir, 1997-; St. Dominic Church, dir Nat Evangelization. **Orgs:** Coordr, Nat Joint Conf, 1998; Black Dominicans Conf, currently. **Special Achievements:** Preached & lectured in US, India, Africa & Europe. **Business Addr:** Director, Blessed Sacrament, 2286 Calvert, Detroit, MI 48206, **Business Phone:** (313)821-1455.

COX, JESSE L
Executive. **Personal:** Born Jun 1, 1946, Bay Minette, AL; son of Jesse Sr and Artensie Wesley; married Mary Walker Cox; children: April, Anwar & Tasia. **Educ:** Ala A&M Univ, BS, 1969; Mercy Col, BS, 1979. **Career:** Alexander's Dept Stores, mgr, 1971-83; consult, Clitee Assocs, 1979-; Buffy Merchandising Corp, gen mgr, 1983-86; Gannett Westchester Rockland Newspaper, dist mgr; United Cerebal Palsy Asn; Westchester Co Inc, teacher, currently; Community Living Corp, currently. **Orgs:** Kappa Alpha Psi Fraternity, 1965-; Jamaican Am Varieties, Lewis Security Corp, 1986-; Legislative Adv Comt, NY City Coun, 1985-; Opengate Inc, counr. **Special Achievements:** Author of cookbook, "Baking with Jesse Cox". Articles published bus & drugs "Parkchester News", 1985. **Military Serv:** AUS, 2 yrs; Bronze Star. **Business Addr:** PO Box 11182, Greenwich, CT 06851.*

COX, JOSEPH MASON ANDREW
Writer, poet. **Personal:** Born Jul 12, 1930, Boston, MA; son of Hiram Cox and Edith Henderson Cox. **Educ:** Columbia Univ, BA, 1949, LLB, 1952; World Univ, Hong Kong, Ph D, art psychol, 1972. **Career:** NY Post, New York, NY, reporter & feature writer, 1958-60; Afro-Asian Purchasing Comn, New York NY, pres, 1961-68; New York Bd Educ, Brooklyn NY, consult, 1969-71; Manhattan Community Col City Univ New York, NY, lectr, 1972-73; Medgar Evers Col City Univ NY, Brooklyn NY, asst prof Eng, 1973-74; Cox & Hopewell Publ Inc, NY NY, pres, 1974; poet & writer; prof City Univ NY, Manhattan Community Col, Bronx Community Col, Medgar Evers Col, New York City Univ Res Ctr, 1975-83; Fed Govt Crime Ins, 1983-88; Poems: The Collected Poetry of Joseph Mason Andrew Cox, 1970; Shore Dimly Seen, 1974; New & Selected Poems, 1979; Unfolding Orchid, 1993; Novels: The Search, 1963; Ode to Dr. Martin Luther King, Jr, 1970; Indestructible Monument, 1974; Great Black Men of Masonry: Qualitative Black Achievers Who Were Freemasons, 1982. **Orgs:** Int Poetry Soc; Int Poets Shrine; United Poets Laureate Int; World Lit Acad; Auth League Am; Poetry Soc Am; Phylaxis Soc; NAACP; Int Acad Arts, Sci & Letters. **Honors/Awds:** International Essay Award, Daniel S Mead Agency, 1964; Great Society writer's award, Pres Lyndon B Johnson, 1965; Master Poets Award, Am Poet Fel Soc, 1970; World Poets Award, World Poetry Fel Soc, 1971; PEN grant, 1972; Humanitarian Award and Gold Medal for poetry, Int Poets Shrine, 1974; United Poet Laureate, Int Gold Crown, 1976; Am Book Award nomination, 1979, for New and Selected Poems; NCP Medal of Distinction, Asbury Park Neptune, 1984; "Statue of Victory" World Culture Prize, Accademia Italia, 1985; Science and Letters Bronze Statue, Int Acad Arts, 1985; Gold Medal, Am Biog Asn, 1987; Gold Medal, Am Biog Asn, 1988.

COX, KEITH
Chief executive officer, manager, president (organization). **Career:** Cox Nissan Inc, owner & chief exec officer, gen mgr & pres, currently. **Orgs:** NY State Automobile Dealers Asn. **Honors/Awds:** Bronx community leader. **Business Addr:** General Manager, President, Cox Nissan Inc, 3700 Boston Rd, Bronx, NY 10460, **Business Phone:** (718)515-7300.*

COX, KEVIN C.
State government official. **Personal:** Born Dec 1, 1949, Oklahoma City, OK; son of Frank and Martina; married Carlise Ann Washington; children: Kenny. **Educ:** Fla A&M Univ, BS, Polit Sci, 1972; Univ GA, MPA, Pub Admin, 1974. **Career:** State OK, field monitor, 1974-77; Energy Conserv & Housing Found, minority bus develop, 1977-80; State OK, Dist 97, state rep, 1981. **Orgs:** Fla A&M Alumni Asn; bd dirs, East side YMCA; Kappa Alpha Psi Frat Inc; NAACP; mem bd dir, Urban League; chmn, Ins Comm; 33 Degree Prince Hall Mason; Prince Hall Shriner; United Native Am, rep. **Honors/Awds:** East side YMCA Volunteer of the Year; Set Club Citizen of the Year; Hon Alumnus Langston Univ.

COX, M. MAURICE
Executive. **Personal:** Born Dec 20, 1951, Dover, NC; son of Nicy Chatmon and Earl E; married Earlene Hardie Cox, Jul 1, 1978; children: Michelle Hardie, Michael M. **Educ:** Univ NC, Greensboro NC, BA, Econ, 1974. **Career:** Greensboro News Co, Greensboro NC, reporter, 1973-74; Assoc Builders & Contractors, Wash, DC, ed, 1975-78, dir commun, 1979-81; Pepsi-Cola Co, Somers, NY, mgr pub rels, 1981-86, dir govt affairs, 1987-91, vpres corp develop & diversity, 1991-. **Orgs:** Black Mgrs Asn, 1986; mentor, White Plains Youth Coun, 1988-; Food Patch, Exec Leadership Coun. **Honors/Awds:** Community Hero Award, Nat Urban League, Ebony Mag list of powerful execs. *

COX, OTIS GRAHAM, JR.
Government official. **Personal:** Born Oct 29, 1941, Winston-Salem, NC; son of Otis (deceased) and Geraldine Cox (deceased); married Wanda Woodlon; children: Wendi, Kevin & Keith. **Educ:** Savannah State Col, GA, BSIA, 1963; FBI Acad Quantico, VA, law enforce cert, 1969; Suffolk Univ Boston, MPA, 1980. **Career:** Baltimore Co, MD, sch teacher 1963-67; Westinghouse Elec Corp, engr writer, 1967-69; FBI, spec agent investr, 1969; FBI, Boston, supr civil rights, 1977; FBI, Wash, DC, adminstr pub, 1979; spec agent supr pub, asst sect chief; St WV, cabinet sec, pub safety, 1997-01; Nat Hwy Traffic Safety Admin, dep adminr, 2003-. **Orgs:** Alpha Phi Alpha Fraternity; Nat Police Asn; MA Assoc Afro Am Policemen; Am Soc Pub Admin; NOBLE; Urban League; Black Exec Exchange Prog; Int Asn Chief Police Inc; deacon Peace of Mind Baptist Church; Rotarian; bd dirs, United Hosp Ctr; exec bd, Boy Scouts Am. **Honors/Awds:** Toland Collier Memorial Award, Savannah State Col, 1961; A A Leadership Award, Alpha Phi Frat Delta Eta, 1963; Cert of Bravery, MA Asn Afro Am Policemen, 1975; Cert Accomplishment, Assessment & Designs Inc, 1975; Achievement Award, Order Eastern Star, 1992; Except Accomplishment Award, The Mountain State Bar Asn, 1992; Exec of the Year, Fraternal Order of Police, 1992; Sigma Pi Phi Frat; Int Speakers Bur. **Business Addr:** Deputy Administrator, West Virginia Highway Safety Program, Capitol Complex Bldg 3 Room 118, Charleston, WV 25301, **Business Phone:** (304)558-6080.

COX, RONALD
Football player. **Personal:** Born Feb 27, 1968, Fresno, CA. **Educ:** Fresno State Univ, BSc, bus mgt. **Career:** Football player (retired); Chicago Bears, linebacker, 1990-95, 1997; Green Bay Packers, 1996; general manager, land dev and construction Co, central Calif; Calif State Univ, football coach; Lake Forest Col, football coach . **Honors/Awds:** Most Valuable player, 1989; Poor Man's Guide, Nat Football League; Defensive Player of the Year, 1989; Fresno Athletic Hall of Fame, 2001.

COX, SANDRA
Executive director. **Career:** SouthCentral RTEC, Los Angeles Anger Mgt Teacher; Palm Springs Life, Couns & Therapist; Coalition Ment Health Profs, exec dir & co founder, 2003-. **Orgs:** Pres, Asn Black Psychol. **Honors/Awds:** Robert Wood Johnson Community Health Leadership Program (CHIP) Award. **Business Addr:** Executive Director, Co Founder, Coalition Mental Health Professionals, 9130 S Figueroa St Suite 100, Los Angeles, CA 90003, **Business Phone:** (323)777-3120.*

COX, SANDRA HICKS
Lawyer. **Personal:** Born Apr 28, 1939, Baton Rouge, LA; daughter of Henry Beecher Sr and Eleanor Victorine Frazier; married Ronald Virgil Cox; children: Michelle Louella, Damien Monroe. **Educ:** Howard Univ, BA, 1959; OH State Univ Col Law, JD, 1962. **Career:** Donald P McCullum, Oakland, CA, coun, 1965; Dixon & White & William C Dixon & Assocs, Oakland, CA, coun, 1965-67; San Francisco Neighborhood Legal Assistance Found, Domestic rels coun, 1967-69; San Francisco Legal Assist Found, chief domestic rels dept, 1969-72; State CA Pub Utilities Comn, Legal Asst pub utilities comnr, 1972-73; Kaiser Found Health Plan, Inc, Coun, 1973-84; Kaiser Found Hosp & Kaiser Found Health Plan Inc, vpres & regional coun. **Orgs:** OH State Bar, 1963-, CA State Bar, 1964-; Agency Rels Coun United Way Inc, 1985-86; Nat Bar Asn; Los Angeles County Bar Asn; Jack & Jill Am, Inc, 1990-93. **Honors/Awds:** Parliamentarian, Delta Sigma Theta Sorority, Inc, 1986-87, 1991; Black Women Achievement Award, NAACP Legal Defense & Educ Fund Inc, 1987; House Counsel Year, John M Langston Bar Asn, 1990; President's Compass Award, Nat Bar Asn, 1990, Sr Advisor to President, Langston Bar Asn, 1994. *

COX, TAYLOR H., SR.
Accountant. **Personal:** Born Feb 28, 1926, Clarksburg, WV; son of Wade (deceased) and Matilda (deceased); married Betty Leftridge, 1947 (died 1963); children: Taylor Jr, Patricia Elam & Nancy Phillips; married Edith Burroughs, 1964; children: Annette Austin & Lamont Seals. **Educ:** WVa Wesleyan Col Buckhannon, BS Bus Econ, 1953; Ind Univ Bloomington, MBA, 1954. **Career:** Accountant (retired); Home Fed Savings & Loan Assoc, Detroit, general mgr, 1954-59; Mich Chronicle, columnist, 1955-79; Detroit Coca-Cola Bottling Co, asst to sales mgr, 1959-64; Motown Records Detroit, dept head-artist mgt, 1964-72; Invictus Records Detroit, vpres artist mgt, 1972-73; New Detroit Inc, proj mgr, 1978-79; Mich Bell Tel Co, dist mgr minority econ develop. **Orgs:** Nat Asn Advan Colored People; Urban League Detroit; Nat Bus League; Am Bridge Asn, 1979-80; Detroit Asn Bus Econ. **Honors/Awds:** Numerous Certificates of Appreciation & Plaques Nat Asn Advan Colored People, Urban League, New Detroit Inc, United Comm Serv. **Special Achievements:** First African-American manager, Detroit Coca-Cola Bottling Co; listed Nat Top 50 List Am Bridge Asn, 1979-80. **Military Serv:** AUS, sgt, 1944-46, 1948-49; Bronze Starr ETO. **Home Addr:** 26836 Summerdale Dr, Southfield, MI 48034. *

COX, TYRONE Y.
Government official, accountant. **Educ:** NC Cent Univ, BBA, acct, 1994. **Career:** Durham City Coun, councilman; NC Off State Auditor; Ty Cox Acct & Bus Serv Inc, pres & chief exec officer; Leonard & Cox PLLC; Cox & Gibbs CPAs PLLC; Cox Gibbs & Thomas CPAs PLLC; Ty Cox & Co CPAs PLLC, managing sr partner, currently. **Orgs:** bd mem, NC Pub Allies; nat bd mem, Nat Asn Black Accts Inc. **Special Achievements:** Youngest person ever elected to the Durham City Council; First Cavalry Baptist Church Boy Scout Troop 108, scout leader. **Business Addr:** Managing senior partner, Ty Cox & Co CPAs PLLC, 1007 Slater Rd Suite 150, Durham, NC 27703, **Business Phone:** (919)403-0353.*

COX, WARREN E.
Lawyer, government official. **Personal:** Born Apr 26, 1936, Brookhaven, MS; son of Pinkie; married Alpha Whiting, Apr 20, 1957; children: Diethra D & Reggie R. **Educ:** Alcorn A&M Col, BSEd, 1957; Southern Ill Univ, MEd, 1966; Univ Miss, JD, 1969. **Career:** US DOL & OFCCP, Jackson, MS, asst dist dir, 1987-91; US Equel Employ Opp Comn, dist coun; Equal Employ Opportunity Comn, sr investigator 1973; Holly Springs, staff atty, 1969-72; Univ Law Sch, res asst, 1966-69; Lincoln's Attendance Ctr, teacher band dir, 1964-69; Gentry High Sch, teacher band dir, 1957-64; pvt practice atty, currently. **Orgs:** Nat Advan Asn Colored People; Miss Dem Pary; Miss Bar Asn; Nat Bar Asn; Am-Bar Asn; Magnolia Bar Asn; Miss Lawyers Asn; Fed Bar Asn; Am Judicate Soc. **Business Addr:** Attorney, 5238 Cloverdale Dr, Jackson, MS 39272, **Business Phone:** (601)373-1161.*

COX, DR. WENDELL
Dentist. **Personal:** Born Nov 7, 1914, Charleston, SC; married Iris; children: Wendell Haley & Iris Marie. **Educ:** Talladega Col, BA; Meharry Col, DDS, 1944; Fisk Univ & Boston Univ, grad courses. **Career:** Radio stations KWK St Louis WCHB-AM & wjzz-FM Detroit, vpres; Pvt Pract Inkster, dentist, 1946-; Georgetown Psychotherapy Group. **Orgs:** Am & Nat Dent Asn; Mayor's Com Human Rels; bd mem, New Detroit Com; Detroit C C; Detroit Inst Arts; Meharry Med Col. **Business Phone:** (202)333-6606.

COY, JOHN T
Private investigator, business owner, police officer. **Personal:** Born Oct 5, 1939, Princeton, NJ; son of John I and Alice Jeanette Douglas; married Faithe Suzanne Parago, Jan 31, 1959; children: Barrie A (deceased), Wendy D, David S, Dhana P & Dawn C. **Educ:** Trenton State Col, Ewing Township NJ, 1973; Mercer County Community Col, W Windsor NJ, 1986; Atlanta Univ, Criminal Justice Inst, 1988. **Career:** Trenton Police Dept, Trenton NJ, patrolman, 1964-70, detective, 1970-78, sergeant, 1978-82, detective sergeant, 1982-93; John T Coy & Assoc, founder & pvt investigator, 1993. **Orgs:** Past pres, Brother Officers Law Enforcement Soc, 1968-; Trenton Superior Officers Asn, 1978-; Mayor's Advisory Comt Affirmative Action, 1981-; bd dir, Carver Youth & Family Ctr, 1983-; Roga Golf Club, 1983; deleg, Nat Black Police Asn, 1983-; pres, Carver Century Club, 1984-; info officer, New Jersey Coun, Nat Black Police 1985-; NAACP, 1985-; info officer, Northeast Region, Nat Black Police Asn, 1987-; mem bd dir, Nat Black Police Asn, 1987—1996; founder & exec dir, NJ Security Officer's Asn; bd dirs, Trenton Downtown Asn, 2004-. **Honors/Awds:** Valor Award, Trenton Police Div, 1980; founder & current pres, Carver Century Club, 1984; founder & current editor, Vanguard ANJ Publication for Black Police Officers, 1984; superior office of the year, City of Trenton, 1985; founder & current editor, Northeast Regional News, Nat Black Police Asn, 1985; member of the year, Nat Black Police Asn Northeast Region, 1986. **Special Achievements:** Author of article on police/community relations in The Police Chief, 1974; author of Police Officer's Handbook for the Trenton Police Division 1980, 1986. **Home Addr:** 513 Eggerts Crossing Rd, Trenton, NJ 08638, **Home Phone:** (609)883-1749. **Business Phone:** (609)393-8900.

COYE, DENA E.
Entrepreneur. **Personal:** Daughter of Ruel (deceased) and Kathleen (deceased). **Educ:** Fordham Univ, MA, Social Sci, 1978; New Sch Social Res, MA, human resource mgt, 1982; MA, Bus Mgt & TV Prod. **Career:** Dena Coye Money Matters, producer & host, TV series; Dena Coye Prod, founder & pres, currently. **Orgs:** Founder & pres, The Mosaic Coun, 1990-; Nat Asn Black Jour, 1989-; Nat Asn Female Exec, 1981-89; Nat Asn Women Bus Owners, 1991; jazz comt, Jackie Robinson Found. **Honors/Awds:** Business Award, Video Ctr Arts Performers, 1991; Rubenesque for Career Achievement, BBI Prod, 1990. **Business Addr:** President, Dena Coye Productions, 163 3rd Ave Suite 133, New York, NY 10003, **Business Phone:** (212)979-8174.*

CRAFT, DR. GUY CALVIN
Librarian. **Personal:** Born Oct 19, 1929, Atlanta, GA; son of Josie Hubert Glass and Guy; married Martha Broadwater, Sep 1972; children: Guy Jr, Audrey, Anthony, Gayle & Scott. **Educ:** Morehouse Col, Atlanta, Ga, AB, 1951; Atlanta Univ, Atlanta, Ga, MSLS, 1961; Southern Ill Univ, Carbondale, Ill, PhD, 1976. **Career:** Florida Memorial Col, St Augustine, Fla, head librn, 1957-63; Elizabeth City State Univ, Elizabeth City, NC, chief cataloger, 1963-65; Albany State Col, Albany, Ga, head librarian, 1965-85; Atlanta Univ Ctr/Robert W Woodruff Libr, Atlanta, Ga, libr dir, 1985-. **Orgs:** Pres, Community Rels Coun, 1976-78; chmn, Chehaw Coun Boy Scouts, 1976-80; bd dirs, CCLC, 1977-; Metrop Atlanta Red Cross, 1986-87; Kiwanis Club, 1987-. **Honors/Awds:** Hon Cert, Morehouse Col, 1976; Hon Cert, Job

Corps, 1977; Honor Cert & Plaque, Boy Scouts, 1978; Resolution Commendation, Ga House Representatives, 1986; Boss of the Year, ABWA, 1988. **Military Serv:** USAF, capt, 1951-56.

CRAFT, SALLY-ANN ROBERTS (SALLY-ANN ROBERTS)
Journalist. **Personal:** Born Feb 14, 1953, Chandler, AZ; married Willie Jerome. **Educ:** Univ Southern Miss, BA, 1976, MS, 1977. **Career:** WXXX Radio Sta Hattiesburg, radio announcer, MS, 1976; WDAM TV Sta Hattiesburg, weathercaster, Reporter, weekend anchor, MS, 1977;WUSM, repoter, announcer, anchor; Community Relations, dir; MS radio sta, announcer & news reporter; Going Live, author, 1998; WWL-TV New Orleans, reporter, 1977-, co-anchor, currently. **Orgs:** MS Press Women, 1977; Am Fed TV & Radio Artists; big sister Big Sisters Greater New Orleans; prog; com mem, St Mark's United Methodlic Church; found, Each One Save One prog, New Orleans. **Honors/Awds:** First place Gen Reporting MS Press Women, 1977; second place Gen Reporting Nat Asn Press Women, 1977; gaines baston mem Award, Am Fed TV & Radio Artists, 1978; TV journalist yr Physically Ltd Asn More Construct Environ, 1979. **Special Achievements:** Author of Going Live: An Anchorwoman Reports Good News. **Business Addr:** Co-Anchor, WWL-TV, 1024 N Rampart St, New Orleans, LA 70116-2487, **Business Phone:** (504)529-6275.

CRAFT, DR. THOMAS J
Educator, administrator, biologist. **Personal:** Born Dec 27, 1924, Monticello, KY; son of Thomas Marion and Wonnie Travis; married Joan Ruth Hunter, Sep 4, 1948; children: Thomas J Jr & Yvonne Diane. **Educ:** Cent State Univ, BS, 1948; Ky State Univ, MA 1950; OH State Univ, PhD, 1963. **Career:** Cent State Univ, Instr, 1950-51, from asst prof to assoc prof 1951-63, prof, 1963-79; Wright State Univ, Med Sch, adj prof, 1973-79; Fla Memorial Col, prog dir DOE energy grant, 1980, natural Scis & math div, dir, 1981, instnl planning dir, 1982, dean fac, 1984-87; Cent State Univ, emer prof, biol, 1979-. **Orgs:** Consult, Nat Sci Found, Gujurat Univ, Ahmedebad, India, 1967; Osmania Univ, Hyderabad, India, 1968; NSF NIH OH State Dept Health ad hoc consulting; investr Res Projs, 1970-77; Exec Comm OH Acad Sci, 1975-77; chmn, Res Resources (NIH) Group Minority BioMed Res, 1976-77; chmn, WSU/Med Sch Anat Fac Search Comm, 1976-77; health sci admin, HEW NIH Div Res Resources, Bethesda, MD, 1977-79; fel, Ohio Acad Sci; mem Adv Panel, Educ Devel Ctr, Newton, MA, 1984-87; bd dirs, children servs bd, Greene County, Ohio, 1989-93; fel AAAS; health subcomt, Gov's Comn Disadvantaged Black Male, 1990; bd dirs, educ comt; Xenia, Ohio Area Chamber Com; chmn, Wilbert Force Planning & Develop Coun, 1990-; bd dirs, Greene Oaks Health Ctr, Xenia, OH, 1993-; chmn, Greene Oaks Health Ctr, 2001-. **Honors/Awds:** Tri-Beta Biological Honor Soc; Sigma Pi Phi Boule; Soc Sigma Xi; Fel, AAAS; Citation for Achievement, OH State Univ, 1979; Emer Prof Biol, Cent State Univ, Ohio; Achivement Hall Of Fame, Cent State Univ, 1993. **Military Serv:** USMCR corporal, 1943-46; Honor Man. **Home Addr:** 1280 Wenofred Dr, PO Box 252, Xenia, OH 45385, **Home Phone:** (937)372-5006.

CRAIG, CARL
Musician. **Personal:** Born May 22, 1969, Detroit, MI; married Hannah Sawtell; children: 1. **Career:** Retro Active Label, cofounder, 1990; Planet E Commun, founder, 1991-; Detroit Electronic Music Festival & Ford Focus, artistic dir, 2000-01; Albums: Psyche; Paper Clip People; 69; Designer Music and Inner zone Orchestra; Bug in a Bassbin, 1992; Land cruising, 1995; More Songs about Food and Revolutionary Art, 1996; Designer Music: The Remixes, 2000; Onsumothasheeat, 2001; The Workout, 2002; The Album Formerly Known As, 2005; "Paris Live", 2007; Sessions, 2008; ReComposed, 2008. **Honors/Awds:** Best Label Award for Planet E, Musik Und Maschine Awards, 2001. **Business Addr:** Musician, Planet E Communications, 4221 Cass Ave Apt 900, Detroit, MI 48201, **Business Phone:** (313)831-8771.*

CRAIG, DAMEYUNE VASHON
Football player, football coach. **Personal:** Born Apr 19, 1974, Mobile, AL. **Educ:** Auburn Col. **Career:** Fotball player (retired); football coach; Carolina Panthers, quarterback, 1998-2001; Scottish Claymores, 1999; Arena Football League, 2002; Indiana Firebirds, 2002; Washington Redskins, 2002; Ottawa Renegades, 2002; Nick Sabanocos LSU staff, grad asst, 2004; Miami Dolphins, asst coach, 2005; Tuskegee Univ, quaterback, 2006-07; Univ SA, running backs coach, currently. *

CRAIG, ELSON L
Physician. **Personal:** Born Nov 27, 1933; divorced; children: Joellyn & Carlton. **Educ:** Ohio State Univ, BS, 1955, MS, 1961, MD, 1966. **Career:** Aff Col Med, OH, opthalmologist, asst dean studs, 1970-; pvt pract, physician; Ohio State Univ, fac, currently. **Orgs:** Acad Me Columbus & Franklin Co; Am Asn Ophthal; AMA; bd dir, Ohio Soc Prev Blindness, 1977; Columbus Asn Physicians & Dentists; Ohio State Med Asn; Nat Med Asn; Electron Mocroscope Soc Am; Nu Sigma Nu; Simga Xi; Soc Heed Fel; Alpha Omega Alpha Med Soc; Landacre Soc. **Military Serv:** AUS, first Lt, 1956-58. **Business Addr:** Faculty of Ophthalmic Pathology General Ophthalmology & Diabetic Eye D, Ohio State University, 456 W 10th Ave, Columbus, OH 43210.

CRAIG, FREDERICK A.
Oral surgeon. **Personal:** Born Apr 28, 1933, Selma, AL; married Leslie J Cyrusd. **Educ:** Fisk Univ, BS, 1954; MS, 1958; Meharry Med Col, DDS, 1963. **Career:** Fisk Univ, instr, 1956-58; US Post Off, 1958; Pvt Dental Pract, 1966-67; Chicago Bd Health, oral surg, 1967-70; Pvt Pract, oral surg; Daniel Hale Williams Neighborhood Health Ctr, dental dir. **Orgs:** Bd dirs, Daniel Hale Williams Heighorhood Health Ctr; Dental Subcom Chicago Heart Asn; IL Soc Oral Surg; Chicago Soc Oral Surg; Am IL Chicago Dental Socs; Alpha Phi Alpha Frat. **Military Serv:** AUS, 1954-56. *

CRAIG, RHONDA PATRICIA
Judge. **Personal:** Born Nov 27, 1953, Gary, IN; daughter of William and Myrtle Glover; married Fulton Smith Jr, Jun 28, 1985; children: Andaiye Spencer, Fulton Douglass Smith. **Educ:** Valparaiso Univ, BA, 1975, Sch Law, JD, 1978. **Career:** Wayne Co Neighborhood Legal Servs, staff atty, 1978-79; Legal Aide & Defender's Off, pub defender, 1979-80; Wayne Co Corp Coun, asst corp coun, 1981; State Mich, admin law examiners, admin law judge, 1982-. **Orgs:** Legal Coun Soc Engrs & Appl Scientists, 1982-; Wolverine Bar Asn, 1982-; Asn Black Judges Mich, 1983-; bd dirs, Legal Aide & Defender's Asn, 1987; Augusta D Straker Bar Asn. **Honors/Awds:** Special Achievement Award, SEAS, 1984. **Business Addr:** Adminstrative Law Judge, State of Michigan, Mich Plz 1200 6th St Suite 540, Detroit, MI 48226-2418, **Business Phone:** (313)256-2063.*

CRAIG, STARLETT RUSSELL
Educator. **Personal:** Born Aug 17, 1947, Asheville, NC; daughter of Robert; divorced; children: Kemi & Karma. **Educ:** Spelman Col, BA, sociol, 1969; Bryn Mawr Grad Sch Social Work & Social Res, MSS, 1971. **Career:** Univ NC, Asheville, dir off aging, 1978-80; Western Carolina Univ, foreign stud adv, asst to vice chancellor stud develop; Clemson Univ, lectr & dir acad progs, currently. **Orgs:** Mem res comn, NC Assn Women Deans, Counselors & Admin, 1982-85; grad adv, Alpha Kappa Alpha Sorority, 1984-85; Nat Assn Foreign Stud Affairs; Jackson Co Coun Status Women. **Honors/Awds:** Field Scholar Spelman Col, 1965-69; Holt Manley Wilburn Young Scholar Alumnus Award, 1965-67; Outstanding Young Women of America, 1983. **Business Addr:** Lecturer, Director of Academic Programs, Clemson University, Acadaemic Outreach Programs, Tillman Hall G11, Clemson, SC 29634-5128, **Business Phone:** (864)656-0676.

CRAIG-RUDD, JOAN
Government official. **Personal:** Born Oct 5, 1931, Flushing, NY; children: Carolyn Hopkins, Michael, Reginald. **Educ:** Immanuel Lutheran Col, 1949, NC Central Univ, 1950, US Army Logistics Mgt Ctr, 1969; Nat Contract Mgrs Assoc, sem, 1978. **Career:** USAF Brooklyn, expeditor, 1958-64; US Army NY City, purchasing agent contract negotiator, 1967-71; Otis Air Force Base, procurement specialist, 1971-72; NY City Off Track Betting Corp, contract adminr, contracts compliance officer, mgr contracts, 1975-. **Orgs:** Credit union loan comn Off Track Betting Corp, 1976-; Nat Contract Mgrs Assoc, 1976-81; OTBC rep NY City Prevailing Wage Coun, 1981-; OTBC Informal Hearing Officer, 1983-; life mem, NAACP, 1985; peer counr, NY Chap Nat Multiple Sclerosis Soc, 1985-. **Honors/Awds:** Service Award, NY Multiple Sclerosis Soc, 1986. *

CRANFORD, DR. SHARON HILL
Executive director. **Personal:** Born Feb 8, 1946, Joaquin, TX; daughter of Rev Garfield (deceased) and Eulalia; married Evies; children: Charlton F, Corey M. **Educ:** TX Woman's Univ, BA, 1966; Atlanta Univ, MA, 1970; Kans State Univ, PhD, 1981. **Career:** TX State Dept Human Resources, coord vol serv, 1976-77; Jarvis Christian Col, dir stud union, 1977-79; Residential Homes Boys, dir, 1983-84; Wichita State Univ, asst prof, 1984-85; Cranford Adult Living-Learning Ctrs Inc, exec dir; Hesston Col, diversity dir, currently. **Orgs:** Corres secy, The Links Inc, 1985-87; pub rels chair, Alpha Kappa Alpha Sor Inc, 1985-87; vpres, City Wichita Pub Libr Bd Dirs, 1985-; Coalition Mental Health; pres, Residential Area Providers Handicapped Serv; Kans State Dept Social Serv Bd, 1987-89; KS Para Transit Coun; grad adv, Alpha Kappa Alpha Sor Inc; soprano & soloist, Calvary Baptist Ch & Choir, 1984-; diversity dir, Hesston Col, currently. **Honors/Awds:** Service to Youth Award, Nat Alliance Bus, 1985; Public Service Award, Omega Psi Phi Frat, 1986. **Business Addr:** Diversity Director, Hesston College, 325 S College Dr, PO Box 3000, Hesston, KS 67062, **Business Phone:** (620)327-8238.

CRAVEN, JUDITH
Educator, public health official. **Educ:** Bowling Green State Univ, BS, 1966; Houston's Univ, MD, 1974, MPH, 1981; Baylor Col Med, MD. **Career:** Sch Allied Health Sci, Houston, TX, dean; City Houston, dir pub health, chief family health serv; Riverside Gen Hosp, chief anesthesia; United Way Tex Gulf Coast, pres; Univ Tex Health Sci Ctr, Houston, prof pub health admin & prof interdisciplinary studies; Baylor Col Med, clin asst prof community med; Shanghai Med Univ, vis prof pub health; Univ Tex Syst, Bd Regents, mem, 2001-; A. H. Belo Corp, bd dir; Luby's Cafeterias Inc, bd dir; SYSCO Corp, bd dir. **Special Achievements:** First African-American to head the Texas Gulf Coast office. **Business Addr:** Regent, University of Texas System, 201 W 7th St Suite 820, Austin, TX 78701-2981, **Business Phone:** (512)499-4402.*

CRAVER, AARON LERENZE
Football player, football coach. **Personal:** Born Dec 18, 1968, Los Angeles, CA; married Dawn, Jun 29, 1991; children: Jalen, Kyndol & Maia. **Educ:** El Camino Jr Col; Fresno State Univ. **Career:** Football player (retired); Football coach; Miami Dolphins, running back, 1991-94; Denver Broncos, 1995-96; San Diego Chargers, 1997; New Orleans Saints, 1998-99; Head Football coach, Artesia High Sch, currently. **Honors/Awds:** Ed Block Courage Award, 1998. *

CRAWFORD, BETTY MARILYN
Manager. **Personal:** Born Sep 25, 1948, Philadelphia, PA; daughter of James and Dolores Fuller. **Educ:** DC Bible Inst, 1987; Gayles Theol Sem, DC, 1988. **Career:** Univ Pa, receptionist; Internal Revenue Serv, temp clerk & typist acct dept, acct maintenance clocker; Internal Revenue Serv, Wash, DC, comput systs analyst, 1977-83; Internal Revenue Serv, prog analyst, 1983-. **Orgs:** Asn Improvement Minorities-Internal Revenue Serv, 1972-; Guildfield Baptist Church, Wash, DC, 1983-; dir Dist Fed Young People DC & Vicinity, 1987-; chmn, Black Employ Prog Mgrs-Internal Revenue Serv, 1988-. **Honors/Awds:** Employee of the year, Internal Revenue Serv, 1989. **Special Achievements:** Profiled in Black Enterprise magazine for career accomplishments in 1987; honored as an outstanding Adopt-A-School Volunteer in 1988. **Business Addr:** Program Analyst, Internal Revenue Service Department Of Treasury, Fields Systems Branch, 550 Main St, Cincinnati, OH 45202, **Business Phone:** (202)622-8001.*

CRAWFORD, BRENITA
Hospital administrator. **Personal:** Born in Amory, MS. **Educ:** Jackson State Univ, BS, biol, chem; Univ Ala, MS, hosp & health admin; Med Univ, SC, Doctorate Degree, currently. **Career:** Univ Miss, Univ NC, joint res team, data collection; LeBonhuer Med Ctr, admis adminr; Reg Med Ctr, exec asst position, vpres; Henry Ford Hosp,assoc adminr, 1987-91; Mercy Hosp, pres & chief exec officer, 1991; Amara Management Resource, Dir; Methodist Health Ctr, exec vpres; Reg Med Ctr, chief operating officer, currently; Univ Memphis, Div Health Admin, asst prof, 2007-. **Orgs:** Warren/Conner Develop asn; Cancer Found; Greater Detroit Area Health Coun; Healthy Detroit; mem, Am Col Health Care Exec; Am Acad Med Adminrs; mem, m Hosp asn; Nat Ctr Health Leadership; adv bd, Sch Health Related Professions; Univ Ala, Birmingham; Tenn Hosp Asn Coun on Diversity; bd,Church Health Ctr; Lifeblood Found bd. **Honors/Awds:** Nat Coun Negro Women, Detroit Chap, Anti-Defamation League Women of Achievement; Community Serv Award, Nat Assn Negro Bus & Prof Women. **Business Phone:** (901)678-5688.

CRAWFORD, DR. CARL M.
School administrator, consultant. **Personal:** Born Nov 14, 1932, Tallahassee, FL; married Pearlie Wilson; children: LeVaughn Harrison. **Educ:** Fla A&M Univ Tallahassee, FL, BA, 1954; Boston Univ, MA, MEd, 1965; Univ Miami Sch Educ Coral Gables, FL, EdD, 1971. **Career:** Battery D 95th Anti-Aircraft Artillery Battalion, Mannheim Germany, exec officer, 1954-56; Dillard Elem Sch Grades 1-6, Ft Lauderdale FL, art,1956-60, grade 6 1960-61, grade 5, 1961-62, art grades, 1-6, 1962-65; S Fla Sch Desegregation Consult Ctr, Sch Educ, Univ Miami, asst consult, 1965-66, assoc consult, 1966-67; Art Ctr Title III ESEA Proj Broward Co Bd Pub Instr, coordr/comt, 1967-70; Psychol & Educ Dept, Miami-Dade Community Col S Campus, Miami FL, chmn, 1970-73, chmn, self-study steering comt, 1972-73; N Campus Broward Comm Col, dean, 1974-75. **Orgs:** Nat & S Regional Coun Black Am Affairs; Nat Asn Black Sch Educrs; Phi Delta Kappa; Fla Asn Community Col; Am Asn Community & Jr Col; Nat Asn Advan Colored People; Urban League; consult, Annual Fest Arts Nat YMCA Week NW Br YMCA Ft Lauderdale, FL, 1963-66; consult, World Work Conf Dept Attendance & Equal Educ Oppor, Palm Beach, FL, 1966; speaker African Art Spring Fest Music/Drama & Art Dillard Comp HS Ft Lauderdale, FL, 1966; consult, Pinellas Co Teachers Asn Human Rel Coun Conf Integration Sch Fac Chinsegut Hill Univ S FL, 1968; speaker African Art Cult Enrichment Series Allapattah Jr HS Miami, FL, 1968; consult, African Art for Intro to Afro-Am Studies Palm Beach Jr Coll Palm Beach, FL, 1969; consult, Miami Springs Jr HS Humanizing the Fac & Studs,1971; chmn Curriculum Com on S As Visiting Com for Eval St Thomas HS Ft Lauderdale, FL, 1971; reactor Synergy in Med Serv sponsored by SAA at Dupont Plaza Hotel Miami, FL, 1971; secy, Fla Arts Coun, 1980; Samuels Campus, provost . **Honors/Awds:** Distinguished Service Award, Prof Educ Broward Co Teachers Asn, 1967; Outstand Achievement & Serv in the Field of Educ Award Piney Grove 1stBapt Ch, 1971; Award for Appreciation Symbolic of Friends of Educ Mrs Susie H Womack Principal, Sunland Park Elem Sch, 1972; Cert of Recog for Serv as a Resource Bank Vol for Enriching the Classroom Exper of Studs in Broward Co Sch, 1974-75; Appreciation for Outstand Contrib in Fostering Better Comm Rel in Broward Co Award Broward Co Off of Comm Rel, 1975; Outstand

Educators of Am in Admin Published by a Div of Fuller & Dees Wash, DC, 1975; Cert of Appreciation for Educ Achievement, The Links Inc, 1975; The Johnnie Ruth Clarke Award for Excell in Comm & Jr Coll Serv S Regional Coun Black Am Affairs Richmond, VA, 1982; Biography in "Black Pioneers of Broward Co" "A acy Revealed" published by The Links Inc The Ft Lauderdale Chap, 1976. **Military Serv:** AUS, lt, 1954-56.

CRAWFORD, CRANFORD L., JR.
Executive. **Personal:** Born Jan 12, 1940, Marshall, TX; married Jennie Henry Crawford (deceased). **Educ:** Tex S Univ, BA, 1963. **Career:** REECO, sr clerk; Zion Univ Meth Church, black comt developer; Juvenile Ctr, probation officer, 1970-73; Prot Serv & Juvenile Prob, supr intake units, 1973-76; Clark City Juvenile Ctr Servs, prog dir, 1976-87, div supr detention, 1987-. **Orgs:** Vpres, NAACP, 1973-77; life mem, Alpha Phi Alpha NV Chapter; Nat Asn Black Soc Workers; Prince Hall Mason; Clark City Comn Christian Social Concerns; Westside Athletic Asn; Alpha Kappa Alpha; grand master, Most Worshipful Prince Hall; MWPH Grand Lodge NV, F&AM 1985-; Scottish Rite Masson 33 degree; hon mem, imperial adviser Ophir Temple; AEAONMS. **Honors/Awds:** Servce to Man kind Award, 1973; Award of Merit, NAACP, Las Vegas, 1973; Afro Unity Festival Award of Merit, 1978, 1980; YMCA Service Awards, 1978, 1981-82; Afro-American of the Year, SOMBER, 1982; Grand Marshal Dr ML King Jr Parade, 1985; Service Award, Sickle Cell Anemia Found, NV, 1986. **Special Achievements:** 100 Most Influential Black in NV 1980. **Business Addr:** Division Supervisor, Clark Company Juvenile Court Service, 3401 E Bonanza Rd, Las Vegas, NV 89191.

CRAWFORD, CURTIS J.
Executive, president (organization), chief executive officer. **Educ:** Gov State Univ, BA, bus admin & comput sci, MA, mkt; DePaul Univ, Charles H Kellstadt Grad Sch Bus, MBA; Capella Univ, PhD, org & mgt. **Career:** IBM, systs engr, 1973, vpres mkt; AT&T Comput Systs, vpres sales, 1988-91;AT&T Microelectronics, vpres & co-chief exec officer, 1991-93, pres, 1993-95; Lucent Technologies, Micro electronics Group, pres, 1995-97, group pres, 1997-98, Intellectual Property Div, pres, 1997-98; Intellectual Property Div, pres, 1997; ZiLOG Inc, pres & chief exec officer, 1998-2001, chmn bd dirs, 1999-2001; ON Semiconductor Corp, chmn bd dirs, 1999-2002; Onix Microsystems Inc, pres & chief exec officer, currently; Xchief exec officer Inc, founder, pres & chief exec officer, currently. **Orgs:** Bd dir, Lyondell Petrochemical Co; bd dirs, I-Stat Corp; Semiconductor Indust Asn; Nat Action Coun Minority Engrs; bd dirs, ITT Indust Inc; bd trustees, DePaul Univ; bd dirs, Agilysys Inc; bd dirs, EI du Pont de Nemours Co; bd dirs, ON Semiconductor Corp, 1999-2002; vice chmn, bd dirs, ZiLOG Inc. **Honors/Awds:** Hon Dr, Govs State Univ, 1996, DePaul Univ, 1999. **Special Achievements:** Selected as one of Black Enterprise's 25 Hottest Black Managers, 1988. **Business Phone:** (408)855-0000.

CRAWFORD, DAN
Basketball executive. **Personal:** Born Nov 23, 1953, Chicago, IL; married Claudia; children: Drew & Lia. **Educ:** Northeastern Col, IL, attended 1976; Cregier, IL. **Career:** Nat Jr Col, official, 1983-84; Chicago land Collegiate Athletic Confs, official; MO Valley, official; Nat Basketball Asn, official, currently. **Honors/Awds:** Hall of Fame, IL; Hall of Fame, Chicago Pub Schs; Wall of Fame, Northeastern Col, IL. **Business Addr:** Official, National Basketball Association, 645 5th Ave 15th Flr, New York, NY 10022-5986.*

CRAWFORD, DAVID
Administrator, manager, vice president (organization). **Personal:** Born Mar 12, 1941, Charlotte, NC; son of Rev Columbus and Margaret Adams; married Joan McGill Crawford, Jul 31, 1965; children: Davaree, Darlisa. **Educ:** Johnson C Smith Univ, Charlotte, NC, BS, 1963; Univ Liverpool, England, 1964; Univ NC, Chapel Hill, MA, 1966; RPI, Hartford, CT, MS, 1983. **Career:** UTC Pratt & Whitney, E Hartford, CT, mgr, manpower planning & devel, 1972-75, divisonal supt, machine shop, 1975-78, exec asst to pres, 1978-80, N Haven, CT, prod mgr, 1980-84, Southington, CT, plant mgr, 1984-91, North Haven, CT, plant mgr, 1991-93; Advan Mfg UTC, Pratt & Whitney, dir, 1993-97; consult, 1997-. **Orgs:** Bd dirs, Conn Pre-Eng Prog, 1990-; vpres, Cheshire Lion Club, 1981-. **Honors/Awds:** UTC Leadership Award, 1987. **Home Addr:** 381 Crestwood Dr, Cheshire, CT 06410. *

CRAWFORD, DEBORAH COLLINS
Educator. **Personal:** Born Oct 6, 1947, San Antonio, TX; divorced; children: Candice Aundrea. **Educ:** Prairie View A&M Col, BS, 1969; Our Lady Lake Univ, MEd, admin cert. **Career:** Educator(retired); St Philips Col, dance instr; Union Carbide, acts recv clk, 1970; Valhalla Sch Dist, pe instr, 1970-71; Summer Camp, White Plains, pe instr, 1971; Alamo Community Col Dist Mgt Workshop, coord insvc, comput literacy instr, 1987; City San Antonio Human Resources, presenter "Why Man Creates"; San Antonio Independent Sch Dist, asst prin, currently. **Orgs:** Am Women Radio & TV; coord, YWCA Sem; lectr, Our Lady Lake Univ Black Hist Activity; Bus & Prof Womens Club; co-emcee, Miss PV Pageant; res person, Nat Asn Advan Colored People State Conv; Links Inc; AKA Sor; Miss Black SAP agent & Choreographer, 1977; Ella Austin Comm Ctrs Bd; St Philips Col Rest Mgt Prog; East side Boys Club; Pine St & Ctr YWCA; Girl Scouts Publicity Com; Nat Asn Advan Colored People publicity com; Youth Philharmonic; Black Expressions Art League; City Fine Arts Comn; Tex State Teachers Asn; Dance Educr Am; Jack & Jill Am; Prairie View A & M Alumni, Nat Convention, publicity chair, 1999. **Honors/Awds:** Distinguished Pub Serv Award, Prairie View A&M, 1974; Award Cause Human Dignity Nat Asn Advan Colored People, 1975; nominee Outstanding Young Woman Am, 1976; Serv Award, Sr Opportunity Serv Ctr, 1975-76; Model Comn Leaders Award, Miss Black SA Bd, 1976; Comm Serv Award Walker-Ford Gospel Singers; mayoral appointment Martin Luther King Jr mem Comn City San Antonio Media Chairperson, 1987; city coun appointment arts & cultural adv bd; citation Mayor Cisneros & Councilman Webb, Pub Serv, 1989; dir,Debbie's Darlings Inc 1989. *

CRAWFORD, ELLA MAE
School administrator. **Personal:** Born Sep 8, 1932, Coffeyville, KS; married Willie E Sr; children: Willie E. **Educ:** Wash State Univ, attended 1980. **Career:** Tacoma Housing Authority, relocation asst, 1954-60; City Tacoma WA, relocation families & individuals, suprv, 1960-68; Tacoma Pub Sch, occup info asst & financial aid officer; LH Bates Voc Tech Inst, coord disadvantaged, 1968-71; Tacoma Urban Coalition, coordr secretarial Improv prog, 1968. **Orgs:** Former mem, Spec Educ Task Force, Wash State Spec Needs; former vchmn, Wash State Develop Disabilities Planning Coun; former secy, Pacific NW Regional Nat Housing & Redevelop Off; Wash State Financial Aid Adminr; Black Prog Educrs Tacoma Pub Schls; Title IX Sex Equity Adv Com; Educ for all Legis, Wash State Dept Soc & Health Serv Coun; United Good Neighbors Planning Coun, 1967-79; UGN Budget Comt, 1967-79; bd mem & chmn, Scholar Com Tacoma Chap, Nat Asn Adv Colored People, 1968-; former pres, Tacoma Altrusa Club, 1968; E B Wilson Civic Club Bethlehem Church, 1975; bd mem, Pierce County Personel Rev Bd, 1978-81; bd mem, City Tacoma Pub Utilities, 1979-85; secy, TacomaModel Cities bd; former mem, Hilltop Improvement Coun; Minority cerns Task Force; Sat Morning Collective; Civic & Prog Asn; Employment Com Wash State Develop Planning Coun; liaison & vpres, Tacoma Urban League Guild. **Honors/Awds:** Citizen Award, OEO Poverty Prog, 1964; Woman of Year, Zeta Phi Beta Sorority, 1972; Outstanding Citizen Award, Tacoma Model Cities Exec Bd,1975; Appreciation Award; Title IX Chmn.

CRAWFORD, HR
Housing developer. **Personal:** Born Jan 18, 1939, Winston-Salem, NC; married Eleanora Braxton; children: Leslie, Hazle, George, Gregory & Lynne. **Educ:** Howard Univ, 1961-63; DC Teachers Col, 1963-65; Am Univ, 1968; Chicago State Univ Polit Sci, BA; NC Archit & Training Univ, hon LLD, 1975. **Career:** Dept Defense, comdr, Navy Yard; Kate Maramont, Rep Victor Degrozia, Chicago, Ill, 1969-73; Nat Asn Home Builders Successful Housing Mgt, lectr, 1969-73; Univ Mich, Taught Successful Housing Mgt, assoc prof, 1969-73; Howard Univ, Sch Archit, assoc prof, 1969-73; Crawford Corp, pres, 1969-73; Kaufman & Broad, vpres & asst mgr, 1971-73; Pollinger & Crawford, vpres & sr mgr, 1972-73; US Dept Housing & Urban Develop, asst secy, 1973-76; Nat Capitol Housing Authority Monteria Ivey, dept dir; Nat Corp Housing Partnership & George DeFranceaux, consult, pres, 1976-79; Mid City Deveop & Eugene Ford, pres, 1976-79; Crawford Edgewood Mgrs Inc, chief exec officer, 1979-, pres, currently; DC Councilman, Ward 7, 1980-92. **Orgs:** Inst Real Estate Mgt, Builders Owners & Mgrs Asn; Nat Asn Housing & Redevel Off; Prof Property Mgrs Asn; Wash Bd Realtors; Wash Planning & Housing Asn; Nat Asn Home Builders; Resident Mgrs Asn; dir, Bonabond Inc; Wash DC Adv Bd Recreation; Anacostia Econ Develop Corp; Frederick Douglass Community Ctr; Cong Heights Asn Serv & Educ; Am Cancer Soc; Jr Citizens Corp Inc; pres, Nat Asn Real Estate Brokers, Wash DC Chapter, 1994-96; chmn, DC Real Estate Comn, 1995-; vpres, Nat Asn Advan Colored People, Wash DC Chap, 1995-97; Kiwanis Club; bd dir, Metro Wash Airport Authority; Mayors Comn Veterans Affairs. **Honors/Awds:** IREM Manager of the Year Award, 1973; Distinguished Serv Award, Nat Real Estate Brokers & Omega Tau Rho; Cherokee Indians Goodwill Award. **Military Serv:** USAF, sgt 1956-65. **Home Addr:** 3195 Westover Dr SE, Washington, DC 20020, **Home Phone:** (202)583-7777. **Business Addr:** Chief Executive Officer, President, Crawford Edgewood Managers Inc, 916 Pennsylvania Ave SE, Washington, DC 20003, **Business Phone:** (202)547-4300.

CRAWFORD, JAMES MAURICE
Administrator. **Personal:** Born Jan 8, 1946, Boligee, AL; son of Maurice and Dollie; married Patricia Jones, Jun 9, 1973; children: Courtney. **Educ:** Ohio Univ, BBA, 1968; Yale Univ, 1970; Occidental Col, MA, 1972. **Career:** Nat League Cities, sr legis coun; US Dept Housing & Urban Develop, spec asst secy; US Dept Health & Human Serv, spec asst secy/dep exec secy; Equitable Life Assurance Soc US, exec asst chief financial off, planning financial mgr; Prin Financial Group, strategic develop, govt rel, dir. **Orgs:** bd mem, C & Families Iowa, 1991-97; bd pres, Found C & Families Iowa, 1990-91; bd mem, Metro Des Moines Young Men's Christian Asn, 1992; bd mem, KAPSI Found, 1991; bd mem, Corinthian Gardens Elderly Housing, 1994; charter mem, Sci Bound Develop Coun, Iowa State Univ, 1996-99; bd mem, W Des Moines Pub Libr, Friends Found, 1996; bd mem, Polk Co Ment Health Serv Inc, 1998; adv mem, Des Moines Area United Negro Col Fund, 1999; bd mem, Am Red Cross, Cent Iowa chap, 2001; comnr, Iowa Col Stud Aid Comn, 2001; cmnr, Clive Planning & Zoning Comn, 2001. **Honors/Awds:** Nat Urban Fel, Ford Found, 1970; Secretary Achievement Award, US Dept Health & Human Serv, 1981; Des Moines Chamber Com, Leadership Inst, 1984; Up & Comer, Des Moines Regist Newspaper, 1985. **Home Addr:** 13545 Village Ct, Clive, IA 50325. *

CRAWFORD, JAYNE SUZANNE
Association executive. **Personal:** Born May 11, 1958, Hartford, CT; daughter of Odell Crawford and Beatrice Crawford. **Educ:** Lincoln Univ, BA, 1980. **Career:** Inquirer Newspaper Grp, reporter 1980-82; Focus Magazine, assoc ed, 1981-83; Crawford-Johnson Assoc, partner, 1981-; Comm Renewal Team, indus organizer, 1983-84, asst to exec dir, vpres direct serv, currently. **Orgs:** Pres, Urban League Guild Greater Hartford, 1982-85; bd dirs, Urban League Greater Hartford 1982-85; Co-chmn, Young Execs, 1983; exec chairperson, New England Urban League Guild Network, 1986-87; Key Issues Leadership Forum/The Hartford Conrant, 1989-; Leadership Greater Hartford Inc. **Honors/Awds:** Co-editor "Beyond Ourselves", Community Renewal Team, 1982. *

CRAWFORD, KEITH
Football player. **Personal:** Born Nov 21, 1970, Palestine, TX. **Educ:** Howard Payne univ. **Career:** NY Giants, wide receiver, 1993; Green Bay Packers, 1995; St Louis Rams, wide receiver, 1996-97; Kans City Chiefs, 1998; Atlanta Falcons, 1998; Green Bay Packers, wide receiver & safety, 1999. *

CRAWFORD, LAWRENCE DOUGLAS
Mayor, dentist. **Personal:** Born Jun 13, 1949, Saginaw, MI; married Winnie Hill; children: Lawrence D Jr & Alan A. **Educ:** Univ Mich, polit sci, 1970, Dent Sch, DDS, 1974. **Career:** Dentist, 1974-; Town Saginaw, city councilman, mayor, 1981-, secy, currently; DBM Technologies, pres & chief exec officer, currently. **Orgs:** Saginaw County Dent Soc; Saginaw Valley Dent Soc; Mich State Dent Asn; Nat Dent Asn; Am Dent Asn; Mid-State Study Club; consult, Univ Mich, Dent Admis Hattie M Strong Found; bd dir, first Ward Community Ctr; commis, E Cent Mich Planning Commis; pres, RCA View Develop Corp; Frontier's Int, Black Businessmen's Asn Saginaw; Alpha Phi Alpha Fraternity; E Side Lions Club; Bethel AME Church; chair bd dirs, Delta Dent Mich; vice chair, Delta Dent Found, currently; Nat Asn Black Automotive Suppliers. **Honors/Awds:** Nat Merit Semifinalist; Public Health Fellowship; Honor Award, 1967; Frontier's Businessman of the Year, Frontier's Int, Saginaw, 1980; Family Members United Meritorious Service Award, 1980; Professional Achievement Award, Zeta Phi Zeta Sorority, 1981. **Business Addr:** President, Chief Executive Officer, DBM Technologies LLC, 140 S Saginaw Suite 725, Pontiac, MI 48342, **Business Phone:** (248)836-4800.

CRAWFORD, MARGARET WARD
Government official. **Personal:** Born Apr 18, 1937, Pontiac, MI; married Samuel Kenneth Crawford Sr; children: Cheryl, Samuel Jr, Gary, Sara Elizabeth & Adrienne Irene. **Educ:** Wayne State Univ, BS. **Career:** Mich Dept Social Serv, social worker, 1960-73; Free Lance Volunteer, counr, facilitator, political, soc activist, 1973-; Schrock Adult Care Homes, admin, asst dir, 1980-; Lincoln Consult Schs, pres brd educ. **Orgs:** Mich Assn Sch Brds, 1974-; trustee, Lincoln Schs Brd Edn, 1974-; Nat Assn Sch Brds, 1975-; instr, Mich Dist Cong Christian Educ, 1979-; Speaker &consult, Studs Rights, Spec Educ, Sch Boards manship, Youth Advocacy, State& Fed Legislation Impacting Youth, Womens Issues 1979-; pres, Lincoln SchsBd Educ, 1981-; Sumpter Housing Rehab Coun, 1981-; brd dir, Corner Health Ctr, 1981-82; Legislative Comn, 1982-84, Wash tenaw County Black Elected Officials, 1983-; designated friend, Corner Health Ctr, 1983-; Sumpter Twp Political Action Comn, 1984-; trustee, church clerk, Mt Hermon Missionary Baptist Church, 1984-; Resolutions Comn, 1985-; ex-officio mem, Sumpter Young Women's Assn, 1985-; Sumpter Nat Assn Advan Colored People; Gifted &Talented Spec Educ Child Advoc; mem delegate, Wash tenaw County Sch Off Assn. **Honors/Awds:** Key Award, Mich Asn Sch Bds, 1984; Certificate, Twp School Dist & NatBlack Child Develop Coun. **Home Addr:** 49372 Arkona Sumpter Twp, Belleville, MI 48111.

CRAWFORD, MARY GREER. **See Obituaries section.**

CRAWFORD, MURIEL C
Executive. **Educ:** Hampton Univ, BS, 1956; Cuyahoga Comn Col, refresher course archit drawing, 1978; Univ WI Sch Engineering & Sci, attended 1979; Case Western Reserve Univ Weatherhead Sch Mgt, course bus planning, 1986. **Career:** York Rd Jr HS, art instr, 1956-57; Cleveland Bd Educ, art instr, 1957-69; Charles Eliot Jr HS, art dept chmn, 1967-69; Self-employed, interior designer, 1969-75; The Halle Bros Co, interior designer, 1975-78; Edith Miller Interiors, interior design, 1978-84; Mgt Off Design Inc, pres, 1982-. **Orgs:** Am Soc Interior Designers; Interior Design Educ Tour Eng Am Soc Interior Designers, 1978; designer, Dining

Rm Hope House Am Cancer Soc Am Society Interior Designers Benefit, 1979; vignette designer, March Dimes Gourmet Gala & ASID Benefit, 1984; speaker, Nat Endowment Arts Recognition Women Design Prof, 1985; juror, Nat Coun Interior Design Qualification Qualifying Exam for Interior Design Prof, 1986. **Business Addr:** President, Management of Office Designers Inc, 16611 Chagrin Lee Plz Suite 202, Shaker Heights, OH 44120, **Business Phone:** (216)991-0498.

CRAWFORD, ODEL
Manager, chief executive officer, president (organization). **Personal:** Born Apr 23, 1952, Brownwood, TX; son of Charles Williams and Jewel Crawford Danner; married Catherine Goodwin, Aug 15, 1972; children: Vanessa Yvonne, Ashanti Monque & Pharren Rene. **Educ:** Abilene Christian Univ, BS, bus mgt, 1974. **Career:** Mutual of Omaha, sales agt, 1976; KMART Corp. asst mgr, 1976-78; TexEmploy Comn, area mgr, 1978-97; Tex Workforce Comn, prog admin & mgr,currently. **Orgs:** Bd mem, Greater Odessa Chamber Com, 1988-; bd secy, Tex Asn Black Chambers Com, 1988-; bd mem, Odessa Boys & Girls Club, 1988-97; bd dirs,pres, chief exec officer, Black Chamber Com, Permian Basin, 1989-; bd mem,Permian Basin Private Indust Coun, 1989-92; classroom consult, bd mem, Jr Achievement, Odessa, 1990-96; bd dirs, pres, W Tex Adult Literacy Coun,1991-95; chmn, bd mem, Bus Devel Bd & Enterprise Zone Comt, 1991-96. **Honors/Awds:** Dean K Phillips Award, Nat Vet Training Inst, 1988; Ebony Bar Award, Black Chamber Com, 1986. **Special Achievements:** Publications: Minorities are Huge Force in Workplace, 1989; Helps to Employers on Hiring and Firing, 1989; Government Provides Many Services to Local and National Small Businesses, 1989. **Home Phone:** (915)580-4423. **Business Phone:** (432)367-3332.*

CRAWFORD, PAM SCOTT (PAMELA D CRAWFORD)
Executive. **Personal:** Born Sep 17, 1969, Nyack, NY; daughter of Wilton and Mary; married Vinson, Nov 6, 1999. **Educ:** Pa State Univ, BS, polit sci, 1991; Georgetown Univ, JD, 1996. **Career:** US Dist Ct, clerk, 1995-96; Tex Senate, atty, legis aide, 1997-99; Tex Coun Admin Spec Educ, asst dir, 1999-2000, exec dir & gen coun, 2000-; Tex Asn Sch Bd, asst dir, currently. **Orgs:** Sigma Gamma Rho, 1988-91; bd mem, Breast Cancer Resource Ctr, 1999-. **Business Addr:** Assistant Director, Texas Association of School Boards, 7703 N Lamar, PO Box 400, Austin, TX 78752, **Business Phone:** (512)467-0222.

CRAWFORD, PAMELA D. See CRAWFORD, PAM SCOTT.

CRAWFORD, RAINEY
Executive. **Career:** Director(retired); Ford Motor Co, dir, regional govt affairs, 2002. **Orgs:** Corporate Round Table; bd mem, Citizenship Sports Alliance; bd mem, Mo Chamber Com; bd mem, Ark State Chamber Com.

CRAWFORD, VANELLA ALISE
Association executive, consultant, social worker. **Personal:** Born Nov 25, 1947, Washington, DC; daughter of James Vance Jackson Jr and Dorothy Samella Raiford Patton; married William Alexander, Apr 1971 (divorced); children: Kahina B. **Educ:** Fisk Univ, 1965-67; Fed City Col, BA, 1973; Howard Univ, MSW, 1975; Wash Sch Psychiat, Cert, 1983. **Career:** Urban Prof Assoc, dir outpatient serv, 1975-79; Lt Joseph P Kennedy Inst, counr, 1977-79; Howard Univ Hosp, psychiat social worker, 1980-86; Cong Nat Black Churches Inc, proj dir, 1986-; Decades Inc, Body Shaping Shoppe, co-owner, 1992-; Vanella Group, pres & chief exec officer, 1988-. **Orgs:** Child Develop Dept, Georgetown Univ, 1978; United Way Am, 1978; Nat Asn Social Workers, 1979; dir, Christian Educ N Brentwood AME Zion Church, 1982-85; Young People's Proj 15-24 Clin, 1985-88; pvt productions/co-owner, Psychol Resource Ctr, 1985-87; trainer, DCPC, 1985; CNBC, 1985; Nat Asn Black Social Workers, 1985; consult, Cong Nat Black Churches, 1986; DC Coalition Social Work Health Care Providers; adv bd, Am Red Cross Adolescent Prog; lead bd/co-chairperson, Duke Ellington Sch Performing Arts. **Honors/Awds:** Alpha Delta Mu Nat Work Honor Soc. **Special Achievements:** Designed nationally acclaimed parent education program, PRAISE: Parents Reclaiming African Information for Spiritual Enhancement, 1980-93. **Home Addr:** 1109 Mich Ave NE, Washington, DC 20017, **Home Phone:** (202)269-0049. **Business Addr:** President & Chief Executive Officer, The Vanella Group, 1109 Mich Ave NE, PO Box 29472, Washington, DC 20017, **Business Phone:** (202)269-0049.

CRAWFORD, VANESSA REESE
Executive, administrator. **Personal:** Born Dec 30, 1952, Petersburg, VA; daughter of Richard A Reese Jr and Esther Elizabeth Taylor Reese (deseased); married Leon Crawford, Jul 11, 1987; children: Latricia, Richard, Roderick, Cornell II, Leon Jr & Courtney. **Educ:** Va Commonwealth Univ, Richmond, Va, BS, 1974. **Career:** Central State Hosp, Petersburg, Va, social worker, 1974-78; Chesterfield Correctional Unit, Chesterfield, Va, counr, 1978-85, asst supt, 1985-87; Dinwiddie Correctional Unit, Church Road, Va, asst supt, 1987-89; New Kent Correctional Unit, Barhamsville, Va, supt, 1989-91; Pocahontas Correctional Unit, Chesterfield County, Va, supt, 1991-99; Va Dept Corrections, Res & Mgt Servs, lead analyst, 2000-03; City Petersburg, sheriff, currently. **Orgs:** Bethany Baptist Ch, 1961; Nat Asn Blacks Criminal Justice, 1980; Am Bus Women's asn, 1987; Petersburgh Chap 33 Order Eastern Star, 1989; secy, Parent & Dist Adv Coun, Petersburg Sch, 1990; Nat Asn Female Executives, 1990-; appointed, Dist 19 Community Adv Bd, Petersburg, Va, 1993-; chair, Camelot Neighborhood Watch asn; Petersberg Symphony Orchestra Women's Comt; mentor, Va Commonwealth Univ; pres, Petersburg High Sch Boosters Club; bd dirs, Town & Country Nursery Sch Found; bd dir, Burger King, Communities Sch; parent advisory coun, Petersburg High Sch; teenage pregnancy coun-Southside Regional Med Ctr; Petersburg Public Sch, Character Educ Task Force; Nat Asn Negro Bus & Prof Women's Club, Petersburg chp, financial secy; Appomatox Reg Governors Sch, bd mem; Petersburg Task Force on Domestic Violence; Am Cancer Bd, Petersburg chp; Petersburg Police Athletic League. **Honors/Awds:** Boss of the Year Award, Am Bus Women's Asn, 1993; Achievement Award for Outstanding Performance, Nat Asn Negro Bus & Prof Women's Club, 1994; African-American Role Model, WTVR Channel 6, 1997; Achievement Award, Delta Sigma Theta. **Special Achievements:** First female sheriff of Pittsburgh. **Business Phone:** (804)733-2369.

CRAWFORD, VERNON
Football player. **Personal:** Born Jun 25, 1974, Texas City, TX. **Educ:** Fla State Univ, Criminology. **Career:** New England Patriots, linebacker, 1997-99; Green Bay Packers,free agent, 2000. *

CRAWFORD, WILLIAM A.
State government official. **Personal:** Born Jan 28, 1936, Indianapolis, IN; son of Kenneth C and Essie L Crouch; married Lennie M (divorced); children: Michael, Daren, Monica & Kim. **Career:** Postal clerk & community organizer; St John's Missionary Baptist Church, Indianapolis IN, youth coordr, 1972-78; Ind Gen Assembly, state rep, 1973-86; Marion Co Clerk, admin asst, 1978; Ind House Reps, D98, state rep, currently; cosult, currently. **Orgs:** Nat Asn Advan Colored People; Urban League; Trans Africa Southern Christian Leadership Conf; Free S Africa Movement. **Military Serv:** Radarman Third Class, USN, 1954-58. **Business Addr:** Representative, Indiana House of Representatives, 200 W Wash St Room 405, Indianapolis, IN 46204, **Business Phone:** (317)232-9600.

CRAWFORD-MAJOR, TONI
Executive director. **Career:** Common Wealth Pa, Dept Community & Econ Develop, Southeast regional dir, currently; Gov Ctr Local Govt Serv, exec dir, currently. **Business Addr:** Southeast Regional Director, Common Wealth of Pa, Department Community & Econ Develop, 1400 Spring Garden St, 1801 State Off Bldg, Philadelphia, PA 19130, **Business Phone:** (215)560-2083.

CRAWLEY, BETTYE JEAN. See BROWN, BETTYE JEAN.

CRAWLEY, DARLINE
Government official. **Personal:** Born Sep 3, 1941, St Louis, MO; married Lou E. **Career:** Real estate entrepreneur; City of Pagedale, MO, alderwoman ward 3. **Orgs:** Women in Leadership; deaconess, Fifth Baptist Church. **Home Addr:** 1835 Ferguson Ave, Saint Louis, MO 63133. *

CRAWLEY, GEORGE CLAUDIUS
Government official. **Personal:** Born Mar 19, 1934, Newport News, VA; married Cynthia Hewitt; children: Judith Crawley Johnson, Jason Claudius. **Educ:** VA State Univ, BA, 1956. **Career:** Government official (retired); Southeastern Tidewater Oppor Project, exec dir, 1966-73; City Norfolk, div social serv dir, 1973-76, dept human resources dir, 1976-83, city mgrs off asst city mgr, 1983-96. **Orgs:** Dir, Legal Serv Corp of VA, United Way Tidewater, Athletic Found Norfolk State Univ, Darden Sch Bus, Univ VA Inst Mgt, Southeastern Tidewater Manpower Auth, Norfolk Investment Corp, STOP Organ; chmn, Hampton Roads Alumni Group Va State Univ; dir, Va State Univ Alumni, adv bd; dir, Girls & Boys Club Hampton Rds VA, St John AME Church; secy, Elizabeth City State Univ. **Honors/Awds:** Distinguished Serv Award, Tidewater Conf Minority Pub Adminrs, 1985; Numerous awards and citations for contributions from governmental, civic, social and religious organisations. **Military Serv:** AUS, lt, 1957-58. **Home Addr:** 1466 Holly Point Rd, Norfolk, VA 23509. *

CRAWLEY, OSCAR LEWIS
Labor relations manager. **Personal:** Born May 19, 1942, Lafayette, AL; son of Katie and Carlton; married Clemestine Clausell; children: Deitra Phernam & Oscar Lewis III. **Educ:** Ala State Univ, BS, psychol, 1963; Univ S Ala, grad study. **Career:** Westpoint Pepperell Inc Fairfax Towel Operation, asst personnel dir, 1972, personnel dir, 1975-; Marengo High Sch & Dixon Mills Ala, teacher, 1963-72; West Point Pepperall Inc, indust rel mgr, 1988-; Bath Prod, Westpoint Stevens, div human resources dir, 1994-; City Lanett, mayor, 2004-. **Orgs:** Alpha Phi Alpha Inc, 1974; comnr Goodwill Inds, 1976; chmn, bd comnr, Lanett City Housing Auth, 1978; dist committee man, George H Lanier Coun Boy Scouts, 1975; chmn, Indust Com Chambers Co Ment Health, 1978; chmn, Aux Com Chambers Co Bd Educ, 1979; gov staff State Ala Gov George C Wallace, 1977; bd mem, Chambers County Heart Asn, 1990; bd dir, Chambers County Libr, 1994. **Honors/Awds:** Chair of the Year, Am Heart Asn, Jailbail, 1992-93; Valley Crime Stoppers, Bd Dir, 1994. **Home Addr:** 611 N 14th St, Lanett, AL 36863. **Business Addr:** Mayor, City of Lanett, 401 N Lanier Ave, Lanett, AL 36863, **Business Phone:** (334)644-5231.

CRAWLEY, SYLVIA
Basketball player. **Personal:** Born Sep 27, 1972, Steubenville, OH; daughter of James and Marie. **Educ:** Univ NC, BA, Commun & Radio, TV & Motion Pictures, 1994. **Career:** Int teams: Rouen, France; Vigo, Spain; Reggio, Italy; Lugo, Spain; ColoXplosion, 1996-97; Portland Power, forward, 1997-98; Am Basketball League, Portland Fire, forward, 2000-02; Univ NC, asst coach, 2000-02; San AntonioSilver Stars, 2003; San Antonio Spurs & Stars, mgt; Fordham Univ, top asst; Korea, player, 2005; Fordham rams, interim head coach, 2006; Ohio Bobcats, Ohio Univ, head coach, 2006; Boston Coll Eagles, Head Coach, currently. **Honors/Awds:** Nat Collegiate Athletic Asn, 1994; Atlantic Coast Conf, 1994; USA Basketball's Female Athlete of the Year, 1995; Most Valuable Player, Prof European League all-star game, 1995. **Special Achievements:** Featured in a Sports Illustrated for Women story on how to dunk; addressed numerous youth groups; first Woman Slam Dunk Champion, 1998. **Business Addr:** Head Coach, Department Athletics, Ohio University, Intercollegiate Athletics, Convocation Ctr, Athens, OH 45701, **Business Phone:** (740)593-1193.*

CRAY, ROBERT
Guitarist, singer, actor. **Personal:** Born Aug 1, 1953, Columbus, GA; son of Henry and Maggie; married Susan Turner. **Career:** The Robert Cray Band, leader, 1974-; Albums: Who's Been Talkin', 1980; Bad Influence, 1983; False Accusations, 1985; Strong Persuader, 1986; Don't Be Afraid Of The Dark, 1988; Midnight Stroll, 1990; I Was Warned, 1992; Shame A Sin, 1993; Some Rainy Morning, 1995; Sweet Potato Pie, 1997; Take Your Shoes Off, 1999; Should a Been Home, 2001; Time Will Tell, 2003; Twenty, 2005; Live From Across The Pond, 2006; Live At The BBC, 2008; This Time, 2009; home video appearances include: Hail! Hail! Rock 'n' Roll, tribute to Chuck Berry, 1988; Break Every Rule, HBO spec with Tina Turner, 1987; 24 Nights, concert video with Eric Clapton, 1991; The Robert Cray Collection, music, videos, live performances, interviews, 1991; Hoodoo U Voodoo live pay per view concert, with the Rolling Stones, 1994; MTV Unplugged: Ballads, 2000; Through Riley's Eyes; 2000; John Lee Hooker: That's My Story, 2001; Lightning in a Bottle, 2004; "Biography", 2004; "The Late Late Show with Craig Ferguson", 2005; "Crossroads Guitar Festival," with Eric Clapton, 2007; film: Animal House, actor; Otis Day & the Knights, actor. **Honors/Awds:** Rolling Stone critics, Best R&B Artist; four Grammy Awards, six additional Grammy nominations; San Francisco Bay Area Music Awards, BAMMIE; numerous awards by Northwest Area Music Asn; numerous W C Handy Awards; Blues Hall of Fame, Showdown!, 1989; platinum & gold status albums worldwide. **Business Phone:** (972)250-1162.

CRAYTON, DR. JAMES EDWARD
Administrator, library administrator. **Personal:** Born Dec 18, 1943, Thomasville, AL; son of Bennie and Ernestine. **Educ:** AL State Univ, BS, 1964; Atlanta Univ, MLS, 1968; CA State Univ Long Beach, MA, 1975; Claremont Grad Sch, PhD Educ & Higher Educ Admin, 1980. **Career:** Milton FL Sch Dist, 1964-65; Cobb Co Bd Educ Austell GA, 1965-67; Anaheim Pub Lib, 1968-70; LA Co Pub Lib, 1970-72; Pasadena City Col, lib 1972-78, teacher & coordr, acquisitions librarian, dir occup educ, 1980-, div dean Community Educ Ctr, currently. **Orgs:** Mem coun, CA Lib Asn; minority adv, 1973-74; chmn, Black Caucus Leg Comm; NAACP LA Urban League. **Business Addr:** Division Dean, Pasadena City Coll, Community Educ Ctr, 1570 E Colorado Blvd, Pasadena, CA 91106-2003, **Business Phone:** (626)585-3000.

CREARY, LUDLOW BARRINGTON
Physician. **Personal:** Born Nov 17, 1930, Kingston, Jamaica; married Lou Jene. **Educ:** Long Island Univ, BS, 1956; Howard Univ, MD, 1960; MPH. **Career:** Wayne Co Hosp Detroit, intern, 1960-61; Ventura Co Hosp CA, resident family pract, 1961-63; Broadway Hosp, chief med, 1969-72; Martin Luther King Jr Hosp, Los Angeles, 1970; W Adams Community Hosp, chief med staff, 1971-72; Charles R Drew Postgrad Med Sch; Drew Med Ctr, chmn & prof, 1981-2000; Pvt Pract, currently; Univ Med & Sci, Univ Calif Los Angeles, prof & chmn, chief serv, Dept Family Med, currently. **Orgs:** Am Acad Family physicians; Los Angeles County Med Asn; bd trustees, Calif Acad family physicians found; Nat Med Asn. **Home Addr:** 1315 Carla Ln, Beverly Hills, CA 90210.

CREFT, BRENDA K
Nurse, military leader. **Educ:** Northwestern State Univ. **Career:** USAF, Wilford Hall Med Ctr, colonel & chief nurse, currently. **Military Serv:** USAF. **Business Phone:** (210)670-7100.

CREIGHTON-ZOLLAR, DR. ANN
Educator. **Personal:** Born Sep 16, 1946, Thomasville, AL; daughter of Thomas E and Jimmie A Gordon; divorced; children: James A & Nicai Q. **Educ:** Univ Ill Chicago, BA, sociol, 1973, MA, sociol, 1976, PhD, sociol, 1980. **Career:** Garfield Park Comprehenisve Comm Health Ctr, supvr res & eval, 1979-80; VaCommonwealth Univ, asst prof sociol, 1981-88, Afro-Am Studies Prog, actgcoordr, 1984-85, Dept Sociol & Anthrop, assoc prof, 1988-, African AmStudies Prog, from interim dir to dir, 1993-98. **Orgs:** Phi Kappa Phi Nat Hon Soc, 1973. **Special Achievements:** A Member of the Family, Strategies For Black Family Continuity, Chicago Nelson Hall, 1985; "The Contribution of Marriage to the Life Satisfaction of Black Adults", J Marriage & Family, 1987; Adolescent Pregnancy & Parenthood, Garland, 1990; The Social Correlates of Infant & Reproductive Mortality in the United States, Garland, 1993; Humanitarian of the Year, Las Amigas Inc, 2003. **Business Addr:** Associate Professor of Sociology, Virginia Commonwealth University, Department of Sociology, Hibbs Bldg, 900 Park Ave, PO Box 842002, Richmond, VA 23284-2002, **Business Phone:** (804)827-0962.

CRENSHAW, REGINALD ANTHONY
Research scientist, college administrator. **Personal:** Born Sep 29, 1956, Mobile, AL; son of Johnnie Mae; married Portia LaVerne Johnson. **Educ:** Morehouse Col, BA, Economics, 1978; Univ S Ala, MPA, Public Admin, 1984; Univ Southern Miss, Phd. **Career:** Mattie T Blount HS, high sch instr, 1978-79; City Prichard, councilman, 1980-88; Bishop State Jr Col, res analyst, instr & dir, student servs, 1980-. **Orgs:** Mem adv bd, Commonwealth Nat Bank, 1982-; bd dirs, Mobile Co Urban League, 1983-; vpres bd dirs, Deaborn St Com Ctr, 1984-; vpres, Beta Omicran Lambda Chap Alpha Phi Alpha Fraternity. **Honors/Awds:** Man of the Year Award, Alpha Phi Alpha Frat, 1980; UNCF Distinguished Leadership Award, 1982 & 1983; Mobilian of the Year Award, Mobile Chap Phi Beta Sigma Frat, 1983; Community Leadership Award, Ladies Auxiliary knights Peter Claver, 1984. **Home Addr:** 1021 Sample St, Prichard, AL 36610. **Business Addr:** Director Student Services, Bishop State Community College, 351 N Broad St, Mobile, AL 36603-5890.

CRENSHAW, WAVERLY DAVID
Lawyer, administrator. **Personal:** Born Dec 17, 1956, Nashville, TN; son of Waverly D, Sr and Corinne Smith. **Educ:** Vanderbilt Univ, Nashville TN, BA, 1978, JD, 1981. **Career:** Chancery Ct, Nashville TN, legal coun chancellors, 1981-82; US Dist Judge John T Nixon, Nashville TN, law clerk, 1982-84; State Tenn, Nashville, TN, asst atty gen 1984-87; pvt law pract, 1987-; Vanderbilt Univ Sch Law, adjunct law fac, 1994; Waller Lansden Dortch & Davis, Nashville, TN, attorney & partner, 1990-. **Orgs:** Civil Justice Reform Act Adv Group, United States Dist Ct, Mid Dist Tenn; comt mem, Bd Prof Responsibility Supreme Ct Tenn; staff mem & Ed bd mem, Vanderbilt J TransNat Law, 1979-81; Panel Selection US Magistrate, 1984; pres, Napier-Looby Bar Asn, 1986-87; bd mem, Nashville Bar Asn Young Lawyers Div, 1986; bd mem, Middle Tenn, Am Civil Liberties Union, 1986-88; bd mem, Nashville Urban League, 1986-90; Chancellor's Comt Women & Minorities, Vanderbilt Univ, 1987; bd mem, Tenn Capital Case Resource Ctr, 1988-92; Harry Phillips Am Inst Ct; Am Bar Asn; Nashville Elec Servs Ethics & Audit Comn, 1992-; bd govs, Nashville Area Chamber Com, 1994-97, legal coun, 1995-96; bd dirs, Nashville Bar Asn, 1994-97; legal coun, 100 Black Men Tenn Inc; legal coun, Nashville Area Chamber Com, 1996; chair, Merit Selection Panel US Magistrate, US Dist Ct, Mid Dist Tenn, 1997-98. life mem, Conf Sixth Judicial Circuit United States; Chair, Labor & Employ Sect, Tenn Bar Asn, 2005; bd dirs, Boys & Girls Clubs Middle Tenn Inc; mayoral appointment, Hosp Authority's bd dirs Nashville; bd dirs, Mid Tenn Workforce Develop Bd; past adj instr pressional ethics, Vanderbilt Univ Sch Law Pressional Licenses; fel, Nashville Bar Found; fel, Tenn Bar Found. **Honors/Awds:** Sylvan Gatchal Award, Vanderbilt Univ, 1978; Whitney Young Jr Award for Excellence in Legal Services, Nashville Urban League, 1996. **Special Achievements:** First African-American Member of Waller Lansden. Recognized and listed in the current edition, Chambers USA America's Leading Business Lawyers. Recognized in the Nashville Business Journal's 2005 "Best of the Bar". Recognized in the current edition of Chambers USA America's Leading Business Lawyers as well as the Nashville Business Journal's 2005 "Best of the Bar"; "Best Lawyers", Tenn Bus J, 2007. **Home Addr:** 895 Oak Valley Lane, Nashville, TN 37220, **Home Phone:** (615)269-8867. **Business Addr:** Attorney, Waller Lansden Dortch & Davis, Nashville City Ctr, 511 Union St Suite 2700, PO Box 198966, Nashville, TN 37219, **Business Phone:** (615)850-8909.

CREUZOT, CHERYL D.
Financial manager. **Personal:** Born May 9, 1959, Washington, DC; daughter of David and Gloria Williams; married Percy P Creuzot III, May 17, 1983; children: Percy P IV, Coline M & Philippe P. **Educ:** BS, 1981; Col Financial Planning, attended 1985; JD, 1992; LLM, 1995. **Career:** AFP Group, financial planner, 1983-99, pres & coo, 1999-2001; Wealth Develop Strategies LP, pres & chief exec officer, 2001-, managing partner, currently. **Orgs:** Financial Planning Asn, 1985-; Million Dollar Round Table, 1989-; bd dir &finance comm, Proj Row Houses, 1991-; State Bar Tex, 1992-; stateco-chairperson, Dem Nat Comms Women Leadership Forum, 1996-; bd dir, African Am Arts Museum, 2000-; bd dir, Ensemble Theatre, 2000-; chair, Univ Houston Alumni Orgn; chair, United Negro Col Fund Black Tie Gala, 2005; the NatCoalition of 100 Black Women; chair, Tex Women's Empowerment Found. **Honors/Awds:** Financial Planner Month, Mutual Funds Mag, 2000; 2001 Super Achiever Award, Greater Houston YMCA, 2001; March of Dimes, 2002, 2004, 2006; National Black MBA (Houston Chapter) Leadership Empowerment Award, 2004; Corporate Sector Achievement Award by the University of Houston Law Alumni Association, 2008. **Special Achievements:** One of the Top Financial Planners in Country, Mutual Funds Mag, 2001. **Business Addr:** Managing Partner, President, Chief Executive Officer, Wealth Development Strategies LP, 5151 San Felipe Rd Suite 2000, Houston, TX 77056, **Business Phone:** (713)561-8100.

CREUZOT, PERCY P.
Hotel executive. **Personal:** Born May 28, 1924, New Orleans, LA; married Sallie Elizabeth Coleman; children: Percy P III, Angele C Williams, John C. **Educ:** Hampton Univ, BS, 1949. **Career:** exec (retired); Pyramid Life Ins Co, vpres, 1949-60; Percy P Creuzot Ins Agency, owner, 1950-59; Free Lance Auto Sales, salesman, 1961-63; Herff Jones Jewelry Co, salesman, 1963-67; Texas Employ Comn, interviewer, 1967-69; Frenchy's Po-Boy Inc, pres. **Orgs:** TX Restaurant Asn; nat Restaurant Asn; private Industry Coun, State TX, 1980-81; regent TX Southern Univ; civil serv comn City Houston TX; adv bd, Houston Restaurant Asn; bd dirs S Main Bank; Private Industry Coun State TX, 1980-81; dir, MacGregor Park Nat Bank, 1984; mem bd dir, Greater Houston Convention & Visitors Coun, 1985. **Honors/Awds:** Man of the Year, Houston Forward Times, 1976; Distinguished Commission Service Award, TX Southern Univ, 1977; Outstanding Alumnus, Hampton Univ, 1982; Humanitarian Award, TX Southern Univ Maroon and Gray Club, 1982; Top 100 Black Bus Black Enterprise Magazine, 1983-85; Distinguish Service Award, TX Southern Univ Superlative Accomplishments Bus & Com, Retailing, Mkt, Franchising, 1983. **Military Serv:** USN, carpenter, 1943-46.

CREW, JOHN L., SR.
Educator, psychologist. **Personal:** Born Nov 2, 1926, Westminister, SC; married Brooksie Wilks; children: John L. **Educ:** Morgan State Univ, BS, 1952; Morgan State Univ, post-19grad, 1953; Am Univ, grad stud, 1954; NY Univ, MA, 1955; Univ MD, PhD, 1968. **Career:** Baltimore Pub Schs, supt, 1975-82, interim supt, 1975-76, dep supt &planning res & eval, 1973-75; Plan Res & Eval, Baltimore City Pub Schs, acting assoc supt, 1972-73, div spec serv, dir, 1969-72. **Orgs:** Prof educ & asn & dir Res West Chester Col, 1968-69; st supv, Res & Eval Md St, Dept Educ, 1966-68; spec asst, Educ Testing Baltimore City Pub Sch, 1955-66; educ psychol, Balt City Pub Sch, 1960-65; psychometrist, Balt City Pub Sch, 1955-60; consultantships, Model Cit Agency Econ Develop Prog, Md St Dept Educ, Spec Educ, Div Archdiocese Baltimore; instr asst, NDEA Inst, Univ Md; res asst, Univ Md; Am Psychol Asn Am Educ Res Asn; ErPer & Guid & Asn Md Sch Psychol Asn; Md Acad Sci; Md Per & Guid Asn; Md, Asn Meas & Eval Guid; Nat Coun Meas Educ; Psi Chi Frat; Md Psychol Asn; Am Asn Sch Admnrs, 1974-; Bd Trustees, Samuel Ready Sch, 1972-73; adv comm Secy, Personnel St Md, 1971-73; vice chmn, St Plan & Adv Coun Develop Disabilities, secy Health & Ment Hygiene; dir, Ment Retard, 1970-73; Adv Coun Ment, Hygiene Secy Health & Comnr Ment. **Special Achievements:** Criterion-Referenced Testing: "Usages in Some Member Systems of the Council of Great City Schools", 1978. **Military Serv:** USN, 1950-52; AUS, res col, 1950-. **Business Addr:** 3 E 25th St, Baltimore, MD 21218.*

CREW, RUDOLPH F.
School administrator. **Educ:** Univ Mass, Amherst; Babson Col, Wellesley, BA. **Career:** San Antonio High Sch, Claremont , CA, adminr; Stupski Found, dir; Inst K12 Leadership, exec dir; Harvard Grad Sch Educ; Calif State Univ, adj asst prof; Lesley Col, adj prof; Wash, Tacoma Schs, supt; NY City Educ Bd, chancellor, 1995-99; Miami-Dade Schs, supt, 2004-. **Orgs:** Lincoln Ctr Performing Arts; New York Philharmonic; Wash Asn Black Sch Educr. **Honors/Awds:** Educational Leadership Award, NAACP; Arthur Ashe Leadership Award; Administrator of the Year Award, Asn Calif Sch Adminr . **Business Addr:** Superintendent, Miami-Dade County Public Schools, 1450 NE 2nd Ave, Miami, FL 33132, **Business Phone:** (305)995-1000.*

CREW, SPENCER R.
Curator, president (organization), chief executive officer. **Personal:** Born Jan 7, 1949, Poughkeepsie, NY; son of R Spencer and Ada L Scott; married Sandra Prioleau, Jun 19, 1971; children: Alika L & Adorn S. **Educ:** Brown Univ, Providence RI, AB, 1971; Rutgers Univ, New Brunswick NJ, MA, 1973, PhD, hist, 1979. **Career:** Univ MD, Baltimore Co, Catonsville MD, asst prof, 1978-81; Smithsonian Inst, Natl Mus Am Hist, Wash DC, historian 1981-87; Nat Mus Am Hist, historian, 1981, Div Community, cur, 1987-89, chair, Dept Social and Cult Hist 1991, dep dir, 1991-92, actg dir, 1992-94; dir, 1994-01; Nat Underground Railroad Freedom Ctr, exec dir, pres & chief exec officer, 2001-07. **Orgs:** Prog chair, 1985-86, exec bd mem, 1986-90, Oral Hist in the Mid-Atlantic Region; mem Oral Hist Assn, 1988-; 2nd vpres African Am Mus Assn, 1988-91; prog co-chair, Oral Hist Assn 1988; comnr & bd mem, Banneker-Douglass Mus, 1989-93; ed bd mem, J of Am Hist 1989-93; prog chair, African Am Mus Assn, 1989; sr youth group coordr, St John Baptist Church, 1989, co-ed, Newsletter for the Am Hist Assn, 1990-; trustee, Brown Univ, 1995-; bd mem Am Assn Mus, 1995-98; chair, Natl Coun Hist Educ, currently; bd mem, Natl Trust Hist Preserv, currently . **Honors/Awds:** Osceola Award, Delta Sigma Theta Sorority, 1988; Cert Award, Smithsonian Inst, 1989-92; Robert A. Brooks Award, Smithsonian Inst, 1994; Serv Award, Asn Study African Am Life & Hist, 1994; Hall of Distinguished Alumni Inductee, Rutgers Univ, 2003; McMickmen Col Distinguished Leadership Award, Univ Cincinnati, 2004. **Special Achievements:** Auth: Field to Factory: Afro-American Migration 1915-40, 1987; Co-cur: "Go Forth and Serve: Black Land Grant Colleges Enter a Second Century," 1990,"African American Images in Postal Service Stamps," 1992; auth, Black Life in Secondary Cities: A Comparative Analysis of the Black Communities of Camden and Elizabeth, NJ, 1860-20, 1993; Published extensively in the areas of African Am Hist & Pub Hist; co-auth, "The American Presidency: A Glorious Burden", 2000; Inducted to the Rutgers Hall of Distinguished Alumni, 2003. **Business Addr:** President, Chief Executive Officer, National Underground Railroad Freedom Center, 50 E Freedom Way, Cincinnati, OH 45202.*

CREWS, DONALD
Writer, illustrator. **Personal:** Born Aug 30, 1938, Newark, NJ; son of Marshanna White Crews and Asa H Crews; married Ann Jonas Crews, Jan 28, 1964; children: Nina Melissa, Amy Marshanna. **Educ:** Cooper Union Advan Sci & Art, NY, cert completion, 1959. **Career:** Dance Mag, NY, asst art dir, 1959-61; Will Burton Studios, NY, staff designer 1961-62; freelance designer for varoius employers, auth & illusr, 1979. **Honors/Awds:** Caldecott Hon Award, Freight Train, 1979, Truck, 1980, Am Library Asn; NYT, Ten Best Illustrated Books for Flying, 1986. **Special Achievements:** Auth: A to Z, Harper & Row, 1967; Ten Black Dots, 1968; Freight Train, 1978; Truck, 1980; Night at the Fair; Bigmama's; Shortcut; Sch Bus, 1984; Sail Away, 1995; Video: Parade, 1983; Fair, 1998; HarperCollins C's Books, currently. **Military Serv:** AUS, pvt first class , Frankfurt, Ger, 1963. **Business Addr:** Author, HarperCollins Childrens Books, 1350 Ave of the Americas, New York, NY 10019-4703.*

CREWS, VICTORIA WILDER
State government official. **Personal:** Born Sep 18, 1946, Brownsville, TN; daughter of Calvin C Sr and Eutropia B; divorced; children: Christine, Charles & Kara. **Educ:** Franklin Univ, bus admin, attended 1985; Ohio Dominican Col, sociol, 1985-87. **Career:** Government official (retired); Ohio Dept Health, ade asst, 1969-87; Ohio Dept Alcohol & Drug Addiction Servs, crd Women's Progs, 1987-90, mgr, prev servs unit, 1990, chief Div Prev Serv, 2000. **Orgs:** Gov Nat Educ Goals, 1991-92; Gov Head Start Collaborative, 1991-92; adv bd, Ohio Prev & Educ Resource Ctr, 1990-92; Gov Drug-Exposed Infants Task Force, 1989-91; Ohio Credentialing Bd Chem Dependency Profs, 1990-92; bd mem, Ohio Chem Dependency Prof Bd, 2006. **Special Achievements:** Nat Drug Prev Network Representative for Ohio, 1990-92.

CREWS, WILLIAM HUNTER
Clergy, executive director. **Personal:** Born Mar 18, 1932, Winston-Salem, NC; married June; children: William H. **Educ:** Virginia Union Univ; New York Univ, MEd; Union Theol Sem NY; George Col Downers Grove Ill. **Career:** Exec dir, Clergy (retired); YMCA Highland Park Branch Detroit, exec dir; Shiloh Baptist church, pastor, 1969-02. **Orgs:** bd dir, Rotary Intl Baptist & Pastors Coun Detoit; bd dir, Mich Mental Health Soc; assoc Prof, YMCA Dir; Omega Psi Phi. **Honors/Awds:** community service award, First Baptist Church, 1970; Outstanding community service award, St Mich, 1973. *

CREWS, WILLIAM SYLVESTER
Executive. **Personal:** Born Mar 5, 1947, Advance, NC; married Belinda Harden; children: David, Angela, William Jr. **Educ:** Winston salem State Univ, BA, 1969. **Career:** Wachovia Bank & Trust, audit & control trainee, 1969-70, asst local auditor, 1970-73, retail credit analyst, 1973-75, mgr, 1975-, vpres, bond opers, sr vpres, currently. **Orgs:** Bankersednl Soc, 1978; Nat Bankers Asn, 1978; Omega Psi Phi Frat, 1967; treas, Nat Sci Ctr, 1979. **Business Addr:** Senior Vice President, Wachovia Bank & Trust NA, PO Box 3099, Winston-Salem, NC 27102.*

CRIBB, JUANITA SANDERS
Government official, consultant, personal trainer. **Personal:** Born Nov 18, 1950, Winston-Salem, NC; married Kenneth Cribb, Jun 1969; children: Darrell, Dawn, Kenya. **Educ:** Carolina Sch Broadcasting & Journ, AAS, 1977. **Career:** Albany Local Develop Corp, GA, exec dir, 1986-88; Crystal Commun Corp, Albany, GA, consult & trainer, 1988-. **Orgs:** Leadership Albany, 1988-89; secy, Black County Comnr Ga, 1988-; Gov Adv Coun Ga Clean & Beautiful, 1989-; dir-at-large, Nat Asn Black County Officials, 1989-; bd dirs, Southwest Ga Community Action Coun, 1989-; Pathways Family Worship Ctr. **Honors/Awds:** Award of Merit, Albany Nat Asn Advan Colored People, Dougherty Chap, 1989; Women Who Make a Difference Award, Minorities &

Women Bus Mag, 1990; Community Leader Award, Delta Sigma Theta Sorority, Albany Alumnae Chap, 1990; Humanitarian Award, Holiday Soc, 1990. **Special Achievements:** Co-host Hour Magazine Talk Show, Fox Television, 1989. **Business Addr:** Consultant, Trainer, Crystal Communications Corporation, PO Box 4636, Albany, GA 31706-4636, **Business Phone:** (912)436-4721.*

CRIDER, EDWARD S., III
Judge. **Personal:** Born Feb 7, 1921, Kimball, WV; married Verdelle Vincson. **Educ:** WVa State Col, BS, 1941; Columbia Univ, attended 1949; Brooklyn Law Sch, JD, 1953; Modern Mgt Tech Long Island Univ, Cert, 1970. **Career:** Sr pub health sanitarian, 1947-67; part time practr law, 1955-; NY City Dept Health, regional dir, 1967-77; NY City Dept Health, spec asst to dir pest control, 1974-77; Dept Health NY, admin law judge. **Orgs:** Pres, Brooklyn Alumni Chap, Kappa Alpha Psi, 1957-59; fel, Food & Drug LawInst, NY Univ Law Sch, 1959; pres, NY Chap, WV Col Alumni Asn, 1975; Y'sMen; secy, Westbury Br, Nat Asn Advan Colored People; Urban League; YMCA;Kimball HS Alumni NY Chap; NY State Trial Lawyers Asn; Nassau Co Bar Asn;NY State Sanitarians Conf. **Military Serv:** AUS, 1st Lt, 1941-45. **Business Addr:** Director of Pest Control, Department Health, 65 Worth St, New York, NY 10013.*

CRIGHT, LOTESS PRIESTLEY
School administrator. **Personal:** Born Dec 3, 1931, Asheville, NC; married George Edward; children: Shaun, Shaniqua, Shannon, George & Wilson. **Educ:** Johnson C Smith Univ, BA, 1953; Brooklyn Col, MS, 1971. **Career:** School administrator (retired). Pub Sch, teacher, 1953-69; City Univ New York, NY Tech Col, reading instr, 1969-71, coordr coun, 1971-77, dir spec serv, 1977; Brooklyn Col, dir stud support serv, 1994, lectr educ servs; Amistad Child Care & Family Ctr, admin dir, 1995. **Home Addr:** 110-15 164th Pl, Jamaica, NY 11433.

CRIM, RODNEY
Executive. **Personal:** Born Jun 29, 1957, Chicago, IL; son of Katie Brown Crim and Elisha Crim. **Educ:** Univ Minesota, Minneapolis, MN, BSB, Acct, 1980; St Thomas Univ, Minneapolis, MN, MBA, 1991. **Career:** CPA; Pillsbury, Minneapolis MN, internal auditor, 1979-81; The Musicland Group, Minneapolis MN, financial analyst, 1981-82; Am Express Financial Servs, Minneapolis MN, gen acct supvr, 1982-83, human resources staffing assoc, 1983-84, mgr financial reporting 1984-87, asst controller, 1987-88, dir controller, 1988-91, dir oper audit, 1991-92; Microtron Inc, Minneapolis, MN, chief financial officer, 1992; St. Louis Development Corp, exec dir, currently. **Orgs:** Pres, Alpha Phi Alpha, Minneapolis MN, 1977-78; teacher, Jr Achievement, 1984; allocation panel mem, United Way, 1985; pres, Nat Asn Black Acct, MN, 1985-87; Leadership Minneapolis Prog, 1987; bd mem, YMCA Bd, Minneapolis MN, 1988-89; Minneapolis Community Col Adv Bd, 1991; Nat Asn Black MBAs; Nat Asn Black Accts. **Honors/Awds:** Vita Tax Assistance, State Bd Accountancy, 1983; Member of the year, Nat Asn Black Accts, 1988. **Business Addr:** Executive Director, St. Louis Development Corp, 1015 Locust St Suite 1200, St Louis, MO 63101, **Business Phone:** (314)622-3400.*

CRIPPENS, DAVID L.
Media executive. **Personal:** Born Sep 23, 1942, Jefferson City, TN; son of Nathaniel and Dorothy; married Eloise Crippens, Aug 4, 1968; children: Gerald. **Educ:** Antioch Col, Yellow Springs OH, BA, 1964; San Diego State Univ, San Diego CA, MSW, 1968. **Career:** KPBS-TV, producer, 1969-71; WQED-TV, Free-lance writer/journalist, 1971-73; KCET, Channel 28, LA CA, dir educ servs, 1973-77, vice pres, 1977-90; Educ Enterprises, sr vpres, currently. **Orgs:** bd trustees, Calif Federation Employment & Disability, Black on Black Crime, Antioch Col; pres, ceo, DLC & Assoc, currently. **Honors/Awds:** Corp for Public Broadcasting fels, 1969; distinguished alumni, Graduate Sch Social Work, San Diego State Univ, 1973; most influential blacks, Pittsburgh Post Gazette, 1973; serv to media award, San Diego chapter NAACP, 1975; minority telecommunications award, Nat Assoc Educ Broadcasters, 1978; commendation, California State Legislature for Voices of Our People, 1983; outstanding service award, Young Advocates, 1986; honored by Nat Assoc Media Women, 1986; 1990 Euclan Award, Sch of Educ, UCLA; National Citation Award, National Sorority of Phi Delta Kappa, 1992; Positive Image Award, Frank D Parent PTA, 1992; Outstanding Educational Leadership Award, National Sorority of Phi Delta Kappa, 1992; Principals Organ Award, Senior Highschools, 1991; Excellence in Educational Commun Award, Cal Poly, 1991. **Business Addr:** Senior Vice President, KCET Pub Television-Educ Enterprises, 4401 Sunset Blvd, Los Angeles, CA 90027, **Business Phone:** (323)666-6500.*

CRISP, DR. ROBERT CARL, JR.
Educator. **Personal:** Born Apr 17, 1947, Sanger, TX; son of Robert and Martella Turner; married Carolyn Tyler, Jan 31, 1970; children: April Nichole & Adria Camille. **Educ:** Langston Univ, Langston, Okla, BA, 1969; Univ Mich, Ann Arbor, Mich, MA, 1971, PhD, 1976. **Career:** Detroit Pub Schs, Detroit, MI, band dir, 1969-84, dept head, 1979-84, music supvr, 1984-94, Off Music Educ, dir, 1994-. **Orgs:** Bd trustees, Messiah Baptist Church, 1979-; Classical Roots Steering Comt, Detroit Symphony, Orchestra, 1985-88; bd trustees, Detroit Chamber Winds, 1987-; bd trustees, Community Treat Ctr, 1989-; nat talent co-chmn, Omega Psi Phi Fraternity, 1990-; bd dirs, Blue Lake Fine Arts Camp, bd dirs, Community Treatment Ctr; bd dirs, Mich Performing Arts Youth Theater; bd dirs, Neighborhood Serv Orgn. **Honors/Awds:** Urban Adult Attitudes Towards Bus & Desegration, University of Michigan, 1976; Distinguished Service Award, Wayne Co Execs, 1985; Testimonial Resolution, Detroit City Coun, 1987; Kappan of the Year, Phi Delta Kappa Int, 1987; Service Award, Omega Psi Phi Fraternity, 1990-; Spirit of Dart Award, Dart City Coun. **Business Addr:** Director, Detroit Public Schools, Office of Fine Arts, 5057 Woodward Rm 850, Detroit, MI 48202, **Business Phone:** (313)494-1075.*

CRISP, SYDNEY A.
Executive. **Career:** FleetBoston Robertson Stephens Inc , sr vpres, global technol serv. **Business Addr:** Senior Vice President of Global Technology Services, FleetBoston Robertson Stephens Inc, 555 California St Suite 2600, San Francisco, CA 94104-1502, **Business Phone:** (415)781-9700.

CRISWELL, ARTHURINE DENTON
Administrator. **Personal:** Born Jan 30, 1953, Memphis, TN; daughter of Arthur and Celia Hambrick; children: Joshua Michael. **Educ:** Park Col, BA 1973; Univ KS, MSW 1981. **Career:** KS City Serv League, social work intern, 1979-80; KS Dept Social & Rehab Serv, grad intern, 1980-81, prog supvr, 1981-84, area mgr, 1984-; Lawrence Area Off, dir, 2004. **Orgs:** Nat Asn Social Workers 1979-; Nat Asn Couples Marriage Enrichment, 1983-; bd mem, Pvt Indust Coun, 1984-85; pres, Junior League Wyandotte & Johnson Counties, 1995. **Honors/Awds:** Outstanding Alumni, Park College, 1995. **Home Addr:** PO Box 12611, Kansas City, KS 66112. **Business Addr:** Supervisor, American Family Insurance, Social & Rehab Servs, PO Box 590, Lawrence, KS 66046.*

CRITTENDEN, RAY
Football player, medical researcher. **Personal:** Born Mar 1, 1970, Washington, DC. **Educ:** Va Tech univ, commun; Barry Univ, MS, biomedical sci. **Career:** Football player (retired); New Eng Patriots, wide receiver, 1993-96; San Diego Chargers, wide receiver, 1997; Horizon Institute, clinical research coordr, currently. **Special Achievements:** Most valuable offensive player of the Metro Invitational Tournament; All-South Atlantic Region honors; Ranked fifth in the AFC kickoff returns as a rookie.

CROCKER, CLINTON C
Art consultant, educator. **Personal:** Born Sep 7, 1928, Norfolk, VA; son of William L and Helen Mae Ford; married Doris Hickson; children: Clinton Jr, Leah Kay, Roger & Ronald. **Educ:** Rider Univ, Trenton, NJ, BMus, 1952; Kean Col, Union, NJ, MA, 1967. **Career:** Educator (retired); Newark, NJ, pub sch teacher, 1955-67; Kean Col, NJ, adj prof, 1959-67; Brookdale Community Col, Lincroft, NJ, exec dean, 1969-72; Rutgers Univ, NJ, univ arts admin, 1972-85; dir, 200th Commemorative Session NJ State Legis, 1983-84; CC Crocker & Co, NJ, pres. **Orgs:** NJ Soc Architects AIA, 1971; founder, Hispanic Arts Inst Rutgers Univ, 1975; United Fund Monmouth Co, 1977; founder & pres, NJ Haiti Partners Am, 1977-83; producer, Rutgers Univ Summer Festival TV Spec, 1980; founding mem & pres, NJ Sch Arts, 1980; bd trustees, Brookdale Community Col, 1987-91; bd trustees, Brookdale Community Col Fedn, 1988-91; founder & pres, African Am Arts & Heritage Festival, Garden State Arts Ctr, 1988; bd dirs, Asn Community Col Trustees, 1990; bd dirs, Monmouth Coun (NJ) Boy Scouts Am, 1995; bd trustees, Rutgers Univ, New Burnswick NJ, currently; vpres, Monmouth Coun, NJ Boy Scouts Am; bd dirs, Count Basie Learning Ctr, Red Bank NJ; bd trustees, NJ State Mus Art; Int Order St John Knights Malta; bishop election comn, Episcopal Diocese NJ; co-founder, Urban League Monmouth County, NJ; NJ State Coun Arts. **Honors/Awds:** Outstanding Public Service Award, Brookdale Community Col, 1972; Brotherhood Award, Nat Conf Christians & Jews, 1994. **Special Achievements:** Selected as one of the 100 Most Influential and Positive Individuals in New Jersey by City News, Plainfield, NJ. **Military Serv:** AUS, E-4, 1952-54. **Home Addr:** 120 Willshire Dr, Tinton Falls, NJ 07724.

CROCKER, CYRIL L.
Educator, physician. **Personal:** Born Aug 21, 1918, New Orleans, LA; married Anna Ruth Smith. **Educ:** Talladega Col, AB, 1939; Howard Univ, MD, 1950; Univ Calif, MPH, 1968. **Career:** Nat Bur Standards, Wash, chemist, 1942-46; Flint Good ridge Hosp, New Orleans, Obstet & Gynec, dir, 1955-56, Family Planning Serv, Dept Obstet Gynec, proj dir, 1970-76, prof, 1976; Howard Univ, instr, 1956-62, from asst prof to prof, 1962-72; Makerere Univ, lectr, 1968-69; Mulago Hosp, Kampala Uganda, E Africa, consult, 1968-69. **Orgs:** Alpha Omega Alpha, 1975; Kappa Pi Honor Soc; Am Col Obstetricians & Gynecologists; Am Col Surgeons; Nat Med Asn; Med Soc DC Medico-chirurgical Soc DC; Am Asn Planned Parenthood Physicans; Howard Univ Med Alumni Asn. **Honors/Awds:** Distinguished Service Award, Chmn DC Met Inter agency Coun, Family Planning, 1975. **Military Serv:** USNR, 1945-46.

CROCKER, DAVID
Chief executive officer, administrator, president (organization). **Career:** Chief executive officer (retired); Crocker Assocs, pres & ceo, 2003. *

CROCKER, WAYNE MARCUS
Library administrator. **Personal:** Born May 26, 1956, Petersburg, VA; son of George and Nancy Cooley; married Sabrina Tucker, Oct 15, 1983; children: Shannon Nicole & Courtney Lynn. **Educ:** Va State Col, Petersburg, VA, BS, 1978; Atlanta Univ, Atlanta, GA, MSLS, 1979. **Career:** Petersburg Pub Libr, Petersburg, VA, page & libr aide, 1973-78; Atlanta Pub Libr, Atlanta, GA, libr asst & libr, 1978-80; Petersburg Pub Libr, Petersburg, VA, Libr Serv, dir, 1980-. **Orgs:** Am Libr Asn, 1980-; Va Libr Asn, 1980-; Alpha Phi Alpha Fraternity, 1985-; pres & bd dirs, Petersburg City Employees Fed Credit Union, 1987; State Networking Users Adv, 1989-; . **Honors/Awds:** Louise Giles Minority Scholar, Am Libr Asn, 1978. **Home Addr:** 101 S Plains Dr, Petersburg, VA 23805. **Business Addr:** Director of library services, Petersburg Public Library, 137 S Sycamore St, Petersburg, VA 23803, **Business Phone:** (804)733-2387.

CROCKETT, DELORES LORAINE
Government official. **Personal:** Born Jun 18, 1947, Daytona Beach, FL; divorced; children: Ayanna T. **Educ:** Spelman Col, BA, psychol, 1969; Altanta Univ, MA, guidance & couns, 1972. **Career:** Minority Women's Employment Prog, proj dir, 1974-77; Avon Products Inc, employment & commun suprv, 1977-79; Nat Alliance Bus, metro dir, 1979; US Dept Labor, reg dir, Women's Bur, reg adminr, currently. **Orgs:** Selected Leadership Atlanta, 1977, Leadership GA, 1978; bd trustees, Leadership Atlanta, 1981; bd dir, Am Red Cross, 1982-; bd dir, Big Brothers/Big Sisters, 1985-; AH Task Force Nat Conf Black Mayors, 1985. **Honors/Awds:** Woman of Achievement, Bus & Prof Women's Clubs Inc, 1977, 1979; Cit Outstanding Comm Serv, Atlanta Women Bus, 1984; Outstanding Alumnae Award, Spelman Col Class of 1969, 1984. **Special Achievements:** One of the Ten Outstanding Young People of Atlanta 1979; Selected by Labor Dept as 1 of 2 reps to serve on Panel III studying Intl Training Prog to Eliminate Sex Imbalances in the Work Place Paris France 1983, 1984. **Business Addr:** Regional Administrator, US Dept Labour, Women's Bur, 200 Constitution Ave NW Rm S 3002, Washington, DC 20210.*

CROCKETT, GEORGE W., III
Judge. **Personal:** Born Dec 23, 1938, Fairmont, WV; son of George William Crockett Jr and Emily Ethelene Jones; divorced; children: Enrique Raul. **Educ:** Morehouse Col, Atlanta, GA, BA, 1961; Wayne State Univ, Detroit, MI, 1959; Detroit Col Law Detroit, MI, JD, 1964. **Career:** Judge (retired); pvt pract, 1965-66; Wayne Co Neighborhood Legal Serv, supv atty, 1967-70; asst corp counsel, 1967; Defenders Off Detroit, dep defender, 1970-76; Third Judicial Circuit Ct, judge, 2003. **Orgs:** Nal Bar Asn; MI State Bar; Wolverine Bar Asn; Asn Black Judges MI; NAACP.

CROCKETT, HENRI
Football player. **Personal:** Born Oct 28, 1974, Pompano Beach, FL. **Educ:** Fla State Univ. **Career:** Football player (retired), Atlanta Falcons, linebacker, 1997-01; Minn Vikings, linebacker, 2002-03. **Orgs:** Team 94; founder, The Crockett Found; Omega Psi Phi Fraternity Inc. **Honors/Awds:** Man of the Yr, Boys & Girls Club. *

CROCKETT, RAY
Football player, television show host. **Personal:** Born Jan 5, 1967, Dallas, TX. **Educ:** Baylor, BA, comput sci, 1992. **Career:** Detroit Lions, defensive back, 1989-93; Denver Broncos, 1994-00; Kans City Chiefs, 2001-03; mem, Fox Sports Net; TV series: "Bound for Glory", 2005; "Identity", 2006; TV & Radio host: "Count down to Kick off"; "Little Big Man"; "30 Days", Nite Tales The Movie, The Hustle, 2008; "Nite Tales: The Series", 2009. **Orgs:** United Way; Crock 39 Found. **Special Achievements:** Two-time Super Bowl champion. **Business Addr:** Member, Fox Sports Net, 10000 Santa Monica Blvd, Los Angeles, CA 90067, **Business Phone:** (310)284-2362.*

CROCKETT, WILLIAM F.
Administrator. **Career:** Ancient Egyptian Arabic Order Nobles Mystic Shrine Inc, imperial potentate. *

CROCKETT, ZACK
Football player. **Personal:** Born Dec 2, 1972, Pompano Beach, FL. **Educ:** Fla State Univ, criminol . **Career:** Indianapolis Colts, running back, 1995-97; Jacksonville Jaguars, 1998; Oakland Raiders, running back, 1999-2006, Tampa Bay Buccaneers, 2007, Dallas Cowboys, 2007. **Orgs:** Omega Psi Phi Fraternity Inc. *

CROCKETT-NTONGA, NOLUTHANDO
Journalist. **Personal:** Born Jul 14, 1950, Chicago, IL; daughter of Leo Crockett and Mae Corbin Williams; children: Adina Gittens. **Educ:** Univ Ill, Chicago, BA, 1972; Northwestern Univ, Medill Sch Journ, MA, 1979; Stanford Univ, Palo Alto, CA, Knight Fellow, 1991. **Career:** WSOC News Radio, producer, reporter, anchor, 1978-79; AP/UPI, Raleigh & Durham, NC, freelance

reporter, 1978-80; WFNC & WQSM, producer, reporter, anchor, 1979-80; Johnson C Smith Univ, vis instr, 1979; Am's Black Forum, panelist, 1980-83; Fayetteville State Univ, vis instr, 1980; Sheridan Broadcasting Network, exec ed & spec correspondent, 1980-81; Howard Univ, panelist & guest lectr; Univ DC, panelist & guest lectr; Stanford Univ, panelist & guest lectr; DC Pub Schs, Fairfax County Pub Schs, 1980-; WTTG-TV, news writer, 1981-82; Nat Pub Radio, reporter, 1981-89, White House correspondent, 1989-91, sr corresp, 1992-; Pac News Serv, freelance reporter, 1984, CNN analyst, 1992-; Black Entertainment Television, analyst, 1987-; C-SPAN Cable TV Network, WHHM-TV, analyst, 1987-. **Orgs:** Nat Asn Black Journalists, 1978-; Sigma Delta Chi, 1979 -; Smithsonian Inst, African Am Adv Comt, 1989-; commun dir, Corp Coun Africa, currently; Nat Newspaper Publ Asn. **Honors/Awds:** Frederick Douglass Award, Nat Asn Black Journalists, 1984; NEA Award, 1988; Robert F Kennedy Award, 1990; Nat Asn Black Journalists Award. **Business Addr:** Communications Director, The Corporate Council on Africa, 1100 17th St NW Suite 1100, **Business Phone:** (202)263-3515.

CROEL, MICHAEL (MIKE CROEL)
Football player, graphic artist. **Personal:** Born Jun 6, 1969, Detroit, MI; married; children: 2. **Educ:** Univ Nebr. **Career:** Football player (retired), Graphic artist; Denver Broncos, defensive end, 1991-94; New York Giants, 1995; Baltimore Ravens, 1996; Seattle Seahawks, line backer, 1998; Los Angeles Xtreme, 2001; Graphic designer, currently. **Honors/Awds:** Defensive Rookie of the Year, AP, 1991; AFL-AFC Rookie of the Year, UPI, 1991.

CROEL, MIKE. See CROEL, MICHAEL.

CROFT, IRA T
Mayor, school administrator. **Personal:** Born Feb 7, 1926, White Hall, AR; son of Effie and Rev E O Croft; married Dorothy Jean Taylor, Feb 10, 1951; children: Sonya Faye Croft & Lisa Juanita Croft. **Educ:** Shorter Col, N Little Rock, AR, BA, sociol, 1951; Fisk Univ, Nashville, TN, advan study sociol, 1951; Ark State Col, Am Hist Inst, Jonesboro, AR, attended 1964; Okla State Univ, Econ Inst, Stillwater, OK, attended 1969. **Career:** Mayor, School administrator (retired); W Memphis Sch Dist, W Memphis, AR, teacher & adminr, 1957-86; City of Edmonson, AR, mayor, 1986-98; Adult Sunday Sch Teacher. **Honors/Awds:** Appointed Chairman of all incorporated towns in Arkansas, Ark Munic League, 1992. **Special Achievements:** First African American instructor with West Memphis High School. **Military Serv:** Veteran of WW II. **Home Addr:** 400 Harrison, PO Box 65, Edmondson, AR 72332.

CROFT, WARDELL C.
Insurance executive, consultant. **Personal:** Born in Gadsden, AL; son of Thomas Croft and Minnie Croft; married Theora; children: Bobbie. **Educ:** Stillman Col; Alexander Hamilton Inst Bus; Univ Mich, Detroit. **Career:** Wright Mutual Ins Co, agency dir, genl mgr, exec vpres, prest, chmn & chief exec officer, 1962-97, chmn emer & consult, 2007-. **Orgs:** Exec comt, United Negro Col Fund, vice chair, 1991-92; vice chmn bd dirs, First Independence Nat Bank One Founders; bd dirs, Physician Drug Ctr,Detroit Renaissance, New Detroit Inc; bd trustees, Stillman Col; bd mem & chair, Life Ins Asn Mich; chmn, Detroit Inst Com; vice chmn, UNCF Exec Comt Mich; bd dirs, Inner-City Coun Alumni UNCF; adv bd mem, Metrop Detroit; Boy Scouts Am; life mem, Nat Asn Advan Colored People Golden Heritage; Detroit Coun Ins Execs. **Honors/Awds:** Michigan Citizen of the Year, Mich Chronicle; S Award, Stillman Col;Citizen Award, Phi Beta Sigma Frat; Silver Beaver Award, Boy Scouts of Am;CC Spaulding Award, Nat Bus League; Mich Ins Hall of Fame. **Military Serv:** AUS, WW II 1st sgt. **Business Phone:** (313)871-2112.

CROMARTIE, ERNEST W., II.
Lawyer, chairperson. **Personal:** Born in Waverly, SC; married Raynette White; children: Ernest W, Antionette. **Educ:** CA Johnson High Sch, attended 1963; Mich State Univ, BA, mkt & bus admin, 1968; George Wash Law Ctr, JD, 1971. **Career:** Cureton & Cromartie, atty, 1974-76; EW Cromartie II, atty, 1976-; City Columbia Dist II, councilman, 1983; Cromartie Law Firm LLP, atty, 1975-; SC Supreme Ct, pract; US Dist Ct, pract; US Ct Appeals 4th Circuit, pract; Charles R Drew Wellness Ctr, chmn, currently. **Orgs:** Zoning Bd Adjustments & Appeals, Mayor City Columbia, 1976-80, 1980-85; chmn, Eau Claire Task Force Community Ctr, 1980-81; nat deleg at large, SC Dem Nat Conv, 1986, 1996; Nat Asn Advan Colored People; Optimist Club; E Columbia Jaycees; United Way Bd Trustees; 32nd Degree Mason; Shriners, Midlands Elks; Townmen Club; Columbia Chamber Com; Housing Comn Greater Columbia, Chamber Com; United Way Gov Bd, Kiwanis Club; Bishop Memorial AME Church; pres usher bd, sunday sch teacher, bd of trustees, chmn bldg fund, Men's Day Activities; SC Bar Asn; Richland City Bar Asn; Am Bar Asn; SC Trial Lawyers Asn; Am Trial Lawyers Asn; SC Youth Serv Bd; Midlands Tech Col Found Bd; Alpha Phi Alpha Fraternity Inc; Richland Kiwanis Club; charter mem, 100 Black Men SC. **Honors/Awds:** Atty of the Yr, 1979; Distinguished Service Award, National Black Caucus; Outstanding Serv Award, SC Chap, Nat Asn Real Estate Brokers; Living Legacy Award, Nat Coun Negro Women; Order of the Palmetto. **Home Addr:** 1607 Harden St, Columbia, SC 29204. **Business Addr:** Attorney, Cromartie Law Firm LLP, 1606 Harden St, Columbia, SC 29204-1058.*

CROMARTIE, EUGENE RUFUS
Association executive. **Personal:** Born Oct 3, 1936, Wabasso, FL; son of Ulysses and Hannah; married Joyce Bell Mims; children: Eugene II, Leonardo, Marcus, Eliseo. **Educ:** Fla Agr & Mech Univ, BS, 1957; Univ Dayton, MS, 1968; US Army Command & Gen Staff Col, attended 1970; Nat War Col, attended 1977. **Career:** Univ Dayton, OH, asst prof military sci; AUS Military Police Sch, staff fac mem; Command & Gen Staff Col, staff fac mem; 82nd Airborne Div, provost marshal; Wash, DC, assignment officer personnel directorate; AUS Criminal Invest Command, spec asst to the commanding gen; AUS Criminal Invest Command Fort Meade, MD, commander first reg; AUS Europe & Seventh Army, dep provost marshal, provost marshal; US Army Military Community Commander Mannheim, Germany; AUS Criminal Invest Command, commanding gen; Int Asn Chiefs of Police, Arlington, VA, dep exec dir & chief staff. **Orgs:** Alpha Phi Alpha Frat, 1954-; Int Fedn Sr Police Officers, 1981-; Nat Coun Law Enforcement Explorer Boy Scouts Am, 1983-; Nat Orgn Black Law Enforcement Exec, 1984-; nat chmn, Law Enforcement Exploring Comm Boy Scouts Am, 1986-; exec dir, chief staff, Int Asn Chiefs Police, 1990-; Military Police Regimental Asn. **Honors/Awds:** Meritorious Achievement Award, Fla Agr & Mech Univ,1982; Outstanding Floridian, Fla State Resolution, 1982; Key to Tallahassee City, 1982; First inductee into Fla Agr & Mech Univ Hall of Fame 1986; Centennial Medallion for Distinguished Service Award Fla Agr & Mech, 1987; Meritorious Service Award, Nat Asn Advan Colored People, 1989; Honorary Doctor of Laws, Fla Agr & Mech Univ, 1990; Public Service Award, Nat Asn Fed Investr, 1989; President's Award, National Sheriffs Assn, 1989. **Special Achievements:** City of Tallahassee & Leon Co declared May 1, 1982 as Brigadier Gen Eugene R Cromartie Day. **Military Serv:** Retired. AUS Major Gen; served over 30 years; Distinguished Service Medal, 2 Bronze Star Medals; 3 Meritorious Serv Medals; 2 Army Commendation Medals; Parachutist Badge. *

CROMBAUGH, HALLIE
Media executive. **Personal:** Born Sep 9, 1949, Indianapolis, IN; married Dennis; children: Trenna, Kendra. **Educ:** Porter Col, 1974; Ind Central Col; St Mary the Woods Col. **Career:** Col & U Corp, auditor, gen acctg dept, 1974-75; Ind Today & Comm, dir, comm affairs, exec producer & host; WISH-TV, asst dir, comn Affairs, 1975-76; Am Fletcher Nat Bank, IBM & opr; Ind Nat Bank, NCR opr. **Orgs:** Chmn by-laws comt, Nat Broadcast Asn Comn Affairs; bd dir, Comn Serv Coun Greater Independent; chmn, Family Violence Task Force; chmn bd dirs, Wishard Mem Hosp Midtown Comm Mental Health Ctr; adv bd, Indianapolis Jr League; vchmn, Queens Selection & Coronation Comt Indianapolis 500 Fest Asn bd dirs,Indianapolis 500 Asn Inc; Gamma Phi Delta Int Sor Inc; asso min St Paul Am Chap IN Conf of 4th Episcopal Dist; ordained deacon Am Chap; chmn adv bd, Auntie Mames CDC. **Honors/Awds:** Outstanding serv award, United Award, 1975-79; media yr award, Marion Co Heart Asn, 1975-76; outstanding serv award, Indianapolis Pre-sch Inc, 1975-79; outstanding serv award, Indianapolis Pub Sch Operation Catch-up, 1977; outstanding serv award, Indy Trade Asn, 1977; outstanding mental health serv award, 1978-79; Golden heart award, Am Heart Asn, 1979.

CROMER, RONNIE E, JR.
Lawyer. **Career:** Law Off Ronnie E Cromer Jr, atty, currently. **Business Addr:** Attorney, Law Offices of Ronnie E Cromer Jr, 26440 Southfield Rd, Southfield, MI 48076, **Business Phone:** (248)559-5353.

CROMWELL, ADELAIDE M.
Educator. **Personal:** Born Nov 27, 1919, Washington, DC; daughter of John W Jr and Yetta M; divorced; children: Anthony C Hill. **Educ:** Smith Col, BA, 1940; Univ PA, MA, 1941; Bryn Mawr, Cert Soc Work, 1952; Radcliffe Col, PhD, 1952. **Career:** Educator (retired); Hunter Col, mem fac, 1942-44; Smith Col, mem fac,1945-46; Boston Univ, prof sociol, 1951-85, dir, Afro-Amer studies, 1953, prof emer sociol. **Orgs:** Adv comt, Corrections Commonwealth, MA, 1955-68; adv comm, Voluntary AID, 1964-80; dir, African Studies Asn, 1966-68; mem, Nat Order Ivory Coast, 1967; Nat Endowment for the Humanities, 1968-70; adv comm dir, IRS; Nat Ctr Afro-Am Artists, 1970-80; African Scholars Coun, 1971-80; bd mem, Wheelock Col, 1971-72; Commonwealth Inst Higher Educ, 1973-74; Nat Fel Fund, 1974-75; Bd Sci & Technol Int Develop, 1984-86; African Studies Asn; Am Social Asn; Asn Study African Am Life & Hist; Acad Arts & Sci; Coun Foreign Rels; Mass Hist Comn, 1993-; Mass Hist Soc, 1997-; exec coun, Am Soc African Cult; Am Negro Leadership Conf; adv coun, Vol Foreign Aid; mem, Phi Beta Kappa, currently; pres, The Heritage Guild Inc. **Honors/Awds:** Alumnae Medal Smith Col, 1971; LHD, Univ Southwestern Mass, 1971;Trans Africa Freedom Award, 1983; Honorary Doctor Humanities, George Washington University, 1989; Honorary Doctor of Humane Letters, Boston Univ, 1995; Distinguished Service & Leadership Award, Black Women in the Acad, 1999; Life Achievement Award, Smithsonian Nat Mus Am Hist, 1999;Citation from the Nat Order of Cote d'Ivoire; Carter G. Woodson Medal, Asn Study African Am Life & Hist. **Special Achievements:** Convened the first conf W African social workers in Ghana, 1960, conf African and African Am scholars & policymakers, 1983; authored : Apropos of Africa: Sentiments of Negro American Leaders Towards Africa from the1800s to 1950s, 1969, The Fulbright Program in Africa, 1946-86, 1986, An Afro-Victorian Feminist: Adelaide Smith Casely Hayford, 1868-1960, 1962. **Home Addr:** 51 Addington Rd, Brookline, MA 02445. *

CROOM, SYLVESTER, JR.
Football coach, football player. **Personal:** Born Sep 25, 1954, Tuscaloosa, AL. **Educ:** Miss State Univ, 1975, MA, 1977. **Career:** Football player (retired); Football coach; Univ Ala, player, 1972-74, centers coach & graduate asst coach, 1976, inside linebackers coach, 1977-81, 1984-86, outside linebackers coach, 1982-83; Tampa Bay Buccaneers, running backs coach, 1987-90; Indianapolis Colts, running backs coach, 1991; San Diego Chargers, running backs coach,1992-96; Detroit Lions, offensive coordinator, 1997-00; Green Bay Packers, running backs coach, 2001-03; Miss State Univ, head coach, 2004-08; Running Backs Coach, st. Louis ram, 2009-. *

CROPP, DWIGHT SHEFFERY
School administrator, educator. **Personal:** Born Aug 5, 1939, Washington, DC; married Linda Washington; children: Allison & Christopher. **Educ:** Howard Univ, BA, MA 1965; Am Univ, MPA, George Washington Univ, EdD. **Career:** US Dept St, res analyst, 1964; DC Pub Schs, educ, 1965; DC City Coun, spec asst chmn, 1971; DC Pub Schs, exec asst to supt, 1971; DC Bd Educ, exec sec; DC Off Intergovernmental Rels, dir; George Washington Univ, assoc prof, Public Policy & Public Admin, Currently. **Orgs:** Am Asn Sch Admin; Urban League. **Military Serv:** AUS, first lt, 1961-63. **Business Addr:** Associate Professor, George Washington University, Public Policy and Public Administration, MPA Bldg 805 21st St NW MPA 601, Washington, DC 20052.

CROSBIE, IVAN
Educator. **Career:** Compton Community Col, asst prof, 1992-. **Orgs:** Marco Antonio Firebaugh; Assemblyman Mervyn Dymally; Congresswoman Linda Sanchez; Congresswoman Lucille Roybal-Allard; Hermandad Mexicana National; Lynwood Unified School District; Los Angeles Unified School District; Wonder of Reading Foundation; Agape Music Institute; San Emigdius High School; Hermandad Mexicana National; Adelante; Plaza Mexico; Tweedy Mile Asn; Huntington Park Chamber of Commerce; Lynwood Chamber of Commerce; Compton Chamber of Commerce; The Salvadorian Chamber of Commerce. **Honors/Awds:** Investigative Series, New Series, Feature Series, Journalism Association of California Community Colleges; Awards and Honorary mentions for Editorials and Opinion pieces; Outstanding Journalist Award, Hearst Community Newspapers; Special Journalism Award, California Newspapers Asn; Outstanding Journalist Award, Cal State Univ, Los Angeles; Special Recognition Award, Cal State Univ, Northridge; First Place Award, Persuasive Speaking,National Phi Rho Pi Assn; First Place Award, Information Speaking, Phi Rho Pi, California Chapter; Resolution of Outstanding Faculty Performance from Compton Community College District; City of Los Angeles Marathon Outstanding Media Performance; City of Huntington Park Chamber of Commerce Outstanding Media Dissemination Community Service; Student Support Award; Faculty Member of the Year; Awards of Merit (ASB of CCCD); Award for Outstanding Academic Senate Service; Outstanding Service Award, National Sickle Cell Anemia Assn; Awards of Excellence as Student Newspapers Advisor. **Business Addr:** Assistant Professor, Compton Community College, Rm F-41 1111 E Artesia Blvd, Compton, CA 90221, **Business Phone:** (310)900-1600.

CROSBY, DR. EDWARD WARREN
School administrator, vice president (organization), educator. **Personal:** Born Nov 4, 1932, Cleveland, OH; son of Fred D and Marion G Naylor; married Shirley Redding, Mar 17, 1956; children: Kofi M Khemet, Darryl M L & E Malcolm. **Educ:** Kent State Univ, BA, 1957, MA, 1959; Univ Kans, PhD, medieval Ger lang &lit & medieval hist, 1965. **Career:** Educator (retired); Educ Resources Inst Inc E St Louis, vpres prog devel, 1968; Southern Ill Univ, Exp Higher Educ, dir educ, 1966-69; Inst African Am Affairs, Kent State Univ, dir, 1969-76; Univ Wash, dir black studiesprog, 1976-78; Kent State Univ, assoc prof, 1969-94, chmn, dept pan-african studies, 1976-94; Network Educ Devel & Enrichment, Kent OH, vpres, 1988; kent Univ, emer chair & prof pan-african studies & Germanic & slavic lang & lit, 1994. **Orgs:** Resident consult, Regional Coun Int Educ; fac, Inst Black World, 1970-72; consult, Peat Marwick Mitchell & Co, 1971-72; pres, NE Ohio Black Studies Consortium, 1974; pres, Ohio Consortium Black Studies, 1980-; bd mem, Harriet Tubman, African Am Mus, 1985-. **Honors/Awds:** Hon Leadership Award, Omicron Delta Kappa, 1976; Hon mem, Alpha Kappa Mu. **Special Achievements:** Published many books including, The Black Experience, An Anthology, 1976; Chronology of Notable Dates in the Hist Africans in the Am & Elsewhere, 1976; The Educ of Black Folk, An Historical Perspective, The Western Journal of Black Studies, 1977; The African Experience in Community Devel, Two Vols 1980; Your History, A Chronology of Notable Events, 1988.

Military Serv: USAF, SCARWAF corporal, 1952-54. **Home Addr:** 437 Silver Meadows Blvd, Kent, OH 44240-1913, **Home Phone:** (330)673-9271. **Business Addr:** Kent, OH 44242.*

CROSBY, FRED CHARLES
Lawyer. **Personal:** Born Dec 12, 1959, Cleveland, OH; son of Fred and Phendalyne; married Carla, Oct 5, 1991; children: Monique Kaitlyn. **Educ:** Northwood Univ, BS, 1982; Cleveland Marshall Col Law, JD, 1987. **Career:** City Cleveland, asst prosecutor, 1988-93; David I Pomerantz, campaign mgr; Pomerantz & Crosby Co, LPA, partner & atty, 1995-; Shaker Heights Munic Ct, actg judge, currently. **Orgs:** Cuyahoga County Criminal Defense Lawyers Asn; Cuyahoga County Certified Grievance Comm; Ohio State Bar Asn; Cleveland Bar Asn; Cuyahoga County Bar Asn; Am Acad Trial Lawyers; Norman S Minon Bar Asn; Ohio Asn Criminial Defense Attys. **Special Achievements:** Legal Editor for City News Newspaper, 1999. **Business Addr:** Attorney, Partner, Pomerantz & Crosby Co LPA, 20676 Southgate Pk Blvd Suite 103, Maple Heights, OH 44137, **Business Phone:** (216)587-1221.

CROSBY, FRED MCCLELLEN
Executive. **Personal:** Born May 17, 1928, Cleveland, OH; son of Fred Douglas and Marion Grace Naylor; married Phendalyne' D Tazewell, Dec 23, 1958; children: Fred C, James R, Llionicia L. **Career:** Crosby Furniture Co Inc, pres, ceo, chmn. **Orgs:** appointee USA, Adv Coun, SBA, 1978-80; gov appointee, State Boxing Commission, 1984-94; bd dirs, First Bank Nat, 1974-90; CBL Economic Develop Corp; Buckeye Exec Club State of OH; ex bd trustee, Greater Cleveland Growth Asn; Auto Club, Ohio Retail Merchants Asn; bd of trustees, Pub TV; Better Bus Bur; Cleveland Cuyahoga Co Port Authority, 1986-90; vice-chair, Ohio Coun Retail Merchants Asn, 1988-91, chmn, 1994-95; chmn, First Inter-City Banc Corp, beginning 1988; bd mem, Cuyahoga Co Loan Review Commission; Cuyahoga Co Community Improvement Corp; trea, Urban League, 1973-74; vpres, NAACP Cleveland Branch, 1971-72; bd trustee, United Black Fund; bd trustee, Am Auto Asn, 1993-98. **Honors/Awds:** Citizens Award, Bel Air Civic Club, 1969; Outstanding Civic Leadership, YMCA, 1971; Sustaining Mem Enrollment BSA, 1972; Bus Man Yr, Mirror Mirror Prod, 1982; Minority Enterprises Develop Award, Mayor George Voinovich, 1985; Ebony Club Award, United Black Fund, 1990. **Military Serv:** AUS, s & sgt, 1950-52. *

CROSBY, JAMES R
Chief executive officer, publisher. **Career:** CityNews Newspaper Group, chief exec officer & publ, currently. **Business Addr:** Chief Executive Officer, Publisher, CityNews Newspaper Group, 1419 E 40th St, Cleveland, OH 44103, **Business Phone:** (216)881-0799.

CROSBY, LORETTA
Administrator. **Personal:** Born Sep 14, 1957, Clover, SC. **Educ:** Lander Col, BS Psychol, 1979; Winthrop Col. **Career:** SC Dept Social Servs, generalist & analyst 1982-86; Richmond County Dept Family & C Servs, county eligibility consult, 1986; Emory Univ, personnel generalist, 1986; Greenville News-Piedmont Co, exec secy, 1986-87; SC Develop Disabilities Counc, exec dir, 1987-. **Orgs:** Vpres & Pres, Lambda Lambda Chap, Alpha Kappa Alpha, 1977-78; treas, Pamoja Club African-Am; Psychol Club Greek Counc; Entertainment Counc rev Mag staff; partic, Poetry People Workshop, 1981. **Honors/Awds:** First place, poetry Lander Col Review Literary Mag, 1979; Published poetry in review, Scribblings, The Bears Tale, News & Views Mag, The Naiad; Published commentary News & Views Mag. **Home Phone:** (704)798-6117. **Business Addr:** Executive Director, SC Developmental Disabilities Council, 4th Fl Edgar Brown Bldg, 1205 Pendelton St, Columbia, SC 29201, **Business Phone:** (803)734-0465.

CROSBY, MARGAREE SEAWRIGHT
Educator. **Personal:** Born Nov 21, 1941, Greenville, SC; daughter of Josie Williams Seawright and Mark Seawright; married Willis H Crosby Jr, Jun 24, 1963; children: Anthony Bernard, Anedra Michelle, Erich Garrett. **Educ:** SC State Univ, BS, 1963; Clemson Univ, MEd, 1973; Univ Mass, EdD, 1976. **Career:** Sch Dist Greenville County, headstart teacher, 1965, 1966, elem teacher, 1964-68, reading resource teacher, 1968-74; Univ Mass, teaching asst, CUETEP coord, 1974-76; Univ SC, Spartanburg, asst prof, 1976-77; Clemson Univ, assoc prof, 1977, prof emer, currently. **Orgs:** Govr Blue Ribbon Com Job Training, 1985; Clemson Univ, Univ self study com, 1986; Affirmative Action Com; Sunbelt Human Advan Resources, Proj RISE adv bd, 1988-; Nat Asn Black Reading & Lang Arts Educrs; chap, nominating com, Greenville Hosp Syst Bd Trustees, 1991-97; Nat Asn Black Educrs, 1991-; Elem Curric Com, chap, 1992, dept head search com, 1985, fac search com, chr, 1988; bd, chap, conf pro comn, SC Coun Int Reading Asn, 1992. **Honors/Awds:** Women in History Who Make a Difference, Am Asn Univ Women, 1982; Order of the Jessamine Award, Greenville News/Hayward Mall, 1991; SC Pageant, 1992; SC Women Achievement Award, The First Award, 1992; Outstanding Educr & Serv Award, Greenville Middle Sch, 1992; Reg Positive Image Award, 1993; Int Citizen of the Year, Omega Psi Phi Fraternity Inc, 1994; Appointed Woman of Achievement, SC Govr Off, 1994. **Special Achievements:** Groomed and trained over 1500 young men and ladies for presentation to soc in Debutante Cotillion, AKA, Beautillion (Jack & Jill), 1968-; trained and developed over 500 AFDC mothers for gainful employment in the hospitality sector, 1984-88; principal investigator, A Survey of Principal Attitudes Toward Ability Grouping/Tracking in the Public Sch of So St, 1991; crd, Multi-Cultural Enhancement Project, 1992; "Cooperative Learning," "Alternatives to Tracking and Ability Grouping," Natl Coun for Teachers of English and the Natl Dropout Prevention Ctr. Fifty Most Influential Black Women of SC, 1992. **Business Addr:** Professor Emeritus, Clemson University, Col Educ, 105 Sikes Hall, PO Box 345124, Clemson, SC 29634-5124, **Business Phone:** (864)656-3311.*

CROSBY, MARY
Chief executive officer. **Educ:** Univ Mich, BS, Electrical Engg, MBA. **Career:** Andersen Consulting; DaimlerChrysler; Univ Mich; FruitfulWorks Inc, chief exec officer, currently. **Business Addr:** Chief Executive Officer, FruitfulWorks Inc, 18701 Grand River 134, Detroit, MI 48223, **Business Phone:** (313)833-3555.*

CROSBY, DR. WILLIS HERMAN
Administrator, executive. **Personal:** Born Jul 31, 1941, Anderson, SC; son of Willis H Crosby and Alwille Hardy Crosby; married Dr Margaree S Crosby, Jun 24, 1963; children: Anthony, Anedra & Erich. **Educ:** SC State Univ, BA, 1963; Furman Univ, MA, 1972; Univ Mass, Amherst, EdD, 1977. **Career:** Spartanburg Sch Dist 7, social studies teacher, 1963-66; Sch Dist Greenville County, social studies teacher, 1966-70, ombudsman, 1970-73; Ford Found Leadership Develop Prog fel, 1973-74; Univ Mass, res asst, 1974-76; Tri-County Tech Col, div chmn, 1976-79; Sunbelt Human Advan Resources Inc, exec dir, 1979-94, pres & chief exec officer, 1994-. **Orgs:** Pres, SC Social Welfare Forum, 1983-85; pres, SC Asn Community Action Agencies, 1986-88; bd mem, Southeastern Asn Community Action Agencies, 1986-; bd mem, SC Educ Resource Ctr Missing & Exploited C, 1990-94; pres, Greater Greenville Pan Hellenic Coun, 1990-92; pres, SC Asn Human Serv Agencies, 1991-93; bd mem, Greater Greenville Chamber Com, 1991-94; voc comt chmn, Greenville Breakfast Rotary Club, 1992-93. **Honors/Awds:** Exceptional Service Award, Southeastern Asn Community Action Agencies, 1992; Dedicated Leadership & Service Award, Greater Greenville Pan Hellenic Coun, 1992; Humanitarian Award, SC Head Start Asn, 1991; Excellence in Leadership, Phillis Wheatley Past Fel Asn, 1988; Meritorious Award, SC CAP Directors Asn, 1987; Humanitarian Award for Social Action, The Greenville Alumnae Chapters, Delta Sigma Theta Sorority, 1994; SC Asn Community Action Partnerships. **Business Addr:** President, Chief Executive Officer, Sunbelt Human Advancement Resources Inc, 1200 Pendleton St, PO Box 10204, Greenville, SC 29611-4832, **Business Phone:** (864)269-0700.

CROSS, DENISE L.
Lawyer, judge. **Personal:** Born May 16, 1953, Cincinnati, OH; daughter of Paul and Julia Martin; married Edward H Cross, IV, Apr 16; children: Vashon, Danielle, Hewitt. **Educ:** Wilberforce Univ, BA, 1975; Univ Akron Law Sch, JD, 1978. **Career:** Erie County Pa, asst pub defender, 1979-87; Legal Aid Soc Dayton, domestic rels supervising atty; Montgomery County Prosecutors Off, asst Prosecuting atty, 1988-90; Montgomery Cty Juvenile Ct, chief magistrate, legal dir, 1990-01; Montgomery County Common Rels Ct, admin judge, currently. **Orgs:** Child Protection Task Force Montgomery County; Delta Sigma Theta Sorority Inc; Thurgood Marshall Law Soc; Ohio Bar Asn; Ohio Asn Magistrates; Girl Scout Leader Troop 69, Buckeye Trails Girl Scout Coun; Supreme Ct Ohio Adv Comt C; Families & Ct; Nat Bar Asn; Dayton Bar Asn Ethics Comt; Nat Asn Women Judges; Nat Asn Ct Mgt; Thurgood Marshall Law Soc; Dayton Bar Asn; Ohio State Bar Asn; Queens Finance; Carrousels Inc Dayton Chap; Delta Sigma Theta Sorority Inc; Dayton Alumnae Chap. **Business Addr:** Judge, Dayton Montgomery County Courts, 301 W 3rd St, PO Box 972, Dayton, OH 45422, **Business Phone:** (937)333-3333.*

CROSS, DR. DOLORES E.
School administrator. **Personal:** Born Aug 29, 1938, Newark, NJ; daughter of Charles Tucker and Ozie Johnson Tucker; divorced; children: Thomas Edwin Jr & Jane Ellen. **Educ:** Seton Hall Univ, BS, educ, 1963; Hofstra Univ, MS, educ, 1968; The Univ Mich, PhD, 1971; Marymount Manhattan, LLD, 1984; Skidmore Col, LLD, 1988; Hofstra Univ, hon degree; Elmhurst Col, hon degree. **Career:** Northwestern Univ, Evanston, IL, asst prof educ & dir MA teaching, 1970-74; Claremont Grad Sch, Claremont, CA, assoc prof educ & dir teacher educ, 1974-78; City Univ NY, vice chancellor stud affairs & spec prog, 1978-81; NY State Higher Educ Serv Corp, Albany, NY, pres, 1981-88; Univ Minn, assoc provost & assoc vpres acad affairs, 1988-90; Chicago State Univ, Chicago, IL, pres, 1990-97; Morris Brown Col, pres, 1998-2002. **Orgs:** Women Exec State Govt; adv bd mem, Asn Black Women Higher Educ; NAACP; Am Educ Res Asn, 1990; vice chmn, Am Asn Higher Educ; vice chair, Campus Compact, sr consult, S Africa Proj; bd mem, Inst Intl Educ, The Nat Ctr Pub Policy, Field Mus; Adelphi Univ Bd Trustees, 2002. **Honors/Awds:** Honorary degrees from Marymount Col, Skidmore Col, Hofstra Univ, and Elmhurst Col; "Breaking the Glass Ceiling" Award from Women Executives in State Government; Muriel Silverberg Award, NAACP, 1987; John Jay Award, NY State Comn Independent Cols & Univs, 1989. **Special Achievements:** Author, autobiography, Breaking Through the Wall: A Marathoner's Story; Chronicle of Higher Education.

CROSS, HAMAN
Clergy. **Personal:** Born Jan 28, 1949, Detroit, MI; son of Haman Sr and Malettor Gause; married Roberta Alexander, Jun 26, 1971; children: Haman III, Gilvonna Corine & Sharryl Lanise. **Educ:** Nyack Missionary Col, Nyack, NY, 1968; William Tyndale Col, BA, 1971. **Career:** Detroit Afro Am Mission, Detroit, MI, dir youth guid, 1971-82; William Tyndale Col, Farmington, MI, varsity basketball coach, 1973-79; Rosedale Park Bapt Church, founder, sr pastor, 1982-. **Orgs:** Bd mem, Carver Foreign Missions; bd mem, Christian Res & Develop; bd mem, Here's Life Black Am; bd dirs, Joy Jesus, 1983; Victory Christian Sch, 1984; consult, Taylor Univ, 1985; consult, World Christian Ctr, 1985; consult, Cedine Bible Mission, 1986; bd dirs, Children's Ctr Detroit, 1986; consult, Justice Fel, 1987; bd dirs, Ctr Black Church, 1987; bd dirs, Black Am Response African Crisis; bd dirs, Carver Foreign Missions; bd dirs, Detroit Afro-Am Mission. **Honors/Awds:** MVP, 1969-73; Honorary Citizen of El Paso, Texas, 1986. **Special Achievements:** Author: Dating & Courtship, God's Honor Roll of Faith, The Life of Moses, all in Christian Research and Development; writer of scripts for the videos Tough Talk on Love, Sex & Dating, Parent/Teen Relationships, & How to Reach & Discipline Black Men. **Home Addr:** 14017 Robson, Detroit, MI 48227. **Business Addr:** Senior Pastor, Rosedale Park Baptist Church, 14179 Evergreen Rd, Detroit, MI 48223, **Business Phone:** (313)538-1180.

CROSS, HOWARD
Football player, television show host. **Personal:** Born Aug 8, 1967, Huntsville, AL; married Pia; children: Isabella & Howard. **Educ:** Univ Ala. **Career:** Football player (retired); NY Giants, tight end, 1989-2001; YES Network, commentator; New York Giants, radio reporter. **Honors/Awds:** Super Bowl, 1990; True Value Man of the Yr, NY Giants, 1995. *

CROSS, JUNE VICTORIA
Journalist, educator. **Personal:** Born Jan 5, 1954, New York, NY; daughter of James Cross and Norma Catherine Storch. **Educ:** Harvard-Radcliffe Col, BA, 1975. **Career:** The Boston Globe, Boston, MA, corresp, 1975-76; WGBH-TV, PBS, Boston, MA, asst dir, 1976-78; WGBH-TV, PBS, Boston, MA, prod mgr, 1977-78; Nac Neil & Lehrer News Hour, reporter urban reg affairs, 1978-80, reporter def & nat secy, 1980-84, reporter politics, 1984-85, producer & corresp, 1985-, producer CBS News, 1987-91; Frontline, producer, sr producer, 2001-; fel, Carnegie-Mellon Univ Sch Urban & Pub Affairs; fel, WEB DuBois Inst Afro-Am Studies, Harvard Univ; Columbia Univ, Grad Sch Jour, assoc prof, currently; Documentary: "This Far By Faith"; "The Old Man & The Show"; "Ashes of the Cold War; Showdown in Haiti; The Confessions of RosaLee"; "A Kid Kills". **Orgs:** Trans Africa, 1979-; founding bd mem, Harvard-Radcliff Black Alumni Assn,NY, 1980, Wash, 1983; judge, Electron Jour Awards Robt F Kennedy Memorial, 1983; Judge, Electron Journalism Awards Nat Urban Coalition, 1984; coun, foreign rels, Nat Press Club; Nat Acad TV Arts & Sci; Nat Assn Black Journalists 1988. **Honors/Awds:** Emmy Award Outstanding Coverage of Breaking News Story, Nat Acad TV Arts &Scis 1983, 1997; Emmy nominee Outstanding Series, 1985; Defense Debate,1986; Joan S Barone Award, Outstanding Reporting Defense Debate; DuPont-Columbia Award, Excellence in Broadcast Jour. **Special Achievements:** Author Of "Secret Daughter", 2006. **Business Addr:** Associate Professor, Columbia University, The Graduate School of Journalism, 2950 Broadway, New York, NY 10027, **Business Phone:** (212)854-0390.

CROSS, DR. ORIS ELIZABETH CARTER
Educator. **Personal:** Born in Martinsville, VA; daughter of Samuel H (deceased) and Fannie M Swanson (deceased); married Winsom (deceased); children: Patsi; married Charles B, May 2002. **Educ:** Va State Col, BA, 1951; Ohio State Univ, MA, 1963, PhD, 1971. **Career:** Va Pub Sch, teacher, 1951-55; Columbus Ohio Pub Sch, teacher, 1963-66;Ohio State Univ, instr, 1966-69; Otterbein Col, asst prof, 1971-75; CountExcept C, pres, 1975; Col Educ, chmn Human Rel Comn, 1975; Wright StateUniv, prof educ, 1975-88; educ development consult, 1988; prof emer educ. **Orgs:** Teachers Adv Comn, State Ohio, 1975; adv, Black Students Otterbein Col,1975; adv bd, Miami Valley Reg Res Ctr; adv bd, Dayton Area UnitedCerebral Palsy Prof Serv; adv bd, Sinclair Community Col Spec Educ; DeltaSigma Theta Sorority; Pi Lambda Theta Women's Hon Educ; Cent Chapel ChurchYellow Springs. **Honors/Awds:** Named Outstanding Educator of Year, 1972; Award for DistinguishedCommunity Service, Delta Sigma Theta Sorority, 1972; Special Award,Service to Black Students, Otterbein Col, 1973; Teacher Excellence Award,Wright State Univ, 1979; Educator of Year, Ohio Fed Coun Except C, 1982;Washington State University Trustees Award, 1987; Greene County Hall ofFame for Women, Greene County, OH, 1988; Ohio Image Maker Award, 1999. **Special Achievements:** Author, poetry book, Life: A Gift to Share, 2000; named one of the Top Ten-Women of Miami Valley, Dayton Daily News, 2001. **Business Addr:** Professor Emeritus of Education, Wright State University, 11319 Nevermore Way, Charlotte, NC 28277.*

CROSS, WILLIAM HOWARD
Clergy. **Personal:** Born Oct 19, 1946, Cincinnati, OH. **Educ:** Univ Cincinnati, 2 yrs; St Gregory's Sem, Ph B; St Mary's Sem, MDiv.

Career: Mt St Mary's Sem, student librn, 1972-73; St James Cathedral Sch, Dayton, OH, religious educ 1973-74; Theol, McNicholas High Sch, teacher, 1980; St Andrew Church, Cincinnati, OH, pastor, 1988; St Joseph Ch & Archdiocese Cincinnati, assoc pastor; St Joseph Cathedral Sch, rel educ coordr; St Margaret Mary Church, Cincinnati, OH, assoc pastor; Social Justice & New Testament Guardian Angels Church, assoc pastor. **Orgs:** Archdiocesan Soc Action Comn; First degree Knights of Columbus; Cincinnati W End Task Force; Nat Office Black Catholics; Nat Black Catholic Clergy Caucus; bd dirs, Jobs People; bd dirs, Nat Asn Advan Colored People, Cincinnati chap. **Special Achievements:** In 1988, Rev . William Cross appointed as the first Black-Archdiocesan priest to be appointed a pastor (St. Andrew Church).

CROSS-BATTLE, TARA
Athlete. **Personal:** Born Sep 16, 1968, Houston, TX; daughter of Ruthie M Tate and Leo O Cross Jr; married Spencer Battle, Sep 8, 1990. **Educ:** Calif State Univ-19Long Beach, 1989. **Career:** Player (retired); Italian Volleyball League, spiker, 1993; Women's Natl & Olympic Volleyball Team, 1990-2004. **Honors/Awds:** NCAA, Player of the Year awarded twice, 1988,1989; Amateur Women's Sports Day, Player of the Year (all sports), 1989; Honda, Honda Award, 1990; US Women's National Team, Coach's Award, 1991-92; Olympics, Bronze Olympic Medal, 1992. *

CROSSE, REV. ST GEORGE IDRIS BRYON, III
Government official, clergy. **Personal:** Born Sep 16, 1939, St Georges, Grenada; son of Winston C and Iris Ernest Thomas; married Delois Bowman; children: Karin Vanessa & Liris Jewel Christina. **Educ:** Univ Md Eastern Shore, BSc, 1964; Coppin State Col, MEd, 1975; Wesley Theol Sem, MDiv, 1980; Univ Baltimore Sch Law, JD, 1970. **Career:** Calvary United Methodist Church, sr pastor, 1975-78; Lewin United Methodist Church, sr pastor, 1978-80; Crosse-Henson & Assoc, pres & ceo, 1979-83; St Matthew's United Methodist Church, sr pastor, 1980; US Dept Housing & Urban Devel, spec adv minority affairs, regional mgr Md, 1987-89; Morgan State Univ, Baltimore, Md, asst to the pres, 1989-; Fallston Fed Hill Charge, United Methodist Church, sr pastor, 1989. **Orgs:** Staff atty, Md Human Rels Comt; founder & pres, Soc Advan Families Everywhere, 1979-85, Baltimore Coalition Against Crime, 1980; nat deleg, Nat Repub Conv, 1980; founder, Md Coalition Against Crime, 1981; Md State Cent Community, 1982; Baltimore Wash Conf United Methodist Church; Md Housing Policy Coun; Regional Planning Coun. **Honors/Awds:** Alumni Scholar, Univ Md, 1964; Scholar of the Year, Omega Psi Phi Fraternity, 1964; Spec Ambassador, Nat St Kitts-Nevis, 1983; Outstanding Alumnus Award, Univ Md Eastern Shore, 1984; Father of the Year, WEBB Charities, 1988; Excellence in Minority Bus, Minority Contractors Md, 1989. **Military Serv:** AUS spec 4 clas 6 yrs; Marksman, Good Conduct Medal, 1964. **Home Addr:** 3509 Kings Point Rd, Randallstown, MD 21133-1605, **Home Phone:** (410)655-0174. *

CROSSLEY, DR. FRANK ALPHONSO
Engineer. **Personal:** Born Feb 19, 1925, Chicago, IL; son of Joseph Buddie and Rosa Lee Brefford; married Elaine J Sherman, Nov 23, 1950 (died 1996); children: Desne Crossley-Hollman. **Educ:** Ill Inst Tech, BS ChE Dean's List, 1945, MS PhD, MetE, 1947, 1950. **Career:** Engineer (retired); TN A&I State Univ, prof dept head, 1950-52; IIT Res Inst, sr scientist, 1952-66; Lockheed Palo Alto Res Lbtry, sr mem, 1966-74; Lockheed Missiles & Space Co, dept mgr, 1974-79, cnltg engr 1979-86; Aerojet Propulsion Res Inst, res dir propulsion mat, 1986-87; Gen Corp Aerojet Tech Syst, dir mat applns, 1987-90, Propulsion Div, tech prin, 1990-91; Museum of Fine Arts, position, develop. **Orgs:** Minerals, Metals & Mat Soc, 1946-; Sigma Xi, 1947-; Nat Mat Adv Bd Ad Hoc Comt Welding High Strength Struct, 1972-74; chmn, Titanium Comt The Metall Soc -Am Inst Motion Engrs, 1974-75; Mat Comt Am Inst Aero & Astro 1979-81; fel, Am Soc Metals, 1978-; fel, African Sci Inst, 2006. **Honors/Awds:** Gen Corp Aerojet R B Young Technical Innovation Award, in quality & manufacturing, 1990; Trailblazer Award, The Northern CA Coun Black Prof Engrs & Nat Soc Black Engrs-Alumni Ext, Silicon Valley Chap, 1994; Leadership Award for Community Serv, S Middlesex Men's Club, 2006; First African-American to receive a doctorate degree in Metal Eng. **Special Achievements:** One of fewer than forty African American integrated USN officers during WW II in an experiment which proved that white military personnel would take orders from black officers; published in various technical jnls and symposia 1951-90; patents 7 issued 1957-83; articles 58 serv Northern CA Coun of Black Prof Engrs 1978. **Military Serv:** UNSR, lt jg, Victory Ribbon WW II, Am Theater, Asiatic-Pacific Theater, 1944-54.

CROSS-MCCLAM, DELORIS NMI
Automotive executive. **Personal:** Born Aug 5, 1952, Lake City, SC; daughter of Louis J and Pauline; divorced; children: LaTarcha D. **Educ:** Prince George's Community Col, AA, 1987; Columbia Union Col, BS, 1991; Mercer Univ, MBA, 1997. **Career:** Ford Motor Co, mkt & sales mgr. **Orgs:** Nat Asn Advan Colored People, 1978-; Howard Univ Scholar Comt, 1986-; Nat Black MBA Asn, 1996. **Honors/Awds:** Hall of Fame, Co Sch Dis, Florence, SC, 1997; SC African American Women's Conference Award, 1994. *

CROSS-WHITE, AGNES
Publisher. **Career:** Charlottesville/Abermale Tribune, publ & ed, currently. **Orgs:** Assoc, African-Am leadership orgn Proj 21a. **Business Phone:** (804)979-0373.

CROUCH, ANDRAE EDWARD
Gospel singer, clergy. **Personal:** Born Jul 1, 1942, Pacoima, CA; son of Benjamin Jerome and Catherine Dorthea Hodnett. **Educ:** Life Bible Col, Los Angeles, CA. **Career:** Gospel ginger, 1954-; The Disciples, organizer, 1968-; Christ Memorial Church God Christ, sr pastor, 1995-; Singles: "My Tribute"; "Soon & Very Soon"; "Jesus Is the Answer"; Albums: Andrae Crouch & the Disciples; His Best; Don't Give Up; Take the Message Everywhere, 2005; Mighty Wind, 2006. **Honors/Awds:** Five Grammy Awards; Gold Record for "Jesus is the Answer"; Soul Gospel Artist, Billboard Mag, 1975, 1977; Dove Award, 1978; Daviticus Awards, 1979; Grammy Award for Best Soul Gospel Performance, 1984; Gospel Music Hall of Fame, Gospel Music Asn, 1998; Hollywood Walk of Fame, 2004; Inaugural Salute to Gospel Music Lifetime Achievement Award, Nat Acad Rec Arts & Sci. **Special Achievements:** Author, Through It All, 1974. **Business Addr:** Senior Pastor, New Christ Memorial Church of God In Christ, 13333 Vaughn St, PO Box 141000, San Fernando, CA 91340, **Business Phone:** (818)361-1087.

CROUCH, ROBERT ALLEN
Government official. **Personal:** Born Aug 9, 1955, St Joseph, MO; son of Robert A Sr and Arvilla Hughes. **Educ:** Southwest Mo State Univ, Springfield, Mo, BS, Psychol, 1978. **Career:** Mo Dept Pub Safety, Jefferson City, Mo, prog specist, 1979-81; Mo Dept Labor & Ind Rel, Jefferson City, Mo, asst dir, 1981-. **Orgs:** Chmn, Black Christian Single Adult Task Force, 1984-; Nat Asn Advan Colored People, Urban League, 1981, Nat Forum Black Pub Adminrs, 1987; Alpha Phi Alpha Fraternity. **Business Addr:** Director, Missouri Department of Labor & Industrial Relations, 3315 W Truman Blvd, Jefferson City, MO 65109, **Business Phone:** (314)751-4091.

CROUTHER, DR. BETTY JEAN
Educator. **Personal:** Born Mar 2, 1950, Carthage, MS; daughter of Eugene Garner and Lee M; divorced; children: Velsie Dione Pate. **Educ:** Jackson State Univ, BS, 1972; Univ Miss, MFA, 1975; Univ Mo, Columbia,PhD, 1985. **Career:** Lincoln Univ, asst prof art, 1978-80; Jackson State Univ, asst prof art,1980-83; Univ Miss, assoc prof art hist, 1983-; Stanford Univ, J Paul Getty postdoctoral fel, 1986. **Orgs:** Col Art Asn; Southeastern Col Art Conf; Nat Art Educ Asn; Miss Art Educ Asn; Phi Kappa Phi Hon Soc; Kappa Pi Int Hon Art Fraternity; Pi Delta Phi Hon Fraternity. **Honors/Awds:** Superior Graduate Achievement Award, Univ Mo, 1985; Award for Excellence in Teaching, Southeastern Col Art Conf, 1994. **Special Achievements:** Juried exhibition, "Images '84," Miss Pavilion, La World Exposition, 1984;contributor, exhibition catalogue "Dean Cornwell, Painter As Illustrator,"Mus Art & Archaeology Univ Mo-Columbia 1978; co-moderator with Dr Joanne VHawks, enrichment prog "Uniting Generations Together, Search Meaning,"1984; author, "Deciphering the Mississippi River Iconography of FrederickOakes Sylvester," MUSE, vol 20, pp 81-9, 1986; reader, Jacob K Javit's FelFund, U S Dept Educ, 1989-90; invited papers: "Diversity in Afro-AmericanArt," Univ Mo, Columbia, 1990; "Iconography of a Henry Gudgell WalkingStick," Southeastern Col Art Conf, Memphis, 1991; "Iconography in the Artof Contemporary African-Americans: Lawrence A Jones & Roger Rice," James APorter Colloquium, Howard Univ, 1992; "Marriage & Social Aspiration in theArt of Rembrandt," Miss Mus Art, 1992; "Images of Peace & African Heritagein the Art of Lawrence A Jones," Southeastern Col Art Conf, Birmingham,AL, 1992; Betty J Crouther, "Iconography of a Henry Gudgell Walking Stick," SECAC REVIEW, p 187-91, 1993; Southeastern College Art Conference,New Orleans, LA, "The Hand as a Symbol for African American Artists," 1994. **Business Addr:** Associate Professor of Art History, The University of Mississippi, The Art Department, 301 Old Chem, PO Box 1848, University, MS 38677, **Business Phone:** (662)915-7647.

CROUTHER, BETTY M.
Educator, elementary school teacher. **Personal:** Born Jun 5, 1931, St Joseph, MO; married Melvin Jr; children: Lou-Ann. **Educ:** Lincoln Univ, BA, 1952; NY Univ, MA, 1953. **Career:** Stephens Sch, Asheville, 1953-54; Newport Sch, 1954; AR Baptist Col, Little Rock, AR, 1954-56; Blewett Sch, St Louis, 1956-61; Garfield Sch, Columbus, OH, 1961-63; Moses Cleveland Sch, teacher, 1963-77; Cleveland Bd Educ, 5th grade enrichment teacher, 1985. **Orgs:** Chmn for vars comm, life mem & past pres, Nat Asn Negro Bus & Prof Women's Clubs; pres, Nat Coun Negro Women; Delta Sigma Theta; Nat Bus League; NOWCuyahoga Co Coalition; Alpha Wives. **Honors/Awds:** Woman of Yr, Baptist Ch, 1972; Ollie C Porter Leadership Award, 1973; Outstanding Elementary Teacher of Am, 1974; Appreciation Award, Cleveland Sr Club, 1976. **Business Addr:** Teacher, Moses Cleaveland School, 4092 E 146 St, Cleveland, OH 44128.*

CROUTHER, MELVIN S., JR.
Association executive. **Personal:** Born Nov 22, 1926, Little Rock, AR; married Betty Madison; children: Lou-Ann. **Educ:** Lincoln Univ, BS; Warren Brown Sch Wash Univ, MSW, 1960. **Career:** Association executive (retired); Cleveland Reg Off, reg dir, 1962-66; Neighborhood Opportunity Ctr, assoc dir, 1966-67, dir, 1967-68; Cuyahoga Hills Boys Sch, dep supt, 1968-71, supt, 1971-74; Ohio Youth Commn Rev Bd, chmn & chief Inst Serv, 1978; Coun Econ Opportunities Greater Cleveland, exec dir, 1979; Cuyahoga County Dept Human Serv, chief, intake Child Abuse & Neglect, 1988. **Orgs:** Pres, Warrensville Kiwanis, 1975; life mem, NAACP; life mem, Alpha Phi Alpha; Lee Rd Bapt Chap; Nat Asn Soc Workers; Acad Cert Soc Workers; Nat Comn Action Agency Exec Dirs Asn; Oh Asn, CA; Lincoln Univ Alumni; Prince Hall Mason 32 degrees Knights Temp; Shriner; Eastern Star; OH Cts & Correction Asn; Nat Coun Crime & Delinq; Police Athletic League; Lee Rd Baptist Church, Bible Study group leader. **Honors/Awds:** Highest Drama Award, Lincoln Univ, 1951; developed 1st state subsidized home for delinquent youth, 1964; selective serv syst, 1971-74; Dist Serv Award, Grand Jury Asn, 1973; Spec Recognition Award, Case Western Res Medicine-Law Acad, 1973. **Military Serv:** USMC, 1945-46. *

CROWDER, WAYNE L
Manager. **Personal:** Born Dec 4, 1966, Grenada, MS; son of Frank and Norma; married Yolanda J, May 2, 1992; children: Jalon DeWayne. **Educ:** Miss State Univ, BS, bus admin, 1988; Jackson State Univ, MS, bus admin, 1998; prof hr cert, 2000. **Career:** Miss Valley Gas Co, mkt rep, 1989-91, tech mkt rep, 1992-97, dist mkt & acct mgr, 1997-98, human resources mgr, 1998-2001, human resources dir, 2001-05. **Orgs:** NW Jackson Optimist Club, 1989-; Miss Asn Partners in Edu, first vpres, 1997-; Capital Area Human Resources asn, 1998; Soc Human Resource Mgt, 1998-. **Honors/Awds:** Titney Jungle Corp, Employee of the Year, 1987.

CROWELL, DR. BERNARD G.
Educator, executive. **Personal:** Born Nov 3, 1930, Chickasha, OK; married Virginia M; children: Bernard Jr & Christopher L. **Educ:** Langston Univ, BS, 1953; Univ OR, MS, 1958; OK State Univ, D.Ed, 1970. **Career:** Educator, Executive (retired); Langston Univ, from exec asst to pres, 1970-75; dir of inst rsch, 1973-75, inst rsch consortium, 1973-75, dirinter discip prog coord Col & univ, 1973-74; dir for admissions & records, 1973-75; TN State Univ, vpres for academic affairs, 1975-84, exec admin intl affairs, beginning, 1984; Tenn State Univ, resolution fac senate, 1984. **Orgs:** Pres Coun Tenn State Univ, 1975-; chmn, Satisfactory Progress Comt Tenn State Univ, 1985-; Faculty Athletics Rep Tenn State Univ, 1986-; pres, Optimist Club 1986-; Nat Collegiate Athletic Asn. **Honors/Awds:** Boss of the Year, Tenn State Univ Secretaries Asn, 1977; Phi Beta Lambda Award, 1981; Distinguished Service Award, Tenn State Univ, 1984. **Home Addr:** 4800 Traceway Dr, Nashville, TN 37221. *

CROWELL, GERMANE L.
Football player. **Personal:** Born Sep 13, 1976, Winston-Salem, NC. **Educ:** Univ Va. **Career:** Detroit Lions, wide receiver, 1998-2002. *

CRUDUP, GWENDOLYN M
Television producer. **Personal:** Born Aug 14, 1961, Lebanon, TN. **Educ:** Univ Tenn, Knoxville, TN, BS, commun, 1983; Univ Mo, Columbia, MA, jour, 1987. **Career:** WAND-TV, Decatur, producer, 1987-88; WTEN-TV, Albany, producer, 1988-90; WPVI-TV, Philadelphia, assoc producer, 1990-. **Orgs:** Soc Prof Journalists, 1987-88; Nat Asn Black Journalists, 1987-; Philadelphia Asn Black Journalists, 1990-92, 1994-95; Nat Asn Female Execs, 1991-92. **Honors/Awds:** Grad & Prof Scholar Recipient, 1985-87. **Business Addr:** Associate Producer, WPVI-TV6/Capital Cities, 4100 City Ave, Philadelphia, PA 19131, **Business Phone:** (215)581-4573.

CRUISE, WARREN MICHAEL
Lawyer, government official. **Personal:** Born Jun 3, 1939, Baltimore, MD; divorced; children: Enid & Wesley. **Educ:** Morgan State Univ, BA, 1963; Howard Univ, Sch Law, JD, 1970, MA, phil, 1996. **Career:** Nat Ed Assn, legal coun, 1985; Neighborhood Legal Serv Prog, staff atty; DC Govt, Off Employee Appeals, admin judge, exec dir, 1980-. **Orgs:** Vpres, brd dir, NEA Credit Union; Retirement Brd, NEA Kappa Alpha Psi Frat; Phi Alpha; Delta Law Frat; NAACP; Nat Bar Asn; Conf Black Lawyers; Am Bar Assn; asst sec, KSEF, 2008. **Honors/Awds:** MJ Naylor Memorial Award. **Business Addr:** Executive Director, DC Govt, Off Employee Appeals, 717 14th St NW 3rd Fl, Washington, DC 20005.*

CRUM, ALBERT B.
Physician, psychiatrist. **Personal:** Born Nov 17, 1931. **Educ:** Univ Redlands, CA, attended 1973; Harvard Med Sch, MD, 1957. **Career:** Columbia Univ Div, Bellevue Hosp, internship, 1957-58; Psychiat Inst Columbia Presby Med Ctr, NY, residency; Am Inst Addictive Disorders, chief psychiat cons; Human Behav Found, med dir, gen ed, chmn. **Orgs:** Am Med Asn; Kings County Med Soc; Delta Alpha Honor Soc; NY State Med Soc; World Med Asn; chmn, Duke Hall Camp Harvard Med Soc; Harvard Club NY; Acad Med Studies, MENSA; Kappa Alpha Psi; bd dir, Univ Redlands Sci Assoc, Hon DSc, Redlands CA 1974. **Honors/Awds:** Brooklyn Young Man of the Year, 1966; diplomat Nat Bd Med Exam; diplomat Pan Am Med Asn. **Military Serv:** USAF, capt. *

CRUMP, ARTHEL EUGENE
Lawyer. **Personal:** Born Oct 19, 1947, New York, NY; son of Walter Eugene and Mary Yeates; married Linda Rose Cooke, Oct

10, 1970; children: Kathryn Rose & Eric Eugene. **Educ:** Nebr Wesleyan Univ, attended 1967; Univ Nebr, Lincoln, BA, sociol, 1973; Univ Nebr Col Law, JD, 1976. **Career:** Legal Serv Southeast Nebr, atty, 1976-82; Nebr Gov Robert Kerrey, legal coun, 1983-85; Nebr Dept Justice, dep atty gen, 1985-91, gen coun, chief dep tax comnr, 1991; Cent Interstate Low-Level Radioactive Waste Comn, exec gen coun, exec dir; Nebr Wesleyan Univ, Criminal Justice Dept, vis instr, 1992, 1995 & 1998; currently, Associate General Counsel, Univ of Nebraska 2001 - present. **Orgs:** Nebr State Bar Asn; Nat Asn Atty Gen; Nat Gov's Asn; bd dir, Univ Nebr Gymnastic Booster Club; bd dir, Family Serv Asn Lincoln; bd dir, United Way Lincoln & Lancaster County; bd dir, Theater Arts Youth; bd dir, Malone Community Ctr; bd dir, Lincoln Community Playhouse; panel mem, Nebr Arts Coun; Touring Artists Progs; Nat Asn Advan Colored People; Nebr Civil Liberties Union; Coalition Black Men; Univ Nebr Booster Club Womens Athletics; bd trustees, Nebr Wesleyan Univ; adv comt, Lincoln Pub Schs Gifted C; adv comt, Lancaster County Child Care; Malone Area Citizens Coun; Lincoln Pub Schs Eval Stud Health Educ Proj; bd dir, Pinewood Bowl Asn; bd dir, Leadership Lincoln; Nebr Supreme Ct Judicial Nomination Comn; Lincoln Bar Asn; Midwest Bar Asn; Nat Low-Level Waste Forum Comn Rep; Lincoln Interfaith Coun; Cornhusker Coun BSA; Crucible Club; Troop 49 Boy Scouts Am, Arborland Dist; Nebr Urban League; bd dir, Found Educ Funding; bd dir, Nebr Wesleyan Univ; Newman United Methodist Church; Bd Higher Educ & Campus Ministry; Nebr United Methodist Church; Community Leaders Am; Foundation for Eucational Services; Nat Student Loan Program; Woods Charitable Fund; Center for People in Need. **Honors/Awds:** Nebr Law Col Scholarship; Kelso Morgan Scholarship; Alumni Achievement Award, Nebr Wesleyan Univ; Silver Key Award, Law Student Div, Am Bar Asn; University of Nebraska-Lincoln Alumni Achievement Award; NAACP, Leonore Lettcher Community Service Award. **Special Achievements:** City of Lincoln Human Rights Commission (Commissioner). **Military Serv:** AUS, sgt, 1967-70; Nat Defense Medal; Good Conduct Medal; Armed Forces Expeditionary Medal. **Home Addr:** 3260 S 31st St, Lincoln, NE 68502. **Business Addr:** Associate General Counsel, University of Nebraska, 241 Varner Hall, PO Box 830745, Lincoln, NE 68583-0745.

CRUMP, BENJAMIN L
President (Organization), lawyer. **Educ:** Fla State Univ, Sch Law, BA, law, 1992; Fla State Univ, JD, 1995. **Career:** Parks & Crump, pres, partner, currently. **Orgs:** Virgil Hawkins Fla Chap, Nat Bar Asn, Tallahassee Barrister's Asn, Am Bar Asn, Acad Fla Trial Lawyers, Civil Trial Lawyers Div, Small Firms & Solo Practitioners Div, Bd Dirs N Fla Legal Servs. **Business Phone:** (850)222-3333.

CRUMP, JANICE RENAE
Manager, executive director. **Personal:** Born Aug 9, 1947, Dragerton, UT; daughter of Jerry Andrew Green Sr and Johnnie Lee Roney Lewis; married Maurice Malone Crump Sr, Sep 14, 1968; children: Maurice Jr, Jason Bernard & Toiya Danielle. **Educ:** Tuskegee Inst, Tuskegee, AL, BS, home econ, 1969; NC Cent Univ, Durham, NC, BA, Eng, 1981; Simmons Grad Sch Mgt, cert, 1986. **Career:** AT&T Southern Bell, Atlanta, GA, 1970; Ga Power Co, Atlanta, GA, customer serv, 1970-72; Delta Airlines, Atlanta, GA, reservationist, 1972-74; Soul City Co, Soul City, NC, pub rels, 1975-80; WTVD II/Cap Cities ABC, Durham, NC, community affairs dir; Cong Black Caucus Found Inc, dir Media Rels & Commun, currently. **Orgs:** Chmn, Warren Co Bd Elections, 1975-82; pres, Northside & Norlina & Warren High PTA's; 1976-88; Gov Small Bus Adv Coun, 1979-81; pres, Warren Co Dem Women, 1982-83; vice chair, Z Smith Reynolds Found, 1988-91. **Honors/Awds:** Volunteer Award, Am Cancer Soc Co; Community Service Award, WTVDII Adv Comm; Parent of the Year Award, Soul City Interfaith Coun, The Silver Bell Award, Ad Coun, Total Sta; Project Award, NBACA. **Home Addr:** PO Box 27, Soul City, NC 27553. **Business Addr:** Director Media Relations and Communications, Congressional Black Caucus Foundation Inc, 1720 Massachusetts Ave NW, Washington, DC 20036, **Business Phone:** (202)263-2800.

CRUMP, NATHANIEL L., SR.
Engineer. **Personal:** Born Jul 18, 1920, Little Rock, AR; married Ruby M Chappell; children: N Lloyd Jr. **Educ:** Lincoln Univ, BS, chem, 1948. **Career:** Engineer (retired); Du Good Micro-analytical Lab, St L, micro-analyst, 1948-52; Universal Match R & D Arma Div, lab asst, proj eng, 1952-59; Hanley Ind, & Pyrotechnics & Explo Chem, proj eng, 1959-61; St Louis Child's Hosp, Cardiol Sec, res asst, 1961-62; Mercury, Gemini, Apollo, Sky Lab Shuttle Progs, unit chief, 1962; McDonnell Douglas Aerospace Co, space eng, 1987. **Orgs:** Am Chem Soc; Soc Aerospace Mat & Process Eng; Am Asn Contam Cont Kappa Alpha Psi Frat; bd mem, Coalition Environ; vpres, St L Co Chap, Civil Int Civic Org; adv comt to vpres Humphrey, Youth Motivation, 1965-68; bd mem, Human Rel Univ City, MO 1972-78; loaned exec, Greater St Louis United Way Dr, 1987-94; loaned exec, Arts & Educ Coun Dr, 1988-93; bd mem, Tower Village Nursing Home, 1992-93; adv bd mem, bd mem, 1995, Mid East Area Agency Aging, 1992-94; bd mem, ABHF, 1993. **Honors/Awds:** Inducted in Greater St Louis Area Amateur Baseball Hall of Fame, 1992; Harris Stowe State Coll, Distinguished Alumnus Award, 1993. **Special Achievements:** Author papers on Organic Micro analyis, Analytical Chemistry, Space System Contam Cont, Aircraft Hydralic System Clean Control. **Military Serv:** AUS, 1942-43; Act Duty, 1943-46. *

CRUMP, WILBERT S
Executive. **Personal:** Born in Portsmouth, VA; married Phyllis Lorraine Archer; children: Deborah D & David P. **Educ:** Howard Univ, Wash DC, BA (Cum Laude), 1965. **Career:** Pfizer Inc NY, suprv prof placement, 1971-73; City Univ NY, LaGuardia Col, adj lectr, 1972-75; Allied Signal Inc, mgr critical manpower admin, 1973-76; Nat Urban League, lectr, black exec exchange prog 1975-; Allied Signal Inc, dir EEO 1976-. **Orgs:** Alpha Phi Alpha Fraternity; Nat Asn Advan Colored People; Edges Group Inc. **Honors/Awds:** Full Scholarship, Howard Univ; recipient, President Cup as Outstanding DMG Graduate Senior, Howard Univ, 1965; Black Achiever in Industry Award, 1976. **Special Achievements:** "Executive Accountability," Ensuring Minority Success in Corporate Management, 1988. **Military Serv:** AUS, capt, 1965-70; Bronze Star Medal, Army Commendation Medal. **Business Addr:** Director, EEO, Allied Signal Inc, 101 Columbia Rd, PO Box 2245R, Morristown, NJ 07960, **Business Phone:** (212)964-5111.

CRUMP-CAINE, LYNN
Executive. **Career:** McDonalds Corp, group vice pres operations, beginning, 1999, exec vpres worldwide systems and operations, 2004, McDonald's Innovation Center, Romeoville, IL, 2004. OutsideIn Consulting, Chief Exec Officer, currently. **Orgs:** Nat Asn Female Exec. **Honors/Awds:** Woman of the Year; Outstanding Georgia Citizen. **Business Addr:** Founder, Chief Executive Officer, OutsideIn Consulting, Concourse Ctr 5 Concourse Pkwy Suite 3000, Atlanta, GA 30328, **Business Phone:** (770)392-3304.*

CRUMPLER, CARLESTER T., JR.
Football player. **Personal:** Born Sep 5, 1971, Greenville, NC; son of Carlester; married Kimberly. **Educ:** E Carolina Univ. **Career:** Football player (retired); Seattle Seahawks, tight end, 1994-98; Minn Vikings, 1999; Banking Group Bank Am, asst vpres, currently. *

CRUMPTON, DR. LESIA
Educator, college administrator. **Educ:** Texas A&M Univ, BS, Indust Engineering, 1988, MS, Human Factors Engineering & ergonomics, safety engineering, 1990, Phd, Human Factors Engineering & Ergonomics, safety engineering, 1993. **Career:** Tex A&M Univ, minority engineering prog, 1987-88, dean engineering & instr, 1990-91; Bryan Independent Sch dist, substitute teacher, 1989; Miss State Univ, assoc dean engineering res & outreach, 1999-2002, assoc prof indust engineering, 1993-99, developer, Ergonomics & Human Performance Res Ctr, dir, 1994-2002; Univ Cent Fla, Dept Indust eng & Mgt syst, chmn & prof, 2002-; ergonomic consult. **Orgs:** Nat Action Coun Minorities Engineering; sr mem, Inst Indust Engrs; newsletter ed, Indust Ergonomics Tech Group Human Factors & Ergonomic Soc; Alpha Pi Mu; Nat Sci Found Indust, 2003-; Sigma Xi. **Honors/Awds:** Outstanding Faculty Award, Mich State Univ Chapter of Alpha Kappa Alpha Sorority, 1994-96; Outstanding Faculty Award, Mich State Univ Golden Key Honor Soc, 1995-96; Outstanding Faculty Award, 1995-97; Outstanding Faculty Award, Mich State Univ Chap Nat Asn Advan Colored People, 1997; and 1996; NSF Presidential Faculty Fellows Award, 1996; Outstanding Women of Color in Science and Technology Award, 1996; Hearin-Hess Distinguished Professor Award, Col Engineering, Miss State Univ, 1996-98; Outstanding Faculty Award, 1997; US Black Engineer of the Year Education Award, 1997; Nat Action Council for Minorities in Engineering Alumni Leadership Award, 1998. **Special Achievements:** First African Am woman to earn an engineering doctorate from Texas A&M Univ; first & only prof from dept indust engineering receive Hearin-Hess Distinguished Prof Award. **Business Addr:** Professor, Department Chair, University of Central Florida, Department Industrial Engineering & Managment Systems, Rm II-308, PO Box 162993, Orlando, FL 32816-2993, **Business Phone:** (407)823-2204.

CRUSOE-INGRAM, CHARLENE
Executive, vice president (organization). **Personal:** Born in New Albany, MS; daughter of Robert and Virginia Simmons; married Earnest. **Educ:** Bradley Univ, BA, sociol fr, 1972, MA, personnel serv, 1975. **Career:** Am Hosp Supply Corp, safety mgr & sr personnel specialist, 1980-82; Abbott Labs, div personnel mgr & corp recruiter, 1983-86; Enterprise Systs, Inc, vpres human resources, 1986-88; Coca-Cola Co, human resources mgr, 1988-91, dir human resources, 1991-94, dir client serv, 1994-95, vpres orgn & people develop, 1995-, Diversity Strategy & Cult, vpres, 2001-. **Orgs:** Bd mem, Inroads, 1995-; Womens Food Serv Forum, 1995-; bd dirs, Nexus Contemp Arts Ctr, 1996-; vol, Literacy Coun, 1994-95; bd trustees, Knoxville Col, 1998; bd dir, Atlanta Women's Found. **Honors/Awds:** Very Important Prestigious Women Award, Dollars & Sense, 1995; Award of Excellence, YWCA, 1995. **Business Addr:** Vice President, Coca-Cola Company, 1 Coca-Cola Plz NW, Atlanta, GA 30301, **Business Phone:** (404)676-2568.*

CRUSTO, MITCHELL FERDINAND
Educator, lawyer. **Personal:** Born Apr 22, 1953, New Orleans, LA; married Ann Marie Walter; children: Eve Michelle & Mia Elizabeth. **Educ:** Yale Univ, New Haven, CT, BA, hist, 1975, PhD Cand, 1977, JD, 1981; Oxford Univ, Oxford, Eng, BA, jurisp, 1980, MA, jurisp, 1985. **Career:** Cravath, Swaine & Moore, New York, NY; Donovan, Leisure, Newton & Irvine, New York, NY, 1981; Hon John M. Wisdom, US Ct Appeals, New Orleans, LA 5th Circuit, advisor, 1981-82; Jones, Walker, Waechter, Pointevent, Carrere & Denegre, New Orleans, LA, atty, 1982-84; Stifel, Nicolaus & Co Inc, St Louis, MO, sr vpres & gen coun, 1984-88; Wash Univ Bus Sch, St Louis, MO, instr, 1985-89; Webster Univ, St Louis, MO, instr, 1986; St Louis Univ Law Sch, St Louis, MO, adj prof, 1987-88; Crusto Capital Resources Inc, St Louis, MO, pres & chief exec officer, 1988-89; US Small Bus Admin, WA, DC, assoc dep adminr finance, investment & procurement, 1989-; Loyola Univ New Orleans, prof law, 2005-; Wash Univ, vis prof law, 2006-. **Orgs:** Vpres, Mo Mutual Funds Asn, 1985-87; dir, Big Brothers & Big Sisters, 1985-89; Securities Indus Asn, Compliance & Legal Div, 1986-88; dir, St Louis Econ Develop Corp, 1987-89; arbitrator, Nat Asn Securties Dealers, 1988-; Am Bar Asn; Fed Bar Asn; Am Corp Coun Asn; Ill Bar Asn; La Bar Asn; Mo Bar Asn; Hon Soc Mid Temple British Barrister Asn. **Special Achievements:** Author: "Reflections on Insider Trading," Sloan Mgt Rev, fall 1987; "Blacks Can Shake Off Their Taken-for-Granted Status," LA Times, October 25, 1988; "Federalism & Civil Rights: The Meredith Incident," the Integration of the Univ Miss by James Meredith in 1963, Tulane Law Sch, Nat Black Law J, summer 1989; "Why Blacks Left the Party of Lincoln," St Louis Dispatch, January 14, 1988; "Mr. Bush & the Plight of Urban African-Ams," Ripon Forum, February, 1989; active in Republican Party. **Business Addr:** Visiting Professor, Washington University Law, Anheuser-Busch Hall Rm 458, St Louis, MO 63130.

CRUTCHER, DR. RONALD ANDREW
School administrator, president (organization). **Personal:** Born Feb 27, 1947, Cincinnati, OH; son of Andrew and Burdella; married Betty Joy Neal; children: Sara Elizabeth. **Educ:** Miami Univ, BA, BM, 1969 (Cum Laude); Yale Univ, MMA, 1972; State Acad Music (Frankfurt W Germany), Dipl, 1976; Yale Univ, DMA (with distinction) 1979. **Career:** Bonn (W Germany) Sch Music, cello instr, 1976-79; Wittenberg Univ, asst prof, 1977-79; UNC Greensboro, asst prof, 1979-83, assoc prof & cordr string area, 1983-88, assoc vchancellor acad affairs, 1988-90; The Cleveland Inst Music, vpres acad affairs, dean conserv, 1990; Wheaton Col, pres, 2004-. **Orgs:** Consul NC Arts Coun, 1981-88; bd dirs, Am Cello Community Coun, 1982-88; founder & pres, Carolina Cello Club, 1983-88; consult, Nat Endowment Arts, 1986-; bd dirs, Greensboro Cerebral Palsy Asn, 1986-88; pres, NC Am String Teachers Asn, 1986-88; bd dirs, Eastern Music Festival, 1988; bd dirs, United Arts Coun Greensboro, 1988; univ coun mem, Case Western Res Univ,1990-; Community Music Proj, 1991-; adv comt mem, Northeast Ohio Jazz Soc, 1990-. **Honors/Awds:** Woodrow Wilson Fel, 1969; Danforth Fellowship Nominee, Miami Univ, 1969; Phi Beta Kappa; Ford Found fel, 1969-72; Fulbright Fel, 1972-74; Outstanding Service to Strings Award, NC Am String Teachers Asn, 1983; Delta Phi Alpha; Pi Kappa Lambda; Omicron Delta Kappa. **Business Addr:** President, Wheaton College, 26 E Main St, Norton, MA 02766-2322.*

CRUTCHER, SIHON HEATH
Engineer. **Personal:** Born Mar 30, 1970, Huntsville, AL; son of James and Catherine; married Deborah Crutcher, Aug 9, 1995. **Educ:** Tuskegee Univ, BS, math & physics, 1972; Kent State Univ, MS, physics, 1994; Univ AL-Huntsville, MS, math, 1999; PhD. **Career:** Univ AL, Huntsville, reaching asst; Nichols Res, syst analyst; Quality Res, senior software engr; Raytheon, group mgr & sr syst engr; US Army, comput engr. **Orgs:** House Raphe; Eagle Wings Ministries; Am Asn Physics Teachers. **Honors/Awds:** Commendation, Dept of the Army, 2000. *

CRUTCHFIELD, JAMES N
Newspaper publisher, executive. **Personal:** Born Dec 7, 1947, McKeesport, PA; son of Charles and Nancy Viola Summers Hill; married Cynthia Lynne Parish; children: Rashida Marie , Kendra Rebecca Edwards & Elena Candace Edwards. **Educ:** Duquesne Univ, BA, 1992; Cleveland State Univ; Oakland Univ. **Career:** Pittsburgh Press, reporter, 1968-71; Pittsburgh Model Cities Prog, pub info officer, 1971; Pittsburgh Post-Gasette, reporter, 1971-76; Detroit Free Press, reporter, 1976-79; US Sen Carl Levin, Wash, DC, press secy, 1979-81; Detroit Free Press, state capital bur chief, asst city ed, dep city ed, city ed, metro ed, Detroit managing ed, 1981-89; Akron Beacon Jour, managing ed, 1989-93; Press-Telegram, Long Beach, CA, sr vpres, exec ed, 1993-97; Philadelphia Newspapers Inc, asst publ, 1998, dir, single copy sales & distrib, 1999; Akron Beacon Jour, gen mgr, 2000-06, pres & publ, 2001-06; Ariz State Univ, student media dir, 2007-; Univ Cronkite Sch Journalism & Mass Commun, Weil Family Prof, currently. **Orgs:** Nat Asn Black Journals, 1983-; Alpha Phi Alpha Fraternity, 1966-; pres, Soc Prof Journals, 1991-93; Akron Art Mus; Weathervane Community Playhouse diversity comt; Summit Educ Initiative; Asian Am Journals Asn, 1998-; Nat Asn Hispanic Journals, 1998-; Am Soc Newspaper Eds, 1993-; Nat Asn Minority Media Execs; Ohio Newspaper Asn; E Akron Community House's 2001-02; fundraising campaign; chair, United Way Summit Co campaign, 2004; bd mem, Duquesne Univ, currently; bd mem, John S & James L Knight Found; 2004-. **Business Addr:**

Director Student Media, Weil Family Professor of Journalism, Walter Cronkite School of Journalism and Mass Communication, Arizona State University, Stauffer Hall A 231, PO Box 871305, Tempe, OH 85287-1305, **Business Phone:** (480)727-6884.

CRUTCHFIELD, LISA
Executive, vice president (organization). **Personal:** Born Mar 21, 1963, Philadelphia, PA; daughter of Johnnie and Ann. **Educ:** Yale Univ, BA, 1985; Harvard Bus Sch, MBA, 1990. **Career:** Philadelphia Nat Bank, com lending officer, 1985-88; Bankers Trust Co, assoc & corp finance, 1990-92; City Philadelphia, dep finance dir, 1992-93; PA PUC, vchmn, 1993-97; TIAA-CREF Southern Serv Ctr, vpres & gen mgr; Duke Energy Corp, vpres; PECO Energy, vpres regulatory & external affairs, 2004-. **Orgs:** bd mem, Mus New S; investment comm, United Way Cent Carolinas Inc, 1998-; bd trustees, Independent Col Fund NC, 1998-; Nat Coalition of 100 Black Women Greater Charlotte; bd dir, TransLink Develop Corp; bd dir, Univ NC; bd dir, Carolinas HealthCare System; Charlotte Chamber Com; bd dir, NC Dept Transp; bd dir, Urban League Philadelphia; American Asn Blacks energy. *

CRUTCHFIELD, SABRINA DAMES. See DAMES, SABRINA A.

CRUTCHFIELD-BAKER, VERDENIA (VERDENIA C BAKER)
Executive, government official. **Personal:** Born Jul 27, 1958, Sylvester, GA; married Joe Thomas. **Educ:** Fla State Univ, BS, 1979, MSPA, 1982. **Career:** Health & Rehabilitative Serv, counr; Sch Bd St Lucie Co, teacher, 1980; Dept Labor Employ Security, interviewer, 1982; Broward City Budget Off, budget analyst; Palm Beach Co, dep co adminr, currently. **Orgs:** Nat Asn Advan Colored People, 1977-79; Delta Sigma Theta, 1977; Am Soc Pub Admin, 1981; Nat Forum Black Pub Admin, 1983. **Honors/Awds:** Service Award, Delta Sigma Theta, 1981; Outstanding Young Women of America, 1982. **Special Achievements:** First Black budget analyst, Broward Co Govt. **Home Addr:** 2231 Ridgewood Cir, Royal Palm Beach, FL 33411-6155. **Business Addr:** Deputy County Administrator, Palm Beach County, 301 N Olive Ave, West Palm Beach, FL 33401, **Business Phone:** (561)355-2030.*

CRUTHIRD, J ROBERT LEE
Educator. **Personal:** Born Dec 10, 1944, Leflore County, MS; son of Harvie and Mary Florence Black; married Jeannett M Williams; children: Robert Lee Jr. **Educ:** Univ Ill, BA, sociol, 1973, MA, sociol, 1976; Chicago State Univ, 1982; Critical Thinking & Acculturation Inst, Univ Chicago, attended 1986; Univ Wis, Madison, summer, attended 1983; Heed Univ, PhD, sociol, 1994. **Career:** IL Dept Corrections, correctional, counr, 1977-78; Kennedy-King Col, dir instnl res, 1982, asst prof sociol, assoc prof sociol, currently, Dept Soc Sci, chmn, 1996-, distinguished prof, 2003-04; Crime & Delinquency Res Training, fel, 1976; Nat Endowment Humanities, fel, 1983; KKC, Title III basic skills develop, 1985-86; City Cols Chicago, Mayor's Summer Youth Employment Prog, site coordr, 1984-86; Acad Support Serv, coordr, 1986-87, Col Advisement Proj, coordr, 1987, asst prof social, 1987; asst dir, MSYEP, 1987-; adv, Phi Theta Kappa, Lambda Rho Chap Kennedy-King Col, currently. **Orgs:** Am Sociol Asn; Asn Inst Res; Asn Study Life & History Afro-Am; consult, Educ Mgmt Assocs, 1981-82; sponsor, Phi Theta Kappa, 1982-; life mem, Univ Ill Chicago Alumni Asn; Nat Asn Develop Educ; Alpha Phi Alpha Fraternity Inc. **Honors/Awds:** Vis scholar, Univ Wis, 1983; Hall Honors IL, Phi Theta Kappa, 1984, 1986, 1988-91; "Black Rural-Urban Migration", ERIC, 1984; "Remedial/Developmental Instructions" ERIC, 1987; honors scholar 23rd Inst, NY, 1990; honors scholar 24th Institute, Minneapolis, 1991; Monarch Award in Education, Alpha Kappa Alpha, 1999. **Military Serv:** AUS specialist E4; Good Conduct Medal, Lett Commendation, 1967. **Home Addr:** 259 E 107th St, Chicago, IL 60628, **Home Phone:** (773)568-8951. **Business Addr:** Associate Professor Social Science, Kennedy-King College, Department Social Science, 6800 S Halsted St, Chicago, IL 60621, **Business Phone:** (773)602-5174.

CRUZ, DR. ILUMINADO ANGELES
School administrator, physician. **Personal:** Born Nov 20, 1936, Navotas, Philippines; son of Dr Iluminado S Cruz Sr and Flora Angeles; married Aurora Bunda, Jun 6, 1962; children: Danny, Eliza & Loralei. **Educ:** Univ Philippines, MD, 1962. **Career:** Howard Univ Col Med, instr, 1968-69, asst prof, 1971-76, assoc prof,1976-92, prof. **Orgs:** Dir, Hemodialysis Unit Howard Univ; fel, Am Col Physicians; Am Soc Nephrology; Int Soc Nephrol; Nat Med Asn; Med Chirurgical Soc DC; DC Med Soc; Am Heart Asn; Nat Capital Med Found. **Business Addr:** Professor, Howard University college of Medicine, 520 W St NW, Washington, DC 20059, **Business Phone:** (202)806-6270.

CRUZ, PATRICIA
Executive director. **Career:** Harlem Stage, exec dir, currently, xAaron Davis Hall Inc, dir, currently. **Business Phone:** (212)650-6900.

CRUZAT, DR. GWENDOLYN S.
Educator, consultant. **Educ:** Fisk Univ, BA, 1951; Atlanta Univ, MLS, 1954; Wayne State Univ, PhD, 1976. **Career:** Fisk Univ, asst librn, 1954-60; Harper Hosp, Detroit, asst librn, 1960-64; Wayne State Univ Sch Med, research librn; Univ Western Ontario, lectr, 1970; Univ Mich, Sch Info, lectr, 1970, from asst prof to prof, 1971-92, prof emer, 1992-; Univ Hawaii Grad Sch Library & Info Studies, vis assoc prof, 1977; Univ Am Sch Library & Info Studies, vis lectr, 1978; Nat Libr Med, regent, 1981-84; Dept Educ, Div Library Prog, consult, 1987; consult, 1987. **Orgs:** Med Library Asn, 1960-, Am Library Asn, 1971-90; Ala Comn Accreditation, 1984-86; Comn Collective Bargaining, chair, 1976-80; Am Soc Info Sci; Am Asn Univ Prof; Spl Libraries Asn; Univ Mich Student Group, adv, 1973-90; Metro Detroit Med Libraries Group; Asn Col & Univ Research Libraries; Asn Library & Info Sci Educ; Univ Mich Alumni Asn; fel Med Lib Asn, 1993. **Honors/Awds:** Gabriel Award Scholarship, Fisk Univ; Beta Phi Mu Honor Soc, 1954-; Distinguished Serv Award Univ MI, 1977; Janet Doe Lectr Med Lib Asn, 1978-79. **Special Achievements:** School's first minority tenure-track faculty member, 1971. **Business Addr:** Professor Emeritus, University of Michigan, Sch Info, 304 W Hall, Ann Arbor, MI 48109-1092.*

CRYER, LINKSTON T.
Dentist. **Personal:** Born Jul 10, 1933, Mt Hermon, LA; married Elizabeth. **Educ:** Southern Univ, BS, 1945; Meharry Med Col, DDS, 1961; Dade Co Res Clinic, endodontics, oral surg, minor tooth movement, periodontal surg. **Career:** Fla State Dental Health Dept, 1961-62; Pvt Pract, dent surgeon, 1962-; Variety C Hosp, staff. **Orgs:** Dade Co Dental Soc, 1961-; pres, S Dade Political Action League, 1965-80; pres, Richmond Enterprises Inc, 1965-; vpres, Dunbar Med Arts Inc, 1971-; pres, Iota Pi Lambda Chap Alpha Phi Alpha, 1972-; Dade Co Dental Res Clinic, 1980-, The Acad Gen Dentistry, 1980-; pres Dade Co Dental Soc, 1985-87; Am & Nat Dental Asn, The Am Inst Hypnosis. **Military Serv:** AUS, 1st lt, 1954-56. **Business Addr:** Dentist, Private Practice, 11350 Dunbar Dr, Miami, FL 33176, **Business Phone:** (305)238-4512.*

CUDJOE, DR. SELWYN REGINALD
Educator, writer. **Personal:** Born Dec 1, 1943, Tacarigua, Trinidad and Tobago; son of Lionel Reginald and Carmen Rose Cudjoe; married Gwendolyn M Long (divorced 1968); children: Frances Louise & Kwamena. **Educ:** Fordham Univ, BA, 1969, MA, 1972; Columbia Univ, attended 1972; Cornell Univ, PhD, 1976. **Career:** Fordham Univ, instr Afro-Am studies, 1970-72; Ithaca Col, asst prof Afro-Am studies, 1973-74; Ohio Univ, assoc prof Afro-Am studies, 1975-76; Harvard Univ, asst prof Afro-Am studies, 1976-81, WEB DuBois Inst AFA Res, vis fel, 1991, vis scholar African-Am studies, 1992-94; Soc Humanities, Cornell Univ, sr lectr, 1980, assoc prof Africana studies, 1981-82, sr fel, 1992; NEH, fel, 1991-92 & 1997-98; Am Coun Learned Soc, fel, 1991-92; Harvard Univ, AFA Studies Dept, vis fel, 1991; Wellesley Col, Marion Butler McLean prof & chmn hist ideas, prof african studies, 1986-, 1995-99; Brandeis Univ, teacher; Auburn State Prison, Auburn, NY, speaker; Bedford-Stuyvesant Youth-in-Action, teacher; Calaloux Res Assocs, pres; Trinidad & Tobago TV, interviewer; Books: Resistance & Caribbean Literature, 1980; Movement the People, 1983; Grenada: Two Essays, 1983; A Just & Moral Society, 1984; VS Naipaul: A Materialist Reading, 1988; Caribbean Women Writers: Essays from the First International Conference, ed, 1990; Eric E Willliams Speaks: Essays on Colonialism & Independence, ed, 1993; Tacarigua: A Village in Trinidad, ed, 1995; CLR James: His Intellectual Legacies, ed, 1995; Maxwell Philip, Emmanuel Appadocca, or, Blighted Life: A Tale of the Boucaneers, ed, 1997; Beyond Boundaries: The Intellectual Tradition of Trinidad & Tobago in the Nineteenth Century, 2002. **Orgs:** Fel Nat Endowment Humanities, 1991-92 & 1994-98. **Business Addr:** Marion Butler McClean Professor of the History of Ideas, Wellesley College, Africana Studies Department, 106 Cent St, Wellesley, MA 02481.

CUFF, GEORGE WAYNE
Clergy. **Personal:** Born Sep 3, 1923, Chester, PA; son of Theodore and Lydia; married Mary Elizabeth; children: Henry Earl Tucker Jr & Selena Cuff Simpson. **Educ:** Lincoln Univ, BA, 1951; Crozer Theol Sem, MDiv, 1955. **Career:** Clergy (retired); pastor, 1955-69; Dover Dist Peninsula Conf, supt, 1969-73; Wilmington Dist Peninsula Conf, supt, 1973-75; Hillcrest Bellefonte, United Methodist Church, Wilmington, DE, pastor, 1975-79; Bd Global Ministries, United Methodist Church, 1979-87; Off Finance & Field Serv, field rep. **Orgs:** Bd trustees, Wesley Col, Dover, DE, 1970-92; bd gov, Wesley Theol Sem, Wash, DC, 1973-80; bd dir, Wilmington Good Will Indust, 1973-79; gen bd mem, Global Ministries United Methodist Church. **Honors/Awds:** Plaque of Appreciation, Methodist Action Prog, Wilmington Dist, 1975; Good Conduct Medal; WWII Medal; Sharp Shooters Medal. **Military Serv:** USN, third class petty officer, 1943-46.

CULBREATH-MANLY, TONGILA M
Executive. **Personal:** Born Jun 9, 1959, Atlanta, GA. **Educ:** Univ Col, Boulder, BA, 1981; Atlanta Univ, MBA, 1987. **Career:** Educ Media Ctr, media tech, 1977-81; H Harper's Design Studios, asst mgr, 1981-82; Sandusky Broadcasting KNUS-AM, tech producer, 1982-84; New City Comn WYAY-FM, acct exec, 1984-88; Summit Commun, WVEE/WAOK, acct exec, 1988-89; WEDR Inc, WEDR-FM, sales mgr, 1989-90; WRIC-TV, acct exec, 1991-. **Orgs:** Nat Black MBA Asn, 1986-87; Exec Women INT. **Business Addr:** Account Executive, WRIC-TV Richmond, Arboretum Pl, Richmond, VA 23228, **Business Phone:** (804)330-8875.

CULLORS, DERRICK SHANE
Football player. **Personal:** Born Dec 26, 1972, Dallas, TX. **Educ:** Murray State univ; Texas Christian Univ. **Career:** Football player(retired); New England Patriots, running back, kickoff return, 1997-98. *

CULPEPPER, BETTY M
Librarian. **Personal:** Born Jan 15, 1941, Lynchburg, VA; daughter of Roosevelt and Agnes Head Witcher. **Educ:** Howard Univ, BA, 1963; Kent State Univ, MA, 1966; Cath Univ, MS, 1969; Howard Univ, MPA, 1981. **Career:** Washington DC Public Libr, reader's adv, 1964-67; Prince George's County Memorial Libr, br librn, 1967-72; Washingtoniana Div DC Public Libr, chief, 1972-77; Moorland-Spingarn Res Ctr, Howard Univ, bibliographer & head ref, 1977-86, asst chief librn, tech serv & auto, 1986-90; Libr Cong, Wash, DC, asst head, 1990-. **Orgs:** Am Libr Asn; Afro-Am Historical & Gen Soc; Nat Advan Asn Colored People; Asn Study Afro-Am Life & History; ALA Caucus Black Librarians; Alpha Kappa Alpha; Historical Soc Wash. **Honors/Awds:** Awarded Scholarship Howard Univ; Fel, Kent State Univ; Scholarship MD Libr Assn. **Business Addr:** Assistant Head, Library of Congress, 101 Independence Ave SE, Washington, DC 20001, **Business Phone:** (202)707-5000.

CULPEPPER, DAUNTE
Football player. **Personal:** Born Jan 28, 1977, Ocala, FL. **Educ:** Cent Fla. **Career:** Minn Vikings, quarterback, 1999-05; Miami Dolphins, 2006. Oakland Raiders, 2007; Detroit Lions 2008-. **Orgs:** AAAA; keynote speaker, United Way Reason To Be Thankful. **Honors/Awds:** Mr. Football, Athletic Coaches Association; Sammy Baugh Natl Passer of the Yr Award, 1998; ESPN Award, ESPN, 2000; NFC Pro Bowl selection, 2000; All-Pro, USA Today, 2000; NFL Quarterback of the Yr, Natl Quarter back Club, 2000; All-NFC, Pro Football Weekly, 2000; NFL's Extra Effort Award, 2003. **Special Achievements:** Drafted by NY Yankees, 1995. **Business Addr:** Professional Football Player, Detroit Lions, 222 Republic Dr, Allen Park, MI 48101, **Business Phone:** (313)262-2002.*

CULPEPPER, DELLIE L.
Manager. **Personal:** Born Mar 24, 1941, Talbotton, GA; daughter of Willie and Daisy. **Educ:** Dimery's Bus Col, Atlanta, GA, ABA, 1963; Atlanta Law Sch, Atlanta, GA, LLB, 1979. **Career:** Southwest Coun Atlanta Chamber Com, mem exec comt, 1978; Traffic Ct, Atlanta, GA, ct admin & dir. **Orgs:** NAACP, 1980; Ida Prather YWCA, 1980; vpres, The Cruisers Fund Raising, 1984; Black Pub Adminr, 1984; Nat Asn Trial Ct Adminr, 1984; Atlanta Chap COMPA, 1985. **Business Phone:** (404)658-6959.*

CULPEPPER, LOUIS S
Chief executive officer. **Educ:** Univ Md, BS; Cent Mich Univ, MBA; Univ Phoenix, PhD; Eastern Ky Univ, Dipl Police Admin & Training; FBI Nat Acad, grad, Quantico, VA. **Career:** Culpepper & Assocs Security Serv, chmn, pres, chief exec officer, currently. **Orgs:** Atlanta Tech Col; Int Asn Chiefs Police; USAF Security Police Asn. **Honors/Awds:** Numerous professional affiliations. **Military Serv:** USAF Security, Comdr. **Business Addr:** Chairman, Chief Executive Officer, Culpepper & Associates Security Service, 1810 Water Pl Suite 180, Atlanta, GA 30339, **Business Phone:** (770)916-0060.

CULPEPPER, LUCY NELL
Physician. **Personal:** Born Jun 11, 1951, Awin, AL; daughter of L C and Lucy Lee Davis; married Joseph Williams (deceased), Jun 30, 1984. **Educ:** Ala A&M Univ, BS, 1973; Meharry Med Col, MD, 1977. **Career:** Martin Luther King Jr Gen Hosp, intern, resident, 1977-80; NHSC, pediatrician med dir, 1980-82; pvt pract, pediatrician, 1982-87; Maude Whatley Health Ctr, pediat, 1988-, med dir, 1989-99. **Orgs:** Zeta Phi Beta Sor Inc, 1972-; active staff mem, DCH Regional Med Ctr, 1980-; Tuscaloosa Co Med Soc, 1982-; Med Asn State Ala, 1982-; youth dir, First Baptist Church, 1984-90; W Ala Pediatric Soc, 1984-, W Ala Med Asn, 1985-, Ala State Med Asn, 1985-; bd dir, W Ala Chap Sickle Cell Disease Asn, 2000-; bd dir, Family Counseling Serv, 2002-; bd dir, DHR, 2000-. **Honors/Awds:** Woman of the Year, Christian Study Ctr, Alabama, 1983. **Home Addr:** 4415 Maple Ln, Northport, AL 35473. **Business Addr:** Medical Director, Maude Whatley Health Ctr, 2731 Martin Luther King Jr Blvd, PO Box 2400, Tuscaloosa, AL 35403, **Business Phone:** (205)758-6647.*

CULVER, RHONDA
Accountant. **Personal:** Born in Phoenix, AZ; daughter of Roscoe and Rose. **Educ:** Ariz State Univ, BS, 1981, MBA, 1986. **Career:** Searle Consumer Prod Div, asst cost acct, 1983-84; Garrett Airline Serv Div, sr acct, 1984-86, acct supvr, 1986-. **Orgs:** Bd dirs & treas, Nat Asn Accountants, Phoenix, 1983-; Asn MBA Execs, 1984, Mayor's Citizen Tax Fairness Comt, 1986; comm chmn, United Negro Col Fund, Phoenix, 1986,87; finance comn, Alpha Kappa Alpha Sor, 1985-87; tech commun coord Focus Software Users Group. **Honors/Awds:** Black Bd of Dirs Honoree Phoenix,

1986; Outstanding Woman, 1987. **Business Addr:** Accounting Supervisor, Garrett Airline Service Division, PO Box 29003, Phoenix, AZ 85038.*

CUMBER, VICTORIA LILLIAN
Columnist, talent agent. **Personal:** Born Feb 5, 1920, San Antonio, TX; daughter of Lora L Johnson and David H Johnson. **Educ:** Phillips Bus Sch, 1936; Metro Bus Sch, 1938. **Career:** Sepia Hollywood Mag, publ, 1941-45; Herald Attractions Agency, mgr, 1949-55; Lil Cumber Attractions Agency, theatrical agt, 1956-; SW Wave Newspaper, columnist, 1967-86; Scoop Newspaper, 1986-. **Orgs:** Life mem, Nat Asn Advan Colored People Hollywood Beverly Hills Br, 1937-; sec Community Actions Comn, 1958-60; co-organizer, Beverly Hills Hollywood Image Awards, 1967. **Honors/Awds:** Plaque Bus & Prof Women's Club, 1967; Black Filmmakers Hall of Fame, 1974; S Calif Motion Picture Coun, 1987, honoree; Special Pioneer Award, Afro American/ Humor Awards, 1990; Beverly Hills/Hollywood 4th ann Theater Trailblazer Award, 1991; Golden Star Halo Award, Motion Picture Coun, 1994; honoree, African-Am Short Film Market Place Short Film Festival, 1998; Sojourner Truth Award, Pan African Film & Arts Festival, 2002. **Special Achievements:** Coorganized the first Com Casting Dirs/Indust Awards saluting honorees who have been voted as an awardee by their peers 1982; First Black Woman Agentin Los Angeles; Am Artists Entertainment Group. **Business Addr:** Consultant, Lil Cumber Attractions Agency, 6363 Sunset Blvd Suite 807, PO Box 3358, Hollywood, CA 90028.

CUMMINGS, AEON L
Banker. **Personal:** Born Jul 5, 1963, Annotto Bay, Jamaica; son of Wilmore and Gladys; married Shawn Lawson, Aug 28, 1993. **Educ:** Hamilton Col, AB, econ & govt, 1985; Brooklyn Col, MA, econ, 1988; Univ VA, Darden Sch Bus, MBA, finance, 1991. **Career:** NYC Bd Educ, eng teacher, 1985-88; NYC Housing Preserv & Develop, analyst, 1989-90; Citibank, NA, vpres, prod mgr; GE Consumer Finance, vpres, currently. **Orgs:** Hamilton Col, alumni recruiting & fund raising, 1985-; Univ VA, Darden Bus Sch, pres, 1990-91; UNCF Citicorp Mentors, mentor, 1991-93; Nat Black MBA, 1993-. **Honors/Awds:** Outstanding Student in Economics, Brooklyn Col, 1988; one of 10 Nat fellows, Citicorp & Citibank Fel, 1990-91; Achievement Award, Fairfield County NBMBAA, 1994. **Special Achievements:** Master Thesis, "The Determinants of Housing Prices in Brooklyn NY," 1988; selected as one of the MBAs of the future by Minority MBA Mag. **Home Addr:** 477 E 24th St, Brooklyn, NY 11210, **Home Phone:** (718)434-5726. **Business Addr:** Vice President, GE Consumer Finance.

CUMMINGS, CARY, III
Physician. **Personal:** Born Jul 13, 1949, Monticello, FL; children: Lindsey. **Educ:** SUNY Binghamton, BS 1972; Meharry Med Col, MD, 1976. **Career:** Univ Rochester, intern, 1976-77; US Pub Health Serv, lt commander, 1977-79; Harrisburg Hosp, residency; Hershey Emergency Med Prog, asst prof dept internal med, 1981-83; Memorial Sloan-Kettering Cornell Univ, fel critical care med, 1983-84; Harrisburg Hosp, asst prof dept internal med, 1984-86; Hershey Medical Ctr, asst prof emergency med & trauma, 1985-86; pvt pract, physician, 1985-; Univ Calif San Francisco, fel, 1990-92; 1992-93; Dialysis Care 2000 Inc, founder & owner, developer; Physiscans Renal Care Inc, chmn bd & chief med officer, currently. **Orgs:** Dauphin Co Med Soc; PA Med Soc; Am Med Asn; Pa Med Soc; Dauphin County Med Soc; Am Soc Internal Med; Int Soc Nephrology. **Business Addr:** Chairman, Chief Medical Director, Physiscans Renal Care Inc, 3971 Linglestown Rd, Harrisburg, PA 17110.*

CUMMINGS, ELIJAH E
Congressperson (U.S. federal government). **Personal:** Born Jan 18, 1951. **Educ:** Howard Univ, BA, polit sci, 1973; Univ Md, JD, 1976. **Career:** Atty; Md House of Delegates, 1983-96; US House Rep, Md seventh Dist, congressman, 1996-. **Orgs:** MD Gov's Comn on Black Males, chair, 1990-; MD Bootcamp Aftercare Prog, founder, 1991-; New Psalmist Baptist Church; Cong Black Caucus, first vice chair, chmn, 2003-; US Naval Acad Bd Visitors; Morgan State Univ Bd Regents, trustee, Maryland Zoo; trustee, Baltimore Aquarium; bd dir, Baltimore Area Coun Boy Scouts Am. **Business Addr:** Congressman, US House of Representative, 2235 Rayburn House Off Bldg, Washington, DC 20515-2007, **Business Phone:** (202)225-4741.

CUMMINGS, FRANCES MCARTHUR
School administrator. **Personal:** Born Feb 2, 1941, Lumberton, NC; children: Isaiah T. **Educ:** Livingstone Col, BS, 1961; NC Cent Univ, MS, 1974; Univ NC Greensboro, Bus & Off Voc Cert, 1976. **Career:** Educator (retired); NC Asn Classroom Teachers, 1978-79; SE Reg Asn Classroom Teachers, pres, 1980; Nat Educ Asn, dir, 1980-87; NC Asn Educ, pres, 1983-84; Lumberton Sr High Sch, teacher; NC Asn Educr, exec dir, 1987-89; House Dist 87, elected NC House Rep, 1992-95. **Orgs:** Hilly Br Baptist Church, 1970-85; chartered mem, Alpha Kappa Alpha, 1974; Robeson City Dem Women, 1979-85, NC Coun Status of Women, 1980-85; bd dir, NC Ctr Pub Policy Res, 1983-86; bd dirs, NC Math & Sci Alliance; chair, Women & Minority Panel, Gov Appt, 1990; Pvt Indus Coun Lumber River comnrs, 1990. **Honors/Awds:** The Order of the Long Leaf Pine Gov's Award, 1983; Gov's Pub Sch Prog of Excellence Gov's Award, 1983; Outstanding Leader of Robeson City, Robeson City Black Caucus, 1983; Par Excellence Service Award, Gen Baptist Conv of NC, 1984; Tar Heel of the Week, News & Observer Raleigh, 1984. **Special Achievements:** The first female member of North Carolinas House of Representatives. Author of " The Girl Who never Quit". *

CUMMINGS, JAMES C., JR.
Executive. **Personal:** Born Sep 22, 1929, Indianapolis, IN; married Norma Lewis; children: Cynthia, James III, Cecilia, Ronald, Claudia. **Educ:** IN Central Univ, BS, 1962; IN Univ, grad work. **Career:** Village Mgt Corp, proj mgr, 1960-66; Bd Fundamental Educ, dir opers, 1966-70; Oxford Develop Co, asst vpres, 1970-71; Urban Advance, pres. **Orgs:** Chmn, Nat Black Rep Coun, exec comt Rep Nat Comn; chmn, IN Black Rep Coun; exec asst chmn, IN Rep State Comt; del Rep, Nat Convocation Fed, 1976; pres, IN Black Expo, 1971-73; former vice chmn, Inst Industrialized Building Oppurtinuty; Pub Works IN; bd mem, Zoning Appeals IN; former mem bd, NAACP. **Honors/Awds:** Disting Hoosier Award, Gov Edgar Whitcomb; Sagamore the Wabash, IN Highest Award, Gov Otis Bowen; Key City Indianapolis, Mayor William Hudnut. **Military Serv:** AUS, corpl, 1951-53.

CUMMINGS, DR. JAY R.
Educator. **Personal:** Born Jan 6, 1942, Jenkins, KY; married Victoria Gerald; children: Darryl, Toi, Jabari, Brandi, Jordan & Trent. **Educ:** Cent State Univ, BS, 1963; Cleveland State Univ, MEd, 1971; Ohio State Univ, Phd, 1974; Tex Women's Univ, post doctoral, 1981. **Career:** Ohio St Univ, Ford Found fel, Urban Educ Lead, 1973; Dallas Independent Sch District, cent adr, 1976-86; St Edward's Univ, adj prof, 1987-90; Tex Educ Agency, asst comnr, 1986-89, dep comnr, 1989-91, exec dep comnr, 1992-95, assoc comnr, 1995-97, asst to Tex comnr, 1997-99; Univ NTex, ColEduc, prof, 1999-2001; Tex Southern Univ, Col Educ, dean, 2001-. **Orgs:** Bd mem, Tex Lead, Educ & Governance, 1987-91; community advs, Austin Jr League, 1987-88; founder & charter mem, Tex Alliance Black Sch Educators, 1989-; KLRU (Public TV), community advisors, 1989-95; exec bd dir, Nat Asn St Dirs Voc Educ Consortium, 1994-98; chair, Nat Alliance Black Sch Educators, Demonstration Sch Inst, 1994-97; Nat CMS African Am Educ, 1998-; voc tech inst comm, chair, CMS Secondary Sch (SACS), 1998-. **Honors/Awds:** Hall of Fame, Cent State Univy, Athletic & Achievement, 1989-90; JohnsHopkins Univ, Sr Exec Residential fellowship, 1993; Black United Fund Tex,Walter Bremond Achievement Award, 1995; Executive Residential fellowship, Duke Univ, 1997; Distinguished Scholar Lecturer, Tex Southern Univ, 1998; Award of Distinction, Ohio State Alumni ASN, Col Educ, 1999. **Special Achievements:** Aspen IST, Games Theory Action Planning, invited participant, 1998; Teritiary Educ in South Africa (USIA), academic specialist, 1993; Nat Teleconference on Educating the Black Child, panelist, 1995; Center for the Development and Study of Effective Pedagogy AA Learners, founder, 1994. **Home Addr:** 10831 Kitty Brook Dr, Houston, TX 77071. **Business Addr:** Dean, Texas Southern University, Rm 200 3100 Cleburne Ave, Houston, TX 77004, **Business Phone:** (713)313-7343.

CUMMINGS, MIDRE ALMERIC
Baseball player. **Personal:** Born Oct 14, 1971, St Croix, Virgin Islands of the United States; married Annette Lewis; children: Mijon & Mikel. **Career:** Baseball player (retired); Pittsburgh Pirates, outfielder, 1993-97; Philadelphia Phillies, 1997.Boston Red Sox, 1998, 2000; Arizona Diamondbacks, 2001; Minnesota Twins, 1999-00; Tampa Bay DevilRays, outfielder, 2004; Baltimore Orioles, 2005. **Honors/Awds:** World Series champion, 2001. *

CUMMINGS, PAT
Writer. **Personal:** Born Nov 9, 1950, Chicago, IL; daughter of Arthur and Christine Taylor; married H Chuku Lee, Dec 27, 1990. **Educ:** Pratt Inst, BFA, 1974. **Career:** Free-lance auth, illusr, 1974-; HarperCollins Publ Inc, auth, illusr, currently; Parsons Sch Design, Manhattan, C bk illus, instr; Books: My Mama Needs Me, illusr; My Aunt Came Back, auth & illusr; Angel Baby, auth & illusr. **Orgs:** Graphic Artists Guild; Soc C Book Writers & Illusr; The Auth Guild; The Writers Guild Am. **Honors/Awds:** Coretta Scott King Award, 1983; Black Women in Publ Illusr Award, 1988; Horn Book Award, Boston Globe, 1992. **Business Addr:** Author, c/o Harper Collins Publ Inc, 10 E 53 St, New York, NY 10022.*

CUMMINGS, ROBERT TERRELL. **See CUMMINGS, TERRY.**

CUMMINGS, TERRY (ROBERT TERRELL CUMMINGS)
Basketball player, president (organization). **Personal:** Born Mar 15, 1961, Chicago, IL; son of John L and Verda; divorced; children: Robert Terrell Jr, Sean & Antonio. **Educ:** DePaul Univ. **Career:** Basketball player (retired), exec; Church of God in Christ, ordainedpentecostal minister; San Diego Clippers, forward, 1983-84; Cummings Entertainment Group, pres, 1984-; Milwaukee Bucks, 1985-89; San Antonio Spurs, 1990-95; Milwaukee Bucks, 1995-96; Seattle Supersonics, 1996-97; NY Knicks, 1997; Philadelphia 76ers, 1998; Golden State Warriors, forward, 1999-00. **Honors/Awds:** NBA Rookie of the Yr, 1983; NBA All-Star, 1985, 1989; Good Guys, Sporting News, 2000; Chicagoland Sports Hall of Fame, 2006. **Special Achievements:** Album, T.C., 2007. **Business Phone:** (210)696-4667.*

CUMMINGS, THERESA FAITH
State government official. **Personal:** Born in Springfield, IL; daughter of Nelson Mark and Mary Jeanette Irvine. **Educ:** Winston-Salem State Univ, BS, educ; Southern Ill Univ, MS, Per, Sch Med, fel, 1979. **Career:** St Louis Pub Sch Syst, teacher, 1957-67; Multi-purpose Neighborhood Serv Ctr Syst Springfield, Sangamon Co Comm Action Agency, proj dir, 1967-69, exec dir, 1969-85; Aband Mine Hands Reclam Coun, asst dir; Ill Dept Natural Resources, chief eeo officer; Cummings Assocs, ceo & owner, currently. **Orgs:** Counr & guid chairperson, Human Develop Corp, 1965-67; planner & counr, Mr.Achievers Summer Inst Banneker Dist St Louis Pub Sch, 1966-67; League Women Voters; Am Asn Univ Women; Nat Coun Negro Women; bd dir, Sangamon CoMarch Dimes; St Paul AME Church; life mem, NAACP; licensing bd, Ill Ambulatory Surg Treat Ctr; vice chairperson, chairperson & state treas, Nat Woman Polit Caucus; adv coun, Fed Reserve Consumer; Bus & Prof Women's Club; treas, pres, dist dir & vpres, State Pres Fed BPW, Women Govt; Women Mgt; pres, Nat Assoc Bus Women Owners; Am Bus Women Club; chairperson, Imperial Credit Union; Iota Phi Lambda Sorority, Inc; pres, Ill Fedn Bus &Prof Women; tres, Ill Affirmative Action officers Asn. **Honors/Awds:** Citation, Gr Lakes Regional Off Econ Opportunity Serv; citation,Springfield Ministerial Alliance Dedication & Devotion Duty; certified for service & contribution to Proj Mainstream Together Inc; cert Consumer Credit Counseling Serv Bd of Dirs; cert Contrib to Comm Develop OH Chapter of NACD; runner-up plaque, Lola M Parker Achievement Award; Medallion, Serv March Dimes; Woman of the Year, Zeta Phi Beta Sorority, 1982; Elizabeth Cady Stanton Awardee, Springfield Women Polit Caucus; Charlotte Danton Award for Government, Women Mgt; Fredda Witherspoon Award; Business Woman of the Year, Iota Phi Lambda Alpha Zeta.

CUNNINGHAM, COURTNEY
Government official. **Personal:** Born Feb 17, 1962, Ocala, FL; son of James Charles Sr and Juanita Perry. **Educ:** Univ Fla, Gainesville, FL, BA, 1983; Univ Fla Col Law, Gainesville, FL, JD, 1986. **Career:** Fisher, Rushmer, Orlando, FL, assoc, 1986-87; Rumberger, Kirk, Orlando, FL, assoc, 1987-89; Republican Nat Community, Wash, DC, dep chief coun, 1989-90; Interstate Com Comn, Wa, DC, atty & adv, 1990-91; Off Cong & Intergovernmental Affairs, Dept Labor, sr legis officer, 1991-93; Am Trucking Asn, sr legis rep, Wash, DC, 1993; Top Wall St firm, officer & investment banker; Miami-Dade County Comn, Off Chairperson, Chief Staff; Miami-Dade County & Miami-Dade County Housing Finance Authority, sr invest banker; Ryder Syst, Inc, dir, govt rels, Miami, FL, 1994; Barreto Cunningham May Dudley Maloy, partner, currently. **Orgs:** Florida Blue Key Fraternity, 1983-86; vice chmn, Justice Campbell Thornal Moot Ct Bd, 1986; Fla Bd Osteopathic Med Examiner, 1988; Am Judicature Soc, 1988; Consult, Nat Republican Inst Intl Affairs, 1990; Univ Fl, Bd Trustees, 2005. **Honors/Awds:** Legal Coun, Fla Republican Conv, 1994-95. **Business Addr:** Partner, Barreto Cunningham May Dudley Maloy, 235 Catalonia Ave, Coral Gables, FL 33134-6704, **Business Phone:** (305)444-4648.*

CUNNINGHAM, DAVID S., JR.
Government official. **Personal:** Born Jun 24, 1935, Chicago, IL; son of David S and Eulah Mae Lawson; married Sylvia AC Krappel; children: David Srumier III, Leslie, Robyn & Amber. **Educ:** Univ Riverside, BA, eco & polit sci, 1962; Occidental Col, MA, urban studies, 1973. **Career:** Cunningham Short Berryman & Asn Inc, consults former partner; Los Angeles City Coun, 1973-; Los Angeles City Council, mayor, 1973; Democratic Nat Comt, state chmn, 1976-86; Dave Cunningham & Assoc; Sr. vpres, Community Housing Equity Corporation, 1988-91. **Orgs:** Chmn, Grants Housing & Community Develop; vice chmn, Finance & Revenue Comn; Police Fire & Pub Safety Comn; authored or co-authored many laws among include establish Mayor's Off Small Bus Asst; reduction minimum age fore firefighters from 21 to 18 yrs; pioneered use fed block grants local govt use; created city's dept aging; created Vista Montoya Los Angele's first subsidized condo proj low & median income families; initiated organ Mid Town Chamber Com & Pico Union Chamber Com; charter mem, CA Minority Employ Coun; Los Angeles Black Agenda; Bd Interracial Coun Bus Affairs; Urban League; bd dirs, Los Angeles Co Sanitation Dist No 1; chmn, Nat Black United Fund; past pres, CORlumni Asn; life mem, Omega Psi Phi FratInc; life mem, NAACP; life mem, Nat Coun Negro Women; col CA Guard; World Affairs Coun; chmn, LA Brotherhood Crusade, 1971-72; South CA Asn Govts Comn & Econ Develop Comn, 1978-79; bd dirs, Nat League Cities, 1981-83. **Honors/Awds:** Man of Tomorrow, Omega Psi Phi, 1973; Los Angeles Brotherhood Crusade,1973, 1976; Honorary Mayor, Baton Rouge LA, 1974; Mid City Chamber Commerce, 1974; Delta Sigma Theta, 1982-84; Dept Navy, 1984; Boy Scouts Am; South CA Fair Housing Congress, 1984; Alex Haley Heritage Award, 1984.

CUNNINGHAM, DON
Business owner, entrepreneur. **Career:** Mayor, Bethlehem, Pennsylvania, Currently; OEM Erie Inc, owner, currently. **Busi-**

ness Addr: Owner, OEM Erie Inc, 1810 W 20th St, Erie, PA 16502, **Business Phone:** (814)459-8024.

CUNNINGHAM, E BRICE
Lawyer. **Personal:** Born Feb 17, 1931, Buffalo, TX; son of Hattie and Tessie Roblow; married Rosie Nell (Portis) Cunningham, Mar 6, 1964; children: LaWanda Kay, Ledner, Michele, Elana Brice. **Educ:** Howard Univ Sch Law, BA, ID, 1960. **Career:** E Brice Cunningham, atty & counr law, City Dallas, munic ct judge, 1971-72; City Dallas, appeals judge; licences minister; atty law, currently. **Orgs:** State Bar Tex, 1960; State Bar Com Coord with Other & Groups; State Bar Pub Affairs Com; State Bar Sub-Com Grievance Com; Dallas Bar Asn; Special Cts Com; Fee Disputes Com Dallas Bar Asn; Courthouse Com; State Bd Code Criminal Pruc Study Com; regional dir, Nat Bar Asn Inc, Region VI; Am Judicature Soc; S Dallas Br YMCA; Grand Atty, United Supreme coun; Past Grand legal Adv, Most Worshipful Prince Hall Grand Lodge F&AM Tex; bd dirs, C Aid Soc; Planning Comn city Dallas, 1973-76; Alpha Phi Alpha Fraternity; Elks; Nat Asn Advan Colored People; Dallas City Planning Comn. **Honors/Awds:** Recipient Award, Law Com 100, 1973; Award for Legal Services, Dallas Tex Nat Asn Advan Colored People, 1977; A. Maceo Smith Community Serv Award, 1979; Black Hist Achievement Award, Aldersgate United Methodist Church; Cert Merit, J L Turner Legal Asn; Cert of Merit, Legislative Black Caucus State Tex, 1981; S Cent Bus & Prof Women's Club, Man Yr Award, 1986; Six Bar Asn Dallas, Dr Martin Luther King Jr Justice Award, 1995; Tex Nat Asn Advan Colored People, Tex Heroes Award, 1997. **Military Serv:** AUS, corpl, 1948-54. **Business Addr:** Attorney, 777 S RL Thornton Freeway Suite 121, Dallas, TX 75203-2951.*

CUNNINGHAM, DR. JAMES J.
Educator, dean (education). **Personal:** Born Apr 19, 1938, Pittsburgh, PA; son of Steve and Roberta; married Lois Vines; children: Lita Denise & James Jr. **Educ:** Va State Col, BA, 1964; George Washington Univ, MS, 1967, EdD, 1971. **Career:** Elem sch teacher, 1964-66; Wash DC, coun & prin, 1966-68; Fed City Col, WADC, 1968-71; assoc Cont Res & Analysis Inc, WA DC, consult, 1969; Fed City Col, dir admis, 1971; HEW & DE, WA DC, consult, 1971; Moton Consortium Admin & Financial Aid, co-dir, 1971-72; Tex Southern Univ, dean studs, prof educ, 1972-74; Mankato State Col, Mankato, MN, vpres stud servs, profeduc, 1974; Tex Southern Univ Houston, spec asst pres, 1986, vpres instadvan, assoc dean, prof educ, currently. **Orgs:** Nat Asn Higher Educ; Personnel Guidance Asn; Asn Col Admin Coun; DC Coun Asn; Elem Classroom Teachers Asn; Nat Teachers Asn; Tex Personnel Serv Adminrs; Minn State Col Stud Asn; Minn Stud Serv Adminr; Nat Asn AdvanColored People. **Military Serv:** USAF, A/1C, 1955-59. **Business Addr:** Professor of Education, Texas Southern University, Grad Educ, 3100 Cleburne St, Houston, TX 77004, **Business Phone:** (713)313-7256.

CUNNINGHAM, JOY VIRGINIA
Judge. **Educ:** City Univ NY, BS; John Marshall Law Sch, JD, 1982. **Career:** French, Rogers, Kezelis & Kominiarek, atty; Circuit Ct, Ill, Judge; Northwestern Mem Hosp, sr vpres & gen coun; Ill Ct, First Dist, 3rd Div, appellate judge, currently. **Orgs:** Nat Asn Advan Colored People; Urban League; Am Bar Asn; Am Health Lawyers Asn; Cook County Bar Asn; Black Women Lawyers Asn; Ill State Bar Asn; Women's Bar Asn Ill; Econ Club Chicago; pres, Chicago Bar Asn, 2004-05. **Special Achievements:** First African-American female president of Chicago Bar Asn, 2004. **Business Addr:** Appellate Judge, Illinois Court, 1004 Columbus St, Ottawa, IL 61350, **Business Phone:** (815)434-5050.

CUNNINGHAM, MALENA ANN
Journalist, television journalist. **Personal:** Born Oct 27, 1958, Laurens, SC; daughter of O'Dell and Betty Brummell. **Educ:** Univ Ga, ABJ, 1980. **Career:** Atlanta Gas Light Co, pub rels assoc, 1980-82; Cable News Network, writer & producer, 1982-86; WTVQ-TV, reporter, 1986-87; WHTM-TV, reporter, 1987-88; WSAV-TV, anchor, 1988-91; WVTM-TV, anchor & reporter, 1992; Strategic Media Rels, owner & pub Rels, currently. **Orgs:** Nat Asn Black Journalists, 1992-; Birmingham Asn Black Journalists, vpres, broadcasting, 1992-; Delta Sigma Theta, 1977-; Jr bd mem, YWCA, 1992-; Birmingham Asn Black Journalists, pres, 1994; co-chair, The Cool Community task force; adv bd, Womens Fund, 2006-. **Honors/Awds:** United Press Intl, First Place, Spot News Reporting, 1988; Second Place, Assoc Press, Spot News Reporting, 1988; Best Newscast, Assoc Press, 1990; Best Newscast, Emmy, 1992; Best Series, Emmy, 1995; Best Spec Project, Emmy, 1996. *

CUNNINGHAM, PATRICK DANTE ROSS. See CUNNINGHAM, RICK.

CUNNINGHAM, PAUL RAYMOND GOLDWYN
Surgeon, educator. **Personal:** Born Jul 28, 1949, Mandeville, Jamaica; son of Winston P Cunningham and Sylvia F Marsh; married Sydney Keniston, Feb 14, 1987; children: Shawn, Rachel, Lucinda, Tifanie. **Educ:** Univ WI, Jamaica, MBBS, 1972. **Career:** Mount Sinai Med Ctr, New York, surgical intern, 1974-75, surgical resident, 1975-79; Joint Disease North General Hospital, New York NY, asst dir of surgery, 1979-81; Bertie Memorial Hosptial, Windsor NC, attending physician, 1981-84; East Carolina Univ, Broody Sch Med, Div surgery, physician, 1984-94, interim dir, prof & chief, 1994-02; Pitt County Memorial Hospital, Greenville, NC, chief of medical staff, 1991; State Univ New York, Upstate Medical Univ, Dept of Surgery, chair, 2002-. **Orgs:** AMA; Nat Med Asn; Southern Med Asn; Am Asn Surgery Trauma; Eastern Asn Surgery Trauma; Southern Surgical Asn; Transplantation Soc; fel Am Col Surgeons; founding mem, Am Soc Minority Health & Transplant Prof; Soc Black Acad Surgeons. **Military Serv:** AUS Reserve, Major, 1990-98. *

CUNNINGHAM, RANDALL
Business owner, football player, clergy. **Personal:** Born Mar 27, 1963, Santa Barbara, CA; son of Samuel and Mabel; married Felicity de Jagar; children: Randall II, Vashti & Grace. **Educ:** Univ Nev, Las Vegas. **Career:** Football player, business owner (retired), pastor; Philadelphia Eagles, quarterback, 1985-95, 2002; TNT Network, TV studio analyst, 1996; Minn Vikings, 1997-99; Dallas Cowboys, 2000; TNT, football analyst, 1999-2000; Baltimore Ravens, 2001; marble & granite bus owner; rec studio & musical group, producer; Remnant Ministries, founder, 2004; pastor & founder, Cupbearer, Las Vegas, 2004-. **Honors/Awds:** Pro Bowl, 1988-90, 1998; Pro Bowl MVP, 1988; NFC Player of the Year, Wash Touchdown Club, 1988, 1990; Bert Bell Award, Maxwell Club, 1988, 1990, 1998; NFL Offensive Player of the Year, 1990; NFC Offensive Player of the Year, 1990; Pro Comeback Player of the Year, Football Weekly, 1992; Player of the Year, Kans City Comn 101, 1998; Player of the Year, Touchdown Club Columbus, 1998; Most Valuable Player, Jim Thorpe Asn & NFL Players Asn, 1998. **Business Addr:** Pastor, Founder, The Cupbearer, 325 E Windmill Rd, Las Vegas, NV 89123, **Business Phone:** (702)269-7803.

CUNNINGHAM, RICK (PATRICK DANTE ROSS CUNNINGHAM)
Football player. **Personal:** Born Jan 4, 1967, Los Angeles, CA; married. **Educ:** Tex A&M Univ, Eng, 1989. **Career:** Indianapolis Colts, Tackle, 1990; Phoneix Thunder, 1992-93; ArizonaCardinals, 1994; Minn Vikings, 1995; Oakland Raiders, 1996-98; MontrealAlouettes, 2000; Edmonton Eskimos, 2000-03; Las Vegas Gladiators, 2003-05. *

CUNNINGHAM, ROBERT SHANNON, JR.
Executive. **Personal:** Born Jan 17, 1958, Columbia, SC; son of Robert Shannon Sr and Dorothy Mae Bell; married Shenita Gilmore, Sep 23, 1989. **Educ:** Johnson C Smith Univ, Charlotte, NC, BS, 1980. **Career:** Union Carbide, Simpsonville, SC, production supvr, 1980; IBM Corp, Charlotte, NC, financial analyst, 1980-89; IBM Corp, Res Triangle Park, NC, bus planner, 1989-91, develop prog mgr, 1991-98, sr prof develop mgr, 1998-. **Orgs:** Vice chmn, Mecklenburg Co Personnel Comn Bd, 1982-88; City Charlotte Cert Develop Bd, 1989; secy, Focus Leadership Bd, 1987; United Way Community Resource Bd, 1981; Urban League, 1985-; numerous positions, Omega Psi Phi Fraternity, 1977. **Honors/Awds:** Man of the Year, Johnson C Smith, Omega Psi Phi Fraternity, RHO Chap, 1979; Citizen of the Year, Pi Phi Chap-Omega Psi Phi Fraternity, 1988; Outstanding Am Award. **Home Addr:** 1008 Sunny Brae Ct, Apex, NC 27502, **Home Phone:** (919)387-7822. **Business Phone:** (919)543-0515.*

CUNNINGHAM, T. J., SR.
Lawyer. **Personal:** Born Feb 6, 1930, Plant City, FL; son of Garrison S and Janette Rome; children: Belinda C. Palmore, Tequesta C. Alston, Yolanda Cunningham Griffin, Kimberly Cunningham, TJ "Jimmy" Cunningham Jr. **Educ:** Fla A&M Univ, Tallahassee, FL, BS, sociol, 1952; Howard Univ Law Sch, Wash, DC, JD, 1957. **Career:** Cunningham & Cunningham, PA, West Palm Beach, FL, owner, 1960-. **Orgs:** Fla Bar; DC Bar Asn; Am Bar Asn; US Ct Appeals; US Supreme Ct; Palm Beach County Bar Asn; Nat Bar Asn; Fla Acad Trial Lawyers; founder/mem, F. Malcolm Cunningham, Sr Bar Asn; Fla Bar Grievance Comt, Palm Beach County; World Peace through Law; Nat Bar Asn; Fla Chapter, Nat Bar Asn; Nat Asn Advan Colored People; Alpha Phi Alpha; Fla Chapter Nat Guardsmen Asn; Forum Club Palm Beaches; Fla State Action Coun; Nat Urban League; adv coun, Fla A&M Univ. **Honors/Awds:** Fla A&M Univ Alumni Leadership Award, Palm Beach County; Leadership Award, 1986; President's Service Award, Fla Chapter NBA, 1981, President's Award, 1975; F. Malcolm Cunningham Sr. Bar Achievement Award, 1981; Chairman Convention Award, Nat Bar Asn, 1972. **Military Serv:** AUS, Corporal, 1952-54; Korea Combat Badge, Purple Heart, Korean Service Award. **Business Addr:** Attorney, Cunningham & Cunningham, PA, 1897 Palm Beach Lakes Blvd, Cross Roads Bldg Ste 201, West Palm Beach, FL 33409.*

CUNNINGHAM, VERNESSA SMALLS-BRANTLEY
Physician. **Personal:** Born Aug 4, 1949, Charleston, SC; married Herman Cunningham. **Educ:** Spelman Col, BS, 1971; Meharry Medical Col, MD, 1975. **Career:** Martland Hosp Newark NJ, resident, 1975-76; Monmouth Med Ctr, Long Branch NJ, resident, 1976-77, fel, 1977-79; Perth Amboy Gen Hosp, dir nurseries, 1980-83; Pvt Pract, pediatrician, 1983-85; Point Pleasant Hosp, dir nursery, 1985-86; Kaiser-Permanente, pediatrician & neonatologist. **Orgs:** Am Acad Pediat, 1983-85; Nat Asn Black Bus & Prof Women, 1985-; Atlanta Med Soc, 1987. **Honors/Awds:** Achievement Award, Nat Coun Negro Women, N Shore Area, 1985. **Military Serv:** USAR, capt, 1 yr. **Business Addr:** Pediatrician, Neonatologist, 1525 Clifton Rd Ne, Atlanta, GA 30322.

CUNNINGHAM, WILLIAM
Business owner. **Personal:** Born Nov 7, 1929, Union County, NC; son of Johnnie Mae Lockhart; divorced. **Educ:** Perry's Bus Col, 1951; Johnson C Smith Univ, 1954; Fla State Univ, Exten, 1972. **Career:** NC Mutual Life Ins Co, debit mgr, 1957-61; SE Bus Col, instr, 1969-70, vpres, admin dean, 1970-72; RSL, assoc dir minority recruiting, 1972-73; Hatchett & Cunningham Assoc, partner, 1973-84; Affordable Used Car, owner, 1987; NC House Rep, rep, 1987-, minority leader, 1995-96; HKL Inc, chief exec officer. **Orgs:** Charlotte C of C; Charlotte BBB; Parkwood Inst CME Chap; YMCA; Retired Veterans Asn; Johnson C Smith Alumni Asn; CLU Civil Liberties Union; contributing mem United Negro Col Fund; Voter Educ Proj; contributing mem Urban League. **Military Serv:** USN, active duty, 20 yrs. *

CUNNINGHAM, WILLIAM
Basketball player. **Personal:** Born Mar 25, 1974, Augusta, GA. **Educ:** Temple Univ. **Career:** CBA, Ft Wayne Fury, prof basketball player; Philadelphia 76ers, ctr, 1997; Utah Jazz, 1998; Toronto Raptors, 1999; NJ Nets, 1999; Atletico Arenas, Uruguay, 2006. *

CUNNINGHAM, DR. WILLIAM DEAN
Educator. **Personal:** Born Aug 9, 1937, Kansas City, MO; divorced; children: Crystal. **Educ:** Univ Kans, BA, 1959; Univ Tex, MLS, 1962; Univ MD, PhD, 1972. **Career:** Educator (retired). Fed Aviation Agency, chief libr serv, 1965-67; Topeka Pub Libr, head adult serv, 1967-68; US Dept Educ, prog officer, 1968-71; Howard Univ, dir univ libr, 1970-73; Univ Md, Col Libr & Info Servs, asst prof, 1973. **Orgs:** Am Libr Asn, 1970, Asn Study Afro-Am Life & Hist, 1974; bd dirs, Soul Journey Enterprises, 1974; Nat Black Heritage Coun, 1984. **Honors/Awds:** Citations from Dept Educ, FAA, ASALA. **Special Achievements:** Author: "Blacks in Performing Arts"; co-author: "Black Guide to Wash". **Military Serv:** USAF, t/sgt, 1954-60. **Home Addr:** 1201 Fairlakes Pl, Bowie, MD 20721. *

CUNNINGHAM, WILLIAM L
Government official, economist. **Personal:** Born Aug 28, 1939, Little Rock, AR; married Annette; children: Karm Joy. **Educ:** Univ Ark Pine Bluff, BS, 1961; St Vincent Med Ctr, Little Rock, assoc, 1964; US Dept Agr, Salt Lake City, mgt cert, 1967; Univ Utah, Salt Lake City, MA, 1972. **Career:** State Utah Anti-discrimination Div, investigator, conciliator & pres; Univ Ark Med Ctr, biochemist, 1964-65; Univ Utah Med Ctr, researcher, 1965-66; US Dept Agr, field adv, 1965-68, agr engr, 1966-68; Univ Wash Med Center, med consult, 1968-69, lab supvr, 1968-70; State Utah, liberal economist, 1970-72, economist adv, 1971-73. **Orgs:** Bd mem, 1957-61, 1993-, third vpres, 1996, first vpres, 1997-, NAACP; officer, 1965-68, bd mem, 1966-67, Elks. **Honors/Awds:** Hon mem cert Am Basketball Asn, 1973; Special Service Award, 1975, Exalted Ruler Award, 1977, Outstanding Citizen Award 1979, Elks; Earnest Turner Day Award, Beehive Elks Lodge, 1991; President Award, NAACP, 1997. **Military Serv:** USAF, a/1c, 1961-63; Special service award, 1962. **Business Addr:** Seniorr Investigator, Conciliator, State Utah, 160 E 300 S, PO Box 146640, Salt Lake City, UT 84114-6640, **Business Phone:** (801)530-6918.

CUNNINGHAM, WILLIAM MICHAEL
Executive. **Personal:** Born Jul 16, 1958, Washington, DC. **Educ:** Howard Univ, BA, econ, 1978; Univ Chicago, MBA, fin, 1983, MA, Econ, 1983. **Career:** Data Resources Inc, mktg rep, 1977-83; Conn Mutual Life, invest anal, 1983-85; Merrill Lynch, instnl sales, 1985-87; Fed Home Loan Mkt Corp, instnl sales, 1987-88; Creative Investment Res Inc, social investment adv, 1989-, chief exec officer; US Securities & Exchange Comn, registered investment adv, 1990-; DC Pub Serv Comn, investment adv, 1994. **Orgs:** Am Friends Serv Comt, fin comn; Social Investment Forum; Asn Investment Mgt & Res; Twin Cities Soc Security Analysts; CFA Inst; The CFA Soc; Social Investment Forum. **Special Achievements:** Testified before US House of Rep Banking Subcomn, 2000; author: "Money & the Sprit," published in Ethisches Investment: Strategien fur Kirchliche Geldan lagen, 2001; Faith-based Mutual Funds, 2001; numerous speaking engagements. **Business Addr:** Social Investment Advisor, Creative Investment Research Inc, PO Box 55793, Minneapolis, MN 55458-0725, **Business Phone:** (866)867-3795.*

CURBEAM, ROBERT L
Astronaut. **Personal:** Born Mar 5, 1962, Baltimore, MD; married Julie Dawn Lein; children: 2. **Educ:** US Naval Acad, BS, aerospace eng, 1984; Naval Postgrad Sch, MS, aeronaut eng, 1990, aeronaut & astronaut eng, 1991. **Career:** Astronaut (retired); USN, naval flight officer, 1984, capt; US Naval Acad, Weapons & Systs Eng Dept, instr, 1994; NASA, astronaut, 1994-2007. **Orgs:** US Naval Acad Alumni Asn; Asn Old Crows. **Honors/Awds:** Fighter Wing One Radar Intercept Officer of the

Year, 1989; US Naval Test Pilot School Best Developmental Thesis (DT-II) Award. **Special Achievements:** Mission specialist on STS-85 assignment, shuttle Discovery, 1997. **Military Serv:** USN, naval flight officer, 1984; 2 Navy Commendation Medals, Navy Meritorious Unit Commendation, Armed Forces Expeditionary Medal, Natl Defense Serv Medal, Navy Battle Efficiency Award, Sea Serv Deployment Ribbon.

CURETON, EARL
Basketball player, basketball coach. **Personal:** Born Sep 3, 1957, Detroit, MI. **Educ:** Robert Morris Col; Univ Detroit. **Career:** Basketball player, (retired), head coach; Philadelphia 76ers, ctr, 1980-83; Detroit Pistons, ctr, 1983-86; Chicago Bulls, ctr, 1986; Los Angeles Clippers, ctr, 1987-88; Charlotte Hornets, ctr, 1988-91; Houston Rockets, ctr, 1994-96; Toronto Raptors, ctr, 1997; Milano, ctr, 1983-84; Philips Milano, ctr, 1989-90; Tours, ctr, 1991-92; Sioux Falls Skyforce, ctr, 1993-94; Long Beach Jam, coach, 2003-04; Orange County Crush, head coach, currently. **Business Phone:** (562)861-6089.

CURETON, JOHN PORTER
Manager, consultant. **Personal:** Born Oct 4, 1936, Oxford, NC; son of John and Marie; married Carolyn Bethea; children: Tonya Yvette & John Porter. **Educ:** Johnson C Smith Univ, BS, Psychol, 1960; Adelphia Univ, postgrad, 1960-61; Univ Pa, attended 1963; Univ Hartford, attended 1980. **Career:** New York State Dept Mental Hygiene, psychiat social worker, 1960-62; Inter-State Staffing Inc, mgt consult, 1962-66; Philco Ford Corp, sr employ rep, 1966-68; Tanatex Div, Sybron Corp, indust rels mgr, 1968-73; US Postal Servs, reg labor rels exec, 1973-75; Heublein Inc Groc Prod Group, mgr employee rels, 1975-78; US Tobacco Co, Indust & Sales Rels, dir, 1978-98. **Orgs:** Nat Asn Market Developers; Employ Mgt Assoc; Inst Rels & Res; Inst Collective Bargaining & Group Rels; Soc Human Resources Mgt; Am Soc Training & Develop; bd mem, Voluntary Action Ctr; Ct UNCF Comn; Kappa Alpha Psi; Nat Urban League; Nat Asn Advan Colored People; Western NE Org Develop Network. **Honors/Awds:** Various awards from UNCF, UL, BNA-Personnel Policies Forum, Kappa Alpha Psi, YMCA.

CURETON, MICHAEL
Police officer, government official. **Personal:** Born Nov 15, 1955, Cincinnati, OH; son of James A Cureton Sr and Dolores J Thomas Rowland; married Jennifer L Horton Cureton, Jun 20, 1987; children: Shana, Mike Jr, Christopher, Angela & Brandon. **Educ:** Univ Cincinnati, AS, 1976. **Career:** City Cincinnati, police cadet, 1973-76; Procter & Gamble Co, security, 1976-78, sales rep, 1978-80; City Cincinnati, police officer, 1980, dist two comdr, asst police chief, 2005-. **Orgs:** Pres, Sentinel Police Asn, 1986-; csteerng comn, Dr Martin Luther King Coalition, 1988-; hairperson ways & means, Nat Black Police Asn Eastern Reg, 1989-; volunteer chair site security, Nat Coun Negro Women Black Family Reunion, Cincinnati Site, 1989-; First Baptist Church Kennedy Heights. **Honors/Awds:** Emerging Leaders for the 90's, Applause Mag, 1990. **Special Achievements:** Brought lawsuit against Cincinnati Police Division, which ultimately promoted minorities into upper levels of police command structure, 1988. **Business Addr:** Assistant Police Chief, Cincinnati Police Division, 3295 Erie Ave, Cincinnati, OH 45208.

CURETON, STEWART CLEVELAND
Clergy, school administrator. **Personal:** Born Mar 24, 1930, Greenville, SC; son of Santee and Martha Henderson; married Claudette Hazel Chapman, Dec 27, 1954; children: Ruthye E Cooley, Stewart C Jr, Santee Charles, Samuel C. **Educ:** Benedict Col, AB, 1953; Starks Sch Theol, BD, 1956; Morris Col, Dr Divinity, 1982; Benedict Col, Dir Divinity 1983. **Career:** North Warren HS, instr, 1956-61; Am Baptist Theol Sem, instr, 1961-85; Beck HS, instr, 1965-82; SC Congress Christian Educ, instr, 1965-83; Reedy River Baptist Church, pastor, currently. **Orgs:** Moderator Reedy River Baptist Asn, 1972-76; state vpres, Nat Baptist Convention, 1977-94; comnr, Human Rels, 1978-84; vpres, E&M Baptist Convention SC; honorary state v pres, NAACP, 1982-84; Urban League Bd Dirs, 1983; treas, SHARE, 1983-85; chmn, Urban League Bd, 1989-90, pres, Bapt Educational & Missionary Convention SC, 1986-91; vpres, At Large, Nat Baptist Convention, USA Inc. **Honors/Awds:** Service Award, Martin Webb Learning Ctr, 1980; Outstanding Citizen, Human Rels, 1983; Outstanding Service, Christian Action Coun, 1984; Outstanding Serv Award, South Carolina State House Reps, 1986; Man of the Year, Urban League, 1990. **Business Addr:** Pastor, Reedy River Baptist Church, PO Box 676, Mauldin, SC 29662, **Business Phone:** (803)277-0364.*

CURRIE, BETTY
Presidential aide. **Personal:** Born Nov 10, 1939, Edwards, MS; daughter of Theodore R and Vivian U Williams. **Educ:** Waukegan Township High Sch's bus course, 1957. **Career:** Presidential aide (retired); Navy Dept, Postal Serv; US Agency Int Develop; Peace Corps & Dept Health & Human Servs, staff; White House, Off Pres, personal secy.

CURRIE, JACKIE L.
Government official. **Personal:** Born Nov 2, 1932, Casscoe, AR; daughter of Dwight Garrison and Lillie Montgomery Cooper; married Charmie, Dec 1949; children: Michael, Gregory, Charmie III & Allen. **Educ:** Wayne State Univ, Detroit, MI, BS, 1974; Univ Mich, Ann Arbor, MI, 1975. **Career:** Wayne State Univ, Detroit, MI, community serv coordr, 1972-; Wayne County Comn, Detroit, MI, comnr, 1976-93, chair pro-tem; City Detroit, city clerk, 1994-2005, chair, currently. **Orgs:** Past chair, Pub Safety & Judiciary Comt; chair, Wayne County Community Adv Bd, 1989-; chair, Comt Airports, Rds, & Pub Serv; bd mem, Detroit E Inc,1980-; Shar House, 1970-; pres, Gamma Phi Delta Sorority Inc, 1990; community develop, Detroit Urban Ctr; devoted work, Boy Scouts Am; Community Serv, Eastside Community Slate; Youth Advocacy Prog, CPAB arrow-Aldridge & Co. **Honors/Awds:** Golden Heritage Award, Civil Serv. **Home Phone:** (313)921-0806. **Business Phone:** (313)224-3460.

CURRY, CHARLES H
Advertising executive. **Career:** Burrell Advert, pres & coo, 1991-93. *

CURRY, CLARENCE F.
Lecturer, management consultant. **Personal:** Born Aug 15, 1943, Hampton, VA; married Agnes A Mason; children: Clarence III & Candace. **Educ:** Lafayette Col, BS, Met Eng, 1965; Univ Pittsburgh, MBA, 1971; Carnegie Mellon Univ, MS, IA, 1973. **Career:** Westinghouse Elec, engr; Univ Pittsburgh Sch Bus, dir Small Bus Devel Ctr, asst vice chancellor; CFC-3 Mgt Serv, prin consult, currently; Pittsburgh Gaming Task Force Mem, Pittsburgh Penguins, currently. **Orgs:** Panelist, Am Arbitration Asn; Minority Bus Opportunity Comm; Int Coun Small Bus; USAS BC; Small Bus Inst Dir Asn. **Honors/Awds:** Pa Minority Bus Advocate, SBA, 1983. **Special Achievements:** International consultant on business development in Brazil, Peru, Poland and Czech Republic and Slovakia; several consulting projects for 500 firms. **Home Addr:** 200 Richland Lane, Pittsburgh, PA 15208, **Home Phone:** (412)243-2084.

CURRY, DELL (WARDELL STEPHEN CURRY)
Executive, basketball player. **Personal:** Born Jun 25, 1964, Harrisonburg, VA; son of Dell; married Sonya; children: Stefan, Seth & Sydell. **Educ:** Va Polytechnic Inst & State Univ, Blacksburg, VA, 1986. **Career:** Basketball player (retired), exec; Utah Jazz, 1986-87; Cleveland Cavaliers, 1987-88; Charlotte Hornets, 1988-98; Milwaukee Bucks, 1998-99; Toronto Raptors, 1999-2002; Charlotte Bobcats, dir player progs, 2003-. **Orgs:** Dell Curry Found, 1998. **Honors/Awds:** NBA Sixth Man of the Year Award; Virginia Sports Hall of Fame, 2004. **Business Addr:** Director of Player Programs, Charlotte Bobcats, 333 E Trade St, Charlotte, NC 28202, **Business Phone:** (704)688-8600.

CURRY, EDDY
Basketball player. **Personal:** Born Dec 5, 1982, Calumet City, IL; son of Eddy Curry Sr. **Career:** Chicago Bulls, ctr, 2001-05; NY Knicks, ctr & forward, 2005-. **Orgs:** Co-chair, Bulls Holiday Heroes prog. **Honors/Awds:** Full athletic scholar, DePaul Univ; Most Valuable Player, McDonalds All-Am Game, 2001; First Team All-Ame, USA Today. **Business Addr:** Professional basketball player, New York Knicks, Madison Square Garden, 2 Penn Plz, New York, NY 10121-0091, **Business Phone:** (212)465-6471.

CURRY, ERIC FELECE
Football player. **Personal:** Born Feb 3, 1970, Thomasville, GA. **Educ:** Univ Ala. **Career:** Football player; Tampa Bay Buccaneers, defensive end, 1993-97; Jacksonville Jaguars, defensive end, 1998-99. **Orgs:** Theta Delta Chapter of Phi Beta Sigma Fraternity Inc. *

CURRY, GLADYS J. See WASHINGTON, GLADYS J.

CURRY, DR. JAMES
Educator. **Educ:** Univ Calif, Berkeley, BA, MS, PhD, 1976. **Career:** Howard Univ, fac; Nat Ctr Atmospheric Res, Boulder, Colorado, postdoctoral fel; Univ Colo, prof appl math, currently, dept chair, currently. **Orgs:** Bd trustee, Colo Univ Found; Colo Ctr Chaos & Complexity.

CURRY, MAJOR GEN. JERRY RALPH
Consultant. **Personal:** Born Sep 7, 1932, McKeesport, PA; son of Mercer and Jesse; married Charlene; children: Charlein, Jerry, Toni & Natasha. **Educ:** Univ Nebr, BA, 1960; Command & Gen Staff Col, attended 1967; Boston Univ, MA, int rels, 1970; Luther Rice Univ, D ministry, 1978; AUS War Col, grad. **Career:** AUS, pvt to maj gen, Test & Eval Command, comndg gen; Carter Admin, mildep asst secy defense; Reagan Admin, Secy Defense, press secy; U.S. Cong, cand, 1988; Nat Hwy Traffic Safety Admin, adminr; mem, Nat Res Coun Transp Res bd; bus consult, currently. **Orgs:** Bd mem, Greater Wash, DC, Bd Trade; bd mem, Am Red Cross; fed trustee, Fed City Coun; Delta Phi Alpha; The Nat Hon German Soc; Phi Alpha Theta; Int Hon Soc Hist; Nat Eagle Scout Asn; chmn Black Revolutionary War Patriots Found; Asn Advan Automotive Med; Soc Automotive Engrs. **Honors/Awds:** Distinguished Alumni, Univ Nebr, 1979; Washingtonian of the Year, Washingtonian Mag, 1982; The Secret Service Honor Award; Order of Orange-Nassau, Queen Beatrix of the Netherlands; received several military & government awards. **Special Achievements:** Author of book "From Private to General: An African-American Rises Through The Rank"s; CD "Generally Singing". **Military Serv:** AUS, major gen, 1950-84; Defense Distinguished Service Medal; Army Distinguished Service Medals; Legion of Merit with Oak Leaf Clusters; Meritorious Service Medals; Bronze Star with V Device; Cross of Gallantry with Palm; Army Commendation Medals; Navy Commendation Medal; Navy Unit Commendation Ribbon; Air Medals; Combat Infantryman Badge. **Business Addr:** Business Consultant, Chateau Antioch, PO Box 407, Haymarket, VA 20168-0407.

CURRY, LEVY HENRY
Administrator, vice president (organization), executive. **Personal:** Born Feb 3, 1949, Buffalo, NY; son of Levi and Cora Marie; married Dianne Curry; children: Tasha. **Educ:** Morehouse Col, BA, 1971; Atlanta Law Sch, JD, 1975. **Career:** Consolidated Mfg Co, plant mgr, 1970-71; Int Harvester, sales mgr, 1971-74; Equal & Employment Opportunity Comn, legal res anal, 1974; Steak & Ale Restaurants Am, dir personnel, 1975-87, dir affirmative action, 1975; Nat Urban League Beep Prog, vis prof, 1977; Hospitality Indust Inc, bd dirs, 1978; Am Fed Bank, sr vpres; 7-Eleven Inc., dir Compensation, Benefits & Employee Rel; Kaiser Found Health Plan Mid-Atlantic States, vpres human resources, currently. **Orgs:** Morris Brown Col Sch Restaurant & Instrumental Mgt, 1977; bd dir, Chain Restaurant Compensation Asn, 1978; Dallas Personnel Asn, 1977; Am Soc Personnel 1977; consult, Jr Achievement Proj Bus, 1979; Morehouse Col Alumni Asn; bd trustees, African Museum Life & Culture; Jr Black Acad Arts & Letters. **Honors/Awds:** Mary C Miller Scholar, Nat Urban League, 1967. **Business Addr:** Vice President of Human Resources, Kaiser Foundation Health Plan of the Mid-Atlantic States Inc, 2101 E Jefferson St, PO Box 6306, Rockville, MD 20852, **Business Phone:** (301)816-2424.*

CURRY, MARK G.
Actor. **Personal:** Born Jun 1, 1961, Oakland, CA. **Educ:** California State Univ, Hayward. **Career:** TV series: "Hangin' With Mr Cooper", 1992-; "Hold This", 2005; "Fat Actress", 2005; TV guest appearances: "Show time at the Apollo", host; 'The Arsenio Hall Show"; "Sinbad and Friends"; "HBO One Night Stand", 1989; "The Jamie Foxx Show", 1997, 1998; "The Drew Carey Show", 2000; "For Your Love", 2000; Films: Panther, 1995; Switchback, 1997; Armageddon, 1998; A Man Is Mostly Water, 1999. Writer: "Def Comedy Jam", 2006; "Comedy Central Presents", 2006; Laffapalooza!, 2008. *

CURRY, MICHAEL
Basketball executive, basketball player. **Personal:** Born Aug 22, 1968, Anniston, AL; married Katrina; children: Xavier, Michael Jr & Crysten. **Educ:** Ga Southern, BA, 1990; Va Commonwealth Univ, MA, 2001. **Career:** Steiner Bayreuth, forward, 1990-91; Capital Region, guard, 1992-93; S Clear, guard, 1993-94; Philadelphia 76ers, guard, 1993; Valvi Girona, guard, 1994-95; Omaha Racers, guard, 1995-96; Wash Bullets, guard, 1996; Detroit Pistons, guard, 1996-97, 1999-2003; Milwaukee Bucks, guard, 1997-99; Toronto Raptors, guard, 2003-04; Ind Pacers, guard, 2004-05; NBA Develop League, vpres, player develop, 2005-06; NBA, vpres basketball opers, 2006-07; Detroit Pistons, asst coach, 2007-. **Honors/Awds:** NBA Community Asst Award, 2003. **Business Addr:** Assistant Coach, Detroit Pistons, 4 Championship Dr, Auburn Hills, MI 48326, **Business Phone:** (864)248-1100.

CURRY, REV. MICHAEL BRUCE
Clergy, bishop. **Personal:** Born Mar 13, 1953, Chicago, IL; son of Kenneth S L and Dorothy A Strayhorne; married Sharon Clement; children: Rachel, Elizabeth. **Educ:** Hobart Col, BA, (with honors), 1975; Yale Univ Divinity Sch, MDiv, 1978. **Career:** St Stephen's Episcopal Church, rector, 1978-82; Diocese Southern Ohio, racism staff, 1982-87; Bethany Sch, chaplain, 1983-88; St Simon Cyrena Church, rector & pastor, 1982-88; St James Episcopal Church, rector & pastor, 1988-00; Episcopal Diocese, NC, bishop, 2000-. **Orgs:** NCP; Union Black Episcopalians; Col Preachers Bd. **Special Achievements:** "Power in the Word," Sermons that Work II; " Servant Woman," Sermons that Work II; first African American elected Episcopal bishop in the South; The first African American bishop to lead a southern diocese of the Episcopal Church; First African-American Episcopal Bishop of North Carolina. **Business Addr:** Minister, St James Episcopal Church, 1020 W Lafayette Ave, Baltimore, MD 21217, **Business Phone:** (410)523-4588.*

CURRY, MITCHELL L
Psychotherapist, clergy. **Personal:** Born Feb 5, 1935, Augusta, GA; son of Walter Lee and Ernestine; married Carolyn D, Sep 11, 1974; children: Rachel M & Michele L (divorced); children: Sonja & Reuben. **Educ:** Morris Brown Col Atlanta GA, BA, 1960; Andover Newton Theol Sch Newton Ctr MA, MDiv, 1964; Univ Louisville, Louisville KY, MSW, 1972; Sch Theol Claremont CA, PhD, 1979. **Career:** Nat Urban League-Western Region, asst reg dir, 1972-75; Lewis Metro Meth Ch LA, minister, 1974-76; Florence Ave Presby Ch LA, minister, 1976-80; LA Co Dept Ment Health, psychotherapist, 1976-86; Allen Am Church San

Bernardino, pastor, 1985-90; psychotherapist pvt pract, currently. **Orgs:** Alpha Phi Alpha Fraternity, 1959; consult, Nat Inst Ment Health, 1972-79; Acad Cert Social Workers, NASW, 1974-; LCSW State Calif, 1975; fel, Am Asn Pastoral Counr, 1979-; bd gov, Nat Coun Church, 1980; lic clin social worker, dipl clin social work, (DCSW), 1984; Bd Cert Dipl. **Honors/Awds:** Scholarship Grant, Am Missionary Asn, 1960-64; Scholarship Grant, Lilly Found, 1961; Scholarship Grant, Nat Inst Ment Health, 1970-72; LHD Reed Christ Col Angeles, 1976. **Military Serv:** AUS, honorably discharged, 1954-56. **Home Addr:** 1809 Virginia Rd, Los Angeles, CA 90019, **Home Phone:** (323)754-7703. **Business Phone:** (323)732-8798.*

CURRY, SADYE BEATRYCE
Educator, physician. **Personal:** Born Jan 1, 1941?, Reidsville, NC; daughter of Charlie Will and Limmmer P. **Educ:** Johnson C Smith Univ, BS, 1963; Howard Univ Col Med, MD, 1967. **Career:** Duke Univ Med Ctr, internship, 1967-68, gastroenterol fel, 1969-72; med instr, 1969-72; VA Hosp, Wash, DC, internal med residency, 1968-69; Howard Univ, asst prof med, 1972-77; Lincoln Hosp, Durham, NC, medical consult;Howard Univ Svc, Wash DC Gen Hosp, asst chief med off, 1973-74; Howard Univ Col Med, asst chief med, 1974-78, assoc prof med, 1978-. **Orgs:** Nat Med Asn; Am Med Asn; Medico-chirurgical Soc DC; DC Med Soc; Nat Inst Arthritis Metabolic & Digestive Diseases Training Grants Com Gastroenterol & Nutrit, NIH, 1972-73; Am Digestive Diseases Soc; Gastrointestinal Drug Adv Comn, FDA, 1975-76; Alpha Kappa Alpha; Beta Kappa Chi; Alpha Kappa Mu;US Friendship Force Ambassador W Berlin, 1980; past pres, Leonidas Berry Soc Digestive Diseases; bd trustees, Lake Land Or Property Owners Asn, Ladysmith VA; Am Soc Internal Med; Leonidas Berry Soc Digestive Diseases. **Honors/Awds:** Student Council Faculty Award, Howard Univ Col Med, 1975; Kaiser-Permanente Award, Howard Univ Col Med, 1978; Woman of the Year Award, Howard Univ Col Med Stud Am Med Women's Asn, 1990. **Special Achievements:** First African American woman postgraduate trainee at Duke University Medical Center in 1969; First African American woman to become a gastroenterologist in the United States in 1972; Only African American to train in the gastroenterology fellowship program at Duke University. **Business Addr:** Associate Professor, Howard University College of Medicine, 2225 Georgia Ave NW, Washington, DC 20059.*

CURRY, THOMAS LEE, SR.
Executive. **Personal:** Born May 20, 1952, Jackson, NC; son of Edward and Mary; married Linda, Oct 4, 1977; children: Tomara, Thomas Jr, Reila & Tailyn. **Educ:** Seton Hall Univ, BS, 1974; Fairleigh Dickinson Univ, MPA, 1986. **Career:** Calvary Baptist Community Ctr Inc, administer, 1975-80, Health Ctr, exec dir, 1980-90, Community Ctr, exec dir, 1990. **Orgs:** Bd dirs, Paterson YMCA, vip, 1975-84; pres, Mayor's Coun Youth, 1976-78; Passaic Valley United Way, Allocation Comt, 1984-86; vip, NJ Asn Community Health Ctrs, 1983-90; chair, Paterson Housing Authority, 1990-99. **Honors/Awds:** Community Service Award, Paterson Br, Nat Asn Advan Colored People, 1981; Service Award, Paterson YMCA, 1984; Man of the Year Award, Calvary Baptist Church, 1997; Outstanding Service Award, Paterson Housing Authority, 1999.

CURRY, REV. VICTOR TYRONE
Radio broadcaster, clergy. **Personal:** Born Mar 8, 1960, Carver Ranches, FL; married Cynthia D Baskin (divorced 1990); children: Victoria, Veronica & Victory. **Educ:** Fla Bible Col, Hollywood, Fla, attended 1981; Fla Mem Col, Miami, Fla, BS, community-clin psychol, 1986; Jacksonville Baptist Theol Sem, MMin, DMin. **Career:** Mt Carmel Missionary Baptist Church, Miami, FL, pastor & adminr, 1984; Dade Co Sch Bd, Miami, FL, classroom teacher, 1987-89; Margolis Broadcasting Co, Miami Beach, FL, radio announcer, talk show host, 1989; WMBM AM Radio AM, 1490, radio host, currently; New Birth Baptist Church Cathedral Faith Int, sr pastor/teacher, currently. **Orgs:** Pres, Miami Christian Improv Asn, 1986; exec comt mem, Nat Asn Advan Colored People Miami Dade Br, 1988-; Omega Psi Phi Fraternity, Sigma Alpha Chap, Miami, Fla, 1989-; vice moderator, Fla East Coast Missionary Baptist Asn; Progressive Race Inspired & Dedicated to Empower. **Honors/Awds:** Numerous honors & awards including Citizen of the Year; Pastor of The Year; Future Leader of America; Humanitarian of The Year; Image Award; JM Family African American Achiever Award for Business & Entrepreneurism; Kool's Achievers Award; Black Achievers Award & DDiv, St Thomas Christian Col, 2004. **Special Achievements:** Books: The Stewardship Test; The Stewardship Task Workbook; Where Your Treasure Is. **Business Addr:** Senior Pastor, Teacher, New Birth Baptist Church Cathedral of Faith International, 2300 NW 135th St Suite 8207, Miami, FL 33167, **Business Phone:** (305)685-3700.

CURRY, WARDELL STEPHEN. See CURRY, DELL.

CURRY, DR. WILLIAM THOMAS
Physician, surgeon, college teacher. **Personal:** Born Jan 4, 1943, Great Neck, NY; married Katherine E Lum, Dec 23, 1967; children: William Jr & Christian. **Educ:** NY Univ, BS, 1964; Howard Univ Col Med, MD, 1968; Am Bd Surg, diplomate,1974. **Career:** George Wash Hosp, surg intern, 1968-69; NY Hosp Cornell Med Ctr, surgresident, 1969-72, chief resident surgeon, 1972-73; Cornell Univ Med Col,asst prof; NY Hosp, attend surgeon, instr surg, 1972-76, fel surg,1969-72; Cornell Univ Med Col, clin asst prof surg, 1976-, asst attend surgeon. **Orgs:** Fel, Am Col Surgeons, 1976; Kappa Alpha Psi Fraternity; Reveille Club NY;bd dir, Music Westchester Symphony Orchestra; Mt Kisco Country Club; chmn,Comt Ins Rev, NY County Med Soc, 1988-; Shinnecock Hills Golf Club. **Honors/Awds:** Teaching Award, Cornell Univ Med College, 2003. **Special Achievements:** Cornell Medical Students, Senior List. **Military Serv:** AUSR, med corps, 1972. **Business Addr:** Surgeon, Clinical Assistant Professor, Cornell University Medical College, Day Hall Lobby, Ithaca, NY 14853, **Business Phone:** (212)628-1681.*

CURSON, THEODORE
Musician, trumpet player. **Personal:** Born Jun 3, 1935, Philadelphia, PA; married Marjorie; children: Charlene & Theodore II. **Educ:** Granoff Mus Conserv, attended 1953. **Career:** PBS TV Show: Jazz Set, star, 1972; NY Univ, concerts; Ted Curson & Co, artist; Composer: "Tears for Dolphy", 1961; "Fliptop", 1977; "Typical Ted", 1977; Albums: Snake Johnson, 1985-86; Mingus at Antibes; Ted Curson Groups; Fire Down Below; Plenty of Horn; Traveling On, 1997; Sugar 'nSpice, 1999; Motion picture soundtracks: Teorema and Brown Bunny, 2003. **Orgs:** Charles Mingus & Jazz Workshop, 1959-60; pres, Nosruc Pub Co, 1961-; Am Fedn Musicians. **Honors/Awds:** New jazz artist, Jazz Podium; Winner, Down Beat Readers Poll, 1978; LI Musicians Soc Award, 1970. **Home Addr:** 8 Lee Pl, Montclair, NJ 07043. *

CURTIN, JOHN T.
Judge. **Personal:** Born Aug 24, 1921, Buffalo, NY; son of John J and Ellen Quigley; married Jane R Good, Aug 9, 1952; children: Ann Elizabeth, John James, Patricia Marie, Eileen Jane, Mary Ellen, MarkAndrew & William Joseph. **Educ:** Canisius Col, BS, 1946; Buffalo Univ, LLB, 1949. **Career:** Pvt pract, Buffalo, NY, atty, 1949-61; US Atty's Off, Western Dist NY, US atty, 1961-67; US Dist Ct, Western Dist NY, sr dist judge, 1967-. **Orgs:** NY State Bar Asn; Am Bar Asn; Erie Co Bar Asn. **Military Serv:** USMC, lt col, 1942-45, USMCR, 1952-54. **Business Addr:** Senior District Judge, United States District Court Western New York, US Courthouse, 68 Court St Room 304, Buffalo, NY 14202-3405, **Business Phone:** (716)551-4221.

CURTIS, BENAY. See CURTIS-BAUER, M BENAY.

CURTIS, CHRISTOPHER PAUL
Writer, government official, automotive industry worker. **Personal:** Born Jan 1, 1954?, Flint, MI; son of Herman and Leslie; married Kaysandra. **Educ:** Univ Mich, Flint, 1996. **Career:** Fisher Body Plant, Flint, MI, assembly line, 1972-85; asst to Senator Don Riegle, Lansing, MI; Automatic Data Processing, Allen park, MI; Books: The Watsons Go to Birmingham, 1963; Bud, Not Buddy, 1999; Bucking the Sarge; Mr. Chickee's Funny Money; Mr. Chickee's Messy Mission. **Honors/Awds:** Newberry Medal, Univ Mich; Hopwood prize for rough draft, Publishers Weekly, Best Books, 1995; Best Books, New York Times, 1995; Newbery honor, Am Libr Asn, 1996; Best Books for Young Adults, 1996; Coretta Scott King Text honor, 1996; Newbery Medal, 2000; Coretta Scott King Award for African American Authors, Am Libr Asn, 2000. **Special Achievements:** His second novel, Bud, Not Buddy, is the first book ever to receive both the Newbery Medal and the Coretta Scott King Author Award. **Business Addr:** Author, Delacorte Press, 1540 Broadway, New York, NY 10036-4094, **Business Phone:** (212)354-6500.*

CURTIS, JAMES
Lawyer, television show host. **Personal:** Born in Los Angeles, CA; married; children: three. **Educ:** Univ Calif, San Diego, BA; Calif Western Sch Law, San Diego, JD. **Career:** State Senate & Govs Off, Calif, 1980-84; Riverside County, Dist Atty's Off, prosecutor, 1989-99; Justice Project Inc, consult, 1999-01; KUCR Radio, host; Court TV, "Closing Arguments", co-anchor, "Curtis Court", host, 2000-01, anchor, commentator, 2001-05; FOX News, "The O'Reilly Factor", commentator; ESPN2, "Cold Pizza", commentator; "Michael Jackson Trial", E Entertainment, host & correspondent, 2005; James Curtis & Assoc law firm, owner, 2005-. **Orgs:** Bd mem, Criminal Law Sect, Calif State Bar Asn. **Honors/Awds:** Beacon Award, 2004; Recognition for Lifetime Commitment to human and civil rights, NAACP, NY. **Special Achievements:** Motivational speaker; television legal commentator; has appeared on: Dateline NBC, ABC's World News Tonight, CNBC, Rivera Live; Appearances as a legal expert and contributor on the following shows: World News Tonight, The Early Show, Dateline, Weekend Today Show, The O'Reilly Factor, Hannity & Colmes, At Large with Geraldo Rivera, Cold Pizza, The Big Idea with Donny Deustch, Hardball with Chris Matthews, The News with Brian Williams, Larry King Live, Nick News Special. **Business Addr:** Owner, James Curtis & Associates, 7121 Magnolia Avenue, Riverside, CA 92504, **Business Phone:** (951)781-2700.*

CURTIS, DR. JAMES L
Physician. **Personal:** Born Apr 27, 1922, Jeffersonville, GA; son of Will and Frances; married Vivian A Rawls; children: Lawrence & Paul. **Educ:** Albion Col, BA, 1943; Univ Mich, MD, 1946. **Career:** State Univ NY, instr, asst prof, 1954-67; Cornell Univ, Med Col, assoc prof, 1968-81; Columbia Univ, Col Physicians & Surgeons, clinic prof psychiatry, 1982-2000, emer prof psychiatry, 2000-; Harlem Hosp Ctr, dir psychiatry. **Orgs:** Fel Am Psychiatric Asn; Am Orthopsychiatric Asn; NY Acad Med; Am Acad Psychoanalysis; AMA; Nat Med Asn; Am Acad Addiction Psychiatrists; Certified Group Psychotherapists. **Special Achievements:** Published, 'Blacks Medical School & Society', 'Affirmative Action in Medicine' & many other publications. **Military Serv:** USAF, capt, 1952-54. **Home Addr:** 17816 Murdock Ave, Jamaica, NY 11434. **Business Addr:** Columbia University, Department of Psychiatry, 180 Ft Wash Ave, New York, NY 10032, **Business Phone:** (212)305-6001.

CURTIS, JEAN TRAWICK
Library administrator. **Personal:** Born in Washington, DC; daughter of Ivory Wilson (deceased) and Dannie May; divorced; children: Karen Elizabeth Phoenix, Jeffrey Lynn Phoenix. **Educ:** Howard Univ, Wash, DC, BA, libr sci, 1958; Univ Md, Col Park, MD, MLS, 1971, Libr Adminrs Develop Prog, 1977. **Career:** Library administrator (retired). DC Pub Libr, Wash, DC, C's librn, 1958-65, reader's advr, 1965-69; Univ Md, Col Park, MD, res asst, 1969-71; Enoch Pratt Free Libr, Baltimore, MD, young adult field worker, 1971-75, regional librn, 1975-78, chief extension div, 1978-85; Detroit Pub Libr, dep dir, 1986-87, dir, 1987. **Orgs:** Am Libr Asn; Mich Libr Asn; dir, Univ Cultural Ctr Asn, 1987-; dir, New Detroit Inc, 1987-; Southeastern Mich League Librs, 1987-; Libr Mich, Libr Servs & Construction Act Adv Commt, Task Force Libr Interdependency & Funding, 1987-90; bd pres, Detroit Assoc Librs Network, 1988-90; Xonta Int, Detroit Chap, 1988-90; Mayor's Trouble Shooting Task Force, 1985. **Honors/Awds:** Michigan Women's Hall of Fame, Hist Honors Comt; Operated campaign to secure community and political endorsements in favor of increase millage to support schools and libraries; reorganized Detroit Public Library administration; speaker at several university seminars on library science; consultant to Information Access Company on strategic planning, 1990. *

CURTIS, MARVIN VERNELL
Educator, musician. **Personal:** Born Feb 12, 1951, Chicago, IL; son of John W Jr and Dorothy Marva; married Sharon Curry Curtis, Jul 19, 1986. **Educ:** N Park Col, BMus, 1972; Presbyterian Sch Christian Educ, MA, 1974; Westminister Choir Col, attended 1978; Juilliard Sch Music, attended 1982; Univ Pacific, EdD, 1990. **Career:** Graham Sch, music teacher, 1975-80; Riverside Church, dir church sch music, 1978-80; Emmanuel Baptist Church, minister music, 1980-84; San Diego State Univ, dir gospel choir, 1984-86; Morse High Sch, chmn music dept, 1985-86; Calif State Univ, Stanislaus, asst prof music educ, 1988-91; Va Union Univ, dir choral activ, 1991-94; Fayetteville State Univ, choral dir & prof, currently; Conductor: Emmanuel Baptist Church Concert, 1983, Va Union Univ Concert Choir, 1992, Alice Tully Hall-Lincoln Center; Richmond Sym, guest conductor & musical adv, currently. **Orgs:** Fac sen, Calif State Univ, Stanislaus, 1989-91; pres, San Joaquin Co Arts Coun, 1989-91; grants panel mem, Calif Arts Coun, 1990-; asst treas, Nat Asn Negro Musicians Inc, 1991-; nat chairperson ethnic & minority concerns, Am Choral Dirs Asn, 1992-94; Cent Va Fac Consortium, 1992-; Music Educrs Nat Conf. **Honors/Awds:** Aubry Award, Outstanding Musical Director, San Diego Asn Community Theatre, 1985; Educator Alumnus of the Year, Univ Pac Sch Educ, 1991; Research Award, Nat Asn Equal Opportunity Higher Educ, 1992; Young Alumni Award, Univ Pac Alumni Asn, 1992; Key to the City, City Savannah, GA, 1992. **Special Achievements:** Published 30 choral compositions, Mark Foster Music Co, 1975-, commissioned by Philander Smith College to compose musical work for Clinton Inaugural Activities, 1992, composed musical work, Clinton Inaugural Activities, 1993, first African-American composer commissioned to write a choral work for a Presidential Inauguration. **Home Phone:** (804)226-6188. **Business Addr:** Choral Director, Professor, Fayetteville State University, Department of Performing & Fine Arts, 1200 Murchison Rd, Fayetteville, NC 28301, **Business Phone:** (910)672-1571.

CURTIS, MARY C
Columnist, editor. **Personal:** Born in Baltimore, MD; daughter of Thomas E and Evelyn C Thomas; married Martin F Olsen, Oct 16, 1976; children: Zane A Curtis-Olsen. **Educ:** Fordham Univ, NY, BA, communs, summa cum laude. **Career:** Assoc Press, NY & Hartford, CT, ed & writer, freelance newspaper & mag reporter, 1977-81; Travelers Ins Co, mkt servs coord, 1977-81; Ariz Daily Star, Tucson, AZ, copy ed, 1981-83; Baltimore Sun, MD, travel ed, asst features ed, 1983-84, arts & entertainment ed, 1984-85; New York Times, copy ed, Cult Dept, 1986-88, from dep ed to ed, 1988-92, Living Arts Sec, ed, Home Sec, 1992-93, educ life ed, 1993-94; Charlotte Observer, exec features ed & columnist, currently; Columns: "The lots may be bare, but I'll be tree-shopping today", 2006, "Merry Christmas, baby — now, go fix your face", 2006; "Christmas past: Shorter lists & wondrous gifts", 2006. **Orgs:** Soc Prof Journalists, 1972-; Nat Asn Black Journalists, 1984-; Am Asn Sunday & Feature Eds, 1994-. **Honors/Awds:** Award for Commentary, Am Asn Sunday & Feature Eds, 1995, 2001; 1st place, NC Press Asn, 2000; Green Eyeshade Award, 2003; Hall of Fame, Region IV, Nat Asn Black Journalists, 2004.

Business Addr: Executive Features Editor, Columnist, Charlotte Observer, 600 S Tryon St, Charlotte, NC 28202, **Business Phone:** (704)358-5000.

CURTIS, SUSAN MANGO. See CURTIS-RIVERS, SUSAN YVONNE.

CURTIS, REV. DR. WILLIAM H.
Clergy. **Personal:** Born in Balitmore, MD. **Educ:** Morgan State Univ, BA, philos; Howard Univ Sch Divinity, Mdiv; United Theol Sem, Dayton, Ohio, DMdiv. **Career:** Mt Ararat Baptist Church, Pittsburgh, Pa, sr pastor, currently. **Orgs:** Bd mem, Urban League of Pittsburgh; African Am Leadership Comt; vpres, Hampton Universitys Ministers Conf; founder, William H Curtis Ministries. **Special Achievements:** featured on WAMO 860 AM. **Business Addr:** Senior Pastor, Mount Ararat Baptist Church, 271 Paulson Ave, Pittsburgh, PA 15206, **Business Phone:** (412)441-1800.*

CURTIS-BAUER, M BENAY (BENAY CURTIS)
Stockbroker. **Personal:** Born Aug 12, 1948, Berkeley, CA; daughter of Emory C and Dorothy A Curtis; married Jon K Bauer, Jul 4, 1988. **Educ:** Univ Calif, Berkeley, BA. **Career:** Morgan Stanley, regist rep, 1991; Alamo Capital, vpres, investment counsr, currently. **Orgs:** St Dominic's Church, Finance Coun. **Business Addr:** Alamo Capital, 1777 Botelho Dr Suite 375, Walnut Creek, CA 94596.

CURTIS-HALL, VONDIE
Actor. **Personal:** Born Sep 30, 1956, Detroit, MI; son of Curtis and Angeline; married Kasi Lemmons; children: Henry. **Educ:** Richmond Col, London. **Career:** Films: Shakedown, 1988; Coming to Am, 1988; Mystery Train, 1989; Black Rain, 1989; Die Hard 2, 1990; One Good Cop, 1991; The Mambo Kings, 1992; Passion Fish, 1992; Falling Down, 1993; Sugar Hill, 1994; Crook lyn, 1994;Clear & Present Danger, 1994; Drop Squad, 1994; Tuesday Morning Ride,1995; Broken Arrow, 1996; Heaven's Prisoners, 1996; Romeo & Juliet, 1996; Gridlock'd, 1997; Eve's Bayou, 1997; Dr. Hugo, 1998; Turn It Up, 2000; Talk to Me TV, 2007; Honeydripper, 2007; Life Is Hot in Cracktown, 2009; Port of Call New Orleans, 2009; films: Heat Wave, 1990; And Then She Was Gone, 1991; What She Doesn't Know, 1992; Murder Without Motive: The Edmund Perry Story, 1992; There Wasa Little Boy, 1993; Keys, 1994; Dead Man's Revenge, 1994; Zooman, 1995; Don King: Only in Am, 1997; Sirens, 1999; Ali: An Am Hero, 2000; Freedom Song, 2000; Deceit, 2004; Dense, 2004; Grid lock'd, dir & writer, 1997; Glitter, dir, 2001; Waist Deep, dir & writer, 2006; TV Series include: CopRock, 1990; Chicago Hope, 1994; ER, 2001; Fastlane, 2001; The Sopranos,2002; 1-800-Missing, 2003; Soul Food, 2004; LAX, 2005; Law & Order, 2006; Second Opinion, 2007; Chance, 2009; "Fear Itself", 2009; Cold Comfort, 2009; "Criminal Minds", 2009; dir currently, Insurgents, 2005; Waist Deep, 2006; "Sleeper Cell", 2006; "Boston Legal", 2008; "The Starter Wife", 2008. **Orgs:** Black Filmmaker Found. **Honors/Awds:** Audelco Award, 1987; Nat Bd of Rev, Excellence in Flimmaking; Golden Satellite Award, 1998; Black Reel Award, 2005. **Special Achievements:** Nominated for Emmy Award in 1995. **Business Addr:** Actor, Director, The Gersh Agency, 232 N Canon Dr, PO Box 5617, Beverly Hills, CA 90210, **Business Phone:** (310)274-6611.*

CURTIS-RIVERS, SUSAN YVONNE (SUSAN MANGO CURTIS)
Journalist. **Personal:** Born Jun 27, 1958, Savannah, GA; daughter of William and Lillain; married James Socrates Rivers, Dec 12, 1992; children: Jasmine DuBignon. **Educ:** Va Commonwealth Univ, BFA design, 1981. **Career:** Nat Rifle Assn, art dir, 1981-84; NUS Corp, graphic supvr, 1984-86; Phillips Publ Inc, art dir, 1986-87; The Wash Post Magazine, asst art dir, 1987-88; Theimes Journal Newspaper, Springfield, designer, 1988-90; The Akron Beacon Journal, asst managing ed, 1990; Northwestern Univ, Medill Sch Jour, asst prof, currently. **Orgs:** Nat Asn Black Journalists; Soc Newspaper Design; Nat Asn Minority Media, 1991-94; Nat Asn Hispanic Journalist; Fla A&M Univ Sch Journalism & Graphic Arts, bd visitors, 1996; pres, Soc News Design; Assoc Press Soc. **Honors/Awds:** Knight-Ridder Entrepreneurial Excellence Award, 1990; The Asniated Press soc of Ohio Award, 1991; Soc Newspaper Design: The Beacon Journal Art Dept Staff won 2 Silver Awards, 1 Bronze Award, and 4 Awards of Excellence, 1992; The Cleveland Press Club Excellence in Journalism, 1993; The Pulitzer Prize Gold Medal for Public Service, 1994; Nat Headliner Award, 1995; Soc Newspaper Design, Staff won 2 Awards of Excellence, 1996. **Special Achievements:** Garth C Reeves Sr Chair, Fla A&M Univ, Sch Journalism & Graphic Arts, 1996. **Home Phone:** (330)645-1408. **Business Addr:** Assistant Professor, Northwestern University, Medill School of Journalism, 1845 Sheridan Rd, Evanston, IL 60208-2101, **Business Phone:** (847)467-2999.

CURVIN, ROBERT
Educator, administrator. **Personal:** Born Feb 23, 1934, Newark, NJ; married Patricia; children: Frank & Nicole. **Educ:** Rutgers, BA 1960, MSW 1967; Princeton Univ, PhD 1975. **Career:** Professor (retired); Essex County Welfare Bd, supvr, 1960-65; League Indus Democracy, dir training Prog, 1965-66; Rutgers Univ, lectr comm develop specialist, 1968-70; Princeton Univ, Wallace Eljabar fel, 1971-73; Brookings Inst, res assoc, 1973-77; CUNY Brooklyn Col, assoc prof, 1974-78; NY Times, ed bd mem, 1978-83; New Sch Social Res, Grad Sch Mgt & Urban Policy, dean, 1984-88; Broad National Bank, dir, 1985-88; Revson Found, dir, 1986-91; Ford found, dir urban poverty prog, 1988-86, vpres commun, 1996-2000, 2002; Greentree Found, pres, 2000-03. **Orgs:** Treas, 21st Century Found, 1977; trustee, Princeton Univ, 1977-81; trustee, Channel 13 WNET, 1977; nat vchmn, CORE; chmn, Newark Essex CORE, 1962-63; Tri-state Reg Planning Comn, 1977; Com Resp Legis, 1977; trustee, Victoria Found, 1976-; trustee, The Revson Found, 1987-91; Newark Beth Israel Hosp, 1998; trustee, Humanity In Action, 2000; trustee, NJ Inst Social Justice, 2000; trustee, RAND, 2001-08. **Honors/Awds:** Outstanding Alumnus, Rutgers, 1991; Service to Nation, Nat Inst Social Sci, 2001. **Military Serv:** AUS, 1st lt, 1953-57. **Home Addr:** 28 Reynolds Pl, Newark, NJ 07106, **Home Phone:** (973)372-5113.

CURWOOD, STEPHEN THOMAS
Writer, television producer. **Personal:** Born Dec 11, 1947, Boston, MA; son of James L Curwood and Sarah Ethel Thomas Curwood; children: Anastasia (Stacy), James. **Educ:** AB Harvard Col, Cambridge, Honors concentration in problems developing societies, 1969; Westtown School, Westtown PA, 1965. **Career:** Bay State Banner, managing editor, 1971-72; Boston Globe, writer, 1972-76, writer/columnist, 1982-89; WGBH TV, producer/ reporter, 1976-79; National Pub Radio, reporter & host, 1979-, senior host, "World of Opera," 1990-, exec producer & host, "Living on Earth," currently. **Orgs:** President, World Media Foundation; Harvard Univ, lecturer; Society of Environmental Journalists; Westtown School; Haverford College, trustee. **Honors/Awds:** Pulitzer Prize for public service, part of Boston Globe team, 1975; Edward R. Murrow Award for radio documentary, 1995; New England Environmental Leadership Award, for work on promoting environmental awareness, 1992. *

CUSHINGBERRY, GEORGE
Clergy, government official. **Personal:** Born Jan 6, 1953, Detroit, MI; son of George Cushingberry Sr and Edna Louise; married Maria Hazel Drew; children: George III & Brandon Drew. **Educ:** Wayne State Univ, BA, 1974; Univ Detroit Law Sch, grad. **Career:** Wayne State Univ, Southend News, ed, vice-chmn Asn Black Students; State Mich, state rep; Wayne Co Bd Comnrs, 1986-2002; ordained minister, currently; Mich House, Lansing Off, rep, currently . **Orgs:** Life mem, NAACP; Founders Soc, Detroit Inst Arts; Mich Ethnic Heritage Ctr; bd trustees, Mus African Am Hist; Mich Humanities Coun. **Honors/Awds:** Superior Cadet Award, Cass Tech High, 1971; Young Man of The Year, Jaycees, 1975; Community Service Award, EBONI Women, 1975; Young Democratic Award, First Cong Dist, 1975; Community Service Award, Together Bros & Sisters, 1975; Man of The Year, Mich Chronicle Newspaper, 1977. **Special Achievements:** Youngest person ever elected to the Michigan House of Representatives (age 21), serving from 1975 to 1982. **Business Addr:** Representative, Michigan Legislature, S0687 House Office Bldg, PO Box 30014, Lansing, MI 48909-7514, **Business Phone:** (517)373-2276.

CUSTIS, ACE
Basketball player. **Personal:** Born May 24, 1974. **Educ:** Va Tech, atttended. **Career:** Dallas Mavericks, forward, 1993-97; Portsmouth Invitational Tournament, 1997; Nike Desert Classic, 1997; Dallas Mavericks, 1997-98; Pennsylvania Valley Dawgs, 1999 & 2000; Dallas Mavericks, 1999; Grand Rapids Hoops, 1999-2000; ASPAC Texmaco Jakarta, 2001; Sporting Al Ryadi, 2001-03; Sporting Al Ryadi Beirut, 2003-04; OSG Phoenix, 2004-05; San Miguel Beer, 2005-06; Matsushita Electric Panasonic Kangaroos, Japan, 2006-07;Panasonic Trians, Japan, 2007-08. **Honors/Awds:** NIT Champion, 1995; USBL Champion, 2001; Philippines PBA Fiesta Conf Champion, 2005. **Business Addr:** Professional Basketball Player, Panasonic Trians.

CUSTIS, ANDREA L.
Administrator, vice president (organization), president (organization). **Educ:** Morgan State Univ, BS; Univ Pa, MS. **Career:** Verizon Enterprise Solutions, vpres, 2001-03; Verizon Ave, pres & chief operating officer, 2003-; Philadelphia Academies Inc, partner. **Orgs:** Bd dirs, Better Bus Bur NY; bd gov, Acad Appl Elec Sci; Verizon's Consortium Info & Telecommunication Exec; Hispanic Support Orgn employee groups; Nat Asn Advan Colored Peoplel; Del Valley Childcare Coun. **Special Achievements:** 25 Influential Black Women in Business, The Network Journal, 2002. *

CUTLER, DONALD
Educator. **Personal:** Born Oct 20, 1943, Tampa, FL; married Rosemary N. **Educ:** Albany State Col, Albany, GA, BS, 1971; GA State Univ. **Career:** WAYX Radio, Waycross, GA, radio announcer, 1965-66; Waycross Jour Herald, Waycross, GA, news corresp, 1965-66; WJIZ Radio, Albany, GA, disc jockey, 1969-70; Goodwill Ind, Albany, GA, dir work adj training, 1971-72; Dougherty Co Pub Sch, educr, 1972; WALB-TV, Albany, GA, sports announcer, weekend anchor, 1973-77; Dougherty Co Albany, co comn bd commrs, 1978-. **Orgs:** Vpres Cong Black Orgn Albany, 1977-; spokesman, Albany Black Caucas, 1979-; NEA/GAE/ DCAE/ Nat Asn Advan Colored People; Ga Easter Seal Soc, 1976; exec comt, SW Ga APDC. **Honors/Awds:** Handicapped Employer of the Year, SW. **Special Achievements:** First Black Commissioner Dougherty Co Commission. **Business Addr:** Pine Ave, PO Box 1827, Albany, GA 31701.*

CUTLIFF, JOHN WILSON
Lawyer. **Personal:** Born Dec 2, 1923, Shreveport, LA; divorced; children: Jennifer C. **Educ:** Southern Univ, BA, 1945; Lincoln Univ, LLB 1948; NY Univ, LLM 1961; Atlanta Univ, MSLS 1968. **Career:** Lawyer (retired); pvt pract, atty, 1980-90; NC Cent Univ, assoc law libr, assoc prof, 1973-79; Media Serv & Fed City Col, assoc dir, assoc prof, 1968-73; Howard Sch Law, assoc law libr, 1965-67; SC State Col, Sch Law, law libr, 1948-65; Chester County Pub Libr, literacy coordr. **Orgs:** SC Bar, 1950; life mem, Nat Asn Advan Colored People; life mem, Kappa Alpha Psi; Unitarian Universalist Asn; Ford Fel, NY Univ, 1959-61. **Home Addr:** 553 Flint St Apt L, PO Box 406, Chester, SC 29706-1861, **Home Phone:** (803)581-8808. *

CUYJET, ALOYSIUS BAXTER
Physician. **Personal:** Born May 20, 1947, Jersey City, NJ; son of Aloysius and Barbara Baxter; married Beverly M Granger, Sep 15, 1990. **Educ:** Brandeis Univ, BA, 1968; NY Univ Sch Med, MD, 1972. **Career:** Harlem Hosp Ctr, intern & resident, 1972-75, cardiol fel, 1975-77; Columbia Univ Col Physicians & Surgeons, asst instr, 1975-77; United Hosps Med Ctr, dir adult critical care med, dir med, currently; NJ Med Sch, dept med, asst prof med, currently. **Orgs:** Asn Black Cardiologists; Am Heart Asn; Soc Critical Care Med; Am Col Cardiol. **Honors/Awds:** Fel, Am Col Cardiol, 1988; dipl, Am Bd Internal Med. *

CUYJET, CYNTHIA K.
Executive, consultant, educator. **Personal:** Born May 16, 1948, Philadelphia, PA; daughter of Esther King and C Jerome. **Educ:** Marymount Col, BA, 1970; Jersey City St Col, MA 1974. **Career:** Marymount Col, Tarrytown, New York, admis counr, 1970-71; Prudential Insurance Co, adult educ instr, 1971-72; Jersey City State Col, asst admis dir, 1972-76; Supermarkets Gen Corp, Selection & Placement Mgr, mgr, 1976-77; Avon Products Inc, supvr mgt develop, 1977, mgr, job opportunity, corporate mgr mgt develop & training 1978-80, div sales mgr 1980-84; Coca-Cola USA, sr proj mgr, mgr mgt training, 1984-87; Cuyjet Mgt Consultants Inc, pres, 1987-93, 1996-; Heller Int, asst vpres employee develop & training, 1993-96; Univ Chicago, Grad Sch Bus, sr assoc dir. **Orgs:** Co-Chairperson, Women Bus Comt, Atlanta Bus League; Atlanta Womens Network; Am Soc Training/ Develop; chair, employ comt, Coalition 100 Black Women; exec bd mem, Coun Concerned Black Executives, 1976-80; exec bd mem, Nj Asn Sickle Cell Anemia; Black Merit Acad, E St Louis, Ill; Black Exec Exchange Prog, Nat Urban League; Am Soc Training & Develop. **Honors/Awds:** Women in Business/Industry Award, NCNW, 1981; participant White House Conf Women Work Force, 1983; Service Award, Inst Jour Educ, 1991. **Special Achievements:** Women in Business/Industry Award, NCNW, 1981; participant White House Conf Women Work Force, 1983; Management Traininng Center Award, Maynard Inst Jour Educ, 1991; Chairman's Club Award for Outstanding Achievement HellerInt, 1994.

CWIKLINSKI, CHERYL A
Executive. **Career:** Technomic Res Assoc, mgr; Telemedia Inc; Blue Cross & Blue Shield; Nat Controls Corp; Xerox Corp; Comprehensive Computerized Bus Serv Inc, chief exec officer & founder, currently; Staffing Partners Int, prin, currently. **Orgs:** Adv bd, DePaul Univ; adv bd, Heartland Alliance. **Honors/Awds:** Numerous awards and honors including Entrepreneur of the Year, Ernst & Young Inc Mag; SBA's Illinois Minority Business Person of the Year. **Business Addr:** Founder, Chief Executive Officer, Comprehensive Computerized Business Service Inc, 2300 N Barrington Suite 400, Hoffman Estates, IL 60169, **Business Phone:** (847)519-7201.

CYRUS-ALBRITTON, SYLVIA
Executive director, association executive. **Career:** Asn Study Afro African Am Life & Hist, exec dir, currently. **Business Addr:** Executive Director, Association for the Study of African American Life & History, CB Powell Bldg, 525 Bryant St NW Suite C142, Washington, DC 20059, **Business Phone:** (202)865-0053.*

D

DABBS, HENRY ERVEN
Executive, arts administrator. **Personal:** Born Oct 15, 1932, Clover, VA; son of Charles and Gertrude; married Loretta D Young; children: Lisa DeLane. **Educ:** Pratt Inst, BFA, 1955. **Career:** Berton Wink Inc, book designer, 1958-62; Afro-Amer History Highlights, author, 1968; Englishtown, publisher, 1968. Fitzgerald Sample NYC, art dir, producer, dancer; USN John F Small Adv Agency, creative dir minority adv, 1975-78; Henry

Dabbs Prod Englishtown NJ, pres, 1977; Cinema & Graphic Design Jersey City St Col, instr, 1977; film: Joshua, producer, directer, 1979. **Orgs:** NAACP; First MultiMedia, audio visual prog Black American. **Honors/Awds:** Humanitarian Award, 1992. **Military Serv:** AUS, Black gens & admirals, 1955-58. *

DABNEY, DAVID HODGES (W DAVID DABNEY)
Lobbyist, psychiatrist. **Personal:** Born Aug 18, 1927, Washington, DC; divorced. **Educ:** Univ Pa, BA, 1949; Howard Med Sch, MD, 1955. **Career:** Mass Participation Lobbyists Asn, legal psychiatrist, reg lobbyist; Forensic Psychiat Res Consult, consult; Harriet Tubman Projs, int lobbyist, 1993-. **Orgs:** Omega Psi Phi, 1946-; expert witness, DC & State, Fed & Mil Ct, 1957-; Am Psychiat Asn; AMA; Am Correctional Asn; DC Med Soc; Wash Psychiat Soc; Medico-Chirurgical Soc; Nat Med Asn; consult, Skidmore Owings & Merrill Chicago; pres, Chance Child Inc; bd dir, Tiber Island Condominium, 1965-70; SW Comm Assy Health & Welfare Task Force, 1965-70; Univ Pa Alumni Fund-Raising & Sec Educ Comts; exec dir, Bethesda Urban Partnership, currently. **Honors/Awds:** Nat winner, Elks Oratorical Contest, "The Negro & Constitution," 1943; author publication voted Best Paper Reha APA Conv, 1963; congional candidate, 1972, 1974; cited, judges US Dist Ct Appeals DC landmark cases. **Home Addr:** 1237 Irving St NE, Washington, DC 20017. **Business Addr:** Executive Director, Bethesda Urban Partnership, 7700 Old Georgetown Rd, Bethesda, MD 20814-3004, **Business Phone:** (301)215-6660.

DABNEY, W DAVID. See DABNEY, DAVID HODGES.

DAGGS, LEON
Automotive executive, manager, president (organization). **Personal:** Born Feb 12, 1941, St Louis, MO; son of Leon and Dorothy Echols; married Saundra Stills Daggs, Apr 19, 1965; children: Christopher. **Educ:** Harris Teachers Col, St Louis, MO, BA, 1964; St Louis Univ, St Louis, MO, MBA, 1971. **Career:** St Louis Bd Educ, St Louis, MO, teacher, 1963-64; Procter-Gamble, St Louis, MO, sales, 1968-70; McDonnel Aircraft, St Louis, MO, mgr, 1970-71; Ford Motor Co, Dearborn, MI, supvr, 1971-85; Hub City Ford-Mercury, Crestview, pres, 1986; Walton Co Ford-Mercury, Defuniak Springs, pres, 1996; Panhandle Automotive Inc, pres, 2002. **Orgs:** Kappa Alpha Psi Fratrnity, 1961-; bd mem, bd dirs, Nat Asn Advan Colored People, 1973-77; dir, Chamber Com, Crestview, 1986-; bd mem, Pvt Indust Coun, 1986-; charter mem, Crestview Rotary Club, 1988-; spec dep, Okaloosa City Sheriff Dept, 1988-; bd dirs, Ford Lincoln-Mercury Minority Dealers Asn, 1994-. **Honors/Awds:** Man of the Year, Kappa Alpha Psi, 1988. **Military Serv:** USN, Lt jg, 1964-68; Naval Flight Officer, 1964. **Business Addr:** President, Panhandle Auto Inc, 4404 Blountstown Hwy, Tallahassee, FL 32304, **Business Phone:** (850)576-8298.

DAILEY, LENORA SHELL
Basketball coach. **Personal:** Born Aug 24, 1963, Fayettville, NC; daughter of Walter and Faye Bollin; married Eric, Aug 10, 2002; children: Eric L Dailey Jr. **Educ:** Univ Tex, Adv Mgt, 1986. **Career:** TCU, asst coach, 1992, head coach, 1993-96; Texas A&M, asst coach, 1997-98; Amer Basketball League, Nashville Noise, asst coach, 1998; Univ SC, asst coach, 1999-03; WNBA, San Antonio Silver Stars, asst coach, interim head coach, 2003-04; Univ Fl women's basketball, asst coach, 2007. **Orgs:** Delta Sigma Theta; Women Basketball Coaches Asn. **Special Achievements:** First Afr Am head coach at TCU. **Home Addr:** 1 Lake Mist Ct, Columbia, SC 29229, **Home Phone:** (803)419-2378. *

DAILEY, QUINTIN
Basketball player. **Personal:** Born Jan 22, 1961, Baltimore, MD. **Educ:** Univ San Francisco, 1981. **Career:** Basketball player (retired); Chicago Bulls, 1982-84; Los Angeles Clippers, 1987-89; CBA, Sioux Falls Skyforce, 1989-90; Seattle Supersonics, 1990-92; Adirondack Wildcats; San Francisco Bay Area Pro City Summer Basketball League, player; Amateur Athletics Union Boy's Basketball Prog, Nevada dir, 2002; Clark County parks & recreation dept, supvr. **Honors/Awds:** Named mem NBA First Team All-Rookie Squad, 1982-83.

DAILEY, THELMA
Association executive, publisher. **Personal:** Born in Baltimore, MD; divorced. **Educ:** BA, AAS. **Career:** Trade Union Women of African Heritage Inc, pres, founder; The Ethnic Woman Int, publ, 1969-. **Orgs:** Bd mem, NCNW; Women's Forum Inc; coordr, Bronx Chap United Nations Asn; Multi-Ethnic Woman Workshop, Fashion Inst Tech; coordr, Inst of Polit Educ Black Women; IWY Tribune; Veteran feminists Am, 1992-; assoc, Women's Inst Freedom of the Press. **Business Addr:** Publisher, The Ethnic Woman International, Cooper Sta, PO Box 1033, New York, NY 10003, **Business Phone:** (718)655-1657.*

DAILY, BYRON
Executive. **Career:** ThreeBM! Internet Syst, Lithonia, GA, prin, currently. **Business Addr:** Principal, 3BM! Internet Systems, 6246 Phillips Lake Way, Lithonia, GA 30058, **Business Phone:** (770)484-9141.*

DAILY, LORI BEARD
Sales manager, advertising executive, public relations executive. **Educ:** Spelman Col, BA, eng, 1985. **Career:** Delta Airlines Employee Media, advert sales rep; Arby[a6]s & Hilton Airport, acct team; LBD Advert Assoc Inc, chief exec officer, currently. **Honors/Awds:** Pulitzer Prize. **Business Addr:** Chief Executive Officer, LBD Advertising Associates Inc, 400 Colony Sq 1201 Peachtree St Suite 200, Atlanta, GA 30361, **Business Phone:** (404)870-9131.*

DAILY, DR. MACEO CRENSHAW
Administrator. **Educ:** Howard Univ, PhD, attended. **Career:** Smith Col, teacher; Howard Univ, teacher; Brown Univ, teacher; Boston Col, teacher; Morgan State Univ, teacher; Spelman Col, teacher; Colby Col, teacher; NY Univ, teacher; Morehouse Col, teacher; Atlanta Hist Ctr & Smithsonian Mus, consult; Univ Tex El Paso, dir, African-Am Studies Dept, assoc prof hist, currently, dir African American Studies, currently. **Orgs:** Bd dirs, Apex Mus & Hammonds House, Atlanta, GA. **Honors/Awds:** Alex W Bealer Prize, Atlanta Historical Soc, 1996. **Special Achievements:** Numerous studies of African-American leaders, such as Emmett Jay Scott, Booker T Washington & W E B Du Bois. **Business Addr:** Director of African American Studies, University of Texas, Department of History, Liberal Arts Bldg Rm 401, El Paso, TX 79968, **Business Phone:** (915)747-8650.

DAIS, LARRY
School administrator. **Personal:** Born Nov 3, 1945, Columbia, SC; son of Wade Dais and Mamie Jeffcoat Dais; married Olga Carter; children: Landon & Larik. **Educ:** Baruch Col, BS, 1974; Columbia Univ Grad Sch Bus, MS, 1976; Cornell NYSSILR & Hofstra Univ Sch Law, cert, 1986. **Career:** Educator (retired), consultant; Grumman Engineering, admin, 1964-68; State Univ Farmingdale, admin, 1968; Leadership Inst Hofstra Univ, asst dir, 1968-69; Columbia Col, Columbia Univ, dir, 1969-81; Columbia Univ, NY, asst vice pres govt rels & dir govt & community affairs, 1981-2007, Athletics Dept, Community Outreach Prog, consult, currently; Abyssinian Develop Corp, chair. **Orgs:** Nat Urban Leagues Comn Standards & Attributes Urban Affiliates; bd dir, NY Urban League; chmn, Whitney M Young Football Classic; bd dir, Harlem USA, LDC, Harlem Commonwealth Coun Inc; bd dir, Harlem Congregations Community Improvements, New York, NY; bd dir, Greater Harlem Chamber Comm, New York, NY; vpres, 100 Black Men Inc, New York, NY; mem, Am Arbitration Asn; chmn & bd mgrs, Harlem YMCA; chmn, St Marys Rehab Ctr C, Ossining, NY; pres & founder, Nat Coun Educ Opportunity Asn, Washington, DC; chmn, TRIO Adv Bd NJ; pres, chmn & bd dirs, Asn Equality & Excellence Educ Inc; pres, Coun Bd Chairpersons, Nat Urban League Affiliates; vice chmn, Harlem Community Develop Corp, New York, NY. **Honors/Awds:** Samuel D Proctor Phoenix Award, Columbia Univ, 1997; Distinguished Trustee Award, United Hosp Fund NY, 1998; Arthuro A Schomburg Distinguished Service Award; CBS Martin Luther King Living The Dream Award; Presidential Service Award, Coun Bd Chair, Nat Urban League Affiliates; Community Service Award, Harlem Athletic Asn; Vision Award, Harlem Congregations Community Improvement; Appreciation Award, Harlem Inst Fashion; Leo B Marsh Leadership Award, Harlem YMCA; Appreciation Award, Greater Harlem Chamber Comm; Educational Award, Greater Harlem Chamber Comm; Founders Award, Nat Coun Educ Opportunity Asn; Presidents Award, Nat Coun Educ Opportunity Asn; Black Accountants Community Service Award, NY Chapter; Distinguished Service Award, NY Urban League; Martin Luther King Humanitarian Award, NY State; Samuel E Proctor Phoenix Award, Abyssinian Develop Corp; Man of the Year Award, YMCA, Greater NY; Educational Service Award, Marquette Univ; President's Award, Nat Coun Educ Asn; Award of Excellence, Asn Equality & Excellence Educ; Outstanding Leadership Award, Leadership Inst, Hofstra Univ. **Military Serv:** AUS, sgt, 1960-63. **Home Addr:** 60 Stuyvesant Plz, Mount Vernon, NY 10552, **Home Phone:** (914)668-4674. **Business Addr:** Consultant, Columbia University, Community Outreach Program, 301 Lowe Libr 116th St & Broadway, New York, NY 10027, **Business Phone:** (212)854-4469.

DALE, BRYANT
Founder (Originator). **Educ:** Univ Bridgeport, BA, acct; Pace Univ, Lubin Grad Sch Bus, MBA, investment mgt. **Career:** Reich & Teng LP, staff, 1989; Dean Witter Morgan Stanley, Mutual Fund Div, 1989-93; Lehman Brothers, Pvt Client Serv, sales assoc, 1993-96; Bryant Group, portfolio mgr, 1996-. **Orgs:** Contribr, Black Enterprise; contribr, KIP Bus Report. **Honors/Awds:** 40 Under 40 Award, Network J; Caribbean Am Chamber of Com & Indust Visionary Award. **Special Achievements:** Has been interviewed on CNNfn, BET.com. **Business Phone:** (212)537-9340.

DALE, CLAMMA CHURITA
Opera singer. **Personal:** Born Jul 4, 1953, Chester, PA; daughter of Granvaul and Clara Robinson; married Terry C Shirk, Dec 19, 1981 (died 1987). **Educ:** Settlement Mus Sch Philadelphia; Juilliard Sch, New York, NY. **Career:** NY City Opera Co, 1975; Houston Opera Co, singer, 1976; Bronx Opera Co, performer; Brooklyn Opera Theatre, performer; Metrop Opera's Mini-Met; Houston Grand Opera Co, 1976-77; Manhattan Theatre Club, 1977; Paris Opera, performer; Berlin Opera, performer; New York City Opera, performer; Opera Co Philadelphia, performer; DAL Prod Ltd, pres, 1989-.Tv appearances: Liberty Weekend, 1986; "Great Performances", 1987. **Honors/Awds:** Cue Golden Apple, 1976; Tony Award, leading actress-musical, 1977; 2Naumburg Awards. **Special Achievements:** Recitals at Avery Fischer Hall & Lincoln Center. *

DALE, DR. LOUIS
School administrator, educator. **Personal:** Born Nov 24, 1935, Birmingham, AL; son of Anne Mae Boykins and Finley; married Gladiola Watts Dale; children: Louis Jr, Valerie Louise, Annice Jeanette & Jonathan David. **Educ:** Miles Col, Birmingham, Ala, BS, 1960; Atlanta Univ, Atlanta, Ga, MS, 1964; Univ Ala, Tuscaloosa, Ala, PhD, 1973. **Career:** Atlanta Univ, Atlanta, Ga, instr, 1964-66; Miles Col, Birmingham, Ala, chmn, Div Natural Sci, 1968-70; acting dean, 1969-73; Interim Dean, 1970-71; Affirmative Action Officer, Sch Natural Sci & Math, 1975-81; Univ Ala Birmingham, Birmingham, Ala, asst prof, 1973-77, prof 1980-, Interim Ch, Dept Math, 1982-84; fassoc dean, 1987-91, dir, Alliance for Minority Participation Proj, 1991-; assoc vpres, Acad Affairs, 1991-95, assoc vpres, Minority & Spec Prog, 1995-97, assoc provost, Minority & Spec Prog, 1997-. **Orgs:** Am Math Soc, 1975-; pres, 1984-88, mem, 1978-88, Birmingham Bd Educ; dir, Ala Alliance Minority Participation Proj, 1991-; bd dir, Ala Asn Sch Bd; rev panelist, Nat Sci Found Proposals, 1988-; Nat Asn Math. **Honors/Awds:** Numerous grants from Nat Sci Found and others. **Military Serv:** AUS, Corporal, 1954-57. **Home Addr:** 663 Dublin Ave, Birmingham, AL 35212. **Business Addr:** Associate Provost for Minority & Special Programs, University of Alabama at Birmingham, Department of Mathematics, 452 Campbell Hall, UAB Station, Birmingham, AL 35294-1170, **Business Phone:** (205)934-8762.

DALE, ROBERT J.
Advertising executive. **Personal:** Born May 2, 1943, Chicago, IL; son of Charles McDearmon and Jessie M; married Shirley J White, Jul 8, 1989; children: Kondo, Yusef, Kareem. **Educ:** Arizona State Univ, BS, bus, 1971; Stanford Univ, CA, MBA, bus & mkt, 1973. **Career:** Kaiser Broadcasting, Chicago, IL, account exec, 1973-74; Field Spot TV Sales, nat account exec, 1974-75; R J Dale & Assocs, consult, 1976-78; Small Bus Admin, mgt consult, 1978-79; Chicago State Univ, asst prof, 1979-84; R J Dale Advertising & Pub Rels Inc, pres, chief exec officer, 1979-. **Orgs:** Am Mkt Asn, 1977-, PUSH Int Trade Bur, 1984-, Nat Black United Front-Chicago, 1984-, Am Asn Advert Agencies, 1986-; co-chair, Chicago State Univ Col Bus Hall Fame Bd, 1987-; advisory bd mem, Black Pub Rels Soc-Chicago, 1988-; bd mem, March Dimes Birth Defects Found, 1989-; pres, IST Positive Educ, 1989; chair, Black Ensemble Theatre CRP, 1990; speaker, 24th Annual Black Bus Students Asn Conf, Stanford Univs Grad Sch Bus. **Honors/Awds:** Outstanding Black Businessman Award, Nat Black United Front, 1986; Pinnacle Award, Being Single Mag, 1989; Col Bus Hall of Fame, Chicago State Univ, 2003. **Special Achievements:** Black Enterprise's list of Top Advertising Agencies, ranked 9th, 1999, 10th, 2000. **Military Serv:** USF, airman 1st class, 1962-66. **Business Addr:** President, Chief Executive Officer, R J Dale Advertising & Public Relations Inc, 211 E Ontario St Suite 200, Chicago, IL 60611-3284.*

DALEY, THELMA THOMAS
Educator. **Personal:** Born in Annapolis, MD; married Guilbert A. **Educ:** Bowie St Col, BS; NY Univ, MA, George Washington Univ, EdD. **Career:** Baltimore County Bd Educ, counr; NC Cent Western Md Col, vis prof; Univ Wisc, vprof; Harvard Univ, vprof. **Orgs:** Nat Asn Advan Colored People; Nat Proj Chmn, 1967-71; Black Adoption Prog, 1968-73; nat treas, Delta Sigma Theta, 1963-67, nat vpres, 1975-79; Natpres, Am Sch Counr Asn, 1971-72; pres, Am Personnel & Guid Asn, 1975-76; chair, Women In Community Services; United Negro Col Fund. **Honors/Awds:** Md Personnel & Guidance Achievement Award, 1972; Life Mem Award, Nat Asn Advan Colored People, 1973. **Special Achievements:** First woman to chair the National Advisory Council on Career Education. *

DALEY-MELESCHI, VALRINE
Manager. **Educ:** Univ Wash, BA, political Science & Econ. **Career:** Montclair Newark Jr League, Prof Develop & Training Chair, 2005-06; Citigroup, practice mgr orgn develop, currently; consulting practice. **Orgs:** Cornell Univ Sch Industrial & labor Rels; City Univ NY; speaker & facilitator: Ford Motor Co; The Financial Women's Asn; Citigroup; YMCA. **Business Addr:** Practice Manager, Citigroup, 399 Park Ave, New York, NY 10043.*

DALFERES, EDWARD R., JR.
Medical researcher, educator. **Personal:** Born Nov 4, 1931, New Orleans, LA; son of Edward Sr and Ray; married Anita Y Bush; children: Edward Rene & Anthony Renard. **Educ:** Xavier Univ, BS, 1956. **Career:** St John Parish Sch Bd, sci teacher, 1956-57; La State Univ Sch Med, med res, 1957-75, instr; Tulane Ctr Cardiovasc Health, instr & res biochem. **Orgs:** La Heart Asn; AAAS; Connective Tissue Soc; Soc Complex Carbohydrates. **Military Serv:** AUS, Med Corps, 1950-52. **Business Addr:** Instructor, Research Biochemist, Tulane Ctr Cardiovasc Health, 1440 Canal St, 18th Fl, New Orleans, LA 70112.*

DALLEY, GEORGE ALBERT
Lawyer, government official, executive. **Personal:** Born Aug 25, 1941, Havana, Cuba; son of Cleveland Ernest and Constance

Joyce; married Pearl Elizabeth Love, Aug 1, 1970; children: Jason Christopher, Benjamin Christian. **Educ:** Columbus Col, BA, econ, 1963; Columbia Univ Sch Law, LLB, 1966; Columbia Univ Grad Sch & Bus, MBA, 1966. **Career:** Metrop Appl Res Ctr, asst pres, 1967-69; Stroock & Stroock & Lavan, assoc couns, 1970-71; US House Reps Comt Judiciary, asst coun, 1971-72; Congressman Charles Rangel, admin asst, 1972-76; US Dept State, dep asst secy state, 1977-79; US Civil Aero Bd, mem, 1980-82; Am Univ Sch Law, adj prof, 1981-85; Mondale Pres, dep camp mgr, 1983-84; Cong Charles Rangel, counr & staff dir, 1985-89; Africare, Transafrica DC Support Group, bd dir; Neill & Co Inc, sr vpres, 1989-93; Neill & Shaw, partner, 1989-93; Holland & Knight, partner, 1993; Apollo Theater Found Inc, asst secy, currently, chmn real estate comt, currently. **Orgs:** Am Bar Asn; Int Law Comt, Nat Bar Asn Fed Bar Asn, 1976-; Transafrica, Nat Asn Advan Colored People; Urban League 1974-; Crestwood Community Asn, 1986-; Apollo Theatre Found; consult, United Nations Develop Prog, 1989-; Am Bar Asn; Coun Foreign Rels; Am Bar Found; DC Judicial Nominating Comn. **Special Achievements:** Published Art Federal Drug Abuse Enforcement 1974; speeches Dem Corp Select Process 1976; various Mags Articles 1977-. **Home Phone:** (202)722-5184. **Business Addr:** Assistant Secretary, Apollo Theater Found Inc, 253 W 125th St, New York, NY 10027, **Business Phone:** (212)531-5300.*

DALTON, DAVID
Chief executive officer. **Educ:** West Virginia Univ, BS, 1971, PhD, pharmacol, 1974. **Career:** Rite Aid Corp, corp vpres, 1971-89; Sherman Mgt Group & Med Ser Agency, chmn & cheif exec officer, 1989-94; MEDNET, exec vpres; Managed Care Rx; Health Resources Inc, founder, pres & chief exec officer; Univec Inc, dir, pres & chief exec officer, curently; Pharmacy Serv Inc, owner, currently. **Orgs:** Essences Nature Asn; Salford Royal NHS Found; Blue Shield Pa; United Way; Nat Health Asn; Nat Asn Chain Drug Stores; bd dir, Nat Coun Prescription Drug Prog. **Honors/Awds:** Medal of Freedom, US Senate; Distinguished alumni and outstanding alumni of School of Pharmacy, WVa Univ. **Special Achievements:** Honored as one of the top ten graduates over a 100 - year span. *

DALTON, RAYMOND ANDREW
School administrator, artist. **Personal:** Born Jan 15, 1942, Chicago, IL; son of Ernest Mitchell and Dorothy Mitchell Hunter; married Alfonsa Vicente (divorced); children: Carlos, Julio & Solange. **Educ:** Ill State Univ, BS, 1964, MS, 1966; Univ San Francisco, doctoral study, 1978; Purdue Univ, W Lafayette, IN, PhD, 1990. **Career:** Antelope Valley High Sch, instr, 1965-67; Lake Hughes, instr, 1967; Drew Jr High Sch, instr, 1967-68; Univ Ill, asst dean, asst prof 1971-84; Purdue fel, 1987-89; Cornell Univ, Ithaca, NY, Minority Educ Affairs & Cosep, dir, 1989-, sr lectr art, 1989-94, exec dir, currently. **Orgs:** Adv, Black Student Organ Archit & Art, 1972-75; co-clrm, Art Comm, 1972; consult, Park Forest Pub Sch Black Art Workshop, 1973; co-adv, Orgn Int Stud, 1975; Prof Orgn Acad Affairs Admin Midwest; Nat Conf Artists; Union Black Artists; Coll Art Asn; Nat Art Educ Asn; Nat Conf Art Admin; Asn Collegiate Registrars & Counrs; Nat Orgn Minority Architects; grad assistantship, Ill State Univ, 1964-65, Purdue Univ, 1984-85; sab lv, Univ Puerto Rico 1977; sab lv, Nigeria, 1982; Gamma Delta Iota Fraternity, 1986-; Omicron Delta Kappa Soc, 1989-; Purdue Circle, 1989-. **Honors/Awds:** Edwards Medal, Ill State Speech Contest, 1965; William H Myers Multicultural Professional Service Award. **Business Addr:** Executive Director, Cornell University, College of Architecture, Art & Planning, Office of Minority Educational Affairs, 100 Barnes Hall, Ithaca, NY 14853, **Business Phone:** (607)255-7000.

DALY, DR. FREDERICA Y
Psychologist. **Personal:** Born Feb 14, 1925, Washington, DC; daughter of Samuel P Young and Geneva A Sharper Young; married Michael E, Mar 15, 1972. **Educ:** Howard Univ, BS, 1947, MS 1949; Cornell Univ, PhD, 1956. **Career:** Psychologist (retired); Howard Univ, instr, 1950; Cornell Univ, teaching asst, 1953-55; Cornell Univ, Cora Smith fel, 1953-54; Cornell Univ, Grant fel, 1954-55; George Jr Repub, clin psychol, 1955-72; State Univ NY, Empire State Col, assoc prof, 1972-80; Univ NMex, Ment Health Prog, clin psychol, 1980-81; Alcohol Prog Va Med Ctr, coordr, 1981-88. **Orgs:** Gov's task force mem, State NMex, 1984; bd mem, Family Serv Agency, 1958-60; NMex Bead Soc; Am Psychol Asn; Inst Noetic Scis; Soc Layerists Multi-media. **Special Achievements:** Perspectives Native Am Women's Racism & Sexism Experiences, paper presented Am Asn Advan Sci, 1990; Poetry pub & one poem to be published in a Russian J; Feminist Press, City Univ NY, Challenging Racism & Sexism. **Home Addr:** 526 Hermosa NE, Albuquerque, NM 87108.

DALY, RONALD EDWIN
Executive. **Personal:** Born Feb 23, 1947, Chicago, IL; son of Edwin W and Ella McCreary Brown; married Dolores, Jul 28, 1978; children: Dawn, Ronald Jr & Erin. **Educ:** Governors State Univ, Univ Park IL, BA, bus admin, 1977; Loyola Univ, Chicago IL, MBA finance, 1980. **Career:** R R Donnelley & Sons, Chicago IL, supvr, 1972-79, mgr, 1980-84, Cherry Hill NJ, gen mgr, 1984-87, Lancaster PA, gen mgr, 1987-88, Chicago IL, div dir; RR Donnelley Norwest Inc, sr vp, Portland, OR, 1991-94; Americas Global Software Servs, sr vpres opers, 1994; Telecommunications Bus Unit, pres, 1995; RR Donnelley Print Solutions, pres, 2001-02; OCE USA Holding Inc, pres & chief exec officer, 2002-04; Supervalu, dir, 2003-. **Orgs:** Trustee, Chicago Symphony; vice chair, bd pres, Environ Law & Policy Ctr; bd mem, Leadership Greater Chicago; adv bd, Loyola (Chicago) Sch Bus; bd dirs, US Cellular Corp, 2004-. **Honors/Awds:** Black Achiever, YMCA, 1977. **Home Addr:** 1418 S Prairie Ave, Chicago, IL 60605, **Home Phone:** (312)945-0511. **Business Addr:** Director, Supervalu, 11840 Valley View Rd, Eden Prairie, MN 60631, **Business Phone:** (952)828-4000.

DAMES, KATHY W.
Executive. **Personal:** Born Jan 22, 1963, Chicago, IL; daughter of Sellers Williams Jr and Katie C Williams. **Educ:** Western Ill Univ, BA, 1984, MA, 1991. **Career:** Ill State Comptrollers Off, asst legislative liaison, 1986-88, chief legislative liaison, 1988-90; Bd Governors Univs, lobbyist, 1990-; Chicago State Univ, dir alumni affairs, 1993-95; Harold Washington Col, asst to pres, 1995; Roosevelt Univ, dir alumni develop, currently. **Orgs:** Chicago Women Gov; Ill Women Gov; Ill Women Adrs; Women's Legislative Network; Asn Black Women Higher Educ Inc; Illinois Comt Black Concerns Higher Educ; Delta Sigma Theta Inc. **Honors/Awds:** Best & Brightest Business & Professional Women, Dollars & Sense Mag, 1991. **Business Addr:** Director of Annual Giving, Alumni Relations, Roosevelt University, 430 S Michigan Ave Rm 124, Chicago, IL 60605, **Business Phone:** (312)341-3725.*

DAMES, SABRINA A. (SABRINA DAMES CRUTCHFIELD)
Television journalist, writer, journalist. **Personal:** Born Nov 9, 1957, Washington, DC; daughter of Anita Mae Wilson Dames and Harold Alexander Dames, Sr; married Curtis A Crutchfield, Jun 4, 1988. **Educ:** Howard Univ, Washington, DC, BA, 1979; Columbia Univ, New York, NY, MS, 1981. **Career:** WTOP Radio, Washington, DC, news writer, 1981-84; CBS News Nightwatch, Washington, DC, news writer, 1984-85; WJLA-TV, Washington, DC, news writer, 1984-86; Black Entertainment TV, Washington, DC, reporter, producer, 1986-. **Orgs:** National Association Black Journalists, currently; AFTRA, 1981-84; Alpha Kappa Alpha Sorority, 1983-; National Television and Radio Correspondents Association, 1986-. **Honors/Awds:** Cable Ace Award Nominee, News Special "Beyond The End," 1995. **Business Addr:** Reporter, Producer, Black Entertainment TV, 1900 W Place NE, Washington, DC 20018.*

DAMPER, RONALD EUGENE
Executive, chief executive officer, president (organization). **Personal:** Born Sep 18, 1946, Birmingham, AL; son of Willie and Ruby; married Patricia Dianne Ward, Jun 7, 1970; children: Ronald Sean & Shevonn Denise. **Educ:** Knoxville Col, BS, math, 1967; NY Univ, attended 1970; Univ Conn,Bridgeport, MBA, 1977. **Career:** GEEC, mkt mgr, 1973-77; Greyhound Leasing, dist mgr, 1977-79; Bankers Trust, v pres, 1979-81; Citi corp, v pres, 1981-84; Visions Entertainment, Blockbuster Video, prin, 1990-; Damron Corp, founder, 1984, pres & chiefexec officer, 1985-, gen mgr, 2001. **Orgs:** Bd trustees, Tea Asn US, 1987; bd dir, Demico Youth Servs, 1988-; bd mem,Community Serv Develop Comt, 1989-93; bd mem, Ill Dept Community Affairs, 1990-; chmn & bd trustees, Montay Col, 1990-; Alliance Bus Leaders &Entrepreneurs, 1992-; chmn, McDonald's Diversity Supplier Coun, 1993-96; leadership mem, Boy Scouts Am, 1992. **Honors/Awds:** Bus Person of the Year, Indust Coun NW Chicago, 1990; Entrepreneur of the Year, finalist, Ernst & Young, 1990. **Military Serv:** USAFR, ssgt, 1968-74. **Business Addr:** President, Chief Executive Officer, Damron Corporation, 4433 W Ohio St, Chicago, IL 60624, **Business Phone:** 800-333-1860.*

DAMPIER, ERICK TREVEZ
Basketball player. **Personal:** Born Jul 14, 1975, Jackson, MS; son of Kenneth and Mary. **Educ:** Miss State Univ, attended 1997. **Career:** Ind Pacers, ctr, 1996-97; Golden State Warriors, 1998-2004; Dallas Mavericks, ctr, 2005-. **Orgs:** Kappa Alpha Psi; founder, Erick Dampier Found. **Special Achievements:** NBA Draft, First round pick, No 10, 1996. **Business Addr:** Professional Basketball Player, Dallas Mavericks, 2909 Taylor St, Dallas, TX 75207, **Business Phone:** (214)747-6287.

DANCE, DR. DARYL CUMBER
Educator. **Personal:** Born Jan 17, 1938, Richmond, VA; daughter of Allen W Cumber and Veronica Bell Cumber; married Warren C; children: Warren C Jr, Allen C & Daryl Lynn. **Educ:** Va State Col, AB, 1957, MA, 1963; Univ Va, PhD, 1971. **Career:** Va State Col, asst prof eng, 1962-72; Va Commonwealth Univ, from asst prof eng to prof eng, 1972-92; Jour W Indian Lit, ed adv, 1986-; Univ Calif, Santa Barbara, vis prof, african-am studies, 1986-87; Univ Richmond, Dept Eng, prof, 1992-. **Orgs:** Danforth Asn, 1964-; adv ed, African Am Rev, 1978-, Ma Comer, 1998-,Callalou, 2000-. **Honors/Awds:** Numerous fellowships & grants; Sister Circle Book Award for Outstanding Anthology, 1999; Storytelling World Award, Freom My People, 2004; The Sojourner Truth Award, The African American Studies Program of George Mason University, 2007. **Special Achievements:** Author: Shuckin' & Jivin, Folklore from Contemporary Black Americans, 1978; Folklore from Contemporary Jamaicans, 1985; Fifty Caribbean Writers, 1986; Long Gone The Mecklen burg Six & The Theme of Escape in Black Literature, 1987; New World Adams: Conversations with West Indian Writers, 1992; Honey, Hush! An Anthology of African American Women's Humor, 1998; The Lineage of Abraham: The Biography of a Free Black Family, 1999; Frommy People: Four Hundred Years of African-American Folklore, 2002. **Business Addr:** Professor of English, University of Richmond, Department of English, 28 Westhampton Way, Ryland Hall 323, Richmond, VA 23173, **Business Phone:** (804)289-8295.

DANCE, HON. ROSALYN R. (ROZ DANCE)
Nurse, mayor. **Personal:** Born Mar 10, 2008, Chesterfield, VA. **Educ:** John Tyler Community Col, AD, nursing, 1975; Va State Univ, BS, nursing, 1986; Va Commonwealth Univ, MPA, 1994; Gen educ develop, dipl. **Career:** Nurse (retired), Mayor; City Petersburg, mayor, 1992-; Va House Deleg, deleg, 2007; South side Va Training Ctr, nurse's aide, head nurse, supt nursing, actg prog dir, dep dir residential serv; Va St Univ, fac; Virginia House Of Delegates, del, currently; Manhattans Restaurant, Richmond, Owner, currently. **Orgs:** Hon mem, Petersburg Chamber Com, 1995; Nat Conf Black Mayors; Sub-Comt,Com Agr & Natural Resources; Sub-Comt, Gen Govt & Technol; Baptist Church; John Tyler Community Col Found; chmn, Southside Va YMCA; chmn, United Way, Southside Opers; Phi Kappa Phi; Petersburg Dem Comt; Petersburg Links Inc;pres, Petersburg Breakfast Rotary; Petersburg Alumnae Chap, Delta Sigma Theta; hon mem, Tri-City Univ Womens Club. **Honors/Awds:** Cert of Appreciation, Va Asn Neighborhoods, 1992; Cert of Appreciation, AmBus Women's Asn, Appomattox Chap, 1992; Golden Apple Award, Petersburg PubSchs, 1992; Citizen of the Yr, Omega Psi Phi Fraternity Inc, Delta Omega Chap, 1993; Cert of Merit, Va State Univ, 1993; Cert of Achievement, Woodstock Job Corps, 1993; Martin Luther King Jr Legacy Award, Alpha Phi Alpha Fraternity Inc, 1994; Outstanding Woman in Govt, YWCA, 1996; Cert of Appreciation, 24th Quartermaster Battalion, 1998; Distinguished Alumni, Va Common wealth Univ, 2003; Inductee, Hall of Fame, Va Community Col, 2003. **Business Addr:** Delegate 63rd District, Virginia House of Delegates, PO Box 2584, Petersburg, VA 23804, **Business Phone:** (804)862-2922.

DANCE, ROZ. **See DANCE, HON. ROSALYN R.**

DANCY, WILLIAM F.
Clergy. **Personal:** Born Nov 6, 1924, Greenville, MS; son of William Pearl and Belle Washington; married Darnell E Pruitt; children: Antonia M, William F, Jr, Winnona D, Darryl B, Kimberly E. **Educ:** Roosevelt Univ; Cent Baptist Theol Sem KCKS. **Career:** Pastored 10 AME churches; presiding elder, KC-Topeka Dist; retired from ministry, 2001; real estate broker; housing admin; licensed insurance broker; election bd comnr; First African Methodist Episcopal Church, assoc pastor. **Orgs:** 3rd Degree Mason; life mem, Nat Asn Advan Colored People; chmn, Oak Pk Soc Serv Orgn. **Honors/Awds:** Hon doctorate, Edward Waters Col. **Military Serv:** US Navy, Liberty Ship Storekeeper 1st Class, 1943-45. **Business Addr:** Associate Pastor, First African Methodist Episcopal Church, 1111 N Eighth St, Kansas City, KS 66101.*

DANDRIDGE, PROF. RITA BERNICE
Educator. **Personal:** Born in Richmond, VA. **Educ:** VA Union Univ, BA, 1961; Howard Univ, MA, 1963, PhD, 1970; Nat Endowment Humanities Study Grant, 1995, 1998, 2001. **Career:** Morgan State Univ, asst prof Eng, 1964-71; Univ Toledo, asst prof Eng, 1971-74; Norfolk State Univ, Dept Eng & Foreign Lang, prof, 1974-. **Orgs:** Subscriber Modern Lang Asn; Col Lang Asn; Multi-ethnic Lit US African Am Rev; Nat Women's Studies Asn; Modern Lang Asn; Col Lang Asn. **Honors/Awds:** Outstanding Teacher of the Year, Norfolk State Univ, 1998; Regional Delegate to MLA, 2003-05; TIAA-CREF Va Outstanding Fac Awards. **Special Achievements:** Selected articles, "But Some of Us Are Brave," Eds Gloria T Hull & Others, Old Westbury, NY, The Feminist Press, 1982; "Louise Meriwether," Dictionary of Literary Biography, Afro-Am Fiction Writers after 1955, Eds Thadious Davis & Trudier Harris, Detroit, Gale Research Co 1984, Vol 33, Pp 182-186; "Josephine Joyce Turpin, Richmond Writer," The Richmond Quarterly 9 Fall 1986 11-13; book "Ann Allen Shockley, An Annotated Primary and Secondary Bibliography," 1987 Greenwood Press Westport CT; book, Black Women's Blues, A Literary Anthology (1934-1988), 1992, GK Hall New York; "Debunking the Beauty Myth" in Terry McMillan's "Waiting to Exhale," Language, Rhythm and Sound, eds Joseph K Adjaye and Adrienne R Andrews, Univ of Pittsburgh Press, 1997; "Debunking the Motherhood Myth in Terry McMillan's Mama," CLA Journal, June, 1998; "The Race, Gender, Romance Connection: A Black Feminist Reading of African-American Women's Historical Romances," in Double Plots, eds Susan Strehle and Mary Carden, Univ Press of MS, 2003. **Business Addr:** Professor, Norfolk State University, Department English & Foreign Language, 106 James Bowser Bldg 700 Pk Ave, Norfolk, VA 23504.

DANDRIDGE, ROBERT L., JR.
Basketball coach, basketball player. **Personal:** Born Nov 15, 1947, Richmond, VA; married Barbara. **Educ:** Norfolk State Univ, attended 1969, Hampton Univ, MA, coun. **Career:** Basketball

player (retired), basketball coach; Milwaukee Bucks, 1969-77;Wash Bullets, 1977-81; Milwaukee Bucks, 1982, Hampton Univ, coach,1987-94; NBA Players Assn, dir, 1996-98; The Am Basketball Asn, LongIsland, head coach, 2005-. **Honors/Awds:** NBA All-Rookie Team, 1970; NBA All Star Team, 1973, 1975, 1976 & 1979; Virginia Sports Hall of Fame. **Business Phone:** (317)844-7502.

DANDY, CLARENCE L.
Clergy, executive. **Personal:** Born Jan 7, 1939, St Petersburg; married Luagussie; children: Cynthia, Louis, Anthony, Jackie, Karlette. **Educ:** Full Gospel Minister Intl Dallas, DD; FL A&M Univ, 1959. **Career:** United Full Gospel Temple, founder, pres; Prayer Twr Raleigh, NC, dir. **Orgs:** Chmn, bd dir Rev C Dandy Evangelistic Asn Raleigh. **Honors/Awds:** Recipient 1st Prize Trophy, Evangelist of the Year, United Full Gospel Temple, 1974. **Military Serv:** AUS, pfc, 1956. **Business Addr:** Founder, UFG Temple Inc of Durham, PO Box 3323, Durham, NC 27705, **Business Phone:** (919)688-0167.*

DANDY, DR. ROSCOE GREER
Government official, educator. **Personal:** Born Dec 20, 1946, Los Angeles, CA; son of Doris L Edwards and Roscoe Conkling; divorced 2003. **Educ:** California State Univ, BA, 1970; Univ Southern Calif, MSW, 1973; Univ Pittsburgh, MPH, 1974, MPA, 1975, DrPH, 1981; Harvard Univ, cert, 1981; Univ Ill, Urbana, IL, 1968; LaSalle Extension Univ, Chicago, Ill, 1968. **Career:** Calif State Youth Authority, youth counr, 1971; Colo State Dept Health, public health intern, 1974; Green Engineering Corp, health planning intern, 1975; Univ Pittsburgh, instr, 1977-80; Kane Hosp, admin health intern, 1979; US Public Health Serv, lt commander, assoc dir out-patient clin, 1980-81; Central Mich Univ, instr, 1981-; Veterans Administration Hosp, asst chief trainee, 1981; Veterans Admin, asst chief med admin, 1983-85, clin social worker, 1985-93; Columbia Inst Psychotherapy, psychotherapist, 1989-91; Columbia Pacific Univ, instr, 1990; Nova Southeastern Univ, instr, 1991; US Public Health Svc, public health analyst/project officer, 1993-. **Orgs:** Consultant Jackson State Univ, Jackson, MS, 1977; mem, Southern Christian Leadership Conf, 1973-; mem, NAACP, 1987-; mem, Am Public Health asn, 1987-; Joint Ctr Political Studies, 1986-; mem, Brookings Inst, 1985; mem, Fed Am Scientists, 1988-. **Honors/Awds:** Fel, Dr Martin Luther King Jr, Woodrow Wilson Found, 1971-73; Outstanding Unit Citation US Public Health Serv Scientist, 1981; author, Board & Care Homes Los Angeles County, 1976; InterNat Directory Distinguished Leadership Award, 1989, Man of the Year, 1990, 1993, Am Biographical Inst Inc; Project Officer of the Year, 1999; Cash Award, 2005; Premier Leadership Training Sem, Nova South Eastern Univ, Ft. Lauderdale FL, 2005; Deployment to Hurricane Katrina in Miss, 2005. **Special Achievements:** Who's Who In America, 2002-04, 2006; Who's Who in the East, 2002. **Military Serv:** USAF, sgt, 1965-68; USMC Reserves, sgt, 1 yr; Air Force/Vietnam Era Veteran Award. **Business Addr:** Senior Public Health Analyst, HRSA/Office of Minority Health, Department of Health and Human Services, 18172 Parklawn Bdg 5600 Fisher Lane, Rockville, MD 20857, **Business Phone:** (301)443-6582.

DANENBERG, SOPHIA
Athlete. **Personal:** Born Jan 1, 1972. **Educ:** Harvard Univ, grad environ sci; Univ Conn, MA, econ. **Career:** Prof mountain climber; Boeing, Seattle, staff. **Special Achievements:** First black woman to climb to the summit of Mount Everest.

DANIEL, BERTHA
College administrator. **Educ:** Valdosta State Col, BS; Troy State Univ, MS. **Career:** Abraham Baldwin Agr Col, assoc prof Criminal Justice, dir col serv & human resources, currently. **Orgs:** Proud Loving Individuals Giving Hand Teens. **Business Addr:** Director of College Services, Abraham Baldwin Agricultural College, ABAC 39 2802 Moore Hwy, Tift Hall Room 23, Tifton, GA 31793-2601, **Business Phone:** (229)391-4890.

DANIEL, CELIA C
Librarian. **Educ:** Concordia Univ, BA, black hist & Eng; McGill Univ, Grad Dipl, educ, MLS, libr & info sci. **Career:** Centennial Regional High Sch, Montreal, Canada, teacher librn; Howard Univ, Founder Libr, assoc librn, currently. **Honors/Awds:** Teacher of the Year Award, 1994. **Business Addr:** Associate Librarian, Howard University, 500 Howard Pl NW, Washington, DC 20059, **Business Phone:** (202)806-7446.

DANIEL, COLENE YVONNE
Health services administrator. **Personal:** Born Apr 23, 1954, Cincinnati, OH; divorced. **Educ:** UNIV Cincinnati, BS, 1977; Texas Woman's UNIV, 1980; Health Care ADMIN Residency, 1979; Johns Hopkins Sch Hygiene & Pub Health, Masters Pub Health, Health Policy, 1996. **Career:** Veterans ADM Med Ctr, health systs specialist, 1980-82; AMR Med Intl Inc, asst hosp dir, 1982-86, mgt assoc, 1986-87; The UNIV Chicago Hosps, assoc dir, 1987-91; John Hopkins Health Syst, vip cre & cot servs, 1991-02, pres's Coun urban Health, co-chair, 1998; Doctors Community Healthcare, regional chief exec officer; D.C. Healthcare Alliance, 2002-03; Maryland gen hosp, pres & chief exec officer, 2004-; KSP Healthcare Group, pres, currently. **Orgs:** Healthcare Forum; Healthcare Forum Jour; AM COL Healthcare EXECs; Johns Hopkins Med Servs Corp, bd trustees, 1995-97; John Hopkins Health Syst, Dome Circle ASO, 1995-97; Johns Hospkins Med & Parking, 1996-98; COL Notre Dame, bd trustees, 1993-99; Health EDUC Resource ORG, bd trustees, 1996-98; The Historic East Baltimore COT Action Coaltion, Inc, bd trustees, 1994-98; The Links, Inc, Harbor City Chap, 1997-00; AFA COM Walters Art Gallery, 1994-97; PULSE COT Prog, bd adv opers, 1992-96. **Honors/Awds:** Maryland House Delegates Citation Excellence Service, 1996; Maryland's Top 100 Women, Finalist, & Maryland's Leading Women EXECs, 1996; Delaware House Delegates Citation Excellence Service, 1996; Winner Healthcare Forum's Emerging Leaders Healthcare Award, 1995; NAT ASN health Servs EXECs, ADR of the Year-Midwest, 1993; Leadership Maryland Fellowship Awarded by the Governor, 1992; numerous others. **Special Achievements:** HTHcare Forum, "Managing Organizational Transition," 1996; AMR CLG of HTHcare EXEs, "COT-Based Primary Care, Assessment and Program," 1995; NAT ASN of HTH Services EXEs, "The Role of Total Quality Mgt in HTHcare Reform," 1993. **Business Addr:** President, Chief Executive Officer, Maryland General Hospital, 827 Linden Ave, Baltimore, MD 21201, **Business Phone:** (410)225-8000.*

DANIEL, DR. ELNORA (ELNORA D DANIEL)
Educator, college administrator, college president. **Personal:** Born Nov 19, 1941, Oxford, NC; married Herman; children: 1. **Educ:** NC A&T Univ, BS, 1964; Teachers Col, Columbia Univ, MEd, 1968, EdD, 1975; The Col William & Mary. **Career:** NY Med Ctr, nurse; Columbia Univ, teaching asst, 1976; Hampton Univ, dean sch nursing, 1980-91, adminr interdisciplinary nursing ctr, 1985, exec vpres & provost, 1995-98; Chicago State Univ, pres, 1998-2008. **Orgs:** Econ Club Chicago; bd dir, Nat Asn Equal Opportunity Higher Educ; bd dir, The Little Company of Mary; bd mem, La Rabida Children's Hospital; bd mem, Womens Bd of the Field Museum and Holds numerous memships. **Honors/Awds:** Citizen of the Year Award, Chatham Lions Club, 2001; holds numerous academic & civic awards; inductee, Gallery of Greats Calendar, Miller Brewing Company, 2003; Tolerance Awards, Annual Peace & Dialogue Awards, 2009. **Special Achievements:** Published numerous articles. **Military Serv:** USAR, col. **Business Addr:** President, Chicago State University, 9501 S King Dr, Chicago, IL 60628-1598, **Business Phone:** (773)995-2000.

DANIEL, ELNORA D. See DANIEL, DR. ELNORA.

DANIEL, EUGENE, JR.
Football player. **Personal:** Born May 4, 1961, Baton Rouge, LA. **Educ:** La State Univ. **Career:** Football player (retired); Indianapolis Colts, defensive back, 1984-96; Baltimore Ravens, defensive back, 1997. **Honors/Awds:** AFC Defensive Player of the Week; Football News All AFC selection, 1985. *

DANIEL, GRISELDA
School administrator. **Personal:** Born Feb 7, 1938, Battle Creek, MI; daughter of Edward and Teritha; children: Cornell A, Gary L, Cheri A, Patrick H. **Educ:** Western Michigan Univ, BS, 1973, MS, 1980. **Career:** School Administrator (retired); Borgess Hosp, surgical nurse, 1958-66; Kalamazoo St Hosp, attendant nurse, 1966-70; Mich Dept Educ; Western Mich Univ, Col Gen Studies, counr & trainer, 1970-73, dir Martin Luther King, Jr prog, 1975-80, asst, vpres acad affrs off & dir spl prog, 1980-88, asst dean, Grad Col, dir grad diversity prog, 1988-06. **Orgs:** Pres, Int Mentoring Asn, 1988-89. **Honors/Awds:** WMU Award Invaluable Contribution Upward Bound Program, 1982; NAACP; Am Asn Univ Adminr; Nat Asn Female Exec; Nat Consortium for Black Prof Devel; Award Outstanding Contribution to Field of Educ, Delta Kappa Gamma , 1981; Creative Programming Award, Continuing Educ Asn, 1989; Outstanding Leadership and Committment, Martin Luther King Jr Program, 1989; Committment to Public Serv Award, Van Buren County Dept Social Serv, 1989; Distinguished Service Award, 1998, 1999. **Special Achievements:** Initiating the University's first merit scholarship program for undergraduate minority students. **Home Addr:** 27847 County Rd 653, Gobles, MI 49055. *

DANIEL, JACK L.
Educator, administrator. **Personal:** Born Jun 9, 1942, Johnstown, PA; married Jerlean Colley; children: Omari & Marijata. **Educ:** Univ Pittsburgh, BS, psychol, 1963, MA, commun, 1965, PhD, commun, 1968;Stanford Univ, Am Coun Educ Fel, post doctoral grad, 1974; Harvard Univ, Inst Educ Mgt, post doctoral grad, 1986. **Career:** Cent Mich Univ, asst prof, 1967-68; Univ Pittsburgh, chmn, assoc prof, 1969-73; Univ Pittsburgh, Col Arts & Sci, assoc dean, 1973-78, Undergrad Studies & Dean Students, assoc provost, 1987-92, vice provost acad affairs, 1992-, prof commun, 1999-, vice provost acad affairs & vice provost & interim dean stud affairs, 2001, vice provost undergrad studies & dean stud, 2002-05, vice provost undergrad studies, 2005. **Orgs:** Numerous memships and positions held in oraganizations including Speech Commun Asn; Int Commun Asn; Soc Intercultural Educ Training & Res; bd mem, Red Cross Educ Ctrs; adv comt mem, Investing Now, 1988-; Louise Child Care Ctr, 1991 & 1992; Fla Educ Fund's Coun Elders, 1995-; bd dirs, Hill House Asn, 1997-; secy, vpres & pres, Nat Commun Asn. **Honors/Awds:** Presidential Award, Nat Commun Asn, 1997; Marting Endowed Lect, Baldwin-Wallace Col, 1998. **Special Achievements:** Numerous speeches and publications including African American Child Rearing: The Context of a Hot Stove, 1999; "Mediation of Ebonics", Jour Black Studies, 2000; AWE Fish, 2000; Guest Editor, Special Issue of the Negro Educational Review, 2001; Guest Editor, Special Issue of the Howard Journal of Communication, 2002; We Fish: The Journey to Fatherhood with Omari C. Daniel, University of Pittsburgh Press, 2003. **Business Addr:** Professor, Vice Provost Academic Affairs, University of Pittsburgh, Undergraduate Studies & Dean Students, 801 Cathedral Learning, Pittsburgh, PA 15260, **Business Phone:** (412)624-4141.

DANIEL, JAMES L.
Consultant, executive. **Personal:** Born Nov 16, 1945, Brunswick, GA; married Brenda; children: James Jr & Tonya. **Educ:** Tuskegee Inst, 1964; Brunswick Col, AS BA, 1976. **Career:** Sears Roebuck & Co, div mgr, 1968-76; Brunswick City, city comnr, 1972-76; Stripe-A-Lot/Precision Pavement Marking & Maintenance Co, owner, 1986-; Southern Bell Tel, acct exec, 1978-80, serv consult, 1980-91, Bell South, sr acct exec, 1991-98, sales mgr, 1998-2000; KMC Telecom, sales mgr, 2000-01, city dir, 2001. **Orgs:** Pres & founder, Leaders Am Dem Soc, 1959; ex-officer, Brunswick Chamber Com, 1972-76. **Honors/Awds:** Frat Order Police 1973; Brunswick City Community Award, 1976; Outstanding Service Award, Christ Mem Baptist Church, 1982. **Military Serv:** USAF amn 1st cl 4 yrs; Expert Marksman Medal, Vietnam Serv Medal, Nat Defense Serv Medal, Pres, Unit Citation, Airforce Unit Commendation, 1964-68. **Home Addr:** 504 Picabo St, Woodstock, GA 30189. *

DANIEL, DR. JESSICA HENDERSON
Psychologist, college teacher, president (organization). **Personal:** Born Aug 2, 1944, San Antonio, TX; daughter of James E and Geraldine Thomas; children: Margaret. **Educ:** Fayetteville State Col, BS, 1964; Univ Ill Urbana, MS, 1967, PhD, 1969. **Career:** Univ Ill, asst prof educ psychiat, 1969-70; Univ Ore, asst prof dept special educ, 1970-72; Boston Col, ast prof educ psychiat, 1972-76; Harvard Med Sch, Postdoctoral Clin fel, 1974-76; Harvard Med Sch, instr psychiat, 1976-91, asst pro psychiat, Harvard Med Sch, 1991-; C's Hosp, res assoc/psychiat, 1972-; Judge Baker C's Ctr, psychologist, 1976-2002; Harvard med Sch, Cambridge, MA, teaching fel, 1989; C's Hosp, co-dir training psychol & assoc dir leadership educ, currently; Judge Baker C'sCtr, sr res assoc, currently; Harvard Univ, adj assoc prof psichiat; asst prof, currently; Boston Univ, Clin Psychol Prog, adj assoc prof psychol, currently. **Orgs:** Vice chmn, Bd Regist Psychologist, State Mass, 1984-89, chmn bd regist, 1989-93; mem bd, Brookline Arts Ctr, 1985-88; Tech Adv Comt Robert Wood Johnson Found, 1986-90; psychol consult Pub Schs Brookline, Cambridge, MA; Charles St AME Church; fel Am Psychol Asn, Mass Psychol Asn; Am Orthopsychiat Asn; cert, Am Bd Clin Psychol, 1999; Univ Ill, Am Psychol Asn, pres, Women's Div, Am Psychol Asn, 2001-02; leadeship coun, Girls Coalition of Greater Boston, 2009. **Honors/Awds:** Black Achiever Greater Boston YMCA, 1984; President's Award, Boston Chap Nat Asn Advan Colored People, 1986; Distinguished Alumni Citation of Yr, Nat Asn Equal Opportunity Higher Educ, 1986; Resource, Harvard Negotiation Proj, Harvard Law Sch, 1989; Woman of Courage & Conviction, Greater Boston Sec, Nat Coun Negro Women, 1995; The Ezra Saul Psychological Service Award, Mass Psychol Asn, 1993; A. Clifford Barger Excellence Mentoring Award, Harvard Med Sch, 1998; Karl F Heiser Presidential Award, Am Psychol Asn, 1999; Kenneth & Mamie Clark Award, Am Psychol Asn Grad Studs, 1999; Univ Ill, Distinguished Education Alumni Award, 2001; Am Psychol Asn, Distinguished Award, Education & Training, 2002; Professional Award, Nat Asn Negro Bus & Prof Women's CLub, Boston & Vicinity Sec, 2003; Charles & Shirley Thomas Mentoring Award, Soc Psychol Study Ethnic Minority Issues(APA), 2003. **Business Addr:** Assistant Professor Co-Director, Associate Director Leadership Education, Children, 300 Longwood Ave, Boston, MA 02115, **Business Phone:** (617)355-6734.

DANIEL, MARTHA (MARTHA V DANIEL)
President (Organization). **Educ:** Calif State Polytech Univ, BS, info systs; Univ La Verne, MBA. **Career:** Aerojet Gen; Bekins Transp; ARCO; IBM; FDIC; Info Mgt Resources Inc, founder, pres & chief exec officer, 1992-. **Orgs:** Bd dirs & founding mem, Women Philanthropy Orange County United Way; chairwoman, Sch Bus Adv Coun (BAC) Calif Polytech Univ; The Trusteeship (an affiliate InterNat Women Forum); Orange County NAWBO; Orange County NAACP. **Honors/Awds:** Numerous awards including, Woman in Business Award, Orange County Bus Jour, 1999; Business & Economic Empowerment Award, 100 Black Men of O.C. Organization, 2000; Nat Asn Women Bus Orange Co & Los Angeles Hall of Fame, 2001; SBA Small Minority Business of the Year, Living History Maker Entrepreneur, Wells Fargo & Turning Pt Mag, 2004. **Special Achievements:** Co-auth: On the Otherside of Midnight 2000, An Executive Guide to the Year 2000 Problem. **Military Serv:** USN. **Business Phone:** (949)852-5101.

DANIEL, MARTHA V. See DANIEL, MARTHA.

DANIEL, MARY REED
Artist. **Personal:** Born Jan 1, 1946?, East St Louis, IL; married William J Daniel Sr; children: William J Jr. **Career:** Black Dimen-

sions Contemp Am Art, publ & artist; Shows: Earl Graves Publ Co Black Enterprise Mag, Art Inst Sales & Rental Gallery, Milliken Rug Design Competition; Galerie Triangle; Lansburgh Ctr; Evans-Tibbs Collection; A Montgomery Ward Gallery; Tweed Mus; Paramaribo Suriname S Am. **Orgs:** Artist Guild Chicago; Artist League Midwest; S Side Community Art Ctr; Old Town Triangle Art Ctr Surface Design Asn; Chicago Artists Coalition. **Honors/Awds:** Listed in Afro-American Artists and Boston Public Library. *

DANIEL, SAMUEL J
Hospital administrator. **Personal:** Born Sep 13, 1950, Leeward Islands, West Indies. **Educ:** Columbia Univ, MD; Am Bd Internal Med & Gastroenterol, dipl, 1989. **Career:** N Gen Hosp, Internal Med Residency Prog, dir & chief Gastroenterol, 1994-99, med dir & dir med, 1998-2001, pres & chief exec officer, 2001-; Mt Sinai Sch Med, assoc clinical prof, currently. **Orgs:** Fel, Am Col Physicians, 1994; fel, Am Col Gastroenterol; Assocs Adv Coun, Am Col Physicians; bd dirs, Boy Scouts Am; bd dirs, Primary Care Develop Corp; bd dirs, League Vol Hosps & Homes; bd gov, Greater NY Hosp Asn; Prof Adv Comt New Horizons Scholars Prog; Selection Comt Lewis & Jack Rudin NY Mem Prize Med Sc; fel, NY Acad Med; bd trustees, Healthcare Asn NY; Heritage Affil Am Heart Asn Bd Trustees-New York Chap; chmn, Bd Dirs Community Health Alliance N Gen; Greater NY Regional Bd Dirs Nat Conf Community & Justice; adv bd, Upper Manhattan Physicians Against Cancer. **Honors/Awds:** The Best Doctors in New York, NY Mag, 2000; Nation's Best Physicians, Network Journal and Black Enterprise Mag, 2001; Leon Bogues Award, Black & Latino Legislative Caucus, 2002; Good Scout Award, Boys Scout Am, 2002. **Business Addr:** President, Chief Executive Officer, North General Hospital, 1879 Madison Ave, New York, NY 10035, **Business Phone:** (212)423-4111.*

DANIEL, SIMMIE CHILDREY
Educator. **Personal:** Born Feb 9, 1934, Shorter, AL; daughter of Luther J (deceased) and Ora M. **Educ:** Ala State Univ, BS, 1957; Ind Univ, MS, 1967; St Louis Univ, Univ Nev, spec stud. **Career:** Albany State Col, Albany Ga, exec sec, 1957-60; St Louis Pub Schs, St Louis Mo, bus teacher, 1963; El Reno Pub Schs, El Reno Okla, Eng teacher, 1963; Clark Co Sch Dist, Las Vegas Nev; Eldorado High Sch, teacher. **Orgs:** Nat Bus Educ Asn; Clark Co Classroom Teachers Asn; Nev State Educ Asn; Nat Vocational Educ Asn; Prof Col Women Asn; Nat Sorority Phi Delta Kappa Inc, 1973; Gamma Phi Delta Sorority, 1975. *

DANIEL, WENDY PALMER (WENDY PALMER)
Basketball player. **Personal:** Born Aug 12, 1974, Timberlake, NC; daughter of Melvin Palmer and Mary Palmer. **Educ:** Univ Va, attended 1996. **Career:** Oveido, Spain, 1996-97; Club DKSK, Hungary, 1997-98; Galatasaray, Turkey, 1998- 99; Utah Starzz, forward, 1997-99; Detroit Shock, 1999-02; Taranto, Italy, 2001-02; Orlando Miracle, forward, 2002; Connecticut Sun, 2003-04; San Antonio Silver Stars, forward, 2005; seattle storm, forward, 2006-07. **Orgs:** Zeta Phi Beta. **Honors/Awds:** Won Gold medal, 1992; ACC Player of the Year, 1995; Kodak All-Am, 1995, 1996; All-WNBA Second Team, 1997; WNBA Most Improved Player Award; 2004. **Business Addr:** Assistant Coach, University of Virginia, PO Box 400821, Charlottesville, VA 22904-4133, **Business Phone:** (434)982-5000.*

DANIEL, WILEY YOUNG
Lawyer. **Personal:** Born Sep 10, 1946, Louisville, KY; son of Lavinia and Wiley; married Ida Seymour; children: Jennifer, Stephanie & Nicole. **Educ:** Howard Univ, BA, 1968; Howard Univ Sch Law, JD, 1971. **Career:** Detroit law firm, Dickinson, atty; Wright McKean & Cudlip, atty, 1971-77; Detroit Col Law, adj prof, 1974-77; Gorsuch Kirgis Campbell Walker & Grover, atty, 1977-88; Univ Colo, Sch Law, adj fac, 1977-80, 2000-; Popham, Haik, Schnobrich & Kaufman, partner & share holder, 1988-95; US Dist Ct, Dist Colo, judge, 1995-. **Orgs:** Nat Bar Asn; Colo Bar Asn, pres-elect, 1991-92, pres, 1992-93; trustee, Denver Bar Asn, 1990-93; Managing Ed Howard LLJ; Delta Theta Phi Law Frat, Alpha Phi Alpha Socl Frat; Sigma Pi Phi Fraternity; Law J, 1970-71; adj facul, Univ Denver Col Law; bd chair, Iliff Sch Theol; Colo State Bd Agr, 1989-95; Am Inst Ct Found; Colo Trial Lawyers Asn. **Honors/Awds:** 1986 Disting Service Award, Sam Cary Bar Asn; Cs Legal Clinic Service Youth Award, 1995; Fel, Am Bar Found; Fel, Colo Bar Found; USA Speaker Aboard, Nigeria, 1995; Speaker Abroad, Russia, 1997; Distinguished Service Award, Kappa Alpha Psi Fraternity, Denver Alumni Chap, 1999. **Special Achievements:** first African Am, US Dist Ct, Dist Colorado. **Business Addr:** Judge, US District Court, DC, Alfred A Arraj US Courthouse 901 19th St Rm A1038, 1929 S tout St, Denver, CO 80294-3589, **Business Phone:** (303)844-2170.

DANIEL, DR. YVONNE
Anthropologist. **Personal:** Born Oct 20, 1940, New York, NY; daughter of Orville and Kibbie Payne; divorced; children: H Douglas III, Kent, Terrence & Todd. **Educ:** Howard Univ; Calif State Univ, Hayward, BA, music, 1972; Mills Col, MA, dance, 1975; Univ Calif, Berkeley, MA, PhD, social & cult anthrop, 1989. **Career:** Calif State Univ, Hayward, lectr, 1973; Mills Col, lectr, 1976-86; Col Alameda, lectr, 1975-77, actg chair, 1977-89; Five Col & Smith Col, asst prof, 1989-91; Five Colege, prof dance, 1991-2001; Mills Col & Women's Leadership Inst, vis prof, 1999-2000; Smith Col, prof Dance & Afro-Am Studies, 2001-04; prof emer Dance & Afro-Am Studies, 2004-. **Orgs:** Congress on Research Dance, 1975-92; Am Anthropologists Asn, 1984-97; fel, Ford Found, 1991-92; World African Diaspora Asn, 1999. **Honors/Awds:** Univ Mass, Amhurst, 2001; Smith Col Black Students Award, 2004. **Special Achievements:** Author, Rumba: Dance & Social Change in Comtemporary Cuba, Univ Ind Press, 1995; Dancing Wisdom: Embodied Knowledge in Haitian Vodou, Cuban Yoruba, and Bahian Candomble, Univ Ill Press; articles published in CORD Dance Research Jour, Black Scholar, & Annals of Tourism; performed with Nat Folklore Ensemble Cuba. **Business Addr:** Professor Emerita of Dance & Afro-American Studies, Smith College, 17 New S St, Northampton, MA 01063, **Business Phone:** (413)585-3870.

DANIELS, A. RAIFORD
Executive. **Personal:** Born Dec 13, 1944, Columbia, SC; son of Willie L and Alma Gordon. **Educ:** Lincoln Univ, BA, 1966; Columbia Univ NY, MBA, 1973; Columbia Univ, EdD, 1997. **Career:** Prudential Ins City Newark, mgt trainee group ins, 1966-67; Citibank, acct officer, Nat Bank Group, 1968-72; Corning Corp, NY, sr financial analyst, 1973-74; Bank Am, San Francisco, vpres, N America Div, 1974-78; Prudential Ins Co, vpres, Capital Markets Group, 1978-88; The Wilalm Group, managing prin & chief exec officer, currently; Bergen Community Col, prof, currently. **Orgs:** Columbia Club; Lincoln Univ Alumni; Minority Interchange NY; The Am Soc CLU & ChFC; Naval Reserve Asn; Nat Asn Advan Colored People; Young Men's Christian Asn; Nat Naval Officers Asn; Newark Chamber Com; Nat Asn Rev Appraisers. **Honors/Awds:** Calder Fel Calder Found NY, 1972; Licensed Cert Gen Real Estate Appraiser, real estate & ins broker; registered invest adv & gen securities rep; Cert Rev Appraiser, register mortgage underwriter & broker. **Military Serv:** USNR, Capt, 1966-. **Business Addr:** Managing Principal, Wilalm Group Ltd, 6 Bleeker St, PO Box 1098, Newark, NJ 07101, **Business Phone:** (201)622-8282.

DANIELS, ALFRED CLAUDE WYNDER
Educator. **Personal:** Born Mar 22, 1934, Philadelphia, PA; married Ginger; children: Carmen & David & Jerry. **Educ:** Ariz State Univ, BS, 1965; Harvard Law Sch, JD, 1975. **Career:** Harvard Law Sch, asst dean, 1975-; NE HH Aerospace Design Co Inc, vpres; pvt pract atty. **Orgs:** Nat Asn Black Mfr; pres, Black Corp Pres New Eng; Urban League; Nat AsnAdvan Colored People. **Military Serv:** USAF, maj, 1952-72.

DANIELS, ANTONIO ROBERT
Basketball player. **Personal:** Born Mar 19, 1975, Columbus, OH; married Sonia; children: Jada. **Educ:** Bowling Green State. **Career:** Vancouver Grizzlies, guard, 1997-98; San Antonio Spurs, 1999-2002; Portland Trail Blazers, 2002-03; Seattle Super Sonics, 2003-05; Wash Wizards, point guard, 2005-08; New Orleans Hornets, guard, currently. **Honors/Awds:** Player of the Year, Mid Am Conf; Freshman of the Year, Mid Am Conf, 1993-94. **Business Phone:** (504)593-4700.

DANIELS, C. MACKEY
Executive, baptist clergy. **Career:** Progressive Nat Baptist Conv Inc, pres; W Chestnut St Baptist Church, pastor, currently. **Business Addr:** Pastor, West Chestnut St Baptist Church, 1725 W Chestnut St, Louisville, KY 40203, **Business Phone:** (502)584-3664.*

DANIELS, CECIL TYRONE
Educator. **Personal:** Born Nov 23, 1941, Miami, FL; married Patricia Ann Robinson; children: Lee Ernest, Letitia Nicole & La Keitha Jonise. **Educ:** Fla A&M Univ, BA, 1964; Univ Northern Colo, MA, 1974. **Career:** Dade County Pub Sch Syst, prin, teacher, 1965-73, asst prin, 1974-76,human rels coordr, 1970; Myrtle Grove Elem Sch, prin, currently. **Orgs:** Natl Alliance Black Sch Educators; Dade County Schs Admin Asn; Dade County Guidance Asn; consult, Univ Northern Colo, 1975-76; Fla A&M Alumni Asn; Univ Northern Colo Alumni Asn; vpres, Lions Club Int, 1977; Phi Delta Kappa; Big Bros Inc; Jack & Jill Am Inc. **Honors/Awds:** Service Award, WJ Bryan Elem PTA, 1976; Service Award, Fulford Elem, PTA, 1977; Service Award, Cub Scouts, 1977; nom Admin of the Year, 1976-77; Certificate for runner-up, Admin of the Yr, 1977; Fulford Comm Award, 1976-77; Administrator of the Year, 1978; Ad Hoc Com Dade Co Sch Sys, 1980. **Military Serv:** Coll ROTC, 1960-64. **Business Addr:** Principal, Myrtle Grove Elementary School, 3125 NW 176th St, Opa Locka, FL 33056.*

DANIELS, CURTIS A.
Salesperson. **Personal:** Born Apr 1, 1941, Italy, TX; married Cynthia A Epps. **Educ:** Bishop Col, BA, 1973. **Career:** Ingham Co Hosp, asst physical therapist, 1961-62; Titche-Goettinger, buyer, 1961-62; Fox & Jacobs, sales rep; Bishop Col, lectr. **Orgs:** Fox & Jacobs' "Million Dollar Circle", 1975; Omega Psi Phi, Mu Gamma Chap. **Military Serv:** USAF; Outstanding Airman.

DANIELS, CYRUS W., II
President (Organization). **Career:** Visions USA Inc, pres & chief exec officer, 2003. *

DANIELS, DARRELL
Administrator, association executive. **Career:** Tampa-Hillsborough Urban League, cheif prog dir & acting chief exec officer, currently. **Orgs:** Greater Tampa Chamber Com Found; Ethiopian N Am Health Professionals Asn, currently. **Business Addr:** Interim President, Tampa Hillsborough Urban League, 1405 Tampa Pk Plz, Tampa, FL 33605, **Business Phone:** (813)229-8117.

DANIELS, DAVID HERBERT, JR.
Physician. **Personal:** Born Sep 1, 1941, Little Rock, AR; married Doris; children: David, Dorothy, Doreen, Danny, Dora. **Educ:** Philander Smith Col, BS, 1968; Univ Ariz Med Sch, MD, 1967; Los Angeles Col Med Ctr, attended 1968. **Career:** Cardiac Ctr Dir Cardiac Pulmonary Serv, physician cardiologist; Montclair & Chino Gen Hosp, physician. **Orgs:** Alpha Kappa Mu Nat Hon Soc, 1962; Beta Kappa Phi Nat Sch Hon Soc, 1962; dir, cardiac chmn, Cardiac Surg Comn Dr's Hosp; Am Col Cardiol; Am Col Physician; Am Col Cert Physicians; cert fel Am Col. **Military Serv:** USAF, major, 1968-74.

DANIELS, EARL HODGES
Journalist, writer. **Personal:** Born May 19, 1963, Tallahassee, FL; son of Earl and Betty. **Educ:** Fla A&M Univ, BS, sociol, 1987; Univ SC, Multicultural Newspaper Workshop, post grad study, 1989. **Career:** Ft Lauderdale Sun-Sentinel, news reporter, 1989-; Fla Times-Union, Jacksonville, staff writer & bus writer, currently. **Orgs:** Nat Asn Black Journalists, 1990-; Kappa Alpha Psi Fraternity, 1982-. **Business Phone:** (904)359-4689.

DANIELS, ELIZABETH
Dentist. **Personal:** Born Sep 23, 1938, Sebastian, FL; daughter of Levi and Addie Blackshear; married Jesse J Robinson; children: Jennifer. **Educ:** Tenn State Univ, BS, biochem, 1958; Howard Univ, MS, 1963; Univ Calif, PhD, 1968; Univ Conn, Sch Dental Med, DMD, 1977. **Career:** Lockheed Propulsion Co, proposal writer, 1963-64; Pfizer Inc, med chemist, 1968-73; Pvt Prac, 1978-; Meharry Med Col, Sch Dent, asst prof, 1977-85, asst dean academic affairs, 1985-88, dept Periodontics, assoc prof, 1988-89; pvt pract, dentist, 1990-. **Orgs:** Nat Dent Asn, 1978-; Am Asn Dent Schs, 1978-89; Golden Heritage mem, Nat Asn Advan Colored People; vice pres, Tenn State Univ Nat Alumni Asn, 1986-88; Howard Univ Alumni Asn; Church & Community Action; Portsmouth City Sch Bd, 1996-04; pres, Nat Asn Advan Colored People, Portsmouth Br, 1997-02; adv bd, Norfolk State Univ, Teacher Recruitment Project, 1998-; VSBA, Legis, Policies & Resolutions comn, 1999-00; bd dirs, Va Sch Bds Asn, 2001-04; Adv Comn Educ Gifted, Commonwealth Va, 2001-04; Nat Soc Dent Practitioners. **Honors/Awds:** NASA Fel, Univ Calif, 1964-68; American Men and Women of Science, 1969; Outstanding Young Women of America, 1970. **Special Achievements:** One of the first elected members of the Portsmouth City School Board in 1996; published an article, "The Effects of Environmental Pollutants on Enamel Hypoplasia and Dental Attrition", Hazard Waste Disposal Journal. **Business Addr:** Dentist, Private Practice, 4259 Greenwood Dr, Portsmouth, VA 23701, **Business Phone:** (757)488-4776.*

DANIELS, FREDERICK L, JR.
Banker, president (organization). **Personal:** Born Oct 9, 1965, Cleveland, OH; son of Gail M Daniels. **Educ:** Univ Va, BA, Econ & Eng, 1987. **Career:** First Nat Bank Atlanta, credit analyst, 1987-89; Wachovia Bank Ga, bus develop mgr, 1989-90, br mgr & banking officer, 1990-93; First Southern Bank, AVP & comm loan officer, 1993-; Citizens Trust Bank, vpres com lending, 1996-97; mgr, loan admin, 1997-2001; DeKalb Co, com lending div mgr, 2002-03, first vpres, sr loan officer, 2003-. **Orgs:** Kappa Alpha Psi, Greenforest Baptist Church, 1980-; South DeKalb Bus Asn, bd dir, 1996-97, vpres, 1998, pres, 1999-00; Partnership COT Action, bd dir, 1998-02; bd chmn, 2002-; DeKalb Med Ctr, Hillandale, bd dir, 2001-. **Honors/Awds:** Grad Leadership, DeKalb, 1999; Grad Leadership, Ga, 2003. **Home Addr:** 6121 Magnolia Ridge, Stone Mountain, GA 30087. **Business Addr:** Vice President, Senior Loan Officer, Citizens Trust Bank, PO Box 4485, Atlanta, GA 30302, **Business Phone:** (678)406-4000.

DANIELS, GERALDINE L.
Government official, politician. **Personal:** Born Sep 9, 1933, Harlem, NY; married Eugene Ray Daniels II (deceased); children: Eugene R III. **Educ:** City Univ NY Queens Col, BA, polit sci; Malcolm-King Harlem Col, AA. **Career:** NY State Legis, standing comn social serv, chair; steering comn, chair, currently; Dem Nat Conv NY, del; NY State Legis Caucus, chairwoman, assembly woman, currently. **Orgs:** Vpres, Inner City Broadcasting Corp; vchair, Harlem Urban Develop Corp; chair, NY Co Dem Comn; treas, Coun Black Elected Dem NYS; dist leader, Martin Luther King Jr Dem Club Cent Harlem; life mem, Nat Asn Advan Colored People; NY state assembly 70th Dist, 1981-92. **Honors/Awds:** Sojourner Truth Award, Negro Bus & Prof Women NY. **Special Achievements:** Raised monies for prev health care progs; Mid-Day-Live, NY City Cable TV. *

DANIELS, GREG
Vice president (organization). **Educ:** Albany State Univ, Ga, BS, maths. **Career:** Ford Motor Co, Wayne Assembly Plant, indust

engr; Nissan N Am Inc, dirprod qual assurance & mfg, vpres mfg & sr vpres US mfg, 1982-2008. **Orgs:** Rutherford County Chamber Com; exec comt, 100 Black Men Middle Tenn;alumnus, Leadership Rutherford County. **Honors/Awds:** Outstanding Young Tennessean, Tenn Jaycees, 1992. **Special Achievements:** First African American to hold the position of senior vice president at Nissan North America Inc.

DANIELS, DR. JEAN E.
Educator. **Personal:** Born in St Louis, MO; daughter of Chester and Maurine David; married James Harrison Bracy. **Educ:** Univ Kans, BA, 1964; Howard Univ, MSW, 1966; UCLA, MPH, 1973, DSW, 1976. **Career:** Neuro psychiatric Ins Univ Calif Los Angeles, psych social worker; various local consults; Found Ford Fellowship, 1975; Calif State Univ, Northridge, Dept Sociol, prof, 1987-; Tokiwa Univ, Japan Lectr 1991. **Orgs:** Am Lung Asn, 1976-93; chmn, Am Pub Health Asn, Social Work Sect, 1984; Nat prog comm Alpha Kappa Alpha Sor, 1982-86; prog dev bd joint policy comt, CA Coun Geriatrics & Gerontol; officer, Nat Women Achievement, Los Angeles Chap, 1987-89; bd mem, Am Lung Asn, 1976-93; bd mem, Am Heart Asn, WValley Region, 1995-96; Nat Asn Social Workers, currently. **Honors/Awds:** Honored Educr, Phi Delta Kappa LA, 1977; Los Angeles County Service Award, Am Lung Asn, 1980; CSUN Faculty Development Award, 1985; Inglewood Chapter Award, Top Ladies of Distinction, 1989; Research Grant, California StateUniv, Northridge 1989-90; Psychology of Aging Awardee, Nat Sci Found, 1992; First Int Conf Black Studies Lect, Accra Ghana, 1993; Phi Kappa Phi Honor Soc, 2000. **Special Achievements:** Niigata, Japan, lectr, International Welfare & Med Col, 1997. **Business Addr:** Professor, California State University, Department Sociology, 18111 Nordhoff St FOB 307, Northridge, CA 91330-8318.

DANIELS, JEROME ALVONNE
Football player. **Personal:** Born Sep 13, 1974, Hartford, CT. **Educ:** Northeastern Univ. **Career:** Ariz Cardinals, tackle, 1998-99; XFL NY/NJ Hitmen, 2000-01.

DANIELS, JESSE
Engineer. **Personal:** Born Oct 14, 1935, Montgomery, AL; son of David M and Prince C Borom; married Ella McCreary; children: Jessica, Kenneth, Eric, Adrienne, Diane & Carl. **Educ:** AL State Univ, BS, 1961; Graduate Credit, Auburn Univ, Emory Univ, Wake Forest Univ, Clemson Univ, GA Southern Col. **Career:** Engineer (retired); Ford Motor Co, design engr. **Orgs:** Eng Soc Detroit, 1963-78, 1978-83; Southeastern Mich Acapella Chorus, 1982-; Screen Actors Guild 1984-; Nat Asn Advan Colored People, 1985-; Kappa Alpha Psi Fraternity; Prince Hall Masons. **Honors/Awds:** Two Nat TV Com Ford Motor Co, 1984; Distinguished Alumnus, AL State Univ, 1986; Narrator, Ford Col Recruiting Video. **Home Addr:** 11360 Auburn St, Detroit, MI 48228. *

DANIELS, JOHN C.
College administrator. **Personal:** Born in Macon, GA; divorced; children: Leslie & John. **Educ:** Cheshire Acad, attended 1956; Villanova Univ, BA, econ, 1960; Nat Urban Fellow, Yale Univ, attended 1971; Occidental Col, MA, 1972. **Career:** Yale Univ, mgr Affirmative Action; West Haven High Sch, teacher 1961-65; EOC, dep dir 1965-67; NH Redevelopment Agy, proj dir, 1967-69; Quinnipiac Col, asst & pres Urban Affairs, 1969-70; Joint Ctr Polit Studies, spec asst, 1970-72; Enterprise Plumbing & Heating Inc, pres, 1987-. State Senate, CT, pres pro tem, 1987-90; City New Haven, CT, aldermen, mayor, 1990-94; deacon, Dixwell Congregational Church, New Haven, currently. **Orgs:** Trustee Hannah Gray Home; YMCA; Dixwell Comn House; Urban League; Family Planning; Nat Asn Advan Colored People; Highland Hts; Prince Hall Masons; Alpha Phi Alpha; assoc fel Trumbull Col; Sigma Fraternity; 33 degree Mason, Prince Hall Masons; Elks Club. **Honors/Awds:** Outstanding Citizens Award 1969; Honorary Degree, Univ New Haven Law,1992; John C. Daniels Elem Sch, named in honor, 2006. **Special Achievements:** NCAA Col Football Official, Big E Conf, 1986; The first African American mayor of New Haven, CT. **Business Addr:** 801 State St, New Haven, CT 06511.*

DANIELS, JOHN W
Lawyer, chairperson. **Personal:** Born Jun 11, 1948, Birmingham, AL; son of John and Kathryn; married Irma, Jun 10, 1972; children: John W III & Inez D. **Educ:** N Cent Col, BA, 1969; Univ Wis, MS, 1972; Harvard Law Sch, JD, 1974. **Career:** Quarles & Brady LLP, assoc, 1974-81, partner, 1981-, chmn, currently; V&J Foods, chmn, dir, currently; Metro Milwaukee Chamber Com, dir, 1990-; N Milwaukee Bancshares, vchmn, 1992-98, chmn; Marshall & Ilsley Corp, dir, currently; Ralph Evinrude Found, dir; Greater Milwaukee Found, dir; Med Col Wis, dir emer; Milwaukee Symphony Orchestra, dir; Boys & Girls Clubs Milwaukee, dir. **Orgs:** Bd Holy Redeemer Christian Acad, 1988-; nat vpres law students div, Am Bar Asn, 1973-74, mem nat coun, 1990-; Med Col Wis, 1991-, secy, 1995-; Am Col Real Estate Lawyers, 1994-96, nat treas, 1996-97, nat vpres, 1997-98, nat pres-elect, 1998-99, nat pres, 1999-2000; trustee, Evinrude Found, 1995-; N Cent Col, 2000-; founder & chair, fel, Golf Open, 2001-; Anglo-Am Real Property Inst, 2002-; Am Col Mortgage Atty, 2002-; Am Col Real Estate Lawyers; State Bar Wis; Milwaukee Bar Asn; pres, Milwaukee Young Lawyers Asn, 1981-82. **Honors/Awds:** Mr Executive USA & Canada, 1965-66; Nat Sci Found fel, 1969; Ford Found fel, 1970-71; Outstanding Young Attny, Milwaukee Jaycees, 1983; Outstanding Alumnus Award, N Cent Col, 1994; Human Relations Award, Nat Conf Christians & Jews, 2001; Award, Wis Asn Aro Lawyers, 2002. **Special Achievements:** Listed in The Best Lawyers in America; Listed in Chambers USA, 2003-; Named Wisconsin Super Lawyer, 2005-; Martindale-Hubbell AV Peer Review Rated. **Business Addr:** Partner, Quarles & Brady LLP, 411 E Wisconsin Ave Suite 2040, Milwaukee, WI 53202-4497, **Business Phone:** (414)277-5103.

DANIELS, JOSEPH
Health services administrator. **Personal:** Born Mar 18, 1931, Linden, NJ; married; children: Joan, Jean. **Educ:** Lincoln Univ PA, BA, 1953; Howard Univ Col Med, MD, 1957. **Career:** NJ Psychiatric Hospital Ancora, attending psych, 1965-66; Salem Out-Patient Clin, Salem NJ, dir, 1966-67; Mental Health Ctr, Wycksoff WI, dir, 1967-70; In-patient Unit, Mt Carmel Guild, dir, 1970-71; NJ Col of Med, chief out-patient, 1971-77; Ctr Growth & Reconciliation Inc, med dir. **Orgs:** Med Ctr Jersey City, internship, 1957-58; Worcester City Hosp MA, 1958-59; Ancora Psychol Hosp, 1962-65; Youth Develop Inc, 1968-73; Northside Addict Rehab Ctr, 1969-71; Victory HSE Inc, 1970-77; NJ Col Med, clin asso prof psych,1970-81; E Orange Bd Educr, consult, 1970-75; Nyack Col, Nyack, NY, bd trustees, 1973-82; Newark Bd Educr, 1977-85; Ministry Reconciliation Inc, pres bd chmn, 1981-85. **Honors/Awds:** Beta Kappa Chi; Nat Sci Hon Soc, 1953; Am Col Student Leaders, 1953; Outsatnding Young Men of America, 1967; Psychodynamics & Psychopathlogy of Racism Publ, 1969. **Military Serv:** AUS, Med Corp, cap, 1959-62. **Business Addr:** Medical Director, Ctr Growth & Reconciliation Inc, 498 William St, East Orange, NJ 07019.

DANIELS, KYSA
Journalist, public speaker. **Personal:** Born Sep 6, 1966, Houston, TX; daughter of Gregory and Judy Hunter; married Derwin Daniels, Aug 30, 1997; children: Ryan Gregory & Nicholas Adam. **Educ:** Tex A & M Univ, BA, jour, 1989; Eastern NMex Univ, MA, mass commun, 1990. **Career:** Houston Defender, reporter, 1990-92; KHOU-AM, news announcer, 1992; KBMT-TV, anchor & reporter, 1992-96; KSLA-TV anchor, 1996-99; CNN, overnight anchor, 2000-01; Clarion Commun, freelance speaker, writer, founder & pres, 2002-; Ga Perimeter Col, adj prof mass media, coordr mkg & pub rels. **Orgs:** Delta Sigma Theta Sorority Inc, 1987-92; Big Brother/ Sister, 1990-92; SE Tex Asn Black Journalists, 1993-96; Nat Asn Black Journalists, 1999-2000; Parent/Teacher Asn, 1999-; sponser, Women Women Int, 2000-; parish vpres, St Vincent de Paul Soc, 2002-; adv, Conyers-Rockdale Coun Arts, 2002-; Toastmasters Int, 2002-. **Honors/Awds:** Presidential Academic Scholar, Tex A & M Univ, 1985-89; Outstanding Mass Comm Grad, Eastern NMex Univ, 1990; Outstanding Young Professional, Spotlight Mag, 1995; Outstanding Journalist, Univ Memphis, 2001. **Special Achievements:** Author of Substance and Spirit (motivational book), 2002, guest columnist, Faith & Values section Atlanta Journal Const, 2002, moderator, Live Satellite Telecast at Centers for Disease Control, 2002, author, Then and Now Black Heritage Retrospect/ perfroming arts, 2002, has been featured in various national publications. **Business Addr:** President, Founder, Clarion Communications, PO Box 1795, Conyers, GA 30012, **Business Phone:** (770)761-3955.

DANIELS, LEE LOUIS
Movie producer. **Personal:** Born Dec 24, 1959, Philadelphia, PA; son of William and Clara Watson; children: Clara Infinity & Liam Samad. **Educ:** Lindenwood Col. **Career:** Nursing agency worker, 1978-79; nursing agency mgr & owner, 1980; casting asst & talent mgr, 1981-; Lion's Gate Films, co-pres; film producer, 2000; Films: A Little Off Mark, 1986; The Woodsman, producer, 2004; Shadowboxer, producer & dir, 2005; Lee Daniels Entertainment, pres, dir, producer & chief exec officer, currently. **Honors/Awds:** Best Picture, Berlin Film Festival, 2002; Golden Globe nominee for Best Picture, 2002; Black Oscar, 2002; Best Picture, Nat Bd Review, 2002. **Special Achievements:** Producer: Monster's Ball, 2001; The Woodsman, 2004. **Business Addr:** Director, Chief Executive Officer, Lee Daniels Entertainment, 39 W 131st St Suite 2, New York, NY 10037, **Business Phone:** (646)548-0930.

DANIELS, LEGREE SYLVIA
Government official. **Personal:** Born Feb 29, 1920, Barnwell, SC; married Oscar Daniels; children: two stepdaughters. **Educ:** Temple Univ & Cent Pa Bus Sch. **Career:** Hugh Scott, former Senate Minority Leader, Staff asst,; Pa State Tax Equalization Bd, Harrisburg, PA, chmn, 1979-85; Pa Bureau Elections, Harrisburg, Pa, comnr, 1985-86; Pa Dept State, Harrisburg, PA, dep secy common wealth, 1986-87; US Dept Educ, Wash, DC, asst secy civil rights, 1987-89; Republican Nat Comt Exec comt; US Postal Serv, Gov, 1990, 1999-. **Orgs:** Former chmn, Nat Black Republican Coun; chmn, Black Voters Reagan & Bush; secy, Republican State Comt, Pa; dir, Pa Coun Republican Women; bd mem, Nat Endowment Democracy; US Army Sci Bd; mem adv bd, US Comn Civil Rights; Joint Cent Political Studies; bd mem, Young Women's Christian Asn; Pa Martin Luther King Comn; past matron, Order Eastern Star; Baptist Missionary Soc; bd dir, Cent Int Enterprise & the Heinz Cent. **Business Addr:** Governor, United States Postal Service, 475 Lenfant Plz SW, Washington, DC 20024, **Business Phone:** 877-275-8777.*

DANIELS, LEMUEL LEE
Administrator, executive, vice president (organization). **Personal:** Born Dec 28, 1945, Montgomery, AL; son of Frank Hudson and Martha Daniels Johnson; children: Quintin Daniels. **Educ:** Univ Illinois, Chicago Circle, Ill, 1963-64; Southeast Col, Chicago, Ill, 1965-67; Southern Ill Univ, Carbondale, Ill, BS, commun, 1971. **Career:** Merrill Lynch,Los Angeles, Calif, regist rep, 1976-78; A G Becker, Los Angeles, Calif, asst vpres, 1978-84; Drexel Burnham, Los Angeles, Calif, vpres, 1984-85; Bear, Stearns & Co, Los Angeles, Calif, assoc dir, 1985-94; Merrill Lynch, first vpres invest, 1994-99; Solomon Smith Barney, first vpres invest, 1999-, treas, currently. **Orgs:** Treas, bd dir, Los Angeles Arts Coun, 1989-; vice chair, Nat Asn Securities Prof, Task Force Rebuild Los Angeles; trustee, exec comt, Cross Roads Arts Acad, 1990-; bd mem, WEB DuBois Sch, 1982-84; chancellor assoc, Univ Calif, La, 1978-80; sect, bd dir, Cottege Bound; bd dir, Greater Los Angeles African Am Chamber Com, 2005-06. **Honors/Awds:** Full Scholar, Southern Ill Univ, 1967; Certificate of Apppreciation, Merrill Lynch, 1976; Broker of the Year, Bear, Stearns & Co Inc, Spec Invest Group, 1985; BET Holdings pub, first African-Am co listed NYSE, 1991. **Special Achievements:** One of two minorities chosen to represent Merrill Lunch in their first Affirmative Action recruitment program, 1975-76. **Military Serv:** AUS, E-5, 1967-69; Platoon Leader, Outstanding Platoon, 1967. **Business Addr:** Director, The Greater Los Angeles African American Chamber of Commerce, 5100 W Goldleaf Circle Suite 203, Los Angeles, CA 90056, **Business Phone:** (323)292-1297.*

DANIELS, LESHUN DARNELL
Football player. **Personal:** Born May 30, 1974, Warren, OH; married Alicia; children: LeShun Jr. **Educ:** Ohio State Univ. **Career:** Minn Vikings, guard, 1997; Jacksonville Jaguars, guard, 2001. *

DANIELS, LINCOLN, SR.
School administrator. **Personal:** Born Feb 17, 1932, Hickman, KY; son of James (deceased) and Viola (deceased); married Robbie L Davis; children: Karen Lee Trice, Lincoln Jr (deceased) & Terence Leon. **Educ:** Philander Smith Col, BA, 1953; Wash Univ, MA, 1969. **Career:** School administrator (retired); St Louis Bd of Educ, elem teacher, 1964-69, res statistician, 1973-75, Div Evaluation, div asst, 1975-80; St Louis Co Social Studies Implementation Proj, master teacher, 1966-69; resasst, St Louis Metro Soc Studies Ctr Wash Univ, 1966-69; Wash Univ, clin assoc, 1967-70, master teacher summer, 1970, supvr elem educ, 1970-73, coordr elem educ summer, 1971; Washington Univ, res adv sum, 1970; StLouis Bd Educ, admin asst, 1980-84, instrnl coordr, 1984-87, elementary principal, 1987-97. **Orgs:** Phi Delta Kappa Ed Leadership Soc; Philander Smith Col Alumni Chap, 1966-68; Community Black Recruitment; Kappa Delta Pi Educ Honor Soc, 1969; pres, 1970-71, historian-reporter, 1971-72, Kappa Delta Pi St Louis; secy, St Louis Philander Smith Col Alumni Chapter, 1970-74; Worshipful Master, Caution Lodge No 23, Prince Hall Masons, 1976; treas, St Louis City Coun, Int Reading Asn, 1976-78; chmn, Block Unit No 375; Nat Urban League Confederation Block Units, 1976-; vpres, Midwest Region Philander Smith Col Nat Alumni Asn, 1977-79; pres-elect, 1978-79, pres, 1980, St Louis City Coun, Int Reading Asn; past pres, Metro-St Louis Philander Smith Col Alumni Chapter; pres, St Louis City Coun, 1979-80; vpres, Congregations Allied Community Improv, 1998-00; bd mem, Metrop Congregations United St.Louis, 1995-. **Honors/Awds:** Service Award, Omega Psi Phi Fraternity, 1968; Community Leaders & Noteworthy Am, 1977; Distinguished Alumnus Award, Philander Smith Col, 1980; Distinguished Service Award, Iota Phi Lambda Sorority Inc, Alpha Zeta Chapter, 1990; Omicron Omega Chapter, Salute to Black Men for Excellence in Education Award, 1991; Meritorious Service Award, UNF, 1985; Hickey Elementary School Exemplary Service Award, 1997; AFSA Award for Outstanding Service to the St Louis Public School & St Louis Community, 1997. **Military Serv:** AUS, para trooper para-medic, 1953-55. **Home Addr:** 4640 Natural Bridge Ave, Saint Louis, MO 63115. *

DANIELS, LLOYD (LLOYD "SWEET PEA" DANIELS)
Basketball player. **Personal:** Born Sep 4, 1967, Brooklyn, NY. **Educ:** Univ Nevada, Las Vegas. **Career:** Basketball player (retired); San Antonio Spurs, guard, 1992-93; Philadelphia 76ers, 1994; Los Angeles Lakers, 1994; Sacramento Kings, 1996; New Jersey Nets, 1996, 1997; Toronto Raptors, 1997.

DANIELS, LLOYD "SWEET PEA". See DANIELS, LLOYD.

DANIELS, MELVIN J.
Basketball player, basketball coach, basketball executive. **Personal:** Born Jul 20, 1944, North Carolina; son of Maceo and Bernice Clemmons; married Cecilia J Martinez. **Educ:** Burlington Jr Col; Univ NM. **Career:** Basketball player (retired), basketball coach; Univ NMex Lobo, player,1964-67; Minn Muskies, forward, 1967-68; Am Basketball Asn, 1967-75; Ind Pacers, ctr, 1968-74, dir player personnel; Memphis Sounds, ctr, 1974-75; NY

Nets, ctr, 1976; Ind State, asst basketball coach, 1978-80, asst coach/scout, 1983. **Orgs:** Am Quarter Horse Farm Circle M Ranch; Am Preview; Dash Cash bred stock Operating, 1972. **Honors/Awds:** Rookie of the Year, Am Basketball Asn, 1967-68; Most Valuable Player, Am Basketball Asn, 1969 & 1971; Naismith Memorial Basketball Hall of Fame. **Home Addr:** 19789 Centennial Rd, Sheridan, IN 46069, **Home Phone:** (317)896-5380. *

DANIELS, PATRICIA ANN
Government official, founder (originator). **Personal:** Born Aug 6, 1940, Kaufman, TX; daughter of James Hiawatha Alexander and Mary Elizabeth Burnett Alexander; married Valjean Daniels, Dec 2, 1964; children: Barry M Alexander & Brette M. **Educ:** Los Angeles Jr Col Bus, Los Angeles CA, AA, 1964; Univ San Francisco, San Francisco CA, BS, 1979. **Career:** City Berkeley, Berkeley, CA, supvr, housing codes, 1968-80, supvr, parking collections, 1981-89, personnel-labor relations trainee, 1989-92, asst bldg & housing inspector; Icanmindyourownbusiness.com, founder & chief exec officer. **Orgs:** Nat regional dir, first vpres, Far Western Region, Nat, 1989-; Gamma Phi Delta Sorority, Vol Serv, 1971-, pres, currently; charter mem, Beta Sigma Chap, 1990-91, Sup First Anti-Basileus, 1992; Calif Fedn Bus & Prof Women, Bay Valley Dist, 1983-, pres, 1990-91; mem, pres-elect, Diversity Task Force, Bay Valley Dist, 1983-; mem, bd dirs, Nat Forum Black Pub Admin, 1985-; charter mem, Nat Coun Negro Women, Alameda County Sect; mem, bd dirs, Local Black Women Organized Polit Action; mem, Women's Missionary Union, prog dir, N Richmond Missionary Baptist Church; vpres, Housing Adv Comn Personnel Bd, City San Pablo; Gamma Phi Delta. **Honors/Awds:** Rose Pin Award, Gamma Phi Delta Sorority, Nat, 1976; Woman of the Year, Far Western Region, Gamma Phi Delta Sorority, 1979; Dedicated Serv, Beta Sigma, 1986; Woman of the Year, Outstanding Community Serv, Nat Forum Black Public Admin, 1987; Local Woman of the Year, District Woman of the Year, Woman of Achievement, California Fedn of Business & Professional Women, 1988; Marks of Excellence, North Richmond Church, 1989. **Special Achievements:** author of two leadership manuals, Gamma Phi Delta Sorority. **Home Addr:** 1810 Hillcrest Rd, San Pablo, CA 94806.

DANIELS, PETER F.
Educator. **Personal:** Born Dec 5, 1928, Pine Bluff, AR; married Ruby; children: Peter Jr, Ronson, Darryl & Connie. **Educ:** Ark A&M Col, BS, 1951; Ind Univ, MSE, 1965. **Career:** Joiner Ark, teacher, 1951; Sherrill Jr High Sch, instr biol; Vaster High Sch, instr biol & sci, 1953-56; prin, 1956-69; Linwood Sch Dist, supt,1969. **Orgs:** Nat Educ Asn; Ark Educ Asn; Jefferson Co Educ Asn; Nat Alliance Black Sch Educr; Ark Admin Asn; Ark Sch Bus Officials; Ark Adv Bd, ESAA & Title; adv bd, Ark Tech Ast Ctr; Jefferson Co Comprehensive Health Bd; Black Adoption Coun; Nat Asn Advan Colored People; Kappa Alpha Psi Frat; deacon,bd mem, St Paul Missionary Bapt Ch. **Home Addr:** 1120 E 34th Ave, Pine Bluff, AR 71601, **Home Phone:** (870)534-7662. *

DANIELS, PHILLIP BERNARD
Football player. **Personal:** Born Mar 4, 1973, Donalsonville, GA. **Educ:** Univ Ga, social work. **Career:** Seattle Seahawks, defensive end, 1996-99; Chicago Bears, 2000-03; Wash Redskins, defensive end, 2004-07. **Orgs:** Phi Beta Sigma Fraternity. **Business Phone:** (703)478-8900.*

DANIELS, PRESTON
Mayor. **Personal:** Married Patty. **Career:** Mayor Des Moines, IA, 1997-04; Ct & Community Rels Employee & Family Resources, dir, currently. **Orgs:** Univ Iowa Adv Bd Addiction Technol; State Iowa Training Adv Bd Substance Abuse; League Cities; Iowa Democratic Party; Metro Solid Waste Agency Bd; Drake Neighborhood Asn; Nat Conf Black Mayors; Nat Conf Mayors. **Honors/Awds:** Professional Achievement Award, Grandview Col. **Special Achievements:** First African American mayor of Des Moines, IA. *

DANIELS, RANDY
Government official, educator. **Educ:** Southern Ill Univ, BS. **Career:** WVON radio, reporter; CBS News, Africa bur chief, 1977; Jacaranda Nigeria Ltd, managing dir; City Col New York, adj prof jour; Columbia Univ's Grad Sch Jour, adj prof jour; New York City Coun, Pres's Off, dir communications, 1986-88; Bahamas, secy to prime minister, 1988; NY State govt, Empire state develop corp, sr vpres; dep comnr Econ Revitalization, 1995; Canyon Johnson Urban Fund, sr vpres, 1999-01; New York Secy of State, 2001-05; bd trustees, State Univ New York, vice chmn, currently. **Orgs:** Co-chair, Comn on Gen Educ & Charter Sch; Exec & Finance Comt, State Univ of New York; Gov Patakiocos Weapons of Mass Destruction Task Force; chair, S Shore Estuary Res Coun; Nat Asn Secretaries State. **Special Achievements:** Named Harlem Hero, New York daily news; one of the leading educ reformers, NY State; Qual Communities Clearinghouse website created under his leadership. *

DANIELS, REBECCA HAYWOOD
Educator. **Personal:** Born Oct 10, 1943, Columbus County, NC; married George; children: Geraldine Renee & Starlin Wynette. **Educ:** Fayetteville State Univ, BS, 1966. **Career:** Richard B Harrison, teacher, 1966-67; S Lumberton Elem, teacher, 1967-69; Acme-Delco Jr Sr High Sch, teacher, 1970-; Coun woman, 1975-77; pro-term, mayor; town clerk, 1974. **Orgs:** NC Asn Classroom Teachers; Bicentennial Community; NC Exten Homemakers Asn; Nat Educ Asn; Nat Cath Educ Asn; PACE; Green Chapel Missionary Baptist Church; Veterans Foreign Wars Aux Post 9003. *

DANIELS, RICHARD BERNARD (DICK DANIELS)
Football player, scout. **Personal:** Born Oct 19, 1944, Portland, OR; married Gloria; children: Sunde & Whitney. **Educ:** Pac Univ. **Career:** Football player (retired), scout; Dallas Cowboys, defensive back, 1966-68; Chicago Bears, 1969-70; Miami Dolphins, 1971, scout, 1972-75; Tampa Bay Buccaneers, head scout, 1975; San Francisco 49ers, scout, 1976-77; Wash Redskins, dir player personnel, 1978-84, 1985-89; USFL, Los Angeles Express, vpres player personnel, 1984; San Diego Chargers, asst gen mgr, 1990-96; Philadelphia Eagles, dir, football oper, 1996; St Louis Rams, col scout, 2000-09.

DANIELS, RICHARD D.
Clergy. **Personal:** Born Jan 27, 1931, Micanopy, FL; married Doris B Bagley. **Educ:** Fl Agr & Mech Univ, BS, 1958. **Career:** St Luke AME, Gainesville, pastor, 1958-59; Silver Springs, 1959-64; St Stephens AME, Leesburg, FL, 1964-71; Mt Zion AME, Ocala, 1971-72. **Orgs:** Deleg, Gen Conf AME Church, 1972; NAACP; Masonic Lodge; Blood Bank Asn, Alachua Co; presiding elder, AME Church, 1973-. **Military Serv:** AUS, Korean Conflict, 1951-53. *

DANIELS, RON D.
Association executive. **Personal:** Children: Malik, Sundiata, Jeannette. **Educ:** Youngstown State, BA, 1965; Rockefeller Sch Pub Affairs, MA, 1967; Union Inst, Pol Sci, 1976. **Career:** Asn Neighborhd Ctr, Hagstrom House, S Side Ctr, Camp Lexington, boys' prog dir, youth & young adult worker, camp counselor, camp prog dir, 1961-64; Youngstown State Univ, educr, 1967-69; Freedom Inc, founder & chmn, 1967-75, exec dir, 1969-74; Perspectives Black, moderator & producer; WYTV, Youngstown OH, Ron Daniels Show, 1968-87; Kent State Univ, educr, ast prof, African American Affairs & Pan-American studies, 1971, & 1981-86; Cornell Univ, educr, visiting prof, 1979-80; Hiram Col, OH, educr 1973, asst prof Pol Sci & Pan-African Studies, 1974-77; Nat Rainbow Coalition, exec dir, 1987; Jesse Jackson Pres Campaign, Southern Regional mgr, 1988; Col Wooster, educr, visiting assoc prof, black studies, 1993; Inst Community Orgn & Develop, Youngstown, OH, exec dir; Ctr Constitutional Rights, exec dir; syndicated columnist; Black media Project Progressive Magazine, editorial opinion writer; Black Collegion & Z Magazine, contributor; American Urban Radio Network, Guest Host, Night Talk. **Orgs:** African Liberation Day Coord Com, 1972; convener OH delegation Nat Black Polit Conv, Gary, IN, 1972; adjunct prof & mem bd dir, OH Inst Practical Pol, 1973; pres, OH Black Pol Assembly; elected pres, Nat Black Pol Assembly, 1974; Pres, Nat Black Political Assembly, 1974-80; Nat co-chmn, Nat Black Independent Political Party, 1981-83; candidate, Mayor, 1977; chmn, 1983-85; exec, Cong African People; founding training & proj eval consult, Episcopal Ch Gen Conv Spec Prog; coordr, Mid-West Regional Coalition; Coun Elders, Fed Pan-African Educ Inst; elder Marcus Garvey Sch; del No, Am Reg Steering Conf, 6th Pan-Africa Conf; Help Us Make A Natio Training Inst; Nat Econ Develop & Law Ctr; bd dirs, Nat Jobs Peace Campaign; bd dirs, Greenpeace USA; bd dirs, Nation Inst; co-chmn, Nat Malcolm X Commemoration Comn; bd dirs, African American Inst Res Empowerment; Nat Chmn, campaign new tomorrow; independent candidate Pres US, 1992; coordinator, NH State Race Conf, 1994; steering comt, Nat African American Ldshop summitt, 1994-96; exec coun, Nat Org comt, The Millian March & Day Action, 1995; founder, the Haiti Support Project, 1995. **Honors/Awds:** Youngstown Black Polit Assembly-Freedom Inc Award 1974; Minority Affairs Dir's Award 1974; Model Cities Citizen Participation Orgn Award 1974; Omega Psi Phi community service award, 1979; McGuffey Center community service award, 1982; African Cultural Weekend Award for dedicated leadership, 1985; Inter-Faith Community Action Committee Award, 1986; Inter-DenominationalClergywomen's Alliance civic award, 1986; First Williams Publishing Co Pioneer Award for outstanding contributions to civil rights in the media, 1988. *

DANIELS, TERRY L
Manager. **Personal:** Born Jul 28, 1951, Shreveport, LA; son of Louis (deceased) and Annie (deceased); married Joyce E Hall, Aug 24, 1972; children: Shemetra Rachel & Nikki Renee. **Educ:** Southern Univ, A&M Col, BS, indust technol, 1973; Webster Col, MA, mgt, 1977. **Career:** General Electric Co, mgr, 1973-88; Eastman Kodak, mgr, mfg, 1988-91, mgr, site mgt, 1991-94; AT&T (GBCS), gen mgr, vpres, 1994-. **Orgs:** Network Northstar Inc, 1991-; Int Facilities Mgt Asn, 1992-; bd, chair, Nat Maintenance Excellence Award, 1992; Alliance Black Telecommunications Workers; Southern Univ Alumni Asn; chair, Boy Scouts Am, West Sect (explorers) Oteciana Coun. **Honors/Awds:** Youth Service Award, Black Achievers, 1984; Peak Award, Nat Maintenance Excellence Award, 1992. **Special Achievements:** Author, Maintenance Technology Magazine, p 24, Jan 1992; Plant Eng Magazine, p 72, September 1992. **Business Addr:** General Manager, Vice President, Denport Mfg-GBCS AT&T, 1200 W 120th Ave, Westminster, CO 80030, **Business Phone:** (303)538-2000.*

DANIELS, WILLIAM JAMES
School administrator. **Personal:** Born Mar 7, 1940, Chicago, IL; son of William Hector McCoy and Ethel Cora Dent; married Fannie Pearl Hudson, Aug 25, 1963; children: Twanda Delois. **Educ:** Upper Iowa Univ, Fayette, IA, BA, 1962; Univ Iowa, MA, 1964, PhD, 1970. **Career:** Woodrow Wilson fel, 1962-63; Union Col, Schenectady, NY, asst prof, 1966-72, assoc prof, 1973-81, prof, 1982-88, assoc dean, 1983-88; Alfred E Smith fel, 1970-71; Fulbright-Hayes fel, Japan, 1973-74; US Supreme Ct, judicial fel, 1978-79; Rochester Inst Technol, Col Liberal Arts, dean, 1988-98, prof polit sci, 1998, emer dean & prof, currently. **Orgs:** Pres, Nat Conf Black Polit Scientists, 1972-73; vpres, Am Polit Sci Asn, 1990-91; Asn Am Col; Am Asn Higher Educ; Nat Urban League Rochester. **Honors/Awds:** George M Pullman Scholarship, 1958-62; Distinguished Service Award, Nat Conf Black Polit Scientists, 1972-73; Liberty Bell Award, Schenectady Co Bar Asn, 1988. **Business Addr:** Emeritus Professor, Dean, Rochester Institute of Technology, College of Liberal Arts, 1 Lomb Mem Dr, PO Box 9887, Rochester, NY 14623-5603, **Business Phone:** (585)475-2938.

DANIELS, WILLIE L
Stockbroker, chief executive officer, founder (originator). **Career:** Bache Securities Inc, stockbroker; United Daniels Securities Inc, chief exec officer & founder, 1984-.

DANIELS-CARTER, VALERIE
President (Organization). **Personal:** Son of John and Katherine. **Educ:** Lincoln Univ, BA, 1978; Cardinal Stritch Col, Milwaukee, MBA, 1982. **Career:** Wis Nat Bank, retail & com lender, 1978; MGIC Invest Corp, auditor, 1981; Pizza Hut restaurants, 1997; V&J Holding Co Inc, pres & ceo, currently; Minority Franchise Assn Burger King Corp, pres, currently. **Orgs:** Star Bank; exec bd mem, Nat Franchisee Asn; Diversity Action Council, Burger King corp; regional minister music, Church God Christ; U.S. Bank; AAA Michigan & Wisconsin Inc; Holy Redeemer Church God Christ; chief financial officer, Auxiliaries Ministries Church God Christ. **Honors/Awds:** Outstanding Bus Leader Award, Nwood Univ; Women of Influence Award, Bus Journal; Peak Performer Award, Jr Achievement; Trailblazer Award, N Milwaukee State Bank; Entrepreneurial Spirit Award; the Heritage Award, Spiritual Perspective; Bus Award, the Nat Rainbow Coalition; Entrepreneur of the Yr, Ernst&Young & Merrill Lynch, 1994; the Sacajawea Award, 1997. **Business Addr:** President, Chief Executive officer, V & J Holding Companies Incorporation, 6933 W Brown Deer Rd, Milwaukee, WI 53226, **Business Phone:** (414)365-9003.*

DANSBY, JESSE L.
College teacher, educator. **Personal:** Born Aug 17, 1942, Bessemer, AL; son of Rev Jesse L Sr and Ora L Martin; divorced; children: Natasha Lynn & Mischa Anita. **Educ:** Tenn State Univ, BS, 1964; Univ Okla, Yale Univ, Cert, Human Resource Mgt, 1973; Univ Okla, MA, 1973; Indust Col Armed Forces, Mgt Cert, 1975; Air Command & Staff Col, Mgt Cert, 1977; Air Force Inst Tech Int Logistics, Mgt Cert, 1977. **Career:** Educator, Col Administrator (retired); Int Logistics Ctr, dir, Mid E & African prog, 1979-80; Defense Electronic Supply Ctr, dir installation serv, 1980-83; Kwang Ju Air Base S Korea, base comdr, 1983-84; HQ AirForce Logistics Command, dir inquiries & govt affairs off inspector gen, 1984-; Ind Univ, Richmond, IN, col adminr, dir diversity & multicultural affairs, 1989; Univ Ark, vis asst prof oper mgt. **Orgs:** Omega Phi Phi, 1962-; Greater Dayton Real Estate Investment Asn, 1980-; bddirs, Girl Scouts Am, 1982-; Indust Rel Asn, 1985-; Ancient EgyptianArabic Order Mystic Shrine. **Honors/Awds:** Outstanding Social Actions Officer, USAF Europe, 1974; PresidentialCitation, Khartoum Sudan, 1979. **Special Achievements:** Author handbook on Equal Opportunity, USAF Europe, 1973; co-authorhandbook "Human Relations in the Military", USAF Europe, 1973; 33 DegreeMason 1988. **Military Serv:** USAF, lt col, 1964-89; Defense Meritorious Service Medal; Efficiency MedalFirst Class (Govt of Sudan); Air Force Meritorious Service Medal with TwoOak Leaf Clusters; Air Force Commendation Medal. **Home Addr:** 685 White Bluff Rd, Fayetteville, AR 72701.

DANTICAT, EDWIDGE
Writer, novelist. **Personal:** Born Jan 19, 1969, Port-Au-Prince, Haiti; daughter of Andre Danticat and Rose. **Educ:** Barnard Col, BA, fre lit, 1990; Brown Univ, MFA, creative writing, 1993. **Career:** Clinica Estetico, prod researcher; auth, currently; Courage & Pain, assoc producer; books: Krik? Krak!, 1996; Breath, Eyes, Memory, 1998; The Farming of Bones, 1998, 1999; A Community of Equals, 1999; Their Eyes Were Watching God, 2000; The Butterfly's Way, 2001; Walking on Fire, 2001; In the Flicker of an Eyelid, 2002; Behind the Mountains, 2002; 2004; After the Dance, 2002; The Royal Diaries, 2005; The Dew Breaker, 2005. **Orgs:** Alpha Kappa Alpha. **Honors/Awds:** Pushcart Short Story Prize, 1995; Essence Fiction Award; Caribbean Writer Fiction Prize; Seventeen Mag Fiction Prize. *

DANTLEY, ADRIAN DELANO
Basketball player, athletic coach. **Personal:** Born Feb 28, 1956, Washington, DC; son of Geraldine Robinson Dantley and Avon

Dantley; married DiNitri; children: Cameron. **Educ:** Univ Notre Dame, bus, 1977. **Career:** Basketball player (retired), Athletic coach: Buffalo Braves, 1976-77; Indiana Pacers, 1977; LA Lakers, 1977-79; Utah Jazz, 1979-86; Detroit Pistons, 1986-88; Dallas Mavericks, 1989-91; Milwaukee Bucks, 1991; Breeze Milano, Italy, 1991-92; Towson Univ, asst coach, 1993-96; Denver Nuggets, asst coach, currently. **Honors/Awds:** Gold medal team, US Olympic basketball, 1976; twice All-Am; Rookie of the Yr, 1976-77; leading scorer NBA, 1980-81; NBA Comeback Player of the Yr Award, 1983-84; NBA All Star Team 1980-82, 1984-86; Basketball Hall of Fame, 2008. **Business Addr:** Assistant Basketball Coach, Denver Nuggets, 1000 Chopper Circle, Denver, CO 80204.*

DANZY, PATRICIA LYNN
Consultant. **Personal:** Born Jul 26, 1958, Canton, OH; daughter of John Ball and Ruth; married Terry, Jul 13, 1996; children: DeWayne, Brian & Jamielle. **Educ:** Am Acad Procedural Coders, CPC, 1997. **Career:** MacDonald Psysicians Inc, client servs analyst, currently. **Orgs:** Coder, Am Acad Prof Coders, 1997. **Honors/Awds:** Good Hands Award, Allstate Ins Co, 1993, Performance Bonus, 1995, 1996. **Business Addr:** Professional Coding Consultant, Danzy Coding Consultants, 808 E Decker Dr, Seven Hills, OH 44131, **Business Phone:** (216)548-6454.

DAPREMONT, DELMONT, JR.
Automotive executive. **Career:** Coastal Ford, Inc, automobile dealer. **Special Achievements:** Named one of the top one hundred auto dealers by Black Enterprise in June, 1988. **Business Addr:** Dealer, Coastal Ford Inc, 7311 Airport Blvd, Mobile, AL 36608.*

DARA, OLU (CHARLES JONES, III)
Musician. **Personal:** Born Jan 12, 1941, Natchez, MS; children: Nasir Jones (Nas). **Educ:** Tenn State Univ. **Career:** Trumpet player & coronetist; Okra Orchestra; Natchezsippi Dance Band; Solo albums: In the World: From Natchez to New York, 1998; Neighborhoods, 2001; Medicated Magic, 2002; Chinatown, 2003. **Honors/Awds:** New York Jazz Award for Stylistic Fusion; France's Django d'Or International Trophy in Blues category; three Audelco Awards; a Drama Desk nomination for "I Am a Man" by OyamO; induction into the Mississippi Musicians Hall of Fame,2003. **Special Achievements:** Played with Art Blakely, Henry Threadgill, David Murray Octet, Don Pullen,Cassandra Wilson; staged "Blues Rooms" to strong acclaim in New York City and Fairfax, VA during the 1990s. **Military Serv:** USN. **Business Addr:** Musician, c/o Atlantic Records, 1290 Avenue of the Americas, New York, NY 10104, **Business Phone:** (212)707-2261.*

DARBY, CASTILLA A., JR.
Physician. **Personal:** Born Jul 17, 1946, Anniston, AL; children: Kimberlynne Michelle. **Educ:** Ala State Univ, BS, 1968; Va Hosp, Tuskegee Inst Ala, Corrective Physical Therapy, 1969; Schiff Scout Reservation Teng Ctr, Mendham, NJ, scout exec, 1970; Meharry Med Col, MD, 1978. **Career:** Woodson HS, biol instr; Ford Greene Elem Sch Nashville, phys educ instr, 1969-70; Boy Scouts Am, Middle Tenn Coun, dist scout exec, 1970-71; Tenn Valley Authority, Nashville, clin physician; Douglas Mem Hosp, Jefferson, TX, med dir, 1980-83; Lake Cliff Hosp, Dallas, TX, chief staff; Pvt Pract, physician, currently. **Orgs:** Nat Asn Advan Colored People, 1986; Meharry Med Col Alumni Asn, 1986-87; Am Med Asn; Nat Fedn Independent Bus, 1986-87; Tex Fedn Sr Citizens, 1987; life mem, Kappa Alpha Psi Fraternity Inc; Tex Med Asn. **Honors/Awds:** Freshman Award for Academic Excellence, Ala State Univ; Jessie S Noyles Scholar Obstetrics & Gynecology, 1978. **Business Addr:** Physician, Private Practice, 1400 Martin Luther King Jr, Dallas, TX 75215.*

DARBY, MATT. **See DARBY, MATTHEW LAMONT.**

DARBY, MATTHEW LAMONT (MATT DARBY)
Football player. **Personal:** Born Nov 19, 1968, Virginia Beach, VA; married Cheryl; children: Matthew & Marcus. **Educ:** Univ Calif, Los Angeles, BS, afro-am studies. **Career:** Buffalo Bills, defensive back, 1992-95; Ariz Cardinals, 1996-97.

DAR DAR, KIRBY DAVID
Football player, businessperson. **Personal:** Born Mar 27, 1972, Morgan City, LA. **Educ:** Syracuse Univ. **Career:** Football player (retired), bus; Miami Dolphins, wide receiver, 1995-98; real estate agent, currently. *

DARDEN, ANTHONY KOJO
Manager. **Personal:** Born Jan 10, 1943, Birmingham, AL; son of Samuel (deceased) and Annie B Harris (deceased); divorced; children: 2. **Educ:** Wayne County Col, assoc arts & liberal arts, 1974; Detroit Inst Tech, BA, psychol, 1976; Wayne State Univ, masters, social work, 1984. **Career:** City Detroit, prin cot service, asst; Enterprising Bus Assoc Mkt, chmn; The Mattah Movement, vpres, currently. **Orgs:** Bd chair, The 24 Hour Store Mkt Assoc; Shrine Black Madonna. **Special Achievements:** Wayne State Univ, real estate, laws & sales, 1973; Omaha Ins Co, ins, rules & law, 1975; Amway Corp, networking mkt, art & sci, 1989; Wayne County Comt Col, Recognition Orgn first student govt struct, managing ed, 1973, pres, 1974, co-organizer "The Open Door"; 25 Year of Service, Shrine of the Black Madonna. **Home Phone:** (313)868-9021. **Business Addr:** Vice President, The Mattah Movement, 4911 Georgia Ave NW, Washington, DC 20011-4525, **Business Phone:** (202)723-3358.

DARDEN, CALVIN
Executive, vice president (organization). **Personal:** Born Feb 5, 1950, Buffalo, NY; married Patricia Gail Darden, Aug 21, 1971; children: Ramarro, Tami, Lorielle. **Educ:** Canisius col, BS, bus mgt, 1972; Emory Univ, Exec Develop Consortium, 1997. **Career:** United Parcel Service ctr, customer service supervisor, 1974, sr exec, district mgr N New Jersey, 1984-86, district mgr Metro Jersey, 1986-91, district mgr Metro District of Columbia, 1991-93, vpres Pacific region, 1993-95, vpres & corporate strategic quality coordinator, 1995-97, sr vpres, 1997-04. **Orgs:** pres, African Am Unity Ctrs; Atlanta Chap, 1996; Nat Urban League, 1997; Nat Urban League Black Exec Exchange Prog; 100 Black Men Metro, atlanta; deacon, Deliverance Temple, Atlanta; United Way Long Beach, CA; target Corp, Coca-Cola Enterprises; target Corp, Atlanta Police Found. **Special Achievements:** carried the Olympic torch in the opening ceremonies of Summer Games in Sydney, Australia, 2000. **Home Addr:** 8155 Sentinae Chase Dr, Roswell, GA 30076, **Home Phone:** (770)993-3511. *

DARDEN, DR. CHRISTINE MANN
Aerospace engineer. **Personal:** Born Sep 10, 1942, Monroe, NC; married Walter L Darden Jr; children: Jeanne Darden Riley & Janet Christine. **Educ:** Hampton Inst, math, 1962; VA State Col, MS, math, 1967; George Wash Univ, DSc, mech eng, 1983. **Career:** Brunswick Co Sch, teacher 1962-63; Portsmouth City Sch VA, teacher 1964-65; VA State Col, math instr, 1966-67; NASA Langley Res Ctr, data analyst, 1967-73, aerospace eng, group leader, sonic boom group, 1989-92, sr proj engr, advan vehicles div, dep proj mgr, HSR TU-144 prog, 1999-2001, dir aero performing, 2002-03, LARC asst dir planning, 2002-04; dir, Off Communs & Educ, NASA Langley, 2004-. **Orgs:** Gamma Upsilon Omega Chap AKA, 1960-; assoc fel, 1973-; Nat Langley Exchange Coun, 1979-; elder Carver Mem Presbyterian Ch 1980-; chmn, boundaries comm Southern VA Presbyterian Church, USA 1983-88; pres, Hampton Roads Chap, Nat Tech Asn, 1984-88; moderator, Synod Mid-Atlantic Presbyterian Churches, 1989-90; chmn, Presbytery Coun, Easter VA Presbytery, 1990-; secy, aerocoustics tech comt, 1990-91, Am Inst Aeronaut & Astronauts; nat secy, Nat Tech Asn, 1990-92. **Honors/Awds:** 20 Year Alumnus Award, Hampton Inst, 1982; Dr AT Weathers Tech Achievement Award, Nat Tech Asn, 1985; Dollars & Sense Mag, 100 Top Black Bus & Professional Women, 1986; Black Engineer of the Year in Government, Mobile Oil Coun Eng Deans, 1988; Technol Transfer, NASA, 1990; Technical Achievements & Humanitarian Efforts, NC State Univ, 1990; NASA, EEO Medal, 1991; Dual Career Ladder Award, NASA Langley Research Center, 1991; Outstanding Women in Government Award, Women Sci & Eng, 1992; Langley Engineering Achievement Award, 1994. **Special Achievements:** Author or co-author of over 54 technical reports and articles. **Business Addr:** Director, Office of Communications & Education, NASA Langley Research Center, Bldg 1216 Rm 211 17 Langley Blvd MS 412, Hampton, VA 23681-0001.

DARDEN, CHRISTOPHER ALLEN
Lawyer. **Personal:** Born Apr 8, 1956, Martinez, CA; son of Eddie and Jean; married Marcia; children: Jenee, Christopher Jr & Tiffany. **Educ:** Calif Univ San Jose, BS, criminal justice admin, 1977; Univ Calif-Hastings Col Law, JD, 1980. **Career:** Nat Labor Rels Bd, atty, 1980-81; Los Angeles Co, asst head dep, Spec Investigations Div, 1981; Los Angeles Co Dist Atty's Off, dep dist atty, 1980-95; Southwestern Univ Sch Law, prof, 1995-99; Darden & Assocs Inc, atty, 2000-. **Orgs:** Los Angeles Co Asn Dep Dist Attys, 1986-87; pres & dir, Loved Ones Homicide Victims, 1987-; Nat Black Prosecutors Asn, 1989; Calif Bar, Criminal Law Sect, Exec Comt, 1994-97; John M Langston Bar Asn, 1995; mem, Alpha Phi Alpha; mem, Greek-letter fraternity. **Honors/Awds:** Alumnus of the Year Award, San Jose State Univ, Dept Admin Justice, 1995; Crystal Heart Award, Loved Ones Homicide Victims. **Special Achievements:** The People vs Orenthal James Simpson, BA097211, part of prosecuting team; co-author: In Contempt, 1996; author: The trials of Nikki Hill; appeared in television movie. **Business Phone:** (310)568-1804.

DARDEN, EDWIN CARLEY
School administrator. **Personal:** Born Sep 13, 1960, New York, NY; son of Eddie and Lee Darden; married Lori, Oct 6, 1984; children: Leandra Ebonique & Jay Spenser. **Educ:** State Univ NY, Col Arts & Sci Geneseo, BA, 1981; Georgetown Univ Law Ctr, JD, 1997. **Career:** Capitol Publ, legal reporter, 1988-89; Georgetown Univ Law Ctr, assoc dir pub rels, 1989-97; Levi, Perry, Simmons & Loots, assoc atty, 1997-98; NY State Sch Brd Assn, sr staff atty, 1998-2002, Ctr Urban Schs Prog, dir; Ed Advocacy, managing partner, currently; Appleseed, educ policy dir, currently; The Session Law Firm P.c, staff, currently. **Orgs:** Fed Bar Assn, 1996-; Am Bar Assn, 1997-; Nat Alliance Black Sch Educr,1998-; Educ Law Assn, 1998-; Va Bar Assn, 1998-; chmn, Fairfax County Coun PTA Educ Comt, 1999-2000, vpres, 2000-; Natl Bar Assn. **Honors/Awds:** Educ Press Award First Place for Service, Educ Press As sn, 1988; Silver Inkwell Award, Intl Assn Bus Communicators, 1991; Coun Advan & Support Educ, Minority Prof Scholar, 1992; Americans United Separation Church & State, Madison-Jefferson Scholar, 1993. **Special Achievements:** Co-ed: Legal Issues & Educ Technol: A Sch Leaders Guide; US Supreme Ct brief: Eisenberg v Montgomery County Schs. **Business Addr:** Education Policy Director, Appleseed, 727 15th St NW 11th Fl, Washington, DC 20005, **Business Phone:** (202)347-7960.

DARDEN, DR. JOSEPH S., JR.
Educator. **Personal:** Born Jul 25, 1925, Pleasantville, NJ; son of Joseph S Sr and Blanche Paige; married; children: Michele Irene Darden Burgess. **Educ:** Lincoln Univ, AB, 1948; NY Univ, MA, 1952, EdD, 1963. **Career:** Clark Col, instr Biol Sci, 1952-55; Albany State Col, asst prof, Biol &Health Educ, 1955-64, chmn sci div, 1959-60; Wagner Col, adj prof,1966-88; Rutgers Univ, adj prof Sex Educ, 1974-75; Mont clair State Col,1975; Kean Col NJ, prof & coordr, Health Educ, 1964-02, chair, Health & Rec Dept, 1979-84; dir, Minority Enrollment, 1988-94, prof emer 2003. **Orgs:** Pres, E Dist Asn AAHPERD, 1974-75; vpres & chmn, Health Educ Div E DistAsn Am Alliance Health Physical Educ Recreation Dance, 1971-72; vpres,Health Educ NJ Asn Am Alliance Health Physical Educ Recreation Dance,1967; mem adv bd, Health Educ Am Alliance Health Physical Educ Recreation Dance, 1973-76; ed bd, The J Sch Health ASHA, 1969-72; gov coun Am Sch Health Asn, 1970-73; author, lecturer, workshop dir, radio & TV panelistsex educ; bd dir, Asn Advan Health Educ, 1975-78; E Dist Rep Alliance Bd,1979-82; founder, NJ Health Educ Coun, 1967; NJ Am Alliance Health Physical Educ Recreation Dance; Am Social Health Asn; SIECUS, Am Asn Sex Educrs, Counrs & Therapists; bd trustees, Planned Parenthood Metrop NJ; dipl, Am Bd Sexology, 1990-2000; founding fellow, Am Asn Health Educ, 1998. **Honors/Awds:** Distinguished Service Award, Am Sch Health Asn, 1971; Hon Fellow Award, NJ Asn Health, Physical Educ & Recreation, 1972; Hon Award, NJ Health Educ Coun, 1975; Distinguished Leadership Award, NJ Asn Health, Physical Educ & Recreation, 1975; Dist Hon Award, E Dist Assn Am Alliance Health Physical Educ Recreation Dance, 1976; Distinguished Service Award, Alpha Alpha Lambda Chap Alpha Phi Alpha, 1975; Alliance Hon Award, Am Alliance Health Physical Educ Recreation Dance, 1985; Outstanding Col & Univ Teacher of the Year, Eastern Dist Asn Am Alliance Health Physical Educ Recreation Dance, 1983; Charles D Henry Award, Am Alliance Health Physical Educ Recreation Dance, 1988; Edwin B Henderson Award, EMC, Am Alliance Health Physical Educ Recreation Dance, 1991; Prof Serv to Health Educ Award, Am Asn Health Educ & Am Alliance Health Physical Educ Recreation Dance, 1990;The Alumni Achievement Award, Lincoln Univ, 1993; Presidential Citation,Am Asn Health Educ & Am Alliance Health Physical Educ Recreation Dance, 1996. **Special Achievements:** Author: Toward A Healthier Sexuality: A Book of Readings, 1996; ed, Critical Health Issues Reader, Dubuque, Iowa 2002, numerous articles publ in state, regional & nat. **Military Serv:** AUS, t/sgt, 1944-46. *

DARITY, JANKI EVANGELIA
Health services administrator. **Personal:** Born in Beirut, Lebanon; daughter of William and Evangeline. **Educ:** Spelman Col, BA, 1980; Univ Tex, Austin Sch Law, JD, 1983; Harvard Univ, Sch Pub Health, MPH, 1984. **Career:** Campbell, Davidson & Morgan, law clerk, 1981-82; Bechtel Group Inc, law clerk, 1982; Southern Union Gas Co, law clerk, 1983; Harper Hosp, admin fel, hosp admin, 1984-87; Mich Hosp Asn, asst dir, legal & regulatory affairs, 1987-89; Henry Ford Hosp, dir urban health initiative, 1989-91; Henry Ford Health Systs, corp dir community health develop, 1992-94; vp community develop, 1994-98, vpres community & bus develop, 1998. **Orgs:** Alpha Kappa Alpha Sorority Inc, 1979; Nat Bar Asn, 1981; Nat Health Lawyers Asn, 1983; Nat Asn Health Serv Execs, 1984; chair, Detroit Rotary Club Int, 1992; Women's Econ Club, 1992; 1st vpres bd dirs, In-Site Horizon Field Trips, Inc, 1992; Leadership Oakland, chair race & ethnic diversity steering community, 1993-97; bd dirs, United Cerebral Palsy Metro Der, 1993-97; Leadership MI, 1993-94; Am Asn Univ Women, 1993; Leadership Am Alumni Asn, 1994; Asn Healthcare Philanthropy, 1994; Jr League Birmingham, 1996; Generation Promise bd dirs, 1996-98; co-chair, Detroit United Negro Col Fund, Walk-A-Thon, 1997-98; chmn, Corp Develop, 1998. **Honors/Awds:** Crain's Detroit Bus, "40 Under 40", 1997. *

DARITY, WILLIAM A.
Educator, lecturer, army officer. **Personal:** Born Jan 15, 1924, Flat Rock, NC; son of Aden Randall (deceased) and Elizabeth Smith (deceased); married Evangeline Royall, Dec 23, 1950 (deceased); children: William Jr, Janki Evangelia; married Trudy L Whisonant, Jul 5, 2002. **Educ:** Shaw Univ, BS, 1948; NC Cent Univ, MSPH, 1949; Univ NC, PhD, 1964. **Career:** Univ Mass, prof, 1965, prof pub health & dean, Sch Health Sci, 1973-89, prof pub health, 1989-91, prof emer pub health, 1989-; World Health Orgn, regional adv, 1953-64, consult, 1971-80; Peace Corps Training Progs, consult dir, 1962-67; Headstart Training Progs, consult lectr, 1965-67; Univ NC, vis prof, 1973; Univ SC, vis prof, 1980; external examiner, Univ Ibadan, Nigeria, & Univ West Indies, 1973-; Nat Cancer Inst, dir & prin investr, Res Cancer & Smoking Black Populations, 1986-91; The Population Coun, NY, sr assoc, posted Cairo, Egypt, 1991-93; Univ NC, decision-maker, 2001.

Orgs: Fel Am Pub Health Asn; fel Soc Pub Health Educ; fel Am Sch Health Asn; Am Nat Coun Health Educ; Int Union Health Educ; Delta Omega; assoc Danforth Found; bd dir, Drug Abuse Coun, 1972-79; bd dir, Planned Parenthood Fed Am, 1967-73; bd dir, SIECUS, 1967-71; pres, Mass Asn Ment Health, 1967-69; pres, Hampshire Pub Health Asn, 1967-70; bd trustees, Univ NC-Chapel Hill, 1985-91; bd Sci Counrs, Nat Cancer Inst, 1986-90; bd dir, Mass Water Resources Authority, 1989-91; Phi Kappa Phi; Sigma Xi; Sigma Pi Phi, (The Boule) 1986-; Omega Psi Phi 1946-; mem & official of many other civic orgns. **Honors/Awds:** Recipient Fellowship World Health Orgn; Hildrus Poindexter Public Health Service Award, BCHW/APHA, 1975; Distinguished Lecture/Chancellor's Medal, Univ Mass, 1989; Dist Alumnus Award, Univ NC, 1996; Alumni Achievement Award, Shaw Univ, 1997. **Military Serv:** AUS, infantry, 1st lt, 1943-47. **Home Addr:** 105 Heatherstone Rd, Amherst, MA 01002, **Home Phone:** (413)253-9861. **Business Addr:** Professor Emeritus, University of Massachusetts, School of Public Health, 129 Arnold House, 715 N Pleasant St, Amherst, MA 01003-9304.*

DARK, LAWRENCE JEROME
School administrator. **Personal:** Born Jan 18, 1953, Americus, GA; son of Charlie Dark and Frances Adrilla Harris Howard; married Okianer B Christian; children: Harrison Edward. **Educ:** Denison Univ, BA 1976; Northwestern Univ, JD 1980. **Career:** Frostburg State Col, from asst to pres, 1979-82; Nat Endowment Humanities fel, 1981; Am Bar Asn Coun Legal Educ Oppor, assoc dir, 1982-85; Claflin Col, dir corp found relns & develop, 1985-86; Am Univ, adj fac mem, 1985; Woodrow Wilson Nat fel, 1985-86; Claflin Col, part-time fac mem, 1985-86; Am Red Cross, corp initiative assoc, 1986-88; Va Coun Human Rights, dir, 1988-90; Va Exec Inst, Gov Educ Prog, 1988;Nat Inst Against Prejudice & Violence, exec dir, 1991; Univ SC, from exec asst to the pres equal opportunity prog, 1992; Urban League Portland, pres, chief exec officer; Campaign Consult Inc; Univ Md, James Macgregor Burns Acad Leadership, exec dir, currently, res assoc, Acad Leadership, currently; Kellogg fel. **Orgs:** Nat Adv Comm Nat Inst Citizen Educ Law, 1986-; Alpha Phi Alpha Fraternity, Iota Upsilon Lambda Chap; bd, Md Humanities Coun, 1980-84, Md State Bd Social Serv, 1982-84; Comm United Way, 1988-; field serv chair, Am Red Cross EOH, 1988-; comm Am Red Cross Vol Commun Campaign Adv Comm, Policy Issues Comm, 1989-; comm Am Soc Pub Admin, 1989-; Nat Forum Black Pub Adminr, Exec Leadership Inst, 1989; Improved Fundraising Capabilites Prog. **Honors/Awds:** Council on Legal Education Opportunity Scholarship; Citation by Sec of the MD Dept of Human Resources for Service on the State Bd for Social Service, 1984; Citation for Service on the MD Humanities Council, 1984; Nat Scholarship Service & Fund for Negro Students Award; United Negro Col Fund Leadership Pin Award, 1986. **Business Addr:** Eexcutive Director, University of Maryland, James Macgregor Burns Academy of Leadership, 1139 Taliaferro Hall, College Park, MD 20742.

DARK, OKIANER CHRISTIAN
Educator. **Personal:** Born Dec 8, 1954, Petersburg, VA; daughter of Marshall Christian Sr and Vivian Louise Rier Christian; married Lawrence, Jun 20, 1981; children: Harrison Edward. **Educ:** Upsala Col, BA, 1976; Rutgers Univ Sch Law, JD, 1979. **Career:** US Dept Justice, Antitrust Div, trial atty, 1979-84, Civil Div, trial atty, 1984; Univ Richmond Law Sch, asst prof, 1984-87, from assoc prof to prof, 1987-90; Am Univ, Wash Col Law, vis prof & scholar, 1991-92; Willamette Univ Col Law, vis prof, 1994-95; US Attorney's Office, asst US atty, 1995-2001; Howard Univ Sch Law, prof, assoc dean acad affairs, 2001-. **Orgs:** Nat Bar Asn; adv bd, NBA Mag, 1988-; bd mem, Daily Planet, 1989-94; St Paul's Baptist Church, 1989-94; bd dirs, Va Black Women Attorneys Asn, 1990-94; Penn State Bar Asn; NJ State Bar Asn; Va State Bar Asn; Ore State Bar Asb; Task Force Gender Fairness; bd trustees, YMCA, Portland, OR; bd dir, NW Health Found; Link, Inc, Silver Spring chap; Mt Olivet Baptist Church, Portland, OR; Montgomery County Comn Health, 2002-05; People's Community Baptist Church, Silver Spring, MD. **Honors/Awds:** Alumni Senior Prize, Rutgers University, 1979; Hope for People Award, 1991; Foundation Distinguished Faculty Award, Va Women Attorneys Asn, 1991; Distinguished Education Award, University Richmond, 1990 & 1993; Distinguished Graduate Award, South Brunswick High School, 1994; Mercedes Diez Award, Ore Women's Bar Assn; Special Achievement Awards, US Dept & Science. **Special Achievements:** First African American to be tenured in the T.C. Williams School of Law at the University of Richmond and the first African American woman to be tenured in the University; Published numerous articles. **Home Addr:** 2504 Locustwood Pl, Silver Spring, MD 20905. **Business Phone:** (202)806-8003.

DARKE, DR. CHARLES B
Dentist. **Personal:** Born Sep 22, 1937, Chicago, IL; son of Paul Olden and Annie Waulene Tennin; married Judith, Dec 15, 1990; married Annetta, Aug 15, 1965 (divorced 1982); children: Charles B Darke II. **Educ:** Wilson Jr Col, AA 1960; Meharry Medical Col, DDS, 1964; Univ Calif, Berkeley, MPH, 1972. **Career:** Dentist (retired); Hosp Appointments: Mt Zion Hosp, St Mary Hosp, San Francisco Gen Hosp; Career Highlights: Dept Labor Job Corp Region 9, dent consult; Univ Calif, Sch Med, asst clin prof; Univ Calif, Sch Dentistry, lectr; San Francisco Gen Hosp, dir dent serv; San Francisco Gen Hosp, asst admin, Satellite Health Ctrs; Opers Officer, San Francisco Health Dept; part time pvt practice, dentist; Calif State Univ, Fullerton, Fullerton, CA, exec dir stud health & coun ctr; Kaiser Found Hosps, sr consult. **Orgs:** State Bd Dent Examiners Calif; dir, Dent Ser San Francisco Gen Hosp, div outpatient & community serv; Am Health Care, consult prepaid health plans; bd dirs, Calif Children's Lobby; field consult, Joint Comn Accreditation Hosps; past pres, Northern Calif, Nat Dent Asn; Yorba Hill Med Ctr, bd dirs; Chapman Univ, sci task force. **Honors/Awds:** 'Outstanding Young Men of America', 1973. **Military Serv:** USAF, Capt, 1965-67. **Home Addr:** 7008 E Columbus Dr, Anaheim, CA 92807-4527, **Home Phone:** (714)281-8316. **Business Addr:** General Dentist, 2175 Hayes St, San Francisco, CA 94117, **Business Phone:** (415)668-8005.

DARKES, LEROY WILLIAM
Electrical engineer. **Personal:** Born Sep 26, 1924, Atlantic City, NJ; son of William E and Isabella Wynder; married Mamie Doris Simpson; children: William S, Leroy S, Lois L Bond & Matthew S. **Educ:** Rutgers Univ, BS, Elec Engr, 1947, MS, 1948. **Career:** Electrical Engineer (retired); Atlantic City Elec Co, elec engr, 1948, distrib engr, 1953, syst planning engr, 1958, mgr var areas, 1965-89. **Orgs:** IEEE, 1948-, Nat Soc Prof Engrs, 1955-, Atlantic City Bd Educ, 1969-87, Atlantic County Planning Bd, 1972-89. **Honors/Awds:** Licensed New Jersey Prof Engr, 1955-. **Military Serv:** AUS, pfc, 1944-46. **Home Addr:** 1915 Grant Ave, Atlantic City, NJ 08401.

DARKINS, CHRIS. **See DARKINS, CHRISTOPHER OJI.**

DARKINS, CHRISTOPHER OJI (CHRIS DARKINS)
Football player. **Personal:** Born Apr 30, 1974, San Francisco, CA; married Paula; children: Andre. **Educ:** Univ Minn. **Career:** Green Bay Packers, running back, 1996-97. *

DARLING, HELEN MARIE
Basketball player. **Personal:** Born Aug 29, 1978, Columbus, OH; daughter of Donald and Patricia Smith. **Educ:** Pa State, educ, 2001. **Career:** Cleveland Rockers, WNBA guard, 2000-03; Minn Lynx, 2004; Univ Memphis, asst coach, 2004-05; Charlotte Sting, guard, 2005-06; San Antonio Silver Stars, guard, 2007-. **Honors/Awds:** Naismith Award small player of the yr; Big Ten Player of the Yr, 1999-00; WNBA Community Asst Award, 2003. **Special Achievements:** Nat spokesperson, March of Dimes. *

DARLING, JAMES JACKSON
Football player. **Personal:** Born Dec 29, 1974, Denver, CO. **Educ:** Wash State Univ. **Career:** Philadelphia Eagles, linebacker, 1997-2000; New York Jets, 2001-02; Ariz Cardinals, linebacker, 2003-06; free agent. **Honors/Awds:** Two-time All-Pacific Ten Conf selection, 1995-96. *

DARNELL, EDWARD BUDDY
Manager. **Personal:** Born Mar 4, 1930, Chicago, IL; son of Edward and Mary; married Gwendolyn Wilson, Aug 19, 1953; children: Glenn T & Gary L. **Educ:** Detroit Inst Technol, BA, psychol, 1968; Wayne State Univ, MSW, social work, 1971; Univ Mich, specialist geront, 1971. **Career:** Ford Motor Co, staff; Detroit Pub Sch Syst, dir; State Mich, social worker; Detroit City Airport, Off Civil Defense, dir, Detroit City Air Port, dep dir. **Orgs:** Imp first ceremonial master, Imp Coun Shriners, 1988; secy, United Supreme Coun, 1977; hon fel, Phylaxis Soc, pres & founder, Great Lakes Chap, Mich;. Detroit Renaissance Lions Club Inc; Am Legion Post; life mem, Nat Asn Advan Colored People; charter mem, Mich Aviation Hall Fame; Govs Air Serv Task Force; United Supreme Coun Benevolent Found, Philadelphia, Penn; bd dir, United Community Serv, Detroit, Mich. **Honors/Awds:** Legion of honor, Prince Hall Shriners, 1973; Scottish Rite Hall of Fame, Prince Hall Scottish Rite, 1984; Humanitarian of the Year Award, Florence Ames Chap, 1990; Lee J Barrett Award, Detroit Metrop Visitors & Conv Bur, 1990, 1997; Seagram's Vanguard Award, 1994; Honorary title of Captain, Capitol Heights Police Dept, Capitol Heights, Md, 1994. **Military Serv:** US Marine Corps, sgt; Pres Unit Citation, 1953.

DARTSON, DR. MYRNA
Educator, physicist. **Educ:** PhD. **Career:** Psychologist, pvt pract, currently; Paul Quinn Col, Dallas, adjunct psychol prof; Univ personal success, fac, currently. **Orgs:** Salesmanship Club. **Business Addr:** Psychologist, 4038 Lemmon Ave, Dallas, TX 75219-3736, **Business Phone:** (214)219-1116.*

DARVIN, DUNKIN. **See HAM, DARVIN.**

DASH, DAMON
Music producer, executive, actor. **Personal:** Born May 3, 1971, Harlem, NY; married Rachel Roy; children: Ava & Talullah Ruth. **Career:** Roc-A-Fella Rec, Co-founder, 1995, ceo 2003-05, consult, currently; Roc-A-Wear clothing line & Roc-A-Fella Films, founder, 1998; Dame Dash Music Group, founder, 2004-; BET, "Ultimate Hustler", producer; Film: Backstage, producer, 2000; Paid In Full, producer & actor, 2002; Death of a Dynasty, producer, actor & dir, 2003; The Woodsman, producer, 2004; Shadowboxer, producer, 2005; Paper Soldiers, dir, 2002; State Property 2, dir & actor, 2005; Highlander: Endgame, actor, 2000; Armadale vodka, owner; America Mag, owner; Pro-Keds sneakers, owner; Team Roc, owner; Tiret Watches, owner; Rachel Roy Clothing Line, owner; Dash Management, owner; Dash Di Bella Boxing, owner; Weapons, co-producer, 2007; Tennessee, exec producer, 2008. **Orgs:** Juvenile Diabetes Res Found; Am Diabetes Asn. **Business Addr:** Chief Excutive Officer, Dame Dash Music Group, 1501 Broadway, New York, NY 10036-5601.*

DASH, DARIEN
Executive. **Personal:** Born Jan 1, 1972?, New York, NY; son of Dennis and Linda; married Deborah; children: three. **Educ:** Univ Southern Calif, BA, polit sci & leadership. **Career:** Digital Music Xpress, vpres sales, 1990; DME Interactive Holdings, founder, chmn & chief exec officer, 1994-. **Orgs:** Making Opportunities Upgrading Schs & Educ. **Honors/Awds:** 40 UNDER 40 Achievement Award, Network J, 2000. **Business Addr:** Founder & Chief Executive Officer, Chairman, DME Interactive Holdings Inc, 39 Broadway, New York, NY 10006.*

DASH, HUGH M. H.
Health services administrator. **Personal:** Born Feb 19, 1943, Brooklyn, NY; married Patricia Morris; children: Angela, Phillip. **Educ:** Morehouse Col, bus admin, 1969; Howard Univ, exec mgt, 1974; Ga State Univ, MA, pub health, 1984, PhD, 1992. **Career:** Citizens Trust Bank, com lending & credit officer, 1972-72; Interracial Coun Bus Opportunity, dep exec dir, 1972-75; Southern Conf Black Mayors, sr econ develop, 1975-76; Enterprises Now Inc, exec vpres, 1976-80; Prudential Health Care, regional dir & qual improv, 1980-. **Orgs:** Leadership Atlanta, 1978-; bd mem & pres, Atlanta Bus League, 1978-79, 1985; treas, White House Conf Small Bus, 1979-80. **Honors/Awds:** Catalyst, Interracial Coun Bus Opportunity, 1977. **Military Serv:** AUS, Sp4/E4; served 3 yrs. **Home Addr:** 1374 Dodson Dr SW, Atlanta, GA 30311. *

DASH, JULIE
Movie producer, movie director. **Personal:** Born Oct 22, 1952, Long Island City, NY; children: Nzinga. **Educ:** City Col NY, BA, film prod, 1974; Am Film Inst, producing & writing fel, 1975, multimedia workshops, 1995; Univ Calif, Los Angeles, MFA, motion picture & tv prod, 1986. **Career:** Director, writer & producer; guest lectures, 1983-2000; Films: Working Models of Success, 1973; Four Women, ed & dir, 1975; Diary of an African Nun, dir & ed, 1977; Illusions, ed, dir, writer & producer, 1982; Daughters of the Dust, dir, writer & producer, 1991; Praise House, 1991; Brothers of the Borderl, 2004; TV series: Women: Stories of Passion, dir & producer, 1997; SUBWAYStories: Tales from the Underground, dir & producer, 1997; Funny Valentines, 1999; Incognito, 1999; Love Song, 2000; The Rosa Parks Story, 2002; Geechee Girls Multimedia, founder, currently. **Orgs:** Alpha Kappa Alpha Sorority. **Honors/Awds:** Numerous honors & awards including Maya Deren Award, AFI; Mirabella's 100 Fearless Women; Delta Sigma Theta Sorority's Lillian Award; Sojourner Truth Award; National Conference of Black Mayor's Literary Award; M.E.N.T.O.R Networks Award; Liberty Bell, The Coalition of 100 Black Women; The Black Oscar; Candace Award, Black Filmmaker's Hall of Fame; Women in Film Dorothy Arzner Award; Cinematography Awar, Sundance Film Festival; Third World Film Festival Award; Oscar Micheaux Award, Black Filmmaker's Hall of Fame; Black Cinema Society Award & Miami International Film Festival-Gold Medal. **Special Achievements:** First African American woman to have a full-length general theatrical release in the United States; Book: Daughters Of The Dust: The Making Of An African American Woman's Film, 1992. **Business Phone:** (212)629-6880.*

DASH, LEON DECOSTA
Journalist, educator. **Personal:** Born Mar 16, 1944, New Bedford, MA; son of Leon Sr and Ruth; children: Darla & Destiny. **Educ:** Howard Univ, BA, 1968. **Career:** The Wash Post, reporter, 1966-71, West African bur chief, 1979-84, investigative reporter, 1984-98; Kenya Peace Corps, teacher, 1968-70; Univ Calif, San Diego, vis prof, 1978; Henry J Kaiser Family Found, fel, 1995-96; Univ Ill, Col Commun, Ctr Advan Studies, fac, 1998-2000, Swanlund Chair prof jour, 2000-, prof, 2003-. **Orgs:** Nat Asn Black Journalist. **Honors/Awds:** Robert F Kennedy Award, 1973; George Polk Award, Overseas Press Club, 1974; Balt-Wash Guild Award, 1974; Reporting Award, Capitol Press Club Intl, 1984; Africare InterNat Reporting Award, 1984; Distinguished Service Award, Md Social Serv Admin, 1986; General News Award, Nat Asn Black Journalists, 1986; First Prize, Public Service Award, Wash-Baltimore Newspaper Guild, 1987; First Place Award, Investigative Reporters & Ed Orgn, 1987; President's Award, Wash Independent Writers, 1989; Special Citation, PEN Martha Albrand Nonfiction for "When Children Want Children"; Pulitzer Prize, Explanatory Jour, 1995; First Prize for Print, Robert F Kennedy Award, 1995; Media Fel, Henry J Kaisr Family Found, 1995-96; Emmy Award, Nat Acad TV Arts & Sci, DC Chap, 1996; first prize, Harry Chapin Best Book Media Award, The World Hunger Year Orgn; Political Book Award, Wash Monthly Mag; Prevention for a Safer Society Literature Award, Nat Coun Crime & Delinquency, 1997; DHL, Lincoln Univ, 1996. **Special Achievements:** Co-author, Shame of Prisons, 1972; author, When

Children Want Children, 1989; Rosa Lee, 1996; Washington Post series, "Rosa Lee's Story," selected one of best 100 works in 20th century American journalism, NYU, 1999; He was one of 44 journalists who founded the National Association of Black Journalists on December 12. **Business Addr:** Swanlund Chair Professor of Journalism, University of Illinois College of Communications, 332 Gregory Hall MC 462 504 E Pa Ave, Champaign, IL 61820, **Business Phone:** (217)265-5055.

DASH, STACEY LAURETTA
Actor. **Personal:** Born Jan 20, 1966, Bronx, NY; married James Maby, Feb 26, 2005 (divorced 2006); married Emmanuel Xuereb, Jan 1, 2007; married Brian Lovell, Jul 16, 1999 (divorced 2005); children: Lola & Austin. **Career:** TV series: "Clueless", 1996-99; "The Strip", 1999; "A Pirate Looks at 15 to 20", 2001; "Eve", 2003; "Duck Dodgers", 2005; Secrets of a Hollywood Nurse, 2008; "American Dad!", 2008; "The Game", 2009; films: Enemy Territory, 1987; Moving, 1988; Tenn Nights, 1989; Mo' Money, 1992; Renaissance Man, 1994; Illegal in Blue, 1995; Cold Around the Heart, 1997; Personals, 1999; Paper Soldiers, 2002; The Painting, 2002; View From the Top, 2003; Gangs of Roses, 2003; Ride or Die, 2003; Lethal Eviction, 2005; Getting Played, 2005; I Could Never Be Your Woman, 2007; Nora's Hair Salon II, 2008; Fashion Victim, 2008;, 2008; Phantom Punch, 2009; Chrome Angels, 2009. **Honors/Awds:** Nominee, Young Artist Award, Best Young Supporting Actress - Feature Film for: Clueless (1995), 1996. **Business Addr:** Actress, PO Box 800487, Santa Clarita, CA 91380-0487.*

DATES, JANNETTE LAKE
Educator, college administrator. **Personal:** Born in Baltimore, MD; daughter of Moses Lake and Iantha Alexander Lake; married Victor H, Dec 17, 1960; children: Karen, Victor Jr, Matthew & Craig. **Educ:** Coppin State Col, BS; Johns Hopkins Univ, MEd; Univ Md, College Park, educ admin, supv & curric, PhD, 1979. **Career:** Baltimore City Pub Sch System, classroom demonstration teacher, 1958-63, tv demonstration teacher, 1964-71; Morgan State Col & Goucher Col, instr, 1971-72; North Star WBAL-TV, exec prod, 1972-73; Morgan State Univ, Commun Arts Prog, instr, 1972-77, coor dr tv proj, 1973-80, Dept Commun & Theater Arts, asst prof, 1977-80; Howard Univ, asst prof, 1981-85, Dept Radio, Television & Film, Sch Commun, sequence coordr, 1981-85; Copp in State Col, Video Prod Serv, dir, 1985-87, Dept Languages, Literature & Jour, assoc prof, 1985-87, video prod serv dir, 1985-87; Howard Univ Sch Commun, assocdean, 1987-92, actg dean, 1993-96, Dept Radio, TV & Film, asst prof, 1981-85, assoc prof, 1990-98, prof 1998-, John H Johnson Sch Commun, assocdean, 1993-96, dean, 1996-. **Orgs:** Comnr, Baltimore City Cable TV Comn, 1979-81; chairwoman, Educ Task Force,1979-81; Baltimore Cable Access Corp, pres, 1982-86, vpres, 1986-88; Mayor's Cable Adv Comn, education task force chairwoman, 1988-90, mem, 1990-94; George Foster Peabody Awards, 1995-2002; chair, Black Col Commun Asn, 1997-2001; Broadcast Educ Asn, bd dir, Finance Comn, 1994, progchair, Nat Conf, 1996, bd dirs, 1997-99, Secy treas bd, 1999-2000, vpres bd, 2000-01, pres bd dirs, 2001-02; Vice-chair, Accrediting Comt, Accrediting Coun Educ Jour & Mass Commun, 1998-99; vpres, Asn Educ Jour &Mass Commun, 2001-02, pres, 2003-04; Nat Black Media Coalition; Nat Commun Asn; Asn Commun Adminr; Speech Nat Commun Asn. **Honors/Awds:** Calif State Univ, Dominquez Hills, Young, Gifted & Black Distinguished Resident Scholar, 1991; Gustavus Myer Award, 1990; Freedom Forum Media Studies Ctr Fel, 1992; George Foster Peabody Awards, Nat Adv Bd, 1995-2002; Ebony's Women in Communications and Marketing Award, 2002; Saluting African American Achievement at the Annual Trumpet Awards, Turner Broadcasting System Inc, 2003; Outstanding Women of 2003; Nat Coalition of100 Black Women Award, 2003. **Special Achievements:** Co-author: Split Image: African Americans in the Mass Media, 1993; author:"African American TV Images Shaped By Others," Crisis magazine, December1992; "Quantity, Not Quality, Suffices for Our TV Images," p 8, Sept30-Oct 6, 1992; "This TV Season Will Be Blacker, But Will It Be Better?"September 13, 1992; reviewer: "A Review of the book Enlightened Racism,"Journal of Broadcasting and Electronic Media, Fall 1993; "A Review ofSaid's Culture and Imperialism," Critical Studies in Mass Communications,Fall 1995; Appeared on TV Shows, "Both Sides with Jesse Jackson-,""Booknotes with Brian Lamb" on CSPAN," "All Things Considered" on NPR,"Close Up" on NPR, "Our Visions" on BET, and "On the Media" on NPR. **Business Addr:** Professor, Dean, Howard University, The John H. Johnson School of Communications, Rm W2 203 G 525 Bryant St NW, Washington, DC 20059, **Business Phone:** (202)806-7690.

DAUGHTRY, HERBERT DANIEL
Clergy, public speaker. **Personal:** Born Jan 13, 1931, Savannah, GA; son of Alonzo Austin and Emmie Cheatham Williams; married Karen Ann Smith, Apr 28, 1962; children: Leah, Sharon, Dawnique, Herbert Jr. **Career:** African Peoples Christian Org, pres, 1982-; Nat Campaign Comm of Rev Jesse Jackson, special asst & confidant, 1983-84; The House of the Lord Churches, nat presiding minister, currently. **Orgs:** bd dir, vice chmn, Bedford Stuyvesant Youth in Action, 1968; vchmn, Oper Breadbasket, 1969; co chmn, Ministers Against Narcotics, 1969; Comn African Solidarity, foudr, 1977; Coalition of Concerned Leaders & Citizens to Save our Children, founder, pres, 1977; bd dir, Randolph Evans Mem Scholarship Fund, 1978-; bd dir, Black United Fund NY, 1980-; bd dir, United African Churches NYS, 1988-; bd dir, Nat Rainbow Coalition, 1985-; chmn, Nat Black United Front, 1979-86, chmn emer, 1986-; chmn, Asn Brooklyn Clergy Comt Devel, 1991-; founder, chmn, African Clergy & Elected Officials, 1991-; comnr, Black Leadership Comn on AIDS, 1989-; Credentials Comt mem, Dem Nat Conv, 2004. **Honors/Awds:** Hon mem, Malik Sigma Psi Fraternity; Doctor of Letters, Seton Hall Univ, 1980. **Special Achievements:** Author, Inside the Storm; No Monopoly on Suffering; Author, Jesus Christ: African in Origin, Revolutionary & Redeeming in Action. **Business Addr:** National Presiding Minister, House of the Lord Penticostal Churches, 415 Atlantic Ave, Brooklyn, NY 11217.*

DAUGHTY, MORRIS. See DAY, MORRIS.

DAUPHIN, BOREL C.
Insurance executive. **Career:** Williams Progressive Life & Accident Ins Co, chief exec.

DAURHAM, ERNEST
Executive, founder (originator). **Educ:** McCoy Barber Col, attended 1969; Dunbar Sch Cosmetol, attended 1969. **Career:** D-Orum Haircare Prod, founder & chief exec officer, 1979; Ernest Daurham Community Found, founder & head, 1991-. **Business Addr:** Founder, Head, Ernest Daurham Community Foundation, 8912 E Pinnacle Peak Rd, Scottsdale, AZ 85255, **Business Phone:** (480)515-0269.

DAUWAY, LOIS MCCULLOUGH
Administrator. **Personal:** Born Jul 30, 1948, Boston, MA; daughter of Eural Allen (deceased) and Pearl Kathleen Griffith. **Educ:** Univ MA; Manhattanville Col, BA. **Career:** Mass State Dept Educ, asst dir, Career Opportunity Prog, 1970-72; Project JESI Univ Mass, project site dir, 1972-74; Nat Div Gen Bd Global Ministries, black community developer, 1974-77; Gen Bd Global Ministries United Methodist Church, secy mission personnel, 1977-82; Nat Coun Churches Christ USA, asst gen secy, community justice & liberation. **Orgs:** Nat training staff Black Community Developers Prog United Methodist Church, 1977-; bd dirs, Nat Black United Fund, 1980-83; Nat Asn Female Execs, 1986-; Black Women's Concerns Prog Initiative Area; women's caucus, Black Methodists Church Renewal, Nat Coun Churches Christ, Theol Am; bd mem, Women's Theol Ctr, Anna Howard Shaw Ctr Boston Univ, Sch Theol; guest lectr, NY Theol Sem; Wash Off Haiti. **Honors/Awds:** Delegate UN End of the Decade for Women NGO Forum Nairobi Kenya; authored Women's Section of the Report of the Futures Task Force UMC; International BPDE Outstanding Leadership in Religious Education, 1977; Outstanding Young Women of America, 1980. **Home Phone:** (212)795-4525. *

DAVALT, DOROTHY B.
Educator. **Personal:** Born Dec 25, 1914, Jacksonville, FL; married Clarence J; children: Clarence J & Vincent P. **Educ:** Fla A&M Univ, BS, 1949. **Career:** Univ Southern Fla, prof; Univ Rochester, prof. **Orgs:** Pres, Escambia County Teachers Fla Educ Asn; Fla Women's Polit Caucus; Nat Asn Advan Colored People; Nat Coun Urban & State Educ Asns; Fla Educ & Voc Asns; Gov's Conf Educ; State Polit Action Comt; Keep Fla Beautiful; Common Cause League Arts; Human Rights Comt, Escambia Educ Asn; Elks; precinct comt woman, Pensacola Chamber Com; Mt Zion Baptist Church. **Honors/Awds:** COPE & NEA convs; effected merger, black/white local teacher assn, 1966-68; Governor's Comn Teacher Training Ctr, 1976. **Business Addr:** Educator, 1305 E Fisher St, Pensacola, FL 32503.*

DAVE, ALFONZO, JR.
Government official, real estate agent. **Personal:** Born Apr 2, 1945, St Louis, MO; son of Alfonzo Sr and Pearl; children: Alfonzo III. **Educ:** Univ Colo, BA, 1967, Univ Calif, graduate study. **Career:** Retired: Lic real estate, CA; Al Dave & Assoc Realty, broker & owner; alt Los Angeles Co Area Admin, state admin youth employ opportunity prog; previous assignments mgr, asst mgr, staff instr, case worker, job develop, employ interviewer; Calif Employ Develop Dept, Deputy Area Admin, div chief. **Orgs:** LA City Pvt Indust Coun, chp Youth & Young Adult Comn, Cent City Exec Comt, Summer Youth Employ Training Prog, Youth Opportunity Unlimited Task Force, Performance Eval Task Force, New Ad Hoc Progs Comn; Cent City Enterprise Zone Bus Adv Coun; Southern Calif Employ Round Table; LA Urban League Data Processing Training Ctr Adv Bd; Intl Asn Personnel Employ Security; Personnel & Industrial Rels Asn Inc; Nat Conf Christians & Jews;Community Rehab Industries; Alpha Kappa Delta; Alpha Phi Alpha; City LA Youth Serv Acad; Community Serv Ctr Prog; Rebuild LA Co-Chairperson Educ & Training Task Force; Los Angeles Demonstration Model Vocational Educ, Workforce LA Steer Comt; Mus Afro-Am Arts; Los Angeles Transp Comn Job Develop & Training Task Force; Rebuild LA Educ & Training & Job, steering comt; Nickerson Gardens Empowerment Prog Adv Coun; New Prog Task Force, Los Angeles City PIC; Community Proj Restoration; vpres, Mus African Am Art, currently. **Honors/Awds:** Commendation, LA Co Probation Dept, 1975; North Hollywood Chamber of Commerce, 1977; Selected participant, 21st Annual Wilhelm Weinberg Seminar, Cornell Univ, 1979; Cash bonuses, State CA Managerial Performance Appraisal Program, 1986, 1988; Certificate, Mgt, Am Mgt Asn, 1974; Certificate, Mgt, State Personnel Bd, 1970; Selected US Conference Mayors make presentation "Remediation in the Inner City", 1988; Commendation, completion & instruction Masters Exec Excellence through EDD, 1988; The Eagle Award, 2001. **Business Phone:** (323)294-7071.*

DAVENPORT, ARTHUR. See FATTAH, CHAKA.

DAVENPORT, C. DENNIS
Lawyer. **Personal:** Born Dec 27, 1946, Lansing, MI; married Roselle Wilson; children: Ronald & Charlene. **Educ:** Mich State Univ, BA, 1969; Mich State Univ, MA, 1970; Univ Mich, JD, 1972. **Career:** Gen Motors Corp, atty, 1972-. **Orgs:** Nat Asn Advan Colored People; Kappa Alpha Psi Frat; Nat Bar Asn, 1973-; Mich State Bar, 1973-; Wolverine Bar Asn, 1973-.

DAVENPORT, CALVIN A.
Educator. **Personal:** Born Jan 15, 1928, Gloucester, VA; son of James Robert Davenport and Carrie Emalia Brooks Davenport; married Beverly Jean Wills; children: Dean Darnell & Lynn Angela. **Educ:** VA State Univ, BS, 1949; MI State Univ, MS, 1950; Nat Univ Mexico, Mexico City, attended 1957; MI State Univ, PhD, 1963; Univ Calif, Berkeley, CA, attended 1966; Harvard Med Sch, attended 1986. **Career:** VA State Col, prof microbiol, 1963-69; MI State Univ, res asst, 1957-62; Michigan Dept Health, Div Labs 1952-53, 1955-56; Letterman Army Hosp San Francisco, med tech, 1953-55; Santa Ana Col, prof Biol; CA State Univ, prof biol, 1969-92, prof emer microbiol, currently; Univ Calif, Irvine Col Bridge Prog Biomed Res, coordr, 1997-2002. **Orgs:** Coordr, Coun Health Sci Educ, 1971-74; chmn, 1974; Accreditation Team Western Asn Schs & Cols, 1973-92; Orange Co Long Beach Health Consortium,1973-83; Am Soc Microbiol, 1963-; CA State Employees Asn, 1973-; Am Public Health Asn, 1968-92; Beta Kappa Chi Nat Sci Hon Soc, 1948-; Kappa Alpha Psi Fraternity; Iota Sigma Lambda Hon Soc; coordr, Health Manpower Educ Proj CA Univ Fullerton, 1974-75; consult, Nat Inst Health Wash, 1973-; Sr Comn Western Asn Sch & Col, 1976-79; evaluation panel bio phys & biochem, Nat Sci Found; reading comm, Danforth Found, 1977-80; secy, Acad Assembly CA Univ & Col Med Tech Progs, 1978-79; Univ Minority Affairs Coun,1981-85; Univ chmn, Acad Affirmative Actioomm, 1982-84; Univ dir incentive grants prog, Nat Action Coun Minorities Eng, 1983-84; dir, Univ " Investment in People" prog, 1983-84; Univ AIDS educ, 1984-92; Minority Biomed Res, Support Adv Comm, Gerontology Res Inst, Univ Inst Health Educ & Training; Univ Health Professions Comm; Dept Long Range Planning Comm, Acad Assembly Calif State Universities & Cols; chair, CA Pub Health Lab Dirs Acad Assembly, 1990-92; chair, Dept Curriculum Comn, 1989-92; Univ Substance Abuse Educ Comn, 1991-92; bd trustees, Charles Drew, Univ Med & Sci, 1994-97. **Honors/Awds:** Babcock Fellow, Michigan State Univ, 1950-51; Awards in recognition of outstanding contributions, CA State Univ Fullerton Black Org Engineers & Scientists, 1982 & CA St Univ Fullerton Affirmative Action Prog, 1983, 1984, 1985. **Military Serv:** AUS, pfc, 1953-55. **Business Addr:** Professor Emeritus, California State University, Department of Biological Sciences, 1 Univ Cir, Turlock, CA 95382.

DAVENPORT, DR. CAROL A.
Educator. **Educ:** Norfolk State Univ, BA, eng, 1992; Old Dominion Univ, MA, eng; Pa State Univ, PhD, educ, PhD, educ, PhD, curric & instr, 2000. **Career:** Norfolk State Univ, asst prof eng, currently. **Business Addr:** Assistant Professor, Norfolk State University, Department of English & Foreign Languages, 218 J Hugo Madison Hall, Norfolk, VA 23504, **Business Phone:** (757)823-2954.

DAVENPORT, CHESTER C
Executive. **Educ:** Univ Ga Sch Law, JD, 1966. **Career:** Transp Policy & Int Affairs, asst secy, 1977-79; GTE Consumer Servs Corp, chmn; Georgetown Partners LLC, founder & managing dir, 1988-; Envirotest Systs Corp, founder & chmn 1990; Davenport Cellular Communs LLC, chmn. **Special Achievements:** Co is ranked No 11 on the Black Enterprise list of Top 100 Industrial & Service company, 1994. **Business Addr:** Managing Director, Georgetown Partners LLC, 6903 Rockledge Dr Suite 214, Bethesda, MD 20817, **Business Phone:** (301)530-8110.

DAVENPORT, CHRISTIAN A.
Educator. **Personal:** Born Jun 4, 1965, New York, NY; son of Donn Davenport and Juliet Seignions. **Educ:** State Univ NY Binghamton, MA, 1989, PhD, 1991. **Career:** Univ Houston, asst prof, 1992-96; Univ Colo, Boulder, assoc prof polit sci, 1996-99; Univ Md Col Pk, sr fel, prof radical info & dir res, 1999-. **Orgs:** Midwest Polit Sci Asn, 1991-; Am Polit Sci Asn, 1991-; Nat Black Polit Sci Asn, 1992-; Shape Cultural Ctr, instr, 1993-95; Nat Popular Culture Asn, 1993-; Nat Coalition of Blacks for Reparations Am, 1993-; ed bd mem, Am Journ Polit Sci, 1994-; West Dallas Detention Ctr, instr, 1995; Comparative Politics Ctr, Univ Colo. **Honors/Awds:** Malcolm X Loves Network, Keeper of the

Flame Award, 1995; Ebony Mag, 50 Young Leaders of Tomorrow, 1996; Nat Asn African-Am Honors Prog, Scholarly Contributions & Leadership, 1996; Nat Sci Found, Res Develop Grant for Minority Scientists & Engrs, 1997. **Special Achievements:** "Multidimensional Threat Perception & State Repression," The American Journal of Political Science, 1995; "Constitutional Promises and Repressive Reality," The Journal of Politics, 1996; "The Weight of the Past," Political Research Quarterly, 1996; "Understanding Rhetoric Under The Gun," The Black Panther Party Reconsidered, 1997; "The Political and Social Relency of Malcolm X," The Journal of Politics, 1997. **Business Addr:** Director of Research, Center for International Development & Conflict Management, University of Maryland, 0145 Tydings Hall, College Park, MD 20742, **Business Phone:** (301)314-7703.*

DAVENPORT, HORACE ALEXANDER
Judge. **Personal:** Born Feb 22, 1919, Newberry, SC; son of William and Julia; married Alice I Latney; children: Alice D Ireland, Beverly A, Horace Jr & Nina D Arnold. **Educ:** Howard Univ, BA, 1946; Univ Pa, Wharton Sch Bus, MA, econs, 1947, LLB, 1950. **Career:** Gerber, Davenport & Wilenzik, atty, Ct Common Pleas Montgomery County 38th Judicial Dist Pa, sr judge, currently. **Orgs:** Former dir, Cent Montgomery County, Bd Am Red Cross; former dir, GW Carver Community Ctr; former dir, Cent Montgomery County Coun Human Rel; former dir, Norristown Community Concerts; Vet Foreign Wars; Hist Soc Montgomery County; Norristown Br Nat Asn Advan Colored People; former mem, Norristown Repub Club; former dir, Norristown Sch Bd; dir, Citizens Coun Montgomery County; former dir, Norristown Art League; former dir, Montgomery County TB & Health Asn; former dir, Montgomery Hosp; former area capt, Salvation Army; former dir, Norristown Sch Bd Lay Rep, Area Voc-Tech Sch; solicitor, Montgomery County Election Bd, 1958-76; solicitor, Norristown Area Sch Dist, 1966-76; solicitor, Norristown Area Sch Authority, 1966-76; solicitor, Cent Montgomery County Area Voc-Tech Sch, 1968-76; dir, Nat Sch Bds Asn, 1969-76; pres, Pa Sch Bd Solicitors Asn, 1972-73, dir, 1969, 1970 & 1971; trustee, Johnson C Smith Univ, Charlotte, NC; solicitor, Montgomery County Tax Claim Bur; Alpha Phi Alpha Fraternity; Sigma Pi Phi Fraternity; 33rd Degree Mason; Philadelphia Trial Lawyers Asn. **Honors/Awds:** Recipient of numerous community awards including the honor with a specialblack and gold stole recognizing his annuity donation to the Johnson C.Smith University by the Kresge Foundation; honorary Doctor Laws, Johnson C Smith Univ, 1979. **Special Achievements:** First African American appointed to the bench in Montgomery County, PA. **Military Serv:** Corps Engr capt. **Business Addr:** Senoir Judge, Court Common Pleasure Montgomery County, 38th Judicial District, PO Box 311, Norristown, PA 19404.*

DAVENPORT, DR. LAWRENCE FRANKLIN
School administrator. **Personal:** Born Oct 13, 1944, Lansing, MI; married Cecelia Jackson; children: Laurence, Anita, Anthony. **Educ:** Mich State Univ, BA, 1966, MA, 1968; Fairleigh Dickinson Univ, PhD, 1975. **Career:** Lansing Community Col Mich, asst dir stud activities, 1968-69; Univ Mich, dir spec proj, 1969-72, asst dean, 1972; Nat Adv Coun Voc Educ, 1970, chmn, 1971; Tuskegee Inst, vpres, 1972-74; San Diego Community Col Educ Cult Complex, pres, 1974-79; San Diego Comm Col Dist, provost, 1979-81; ACTION Agency, assoc dir domestic & anti-poverty opers, 1981-82; Fla Atlantic Univ, exec vpres & chief operating officer, currently; Fla AU Found Inc, exec dir, currently. **Orgs:** Comt, Martin Luther King Jr Fed Holiday Comt, 1985-86. **Honors/Awds:** Outstanding Young Citizen of San Diego, San Diego Jaycees, 1978. **Special Achievements:** Nomination as Asst Secy for Elem & Sec Educ, Dept Educ. **Business Phone:** (561)297-4030.

DAVENPORT, REGINALD
Newspaper executive, auditor. **Personal:** Born Apr 5, 1948, Chicago, IL; son of Myrtle and Reginald C; married Stevelena, May 24, 1969. **Educ:** Southern Univ, BS, 1969; cert pub acct, IL, 1972. **Career:** Coopers & Lybrand, auditor, 1969-72; Beatrice Foods Co, internal audit supvr, 1972-74; NY Times Reg Newspaper Group, group controller, 1974-83, sr vpres, 1983-93, exec vpres opers, 1993. **Orgs:** bd dirs, Assoc Press, 1994-98. *

DAVENPORT, RHONDA
Executive. **Career:** Comerica Bank, Detroit, MI, vpres, currently. *

DAVENPORT, RONALD R., SR.
Executive. **Personal:** Born May 21, 1936, Philadelphia, PA; son of James and Beatrice McLemore; married Judith Loftin Davenport, Aug 4, 1962; children: Ronald R Jr, Judith Allison, Susan Ross. **Educ:** PA State Univ, State Col, PA, BS, 1958; Temple Univ Sch Law, Philadelphia, PA, LLB, 1962; Yale Law Sch, New Haven, CT, LLM, 1963. **Career:** Duquesne Univ Sch Law, Pittsburgh, PA, prof, 1963-70, dean, 1970-81; Buchanan Ingersoll, PC, Pittsburgh, PA, partner, 1982-84; Sheridan Broadcasting Corp, Pittsburgh, PA, founder, chief exec officer, 1972, chmn, currently; Am Urban Radio, co-chmn. **Orgs:** Trustee, Comt Econ Develop, 1975-; bd mem, Allegheny Gen Hosp; bd mem, Nat Urban League; bd mem, Colgate Univ; bd mem, Boys & Girls Club. **Honors/Awds:** Hon Degrees: Point Park Col, LLD, 1971; Allegheny Col, LLD, 1978; Distinguished Alumni Award, Penn State Univ, 1975. **Business Addr:** Co-Chairman, Am Urban Radio Network, 432 Park Ave Fl 9, New York, NY 10016.*

DAVID, ARTHUR LACURTISS
Educator, dean (education). **Personal:** Born Apr 13, 1938, Chicago, IL; son of Carey H David Sr and Annetta; married Martha Barham; children: Alexis R Womack & Sean. **Educ:** Lane Col, BA, 1960; Phillips Sch Theol, BD, 1963; NE Univ, MA, 1970; ITC,MDiv, 1971; Middle Tenn State Univ, Arts D, 1973. **Career:** Soc Sci Div Lane Col, chmn; Lane Col, prof hist, 1963-67, 69-77; NE Wesleyan Univ, 1967-69; Motlow State Community Col, 1972-73; Lane Col, dean, 1979-93, prof hist, 1993-. **Orgs:** Soc Hist Asn; Am Hist Asn; Orgn Am Hist; Pi Gamma Mu Soc Sci, Hon Soc; Phi Alpha Theta Hist Hon Soc; Sigma Theta Epsilon Hon Soc Clergymen; Kappa Kappa Psi Hon Band Frat; Alpha Phi Alpha Frat Inc. **Special Achievements:** Dissertation "The Involvement of the Black Man in the Teaching of Western Civilization a Study of Black Colleges & Univs" 1973; You Can Fool Me But You Can't Fool God, 1976; An Anthology of a Minister's Thoughts, 1977; He Touched Me, 1992. **Home Addr:** 28 Gold Medal Rd, Milan, TN 38358, **Home Phone:** (731)686-3293. **Business Addr:** Interim President, Lane College, 545 Lane Ave, Jackson, TN 38301, **Business Phone:** (731)426-7635.*

DAVID, GEORGE F., III
Executive. **Personal:** Born Nov 6, 1923, Wilberforce, OH; son of George F II and Olivette Poole; divorced; children: George F IV, Lynn David Irby. **Educ:** Wilberforce Univ, BS, 1943; St Andrews Univ Scotland, 1946. **Career:** Glidden Co, chemist, 1950-52; Oscar Mayer & Co, food technologist, plant mgr, 1952-60; Sinai Kosher Sausage Co, plant supt, 1960-62; Superior Meat Co, plant supt, 1962-63; Superiors Brand Meats, mgr & asst opers mgr, 1962-68; Parks Sausage Co, vpres & dir, 1968-88. **Orgs:** Bd mem, USO-Central MD, 1982-; Girl Scouts-Central MD, 1984-92; pres, Hilltop Comt Org, Woodlawn MD, 1974-76; bd mem, Combined Health Agencies, 1986-88; treas, Mutual Housing Asn Baltimore, 1997-; 100 Black Men MD; chmn, Sr Kappas Comt, Kappa Alpha Psi Found; chmn, Nat Sr Kappa Affairs, 2000-. **Honors/Awds:** Achievement Award, Eastern Province Kappa Alpha Psi, 1976 & 1980; Wm "Box" Harris Award, 1986; William L Crump History Award, 1991, 1995. *

DAVID, GERALDINE R.
Government official. **Personal:** Born Sep 15, 1938, Helena, AR; married Odell Davis Jr; children: Cheryl, Vivian, Odel III, Eva, Darin, Vivian L Ross & Eva Gammon. **Educ:** Univ Pine Bluff; Rust Col, Holly Springs, MS; Phillips County Community Col. **Career:** Elaine Jr HS, librn asst, 1967; Lake View Coop Assoc, bookkeeper, 1970; Lake View Elem Sch, librn asst, 1974; City Lake View, secy & treas, 1978-. **Orgs:** Bd dir, City Exec Comt, Lake View Med Clinic, 1980-, E Ariz Area Aging, 1980-. **Honors/ Awds:** Governors Office Volunteer Award, Govs Off, 1980; Volunteer Tax Award, Fed Income Tax Off, 1980; Tri-City Leadership, 1980; Mid-Delta Community Service Volunteer Award for Community Service, 1980; Phillips City Notary Secy State Off. **Home Addr:** Rte 2, PO Box 350 A, Lexa, AR 72355. **Business Addr:** Secretary, Treasurer, City of Lake View, Rte 1, PO Box 221 A, Helena, AR 72342.

DAVID, KEITH (KEITH DAVID WILLIAMS)
Actor. **Personal:** Born Jun 4, 1956, Harlem, NY; son of Lester Williams and Delores Tittley Dickinson; married Margit Edwards Williams, Sep 22, 1990. **Educ:** Juilliard Sch, New York, NY, BFA, 1979. **Career:** Films: The Thing, 1982; Platoon, 1986; They Live, 1988; Road House, 1989; Men at Work, 1990; Marked for Death, 1990; Dead Presidents, 1995; The Quick and the Dead, 1995; Volcano, 1997; Armageddon, 1998; There's Something About Mary, 1998; Pitch Black, 2000; Requiem for a Dream, 2000; Barbershop, 2002; Agent Cody Banks, 2003; The Chronicles of Riddick, 2004; Crash, 2004; Mr & Mrs Smith, 2005; ATL, 2006; Delta Farce, 2007; voice work: Christmas In Tatter town, 1987; 3x3 Eyes, 1991; Fantastic Four, 1995; Yellowstone: Realm of the Coyote, 1995; Gargoyles, 1994-97; Hercules,1997; Spawn: The Animation, 1997; Princess Mononoke, 1997; Fallout, 1997; Hercules The Animated Series, 1998; Spawn 3: Ultimate Battle, 1999; Plan escape: Torment, 1999; The Legend of Tarzan, 2001; Final Fantasy: The Spirits Within, 2001; House of Mouse, 2001-02; PBS Hollywood Presents, 2001; Tales From the Crypt: Fare Tonight, Followed by Increasing Clottiness!, 2002; Lords of Ever quest, 2003; Justice League, 2003; Spider-Man: The New Animated Series, 2003; Kaena: The Prophecy, 2003; BeefII, 2004; The Chronicles of Riddick: Dark Fury, 2004; Teen Titans, 2004; Halo 2, 2004; City Confidential, 2004; The Proud Family Movie, 2005; Saints Row, 2006; Walking the Bible, 2006; Halo 3, 2007; Primeval, 2007; Transformers: The Game, 2007; Mass Effect, 2007. Beautiful Loser, 2008; First Sunday, 2008; Superhero Movie, 2008; Chasing 3000, 2008; My Mom's New Boyfriend, 2008; The Sensei, 2008; Behind Enemy Lines: Colombia, 2009; Against the Dark, 2009; Don McKay, 2009. **Honors/Awds:** Image Award Nomination, Nat Asn Advan Colored People, 1982; Sinclair Bay field Award Best Performance, Actors Equity, 1989; Emmy award, 2005. Prime time Emmy Award for Outstanding Voice-Over Performance, 2008. **Business Addr:** Actor, Abrams Artists Agency, 9200 W Sunset Blvd Suite 1130, West Hollywood, CA 90069.*

DAVIDDS-GARRIDO, NORBERT
Football player. **Personal:** Born Oct 4, 1972, La Puente, CA; married Yasmin. **Educ:** Univ Southern Calif. **Career:** Football player-(retired), Carolina Panthers, tackle, 1996-99; Ariz Cardinals, tackle, 2000. **Honors/Awds:** All-Rookie Team, Football Weekly, 1996. *

DAVIDSON, ALPHONZO LOWELL, SR.
Dentist. **Personal:** Born Dec 12, 1941, Fredericksburg, VA; married Carolyn; children: Alphonzo Jr, Stephanie. **Educ:** Howard Univ, BS, 1964, DDS 1968, cert oral surg, 1973. **Career:** Howard Univ, Dept Oral Surg, asst prof; Howard Univ Hosp, attend oral surgeon; Prince George Co Hosp, asso staff mem, Pvt Pract, currently. **Orgs:** Chi Delta Mu Fraternity, 1967; Oral Cancer Soc, 1968-80; Am Dent Soc, 1969; Robert T Freedman Dent Soc; Nat Dent Soc, 1969; Asn Mil Surgeons, 1970; Asn Interns & Residents Freedmen's Hosp, 1972; Am Soc Oral Surg, 1975; Am Bd Oral Surg, 1976; Dent Soc Anesthesiol, 1978; Pres, DC Oral Surg Soc, 1979-80; Omicron Kappa Upsilon Pi Pi Chap, 1979-80; Sigma Phi Sigma; DC Dent Soc. **Military Serv:** USAF, capt, 1968-70. **Business Addr:** Dentist, 2811 Pa Ave SE, Washington, DC 20020.

DAVIDSON, ARTHUR B
Administrator. **Personal:** Born Dec 5, 1929, Detroit, MI; son of Arthur B and Idella; married Edith. **Educ:** Detroit Inst Technol, BA, 1964; Wayne State Univ, Pub Admin, 1970. **Career:** Human Resources Develop, area admin, 1964-68; Butzel Family Ctr Co-ord Serv, dir, 1968-70; City Detroit, planning admin, 1970-81, opers & mgt serv admin, 1981-82, dir admin serv & weatherization, 1982-88, asst dir, 1988; Dept Human Serv, interim dep dir, 2002-. **Orgs:** Nat Asn Housing & Redevelop & Off, 1964; New Detroit Inc, 1970; treas, chmn finance, exec comt, OmniCare Health Plan Bd Trustees. **Honors/Awds:** Cert excellence, Urban League, 1965; cert recognition, Greater Macedonia Baptist Church, 1965. **Military Serv:** AUS, 1951-53. **Business Addr:** Interim Deputy Director, City of Detroit, Department of Human Services, 5031 Grandy Ave, Detroit, MI 48211, **Business Phone:** (313)852-5609.

DAVIDSON, ARTHUR TURNER
Physician, lawyer. **Personal:** Born Jul 30, 1923; son of Robert J; married Ezeria Jennie White; children: Arthur T Jr, Ronald W, Michael G, Kathie E. **Educ:** Howard Univ Sch Med, MD, 1945; St John's Univ Sch Law, JD, 1974. **Career:** Downstate Med Ctr, Brooklyn, asst clinical prof surg; Columbia Univ, Col Physicians & Surgeons, NY, asst clinical prof surg; Yeshiva Univ, Albert Einstein Col Med, Dept Surg, asst clinical prof; pvt pract, physician & atty. **Orgs:** Am Med Asn; Nat Med Asn; Am Bar Asn. **Special Achievements:** Publ, "Mech Small Bowel Obstruction Gangrene Presenting Narrowing Pulse Pressure A New Diagnostic Sign", JNMA 56 393, 1964; "Thymotropic Action Vitamin A", Fed Proc Am Soc exp Biologists, 1973; "Enhanced Lymphocytic Action Breast Tumor", JNMA 66 472, 1974. **Military Serv:** AUS, med corps capt, 1951-53. **Business Addr:** Physician, Attorney, Private Practice, 1378 President St, Brooklyn, NY 11213, **Business Phone:** (718)756-1708.*

DAVIDSON, DR. CHARLES ODELL
Physician. **Personal:** Born Nov 12, 1935, Pine Bluff, AR; married Fredricka Cooper; children: Harryl & Darryl. **Educ:** Howard Univ Med Sch, MD, 1961; Homer G Phillips Hosp, Internship, 1961-62; Homer G Phillips Hosp, Resident, Chief Resident, 1962-65. **Career:** Obstet-Gynec, Pvt practice, currently; The Methodist Hosp Gary Inc Med Staff, pres, 1980-81; coordr, Performance Improvement, Resource Utilization, 2000. **Orgs:** Bd trustee, Methodist Hosp Gary Inc; bd dirs, Gary Bd Health, 1978-; chmn, Obstet-Gynec Gary Merrillville Methodist Hosp; pvt practice, 1968-77; hosp comdr, Malstrom AFB, 1967-68; chmn, OB-GYN Malstrom AFB, 1966-68; supr, OB-GYN Homer G Phillips St Louis, 1965-66; secy-treas, Gary Med Specialists Inc; chmn, NW IN Planned Parenthood Med Adv Council; Am Fertility Sox; Asn Am Gynec Laparoscopists Diplomat Am; bd OB-GYN, 1967; Fel, Am Col OB-GYN, 1972. **Honors/Awds:** Dudley Turner Community Service Award, 1989. **Military Serv:** USAF, maj. **Business Addr:** Physician, 2200 Grant St, Gary, IN 46311, **Business Phone:** (219)944-7565.

DAVIDSON, CLEATUS LAVON
Baseball player. **Personal:** Born Nov 1, 1976, Bartow, FL. **Career:** Minn Twins, 1999; Elmira Pioneers, infielder, 2003-04; N Shore Spirit, 2005; Long Beach Armada, 2008. *

DAVIDSON, EARNEST JEFFERSON
Educator, sculptor. **Personal:** Born Aug 16, 1946, Little Rock, AR; son of Alice Sanders and Earnest Jefferson Davidson Sr; children: Tamara S & Earnest III. **Educ:** Philander Smith Col, BA, Ark Art Ctr, 1969; Syracuse Univ, MFA, 1972; UnivArk, Little Rock, attended 1975. **Career:** Adventures in Ed Syracuse, NY, woodwork Specialist, 1972; Lomax Hanna Jr Col, teach arts & crafts, 1978; Southeast Art & Sci Ctr, teach pottery, 1984; Ark Art Ctr, teach sculpture, 1984; Univ Ark, Pine Bluff, assoc prof, 1972-

92, prof, 1992-, Standing Comt Student Appeals (Adademic Evaluation), chmn; Pine Tech Col, adj prof, 1994-98; Univ Ark, Pine Bluff, prof sculpture & ceramics, currently. **Orgs:** Chairperson, Visual Arts Com Arts & Sci Ctr, 1985; Emergency School Aid Act Artist-In-Residence Selection Committee, 1976-82; mem, Int Sculpture asn, 1988-, Am Foundrymen Soc, 1988-; potter consult, bd trustees, SE Ark Arts & Sci Ctr, 1990-; Martin L King, Jr Comn, 1998-2003; chair, Academic Prog Review Comm, Univ Ark, Pine Bluff, 1998; pres, Am Asn Univ Prof, (AAUP), 1998. **Honors/Awds:** Gov Award Little Rock Arts & Crafts Fair, 1974; Title III Grant Univ of Ark, Little Rock, 1975; Under grad ad Omega Psi Phi Te, 1985-87; Apprentice in the Arts Grant, 1982; Commissioned to create bronze statue Martin Luther King, Student Assn Northern Univ Ill, Dekalb, 1985-86; Title III Grant Univ Ark, Little Rock, 1986; Pine Bluff, Bus for the Arts Award, 1988; One of three finalists for the Arkansas Vietnam Veterans Memorial, 1987; Arkansas Art Registry; Distinguished Faculty Award, Arts & Science, Univ Ark, Pine Bluff, 1990; Purchase Award, Ceramic Sculpture, Hendrix Col, 1990; Golden Citation, Trilogy of South Africa Philander Smith Col, 1990; Ancestral Visions Series, Ceramic Sculpture on the Cove of African American Folktales for Young Readers, August House, 1993; Comcast Cable, Studio 14, Learning About Art, talk show host, 1993-; Arkansas State Capitol, Distinguish Arkansas Collection, commissioned work of fourceramic clay busts, Dr Elijah Coleman, 1995, Dr Jerry Jewell, 1995, Dr William Townsend, 1994, Prof Henry Wilkins, 1993; Rap Grant, Regional Artist Prog Award, 1997; Commission, Ceramic Sculpture, 1997; Commissioned Parks Project, 2003.

DAVIDSON, DR. ELVYN VERONE
Surgeon. **Personal:** Born Sep 6, 1923, New York, NY; son of John A H and Hattie Olizabeth Hargraves; married Esther M Johnson, Jun 9, 1953 (deceased); children: Pamela D Branner, Evelyne M & Elvyn V II. **Educ:** Lincoln Univ, PA, AB, 1949; Meharry Med Col, MD, 1953; New York Univ, Post Grad Sch Med, certificate surg, 1954. **Career:** Surgeon (retired); Univ Tenn, Meharry Med Col & Hosp, Knoxville, instr surg, 1959-70, asst prof, 1970-91; Am Soc Abdominal Surg fel, 1968; East Tenn Baptist Hosp, Knoxville, chief surg, 1974-76; Knox County, dep med examr, 1979. **Orgs:** AMA; Nat Med Asn; Ky Med Asn; VSMA; Tex Med Asn; Am Heart Asn; CSS; SMA; Am Cancer Soc; Century Club UMCA, NAACP; bas, Omega Psi Frat; bd dir, VIP Home Health Asn, 1983; grant knight, Knights Columbus, 1982-83; dist dep, Knights Columbus; bd dir, Columbus Home. **Military Serv:** AUS, tech sgt, 1942-46; Purple Heart Combat Inf Award. **Home Addr:** PO Box 14144, Knoxville, TN 37914-1144, **Home Phone:** (615)522-3559.

DAVIDSON, EZRA C.
Educator, dean (education). **Personal:** Born Oct 21, 1933, Water Valley, MS; son of Ezra C Sr and Theresa; divorced; children: Pamela, Gwendolyn, Marc & Ezra K. **Educ:** Morehouse Col, BS, 1954; Meharry Med Sch, MD, 1958. **Career:** LA Co Univ So CA Med Ctr, 1970-80; Martin Luther King Gen Hosp, chief serv, 1971-96; Univ So Calif Sch Med, prof, 1971-80; Univ Calif Los Angeles, chmn & chief-to-staff, 1971-96, prof, 1979-; Charles R Drew Univ Med & Sci, prof, 1971-, chmn dept ob & gynec 1971-96, assoc dean primary care, currently. **Orgs:** Consult, Nat Found March Dimes, 1970-77; bd consult, Int Childbirth Educ Asn Inc, 1973-80; Nat Med Adv Com Nat Found March Dimes Inc, 1972-77; bd dir, Prof Staff Asn Found Martin Luther King Jr Gen Hosp, 1972-; examiner,Am Bd Ob & Gynec, 1973-; Sec Adv Comt Pop Affairs, 1974-77; chmn, Serv Task Force, 1975-77; bd dir, Nat Alliance Sch Age Parents, 1975-80; bd trustees, 1989-, nat chmn, sec, 1975-77; Alpha Omega Alpha Honor Soc; fel,Robert Woods Johnson Health Policy Inst Med Wash, DC, 1979-80; Ob & Gynec Nat Med Asn; pres Assoc Profs Gynec & Ob, 1987-88; pres, Golden State Med Asn, 1989-90; sec, Am Col Ob & Gynec, 1983-89, pres-elect, 1989-90, pres,1990-91; chmn, Obstetrical & Gynec Asn Southern CA, 1988-89; Food & DrugAdm, chair, adv com fertility & maternal health drugs, 1992-96; chair &sec's adv com infant mortality, Dept Health & Human Serv, 1992-95; Nat Acad Scis, Inst Med, 1991-; fel Am Col Ob-Gynec; fel Am Col Surg; fel LAOb-Gynec Soc Inc; bd dir, Children's? Bur Southern Calif, pres, 1999-2002;bd dir, Calif Wellness Found, chair, 1998-2000. **Honors/Awds:** Black Hall of Fame, Nat Black Alumni Asn, 1990; Alumnus of Year, Chicago Chap, Mc Harry Alumni, 1990; Citation of Merit, City Los Angeles, 1990;Royal Col Obstetricians-Gynecologists, Fellow ad eundem, 1991; honorary mem, Perinatology Section, Am Acad pediats, 1999. **Special Achievements:** First black president of the America College Obstetricians &Gynecologists, 1990; published number of articles. **Military Serv:** USAF, capt, 1959-63. **Home Addr:** 800 W 1st St, Los Angeles, CA 90012, **Home Phone:** (213)680-9532. **Business Addr:** Associate Dean, Professor, Charles R Drew University of Medicine & Science, Department of Obstetrics and Gynecology, 1731 E 120th St, Los Angeles, CA 90059, **Business Phone:** (323)563-4800.

DAVIDSON, FLETCHER VERNON, JR.
Automotive executive. **Personal:** Born Feb 23, 1947, Portland, OR; son of Fletcher V Sr and Stella M; married Rosie Lee Tucker, Sep 10, 1967; children: Fletcher V III, Damion R, Crystal N. **Educ:** Los Angeles City Clg, AA, tech engineering, 1966; Calif State Univ, Long Beach, BS, indust tech, 1972; Univ Southern calif, MS, mgt sci, 1976. **Career:** McDonnell-Douglas Corp, draftsman, 1966-70, sr engr & syst analyst, 1970-73; Toyota Motor Sales USA Inc, planning analyst, 1973-76, systs develop mgr, 1977-83, nat supply mgr, 1984-90, nat logistics planning mgr, 1991-92, vpres distrib & financial opers, 2001-; N Am parts Logistics Div, corp mgr, 1993-99. **Business Addr:** Vice President, Toyota Motor Sales USA Inc, 19001 S Western Ave, Torrance, CA 90509, **Business Phone:** (310)468-4953.*

DAVIDSON, HEZEKIAH MILES
Executive. **Personal:** Born Jan 1, 1970. **Career:** Right Hand Mgt & Prod Inc, chief exec officer, currently. **Honors/Awds:** 26 Best Bachelors of the Year, Ebony, 2003. **Business Addr:** Chief Executive Officer, Right Hand Management & Productions Inc, PO Box 2112, Akron, OH 44309-2112, **Business Phone:** (330)535-5431.

DAVIDSON, DR. KERRY
State government official. **Personal:** Born May 1, 1935, Water Valley, MS; married Betty Vanover; children: Mary Jaures & Elizabeth Jeanette. **Educ:** Morehouse Col; Univ Iowa, pol sci; Tulane Univ, PhD. **Career:** Southern Univ New Orleans, former chmn dept hist; Fisk Univ, former chmn; La Bd Regents, comnr acad affairs, Sponsored Progs, dep comnr & proj dir, currently. **Honors/Awds:** Danforth Grant. **Special Achievements:** Author of 20th Century Civilization. **Business Addr:** Deputy Commissioner for Sponsored Programs, Louisiana Board of Regents, Office of Sponsored Programs, PO Box 3677, Baton Rouge, LA 70801-3677, **Business Phone:** (225)342-4253.

DAVIDSON, LURLEAN G.
Administrator. **Personal:** Born May 3, 1931, West Point, GA; married Ogletree; children: Marzette, Jerome, John, Darlene & Mary. **Educ:** Case Western Res; OH Univ; Cleveland State Univ. **Career:** Parent Resource Ctrs Cleveland Bd Educ, dir; Sol Victory Mutual Life Ins, 1958-60; auditor; interviewer; election clerk; Cleveland Bd Ed, teacher; Davidson's Construction Co, secy, treas; Inner City Pride, pres. **Orgs:** Parent Adv Bd YMCA; Precinct Committee woman, 1960-73; Glenville Area Coun Phyllis Wheatley Asn; Nat Asn Advan Colored People; Urban League; Jewish Coun; life mem, PTA, 1965. **Honors/Awds:** Outstanding Service Award, 1961; Outstanding Social Award, Certificate of Merit, Nat Asn Advan Colored People, 1962; Community Leadership Award, Coun City Cleveland, 1981. **Business Addr:** Staff, Joseph F Landis School, 10118 Hampden Ave, Cleveland, OH 44108.*

DAVIDSON, RICK BERNARD
Banker. **Personal:** Born Oct 6, 1951, Nashville, TN; son of Robert and Beula Jones; married Izola Putnam, Sep 22, 1979; children: Sandra Putnam & Robert Derrick. **Educ:** Tenn Sch Banking, Nashville, TN, dipl, 1980; Univ Okla, ABA Com Sch Lending, dipl, 1983; La State Univ, Grad Sch Banking S, Baton Rouge LA, cert, 1989; Tenn Com Lending Sch, Nashville TN, cert, 1988. **Career:** Third Nat Bank, Nashville, TN, asst mgr, 1969-78; Com Union Bank, Nashville, TN, mgr, 1978-80; Com Union Bank, Nashville, TN, asst vpres & comn lending Officer, 1981-84; Nashville City Bank, Nashville, TN, loan review specialist, 1984; Citizens Bank, Nashville, TN, first vpres, 1985-88, pres & chief exec officer, 1988-95. **Orgs:** Dir, Bethlehem Ctr, 1985-89, treas, 1986-88; pres, Middle Tenn Chap, Am Inst Banking, 1986-87; pres, Am Inst Banking, 1986-87; comnr, Tenn Serv Bd, 1987; treas, Uptown Nashville, 1989; dir, Proj Pencil, 1989; Legis Comn, 1989.

DAVIDSON, ROBERT C., JR.
Executive. **Personal:** Born Oct 3, 1945, Memphis, TN; son of Robert C Sr and Thelma; married Alice Faye Davidson, Jan 5, 1978; children: Robert C Davidson, III, John R Davidson, Julian L Davidson. **Educ:** Morehouse Col, BA, 1967; Grad Sch Bus Univ Chicago, MBA, 1969. **Career:** Cresap, McCormack & Paget, sr assoc consult, 1969-72; Urban Nat Corp, vpres, 1972-74; Avant Garde Enterprises, exec vpres, 1974-75; R Davidson & Assoc, consult, 1975-78; Surface Protection Industs Inc, pres, chief exec officer & chmn, 1978-. **Orgs:** Bd dirs, Los Angeles Chamber Orchestra; bd dirs, C's Hosp Los Angeles; Young Pres's Orgn; Nat Asn Investment Cos. **Honors/Awds:** Black Businessman of the Year, Los Angeles Chap, Black MBA Asn, 1988; Business listed as No. 21 in Black Enterprise's list of top 100 black firms, 1989; Outstanding Entrepreneur, Nat Asn Investment Cos, 1990. **Business Addr:** President, Chairman, Surface Protection Industries Inc, 3411 E 15th St, Los Angeles, CA 90023, **Business Phone:** (323)980-1250.*

DAVIDSON, RUDOLPH DOUGLAS
Government official. **Personal:** Born Jul 19, 1941, Louisville, KY; son of Nathaniel and Catherine Ruffins; married Jean Slater Davidson, Feb 12, 1988. **Educ:** Univ Louisville, KY, 1972. **Career:** Westinghouse Learning Corp, Louisville, KY, mgr, 1966-70; Model Cities Prog, Louisville, KY, dir, oper mainstream, 1970-73; City Louisville, Louisville, KY, dir, Lou & Jeff County, directions opport, 1973-77, dir, Louisville, Jeff County, WEP, 1977-79, exec dir, Lou & Jeff County, CAA, 1979-83, dir solid waste mgt & serv, 1983-. **Orgs:** Lou & Jeff County Community Action Agency, 1983-; Jeff County Solid Waste Mgt Bd, 1985-; Nat Forum Black Pub Adminrs, 1989-; chmn, Mayor Jerry Abramson's Recycling Comt, 1989-; chmn, Mayor Jerry Abramson's Resource Recovery Project Comn, 1990-; Munic Waste Mgt Asn exec comt; pres, Ky Bluegrass Chap, Solid Waste Asn N Am; vpres, US Conf Mayors, Munic Waste Mgt Asn; vpres, W End Clubs Develo Ctr Bd; Cabinet Pub Works & Servs, Louisville-Jefferson County. **Honors/Awds:** Fleur De Lis Award for Meritorious Service, Mayor William Stansbury, 1977-82; Certificate of Merit, Louisville, Bd Alderman, 1983; Distinguished Citizen Award, Mayor Harvey Sloane, 1983; Outstanding Community, County Judge, Exec Mitch McConnell, 1983; Commissioned KY Colonel, Gov, John Y Brown, 1983; Black Achiever, 1984; Public Works Leaders of the Year, Am Pub Works Asn, 1997. **Military Serv:** Army, E-4, 1963-65, Honorable Discharge, 1965. **Home Addr:** 108 Fontaine Landing Ct, Louisville, KY 40212.

DAVIDSON, TOMMY
Comedian, actor. **Personal:** Born Nov 10, 1963?, Washington, DC. **Career:** Standup comedian, currently; actor, currently; Films: Strictly Business, 1991; CB4, 1993; Ace Ventura: When Nature Calls, 1995; Booty Call, 1997; Plump Fiction, 1997; Woo, 1998; Pros & Cons, 1999; Bamboozled, 2000; Juwanna Mann, 2002; Funky Monkey, 2004; Black Dynamite, 2009; TV Series: "CBS Summer Playhouse", 1989; "In Living Color", 1990-94; "Tommy Davidson: Illin' in Philly", 1991; "The Best of Robert Townsend & His Partners in Crime", 1991; "Roc", 1992; "The 6th Annual Soul Train Music Awards", 1992; "The Commish", 1993; "Martin", 1993; "Yuletide in the 'hood", voice, 1993; "Mo' Funny: Black Comedy in America", 1993; "Soul Train Comedy Awards", 1993; "A Cool Like That Christmas", voice, 1994; "Duckman: Private Dick/Family Man", 1994; "Boston Common", 1997; "Between Brothers", 1997; "Mad TV", 1997; "Space Ghost Coast to Coast", 1997; "Premium Blend", 1997; "Tonight at the House of Blues", 1998; "The Magic Hour", 1998; "Happily Ever After: Fairy Talesfor Every Child", 1999; "Malcolm & Eddie", 1999-2000; "All That", 1999; "Santa Who?", 2000; "The Proud Family", 2001-05; "Weakest Link", 2001; "Comedy Central Presents: The N.Y. Friars Club Roast of Hugh Hefner", 2001; "The Scream Team", 2002; "Platinum Comedy Series: Roasting Shaquille O'Neal", 2002; "The View", 2002; "Mad TV", 2003; "Hollywood Squares", 2003; "The Tonight Show with Jay Leno", 2003; "The Bernie Mac Show", 2004-05; "TV in Black: The First Fifty Years", voice, 2004; "The Sharon Osbourne Show", 2004; "Last Call with Carson Daly", 2004-05; "Inked", 2005; "Lilo & Stitch: The Series", 2005; "The Proud Family Movie", voice, 2005; "I Love the '90s: Part Deux", 2005; "In the Mix", 2006; "Comics Unleashed", 2006; "Live at Gotham", 2008. **Honors/Awds:** Voted one of the Rising Stars of Comedy, 1990. **Business Addr:** Actor, c/o William Morris Agency, 151 El Camino Dr, Beverly Hills, CA 90212-2775, **Business Phone:** (310)274-7451.*

DAVIDSON, U S, JR.
Educator. **Personal:** Born Oct 28, 1954, Fulton, MS; son of U S Davidson Sr and Juanita; married Jacqueline J Martin, Aug 29, 1980 (divorced); children: Brian Anthony. **Educ:** Parkland Community Col, AA, univ studies, 1975; NDK State Univ, BS, sec educ, 1978; Eastern Ill Univ, Masters, guidance/coun, 1983, type 75, adm endorsement, 1986. **Career:** Champaign Community Unit District #4, instructional aide, 1978-79, spec educ teacher, 1979-81, physical educ teacher, 1981-85, counr, 1985-88, dean studs, 1988-90, asst prin, 1990, prin, 1990; Osborne High Sch, prin, currently. **Orgs:** Kappa Alpha Psi, 1974-; Phi Delta Kappa, 1983-; Asn Ill Middle Sch, 1990-; Champaign Human Rels Comn, 1990-; Champaign County Urban League, 1985-; Minority Teacher Recruitment Team, 1989-; Ill Middle Grades Planning Initiative Comt, 1991-; Comt Identify Minorities for Bds & Comns, 1992-. **Business Phone:** (770)319-3791.

DAVIDSON-HARGER, JOAN CAROLE
Lawyer. **Educ:** Univ Mich, 1965-66; Univ Detroit, BA, 1975; Detroit Col Law, JD, 1983. **Career:** Detroit Bd Educ, urban adult teacher math, 1975-76; Ford Motor Co, NAAO, analyst, 1976-89; sole practitioner, atty, 1987-90; UAW Legal Serv, staff atty, 1990-91; Bloomfield Law Ctr, atty, 1991-. **Orgs:** Phi Alpha Theta, Hist Hon Soc, 1974; Nat Bar Asn, 1983-; vpres, secy, United Methodist Women, 1985-90; leader/sponsor, Magnolia United Methodist Youth Group, 1985-89; Oakland Co Bar Asn, 1987-88; State Bar Mich, 1987-; Detroit Metrop Black United Methodist Scholar Fund, 1988-90; D Augustus Straker Bar Asn, 1991-. **Honors/Awds:** Service Award, United Methodist Women, 1988. **Business Phone:** (248)332-0222.

DAVIE, DAMON JONATHON
Automotive executive. **Personal:** Born May 8, 1964, Detroit, MI; son of William and Alice; married Ruthanne, May 14, 1988; children: Damon & Daniel. **Educ:** Drake Univ, attended 1985; Western Ill Univ, Communs. **Career:** Pepsi Cola Co, mgt trainee, 1989-90; Rent-A-Center, acct mgr, 1990-91; AAA Mich, 1991-. **Orgs:** Vpres, Omega Psi Phi Fraternity Inc, Epsilon Beta Chap, 1987; New Detroit Inc, comt mem, 1996. **Business Phone:** (313)336-1545.

DAVIE, TIMOTHY M
Government official. **Personal:** Born Oct 14, 1955, Hopkinsville, KY; son of Barker W Sr; married Chloretha, May 7, 1983. **Educ:**

Ind Wesleyan Univ, BS (cum laude), bus mgt. **Career:** Government Official (retired); Ft Wayne Fire Dept, fire fighter, 1981-84, lt, opers div, 1984-88, inspector, 1986-96, fire marshal, 1996-2000, fire chief, 2000-07. **Orgs:** NFPA; Am Lung Asn, Regional Coun II, 1999-; ICBO; Ind Fire Inspectors Asn; bd mem, Friends Lincoln Museum; Greater Progressive Baptist Church, Men Vision; comnr, Safety Village Survive Alive; bd dir, Am Heart Asn; Ind Fire Chiefs Asn; Int Asn Fire Chiefs; Nat Fire Protection Asn; bd dir, Parkview YMCA; bd dir, Ind State Emergency Med Servs Comn, Lutheran Hosp Bd Dirs, Pres Friends Lincoln Mus; chmn bd, Ind Fire Chiefs Asn; Paul Harris Fel; Allen County Community Libr. **Honors/Awds:** Golden Apple Award, East Allen County Schs, 1994; Order of Life Safety Servants' Knight.

DAVIES, REV. LAWRENCE A.
Mayor, clergy. **Personal:** Born Jul 7, 1930, Houston, TX; son of Lawrence A Davies Sr and Autrey Thomas Davies Miller; married Janice J Pryde; children: Lauren A, Karen M & Sharron L. **Educ:** Prairie View A&M Col, BS, 1949; Howard Univ Sch Relig, MDiv, 1957; Wesley Theol Sem, STM, 1961; Fredericksburg Bible Inst & Sem, DDiv, 1985. **Career:** Good Samaritan Baptist Church WA DC, pastor, 1956-60; Shiloh Baptist Church WA DC, asst pastor & relig ed dir, 1960-62; Shiloh Baptist Church, Fredericksburg, VA, pastor, 1962-; City Fredericksburg, city councilman, 1966-76, mayor, 1976. **Orgs:** Pres, Fredericksburg Area Ministerial Asn, 1965-66; Fredericksburg Baptist Ministers Conf, 1969-70; Rappahannock Citizen Corp, 1968-; VA Asn Ment Health, 1974-76; adv dir, Perpetual Am Bank, 1975-88; bd dir, Nat Conf Black Mayors, 1977-86, Nat Kidney Found VA, 1984-86; pres, VA Munic League, 1984-85, VA Conf Black Mayors, 1985-; founder, Fredericksburg Area Sickle Cell Asn; Fredericksburg Lions Club, Alpha Phi Alpha Frat, Prince Hall Masons, Gov's Comn Transp in the 21st Century, 1986-88; bd visitors, Mary Wash Col, 1986-90; Commonwealth Transp Bd, 1990-. **Honors/Awds:** Young Man of the Year, Fredericksburg Jaycees, 1966; Citizen of the Year, Omega Psi Phi Frat, 1966; Citizenship Award, Fredericksburg Area Chamber Com, 1976; Man of the Year, VFW No 3103, 1977; Outstanding Service Award, Nat Asn Ment Health, 1979; Humanitarian of the Year Award, Mt Bethel Baptist Asn, 1984; Citizen of the Year, Alpha Kappa Alpha Sorority, Mid-Atlantic Region, 1990. **Special Achievements:** First African American mayor of City of Fredericksburg. **Business Addr:** Pastor, Shiloh Baptist Church, 801 Sophia St, Fredericksburg, VA 22401, **Business Phone:** (540)373-8701.

DAVIS, ABRAHAM
Educator. **Personal:** Born May 14, 1923, Beaufort, SC; son of Abraham and Everlena; married Jennie Howard; children: Silena Davis, Wilkins Garrett Jr, James Wright & Joya Wright. **Educ:** Lancaster Sch Bible & Theol, diplo Bible & Theol, 1949; Houghton Col, BA, 1955; Temple Univ, MA, 1956; Univ Iowa, Penn State Univ, Western Reserve Univ, attended 1960; Ind Univ Bloomington, PhD, 1971. **Career:** Educator (retired); Positive Ethnic Models & Ethnic Integration Col Curricula, lect, rhetorician; SC State Col Neg, speech therpst & instr, Orange, SC, 1956-58; Greenville Co Negro Pub Sch, co speech therpst, 1958-61; Houghton Col, instr Speech & English Compos, 1961-65; Ind Univ Bloomington, assoc teacher pub speaking, 1965-67; Houghton Col, assoc prof, prof speech, 1967-72; sabbatical lect, oral inter Afro-Am Lit & Rhetoric, 1972-73; Messiah Col, acting dean, Philadelphia PA, 1973-74; Asbury Col,vis prof, 1973-74, Philadelphia PA; Messiah Col, admin acad dean, 1975-80; Eastern Mennonite Col, Cross Cult Comn, coordr, prof, 1980-85; Ctr Urban Theol Studies,prof speech & basic writing, Philadelphia, PA, 1986-87; Calvin Col, Grand Rapids, vis prof dept comn arts & sci, 1987-88. **Orgs:** Volunt various organs. **Honors/Awds:** Pub Doctoral Dissertation & Abstract, An Accelerated Speech Curriculum for Selected Educational Disadvtd Negros, Dissertation Abstract, 1971; Speaker Regional & Nat Professional Speech Comm Assn 1972; Speaker Nat Coun Teachers Eng, 1973; vis lectr, The Fundamentals of Oral & Written Commun, 1976; Speaker & oral interpreter of Afro-Am lit & rhetoric various chs, comm groups, pub assemblies, faculty In Serv. **Special Achievements:** Published books: Review of Your God is Too White Journal of Am Sci Affiliation, 1971; The Oratory of Negro Leaders 1900-1960 for Ethnic and Minoirty Studies Newsletter of WI State 1972; Black Jargon in White Am Journal of Am Sci Affiliation; Article: Evangelicals Listen, Please Listen Bridge 1976. **Home Addr:** 1285 Shank Dr Suite 321, Harrisonburg, VA 22802-5534, **Home Phone:** (540)432-7295.

DAVIS, ADRIAN
President (Organization), administrator. **Career:** Nat Coun Social Studies, pres, 2001-02, Nominations & Elections Comt, mem, currently. **Orgs:** Nat Alliance Civic Educ.

DAVIS, ADRIANNE
Government official. **Personal:** Born Sep 6, 1945, Newark, NJ. **Educ:** Montclair St Col, BA, bus educ, MA, 1967. **Career:** W Side HS, NJ, instr 1967-73; N Ward Ctr Inc, NJ, adminr, 1973; Essex Co NJ, free holder large, 1982-87; County Col Morris, adj prof; Caucus Educ Corp, secy. **Orgs:** Consult, John Hay Whitney Found, 1973-74; chair, Essex County Col Personnel Communs, 1979; Essex Vty Col Bd Trustees, 1979-80; Essex County Bd Freeholders, 1982, Budget Review Comn, Essex County Bd Freeholders, 1983; Essex County Econ Develop Corp, 1983; vpres, Essex County Bd Educ, 2007. **Honors/Awds:** Distingushed Service Award, Theatre Universal Images, 1980; Appreciation Award, Essex County Col, 1980; Citizens Appreciation Award, Community Womens Concerns Essex County, 1980; Dr Martin Luther King Recogonition Award, N Ward Ctr, 1983. *

DAVIS, AGNES MARIA
Manager, registered nurse. **Personal:** Born Jun 3, 1927, Republic of Panama, Panama; daughter of Frederick (deceased) and Ellen (deceased); married Samuel Huntley, Mar 17, 1972; children: Alexander Dunker Jr & Ann Maria Dunker. **Educ:** St Francis Col, BS, 1984; Long Island Univ, MS, 1987; Sch Nursing, Jewish Hosp & Med Ctr Brooklyn. **Career:** Jewish Hosp & Med Ctr Brooklyn, supvr, 1961-65; Interfaith Med Ctr, full-time asst dir nursing, 1985-88; Clove Lakes Nursing Home, part-time supvr, 1992-; Senga Travel Inc, pres, currently. **Orgs:** Nursing Alumnae Bd, 1973-; exec bd mem, Staten Island Chamber Com, 1992-; chairperson, NAACOG. **Special Achievements:** Author: Fetal Alcohol Syndrome (In The Neonates), 1978. **Business Phone:** (718)816-1608.

DAVIS, ALFRED C., SR.
Commissioner, clergy, administrator. **Personal:** Born Mar 11, 1938, Vaiden, MS; married Mary L Mack; children: Alfred C Jr, Darlene, Frederick Jerome, Angel Aleeta. **Educ:** NW Training Center OR State, 1969; Tacoma Vocational Tech, 1970; Trinity Hall Col & Seminary York, PA, DD, 1980. **Career:** New Jerusalem, asst pastor, 1958-61; Altheimer Meml Ch, asst pastor, 1961-64; Eastside Comm Church, pastor & founder, 1964-, minister, currently; Multi Serv Ctr, Eastside, ODI, asst dir, 1965; Eastside Comm Day Care Ctr, founder & admin, 1972-; Tacoma Housing Authority, minister. **Orgs:** Pres & exec officer, FORCE, 1973-; founder, majestic Aires Rehab Farm Yelm, 1975-; past chmn, bd of commr Tacoma Housing Authority, 1977-; pres, Tacoma Ministerial Alliance, 1978-80; bd mem, Nat Commn ERS Com of Nahro's, 1979-; charter mem, The Tacoma Club; NAACP; Tacoma Urban League; chmn, Ministrial Alliance; evangelism & mem, Adv Bd to the TMA Pres. **Honors/Awds:** Service to Mankind Award, Puget Sound Sertoma Club, 1980; Dist Serv to Mankind Award, BC-WA Dist NW Region Sertoma, 1980; Key to City of Tacoma, WA from Mayor Mike Parker, 1980. **Military Serv:** USAF, Good Conduct Medal, 1960. **Business Addr:** Pastor, Eastside Community Church, 4420 E Portland Ave, Tacoma, WA 98404, **Business Phone:** (253)472-3552.*

DAVIS, ALGENITA SCOTT
Lawyer, vice president (organization). **Personal:** Born Oct 1, 1950, Houston, TX; daughter of Althea Lewis and CB Scott; married John W Davis III (died 1977); children: Marthea & John IV. **Educ:** Howard Univ, BBA, 1971, JD, 1974. **Career:** US Govt Printing Off, clerk-typist, 1969-70, 71; Howard Univ Dept Residence Life, grad fel, 1971-74; US General Acct Off, legal intern, 1972; Shell Oil Co, tax serv mgr, tax compliance dept, 1974-77, off legislation & indust affairs, mgr, 1977-79, tax atty, tax compliance dept, 1979; Burney Edwards Hall Hartsfield & Scott, partner, 1975-78; Port Houston Authority, counsel, 1979-89; Tex Commerce Bancshares, vpres, community affairs officers, sr vpres, community affairs officers; J P Morgan Chase & Co, mgr, sr vpres & community affairs officer, currently. **Orgs:** State Bar Tex, US Tax Court, US Southern Dist Court & Fifth Circuit Ct Appeals, US Supreme Ct, Interstate Comm Commn, Fed Maritime Comn; charter mem, Nat Bar Inst; polit action comm, 1975-76, bd dir, 1976-77, 1985-88, pres, 1988-89; Houston Lawyers Asn; Black Women Lawyers Assoc; Judicial Campaign Worker Domestic Relations Ct Candidate, 1976; Speakers Bureau Houston Bar Asn, 1978-79; rep Single Mem Dist Coalition Houston Lawyers Asn, 1979; NBA Invest Corp, 1984-; fundraising chair, Committee-to-re-Elect Judson Robinson Counman-at-Large Position 5, 1985; NBA Women's Div vpres, 1987-89; Third Ward Redevelopment Coun, chair, bd dir; Houston Urban League; Houston Chamber Commerce; Zeta Phi Beta; Nat Coun Negro Women; Links Inc; Jack 'n Jill Am. **Honors/Awds:** Distinguished Christian Serv, Sloan Methodist Ch, 1977; Distinguished Comm Serv, Trinity Methodist Ch, 1978; Distinguished Serv Award, Nat Bar Asn, 1982; One of Houston's Most Influential Black Women, Black Experience Mag, 1984; Houston Lawyers Asn Serv Award, 1985, 1987, 1988; Human Enrichment of Life Program Inc, Young Achievers Award, 1986, 1990; Woman of Distinction, Ebony Man Mag; Named one of 5 Outstanding Young Houstonian & Texan Designers, 1989; Ebony Mag, 100 Most Influential African Americans, 1991; Woman of Distinction, 1992; Woman on the Move, 1994; Human Enrichment of Life Prog, Super Achiever, 1997; Houston Bus & Prof Men's Club, Comm Service Award, 1997; Comm Service Award, 1997. **Special Achievements:** Founding Chair, Houston Downtown Management District; founder, William A Lawson Institute for Peace & Prosperty. **Business Addr:** Senior Vice President, Community Affairs Officer, J P Morgan Chase & Co, 712 Main St Chase Bank Bldg E 7th Fl E, Houston, TX 77002, **Business Phone:** (713)216-4057.

DAVIS, ALISHA
Television news anchorperson. **Educ:** Harvard Univ, BA, afro-american studies, 1996. **Career:** Newsweek, reporter, 1997-2001; CNN Int, guest commentator; MSNBC, guest commentator; Fox News Channel, gen assignment corresp; Oxygen, guest commentator; CNN Headlines News, anchor, 2001-05; MTV News, news reporter, currently. **Business Addr:** News reporter, MTV Networks, MTV News, 1515 Broadway, New York, NY 10036, **Business Phone:** (212)258-8000.*

DAVIS, ALONZO J
Artist. **Personal:** Born Feb 2, 1942, Tuskegee, AL. **Educ:** BFA, 1971; Otis Art Inst, MFA, 1973; Univ Calif, Los Angeles, post-grad, 1966; Pepperdine Col, BA, 1964. **Career:** La Unified SchD-dist, instr, 1962-70; Contemp Crafts Inc, consult, 1968-70; Mt San Antonio Col, instr, 1971-73; Padasena City Col, instr, 1971; Univ Calif, Los Angeles, lectr, 1973; Watts Towers & Art Ctr, consult, 1976-; Los Angeles Col Mus Art, consult, 1976; Calif State Univ, instr, 1976-; artist, currenlt. **Orgs:** Owner & co-dir, Brockman Gallery, 1967-73; exec dir, Brockman Gallery Prod, 1973-; bd mem, Calif Confederation Arts, 1976-; bd mem, Comm Arts Develop Group, 1976-77; founder, Support The Arts, 1976-; bd mem, Cult News Serv, 1977-; bd mem, Artists Econ Action; ed, Neworld Mag, 1977. **Honors/Awds:** Grants, NEA, 1973-77; Inner City Mural Grant, 1974; Excellence in Celebrating Bamboo, Arts & Crafts Competition, Am Bamboo Soc, 2006. **Special Achievements:** Numerous exhibits; published "Black Artists of the New Generation", 1977. **Business Phone:** (301)454-0433.

DAVIS, ANGELA YVONNE
Activist, writer, educator. **Personal:** Born Jan 26, 1944, Birmingham, AL; daughter of B Frank and Sallye E. **Educ:** Univ Paris, attended 1964; Brandeis Univ, BA, 1965; Univ Frankfurt, attended 1967; Univ Calif, San Diego, MA, 1968; Lenin Univ, PhD. **Career:** Univ Calif, Los Angeles, asst prof, 1969-70; San Francisco State Univ &San Francisco Art Inst, prof; Univ Calif, Santa Cruz, prof histconsciousness, 1991-. Books: If They Come in the Morning: Voices ofResistance, 1971; Angela Davis: An Autobiography, 1974; Women, Race, &Class, 1981; Women, Culture, & Politics, 1989; The Angela Y Davis Reader,1999; Are Prisons Obsolete?, 2003. **Orgs:** Founder/co-chairperson, Nat Alliance Against Racist & Polit Repression; nat bd dir, Nat Polit Cong Black Women; nat bd mem, Nat Black Womens Health Proj; Che-Lumumba Club; Phi Beta Kappa; Black Panthers; Cent Comn, Communist Party; Black Panther Party; mem, Adv Bd Prison Activist Resource Ctr. **Honors/Awds:** Lenin Peace Prize, USSR, 1979. **Business Addr:** Professor of History of Consciousness, University of California Santa Cruz, 1156 High St, Santa Cruz, CA 95064, **Business Phone:** (831)459-2813.

DAVIS, ANITA LOUISE
County government official, association executive. **Personal:** Born Oct 3, 1936, Williamsport, PA; daughter of Malcolm Porter and Jessie Porter; married Morris S, 1962; children: Lynn M, Lyles Jeyious, Wayne D Lyles & Mark E Lyles. **Educ:** Buffalo State Col, attended 1955 & 1979; Univ NDak, Grand Forks, AFB, 1969; Univ NH, Pease AFB, 1971; Univ Buffalo, attended 1972; Tallahasee Community Col; Fla A&M Univ, BS, criminal justice, 1990. **Career:** Association Executive (retired); Health & Rehab Servs Leon Start Ctr, adminr asst III, 1979-83; Fla Dept Labor, employ spec, 1983-87, civil rights specialist II, 1987-89; Re-elected Leon City Bd Commissioners Dist I, 1994; Nat Asn County Orgn, Elder Serv Inc, vol; Pride Ct Colanthes, Community/Civic Comt, vice chair; Leon County, Proj Community Task Force Drugs & Crime, comnr, dir community enrichment, chmn, BSA Suwanne Dist Risk Kids Coun, Leon County Bd Commissioners, chmn. **Orgs:** Pres, Tallahassee Br, Nat Asn Advan Colored People, 1981-90; pres, Regional/Local Int Philo Coord, Philos Sigma Gamma Rho Sorority, Beta Delta Chap, 1982-88 & 1990-; vpres, Fla State Conf Nat Asn Advan Colored People Br, 1986-99; reporter, Beta Delta Sigma Chap, 1992; Nat Hookup Black Women; FSU Leadership Conf; Capital Women's Polit Caucus; pres, Capital City Dem Women's Club; coun mem, Suwanne Area Boy Scouts Am. treas & bd dirs, Black Develop Found; first vpres & comt chmn, CAO Head Start Overall Policy Coun; Criminal Justice Comn, BUILD Buffalo Inc; criminal justice chairperson, Nat Asn Advan Colored People; social dir, AD Price & Perry Sr Citizens; coordr, Masten Dist Block Club Asn. **Honors/Awds:** Lifetime Achievement Award, Acad Fla Trial Lawyers, 1987; Nat Leadership Award, Nat Asn Advan Colored People, 1989 & 1990; Martin Luter King Jr Community Leadership Award, Fla A&M Univ, 1991; Community Service Award, Fla Comn Human Rels Community, 1994. **Home Addr:** 708 Bragg Dr, Tallahassee, FL 32305-6708.

DAVIS, ANTHONY D.
Football coach. **Personal:** Born Mar 7, 1969, Kennewick, WA. **Educ:** Univ Utah. **Career:** Football player(retired), Seattle Sea hawks, linebacker, 1993; Kansas City Chiefs, 1994-98; Green Bay Packers,1999; Baltimore Ravens. 2000; coaching staff at MidAmerica Naz Univ, linebackers, currently. *

DAVIS, ANTHONY EBONEY
School administrator. **Personal:** Born in Paterson, NJ; son of Thomas and Dorothy. **Educ:** Cheyney Univ, BS, 1999; Rutgers Univ, Sch Social Work, attending. **Career:** Devernex Found, recreation counr, 1987-89; Chester County Prison,correction officer, 1989-90; Comar Inc, ment health counr, 1990-91; Resource Human Develop, supvr, 1990-96; N Philadelphia Health Syst,

drug, alcohol counr, 1991-93; N Philadelphia Health Syst, clin counr, 1992-96; St Joseph's Hosp, Psychiatry Dept, family clinician, caseworker, 1996-2001; Passaic County Community Col, SMT Col Bound Prog, asst dir, currently. **Orgs:** Chair, Omega Psi Phi, Omega Teens, 1987-; founder, Concerned Role Model Scholarship, 1989-; Cheyney Univ, Nat Alumni Asn, 1990-, Mentoring Prog, 1990-; treas, Caribbean Empowerment NJ, 1996-; County Comt, 1998-; East side HS Mentoring Prog, 1998; comnr, Paterson Bd Educ, 2000-; comnr, Paterson Rent Leveling Bd, 2000-. **Honors/Awds:** Congressional Record, House Rep, 2000; Resolution of the City, City Coun, 2000; Civilian Citation, Paterson Fire Dept, 2000; NJ Meritorious Service Award, UNCF, 2000; Caring Indeed Award, St Joseph's Hosp Psychiatry Dept, 2000. **Special Achievements:** Volunteer to Feed Paterson's homeless citizens. **Home Addr:** 125 Presidential Blvd 12H, Paterson, NJ 07522, **Home Phone:** (973)956-1529. **Business Addr:** Assistant Director, Club Advisor, Passaic County College, carbbean club, 1 Col Blvd 155 Mkt St 3rd Fl, Paterson, NJ 07505, **Business Phone:** (973)684-5223.

DAVIS, ANTHONY R.
Personal: Born Aug 24, 1957, New Orleans, LA; son of Donald and Anna; married Theresa, Jun 19, 1982; children: Brittany Nicole, Bliss Monique. **Educ:** Southern Univ, BS, comput sci, 1980; Univ Colo, MS, telecommunications, 1997. **Career:** Am Bank, night transit operator, 1976-79, asst supv, transit opers, 1979-80; Western Elec, software developer, 1980-82; Honeywell, TID, programmer, 1982-85; AT&T Bell Labs, software engr, 1985-96; Lucent Technologies, software engr, 1996-. **Orgs:** Col Asn Black Prof Engrs & Scientists, 1986-; IEEE Comput Soc, 1998-. **Special Achievements:** "Virtual Local Area Networks: The New LAN Paradigm", thesis, 1997. **Home Addr:** 3707 S Truckee Way, Aurora, CO 80013-3457. *

DAVIS, ANTONE EUGENE
Football player, business owner. **Personal:** Born Feb 28, 1967, Sweetwater, TN; married Carrie; children: Cailyn Marie, Dakota, Braden. **Educ:** Tenn. **Career:** Philadelphia Eagles, tackle, 1991-95; Atlanta Falcons, 1996-98; Green Bay Packers, 2000; Northwestern Mutual Financial Network, financial representative; Rocky Top Holdings LLC, owner, currently. **Orgs:** Am Cancer Soc; Special Olympics; Campus Crusade for Christ; Jr Achievement & the Community Found; Christian Athletes & S Lake Kids Hope USA. **Honors/Awds:** Jacobs Trophy, Univ Tenn, 1990; best blocker, southeastern Conference. **Special Achievements:** named to the Consensus All-America team.

DAVIS, ANTONIO CAMERON. **See ANDREWS, REAL.**

DAVIS, ANTONIO LEE
Basketball player. **Personal:** Born Oct 31, 1968, Oakland, CA; married Kendra; children: 2. **Educ:** Univ Tex, El Paso, attended 1990. **Career:** Basketball player (retired); Panathinaikos, 1990-92; Philips Milano Italian league, 1992-93; Ind Pacers, forward-ctr, 1994-99; Toronto Raptors, 1999-2003, 2006; Chicago Bulls, power forward, 2003-05; New York Knicks, 2005-06. **Orgs:** Pres, NBA Players Asn, 2005. **Honors/Awds:** NBA All-Star Award.

DAVIS, ARNOR S.
Educator, clergy. **Personal:** Born Dec 19, 1919, Patterson, GA; married; children: 3. **Educ:** Savannah State Col, BS; Howard Univ Sch Relig, BD, Wash DC; Howard Univ, MA. **Career:** Zion Baptist Church, asst minister, Wash, DC, 1950-52; New Bethel Baptist Church, dir relig educ, Wash, DC, 1960-75; Inst Rels DC Redevel Land Agency, asst area dir, Wash, DC; Antioch Baptist Church, asst minister, Wash, DC, 1975. **Orgs:** Exec dir, Second Precinct Clergymens Asn,1948-74; Savannah State Alumni Asn DC Chap, 1948-74; Howard Univ Alumni Asn; Bapt Ministers Conf, 1960-74; bd dir, Mt Ethel Bapt Training Union, 1969-74; pres, bd dir, Nat Med Asn Found, 1967-74; bd dir, Lincoln-Westmoreland Non-Profit Housing Corp; bd dir, DC Citizens Better Educ, 1970-74; Nat Asn Advan Colored People, 1970-74; bd dir, Hillcrest C Ctr, 1971-74; Bd dir, local coun Churches; Housing Task Force Coun Churches. **Honors/Awds:** Publs A Guide to Chs & Institutions in the Shaw & Urban Renewal Area 1974; A Guide SAC Area Schs & Non-profit Sponsorships 1975. **Special Achievements:** Auth: The Pentecostal Movement in Black Christianity. **Military Serv:** AUS, 1941-46. **Business Addr:** Pastor, Antioch Baptist Church, 1105 50th St NE, Washington, DC 20019, **Business Phone:** (202)526-9380.*

DAVIS, HON. ARRIE W.
State government official, educator. **Personal:** Born Jul 21, 1940, Baltimore, MD; children: Joanne & Aria. **Educ:** Morgan State Col, BA, 1963; NY Univ, MA, 1966; Univ Baltimore, JD, 1969. **Career:** Baltimore City Pub Sch, Eng instr, swimming coach, 1964-69; Supreme Bench Baltimore, bailiff, 1968-69; Judge Joseph Carter & Master Harry Sachs, law clerk, 1968-69; Baltimore City, asst atty gen, Criminal Appeals Div, 1971-79; Morgan State Univ, bus law instr, 1971-81; Villa Julie Col, law instr, 1972-80; Baltimore City, Dept Pub Safety & Correctional Serv, Div Correction, coun, 1979-81; Baltimore City, Dist Court Md, Dist 1, assoc judge, 1981-83; Baltimore City, Legis Comt mem, 1989-91, Exec Comt, 1995-97, Civil Law & Procedure Comt, 1998-01; Judicial Inst Md, bd dir & Instr, 2000-; Baltimore City Circuit Court, 8th Judicial Circuit, assoc judge, 1983-90; City Baltimore, Ct Spec Appeals Md, judge, 1990-. **Orgs:** Baltimore City Bar Asn; Md State Bar Asn; Am Bar Asn; Nat Bar Asn; Comt Study Sentencing & Correctional Alternatives Women Convicted Crime, 1987-88; Monumental Bar Asn; Baltimore City Bar Found; Wranglers Law Club, 1998-; Chair, Harry A. Cole Judicial Coun; Maryland Bar Found, 1999-; State Comn Criminal Sentencing Policy, 2000-; Bd Dirs, Judicial Inst Md, 2000-. **Honors/Awds:** Legal Excellence Award, Waring Mitchell Law Society of Howard County, 1994; Legacy for Excellence in Litigation Award, Snyder Center, Univ Baltimore Sch of Law, 2003; Legal Excellence Award, J. Franklyn Bourne Bar Asn, 2004; Alumnus of the Year, Univ of Baltimore Sch of Law, 2004; Recognized as Distinguished Alumnus of Frederick Douglass Senior High School, Baltimore City Council, 2005. *

DAVIS, ARTHUR
City planner, educator, consultant. **Personal:** Born Nov 12, 1942, Sampson County, NC; son of Arthur Davis; divorced; children: Arthur Paris. **Educ:** Morehouse Col, BA, 1965; Carnegie-Mellon Univ, MA, 1966; Univ Pittsburgh, MPA, 1967. **Career:** City Planner (retired), Educator, Consultant: A&T State Univ, asst prof 1967-68, 1990-95; City Greensboro, sr planner, 1969-2005; Guilford Col, lectr, 1975-81; Consult 1975-; A&T State Univ, asst prof, planning & design, consult assoc; Carolina Evaluation Res Ctr, city, corp, church planner. **Orgs:** Bd NC Fellows Bd, 1971-84; Nat Greene Sertoma pres & bd, 1971; bd & pres, Greensboro Interclub Coun, 1971-98; pres bd, Greensboro Credit Union, 1978; bd chmn, Greensboro Emp Comem, 1978-82; Gen Greene Coun BSA, 1980-; secy, NC APA, 1980-86; Grimsley PTA bd, 1982-86; bd secy, Am Planning Orgn, 1981-85; United Arts Coun Bd, 1983-85; USOA Bd, 1985-90; Greensboro Visions I & II 1986-92; bd mem, NC ASPA, 1987-; staff adv, Ole Asheboro Neighborhood Asn, 1989-; COM 100, 1989-; bd, Human Serv IST, 1989-95; adv brd GTCC, 1989-; County Resource Housing Bd, 1990-94; Minority Women Bus deveop Coun, 1990-; pres, Am Soc Pub Admin, 1991-92; BSA Eagle Rev Bd, 1991-; Ctr City Coun, 1995-; Morehouse Col Alumni Club; area rep, Exec Comt, Greensboro Neighborhood Cong. **Honors/Awds:** Community Service Award, A&T, 1974, 1975; Univ S Jaycees, Am Plng Asn, A&T Univ, 1975; Men of Achievement, 1976; award Greensboro, YMCA, 1978; Comm Serv Sertoma Int, 1981; numerous citations US Dept of Comm, President Leadership Award 1983; Sertoman of the Year Sertoma InterNat, 1998; Greensboro 100 Award 1991; NBFPA Service Award Outstanding Citizen, 1992; Outstanding 100 Citizens 1992; Carolina Peacemaker Award, 1993; Technology/ Strategic Planning, 1997; Leadership 2000, 1996-98; City Service Award, 1995; ASPA Outstanding Service Award, 1992; Sertoma Award, 1993; Ole Asheboro Award, 1994; YPL Award, 1993; NC Credit Union Volunteer, 1994; Comm of 100 Service Award, 1997; NAACP Award, 1998; Employee of the Yr, 1998; NAHRN award, 1998, Hayes Taylor YMCA, 1999; City Service Award, 1999; Sertoma Award, 1999; Hayes Taylor YMCA, 2000; President's Award, NFBPA, 2001; Nat Green Sertoma, 2001; NC Neighbors Award, 2003; Carolina Peacemaker, 2002. **Home Addr:** 910 Ross Ave, Greensboro, NC 27406-2414. **Business Addr:** 910 Ross Ave, Greensboro, NC 27406-2414, **Business Phone:** (336)373-2761.

DAVIS, ARTHUR, JR.
Educator. **Personal:** Born Apr 17, 1933, Bessemer, AL; married Loretta J; children: Arthur III, Deborah & Sarah. **Educ:** Ala A&M, BS, 1955; Univ Ill, MA, 1968, PhD, 1970. **Career:** Aero-space Equip Br, civil training instr, ground support, 1959-61; Aerospace Ground Equip Br, civ aircraft & missle ground support equipment repairman tech, 1961-63; Dept Air Force, Chanute Tech Training Ctr, civilian elec electron, training instr, 1963-66; Northeastern Univ, dir, asst dir, 1966-70; asst prof, 1970-76; assoc prof educ, 1976-77; prof, 2004; Ky State Univ, Univ Ill. **Orgs:** Consult, Urbana Pub Sch, 1966; consult, dean, Stud Loc Urban Comn Needs & Prob, 1968-69; asst coordr, State Univ NY, 1970-73; consult Rochester, NY, Model Cities Prog, 1971; pres, Wright way Ed Consult Ltd, 1972-76; consult Univ Ill, Pal Prog; consult, Parents Adv Com Title, ESEA, 1972; consult, Univ Ill, 1977; consult, Univ Col Educ, 1977; Admin Oper & Comm; Univ Cabinet; Steering Comt Ath; Black Recruit Adv Comt; Search Comm, Dean ColEduc; Univ Cabinet; Task Force Compensatory Educ; Adv Comn Arts. **Special Achievements:** Publ: Racial Crisis in Pubic Education A Quest for Social Order, 1975; presently writing 2 books, The Pedagogic of the African American Studies &The Educ of the American Negro from Slavery to the Present; sev articles & ed 2 other books; num art publ. **Military Serv:** AUS, 1955-57. **Business Addr:** Professor, Northeastern University, Col Educ, 360 Huntington Ave, Boston, MA 02115, **Business Phone:** (617)373-2000.*

DAVIS, DR. ARTHUR DAVID
Educator, psychologist, musician. **Personal:** Married Gladys (deceased) (deceased); children: Kimaili & Mureithi. **Educ:** Hunter Col, BA, psychol, mus (summa cum laude), 1973; City Col, MA, 1976; NY Univ, MA, 1976; NY Univ, PhD, 1982. **Career:** Composer, musician & educr, 1958-; Borough Manhattan Comm Col, asst adj prof, 1972-86; Univ Bridgeport, prof, 1979-82; mgr, Little League Inc, 1979-82; Head Start, consult, psychologist, 1981-82; Lincoln Med & Ment Health Ctr, clin psychologist, 1982-85; NY Med Col, instr, 1983-86; Lakeside UFSD, psychologist, 1985-86; pvt pract, 1986-; Orange Coast Col, fac, 1987-; psychologist, assoc prof; Calif St Univ, Fullerton, prof, 1988-90; Orange Co AIDS, 1988; Orange County Urban League Inc, bd dirs, 1992-96; Chancellor's distinguished lectr, Univ Calif, Irvine, 1992-93; Univ Calif Irvine, fac, 1999-2001; Guiden W Col, 1999-2001; ARKIMU Inc, author, currently; from consult to ment health serv, from consult to music proj. **Orgs:** Am Soc Authors Composers & Publ, 1976-; Am Psychol Asn, 1977-; Am Asn Black Psychologists, 1983-97; NYAcad Sci, 1984-; exec bd mem, Local 802 Jazz Musicians Found, 1984-86; adv, William Grant Still Mus, 1988-96; Orange County Psychol Asn, 1989-96; dir, Local 47 Musician's Union, Los Angeles, 1993-98; pres, ceo, Better Advantages Stud & Soc, 1993. **Honors/Awds:** Named No 1 Bassist Downbeat Intl Critics Poll, 1962; World's Foremost Double Bassist Dict of Inter Nat Biographer 1969-; Phi Beta Kappa, Psi Chi Nat Honor Socs; cited for music in Chap 9 of "Music; Black, White & Blue"1972; Life Patron Intercontinental Biographical Asn, 1974-; The Arthur Davis System For Double Bass, Arkimu Publ, 1976; Reemergence Art Davis, Interplay Rec, IP7728, 1980; Dr Art Davis Live, 1984; Gold Note Jazz Award LION, Nat Black MBA Asn, 1985; cited in NY Times as one of the world's top gourmet chefs; Morrow Publ; music album: "Art Davis Quartet, Life" Soulnote 1443, 1987; Annual Doctor, Art Davis Scholar; Gladys Davis Memorial Scholarship; A Brief History of Jazz, Arkimu Publ Co, 1993; A Time Remembered, Jazz Planet, 1996; Puttin' on the Ritz, Arkimo Rec, 2002; one of the 129 Greatest Bands of Orange Co, Orange Co Weekly; Certification of Specialisation Cong Recognition, 2002; ASCAP Award, Am Soc Composers; Certificate of Special Congressional Recognition, 2002. **Special Achievements:** Published numerous books and released many albums. **Business Addr:** Author, ARKIMU Inc, 3535 E Coast Hwy Suite 50, Corona Del Mar, CA 92625.

DAVIS, ARTUR
Government official. **Personal:** Born Oct 9, 1967, Montgomery, AL. **Educ:** Harvard Univ, BA, 1990; Harvard Law Sch, JD, 1993. **Career:** Mid Dist Ala, asst to US atty, 1994-98; Southern Poverty Law Ctr, intern; pvt pract, civil rights law; FOX Network, Birmingham, legal & polit commentator; US House Rep, Ala 7th Cong Dist, dem mem, 2003-. **Orgs:** Cong Black Caucus; Dem Cong Campaign Comt. **Honors/Awds:** Best Oralist Award, Harvard Law Sch. **Business Addr:** US House Rep, 208 Canon House Off Bldg, Washington, DC 20515.*

DAVIS, BARBARA D
Executive. **Educ:** St Joseph Calumet Col; Ind Univ; Univ Wis. **Career:** Insland Steel Proj, off mgr, 1976-77, recruiter-counr, 1977-78, asst proj dir, 1978-79, dir, 1980; Gilbane Bldg Co, equal employ opportunity officer, 1982, corp affirmative action specialist, 1984-. **Orgs:** Ill Affirmative Action Officers Asn; chairperson, IAAOA Conf, 1985; liaison Black Contractors United/Chicago Urban League; consult, World's Fair Plan on Affirmative Action; pres, Women in Construct; consult Int Women Econ Develop Corp; Ind Civil Rights Comn; vpres, Fair Share Orgn; consult Women's League State Affil; Nat Asn Advan Colored People. **Honors/Awds:** Union Counselor Award, AFL-CIO Lake Co Cent Labor Union & United Steel Workers Am Local 1010; Affirmative Action Officer of the Year Award, Black Contractors United; Dedicated Service Award, Nat Coun Black Child Develop NY; Spec Award, Black Contractors United, 1985. **Business Addr:** Corporate Affirm Action Officer, 200 W Madison St Suite 700, Chicago, IL 60606.

DAVIS, BELVA
Television show host. **Personal:** Born Oct 13, 1933, Monroe, LA; daughter of John Melton and Florence Howard Mays; married William Vince Moore; children: Steven Eugene, Darolyn Denise. **Educ:** Oakland City Col; San Francisco State Univ. **Career:** Jet, freelence writer; KSAN, news reader; Bay Area Independent; KDIA; Sun Reporter Newspaper, San Francisco, CA, womens ed, 1963-68; KPIX-TV, San Fancisco, anchor & prog host, 1967-77; KQED-TV, San Francisco, anchor & reporter, 1977-81; KRON-TV, urban affairs specialist & prog host, 1981-99, spec proj reporter, currently. **Orgs:** Awards Comt, San Francisco Found, 1982-88; nat vpres, Am Fedn TV & Radio Artists, 1984-; bd mem, Howard Thurman Found; bd mem, Black Filmmakers Hall of Fame; Links; bd mem, Commonwealth Club Calif, 1991-; bd mem, Blue Shield Calif, 1992-; bd mem, Metro YMCA. **Honors/Awds:** 6 Emmy's No Cal TV Acad; National Journal Award, Nat Urban Coalition, 1985; Nat Journal Award, Ohio State Univ, 1985; Outstanding Journalism, Sigma Delta Chi, 1990; Governor's Award, NC Chap, Nat Acad TV Arts & Sci, 1996; Lifetime Achievement Award, Nat Acad TV Arts & Sci. **Special Achievements:** First black female at KSAN; first female African American television reporter on the West Coast. **Business Addr:** Special Projects Reporter, KRON Channel 4, 1001 Van Ness Ave, San Francisco, CA 94109, **Business Phone:** (415)441-4444.*

DAVIS, BEN JEROME
Basketball player. **Personal:** Born Dec 26, 1972, Vero Beach, FL. **Educ:** Univ Ariz, attended 1996. **Career:** Phoenix Suns, 1997, 2000; NY Knics, 1998-99; Houston Rockets, 2003-04; Paysandu, 2006; Lichief exec officer de Costa Rica, 2008-. **Honors/Awds:** Virginia Player of the Year, Oak Hill Acad.

DAVIS, BENNIE L.
Physician. **Personal:** Born Dec 7, 1927, Muskogee, OK; married; children: Benjamin & Duane. **Educ:** Samuel Huston Col, BS, 1947; Howard Univ, MD, 1952. **Career:** Homer G Philips Hosp St Louis, internship, 1952-53; Terre Haute IN, gen practice, 1953-54; Homer G Phillips Hosp, surgery resident, 1953-55; urology resident, 1954-58; Pvt Pract Indianapolis IN, urologist, 1960. **Orgs:** Am Med Asn; Nat Med Asn; Alpha Phi Alpha Frat; Chi Delta Mu Sci Frat; Sigma P Phi Frat; Am Urol Asn; Ind Univ Med Ctr; Rotarty Club; Our Savior Luthern Church; Div Urol Meth Hosp Grad Med Ctr; Urol Sec Nat Med Asn. **Honors/Awds:** Diplomate, Am Bd Urol, 1961; fel Am Col Surgeons, 1963. **Military Serv:** USAF, urologist, 1958-60. **Business Addr:** 2615 N Capitol Ave, Indianapolis, IN 46208.

DAVIS, DR. BERTHA LANE
Educator. **Personal:** Born Sep 3, 1950, Mobile, AL; daughter of James Lane; married George W; children: Geoffrey J. **Educ:** Tuskegee Univ, BS, 1972; Coppin State Col, MEd, 1975; Univ Md, MS, 1976; Wash State Univ, PhD, 1983; Univ Pa, further study. **Career:** Hampton Univ, prof, asst dean res, chairperson, 1998-. **Orgs:** Chi Eta Phi Nursing Sorority, 1976-; Sigma Theta Tau, newsletter ed,1981-; Am Nurses Asn, 1981-; Am Acad Nursing, 1991-. **Honors/Awds:** Endowed University Professor, Hampton Univ, 1986; Isabelle Steward Award, Nat League Nursing, 1997; One of 99 Distinguished Nurses in Va, 1999; Outstanding Nurse of the Year, 1999; Delta Distinguished Endowed Chair, 2000. **Special Achievements:** State Va, Senate Resolution commendation for commitment to nursing, 2004. **Military Serv:** USAR, Nurse Corps, LTC, 1988-; Army Achievement Medal, 1977; Army Command & General Staff Col, 1997; Naval War Col, 2001. **Home Addr:** 116 Glascow Way, Hampton, VA 23669. **Business Addr:** Assistant Dean for Research, Hampton University, School of Nursing, William Freeman Hall, Hampton, VA 23668, **Business Phone:** (757)727-5762.

DAVIS, BETTYE J
State government official, social worker. **Personal:** Born May 17, 1938, Homer, LA; daughter of Rosylind Daniel Ivory and Dan Ivory; married Troy J, Jan 21, 1959 (deceased); children: Anthony B & Sonja Davis-Wade. **Educ:** St Anthony Sch Practical Nursing, GN, 1961; Grambling State Univ, BSW, 1971; Univ Alaska, attended; UA Anchorage, Post Grad, 1977. **Career:** YWCA San Bernardino, asst dir, 1971-72; DFYS Anchorage, child care specialist, 1975-80; Alaska Black Leadership Educ Prog, dir, 1979-82; Anchorage Youth Serv Div Family, social worker, 1980; Anchorage Div Soc Serv, foster care coordr; elected Off at large, 1982-89; Anchorage Bd Ed, vpres; State Alaska Div Family & Youth Servs, foster care coordr, 1982-87; Alaska State Legis, Juneau, Alaska, rep, 1990-, sen, 2000-; NCSL Health Comt, Nat Conf State Legislatures, presiding officer, 2007-08. **Orgs:** N Future BPW Club Inc, 1978-79; pres, Anchorage Chap Delta Sigma Theta, 1979-80; bd dirs, March Dimes, 1983-85; bd dirs, Nat Caucus Black Sch Bd Mem, 1987-89; pres, Nat Sch Bd Asn, 1989-91; bd mem, YWCA Anchorage, 1989-90; bd dirs, Alaska 2000, 1991-; bd dirs, Winning with Stronger Educ, 1991-; bd dirs, Anchorage Ctr Families, 1992-; Anchorage Sch Bd: 1998-; pres, Alaska Fed Bus & Prof Women, 1999-; Alaska Black Leadership Conference; treas, Alaska Women's Lobby; Blacks Govt; chairperson, Alaska Black Caucus; Anchorage Br Nat Asn Advan Colored People; League Women Voters; Alaska Women's Polit Caucus; Nat Asn Advan Colored People; Anchorage Zonta Club; life mem Delta Sigma Theta Sorority; life mem Bus & Prof Women. **Honors/Awds:** Woman of the Year, Alaska Colored Womens Club, 1981; Social Worker of the Year, Nat Foster Parents Asn, 1983; Child Care Worker of the Year, Alaska Foster Parent Asn, 1983; Political Awareness Award of the Year, Alaska Black Caucus, 1984; Outstanding Achievement Award in Education, Alaska Colored Womens Club, 1985; Outstanding Women in Education, Zeta Phi Beta 1985; Outstanding Service Award, Alaska Black Caucus 1986; Outstanding Political Awareness Award, Alaska Black Caucus 1986; Community Service Award, Alaska Black Leadership, 1986; Caucus Member of the Year, Alaska Black Caucus, 1987; Boardsmanship Award, Asn Alaska Sch Boards, 1989; Outstanding Board Member Award, Asn Alaska Sch Boards, 1990; Woman of the Year, Alaska Bus & Prof Womens Club, 1990; Woman of Achievement Award, YWCA, 1991; Henry Toll Fellowship, Toll Fel, 1992; Outstanding Leadership Award, California Assembly, 1992. **Home Addr:** 2240 Foxhall Dr, Anchorage, AK 99504. **Business Addr:** Senator, Alaska State Legislature, District K, State Capitol Rm 30, Juneau, AK 99801-1182, **Business Phone:** (907)465-3822.

DAVIS, BILLY. See DAVIS, WILLIAM AUGUSTA, III.

DAVIS, BILLY
Entertainer, singer. **Personal:** Born Jun 26, 1940, St Louis, MO; married Marilyn; children: Steven. **Career:** Professional singer, rec artist, entertainer; Fifth Dimension, mem, 1965-75; solo artist, 1975-; performed as duet act, Marilyn McCoo & BillyDavis Jr, 1976-80; variety show: "The Marilyn McCoo & Billy Davis Jr-Show," CBS-TV, 1977; numerous tv & stage appearances; Let Me Have A Dream, 1982; Grizzly Adams & the Legend of Dark Mountain, 1999; Thank You, GoodNight, 2001; "The Jamie Foxx Show", 2001; "Pyramid", 2003; "Tavis Smiley", 2004; Miss Rising, 2005; The Billy Davis Rhythm Machine, head, currently. **Orgs:** Bill Glass Ministries; The Billy Graham & Luis Palau Ministries. **Honors/Awds:** Grammy Award, with Marilyn McCoo, "You Don't Have To Be A Star," 1977;Tokyo Music Festival, Grand Prize, with Marilyn McCoo; mem of 5th Dimension: six Grammy Awards; Star on the Hollywood Walk of Fame; 14 Gold Records. **Special Achievements:** Guest appearance, The Trinity Broadcasting Network; Author: Up Up and AwayHow We Found Love; Faith and Lasting Marriage in the Entertainment World. **Business Addr:** Entertainer, William Morris Agency, 1325 Avenue of the Americas, New York, NY 10019, **Business Phone:** (212)586-5100.

DAVIS, DR. BRENDA LIGHTSEY-HENDRICKS
School administrator, president (organization). **Personal:** Born Dec 21, 1943, Fairfield, AL; daughter of Guy and Flora; married William R David MD; children: Tonia D Kelly, William R Jr, Scott, Frank B & Joye Lynn. **Educ:** Harlem Hosp Sch Nursing, dipl, 1964; Teachers Col Columbia Univ, BS,nursing, 1969, MEd, psychiat, 1972, EdD, curric & teaching, 1976. **Career:** Riverside Community Col, dir & chairperson nursing, dean nursing educ,dean occup educ, dean grants & contract educ, Norco Campus, provost, pres, 2006-. **Orgs:** Nat League Nurses, 1975-; Calif Community Col Adminrs, 1984-; AmVocational Educ Asn, 1984-; Diamond Bar Black Women's Asn, 1985-; Nat Black Nurses' Asn, 1985-; pres, Inland Empire Black Nurses' Asn, 1986-; adv comt mem, Calif State Univ, San Bernardino, 1986; Black Hist ProgComt, DBBWA, 1986-. **Honors/Awds:** Training Grant NY State, 1968-69; Minority Scholarship Teachers Col Columbia, 1970; Training Grant Nat Inst Ment Health, 1971-75. **Home Addr:** 2149 S Indian Creek Rd, Diamond Bar, CA 91765. **Business Addr:** President, Riverside Community College, Norco Campus, 2001 3rd St, Norco, CA 92860-2600.*

DAVIS, BRIAN KEITH
Basketball player, businessperson. **Personal:** Born Jun 21, 1970, Atlantic City, NJ; married Marsha; children: Brian Jr. **Educ:** Duke Univ, attended 1992. **Career:** Basketball player (retired), businessperson; French League, Pau Orthez, 1992-93; NBA, Minn Timberwolves, 1993-94; Pan-American Games team, 1994; Blue Devil Ventures, managing partner, currently. **Orgs:** Nat Historic Trust. **Honors/Awds:** First Team All-ACC Tournament, 1992. **Special Achievements:** Only African American in NCAA history to play in four consecutive Final Four tournaments. **Business Addr:** Managing Partner, Devil Ventures, 604 W Morgan St Suite B3, Durham, NC 27701, **Business Phone:** (919)956-5957.

DAVIS, BROWNIE W
Insurance executive. **Personal:** Born Mar 13, 1933, Philadelphia, PA; son of Brownie and Eloise; married Elba, Feb 14, 1997; children: Brenda & Bruce. **Educ:** City Col, NY, BA, 1957; Life Underwriter Training Coun, grad advan underwriting & health ins. **Career:** Va Hosp Brooklyn, radioisotope tech; Farmingdale LI Unit, repub aviation supvr; Williamsburgh Steel Prod Co, draftsman off mgr; Macy's Rego Park, mgr in-charge, housewares; NY Life Ins Co, field underwriter; Guardian Life Ins Co Am, dist agency mgr; Manhattan Community Col, adj prof, 1986-; LaGuardia Community Col, adj prof, 1989; Brownie W Davis Agency Corp, pres, currently. **Orgs:** Pres, Queens Br First Nat Asn Life Underwriters; past mem, NY Life Agent Adv Coun, 1973-74; adv bd mem, Minority Bus Coun; Queens Chamber Com; bonding chmn, vpres, Asn Minority Bus Enterprises; pres, Cedar Manor Co-op, 1967-70; bd mem, NY Housing Auth, Symphony Orchestra; exec vpres, Nat Minority Bus Coun; Aetna Great Performance Club, 1986-88; bd mem, United Blackmen Queens; Black Achiever in Industry Harlem Y.M.C.A, 1974, chmn Bd Mgrs, 1979-82. **Honors/Awds:** Centurion, 1967-; Health Ins Leader, 1967-75; Nat Quality Award for Life-Health, 1972-75; Group Ins Leader, 1973; Company Honor Roll over 100 Consecutive Months; Black Achiever in Indiana, 1974; Leader Aetna Life & Casualty Region; Leadership Award, York Col, 1989. **Business Addr:** President, Brownie W Davis Agency Corp, PO Box 593, Lawrence, NY 11559, **Business Phone:** (516)569-7979.

DAVIS, BRUCE
Executive. **Personal:** Born Dec 27, 1963, Cordele, GA; son of Andrew Carter West and Eddie Mae; married Shawn Watson Davis, Aug 19, 1993; children: Bruce Randall Davis II & Br. **Educ:** Clark Col, BA, 1986; Atlanta Univ, MBA, 1988. **Career:** Marathon Oil Co, staff acct, 1984-85; Bank One, corp credit analyst, 1987; Bank Am, lender & asst vpres, 1988-93; Nat City Bank, city exec & pres, 1993-; Community State Bank, vpres & invest officer. **Orgs:** Golf comm chmn, Greater Jackson Chamber Community, 2002-; dir, finance comm, Jackson Non-Profit Support Ctr, 2002-; dir, mkt workgroup, Foote Hosp HIO Community, 2002-; dir, funding comm, Junior Achievement, 2003-. **Honors/Awds:** Man of the Year, Clark Col, 1986; Minority Businessperson of the Year, Lansing (MI) Chamber Com, 1995. **Special Achievements:** Passed the Uniform Certified Public Accounting (CPA) examination, 1992. **Home Addr:** 3720 Colchester Rd, Lansing, MI 48906, **Home Phone:** (517)321-4520. **Business Addr:** President, National City Bank of Jackson, Corporate Banking Center, 101 E Michigan Ave, Jackson, MI 49201-1434, **Business Phone:** (517)780-0507.

DAVIS, BUNNY COLEMAN
Librarian. **Personal:** Born Mar 21, 1946, New Orleans, LA; daughter of Joseph and Elberta Plummer; divorced; children: Sean & Mark. **Educ:** Memphis State Univ, BS, Educ, 1972; George Peabody Col Vanderbilt Univ, MLS, 1975. **Career:** Memphis City Schs, librn, 1972-85; State Dept Educ, evaluator, 1985-88; Memphis City Schs, librn, 1988-. **Orgs:** Nat Educ Asn; Alpha Kappa Alpha Sor Inc; Holy Rosary Outreach Prog. **Honors/Awds:** Rotary Award for Teacher Excellence, 1998. **Home Addr:** 5020 Pheasant Run Lane, Memphis, TN 38141.

DAVIS, CAL DELEANOR
Executive. **Personal:** Born Nov 4, 1940, Tulsa, OK; son of Joseph Jr and Retha; widowed; children: Byron, Marvin & Erica. **Educ:** Calif State Univ, Los Angeles, BS, 1967; Golden Gate Univ, MS, 1987. **Career:** TRW Systs Inc, sr acct, 1967-68; FS Moultrie & Co, CPA-auditor, 1968-70; Peat, Marwick & Mitchell, CPA-auditor, 1970-72; Cert Pub Acct, 1972; Morris, Davis & Co, partner, 1972; DEMANCO Inc, treas, chief fin officer, currently. **Orgs:** Bd dirs, Bay Area black Consortium Quality Health Care, 1991-93; adv bd mem, Bank Oakland, 1992; adv bd mem, Nat Marrow Donor Prog Patient Advocacy Comn, 1992-93; Chabot Col Mentor Prog DARAJA Proj, 1992-93; pres, Judie Davis Marrow Donor Recruitment Prog, beginning 1992; co-chair, 100 Black Men the Bay Area Inc, currently. **Honors/Awds:** Outstanding Local Small Bus Leader, State Calif Assembly Woman Barbara Lee, 1992; Man of the Year, Distinguished & Devoted Serv From East Bay Area Club, 1992; Strong Achiever Award, Nat Asn Negro Bus & Pro Women's Clubs Inc, By Wild 107 FM Radio Station, 1993; Pinnacle Award, Being Single Mag & Gillette, 1993; Sigma Gamma Rho Sorority Inc, Sigma Sigma Chap, Quality Life Award, 1994. **Military Serv:** USAF, airman second class, 1958-62. **Business Addr:** Chief Financial Officer, DEMANCO Inc, 1734 Martin L King Jr Way, PO Box 71761, Oakland, CA 94612, **Business Phone:** (510)428-9798.

DAVIS, DR. CARRIE L FILER
Educator. **Personal:** Born Oct 19, 1924, Marianna, AR; married Wm; children: Arthur, Norma, Helen & Gina. **Educ:** Univ Ark, BA, 1948; NE Ill Univ, MA, 1971; NW Univ, grad study; Univ Sarasota, EdD 1982. **Career:** Educator (retired); Robert Morton High Sch, educr, 1948-55; Crest Finishing Sch, co dir 1956-60; Englewood High Sch Chicago, counr, 1961-72; Chicago Bd Educ, co compiler curric guide drama, admin dist 19, instructional serv coord dist 27, adminr dist 19, 1973; Chicago Schs, educ consult, 1997. **Orgs:** Sigma Gamma Rho Sorority, 1943-; campus coord, Central Region, 1972-74, dir, 1974; grand epistoleus, Sigma Gamma Rho Sorority, 1980-84; pres, Roseland Community Hosp; chmn, Calumet Dist United Charities Educ Comt; Good Citizenship Club Inc; Nat Scholarship Comt; Altgeld Urban Prog Ctr Educ Com; com chairperson, Afro-Am Family Serv; Quinn Chapel AME Church; Sshore YMCA; sub com, White House Conf Youth; St Luke AME Ch; nat pres, Nat Women Achievement Inc; bd trustees, Univ Sarasota. **Honors/Awds:** Citizenship Award, 1971; Outstanding Drama Coordinator, 1978; Outstanding Admin, 1979; Outstanding Service to Community Award, Sigma Gamma Rho Sorority; Judge IL Speech Association Award; Governor of Arkansas Award, 1986; Outstanding Alumni Award, Robert Moton High Sch, Marianna Ar, 1997; Community Service Award, Roseland Comt Hosp 1997; Senior Citizen Hall of Fame Award, Mayor Daley, Chicago, 1997; Community Educational Service to Youth, LeMoyne Col Alumni Award, 1997. **Special Achievements:** Woman of the Year, Creast Finishing School, 1973; co-author, Curriculum Guide & Activities for Proficiency in Basic Skills, 1977; co-author, Curriculum Guide for Drama Classes.

DAVIS, CHARLES
Athletic director, athlete. **Educ:** Wake Forest Univ, BA, English, 1971, MA, liberal science, 1997. **Career:** Athletic player (retired), Athletic director; Wake Forest Univ, sports marketer and acct exec, 1989, dir community programs, 1991-94, asst athletic dir, 1995-99; Bowie State Univ, athletics dir, 2000-02; NC A&T State Univ, athletics dir, 2002-04. **Orgs:** Millennium Fund. **Honors/Awds:** ACC Player of the Year, 1971. *

DAVIS, CHARLES
Government official. **Personal:** Born Sep 4, 1944, Seattle, WA; married Lonear W Heard; children: Charles II & Jenise A. **Educ:** Calif State Univ, BS, 1972. **Career:** Government official (retired); Hughes Aircraft Co Culver City CA, contract adm acct, 1966-73; City Compton, clerk. **Orgs:** Int Inst Municipal Clerks, 1973-; Am Records Mgt Asn, 1973-; Am Mgt Asn Adv Bd Compton & Br Salvation Army; exec bd, YMCA; South East Area Planning Coun. **Honors/Awds:** Air force Craftmanship Award, Hughes Aircraft Co, 1971; Community Service Award, Compton Model Cities, 1974; Merit Award, Inner City Challenge Inc, 1974; Council Resolution of Appreciation, 1975. **Special Achievements:** First black to receive "Certified Municipal Clerk" designation in the US, 1976. **Military Serv:** USAF, 1963-66. *

DAVIS, DR. CHARLES (CHUCK DAVIS)
Dancer, founder (originator), artistic director. **Personal:** Born Jan 1, 1937, Raleigh, NC; son of Tony and Ethel. **Educ:** Howard Univ, attended 1962. **Career:** Babatunde Olatunji's Dance Co, dancer; Eleo Pomare's Dance Troupe, dancer; Bernice Johnson Dance Co, dancer; Chuck Davis Dance Co, founder, 1967; Am Dance Festival, Durham, artist-in-residence; African Am Dance

Ensemble, founder & artistic dir, 1984-; Moments Black Inc; Am Dance Festival, Balasaraswati Joy Ann Dewey Endowed Chair, 2006; Cult Arts Safari, founder & facilitator. **Orgs:** Nat Asn Advan Colored People; bd mem, Int Asn Blacks Dance; NC Arts Coun, 1991; Brooklyn Acad Music, Brooklyn; Nat Endowment Arts; Honorary Doctorate Fine Arts, Medgar Evers Col, 1998. **Honors/Awds:** NC Artist Award, 1990; NC Award Fine Arts, 1992; NY Bessie Award; Brooklyn Acad Music Award; Dance for the Planet Award, 1998 & 2001; Nat Gov Award, 2000 & 2002; Kathryn H Wallace Award, 2000; The Advocacy Award, Durham Human Rels Comn, 2002; NC Dance Alliance Award, 2002; Commonwealth of Pennsylvania Legislative Black Caucus Award; Certicate of Excellence, AARP; NC Order of the Long Leaf Pine; Dance Magazine Award, 2004; Spirit of Hayti Trail Blazer Award, 2004. **Special Achievements:** Recognized by the Dance Heritage Coalition as one of the first 100 Irreplaceable Dance Treasurers in the US, 2000; Chuck Davis Day, declared in recognition on August 5, 2002 & January 1, 2007. His biographical profile was chronicled in The North Carolina Century: "Tar Heels Who Made a Difference 1900-2000". **Business Addr:** Founder, Artistic Director, African American Dance Ensemble, 120 Morris St, Durham, NC 27701, **Business Phone:** (919)560-2729.*

DAVIS, CHARLES A
Executive. **Personal:** Born Sep 29, 1922, Mobile, AL; son of Robert and Clara. **Educ:** WV State Col, 1944; Roosevelt Univ Chicago, polit sci, 1953. **Career:** Dir advertising, dir pub rel, city ed, sportswriter, reporter, Chicago Defender, 1946-59; Jayson Bldg Assoc, gen partner; Adco Assoc, gen partner; ADCO II, partner; Charles A Davis & Assoc Inc, pres, currently. **Orgs:** Econ Club; life mem, Nat Asn Advan Colored People; Chicago Urban League; Alpha Phi Alpha Fraternity. **Honors/Awds:** Hon Doctor Human Serv, Gov State Univ, 1967; Citations, Contributor Minority Bus Chicago Comm Human Rel, 1974; Gold Oil Can Award, Chicago Econ Develop Corp Chamber Com; Spaulding Ins Award, Nat Bus League. **Military Serv:** US Quartermaster Corps, tech sgt, 1943-46. **Business Addr:** President, Charles A Davis & Associates LLC, 29340 Indust Way Unit D401, Evergreen, CO 80439.

DAVIS, CHARLES FRANKLIN
Sports manager. **Personal:** Born Nov 14, 1964, Elizabethton, TN; son of Franklin and Hildred; married Lisa Hales, Nov 24, 1990. **Educ:** Univ Tenn, Knoxville, BA, polit sci, 1986, MA, hist, 1989. **Career:** South eastern Conf, fellowship, 1988; Univ Pacific, asst football coach, 1989-90; USS Olympic Comt, asst to exec dir, 1990, dir, USS Olympic Training Ctr, 1990-94; Stanford Univ, asst athletic dir, 1994-96; broadcaster, Turner Sports & NBC Sports; sport analyst, ESPN, 2004; Fox Sports South & Sunshine Network, analyst. **Orgs:** Colorado Springs Opera Festival, bd, 1991-94; Colorado Springs Non Profit Ctr, bd, 1992-94. *

DAVIS, CHARLES THEODORE. **See DAVIS, CHILI.**

DAVIS, CHILI (CHARLES THEODORE DAVIS)
Baseball player. **Personal:** Born Jan 17, 1960, Kingston, Jamaica. **Career:** Baseball player (retired); San Francisco Giants, outfielder, 1981-87; Calif Angels, outfielder, 1988-90, 1993-96; Minn Twins, outfielder, 1991-92; Kans City Royals, 1997; NY Yankees, outfielder, 1998-99; Ariz Diamondbacks, hitting instr & coach. **Honors/Awds:** All-Rookie Squad, Baseball Digest, 1982; Nat League All-Star Team, 1984, 1986, 1994; World Series champion, 1991, 1998, 1999. *

DAVIS, CHRISTINE R.
Executive, government official. **Personal:** Born in Nashville, TN; married Steve G; children: Pamela E. **Educ:** Fisk Univ; Tenn State Univ; Boston Bus Col; Catholic Univ Am. **Career:** Wash Bur Tuesday Pub Inc, dir; US Mem Congress, admn asst; Dem Nat Com, exec asst vice chrm; Comn Govt Operations House Representatives, staff dir. **Orgs:** Links Inc; Girl Friends Inc; Nat Press Club; Nat Coun Negro Women; Nat Coun of Women; Delta Sigma Theta Sorority. **Honors/Awds:** Numerous awards from national, religious, educational, political, civic and congressional organizations. *

DAVIS, CHUCK. **See DAVIS, DR. CHARLES.**

DAVIS, CLARENCE
Photojournalist. **Personal:** Born Dec 17, 1939, Atlanta, GA; son of Clarence and Trudie Goolsby; married Carol Venuto Davis, Aug 15, 1968 (divorced); children: Hazel C, Amanda Lael; married Jean Gaffley Chitiva Davis, Dec 30, 1991. **Educ:** City Col, New York, NY, 1988; Temple Univ, attended 1958. **Career:** Columbia Univ, New York, NY, photogr asst, 1965-68; Journal News, Nyack, NY, staff photogr, 1968-72; Bergen Rec, photojournalist, 1972; NY Daily News, photojournalist, 1972-; Amsterdam News, New York, NY, photo consult, 1977-79; Rockland Community Col, photo teacher, 1984-87; The Africa Proj Inc, founder & dir, 1987-. **Orgs:** Arts Coun Rockland; bd directors, Arts in Public Places, 1987-90; mem, New York Press Photogr Asn; US Senate News Galleries. **Honors/Awds:** Nat Black Achievers Award, 1988; The Daily News Photojournalism Award, 1987; NY PBA Award, 1985; Bergen Record Insight Award, 1972; New York State AP Award, 1971. **Special Achievements:** First, second, & third place, NY Press Photogr Asn, 1990, third place & honorable mention, 1989, first & second place, 1988, third place, 1987, honorable mention, 1986, 1985; first place, New York Daily News Photo Contest, 1977; Three Pulitzer Prize nominations. **Home Addr:** 4 Dogwood Pl, Pomona, NY 10970. *

DAVIS, CLARENCE
State government official, educator. **Personal:** Born Sep 25, 1942, Wilkes County, GA; son of Clement Sr and Lola M McLendon; married Barbara J Holder; children: Wayne C, Clarence R, Cherylle M & Dawn T. **Educ:** Morgan State Univ, Baltimore, MD, BA, Polit Sci, 1968, MA, hist & social Sci, 1978, currently pursuing doctorate in educ. **Career:** Exec dir, Hamilton Court Improv Assoc, 1968; suprv St Bernadine Comm Serv Ctr, 1971-72; res asst Friends Psychiat Res, 1972-75; Ways & Means Committee, 1983-2007; bd mem Nat Assoc Sickle Cell Disease, 1984-87; steering comn, Nat Assoc Black Soc Wk, 1984-86; command coun mem Nat Asn Black Vets; Dorie Miller Veterans Foreign Wars Post, IBPOE W No 1043; vice chmn, Md Legis Black Caucus, 2001-07; Nat Asn Concerned Veterans; Nat Asn Advan Colored People. **Orgs:** Exec dir, Hamilton Court Improv Assoc, 1968; suprv St Bernadine Comm Serv Ctr, 1971-72; res asst Friends Psychiat Res, 1972-75; bd mem Nat Assoc Sickle Cell Disease, 1984-87; steering comn, Nat Assoc Black Soc Wk, 1984-86; command coun mem Nat Asn Black Vets; Dorie Miller Veterans Foreign Wars Post, IBPOE W No 1043; vice chmn, Md Legis Black Caucus, 2001-07; Nat Asn Concerned Veterans; Nat Asn Advan Colored People. **Honors/Awds:** Goldseker Fellow. **Military Serv:** USAF E-4 1960-64; Md Line, Md Nat Guard, col. **Home Addr:** PO Box 33167, Baltimore, MD 21218, **Home Phone:** (410)366-0483.

DAVIS, CLARENCE A.
Consultant, executive. **Personal:** Born Nov 29, 1941, New York, NY; children: Todd. **Educ:** Long Island Univ, BS, Acct, 1967; cert pub acct, 1975. **Career:** Spicer & Oppenheim, sr partner, 1967-90; NY Inst Clarence A Davis, fac, 1973-79; LIU Brooklyn Ctr, fac, 1974-80; St Brigid's Elem Sch, chmn sch brd; St Brigid's CYO Track Team, track coach; Oppenheim, Appel, Dixon & Co,mgr, 1976, partnership, 1979, audit partner; Cub Scout Pack 999,cubmaster, 1977-81; Am Inst CPA Minority Recruitment Equal Opporturnity Comn, chmn, 1977-83; Boy Scout Troop 999, asst scoutmaster; Clarence A Davis Enterprises Inc, prin, 1990-98; AICPA, cfo, 1998-2000; ceo, 2000-05, chief operating officer; Oneida Ltd, brd dir, 2005-; Nester Inc, ceo, 2007-09; Sonesta International Hotels Corporation, dir nominee; Pennichuck Corporation, dir nominee; Telephone & Data Sys Inc, dir nominee; Gabelli SRI Fund & Gabelli mutual Fund, currently. **Orgs:** NY State Brd Pub Acct, 1984-; Am Inst CPA Future Issues Comn, 1984; NY St Soc CPA; Am Inst CPA; Nat Assn Black Acct; 100 Black Men; Kappa Alpha Psi Frat; Acct Pub Interest. **Honors/Awds:** Elected Archbishop Molloy High Sch Alumni Hall of Fame, 1984. **Special Achievements:** Article: "Accounting & Auditing Careers", The Black Collegian Mag, 1982. **Military Serv:** USMC, corp, 1960-64. **Business Addr:** Chief Executive Officer, Gabelli SRI Fund & Gabelli Mutual Fund, 1 Corporate Center, PO Box 1, Rye, NY 10580-1422, **Business Phone:** (914)921-5100.*

DAVIS, REV. CLIFTON DUNCAN
Singer, school administrator, actor. **Personal:** Born Oct 4, 1945, Chicago, IL; son of Toussaint L and Thelma; married Ann Taylor, Jan 1, 1984 (divorced); children: Noel & Holly; married Monica Durant, Jan 1, 2000. **Educ:** Oakwood Col, BA, theol, 1984; Andrews Univ, MDiv, 1988; Lincoln Univ, PhD. **Career:** Actor, singer, songwriter, minister, speaker; Elizabeth City State Univ, interim vice chancellor, 1995-96; Welcome Christ Ctr, Huntington Beach, co pastor, 1999-2001; Clifton Davis Prods, founder; Welcome Am Inc, chief exec officer; Clifton Davis Ministry, pastor, currently; TV appearances include: "Love, American Style", 1971; "The Melba Moore-Clifton Davis Show", 1972; "That's My Mama", 1974-75; "Amen", 1986-;"Half & Half"; "American Dreams", 2002; "Halloweentown High", 2004; Stage appearances include: Scuba Duba, 1967; Horseman Pass By, 1969; Look to the Lilies, 1970; The Engagement Baby, 1970; Two Gentlemen of Verona, 1971;Films: The Landlord, 1970; Gus, Together for Days, 1972; Lost in the Stars, 1974; Scott Joplin, 1977; Any Given Sunday, 1999; The Painting,2001; Kingdom Come, 2001; Max Keeble's Big Move, 2002; The Climb, 2002; The Engagement: My Phamily BBQ 2, 2006; Christian Lifestyle Mag TV Prog, co-host; Trinity Broadcast Network, frequent guest host,. **Orgs:** Actor's Equity; Am Fedn TV & Radio Artists; Screen Actors Guild; SCLC;NCF; Nat Am Advan Colored People; Freedom Fund SC, Nat Black Meeting Planners; 100 Black Men Am, Nat Black Educrs. **Honors/Awds:** Theater World Award, 1971; Gold Record for Never Can Say Goodbye, 1971; Heart Torch Award, Am Heart Asn, 1975; Hon doctorate: Dr, Trinity Int Univ; DHL, Lincoln Col, Paine Col & Edward Waters Col. **Special Achievements:** Grammy nomination for "Never Can Say Goodbye"; Tony Award nomination for Two Gentlemen of Verona; co-author of Lookin' Through The Windows; author, autobiographical essay, A Mason Dixon Memory. **Military Serv:** USAF. **Business Addr:** Pastor, Clifton Davis Ministry, 10624 S Eastern Ave Suite A224, Henderson, NV 89052.

DAVIS, CORA BOWIE
Executive. **Career:** Wal Mart Stores Inc, vpres & div merchandise mgr, 2004. **Business Addr:** Vice Pesident, Divisional Merchandise Manager, WalMart Stores, Division of Wal-Mart Stores Inc, 702 SW 8th St, Bentonville, AR 72716-0230, **Business Phone:** (479)277-2810.

DAVIS, CYPRIAN
Educator, clergy. **Personal:** Born Sep 9, 1930, Washington, DC; son of Clarence William and Evelyn Theresa Jackson. **Educ:** St Meinrad Col, BA, 1953; Catholic Univ Am, STL, 1957; Catholic Univ Louvain, Belgium, Lic en Sci Hist, 1963, Doctorat en Sci Hist, 1977. **Career:** St Meinrad Sem, St Meinrad, IN, instr, 1963-68, assoc prof, 1971-82, prof, 1982-; St Meinrad Archabbey, archivist, 1984-. **Orgs:** Archivist, Nat Black Catholic Clergy Caucus, 1968-. **Honors/Awds:** John Gilmary Shea Award, book: The History of Black Catholics in the USS, 1991; Catholic University's Johannes Quasten Medal, 2002. **Special Achievements:** Author several articles, Black Catholic hist, Black spirituality; author textbook Church History, "The Church a Living Heritage," "Black Spirituality, a Roman Catholic Perspective," review & expositor, "Black Catholics in Nineteenth-Century America," US Catholic Historian "Evangelization United States Since Vatican Coun II," Catholic Evangelization Today New Pentecost United States; "The Holy See and American Blacks, A Forgotten Chapter Hist Am Church", US Catholic Historian, 7 157-181, 1988; author, Hist Black Catholics US, Crossroad, 1990; "The Didache & Early Monasticism East & West," in The Didache Context, Essays Text, Hist & Transmission, edited Clayton N Jefford, Leiden: EJ Brill, p 352-367, 1995. **Business Addr:** Professor of Church History, Saint Meinrad School of Theology, Department History, 200 Hill Dr, St Meinrad, IN 47577, **Business Phone:** (812)357-6632.*

DAVIS, DALE (ELLIOTT LYDELL DAVIS)
Basketball player. **Personal:** Born Mar 25, 1969, Toccoa, GA. **Educ:** Clemson Univ, bus mgt, 1991. **Career:** Basketball player (retired); Ind Pacers, forward, 1991-2000; Portland Trail Blazers, 2000-04; Golden State Warriors, 2004-05; Detroit Pistons, 2005-07. **Orgs:** Founder, Dale Davis Found. **Honors/Awds:** Clemson Ring of Honor, 2000. **Special Achievements:** Ind Pacers, first round draft pick, 13th overall, NBA Draft, 1991; produced movie Playas Bal.

DAVIS, DANNY K.
Congressperson (u.s. federal government). **Personal:** Born Sep 6, 1941, Parkdale, AR; son of Mazzie and H D; married Vera Garner; children: Jonathan & Stacey. **Educ:** Ark AM&N Col, BA, 1961; Chicago State Univ, MS, 1968; Union Inst, PhD,1977. **Career:** US Postal Serv, clerk, 1961-62; Chicago Bd Educ, teacher, counr, 1962-69; Greater Lawndale Conserv Comn, exec dir, 1969; Martin Luther King & Neighborhood Health Ctr, Chicago, dir training, 1969-71; W Side Health Planning Orgn, manpower consult, 1971-72; Miles Square Community Health Ctr, spec asst pres, 1976; W Side Health Planning Orgn, exec dir, 1972-; 29th Ward City Chicago, alderman, chmn comn health, chmn comn zoning, alderman, 1979-90; Cook County, comnr, 1990-96; US House Rep, congressman,7th Cong Dist Ill, rep & congressman, 1996-. **Orgs:** Feelance consult, 1970-; lectr, Malcolm X Col, 1972-74; pres, W Side Asn Community Action, 1972-; Organizing Group W Side State Bank Chicago, 1973-; pres, Nat Asn Communty Health Ctr, 1977; mid-west rep, Speaker House Nat Asn Neighborhood Health Centers; Am Pub Health Asn; Lawndale People's Planning & Action Conf; comnr, Chicago Health Systems Agency; Congressional Asian Pac Am Caucus; Congressional Art Caucus; Congressional Cancer Caucus; Congressional C's Caucus; Congressional Heart & Stroke Caucus; Congressional Labor & Working Families Caucus; Congressional Iraq Fallen Heroes Caucus; Congressional Mental Health Caucus; Congressional Pakistani Caucus; Rural Health Caucus; Congressional Ukrainian Caucus;Congressional Caucus Hellenic Issues; chair, Congressional Postal Caucus; regional whip, Democratic Caucus; mem, Alpha Phi Alpha. **Honors/Awds:** Achievement Award, Mont ford Pt Marine Asn, 1972; Certificate of Merit, Pres Task force Youth Motivation, 1970; Community Service Award, United Concerned Parents, 1973; Best Alderman Award, IVI-IPO; Leon Des Press Award. **Home Phone:** (312)261-3164. **Business Addr:** Congressman, Representative, Illinois 7th District, 3333 W Arthington St Suite 130, Chicago, IL 60624, **Business Phone:** (773)533-7520.

DAVIS, DARLENE ROSE
Secretary (office). **Personal:** Born Mar 9, 1959, New Orleans, LA; daughter of Benjamin Joseph and Estelle Cornish. **Educ:** Univ Grenoble, France; Univ New Orleans, BA; Tulane Univ, JD; Univ Baltimore, grad tax prog, currently. **Career:** US House Rep; Fed Judicial Ctr; EEO CMS; US Dist Ct New Orleans, Off Hon Louis Moore Jr; Off Rep Jefferson, legis staff asst, 1993-. **Orgs:** LOU State Bar Asn; NBA; League Women Voters; Alpha Theta Epsilon. **Honors/Awds:** Moot Ct Trial Team Mem; Int Law Jurisdiction, Highest Grade. **Special Achievements:** Contributor: Judicial Evaluations, FJC publ. **Business Addr:** Legislative Staff Assistant, Off Rep Jefferson, 428 Cannon Bldg, Washington, DC 20515, **Business Phone:** (202)225-6636.

DAVIS, DENICE FAYE
Executive. **Personal:** Born Mar 4, 1953, Flint, MI; daughter of Raymond Leverne Sr and Nita Jean Grier; married Kendall Blake

Williams (divorced 1979). **Educ:** Fisk Univ, Nashville, TN, attended 1972; Univ Detroit, Detroit, MI, BA, 1975; Univ Mich, Ann Arbor, MI, JD, 1978; Am Managed Care Review Asn, Exec Leadership Prog, 1992. **Career:** Equitable Life Assurance Soc US, Equitable Real Estate Investment & Managing Co, contract specialist, 1979-84, real estate investment trainee, 1982-84; Denice Davis & Assoc, bus consult, lectr, 1984-87; Metmor Financial Inc, mgr, electronic fund transfer dept, 1988-89; United Am Healthcare Corp, Detroit, MI, dir planning & develop, 1990-91, vpres, planning & develop, 1991-93, sr vpres, planning & develop. **Orgs:** Founder & mem, Alpha Kappa Alpha Sorority, 1974-; bd mem & head finance comt, Crenshaw Christian Center Alumni Asn, 1987-89; chaplain, parlamentarian, Pierians, 1990-; Bus Policy Review Coun; Detroit Inst Arts; In Roads Metrop Detroit; founder & mem, Theta Tau Chaper; Detroit Athletic Club. **Honors/Awds:** Man of Year Achievers Award, YMCA, 1992.

DAVIS, DENISE
Lawyer. **Personal:** Born in Lubbock, TX; married Ian Hancock; children: Colin & Chloe. **Educ:** Univ Texas, BA; Law Sch, 1993. **Career:** Legis Coun; Senate Jurisprudence Comt, gen coun; Tex Judicial Coun, dir & coun; Office Lt Governor, gen coun; Tex House Reps, dep parliamentarian & spec coun, 2003-04, parliamentarian, 2004-07; Baker Botts LLP, spec coun, 2007-. **Orgs:** Town & Gown Club; Dyslexia Res Found; Links Inc; vol, Red Cross; chair, Task Force Ensure Judicial Readiness Times Emergency. **Special Achievements:** One of the "Top 40 Under 40", Eclipse Magazine & featured in Austin Woman Magazine. **Business Phone:** (512)322-2643.*

DAVIS, DENYVETTA
Library administrator. **Personal:** Born Jul 26, 1949, Muskogee, OK; daughter of Denyfeaus Elliott and Hattie Bell Shipp Elliott; divorced; children: Melvin & Erma. **Educ:** Cent State Univ, Edmond, BS, 1971, MEd, 1977; Atlanta Univ, Atlanta, MSLS, 1974; Univ Okla, Norman, attended 1990-. **Career:** Langston Univ, Langston, curator, 1974-77; Okla Community Col, Okla City, librn, 1977-82; Ralph Ellison Libr, Metro Libr Syst, Okla City, librn, 1982-84; D'Ermel Enterprises, pres, 1984-; Metro Libr Syst, dir, 1984-; Univ Okla, adj, 1990-. **Orgs:** Leadership Okla City, 1987-; pres, Literacy Coalition, 1989-90; vpres, NE Okla City Lioness Club, 1989-91; secy, Pub Libr Div, Okla Libr Asn, 1990-91; chair, deleg elect comt, Govs Conf Libraries, 1991. **Honors/ Awds:** John Cotton Dana Public Relations Award, 1986, Young Visionary Leader, 1987, American Library Asn; Celebrate Literacy Award, International Reading Asn, 1988; Finer Womanhood Award, Zeta Phi Beta Sorority, 1988; Outstanding Community Service, Assault Illiteracy, 1988; Outstanding Community Service, HARAMBEE Inc, 1990; Governor's Community Service Award, 1999.

DAVIS, DIANA L.
Educator. **Personal:** Born Aug 9, 1952, Akron, OH; daughter of Walter Sims and Margaret; married Dr Henry Vance, Jun 23, 2001; children: Leon, Makeba, Kilemo, Ada & Henry. **Educ:** Cent State Univ, BA, 1974; Howard Univ, MA, 1983. **Career:** Prince George's County Pub Sch, social studies teacher, 1975-88, social studies coordr, 1988-91, prog coordr, 1991-95, community instr specialist, 1995-99, elem sch prin, 1999-2001; Houghton Mifflin, teacher consult, 1986; Ramapo Col, NJ, asst prof edu, prof, currently. **Orgs:** Nat Coun Social Studies, 1989; Nat Alliance Black Sch Educr; ed, Asn Afro-Am Life & History Black Studies Kit, 1997-98. **Business Addr:** Professor, Ramapo College of New Jersey, Social Science Human Services, 505 Ramapo Valley Rd, Mahwah, NJ 07430, **Business Phone:** (201)684-7500.

DAVIS, DIANE LYNN
Executive. **Personal:** Born Apr 11, 1954, Detroit, MI; daughter of S Davis and V Davis. **Educ:** Wayne State Univ, Detroit, BS, 1981. **Career:** LI Farris Investment, Detroit, consult; Dow Chem Co, Midland, progmr, analyst; Candid Logic, Hazel Park, progmr; Gen Motors Corp, Warren, software engr; Electronic Data Systs, Detroit, syst engr mgr; Digital Equip Corp, Novi, info support systs, tele commun mgr; Fairfield Group, consult; Univ Detroit, Mercy, instr, 1987-. **Orgs:** Wayne State Univ Alumni Asn, 1981-; CYTCIP Adv Coun, 1988-, Detroit Urban League, 1989-; nat pres, Black Data Processing Assoc, 1992-. **Honors/Awds:** member of the Year, Black Data Processing Asn, 1987. **Home Addr:** 19020 Fairfield, Detroit, MI 48221, **Home Phone:** (313)861-2610.

DAVIS, DON. See DAVIS, DONALD EARL, JR.

DAVIS, DONALD
Executive. **Career:** Barclay Ltd Develop Co, partner, currently; United Sound Systs Rec Studio, owner, currently; First Independence Bank, chief exec officer & chmn, currently. **Orgs:** Bd Mem, Detroit Renaissance. **Business Addr:** Chairman, First Independence Bank, 44 Mich Ave, Detroit, MI 48226, **Business Phone:** (313)256-8400.*

DAVIS, DONALD EARL, JR. (DON DAVIS)
Football player. **Personal:** Born Dec 17, 1972, Olathe, KS; married Yannette; children: Dominique. **Educ:** Univ Kans, human develop, 1995. **Career:** Football player (retired), football coach; New Orleans Saints, linebacker, 1996-98; Tampa Bay Buccaneers, 1998-2000; St. Louis Rams, 2001-02; New Eng Patriots, 2003-06, asst strength & conditioning coach, 2007. **Honors/Awds:** Super Bowl XXXVI, 2001; Super Bowls XXXVIII, 2003; Super Bowls XXXIX, 2004; Ernie Tavila Award, Athletes Action org, 2004. *

DAVIS, DR. DONALD FRED
Artist, educator. **Personal:** Born Jan 14, 1935, Baton Rouge, LA; son of Bennie Davis and Annabelle Davis; married Anna Mae Eames; children: Anthony, Angela, Derek, Miriam & Michael. **Educ:** Southern Univ, BA, 1959, MEd, 1966; Ariz State Univ, PhD, 1983. **Career:** Scotlandville High Sch, art instr, 1959-69; Istrouma High Sch, art instr, 1969-71; La State Univ Lab Sch, art instr, 1972-87, Col Ed, 1987-89, Livingston Head Start, dir, 1990-95. **Orgs:** Nat Art Ed Asn; La Art Ed Asn; Phi Delta Kappa; Nat Asn Advan Colored People; United Methodist Church. **Honors/ Awds:** Outstanding Contribution, Links Inc, 1972. **Special Achievements:** Authored "Contributions of four Blacks to art education in the South, 1920-70", 1983. **Military Serv:** USN, pn3, 1952-56; Good Conduct, Korean Service, Nat Defense. **Home Addr:** 3116 Madison, Baton Rouge, LA 70802.

DAVIS, DONALD GENE
Government official, educator, naval officer. **Personal:** Born Aug 29, 1971, Snow Hill, NC; son of Amos Artis and Mary Patricia. **Educ:** US Air Force Acad, BS, Social Sci, 1994; Cent Mich Univ, MS, Admin, 1996; E Carolina Univ, EdD , 2001. **Career:** USAF Acad, admis adv, 1994-95; Andrews Air Force Base, services officer , 1995-96, exec officer, 1996-97, 89th Airlift Wing, protocol duty officer, protocol flight line duty officer, 1997-98; Air Force Reserve Officer Training Corps Detachment 600, asst prof aerospace Studies & commandant cadets, 1998-01; Snow Hill, mayor, currenlty; E Carolina Univ, prof dept sociol, currently; Lenoir Community Col, sociol instr, currently. **Orgs:** Nat Asn Advan Colored People, 1997-00; USAF Acad Asn Grad, 1994-00; air force cadet officer, Mentor Action Prog, 1995-97; Democratic Nat Comn, 1997-00; prog dir, Reach Tomorrow, 1992-00; liaison officer, Metrop Admis Liaison, 1995-97; pres, African Heritage Asn, 1994-97; Greene County Interfaith Volunteers, 2001; Saint James Presbyterian Church, Snow Hill, 2003; bd dirs, NC League Municipalities; Z Smith Reynolds Found Adv Panel; bd visitors, E Carolina Univ; NC Code Officials Qualification Bd, 2005. **Honors/Awds:** 50 Top Leaders of Tomorrow, Ebony Mag, 1995; Teaching Award for outstanding instruction, E Carolina Univ & Lenoir Community Col, 2004. **Special Achievements:** African American and youngest mayor in the 173-year history of Snow Hill. **Military Serv:** USAF, capt, 89th Services Squadron Co; Grade Officer of the Year, 1996. **Business Phone:** (252)747-3414.*

DAVIS, DONALD W.
Lawyer. **Personal:** Born Feb 1, 1934, Oklahoma; married Marjorie D Williams; children: Lawrence, Wayne, Robert, Marjean. **Educ:** Univ Colo, BA; Univ WVa. **Career:** US Dept Interior; US Dept Lbr; Mntn Sts Tel Co, Denver; priv pract, atty. **Orgs:** Nat Bar Asn; Nat Bar Found; Am Bar Asn; Am Judictor Soc; lawyer Referral Comn; Com & Credit Comn, Okla Bar Asn; vice-chmn, JJ Bruce Law Soc; Masons; Nat Asn Advan Colored People; bd dir, Urban League; coalition Civ Leadership; Baptist Church. **Military Serv:** USAF.

DAVIS, DR. DORIS ANN
President (organization), teacher. **Personal:** Divorced; children: John, Rick, Kennedy & Shedrick. **Educ:** Univ Ill, BA; Northwestern Univ, MA; Univ Calif, Los Angeles, Phd. **Career:** Chicago & LA, teacher; City Compton, elected city clerk, 1965-73, mayor,1973-77; Daisy Child Develop Ctr, dir; Heritage Unlimited Inc, owner,chief exec officer, 1980-. **Orgs:** Bd dir,Southern Calif Clers Asn; Calif Teachers Asn; Southern Calif Clerk Asn, 1967-97; Int Muncpl Clerk Asn; Dem nat Policy Coun; St Calif Jnt Comn Rev Election Laws; educ res SWRL; pres, Davis Edgerton Asn; adv bd, Water Reclamation & Resource Recovery State Calif; chair bd dir, Welfare Info Serv; Calif Museum Sci & Indust; bd dir, Nat Advan Asn Colored People; Nat Urban League; Conf Negro Elected Officials; Phi Beta Kappa; Iota Lambda Phi; del, Calif 1972 Dem Conv; Links Int League Women Voters; Welfare Info Serv; Med-Dental & Pharmaceutical Aux; St Calif State Bar Ct; Int Studies Community; pres, La Chap, Nat Congress Black Political Women; founder,Links, Harbor City; founder, Comn Status Women. **Honors/Awds:** Inductee Hall of Fame; Ron H Brown Award, African Am Trailblazers. **Special Achievements:** First Black woman to govern a metrop city as the mayor of Compton, CA. **Business Addr:** President, Heritage Unlimited Inc, 2221 E Rosecrans Ave, Compton, CA 90221, **Business Phone:** (310)639-1596.*

DAVIS, DUPREE DANIEL
Lawyer. **Personal:** Born Mar 18, 1908, Jackson, TN; married Cleo. **Educ:** Morehouse Col, AB, 1930; Tenn State Univ, BS, 1933; La Salle Univ, LLB,1944; Iowa State Univ, JD, 1944; Harvard Law Sch, attended 1945; Wash Univ, attended 1956. **Career:** Tenn Pub Sch Syst, teacher; St Clair County, Ill, atty asst state's atty; State Ill, spec asst atty gen; City E St Louis, Ill, city atty, corp counr. **Orgs:** Legal coun, Nat Asn Advan Colored People, Hanford, Wash area, 1944-45; bd auditors, E St Louis Twp.

DAVIS, EARL S.
Educator. **Personal:** Born in New York, NY; son of Maurice and Evelyn Bryan; divorced. **Educ:** NC Cent Univ, Durham, NC, BA, 1951; NY Univ, NY, MSS, 1957; Long Island Consult Ctr, NY, cert, Psychoanal Psychother, 1968. **Career:** Educator (retired); Dept Social Serv, NY, supvr, spec family coun, 1959-62; Travelers Aid Soc, NY, airport supvr, JFK, 1962-64; Lutheran Community Serv, NY, caseworker, dir group homes, 1964-68, dir social serv, 1968-71; St Christophers Sch, Dobbs Ferry, NY, dir treatment serv, 1971-72; NY Univ, asst dean, SSW, 1973-79, dir, IAAA, 1979-94; NYW Shirley M Ehrenkrenz, Sch Soc Work, consult spec prog, 1995. **Orgs:** Bd dirs, New Fed Theatre, 1990; bd dir, Carib Arts Festival Ensemble, 1989; bd dirs, Rod Rogers Dance Co, 1986; One Hundred Black Men, NY City, 1973; UNESCO, 1982-84. **Honors/Awds:** Outstanding Community Service, Peoples Alliance Community Orgn, 1990; Outstanding Service Award, Black Women Higher Educ, 1988; Service & Dedication, NY Univ Black Fac, Adminrs, 1987; Citation of Appreciation, Community Serv, Abyssinian Baptist Church, 1983; Outstanding Fac, Adminr, Black Stud Caucus, NY Univ, 1981. **Military Serv:** AUS, 1st Lt, 1951-54. **Home Addr:** 401 1st Ave, New York, NY 10010. *

DAVIS, DR. EARLEAN
Educator. **Personal:** Born Dec 13, 1947, Sawyerville, AL; daughter of Roosevelt and Rosa Rutley; married Jimmy L Davis, Nov 6, 1970; children: Patrice, Jesse, Jermaine. **Educ:** Stillman Col, BA, elem educ, 1969; Oakland Univ, teaching in reading, 1976; Logos Grad Col, christian coun, 1998, PhD, philosophy & human develop, 1998. **Career:** Pontiac Bd of Educ, teacher, 1969-94; stud advocate, 1994-96, consult, 1996-99; Edison schs, asst prin, 1997-00, prin, 2000-. **Orgs:** Nat Asn Advan Colored People; Int Reading Asn; Pontiac Educ Asn; Mich Educ Asn; Nat Educ Asn; Oakland County Reading Coun; Asn Supvr & Curric Develop; Pontiac Asn Sch Adminrs. **Honors/Awds:** Teacher of the Year, Pontiac PTA, 1991; Child Advocate Award, Oakland County, 1994;Achiever of the Yr, Negro Bus & Prof Black Woman, 1997; Woman of the Yr, Zeta Sorority, 1997. **Special Achievements:** Publications: Poetry Reading In The Elementary Classroom; poems: "Are You Listening", "Twas The Day Before Graduation". *

DAVIS, EDWARD
Salesperson. **Personal:** Born Aug 6, 1935, Tennessee; married Henrene Cannon; children: Dara Dene, Debra Donne & Edward Jr. **Educ:** Tenn State Univ, Nashville, attended 1957. **Career:** Life Ins salesman, 1957; teacher, 1960; Edward Davis & Co, ins & real estate broker, 1964; Tenn Dist 33, state senator, 1978. **Orgs:** Kappa Alpha Psi. Bd Zoning Appeals, Hamblen Co, TN.

DAVIS, DR. EDWARD L.
Educator. **Personal:** Born Dec 6, 1943, Union Bridge, MD; married Carol Johnson; children: Tanya Lynn & Brian Patrick. **Educ:** Morgan State Univ, BS, 1965; Ohio Univ, MS, 1967; Johns Hopkins Univ, MS, 1973; NC State Univ, PhD, 1977. **Career:** MD Sen fel, 1961-65; Morgan State Univ, Math Dept, instr, 1970-73; Univ Cincinnati, Col Bus, asst prof, 1976-80; Atlanta Univ, Grad Sch Bus, assoc prof, 1980-88; NC A&T State Univ, asst prof; NC Cent Univ, vis prof; AUS Air Defense Sch, Missile Sci Div, instr math; Univ Tex, El Paso, vis lectr; Ohio State Univ, teaching asst; Bell Telephone Lab, engr; Clark Atlanta Univ, Decision Sci Dept, prof decision sci, 1980-, chmn, 1988-95, Bus Sch, actg dean, 1995-99, dean, 1999-2004, interim dean, 2007-. **Orgs:** Alpha Phi Alpha Fraternity, 1961-; Opers Res Soc Am, 1973-; Southern Fel Found, 1973-76; Am Inst Decision Sci, 1980-; Transp Res Bd, 1980-; taskforce mem, Atlanta C C, 1982-. **Honors/Awds:** Balt Colt Found Scholar, 1961-65; Volunteer of the Year, City Raleigh, 1974; Teaching & Research Scholar, Univ Tex, Austin. **Special Achievements:** Author of Forecasting Inflation of Seven Asian Countries using Time Series Methods, An Empirical Comparison of Simple versus ARIMA models for the Foreign Sector of the U.S Economy, An Empirical Comparison of Foreign Trade Forecasts of Six Industrialized Nations, MARTA: A Stimulate to Atlanta Development?, Forecasting GNP/GDP of Six Industrialized Countries with Simple, Box-Jenkins and Combination Methods. **Military Serv:** AUS, first lt, 1967-69. **Home Addr:** 1424 Niskey Lake Trail SW, Atlanta, GA 30331, **Home Phone:** (404)346-3837. **Business Addr:** Dean, Professor of Decision Sciences, Clark Atlanta University, Rm 100 223 James P Brawley Dr SW, Atlanta, GA 30314, **Business Phone:** (404)880-8451.

DAVIS, DR. ELAINE CARSLEY (ELAINE O CARSLEY)
Educator. **Personal:** Born Apr 15, 1921, Baltimore, MD; daughter of Stanley Carsley (deceased) and Corinne Baker Carsley (deceased); married R Clarke (deceased); children: R Clarke Jr & Lisa. **Educ:** Coppin State Col, BS, 1942; Morgan State Col, BS, 1943; Univ Md, LLB,1950; Johns Hopkins Univ, MEd, 1955, PhD, 1958. **Career:** Baltimore City Pub Schs, 1942-74; Morgan State Col, instr, 1959-73; Baltimore Jr Col, instr, 1963-68; Loyola Col, instr, 1963-66; Johns Hopkins Univ, instr, 1964; assoc prof, dir educ, 1974-86. **Orgs:** Bd trustees, Morgan State Col, 1965-67; chmn, bd trustees, Md State Col, 1967-73; bd trustees, Goucher Col, 1972-75; nat vpres, Pi Lambda Theta, 1973-78; Delta Sigma Theta; bd dir, Rouse Co, 1978-91. **Honors/Awds:** Elected to Law Review Staff, Univ Md, 1948; Fel Am Asn Univ Women, 1957, John Hay Whitney, 1957, George Peabody, 1956-57; Phi Beta

Kappa, 1958; citations from Iota Phi Lambda, 1972; Urban League, 1947; Delta Sigma Theta; United Negro Coll Fund, 1970; Distinguished Alumni of the Year, Nat Asn for Equal Opportunity Higher Educ, 1982; Alumni Award, Coppin State Col, 1965. *

DAVIS, ELLIOTT LYDELL. See DAVIS, DALE.

DAVIS, EMANUAL
Basketball player. **Personal:** Born Aug 27, 1968, Philadelphia, PA; children: Jennifer & Tiffany. **Educ:** Del State Univ, attended 1991. **Career:** Basketball player (retired); Houston Rockets, guard, 1996-98; Seattle Supersonics, 1999-2001; Atlanta Hawks, guard, 2001-03. **Honors/Awds:** Rookie of the Year, 1996; CBA Defensive Player of the Year Award.

DAVIS, ERELLON BEN
Athlete. **Personal:** Born Feb 19, 1912, Pensacola, FL; son of Bell Coker Davis and Ellis Davis; married Ruby Nell Day, Apr 19, 1952. **Career:** Athlete (retired); Golf instr; Rackham Golf Course, head prof golfer. **Orgs:** Cotillian Club. **Honors/Awds:** Senior Champ, PGA MI Sectional, 1974; testimonial resolution, Common Coun, 1986; proclamation, Detroit Mayor Coleman Young, 1986; inductee, Black Hall of Fame, 1988; Michigan Golf Hall of Fame, 1992. **Special Achievements:** Scholarship fund, Oakland Univ, 1978. **Home Addr:** 1601 Robert Bradby Dr Apt 413, Detroit, MI 48207, **Home Phone:** (313)259-1973. *

DAVIS, ERIC KEITH
Business owner, baseball player. **Personal:** Born May 29, 1962, Los Angeles, CA; married Sherrie; children: Erica & Sacha. **Career:** Baseball player (retired), business owner; Cincinnati Reds, outfielder, 1984-91; Los Angeles Dodgers, outfielder, 1992-93; Detroit Tigers, 1993-94; Cincinnati Reds, 1996; Baltimore Orioles, 1997-98; StLouis Cardinals, 1999-2000; San Francisco Giants, 2001; Hitting From The Heart Productions LLC, owner & founder, currently. **Orgs:** Eric Davis Youth Org; RBI Reviving Baseball Inner City; hon bd mem, Multiple Myeloma Res Found. **Honors/Awds:** NL Gold Glove-CF, 1987-89; NL All-Star Team, 1987, 1989; NL Comeback Player of the Year, 1996; True Value Roberto Clemente Award, 1997; Jack Dunn Award, 1997; Fred Hutchinson Cancer Research Center, Hutch Award, 1997; Boston BBWAA, Tony Conigliaro Award, 1997; New York BBWAA, You Gotta Have Heart Award, 1997; Arete Award, 1997; Bob Chandler Courage Award, 1997; AL Comeback Player of the Year, 1998; Bob Bauman Physical Comeback Award, 1998; Espy Award as Comeback Athlete of 1998; inducted, Cincinnati Reds Hall of Fame, 2005. **Special Achievements:** Author: Born to Play: The Eric Davis Story, 1999; DVD: "Hitting from the Heart".

DAVIS, ERIC WAYNE
Football player. **Personal:** Born Jan 26, 1968, Anniston, AL; married Serena; children: Kevin, Nicolas, Daniel & Erica. **Educ:** Jacksonville State Univ, attended. **Career:** Football player (retired); San Francisco 49ers, defensive back, 1990-95; Carolina Panthers, cornerback, 1996-2000; Denver Broncos, 2001; Detroit Lions, 2002. **Honors/Awds:** Pro Bowl hon, 1996. **Special Achievements:** The highest drafted player in Jacksonville State history; named to the NFC Defensive Player of the Month, 1993. *

DAVIS, DR. ERNESTINE
Educator. **Personal:** Daughter of Henry B and Martha; widowed 1997; children: Ella Michelle & Luther III. **Educ:** Tuskegee Univ, BSN, 1965; Med Col, Ga, MSN, 1973; Univ Ala, Ed.D, 1979. **Career:** Orange County Med Ctr, supvr, 1969-71; Tuskegee Univ, pt instr, 1971-72; JA rew, obstetrics, maternal consult, 1973; Tuskegee Univ, instr, 1973-77; Univ Ala Weekend Col, asst prof, 1977-80; Univ Ala Capstone, asst prof, 1978-80; Univ N Ala, Col Nursing & Allied Health, prof, 1980-, RN & BSN, coord, currently, Presidential Mentors Prog, coordr. **Orgs:** Am Nurses Asn, 1965-; Medical Col Geo Alumni Asn, 1973-; phi kappa phi honor soc, banquet com, 1984-; Ala State Nurses Asn, chap human rights comn, 1985-89; Univ N Ala, nursing honor soc, treas, 1986-; Soc Prof nurses, 1988. **Honors/Awds:** Lillian Harvey Award, 1987; Certificates of Recognition, Alabama Nurses Asn, 1988-89; Una Nursing Honor Soc Award, 1992. **Special Achievements:** Awarded Grant, "Students Perceptions of Minority Faculty and Admin in Coland Universities in Southeast Region," UNA, 1989-92; author, Integration of Cultural Concepts into Schools of Nursing Curriculum, 1987-90, Alabama State Nurses Asn, 1990; contributing editor, Guide to Nursing Management & Leadership, 2000. **Business Addr:** Professor, Traditional Option, Nursing, University of North Alabama College of Nursing & Allied Health, Department of Nursing, 2nd Fl 203 Stevens Hall, UNA Box 5043/5155, Florence, AL 35632-0001, **Business Phone:** (256)765-4583.

DAVIS, DR. ERNESTINE BADY
Educator. **Personal:** Born Apr 8, 1943, Atlanta, GA; daughter of Henry B and Martha; married Luther Davis Jr, Aug 14, 1965 (died 1997); children: Ella Michelle & Luther III. **Educ:** Tuskegee Univ, BSN, 1965; Med Col, Ga, MSN, 1973; Univ Ala, EdD, 1979. **Career:** Orange County Med Ctr, supvr, 1969-71; Tuskegee Univ, pt instr, 1971-72; JA rew, obstetrics, maternal consult, 1973; Tuskegee Univ, instr, 1973-77; Univ Ala Weekend Col, asst prof, 1977-80; Univ Ala Capstone, asst prof, 1978-80; Univ N Ala, Col Nursing, prof, 1980-, RN & BSN coord, currently. **Orgs:** Am Nurses Asn, 1965-; dist, 1971-; Medical Col Geo Alumni Asn, 1973-; phikappa phi honor soc, banquet com, 1984-; Ala St Nurses Asn, chap human rights comn, 1985-89; Univ N Ala, nursing honor soc, treas, 1986-; Soc Prof nurses, 1988. **Honors/Awds:** Lillian Harvey Award, 1987; Certificates of Recognition by Alabama Nurses Asn, 1988-89; Una Nursing Honor Soc Award, 1992. **Special Achievements:** Awarded Grant, "Students Perceptions of Minority Faculty and Admin in Coland Universities in Southeast Region," UNA, 1989-92; author, Integration of Cultural Concepts into Schools of Nursing Curriculum, 1987-90, ASNA, 1990; contributing editor, Guide to Nursing Management & Leadership, 2000. **Home Addr:** 110 Colonial Dr, Florence, AL 35633, **Home Phone:** (256)767-5756. **Business Addr:** Professor, Coordinator, University North Alabama College Nursing, Presidential Mentors Program, PO Box 5155, Florence, AL 35632-0001, **Business Phone:** (256)765-4583.

DAVIS, ERROLL B., JR.
Executive. **Personal:** Married; children: two. **Educ:** Carnegie-Mellon Univ, BSEE, 1965; Univ Chicago, MBA, 1967. **Career:** Ford Motor Co, Detroit, corp finance staff, 1969-73; Xerox Corp Rochesterm, NY, 1973-78; Wis Power & Light Co, vpres finance, 1978-82, vpres, finance & pub affairs, 1982-84, exec vpres, 1984-87, pres, 1987-, chief exec off, 1988-; WPL Holdings, pres & chief exec, 1990-98; Alliant Energy Corp Serv Inc, pres & chief exec officer, 1998-05; Univ Syst Ga, chancelor, 2006-. **Orgs:** Selective Serv Appeal bd, 1982-01; adv bd, 1984-89, chair, 1987, campaign chmn, 1992, United Way; bd dirs, Sentry Ins Co, 1988-97; bd dirs, BP PLC, 1991-; bd dirs, Asn Edison Illum Cos, 1993-; bd dirs, PPG Industs, 1994-; bd mem, 1986-, chair, 1994-95, Wisc Asn Mfrs & Com; bd dirs, 1995-, chair, 2002, Edison Electric Inst; Univ Wis, bd regents, 1987-94; bd mem, Competitive Wis, 1989-; life trustee, chmn, bd trustees, 1989-, Carnegie Mellon Univ; bd dirs, Am Gas Asn, 1990-95; bd dirs, Electric Power Res Inst, 1990-; chmn, Start Smart Dane Co, Dane Co; Am Soc Corp Execs, 1998-; adv bd, Fed Res Bank Chicago. **Honors/Awds:** Black Engineer of the Yer Award, 1988; Distinguished Alumnus Award, Univ Chicagos Grad Sch Bus, 1993; CEO of the Year, Bronze Medal winner, Financial World, 1993; Executive of the Year, Sales & Marketing, 1995; named one of the Top 50 Blacks, Black Enterprise, 2000; Ellis Island Medal of Honor, 2001; Dr Martin Luther King Jr Awd, Dane County/City of Madison, 2001; Fortune Magazine's 50 Best Most Powerful Black Executives in Am. **Business Addr:** Chancellor, University System of Georgia, 270 Washington St SW, Atlanta, GA 30334, **Business Phone:** (404)656-2250.*

DAVIS, ESTHER GREGG
School administrator. **Personal:** Born Oct 16, 1934, Chicago, IL; married Fred A Cooper. **Educ:** Hofstra Univ, BS, 1966; N western Univ, MA, 1972; N western Univ, PhD, 1974. **Career:** VA Tech, vis prof Educ, 1979-; VA Common wealth Univ, asst prof Educ, 1976-; Blue Cross Asn, dir assessment ctr, 1974-75; Chicago Bd Educ, teacher, 1970-71; NY Bd Educ, teacher, 1966-67; Richmond Pub Sch, ESEATTLE I Proj, consult, 1976-; Danforth Found, consult, 1976-77; Mgt Ctr VA Common wealth Univ, cons, 1977-. **Orgs:** Phi Delta Kappa, 1973-; Am Mgt Asn, 1979; Mat Alliance Black Sch Educators, 1979. **Special Achievements:** Publ; "Intern Perception of Supervisory Support" ERIC, 1974; "Classroom Mgmt" Kappa Delta Pi Record, 1980-81; "Living Patterns of Urban Sch Adminstrs"; "Lewin's Force Field Theory a model for decision making". **Business Addr:** AUS Med Dept Personnel Sup Agency, VA Commonwealth University, Richmond, VA 23284.

DAVIS, ETHELDRA S.
Educator, school administrator, consultant. **Personal:** Born May 11, 1931, Marianne, AR; daughter of Luther Sampson and Fannie Sampson; widowed; children: Andrea & Robert. **Educ:** Los Angeles City Col, AA, 1951; Los Angeles St Col, BA, 1953; Univ AK, MA, 1964; Newport Univ, PhD, 1980. **Career:** Educator, school administrator, consultant (retired); Los Angeles Sch, teacher, 1953-58; Anchorage Sch, from teacher to asst prin, 1958-66, prin, 1967-80; Hew Region ten, field reader, 1967-70; Western Region, oeo consult, 1967-70; Juvenile Diversion Prog, exec dir, founder. **Orgs:** Alpha Kappa Alpha, NEA; ACPNA; NAESP; IS-CPP; pres, Pan-Hellenic Coun Club Anchorage, 1960; dir, Child Develop Ctr Anchorage Community Action Agency; teacher, arts & crafts, YMCA; Home un-wed Mothers; Mayor's Adv Bd, 1968; Parks & Recreation Bd; bd dir, Camp fire; founder, United League Girls;Boy Scouts Am & Girls Scouts Am; Anchorage Neighborhood Watch, 1982-; founder, Nat Asn Advan Colored People, Youth Chapter. **Honors/Awds:** Woman of the year, Northern Lights Club, 1969; Most Outstanding Educator,1970; Certificate of Merit, Anchorage Post Office, 1969; Honor Award, Nat Asn Advan Colored People; Volunteer of the year, Nat Crime Prev Coun. **Special Achievements:** First African american women to become school principal, Anchorage, Alaska.

DAVIS, EUNICE J.
School principal. **Career:** N Dade Middle Sch, prin, currently. **Honors/Awds:** Principal of the Yr, Access Ctr I Winner. **Business Addr:** Principal, North Dade Middle School, 1840 NW 157 St, Miami, FL 33054, **Business Phone:** (305)624-8415.

DAVIS, FRANCE ALBERT
Clergy, educator. **Personal:** Born Dec 5, 1946, Gough, GA; son of John H and Julia Cooper; married Willene Witt; children: Carolyn Marie, Grace Elaine, France II. **Educ:** Tuskegee Inst; Laney Col, AA, arts & humanities, 1971; Merritt Col, AA, afro-am studies, 1972; Univ CA, BA, rhetoric, 1972; Westminster Col, BS, relig & philos, 1977; Univ UT, MA, mass commun, 1978; NW Nazarene Col, Master of ministry, 1994. **Career:** Univ Utah, instr, 1972-; Calvary Baptist Church, pastor, 1973-. **Orgs:** Bd chmn, UT Bd Corr, 1982-, bd mem, 1975-; bd chmn, UT Opportunities Industrialization Ctr, 1974-; exec bd, DIC/A; 1982 chmn, Tribune Common Carrier Ed Bd, 1982; Albert Henry Educational Found, 1976-; bd mem, Nat Asn Advan Colored People Salt Lake Br, 1975-77, 1985-; chmn, Martin Luther King Jr Holiday Comm Utah, 1985-86; chmn, Mignon Richmond Park Comn, 1985-86. **Honors/Awds:** Pres award, Salt Lake, Nat Asn Advan Colored People, 1975; Serv award, Beehive Elks, 1975; torch bearer, OIC/A, 1979; OIC Torchbearer Award, 1979; civil rights worker, Salt Lake Nat Asn Advan Colored People, 1984; Black Scholars Outstanding Image Maker, 1986; Salt Lake Ambassadors, Salt Lake Conv & Visitors Bur, 1991; Univ Utah, Hon DHL, 1993. **Special Achievements:** Authour, "Light in the Midst of Zion". **Military Serv:** USAF, aircraft mechanic, 1966-70, staff seargeant commendation award, Vietnam service award. **Business Addr:** Pastor, Calvary Baptist Church, 1090 S State St, Salt Lake City, UT 84111-4521.*

DAVIS, FRANK
Law enforcement officer. **Personal:** Born Mar 22, 1947, Claiborne County, MS; son of Green Lee and Mary Lee Barnes Triplett; divorced; children: Tracy, Gary. **Educ:** Alcorn State Univ, BS, phys educ, 1972; Southern Univ, criminal justice, 1973. **Career:** AUS, 1966-68; Port Gibson, MS, dep sheriff, 1968-78; Claiborne County, civil defense dir, 1978-79, Port Gibson Police Dept, asst chief police, 1978-79, sheriff, 1980-. **Orgs:** Treas, New Zion Lodge, 1976; hon mem, FBLA, 1980; Kiwanis Club, 1980; prof mem, Am Correctional Assoc, 1983; Miss Sheriff's Asn; pres, NOBLE, MS chap, 1997; Police Pusuit Bd, 2003. **Honors/Awds:** Civil Defense Council, MS Civil Defense, 1978; Certificate of Merit, Aide-de-Camp, 1979; Mississippi Sheriff's Asn 1988; MS Pkwy Commission Bd; MS Heritage Corridor Bd; Governor of the State of Missisippi, 1990; Citizenship Award, 1991. **Special Achievements:** First black president of the Mississippi Sheriff Asn, 2000-01. **Military Serv:** AUS, E-6, 1966-68. **Business Addr:** Sheriff, Claiborne County, 410 Main St, PO Box 427, Port Gibson, MS 39150.*

DAVIS, FRANK ALLEN
Chief executive officer, president (organization). **Personal:** Born Nov 17, 1960, Washington, DC; son of Joan A Johnson Davis and Eugene N Davis; married Elena Labarrere, Sep 25, 1983; children: Michael Allen. **Educ:** Bucknell Univ, BSEE, 1982; Univ Ala, Birmingham, MBA, 1989; Tuck Sch Bus, Dartmouth, MBEP, 2004. **Career:** Westinghouse Control Div, div sales engr, 1982-85; Westinghouse Industries Mkt, asst sales engr, 1985-86, personnel consult, 1985-89, industrial sls engr, 1987-89; Honeywell Inc, sr mkt spec, 1989-92, nat distributor sls mgr, 1992-93; Siebe PLC Ltd, sr prod mkt mgr, 1993-94; Johnson Controls, nat end user sls & mktg mgr, 1994-95; Delco Ventures, vpres, 1994-; Johnson Controls, group gen mgr, 1997-98, Dir strategic planning, 1998-2000; Horizon Group Co, pres & chief exec officer, 2001-. **Orgs:** Alpha Phi Omega, 1984-; Nat Black MBA Asn, 1986-; Am Mkt Asn, 1987-; Open Pit Mining Asn, 1987-89; Am Cancer Soc, 1990-91; Rockford Asn Minority Mgt, 1991-97; Northern Ill Minority Contractors Asn, 1995-97; Leaders Forum Milwaukee, 1997-98; Greater Atlanta Chamber Com, 1999-; S Reg Minority Bus Coun, 2002-; Ga Minority Supplier Develop Coun, 2005-; Inst Supply Mgt, 2005-06; The Georgian Club, 2006-; Vindus, 2008-; bd dir, Bucknell Univ Alumni Asn, 2008-. **Honors/Awds:** William Randolph Hearst United State Sen Youth Scholar; winner, Susan Thomas Hensinger Prize; Hon Alpha Mu Alpha Nat Mkt; Johnson Controls Inner Circle Award. **Home Addr:** 1927 Westover Lane NW, Kennesaw, GA 30152. **Business Addr:** President, Chief Executive Officer, Horizon Services Corporation, 5346 Stadium Trace Parkway Suite 212, Birmingham, AL 35242, **Business Phone:** (205)249-8033.

DAVIS, FREDERICK D.
Labor activist. **Personal:** Born Aug 6, 1935, Tulsa, OK; married Patricia; children: Grant Anthony, Frederick Douglass II, Mwindaace N Gai. **Educ:** Okla Univ. **Career:** McDonnell Douglas Aircraft Corp, 1956-, Equal Oppurtunity Prog, chmn, 1974-75. **Orgs:** Pres, Nat Asn Advancement Colored People, Tulsa; pres, bd dirs, Tulsa Area United Way; pub rel dir, Prince Hall Free & Accepted Masons; UAW Constl & Convention Delegate, 1975-; Paradise Baptist Church; Coal Creek 88 Masonic Lodge; pres, Tulsa Community Recreation Coun, 1972-74; Police Community Rels; Air Force Mem Found. **Special Achievements:** First Black/minority major developer in the state of Oklahoma. *

DAVIS, GENE A.
Executive. **Personal:** Born Jun 29, 1939, Philadelphia, PA; married Jonna Bjorkefall; children: Peter, Philip. **Educ:** Philadelphia Mus Sch Art, adv design & undergrad, 1960; New York Col, advert copy, 1965. **Career:** CBS Columbia Records, adv prod

mgr, 1966-68; Westinghouse Group W, mgr, 1968-72; WNEW Radio NY, creative dir, 1972-74; STOP TV Wash, mgr, 1974-76; WMAQTV, mgr, 1976-79; Corinthian Broadcasting Corp, vpres, adv & Pub rel, 1979-81; Essence Comm Inc, dir corp creat serv, 1983. **Orgs:** BPA Awards; MI State Awards, 1974-77; Addy Awards, Am Advert Fed, 1977-79; treas & secy, Broadcasters Promotion Asn Inc, 1978-79; Intl Radio & TV Soc, 1978-. **Honors/Awds:** US TV Commercial Award, TV Advert, 1978; Cable Marketing Award, 1981. *

DAVIS, GEORGE B.
Educator, writer. **Personal:** Born Nov 29, 1939, Shepherdstown, WV; married Mary Cornelius, Aug 31, 1963; children: Pamela & George. **Educ:** Colgate Univ, BA, 1961; Columbia Univ, MFA, 1971. **Career:** Wash Post, DC, staff writer, 1968-69; NY Times, NY, deskman, 1969-70; Bronx Community Col, City Univ NY, Bronx, asst prof, 1974-78; Rutgers Univ, NJ, asst prof, 1978, Dept Eng, assoc prof, currently; freelance writer various publ; Columbia Univ & Green haven Prison, teacher writing workshops; Black Swan Commun, co-founder & pres; Author: Coming Home, Random House, 1971; Love, Black Love, Doubleday, 1978; Black Life in Corporate America: Swimming in the Mainstream, Doubleday, 1982; Soul Vibrations Astrology for African Americans, 1996; Alex, currently. **Orgs:** Author's Guild; Grant NY Coun Arts; Nat Endowment Humanities; mem, AuthorsLeague Am. **Military Serv:** USAF, capt, 1961-68; Air Medal. **Business Addr:** Associate Professor, Rutgers University, Department of English, Hill Hall Room 501, Newark, NJ 07102-1801, **Business Phone:** (973)353-5279.*

DAVIS, GEORGE NELSON, JR.
Administrator, association executive. **Personal:** Born Sep 17, 1936, Somerville, TN; son of George N and Jennie Burr; married Ruth J Hayes (divorced 1989); children: Judy Elaine. **Career:** Association executive, administrator (retired); US Postal Serv, Memphis, TN, letter carrier, 1960-70; br 27 NALC, Memphis, TN, vpres, 1970-78, pres, 1978-85; Nat Asn Letter Carriers, Wash, DC, bd trustees, 1978-85, chmn & bd trustees, 1981-85, dir safety & health, 1986.

DAVIS, GLEN ANTHONY
Physician. **Personal:** Born Mar 18, 1972, Kalamazoo, MI; son of Charles and Clemetine (deceased). **Educ:** Univ Mich, BS, 1994; Univ Mich Med Sch, MD, 1998. **Career:** Upjohn Co, lab asst, 1990; Children's Hosp Mich, resident physician, 1998-01; Bristol St Pediat, physician, 2001-; ProMed Physician, pediatrician; S Bend Clinic, pediatrician, currently. **Orgs:** Golden Key Nat Honor Soc, 1991; Black Med Asn, 1994-98; Am Med Asn, 1994-; Am Acad Pediat, 1998-. **Honors/Awds:** Ralph Gibson Award, Univ Mich Med Sch, 1998. **Business Addr:** Pediatrician, South Bend Clinic, 211 Eddy St, South Bend, IN 46617.*

DAVIS, GLENN
President (organization). **Career:** Acct mgr; proj mgr; sr consult; Bran Core Technologies, pres & chief exec officer, 1986-. **Orgs:** Bd dirs, GRTC; bd dirs, Va Commonwealth Univ Alumni; Asn dir, pres, & vpres, Asn Info Technol Profs; Comput Adv Comt Garfield Childs Mem Fund; VCU Adv Adopt-A-School Prog & ECPI. **Honors/Awds:** Entrepreneur of the year Award, Va Minority Supplier Develop Coun, 2004; Technology Award, Greater Richmond Technol Coun, 2003, 2004, 2005, & 2006; IBM Leadership Award; Information Systems Alumnus of the Year Award, Va Commonwealth Univ. **Business Addr:** President, Chief Executive Officer, Bran Core Technologies, 501 E Franklin St Suite 724, Richmond, VA 23219-2323, **Business Phone:** (804)521-4041.

DAVIS, DR. GLORIA-JEANNE
School administrator, administrator. **Personal:** Born Feb 6, 1945, Gary, IN; daughter of Rixie Hardin McCarroll and Gloria Lavern Cummings McCarroll; married Wilbert Douglas Davis; children: Wilbert Douglas II & Rixie Hardin. **Educ:** Eastern Ky Univ, BBA, 1970, MBA 1971; Ill State Univ, PhD, 1986. **Career:** Sch administrator & Administrator (retired); Caterpillar Tractor Co, analyst & machine shop training, 1974-78; Bloomington City Hall, financial adv, 1978-84; Ill Comt Black Concerns Higher Educ, steering community secy, 1984-93, steering comt, 1994-96, co chair annual conf, 1993; Ill Cent Col, instr & bus dept, 1986; Ill State Univ, univ affirmative action officer, asst pres affirmative action & equal opportunity, 1988-96; Mitsubishi Motor mfg Am, dir opportunity prog. **Orgs:** Pres, ISU Toastmasters; pres, Ill Affirmative Action Officers Asn, 1986-88; pres, Asn Black Acad Employ, 1987-91; chair, ISU Recruitment & Retention Comt, 1988-96; Admin Prof Grievance Panel; campus liaison, Ill State Univ Black Colleagues Asn; N Cent Asn Col & Sch Self Study, 1993-96; Nat Collegiate Athletic Asn Self Study, 1993-96; bd dirs, McLean City AIDS Task Force; bd dir, Inst Collaborative Solutions; comnr, Bloomington Liquor Comn; adv bd, Ill State Univ, Col Arts & Sci. **Honors/Awds:** Administrator of the Year Award, Black Stud Union, 1987; Recognition Award, Educ Admin & Found Adv Coun, 1990; Distinguished Service Award, Admin Prof Staff, 1991; Civil Rights Award, MacMurray Col, Nat Advan Asn Colored People, 1994.

DAVIS, GOLIATH J., III
Law enforcement officer. **Educ:** Rollins Col, BS Behav Sci; Univ S Fla, MS, criminal justice; Fla State Univ, PhD, criminol; Harvard Univ's John F. Kennedy Sch Govt, grad. **Career:** St Petersburg, Fla, Police Dept, asst chief admin serv bur, 1997, chief police, 1997-01; Univ S Fla, adj prof criminol, currently; Midtown econ develop, dep mayor Midtown econ develop, 2003-. **Honors/Awds:** Tampa Bay Ethics Award, Univ Tampa Ctr Ethics; Alumni Achievement Award in Law Enforcement, Rollins Col; Distinguished Alumni Award, Univ S Fla Pinellas County; Distinguished Citizen Award, Boy Scouts Am. **Special Achievements:** First African Am police chief St Petersburg, Fla. **Business Addr:** Deputy Mayor, Midtown Econ Develop, 175 5th St N, St Petersburg, FL 33701.*

DAVIS, GRACE E
Software developer. **Educ:** Grambling State Univ, BS, 1998; Univ Utah; Utah State Univ. **Career:** Tex Schs, Garland, teacher, 1999-2000; Salt Lake Conv & Visitors Bur, res asst, 1994-96; Baylor Univ Med Ctr, Dallas, TX, police officer, 2001; Waterford Inst, educ software designer, currently. **Orgs:** Pub rels chair, Blacks Collegiates & Assocs United, Utah State Univ, 1992-95; vol, Head Start, 1995; asst dir, Calvary Baptist Church, Saturday Sch Comput Reading Prog, 1998. **Honors/Awds:** Grambling State Univ, President's List, 1998. **Home Addr:** 1912 Meadow Dr, Salt Lake City, UT 84121, **Home Phone:** (801)943-6145. **Business Addr:** Teacher, Waterford Institute, 1590 E 9400 S, Sandy, UT 84093, **Business Phone:** (801)576-4900.*

DAVIS, GREGORY T
Media executive. **Career:** WRR Class 101.1 FM, gen mgr, 2004-. **Business Addr:** General Manager, WRR Classical 101.1 FM, 1516 1st Ave, PO Box 159001, Dallas, TX 75315-9001, **Business Phone:** (214)670-8888.

DAVIS, GUY
Composer, guitarist, actor. **Personal:** Born May 12, 1952, New York, NY; son of Ossie Davis and Ruby Dee. **Career:** Films: Beat Street, 1984; tv series: "One Life to Live"; stage: Cotton Comes to Harlem; Mulebone, 1991; Trick the Devil, 1993; Ideas, 2004; albums: Stomp Down Rider, 1995; Call Down the Thunder, 1996; You Don't Know My Mind, 1998; Butt Naked Free, 2000; Give In Kind, 2002, Chocolate to the Bone, 2003; Legacy, 2004; Skunkmello, 2006; Down At The Sea, 2007; Guy Davis On Air, 2007; Sweetheart Like You, 2009. **Honors/Awds:** Best Acoustic Album of the Year; Best Acoustic Artist of the Year; Best Instrumentalist. *

DAVIS, H. BERNARD
Automotive executive. **Personal:** Born Apr 30, 1945, Burnsville, AL; son of Leslie Holmes and Roxie Davis Price; married Delphine Handley Davis, Oct 18, 1964; children: Jason Henry, Jeanine Kianga. **Educ:** Mott Community Col, Flint, MI, AD, data processing, 1970; Univ Mich, Flint, MI, BBA, 1976; Mich State Univ, E Lansing, MI, MBA, 1984; Pa State Univ, Col Park, PA, exec mgt prog, 1989. **Career:** Gen Motors Corp, Corp Finance Staff, Detroit, MI, dir prod cost anal, 1979-81; Gen Motors Corp, Oldsmobile Div, Lansing, MI, from asst div comptroller to div comptroller, 1981-88; Powertrain Div B-O-C, Brighton, MI, dir finance & bus planning, 1988-90; GM Engine Div, Brighton, MI, div comptroller; Gen Motors Corp, Global Financial Shared Serv, exec dir, currently. **Orgs:** Treas, mem, bd dirs, Black Child & Family Inst, 1987-89; sr pastor, Alexander St Church of God, 1988-89; vice chmn, Capital Area United Way, 1987; bd dirs, Capital Area Found, 1987-89. **Home Addr:** 7719 Flemingwood Ct, Sanford, FL 32771-8105. **Business Addr:** Executive Director, General Motors Corporation, Global Financial Shared Services, 300 Renaissance Ctr, Detroit, MI 48265-3000.*

DAVIS, HAROLD
Government official. **Personal:** Born Feb 29, 1932, New Orleans, LA; son of T D Davis and Myrtle L Royal; married Barbara M, Aug 20, 1955; children: Harold Jr, Deborah Davis-Gillespie. **Educ:** Southern Univ, BA, 1952; Univ Calif, MPA, 1957; Am Baptist Sem The W, LLD. **Career:** Alameda Co, CA, Redevelopment Agency, relocation officer, 1961-63, asst exec dir, 1963-65, exec dir, 1965-68, chief asst welfare dir, 1968-72; Oakland Housing Authority, ceo, exec dir emer, currently. **Orgs:** life mem, Alpha Phi Alpha; Nat Asn Housing & Redevelopment Off, 1962; bd mem, Grad Theol Union, 1970 & 1994; pres, Am Baptist Churches, 1988-89; chmn, Nat bd dirs & pres, YMCA, 1989-90; chmn bd dir, C Hosp & res Ctr, Oakland, 1993-; life mem, Nat Advan Asn Colored People; Sigma Pi Phi Boule; Sire Archon, 1994-96; bd dir, Toastmasters Int; chmn bd trustees, Am Baptist Seminary. **Honors/Awds:** Distinguished Serv, Alpha Phi Alpha, 1987 & 1988; Outstanding Pub Adminr, Nat Forum Black Pub Adminrs, 1988; Outstanding Pub Adminr, Am Soc Pub Admin, 1989; National Treasurer Award, YMCA, 1993; Williford Award, C Hosp Oakland, 1996; Legend Award, YMCA, Berkeley CA, 1996. **Military Serv:** AUS, first Lt, 1952-54, hon discharge. **Business Addr:** Executive Director Emeritus, Oakland Housing Authority, 1619 Harrison St, Oakland, CA 94612, **Business Phone:** (510)874-1500.*

DAVIS, HAROLD R.
Executive. **Personal:** Born Mar 25, 1926, High Point, NC; married Marva Lane; children: Stpehen, Craig, Brenda, Peggy J Slaughter. **Educ:** US Sch Admin, CLU, Am Col Life Underwriters, 1970; FLMI, Life Off mgt courses, 1976. **Career:** exec (retired); dist mgr, 1966-69; asst agency dir, 1969-72; self emp ins consult, Davis Financial Serv; regnl agency dir, 1973-77; vpres field opers, 1978-84; vpres mkt servs, 1984-88; NC Mutual Life Ins Co, 1988. **Orgs:** Am Soc CLU; vpres, Nat Ins Asn; bd dir, Durham, YMCA, 1979-83; bd dir, Life Ins Mkt & Res Asn, 1982-84. **Military Serv:** USNA, pfc, 1945-46. *

DAVIS, HERMAN E.
Chief executive officer, educator. **Personal:** Born Mar 3, 1935, Carlton, AL; married Thelma; children: Millicent, Chiaka, Jennifer & Holly. **Educ:** BEd, 1962. **Career:** New Direction Budgeting & Financial Serv Ctr Inc, pres; Du Sable High Sch, Chicago, teacher; Waddell & Reed Inc, rep; Chicago Pub Sch Syst, teacher; Gary Community Sch Syst, teacher; City coun Coopertown, TN, vmayor, mayor; Nashville Game Co, founder & ceo, currently. **Orgs:** Pres, Asn Distrib Educ Coordinators, 1966; pres, Bryn Mawr & West Area Coun; S Shore Comn; chmn, Finance Comt S Shore Comn; Sigma Omega Chap Omega Psi Phi. **Honors/Awds:** Award of Merit, US Small Bus Admin & Cosmopolitan Club Children, 1968; Sales Champion Award, Waddell & Reed Inc, 1968; Certificate of Excellence Cosmopolitan Club Children, 1969-70. **Military Serv:** AUS, security agency, sp2, 1954-57. **Business Addr:** Chief Executive officer, Nashville Game Co, 340 W Trinity Lane, Nashville, TN 37207, **Business Phone:** (615)262-5139.

DAVIS, HOWLIE R
Executive. **Personal:** Born Sep 14, 1957, Charlotte, NC; son of Harry and Hattie B; divorced. **Educ:** Morehouse Col, BS, bus, 1979; Atlanta Univ, Sch Bus, 1980. **Career:** Clinton-Gore Presidential Transition Comm, 1992-93; The White House, assoc dir personnel, 1993; US Dept of Energy, White House liaison, 1993-96; Democratic Nat Convention, dir security, 1996; Citizenship Education Fund, proj dir, 1996; Presidential Inaugural Comm, dir special services until 1997; Public Private Partnership, Inc, managing partner, 1997-98; CH2MHILL, sr vpres & dir local govt affairs, currently. **Orgs:** Alpha Phi Alpha Fraternity Inc. **Honors/Awds:** Best & Brightest in African-Am Achievement, Dollars & Sense Mag. **Business Addr:** Senior Vice President, CH2MHILL, 13921 Pk Ctr Rd Suite 600, Herndon, VA 20171-5416, **Business Phone:** (703)471-1441.

DAVIS, HUBERT IRA
Basketball player, entertainer. **Personal:** Born May 17, 1970, Winston-Salem, NC; son of Hubert Davis Sr. **Educ:** Univ NC, Bachelor's Degree, criminal justice, 1992. **Career:** Basketball player (retired), color analyst; NY Knicks, guard, 1992-96; Toronto Raptors, 1996-97; Dallas Mavericks, 1998-2001; Wash Wizards, 2001-02; Detroit Pistons, 2003-04; NJ Nets, guard, 2004; ESPN's col basketball broadcasts, color analyst, currently. **Special Achievements:** First round pick, No 20, NBA Draft, 1992. **Business Addr:** Color Analyst, ESPN, ESPN Plaza 935 Middle St, Bristol, CT 06010, **Business Phone:** (860)766-2000.

DAVIS, ISAAC
Football player, football coach. **Personal:** Born Apr 8, 1972, Malvern, AR; son of John Davis and Theresa Davis; married Chandra; children: Gabrielle Nicole & Gisele Marie. **Educ:** Univ Ark. **Career:** NFL: Ar Razorbacks, guard, 1990-93; San Diego Chargers, guard, 1994-97; New Orleans St, guard, 1997-98; Minn Vikings, guard, 1998; XFL: Las Vegas Outlaws, 2001; Chicago Enforcers, 2001; Memphis Maniax, 2001; John Horn High Sch, defensive line & track coach; Arkans Baptist Col Buffaloes, Offensive asst coach, 2007-. **Orgs:** Athletes for Educ Prog; founder, Block Against Hunger Found. **Business Phone:** (501)244-5168.*

DAVIS, J MASON
Lawyer. **Personal:** Born Jul 30, 1935, Birmingham, AL; son of Madeline Harris and J Mason; married June Carolyn Fox; children: Karen M & J Mason III. **Educ:** Talladega Col, BA, 1956; State Univ NY Law Sch, JD, 1959. **Career:** Sirote & Permutt PC, atty, 1960-, sr partner, currently; Univ Ala, Sch Law, adj prof ins & damages, 1972-97; Protective Indust Ins Co Ala Inc, chmn bd dir, 1988-. **Orgs:** Gen Counsel Nat Ins Asn, 1962-77; exec comn mem, Ala Democratic Party, 1970-; exec Comn Birmingham Bar Asn, 1974-77; secy, Birmingham Bar Asn, 1978-79; pres, Nat Ins Asn, 1978-79; secy, Ala Dem Party, 1978-; chmn, bd dir, Nat Ins Asn, 1979-81; Alpha Phi Alpha Fraternity, Nat Asn Advan Colored People, Sigma Pi Phi, Omicron Delta Kappa; chmn bd trustees, Talladega Col, 1981-88; pres, Birmingham Bar Assoc, 1985-86; vice chmn Birmingham Airport Authority. **Honors/Awds:** Pres Citation Frontiers Am, 1962; Man of the Year, Alpha Phi Alpha Fraternity, 1973; Outstanding Serv Comm Serv Coun, 1973; Outdoor Recreation Achievement Award, US Dept Comm, 1975; Ala Recreation Parks Soc Lay Award, 1975; Outstanding Serv Univ Ala, Sch Law, 1977; Exemplary Dedication Higher Educ Ala Asn Col & Univ, 1982. **Business Addr:** Attorney, Sirote & Permutt PC, 2311 Highland Ave S, PO Box 55727, Birmingham, AL 35255-5727, **Business Phone:** (205)930-5134.

DAVIS, JACKIE SOWELL
Educator, high school principal. **Career:** Principal (retired); PM High Sch, prin. *

DAVIS, JACKLEAN ANDREA
Law enforcement officer. **Personal:** Born Feb 6, 1957, Cleveland, OH; daughter of Fredrick and LaFrench; children: Christina

Katherine. **Educ:** Univ New Orleans. **Career:** Law Enforcement Officer (retired); New Orleans Police Dept, patrol officer, 1981-82, first dist, 1982, sixth dist, 1982-83, narcotic & drug abuse unit & vice unit, 1983-86, investr rape unit, 1984-86, investr homicide unit, 1986-91, sgt, 1991, lt. **Orgs:** Black Orgn Police; Nat Orgn Black Law Enforcement Exec; Int Asn Women Police; Int Asn Chiefs; Martha Grand Chap Order Eastern Stars. **Honors/Awds:** Officer of the Year, Black Orgn Police, 1989; Law Enforcement Officer of the Year, Int Orgn Women, 1992. **Home Addr:** 4743 Knight Dr, New Orleans, LA 70127, **Home Phone:** (504)246-0601.

DAVIS, JAMES EDGAR
Association executive, engineer. **Personal:** Born Apr 30, 1948, Augusta, GA; son of Sarah N Davis; married Kathleen Stitt, Feb 1998; children: Esa, Veronica. **Educ:** NC State Univ, BS, Civil Engg, 1970, MS, Civil Engg, 1972; Univ NC, Master Regional Planning, 1972; Univ Md, PhD course Req, 1976; Fedn Exec Inst, 1982, Synectics, 1989, Univ Pa, 1991, Harvard Univ, attended 1992. **Career:** Southern Railway Co, mgt trainee, 1970-72; Barton-Aschman Assocs, assoc, 1972-73; The MITRE Corp, tech staff, 1973-74; US Dept Transp, chief pre-award rev br, 1974-75, sr prog ayalyst, 1976-77, dir off grants asst, 1978-82, dep assoc adminr grants mgt, 1982-83, urban mass transp admin, 1974-83; Port Authority NY & NJ, asst dir rail transp, 1983-84; Sea-land Serv Inc, dir opers res, 1985-89; Am Soc Civil Engrs, asst exec dir, exec dir & chief exec officer. **Orgs:** Fedn Sr Exec Serv; Can Sr Transp Mgt Prog, 1980; Am Mgt Asn; Am Soc Asn Exec; Greater Wash Soc Asn Exec; Coun Engg & Scientific Soc Exec, Am Soc Civil Engrs. **Honors/Awds:** Silver Medal of Meritorious Achievement, The Secy Transp; The UMTA Adminr Bronze Medal Super Achievement; Represented USDOT in Riyadh, Saudi Arabia, 1978. *

DAVIS, JAMES F.
School administrator. **Personal:** Born Jan 29, 1943, Marion, SC; married Beverly A Hemmingway; children: Shean Askia & Donald Affonso. **Educ:** Johnson C Smith Univ, BA, 1964; Pepperdine Univ, MBA, 1977. **Career:** EF Hutton & Co Inc, super, 1968-71; SC Natl Bank, asst vpres 1971-78; Rice Col, fac mem, 1978-79; Benedict Col, assoc vpres stud affair, 1979-, dean students, currently. **Orgs:** Columbia Chamber Com, 1979; trustee mem, Benedict Col Fed Credit Union, 1979-; AUS Asn, 1979; Nat Assoc Col Deans Registrars & Admissions Officers, 1984; Am Asn Col Registrars & Admis Officers; Steering ComtAssessment Stud Acad Achievement; Nat Asn Stud Financial Aid Adminrs; NAPW. **Honors/Awds:** Outstanding Volunteer, Worker Bibleway Child Develop Ctr, 1984. **Special Achievements:** Columbia Chamber Com, 1979; trustee mem, Benedict Col Fed Credit Union, 1979-; AUS Asn, 1979; Nat Assoc Col Deans Registrars & Admissions Officers, 1984; Am Asn Col Registrars & Admis Officers; Steering ComtAssessment Stud Acad Achievement; Nat Asn Stud Financial Aid Adminrs; NAPW. **Military Serv:** AUS, private class, 9 months. **Business Addr:** Associate Vice President, Dean of Students, Benedict College, 1600 Harden St, Admin Bldg 104, Columbia, SC 29204.*

DAVIS, JAMES R.
School superintendent. **Career:** Hattiesburg Pub Sch Dist, supt, currently. **Orgs:** pres, Nat Bd Educ Sci, US Dept Educ. **Business Addr:** Superintendent, Hattiesburg Pub Sch Dist, Camp Admin Off Bldg Suite A, 301 Mamie St, Hattiesburg, MS 39401-4200, **Business Phone:** (601)582-5078.*

DAVIS, JEAN E.
Consultant, lawyer, research administrator. **Personal:** Born in New York, NY; daughter of Cynthia and Martin. **Educ:** Hunter Col, New York, NY, BS, 1961; Teachers Col, Columbia Univ, New York,NY, MEd, 1966; Univ Wis Law Sch, Madison, Wis, JD, 1976; Boston Col. **Career:** Lincoln Hosp, Yeshiva Univ, Bronx, NY, cord, 1966-67; Maimonides Hosp,Brooklyn, NY, supvr, 1967-69; City Col, New York, NY, supv, counr, 1969-74; Off Solicitor, US Dept Labor, Civil Rights Div, Wash, DC, asst counsel, atty, adv, 1977-88, counsel, interpretations & advice, 1988-90; Drexel Univ, Philadelphia, Pa, sr adv pres, 1990, chief staff & exec asst pres, Int Students & Scholars, dir;.

DAVIS, DR. JEWELNEL
Executive, educator. **Personal:** Born in Brooklyn, NY. **Educ:** Brown Univ, BA, religious studies, 1979; Yale Univ Divinity Sch, Mdiv; Univ Conn Sch Social Work, MSW. **Career:** Carleton Col, Northfield, MN, col chaplain; Colgate Univ, assoc univ chaplain; Columbia Univ, univ chaplain & assoc provost, Earl Hall Ctr, dir, currently. **Orgs:** Pres, Coun Stud Affairs; Presidential Adv Comt, Sexual Assault; Harlem Congregations Community Improv Brd. **Honors/Awds:** DHL, Carleton Col, 2005; Hon doc by Carlton college, 2005. **Business Addr:** University Chaplain & Associate Provost, Director, Columbia University, 2980 Broadway, 202 Earl Hall MC 2008, New York, NY 10027, **Business Phone:** (212)854-1493.

DAVIS, JOAN Y. (JOAN YVETTE DAVIS)
Educator. **Educ:** JD. **Career:** Ala Dept Post secondary Educ, gen coun & vice chancellor legal & human resources, actg dir, Ala Col Syst, chancellor, currently. **Business Addr:** Acting Director, Alabama Department of Postsecondary Education, 401 Adams Ave, PO Box 302130, Montgomery, AL 36130.

DAVIS, JOAN YVETTE. **See DAVIS, JOAN Y.**

DAVIS, JOHN (JOHN LEONARD)
Football player. **Personal:** Born May 14, 1973, Jasper, TX. **Educ:** Emporia State. **Career:** Dallas Cowboys, 1995; Tampa Bay Buccaneers, tight end, 1997-99, Minn Vikings, tight end, 2000; Chicago Bears, tight end, 2001-03. *

DAVIS, DR. JOHN ALBERT
Educator. **Personal:** Born Jan 6, 1935, La Grange, GA; widowed; children: Greg, Deanna & Keith. **Educ:** Univ Calif, Los Angeles, BA, 1963, MA, 1965, PhD, 1971. **Career:** Educator (retired); Social Action Training Ctr, dir res, 1965; Univ Calif, asst prof, 1968; Univ Calif, Berkely, vis prof, 1971; Off Minority Affairs, Univ Southern Calif, 1972; Loyola Marymount Univ, assoc prof, sociol, chairperson African Am Studies, prof. **Orgs:** Alpha Sigma Nu Soc Sci Hon Soc, 1970; mem bd, Los Angeles Childrens Bureau, 1983-90, Milton F Williams Fund, 1980-86; pres, Crenshaw Neighbors, 1981-83. **Honors/Awds:** LA Times "Understanding Black & Chicano Groups", 1978. **Military Serv:** AUS, 1959-61. **Home Addr:** 4501 Circle view Blvd, Los Angeles, CA 90043.

DAVIS, JOHN ALEXANDER
Civil rights activist. **Personal:** Born Jun 2, 1960, Bronx, NY. **Educ:** Columbia Univ NY, BA, 1982; Rutgers Law Sch Newark. **Career:** Century Pacific Investment Corp, law clerk, 1985; Cohn & Lifland, law clerk, 1985-86; Integrity Life Ins, paralegal, 1986; NAACP, nat youth dir, 1986-. **Orgs:** Trustee, bd governors DeWitt Clinton Alumni Org, 1978-; nat bd mem, NAACP Nat Bd Dirs, 1980-86; alumni officer, Columbia Univ, 1982-87. **Honors/Awds:** Roy Wilkins Scholarship, NAACP, 1978; One of Fifty Future Black Leaders, Ebony Magazine, 1982; Best Legal Brief Frederick Douglass Moot Ct Competition BALSA, 1985. **Business Addr:** Director of Youth, College Division, National Association for the Advancement of Colored People, 4805 Mt Hope Dr, Baltimore, MD 21215-3297, **Business Phone:** (410)358-8900.

DAVIS, JOHN W., JR.
Church historian, executive director, executive director. **Career:** Faith MB Church; Gen Missionary Baptist State Convention, pub rel dir, currently. **Business Phone:** (228)392-3718.*

DAVIS, JOHN W., III
Financial manager, government official. **Personal:** Born Oct 29, 1958, Cincinnati, OH. **Educ:** Georgetown Univ, BS, 1980; ICMA City Mgt Sch; Harvard Univ; Ind Univ, attended 1986. **Career:** Georgetown Univ, assoc prof, 1979-80; Cincinnati City, contract acct,1980-82; Dun & Bradstreet, financial analyst, 1981; Queen City Metro, comput programmer, 1982-85; SORTA, supt capital; Silverton City, chief financial officer, 1982-87. **Orgs:** Nat Asn Accountants, 1982-87; Munic Fin Off Asn, 1982-87; Nat Asn Advan Colored People, 1983-87; Notary Pub State Ohio, 1984-87; bd trustee, OKI, 1984-85; Nat Budget Review Bd; Nat Cash Mgt Comt; bd trustees, Cincinnati Br, Nat Asn Advan Colored People. **Honors/Awds:** Bachelor of the Year, Ebony Mag, 1983; Leader of the Future, Ebony Mag,1983; Outstanding Young Person Under 30 Cincinnati Enquirer, 1983; Hon Recruiter US Army 1984; Distinguish Budget Award, 1986.

DAVIS, JOHN WESLEY
Lawyer. **Personal:** Born Nov 1, 1943, Detroit, MI; son of Dorris Miller; married Lorraine F Davis, Mar 30, 1966; children: Aisha, Kiilu. **Educ:** Wabash Col, AB, 1964; Univ Denver, JD, 1971. **Career:** Int Asn Human Rights, EEO Prog, dir, 1975-76; Nat Bar Assn, EEO Prog, exec dir, 1976-78; Howard Univ, Reggie Prog, exec dir, 1980-84, law prof, 1978-85; Self Employed, atty, 1985-. **Orgs:** life mem, Nat Bar Asn, NBA jour ed bd; Nat Asn Advan Colored People, life mem, 1979-, coop atty, 1977-;bd mem, DC Neighborhood Legal Serv, 1992-. **Honors/Awds:** Award Merit, Nat Asn Advan Colored People, 1975; Equal Justice Award, Nat Bar Asn, 1977; Cert Appreciation, 1980. **Special Achievements:** Law Review Article, NCCU Law Journal, The Supreme Court Rationale for Racism, 1976. Employment Discrimination Litigation Manual, 1977. **Home Phone:** (703)780-5044. **Business Addr:** Attorney, 1003 K St NW, Washington, DC 20001, **Business Phone:** (202)783-3705.*

DAVIS, JOHN WESLEY, SR.
Clergy, president (organization). **Personal:** Born Aug 10, 1934, Laurel, MS; son of Willie and Mary Alice Wright; married Virgie Louise Sumlin, Jul 4, 1958; children: John W Jr, Maurice Benard. **Educ:** Jackson State Univ, BME, 1960; Am Bible Col, BPhB, 1963, MPhB, 1965, DD, 1968. **Career:** Jackson S Univ, scholar, 1956-60; Mt Olive D Cong, pres, 1968-80; Greater Antioch MB Church, pastor, 1981-. **Orgs:** Trustee, Mich Col Inst W Point, 1975-85; Nat Asn Adv Colored People, 1981-; SCLC, 1981-; adv bd, Judge Baker, 1982; bd dirs, Nat Baptist Conv Inc; pres, New Educ State Conv; pres, Dist Cong; vpres, New Educ State Cong; parliametarian, Shiloh Dist Asn; adv bd, Gov MS Ceta Prog; vpres, Mt Olive Dist Cong Alumni Asn; Ministerial Biracial Alliance; adv bd, Miss Coop Exten Serv; Interdenominational Ministerial Alliance; Youth Court Adv Bd; adv bd, Salvation Army Domestic Violence Shelter; Salvation Army; bd dirs, Am Cancer Soc; counr, Youth Prison Ministry; chair, Pres Coun, NBC, USA Inc; pres, Jackson Co Interdemominational Ministerial Alliance. **Honors/Awds:** Outstanding Minister of the Yr, 1994; Vol of the Yr, 1994; Community Serv Award, Jackson County Nat Asn Adv Colored People, 1994; received numerous awards. **Special Achievements:** Recording artist known nationally & internationally. **Business Addr:** Pastor, The Greater Antioch MB Church, 1028 Denny Ave, Pascagoula, MS 39567.*

DAVIS, JOHNETTA GARNER
Pathologist, school administrator, educator. **Personal:** Born Nov 1, 1939, Warrenton, VA. **Educ:** Teachers Col, BS, 1961; George Wash Univ, MA, 1969; Howard Univ, PhD, 1976. **Career:** Howard Univ, assoc dean, grad prof, 1978-96, assoc prof, prof 1972-78; Am Speech & Hearing Asn, asst sec, prog develop, 1971-72; Fed City Col, asst prof, 1970-71; Teachers Col, instr, 1969-71; Wash DC Pub Schs, speech pathologist, 1961-68; Univ Md Col Pk, Grad Sch & Off Grad Recruitment, Retention & Diversity, assoc dean & dir, 1993-, lectr grad studies, lectr family studies, currently. **Orgs:** Fed City Alumnae Chap Dist Sorority; Wash DC chap, The Soc Inc; Potomac Chap Links Inc; Am Speech-Lang & Hearing Asn, 1961-; DC Speech, Lang & Hearing, 1963-; task force on int grad educ Coun Grad Schs Task Force on MNY Educ; bd Stoddard Bapt Home, 1977-82; Sunday sch teacher, Mt Sinai Baptist Church, 1977-82. **Honors/Awds:** CCC-SP-L, Am Speech-Lang Hearing Asn, cert, 1962; US Office Educ, Fel, 1967; Outstanding Junior Faculty Award, DC Teachers Col, 1971; Outstanding faculty citation Students at DC Teachers Col, 1971; Frederick Douglass Honor Soc Howard Univ Chap, 1974; Outstanding Young Women in America, 1976; Outstanding Alumni Award, Howard Univ, Sch Communs, 1986; Howard Univ, establishment of the Johnetta G Davis Award for Best Mentor of Graduate Students, 1993; Administrator of the Year, Grad Stud Coun, 1992; Distinguished Service Awards, 1978-80, 1982, 1986, 1988, 1990; Prof Emerita, Howard Univ, 1996; Editors Award, J Contemporary Issues in Commun Scis & Disorders, 2000; Service Award, Univ Md, Grad Stud Govt, 2000; Merit Award, Univ Md, Black Fac & Staff Asn, 2000; President's Distinguished Service Award, 2006; ASHA Award, Am Speech-Lang-Hearing Asn, 2009. **Home Addr:** 519 Brummel Ct NW, Washington, DC 20012. **Business Phone:** (301)405-4183.

DAVIS, JOHNNY REGINALD
Basketball player, basketball coach. **Personal:** Born Oct 21, 1955, Detroit, MI; married Lezli; children: Reginald & Austin. **Educ:** Univ Dayton, attended 1976; Ga State Univ, BS, community develop, 1987; Union Inst & Univ VT Col, MA, sports psychol. **Career:** Basketball player (retired), basketball coach; Portland Trail Blazers, guard, 1976-78, asst coach, 1994-96; Ind Pacers, guard, 1978-82; Atlanta Hawks, guard, 1982-84, 1986, dir community affairs, 1986-89, asst to pres, 1989-90, asst coach, 1990-93; Cleveland Cavaliers, guard, 1984-85; Los Angeles Clippers, asst coach, 1993-94; Philadelphia 76ers, head coach, 1996-97; Orlando Magic, head coach, 2003-05; Minn Timber wolves, asst coach, 2005-06; Memphis Grizzlies, asst coach, 2007-. **Special Achievements:** Championship, NBA, 1977. **Business Addr:** Assistant Coach, Memphis Grizzlies, 191 Beale St, Memphis, TN 38103, **Business Phone:** (901)888-4667.

DAVIS, JOSEPH SOLOMON
College administrator. **Personal:** Born Apr 8, 1938, Macon, GA; married Sarah Frances Striggles; children: Joan Yvette & Oscar Wendall. **Educ:** Tuskegee Inst, BS, MEd, 1968. **Career:** College administrator (retired); Boggs Acad, teacher ind arts, 1961-65; guid dir, 1965-67; Southern Asn Sec Sch, fel, 1967; Stillman Col, dir, financial aid, 1967-76, 1981-95; dir, coun serv, 1976-81. **Orgs:** W Tuscaloosa Optimist Club, 1980-. **Honors/Awds:** Keyman Service United Way Award, 1978. **Home Addr:** 2608 32nd St, Northport, AL 35476, **Home Phone:** (205)333-5529. *

DAVIS, JULIA H.
Association executive, president (organization). **Personal:** Born in Fort Lauderdale, FL. **Career:** Eta Phi Beta Sorority Inc, nat pres, 1994-98. *

DAVIS, DR. KATIE CAMPBELL
Educator. **Personal:** Born Sep 11, 1936, Lumber City, GA; married Ernest Davis Jr; children: Theresa Lynn. **Educ:** Tenn State Univ, BA, 1957; Tenn State Univ, MA, 1968; Univ Ill, PhD, 1974. **Career:** Teacher various pub sch; commun consult; Norfolk State Univ, prof speech & Eng, theatre arts. **Orgs:** Speech Comm Asn; Nat Advan Asn Colored People; Alpha Kappa Alpha Sorority; Am Asn Univ Women. **Honors/Awds:** National Consortium of Doctors' Perseverance Award, 1992. *

DAVIS, KERY
Executive. **Educ:** Cornell Law Sch. **Career:** HBO, sr vpres sports prog, currently. **Business Addr:** Senior Vice President, HBO Sports Programming, 1100 Avenue of the Americas, New York, NY 10036, **Business Phone:** (212)512-1168.*

DAVIS, L. CLIFFORD
Lawyer, judge, educator. **Personal:** Born Oct 12, 1925, Wilton, AR; son of Augustus and Dora Duckett; married Ethel R Weaver,

Nov 14, 1955; children: Karen Renae & Avis Janeth. **Educ:** Philander Smith Col, BA, 1945; Atlanta Univ, Grad Studies Econs, 1946; Howard Univ, law sch, JD, 1949. **Career:** Davis Sturns & Johns, atty, 1949-; Gen Practioner Law, Ark, 1949-52; Paul Quinn Col, Waco, Tx, asst prof Bus, 1952-54; gen practitioner law, 1953-83, 2003-; Criminal Dist No. 2, judge, 1983-88; Johnson, Vaughn & Heiskell, gen counsel, 1989-; Dist Judge, 1989-96; Tarrant County, sr dist judge, Tarrant County, 1994-2003. **Orgs:** Omega Psi Phi Frat; past trustee, St Andrews United Methodist Church; pastmem bd, Tarrant Co Unit Fund; Tarrant County & Prec Worker's Coun; charter revision com City Ft Worth TX; adv coun, Tex Legal Serv Corp; Young Men Christian Asn; Nat Asn Advan Colored People; State Bar Texas; US Ct Appeals Fifth & Eighth Circuits; life mem, Nat Bar Asn; Tex Bar Found Fel; Col State Bar Texas; Tarrant Co & Ft Worth/Tarrant Co Black Bar Asn. **Honors/Awds:** Hall Fame, Nat Bar Asn; Outstanding Achiever Award, Philander Smith Univ Alumni Asn, 1994; Living Legend in the Law, Jr Black Acad Arts & Letters, 1994; Marion Brooks' Living Legend Award, 1995; KRLD Radio Appreciation Community Service Award, 1996; Silver Gaval Award, Tarrant County Bar Asn, 1997; Arkansas Black Hall of Fame, 2007. **Special Achievements:** Opened first African Am law office Tx; Living Legend in the Law presented by the Junior Black Academy of Arts & Letters, 1994. **Military Serv:** AUS, E-2, 1954-55. **Home Addr:** 2101 Fleming Dr, Ft Worth, TX 76112. **Business Addr:** General Counselor, Johnson, Vaughn & Heiskell, 5601Bridge St Suite 220, Ft Worth, TX 76112, **Business Phone:** (817)457-2999.

DAVIS, LANCE ROOSEVELT
Executive. **Personal:** Born Dec 21, 1962, Orange, NJ; son of Roosevelt Jr and Joan Henson Roach. **Educ:** Johson & Wales Univ, ASc, culinary arts, 1982, BA, food serv mgt, 1984. **Career:** APO Catering, owner & chief operator, 1983-84; Hyatt Regency, NB, corp mgr trainee, 1984-85, beverage mgr, exec steward, 1985-86, gourmet restaurant mgr, 1986-88, freelance food & beverage consult, 1987-89, Kans city, banquet mgr, 1988-89; Harrison CNF Ctr, from asst food & beverage dir to food & beverage dir, 1989-92; Lackmann Food Serv, Food Serv dir. **Orgs:** Pres, Distrib Educ Club AME, Stanhope, NJ, 1979-80; founding father, Alpha Pi Omega Fraternity Inc, 1983; founding father, Omega Phi Delta Fraternity, 1984; bd mem, City CNL Glen Cove, NY, 1989-90; Bus Vols Arts, Middlesex County, 1984-85; Glen Cove Citizens Against Substance Abuse Inc, 1989-90; pres, Nat Asn Black Hospity Profs NY Chap, 1992-. **Honors/Awds:** Certificate of Appreciation, United Cerebal Palsy, RI, 1984. **Home Phone:** (516)676-3551.

DAVIS, DR. LARRY EARL
Educational psychologist, dean (education). **Personal:** Born May 11, 1946, Saginaw, MI; son of Kires and Clara. **Educ:** Delta Col Bay City, Mich, attended 1966; Mich State Univ, BS, psychol, 1968; Univ Mich, MSW, 1973, MA, psychol, 1975, PhD, soc work & psychol, 1977. **Career:** VISTA, New York City, vol, 1969-72; Wash Univ, asst prof soc work & psychol, 1977-; Univ Hawaii, sabbatical, 1988; Norfolk State Univ, adj fac, 1995-97; Univ Pittsburgh, Sch Soc Work, Donald M Henderson Prof, currenlty, dean & Sandra Wexler dir, currently, Ctr Race & Social Prob, dir; Washington Univ, George Warren Brown Sch Social Work, fac mem; Ethnic & Racial Diversity, prof social work & psychol & E Desmond Lee chmn, E Desmond Lee Prof, 1998. **Orgs:** Asn Black Psychologists, 1977-; Nat Asn Black Social Workers, 1977-; Nat Asn Social Workers, 1977-; Leadership St Louis, 1986; Coun Social Work Educ; Soc Social Work Res. **Honors/Awds:** Chancellor's 2007 Affirmative Action Award, 2007. **Special Achievements:** Published and co-published numerous articles, including "Racial Composition of Groups," Social Work MA, 1979; "Racial Balance, A Psychological Issue," Social Work With Groups, 1980; "Minority Content in Social Work Educ, A Question of Objectives," Journal of Educ for Social Work, 1983; co-author, Race, Gender and Class: Guidelines for Practice with Individuals, Families, and Groups, Prentice-Hall, 1989; co-editor, Ethnic Issues in Adolescent Mental Health, Newbury Park, CA, Sage, 1990; Black & Single: Finding & Choosing a Partner Who is Right for You, Ballantine, 1998; Too Many Blacks, Too Many Whites: Is There A Racial Balance? Basic and Applied Social Psychology, 1995; Working with African-American Males: A Guide to Practice, Sage, 1999. **Home Addr:** 944 N Sheridan Ave, Pittsburgh, PA 15206, **Home Phone:** (412)441-6602. **Business Addr:** Dean, Donald M Henderson Professor, University Pittsburgh, School Social Work, 2117 Cathedral Learning, Pittsburgh, PA 15260, **Business Phone:** (412)624-6304.

DAVIS, LATINA
Basketball player, security consultant. **Personal:** Born Oct 8, 1974. **Educ:** Univ Tenn, 1996. **Career:** Tenn Maryville, teaching & running basketball camps; Atlanta,1996-97; New England, 1996-97; Columbus Quest, guard, 1997-99; Unicoi Co High Sch, asst coach; Watauga High Sch, basketball coach, 2003; security officer. **Honors/Awds:** Silver medal, World Univ Games, 1995.

DAVIS, LAWRENCE ARNETTE, JR.
Educator, college administrator. **Personal:** Born May 13, 1937, Pine Bluff, AR; married Ethel Louise Grant; children: Sonya, Lawrence III & Catherine. **Educ:** AM & N Col, BS, math, 1958; Univ Ark, Fayetteville, MS, math, 1960; IAState Univ, PhD, engineering math, 1973. **Career:** MS Valley St Col, instr, 1960; AM & N Col, prof, 1961-68; NASA Advanced Res & Technol summers, 1964, 1965; NSF In-service Inst, AM & N Col, dir, 1967-68; IA State Univ, grad teaching asst, 1969-71; IA State Univ, Engr Res Inst, res asst, 1971-73; NASA Res Proj, Univ AR, dir, 1973-74; NASA Off Advan Res & Technol, admin specialist; Univ Ark, Pine Bluff, chmn math & physics, prof math & physics, 1976-, dean arts & sci, dean sci & technol, pres, chancellor, 1991-. **Orgs:** Soc Indust & Appl Mathematicians; Math Asn Am; Nat Asn Mathematicians; AR Acad Sci, 1966-68; AAAS; Am Asn Univ Prof; Am Asn Physics Teachers; BetaKappi Chi; Alpha Kappa Mu; bd mem, Jefferson County Industrial Found; bd mem, Southern Regional Educ; bd mem, Fed Res Bd St. Louis (Little Rock-Branch); bd dir, Jefferson Regional Med Ctr; bd dirs, Ark Land & Farm Develop; pres bd advisors, Historically Black Cols & Univs. **Honors/Awds:** Chancellors medal, Univ Ark, 1994; NAACP award outstanding contrib educ; Nat distinguished leadership award. **Special Achievements:** Appointed as a member in the President's Board of Advisors on Historically Black Colleges and Universities; Included in the Citation of Distinguished Alumni (CDA) by the Arkansas Alumni Association. **Business Addr:** Chancellor, University of Arkansas at Pine Bluff, Department Math & Physics, 1200 N Univ Dr, Pine Bluff, AR 71611, **Business Phone:** (870)575-8000.*

DAVIS, LELIA KASENIA
Executive. **Personal:** Born Nov 7, 1941, Taft, OK; daughter of Willie Smith and Canzaty; married David Earl Davis, Nov 22; children: Mark, Kasandra, Starla Smith Phillips, Canraty, Derrick. **Career:** Am Technical Inst, Muskogee OK, admin counr; City Taft, Taft OK, mayor. **Orgs:** Bd dir, Eastern Okla Develop Dist; pres, LeCon Org; chairwoman, Taft Parade Comn; adv bd dir, Dept Corrections. **Honors/Awds:** First Black Elected Female Mayor, 1973; Am Ten Outstanding Young Women, 1974; Muskogee League Hall of Fame. *

DAVIS, LEODIS
Educator. **Personal:** Born Sep 25, 1933, Stamps, AK; married N June Wilson; children: Melonie & Leon. **Educ:** Victor Wilson Sch, Univ Mo Kans City, BS, Chem, 1956; IA State Univ, MS, Chem, 1958, PhD, Biochem, 1960. **Career:** Tenn State Univ, asst prof chem, 1961-62; Howard Univ Med Col, asst prof biochem, 1962-67, assoc prof biochem, 1967-69; Iowa State Univ, res assoc, 1960-61, vis assoc prof, 1969, assoc prof biochem, 1969-76, prof chem, 1976-97, chmn chem dept, 1979-87, actg dean, Grad Col, 1988-89, assoc vpres, Acad Affairs, 1989-94, dir summer session, 1992-94, prof emer, 1997-; Oakdale Res Park Bd Dir, pres. **Orgs:** Soc Sigma XI, 1960; biochem study sect Ad Hoc Consult, 1970-; chem community minority affairs, Am Soc Biol, 1973; Aging Rev Comn, 1976-80; NIH Biochem Study Sect 1976-81; Nat Res Coun Rev NSF Grad Fel, 1977-80; bd dir, Univ IA Credit Union, 1986-; Celluar & Molecular Basis Dis Rev Comm, 1986-90; Div Res Grants Adv Comm, 1993-97; HEW NIH Min Biomed Supp. **Honors/Awds:** One of ten med school faculty mem in US awarded Lederle Med Fac Award, 1967; Gen Elec Conf for Prof of Chem & Chem Eng, 1973; Fogarty InterNat Research Collaboration Award, Special Rev Community, 1992-93. **Home Addr:** 12012 Grand Ave, Kansas City, MO 64145-1493. **Business Phone:** (319)384-0000.

DAVIS, LEON. See Obituaries section.

DAVIS, LEONARD HARRY
Manager. **Personal:** Born Sep 3, 1927, Indianapolis, IN; married Erla Darling Robinson (deceased); children: Kevin L, Gail D, Janna L, Aaron L (deceased), Barry C; married Virginia Mae Griffin, Apr 26, 1997. **Educ:** Univ IL Sch Fine & Applied Arts Champaign, BS, BA, 1952. **Career:** Retired: Naval Ordinance Facility Indianapolis, asst art dir, 1952-57; Indust Arts & Engg Co San Diego, asst dir, 1957-62; Cubic Corp, mgr graphic & promotional arts. **Orgs:** Indus photographer Indus Art & Engg Co San Diego, 1957-62; past secy, Kappa Alpha Psi Champaign, 1949-52; pres, Cubic Mgt Assoc, 1977-79; past pres, San Diego Area Coun, 1980-81. **Honors/Awds:** Numerous 1st through 3rd places art exhibits, 1948-65; Member of the Year, Cubic Mgt Assoc, 1979. **Military Serv:** AUS, corpl, 1944-48. *

DAVIS, DR. LEROY
Administrator, executive. **Educ:** Purdue Univ, PhD, molecular biol, 1973. **Career:** SC State Univ, pres, 1996-. **Orgs:** Am Coun Educ. **Business Addr:** President, South Carolina State University, 300 College Ave NE, PO Box 7008, Orangeburg, SC 29117, **Business Phone:** (803)536-7013.*

DAVIS, LESTER E.
Consultant, engineer. **Personal:** Born Aug 5, 1918, Tunica, MS; son of Emanuel and Carrie Ruth Jackson; married Annie B Debro; children: Dorothy Wakefield. **Educ:** Kans State Univ, BS, archit eng, 1950; Lincoln Univ, attended 1946. **Career:** USN Dept Naval Ship Yard, Vallejo, naval architect/struct, 1950-53; StateCalif Dept Transp, bridge engr, 1953-75; Bay Area Rapid Transit Dist Ca-,supr engr, struct/civil, 1975-86. **Orgs:** Life mem, Am Soc Civil Engrs; N Calif Coun Black Pr Engrs; regist pr engr Civil Br St CA; life mem, Alpha Phi Alpha Fraternity; E Bay Struct Engrs Soc; Active local church & civic Asn. **Military Serv:** USAF, 1943-46.

DAVIS, LISA E
Lawyer. **Personal:** Born Feb 6, 1960, Queens, NY; married Anthony Jamison, Oct 15, 1994; children: Marcus & Noelle. **Educ:** Harvard Univ, AB, 1981; NY Univ, JD, 1985. **Career:** Hon Constance Baker Motley, law clerk, 1985-86; Kramer Levin Naftalis & Frankel LLP, assoc, 1986-88; New York Univ Law Rev, staff mem; Frankfurt Kurnit Klein & Selz PC, assoc, 1988-93, partner, 1994-. **Orgs:** Intellectual Property Sect, Nat Bar Asn, 1993-; Black Entertainment & Sports Lawyers Asn; New York City Bar. **Honors/Awds:** Top 50 Black Power Brokers in Entertainment, Black Lawyers, Black Enterprise Mag, 2002; America's Top Black Lawyers, Black Enterprise Mag, 2003; Jacob K Javits Achievement Award, Bedford Stuyvesant Restoration Corp, 2003. **Business Addr:** Partner, Frankfurt Kurnit Klein & Selz PC, 488 Madison Ave 9th Fl, New York, NY 10022, **Business Phone:** (212)826-5530.

DAVIS, LISA R
Executive. **Personal:** Born Dec 2, 1961, Washington, DC; daughter of Doris and Lorenzo. **Educ:** Univ NC, Greensboro, BA, 1983; Howard Univ, MBA, MPA, 1988. **Career:** Nat Bar Asn, communs dir, 1986-89; Am Bar Asn, staff dir, media & prof servs, 1989-93; Democratic Leadership Coun, press secy, 1993-96; Clinton/Gore Campaign, nat dep press secy, 1996; AARP, acting dep dir & dir commun; AstraZeneca Pharmaceut LP, vpres corp communs, currently. **Orgs:** Nat Press Club; Pub Rels Soc Am; Delta Sigma Theta, 1983-. **Business Addr:** Vice President Corporate Communications, AstraZeneca Pharmaceuticals LP, 1800 Concord Pke, PO Box 15437, Wilmington, DE 19803-2902, **Business Phone:** 800-236-9933.

DAVIS, LOUIS GARLAND. See Obituaries section.

DAVIS, LUTHER CHARLES
Consultant, sales manager. **Personal:** Born Sep 21, 1948, Key West, FL; son of Earl and Carol; married Sharon Ann Williams; children: Jason. **Educ:** Cornell Univ, BA, 1970. **Career:** Jewel Co Inc, buyer, 1977; Kraft Inc, Dairy Group, dist sales mgr 1984; Mellin Ice Cream Co, vpres, 1985; Wisconsin Milk Mkt Bd, regional mkt mgr. **Orgs:** Pres, Randallstown Optimist, 1990-91. **Home Addr:** 260 Iacuele Dr S, Kingston, RI 02879. **Business Addr:** Managing Partner, Eccleston Davis Consulting, 1 Noank Rd, Mystic, CT 06355.

DAVIS, MAJOR
Administrator, association executive. **Personal:** Born Nov 6, 1931, Hartsville, SC; married Elsie M Luck; children: Shynethia Catrice & Trent Damone. **Educ:** Maricopa Tech Comm Col, AA, 1973; Phoenix Col, AA, 1975; AZ State Univ, BA, 1979. **Career:** USAF, jet test flight engr, 1951-72; ed, pub Phoenix Chronicle Newspaper, 1969; Youth Together Inc, founder & owner, 1970-; Miss Black Ariz Pageant, dir, 1971-; Miss Galaxy Int Pageant, nat dir, 1975-. **Orgs:** USAF Worlds Southern Hemisphere, 1968; Nat Asn Advan Colored People, 1970-; grand master, Alpha Grand Lodge, 1974-75; Phoenix Advert Club, 1976; Ariz Newspaper Asn, 1978; Phoenix Chamber Com, 1978. **Honors/Awds:** 33rd Degree Mason Ivanhoe Grand Lodge, AF&AM Denver, 1964; Black & Gold Service Award, Maricopa Tech Col, 1973; Key to the City, Austin, Tex, 1979, Key to the City, Las Vegas, Nev, 1981. **Special Achievements:** Founder of the first private state sickle cell anemia foundation in Phoenix. **Military Serv:** USAF, t/sgt 21 yrs; 15 Decorations. **Home Addr:** 4310 W Verde Lane, Phoenix, AZ 85031, **Home Phone:** (602)272-5496. **Business Addr:** Owner, Youth Together Inc, 4310 W Verde Lane, Phoenix, AZ 85031, **Business Phone:** (602)272-5496.*

DAVIS, MARCIA
Editor, writer. **Career:** Wash Post, journalist & ed, 2004, writer, currently. **Business Addr:** Writer, Washington Post, 1150 15th St NW, Washington, DC 20071, **Business Phone:** (202)334-6000.*

DAVIS, DR. MARIANNA WHITE
Educator. **Personal:** Born Jan 8, 1929, Philadelphia, PA; daughter of Albert McNeil White and Laura Bowman Frederick; widowed; children: Kenneth Renay. **Educ:** SC State Col, BA, Eng, 1949; NY Univ, MA, Eng, 1953; Boston Univ, DEd,Eng, 1966. **Career:** SC Pub Sch, teacher, 1949-51, 1955-56, 1986-96; SC State Col, asst prof, 1956-64; Claflin Col, prof, 1966-69; Voorhees Col, vis prof, 1966-68; Boston Univ, vis prof, 1967; Univ TN, vis prof, 1969; Benedict Col, Eng prof & res, 1969-82; ABC Devel Corp, cofounder & secy, 1972; Denmark Tech Col, acting pres, 1985-86; Davis & Assocs, pres, 1980-; N eastern Univ, Training Proj, coord, 1992-94; Benedict Col, spl asst pres, 1996-; lectr,Ger, 1998, Italy, 2000. **Orgs:** Bd dir, Nat Coun Teachers Eng, 1958-80; exec comt, ADE Modern Language Asn, 1976-79; commr SC Educ TV, 1980-95; Pub Broadcasting Syst Adv Bd, 1981-83; Francis Burns United Methodist Ch; bd chmn, Columbia Urban League Bd, 1981-82; Nat Coun Negro Women; YWCA; life mem NAACP; The Moles; coord, Coalition Concerns Blacks Post Sec Educ SC; Alpha Kappa Alpha Sor; Order of Eastern Star; chmn, SC Int Women's Yr Comn; founder, VICOS Women's League Comt Action; TISAWS; Civil Rights Comn Adv Bd, 1985-; Nat Publicity chair, The Moles, 1988-92; bd educ, SC United Methodist Church 1988-96; bd mem, bd visitors, Claflin Col. **Honors/Awds:** SC State Col Alumni Scholar; Crusade Scholar doctoral studies, 1964-66; Outstanding Educator of Am, 1970-71; Outstanding Educ Award, Kappa Alpha Psi Frat, Athens, GA, 1974; Educators

Round table Award, 1976; Outstanding Award, Omega Psi Phi Frat, 1977; Emory O Jackson Journalism Award, 1978 &1996; Distinguished Res Award, NAFEO, 1980; Distinguished Fac Award, Benedict Col, 1980; Distinguished Serv Award, Columbia Urban League, 1981; Distinguished Alumni Award, Boston Univ, 1981; Distinguished Alumni Award, SC State Col, 1981; Par Excellence Award in Educ Operation PUSH, 1982; Outstanding Citizen Award, Cleveland, OH, 1984; Kappa Alpha Psi of SC Outstanding Black Woman Award 1987; Jacob Javits Fellowship Bd, Presidential Appointment, 1993; Governor's Award, Outstanding Achievement, 1995; Belle Ringer Role Model Award, Bennett Col, 1996; Gerber Award for Distinguished Service, Nat Coun Teachers Eng, 1999; Hall of Fame, 100 Black Men of SC, 1999; Most Outstanding African Am Woman, Nat Asn Colored Women & Youth Clubs, 2000. **Special Achievements:** Contributed papers to Boston Univ Mugar Mem Library, 1989; exec producer, "The Struggle Continues," black history tele conf, PBS, 1986-; author, 20 books, numerous articles. **Business Addr:** Special Assistant to the President, Benedict College, PO Box 3097, Columbia, SC 29230.*

DAVIS, MARIE H.
President (Organization), politician. **Career:** Foster City, elected mem. **Orgs:** Pres, Nat Asn Advan Colored People, San Mateo County. **Honors/Awds:** San Mateo County Women's Hall of Fame. *

DAVIS, DR. MARILYN ANN CHERRY
Educator. **Personal:** Born Mar 26, 1951, Aiken, SC; daughter of Council Christopher and Sara Wilhelmena Walton; married Charles Douglas Davis, Aug 19, 1975; children: Cheryl Maria Davis. **Educ:** Hampton Inst, Hampton, VA, BA, 1973; Atlanta Univ, Atlanta, GA, MA, 1977, PhD (polit sci), 1979. **Career:** Atlanta Jr Col, Atlanta, GA, instr polit sci, 1977-79; Tuskegee Inst, Tuskegee, AL, asst prof polit sci, 1980; Bennett Col, Greensboro, NC, asst prof polit sci, 1980-81; Spelman Col, fac, 1981-, chair, 1984-85 & 1988-90, assoc prof polit sci, 1981-. **Orgs:** Am Polit Sci Asn, 1981-; Southern Polit Sci Asn, 1981-; Ga Polit Sci Asn, 1981-; Nat Conf Black Polit Scientists, 1981-; hon mem, Golden Key Nat Honor Soc. **Honors/Awds:** Valedictorian, Martha Schofield High Sch, 1969; Sears Roebuck Foundation Award, Excellence in Teaching and Campus Leadership, 1990; Named Best Professor, Spelman Col, 2004. **Special Achievements:** Contributing author to an anthology: Dilemmas in Black Politics, HarperCollins, 1992; author, Student Guide to Practicing American Politics, Worth Publishers, 1998; anthology contributor, Beyond the Color Line? Race, Redistricting, and Community in the New Century, NY Law Sch Press, 2002. **Home Addr:** 4140 Welcome All Terr, College Park, GA 30349. **Business Addr:** Associate Professor, Spelman College, Department of Political Science, 350 Spelman Lane SW, Giles Hall Rm 216, Atlanta, GA 30314-4399, **Business Phone:** (404)270-5649.

DAVIS, MARILYNN A.
Government official. **Personal:** Born Oct 30, 1952, Little Rock, AR; daughter of James Edward and Erma Lee Glasco. **Educ:** Smith Col, BA, 1973; Univ Mich, MA, econ, 1976; Wash Univ, St Louis, MA, econ, 1980; Harvard Grad Sch Bus Admin, MBA, 1982. **Career:** State Street Bank, Boston, sr credit analyst, 1981; Gen Motors Corp, Detroit, analyst, cent off financial staff, 1982-83; Gen Motors Corp, NY, sr financial analyst, overseas borrowing sect, 1984, sr financial analyst, financing, investment & financial planning sect, 1984, asst to GM group vpres, chief economist, 1984-86; Am Express Co, NY, vpres, risk financing, 1987; NY Housing Authority, dep gen mgr finance, 1993; US Dept Housing & Urban Develop, asst secy admin, 1993-; Fleet Boston Financial Corp, exec vpres & mgr consumer banking, 2002. **Orgs:** Bd trustees, Studio Mus Harlem; chair, comt residence, Bd Counrs Smith Col; bd dirs, Queensboro Soc Prev Cruelty to C; mgt assistance comt, Greater NY Fund/United Way. **Honors/Awds:** Black Achievers Award, Harlem YMCA, 1989. **Special Achievements:** Named to 100 Top Black Business and Professional Women list, 1988. "The consistent theme for me," is that a liberal arts background is extremely helpful in business today. **Home Phone:** (202)364-6943. **Business Addr:** Executive Vice President, Manager, Fleet Boston Financial Corp, 100 Federal St, Boston, MA 02110.*

DAVIS, MARION HARRIS
Administrator. **Personal:** Born Jul 27, 1938, Washington, DC; married Charles B; children: Alan Edward. **Educ:** Univ Pittsburgh, Grad Sch Public & Int Affairs, MPA, 1971; Am Univ Wash DC, attended 1970. **Career:** US Dept Housing & Urban Develop, Area Off Detroit, deputy dir housing mgmt div; Off Secy Dept Housing & Urban Develop, Wash, DC, conf asst congr rltns officer, 1967-69. FHA Dept Housing & Urban Develop, Wash, DC,housing prog specialist mgt asst, 1969-70; Westinghouse Elec Corp, sr mgt consult, 1970-71; Dept Urban Renewal & Economic Develop, Rochester, NY, dir program planning, 1971-72; Co Housing Off, Fairfax, VA, exec dir comt develop authority, 1972. **Orgs:** Nat Asn Housing & Redevelop Officials; Nat Inst Real Estate Mgt; Am Soc Planning Officials. **Honors/Awds:** Recip Carnegie Mid-Career Fellow Grad Sch of Pub & Internatl Affairs, Univ Pittsburgh, 1970-71; Travel Study Award $3,000, Grad Sch Ford Found,1970-71. **Business Addr:** Deputy director, US Department Housing & Urban Dev, 660 Woodward Ave, Detroit, MI 48226.

DAVIS, MARK ANTHONY
Basketball player. **Personal:** Born Apr 26, 1973, Thibodaux, LA. **Educ:** Howard Col; Tex Tech Univ. **Career:** Minn Timberwolves, guard-forward, 1995-96; Philadelphia 76ers, guard-forward, 1996-98; Golden State Warriors, guard-forward, 1999-2000; Wonju Dongbu Promy, guard-forward, 2005-06; Science City Jena, 2007-. **Business Addr:** Professional Basketball Player, Science City Jena, Abteilung Basketball, 07705 Jena, Germany.

DAVIS, MARTIN
Clergy, teacher. **Educ:** Point Park Col, BA. **Career:** Capuchin Franciscan Order, Soleman prof, 1964; St Augustine's Capuchin Franciscan Province, brother, 1968-; Moor Cath Parish, 1970; Lwrncvll Hawks Basketball Team, organizer; St Brigid/St Benedict, brother; BlackInner-City Parochial Schs, teacher; Univ Md. **Orgs:** Nat Black Cath Clergy Caucus; Pittsburgh Dance Coun.

DAVIS, MARVA ALEXIS
Lawyer. **Personal:** Born May 19, 1952, Gretna, FL; daughter of Harold Kenon and Thelma Kenon Robinson; married Joseph E Roberts, Jun 20, 1998; children: Sheletha. **Educ:** Lincoln Univ, BA, 1974; Fla State Univ, JD, 1977. **Career:** Pub Defender's Off, asst pub defender, 1977-85; atty pvt practice, 1980-; CEDO, gen coun, 1986-91; City Midway, city atty, 1986-87, 1992-02; Fla A&M Univ, assoc gen coun, 1991. **Orgs:** Past pres, The Barristers Asn; past bd mem, Tallahassee Women Lawyers Asn; past bd mem, Big Bend Hospice; bd mem, C Home Soc; Fla Bar Asn; Nat Bar Asn, 1977-; Acad Fla Trial Lawyers, 1983-. **Honors/Awds:** Outstanding Leadership, Capital Area Cot Action Agency, 1996. **Business Addr:** Attorney, 121 S Madison St, PO Box 551, Quincy, FL 32353, **Business Phone:** (850)875-9300.*

DAVIS, MARY AGNES MILLER
Association executive, social worker. **Personal:** Born in Montgomery, AL; daughter of Mollie Ingersoll Miller and George Joseph Miller; married Edward. **Educ:** Wayne State Univ, BA; Univ Mich, MSW. **Career:** Catholic Social Serv, caseworker & supvr stud, 1947-48; Wayne Co Juvenile Ct, foster homes officer, 1953-57; League Catholic Women Youth Serv Bur, caseworker, 1957-59; City Detroit Youth Agency, consult & analyst, 1963; Co-Ette Club Inc, founder, nat dir, adminr, currently; Metrop Detroit Teen Conf Coalition, found & dir. **Orgs:** Pres, Keep Detroit Beautiful Inc, 1973-77; chmn, ARC Cent Region Recognition Ceremony, 1980; bd dir, Carmel Hall; Franklin-Wright Settlements; chmn, Personnel Practices-Bylaws; League Catholic Women; St Francis Home Boys; Heartline Inc; Oper Understanding Brewster-Douglas Housing Proj; nominating comn, Detroit Chap Am Red Cross; Nat Coun US Women Inc; Women's Asn Detroit Symphony Orch; sec, social work admr, Edward Davis Asn Inc, currently; Detroit Area Chmn, Meadowbrook Festival Com, Oakland Univ; educ comt, Detroit Opera Asn; bd dirs, Merrill Palmer Inst; Nat Coun Women US Inc; Nat vpres, prog chmn USA; bd dirs, Catholic Youth Orgn; Alpha Kappa Alpha Sorority; The Girl Friends Inc; life mem, Am Red Cross; Meadow Brook Music Festival; co-found, Metro Teen Conf. **Honors/Awds:** NCW Woman of Conscious Award, 1984; One Hundred Most Distinguished Black Women In The USA, 1988; Co-Ette Club Alumnus, 50th Anniversary Tribute Luncheon Honoree, 1990; Top Lady of Distinction Award, Outstanding Civic Leadership, 1993; Civic Community Leadership Award, Merrill-Palmer Inst, Wayne State Univ, 1999; Greater Detroit Chamber Com Award; City Detroit Common Coun Leadership Award; One of Detroit's 12 Most Outstanding Women Award, Detroit Bicentennial Comn; Nat Community Leadership Award, Nat Coun US Women Inc. **Business Addr:** Founder, Administrator, Co-Ette Club Inc, 2020 W Chicago Blvd, Detroit, MI 48206, **Business Phone:** (313)867-0880.

DAVIS, MATILDA LAVERNE
Physician. **Personal:** Born Sep 23, 1926, Elizabeth, NJ; daughter of James T and Martha Hilton; married Robert M Cunningham, Aug 15, 1950; children: Robert Davis, Dellena M, William E. **Educ:** Howard Univ, Wash DC, BS, 1948, MD, 1951. **Career:** Harlem Hosp NYC, intern, 1951-52; Karen Horney Horney Clin, postdoctorate psychiat, 1967-71; FAAFP Cunningham-Davis MD PA, dir, 1971-; Vet Admin Hsop, Newark, NJ, adjudication physician. **Orgs:** Am Med Asn; alumni mem, Howard Univ Med Sch; Nat Med Asn; life mem, Nat Asn Advan Colored People; charter mem, Howard Univ Med Alumni Asn; Nat Carrousels; Nat Contempo. **Honors/Awds:** charter fellow, Am Acad Family Physicians, 1974; Physicians Recognition Award, Am Med Asn, 1980. **Special Achievements:** First women in the East in tennis 45 yrs & Older, Tennis Players 1979. *

DAVIS, MELVIN LLOYD
Executive. **Personal:** Born Mar 29, 1917, Richmond, VA; son of Adelaide Turner and Thornton F; married Helen Randolph Davis, May 22, 1939; children: Melvin Jr, Langston, Adelaide Flamer, Carolyn Harris, Wendell F, Kermit M, Nancy Elam, Anna Hudson, Leon V, Revell R, Deborah N Davis. **Educ:** John Tyer Community Col, 1949. **Career:** Thorton F Davis, laborer, 1931-35; Thornton J Davis Jr, painter, 1935-42; US Navy, painter, 1942-45; Davis & Myers Bldg Co, painter, 1945-60; Melvin L Davis Gen Contractor, owner, 1960-68; Davis Bros Construct Co, pres, 1968-. **Orgs:** Sunday school supt, Troop Providence Baptist Church, 1945-50. **Business Addr:** President, Davis Bros Construct Co, 2410 Chamberlayne Ave, Richmond, VA 23222.*

DAVIS, MICHAEL JAMES
Judge. **Personal:** Born Jul 21, 1947, Cincinnati, OH; son of Chester L and Doris R Smith; married Sara Wahl, Sep 6, 1980; children: Michael, Alexander. **Educ:** Macalester Col, St Paul, BA, 1969; Univ Minn Law Sch, Minneapolis, JD, 1972; Macalester Col, Honorary Doctor Laws degree, 2001. **Career:** US Dept Health, Educ & Welfare, Off Gen Coun, Litigation Div, atty, 1973; Neighborhood Justice Ctr, Legal Rights Ctr, Minneapolis, criminal defense atty, 1974, mem bd; Legal Rights Ctr, criminal defense atty, 1975-78; Hennepin County Pub Defender's Off, asst pub defender, 1978-83; Univ Minn Law Sch, adj prof, 1982-; Hennepin County Munic Ct, judge, 1983-84; Hennepin Cty Dist Ct, judge, 1984-94; US Dist Ct, judge, 1994-. **Orgs:** MN Civil Rights Comn, 1977-82; Am Inns Ct, 1992-; MN Minority Lawyers Asn, 1980-; Nat Bar Asn, 1990-; Hennepin Cty Bar Asn, 1986; MN State Bar Asn, 1986; MN Lawyers Int Human Rights Comn, 1983-85; MN Supreme Ct Racial Bias Task Force, 1990-93; MN Supreme Ct, Closed Circuit TV Task Force, 1991; Atty Gen's Task Force Prevention Sexual Violence Against Women, 1988-89; Hennepin Dist Cts, Fourth Judicial Dist, 1984-; Int Acad Trial Judges, 1996-; bd mem, Nat Asn Pub Interest Law Fellowships for Equal Justice, 1997-; Eighth Circuit Jury Instruction Comn, 1997-; US Asn Constitutional Law, 1997-; Fed Bar Asn, 1994-; Fed Judges Asn, 1994-; Jack & Jill Am Inc, Rites Passage prog, youth mentor, 1998. **Honors/Awds:** Outstanding Alumni Award, Macalester, 1989; Good Neighbor Award, WCCO Radio,1989; Honorary Black Achievers Award; Law Student Scholarship in Judge Michael J Davis' Name, Minnesota Minority Lawyers Assn; Distinguished Service Award, William Mitchell Col Law, 2000. **Special Achievements:** Published "Strategies and Techniques: Court's Role in Promoting Settlement;" Civil Pretrial Practice Inst, MN Inst of Legal Education, 1993; "Jury Challenges Involving Issues of Race," MN Developments and US Supreme Ct Updates, MN State Bar Assn Continuint Legal Education, 1993; "Nominated for appointment: Judge Pamela Alexander," 62 Hennepin Lawyer 11, May-June 1993; MN Supreme Court Closed-Circuit TV Task Force, writer of report adopted by the ct, 1991; "Civil Rights Advocate Doug Hall Retires from Legal Rights Center," 54 Hennepin Lawyer, July-August 1985. **Home Addr:** Henn Co Govt Ctr, Minneapolis, MN 55401, **Home Phone:** (612)348-3677. **Business Addr:** Judge, US District Court, 14E US Courthouse, 300 S Fourth St, Minneapolis, MN 55415, **Business Phone:** (612)664-5070.*

DAVIS, MIKE
Basketball coach, basketball player. **Personal:** Born Sep 15, 1960, Fayette, AL; married Theresa (divorced); children: Mike Jr & Nicole (deceased); married Tamilya; children: Lateesha & Antoine. **Educ:** Ala Univ, attended 1983; Thomas Edison Col, BA, communs, 1995. **Career:** Pro basketball player, Switzerland & Italy, CBA, 1984-89; Miles Col, asst coach, 1989-90; Venezuela, 1990-91; Wichita Falls Texans, asst coach, 1990-94; Chicago Rockers, player & coach, 1994-95; AL Univ, asst coach, 1995-97; IN Univ, asst coach, 1997-2000, Dept Intercollegiate Athletics, head coach, 2000-06; UAB blazers, Univ Al, Birmingham, head coach, 2007-. **Honors/Awds:** SE Conference All-Defensive Team, 1983; Major Taylor Award, 2002; Big Ten Regular Season Championship. **Special Achievements:** Led IU to Regional title, Final Four & Nat Championship Game appearance in 2002. **Business Addr:** Head Coach, UAB blazers, Univ of Alabama at Birmingham, 1530 3 Ave S, Bartow East Tower, Birmingham, AL 35294-1160.*

DAVIS, MILTON C.
Lawyer, association executive. **Personal:** Married Myrtle Goore; children: Milton, Warren. **Educ:** Tuskegee Univ, BS, 1971; Univ Iowa Sch Law, JD, 1974. **Career:** State Ala, asst atty gen, 1977; pvt pract, atty, 1977-; Herman Lehman Found Scholar. **Orgs:** Pres, Alpha Phi Alpha Fraternity, 1993-96; Nat Bar Asn; Sigma Pi Phi Boule; fel Am Polit Sci Found; fel Ford Found. **Special Achievements:** First Ala resident elected as head of Alpha Phi Alpha; the oldest African-Am fraternity in the US. **Business Addr:** Attorney, Private Practice, 304 N Main St, Tuskegee, AL 36083, **Business Phone:** (334)727-6500.*

DAVIS, MONIQUE DEON
State government official. **Personal:** Born Aug 19, 1936, Chicago, IL; daughter of James McKay and Constance McKay; divorced; children: Robert A Davis & Monique C Conway. **Educ:** Chicago State Univ, BS, elem educ, 1967, MS, 1975; Univ Ill; DePaul Univ. **Career:** Chicago Bd Educ, teacher, 1967-86; City Cols Chicago, teacher, 1976-84; Chicago Bd Educ, coordr & adminr, 1986-; Ill Gen Assembly, Dist 27, state rep, 1986-. **Orgs:** Chmn, Southside Chap IVI-IPO, 1980-84; chmn, Legis Comt Chicago Area Alliance Black Sch Educators, 1981-83; coordr, Chicago Bd Educ, 1986-; bd mem, Christian Bd Trinity United Church Christ; Chicago State Univ, Alumni Bd, 1992-94; Nat Asn Advan Colored People; Phi Delta Kappa; Beverly Area Planning Asn. **Honors/Awds:** Teacher of the Year Award, Gresham Sch, 1978; Teacher Who Makes a Difference Center for New Schools; Excellent Legislator, Dept Aging, 1988; Excellent Legislator, Oper PUSH, 1989; Presidential Award, Nat Asn Equal Opportunity Higher

Educ; Legislative Award, Ill Bd Regents Comt; Best & Brightest Award, Dollars & Sense Mag; Women for Work & Dedication to Education Award, Second Congressional Dist. **Business Addr:** State Representative, Illinois General Assembly, 27th District, 1234 W 95th St, Chicago, IL 60643, **Business Phone:** (773)445-9700.

DAVIS, MORRIS E
Lawyer, educator, manager. **Personal:** Born Aug 9, 1945, Wilmington, NC. **Educ:** NC A&T State Univ, BS, 1967; Univ Iowa, Col Law, JD, 1970; Univ Calif, Sch Pub Health, MPH, 1973. **Career:** Dept Housing & Urban Devel, San Francisco, atty adv, 1970-72; J Black Health Perspectives, managing ed, 1973-74; Univ Calif, Berkeley, Inst Indust Rels, Labor Occup Health Prog, exec dir, 1974-80; US Merit Systs Protection Bd, admin judge, 1980-85; Law Off David P Corsi, atty law, 1986-88; abritrator & mediator, atty, 1986-. **Orgs:** Calif Bar Asn; Iowa Bar Asn; Am Abritrator Asn; Am Pub Health Asn. **Business Addr:** Attorney, American Arbitrator Association, Arbitrator-Mediator, 417 Montgomery St 5th Fl, San Francisco, CA 94104-1113, **Business Phone:** (510)635-4509.

DAVIS, MYRTLE A.
College teacher. **Career:** Univ Maryland Sch Med, asst prof, 2002. *

DAVIS, MYRTLE HILLIARD
Executive, chief executive officer, president (organization). **Personal:** Born Jun 13, 1926, Texarkana, AR; daughter of Thelma Hacker and Arthur L (deceased); divorced; children: Drew Hillard. **Educ:** Homer G Phillips Hosp, RN, 1955; Univ Cincinnati, MS, health planning admin, 1977. **Career:** Harvard St Health Ctr Boston, MA, pres, 1982-83; Myrtle Hilliard Davis Comprehensive Health Ctr, admin, 1969-82, pres & ceo. **Orgs:** Top Ladies Distinct St Louis Chap, 1974-; Co chair, finance comt; bd dir,St Louis Metro Urban League, 1983-; chmn, personnel comt, bd dir, Tower Vill Geriatric Ctr, 1984-; treas & bd dir, MO Coalition Amb Care Ctrs, 1984-, secy & bd dir, 1983-, chmn & bd dirs, 1987-, Primary Care CounGreater St Louis; Spec Proj Comn, St Louis ambassadors, 1985-; secy, Gateway Chapter Links, 1986; pres& bd dirs, Tower Village Nursing CareCtr, 1987-; pres & chmn, Health Med Adv Comn, St Louis Urban League, 1987-; Black Leadership Round Table, 1989. **Honors/Awds:** Certificate of Appreciation, MO Senate; Distinguished Citizen, St Louis Argus Newspaper; Distinguished Public Service, Culinary Arts Club; Leadership, Publ Relations Order Eastern Star; Woman of Achievement,Suburban Journals/radio station KMOX, 1989; Black Women Who Make Things Happen Award, Nat Coun Negro Women, Frito Lay, 1988; Women in Leadership Award, YWCA, Non Profit Management, 1993. *

DAVIS, MYRTLE V.
Nurse. **Personal:** Born Aug 23, 1930, Niles, OH; daughter of Willa Mae Smith and Anthony B Smith; married Frank T; children: Robin C. **Educ:** St Elizabeth Hosp Sch Nursing, Youngstown, Ohio, RN, 1952; Youngstown State Univ, BS, 1957; Ky State Univ, Ky, Ohio, MEd; Tex Woman's Univ, MS, 1980. **Career:** Nurse (retired); RN 1952-54; St Elizabeth Hosp, Youngstown, Ohio, asst head nurse, 1954-56, head nurse, 1956-62; Choffin Sch Practical Nursing,instr, 1963-71; Youngstown Bd Educ, dir, 1971-76; Youngstown State Univ, instr, 1976-81; various health care agencies, Youngstown, Ohio, staff nurse, med surgical nursing, 1981-90. **Orgs:** Youngstown Supvr Personnel Asn; adv bd, St Elizabeth Hosp Sch Nursing; adv comn bd, Lic Practical Nurse Asn Ohio; Am Nurses Asn; Delta Sigma Theta; Youngstown chap Links Inc; Negro Bus & Prof Women's Club; life mem Ohio Voc Asn; Am Voc Asn; 3rd Baptist Church. **Special Achievements:** First black director of school of practical nursing, State of Ohio, 1971. **Home Addr:** 5889 Oak St Ext, Lowellville, OH 44436.

DAVIS, DR. NATHAN TATE
Educator, saxophonist. **Personal:** Born Feb 15, 1937, Kansas City, KS; son of Rosemary Green and Raymond E; married Ursula Broschke; children: Joyce Nathalie & Pierre Marc. **Educ:** Univ Kans, BME, 1960; Wesleyan Univ, CT, PhD, Ethnomusicology, 1974. **Career:** Educator, Musician: Club St Germain, Paris, prof debut, Kenny Clark, 1963; Donald Byrd, Blue Note Club Paris, 1963; Chat Que Peche, Eric Dolphy, Paris, 1964; Europe; Belg Radio-TV, staff composer; Univ Pittsburgh, Dept Music, prof music & dir, Jazz Studies, 1969-; Penn Coun Arts fel, 1984; Recordings: Happy Girl, 1965; Nathan Davis Sextet Peace Treaty, 1965; The Hip Walk, 1966; Nathan Davis Quartet Rules of Freedom, 1968; Nathan Davis Quartet: Jazz Concert In A Benedictine Monestary, 1969; Makatuka, 1970; The 6th Sense in the 11th House, 1972; If, 1976; Suite for Dr. Martin Luther King, Jr, 1977; Faces of Love, 1982; London By Night, 1987; I'm A Fool To Want You, 1995; Two Originals, 1998; The Other Side of Morning, 2004. **Orgs:** SACEM, Soc Composers, Paris, France; co-chmn ed com Inst Black Am Music; mem, Afro Am Bi Cen Hall Fame; founder, Int Acad Jazz Hall Fame & Sonny Rollins Int Jazz Archives, Univ Pittsburgh; dir, John F Kennedy Ctr's Jazz Ahead Prog. **Honors/Awds:** Robert M Frankel Award of City Theatre, Pittsburgh, 1995; DHL, Florida Mem Col. **Special Achievements:** Created PhD deg prog Ethnomusicology, Univ Pittsburgh; created Jazz Prog, Univ Pittsburgh; created Jazz Prog Paris-Am Acad Paris. **Military Serv:** AUS, 298 army band, Berlin, 1960-62. **Business Addr:** Professor, Director of Jazz Studies, University Pittsburgh, Department of Music, 130 Music Bldg, Pittsburgh, PA 15260, **Business Phone:** (412)624-4187.

DAVIS, NATHAN W., JR.
Lawyer. **Personal:** Born Dec 24, 1936, Ocean City, NJ; son of Nathan and Louisa; married Emma, Jul 21, 1962; children: Melode, Carla, Nathan III. **Educ:** Rutgers Univ, BA, 1959; Howard Univ, Sch Law, JD, 1962. **Career:** Self-Employed, atty, 1974-84; State NJ, dep pub defender, 1984-. **Orgs:** Lay leader, Macedonia Methodist Church, 1974-; pres, Egg Harbor Township Bd Educ, 1984-; Atlantic Co Bar Asn, 1975-; chmn, Munic Utilities Authority, 1991-. **Honors/Awds:** Service Award, Bd Educ, Egg Harbor Township, 1991 & 1992.

DAVIS, NATHANIEL ALONZO
Executive, president (organization), chief executive officer. **Personal:** Born Jan 25, 1954, Fort McClelland, AL; son of Laura M Davis and Jesse Davis Jr; married Al Gene Redding, Jun 11, 1983; children: Taylor, Darren & Jasmine. **Educ:** Stevens Inst Technol, BE, 1976; Univ Pa, Moore Sch Elec Engineering, MSEE, 1982; Univ Pa, Wharton Sch Bus, MBA, 1982. **Career:** AT&T Telecom Long Lines, engr, staff supvr, various other positions, 1976-81; MCI Telecommunications, dir, network engineering, 1983-86, vpres, financial oper, 1986-88, vpres, syst engineering, 1988-90, sr vpres, finance, 1990-92, sr vpres, access serv, 1992-98; Nextel Commun, exec vpres, 1998-99; XO Commun Inc, pres & ceo, 2000-03; Vibrant Solutions, dir; Mutual Am Capital Mgmt Corp, dir; Columbia Capital L.L.C, Exec Residence, 2003-; RANND Adv Group, managing dir, 2003-05; Charter Commun, former Independent dir & mem audit Comt, 2005-08, dir, 2005-; XM Satellite Radio Holdings Class A, dir, 1999-, chief operating officer, 2006-07, pres & ceo, 2007-. **Orgs:** Black MBA Asn, 1987; Black Data Proc Asn, 1988-90; Wharton Alumni Asn, 1989-. **Home Addr:** 2609 Geneva Hill Ct, Oakton, VA 22124-1534. **Business Addr:** President, Chief Executive Officer, XM Satellite Radio Holdings Class A, 1500 Eckington Place NE, Washington, DC 20002, **Business Phone:** (202)380-4000.

DAVIS, NIGEL S
Banker. **Personal:** Born Oct 1, 1955, Bastrop, LA; son of Charles and Gladys. **Educ:** Grambling State Univ, attended 1976. **Career:** Fed Res Bank Kans City, asst bank examr, 1977-82, bank examr, 1982-86, sr bank examr & managing examr, 1986-, asst vpres, currently. **Orgs:** Youth task group vol full employ Coun, 1990; vol, Women's Employ Network. **Home Addr:** 8726 Ridgeway Ct, Kansas City, MO 64138. **Business Addr:** Assistant Vice President, The Federal Reserve Bank of Kansas City, 925 Grand Blvd, Kansas City, MO 64198-0001, **Business Phone:** 800-333-1010.

DAVIS, NORMA JUNE (NORMA JUNE WILSON)
School administrator, educator. **Personal:** Born May 1, 1940, Jacksonville, FL; daughter of Myra and Maxie; married Leodis, Apr 27, 1962; children: Melonie Jones & L Elliott. **Educ:** Spelman Col, BA, 1961. **Career:** Educator (retired); SNCC Atlanta, chmn, 1960; IA City Parks & Rec Comn, vchmn, 1972-76; Univ Iowa, Admin Serv Dept, coordr info, 1975-76, coordr residence serv, 1976-84, asst dir residence serv, 1984-86, Affirmative Action, acting dir, 1985-86, asst to vpres fin, 1986-91, asst vpres fin & univ servs, 1991-98, Continuous Qual Improv, qual coordr. **Orgs:** Ad Hoc Commn Racism, Iowa City Sch Bd, 1971-72; secy & treas, Cedar Rapids Chap Links Inc, 1974-77; Kans City Friends Alvin Ailey, 2000-; Univ Ia African Am Coun. **Honors/Awds:** Distinguished Achievement Award, Univ Iowa, 1996. **Home Addr:** 12012 Grand Ave, Kansas City, MO 64145, **Home Phone:** (816)941-3091.

DAVIS, NORMAN EMANUEL
Association executive. **Personal:** Born Apr 6, 1941, Waycross, GA; married Mineola James Davis; children: Norman, Anthony, Corey V. **Educ:** Tuskegee Inst, BS, Commercial Industries, 1966. **Career:** Dial-A-Maid Inc, pres, 1978-80; Migrant & Seasonal Farmworkers, exec dir, 1980-; Young Volunteer Action, dir; MECRR Activity Center, adjustment instr; Davis Mkt and Assoc Inc; Tuskegee Model City, Human resources Develop; Children Trust Fund, program asst & planning & econ develop; Waycross City, Comnr, currently. **Orgs:** Staff planner, Planning Comn; exec dir, City Tuskegee Migrant & Seasonally Employed Farmworkers; city recreation projects City Tuskegee; F&A Mason 32nd Degree, Shriner, Tuskegee Jaycees, Electrolex Club, Elks Lodge, Intl Guild Res Develop, Am Soc Planning Officials, Am Legion, Macon City Retardation & Rehab Exec Bd; adv bd, Macon Cty Medicare & Medicaid; Talent Search Adv Bd; Macon Cty Mental Health Bd; Tuskegee Planning Comn; Macon Cty Monumental & Historical Soc; Tuskegee-Macon Cty Youth Coun; Omega Psi Phi; served 2 yrs pres Washington Pub Sch PTA; pres, City Wide PTA; elected, 6 yrs to Macon Co Bd Educ; Model Cities soc planner City Tuskegee, 1969-78; dir & planner, Rec Dept; Young Volunteers & Action Prog; Migrant Worker Prog. **Honors/Awds:** Legionnaire of the Year; Social Work Certificate for Suprvisions; State Mental Health Service Award; Youth Council Cert; Red Cross Campaign Fund Raising Certificate; Outstanding Achievement Award, City Tuskegee; Jaycees Scotman Award; Outstanding Achievement Award, Pro Plan Intl; Jaycees Outstanding Business Award, Outstanding Young Man of the Year; Macon City Council Retardation & Rehab Appreciation Certificate; Macon Cty 4 H Leadership Certificate. **Special Achievements:** designed, develop & implemented several community programs; Parenting Facilitator. *

DAVIS, PATRICIA C.
Association executive. **Personal:** Born Jul 25, 1943, Grand Rapids, MI; married Frederick Douglass; children: Grant Anthony, Frederick Douglass II, Mwindaace N' Gai. **Educ:** Detroit Inst Commerce, 1969. **Career:** NAACP, exec secy; Amoco Production Co, admin secy, 1970-73; UAW Fai Practices & Anti-discrimination Dept, secy, 1969-70; League Life Ins Co, stenographer, 1964-69; US Army Detroit Procurement Dist, clerk stenographer, 1963; Burroughs Corp, clerk typist, 1962-63. **Orgs:** Lay mem, Paradise Bapt Ch; Immaculate Conception Christian Bd Of Edn; asst secy, OK St Conf of Branches NAACP; asst secy, Tulsa Br NAACP; exec secy, Tula Br, NAACP, 1970-76. *

DAVIS, PERNELL
Football player. **Personal:** Born May 19, 1976, Birmingham, AL; son of George and Betty. **Educ:** Univ Ala, Birmingham, english. **Career:** Philadelphia Eagles, defensive tackle, 1999-01; Cincinnati Bengals, 2002; Scottish Claymores, Scotland, defensive back, 2002. *

DAVIS, PRESTON A
Executive, president (organization). **Personal:** Born in Norfolk, VA; married Michelle; children: Ashley & Preston III. **Career:** Am Broadcasting Co Inc, ABC TV Network Group, engr, 1976, TV Opers E Coast, vpres, 1988-92, Broadcast Opers & Eng, pres, 1993-. **Orgs:** Bd mem, Jr Achievement; bd dirs, Minorities Media; bd dir, Found Minority Interests Media Inc; Tech Adv Comn, Mus TV & Radio; Pres Coun Cooper Union Col Sci & Art. **Military Serv:** AUS, specialist commun technol, Vietnam War. **Business Addr:** President of Broadcast Operations & Engineering, American Broadcasting Companies Inc, 500 S Buena Vista St, Burbank, CA 91521-4551, **Business Phone:** (818)460-7477.

DAVIS, PRESTON AUGUSTUS
Association executive. **Personal:** Born in Norfolk, VA; son of Charles A and Mattie E; married Mary Pierson, Aug 22, 1971; married Helen G, Sep 7, 1946 (divorced 1970); children: Gwendolyn Dyess, Preston A Jr, Karen Heggs & June Kimbrugh. **Educ:** WV State Col, BS, bus admin, 1949; Command & Gen Staff Col, MS, exec mgt, 1965; George Wash Univ, MSA, 1974. **Career:** Fairmicco Indust, vpres & gen mgr, 1969-70; Morgan State Univ, vpres develop, 1970-71; USDA, sr mgt analyst, 1971-78, spec asst to asst sec adminr, 1978-79, dir small & disadvantaged bus utilization, 1979-87; Grad Sch & No VA Community Col, prof 1974-94; Davis & Davis Consult Asn, 1989-. **Orgs:** Omega Psi Phi Fraternity, 1947-; Masonic Lodge, 1949-; bd dir & com chmn, Agr Fed Credit Union, 1972-99; Phi Delta Kappa 1978-92; Kiwanis: gov, 1988-89 (1st black in south), int chmn, young children's priority one progs, 1990-93, Kiwanis Int UNICEF, cabinet chmn worldwide serv prog, 1993-95, ambassador worldwide serv proj, 1995-2000, trustee, Kiwanis Found, 1998-2001. **Honors/Awds:** Distinguished Mil Graduate WV State Col, 1949; Outstanding Achievement Award, Salvation Army Wash, DC, 1976; Certificate of Merit for Outstanding Performance, USDA, 1979; NAFEO Distinguished Alumni Award, 1983; Hall of Fame, West VA State Col, 1983; Small Business Administration's Award for Excellence, 1984; Alumnus of the Year, West VA State Col, 1990. **Military Serv:** RA, lt col, 1949-70; Bronze Star; Army Commendation Medal; Purple Heart; Army Meritorious Service Award; 17 other medals & combat ribbons. **Business Addr:** CEO, Davis & Davis Consultant Associates, 600 6th Pl SW, Washington, DC 20024.

DAVIS, RAOUL A. See Obituaries section.

DAVIS, REGINALD FRANCIS
Journalist, lecturer, writer. **Personal:** Born Aug 18, 1951, East Chicago, IN; son of James William Davis and Frances Vivian Hyman Ford; married Toni Diane Holliday, May 11, 1980 (divorced 1994); children: Michael, Andrea & Paul. **Educ:** Purdue Univ, West Lafayette, IN, BA; Northwestern Univ, Evanston, IL, MA, Mgt, 1997. **Career:** The Times, Hammond, IN, reporter, 1973-76; The Charlotte Observer, Charlotte, NC, copy ed, 1976-78; The Chicago Tribune, Chicago, IL, 1978-, dep metro ed, 1987-92, assoc managing ed & mem ed bd; ABA Jour, Medill News Serv, asst managing ed, currently; Northwestern Univ, adj lectr, currently; Author: Contemporary Books, 1997; The Solo Dad Survival Guide, 1998; Raising Your Kids on Your Own. **Orgs:** Chicago Asn Black Journalists, 1988-; Nat Asn Black Journalists; Soc Newspaper Design. **Honors/Awds:** Academic Honorary, Phi Kappa Phi, 1973; Best Commentary Writing, Chicago Asn Black Journalists, 1994; Apex Awards, 2004, 2005 & 2006; Silver Award, Am Soc Bus Publs Eds, 2005. **Business Phone:** (312)503-3800.

DAVIS, REUBEN CORDELL
Football player. **Personal:** Born May 7, 1965, Greensboro, NC. **Educ:** Univ NC. **Career:** Football player (Retired); Tampa Bay

Buccaneers, defensive end, 1988-92; Phoenix Cardinals, 1992-93; San Diego Chargers, defensive end, 1994-96. *

DAVIS, REUBEN K.
Judge. **Personal:** Born Jul 26, 1920, Columbus, MS; son of Reuben B and Leola H Adkins; married Elizabeth Zangerle; children: Jennifer, Andrea & Mark. **Educ:** Va State Col, BA, 1946; Boston Univ Law Sch, LLB, 1949. **Career:** Hurst Davis & King, atty, 1955-66; Rochester City, dep corp coun, 1966-68, community bldg, 1968-72; Rochester City Ct, judge, 1967; Stewart & Bennett Inc, gen coun, 1972-74; Assoc Justice, Appellate div, New York Supreme Ct, fourth Judicial Dept, judge (retired), 1987-96; Unified Ct Syst, judicial hearing officer, currently. **Orgs:** Trustee, AME Zion Church, 1958-; Monroe County Bar Asn, 1966; chmn, Monroe County Human Rel Comn, 1966-69; trustee, Community Savings Bank, 1969-74; bd dir, YMCA, 1976-; New York State & Monroe County Bar Asn. **Honors/Awds:** Rodenbeck Award, 2005. **Military Serv:** AUS, Lt, 1943-46. **Business Addr:** Judicial Hearing Officer, Rochester City Court, Seventh Judicial District, 6 Justice Hall, New York, NY 14614, **Business Phone:** (585)428-2450.

DAVIS, RICHARD
Lawyer. **Personal:** Born Sep 12, 1943, Miami, FL; married Doreen D; children: LaRonda R, Richard QuinRo. **Educ:** Univ AZ, BS, Publ Admin, 1969, JD, 1972. **Career:** Univ AZ, Col Law, lectr, 1973-; Chandle Tullar Udall & Redhair, assoc atty, 1972-80, partner, 1980; Mesch Clark & Rothschild P C, chmn & partner, currently. **Orgs:** Am Bar Asn, 1972-, AZ Bar Asn, 1972-; bd dir, Soc AZ Legal Aid Soc, 1975-, Tucson Urban League, 1975-, Ododo Theatre, 1975-; comnr, AZ Athletic Comn, 1977-81; AZ Civil Rights Comn, 1977-78; pres, Tucson Urban League, 1977-78; bd dir, Pima City Bar Asn, 1978-80; Am Red Cross, 1980-83; YMCA, 1983-; Am Col Trial Lawyers; Sr Coun, Am Col Barristers. **Honors/Awds:** Fellow, Woodrow Wilson Nat ship, 1969-72; Distinguished Citizen Award, NAACP Tucson, 1982. **Military Serv:** USAF, E 4, 4 yrs. **Business Addr:** Partner, Chairman, Mesch Clark & Rothschild P C, 259 N Meyer Ave, Tucson, AZ 85701-1090, **Business Phone:** (520)624-8886.*

DAVIS, RICHARD C.
Educator. **Personal:** Born Sep 6, 1925, Los Angeles, CA; married Dolores Parks; children: Saundra, Marilyn & Jacqueline. **Educ:** Compton Col, AA, 1949; Geo Pepperdine Col, Los Angeles, BA, 1952. **Career:** Los Angeles County Dept Parks & Recreation, recreation dir, 1948-52; Willow brook Jr High Sch, 1952-57; Ralph Bunche Jr High Sch, teacher, 1957-65; Tubman High Sch, continuing educ guid counr, 1965-66; Compton Sr High Sch, voc educ coun, 1966-67; Compton Union Sch Dist, 1967-70; C Welfare & Attend, Compton Unified Sch Dist, supt, 1970-74; Sacramento County, Off Educ, Child Welfare & Attendance Servs, consult. **Orgs:** Pres elect, Calif Asn Supervisors Child Welfare; Nat Educ Asn; Compton Sec Teachers Asn; Calif Continuing Educ Asn; Asn Compton Sch Adminr; Los Angeles County Dist Atty Adv Coun; cit adv com, Reg Planning Comn; agency exec Com, Welfare Planning Coun; chmn, Vandalism Prev Task Force; chmn, Feasibility Study YMCA; Del Am Home Owners Asn; PTA; pres Grant, Univ Calif Los Angeles, 1968. **Honors/Awds:** National Junior College Track & Field Award; All Pacific Island Champ Football Award. **Military Serv:** USMC, corpl, 1943-46. **Business Addr:** 1623 E 118 St, Los Angeles, CA 90059.

DAVIS, RICHARD O.
Automotive executive. **Personal:** Son of Richard and Katherine. **Career:** Davis Buick-Jeep Eagle Inc, chief exec officer; Davis Automotive Inc, pres, currently. **Honors/Awds:** BE Auto Dealer of the Year, 1998. **Business Addr:** Owner, President, Davis Automotive Inc, 226 N Greenville Ave, Richardson, TX 75081, **Business Phone:** (972)235-1977.*

DAVIS, RICKY (TYREE RICARDO DAVIS)
Basketball player. **Personal:** Born Sep 23, 1979, Las Vegas, NV; son of Tyree III Davis and Linda; children: Tyree Ricky Davis V, Terez & Racquel Natale. **Educ:** Unic Iowa, attended 2001. **Career:** Charlotte Hornets, 1998-2000; Miami Heat, 2000-01; Cleveland Cavaliers, 2001-04; Boston Celtics, forward, 2003-06; Minnesota Timberwolves, guard, 2006-07; Miami Heat, 2007-08; Los Angeles Clippers, 2009-. **Orgs:** Owner, The Ricky Davis Found. **Business Phone:** (612)673-1600.*

DAVIS, ROB (ROBERT EMMETT DAVIS)
Football player. **Personal:** Born Dec 10, 1968, Washington, DC. **Educ:** Shippensburg Univ, criminal justice, 1992. **Career:** New York Jets, pract squad mem, 1993-94; Baltimore Stallions, 1995; Kansas City Chiefs, pract squad mem, 1996; Chicago Bears, defensive tackle, 1996; Green Bay Packers, 1997-2001, captain, 2001-04, dir player develop, 2008-. **Honors/Awds:** Community Service Award, Green Bay Chamber Com, 1999; Athletic Hall of Fame, Shippensburg Univ, 2003. **Special Achievements:** USA Today All-Joe Team, 2006. **Business Addr:** Director of Player Development, Green Bay Packers, PO Box 10628, Green Bay, WI 54307, **Business Phone:** (920)496-5700.*

DAVIS, ROBERT ALAN
Government official. **Personal:** Born in Detroit, MI; married Sheela Davis. **Educ:** Univ MI, BA, econs, 1981; Univ Detroit, MPA, 1983; Drew Theological Sch, DMin. **Career:** Planner, 1984-86, dir human resources, 1986-97, exec asst mayor, City Detroit; Wayne County, Commun & Faith Based Initiatives dep dir; Gov Off, Southeast Mich, sr adv & dir, currently. **Orgs:** Child Care Coord Coun, pres, 1995-; pres, NW Activities Ctr, 1998-; pres, Univ Dist Community Asn, currently. **Home Addr:** 18255 Oak Dr, Detroit, MI 48221, **Home Phone:** (313)342-0724. **Business Addr:** Director, Office of Governor, SE Michigan Office, 3022 W Grand Bld Suite 14-150, Detroit, MI 48202, **Business Phone:** (313)456-0010.

DAVIS, ROBERT E.
Government official. **Personal:** Born Nov 21, 1908, Kenansville, NC; married Bernice Shaw; children: Sandra Roberta. **Educ:** Fayetteville State Univ, BS, 1936. **Career:** Robesou Co Bd Educ, teacher, 1930-43; David Bros Wholesale Grocers, co-owner, 1940; City Maxton, city councilman, 1972-78; St NC, rep, 1978-80. **Orgs:** Master Masonic Lodge 86 Maxton, 1950-54; illustrous potentate Ouda Temple 147 Shriner, 1952-56. **Business Addr:** Government Officer, Davis Bros Wholesale Grocers, Wilmington St, Maxton, NC 28364.

DAVIS, ROBERT N
Judge. **Personal:** Born Sep 20, 1953, Kewanee, IL; son of Robert Ezekiel and Rose; married Linda M Williams, Aug 28, 1982; children: Robert L. **Educ:** Univ Hartford, BA, 1975; Georgetown Univ Law Sch, JD, 1978. **Career:** US Dept Educ, atty; US Atty, spec asst; CFTC, atty; Univ Miss, Sch Law, prof; Georgetown Univ, prof; J Nat Security Law, founder, currently; Stetson Univ Col Law, prof, 2001-04; US Ct Appeals Veterans Claims, judge, 2004-. **Orgs:** Am Arbitration Asn. **Honors/Awds:** Teacher of the Year, 1990; Scholar in Residence, Office of Gen Coun, US Olympic Comt, 1996. **Military Serv:** USN, lt cmdr, 1987-. **Business Addr:** Judge, United States Court of Appeals for Veterans Claims, 625 Ind Ave NW Suite 900, Washington, DC 20004-2950, **Business Phone:** (202)501-5970.

DAVIS, RONALD
Executive, chief executive officer. **Career:** Tri-State Design Construct Co Inc, chief exec officer, currently. **Business Phone:** (215)782-8200.

DAVIS, RONALD (RONALD L DAVIS)
Executive, police officer. **Personal:** Born Sep 18, 1963, Columbus, OH; son of Arthur and Marva Berry; married Janeith, Aug 24, 1996; children: Veronica, Glenn & Destiny. **Educ:** Community Col Air Force, attended 1985; Univ Phoenix, attended 1989-90; Southern Ill Univ, attended 2001. **Career:** Oakland Police Dept, police officer, 1986-92, sergeant, 1992-97, lt, 1997-99, police acad dir, area comdr, capt, 1999-; US House of Representatives, mem; US Senate, mem; Diversity Expert Serv LLC, pres & ceo, 2002-05; East Palo Alto Police Dept, police chief, 2005-. **Orgs:** Pres, 1999, region vpres, 1999-02, San Francisco-Bay Area chap;chair, Nat Racial Profiling Task Force, 2000-02; Nat Org Black Law Enforcement Exec; Nat Comn Police Integrity, 2002-; Nat Conf State Legis. **Honors/Awds:** Medal of Merit, Oakland Police Dept, 1996, 2000; NOBLE, pres citation, 2001; Civil Rights Award, 2001; Robert Lamb Humanitarian Award, 2001. **Special Achievements:** Developed & presented first "Bias-Based Policing" training course in the country; pub the following articles: Racial Profiling: A Symptom of Bias-Based Policing, 2000; Racial Profiling: What Does the Data Mean, 2001; TV & Mag appearances: JET Mag; Assoc Press; Black Entertainment TV; Ct TV, 2002. **Military Serv:** USAAF, E4, Good Conduct Medal, 1981-85. **Business Addr:** Chief of Police, East Palo Alto Police Department, 2415 University Ave, East Palo Alto, CA 94303, **Business Phone:** (650)853-3171.

DAVIS, RONALD L. **See DAVIS, RONALD.**

DAVIS, RONALD R.
Association executive. **Personal:** Born Feb 5, 1942, Harlem, NY; son of Stanley A and Lauribel Diana; married Jean Williams Davis; children: Yvette, Pamela. **Educ:** City Col. **Career:** US Track & Field, mem; RCA, sect mgr; Afro-Am Vegetarian Soc, NY, pres, 1976, vegetarian activist; defensive driving instr, currently. **Special Achievements:** Author, Cdl Workbook: Everything You Need to Know to Pass Your Test. *

DAVIS, RONALD WESTON
Football executive, football player, vice president (organization). **Personal:** Born Sep 16, 1950, Camden, NJ; son of Arthur and Emma; married Willabel; children: Ronald W II. **Educ:** Va State Univ, BS, 1972, MED, 1975; Richard Bland Col, conv mkt & tourism mkt. **Career:** Football player(retired); San Fran 49ers, football palyer, 1972; St Louis Cardinals, football player, 1972-76; United Va Bank, retail & oper officer, 1976-84; Metro Richmond Conv & Vis Bur, dep exec dir; Western Asn Conv & Visitors Bur, pres; Calif Conv & Visitors Bur, pres & chief exec officer; San Mateo County Conv & Visitors Bur, v pres; Pa Conv Ctr Authority, sr vpres sales &customer rels, 2001-. **Orgs:** Nat Football League Players Asn, 1976-85; bd dir, Metrop Bus League, 1977-84; pres & bd dir, Va State Univ Found, 1979-85; Guil field Church Finance Bd, 1985-89; Sr Community Develop Corp; The Rotary Club; Guilfield Baptist Church; Kappa Alpha Psi Fraternity. Active mem in numerous Soc &Orgn. **Honors/Awds:** Man of the Year, Health Phys Educ & Recreation, 1972; Top ten Richmond, Richmond Surroundings Mag; Va State Univ Sports Hall Fame, 1989; Outstanding Achievement Award, City Richmond; Imperial Potentates Humanitarian Award, Prince Hall Shiners Worldwide; Polemarchs Award, Kappa Alpha Psi fraternity. Has earned numerous awards for his service. **Business Phone:** (215)418-4700.

DAVIS, RUSSELL ANDRE
School administrator. **Personal:** Born Sep 16, 1958, Wilmington, DE; son of Warren and Alberta. **Educ:** Hampton Univ, BA, 1980, MA, 1982; Univ Md, MEd, 1989, EdD, 1992. **Career:** The Wash Sch Secretaries, dean studs, 1983-86; Howard Univ, instr Eng, 1986-88; Bowie State Univ, adj fac, Eng dept, 1988-, coordr psychol servs, 1989-90, dir coun & stud develop, 1990-92; Morgan State Univ, res assoc; Cecil Community Col, dir advising; Gloucester Co Col, vpres stud serv & interim pres currently. **Orgs:** Nat Educ Asn, 1980-; Nat Coun Teachers Eng, 1986-; chair, Am Col Testing Coun, 1986-; pres, Md Asn Multicultural Coun & Develop, 1988-92; Health Care Homeless, 1993-; bd dir, Nat Coun on Black Am Affairs, A Coun the Am Asn Community College, 2006-07. **Honors/Awds:** Instructor of the Year, Wash Sch Secretaries, 1984; Prince George's Community Col, Master Teacher's of English Distinction, 1992; Outstanding Male Administrator, Bowie State Univ, 1994. **Business Addr:** Vice President Student Services, Interim President, Gloucester County College, 1400 Tanyard Rd, Sewell, NJ 08080.

DAVIS, RUTH A.
Government official. **Personal:** Born May 28, 1943, Phoenix, AZ; daughter of Anderson and Edith. **Educ:** Spelman Col, BS, 1966; Univ Calif, Berkeley, MSW, 1968; 34th Class Senior Seminar, US Gov, grad, 1993; Aspen Inst, Colo, grad. **Career:** Agency Int Develop, Pop Div, staff; Univ Calif, Berkeley, res asst; Foreign Serv, 1968-; consular off: Kinshasa, Zaire, 1969-71; Nairobi, Kenya, 1971-73; Tokyo, Japan, 1973-76; Naples, Italy, 1976-80; City Wash, DC, spec adv Int Affairs, 1980-82; State Dept's Oper Ctr, sr watch officer, 1982-84; Bur Pers, chief training & liaison, 1984-87; consult gen, Barcelona, Spain, 1987-91; ambassador to Republic of Benin, 1992-95; Consular Affairs, prin dep asst secy, 1995-97; Foreign Serv Inst, dir, 1997-01; US Foreign Serv, dir gen & dir human resources, 2001-03; Howard Univ, Diplomat-in-Residence Int Affairs, Distinguished Advisor, 2004. **Orgs:** Pres, Thursday Luncheon Group. **Honors/Awds:** Honorary Doctorate of Laws, Spelman Col, 1998; Presidential Distinguished Service Award, 1999; Arnold L Raphel Memorial Award, State Dept, 1999; Superior Honor Award, State Dept; Honorary Doctorate of Laws, Middlebury Col, 2000; The Secretary's Distinguished Award, 2003; Friend of Advanced Language Study Award, Coalition of Distinguished Language Centers, 2003. **Special Achievements:** First African American woman to direct Foreign Service Institute; significant role in the organization of the 1992 Barcelona Olympic games. *

DAVIS, SAMMY, JR. **See Obituaries section.**

DAVIS, SAMUEL C
Journalist. **Personal:** Born Dec 10, 1959, Baltimore, MD; son of Sam Jr and Mammie Lee; married Gina Marie, Oct 8, 1994. **Educ:** Community Col, Baltimore, 1981; Coppin State Col, 1983. **Career:** Baltimore Sun, ed asst, 1980, sports reporter, 1984, local sports ed, 1992, asst sports ed, 1994, dep sports ed, 1996, exec sports ed, 1998, asst managing ed-sports, 2001, asst managing ed-recruitment & staff develop, currently. **Orgs:** Trustee, Christian Mem Church; Nat Asn Black Journalists. **Honors/Awds:** Carver High Sch, Hall of Fame. **Business Addr:** Assistant Managing Editor - Recruitment & Staff Development, The Baltimore Sun, 501 N Calvert St, Baltimore, MD 21278-0001, **Business Phone:** (410)332-6534.

DAVIS, SHANI
Speed skater. **Personal:** Born Aug 13, 1982, Chicago, IL; son of Reginald Shuck and Sherry. **Educ:** Northern Mich Univ. **Career:** Evanston Speedskating Club, Speedskater, 1988-. **Honors/Awds:** US Allround Champion, US Championships, 2003, 2004, 2005; Silver Medal, World Allround Long Track Championships, 2004; 1500 Meters World Champion, World Single Distance Championships, 2004; Bronze Medal, World Short Track Relay Team, World Short Track Championships, 2005; Silver Medal 1000 Meters, World Sprint Championships, 2005; 1000 Meters World Record Holder, 2005; World Champion, World Allround Long Track Championships, 2005, 2006; 1000m Olympic Gold Medal, Olympic Winter Games, 2006. **Special Achievements:** First African American to qualify for the Olympic Short Track Team; First black athlete to win a Winter Games Olympic Gold Medal in an individual event. **Home Addr:** Calgary, AB, Canada. **Business Addr:** Speedskater, Evanston Speedskating Club, Team Shani Davis, 815 Dempster St, Evanston, IL 60201.

DAVIS, DR. SHEILA PARHAM
Educator. **Personal:** Born Nov 30, 1954, Sumter, SC; daughter of James Franklin Sr and Mattie Mae Garvin; married Melvin, Aug 19, 1973; children: Deia Deneace & Danyetta Denise. **Educ:** Univ

SC, ASN, 1975; Univ Ala, Huntsville, BSN, 1984; Univ Ala, Birmingham, MSN, cardiovascular nursing, 1985; Ga State Univ, Atlanta, PhD, nursing educ, 1993. **Career:** Huntsville Hosp, Huntsville, AL, critical care nurse, 1983-85; Univ Ala, Birmingham, AL, instr, 1985-89, asst prof, 1989-; Oakwood Col, Dept Nursing, chair, 1991-; Univ Miss Med Ctr, Jackson, MI, prof nursing & asst dean doctoral studies specialties, currently. **Orgs:** Sigma Theta Tau, 1984; dir at Large, S Central Asn Black SDA Nurses, 1988-; educ comt chair, Ala League Nurses, 1988-90; med temperance leader, S Park SAC Church, 1988-; fel Am Nurses Asn, 1989-; publ commun comt mem, Asn Black Nurses Higher Ed, 1989-; inductee, Nat Hon Soc Nurses. **Honors/Awds:** Faculty Recognition Award, Univ Ala, Birmingham, 1988; Alumni of Achievement, Univ Ala Huntsville, 2006; Young Publication Award, ABNF; Distinguished Service Award, Oakwood Col. **Business Addr:** Professor of Nursing, Assistant Dean for Doctoral Studies, University of Mississippi Medical Center, 2500 N State St, Jackson, MS 39216, **Business Phone:** (601)815-4010.

DAVIS, SIDNEY LOUIS
Scientist. **Personal:** Born Jan 3, 1953, Kittery, ME; son of Sidney Louis Davis and Wilhelmina Irene Ramsay; divorced; children: Jesse A Davis & Joshua J Davis. **Educ:** Bernadean Univ, ND, 1977; Anglo Am Inst Drugless Ther, ND, 1978; Univ State New York, BS, 1990. **Career:** Naturopathic physician; USN, advan lab tech, 1983-2003. **Orgs:** Ed, Proclaiming Sabbath More Fully, 1998-; knight, Imperial House Sellassie, 1999-; Sodality Ark Int, 1999-; pres, Bible Sabbath Asn, 1999, bd dirs, currently,; Sabbath Africa Proj, 2000; Southern African Missiological Soc, 2001-. **Honors/Awds:** Knight de Bryan, 1999; Meritorious Ethiopian Order the Lion Judah, Imperial House Sellassie Solomonic Dynasty, 1999. **Special Achievements:** Proclaiming the Sabbath More Fully Sabbath Conferences, founder, 1998-; Seventh-day Adventist Feast day Internet Forum, founder, moderator, 2001; Sabbath in Africa Internet Forum, co-moderator, 2001. **Military Serv:** USN, EG, 1983-03; Nat Defense medal, 1983, 2001; Expert Pistol Shot medal, 1985; Good Conduct medal, 1987, 1991, 1995, 1999, 2003; Kuwait Liberation medal, 1992; Meritorious Unit commendation, 1992, 1994; SW Asia Serv medal, 1992; Navy Achievement medal, 1992, 1998, 2001; Armed Forces Exemplary medal, 1992; Navy "E" Ribbon, 1993; Overseas Serv Ribbon, 1993; Sea Serv Deployment Ribbon, 1994; Mil Outstanding Volunteer Serv medal, 2001. **Business Addr:** Director, Bible Sabbath Association, 2940 E Wisconsin Apt J, Great Lakes, IL 60088, **Business Phone:** (847)785-0315.

DAVIS, SONIA
Vice president (Organization). **Career:** Northern Trust Bank, vpres, currently. **Orgs:** Co-chair, HRIR Alumni Asn. **Business Addr:** Vice President, Northern Trust Bank, 50 S LaSalle M-6, Chicago, IL 60675, **Business Phone:** (312)630-6000.

DAVIS, STACEY H
Executive. **Educ:** Georgetown Univ, MBA. **Career:** Fannie Mae Found, Housing & Community Develop, dir, SE regional vpres, pres & chief exec officer, currently. **Business Addr:** President, Chief Executive Officer, Fannie Mae Foundation, 4000 Wisconsin Ave NW, Washington, DC 20016-2804, **Business Phone:** (202)274-8000.

DAVIS, STEPHEN
Football player. **Personal:** Born Mar 1, 1974, Spartanburg, SC. **Educ:** Auburn col. **Career:** Wash Redskins, running back, 1996-2002; Carolina Panthers, running back, 2003-05; St. Louis Rams, Running back, 2006-07; Carolina, 2008; Wash Redskins, 2009-. **Honors/Awds:** Three times Pro Bowl selection, 1999, 2000, 2003; One time All-Pro selection, 1999. *

DAVIS, SUSAN D
Judge. **Educ:** Norfolk State Univ; Col William & Mary, Marshall Wythe Sch Law, JD. **Career:** Judge (retired); Judge Lawrence M Lawson, Monmouth Co Superior Ct, law clerk, 1987-88; Giordano, Halleran & Ciesla, PC, 1988-96, partner, 1996; City Asbury Park, pub defender, 1989-93; US Dist Ct, Dist NJ, US magistrate judge. **Orgs:** Dist IX, Ethics Comt, 1991-94, chair, 1995; Supreme Ct, Adv Comt Prof Ethics. **Honors/Awds:** Susan D Davis Endowed Scholarship, named in honor, 2003. **Special Achievements:** First African American female US magistrate in NJ; second woman US magistrate in NJ; youngest judge appointed to federal bench in NJ.

DAVIS, TERRELL
Football player, media executive. **Personal:** Born Oct 28, 1972, San Diego, CA. **Educ:** Univ Ga, BS, consumer econ. **Career:** Football player (retired), Media executive; Denver Broncos, running back, 1995-2002; NFL Network, analyst, currently. **Honors/Awds:** Rookie of the Year, Football Digest, 1995; NFL Offensive Player of theYear, Assoc Press; NFL Player of the Year, Sports Illustrated; NFL Player of the Year, UPI; Most Valuable Player, Associated Press, 1998, Offensive Player of the Year, 1998; Espy Award for best NFL player, 1999; Pro Football Hall of Fame, 2007. **Business Phone:** (212)450-2000.*

DAVIS, THEODIS C.
Marketing executive. **Personal:** Born Aug 19, 1946, Little Rock, AR; son of Tommy B and Matilda; married Faye E Davis, Dec 26, 1966; children: Jessica, Ericka, Alyson. **Educ:** Indiana Univ, masters, 1976. **Career:** Hankscrafts Motors, gen mgr; Gerber Prods, area mgr, Chicago dist, dir sales baby care, dir mktg baby care, vpres, baby care mktg. **Orgs:** Bd chmn, Urban League, Muskegon, MI; Kappa Alpha Psi Fraternity; Frontiers Intl Serv Club; Kiwanis Intl; bd mem, West Shore Symphony. **Honors/Awds:** Numerous service & professional awards. **Military Serv:** US Air Force, staff sgt, 1964-68. *

DAVIS, THURMAN M, SR.
Government official. **Personal:** Born Oct 11, 1936, Raleigh, NC; son of John C and Elizabeth Davis Sr; married Loretta White, Jun 24, 1965; children: Thurman Jr, Cynthia & Stephanie. **Educ:** Hampton Univ, attended, 1960; US Army Engineering Sch; Fed Exec Inst. **Career:** US Gen Serv Admin, proj dir; Dalton Dalton Little Newport, proj mgr, assoc, 1973-79; US Gen Serv Admin, exec asst comnr, PBS, 1979-83, real property operations, 1983-84, asst regional admin, 1984-94, regional admin, 1994-96, dep admin, 1996; Archit & Transp Barriers Compliance Bd, chmn; LoZart & Assoc LLC, managing dir, currently. **Orgs:** Life mem, Alpha Phi Alpha Frat Inc, 1958-; Nat Am Soc Pub Admin, 1989-; Nat Forum Black Pub Adminr, 1993-; 100 Black Men Greater Wash, DC, 1995-; bd adv, Am Defense Int Inc; chmn, Found Advan Music & Educ, currently. **Honors/Awds:** Meritorious & Distinguished Presidential Rank Award, pres US, 1988, 1994 & 1997. **Military Serv:** AUS, first lt, 1960-61. **Home Addr:** 14924 Emory Lane, Rockville, MD 20853, **Home Phone:** (301)460-1050. **Business Addr:** Chairman, The Foundation for Advancement of Music & Education Inc, PO Box 2228, Bowie, MD 20718-2228, **Business Phone:** (301)805-5358.

DAVIS, TRAMAINE. See HAWKINS, TRAMAINE.

DAVIS, TRAVIS. See JOHNSON, MELVIN CARLTON, III.

DAVIS, TRAVIS HORACE
Football player. **Personal:** Born Jan 10, 1973, Harbor City, CA; children: David. **Educ:** Univ Notre Dame, psychol, 1997. **Career:** Football player (retired); Jacksonville Jaguars, defensive back, 1995-98; Pittsburgh Steelers, 1999. **Honors/Awds:** Rookie of the Year, 1995. *

DAVIS, TROY
Football player. **Personal:** Born Sep 14, 1975, Miami, FL. **Educ:** Iowa State Univ. **Career:** New Orleans Saints, running back, 1997-99; Hamilton Tiger Cats, Canadian Football League, running back, 2003-05; Canadian Football League, Edmonton Eskimos, running back, 2005-07. **Honors/Awds:** Big 12 Offensive Player of the Yr, 1996; E Div All-Star; All-Star; Grey Cup champion, 2005. **Special Achievements:** First and only running back in NCAA football history to rush for 2,000 yards. *

DAVIS, TYREE RICARDO. See DAVIS, RICKY.

DAVIS, TYRONE
Football player. **Personal:** Born Jun 30, 1972, Halifax, VA. **Educ:** Va Univ. **Career:** Football player (retired); New York Jets, tight end, 1995-96; Green Bay Packers, 1997-2002. *

DAVIS, REV. TYRONE THEOPHILUS
Executive. **Personal:** Born Dec 10, 1948, Kansas City, KS; son of Morris T and Sara A Richardson; widowed; children: Monette M, Natalie R & Tyrena E. **Educ:** Univ Cincinnati, BBA, 1970; Lexington Theol Sem, M Divinity, 1976. **Career:** Lexington-Fayette Co, exec dir, 1972-74; Phillips Mem CME Church, sr pastor, 1972-76; Urban League of St Louis, acct, 1977-82; Parrish Temple CME Church, sr pastor, 1976-79; Jamison Mem CME Church, sr pastor, 1979-82; CME Church, admin coord, 1982-86; Wesley CME Church, sr pastor, 1986-88; Cong Nat Black Churches, comptroller, 1988; Gen Bd Personnel Servs Inc, gen secy, currently, Zion Community Project Inc, pres, currently. **Orgs:** Life mem, Alpha Phi Alpha Frat 1968-; Lexington Fayette County, 1973-76; treas, KY Coun Churches, 1974-76; former treas, KY Conf Nat Asn Advan Colored People Chapts, 1975-76; Nat Asn Black Acct, 1981-91; treas, Beloit Br, Nat Asn Advan Colored People, 1986-; pres, Beloit Comm Ministers Fel, 1987-88. **Honors/Awds:** 110% Award Merit Alpha Phi Alpha Frat, 1976; GW Carver Award, Sigma Gamma Rho Sor, 1984. **Business Addr:** President, Zion Community Project Inc., PO Box 74, Memphis, TN 38101-0074, **Business Phone:** (901)261-3228.

DAVIS, VIOLA
Actor. **Personal:** Born Aug 11, 1965, Saint Matthews, SC; daughter of Dan and Mary. **Educ:** RI Col, BA, theater, 1988; Julliard Sch Performing Arts, NY, NY, certactg, 1994. **Career:** Plays: Broadway: King Hedley Two, Seven Guitars; NY Shakespeare Fest: Everybody's Ruby, Pericles, As You Like It; OffBroadway: God's Heart; TV Series: "City of Angels", 2000; "Judging Amy", 2000; "Traffic", 2000; "Providence", 2001; "The Guardian", 2001; "Third Watch", 2001; "Amy & Isabelle", 2001; "The Shrink Is In", 2001; "Kate & Leopold", 2001; "Law & Order: Criminal Intent", 2002; "The Division", 2002, "CSI: Crime Scene Investigation", 2002; "Far from Heaven", 2002; "Antwone Fisher", 2002; "Solaris", 2002; "Hack", 2003; "The Practice", 2003; "Century City", 2004; "Threshold", 2005; "Stone Cold", 2005; "Get Rich or Die Tryin'", 2005;"Jesse Stone: Night Passage", 2006; "Life Is Not a Fairytale: The Fantasia Barrino Story", 2006; "Jesse Stone: Sea Change", 2007; "Traveler", 2007; Brothers & Sisters, 2008; The Andromeda Strain, 2008; Law & Order: Special Victims Unit, 2008; Films: The Substance of Fire. 1996; Out of Sight, 1998; Traffic, 2000; The Shrink Is In, 2001; Kate & Leopold, 2001, Far from Heaven, 2002; Antwone Fisher, 2002; Solaris, 2002; Get Rich or Die Tryin, 2005; Syriana, 2005; World Trade Center. 2006; The Architect. 2006; Disturbia, 2007; Nights in Rodanthe, 2008, Doubt, 2008; Madea Goes to Jail, 2009; State of Play, 2009; Law Abiding Citizen, 2009. **Honors/Awds:** Tony Award, 2001; Los Angeles Drama Critics Circle Award, 2004. **Business Addr:** Actor, Agency Performing Arts, 9200 Sunset Blvd Suite 900, Los Angeles, CA 90069, **Business Phone:** (310)273-0744.*

DAVIS, WALTER PAUL
Public relations executive, basketball player. **Personal:** Born Sep 9, 1954, Pineville, NC; married Susan Hatter; children: Hillary Elyse & Jordan Elizabeth. **Educ:** Univ NC, attended 1977. **Career:** Basketball player (retired), public relations exec; Phoenix Suns, guard, 1977-88; Denver Nuggets, guard, 1989-91, 1992; Portland Trail Blazers, 1991; ESPN Classic, broadcaster; Wash Wizards, adv scout; Denver Nuggets, community ambassador, 1992-. **Honors/Awds:** Gold Medal, Olympic Games, Montreal, 1976; NBA Rookie of the Year, 1978; Pro Athlete of Year, Phoenix Press Box Asn, 1979; 5-time mem, Western Conf All-Star Team; 37th National Basketball Association All Star Team. *

DAVIS, WARREN B
Educator. **Personal:** Born Sep 16, 1947, Gary, IN; son of Richard and Armenta; children: Kwame Inhatep & Ida Aisha. **Educ:** Bowling Green State Univ, BA, 1970, MA, 1971; Defiance Col, BA, 1970; Appalachian State Univ, Develop Educ Specialists, 1984. **Career:** Mid-town Coffee Hse, Gary Youth Activities, prog dir, Trends Afro-Am Thought, teacher, 1969; USS Steel, laborer part time, 1967-69; Stud Develop Prog, coun, 1971-72; Bowling Green State Univ, assoc dir stud develop; Stud Develop Prog, coord coun serv, 1973; Defiance Col, instr, Afro-Am Hist II, 1973; Neighborhood Youth Corps, supvr; Coord Univ Toledo Tutorial Servs, Career Planning Ctr, supvr; Acad Support Serv, asst dir; Univ Toledo, dir stud develop, Stud Develop Ctr, sr dir stud develop, currently. **Orgs:** Am Pers & Guid Asn, 1971; Asn Counr Educ & Supvision 1971; Minority Educ Serv Asn, Ohio; Nat Asn Develop Educ; bd dir, Coalition Qual Integrated Educ. **Honors/Awds:** Recipient Service Award, Minority Studs; Service Award, Bowling Green State Univ, 1977; Administrator of the Year, Boise State Univ, 1983. **Business Addr:** Senior Director of Student Development, University of Toledo Scott Park Campus, Student Develop Services, Rm LR 212 2030 Univ Hall, Toledo, OH 43606, **Business Phone:** (419)530-6290.

DAVIS, WENDELL
Football player. **Personal:** Born Jun 27, 1973, Wichita, KS. **Educ:** Univ Okla, sociol. **Career:** Dallas Cowboys, wide receiver, 1996-99; Can Football League, Calgary Stampeders, 2001; XFL, San Francisco Demons, 2001; Arena Football League, San Jose Saber Cats, 2002-05; Grand Rapids Rampage, 2005; Ariz Rattlers, 2005. **Honors/Awds:** Arena Bowl title, 2002, 2004. *

DAVIS, DR. WILEY M.
School administrator, educator. **Personal:** Born Dec 4, 1927, Meadowview, VA; son of William Jackson and Pearl Fitzsimmons; married Mary Hargrove; children: Wiley Jr. **Educ:** Swift Jr Col, AA; St Augustines Col, BA; Springfield Col, MEd; Brigham Young Univ, DEd. **Career:** School administrator, educator (retired); Meadow view Elem Sch, teacher,1947; hist instr, 1952; Douglas High Sch, teacher, 1956; prin, 1960; St Augustine's Col, dean stud, 1960, admin asst to pres, 1970, vpres admin,1973; vpres studt affairs, 1974. **Orgs:** Secy, Elizabethton Prin Asn; treas & pres, Phi Beta Sigma; Raleigh, NC Community Action Coun; Govt Comn Employ Handicapped; Phi Delta Kappa HonSoc; NC Cemetery Comn; Hospice Wake County; deacon, Martin St Baptist Church; Garner Rd YMCA; bd dirs, Haven House; Arts Coun Wake County; Wake County Habitat Humanity; Col Found Inc; exec dir, St Augustine's Col Nat Alumni Asn. **Honors/Awds:** Honorary member, St Augustines Col Vet Club; Phi Beta Sigma Achievement Award; Henry St Settlement's Thomas Higgs Oper Athlete Education Award. **Military Serv:** AUS, 1951-53. *

DAVIS, DR. WILLIAM (WILLIAM C DAVIS)
Educator. **Educ:** Talladega Col, attended; Tuskegee Univ, attended; Univ Idaho, Phd. **Career:** Wash State Univ, Div Indust Res; Univ Tex Health Sci Ctr, pharmaceut dept; St Philip's Col, Natural Sci Dept, chmn & prof; Natural Sci Dept, prof, currently.

DAVIS, WILLIAM AUGUSTA, III (BILLY DAVIS)
Football player. **Personal:** Born Jul 6, 1972, El Paso, TX. **Educ:** Univ Pittsburgh. **Career:** Dallas Cowboys, wide receiver, 1995-98; Baltimore Ravens, wide receiver, 1999-2000. **Honors/Awds:** Two-time SuperBowl champion.

DAVIS, WILLIAM C. See DAVIS, DR. WILLIAM.

DAVIS, WILLIAM DELFORD
Executive, president (organization), chief executive officer. **Personal:** Born Jul 24, 1934, Lisbon, LA; son of Nodie; married

Ann; children: 2. **Educ:** Grambling Col, BS, 1956; Univ Chicago, MBA. **Career:** City of Cleveland, teacher; Cleveland Browns; Green Bay Packers; Joseph Schlitz Brewing co, sales & pub rels, 1964; Willie Davis Distributing Co, owner; All-Pro Broadcasting Inc, pres & ceo, 1976-. **Orgs:** Bd of dir, Jos Schlitz Brewing Co; charter mem & dir, Exec Savings & Loan Asn; color analyst, KNBC Football Telecast; pub rel & promotion work, Chrysler Corp; LA Co Spec Task Force; pres & dir, LA Urban League; dir &bd mem, W Adams Comm Hosp; chmn, Cent Div LA Explorers, BSA; Career Coun Group; So CA Businessmen's Assn; adv bd, Black Peace Officers Assn; Bicentennial Black Achievement Exhibit; Spl LA Co Study Comn; toured Vietnam for St Dept, 1966; bd dirs, Sara Lee Corp; bd dirs, KMart Corp; bd dirs, Dow Chem; trustee Marquette Univ; Emeritus Trustee, Univ Chicago. **Honors/Awds:** Selected, All-Pro teams; Byron "Whizzer" White Award; Hall of Fame, NAIA; Hall of Fame, Green Bay Packers, 1975; Man of Year, NAACP, 1978; Part of 6 Div Championships, 5 World Championships; Black Enterprise list of Top 100 Black Businesses; Pro NFL Hall of Fame, 1981. **Military Serv:** AUS, spec-5, 1956-58. **Business Addr:** President, Chief Executive Officer, All Pro Broadcasting Inc, 161 N La Brea Ave, Inglewood, CA 90301, **Business Phone:** (310)330-3123.*

DAVIS, WILLIAM E., SR.
Architect, city planner. **Personal:** Born Dec 1, 1930, Camden, SC; son of Clarence Davis Sr (deceased) and Margaret White (deceased); married Jacqueline Hawkins (divorced); children: William, Jr, Aia, Noma, Victor (deceased), Brian. **Educ:** Howard Univ, BA, 1967; Columbia Univ, Pratt Inst NY, Mass Inst Tech, grad studies; City & Regional Planning Pratt Inst, MS, 1976. **Career:** US Treas Dept, 1958-66; RC Architects & Assocs, des & off mgr, 1967-68; F&M Shaefer Corp Brooklyn, arch designer, 1968-69; Brownsville Adv Planning Agency, planner, 1969-70; Urban Consultants Inc, vpres, 1969-75; Volmer Assocs NY, arch & planner, 1971; City Boston Model City Admin, chief phys planning, 1972-75; Boston Model City, asst adminst, 1975; Onyx Consultants Inc, pres, 1975-76; Mass Dept Pub Works, Bur Transport & Planning Develop, regional planner, 1976; US Dept Housing & Urban Develop, loan specialist, 1977-80; US Dept of Transport Fed Trans Admin, comm planner, 1980-87, prog mgr 1987-; Manchester Cult Diversity Taskforce, pres. **Orgs:** Nat Tech Asn, 1968-75; Am Soc Planning Officials, 1969-77; founder, chair grad stud, Black Planners Network NY, 1970; Community Vol Asn Educ Adv C, 1971; prog mgr, SW Corridor Land Develop Coalition Proj Boston, 1971-75; Conf MA Planning Dirs, 1973-75; housing chmn, Roxbury Neighborhood Develop Coun, Boston, 1975; Dedham MA town mem Title I Educ Adv Coun, 1975-76; Greater Manchester Br Nat Asn Advan Colored People; vpres, Greater Manchester Black Scholar Found, 1987-; Martin Luther King Jr Speakers Bur, 1987-89; planning bd, Town of Auburn, NH, 1987-89; pres, Levi & Penelopia Kirkland Family Asn, 1990-94. **Honors/Awds:** Martin L King Fel 1969-71; Commendation Urban Planning & Develop, Boston; Volpe Nat Transport Ctr, Dirs Award for EEO; Adminir Award, Am Turkish Friendship Asn, 1994; vpres, Gore Award, Superior Work Toward Reinventing Govt, 1994. **Military Serv:** AUS, 1955-57. *

DAVIS, WILLIAM HAYES, SR.
School administrator. **Personal:** Born Jun 13, 1947, Richmond, VA; married Ivy P West; children: William Jr. **Educ:** Virginia State Univ, BA, 1970; Virginia Commonwealth Univ, MEd, 1983. **Career:** Gooehland Pub Schs, teacher, 1972-73; Commonwealth Psychiatric Ctr, ed therapist, 1974-79; St Joseph's Villa, ed therapist, 1979-81; Garfield Childs Memorial Fund, prog dir, 1983-85; VA State Univ, spec educ Col instr, 1986-; Richmond Pub Schs, clinical teacher; Virginia pub schs, educ consult. **Orgs:** NAACP, 1980-; guide right prog dir, 1980-84, asst keeper records, 1984-85, Kappa Alpha Psi Inc Rich Alumni; co owner Assessment Then Remediation 1986-; Bd Visitors, Norfolk State Univ. **Honors/Awds:** Outstanding Leadership Guide, Right Kappa Alpha Psi Rich Alumni, 1982; Service to the Fraternity Achievement Award, Kappa Alpha Psi Rich Alumni, 1983; Institute for Eduction Leadership Award, Rich Pub Schs, 1984-85. **Military Serv:** ANG, sp4, 1970-76; Certificate Training Achievement, Outstanding Performance Duty, 1970.

DAVIS, DR. WILLIAM L.
Association executive. **Personal:** Born Dec 30, 1933, Hopewell, VA; married Glenice Claiborne; children: Kevin & Todd. **Educ:** Morgan State Col, AB, 1955; Howard Univ, JD, 1961. **Career:** US Dept Navy, law clerk gen coun, 1960; US Dept Justice DC, trial atty, 1961-65; US Atty, asst, 1965-68; NLSP, desp dir, 1968-69; Neighborhood Legal Serv Prog Inc & Wash, acting exec dir, 1969-70; United Planning Orgn, exec dir; UPO Wash DC, gen coun, 1970-73; Howard Univ, prof law, 1972. **Orgs:** Washington Bar Asn; Howard Law Sch Alumni Asn; mem bd dir, Independence Serv Corp; mem bd dir, Nat Children's Island Inc; mem Bd dir, UPO Enterprises Inc; mem bd dir, Ed chief, UPO Comn Develop Corp; Howard Law Journal, 1960-61; Class Pres, 1960. **Honors/ Awds:** Bureau of National Affairs Award; Bancroft-whitney Co & Lawyer's Cooperative Publishing Co Award.

DAVIS, WILLIAM R.
Educator. **Personal:** Born Apr 28, 1921, Cincinnati, OH; son of William and Florence; married Gladys Hamilton; children: William R Jr. **Educ:** Univ Cincinnati, BS, 1950; Ohio State Univ, MA, 1951; Northeastern IllUniv, MA, 1969; Loyola Univ. **Career:** Cincinnati Pub Recreation Comn, 1947-54; Chicago Pub Schs, from teacher toasst prin; Oldtown Chicago Boys Club, athletic dir & prog dir, 1954-68;Loyola Univ Chicago, dir Project Upward Bound, instr, curric & instr,1969-. **Orgs:** Nat Upward Bound Steering Comt, 1970-72; pres, Coun Col Attend, 1970-74;chmn, Chicago Nat Col Fair (NACAC), 1973-75 & 1978-80; mem bd dir, Ill AsnCol Admis Coun, 1974-76; pres, Ill Asn Non-White Concerns Pers & Guidance,1977-78; pres, Ill Asn Col Admis Counr, 1981-82; Am Sch Health Asn; Am AsnUniv Profs; Nat Asn Higher Edn; Nat Asn Col Admis Counr; Phi EpsilonKappa; Phi Delta Kappa; Asn Supv & Curric Develop; Am Asn Coun & Develop(APGA); midwest reg rep Asn Non-White Concerns Coun & Develop; Ill StateBd Educ Adv Bd Pupil Personnel Serv. **Honors/ Awds:** Presidential Award, Mid-Am Asn Educ Opportunity Prog Personnel, 1979;Presidential Award, Ill Asn Col Admis Counrs, 1982; Presidential Citation,Asn Multicultural Coun & Develop, 1984; Human Relations Award, Nat Asn ColAdmis Counrs, 1984; Hon Degree Doctor of Humanities, Monrovia Col MonroviaLiberia W Africa 1986. **Military Serv:** AUS, corpl, 1942-46; USAR, first Lt, 1950-64.

DAVIS, WILLIAM R.
Physician. **Personal:** Born Oct 4, 1934, Newport News, VA; son of Mollie Davis Clarke; married Brenda Lightsay Davis; children: William Jr, Cardis, Tonia Kelly, Frank, Joye. **Educ:** Hampton Inst, BS, 1956; Med Col Va, MD, 1964. **Career:** Fitzsimons Hosp, Denver, intern; Brooke Army Med Ctr, San Antonio, resident; Dept Navy, res chemist, 1956-60; DeWitt Army Hosp, asst chief pediats, 1967-68; Howard Univ Col Med, asst clin prof, pediat, 1968-69; Baltimore, pvt prac Pediats, 1969; Johns Hopkins Med Sch, instr pediat, 1972; Univ Southern Calif, res fel, allergy immunol, 1985; Loma Linda Univ Sch Med, asst prof; Vet Admin Hosp, chief, allergy & immunol sect. **Orgs:** Omega Psi Phi Frat; Chi Delta Mu Frat; hon, Alumnus Johns Hopkins Univ; Beta Kappa Chi; hon, Scienlike Soc; dipl, Nat Bd Med Examiners; diplomate, Am Bd Pediats; fel, Am Acad Pediats, Nat Med Asn; fel, Am Allergy & Immunol; fel, Am Asn Certified Allergists. **Honors/Awds:** Award for Meritorius Service; Provid Comp Health Ctr, 1971. **Military Serv:** AUS, maj, 1964-72. **Home Addr:** 2149 S Indian Creek Rd, Diamond Bar, CA 91765. *

DAVIS, WILLIAM W
Computer executive, chairperson. **Educ:** Southern Univ, BS, MBA; Dartmouth Col & Univ Miami, exec mgt prog. **Career:** Pulsar Data Syst Inc, founder, chief exec officer, 1983-99, pres, chief operating officer, 1999-2000; Liberty Lending, co-founder, chief finance officer; Dupont, staff; Chevron, staff; Occidental Petrol Corp, staff; Spectrum Solutions Group Inc, prin & chmn, currently. **Business Addr:** Chairman, Principal, Spectrum Solutions Group Inc, 1921 Gallows Rd Suite 360, Vienna, VA 22182, **Business Phone:** (703)752-3261.

DAVIS, DR. WILLIE (BABAKUBWA KWEKU)
Educator, museum director. **Personal:** Born Oct 30, 1945, Memphis, TN; son of Willie and Mary Davis; divorced; children: Willie Dell Davis IV, Wendolyn Delores Davis, Ayana Kai Davis, LarrySmith, Lori Smith, Jackie Smith (Cannon), Kathy Smith, Eric Smith & DebraRoper. **Educ:** Grand Valley State Univ, BS, 1971; Western Mich Univ, MA, 1974; Mich State Univ, PhD, 1982. **Career:** City Grand Rapids, maintenance worker, 1965-71; Grand Rapids Sch Dist, social studies teacher, 1971-76; Lansing Sch Dist Urban League, educ consult, 1976-80; Mich Dept Community Health, pub health consult, 1980-97;Walker French Acad High Sch, teacher, 1998-2002; Davenport Univ, adj prof, 1994-; Lansing Community Col, adj prof, 1981-; All Around African World Mus, dir, 2000-; Dianex Ltd, pres & chief exec officer, currently. **Orgs:** Pres, Black Asn State Employment, 1980-; Nat Asn Advan Colored People, Urban League, 1990-; pres, Nat Afr Am Historical Soc, 1992-; secy, EventLansing Regional Sister Cities Comm, 1995-; Asn Study Classical African Civilizations, 1995-; chair health task force, Nat Asn Black Social Workers, 1995-; bd mem & secy, El Hajj Malik El Shabazz Acad, 1995-; pres, Nat Black United Front, Lansing chapter, 1999-; Black Data Processing Asn; co-chair, Ghana Comt, Lansing Regional Sister City Comn; founder, Greater Lansing Minority Bus Asn; cofounded, Potter & Walsh Neighborhood Asn; past-pres, Neighborhood Youth & Parent Partnership Prog. **Honors/Awds:** Community Service Award, Negro Bus & Prof Women, 1992; Monty Award, Parent Support Network, 1993; Award of Appreciation, Mich St Univ, 1993; Certificate of Appreciation, Howard Univ, 2000. **Business Addr:** Director, All Around African World Museum & Resource Center, 1134-36 Shepard, Lansing, MI 48912, **Business Phone:** (517)484-7480.

DAVIS, WILLIE A.
Educator, athletic coach. **Personal:** Born Dec 10, 1948, Marks, MS; married Barbara M Landry. **Educ:** Coahoma Jr Col, AA; Jackson State Univ, BA, MS, 1967; Univ MI, MA, 1974, MS, 1970. **Career:** Neighborhood Youth Core, Jackson MS, summer coun, 1970; Jackson Pub Schs, Mar-Jun teacher, 1970; Albion Pub Schs, Albion MI, teacher, coach Football & Track, summers, 1973-74. **Orgs:** Pres, NAACP Albion Branch; Albion Educ Asn; Educ Asn; Twin Athletic Asn; High Sch Coaches Asn; Albion United Fund Bd; mem & pres, Albion NAACP; US Jaycees; Big Brothers Am; SS Supt Teacher Behtl Bapt Ch; Phi Beta Sigma Frat. **Honors/Awds:** Honor student Quitman County High Sch, 1961-65; honor student Coahma Jr Col, 1965-67; honor student Jackson State Univ, 1967-70; 1974 Nominee Educator of the Year; Albion Distinguished Serv Award nominee, 1974; Albions Distinguished Serv Award, 1975. **Business Addr:** Football Coach, Albion Sr HS, 225 Watson St, Albion, MI 49224.

DAVIS, WILLIE CLARK
Football player. **Personal:** Born Oct 10, 1967, Little Rock, AR; married Veronica; children: Tiana, Jeremy & William. **Educ:** Cent Ark. **Career:** Kansas City Chiefs, wide receiver, 1991-95; Houston Oilers, wide receiver,1996; Tenn Oilers, wide receiver, 1997-98, scout, chiefs club, currently. **Honors/Awds:** Winning touchdown, Mile High Stadium, Chiefs' victory Denver, 1994. *

DAVIS, REV. WILLIE FLOYD, JR.
Clergy. **Personal:** Born Sep 16, 1963, Bainbridge, GA; son of Willie Sr and Mary Beard; married Michelle R, Aug 24, 1985; children: Leslie Ann & Ashley LaShae. **Educ:** Monroe Comm Col, attended 1983; State Univ New York, Brockport, BA, 1986; Rochester Real Estate Training Ctr, cert real estate sales, 1986; Children's Aid Soc, Nat Training Inst, cert human & teen sexuality training, 1991; New York State AIDS Inst, cert HIV/AIDS counsel, 1992; Monroe City Health, cert HIV/AIDS Prev Educ, 1993; Univ NC, cert continuing educ, 1993; Univ Rochester, cert crisis mgt resp, 1994; John Hopkins Univ, cert Formative Res, 1992. **Career:** Mt Olive Baptist Church, assoc minister, minister music, 1985-86; Pentecostal Memorial Baptist Church, assoc minister, minister music, 1986-91; Action Better COT, proj coordr, case mgr, housing coordr, 1989-92; Emmanuel Missionary Baptist Church, pastoral asst, assoc minister, minister music, dir christian educ, 1991-; Puerto Rican Youth Develop & Resource Ctr, dir prog opers, sr counr, 1992-94; Catholic Family Ctr, Catholic youth orgn, prog dir, resource coordr, 1994-95; Baden St Settlement Rochester, Inc, assoc exec dir, 1995-; Church Covenant United Church Christ, sr pastor, teacher, 1996-. **Orgs:** Exec dir, Monroe Coun Teen Pregnancy, 1989-; bd dirs, Rochester Area Task Force AIDS, 1992-; sch health adv bd, John Marshall High Sch, 1994-; CHHA prof adv bd, Monroe City Health Dept, 1995-; bd dir, Zion Hill Found, 1995-; bd dirs, CHANGE Collaborative, 1996-; bd dirs, United Way Greater Rochester, 1996-; pres, chair, Black Leadership Comn AIDS, 1996-; Youth Services Qual Coun, 1996; adv bd, Catholic Family Ctr, 1997; New York State Gov Task Force, Out-of-Wedlock Births & Poverty, 1997-; Religious & Public Values Task Force, 1998-; bd dir, Action Better COT, 1998; Nat Campaign Prevent Teen Pregnancy. **Business Addr:** Executive Director, Monroe Council on Teen Pregnancy, 585 Joseph Ave, Rochester, NY 14621, **Business Phone:** (716)325-8123.

DAVIS, WILLIE J.
Lawyer, businessperson. **Personal:** Born Sep 29, 1935, Fort Valley, GA; married Carolyn Scoggins; children: Kristen & Roland. **Educ:** Morehouse Col, BA, 1956; New England Sch Law, JD, 1963. **Career:** Mass Comn Against Discrimination, field rep, 1963; Commonwealth Mass, asst atty gen, 1964-69; Dist Mass, asst US atty, 1969-71, US magistrate, 1971-76; pvt pract atty; Davis Robinson & White LLP, atty & sr partner,currently; bd mem, Mass Bay Transp Authority, currently; chmn bd trustees, Morehouse Col, currently. **Orgs:** Am Bar Asn; Am Judicature Soc; Alpha Phi Alpha; Sigma Phi Fraternity; Nat Asn Guardsmen; pres emer, Morehouse Col Nat Alumni Asn; vice chmn & chmn,Morehouse Col Bd Trustees; bd mem, Comt Pub Coun Servs, Commonwealth Mass; chmn, Comt Pub Coun Servs, Commonwealth Mass. **Honors/Awds:** Ten Outstanding Young Men Award, Boston Jr C C, 1971; Hon Deg JD, New England Sch Law, 1972; Hon Deg DSc, Lowell Tech Inst, 1973; Southern Inter collegiate Athletic Conference Hall of Fame, 1998; Presidential Award of Distinction, Morehouse Col, 1999; Bennie Trailblazer Award, Morehouse Col, 2003. **Military Serv:** AUS, sp4, 1958-60. **Home Addr:** 61 Westbourne Rd, Newton Center, MA 02459-1617, **Home Phone:** (617)332-1571. **Business Addr:** Attorney, Davis Robinson & White LLP, 1 Faneuil Hall Mkt Pl 3rd Fl S Mkt Bldg, Boston, MA 02109-1646, **Business Phone:** (617)723-7339.*

DAVIS, WILLIS H.
School administrator. **Personal:** Born Jun 30, 1937, Greer, SC. **Educ:** DePauw Univ, Greencastle, IN, BA, 1959; Dayton Art Inst, 1965; Miami Univ, Oxford, OH, MEd, 1967; Grad Study, Ind State Univ, 1976. **Career:** DePauw Univ, asst prof art, 1971-76; Coord Black Studies, 1971; Wright State Univ, Dayton, OH, art instr, 1969-71; ESEA Title & III Living Arts Ctr, Dayton, OH, art dir, 1967-71; Dayton Ohio Pub Schs, teacher, 1957-67; Black Hist & Cultural Workshops, German Town, OH, vis artist & lectr series, 1968; Bergamo Ctr, 1968-69, 70; VISTA Prog; Auburn Univ, AL, 1969; Miami Univ, assist dean grad sch, assoc prof art, 1976-78; Paul Robeson Cult & Perf Arts Ctr, Dir, 1978-84; Cent State Univ, chmn art dept, 1978; Nat Conf Artists, chmn, currently. **Orgs:** Ohio Sec & Sr High Prins Assn Conf, Cleveland, 1970; Western Arts Asn, NAEA, Milwaukee, 1970; Black Studies Inst, Miami Univ, 1970; Va State Univ, Norfolk, 1970; Univ Cincinnati, Blue Ash Raymond Walters Br, 1972; HEW Inst Afro-Am Studies, Earlham Col, Richmond, 1972; Living Arts Prog, Dayton, 1972;

Archdiocese Cincinnati Dayton Area Cath Schs, 1972; Purdue Univ, Lafayette, IN, 1972; Univ Mass, 1972; Gov State Univ Nat & Endowment Arts Prog, 1972; Ind Pub Schs, Shortrigde High Sch, Ind Arts Coun, 1972; Lafayette Community Ctr, Summer Arts Prog, Ind Arts Coun, 1972; Montgomery County Regional Arts & Cultural Dist, Trustee, 1990-; Asn Am Cultures, SanAntonio, TX, 1994; Ctr Study & Develop Effective Pedag African-Am Learner, Tex Southern Univ, Houston, TX, 1994; African-Am Art Collectors Soc, Dayton Art Inst, 1995. **Honors/Awds:** Honourable Doctorate of Fine Arts, Depauw Univ, 1997; Ohio Art Educator of the Year, Ohio Art Educ Asn, 1996; Opus Award, 1996; Walk of Fame Award, Dayton, OH, 1996. **Special Achievements:** Publications: Communications LaRevue Moderne Mag article Paris, 1967; Mural Panorama on Black Hist Dayton Daily Newspaper, 1968; Cover Designfor Educ Booklet on Black Hist Geo A Pflaum Pub, 1968; Calendar Illus for Nat Office for Black Cath, Washington, DC, 1972; represented in book"Black Artists on Art", 1972; Black Artist Documentary "Color It Black"Channel 13 WLWI-TV Indianapolis, 1972. Ceremony & Ritual: The Art pf Bing-Davis Retrospective Exhibit, Dayton, OH, 1996; Work shown in group juried competitive exhibitions one-man shows priv collections permanent museum collections. *

DAVIS ANTHONY, VERNICE
Health services administrator. **Personal:** Born Jan 10, 1945; daughter of Leonard Chambers and Vernice Bradford Chambers; married Eddie Anthony (died 1993); children: Dana, Dara & Todd. **Educ:** Wayne State Univ, BS, 1970; Univ Mich, Ann Arbor, MPH, 1976. **Career:** City Detroit, serv, chief, pub health nursing, field prog, 1971-79; State Mich, Develop & Eval, local health serv admn, community health field, 1979-83; Wayne Co, co health officer chief, off policy, 1983-91; State Mich, dir Mich dept pub health, 1991-95; St John Health Syst, sr vpres, Corp Affairs, 1995; Western Mich Univ, vice chairperson; Greater Detroit Area Health Coun, pres & chief exec officer, currently. **Orgs:** Chair bd trustees, Western Mich Univ; Cyberstate Organizational Bd; Mich Res Coun; Mich Neighborhood Partnership; exec bd, Voices Detroit; S E Mich Health Improv Coun. **Honors/Awds:** Distinguished Alumni Award, Wayne St Univ; Distinguished Alumni Award, Univ Mich Sch Pub Health; Distinguished Service Award, Mich Pub Health Asn; Women of Wayne Headliner Award; Girls Role Model Award; Mich Asn Bus & Prof Women Award; Michigan Womens Found Humanitarian Award; Anti Defamation League Humanitarian Award. **Special Achievements:** Crains Detroit Bus Most Influential Women & Most Influential Blacks Top 100. **Business Addr:** President, Chief Executive Officer, Greater Detroit Area Health Council, Inc, 333 W Fort St Suite 1230, Detroit, MI 48226.

DAVIS-CARTER, HOLLY
Entrepreneur. **Career:** Agency W Entertainment, Releve Entertainment, owner & prin agt, 2004-. **Business Addr:** Owner, Principal Agent, Agency West Entertainment, Releve Entertainment, 6255 W Sunset Blvd Suite 923, Los Angeles, CA 90028, **Business Phone:** (323)468-9470.*

DAVIS-HALEY, DR. RACHEL T
College teacher, educator. **Educ:** Loyola Univ, BS, educ, 1989; Xavier Univ, MS, curric & instr, 1993; Univ Md, Col Park, PhD, curric & instr, 1998. **Career:** Univ GA, Col Educ, asst prof, prof; Univ New Orleans, Col Educ & human Develop, asst prof, currently. **Business Phone:** (504)280-5558.

DAVIS-HOWARD, VALERIE V.
Executive, consultant. **Educ:** Spelman Col, Atlanta, econ; Univ IA, MBA. **Career:** The Chase Manhattan Bank, asst vpres org develop; State Mich, training consult; Kaleel Jamison Consult Group Inc, 1998, mgr, vpres, sr consult, 2000-. **Orgs:** Am Soc Training & Develop; Nat Black MBA Asn; Org Develop Network. **Honors/Awds:** Guard, Am Soc Training & Develop, 2002. **Business Addr:** Senior Consultant, Kaleel Jamison Consult Group Inc, 279 River St Suite 401, Troy, NY 12180, **Business Phone:** (518)271-7000.*

DAVIS-MCFARLAND, DR. E. ELISE
College administrator. **Personal:** Born Oct 18, 1946, Greensboro, NC; married Arthur C; children: Kira Jihan & William Joseph. **Educ:** Univ NC, BA, 1968; Univ Va, MEd, 1971; Univ Wis, european study prog, 1971; Harvard Univ, vis scholars prog, 1975; Univ Pittsburgh, PhD, 1976. **Career:** Va State Univ, Dept Eng, instr, 1971-73; Univ Pittsburgh, Dept Psychol, res asst, 1973-76; Univ Houston, Dept Speech Pathol, asst prof, 1976-79; Col Charleston, Univ Affiliated Facilities Prog, asst dir, 1978-79; Charleston Higher Educ Consortium, Educ Opportunity Ctr, dir, 1979-82; Charleston Trident Chamber Com, staff vpres, 1982-86; Citadel, dir in stres, 1985-93; Med Univ SC, assoc prof & prog dir, 1993-2002; Trident TechCol, vpres stud serv, 2002-. **Orgs:** SC Health & Human Serv Finance Comn, 1984-; secy, SC Asn Elected &Appointed Women Officials, 1984-; bd mem, Nat Rural Develop Finance Corp, 1985-; Am Speech-Lang Hearing Asn; Nat Asn Stud Personnel Admin; Am Col Personnel Asn; Nat Black Asn Speech Lang & Hearing; fel Am Speech Lang & Hearing Asn. **Honors/Awds:** Outstanding Young Women of America, 1982-83; Hall of Fame, Nat Black Asn Speech Lang & Hearing; Distinguished Educator Award, Prince Hall Masons; Tribute to Women in Industry Honoree, YWCA; Community Service Award, Nat Coun Negro Women; Distinguished Teaching Award, Med Univ SC; Teaching Excellence Award, MUSC Health Sci Found. **Special Achievements:** First Black Vice President of Chamber of Commerce in South Carolina, 1982. **Home Addr:** 204 Grove St, Charleston, SC 29403. **Business Addr:** Vice President for Student Services, Trident Technical College, PO Box 118067, Charleston, SC 29423-8067, **Business Phone:** (843)574-6010.

DAVISON, EDWARD L.
Lawyer. **Personal:** Born May 10, 1943, Akron, OH; son of Edward Davison (deceased) and Marie Mapp Gordon; married Willa Rebecca Branham; children: Rebecca Marie, Christopher Larry. **Educ:** Univ Akron, Assoc Degree, 1967, BS, Natural Sci, 1973, JD, 1977. **Career:** Westinghouse R & D, lab technician, 1963-64; Gen Tire R & D, lab technician, 1964-67; Babcock & Wilcox, perf engineer, 1967-76; Babcock & Wilcox CRD, cont mgr, 1976-89, sr cont mgr, 1989-. **Orgs:** Davison & Greene; treasurer, pres, United Coun Corvette Clubs, 1983-91; pres, treasurer, planning & allocation Summit County United Way, 1984-89. **Honors/Awds:** Award of Merit, Summit County United Way, 1980; Outstanding Achievement, Summit County Democratic Party, 1978; Outstanding Achievement, United Coun Corvette Clubs, 1986. **Business Addr:** Attorney, 1562 Beeson St, Alliance, OH 44601, **Business Phone:** (330)829-7617.*

DAVISON, JAMES, JR.
Physician, psychologist. **Educ:** PhD. **Career:** Calif State Prison syst, criminal justice syst; Pvt Pract, psychologist, currently. **Special Achievements:** Author, Prisoners of Our Past. **Business Addr:** Psychologist, 3075 Fulton Ave Suite 2, Sacramento, CA 95821-4442.

DAVIS STEED, STACEY D.
President (Organization). **Educ:** Georgetown Univ, AB, econ; Univ Mich, MBA. **Career:** Merrill Lynch, pub finance div, invest banker; McClendon Counts, Atlanta, GA, vpres; Fanny Mae Found, dir regional pub affairs Southeastern region, 1992-95, vpres Housing & Community Develop Southeastern region, 1995-99, pres & chief exec officer, 1999-07, sr vpres, currently. **Business Addr:** Senior Vice President, Fanny Mae Foundation, 3900 Wisconsin Ave NW, Washington, DC 20016-2892, **Business Phone:** (202)752-7000.*

DAVIS-WRIGHTSIL, CLARISSA
Basketball player. **Personal:** Born Jun 4, 1967; married Jerald Wrightsil. **Educ:** Univ Tex, 1998. **Career:** Basketball player(retired); Italy, 1990- 91; Japan, 1992- 93; Turkey, 199496; New Eng Blizzard, forward, 1996; Long Beach Stingrays, 1997-98; San Jose Lasers, 1998, Fenerbahce, Turkey, 1998- 99; WNBA, San Antonio Spurs, dir devel, 1999-2002, WNBA, San Antonio Silver Stars, chief operating officer, 2002-06; Univ Tex Longhorns, asst coach, 2006-07; Rutgers Univ, asst coach, 2008-. **Orgs:** Spurs Found; pres & founder & ceo, Team xpress Found. **Honors/Awds:** Naismith Player of the Year, 1987, 1989; Womens Basketball Hall of Fame, 2006; Kodak All-American. **Business Phone:** (512)619-0080.

DAVY, DR. FREDDYE TURNER
Educator. **Personal:** Born Apr 8, 1933, Roston, AR; daughter of Frederick C and Ercerene Lea Turner; married Earl L Davy (deceased), Apr 26, 1953 (deceased); children: Earl L Jr, Sue Davy Witherspoon & Frederick C. **Educ:** Philander Smith Col, BA, 1953; Univ Md, MA, 1965; Vanderbilt Univ, EdD, 1985. **Career:** Negro Boys Indust Sch, teacher, 1953-54; Pulaski County Pub Sch, teacher, 1954-56; Little Rock, AR, Pub Schs, teacher, 1956-60; DC Pub Schs, teacher, 1960-63; Montgomery County Pub Schs, teacher, 1963-87; Benedict Col, prof, dir, elem educ, 1987-94; Hampton Univ, Hons Col, dir, 1994-. **Orgs:** Nat Alliance Black Sch Educr, Comn Instrnl Support, chair, bd dirs, 1981-83, life mem; pres, Nat Asn African Am Hons Prog, 1996; asst secy, Downing Gross Cult Arts Found, 1997-; Nat Asn Univ Women, 1998-; Aka Sorority; elder, Carver Presbyterian Church; Southern Regional Hons Coun; trustee, Philander Smith Col Bd Trustees; exec dir, Nat WEB Bois Hon Soc, 2001-. **Honors/Awds:** Outstanding Teacher, Montgomery County Pub Sch, 1987; Distinguished Professor, Benedict Col, 1990; Governor's Distinguished Professor, SC, 1990; Outstanding Service, Newport News Pub Sch, 1998; Endowed Univ prof, 2000. **Home Addr:** 7501 River Rd Suite 10G, Newport News, VA 23607, **Home Phone:** (757)245-2114. **Business Addr:** Director, Hampton University, Honors College, WEB DuBois Hall, PO Box 6174, Hampton, VA 23668, **Business Phone:** (757)727-5076.

DAVY, GLORIA (GLORIA DAVY PENNINGSFELD)
Opera singer, educator. **Personal:** Born Mar 29, 1937, Brooklyn, NY; daughter of George Timson and Lucy Crick; divorced; children: Jean-Marc Penningsfeld. **Educ:** Juilliard Sch Music, BS, 1954. **Career:** Educator (retired), opera singer; Little Orch Soc Town Hall, debut, 1954; Nice Opera, 1957; Metropolitan Opera, 1958-62; Vienna State Opera, 1959; Convent Garden Opera Co, 1961; La Scala Milan, guest performer; San Carlo; Naples; Teatro Communale, Bologna; Teatro Massimo, Palermo; Teatre Reggio, Parma; Deutsche Opera, Berlin, guest contract, 1961-69; Indiana Univ Sch Music, prof, 2001; Concerts: AME Capriccio, R Straus, Juilliard, 1954; New York Premiere Anna Bolena, Donizetti, 1957; Am Premiere Daphne, Strauss, 1960; Homage to Gershwin conductor Giorgio Gaslini Orchestra, 1985-87. **Orgs:** Hon mem, Nat Soc Arts & Letters. **Honors/Awds:** Marian Anderson Award, 1953; Marian Anderson Special Award, 1954; Music Education League Award, New York, 1954; Legacy Award, Nat Opera Asn, 1999. **Special Achievements:** First black artist to sing in Aida at the New York Metropolitan Opera on February 1958; Created integral work Karl Heinz Stockhausen's "Momente," Beethoven Hall, Bonn, 1972; first performances Festival Hall London/ Brussells Opera/Theatre De La Ville Paris/Beethoven Halle-Bonn, 1973; created "Vortrag Uber Hu" Stockhausen Donauschingen Festival, 1974. *

DAWES, DOMINIQUE MARGAUX
Gymnast, business owner. **Personal:** Born Nov 20, 1976, Silver Spring, MD; daughter of Don Arnold and Loretta Florence. **Educ:** Stanford Univ; Univ Md. **Career:** Gymnast; gymnastics TV commentator; Hill's Gymnastics, instr; Dominique Dawes LLC, pres, currently. **Orgs:** Hill's Gymnastics, elite, 1988-93; pres, Women's Sports Fedn. **Honors/Awds:** Most Outstanding, Hill's Gym, 1990-92; Bronze Medal Gymnastics, Olympic Games, 1992; World Gymnastics Championships Competition, Birmingham, Eng, Silver Medals (2), 1993; Silver Medalist, team competition, World Championship, 1994; Henry P Iba Citizen Award, 1995; Bronze Medalist, Atlanta Olympics, 1996; USA Gymnastics Hall of Fame, 1998; Women of Distinction Award, AAUW, 2004; Gymnastics Hall of Fame Induction, 2005. **Special Achievements:** First African American on US National gymnastics team, 1988, and on US Olympic gymnastics team, 1992; First African American to win individual Olympic medal in gymnastics, 1996. **Business Addr:** President, Dominique Dawes LLC, 5284 Randolph Rd, PO Box 212, Rockville, MD 20852, **Business Phone:** (301)404-8010.

DAWKINS, BRIAN PATRICK
Football player. **Personal:** Born Oct 13, 1973, Jacksonville, FL; married Connie; children: Brian Jr. **Educ:** Clemson. **Career:** Philadelphia Eagles, defensive back, 1996-2008; Denver Broncos, 2009-. **Honors/Awds:** NFC Defensive Player of the Month award, 2006; Seven Times Pro Bowler Selection, 1999, 2001, 2002, 2004, 2005, 2006, 2008; Five Times First Team All Pro Selection, 1999, 2001, 2002, 2004, 2006; Philadelphia Eagles 75th Anniversary Team. **Business Addr:** Professional Football Player, Philadelphia Eagles, Nova Care Complex, 1 Novacare Way, Philadelphia, PA 19145-5996, **Business Phone:** (215)463-2500.*

DAWKINS, DARRYL
Basketball player, basketball coach. **Personal:** Born Jan 11, 1957, Orlando, FL; married Kelly Barnes (deceased). **Career:** Basketball player (retired), basketball coach: Philadelphia 76'ers, 1976-82; NJ Nets, 1983-87; Utah Jazz, 1988; Detroit Pistons, 1988-89; Phillips Milan, Italy; Harlem Globetrotters; Winnipeg Cyclone, head coach; American Basketball Association, head coach; PA Valley Dawgs, coach, Head coach, Lehigh Carbon Community Col, 2009-. **Special Achievements:** Co-author, Chocolate Thunder: The Uncensored Life & Times of the NBA's Original Showman, 2003; Author, Chocolate Thunder: The In-Your-Face, All-Over-The-Place, Death-Defyin, Mesmerizin, Slam-Jam Adventures of Double-D. *

DAWKINS, JOHNNY EARL, JR.
Basketball player. **Personal:** Born Sep 28, 1963, Washington, DC; married Tracy; children: Aubrey, Gillian, Blair & Sean. **Educ:** Duke Univ, BA, polit sci, 1986. **Career:** Basketball player (retired), basketball coach; San Antonio Spurs, guard, 1986-89; Philadelphia 76ers, guard, 1989-94; Detroit Pistons, guard, 1994-95; Duke Univ, mens basketball, asst coach, 1998-99, assoc head-coach, 2000-08, player personnel dir, 2006-08; Duke games, Capitol Sports Network, radio color anal; Stanford Cardinal, head coach, 2008-. **Honors/Awds:** MVP ACC Tournament, 1986; Nat Player of the Year, Naismith Col, 1986; Duke Sports Hall of Fame, 1996; CAA East Regional MVP, 1986; Consensus All-American, 1985 & 1986; Freshman All-American, 1983; Duke Team MVP, 1983, 1984, 1985 & 1986. **Business Addr:** Head Coach, Stanford Cardinal, Stanford University, Department of Athletics, Arrillaga Family Sports Ctr, 641 East Campus Dr, Stanford, CA 94305-6150, **Business Phone:** (650)723-4591.

DAWKINS, MICHAEL JAMES
Engineer. **Personal:** Born Nov 11, 1953, Chicago, IL; son of Willie James and Willie Mae; married Cornelia A Long, May 26, 1985; children: Erika Michelle & Michael James Jr. **Educ:** Univ Ill, Chicago, BS, 1978, MS, 1979. **Career:** Dow Chem, res engr, 1979-83; sr res engr, 1983-86, project leader, 1986-87; res leader, 1987-90, res assoc, 1990-. **Orgs:** AIChE, 1976-; adv bd, Soc Black Engrs LSU, 1982-; chmn, LSU SBE Adv Bd, 1982-84; minority liason for Georgia Tech & LSU/Dow, 1983-; contact, Educ Enhancement/Dow, 1984-86; NOBCCHE. **Honors/Awds:** EIT Certification La, 1985. **Military Serv:** AUS, spl/5 3 yrs. **Business Addr:** Research Associate, Dow Chemical Company, Bldg 2513, PO Box 150, Plaquemine, LA 70765, **Business Phone:** (504)389-6507.

DAWKINS, MILLER J.
City commissioner, educator. **Personal:** Born Mar 10, 1925, Ocala, FL; son of Miller James Sr and Gertrude Ulmer; married

Nancy Sidney; children: Myron. **Educ:** Fla A&M Univ, 1955; Fla Mem Col, BS, soc sci, 1971; Univ N Colo, MA, soc sci, 1974. **Career:** Miami-Dade Comm Col, chair person contin ed dept, 1977-78; Dade Cty Correctional Ctrs, dir ed prog, 1977-82; Miami-Dade Community Col, prof/admin; City Miami, city comnr, 1981-97. **Orgs:** Supvr, Aircraft Serv Inc, 1966-68; voc counr, Youth Ind Inc, 1966-68; admin officer, Dade Cty Model City's Prog, 1969-71; Omega Psi Phi; AARP. **Honors/Awds:** Received many awards from clubs, Bus & schs. **Military Serv:** AUS, Pvt, 1950-52. **Home Addr:** 1385 NW 50 St, Miami, FL 33142, **Home Phone:** (305)633-1163.

DAWKINS, SEAN RUSSELL
Football player, real estate agent. **Personal:** Born Feb 3, 1971, Red Bank, NJ. **Educ:** Univ Calif. **Career:** Football player (retired); Indianapolis Colts, wide receiver, 1993-97; New Orleans Saints, 1998-99; Seattle Sea hawks, 1999-00; Jacksonville Jaguars, 2001; Minn Vikings, 2002; real estate, 2003. *

DAWKINS, STAN BARRINGTON BANCROFT
Dentist. **Personal:** Born Jul 11, 1933, Jamaica, WI. **Educ:** City Col NY, BS, 1959; New York Univ Col Dent, DDS & MSD, 1963; FACD, 1990. **Career:** Self-employed, dentist; Bird S Coler Metropolitan Hosp, chief prosthetics; New York Univ Col Dentistry, asst prof, assoc prof, currently. **Orgs:** ADA; NE Gnathological Soc; Am Radiol Soc; co-chair comm, Encourage Blacks to Enter Med Prof; capt, City Col Track Team, 1957-59; capt, City Col Soccer Team, 1959; Greater New York Acad Prosthododtics; Am Prosthodontic Soc; New York Acad Dentistry; vpres, OKU, 1995. **Honors/Awds:** Outstanding Athlete Award, CCNY, 1959; CCNY Hall of Fame, 1974. **Military Serv:** USAF, sgt, 1952-56, Distinguished service medal; Good conduct medal. **Business Addr:** Prosthodontist, 186 W 135th St, New York, NY 10030, **Business Phone:** (212)926-4600.

DAWKINS, DR. STEPHEN A
Physician. **Personal:** Born Feb 27, 1960, Nashville, TN; son of Wilbert L Sr and Tinye L; married Arnika G Dawkins, Dec 17, 1983; children: Brandon, Morgan-Brien & Paige-Nichette. **Educ:** Ga Inst Technol, BS, 1982; Morehouse Sch Med, MD, 1987; Columbia Univ, MPH, 1990. **Career:** Consult, 1987; Occup Health Serv, resident, 1988; NJ Dept Health, consult, 1988-90; NJ Bell, Med dir, 1989-90; Arkins Corp, owner, 1980-90; Occup Safety & Health Admin, occup med physician, 1990; Occup Health Int, Atlanta, physician, 1990-, Occup Med, dir, 2000; Caduceus Occup Med, Atlanta Med Ctr, med dir, currently. **Orgs:** Am Col Occup & Environ Med, Ga Chap; AMA; Med Asn Ga; Am Diabetes Asn; Arthritis Found; State Bd Worker's Compensation. **Special Achievements:** Numerous presentations including, Opportunities in Occupational Medicine, 1991; Asbestos Exposure & Clean Air, 1991; Workplace Drug Testing: Implementation Guidelines for Employers, 1992; The Americans With Disabilities Act: Medical Implications and Employer Considerations, 1992. **Business Phone:** (404)607-7677.

DAWKINS, TAMMY C.
Educator. **Personal:** Born Aug 30, 1960, Washington, DC; daughter of Dan Lee Jenkins and Alfreda F Jenkins; married Fitzroy W, Apr 4, 1987; children: Danielle Charisse & Ayana Noelle. **Educ:** Howard Univ, BS, pharm, 1983; State Univ NY, Buffalo, DPharm, 1986. **Career:** Erie Co Med Ctr, staff develop pharmacist, 1987-88; Howard Univ, asst prof pharm pract, 1988-, Howard Univ Hosp, Pediatric AIDS Clin Trials Group, pharmacist, currently; Dist Columbia AIDS Drug Awareness Prog, currently; NIH, resident. **Orgs:** Am Soc Hosp Pharmacists, 1988-; Am Asn Col Pharm, 1989-90. **Honors/Awds:** Student Achievement Award, Association Black Hospital Pharmacists, 1985; Rho Chi Nat Pharmacy Honor Soc, 1982. **Business Addr:** Assistant Professor, Howard University, College Pharmacy, Chauncey Cooper Hall, 2300 4th St NW, Washington, DC 20059, **Business Phone:** (202)806-7960.*

DAWKINS, WAYNE J
Journalist. **Personal:** Born Sep 19, 1955, New York, NY; son of Edward H and Iris C McFarquhar; married Allie Crump, Apr 29, 1988; children: Carmen Jamila Dawkins. **Educ:** Long Island Univ, Brooklyn, NY, BA, 1977; Columbia Univ, Grad Sch Jour, New York, NY, MS, 1980. **Career:** Trans-Urban News Serv, Brooklyn, NY, intern/reporter, 1978-79; The Daily Argus, Mount Vernon, NY, reporter, 1980-84; Courier-Post, Cherry Hill, NJ, reporter, 1984-88, ed writer, 1988-, columnist, 1991-96; Post-Tribune, Gary IN, deputy south lake ed, 1996-98; Daily Press, assoc edi, 1998-2003, August Press, pres, 1992-; Auth, Black Journalists: The NABJ Story, August Press, 1997; Rugged Waters: Black Journalists Swim the Mainstream, August Press, 2003; Ed, Black Voices in Commentary: The Trotter Group, August Press, 2006. **Orgs:** Ed, co-founder, Black Alumni Network, 1980-; regional dir, 1984-89, mem, 1981-, Nat Asn Black Journalists; co-founder, pres, treas, Garden State NJ, ABJ NABJ Affil, 1988-; Jour Alumni Asn, Columbia Univ, 1981-84; The Trotter Group, 1992-; Publishers Marketing Asn, 1994. **Honors/Awds:** Robert Harron Award, Columbia University GSJ, 1980; First-Place Award, NY State Asn Press, 1983; First-Place Award, NJ Press Asn, 1987; Journalism Alumni Award, Columbia University, 1990; Alumni Asn Award, Columbia Sch Jour, 1990; T Thomas Fortune Lifetime Achievement Awd, Golden State Asn of Black Journalists, 1994. **Special Achievements:** Author, Black Journalists: The NABJ Story, August Press, 1993. **Business Addr:** President, August Press, 108 Terrell Rd, PO Box 6693, Newport News, VA 23606, **Business Phone:** 800-268-4338.

DAWSEY, LAWRENCE LENEIR
Football player, football coach. **Personal:** Born Nov 16, 1967, Dothan, AL; married Chantal; children: Lawrence Jr & Dominque Arce. **Educ:** Fla State. **Career:** Tampa Bay Buccaneers, wide receiver, 1991-95; New York Giants, 1996; Miami Dolphins, 1997; Tampa Catholic High Sch, receivers Coach, 1998; New Orleans Saints, 1999-; St Louis Rams, training camp asst, 2001; Tampa Blake High Sch, receivers Coach, 2002; La State Univ, grad asst, 2003; Univ S Fla, seminoles, receivers coach, 2004-06. **Honors/Awds:** UPI NFL-NFC Rookie of the Year award, 1991; NFL Rookie of the Yr, Sports Illustrated & USA Today, 1991; Graduate Assistant at LSU on Nick Saban's staff, 2003. **Business Phone:** (863)667-7000.*

DAWSON, DR. ALMA
Educator, librarian. **Educ:** Grambling State Univ, BS, 1963; Univ Ore, MLS; Univ Mich, Ann Arbor, MI, AMLS, Libr Sci, 1974; Tex Women Univ, Denton, TX, PhD (libr sci), 1996. **Career:** Natchitoches Parish La Sch syst, teacher & librn, 1964-69; Univ Mich, Mich, libr assoc, 1972-74; Prairie View A & M Univ, libr assoc, 1969-72, head serials dept, 1974-82, Dept Educ Technol, instr, 1980-82; La State Univ, head librn, 1982 -94, from instr to assoc prof, 1994-2006, Sch Libr & Info Sci, Russell B Long prof, 2003-, prof, 2006-. **Orgs:** Beta Zeta Chap, Beta Phi Mu Nat Honor Soc; Phi Delta Kappa Honor Soc; Asn Col & Res Librns; Am Libr Asn; Asn Libr & Info Sci Educ; Lo Libr Asn; Asn Libr Collections & Tech Servs; Libr Res Round Table. **Honors/Awds:** fel, Tex womens univ, Denton, 1990-91; Beta Phi Mu Nat Honor Socy Libr & Info Sci, inducted Beta Zeta Chap, October 1996; Am Libr Asn Equality Award, 2005. **Business Addr:** Professor, Louisiana State University, School of Library and Information Science, 267 Coates Hall, Baton Rouge, LA 70803, **Business Phone:** (225)578-3158.

DAWSON, ANDRE NOLAN
Baseball player, baseball executive. **Personal:** Born Jul 10, 1954, Miami, FL; married Vanessa Turner; children: Darius. **Career:** Baseball player (retired), baseball executive; Montreal Expos, outfielder, 1976-86; Chicago Cubs, outfielder, 1987-92; Boston Red Sox, 1993-94; Fla Marlins, outfielder, 1995-96, spec asst pres, currently. **Orgs:** Fla A&M Univ Nat Alumni Asn. **Honors/Awds:** Nat League Most Valuable Player, Baseball Writers' Asn Am, 1977, 1987; Nat League Rookie of the Year, Baseball Writers' Asn Am, 1977; Silver Slugger Award, 1980, 1981, 1983, 1987; Gold Glove Award, 1980-85, 1987, 1988; Nat League All-Star Team, 1981-83, 1987-90. **Special Achievements:** TV appearance: "The Cap", 1984; "The Story of America's Classic Ballpark", 1991. **Business Addr:** Special Assistant to the President, Florida Marlins, 2267 NW 199th St, Miami, FL 33056, **Business Phone:** (305)626-7470.

DAWSON, DR. B. W.
College administrator, college president. **Career:** Selma Univ, Selma, AL, pres, 1985-94.

DAWSON, BOBBY H
Automotive executive, business owner. **Career:** Freedom Ford Lincoln-Mercury Inc, pres & chief exec officer, currently. **Orgs:** Community Bus Partners. **Honors/Awds:** Company is 84 on Black Enterprise magazine's list of top 100 auto dealers, 1992. **Business Addr:** President, Chief Executive Officer, Freedom Ford Lincoln-Mercury Inc, 149 Woodland Dr, PO Box 3419, Wise, VA 24293, **Business Phone:** (703)328-2686.

DAWSON, ERIC EMMANUEL
Government official. **Personal:** Born Dec 26, 1937, St Thomas, Virgin Islands of the United States; son of Joseph E and Ann Olivia Forbes; married Betty Vanterpool, Jun 11, 1966; children: David, Diane, Eric Jr. **Educ:** NY Univ, BS, bus; Howard Univ, JD. **Career:** Senate VI, exec secy, 1965-67, 1968-71; Spec Asst to Governor, 1967-68; Sales Exec, 1971-72; Govt VI , senator, 1973-79, chief legal coun senate, 1983-84, senator, 1985-87, comnr econ develop & agr. **Orgs:** Caribbean Travel Orgn, 3rd vpres; VI Bar Asn, 1982-. **Military Serv:** Army Nat Guard, col, 1969-; Army Commendation, Nat Defense, Army Achievement. *

DAWSON, HAROLD A., SR.
Chief executive officer, administrator. **Personal:** Born Mar 5, 1935. **Educ:** Morehouse Col, BS, bus admin, 1963. **Career:** Alexander Dawson & Assocs, pres; Harold A Dawson Co Inc, chmn & chief exec officer, currently. **Orgs:** Ga Real Estate Comn; pres, Nat Asn Real Estate License Law Officials; pres, Empire Bd Realtists; pres, Nat Asn Real Estate Brokers. **Honors/Awds:** Numerous awards and recogitions from civic, religious, educational, and business organizations. **Business Phone:** (404)347-8030.*

DAWSON, HORACE G
Lawyer, food service manager. **Personal:** Born Oct 23, 1954, Durham, NC; son of Horace G Dawson Jr and Lula Cole Dawson; married Mildred L Dawson, Sep 15, 1985; children: H Greeley Dawson III & Mia Karisa Dawson. **Educ:** Harvard Col, BA, 1976; Harvard Bus Sch, MBA, 1980; Harvard Law Sch, JD, 1980. **Career:** Baker & McKenzie, assoc, 1980-82; Summit Rovins & Feldesman, assoc, 1982-86; Reliance Group Holdings, staff coun, 1986-87; Telemundo Group Inc, vpres & asst gen coun, 1987-96; Hard Rock Cafe Int Inc, sr dir bus affairs, vpres bus affairs, 1996-2001; Akerman Senterfitt & Eidson, coun, 2001-03; Darden Restaurants Inc, sr assoc gen coun, currently. **Orgs:** Am Bar Asn, 1980-; NY State Bar, 1980-; NY City Bar, 1980-; Coun Foreign Rels, 1989-96; Fla State Bar, 1994-. **Business Addr:** Senior Associate General Counsel, Darden Restaurants Inc, 5900 Lake Ellenor Dr, PO Box 59330, Orlando, FL 32859-3330, **Business Phone:** (407)245-4000.

DAWSON, HORACE GREELEY
Government official. **Personal:** Born Jan 30, 1926, Augusta, GA; son of Horace Greeley Dawson; married Lula M Cole, Aug 30, 1953; children: Horace G III & H Gregory. **Educ:** Lincoln Univ Pa, AB, 1949; Columbia Univ, AM, 1950; State Univ Iowa, PhD, 1961. **Career:** Southern Univ Baton Rouge, instr eng, 1950-53; NC Cent Univ, Durham, assoc prof, dir pub rels, 1953-62; Uganda, cultural affairs officer, 1962; Nigeria, cultural affairs officer, 1964; Univ Lagos, Nigeria, vis prof,1966-67; Liberia, pub affairs officer, 1967; US Dept State, sr seminar foreign policy, 1970, cultural affairs advisor, 1970-71; USIA/Africa, asst dir, dir, 1971-76; Univ Md, vis prof, 1971-79; US Dept State, Botswana, ambassador extraordinary, plenipotentiary, 1979-83; Bd Examiners Foreign Serv, 1983-85; US Info agency, advisor dir, Off Equal Employ Opport &Civil Rights, dir, 1985-89; Howard Univ, PACE Prog, dir, 1989-91, Patricia Roberts Harris Pub Affairs Prog, dir, 1990-, Ctr Int Affairs, interim dir,1993-94, asst pres Pub Affairs, 1994-95, Ralph J Bunche Int Affairs Ctr, acting dir, 1992, dir, 1997-. **Orgs:** Nat Asn Advan Colored People; Am Legion; vice chair, APA World Affairs Coun; sr bd stewards, Metrop Am Church; Asn Black Am Ambassadors; Coun Foreign Rels; World Affairs Coun, mem Alpha Phi Alpha. **Honors/Awds:** Superior Honor Award, USIA, 1965 & 1989; honorary doctorate, Lincoln Univ,1990. **Special Achievements:** Author: "New Dimensions in Higher Education", 1961; "Handbook for High School Newspaper Advisors", 1961; "Race As A Factor in Cultural Exchange","Exporting America", 1993; "First Black Diplomat," Foreign Serv J, Jan1993; numerous others. **Military Serv:** USY, ssgt, 1944-46. **Business Addr:** Director, Ralph J Bunche International Affairs Center, Howard University, 2218 6th St NW, Washington, DC 20059, **Business Phone:** (202)806-4363.

DAWSON, LAKE
Football player, football executive. **Personal:** Born Jan 2, 1972, Boston, MA; married Lori. **Educ:** Univ Notre Dame, telecommunications. **Career:** Football player (retired), football executive; Kans City Chiefs, wide receiver, 1994-99; Indianapolis Colts, 2001; Seattle Seahawks, from propersonnel asst to asst dir pro personnel; TN Titans, dir pro personnel, 2007-. **Business Addr:** Director of Pro Personnel, Tennessee Titans, 460 Great Circle Rd, Nashville, TN 37228, **Business Phone:** (615)565-4000.*

DAWSON, DR. LAWRENCE E
College administrator, school administrator, president (organization). **Career:** Am Coun Educ, dir, mgt prog; Voorhees Col, pres, 1985. **Orgs:** Chair, Voorhees Col Bd Trustees.

DAWSON, LEONARD ERVIN
Educational consultant, college president. **Personal:** Born Feb 5, 1934, Augusta, GA; married Laura R Dawson; children: Michael, Randall (deceased), Lavinia & Stephanie. **Educ:** Morris Brown Col, BA, Eng, 1954; Columbia Univ, MA, 1961, dipl, 1964; George Washington Univ, EdD, 1974. **Career:** Educator (retired), consultant; Carver High Sch, teacher, 1956; Johnson Jr High Sch, head counr, 1964-67; Paine Col, prof, 1967-69, acad dean, 1969-70; US Dept Educ, educ prog specialist, 1970-71; RR Moton Memorial Inst, sr prog officer, 1971-77, exec vp, 1977-80; United Negro Col Fund, dir spec proj, 1980-85; Voorhees Col, pres, 1985-2001; White House Initiative, sr consult, 2001-, dep counr, 2004-. **Orgs:** Am Coun Educ; Am Mgt Asn; HBCU Capital Financing Adv Bd; United Negro Col Fund; Am Asn Higher Educ; bd trustees, Asn Episcopal Cols; Phi Delta Kappa; Alpha Phi Alpha; NAACP. **Honors/Awds:** Distinguished Alumni Award, Morris Brown Col, 1981, 1999; Awarded Order of the Palmetto by President of SC, 2001. **Special Achievements:** Author: "The Role of the Counselor," The Columbia Owl, 1964; "Accountability and Federal Programs," United Board for Col Develop, 1976; "Goverance and the Small, Liberal Arts College," Moton Col Serv Bur, 1977; "Integrated Management Systems in United Negro College Fund Institutions," 1984; "The Next Ten Years: Who Should Benefit from Federal Support Available for Higher Education," a report prepared for the United Negro Col Fund, 1984. **Military Serv:** AUS, pfc, 1956-58. **Business Addr:** Senior Consultant, White House Initiative on Historically Black Colleges and Universities, US Department of Education, 400 Maryland Ave SW, Washington, DC 20202, **Business Phone:** (202)502-7889.

DAWSON, LUMELL HERBERT
Government official, executive director. **Personal:** Born Sep 5, 1934, Harrisburg, PA; married Jacquelyn Bourne; children: Anegla

Lynn, Jeffrey Bourne. **Educ:** WVa State Col, BA, 1961. **Career:** NY City Dept Human Resources, supv caseworker, 1962-65; Voc Educ & Ext Bd, dir soc serv, 1965-70; Nassau County Comn Human Rights, assoc dir, 1970-; WVa State Col, recruiter, 1980-. **Orgs:** Omega Psi Phi Fraternity, 1958-; voc adv bd mem, State Univ NY, Farmingdale, 1979-85; voc adv bd mem, Hempstead High Sch, NY 1980-; chair, Fund Raising Comn, Long Island Coalition Full Employ, 1980-; adv bd mem, Leadership Training Inst, 1982-; EDGES Group, 1985-; Christ First Presby Church, Hempstead, NY, 1987. **Honors/Awds:** Spec Recognition, Nassau County Comn Human Rights, 1983; Alumni Award, WVa State Col, 1986; Outstanding Contrib & Support, Oper Get Ahead, 1986; Achievement Award, Nat Asn Counties, 1986. **Business Addr:** Associate Director, Nassau County Commission Human Rights, 320 Old Country Rd, Garden City, NY 11530.

DAWSON, MARTHA E
Educator, executive. **Personal:** Born Jan 12, 1922, Richmond, VA; daughter of John Eaton and Sarah Eaton; divorced; children: Greer Dawson Wilson, Martina M & James M. **Educ:** VA State Col, BS, 1943; Ind Univ, MS, 1954, EdD, 1956. **Career:** Richmond Pub Schs, teacher, supr; Multi-Cultural Educ Ctr, dir; Ind Univ, speaker, writer, cons, numerous publs in field; Hampton Inst, chmn dept elem educ, 1960-70, vpres acad affairs, exec leadership summit coordr; Va State Univ, provost & vpres acad affairs, 1993-99, provost emer; 4M Exec Coaching Team Inc, chief exec officer, currently. **Orgs:** Delta Kappa Gamma Hon Soc, 1971; Phi Delta Kappa, 1975; bd visitors, Defense Opportunity Mgt Inst, 1987-90; pres, Ind Univ Sch Educ Alumni Bd, 1989-90; bd visitors, Sch Educ, Ind Univ, 1990-93. **Honors/Awds:** Distinguished Teacher, Hampton Inst, 1967; Certified Nat Council of Negro Women 1970; Harbison Distinguished Teacher, finalist Danforth Found, 1970; Outstanding Women of the 70s, 1972; visiting scholar, Southern Univ 1974; Outstanding Achievement Award in Higher Educ, Zeta Phi Beta Sorority, 1984; Old Masters Honoree, Purdue Univ, 1984; Distinguished Alumni Service Award, Ind Univ, 1980; Brother/Sisterhood Award, Nat Conference Christians & Jews, 1991; President's Citizenship Award, 2001. **Business Addr:** Cheif Executive Officer, 4m Executive Coaching Team Inc, 13 Howe Rd, Hampton, VA 23669.

DAWSON, MICHAEL C
Educator. **Personal:** Born Jan 1, 1951; married Alice Furumato-Dawson. **Educ:** Univ Calif, Berkeley, BA, 1982; Harvard Univ, PhD, 1986. **Career:** Univ Chicago, assoc prof, polit sci prof & chair, Ctr Study Race, Politics & Cult, founding dir & investr, William R Kenan Jr prof, 2001; Harvard Univ, Dept Govt & African Studies, prof, 2002-05; Univ Chicago, Dept Polit Sci, John D MacArthur prof, John D MacArthur distinguished serv prof currently. **Orgs:** Bd dir, Social Sci Res Coun; Am Acad Arts & Sci; Black Civil Soc. **Special Achievements:** Publications: Behind the Mule: Race, Class and African American Politics (Princeton University Press, 1994) and Black Visions: The Roots of Contemporary African American Mass Political Ideologies (University of Chicago Press, 2001). *

DAWSON, PETER EDWARD
Physician. **Personal:** Born Nov 18, 1931, Plaquemine, LA; married Jean Lezama; children: Jonathan, Patricia. **Educ:** Xavier Univ, BS, 1954; Meharry Med Col, 1962. **Career:** St Joseph Hosp, internship res. **Orgs:** Charter mem, Am Acad Family Physicians; asst dir, So Infirmary; assoc prof, family med LSU Sch Med; past pres, Plaquemine Br; NAACP 1966-76; 32nd degree Mason; chmn, test My Syremem BC; Alpha Phi Alpha Frat. **Honors/Awds:** Physician Recognition Award, 1969, 1972, 1975. **Military Serv:** AUS, sp 2, 1954-57. **Business Addr:** Family Practice Physician, Private Practitioner, 58434 Meriam St, Plaquemine, LA 70764.

DAWSON, RALPH C
Lawyer. **Educ:** Yale Univ, BA, 1973; Columbia Univ Law Sch, JD, 1976. **Career:** Fulbright & Jaworski LLP, atty & partner, currently. **Orgs:** Am Bar Asn; NY State Bar Asn. **Business Addr:** Attorney, Partner, Fulbright & Jaworski LLP, 666 5th Ave, New York, NY 10103-3198, **Business Phone:** (212)318-3000.

DAWSON, DR. ROBERT EDWARD
Physician. **Personal:** Born Feb 23, 1918, Rocky Mount, NC; son of William and Daisy Wright; married Julia Davis; children: Dianne Elizabeth, Janice Elaine, Robert Edward & Melanie Lorraine. **Educ:** Clark Col, BS, 1939; Meharry Med Col, MD, 1943; Am Bd Ophthalmol, dipl. **Career:** Physician (retired); Homer G Phillips Hosp St Louis, internship 1943-44, resident 1944-46; Lincoln Hosp Ophthalmol Dept, attending staff, 1946-55; Duke Univ, preceptorship, 1946; NC Central Univ Health Serv, consult ophthalmol, 1950-64; 3310 Hosp Scott AFB, chief ophthalmol & otolaryngology, 1955-57; Armed Forces Inst Path, ophthalmic path, 1956; Lincoln Hosp, chief ophthal & otolaryng, 1959-76; NY Inst Ophthalmol, 1962; NY Eye & Ear Infirmary, 1963; Watts Hosp, attend staff, 1966; Duke Univ, clinical instr ophthalmol, 1968; Durham Co Gen Hosp, attend staff, 1976; DCGH, vpres staff, 1976-77; Duke Univ, clin asst prof ophthalmol; scholar in residence. **Orgs:** Fel Am Col Surgeons; fel Acad Ophthalmol & Otolaryngol; Am Asn Ophthalmol; diplomate Pan Am Nat Asn; Nat Med Asn; pres, Chi Delta Mu Sci Frat; Soc Eye Surgeons; AMA; bd trustees, Meharry Med Col; exec com chmn, Hosp & Health Affairs Comt; bd trustees, Nat Med Asn; bd trustees, NC Central Univ; chmn, Faculty-Trustee Rel Com NC Cent Univ; regional surgical dir, Eye Bank Asn Am; bd dirs, Better Health Found, 1960-66; bd dirs, Lincoln Comm Health Ctr; bd trustees, Durham Acad, 1969-72; bd dir, Nat Soc Prevent Blindness; bd dir, Am Cancer Soc; adv bd, NC State Comn Blind, 1970-78; pres, Sigma Pi Phi Frat; President's Comn Employment Handicapped; bd dir, Nat Prevent Blindness; St Joseph's AME Ch; Nat Am Advan Colored People; bd visitors, Clark Col; Alpha Omega Alpha Hon Soc; pres, AOA NMA; bd visitors, Greensboro Col; 33rd degree Mason. **Honors/Awds:** Recipient Physician of the Year Award, 1969; Distinguished Service Award, Nat Med Asn, 1982; Distinguished Service Award, Nat Asn Equal Opportunity Higher Educ; Distinguished Service Award, Clark Col, 1983; Trailblazer in Opthemology, 2001; Community Service Award, City Durham, 2002; City Med, 2002; Duke Univ Award, 2002; Outstanding Community Service Award. **Special Achievements:** Publications, Journal of the Nat Med Asn, "Equal Access to Health Care Delivery for Blacks, A Challenge for the NMA", Jan, 1981; "Crisis in the Medical Arena, A Challenge for the Black Physician", Dec, 1979; "Bedside Manner of a Computer", March, 1980; "Federal Impact on Medical Care", June, 1980. **Military Serv:** USAF, Major, 1955-57. **Home Addr:** 817 E Lawson St, Durham, NC 27701, **Home Phone:** (919)682-4155.

DAWSON, ROSARIO
Actor. **Personal:** Born May 9, 1979, New York, NY. **Career:** Films include: Kids, 1995; Side Sts, 1997; Girls Night Out, 1997; He Got Game, 1998; Light It Up, 1999; Down to You, 2000; Sidewalks of New York, 2000; Josie & the Pussycats, 2001; Trigger Happy, 2001; Chelsea Walls, 2001; King of the Jungle, 2001; Love in the Time of Money, 2002; Ash Wednesday, 2002; Men in Black II, 2002; The Adventures of Pluto Nash, 2002; 25th Hour, 2002; Helldorado, 2002; This Girl's Life, 2003; Shattered Glass, 2003; The Rundown, 2003; This Revolution, 2005; Sin City, 2005; Little Black Dress, 2005; Rent, 2005; A Guide to Recognizing Your Saints, 2005; Sin City 2, 2006; Killshot, 2006; Clerks II, 2006; A Guide to Recognizing Your Saints, 2006; Grindhouse: Death Proof, 2007; Descent, 2007, Killshot, 2007. **Honors/Awds:** Rising Star Award Won, Am Black Film Festival, 2004. **Business Addr:** Actress, Robbie Reed & Associates, 1635 N Cahuenga Fl 5, Los Angeles, CA 90028, **Business Phone:** (323)769-2455.

DAWSON, SHED, JR.
Educator. **Personal:** Born Oct 6, 1973, Philadelphia, PA. **Educ:** Savannah State Univ, BS, sociol & psychol, 1995, MPA, leadership & human resources mgt, 2005. **Career:** Family Dollar Stores, store mgr, 1991-96; Ga State Bd Pardons & Paroles, parole officer, 1996-97; Books-A-Million, receiving distrib mgr, 1996-98; Savannah State Univ, enrollment mgt specialist, 1998-2005, dir Acad Serv & Champ & Life Skills, 2005-, asst athletic dir, 2005-. **Orgs:** Beta Phi Lambda-Community Serv chair, Alpha Phi Alpha Fraternity Inc, 1995-; Prince Hall Mason, Sr Decon-Pythagoras Lodge noll, 1996-; Chap adv, Nat Asn Advan Colored People, Savannah Br Exec Comt, 1998-; March Dimes East Ga Div, Community Serv Comt, 1998-; staff coun exec comt-parliamentarian, Savannah State Univ, 2000-; Nat Col Testing Asn, 2000-; Mens Health adv bd, St Joseph Camdler Hosp, 2001-; chmn, Cult Competency & Diversity Comt; Ga Dist bd dir, 2003-. **Honors/Awds:** Profession Preparation in Research Award, Univ Ga, 1994; Professional Preparation in Research Award, Emory Univ, 1995; Int Dean' List, 1995; All American Scholar Award, 1995. **Home Addr:** 12409 Largo Dr, PO Box 15172, Savannah, GA 31419. **Business Addr:** Assistant Athletic Director for Academic Services, Savannah State University, 3219 College St, Savannah, GA 31404-5255, **Business Phone:** (912)303-1863.

DAWSON, SIDNEY L., JR.
School administrator. **Personal:** Born Dec 27, 1920, Kansas City, MO; married Etta Mae Jackson; children: Sandra Kaye & Sidney L III. **Educ:** Univ KA, BME, 1948; Univ AZ, MME, 1956; Educ Admin Cert, 1968. **Career:** School administrator (retired); Tucson Educ Asn, pres, 1963-64; Ariz Educ Asn, pres, 1970-71; High Sch, prin, 1973-79; Catalina High Sch, asst prin stud activ, 1979-84. **Orgs:** Phi Delta Kappa, 1956; pres, Rincon Rotary Int, 1979-80; pole march Alumni Chaps, Kappa Alpha Psi, 1980-81; chairperson, Tucson Police Adv Comm, 1983-. **Honors/Awds:** Pusic Phi Mu Alpha, 1948. **Military Serv:** AUS, sgt, 1943-46; Hon Discharge, 1946. *

DAWSON, WARREN HOPE
Lawyer. **Personal:** Born Oct 17, 1939, Mulberry, FL; married Joan Delores; children: Wendy Hope. **Educ:** Fla A&M Univ, BA, 1961; Howard Univ Sch Law, JD, 1966. **Career:** Warren Hope Dawson & Assoc, atty. **Orgs:** Pres, Fla Chap Nat Bar Asn, 1979; Nat Bar Asn, 1979; vpres, Tampa Chap Frontiers Int; Fla Bar Asn, 1980; standing comt legal asst, Am Bar Asn, 1980; adv bd dir, Tampa Bay Buccaneers, 1980; chmn, Hillbro County Civil Serv Bd. **Honors/Awds:** Whitney M Young Memorial Award, Tampa Urban League, 1979. **Military Serv:** AUS, co comdr, 1961-63. **Business Addr:** Lawyer, Warren Hope Dawson & Associates, 1467 Tampa Park Plaza, Tampa, FL 33605-4821.*

DAWSON BOYD, DR. CANDY
Educator. **Personal:** Born Aug 8, 1946, Chicago, IL; daughter of Mary Ruth Ridley and Julian; divorced. **Educ:** Northeastern Ill State Univ, BA, educ, 1967; Univ Calif, Berkeley, CA, MA,reading educ, 1978, PhD, curric & instr, 1982. **Career:** Overton Elementary Sch, Chicago, Ill, teacher, 1968-71; Longfellow Sch, Berkeley, Calif, teacher, 1971-73; Univ Calif, Berkeley, Calif, ext instr lang arts, 1972-79; Berkeley Unified Sch Dist, Berkeley, Calif, dist teacher trainer reading & commun skills, 1973-76; St Mary's Col Calif, Moraga, Calif, ext instr lang arts, 1972-79, lectr asst prof, 1976-83, Reading Leadership Elem Educ & Teacher Effectiveness Prog, chair, 1976-87, tenured assoc prof, 1983-91, prof, 1991-94, Masters Progs Reading & Spec Educ, chair, 1994-, Multicultural Lit Collection, dir, currently. **Orgs:** St Mary's Col Rank & Tenure Comt, 1984-87; Multiple Subj Waiver Progs Comt, Rev Comn, State Calif Comn Teacher Credentialing, 1985-; adv comt, Multiple Subj Credential Childhood Emphasis, State Calif Comn Teacher Credentialing, 1986-87; co- founder, Common Lit Cult. **Honors/Awds:** Coretta Scott King Award Honor Book for Circle of Gold, Am Libr Asn, 1985; Outstanding Bay Area Woman, Delta Sigma Theta, 1986; First Distinguished Professor of the Year, St Mary's Col, 1992; Spotlight on Literature Program, McGraw-Hill, 1995. **Special Achievements:** Author Circle of Gold, Scholastic, 1984; Breadsticks and Blessing Places, Macmillan, 1985, published in paperback as Forever Friends, Viking, 1986; Charlie Pippin, Macmillan, 1987; Chevrolet Saturdays, Macmillan, 1993; Author, Fall Secrets, Puffin, 1994; A Different Beat, 1994; Daddy, Daddy, Be There, Philomel, 1995. **Home Addr:** 1416 Madrone Way, San Pablo, CA 94806. **Business Addr:** Professor, Director Multicultural Literature Collection, Saint Marys College of California, School of Education, 1928 St Marys Rd, PO Box 4350, Moraga, CA 94556, **Business Phone:** (925)631-4000.

DAY, ERIC THERANDER
Law enforcement officer. **Personal:** Born Dec 15, 1952, Mobile, AL; son of Joseph and Ruby James; married Valerie Jones, Mar 30, 1974; children: Eric Therander Jr, Joaquin Kyron. **Educ:** Univ S Ala, BA, Criminal Justice, 1977, MEd, 1979. **Career:** Mobile Co Sheriff Dept, asst dir work release, 1977-79, dir work release, 1979-80, asst warden, 1980-81, asst planning officer, 1981-84, dir victim witness prog, 1984-85, dep sheriff, 1985-88; US Atty Off, Law Enforcement, Victim Witness, coordr, 1988-. **Orgs:** Southern States Correctional Asn; Lambda Alpha Epsilon; Alpha Phi Sigma; Ala Peace Officer Asn; Am Correctional Asn; vpres, Fel Christian Law Enforcement Officers; bd mem, 2nd vpres, Gulf Coast Federal Credit Union, 1985; chaplain, Southern Region Nat Black Police Asn, 1987; bd mem, Epilepsy Chap Mobile & Gulf Coast, 1988; Mobile United, 1989; Coalition Drug Free Mobile, 1990; Challenge 200, 1990; vchmn, Summit Advan Values & Ethics, 1990; vpres, Blacks Govt, 1987; pres, Mobile Co Criminal Justice Soc, 1984-88; Mobile United; chmn, Human Resources Comt, 1992; Coalition Drug Free Mobile, 1992; chmn, bd mem, Youth Concerns Comn; chmn, Summit Advan Values & Ethics, 1992-93. **Honors/Awds:** Man of the Year, Alpha Phi Alpha Frat, 1977; Outstanding Victim Advocate, Ala, 1990, 1992; Outstanding Service Victims Commendation, Dept Justice, Off Victims Crimes, 1992; Outstanding Young Men of America. **Military Serv:** AUS, sgt, 1972-74; Nat Defense Medal, 1972; Good Conduct Medal, 1974. **Business Addr:** Law Enforcement Victim Witness Coordinator, United States Attorney Office, 310 Cummings St Suite A, Abingdon, VA 36602.*

DAY, JOHN
Entrepreneur, business owner. **Personal:** Born Jan 1, 1965?; married Angela. **Career:** Helping Our Brothas Out Shop, owner, 1996-. **Business Phone:** (301)735-7444.

DAY, JOHN H
Physicist. **Personal:** Born Jun 5, 1952, Savannah, GA; son of John H and Elsie M; married Agnes A Lasiter, 1973 (divorced 2002); children: Teresa; married Yardyne Jackson, Feb 25, 2006; children: Gregory Proctor. **Educ:** Bethune-Cookman Col, BS, physics, 1973; Howard Univ, MS, physics, 1976, PhD, physics, 1982. **Career:** Martin Marietta Corp, Engr, laser optics div, 1973; Dept Com, physicist, Nat bur stand, 1974-78; Dept Interior, physicist, US Geol surv, 1979-82; NASA, Goddard Space Ctr, Engr, energy conversion sect, 1982-88, sect head, energy conversion sect, 1988-90, asst br head, space power br, 1990-92, br head, space power br, 1992-98, chief technologist, Appl Engineering & Technol dir, 1998-99, Elec Eng Div, chief, 1999-; Tex A&M Ctr Space power, adv bd, 1994-99; Capital Col Engineering, Dept Adv Bd, fac. **Orgs:** Interagency Advan Power Group; Am Inst Aeronaut & Astronaut; Inst Elec & Electronic Engrs; AAAS; Am Phys Soc; Nat Soc Black Physicists; Sigma Pi Sigma Physics Hon Soc; Alpha Kappa Mu; Nat Hon Soc; Phi Beta Sigma Fraternity. **Honors/Awds:** Nat Science Foundation Fellowship Award, 1976-78; Graduate Fellowship Award, Howard Univ, 1979-81; Terminal Fellowship Award, Howard Univ 1980-82; NASA Outstanding Performance Awards, 1984-85, 1987, 1992-96; InterNat Cometary Explorer Group Award, 1985; InterNat Sun Earth Explorer Group Award, 1987; NASA Performance Management & Recognition System Awards, 1989-94; Gamma Ray Observatory Group Award, 1992; Goddard Exceptional Achievement Award, 1993; Upper Atmosphere Research Satellite Achievement Award, 1993; Geostationary Operational Environmental Satellite Group Award, 1994; Global Geospace Sci Satellite PSE Review Team Award, 1994; Hubble Space Telescope Servicing Mission Group Award,

1994; Landsat 7 Design Review Streamlining Team Award, 1995; X-Ray Timing Explorer Team Award, 1996; Tropical Rainfall Measuring Mission Team Award, 1998; NASA Medal of Exceptional Service, 1998; NASA Medal for Exceptional Service, 1998; Tropical Rainfall Measuring Mission Group Achievement Award, 1998, Presdiential Meritorious Executive Award, 2004. **Special Achievements:** NASA Space Photovoltaics Research & Technology Conference, 1983 & 1994; Presentations and publications include: Intersociety Energy Conversion Engineering Conference, 1987; Inst Elec & Electronic Engrs Photovoltaics Conf, 1987; Am Inst Aeronaut & Astronaut Small Satellite Symposium, 1993. **Home Addr:** 14507 Briercrest Rd, Bowie, MD 20720, **Home Phone:** (301)464-4139. **Business Addr:** Chief, NASA Goddard Space Flight Center, Electrical Engineering Division, Mail Code 560 Bldg 23 Rm S-120, Greenbelt, MD 20771.

DAY, MORRIS (MORRIS DAUGHTY)
Musician, actor. **Personal:** Born Dec 13, 1957; married Judith; children: Evan, Derran & Tionna. **Career:** Films: Purple Rain, actor, 1984; Moving, actor, 1988; A Woman Like That, actor, 1997; Boys Klub, actor, 2001; West from North Goes South, actor,2004; Moesha; The Adventures of Ford Fairlane; Jay & Silent Bob Strike Back; TV series: "A New Attitude", 1990; "Da Boom Crew", 2004; "Eve",2004; "I Love the '90s: Part Deux", 2005; Singles: "Color of Success"; "The Oak Tree"; "Daydreaming"; "The Character"; "Fishnet" 1988, #23; "Lovels a Game"; "Gimme Watcha Got"; "Circle of Love"; "777-9311"; "Gigolos Get Lonely Too"; "Jungle Love"; "Jerk Out"; "The Bird". **Business Addr:** Actor, Singer, Reprise Records, Warner Bros, 3300 Warner Blvd, Burbank, CA 91510.

DAY, TERRY
Football player. **Personal:** Born Sep 18, 1974, Pickens, MS. **Educ:** Miss State Univ; Holmes CC. **Career:** NY Jets, defensive end, 1997. **Honors/Awds:** Hall of Fame Mem, Dedicated Football League, 2004.

DAY, TODD FITZGERALD
Basketball player. **Personal:** Born Jan 7, 1970, Decatur, IL. **Educ:** Univ Ark. **Career:** Basketball player (retired), basketball coach; Milwaukee Bucks, guard/forward, 1992-95; Boston Celtics, 1995-97; Miami Heat, 1997-98; Phoenix Suns, 1999-2000; Minn Timberwolves, 2000-01; Blue Stars, 2006-07; Premier Basketball League, Ark Impact, head coach, currently. **Orgs:** Alpha Phi Alpha. **Special Achievements:** NBA Draft, First round pick, No 8, 1992. **Business Phone:** (301)424-8612.

DAYE, CHARLES EDWARD
Educator, lecturer. **Personal:** Born May 14, 1944, Durham, NC; son of Addie R and Eccleasiastes; married Norma S; children: Clarence L Hill III & Tammy H Roundtree. **Educ:** NC Cent Univ, BA, magna cum laude, 1966; Columbia Univ, JD, cum laude, 1969. **Career:** US Ct of Appeals for the Sixth Circuit, law clerk to chief judge; Covington & Burling, Wash, assoc; Univ NC, Chapel Hill, fac law, 1972; Univ NC Chapel Hill Sch Law, prof, 1972-81; NC Cent Univ Sch Law, vis prof, 1980-81, dean & prof, 1981-85; UNC Chapel Hill Sch Law, prof, 1985-; Henry P Brandis Dist, Prof of law, 1991-. **Orgs:** Pres, NC Asn Black Lawyers, 1976-78; exec secy, NC Asn Black Lawyers, 1979-99; bars mem, US Supreme Ct, NY, DC, NC; Triangle Housing Devel Corp,1977-; chmn, Triangle Housing Devel Corp, 1979-91; bd dir, United Way Greater Durham, 1984-88; pres, Law Sch Admis Coun, 1991-93; Am Bar Asn; NC State Bar; NC Bar Asn; chair, Asn Am Law Sch; chair bd, NC Fair Housing Ctr; chair, NC Poverty Proj. **Honors/Awds:** Lawyer of the Year, NC Asn Black Lawyers, 1980; Civic Award, Durham Community Affairs Black People, 1981; co-auth, Casebook Housing & Community Devel, 1999; Hon Dr Laws degree, Suffolk Univ, 1999; co-auth, NC Law Torts; auth, Articles in Prof J; Hon Order of the Coif. **Special Achievements:** Published numerous articles; the first African American to serve as a law clerk in US Ct of Appeals for the Sixth Circuit; the first African American to hold a tenure-track position on the law faculty, Univ NC, Chapel Hill. **Home Addr:** 3400 Cambridge Rd, Durham, NC 27707. **Business Addr:** Professor of Law, University North Carolina, School of Law, 5121 Van Hecke-Wettach Hall, 160 Ridge Road, PO Box 3380, Chapel Hill, NC 27599-3380, **Business Phone:** (919)962-7004.*

DAYS, BERTRAM MAURICE
Executive. **Personal:** Born Oct 1, 1952, Mobile, AL; son of Raymond N Days Sr and Hattie M Days; married Ava, Aug 10, 1973; children: Marcia Y Burke. **Educ:** Macalester Col, BA, 1974; Univ Rochester, MBA, 1976. **Career:** Cummins Engine Co, corp financial planning, 1976-80, mgr, financial admin, 1980-82, controller, service products, 1982-85, dir, bus development, 1985-90, gen mgr, 1990-93; Hunter Industries, vp/gen mgr, 1993-. **Orgs:** Big Brother/Big Sister, 1982-85; William Laws Scholarship Fndn, pres, 1985-88; Asn for Quality & Participation, 1996-2001; Wake County Schls/Bus Partnership, 2000-02; Am Mgt Asn, 2002-; Raleigh Chamber Com bd dirs, 2003-. **Home Addr:** 116 Bromfield Way, Cary, NC 27519. **Business Phone:** (919)467-7100.

DAYS, DREW SAUNDERS
Government official, educator. **Personal:** Born Aug 29, 1941, Atlanta, GA; son of Drew S Jr and Dorothea Jamerson; married Ann Ramsay Langdon; children: Alison Langdon & Elizabeth Jamerson. **Educ:** Hamilton Col, Clinton, NY, BA, 1963; Yale Law Sch, New Haven, CT, LLB,1966. **Career:** Cotton Watt Jones King & Bowlus, Chicago, IL, law assoc, 1966-67; Ill Civil Liberties Union, vol atty, 1966-67; Comayagua Honduras, peace cor psvol, 1967-69; NAACP Legal Defense & Educ & Educ Fund Inc, first asst coun, 1967-77; Agency Internal Develop Honduras, consult prog writer, 1968-69; Rockefeller Comn Latin Am, interpreter, 1969; Temple Univ & Philadelphia, asso prof of Law 1973-75; SUS Dept Justice, asst atty gen, solicitor gen;Yale Law Sch, fac, 1981-, Alfred M Rankin Prof Law, 1992-; Gen US, Solicitor, 1993-96. **Orgs:** Numerous memships including Cong Black Caucus & Nat Conf Educ Blacks, 1972; trustee, Edna McConnell Clark Found, 1988-93; bd dirs, John D &Catherine T MacArthur Found; trustee, Hamilton Col; bd dirs, Petra Found; Reginald Heber Smith Lawyer Fel Prog; Nat Asn Advan Colored People Legal Defense Fund. **Honors/Awds:** Fel, Am Acad Arts & Sci; Alfred M Rankin Professor of Law, Yale Law Sch,1992-; Spirit of Excellence Award, Am Bar Asn, 1997; Hon Doctoral Degree, Univ NC Chapel Hill, 2003; Judge Robert F Kennedy Memorial Human Rights Award, 1990. **Special Achievements:** Publ "Materials on Police Misconduct Litigation"; co-editor "Federal Civil Rights Litigation", Practising Law Inst 1977. **Business Addr:** Alfred M Rankin Professor, Yale Law School, 127 Wall St, PO Box 208215, New Haven, CT 06511, **Business Phone:** (203)432-4992.

DAYS, MICHAEL IRVIN
Journalist, editor. **Personal:** Born Aug 2, 1953, Philadelphia, PA; son of Helen Boles Days and Morris Days; married Angela P Dodson, Apr 17, 1982; children: Edward, Adrian, Andrew & Umi. **Educ:** Col Holy Cross, BA, 1975; Univ MSR Sch Jour, MA, 1976. **Career:** Rochester Gannett Newspaper, reporter, 1978-80; Louisville Courier-Jour, reporter, 1980-84; Wall Street Jour, reporter, 1984-86; Philadelphia Daily News, city hall, educ reporter, 1986-88, asst city ed, 1988-89, bus ed, 1989-91, asst managing ed, 1991-98, dep managing ed, 1998, managing ed, currently; McCormick Tribune fel, 2002. **Orgs:** Pres, Louisville Asn Black Communicators, 1983; Nat Asn Black Journalists, 1985-87; pres, Philadelphia Asn Black Journalists, 1987-88; bd mem, PA SOC Newspaper Eds, 1991-93; Knight Ctr Specized Jour, 1998-. **Business Addr:** Managing Editor, Philadelphia Daily News, 400 N Broad St, PO Box 7788, Philadelphia, PA 19101, **Business Phone:** (215)854-5984.

DAYS, ROSETTA HILL
School administrator. **Personal:** Born in Gibsland, LA; married James; children: Yanise & Regiuel. **Educ:** Grambling Col, BS, 1957; Univ Mich, MS, 1965. **Career:** Wilerson's Home srv Inst, home econ lectr, 1957-60; Webster Parish Sch, teacher, 1960-65, counr, 1965-67; Grambling Col, chief counr, 1967, asstprof & acad counr, 1967-70, asst prof & dir, prof Rescue, 1970; La & US-Cols, grants admin & Equal Opportunity Officer; Grambling St Univ, chmn Counseling & Testing Dept, 1972-73, dean & dir, 2001; La Asn Stud AsstProgs, 1974-75. **Orgs:** Bd dir SW Asn Stud Asst Progs, 1974-75; vice chmn La State Adv Coun, Ment Health; bd dir, Nat Asn Women Criminal Justice; reg adv coun, Emergency Med Serv Sys; Am Personnl Guid Asn; Asn Counr Ed & Supv; Asn Non-White Counr; Am Col Personnel Asn; La Educ Asn; La Asn Measrement & Eval Guid Admin, Grambling, LA; sec-treas League Womn Voters, 1972; chap VP MentelHealth Asn, 1973-74, pres 1974-75; Chap pres Delta Sigma Theta Inc, 1971-73; Nat Coun Negro Women; Bd Dir Lincoln Sickle Cell Asn, 1974-75; VP Lincoln Parish Black Elected Coord Comt, 1974-75; Grambling St Univ. **Honors/Awds:** Scroll of Honor Omega Psi Phi Frat, 1973-74; Lewis Temple CME Church Womn's Day Citation, 1972; Alpha Kappa Mu Nat Hon Soc. **Business Addr:** Project Director, Dean, Grambling State University, 100 Main St, PO Box 8, Grambling, LA 71245.*

DEAN, ANGELA
Executive, fashion designer. **Career:** Deanzign Design Co, celebrity designer & bus owner, currently. **Business Phone:** (323)230-6761.

DEAN, CLARA RUSSELL
School administrator. **Personal:** Born Sep 11, 1927, Greenville, SC; married Miles; children: Miles Jr, Angela, Jacquelynn, Barbara, Wanda & Patricia. **Educ:** Essex County Col, AAS, 1970; Rutgers, BA, psychol, 1970, MA, 1972; Felician Col, ASRN, 1972; Jersey City State, Nursing Sch, attended 1973. **Career:** Col Hosp Coun, bd mem & chair affirm action, 1975-79; Col Med & Dent NJ, supv implimented dent clinic, 1977; Essex County, long range planning bd, 1983-; Bethune Acad, dir, 1984-. **Orgs:** Life mem, Nat Asn Advan Colored People; pres, Clara Dean Civic Asn, 1976-; Asn Bus & Prof Women, 1978-; ed comn, Greater Abyssian Church, 1980-; chairperson, Three City Wide Health Fairs, 1982-84; 100 Black Woman, 1982. **Honors/Awds:** Achievement Award, PATCH-Newark 1981; Recognition Award, NAACP, Newark Br, 1983; Recognition Award, NJ State Commn for the Blind, 1985.

DEAN, CURTIS
Hotel executive. **Career:** Philadelphia Marriott Hotel, mgr, 1995-; Los Angeles Marriott Hotel, mgr; Marriott Hotel, gen mgr, currently. **Business Addr:** General Manager, Marriott Hotel, 1143 NH Ave NW, Washington, DC 20037, **Business Phone:** (202)775-0800.*

DEAN, DANIEL R.
Executive. **Personal:** Born Jan 23, 1941, Atlantic City, NJ; son of Edward and Cora L Harris; married Edna Geraldine Jeter; children: Tracey & Kevin. **Educ:** WVa State Col, BS, Bus Admin, attended 1963; Rutgers Univ, attended 1968; Pace Univ, attended 1977; Stonier Grad Sch Banking, attended 1983. **Career:** Citibank, NA New York, NY, oper officer, 1972-76, oper mgr, 1976-78, oper head, 1978-84; Citicorp USA Inc Atlanta, relationship team mgr, 1984-89; D & E Floor Serv Inc, pres, currently. **Orgs:** Chmn bd dir, Frederick Douglas Liberation Library, 1969-75; treas, Somerset County Comn Action Prog, 1973-76; trustee, Franklin Township Library Bd, 1975-78; pres, Superior Golf Assoc, 1983-84; pres, SouthernSnow Seekers Ski Club, 1985-88. **Military Serv:** AUS, 1st/lt, 1963-65. **Business Addr:** President, D & E Floor Serv Inc, 2501 Old Sewell Rd, Marietta, GA 30068, **Business Phone:** (770)973-5029.*

DEAN, DIANE D
Consultant, educator. **Personal:** Born Aug 26, 1949, Detroit, MI; daughter of Ada Spann and Edward Lesley. **Educ:** Mich State Univ, attended 1968; NC A&T State Univ, BS, 1971; Ind Univ, MS, 1973; Univ Calif Los Angeles, attended 1983; Stanford Univ, Summer Inst, 1981; Case Western Reserve, cert, 1991; Harvard Grad Sch Educ, atteneded 1995; Cornell Univ, mgt develop cert, 2000. **Career:** Univ Miami, area coordr, 1973-75; Occidental Col, dir housing, 1975-78; Univ Southern Calif, asst dir admis, assistance & sch rels, 1978-80; Univ Calif Los Angeles, from asst dir admis to assoc dir admis, 1980-85; Leadership Educ & Develop, dir operations, 1983-85; Nat Action Coun Minorities Engineering, dir incentive grants & educ & training scholar progs, 1985-90; Girl Scouts USA, mgt consult, 1990-95, develop consult educ & training; Columbia Bus Sch, Inst Nonprofit Mgt, fac, 1998-. **Orgs:** Co-facilitator mgt inst, Calif Asn Col, Univ Housing Officers, 1975-78; standing Comt, Nat Asn Col Admis Counr, 1979-86; Black Womens Forum Los Angeles, 1980-; rep, Grad Mgt Admis Coun, 1981-85; Alpha Kappa Alpha; Caif Mus Afro-Am Art, 1984-; Studio Mus, Harlem, 1985-, co-chair, Region VI Nat Asn Stud Personnel Admin, 1985; Schomburg Soc, 1986-; Coun Concerned Black Execs, 1986; lifetime mem, Univ Calif Los Angeles Alumni Asn; NC A&T Alumni Asn, Urban League; lifetime mem, Cass Tech Alumni Asn; Nat Asn Advan Colored People; Corporate Womens Network; Literary Soc, 1989-; Coalition 100 Black Women, 1991-; Nat Soc Fund Raising Execs; Am Soc Training & Develop; Nat Asn Female Exes; lifetime mem, Girl Scouts; Asn Girl Scouts Exec Staff, 1994-. **Honors/Awds:** J&B Winners Circle Award, Paddington Corp, 1984. **Business Addr:** Faculty, Columbia Business School, Institute for Not-for-Profit Management, 2880 Broadway, New York, NY 10025, **Business Phone:** (212)854-6018.

DEAN, JAMES EDWARD
Educator, social worker, state government official. **Personal:** Born Mar 14, 1944, Atlanta, GA; son of Steve Dean, Sr and Dorothy Cox Dean; married Vyvyan A Coleman; children: Sonya V & Monica A. **Educ:** Clark Col, BA, 1966; San Francisco City Col, 1966; Fisk Univ, 1967; Atlanta Univ Sch Soc Work, MSW, 1968; Univ Ga, post grad studies, 1968; Emory Univ, post grad studies, 1975-76. **Career:** Econ Opport Atlanta Inc, human res, 1965-66; Ga Gen Assembly, state rep, 1968-75; Clark Col, Atlanta, GA, dir alumni affairs, 1971-78; MBO, contract procurement specialist, 1978-80; Nat Urban League Inc, asst dir, 1980-82; BMC Realty Co, Atlanta, GA, mgt rep, 1982; State Ga Dept Transp, equal employ opportunity off, 1982-88, equal employ opportunity review off, 1988-. **Orgs:** Atlanta Daily World Newspaper, 1960-70; Atlanta Inquirer Newspaper,1962-68; vpres Comm Serv Inc, Atlanta GA, 1982-89; sec & gov bd mem, Pine Acres Town & Country Club 1989; mem, Ctr Study Presidency, New York, 1988-89; mem, Am Fedn Police; mem, Nat Asn Social Workers; mem, Nat Tech Asn; mem, Southern Ctr Intl Studies; mem, Acad Cert Soc Workers; mem, Leadership Ga Prog Found; Friendship Baptist Church; Alpha Phi Alpha Inc, life mem; HR Butler Lodge, Prince Hall Masonic Order; Atlanta Area Tech Sch Off-Campus Adv Comm; Atlanta Hist Socy; Frontiers Int Inc; Clark Atlanta Univ Alumni Asn, Atlanta Chap; Clark Atlanta Univ Nat Alumni Asn; Minority Worker Training Prog Clark Atlanta Univ; Joymen Club; bd dirs, Atlanta Chapter Univ N Asn; Hunter hills volunteers crime, pres, 2004. **Honors/Awds:** Nat Urban League Fel; Atlanta Univ Multi-Purpose Scholar Award; Alpha Kappa Delta Nat Soc Honour Soc, 1968; Coun Religion & Int Affairs Fel; Outstanding Young Men Atlanta, Atlanta Jaycees; Souther Ctr Int Studies, Atlanta Black/Jewish Coalition; Spec Achievement Award, Dept Transp State GA, 1986, 1988, 1996; A Study Comm Organizaton Techniques Utilized Three Self-Help Projects Securing Low-Income Involvement 1968; Award Political Leadership, Price High Sch; Presidential Citation, Clark Col; Social Action Leadership Award, N Ga Chap, Natl Assn Soc Workers, Inc; Honorary State Trooper; Gov Ga, Lt Colonel Aide de Camp, 1979, 1983, 1991; Gov Ga, Admiral Ga Navy, 1971; Community Service Award, Women Morris Brown Col . **Home Addr:** 87 Burbank Dr NW, Atlanta, GA 30314-2450, **Home Phone:** (404)752-5427. **Business Addr:** District EEO Review Officer, State Georgia Department Transport, Atlanta, GA 30314, **Business Phone:** (404)755-8518.*

DEAN, DR. MARK E
Executive. **Personal:** Born Mar 2, 1957, Jefferson City, TN; son of James and Barbara; married Denise Dean. **Educ:** Univ Tenn, BS, 1979; Fla Atlantic Univ, MSEE, 1982; Stanford Univ, PhD, elec engineering, 1992. **Career:** IBM Corp, dir archit, Power Personal Systs Div, 1993-94, vpres syst platforms, Interactive Broadband Systs, 1994-95, IBM fel & vpres, syst archit & performance, RS/6000 Div, 1995-97, IBM fel & dir, IBM Enterprise Server Group, Advan Tech Dev, 1997-2000, IBM TJ Watson Res Ctr, IBM fel & vpres systs, 2000-. **Orgs:** Bd trustees, Houston-Tillotson Col, 1977-; bd dir, Inroads Inc; bd advrs, Univ Tenn, Sch Engineering; bd advrs, Ga Tech. **Honors/Awds:** Ronald H Brown Am Innovators Award, 1977; Nat Soc Black Engrs, Distinguished Engineer Award, 1999; Founders Day Medal, Univ Tenn, 1999; Career Communs Group, Black Engineer of the Year Award, 2000; Calif African Amer Museum, 50 Most Important African Americans in Tech Award, 2000; IEEE fel, 2001; NAE Member, 2002; Am Acad Arts & Sci, Fel, 2004. **Special Achievements:** Reciverd 30 patents and publications including papers published in the IEEE Computer Society Press, MIT Press, and IBM Technical Disclosure Bulletin. **Business Addr:** IBM Fellow, Vice President, IBM TJ Watson Research Center, IBM, PO Box 704, Yorktown Heights, NY 10598-0218, **Business Phone:** (914)945-1200.

DEAN, TERRANCE
Founder (Originator), spiritualist. **Educ:** Fisk Univ, grad. **Career:** MTV; Men's Empowerment, founder & creator, currently; Young Men's Empowerment, founder & creator, currently; Young Women's Empowerment, founder & creator, currently; co-creator, "The Gathering of Men", with Adeyemi Bandele. **Special Achievements:** Author, 'Be Empowered - 30 Days of Meditation for Men of Color ', 2001, Reclaim Your Power.

DEAN, VYVYAN ARDENA COLEMAN
School administrator, educator. **Personal:** Born Jun 11, 1945, Fort Benning, GA; daughter of Clarence and Dorothy Sims; married James Edward Dean, Jun 12, 1966; children: Sonya V & Monica A. **Educ:** Palmer Memorial Inst, Sedalia, NC, dipl, 1962; Clark Col, BA, 1966; Atlanta Univ, MA, 1973; Ga State Univ, postgrad advan studies, 1987; Atlanta Univ, postgrad advan studies, 1987. **Career:** Atlanta Pub Sch Syst, Atlanta, GA, teacher, 1966-, Atlanta Metrop Col, GED teacher, 1966-, John B Gordon Elementary Sch & Charles R Drew Elementary Sch, curriculum specialist, 1992-97; Marylin Elementary Sch, curriculum specialist, 1997-98; SIA, City Atlanta Parks & Recreation, Atlanta, GA, summer reading prog dir; Atlanta Pub Schs, SIA liaison, specialist, 1999-. **Orgs:** Vpres, Decatur/DeKalb Chap, The Drifters, 1989-91, pres, currently; Nat Asn Educ Young C; Int Reading Asn; Ga Asn Educators; Nat Asn Educators; Atlanta Asn Educators; Curriculum & Supv Develop Asn; Pals, LINKS Interest Group; treas, Atlanta Chap, Circle Lets, 1982-91, pres, 1998-99; corresponding secy, The Inquirers Literary Club, 1983-91; Delta Sigma Theta Sorority, 1969-, sgt arms; AAE, AFT & Ga Adult Literacy Asn, 1970-; Friendship Babtist Church; Delta Sigma Theta; NAACP; volunteer, United Negro Col Fund. **Honors/Awds:** Outstanding Teacher of Children, Atlanta Pub Sch, 1990; Spl Recognition for Outstanding Teaching of Adults, 1989; Special Recognition, DeKalb Housing Resources Comt; Governor's Staff Appointment, Lieutenant Colonel, Aide De Camp, Governor's Staff, Outstanding Elementary Teaching in America, 1975. **Home Addr:** 87 Burbank Dr NW, Atlanta, GA 30314-2850. **Business Addr:** Department of Literacy and Resource Services, Atlanta Public Schools, 2250 Perry Blvd NW Suite 331, Atlanta, GA 30310, **Business Phone:** (404)792-5765.

DEAN, WALTER R
School administrator. **Personal:** Born Dec 12, 1934, Baltimore, MD. **Educ:** Morgan State Col, BA, 1962; Univ MD, MSW, 1969. **Career:** Afro-Am Newspapers Baltimore, reporter, 1962-64; St Club Worker Bur Recreation, 1964-66; Health & Welfare Coun Baltimore, assoc soc res, 1968-69; Legis Dist 41, house rep, 1971-82; Baltimore City Community Col, chairperson, soc & behavioral sci, affairs, coord human serv asst, 1969-, assoc prof soc & behavioral sci, 1998-. **Military Serv:** USAF, airman 1st class. **Business Addr:** Associate Professor, Baltimore City Community College, Department Social & Behavioral Science, 2901 Liberty Heights Ave, Baltimore, MD 21215-7893, **Business Phone:** (410)462-7675.

DEAN, WILLIE B
Association executive. **Personal:** Born Mar 15, 1951, Potts Camp, MS; son of Mattie Delyta Brown and Eddie B; married Pamela Williamson Dean, Oct 25, 1985; children: Cedric Lamont, Jarrod Wilberforce & Matthew Alexander. **Educ:** Univ Memphis, BS; Univ Nebr, MBA; Univ Minn, PhD. **Career:** Glenview YMCA, Memphis, Tenn, prog dir, 1974-75; McDonald YMCA, Ft Worth, Tex, exec dir, 1975-81; Mondanto YMCA, St Louis, Mo, vpres & exec dir, 1981-; Monsanto Co, vpres; Univ Minn, teching asst; YMCA Greater Cleveland, sr vpres opers & chief operating officer, currently. **Orgs:** Jennings-N St Louis Kiwanis Club, 1981-89, pres, 1985; prog chmn, 100 Black Men Metro St Louis, 1983-89; Omega Psi Phi Frat Inc, 1983-89. **Honors/Awds:** Father of the Year, 100 Black Men off St Louis, 1985; Yes I Can Award, Metro Sentinel Newspaper, 1988. **Business Addr:** Senior Vice President, Chief Operating Officer, YMCA of Greater Cleveland, 2200 Prospect Ave Suite, Cleveland, OH 44115-2697, **Business Phone:** (216)344-0095.

DEANDA, PETER
Actor. **Personal:** Born Mar 10, 1938, Pittsburgh, PA; married Fatima Salik, Apr 23, 1960 (divorced 1977); children: Allison & Peter; married Jacqueline Alexander, Nov 11, 1980 (divorced 1982); married Aeros Terra, Jun 21, 1987 (divorced 1992). **Educ:** Actors' Workshop. **Career:** Pittsburgh Playhouse; Weslin Productions; Nasara Productions Labor & IndCom Beverly Hills, founder; Films: The Cool World, 1964; La Mortadella, 1971; The New Centurions, Come Back, Charleston Blue, 1972; Banged Up, 2003; TV series: "One Life to Live", 1968; "Cutter", 1972; "The Deadly Conspiracy", 1975; "The Death Volley", 1975; "The Deadly Conspiracy", 1975; "The Death of a Dream", 1976; "Advice to the Lovelorn", 1981; "Sorority Sisters", 1986; "I Wanna Reach Right Out & Grab Ya, Patterns of the Soul", 1999; "One Life to Live", 1968; "Beulah Land", 1980; "Crusade", 1999; Strong Medicine, 2003. **Orgs:** Nat Asn Advan Colored People; Actors Equity Asn. **Honors/Awds:** Image Awards, Com Publ Black Drama Anthology, 1971. **Special Achievements:** Author of the Play "Ladies in Waiting". **Military Serv:** USAF, 1955-59. **Business Addr:** Actor, William Morris Agency, 1 William Morris Pl, Beverly Hills, CA 90212, **Business Phone:** (310)285-9000.*

DEANE, MORGAN R.
Dentist. **Personal:** Born Sep 17, 1922, Lawrenceville, VA; son of Robert; married Lela W; children: Frances, Judith, Morgan Jr. **Educ:** WV State Col, BA, 1949; Howard Univ, DDS, 1953. **Career:** Cincinnati Health Dept, 1953-74; Health Serv Dir W End Health Ctr, dent dir, 1975; dentist, pvt pract, currently. **Orgs:** OH Valley Dent Soc; Cincinnati Dent Soc; OH State Dent Asn; Am Dent Asn; Am Soc Clin Hypnosis. **Honors/Awds:** Omega Psi Phi Fraternity; Westley Smith Lodge; KY Col. **Military Serv:** World War II, active 3 yrs, inactive 8 yrs. **Business Addr:** Dentist, Private Practitioner, 6186 Lakota Dr, Cincinnati, OH 45243, **Business Phone:** (513)271-3000.*

DEAR, ALICE
Executive director. **Career:** African Develop Bank, exec dir, currently. **Business Addr:** Executive Director, African Development Bank, BP 1387, Abidjan 01 Cote DIvoire, Abidjan, Cote d'Ivoire, **Business Phone:** (225)20—4015.*

DEARMAN, JOHN EDWARD
Judge. **Personal:** Born Mar 28, 1931, Troy, TX; son of Melvin Dearman and Jessie Mae Banks-Evans (deceased); married Ina Patricia Flemming, Dec 22, 1960; children: Tracy, Kelly, Jonathan, Jason. **Educ:** Wiley Col, BA soc studies, 1950; Wayne State Law Sch, JD 1954; Univ Calif, Cert Labor Arbitrator, 1973. **Career:** City of Detroit, soc worker, 1957-58; Pvt Pract, atty, 1957-59, 1961-77; State Calif, judge; San Francisco Super Ct, judge, currently. **Orgs:** Nat Asn Advan Colored People; dir, Golden Gate Bridge Bd, 1966-70; comnr, metropolitan Transport Comn, 1970-75; dir, vpres, Family Serv Asn Am, 1968-72; pres of bd, Family Serv Agency of San Francisco, 1968-72. **Honors/Awds:** Judge of the Yr, SF Trial Lawyers Asn, 1984; Humanitarian Judge of the Yr, Calif Trial Lawyers Asn, 1984. **Business Addr:** Judge, San Francisco Superior Court, 400 McAllister St Rm 204, San Francisco, CA 94102-4514, **Business Phone:** (415)551-4000.*

DEBARGE, CHICO (JONATHAN ARTHUR DEBARGE)
Singer. **Personal:** Born Jun 23, 1966, Grand Rapids, MI. **Career:** Motown Rec, solo artist; Koch Rec, rec artist; Albums: Chico DeBarge, 1986; Talk to Me, 1986; Kiss Serious, 1988; Long Time No See, 1997; The Game, 1999; Free, 2003; Addiction, 2009; Songs: "Talk To Me", 1986; "The Girl Next Door",1987; "Rainy Night", 1987; "Iggin' Me", 1997; Love Still Good, 1997; No Guarantee, 1998; Virgin, 1998; Soopa man Lover, 1999; Give You What You Want, 1999; Listen to Your Man, 2000; Playa Hater, 2000; Home Alone, 2003; Oh No, 2009. **Business Addr:** Recording Artist, Koch Records, Koch Entertainment LLC, 740 Broadway 7th Fl, New York, NY 10003, **Business Phone:** (212)353-8800.*

DEBARGE, EL (ELDRA DEBARGE)
Singer, actor. **Personal:** Born Jun 4, 1961, Grand Rapids, MI. **Career:** DeBarge Musical Group, vocalist, 1978-86; solo artist, 1986-; Solo Albums: El DeBarge, 1986; Gemini, 1989; In the Storm, 1992; Heart Mind & Soul, 1994; Paid in Full, 2002; Ultimate Collection, 2003; Kicking it old school, 2007; Who's Johnny?; All This Love; Love Me in a Special Way; Who's Holding Donna Now; Rhythm of the Night; Album appearances: The Secret Garden, 1990; TV Series: "Motown25: Yesterday, Today, Forever", 1983; "The 11th Annual American Music Awards", 1984; "Motown Returns to the Apollo", 1985; "Bandstand", 1985;"The Facts of Life", 1985; "Miami Vice", 1985; "The 13th Annual American Music Awards", 1986; "Soul Train", 1989; "The 4th Annual Soul Train Music Awards", 1990; "The 6th Annual Soul Train Music Awards", 1992. **Special Achievements:** Hit "Who's Johnny?" featured in film, Short Circuit. **Business Phone:** (818)846-9090.*

DEBARGE, ELDRA. See DEBARGE, EL.

DEBARGE, JONATHAN ARTHUR. See DEBARGE, CHICO.

DEBAS, DR. HAILE T.
Surgeon, educator. **Personal:** Born Feb 25, 1937; married Ignacia Kim. **Educ:** Univ Col Addis Ababa Ethiopia, BS, 1958; McGill Univ, Montreal, Canada, MD, 1963; Ottawa Civic Hosp, Internship, 1964; Vancouver Gen Hosp, Surgical Residency, 1969. **Career:** Univ British Columbia, res fel, 1965-66, 1969-70, asst prof surgery,1971-75; Univ Calif, Los Angeles & Wadsworth Va Med Ctr, res fel, 1972-74, prof surgery, 1981-85; Univ British Columbia, assoc prof surgery, 1976-80; Univ Wash, Seattle, prof surgery, chief gastrointestinal surgery, 1985-87; UCSF, AOA vis prof, 1989; Univ Calif, prof & chmn surgery, 1987-93; UnivTex Med Br, Galveston, vis prof, 1980; Univ Calif, San Francisco, dean, Sch Med, 1993-, chancellor, 1997-98, vice chancellor med affairs, 1998-, Dept Global Health Sci, exec dir, currently; Maurice Galante distinguished prof surg currently; vice chancellor emer med affairs currently; chancellor emer currently; UCSF Global Health Sci, Exec Dir, currently. **Orgs:** Fel, Royal Col Physicians & Surgeons, Canada, 1969-; Am Col Surgeons,1984-; mem, Am Gastroenterological asn, 1974-; mem, Pacific Coast Surgical asn, 1982-; pres, Soc Black Academic Surgeons, 1998-99; mem, Soc Surgical,1987-; dir, Am Bd Surgery, 1990-97; mem, Inst Med, 1990-; pres InterNat Hepato-Biliary-Pancreatic Assoc, 1991-92; fell AAAS, 1992; pres, Am Surgical asn, 2001-02; Inst Med. **Honors/Awds:** British Columbia Surgical Soc Essay Award, 1965; Med Res Coun Canada Fel,1972-74; William H Rorer Res Prize for Original Res So Calif Soc Gastroenterology, 1973; Golden Scalpel Award, Teaching Excellence Div of General Surgery UCLA Sch Med, 1981; Kaiser Award Excellence in Teaching, UCSF Sch Med, 1991; fell, The Rockefeller Found, Bellagio Study &Conference Ctr; Academy was named in honor of Haile T Debas; Abraham Flexner Award, 2004. **Business Addr:** Dean Emeritus, University of California, School of Medicine, 3333 California St, PO Box 0443, San Francisco, CA 94143-0443, **Business Phone:** (415)353-2161.

DEBERRY, ANDRE
Mayor. **Educ:** Jackson State Univ, BA, polit sci. **Career:** Motivational speaker; motivational teacher & trainer; baptist preacher; DeBerry & Bean Ins, owner; City Holly Springs, mayor, currently. **Orgs:** Holly Springs Chamber Com. **Business Addr:** Mayor, City of Holly Springs, 160 S Memphis St, Holly Springs, MS 38635, **Business Phone:** (662)252-4280.

DEBERRY, DONNA
Executive. **Educ:** Calif State Univ, attended. **Career:** Wyndham Int hospity Inc, sr vpres diversity & corp, exec vpres diversity & corp, asst chmn, currently; DRP International, chief exec officer & founder; Nike, vpres diversity, 2006-. **Orgs:** Multicultural Food Service & Hospitality Alliance; Asn Black Hotel Owners, Operators & Develop; Nat Hisp Corp Coun; United States Hisp Chamber Com; Nat Coalition Black Meeting Planners; Nat Asn Black Hotel Owners, Operators and Develop; mem adv coun, eWomen Network Found; Nat Football League; US Olympic Comt. **Special Achievements:** Featured in magazines as Fortune, Time, Essence, Black Enterprise, and Diversity Inc; Served as highest-ranking African American in the hotel and hospitality industry. **Business Addr:** Vice President of Diversity, Nike, 1 Bowerman Dr, Beaverton, OR 75207, **Business Phone:** (503)671-6453.*

DEBERRY, LOIS MARIE
State government official. **Personal:** Born May 5, 1945, Memphis, TN; married Charles Traughber; children: Michael Boyer. **Educ:** Lemoyne-Owen Col, Memphis,TN, BA, 1971. **Career:** Tenn House Rep, Dist 91, state rep, 1972-; Speaker Pro Tempore Tenn House Reps, 1986. **Orgs:** Pres emer, Nat Black Caucus State Legislators; bd dirs, State Legis Leaders Found; pres, bd dirs, Women Govt; Nat Conf State Legislators; founder & chmn, Annual Legis Retreat Tenn Black Caucus; Nat Asn Advan Colored People; Delta Sigma Theta Sorority; Memphis Chap Links. **Honors/Awds:** Tri State Woman of the Year, 1972; Outstanding Woman of the Year, KWAM Gospel, 1973; Glorification of the Image of Black WomanHood Award, 1975; Social Service Award, Memphis Chap Links, 1975; Outstanding Women in Community Service Award, Epsilon, Epsilon Chap Alpha Kappa Alpha Sorority, 1975; The Lois DeBerry Correctional Institute for Special Need Offenders, named in hon, 1977; Outstanding Woman in Corrections Award, Shelby State Community Col, 1979; Martin Luther King Drum Major Award, 1990; NBCSL Legislator of the Year, 1994; Pioneer Award, Nat Polit Cong Black Women Inc, 1996; The Harold Bradley Legislative Leadership Award, 1997; The Kansas City Globe 100 Most Influential African-Americans, 1997; Arthur S Holman Lifetime Achievement Award, 1998; Dr Henry Logan Starks Distinguished Service Award, 1999; Alumni Hall of Fame, Memphis City Schs, 1999; William M Bulger Excel-

lence in State Legislative Leadership Awd, 2000. **Special Achievements:** First African-American woman elected to House of Representatives from city of Memphis; First African-American woman elected speaker pro tempore of the House of Representatives. **Business Addr:** State Representative, Tennessee House of Representatives, District 91 - Part of Shelby county, 15 Legis Plz, Nashville, TN 37243-0191, **Business Phone:** (615)741-3830.

DEBERRY, VIRGINIA
Novelist, fashion model, vice president (organization). **Personal:** Daughter of John and Juanita. **Educ:** State Univ NY, BA 1972; Fisk Univ, attended. **Career:** Model (retired), novelist, executive; Eng teacher, Buffalo, NY; modelling; BB/LW, acting vpres; Hanes hosiery, spokeswoman; Great Dimensions newsletter, fashion ed; Maxima Magazine, cofounder & ed chief; Maxima, chief ed; Co-author: St. Martin's Press, author: Tryin' to Sleep in the Bed You Made, Far From the Tree, & Better Than I Know Myself; Warner Books-Exposures (as Marie Joyce); Gotta Keep on Tryin', What Doesn't Kill You, Simon & Schuster. **Honors/Awds:** African American Literature Award, 2004; Fiction Award, Black Caucus Am Library Asn, 1998. **Business Addr:** Novelist, DeBerry & Grant, PO Box 5224, Kendall Park, NJ 08824.

DEBNAM, CHAD. See DEBNAM, CHADWICK BASIL.

DEBNAM, CHADWICK BASIL (CHAD DEBNAM)
Consultant, association executive, president (organization). **Personal:** Born May 10, 1950, Clayton, NC; son of Clarence and Madie; married Mauria Fletcher, May 1, 1979; children: Andrea Dione. **Educ:** Pac Univ, Forest Grove, BS, polit sci, 1972; Portland State Univ, post grad studies, 1973. **Career:** Mary Acheson House, prog dir, 1972-75; Urban Redevelop Corp, mkt dir, 1976-78; Three Sixty Degree Publ, pres, 1979-82; B Chadwick Ltd, pres, 1982; King Neighborhood Asn, chair, pres, currently. **Orgs:** Bd mem, Multnomah Co Charter Rev, 1982-84; chmn, Adv Steering Comt Inner NE YMCA, 1983-85; Albina Lions Club, 1983-; pres, Ore Bus League, 1984-87; Am Mkt Asn, 1986-87; chmn, Black Republican Coun Ore, 1986-88. **Honors/Awds:** Keynote speaker, Annual Banquet Scottish Rites Masons, 1984; Century Award, Portland Metro YMCA, 1984-85; Businessman of Month, MBE Torch Award, Am Contractor Pub, 1985; guest lectr, Camp Enterprise Downtown Rotary, 1986. **Home Addr:** 5215 NE Mallory, Portland, OR 97201, **Home Phone:** (503)281-6315. **Business Phone:** (503)281-6315.

DEBRO, JOSEPH ROLLINS
Executive. **Personal:** Born Nov 27, 1928, Jackson, MS; married Anita English; children: Keith, Karl, Kraig. **Educ:** Univ CA, Berkeley, BA, MS, 1959. **Career:** Model Cities, Oakland, CA, dir; Oakland Small Bus Develop Ctr, dir; NASA, res scientist; Producers Cotton Oil Co, chem engr; Nal Asn Minority Contractors, exec dir; trans Bay Engr & Builders, CFO, 2002-. **Orgs:** pres, Reca Inc; pres, Housing Assistance Coun; pres, JDA Consult Group Inc; pres, Gaylor Construction Co; chmn, minority Bus Enterprise Task Force Inc; vpres, Trans Bay Engrs & Builders, Sigma Xi; Alpha Phi Alpha; publ, More Than 25 Articles Scientific Bus J. **Business Addr:** Chief Financial Officer, Transbay Engineering & Builders, 1025 Vermont Ave NW Suite 606, Washington, DC 20005, **Business Phone:** (202)842-8600.*

DEBRO, DR. JULIUS
School administrator. **Personal:** Born Sep 25, 1931, Jackson, MS; son of Joseph and Seleana; married Darlene Conley; children: Blair & Renee. **Educ:** Univ San Francisco, CA, BA, polit sci, 1953; Univ San Francisco Law Sch, attended 1957; San Jose State Univ, MA, sociol, 1967; Univ Calif, Berkeley, PhD, 1975. **Career:** NIH, fel, 1969-70; Narcotic & Drug Res Inc, res assoc, 1989-90; Univ Md, Inst Crim Justice & Criminol, asst prof, 1971-79; Comn Criminol & Criminal Justice Educ, Wash DC, prin investr, 1978-79; Dept Pub Admin, chmn, 1979-80; Clark Atlanta Univ, Dept Criminal Justice, dir 1979-, profcriminol, chmn, 1985-86, chmn criminal justice admin, 1986-91; acting asst provost, 1992; Justice Quarterly dep ed; Univ Wash Grad Sch, Col Arts &Sci, Seattle, WA, assoc dean, 1991-99, adj prof am ethnic studies, Law Soc& Justice Prog, prof, currently. **Orgs:** Dir, Spec Opportunity Prog, Univ Calif, Berkeley, 1968-70; bd mem, Metrop Atlanta Crime Comn, 1984-; Citizen's Review Bd, Atlanta, GA, 1985-; Cent Atlanta Progress Study Comn, 1986-87; Atlanta Anti-Crime Bd, 1987; chmn, Metrop Atlanta Crime Comn, 1987-88; investigative panel, Ga Bar Asn, 1988-90; fel Western Soc Criminol; Coun Higher Educ Criminal Justice; Alpha Phi Alpha; chmn, Drug Task Force, Fulton County, GA; Am Soc Criminol. **Honors/Awds:** Herbert Bloch Award, Am Soc Criminol. **Military Serv:** AUS, col; Korean Victory Medal. **Business Addr:** Professor, University of Washington, Department Sociology, Gowen 107 202 Savery Hall, PO Box 353340, Seattle, WA 98195-3340.

DECARAVA, ROY RUDOLPH
Photographer, educator. **Personal:** Born Dec 9, 1919, New York, NY; son of Andrew and Elfreda; married Sherry, Sep 4, 1970; children: Susan, Wendy & Laura. **Educ:** Cooper Union Inst, attended 1940; Harlem Art Ctr, attended 1942; George Wash Carver Art Sch, NY, attended 1945. **Career:** Berman Studios, illustrator, 1943-58; free-lance photographer, 1958-65; Sports Illustrated Mag, photographer, 1965-75; Look mag, photographer; Newsweek mag, photographer; Time mag, photographer; Life mag, photographer; Cooper Union, adjunct prof art, 1970-73; Hunter Col, City Univ NY, assoc prof, 1975-78, prof, 1978-88, distinguished prof art, 1988-. **Orgs:** Chair, Am Soc Mag Photographers. **Honors/Awds:** Art Service Award, Mt. Morris United Presby Church, NY, 1969; Benin Creative Photography Award, 1972; honorary citizen of Houston, Texas, 1975; Artistic & Cultural Achievement Award, Community Mus Brooklyn, NY, 1979; Honorary DFA, RI Inst Fine Arts, 1985; Honorary DFA, The Md Inst, 1986; Distinguished Career in Photography Award, Friends of Photography, 1991; Special Citation for Photographic Journalism, Am Soc Mag Photographers, 1991; Honorary DFA, Wesleyan Univ, 1992; Nat Medal of Arts, 2006. **Special Achievements:** In 1952 DeCarava became the first African-American recipient of a John Simon Guggenheim Memorial Fellowship; Publications: The Sound I Saw, book of jazz photos, 1983; Roy DeCarava-Photographs, 1981; exhibition, "The Sweet Flypaper of Life," Roy DeCarava and Langston Hughes, shown throughout the US and overseas. **Military Serv:** AUS, topographical draftsman, 1943.

DECOSTA, HERBERT ALEXANDER, JR.
Executive. **Personal:** Born Mar 17, 1923, Charleston, SC; son of Herbert and Julia Craft; married Emily Spencer; children: Gail D. **Educ:** IA State Univ, BS, Architectural Engineering, 1944. **Career:** exec (retired); Nat Adv Com Aeronautics Langley Field, architectural Engr, 1944-47; H A DeCosta Co Gen Contractors, vpres, 1948-60, pres, 1960-90. **Orgs:** bd mem, United Way Charleston County; bd mem Charleston Trident Chamber com; bd mem, SC State Bd for Technical & Comprehensive Educ; founding bd mem, Charleston Bus & Prof Assoc; Nat Assoc Minority Contractors; bd mem Nat Assoc Home Builders; SC Chamber Com, Benedict Col Trustee Bd; SC State Historic Preservation Review Bd; City charleston bd of architectural review; city charleston planning & zoning comn; carolina art assoc; Sr Warden St Marks Episcopal Ch Charleston; bd mem Historic Charleston Found; Penn Community Serv inc; bd, Spoleto Festival; SC Archives & History Found; the Art Forms & Theatre Concepts; the SC African American Heritage Coun; Cannon St YMCA; Trustee, Col Building Arts Charleston. **Honors/Awds:** Man of the year, Alpha Phi Alpha Frat, 1970; silver beaver award, Coastal Carolina Coun Boy Scouts Am, 1972; American Institute of Architects Award, Mayor Charleston; SC Governor Award, 1998; the Frances R. Edmunds Award, Historic Charleston Found, 2002; Three Sisters Award, Committee Save city, 2004. *

DECOSTA-WILLIS, DR. MIRIAM
Educator. **Personal:** Born Nov 1, 1934, Florence, AL; daughter of Frank A and Beautine Hubertt; married Archie W Willis Jr, Oct 20, 1972 (deceased); children: Tarik Sugarmon, Elena S Williamson, Erika S Echols & Monique A Sugarmon. **Educ:** Wellesley Col, BA, 1956; Johns Hopkins Univ, MA, 1960, PhD, 1967. **Career:** Educator (retired); Owen Col, instr, 1960-66; Memphis State Univ, assoc prof Spanish, 1966-70; Howard Univ, assoc prof Spanish, 1970-74, prof & chmn dept, 1974-76; LeMoyne-Owen Col, prof, Romance Lang, prof Spanish &dir Du Bois prog, 1979-88; Univ Md, emer Prof. **Orgs:** Coll Language Assn; bd of dirs, MSU Center for Rsch on Women; chair TN Humanities Coun; bd Federation of State Humanities Couns; editorial bd Sage & Afro-Hispanic Review; life mem NAACP; chmn, Exec bd/mem, TN Humanities Coun, 1981-87; chmn & founding mem, Memphis Black Writers Workshop. **Honors/Awds:** Phi Beta Kappa 1956; Johns Hopkins Fellowship 1965; editor Blacks in Hispanic Literature Kennikat Pr 1977; articles in CLAJ, Journal of Negro History, Black World Negro History Bulletin, Revista Inter americana, Caribbean Quart; Sage Afro-Hispanic Review; Outstanding Faculty Mem of the Year, Le Moyne-Owen Coll, 1982; Homespun Images: An Anthology of Black Memphis Writers & Artists, 1988; editor, The Memphis Diary of Ida B Wells, Beacon Press, 1994. **Special Achievements:** First African American faculty member of Memphis State University; books: Daughters of the Diaspora; Afra-Hispanic Writers. *

DEE, MERRI
Talk show host, radio broadcaster. **Personal:** Born Oct 30, 1936, Chicago, IL; daughter of John Blouin and Agnes Blouin; children: Toya Dorham. **Educ:** St Xavier Univ, bus admin. **Career:** WBEE Radio, news hostess of talk-music prog women's ed, 1966-72; WSDM-FM radio, hostess, 1968-69; WSNS-TV, hostess TV talk show, 1971-72; Cont Bank, spokesperson, 1972-76; WGN-TV, news announcer, ed & spokesperson, 1972-76; WGN-Radio, news announcer, ed & spokesperson, 1972-76; Hillman's Foods, consumer adv, 1974-75; Kraft Foods, nutrit spokesperson, 1975-76 & 1979-80; WGN Broadcasting, newscaster & announcer; WGN-TV, dir community rels, currently. **Orgs:** Dir & co-founder, Athletes Better Educ; host, United Negro Col Fund, Telethon Chicago; Am Fedn TV & Radio Announcers; Ronald McDonald House Charities; Assoc Col Ill; Adoptions Unlimited; Junior Achievement; Gateway Charitable Found; Nat Tree Trust Found; Chinese Am Serv League; Ill Atty Gen's Violent Crime Victims Comn; States Atty's Adv Coun violence. **Honors/Awds:** Muscular Dystrophy Fundraising Trophy; National Association of Media Women Award; National Association of Black Accountants Recognition Award; Woman of the Year, Chicago Church Women's Fedn; Frederick D. Patterson Award, United Negro Col Fund, 1990; Little City Foundation Award, 1995; President's Award, Nat Asn Negro Bus & Prof Women's Club, 1995; Bethany Christian Service Award, 1995; Outstanding Media Person, AT&T; Outstanding Community Role Model, Kellogg's Corp; National Voice Award; Adoption Spokesperson Award, YMCA Metro Chicago; Outstanding Leadership Award; Woman of the Year, Today's Chicago Woman News; Mercedes Mentor Award, Chicago Mag; History Maker Award, Nat Hist Makers Asn. **Business Addr:** Director, Manager, WGN-TV Children's Charities, Community Relations, 2501 W Bradley Pl, Chicago, IL 60618, **Business Phone:** (773)528-2311.*

DEE, RUBY (RUBY ANN WALLACE)
Actor. **Personal:** Born Oct 27, 1924, Cleveland, OH; married Ossie Davis, Jan 1, 1948 (died 2005); children: Nora, Guy & Hasna; married Frank Dee Brown, Jan 1, 1941 (divorced 1945). **Educ:** Hunter Col, BA, 1945; Am Negro Theatre, apprentice, 1944. **Career:** Films: What a Guy, 1939; Jackie Robinson Story, 1950; The St Louis Blues,1958; A Raisin in the Sun, 1961; Gone Are the Days, 1963; Buck & the Preacher, 1972; Do the Right Thing, 1989; Cop & a Half, 1993; Just Cause,1995; A Simple Wish, 1997; Baby Geniuses, 1999; Baby of the Family, 2002; Dream St, 2005; No 2, 2006; The Way Back Home, 2006; Steam, 2007; American Gangster, 2007; All About Us, 2007; TV series: "The Stand", 1994; "Having Our Say: The Delany Sisters' First 100 Years", 1999; "PassingGlory", 1999; "My One Good Nerve: A Visit With Ruby Dee", 1999; "A Stormin Summer", 2000; "Finding Buck McHenry", 2000; "Taking Back Our Town", 2001; "Their Eyes Were Watching God", 2005; "CSI: Crime SceneInvestigation", 2007. **Orgs:** Nat Asn Advan Colored People; Southern Christian Leadership Conf; Delta Sigma Theta. **Honors/Awds:** Obie Award, 1971; Martin Luther King Jr Award, Operation PUSH 1972; Frederick Douglass Award, NY Urban League, 1970; Drama Desk Award, 1974; Theater Hall of Fame, 1988; Best Performance by an Actress, NAACP Image Award, 1989; NAACP Image Awards, Hall of Fame, 1989; Literary Guild Award,1989; Monarch Award, 1990; Emmy Award, Best Supporting Actress, Decoration Day, 1991; Screen Actors Guild Awards, Lifetime Achievement Award, 2001; Kennedy Center Honor, 2004. **Special Achievements:** Author: Take It From the Top; My One Good Nerve; Two Ways to Count to Ten; Tower to Heaven; Glowchild; co-author: With Ossie & Ruby: In This Life Together. **Business Addr:** Actor, The Artist Agency, 10000 Santa Monica Blvd, Los Angeles, CA 90067.

DEESE, DERRICK LYNN, SR.
Football player. **Personal:** Born May 17, 1970, Culver City, CA; married Felicia; children: Drew, Dante & Derrick Lynn Jr. **Educ:** El Camino Col, torrance, CA; S Calif. **Career:** Football player (retired); San Francisco 49ers, tackle, 1992-03; Tampa Bay Buccaneers, offensive tackle, 2004-05; fox sports radio, 2004. **Honors/Awds:** Super Bowl champion, XXIX. *

DEESE, GLENDA
Government official. **Personal:** Born in Selma, AL; married; children: 3. **Educ:** Concordia Col, AA, bus mgt, 2003. **Career:** Ala Dept Pub Safety, state trooper, 1980; Ala Dept Pub Safety, Hwy Patrol Div, trooper, 1981; Ala Criminal Justice Training Ctr, asst basic training coordr, 1988, asst comdr, spec proj coordr, 2006-; Ala Dept of Pub Safety, capt, 1997; Ala Dept Pub Safety Admin Div, major; Ala Dept Pub Safety, asst dir, 2003-05. **Special Achievements:** first African-American woman to complete the trooper cadet program; first woman to hold the second highest position in the state troopers; first Major to ever be assigned at the Alabama Criminal Justice Training Center in Selma. **Business Addr:** Special Projects Coordinator, Major, Alabama Criminal Justice Training Center, Craig Field, 349 Ave C, Selma, AL 36701, **Business Phone:** (334)872-0435.*

DEESE, MANUEL
Government official. **Personal:** Born Nov 8, 1941, Toomsboro, GA; married Jean Matthews; children: Eric & Byron. **Educ:** Morgan State Univ, BA, Polit Sci; Am Univ Sch Govt & Pub Admin, MPA. **Career:** Nat League Cities DC, policy analyst, 1969-71; City Alexandria, asst to city mgr, 1971-74; City Richmond, asst city mgr admin, 1974-77, asst city mgr opers, 1977-79, city mgr, 1979; Deese, Hastings & Miller, managing partner, currently. **Orgs:** Pres, Nat Forum Black Pub Admr, 1983-85; governing bd, Am Asn for Pub Admin; bd dir, Richmond Regional Criminal Justice Training Ctr; bd, Intl City Mgt Asn. **Honors/Awds:** Alumnus of the Year, Morgan State Univ, 1981; Recipient of numerous awards for leadership in govt & civic affairs. **Business Addr:** Managing Partner, Deese, Hastings, & Miller, 700 E Main St Suite 1600, Richmond, VA 23219, **Business Phone:** (804)649-1121.

DEFRANTZ, ANITA L.
Association executive. **Personal:** Born Oct 4, 1952, Philadelphia, PA; daughter of Robert D (deceased) and Anita P. **Educ:** Conn Col, BA, polit philos, 1974; Univ Pa Sch Law, JD, 1977. **Career:** US Women's Rowing Team, 1975-80, team capt, 1976 Olympics, Montreal; juv Law Ct Philadelphia, atty, 1977-79; World Rowing

Championships, 1978; Princeton Univ, adminr, 1979-81; Corp Enterprise Develop, coun, 1980-81; Los Angeles Olympic Organizing Comt, vpres, 1981-84; Int Olympic Comt, 1986, exec bd, 1992, vpres, 1997; Amateur Athletic Found, pres, currently. **Orgs:** Int Olympic Comt, 1986-, exec bd, 1992-01, vpres, 1997-00, Women & Sport Working Group, chmn; trustee, emer, Connecticut Col; bd dirs, exec comt, US Olympic Comt; Int Comt Fair Play; Acad Sports; bd dir, Salt Lake City Olympic, Organizing Comt; Women's World Cup 1989, vpres, Children NOW, Fed Int Socs d'Aviron; pres, bd mem, Kids in Sports; bd mem, Vesper Rowing Club; bd mem, US Rowing Asn; trustee, Women's Sports Found; vpres, Int Rowing Fed, 1993; pres & mem, LA84 Found Bd Dirs. **Honors/Awds:** Black Women of Achievement Award, Nat Asn Adv Colored People Legal Defense & Educ Fund; Award for Sports, Essence Mag; Silver Achievement Award for Pub Serv, Los Angeles YWCA; Olympic Torch Award, US Olympic Comt, 1988; honourable Doctor of Laws, Univ Rhode Island, 1989; Hall of Fame inductee, Conn Col, 1989; Major Taylor Award, 1989; Metrop Los Angeles YMCA, Martin Luther King Jr Brotherhood Award, 1990; Hon Award, Natl Assn of Women Collegiate Athletic Adminr, 1991; Jack Kelly Award, US Rowing's Bd Dirs, 1991; Doctor of Philanthropy Degree, Pepperdine Univ, 1992; Award of Excellence, Sports Lawyers Asn, 1992; Turner Broadcasting Trumpet Award, 1993; Billie Jean King, Contribution Award, 1996; Medal of Hon, Int Softball Fed; Doctor of Laws, Mills Col, 1998; Doctor of Laws, Mount Holyoke Col, 1998; numerous other awards. **Special Achievements:** One of the 100 Most Powerful People in Sports, The Sporting News, 1991-97; one of Southern California's "Rising Stars", Los Angeles Times Mag, 1988; one of America's 100 Most Important Women, Ladies Home J; Rowing Awards: Bronze Medal, Olympic Games, 1976; Silver Medal, World Championships, 1978; Six National Championships; Olympic Order Bronze Medal, 1980; first American woman and first African American to serve as vice president of the International Olympic Committee; 101 Most Influential Minorities in Sports, Sports Illustrated, 2003. **Business Addr:** President, Amateur Athletic Foundation, 2141 W Adams Blvd, Los Angeles, CA 90018, **Business Phone:** (323)730-4600.*

DEGENESTE, HENRY IRVING (HANK DEGENESTE)
Manager, vice president (organization). **Personal:** Born Aug 16, 1940, Newark, NJ; son of William Henry and Olive Pansy Lopes; divorced; children: Michelle, Rene & Henry Jr. **Educ:** Fairleigh Dickinson Univ, attended 1962; Rutgers Univ, cert criminal justice planning & res, 1975; Fed Bur Invest, cert exec mgt, 1976; Columbia Univ, cert exec mgt criminal justice syst, 1976; Adelphi Univ, BA, bus admin, 1976; John Jay Col, MPA. **Career:** Edmond Assocs, draftsman, 1962-65; Newark Pub Schs, sch teacher, 1962-65; US Postal Serv, staff, 1965-67; Port Authority of NY & NJ, Law Enforcement, police officer, 1967-74, police sgt, 1974-76, police lt, 1976-78, police capt, 1978-81, supt of police, 1984-88, dir pub safety & supt police, 1988-90; Prudential Securities, sr vpres & dir corp security & treas, 1990-2005; iJET Intelligent Risk Systs, vpres risk mgt, currently. **Orgs:** Pres, Nat Orgn Black Law Enforcement Execs, 1982-83; pres, Hudson County, NJ Chief Police, 1987-88; chmn, Tri-State Radio Planning Comt, 1988-90; pres, Am Acad Prof Law Enforcement, 1989-91; NJ Coun Corrections, 1990; bd mem, NY & NJ Cargo Security Coun; bd mem, NJ Spec Olympics; bd mem, Mott Hall Sch Math, Sci & Tech Gifted & Talented Stud; bd mem, Police Exec Res Forum; Am Soc Pub Admin; Am Mgt Asn; Criminal Justice Educrs NY; Am Soc Indust Sec. **Honors/Awds:** New Jersey Pride Award, 1986; Three Police Commendation Medals;Meritorious Police Duty Medal; Port Authority Executive Director's UnitCitations; Whitney M Young Jr Award, Nat Urban League; Two Black Achieversin Industry Award, Harlem YMCA; United Nations Peace Medal. **Special Achievements:** Author, EMS and the Police Response to Terrorism, The Police Chief, May 1987; Urban Transit Center: Where Crime and the Homeless Meet, Law Enforcement News, 1987; Policing Transportation Facilities, Charles CThomas, Publisher, 1994. **Home Addr:** 40 Conger St, Bloomfield, NJ 07003, **Home Phone:** (201)748-2373. **Business Addr:** Vice President of Risk Management, iJET Intelligent Risk Systems, 910F Bestgate Rd, Annapolis, MD 21401, **Business Phone:** (410)573-3860.

DE GRAFF, JACQUES ANDRE
Executive. **Personal:** Born Nov 11, 1949, New York, NY; son of Beryl Hay and James Augustus; married Jacqueline Riley, Sep 29, 1974; children: Danielle Janet. **Educ:** Queensborough Community Col, Astoria, AA, 1971; Hunter Col, NY, BA, 1975; Develop Real Property, attended 1980; NY Univ, Real Estate Inst, attended 1981; Harvard Univ Community Develop Finance, attended 1981; NY Theol Sem, Mdiv, currently. **Career:** NY State Urban Develop Corp, New York, vpres finance, 1979-83; Packard Press Inc, NY, nat acct rep, 1985-86; Securities Press Inc, NY, vpres, 1986-88; De Graff Unlimited Inc, NY, managing partner, 1988-90; Blueberry Treatment Ctrs Inc, Brooklyn, exec dir, 1990; Rev Al Sharpton Mayor, NY, campaign mgr, campaign coord, Nat Action Network, pres, currently. **Orgs:** Vice chmn, Adv Bd, Manhattan Urban League, 1987-; friend, Studio Mus, 1986-; 3rd vpres, Nat 100 Black Men NY Chap. **Honors/Awds:** Community Service Award, Caribbean Am Legal Inst, 1980; Governor's Citation, Gov NY, 1982; National Leader Service Award, 1983; Businessman of the Year, DRIVE, 1988. **Home Addr:** 60 Harbor Key Harmon Cove, Secaucus, NJ 07094, **Home Phone:** (201)866-5017. **Business Addr:** President, Rev Al Sharpton for Mayor, National Action Network, 16 Ct St 3rd Fl, Brooklyn, NY 11241, **Business Phone:** (718)834-4880.

DEGRAFFENREIDT, ANDREW. See Obituaries section.

DEGRAFFENREIDT, JAMES H
Executive, lawyer, chairperson. **Educ:** Yale Col, BA, 1974; Columbia Univ, JD & MBA, 1978. **Career:** Md, asst people's counsel; Hart, Carroll & Chavers, partner; Wash Gas Light Co, sr managing atty, 1986, vpres rates & regulatory affairs, 1991, sr vpres rates & regulatory affairs, pres & chief oper officer, 1994-98, pres, chief exec officer, 1998; WGL Holdings, bd dir, 2000-, chmn & chief exec officer, currently. **Orgs:** Bd mem, Harbor Bankshares Corp; Mass Mutual Financial Group; chmn, Am Gas Asn, 2007-; Alliance to Save Energy; coach, St Matthews Athletic Asn; coach, Northwood Baseball League; vpres, Walters Art Mus; Md Sci Ctr; Alliance to Save Energy; MedStar Health; Harbor Bankshares Corp; Greater Wash Bd Trade. **Business Addr:** Chairman, Chief Executive Officer, WGL Holdings Inc, 101 Constitution Ave NW, Washington, DC 20080, **Business Phone:** (703)750-2000.

DEHART, HENRY R.
Engineer. **Personal:** Born Nov 11, 1931, Staten Island, NY; married Panzy Hawk; children: Henry, Linda. **Educ:** Polytech Inst NY, BCE, 1958. **Career:** Engineer (retired). NY City Dept Traffic, dir hwy design, 1992. **Orgs:** Licensed prof engr, NY; past warden, past dir, SS; licensed lay reader, St Gabriels PE Church; past pres, Staten Island Br Nat Asn Advan Colored People, 1965; past comdr, Am Legion, 1966; acolyte master, St Gabriels Church. **Honors/Awds:** Friend of Howard Adward NY Club, Howard Univ Alumni, 1975; Past President Award, Staten Island Br, Nat Asn Advan Colored People, 1986; Bishop Cross Long Island Diocese, 1987; Meritorious Award for Community Service, 1987. **Military Serv:** USAF, 1952-56. **Home Addr:** 11006 214 St, Queens Village, NY 11429, **Home Phone:** (718)479-8315. *

DEHART, DR. PANZY H
Social worker. **Personal:** Born May 18, 1934, Cleveland County, NC; daughter of Henry Kilgore and Sallie Maude Hawk Owens; married Henry Ross; children: Henry Jr & Linda. **Educ:** Howard Univ, BA, 1956, MSW, 1958; George Mercer Sch Theol, Cert Christian Theol, 1997; NYU Grad Sch Social Work, PhD, 1999. **Career:** Social worker (retired); DC Dept Welfare, child welfare social worker, 1958-61; Vets Admin, clin social worker, 1961-65; NY City Dept Health, consult, 1968-70; Inwood House, supvr, 1966-68, 1970-72; NY Univ Med Ctr, rehab social worker, 1976-96. **Orgs:** Pres, Howard Univ Alumni Club, New York City, 1970-74; bd dir, Parent Preparation Inc, 1970-75; Queens Chap Jack & Jill Am Inc, 1973-87; dir, Jack & Jill Comput Assisted Lab, 1985-87; Concerned Citizens S Queens, 1987; Partnership for the Homeless, 1991-; Psychoanalytic Res Soc Sect VI, Am Psychol Asn, 1992-99; bd dirs, Episcopal Charities, 1996-; St Gabriel's Episcopal Church, Hollis, Queens. **Honors/Awds:** Serv Award, Howard Univ Alumni Club, 1972; Nat Achievement Award, Lambda Kappa Mu Sorority, 1974; Serv Award, Jack & Jill Am Inc, Queens Chap, 1986. **Home Addr:** 110-06 214th St, Queens Village, NY 11429, **Home Phone:** (718)479-8315.

DEHERE, TERRY
Basketball player. **Personal:** Born Sep 12, 1971, New York, NY. **Educ:** Seton Hall Univ. **Career:** Los Angeles Clippers, guard, 1993-97; Sacramento Kings, 1997-99; Vancouver Grizzlies, 1999; N Charleston Lowgators, 2001-02, Jersey City Bd Ed, 2007-. **Honors/Awds:** Big East Men's Basketball Player of the Year, 1993.

DEJESUS, EDWARD
Founder (Originator). **Educ:** Fordham Univ, BA; New Sch Social Res, MA; Rutgers Univ, Ctr Strategic Urban Community Leadership Prog, attended. **Career:** Youth Develop & Res Fund, founder & pres, currently; WK Kellogg Found, nat fel. **Orgs:** Vice chair, Nat Youth Employ Coalition, currently; Sar Levitan Ctr Youth Policies, John Hopkins Univ. **Honors/Awds:** Eli and May Rudin Community Service Award, 1993; One of the top 40 under 40 in the Wash Metrop Area, 2000; October 12th Ed DeJesus Day, named in honor, 2003. **Business Addr:** Founder, President, Youth Development & Research Fund, 20405 Studio Pl, Gaithersburg, MD 20886, **Business Phone:** (301)215-2566.

DEJOIE, CAROLYN BARNES MILANES
Educator, counselor. **Personal:** Born in New Orleans, LA; daughter of Edward Franklin Barnes and Alice Milanes Barnes; children: Deirdre Jeanelle, Prudhomme III & Duan Kendall. **Educ:** Xavier Univ La, BA; Nat Univ Mex, MA, 1962; Univ Wis, MSW, 1970; Union Grad Sch, PhD, 1976. **Career:** Wis cert marriage & family therapist, clinical social worker; Southern Univ, instr, 1962-63; Va State Col, asst prof, 1963-66; Univ Wis Ext, admin specialist, 1967-68, asst pres, 1970-73, prof continuing educ & prof develop, 1973-92, prof emeritus currently; Human Rels Coun Serv, owner, dir, 1980-; psychotherapist Pvt Pract, 1980-; Sun & Shadows Publishing Co, owner, 1987-; Lectura, 1994-; Itinerant Journalistic reporter, 1996-; Univ Havana, Socio-Economic Aspects Cuban Life, investr, 1996-97; Secular Humanists, Madison, WI, founder, dir; Wis Bd Bar Examiners, rep, currently. **Orgs:** Foreign language consult, Travenol de Mexico Am British Cowdray Hosp Mex, 1959-62; exec dir, Centro Hispano-Americano Madison, 1978-79; ed adv bd mem, Jour Negro Educ, 1985-; exec bd, Nat Asn Advan Colored People, Madison WI, 1987-; exec bd mem, Negro Educ Rev, 1988-; vpres, Nat Asn Media Women, 1989-90; crespar, Johns Hopkins Univ, 1996-; Univ League, 1995-. **Honors/Awds:** Fulbright US Govt, 1966; Achievement Against Odds Award, Wis Humanities Comn, Smithsonian Inst Exhibit, 1983; Outstanding Contribution, Soc Alpha Kappa Alpha, 1984; Wisconsin Governor's Award, 1984; Woman of the Year Award, Nat Asn Media Women, 1985; Recognition of Service Award, Nat Asn Negro Bus & Prof Women, 1986; Bd Commissioners Genessee County MI Laudatory Resolution, 1986; Golden Egg Award, Nat Asn Media Women, 1987; Appreciation Award, City New Orleans, 1988; Unsung Heroine Award, Nat Asn Advan Colored People - Madison, WI, 1988; Louisiana Black Heritage Award, For Get Me Knots Inc, 1990; Outstanding Professional Woman & Role Model, Dollars & Sense, 1991; Certificate of Recognition of Emerita Status, Univ Wis Madison, 1992; Consortium of Doctor's Award, 1993. **Special Achievements:** Publications, Students Speak Out: Racial Problems and What Students Can Do About Them; Blackness Amidst Whiteness in Educ, 1978; Varied Views of Death, 1978; Readings from a Black Perspective An Anthology, 1984, 1986; Racism-sexism, The Interlock of Racist and Sexist Social Problems, 1986, 1988. **Business Addr:** Director, Carolyn Dejoie & Assocs, 5322 Fairway Dr, Madison, WI 53711-0000, **Business Phone:** (608)274-2152.

DEJOIE, MICHAEL C
Executive. **Personal:** Born Apr 25, 1947, New Orleans, LA; son of Constant C Jr and Julia B; divorced. **Educ:** Grinnell Col, AB, 1968; Loyola Inst Polit, fel, 1970; Columbia Univ, Grad Sch Bus, MBA, 1977. **Career:** WWL-TV, consumer affairs reporter, 1968-70; CBS News, assoc producer, ed, 1970-78; AT&T Long Lines, Mgr, int & pub serv advert, 1978-79, AT&T Long Lines AT&T Communs, Mgr, bus advert, 1979-84, AT&T Communs, Southern Region Media Ctr, Mgr, 1984-85; MCD Communs Consults Inc, owner, consult, 1986-; Southern Christian Leadership CNF, dir, Communs, 1991-94; Am Asn Retired Persons, Communs rep, currently. **Orgs:** Shop steward, Writers Guild Am E, 1970-78; Atlanta Asn Black Journalists, 1987, 1992-; Int Asn Bus Communicators, 1987-; Am Fed TV & Radio Artists, 1968-70; bd mem, Black Pub Rels SOC Atlanta, 1988-90; bd mem, Coord Coun Atlanta Pub Rels Orgs, 1989. **Honors/Awds:** various advertising awards, 1978-84; Silver Quill for Best Video Prod, IABC, Operator, 1985; Best Ed, Asn Black Journalist, 1994. **Special Achievements:** Assoc Producer Midwest Bureau, CBS Weekend News with Dan Rather, 1974-76; editor: SCLC Magazine, 1991-94; Producer: "What's Going On? with Joseph Lowery," WIGO-TV, 1992-94. **Military Serv:** AFROTC, USF Reserves, squadron first sgt, 1964-67; Good Conduct, Corps Photographer & Illusr, Color Guard comdr. **Business Addr:** Communications Representative, American Association of Retired Persons, 999 Peachtree St NE Suite 1650, Atlanta, GA 30309, **Business Phone:** (404)888-0077.

DE JONGH, PROF. JAMES LAURENCE
Educator. **Personal:** Born Sep 23, 1942, St Thomas, Virgin Islands of the United States; son of Mavis Elizabeth Bentlage and Percy Leo. **Educ:** Williams Col, BA, 1964; Yale Univ, MA, 1967; New York Univ, PhD, 1983. **Career:** Rutgers Univ Newark, instr, 1969-70; City Col City Univ NY, prof, 1970-; CUNY Inst Res African Diapora Americas Caribbean, IRADAC, prof, eng, dir, 1997-. **Orgs:** Dramatists Guild; Writers Guild Am East; Modern Language Assn; Harlem Writers Guild; Zeta Psi Frat. **Honors/Awds:** Fel, Ctr Black Studies Univ Calif Santa Barbara, 1981; Outstanding Achievement Award, Black Action Coun City Col New York, 1982; Audelco Recognition Award Outstanding Musical Creator, 1984; Hon Fel, Brookdale Ctr Aging Hunger Col, 1985; Nat Endowment Humanities Fel Col Teachers,1986; major plays & pub "Hail Hail the Gangs!" w Carles Cleveland produced NY Theatre Ensemble Inc, 1976; "City Cool, A Ritual ofBelonging," w Carles Cleveland Random House, 1978; "Do Lord Remember Me "Off-Broadway Premier, produced Wynn Handman Am Place Theater, 1982; "Playto Win, Jackie Robinson" w Carles Cleveland Nat sch tour, 1984-86; Vicious Modernism: Black Harlem & Lit Imagination, Cambridge Univ Press, 1990. **Business Addr:** Professor, Director IRADAC, The City University of New York, The Graduate Center, Rm 7114 365 5th Ave, New York, NY 10016-4309, **Business Phone:** (212)817-2071.

DELANEY, DALLAS
Executive, manager. **Educ:** Univ Kans, elec eng. **Career:** AT&T Technologies, 1985; Hallmark Cards, proj leader; Windy City, chem & agr prods controls engr; Abbott Pk Finishing Goods Mfg, Global Pharma Opers, opers mgr, currently. **Honors/Awds:** Abbott Chmn's Award; Abbott Pres's Award; Black Engr of the Yr, Black Engr mag, 2004. **Special Achievements:** The 50 Most Important Blacks in Technol, 2005. **Business Addr:** Operations

Manager, Abbott Laboratories, 100 Abbott Pk Rd, Abbott Pk, IL 60064, **Business Phone:** (847)937-6100.*

DELANEY, DUANE B.
Government official. **Personal:** Born in Washington, DC. **Educ:** Howard Univ, BA, (magna cum laude), sociol, 1977; Am Univ, MA, judicial admin, 1979; Georgetown Univ Law Ctr, JD, 1989. **Career:** Superior Ct DC, spec asst clerk ct, 1989-91, dep clerk ct, 1991, dir civil div, 1991-93; acting dir social serv div, 1993-94; Superior Court of the Dist of Columbia, Clerk, 1994-. **Orgs:** DC Bar Asn; Nat Asn Ct Mgt; Phi Beta Kappa. **Business Addr:** Clerk of Court, Superior Court of the District of Columbia, Moultrie Courthouse, 500 Indiana Ave NW Room 2500, Washington, DC 20001, **Business Phone:** (202)879-1400.

DELANEY, JOHN PAUL
Journalist. **Personal:** Born Jan 13, 1933, Montgomery, AL; married Anita Jackson; children: John Paul III, David Allen. **Educ:** Ohio State Univ, BA, jour, 1958. **Career:** Atlanta Daily World, 1959-61; Atlanta Munic Ct, probation officer, 1961-63; Dayton, OH, Daily News, 1963-67; Wash Star, reporter, 1967-69; NY Times, corresp, Wash Bur, 1969-74, Chicago bur, 1974-77, corresp, asst nat ed, 1977-80, dep nat ed, 1980-86, chief Madrid bur, 1987-89, sr ed; Univ Ala, chair, jour dept, currently. **Orgs:** Publ Comn, Atlanta Br, Nat Asn Advan Colored People, 1961-63; Robert F Kennedy Journ Awards Comt, 1973-75, chmn, 1975; founding mem, Nat Asn Black Journalists; bd chmn. **Honors/Awds:** Recipient of Special Scholarship, Ohio State Univ, 1957; First Place, Baltimore-Washington Newspaper Guild, 1968; Lifetime Achievement Award, NY Asn Black Journalists, 1992. **Military Serv:** AUS, Corpl, 1953-55. **Business Addr:** Chairman, University of Alabama, College of Communications Department of Journalism, PO Box 870172, Tuscaloosa, AL 35487-0172.*

DELANEY, WILLI
Government official. **Personal:** Born Mar 23, 1947, Washington, DC; divorced; children: Damon. **Educ:** Cath Univ Am; Atlanta Univ. **Career:** Women's Bur, spec asst dir; White House Pres Speechwriting Off; CarterCampaign Pres, nat dir vol; City Atlanta Off Consumer Affairs, counr;Voter Educ Proj Atlanta, res asst. **Orgs:** Washington Women's Forum, 1977; Metro Dem Women's Club, 1977; Nat Hook-upBlack Women Inc, 1977. **Business Addr:** Staff, US Department of Labor, Washington, DC 20210.

DELANEY, WILMA I.
Executive, vice president (organization). **Educ:** Prairie View A&M Univ, BS. **Career:** Dow's Midland, Mich, Global Environ Technol Ctr, mgr; Dow N Am, Environ Qual, dir; Dow's pub policy rel; US Geog Leadership Team; Pub Affairs Leadership team; Dow Chem Co, environ & regulatory affairs, vpres; Dow Chem Co, Fed & State Govt Affairs, vpres, 2002; Mickey Leland Natl Urban Air Toxic Res Ctr, bd dirs, currently. **Orgs:** EPA's Nat Adv Coun Environ Policy & Technol. **Special Achievements:** Named to the US-S Africa Bi-Natl Comns Environ Mgt & Pollution Wing; appointed to State Of Mich Study Tour For Solid Waste Mgt In Europe; appointed to Mich Natural Resources & Environ Leadership Inst. **Business Addr:** Board of Directors, The Mickey Leland National Urban Air Toxics Research Center, 7000 Fannin Street Suite 700, Houston, TX 77030, **Business Phone:** (713)500-3450.*

DELANY, SAMUEL RAY (K LESLIE STEINER)
Educator, writer. **Personal:** Born Apr 1, 1942, New York, NY; son of Samuel Ray and Margaret Cary Boyd; married Marilyn Hacker, Aug 24, 1961 (divorced 1980); children: Iva Alyxander Hacker-Delany. **Educ:** Col City New York, 1961. **Career:** Novels: Out of the Dead City, 1963; The Towers of Toron, 1964; City of a Thousand Suns, 1965; The Ballad of Beta-2, 1965; Babel-17, 1966; Empire Star, 1966; The Einstein Intersection, 1967; Nova, 1968; Dhalgren, 1975; Triton, 1976; Three Tales, 1993; They Fly at Ciron, 1993; The Mad Man, 1994; Stars in My Pocket Like Grains of Sand, 1994; Hogg, 1995; Longer Views, 1996; The Motion of Light in Water, 1998; Shorter Views, 1999; Phallos, 2004; About Writing, 2005; Dark Reflections, 2007; Univ Mass, prof comparative lit, 1988-99; Temple Univ, Col Lib Arts, PA, prof eng, 2001-. **Honors/Awds:** World Science Fiction Achievement, Hugo, 1968, 1989; Nebula Award of the Science Fiction Writers of America, 1966-68; Pilgrim Award, Science Fiction Research Assn, Excellence in SF related Scholarship, 1984; William Whitehead Memorial Award, Lifetime Contribution to Lesbian & Gay Writing, 1993. **Home Addr:** 184 West 82nd St, New York, NY 10024, **Home Phone:** (212)580-1943. **Business Phone:** (215)204-7561.

DELAUDER, DR. WILLIAM B.
College president. **Educ:** Morgan State Univ, BS, chem; Wayne State Univ, PhD, phys chem. **Career:** NC A&T State Univ, Col Arts & Sci, prof chem. & chair, dean, 1981-87; Del State Univ, Dover, pres, 1987-2003, pres emer, currently. **Orgs:** Exec dir, Abraham Lincoln Study Abroad Fellowship Prog, 2004; bd mem, Int Food & Agr Develop; Adv Comt Educ & Human Resources Dirate NSF; sr coun, Del State Chamber Com; bd dir, United Way Del; chair, NASULGC Task ForceInt Educ; NC Bd Sci & Technol; MARC Review Comt; Nat Adv Coun; Nat Inst Gen Med Sci NIH; bd mem, Agr Nat Res Coun; bd dir, Nat Asn State Univs &Land-Grant Cols; bd dir, Coun Higher Educ Accreditation. **Honors/Awds:** Thurgood Marshall Scholarship Fund Education Leadership Award, 2001; Order of the First State Award, Ruth Ann Minner, 2002; Wesley Medal, Wesley Col, 2005; hon degree, Kent State Univ; hon degree, Univ Del. **Military Serv:** AUS, capt, 5 yrs. **Business Addr:** President Emeritus, Delaware State University, 1200 N DuPont Hwy, Dover, DE 19901, **Business Phone:** (302)857-6060.

DELCO, DR. EXALTON ALFONSO, JR.
Educator. **Personal:** Born Sep 4, 1929, Houston, TX; son of Exalton and Pauline Broussard; married Wilhelmina R, Aug 23, 1952; children: Deborah, Exalton III, Loretta & Cheryl. **Educ:** Fisk Univ, BA, 1949; Univ Mich, MS, 1950; Univ Tex, PhD, 1962. **Career:** Educator (retired); Tes Southern Univ, instr, 1950-55, asst prof, 1957-60, res asst, 1958-62; Huston-Tillotson Col, assoc prof, 1963-66; Prairie View A & M Col, guest prof, 1964; Huston-Tillotson Col, head, biol dept, prof biol, 1966-68, vpres acad affairs, 1967-85; Austin County Col, vpres acad affairs, 1985-93, Univ Tex-Austin, spec asst, Office Pres, 1995-96. **Orgs:** Fel, AAAS; Am Inst Biol Sci; vpres, exec secy, mem coun, Beta Kappa Chi Sci Honor Soc, 1962-68; dist comnr, Eagle Dist Boy Scouts Am, 1967-68; pres, St Vincent de Paul Soc Holy Cross Church, 1968; vpres, pres, Phi Delta Kappa, 1969-72; Am Fisheries Soc; Am Soc Ichthyologists & Herpetologists; Am Soc Limnol & Oceanog; Soc Sigma Xi; NY Acad Sci; Tex Acad Sci; Austin Housing Auth Comn, 1967-69; Travis Co Grand Jury Assoc, Community Coun Austin & Travis Co, 1968-70, pres, 1982-85; Family Prac Residency Adv Comn Tex, 1968-84. **Honors/Awds:** Stoye Prize, Am Soc Ichthyologists & Herpetologists, 1960; Danforth Assoc Huston-Tillotson Col Campus, 1966; Nominated Harbison Award, Danforth Found, 1966; Piper Prof, 1967; Nat Urban League Summer Fel, Allied Chem Co, 1969; Outstanding Educator of America. **Military Serv:** Surgical tech in 46th MASH unit in Germany, 1955-56; rank, SP3. *

DELCO, WILHELMINA R.
State government official, educator. **Personal:** Born Jul 16, 1929, Chicago, IL; daughter of William P Fitzgerald and Juanita Heath Watson; married Exalton A Jr, Aug 23, 1952; children: Deborah Diane Agbottah, Exalton A III, Loretta Elmirle Edelen & CherylPauline. **Educ:** Fisk Univ, BA, sociol, 1950. **Career:** St Government Official (retired), Educator; Prov Hosp, rec clerk; Ill Bell Telephone, serv rep; Teachers St Asn, TX, clerk; St Tex House Reps, rep, speaker pro tempore, 1991-95; Univ Tex, adj prof, currently. **Orgs:** Secy, Austin Ind School Dist, 1972-74; deleg, Tex Cath Conf, 1972-; deleg,Tex Asn Sch Bds, 1973; mem bd trust, secy, Aus Community Col, 1973-74;chmn, Higher Educ Comt, Tex House Rep, 1979; secy, vice chmn, Citizens AdvComt Juv Ct; City Austin Hum Rels Comt; Vol Soc Worker, Travis Cty Welfare Dept; bd mem, Vol Bur, Key Trnr; Well-Child Conf, Austin League Women Voters; mem adv comt mem, Tex Employ Comt, Tex Comt Human & Publ Pol; chmn, leg adv coun, mem exec comt, Southern Reg Ed; mem steering comt, exec comt, Ed Comt, States; vice chmn, State-Fed Assembly Nat Conf State Legis; vice chmn, bd trustees, Ed Testing Serv; vice chmn, Nat BlackCaucus State Legis; Comn Standards Southern Asn Cols & Schs; chmn & bd trustee, ETS; chmn assembly legis, Nat Conf State Legis; trustee, Southern Ed Found. **Honors/Awds:** Outstanding Woman Austin American Statesman, 1969; Liberty Bell Award, Austin Jr Bar Asn, 1969; Public School Service Award, Zeta Phi Beta, 1970; Public Service Merit Award, Omega Psi Phi, 1971; Appreciation Arthur DeWitty Award, 1971; Coronat Medal, St Edwards Univ, 1972; Service Award, Tex Congress Parents & Teachers, 1973; Appreciation Award Blanton School, 1973; Service Award, Sakarrah Temple, 1973; Service Citation, Optimist Club E Austin, 1973; Tex Women's Hall of Fame, 1986; building named for her, Prairie A&M Univ, 1996; Legends of Texas, 1999; Recieved various honorary degrees from St Edward Univ, Lee Col, Southwestern Univ, Houston-Tillotson Col & Wiley Col. **Special Achievements:** First woman and the second African American to hold the second highest position in the Texas House of Representatives until 1993. **Home Addr:** 1805 Astor Pl, Austin, TX 78721, **Home Phone:** (512)926-2424. **Business Addr:** Adjunct Professor, The University of Texas at Austin, College of Education, Department Educational Administration, 1 Univ Sta D5400, Austin, TX 78712, **Business Phone:** (512)471-7551.

DELE, BISON (BRIAN CARSON WILLIAMS)
Basketball player. **Personal:** Born Apr 6, 1969, Fresno, CA; son of Tony Williams and Patricia A Phillips. **Educ:** Md; Ariz. **Career:** Basketball player (retired); Orlando Magic, forward/ctr, 1991-93; Denver Nuggets, 1993-95; Los Angeles Clippers, 1995-96; Chicago Bulls, 1996-97; Detroit Pistons, 1997-99. **Special Achievements:** NBA Draft, First round pick, No 10, 1991; NBA Championship, Chicago Bulls, 1997.

DELEON, CHESTARO. **See DELEON, JOSE.**

DELEON, JOSE (CHESTARO DELEON)
Baseball player. **Personal:** Born Dec 20, 1960, Rancho Viejo, Dominican Republic. **Career:** Baseball player (retired); Pittsburgh Pirates, pitcher, 1983-86; Chicago White Sox, pitcher, 1986-87, 1993-95; St Louis Cardinals, pitcher, 1988-92; Philadelphia Phillies, 1992-93; Montreal Expos, 1995. **Honors/Awds:** Nat League Strikeout Champion, 1989. **Special Achievements:** First Cards pitcher since 1972 to record 200 strikeouts.

DE'LEON, LUNDEN
Actor, fashion model, chief executive officer. **Personal:** Born in Barbados. **Career:** Films: Surviving Paradise, 2000; Faux Pas, 2001; Cryptz, 2002; Deathbed,2002; Ronny Camaro & Seven Angry Women, 2003; Pure, 2004; Irrebuttable Presumption, exec producer, 2004; Stifle, exec producer, 2009; Space Girls in Beverly Hills, 2009. TV series: Herzflimmern, 1998; Livin'with Shuganah Shiksa; Vital Signs; Fury; Just Shoot Me; "Undercover", exec producer; "Veronica's Secret", exec producer; Dirrty Records, founder & ceo, 2003-. **Honors/Awds:** Caribbean Hall of Fame, 2004. **Special Achievements:** First Black Actress to Star in an Online Series; "One of the Most Significant Women In Entertainment", Ave Mag. **Business Addr:** Chief Executive officer, Dirrty Records, 468 N Camden Dr Suite 200, Beverly Hills, CA 90210, **Business Phone:** (310)860-5609.*

DELEON, PRISCILLA
Executive. **Personal:** Born Apr 5, 1958, Watsonville, CA; daughter of Federico and Jessie; married Douglas Carter, Oct 10, 1987; children: Aaron Carter. **Educ:** San Jose State Univ, BS. **Career:** Security Pacific Book, opers mgr, 1981; Atari, Inc, travel cood, 1982-83; Sheraton Sunnyvale, mgt coord, 1983-86; San Jose Conv & Visitors Bur, sales res, 1986, sales mgr, 1986-96, natl sales mgr, 1996; The Expo Group, San Jose, assoc dir sales, 2002-. **Orgs:** Nat Coalition Black Meeting Planners; Hotel Sales & Mktg Asn Int. **Business Addr:** Associate Director of Sales, The Expo Group, 2239 Moorpark Ave Suite 202, San Jose, CA 95128, **Business Phone:** (408)297-2600.

DELEON-JONES, FRANK A., JR.
Psychiatrist. **Personal:** Born May 6, 1937, Colon, Panama; married Silvia Cavallaro; children: Karen, Elizabeth. **Educ:** Nat Inst Panama, BS highest hon, 1958; Univ Rome, Italy, MD Surgery, 1964; IL State Psychiatric Inst, Psychiatric Residency, 1970. **Career:** VA Westside Hosp Chicago, chief psychiatry; IL State Psychiatric Inst, assoc dir res, 1973-75, chief, metabolic res units, 1971-73, res assoc, 1970-71; Psychiatry Abraham Lincoln Sch Med Univ IL, assoc prof; pract Psychoanalist; Chicago Inst Psychoanalysis, grad; Jones Therapy Partners, currently. **Orgs:** Am Psychiatric Asn; Am Asn Advancement Sci; Am Psychoanalytic Asn; interested psycho pharmacology depression, schizophrenia, drug addiction, other psychiatric disturbances. **Honors/Awds:** Ginsburg Fellow, Troup Advancement Psychiatry, 1968-70. **Business Phone:** (732)422-0800.

DELIBERO, SHIRLEY A.
Executive. **Career:** Green Line, Mass Bay Transp Authority, proj mgr & supt, 1976; Wash Metrop Area Transit Authority, dir bus serv, gen mgr; Dallas Area Rapid Transit, dep exec dir, NJ Transit, exec dir, 1999; Metrop Transit Authority Harris Co, pres & chief exec officer, 1999-2004; DeLibero Transp Strategies LLC, pres, currently. **Orgs:** Adv bd, Newark Performing Arts; Urban League; YMCA Black Achievers; Woman State Govt; Women Transit; vice chair & bd dir, Am Pub Transp Asn; nat chair, Conf Minority Transp Off. **Honors/Awds:** Lifetime Achievement Award, Am Pub Transp Asn; Public Officials Of The Year, Governings, 1999; Outstanding Community Service Award, 2002; Distinguished Leadership Award in Transportation, 2002; Thomas G. Neusom Founder's Award, Conf Minority Transp Off, 2003; Hall Of Fame, Am Pub Transit Asn, 2006. **Special Achievements:** First African-American woman to hold the transit industry's highest honorary post as Chair of Am Pub Transit Asn; Received numerous awards from Conf Minority Transp Off; One Of The Top 10 Women In US govt. *

DELICE, RONALD
Fashion designer. **Personal:** Married Shelly Meridith; children: Maude, Ioan & Zinedine. **Educ:** Fashion Inst Tech, NY, fashion merchandising & accessories design. **Career:** Ron & Ron Boutiques, co-founder & owner, 1997-. **Honors/Awds:** The Rising Star Award, Fashion Group Int. **Business Addr:** Founder, Co-owner, Ron & Ron Boutiques, 55 Mercer St 4th Fl, New York, NY 10013, **Business Phone:** (212)941-1905.

DELILLY, MAYO RALPH, III
Pediatrician. **Personal:** Born Apr 3, 1953, Los Angeles, CA; son of Mayo R DeLilly Jr and Irene Wood; married Carol Covyeau DeLilly, Jun 28, 1986; children: Irene Rose, Lauren Marie. **Educ:** Williams Col, BA, biol, 1974; Howard Univ Col Med, MD, 1978. **Career:** Martin Luther King Gen Hosp, intern/resident, 1978-81; pvt pract, pediatrician, currently. **Orgs:** LA Pediat Soc, 1981; Big Bros Greater Los Angeles, 1981-90; med adv, Sheenway Sch, Los Angeles, 1983; Am Acad Pediat. **Honors/Awds:** Acad Achievement Award, Howard Univ Med Sch, 1976; Med Alumni Award, Howard Univ Med Sch, 1978; Alpha Omega Alpha Hon Med Soc; fel Am Acad Pediatrics, 1984; vchmn, Pediat Comn, Calif Med Ctr, 1988. **Business Addr:** Pediatrician, Private Practice, 1818 S Western Ave Suite 207, Los Angeles, CA 90006-5808.*

DELK, JAMES F, JR.
Automotive executive. **Personal:** Born Sep 10, 1948, Smithfield, VA; son of James and Edith Majors; married Thelma Garvin Delk,

Sep 21, 1985; children: Darlene, Kim, Timothy & James. **Educ:** Temple Univ, Philadelphia, PA, assocs, elec eng, 1969. **Career:** IBM, Philadelphia, PA, customer eng, 1969-71; William H Porter, Newark, DE, salesman, 1971-74; Vans Chevrolet, New Castle, DE, sales mgr, 1974-82; Fairlane Ford Inc, Pottsville PA, ceo & owner, currently. **Orgs:** Alpha Phi Alpha, 1967-; pres, Schuylkill County Dealer Asn, 1991-92; regional mgr, Black Ford & Lincoln Mercury Dealers Asn, 1991-93. **Business Addr:** President, Fairlane Ford Sales Inc, 440 N Claude A Lord Blvd, Pottsville, PA 17901, **Business Phone:** (717)622-1991.

DELK, OLIVER RAHN
Educator, executive director. **Personal:** Born Feb 4, 1948, Staten Island, NY; son of James and Mary Dixon. **Educ:** Ind Univ, BA, psychol, 1974; Ga State Univ, MS, criminal justice, 1976. **Career:** Sears, Roebuck & Co, asst mgr, 1974-76; Southeast Branch YMCA, Atlanta, community prog dir, 1976-77; Off Mayor Atlanta, tech assist specialist, 1977-79; Morehouse Col, dir govt rels; Communities Joined Action, bd dir, currently. **Orgs:** Nat Asn Equal Opportunities Higher Educ, 1979-; Nat Asn Advan Colored People, 1979-; Omega Psi Phi Frat, 1979-; SCLC, 1979-; pres, Asn Fund-Raising Officers 1985; chmn, Budget & Fin, Water, Waste Water Treat Operators, 1985. **Honors/Awds:** Youth Services Award, WAOK Radio, 1978; Outstanding Young Man of America, US Jaycees, 1979; Public Speaking Award, Ga State Univ, 1979; Fulbright Scholar; Outstanding Personalities of the South. **Business Phone:** (360)493-5762.

DELK, TONY LORENZO
Basketball player. **Personal:** Born Jan 28, 1974, Covington, TN. **Educ:** Univ Ky, attended 1986. **Career:** Charlotte Hornets, 1997-98; Golden State Warriors, guard, 1998-99; Sacramento Kings, 2000; Phoenix Suns, 2001-02; Boston Celtics, 2002-03; Dallas Mavericks, 2004; Atlanta Hawks, 2005-06; Detroit Pistons, 2006; Panathinaikos Athens, Greece, 2006-07. **Orgs:** Omega Psi Phi Fraternity. **Honors/Awds:** Most Outstanding Player, NCAA-Div I, 1996; Player of the Year, SEC.

DELK, YVONNE V
Clergy. **Personal:** Born Apr 15, 1939, Norfolk, VA; daughter of Marcus T. **Educ:** Norfolk State Col, Norfolk, VA, BA, sociol, 1961; Andover Newton Theol Sem, Newton Ctr, MA, MRE, 1963; Cincinnati Univ, Cincinnati, OH, attended 1966; New York Theol Sem, New York, NY, ministry doctor, 1978. **Career:** United Church Christ, Bd Homeland Ministries, Boston, MA, Philadelphia, PA, secy urban & black church, 1969-76; Harvard Divinity Sch, Cambridge, MA, visiting lectr, 1976-77; United Church Christ, New York, NY, assoc constituency develop off church soc, 1978-79, affirmative action officer, 1980-81, exec dir, off church soc, 1981-90; Community Renewal Soc, exec dir. **Orgs:** Bd dirs, Proj Equality; mem prog combat racism, World Coun Churches; adv comn, World Coun Churches Conv Justice, Peace & Integrity Creation; Nat Planning Comt C Poverty; coordinating comt mem, Choose Peace. **Honors/Awds:** Antoinette Brown Award, United Church of Christ, 1979; Doctor of Divinity, Chicago Theological Seminary, 1986; Doctor of Divinity, Ursinus College, 1986; Excellence in Field of Religion, Howard University, 1987; Leadership & Service Award, Project Equality, 1988. **Special Achievements:** In 1974, she became the first African-American woman to be ordained in the United Church of Christ.

DELL, WILLIE J.
Government official. **Personal:** Born May 8, 1930, Weldon, NC; daughter of Willie Aikens and Emma F Grant; married Nathan; children: Wayne & Arthur Jones. **Educ:** St Augustines Col, BA, 1952; Richmond Prof Inst Col William & Mary, MSW, 1960. **Career:** Government official (retired); Social Serv Bur, social worker, 1953-58; Med Col Va, med social worker, 1961-66; Richmond Pub Health Dept, chief med soc worker, 1966-68; Va Commonwealth Univ, asst prof, 1968-74; JJ & W assoc, exec dir; Richmond Comm Sr Ctr, exec dir, 1976-95; adj prof, Univ Richmond, 1978-96; Va St Conf, Nat Asn Advan Colored People, Voter Empowerment Coord, 2000. **Orgs:** City coun mem, City Richmond Va, 1975; Pres, Richmond Chapter Nat Asn Social Workers, 1975; bd mem, Commonwealth Psychol; bd mem, Richmond Chapter ARC & Fam C Serv, Nat League Cities; VCU Grad Sch; Richmond Community Hosp; Proj Jump St, 1975-80; co-owner, JJ & W Assoc Consult; Nat Asn Advan Colored People; North Side Civil Asn; pres, Black Ed Assoc, 1973-75; St Augustines Chap; Nat Assoc Black Soc Workers; past chmn Reg III NBC Leo; Va Coun Soc Welfare Coun Human Rel; Del Ver Women Clubs, Delta Sigma Theta; pres, Nat Black Presby Caucus; pres, Richmond Chap Nat Causes Black Aged, 1980-89; pres, Richmond Urban Inst, 1984-88; Bd Southern Regional Coun, 1980-99; Diocese Richmond, Haitian Comn, 1990-95; Nat Presby Hunger Adv Comt, 1994-99; Heifer Proj Int, bd mem, 1996-; bd, St Joseph's Home, Port-Au-Prince, Haiti. **Honors/Awds:** Omega Citizen Yr Award, 1974; Govt Award, Metro Bus League, 1975; Delta's Civic & Polit Involvement Award, 1975; Distinguished Serv Award, St Augustine's Col, 1982; Outstanding Woman Award, Govt YMCA, 1982; Good Govt Award Eta Tau Chapter, 1982; Outstanding Vol, Powhatan Correctional Ctr, 1988. **Special Achievements:** First black woman elected to Richmond City Coun, Richmond, Va, where she served from 1973-82. **Home Addr:** 2956 Hathaway Rd, Richmond, VA 23225. *

DELLUMS, LEOLA HIGGS (ROSCOE DELLUMS)
Lawyer. **Personal:** Born Dec 12, 1941, Berkeley, CA; daughter of Esther Lee and Leo C; married Ronald V Dellums, Jan 20, 1962 (divorced 1999); children: Ronald Brandon, Erik Todd & Piper Dellums Ross. **Educ:** San Francisco State Univ, BA, sociol, 1966; Calif State Teaching Credential, adult educ, 1967; Georgetown Univ Law Ctr, JD, 1982. **Career:** Inst Servs Educ, consult, 1976; ACL, develop dir, publicist, 1976-78; Zuko Interior Designs, Pub Rels, advert mgr, 1978-79; Congressman Mickey Leland, spec asst, 1983; Super Ct Dist, judicial law clerk, 1984-85; Assembly Calif Legis, prin consult, Assembly Office Res, Wash, Dist, rep, 1985-92; Wash & Christian, atty law, 1993-96; US Dept Com, 1996-97; sole practr atty, 1997-. **Orgs:** Nat Bar Asn; PEN Bar; Calif State Soc; Am Bar Asn; Potomac Chap Links Inc; AKA Sorority; Congressional Club; Am Soc Composers, Authors & Publishers; Berkeley High Sch Alumni Asn; US Supreme Court Bar; DC Court Appeals Bar; US Dist Court, DC Bar; Nat Bd Trustees, Ctr Prevent Handgun Violence, Sasha Bruce Youth Work; Regional Addiction Prevention Inc, Advisory Bd; Rise Sister Support Coun For the Minority Breast Cancer Resource Ctr. **Honors/Awds:** The Ella Hill Hutch Award, Black Women Organized for Political Action, 1992; Inductee Berkeley High School Hall of Fame; The Sojourner Truth Meritorious Service Award, Nat Asn Negro Bus & Prof Women's Club Inc, 1991; AT&T Volunteer Activist Award of Wash DC, Area, 1985; Congressional recognition for efforts in attaining passage of HR 1580; Annual Solid Image Award, 1999; Outstanding Leadership Award, Black Women Organized for Political action, 1999; Nat Sojourner Truth Meritorious Service Award. **Special Achievements:** First black Pom-pom girl & the first black on the Homecoming Queen Court; Songs published under RREPCO Publishing Company; poetry published in "The Sheet"; prescriptive diagnostic research paper, "Teaching English as a Second Language to Native Born"; hosted local Emmy award-winning television show "Cloth-A-Thon," WGLA; co-hosted local Emmy award-winning television show, "The Place," WRC; published "Something More," 1999. **Business Phone:** (202)686-5156.

DELLUMS, RONALD V
Civil rights activist, congressperson (u.s. federal government), mayor. **Personal:** Born Nov 24, 1935, Oakland, CA; son of Verney and Willa; married Leola Roscoe Higgs, Jan 1962; children: Brandy, Erik & Piper. **Educ:** Oakland City Col, AA, 1958; San Francisco State Col, BA, 1960; Univ Calif, Berkeley, MSW, 1962; Wilberforce Univ, Dl (hons), 1975. **Career:** Congressperson (retired), President of organization; Calif Dept Mental Hygiene, psychiatric social worker, 1962-64; Bayview Community Center, prog dir, 1964-65; Hunters Point Youth Opportunity Ctr, assoc dir, dir, 1965-66; Bay Area Social Planning Coun, planning consult, 1966-67; San Francisco Economic Opportunity Coun, Concentrated Employment Prog, dir, 1967-68; Social Dynamics Inc, sr consult, 1968-70; Berkeley City Coun, 1967-71; US House Rep, 9th Dist Calif, democrat, 1971-98; Healthcare Int Mgt Co, pres, City of Oakland, Mayor, currently. **Orgs:** Ranking mem, House Committee on Nat Security, 1973; Mil Procurement Subcomt; former chair, Congressional Black Caucus; former chair, House Comt Dist Columbia; former chair, House Armed Svcs Comt; former mem, Permanent Select Comt Intel; Berkeley City Coun. **Special Achievements:** Author, Defense Sense: The Search for a Rational Military Policy, 1983. **Military Serv:** USMC, active duty, 1954-56.

DELLUMS, ROSCOE. **See DELLUMS, LEOLA HIGGS.**

DELOACH, WENDELIN W.
Attorney general (u.s. federal government). **Educ:** Roosevelt Univ, BS, BA; Univ Denver, JD, 1987. **Career:** DeLoach Law Firm, atty, currently. **Orgs:** Bd mem, Colo Sch Family Ther, currently. **Business Addr:** Attorney, DeLoach Law Firm, 3773 Cherry Creek Dr N Suite 575, Denver, CO 80209, **Business Phone:** (303)344-4441.

DELOATCH, DR. EUGENE
College administrator. **Career:** Morgan State Univ, Sch eng, Baltimore, Md, dean, currently. **Business Addr:** Dean, Morgan State University, School of Engineering, 1700 E Cold Spring Lane, Baltimore, MD 21251, **Business Phone:** (443)885-4226.*

DELOATCH, MYRNA SPENCER
Association executive. **Personal:** Born in Tarboro, NC; married Johnnie W Deloatch; children: Chris, Tamyra, Ivan. **Educ:** Ag & Tech Univ, BS, Home Econ; Purdue Univ, Spec Cert. **Career:** Rural Ed Inst Chillan S Am, teacher; La Guardia House NY, dir food serv; Farmers Home Admin, home supvr; Rich Square Training Ctr, home econ teacher; Telamon Corp, employ training specialist; Edgecombe Co Dept Social Serv, human servs coord, Family & Consumer Sci Comm mem, currently. **Orgs:** pres, Ebonette Club; employ interviewer, Employ Sec Commn, 1976-81; Tarboro Housing & Comm Develop Adv Bd, 1979-84; Tarboro Arts Coun; Tarboro City Sch Bd Educ, 1979-85; Tarboro Community Outreach, bd dir; Delta Sigma Theta Sorority, 1959; NC Cooperative Extension Serv, advisory bd. **Honors/Awds:** Outstanding Citizenship, E Tarboro Citizen League, 1978; Past Presidet Award, Ebonette Club, 1980; Meritorious Service, East Tarboro Citizens League, 1981; special Service Award, Black Voices, 1982; Meritorious Service Award, E Tarboro Citizens League, 1985. **Business Addr:** Member, Edgecomb County, Family & Consumer Sci Committee, Edgecombe County Administrative Bldg, 201 St Andrew St, Tarboro, NC 27886, **Business Phone:** (252)641-7821.*

DE LOATCH, RAVEN L.
Hospital administrator. **Educ:** East Carolina Univ Sch Med, MD. **Career:** Halifax Regional Hosp, chief staff, pvt pract, currently. **Special Achievements:** First African Am chief of staff in Roanoke Rapids, NC. *

DELOATCH, SANDRA
Dean (Education). **Career:** Norfolk State Univ, interim dean, Sch Sci & Technol, dean, currently. **Orgs:** AAAS; Asn Comput Mach. **Special Achievements:** Guest on the radio program "With Good Reason". **Business Addr:** Dean, Norfolk State University, Sch Sci Technol, 700 Park Ave, Norfolk, VA 23504, **Business Phone:** (757)823-8180.*

DELOATCH, DR. SANDRA J
College administrator. **Personal:** Born in Suffolk, VA; daughter of David and Essie DeLoatch. **Educ:** Howard Univ, BS, 1971; Univ Mich, MA, 1972; Ind Univ, PhD, 1977; Col William & Mary, MS, 1995. **Career:** Norfolk State Univ, Math Dept, instr, asst prof, 1972-83, prof & comput sci prog coord, 1983-91, Comput Sci Dept, prof & chair, 1991-99, Sch Sci & Technol, prof comput sci & dean, 2000-. **Orgs:** Phi Beta Kappa, 1971-; team chair, Comput Sci Accreditation Comn, 1987-98; bd dirs & chair, technol task force, Girl Scout Coun Colonial Coast, 2001-; bd zoning appeals, City Suffolk, 2002-; Asn Comput Mach; Inst Elec & Electronics Engrs Comput Soc; Va Modeling Anal & Simulation Ctr; bd mem, Ctr Excellence Space Data & Info Sci Space Coun. **Honors/Awds:** Teacher of the Year, Norfolk State Univ, 1983; Technical Achiever of the Year, Nat Technical Asn, 2001; Administrator of the Year, Norfolk St Univ, 2001; Woman of Distinction Award, Girl Scout Coun Colonial Coast, 2003. **Special Achievements:** Co-author: Mathematics for College Students, 1985; Author: MACSYMA Usage at Langley, 1987; Inegrated Prototyping System, 1991; Computer Aided Software Engineering Tools, 1991. **Business Addr:** Dean, Professor of Computer Science, Norfolk State University, School of Science & Technology, 700 Pk Ave, Norfolk, VA 23504, **Business Phone:** (757)823-8180.

DELPHIN, DR. JACQUES MERCIER
Physician. **Personal:** Born Apr 26, 1929, Cap Haitien, Haiti; married Marlene M (divorced 1997); children: Patrick, Barthold, Beverly, Miriam, Matthew & Janice. **Educ:** Grad Secondary Studies, BS, 1950; Univ Haiti, W Indies, med sch, 1957; Sch Med State Univ, MD. **Career:** St Cabrini Home W Park, NY, medical dir 1974-; St Francis Hosp Poughkeepsie, NY, attending physician, 1968-; Ad Interim, comm mental health, 1973-74; Dutchess Co Dept Mental Hygiene, psychiatric dir, 1969-73; Hudson River Psychiatric Ctr, psychiatric dir partial hosp, 1966-69; Spectrum Behavioral Health, medical dir, 1998-; pvt pract, currently. **Orgs:** Past pres, Mid-hudson Br Psychiatric Asn, 1972; fel, APA, 1972; med license NY State, 1967; AAPA; ACA Forensic Psychiatry; Am Asn Adolescent Psychiatry. **Home Addr:** 132 N Ave Apt Suite 104, Pleasant Valley, NY 12569, **Home Phone:** (845)635-3942. **Business Phone:** (845)485-9098.

DEL PINO, JEROME KING
Clergy. **Personal:** Born Sep 12, 1946, Savannah, GA; son of Rev Jerome Frank and Flossie Mae Childs; married Kathleen Joy Peterson Del Pino, Aug 25, 1968; children: Jerome Curtis, Emily Kathleen. **Educ:** Gustavus Adolphus Col, BA, 1969; Boston Univ Sch Theol, ThM, 1972; Boston Univ Grad Sch, PhD, 1976. **Career:** Union United Methodist Church, Boston, asst pastor, 1968-69; Emerson Col, Boston, lectr, 1971-72; St Andrew's United Methodist Church, Worcester, co-pastor, 1971-72; Greenwood Memorial United Methodist Church, Dorchester, pastor, 1973-76; Wesley United Methodist Church, Springfield, pastor, 1978-89; Wesley United Methodist Church, Springfield, pastor, 1978; Boston Univ Sch Theology, visiting lectr, 1980-82; Luther & Northwestern Theol Sem, St Paul, visiting lectr, 1984-85; Crawford Memorial United Methodist Church, Winchester, pastor, starting 1989; United Methodist Church, pastor, 1993-98; Metrop United Methodist Church, sr pastor, 1998; Gen Bd Higher Educ & Ministry, Gen Secy, currently. **Orgs:** Am Soc Church Hist, 1971; deleg, Gen Conf UMC, 1976, 1980, 1984, 1988; NE Jurisdictional Conf, UMC, 1976, 1980, 1984; dir gen, Bd Higher Educ & Minstry, UMC, 1980-88; Div Ordained Ministry, UMC, 1980-88; pres, Black Ecumenical Comn MA, 1983-85; adv coun, Word & World Journ, 1985; gov, Gen Bd Discipleship, United Methodist Church, 1988; gov, Gen Coun Ministries, United Methodist Church, 1988-. **Honors/Awds:** Rockefeller Fellow, Fund Theol Educ Princeton, 1971-73; fellow, Inst Reformation Res St Louis MO, 1973; North American Black Doctrate Fellow, Fund Theol Educ, 1976-77; 1st Decade Alumni Achievemnt Award, Gustavus Adolphus Col St Peter MN, 1978. **Business Addr:** General Secretary, General Board of Higher Education and Ministry, 1001 Nineteenth Ave S, PO Box 340007, Nashville, TN 37203-0007, **Business Phone:** (615)340-7400.*

DELPIT, JOSEPH A.
State government official, restaurateur, president (organization). **Personal:** Born Jan 9, 1940, Baton Rouge, LA; son of Thomas H

(deceased) and Edmae Butler; married Precious Robinson; children: Joseph Jr, Thomas, Deidre, Desiree & Derrick. **Educ:** Southern Univ, Baton Rouge, bus admin, food & nutrit. **Career:** Chicken Shack Restaurant, owner/operator; Gr Baton Rouge Develop Corp; Gen United Life Ins Co; Sports Unlimited Inc, co-owner; Baton Rouge City, city councilman, 1968-75; La House Rep, state rep; Joe Delpit Enterprises Inc, owner, currently; Chicken Shack Syts Inc, pres, currently; D & W Health Servs Inc, pres, currently; W T B Inc, secy, treas & chief financial officer, currently. **Orgs:** Mem bd dirs, People's Savings & Loan Co; bd mem, St Francis Xavier Cath Church; bd mgt, Baranco Clark YMCA; pres, Baton Rouge Chap, Nat Asn Advan Colored People, life mem; City Parish Bi-racial Comt; Cath Lay Congress; bd dirs, Op Upgrade; bd mgt, Ment Health Soc; Capital Region Planning Comn; Mason; Shriner Hon mem, John B Frazier Hon Soc, 1974; founder, LaLegis Black Caucus; life mem, McKinley High Sch Alumni Asn; bd dirs, Capital City Kids Baseball Clin; chmn, Old McKinley Bldg Proj. **Honors/Awds:** Outstanding Service Award, Baranco Clark YMCA, 1960; Baton Rouge Businessman of Year, News Leader, 1961; McKinley High Alumni Award, 1968; Outstanding Academic Support, Southern Univ Am Women Soc, 1970; Nat Freedom Award, Nat Asn Advan Colored People, 1970; Outstanding Leadershipin Business and Civic Community Service, Omega Psi Phi Frat Inc, 1971; Outstanding Service, Southern Univ Alumni Fed, 1973; Businessman of Year, 1973; Shriver Award for dedicated service to the poor, Off Econ Opportunity, 1973; La Educ Asn Award; Alpha Kappa Alpha Sorority Award. **Special Achievements:** First black councilman, Baton Rouge; Listed in Outstanding Young Men of America. **Home Addr:** 2323 Iowa St, Baton Rouge, LA 70802, **Home Phone:** (225)344-6046. **Business Addr:** Owner, Joe Delpit Enterprises Inc, 725 Lettsworth St, Baton Rouge, LA 70802, **Business Phone:** (225)343-1687.

DELPIT, LISA DENISE
Educator. **Personal:** Born May 23, 1952, Baton Rouge, LA; daughter of Thomas H and Edmae Butler; children: Maya. **Educ:** Antioch Col, BA, 1974; Harvard Univ, MEd, 1980, EdD, 1984. **Career:** Durham Child Develop Ctr, teacher, admin asst, 1972-77; N Solomons Provincial Govt, consult, 1982-83; Atari Research Lab, consult, 1983-84; Univ Alaska, asst prof, reading, language, & literature, 1984-88, Teacher Educ Prog, coordr, 1987-88; Mich State Univ, Sch Educ, assoc prof, 1988-91; Morgan State Univ, Inst Urban Res, sr res assoc, 1988-94; Ga State Univ, Benjamin E Mays Prof & chmn, currently, Ctr Urban Educ Excellence, dir, 1994-; Fla Int Univ, Miami, Fla, Ctr Urban Educ & Innovation, exec dir & eminent scholar, currently. **Orgs:** Res support, Nat Black Child Develop Inst, Baltimore Chap, 1990-91; literacy comt, vchmn, Nat Bd Prof Teaching Stds; African & African-Am Curriculum Infusion Comt Baltimore PS, co-chair; Int Reading Asn; Phi Delta Kappa; Nat Coun Teaching Eng; Am Educ Res Asn; Ctr Collaborative Educ. **Honors/Awds:** MacArthur Fellowship, 1990; Nat Acad Educ Spencer Fel, 1988; Dissertation Fel, Am Assn Univ Women Educ Found, 1984; Am Educ Research Assn Raymond Cattell Award, 1994; Alumni Award for Outstanding Contribution to Education, Harvard Univ, 1993. **Special Achievements:** "The Silenced Dialogue: Power and Pedagogy in Educating Other People's Children," Harvard Educational Review, 1988; "Skills and Other Dilemmas of a Progressive Black Educator," Harvard Educational Review, 1986; author, "Other People's Children," The New Press, 1995; winner of several national awards; numerous other articles. **Business Addr:** Executive Director, Florida International University, Center for Urban Education & Innovation, 11200 SW 8th St, Miami, FL 33199, **Business Phone:** (305)223-9412.

DELSARTE, LOUIS
Artist, college teacher. **Personal:** Born Sep 1, 1944, Brooklyn, NY. **Educ:** NY Univ, Pratt Inst, BFA, 1967; Univ Ariz, MFA, 1977. **Career:** Col New Rochelle, adj prof, 1988-92; Morris Brown Col, asst prof, 1992, prof, 2003; Spelman Col, adj prof, 1992-94; Morehouse Col, Altanta, GA, prof fine arts & humanities, currently; Stella Jones Gallery, New Orleans. **Orgs:** Commun, NY Metrop Transit Authority, 2000-01; artist-in-residence, Howard Univ. **Honors/Awds:** Otto M Burkhardt Trust Award; Purchase Award, Atlanta Life Ins Co, 1989. **Home Phone:** (404)524-3245. **Business Addr:** Professor of Fine Arts & Humanities, Morehouse College, 830 Westview Dr, Atlanta, GA 30314, **Business Phone:** (404)681-2800.

DEMAS, DR. WILLIAM F.
Educator. **Educ:** St Univ NY, MD, attended; Kings County Univ Hosp Med Ctr, residency, attended. **Career:** MD Anderson Hosp & Tumor Inst, fel; Univ Tex Houston Br, instr; Akron City Hosp, Summa Health Syst, Div Radiotherapy, chief, currently, Radiation Ther Oncol Group, prin investr, currently; Northeastern Ohio Univs ColMed, prof radiol, currently; Cancer Care Ctr, pres & chief exec officer, currently. **Orgs:** Am Bd Radiol; chair, Personnel & Compensation Comt; trustee, Akron Community Found; bd trustee, Northeastern Ohio Univ Col Med. **Business Addr:** Chief, Radition Oncology, Akron City Hospital, Summa Health Systems, 525 E Market St, Akron, OH 44304, **Business Phone:** (330)375-3557.

DEMBER, JEAN WILKINS
Counselor. **Personal:** Born Jan 29, 1930, Brooklyn, NY; daughter of William H Wilkins Sr and Martha Marie Benson; married Clarence Robert Dember; children: Clarence Jr, Judith, Regina, Lila, Theresa, Zelie. **Educ:** Lincoln Schl Nurses, 1950; Manhattan Bus Inst, cert secy, 1952; Empire State Col, Old Westbury, 1983; Lincoln Univ, PA, MHS, 1988. **Career:** NY State Delegation Black Political Assem, 1972, pres, 1981-82; Webb-Dember African Am Heritage, curator & co-founder, 1975-; Black History Cult Prog, presentor designer, 1978-; Nat Black Polit Assembly, Comn Prisons & Genocide, org vol 1982-83; Nassau Community Col, Black Women Studies, adj prof, 1983-02; Nat Urban League Long Island, career counr, Structured Educ Support Prog, 1989-92. **Orgs:** Adv bd mem, Nat Black Lay Cath Caucus, 1970-85; Econ Opport Coun Suffolk, 1972-84; founding mem, Tri Community Health Coun, 1974-82; designer White Racism Mental Health Comm SC Div Mental Health, 1977-82; State Youth Advocacy, 1980-84; Evangelization Community Nat Off Black Catholics, 1982-84; Uganda Human Rights League, 1982-86; chairperson, Long Island Day Care Serv, 1986-88; Lincoln Univ Alumni Asn; NY State Multicultural Adv Comt, 1984-91; African Cult Ctr, Los Angeles; Nat Black Alcoholism Coun, 1987-89; pres, LI Catholic Interracial Coun, 1988-91; Reform Mental Health, address Racist, White Supremist & Police Brutality & Murders Psychosocial Pathol; founder, Afrikans United Sanity Now, 1992-; Shape Ctr Harambee Coun Elders, 1992-; consult, Inst African Wisdom IFA ORISHA Educ Ctr, Inst Interracial Harmony. **Honors/Awds:** Am Beautiful grant community prog, 1981; Nat Off Black Cath Evangelization Award, 1982; Citizen of Yr, Chi Rho Chprt Omega Psi Phi Frat Inc, 1982; Martin L King Award, Pilgrim State Human Rights Comn, 1983; vol advocate African Relief Cath Church & broader community; Suffolk County, Jack & Jill Award, 1990; Nat Asn Negro Bus & Prof Women's Clubs Inc, Nat Sojourner Truth Award, Meritorious Serv, 1991; Outstanding Serv, Asn Community Rels, 1992; Nat Asn Advan Colored People Serv Award, Auburn Prison, 1992; Natl Black Service Award, Alcohol & Substance Abuse, Long Island Chap, Cosco Williams, pres; Cert Serv, Kazi Shule & SHAPE Ctr, 1995-96; Cert Appreciation, Million Man March LOC, 1996; Houston, Tex Cert Appreciation, Foster Elementary Sch, 1996; various nominations, ABI, 1997-01. *

DEMBY, JAMES E.
Electrical engineer. **Personal:** Born Dec 24, 1936, Chesapeake, VA; married Mavis A Smith; children: James Jr, Ken, Len. **Educ:** Tuskegee Inst, attended 1957; Howard Univ, BS, 1961. **Career:** Norfolk Naval Shipyard, advancing positions, 1961-; Norfolk Naval Shipyard, supvry elec engr, 1973-. **Orgs:** Vpres, United Civic League, 1963-64; asst dist comnr, Tidewater Coun BSA, 1966; Naval Civilian Admin Asn; Nat Asn Naval Tech & Supvr; Chesapeake Chap, Nat Tots & Teens. **Honors/Awds:** Super Performance Award, 1971; Beneficial Suggestion Award, 1971; Cert of Merit, 1971; Scout Exec Award, 1970; Arrowhead Honor, 1971; Scouter's Key, 1971; Order of the Arrow, 1972. *

DEMBY, PROF. WILLIAM E.
Educator, novelist. **Personal:** Born Dec 25, 1922, Pittsburgh, PA; son of William E and Gertrude Lulu Hendrick; married Barbara Harris, Jan 1, 2004; married Lucia Drudi (died 1995); children: James Gabriel. **Educ:** Fisk Univ, Nashville, TN, BA, 1947; Univ Rome. **Career:** Educator (retired), novelist; Col Staten Island, asst prof eng, 1969-89; Novels: Beetlecreek, 1950; The Catacombs, 1965; Love Story Black, Blueboy, 1978. **Military Serv:** AUS, 1942-45. **Home Addr:** 17 Bittersweet Lane, PO Box 363, Sag Harbor, NY 11963.

DEMERITTE, DR. EDWIN T.
Insurance executive, government official. **Personal:** Born Jun 25, 1935, Miami, FL; son of Arnold and Daisy; children: Edwin Jr, Kathy Wynn, Deborah Renee, Dianne Marie & Michelle. **Educ:** Fla A&M Univ, BS, MEdn; grad work guid & coun Barry Col Miami; grad work admin & supr Fla Atlantic Univ; Doc Prog Nat Educ D Prog Nova Univ. **Career:** N Dade Sr HS, teacher, 1958-63, dept head, 1963-65; Miami NW Sr High Sch, guid counr, 1966-67; Miami NW Adult Educ Cent, instr, 1966-69; Miami Edison Sr High Sch, asst prin guid, 1969-70; Hialeah Jr High Sch, prin 1/2 quinmester prog, 1973; Metropolitan Life Ins Co, sales rep sr acct exec; Dade County Pub Sch Syst, Miami, FL, dir, 1976-81; Kovack Securities, registered rep, govt rels chmn, currently; Conf Metrop life, pres, 1988, 1994-97. **Orgs:** Nat Conf Chris & Jews on Violence & Youth, 1969; Nat Inst Pol & Commun Rel, 1970; Nat Asn Sec Sch Prin Annual Meeting, 1971-73; Nat Asn Life Underwriters, 1981-; Miami Asn Life Underwiters, 1981-; Fla Asn Life Underwriters, 1981-; Million Dollar Round Table, 1984-2003; trustee, Presbyterian Church USA Found, 1991-96; treas, advocacy & govt rels chair, Miami Dade Asn Insu & Financial Adv; consult, S Region Educ Bd. **Honors/Awds:** Metro Ins Co policies placed over 200 policy contacts 1983 Award; Three Metropolitan SE Territory Award, 1983; 1984 Qualifying Life Member of the Million Dollar Roundtable; Kiwanis Fellow, Guidance Counseling; Boy Scouting Award, Community Serv Recognition; Dade Co School Board Award, Commendable Contribution Educ; Nat Sales Award, NALU, 1988, 1994-97; Nat Quality Awards, NALU, 1988, 1993-97; awarded The LUTCF Designation, 1998; Nat Sales Achievement Award, 1998; Nat Quality Award, 1998; Million Dollar Round Table Honor Roll, 1998. **Special Achievements:** Million Dollar Roundtable, 1999, 2003. **Home Addr:** 5301 NW 18 Ave, Miami, FL 33142, **Home Phone:** (305)696-2677. **Business Addr:** Government Relations Chairman, Kovack Securities, 5301 NW 18 Ave, PO Box 680098, Miami, FL 33142, **Business Phone:** (305)696-2677.

DEMERSON, CONNIE MARIE
Administrator. **Personal:** Born Nov 7, 1936, Belton, TX; son of Charlie and Connaola Sweeney; married Elbert Eugene, Jun 22, 1961; children: Bryan Avery Sweeney, Marion Eugene Demerson, Robin Smith, Deidra Lynn Nolan. **Educ:** Prairie View A&M, attended 1956. **Career:** Administrator (retired); Olin E Teague Va Ctr, nursing asst, 1967-94. **Orgs:** Pres, West-Belton-Harris High Ex-Students Asn, 1986-99; Nat Asn Advan Colored People, 1989-99; lay leader, treas, Mt Zion United Methodist Church, 1994-99; bd mem, sch site chair, Am Heart Asn, 1996-99; bd trustees, Belton Independent Sch Dist. **Honors/Awds:** Appreciation for Contribution, United Methodist Women, 1998; Belton Area Chamber of Commerce Beltonian Award, 2007. **Special Achievements:** First Black woman elected to the Board of Trustees of the Belton Independent School District; first Black woman to receive the award. **Home Addr:** 210 Smith St, Belton, TX 76513. *

DEMESME, RUBY B
Military leader. **Career:** Air Force, asst secy, currently. **Orgs:** Women in Defense; SES Women's Appointees; Subgroup on Women & C; Sen Black Legis Staff (Caucus); Nat Military Family Asn; Delta Sigma Theta Sorority. **Honors/Awds:** Outstanding Students Teachers Award, 1968; Outstanding Performance & Cash Awards, 1985-97; Commanders Award for Exceptional Service, 1984; Superior Civilian Service, 1991; Meritorious Civilian Service Award, 1994-98; Air Force Orgnal Excellence Award, 1997; Cert Achievement, Secy Army, 1997; 25th Anniversary All Volunteer Force Award, 1998; Distinguished Alumni Award, Univ NCA, 1998; Distinguished Leader Award, Air Force Asn, 1998; Distinguished Service Award, Tuskegee Airmen, 1999; Distinguished Alumni Award, St Augustine's Col, 2000; Meritorious Civilian Service, 2001. **Business Addr:** Assistant Secretary of the Air Force, SAF/MI, 1660 Air Force Pentagon Rm 4E1020, Washington, DC 20330-1660, **Business Phone:** (202)697-2302.

DEMILLE, DR. VALERIE CECILIA
Businessperson, medical researcher, consultant. **Personal:** Born Jun 2, 1949, New York, NY; daughter of Arnold C and Annie M Clark. **Educ:** NC Cent Univ, BS, 1972, MS, 1974, Meharry Med Col, MD, 1977; Baruch Col, New York, NY, MPA, 1991. **Career:** USAF Sheppard AFB, staff psychiatrist, 1981-83; USAF Vandenberg AFB, chief ment health serv, 1983-84; Woodhull Hosp, staff psychiatrist, 1985; NY Med Col & Lincoln Hosp, New York, NY, unit chief, 1985-87, staff psychiatrist, 1987-88; New York City Dept Ment Health, New York, NY, staff assoc anal, 1990-91; Upper Manhattan Ment Health ctr, exec dir, 1992; Life Mgt, consultant, 1993-99; Stress Mgt Asn, Harlem & the deMille Consult Agency, founder; Pet Groomer, 2000; New York Bureau, chief. **Orgs:** LomPoc bus Women Network; dir press rel, NAACP Legal Defense Fund. **Military Serv:** USAF, major.

DE MORSELLA, TRACEY. **See MINOR, TRACEY L.**

DEMPSEY, REV. DR. JOSEPH PAGE
Clergy, school administrator. **Personal:** Born Mar 8, 1930, Nashville, NC; son of Sidney H (deceased) and Irene Alice Vick (deceased); married Evelyntyne Humphrey, May 31, 1958; children: Denise P, Joseph T, Eric H & Kathy D. **Educ:** Fayetteville State Univ, BS, 1958; Shaw Div Sch, BD, 1964; NC Cen Univ, MA, 1971; Shaw Div Sch, MDiv, 1972; Jacksonville Theol Sem, FL, DTh, 1982; Faith Evangelical Lutheran Sem, Tacoma WA, DMin, 1988. **Career:** Pastor various locations since, 1961; NC Cen Univ, instr, 1971-, assoc dir, 1988-; Pine Grove Baptist Church, Creedmoor NC, pastor, 1986-87; Elem & High Sch, instr; Worthdale United Baptist Church Raleigh, NC, pastor; NC Cent Univ Coun Ctr, assoc dir, currently; NC Cent Univ, Grad Sch Educ, adj asst prof, 1991-. **Orgs:** Min Bd, Wake Baptist Asn, 1964; NC Personnel & Guide Asn; Am Personnel & Guid Asn; Exec Com, Wake Co Dem Party; bd dir, NC Gen Baptist Con, bd dir, YMCA, 1967-; bd dir, Comm Day Carde Ctr; Goals Raleigh Educ Outreach; The Raleigh-Wake Martin Luther King Celebration Comt, 1989. **Honors/Awds:** Teacher of the Yr, 1967; Raleigh, NC Christian Family of the Yr, 1972; Outstanding Serv Award, NC Cent Univ, 1973-74. **Home Addr:** 1409 E Martin St, Raleigh, NC 27610-2611. **Business Addr:** Adjunct Assistant Professor, NC Central University, Grad Sch Educ, PO Box 19688, Durham, NC 27707, **Business Phone:** (919)560-6466.*

DENMARK, LEON
Vice president (Organization), executive director. **Career:** Apollo Theater Harlem, exec dir; NJ Performing Arts Ctr, vpres, currently. **Business Addr:** Vice president, New Jersey Performing Arts Center, 1 Center St, Newark, NJ 07102, **Business Phone:** (973)642-8989.*

DENMARK, ROBERT RICHARD
Manager. **Personal:** Born Apr 1, 1930, Savannah, GA; son of Robert and Gladys Church; married Mamie E Sampson-Denmark, Aug 14, 1971; children: Gladys Denmark-Reed. **Educ:** MTI Bus Col, Cert Comput Sci, 1978; Am River Col, AA, 1980; Univ San

Francisco, BS, 1982. **Career:** Manager (retired). Fed Aviation Admin, air traffic control, 1969-71; Prudential Ins Co Am, spec agt, 1971-74; Dept Interior US Bur Reclamation, comput analyst & programmer, 1974-84, adp contract adminr, 1984; US Dept Interior Div Info Resources, comput consult, 1980-84; comput security mgr, 1988-94. **Orgs:** Chief Rabban Ancient Arabic Order Nobles Mystic Shrine N & S Am, 1982-; pres, Sphinx Club Alpha Phi Alpha Frat Inc, 1985; clusterleader Sacramento Area Strategy Team Lutheran Church Am, 1985-87; Zeta Beta Lambda Chap Alpha Phi Alpha, secy, 1987, pres, 1988-92; pres, First Eng Lutheran Church Coun, 1987-; Nat Asn Adv Colored People, Black Data Processing Asn; mem exec bd, Div Aging; 32 Degree Mason Ancient Free & Accepted Masonic Cong; exec bd mem, Sierra Pac Synod, Evangelical Lutheran Church, 1991-; Sierra Pacific Synod Coun, Evangelical Lutheran Church Am, 1991-94; bd dirs, Sacramento Lutheran High Sch, 1994-97. **Honors/Awds:** Res proj, Univ San Francisco, A Study of the Potential of Off Automation, 1982; Outstanding Leadership Award, Lutheran Church Am First Eng Lutheran Church, 1982-84; Special Achievement Award, US Dept Interior, 1985-86; Outstanding Service Award, Div Data Processing Bur Reclamation, 1987; Meritorious Service, Zeta Beta Lambda Chap, Alpha Phi Alpha Fraternity Inc, 1988; Outstanding Serv, Sacramento Area Lutheran Ministry, Evangelical Lutheran Church Am, 1988; Performance Award, US Bur Reclamation, Dept Interior, 1988; Alpha Phi Alpha Man of the Year, Zeta Beta Lambda Chap, 1990; Outstanding Service Award, Bur Reclamation, 1991-92. **Military Serv:** USAF, master sgt, 20 yrs; Highest Award, Air Force Commendation Medal, 1969, Outstanding NCO of the Year, 1963-64. **Home Addr:** 1043 Lake Glen Way, Sacramento, CA 95822, **Home Phone:** (916)422-5517. *

DENNARD, BRAZEAL WAYNE
Musician, educator, consultant. **Personal:** Born Jan 1, 1929, Detroit, MI; son of Ezekiel and Bertha Brazeal; married Murdice Vallery Dennard, Oct 10, 1959 (died 1988). **Educ:** Highland Park Junior Col, Highland Park, MI, 1956; Wayne State Univ, Detroit, MI, BS, 1959, M, Mus, 1962. **Career:** Detroit Bd Educ, Detroit, MI, teacher, 1959-71, fine arts dept head, 1971-83, music supvr, 1983-89; Brazeal Dennard Chorale, Detroit, MI, artistic dir, 1972-, founder & leader, currently; Wayne State Univ, Detroit, MI, music instr, 1984, adj prof; Detroit Pub Schs, supvr vocal music, 2000. **Orgs:** Pres, Detroit musicians Asn, 1974-88; pres, Nat Asn Negro Mus Inc, 1975-79; chorale panel, Nat Endowment Arts, 1985-87; Arts Educ, Nat Endowment for the Arts, 1986-88; consult, Music Educrs Nat Conf, 1989; Master Panalist; Cult Affairs Dept, City Detroit, 1990-. **Honors/Awds:** Vocal Teacher of the Year, Mich Sch Vocal Asn, 1990; Choral Performance, Am Choral Dir Asn, 1989; Distinguished Achievement Award, Arts Found Mich, 1989; Outstanding Service Award, Detroit Pub Schs, 1989; Distinguished Alumni Award, Wayne State Univ, 1986; Dr. Alain Locke Award, The Detroit Inst Arts Founders Soc, Friends African-Am Art; Maynard Klein Award, Mich chapter, Am choral Drrs Asn; Teacher of the year, Mich Sch Vocal Asn; Mus Afa Hist Award for Excellence in Arts/Music; 1st Annual Brazeal Dennard Arts Heritage Award, presented by the Bd Dir, Brazeal Dennard Choral Ensembles; Hon Doctor Music Olivet Col, 2000; lifetime achievement award, Detroit Symphony Orchestra; fdr of "Classical Roots" Brazeal Dennard Chorale & Detroit Symphony Orchestra. **Military Serv:** Army, cpl, 1951-53. **Home Addr:** 4330 Fullerton, Detroit, MI 48238. *

DENNARD, DARRYL W.
Television journalist. **Personal:** Born Sep 18, 1957, New York, NY; son of Eleanor Adamson and Glenn W; married Darlene Gray Dennard, Jul 13, 1979; children: Autumn Simone Dennard. **Educ:** Fordham Univ, Bronx, NY, attended 1985; State Univ Col Buffalo, NY, BA, broadcasting, 1981. **Career:** US Customs Serv, Buffalo, NY, import specialist trainee, 1977-79; WGR-TV, Buffalo, NY, prod asst, 1980-83; WGRZ-TV, Buffalo, NY, news reporter, 1983-87; Johnson Publ Co, Chicago, IL, TV co-host, 1987; Black Enterprise Report, co-host; Minority Bus Report, WGN-TV, host, currently. **Orgs:** Nat Black Media Coalition, 1983-87; bd mem, Buffalo Urban League, 1985-87; State Univ NY Col Buffalo Alumni Asn, 1985-86; community advisory bd, Community Dept, SUNY Col Buffalo, 1987. **Honors/Awds:** Best Public Affairs Program, New York State Broadcasters, 1985; Best Newscast of the Year Award, United Press Int, 1986; Black Leadership Award, 1490 Enterprises, 1986; Young Pioneer Award, Northern Region Black Political Caucus, 1986; Media Award, Buffalo Public Schs, 1987; Special Service Award, Seek/EOP SUNY Col Buffalo, 1988; Merit Award, United Negro Col Fund, 1989. **Business Addr:** Host, WGN-TV, Minority Business Report, 2501 W Bradley Place, Chicago, IL 60618-4718.*

DENNARD, GLORIA
Executive. **Personal:** Married. **Educ:** Stillman Col, attended 1965. **Career:** Birmingham Civil Rights Inst, bd dirs; Jefferson County Pub Schs, dir libr serv; Jefferson County Bd Educ, dir media serv, currently. **Orgs:** Immediate past pres, Nat Alumni Asn Stillman Col. **Home Addr:** 212 Westmoreland Circle, Fairfield, AL 35064. **Business Addr:** Director of Media Services, Jefferson County Board of Education, 2100 S 18th St, Homewood, AL 35209.

DENNING, DR. BERNADINE NEWSOM
School administrator, executive. **Personal:** Born Aug 17, 1930, Detroit, MI; married Blaine; children: Blaine Jr. **Educ:** Mich State Normal EMU, BS, 1951; Wayne State Univ, MA, 1956, MA & 30 Specialist, 1960, EdD, 1970. **Career:** Educator (retired); Detroit Pub Sch, teacher, 1951-62, counr, 1962-70; Univ Mich, asst prof, 1970-75; Title IV Civil Rights, dir, 1975-77; Off Revenue Sharing Dept Treas, dir, 1977-79; Detroit Pub Sch, asst supt; Urban Edu Prog, dir; Human Rights Off, dir. **Orgs:** Trustee, Cent MI Univ, 1980-90, chmn, 1985; secy Mich Atty Discipline Bd, 1983-; Mich Women's Comn, 1975-77, vice chmn, 1976-78, chmn, 1981-87; YWCA USA Bd, 1973-85; vice chmn, Black United Fund, 1984-90; Black Family Develop Bd, 1981-90; secy, C's Aid Soc, 1983-90; vice chmnr, Skillman Found, 1985-01. **Honors/Awds:** Michigan Women's Hall of Fame, 1985; Emma V Kelly Award Daughters of IBPOE of W, 1983; Distinguished Award, US Coast Guard Acad, 1982; Lifetime Achievement Award, YWCA 1984; Negro Bus & Prof Award, 1978; Distinguished Warriors, Urban League, 2001. **Home Addr:** 3309 Leslie, Detroit, MI 48238.

DENNING, JOE WILLIAM
Government official. **Personal:** Born Nov 30, 1945, Bowling Green, KY; son of Marion E and Evelyn Huskey; divorced; children: Kita Denning Clements & Larecia Denning Bell. **Educ:** Ky State Police Acad, 1970; Western KY Univ. **Career:** Bowling Green Ind Sch Dist, mem, 1975-92; City Bowling, city comnr, 1992-04, 2007-. **Orgs:** BG Warren County Chamber Comt; KY League Cities; Nat League Cities; Bowling Green Chamber Comt. *

DENNIS, ANDRE L
Lawyer. **Personal:** Born May 15, 1943, Burton-On-Trent, England; married Julie B Carpenter; children: Matthew. **Educ:** Cheyney Univ, BA, 1966; Howard Univ Sch Law, JD, 1969. **Career:** Stradley Ronon Stevens & Young LLP, assoc, 1969-76, partner, 1976-. **Orgs:** Bd mem, Independence Found, 1997-; bd mem, Nat Sr Citizens Law Ctr, 1995; bd mem, Phil Facilities Mgt Corp, 1994-99; pres, Pa Capital Case Resource Ctr, 1993; chancellor, Philadelphia Bar Asn, 1993; pres, 1990-91, bd Govs, chair, 1986, Vol Indigent Prog; bd trustees, Community Legal Servs, 1973-84; Pa Bar Asn House Delegs, 1988-; fel, Am Col Trial Lawyers, 1994-; bd adv, Phil Lawyer Chap; fel, Am Bar Asn; Nat Bar Asn; Pa Bar Asn; fal, Am Col Trial Lawyers. **Honors/Awds:** Pro Bono Serv Award, Pa Bar Asn, 1991-92; Appreciation Award, BWEA, Montgomery County Chap, 1992; Equal Justice Award, Community Legal Servs, 1992; Cheyney Univ, Honorary Doctor of Laws, 1993; ML King Jr Humanitarian Award, Salem Baptist Church, 1993; Pro Bono Pub Award, Am Bar Asn, 1994; Alumni Achievement Award, Howard Univ, 1996; Civil Liberties Award, Am Civil Liberties Union Found, 1997; Hon fel, Univ Pa, 1999; Region III Advocacy Award, Nat Bar Asn; named a "Pennsylvania Super Lawyer, 2007. **Business Addr:** Partner, Stradley Ronon Stevens & Young LLP, 2600 One Commerce Sq, Philadelphia, PA 19103-7098, **Business Phone:** (215)564-8034.

DENNIS, BARBARA RODGERS. See RODGERS, BARBARA LORRAINE.

DENNIS, CAROLYN K
Executive. **Personal:** Born Nov 12, 1948, Hickory, NC; daughter of George Killian and Naomi Killian; married Michael, Feb 21, 1986; children: Brandon Thompson & Christopher. **Educ:** North Carolina A&T State Univ, BS, acct, 1971; Univ Wis, MBA, 1998. **Career:** Executive (retired); Gen Motors, acct supvr, 1972-76; Ford Motor Co, acct supvr, 1976-80; Miller Brewing Co, acct supvr, 1981-87, acct mgr, 1987-94, brewery controller, 1994-97, group dir opers & finance, 1997-2005. **Orgs:** Adv bd, Univ Wis, Sch Educ, 1998; YWCA, financial comt, 2000; adv bd, UWM Sch Educ. **Honors/Awds:** UWM School of Business GOLD Award, 2005. **Home Addr:** 3321 W Burgundy Ct, Thiensville, WI 53092, **Home Phone:** (262)242-9463.

DENNIS, CECELIA GRIFFITH
Educator. **Personal:** Born Sep 23, 1943, Raleigh, NC; daughter of Cecil and Sadie; married William Thomas, Jul 18, 1970; children: Jason Maurice. **Educ:** St Augustines Col, BA, 1966. **Career:** Educator (retired); Somerset Co Bd Educ, teacher, 1966-74; Worcester Co Bd Educ, teacher, 1974-2000, coordr teacher recruitment, 2000. **Orgs:** Delta Sigma Theta, 1963-2003; Nat Asn Advan Colored People, Wicomico Br, 1985-2002; bd mem, Community Found Eastern Shore, 1972-2003; Delta Kappa Gamma, 1989-2000; secy, Wicomico Co Liquor Control Bd, 1990-2003; Dem Club Wicomico Co, 1990-2003; secy, YMCA Mid Shore, Corp Bd, 1990-2003; Worcester Co Retired Teachers Asn, 2000-02; Independent Retired Persons; AARP; Chesapeake Forestry Adv Bd; Rural Legacy Adv Bd; Deacon Bd, Wicomico Presbyterian Church; St Augustines Col Alumni; Human Rels Comt. **Honors/Awds:** Outstanding Educator, Am Asn Univ Women, 1985; Worcester County Teacher of the Year, 1988; Sustaining Campaign Award, YWCA, 1991; Achievement Award, Worcester Co Nat Asn Advan Colored People, 2001; Black Achievement Award, Omega Psi Phi, 2001; Hall of Fame, WICOWICO Co CMS Women, 2003; Chair Award for Excellence for Community Achievement, Md State Dept Edu, 2003; Rev Dr MLK Jr Achievement Award for Humanitarian Services, 2003; Delta Sigma Theta Service Award. **Special Achievements:** First African American to integrate faculty at Marion High School, 1960. **Home Addr:** 1004 S Delano Ave, Salisbury, MD 21801.

DENNIS, EDWARD S G, JR. (EDWARD SPENCER GALE DENNIS)
Lawyer. **Personal:** Born Jan 24, 1945, Salisbury, MD; son of Virginia Monroe and Edward S; married Lois Juliette Young, Dec 27, 1969; children: Edward Brookfield. **Educ:** US Merchant Marine Acad, BS, 1967; Univ Pa Law Sch, JD, 1973. **Career:** Lawyer (retired); US Dist Ct, from law clerk to Judge A Leon Higginbotham Jr, 1973-75; Eastern Dist Pia, asst US atty, 1975-80; US Dept Justice, Criminal Div Narcotic & Dangerous Drug Sect, dep chief, 1978-80, chief, 1980-83, Eastern Dist Pa, US atty, 1983-88, asst atty gen, 1988-90, actg dep atty gen US, 1989-2002; Morgan, Lewis & Bockius, senior partner, 1990. **Orgs:** Bd dir, Pub Broadcasting Sta, WHYY Inc, 1990; Citizens Crime Comn, 1990-; fel Int Soc Barristers, 1991; Am Col Trial Lawyers. **Honors/Awds:** Citizen of the Year, Omega Psi Phi Fraternity, 1987; Edmund J Randolf Award, atty gen US, 1988; Hobart C Jackson Award, Philadelphia Inter-Alumni Coun United Negro Col Fund, 1988; Reverend Dr Martin Luther King Award, Educr Roundtable Inc, 1988; Religious Liberty Award, Am Jewish Cong, 1990. **Military Serv:** US Naval Reserve, Lt, 1967-82. **Home Addr:** 448 Darlington Rd, Media, PA 19063, **Home Phone:** (215)558-5975.

DENNIS, EDWARD SPENCER GALE. See DENNIS, EDWARD S G, JR.

DENNIS, DR. EVIE GARRETT
School administrator, government official. **Personal:** Born Sep 8, 1924, Canton, MS; daughter of Eugene Garrett and Ola Brown Garrett; divorced; children: Pia E Dennis. **Educ:** St Louis Univ, BS, 1953; Univ Colo, MA, 1971; Nova Univ, EdD, 1976. **Career:** Sch administrator (retired), government official; Childrens Asthma Res Inst & Hosp, from res asst to res chief, 1958-66, Denver Pub Schs, Lake Jr High Sch, counr, teacher, 1966-71, community specialist, starting 1971; Denver Vocational Guidance Inst, cons, 1971-72; Metro State Col, teacher, 1974; Denver Pub Schs, supt. **Orgs:** Alpha Kappa Alpha; US Olympic Comt; bd trustees, US Sports Acad; US Track & Field Inc; delegate, Int Amateur Athletic Fed. **Honors/Awds:** Congressional Gold Medal, US Olympic Team, 1990; Olympic Order; Asn Nat Olympic Commission Award; Salute to Excellence Award, Colo Black Women Polit Action, 1994; Appreciation for Service Award, Nation Islam, 1994; Service Appreciation Award, Escolites Drill Team, 1994; Service Recognition Award, Colo Asn Sch Execs, 1995;.

DENNIS, HUGO, JR.
Educator. **Personal:** Born Aug 5, 1936, Tortola, British Virgin Islands; married Carmen Lydia Marrero; children: Tony, Hugh, Jancie, Reynaldo & Alex. **Educ:** Hampton Inst, BS, 1959; Univ CT, 1968. **Career:** VI Pub Schs, math teacher, 1960; St Thomas-St John Fedn Teacher, pres,1967; Cent Labor Coun VI, pres, 1976; VI legis, pres, 1983-84; VI Govt, acting comnr housing, 1986-; AARP VI, pres,currently. **Orgs:** Deleg, Third Const Conv VI, 1978; rep, Study Tour SAfrica, 1980. **Business Addr:** President, Virgin Islands Government, PO Box 960, St Thomas, Virgin Islands of the United States 00801.

DENNIS, JAMES CARLOS
Marketing executive. **Personal:** Born Jun 21, 1947, Washington, DC; son of Sadie; married Tonya Redding, Jul 1980; children: James Stratford. **Educ:** Fairfield Univ, Fairfield, CT, BS, mgt, 1969; USN, Officer Cand Sch, Newport, RI, comn lt, 1969; Harvard Bus Sch, Soldiers Field, MA, MBA, 1974. **Career:** Gen Foods Corp, White Plains, NY, brand mgr, 1974-78; Warner-Lambert Co, Morris Plains, NJ, sr prod mgr, 1978-81; Heublein Spirits Group, Hartford, CT, vpres mkt, 1981-83; Hewlett-Packard, Palo Alto, CA, dir mkt communs, 1983-89; Travelers Co, Hartford, CT, vpres mkt corp commun, 1989; Northeast Client Serv, sr vpres; Paymap, chief operating officer; Cendant Mem Serv, chief mkt officer & unit gen mgr; Citigroup, sr corp mkt; AXA Equitable Life Ins Co, sr vpres customer mkt, currently. **Orgs:** Omega Psi Phi Fraternity, 1969-; bd mem, Conn Spec Olympics, 1990-; bd mem, Hartford Stage Co, 1990-. **Military Serv:** USN, lt, 1969-72; Meritorious Unit Commendation. **Business Phone:** (212)554-1234.

DENNIS, KAREN
Athletic coach. **Personal:** Born in Detroit, MI; married; children: Ebony. **Educ:** Mich state univ, BA, public affairs, 1977; MA, phys educ, 1979. **Career:** Spartans womens track & field, asst coach, 1977; US Sports Festival, coach, 1985; World Univ Championships, asst coach, Duisburg, Ger, 1989; Pan Am Games, coach, Havana, cuba; 1991; World Championships squad, asst coach, Gotteberg, Sweden, 1995; Univ Nevada-Los Vagas, track coach; Ohio State's, women's head coach; Buckeyes, head coach. **Orgs:** Black Coaches Assn; mem, USA Track & Field Intl Competition Comm; past pres, Athletic Cong Womens Track Coaches Assn; mem, NCAA Womens Track &Field Comm; mem, NCAA Track Coaches Assn. **Honors/Awds:** District VIII, Coach Yr, 1992; US-ATF Pres Award, 1993; Dennis Conference Coach Yr hons. **Special Achievements:** Olympic Games, womens head coach, Sydney, Australia, 2000; Mich State Univ track & field prog, head coach, 1981; District IV Coach Yr, 1982. **Business Addr:** Women's Head Coach, The Ohio State University, Jerome Schottenstein Center, 555 Borror Dr, Columbus, OH 43210, **Business Phone:** (614)292-2624.*

DENNIS, MICHAEL A.
Executive, vice president (organization), administrator. **Educ:** Dartmouth Col, BS; Univ VA, Darden Sch Bus, exec prog; Haas

Bus Sch. **Career:** AT&T, Corp Data Ctr, syst admin, 1981; Lucent Technologies, vpres US serv bus commun syst group, 1999. **Orgs:** bd dirs, INROADS, Cent NJ. *

DENNIS, PHILIP H.
Physician, neurologist. **Personal:** Born Dec 1, 1925, St Louis, MO; son of Herman and Nellie Helena Watters Holton; married Patricia; children: Pia Evene, Lisette Marie, Philip Herman, Michael Marion. **Educ:** Lincoln Univ, attended 1947; St Louis Univ, attended 1953; Meharry Med Col, attended 1957; Cook County Grad Sch Med, 1972, 1979, 1980, 1982, 1985, 1986, APA (CME), 1988. **Career:** City Hosp St Louis, internship, 1957-58; Homer G. Phillips, Renard, & Cochran Hosp, psychiat resident, 1972, 1979, 1980, 1982, 1985, 1986; Southern Ill Community Col, instr, 1971-74; SIU Edwardsville, coun, 1982-; Ment Health Ctr, dir, 1980-; pvt pract, currently. **Orgs:** Consult psychiat, Ill Retirement Syst, Southern Illi Univ, Edwardsville; Family Serv Agency; Chamber Com, Kiwanis, Am Soc Clinical Hypn. **Honors/Awds:** NIMH fel, 1958-59; Lovejoy Award; Golden Rule Award; Host for KATZ radio "Open Mike" 1968-81; Developer Pleasingly Soft Prods, 1982; Exhibitor one man art & sculpture show. **Business Addr:** Neuropsychiatrist, 100 N 8th St Suite 200, East St Louis, IL 62201.*

DENNIS, DR. RODNEY HOWARD
Psychiatrist. **Personal:** Born Oct 3, 1936, Tampa, FL; son of Huerta W and Gussie Harris. **Educ:** NY Univ, Col Arts & Sci, BA, 1958; Howard Univ, Col Med, MD, 1962; Kings County Hosp, Brooklyn, NY, Rotating Internship, 1962-63; New York Sch Psychiatry, Brooklyn State Hosp, Psychiatric Resident, 1970-73. **Career:** Letterman Gen Hosp, gen med officer, 1964-65; Univ Calif, LA, Brentwood Va Hosp, psychiat res, 1965-67; Metropolitan State Hosp, Norwalk, CA, physician, 1968-69; Kingsboro Psychiat Ctr, Brooklyn State Hosp, psychiat, 1973-83; Woodhull Med & Ment Health Ctr, consult & liaison serv, attending physician dept psychiat, 1986-. **Orgs:** Am Psychiatric Asn; The Brooklyn Psychiatric Soc; The NY Acad Sci; NY Univ Alumni Asn; Asn NY State Mental Hygiene Phys & Dentists; AAAS, Acad Psychosomatic Med, Pi Lambda Phi Frat. **Military Serv:** AUS, capt, med corps, 1962-65. **Home Addr:** 307 Decatur St, Brooklyn, NY 11233. **Business Addr:** Attending Physician, Medical Associates Woodhull PC, Department of Psychiatry, Consultant & Liaison Service, 760 Broadway, Brooklyn, NY 11206, **Business Phone:** (718)963-5841.

DENNIS, DR. RUTLEDGE M.
Educator, sociologist. **Personal:** Born Aug 16, 1939, Charleston, SC; son of Ora Porcher and David Dennis Sr; married Sarah Helen Bankhead; children: Shay T, Imaro, Kimya & Zuri. **Educ:** SC State Col, BA, Social Sci, 1966; Wash State Univ, MA, Sociol, 1969, PhD, Sociol, 1975. **Career:** Va Commonwealth Univ, Dept Sociol & Anthrop, coord Afro-Am studies, 1971-78, assoc prof sociol dept, 1981-83, assoc chmn, sociol dept,1981-83; George Mason Univ, Dept Sociol & Anthrop, vis commonwealth prof, 1989-91, prof, 1991-; Wash State Univ, Dept Sociol, teaching assoc. **Orgs:** Adv, Alpha Kappa Delta Chapt, George Mason Univ, 1991-; co-coordinator, Grad Prog, sociol dept, George Mason Univ, 1991-; pres, Asn Black Sociologists, 1981-83; pres, Black Educ Asn, 1974-75; comnr, Richmond Redevelopment & Housing Authority, 1979-81; NY Acad Sci; Am Sociol Asn; Southern Sociol Asn; Ba'Alay Keriyah Soc; chair, African-Am Acad, 1999-; life mem, Nat Asn Advan Colored People; life mem, Asn Black Sociologists; Am Asn Univ Prof; George Mason Univ. **Honors/Awds:** Outstanding Educator of America, 1975Reise-Melton Award, Va Commonwealth Univ, Cultural Award, 1981; Boys Club Citizen Award, Richmond Boys Club,1980; Distinguished Community Educ Award, Alpha Phi Alpha Frat, 1985; Alpha Kappa Mu Honor Soc, 1966; Initiated into Omicron Delta Kappa, 1986; Jewish Educators Award, 1998; President's Award, SC State Univ, 1966; Sigma Rho Sigma Research Award, 1965; Fenwick Fel, 2005-06, George Mason Univ; Nat Monitor Family & Community Award, 1985; Ford Foundation Award, 1970; co-coordinator, Southeastern Regional African Seminar, 1973-76; Distinguished Leadership Award, Afro-American Studies Prog, Va Commonwealth Univ, 1991; Joseph Himes Distinguished Scholarship Award, 2001; DuBois-Johnson-Frazier Award, 2006. **Special Achievements:** Co-editor, The Afro-American, 1976; co-author, The Politics of Annexation:Oligarchic Power in a Southern City, 1982; editor, JAI Press Series in Race and Ethnic Relations, 1990-; co-editor,Race & Ethnicity in Research Methods, 1993; Racial & Ethnic Politics, 1994; The Black Middle Class, 1995; WEB DuBois:The Scholar as Activist, 1996; The Scholar as Activist, 1996; The Black Intellectuals, 1997; co-editor,Race and Ethnicity-comparative and theoretical Approaches, 2003; Marginality: Race, Class and Gender, 2005. **Military Serv:** AUS sp 4. **Home Addr:** 3015 Sunset Ave, Richmond, VA 23221, **Home Phone:** (804)358-8198. **Business Addr:** Professor, George Mason University, Department of Sociology & Anthropology, 320 B Robinson Hall, Fairfax, VA 22030, **Business Phone:** (703)993-1431.

DENNIS, SHIRLEY M
Government official, chairperson, vice president (organization). **Personal:** Born Feb 26, 1938, Omaha, NE; married William D C; children: Pamela, Robin & Sherrie. **Educ:** Cheyney State Col, 1955-56; Real Estate Inst, 1959; Am Inst Planner, 1970; Temple Univ, AS 1985; Lincoln Univ, hon doctorate laws, 1986; Morris Brown Col, hon doctorate humane letters, 1988; Cabrini Col, BA, orgn mgt, 1996; West Chester Univ PA, MBA, bus admin, 1998. **Career:** Government official, Chairperson, Vice president (retired); Tucker & Tucker, Philadelphia, sales & Off mgr, 1961-67; Redevelop Authority, Philadelphia, equal opportunity specialist, 1967-68; Urban League Philadelphia, housing dir, 1969-71; Housing Asn Del Valley, managing dir, 1971-79; Pa Dept Community Affairs, exec dep secy, 1979, actg secy, 1979-80, secretary, 1980-86; Women's Bur, US Dept Labor, dir, 1986-88; PECO Energy Co, Prgms & Dev, dir corp sponsorships, 1991-99; Cheyney Univ Pa, Instnl Advan, vpres, 1999-2001. **Orgs:** Philadelphia Tribune Charities, 1978; co-chairperson, Philadelphia Housing Task force, 1978; chairperson, PA Housing Finance Agency, 1979-86; exec bd mem, Coun State Community Affairs, 1980-86; exec comt, Nat State Housing Finance, 1982-86; Coalition 100 Black Women, 1982-; founding mem, Abington Memorial Hosp, MLK COM, 1982; bd mem, Philadelphia Martin Luther King, Jr Asn Inc, 1985; pres, NAACP Willow Grove Br, 1972-79; exec bd mem, PA State Conf NCP, 1974-80; chair, Regional Performing Arts Ctr Oversight Comt, 1996-00; bd mem, Health Partners, 1993-01; United Negro Col Fund, Philadelphia Regional Telethon, 1996; Mayors Comn on Aging, 1994-00; Willow Grove Sr Citizens Ctr, 1990-00; Distinguished Daughters PEN, 1998-. **Honors/Awds:** Redbook Magazine one of 12 outstanding women in Penna, 1977; Black Journalist Award, 1978; Public Service Award, PA Federation of Business & Prof Women's Club, 1980; Service Award, NAACP, 1980; Appreciation Award, Carlisle OIC, 1981; Community Serv Award, Nat Asn Negro Business & Prof Women, 1981; John F Kennedy School of Govt fellowship, Harvard Univ, Inst of Politics, 1988; Pioneering Women's Hall of Fame, inductee, SW Belmont YWCA of Philadelphia, 1989; Martin Luther King Award for Public Service, Abington Township, PA, 1990; Shirley Dennis Public Sector Award, created in her honor, Community Action Development Commission of Montgomery County, 1995; Barristers' Assn Community Service Award, 1996; The Intelligencer, One of Top 100 People of the Century, 1999. **Special Achievements:** Travelled extensively in support of human rights, including United Nations Decade for Women Conference, Nairobi, Kenya, Zaire, Congo, Zimbabwe, Botswana, South Africa, Senegal. First female to chair the United Negro College Fund in 1996.

DENNISTON, PROF. DOROTHY L.
Educator. **Personal:** Born Aug 10, 1944, Springfield, MA; daughter of James H Hamer and Irma L Washington Hamer; divorced. **Educ:** Northeastern Univ, BA, 1967; Simmons Col, MA, 1975; Brown Univ, PhD, 1983. **Career:** Sec Schs, teacher Eng, 1967-71; Simmons Col, asst dir admis, 1971-72,instr Eng, 1973-74, assoc dean, 1974-76, 79-80; Univ Tenn, asst prof Eng, 1983-86; Brown Univ, Dorothy Danforth Compton Fel, 1981-82, howard post doc fel, 1986-87, vis asst prof Eng, 1987-88, asst prof, 1988-94, assoc prof Eng, 1994, assoc dean col, 1995-96, 1999-2000, assoc prof Africana Studies, 2000-, Wriston Fel; Wheaton Col, vis cole Jr prof, 1993. **Orgs:** Alpha Kappa Alpha Sorority, 1963-67; Nat Asn Foreign Stud Affairs, 1972; Assn Study Negro Life & Hist, 1972-; Modern Lang Assn, 1975-; adv com scholars-internship prog, Martin L King Jr Ctr Social Change, 1976-; Natl Assn Inter discipliny Ethnic Studies, 1977-; standing comt black studies.Col Lang Asn, 1983-86; SE Lang Asn, 1984-86; col bd, Eng Compos Test Comt,1984-87; Col Lang Asn, 1984-; Langston Hughes Ctr Arts, 1988-; NE Lang Assn, 1991-. **Honors/Awds:** Omega Psi Phi Fraternity Scholarship Boston Chap, 1962; J Rosen Scholarship Award, Boston Chap NE Univ, 1965; Fellow Nat Fellowship Fund,1976-79; J Hodges Faculty Research Award, Univ Tenn, 1984; Outstanding Service & Dedication Community Award, Brown Univ, 1991; Wriston Fellowship Award, Brown Univ, 1991; Fel, Ford Found, Summer Seminar Col Prof, 1993; Excellence Teaching Award, Brown Univ, 1999, 2000; Faculty Mentor,Alliance Int Res Minority Scholars, 2000; Faculty Mentor Book Award, Brown Univ, 2003, 2004, 2005; Exemplary Leadership Award, 2004. **Special Achievements:** Author, The Fiction of Paule Marshall: History, Culture & Gender, Univ of Tennessee Press, 1995; "Paule Marshall," American Women Writers from Colonial Times to Present, 1980, updated 1992; associate editor, Langston Hughes Review; associate editor, Abafazi: The Simmons College Review of Women of African Descent; "Paule Marshall," Black Women in America: An Historical Encyclopedia, 1992; "Early Short Fiction by Paule Marshall,"Short Story Criticism, 1990; "Faulkner's Image of Blacks in Go Down Moses," Phylon, March, 1983. **Business Addr:** Associate Professor, Brown University, Department English, 70 Brown St Room 336, PO Box 1852, Providence, RI 02912, **Business Phone:** (401)863-3739.

DENSON, ANDRE B.
Educator. **Educ:** Univ Nev, PhD, Las Vegas, 1995. **Career:** Mojave High Sch, Clark County Sch Dist, prin & region supt, currently.

DENSON, AUTRY
Football player. **Personal:** Born Dec 8, 1976, Lauderhill, FL; son of Janice Franklin. **Educ:** Notre Dame. **Career:** Football player-(retired); Tampa Bay Buccaneers, 1999; miami dolphins, 1999-00; Chicago Bears, 2001; Detroit Lions, running back, 2002. **Orgs:** Founder, The Autry L Denson Run For Your Goal Foundation, 1999. **Honors/Awds:** Rookie of the year, 1999. **Special Achievements:** Sixth player in Notre Dame history to reach the 1,000-yard mark in a season; Reached 1,176 yards mark in 1998 & ranked seventh in Irish history. **Business Addr:** Founder, Run For Your Goal Foundation, 5379 Lyons Rd, Coconut Creek, FL 33073, **Business Phone:** 800-307-8130.*

DENSON, DAMON
Football player. **Personal:** Born Feb 8, 1975, Pittsburgh, PA; married Camille; children: 1. **Educ:** Univ Mich, physic educ. **Career:** Football player (retired); New Eng Patriots, guard, 1997-99; Baltimore Ravens, 2000; Assoc Pastor, Life International Church, currently. *

DENSON, FRED L
Lawyer. **Personal:** Born Jul 19, 1937, New Brighton, PA; married Catherine; children: Terry, Kelly & Kendra. **Educ:** Rensselaer Polytech Inst, BE, chem eng, 1959; Georgetown Univ, JD, 1966. **Career:** WOKR-TV ABC, host black dimensions, 1972-; Urban League, Rochester, exec dir, 1970-71; Eastman Kodak Co, atty, 1967-70; Law Off Fred L Denson, atty, currently. **Orgs:** Bd mem, NY Pub Employ Rels Bd; exec dir, Nat Patent Law Asn; dir, Armarco Mkg; pres, Genessee Region Home Care Asn; chmn, adv coun, NY Div Human Rights Am Bar Asn; Nat Bar Asn; Monroe Co Bar Asn; Nat Patent Law Asn; Am Arbit Asn. **Honors/Awds:** Rochester Community Service Award, 1974-76. **Special Achievements:** Author, Know Your Town Justice Court. **Military Serv:** AUS, first lt, 1960-61. **Business Addr:** Attorney, Law Office Fred L Denson, 14 E Main St, PO Box 801, Webster, NY 14580, **Business Phone:** (585)265-2710.

DENT, DR. ANTHONY L
Scientist, college teacher. **Personal:** Born Apr 19, 1943, Indian Head, MD; married Joyce P Chesley-Dent; children: Antonette, Robert & Christopher. **Educ:** Morgan State Col, BS, 1966; Johns Hopkins Univ, PhD, 1970. **Career:** Carnegie Mellon Univ, asst prof, assoc prof chem eng, 1970-78; DuPont Co, res engr, 1972; PQ Corp, Mat Sci Dept, sr chemist, 1979-80; res & develop supvr, 1981-83; res & develop mgr, 1983-85; Silica Catalyst Res & Develop Dept, res & develop assoc, 1985-87, prin scientist, Silica Catalyst Res & Develop Dept, sr res fel, 1987-95, Explor Dept, sr res fel, 1995-2000; NOBCCHE News Mag, ed, 2004-, pres; PQ Intranet websites, webmaster; Cheyney Univ Pa, fac. **Orgs:** Beta Kappa Chi Hon Soc, 1963; Phi Lambda Upslon, 1967; Sigma Xi, 1968; Phi Beta Kappa, 1969; CMU Facil Senate, 1971-75; secy, treas, pres, dir, Pitts Catalyst Soc, 1972-81; chmn, Sch Admis Comt Western PA Chap, John Hopkins Univ, 1972-75; pres, Pitts Chap, Alumni Asn, 1976-77; vice chmn, 5th N Am Catalyst Soc, 1977; secy-treas, dir, Philadelphia Catalysis Club, 1981-83; pres & regional chmn, Del Valley Chap NOBCCHE, 1983-89, 1989-93; fel Am Inst Chemists, 1986; bd dir, NOBCChE, 1997-; chmn, Nat Sci Bowl, 1999-; AAAS, 1999-2000; Nat Res Coun Comt; Identification Adv Serv; co-chmn, I & EC Ann Chem Engr Symp; Am Inst Chem Engrs. **Honors/Awds:** Meritorious Service Award, NOBCChE, 1988, 1994.

DENT, DAVID
Educator, journalist. **Educ:** Morehouse Col, BA, polit sci, 1981; Columbia Univ Grad Sch Journ, MS,1982. **Career:** New York Univ, assoc prof jour & mass commun, Dept Social & Cultural Anal, prof journ, currently; auth: Whose Reality: Million Man March. Black Renaissance Noire, 1996; In Search of Black America, Discovering the African American Dream, Simon & Schuster, 2000. **Orgs:** Adv, Univ's Fac Resource Network; brd, The Calhoun Sch. **Honors/Awds:** Freedom Forum Foundation Grant for Journalists in Education, to research the growth of black private elementary & secondary schools, 1990; Natl Assn of Black Journalists Award of Excellence for television news series Brothers in Arms, 1990; Griot Award, New York Assn Black Journalists Award for Excellence in Magazine Journalism for "The New Black Suburbs," 1992; Teaching Fellowship for Outstanding Broadcast Journalism Professors, Poynter Institute for Media Studies, 1992; Lincoln University Journalism Award for Excellence in Reporting, Print/Minority Audience, Jefferson City, 1993; Golden Dozen Award for Excellence in Teaching & Service, New York Univ, spring 1993.

DENT, GARY KEVER
Executive, administrator. **Personal:** Born Nov 18, 1950, Norfolk, VA; son of Kever H and Geraldine Brown; married Carman Stroud Dent, May 29, 1982; children: Katina Arne & Travis Damon. **Educ:** Norfolk State Univ, BS, 1972; Cent Mich Univ, MA, mgt & supv, 1983. **Career:** Detroit Diesel Allison-GMC, service training rep, 1974-76; Gen Motors Educ & Training, regional mgr, 1977-85; Gen Motors Personnel Programs & Serv, mgr, 1985-89; Gen Motors Cent Off Personnel, 1989-93; City Detroit, Human Resource Dept, dir, assoc vpres; Wayne State Univ, asst vpres human resource; Univ Cincinnati, assoc vpres, chief human resources officer & sr assoc vpres, currently. **Orgs:** Co-chairperson, Nat Asn Advan Colored People, 1980-; Aircraft Owner & Pilots Asn, 1985-; pres, Nat Black MBA Asn, Detroit; chairperson, Boy Scouts Am, Cent Sec, 1988-. **Honors/Awds:** Outstanding Citizen Award, City Dayton Priority Bd, 1985; Outstanding Alumnus, Norfolk State Univ, 1987; Presidential

Citation, Nat Asn Equal Opportunity Educ, 1987; Nat Quality Section Award, Boy Scouts Am, 1989, 1990; Presidents Award, Nat Black MBA Asn, Detroit chap, 1990. **Military Serv:** AUS, capt, 1972-85; Army Commendation Medal, Indiana & Ohio Commendation Medals. **Business Addr:** Chief Human Resources Officer, Senior Associate Vice President, University of Cincinnati, Office of the Senior Associate Vice President for Human Resources, 51 Goodman Dr, PO Box 210087, Cincinnati, OH 45221-0087.

DENT, DR. PRESTON L.
Educator, businessperson, psychologist. **Personal:** Born Apr 30, 1939, Philadelphia, PA; son of William Preston and Alice Livingston; married Imelda Velasco; children: David-Preston & Robyn Lynn. **Educ:** Pa State Univ, BS, psychol, 1961; San Francisco State Univ, MA, psychol, 1963; Univ Calif, Santa Barbara, PhD, educ psychol, 1971. **Career:** San Francisco City Col, Dept Psychol, grad instr, 1966-67; STIR Facil, Bunker-Ramo Corp, simulator flight contrl prog eng, 1966-67; TRW Systems Inc, Indus Rels Div, trainer, counr, equal opport prog off, 1967-68; Pierce Col, psychol instr, 1967-72; Univ Calif, Santa Barbara, asst chancellor, 1969-72; Col Letters Arts Sci, assoc dean, dir develop & sponsored res; Univ Southern Calif, prof higher educ, 1972-86; Dent-Glasser Corp, pres, chief exec officer, 1984-. **Orgs:** Int Coun Psychol; Am Psychol Soc; AAAS; Am Asn Univ Admin; UN Asn; Golden State Found; comnr, City Los Angeles, 1981-82; fel, Am Coun Educ, 1971-72; dir, Los Angeles Child Guidance Clinic; consult, MacNeal-Schwendler Corp; bd advrs, Am Int Nat Bank; trustee, Paine Col. **Honors/Awds:** Outstanding Young Men of America Award, US Chamber Com, 1970; Kappa Delta Pi Ed Hon, Phi Delta Kappa Ed Hon; Distinguished Service Award, City Los Angeles; Sigma Xi. **Special Achievements:** Author: "A Study of Faculty and Student Opinions on Teaching Effectiveness Ratings", 1980. **Military Serv:** USAF, first lt, 1963-66. **Business Addr:** President, The Dent-Glasser Corporation, 606 El Segundo Blvd Suite A, Los Angeles, CA 90061, **Business Phone:** (310)516-9604.*

DENT, RICHARD LAMAR
Football player, chief executive officer, football coach. **Personal:** Born Dec 13, 1960, Atlanta, GA; married Leslie; children: Mary Francis & Sarah. **Educ:** Tenn State Univ. **Career:** Football player (retired), asst coach,chief exec off: Chicago Bears, def end, 1983-93, 1995; San Francisco 49ers,def end, 1994; Indianapolis Colts, 1996; Philadelphia Eagles,def end,1997; Chicago Bears, asst coach, 2003; RLD Resources LLC,ceo,1999-. **Orgs:** Bd mem: Natl Col Found,Illinois Col Hall of Fame,Illinois Literacy prog, Chicago Park Dist,Better Boys Found. **Honors/Awds:** NFC Defensive Player of Week, hons & game ball; first team, Col & Pro Football Weekly; All-NFC; Most Valuable Player, Super Bowl XX, 1985; Pro Bowl, 1984, 1985, 1990, 1993. **Special Achievements:** Bears all-time sack leader with 112; 10.5 playoff sacks is best in Natl Football League hist. *

DENTON, SANDI (SANDRA DENTON)
Singer, actor. **Personal:** Born Nov 9, 1969, Kingston, Jamaica; married Anthony Criss, Jul 24, 1999 (divorced 2001); children: Tyran & Egypt. **Educ:** Queensborough Community Col, nursing. **Career:** Singer & actress; Salt-N-Pepa, rap group, mem, 1985-2002; actor, currently; Albums: Hot, Cool, & Vicious, 1986; A Salt with a Deadly Pepa,1988; Brand New, 1998; Films: Stay Tuned, 1992; Who's the Man?, 1993; Jason's Lyric, 1994; Joe's Apartment, 1996; 3 A.M., 2001; Love & a Bullet, 2002; The Perfect Holiday, 2007; TV Series: "Saturday Night Live", 1994; First Time Felon, 1997; Linc's, 2000; "Oz", 2000-03. **Honors/Awds:** Push-It was #37 on VH1 Hundred Greatest Dance Songs. **Special Achievements:** First female rapper to have a gold album; Ranked #83 on VH1's Greatest Women of Rock N Roll. **Business Phone:** (310)859-4000.

DENTON, TIMOTHY JEROME, SR.
Football player. **Personal:** Born Feb 2, 1973, Galveston, TX. **Educ:** Sam Houston State Univ; Blinn JC; Univ Okla. **Career:** Atlanta Falcons, defensive back, 1996; Wash Redskins, defensive back,1998-99; San Diego Chargers, defensive back, 2000; Arena football league, Dallas Desperados, 2002-03.

DENYE, BLAINE A.
Educator, teacher, vice president (organization). **Personal:** Born Jun 27, 1933, Chicago, IL; son of Julius and Gladys; married Doris L Thornton; children: Paul & Iva. **Educ:** Roosevelt Univ, BA, 1960; Chicago Teachers Col, MEd, 1964. **Career:** Teacher, 1960-63; coun, 1963-69; Educ Prog Planning, dir, 1969-70; Model Cities Prog, dir, 1969-73; Manley HS Chicago, prin, 1973-86; Dist Ten, supt, 1986-89. **Orgs:** Chmn, Diaconate Bd, 1966; chmn exec coun, Trinity United Church Christ,1973-75; chmn, Bldg Comt, 1974-80; chmn, Bd Long Range Planning; Phi Delta Kappa; vice pres bd dirs, Trinity; pres, Trinity Community Housing Corp; pres, Trinity Acres Housing Corp. **Honors/Awds:** Phi Delta Kappa Educator of the Year; Ora Higgins Youth Found. **Military Serv:** AUS, 1st lt, 1953-58. *

DE PASSE, SUZANNE
Television producer, chairperson, chief executive officer. **Personal:** Born Jul 1, 1947?, New York, NY; married Paul Le Mat, Jan 1, 1978. **Educ:** Manhattan Community Col. **Career:** Motown Industs, asst exec, 1968, pres, 1980-; Lady Sings the Blues, co-author; Motown 25: Yesterday, Today, Forever, producer & writer, 1983;De Passe Entertainment Inc, chmn & chief exec officer, 1992-; Motown 40:The Music Is Forever, producer & writer, 1998; The Loretta Claiborne Story, producer, 2000; Cheaters, producer, 2000; Zenon: The Zequel, producer, 2001; 32nd Nat Asn Advan Colored People Image Awards, producer, 2001; Essence Awards, producer, 2002; It's Show time at the Apollo, producer, 2002; Essence Awards, producer, 2003; 34th Nat Asn Advan Colored People Image Awards, producer, 2003; Soluna Proj, producer, 2004; Zenon: Z3, producer, 2004; The Black Movie Awards, producer & writer, 2005; The2006 Black Movie Awards, exec producer, 2006. **Orgs:** Alpha Kappa Alpha Sorority Inc. **Business Addr:** Chairman, Chief Executive Officer, De Passe Entertainment Inc, 5750 Wilshire Blvd Suite 640, Los Angeles, CA 90036, **Business Phone:** (323)965-2580.

DEPILLARS, MURRY NORMAN
Educator, artist. **Personal:** Born Dec 21, 1938, Chicago, IL; son of Mary Taylor; married Mary L. **Educ:** Kennedy-King Community Col, AA, fine arts, 1966; Roosevelt Univ, BA, art educ, 1968, MA, urban studies, 1970; Pa State Univ, PhD, art educ, 1976. **Career:** Educator (retired), artist; Mast Inst, Chicago comm urban opportunity, div training 1968; Univ Ill, educ asst prog asst dir, 1968-71; Va Commonwealth Univ, dean sch art, 1976-95; Chicago State Univ, exec vpres planning & mgt, Art & Design, prof, 1998; artist, currently. **Orgs:** Bd dir & illusr, 3rd World Press Chicago; bd dir & art dir, Kuumba Workshop Chicago, 1969; bd dir & contrib ed, Inst Positive Educ, Chicago, 1970; adv bd, J Negro Educ, WA, 1973; bd dir, N Am Zone; co-chmn, Upper So Region 2nd World Black & African Festival Arts & Cult, 1973-74; pres, Nat Conf Artists, 1973-77; Int Coun Fine Arts Deans, 1976; chmn bd, Nat Conf Artists, 1977; Nat Asn State Univ & Land Grant Col, 1981-88; consult, Nat Endowment Humanities, 1982-84; cons, Corp Pub Broadcasting & Annenberg Sch Commun, 1983; Ohio Eminent Scholars Prog Panel, Ohio Bd Regents, 1983-84; consult, The O Paul GetTrust, 1984; Nat Endowment for the Arts Expansion Arts Prog, 1985; Nat Jazz Serv Orgn, 1985; US Info Agency Acad Specialist to Malaysia, 1985; Africobra, 1985; arts adv bd, Col Bd, 1984-85; chmn, coordr comm, The Richmond Jazz Festival, 1984; art & archit review bd, Commonwealth Va, 1986. **Honors/Awds:** Elizabeth Catlett Mora Award of Excellence, Nat Conf Artists, 1977; Spec Arts Award & Art Educ Award Branches for the Arts, 1980; Man of Excellence Plaque, Ministry of Educ Republic of China, 1980; Excellence Educ Preservation & Promotion of Jazz, Richmond Jazz Soc, 1981; Outstanding Admin Award, Black Stud Alliance, 1982; Outstanding Achievement in the Arts Branches for the Arts, 1982; Alumni Fel Penn State Univ, 1989. **Military Serv:** AUS, pfc, 1962-63. *

DEPREIST, JAMES ANDERSON
Conductor (music). **Personal:** Born Nov 21, 1936, Philadelphia, PA; son of James Henry and Ethel Anderson; married Ginette Grenier; children: Tracy Elisabeth & Jennifer Anne. **Educ:** Univ Pa, BA, 1958, MA, 1961; Philadelphia Conservatory Music attended 1961. **Career:** State Dept, Am specialist music, 1962-63; NY Philharmonic, Am debut, 1964; NY Philharmonic Orchestra, asst conductor to Leonard Bernstein, 1965-66; Symphony of New World, prin guest conductor, 1968-70; Rotterdam Philharmonic, European debut, 1969; Natl Symphony Orchestra Washington, assoc conductor, 1971-75, Philadelphia Orchestra, 1972; Chicago Symphony,1973; Cleveland Orchestra, 1974; prin guest conductor, 1975-76; L'Orchestre Symphonique de Que, mus dir, 1976-83; Oregon Symphony, laureate music dir, 1980-2003; Laureate Music Dir, currently; Julliard Sch, dir conducting & orchestral Studies, 2004-; Tokyo Metrop Symphony Orchestra, conductor, 2005-; composed ballet scores for, "Vision of America" 1960; "Tendrils" 1961; "A Sprig of Lilac" 1964; concert "Requiem"1965. **Orgs:** Trustee, Lewis & Clark Col, 1983-; Sigma Pi Phi. **Honors/Awds:** First Prize Gold Medal, Dimitri Mitropoulos Int Music Competition for Conductors, 1964; Merit Citation, City Philadelphia, 1969; grantee, Martha Baird Rockefeller Fund for Music, 1969; Medal of City of Que, 1983; honorary degrees: Univ of Pennsylvania, LHD, 1976; Laval Univ, DMus, 1980; Univ of Portland, DFA, 1983; Pacific Univ, DFA, 1985; St Mary's Col-l,Doctor of Arts & Letters, 1985; Lewis & Clark Coll, Doctor in Humanities,1986; Linfield Coll, DMus, 1986; Willamette Univ, DFA, 1987; Drexel Univ,DFA, 1989; Reed Col, Doctor of Letters, 1990; Oregon State University,DFA, 1990; Nat Medal of Arts, 2005; fellow, Royal Swedish Academy of Music. **Special Achievements:** Author: This Precipice Garden; The Distant Siren. **Business Phone:** (503)228-4294.

DEPRIEST, DARRYL LAWRENCE
Lawyer. **Personal:** Born Sep 23, 1954, Chicago, IL; son of W LaVerne and Bertha Williams; married Colleen K Connell, May 19, 1987; children: Brennan Connell, Carlyle Ann. **Educ:** Harvard Col, Cambridge, MA, BA, cum laude, govt, 1976; Harvard Law Sch, Cambridge, MA, JD, 1979; Nat Inst Trial Advocacy, Boulder, Col, 1983. **Career:** Honorable Robert E Keeton, USDJ, Boston, MA, law clerk, 1979-80; Jenner & Block, Chicago, IL, partner, 1980-88; Am Bar Asn, Chicago, IL, gen coun, 1988-. **Orgs:** Am Bar Asn; Nat Bar Asn; Ill State Bar Asn; Cook County Bar Asn; Chicago Bar Asn; Am Corporate Coun Asn; Am Soc Asn Execs; Chicago Soc Asn Execs; Chicago Bd Ethics; bd dirs, Chicago Pub Schs Alumni Asn; bd dirs, 1981-85, Schs & Scholarship Comt, 1980-, Harvard Club Chicago; Harvard Club Boston; Assoc Harvard Alumni; bd dirs, Leadership Greater Chicago, pres, 1995-96. **Honors/Awds:** Leadership Greater Chicago, 1987-88; 40 Under 40, Crain's Chicago Bus, 1989; America's Best & Brightest Young Business & Professional Men, Dollars & Sense Mag, 1989; Monarch Award, Achievement Law, Xi Nu Omega Chapter, Alpha Kappa Alpha Sorority, 1989. **Business Addr:** General Counsel, American Bar Association Center for Professional Responsibility, 14th Fl, 541 N Fairbanks Ct, Chicago, IL 60611-3314, **Business Phone:** (312)988-5304.*

DERAMUS, BETTY
Columnist, writer. **Career:** Columnist, Writer: Wayne State, Detroit, instr, eng & Africana studies; Eugene Pulliam fel, 1986; BBC, commentator; Detroit News, columnist, 2002; Auth: Forbidden Fruit: Love Stories from the Underground Railroad. **Honors/Awds:** Distinguished Journalism Citation, Howard Found, 1980; First Prize for Education Reporting, Stewart Mott Found, 1980; First prize for commentary, Overseas Press Club Am, 1980; Deems Taylor Award, Am Soc Composers, Authors & Publishers, 1983; Pulitzer Prize finalist for commentary, 1993. **Home Addr:** 1300 E Lafayette St, Detroit, MI 48207, **Home Phone:** (313)259-0485. **Business Addr:** Columnist, c/o Detroit News, 615 W Lafayette, Detroit, MI 48226, **Business Phone:** (313)222-2296.

DERAMUS, BILL R.
Businessperson. **Personal:** Born Jul 10, 1938, Timpson, TX; son of Lafayette and T J; children: William. **Educ:** Prairie View A&M Univ, BS, 1961; Webster Univ, MS, 1983. **Career:** Marriott, regional mgr, 1991-96, franchisee, currently. **Orgs:** Alpha Phi Alpha; Nat Am Advan Colored People; Nat Black MBA. **Honors/Awds:** Regional Manager of the Year, 1995. **Special Achievements:** First African Am franchisee for Marriott Intl. **Military Serv:** AUS, ltc, 1961-86; Legion of Merit, 1986; Bronze Star, 1967; 3 MSM; 2ARCOM. **Business Addr:** Business Owner, Courtyard Marriott, 4949 Regent Blvd, Irving, TX 75063, **Business Phone:** (972)929-4004.

DERBIGNY, RHODA L
Marketing executive. **Personal:** Born Jul 19, 1960, Hagerstown, MD; daughter of Maylon A Campher Sr and Gloria M Weathers; married Curtis E, Jul 27, 1985; children: Dominique M Derbigny. **Educ:** Hagerstown Jr Col, Hagerstown, AA, bus admin, 1981; Towson State Univ, BS, bus admin, 1984. **Career:** Household Finance Corp, Hagerstown, asst mgr, 1984-86; Goodwill Indust Inc, Hagerstown, dir community based serv, 1986-87; Citicorp, Hagerstown, unit mgr, 1987-89; Corning Inc, mkt develop specialist, nat sales mgr, 1989-. **Orgs:** Nat Asn Advan Colored People, 1987-89; bd mem, Southern Tier Asn Blind, 1990-; Soc Black Prof, 1990-. **Business Phone:** (607)974-7823.

DERRICK, KEITH. **See MCKENZIE, KEITH.**

DERRICOTTE, C. BRUCE
Executive. **Personal:** Born Jun 22, 1928, Fostoria, OH; married Toinette Webster; children: Anthony. **Educ:** Defiance Col, BS; MI Univ, EE, 1955. **Career:** Detroit Arsenal Centerline MI, instrument engr, 1955-60; IT&T NJ labs, product line mgr, 1960-68; NY Dist & Control Data Corp, mgr, 1968-73; The Chase Manhattan Bank NA NYC, Systems Planning Div, vpres exec. **Orgs:** Am Bankers Asn; Nat Planning Asn; Aircraft Owners & Pilots Asn; Nat Exec Res, 1966-68; VP Task Force Youth Motivation. **Military Serv:** AUS, corpl, 1950-52.

DERRICOTTE, EUGENE ANDREW
Dentist. **Personal:** Born Jun 14, 1926, Fostoria, OH; son of Clarence C and Bessie M Anderson; married Jeanne E Hagans; children: Robert. **Educ:** Univ Mich, BS, pharm, 1950, DDS, 1958. **Career:** Dentist (retired). USAF, dent surgeon/chief dent surgeon various air force bases, 1971-79; USAF Acad, command dent surgeon, 1979-84; USAF Hosp Chanute AFB, dir dent serv, 1984-85; Univ Tex Health Sci Ctr, San Antonio, asst prof, 1985-02. **Orgs:** Am Dent Asn; Alpha Phi Alpha; Air Force Memorial Found. **Honors/Awds:** Hall of Honor, Univ Mich, 1987. **Military Serv:** AUS Air Corps, 1944-46; US Air Force, colonel, 1962-85; Bronze Star Medal; Meritorious Serv Medal; USAF Commendation Medal w/1 Oak Leaf Cluster; AUS Commendation Medal; Good Conduct Medal; WW II Victory Medal; Nat Def Serv Medal; USAF Longevity Serv Awd w/2 Oak Leaf Clusters; Vietnam Serv Medal w/2 Bronze Serv Stars; Republic of Vietnam Campaign Medal; Legion of Merit, 1985. **Home Addr:** 3718 Morning Mist, San Antonio, TX 78230-2129. *

DERRICOTTE, TOI
Educator, poet. **Personal:** Born Apr 12, 1941, Detroit, MI. **Educ:** Wayne State Univ, BA, spec educ, 1965; NY Univ, MA, Eng lit & creative writing, 1984. **Career:** NJ State Coun Arts & Md State Arts Coun, master teacher, 1973-88; Columbia Univ, educ consult, 1979-82; MacDowell, fel, 1984; Writers Voice Series Manhattan, poetry teacher, 1985-86; Old Dominion Univ, assoc prof Eng lit, 1988-90; George Mason Univ, commonwealth prof Eng dept, 1990-91; Univ Pittsburgh, Eng Dept, prof Eng, 1991-; NY Univ,

Creative Writing Prog, vis prof, 1992; Cave Canem, Hist Workshop & Retreat African-Am Poets, co-founder, 1996; Mills Col, distinguised vis poet, 1998; Xavier, Delta Sigma Theta, endowed chair poetry, 1999-2000; MFA NY Univ, prof, currently. **Orgs:** Fel poetry Nat Endowment Arts, 1984; Grad Admin Comt; Pedag & Difference Comt. **Honors/Awds:** Lucille Medwick Memorial Award, Poetry Soc Am, 1985; Pushcart Prize, 1989, 1998; Poetry Committee Book Award, Floger Shakespeare Libr, Washington, DC, 1990; Distinguished Pioneering of the Arts Award, United Black Artists Inc, 1993; Award in Non-fiction, Black Caucus Am Libr Asn, 1998; Annisfield-Wolf Award Non-fiction, 1998; Paterson Poetry Prize, 1998. **Special Achievements:** The Black Notebooks, WW Norton & Co, 1997, listed in "Notable Books of the Year" 1997, NY Times Book Review; Tender, Univ Pittsburgh Press, 1997; Captivity, Univ Pittsburgh Press, Oct 1989, 2nd printing, Oct 1991, 3rd printing, Jan 1993, 4th printing, Dec 1995; Natural Birth, The Crossing Press, 1983; The Empress of the Death House, Lotus Press, 1978, 2nd printing, 1989; Creative Writing: A Manual for Teachers, New Jersey State Council on the Arts, 1985; hundreds of poems published in anthologies and journals including: The Garden Thrives: 20th Century African-American Poetry, My Soul Is A Witness, One World Many Cultures, 2nd edition, I Hear A Symphony: African Americans Celebrate Love, In Search of Color Everywhere; A Collection of African-American Poetry, Unsettling America: Race and Ethnicity in Contemporary American Poetry; and many others. **Business Addr:** Professor of English, University of Pittsburgh, Department of English, CL 517-D Cathedral Learning 4200 5th Ave, Pittsburgh, PA 15260, **Business Phone:** (412)624-6527.

DERRYCK, VIVIAN LOWERY
Government official. **Personal:** Born Jan 30, 1945, Cleveland, OH; daughter of Collins and Mary; married Robert Berg, Jun 24, 1989; children: David P, Amanda Derryck Castel & Belinda Z Berg (stepdaughter). **Educ:** Chatham Col, BA, 1967; Columbia Univ, masters, int affairs, 1969. **Career:** US Dept State, dep asst secy, 1980-82; Nat Coun Negro Women, exec vp, 1982-84; Nat Democratic Inst Int Affairs, vpres, 1984-88; Wash Int Ctr, exec dir, 1988-89; African Am Inst, pres, 1989-95; African Leadership Forum, sr advr, 1996-98; Acad Develop, sr vpres, 1997-98; US Agency Int Develop, asst adminr & AFR; Acad Edu Develop, sr vpres & dir, currently; African Am Inst, pres, currently. **Orgs:** Intl Develop Conf, bd dirs, 1983-; African Ctr Develop & Stategic Studies, bd trustees, 1991-; Constituency for Africa, bd dirs, 1993-; US Agency for Int Develop, adv comn voluntary foreign aid, 1993-97; Ctr for Preventive Action, 1994-97; Meridian Int Ctr, bd dirs, 1998-; Coun Foreign Rels; Bretton Woods Comt; exec vpres, Nat Coun Negro Women, currently. **Honors/Awds:** Woman of the Year, Sierra Leone, 1991; UNICEF African Partnership Award, 1995; hon doctorate, Chatham Col, 1995; Guggenheim Museum Humanitarian Award, 1996; Martin Luther King Nat Service Award, 1998. **Special Achievements:** "Post-Conflict Africa: Three Essentials for Recovery," Africa Report, March/April 1995; "Nigeria: Democracy Delayed, Development on Hold," IDC Policy Policy Bulletin, Nov 1996; "Black Women's International Agenda for the Twenty-First Century," Voices of Vision. Nat Coun Negro Women, 1996. **Home Addr:** 3027 Univ Ter NW, Washington, DC 20016, **Home Phone:** (202)244-7474. **Business Phone:** (202)712-4320.

DESANDIES, DR. KENNETH ANDRE
Physician. **Personal:** Born Feb 16, 1948, New York, NY; son of Conrad and Elsie; married Karen Yvonne Grant; children: Kisha & Kanika. **Educ:** Hampton Inst, BA, 1969; Meharry Med Col, MD, 1973. **Career:** Hurley Hosp, intern, 1973-74; King's Co Hosp, resident obstet & gynec, 1974-78; Group Health Asn, obstet & gynec attend, 1978-81; Pvt Pract, 1981. **Orgs:** Fel Am Col Obstet & Gynec, 1981; Nat Med Asn; Alfred St Baptist Church; pres, Northern Va Med Soc. **Honors/Awds:** Board Certificate, Am Col Obstet & Gynec, 1980; Am Col Obstet & Gynec Award, 1980, 1998; Physician Recognition Award, Am Med Asn, 1983-98. **Home Addr:** 4600 Duke St Suite 332, Alexandria, VA 22304-2516. **Business Addr:** Physician, 4600 Duke St Suite 332, Alexandria, VA 22304-2516, **Business Phone:** (703)823-5656.

DESASSURE, CHARLES
Computer scientist, educator. **Personal:** Born Apr 19, 1961, Eutawville, SC; son of Moses and Emma Dessesso; married Gloria Sumpter, Apr 26, 1997. **Educ:** Claflin Col, BS, 1984; Orangeburg-Calhoun Tech Col, AS, 1989; Webster Univ, MA, 2000. **Career:** Tarrant County Col, Compensatory, remedial educ teacher, 1984-87, coordr, comput instr, 1988-90, Micro Comput Specialist, programmer, 1990-93, LAN adminr, 1993-96, Comput Field Technol, analyst, 1996-98, Marcus Cabler, info syst mgr, 1998-2001; Comput Sci & Info Technol, instr, 2000-. **Orgs:** Bd dirs, former mem, St Jones Baptist Church; Phi Beta Sigma Fraternity Inc, 1981-; Pres, SC Youth & Col Conf, NAACP, 1981-83; bd mem, El Ctr Col Comput Technol Adv Comt, 1993-97; Asn Corp Comput Tech Prof, 1997-; NAACP; former mem, Orangeburg Calhoun Tech Col Adv Bd; Arlington City Youth & Families Bd, 1998-; Arlington-Sundown Kiwanis Club, 2000-. **Honors/Awds:** Creative Writing Contest Award, Claflin Col, 1981; Leadership Award Nat, Phi Beta Sigma, 1982; Outstanding Undergraduate of the Year, Southeastern Region, Phi Beta Sigma Fraternity Inc, 1982-83; Editor-in-Chief Leadership Award, Clafin Col, 1983; Outstanding Teacher of the Year, Mansfield Bus Col, Columbia, SC, 1988-89; American Legion Bronze Medal, Dept SC, 1993; Presidential Award for Leadership, SC NAACP Conf, 1993. **Special Achievements:** Cert Novell Adminr, CNA, 1995. **Business Addr:** Instructor of Business & Technology Division, Tarrant County College, Computer Science & Information Technology, 1500 Houston St, Fort Worth, TX 76102, **Business Phone:** (817)515-3747.

DESERT, ALEX
Actor, singer, writer. **Personal:** Born Jul 18, 1968. **Career:** TV 101, 1988; "Free Spirit", 1989; "A Different World", 1990; The Flash, 1990; "Beverly Hills, 90210", 1990; "The Flash", 1991; "The Heights", 1992; Lush Life, 1993; The Ticket, 1994; Galaxy Beat, 1994; PCU, 1994; Swingers, 1996; Playing God, 1997; High Fidelity, 2000; "Boy Meets World", 2000; Masked and Anonymous, 2003; Chicken Party, 2003; "Becker", 2003; "Harry Green and Eugene", 2004; Death of the Day, 2004; Pretty Persuasion, 2005; Tomb Raider: Legend, 2006; Scarface: The World Is Yours, 2006; "The Sarah Silverman Program.", 2007; Tomb Raider: Underworld, 2008; "Wolverine and the X-Men", 2008; "Rita Rocks", 2008; Bob Funk, 2009. **Business Addr:** Actor, c/o CBS Television Network, 51 W 52nd St, New York, NY 10019, **Business Phone:** (212)975-3247.*

DESHIELDS, DELINO LAMONT
Baseball player, baseball executive. **Personal:** Born Jan 15, 1969, Seaford, DE; married Tisha Milligan, Dec 15, 1990; children: Delino DeShielda Jr & 3 children. **Career:** Baseball player (retired), baseball executive; Montreal Player (retired); Expos, infielder, 1990-93; Los Angeles Dodgers, 1994-96; St Louis Cardinals, 1997-98; Baltimore Orioles, 1999-2001; Chicago Cubs, 2001-02; Urban Baseball League, co-founder & vpres, 2007-; Billings Mustangs, hitting coach, curently. **Honors/Awds:** Rookie of the Year Award, 1990.

DESKINS, DONALD R., JR.
Educator. **Personal:** Born May 10, 1932, Brooklyn, NY; married Lois Jackson; children: Sharon, Sheila & Sharlene. **Educ:** Univ Mich, BA, 1960, MS, 1963, PhD, 1971. **Career:** Univ Mich, teaching fel, 1963-65, fac counr, 1968-69, lectr, 1968-70, from asst prof to assoc prof geog, 1970-80, from assoc chair to chair geog,1973-79, Urban & Regional Planning PhD Prog, assoc prof, 1973-80, Urban Geog & Social, assoc prof, 1973, act chmn, 1974-75, assoc res scientist geog, 1974-75, chmn, 1975-, Horace H Rackham Sch Grad Studies, assoc dean, 1979-85; Urban & Regional Planning PhD Prog, prof, 1980-82, prof, 1982-2002, fac assoc, 1986-, assoc chair & dir grad studies, 1988-91, prin investr, 1995-96, prof emer 2002-; BOR US Dept Interior, supvry recreation resource specialist, 1964-68; Comn Geograp & Afro-Am, Assn Am Geogr, dir,1969-78; Chautaugua Type Short Courses, course dir, 1973-76; Oberlin Col, vis prof sociol, 1986; Vassar Col, distinguished Randolph vis prof, 1992; Ill State Univ, scholar residence, 1993. **Orgs:** Dir, Comn Geog & Afro-Am, 1968-69; Task Force Minority Res, 1970-71; Zoning brd appeals City Ann Arbor, 1971-73; counr, E Lakes Div, 1973-76,chmn; GRE Advan Geog Test Comn; Educ Testing Serv; Assn Am Geog; Pub Comn;mem exec brd Assn Social & Behavoiral Sci; Natl Sci Found; Assn Am Geogrs; Am Geog Soc; Asn Social & Behav Sci; Pop Asn Am; Regional Sci Assn; Natl Coun Geog Educ; AAAS; Western Regional Sci Assn; Natl Coun Geog Educ; Am Sociol Assn; Assn Social & Behav Scientists; Sigma Xi; Gamma Theta Upsilon; Kappa Phi Honor Soc. **Honors/Awds:** Senior honors, Univ Mich, 1959, Fielding H Yost Honor Award, 1959, Faculty Recognition Award, 1980, Leonard F Sain Esteemed Alumni Award, 1986, Dream keeper Award, 1992, Harold R Johnson Diversity Award, 1996, Charles DMoody Higher Achievement Award, 1997, Distinguished Faculty-Graduate Student Seminar Award, 1998, Award for Service, 2001; Award of Appreciation, Mich State Univ, 1993; Honors Award, Assn Am Geogrs, 1994;Distinguished Mentor Award, Natl Coun Geog Educ, 1996; Spencer Foundation Mentor Award, 1999. **Special Achievements:** Published numerous books and articles. **Military Serv:** USMC, drill instr & inf right guide, 1953-57. **Business Addr:** Professor Emeritus of of Urban Geography and Sociology, University of Michigan, School of Social Work, Department of Sociology, 1080 S Univ Ave, Ann Arbor, MI 48109-1106, **Business Phone:** (313)764-0340.

DESOUSA, D. JASON
School administrator, vice president (organization). **Personal:** Born Sep 12, 1964, New York, NY; son of William and Catherine. **Educ:** Morgan State Univ, BS, sports admin, 1987; Bowling Green State Univ, MA, col stud personnel, 1989; Ind Univ, EdD, higher educ admin, 1989. **Career:** Tuskee Univ, dir career develop, 1994-95; Ala State Univ, asst vpres stud affairs, 1995-99; Savannah State Univ, vpres stud affairs; Morgan State Univ, asst vpres acad affairs, 2002-; ed bd, NASAP J, currently. **Orgs:** Stud regent, Morgan State Univ Bd Regents, 1986-87; nat bd dirs, Kappa Alpha Psi Fraternity Inc, 1986-88; Am Col Stud Personnel Asn, 1989-; fel Ford Found, 1990-91; pres, Nat Asn Stud Affairs Prof. **Honors/Awds:** Nat Col Merit Award, 1988; Guy L Grant Medallion, Kappa Alpha Psi Fraternity, 1988; Benjamin L Perry Award. **Special Achievements:** Co-author, "Are White Students Really More Involved in Collegiate Experiences Than Black Students," Journal of College Student Development, 1992; author, "Re-examine the Educational Pipeline for African American Students," 2001; selected participant, Millennium Leadership Institute, AASCU, 2001. **Business Addr:** Assistant Vice President, Morgan State University, 1700 E Cold Spring Lane, Baltimore, MD 21251, **Business Phone:** (443)885-3333.*

DESSASO-GORDON, JANICE MARIE
Government official, consultant. **Personal:** Born Apr 10, 1942, Washington, DC; daughter of John F Ford (deceased) and Marie E Sheppard; married Harold J, Aug 8, 1987; children: Eugene C & Michael A. **Educ:** Univ DC, Wash, DC, BA, 1977. **Career:** Various fed govt agencies, Washington, DC, secy, 1960-70; US Dept Com,Wash, DC, prog analyst, 1971-76, Minority Bus Develop Agency, prog mgr; JD Consulting Inc, consult, currently. **Orgs:** Exec vpres, Holy Comforter-St Cyprian Community Action Group, 1988-; Bus & Prof Women's Asn, 1988-; Nat Asn Female Execs. **Honors/Awds:** Outstanding Performance Award, US Dept Com, 1973, 1979, 1984, 1986, 1988 & 1990-94; Certificate of Appreciation, Nat Minority Supplier Develop Coun, 1981; Outstanding Service Award, Nat Minority Supplier Develop Coun, 1985 & 1987; Appreciation Award, Nev Econ Develop Co, 1988; One of the 25 individuals honored for NMSDCs 25th Anniversary, 1997. **Special Achievements:** Annual 30-hour dancer, Washington DC Special Olympics for Mentally Retarded-Dance Marathon, 1983-89. **Business Addr:** Consultant, JD Consulting Inc, 347 11th St SE, Washington, DC 20003, **Business Phone:** (202)546-1607.

DESSELLE, NATALIE (NATALIE DESSELLE-REID)
Actor. **Personal:** Born in Alexandria, LA; married Leonard Reid, Apr 6, 2003; children: 3. **Educ:** Grambling State Univ. **Career:** Films: Set It Off, 1996; BAPS, 1997; How to Be a Player, 1997; Sweet Hideaway, 2003; TV Series: "Built to Last", 1997; "Getting Personal", 1998; "For Your Love", 1998-2000; "Yes, Dear", 2002; "ER", 2003; "Sweet Hideaway", 2003; "Eve", 2003-06; "Resident Aliens", 2005; TV films: "Cinderella", 1997. *

DESTINE, JEAN-LEON
Dancer, choreographer, educator. **Personal:** Born Mar 26, 1928, St Marc, Haiti; son of Leon Destine Sr and Lucienne; children: Gerard, Ernest, Carlo. **Educ:** Lycee Petion Haiti, attended 1943; Howard Univ, Wash, DC, attended 1944; Columbia Univ, New York, attended 1944. **Career:** New Dance Group Studio, New York, teacher,1948; Haiti's First Troupe Nationale Folklorique, founder & dir, 1950; Destine Afro-Haitian Dance Co, dir, 1951-; Repub Haiti, US, Cult Attache, 1960; Alvin Ailey Dance Ctr, guest artist, 1960-68; Destine Dance Found, pres, choreographer, dancer, teacher & lectr, 1975-; New York Univ, Sch Arts, fac mem; Lezly Dance Studio, New Yock, fac mem, currently; Nat Endowment Arts, choreography fel. Film: In the Mirror of Maya Deren, actor, 2003. **Orgs:** Haitian-Am Cult Orgn, 1988. **Honors/Awds:** Award of Merit, Haitian-Am Soc, 1970, 1975; Distinguished Visitor, Metropolitan Dade County, FL, 1986; Officier de l'Ordre National "Honneur et Merite". **Special Achievements:** Appeared in the Dance World Festival in Poland in 1999. **Business Addr:** Choreographer, Dancer, Destine Dance Foundation, 676 Riverside Dr, New York, NY.*

DEVARD, JERRI
Executive. **Educ:** Spelman Col, BA, econ; Clark Atlanta Univ Grad Sch Mgt, MBA, mkt. **Career:** Pillsbury Co, brand mgt position; Harrah's Entertainment, vpres mkt; Revlon, vpres mkt color cosmetics; Citigroup, chief mkt officer; Verizon Commun, Brand Mgt & Mkt Communs, sr vpres, 2003-05, Mkt & Brand Mgt, sr vpres, 2005-. **Orgs:** Bd, Pepsi African-Am Adv; bd dir, Asn Nat Advertisers; exec comt, Am Advert Fed Bd; bd mem, Exec Leadership Coun; bd trustees, Spelman Col; bd dir, Tommy Hilfiger Corp, currently. **Special Achievements:** Named as one of Black Enterprise magazine's "75 Most Powerful African-Americans in Corporate America" in February 2005. **Business Addr:** Senior Vice President of Marketing & Brand Management, Verizon Communications, 1095 Ave of the Americas, New York, NY 10036, **Business Phone:** (212)395-1470.

DEVAUGHN-TIDLINE, DONNA MICHELLE
Health services administrator. **Personal:** Born Sep 20, 1954, Houston, TX; daughter of Louise Robinson DeVaughn and Canary DeVaughn; married Eric, Aug 27, 1988; children: Joseph W. **Educ:** Southern Methodist Univ, BBA, 1977. **Career:** Prudential Health Care Plan Inc, admin mgr claims, 1983-84, dir admin HMO, 1984-86; Prudential Ins Co Inc, assoc mgr acct, 1980-83, dir health care mgt, 1987-. **Orgs:** Nat Asn Female Execs; vol, Big Brothers, Big Sisters; Delta Sigma Theta. **Honors/Awds:** 100 Most Promising Corporate Executives, Ebony Mag, 1991. **Business Addr:** Director, Prudential Insurance Company Inc, 5170 Sanderlin Ave, Memphis, TN 38117, **Business Phone:** (901)685-9071.

DE VEAUX, ALEXIS
Educator, writer. **Personal:** Born Sep 24, 1948, New York, NY; daughter of Mae De Veaux and Richard Hill. **Educ:** Empire State College, BA, 1976; SUNY at Buffalo, MA, 1989, PhD, 1992. **Career:** New Haven Board of Education, master artist, 1974-75; Sarah Lawrence College, adjunct lecturer, 1979-80; Norwich

University, associate faculty, 1984-85; Wabash College, Owen Dutson visiting scholar, 1986-87; Essence Magazine, editor-at-large, 1978-90; State Univ NY, Buffalo, NY, visiting assistant professor, 1991-92, assistant professor, beginning 1992, Dept Women's Studies, assoc prof & chair, currently. **Orgs:** Organization of Women Writers of Africa, Inc (OWWA). **Honors/Awds:** Drew Child Development Corp., Lorraine Hansberry Award, 1991; American Library Association, Coretta Scott King Award, 1981, 1988; MADRE, Humanitarian Award, 1984; Medgar Evers College, Fannie Lou Hamer Award, 1984; Lincoln University, Unity in Media Award, 1982, 1983; Brooklyn Museum, Art Books for Children Award, 1974, 1975; numerous others. **Special Achievements:** Author: An Enchanted Hair Tale, 1987, Don't Explain: A Song of Billie Holiday, 1980, Na-Ni, 1973, (all Harper & Row); Blue Heat, Poems, Diva Publishing, 1985; Spirits In The Street, Doubleday, 1973; writer: "Walking into Freedom with Nelson and Winnie Mandela," June 1990, "Forty Fine: A Writer Reflects on Turning Forty," Jan 1990, "Alice Walker: Rebel With A Cause," Sept 1989, (all Essence Magazine); numerous other poems, short stories and plays. **Business Addr:** Associate Professor, State University NY, Col Arts & Sci, Dept Womens Studies, 712 Clemens Hall, Buffalo, NY 14260-4630, **Business Phone:** (716)645-2327.*

DE VEAUX, STUART SAMUEL
Political consultant. **Personal:** Born May 19, 1970, Bronx, NY; son of Stuart De Veaux and Jean. **Career:** Republican Nat Comt, spec asst co-chair; Calif Republican Party, spokesperson, commun dir, currently. **Business Addr:** Spokesperson, Communication Director, California Republican Party, 1903 W Magnolia Blvd, Burbank, CA 91506, **Business Phone:** (818)841-5210.

DEVEREUEAWAX, JOHN L., III
Government official. **Personal:** Born Oct 19, 1953, Flowood, MS; children: Andre, John IV, Marie Janet, Jonathan, Domonique Javelle & Brandi. **Educ:** Jackson State Univ, BA, 1976. **Career:** Rockford Comn Asn, exec dir 1981-; City Rockford, alderman, 1993; Rockford Public Schs; CETA, mgr. **Orgs:** Pres, RKF Area MS Club, 1980-; assoc mem, Nat Coun Negro Women, 1984-; NatAsn Advan Colored People. **Honors/Awds:** Outstanding Young Am, 1984.

DEVERS, GAIL
Entrepreneur, athlete. **Personal:** Born Nov 19, 1966, Seattle, WA; daughter of Larry and Adele; married Ron Roberts (divorced); married Mike Phillips. **Educ:** Univ Calif Los Angeles, BA, sociol. **Career:** US Olympic Team, track & field, 1988, 1992, 1996, 2000; Gail Force Inc, owner, currently; Phil Prod LLC, co-owner, currently. **Orgs:** Founder, Gail Devers Found. **Honors/Awds:** Silver Medalist, World Championship Games, 1992; Gold Medalist, Olympic Games, 1992, 1996; Gold Medalist, 1993. **Special Achievements:** Named the world's No. 1 100-meter hurdles for two consecutive years in 2001 and 2002. **Business Addr:** Owner, Gail Force Inc, 950 Herrington Rd Suite C, PO Box 217, Lawrenceville, GA 30044-7217, **Business Phone:** (770)822-5641.

DEVINE, FRANK E.
School principal. **Career:** Charter Sch Philadelphia, prin, currently. *

DEVINE, JAMIE
Manager. **Personal:** Married Tameika Isaac. **Educ:** Benedict Col. **Career:** Columbia Housing Authority, mgr, currently; licensed realtor. **Orgs:** Greater Columbia Chamber Com. **Business Addr:** Manager, Columbia Housing Authority, 1917 Harden St, Columbia, SC 29204, **Business Phone:** (803)254-3886.*

DEVINE, LORETTA
Actor. **Personal:** Born Aug 21, 1949, Houston, TX; daughter of James Devine and Eunice O'Neal. **Educ:** Univ Houston, BA, speech & drama educ, 1971; Brandeis Univ, MFA, theatre arts, 1976. **Career:** Films: Will, 1981; Little Nikita, 1988; Sugar and Spice, 1990; Livin'Large, 1991; Caged Fear, 1992; Amos & Andrew, 1993; The Hard Truth, 1994; Waiting to Exhale, 1995; The Preacher's Wife, 1996; Hoodlum, 1997; Lover Girl, 1997; The Price of Kissing, 1997; Urban Legend, 1998; Book of Love, 1999; Oper Splitsville, 1999; Urban Legends: Final Cut, 2000; What Women Want, 2000; Kingdom Come, 2001; I Am Sam, 2001; Book of Love, 2002; The Script, 2002; Baby of the Family, 2002; Dreamgirls, 2006; This Christmas, 2007; First Sunday, 2008; Spring Breakdown, 2009; TV series: "A Different World", 1987-88; "The PJs", 1999-2008; "Introducing Dorothy Dandridge", 1999; "Boston Pub", 2000; "Life Is Not a Fairy Tale", 2006; Cable series: "Clover", 1997; "Don King: Only in Am", 1997; "Down in the Delta", 1998; "Funny Valentines", 1999; "As We Know It (Part II)", 2006; "Grey's Anatomy", 2005-09; "Eli Stone", 2008-09. **Orgs:** Alpha Kappa Alpha Sorority Inc. **Honors/Awds:** Image Award, Nat Asn Advan Colored People, 2001; Image Award for Outstanding Supporting Actress in a Drama Series, 2001, 2003, 2004; Black Reel Award, 2006. **Special Achievements:** Has earned an Image Award nomination and an Independent Spirit Award nomination for her work in the 2004 film Woman Thou Art Loosed; also nominated for Black Movie Award and Satellite Awards. *

DEVOE, RONALD BOYD, JR. (RONNIE DEVOE)
Singer, real estate executive. **Personal:** Born Nov 17, 1967, Roxbury, MA; son of Ronald Sr and Florence E; married Shamari Fears. **Career:** New Ed, singer, 1983; Bell Biv DeVoe, singer, 1990-; Albums: Poison, 1990; Bel Biv DeVoe—Greatest Hits, 2000; BBD, 2001; RE/MAX Real Estate agency, owner, currently. **Honors/Awds:** Billboard Top Ten, Candy Girl, 1983. **Home Phone:** (818)340-2300. **Business Phone:** (818)340-2300.*

DEVOE, RONNIE. **See DEVOE, RONALD BOYD, JR.**

DEVORE MITCHELL, OPHELIA
Executive, chief executive officer. **Personal:** Born Aug 12, 1922, South Carolina; daughter of John Walter and Mary Emma Strother; married Harold Cater, Jan 1, 1941 (divorced); married Vernon Mitchell, Jan 1, 1968 (deceased). **Educ:** NY Col; Vogue Sch Modeling; Hunter Col High Sch, BA, MA, math, 1938. **Career:** Grace Del Marco Agency, founder, 1946; Ophelia De Vore Assoc Inc, chmn bd, model agency, self-develop, charm sch, 1948; Columbus Times, ceo & publ, currently. **Orgs:** Am Women Radio & TV; Nat Asn Market Develop; Nat Bus League. **Special Achievements:** One of the first African-American fashion models. **Business Addr:** Chief Executive Officer, Publisher, Columbus Times, 2230 Buena Vista Rd, PO Box 2845, Columbus, GA 31909, **Business Phone:** (706)324-2404.*

DEVROUAX, PAUL S., JR.
Architect, president (organization). **Personal:** Born Oct 4, 1942, New Orleans, LA; son of Paul Sr and Freddie Warner; married Branda Stallworth, Sep 9, 1972; children: Lesley S. **Educ:** Southern Univ, Baton Rouge, LA, BArch, 1966. **Career:** Nolan Norman & Nolan Architects, New Orleans, LA, proj architects, 1968-69; Urban Planners Inc, Arlington, VA, dir design, 1969-72; DiSilvestro & Phelps Architects, Miami, FL, assoc & designer, 1972-73; Paul Devrouax & Assocs, 1973-78; Devrouax & Purnell, Architects, Washington, DC, pres & architect, 1978-. **Orgs:** Mayor's Comn Handicapped, Washington, DC, 1976-79; Am Inst Architects, 1980-; pres, Nat Org Minority Architects, 1980-81; bd mem, DC Chamber Com, 1982-; DC Archit Rev Panel, 1983-; Am Arbit Asn, 1985-; chmn, AIA, Mid-Atlantic Region, 1986-87; sr dir, AIA, Wash Chap, 1986; DC Bicentennial Comn, 1987-92; bd dir, Wash Proj Arts, 1987-94; Leadership Wash, 1991; Col fel, FAIA, 1991; Lambda Alpha Int, 1991; Bus Reulatory Reform Comn. **Honors/Awds:** Hist Preserv & Archit Design Excellence, AIA, Wash Chap, 4 Logan Circle, 1981; Citation Award, AIA, Wash Chap, Iowa Complex, 1981; Design Award, Nat Orgn Minority Architects, Nat Award Prog, Carter Beach House, 1984; Prof Serv of the Year, Minority Enterprise Devel Community Award, Washington, DC, 1986; Archit Serv Citation, Howard Univ, Washington, DC, 1989. **Special Achievements:** Features spokesperson, Washington Urban League, Focus: "Design within an Urban Environment". **Military Serv:** AUS, sergeant, E-5, 1966-68. **Business Addr:** President, Architect, Devrouax & Purnell Architects, 717 D St NW, Ste 500, Washington, DC 20004.*

DEWBERRY-WILLIAMS, MADELINA DENISE
Manager. **Personal:** Born Oct 18, 1958, Los Angeles, CA; daughter of Johnnie Mae Lemons Dewberry and Clarence Dewberry; married Ja Daun Williams, May 9, 1992. **Educ:** San Jose State Univ, attended 1981. **Career:** San Jose Unified Sch Dist, teacher, 1980-81; Santa Clara Junvenile Hall, counr, 1981; National Med Enterprises, personnel coordr, 1981-87; Am Express TRS, mgr, human resources; Silicon Graphic Comput Syst, mgr, employment progs, 1993; Advo Inc, regional dir, human resources, 1999-. **Orgs:** Vpres, 1986-87, National affirmative action, 1986-87; National conf, 1987-88; Int Asn Personnel Women; co-chair, United Christian Network, 1986-; dir Spirit Connections 1986-; bd mem, Cities in Schs, 1990-91. **Honors/Awds:** Outstanding Woman in Health Care, YWCA, 1986. **Home Addr:** 1356 Eagle St, Tracy, CA 95376.

DEWEY, GEORGE
Executive director. **Educ:** Morehouse Col, attended 1986; Vassar Col, attended 1988; Harvard Bus Sch, MBA, 1994. **Career:** Citigroup Global Markets Inc, invest banking dir, 1998-2005; Royal Bank Scotland, Managing Dir, 2005-. **Orgs:** Hentor, Harvard Bus Sch- Community Partners BMAD; bd mem, 100 Black Men the Bay Area. **Business Addr:** Managing Director, Royal Bank of Scotland, 150 Spear St, San Francisco, CA 94105, **Business Phone:** (415)644-9759.*

DEWITT, FRANKLIN ROOSEVELT
Lawyer. **Personal:** Born May 25, 1936, Conway, SC; son of Matthew A and Rebecca Hughes; married Willa Waylis Johnson; children: Rosalyn Abrevaya, Sharolyn Renee. **Educ:** SC State Univ, BS, Bus Admin, 1962, JD, 1964; Ga State Univ, Cert Housing Mgt, 1973. **Career:** US Justice Dept, summer law clerk, 1963; US Civil Serv Comn, Wash, DC, trial attny, 1965-67; Atlantic Beach SC, town attny; Nat Football League Players Asn, contract adv; pvt practice, atty, currently. **Orgs:** Municipal consult, Glenarden, Md, 1965-67; Conway SC City Coun, 1969-84; del, Nat Dem Party Conv, Miami Beach, FL, 1972; US Ct Appeals Fourth Circuit, Wash, DC Bar; US Supreme Ct; SC State Bar Asn; Am Bar Asn, Fed Bar Asn; chmn, bd dir, Horry-Georgetown Ment Health Clinic; life mem, Nat Advan Asn Colored People; contract adv, Nat Football League Player Asn; del, Nat Dem Party Conv, 1980; Nat Bar Asn; Kappa Alpha Psi. **Honors/Awds:** Usher of the Year, Cherry Hill Baptist Church, 1978; Executive of the Year, 1998. **Special Achievements:** Books: Super Redskins Pay Bills in Full, 1992; Washington Just Super, Super Bowl, 1988; History of a Family from Slavery to Freedom, 1985; Changed the death penalty law in SC for murder in the case of the State of SC vs Archie Allen. **Military Serv:** USAF, a/1c, 1955-59, Active Reserve, 1959-61; Good Conduct Ribbon, USAF, 1957. *

DIANA, DIANA
Cosmetics executive, consultant. **Personal:** Born Mar 6, 1948, Jamaica, NY; daughter of William Griffin and Corinne; divorced. **Educ:** Northern Essex Community Col, assoc degree, child care & special educ, 1971; Midlands Tech. **Career:** Black Angels Dive Club, pres, 1975-; DiAna's Hair Ego salon, owner, 1977-; SC AIDS Educ Network Inc, exec dir, 1986-2000. **Orgs:** Nat Minority AIDS Coun, 1986-; Women's Callaborative Work Group, 1999; SC African Am HIV Coun. **Honors/Awds:** Black Maria Film & Video Festival, Juror's Award; Am Film Festival Awards; 11 other awards. **Special Achievements:** Author: Bacteriology & Sanitation for the Personal Care Worker, 1988; AIDS & the Law, 1988; AIDS in the Workplace, 1990; Curlers & Condoms, 2003. **Business Addr:** Cosmetologist, Owner, DiAna's Hair Ego Salon, 7222 Highview Dr, Columbia, SC 29223.

DIANE, MAMADI
Shipping executive, president (organization). **Personal:** Born May 16, 1947, Conakry, Guinea; son of Ibrahima and Nankoria; married Cynthia Horthense, Jul 16, 1977; children: Mori. **Educ:** Richer Col, Houlton, Maine, BA, 1970; George Washington Univ, MBA, 1982. **Career:** St John Int, Wash, DC, vpres, 1972-82; AMEX Int Inc, Wash, DC, founder &pres, 1983-. **Orgs:** Bd dirs, US World Cup Organising Comt, 1994-; mem, US Indust Policy Adv Comt, 1995; adv bd mem, Salam Sudan Found. **Honors/Awds:** Congresional Award, Cong Mervyn Dymally, 1988; Hon Mem, Natl Conf Black Mayors, 1989; Chevalier Odre, Natl du Leopard, Govt Zaire, 1990. **Business Addr:** President, AMEX International Inc, 1615 L St NW Suite 340, Washington, DC 20036.*

DIAZ, F LOUISE
Educator. **Personal:** Born Dec 25, 1939, Jersey City, NJ; daughter of Antonio and Pearl Diaz; married Joseph W Jenkins, Aug 10, 1991; children: Tia Sinclair, William Perkins & Grantlin Perkins. **Educ:** St Peter's Col, BA, 1974; Trenton State Col, MED, 1976. **Career:** Thomas A Edison Col, asst dir, 1975-80; NJ City Univ, dir, 1981-. **Orgs:** Asn Col Bound Progs, 1989-, pres, 1998-2001; Kenmare HS, bd trustees, 1995-2001, pres, 2000-01; Hudson County Perinatal Consortium, 1995-97; First Unitarian Universalist Church Essex County, bd mem, 1998-2001. **Honors/Awds:** Sojourner Truth Award, Action Sickle Cell Anemia Hudson County, 1988; Community Service Award New Jersy, Nat Coun NW, 1995; Martin Luther King Jr Community Service Award, Leehagan African Studies Ctr, 1999. **Special Achievements:** Keynote Speaker, Jersey City School District Student Leadership Forum, 2001. **Business Addr:** Director Upward Bound, New Jersey City University, Vodra Hall 2039 Kennedy Blvd Suite 203, Jersey City, NJ 07305, **Business Phone:** (201)200-2347.

DICK, GEORGE ALBERT
Manager. **Personal:** Born Jan 31, 1940, Lloyds, St Thomas, Jamaica; son of Cleveland and Ruby Drummond; married Margaret Wesley, Aug 29, 1981; children: Pete Dick, Dave Dick, Charmaine Dick & Sharon Dick. **Educ:** Bellevue Sch Nursing, Kingston Jamaica, RMN, 1962. **Career:** Bellevue Hosp, Kingston, Jamaica, stud nurse, 1959-62, staff nurse nurse, 1962-67; Beverly Hills Hosp, Dallas, TX, staff nurse, supvr, 1967-77, Southwest Airlines Co, Dallas, TX, ramp agent, 1977-79, flight info agt, 1979-83, flight info supvr, 1983-86, mgr, currently. **Orgs:** Opers Comn Southwest Airlines, 1986-; pres, Third World Sports & Social Asn, 1974-76. **Home Addr:** 732 Havenwood, Dallas, TX 75232. **Business Phone:** (214)904-4455.

DICKENS, JACOBY
Banker. **Personal:** Born Jun 19, 1931, Panama City, FL; son of Jacoby and Marie Jackson; married Veranda; children: Karen. **Educ:** Roosevelt Univ, Chicago, 1954. **Career:** Chicago Bd Educ, Chicago, IL, engr, 1959-71; Seaway Nat Bank, Chicago, IL, vice chmn, 1979, chmn, 1983-; Chicago State Univ, dir, currently. **Orgs:** Comnr, Econ Develop Comn-Chicago, 1986; bd dirs, United Way, 1986-; vice chmn, Chicago Urban League, 1986; bd mem, Roundtable Fla A&M Univ, 1987; exec comt mem, Econ Club Chicago, 1986; bd mem, Chicago State Univ, 1997. **Honors/Awds:** Hall of Fame, Sch Bus, Chicago State Univ, 1990; Humanitarian of the Year, Coalition for United Community Action, 1984; Par Excellence Award, Mayor Harold Wash, 1987. **Special Achievements:** 20 People Who Made a Difference, Chicago Mag, 1990; Distinguished American, Dollars & Sense Mag, 1991. **Military Serv:** Army, Corporal, 1952-54; Battle Star. **Business Addr:** Chairman, Seaway National Bank, 645 E 87th St, Chicago, IL 60619-6127, **Business Phone:** (773)487-4800.*

DICKENS, SAMUEL
Executive, chief executive officer. **Career:** Uchs Inc, vpres & coo; Premier Circuit Assembly Inc, pres & chief exec officer, currently. **Orgs:** Bd trustees mem, NC Asn Community Col Trustees.

DICKERSON, DR. BETTE JEANNE
Educator. **Personal:** Born May 21, 1951, Philadelphia, PA; daughter of Rosa Anthony Dickerson. **Educ:** Morehead State

Univ, BA, Sociol, 1972; Univ Louisville, MEd, Special Educ, 1975; Wash State Univ, PhD, Sociol, 1986. **Career:** Louisville Jefferson Co Bd Educ, teacher, 1972-78; Wash State Univ, res asst, 1978-81; Nat Urban League, intern prog dir, 1981-82; WK Kellogg Found, prog assoc, 1982-86; Delta Sigma Theta Sor Inc, found dir, 1986-90; Am Univ, dept chair, 1999, assoc prof, currently; Women's & Gender Studies Prog dir, currently; co prin investr Am Univ Ronald E.McNair Post baccalaureate Achievement Prog currently. **Orgs:** Am Sociol Asn; pres, Asn Black Sociologists, 1990-2000; Eastern Sociol Soc; Delta Sigma Theta Sor Inc; Phi Kappa Phi Honor Soc; Sociologists Women Soc; DC Sociol Soc. **Honors/Awds:** George Edmund Haynes Fellowship, Nat Urban League, 1981; Community Service Award, Washington Heights Comm Ministeries, 1984; Women In Leadership, Junior League Washington DC, 1989; Outstanding Teacher, Office of Minority Affairs, The American University, 1992; Outstanding Educator & Administrator, DC Council Administrative Women in Education, 1992; Chesepeake Regional Scholar in African American Studies, Univ Virginia; A.Wade Smith Award, Asn Black Sociol. **Special Achievements:** Publ: African American Single Mothers: Understanding Their Lives and Families, Blooming in the Noise of the Whirlwind: the Roots of the Association of Black Sociologists" in Diverse Histories of American Sociology, Brill, 2005. **Business Addr:** Associate Professor, American University, Department Sociology, 4400 Massachusetts Ave NW, 230 McCabe Hall Battelle-Thompkins T-20, Washington, DC 20016, **Business Phone:** (202)885-2479.

DICKERSON, PROF. DENNIS CLARK
Educator, clergy. **Personal:** Born Aug 12, 1949, McKeesport, PA; son of Carl O and Oswanna Wheeler; married Mary Anne Eubanks; children: Nicole, Valerie, Christina & Dennis Jr. **Educ:** Lincoln Univ, BA, 1971; Wash Univ, MA, 1974, PhD, 1978; Hartford Sem, addn study; Morris Brown Col, LHD, 1990; Vanderbilt Univ, MDiv, 2007. **Career:** Forest Pk Community Col, instr, 1974; Penn State Univ, Ogontz Campus, instr, 1975-76; Williams Col, from asst prof hist to assoc prof hist, 1976-85; Payne AME Church Chatham NY, pastor, 1980-85; St Mark AME Church, Munford, TN, pastor, 1985-87; Rhodes Col, assoc prof hist, 1985-87; Carter Woodson Inst, Univ Va, vis scholar, 1987-88; Williams Col, assoc prof hist, 1987-88, prof; African Methodist Episcopal Church, historiographer, 1988-, gen off coun, currently; Stanfield prof hist, 1992-; Gen Officers Coun, secy; Payne Theolo Sem, vis prof, 1992, 1996, 1998; Yale Divinity Sch, vis prof am relig hist, 1995; Vanderbilt Univ, James M Lawson Jr prof hist, currently. **Orgs:** IBPOEW; Alpha Phi Alpha Fraternity; NAACP; GRE Hist Comm Educ Testing Serv, 1990-96; bd corporators, Williamstown Savings Bank, 1992-; bd trustees, N Adams State Col, 1992-95; Am Soc Church Hist; Orgn Am Historians; Am Hist Asn; Southern Hist Asn; World Methodist Hist Soc; Wesley Hist Soc; bd trustees, Am Bible Study Soc, 1995-. **Honors/Awds:** Fel Nat Endowment for the Humanities, 1982; Apostles at Home & Abroad, GK Hall 1982; Moody Grant Lyndon B Johnson Found, 1983; Grant-in-aid Am Coun Learned Soc, 1983-84. **Special Achievements:** Articles in New Jersey Hist, Church Hist, Pa Heritage, New York State J Med, Methodist Hist, Western PA Hist Mag, AME Church Rev; J Presby Hist; contributing auth: Encyclopedia of Am Bus Hist & Biography: Iron & Steel in the 20th Century, Bruccoli Clark Layman Boo, 1994, Hist Dictionary of Methodism, Scarecrow Press, 1996; Blackwell Dictionary of Evangelical Biography, Blackwell Publishers, 1995; Black Encyclopedia of Southern Culture, University of North Carolina Press, 1989; Biographical Dictionary Amer Social Welfare, Greenwood Press 1986; Life and Labor, SUNY Press 1986; author "Out of the Crucible, Black Steelworkers in Western Pennsylvania 1875-1980," Alb State Univ of NY Press 1986; author, Religion, Race and Region: Research Notes on AME Church History, Nashville AME Sunday School Union, 1995; Militant Mediator: Whitney M Young, Jr, Univ Press of Kentucky, 1998. **Business Addr:** James M Lawson Jr Professor of History, Vanderbilt University, Graduate Department of Religion, 2201 W End Ave, Nashville, TN 37235, **Business Phone:** (615)343-4329.

DICKERSON, ERIC DEMETRIC
Football player, television show host, business owner. **Personal:** Born Sep 2, 1960, Sealy, TX; son of Richard Seal and Helen. **Educ:** Southern Methodist Univ. **Career:** Football player (retired), TV show host; Los Angeles Rams, running back, 1983-87; Indianapolis Colts, 1987-92; Los Angeles Raiders, 1992-93; Atlanta Falcons, 1993; ABC, Monday Night Football, sideline reporter, 2000; Original Mini's Inc, founder & co-owner, 2005-; KCBS, Sports Cent Team, commentator & analyst. **Orgs:** Spokesperson, Just Say No; nat chmn, Nat Lung Asn. **Honors/Awds:** Pro Bowl, 1982, 1983, 1987; AP NFL Offensive Rookie of the Year, 1983; Rams Rookie of the Year Award, 1983; All-Pro, 1983, 1984, 1986, 1987, 1988; Rams Most Valuable Player Award, 1983-84, 1986; NFC Player of Year by UPI, Football News, USA Today, Washington DC Touchdown Club, Atlanta Touchdown Club, Columbus OH Touchdown Club & Kansas City Comt 101, 1984; Daniel F Reeves Member Award; Pro Football Hall of Fame, 1999. **Special Achievements:** First player in NFL hist to gain more than 1000 yards. **Business Phone:** (714)828-0018.

DICKERSON, ERNEST ROSCOE
Movie director, cinematographer, writer. **Personal:** Born Jun 25, 1951, Newark, NJ. **Educ:** Howard Univ, Washington, DC; New York Univ, Tisch Sch Arts, New York, NY, MFA, film, 1982. **Career:** New Line Cinema, dir & cinematographer; TV series: "Blind Faith," 1998; "Strange Justice", 1999; "Never Die Alone", 2004; "The Cradle", 2005; "The Evidence", 2006; Movies: Krush Groove, 1985; She's Gotta Have It, 1986; School Daze, 1988; Do the Right Thing, 1989; Mo' Better Blues, 1990; Law & Order, 1990; Jungle Fever, 1991; Juice, 1992; Malcolm X, 1992; Surviving the Game, 1994; Tales from the Crypt Presents Demon Knight, 1995; Bulletproof, 1996; Bones, 2001; The Wire, 2002; Never Die Alone, 2004; Miracle's Boys, 2005. **Honors/Awds:** New York Film Critics Circle Award for Best Cinematography, 1989; IFP Gotham Award for Cinematography, 1991; Austin Gay & Lesbian International Film Festival Award, 1999; Grand Jury Award, 1999; Daytime Emmy Award, 2003. **Special Achievements:** Nominated for Mystfest Award, 1993; Black Reel Awards, 2000, 2004, 2005, 2006. **Business Addr:** Director, Cinematographer, New Line Cinema, 116 N Robertson, Los Angeles, CA 90048.*

DICKERSON, HARVEY G, JR.
Army officer, business owner, presbyterian clergy. **Personal:** Born Oct 21, 1926, Prairie View, TX; son of Ada Taminia Kilpatrick and Harvey G; married Gerthyl Raye Sanders, Jan 13, 1944; children: Glenda Joy & Harvey G III. **Educ:** Prairie View A&M Col, BS, 1947; Syracuse Univ, MBA, 1961. **Career:** Army Officer (retired), business executive; AUS, officer, 1948-77; financial adv, 1977-80 & 1985-90; Corp Pub Broadcasting, vpres, 1980-85; Prairie View A&M Univ, dir inst develop & asst pres, 1990-; Dickerson & Assocs Inc, pres, currently. **Orgs:** Asn Syracuse Comptrollers, 1962-; Asn Govt Comptrollers, 1963-; APA Frate Inc, 1975-; pres, Rocks Inc, 1975-; Am Soc C/U & CHFC, 1985-; Nat Bus League Southern Mar, 1985-90. **Military Serv:** Retired. AUS, Army Artillery, col, 1948-77; Legion of Merit with Oak Leaf Cluster, 1977, nine other citations. **Home Addr:** 12204 Dillard Place, Fort Washington, MD 20744. **Business Addr:** President, Dickerson & Associates Inc., 12204 Dillard Pl, Fort Washington, MD 77446, **Business Phone:** (301)292-5332.

DICKERSON, JANET SMITH
Educator, school administrator. **Personal:** Born Feb 13, 1944, New York, NY; married J Paul Stephens; children: Jill, Karin & Dawn Stephens. **Educ:** Western Col Women, BA, 1965; Xavier Univ, MEd, 1968; Univ Pa, attended; Harvard Univ Inst Exec Mgt, cert, 1982. **Career:** Cincinnati Pub Schs, Ach Jr High Sch, Eng teacher, 1965-68; Sawyer & BloomJr High Schs, guidance counr, 1968-71; Univ Cincinnati, Educ Develop Prog, teacher, counr, 1971; Earlham Col, Richmond, IN, dir supportive serv &asst prof, 1971-76; Swarthmore Col, assoc dean, 1976-81, dean col,1981-91; Duke Univ, vpres stud affairs, 1991-2000; Princeton Univ, vpres campus life, 2000-. **Orgs:** Bd mem, Valentine Found, 1990-95; bd mem, NC Equity, 1992-95; Durham Chamber Com, human relations comt; Links Inc, 1993-; brd trustee, Guilford Col, 1993-; Reader, HWE proposals, 1978-81; Wallingford-Swarthmore Sch Brd,1988-91; bd mem, Client Security Fund Commonwealth PA,1983-88; consult, Davidson, Oberlin; consult, Scripps; consult, Brown; consult, Barnard; consult, Wesleyan; consult, Haverford; consult, Bowdoin; elder, Witherspoon Street Presbyterian Church; pres, central NJ chapter of the Links, Inc. **Honors/Awds:** WASC accreditation teams, Mills, Occidential, UCSD; LHD, Xavier Univ,1990; LLD, Swarthmore Col, 1992; Princeton's Tribute to Women Awrd, 2009. **Business Addr:** Vice President for Campus Life, Princeton University, 220 Nassau Hall, Princeton, NJ 08544, **Business Phone:** (609)258-3056.

DICKERSON, LOWELL DWIGHT
Musician, educator. **Personal:** Born Dec 26, 1944, Los Angeles, CA; son of Charles Edward and Ethel Hartie (deceased). **Educ:** Calif State Univ, Los Angeles, BA, music, 1973; Boston Univ Berkley Col Music; pvt lessons Ray Santisi & Margaret Chaloff; Univ Southern Calif, masters music, 1989; Univ Southern Calif, MM, jazz studies, 1990; Univ Calif, Los Angeles, C Ph1, PhD, ethnomusicology, 1995. **Career:** Albums: Sooner or Later, 1990; Dwights's Right's, 1992; Windows; Los Angeles Musicians Union, piano musician; Am Univ Sharjah, Col Arts & Sci, vis prof, currently. **Orgs:** Pi Kappa Lambda, 1989. **Business Addr:** Visting Professor, American University of Sharjah, College of Arts and Science, PO Box 26666, Sharjah, United Arab Emirates, **Business Phone:** (971)6515-5555.

DICKERSON, MICHAEL (MICHAEL DEANGELO DICKERSON)
Basketball player. **Personal:** Born Jun 25, 1975, Greenville, SC. **Educ:** Univ Ariz, attended 1998. **Career:** Basketball player (retired); Houston Rockets, guard, 1999; Vancouver Grizzlies, guard, 2000-01; Memphis Grizzlies, guard, 2002-03.

DICKERSON, MICHAEL DEANGELO. **See DICKERSON, MICHAEL.**

DICKERSON, RALPH
Association executive, president (organization). **Educ:** Southern Ill Univ, BS, bus admin, 1969; Univ Wis, MBA. **Career:** Executive (retired); United Way, St Louis, MO, staff, 1970-76; United Way, Madison, staff, 1977-81; United Way, Cleveland, OH, staff, 1981-84; United Way, Pittsburgh, PA, staff, 1984-88; United Way New York City, pres & chief professional officer, 1988-2004. **Orgs:** Dir, Civic & Corp Orgn; Alpha Kappa Psi Honorary Bus Fraternity; bd dir, Faith Ctr Community Develop; Visitors Comt, Sch Mgt & Urban Affairs, New Sch Social Res. **Honors/Awds:** Gorgeous Mosaic Award, NY Urban Coalition; Medal of Life, Pius XII Found; Frederick Douglass Award, NY Urban League.

DICKERSON, RON, SR.
Football coach. **Personal:** Born Jan 1, 1948?; married Jeannie; children: Ron Dickerson Jr, Rashawn Dickerson & Causey. **Educ:** Univ Ark, attended 1996. **Career:** Miami Dolphins, 1972; Clemson Univ Football Team, defensive coordr, ending 1992; Temple Univ Football Team, head football coach, 1993-97; Southwest Mo State Univ, asst Coach; US Sports Acad, chair of sport coaching; Ala state Univ, interim dirof athletics, currently. **Orgs:** Black Coaches Asn. **Business Phone:** (334)229-4100.*

DICKERSON, THOMAS L, JR.
Television journalist. **Personal:** Born Mar 1, 1949, Houston, TX; son of Thomas Dickerson Sr and Della Dervis Collins; married Peggy Lou Deale (divorced 1991); children: Traci Lauren & Troy Lewis. **Educ:** Baker Univ, Baldwin City, BA, jour, 1971. **Career:** Radio News, KPRC-AM, reporter, KLOL-FM, news dir, KCOH, KWTV-TV, Oklahoma City, news reporter & anchor, 1973-75; KTRK-TV, news reporter, 1975-77; WJLA-TV, Albritton Commun, news reporter, 1977-79; KTRK-TV, Cap Cities ABC, Houston, news reporter outdoors ed, 1979-. **Orgs:** Houston Asn Black Journalists, 1986-; Nat Asn Black Journalists, 1987-91; Int Asn Firefighters, 1990. **Honors/Awds:** Robert F Kennedy, Requiem Dying Neighborhood, 1978; Austin Headliner, Parole Series, 1991. **Business Addr:** Outdoors News Editor, KTRK-TV, PO Box 13, Houston, TX 77001, **Business Phone:** (713)663-4559.

DICKERSON, TYRONE EDWARD
Certified public accountant. **Personal:** Born Dec 18, 1943, Abington, PA; married Denise P Dickerson. **Educ:** Central State Univ, BS, 1965; Harvard Grad Sch Bus, MBA, 1970. **Career:** Lucas Tucker & Co, CPA's, 1971-74; Urban Nat, vpres, 1974-77; Mitchell & Titus CPA, partner, 1977-80; Tyrone E Dickerson CPA, owner, 1984-. **Orgs:** Kappa Alpha Psi, 1962-; Nat Asn Black Accts, 1971-; Am Inst Cert Pub Accts, 1974-; NY State Soc CPA's, 1975-; bd mem, Va Soc of CPA's, 1980-. **Business Phone:** (804)272-1250.*

DICKERSON, DR. WARNER LEE
Educator. **Personal:** Born Jun 18, 1937, Brownsville, TN; son of George and Mary; married Arcola Leavell, Apr 11, 1936; children: Jarvis Fernando & Arletrice Mechele. **Educ:** Tenn State Univ, BS, math, 1961; Memphis State Univ, MS, math, 1969; Univ Sarasota, EdD, voc ed, 1979. **Career:** Educator (retired); Memphis City Sch, teacher, 1961-70; State Tech Inc,teacher, 1970-74, vpres, 1970-81; dept head develop studies, 1974-76; ed admin, 1976-78; dir admin affairs, 1978-81; comnr voc educ, Tenn State Dept Educ, Nashville, 1981-84; educ consult, Tenn State Dept Educ, Memphis, 1984-86; supt, Fayette Co Bd Educ, Somerville, Tenn, 1986-91; Prudential Memphis, affil broker, 1992-94. **Orgs:** Vice pres, Memphis Br, Nat Asn Advan Colored People, 1977-79, 2nd vpres, Tenn State Conf, currently; pres, OIC Memphis Br, 1977-81; bd dir, Am Voc Asn, 1980-83; Nat Asn Advan Black Am Voc Educ, 1982-84; Am Voc Tech Asn; Tenn Voc Asn; bd dir, Fayette Co, 1988; Phi Beta Kappa. **Honors/Awds:** Distinguished Teacher Award, State Tech Ins, 1971. **Business Addr:** Second Vice President, National Association for the Advancement of Colored People, Tennessee State Conference, 27 Brentshire Sq Suite A, Jackson, TN 38305, **Business Phone:** (731)660-5580.

DICKEY, BERNESTINE D.
Aerospace engineer, manager. **Personal:** Born Jun 25, 1947, Redwater, TX; married William Dickey; children: Carl Vashun, William Shane. **Educ:** Prairie View A&M Univ, BS, phyiscs/math, 1969; TX A&M Univ, ME, indust eng. **Career:** Dept Defense, Red River Army Depot, maintainability engr, 1970-74; US Aviation Syst Command, indust engr, 1974-77; Ford Aerospace, quality engr, 1977-82; Gen Elec Co, instrnl design specialist, manned space flight, 1982-93; Johnson Space Ctr, spacelab payload crew training mgr, spacelab mission mgr, aerospace engr, 1993-97; Lyndon B Johnson Space Ctr, int space st launch package mgr, 1997-. **Orgs:** Delta Sigma Theta; LaMarque chap, Nat Asn Advan Colored People; Tex City Music Hall of Fame. **Honors/Awds:** Outstanding Performance Award Spacelab Life Sci Mission, 1991; Lyndon B Johnson Cert of Commendation, 1992; Outstanding Performance Rating Award, 1993, 1995-99; Cert Readiness Group Achievement Award, 1994; Exceptional Serv Medal, NASA, 1995,1999; Lauch Package Group Achievement Award, Flight 5A.1, 2001; Multipurpose Logistics Module Group Achievement Award, Marshall Space Flight Ctr, 2001; STS Flight Crew Recognition Award, 2001. *

DICKEY, ERIC JEROME
Novelist, screenwriter. **Personal:** Born Jul 7, 1961, Memphis, TN. **Educ:** Univ Memphis, BS engineering tech, 1983; UCLA, attended 1997. **Career:** Aerospace Indus, software developer; Rockwell Int, software develop, 1983-92; Rowland Unified Sch Dist,

educator, 1994-97; writer, novelist, 1992-; Published novels: Sister, Sister, 1996; Friends & Lovers, "Thirteen, 1997; Milk in My Coffee, 1998; Cheaters, 1999; Cappuccino, screenplay, 1997; Liar's Game, 2000; Between Lovers, 2001; Thieves Paradise, 2002; contributor: Got To Be Real, 2000; Mothers & Sons, 2000; Between Lovers, 2001; Griots Beneath the Baobab: Tales from Los Angeles, 2002; Black Silk, 2002; Thieves' Paradise, 2002Gumbo: A Celebration of African American Writing, 2002; The Other Woman, 2003; Naughty or Nice, 2003; Drive Me Crazy, 2004; Genevieve, 2005; Voices from the Other Side: Dark Dreams II, 2006; Chasing Destiny, 2006; Storm, 2006; Sleeping With Strangers, 2007; Waking With Enemies, 2007. **Orgs:** Alpha Phi Alpha, 1980-; Intl Black Writers & Artists, (IBWA/LA), 1993-; Project Reach, mentor, 1996-. **Honors/Awds:** City of Pomona, CA, Proclamation, 1998; Edna Crotchfield Founders Award, Commitment as Literary Artist, 1995; Blackboard Bestsellers, Sister, Sister, 1996, Friends & Lovers, 1997; NAACP Image Awd, nominee, for literature, Liar's Game, 2001. **Special Achievements:** NAACP Image Award, Nominee for Literature, Thieves Paradise, 2002; The Other Women, 2003.

DICKEY, LEONEL
Dentist. **Educ:** San Francisco State Col, clin psychol; Meharry Med Col, DDS; Tex Col, BA. **Career:** Life Sci, col teacher; High Sch prin; teacher sci math; coach sports; Pvt Pract, dentist, currently. **Orgs:** Pres, organizer & founder, Golden State Dental Asn; mem bd dirs, San Francisco Dental Care Found; pres, N Calif Chap Meharry Med Col Alumni Asn; chmn coord, Meharry Med Col Western Regional Mounting & Fund Raising Event; pres, Parents Adv Comt-pacific Heights Elem Sch; chmn, Benj Franklin Jr High Sch Parents Adv Comt Implementing Fresno Plan; mem, N Calif Chap Nat Dental Asn; chmn state coord, Meharry Alumni $88 Million Campaign Fund Drive; organizer, Bay Area Tex Col Alumni Asn. **Honors/Awds:** Outstanding Alumnus Award, Meharry Med & Moll Tex Col; Community Service Award, Bay Area Howard Univ Alumni. **Special Achievements:** Author of several outstanding scientific papers. **Military Serv:** AUS, capt, WW II chief surgical tech; Korean War, chief oral surgery & Prosthetics.

DICKINSON, DR. GLORIA HARPER
School administrator. **Personal:** Born Aug 5, 1947, New York, NY; daughter of Clifford Horace and Martha Louis Sinton; married Arthur Clinton. **Educ:** City Col NY, BA, European Hist, 1968; Howard Univ, MA African Studies, 1970, PhD, African Stud, 1978. **Career:** Camden High Sch Camden NJ, geog, social studies teacher, 1970-71; Eng Dept Trenton State Col, instr, 1971-73; Col NJ, Trenton State Col, Dept African-Am Studies, chmn, assoc prof, 1973-. **Orgs:** Ed bd, Jour Negro Hist, 1983-93; NJ Comt The Humanities 1984-90; Asn Study African Am Life & Hist; ASA; AHSA; NCBS; Nat Coun Negro Women; fac adv, Zeta Sigma Chapter Alpha Kappa Alpha, 1972-; contrib scholar NJ Women's Proj, 1984; proj dir, TSC Summer Study Tours Africa, 1984-; NJ Historic Trust, 1986-89; Alpha Kappa Alpha Sorority, chair, Int Nominating Comt, 1988-92, archives comm, 1994-98; Supreme Grammateus, 1998-2000; secy, Alpha Kappa Alpha Sorority Inc, 1998-2002; nat pres, Asn Study African Am Life & Hist, 2001-03; life mem, Asn Black Women Hist; adv bd, Am Studies Asn Crossroads Proj, 2002-. **Honors/Awds:** NEH summer fellowship, col fac, Univ Iowa, 1977, NY Univ Sch Bus, 1979, Univ Penn, 1981, Princeton Univ, 1984; Faculty Member of the Year, Trenton State Col, 1984; Proj Dir, NEH Summer Inst in African-Am Cult Trenton State Col, 1987; Blue Key Honor Society, Trenton State Col, 1989; Mentor of the Year, Trenton State Col Minority Scholars, 1990. **Business Addr:** Chairman, Associate Professor, College NJ, Trenton State College, Department African-Am Studies, 2000 Pennington Rd, PO Box 7718, Ewing, NJ 08628-0718, **Business Phone:** (609)771-2138.

DICKSON, CHARLES. See DICKSON, DR. CHARLIE JONES.

DICKSON, DR. CHARLIE JONES (CHARLES DICKSON)
Educator. **Personal:** Born in Alabama; daughter of Edward Jones and Tommie A Jones; married Joe N, Apr 2, 1970; children: Jonathan, Chari & Jori. **Educ:** Tuskegee Inst, BS, 1966; Ohio State Univ, MS, 1969; Univ Ala, EdD, 1984. **Career:** Lawson State Jr Col, chair dept nursing, 1969-70; Tuskegee Inst, instr, 1970-73; Univ Ala-Birmingham, prof, 1973, sch nursing, prof emer, currently. **Orgs:** Am Nurses Asn, 1975-; Ala State Nurses Asn, 1975-; bd dir, Shelby Med Ctr, 1987-93; bd mem, Shelby County Red Cross, 1990-91; bd, Nat Coun State Bd Nursing Inc, area III dir, 1990-91; Delta Sigma Theta Sorority Inc; pres, Ala Bd Nursing, 1990-91, chairperson, continued competence & continuing educ comt, 2001; Ala Respiratory Prog, 1991; Am Acad Nursing. **Honors/Awds:** Outstanding Instr, 1980; Professionalism Award, Univ Ala Sch Nursing, 1984; Class of 87 Award, Tuskegee Univ, 1987; Outstanding Leadership, Ala bd Nursing, 1992; R Louise McManus Award . **Special Achievements:** First African American Registered Nurse to serve as president of the Alabama Board of Nursing. **Military Serv:** USAFR, capt, 1966-68. **Business Phone:** (205)934-5428.

DICKSON, DARYL M.
Executive, consultant. **Personal:** Born in Detroit. **Educ:** Univ Mich, PhD. **Career:** Allied Signal Inc, dir mgt, 1991-1993; Quaker Oats Co, vpres human resources, 1993-1996; Bausch & Lomb, sr vpres human resources, 1996-2003; Dickson Consult, prin, currently. **Orgs:** Mem bd dir, Wilson Commencement Park. **Special Achievements:** First African American on Bausch & Lomb's Management Executive Commitee. **Home Addr:** 34 Paige St, Rochester, NY 14619. **Business Phone:** (716)338-6000.*

DICKSON, FRED
Executive. **Educ:** Univ Minn, BA, math & comput Sci; Univ St Thomas, exec leadership prog. **Career:** Prudential Ins Co; The Pillsbury Co; Blue Cross & Blue Shield Minn, vpres customer relationship mgt systems, technol & chief info officer, vpres1999-. **Orgs:** Sabathani Community Ctr; Eagan Technol Task Force. **Business Addr:** Chief Information Officer, Vice president, Blue Cross and Blue Shield of Minnesota, 3535 Blue Cross Rd, Saint Paul, MN 55122, **Business Phone:** (651)662-8000.*

DICKSON, ONIAS D, JR.
Activist, research scientist. **Personal:** Born Jun 18, 1958, Washington, DC; children: Jennifer & O Timothy. **Educ:** Hobart & William Smith, BA, 1981; Univ Notre Dame, MA, 1983. **Career:** St Martins Parochial Sch, jr high Sch teacher, 1983; Am Greetings, biog researcher, 1984; Westat Res Corp, freelance investr, 1985; Nat Asn Advan Colored People, nat res coord. **Orgs:** Preime minister, Third World Coalition Hobart & Wm Sm, 1980; founder, Hobart & William Smith Scuba Diving Asn, 1980-81; founder, Black Grad Stud Orgn, Univ Notre Dame, 1981-83; chmn, Govt Grad Stud Orgn, Univ Notre Dame, 1982-83; grad stud govt rep, Univ Notre Dame, 1983; Nat Asn Advan Colored People. **Honors/Awds:** Teacher's Asst, Hobart & William Smith, 1980-81; Dorothy Danforth-Compton Grad Fel Award, 1981,82; Nat Conf Black Polit Scientist Grad Asst Award, 1982-83. **Special Achievements:** Staff writer, Herald Weekly Newspaper, Hobart & William Smith, 1980-81. **Home Addr:** 4805 Mt Hope Dr, Baltimore, MD 21215. **Business Addr:** National Reserch Coordinator, National Association for the Advancement of Colored People, 4805 Mt Hope Dr, Baltimore, MD 21215, **Business Phone:** (410)358-8900.

DICKSON, REGINALD D.
Association executive. **Personal:** Born Apr 28, 1946, Oakland, TN; son of Louis Smith and Mildred Smith; married Illona White; children: Kia, Brandon, Rachel. **Educ:** Univ MO, Columbia, 1966; Harris Tchrs Col, Elementary Educ 1969; Wash Univ, Bus Admin, 1978; St Louis Univ, attended 1978. **Career:** St Louis Public Sch Syst, tchr, 1969-73; INROADS, Inc, dir, 1973-76, regional dir, 1976-80, exec vice pres, 1980-83, pres, ceo, 1983; Buford, Dickson, Harper & Sparrow, Inc, Chmn & owner, currently. **Orgs:** Co-chmn Salvation Army Tree Lights St Louis, 1977-78; area coordr, Boy Scouts Am, 1978; Metro Develop Comt Red Cross, 1980; chmn, exec comn Child Guidance Ctr, 1982-83; bd dirs, First Am Bank, 1981-; bd dirs, Conf Educ, 1982-; Statewide Task Force Educ, 1984-; Urban League, 1986-, CORO Found, 1986-, Confluence St Louis, 1986-; adv bd trustees, The Found Student Communs; life memship comt mem, NAACP. **Honors/Awds:** Participant Danforth Leadership Program St Louis, 1978-79; Distinguished Service Award, INROADS Inc St Louis, 1984; Distinguished Alumni Award, Harris-Stowe State Col, 1985; judge, Washington University's first annual John M. Olin Cup competition, 1989. **Business Addr:** Chairman, Owner, Buford, Dickson, Harper & Sparrow, Inc, 211 N Broadway Suite 2080, 1 Metropolitan Square, Saint Louis, MO 63105, **Business Phone:** (314)725-5445.*

DIDDLEY, BO. See Obituaries section.

DIDLICK, WELLS S.
Educator. **Personal:** Born Jun 16, 1925, Middletown, OH; son of Brack and Lena; married Beverly Chavis; children: 4. **Educ:** Miami Univ, BA, 1952. **Career:** Educator (Retired); Campus Inter-Racial Club Miami Univ, pres 1950-51, pres student fac coun 1951-52; Woodlawn Planning Comm, comnr; WoodlawnOhio, councilman 8 years; Cincinnati Bd Ed, teacher. **Orgs:** Nat Asn Advan Colored People; Zoning Bd Appeals Village Woodlawn, 1979; Gov Task Force Sch Discipline Cincinnati Sch Syst, 1979; Indus Rel Comm Village Woodlawn, 1980. **Military Serv:** USN, seaman 1/c, 1943-46.

DIESEL, VIN (MARK SINCLAIR VINCENT)
Actor. **Personal:** Born Jul 18, 1967, New York, NY; son of Delora. **Educ:** Theater for the New City; Hunter Col. **Career:** Films: Multi-Facial, 1994; Strays, 1997; Saving Pvt Ryan, 1998; The Iron Giant, 1999; Into Pitch Black, 2000; Boiler Room, 2000; Pitch Black, 2000; Knockaround Guys, 2001; The Fast & the Furious, 2001; A Man Apart, 2003; The Chronicles of Riddick: Escape from Butcher Bay, 2004; The Chronicles of Riddick: Dark Fury, 2004; The Pacifierm, 2005; Find Me Guilty, 2006; The Fast & the Furious: Tokyo Drift, 2006; Babylon A.D, 2008; Rockfish, 2008; OneRace Films, founder, currently; Tigon Studios, founder, currently. **Honors/Awds:** OFCS Award, 1999; MTV Movie Award, Best On-Screen Team, 2002. **Business Addr:** Actor, International Business Management, 9696 Culver Blvd Suite 203, Culver City, CA 90232.

DIGGA, RAH (RASHIYA FISHER)
Rap musician. **Personal:** Born Dec 18, 1972, Newark, NJ; daughter of Al Fisher and Brenda. **Educ:** NJ Inst Technol, elec engineering. **Career:** The Outsidaz & The Flip mode Squad, group mem; Albums: Dirty Harriet, 1999; Everything Is a Story, 2004; TV appearances: "Da Hip Hop Witch", 2000; "Michael Jackson 30th Anniversary Celebration", 2001; "Carmen: A Hip Hopera", MTV, 2001; "The Making of Thir13en Ghosts", 2002; "Its Black Entertainment", 2002; "Hip-Hop VIPs", 2002; "Queens of Hip Hop", 2003; "Dennis Miller", 2004; Say My Name, 2009; Michael Jackson NRJ 12 Tribute, 2009; Films: Da Hip Hop Witch, 2000; 13 Ghosts, 2001; Songs: "Tight", 1999; "Imperial", 2000; "Tight", 2000; "Break Fool", 2000; "Party and Bullshit", 2003; Breakin' All the Rules, 2004. **Special Achievements:** Nominee, Best Female Hip-Hop Artist, 2002, 2004; Nominee, People's Champ Award, 2006. *

DIGGS, CHRISTIAN EMANUEL
Founder (Originator), entrepreneur. **Personal:** Son of Clarence Diggs and Liz. **Career:** SandoteWebsites.com, chief exec officer & founder, 1997-. **Honors/Awds:** Kidpreneurs Award, Black Enterprises Entrepreneurs Conf, 2001. **Business Phone:** (972)709-1494.

DIGGS, DEBORAH DOLSEY
Executive. **Career:** United Negro Col Fund, dir, 2001-. **Business Addr:** Director, United Negro College Fund Inc, 3031 W Grand Blvd Suite 531, Detroit, MI 48202, **Business Phone:** (313)873-1500.

DIGGS, ESTELLA B.
State government official. **Personal:** Born Apr 21, 1916, St Louis, MO; divorced; children: Edward A, Lawrence C & Joyce D. **Educ:** NY Inst Dietetics, grad; Pace Col; CCNY; NY Univ; Adult Continuing Ed Queens Col. **Career:** NY State, comt woman; real estate dealer; freelance writer; career counr; catering bus owner; pres; State NY, legislator, assembly woman, 1973-80. **Orgs:** Chmn, Neighborhood Girl Scouts; Rosary Soc St Augustines Roman Cath Church; chmn, March Dimes; founder & chmn Bronx Cit Comm; bd mem, Comm Planning Bd 3, Forest House Day Care, Morrisania Pioneer Sr Citizens; charter mem, Prof Women Bronx Chapt, Pride Inc; mem Nat Coun Negro Women; Cath Interracial Coun Bronx; Womans Grand Jury Asn; bd dir, Halfway House Women; exec mem, Prison Rehab Bedford Hills Corr Inst. **Honors/Awds:** Hon Parade Marshal Afro-Am Day Parade, Jackson Dem Club; Special Salesmanship Award, Cushman Baker Co; Confidential Aid to Judge Donald J Sullivan Supreme Ct; Seagram Van Guard Soc Award, 1974; Ecumenical Award, Coun Churches, New York, 1973. **Home Addr:** 592 E 167 St, Bronx, NY 10456.

DIGGS, LAWRENCE J
President (Organization). **Personal:** Born Nov 2, 1947, Houston, TX; son of Louis Maurine. **Educ:** Antioch Univ, BA, 1987. **Career:** KFRC, announcer, 1968-70; KSFO, announcer, producer & reporter, 1970-72; KSFX, announcer; Quiet Storm Trading Co; Vinegar Connoisseurs Int, pres & founder, 1972-; Int Vinegar Mus, founder & cur. **Orgs:** Med vol, Peace Corps, 1979-81; pres, Zen Yukai, 1982-83; Lions Club, 1992-; Am Fedn Radio & TV Artists; Media Alliance; Micros Soc; Nat Coun Returned Peace Corps Vol; bd dirs, Soto Zen Mission; Int Vinegar Mus; founder, Int Vinegar Res Inst. **Honors/Awds:** California Senate, Commendation, 1973; California Assembly, Commendation, 1973; Beyond War Award. **Special Achievements:** Author: Vinegar, The Standard Reference, 1989; Suihanki Cooking; Introduction to Men's Issues, 1992; Facts About Blacks, 1971; Author, "Allies: A Positive Approach to Racial Reconciliation," 1998. **Business Addr:** Founder, President, Vinegar Connoisseurs International, 104 W Carlton Ave, PO Box 41, Roslyn, SD 57261, **Business Phone:** 877-486-0075.

DIGGS, ROY DALTON, JR.
Physician. **Personal:** Born Mar 29, 1929, Detroit, MI; married Johnella Smith. **Educ:** Wayne State Univ, attended 1949; Meharry Med Sch, MD 1953. **Career:** Hurley Hosp, intern, 1953-54; KS City Gen Hosp, resident, 1954-56; VA Hosp Buffalo NY, resident, 1958-61; Lapeer St Home, surgeon, 1961-63; pvt pract, gen surgeon; Hurley Med Ctr, gen surgeon, currently. **Orgs:** Am Bd Surgery; fel Am Col Surgeons; Flint Acad Surgery; fel Am Col Emergency Physicians; Mich State Col Human Med; Am Med Asn; Nat Asn Advan Colored People; Nat Urban League; Foss Ave Christian Sch; Flint Urban League; Omega Psi Phi Frat. **Honors/Awds:** Humanitarian Award Flint, Human Rels Comt, 1977. **Military Serv:** USMC captain 1956-58. **Business Addr:** General Surgeon, Hurley Med Ctr, 4250 N Saginaw St, Flint, MI 48505.*

DIGGS, SCOTT L. See DIGGS, TAYE.

DIGGS, TAYE (SCOTT L DIGGS)
Actor. **Personal:** Born Jan 2, 1972, Rochester, NY; married Idina Menzel, Jan 11, 2003. **Educ:** Syracuse Univ, BFA, musical theater. **Career:** Films: How Stella Got Her Groove Back, 1998; The Best Man, 1999; House on Haunted Hill, 1999; Go, 1999; The Wood, 1999; The Way of the Gun, 2000;Mary Jane's Last Dance, 2001; Equilibrium, 2002; Brown Sugar, 2002; New Best Friend, 2002; Just a Kiss, 2002; Chicago, 2002; Malibu's Most Wanted,2003; Basic, 2003; Drum, 2004; Rent, 2005; Cake, 2005; Slow Burn, 2005; 30Days, 2006; Days of Wrath, 2008; TV series: "Law &

Order", 1996; "New York Undercover", 1996;"Ally McBeal", 1997; "101 Dalmatians: The Series", 1997; "The Guiding Light", 1997; "The West Wing", 1999; "The Martin Short Show", 1999; "Ed",2000; "Ally McBeal", 2001; "Punk'd", 2003; "The West Wing", 2003; "Kevin Hill", 2004-05; "Will & Grace", 2006; "Day Break", producer & actor, 2006-07; "Grey's Anatomy", 2007; "Private Practice", 2007-09. **Honors/Awds:** Blockbuster Entertainment Award, 2000; Critics Choice Award, 2003;Excellence in Film making Award, Chicago Int Film Festival, 2003; Screen Actors Guild Award, 2003; Image Award, 2005, 2009. **Business Addr:** Actor, c/o Burton Goldstein Co, 156 W 56th Suite 1803, New York, NY 10019-3878, **Business Phone:** (212)582-9700.*

DIGGS, WILLIAM P., JR.
Clergy, educator, teacher. **Personal:** Born Oct 19, 1926, Columbia, SC; married Clotilda J Daniels; children: Mary Lynne, William jr. **Educ:** Friendship Jr Col, Rock Hill, SC, attended 1943; Morehouse Col, AB, 1949; Atlanta Univ, MA, 1951; Colgate-Rochester Div Sch, BD, 1955; MDiv, 1972; Friendship Jr Col, DD, 1973; Morris Col, LHD, 1973. **Career:** Friendship Jr Col, Rock Hill, SC, instr, 1950-52, instr sociol, 1955-61; Second Baptist Church, Leroy, NY, student pastor, 1954-55; Galilee Baptist Church, pastor, 1955-62; Benedict Col, Columbia, SC, asst prof sociol, 1964-74; Morris Col, Sumter, SC, minister, asst prof sociol; Trinity Baptist Church, Florence, SC. **Orgs:** Pres, Florence Br, Nat Asn Adv Colored People, 1970-74; Am Asn Univ Prof; Alpha Kappa Delta Hon Sociol Soc; Community Rels Comn, Florence, SC; chmn, Community Action Agency, Florence, Co; Area Manpower Bd; Florence County Bd Health; trustee bd, Friendship Jr Col; trustee bd, Morris Col; bd mem, Morehouse Col; bd mem, ITC. **Honors/Awds:** Recognition Dedicated Serv, Church & Community, 1969; Florence Outstanding Leadership Civic Econ Community Involvement, 1971; Citzen of the Yr, Chi Iota Chap, Omega Psi Phi Fraternity, 1976; Outstanding Achievement & Serv, Omega Psi Phi Fraternity, 1976; Valedictorian, High Sch Class; Honored, Trinity Baptist Church, Florence; Honored, Zeta Phi Beta Sorority. **Military Serv:** AUS, t/5, 1945-47. **Business Addr:** Pastor, Trinity Baptist Church, 124 W Darlington St, Florence, SC 29501.*

DIJI, DR. AUGUSTINE EBUN
Psychiatrist. **Personal:** Born Jun 27, 1932; son of James Sogo and Cecelia Oyeloye Sogo; married Celestine Gavor; children: Augustine & Angela. **Educ:** Queen's Univ Belfast, BS, 1958; Queen's Univ Belfast, MD, 1961; Royal Victoria Hosp Belfast, intern, 1962-63; Queen's Univ Belfast, resd, 1963-67. **Career:** Ghana Med Sch, instr physiology 1967-69; Erie County Medical Ctr, special flwsp, 1969-70; Buffalo General Hosp, staff 1971-; Part-time Pvt Pract, psychiat, 1971-; State Univ NY, Buffalo, clinical asst prof, 1975-; Geneva B Scruggs Com Health Care Ctr, Buffalo, consult psychiat, 1985-89; Buffalo Psychiat Ctr, staff psychiat, 1970-72, unit chief, 1972-78, acting dept clin dir, 1978-79, acting dir, 1979, med dir, 1980-; Univ Ny, Buffalo, asst prof emer & psychiat, currently; pvt pract, currently. **Orgs:** British Med Asn, 1963-76; Royal Col Physicians, 1966-; Royal Col Psychiats 1966-; AMA 1970-; Am Psychiat Asn, 1970-; Nat Med Asn, 1971-; World Asn Soc Psychiat, 1976-; pres, Med & Dent Staff Buffalo Psychiat Ctr, 1985-88, 1976-77. **Honors/Awds:** Belfast scholar, Queen's Univ, 1955-61, Milroy Medal, 1957; Hutchinson's Scholar, 1957-58. **Special Achievements:** publ "Local Vasodilation Action of Carbon Dioxide on Blood Vessels of Hand" Queen's Univ 1959; "The Local Effects of Carbon Dioxide on Human Blood Vessels" Queen's Univ 1960; dissertation "A Survey of the Incidence of Mental Disorder in the Mentally Subnormal" 1965; First black psychiatrists to open a private practice in the city of Buffalo. **Home Phone:** (716)832-9777. **Business Addr:** Physician, 655 Hertel Ave, Buffalo, NY 14207, **Business Phone:** (716)874-4975.*

DILDAY, HON. JUDITH NELSON
Judge. **Personal:** Born Mar 28, 1943, Pittsburgh, PA; daughter of Alberta Nelson and Frank Nelson; married James S, Dec 1972; children: Ayana, Sekou & Zakia. **Educ:** Univ Pittsburgh, BA, 1966; Millersville State Col, grad credits french; Boston Univ Sch Law, JD, 1974. **Career:** Pittsburgh Bd Educ, Fr teacher, 1966-70; Boston Model City, educ counr, 1970-71; Suffolk County Dist Atty, asst dist atty, 1974-75; Specialized Training/Advocacy Proj, coun, 1977; Stern & Shapiro, atty 1977-80; Off Solicitor US Dept Interior, atty adv, 1980-81; pvt pract counr law, 1981-82; Mass Bay Transp Authority, asst gen coun, 1982-89; Burnham, Hines & Dilday, partner, 1989-93; Probate & Family Ct Mass, assoc justice, circuit judge, 1993-98; Probate & Family Ct, Middlesex County Div, judge, 1998-. **Orgs:** Bd mem, Mass Black Lawyers Asn, 1980-84; Steering Comt, Lawyer's Comt Civil Rights, 1980-; vpres, Psi Omega Chap, Alpha Kappa Alpha, 1984-86; bd dirs, Women's Bar Asn, 1984-; deleg, State Dem Convention, 1986; Mass Bar Asn; treas, Nat Bar Asn Region I; Mass Black Women Attorneys, League Afro-Am Women; pres elect, Women's Bar Asn; 1989; deleg, State Dem Convention, 1987-89; secy bd dir, Daniel Marr Boy's Club; pres, Women's Bar Asn, 1990-91; gen coun, 100 Black Women, 1992; Nat Asn Women Judges; Mass Black Judges Asn; Boston Black Women's Lit Club; eucharistic minister, St Cyprian's Episcopal Church. **Honors/Awds:** Woman of the Year, Cambridge, YWCA, 1989; Legal Services Achievement Award, League Afro-American Women, 1991; Silver Shingle Alumni Award, Boston Univ Sch Law, 1991; Sojourner Truth Legal Service Award, Nat Asn Negro Bus & Prof Women, 1991; Drum Major for Justice MLK Award, 2001. **Special Achievements:** First African American to serve on the Probate and Family Court; First black female to serve as Assistant District Attorney for Suffolk County; one of four African American female judges in the Massachusettes judiciary. **Home Addr:** 9 Larchmont St, Boston, MA 02124. **Business Phone:** (617)788-6600.

DILDAY, WILLIAM HORACE, JR.
Advertising executive, business owner. **Personal:** Born Sep 14, 1937, Boston, MA; son of William Horace and Alease Virginia Scott; married Maxine Carol Wiggins, Nov 6, 1966; children: Scott, Erika & Kenya. **Educ:** Boston Univ, BS, BA, 1960. **Career:** Int Bus Mach, supvr, 1964-68; EG&G Roxbury, 1968-69; WHDH Inc, dir personnel, 1969-72; WLBT-TV, gen mgr, 1972-84; WJTV, exec vp, gen mgr, 1985-89; News, Press & Gazette, Broad Div, corp vpres, 1989-93; Kerimax Communications, pres & owner, 1994-. **Orgs:** Bd dirs, NBC TV Affilitaed Bd; bd dirs, Nat Asn Broadcasters; bd dirs, Jackson-Hinds Comprehensive Health Ctr; bd dirs, Miss Ment Health Asn, Jackson; past pres, Jackson Urban League, 1978-79; bd dirs, Pvt Indust Coun; bd dirs, Congress Black Caucus' Comn Brain Trust; finance chairperson, Boy Scouts Am, Seminole Dist, 1988-89; bd mem, Junior Achievement, 1988-89; bd mem, United Way, 1988-89; vpres, 100 Black Men of Jackson, 1991. **Special Achievements:** First African American General Manager Commercial TeleVision Station; First African American elected to a Television network affiliate board of directors; First African American elected to National Association of Broadcasters Board of Directors. **Military Serv:** AUS, Sp4, 1960-62. **Business Addr:** Owner, Kerimax Communications, 855 Rutherford Dr, PO Box 68248, Jackson, MS 39286, **Business Phone:** (601)955-7558.

DILDY, CATHERINE GREENE
Educator, executive. **Personal:** Born Nov 21, 1940, Dinwiddie, VA; daughter of Bruce Greene Sr and Cora H Greene; married Alvin V, 1982; children: Jewel D Trotman. **Educ:** Elizabeth City State Univ, BS, 1964; Univ Va, 1966-68, 1988-90; Norfolk State Univ, 1980-81, 1988-89; Old Dominion Univ, 1970-71, 1976-77, 1978-80, 1986-90. **Career:** Norfolk Pub Schs, physical educ resource, elem, 1964-70, health & physical educ, jr, 1970-79, health & physical educ, 1979-, driver educ coordr, intramural dir, city-wide health fair chmn, 1979-92, dance group sponsor, 1979-92; Tri City Tours, vpres. **Orgs:** Nat Educ Asn, 1964-; Va Educ Asn, 1964-; Norfolk Educ Asn, 1964-; Dist Sorority, pres, fin secy, 1960-, chair budget, May Week Social; Norfolk Chap Drifters Inc, pres treas, 1969-; Va Beach Chap Pinochle Bugs, fin treas, 1980-; Norfolk Chap Nat Epicurean, fin secy, 1988-. **Honors/Awds:** National Champion, Nat Pinochle Bugs Inc, 1988; Apple For The Teacher, Iota Phi Lambda, 1990. **Special Achievements:** Comt Involvement Team for Family Life Educ, 1990; contributed to the develop Curric Guide Family Life; contributed to the develop of the Health & Physical Educ Guide; Norfolk Pub Schs, HTH Educ Fair, co-chairperson. **Home Addr:** 5524 Connie Lane, Virginia Beach, VA 23462, **Home Phone:** (804)497-8609. **Business Addr:** Vice President, Tri City Tours, 5524 Connie Lane, Virginia Beach, VA 23462, **Business Phone:** (804)499-4335.

DILL, DR. BONNIE THORNTON
Educator. **Personal:** Born Oct 5, 1944, Chicago, IL; daughter of Irwin Stanley Thornton and Hilda Branch Thornton; married Jack C Shuler, Aug 29, 2008; children: Allen Richard Kamau, Anika Hillary & Nandi Elizabeth. **Educ:** Univ Rochester, BA, 1965; NY Univ, MA, 1970, PhD, 1979. **Career:** Off of Equal Opportunity-Northeast Region, field rep, 1965-67; City New York Community Develop Agency, community organizer & prog officer, 1967-68; City New York Human Resources Admin, prog develop & field supvr, 1968-70; New York Univ Ctr Human Rel, trainer (part-time), 1969-71; Bernard M Baruch Col, Dept Compensatory Prog, lecturer & coun, 1970-77; Bernard M Baruch Col, Black & Hisp Studies Prog, adjunct lectr, 1972-73; New York Univ Sociol Dept, teaching asst, 1974-75, adj instr, 1976-77; Memphis St Univ, asst prof sociol, 1978-83, Ctr Res Women, dir & founder, 1982-88, assoc prof sociol, 1983-90, prof sociol, 1990-91; Univ Md-Col Pk, prof women's studies & affil prof sociol, 1991-; Univ MD, Consortium Race, Gender & Ethnicity, founding dir; Women's Studies, prof & chair, 2003-; Princeton Univ, vis prof distinguished teaching, 2009-. **Orgs:** Vpres, Am Sociol Asn, 2005-08; Soc Study Social Problems; Asn Black Sociol; Sociol Women Soc; Nat Women's Studies Asn; Nat Coun Res Women. **Honors/Awds:** Robin M Williams, Jr lectr, Eastern Sociological Society, 2001-02; Jessie Bernard Award & Distinguished Contributions to Teaching Award, Am Sociol Asn, 1993; Summer Research Award, Univ MD, 1992; Superior Performance in Univ Res Award, Memphis State Univ, 1984-87, 1990, Mid year Raise for Merit in Res & Scholarly Productivity, 1985; Women of Achievement Award for Vision, Memphis Women's Network, 1985; Women's Rights Award, Nat Conf Christians & Jews, Memphis Chap, 1984. **Special Achievements:** Co-ed, Emerging Intersections: Race, Class and Gender in Theory, Policy and Practice, Rutgers University Press, 2008; co-ed, Women of Color in US Society, Temple Univ Press, 1993; Author: Across the Boundaries of Race and Class: An Exploration of Work and Family Among Black Female Domestic Servants, Garland Pub, 1993, "Theorizing Difference from Multi Racial Feminism" in Feminist Studies 22:2, 1996; "Race, Family Values & Welfare Reform" in A Re-Introduction to Poverty, New York Univ Press, 1998; "Race, Gender and Poverty in the Rural South: African American Single Mothers," in Rural Poverty in America, Auburn House, 1992;Co-author, "To Be Mature, Tenured, and Black: Reflections of Twenty Years of Academic Partnership" in Change, 22:2, p 30-33, 1990; Between a Rackand a Hard Place: Motherhood, Choice and Welfare in the Rural South are the recent publications. **Business Addr:** Professor, Chair, University of Maryland, Department of Women's Studies, 2101 Woods Hall, College Park, MD 20742, **Business Phone:** (301)405-6877.

DILL, GREGORY
College administrator, school administrator. **Personal:** Born Dec 8, 1958, Flint, MI; son of Charles and Doris Dill. **Educ:** Eastern Mich Univ, BBA, 1988, MBA, 1997. **Career:** Catherine McAuley Health Sys, mgr, 1989-93; Eastern Mich Univ, gen foreman, 1993-95, mgr, stud org adv; Oak Park Dist Sch, chief of staff, currently. **Orgs:** Alpha Phi Alpha, 1984-. **Honors/Awds:** Gold Medallion Award, Mich Univ,1999. **Business Addr:** Chief of staff, Oak Park School District, 13900 Granzon, Oak Park, MI 48237, **Business Phone:** (248)336-7700.

DILLARD, HOWARD LEE
Government official. **Personal:** Born Jan 21, 1946, Clinton, KY; son of Samuel William and Rosie Pearl Smith; married Frances Louise Piper, Aug 20, 1970; children: Wynita M, Christina M, Howard L Jr & Tamra Deann. **Educ:** Draughon's Col, attended 1982. **Career:** Dillard & Hunt, Clinton, KY, partner & mgr, 1980-82; Dillard Contractors, Clinton, KY, owner, 1982-88; Excel Industs, Fulton, KY, staff, 1988-. **Orgs:** Exec comt mem, Hickman Co Parks & Recreation Bd, 1984; treas, Hickman County Dem Exec Comt, 1988-; bd dirs, Hickman County Sr Citizens, 1988-; Clinton Ky City Coun, 1988-; Worshipful Master, Prince Hall Masons, 1991-. **Military Serv:** AUS, SP/4; Vietnam Serv Medal, Vietnam Campaign Medal; Vietnam Occup Medal. **Home Addr:** 319 Blair St A, Clinton, KY 42031. **Business Addr:** Staff, Excel Industries, 600 College St, Fulton, KY 42041.

DILLARD, JUNE WHITE
Lawyer. **Personal:** Born Sep 26, 1937, Youngstown, OH; daughter of Dr John Ira; married Martin Gregory Dillard, Nov 29, 1958 (divorced 1978); children: Belinda Louise, Brian Martin, Stephen Jeffrey; married John Vartou Lian, Jul 31, 1988. **Educ:** Univ Chicago, AB, 1958; Chicago Teachers Col, MA, 1964; Howard Univ Sch Law, JD, 1975. **Career:** Chicago Pub Schs, teacher, 1958-61; Off Econ Oppor, field rep, 1967-70; Securities & Exchange Comn, clerk, 1975-76; Taylor & Overby, assoc, 1978-80; JW Dillard Esquire, atty, 1980-; Dillard & Assoc PC, atty. **Orgs:** Exec Dir NAACP, Prince Georges County br; pres, Prince Georges Arts Coun; bd dir, Harriets List; bd dir, Alpha Kappa Alpha Sorority, Inc. **Honors/Awds:** Top Ladies Distinction; Cable TV Commissoner; Service Award, Coalition Black Affairs; Outstanding Contribution Legal Community, Nat Bar Asn; Disting mem Award, Nat Bus League Southern MD; Frederic Douglass Civic Achievement Award, MD Black Repub Coun; President Award, NAACP; Outstanding Service Award, Prince Georges County Govt. *

DILLARD, DR. MARTIN GREGORY
Physician, educator. **Personal:** Born Jul 7, 1935, Chicago, IL; son of Manny Martin and Evelyn Farmer; married Patricia Rachelle Cheek; children: Belinda, Brian & Stephen. **Educ:** Univ Chicago, BA, 1956, BS, 1957; Howard Univ Med Sch, MD, 1965. **Career:** US Pub Health Serv, fel, 1969-70; Howard Univ Col Med, asst prof med, 1970-74, Admin, Planning & Exec Comt, 1976-, asst dean & clin affairs,1984-; Howard Univ Hosp, Hemodialysis Unit, chief, 1970-76; Howard Univ Hosp, Dept Med, asst chmn educ, 1973-76; Health Care Coalition Nat Capitol Area, bd dir, 1982-; Howard Univ Hosp, assoc prof med, Div Nephrol, chief, physician, currently; Howard Univ, prof med, Nephrol Div, med dir & asst dean clin affairs. **Orgs:** Alpha Omega Alpha Honor Med Soc, 1965; Nat Bd Med Examiner, 1966; Am Bd Internal Med, 1972; Am Bd Internal Med Nephrol, 1978. **Military Serv:** AUS, e-4. **Business Addr:** Physician, Howard University Hospital, 2041 Ga Ave NW Room 5113, Washington, DC 20060, **Business Phone:** (202)865-6100.*

DILLARD, DR. MELVIN RUBIN
Administrator. **Personal:** Born Feb 26, 1941, Kendleton, TX; son of Ruby Lee Taylor and Vellas; children: Melvin II, Melvia & Melvis. **Educ:** Huston-Tillotson Col, BA, 1964; Prairie View A&M Univ, MA, 1973; Life Underwriters Training Coun, 1984. **Career:** Life Underwriter Training Coun, moderator, 1979-86; Nat Western Life, gen agt, 1975-81, div mgr, 1975-97. **Orgs:** Tex Leaders Round Table, 1970-91; E Million Dollar Round Table, 1977-97; Lone Star Leader, 1983-87; pres-elect, San Jacinto Asn Life Underwriters, 1991-; bd mem, Houston Asn Life Underwriters; nat pres, Huston-Tillotson Alumni; bd mem, Tex Comt Corp, United Methodist Church Mission Bd & Pension Bd; Regional 4 Dir, Tex Asn Life Underwriters, TALU; dist lay leader, United Methodist Ch-South Dist; Asn Health Ins Agt; Houston Asn

Health Underwriters; Bd Ordained Ministry, United Methodist Church; vice chmn, Houston Tillotson Col, bd trustees; bd mem, Coppertree Asn, treas; past bd mem, Tex Community Corp; chmn, TALU Community Serv. **Honors/Awds:** Presidential Citation Nat Asn Equal Opportunity, 1983; Doctorate Deg, Huston Tillotson Col, 1984; LUTCF, Life Underwriters Training Coun & Nat Asn Life Underwriters, 1984. **Special Achievements:** Articles publ, Tex Asn News Mag, 1979, Salesman Mag, 1980. **Home Addr:** 12039 Willow Trail, Houston, TX 77035. **Business Addr:** Divisional Manager, National Western Life Insurance, 2656 S Loop W Suite 585, Houston, TX 77054, **Business Phone:** (713)669-9313.

DILLARD, THELMA DELORIS
Government official, educator. **Personal:** Born Jan 6, 1946, Macon, GA; daughter of Hester Lou Newberry Bivins; divorced; children: Cartese. **Educ:** Ft Valley St Col, BS, Bus Educ, 1966; Ga Col, Spec Educ, 1975, Bus Educ, 1978. **Career:** Macon Nat Asn Advan Colored People, secy, 1965-, pres, 1995-97; Ft Valley St Col, teacher, 1970; Ga St Nat Asn Advan Colored People, asst secy, 1978, parliamentarian, 1982; Area Planning & Develop Comn, bd dir, 1980-; Democratic St Comn Ga, appointed mem, 1983-; Central High sch, educr; Bibb Bd Educ, Macon, Ga, chmn, spec educ dept, 1986-. **Orgs:** Zeta Phi Beta, 1965-; secy, Nat Asn Advan Colored People, 1965-, vpres, 1991; Ga Coalition Black Women, 1980-; chmn, Rules Comn Macon City Coun, 1980-; asst secy, Ga Asn Black Officials, 1980-, vice chmn, 1983, chmn, 1987-; mem, Jack & Jill Am, 1948; chmn, Cherry Blossom Think Pink Comn, 1990-91; assoc mem, Jack & Jill, 1990-; chmn, Pub Property Comn, City Macon, 1992-. **Honors/Awds:** Fifty Most Influential Women, Nat Asn Advan Colored People Macon & Informer Mag, 1981; Outstanding Woman of the Year, Nat Asn Advan Colored People, 1983; 50 Most Influential Women, GA Coalition Black Women, 1984; Several Comn Service Awards from many orgn. **Business Addr:** Chairman, Bibb County Public Schools, 484 Mulberry St, Macon, GA 31201, **Business Phone:** (478)765-8711.

DILLARD, VICTORIA
Actor. **Personal:** Born Sep 20, 1969, New York, NY. **Career:** Films: Star Trek:The Next Generation; Murder in Mississippi, Coming to America, 1988; Porgy & Bess; Internal Affairs, 1990; Ricochet, 1991; Deep Cover,1992; The Glass Shield, 1994; Killing Obsession, 1994; Out-of-Sync, 1995; Statistically Speaking, 1995; The Best Man, 1999; Ali, 2001; TV : "Seinfeld", 1993; "L. A Law", 1994; ; "Chicago Hope", 1994; "LA Law", 1994; "Martin",1995; "Moesha", 1996; "Spin City", 1996-2000; "The Ditch digger's Daughters", 1997; "Laugh-In";"Family Law", 1999; "Commitments", 2001; "Law & Order", 2006. **Business Addr:** Actress, ABC - TV, Dorfman, Craig & Associate, 6100 Wilshire Blvd Suite 310, Los Angeles, CA 90048, **Business Phone:** (323)937-8600.*

DILLARD, WANDA J
Administrator. **Personal:** Born Apr 19, 1953, Bluefield, VA; daughter of Robert and Louise Dillard; children: Micah C. **Educ:** Columbus Univ, AS, 1980; Otterbein Col, BS, 1983; Central Mich Univ, MS, 1988. **Career:** Riverside Methodist Hosp Dir Minority Health, adr, 1980-93; Ohio State Univ Med Ctr, community develop dir, currently. **Orgs:** Columbus Black Women's Health Proj, bd/steering comt; bd dirs, Livington Ave Collaborate, 1996-; coun, United Way Franklin County, Health Vision, 1996-; bd dirs, Hannah Neil, 1998-; bd trustees, Columbus Compact. **Honors/Awds:** President's Award, Riverside Methodist Hosp, 1988; Women Making a Difference, Ohio Dept Health, 1998; Diversity Award, Ohio State Univ, 1998; Community Award, Columbus Urban League, 1999. **Military Serv:** Ohio Nat Guard, lt col, 1974-98. **Home Addr:** 1089 Wildwood Ave, Columbus, OH 43219. **Business Addr:** Director Community Development, The Ohio State University Medical Center, 370 W 9th Ave, 200 Meiling Hall, Columbus, OH 43210, **Business Phone:** (614)292-5062.

DILLENBERGER, R. JEAN
Government official. **Personal:** Born May 6, 1931, Maywood, IL; married John; children: Tsan. **Educ:** San Francisco State Univ, BA, 1963, MA, 1978. **Career:** Government Official (retired); San Francisco St Univ, serv to minority stud; Ford Found, proj dir; Off Civil Rights, chief oper; US Dept Educ, acting dir higher educ div & dir elem & sec educ div regional off civil rights; dep regional dir, 1987-94. **Orgs:** Dir, Advocates Women, 1973-77; dir & treas, Consumers Coop Berkeley, 1977-83; dir & pres, Consumers Group Legal Serv, 1973-76; adv bd, Women Orgn Employ; Asn Fed Women Execs Speaking Engagements, Higher Educ Br, Off Civil Rights, HEW. **Honors/Awds:** Published "70 Soul Secrets of Sapphire," "Toward Viable Directions in Post secondary Education".

DILLIHAY, TANYA CLARKSON
Psychiatrist. **Personal:** Born Aug 8, 1958, Columbia, SC; daughter of Zack C and Rachel Scott; married Otha R Dillihay Sr; children: Otha R II, Elliot Clarkson, Adam Scott. **Educ:** Spelman Col, BS, Biol, 1979; Meharry Med Col, MD, 1983. **Career:** Wm S Hall Psychiat Inst, resident training, 1983-87; SC State Hosp, psychiat serv chief, pvt practice. **Orgs:** Treas, Afro-Amer Psychiatrists SC, 1986, 1987; chief resident, psycho-social rehabilitation WSHPI, 1987; Ladson Pres Ch Columbia SC; Spelman Col Club; Congaree Med Asn; Delta Sigma Theta Sorority. **Special Achievements:** "Suicide in Black Children" published in Psychiatric Forum, 1989. **Business Addr:** 20 Powderhorn Rd, PO Box 119, Columbia, SC 29201.*

DILLON, AUBREY
Educator. **Personal:** Born Jan 25, 1938, Prentiss, MS; son of Louella Barnes Quinn. **Educ:** Edinboro State Col, BS, social studies, 1961, MEd, 1964. **Career:** Educator (retired); Playground dir, 1961-63; Erie, PA Sch Dist, teacher, guid counr, 1961-69; Erie Tech High Sch, tennis coach, 1965-68; basic adult educ coord, 1966-68; Edinboro State Col, assoc dean men, 1969-93, Edinboro Univ Penn, prof emer, 1993, educ consult, jazzie bd dirs. **Orgs:** Pa State Educ Asn; dir, Human Awareness Lab, Edinboro, 1965; YMCA asst boy's work, dir, 1964-66; supr student teachers; chmn, Black Studies Comn Edinboro, 1969-72; PA Govs Justice Comn; bd Incorporators, WQLN Educ TV; Erie ACT Community Ctr Bd; Presque Isle Jaycees; Erie Human Rel Educ Com; Erie Urban Coalition; Kappa Delta Phi; Nat Educ Fraternity; Alpha Phi Alpha Soc Fraterniyt; bd dir, Meadville, PA Unity Ctr; NATO Community Educ Comn; Booker T Washington Community Ctr Scoutmaster; bd dir, Citizen Scholarship Found; PA Black Conf Higher Educ; Inner-Frat Coun Adv; Phi Delta Kappa Edinboro Univ PA; Edinboro Univ Human Rels Comn; pres, Phi Delta Kappa Beta Nu Chapter, 1987-88; bd dir, Jazz Erie; bd dir, Bay front Ctr Maritime Studies; bd dir, Pennbriar Tennis & Health Club; bd dir, Presque Marina Asn; bd dir, Roadhouse Theatre; bd dir, Edinboro Univ Pa Alumini Asn. **Honors/Awds:** Jaycee of the Month, 1966; Runner-up Jaycee Man of the Year, 1967; Alpha Kappa Alpha Sor Sweetheart, 1971; Freshman Advocate Nominee, First Year Experience, Univ SC, 1990-91. **Home Addr:** 222 Beech Lakeside, PO Box 506, Edinboro, PA 16412, **Home Phone:** (814)734-3417. *

DILLON, COREY
Football player. **Personal:** Born Oct 24, 1974, Seattle, WA. **Educ:** Univ Wash. **Career:** Football player(retired); Cincinnati Bengals, running back, 1997-03; New Eng Patriots, 2004-06. **Honors/Awds:** All-Metro Player of the Year; NFL Players Asn, AFC Rookie of the Yr, 1997. **Special Achievements:** Record holder for top rushing game in NFL history, 278 yards vs. Denver in 2000. *

DILLON, VERMON LEMAR
Government official. **Personal:** Born Jun 5, 1958, New Orleans, LA; son of Willie L Dillon (deceased) and Ruby Mary Cross Dillon (deceased); married Gloria Wade, Apr 27, 1990; children: Charles A Wade & Micah Lemar Dillon. **Educ:** La State Univ, BS, 1981; Southern Univ, MS, 1983. **Career:** Nicholls State Univ, equipment mgr athletics, 1981-82; Southern Univ, grad asst athletics, 1982-83; Bogalusa City Schs, teacher, 1984; La State Univ, asst athletic dir, 1984-85; Univ New Orleans, dept athletics equipment mgr, 1985-86; Cent State Univ, dept athletics equipment Mgr, 1986-90; Off Youth Develop, Baton Rouge Parish, probation officer II, 1990. **Orgs:** Founder, JC Crump & JJ Piper Memorial, 1979-; Phi Beta Sigma Fraternity; Shiloh Baptist Church Brotherhood, 1990-; comt leader, Undershepherd Shiloh Baptist Church, 1991-; pres elect, Prince Hall Masons; Kiwanis, 1992. **Honors/Awds:** Sigma of the Year, Phi Beta Sigma, 1981. **Special Achievements:** Kool Achiever Awards, nominee, 1992. **Home Phone:** (513)769-5277.

DILWORTH, DR. MARY ELIZABETH
Educator. **Personal:** Born Feb 7, 1950, New York, NY; daughter of Tom and Martha Lina Williams; married Clyde C Aveilhe. **Educ:** Howard Univ, BA, 1972, MA, 1974; Catholic Univ Am, EdD, 1981. **Career:** Nat Adv Coun Educ Pr Develop, educ res analyst, 1974-76; Nat Inst Advan Studies, sr prog analyst, 1978-82; Inst Study Educ Policy, res assoc, 1983-85; Howard Univ Hosp, coord educ & training; ERIC Clearinghouse Teacher Educ, dir, 1987-; Am Asn Cols Teacher Educ, Wash, sr vpres, 1987-2005, dir; Howard Univ, Washington, DC, adjunct faculty, sch educ, 1989-90; Nat Bd Prof Teaching Stand, Higher Educ Initiatives & Res, vpres, 2005-. **Orgs:** Am Educ Res Asn; bd mem, Nat Ctr Res Teacher Educ; Phi Delta Kappa; prog chair, Nat Coun Negro Women; NAACP Task Force Teacher Training & assessment; secy, Div K, Am Educ Res Asn, 1991-92; ETS Vis Panel Res, 2001-; bd dir, Holmes Partnership. **Honors/Awds:** Black Woman Achiever Award, NCNW/Frito Lay, 1985; Mary McLeod Bethune Recognition Award, 1985; Outstanding Community Service Award, 1979; Howard Univ Urban Affairs, 1985. **Special Achievements:** Publications: "Teachers' Totter, A Report on Teacher Certification Issues," 1984; "Reading Between the Lines: Teachers and Their Racial Ethnic Cultures," 1990; Diversity in Teacher Education: New Expectations, editor, 1992; "Being Responsive to Cultural Differences: How Teachers Learn,", 1998, editor.

DIMRY, CHARLES LOUIS, III
Football player. **Personal:** Born Jan 31, 1966, San Diego, CA; married Erin; married Francine (deceased); children: Erin, Carlee & Christopher. **Educ:** Univ Nev Las Vegas. **Career:** Football player(retired); Atlanta Falcons, defensive back, 1988-90; Denver Broncos, 1991-93; Tampa Bay Buccaneers, 1994-96; Philadelphia Eagles, 1997; San Diego Chargers, 1998-99; defensive backs' coach, San Diego col, 2004. **Honors/Awds:** Ed Block Courage Award, 1996. **Business Addr:** 6070 Avenida Encinas, Carlsbad, CA 92011, **Business Phone:** (760)444-0100.*

DINES, GEORGE B
Manager, administrator. **Personal:** Born Feb 28, 1931, Washington, DC; married Dorothy L Baham; children: George Jr, Kedric & Christopher. **Educ:** Yale Univ, exchange stud; Howard Univ, grad studies; Harvard Univ, grad sch bus; various short courses, 1973. **Career:** Sr adv (retired), bd dir; Int Health Affairs, sr adv; Health Resources & Serv Admin, Dept Health & Human Serv, assoc admin, sr adv; Off Sub-Saharan Africa & Off Int Health Off Asst Sec Health, Dept Health & Human Serv, dir; Div org Anal & Develop, Off Org Develop, Bur Comm Health Serv, Dept Health, Educ, & Welfare, dir; Div Health Care Servs CHS, Dept Health, Educ, & Welfare, spec asst dir; Off Prog Eval Div Health Care Servs, Dept Health, Educ, & Welfare, chief; Off Health Affairs Off Eco Opportunity, dep dir; US Peace Corps Sierra Leone W Africa, regional dir; US Peace Corps No Nigeria; Med Care Develop Inc, bd dir, currently. **Orgs:** Am Pub Health Asn; Nat Asn Comn Develop; Nat Asn Neighborhood Health Ctrs; Nat Coun Int Health; Nat Asn Health Serv Execs; AFRICARE; Am Asn World Health; Blacks Govt; Harvard Univ Bus Sch Club Wash; Pi Sigma Alpha Honorary Soc; Comnr, Housing Opportunities Comn Mont county; Pub Mgt Asn; Friends Chapel; pres bd dir, Howard Univ; Woodlawn Cemetery Asn; chmn, Minority Rels Monitoring Comn, TransAfrica; Kappa Alpha Psi; Nat Asn Advan Colored People; Boys & Girls Homes; Woodlawn Cemetery Assoc, pres. **Honors/Awds:** Admin Award for Excellence, Dept Health & Human Serv, Public Health Service, Health Resources & Serv Admin, 1987; Superior Service Award, Dept Health & Human Serv, Public Health Service, 1990, 1992, 1994; Recognition, Medical Care Develop Int Cert Appreciation, Nat Asn Health Care Execs; recipient of numerous awards and recognition of outstanding contributions in the field of health services design and delivery. **Military Serv:** Infantry, cap, 1954-59. **Business Addr:** president, Medical Care Development Inc, 11 Parkwood Dr, Augusta, ME 04330, **Business Phone:** (207)622-7566.

DINES, STEVE
Entrepreneur, executive. **Educ:** Univ Leeds, BS, elec engineering; Univ Manchester Inst Sci & Technol, MSc, commun. **Career:** Cirrus Logic, officer corp; Bandwidth Corp, pres & chief exec officer; Azanda Network Devices, pres & chief exec officer, 2001-. **Business Addr:** President, Chief Executive Officer, Azanda Network Devices, 250 Santa Ana Ct, Sunnyvale, CA 94085, **Business Phone:** (408)720-3100.*

DINIZULU, YAO O
Lawyer. **Personal:** Born Jan 1, 1973. **Educ:** Fla A&M Univ, BS, 1994; Univ Ill Col Law, JD, 1997. **Career:** Price Waterhouse LLP, staff; Harris, Mitchell & Dinizulu LLC, founder & atty, 2000-. **Orgs:** Supreme Ct Ill; Asn Trial Lawyers Am; bd dir, Bethel New Life Inc; Kappa Alpha Psi Fraternity; exec bd, Nat Black Law Student Asn. **Honors/Awds:** James Benton Parsons Scholarship Award, Just Beginning Found; Public Service & Academic Achievement, Nat Bar Asn Judicial Coun; Best Bachelor of the Year, Ebony, 2003. **Business Addr:** Founder, Attorney, Horris, Mitchell & Dinizulu LLC, 205 W Randolph St Suite 410, Chicago, IL 60606, **Business Phone:** (312)236-2900.

DINKINS, DAVID N.
Educator, mayor. **Personal:** Born Jul 10, 1927, Trenton, NJ; married Joyce Burrows; children: David Jr. **Educ:** Howard Univ, BS, maths, 1950; Brooklyn Law Sch, JD, 1956. **Career:** Dyett, Alexander, Dinkins, Patterson, Michael, Dinkins, Jones,atty-partner, 1956-75; NY State Dem Party, dist leader, 1967-; NY State Assembly, state assemblyman, 1966; City New York, pres bd elections, 1972-73, city clerk, 1975-85, Manhattan borough, pres, 1986-90, mayor, 1990-93; Columbia Univ, Sch Int & Pub Affairs, prof pract pub affairs, 1993-, bd adv, professorship, 2003-. **Orgs:** Bd dir, NY State Am Dem Action; Urban League; bd dir, 100 Black Men; bd dir, March Dimes; bd dir, mem steering comt, Asn Better NY; Manhattan Women's Polit Caucus; NAACP; Black-Jewish Coalition; Vera Inst Justice; Nova Anorca & NY State Urban Develop Corp; bd trustees, Malcolm King Harlem Col; pres adv coun, Marymount Manhattan Col; exec comt, Asn Bar City NY; bd dirs, Upper Manhattan Empowerment Zone; Honorary Life Trustee, Community Service Society of New York; Hon trustee,Harlem Hospital. **Honors/Awds:** Pioneer of Excellence, World Inst Black Commun, 1986; Righteous Man Award, NY Bd Rabbis, 1986; Man of the Year Award, Corrections Guardians Asn, 1986; Distinguished Service Award, Fedn Negro Civil Serv Orgn, 1986; Man of the Year Award, Asn Negro Bus & Prof Women's Clubs; Father of the Year Award, Metropolitan Chap, Jack & Jill Am Inc, 1989. **Special Achievements:** First black mayor of New York City. **Business Addr:** Professor, Columbia University, School of International & Public Affairs, Int Affairs Bldg Room 1430, New York, NY 10027, **Business Phone:** (212)854-4253.

DINKINS, TRACI
Advertising executive. **Career:** Starcom MediaVest Group, GM Planworks, diversity group dir, 2003-; Spike DDB, assoc media

dir, media dir; African-American Advert, pres; Omnicom Group. **Honors/Awds:** Outstanding Women in Marketing & Communication, Ebony Mag, 2003. **Business Addr:** Diversity Group Director, Starcom MediaVest Group, GM Planworks, 1 E Wacker Dr Suite 1500, Chicago, IL 60601, **Business Phone:** (312)494-4002.

DISHER, SPENCER C, III
Executive. **Personal:** Born Sep 30, 1957, Florence, SC; son of Spencer C Jr and Georgia G Montgomery; married Katherine Dowdell, Oct 8, 1989. **Educ:** Univ Wis-Madison, BSCE, 1980; Northwestern Univ, JL Kellogg Grad Sch Mgt, MBA, 1986. **Career:** Mobil Oil Co, proj engr, 1980-84; Continental Bank, pub finance assoc, 1985-86; Chevron fel, 1985; Citicorp Investment Bank, assoc, 1986-87; BT Securities, NY, assoc, 1987-88; Credit Nat, vpres. **Orgs:** Toastmasters, 1984-86; Nat Black MBA Asn, 1985-; Nat Asn Advan Colored people; founder, Wis Black Engr Stud Soc. *

DISHMAN, CRIS EDWARD
Football player, football coach. **Personal:** Born Aug 13, 1965, Louisville, KY; married Carmen; children: Bianca. **Educ:** Purdue Univ. **Career:** Football player (retired), football coach; Houston Oilers, defensive back, 1988-96; Wash Redskins, 1997-98; Kansas City Chiefs, 1998-99; Minn Vikings, football player, 2000; Miami Dolphins, coach, 2006; Menlo Col, defensive back, currently; Oakland Raiders, coach, 2007; ass defensive backs coach, San Diego Chargers, 2009-. **Honors/Awds:** All-Pro selection, 1991; Pro Bowl, 199, 1997.

DISMUKE, LEROY
Educator, school administrator. **Personal:** Born Aug 18, 1937, Camden, AR; son of Roy and Edna Mae Bragg Byrd; married Gladys M; children: Alan Roy. **Educ:** Lane Col, BA, 1960; Eastern Mich Univ, MA, 1965 & 1977, EdS, 1983. **Career:** Flint Educ Asn, 1966-69; United Teachers Flint Exec Bd, 1969-87; Flint BdEduc, Spec Educ Dept, consult; consult, currently. **Orgs:** Flint Educ Asn, 1961-69; Prof Negotiation Team, 1967-73; United Teachers Flint, 1969-87; Mich Fedn & Teachers, 1969-74; Am Fedn Teachers, 1969-74; Black Caucus, Nat Educ Asn, 1970-; rep, NEA, 1971-91; treas, Nat Asn Advan Colored People, 1983-89; Flint Cong Adminr, 1991-. **Honors/Awds:** Fifteen years Service Award, Big Brothers, 1972; Central Flint Optimist Award, 1985-86; Kappa Alpha Psi, 1985-86; Educator of the Year, Flint Coun Exceptional Chidren, 1989; Man of the Year, Flint Alumni Chap, Kappa Alpha Psi Fraternity, 1990; Achievement Award, Phi Delta Kappa, 1992; Achievement Award, Kappa Alpha Psi Fraternity, 1994, 1999; Region Educators Hall of Fame, 2000. **Home Addr:** 1701 Laurel Oak Dr, Flint, MI 48507-2210, **Home Phone:** (810)239-8024. **Business Addr:** Consultant, 1701 Laurel Oak Dr, Flint, MI 48507, **Business Phone:** (810)239-8024.*

DISMUKE, MARY EUNICE
Association executive. **Personal:** Born Feb 5, 1942, West Point, GA; daughter of Hattie Snow Pelleccitti and Hubert Hazes Moss; married Olin Dismuke (divorced); children: Sonja, Monica. **Educ:** Ga State Univ, Atlanta, GA, BS; Wayne State Univ, Detroit, MI, MSW. **Career:** Detroit Compact, Detroit, MI, dir; Mich Dept Labor, Detroit, MI, dir, urban affairs, Detroit Associate Black Org, Detroit, MI, exec dir. **Orgs:** Exec bd mem, Detroit Asn lack Social Worker; secy, Coalition Black Trade Unionists. **Honors/Awds:** Outstanding Leadership, Detroit Asn Black Social Workers, 1970; Leadership Am, 1985; Harriet Tubman Award, A Philip Randolph Inst & Coalition Black Trade Unionists, 1989. *

DIUGUID, LEWIS WALTER
Newspaper executive. **Personal:** Born Jul 17, 1955, St Louis, MO; son of Lincoln I and Nancy Ruth Greenlee; married Valerie Gale Words, Oct 25, 1977; children: Adrianne Renee & Leslie Ellen. **Educ:** Univ Mo-Columbia, Sch Jour, BJ, 1977; Univ Ariz-Tucson, attended 1984; Maynard Inst Jour Educ, Editing Prog Minority Journalists. **Career:** Kans City Times, reporter, photogr, 1977-80, gen assignment reporter, surburban reporter, 1980-82, Jackson County courthouse reporter, 1982-84, copy ed, automotive ed, 1984-85; Kans City Star, asst bur chief, Johnson County, 1985-87, Southland Bur chief & columnist, 1987-92, asst city ed & columnist, 1993-94, assoc ed, Metro Columnist, 1994-, diversity co-chair, asst minority recruiter, 1995-, vpres community resources, currently. **Orgs:** The Kansas City Asn Black Journalists; Nat Asn Black Journalists, 1985-; Nat Soc Newspaper Columnists; Trotter Group Black Voices Commentary; bd dirs, Missourian Publishing Asn, Univ Mo-Columbia; bd trustees, William Allen White Found, William Allen White Sch Jour & Mass Commun, Univ Kansas-Lawrence. **Honors/Awds:** Unity Award, Lincoln University, 1979; Ark of Friends Award, 1990-92; Urban League, Difference Maker Award, 1992; Mental Health Award, Missouri Dept of Mental Health, 1991; Research Mental Health Service, Media Award, 1992; First Place Opinion Column Award, Kansas City Press Club, 1993; Ark of Friends Media Professional Award, 1993; Asn Media Award, Mo Community Col, 1993; Journalism Award, Wayside Waifs Humane Society, 1993; Mental Health Awareness Award, Mental Health Asn Kansas City, 1993; Public Affairs/Social Issues Unity Award, Lincoln Univ, 1993; Ark of Friends of Greater Kansas City Media Professional Award, 1994; Harmony Encourages Awareness, Responsibility, Togetherness Award, 1995; SCLC Evelyn Wasserstorm Award, Commitment to Causes of Freedom, 1996; Project Equality Individual Achievement Award, 1997; Black Achievers in Industry Award, 1997; James K Batten Knight-Ridder Excellence Award, 1998; MO Honor Medal for distinguished Service, Univ MO Columbia School of Journalism, 2000; Millennium Award, NAACP Branch 4071, 2000; Missouri Asn Social Welfare Community Service Award, 2001; Charles E Bebb Peace Merit Award, 2002; Peace Alliance Award, Kansas City Institute, 2002; Media Award, Kansas Correctional Asn, 2002; Journalism Award, Current Peace Society, 2002; Gail & Irving Achtenburg Civil Libertarian of the Year Award, 2002; Mary Lona Diversity Award, Black Chamber of Commerce of Greater Kansas City, 2003; Soldier Award, NAACP Branch 4071 in Moberly, MO, 2004; Award for Unwavering Support & Good Work, Kansas City Federation of Teachers & School-Related Personnel, Local 691, 2005; First African American Achievement Award for Literary Contributions, United Govt Wyandotte County/Kans, KS, 2005; Courage Award, Kansas City Task Force for a Season for Nonviolence, 2005; Toast for the Children Award, 2006; Mayors Committee for People with Disabilities Media Leadership Award, 2006; Maxey DuPree Humanitarian Kindest Kansas Citian Award, 2007; Spotlight Award for Outstanding Media Coverage of Social Welfare Issues, Mo Asn Social Welfare, Kans Chapter, 2007; University of Missouri-Columbia Faculty-Alumni Award, 2007. **Special Achievements:** 100 Most Influential African-Americans in Greater Kansas City, 1992-97; Author, A Teacher's Cry: Expose the Truth About Education Today, 2004; Discovering the Real America: Toward a More Perfect Union, 2007. **Business Addr:** Vice President for Community Resources, Editorial Board Member & Columnist, The Kansas City Star, 1729 Grand Blvd, Kansas City, MO 64108, **Business Phone:** (816)234-4723.

DIUGUID, DR. LINCOLN I.
Educator, administrator. **Personal:** Born Feb 6, 1917, Lynchburg, VA; married Nancy Ruth Greenlee (deceased); children: David, Lewis, Renee & Vincent. **Educ:** WVa State Col, BS, chem, 1938; Cornell Univ, MS, chem, 1939, PhD, chem, 1945, post doctorate organic chem, 1947. **Career:** AM & N Col Pine Bluff Ark, head chem dept, 1939-43, prof chem, 1939-43, consult sci, 1949-55; Pine Bluff Arsenal, analytical chem, 1942-43; Cornell Univ, Ithaca, NY, res asst organic chem, 1945-46, res assoc organic chem, 1946-47; Stowe Teachers Col, St Louis, prof chem, 1949-55; Harris Stowe State Col, prof chem & chmn phys sci dept, 1955-82, prof emer, 1982-; Jewish Hosp, res assoc, 1959-61; Leukemia Guild Mo & Ill, res dir, 1961-63; Wash Univ St Louis, vis prof chem, 1966-68; Du-Good Chem Lab & Mfrs, dir, 1947-, pres, currently. **Orgs:** Sigma Xi; Am Chem Soc; Nat Educ Asn; Phi Kappa Phi; Am Asn Univ Prof; Mo State Teachers Asn; Asn Consult Chem & Chem Engrs; Fla Am Inst Chemists; Omega Psi Phi Frat; mem bd dir, vpres 1963, Leukemia Guild Mo & Ill. **Honors/Awds:** Man of Year Award, Omega Psi Phi 1960; Carver Civic Award, 1979; MeritAward, St Louis Am Newspaper, 1992; American Chemical Society Award,Salute Excellence, 2000. **Special Achievements:** Book: "The Use of Amalgated Aluminum as a Catalyst in the Friedd & Crafts Reaction, JACS 63", 1941; Ref, In Organic Reactions vol III 1946,"Synthetic Organic Chemistry", 1953; "Benzothiazoles II Nuclear Chlorination in the Hertz Process", 1947; "Joint Symposium on Micro Chem & Pet Industry", 1949; "Synthesis of Long Straight Chain Dicarboxylic Acidsvia the Ketene Synthesis", 1952; "Methods for the Micro Determination of Mixed Halogens & Amide Group", 1952; "Synthesis of Large Carbon Ring Ketones", 1953; "Synthesis of Plastizing Agents from the Reaction of Olefins & Formaldehyde Condensation", 1957; "Micro Determination of Sulfur& Phosphorus in Organic Compounds by Perchloric Acid Digestion"; co-authored chapter on Thygroxine Research in "Radioassay in Clinical Medicine," by CC Thomas, Springfield, Ill. **Business Addr:** President, Du-Good Chem Labs & Mfrs, 1215 S Jefferson Ave, Saint Louis, MO 63104.*

DIVINS, CHARLES
Actor, fashion model. **Personal:** Born Jan 29, 1976, Dallas, TX. **Career:** Tommy Hilfiger, model; Films: Passions; Till We Stop Having Fun, 2007; TV Series: "Family Feud", 1999; "Passions", 1999; "Half & Half", 2002; "Passion for the Game", 2005; "Ben Masters"; Episode dated 24 March 2003, 2003; "Soap Talk", 2003-06, "The Turn On", 2006; "Your LA", 2006, Dinner Party, 2008; "My Boys", 2008; TV Shows: "50 Steamiest Southern Stars", 2005; "The 19th Annual Soul Train Music Awards", 2005; "101 Incredible Celebrity Slim downs", 2006. **Honors/Awds:** Winner, Male Spokesmodel. **Special Achievements:** Featured in commercials including GQ, Glamour, Cosmopolitan, Gear;appeared in the 2003 Alaye calendar. *

DIX, HENRY
Postmaster general, manager. **Career:** US Postal Serv, clerk, 1976, postmaster, post off opers, sr mgr, dist mgr & lead exec, currently. **Business Phone:** (215)895-8000.*

DIXON, ARDENA S
Educator. **Personal:** Born Feb 24, 1927, Baltimore, MD; daughter of Albert E Simmons Sr and Sedonia Parker Simmons; married Daniel E Dixon Jr, Jan 24, 1948 (deceased); children: Deidre I (deceased), Stephanie Dixon-Barham & Eris I. **Educ:** Coppin State Col, BS, 1963; Loyola Col, MS, 1971. **Career:** Educator (retired); Baltimore City Pub Schs, classroom teacher, 1963-69, reading specialist, 1969-73; Baltimore City Dept Social Serv, social work asst II, 1965-78, SWAII, supvr, 1969-71; Baltimore City Pub Schs, edual specialist, 1973-74, asst prin, 1974-79, prin, 1979-98; Md State Foster Care Review Bd, chairperson SWII bd, 1988. **Orgs:** PSASA, 1973-; MAESA/NEA, 1973-; eastern regional dir, Phi Delta Kappa Sorority, Inc, 1983-87, chairperson, eastern region Xinos, 1992-93, supreme basileus, 1997-2001; NC-NVV, 1983-; ASCD, 1985-; Urban League Perpetual Guild, 1987-; life mem, Nat Asn Advan Colored People, 1987-; vpres, Pinochle Bugs Social/Civic Club, Baltimore Co, 1988-; NANBPWC, 1992-; pres, Perpetual Scholar Found, 1993-; Nat Sorority, Phi Delta Kappa; chairperson, Southwest Region Bd No 2, Citizen Review Bd C, Baltimore, MD, 2004. **Home Addr:** 1410 N Ellwood Ave, Baltimore, MD 21213, **Home Phone:** (410)675-1573.

DIXON, DR. ARMENDIA P.
School administrator. **Personal:** Born in Laurel, MS; daughter of L E Pierce; married Harrison D Dixon Jr; children: Harrison D III. **Educ:** Jackson State Univ, BA, Eng; Edin boro Univ PA, MEd, sch admin; Kent State Univ, PhD, curriculum, instrnl & supv, 1993. **Career:** Kent State Univ, adj prof, 1984-85; Crawford Cent Sch, asst prin, 1985-90, prin, 1992-93; Erie Pub Sch, Sec Edu, dir, 1993-; Edinboro Univ PA, Dr.Gerald P. Jackson Dept Acad Support Services, dept chair, currently. **Orgs:** Dr. Martin Luther King, Jr Scholar Found, 1980-; bd mem, United Way, Meadville, 1984-95; bd mem, Am Red Cross, 1989-95; chair, AKA Scholarships, 1989; Edinboro Univ Alumni Bd, 1990-. **Honors/Awds:** Urban Teachers Award, 1985; Citizenship Award, 1993; Numerous Service Awards.

DIXON, ARRINGTON LIGGINS
Executive. **Personal:** Born Dec 3, 1942, Washington, DC; son of James and Sallie; married Sharon Pratt, Jul 7, 1967 (divorced); children: Aimee, Drew. **Educ:** Howard Univ, BA, 1966; George Wash Univ, JD, 1972; Command & Gen Stall Col, 1989. **Career:** Univ DC, assoc prof, 1967-74; Mgt Info Syst, pres, 1967-74; Coun DC, chmn, mem, 1975-82; The Brookings Inst, guest scholar, 1983; Planning Res Corp, vpres, 1983-85; Arrington Dixon & Assoc Inc, pres, currently. **Orgs:** Bd mem, Wash Ctr, 1983-86; advan studies, adv comt, The Brookings Inst, 1983-; bd mem, Greater SE Comt Hosp Found, 1983-84, Anacostia Museum, 1984-; Chmn, Anacostia Coordr Coun; life Mem, Comt 100 Federal City. **Honors/Awds:** Congressional Appt US Air Force Acad, 1963-65; Software, Statutes & Stare Decisis Howard Univ Law Journal 420, 1967; Scholarship, George Wash Univ Law, 1969-72. **Special Achievements:** Mr. Dixon appointed, Commission by Mayor Adrian Fenty. **Military Serv:** AUS Reserves, LTC, 16 yrs. **Business Phone:** (202)889-0123.*

DIXON, DR. BENJAMIN
School administrator. **Personal:** Born Apr 18, 1939, Hartford, CT; son of Rose Carter Brown and Cue Benjamin; married Carolyn Holmes; children: Kevin, Kyle & Kimberly; married Carolyn. **Educ:** Howard Univ, BS, music educ, 1962; Harvard Univ, MAT, 1963; Univ Mass, Ed.D, 1977. **Career:** Hartford CT Pub Schs, teacher, 1963-69; Westledge Sch, West Simsburg CT,teacher & adv, 1969-71; Educ & Instr Inc, Hartford, CT, co-dir, 1971-73; Bloomfield Pub Schs CT, asst supt, 1974-87; Capitol Region Educ Coun, Windsor, CT, asst exec dir, 1987-89; The Travelers, Hartford, CT, dir Human Resouces, 1989-92; CT State Dept Educ Hartford, CT, dep comnr Educ, 1992-98; Va Tech Univ, Blacksburg, Va, vpres, off Multicultural Affairs, 1998-2006, vpres emer, 2006-. **Orgs:** Pres, CT Assoc Pupil Personnel Administr, 1983-84; bd dir, Univ MA SchEduc Alumni Assoc; sec bd trustees, Stowe Sch; mem, CT State Adv Comn Mastery Testing, Spec Educ, Gifted & Talented; treas bd dir, Hartford Dist Catholic Family Servs; gov's appointee CT Children's Trust Fund Coun; bd dir Educ & Instruction Inc; bd trustees Metro AME Zion Church; Am Mgt Asn,1989; Am Soc Personnel Admins, 1989; pres Study Comn, Coun Chief State Sch Officers, WA, DC; chair, Capitol Community-Technical Col Found, Hartford, CT; Black Men's Soc, Hartford, CT; CT Awards Excellence Bd; CT Comn African-Am Affairs; Pi Kappa Lambda Nat Honor Soc. **Honors/Awds:** Achievement & Service Award, Bloomfield Concerned Black Parents for Quality Educ, 1987. **Special Achievements:** Virginia Tech's first vice president for multicultural affairs; co-author "Stress and Burnout, A Primer Spec Educ & Special Servs Personnel", 1981. **Business Addr:** Vice President Emeritus, Office of Multicultural Affairs, Virginia Tech, 332 Burruss Hall, Blacksburg, VA 24061, **Business Phone:** (540)231-1820.

DIXON, CAROLYN D. **See FAULKNER, CAROLYN D.**

DIXON, CHERYL MCKAY
Educator. **Career:** Mus African Am Art, exec dir; Dillard Univ, Art Dept, chmn, asst prof art, art area coordr; La State Univ Mus Art, mem, currently. **Business Addr:** Member, Louisiana State University Museum of Art, Shaw Center for the Arts, 100 Lafayette St, Baton Rouge, LA 70801.

DIXON, DIANE L.
Athlete, executive. **Personal:** Born Sep 23, 1964, Brooklyn, NY; daughter of David and Beverly. **Educ:** Howard univ, B.A, sociol;

Bernard M Baruch Col, BBA, 1988; M.Ed, Loyola Col. Wash Univ, Ed.D. **Career:** George Steinbrenner, pub rels, 1989-91; Fitness consult, 1993; People Mag & Time Inc, special events, 1993-94; Diane Dixon Inc, ceo, managing Prin, currently. **Orgs:** Womens Sports Found, spec guest, 1986; Int Spec Olympics, supporter, spec guest, 1988; Multiple Sclerosis Soc, supporter, spec guest, 1990. **Honors/Awds:** Nat US Indoor Champion, 1982-92; Gold Medal, Olympics, 1984; Athlete of the Year, Metrop Athletics Cong, 1985-91; Overall Indoor Champion, MobilCorp, 1986-91; Olympics, Silver Medal, 1988; Victor Awards, Sports mens Club for the City of Hope, 1991; Athlete of the Year, Wheelchair Charities, 1991; World Indoor Champion, 1991. **Special Achievements:** Nominee of Jesse Owens Award, 1986; Am Indoor Record Holder, 1991; World Indoor Record Holder, 1991. **Business Phone:** (410)997-3340.*

DIXON, ERNEST
Football player. **Personal:** Born Oct 17, 1971, Fort Mill, SC. **Educ:** SC, BA, psychol. **Career:** Football player (retired); New Orleans Saints, linebacker, 1994-97; Oakland Raiders, 1998; Kansas City Chiefs, 1998. *

DIXON, GERALD SCOTT. See DIXON, GERALD SCOTT.

DIXON, GERALD SCOTT (GERALD SCOTT DIXON)
Football player. **Personal:** Born Jun 20, 1969, Charlotte, NC. **Educ:** Garden City Comm Col; Univ SC. **Career:** Football player (Retired); Cleveland Browns, linebacker, 1993-95; Cincinnati Bengals, 1996-97; SanDiego Chargers, 1998-2001. *

DIXON, ISAIAH, JR.
Executive. **Personal:** Born Dec 23, 1922, Baltimore, MD; married Miriam Millard. **Educ:** Howard Univ. **Career:** Gen Assembly MD, ins broker realtor delegate. **Orgs:** Maryland House Delegates, 1967-; Peoples Dem Orgn; NAACP; Kappa Alpha Psi Frat; del Dem Mini-Conv KC MO, 1974; del Dem Nat Conv New York City, 1976. **Honors/Awds:** Certificate of honor, NAACP, 1970; certificate of merit, Calverton Jr High Sch, 1972; certificate, Trng & mgt Joint Ctr for Polit Studies. **Military Serv:** AUS, pfc. *

DIXON, JAMES WALLACE EDWIN, II
Clergy. **Personal:** Born Nov 12, 1962, Houston, TX; son of James Sr and Carrol; married Linda, Nov 29, 1997. **Educ:** Oikodome Sch Biblical Studies, BA; Houston Baptist Univ; Texas Southern Univ; Houston Grad Sch Theol. **Career:** Northwest Community Baptist Church, sr pastor; GOOD GANG USA , Inc, founder & exec dir; Dominion Acad, Founder & pres, currently. **Orgs:** bd mem, Fellowship Christian Athletes; bd mem, United Way Texas Gulf Coast; pres ministers conf, pres social justice comn, Nat Baptist Conv Am; NAACP; bd dirs, Metrop Transit Auth; founder, James Dixon Ministries Inc; bd mem, METRO Univ Corridor Details & Drawings; Third VPres, NAACP Houston Br Bd Mems. **Honors/Awds:** Humanitarian Award, Prairie View A & M Univ, 1986; TX Gospel Music Awards, Outstanding Community Serv; Olympic Games Touchbearer, 1996. **Business Addr:** President, Founder, Dominion Academy, 835 Lee Ave Sw, Leesburg, VA 20175, **Business Phone:** (703)737-0157.*

DIXON, JIMMY
Government official, chairperson. **Personal:** Born Dec 9, 1943, Devereux, GA; divorced; children: Glenda, Thaddeus & Taranda. **Educ:** Ga Mil, 1972, 1974, 1976; Univ Ga, attended 1978; Ga Col, attended 1981. **Career:** Cent St Hosp, supvr, 1964-74; Sparta Parks & Recreation, dir, 1975-79; Hancock County Bd Educ, chmn, 1978-; Rheem Air Condition Div, storekeeper, 1979-. **Orgs:** Supt Jones Chapel AME Sunday Sch, 1971-; Jones Chapel AME Steward Bd, 1974-, Ga Sch Bd Asn, 1975-; Stolkin Temple 22, 1976-; Lebar Consistory 28, 1976; GSBA Positions & Resolutions Comn, 1979-; comt mem, Dem Party Ga, 1982-85; CAES Adv Coun, Univ Ga. **Honors/Awds:** Appreciation Plaque Blackstone, Shrine Club, 1977. **Home Addr:** 728 Reynolds Cemetary Rd, Sparta, GA 31087.

DIXON, JOHN FREDERICK
Marketing executive. **Personal:** Born Feb 19, 1949, Boston, MA. **Educ:** Howard Univ, BA, 1971; Columbia Univ Grad Bus Sch, MBA, 1973; Columbia Univ Teacher's Col, PhD. **Career:** Essence Commun Inc, mkt & res serv dir; US Dept Agr, agr mkt specialist, 1971; fel, Columbia Univ, 1971-73; Xerox Corp, sales rep, 1973-74; Stand Brands Inc, asst prod mgr, 1974-76; Red-T Productions, co-founder, 1975-; Black Sports Mag, mkt dir, 1976-78. **Orgs:** World mem Int House, 1971-; African-Am Inst, 1973-; Alliance Francaise-French Inst, 1975-78; Consult, Africa Mag, 1976; consult, Horn of Africa Mag, 1977-78; Am Mkt Asn, 1978-; Advert Res Found, 1978-; Media Res Dirs Asn 1979-; NAACP, 1979-. **Honors/Awds:** co-inventor "Claim to Fame" Black History Game, 1977; pub "Pony Goes After Young Blacks with 'follow the Leader' Tack", 1977; creator "Battle of New Orleans" 64-page fight Prog, Muhammad Ali vs Leon Spinks, 1978; established In-House Essential Media Ad Agency Essence Mag; distinguished serv Award, Harlem Teams for Self-Help, 1979. *

DIXON, JOHN M.
Executive, chairperson. **Personal:** Born Jan 25, 1938, Chicago, IL; divorced; children: Kwane Dubois. **Educ:** Univ MT, BS, 1959; New England Sch Law, JD, 1966; Boston Univ, MBA, 1976. **Career:** Sonesta NY, regional sales mgr, 1968-70; Sheraton Mtr Inns, dir promotion, 1970-73; Hyatt Regency O'Hare, exec asst mgr, 1973; Burlingame CA, gen mgr, 1973; Hyatt Regency, resident mgr, 1974-; Hyatt Regency Cambridge, gen mgr, 1975-; J.W. Marriott Hotel, owner, Wash; Univ Md, Sch Bus & Technol, Dept Hotel & Restaurant Mgt,chmn, 2000-. **Honors/Awds:** Distinguished Alumni Awards, Univ Montana, 1999. **Military Serv:** AUS, 1962-64. **Business Addr:** Chairman, Department of Hotel and Restaurant Management, University of Maryland Eastern Shore, Princess Anne, **Business Phone:** (410)651-2200.

DIXON, JULIUS B.
Executive. **Career:** Astra Zeneca LP, Cardiovasular Therapeut Area, regional sales dir, area sales dir, 2003. *

DIXON, LEON MARTIN
Health services administrator, physician. **Personal:** Born Nov 12, 1927, Brooklyn, NY; son of Leon M and Helen Moody; married Alfonso Baxter; children: Deborah, Carolyn Knight, Cynthia, Suzanne, Leon II. **Educ:** Howard Univ, BS, 1949, MD, 1953. **Career:** Med/Cardiol Colorado Univ Sch Med, instr, 1963-65; US Walson Army Hosp, hosp comdr, 1973-77; Reynolds Metals Co, dir Macmillan Med Ctr, 1977-97; Commonwealth Occup Safety & Health Asns, staff physician, currently. **Orgs:** Consultation Disaster Planning, Reynolds Metal, 1977-91; Cardiol Med First Army Area, 1965-69; chmn, Pub Health Prevention Med Richmond Acad Med, 1980-81; Chesterfield County Drug Abuse Adv Comn, 1979-80; Med Soc Va. **Honors/Awds:** Physician for Astronantical Program, Gemini Mercury, NASA, 1965-69; articles published in Physiology of Heart Meningitis, Congenital Heart Disease, Chemotherapy of Tumors. **Military Serv:** AUS col; Legion of Merit Two Oak Leaf Clusters 1969, 1971, 1977. **Business Addr:** Staff Physician, Commonwealth Occupational Safety & Health Associations, 3800 Meadow Dale Blvd, Richmond, VA 23234-5750.*

DIXON, LEONARD BILL
Executive. **Personal:** Born Aug 1, 1956, Albany, GA; son of Clarence and Ruby; married Adrian, May 25, 1980; children: Joseph & Rosalind. **Educ:** Southwest Baptist Univ, BA, sociol & psychol, 1980; Nova Univ, masters degree, child & youth care admin, 1990; State Fair Community Col, Asn Arts Degree, educ. **Career:** Dept Health & Rehab Servs, group leader, 1980-82, supvr, 1982-85, supt, 1985-90; Dep Juv Justice Serv, prog opers adminr, 1990-95; Wayne County Community Col, adj prof, 1995-; Dept Community Justice, exec dir, 1995-2004; Mich Dept Human Serv, Bur Juv Justice, dir, currently. **Orgs:** Nat Juv Detention Asn; Am Correctional Asn; adj staff mem, Nova Univ; Nat Juv Jus Group-Children's Defense Fund; EEOC-Dade County; The Wellington Group; ACA Comt Florida District XI; Community Tree House, Detroit Michigan. **Special Achievements:** First African-American president of the National Juvenile Detention Association (NJDA); US Congressional Senators, Juv Jus Reform Paper Presentor; Southwest Baptist University, MO, Athletic Scholarship; All American High School Basketball Team. **Business Addr:** Director, Department of Human Services, Bureau of Juvenile Justice, PO Box 30037, Lansing, MI 48909, **Business Phone:** (517)373-2035.

DIXON, DR. LOUIS TENNYSON
Manager. **Personal:** Born Dec 13, 1941; son of Eitel V and Enid L; married Lora M; children: Michael. **Educ:** Howard Univ, BS 1968; Johns Hopkins Univ, PhD 1973. **Career:** Ford Motor Co, prin res scientist, sr resscientist, 1973-76, mgr chem dept, 1976-78, prin staff engr, 1978-86, engineering assoc, l986-89, mgr; pres, Nat Coop Lab Accreditation. **Orgs:** Am Chem Soc; Soc Automotive Engrs; Soc Mfg Engrs; Standards Engineering Soc; Vpres, Int Club, 1966-67; chmn, People-To-People, 1967-68; pres, Phi Lambda Upsilon 1972-73; SAE Int, currently. **Honors/Awds:** Publ, "Infrared Studies of Isotope Effects for Hydrogen Absorption on Zinc Oxide" Journal of Amer Chem Soc 1972; "The Nature of Molecular Hydrogen Absorbed on Zinc Oxide" Journal of Physical Chem 1973; "Infrared Active Species of Hydrogen Absorbed by Alumina-Supported Platium" Journal of Catalysis 1975; "Hydrogen Absorption by Alumina-Supported Supported Platinum" Journal of Catalysis 1975; "Foaming & Air Entrainment in Automatic Transmission Fluids" Soc of Auto Engr 1976; "Fuel Economy -Contributor of the Rear Axle Lubricant" Soc Auto Engr 1977. **Business Addr:** Chairman, Finance Committee, SAE International, 400 Commonwealth Dr, Warrendale, PA 15096-0001.

DIXON, MARGARET A
Association executive, teacher, president (organization). **Personal:** Born Jan 1, 1920, Columbia, SC; married Octavius; children: Kevin, Karen & Edith. **Educ:** Allen Univ, BS, educ; Hunter Col, Mass; NYU, Mass; Fordham Univ, prof dipl educ leadership; Nova Southeastern Univ, PhD. **Career:** New York Sch, teacher, 1954-80; Brooklyn Col Teacher Educ prog, supv prin; Brooklyn Col, supv prin; SC State Dept Educ, consult, 1981-86; Ford Found Fel; US Office Educ graduate fel; Allen Univ, assoc prof & dir teacher educ, 1981-86; Am Assn of Retired Persons, pres, 1996-. **Orgs:** AARP, Minority Affairs Initiative, spokesperson, 1988-92, vpres, 1992-94, pres-elect, 1994-96; AARP Exec & Finance Comm, nat legis coun, Andrus Found; bd strategic planning comm; Nat Retired Teachers Asn Task Force; literacy tutor; vol, Meals-on-Wheels; bd mem, Am Asn Homes & Servs for the Aging, 1998-. **Honors/Awds:** Living Legacy Award for Outstanding Community Serv, Delta Sigma Theta; Alumni Achievement Award, Fordham Univ; Alumni Hall of Fame, Hunter Col; Living Legacy Award, Nat Caucus & Ctr on Black Aged; Nation Builder Award, Natl Black Caucus of State Legislators; Hon Doctor of Humane Letters, Hunter Col, 1998; Women of Courage and Distinction Award, Nat Asn Colored Women's Clubs Inc. **Special Achievements:** First African-Am pres of AARP.

DIXON, ORA WRIGHT
Administrator. **Career:** US Fish & Wildlife Serv, Conserv Training Ctr, Nat Girl Scout coordr & course leader div educ outreach, currently. **Orgs:** US Environ Protection Agency.

DIXON, RAYMOND
Chief executive officer. **Career:** Family Automobile Group, chief exec officer, 1996-. **Business Addr:** Chief Executive Officer, Family Automotive Group, 33395 Camino Capistrano, San Juan Capistrano, CA 92675, **Business Phone:** (949)493-4100.*

DIXON, RICHARD CLAY
Government official, mayor, politician. **Career:** City Dayton, OH, city comnr, mayor, 1987-93; Ohio Dem party, politician. **Orgs:** Trustee, Greater Dayton Reg Transit Authority; adv coun, Great Pk Conservancy. **Special Achievements:** Second African-American person to serve as mayor of Dayton.

DIXON, RICHARD NATHANIEL
State government official. **Personal:** Born Apr 17, 1938, Westminster, MD; married Grayson Lee; children: Timothy A & Richard N. **Educ:** Morgan State Col, BS, 1960, MBA, 1975. **Career:** Provident Hosp, hosp admin, 1968-69; Morgan State Univ, asst prof sch bus,1976-; Merrill Lynch, delegate & stock broker, asst vpres; Md Dept Treas,treas, 1996-02. **Orgs:** Bd Educ, 1970-78; pres, former stud, Robert M Sch, 1970; secy, Md Asn Bd Educ, 1973-74; chair, Nat Sch Bds Conv, 1974; Morgan State Univ Found,1975-; pres & first black County Sch Bd, 1975-76; trustee, Middle State Asn Cols & Schs; chmn, Budget & Audit Comn; House Delegates, Md HousePensions; chmn, Joint Comt Pensions, Md House Delegates; chair, CapitalDebt Affordability Comt, 1996-02; Md Agr Land Preservation Found, 1996-02;Bd Pub Works, 1996-02; Bd State Canvassers, 1996-02; Gov's Salary Comn,1996-02; Hall Recs Comn, 1996-02; Md Health & Higher Educ FacilsAuthority, 1996-02; Md Higher Educ Investment Prog Bd, 1997-02; AircraftOwners & Pilots Asn. **Honors/Awds:** First black Board of Education; first black president of County School-Board of Maryland; selected top 5 of 50 new delegates, 1984; selected tobe among top 25 members, House of Delegates; Honorary Doctor of Laws,Western Md Col, 1988; Honorary Doctor of Public Service, Carroll CountyCommunity Col, 1994; honorary degrees, Villa Julie Col & Morgan StateUniv, 1997; First Citizen Award, Md Senate, 2002. **Special Achievements:** First African American state treasurer of Maryland; Future Black Leader inBaltimore, Baltimore Sunpapers, 1979. **Military Serv:** AUS, capt med serv corps, 1960-68. *

DIXON, RODRICK
Singer, composer. **Personal:** Born Jan 1, 1967?. **Educ:** Mannes Col Music, New York, BA, MA. **Career:** Lyric Opera Chicago, performer; Portland Opera, performer; Virginia Opera, performer; Columbus Opera, performer; Album: In Concert; Follow the Star; Sacred Land; Three Mo Tenors, 2001; Cook, Dixon & Young Volume One, 2005; Liam Lawtons Sacred Land, 2006. **Honors/Awds:** Richard F. Gold Career Grant, Shoshana Found; "Tenor of the Year" Award, Mary Dawson Art Guild. **Special Achievements:** Appeared on Great Performances, PBS, 2001; earned rave reviews for his Dame Myra Hess Memorial Concert broadcast honoring Roland Hayes on WFMT-FM Chicago. **Business Phone:** (301)423-6505.

DIXON, RONNIE CHRISTOPHER
Football player. **Personal:** Born May 10, 1971, Clinton, NC. **Educ:** Univ Cincinnati, criminal justice. **Career:** New Orleans Saints, defensive tackle, 1993; Philadelphia Eagles, 1995-96; New York Jets, 1997; Kans City Chiefs, 1998.

DIXON, DR. RUTH F.
Educator. **Personal:** Born Sep 22, 1931, Camden, NJ; married George Dixon Jr; children: Cheryl Yvette & Brian Duane. **Educ:** Rowan Univ, NJ, BS, 1953, MA, 1965; Pa, EdD, 1977. **Career:** Educator (retired); Camden City Schs, elem & sec teacher, admin; NJ St Dept Educ, supvr; Rutgers Univ, assoc prof educ, Acad Found Dept, prof &chair, 1971-98. **Orgs:** Educ consult, St Col, 1965-71; State Asn Adult Educ, 1965-; exec bd, Black Peoples Unity Movement, 1973-; exec bd, educ opport fund prog, 1971-; mayors adv coun, 1974-; bd educ, Lay Comn, 1972-; Kappa Delta Pi, 1976; bd trustees, Camden City Col, 1984; coun, Camden City Pvt Indust, 1983, Nat Asn Notaries, 1984; bd dir, Soc Educ & Scholars, 1984; NJ AsnBlack Educrs, 1978-, Our Lady Lourdes Commuity Adv Comt, 1984; BPUM Child Develop Ctrs Adv

Comt, 1983; dir, Distinguished Am Educ & Community Serv,1980; Cable Adv Bd, City Spokane, 2003-06. **Honors/Awds:** Community Award, BPUM-EDC, 1973; Kappa Delta Pi; BPUM Special Award for Outstanding Education, 1976; Soc Educ & Sch, Phi Delta Kappa Nat HonorSoc, 1975; Pi Lambda Theta Nat Honor Soc, 1975; prof emerita, Rutgers Univ. *

DIXON, SHEILA
Government official. **Personal:** Born Dec 27, 1953, Baltimore, MD; daughter of Phillip Dixon Sr and Winona; married Thomas Hampton, Sep 3, 1986; children: Joshua & Jasmine. **Educ:** Towson State Univ, BA, Early Childhood Educ, 1976; Johns Hopkins Univ, MS, Educ Mgt, 1985. **Career:** Tillman Learning Ctr, adult learning specialist, 1983-84; Quazar Int, int sales mgr, 1983-84; Md Dept Bus & Econ Develop, int trade specialist, 1986-99; Dem State Cent Comt, mem, 40th legis dist, 1986; Baltimore City Coun, mem, 4th dist, 1987-99, pres, 1999-2007, mayor, 2007-. **Orgs:** Fel, Urban Health Initiative; Baltimore City Tobacco Community Health Coalition; lifetime mem, NAACP; Afr-Am Women's Caucus; hon chair, HERO AIDS WALK; Nat Black Caucus Elected Officials; co-founder Bethel AME Food Coop; Retired Sr Volunteers Prog Adv Coun. **Honors/Awds:** Maryland's Top 100 Women, Warfield's Bus Rec, 1996 & 1999; Most Influential Baltimoreans, Baltimore Bus J, 2000; Service Above Self Award, Rotary Club, 2001; Founder's Award, David Horner Black Educ AIDS Proj, 2001. **Special Achievements:** Studied karate for 15 years, First degree Black Belt; studied photography; collector of int art; First African-Am woman ever elected to the position of Baltimore City Coun Pres. **Business Addr:** Mayor, Baltimore City Council, City Hall Rm 250 100 N Holliday St, Baltimore, MD 21202, **Business Phone:** (410)396-3835.

DIXON, TAMECKA MICHELLE
Basketball player. **Personal:** Born Dec 14, 1975, Linden, NJ; daughter of Russell. **Educ:** Univ Kans, BA, child psychol, 1998. **Career:** Istanbul; Turkey; Los Angeles Sparks, guard, 1997-05; Houston comets, 2006-08; Indiana Fever, 2009-. **Honors/Awds:** Phillips 66 Big Eight All-Acad hon mention, 1994; Bronze Medal, US Olympic Festival, 1994; Asc Press All-Am hon, 1996; Big Eight Player of the Yr,1996; Big 12 Conf Player of the Yr, 1997, Gold Medal, FIBA World Championship, 2002; Gold Medal, Opals World Challenge, 2002. *

DIXON, TOM L.
Educator. **Personal:** Born Jan 29, 1932, Shreveport, LA; married Sarah Hunter; children: Abigail & Cleon. **Educ:** Gramblins State Univ, BS, 1959; Bradley Univ, MS, 1968; Prairie View A&M Univ. **Career:** Walnut Hill High Sch, teacher, 1959; JS Clark Jr High Sch, teacher, 1960-61; Linear High Sch, teacher, 1961-71; Green Oaks High Sch, teacher; Caddo Parish Sch Bd, supr Voc Educ. **Orgs:** Caddo Educ Asn; LA Educ Asn; Nat Educ Asn; chmn, LA Indust Arts Conf, 1976; chmn Banquet LTAA, 1975; Indust Arts Curriculum Planning Comn; Am Indust Arts Asn; pres, North Shreveport Kiwanis Club, 1973-74; pres, Phi Beta Sigma Frat; bd dir, YMCA. **Honors/Awds:** Am Legion Indust Arts Teacher Award, North western State Univ, 1968-69; Shreveport Times Educator of the Year Award; Kiwanis Club Award Outstanding Leadership. **Special Achievements:** First black president of North Shreveport Kiwanis Club. **Military Serv:** AUS, corpl, 1953-55. **Business Addr:** Supervisor, Caddo Parish School Board, PO Box 37000, Shreveport, LA 71103.*

DIXON, TYNNA G
Executive. **Personal:** Born Jul 16, 1969, Temple, TX; daughter of M C and Sandra Thomas; divorced; children: Andre & Daylan. **Educ:** Temple Col, attended 1989; Univ Mary Hardin Baylor, attended 1995. **Career:** First Natl Bank, data entry/customer service rep, 1989-93; TX Dept of Human Services, eligibility specialist, 1993-95; TX Workforce Comm, case mgr, 1995-97; Cent Tex Worforce Ctr, workforce develop specialist, 1997-. **Orgs:** Temple High South Prep Advy Cou, 1997-; Temple Health & Human Services, 1997-; Bell County Transportation Alliance, 1997-; Child Care mgt Adv Coun, 1998-99; Ebony Cult Soc, 1998-; Nat Asn Advan Colored People, 1999-2000. **Business Addr:** Workforce Development Specialist, Cent Tex Workforce Ctr, 102 E Central Ave Suite 300, Temple, TX 76501, **Business Phone:** (254)771-2555.

DIXON, VALENA ALICE
Executive, administrator. **Personal:** Born Jan 11, 1953, Philadelphia, PA; daughter of James and Alice; children: James. **Educ:** St Joseph Univ; Univ South Ala, attended 1976; Westchester State Univ, BSEd, 1974; Temple Univ, attended 1979. **Career:** Mobile County Pub Schs, ed, 1974-79; Reading Sch Dist, ed, 1974-79; Urban League, Philadelphia Chapter, employ counr, 1979-81; Temple Univ, cot resource spt, 1981-82; Crisis Intervention Network Inc, prog mgr, 1982-87; Greater Media Cable Philadelphia, community rels mgr, 1987-92; Philadelphia Housing Authority, pub affairs dir, 1992-98; Richmond Redevelopment & Housing Authority, commun dir, currently. **Orgs:** Bd mem, Ctr for Literacy, 1990-94; Philadelphia Pub Rels Asn, 1990-; Philadelphia Asn Black Journalists, 1990-93; Nat Black Media Coalition, 1990-92; bd mem, Korean & Am Friendship Asn, 1991-; pres, Am Women Radio & TV, Philadelphia Chapter, 1992-; Nat Forum Black Pub Adminr, 1992-; Linda Creed Breast Cancer Found, 1993-. **Honors/Awds:** Community Service, CORPP, 1989; Community Service Awards, Mayor's off Community Ser, 1989-91; Outstanding Community Service, NCP, 1991; Community Service Award, WUSL Radio, 1993; Recognition, Nat Polit Cong Black Women. **Home Addr:** 205 Beaufont Ct, Richmond, VA 23225-5811. **Business Addr:** Communications Director, Richmond Redevelopment & Housing Authority, 901 Chamberlayne Pkwy, PO Box 26887, Richmond, VA 23261-6887.

DIXON, WILLIAM R.
Composer, musician. **Personal:** Born Oct 5, 1925, Nantucket, MA; son of William Robert and Louise Wade; divorced; children: William Jr, Claudia Gayle & William II. **Educ:** Hartnette Conserv Music, diploma, 1951. **Career:** UN Secretariat NYC, clerk int civil servant, 1956-62; NYC, freelance musician composer, 1962-67; Columbia Univ Teachers Col, 1967-70; George Wash Univ, composer-in-residence, 1967; Conserv Univ Streets NYC, dir, 1967-68; Ohio State Univ, guest artist in residence, 1967; Bennington Col VT, mem fac dept dance, 1968-95, chmn, black music div, 1973-85; vis prof, Univ Wis Madison, 1971-72; lectr painting & music, Museum Modern Art Verona, Italy, 1982; Bill Dixon Inc, founder, currently; recordings: "November 1981", 1981; "Bill Dixon: 1970-73", 1982; "Collection", 1985; "Thoughts", 1987; "Son of Sisyphus", 1990;" Vade Mecum", 1994: "The Enchanted Messenger", 1996; "VADE Mecum II", 1997; "Papyrus", 1999; "Berlin Abbozzi", 2000; "Odyssey:The Art of the Trumpet", 2001; Victo CD082, 2002; Search of a Sound:Darfur. Aum Fidelity, 2008. **Orgs:** Found UN Jazz Soc NYC; arch Jazz Composers Guild Performance Contemp Am Black Music; organizer, OctoberRevolution: a Concert Series; Bill Dixon 7-Tette, 1963; Intents &Purposes: The Bill Dixon Orchestra, 1967; For Franz, 1976; New MusicSecond Wave, 1979; Bill Dixon in Italy, 1980; considerations 1 & 2 BillDixon 1980, 1982; Bill Dixon in the Labrinth, 1983; paintings exhibitedFerrari Gallery Verona, Italy, 1982; exhibited paintings, MultimediaContemp Art Gallery Brescia, Italy, 1982; Am Fedn Musicians; adv comm mem,New Eng Found Arts, 1988-91; panel mem, Nat Endowment Arts, 1990-; fel,Vermont Acad Arts & Sci. **Honors/Awds:** Hon mem, Duke Ellington Soc; Musician of the Year, Jazz Mag, 1976;Giancarlo Testoni Award, 1981; Jazz Pioneer Award, Broadcast Music Inc,1984; Distinguished Visitor in the Arts, Middlebur Col, 1986. **Special Achievements:** Subject in Documentary Film, Imagine The Sound, Toronto Canada, 1982,Conducted Orchestra Workshop in: Vienna, Austria, 1985, author of L'Opera:A Collection of Writings and Letters, Etc, 1986, International Trumpet-Guild Recording: VADE MECUm, 1994, Exhibition of Lithographs, NYC, 1988,Israel, 1990, Pori Finland, 1991, Chittenden Bank, Bennington VT, 1994-95,Workshop in Improvisation/Music, Federal Republic of Germany, 1990,Exhibition of Paintings, Ufer Palast, Furth, Nurembert, Germany, 1990,Trumpet Soloist, Celebration Orchestra, Conducted by Tony Oxley, Berlin,1994, Master Class in Improvisation/Music, Villeurbanne, France, 1994,Exhibition of Lithographs in Villeurbanne, France, 1994, Exhibition ofLithographs, Skoto Gallery, NYC, 1996, composed & conducted "Index: A Workfor the Orchestra," Visions Orchestra, 2000, three lithographs exhibitedat Total Music Events, Berlin, Germany, Nov 2001, conducted Master Classin Music performance, New School Univ, NYC, spring 2001, concert,Victoriaville, Canada, recording issued with his paintings on front & backcovers, 2002, "Qwhortette No 3," composition performed in Vienna, 2002,two concerts with Cecil Tayolr & Tony Oxley, Paris, France, 2002, listedin Who's Who in America, Who's Who Among Black Americans. **Military Serv:** AUS, 1944-46. **Business Addr:** Founder, Bill Dixon Inc, PO Box 215, North Bennington, VT 05257-0215, **Business Phone:** (802)442-4509.

DIXON, WILLIE L.
Government official. **Career:** Teledyne-Brown Corp, Jackson, supvr; Wash County Dist 5, comnr, 1992-. **Orgs:** Mobile Community Action Bd Dirs; ACCA Transportation Bd. **Business Addr:** Commissioner, Washington County District 5, Hwy 43, PO Box 146, Wagarville, AL 36585, **Business Phone:** (251)246-6670.*

DIXON, YVONNE T
Government official, executive. **Personal:** Born in Washington, DC. **Educ:** Earlham Col, BS, 1971; New York Univ Sch Law, JD, 1974. **Career:** Nat Labor Rels Bd, atty advisor, spec asst to gen coun, spec coun to gen coun, dep asst gen coun, asst gen coun, actg dep gen coun, 1992-93, Off Appeals, dir, currently. **Special Achievements:** First African-American woman to head NLRB'S Office of Appeals. **Business Addr:** Director, National Labor relations Board, 1099 14th St, Washington, DC 20570-0001, **Business Phone:** (202)273-3760.

DOAN, LURITA
Executive, founder (originator). **Personal:** Born Jan 4, 1958. **Educ:** Vassar Col, eng; Univ Tennessee, Knoxville, MA, renaissance lit, 1983. **Career:** Col, La & Va,adj prof, 1984; Unisys, technician, 1986; New Technol Mgt Inc, pres, founder & cheif exec officer, 1990-; US Gen Serv Admin, adminr, 2006. **Orgs:** Enterprising Women Soc; Am Constitution Soc; Security Indust Asn; Am Red Cross; Nat Women Bus Ctr, DC; Rape Crisis Ctr; United Negro Col Found; Am Women Bus Ctrs; Cystic Fibrosis Found; Whitman Walker Clinic; Vassar Col Bd Trustees; Shakespeare Theatre Wash, DC Bd Trustees; The Comt 200; Coun Competitiveness; Nat Asn Women Bus Owners; Nat Asn Female Exec; Women Technol Int; Minority Bus Network; Northern Va Technol Coun. **Special Achievements:** First woman to hold the position in US Gen Admin; first African Americans to integrate into the private school system in New Orleans in the early 1960s; nominated by President George W. Bush to lead the GSA. **Business Phone:** (703)390-5560.*

DOANES-BERGIN, SHARYN F
Executive. **Personal:** Born in Atlanta, GA; daughter of Onzelo Doanes; married Michael; children: Jennifer & Jessica. **Educ:** Paine Col, BA, 1969; Atlanta Law Sch, JD, 1978, ML, 1979; Cent Mich Univ, MPA, 1983. **Career:** Executive (retired); Honeywell Info Syst, employee rels mgr; NY Times Regional Newspaper Group, Atlanta, employee rels mgr; Atlanta Ballet Inc, vpres human resources. **Orgs:** Ga Exec Women, 1980-87; vpres, Paine Col Alumni, 1982-87; vpres, Ga Leukemia Soc, 1984-87; trustee, Paine Col, 1983-88; Odyssey, 1985-. **Honors/Awds:** Black Achiever Award, Harlem YMCA, 1992. **Home Phone:** (404)964-9921.

DOBARD, RAYMOND G
Educator. **Educ:** Xavier Univ, La, BA, 1970; Johns Hopkins Univ, MA, 1973, PhD, hist art, 1975. **Career:** Howard Univ, Col Arts & Sci, prof art, currently; Univ Nebraska, adj fac mem & Quilt Study Ctr fel, currently. **Orgs:** Founding mem, Bd Dirs, Va Quilt Mus, Harrisonburg, 1992-96; adv bd, Textile Mus, Wash, DC, 1993-96; adv bd, Int Quilt Study Ctr, UNiv Nebr, Lincoln, 1997-98; adv, New African Am Art Museum, Baltimore, MD, currently. **Honors/Awds:** Recipient of several fellowships from such granting organizations including Johns Hopkins Univ, John Hay Whitney Found & Leopold Schepp Found; Thomas Mann Fellowship as Artist-in-Residence, city Lubeck, Ger, 1986. **Special Achievements:** Co author: Hidden In Plain View: A Secret Story of Quilts and the Underground Railroad, 1999; appeared on C-Span Book TV, March 2002; Numerous publications including "A Knowing Hands: Binding Heritage in African American Quilts", 2001; "Signs and Symbols", 2003. **Business Addr:** Professor, Howard University, Art Department, 2455 6th St NW, Washington, DC 20059, **Business Phone:** (202)806-7047.

DOBBINS, LUCILLE R.
Executive. **Personal:** Married George; children: Diane. **Educ:** Roosevelt Univ, acct, 1968; Ill Cert Pub Acct Cert, 1970. **Career:** Hyde Park Fed Savings & Loan, asst treas, 1963-69; Blackman Kallick & Co, auditor, 1969-73; Harris Trust & Savings Bank, vpres, 1974-84; City Chicago Dept Plng, dep comnr, 1984-86; City Chicago Mayor's Off, chief financial planning officer; Resolution Resources, pres, currently. **Orgs:** Nat Soc Cert Pub Acct, Ill Soc Cert Pub Acct; nat adv bd, Black Career Women Inc, Lambda Alpha Intl Hon Land Econ Soc. **Honors/Awds:** Entrepreneur of the Year, 1994. *

DOBBS, DR. JOHN WESLEY
Educator. **Personal:** Born Oct 8, 1931, Grenada, MS; married Mildred; children: Kiley & Kelly. **Educ:** Western Mich Univ, BA, 1954; Wayne State Univ, ME, 1960; Mich State Univ,PhD, 1975. **Career:** Hemp seatd Pub Schs, supvr schs; Mich Dept Educ, asst supt; Detroit Sch Syst, teacher, counr, asst prin, prin. **Orgs:** St Adv Coun Equal Educ Opportunity; St Task Force Coun Guid; coordr, Task Force Out of Sch Out of Work Youth; rep, Mich Comn Criminal Justice; ad com, Mich Hum Serv Network; Am Asn Sch Adminr; Nat Asn Advan Colored People; Urban League; Nat Alliance Black Sch Educr; Eastern Mich Univ; bd dir, Metro Detroit Youth Found. **Honors/Awds:** President Award, Nat Alliance Black Sch Educr; Outstanding Admin Award,Detroit Soc Black Educr; Resolution of Appreciation, State Mich Concurrent House of Rep, 1983; Outstanding Eductor, Leader & Humanitarian Award, Hemp stead, NY Bd Educ, 1986; Distinguish Educator in Support of Black Children Award Leadership & Training Inst Hemp stead, 1986; Mayor's Proclamation Outstanding Community Leader Village of Hemp stead Long Island, 1986. **Military Serv:** AUS, spec-5, 1956-58. **Home Addr:** 1448 Farwood Dr, East Lansing, MI 48823, **Home Phone:** (517)351-7478. *

DOBBS, MATTIWILDA
Educator, opera singer. **Personal:** Born Jul 11, 1925, Atlanta, GA; daughter of John Wesley and Irene; married Bengt Janzon, Dec 23, 1957 (deceased); married Luis Rodriguez (deceased). **Educ:** Spelman Col, Atlanta, GA, BA (with honors) 1946; Teachers Col, Columbia, MA, 1948; studied voice under Mme Lotte Leham, New York City, 1946-50; Mannes Music Col, 1948-49; Berkshire Music Festival, 1949; studied French music Pierre Bernac, Paris, France, 1950-52. **Career:** Opera singer, educator (retired); Appeared Dutch Opera Holland Festival, 1952; numerous recitals Paris, Stockholm, Holland, & La Scala, 1953; concerts Scandinavia, Austria, England, France, Italy & Belgium; command performance, Covent Garden, London, 1954; concert tour, US, 1954; concert tour, Australia, 1955, 1959, 1972; concert tour, Israel, 1957, 1959; concert tour, USSR, 1959; concert tour, Hamburg State Opera, 1961-62; Amoperatic debut, San Francisco Opera, 1955; Metrop Opera debut, 1956; recitals Philadephia, PA, NC, Fla, Al, Ga, La, New York City, & the Midwest, 1972-75;

Univ Tex, performing voice prof, 1973-74; Howard Univ, prof voice; Univ IL Champaign-Urbana, fac mem; Spelman Col, artist-in-residence; released recs, most recent, Arias & Songs, 2000. **Orgs:** Metropolitan Opera Asn, Order N Star Sweden, 1954. **Honors/Awds:** Recipient, second prize, Marian Anderson Award, 1947; John Hay Whitney Fellowship Award, Paris 1950; first prize, Int Competition Music, Geneva Conservatory Music, 1951; James Weldon Johnson Award Fine Arts, Nat Asn Adv Colored People, 1983; Spelman Col, honorary doctor fine arts degree. **Special Achievements:** Libr Cong, exhibit about career; First African American to sing a romantic lead at the Metropolitan Opera; First African American to sing at La Scalain Milan, Italy; First African American faculty on the faculty of University of Texas. **Home Phone:** (703)892-5234.

DOBSON, BYRON EUGENE
Journalist, editor. **Personal:** Born Jan 26, 1957, Easton, MD; son of William Edward and Elizabeth Young. **Educ:** Bowie State Univ, Bowie, MD, BA, communs, 1979; Univ Ariz, Ed Prog, Minority Journalists, grad fel, 1985. **Career:** WEMD-Radio, Easton, MD, news asst, 1979-80; Boca Raton News, Boca Raton, FL, reporter, asst city ed, city ed, 1980-90; Tallahassee Democrat, Tallahassee, FL, night city ed, 1990-, religion ed, community news ed, metro ed, currently. **Orgs:** Past pres, charter mem, Palm Beach Asn Black Journalists, 1988-90; Nat Asn Black Journalists, 1990-; Kappa Alpha Psi Fraternity Inc, 1984-; Blacks Communs, 1990-. **Honors/Awds:** Featured in The Bulletin, Minorities in the Newsroom, May-June, 1987; Corene J Elam Communications Award, Bowie State Univ, 1979. **Home Phone:** (850)942-6916. **Business Addr:** Community News Editor, The Tallahassee Democrat, 277 N Magnolia Dr, PO Box 990, Tallahassee, FL 32301, **Business Phone:** (850)599-2100.

DOBSON, DOROTHY ANN
Social worker. **Personal:** Born May 10, 1934, Chester, VA; daughter of Alfred and Julia Morton; married James, Oct 16, 1957; children: Jacquelyn, Kimberley & Gina. **Educ:** NC A&T State Univ, Greensboro, NC, BS, 1957. **Career:** Social worker (retired); Monroe County Dept Social Serv, Rochester, NY, adult protection caseworker, 1958-89. **Orgs:** Pres, Jack & Jill Am Inc, 1964-66; bd dirs & comt, Girl Scouts Genesee Alley, 1970-80; bd dirs, United Way Rochester, eval comt, 1975-; bd dirs, YWCA, 1975-81; pres, NC A&T Alumni Asn, 1980-82; pres & founder, Greater Rochester AARP, 1989-; deleg, NY State, AARP Biennial Conv, San Antonio, 1992; deleg, Black Cath Cong, New Orleans, 1992. **Honors/Awds:** Urban League of Rochester Community Service Award, 1977; Monroe County Human Relations Community Services, 1982; Black Catholic Family Award, 1983; Volunteer Service Award United Way of Rochester, 1984; Dedicated Service Award NC A&T State University, 1987. **Business Addr:** Social Worker, c/o Emmelyn Logan-Baldwin, 171 State St, Rochester, NY 14614.

DOBY, ALLEN E
Government official, executive director. **Personal:** Born Oct 26, 1934, Mississippi; son of A Doby; married LaFaye Ealy. **Educ:** Calif State Univ, Northridge, BS, 1973; MPA prog. **Career:** County Los Angeles, dist dir, 1959-75; lectr, Calif Community Col Syst, 1973-75; City Compton, dir parks & rec, 1975-80; City Santa Ana, exec dir, 1980-. **Orgs:** Calif Parks Rec Soc 1961-; bd dirs, Nat Recreation Parks Assoc, 1971-; bd dirs, NRPA Ethnic Minority Soc, 1971-. **Honors/Awds:** Administrator of Year, Ethnic Minority Soc, 1977; Administrator of the Year, Calif Parks & Recreation Soc, 1988; elected to bd Trustees, Nat Recreation & Parks Asn. **Military Serv:** USY Army E5, 1955-57; Good Conduct & Service Medal. **Business Phone:** (714)571-4202.

DODD, GERALDA
Business owner. **Personal:** Born Jul 4, 1957, Toledo, OH; married T Edward Sellers, 1991. **Educ:** Univ Toledo. **Career:** Integrated Steel, owner & ceo, 1990; HS Automotive, chief exec officer, 1991; Heidtman Steel Prod, receptionist, inventory control mgr, purchasing mgr, vpres purchasing & admin; Thomas Madison Inc, ceo, currently. **Orgs:** Past bd dir, Cent Mich Univ. **Special Achievements:** First African-American woman to break through the gender barrier in the traditionally male-dominated business of steel and metal stamping. **Business Addr:** Chief Executive Officer, Thomas Madison Inc, 2301 Hubbell St, Detroit, MI 48227, **Business Phone:** (313)273-4000.*

DODDS, R. HARCOURT. **See Obituaries section.**

DODDY, REGINALD NATHANIEL
Software developer. **Personal:** Born Jul 2, 1952, Cincinnati, OH; son of Nathan and Mildred Peek. **Educ:** Northwestern Univ, BSEE, 1975. **Career:** Eastman Kodak Co, mfg engr, 1975-77; Mead Corp, mfg engr, 1977-79; RCA Corp, assoc mem staff engr, 1979-84; Cincinnati Milacron, systs engr, 1984-94; Software Engineering, supvr, 1994-. **Orgs:** Toastmasters Club, 1976-77; Inst Elect & Elect Engr, 1977-; tech dir, RCA Minority Engineering Prog, 1980-83. **Honors/Awds:** Nomination Outstanding Young Men of America, 1982-83; Community Service Award, Indianapolis Ctr Leadership Develop, 1982. **Home Addr:** 3595 Wilson Ave, Cincinnati, OH 45229. **Business Addr:** Software Engineer Supervisor, Cincinnati Milacron, 4165 Halfacre Rd, Batavia, OH 45103, **Business Phone:** (513)536-3311.

DODGE, DEDRICK ALLEN
Football player. **Personal:** Born Jun 14, 1967, Neptune, NJ; married Patrice; children: Chante, Dedrick Jr & Nyla. **Educ:** Fla State,criminol. **Career:** Seattle Sea hawks, defensive back, 1991, corner back, 1992; San Francisco49ers, 1994-96; Denver Broncos, 1997; San Diego Chargers, safety, 1998. **Special Achievements:** Super Bowl XXIX for the San Francisco 49ers, Super Bowl XXXII for the Denver Broncos. *

DODSON, ANGELA PEARL
Editor. **Personal:** Born May 24, 1951, Beckley, WV; daughter of William Alfred Dodson Sr and Kira Evelyn; married Michael Irvin Days, Apr 17, 1982. **Educ:** Marshall Univ, Huntington, W VA, BA, 1973; Am Univ, Wash, DC, MA, 1979. **Career:** Charleston Gazette, intern, Charleston, WV, 1972; The Huntington Advertiser, Huntington, WV, reporter, 1972-74; Gannett News Serv, Wash, DC, corresp, 1974-77, asst news/feature ed, 1977-79; Rochester Times Union, Rochester, NY, asst city ed, 1979-80; Wash Star, Wash, DC, night slot/features ed, 1980-81; Courier J, Louisville, KY, copy ed, 1981-82; Diocese Trenton, Black Caths, radio host, 1999; New York Times, New York, NY, copy ed, dep ed living sect, ed living sect, ed style dept, 1983-95, sr ed, news admin, consult/ed, 1995-2003; freelance consult/ed, exec ed; Black Issues Book Review Mag, freelance ed/write, 1999-2003, exec ed, 2003-. **Orgs:** Alpha Kappa Alpha, chap founder, mem, Marshall Univ, 1971-75; Nat Asn Black Journalists, 1977-, former nat secy; Editing Prog Minority Journalists, faculty mem & adv bd mem, 1982 - . **Honors/Awds:** Black Alumna of the Year, Sons Marshall, 1988; Distinguished Alumna, Sch Jour, Marshall Univ, 1989; Black Achiever in Industry, Harlem YMCA, 1990; New York Asn Black Journalists, Feature Writing Award, 2000. **Business Addr:** Executive Editor, Black Issues Book Review, 350 5th Ave Empire State Bldg Suite 1522, New York, NY 10118-0165, **Business Phone:** (212)947-8515.

DODSON, HOWARD, JR.
Executive, educator. **Personal:** Born Jun 1, 1939, Chester, PA; divorced; children: Alyce Christine & David Primus Luta. **Educ:** W Chester State Col, BS, 1961; UCLA, Additional Study, 1964; Villanova Univ, MA, 1964; UC Berkeley, ABD, 1974. **Career:** Peace Corps, recruiter, 1966-67, dir spec recruiting, 1967-68, trng officer, 1968; CA State Col, assoc prof, 1970; Shaw Univ, adjunct prof, 1975; Emory Univ, lectr, 1976; Inst Black World, prog dir, 1973-74, exec dir, 1974-79; Nat Endowment Humanities, asst to chmn, 1980-82; The Schomburg Ctr Res Black Culture, chief, 1984-, dir library, currently, proj cur, currently. **Orgs:** Alpha Phi Alpha, 1959-64, SC Hist Soc, Peace Corps Vol, 1964-66, Oakland Black Caucus, 1969-73; consult, Nat Endowment Humanities, 1979-80; chmn,ceo, Black Theol Proj, 1982-84; bd dir, Inst Black World, Atlanta Assoc Intl Ed; Ed Brain Trust Congressional Black Caucus, Atlanta Univ Sch Soc Work, Nat Comn Citizens Educ, GA Assoc Black Elected Officials, ESEA, NatCredit Union Fed Edcur; African Heritage Studies Assoc, Assoc the Study Afro-Am Hist, So Hist Assoc; bd overseers Lang Col New Sch Social Res; bddirs, NCBS, AHSA, Caribbean Res Ctr. **Honors/Awds:** PICCO Scholar, 1959-61; Grad Fel UC Berkeley, 1969-73; Res Fel Inst Black World, 1970-71; ASALH Service Award, 1976; Governor's Award for African Am Distinction, 1982; Doctor Humane Letters, Widner Univ, 1987. **Business Addr:** Chief, Schomburg Center for Research in Black Culture, 515 Malcolm X Blvd, 135th St, New York, NY 10037-1801, **Business Phone:** (212)491-2200.*

DODSON, DR. JUALYNNE E.
School administrator, educator. **Personal:** Born Jan 4, 1942, Pensacola, FL; daughter of Benjamin White and Flora White; married Howard; children: Alyce Christine & David Primus Luta. **Educ:** Univ Calif, Berkeley, BS, 1969, MA, 1972, PhD, 1984; Warren Deem Inst, Educ Mgt Columbia Univ Sch Bus, 1985. **Career:** Atlanta Univ Sch Social Work, instr, 1973-74, res proj dir, 1973-81, dir res ctr, 1974-80, from asst prof to assoc prof, 1974-82, chair Dept Child & Family Serv, 1980-82; Am Sociol Asn, res fel appl social, 1980; Black Theol Proj, exec dir, 1985-88; Union Theol Sem, dean sem life, 1982-87; Hunter Col, City Univ NY, sociol dept, vis assoc prof, 1987-88; Yale Univ, sr res assoc, African & African-Am Studies, 1988-90; Princeton Univ, Ctr Studies American Religion, 1991-92; Univ Colo, religious studies, African Am studies, sociol, assoc prof, 2001; Michigan State Univ, African Am & African Studies, fac, dir, Dept Sociol prof, 2002-. **Orgs:** Elected delegate Coun, Social Work Educ, 1979-82; Am Acad Religion, 1981, 1983, 1984, 1987; Nat Coun Convenor Feminist Theol Inst, 1982-83; Soc Sci Study Religion, 1982, 1983, 1986; consult, Nat Child Welfare Training Ctr, Ann Arbor, MI,1983-85; chair & bd dirs, Black Theol Proj, 1983-84; Nat Coalition 100 Black Women, 1984; NY State Black & Puerto Rican Legis Caucus Women's Conf, 1985; NY State Affirmative Action Adv Coun, 1985-86; leader, Black Church Studies & Stud Caucus Retreat Colgate Rochester Divinity Sch, 1985; adv bd, Asn Black Women in Higher Educ, 1985-88; Soc Am Archivists, 1986. **Honors/Awds:** Gubernatorial Appointee White House Conf on Families, 1980; Lucy Craft Laney Award, Black Presbyterians United UPCUSA, 1982; Spivack Fel, Am Sociol Asn, 1983; Medal of Honor, Outstanding Community Service One Church One Child Prog, Indianapolis, 1986; delegate Intl Conf, Ecumenical Sharing Nanjing, China, 1986; Global Competency award, 2009. **Special Achievements:** Author: A Source book in Child Welfare, National Child Welfare Training Center, 1982; "An Afro-Centric Educational Manual," University of Tennessee Press, Knoxville, 1983; African Religious Traditions of Cuba. **Business Addr:** Director, Professor, Michigan State University, African American and African Studies, 1 Morrill Hall, East Lansing, East Lansing, MI 48824.

DODSON, SELMA L
Executive. **Personal:** Born May 21, 1955, Chicago, IL; daughter of Robert W and Juanita L. **Educ:** Northwestern Univ, BS, 1977. **Career:** WZGC Radio, promotions dir/public affairs, 1977-81; KFMK Radio, acct exec, 1981-84; KO5HU TV, sales mgr, 1984-86; KMJQ/KYOK, acct exec, 1986-88, local sales mgr, 1988-92, gen sales mgr; Clear Channel Works, gen mgr, 2000. **Orgs:** Houston Nat Asn Advan Colored People, chp publicity/comm Annual Freedom Fund Banquet, 1989, 1990, 1991, 1992; Houston Coalition of 100 Black Women, 1989; Am Mkt Asn, 1984-85; Am Women Radio/TV, 1981-83; Am Women Radio/TV, historian, 1979-81. **Honors/Awds:** Human Enrichment for Life Program, Young Black Achiever, 1988. **Business Addr:** General Sales Manager, Clear Channel Works, 11508 E Quartz Rock Rd, Scottsdale, AZ 85255, **Business Phone:** (480)473-3058.*

DODSON, VIVIAN M
Government official, mayor. **Personal:** Born Jan 22, 1934, Washington, DC; daughter of Brevard and Maefield Wilson; married Barke M, Dec 24, 1958 (died 1991); children: Tangie B & Kaphree A. **Educ:** Wash Col Music, Wash DC, AA, 1956. **Career:** Government official, Mayor (retired); Prince Georges County Communs, Upper Marlboro, MD, communs oper, 1973-89; Town Capitol Heights, Capitol Heights, MD, councilwoman, 1982-86, mayor, 1986-2004. **Orgs:** Girl Scouts Am, 1971, retired; pres, Prince Georges Municipal Elective Women, 1992-; dir, Recreation for Capitol Heights, 1982-; bd mem, Prince Georges County Municipal League, 1983-; Mothers On The Move, 1984-; Citizen on The Move, 1986; Mid-County Youth Services; Coun Black Mayors; Nat Coun Black Women; Prince Georges Municipal Mayors; Nat Polit Cong Black Women, 1991; Governor Parris N. Glendening[a6]s Comn, State Block Grants. **Honors/Awds:** Citizen on the Move. **Special Achievements:** First black and first female Mayor of the Town of Capitol Heights. **Home Addr:** 5635 Southern Ave, Capitol Heights, MD 20743.

DODSON, WILLIAM ALFRED
Administrator. **Personal:** Born Feb 9, 1950, Beckley, WV; son of William A Dodson Sr and Kira E Walthall; married Judythe Irene Taylor, Jul 27, 1975; children: Daymon. **Educ:** Marshall Univ Huntington, WV, BA, sociol, 1973; OH State Univ Columbus, OH, MA Public Admin, 1981; Ohio Real Estate Sales License, 1997. **Career:** Tri-state OIC Huntington, WV, instr, 1972-73; ACF Ind Huntington, WV, instrl rel repr 1973-75; Off Human Serv, ODOD, field rep, 1975-77; Office Appalachia ODOD, housing rep, 1977-82; WCVO-FM New Albany, OH, vol announcer, 1980-96; Off Local Gov Serv, ODOD, field rep/devel specialist, 1982-86; Columbus Metro Housing Authority, asst dir housing prog, 1986-88, MIS mgr, 1988-89, mgt analyst, 1989-93; Rhema Christian Ctr, exec vp, 1992-; Dayspring Christian CDC, exec dir, 1993-; licensed realtor, 1997-2005. **Orgs:** Elder, Rhema Christian Ctr, 1982, exec vp, 1992-; chmn, Neighborhood Serv Adv Coun, Columbus, 1989-90, 1993-94, vp, 1991-93, bd dirs, 1986-93; bd mem, Asn Developmentally Disabled, 1986-99; Directions Youth, pres, 1992-93; Christian Management Asn, 1993-, chair, 1999-; Christian Comm Dev Assoc, 1993-; vice chmn, Northeast Area Comm, 1993-96, chair, 1996-98; pres, Nat Asn Church Bus Admin, 1994-96; vice chmn, Columbus State Community Col, 1994-99, chmn, 1998-99; trustee, Columbus Compact Corp, 1995-97; Urban Concern, 1995-; I-670 Development Corp, 1996-98; bd trustees, Columbus Metro Area Community Action Org, 1998-, chair, 2000. **Honors/Awds:** Nat Achievement Scholar, Nat Merit ETS, 1968; Outstanding Participant, Nat Alliance Bus Jobs Campaign Huntington Metro, 1975; Certified Public Housing Mgr, 1987; Certified Economic Development Specialist, Nat Dev Council, 1984; Community Achievement Award, Marshall Univ Alumni Asn, 1996; Church Manager certificate, Christian Mgt Asn, 1997; Soldier Faith Award, Unity Economic Summit, 1999; Harvard Divinity Sch, Summer Leadership Inst, 2000. **Home Addr:** 5362 Pk Lane Dr, Columbus, OH 43231, **Home Phone:** (614)901-0870. **Business Addr:** Executive Vice President, Rhema Christian Center, 2100 Agler Rd, PO Box 247198, Columbus, OH 43224, **Business Phone:** (614)471-0816.

DOGGETT, JOHN NELSON
Educator. **Personal:** Married. **Educ:** Claremont Mens Col, BA, 1969; Yale Univ, JD, 1972; Harvard Univ, MBA, 1981. **Career:** Legal serv litigator, 1972-74; State Bar Calif, Legal Serv Dept, dir, 1975-79; McKinsey & Co, US & Scandinavia, mgt consult, 1981-83; mgt5 consult, 1983-93; Univ Tex, Red McCombs Sch Bus, Dept Mgt, codir, srlectr, currently; Univ Tex IC2 Inst, sr res fel, currently; IMA DEC Univ, Sch Bus, vis prof; Aoyama Gakuin Univ, vis prof; Thammasat Univ, vis prof. **Orgs:** Bd mem, Gnumber Inc. **Honors/Awds:** Outstanding Elective Professor, MBA Class 2004, Mccombs Sch Bus, Texas Exec MBA Prog, Class

2004, Univ Tex Austin; Outstanding Professsor, UnivTex Austin; Outstanding Faculty Award, Exec Engineering Mgt Prog, Univ Tex Austin; Outstanding Professor in a Elective Course in Fall, 1997, Tex Grad Sch Bus, Univ Tex Austin. **Special Achievements:** Was selected by Business 2.0 as one of the top two professors at Mc Combs. **Business Addr:** Senior Lecturer, The University of Texas, Red McCombs School of Business, Management Department, 1 University Station B6300, Austin, TX 78712-1178.

DOGGETT, DR. JOHN NELSON
Clergy. **Personal:** Born Apr 3, 1918, Philadelphia, PA; son of John Nelson Jr and Winola Ballard; married Juanita Toley, Aug 3, 1973; children: John N, Lorraine F, John III, William II & Kenneth Riddick. **Educ:** Lincoln Univ, BA, 1942; Union Theol Sem, MDiv, 1945; Saint Louis Univ,MEduc, 1969, PhD, 1971. **Career:** Union Memorial United Methodist Church, sr pastor, 1964-76; Harris-StoweState Col, instr educ 1973-76; Metro Col, St Louis Univ, assoc prof,1976-78; UM Church, St Louis Area, dist supt, 1976-82; Grace UnitedMethodist Church, sr minister, 1982-85; Cabanne United Methodist Church,minister, 1985-89; Cen Med Ctr, St Louis, chmn, bd dirs, 1975-87, chmnemeritus, 1987-; CMC Retirement Home, chmn, bd dirs, 1985-; Limelight Mag,Univ City, MO, assoc publisher/staff writer, 1988-; Mid-West Consultants, pres. **Orgs:** Staff counr, Pastoral CounInst, St Louis, 1968-88; pres, St LouisBr, NAACP, 1973-80; citizens comn, Mont Dept Corrections, 1974-80; bddirs, United Way Greater St Louis, 1974-81; bd dirs, Nat Coun ChurchesChrist, 1976-80; St Louis Ambassadors & RCGA, 1980-90; bd dir, Am Lung AsnEastern MO, 1985-88; Family Planning Asn, MO, 1986-88; ACLU; UNA, 1986-88,Metro Clergy Coalition; founder, JN Doggett Scholar Found; Lincoln PAAlumni Asn, St Louis Conf Educ; Confluence Focus St Louis Nat ConfChristians; bd trustees, exec comn, Miss Hist Soc Inc, 1987-; UnitedMethodist Hist Soc, 1988-96; NAACP; exec officer, Union Memorial Leaders &Church Coun, currently; life trustee, Mo Hist Mus. **Honors/Awds:** Natl Chaplain's Awd Alpha Phi Alpha Fraternity 1973,79,86,87; OutstandingAlumni Awd St Louis Univ 1981; Martin Luther King Awd Alpha &Anheuser-Busch Project 1987; "Effect of Community School Achievement" StLouis Univ edition 1971; "Black Religious Experience" Gammon TheolSeminary Press GA 1973; Regional Hall of Fame Alpha Phi Alpha Fraternity1988; Outstanding Service Award, Elijah Parish Lovejoy Society 1989; JobCorp Martin Luther King Excellence Award, 1990; Citizenship Service-Certificate, St Louis Public Schools, 1988; Leadership Trainer Award,Kansas City Blacks Against AIDS, 1989; NAACP, Lifetime Achievement Award,1992; Urban League, Lifetime Achievement Award, 1993; Alpha Kappa Alpha,Lifetime Achievement Award, 1994; Education Honor, Two Trees in TowerGrove Park, 1999. **Military Serv:** USNG chaplain first lt 119, Artillary Bn, 1946-50. **Home Addr:** 4466 W Pine Blvd Apt 2C, St Louis, MO 63108. **Business Addr:** Board of Trustee, Missouri Historical Society, PO Box 11940, St Louis, MO 63112-0040, **Business Phone:** (314)361-7229.

DOGINS, KEVIN RAY
Football player. **Personal:** Born Dec 7, 1972, Eagle Lake, TX; married Erica. **Educ:** Tex A& M- Kingsville. **Career:** Football player(retired); Tampa Bay Buccaneers, ctr, 1996-2000, Chicago Bears, 2001-02; Atlanta Falcons, ctr, 2003. *

DOIG, ELMO H.
Executive. **Personal:** Born Aug 14, 1927, Panama City, Panama; son of Henry C and Fortunee Andree; married Silvia Doran, Nov 8, 1952; children: Elmo Jr, Yvette. **Educ:** Am Sch, Col prep, 1959; City Col, BBS & MBA, 1969. **Career:** Executive (retired); Ordinance Corps Panama, supr supply shop, 1942-58; Bezozi Corp, supr billing dept, 1958-62; Flower Fifth Ave Hosp NY, head payroll & accts payable dept, 1963-64; Manufacturers Hanover Trust Co, branch mgr, asst vp. **Orgs:** Treas, financial secy, Bronx Lions Club Bronx, NY, 1971; financial comt, 100 Black Men, NY, 1975; treas, Mt Kisco Village Condominium, 1979; dir, Catholic Youth Org, NY, 1984-86; dir, Sandpaper Bay Homeowners Asn PSL-FL, 1991-95, pres, 1995-97. **Honors/Awds:** Am Sch Scholar, Chicago, 1960; Black achievers in industry, Greater NY, YMCA 1972; banking & finance Grodon Heights Comm City Tabernacle Church Seventh-day Adventist NY, 1978. **Home Addr:** 233 NW Chimere Ln, Port St Lucie, FL 34986.

DOLBY, EDWARD C.
Banker. **Personal:** Married Dee; children: Ed, Terius, Jarvone. **Educ:** Shaw Univ, sociol, 1966. **Career:** NC Nat Bank, consumer bank exec; Bank Am Carolinas, pres, 1997-01; NationsBank Carolinas, pres, 1998; US Securities & Exchange Comn, dir, 2003; Edward C Dolby Strategic Consult Group LLC, pres, 2002-. **Orgs:** incoming chmn, Audit Comt, US Securities & Exchange Comn; Charlotte Chamber; Shaw Univ Bd Trustees; Audit & Compensation Comt. **Special Achievements:** Highest ranking African Am line mgr for NationsBank. *

DOLEY, AMBASSADOR HAROLD E
Executive. **Personal:** Born Mar 8, 1947, New Orleans, LA; married Helena Cobette; children: Harold III & Aaron. **Educ:** Xavier Univ, BS; Harvard Univ, Grad Sch Bus, PM. **Career:** Doley Properties, pres; Southern Univ New Orleans, instr; Bache Halsey Stuart Inc, acct exec; Howard Weil Labouisse & Friedrichs Inc, asst vpres, 1974-75; Minerals Mgmt Servs, dir, 1982-83; African Development Bank, exec dir, 1983-85; Doley Securities Inc, chmn, pres, founder, 1973-. **Orgs:** NY Stock Exchange; Pub Broadcast Syst WYES-TV; Inter-racial Coun Bus & Opp; AFA IST; former bd mem, OIC Adv Bd; Lloyds London; Zeta Boule; NY Options Exchange; trustee, Clark-Atlanta Univ; trustee, Shaw Univ; LA Weekly Bd; US Africa COC; Population Resource CTR; LA State Mineral Bd. **Honors/Awds:** Outstanding Stockbrokers, Shareholders Mgt Co, 1982; Harvard Mgt Grad Sch of Bus; Stock Picker Contest Winner, Wall St J, 1989; Honorary Degrees: Clark-Atlanta Univ, Bishop CLG, Shaw Univ. **Special Achievements:** TV guest appearances: "The Today Show"; CNN; CNBC; FNN; "Wall St Week"; "NYK Times Spotlight"; NY Times Profile. **Business Addr:** Founder, Doley Securities Inc, 616 Baronne St Suite 300, New Orleans, LA 70113.

DOLPHIN, DERRICK
Business owner. **Personal:** Born Jan 1, 1971?. **Career:** Youth Develop & Res Fund, co-owner, 1997-, exec producer, currently. **Orgs:** Am Youth Policy Forum; NY Asn Training & Employment Prof Inc. **Business Addr:** Co-owner, Executive Producer, Youth Development and Research Fund, 20405 Studio Pl, Gaithersburg, MD 20886, **Business Phone:** (301)216-2566.

DOMINIC, IRWING
Manager. **Personal:** Born Aug 12, 1930, Spartanburg, SC; son of Irvin and Jessie M Hall Hunt; married Catherine Virginia Chapman Dominic, Jun 14, 1956; children: Duane, Dwight, Denice, Deirdre, Deland, Damian. **Educ:** Bellevue Univ, BA, Sociol, 1978; Univ Nebr-19Omaha, attended 1979, Creighton Univ Omaha, attended 1980. **Career:** Manager (retired); US Postal Serv, Omaha NE, mail handler, 1974-79, assoc training & develop specialist eas-14, 1979-80, training & develop spec eas-16, 1980-83, Cleveland mgr training, EAS-21, 1983-86, Hicksville NY mgr employ & develop, EAS-23, 1986-88, Akron OH, mgr training & develop. **Orgs:** Founding mem, Blacks Govt Omaha NE Chap, 1981-82; Knights Columbus, fourth degree, 1980; Phoenix Rising Toastmasters, 1982; A Plus, 1988; educ adv, Nat Asn Postal Supvr, 1983; Phoenix Postal Supvr, 1983. **Honors/Awds:** Super Performance Award, US Postal Serv, 1979, Managers Recognition Award, 1982, Spot Awards, 1996, Far Exceeds Merit Award, 1997. **Military Serv:** USAF, radio oper & electronic analyst, 1949-74; Korean & Vietnam Serv, Sr Crew Mem Badge; Meritorious Service Award. *

DOMINO, ANTOINE DOMINIQUE. See DOMINO, FATS.

DOMINO, FATS (ANTOINE DOMINIQUE DOMINO)
Musician. **Personal:** Born Feb 26, 1928, New Orleans, LA; married Rosemary; children: Antoinette, Antoine III, Andrea, Anatole, Anola, Adonica, Antonio & Andre. **Career:** Rock & roll singer; songwriter; pianist; musician & concert performer,1950-; Composer: Let the Four Winds Blow; Walking to New Orleans; Ain't That a Shame; Blue Monday; The Fat Man; I Want to Walk You Home; I'm Gonna Be a Wheel Someday; I'm Walking; Whole Lotta Loving; Alive & Kickin',2006; hit records include: Blueberry Hill; Margie; Lady Madonna; Dick Clark Productions, partner, 1995-; Grabow & Assocs, entertainer, currently. **Honors/Awds:** Awarded more than 20 Gold Records; Rock & Roll Hall of Fame, 1986; Grammy Lifetime Achievement Award, 1987; American Nat Medal of the Arts, Nat Endowment Arts, 1998; Lifetime Achievement Award, OffBeat Mag, 2007; Inducted to Louisiana Music Hall Fame, 2007; Inducted to Hit Parade Hall Fame, 2007. **Special Achievements:** The 25th Greatest Rock 'n' Roll Artist of all time by Rolling Stone; appeared in numerous movies &TV shows including: The Big Beat, 1958; "Ricky Nelson& Fats Domino: Live at the Universal Amphitheatre", 1985; Biography, "Blue Monday, Fats Domino & the Lost Dawn Of Rock 'n' Roll", written by Rick Coleman, Da Capo Press, 2006; "Statue of Fats Domino", French Quarter of New Orleans. **Business Phone:** (972)250-1162.

DONAHUE, WILLIAM T.
Government official. **Personal:** Born May 31, 1943, San Antonio, TX; married Monica Lechowick; children: Erin Michelle, Mark Pittman. **Educ:** San Antonio Jr Col. **Career:** Human Resources & Servs, dir, 1972-82; City San Antonio, asst city mgr; County Bd Arlington, county mgr, currently. **Orgs:** Vol, US Peace Corps, 1965-67; past pres, US Conf City Human Servs; Official Adv Comt United Negro Col Fund; life mem, NAACP; co-chair, 1980, UNCF Radiothon; deleg Pres Conf Children & Youth; 1st Black Asst City Mgr City San Antonio; bd dir, Nat Forum Black Pub Admin, 1982-; vice chair, TX Emergency Serv Adv Coun; Commissioned Admin TX Navy; D Law Univ TX, San Antonio; Intl City Mgr's Asn; Achievement Award, S Cent Region AKA Sorority; TX City Mgrs Asn; Outstanding Texan TX Legislative Black Caucus. **Business Addr:** County Manager, Office County Manager, Arlington County, 2100 Clarendon Blvd Suite 302, Arlington, VA 22201, **Business Phone:** (703)228-3120.*

DONALD, ARNOLD WAYNE
Executive. **Personal:** Born Dec 17, 1954, New Orleans, LA; son of Warren Joseph Sr and Hilda Aline (Melancon); married Hazel Alethea (Roberts) Donald, May 18, 1974; children: Radiah Alethea, Alicia Aline, Stephen Zachary. **Educ:** Carleton Col, BA, econ, 1976; Wash Univ, BS, mech eng, 1977; Univ Chicago, MBA, finance, 1980. **Career:** Monsanto, sr mkt analyst, 1980-81, mkt res supvr, 1981-82, prod supvr, 1982-83, round-up prod mgr, 1983, mkt mgr, 1983-86, prod dir, 1986; specialty crops dir, 1986-87; lawn & garden bus dir, 1987-91, Residential Prod Div, vpres, 1991-92; Crop Protection Prod Div, vpres/gen mgr, 1992-93; NA Div, Crop Protection Unit, group vpres & gen mgr, pres, 1995, sr vice pres, 1998; Merisant Co, chmn & chief exec officer, 2000-2005; Juv Diabetes Res Found Int, pres & chief exec officer, 2005-. **Orgs:** Can Agr Chem Asn, 1983-86; Nat Lawn & Garden Distribr Asn, 1988-91; team capt, 1988-89, bd mem, 1989-91, Monsanto YMCA; bd vpres, 1990-93, pres bd, 1993, Leadership St Louis; bd mem, Theater Proj Co, 1989-91; bd mem, Ecumenical Housing Prod Corp, 1990-98; bd mem, 1991-93, exec comt, currently, Lindenwood Col; bd mem, John Burroughs Sch, 1992-93; comt mem, United Way of Greater St Louis, 1991-93; pres, Leadership Ctr Greater St Louis; exec comt, Brit Am Proj; Jr League Adv Bd; Nat Adv Coun Wash Univ Sch Engineering; Elliot Soc; Am Col Personnel Asn; Future Farmers Am; 4-H Club. **Honors/Awds:** Nat Achievement Scholar, Carleton Col, 1972-76; Dave Okada Memorial Award, Carleton Col, 1976; Outstanding Young Alumni Award, Wash Univ Sch Engineering & Appl Sci, 1994; Nat Black Alumni Award, Nat Black Alumni Coun, Wash Univ, 1994; Black Enterprise Executive of the Year, 1997; Agri-Marketer of the Year, Nat Agri-Marketing Asn, 1997; Founders Award, Wash Univ, 1998. **Special Achievements:** one of Fortune magazine's "50 Most Powerful Black Executives in America". **Business Addr:** President, Chief Executive Officer, Juvenile Diabetes Research Foundation International, 120 Wall St, New York, NY 10005-4001, **Business Phone:** 800-533-2873.*

DONALD, DR. BERNICE BOUIE
Judge. **Personal:** Born Sep 17, 1951, DeSoto Co, MS; daughter of Perry Bowie; married W L. **Educ:** Memphis State Univ, BA, 1974; Memphis State Univ Sch Law, JD, 1979; Nat Judicial Col, Evidence Cert, 1984. **Career:** S Cent Bell, clerk's mgr, 1971-79; Memphis Area Legal Serv, atty, 1979-80; Shelby Co Govt Pub Defenders Off, asst pub defender, 1980-82; Gen Sessions Ct, judge, 1982-88; Shelby State Community Col, adj prof, 1984-89; S Bankruptcy Ct, Western Dist Tenn, judge, 1988-96; US Dist, Western Dist Tenn, judge, 1996-. **Orgs:** Memphis Bar Asn; Tenn Bar Asn; co-chair, Courts Comt Memphis & Shelby County Bar Asn; Ben F Jones Chap Nat Bar Asn; Asn Women Attys; Nat Asn Women Judges, 1983-; Am Judges Asn, 1983-; chair, Gen Sessions Judges Conf Educ, 1987; Bd Dirs, Memphis State Univ Law Alumni; chair, Comt Excellence Legal Educ; Zeta Phi Beta Sor, Alpha Eta Zeta Chap; Bd dirs, Shelby State Community Col, Criminal Justice Panel, Nat Conf Negro Women, Bus & Prof Women Clubs; assoc mem, Nat Ctr State Courts; JAD Div Am Bar Asn; chair, Comn Opportunities Minorities, ABA, Am Trial Lawyers Asn; Conf Spec Court Judges; pres, Asn Women Attys, 1990; Nat Conf Bankruptcy Jes, 1988; Found Womens Rights Adv Bd; secy, Am Bar Asn, 2008-. **Honors/Awds:** Young Careerist Award, State Tenn Raleigh Bur Prof Women; Woman of the Year, Pentecostal Church of God in Christ; Martin Luther King Community Service Award; Citizen of the Year, Excelsior Chap Eastern Star; Community Service Award, Youth-Nat Conf Christians & Jews, 1986. **Special Achievements:** First African-American woman to hold an officer position in the American Bar Association; First black female in US to serve on Bankruptcy Court; elected first black female judge in the history of the State of TN; Featured in Essence, Ebony, Jet, Dollar & Sense, and Memphis Magazine; participated on numerous TV shows to discuss legal and judicial issues; participated on numerous panels and forums dealing with legal process and the judiciary. **Business Phone:** (901)495-1276.

DONALD, ELVAH T
Broker, executive, business owner. **Personal:** Born in Pine Bluff, AR; daughter of Leon F Sr and Evelyn S; married Robert E Donald, Sep 26, 1980. **Educ:** Univ Toledo, BEd, 1970; Ohio State Univ, attended 1972; Mich State Grad Sch Bus, 1977. **Career:** NAB Exec Loan Prog, Col/Ind, dir, 1976-78; Toledo Bd Edu, teacher, 1970-71; Owens-Corning Fiberglas Corp, Human Resources, mgr, Logistics & Planning, mgr, 1971-83; Reynolds Real Estate Co, sales assoc, 1984-86; Loss Realty Group, assoc broker, 1986-92; Donald Co, realtors, pres, owner & broker, 1992-. **Orgs:** Founder & organizer, The Gathering Profs, 1996-; pres, Bus Ladies in Session, 1972-79; bd mem, Mid Am Bank, 1984-94; exec bd, Nat Asn Advan Colored People, Toledo Br, 1975-77; bd mem, WGTE Pub Broadcasting, 1992-94; chair, Preferred Properties, Inc, 1989-95; Columbus Bd Realtors, chair, Communs, 1997-; Toledo Bd Realtors, Prof Standards, 1993-; bd mem, United Way Central Ohio; Nat Asn Realtors & HUD, instr, "At Home With Diversity;" IBA Central Ohio, pres, 2002-04; New Albany Chamber Com. **Honors/Awds:** Business Award, Blue Chip Found, 1999; Lifeline Award, Preferred Properties, 1995; Service Award, Mid Am Bank, 1993. **Business Addr:** President, Broker, Owner, The Donald Company, Realtors, 2931 E Dublin-Granville Rd, Columbus, OH 43231, **Business Phone:** (614)899-0094 Ext 71.

DONALD, JAMES E
Commissioner. **Personal:** Married August; children: Jeff & Cheryl. **Educ:** Univ Miss, BA, 1970; Univ Mo, MPA, 1983.

Career: Ga Dept corrections, Off Ombudsman & Family Advocacy, corrections comnr, currently. **Military Serv:** USAF, 1970-2003. **Business Addr:** Corrections Commissioner, Georgia Department of corrections, Office of the Ombudsman & Family Advocacy, 2 Martin Luther King Jr Dr Suite 954 E Twr, Atlanta, GA 30334, **Business Phone:** (404)656-9772.*

DONALDSON, JAMES LEE, III
Basketball player, businessperson. **Personal:** Born Aug 16, 1957, Heachem, England. **Educ:** Wash State Univ, attended 1979. **Career:** Basketball player (retired), Business person; Seattle Super Sonics,1981-83; San Diego Clippers, 1984; Los Angeles Clippers, 1985-86; Dallas Mavericks, 1986-92; New York Knicks, 1992; Utah Jazz, 1993-95; The Donaldson Clinic, owner, 1990-. **Orgs:** Boy Scouts of Am; Chmn, Central Area Senior Center Christian Brotherhood Academy; Columbia Tower Club; Communities In Schools; Greater Seattle Chamber of Commerce; bd mem, Magnolia Community Advisory Coun; bd mem, Mill Creek Business Asn; bd mem, Mount Zion Baptist Church Scholarship Committee; bd mem, Mukilteo Chamber Of Commerce, bd mem, NAACP Tacoma; bd mem, Northwest Minority Bus Coun; spokesperson, Sno King Youth Club; Sound Transit Diversity Oversight Committe; South Snohomish County Chamber of Commerce; bd mem; Tacoma Pierce County Black Collective; bd mem, exec comt, Washington State Mentors; Washington State University Gray; Werlin Reading Program. **Honors/Awds:** Pac 10 Sports Hall of Fame; Washington St University Athletic Hall of Fame; Hon Cmndr Of McCord Air Force Base; Jen McDonald Community Service Award, 2005. **Special Achievements:** Was one of only two players on the Clippers to have played in all 82 games of the year; set a Clipper club record for highest field goal percentage. **Business Addr:** Owner, Physical Therapy, The Donaldson Clinic, 16030 Bothell-Everett Hwy Suite 200, Mill Creek, WA 98012, **Business Phone:** (425)745-4910.

DONALDSON, LEON MATTHEW
Educator. **Personal:** Born Aug 16, 1933, Burton, SC; married Merita Worthy; children: Carter & TaJuania. **Educ:** Ala State Univ, BS 1963; Southern Univ, MS, 1966; Rutgers Univ, EdD, 1973; Auburn Univ, attended; George Wash Univ, attended; NC Cent Univ, attended. **Career:** NASA, res assoc; TV McCoo High Sch, teacher, 1963-70; Corning Glass Works, chem eng, 1970-71; Stauffer Chem Corp, chemist; IBM Corp, eng; Morgan State Univ, assoc prof chem, currently, fac athletics rep, currently. **Orgs:** Nat Asn Advan Colored People; Nat Educ Asn; Nat Sci Teachers Asn; Nat Coun Teachers Math; Ala Educ Asn; SC Educ Asn; Civitan Int; Fla & AM; Kappa Alpha Psi Fraternity Inc; NSF fel, Ala State Univ, NC Cent Univ; NSF fel, Southern Univ; EPDA fel, Rutgers Univ. **Military Serv:** AUS, sp5, 1957-60. **Business Addr:** Faculty Athletic Representative, Associate Professor, Morgan State University, 1700 E Coldspring Lane, Baltimore, MD 21251, **Business Phone:** (443)885-3344.

DONALDSON, SHAWN RIVA
Educator. **Personal:** Born May 6, 1957, Camden, NJ; daughter of Richard and Cammee; divorced; children: Ayanna Bernice Polk, Layla Callie Polk. **Educ:** Univ Penn, BA, 1979, MA, 1979; Rutgers Univ, PhD, 1990. **Career:** Stockton Col, instr, 1980-90, asst prof, 1990-96, assoc prof, 1996-05. **Orgs:** Vpres, pres, found bd mem, RSC NJ, Coun Black Faculty & Staff, 1987-88, 2002-03, 2004-; family selection comt, Habitat Humanity, Atlantic County. **Honors/Awds:** Key to the City, City Pleasantville, 1994; Council of Black Faculty & Staff Merit Award, ESCNJ, 1994; Women Helping Women Award, Soroptimist Soro, 2001; International Educator of the Year, Int Biographical Ctr, 2003. **Special Achievements:** Book: North Carolina Inerracial Rape Cases, 1837-56; South Africa, Women's Rights Entries in Karl Max, Phila Negro, Web Dubois Encyc; The Progressional and Personal of Oral History Projects: Atribute to Bernice Fanny Walker. *

DONAPHIN, ALEXA B.
Architect, administrator. **Educ:** Howard Univ; Harvard Univ; Dartmouth Col, MBA. **Career:** Archit Health Sci & Com, architect, currently. **Orgs:** Am Inst Architects. *

DONAWA, DR. MARIA ELENA
Pathologist, consultant. **Personal:** Born May 13, 1948, Detroit, MI; daughter of Milton Solese and Helen Solese; married John R Lupien. **Educ:** Howard Univ Col Pharm, BS, Pharm 1971; Howard Univ Col Med, MD, 1976. **Career:** Marco Pharm, pharmacist, 1971-72; Peoples Drug Stores Inc, registered pharmacist, 1972-73; Howard Univ Hosp, resident, 1976-80, chief resident, 1979-80; Abel Labs Inc, staff pathologist, 1980; Food & Drug Admin Bureau Med Devices, special med consult, 1980-83, assoc dir stands, 1983-86; Food& Drug Admin Ctr Devices & Radiol Health, asst dir device safety & risk mgt, 1980-86; Metro Lab, path dir, 1982-83; United Kingdom Inst Qual Assurance, lead auditor; Med Device Technol mag, columnist;Technion Commns, prog mgr, 2003-06; Orbis Global solns, 2006-08; Donawa & Assoc Ltd, Rome, Italy, pres, currently. **Orgs:** Precinct chairperson Democratic Party 1978-79; bd trustees 1979-86,chairperson quality control comm 1983-86, sec & mem exec comm, 1985-86, DC-Gen Hosp; Global Harmonization Task Force; brd Dirs, Regulatory Affairs Prof Soc; ISO TC 210. **Honors/Awds:** US Public Health Serv Achievement Award, 1983, Unit Commendation, 1985. **Special Achievements:** Network TV interview ABC News (World News Tonight) TSS, Tampons & FDA May2, 1984 and June 21, 1982; selected media interviews; "The Case of Toxic Shock Syndrome," Knowledge Transfer Round table US Public Health Serv 1984; Report Panel Presentations; articles "Toxic Shock Syndrome, Chronology of State & Federal Epidemiologic Studies and Regulatory Decision Making" with G Schmid, M Osterholm Public Health Reports Vol 99 No 4 1984. **Business Addr:** President, Donawa & Associates, Via Fonte di Fauno 22, I-00153 Rome, Italy.

DONEGAN, CHARLES EDWARD
Lawyer, educator. **Personal:** Born Apr 10, 1933, Chicago, IL; son of Arthur C Jr and Odessa Arnold; married Patty L Harris; children: Carter Edward. **Educ:** Wilson Jr Col, BA, 1953; Roosevelt, BSC, 1954; Loyola, MSIR, 1959; Howard, JD, 1967; Columbia, LLM, 1970. **Career:** US Comn Civil Rights, legal intern, 1966; Poor Peoples Campaign, legal counsel, 1968; F B McKissick Enterprises, staff counsel, 1969; SUNY Buffalo, first asst prof law, 1970-73; Ford Fellow Columbia Univ Law Sch, 1972-73; NEH Post Doctoral Fellow Afro Am Studies Yale Univ, 1972-73; Howard Univ, assoc prof law, 1973-77; Ohio State Univ, vis assoc prof, 1977-78; First US EPA, asst reg counsel, 1978-80; Southern Univ, prof law1980-84, vis prof law, 1992; CE Donegan & Assoc, atty law; LA State Univ, Law Sch, vis prof, 1981; NC Ctrl Univ Law Sch, vis prof 1988-89; Cook County, Circuit Ct Judge Cand, 2000; Atty Law, 2003. **Orgs:** Labor arbitrator Steel Inds Postal AAA, 1971-; consult US Dept Ag, 1972; asst counsel, Nat Asn Advan Colored People, Legal Defense Fund Inc1967-69; hiring officer Various Govt Agy, 1975-; Am Nat DC Chicago Bar Asn; Nat Asn Advan Colored People Urban League; Alpha Phi Alpha; Phi Alpha Delta; Phi Alpha Kappa; labor arbitrator, AAA, 1978; labor arbitrator FMCS, 1985; consult DC Govt Dept Pub Works; DC Consumer Claims Arbit bd;chmn, legal educ comt, Wash Bar Asn, 1984-91; DC Atty-Client Arbit Bd, 1990-91; DC Superior Court; adv comt, DC Educ, Ward 4, 1991; moot court judge, Georgetown, Howard, Balsa, 1987-; vp, Columbia Law Alumni Asn, Wash DC, 1994-; pres, vp, mem, Soc Labor Rels Prof, 1987-; Nat Bar Asn, Arbit Sect, chair; NBA Arbit Sect News letter, Ed, 1997-; Nat Asn Securities Dealers; Nat Futures Asn; NY Stock Exchange; Nat Conf Black Lawyers; Wash Bar Asn; Indust Rels Res Asn; Soc Prof Dispute Resolution. **Honors/Awds:** Most outstanding Prof, Southern Univ Law Sch, 1982. **Special Achievements:** First Black member elected to the DC, Labor & Employment Law Section, steering comt, 1995-98; Donated papers to Amistad Res Ctr, Tulane Univ, New Orleans, LA; pub numerous articles in professional journals; Speaker & Participant at Nat & Regional Conf, Named one of top 45, 42, 56, 61 Lawyers in Wash DC Area, Wash Afro-Am Newspaper, 1993-96. **Home Addr:** 4315 Argyle Terr N W, Washington, DC 20011. **Business Addr:** Attorney, Arbitrator, 601 Pennsylvania Ave NW Suite 900 S Bldg, Washington, DC 20005, **Business Phone:** (202)434-8210.*

DONOVAN, KEVIN. See BAMBAATAA, AFRIKA.

DOOMES, DR. EARL
Educator. **Personal:** Born Feb 8, 1943, Washington, LA; son of Othus Sr; married Mazie Marie LeDeaux; children: Elizabeth Denise, Edward Earl & Elliot Doyle. **Educ:** Southern Univ Baton Rouge, BS, 1964; Univ NE Lincoln, PhD, 1969. **Career:** Univ NC, NSF trainee, 1967-68; Northwestern Univ, post doctoral res, 1968-69; Macalester Col, from asst prof to assoc prof, 1969-77; reviewer, Petroleum Res Fund Grant Proposal, 1970-80; Fla State Univ, res assoc, 1975-76; La State Univ, Nat Sci Found Fac, Sci fel, 1975-76; Southern Univ, Baton Rouge, assoc prof, 1977-82, prof chem, 1982-87, chmn, 1987-92, Col Sci, dean, 1992-99, assoc vice chancellor, 1999, training & mentoring, dir, 2003-06, prof emer, 2006-; consult, Minority Biomed Re Sport Prog Nat Inst Health, 1979-92. **Orgs:** NSF Grants Prog, 1985. **Honors/Awds:** Merck Sharpe & Dohme Award, Univ Northeast Lincoln, 1968; Faculty Excellence in Science and Technology, White House Initiative HBCU's, 1988;Charles E Coates Memorial Award, 1997. **Home Addr:** 13302 London Dr, Baker, LA 70714, **Home Phone:** (225)774-8284. **Business Addr:** Professor Emeritus, Southern University-Baton Rouge, Office of Academic Affairs, 3rd Fl J S Clark Admin Bldg, PO Box 9820, Baton Rouge, LA 70813, **Business Phone:** (225)771-2360.

DORMAN, HATTIE LAWRENCE
Management consultant, college teacher, president (organization). **Personal:** Born Jul 22, 1932, Cleveland, OH; daughter of James Lyman Lawrence (deceased) and Claire Correa Lenoir (deceased); married James W L; children: Lydia Dorman, Lynda & James Larry. **Educ:** Fenn Col, Cleveland State Univ, attended 1958; DC Teacher's Col, attended 1964; Howard Univ, BA, 1987. **Career:** IRS, 1954-79; US Treas, from spec asst to deputy asst secy, 1978-79; Inter agency Comn Women's Bus Enterprise, US Small Bus Admin, dep dir, 1979-83; US Small Bus Admin Off Comn & Govt Support, dir, 1983-85; Dorman & Assocs, mgt consult, trainer, 1985-; Univ DC, assoc prof continuing educ; Howard Univ, guest lectr continuing educ; presial Transition Team, chief staff dep dir, 1992-93. **Orgs:** Trainer Nation's Capital Girl Scout Coun, 1972-; Pres Task Force Women Bus Enterprise, 1978-79; Nat Asn Female Execs; Am Asn Black Women Entrepreneurs; Black Career Women Inc; sr exec assoc, Fed Exec Inst Alumni Asn; Am Sociol Asn; Nat Coun Negro Women; golden life mem, Delta Sigma Theta Sorority Inc; Nat Urban League; bd dirs, Girl Scouts USA; Wider Opportunity Women; Am Soc Training & Develop; Howard Univ Alumni Asn. **Honors/Awds:** Monetary Performance Award, IRS, 1970-78; Mary McLeod Bethune Centennial Award, Nat Coun Negro Women; Monetary Performance Award, US Small Bus Admin, 1980, 1984, 1985; Boss of the Year Award, Am Bus Women's Asn L'Enfant Chap, 1981; other award & citations: Delta Sigma Theta; PTA's; Am Asn Black Women Entrepreneurs; Nat Asn Minority Women; Articles: "Survey of Support Patterns", Black Orgn Black Polit Appointees Benjamin E Mays Monogr ser, 1988; "Field of Small Bus Develop". *

DORMAN, LINNEAUS C.
Scientist, chemist. **Personal:** Born Jun 28, 1935, Orangeburg, SC; son of John A Sr (deceased) and Georgia (deceased); married Phae Hubble; children: Evelyn S, John A. **Educ:** Bradley Univ, BS, 1956; Ind Univ, PhD, org chem, 1961. **Career:** Chemist, scientist (retired); Regional Res Lab, chemist, summers, 1956-59; Dow Chem Co, res chemist, 1960-68, res specialist, 1968-76, sr res assoc, 1976-83, assoc scientist, 1983-92, sr assoc scientist, 1993-94. **Orgs:** Bd dir, Comerica Bank-Midland 1982-95; Am Chem Soc, 1971-92; bd fel, Saginaw Valley State Col, 1976-87; Nat Org Black Chemist & Chem Engrs, 1978-; pres, Midland Rotary Club, 1982-83; chmn, Midland Black Coalition, 1973, 1977; Saginaw Valley Torch Club, 1995-; bd trustees, Midland Found, 1981-90; United Negro Col Fund; chmn, Midland Area Campaign, 1981-84; life mem, Nat Asn Advan Colored People; vpres, Midland Found, 1988-90; Elected to Bradley Univ, Centurion Soc, 1993; Bradley Univ Coun, 1994; bd financial advisers, Ind Univ, Dept Chem, 1994; bd mem, Midland County Hist Soc, 2001-; bd Managers, Midland County Hist Soc, 2001; exec coun, Ind Univ Alumni Asn, 2002. **Honors/Awds:** Dow Research Fellow, Ind Univ, 1959-60; Bond Award, Am Oil Chemist Soc, 1960; Central Research Inventor of the Year, Dow Chem Co, 1983; Honorary Doctor Science, Saginaw Valley State Univ, 1988; Outstanding Service, Am chem Soc, 1990; Percy L Julian Award, Nat Org Black Chemist & Chem Engrs, 1999; Distinguished Service Medallion, Saginaw Valley State Univ, 2002. **Special Achievements:** received twenty-six U.S. patents for his inventions. **Home Addr:** 2452 N Deer Valley Dr, PO Box 1732, Midland, MI 48642, **Home Phone:** (989)631-0213. *

DORN, MICHAEL
Administrator, actor. **Personal:** Born Dec 9, 1952, Luling, TX. **Career:** TV Series: "CHIPS", 1979-82; "Days of Our Lives", 1986-87; "Star Trek: The Next Generation", 1987-94; "Aladdin", animated, 1993; "Gargoyles", animated, 1994; "Superman", animated, 1996; "Cow & Chicken", animated, 1997; "Johnny Bravo", animated, 1997; "I Am Weasel", animated, 1999; "Spider man: The Animated Series", 2002; "Duck Dodgers", 2005; "Justice League", 2005; "Danny Phantom", 2005; "Without a Trace", 2007; "Ben 10", 2007; Films: Jagged Edge, 1985; Star Trek: Generations, 1994; Time master,1995; Star Trek: First Contact, 1996; Menno's Mind, 1996; Trekkies, 1997; Star Trek: Insurrection, 1998; The Prophet's Game, 1999; Mach 2, 2000; Ali, 2001; The Gristle, 2001; Face Value, 2001; The Santa Clause 2, 2002; Star Trek: Nemesis, 2002; Shade, 2003; Writer: Through the Fire, 2002; Director: episodes of Star Trek: Deep Space Nine, 1993; episode of Enterprise, 2001; Walking on Water, assoc producer, 2004; TV Episode voice: Good Duck Hunting & Consumption Overruled, Diamond Boogie & Corporate Pig fall, The Kids Are All Wrong & Win, Lose or Duck,Villain struck & Just the Two of Us, Diva Delivery & Castle High, The Ultimate Enemy, Reign Storm, Fright Knight, 2005; Heart of the Beholder, 2005; Descent, 2005; The Santa Clause 3: The Escape Clause, 2006; A.I. Assault, 2006; All You have Got, 2006; Fallen Angels, 2006; The Deep Below, 2007; Night Skies, 2007; Saints Row 2, 2008; Bionicle: The Legend Reborn, 2009; Superman/Batman: Public Enemies, 2009. **Orgs:** Air Force Aviation Heritage Found. **Military Serv:** USAAF. **Business Addr:** Actor, Agency Performing Arts, 9000 Sunset Blvd Suite 1200, Los Angeles, CA 90069, **Business Phone:** (310)273-0744.

DORN, ROOSEVELT F
Judge, clergy, mayor. **Personal:** Born Oct 29, 1935, Checotah, OK; married Joyce Evelyn Glosson, 1965; children: Bryan Keith, Renee Felicia & Rochelle Francine. **Educ:** Univ Calif Sch Law, Berkeley; Whittier Law, JD, 1969; Calif Judicial Col; Earl Warren Legal Inst, 1979, 1982. **Career:** Los Angeles County, dep sheriff super ct bailiff, 1961-69; Los Angeles, asst city atty 1970-79; Inglewood Jud Dist CA, Munic ct judge 1979-80; Los Angeles County Supe Court, judge 1980-99; Inglewood City, CA, mayor, 1997-. **Orgs:** Founder, First pres Inglewood Dem Club, 1977-79; Nat Asn Advan Colored People; Urban League; LA Co Bar Asn; Langston Bar Asn; Calif Black Lawyers Asn; Am Bar Asn; Lions Club; assoc minister, Atherton Baptist Church, Inglewood, CA; Calif Judges Asn; Nat Bar Asn; Los Angeles Trial Lawyers Asn; 100 Black Men Los Angeles Inc; John M Langston Bar Asn Judges Div; Nat Conf Black Mayors. **Honors/Awds:** Commendation for Outstanding Community Service, Senate CA Legislature, 1978; Commendation for Outstanding Service, CA State Assembly, 1979; Commendation for Outstanding Achievement, New Frontier Dem Club Inglewood Dem Club, 1979; Outstanding Service

Award, field Juvenile Justice Nat Sor Phi Delta Kappa Inc Delta Kappa Chap, 1983; Outstanding Contributions Support & Leadership for Youth Award, RDM Scholarship Fund Inc, 1984, 1985; Meritorious Service Youth Award, The Inglewood Teachers Asn, 1986; Dedicated Service & Guidance Award, Inglewood High School Student Body; Nat Top Ladies Distinction Humanitarian Award, 1987; Outstanding Service Award, Prairie View A&M Univ Alumni Assn, 1989; Most Valuable Judge Certificate, Los Angeles County, Central District, 1991-93; Commendation for Outstanding Leadership, Los Angeles Chief of Police, Willie L Williams, 1992; FAME Award, First African Methodist Episcopal Church, 1992; Distinguished Service Award, Nat Bar Asn Judicial Coun; Certificate of Appreciation, Los Angeles Southwest Col; Nat Honoree, Los Angeles Sentinel's Highest Award; Man of the Year Award, Because I Love You. **Military Serv:** USAF, airman first class, 1954-58. **Business Phone:** (310)412-5300.

DORRELL, KARL
Football coach, football player. **Personal:** Born Dec 18, 1963, Alameda, CA; married Kim; children: Chandler & Lauren. **Educ:** Univ Calif, BS, Los Angeles, 1986. **Career:** Dallas Cowboys, 1987; Univ Calif, Los Angeles, graduate asst, 1988, Head Coach, 2003-; Univ Cent Fla, Wide Receivers Coach, 1989; Univ N Ariz, Offensive Coordinator & Wide Receivers Coach, 1990-91; Univ Colo, Wide Receivers Coach, 1992-93, Offensive Coordinator & Wide Receivers Coach, 1995-98; Univ Ariz State, Wide Receivers Coach, 1994; Univ Wash, Offensive Coordinator & Wide Receivers Coach, 1999; Denver Broncos, Wide Receivers Coach, 2000-02; Wide Receivers Coach, UCLA, 2003-07; Wide Receivers Coach, Miami Dolphins; 2008-. **Honors/Awds:** Freedom Bowl, 1986.; PAC-10 championship, 2005. **Special Achievements:** First African American head coach in the history of the UCLA Bruins college football team. *

DORSE, EARNESTINE HUNT
Judge. **Personal:** Born Jun 29, 1952, Memphis, TN; daughter of William Ernest and Jennie Hunt; married Fred O Dorse, Apr 6, 1991; children: Sharon, Denee A Spencer, Dionne Hunt, William Keys, Larry Benson & Yolanda Hunt. **Educ:** Clark Col, Cum Laude, BA, 1974; Exchange Stud, Geneva, Switz, Vienna, Austria, Paris, France, Luxemburg, Ger; Memphis State Univ, JD, 1984. **Career:** Sonnenschein, Carlin, Nath & Rosenthal, litigation paralegal, 1981-82; Memphis Area Legal Servs Inc, Family Unit, law clerk, 1983-84; Evans, Willis, Stotts, Kyles, independent legal asst, 1984-86; Perkins, Hanna & Assocs, Gen civil pract, 1986-87; Shelby County Pub Defender, asst pub defender, 1986-90; Nat Acad Paralegal Studies, 1989-90; Div I, City Ct, Memphis, judge, 1990-. **Orgs:** S Am Bar Asn; dir, Nat Bar Asn, Judicial Coun, Region VI, 1991-93; Nat Asn Women Judges; TN Bar Asn; Ben F Jones Chap Nat Bar Asn; past pres bd, Memphis St Law; bd dir, Nat Coun Community Behavioral Healthcare; atty, Asn Women Attys. **Honors/Awds:** Zeta Achiever Award, Zeta Phi Beta Sorority Inc, 1990-91; Tennessee Asn of Blacks in Criminal Justice, Maybelline Shades of You, Nat Council of Negro Women, 10 Best Dressed, 1991; Sr Outstanding Community Service, AA Latting, 1992. **Special Achievements:** Researched and wrote the History of the Memphis Urban League, 1945-75. **Business Addr:** Judge, Administrative, City Ct Memphis, 201 Poplar LL-80, Memphis, TN 38103, **Business Phone:** (901)545-5410.

DORSETT, ANTHONY DREW, JR.
Football player. **Personal:** Born Sep 14, 1973, Aliquippa, PA; son of Tony. **Educ:** Univ Pittsburgh. **Career:** Houston Oilers, defensive back, 1996; Tennessee Oilers, 1997-99; Tennessee Titans; Oakland Raiders, defensive back, 2000-03. *

DORSETT, DR. KATIE GRAYS
State government official. **Personal:** Born Jul 8, 1932, Shaw, MS; daughter of Willie Grays and Elizabeth Grays; married Warren G Dorsett; children: Valerie. **Educ:** Alcorn State Univ, BS, 1953; Ind Univ Bloomington, MS, 1955; Univ NC Greensboro, EdD, 1975; State Univ New York Buffalo, attended 1981; Univ Md Col Park, attended 1983. **Career:** NC A&T St Univ, Sch Bus & Econ, assoc prof, 1955-87; Greensboro City Coun 1983-86; Guilford County Comn, 1986-92; Transp Inst NC A&T, res assoc, 1983-87; Dept Admin, State North Carolina, secy, 1993-2001, senator, 2002-, 28th Dist, State Sen, currently. **Orgs:** Bd mem, Guilford Tech Comm Col 1978-, trustee, 1983-93; exec bd, Gen Greene Coun Boy Scouts, 1980-; Greensboro Citizens Asn; Nat Asn Advan Colored People; League Women Voters; bd mem, Greensboro Nat Bank; bd mem, MDC Corp; NC Gene Assembly; comt mem & bd mem, Nat Asn Counties, 1991-93; bd mem, Sickle Cell Disease Asn Am, 1993-; bd mem, NC Asn County Comnrs, 1997-99; pres, Nat Asn State Cheif Admin, 1999-2000; trustee, NC A & T State Univ, 2001-; nat chair, Sickle Cell Disease Asn Am, 2002-. **Honors/Awds:** Outstanding Civic Leader, Greensboro Interclub Coun, 1978; TV Citizen of the Week, WGHP TV, 1978; One Comm Award, Feb One Soc, 1982; Outstanding Citizen Award, Negro Business & Prof Women, 1983; Outstanding Comm Leader, Mt Zion Baptist Church, 1983; Leader of the Year, Omega Psi Phi, 1983; Woman of the Year, Mt Zion African Methodist Espicol Church, 1984; Sojourner Truth Award, Negro Bus & Prof Women, 1985; Leadership Award, Negro Bus & Prof Women, 1986; Distinguished Alumni, Nat Asn Equal Opportunity, 1987; Leadership Award, Sigma Gamma Rho, 1987; Silver Anniversary Service Award, NC Community Col, 1989; Woman of Year, Nat Asn Advan Colored People, 1989; Strong Men and Women, Virginia Power, 1998; Distinguished Service Award, NC Asn Black Cty Comnrs, 1995. **Special Achievements:** First African American woman ever elected for Greensboro City Council; first African American woman to hold a North Carolina Cabinet post; 10 publications including "A Study of Levels of Job Satisfaction and Job Aspirations Among Black Clerical Employees in Greensboro & Guilford Co, North Carolina" 1976; "Training & Career Opportunities for Minorities & Women" Proceedings, 1984. **Home Addr:** 1000 N Eng St, Greensboro, NC 27405, **Home Phone:** (336)275-0628. **Business Addr:** State Senator, 28th Dist, Rm 2106 2106 Legis Bldg 16 W Jones St, Raleigh, NC 27601-2808, **Business Phone:** (919)715-3042.

DORSETT, MARY ALICE
Consultant. **Personal:** Born Feb 4, 1926, Dade City, FL; daughter of James and Nannie Mae Johnson; divorced; children: Dwayne Oswald Hill, Countess Charisse Clarke. **Educ:** Paine Col, 1946; Nat Trade & Prof Sch Women & Girls, 1950. **Career:** Self-employed, 1951-; Prof Bailbonds; Gen Employ Agency; Income Tax consult. **Orgs:** Nat Asn Advan Colored People, 1950-; Urban League, Tampa br, 1950-; Nat Coun Negro Women, 1965-; Tampa Orgn Black Affairs, 1999-. **Honors/Awds:** Plaque, Tampa Org on Black Affairs, 1983; plaque, Links, 1986, 1994, 2001; plaque, Hills Jr Coll, 1991; Susie Padgett Award, 1996; plaque, Hillsborough County Sheriff Dept, 1996; Dr King Drum Major Award, 1998; plaque, SDA Church, 1999; plaque, NAACP, 2001. **Special Achievements:** Building named in her honor, 2001. *

DORSETT, TONY DREW
Football player. **Personal:** Born Apr 7, 1954, Rochester, PA; son of West and Myrtle; married Janet Simon, Jan 1, 1981; children: Shukura & Anthony Jr. **Educ:** Univ Pittsburgh. **Career:** Football player (retired), sports speaker; Dallas Cowboys, running back, 1977-87; Denver Broncos, running back, 1988; Southwestern Drilling Mud Co, Midland TX, partner; Brooks Intl Speakers Bur, sports speaker, currently. **Orgs:** Nat Easter Seals Sports Coun; chmn, Am Heart Asn; Jump-Rope-A-Thon, 1980; United Way; United Negro Col Fund; TX Dept Hwys & Pub Trans Seat Belt Prog, Dallas Civic Opera. **Honors/Awds:** Heisman Trophy 1976; established record for longest run from scrimmage (99yards), 1983; Rookie of the Year, Sporting News, 1977; NFC Player of the Year 1981; holds numerous team (Dallas) records; played in Pro Bowl,1978-81, 1983; inducted into the Professional Football Hall of Fame, 1994. **Special Achievements:** First player in NCAA history with four 1000 yard seasons; appeared in films including: Necessary Roughness, 1991; Kill Zone, 1993; The Big Bounce, 2004. **Business Phone:** (303)825-8700.

DORSEY, DR. CAROLYN ANN
Educator. **Personal:** Born in Dayton, OH; daughter of James J and Lorana Madeline Webb. **Educ:** Kent State Univ, BS, 1956, MEd, 1961; New York Univ, PhD, 1976. **Career:** Educator (retired); Cleveland Pub Schs, teacher, 1956-62; Tabora Girls Sch, Tanzania, E Africa, teacher, 1962-64; Cleveland Job Corps Ctr, social studies dept chair & teacher, 1965-67; Southern Ill, Univ Expert Higher Educ Prog, curric spec & instr, 1967-69; Yale Univ Transitional Yr Prog, assoc dir & teacher, 1969-70; Yale Univ, Danforth Found black studies fel, 1969-70; NY Univ Inst Afro-Am Affairs, jr fel, 1970-74; Ind State Univ, asst prof, afro-Am studies, 1976-77; Univ Mo, coordr black studies, from asst prof higher educ to assoc prof higher educ, 1977-85, assoc prof higher educ, 1985-95, grad studies, dir, 1986-91. **Orgs:** Stephens Col Bd, 1981-91; Am Asn Higher Educ, Nat Coun Black Studies; Phi Delta Kappa; Phi Lambda Theta; Asn Study Afro-Am Life & Hist; Alpha Kappa Alpha Sorority; bias panel, Am Col Testing Prog Tests, 1982-; Psychol Corp Stanford Achievement Test. **Honors/Awds:** Danforth Found Associate, 1980-86; resident participant, Summer Inst Women Higher Educ Admin, Bryn Mawr Col, 1989; Faculty Award, Univ Mo, 1990; Alumnae Anniversary Award, Univ Mo, 1990; Carolyn A. Dorsey Minority Fellowship Fund, named in honor, Univ Missouri. **Special Achievements:** One of the first African American faculty members in the College of Education, Univ Missouri.

DORSEY, CLINTON GEORGE
Educator, clergy. **Personal:** Born Oct 29, 1931, New York, NY. **Educ:** Wilberforce Univ, Ohio, BS, educ, 1966; United Theol Sem Dayton, Ohio, Mdiv, 1970; Wright State Univ, Dayton, Ohio. **Career:** Educator (retired); AME Church, United Church Christ, 1962-68; Wright Patterson Air Force Base, Dayton, Ohio, W Ohio Conf, United Methodist Church, pastor, 1969-74; Troy High Sch, Troy, Ohio, counr, 1975-92. **Orgs:** Pres, Clinton G Dorsey Assoc Motivational Human Devel; dist rep, Ohio Sch Counselors Asn, 1971-76; consult, Dem Nom US Rep Fourth Cong Dist Ohio,1976; bd mem, Miami County Ment Assn, 1976; adv brd criminal justice comn, Edison State Community Col, 1979; APGA leg prog proj trainer Amer Personnel & Guid Assn, 1980; bd mem, Miami County Habitat Humanity, 1992; chmn, Miami County Dem Party; Troy Civil Serv Comn. **Military Serv:** USAF, a1/c, 1949-53. **Home Addr:** 1334 Custer Ct, Troy, OH 45373, **Home Phone:** (937)339-5028.

DORSEY, DENISE
Graphic artist. **Personal:** Born Apr 24, 1953, Washington, DC; daughter of Lillian Miles and Willie K. **Educ:** Univ MD, Col Park, BS, 1975. **Career:** Young Women Christian Asn, Baltimore, MD, aerobic instr, 1981-91; Afro-Am Newspapers, Baltimore, MD, graphic artist, prod mgr, currently. **Orgs:** Bd dir, Charles St Dancers, 1991; secy & treas, United Paperworkers Int Union, Local 111, 1988-95. **Business Addr:** Production Manager, Afro-Am Newspapers, 2519 N Charles St, Baltimore, MD 21218, **Business Phone:** (410)554-8288.

DORSEY, ELBERT
Lawyer, library administrator, teacher. **Personal:** Born Oct 4, 1941, St Louis, MO; son of Velmer and Juanita Jarrett Green; married Diane Elaine; children: Elbert Todd, Donielle Elaine, Daniel Christopher, Joseff Alexander. **Educ:** Harris-Stowe State Col, BA, 1966; St Louis Univ Sch Law, JD, 1973. **Career:** St Louis Community Col Dist, asst librn, 1965-66; St Louis Bd Educ, teacher, 1966-70; St Louis Legal Aid Soc, law clerk, 1971-72; Small Bus Admin, loan officer & atty, 1973-74; Collier, Dorsey & Williams, atty; Smith & Dorsey, atty, currently. **Orgs:** Historian Mound City Bar Asn; Judicial Conf Adv Comt, Eighth Circuit Ct Appeals; chmn/bd dir, Yeatman/Union-Sarah Joint Comn Health; Polemarch St Louis Alumni Chap Kappa Alpha Psi Frat; chmn, adv bd, St Louis Comprehensive Health Ctr Home Health Bd. **Honors/Awds:** Ford Fel World Conf Peace, 1973; Dedication Award, Mound City Bar Asn St Louis, 1983; Humanitarian Award, St Louis Alumni Chap Kappa Alpha Psi, 1985. *

DORSEY, HAROLD AARON
Chief executive officer. **Personal:** Born Jun 22, 1933, Louisville, KY; married Julia Anita Willis; children: Michelle, Harold II & Michael. **Educ:** Ohio Univ, Athens, BA, Pol Sci, 1965; Ohio State Univ, Columbus, MA, 1971. **Career:** Community Action Agency, asst dir, 1965-69; Grad Sch Ohio State Dept Soc, res asst, 1968-70; Community Action Agency, acting dir, 1970; Ohio State Univ, teaching asst, 1970-71; Mansfield OIC, exec dir. **Orgs:** Pres, Mansfield, NAACP, 1974; chmn, Ninth City Manpower Adv Coun, 1975; bd dir, Mansfield Area C C, 1977-80; pres, Nat Black Prof Asn, 1977-80. **Honors/Awds:** Personality of the Week Local Newspaper, Mansfield News Journ; Businessman of Week Local Radio Sta; Ed Bd, Gerontologist. **Military Serv:** USAF, a/1c. *

DORSEY, HERMAN SHERWOOD, JR.
Consultant. **Personal:** Born Apr 5, 1945, Brooklyn, NY; son of Herman Sherwood Sr and Loretta Rosa Kenney; married Maria Teresa Miller Dorsey, Feb 19, 1966; children: Donna Michelle, Bryan Sherwood. **Educ:** NY City Community Col, Brooklyn, NY, AA, mech tech, 1966; Brooklyn Polytechnic Inst, Brooklyn, NY, BS, mech engineering, 1972; NY Univ, Bronx, NY, BS, mech engineering, 1972; Duke Univ, Durham, NC, cert, exec mgt, 1988. **Career:** Consolidated Edison Co, NY, technician, 1966-72, engr, 1972-78, sr engr, 1978-83, subsection mgr, 1983-86, mgr, steam generation planning, 1986-91, tech supt, 1991-93, Steam & Electric Sta, 1994, plant mgr, currently; pvt int consult, 1992-; motivational speaker, 1995. **Orgs:** DOE, cand prin asst secy, 1993; IDEA, Nat Planning Comt, 1991-93; US Trade & Develop Team, 1995; Nat Action Coun Minorities Eng, liaison, 1989-98; nat chair, Am Asn Blacks Energy, 1996-98; vpres, bd mem, Tamiment Resort POA, 1991-94; chr, Steam Integrated Resource Plan, Consolidated Edison, 1992; Am Soc Mech Engrs, 1972; Nat Republican Cong Comm & Frederick Douglass Republican Coun, 1990-. **Honors/Awds:** Cert Vis Prof, Black Exec Exchange Prog, Nat Urban League & Asn Cols, 1976, 1977, 1980-89; Black Achiever in Indust, YMCA-Harlem Br, 1975; Cert, Shaping the Minds of Young Adults, Consolidated Edison, 1988; Pi Tau Sigma, Scholastic Achievement, Pi Tau Sigma-Hon Mech Engineering Soc, 1972; Ms Am Pageant judge, 1995; Consult Gingdao, China Power Co, 1995. **Special Achievements:** Three technical papers published internationally, Int Dist Heating & Cooling Asn, 1988, 1989, 1991. **Business Addr:** Plant Manager, Consolidated Edison Co, 850 12th Ave, New York, NY 10019.*

DORSEY, IVORY
Public speaker, writer, executive. **Personal:** Born Apr 29, 1947, DeQuincy, LA; daughter of Walter E Wood and Mary L Wood; divorced; children: Edward Douglas Dorsey (deceased). **Educ:** Southern Univ, BS, bus ed, 1970; Xerox Int Ctr Training & Mgt Develop. **Career:** Xerox Corp, customer rep, Houston, 1974-75, high volume syst rep, 1975-76, region prog support, Dallas, 1976-77, field sales exec, 1977-79, field sales Mgr, Atlanta, 1979-81, Mgr Xerox store, Atlanta, 1981-84; teacher, pub schs; Golden Eagle Bus Servs Inc, pres & owner, 1984-; pub speaker, trainer, facilitator & author; Book: Universal Appeal: The Bottom Line Benefit of Diversity, 1994; Soft Skills for Hard Times: A Handbook for High Achievers, 2004. **Orgs:** Pres, Am Soc Training & Develop, 1992; adv bd, Atlanta Chamber Com Partners Bus & Ed, 1992; Gov's Small & Minority Bus Adv Comt, vice-chairwoman, 1992; Nat Speakers Asn, Ga. **Honors/Awds:** Atlanta Tribune, Annual Salute Bus Owners, 1990; Distinguished Past Resident, DeQuincy Chamber Com, 1991; Distinguished Alumni Award, Southern Univ, 1998; Delta Sigma Theta Leadership Award, 2005; Professional Development Award, ASTD. **Business Phone:** (404)881-6777.

DORSEY, JOHN L.
Lawyer. **Personal:** Born Sep 24, 1935, New Orleans, LA; married Evelyn. **Educ:** Dillard Univ, BA, 1963; Loyola Univ, Law Sch,

JD, 1969. **Career:** New Orleans Legal Assistance Corp, atty, 1968-70; Dorsey & Marks, New Orleans, atty, 1970-; atty, pvt pract, currently. **Orgs:** Nat Bar Asn; New Orleans Criminal Ct Bar Asn; Am Bar Asn; Nat Asn Advan Colored People; New Orleans Urban League; Lower & Ninth Ward Neighborhood Coun; Comt Alcholism & Drug Abuse Greater New Orleans; All Conf Football, 1961. **Military Serv:** USAF, a/1c, 1955-59. **Business Addr:** Attorney, Private Practice, 4948 Chef Menteur Hwy Suite 519, New Orleans, LA 70126.*

DORSEY, JOSEPH A.
School administrator, physical therapist. **Personal:** Born Apr 19, 1932, Baltimore, MD; married Alma K Edmonds; children: Dwain Kevin, Kyle Joseph. **Educ:** Springfield Col, BS, 1958; NY Univ, Cert Advan Grad Studies, 1959; Northeastern Univ, MEd, 1966; Boston Univ, DEd, 1976. **Career:** Univ Lowell Dept Health, prof, chmn, 1976-; Boston State Col, Dept Phys Educ, assoc prof, chmn, 1968-76; Andover Sch Syst, teacher & coach, 1960-68; Wayne County Gen Hosp, Detroit, phys therapist, 1959-60; Lawrence Gen Hosp, phys therapist, 1960-66; Pvt Pract, phys therapist, 1960-; Andover Bd Health & Sch Syst, consult, 1977-78. **Orgs:** Bd dir, Andover ABC, 1977-; fel Am Col Sports Med; comt mem, Merrimack Valley Health Coun, 1978-. **Honors/Awds:** Coach of the Year, MA Asn Gymnastic Coaches, 1967-68; citations State Rep & State Sen 1968 & 1977; Andover Hall of Fame, Andover Sch System 1977. **Military Serv:** USMC sgt 1951-54; Good Conduct Medal/UN Serv Medal/Korean Serv Medal W/3 Stars/ Nat Defense Medal USMC. **Business Addr:** 1 Rolfe St, Lowell, MA 01854.*

DORSEY, L. C.
Executive. **Personal:** Born Dec 17, 1938, Tribbett, MS; daughter of Mary Davis and Abraham Warren; married Hildery Dorsey Sr, Feb 17, 1956 (divorced); children: Cynthia Dorsey Smith, Norma Dorsey, Anita Dorsey Word, Michael Dorsey, Adriane Dorsey, Hildery Dorsey Jr. **Educ:** Mary Holmes Col, 1971; Worker Col Tel Aviv Israel, 1970; State Univ NY Stony Brook NY, MSW, 1973, Howard Univ, DSW, 1988. **Career:** Oper Headstart, teacher, 1966-67; No Bolivar Co Farm Coop, dir, 1968-71; Wash Co Opportunities Inc, dir social serv, 1974; So Coalition Jails & Prisons Inc, asso dir, 1975-83; Delta Ministry, asso dir, 1977-83; Lutheran Social Servs Wash DC, Advocacy & Educ, dir, 1983-85; Memphis health CTR, asst to Chief Health Officer, 1986-88; Delta Health Ctr Inc, exec dir, 1988-95; Univ Miss, res asst prof, 1988; Jackson State Univ, Sch Soc Work, asst prof; Univ Miss Med Ctr, clinical assoc prof. **Orgs:** MS Conf Soc Welfare 1976-; pres, Jackson chap NABSW, 1976-78, 1980-82; chmn, polit action com, Stte NAACP 1979; New Bethel MB Ch choir, 1975-80; First Christian Church, 1988-; writer, bd mem, Jackson Adv, 1978-80; poet, founding mem, Black Women's Art Collective, 1978-80; Presidential Comn, Nat Adv, Coun Econ Opportunities, WASH DC, 1978-80; Governor's Comn Children & Youth, Jackson MS, 1980; Governor's Task Force Indigent Health Care, Jackson MS, 1988-89; life mem, NAACP; Nat Coun Negro Women, 1971-; Am Pub Health Asn, 1989-; NASW, 1995-; ACLU MS, 1989-; Southern Regional Coun, 1997-; Pres, Clinton's Health Prof Comn, Health Care Reform, 1994-96; chair, Mayor's Task Force Human & Cultural Service, 1997-. **Honors/Awds:** Meritorious Service Awards, Nat Med Asn, Women's Aux 1970; Woman of the Year, New York City Utility Club, 1971; Fellowship Black Women's Community Develop Found, 1971-72; Fannie Lou Hamer Award, Urban League Jackson, 1978; Fellow, MATCH Program, Nat Asn Community Health Ctrs, 1986-87; The Significance Jealousy & Addictive Love Acts Homicide Among Black Women, 1987; Not In Our Names, 1984; Cold Steel, 1982; If Bars Could Talk, 1980; Freedom Came to Mississippi, 1978; Harriet Tubman Award, Magnolia Bar Asn, 1998. **Business Addr:** Assistant Professor School of Social Work, Jackson State University, 1400 John R Lynch St, Administration Tower, Jackson, MS 39217-0280, **Business Phone:** 800-848-6817.*

DORSEY, SANDRA
Association executive. **Personal:** Children: Kellee. **Career:** ABC TV, staff; Am Women Radio & TV, pres; Found Minority Interests Media, W Coast Regional Off, dir, currently, Eastern Region, vpres, currently; Emma Bowen Found Minority Interests Media, vpres, currently. **Orgs:** Am Women Radio & TV (AWRT), pres, 1997. **Honors/Awds:** Everett C Parker Award, Minority Media & Telecommunications Ctr, 2002. **Business Addr:** Vice President, Emma Bowen Found Minority Interests Media, 524 W 57th St, New York, NY 10019, **Business Phone:** (212)975-2545.

DORSEY, TREDELL
Athletic coach. **Personal:** Married Makasha; children: Justin. **Educ:** Univ RI, BS, exercise sci & phys educ, 1998; Springfield Col, MS, applied exercise sci. **Career:** Gateway High Sch, asst defensive backs coach, 1999-2000; Discovery Intermediate Middle Sch, head phys educ coach, track coach & health teacher; Amherst Col, strength & conditioning coach; Velocity Sports Performance, dir sports performance; Holy Cross, strength and conditioning coach; Ga Tech Univ, asst dir player develop, 2000-04, Ga State Panther Athletics, head strength & conditioning coach, 2005-. **Business Addr:** Head Strength, Conditioning Coach, Georgia State University, Georgia State Panther Athletics, 125 Decatur St Suite 201, Atlanta, GA 30303, **Business Phone:** (404)413-4020.

DORTCH, HEYWARD
Executive. **Personal:** Born Jun 25, 1939, Camden, AL; son of Clarence and Alice; married Amelia, Jul 3, 1966; children: Derrick. **Educ:** Tenn State Univ, BS, 1966. **Career:** Mich Consol-Gas Company's Annual Jobs & Careers Seminar, founder & chairperson, 1982-94; Diversa Group Inc, pres, founder & chief exec officer, currently. **Orgs:** Bd trustees, financial secy, chief fiscal officer, chairperson/insurance & real estate comt bd, non-profit housing corp, Ebenezer AME Church; facilities mgt advisory bd, Eastern Mich Univ, Col Technol; bd chair, Phenix Inc; entrepreneurship adv coun & chair, Northern High Sch; vpres, Ebenezer A M E Church Non-Profit Housing Corp; vpres, Robert L Phillips Housing Corp; vpres, Robert Thomas Ltd Dividend Housing Asn Ltd Partnership; founder & coordr, Ebenezer AME Church Tutorial Prog. **Honors/Awds:** Minority Achiever in Indust, Young Men's Christian Asn Metro Detroit, 1980; Strong Achiever Award, Radio Sta WJLB, 1990. **Special Achievements:** Nat Asn Negro Bus & Prof Women's Club, Outstanding Dedication and Work with Youth, 1990; Detroit City Coun, Testimonial Resolution For Contributions to the City of Detroit, 1991; Serves as a mentor at various schools working primarily with young male students; Author, Preparing for Your Career, A Resource Handbook; Author, Fundamentals of Entrepreneurship. **Home Addr:** 15537 Thatcher, Detroit, MI 48235, **Home Phone:** (313)273-0904. **Business Addr:** President, Chief Executive Officer, Diversa Group Inc, 17515 W 9 Mile Rd, Southfield, MI 48075, **Business Phone:** (248)559-2066.*

DORTCH, THOMAS W., JR.
Executive, entrepreneur, writer. **Personal:** Born Apr 12, 1950, Toccoa, GA; son of Thomas Wesley Sr and Lizzie Porter; married Carol Warren, Sep 16, 1985; children: Five. **Educ:** Fort Valley State Col, BA, sociol, 1972; Clark Atlanta Univ, MA, criminal justice admin, 1985. **Career:** Democratic Party Ga, Atlanta, assoc dir, 1974-78; Office US Sen Sam Nunn, Atlanta, admin aide, 1978-86, state exec asst, 1986-90, state dir, 1990-94; 100 Black Men Am, chmn bd, 1994-05; Atlanta Transp Systs, Inc, founder & chief exec officer, 1995-; TWD Inc, Atlanta, founder & chief exec officer, 1995-. **Orgs:** bd mem, Ga Asn Minority Entrepreneurs; adv bd mem, Ga Asn Black Elected officials; founder, Nat Black Col Alumni Hall Fame Found; Assault Illiteracy Prog; Atlanta Jewish/ Black Coalition; bd mem, Friendship Force Int. **Honors/Awds:** Ford Fel, Ga State Univ, 1972-74; Humanitarian Award, Ga Asn Black Elected officials, 1989; Pres Citation Volunteerism, Pres George Bush, 1990; Nation Builder's Award, Nat Black Caucus State Legislators, 2002; Distinguished Phoenix Award, Cong Black Caucus Found, 2004; Man of the Decade, 100 Black Men Am Inc, 2004; John E Jacobs Community Serv Award, Anheuser Busch Co, 2004; Distinguished Serv Award, Martin Luther King Jr; Hall of Fame, inductee, Fort Valley State Col Alumni; Dr, Fayetteville State Univ & Jarvis Christian Col. **Special Achievements:** Founded National Black College Alumni Hall of Fame Found, Inc; Author: The Miracles of Mentoring: The Joy of Investing in Our Future, 2000. *

DOSS, CONYA
Singer. **Personal:** Born in Cleveland, OH. **Career:** Cleveland pub sch syst, teacher; Albums: A Poem About Ms. Doss, 2002; Just Because, 2004; Love Rain Down, 2006; Still, 2008. **Honors/ Awds:** Soultracks Award, 2008. **Business Addr:** Singer, c/o Heliocentric Public Relations, 7137 Alvern St Suite 212, Los Angeles, CA 90045, **Business Phone:** (310)645-4246.*

DOSS, DR. JUANITA KING
Clinical psychologist. **Personal:** Born Jan 5, 1942, Baltimore, MD; daughter of Charles and Helen; divorced 1975; children: Charles Doss & Lawry Doss. **Educ:** Howard Univ, Wash, DC, BS, 1963; Wayne State Univ, Detroit, MI, MSW, 1972; Union Inst, Cincinnati, OH, PhD, 1988. **Career:** Allied Health Serv, MI, assoc dir, 1972-78; Southwest Detroit Hosp, MI, dir planning & develop, 1978-80; Psychol serv clin, co-founder & principal partner, currently; Burdette & Doss Assocs, MI, co-owner & clin dir, 1980-. **Business Phone:** (248)559-0730.

DOSS, LAROY SAMUEL
Automotive executive. **Personal:** Born Oct 6, 1936, San Francisco, CA; son of Samuel Doss Jr and Louvonia Smith; married Mary Joyce Piper; children: Gwendolyn Marie. **Educ:** St Marys Col Calif, BA, psychol, 1959. **Career:** Crown Zellerback, warehouseman, 1959-61; SF, playground dir, 1961-63; Geary Ford, salesman, 1963, fleet mgr, 1968-69, truck sales mgr, 1969-71, used car mgr, 1974; Pittsburg Ford Inc, pres & owner, 1974-. **Orgs:** Vpres & bd dir, St Marys Coll Alumni, 1963-; Proj Inside & Out San Quentin Prison, 1967-71; vpres, Optimist Club, 1972-74; pres Pittsburg C of C, 1976-; bd dir, E Contra Costa YMCA, 1977-; dir, Sr Citizens Home Aging Bldg Fund, 1977-; Black Political Asn; Pittsburg Rotary Club, 1975-; Pittsburg Bus & Prof Asn; bd trustees, St Marys Col 1980-; pres, Easter Seals Soc Contra Costa Solano City, 1983-84; bd regents, St Mary's Col Moraga, Ca, 1986-; chmn bd, Black Ford-Lincoln-Mercury Dealers Asn, 1988-89. **Honors/Awds:** Invited, White House ceremony, President Jimmy Carter; Most Successful 100 Black Businesses in Am, Black Enterprise Mag; received numerous awards contributions & serv community. **Business Addr:** President, Owner, Pittsburg Ford Inc, 2575 Railroad Ave, Pittsburg, CA 94565, **Business Phone:** (925)676-6400.*

DOSS, ROD
Publisher. **Career:** New Pittsbugh Courier, ed & publ, currently. **Business Addr:** Editor, Publisher, New Pittsbugh Courier, 315 E Carson St, Pittsburgh, PA 15219, **Business Phone:** (412)481-8302 Ext 138.*

DOSS, HON. THERESA
Judge. **Personal:** Daughter of Eddie E and Ida Richards; married James T Wahls; children: James Christopher Doss Wahls. **Educ:** Ohio Univ, Athens, OH, AB, 1961; OH State Univ Col Law, JD, 1964; Wayne State Univ, MA, 2000. **Career:** Judge (retired); Cleveland Pub Sch, teacher, 1961; State Mich, law librn, 1964-65; Archdiocesan Opportunity Prog, 1965-66; State Mich, asst atty-gen, 1966-76; Detroit Lighting Comn, comnr, 1974-76; Common Pleas Ct, City Detroit, judge, 1976-81; State Mich Thirty sixth Dist, judge, 1981-2003; Mich Judicial Tenure Comn, comnr, 1995-2001; vice chair, 2001. **Orgs:** Secy, Wolverine Bar Asn, 1967-68; jour adv comn, State Bar MI, 1971-77, rep assembly, 1975-81, Wayne County character & fitness comt, 1971-75; pres, Nat Bar Asn, Women Sect, 1975-76; pres, Women's Lawyers Asn Mich, 1973-74; Mich Metro Girl Scouts Coun; Neighborhood Serv Orgn, 1977-87; pres, Mich Dist Judges Asn, 1991; Wayne County Dist Judges Asn; trustee, Tabernacle Missionary Baptist Church; NAACP; Nat Coun Negro Women. **Honors/Awds:** Certificate of Distinction, Ohio State University Col of Law Alumni Assn, 1983; Nat Council of Negro Women, Outstanding Achievement in Law, 1976; United Methodist Women of Second Grace Methodist Church, Meritorious Achievement of Community Service in Jurisprudence, 1976; Rosa L Gragg Educational & Civic Club, Humantarian Service Award, 1986; honored as Founding Member, Women Division of Nat Bar Assn, 1992; Natl Bar Assn, scroll of distinguished women lawyers award, 2001.

DOSSMAN, CURLEY M, JR.
President (Organization). **Personal:** Married Jennifer; children: Jonathan. **Educ:** Morehouse Col, Atlanta, BA, 1973; Washington Univ Sch Law, JD, 1976. **Career:** Office Fed Affairs & Spec Projects, inter-agency liaison officer, 1976; La State Planning Office,asst dir,1978; AT&T, regional atty,1984; Georgia-Pacific Found, sr dir, Community Progs Dept, pres, currently. **Orgs:** Chair, AAMI task force subcommittee; Brown V Bd Educ; Phi Beta Kappa; pres, Morehouse Stud Gov Asn; Nal Bd Dir & Exec Comn; 100 Black Men Am Inc; La Bar Asn; Nat Bar Asn; Am Bar Asn; Prof Asn Ga Educrs; High Mus Art. **Honors/Awds:** AT&T External Affairs Pacesetter Award for Excellence in Performance,1989. **Special Achievements:** Outstanding Youth Man of America by the US Jaycees, 1977. **Business Addr:** President, Georgia-Pacific Foundation, 133 Peachtree St NE, Atlanta, GA 30303, **Business Phone:** (404)652-4182.*

DOTSON, ALBERT E., JR.
Lawyer. **Personal:** Born in Detroit, MI; married Gail Ash Dotson; children: Ashley, Albert III. **Educ:** Dartmouth College, Economics and History; Vanderbilt University, JD; Universidad de Granada. **Career:** Bilzin Sumberg Baena Price & Axelrod LLP, Attorney and Equity Partner. **Orgs:** Chairman of the Board, 100 Black Men of America; President, Orange Bowl Committee; Chairman, Miami Dade College Foundation Board of Trustees; Board of Governors, Big Brothers/Big Sisters of Greater Miami. **Honors/Awds:** Bennett Douglas Bell Memorial Prize; 40 Business Leaders in South Florida Under 40; Daily Business Review's Most Effective Lawyer; Certificate of Special Congressional Recognition. **Home Addr:** 004850. *

DOTSON, BETTY LOU
Management consultant, president (organization). **Personal:** Born Jun 29, 1930, Chicago, IL; daughter of Heber T and Christine Price. **Educ:** Ohio Wesleyan Univ, BA, 1950; Lincoln Univ, JD, 1954. **Career:** Dept Urban Renewal, 1963; Cook County Dept Pub Welfare, caseworker-cons, 1964-66; First Nat Bank Chicago, legal serv trust dept, 1966-68; US Dept Agr Food & Nutrit Serv, dir civil rights, 1970-75; Dept Health & Human Serv, Wash, DC, dir, office for civil rights, 1981-87; BLD & Assoc, pres, currently; Houston Community Col, instr. **Orgs:** From asst dir to dir, Equal Oppty Action, 1975-79; sr staff assoc, Joint Ctr Polit Studies 1979-80; chief adjudications USDA Equal Oppty Office, 1980-81; bd dir, Nat Capital YWCA, 1981-84; Alpha Kappa Alpha; steeering comm Black Am Nixon/Agnew, 1968; advisory bd, Arneson Inst Practical Politics, Ohio Weslegan Univ, 1989-; bd trustees, Ohio Wesleyan Univ, Delaware, trustee, 1994-03. **Honors/Awds:** Administration Assistant Office of President elect Nixon, 1969. **Business Addr:** President, BLD & Associates, PO Box 331143, Houston, TX 77233-1143, **Business Phone:** (713)734-1807.

DOTSON, EARL CHRISTOPHER
Football player. **Personal:** Born Dec 17, 1970, Beaumont, TX; married Janell; children: Jared. **Educ:** Tex A&M Univ, Kingsville. **Career:** Football player (retired); Green Bay Packers, offensive tackle, 1993-02. **Honors/Awds:** Super Bowl champion (XXXI). *

DOTSON, HOWARD
Association executive. **Career:** Schomburg Ctr Res Black Cult, coordr, chief, dir, currently. **Special Achievements:** Published numerous articles. **Business Addr:** Director, Schomburg Center

for Research in Black Culture, 515 Malcolm C Blvd, New York, NY 10037-1801, **Business Phone:** (212)491-2263.*

DOTSON, HON. NORMA Y
Executive director, judge. **Educ:** Wayne State Univ, Detroit, MI, BS, MEd, JD. **Career:** Detroit Pub Schs, teacher; Norma Y Dotson, PC, atty; Patterson, Phifer & Phillips, coun; 36th Dist Ct, judge, currently. **Orgs:** State Bar Mich; Asn Black Judges Mich; Mich Dist Judges Asn; Nat Bar Asn; Wolverine Bar Asn; NAACP; Detroit Fedn Teachers; Wayne State Univ Alumni Asn; Phi Alpha Delta; Delta Sigma Theta Inc; Phi Delta Kappa; bd mem, Nat Conf Artists; bd dirs, Nat Healthcare Scholars Found, currently. **Business Addr:** Judge, State of Michigan District Court, 36th District, Rm 3070 Madison Ctr 421 Madison Ave, Detroit, MI 48226-2358, **Business Phone:** (313)965-8728.

DOTSON, PHILIP RANDOLPH
Educator. **Personal:** Born Oct 10, 1948, Carthage, MS; son of Jim O R Dotson and Velma Ernest Dotson; married Judith Kerr Dotson, May 19, 1973; children: Philip T R, Tiffany M & Brian R. **Educ:** Jackson State Univ, Jackson, Miss, BS, art educ, 1970; Univ Miss, Oxford, MS, MFA painting, 1972. **Career:** Memphis Jack & Jill Exhibition, curator, 1983-84; Spirit of African Art in the South, Memphis State Univ, curator, 1983; LeMoyne-Owen Col, Dept Art, chmn, 1972-87, chmn, div fine arts & humanities, 1988-96; LeMoyne-Owen Col, prof, currently. **Orgs:** Sponsor, Cotton Carnival Asn, 1972-83; Planning mem, Memphis May Int Festival, 1972-73; review mem, Tenn Arts Comn, 1975-76; Religious Comm Arts & Am Revolution, 1976, Chamber Com; arts adv bd, Mallory Knights Charitable Orgn, 1976-80; Col Art Asn, 1978-80; bd mem, Artist in Sch Prog Arts Coun; bd dir, Round Table Memphis Mus Dir, 1982-; bd mem, Memphis Arts Coun, 1986-; bd mem, Memphis Arts Festival, 1989-. **Honors/Awds:** Hon Mention, Nat Conf Artists, 1969; Phi Kappa Phi, Univ Miss, 1972; Art Work Permanent Collection in Nigeria Africa, 1981; Permanent Collection Memphis Brooks Mus, 1982; Video Tape in Collection State Dept of Archives; illus in three med books, 1983; oil painting Anthropomorphic Psychosis, permanent collection, Memphis Brooks Mus of Art. **Special Achievements:** Co-edited Homespun Images: An Anthology of Black Memphis Writers & Artists. **Business Phone:** (901)942-6407.

DOTSON-WILLIAMS, HENRIETTA
Government official. **Personal:** Born May 27, 1940, Valden, MS; daughter of Fred Perteete and Woodsy; married Michael J Williams; children: Johnice, Mike, Angela Woodson, Earl Dotson Jr , Dennis & Clifford. **Educ:** Ill Extn Univ, 1960. **Career:** Government official (retired); Ill Bell Telephone Co, operator spec eng clerk, 1960-68; N Ill Women's & Ctr, coun, 1974-; Secy State, fac serv clerk; "Black Corner" Monthly TV Prog, former moderator; Winnebago County Bd Dist 12, suprv, 1972; comm, Rockford Fire & Police commission, 2008-. **Orgs:** Pres, Winnebago County Bd Health, 1983-85; Ill Asn Bd Health, 1984-86; secy, Burpee Museum, bd dirs; bd dirs, Klehm Arboretum & Botanical Gardens; chmn, Winnebago County Intergovernmental Affairs Comn; bd mem, Fire and Police Com, Ill. **Honors/Awds:** Finalist Excalibur nomination, 2008. **Special Achievements:** Woman of the Month, Essence Mag, 1978; nominee for Woman of the Year, Young Women's Christian Asn, 1982 & 1986; Led an Effort to Retain Dr ML King's Birthday as a Legal Holiday for Winnebago County Employees. **Home Addr:** 1202 Kent St, Rockford, IL 61102. *

DOTTIN, DR. ROBERT PHILIP
Educator, scientist. **Personal:** Born May 23, 1943, Trinidad, West Indies; son of William Dottin and Lena Dottin; married Gail, May 1990; children: Melissa & Garreth. **Educ:** Univ Toronto, BS, 1968, MS, 1970, PhD, 1974; Univ mass, post doc, 1974-76. **Career:** MIT, Post Doctoral, 1974-76; Univ Copenhagen, vis prof, 1975; MIT, Johns Hopkins Univ, asst prof, 1976-82, assoc prof, 1982-87; Hunter Col, CUNY, New York, NY, Dept Biol, prof, 1986-, prog dir, ctr gene struct & function, currently. **Orgs:** Genetics Study Sect; grantee, Nat Inst Health, 1984-; Am Soc Cell Biol-;Nat Sci Found; Am Heart Asn; Am Soc Human Genetics, 1986; Am Soc Biochem &Molecular Biol, 1985; ed, publ, Coalition Advan Blacks BioMed Scis, CABBS,A Resource Diry; Sigma Xi, exec comt. **Honors/Awds:** Govs Gens Canada Medal, 1968; Med Res Coun Canada Fel, 1974-76; NATO Travel Fel, 1991-93; Fogarty Sr Int Fel, 1991-92; Fogarty Int Sr Colaboration Award, 1992-95; Distinguished Scientist, Univ Calif, 1996; Distinguished Scientist, Howard Univ, 1997. **Business Addr:** Professor of Biology, Program Director, Hunter College, Center for Study of Gene Structure and Function, Hunter Col N Bldg Room 932, 695 Pk Ave, New York, NY 10021, **Business Phone:** (212)772-5171.

DOTTIN, ROGER ALLEN
Executive. **Personal:** Born Jul 13, 1945, Cambridge, MA; son of Reuben and Eunice; married Marilyn Ames, Apr 9, 1989. **Educ:** Cambridge Sch Bus, Dipl, 1965; Grahm Jr Col. **Career:** Econ Opportunity Atlanta Inc, ctr dir, 1970-73; City Atlanta Community Rels Comn, asst dir, 1974-76; Metro Atlanta Rapid Transit Authority, sr comm rels spec, 1976-84, mgr community rels, 1984-86; Dallas Area Rapid Transit, mgr cust servs, 1986-90; Metrop Atlanta Rapid Transit Authority, mgr & community coordr, 1990-. **Orgs:** Vice chair, Sponsor-A-Family Proj Atlanta, 1983-87; Atlanta Pub Schs Safety & Emergency Mgt Adv-Coun, 1984-86; co-chair, Atlanta Br Nat Asn Advan Colored People; Afro-Acad Cult Tech Sci Olympics, 1984-86; Conf Minority Transp Offs, 1985-; past pres, Int Cust Serv Asn; ampbellton/Cascade Y's Men; Local Coord Coun Fulton Co Pvt Indust Coun. **Honors/Awds:** Outstanding Servce Award, John Harland Boys Club Atlanta, 1982; Community Service Award, NAACP Atlanta Br, 1984; Outstanding & Dedicated Service, NAACP Atlanta Br, 1986; YMCA Minority Achievers Prog, Dallas YMCA, 1988; Jondelle Harris Johnson Humanitarian Award, NAACP, Atlanta, 2001. **Military Serv:** AUS, E-2 1 1/2 yrs; Hon Discharge. **Business Addr:** Community Coordinator, Metrop Atlanta Rapid Transit Authority, 2424 Piedmont Rd, Atlanta, GA 30324, **Business Phone:** (404)848-4266.

DOUG, DOUG E. (DOUGLAS BOURNE)
Actor. **Personal:** Born Jan 7, 1970, Brooklyn, NY. **Career:** Films: Mo' Better Blues, 1990; Hangin' With the Homeboys, 1991; Jungle Fever, 1991; Class Act, 1992; Cool Runnings, 1993; Operation Dumbo Drop, 1995; That Darn Cat, 1997; Rusty: A Dog's Tale, 1997; Everything's Jake, 2000; Citizen James, 2000; Eight-Legged Freaks, 2002; Shark Tale, Voice, 2004; TV series: "Where I Live", 1993; "Cosby", 1996-2000; "Citizen James", dir, writer & producer, 2000; "Wyclef Jean in America", 2006; "Pilot", 2006. **Honors/Awds:** Nominee, Image Award, 1998, 1999, 2000; Nominee, Independent Spirit Award, 1992; Nominee, Young Artist Award, 1994. **Business Addr:** Actor, William Morris Agency, Attn: Norman Brokaw, 151 El Camino Dr, Beverly Hills, CA 90212.*

DOUGLAS, ARTHUR E. See Obituaries section.

DOUGLAS, ASHANTI SHEQUOIYA
Singer, actor, writer. **Personal:** Born Oct 13, 1980, Glen Cove, NY; daughter of Thomas Kincaid Douglas and Tina. **Career:** Albums: Ashanti, 2002; Chapter II, 2003; Ashanti's Christmas, 2003; Concrete Rose, 2004; Collectables by Ashanti, 2005; The Declaration, 2007; Films: Bride and Prejudice, 2004; Coach Carter, 2005; John Tucker Must Die, 2006; Resident Evil: Extinction, 2007; You're Nobody till Somebody Kills You, 2007; tv: " American Dreams", 2002; "Sabrina, The Teenage Witch", 2002; "Buffy The Vampire Slayer", 2003; "Punk'd", 2004; "The Muppets' Wizard of Oz", 2005; "Oprah Winfrey's Legends Ball", 2006; "What Perez Sez", 2007; "Access Granted", 2009; "The Morning Show with Mike & Juliet", 2009; "The Tonight Show with Conan O'Brien". **Honors/Awds:** Grammy Award, Best Contemporary R&B Album, 2003; American Music Award, 2003; Teen Choice Award; Soul Train Lady of Soul Award. **Special Achievements:** Ranked as No 81 in FHM's "100 Sexiest Women in the World 2005" special supplement, 2005;Named #13 on the Maxim magazine Hot 100 of 2005 list; Ranked #37 on the Maxim magazine Hot 100 of 2008 list. **Business Addr:** Artist, c/o Murder Inc Records, PO Box 538, Glen Oaks, NY 11004.*

DOUGLAS, AUBRY CARTER
Physician, orthopedic surgeon. **Personal:** Born Feb 1, 1943, Onalaska, TX; son of Desso and Mary; married Janice Sanchez; children: Mary, Ronald, Jenniffer, Anitra. **Educ:** Fisk Univ, BS, bio, 1964; Meharry Med Col, Doctorate Med degree, 1968. **Career:** Howard Univ, resident orthopaedics, 1973-76; George Hubbard Hosp, resident gen surg, 1970-71; Fisk Univ, lab asst, 1962-63; pvt pract, currently. **Orgs:** Life scout, BSA; Kappa Alpha Psi; Beta Kappa Chi; Harris & Co Med Soc; Houston Med Forum; Meharry Med Col Alumni asn; Am Med Asn; Texas Med Asn; Houston Med Asn; Harris County Med Soc; Houston Med Forum; 100 Black Men Metropolitan. **Military Serv:** AUS, maj, 1971-73. **Business Addr:** Private Practitioner, 2000 Crawford Suite 860, Houston, TX 77002, **Business Phone:** (713)659-4401.*

DOUGLAS, BETTY. See DOUGLAS, ELIZABETH (BETTY) ASCHE.

DOUGLAS, BUSTER. See DOUGLAS, JAMES.

DOUGLAS, CARL E
Lawyer. **Educ:** Northwestern Univ, undergrad deg, 1977; Univ Calif, Boalt Hall Sch Law, law degree, 1980. **Career:** Fed Commun Comn; Fed Pub Defender's Off, Los Angeles, trial atty; Law Offs Johnnie Cochran, managing atty; Law Offices Carl E Douglas, atty, 1998-. **Orgs:** State Bar Calif; John M Langston Bar Asn; Consumer Attorneys Asn Los Angeles. **Honors/Awds:** Loren Miller Lawyer of the Year, John M Langston Bar Asn, 1994; Trial Lawyer of the Year, Consumer Attorneys Asn Los Angeles, 2006. **Special Achievements:** Atty of Orenthal James Simpson, 1994-95. **Business Phone:** (310)277-9595.

DOUGLAS, ELIZABETH (BETTY) ASCHE (BETTY DOUGLAS)
Artist, educator. **Personal:** Born Dec 22, 1930, Rochester, PA; daughter of Charles F and Irma M Edmonds; married William R, Dec 28, 1957 (died 1997); children: Andrea Hanford, Vicki Gaddy & Nanette. **Educ:** Carnegie Inst Tech, BFA, 1951; Univ Pittsburgh, MA, 1956; Univ Pa, 1979. **Career:** Tex Col, Tyler, TX, asst prof, 1955-58; Good Publ Co, Ft Worth, TX, art dir, 1958-61; Beaver (PA) Schls, Rochester (PA) Schs, teacher art, 1962-66; Geneva Col, Beaver Falls, PA, asst prof, assoc prof, prof, coord humanities, 1966-96, emerita, 1996-; Douglas Art Gallery, artist & owner, 1975-. **Orgs:** Col Art Asn, 1969-2000; chairperson, Rochester Area Human Rel Comm, 1973-74; Arts rev Christian Scholars Rev, 1973-; co-chairperson, task force Juv Delinq SW Reg Planning Comm Govs Justice Comm, 1976-78; prog chmn, Brodhead Cult Ctr, 1977-78; secy & treas, Found Art, Theory & Educ (FATE), 1979-80; art comm, Merrick Art Gallery Assoc, 1980-; Nat Conf Artists, 1980-2000; bd mem, Christian Scholars Revolution, 1983-95; Asn Integrative Studies, 1985-99; Hofstra Univ Conf Avant-Garde Lit/Art, 1985; bd mem, Christians Visual Art, 1985-89, 1991-99; chmn, Merrick Art Gallery Asn Catalog Comm; auth & ed, Catalogue Merrick Art Gallery, 1988; bd mem, Greater Beaver Valley Cult Alliance, 1989-92; bd mem, Northland Pub Libr Found, 1989-92; bd mem, Asn Integrative Studies, 1991-94; bd mem, 1992, pres, 1997-, Merrick Art Gallery; bd mem, Sweetwater Ctr Arts, 1996-; Trinity Episcopal Sch Ministry, 1997-99; resource artist, Intergenerational Arts Proj; butler, Lawrence & Mercer Counties, PA; Beaver chap, Women's Bus Network; bd mem, 2001-, chairperson, 2001-02, Beaver Valley Int Arts Festival; bd mem, Rochester Chamber Com; Beaver County Chamber Com; Guild Coun Pittsburgh Ctr Arts; Am Fed Musicians Beaver Chap. **Honors/Awds:** Achievement Award, Beaver Valley Service Club, 1978; Scholar of the Year, Geneva Col Fac, 1985; Woman of Distinction in the Arts, Beaver-Castle Girl Scouts Coun, 1989; Woman of Eminence, Hawthorne Club, 1999; Athena Award Nominee, Beaver County, 2000, 2002; Hall of Fame inductee, Am Fedn Musicians, Beaver Valley Chap, 2003; Elizabeth Asche Douglas Fund, Geneva Col, named in honor, 2003. **Special Achievements:** Articles published in CIVA (Christians in Visual Arts) numerous times, 1983-, papers delivered annual meetings FATE Toronto 1984, Assoc Integrative Studies 1984, article published Leonardo's Last Supper, Christian Scholar's Review 1988, career documented in Archives of National Museum for Women in the Arts, biography referenced in Who's Who in the World, Who's Who Among African Americans, Who's Who in the East, the National Registry of Who's Who, the International Directory of Women in the Arts, Outstanding Educators of American, The International Biographical Centre, Cambridge, U.K., Outstanding Achievers of the 21 Century. **Business Addr:** Artist, Owner, Douglas Art Gallery, 491-3 McKinley St, Rochester, PA 15074-1663, **Business Phone:** (724)775-4618.

DOUGLAS, FLORENCE M
Physician. **Personal:** Born Mar 26, 1933; married Franklin E Mcfarlane; children: Valerie, Angela & Alychandra. **Educ:** Hunter Col NY, BA, 1955; Howard Univ Col Med, MD, 1959. **Career:** Los Angeles Co Gen Hosp, intership 1959-60, residency gen psychiat, 1960-62, residency child psychiat, 1963-65; pvt pract, 1965-; Los Angeles Co Gen Hosp Sch Nursing, consult, 1960-62; Los Angeles Co Juvenile Hall, consult, 1960-62; Montefiore Hosp NY, residency gen psychiatry 1962; Episcopal Ch Home for Children Pasadena, CA, consult, 1963-67; Huntington Meml Hosp Pasadena, consult, 1965-66; Los Angeles Co Mental Health Arcardia Sch System, consult, 1965-67; Univ Calif, Irvine, assoc clin prof, 1989. **Orgs:** Southern Calif Psychiat Soc; AMA; Los Angeles Co Med Asn; Am Psychiat Asn; Nat Med Asn; Am Asn for Adolescent Psychiat; Am & Orthopsychiatric Asn; Calif Med Asn; Black Psychiat So CA; Black Psychiat Am; Mental Health Develop Comt, United Way; bd mem, Calif Dept Rehab; former mem, Southern Calif Psychoanalytic Asn; Am Asn Group Psychotheraphy; Col Psychol & Soc Studies; bd mem, Model Cities Child Care Ctr; Johnny Tillmon Child Develop Ctr, New Careerists; Inner City Students; Urban Corp Students; Mshauri Students; Medex Prog; diplomate Am Bd Psychol & Neurol; bd certified Child & Adolescent Psychiat; examiner Am Bd Psychiat & Neurol; attending physician medical staff DelAmo Hosp, Little Co Mary Hosp, Torrance Memorial Hosp; Riviera Hosp; Fel Am Acad Child & Psychiat; bd cert & fel Forensic Med & Forensic Examiner, 1997. **Honors/Awds:** Anna Bartsche Dunne Scholarship, Howard Univ Col Med, 1956-58; Distinguished Public Service Award, 1998.

DOUGLAS, HARRY E., III
Educator. **Personal:** Born Nov 8, 1938; children: 2. **Educ:** Univ Denver, BA, 1959; Univ Calif LA, MPA, Personnel, 1971; Univ Southern Calif, MPA, Health Serv, 1981, DPA, Health Admin & Policy, 1983. **Career:** Dept Pub Social Servs, proj dir, sr prog asst, mgt trainee, social worker, 1960-68; Univ Southern Calif, training officer, 1968; Martin Luther King & Charles R Drew Med Ctr, personnel officer, 1969-71, dir allied healthtraining, 1971-73; Cedars-Sinai Med Ctr, dir manpower training & develop, 1973-74; Calif Reg Med Prog, prog dir HS & EP, 1974-75; Howard Univ Col, Allied Health Sci, assoc dean, assoc prof, 1975-83; Charles R Drew Postgrad Med Sch, Sch Allied Health, dean, 1983-94, Charles R Drew UnivMed & Sci, vpres acad affairs, exec vpres, Interim Pres. **Orgs:** Consult, DHEW Div Health Manpower; adv & coun Am Soc Allied Health Prof Nat Data Gathering Proj; health brain trust mem, Cong Black Caucus; mgt progs, nursing personnel George Wash Univ; tech review comn, Calif Community Reg Med Progs; Calif St Dept Ed; ad hoc adv comn, Career Educ Health Occupations; Am Assoc Comn & Jr Col; Sch Allied Health Study; Charles R Drew Postgrad Med Sch; San Francisco Personnel Dept; Nat Inst Ment Health; Orange City

Personnel Dept; Univ Calif, Los Angeles; Proj Allied Health Prof; bd dir, DC Coalition Health Advocates; treas, bd mem,Nat Assoc Allied Health; Dietetic Manpower Demand Study; Child-Find & Advocacdv Comn; chmn, Am Soc Allied Prof; DC Adv Comn Magnet Sch HealthCareers; assoc coord, Reg Leadership Ctr Allied Health Educ; Am Soc PubAdmin; Am Pub Health Assoc; Nat Soc Allied Health. **Special Achievements:** Numerous presentations & publs. *

DOUGLAS, HERBERT P., JR.
Consultant. **Personal:** Born Mar 9, 1922, Pittsburgh, PA; married Rozell; children: Barbara Joy Ralston & Herbert III. **Educ:** Xavier Univ, 1942; Univ Pittsburgh, BS, 1948, MEd, 1950. **Career:** Managed night bus, fathers auto bus, 1942-45; Pabst Brewing Co, sales rep dist mgr, 1950-63; Schieffelin & Co NYC, sales rep, 1963-65, Nat Spec Mkt Mgr, 1965-68; Nat Spec Mkts, vpres, 1968-; Nat Asn Mkt Develop, vpres; Schieffelin & Somerset Co, vpres (retired); Urban Mkt Develop, 1977-80, consult, 2005. **Orgs:** Track & Field Club; Optimist Club; Philadelphia Pioneer Club; Nat Asn Advan Colored People; Nat Urban League; Omega Psi Phi Frat; Chris Atlete Club; Ebenezer Bapt Church; Sales Exec Club; Int Amateur Athletic Asn Inc,pres & founder, 1980-; emer trustees, Univ Pittsburgh. **Honors/Awds:** Black Athletes Hall of Fame, 1974; Beverage Ind Award Urban League Guild, 1974; Jesse Owens Int Trophy Award, 1980; Univ Pittsburgh, Lettermen of Distinction Award, 1980-; Univ Bicentennial Award, 1987; Black Achievement Award, 1987; Western Pa Sports Hall of Fame, 1988; Pa Sports Hall of Fame, 1992; Legacy Award, Univ Pittsburgh, 2000. **Special Achievements:** Selected by Ebony success libr one of top 1000 Successful Blacks in US;Olympic Games, long jump Bronze medal, 1948; currently last athlete fromPittsburgh to win a medal in Olympic Games. *

DOUGLAS, HUGH LAMONT
Football player. **Personal:** Born Aug 23, 1971, Mansfield, OH; married Ayanna; children: Kayla Rachelle & Brianna Syann. **Educ:** Cent State Univ. **Career:** NY Jets, defensive end, 1995-97; Philadelphia Eagles, football player, 1998-02; Jacksonville Jaguars, 2003; Philadelphia Eagles, 2004. **Orgs:** Founder, Hugh Douglas Found, 1999. **Honors/Awds:** AP NFL Defensive Rookie of the Year, 1995; Jack Edelstein Memorial Award, 2000, 2001. *

DOUGLAS, JAMES (BUSTER DOUGLAS)
Boxer. **Personal:** Born Apr 7, 1960, Columbus, OH; son of William Douglas Jr and Lula Pearl McCauley Douglas; married Bertha Paige, Jul 2, 1987; children: LaMar & Cardae. **Educ:** Mercy hurst Col; Coffey ville Community Col; Dayton Sinclair Community Col. **Career:** Prof boxer (retired). **Orgs:** Pres, Lula Pearl Douglas Found. **Honors/Awds:** Heavyweight Champion of the World, WBA, WBC, IBF, 1990. **Special Achievements:** Special guest referee for the Hulk Hogan vs Randy Savage match at WWF's The Main Event III; Star of the Video Game James 'Buster' Douglas Knockout Boxing; Film Appearance, Pluto's Plight; 2007; Appeared on an episode of the game show Identity, 2007.

DOUGLAS, JAMES MATTHEW
Educator, college administrator. **Personal:** Born Feb 11, 1944, Onalaska, TX; son of Desso D and Mary L; married Keryl; children: DeLicia & James. **Educ:** Tex Southern Univ, BA, Math, 1966, JD Law, 1970; Stanford Univ, JSM Law, 1971. **Career:** Singer General Precision, programmer analyst, 1966-72; Tex Southern Univ,Thurgood Marshall Sch Law, asst prof law, 1971-72, prof law, 1981-95, interim provost & vp acad affairs, 1995, pres, 1995-99, distinguished proflaw, 1999-, pres, 2002-; Cleveland State Univ, Cleveland-Marshall Col Law, asst prof law, 1972-75, asst dean stud affairs, 1974-75; Syracuse Univ ColLaw, assoc prof law & assoc dean, 1975-80; Northeastern Univ Sch Law, proflaw, 1980-81; Tex Southern Univ, dean & prof, 1981-95, interim provost & sr vpres acad affairs, 1995, interim pres, 1995, pres, 1995-99. **Orgs:** State Bar Tex; Houston Jr Bar Asn; Chmn Educ Comm Sci & Tech Sect; Am Bar Asn; bd dir, Hiscock Legal Soc; fac adv, Nat Bd Black Am Law Students; bd dirs, Gulf Coast Legal Found; Nat Bar Asn Comm Legal Educ; ed bd, Tex Lawyer; life mem, Houston Chamber Comm; bd dirs, Law Sch Admission Coun;chmn, Minority Affairs Comt, Law Sch Admission Coun; fel Am Bar Found; fel Tex Bar Found; fel Nat Bar Found; fel Houston Bar Found; Parlimentarian Stud Bar Asn; adv, Alpha Phi Alpha Soc Fraternity; pres, Sophomore Class; pres, Student Body; pres, Alpha Phi Alpha Soc Fraternity. **Honors/Awds:** Most Outstanding third Year Student; Winner ten Am Juris prudence Awards;Sch Moot Ct Team; Outstanding Alumnus Tex Southern Univ, 1972; outstanding Young Men of America, 1976; Outstanding Contribution to Legal Educ Tex Bar Found, 1986; Distinguished Serv Award, Nat Bar Asn, 1991; Member of the Year, Diamond Club, 1991; Mickey LeLand Humanitarian Award, Profiles of Prominence Award, 1994; President Award, Nat Asn Advan Colored People, 1995. **Special Achievements:** Published: "Some Ideas on the Computer and Law" Tex Souther Univ Law Review 20 1971; work in prog "Cases & Materials on Contracts". contributed few publications. **Home Addr:** 5318 Calhoun Rd, Houston, TX 77021, **Home Phone:** (713)747-4737. **Business Addr:** President, Distinguished professor of Law, Texas Southern University, 220 Hannah Hall 3100 Cleburne Ave, Houston, TX 77004, **Business Phone:** (713)313-7036.

DOUGLAS, DR. JANICE GREEN
Physician, educator. **Personal:** Born Mar 19, 1943; daughter of Louis and Electa Green. **Educ:** Meharry Med Sch, Nashville, Tenn, MD, DDS; Vanderbilt Univ, Nat Inst Health, fel endocrinol, 1973. **Career:** Nat Inst Health, sr staff fel; Case Western Res Univ Sch Med, dir div Hypertension, 1993-, prof med & prof physiol & biophys, 1984-; Univ Hosp Cleveland, corres, 2003, dir hypertension. **Orgs:** Inst Med; Am Soc Clin Invest; Asn Am Physicians; fel Am Heart Asn; bd dir, Am Bd Internal Med; Int Soc Hypertension Blacks. **Special Achievements:** First woman promoted to or appointed to the rank of professor of Medicine at Case Western Reserve University Medical School; Co-Authored : Pathophysiology of Hypertension in Blacks, Hypertension in Ethnic Populations. **Business Addr:** Professor, Case Western Reserve University, Division of Hypertension School of Medicine, 10900 Euclid Ave, Cleveland, OH 44106, **Business Phone:** (216)368-4340.

DOUGLAS, JOE, JR.
Government official, firefighter. **Personal:** Born Jun 9, 1928, Topeka, KS; married Nathalia Washington; children: Shelley Jolana Douglas Wilder. **Educ:** Washburn Univ, attended 1949. **Career:** Firefighter (retired); City Topeka, firefighter, 39 yrs, appointed fire chief, 1983; USD No 501, bd mem, 1977-85. **Orgs:** Topeka Coun Churches; First Conf Chair KS East Conf Clomm on Relig & Race United Methodist Ch; bd dir, Boys Club Am, 1971-73; chmn, comt Adv, Comn on Educ, 1975-76; bd pres, USD No 501, 1980-81 & 1983-84; bd dir, Boy Scouts Am; Mayor's Disaster Adv Coun, Mayor's Task Force on Illiteracy, Sunset Optimists; Topeka YWCA. **Honors/Awds:** Dean, United Methodist Youth Fel Inst, 1971-73; Presidential Citation for Extraordinary Serv Boys Club Am, 1972-73; Kans Friends Educ plaque winner; Annual Local Govt Official Category, 1986. **Military Serv:** AUS, pvt first class, 18 months. *

DOUGLAS, JOHN DANIEL
Government official, educator. **Personal:** Born Aug 18, 1945, Richburg, SC; son of James E and Alberta Cousar; married Mildred Barber, Feb 12, 1970; children: Maurice, Jermel, GiGi & LaShawn. **Educ:** Morris Col, BS, 1967; Winthrop Col, MEduc, 1976. **Career:** Chester Co Schs, teacher, 1967-68; Carolina Community Actions Inc, Head Start dir, 1968-70; York County Family Ct, chief probation officer, 1970-75; Charlotte-Mecklinburg Sch, teacher, 1975-80; Rock Hill Sch Dist No 3, teacher, 1980-; York County, councilman; Union County Sch, NC, 1988-. **Orgs:** Pres, Rock Hill Nat Asn Advan Colored People, 1976-81; pol action chmn, Menzel Shiner, 1980-; Counman, York County Dist No 4, 1980-; chmn, Destinations Human Serv Trans, 1982-; chmn, Pub Works York County, 1982-; financial secy, Sterling Elk Lodge, 1983-; bd dirs, SC Asn Counties, 1986; exec admin asst, SC Asn Elks, 1986; chair, N Cent Med Clinic, 1999-01. **Honors/Awds:** Service to Mankind, Rock Hill Nat Asn Advan Colored People, 1979; Community Service Award, Elk-Sterling Lodge No 344 Rock Hill, 1980; Scroll of Honor, Omega Psi Phi Fraternity, 1983; Humanitarian Menzel Shiner, 1984; Elk of the Year, 1986; Man of the Year, Rock Grove AME Zion Church, 1986; Man of the Year, Elks, 1988; ID Quincy New man Award for Outstanding Service, 1991. **Business Addr:** Councilman, PO Box 11578, Rock Hill, SC 29731.*

DOUGLAS, JOSEPH FRANCIS
Educator. **Personal:** Born Oct 31, 1926, Indianapolis, IN; son of Louis Joseph (deceased) and Marion Elizabeth Brabham (deceased); married Edna J Nichols, Apr 9, 1950; children: Marian E, Joseph Jr, Marie A & Barbara J. **Educ:** Purdue Univ, BSEE, 1948; Univ Mo, MSEE, 1962. **Career:** Educator (retired). Rural Electrification Admin, 1948-56; Southern Univ,1956-64; Am Mach & Foundry Co, 1964-66; Pa State Univ, engr instr, 1966-70, assoc prof, 1970-87; engr consult, 1987-92; Ministry Educ, Sci & Technol, math teacher. **Orgs:** Inst Elect & Electronics Engrs, 1949-; Am Soc Engineering Educ, 1969-80, reg prof engr, 1954-96; Nat Asn Adv Colored People; Human Rel Adv Coun;York-Adams Area Coun; Boy Scouts Am; Community Action Prog; bd dir, York Hosp, PA, 1982-92; adv bd, Pa State York, 1986-96. **Honors/Awds:** The Role of the Engineering Teacher, Conf Rec, Tucson, 1972; Lind back Award for Distinguished Teaching, 1972; Recipient of a Centennial Medal of the IEEE in 1984. **Special Achievements:** Contributor, "Understanding Batteries," technical paper, Volunteers in Technical Assistance Publication (VITA), 1985; special biography, included in various publications on outstanding African American scientists. **Military Serv:** USY, Air Corps, aviation cadet, 1944-45. **Home Addr:** 2755 Trout Run Rd, York, PA 17402. *

DOUGLAS, MAE ALICE
Executive. **Personal:** Born Dec 26, 1951, Rowland, NC. **Educ:** Univ NC, Greensboro, NC, BA, 1972. **Career:** Comn Status women, adminr, 1973-74; CIBA-GEIGY Corp, eeo coord, 1974-77, personnel mgr, mgr human resources, 1983-86, dir human resources; Ciba-Geigy Corp; CableRep Cox, Mgr Employ Rels, 1995, dir Employ Rel, 1998, Regional vpres, 1999; Cox Commun Inc, mgr, sr vpres & chief people officer, 2000-. **Orgs:** Leadership Greensboro Chamber Com, 1979-80; planning div United Way, 1980; prof review comt State Dept Pub Instr, 1981-82; Am Soc Personnel Admin; mem Women's Prof Forum;bd mem, Women Cable Telecommun Found; Society Human Resources Mgt, Nat Asn African Am Human Resources; Grady Health System Found; bd dir, NAMIC, currently. **Honors/Awds:** Outstanding Young Women of America, 1975; Outstanding Young Woman Greensboro Jaycettes, 1978; Outstanding Woman in Business, YWCA, 1980; Best Operator Women, Working Mother Media, 2003, 2004, and 2005; first Pioneer award, NAMIC, 2005. **Business Phone:** (404)843-5000.*

DOUGLAS, MANSFIELD, III. **See Obituaries section.**

DOUGLAS, NICHOLAS
Government official, manager. **Career:** Bur Land Mgt, Bakersfield, CA, div minerals chief; Bur Land Mgt, Anchorage, AK, field mgr, sr policy adv, Minerals, Realty & Resources Protection, dist mgr, currently. **Orgs:** Sr Exec Asn; Soc Petrol Engrs AIME. **Honors/Awds:** Special Achievement Awards; Nat Performance Rev, 1995. **Special Achievements:** First African American district manager for the Bureau of Land Management. **Business Phone:** (907)267-1246.

DOUGLAS, OMAR
Football player. **Personal:** Born Jun 3, 1972, New Orleans, LA. **Educ:** Univ Minn. **Career:** New York Giants, wide receiver, 1994-96. **Honors/Awds:** Athlete of the Year, 1994. *

DOUGLAS, SAMUEL HORACE
Educator. **Personal:** Born May 10, 1928, Ardmore, OK; divorced; children: Carman Irving, Samuel & Emanuel. **Educ:** Bishop Col, BS, 1950; Okla State Univ, BS, 1959; MS, 1963; PhD, 1967. **Career:** Praire View A&M Univ Tex, asst prof Math, 1959-63; dept chmn, 1962-63; felSci Fac, 1963-67; Grambling Col La, math prof, 1967-; dept chmn, 1967-. **Orgs:** Mem Panel Spl & Probs Minority Groups; Am Math Soc; London Math Soc; Math Asn Am; consult Com Undergrad Prog Math dir summer & inservice Insts Math, NSF-Grambling Col 1968-71; vis lectr, vice chmn, La-Ms sect, Math Asn Am; Pi Mu Epsilon; Alpha Phi Alpha. **Honors/Awds:** Distinguished Service Award, Pi Mu Epsilon, 1970. **Military Serv:** AUS 1943-46.

DOUGLAS, SHANNON
Executive, founder (originator). **Career:** First Impressions Group, founder, 1999-. **Business Addr:** Founder, First Impressions Group, 1249 Washington Blvd Suite 1210, Detroit, MI 48226, **Business Phone:** 888-716-5718.*

DOUGLAS, SHERMAN
Basketball player. **Personal:** Born Sep 15, 1966, Washington, DC; married Denise; children: Demi. **Educ:** Syracuse Univ, Syracuse, NY, attended 1989. **Career:** Basketball player (retired); Miami Heat, guard, 1989-92; Dolpher's Dolphins, 1994-95; Boston Celtics,1992-96; MBA, Milwaukee Bucks, 1996-97; Cleveland Cavaliers, 1997; Los Angeles Clippers, 1998-99; NJ Nets, 1997-98, 1999-2001. **Honors/Awds:** Most Valuable Player, Miami Heat, 1991; Victor Hanson Medal of Excellence, 2003.

DOUGLAS, SUZZANNE
Actor. **Personal:** Born Apr 12, 1957, Chicago, IL; daughter of Donald Sr and Lois Mae; married Dr Roy Jonathan Cobb, Feb 11, 1989; children: Jordan & Victoria. **Educ:** Ill State Univ, attended 1978. **Career:** The Last Weekend, producer, 1998; Stage roles: Three Penny Opera, Broadway, co-star with Sting; Drowning Crow, world premiere; A Night in Tunisia; Jar the Floor, Charlotte Repertory Theatre; Agnes of God, George Street Playhouse; tv movies: Shadow of Love; Condition Critical; Search For Grace; Hallelujah; tv series: "Against the Law", "series regular"; The Parent Hood, lead role; The Parkers, recurring; Law & Order Special Victims Unit, guest star; films: Tap; I'll Do Anything; Chain of Desire; How Stella Got Her Groove Back; Inkwell; Jason's Lyric; The School of Rock, 2003. co-starred with Forrest Whittaker; Inkwell, featured lead, co-starred with Joe Morton; Touched By An Angel; The Parkers, recurring; stage role, Drowning Crow, world premiere; Sounder, The School of Rock; stage, A Night in Tunisia; "Law & Order: Criminal Intent", 2004; "Mad Hops", 2004; film; Sunday on the Rocks, 2004. **Orgs:** Camp Giddiup; Athletes Against Abuse; Jackie Robinson Found; Marylawn Oranges Acad, 1995; Royce Clayton Found Sickle Cell; UNCF; trustee, George St Playhouse, 2001-02; USTA, community spec populations; Honorary mem, Delta Sigma Theta Sorority Inc. **Honors/Awds:** Nat Asn Advan Colored People Image Award, Tap, 1989; Mary Martin Award, 1987; Athletes Against Drugs. **Special Achievements:** First African Am to play the head role in Wit, NJ Premiere, George St Playhouse. **Business Addr:** Actress, 13400 Chandller Blvd, Sherman Oaks, CA 91401, **Business Phone:** (818)990-4706.*

DOUGLAS, WALTER EDMOND
Association executive, car dealer. **Personal:** Born Aug 22, 1933, Hamlet, NC; married Retha Hughes; children: Petra, Walter Jr & Mark. **Educ:** NC Cent Univ, BS, 1954, MS, 1955. **Career:** Int Revenue Serv Data Ctr, br chief, 1968-69, asst chief syst div, 1969-70, chief mgt staff, 1970-71, asst dir, 1971-72; New Detroit, from, vpres to pres, 1972-85; DHT Tranp Inc, pres, 1979-2002; Federal Home Loan Bank, Indianapolis, dir; Avis Ford Inc, chmn,

currently; vchmn, Henry Ford Health System. **Orgs:** Chair, Health Alliance Plan, United Way; bd mem, Detroit Symphony Orchestra Hall, 1980-; bd dir, former chmn, Skillman Found; bd dir, Oakland Univ Found; bd dir, NCCU Found; bd dir, AAA; bd dir, Henry Health Ford Syst; Found Southeast Mich; bd, Tiger Woods Found; chmn, Auto Club Group; chmn, external affairs comt, Charles H Wright MusAfrican Am Hist; Wayne State Univ Found. **Honors/ Awds:** Liberty Bell Award, Detroit Bar Asn, 1975; Award from President Reagan Exemplary Youth Development Program, 1984; Honorary Doctorate, NC Cent Univ. **Military Serv:** AUS. **Home Addr:** 1189 Lone Pine Wds Dr, Bloomfield Hills, MI 48302. **Business Addr:** Chairman, Avis Ford Inc, 29200 Telegraph Rd, Southfield, MI 48034.

DOUGLAS, WILLARD H

Judge. **Personal:** Born Feb 4, 1932, Amherst, VA; married Jane O Eggleston; children: Willard III & Wendelin Janna. **Educ:** Va Union Univ, AB, 1957; Howard Univ Sch Law, JD, 1960. **Career:** Judge (retired); Teamsters Union, admin asst bd monitors, 1960-61; US Copyright Off, staff atty, 1961-62; US Comn Civil Rights, staff atty, 1962-65; Pvt Pract, 1965-69; asst Commonwealth atty, 1969-74; Juv & Domestic Rels Dist Ct Commonwealth Va, chief judge, 1974-89. **Orgs:** Am Bar Asn; Va State Bar; Old Dominion Bar Asn; Richmond Criminal Law Asn; Richmond Trial Lawyers Asn; Va Trial Lawyers Asn; Kappa Alpha Psi Frat Bd Richmond Area Psychiat Clin; Richmond Epilepsy Found; Big Bros Ferrum Col Va Wesleyan Col; Lay Leader Wesley Memorial United Methodist Church; Asn Lay Leader Va Conf Bd Laity & Richmond Dist Eastern Province; bd mem, Nat Coun Juv & Family Ct Judges, 1986-89; United Methodist Church, Judicial Coun, 1984-92; exec comt, World Methodist Coun, 2001-06. **Honors/ Awds:** Achievement Award, Richmond Alumni & Petersburg Alumni, 1974; Man of the Year, Richmond Alumnae Delta Sigma Theta, 1974. **Special Achievements:** First African-American judge in Virginia. **Military Serv:** USMC, Sgt, 1951-54. **Home Addr:** 606 Edgehill Rd, Richmond, VA 23222, **Home Phone:** (804)321-4222.

DOUGLASS, JOHN W.

State government official. **Educ:** Lincoln Univ, BA, 1964; Johns Hopkins Univ, MA, 1966. **Career:** Rohm & Hass, fel, 1964; Gilman, fel, 1964; Morgan State Col, instr, 1966-68; Mutual Funds, salesman, 1967-68; RL Johnson Realty Co; Baltimore City Coun, clerk, 1967-68; Balitmore City Planning Dept, consult, 1970-71; Md House Delegates, mem, 1971-94; Md Dept Assessments & Taxation, dep dir, 1995-2003; State Retirement & Pension Syst Md, employee systs rep, 2004-, bd trustee, 2007-; Ideal Fed Savings Bank, Baltimore, Md, vpres, currently. **Orgs:** New Dem Club, 1968-; Adj Neighborhood Improvement Asn, 1969-; bd trustees, Md State Retirement & Pension Syst. **Honors/Awds:** Am Legion Award, 1956; Am Chem Soc Award, 1964; Norman E Gaskin's Prize, 1964; Eastern LI Ward, 1964; Certificate of Achievement, Morgan State Col, 1968, 1969. **Business Phone:** (410)625-5555.

DOUGLASS, HON. LEWIS LLOYD

Judge. **Personal:** Born Dec 12, 1930, Brooklyn, NY; son of Lloyd and Cornelia; married Doris Wildy; children: David & Lori. **Educ:** Brooklyn Col, BS, 1953; St John's Law Sch, JD, 1956. **Career:** Judge (retired); Fed Prosecutor's Off, asst US atty, 1961-65; Housing Redevelop Agency, exec dept dir, 1965-68; Housing Develop Orgn, gen coun, 1968-71; Black Enterprise Mag, exec vpres, 1971-75; NY State Prison Syst, exec deputy comnr, 1975-78; NY Criminal Ct, judge, 1978-82; NY Ct Claims, 1982-99; Supreme Ct NY, judge, 1999. **Orgs:** Chair, NY State Comn Minorities; Phi Beta Sigma. **Special Achievements:** Publication: "Investing in Real Estate", Black Enterprise, 1972.

DOUGLASS, M LORAYNE

Educator. **Personal:** Born May 11, 1927, Fort Gibson, OK; daughter of Wallace McNac and Ollie Nivens McNac; married Carlton R, Jan 30, 1954 (divorced). **Educ:** Langston Univ, BA, 1948; Olkahoma Univ, MEd, 1956. **Career:** Educator (retired); Ponca City Okla Schs, classroom teacher, 1950-54; Oklahoma City Schs, classroom teacher, 1954-63; Los Angeles Unified Sch Dist, coordr, consult, parent educ coordr & conf planner, curric adv, resource teacher, classroom teacher, 1963-87. **Orgs:** United Teachers Los Angeles, 1963-87; Founders Church Religious Sci, 1965-; Nat Sorority Phi Delta Kappa, Far Western, regional dir, 1983-87; life mem, Nat Asn Advan Colored People, 1987. **Honors/Awds:** Service Award, Calif Asn Compensatory Ed, 1979; Model Excellence Award, Nat Sorority, Phi Delta Kappa, Delta Kappa Chap, 1991. **Home Addr:** 3501 Floresta Ave, Los Angeles, CA 90043, **Home Phone:** (323)291-1830.

DOUGLASS, MAURICE GERRARD

Football player, football coach. **Personal:** Born Feb 12, 1964, Muncie, IN; married Camela; children: Shiloh, Moses & Maurice. **Educ:** Coffeyville Community Col; Univ Ky. **Career:** Football player (retired), Football coach; Chicago Bears, defensive back, 1986-94; New York Giants, 1995-96; Trotwood-Madison High Sch, head coach, currently. **Business Phone:** (937)854-0878.*

DOUGLASS, MELVIN ISADORE

Educator, clergy. **Personal:** Born Jul 21, 1948, Manhattan, NY; son of Isadore and Esther Tripp. **Educ:** Vincinnes Univ, AS, 1970; Tuskegee Inst, BS, 1973; Morgan State Univ, MS, 1975; NY Univ, MA, 1977; Columbia Univ, EdM, 1978, EdD, 1981. **Career:** Queensboro Soc Prev Cruelty C Inc, child care worker, 1973-75; Pub Sch 401-X, dean stud & teacher, 1973-75; Amistad Child Day Care Ctr, sch age prog dir, 1976-77; Beck Mem Day Care Ctr, admin dir, 1983-84; Dept Juvenile Justice, primary sch dept chair, 1984-85, ombudsman, 1985-88; John Jay Col Criminal Justice, adj instr, 1988-89; Stimson Middle Sch, chmn, 1988-; Col New Rochelle, instr, 1993-; Long Island Inst Prof Studies, instr educ, 1998-; Metropolitan Col NY, adj prof social sci, 1999-; Minority Educr Network Inc, pres & chief exec office, 1999-. **Orgs:** Pres, fed Jamaica Track Club, 1973-; bd dirs, Nu Omicron Chap OPP Day Care Ctr, 1984-; Prince Hall Masonry; 100 Hundred Black Men; pres bd dirs, NY Transit Br NCP, 1984-90; co-chp Educ Comm NY State Conf of NCP 1986-89; chp Anti-Drug Comm Metro Coun Nat Asn Advan Colored People Br, 1986-89; Jamaica EW Adolescent Pregnancy Prev Consortium, 1986-89; basileus Nu Omicron Chap OPP Frat, 1987-88; bd dir, Queens Coun Arts, 1983-86; bd dirs Black Experimental Theatre, 1982-; bd dirs, The United Black Men of Queens County Inc, 1986-89; asst pastor, Calvary Baptist Church, 1987-91; S Huntington Chmns' Asn, 1988-; Queens adv bd, NY Urban League, 1988-93; Am Fedn Sch Adminrs, 1988-; Coun Adminrs & Supvrs, 1988-; Nat Black Child Devel Inst, 1982-; Nat Educ Asn, 1973-; community adv bd, The City of NY Dept of Correction, The Queens House of Detention for Men, 1991-94; community adv bd, Pub Sch 40, Queens, NY, 1992-97; bd dirs Long Island Tuskegee Alumni Asn, 1986-, vpres, 1987-89; bd dirs, Dance Explosion, 1987-97; area policy bd no 12, Subunit 2, 1987-99; Ancient Arabic Order of Nobles of the Mystic Shrine; Omega Psi Phi Fraternity, Phi Delta Kappa Fraternity; SPP Fraternity. **Honors/Awds:** Grad Scholarship Columbia Univ, 1978; Kappa Delta Pi Honor Soc in Educ inducted, 1978; Service Award, NY City Transit Br Nat Asn Advan Colored People, 1986; Citation for Comm Serv NYS Govr Mario Cuomo, 1986; Citation Award, NY City Mayor Edward Koch, 1986; Citation Honor Queens Borough Pres Claire Shulman, 1986; City Coun Citation Award, NY City Councilman Archie Spigner, 1986; Civil Rights Award, NY City Transit Br Nat Asn Advan Colored People, 1988; auth, Black Winners: A Hist Spingarn Medalists, 1984; auth, Famous Black Men of Harvard, 1988; Jefferson Award, American Inst Publ Service, 1987; Omega Man of the Year Award, Nu Omicron Chap, 1987; Licensed to preach, Calvary Baptist Church, Jamaica, NY, 1989; Cert of Ordination, Cross Roads Baptist Church, NY, 1990; State NY Legis Resolution, Senator Alton R Waldon Jr, 1991; Alumni Faculty Citation Award, Vincennes Univ, 1991; Wyandanch Mem HS, Service Award, 1994; Service Award, Eastern Shore Chap the Links Inc, 2001; Huntington Town Bd, Certif of Recognition, 1998; NY State Assembly Citation, 1999; Henry M Minton Fel Award. **Special Achievements:** Written numerous publications, including: "William Montague Cobb: The Principal Historian of Afro-Americans in Medicine," The Crisis, Jan 1991; "Dr Louis Tompkins Wright" African-Americans in New York Life and History, Jan 1993; "Gerald W Deas, MD, MPH," JNMA, Nov 1996; "Dr Aubre de Lambert Maynard" JNMA, April, 2000. **Home Addr:** 395 Stuyvesant Ave, Brooklyn, NY 11233. *

DOUGLASS, ROBERT LEE

State government official. **Personal:** Born Jun 23, 1928, Winnsboro, SC; son of John and Jannie B Stevenson; married Bernice Viola Sales, 1947; children: Beverly, Ronald K, Eric L & Loren R. **Educ:** Morgan State Col, BS, math, 1953; John Hopkins Univ, BS, elect eng, 1962. **Career:** State Government Official (retired); Baltimore City Pub Schs, teacher, 1955-64; Bendix Corp, elec design engr, 1962-64; IBM, systs engr, 1965-67; Baltimore Electronics Assn, pres & founder, 1968-88; Baltimore City Coun, councilman, 1967-74; MD State Senate, senator, 1975-82; Maryland Legis Black Caucus, chair, 1976-77, 1978-80. **Orgs:** E Baltimore Comm Corp; Nat Assn Black Manufacturers; Baltimore Urban Coalition; Nat Assn Advan Colored People; Baltimore City Coun. **Special Achievements:** First black to hold a council seat for the 2nd District. **Military Serv:** AUS, 1st lt, 1953-55.

DOURDAN, GARY (GARY ROBERT DURDIN)

Actor. **Personal:** Born Dec 11, 1966, Philadelphia, PA; son of Robert Durdin and Sandy; married Roshumba Williams, 1992 (divorced 1994); children: Nyla & Lyric. **Career:** Actor, currently; Films: Weekend at Bernie's II, 1993; The Paper, 1994; Sunset Park, 1996; Playing God, 1997; Alien: Resurrection, 1997; Get That Number, 1997; Thursday, 1998; Scar City, 1998; The Weekend, 1999; Trois, 2000; Dancing in September, 2000; Imposter, 2002; Slipping Into Darkness, 2003; Black August, 2007; Perfect Stranger, 2007; TV films: The Good Fight, 1992; Laurel Avenue, 1993; Keys, 1994; Rendezvous, 1999; King of the World, 2000; TV series: "A Different World", 1991-93; "Swift Justice", 1996; "Lyric Cafe", 2002; "Loco Motives", 2006; "Leaving Las Vegas", 2007; TV guest appearances: "New York Undercover", 1994; "Lois & Clark", 1996; "Seven Days", 1999; "Soul Food", 2000; "CSI", 2000-08. **Honors/Awds:** Seattle Int Film Fest Citation Excellence Ensemble Cast Performance, New American Cinema Award, 2000; Image Award, Outstanding Supporting Actor Drama, 2003. **Business Addr:** Actor, Paradigm, 10100 Santa Monica Blvd Suite 2500, Los Angeles, CA 90067.

DOVE, DR. PEARLIE C.

Educator. **Personal:** Born in Atlanta, GA; daughter of Dan Cecile Craft and Lizzie Dyer Craft; married Chaplain Jackson B (deceased); children: Carol Ann Dove Kotcha. **Educ:** Clark Col, BA, 1941; Atlanta Univ, MA, 1943; Univ Colo, EdD, 1959. **Career:** Atlanta bus & prof secy, Phyllis Wheatley Br, Young Men's Christian Asn, 1943-45; Clark Col, dir, stud teaching, 1949-62, chmn, Dept Educ, 1963-85, dist prof, 1975-86; Assoc Chair, Consol Steering Comt, Clark Atlanta Univ, 1988-89; Atlanta Proj, cluster coordr, 1992-96. **Orgs:** Bd dir, Ga Stud Fin Comn, 1981-87; elem comn, Southern Asn Col & Schs, 1975-81; bd dir, Am Asn Col Teacher Educ, 1972-75; natl exe comn, Asn Teacher Educrs, 1970-73; pres, Clark Col, Am Assoc Univ Profs, 1978-80, 1983-87; pres, Atlanta Pan-Hellenic Coun, 1960-64; pres, Atlanta Alumni Delta Sigma Theta Sor, 1962-63; adv coun, Fulton High Sch, Ctr Teaching, 1990-91; bd dirs, Helping Teens Succeed Inc, 2000-. **Honors/Awds:** Chairman's Award, State Comn Life & Hist Black Georgians, 1979; ServiceAward, Atlanta Alumnae, Delta Sigma Theta Sorority, 1963; Woman of theYear Education, Iota Phi Lambda Sorority, 1962; Delta Torch Award, DeltaSigma Theta Sorority Inc, 1989; Distinguished Alumni Achievement Award-,Clark Col, 1989; Included, 1990-91, Calendar Atlanta Black History, Southern Bell: A Bell South Co, 1990-91; Lt Colonel, Aide De Camp, GovsStaff, 1991; Honorary Rosalynn Carter Fel, Inst Women's Studies, Emory Univ, 1993-95; Local Community Service Award, Spelman Col, 2001; Neighborhood Planning Unit K Legacy Award, 2002. *

DOVE, RITA FRANCES

Poet, educator, writer. **Personal:** Born Aug 28, 1952, Akron, OH; daughter of Ray A and Elvira E; married Fred Viebahn, Mar 23, 1979; children: Aviva Chantal Tamu. **Educ:** Miami Univ, Oxford, OH, BA, 1973; Univ Tubingen West Germany, attended 1975; Univ IA, MFA, 1977. **Career:** Tuskegee Inst, writer in residence, 1982; AZ State Univ, asst prof, 1981-84, assoc prof, 1984-87, full prof, 1987-89; Univ Va, full prof Eng, 1989-93, Commonwealth prof Eng, 1993-; Univ Va, Shannon Ctr Advan Studies, fel, 1995-; poet laureate, US, 1993-95; spec cons Poetry, Lib Congress Bicentennial, 1999-2000; poet laurate, VA, 2004-06; Poems: Ten Poems, 1977; The Only Dark Spot In The Sky, 1980; The Yellow House on the Corner, 1980; Mandolin, 1982; Museum, 1983; Thomas & Beulah, 1986; The Other Side of the House, 1988; Grace Notes, 1989; Selected Poems, 1993; Lady Freedom Among Us, 1994; Mother Love, 1995; On the Bus with Rosa Parks, 1999; American Smooth, 2004; Short Stories: Fifth Sunday, 1985; Novels: Through The Ivory Gate, 1992; Drama: The Darker Face of the Earth, 1994; Essays: The Poet's World, 1995; "The Poet's Choice", The Washington Post, columnist, 2000-02. **Orgs:** Bd mem, Nat Forum Phi Kappa Phi Jour, 1984-89; lit adv panel, Nat Endowment Arts, 1984-86; chair, Poetry Grants Panel, Nat Endowment Arts, 1985; bd dir, Asn Writing Prog, 1985-88; pres, Asn Writing Prog, 1986-87; assoc ed, Callaloo Jour Afro-Am Arts & Letters, 1986-98, adv ed, Gettysburg Rev, 1987-, TriQuarterly 1988-, Ploughshares, 1992-, Ga Review, 1994-, Bellingham Review, 1996-, Int Quarterly, 1997-, Poetry Int, 1997-, Callaloo Jour Afro-Am Arts & Letters, 1998-, Mid-Am Review, 1998-, Hunger Mountain, 2003-, Am Poetry Review, 2005-; comnr, Schomburg Ctr Res Black Cult, 1987-; PEN Club Am Ctr; ed bd, Iris, 1989-; cont ed Meridian, 1989-; Acad Am Poets, 1990; adv bd, NC Writers' Network, 1991-99; Afro-Am Studies Vis Comt, Harvard Univ, 1992-; Poet's Corner, Cathedral St John Divine, elector, 1991-2002; adv bd, Thomas Jefferson Ctr Freedom Expression, 1994-; adv bd, VA Ctr Creative Arts, 1994-; adv bd, Live Arts, Charlottesville, 1994-; adv bd, Civilization, Mag Libr Cong, 1994-97; Coun Scholars, Libr Cong, 1994-; PEN Am Ctr, 1994; consult, Woman to Woman on Lifetime, Lifetime TV, 1994; Phi Beta Kappa, 1994-2000; bd mem, Charlottesville-Albemarle Opera Soc, 1995; adv bd, US Civil War Ctr, 1995-99; bd gov, Univ CA, Humanities Res Inst, 1996-2000; adv bd, MacDowell Colony, 1997-; chair, poetry jury, Pulitzer Bd Columbia Univ, 1997; bd dir, Poetry Daily, 2002-; Am Heritage Dict Usage Panel, 2002-; adv bd, Student Achievement & Advocacy Serv, 2002-; adv bd, DuBois Ctr Am Hist & Culture, 2005-; adv bd, Givens Found Afr Am Lit, 2005-; chancellor, Ac Am Poets, 2006-. **Honors/Awds:** Presidential Scholar, The Pres US Am, 1970; Fulbright Scholar, US Govt, 1974-75; Literature Grant, Nat Endowment Arts, 1978, 1989; Portia Pittman Fel, Nat Endowment Arts, 1982; Guggenheim Fel, Guggenheim Found, 1983-84; Callaloo Award, 1986; Lavan Younger Poet Award, The Acad Am Poets, 1986; Pulitzer Prize for Poetry, Pulitzer Bd Columbia Univ, 1987; General Electric Foundation Award for Younger Writers, 1987; Ohio Governor's Award, 1988; Bellagio Residency, Rockefeller Found, 1988; Andrew W Mellon Sr Fel, Nat Humanities Ctr, NC, 1988-89; Fel, Ctr Advanced Studies, Univ Va, 1989-92; Ohioana Book Award for Grace Notes, 1990; Literary Lion, NY Pub Libr, 1991; Ohio Women's Hall of Fame, 1991; Phi Beta Kappa Poet, Harvard Univ, 1993; Poetry Reading at The White House, State Dinner in honor of Nat Medal of Arts recipients, 1993; Va Col Stores Asn Book Award for Through the Ivory Gate, 1993; Woman of the Year Award, Glamour Mag, 1993; NAACP Great American Artist Award, NAACP, 1993; Renaissance Forum Award, Leadership Lit Arts, Folger Shakespeare Libr, Wash DC, 1994; Ohioana Book Award for Selected Poems, 1994; Distinguished Achievement Medal, Miami Univ Alumni Asn, 1994; Golden Plate Award, Am Acad Achievement, 1994; Carl Sandburg Award, Intl Platform Asn, 1994; The Kennedy Ctr Fund for New American Plays Award, 1995; Heinz Award in Arts & Humanities, 1996; Charles Frankel prize, US Pres, 1996; Literary Lion, NY Pub Libr, 1996; Honorary Doctor of Letters, Univ Pa, 1996; Honorary Doctor of

Letters, Spelman Col, 1996; Honorary Doctor of Letters, Univ NC, 1997; Honorary Doctor of Letters, Univ Notre Dame, 1997; Honorary Doctor of Letters, Northeastern Univ, 1997; Sara Lee Frontrunner Award, 1997; Writers for Writers Award, Barnes & Noble, 1997; Distinguished Woman Award, Nat Asn Women Educ, 1997; featured author on Ugandan postage stamp, 1997; Levinson Prize, Poetry Mag, 1998; Honorary Doctor of Letters, Columbia Univ, 1998; Honorary Doctor of Letters, SUNY Brockport, 1999; Honorary Doctor of Letters, Washington & Lee Univ, 1999; John Frederick Nims Translation Prize, with Fred Viebahn, 1999; Library Lion, NY Pub Libr, 2000; Duke Ellington Lifetime Achievement Award, 2001; Honorary Doctor of Letters, Howard Univ, 2001; Honorary Doctor of Letters, Pratt Ins, 2001; Emily Couric Women's Leadership Award, 2003; Honorary Doctor of Letters, Skidmore Col, 2004; Common Wealth Award of Distinguished Service, 2006. **Special Achievements:** Youngest & first African-American Poet Laureate, 1993-95; Second African-American to win Pulitzer Prize in Poetry. **Business Addr:** Commonwealth Professor, University of Virginia, English Department, 219 Byran Hall, PO Box 400121, Charlottesville, VA 22904-4121, **Business Phone:** (434)924-6618.

DOVE, DR. SHIRLEY
Executive. **Career:** Lenoir Community Col, vpres acad & stud serv, currently. **Orgs:** Steering comt, NC Asn Community Col Instrnl Adminir. **Business Addr:** Vice President of Academic & Student Services, Lenoir Community College, 231 Hwy 58 S Admin Bldg 104, PO Box 188, Kinston, NC 28502-0188, **Business Phone:** (252)527-6223.

DOWD, MARIA DENISE
Executive, writer. **Personal:** Born in California; children: 2. **Career:** African Am Women Tour, founder & exec producer, 1991-; Warm Spirit, dir, 2002-; Soul Journeys Inc, pres & founder, currently; PROMOTrends Inc, pres. **Orgs:** Presenter, Divinity Christian Church Retreat; health & wellness columnist, Turning Point Mag. **Honors/Awds:** The Spirit of Madam CJ Walker Award. **Business Addr:** Founder, Executive Producer, African American Women On Tour, PO Box 152107, San Diego, CA 92195-2107, **Business Phone:** (619)229-7766.

DOWDELL, DENNIS, JR.
Manager. **Personal:** Born Mar 8, 1945; son of Marjorie Dowdell and Dennis Dowdell; married Equinetta Cox, Aug 22, 1970; children: Malaika, Arianne, Cicely. **Educ:** Central State Univ, BS, history & polit sci, cum laude, LHD; Cleveland State Univ Col Law, JD. **Career:** Cleveland Bd Educ, teacher, 1968-71; Legal Serv Org Indianapolis Inc, staff atty, 1971-72; US Dept Labor, Off Solicitor, trial atty, 1972-76, asst coun, OSHA, 1976-78, co-counsel, Black Lung, 1978-80; Am Can Co, Compliance Plans & Litigation, dir, 1980-84; Am Nat Can, Performance Plastics Div, v pres human resources, 1985-91; Henry Ford Health Syst, corp vpres human resources; The Longaberger Co; LANYAP SQUARED LLC, pres; Nat Asn Black Automotive Suppliers; Exec Leadership Coun, Inst Leadership develop & res, exec dir, 2004, pres; Memorial Sloan Kettering Cancer Ctr, chief human resources, vpres. **Orgs:** chmn, pres coun, Central State Univ; bd dir, Nat Urban League, Black Exec Exchange Prog; Nat Urban League; NAACP; Am Bar Asn; Nat Bar Asn; past nat pres, Central State Univ Nat Alumni Asn; exec leadership council, Omega Psi Phi Frat; Central State Univ Found; Leadership Detroit; Detroit Urban League; nat bd dirs, Alzheimer's Disease and Related Disorders Asn Inc; pres, 100 Black Men Greater Detroit; bd dir, Exec Leadership Found. **Honors/Awds:** Donald McGannon Award, Nat Urban League, 1998; David McGannon Award, Nat Urban League; Corporate Award, Exec Leadership Coun. **Business Addr:** Vice President, Human Resources, Memorial Sloan-Kettering Cancer Center, 1275 York Ave, New York, NY 10021, **Business Phone:** (212)639-2000.*

DOWDELL, KEVIN CRAWFORD
Chief executive officer. **Personal:** Born Oct 7, 1961, Schenectady, NY; son of Crawford and Doris. **Educ:** Princeton Univ, BSE, mgt syst eng, 1983; Wharton Bus Sch, MBA, finance & mkt, 1985. **Career:** Gen Elec Co, eng fel, 1979-80; Johnson & Johnson, leadership fel, Wharton, 1983-85; Strategic Planning Assocs, sr assoc & sr consult, 1985-89; Safe Passage Found, Wash, DC, exec dir, 1989-93; Home Box Off, dept head & vpres new bus develop, 1994-2001; Volume Media LLC, founder & cheif exec officer, 2001-03; Boys & Girls Club, Wash, DC, chief exec officer, 2006-. **Orgs:** Pres, Princeton Soc Black Engrs, 1982-83; vice chmn, Whitney Young Conf, Wharton, 1984-85; co-founder, Arthur Ashe's Safe Passage Found, 1989; chair, US Tennis Asn Nat Jr Tennis League, 2006-. **Honors/Awds:** Joseph Clifton Elgin Prize, Princeton, 1983. **Special Achievements:** Highly ranked tennis player. **Business Addr:** Chief Operating Officer, Boys & Girls Club Of Greater Washington, 8380 Colesville Rd Suite 600, Silver Spring, MD 20910, **Business Phone:** (301)562-2000.

DOWDY, JAMES H
Executive. **Personal:** Born Jun 3, 1932, New York, NY; son of Gertrude Dowdy and Edward Dowdy; married Elsia M; children: James Jr. **Educ:** D&B Bus Sch. **Career:** Limosine Serv; Real Estate firm; Vending Co; Contracting Co, 1962; Harlem Commonwealth Coun, exec dir; Commonwealth Holding Co, pres, CEO 1970-92; Eastcoast Devel Corp, pres, chief exec officer; Eastcoast Develop Community Tech Serv Inc, pres, currently. **Orgs:** Chmn, Vanguard Nat Bank; bd dirs, Freedom Nat Bank, New York; bd mem, Harlem Interfaith Coun Serv; Presidential Task Force, 100 Black Men; bd mem, Cathedral Church St John Devine; chmn, Boys Choir Harlem. **Honors/Awds:** First Community Service Award, Gov VI; Martin L King Award. **Business Addr:** President, Eastcoast Development Community Technical Services Inc, 1250 Md Ave SW Suite C10, Washington, DC 20024-2166, **Business Phone:** (202)554-1970.

DOWDY, DR. JOANNE KILGOUR
Educator. **Personal:** Born in port of spain, Trinidad and Tobago; daughter of Lennox Kilgour and Kathleen Kilgour. **Educ:** Teachers Col, Masters degree; Columbia Univ, attended; Univ NC, PhD. **Career:** Kent State Univ, Col Educ, prof, lead & curri studs, currently. **Honors/Awds:** Diversity Leadership Faculty/Research Award, Kent State Univ; Research and Narrative Outstanding Book Award, Am Educ Res Asn Spec Interest Grp, 2009. **Special Achievements:** Author: The Skin that We Speak: Thoughts on Language and Culture in the Classroom, GED Stories:Black Women & Their Struggle for Social Equity, 2003; Readers of the Quilt: Black Women and Literacy, 2005; Ph.D. Stories: Conversations with My Sisters, 2008; Ovuh Dyuh.

DOWELL, CLYDE DONALD
Government official. **Personal:** Born Aug 19, 1938, Gordonsville, TN; son of Frances and LC; married Daisy Dowell, Oct 14, 1958; children: Sherry Green, Clyde D II, Marilyn Barnes, Tonja Hale. **Educ:** Wayne State Univ, BS, 1971; MBA, 1975. **Career:** City Detroit, jr typist, 1962-, jr acct, 1971-73, sr acct, 1973-74, prin acct, 1974-79; head acct, 1979-85, acct mgr, 1985-86, dep budget dir, 1986-93, dir pub works, 1994-00. **Orgs:** Am Pub Works Asn; Detroit Zool Soc; Founder's Soc-Detroit Inst Arts; Nat Asn Assessing officers, 1979-85; Nat Asn Advan Colored People, 1981. **Special Achievements:** Ran & Completed 3 Marathons, 1983-85. **Military Serv:** AUS, spec-4, 1958-61. **Home Addr:** 20429 Ardmore, Detroit, MI 48235-1510, **Home Phone:** (313)864-1849. **Business Addr:** Director Public Works, City of Detroit, 513 Coleman A Young Munic Ctr, Detroit, MI 48226, **Business Phone:** (313)224-3900.*

DOWELL-CERASOLI, PATRICIA R
Government official. **Personal:** Born May 13, 1957, Bethpage, NY; daughter of Norman and Kathryn; married Paul; children: Justin David. **Educ:** Univ Rochester, Rochester, NY, BA, 1978; Univ Chicago, Chicago, Ill, MA, 1980. **Career:** Dept Planning, City Chicago, Chicago, Ill, city planner, 1981-86; Mayor Off, City Chicago, Chicago, Ill, develop subcabinet staff dir, 1987-89; Dept Planning City Chicago, Chicago, Ill, dep comnr, 1989-. **Orgs:** Bd mem, Midwest Ctr Labor Res, 1989-; Lambda Alpha Land Econ Soc, 1990-; Nat Forum Black Pub Adminrs, 1990-; exec dir, Mid-South Planning & Develop Comn. **Honors/Awds:** Leadership Fel, Leadership Greater Chicago, 1988-89. **Business Addr:** Deputy Commissioner, Department of Planning & Development, 121 N LaSalle St Rm 1006, Chicago, IL 60602, **Business Phone:** (312)744-4565.

DOWERY, MARY
Educator. **Personal:** Born in Kentucky; divorced. **Educ:** Knoxville Col, 1950; Atlanta Univ, MSW, 1952; Columbia Univ, 1964; NY Univ, 1965; Psychoanal Inst Training & Res, 1945; Tulane Univ, 1975; Union Grad Sch. **Career:** Ball St Univ, asst prof; Arch, 1971-74; Einstein Med Col; Comm Ment Col; Comm Ment Health; Urban Renewal, Mobilization Youth Inc; Residential Treat Adolescent Girls; Calif Youth Authority; NY City Bd Educ; NY City, protestant cnc; Social Worker, 1953-65; Personnel By Dowery, founder & operator, 1965-71; Black Greeting Card "Uhuru", orgn publ, 1968-71. **Orgs:** Delta Sigma Theta; Asn Personnel Agys, NY City, 1965-69; Am Mgt Asn; Nat Asn Social Workers; Coun Social Work Educ; 100 Black Women, 1975-77; League Women Voters; NY Soc Sickle Cell Anemia; AU Alumni; Knoxville Col Alumni Asn; United Day Care Ctr; Bethel Home Boys; reviewer Nat Endowment of Humanities. **Special Achievements:** Partic Mike Wallace Show, 1964; publ Greeting Card Mag, 1970; publ Et Cetero Mag 1964; Black Enter, 1970; Income Mag, 1970; Daily News 1972; BusWeek Peps 1969. **Business Addr:** 710 N Mc Kinley Ave, Muncie, IN 47303.*

DOWKINGS, WENDY LANELL
Editor. **Personal:** Born Jun 24, 1964, Fort Meade, MD; daughter of Bennie and Jessie Marbury. **Educ:** Univ Tex, El Paso, TX, 1984; Univ Texas, Austin, TX, BA, jour, 1986. **Career:** Fort Worth Star Telegram, Fort Worth, TX, intern reporting, 1985; Austin Am Statesman, TX, copy ed, 1985-86; Hartford Courant, Hartford, CT, copy ed, 1986-89; Philadelphia Inquirer, Philadelphia, PA, copy ed, 1989-. **Orgs:** Nat Asn Black Journalists, 1986-; vol fair coordr, Hartford Neighborhood Housing Asn, 1988-89; Conn Asn Black Communicators, 1988-89; Philadelphia Asn Black Journalists, 1991-. **Business Addr:** Copy Editor, Philadelphia Inquirer, 400 N Broad St, Philadelphia, PA 19130, **Business Phone:** (215)854-2432.*

DOWNES, DWIGHT. See Obituaries section.

DOWNIE, DR. WINSOME ANGELA
Educator. **Personal:** Born Apr 14, 1948, Kingston, Jamaica; daughter of Frank G and Marie Angela Crarey; married Norbert W Rainford, Jun 28, 1980; children: Damien & Ayana. **Educ:** Barnard Col, New York, NY, AB, 1970; Columbia Univ, New York, NY, Pres's Fel, 1974, MA, 1977, MPhil, 1977, PhD, 1985. **Career:** Kingsborough Community Col, instr, 1975-78; State Univ, New York, New Paltz, NY, instr, 1978; Manhattan Col, Dept Govt, asst prof gov, 1978-, chairperson, currently. **Orgs:** Bd dirs, Martin Luther King Ctr, 1988-92; chair, Church & Soc Work Area, United Methodist Church, 1990-; exec bd, Jamaican Cult & Civic Asn Rockland, 1991-; comt mem, Jack & Jill Rockland County; chair, Compact Team Viola Sch, Suffern, Rockland, NY. **Honors/Awds:** Summer Grant, Manhattan Col, 1991; Sabbatical Leave MLK-Center Service Award, 1995. **Special Achievements:** Author of several articles on the politics of development in post-colonial Jamaica and the Caribbean and on women in politics in Jamaica, the USA, the Caribbean, South Africa and other areas of Africa and the African diaspora. **Business Addr:** Assistant Professor of Government, Chairperson, Manhattan College, Department of Government, Manhattan Col Pkwy, Miguel 415, Riverdale, NY 10471, **Business Phone:** (718)862-7292.

DOWNING, DR. BEVERLY
Educational consultant. **Career:** St Augustines Col, Div Educ, chmn, currently. **Business Phone:** (919)516-4096.

DOWNING, DR. JOHN WILLIAM, JR.
Educator, physician. **Personal:** Born Mar 13, 1936, Phoebus, VA; son of John W Downing Sr and Alice B; married Bessie; children: Kevin & Kimberlynn. **Educ:** More house Col, BS, 1957; Meharry Med Col, MD, 1961. **Career:** Cincinnati Children's Med Ctr, fel pediat cardiol, 1967-70; Univ Cincinnati, instr Pediat, 1969-70; Howard Univ, asst prof, 1970-74, assoc prof, 1974-80, prof, 1980-, chmn, dept pediat, 1986-94. **Orgs:** Dir, Pediat Cardiac Clin Howard Univ Hosp; consult, DC Gen Hosp; chmn profed, comn Am Heart Asn Nations Capital Affil; DC Med Soc; Am Heart Asn, 1974-; ch coun, Third St Ch God, 1974-; bd dir, Am Heart Asn Nations Capital Affiliate; dipl, Am Bd Pediats; fel, Am Col Cardiol. **Honors/Awds:** Alpha Omega Alpha Honor Medical Society. **Special Achievements:** Several publications in medical literature. **Military Serv:** AUS, Med corp, capt, 1964-67. **Business Addr:** Professor, Howard University, 2041 Ga Ave NW, Washington, DC 20060.*

DOWNING, STEPHEN
Athletic director. **Personal:** Born May 28, 1950, Indianapolis, IN; son of William Downing and Evana Downing; married Doris. **Educ:** Ind Univ, BS 1973; IUPUI, MS, Coun & Guid, 1978. **Career:** IN U, adminstrator asst to athletic dir 1978-; Boston Celtics, former bskbll prof; Texas Tech Univ, sr assoc athletic dir. **Orgs:** Active childrens summer groups; first draft Boston, 1973. **Honors/Awds:** Most Valuable Player Big Ten; Converse All-Amer Team; NCAA 3rd place team; HS All-Amer; Indiana Hall of Fame, 1996. **Home Addr:** 6433 Lakeside Woods Cir, Indianapolis, IN 46278.

DOWNING, WILL
Singer. **Personal:** Born Jan 1, 1961, Brooklyn, NY; married Audrey Wheeler, 2002. **Educ:** Va Union Univ. **Career:** Albums: Will Downing, 1988; Come Together as One, 1989; A Dream Fulfilled, 1991; Love's the Place to Be, 1993; Moods, 1995; Invitation Only, 1997; Pleasures of the Night, 1998; All the Man You Need, 2000; Greatest Love Songs, 2002; Sensual Journey, 2002; Emotions, 2003; Christmas Love & you, 2004; Soul Symphony, 2005; The Best Of Will Downing: The Millennium Collection, 2006; After Tonight, 2007; Classique, 2009; Songs: "Sorry I"; "If She Knew"; "The Rhythm of you & me"; "Nothing has ever felt like this"; "When you need me"; "Where is the Love". **Orgs:** Spokesperson, Am Stoke Assn. **Honors/Awds:** Best Album of the Year, Blues & Soul Mag; Vocalist of the Year; Best Live Performer, 1992; NAACP Image awards; International Association of African American Music Diamond Award, 2002. **Special Achievements:** Sang background vocals for artists such as: Nona Hendryx, Jennifer Holliday; Najee; Stephanie Mills; David Peaston; Billy Ocean; Art Porter; sang duets with Rachelle Ferrell, Mica Paris; performed for Prince Charles and Princess Diana at the Prince's Trust Concert; nominated for Soul Train Music Awards; Recognized by the Grammys (All the Man you need) & the National Association for the Advancement of Colored People Image awards for his excellence on the stage & in studio; Published a book: UNVEILED, 2005; conducts a charity bowling event called Strike against Stroke to raise funds toward greater stroke awareness & educ in the African American Community. **Business Phone:** 800-551-5299.*

DOWNS, CRYSTAL
Consultant, writer. **Personal:** Born Dec 29, 1964, Chicago, IL; daughter of Charles Edmond and Queen Esta Taylor. **Educ:** Chicago State Univ, Chicago, attended 1987; Columbia Col, Chicago, BA, 1989. **Career:** Am Jour Reprod Immunol & Microbiol, Chicago, ed intern, 1987-88; Essence Mag, New York, summer intern, summer, 1988; Alpha Kappa Alpha Sorority, Chicago, asst dir, assoc ed, 1989-92; self-employed, writer, ed consult, 1992-95; Chicago State Univ, Chicago, from exec asst to the pres, 1995-. **Orgs:** Nat Asn Black Journalists, 1990-; Alpha Kappa Alpha Sorority, 1984-; CASE; bd, Pub Allies; Women's Adv

Group. **Special Achievements:** Mag Publ Procedures Course, Howard Univ & Mag Publ of Am, 1990; Univ Chicago Publ Prog, 1994. **Business Addr:** Executive Assistant President, Chicago State University, 9501 S King Dr ADM 300, Chicago, IL 60628, **Business Phone:** (773)995-3608.

DOXIE, MARVIN LEON
Marketing executive, executive director. **Personal:** Born May 15, 1943, Youngstown, OH; son of Melvin and E Beatrice Boyd Doxie; married Beverly Owens, Feb 27, 1965; children: Monica Yvette & Marvin Leon Jr. **Educ:** Youngstown State Univ, attended; Ohio Univ, attended; Howard Univ, Sch Bus & Pub Admin, attended 1975; Prince George's Col, attended 1995. **Career:** Greater Wash Bus Ctr, vpres, 1973-82; Raven Systs & Res, Bus Develop, dir, 1982-83; DC Govt, Minority Bus Opportunity Comn, mkt mgr, 1983-85; Automated Sci Group Inc, mkt support dir, 1985-94; M L Doxie & Assocs, pres, 1994-95; Delon Hampton & Assocs, chartered, client rels, dir; C C Johnson & Malhotra Engrs Ltd, Corp Bus Develop, dir, currently. **Orgs:** Montgomery C High Technol Coun, 1989-95; Silver Spring Chamber Com, bd dir, 1990-95; AFCEA, 1989-95; DC Chamber Com, 1975; MD/DC Minority Supplier Develop Coun, 1989; Am Mkt Asn; Architect/Eng Coun, dir, 1996. **Honors/Awds:** Appreciation Award, DC Govt, 1985; Cert Appreciation, White House Conf Small Bus, 1986; Cert Appreciation, Montgomery C, MD Govt, 1997. **Home Addr:** 7202 Wendover Dr, District Heights, MD 20747-1742, **Home Phone:** (301)336-6136. **Business Addr:** Director Corporate Business Development, C C Johnson & Malhotra Engineers Ltd, 3700 Koppers St Suite 109, Baltimore, MD 21227-1020, **Business Phone:** (410)644-0130.

DOZIER, LAMONT
Songwriter. **Personal:** Born Jun 16, 1941, Detroit, MI; married Barbara, Nov 20, 1980; children: Beau Alexandre, Paris Ray & Desiree Starr. **Career:** Songwriter, currently; Albums: Inside Seduction; Bigger Than Life; Lamont; Working On You; Bittersweet; Peddling Music On The Side; Right There; Black Bach; Out Here On My Own; Lamont Dozier - Reflections of; Ain't Got No Stop Button. **Honors/Awds:** Numerous honors & awards including Grammy Award, Best Song Written Specifically for a Motion Picture or Television, for "Two Hearts," 1988; Rock & Roll Hall of Fame, 1990; BMI Icon Award, 2003; Billboard Magazine Award; SongWriter's Hall of Fame; Brit Award; BMI ICON Awards; Pioneer Award, Rhythm & Blues Found. **Business Addr:** Songwriter, Holland Group Productions, 1800 N Highland Ave, Hollywood, CA 90028, **Business Phone:** (323)463-2391.*

DOZIER, MORRIS, SR.
Insurance executive, military engineer. **Personal:** Born Nov 30, 1921, Americus, GA; son of Charlie and Minnie M; married Mary Lois Strawn; children: Morris Jr, Yolonda Maria. **Educ:** KS State Univ, attended 1963; Brown Mackie Bus Col, 1965. **Career:** mil (retired), ins exec; Civilian Conservation Clerk, admin clerk, 1941-42; US Army, sr clerk typist, 1942-44, command sgt major 1944-51, military personnel off, 1951-62; US Govt Ft Riley, independent contractor, 1967-78; Universal Insurance Service, owner & operator 1965-80; Geary Co, comm 1973-85. **Orgs:** Pres, PTA Westwood Elem Sch, 1966; vpres, Kawanis S, Jct City, 1970; chmn, Advisory Comn Sickle Cell Anemia Educ & Screening Prog; lay leader, Ch Our Savior United Methodist; bd dir, chmn, Geary County Sr Citizens; treas, Hunger Comn, Kansas E Conf, United Methodist Ch. **Honors/Awds:** Comm Medal 1957, 1st Oak Leaf Cluster 1962 US Army; Disting Citizen of the Yr Awd Omega Psi Phi Frat 1979; Plaque of Recognition for Outstanding Serv of State JTPA Prog Honorable John Carlin Gov State of KS 1983. **Military Serv:** AUS, chief warrant officer, w3 20 yrs; Good Conduct Medal, Nat Defense Medal, Asiatic Pacific Medal; Philippine Liberation Medal, 1943-45; Army Occupation Medals, Japan 1945, Italy 1946. *

DOZIER, MORRIS CICERO
Architect. **Personal:** Born Dec 24, 1953, Heildelburg, Germany; son of Morris and Mary; married Patricia A, Sep 3, 1977; children: Tiffany, Yannic & Sakai. **Educ:** Kans State univ, BArch, 1978; Fla Inst Technol, MBA, 1986. **Career:** Blue Dot Energy Co, proj mgr, 1996-2000; Bruce McMillan AIA Architects PA, architect, 2000-, pres, currently. **Orgs:** Gideons, 1998-; Am Inst Architects, 2000-; Nat Coun Archit Registration Bds, 2002-. **Military Serv:** Air Force, lt col, 1974-96; Commendation Medal, IT Serv Medal, 1991; Meritorious Serv Medal Second Oak Leaf Cluster, 1996. **Home Addr:** 226 W 14th St, Junction City, KS 66441, **Home Phone:** (785)238-6816. **Business Addr:** President, Architect, Bruce McMillan AIA Architect PA, 555 Poyntz Ave Suite 295, Manhattan, KS 66502, **Business Phone:** (785)776-1011.

DOZIER, RICHARD K.
Architect, school administrator. **Personal:** Born Jan 18, 1939, Buffalo, NY. **Educ:** La Tech Col, AA, 1962; Yale Sch Archit, BA, 1969, MA, 1970; Univ Mich, doctor archit hist, 1990. **Career:** Historic Preserv Archit Tuskegee Inst Ala, pvt prac; The Archit Off New Haven, Conn, pvt prac; Tuskegee Inst, chmn dept archit, 1976-79, prof archit hist, 1979-87; Yale Univ, prof archit, 1970-76; Archit various firms; Hist Afro-Am Archit & Archit, teaching & prof specialization; Morgan State Univ, prof archit, 1987-91; Fla A&M Univ, assoc dean, sch archit, 1991-96, prof archit, 1996-. **Orgs:** Am Inst Architects; Nat Orgn Minority Architects; African Am preservation orgn; Ala Black Heritage Coun. **Honors/Awds:** Nat Book Award, 1953; Leadership Award, Yale Univ, 1969, Honor Award, 1970; Res Fellow, Graham Found, 1970; Nat Endowment Arts Award; CT Found Arts; Dissertation Award, Nat Educ Health, 1986. **Military Serv:** USN, radarman E-5, 1956-60. **Home Addr:** 3446 Paces Ferry Rd, Tallahassee, FL 32309, **Home Phone:** (850)894-2691. **Business Addr:** Professor, Florida A & M University, Room 112 FHAC, Tallahassee, FL 32307, **Business Phone:** (904)599-3894.*

DRAHER, DODIE. See WALBEY, THEODOSIA EMMA DRAHER.

DRAIN, GERSHWIN A
Judge. **Educ:** Western Mich Univ, BS, 1970; Univ Mich Law Sch, JD, 1972; Univ Nev, Reno, Nat Judicial Col, MJS, 1991. **Career:** Thirty Sixth Dist Ct, Detroit, judge, 1986; Recorder's Ct, Detroit, judge, 1987; Wayne County Circuit Ct, judge, 1997-. **Orgs:** Numerous orgn including, Mich Judges Asn; Wolverine Bar Asn; Asn Black Judges Mich; Mich Bar Asn; Mic Judges Asn. **Honors/Awds:** Michiganian of the Year, Detroit News, 1997; Citizen of the Week, WWJ 950 AM. **Special Achievements:** The sec Mich judge to receive a MJS degree. **Business Addr:** Judge, Wayne County Circuit Court, 2 Woodward Ave Rm 1519, Coleman A Young Munic Ctr, Detroit, MI 48226, **Business Phone:** (313)224-2474.

DRAINE, MICHAEL
Pharmacologist. **Career:** Novartis Pharmaceuticals, Sales Representative, 1983; AstraZeneca Pharmaceuticals, Senior Director of Federal Government Affairs. **Orgs:** Member, Congressional Black Caucus Foundation, Inc. *

DRAKE, JERRY
Football player. **Personal:** Born Jul 9, 1969, Kingston, NY. **Educ:** Ulster County Community Col; Hastings Col. **Career:** Ariz Cardinals, defensive tackle, 1995-99; free agent, currently. *

DRAKE, LARRY. See DRAKE, LAWRENCE M, II.

DRAKE, LAWRENCE M, II (LARRY DRAKE)
Executive, president (organization). **Personal:** Born Jun 10, 1954, Pittsburgh, PA; son of Lawrence M II and Jean Williamson; married Sharon Martin, Sep 3, 1994; children: Kia Nichol & Kory Lawrence. **Educ:** Ga State Univ, BS, 1977; Rockhurst Col, MBA, 1990. **Career:** Coca-Cola USA, region mgr, KC Region, 1985-87, acct group mgr, CCE liaison, 1987-88, group dir, NY Acct Group, 1990-91, vpres north, vpres mide-cent, 1999-2004, Coca-Cola Nigeria & Equatorial Africa, pres, currently; KFC, Div Pepsico Inc, vpres, admin, asst to pres, 1990-91, vpres, general mgr, N Ctr Div, 1991-93, New Bus Develop, vpres, KFC Express Concepts, 1993-95; Cablevision Systems Corp, sr vpres & gen mgr, 1995-96; Dolman Technologies Group, exec vpres, coo, 1996-. **Orgs:** Alpha Phi Alpha Fraternity Inc, 1974-; Ga State Univ Alumnae Asn, 1985-; Rockhurst Exec Fels Asn, 1990-; bd dir, MAI Inc, 1990-; Exec Leadership Coun, 1991-; Nat Black MBA Asn, 1991-; Nat Conf of Christian & Jews; Leadership Cleveland; Cleveland Bus Roundtable; Calif Sciences Ctr; Coca-Cola Africa Found. **Business Phone:** 800-438-2653.

DRAKE, LEONARD
Basketball coach. **Personal:** Born Jul 16, 1954, Chicago, IL; son of Charles Drake and Ruth; married Rhonda Denise, Apr 19, 1986; children: Jared Leonard & Enjoli Desiree. **Educ:** Cent Mich Univ, BS, educ, 1978, MA, phys educ, 1983. **Career:** Basketball coach (retired); Cent Mich Univ, asst coach, 1978-79, head basketball coach, 1993-97; Xavier Univ, asst coach, 1979-84, head women's basketball coach, 1984-85; Ball State Univ, assoc basketball coach, 1985-93; Cent Mich, head coach, 1993-97; Lamar Univ, asst staff, men's basketball team; Lady Cardinal basketball Team, head coach, 2002-07; E Mich Univ, EMUEagles, asst. Women's Basketball coach, currently. **Orgs:** Nat Asn Basketball Coaches; Black Coaches Asn. **Honors/Awds:** Most Valuable Player Hons, 1976; Athlete of the Yr, 1977. **Business Addr:** Head Coach, Lamar University Intercollegiate Athletics, 4400 MLK Blvd, PO Box 10066, Beaumont, TX 77710-0066, **Business Phone:** (734)487-0481.*

DRAKE, MAGGIE W.
Judge. **Personal:** Daughter of Arthur and Margaret K Williams. **Educ:** Highland Park Col, AA, 1971; Mercy Col Detroit, BS, 1976; Univ Detroit, JD, 1981; Judicial Col, DP, 1993. **Career:** Detroit Police Dept, sergeant, 1974-92; Corp Coun, asst, 1982-92; Detroit Recorders Ct, 1992-97; Wayne County Circuit Ct, third judicial circuit, 1997-2007. **Orgs:** Michigan Judges Asn, 1993-; Black Judges Asn, 1993-; Asn Trial Judges, 1993-; Wolverine Bar Asn, 1993-. **Honors/Awds:** Community Treatment Ctr, Distinguished leader, 1996-97; Blacks in Blue Award, Detroit Police Asn, Distinguished Leader, 1997; BM&E State Convention, Women Auxiliary, Distinguished Leader Award, 1996. **Business Addr:** Judge, Wayne Co Circuit Ct, Third Judicial Circuit, 1441 St Antoine, Courtroom 703, Detroit, MI 48226, **Business Phone:** (313)224-2481.*

DRAKE, PAULINE LILIE
Association executive, government official. **Personal:** Born Jul 20, 1926, Cliffwood, NJ; daughter of Gabriel David Robinson and Daisy Etta Brown; married Howard William Drake; children: Sidney Howard. **Educ:** NY Univ, attended 1946; Brookdale Community Col, NJ, attended 1985. Veterans Foreign Wars. **Career:** Providence Baptist Church Cliffwood, church clerk, 1957-65, youth chair dir, 1960-72; Order Eastern Star AF&AM, worthy matron, 1994-97, Monmouth, county dep, 1960-71; Order Sunbeam Youth Dept OES AF&AM, dep, 1972-82. **Orgs:** Vol, USO, 1942-45; Pres, Matawan, Hadassah, NJ, 1979-81; pres, Monmouth County Veterans Foreign Wars Aux NJ, 1980-81; cert chmn, Southern NJ Reg Hadassah, 1981-85; publicity chmn, State NJ Ladies Aux Veterans Foreign Wars , 1981-82, 1988-89; jr girls unit chmn, NJ Ladies Aux Veterans Foreign Wars , 1982-83; safety chmn, NJ Ladies AuxVeterans Foreign Wars , 1983-84; voice of democracy & youth activity chmn, Ladies Aux Veterans Foreign Wars , 1984-85; safety chmn, 1986-87, guard, 1986-87, conductress, 1987-88, Dept of NJ Ladies Aux Veterans Foreign Wars ; transfer and trackdown chmn, Southern NJ Region Hadassah, 1987-90; chaplain, 1988; jr vpres, NJ Ladies Aux Veterans Foreign Wars , 1988-90, rehab chmn, 1988-89; JNF chairperson, Southern NJ Region Hadassah, 1990-91; sr vpres, NJ Veterans Foreign Wars, 1990-91; community activity chairperson, state pres, NJ Ladies Aux Veterans Foreign Wars , 1991-92; grand conductress, Military Order Cooties, 1994-95; second vpres, Madison Twp Historical Soc, 1994-96; Monmouth County Park Afro Am Comt; Aberdeen Twp Community Develop Comt; Concerned Citizens Aberdeen; grand senior vpres,Ladies Auxiliary MOC, NJ, 1995-96; pres, Madison Twp Historical Soc, 1996-02; bd dir, Ctr Holocaust Studies Brookdale Community Col, Lincroft, 1996-03; grand pres, Ladies Auxilairy MOC, NJ, 1997-98; pres, Matawan Women's Club, 2000-02; chair, E States Conf,Veterans Foreign Wars Rehab, 2002-03. **Honors/Awds:** Woman of the Year, Matawan, Hadassah, 1979; Presidential Award, Nat Hadassah, 1981; Humanitarian of the Year Award, Adath Israel Congregation Sisterhood and Men's Club, 1995. **Special Achievements:** Citation for Runner Up State President, 1991-92; Citation Bayshore Recreation & Economic Develop 1979; NJ Publicity 1st Place Natl Veterans Foreign Wars Aux Kansas 1982; NJ Jr Girls Unit 2nd Place Natl VFW Kansas 1984; NJ Safety Cert Natl VFW KS 1984; 15 Yr Pin Keyport Aux to VFW NJ 1985; NJ Publicity 1st place Natl VFWA 1988; Runner Up, Rehabilitation National Convention, 1990. **Home Addr:** 85 Kennedy Ave, Cliffwood, NJ 07721. *

DRAKEFORD, JACK
Government official. **Personal:** Born May 14, 1937, Englewood, NJ; son of Margaret Harris; married Virginia Finley, Sep 16, 1975; children: Gina & Nancy. **Educ:** NY Univ, New York, NY, bus admin; Syracuse Univ, Syracuse, NY, pub admin. **Career:** City Englewood, firefighter, 1959-73; James E Hanson, Hackensack, NJ, ins broker & real estate agent, 1973-77; City Englewood, city clerk, 1977-85; Englewood City Council, pres, 1976, 1999, 2002, 2004; DPW, act dir & act pub safety dir; City Of Englewood, counc man, currently; Labor Union Local 108 RWDSU, consult, currently. **Orgs:** Englewood Hospital Brd Trustees; comnr, Bergen County Housing Authority;chmn, bd mem, Northern Valley Dist Bergen County Boy Scouts; exec bd mem, Bergen County Girl Scouts; brd pres, Bergen County Tech Schs; mem, Brd Habitat for humanity of Bergen County; mem, Englewood Housing Authority; brd pres, Bergen County Technical School. **Honors/Awds:** Received approximately 20 awards from various organizations including: Englewood Chamber Com; Bergen County NAACP; Bergen County Boy Scouts Am;Bergen County Urban League; Bergan County Black Bus & Prof Women. **Special Achievements:** First African American City Clerk and the First African American City Manager. **Military Serv:** AUS, Spec/4, 1960-62. **Business Addr:** President of Board, Bergen County Technical Schools, 200 Hackensack Ave, Hackensack, NJ 07601, **Business Phone:** (201)343-6000.

DRAKEFORD, TYRONNE JAMES
Football player. **Personal:** Born Jun 21, 1971, Camden, SC; married Cindi; children: Julian James & Justus T. **Educ:** Va Tech, Bachelor's Degree, finance. **Career:** Football player (retired); San Francisco 49ers, defensive back, 1994-97, 2001; New Orleans Saints, 1998-99; Washington Redskins, 2000. **Honors/Awds:** Champion, SuperBowl, 1995. *

DRAKES, MURIEL B.
State government official. **Personal:** Born Nov 25, 1935, Bronx, NY; daughter of Alphonso and Frances. **Educ:** Del State Col, BS, 1958; Columbia Teacher Col, MA, 1963. **Career:** NY City Childrens Aid Soc, vis lectr, 1957-60; Faming dale Pub Sch, teacher, 1958-65; Bedford Stuyvesant Comn Corp, dir, educ explt prog, 1965-69; NY Sch Social Res, vis guest speaker, 1968; Comn Corp, assoc dir prog, 1969-72; Dahomey W Africa, vis guest lectr, 1971; Manpower Develop Com Labor Ind Corp, asst vpres, 1972-74; Dept Com & Ind, dep comnr, 1974-75; NY State Lottery Pub Rels, consult, 1976; NY State Off Gen Serv, dir promotion & pub affairs, 1976-; NY State Environ Conserv, dir EEO, 1987-. **Orgs:** Delta Sigma Theta Sor; NEA; vpres, Brooklyn Kings Co Judiciary Sect Comn Bldg; C of C Brooklyn Managerial Club; Int Ind Mkt Club; Albany Womens Press Club; pres, Eleanor Roosevelt Educ Action Prog. **Honors/Awds:** Achievement Excellence, Black Photographers Asn, 1974; Outstanding Leadership Civic Asn Jersey City, 1974; Brooklyn Distinguished Coun, Negro Women,

1975; Outstanding effort & Achievement Inter Ethnic Civic Asn, 1975; Distinguished Citizen Award, Concord Bapt Church; Willoughy Walk Tenants Coun Recipient; Woman of the Year, Albany, YWCA, 1987; Outstanding Leadership, Albany Cap Dist Ethnic Heritage Orgs (28), 1987. **Special Achievements:** Author "1965 Proposal of Bed ford Stuyvesant Comm Corp on the Homework Study Program". *

DRAPER, DR. EDGAR DANIEL
Educator. **Personal:** Born Aug 29, 1921, Brooklyn, MD; son of Andrew J Sr and Anniebelle Saunders; married Emma J Williams, Dec 29, 1948; children: Marie E, Yvonne T & Edgar D Jr. **Educ:** Howard Univ, BA, 1943; NY Univ, MPA, 1948, PhD, 1967. **Career:** Educator (retired); Tex Southern Univ, dir, instr, 1948-49; Tubman Col, pres, 1949-51; Baltimore Housing Authority, asst mgr, 1951-52; Morgan State Col, bus mgr, from asst to the pres, 1952-60; Conf African Resources NY Univ, asst dir, 1960-61; African-Am Trade Develop Asn, exec secy, 1961-62; UN Inst Pub Admin, dep chief 1962-63; Gov Nelson Rockefeller, prog asst, 1963-66; Borough Manhattan Comm Col, assoc dean, dean col, fac, 1967-70, pres, 1970-84. **Orgs:** Met Chap Am Asn Pub Admin; NY Plan; Nat Conf Christs Jews, 1970-; Coun Higher Educ Inst, 1972-; Pr Training Com & Com; BSA; Nat African Studies; Nat Ed Asn; Comparative Ed Soc; Am Asn Comm & Jr Col; Asn Asst Negro Bus; Urban League; Gov Libr Com; Interstate Compact Ed; Joint Legislative Com; Host Radio WNYC-AM Open Door, 1973-74; chmn, 4th Round Table Conf Perspectives Pub Admin Sudan; NY St Gov Com Manpower, 1966; Am Soc Pub Admin; Baltimore Urban League; NY Univ Alumni Asn; Nat Asn Advan Colored People; Metropolitan Educ Coalition; mem of phi beta sigma bro org; Baltimore Counon Foreign Affairs; task force, Baltimore City Pub Sch. **Honors/Awds:** Founders Day Award, NY Univ. **Military Serv:** AUS, pfc, 1946-47. **Home Addr:** 2728 Longwood St, Baltimore, MD 21216.

DRAPER, REV. FRANCES MURPHY
Newspaper executive, clergy. **Personal:** Born Dec 18, 1947, Baltimore, MD; daughter of James E Wood Sr and Frances L Murphy II; married Andre Reginald; children: Kevin E Peck, Andre D, Andrea J & Aaron R. **Educ:** Morgan State Univ, BA, spanish educ, 1969; The Johns Hopkins Univ, MEd, bus admin & pastoral coun 1973; Univ Baltimore, Grad Cert Mgmt, 1979, MBA, 1981; Loyola Col, MS, 1996; St. Mary's Seminary, theol; Dr Ministry degree, United Theol Seminary. **Career:** Baltimore City Pub Schs, teacher, 1969-73; New Jersey Afro-Am, mgr, 1973-76; Merrill Lynch Pierce Fenner & Smith, acct exec, 1976-78; Morgan State Univ, asst vpres develop, instr, 1978-84; Afro-Am Newspapers, pres, 1986-99, treas & bd mem; Nat cert counr; partor, John Wesley AME Zion Church, Baltimore, MD, partor, 2002-. **Orgs:** Delta Sigma Theta Sor Inc, 1968-; dir, Afro-Am Newspapers, 1976-; vice chair, City Baltimore's Literacy Found, 1988-94, chair, 1995-; Nat Coalition 100 Black Women, 1989-; bd mem, United Way Cent MD, 1994-97; bd mem, Balitmore City Chamber Com, 1994-97; bd regents, Morgan State Univ, trustee; bd trustees, Loyola Col; pastoral counr, Brantley Group; elder, AME Zion Church; cofounder, Gods Love Ministry; Network 2000. **Honors/Awds:** Woman of the Year in Business, Zeta Phi Beta Sorority Inc, 1990; AFRAM, one of 15 women honored, 1992; The New Daily Record, Maryland's Top 100 Women, 1996, 1998; 21st Century Award, The InterNat Alliance for Women, 1998; Carroll Award, Loyola Col, 1998; Distinguished Black Marylanders Award, Towson State Univ. **Special Achievements:** one of the "Area's Most Influential Women," , Baltimore Magazine, 1983; USA Today, one of the "People to Watch," 1987. **Business Addr:** Pastor, John Wesley Ame Zion Church, 1923 Ashland Ave, Baltimore, MD 21205-1535, **Business Phone:** (410)732-7020.

DRAPER, FREDERICK WEBSTER
Educator. **Personal:** Born Jul 10, 1945, St Louis, MO; married Carrie Todd; children: Fred W II & Angela. **Educ:** Ind State Univ, BS, 1968, MS, PE, 1969, MS, personnel admin, 1972, EdD, 1976. **Career:** Project Upswing IN, asst dir, 1969; GED Prog Off Econ Opport, supvr, 1972-73; asst phys educ & head cross country coach, 1969-, dir ed progs; Sch HPER, IN, State Univ, dir educ opportunity progs, prof; Global Net Solutions, pres/chief exec officer, currently. **Orgs:** Chmn Black Freshmen Orientation Prog, Ind State Univ, 1971-74; internship vpres, Ind State Univ, Stud Affairs, 1972-73; bd vpres, Ind State Black Expo; bd dir, Hyte Community Ctr; bd dir & treas, Ind Airport; fac adv, Kappa Alpha Psi; City Human Rel Comn; Sch Human Rel Comn; Boy Scout Troup Leader; pres, Hulman Reg Airport; bd dir, Civil Rights Comn; chmn bd, Ind Black Expo. **Honors/Awds:** Outstanding Black Faculty Award, Ind State Univ, 1972-73; Dean's List1968; Alumni Club; All-conf intrack every year as an undergrad. **Special Achievements:** One of Nations Most Eligible Bachelors, Ebony Mag, 1969. **Business Addr:** President, Chief Executive Officer, Global Net Solutions, 2626 E 46th St Suite 200, Indianapolis, IN 46205.*

DRAPER, SHARON MILLS
Educator. **Personal:** Born Aug 21, 1948, Cleveland, OH; daughter of Vick and Catherine; married Larry E Draper, Jul 25, 1970; children: Wendy, Damon, Cory & Crystal. **Educ:** Pepperdine Univ, BA, 1970; Miami Univ, MA, 1972. **Career:** Cincinnati Bd Educ, teacher, 1972-97; Mayerson Acad, Nat Teacher Yr Prog, assoc, currently; Author: Tears of a Tiger, 1994; Forged by Fire, 1997; Romiette & Julio, 1999; Teaching from the Heart, 1999; Darkness Before Dawn, 2001; Not Quite Burned Out, But Crispy around the Edges, 2001; Double Dutch, 2002; The Battle of Jericho, 2003; We Beat the Street, 2005; Copper Sun, 2006; Fire from the Rock, 2006; November Blues, 2007. **Orgs:** Bd dirs, Nat Bd Prof Teaching Stands, 1995; Women's City Club; Nat Coun Teachers Eng; Ohio Coun Teachers Eng Lang Arts; Conf Eng Leadership; Am Fedn Teachers; Int Reading Asn; Delta Kappa Gamma. **Honors/Awds:** Ebony Mag, First Prize in Literary Contest, 1991; Fiction Work, "Tears of A Tiger," honored by Am Language Assn, Best Book for Young Adults, 1995; Genesis Award Am Libr Asn, 1995; Coretta Scott King Literary Award; Outstanding High Sch Language Arts Educr, 1995; Excellence in Teaching Award, Nat Coun Negro Women, 1996; Nat Teacher of the Year, 1997; Ohio Teacher of the Year, 1997; Excellence in Education Award, 1997; Milken Family Found, Nat Educator Award, 1997; YWCA, Career Women of Achievement, 1997; Nat Teacher of the Year, 1997; Dean's Award, Howard Univ Sch Educ; Distinguished Alumnus Award, Pepperdine Univ; Educ Excellence Award, Marva Collins; Gov's Educational Leadership Award, Gov Ohio. **Special Achievements:** One of the first teachers in the nation to achieve Nat Bd Certification in Eng/Lang Arts, & is one of only three Eng teachers in Ohio to be cert; Award winning essay on educ was publ in: "What Govs Need to Know About Educ. **Business Phone:** (513)475-4100.

DRAYTON, TROY ANTHONY
Football player, real estate executive. **Personal:** Born Jun 29, 1970, Harrisburg, PA; son of Stella. **Educ:** Pa State Univ, attended. **Career:** Football player (retired); Los Angeles Rams, 1993-94; St Louis Rams, tight end, 1995-96; Miami Dolphins, 1996-99; Kans City Chiefs, 1999-00; Green Bay Packers, 2001, real estate, currently. **Honors/Awds:** Pro Bowl alternate, 1994. *

DRE (ANDRE RAMELLE YOUNG)
Rap musician, music producer. **Personal:** Born Feb 18, 1965, Compton, CA; married; children: 3. **Career:** Rap artist, currently; rec producer for various artists; Death Row Recs, co-founder, 1991; Niggaz4Life: The Only Home Video, 1992; Set It Off, 1994; Aftermath Rec, founder, 1996-; Up In Smoke Tour, 2000; The Wash, 2001; Training Day, 2001; Hollywood Homicide, 2003; The Game: Documentary, 2005; 50 Cent:The Massacre - Spec Edition, 2005; Tupac Is Not Dead, 2006; Solo albums include: The Chronic, 1993; Dr Dre Presents The Aftermath, 1996; Dr Dre, 2001; released two albums as mem of World Class Wreckin Cru; released three albums, one EP, as mem of NWA. **Honors/Awds:** Grammy Award for Best Rap Solo Performance, 1993; Grammy Award, 1994; Source award for best producer, solo artist, & album, 1994; Grammy, Producer of the Year, 2000. **Business Phone:** (818)385-0024.

DRENNEN, GORDON
Auditor. **Personal:** Born Jul 15, 1947, Atlanta, GA; son of Gordon D Sr and Eliza Harris; married Diane Hatcher, Mar 17, 1978; children: Kimberly. **Educ:** Fort Valley State Col, BS, 1970; TX Southern Univ, MBA, 1971. **Career:** Wolf & Co CPA's, staff acct, 1971-73, sr acct, 1973-78; Tarica & Co CPA's, supvr, 1978-80, mgr. **Orgs:** Dir, Am Civil Liberties Union GA, 1986-; finance chmn, Ft Valley State Col Alumni Asn, 1986-; GA State Soc CPA's; consult, Nat Asn Community Health Ctrs, GA Asn Primary Health Care Inc; Kappa Alpha Psi Frat; vice chair, finance comt, Nat Black Col Alumni Hall Fame Found Inc, 1990-; selection comt, chair, Georgia Asn Minority Entrepreneurs, 1987-; Nat Asn Black Accts, 1973-; Bd Dir, Georgia Advocacy Off Inc. **Honors/Awds:** Distinguished Alumni Citation of Year, Nat Asn Equal Opportunity Higher Educ; Grad Fellowship, Texas Southern Univ, 1970-71. *

DREW, KENNETH R.
Publisher, commissioner. **Career:** Commissioner (retired); Human right Comnr; New Voice NY, publ, 2003. *

DREW, LARRY DONELLE
Basketball player, basketball coach. **Personal:** Born Apr 2, 1958, Kansas City, KS; married Sharon; children: Larry, Landon & Lindsey. **Educ:** Univ Mo, 1980. **Career:** Basketball player (retired), basketball coach: Pkp on various teams: Detroit Pistons, 1980-81; Kansas City Kings, 1982-85; Sacramento Kings, 1986; Los Angeles Clippers, 1987-88; Los Angeles Lakers, 1990-91; Los Angeles Lakers, asst coach; Detroit pistons, asst coach, 1999-2000; NJ Nets, asst, 2000-03; Atlanta Hawks Basketball Inc, asst coach, 2004-. **Orgs:** Bd mem, KC K's Red Cross; teacher, basketball camps, Kansas, Missouri. **Honors/Awds:** All Big 8 Honorable Mention; ranked 9th, NBA in asst, 1984-85. *

DREW, STEPHEN RICHARD
Lawyer. **Personal:** Born May 25, 1949, Detroit, MI; son of Richard T and Gwendolyn Mae Johnson; married Clarice Smith Drew, Apr 22, 1989; children: Richard, Stephen, Anthony, Thomas & Sahara. **Educ:** Univ Mich, BA, 1971; Univ Mich Law Sch, JD, 1974. **Career:** Williams Klukowski Drew & Fotieo, assoc, 1974-77, partner, 1977-87; Drew, Cooper & Anding, Grand Rapids, Mich, partner, 1991-. **Orgs:** Chmn, City Grand Rapids Comn Rels Comn, 1984-85; consult, spec investigator, Saginaw Police Dept, 1985-86; Sigma Pi Phi, 1985-; judicial merit selection panel mem, US Ct Appeals 6th Circuit, 1986-; legal redress comn, Nat Asn Advan Colored People Grand Rapids Chap, 1987-; trustee, 1987, judicial rev comt, Grand Rapids Bar Asn, vpres, 1990-91, pres elect, 1991-92, pres, 1992-93; Am Bar Asn; Nat Bar Asn; Mich Trial Lawyers Asn; Am Trial Lawyers Asn; fel State Bar Mich; pres, Floyd Skinner Bar Asn; civil justice reform adv comt, United States Dist Ct, 1991-. **Honors/Awds:** Outstanding Volunteer Award, Nat Asn Advan Colored People Grand Rapids Chap, 1982; Patriotic Service Award, Secy US Treas, 1986; Grand Rapids Giant Award Justice; Civil Libertarian Year, W Mich Am Civil Liberties Union, 1989; Giant Giants Award, 1999. **Business Addr:** Partner, Drew, Cooper & Anding, 125 Ottawa Ave NW, Ledyard Bldg 125 Ottawa Ave NW Suite 300, Grand Rapids, MI 49503-2898, **Business Phone:** (616)454-8300.

DREW, THELMA LUCILLE
Government official, secretary (government). **Personal:** Born in Flushing, NY; married Archer S Drew Jr; children: Richard Michael, Kenneth Edward, Joanne Michelle, Sheryln Liane & KimberlyTerese. **Educ:** Queens Col, NY, Eng, attended 1949; Am Inst Banking, mgt, attended 1972; Empire State Col, NY, pub admin, attended 1980; Hofstra Univ, Hempstead, NY, cert in mus studies, 1985. **Career:** Secretary (retired) NY Tele Co, bus off rep, 1949-58; Smithtown Twp, town rec leader (1st black), 1965-69; Nat Bank N Am, banker & mgt, 1969-73;Suffolk Co Dept Soc Servs, social welfare examiner, 1973-77; SuffolkCo, Human Rights Comm, sr investr, 1977-82, Dept Consumer Affairs, asst dir. **Orgs:** NYS Div of Human Rights Coun, 1983-; bd dir, Long Isl Affirmative Act Plan, 1980-, Victims Inf Bur, 1980-, Inst Labor/Mgmnt Studies, 1979-; founding mem, 100 Black Women LI, 1980-; Nat Asn Female Exec, 1982-, NatAsn Consumer Prot, 1982-; pres & chairperson, Suffolk County Black HistAsn, 1982-; pres, secy & founding mem, Long Island Minority Coalition,1982-; orgn mem, Womens Equal Oppty Coun, 1980-, Womens Equal Rights Cong,1980-82; pres & orgn mem, Nat Asn Advan Colored People Smithtown Br, 1966-82; secy, Suffolk County, 1991; Suffolk Coalition, 2005. **Honors/Awds:** Woman of the Year, Womens Equal Rights comn, 1984; Community Serv Award,Nat Coun Oppty Coun LI, 1983; Community Serv Award, Nat Asn Counties/LIAAO, 1983; Leadership Award, Nat Coun Christ & Jews/LI, 1982;comn, Serv Human Rights Comn, Suffolk County, 1981; candidate for presrecognisation Award, vlnt Rsm/Suffolk, 1984. **Business Addr:** Smithtown, NY 11787.

DREW, WELDON
Educator, basketball coach. **Personal:** Born Apr 22, 1935, Silsbee, TX; married Gloria Marie McIntosh. **Educ:** Fisk Univ, BS, 1957; Tex So Univ, MS, 1973. **Career:** Houston Independant Sch Dist, teacher & coach, 1957-75; NMex St Univ, head basketball coach, 1975-85. **Orgs:** Sponsor, KAY; Nat Advan Asn Colored People; Nat Asn BasketBall, 1975-80. **Honors/Awds:** Coach of the Year, Texas High School, 1974-75; Coach of the Yr, Houston High School, 1974-75; National Achievement Award, Nat Asn Basketball, 1974-75; Coca-Cola Award, Houston, 1974-75.

DREW-PEEPLES, BRENDA
Lawyer. **Personal:** Born Feb 28, 1947, Fresno, CA; daughter of Gladys Drew and Jesse Drew; married Horace Peeples, May 20, 1989; children: Cranford Thomas, Vanessa Leigh. **Educ:** Des Moines Area Community Col, AA, 1973; Drake Univ, BS, bus admin, 1975; Univ Iowa Col Law, JD, 1978. **Career:** Iowa City Atty's Office, legal intern, 1978; Aetna Life & Casualty Ins Des Moines, claim rep, 1979; Legal Serv Corp, Iowa, atty, 1979-81; Polk Co Atty Off, asst co atty, 1981-83; Davenport Civil Rights Comn, dir & atty, coun & exec dir; Pvt Pract, currently. **Orgs:** Iowa State Bar Asn, 1980-; moderator Davenport Comm Forum, 1985; Quad Cities Vision for the Future; League United Latin Am Citizens CLub; Nat Asn Advan Colored People; St Louis County Libr; Poor People's Campaign Steering Comt; East Side Adv Bd; Nat Youth Sports Adv Bd; Quad Cities Merit Employ Coun; Women's Encouragement Bd; Davenport Civil Serv Comn; Iowa Asn Human Rights Agencies; Int Asn Official Human Rights Agencies; Nat Asn Human Rights Workers; Greater Quad Cities Telecomm Corp Bd; Maternal Health Ctr Bd; Scott County Bar Asn. **Business Addr:** Lawyer, Private Practice, 125 Kirkwood Blvd, Davenport, IA 52803, **Business Phone:** (563)344-9765.*

DREWRY, CECELIA HODGES
Educator, actor. **Personal:** Born in New York, NY; married Henry N. **Educ:** Hunter Col, AB, 1945; Columbia Univ, AM, 1948; Shakespeare Univ, Birmingham, Eng, Cert, 1949; Northwestern Univ, PhD, 1967; Univ Ghana, Cert, 1969. **Career:** Educator(retired); Talladega Col, instr, 1945-47; Pent house Dance & Drama Theatre, NY, dir speech, 1948-52; High Sch Performing Arts, NY, teacher, 1952-59; Princeton High Sch, teacher, 1959-61; Rutgers Univ, assoc prof, 1962-70; Teachers Col Columbia Univ, vis instr, 1968; African & Afro-Am Studies Prog, chair person, 1969-70; Princeton Univ, asst dean, asst prof; Haverford Col, vis prof eng; various theatre appearances, 1977-89. **Orgs:** AAVP; Am Asn Univ Women; MLA; SCA; trustee, Cedar Crest Col, PA; Carnegie Found Advan Teaching; Nat Asn Advan Colored People; Nat Coun Negro Women;Princeton Asn Human Rights; life mem, NACCP. **Honors/Awds:** Award for excellence in oral interpretation of

literature, N western Univ Sch of Speech; Alpha Psi Omega Hon Soc; Danforth Assn; Honoree, Phi Delta Kappa; Distinguished Women Award, Delaware-Raritan Girl Scouts. *

DREWRY, HENRY NATHANIEL
Educator. **Personal:** Born Feb 8, 1924, Topeka, KS; son of Leonard E and Bessie Boyd; married Cecelia Hodges (divorced). **Educ:** Talladega Col, AB, 1948; Teachers Col, Columbia Univ, MA, 1949. **Career:** Educator (retired); A&T Col, Greensboro, NC, inst, 1949-51; Social Security Admin, claims asst, 1952-54; Princeton NJ High Sch teacher, 1954-60; Princeton High Sch, History Dept Chmn, 1960-68; Princeton Univ, dir Teacher Prep & Placement, lecturer, prof, 1968-89; Andrew Mellon Found, prog assoc & sr adv, 1988-2001, sr adv, currently. **Orgs:** NJ Historical Comn, 1977-96; mem, bd trustees Talladega Col, 1965-85, Groton Sch, 1977-91, Manhattan Country Sch, 1994-96; mem, NY Historical Soc, 1986-89; Coun Basic Educ, 1975-85. **Honors/Awds:** Fel, John Hays Fellos Prof, 1964; Distinguished Secondary School Teacher Award, Harvard Univ, 1964; Outstanding alumnus UNCF, NJ State Org, 1978; Honorary Doctorate, Talladega Col, 1995, Taugaloo Col, 1997. **Special Achievements:** Author : Stand and Prosper: Private Black Colleges and Their Students. **Military Serv:** USAF, 1943-46. **Home Addr:** 2 Bellaire Dr, Princeton, NJ 08540, **Home Phone:** (609)936-8486.

DREXLER, CLYDE
Basketball player, basketball coach, broadcaster. **Personal:** Born Jun 22, 1962, New Orleans, LA; son of James Drexler Sr and Eunice Prevost; married Gaynell Floyd, Dec 30, 1988; children: Clyde Austin, Kathryn Elise & Adam Eugene; children: Erica. **Educ:** Univ Houston, attended 1983. **Career:** Basketball player (retired), basketball coach, broadcaster; Portland Trail Blazers, forward, 1983-95; Houston Rockets, forward, 1995-98, color commentator, currently; Univ Houston, head coach, 1998-2000; Drexler Holdings LLC, mgr. **Orgs:** Chmn, Blazer, Avia Reading Prog, 1988-; hon chmn, UNCF, Portland Region, 1988-91; Houston's Phi Slama Jama Dunking Fraternity. **Honors/Awds:** Newcomer of the Year, Southwest Conf, 1981; Houstons Most Valuable Player; Southwest Conference Player of the Year; Gold Medal, Olympics, 1992; NBA Championship, 1995; Oregon Sports Hall of Fame, 2001; Naismith Memorial Basketball Hall of Fame, 2004. **Special Achievements:** Selected as one of the 50 Greatest Players in NBA History, 1996; co-authored his biography, Clyde the Glide.

DREYFUSS, JOEL P
Writer, editor. **Personal:** Born Sep 17, 1945, Port-au-Prince, Haiti; son of Roger and Anne-Marie; married Veronica Pollard, Oct 4, 1980; children: Justin. **Educ:** City Univ NY, BS; Univ Chicago, urban jour fel. **Career:** NY Post, reporter, 1969-73; Associated Press, reporter, 1969-71; Wash Post, reporter 1971-76; AP, reporter, 1973-76; Black Enterprise, exec editor, 1980-83; Emerge, contributing ed; Fortune, assoc ed, 1983-90; Tokyo bur chief, 1986-88; Bus Tokyo, New York, NY, managing ed, 1990-91; PC Mag, New York, ed, 1991-94; Info Week, ed-in-chief, 1993-96; Our World News, ed-in-chief, 1996-97; CMP Publ Inc, ed-in-chief; Red Herrings Inc, ed-in-chief, currently. **Orgs:** Coun Foreign Rels, 1986-; Japan Soc, 1988-; founding mem, Nat Asn Black Journalists, 1975-. **Honors/Awds:** Urban journalism fel, Univ Chicago, 1973; coauthor (with Charles Lawrence III), The Bakke Case: The Politics of Inequality; founder, Nat Asn Black Journalists; Coun Foreign Rel. **Business Addr:** Editor-in-chief, Red Herring Inc, 19 Davis Dr, Belmont, CA 94002, **Business Phone:** (650)428-2900.

DRIESSEN, DANIEL
Baseball player. **Personal:** Born Jul 29, 1951, Hilton Head Island, SC; married Bonnie; children: Dominique & Devon. **Career:** Baseball player (retired); Cincinnati Reds, infielder, 1973-84; Montreal Expos, infielder, 1984-85; San Francisco Giants, infielder, 1985-86; Houston Astros, infielder, 1986; St Louis Cardinals, infielder, 1987. **Honors/Awds:** Nat League Rookie of the Yr balloting. **Special Achievements:** National League's first ever designated hitter in the World Series, 1976. *

DRIESSEN, HENRY, JR.
Government official. **Personal:** Born Sep 28, 1927, Hilton Head Island, SC; married Phoebe; children: Leon, Ann J, Bernard. **Educ:** Savannah State Col, BA, 1957. **Career:** Government official (retired); Driessen Groc & Serv Stat & Bottle Shop, merchant, 1958; Town of Hilton Head, councilman. **Orgs:** Teacher Screven County High Sch, 1957-58; area dir, Bank Beaufort; dir, Palmetto Electric Coop Inc; past vpres, Hilton Head Island med Clin; past master, Happy Home Lodge No 125; past pres, Hilton Head Elem Sch PTA; past pres, McCracken High Sch; past dir, Hilton Head Island Chamber Com. **Honors/Awds:** Islander of the Month, Hilton Head Island Chamber Com; Business Community Service Award, Island Bus & Community Affairs Asn, 2005. **Military Serv:** AUS, corpl, 2 yrs. **Home Addr:** Hwy 278, Hilton Head Island, SC 29926. *

DRIGGRISS, DAPHNE BERNICE SUTHERLAND
School administrator. **Personal:** Born in New York, NY; married Harvey Driggriss Sr (deceased); children: Harvey William Jr. **Educ:** NY Univ, attended 1944; Queens Col-19 City Univ NY, 1950; Adel phi Col univ, BS, 1963; Adel phi Univ, MA, 1971; Pace Univ, cert & MS, 1973. **Career:** Pub Sch 136 Queens, NY, asst prin, 1970; Pub Sch 116 Queens, NY, asst prin, 1974-78; Pub Sch 35 Queens, NY, asst prin, 1976-77; Pub Sch 132 Queens, NY, prin, 1978-. **Orgs:** NAACP-JAMAICA, NY, 1950; Beta Omicron Chap Nat Sor Phi Delta Kappa Inc,1966-; basileus Nat Sor Phi Delta Kappa Inc Beta Omicron Chap, 1975-77; Dist 29 treas Coun Spvrs & Adminrs, 1976-; NY City Elem Sch Prins Asn, 1979-; exec advisr, 1977-79; nat coordr int proj Nat Sor Phi DK Inc, 1981-; constitution chairperson Eastern Reg, 1984-. **Honors/Awds:** Asst Prin Achievement Award, PTA PS #116 Queens, NY, 1977. **Business Addr:** Principal, Public School 132 Queens, 132 15 218 St, Springfield Gardens, NY 11413.*

DRINKARD HOUSTON, EMILY CISSY. See HOUSTON, CISSY.

DRISKELL, CLAUDE EVANS
Dentist. **Personal:** Born Jan 13, 1926, Chicago, IL; son of James Ernest Sr and Helen Elizabeth Perry; married Naomi Roberts Driskell, Sep 28, 1953; children: Yvette Michele, Isaiah, Ruth, Reginald, Elaine. **Educ:** Roosevelt Univ, BS, 1950; Univ Ill Col Dent, BS, 1952, DDS, 1954. **Career:** Lincoln Dental Soc, ed, 1966-; Nat Dental Asn, dir publicity, 1968-76, asst ed; Chicago State Univ, adj prof; Ill Inst Technol, adj prof, 1970-79; Chicago Bd Educ, dent consult, 1972-76; Pvt Pract, dentist. **Orgs:** Omega Psi Phi Fraternity, 1948-77; fel Acad Gen Dent, 1973; Am Dental Asn; Chicago Dent Soc; vpres, Jackson Park Asn; Dean's Com Black Students Univ Ill, Col Dent; life mem, Chicago Inst Art; Am Sch Health Asn; Intercontinental Bio Asn; adj off-campus prof, pre-dental students, Chicago State Univ; Ill Inst Technol, 1986-87; Int Asn Anesthesiologists, 1952-91; Ill State Dent Soc, 1954-; Am Dent Asn; Chicago Dent Soc. **Honors/Awds:** Editorial Award, Nat Dent Asn, 1968-72. **Special Achievements:** Publications: "The Seventy-Fifth Anniversary of the Incorporation of the Original Forty Club of Chicago, 1920-1995;" "The History of the Negro in Dentistry," 1968; "The Influence of the Halogen Elements Upon the Hydrocarbon & Their Effect on General Anesthesia," 1970; "The Chicago Black Dental Profs 1850-1983;" Lincoln Dental Soc, 1967-75; Fellowship Acad General Dentistry, 1973; editor/author, The 75th Anniversary Edition of Incorporation of the Original Forty Club of Chicago, 1920-96. **Military Serv:** AUS, company clerk, 1944-46; European-African-Middle E Campaign Medal; Asiatic-Pacific Campaign Medal; 4 Battle Stars. **Business Addr:** Dentist, 11139 S Halsted St, Chicago, IL 60628.*

DRISKELL, DAVID C.
Artist, educator. **Personal:** Born Jun 7, 1931, Eatonton, GA; son of George W and Mary L Cloud; married Thelma G Deloatch Driskell, Jan 9, 1952. **Educ:** Skowhegan Sch Painting & Sculpture, Maine, cert, 1953; Howard Univ, AB, 1955; Cath Univ, MFA, 1962; Ricksbureau unsthistoriches Den Haag, Holland, 1964. **Career:** Talladega Col, assoc prof, 1955-62; Howard Univ, assoc prof, 1962-66; Fisk Univ, prof & chmn dept art, 1966-76; Univ Ife, Nigeria, vis prof, 1970; Univ Md, chmn dept art, 1978-83; Amistad Res Ctr, curator Aaron Douglas collection, 1977-; Univ Md, prof art, 1977-98, prof emer, currently. **Orgs:** Coll Art Asn Am; SE Mus Conf; Am Asn Mus; Am Fedn Arts; bd dirs, Nat Mus African Art; bd dirs, Am Fedn Arts. **Honors/Awds:** Purchase Awards, Birmingham Mus Art, 1972; Tougaloo Col Gallery, 1973; Honorary Doctor of Humane Letters, Daniel Payne Col, 1977, Rust Col, 1991; Honorary Doctor of Fine Arts, Tougaloo Col, 1977, Bowdoin Col, 1989, State Univ NY, Old Westburg, 1989; Distinguished University Professor, Univ Md, College Park; Distinguished Alumni Awards in Art, Howard Univ, 198; National Humanities Medal, 2000; Rockefeller Foundation Fellowships; Danforth Foundation Fellowship; Harmon Foundation Fellowship. **Military Serv:** AUS, 1st lt, 1957-65. **Business Addr:** Professor Emeritus of Art, University of Maryland, 1202 Art Sociol Bldg, College Park, MD 20742.*

DRIVER, DAVID E
Publishing executive. **Personal:** Born Oct 17, 1955, Chicago, IL; son of Edward and Esther. **Educ:** Bradley Univ, BA, 1976; Univ Chicago, MBA, 1986. **Career:** Arthur Young, mgr, 1977-79; Merrill Lynch, vpres, 1979-88; Noble Press, pres & publ, 1988-. **Orgs:** Bd mem, Better Boys Found, 1987-89; Points Light Found, adv coun, 1989-91; recruitment chmn, United Way Volunteer Ctr, 1990-92; bd mem, Breakaway, 1991-92; Black Literary Soc; Nat Asn Black Book Publ. **Special Achievements:** The Good Heart Book: A Guide to Volunteering, Noble Press, 1989; Defending the Left, nonfiction book, Noble Press, 1991. **Business Addr:** President, Publisher, Noble Press Inc, 880 N Lima Rd, Kendallville, IN 46755, **Business Phone:** (260)347-0407.

DRIVER, DONALD JEROME
Football player. **Personal:** Born Feb 2, 1975, Houston, TX; son of Marvin Driver and Faye Gray. **Educ:** Alcorn State Univ, BS, acct, MCS. **Career:** Green Bay Packers, wide receiver & defensive back, 1999-; Marco Rivera,instr, 2002. **Orgs:** Founder, Donald Driver Found, 2001. **Honors/Awds:** Conf Athlete of the Yr Award; Nice Guy Award, 2000; Community Serv Award,Green Bay Chamber Com, 2001; Most Valuable Player, Green Bay Packers,2002; Walter Payton Man of the Yr, NFL, 2002; Professional Achievement Award, the sixth annual Lee Remmel Sports Awards, 2003; Ed Block Courage Award, 2005. **Special Achievements:** TV show: Host, "Inside the Huddle with Donald Driver"; host, annual Offense vs. Defense softball game. **Business Addr:** Professional Football Player, Green Bay Packers, 1265 Lombardi Ave, PO Box 10628, Green Bay, WI 54307-0628, **Business Phone:** (920)569-7500.*

DRIVER, JOHNIE M
Engineer. **Personal:** Born May 8, 1933, Centerville, AL; son of McKelway and Daisy B Richard; married Odessa Wright, Apr 12, 1952; children: Dwaine Stuart & Courtney LaShay. **Educ:** Univ IL, BS, elec eng, 1961, MS, elec eng, 1963. **Career:** Sperry UT Co, Salt Lake City, UT, proj engr, 1963-66; Jet Propulsion Lab Systs Div, mem, tech staff, 1966-99; self-employed, Software Oper Engr, currently. **Orgs:** Pres, Salt Lake City Nat Advan Asn Colored People, 1965-66; UT State Civil Rights Comn, 1965; Pasadena, CA Nat Advan Asn Colored People; deacon, chmn, teacher Bible, SS Admin, leadership, Metrop Baptist Ch. **Special Achievements:** First Black to address Joint Session UT State Legislature, 1965. **Military Serv:** USAF, s/sgt, 1950-58. **Business Addr:** Software Operations Engineer, 3002 Grandeur Ave, Altadena, CA 91001, **Business Phone:** (626)797-6393.*

DRIVER, PAT. See CHATMAN-DRIVER, PATRICIA ANN.

DRIVER, RICHARD SONNY, JR.
Editor, publisher. **Personal:** Born Aug 16, 1926, Philadelphia, PA; son of Richard E Sr and Helen Birchett. **Career:** Free-lance advert & pub rels; Scoop USA, Newspaper ed, publ & owner. **Orgs:** Nat Asn Advan Colored People; consult, United Black Bus Asn; bd mem, Black United Fund. **Honors/Awds:** Distinguished Award, Nat Asn Advan Colored People, 1962; Citation Jazz, Home Club Am, 1971; Advertising Award, Lancaster Ave Bus Asn, 1973; City of Philadelphia Citation, City Philadelphia, 1995; Four Chaplains Legion of Honor Award, Chapel Four Chaplains, 1989; Service Award, Senator Pa, Pa legis Black Caucus, 1992; Service Award, Philadelphia City Coun, Mayor Philadelphia, 1995; US House of Representatives Citation, 1995; Pa State House of Representation Citation, 1995. **Military Serv:** USY, 1944-46. **Home Addr:** 1220 N Broad St, Philadelphia, PA 19121. **Business Addr:** Publisher, Scoop USA, 942 N Watts St, Philadelphia, PA 19122, **Business Phone:** (215)232-5974.

DRIVER, ROGERS W.
Clergy, executive. **Personal:** Born Jun 14, 1921, Elkton, TN; son of Rogers W Sr and Louetta; married Mackie L Baker; children: John R & William B. **Educ:** Univ Hawaii, attended 1944; Tenn State Univ, BS, 1948; TN Univ, attended 1969; Am Baptist Theol Sem, BTH, 1987. **Career:** Executive (retired), Clergy: Triangle Chem Co, sales rep, 1948-66; Pearl Voc Sch, instr, 1951-52; Gen Spec Co, owner mgr, 1952-66; Triangle Chem Co, spec sales consult, 1966-74, sales mgr, 1974, buyer HBA, 1978, 1989; Gladeville Circuit Churches, North Nashville AME, pastor; Lee Chapel AME, minister, 1986; AME Church, ordained elder, 1989. **Orgs:** Vpres, Nashville Asn Black Salesmen, 1971; Nat Asn Mkt Develop, 1972-; Nat Bus League; Mid Tenn Bus Asn; Nat Asn Advan Colored People, Nashville Model Cities Cit Coord Comt; Econ Develop Comt; Tenn State Univ Alumni Asn; Urban League; Chamber Com; Am Voc Asn; Nat Asn Advan Black Am Voc Educ; Nashville Job Serv Employer Comm State Tenn; Inter-Faith Asn; exec comt, Nashville Area Rep Lee Chapel AME 1984. **Honors/Awds:** Minority Bus Serv Award, Frito-Lay Inc, 1966; Spec Award, Bus Tenn State Univ, 1968; Outstanding Citation Award, WVOL Radio, 1953; Cit Month Award, Emmas Florist, 1962; JC Napier Award, Mid Tenn Bus Asn, 1974; Fisk Univ Award, 100% Right Comn, 1974; apt Hon Sgt-at-Arms, Tenn House Rep, 1974; Comn Hon Dep Sheriff Davidson Co Tenn, 1975; comn serv mem, Tenn Adv Coun Voc Educ; Sales Training Course Best Pitch book Award, 1979; inducted in Vintagers Club, TSU, 1988. **Home Addr:** 3501 Geneva Cir, Nashville, TN 37209-2524. *

DRUITT, ATTY. BEVERLY F
Lawyer. **Personal:** Born Jun 5, 1947, Buffalo, NY; daughter of James and Florence; divorced. **Educ:** Edna G Dyett Sch Practical Nursing, Millard Fillmore Hosp, Buffalo New York, LPN, 1966; State Univ NY, Buffalo, BA, 1971; Rutgers Univ Sch Law, Newark, NJ, JD, 1974. **Career:** N Miss Rural Legal Servs, Oxford, Miss, managing atty, 1975-77; NLRB, field atty, 1977-80, sr atty, 1980-. **Orgs:** Pres, Nat Labor Relations Bd Profs Asn, 1990-97; Nat chairperson, Bar Asn, govt lawyers div, chair 2004-06; 1997-2001; Vice-chair 2006-08; 1993-97; treas, Nat Bar Asn, labor law sect, 1988-97; Nat Bar Asn, treas, arbitration section, 2002-04. **Honors/Awds:** Special Act Award, NLRB, 1996, 2000, 2005, 2006, 2007. **Business Addr:** Senior Attorney (Labor), National Labor Relations Board, Division of Enforcement Litigation Office of Appeals, 1099 14th St NW Suite 8710, Washington, DC 20005, **Business Phone:** (202)273-3758.

DRUMMING, SAUNDRA T
Educator. **Educ:** Fla A&M Univ, BS; Univ Ill, MAS; Univ Wis, PhD, 1983. **Career:** Fla A&M Univ, assoc prof acct, prof, currently. **Honors/Awds:** Employee of the Year, Fla A&M Univ. **Business Addr:** Professor, Florida A&M University, 682 Gamble St, Tallahassee, FL 32307, **Business Phone:** (850)599-3000.

DRUMMOND, DAVID C.
Executive. **Educ:** Santa Clara Univ, BA, hist; Stanford Law Sch, JD. **Career:** SmartForce, exec vpres finance & chief financial of-

ficer; Google Inc, partner, Corp Coun Off, sr vpres, 2002-. **Business Addr:** Senior Vice President of Corporate Development, Google Inc, Corporate Counsel Office, 1600 Amphitheatre Pkwy, Mountain View, CA 94043, **Business Phone:** (650)623-4000.*

DRUMMOND, WILLIAM JOE
Educator, journalist. **Personal:** Born Sep 29, 1944, Oakland, CA; son of Jack Martin Drummond Sr and Mary Louise Tompkins; married Faith Boykin, Jun 22, 1962; children: Tammerlin & Sean. **Educ:** Univ Calif, BA 1965; Columbia Univ, Grad Sch Jour, MS 1966; Univ Calif, LA, attended 1971. **Career:** Courier-Jour, Louisville, KY, staff writer 1966-67; Los Angeles Times, staff writer 1967-70, asst metropolitan ed, 1970-71, bur chief New Delhi, India, 1971-74, bur chief Jerusalem, Israel, 1974-76, Wash Bur, staff writer, 1977-79, reporter; Nat Pub Radio, corresp, 1979-83; Univ Calif, Berkeley, jour prof 1983-; Christian Sci Monitor, special corresp, 1992-97. **Orgs:** Nat Asn Black Journalists; Soc Prof Journalists. **Honors/Awds:** Journalism Award, Vision Mag, 1966; Edward M Hood Award, Nat Press Club, Wash, DC, 1982; Chancellor's Dist Lectr, Univ Calif, Berkeley, 1983; Sidney Hillman Foundation Award for Journalism Excellence, 1986; Award for Outstanding Coverage of the Black Condition, Nat Asn Black Journalists, 1989; Roy W Howard Award, Scripps Howard Found, 1991; Jack R Howard Award for Broadcasting Excellence, Scripps Howard Found, 1992; Excellence in Journalism Award, Soc Prof Journalists Northern Calif Chap, 1994. **Business Addr:** Professor of Journalism, University of California, Berkely Graduate School of Journalism, 121 N Gate Hall Suite 5860, Berkeley, CA 94720-5860, **Business Phone:** (510)642-5710.

DUAL, J. FRED, JR.
Executive, entrepreneur, president (organization). **Personal:** Born Apr 10, 1942, Chicago, IL; son of Joseph Frederick and Dorothy Marie Bowie; married Joyce Faye Metoyer, 1962 (divorced 1978); children: Leah, Joseph F III, Karen; married Mindy Lou Good, Sep 9, 1990. **Educ:** Northern Va Community Col, Annandale, VA, AA, 1974; Am Univ, Wash, DC, BA & BS, 1981; George Wash Univ, Wash, DC, 1982; Owner Pres Mgt Prog, Harvard, Cambridge, MA, 1991. **Career:** Booz Allen & Hamilton, Arlington, VA, assoc, 1981-85; Dual Inc, Arlington, Va, founder, pres & chief exec officer, 1983-. **Orgs:** Prof Servs Coun, 1990-91; Navy League US, 1988-95; Nat Training Systs Asn, 1993-; Nat Space Club, 1994-; Am Defense Preparedness Asn, 1995-. **Honors/Awds:** Entrepreneur of Year Finalist, KPMG Peat Marwick, 1990; EEO Person of Year, Naval Aviation Engg Servs Unit, Philadelphia, 1979; NASA Minority Contractor of the Yr, 1989; Black Enterprise, Listed as no 75 of Top 100 Black Bus, 1994. **Military Serv:** US Navy, C Warrant Officer, 1960-79; Navy Commend, 1978; Navy Achievement Medal, 1977; Nat Serv Medal, 1965. **Business Phone:** (240)462-0225.*

DUAL, PETER A.
Educator. **Educ:** Lake Michigan Col, AA, 1966; Western MI Univ, BS, 1969, MA, 1971; MI State Univ, PhD, 1973; Univ TX, MPH, 1975. **Career:** Univ TX, asst prof, 1973-75; assoc dir African-American Studies, 1973-75, Nat Pub Haelth fel, 1974-75; Univ MI, Grad Sch Pub Health, asst prof health behavior, dir, Ctr Prof Ed Pub Health Professionals, asst prof health behavior 1975-80, Martin Luther King & Rosa Parks distinguished vis prof, 1987-88; Eastern MI Univ, Col health human serv, dean, prof health admin & pub health, 1980-82; San Diego State Univ, dean Col HTH, prof health serv, 1982-93; Panama Proj Hope, sr consult, 1985; Chinese Med Asn ROC, distinguished guest lectr, 1986; CAP Hahnnemahn Med Ctr, Philadelphia, provost, 1993-95; San Diego State Univ, teacher intl health, 1995-96, Sch Pub Health, grad prof pub health; CA State Polytech Univ, Sch Educ & Intergrative Studies, prof, Col Lett Arts & Social Sci, prof kinesiology, vpres acad affairs, Pomona, CA, 1996-00; E Washington Univ, provost & vpres acad affairs, 2000-02; Bethel AME Church Emmanuel Ctr, sr res scholar, 2002-, ceo & sr res scholar, currently; chmn bd dir, Richard Allen Enterprises. **Orgs:** Am Asn Higher Educ; Am Pub Health Asn, 1971-; USAID; Alpha Pi Boule Chap; Sigma Pi Phi Frat; Phi Beta Delta Honor Soc Intl Scholars; bd dir, Joint-Health Policy, Scripps Res Found Inst, SDSU, 1988-93; Nat Coun Community & Edu Partnership. **Honors/Awds:** Confucius Award, Ministry Educ, Repub China; Charles Beckwith Distinguished Alumnus Award, Lake MI Col, 1986; Distinguished Alumnus Award, Col Educ, MI State Univ, 1988; Nat Millenium Leadership Fel, Am Asn State Cols & Univ, 2001. **Special Achievements:** Published "The Case for a COT Based School of Public Health," for Sun Valley National Health Policy Forum, Univ of WA, Asn for Academic Health Ctrs, 1995; First Bi-National Conf for Environmental Protection, China, Taiwan, co-host, 1989; First black academic dean in history of Eastern MI Univ 1980; First black academic dean in history of San Diego State Univ 1983; First Intl Conf on Aging, United Nations, State Univ, San Diego, CA, co-host, 1992; Lecturer Citation Beijing & Health Bureau; Citation Chinese Medical Asn Republic of China 1986; first black and non MD to deliver keynote address at Chinese Medical Asn in 1987; travelled and worked abroad: Zimbabwe, Tanzania, Kenya, Japan, Thailand. *

DUBE, THOMAS M T
Educator. **Personal:** Born Dec 25, 1938, Essexvale, Zimbabwe; married Ruth; children: Cengubuqotho & Thina. **Educ:** Univ Lesotho, BA, 1958; Univ S Africa, UED, 1960; CW Post Col Long Island Univ, MS, 1963; Univ Chicago, MA, 1972; Mich State Univ, MA, 1974; Univ Rochester, EdD, 1969; Cooley Law Sch, JD. **Career:** Western Mich Univ, asst prof social sci; Geneva Col Pa, asst prof; Rochester, NY, pre-sch teacher; Ministry African Educ, Rhodesia Africa, high sch teacher & elem sch teacher. **Orgs:** Rhodesian African Teachers Asn; Asn African Studies Am; founder mem, JairosJiri Inst Physically-Handicapped; founder, asst prin Mpopoma African Community High Sch.

DUBENION, ELBERT
Scout, football player. **Personal:** Born Feb 16, 1933, Griffin, GA; married Marilyn Earl; children: Debra Lynn, Carolyn Ann, Susan Marie & Lisa Renee. **Educ:** Bluffton Col, BS, 1959. **Career:** Football player (retired), Scout; Columbus Recreation Dept, 1960-67; Ohio Malleable Co Columbus, attendance dir, 1963-64; Buffalo Bills, prof player& guard, 1960-68; Atlanta Falcons, col scout, currently. **Orgs:** Charter mem, Am Football League Hall Fame; Bills Silver Anniversary All-Time team. **Honors/Awds:** Most Popular Man May Day, 1959; Voted MVP three times Buffalo; All-AFL; AFL All-Star Game, 1964 & 1965; Bill's most-valuable-Player Rookie, 1960; Greater Buffalo Hall of Fame, 1993. **Special Achievements:** The first player franchise hist to gain 1,000 receiving yards in a season; The eighth person selected for the Bill's Wall of Fame, 1993. **Military Serv:** AUS, spec serv pfc, 1953-55.

DUBOIS, JOSHUA
Government Official, Minister, Religious Leader. **Personal:** Born in Bar Harbor, ME. **Educ:** Boston Univ, BA, cum laude, 2003; Master's degree in Public Affairs from Princeton Univ. **Career:** Aide to US Rep Rush Holt and served as a fellow in the office of US Rep Charles Rangel; Associate Pastor at Calvary Praise and Worship Center in Cambridge, MA; Head of the Office of Faith Based and Neighborhood Partnerships, 2009-. **Orgs:** Big Brother mentor;. **Special Achievements:** Helped engineer Obama's participation in Rick Warren's Presidential Forum during the campaign, decision to use Saddleback church pastor for Obama's Inaugural invocation. **Business Addr:** The White House, Office of Faith Based and Neighborhood Partnerships, 1600 Pennsylvania Ave, NW, Washington, DC 20500, **Business Phone:** (202)456-1414.*

DUBOSE, CULLEN LANIER
Administrator. **Personal:** Born Jul 5, 1935, Moss Point, MS; married Helena Joyce; children: Cheri, Cullen, Freddie. **Educ:** Tougaloo Col, 1956; Tri State Col, BS, 1958. **Career:** State MI, bridge design engr, 1958-70; State MI Housing Develop Authority, civil Engr, 1970; dir rehab, 1971-72; dir constr, 1972- 73; dir mgt & mkt, 1974. **Orgs:** Tri State Col Alumni Club; West Side Action Ctr; Lansing Civic Ctr Bd; Omega Psi Phi Frat Inc; NAACP; dir housing comt; Big Bro Lansing; Model Cities Policy Bd; past pres, Gov Milliken's Task Force Oper Break Through, 1970-71. **Honors/Awds:** Omega Psi Phi Citizens Award, 1966; NAACP Citizen Award, 1967. **Military Serv:** Mil serv, 1957-58.

DU BOSE, ROBERT EARL, JR.
Clergy. **Personal:** Born Oct 9, 1927, Birmingham, AL; married Angela Grace Edwards; children: Robert III, Audrice, Gerald, Lucy, Angela. **Educ:** St Augustine's Col Raleigh, NC, BA/BS, 1950; Seabury-Western Theol Sem Evanston, IL, LTh, 1953; St Augustine's Col, Hon DCL, 1979. **Career:** St Andrew's Tuskegee, AL, vicar, 1953-56; Church of the Good Shepherd Montgomery, AL, vicar, 1956-61; Historic St Thomas' Epis Ch Phila, PA, curate, 1961-62; St Cyprian's Epis Ch Phila, PA, vicar, 1962-64; St Barnabas Epis Ch Phila, PA, assoc rector, 1964-66; House of Prayer Epis Church Phila, PA, rector, 1966-76; Gen Conv of the Epis Ch, spl rep, 1970; Historic St Thomas' Episcopal & Ch, rector, 1977-. **Orgs:** Active Qparticipant Bus Protest & Sit Ins With Dr M L King Montgomery AL, 1956-61; active participant, Selective Patronage Prog with Dr Leon Sullivan, 1961-64; one of the founders Opport Indsl & Ctrs of Am & Int 1964 & 67; Comn Finance of Property Epis Diocese of PA, 1974-; Bishop's Task Force on Housing Epis Diocese of PA, 1979-. **Honors/Awds:** Key Award Opport Indsl Ctr Phila, PA, 1969; Nat Distinguished Service Award, Alpha Phi Alpha Frat, 1970; Outstanding Service Award, Greater W Oak Ln Coord Coun, 1970-71; Service Award, The Sch Dist of Philadelphia Wagner Hr High Sch, 1974. **Business Addr:** Historic Saint Thomas' Episcap, 52nd Parrish St, Philadelphia, PA 19139.*

DUBRIEL, LISA M.
Executive. **Career:** Antioch Ford Auto Ctr, pres & owner, currently. **Honors/Awds:** Ford's Blue Oval Certification. **Business Addr:** President, Owner, Antioch Ford Auto Center, 1400 W 10th St, Antioch, CA 94509-1438, **Business Phone:** (925)757-1771.*

DUCKETT, ESQ. GREGORY MORRIS
Executive. **Personal:** Born Jan 26, 1960, Memphis, TN; son of Lavance Harris and Ocie; married Brenda Parker, Oct 11, 1986; children: Stephen Gregory & Kelsey Breanna. **Educ:** Carnegie-Mellon Univ, Pittsburgh, attended 1981; Oberlin Col, Oberlin, BA, 1982; Memphis State Univ, Memphis, TN, JD, 1985. **Career:** US Congressman Harold Ford, Memphis, TN, staff asst, 1983-84; Shelby County Criminal Ct, Memphis, TN, judicial law clerk, 1984-85; US Senator Albert Gore Jr, Memphis, TN, staff asst, 1985, staff atty, 1985-86, state coun, 1986-87; City Memphis, Memphis, TN, dir, div pub serv, 1988, dir, Div Housing & Community Develop, 1988-; City Memphis, chief ade officer, 1991; Baptist Mem Health Care, sr vpres & corp coun, 1992-; Clinton/Gore Transition Team, appointee, 1992. **Orgs:** Pres, Memphis State Univ Sch Law Student Bar Asn, 1985; bd mem, Youth Villages, 1988-; bd mem, Leadership Memphis, 1989-; Tenn Adv Comt Lower Miss Delta Develop Comn, 1989; bd mem, Memphis Col Art, 1990-; bd dirs, WONDERS; St Jude Liberty Bowl; bd mem, Fed Res Bank St Louis, Memphis Br; Memphis Col Art; Nat Civil Rights Mus & Liberty Bowl Festival Asn; bd mem, Am Health Lawyers Asn & Health Servs Develop Agency; bd mem, Memphis Zool Soc. **Honors/Awds:** First Place, Champion Coun, Memphis State Univ, Advan Appellate Moot Ct Competition, 1983; Outstanding Young Men of America, US Jaycees, 1984, 1985. **Home Addr:** 9435 Forest Wind Cove, Collierville, TN 38017. **Business Addr:** Senior Vice President, Corporate Counsel, Baptist Memorial Health Care, 350 N Humphreys Blvd EAGLB2 5th Fl, Memphis, TN 38120-2177, **Business Phone:** (901)227-5233.

DUCKETT, KAREN IRENE
Executive, president (organization), chief executive officer. **Personal:** Born Jun 12, 1947, Rochester, NY; daughter of Albert and Ann Maass; married Wardell Duckett, Dec 28, 1973; children: Chioke, Shani, Makiri. **Educ:** Ohio Univ, BFA, 1969; Yale Univ, Occidental Col, MA, 1974; Woodrow Wilson Col Law, JD, 1981. **Career:** Xerox Corp, facil mgr, 1969-73; City Flint, dir planning, 1974-75; City Atlanta, phys develop adminr, 1976-78; Duckett VanDevere & Assocs Inc, pres, chief exec officer, 1985-03; Duckett Design Group, pres & chief exec officer, 2003-. **Orgs:** pres, Metro Atlanta Coalition 100 Black Women, 1987-96; Exec Comt, Leadership Atlanta, 1987-91, 1996; Nat Orgn Minority Architects, 1990-; treas, Jack & Jill Am, 1990-; bd mem, Atlanta Chamber Commerce, 1993-96; Women's Econ Develop Agency, bd mem, 1994-, chair, 1995-96; bd mem, Atlanta Bus League, 1995-98; Harvard Black Law Students Asn. **Honors/Awds:** Small Business Person of the Year, Atlanta Chamber Com, 1989; Super-Tuesday Salute-Non-Traditional Award, Atlanta Bus League, 1994; Women of Achievement, YWCA, 1996; Atlanta's Top Women of Influence, Atlanta Bus League, 1996; Blueprint for Success Award, Women Looking Ahead Mag, 1996. **Special Achievements:** First African American female to head planning department of a city over 300,000; First African American female licensed as a registered designer in state of Georgia; Presidential representative to 1996 Olympic Games. **Business Addr:** President, Chief Executive Officer, Duckett Design Group, 1632 Ware Ave, East Point, GA 30344, **Business Phone:** (404)592-4539.*

DUCKSWORTH, MARILYN JACOBY
Publishing executive. **Personal:** Born in Stamford, CT. **Educ:** Tufts Univ, BA, 1978, MA, Eng, 1979; Tufts Univ London England, 1977. **Career:** Doubleday & Co Inc, publicity asst, 1979-80, assoc publicist, 1980-82, sr publicist, 1982-83, mgr publicity, 1983-85; GP Putnam's Sons, mgr publicity, 1985, dir publicity, 1985-87; GP Putnam's Sons & The Putnam & Grosset Group, exec dir publicity, vp, assoc publ, 1987, sr vpres corp commun. **Orgs:** Col Language Asn; Pub Publicity Assoc; The Women's Media Group. **Honors/Awds:** Scholastic Achievement Award, Black Educators Stamford, 1974; Nat Honor, Soc Hon Soc Sec Sch, 1974; Dean's List Tufts Univ, 1974-78; Langston Hughes Literary Award, Tufts Univ, 1978; Black Mgr Publicity, Doubleday & Co Inc, 1983-85; Black exec dir publicity, GP Putnam's Sons. *

DUDLEY, CHARLES EDWARD
President (Organization), clergy. **Personal:** Born Feb 27, 1927, South Bend, IN; son of Joseph Sr and Julia Talley; married Etta Mae Maycock, Dec 28, 1947; children: Bonita Andrea, Charles Edward II, Albert Leroy Sr, Benson Mugemancuro, Seth Bardu. **Educ:** Emmanuel Mission Col, attended 1945; Oakwood Col, attended 1947; Baptist Theol Sem, LLD, 1969; Union Baptist Sem, LLD, 1969; London Inst Applied Res, DDiv, 1973; Andrews SDA Univ, DDiv, 1992; Oakwood Col, Huntsville, AL, BA, relig. **Career:** S Cent Conf, Seventh Day Adventists Church, pastor, 1947-54, pres, 1962-93; TN, AL, LA, TX, pastor. **Orgs:** Nat Asn Advan Colored People. **Honors/Awds:** Pi Lambda Sigma Award, 1964; Merit of Hon, OC Nat Alumni Asn, 1977; Inst Church Ministry Award, Andrews Univ, 1983; Breath of Life Award, 1984; Annual Ministers Conf Award, Int Regional Evangelis Coun, 1990; Award of Merit, Allegheny W Conf, 1993; Golden Heritage Life Membership Award, Nat Asn Advan Colored People, 1993; Award of Distinction, Lake Region Conf Seventh-day Adventists, 1993; Citation of Excellence Award, Pres George Bush; Citation of Excellence Award, Pres William Clinton; Hon Leader Award, Miss Mass Choir. **Special Achievements:** Publications: Four Volumes, "Thou Who Hath Brought Us"; author, "Growth & Development of African-Am in the Seventh-Day Advent Denom", "Geneology of Ellen G. White", "Thou Who Hath Brought Us".

Business Addr: Pastor, Seventh Day Adventists Church, 715 Youngs Lane, Nashville, TN 37207.*

DUDLEY, CRAYTON T.
Clergy. **Personal:** Born Feb 23, 1928, Atlanta, GA; married Allegra Lewis; children: Angus Clement, Karen Yvette. **Educ:** Clark Col, Atlanta, AB, 1950; Gammon Theol Sem, Atlanta, BD, 1961; MDiv, attended 1973; Univ Pitts, MLS, 1965; Atlanta Univ, Am Univ, Grad Study. **Career:** Clergy (retired); Interdenom Theol Ctr, Atlanta, asst libr, 1961-64; Rel & Phil Enoch Pratt Free Libr, Baltimore, sub specialist, 1965-68; Coppin State Col, Baltimore, asso dir libr, 1968-72; Montrose Training Sch Girls State, MD, chaplian, 1968-72; St James Episcopic Church, Baltimore, worker priest, 1968-72; asn prof philosophy, 1972-74; St James, asst priest, 1972-74; TN St Univ, collections develop librn, 1976; Holy Trinity Episcopic Church, Nashville, rector; Vicar, St Augustine, 1980-87; St Marks, rector, 1987-93. **Orgs:** Life mem, Phi Beta Sigma Frat; NAACP; Boy Scouts Am, 1972-74; coun chaplian mem, Am Libr Asn; Am Theol Libr Asn; historiographer Diocese, MD, 1972-74; bd mem, Grace Eaton Day Ctr, 1974; vice chmn, Urban Min Diocese TN, 1977. **Military Serv:** AUS, sgt, 1945-46, 1950-53, 1956-62. *

DUDLEY, EUNICE MOSLEY
Executive. **Personal:** Born in Selma, AL; daughter of Andrew M Mosley Sr and Eva O Murdoch Mosley; married Joe Louis Dudley Sr; children: Joe Jr, Ursula, Genea. **Career:** Dudley Cosmetology Univ, Kernersville, NC, dir; Dudley Prod Inc, Kernersville, NC, chief financial officer, currently. **Orgs:** Boy Scout Camp, Winston Salem; Girl Scout Camp, Keyauwee; United Negro Col Fund; Bennett Col Scholar; NC Agr & Tech Univ; E Forsyth Citizens Human Servs.; Providence Baptist Church, Greensboro, NC; comt organizing sch mgt, Africa Univ. **Honors/Awds:** The Kernersville First Citizens of The Year Award, 1993; DHL, Bennett Col; The Athena Award, Greensboro Area Chamber Com; The Crystal Award, Nat Asn Negro Bus & Prof Womens Clubs. **Business Phone:** (336)993-8800.*

DUDLEY, GODFREY D.
Lawyer, executive director. **Personal:** Born Mar 14, 1944, Newborn, AL; married. **Educ:** Tuskegee Inst, BS, 1967; Univ Mich, attended 1966; Howard Univ, JD, 1970. **Career:** Tuskegee Inst Community Educ Prog, teacher coordr, 1965; Birmingham Dist Off, equal employ officer, 1970; Labor Adv Nat Labor Rels Bd, atty, 1970-; DC Off NLRB Atlanta Regional Off, field atty, 1972; instr new attys & field examr, 1975, 1979; Nat Labor Rels Bd, dep asst gen coun, 1979-; dep asst gen coun, 1979-88; Equal Employ Opportunity Comn, Field Mgt Progs East, dir, 1988-95, dir, Field Mgt Progs, 1996-99; Housing & Urban Develop Agency, Denver. **Orgs:** DC Bar Asn; Bar Asn DC; Am Bar Asn; Nat Bar Asn; Ala Bar Asn; Phi Alpha Delta Law Fraternity; Nat Asn Advan Colored People, Urban League. **Honors/Awds:** Cert Commendations, Gen Coun NLRB, 1973-74; Qual Work Performance Award, 1973-74, 1978-79. *

DUDLEY, HERMAN T.
Government official. **Personal:** Born Apr 4, 1924, Richmond, KY; married Ruth. **Educ:** BS, 1956. **Career:** Government Official (retired); Detroit Engr Off Bur Archit, dir. **Orgs:** Regist architect, State Mich. **Military Serv:** US Marine Corps, corporal, 1943-46. Detroit Engr Off Bur.

DUDLEY, JOE LOUIS
Entrepreneur, chief executive officer, salesperson. **Personal:** Born May 9, 1937, Aurora, NC; son of Gilmer L and Clara Yeates; married Eunice Mosley; children: Joe Jr, Ursula & Genea. **Educ:** NC A&T State Univ, BS, bus admin, 1967. **Career:** Fuller Products, staff, 1962, distribr, 1967, pres, 1976-94; Dudley Prod Inc, pres & chief exec officer, 1975-; Dudley Cosmetol Univ, founder, 1989-; DCU Inn, 1990; Dudley Beauty Sch Syst, owner, currently. **Orgs:** Direct Selling Asn; Joe Dudley Fel; Dudley Ladies; ComPASS; bd dirs, Am Health & Beauty Aids Inst; bd dirs, Br Banking & Trust Financial Corp. **Honors/Awds:** Alumni Excellence Award, NC A & T Univ, 1987; Economic Development Award, Greensboro Nat Asn Advan Colored People, 1987; Vision for Tomorrow Award, Direct Selling Asn, 1991; 467th Daily Point of Light Award, Pres George Bush, 1991; Maya Angelou Tribute To Achievement Award, 1992; NC Master Entrepreneur Award, Inc Mag, 1993; Medallion Award, Nat Beta Gamma Sigma, 1993; Award For Excellence, Minorities & Women In Business Mag, 1993; J C Penney's Non-Merchandise Supplier Grand Award, 1994; Alumni Hall of Fame, Nat Black Col, 1995; hon doctorate, NC A&T Univ & Edward Waters Col. **Business Addr:** Chief Executive Officer, President, Dudley Products Inc., 1080 Old Greensboro Rd, Kernersville, NC 27284, **Business Phone:** (336)993-8800.

DUDLEY, JUANITA C.
Social worker, administrator. **Personal:** Born Apr 14, 1929, Talladega, AL; daughter of Walter Thomas Strickland and Fannie Tanner; married Calmeze Henike Dudley, Jun 30, 1964; children: Rhonda Carroll Le Grice. **Educ:** Talladega Col, AL, BA, 1950; Atlanta Univ, GA, MSW, 1954; Southwestern Univ Law Sch, Los Angeles, CA, 1967. **Career:** Dr C H Dudley, Los Angeles, CA, psychiat soc worker, 1954-; Govt VI, St Thomas, supvr pub assistance, 1957-59; Los Angeles County, adoption consult, 1963-66; Nat Urban League Inc, Los Angeles, asst regional dir, 1966-73; Los Angeles County Hosp Asn, consult, 1975-76; Los Angeles County Grand Jury, CA, 1982-83. **Orgs:** Nat vpres, The Girlfriends Inc; The Wilfandel Club Inc; The Circlelets Inc. **Honors/Awds:** Woman of Year, Auxiliary Nat Med Asn; Woman of Year, Women on Target, 1990. *

DUDLEY, RICKEY D.
Football player. **Personal:** Born Jul 15, 1972, Henderson, TX. **Educ:** Ohio State Univ. **Career:** Football player (retired); Oakland Raiders, tight end, 1996-2000; Cleveland Browns, 2001; Tampa Bay Buccaneers, 2002-04; NFL, Free Agt, currently. *

DUDLEY-WASHINGTON, LOISE
Educator. **Personal:** Born Nov 1, 1944, Ft Lauderdale, FL; daughter of Thomas and Clara Kirkland Morley; divorced; children: Keith & Renee. **Educ:** City Col NY, BS, 1978, MS, 1980, PhD, 1990-. **Career:** MLK Health Ctr, mgr, MIS analyst, 1969-89; G&S Res Analyst, statistian, 1981-82; Childrens Cir Daycare Ctr, spec ed coord, 1982-88; Children's Cir Daycare Ctr, dir/proj Giant Step, 1989-90; St Mary's Sch, spec educ teacher, 1990-92; NYC Sch Bd, Dist 9, pres, 1992-. **Orgs:** Vpres, NYC Sch Bd, Dist 9, 1983-92; consult, Hosp Billing Syst; dir, Bronx Youth Action, 1985-. **Honors/Awds:** Outstanding Community School Board Member Bronx Democratic Club, 1985; Excellence in Education, NYS Coun Black Republicans, 1986, 1987; Community Service Award, Montefiore Health Ctr, 1988. **Home Addr:** 540 E 169th St, Bronx, NY 10456. **Business Addr:** Early Intervention Official Designee, Health & Hospital Corp, 1805 Williamsbridge Rd, Bronx, NY 10462.

DUE, TANANARIVE
Writer. **Personal:** Born Jan 1, 1966, Tallahassee, FL; daughter of John Dorsey Jr and Patricia Stevens; married Steven Barnes; children: Jason. **Educ:** Northwestern Univ, BS, jour; Univ Leeds, MA, Eng lit. **Career:** Journalist & novelist; The Miami Herald, feature writer & columnist, 1988-98; Author of the novels: The Between, 1995; My Soul to Keep, 1997; The Black Rose, 2000; The Living Blood, 2001; The Good House, 2003; Freedom in the Family, 2003; Joplin's Ghost, 2005; Casanegra: A Tennyson Hardwick Story, 2007; Blood Colony, 2008; contributor to Naked Came the Manatee, 1997. **Honors/Awds:** Afro-Am Cultural, Technological & Scientific Olympics, gold, silver, & bronze medals for essay & play writing, & oratory, 1982-83; Horror Writers Asn Bram Stoker Award for Outstanding Achievement in a First Novel, finalist, for The Between, 1995; NAACP King of Clubs of Greater Miami President's Award, 1998; American Book Award, 2002. **Business Addr:** Author, Simon & Schuster, Pocket Books, 1230 Ave of the Americas, New York, NY 10020.

DUERSON, DAVID R
Football player, business owner. **Personal:** Born Nov 28, 1960, Muncie, IN. **Educ:** Univ Notre Dame, BA, econ, 1983; Harvard Bus Sch, Entrepreneurial Mgt, 2001. **Career:** Chicago Bears, 1983-90; NY Giants, 1990; Phoenix Cardinals, 1991-93; McDonald's franchises, owner; Fair Oaks Farms LLC, owner; Duerson Foods LLC, pres, chief exec officer & founder, 2002-. **Orgs:** Pres, Chicago Econ Develop Corp; Notre Dame Col Bus Admin; Notre Dame Nat Monogram Club; Ronald McDonald House Charities Worldwide Bd; Maryville Acad Bd; ILAD Bd; YPO; Omega Psi Phi Fraternity; bd dir, Carthage Col; Omega Psi Phi Fraternity. **Honors/Awds:** Pres, Chicago Econ Develop Corp; Notre Dame Col Bus Admin; Notre Dame Nat Monogram Club; Ronald McDonald House Charities Worldwide Bd; Maryville Acad Bd; ILAD Bd; YPO; Omega Psi Phi Fraternity; bd dir, Carthage Col; Sigma Pi Phi Fraternity. **Special Achievements:** Played in two Super Bowls & four Pro Bowls; Co ranked fourty eighth, Black Enterprise mag, 1997. **Business Addr:** President, Chief Executive Officer, Duerson Foods LLC, 8922 102nd St, Pleasant Prairie, WI 53158, **Business Phone:** (262)947-0218.

DUFF, JAMAL EDWIN
Football player, actor. **Personal:** Born Mar 11, 1972, Columbus, OH. **Educ:** San Diego State Univ. **Career:** New York Giants, defensive end, 1995; Washington Redskins, prof football player, 1997-98; film: S.W.A.T, 2003; The Rundown, 2003; The Eliminator, 2004; Dodgeball: A True Underdog story, 2004; The Marine, 2006; The Lords Of The Underworld, 2007; The Game Plan, 2007; Blood:The Last Vampire, 2009; TV: "CSI: Crime Scene Investigation, 2006; "All Of Us", 2006; "In Justice", 2006; "The Game", 2007. **Honors/Awds:** Aztecs Outstanding Def Player Of The Year Awd, San Diegfo Univ. *

DUFFOO, DR. FRANTZ MICHEL
Scientist, physician. **Personal:** Born Mar 5, 1954, Port-au-Prince, Haiti; son of Franck and Leonie Narcisse; married Marcia Sylvester; children: Brian Anthony, Christian Jason & Ashley Gabrielle. **Educ:** City Col NY, BS, 1977; Meharry Medical Col, MD, 1979. **Career:** Brookdale Hosp Med Ctr, resident internal med, 1979-82; Montefiore Med Ctr, clinical fel, 1982-83, res fel, 1983-84; Internal Med Am Bd Internal Med, diplomate, 1984-; Woodhull Med & Mental Health Ctr, attend physician & consult nephrol, 1984-92, chief nephrology associate dir med, 1990-92; Am Bd Internal Med, diplomate, 1986; State Univ NY Health Sci Ctr, Brooklyn, instr med, 1985-88, asst prof med, 1988-; New York Univ, adj asst prof, 1990-; St Mary's Hosp, dir internal med residency prog, dir med, 1992-97, secy, 1992; Cath Med Ctrs, Internal Med Residency Prog, dir, 1997; St Vincent Cath Med Ctr, physician, pvt prac, currently. Caritas Health Care Inc, physician. **Orgs:** New York Acad Scis, 1981-88; Am Col Physicians, 1985-92; Am Soc Nephrology, 1985-; Int Soc Nephrol, 1985-; New York Soc Nephrol; charter mem, Am Soc Hypertension, 1986-; charter mem, Int Soc Hypertension Blacks; Nat Kidney Found, 1989-. **Honors/Awds:** Physician's Recognition Award, Am Med Asn, 1982, 1988; The Editorial Research Bd, The Physician and Sportsmedicine, 1982; abstract selected for presentation, New York Soc of Nephrology, 1984; Woodhall Medical and Mental Health Center, Secretary of the Medical Staff, 1989, Vice President of Medical Staff, 1990, President of Medical Staff, 1991; Fellow, American Col of Physicians, 1992. **Business Addr:** Private Practice, Physician, 8825 153rd St, Jamaica, NY 11432.

DUFFY, EUGENE JONES
Executive. **Personal:** Born Aug 25, 1954, Columbus, OH; son of Franklin V and Helen Jones; married Norrene Johnson, Apr 19, 1986; children: Josie Helen, Rosa Patrice. **Educ:** Univ Ibadan Nigeria; Morehouse Col, BA, 1976. **Career:** Dept Parks Recreation & Cultural Affairs, deputy comr; Office Contract Compliance, dir; Office Mayor, deputy chief admin officer; H J Russel & Co, Atlanta, GA, sr vpres, 1990-94; Albritton Capital Mgt, exec vpres; Paradigm Asset Mgt co, Exec VPres Mkt, currently. **Orgs:** Nat League Cities, Nat Conf Black Pub Admins; trustee, Morehouse Col; YMCA; pres, Atlanta Univ Ctr Student Coun; founding mem, 100 Black Men atlanta; Urban Consortium. **Honors/Awds:** Charles E Merrill Foreign Study Scholar, Univ Ibadan. **Business Addr:** Executive Vice President, Paradigm Asset Managment company, 445 Hamilton Ave, White Plains, NY 10601, **Business Phone:** (212)771-6100.*

DUGAS, A JEFFREY ALAN, SR.
Physician. **Personal:** Born Aug 6, 1953; son of Lester and Laurenetta; divorced; children: Andrea & Jeffrey Jr. **Educ:** Morehouse Col, BA, biol, 1972-76; Atlanta Univ, attended 1976-77; Roosevelt Univ, attended 1977-79; Morehouse Col Sch Med, attended 1979-82; Rush Medical Col, MD, 1984; Rush-Presbyterian St Lukes Med Ctr, internship, 1984-85, residency, 1985-87. **Career:** Michael Reese Hosp & Med Ctr, community relations mental health representative, 1978-79; Morehouse Sch Med, res asst, 1981-82; Coastal Emergency Servs, independent contractor, 1986-87; Provident Med Ctr, attending 1987; Rush-Presbyterian St Luke's Med Ctr, instr med, 1987-, attending 1987-; City Chicago, Bd Health, physician, 1988-91; Rush Med Col, asst prof, 1991-; William L Dawson Nursing Ctr, med dir, 1991-; pvt pract, currently. **Orgs:** Chicago Med Soc; Ill State Med Soc; Am Col Physicians; Am Med Asn; Nat Med Asn, Cook County Physicians Asn; Crescent Counties Found Med Care; Southside YMCA, bd, vchair. **Special Achievements:** Leading Young Black Doctor, Dollars and Sense Magazine. **Home Addr:** 401 W Ontario St Suite 220, Chicago, IL 60610, **Home Phone:** (312)255-1580. **Business Phone:** (312)733-6968.

DUGGER, CLINTON GEORGE
Clergy. **Personal:** Born Sep 8, 1929, Beacon, NY; son of William and Mary Anderson; married Virginia McLean, Nov 24, 1962; children: Michael Kerwin. **Educ:** St Augustine's Col, BA, 1959; Philadelphia Divinity Sch, MDiv, 1962; State Univ New York Albany, MSW, 1967. **Career:** Clergy (retired); Trinity Church, cur, 1962-65; Diocese Albany, diocesan officer, 1965-67; Berkshire Farm Boys, chaplain, 1967-81; St Luke's vicar, 1973-85; Hoosac Sch, chaplain, 1981-85; Church Redeemer, rector. **Orgs:** Lebanon Valley Lions Club; Rensselaer Comm Ctr Bd; Troy Church Home Bd; bd dir, Gould Farm, MA; bd mem, Episcopal Church Coun Ctr, 1986-92; Am Legion Post No 1683. **Honors/Awds:** Man of the Yr, Rotary, 1975; Chaplain Emer, Hoosac Sch, 1987; Dean of the Metrop Deanery, Diocese, 1987; Chaplain of Fire Dept, Rensselaer, 1992. **Military Serv:** AUS, cpl, 1952-54. *

DUGGER, EDWARD, III
Executive. **Personal:** Born Apr 14, 1949, Dayton, OH; son of Edward Jr and Wertha; married Elizabeth Harris; children: Cyrus Edward, Langston Reid, Chloe D'jenne. **Educ:** Harvard Col, AB, 1971; Princeton Univ, MPA UP, 1973. **Career:** Irwin Mgt Co Inc, mgr real estate div, 1973-74; UNC Partners Inc, pres & chief exec officer, 1974-. **Orgs:** Greater Boston YMCA, 1981-92; United Way MA Bay, 1981-87; Federal Reserve Bank Boston, corp bd, 1994-; chair, UNC Media Inc, 1991-97; Envirotest Syst Co, corp bd, 1990-98; US Radio, LP, adv comt, 1990-96; Granite Broadcasting Co, corp bd, 1989-; San Francisco Med Ctr, mgt comn, 1989-; UNC Ventures Inc, corp bd, 1978-97; Boys & Girls Club Boston, bd dirs, 1993-; Beth Israel Hosp, Boston MA, bd dirs, 1991-96; New England Aquarium, bd dirs, 1988-; The Partnership, bd dirs, 1988-95; NAACP Legal Defense Fund, New England, bd dirs, 1985-; The Boston Club, 1994-; MA Bus Roundtable, 1994-; Social Venture Network, 1994-; Students Responsible Bus, 1994-; The Children's Museum, 1988-95; Harvard Univ, comt univ res, 1985-. **Honors/Awds:** Greater Boston's 100 Most Influential Business People 20th Century, Boston Bus Journal, 1999; Social Venture Pioneer Award, Investor's Circle,

1993; Achievement Award, ONE, 1988; Outstanding Bus Prof, Nat Urban Bankers, 1985; Esquire Register, 1984. **Special Achievements:** Articles: Esquire, 1984; New England Business, 1987; Wall Street Journal, 1983, 1994; Black Enterprise, 1990, 1994; Bay State Banner, 1994; Boston Globe, 1994; Boston Business Journal, 1994; Pension & Investments, 1994. **Business Addr:** President, Chief Executive Officer, UNC Partners Inc, 54 Burroughs St, Boston, MA 02130, **Business Phone:** (617)522-2160.*

DUHANEY, TREVOR
Automotive executive. **Career:** Nova Scotia Jamaica Ltd, br mgr, 1971-74; Deel Ford, sales assoc, sales mgr & gen mgr, 1974-78; Newport Lincoln Mercury, partner & gen mgr, 1978-80; Anthony Abraham Chevrolet, sales assoc, 1980-83; Potamkin Chevrolet, sales mgr & sales assoc, 1983-85; Potamkin World Ctr, partner & gen mgr, 1985-89; Duhaney Auto Sales, pres & chief exec officer, 1989-93; Duhaney Pontiac Buick GMC, pres & chief exec officer, 1993-04; Duhaney Motors, pres & chief exec officer, 2004-. **Orgs:** Bd gov, Greater Miami Chamber Com; Rainbow PUSH Coalition; Nat Minority Automobile Asn; S Fla Automobile Asn. **Honors/Awds:** Honoree, 9th Annual African-Am Achievers awards; Award for Excellennce Bus, Fla A & M Univ, Nat Alumni Asn, 2002. **Business Phone:** (305)751-9621.*

DUHART, HAROLD B.
Manager. **Personal:** Born Dec 15, 1938, Macon, GA; married Margaret Roberts; children: Bobby, Lori. **Educ:** NC Agr & Tech Univ, BS, 1963; GA Inst Tech, advan study. **Career:** City Durham NC, eng redevelopment officer, 1964-65; US Army Corps Engrs, space facilities design Engr, 1964-68; Dept HUD, eng munic proj mgr, 1968-70; US Environ Protection Agency, NC State proj mgr. **Orgs:** Pres, Duhart Bros Enterprises Macon, GA, 1974-; Fed Water Pollution Control Asn; Equal Opportunity Comn EPA; assoc mem, ASCE; PTA; Task force Minority Bus for EPA prog; YMCA; SW Atlanta Comn Asn; SABFO. **Honors/Awds:** Membership campaign Award, YMCA; spec achievement Award, EPA 1973. **Military Serv:** AUS, NATO, 1961-63.

DUKE, BILL (WILLIAM HENRY DUKE, JR.)
Administrator, movie director, actor. **Personal:** Born Feb 26, 1943, Poughkeepsie, NY; son of William Henry Sr and Ethel Louise Douglas. **Educ:** Boston Univ, BA, 1964; NY Univ, MA, 1968; Am Film Inst, MA, 1971. **Career:** Films: Car Wash, 1976; Am Gigilo, 1980; Commando, 1985; Predator, 1987; No Man's Land, 1987; Action Jackson, 1988; St of No Return, 1989; Bird on a Wire, 1990; Rage In Harlem, dir, 1991; Deep Cover, dir, 1992; Menace II Soc, 1993; Cemetary Club, dir, 1993; Sister Act 2, 1993; Sweet Potato Ride, exec producer, 1996; Hoodlum, exec producer, 1997; Susan's Plan, 1998; Payback, 1999; Foolish, 1999; The Limey, 1999; Fever, 1999; Never Again, 2001; Exit Wounds, 2001; Love & a Bullet, 2002; Red Dragon, 2002; National Security, 2003; Twisted, 2004; Yellow, 2006; X-Men: The Last Stand, 2006; The Pact, exec producer, 2006; Yellow, 2006; The Go-Getter, 2007; Prince Among Slaves, recreations dir, 2008; Cover, dir & producer, 2008; TV Series: "American Playhouse", dir, 1989; "Raisin In The Sun", dir, 1989; "Karen Sisco", 2003-04; "Lost", 2006; "Every Man for Himself", 2006; "Battlestar Galactica", 2006; "Black Market", 2006; Am Playhouse, Killing, dir; The Meeting, dir; Miracle's Boys; Get Rich or Die Tryin, 2005; "Battlestar Galactica", 2006; Howard Univ, Dept Radio, TV, & Film, chmn, 2000. **Orgs:** Sundance Film Festival, 1992; Artist Against Homelessness; Dirs Guild Am; Writers Guild Am; Screen Actors Guild. **Honors/Awds:** Special Jury Prize, 1985; New Vision Award, Black Filmmakers Hall of Fame, 1990; Nat Asn Advan Colored People Image Award, 1991; Star Bright Award, Black Am Soc, 1991; Career Achievement Award, 1997; Black Reel Award, 2004. **Special Achievements:** First Time Warner Professor at the School of Communications, Howard Univ. **Business Phone:** (310)230-4040.

DUKE, GEORGE M. (DAWILLI GONGA)
Singer. **Personal:** Born Jan 12, 1946, San Rafael, CA; married Corine Ann Salanga; children: Rashid Amon & John Lee Shiffer. **Educ:** San Francisco Conserv Music, BA, music, 1967; San Francisco St Col, MA, 1970; Merritt Jr Col, MA, am cult. **Career:** George Duke Band, Epic Recs, leader, 1977-; Billy Cobham-George Duke Band, Atlantic, co-leader, 1976-77; Frank Zappa, Warner Bros, keyboardist, 1970-72, 1973-76; Julian Cannonball Adderly, Capital & Fantasy, keyboardist, composer & arranger, 1971-72; Jean-Luc Ponty, United Artists, pianist, 1969-70; MPS/BASF Recs, recartist (solo), 1973-76; Epic Recs, solo rec artist, 1976-; George Duke Enterprises, owner, currently; Capital Rec/G Duke Prod, A Taste of Honey "Twice As Sweet", 1980; Songs: "From MeTo You", 1978; "Stay With Me Tonight"; "On The Wings Of Love"; "SweetBaby"; Albums: A Taste Of Honey; The Calling, 2001; Duke, 2005; In A Mellow Tone, 2006; Dukey Treats, 2008. **Orgs:** Pres, founder & mem, Mycenae Music Publ Co, 1968-; pres & founder, George Duke Enterprises Inc, 1976-; consult, Contemp KeyBd Mag, 1977-; NAACP, 1979-; BMA, 1979-. **Honors/Awds:** Gold Record, "Reach For It", RIAA, 1978; Gold Record, "Dukey Stick", RIAA, 1979; Hit Record Awards, ASCAP, 1979-80; R&B Keyboardist Of The Year; Keyboard Mag, 1990; All That Jazz Award, Am Soc Young Musicians; Prism Lifetime Achievment Award, Minoritys Bus Mag; Milley Creative Achievment Award, Mill Valley Outdoor Art Club; Living Legend Award, Nat Alliance Black Sch Edu; Pinnacle Of Musical Excellence Award, Harry A. Mier Center Ability First; Edison Life Time Achievement Award, 2005; Jay McShann Lifetime Achievement Award, Ok Jazz Hall Fame; Judge for 2nd Independent Music Awards. **Business Addr:** Musician, George Duke Enterprises Business Office, Bpm Records, 7095 Hollywood Blvd Suite 657, Los Angeles, CA 90028-8903, **Business Phone:** (323)467-0823.

DUKE, DR. LESLIE DOWLING, SR.
Physician. **Personal:** Born Mar 21, 1924, Washington, DC; married Dolores Douglass; children: Leslie Jr & Lori. **Educ:** Howard Univ, BS, zool, 1950; Howard Univ, MD, 1957. **Career:** Physician (retired); Ft Meade, med officer, 1959-62; Walter Reed Gen Hosp,phy, 1962-77; pvt pratice, 1998. **Orgs:** Nat Med Asn; Pro-Duffers golf club. **Military Serv:** AUS, sgt, 1943-46. **Home Addr:** 101 Shaw Ave, Silver Spring, MD 20904, **Home Phone:** (301)622-0723. *

DUKE, RUTH WHITE
Educator. **Personal:** Born Dec 12, 1927, Hampton, VA; daughter of George David (deceased) and Lucille Lowry (deceased); married Everette L Duke, Jun 27, 1953; children: Everette L Jr & Cecil Q. **Educ:** Va State Univ, BS, 1948; NY Univ, MA, 1951; James Madison Univ, 1970; Old Dominion Univ, 1972; Norfolk State Univ, 1973; Va Polytechnic Ist & State Univ, 1975. **Career:** Educator (retired); Lunenburg High Sch, bus teacher, 1949-52; Sumner & Vashon High Sch, bus teacher, 1952-54; Norfolk State Univ, bus teacher, 1955-56; BT Wash High Sch, bus teacher, 1956-57; US Govt, civil serv worker, 1957-59; Jacox Junior High Sch, bus teacher, 1961-65; Norview High Sch, bus teacher, dept chp, 1965-86; Old Dominion Univ, supvr social studies stud teachers, 1989-91. **Orgs:** Pres, vpres, corresp secy, Va Beach Pinchole Bugs, 1972-96; secy church meetings, Bank St Mem Church, 1974-94; bd, chair by-laws, Girls Inc Tidewater, 1975-93; nat fin secy, Pinochle Bugs Social & Civic Club, 1980-84, nat treas, 1988-92; volunteer admin off, Norfolk Cot Hosp, 1990-96; Pinochle Bugs Social & Civic Club, Inc, Nat exec sec; treas nat exec sec, L & J Gardens. **Honors/Awds:** Certificate for Volunteer Service, Meals on Wheels. **Home Addr:** 1036 Fairlawn Ave, Virginia Beach, VA 23455, **Home Phone:** (757)461-2908. **Business Phone:** (804)461-2908.*

DUKE, WILLIAM HENRY, JR. See DUKE, BILL.

DUKES, CARL R
Automotive executive, founder (originator). **Educ:** Mich State Univ. **Career:** Joliet Dodge Inc, pres, owner, 1990-. **Orgs:** Bd dir, Joliet Region Chamber Com. **Business Addr:** President, Owner, Joliet Dodge Inc, 2617 W Jefferson St, Joliet, IL 60435, **Business Phone:** (815)729-3343.

DUKES, HAZEL NELL
Government official. **Personal:** Born Mar 17, 1932, Montgomery, AL; daughter of Edward and Alice; divorced; children: Ronald. **Educ:** Ala State Tchr Col, AA, 1950; Adelphi Univ, advance master prgm Adelphi Univ, Grad, 1978. **Career:** Macys Dept Store, staff, 1950; Nassau Co Atty Off, community organizer; Dem Natl Conv, New York, deleg, 1976, 1980; New York Off-Track Betting Corp, pres, 1990-92; Presidential Elector, New York, 1992; NY Nat Asn Advan Colored People, pres, 1999-. **Orgs:** Metro-LINKS; bd dirs, Coalition 100 Black Women; bd dirs, St NY Martin Luther King Jr. Comn; Nat Bd, 1977-, pres, 1990-, NAACP; mem, bd trustees, St Univ New York; Westbury Negro Bus & Prof Women's Club; secy, Coun Black Elected Democrats NY; mem, Dem Nat Comt; pres, NY NAACP. **Honors/Awds:** Social Action Award, Delta Sigma Theta Sor Inc, 1976; Sojurner Truth Award, Nat Asn Negro Bus & Prof Women's Clubs Inc, 1977; Comm Service Award, New York OIC, 1976; Salute to African American Women, Dollar and Sense Magazine, 1989; Award for Outstanding Contribution to Social Justice, New York Human Rights Comn, 1985; Award for Promoting Justice & Interracial Harmony, B'nai B'rith, 1990; hon doc, Queens Col, 1990. **Special Achievements:** First black American to work for the Nassau County attorney's office. **Home Addr:** 10 W 135 St, New York, NY 10037-2610, **Home Phone:** (212)281-1215. **Business Addr:** President, National Association for the Advancement of Colored People, 39 Broadway Suite 2201, New York, NY 10006, **Business Phone:** (212)344-7474.

DUKES, OFIELD
Public relations executive, consultant, president (organization). **Personal:** Born Aug 8, 1932, Rutledge, AL; son of Violet Stringer and Garfield; married Elaine Robinson, Aug 3, 1991; children: Roxi Anica Trapp; married Elaine Robinson, Aug 3, 1991. **Educ:** Wayne State Univ, BA, 1958. **Career:** WCHB Radio, news dir, 1958-61; Mich Chronicle, asst ed, gen mgr, 1961-64; President's Comt Equal Employ Opportunity & Plans Progress, dep dir, 1964-65; White House Conf Fulfill These Rights, dep dir pub affairs, 1965-69; Hubert H Humphrey, asst, vpres, 1966-69; Ofield Dukes & Assoc Inc, pres 1969-; Howard Univ, adj prof, 1972-83; Am Univ, Sch Commun, adj prof, 1993-2001; Howard Univ Sch Commun, co-chmn, currently; John H Johnson Sch Commun, co-chmn, currently; Bethune-DuBois Inst, Washington, DC, pres, currently. **Orgs:** Pub Rel Soc Am; bd mem, Nat Coalition Black Voter Partic; bd mem, PeoplesInvolvement Corp; founder, Black Pub Rels Soc Washington; co-chair, John H. Johnson School of Communications. **Honors/Awds:** Male Decision Maker, Nat Asn Media Women, 1971; Silver Anvil Award, Pub Rels Soc Am, 1974; Frederick Douglass Award, Howard Univ Sch Commun, 1974; Outstanding Faculty Award, Howard Univ Sch Commun, 1978; Eagle LeadershipAward, Bethune-DuBois Fund, 1991; Moss Kendrick Award of Excellence, Capital Press Club, 1994; D Parke Gibson Pioneer Award, PRSA Multicultural Affairs, 1995; Founder's Award, Nat Black Pub Rels, 1999; Torch Award, Nat Newspaper Publishers Asn, 1999; Hall of Fame, Pub Rels Soc, Washington, DC, 1999; Gold Anvil Award, Pub Rels Soc Am, 2001; Nat Public Relations Achievement Award, Ball State Univ, 2003; inductee, Virginia Communications Hall of Fame, 2003. **Military Serv:** AUS, 1952-54. **Business Addr:** President, Ofield Dukes & Associates, 1424 Carrolsburg Pl SW, Washington, DC 20024, **Business Phone:** (202)488-4948.

DUKES, RONALD
Consultant. **Personal:** Born 1943, Neelyville, MO; married Albertine A Elliott; children: Barry Girard. **Educ:** Lincoln Univ, MO, BS, 1964. **Career:** Continental Can Co, training supvr, 1969-71; Emerson Electric Co, sr corp recruiter, 1971-74; Am Motors Corp, corp dir recruiting & mgmt develop, 1974-78; Booz Allen & Hamilton, assoc, 1978-80; Heidrick & Struggles Inc, partner, shareholder, bd dirs, 1980-99; Ronald Dukes Assoc LLC, pres, 1999-. **Orgs:** Phi Beta Sigma Fraternity; Chicago Youth Ctrs, 1987, Chmn Bd, 1995-97, currently exec comt mem; bd dirs, chair audit comt, First Non-Profit Ins Co; Chicago United Way/Crusade Mercy Pension Subcomt, 1995-2005; bd visitors, Peter F Drucker Graduate Mgt Ctr. **Special Achievements:** Listed in the 1990 Harper and Row Book, "The Career Makers: America's Top 100 Recruiters". **Military Serv:** AUS, capt, 1966; Commendation Medal, Combat Badge, 1967, Vietnam Serv. **Home Addr:** 1105 Alden Lane, Buffalo Grove, IL 60089. **Business Addr:** President, Ronald Dukes Associates LLC, 20 N Wacker Dr Suite 2010, Chicago, IL 60606, **Business Phone:** (312)357-2895.

DUKES, DR. WALTER L
Association executive. **Personal:** Born Jun 23, 1933, Youngstown, OH. **Educ:** Seton Hall Univ, BS, Econ, 1953; NY Univ, MBA, 1956; NY Law Sch, LLB, 1959; NY Law Sch, Dr Law, 1968; Hunter Col, MVP, 1981. **Career:** Vista Travel Serv, vpres, 1963-67; US Labor Dept, atty, 1967-69; Civil Disorder, nat adv comn, 1969-70; King-Kennedy Develop Found Inc, pres, 1970-. **Orgs:** Nat Asn Advan Colored People, 1951-; vpres, Nat Orgn Boys Scouts, 1960-; Am Bar Asn, 1961-; Mich Bar Asn, 1968-; Nat Mkt Club, 1970-; mem Urban Planners 1980-; Vpres, Boy's of Yester Year, 1975-91; Nat Youth Dir NAACP, dir, 1953-54; Alliance Franchise, vice pres, 1975-84; pres, Nat Bar Asn, 1984-91. **Honors/Awds:** Athletic of the Year US Writers Guild, 1953. **Special Achievements:** Charter Life Underwriters Philly PA CLU. **Business Addr:** President, King-Kennedy Develop Found Inc., Church St Sta, PO Box 756, New York, NY 10008.

DULANEY, MICHAEL FAULKERSON
Personal: Born Sep 9, 1970, Kingsport, TN; married Alisia. **Educ:** Univ NC. **Career:** NY Firebirds, Arena Football League; Chicago Bears, running back, 1995-97; Carolina Panthers, fullback, 1998.Pract Solns, treasurer,currently.

DULIN, JOSEPH
School administrator. **Personal:** Born Aug 10, 1935, Evansville, IN; son of Charles and Alberta Cooksey; married Yvonne, Aug 14, 1976; children: Tierre Porter, Charles, Joseph II, Doris Fields & Kasner L Will is. **Educ:** St Josephs Col, BS, 1957; Ind State Univ, MS, admin, 1963; Eastern Mich &Western Ill Univs addn studies. **Career:** St Marys High Sch, W Point, IA, teacher-coach, 1958-64; St Martin De Porres High Sch, prin, 1967-72; Detroit Pub Schs, teacher, 1964-67; Friends Sch, Detroit, asst headmaster, 1972-73; Neighborhood Serv Orgn, community organizer, 1973-74; Roberto Clemente, Stud Develop Ctr, Ann Arbor Pub Schs, prin, 1974. **Orgs:** Founding Pres, Nat Black Lay Catholic Caucus, 1970; United Comm Negro Hist Inc, Educ & Comm Serv, 1971; pres & bd dirs, Saturday Acad African Am Studies, 1992; bd mem, Ann Arbor Comm Found, 1993; Founder, NAAPID, 1995-;life mem, NABSE; MDABSE; adv bd, Ann Arbor African Am Festival, 1996; vpres, Washte naw Co Comm Ment Health, 1996; vice chairperson, Cope OBrien, 1996-; bd trustees, Huron Valley Ambulance; co-chairperson, Ann Arbor Black Adminrs Asn; co-chairperson, Ann Arbor Achievement Initiatives; bd mem, Ann Arbor Hands-On Museum; bd mem, Washte naw Housing Alliance. **Honors/Awds:** Hall of Fame, NABSE; Distinguished Achievement Award Parenting, Nat Parent Day Coalition, 1996; UNCF Eugene Powers Comm Service Award, 1993; Distinguished Alumni Merit, St Josephs Col, 1969; Black Lay Catholic Caucus Leadership Award, 1973; Hall of Fame, Nat Alliance Black Sch Educrs, 1997; Alumni Achievement Award, St Joseph Col, 1998; Distinguished Alumni Award, Ind State Univ, 1998; Leadership Award, COPE OBrien Ctr; Appreciation Award, NAAPID Initiative, Washte naw Co Comm Action Bd. **Special Achievements:** First African American Lay Prin Catholic School Nation, 1967, TV & Press appearances, NBC, CBS, ABC & BET, 1995, spec advisor, presidential cand AlGore, 2000; Consult Motivational Speaker, 1996. **Military Serv:** AUS, pvt, 1957-58, 1961-62. **Home Addr:** 439 Sumark Way, Ann Arbor, MI 48103, **Home Phone:** (734)747-6671.

DULIN, ROBERT O., JR.
Clergy. **Personal:** Born Mar 24, 1941, Lawrence, KS; married C Hawice Allen; children: Shannon E, Robert O, III. **Educ:** Anderson Col, BA, 1963; Cent Bapt Theol Sem, BD, 1967. **Career:** Third St Church God, assoc minister, 1964-66; First Church God, pastor, 1967-69; Nat Bd Christian Educ, assoc secy, 1969-74; Metrop Church God, sr minister, Reverend, currently. **Orgs:** Life mem, Nat Asn Advan Colored People, 1979; vchmn, bd dirs, Charles H. Wright Mus African Am Hist, currently; bd dirs, Youth Sports & Recreation Comn; bd dirs, Franklin Wright Settlements; Mid-Night Golf Inc; Metrop Organizing Strategy Enabling Strength (MOSES). **Honors/Awds:** Alumni Achievement Award, Cent Baptist Theol Sem, 1974; Distinguished Alumni Award, Anderson Univ, 1997; DDiv, Anderson University, 2005. **Home Addr:** 14565 Whitcomb St, Detroit, MI 48227, **Home Phone:** (313)493-0478. **Business Addr:** Reverend, Metropolitan Church God, 13400 Schaefer Hwy, Detroit, MI 48227-3539, **Business Phone:** (313)273-5580.*

DUMARS, JOE
Basketball executive, basketball player. **Personal:** Born May 24, 1963, Shreveport, LA; son of Joe and Ophelia; married Debbie; children: Jordan Taylor & Aren. **Educ:** McNeese State Univ, 1981-85. **Career:** Detroit Pistons, guard, 1985-99, vpres player personnel, pres basketball opers, currently; Detroit Technologies, chief exec officer & pres, 1996-2006; Joe Dumars Field house, owner, currently; First Mich Bank, bd dirs, currently. **Honors/Awds:** NBA Finals MVP, 1989; World Championship Gold Medal, 1994; J Walter Kennedy Citizenship Award, 1994; NBA Sportsmanship Award, 1996; Naismith Memorial Basketball Hall of Fame, 2006; NBA Sportsmanship Award has been named the Joe Dumars Trophy. **Special Achievements:** First recipient of the NBA Sportsmanship Award. **Business Addr:** President of Basketball Operations, Detroit Pistons, 4 Championship Dr, Auburn Hills, MI 48326, **Business Phone:** (248)377-0100.

DUMAS, KAREN MARIE
Municipal government official, executive. **Personal:** Born Oct 22, 1962, Detroit, MI; married Timothy L Cook; children: Kirby & Jason. **Educ:** Mich State Univ, East Lansing, MI, BS, 1986. **Career:** Marx & Co, Bloomfield Hills, MI, acct asst & media rels, 1986-87; City Highland Park, Highland Park, MI, dir pub info, 1987-88; Images & Ideas, Detroit, MI, pres, 1988-; Athletes Exclusive Sports Mkt, assoc partner, 1996-; Mich Front Page, columnist, 2000-; Off Mayor, City Detroit, exec dir community rels, 2002-03; Detroit Dept Cult, Arts & Tourism, dir; Mich Chronicle, columnist; Next Detroit, prog host; Artifacts & Jazz at the Center, TV prog co host; Images & Ideas Inc, pres, currently. **Orgs:** Nat Asn Advan Colored People, 1983-; Riverfront Community Orgn, 1986-; Adcraft Club Detroit, 1987-; bd dirs, ALERT, 1987-; Civic Searchlight Comn, 1990-; bd dirs, Sickle Cell Detection Comn, 1990-; Nat Asn Black Journalists, Detroit Chap, 1991-; Black Advertising, Radio & Tv, 1991-; bd dirs, Sphinix Orgn, 2001-; Mich Film Comn; Arts League Mich; Tourism Econ Deveolp Ctr; commun comt mem, Detroit Riverfront Conservancy. **Honors/Awds:** Profiles of Success Award, State Mich, Dept Com, MBE, 1991; 25 Most Influential Women in Detroit, Women's Informal Network, 2001. **Business Phone:** (866)330-4585.

DUMAS, MICHAEL DION (MIKE DION DUMAS)
Football player, football coach. **Personal:** Born Mar 18, 1969, Grand Rapids, MI. **Educ:** Indiana Univ, sports marketing. **Career:** Football player (retired), coach; Houston Oilers, 1991-92; Buffalo Bills, 1994; Jacksonville Jaguars, 1995;San Diego Chargers, 1997-2000; Miami Dolphins, defensive coach, currently. *

DUMAS, MIKE DION. See DUMAS, MICHAEL DION.

DUMAS, TONY
Basketball player. **Personal:** Born Aug 25, 1972, Chicago, IL. **Educ:** Univ Miss-Kans City. **Career:** Basketball player (retired); Dallas Mavericks, guard, 1995-96; Phoenix Suns, 1997; Cleveland Cavaliers, guard, 1998. **Special Achievements:** First round pick, No 19, NBA Draft, 1994. Only player in University of Missouri-Kansas City history to be drafted into the NBA.

DUMAS, TROY
Football player, football coach. **Personal:** Born Sep 30, 1972, Cheyenne, WY. **Educ:** Univ Nebr-Lincoln, Human Resources and Family Sci, 1995. **Career:** Football player (retired), football player coach; Kans City Chiefs, linebacker, 1996-97; St Louis Rams, 1997; Denver Broncos; Orlando Pradators, linebacker, 2000; Edmonton Eskimos, linebacker, 2001; Cheyenne Cent High Sch, coach; Doane Col, asst coach; Huskers.net, line backers coach, currently. **Honors/Awds:** All-Am hons; Semi-finalist for the Butkus Award. **Business Phone:** (402)472-4224.

DUMMETT, CLIFTON ORRIN. See Obituaries section.

DUMMETT, DR. JOCELYN ANGELA
Pediatrician. **Personal:** Born Sep 15, 1956, Leicester, England; daughter of Kenneth J and Sheila A Waterman; children: Richard Anthony Hunte, Ryan William Hunte. **Educ:** Howard Univ Col Med, MD, 1980. **Career:** Downstate Med Ctr, clini instr, 1983-85; LBJ Sch Health Prog, preceptor; Health Sci Ctr Brooklyn, asst clinic prof; Javican Pediatric Assocs, co-founder, 1985-87. **Orgs:** Fellow, Am Acad Pediatrics; Brooklyn Pediatric Soc; Nat Med Assoc; recording secy, Provident Clinical Soc, 1984-88; med secy, Hanson Place Seventh-day Adventist Ch, 1986. **Honors/Awds:** Excellence in Pediatrics, Howard Univ, Col Med, 1980; Recoginition Award, Nat Health Serv Corps, 1985. **Business Addr:** Physician, PO BOX 696, Pine Bush, NY 12566.*

DUMPSON, DR. JAMES R.
Educator, consultant, administrator. **Personal:** Born in Philadelphia, PA; son of James T (deceased) and Edythe Francis Smith (deceased). **Educ:** State Teachers Col, BS, 1932; New Sch Social Res, AB, 1947; Univ Pa, Sch Social Work, 1938, 1944, 1947; Fordham Univ, Sch Social Serv, 1944, New Sch Social Res, MA, 1950; Univ Dacca, PhD, 1955. **Career:** Teacher, Oxford, PA, 1932-37; Supvr, Dept Pub Assistance, Philadelphia, PA, 1937-40; NY City Dept Welfare, first dep comn, 1957-59; NY City Dept Welfare, comn, 1959-65; Hunter Col, Sch Social Work, prof assoc dean, 1965-67; Fordham Univ, Grad Sch Social Servs, dean, prof, 1967-74, prof, Chair Family & Child Welfare, 1989-; NY City, comn social serv & admin human resources, 1974-76; NY Community Trust, vpres, 1976, sr consult, currently; City NY, health servs adminr, 1990-94, chair, NY City Health & Hosp Corp, 1990-94, spec asst mayor, 1990-94; dir, Bur Child Welfare NYC, consult NY City Welfare Coun; cons, supvr, Cs Aid Soc NYC; supvr, Philadelphia, Dept Pub Asst; teacher, pub sch Oxford PA; Gov Carey's Task Force Human Resources;UN adv, Chief Training Soc Welfare Gov Pakistan; consult, Pakistan Asia Found. **Orgs:** Chmn, Mayor Lindsay Anti-Poverty Coun & Anti-Poverty Oper Bd; mem bd, Dept Juv Justice NYC, chmn Mayors Task Force Foster Care; pres, Kennedy's Comn Narcotics & Drug Abuses; Pres Johnson's Comn Alcoholism; bd mem, Fedn Protestant Welfare Agencies, 1987-; chair, US Comt Int Coun Social Welfare, 1987-; chair, Black Leadership Comn AIDS, 1989-92; Gov Cuomo'sAdv Coun AIDS, 1989-; bd mem, United Way NY City, 1986-; bd mem, Assoc Black Charities, 1984-; United Way NY City, 1990-; bd mem, N Gen Hosp, 1994-; founding pres, Nat Black Leadership Comn AIDS, 1990-95, comnr, 1995-; Nat Asn Social Workers, NY Chap, currently. **Honors/Awds:** James R. Dumpson Chair in Family & Child Welfare, Fordham Univ, 1990-; Honorary LLD, Tuskegee Univ; Honorary LLD, Fordham Univ; Honorary LHD, St Peters Col; Honorary LLD, Howard Univ; Honorary LHD, City Univ NY; installed as Nana Bonso Ababio I, Repub Ghana. **Business Addr:** Senior Consultant, New York Community Trust, 909 Third Ave 22nd Fl, New York, NY 10022.*

DUNBAR, ANNE CYNTHIA
Administrator. **Personal:** Born Sep 24, 1938, New York, NY; divorced; children: Christopher. **Educ:** Borough Manhattan Community Col, AA, 1967; Brooklyn Col, BA, 1975, MS, 1977; Columbia Univ Sch Pub & Int Affairs, Cert, 1985. **Career:** Citi-Bank/Canal St Training Ctr, asst, master, 1968-69; 1st Venture Corp NY, asst, vpres, 1969-70; Hunter Col, SEEK Financial Aid Prog, dir, 1970-76; founder, Ford-Whitfield-Young Scholarship Fund Hunter Col, City Univ NY, 1975; NY State Dept Correctional Servs, dir comt rel, 1976-; consult, Dept HEW NIH Sickle Blood Dis Prog, 1977-79; trustee, Bronx Museum, 1981-; instr, City Univ NY. **Orgs:** volunteer, Womens Div Gov Off, 1969-71; chairperson, Spec Progs Handicapped Community Sch Bd 12, 1977-; chmn bd, NY Urban League, 1983-; Am Personnel & Guid Asn; founder pres, Break Thru Art; pres, NAACP Parkchester Br; adv mem, NY City Businessman Coun Employ Ex-offender; educ sponsor, Coalition 100 Black Women; mem bd dir, Bronx Boys Clubs; NY State Catholic Conf Criminal Justice Adv Comt; Comt Sch Bd 12; Brooklyn Col Alumni Asn; Borough Manhattan Community Col Alumni Asn; Bronx Coun Arts; Womens City Club NY. **Honors/Awds:** Citation Comt Coord & Devel Northside Ctr Child Develop, 1972; "Ambassador of Love" Val-to-me Productions, 1974; Citation Achievement Eastern NY Correctional Facil Jaycees, 1974; Citation Activ Penal Reform Gamblers Anonymous Greenhaven Prison Chap, 1974; Cert Appreciation, Eastern NY Correctional Facil, 1975; Claire Joseph King Mem Citation, 1975; Each One Teach One Comt Serv Award, Harlem Prof & John Hunter Mem Camp Fund, 1975; Outstanding Serv Award, Eastern Br NAACP, 1975; honoree, Int Women's Year Nat Coun Negro Women Inc, Flatbush Sect, 1975; Citation Distinguished Servs Handicapped C; Community Serv Award, Schaefer Brewry Co, 1978; Citizen Year Award, Bronx Boys Clubs, 1979; Humanitarian Award, Parkchester Cardiac Diag Med Ctr, 1979; Leadership Award, City Coun NY, 1983; Distinguish Community Serv Coun Churches NY; Commun Serv Award, Consolidated Edison NY; Congressional Citation Rep Mario Biaggi, 1978. **Home Addr:** 1940 E Tremont Ave, Bronx, NY 10462.

DUNBAR, JOSEPH C.
Educator, scientist. **Personal:** Born Aug 27, 1944, Vicksburg, MS; son of J C Dunbar Sr and Henrienne M Watkins; married Agnes Estorge, Jul 1, 1967; children: Andrea, Erica. **Educ:** Alcorn Col, Lorman, MS, BS, biol, 1963; Tex Southern, Houston, TX, MS, zool, 1966; Wayne State Univ, Detroit, MI, PhD, physiol & pharmacol, 1970. **Career:** Tex Southern, Houston, TX, instr biol, 1966-67; Sinai Hosp Detroit, MI, res assoc, 1972-81; Wayne State Univ, Detroit, MI, from asst prof to assoc prof physiol, 1972-85, prof physiol, 1985-, assoc chmn, 1995-97, chmn physiol, 1998-. **Honors/Awds:** Author of 100 publications; Distinguished Fac Fel; Outstanding Graduate Mentor; Medical Service Award. **Business Addr:** Chairman, Professor, Wayne State University, Department of Physiology, 540 E Canfield, 5275 Scott Hall, Detroit, MI 48201, **Business Phone:** (313)577-1520.*

DUNBAR, ROCKMOND
Actor. **Personal:** Born Jan 11, 1974, Oakland, CA; married Ivy Holmes, Sep 19, 2003 (divorced 2006). **Career:** Films: Misery Loves Company, 1993; Punks, 2000; All About You, 2001; Kiss Kiss Bang Bang, 2005; Dirty Laundry, producer, 2006; Jada, 2008; The Family That Preys, 2008; Alien Raiders, 2008; Pastor Brown, 2009; TV series: "Earth 2", 1994-95; "The Good News", 1997; "The Wayans Bros.", 1998; "Two Guys, a Girl & a Pizza Place", 1998; "Pacific Blue", 1999; "The Practice", 1999; "The Pretender", 1999; "Felicity", 1999; "G vs E", 2000; "Soul Food", 2000-04; "Girlfriends", 2003-04; Hollywood Division, 2004; "North Shore", 2004; "Head Cases", 2005; "Prison Break", 2005-07; Heartland, 2007; "Grey's Anatomy", 2007; "CSI: Miami", 2007; "The Game", 2009; Director: The Great Commission, producer, 2003; Behind the Scenes: The Great Commission, 2003; Pastor Brown, 2009. **Honors/Awds:** Black Reel Award, 2002. **Special Achievements:** Named one of "Television's 50 Sexiest Stars of All Time" by TV Guide. **Business Addr:** Actor, Showtime Networks Inc, 1633 E Broadway, New York, NY 10019, **Business Phone:** (212)708-1600.*

DUNBAR, THOMAS JEROME (TOM DUNBAR)
Sports manager, baseball player. **Personal:** Born Nov 24, 1959, Aiken, SC; son of George and Rosa Lee; married Tjwana Delph, Jul 4, 1985; children: Tia & Tyson. **Career:** Baseball player (retired), sports manager; Tex Rangers, outfielder, 1983-86; Pittsburgh Pirates, 1987; Atlanta Braves, 1988-89; Kans City Royals, 1989-91; Princeton Reds, mgr, currently. **Honors/Awds:** Minor League Rookie of the Year, Tex Rangers, 1984; American Asn Batting Title, Okla City, Tex Rangers, 1984. **Home Addr:** 558 Palm Dr S, Aiken, SC 29803, **Home Phone:** (803)642-8436. **Business Addr:** Professional Baseball Manager, Princeton Reds, Cincinnati Reds, 100 Riverfront Stadium, Cincinnati, OH 45202, **Business Phone:** (513)421-4510.

DUNBAR, TOM. See DUNBAR, THOMAS JEROME.

DUNCAN, GENEVA
Administrator. **Personal:** Born Aug 21, 1935, Cleveland, OH; married Dave L Sr; children: Jolette, Dave jr, Brenda, Darnell, Darlynn & Kevin. **Educ:** Feen Col; Cleveland State Univ. **Career:** Ministerial Day Care Asn, dir social serv. **Orgs:** Crest Found; bd, HADC; Cuyahoga County Welfare Dept; Fed Comn & Planning; Comn Christmas bur; dir Pub Rels; Mt Nebo Baptist Church; Hough Area Coun; Glenville Area Coun; Hough Area Devel Corp; Crest Found. **Business Addr:** Administrator, 2521 E 61 St, Cleveland, OH 44104.

DUNCAN, JAMIE (JAMIE ROBERT DUNCAN)
Football player. **Personal:** Born Jul 20, 1975, Wilmington, DE. **Educ:** Vanderbilt univ, BA, human & orgn develop. **Career:** Football player (retired); Tampa Bay Buccaneers, linebacker, 1998-2001; St Louis Rams, linebacker, 2002-03; Atlanta Falcons, linebacker, 2004; Business currently. **Orgs:** Bus Prof Am; Stud Promoting African-Am Cult. **Honors/Awds:** First-team all-SEC hon. **Special Achievements:** Featured on a poster promoting the importance of educ titled. *

DUNCAN, JAMIE ROBERT. See DUNCAN, JAMIE.

DUNCAN, JOAN A.
Government official, executive director. **Personal:** Born Sep 8, 1939, Butte, MT; daughter of Dr Walter E and Alyce M Driver. **Educ:** Syracuse Univ, attended 1958; Carroll Col, 1957. **Career:** Carroll Col, asst dean women, 1961-67; RDMC Comn Action Agency; dir, Foster Grandparent Prog, 1969-75; MT Dept Labor & Indust, Chief Women's Bur, 1975-81; City Helena, city comnr, 1982-86; MT Legis, 1983-87; Helena Food Share Inc, exec dir, 1987-91; Hennesys Dept Store, promotions dir & personnal shopper, 1992-. **Orgs:** Bd dir, Model Cities, 1972-74; dir, Helena Area Econ Develop Inc, 1985-87, Rocky Develop Coun Inc, 1982-86, United Way, 1973-89; writer producer host Leg, 1979-, TV Prog, 1979, Women's Window R Dio 52 Stations, 1981, 51%, 1976-81, Guardian Culch TV Prog, 1982-86; Last Chance Press Club, 1976-, MT Dem Party, 1980-, Lewis & Clark Health Bd, 1983-86; Lewis & Clark County Tax Appeals Bd; MT Communities Found; co-chmn, Proj Progress, Jobs for Helena's Future, 1990-; MT Food Bank Network, exec dir, 1991-92. **Honors/Awds:** Outstanding Young Women of America, 1970; Montana Carrying the Torchin Troubled Times, 1974. *

DUNCAN, DR. LOUIS DAVIDSON, JR.
Physician. **Personal:** Born Oct 26, 1932, Lancaster, SC; son of Louis and Minnie. **Educ:** Howard Univ, BS, 1954; Howard Univ Sch Med, MD, 1958. **Career:** pvt practice physician, currently. **Orgs:** Med Surgical Soc DC Inc; Nat Med Asn Mt Airy Baptist

Ch; Phi Beta Kappa. **Business Addr:** physician, 1105 Buchanan St, Washington, DC 20011, **Business Phone:** (202)882-3221.*

DUNCAN, LYNDA J
Government official. **Educ:** Motlow State Comm Col, AS, 1984. **Career:** Ray Belue & Assocs, model & actress, 1974-77; Univ Tenn, contract coord, 1978-81; City Tullahoma, ct clerk, 1982-86; WKQD FM/AM, mkt consult & copywriter, 1986-. **Orgs:** Circle Player, Atlanta, 1974-76; fund raiser Comm Action Guild, 1977-79; coord, youth activ Mt Zion Baptist Church, 1977-79; sponsor, Black Hist Club Tullahoma HS, 1978-79; treas, bd dir Tullahoma Day Care Ctr, 1979-81; chair, C&D Stamps Scholar Fund, 1982-86; bd dirs, TENCO Develop Inc, 1986-. **Special Achievements:** Has appeared as a model in Ebony-Essence-GQ-Madamoiselle, 1974-79. Appeared as prin character in numerous natlly distrib commercials. **Business Addr:** Marketing Consultant, Copywriter, WKQD FM/AM, Westside Dr, Tullahoma, TN 37388.

DUNCAN, MARVIN E.
Educator, manager, executive. **Personal:** Born Nov 23, 1939, Greenville, NC; son of Leroy (deceased); married Sandra Fields Duncan, Mar 25, 1981; children: Crystal Lynn, Catayah Angelia. **Educ:** NC Col, Durham NC, BA, Math, 1962, MA, Educ, 1963; Univ Va, Charlottesville Va, attended 1970; Mich State Univ, E Lansing Mich, PhD, Inst Develop & Educ Psychol, 1972. **Career:** NC Central Univ, asst dir, Learning Resources Ctr, 1963-70, dir, Learning Resources Ctr, prof educ. **Orgs:** Evaluation consult, Ohio State Univ, 1971; test consult, Stanford Res Inst, Menlo Pk Calif; chmn, Durham Chamber Com Leadership Develop Community, 1981; planning consult, NC Schs & Cols; bd dir, Edgemont Community Ctr, Durham NC, 1986-87; bd mem, Child Care Food & Nutrition Network, 1986-87; NC Ment Health Asn, 1986-87, Alpha Phi Alpha Frat; Asn Educ Commun Technol; NC Asn Educ. **Honors/Awds:** Outstanding Research Award, NC Cent Univ, 1988; Distinguished Service Award, NC Cent Univ, 1988. **Special Achievements:** Author of 17 publications in the field of educ. *

DUNCAN, MICHAEL CLARKE
Actor. **Personal:** Born Dec 10, 1957, Chicago, IL; son of Jean. **Educ:** Alcorn State Univ; Kankakee Community Col. **Career:** People's Gas Co, ditch digger; nightclub bouncer; body guard for Will Smith & Martin Lawrence; Films: Friday, 1995; Back In Business, 1997; Caught Up, 1998; The Players Club, 1998; Bulworth, 1998; Armageddon, 1998; A Night At Roxburt, 1988; Breakfast of Champions, 1999; The Green Mile, 1999; The Whole Nine Yards, 2000; Soldier of Fortune (voice), 2000; See Spot Run, 2001; Cats & Dogs (voice), 2001; Planet of the Apes, 2001; The Scorpion King, 2002; Daredevil, 2003; George of the Jungle 2 (voice), 2003; Brother Bear (voice), 2003; SOCOM II: US Navy SEALS (voice), 2003; George & the Dragon, 2004; Pursued, 2004; The Island, 2005; Talladega Nights: The Ballad of Ricky Bobby, 2006; Sch for Scoundrels, 2006; One Way, 2006; American Crude, 2007; The Last Mimzy, 2007; Slipstream, 2007; Welcome Home, Roscoe Jenkins, 2008; TV Film: They Call Me Sirr, 2001; Kim Possible: A Sitch in Time (voice), 2003; Racing Stripes, 2005; "Teen Titans", 2005; The Suffering: Ties That Bind, 2005; "Beyond the Glory", 2005; "Loonatics Unleashed", 2005; Saints Row, 2006. **Honors/Awds:** Golden Globe Award, Best Supporting Actor, for The Green Mile, 2000; Screen Actors Guild Award, Best Supporting Actor, for The Green Mile, 2000; Nominee for Oscar for Best Actor in a Supporting Role, 2000; Saturn Award for Best Supporting Actor, 2000; Black Reel Award for Theatrical-Best Supporting Actor, 2000; BFCA Award for Best Supporting Actor, 2000; Nominee for Golden Globe Award for Best Performance by an Actor in a Supporting Role in a Motion Picture, 2000; Nat Asn Advan Colored People Image Award. **Business Addr:** Actor, Delores Robinson Entertainment, 112 S Almont Dr, Los Angeles, CA 90048-2911, **Business Phone:** (310)777-8777.

DUNCAN, PEGGY
Entrepreneur, consultant. **Educ:** Ga State Univ, Atlanta, BS, mkt. **Career:** Duncan Resource Group Inc, chief exec officer, currently; consult, currently. **Orgs:** Nat Asn for Female Executives. **Honors/Awds:** Best & brightest entrepreneurs, Who's Who in Black Atlanta, 2004, 2005 & 2006. **Special Achievements:** Author: Just Show Me Which Button to Click! in PowerPoint 2003; Put Time Management to Work and Live the Life You Want; and Conquer Email Overload with Better Habits, Etiquette, and Outlook Tips and Tricks. **Business Addr:** Chief Executive Officer, Duncan Resource Group Inc, 1010 Pine Tree Trl, Atlanta, GA 30349, **Business Phone:** (770)907-8868.

DUNCAN, ROBERT M
Lawyer. **Personal:** Born Aug 24, 1927, Urbana, OH; son of Benjamin A and Kathleen Wanda; married Shirley A Duncan; children: Linn, Vincent & Tracy. **Educ:** Ohio State Univ, BS, 1948, JD, 1952, LLD, 1979. **Career:** Gen law pract, Columbus OH, 1954-57; State Ohio, asst atty gen, 1957-59; Bur Workmen's Compensation, atty examiner, 1959-60; City Columbus OH, asst city atty, 1960-63; chief, workmen's compensation section, 1963-65; atty gen Ohio, chief coun, 1965-66; Franklin County Municipal Ct, judge, 1966-69; Supreme Ct Ohio, justice, 1969-71; US Ct Military Appeals, judge, 1971-74, chief judge, 1974; US Dist Ct Southern Dist Ohio, Columbus OH, judge, 1974-85; Jones, Day, Reavis & Pogue, Columbus OH, partner, 1985-92; Ohio State Univ, vpres & gen coun, 1992-96, vpres emer, 1996-, col Law Jurist residence, 1996;The Ohio State Univ, Acad & Stud Affairs Comm, vice chair, currently. **Orgs:** Am Bar asn; Ohio State Bar asn; Columbus Bar asn; Columbus Bar Found; Fed Bar asn; Sixth Circuit Judicial Conf fel Am Col Trial Lawyers; judicial panel mem, Ctr Public Resources; Nat Ctr State Courts; Ohio State Univ Col Law Alumni asn; bd visitors, Wake Forest Law Sch; chair, Nat Coun Ohio State Univ Col Law; US Ct Military Appeals Ct Committee; Phi Delta Phi; Kappa Alpha Psi; Sigma Pi Phi; chair, Ohio State Univ Bd Trustees. **Honors/Awds:** Franklin Univ Law Sch Liberty Bell Award, 1969; Ohio State Univ Alumni Centennial Award, 1970; Columbus Urban League Equal Opportunity Award, 1978; Alpha Kappa Alpha Humanitarian Award, 1980; Omega Psi Phi Fraternity Citizen of the Year, 1984; Columbus Education Assn Martin Luther King Award, 1984; Ohio Bar Medal for unusually meritorious service, 1985; Ohio State Univ Ralph Davenport Mershon Award, 1986; ACLU Award, 1986; Christopher Columbus Achievement Award, 1986; HDL, Ohio State Univ, Central State Univ, Wilberforce Univ, & Ohio Northen Univ. **Military Serv:** AUS, 1952-54. **Business Addr:** Vice Chairman, The Ohio State University Board of Trustees, Academic & Student Affairs Committee, 154 W 12th Ave Enarson Hall, Columbus, OH 43210, **Business Phone:** (614)292-6446.

DUNCAN, SANDRA RHODES
Executive, president (organization). **Personal:** Born Nov 16, 1944, Chicago, IL; daughter of Duplain W Rhodes Jr and Doris Millaud; divorced; children: Sabrina, Otis Jr, Orrin, Omar, Ashea Duncan. **Educ:** Commonwealth Col Mortuary Sci, 1969; La State Univ, exec mgt, 1991. **Career:** Duplin W Rhodes Funeral Home Inc, lic, funeral dir, 1962-; Airport Rhodes Transp Inc, pres, 1986-91; Rhodes Enterprises, pres, 1991-. **Orgs:** chairwoman, Jr Achievement, 1992-93; Bus Coun New Orleans & The River Region; World Trade Ctr; La Coun Fiscal Reform, Amistad Resh Ctr; New Orleans Ctr Creative Arts; New Orleans Chap Links; mem bd, Dryades Savings Bank, FSB. **Honors/Awds:** Certificate of Merit for Outstanding Service, City New Orleans, 1988; National Business League Award, 1988; Humanitarian Award, St Mark Missionary Baptist Church, 1989; Certificate of Appreciation, City New Orleans, 1986-92; Certificate of Appreciation, The Good Samaritan Comt, 1992. **Business Addr:** President, Rhodes Enterprises, 1716 N Claiborne Ave, New Orleans, LA 70116, **Business Phone:** (504)943-6621.*

DUNCAN, SYDNEY REE
Executive. **Personal:** Born Sep 29, 1937, Dallas, TX; daughter of Elijah L and Fannie Earl Carter; divorced; children: Shirley, Michelle & Walter Duncan. **Educ:** Tex Southern Univ, BA, 1959; Univ Wis, attended 1961; Wayne State Univ, MSW, 1996. **Career:** Executive (retired); Pontiac Pub Sch, social worker, 1966-69; Homes Black C, prog dir, 1969-71, pres & chief exec officer, 1972. **Orgs:** Academy Certified Social Workers; Nat Ctr on Permanency for African Am Children, founding mem, advisory bd; Foundation for Community Encouragement, bd dirs; 15th Congressional dist, Community Advisory Bd; White House Task Force on the Black Family, participant, 1994. **Honors/Awds:** North American Council on Adoptable Children, Advocate for the Year Award, 1989. **Special Achievements:** Detroit Historical Museum, exihibit, "Black Women in MI History," 1984-85; published "Healing Old Wounds," Parenting Resource Manual, 1988.

DUNCAN, TIM
Basketball player. **Personal:** Born Apr 25, 1976, St. Croix, VI; son of William duncan and Lone duncan. **Educ:** Wake Forest, BA psychol. **Career:** San Antonio Spurs, ctr & forward, 1997-. **Orgs:** Founder, Tim Duncan Found; Tim Duncan's Character Prog, Spurs Found. **Honors/Awds:** John Wooden Award, 1997; Rookie of the Yr, NBA, 1997; NBA All-Star, 1998;NBA Champion, 1999, 2003, 2005; NBA Most Valuable Player, 1999, 2001-03;co-Most Valuable Player, All-Star Game, 2000; Athens Olympic Game Medalist, 2004. **Special Achievements:** The 2nd player in NBA hist to be named to both an All-NBA Team & an All-Defensive Team. **Business Addr:** Professional Basketball Player, San Antonio Spurs, 1 SBC Ctr, San Antonio, TX 78219, **Business Phone:** (210)444-5000.*

DUNCAN, VERDELL
Executive, government official, labor relations manager. **Personal:** Born May 9, 1946, Arkadelphia, AR; children: Constanc Regina, Cameron Chad & Jacobi Edwin. **Educ:** Henderson State Univ, BSE, 1968; Eastern Mich Univ, MA, 1974, MA, 1976. **Career:** Greater Flint OIC, dir training, 1972-73; City of Flint, flint police officer, 1973-77; City of Flint Retirement, trustee retirement bd, 1977-79; CON-CAM Publ Corp, owner; City of Flint Hurley Med Ctr, 1st ward councilman, adminr Cult Diversity; Acad Flint Charter Sch, dir, currently; Ctr Educ Performance & Info, prin, currently. **Orgs:** Urban League; Nat Asn Advan Colored People; Coun liason, City Flint Human Rels Comn; Mich Asn Hosp Personnel Dirs; bd mem, Partner In Progress; secy, Mich Asn Affirmative Action Off; pres/owner, Twin & Assoc, 1983-; Omega Psi Phi Fraternity; coordr, Hurley Med Ctr Employee Assistance Prog; bd mem, Community Recovery Ctr; bd mem, Community Coalition; bd mem, Genesee County Fedn Blind. **Military Serv:** AUS, spec 4, 1969-71; Combat Med Badge; Nat Defense Medal. **Home Addr:** 6906 Daryll Dr, Flint, MI 48505. **Business Addr:** Director, Academy of Flint Charter School, 4100 W Coldwater, Flint, MI 48504.

DUNGEE, MARGARET R.
Teacher. **Personal:** Born in Richmond, VA; married Winfred A; children: Veronica Dungee Abrams. **Educ:** Va Union Univ, BA, 1962; Va Commonwealth Univ, MA, 1971; Howard Univ; Univ Va. **Career:** Teacher (retired); Fairmount Sch, teacher, 1962-69; John B Caly Sch, 1969-70; Southampton, resource teacher, 1971-72; Westhampton, diag prescriptive teacher, 1972-74; Richmond Pub Schs, human rels adv specialist, 1974-; Thirteen Acres Residential Sch, spec educ 1981-86; Richmond Pub Schs Clark Springs, teacher, 1986-94; Va Union Univ, reading instr, 1994-2001. **Orgs:** Pres & vpres, PTA Fairmont Elem Sch, 1959-61; pres, Richmond Educ Asn, 1973-74; pres, Delta Sigma Theta, 1979-81; vol, McGuire Community Hosp; advanced gift chmn, Va Fund Renewal Conf Am Bapt Church & Progressive Nat Bapt; pres, sr chair, 5th Baptist Church; pres, Mission Soc 5th Baptist Church; tutor reading, vol; BGC; ABCOTS; ABCOT USA; Church WM United. **Honors/Awds:** Ten Year trophy, PTA Serv, 1969; Teacher of the Year, 1991.

DUNGEY, MERRIN
Actor. **Personal:** Born Aug 6, 1971, Sacramento, CA. **Educ:** Univ Calif, Los Angeles, BA. **Career:** TV Show: "Black Like Who?"; film: Deep Impact, 1998; TV series: "Party Girl", 1996; "King of Queens", 1998; "ED tv", 1999; "Malcolm in the Middle", 2000; "The Sky Is Falling", 2000; "Alias", 2001-06; "Scream at the Sound of the Beep", 2002; "Summer land", 2004-05; "Beyond", 2006; "The King of Queens", 1999-2007; "Grey's Anatomy", 2007; "Angel of Death", 2007, "Grey's Anatomy", 2007; "Surviving Suburbia", 2009; "Better Off Ted", 2009. **Honors/Awds:** UCLA Acting Award. **Business Addr:** Actress, C/o The Disney Studios, 500 S Buena Vista St, Burbank, CA 91521.*

DUNGIE, RUTH SPIGNER
Consultant. **Personal:** Born in New York, NY; daughter of William M Spigner and Fannie W Spigner; married Elias; children: Christopher David. **Educ:** Col New Rochelle, BA, 1975; New Sch Social Res, MA, 1980; Univ New Haven, MBA, 2002. **Career:** ROLM Co, Norwalk, Conn, mgr, employee rels, 1989-92; IBM, personnel prog admin, 1981-83, corp litigation mgr, 1983-85, EEO prog adminr, 1985-86, personnel res surv adminr, 1987-89, Global Employee Res, sr HR consult, 1992-. **Orgs:** Alpha Kappa Alpha Sor; Nat Black MBA; Greater Hudson Valley Chap Links Inc; Soc Human Resource Mgt. **Home Addr:** 205 Langdon Ave, Mount Vernon, NY 10553, **Home Phone:** (914)667-8070. **Business Addr:** Senior Human Resource Consultant, IBM Corporation, 1 New Orchard Rd, Armonk, NY 10504-1722, **Business Phone:** (914)765-4283.

DUNGY, DR. CLAIBOURNE I.
Physician, educator. **Personal:** Born Jan 1, 1938?, Chicago, IL; married Madgetta T; children: Kathryn & Camille. **Educ:** Eastern Ill Univ, BS, 1962; Univ Ill, MD 1967; Johns Hopkins Univ, MPH, 1971. **Career:** Univ Colo, Dept Pediats, 1971-75; Univ Calif, Irvine, Dept Pediats, 1975-88, Div Gen Pediats, chief, 1976-80, 1985-88; consult, KOCE TV, 1980-88; Univ Iowa, Nat Health Law & Policy Resource Ctr, sr assoc dir, currently, Dept Pediat, prof pediat & epidemiol, 1988-, Div Gen Pediat & Adolescent Med, dir, currently. **Orgs:** Am Pub Health Asn, 1971-; Ambulatory Pediat Asn, 1973-; reg dir, Region XIII AAP Head Start Prog, 1974-75; Calif State Child Health Bd, 1977-82;consult, Brookhaven Nat Labs Marshall Islands, 1982-; bd, Urban League Orange County Chap, 1982-88; co chair, APA Region IX, 1987-88, Region VI, 1993-95; Asn Acad Minority Physicians, 1991-2004; bd dirs, Goodwill Southeast Iowa, 1993-2003, bd chair, 2000-02; Am Pediat Soc, 1994-; Am Acad Pediat, 1975-, comt pediat res, 1995-2001, coun gov affairs, 1996-99; ed bd, Archives Pediat & Adolescent Med, 1996-2002; bd dirs, Ambulatory Pediat Asn, 1996-99, Am Bd Pediat, 1999-; pres elect, 2005-06, pres, 2006-07. **Honors/Awds:** Distinguished Alumnus, Eastern Ill Univ, 1979; Minority Alumni Hall of Fame, Eastern Ill Univ, 1994. **Military Serv:** AUS, 1956-58. **Business Addr:** Professor Pediatrics, Director Division of General Pediatrics and Adolescent Medicine, University Iowa, The Children's Hospital of Iowa at UIHC, 2627 JCP 200 Hawkins Dr, Iowa City, IA 52242-1083.

DUNGY, MADGETTA THORNTON
Educator, school administrator. **Personal:** Born Jan 1, 1942, Lynchburg, VA; daughter of Edgar T and Madge Meadors; married Claibourne I; children: Kathryn & Camille. **Educ:** Cornell Col, IA, BA, polit sci, 1964; Univ Colo, Boulder, MA, educ, 1974; Univ Iowa Col Educ, PhD, 1997. **Career:** Educator, school administrator (retired); Chicago Urban Renewal Comn, field rep, 1964; Chicago Sch Bd, high sch teacher-counr, 1964-67; Univ Utah, admis counr, 1967-68; Stanford Univ, financial aids officer, 1968-70; Girl Scout Coun, dir mem serv, 1979-86, counr summer bridge prog; Univ Calif-Irvine, student affairs officer; Univ Iowa Carver Col Med, assoc, stud affairs, dir, minority progs, 1988, asst dean fac affairs & develop, 2000-05. **Orgs:** Nat Asn Stud Person-

nel Admin, 1973-; Calif Asn Coun & Develop, 1975-88; Orange City Vis Nurses Asn, 1976-81; adv bd coun, Gifted & Talented, 1978-; Dirs Vols Agencies, 1979-86; charter mem, Jack & Jill Am, 1980-88; Links Inc, 1982-88; citizens adv coun, KOCE TV, 1983; Nat Asn Med Minority Educr Inc, 1989-; golden life mem, Delta Sigma Theta Sorority Inc; vpres, Orange City Chapter; bd mem, IA Women's Found; Am Asn Higher Educ.

DUNGY, TONY
Football player, football coach. **Personal:** Born Oct 6, 1955, Jackson, MI; son of Wilbur and Cleomae Dungy; married Lauren; children: Tiara, Jade, Eric, Jordan, Justin & James (deceased). **Educ:** Univ Minn, BA, 1977. **Career:** Football player (retired), football coach; Pittsburgh Steelers, safety, 1977-78; San Francisco 49ers, 1979; NY Giants, 1980; Univ Minn, defensive backs coach, 1980; Pittsburgh Steelers, defensive asst, 1981, defensive backs coach, 1982-83, defensive coordr, 1984-88; Kans City Chiefs, defensive backs coach, 1989-91; Minn Vikings, defensive coordr, 1992-95; Tampa Bay Buccaneers, head coach, 1996-2001; Indianapolis Colts, head coach, 2002-. **Orgs:** Nat spokesperson, Am Diabetes Asn, African Am Prog & Sch Walk Diabetes campaign, 2003. **Honors/Awds:** Prof Coach of the Yr, Maxwell Football Club, 1997; Fatherhood Award, Nat Fatherhood Initiative, 2002; Coach of 2007. **Special Achievements:** First African American coach to win SuperBowl; Youngest assistant coach in NFL history; Author: Quiet Strength. **Business Addr:** Head Coach, Indianapolis Colts, 7001 W 56th St, Indianapolis, IN 46254, **Business Phone:** (317)297-2658.

DUNHAM, CLARENCE E.
Consultant. **Personal:** Born Aug 29, 1934, Syracuse, NY; son of Clarence and Leona Shepard; divorced; children: Audrey, Tracey, Joi & Roderick Stubbs. **Educ:** Syracuse Univ, 1953; AUS, Comm Tech Teletype Sch, 1959. **Career:** Consultant (retired). W Elec Co Inc, 1953-69; NY Telephone Co, commun consult, 1969-83; AT & T, asst mgr, 1983-87; Syracuse Cty Legislator, 2007. **Orgs:** Past coun mem, Syracuse Neighbourhood Health Ctr; bd dir, Dunbar Ctr social serv & facil; pres, Grand St Boys; adv, Jr Achievement Orgn, 1972-73; Co Legislator, 1973; bd dir, PEACE Inc, 1974; bd dir, WCNY TV, 1974; adv bd, Bishop Foery Found, 1974; bd dir, Onondaga Neighborhood Leg Serv, 1975; bd dir, Metro Syracuse Bus Ind Educ Coun, 1975; exec com, Northern Region Black Pol Caucus; pres, Southwest Community Ctr, 1989. **Honors/Awds:** Citation from Jr Achievement, 1972; First runner-up in YMCA Black Achievement Award, 1973; YMCA Black Achievement Award, 1975. **Military Serv:** AUS, 1957-59. **Home Addr:** 824 S Ave, Syracuse, NY 13207-1817, **Home Phone:** (315)478-1058. *

DUNHAM, ROBERT
Restaurateur. **Personal:** Born Jan 1, 1932?, Kannapolis, NC; married. **Career:** NY Waldorf-Astoria Hotel, salad man; McDonald's Franchise Harlem, pres. **Military Serv:** USAF.

DUNIGAN, MAYME O.
Manager, teacher, counselor. **Personal:** Born Oct 4, 1921, Darling, MS; daughter of George W Simmons and Corrie Cade; married Charles Dunigan; children: 5. **Educ:** Lincoln Univ; Wayne State Univ; Merrill Palmer Inst, Cert Home Mgt; Wayne State Univ, BS. **Career:** Manager, Counselor, Teacher (retired); MO Pub Sch, teacher; Mayors Comn Human Resources Develop, City Detroit, home mgt adv, 1965-70; Mayors Comn Human Resources Develop, social planner, 1970-76; Neighborhood Serv Dept, City Detroit, counr. **Orgs:** Founding mem, 1st Independence Bank Detroit; Womens Guild 1st Independence Bank; secy, Lincoln Univ Alumni Assoc Detroit Chap, 1965-67, 1970-72, pres, 1972-74, chmn, 1973-79; Mayors Task Force on Hunger & Malnutrition 1972-75, Interim Comm Nutrition Prog 1973, Nat Adv Coun, Lincoln Univ Alumni Asn; Crime & Justice Task Force, Womens Conf Concerns, 1975-78; mem bd trustees, Gr Macedonia Bapt Church, 1978, chmn Budget Comt & Scholar Comt, 1978-79; bd dir, Transformation Employ, 1989-90; mem, bd dir, Boston MacFarlane Neighborhood Asn, 1997, 2002; Equal Justice Coun; pres, United Total Comm Deaf Met Detroit; mem bd trustees, C Hosp Mich; Women's Conf Concerns, Greater Macedonia Bapt Church; Mich State Mental Health Adv Coun Deafness; Unity of Hands Deaf Chorale Bd Dir; chair, Home Repair Proj; chair, Crime & Justice Taskforce. **Honors/Awds:** Achievement Mem Dr, NAACP, 1972; Chronicle Mother of the Year 1974; Distinguished Alumni Award, Lincoln Univ, 1976; nominated for "Heart of Gold" 1984. **Home Addr:** 8519 Kentucky St, Detroit, MI 48204, **Home Phone:** (313)491-4886. *

DUNLAP, ERICKA
Entertainer. **Personal:** Born Dec 29, 1981; married Brian Kleinschmidt, Feb 18, 2007. **Educ:** Univ Cent Fla. **Career:** The Miss Am Orgn, beauty contestant, Career in Country Music, currently. **Orgs:** Delta Sigma Theta Sorority. **Honors/Awds:** Miss Orlando, 2001; Miss Heart Florida, 2002; Miss City Beautiful, 2003; Miss Florida, 2003; Miss America, 2003, 2004. **Special Achievements:** The first African American woman to be crowned Miss Florida. *

DUNLAP, DR. KAREN F BROWN
Journalist, president (organization), educator. **Personal:** Born Jul 13, 1951, Nashville, TN; daughter of Charles Fitzgerald and Mary Shute; married Tony Brown (divorced); children: Asim, Christopher & Asha; married Henry L Dunlap. **Educ:** Mich State Univ, E Lansing, BA, 1971; Tenn State Univ, Nashville, MS, 1976; Univ Tenn, Knoxville, PhD, jour, 1982. **Career:** Nashville Banner, Nashville, TN, staff writer, 1969-71; Warner Robins Enterprise, Warner Robins, GA, ed, 1973; Macon News, Macon, GA, reporter, 1973-74; Tenn State Univ, Nashville, TN, asst prof com, 1975-85; Bickel Found, Karl A & Madira Bickel fel, 1979-80; Nashville Banner, assoc ed, 1983-85; Univ S Fla, Sch Mass Commun, Tampa, FL, asst prof, 1985-2003; St Petersburg Times, staff writer, 1986-92; Fla Endowment Fund, McKnight fel, 1986-87; Poynter Inst, St Petersburg, FL, assoc dir, 1989, dean & reporting, writing & editing fac, 1991, pres & managing dir, currently. **Orgs:** Soc Prof Journalists, 1980-; Asn Educrs Jour & Mass Communs, 1981-; Delta Sigma Theta Sorority, 1982-; Nat Asn Black Journalists, 1985-. **Business Addr:** President, Managing Director, Poynter Institute of Media Studies, 801 3rd St S, St Petersburg, FL 33701, **Business Phone:** (813)821-9494.

DUNLAP KING, VIRGIE M
Educator. **Personal:** Born Oct 9, 1940, Fayette, MS; daughter of Edward Lee and Luetter Massie Hunt; divorced; children: Rufus Daniel Jr & Jessica Chase. **Educ:** Jackson State Univ, Jackson, MS, BS, language arts, 1963; Univ Southern Calif, Los Angeles, CA, MA, educ, 1971; Univ Alaska, Fairbanks, AK, admin, 1982. **Career:** Educator (retired); FBNSBSD, Fairbanks, Alaska, teacher, 1973-97. **Orgs:** Alaska Juvenile Justice Adv Comt, N Star Youth Ct, 1997-; PGWM Prince Hall Grand Chap, OES; imperial dep, Desert D I; state loyal lady ruler, Heroines Jericho; chairperson, FEA Minority Caucus; chairperson, Alaska State Human Rights Comn; chair, NEAT Bd; life mem & pres, Nat Asn Advan Colored People; life mem, Jackson State Univ Alumni; Corinthian Baptist Church. **Honors/Awds:** Williard Bowman Award for Human Rights, NEA-Alaska, 1985; H Council Trenholm Memorial Award for Human Rights, NEA, Washington, DC, 1985; Martin Luther King, Jr Award, Community Services, Chap Martin Luther King Community, 1992. **Home Addr:** 4010 Dunlap Ave, Fairbanks, AK 99709.

DUNMORE, CHARLOTTE J.
Educator, social worker. **Personal:** Born Nov 16, 1926, Philadelphia, PA. **Educ:** Univ Pa, BS, 1949; Columbia Univ, MSSW, 1954; Brandeis Univ Florence Heller Sch, PhD, 1968. **Career:** Boston Childrens Serv Asn, supvr adoption dept, 1957-62; Episcopal Comn Serv, social worker, 1962-64; Simmons Col, Sch Soc Work, assoc prof,1967-77; Ment Health Ctr, consult, 1974; NIH, consult, 1975; Univ Pittsburgh, Sch Social Work, prof, 1977. **Orgs:** Bd mem, Nat Conf Social Welfare NIMH Fellowship, 1964-67; bd mem, New EngMed Ctr Accreditation Comn Coun Social Work Educ, 1976-79; rev panel, Coun Int Exchange Scholars, 1976. **Honors/Awds:** Career Scientist Development Award, Nat Inst Ment Health, 1972-77. **Home Addr:** 144 N Dithridge St, Pittsburgh, PA 15213, **Home Phone:** (412)621-2097. *

DUNMORE, GREG. **See DUNMORE, GREGORY CHARLES.**

DUNMORE, GREGORY CHARLES (GREG DUNMORE)
Journalist, fashion designer. **Personal:** Born Mar 24, 1958, Detroit, MI; son of Albert J and Jo Thompson. **Educ:** NAT UNIV Mexico, BA, spanish, 1979; Cornell UNIV, BS, indust & labor rels, 1980. **Career:** Jo Thompson Productions Inc, dir, fashion designer, 1985-; MIC Chronicle Newspaper Agency, columnist, 1987-; Black Entertainment Television, On Line Productions, entertainment reporter; Michigan Chronicle, Columnist, currently. **Orgs:** INT IST Metro Detroit, vip pub rels, bd, 1990-; NAB, 1987-; APA, 1989-; Harmonie Park Playhouse, adv bd, 1987-. **Honors/Awds:** Bachelor of the Year, Essence Magazine, 1992; MIC Winner, Beefeater Gin's Fashion & Jazz Competition; Fellow, MIC Opera Theatre; , Congressional Intern Fellow, Congressman Crockett. **Special Achievements:** Producer, writer, director: "Jo Thompson: This Is My Life-Melodies and Madness!!!" one-woman show, Carnegie Hall, 1991; "Jo Thompson Show," New York's legendary Michael's Pub, 1992; fashion designer: Carlos Nina Haute Couture label. **Business Addr:** Columnist, Michigan Chronicle, 479 Ledyard St, Detroit, MI 48201, **Business Phone:** (313)963-5522.*

DUNMORE, LAWRENCE A., JR.
Physician. **Personal:** Born May 17, 1923, Georgetown, SC; married Gloria Parker; children: Gwendolyn, Jacquelyn, Lawrence, III. **Educ:** SC State Col, BS; Howard Univ, MD; Johns Hopkins Univ, MPH, 1970. **Career:** DC Gen Hosp; DC Govt Sec Stand Investments & Stand Ltd Partnership, exec dir. **Orgs:** Health Adv Planning Comt; adv bd, Shaw Health Ctr; Health Priorities Subcomt; DC Govt Adv Bd, Phys Asst Sch Allied Health Howard Univ. **Honors/Awds:** Distinguished Public Service Award, Govt DC, 1973; Outstanding Performance Award, Dept Human Resources, DC, 1974. **Military Serv:** AUS. **Home Addr:** 1911 Sudbury Rd NW, Washington, DC 20012. *

DUNN, ALMEDA EFFIE
Executive. **Personal:** Born Sep 22, 1940, Chicago, IL; daughter of Donald L Barksdale and Vivian V Wilson; married Erwin Dunn, Jan 6, 1968; children: Volora V Watson & Dominique A. **Educ:** BS, criminal social justice, 1988, MS, criminal social justice, 1990. **Career:** US PO, Berkeley, CA, mail sorter; Chicago Police Dept, police officer; Star Detective & Security Agency Inc, corp sec, pres & chief exec officer, 1999-. **Orgs:** Vice chmn pvt detective bd, State Ill Dept Prof Regulation; vice chmn, Dept Employ Security Ill Employer Coun; Ill Employ Coun; W 76th St Area Coalition; dir, Nat Black Police Asn; dir, Nat Coun Invest Serv Inc; Ill Asn Detectives; Ill Security Chiefs Asn; bd dirs, Roseland Community Hosp. **Honors/Awds:** Outstanding Minority Owned Co, Minority Business News, 1999; Bus Excellence Awards, 1999; Top 100 by Minority Business News, USA, Ebony Magazine. **Military Serv:** USN, E-4, 1959-61; Good Behavior. **Business Addr:** President, Chief Executive Officer, Star Detective & Security Agency Inc, 813 E 75th St, Chicago, IL 60619, **Business Phone:** (773)874-1900.

DUNN, DAVID
Football player. **Personal:** Born Jun 10, 1972, San Diego, CA. **Educ:** Fresno State Univ. **Career:** Football player(retired); Cincinnati Bengals, wide receiver, 1995-98; Pittsburgh Steelers, 1998; Cleveland Browns, 1999; Oakland Raiders, 2000-01. *

DUNN, DAX
Executive. **Career:** Am Mortgage Inc; RAD Financial Services Inc, founder, pres & dir, currently. **Business Addr:** Founder & President, Director, RAD Financial Services Inc, 1060 Sunset Strip Ave Suite A, Sunrise, FL 33313, **Business Phone:** (954)587-2662.*

DUNN, JAMES EARL
Educator, real estate agent. **Personal:** Born Apr 7, 1955, Tunica, MS; son of Robert and Helen; married Dorothy Mae Collier. **Educ:** NW Jr Col, attended 1975; Ft Gordon Ga Community Sch, dipl, 1978; Ft Sill Field Artillery Sch, dipl, 1981; Delta State Univ, BS, 1978, MA, 1983. **Career:** Tunica Jr High Sch, sch teacher, 1978-; County Tunica, co supvr, currently; licensed realtor & real estate agt, currently. **Orgs:** Nat Guard Asn, 1978; Nat Asn Advan Colored People, 1980; Tunica County PTA, 1983; Miss Asn Supvrs, 1984; bd dir, Delta Coun; treas, Tunica Educ Asn, 1983-; bd dirs, N Delta Planning & Develop Dist, 1987; NW Miss Asn Realtors. **Honors/Awds:** US Jaycees, 1981; Man of the Year, United Voters of Tunica-Tunica County, 1983. **Military Serv:** ANG, capt, 1986. **Home Addr:** 1175 Hollywood Rd, PO Box 1463, Tunica, MS 38676.

DUNN, JASON (JASON ADAM DUNN)
Football player. **Personal:** Born Nov 15, 1973, Harrodsburg, KY. **Educ:** Eastern Ky Univ. **Career:** Football player (retired); Philadelphia Eagles, tight end, 1996-99; Kans City Chiefs, tight end, 2000-07; Free agt, currently. **Orgs:** Dunn 4 Kids Found. **Business Addr:** Free Agent, 101 State Place Suite F, Escondido, CA 92029, **Business Phone:** (760)743-4600.*

DUNN, JASON ADAM. **See DUNN, JASON.**

DUNN, JERRY MICHAEL
Basketball coach. **Personal:** Born May 6, 1953, Raleigh, NC; son of Maelene Dunn Leake; married Gwendolyn, Apr 10, 1977; children: Nichole, Taylor & Morgan. **Educ:** Wyo Jr Col, assoc degree; George Mason Univ, BS, educ, 1980. **Career:** George Mason Univ, asst coach, men's basketball, 1979-83; Penn State Univ, asst coach, men's basketball, 1983-96, head basketball coach,1996; West Va Univ, asst coach, 2003-07; Michigan Wolverine program, asst coach, 2007-. **Orgs:** Natl Asst Basketball Coaches; Black Coaches Asn; bd dirs, Second Mile Charity Organizer. **Honors/Awds:** NABC Coach of the Yr, District No 3, 1996. **Special Achievements:** Natl Clinician, USA Basketball Clins, 1996; Natl Camp Speaker coll, 1996. *

DUNN, LINDA SPRADLEY
Publisher. **Educ:** George Washington Univ; Harvard Univ, MBA Prog. **Career:** Int Bus Machines Corp, staff, 1983-94, bus unit mgr, Health Indust Mkt & Sales Support Strategy, mgr & founder; Women's Leadership Exchange, pres & ceo; Idamar Enterprises Inc, founder, pres & chief exec officer; Odyssey Media, chief exec officer & publ, currently. **Orgs:** Bd mem, NJ Performing Arts Women's Bd; bd mem, Essex County Col Found Bd; bd mem, United Way Essex. **Honors/Awds:** National Black Achievers Award; Newark's Female Entrepreneur of the Year. **Special Achievements:** First African American & Female Chair of United Way of Essex County; featured in Working Women Magazine, Essence Magazine, The Asian Times, O Magazine. **Business Addr:** Chief Executive Officer, Publisher, Odyssey Media, PO Box 10086, Singer Island, FL 33419, **Business Phone:** (561)881-0351.*

DUNN, MARVIN
Educator, psychologist. **Personal:** Born Jun 27, 1940, De Land, FL; married Linda Irene Lacy; children: Wanda, Fredrick, Kimberly, Jafari & Dierdre. **Educ:** Morehouse Col, BA, 1961; Roosevelt Univ, MA, 1965; Univ Tenn, Knoxville, PhD, psychol, 1972. **Career:** Educator (retired), executive; Miami, psychologist, 1970-71; Cult & Human Interaction Ctr, dir, founder, 1973-; Fla

Int Univ, Dept Psychol, from asst prof to assoc prof, 1972-2006; Acad Community Educ, founder & dir, 1981-; keynote speaker, US Info Serv, 1994; Overtown Community Garden, dir, 1999-; tech asst, Overtown Neighborhood Partnerships Proj; Roots in the City Proj, 2009. **Orgs:** Treas, Fla State Asn Dist Ment Health Bd, 1975-76; bd dir, Dade Co Found Emotionally Disturbed Youth, 1975; bd dir, Transition Inc, 1976-; pres bd, Driver Improv Prog, 1976-; comnr, Eleventh Judicial Circuit Nominating Comn, 1977; pres & bd mem, Human Inter-Action Potential Inc; consult, HEWOCD Ford Found Early Admin Col Scholar; Nat Asn Black Psychologists; Dade Co Psychol Asn; vpres, Dade Co Ment Health Asn; vpres, Dade-Monroe Dist Ment Health Dept; bd dir, Ctr Dialogue; Fla Coun Community Ment Health; Goldberg Comn Violence, South Africa. **Honors/Awds:** Award, KAY SE Region, 1957; Academic Scholar, 1969-61; Achiever of the Year, Achievers Greater Miami Inc, 1977; Educator of the Year, Fla Civil Rights Comm, 1989; Garden Crusader Winners, 2006. **Special Achievements:** Film: Murder on the Suwannee River: The Willie James Howard Story, director & producer. **Military Serv:** USN, lt, 1962-67; USS Kitty Hawk, officer aboard; USS Saratoga, officer aboard; US Naval Recruit Training Command, 14th Battalion, comdr. **Home Addr:** 3530 Crystal View Ct, Miami, FL 33133, **Home Phone:** (305)857-9701.

DUNN, REGINALD ARTHUR
Judge. **Career:** Judge (retired); Los Angeles County Super Ct, judge, 2002.

DUNN, ROSS
Executive. **Personal:** Married Rosa Lee; children: Martin De Rosseau, Rosephanye Tolandra, Kennedy Fitzgerald, Wilfred Julian. **Educ:** Ala State Univ, BS, M admin supvr. **Career:** Executive (retired); Dunbar Elementary Sch, Pine Mtn GA, teacher; Johnson Elem Sch, Whitesville GA, teacher; Laney Elem Sch, Waverly Hall GA, teacher; Johnson Elem Sch, West Point GA, prin; Macon County Sch Syst, asst supt; Muscogee County Sch Dist, admin asst; W Point Pepperell, personnel asst, personnel rels dept, 1974. **Orgs:** Nat Educ Asn; Muscogee County Asn; GA Educ Asn; AL Educ Asn; Textile Ind; pres, org, Chambers Cty Valley Br, NAACP; dir, pres, Huguley Water Syst; dir, Drew Rec Ctr; Goodwill Ind; AL Health Syst Agency; Chattahoochee Valley Area Asn Retarded C; bd mem, Chambers Cty Pensions & Security; Jr Achievement; Am Red Cross; Gov Staff, Montgomery AL; exec bd, George H Lanier Coun BSA; co-chmn, Chambers Co Child Abuse; Valley Chamber Com; Valley Chap, Ala State Univ Alumni; bd trustees, Ala State Univ; org, Chambers Cty Voter Reg, responsible 75 per cent Black registered voters; Chambers County CMS, 1988-93, reelected, 1992-96. **Honors/Awds:** Outstanding Serv, Boy Scouts Am, 1968; Outstanding 4-H Leader, 1969; Man of the Yr, 1970-71; Essie Handy Award, 1971; Administrative Spirit Award, 1972; NAACP Citation Award, 1973; Democratic Club Alabama Award, 1974; President's Award, NAACP, 1975; 100 Membership Award, NAACP, 1976-79; Responsible revamping elections, Chambers City Comn & Chambers City Bd Ed, 1976; Dist Award Merit, BSA, 1977; BSA Silver Beaver Award, 1978. **Special Achievements:** First Black elected, Chambers County CMS, Dist 1. *

DUNN, TRACI
President (Organization). **Educ:** Univ N Tex, Sch Merchandising & Hospitality Mgt, BS, 1994; Dallas Baptist Univ, orgn mgt. **Career:** Four Seasons Hotels & Resorts, human resorce mgr, 1995-98; Accenture, diversity specialist, 1998-2002; Compass Group, dir diversity, 2002-04; Dunn & Assocs, pres, 2004-. **Orgs:** Bd & conf chair, Diversity Coun Carolinas; charlotte chap pres, Nat Asn African Am Human Resources; Leadership Comt, Univ City Community Bldg Proj; co-chair, Charlotte Chamber Black Prof Network; Diversity Best Pract Comt, Charlotte Chamber. **Special Achievements:** Top 40 Under 40 Selectee by the Charlotte Business Journal. **Business Addr:** President, Dunn & Associates, PO Box 26175, Charlotte, NC 28221, **Business Phone:** (704)307-2650.*

DUNN, W PAUL
Aerospace engineer, administrator. **Personal:** Born Oct 2, 1938, Fort Worth, TX; son of Lillian and Willie; married Alnita Frances Rettig, Jun 2, 1962; children: Sheri & Brian. **Educ:** Univ TX, Austin, BS, Civil Engr, 1962; Calif State Univ, Los Angeles, MS, Civil Engr, 1969; Calif State Univ, Dominguez Hills, MBA, Bus Admin, 1976. **Career:** Rocketdyne, res engr, 1962-66; TRW Systs Group, mem tech staff, 1966-71; Northrop Corp, mgr engr, 1971-77; The Aerospace Corp, Launch Systs Anal Directorate, prin dir, currently. **Orgs:** Consult, Hi-shear Corp, 1970; adv bd mem, Calif State Univ, Los Angeles, Minority Engr Prog, 1983-86; chmn, Civil Engineering Vis Comt, 1987-88; charter mem, UT Austin Civil Engineering Dept, Acad Visting Alumni, 2003-. **Honors/Awds:** Public Service Award, Vpres US, 1966; Manned Space Awareness Award, NASA, 1968; Award of Record, TRW Systems Group, 1969; Specail Achievement Award, Sickle Cell Anemia Asn TX, 1979; Robert H Herndon Black Image Award, 1985; Distinguished Grad, Univ Tex, Austin, 1993. **Home Addr:** 5625 Glenford St, Los Angeles, CA 90008. **Business Addr:** Principal Director, Aerospace Corporation, 2350 E El Segundo Blvd M1/553, El Segundo, CA 90245, **Business Phone:** (310)336-5648.

DUNN, WARRICK DE'MON
Football player. **Personal:** Born Jan 5, 1975, Baton Rouge, LA. **Educ:** Fla State Univ, BS, info studies, 1997. **Career:** Tampa Bay Buccaneers, running back, 1997-01; Atlanta Falcons, running back, 2002-07. Tampa Bay Buccaneers, 2008. **Orgs:** Founder, Warrick Dunn Foundation. **Honors/Awds:** Named NFL Rookie of the Year by Football News, Pro Football Weekly, and Sports Illustrated, 1997; named Offensive Rookie of the Year by the Associated Press, Football Digest, and College and Pro Football Newsweekly, 1997; Pro Bowl, 1997; Walter Payton Man of the Year Award; Giant Steps Award; Jessie Tuggle Humanitarian Award, 2004; No. 1 Good Guy Award, Sporting News. Walter Payton Man of the Year Award, 2004; Bart Starr Award. 2009. **Business Addr:** Founder, Warrick Dunn Foundation, 3413 W Fletcher Ave, Tampa, FL 33618, **Business Phone:** (813)964-0100.*

DUNN, WILLIAM L. See Obituaries section.

DUNN-BARKER, LILLIAN JOYCE
Educator, counselor. **Personal:** Born Aug 9, 1938, Robbins, IL; daughter of Douglas Ivory Daniels and Margie Moore Wesley; married Timothy T, Aug 7, 1988; children: Darrin Douglas Dunn. **Educ:** St Augustine's Col, BA, 1960; Chicago State Univ, MS, 1976; Urban Sch Admin, endorsement prog, 1977. **Career:** Cert voc eval specialist; Mission Union Aid Soc, secy, 1956-91; Chicago Bd Educ, teacher eng & fr, 1960-76; Chicago Bd Educ, guid counr; Simeon Voc High Sch, Guid Dept, 1976; Chicago Bd Educ, chairperson, 1986; comnr. **Orgs:** Secy, Posen Robbins Sch Bd, 1983-85; secy, Robbins Ambulance Fund Comt, 1984-85; ruler, Pride Tobbins Temple No 915, 1988-91; adv, Chicago Bd Educ Peer Counr, 1991; Simeon, Chicago Bd Educ, Drug Free Schs Prog, 1991; secy, Ill Wis State Asn, Improved Benevolent Protective Order Elks World, Election Comt, 1991; Ill Fire & Police Commissioners Asn, Robbins, Ill, 1991-; Comn Cert Work Adjustment & Voc Eval Specialist; Phi Delta Kappa Prof Educ Fraternity; pres, Chicago State Univ, St Augustine's Col Alumni Asn; Alpha Kappa Alpha Sorority; Pride of Robbins Temple No 915 Elks, Improved Benevolent Protective Order Elks World. **Honors/Awds:** Grand Daughter Ruler Elks, 1974; Teacher's Award, Certificate Suburban Fed Credit Union, 1977. **Special Achievements:** One of the First Women on School Bd Dist 143 1/2; First Woman Secretary, 1983. **Home Addr:** 13735 S Trumbull St, Robbins, IL 60472.

DUNNER, DR. LESLIE BYRON
Conductor (music). **Personal:** Born Jan 5, 1956, New York, NY; son of Lloyd Bertram Dunner and Audrey Hemmings Dunner. **Educ:** Univ Rochester, Eastman Sch Music, Rochester, NY, BA, 1978; Queens Col, New York, NY, MA, 1979; Univ Cincinnati, Col Conservatory Music, Cincinnati, Ph.D, 1982. **Career:** Carleton Col, Northfield, MN, asst prof, 1982-86; Dance Theatre Harlem, New York, NY, princ guest coductor, 1986-99; Detroit Symphony, MI, resident conductor, 1987-99; Symphony Nova Scotia, music dir, 1996-99; Annapolis Symphony Orchestra, music dir, 1998; Joffrey Ballet, music dir & prin conductor, 2003-. **Orgs:** Bd dirs, Am Music Ctr, 1991-; music dir, 1998-. **Honors/Awds:** Third Prize, Arturo Toscanini Inter Nat Conducting Competition, 1986; Spirit of Detroit award, 1988; Named Man of the Year, Delta Phi Beta, Detroit, 1988; James Weldon Johnson Award, Nat Am Advan Colored People, 1991; American Symphony Orchestra League Award, 1994; Distinguished Young Alumnus Award, Univ Cincinnati, 1996. **Home Phone:** (410)295-0927. **Business Phone:** (312)739-0120.

DUNNIGAN, JERRY
Educator, artist. **Personal:** Born Jul 28, 1941, Cleveland, OH; married Roberta; children: James, Jerome, Jeffrey. **Educ:** Dayton Art Inst, Univ Dayton, BS, 1965; Ky State Univ, MA, 1970. **Career:** Linden Ctr, instr, 1964-65; Akron Art Inst, art instr, 1969-70; E Tech High Sch Black Acculturation Prog, instr Black Art, 1970-71; Nathan Hale Jr High Sch, dept chmn. **Orgs:** Nat Conf Artists; numerous exhibitions Comt Chmn, OH; Div World Festival Black Art, 1975. **Honors/Awds:** Scholarships, Columbus Col Art & Design, 1960-63; Univ Dayton, 1963-65; Martha Holden Jennings Found Teacher Leadership Award, 1973. **Business Addr:** 3588 East Blvd, Cleveland, OH 44105.

DUNNINGS, STUART
Lawyer. **Personal:** Born Oct 29, 1952, Lansing, MI; son of Stuart J and Janet Taylor; married Cynthia Marie, Oct 22, 1977; children: Courtney R & Coral S M. **Educ:** Amherst Col, BA, 1974; Univ Mich Sch Law, JD, 1979. **Career:** Dunnings & Frawley PC, atty, 1980-96; Ingham County, prosecuting atty, 1997-, prosecutor, currently. **Orgs:** Standing comt character & fitness, State Bar Mich, 1988-; secon vpres, Nat Asn Advan Colored People, Lansing Br, 1993; Prosecuting Attys Asn Mich; Trinity AME Church; Cath Educ Found; bd mem, Girl Scouts Mich Capitol Coun; bd mem, Mich State Univ Col Law; Youth Violence Prev Coalition. **Business Addr:** Prosecuting Attorney, Prosecutor, Ingham County, 303 W Kalamazoo St, Lansing, MI 48923, **Business Phone:** (517)483-6272.

DUNSON, DR. CARRIE LEE
School administrator. **Personal:** Born Apr 19, 1946, Kansas City, MO; daughter of Walter and Roberta King; divorced; children: Anthony & Darren Harris. **Educ:** Lincoln Univ, Jefferson City, MO, BS, Psychol, 1974; Cent MO State Univ, Warrensburg, MS

Corrections, 1975, Educ Spec, 1976; Univ MO, Ka, PhD, 1992. **Career:** Educator (retired); USMC, Kansas City MO, mail clerk supvr, 1967; Wash DC Police Dept, supvr documents, 1971; MO Div of Ins, Jefferson City, sec,test examiner 1973; Cent Mo State Univ, Warrensburg, instr criminal justice, 1975, asst prof indus security, 1978, dir equal employ, 1978-88, assoc prof criminal justice, 1992-2005. **Orgs:** Sponsor Sigma Gamma Rho Sorority, 1975; Asn Black Collegiates, 1975; Am Soc Indus Sect, 1978; Order Eastern Star KS Chap, 1973; Comn Human Rights,MO Comn Human Rights, 1976; co-chmn, Comn MO Affirmative Action Asn, 1979; Asn Black Women in Higher Educ, 1980; adv, LAE Club, 1998-. **Honors/Awds:** Hon Mention in Scholarship, Ford Found 1971; Outstanding Young Women of America, Montgomery, AL, 1978; Certificate of Appreciation, Jericho Rd Award MLK, 1979-80; Shirley Chisholm Leadership Award. **Special Achievements:** First African American female professor to retire from Central Missouri State University. **Home Addr:** 4939 College Ave, Kansas City, MO 64130, **Home Phone:** (816)923-9638.

DUNSTON, SHAWON DONNELL
Baseball player, athletic coach. **Personal:** Born Mar 21, 1963, Brooklyn, NY. **Career:** Baseball player (retired), coach; Chicago Cubs, infielder, 1985-95, guest coach; San Francisco Giants, 1996, spring instr, 2001-02; Chicago Cubs, 1997; Pittsburgh Pirates, 1997; Cleveland Indians, 1998; San Francisco Giants, 1998; St Louis Cardinals, 1999-2000; New York Mets, 1999; San Francisco Giants, spring instr, 2001-02; Dusty Baker Academy, instr, currently. **Honors/Awds:** Nat League All-Star Team, 1988 & 1990. **Business Addr:** Instructor, Dusty Baker International Baseball Academy, PO Box 1461, Pollock Pines, CA 95726, **Business Phone:** (480)644-6372.

DUNSTON, WALTER T.
Dentist, secretary of the navy, teacher. **Personal:** Born Jun 3, 1935, Williamsport, PA; children: Walter Jr, Michelle, Connie, Mark. **Educ:** Lycoming Col, BS, 1956; Temple Univ Dental School, DDS, 1960. **Career:** Secretary of the navy (retired), dentist, teacher; Temple Univ Dent Sch, instr, 1965-67; Univ PA Dent Sch, instr; Dent Serv Inst Pa Hosp, chief; pvt practice, dentist, currently. **Orgs:** bd trustees Lycoming Col; Am Dent Assoc; Nat Dent Assoc; PA State Dent Assoc; Fellow, Royal Sci Health London England; New Era Dent Sch of Philadelphia; pres, E Coast Investment Corp; commanding officer, Naval Reserve Dent Co 4-1; emm Naval Reserve Assoc, Philadelphia City Dent Soc. **Military Serv:** USN, Dent Corp, 31 yrs; navy capt, retired. **Business Addr:** Dentist, 2596 Balwynne Pk Rd, Philadelphia, PA 19131, **Business Phone:** (215)878-6744.*

DUPER, MARK SUPER
Football player. **Personal:** Born Jan 25, 1959, Moreauville, LA; married Renee; children: Tracy, Stacey, Mark II, Alexandria & Kirby. **Educ:** Northwestern State Univ-La. **Career:** Football player (retired); Miami Dolphins, wide receiver, 1982-92; Miami Hooters, 1994. **Orgs:** Omega Psi Phi Fraternity Inc. **Special Achievements:** Rated as number one receiver in AFC & number two in NFL by Sportsgames computer rating system.

DUPRE, DR. JOHN LIONEL
Psychiatrist. **Personal:** Born Dec 6, 1953, New Orleans, LA; son of Antoine Joseph Jr and Leverne Boutte; married Yadira Gisella McGrath Dupre, Sep 2, 1984; children: Joya Gabrielle Dupre. **Educ:** Tulane Univ, New Orleans, LA, BS, 1975; Tulane Med Sch ,MD, 1979; Univ Calif, San Francisco, CA, Residency Prog, 1983. **Career:** San Quentin State Prison, San Quentin, CA, staff psychiatrist, 1983-; pvt practice, Psychiatrist, San Francisco, CA, 1983-. **Orgs:** Former pres, Black Psychiatrists NC, 1985-89; Am Psychol Asn; NAMA. *

DUPREE, DAVID H.
Lawyer, educator. **Personal:** Born Aug 18, 1959, Knoxville, TN; son of William F and Eloise Edwards; married Aleathea A, Feb 18, 2000. **Educ:** Howard Univ Sch Bus & Pub Admin, BBA, 1981; Howard Univ Sch Law, JD, 1984. **Career:** Howard Univ Academic Computing Servs, student res asst, 1978-84, systems analyst, 1985-87; Self-Employed, res methodologist, 1979-; Law Off David Dupree, atty, 1985-; Howard Univ Sch Bus, instructor, 1990-94; pvt pract,atty, currently. **Orgs:** Computer Law assn, 1985-; DC Computer Law Forum, 1985-; Pa Bar assn, 1985;Pa Supreme Ct Bar 1985-; mem, Am Judicature Soc 1986; DC Bar assn, 1986,Tax Ct US, 1986-; Am Bar assn, 1986, DC Ct Appeals, 1986-; bd mem, Achievement Scholarship Prog, 1986-; mem, trustee bd, Greater Mt Calvary Holy Ch, 1988-; mem, US District Ct, DC, 1989-; mem, Delta Sigma Pi Bus Fraternity, 1980-; mem, Phi Alpha Delta Legal Fraternity, 1984-. **Honors/Awds:** Special Serv Award, Howard Univ Comp & Info System Soc, 1982; Meritorious Serv Award, Howard Univ Acad Computing, 1984; co-author, Affect Parent Practices on Reading Achievement, 1983; Does Rosen Still Live, An Analysis Gift Tax Income Exclusion on Non-income Producing Property, 1984.

DUPREE, EDWARD A
Administrator, executive. **Personal:** Born Mar 24, 1943, Farmville, NC; son of David and Nellie Fields Lunsford; married Helen

Roberts, Aug 14, 1965; children: Davido M. **Educ:** NC Cent Univ, BA, 1965; Howard Univ Sch Social Work, MA, social work, 1968. **Career:** Baltimore City Dept Social Serv, casework supvr, 1968-70; Model Cities Agency, Community Info Div, Baltimore, MD, chief, 1970-80; Urban Serv Agency, Baltimore, MD, Energy & Housing Progs, chief, 1980-. **Orgs:** NC Cent Univ Alumni Asn, 1966-; Howard Univ Alumni Asn, 1968-; Am Asn Blacks Energy, 1980-; House Resolution, Md House Deleg, 1980; City Coun Baltimore Resolution, Baltimore City Coun, 1982, 1987; Md Energy Dirs Asn, 1984-; Nat Forum Black Pub Admins, 1989-. **Honors/Awds:** Outstanding Md Energy Assistance Prog Dir, Md Dept Human Resources, 1987; Citizen Citation, City Baltimore, 1990; Vpres Citation, Vpres City Coun Baltimore, 1990. **Business Addr:** Chief, Urban Services Agency, 501 E Fayette St Lower Level, Baltimore, MD 21202, **Business Phone:** (410)396-8413.*

DUPREE, KIA
College teacher, writer. **Career:** Hampton Univ, prof english dept, currently. staff Dept Univ Relations, currently. **Special Achievements:** Written and co-authored many books. *

DUPREE, SANDRA KAY (SANDRA DUPREE CAMPBELL)
Librarian. **Personal:** Born Jul 17, 1956, Warren, AR; daughter of Asibear and Erie Ingram; married Bobby Charles Campbel; children: David Dupree Russell. **Educ:** Univ Ark, Pine Bluff, AR, BA, 1978; Atlanta Univ, Atlanta, GA, MSLS, 1979; Texas Woman's Univ, Denton, TX, 1985. **Career:** Pub Libr, Columbus & Franklin Co, Columbus, OH, intern, 1979-80; Bradley Co Libr, Warren, AR, dir, 1980-81; Univ Ark, Pine Bluff, AR, instr, 1982; SE Ark Regional Libr, Monticello, AR, specialist, 1982-83; Univ Ark, Monticello, AR, asst librn, 1984-97, assoc librn, beginning 1997, dir, currently. **Orgs:** Am Libr Asn, 1980-; Ark Libr Asn, 1980-; head nominating comt, Southeast Ark Concert Arts, 1987-98; bd mem, Friends of Monticello Br Libr, 1988-; bd mem, Ark Endowment Humanities, 1986-89. **Honors/Awds:** Honorary Member, Phi Kappa Delta, 1987. **Home Addr:** PO Box 312, Monticello, AR 71655, **Home Phone:** (870)367-2234. **Business Addr:** Director, University of Arkansas-Monticello, 514 Univ Dr, PO Box 3599, Monticello, AR 71656, **Business Phone:** (870)460-1180.*

DUPREE, PROF. SHERRY SHERROD
Religious scholar, bibliographer, educator. **Personal:** Born Nov 25, 1946, Raleigh, NC; daughter of Matthew Needham and Elouise Heartley; married Herbert Clarence, Jan 11, 1975; children: Amil, Andre & Andrew. **Educ:** NC Cent Univ, BS, Voc Home Econs, 1968, MA, Educ Media, 1969; Univ Fla. **Career:** Eastern Mich Univ, vis prof educ media, 1974; Ann Arbor Pub Schs, media specialist, 1970-76; Univ fla, assoc ref librn, 1977-83; Inst Black Cult, proj dir, 1982-92; Santa Fe Community col, ref librn, 1983-99, libr user serv coorde, 1999-2002, prof behavior sci, 2002, prof, stud develop instr, currently; Gospel Music Hall Fame & Mus, Detroit, archivist, 1995-; Gospel Music Traveling Exhibit, curator, 1994-; Fla Humanities Coun, exhibit consult; Books & articles: "Library Media Center & Classroom Displays", w/Hertha Jenkins, Media Spectrum, 1976; "Mini-Course in Library Skills", Univ Fla, 1983; "What You Always Wanted to Know About Card Catalog But Was Afraid to Ask", 3rd ed rev Displays for Schs Inc, 1987; African-American Holiness Pentecostal Movement: An Annotated Bibliography, Garland Publ, NY, 1996; African-American Good News (Gospel) Music, w/Herbert C DuPree, Middle Atlantic Regional Press, 1993; Exposed !!!: FDL Bureau Investigation (FBI) Unclassified Reports on Churches & Church Leaders, w/Herbert C DuPree, Middle Atlantic Regional Press, 1993; Biographical Dictionary African-American Holiness Pentecostals: 1880-1990, 1989; African American Holiness Pentecostal movement: Annotated bibliography Garland Library Social Sci, 1996; The Silent Spokesman Bishop Robert Clarence Lawson/Stewart & DuPree, 1998; A project of the Vanderbilt Divinity Library funded by the Association of Theological Schs with cooperation from the archivists of the Society for Pentecostal Studies, web site, 1999. Organizing Black Am: An Encyclopedia African American Associations/Mjagkij, 2001; New International Dictionary Pentecostal & Charismatic Movements/Burgess, 2002; League Innovations Presentation 2004; Encyclopedia of American Gospel Music/McNeil, 2006; Encyclopedia of Religious Revivals/ McClymond 2007; The Encyclopedia of Christian Civilization/ Kurian, 2008; Advisory Board member for the textbook Becoming A Master Student/Ellis, 2009; Library Credit Workshop, Roadmap to African American Reference Resources; spec collection, African-American Pentecostal & Holiness Collection. **Orgs:** MZeta Phi Beta Sorority Inc, 1967-; NAACP 1977-; Alachua Libr League 1977-; Williams Temple Church God Christ; Fla Libr Asn, 1980-; pres, Univ Fla Libr Asn, 1981-82; Fla Asn Community Cols, 1983-; Am Libr Asn; Asn Col & Res Libraries Fla Chapt; Black FOCUS; Soc Am Archivists, 1986-; Middle Atlantic Regional Gospel Ministries 1987-; Soc for Pentecostal Studies, 1987-; Black Family Develop, 1990-; Int Platform Asn; chair, Rosewood Massacre Forum, 1994-; Alachua Regional Marine Inst (ARMI), 1994-; Religion Caucus, Fla Libr Asn, chair, 1994-96; ed bd, 1994-, pres, 2000-01, Soc for Pentecostal Studies; Fla Asn Christian Librarians, 1996-; bd mem, Alachua County Hist Trust/ Matheson Mus, 1996-2001; Gospel Music Hall Fame & Mus Inc, archivist, 1996-; Univ Fla Ctr Autism & Related Disabilities (CARD), 1996-; pub serv rep, Col Ctr for Libr Automation (CCLA), 1998-2002; Black Caucus Am Libr Asn Newsletter; Fla Dept State, State Hist Marker Coun, 1999-2001; Friends Marjorie Kinnan Rawlings Farms Inc, 2000-; consult, Mission Agencies Who Preserve Church Archives; 2000-01; Fla State Geneal Soc, 2005-; Fla Storytelling Guild, 2006-. **Honors/Awds:** Procter & Gamble Award, NC Cent Univ, 1968, Grad Fel, 1968-69; Govt's Award for Outstanding Florida Citizen, State fla, 1986; Sojourner Truth Award, Int Women's Day, 19951; Humanitarian Award, Marion County Teen Cts, 1999; Honored, Libr Cong Bicentennial & Local Legacy Celebration, 2000; Santa Fe Community Col Wall Fame, 2000-01. **Special Achievements:** Exhibit designer of "The Rosewood Exhibit entitled: The Beginning That Never Ends.."; known as an exhibit designer of gospel music, dolls, Rosewood and other cultural exhibits; Known for libr prof credit workshop entitled, A Roadmap to African-American and Multicultural Resources (ARAAMR). **Business Addr:** Professor, Bibliographer, Santa Fe Community College, 3000 NW 83rd St, Student Serv S-212, Gainesville, FL 32606, **Business Phone:** (352)395-5407.

DUPRI, JERMAINE (JERMAINE DUPRI MAULDIN)
Executive. **Personal:** Born Sep 23, 1972, Asheville, NC; children: Shaniah. **Career:** Arista Records, sr vpres, 2003-; albums: Life in 1472, 1998; Instructions, 2001; Welcome to Atlanta, 2001; Green Light, 2004; Get Your Number, 2005; Gotta Getcha, 2005; TLC's CrazySexyCool; Mariah Carey's Daydream; tv movie: Carmen: A Hip Hopera, MTV, 2001; So So Def Recordings, CEO, currently. **Honors/Awds:** Songwriter of the Year, ASCAP, 1999. **Special Achievements:** Label acts include: Kriss Kross, Xscape, Da Brat, Yvette Michele; written and produced for: TLC, Mariah Carey, The Notorious B.I.G., Sylk Times Leather.:Listed top ten richest people in Hip-Hop; Top 25 greatest southern artists by Ozone Magazine. **Business Addr:** Chief Executive Officer, So-So Def Recordings, 685 Lambert Dr NE, Atlanta, GA 30324, **Business Phone:** (404)888-9900.

DURAND, HENRY J., JR.
Educator. **Personal:** Born Jun 14, 1948, Griffith, GA; son of Henry J Sr and Mildred C; married Bonita Ruth Cobb, Nov 12, 1979; children: Anitra R, Kendra N, Aprille L, Leroy Alan Larkin. **Educ:** Denison Univ, BA, sociol, 1971; Xavier Univ, MEd, 1976; Univ Cincinnati, EdD, 1988. **Career:** Cincinnati Bd Educ, classroom teacher, reading spt, 1974-76; Univ Cincinnati, inr, actg dir, reading & study skills prog, 1976-80, Col Med, dir, learning resources, 1980-82; Bushido Training Prog, training dir, 1982-86; Northern Ken Univ, asst prof, sociol, 1987-90; State Univ NY Buffalo, Ctr Appl Pub Affairs, sr res assoc, 1990, Ctr Acad Develop, dir, 1990; Educ Opportunity Prog, currently. **Orgs:** Am Educ Res Asn; Am Asn Higher Educ; Am Asn Univ Adrs; Am soc Training & Develop; United Univ Professions. **Home Addr:** 153 Winspear, Buffalo, NY 14215, **Home Phone:** (716)835-8244. **Business Addr:** Director, State University NY Buffalo, Ctr Acad Develop Serv, 208 Norton Hall, Buffalo, NY 14260, **Business Phone:** (716)645-3072.*

DURAND, WINSLEY, JR.
Consultant, engineer. **Personal:** Born Jul 29, 1941, Bunkie, LA; son of Winsley Sr (deceased) and Enola (Deceased); married Sonya Marie; children: Winsley III & Janay. **Educ:** USL, attended 1963; Southern Univ, BS, 1968; Bradley Univ, attended 1974; Univ Ill, MBA, 1987. **Career:** Caterpillar Tractor Co, jr sales develop engr, 1968-70, app engr, rels rep mgr, 1974-, equal employ cord, 1977-, mgr tech recruiting, 1987-; Western Engg, Acct cord, 1970-71, sales develop engr,1971-72, Sales, spec assignment employee rels, 1973; Caterpillar Inc, Peoria, Ill, quality improvement cord, 1988, Off Bus Practices, consult,currently; pvt investor. **Orgs:** Civil Rights Movement, 1960-65; pres, Peoria Black Polit Assembly, 1974-75; chmn, Voter Reg Dr, 1976; bd mem, Tri Co Labor Educ & Indust Coun, 1977; pres, Greater Peoria Big Brother/Big Sister, 1982; brd adv, Greater Peoria Found, 1986; bd mem, Peoria Pub Libr, 1987; pres, greater Peoria Libr Brd, 1992; pres, Greater Peoria Pvt Indust Coun, 1993-95. **Honors/Awds:** Outstanding New manite for Leadership, 1963; Outstanding Marine of Year Award, 1965; Dress Blue & Leather Neck Award, 1965; Outstanding Marine Award, Outstanding Leadership in Civilian Work Marines, 1969. **Military Serv:** USM, sgt.

DURANT, CELESTE MILLICENT
Media executive, executive. **Personal:** Born Apr 23, 1947, New York, NY. **Educ:** Grinnell Col, BA, Hist, 1968;Columbia Jour, MSJ, 1970. **Career:** Life Mag, publicity asst, 1968-70; Dayton J Herald, staff writer, 1970-72; La Times, staff writer, 1972; freelance writer; KCOP, exec producer; Univ Calif, Riverside, campus commun officer, currently, sr pub info officer, currently. **Honors/Awds:** Ohio Newspaper, Women's Feature Writing Award, 1971; Recip, La Press Club Award, 1974. **Business Addr:** Campus Communications Officer, University of California, A140 Highlander Hall 900 Univ Ave, Riverside, CA 92521, **Business Phone:** (951)827-7847.

DURANT, KAREN
Executive. **Personal:** Born in New York, NY; daughter of Frank and Frankie Jackson; divorced; children: Darren Emil Simon. **Career:** CBS Records, mgr, 1978-88; Jive Records Zomba Music, mgr, 1988-90; EMI Records, dir, 1992-94; Rondor Music, creative mgr, 1992, exec dir, gen mgr, 1994-. **Orgs:** Nat Acad Rec Arts & Sci. **Business Addr:** Executive Director, General Manager, Rondor Music International, 2440 Sepulveda Blvd Suite 119, Los Angeles, CA 90064.*

DURANT, NAOMI C.
Clergy. **Personal:** Born Jun 23, 1938, Baltimore, MD; daughter of Bishop Clem Williamson and Ruth Martin; married Albert; children: George, Victoria, Rodney, Hope. **Educ:** Baltimore Col the Bible, DD, 1970. **Career:** New Refuge Deliverance Holiness Church Inc, bishop founder, 1967-; 4 Churches Baltimore & Wash Area, overseer bishop; Radio Stations WEBB WSID WUST, gospel disc jockey, 1968-73. **Orgs:** Advocates Baltimore, 1971; Ada Chaplian 1 Order Eastern Star. **Honors/Awds:** Recipient honor BTH degree, MD Bible Col, 1972. **Business Addr:** Senior Pastor, Founder Archbishop, New Refuge Deliverance Holiness Church Inc, 1100 St Paul St Bishop DuRants Way, Baltimore, MD 21202, **Business Phone:** (410)752-6524.

DURANT, DR. THOMAS JAMES
College teacher. **Personal:** Born Apr 9, 1941, Mansfield, LA; son of Thomas J Sr and Lena B Jones; married Mary C Peyton; children: Thomas III, Timothee & Tyrone. **Educ:** Grambling State Univ, BS, 1963; Tuskegee Inst, MS, 1966; Univ Wis, Madison, PhD (rural sociol), 1973. **Career:** US Peace Corps St Lucia Proj, agr exten, 1963-65; Tuskegee Inst, res assoc, 1966-68; Univ Wis, res asst, applied demog lab, 1968-72; madison area tech col, adult basic educ recruiter, 1969; Va State Univ, assoc prof, 1972-73; La State Univ, assoc prof sociol, 1973-95, dir African & African Am Studies, 1997-2001, prof sociol, 1995-; ed, Sociol Spectrum Sociol Jour, 1984 & 1995. **Orgs:** Phi Beta Sigma Frat Inc, Omicron Beta Sigma, 1961-; Gamma Sigma Delta Hon Soc, La State Univ, 1979-86; Omicron Delta Kappa Leadership Soc, La State Univ Chap, 1986; NAACP; Am Sociol Asn; Southern Sociol Soc; Rural Southwestern Mid-South & Southwestern Societies; Mid-South Sociol Asn; Rural Sociol Soc; Southern Rural Soc. **Honors/Awds:** Beyond War Award, US Peace Corps Vol, 1987; Service Appreciation Award, La Asn Minority Criminal Justice, 1997 & 1999; Outstanding Teaching Award, La State Univ, 1998; Sociology Club Service Appreciation Award, African Stud orgn, 2001; Outstanding Educr & Community Service Award, Shiloh Baptist Church, 2002; Outstanding Service Award, Baton Rouge Kiwanis, 2002; received numerous other awards. **Special Achievements:** Author: Plantation Soc & Race Rels: The Origins of Inequality Westport, CT, 1999; Our Roots Run Deep: Hist of The River Road African Am Mus, Virginia Beach, VA, 2002; Numerous publications including "Sub-Saharan Africa: Prospects of Development in the New Millennium.", 1998; "Sociology and Public Health: Toward an Integrated Paradigm for Research on Violence.", 1999. **Home Addr:** 7826 Wimbledon Ave, Baton Rouge, LA 70810, **Home Phone:** (225)766-8233. **Business Addr:** Professor, Louisiana State University, Department of Sociology, 125 Stubbs Hall, Baton Rouge, LA 70803, **Business Phone:** (225)578-5315.

DURANT-PAIGE, BEVERLY
Public relations executive, music publisher. **Personal:** Born in New York, NY; daughter of Eunice Fuller and Wesley Durant; divorced; children: Desiree Spirit & Danielle Carrington. **Educ:** Hunter Col, attended 1974. **Career:** CBS Rec, New York, mgr publicity, 1978; Howard Bloom Pub Rels, New York, sr acct exec, 1983; PAIGE ONE Pub Rels, New York, pres/chief exec officer, 1985; Polygram Inc, sr dir nat publicity; Interscope Rec, vpres-,publicity, black music, Island Black Music, vp media rels, 1998; Island/Def Jam Music Group, vpres, 2000; PMTPR, pres, currently. **Orgs:** Pub Rels Soc New York; life mem, NAACP. **Honors/Awds:** The Lillian Award, Delta Sigma Theta, 1988; Award of Appreciation, New York Police Dept, 1989; Industry's Top Publicists, Ebony Mag. **Business Phone:** (845)659-1271.

DURDEN, EARNEL
Football coach, automotive executive. **Personal:** Born Jan 24, 1937, Los Angeles, CA; married June Pecot; children: Mike, Kevin & Allan. **Educ:** OR State Univ, BS, 1959; Calif State Univ, Long Beach, MA, 1969; Calif State Bd Educ, Life Diploma. **Career:** Football Coach, Automoative Executive (retired); LA Co Pks & Rec, dir, 1959-60; Jr High Sch, teacher coach entrpreners, 1960-63; Compton High Sch, backfield coach wrestling coach, 1963-66; Compton Col, defensive backfield coach, 1966-68; Versity Long Beach Calif State Univ, head fresh coach asst defensive backfield coach, 1968-69; Univ calif, off backfield coach, 1969-71; LA Rams, off backfield 1971-73; Houston Oilers, off backfield 1973-74; Gen Motors automobile dealer; San Diego Chargers, backfield rec, 1974-87, offensive backfield coach; Spec Sport Prog Young Men, spec asst dir & organizer. **Special Achievements:** Reciptant first black Joe Col OR State Univ, 1956-57; first black football coach California State University in Long Beach; first black coach La Rams; first black coach Houston Oilers; first team Pacfic Coast Conference, 1956-57.

DURDIN, GARY ROBERT. See DOURDAN, GARY.

DURE, GERARD
Beautician. **Career:** Gerard Dure Salon, owner & celebrity hairstylist, currently. **Business Addr:** Owner, Celebrity Hairstyl-

ist, Gerard Dure Salon, 635 W 125th St Second Fl, New York, NY 10027, **Business Phone:** (212)865-0201.*

DURHAM, C. SHELBY
Health services administrator, chief executive officer, president (organization). **Personal:** Born Jul 25, 1960, Crawl Hill, Bermuda; daughter of Coolidge and Julia L; married Melvin T Jackson, Sep 4, 1993. **Educ:** Bermuda Col, general cert educ, 1977; NC Agr & Tech State Univ, BA, 1981; Howard Univ, MS, 1983. **Career:** Dept Education, Bermuda, c devel diagnostician, 1981; Ministry Health & Social Servs, Bermuda, speech therapy intern, 1983; Howard Univ, teaching asst, 1983-84; In Speech, Inc, speech pathologist, 1984-86; Keystone Rehabilitation Systs, speech pathologist, 1986-87, dist dir, 1987-92; ROI HealthCare Continuum, pres & chief exec officer, 1992-99; At Home Health Inc, pres & chief exec officer, 1996-. **Orgs:** ASHA, 1983-96; NAWBO, 1995-96; NAFE, 1995-96; NCNW Inc, 1995-96. **Honors/Awds:** Recognition Award, Nat Coalition of 100 Black Women, 1993; Women to Watch, Bus Philadelphia & NAWBO, 1995; Small Bus of the Year, African-Am Chamber Com, 1995; 10 Making a Difference, The Philadelphia Inquirer, 1996; 25 Women of Distinction, Philadelphia Bus Jour's, 1998. **Business Phone:** (215)222-3325.*

DURHAM, REV. EDDIE L, SR.
Government official, clergy. **Personal:** Born Mar 17, 1946, Newellton, LA; son of Rev Albert E and Annie B Emerson; married Fannie Henderson, Dec 14, 1966; children: Eddie Jr & Robert. **Educ:** Southern Univ, Baton Rouge, LA, BA, eng, 1968; Harvard Univ, Cambridge, MA, attended 1967; Univ Utah, Salt Lake City, Utah, MS, admin, 1974. **Career:** Stauffer Chem Co, Dayton, NJ, mgt trainee, 1969-70; Agway Chem Co, Yardville, NJ, asst plant mgr, 1970-71; NJ Dept Labor, Trenton, NJ, claims reviewer, 1971-72, personnel asst, 1972-74, chief admin, 1974-76, admin dir, 1976-; Red Hot Publ Co, pres, 1989-; Home Income Reporter, newsletter, ed & publ, 1990-; Success Inc, pres, 1992; Saints Memorial Community Church, pastor, currently. **Orgs:** Polit Action Comn Willingboro, 1975-82; pres, Am Soc Pub Admin, NJ, 1976-77; dir, First Peoples Bank NJ, 1977-82; Willingboro Township Coun, 1977-82; dir, Saints' Memorial Community Church, 1979-; Blacks Govt, 1984-; Forum Black Pub Admin, 1986-; dir, Better Day Care Ctr, 1986-. **Honors/Awds:** Service Award, Saints' Memorial Community Church, 1983 & 1984; Service Award, Cathedral Love, 1989. **Special Achievements:** Editor/publisher, Home Income Reporter Newsletter, 1990-. **Business Phone:** (609)871-4779.

DURHAM, DR. JOSEPH THOMAS
College teacher. **Personal:** Born Nov 26, 1923, Raleigh, NC; son of Watt Sr and Serena Hooker; married Alice Spruill; children: LaDonna D Stamper & LaVerne. **Educ:** Morgan State Col, AB, 1948; Temple Univ, Ed.M, 1949; Columbia Univ, Ed.D,1963. **Career:** New Lincoln Sch, teacher, 1956-58; Southern Univ, prof, 1958-60; Coppin State Col, chmn educ, 1960-63, dean col, 1965-68, dean of educ 1975-76, lectr, adj prof; Albany State Col, dean & prof, 1963-65; Univ NH, vis prof, 1966; Ill State Univ, assoc dean educ, 1968-72; Howard Univ, dean sch educ, 1972-75; Md State Bd Higher Educ, dir inst approval; Community Col Baltimore, pres, 1985-90, pres emer; Morgan State Univ, prof; United Holy Church Am Inc, Holiness Union, ed, 1980-00; Montgomery County Human Rels, comnr, 1983-86. **Orgs:** Phi Delta Kappa; Alpha Phi Alpha. **Honors/Awds:** Fel Gen Educ Bd, 1953-54; Fel Dan forth Found, 1975; Presidential Leadership Medallion, Univ Tex, 1989. **Special Achievements:** The Story of Civil Rights as Seen by the Black Church, DC Cook Publishing Co, 1971. **Military Serv:** USAF sgt 3 yrs; Good Conduct Medal; Philippine Liberation Medal; Pacific Theater Medal. **Home Addr:** 13102 Morningside Ln, Silver Spring, MD 20904. *

DURHAM, LEON
Baseball player, baseball manager. **Personal:** Born Jul 31, 1957, Cincinnati, OH; married Angela; children: Loren, Ian & Lance. **Career:** Baseball player (retired), baseball coach, Film; St Louis Cardinals, outfielder& infielder, 1980, 1989; Chicago Cubs, outfielder & infielder, 1981-88; Cincinnati Reds, infielder, 1988; St Louis Cardinals, infielder, 1989; Lake Elsinore Storm, Calif League, coach, 1996; Vancouver Canadians, Pacific Coast League, coach; Edmonton Trappers, coach; Anaheim Angels, coach; Toledo Mud Hens, hitting coach, 2001-. **Orgs:** Chicago Pub High Sch Athletic Prog. **Honors/Awds:** Rookie of the Yr, Am Assn, 1979; Ken Hubbs Mem Award, Chicago Chaps Baseball Writers Assn Am;Silver Slugger award, 1982; Natl League All-Star Game, 1983. **Business Addr:** Hitting Coach, Toledo Mud Hens Baseball Club Inc, 406 Washington St, Toledo, OH 43604, **Business Phone:** (419)725-4367.*

DURHAM, RAY
Baseball player. **Personal:** Born Nov 30, 1971, Charlotte, NC; married Crystal Hedgecoe; children: Kendra Amber & Trent Austin. **Career:** Chicago White Sox, infielder, 1995-2002; Oakland Athletics, 2002; San Francisco Giants, infielder, 2003-08; Milwaukee Brewers, 2008; free agent, currently. **Honors/Awds:** Am League All-Star Team, 1998; All-Am defensive back hons. *

DURR, MARLESE
Sociologist. **Personal:** Born in Albany, NY; daughter of Moses and Mary. **Educ:** Univ Detroit, BS, lib studies, 1978; State Univ NY-Albany, MA, african & afro-am studies, 1979; MA, sociol, 1985, PhD, sociol, 1993. **Career:** Wright State Univ, asst prof sociol, 1994-2000, assoc prof sociol, 2000-, Womens Studies Prog, dir, 2001-04. **Orgs:** Asn Black Sociologists; Am Sociol Asn; Nat Asn Black Bus & Prof Women, Orgn, Occup & Work Sect Grad Comn; Eastern Sociol Soc; Asn Black Sociologist, 1998-2001; Sociologist Women Soc, 1998-2002; Am Sociol Soc; 2004-07; adv bd, Jour Southern Sociol Soc, 2004-07; Soc Study Social Probs, 2006-09. **Special Achievements:** Has published articles on topics such as Racial Submarkets for Employment, Social Cost and Entrepreneurship, Politics of Race, and Needs of Urban Entrepreneurs; Published Race, Work, and Family in the Lives of African American Men and Women; Textbook/Reader, edited by Marlese Durr and Shirley A. Hill. New York: Rowman & Littlefield; and The New Politics of Race: From Du Bois to The 21st Century; edited by Marlese Durr; West Port, Connecticut: Praeger Press; "The New Politics of Race: Du Bois to the 21st Century and Race, Work; "African American Women: Gender Relations, Work, and The Political Economy in The Twenty-First Century." Gender & Society, Vol. 16. No. 4. with Shirley A. Hill; Family-Work Interface.? in Race, Work, and Family in the Lives of African American Men and Women with Shirley A. Hill; "Social Networks and Occupational Mobility? Pp. 55-71 in The New Politics of Race: From Du Bois to the 21st Century. edited by Marlese Durr. West Port, Connecticut: Praeger Press; "Sex, Drugs, and HIV: Sisters of the Laundromat?; Gender & Society, Vol. 19. No. 6; "Identifying the Unique Needs of the Urban Entrepreneurs: African American Skill Set Development." Race & Society, Vol. 2, No. 2, with Thomas S. Lyons and Gregg A. Lichtenstein; "Does Race Matter?: The Determinants and Consequences"; Race & Society, Vol. 1, No, 2 With Cedric Herring, Hayward D. Horton, and Melvin E. Thomas.; "Social Costs and Inner-city Entrepreneurship". National Journal of Sociology Vol. No. with Thomas S. Lyons and Katharine Cornwell; "Racial Submarkets in Government Employment: African American Professionals in New York State.? Sociological Forum Vol. 12, No. 3, with John R. Logan. *

DUSTER, BENJAMIN C., III
Consultant. **Personal:** Born Mar 15, 1927, Chicago, IL; son of Benjamin C Sr (deceased) and Alfreda Barnett (deceased); married Murrell Higgins, Aug 22, 1954; children: Alice Duster Pennamon, Benjamin C IV & Karen Duster Reynolds & MurielDuster DeVore. **Educ:** DePaul Univ, JD 1954; Grad Sch Bus Univ Chicago, MBA exec prog, 1968. **Career:** Pvt pract, atty, 1955-68, atty, 1979-; GH Walker & Co, stockbroker, 1968-71; Chicago Community Ventures Inc, pres, chief exec officer,1971-79; Williams Rux Hill Whitefield Ltd, spec coun finance invest, 1979-80; Cimply Complex Commun, founder, pres, 1980-. **Orgs:** Gen coun, Chatham Village Asn, 1957-; vpres bd trustees, Allendale Sch-Boys, 1968-; chmn, Ill Comn Human Rels, 1971-73. **Military Serv:** AUS, pfc, 1951-53. **Home Addr:** 8952 S King Dr, Chicago, IL 60619. **Business Addr:** President, Cimply Complex Communications, 7459 S Cottage Grove Ave, Chicago, IL 60619-1911, **Business Phone:** (773)651-9310.

DUSTER, BENJAMIN C, IV
Executive. **Personal:** Born in Chicago, IL. **Educ:** Yale Univ, 1981; Harvard Univ, law & bus, 1985. **Career:** Masson & Co LLC, partner; Salomon Brothers, vpres; Leveraged Finance Group, exec; Watermark Advisors LLC, owner, currently; Algoma Steel Inc, chmn bd, currently. **Orgs:** Adv bd mem, Neenah Foundry Co, 1997-2001; Ill Bar Asn. **Business Phone:** (864)527-5960.

DUSTER, DONALD LEON
Executive. **Personal:** Born Feb 10, 1932, Chicago, IL; son of Benjamin and Alfreda; married Maxine Porter; children: Michelle, David, Daniel. **Educ:** Univ Ill, BS, math, 1953; DePaul Univ, MBA, 1977. **Career:** Commonwealth Edison Co, exec, 1962-87; Chicago Commons Asn, pres, 1970-72; Northern Ill Univ, Dept Bus & Econ Develop, dir, 1977-79; Chicago Commons Asn, asst exec dir, 2002; Corn-Ed's 350 Million Pension Fund, financial analyst; Ill Bus & Labor Adv Coun, dir. **Orgs:** Gov Thompsons Cabinet, 1977; bd mem, Chicago Commons Asn; bd mem, USS Africa Leader Exchange Prog; exec comt, Adlai Stevenson Ctr, Univ Chicago; Econ Club Chicago; Investment Analyst Soc Chicago. **Honors/Awds:** Outstanding Achievemet Award, Nat Fed Settlements, 1976. **Military Serv:** Lt exec officer. *

DUSTER, TROY
Educator. **Personal:** Born Jul 11, 1936, Chicago, IL; son of Benjamin Cecil Duster and Alfreda M Barnett; married Ellen Marie Johansson, May 16, 1964. **Educ:** Northwestern Univ, BS, jour, 1957, PhD, sociol, 1962; Univ Calif, MA, sociol, 1959. **Career:** Northwestern Univ, lectr, 1962; Univ Calif Berkeley, res sociol, 1966-71, from asst prof to assoc prof, 1967-78, dir Inst Study Social Change, 1979-97, prof, 1979-99, chmn, Dept Sociol, 1985-88; Univ Calif, Riverside, asst prof, 1963-65; Stockholm Univ, res sociologist, 1966-67; Am Sociol Asn, asn ed, 1968-70, 1974; Univ BC, vis assoc prof, 1969; London Sch Economics, Guggenheim Fel, 1971-72; Rose Monograph Series; Comtemporary Sociol asn ed, 1974-76; Ford Found, Sr Res Fel, 1980; NY Univ, Dept Sociol, prof, 1999-. **Orgs:** Dir, Nat Inst Ment Health Training Grant, 1971; Assembly Behav & Social Sci Nat Rsch Coun Wash, 1973, Community Clin Eval Narcotic Antagonists, Nat Acad Sci, 1973; pres, Am Sociol Assoc, 2005, AAAS. **Honors/Awds:** Res Reports Sociology; 1963; Our Children's Burden, 1968; Am Behavioral Scientist, 1968; Social Psychiatry, 1968; Changing Perspectives Ment Illness, 1969; The State Univ, 1970; Sanctions Evil, 1971; The Encyc Ed, 1971; Crime Am Soc, 1971; Guggenheim Fellowship, London School of Econ, 1971; The Liberal Univ Under Attack, 1971; Issues in the Classification of Children, 1975; Social Policy & Sociol, 1975; Am Sociologist, 1976; co-ed with Karen Garrett Cultural Perspectives on Biological Knowledge, 1984; Doctor of Letter, Williams Col, 1991; DuBois-Johnson-Frazier Award, Am Sociol Asn, 2001; Hatfield Scholars Award, 2002; Doctor of Science, Northwestern Univ, 2005. **Business Addr:** Professor, New York University, Department Sociology, Rm 4143 295 Lafayette St, New York, NY 10003, **Business Phone:** (212)998-8882.

DUTTON, CHARLES S.
Movie director, actor. **Personal:** Born Jan 30, 1951, Baltimore, MD; married Debbi Morgan, Jan 1, 1994 (divorced 1994). **Educ:** Towson State Univ, BA, theatre drama, 1978; Yale Univ,MA, Drama, 1983. **Career:** Plays:" Ma Rainey's Black Bottom", 1984; " Pantomime", 1986; "Fried Chicken Invisibility", 1987; "Joe Turner's Come & Gone", 1987; " Splendid Mummer", 1988; "The Piano Lesson", 1990; "Ma Rainey's Black Bottom", 2003; TV: "Equal Justice;The Trial of Mary Phagan", 1987; "Roc", 1991-95; "True Women", 1997; "First-Time Felon", dir, 1997; "Aftershock: Earthquake in New York", 1999; "For Love or Country: The Arturo Sandoval Story", 2000; "10,000 Black Men Named George", 2002; "Conviction", 2002; "DC Sniper: 23 Days of Fear", 2003; "Something the Lord Made", 2004; "Land Ahoy", 2005; "The Fly Guys, singing group mgr"; Film:Crocodile Dundee II, actor, 1988; Q&A; Mississippi Masala, actor, 1991; Alien 3, actor, 1992; Distinguished Gentlemen, actor, 1992; A Low Down Dirty Shame, actor, 1995; Time to Kill, actor, 1996; Mimic, actor, 1997; Blind Faith, actor, 1998; Black Dog, actor, 1998; Cookie's Fortune, actor,1999; Random Hearts, actor, 1999; D-Tox, actor, 2002; Against the Ropes, actor & dir, 2004; Ma Rainey's Black Bottom, actor, 2003; Gothika, actor,2003; Against the Ropes, actor & dir, 2004; Secret Window, actor, 2004; The L.A. Riot Spectacular, actor, 2005; The Third Nail, actor, 2008; Racing for Time, actor, 2008; The Express, actor, 2009; Legion, actor,2009. **Honors/Awds:** Yale School of Drama, class marshal, 1983; Outer Critics' Circle nomination, 1985; Drama Desk Award, 1985; Theatre World Award, 1985; Tony nomination, Ma Rainey's Black Bottom; Tony nomination, The Piano Lesson,1990; Emmy Award, Best Director, "The Corner," 2000; Black Reel award for Best Director, Network/Cable, 2001; 2002 Won Emmy award for Out standing Guest Actor in a Drama Series, 2002; 2003 Won Emmy award for Out standing Guest Actor in a Drama Series, 2003; 2003 Won Black Reel award for Best Supporting Actor, Network/Cable, 2003. **Business Addr:** Actor, William Morris Agency, 151 EI Camino Dr, Beverly Hills, CA 90212-2775.

DUTTON BROWN, MARIE
Publisher. **Personal:** Born Oct 4, 1940, Philadelphia, PA; daughter of Benson L and Josephine; married Kenneth, Sep 6, 1969 (died 2004); children: Laini. **Educ:** Penn State Univ, BS, psychol, 1962. **Career:** Wagner High Sch, PA, teacher, 1962-65; Bronze Books, bookstore mgr, 1970-71; Doubleday & Co, from assoc ed to ed & sr ed, 1972-81; Frederick Douglass Creative Arts Ctr, 1979-2004; Elan Mag, ed-in-chief, 1981-82; Endicott Bookseller, bookseller, asst buyer, asst mgr & consult, 1982-84; Marie Brown Assoc, founder, pres & lit agent, 1984-; Allison & Busby Ltd, founder & ed dir; USA Weekend, lit agent & ed. **Orgs:** Studio Mus Harlem, 1984-2004; Coun Lit Mag & Presses, 1989-2004; Poets House, 1994-2001; Hurston Wright Found, 1999-2002; Calabash Lit Festival, 2001-; Caribbean Cult Ctr, 2003-. **Honors/Awds:** Legacy Award, Hurston Wright Found, 2005. **Business Addr:** Founder, President, Marie Brown Associates, 412 W 154th St, New York, NY 10032, **Business Phone:** (212)939-9725.

DUVALL, HENRY F
Public relations executive. **Personal:** Born Jan 3, 1949, Washington, DC; son of Henry F Duvall Sr and Ruth C; married Deborah Hawkins, Aug 12, 1975; children: Cherie. **Educ:** Univ Md, BS, 1975. **Career:** Albuquerque Jour, copy ed, 1975-76; Univ Md, staff writer, 1976-77; Potomac Elec Power Co, writer, 1978; Howard Univ, ed, 1978-81, media coordr, 1981-89, info officer, 1989-91; Am Red Cross, media rels assoc, 1991-92; Coun Great City Schs, dir commun, 1992-. **Orgs:** Nat Press Club, 1993-; Nat Asn Black Journalists, 1977-; Educ Writers Asn, 1993-; Capital Press Club, 1978-; Nat Sch Pub Rels Asn, 1993-; Am Soc Asn Execs, 1993-; Inst Educ Leadership, Commun Execs Group, 1992-. **Honors/Awds:** Scholarship, Am Newspaper Publ Asn, 1974; multiple awards, Coun Great City Sch. **Special Achievements:** Established Communications Dept, Council of the Great City Schools, 1992, launched a national news service, Howard University, 1981. **Military Serv:** USN, petty officer, 1968-70 (active), 1970-75 (ready reserve). **Business Addr:** Director of Communications, Council of the Great City Schools, 1301 Pennsylvania Ave NW Suite 702, Washington, DC 20004, **Business Phone:** (202)393-2427.

DYAS, PATRICIA ANN
Firefighter, government official. **Personal:** Born Dec 6, 1952, Shreveport, LA; daughter of Henry and Martile; children: Patrick,

Matthew, Elizabeth & William. **Educ:** Southern Univ, BS, 1976; Va Hosp Tuskegee, AL, clinic training, graduated, 1976. **Career:** Shreveport Fire Dept, Shreveport, LA, firefighter, emergency med technician & fire inspector, 1981-, asst dir, fire prev, 1999-, chief; licensed realtor. **Orgs:** Red Cross Safety Bd; bd mem, YWCA; Greater Shreveport Optimists Club; Shreveport Black Chamber Com. **Honors/Awds:** Outstanding Young Firefighter, Shreveport, 1987; Outstanding community service award, 1987-88; Outstanding Woman of the Year, Zeta Phi Beta, 1987; Distinguished Black Female award, Traveleers Coalition, 1988; St Abraham Baptist Church Outstanding young Christian woman, 1988. **Military Serv:** US Marine Corps, LCol, 1978-80. **Home Addr:** 2526 E Galloway Blvd C, Shreveport, LA 71104, **Home Phone:** (318)424-4335. **Business Addr:** Chief, Bureau of Fire Prevention, 505 Travis St Suite 510, Shreveport, LA 71101, **Business Phone:** (318)673-6740.

DYCE, BARBARA J.
Biochemist, educator, president (organization). **Personal:** Born in Chicago, IL; daughter of Webster S Thompson III and Carolyn Goin; divorced; children: Sigidi Abdullah. **Educ:** Loyola Univ, attended; Evansville Col, attended; Univ Ill, attended; Univ Chicago, attended; Univ Ill Med Sch, attended; Univ Southern Calif Sch Med, Msc, 1971. **Career:** Central Adult High Sch, instr; Trade Tech Comm Col, instr; Univ Southern Calif Med Sch, asst prof pharmacology; Crenshaw Adult Sch, adult basic educ instr; Radio immuno assay Lab So CA, pres, tech dir. **Orgs:** AAAS; past pres, Feminine Touch Inc; Urban League; NAACP; Alpha Kappa Alpha; Top Ladies of Distinction, Inglewood Branch; bd dir, Crenshaw Adult Sch; Concerned Citizens Commission. **Honors/Awds:** Numerous papers published in scientific journals.

DYE, CLINTON ELWORTH, JR.
Association executive. **Personal:** Born Apr 9, 1942, Atlanta, GA; married Myrtice Willis; children: Clinton E III, Trevin Gerard. **Educ:** Morehouse Clge, AB, 1965; Atlanta Univ Schl Soc Work, MSW, 1969; Atlanta Univ Schs Soc Work & Bus Admin, PhD & MBA, attended 1983. **Career:** Economic Oppor Atlanta, dir drug recov prog, 1971-73; Atlanta Regional Comn, coord drug & alcohol planning, 1973-76; Atlanta Urban League Inc, dir comn srv, 1976-79, deputy exec dir, 1979-, pres & chief exec officer, currently. **Orgs:** Governor's Adv Coun Mental Health, 1975-76; Bd Visitors Grady Hosp, 1983-, Leadership Atlanta, 1971-; vchmn bd, Metro Atlanta Pvt Industry Owner, 1983-; bd mem, N Cent GA Health System Agency, 1981-84; Regional Devel Coun, 1979-83; Regional Educ Policy Comt, 2007. **Home Addr:** 405 Ivy Glen Ct SW, Atlanta, GA 30331. **Business Addr:** President, Chief Executive Officer, Atlanta Urban League Inc, 100 Edgewood Ave NE Suite 600, Atlanta, GA 30303, **Business Phone:** (404)659-1150.*

DYE, ERNEST THADDEUS
Football player. **Personal:** Born Jul 15, 1971, Greenwood, SC; married Rhonda; children: Ariel. **Educ:** SC. **Career:** Football player (retired), Phoenix Cardinals, 1993; Arizona Cardinals, tackle, 1994-96; St Louis Rams, 1997-99. *

DYE, JERMAINE TERRELL
Baseball player. **Personal:** Born Jan 28, 1974, Vacaville, CA. **Educ:** Cosumnes River Col. **Career:** Atlanta Braves, outfielder, 1996; Kansas City Royals, 1997-01; Oakland Athletics, 2001-04; Chicago White Sox, outfielder, 2005-. **Honors/Awds:** Les Milgram Royals Player of the Yr, 1999; Players Choice Award, 2006; Silver Slugger Award; Roberto Clemente Award, 2006; AL Player of the Week honor, 2006. **Special Achievements:** Hit a two-run homer against the Detroit Tigers, 2009. **Business Addr:** Professional Baseball Player, Chicago White Sox, US Cellular Field, 333 W 35th St, Chicago, IL 60616, **Business Phone:** (312)674-1000.*

DYE, HON. LUTHER V
Judge. **Personal:** Born Sep 26, 1933, Winston-Salem, NC; son of Luther William and Mattie Harpe; children: Barry, Bryan, Lisa & Blake. **Educ:** Brooklyn Law Sch, LLB, 1960; State Univ, BS, NC A&T, 1955. **Career:** Chicago Title Ins Co, title officer, 1958-69; Demov Morris Levin & Shein, assoc atty, 1969-73; NY Life Ins Co, assoc coun off gen coun, 1974-86; pvt law pract, 1986-88; Civil Ct City New York, judge, 1988-94; Justice Supreme Ct, 2003. **Orgs:** Macon B Allen Black Bar Asn; NY State Bar Asn; exec mem, Real Property Law Sect; Queens Co Bar Asn; Real Property Com Civil Rights Com & Admis Comn; Grievance Comn; Local Draft Bd Selective Serv Syst; Brooklyn Law Sch Alumni Asn; trustee, Housing Develop Corp Coun Churches. **Honors/Awds:** Elected to US Supreme Ct & US Dist Ct, elected to Civil Ct, 1988, elected to Supreme Ct, 1994. **Home Addr:** 19614 McLaughlin Ave, Holliswood, NY 11483, **Home Phone:** (718)464-3580.

DYER, BERNARD JOEL
Publisher. **Personal:** Born Mar 23, 1933, Bronx, NY; son of Joel and Miariam Samuels; divorced; children: Ethelda, Bertha, Minia & Joel. **Educ:** NY Community Col, technol, 1957. **Career:** CDM Neighborhood Develop Inst, exec dir; Miami Weekly, Journey Mag, publ; Third World Media Corp, pres & chief exec officer. **Orgs:** Phi Tau, vpres, 1955-57. **Honors/Awds:** Dade Co Award, 1969; Nat Coun Churches, Nations Best Community Org, 1967; Hon Dr, Community Org; Leadership Fel, Ford Found, 1979. **Military Serv:** AUS, pvt first class, 1953-55.

DYER, DR. CHARLES AUSTEN
Manager. **Personal:** Born Jul 24, 1936, St Ann, Jamaica; son of Jacob Alexander and Marjorie Emma Lewis; married Edwina Weston; children: M Hakim & Adam L. **Educ:** Pratt Inst, Bachelor Indust Design, 1957; Yeshiva Univ, MS, 1962; City Univ New York, PhD, 1980. **Career:** Digital Equip Corp, computers educ, artificial intelligence; Charles A Dyer Assocs, owner, currently. **Orgs:** Bd dir, Harmony Grove Res Ctr African Diaspora Inc. **Special Achievements:** Author of Preparing for Computer Assisted Instruction 1972; Teaching Aid patented 1973; Articles & papers on artificial intelligence & computer-assisted instruction 1980-. **Military Serv:** USAR, Infantry, capt, 1957-66. **Home Addr:** 203 Grove St, Framingham, MA 01701.

DYER, JOE, JR.
Executive, journalist. **Personal:** Born Sep 24, 1934, Bogalusa, LA; son of Joe Sr and Barbara Fletcher Brooks; married Doris Dillon, Dec 29, 1960; children: Monica, Kimberly, Karen, Joseph III & Dillon. **Educ:** Grambling Col, BA, 1957. **Career:** Executive (retired), journalist; Sickle Cell, LA, first telethon co-prod; United High Blood Pressure Found, co-founder; Black TV Community Org; Avalon Carver Community Ctr, first maj & fundraiser coordr; La City Coun, asst coordr; La, mayor; KCBS-TV, journalist, dir community affairs, 1965-95, mgr community affairs, dir community on-air coordn. **Orgs:** Pres, Sickle Cell Disease Res Found; High Blood Pressure Found; exec bd mem, KNXT Sugar Ray Robinson Youth Found; pub rels adv, Watts Summer Festival; Festivalin Black; IMPACT; S Cent Area Improv Coun; bd mem, Alcoholism Coun Greater La; corp bd mem, United Way Region 5; bd mem, Avalon-Carver Community Ctr; Protestant Community Serv; adv bd mem, SW Col; bd mem, Willing Workers Mentally Retarded; planning comn mem, Chinese New Year's Celebration; bd mem, Oper PUSH; La Chap Media Women; La Urban League; Dept Sr Citizen; Sch Vol Prog; Nat Asn Jr Col; Alpha Chi Pi Omega Sorority; Nat Acad Motion Pictures & TV; Teen Posts Inc; Ann Festival Black Com; Lions; Rotaries; Kiwanis; bd mem, Community Youth Gang Serv; corp bd, Corp Comn Human Rels; bd mem, Crossroads Acad; Greater Los Angeles Urban League; bd mem, S Los Angeles Develop Corp. **Honors/Awds:** National Abe Lincoln Award, Sickle Cell Anemia; Award, Nat Asn Media Women; John Anson Ford Award, Co Human Rels Comn; Image Award, Nat Asn Advan Colored People; Chinatown Firecracker Award; Received more than 83 awards. **Special Achievements:** First African-American Journalist in KCBS-TV. **Military Serv:** USAF, Airman 1st Class, 1957-61; Airman of the Month, Airman of the Year.

DYER-GOODE, PAMELA THERESA
Physician, gynecologist. **Personal:** Born Oct 7, 1950, Philadelphia, PA; daughter of Kirby and Mabel Clyatt; children: Lisa, Shonn, Erica, Brian. **Educ:** Cheyney State Col, BS Biol, BS Chem, 1971; Temple Univ Med Sch, MD 1977; Temple Univ, attended 1985. **Career:** Planned Parenthood, physician/ambulatory, 1978-80; Gruiffree Med Ctr, physician/ambulatory care 1980-82; Broad St Hosp, ambulatory care physician, 1982-84; SEPTA, indust med & claims specialist, 1986; pvt family pract, 1986-. **Orgs:** NOW, Coalition 100 Black Women, Pa Med Soc, Am Med Asn, Nat Med Asn, Friends PA Ballet Co. **Honors/Awds:** Distinguished Alumna Award Cheyney State Col, 1986; Outstanding Alumna St Maria Goretti High Sch, 1986; Philadelphia New Observer "Women on the Move" ed presentation. **Home Addr:** 305 Penbree Cir, Bala Cynwyd, PA 19004. *

DYKES, DEWITT S.
Educator. **Personal:** Born Jan 2, 1938, Chattanooga, TN; son of De Witt S Dykes Sr and Violet T Anderson; married Marie Draper; children: Laura Marie Christine. **Educ:** Fisk Univ, BA (Summa Cum Laude), 1960; Univ Mich, MA, 1961, PhD cand 1965. **Career:** Mich St Univ, instr, Am Thought & Lang, 1965-69; Oakland Univ, asst prof hist, 1969-73, assoc prof hist, 1973-, dean's asst for affirmative action, 1975-78, coordr Afro-Amer studies 1975-83; Univ SC Sch Pub Health, consult 1977. **Orgs:** African Heritage Studies Asn, 1970; Asn Study Afro-Am Life & Hist; charter mem, Afro-Am Hist & Geneal Soc, 1978; Alpha Phi Alpha Fraternity; bd ed, Detroit Perspective, A Jour Regional Hist, 1978-84; vchmn, HistDesignation Adv Bd City, 1980-82, chmn, 1982-84; book rev ed, Jour Afro-Am Hist & Geneal Soc, 1981-85; pres, Fred Hart Williams Geneal Soc, 1980-86; bd trustees, Hist Soc Mich, 1983-; bd trustees, Hist Soc Mich, 1983-89; Nat Endowment Humanities, 1985; pres, Mich Black Hist Network 1986-; pres,Mich Black Hist Network, 1986-88. **Honors/Awds:** Phi Beta Kappa, Honorary Fraternity, 1969. **Special Achievements:** Published "Mary McLeod Bethune"; "Ida Gray Nelson Rollins DDS" Profiles of the Negro in Amer Dentistry 1979; "Augusta Savage"; "Jerome Cavanagh & Roman Gribbs"; "Amer Blacks as Perpetual Victims, An Historical Overview", Victimization of the Weak, 1982; "The Black Population in MI, Growth, Distribution & Public Office 1800-1983", Ethnic Groups in MI Vol 2, 1983; "The Search for Community: Mich Soc & Educ, 1945-80" in MI: Visions of our Past, 1989.

DYMALLY, LYNN V
Government official, educator. **Personal:** Born Sep 8, 1958, Los Angeles, CA. **Educ:** Univ Calif, San Diego, BA Commun, Sociol, 1979; Univ Redlands, MA, Bus Mgmt, 1987; Whittier Col, Sch Law, 1988. **Career:** Network Data Processing, vpres, 1979-80; Drew Postgrad Med Sch, Prog Int Health & Develop, admin analyst, 1980-81; KBRT Radio, bus mgr, 1981-85; Compton Unified Sch Dist, bd trustee; Calif State Univ, Long Beach, CA, lectr, currently. **Orgs:** Spec asst, Calif State Museum Sci, Summer Break & Ind, 1973-78; analyst, consult, Aid to Needy Children Mother's Anonymous Inc, Calif State Social Serv Prog, 1979-; Calif League Women Voter, 1983-; staff, Youth for Christ 1983-; statewide co-chmn, Calif Rainbow Youth Coalition Jackson for Pres, 1984. **Honors/Awds:** Co-instr, The Presidential Classroom, 1985. **Business Addr:** Lecturer, California State University, CBA - 449, Long Beach, CA 90840, **Business Phone:** (562)985-4830.

DYMALLY, MERVYN MALCOLM
Congressperson (u.s. federal government), educator, senator (u.s. federal government). **Personal:** Born May 12, 1926, Cedros, Trinidad and Tobago; son of Andreid Richardson and Hamid Dymally; married Alice M Gueno; children: Mark & Lynn. **Educ:** Lincoln Univ, 1946; Calif State Univ, BA, educ, 1954, MA, govt, 1969; US Int Univ, San Diego, PhD, human behav, 1978. **Career:** The Vanguard, reporter; Los Angeles Unified Sch Dist, teacher exceptional c, 1955-61; Univ Calif, lectr; Whittier Col, lectr; Pomona Col, lectr; Claremont Grad Sch, lecturer; Charles R Drew Univ Med & Sci, Los Angeles, lectr; Cent State Univ, lectr; Golden Gate Univ, adj prof; State Calif, coordr disaster off, 1961-62; Calif State Assembly, mem, 1963-66; Calif State Senate, mem, 1967-75; State Calif, lt gov, 1975-79; John F Kennedy Campaign, field coordr; Mervyn M Dymally Co Inc, pres, 1981-; US House Representatives, mem, 1981-93; Surplus Book Found, past pres; Calif State Assembly, 52 Dis, assemblyman, chief protocol officer, currently; Repub Benin, W Africa, hon consult, currently. **Orgs:** Chmn, Caribbean Am Res Inst; bd mem, Joint Ctr Polit Studies; chmn, Thirty First Cong Dist Adv Comn; pres, Res Inst Space Sci & Tech; Task Force Missing Action, US House Reps; Calif Dem State Cent Comt; Arab Am Affairs Coun; Jewish Labor Comt; Japanese Am Citizens League; Chinese Am Asn; Korean Am Polit Asn; Mexican-Am Polit Asn; Asian Dem Caucus; Urban League; Am Civil Liberties Union; NAACP, Wash DC Comn Crime Prevention; Am Asn Univ Professors; AAAS; Am Polit Sci Asn; Am Acad Polit Sci; Am Acad Polit & Social Sci; Kappa Alpha Psi Frat; adv, United Nat Coun; La County Water Appeals Bd; chair, Robert Smith Water Inst. **Honors/Awds:** Hon Soc Phi Kappa Phi; Solomon Carter Fuller Award, Black Psychiatrist Am, 1975; Adam Clayton Powell Award, Cong Black Caucus, 1975; Chaconia Medal, Class 1 Order Trinity for Public Service, Govt Trinidad & Tobago, 1975; Distinguished Citizen Award, Lincoln Univ; LLD, W Los Angeles Univ, Calif Col Law, 1976, City Univ Los Angeles, 1976; JD, Lincoln Law Univ, Sacramento, 1975; HLD, Shaw Univ, 1981. **Special Achievements:** Auth, The Black Politician: His Struggle for Power, Duxbury Press, 1971; First African American to serve in the State Senate; First of two African American Lieutenant Governors in the United States, 1974; First person of African and Indian origin to serve in the U.S. Congress; Along with George L. Brown of Colorado, he was also elected a lieutenant governor in 1974; First black elected to any statewide office in any state since Reconstruction. **Business Addr:** Assemblyman, California State Assembly, 322 W Compton Blvd Suite 100, Compton, CA 90220, **Business Phone:** (310)223-1201.

DYSON, MICHAEL ERIC
Educator, baptist clergy. **Personal:** Born Oct 23, 1958, Detroit, MI; son of Addie Mae; married Marcia Louise, Jun 24, 1992; children: Michael II & Maisha; married Brenda Joyce (divorced 1992) (divorced). **Educ:** Carson-Newman, BA, 1982; Princeton Univ, MA, 1991, PhD, 1993. **Career:** Princeton Univ, Mathy Col, asst master; Hartford Seminary, fac mem; Chicago Theol Seminary, instr, asst prof; Brown Univ, asst prof; Univ NC, Prof Comm; Columbia Univ, vis prof African Am studies, 1997-99; DePaul Univ, Ida B Wells-Barnett prof relig studies, 1999-2002; Univ Penn, Avalon Found prof humanities, 2002-; ordained Baptist minister, currently. **Orgs:** Democratic Socialist Am. **Honors/Awds:** Nat Asn Black Journalists, Nat Mag Award, 1992. **Special Achievements:** Author: Reflecting Black: African-American Cultural Criticism, 1993; Black History Booklet, A Collection of 20 Essays; The Second Coming of Malcolm X, liner notes for RCA Records; Making Malcolm: The Myth and Meaning of Malcolm X, Oxford Univ Press, 1994; Between God and Gangsta' Rap, collection of essays, Oxford Univ Press, 1995; Race Rules: Navigating the Color Line, Addison Wesley, 1996; I May Not Get There With You: The True Martin Luther King Jr, Free Press, 2000; Hollar if You Hear Me: Searching for Tupac Shakur, Basic Civitas, 2001; Why I Love Black Women, Basic Civitas, 2003; Open Mike: Reflections on Philosophy, Race, Sex, Culture and Religion, Basic Civitas, 2003; Mercy, Mercy Me: The Art, Loves & Demons of Marvin Gaye, 2004; named as the first Ida B Wells Barnett University Professor at DePaul University. **Business Addr:** Avalon Foundation Professor, University of Pennsylvania, Department Humanities, 226 Logan Hall 249 S 36th St, Philadelphia, PA 19104-6304.

DYSON, WILLIAM RILEY
State government official, educator. **Personal:** Born Jul 12, 1940, Waycross, GA; son of Edward James and Lula Lorene Williams; divorced; children: Sonia, Wilfred, Erick & Michael. **Educ:** Mor-

ris Col, BA, soc studies, 1962; Southern Conn State Univ, MA, urban Studies, 1976, Sixth-Yr Degree, Admin & Supv, 1982. **Career:** Educator, state representative; New Haven, Conn, teacher; Douglas GA, Blackshear GA, teacher; State Conn, 94th Assembly Dist, House Representatives, state rep, 1976-. **Orgs:** Hillary's Conn Steering Comt. **Business Addr:** State Representative, State of Connecticut, 94th Assembly District, Legis Off Bldg Rm 4032, Hartford, CT 06106-1591, **Business Phone:** (860)240-8585.

E

E-40, E (EARL STEVENS)
Rap musician. **Personal:** Born Nov 15, 1967, Vellejo, CA. **Career:** Albums: Federal, 1994; The Mail Man, 1994; In a Major Way, 1995; The Hall of Game, 1996; The Element of Surprise, 1998; Charlie Hustle, 1999; Loyalty & Betrayal, 2000; Grit & Grind, 2002; Breakin News, 2003; That Fire, 2004; The Best of E-40: Yesterday, Today, & Tomorrow, 2004; The Bay Bridges Compilation, 2005; My Ghetto Report Card, 2006; My Ghetto Report Card, 2006; Films: The Breaks, 1999; Charlie Hustle, 1999; Obstacles, 2000; three Strikes, 2000; Malibooty, voice, 2003; Survival of the Illest, 2004; Hair Show, 2004, Lil Jon Makes a Video: Snap Yo Fingers, 2006; Dead Heist, 2007; Sick Wid It Recs, co-founder; Cloud 9, owner. **Special Achievements:** author, E-40's book of slang, Warner Books, 2005. **Business Addr:** Recording Artist, Jive Recs, 137-137 West 25th St Fl 11, New York, NY 10001, **Business Phone:** (212)727-0016.

EADY, CORNELIUS
Poet, educator. **Personal:** Born Jan 1, 1954?, Rochester, NY. **Educ:** Monroe Community Col; Empire St Col; Warren Wilson Col, MFA, 1986. **Career:** St Univ NY, Stony Brook, assoc prof eng, dir, Poetry Ctr; Sarah Lawrence Col; NY Univ; City Col NY; Col William & Mary; Sweet Briar Col, Univ Notre Dame, assoc prof, currently, Creative Writing Prog, dir, currently; Poems: Kartunes, 1980; Victims of the Latest Dance Craze, 1985; BOOM BOOM BOOM, 1988; The Gathering of My Name, 1991; You Don't Miss Your Water, 1995; Brutal Imagination, Putnam, 2001. **Orgs:** Founder, Cave Canem. **Honors/Awds:** George Oppenheimer Award, Newsday, 2002; Pulitzer Prize nominee; Lamont Poetry Selection, Acad Am Poets Victims Latest Dance Craze; Strousse Award, Prairie Schooner; fel, from the Guggenheim Found; fel, Nat Endowment Arts; fel, Rockefeller Found; fel, Lila Wallace-Reader Digest Found.

EADY, KERMIT
President (Organization), chief executive officer, entrepreneur. **Educ:** Morgan State Univ, BA; NY Univ, MSW. **Career:** Medger Evers Col, asst prof; Norfolk State Univ Grad Sch Social Work, dir admis & recruitment; Black United Fund, NY, founder, 1979-, pres & chief exec officer; Eady Assocs, pres & founder, 2003-. **Business Addr:** President, Chief Executive Officer, Eady Associates, PO Box 70 1021, Jackson Heights, NY 11370, **Business Phone:** (917)642-1878.

EADY, LYDIA DAVIS
Vice president (Organization), president (organization), marketing executive. **Personal:** Born May 4, 1958, Indiana; daughter of Henderson S and Ruth V; married Jacques Wayne; children: Andrew Jacques & Matthew John. **Educ:** Howard Univ, BA, broadcast mgt, Magna Cum Laude, 1980. **Career:** WRTV ABC Indianapolis, IN, news reporter, 1980-81; Johnson Publ Co, asst dir pub rels, 1981-83, dir prom, 1983-85, vpres, 1985-2004; Ebony & Jet Celebrity Showcase, assoc producer; American Black Achievment Awards, prog coord exec; Joy Communs, pres, 2004-. **Orgs:** Quinn Chapel AME Ch Chicago, IL; Execs Club Chicago; League Black Women; Women's Advert Club Chicago; Chicago Asn Black Journalists; trustee, Alder Sch Prof Psychol; bd adv, Jad Communs; Woman Substance Award. **Honors/Awds:** Folio Circulation Direct Mail Award of merit; CEBA Award for Merit; listed in: Who's Who in the World; Who's Who of Am Women; Who's Who of Black Ams; Woman Of Substance Award, men committed better community. **Special Achievements:** EBONY Guide To Historically Black Coll & Univs, author; mag articles spec events & press releases; represented Co at the White House; ABC-TV network special, Celebrate The Dream: 50 Years Of EBONY; associate producer of EBONY/JET Celebrity Showcase. **Home Addr:** 1137 S Pk Terr, Chicago, IL 60605, **Home Phone:** (312)427-0207.

EADY, MARVIN P.
Dentist. **Career:** Dr Eady Family Dent PC, dentist, currently. *

EADY, MARY E
School administrator. **Personal:** Born in Waterbury, CT; married Eugene H Eady; children: Mary Vienassa, Alan, Larry, Barry, Audrey, John & Carol. **Educ:** Bridgeport Hosp, lpn, 1967; Housatonic Community Col, AS, drug & alcohol couns, 1977; Sacred Heart Univ, BS, psychol, 1977; Southern CT State Col, MA, couns, 1978. **Career:** St Joseph's Manor, ward charge nurse, 1967-74; Greater Baptist Methadone Ctr, staff nurse, 1974-75; Dinan Mem Ctr, ward charge nurse, 1975-76; Greater Baptist Ment Health Ctr, counr, 1976-78; Housatonic Community Col, proj dir spec serv prog, 1979-. **Orgs:** Nat Asn Advan Colored People Police & Community Rels Comn, 1973; Univ Bridgeport Oper Open Doors Prog, 1975; chairperson, Bridgeport Sr Citizens Activities Week, 1976; Community Counr Asn, 1980-; volunteer counsr, St George's Church Ment Health Social Group, 1980-; pres, Housatonic Community Col Alumni Asn, 1982-; vol, Sch Vol Asn City Baptist, 1983-; New Eng Asn Ed Opport Prog; Nat Asn Advan Colored People Polit Action Comn; N End Neighborhood Coun; Bridgeport Bar Asn Support Improve Correctional Serv Comn; Nat Asn Advan Colored People Voter Reg Comn. **Business Phone:** (203)332-5037.

EAGAN, CATHERINE B
Banker. **Personal:** Born Jan 14, 1954, New York, NY; daughter of James Doyle Davis and Adele Helen Dixon Cartey; married Jay Victor Eagan. **Educ:** Simmons Col, Boston, BA, MA, 1975, Grad Sch Mgt, cert, 1996; Harvard Univ, Cambridge, MA, EdM, 1978; Am Inst Banking, Wayne State Univ, 1980; Word Faith Bible Training Ctr, grad (summa cum laude), 2000. **Career:** Metrop Coun Educ, Roxbury, MA, Support serv dir, 1975-78; United Community Serv Detroit, MI, prog consult, 1978-80; Nat Bank Detroit, Detroit, MI, com credit analyst, 1980-82; Detroit Econ Growth Corp, dir, 1982-93; Pvt Banking Div, Mich Nat Bank, vpres, 1993-98; Workplace Wisdom Publ, founder, 1999-; William Tyndale Col, chmn dept continuing educ & assoc prof prof studies, 1999-; Catherine Eagan Ministries, founder; Catherine Eagan Enterprises LLC, vpres, currently. **Orgs:** Life mem, Nat Asn Advan Colored People, 1982-; Harvard Club Eastern Mich, 1982; Women's Econ Club, 1983-; Econ Club Detroit, 1984; role model, Detroit Pub Sch Stud Motivation Prog, 1986-; finance chairperson, United Negro Col Fund Walkathon, 1986-; finance chairperson, Detroit Area Agency Aging, 1990-; Nat Speakers Asn, Christian Booksellers Asn, Women's Exec Golf Club. **Honors/Awds:** Certificate of Nat Recognition for Trapper's Alley Project; Award of Nat Excellence, Va Park Shopping Ctr, US Dept Housing & Urban Develop; Certificate of Participation, Business Role Model, Detroit Pub Schs Stud Motivational Prog 1985, 1987, 1988, 1989, 1990; African-American Business & professional Women's Award, Dollars & Sense Magazine, 1991; Testimonial Resolution from the Detroit City Council, 1993; Proclamation from Mayor Coleman A Young for her work in the City of Detroit, 1993. **Special Achievements:** Numerous speaking engagements, coauthor of dominating money & How to discover our purpose in ten days. **Business Addr:** Vice President, Catherine Eagan Enterprises LLC, The Wealthy Women Club, 3200 N Fed Hwy Suite 222, Boca Raton, FL 33431, **Business Phone:** (561)338-0009.

EAGAN, EMMA LOUISE
Dentist. **Personal:** Born Oct 12, 1928, Cartersville, GA; married John D; children: 3. **Educ:** Spelman Col, BA, 1948; Meharry Med Col, diploma, 1953. **Career:** Working for Husband, orthodontist hygienist; Dr Earl Renfroe Chicago, hygienist; GA Sch Sys, sch teacher. **Orgs:** Delta Sigma Theta Sor; AAVW; Jack n' Jill Am; Dental Wives Orgn meharry alumni asn; vol worker MI cancer fund; moles sunday Sch Teacher Orgn; Spellman Col Alumni Club; League Women Voters; Nat Dent Hyg Asn; Dent Hygiene Hon. **Honors/Awds:** Recipient scholarship achievement Medal Arts Award, Meharry Col; dent hygiene hon soc Sigma Phi Alpha, 1962. **Special Achievements:** Cover girl nat write-up on dental hygiene, Jet Mag, 1958; honored achievements Spelman Alumni Club Civic & Professional, 1960. **Business Addr:** 1130 Woodward Ave, Detroit, MI 48226.

EAGLE, ARNOLD ELLIOTT
Labor relations manager. **Personal:** Born Jul 7, 1941, Brooklyn, NY; son of Porter and Gwendolyn Saunders; divorced; children: Todd. **Educ:** VA State Col, BS, 1964; VA State Univ, BS, 1964; NY Univ, MA, 1975. **Career:** Manufacturers Hanover Trust, personnel interviewer, 1966-69; Colgate-Palmolive Co, employment mgr, 1969-73; Bristol-Myers Int, dir human resources, finance & hq admin; Am Coun Int Personnel, mem bd dir, vpres bd dir, 1982, pres, 1987-. **Orgs:** Black Retail Action Group, 1974-; Am Mgt Asn, 1974-; Am Coun Int Personnel, 1975-; Employment Managers Asn, 1975-; bd dir, Omega Psi Phi Fed Credit Union, 1986; Employee Relocation Coun, 1988-; Bus & Indus Comn, Omega Psi Phi; vpres, Omega Psi Phi Fraternity Fed Credit Union, 1989-; Basileus Omega Psi Phi Fraternity Iota Xi Chap; Bus & Indust Comm Omega Psi Phi. **Honors/Awds:** Omega Citizen of the Year, 1976; Omega Man of the Year, 1983. **Military Serv:** AUS, 1st lt, 1964-66. **Home Addr:** 40 Waterside Plz, PO Box 28 305 E, New York, NY 10016. **Business Addr:** President, American Council on International Personnel Inc, 515 Madison Ave 6th Fl, New York, NY 10022-5403, **Business Phone:** (212)688-2437.

EAGLIN, FULTON B.
Lawyer. **Personal:** Born Nov 23, 1941, Ann Arbor, MI; son of Simon P and Marguerite Davis; married Jan Collins Eaglin, Jun 30, 1979; children: Fulton Christopher, Jennifer Naomi, Jessica Marguerite. **Educ:** Eastern Mich Univ, Ypsilanti, MI, BS, 1963; Harvard Sch Bus, Cambridge, MA, 1969; Harvard Law Sch, Cambridge, MA, JD, 1969. **Career:** Harvard Univ, Cambridge, MA, 1969-72; self employed atty, Ypsilanti, MI, 1975-80; Eaglin, Drukis & Green, Ann Arbor, MI, 1980-. **Orgs:** Mich Bar Asn; Ypsilanti & Washtenaw County Bar Asn; trustee, Washtenaw Community Col, 1976; chmn, bd dirs, United Way Mich, 1988; bd governors, United Way Am, 1992-99; Kiwanis Int; bd dir, Am Red Cross, Washtenaw County Chap, 1985-87; treasurer, bd dir, Child Family Serv Washtenaw County, 1975-77; Alpha Phi Alpha Fraternity; Sire Archon 1990-92; Gamma Rho Chap; Sigma Pi Phi Fraternity. **Military Serv:** AUS, Lt, 1963-66; Combat Infantryman's Badge, 1965, Airborne, 1963, Ranger, 1964. **Business Addr:** Attorney, Eaglin Drukis and Green, City Center Bldg 220 E Huron Suite 705, Ann Arbor, MI 48104-1907, **Business Phone:** (734)665-5355.*

EAGLIN, RUTH
Government official. **Career:** US Dept Transp, White House Liaison, 2000; White House Off, exec asst dir presial Personnel, currently. **Business Phone:** (202)456-6676.*

EALEY, MARK E
Social worker. **Personal:** Born Jun 13, 1926, Oklahoma City, OK; married Ruth Keenan; children: Michael K, Marquetta E & Roger K. **Educ:** Howard Univ, BS, 1950; Howard Univ, MSW, 1952. **Career:** Clinic social worker; Pvt Practice, psychother; Howard Univ, Richard Welling fel, 1951; San Diego Co Pub Welfare Dept, social worker, 1952-53; Dept Corrections, social worker, 1953-60; Univ Calif, Berkeley, CA, instr, 1960-69; Univ Calif, fac, 1966-67; Univ Pac, chmn black studies dept, 1969-, prof emer, 1990-; Probation Off, Solano Co, CA, consult, 1971; Vallejo Unified Sch Dist, consult, 1973; Vallejo Counseling Ctr, owner, currently. **Orgs:** Nat Asn Advan Colored People, 1946-; Nat Asn Social Workers, 1952; Calif Probations Parole & Correctional Asn, 1955-72; prin speaker, Symposium By Area Correctonal Workers Oakland, 1957; Nat Coun Crime & Delinquency; Nat Coun Social Work Educ; Am Asn Univ Profs; Inst Race Culture & Human Dignity; adv coun, Community Affairs, Dept KTVU-TV; Ctr African & African-Am Studies; dir, Univ Travel Tour Courses to W & E Africa, 1973, 1975, 1977, 1979 & 1981; fed & exec bd mem, Nat Coun Black Studies, 1975-. **Honors/Awds:** Outstanding professional in human service, Am Acad Human Serv, 1974. **Military Serv:** USN, steward 3/c, 1944-46. **Business Addr:** Owner, Vallejo Counseling Center, 301 Georgia St Suite 105, Vallejo, CA 94590-5937, **Business Phone:** (707)644-0282.

EALY, MARY NEWCOMB
Educator, financial manager. **Personal:** Born Aug 26, 1948, Charleston, MO; daughter of Gussie E Newcomb and Susie M Williams; married Willie R, Jun 17, 1978 (divorced 1999); children: Lisa Denise. **Educ:** Lake Mich Col, AA, 1968; Western Mich Univ, BS, 1972. **Career:** Fox's Jewelry, ed mgr, 1969-70; Shifren & Willens Jewelry, off coord, 1969; Benton Harbor Area Sch, secy, 1970-71, dept head, Unit Coord Social Studies, 1973, teacher, 2004; Mich State Dept Educ, reviewer, 1975-; Sch Curr & Educ Leadership, res; Jordan Col Berrien Campus, adj prof, 1987-; La'Nise Productions, vpres, currently. **Orgs:** Pres, Essence Blackness, 1974-; Mich & Nat Educ Asn Rep Assembly, 1974-; Nat Educ Asn, Off Black Caucus, 1974-; adv, Excelsior Chap, Nat Jr Hon Soc, 1975-; Exec comm, MEA, 1976-77; Phi Delta Kappa, 1976; Andrews Unit Chap; Am Asn Col Pharm; Delta Sigma Theta Sorority Inc, BH-SJ Alumnae Chap, 1983-; coord, Close-up Found, 1985-; vpres, Benton Harbor-St Joseph Alumnae Chap, Delta Sigma Theta, 1987-89. **Honors/Awds:** Outstanding Teacher Award, MI Dept Educ, 1976, Cert Merit, 1976; Nunn-Williams Family History, 1986; Teacher of the Year, Benton Harbor High Sch, 1987. **Special Achievements:** First Vice president of Benton Harbor-St Joseph Alumnae Chapter. **Business Addr:** Vice President, La'Nise Productions, PO Box 844, Benton Harbor, MI 49023.

EALY, MICHAEL (MICHAEL BROWN)
Actor. **Personal:** Born Aug 3, 1973, Silver Spring, MD. **Educ:** Univ Md, College Park. **Career:** Stage productions: Joe Fearless & Whoa-Jack; Films: The Lush Life, 2000; Kissing Jessica Stein, 2001; Barbershop, 2002; Bad Company, 2002; Justice, 2003; 2 Fast 2 Furious, 2003; November, 2004; Never Die Alone, 2004; Barbershop 2: Back in Business, 2004; Jellysmoke, 2005; Suspect, 2007; Put it in a Book, 2007; Miracle at St Anna, 2008; Seven Pounds, 2008; TV Episode: Metropolis, 2000; Law & Order, 2000; Madigan Men, 2000; Soul Food, 2001; ER, 2002-03; Their Eyes Were Watching God, 2005; Sleeper Cell, 2005-06; Suspect, 2007. **Honors/Awds:** Best Actor in TV Series Eyes Were Watching God, 2005; Black Reel Award, 2006; Nominee, Golden Globe Award, 2007; Nominee, Black Reel Award, 2008. **Business Addr:** Actor, c/o Vic Ramos Management, 49 W 9th St Suite 5B, New York, NY 10011, **Business Phone:** (212)473-2610.*

EARL, ACIE BOYD
Executive, basketball player, business owner. **Personal:** Born Jun 23, 1970, Peoria, IL; son of Acie and Carolyn. **Educ:** Univ Iowa, BS, Leisure studies, 1992. **Career:** Basketball player (retired), executive, business owner; Boston Celtics, 1993-95; Toronto Raptors, 1995-96, Milwaukee Bucks, 1996; played probasketball France, Australia, China & Turkey, 1997-2000; Ace Promotion &Mkt, vpres, 1993; Coach; Tijuana Dragons, 2005; freshman boys basketball, Solon High Sch, currently; Venom Productions, owner,

1993-. **Orgs:** Vpres, Ace Award, 1993-; camp dir, WAM-JAM basketball camp, 1994; VenoSports Mgt, 1999; Nation Islam. **Honors/Awds:** Pre-season All Am, Playboy Mag, 1992-93; Big Ten Defensive Player of the Year, 1992; nominee, John Wooden Award, 1992-93. **Special Achievements:** NBA Draft, First round pick, 1993. **Home Phone:** (319)338-1460. **Business Addr:** Owner, Venom Productions, PO Box 1685, Moline, IL 61265, **Business Phone:** 888-836-6649.

EARL, DR. ARCHIE WILLIAM
Educator. **Personal:** Born Nov 28, 1946, Suffolk, VA; son of Rev Edward Earl Jr and Thelma Virginia Gertude Williams; married Doristine Gause; children: Karen, Archie Jr & Keisha. **Educ:** Norfolk State Univ, BS 1971; Hampton Univ, MA 1976; Col William & Mary, CAS 1986; Col William & Mary, EdD 1986. **Career:** Hampton Univ, statistics instr, 1983; Col William & Mary, grad asst, 1983-85; Family Inns Amer, night auditor, 1985-86; City Col Chicago, math lectr, 1986; Saudi Arabian Govt, Dammam Saudi Arabia, Math instr, 1987; Christopher Newport Col, Newport News VA, asst prof Math, 1987-90; Norfolk State Univ, asst prof math, 1991, assoc prof, currently; IEIC Press, author, publisher, 1993-. **Orgs:** Deacon & treas, Mt Pleasant Baptist Church, Williams burgs, 1983-86; Asn Study Higher Educ 1986-, Am Statist Asn, 1991; Math Asn Am, 1988-; Am Math Soc 1988-; Am Asn Univ Prof, 1997-. **Honors/Awds:** NSF fel & grants, grad study, Hampton Univ, 1972-74; "2000 Outstanding Intellectuals of the 20th Century", 1999. **Special Achievements:** Author: Univ Services and Auxiliary Enterprises; Higher Education and the Student; What Every Prospective College Student Should Know; What Every Prospective Grad Student Should Know; High Tech Higher Education; Business Statistics with Computer Applications; Probability and Statistics for the Sciences with Computer Applications; Probability and Statistics for Educators and Social Scientists with Computer Applications; author "The Budget Information Systems of Selected Colleges & Universities in the State of VA as Described and Perceived by Budget Managers," College of Wm& Mary 1986; Elementary Probability and Statistics with Computer Applications; Ed-in-chief, Increasing Americas Knowledge of Aviation through the Mathematics Curriculum; Co-author "A Preliminary Planning Study for a New College," College of Wm & Mary 1983; co-author, The American Far West in the Twentieth Century (The Lamar Series in Western History), 2008. **Military Serv:** Private E-1, USAR, 1966-68. **Business Addr:** Associate Professor of Mathematics, Mathematics Department, Norfolk State University, 700 Pk Ave, Norfolk, VA 23504, **Business Phone:** (757)823-9564.

EARLES, DR. JULIAN
Executive. **Personal:** Born in Portsmouth, VA. **Educ:** Norfolk State Univ, BS, physics; Univ Rochester Sch of Med, MS, radiation biol; Univ Mich, PhD, radiation physics; Univ Mich, environl health; Harvard Bus Schs, Mgt Develop. **Career:** Rock & Roll Hall of Fame, mem of the Adv Bd; NASA's Glenn Res, dep dir of opers; NASA's Glenn Res, ctr dir, 2003-. **Orgs:** NMCP; Kappa Alpha Psi Fraternity. **Honors/Awds:** Excep achievement & outstanding leadership medals, NASA; Presidential Rank Award of Meritorious Exec; Distinguished Scholar Lectr, Jennings Found; Col Aeronaut, NY, DSc; Nova Southeastern Univ, Doctor of Pedagogy; NC A&T State Univ, DHL; Distinguished Honors Visiting Professor at numerous universities throughout the Nation. **Special Achievements:** Guest speaker, Black Hist month closing ceremony; over 28 publ, tech & educ; run over 10,000 miles in the past 5 years & successfully completed 22 marathons incl the Boston Marathon. **Business Addr:** Director, NASA-Glenn Research Center, 21000 Brookpark Rd, Cleveland, OH 44135.

EARLES, DR. RENE MARTIN
Physician, executive. **Personal:** Born Oct 31, 1940, New Orleans, LA; married Eve Evans; children: Robert & Andrea. **Educ:** Howard Univ, BS, 1963; Howard Univ, Col Med, MD, 1967. **Career:** Pvt pract, dermatologist; Rush Med Ctr, residency, 1972-75; Univ Wash, preceptorship, 1970-72; resident surgery, 1968-70; Kemo Health Ctr, Chicago Ill, chief dermatologist; Dr Earles LLC, chmn & head product develop, 2001-. **Orgs:** Chmn, Div Dermatol, Mt Sinai Med Ctr, Chicago Ill; bd dir, Region Four, Ill; Am Cancer Soc; past pres, Howard Univ, Alumni asn, Chicago; frat life, Kappa Alpha Psi; Sigma Pi Phi; Chicagoans; Saracens; Am Acad Dermat; Chicago Dermat Soc; Soc Investigative Dermat; Cook County Physicians Asn. **Special Achievements:** Featured as one of top 100 African - American Doctors in the United States in Black Enterprise Magazine. **Military Serv:** USN LCDR 1970-72. **Business Addr:** Chairman, Head of Product Development, Dr Earles LLC, 2930 S Mich Ave Suite 102, Chicago, IL 60616, **Business Phone:** (312)225-7200.

EARLEY, KEITH H.
Lawyer. **Personal:** Born Feb 3, 1952, New York, NY; son of Charles and Wilma; divorced; children: Khary. **Educ:** Cornell Univ, BA, 1974; Rutgers Law Sch, JD, 1977. **Career:** Fed Home Loan Mortgage Corp, assoc gen coun, currently. **Orgs:** Chmn, Am Bar Asn Minority In-house Coun Group. **Home Addr:** 1640 Martha Terr, Rockville, MD 20852. *

EARLEY, DR. STANLEY ARMSTEAD, JR. See Obituaries section.

EARLS, DR. JULIAN MANLY
Association executive. **Personal:** Born Nov 22, 1942, Portsmouth, VA; son of James and Ida; married Zenobia N Gregory; children: Julian Jr & Gregory. **Educ:** Norfolk State Col, BS, phys, 1964; Univ Rochester, MS, radiation biol, 1965; Univ Mich, MPH, 1972, PHD, environ health, 1973; Harvard Univ Grad Sch Bus, PMD, admin, 1979. **Career:** Cuyahoga Comm Col, adj math, 1966; NASA, physicist, 1965-67, Health Safety & Security Div, chief, 1983-88, Off Health Serv, dir, 1988, Glenn Res Ctr, dep dir, dir, 2003-05; US Nuclear Regulatory Agency, radiation specialist, 1967-68; Cleveland State Univ, adj prof, 1973, Nance Col Bus Admin, exec-in-residence, 2006-; Capital Univ, adj prof, 1984. **Orgs:** Kappa Alpha Psi Frat Inc, 1963-; fel, US Atomic Energy, 1964; Am Health Phys Soc Pub Info Comm, 1966-73; Am Nuclear Soc, 1966-; health phys consult, 1970-; Environ Pollution Cont Bd NASA, 1970-; US Nuclear Reg Comm Radiation Emergency Team, 1971-; chmn, Norfolk State Col Alumni Assoc, 1971-72; exec safety bd, NASA, 1972-; Nat Urban League Black Exec Exchange Prog, 1973-; bd trustees, Inner City Protestant Par 1974-76, Cuyahoga Community Col, 1987-; Ohio Environ Manpower Symp Strgn Comm, 1974-; pres, orgn Cleveland Chap NTA Inc, 1974-76; visiting comm, Case Western Res, 1975-; chmn, Cleveland Bd Educ Occup Work Exp Adv Bd, 1975-77; nat pres, Nat Tech Asn Inc, 1976-77; bd overseers, Case Western Res, 1977-; Mayors Coun CETA Funded Prog, Cleveland 1980-; bd dir Opportunity Ind Ctr Inc, Nat Black Col Alumni Hall Fame, 1986-. **Honors/Awds:** Certificate of Merit, Fed Exec Bd, 1973; Award for BEEP, Nat Urban League, 1973-74; Distinguished Alumnus Award, Norfolk State Col, 1974; OIC Service Award, 1974; EO Award & Med NASA, 1974; Beta Kappa Chi Sci Hon Soc; Alpha Kappa Mu Honor; resolution passed by Cleveland City Council for Service to Community, 1978; Tech Achievement Award, Soc Black Mfg Engrs & Tech, 1978; Distinguished Service Award, Cleveland Jaycees; Distinguished Service Award, Nat Tech Asn, 1981; Humanitarian Award, Wittenberg Univ, 1983; Distinguished Service Award, Nat Asn Black Accts, 1984; Nat Black Col Alumni Hall of Fame, 1986; Black Col Graduate of Distinction, Nat Urban League, 1987; Technical Achievement Award, Nat Technical Asn, 1987; Acad Excellence Commendation, Univ Miss, 1989; Distinguished Book In Science, Africa-Sci Inst, 1990; Sons of Mandela Award, Cleveland, Nat Asn Advan Colored People, 1990; NASA Medal for Exceptional Achievement, 1995; Strong Men and Women Excellence in Leadership, 1996; Cleveland All Star Salute, 1997; Honorary Doctor of Aeronautics Degree, 1999; Honorary Doctor of Pedagogy Degree, 2000; Salt Lake Olympics Torch Bearer, 2002; Honorary Doctor of Humane Letters, 2003; Presidential Rank Award of Meritorious Executive. **Home Addr:** 2566 Richmond Rd, Beachwood, OH 44122, **Home Phone:** (216)765-0828. **Business Addr:** Executive-in-Residence, Cleveland State University, Nance College of Business Administration, 2121 Euclid Ave, Cleveland, OH 44115-2214, **Business Phone:** (216)687-2000.

EARLY, DELLAREESE PATRICIA. See REESE, DELLA.

EARLY, EZZARD DALE
Automotive executive. **Personal:** Born Aug 15, 1953, Memphis, TN; son of Johne and Nicula B; married Joan, Dec 23, 1977; children: Ashley. **Educ:** Univ Tenn, BS, 1975; Univ St Thomas, MBA, 1984. **Career:** Mo Pac Railroad, asst tech mgr, 1976-77; Conoco Inc, rail fleet super, 1978-84; Vista Chem Co, rail fleet mgr, 1984-85; Deerbrook Forest Chrysler-Jeep Inc, pres, 1987-. **Orgs:** mem-at-large, Nat Automotive Dealers Asn, 2004-; pres, Conrad O Johnson Fines Arts Found; Lake Houston Cult Arts Coun; Rotary Club. **Business Addr:** President, Deerbrook Forest Chrysler-Jeep Inc, 22655 Hwy 59 N, Kingwood, TX 77339, **Business Phone:** (281)359-4000.*

EARLY, DR. GERALD
Writer, educator. **Personal:** Born Apr 21, 1952, Philadelphia, PA; son of Florence Fernandez Oglesby and Henry Early; married Ida Haynes, Aug 27, 1977; children: Linnet Kristen Haynes & Rosalind Lenora Haynes. **Educ:** Univ Pa, Philadelphia, PA, BA, eng lit, 1974; Cornell Univ, Ithaca, NY,MA, eng lit, 1982, PhD, eng lit, 1982. **Career:** Wash Univ, St Louis, MO, instr, Am Cult Studies Prog, dir & co-dir,1991-96, African & Afro-Am Studies Prog, dir, 1992-99, Merle Kling prof modern letters, currently, Ctr Humanities, dir, currently, Ctr Joint Proj Humanities & Social Scis, dir, currently, prof eng, currently, prof Am Cult Studies, currently, prof African & African Am Studies, currently; Minority fel, Univ Kans, 1985-87; Randolph Macon Col Women, Lynchburg, VA,writer residence, 1990. **Orgs:** Fel Am Acad Arts & Sci; invited fel, Nat Humanities Ctr, 2001-02. **Honors/Awds:** The Passing of Jazz's Old Guard, Best American Essays, 1986; Whiting Foundation Writer's Award, Whiting Found, 1988; CCLM/General Electric Foundation Award for Younger Writers, 1988; National Book Critics Circle Award, 1994; Phi Beta Kappa Award for Distinguished Service to the Humanities, Phi Beta Kappa Soc, 2006; 2 times nominated, Grammy Award; Honored, Washington Univ, 2007. **Special Achievements:** Daughters: On Family and Fatherhood, Addison-Wesley, 1994; Auth: How the War in the Streets Is Won Poems on the Quest of Love and Faith; The Culture of Bruising: Essays on Prizefighting, Literature, and Modern American Culture. **Business Addr:** Professor African & Afro-American Studies, Merle Kling Professor of Modern Letters, Washington University, Department of African & African American Studies, McMillan Hall S102 One Brookings Dr, PO Box 1109, St Louis, MO 63130, **Business Phone:** (314)935-5576.

EARLY, IDA H.
School administrator. **Personal:** Born Nov 3, 1952, Dallas, TX; daughter of Oscar E Haynes and Thalia M Ephraim Haynes; married Gerald L, Aug 27, 1977; children: Linnet Kristin Haynes Husi & Rosalind Lenora Haynes. **Educ:** Univ Pa, BA, 1974; Cornell Univ, 1979. **Career:** Univ Pa, asst to the vice provost, 1975-77; Cornell Univ, admin asst to dir, 1980-82; Washington Univ, spec proj, info & found, dir, 1982-93, alumni & develop progs dir, 1993-98, dir progs, 1998-2001, sr assoc dir, alumni & develop, 2001-07, secy bd trustees, 2007-. **Orgs:** Alpha Kappa Alpha, 1974-; bd mem, Washington Univ, Campus YMCA/YWCA, 1987-95; vpres fundraising, 1991-93, pres, 1996-98, Jr League St Louis; bd mem, UN Assoc, 1992-94; United Way Greater St Louis Allocations Panel, 1992-94; bd mem, Epworth C & Family Serv, 1993-99, 2001-05; bd mem, Eden Sem, 1993-2005; bd mem, Dance St Louis, 1993-; bd mem, Asn Jr Leagues Int Inc, 1993-95; Zoo Friends, 2004-; bd mem, Girls Inc, 2005-; bd mem, Webster Community Arts Found, 2003-; bd mem, St Louis Woman's Club, 2007-. **Honors/Awds:** First Year Minority Grad Fel, Cornell Univ, 1977; Difference Maker's Award, Bar Asn Metrop St Louis, 2001. **Special Achievements:** Co-author, "The Consortium for Graduate Study in Management", Selections, The Magazine of the Graduate Management Admission Council, winter 1986, p14-17. **Business Addr:** Secretary to the Board of Trustees, Washington University, 1 Brookings Dr, Campus Box 1081, Saint Louis, MO 63130, **Business Phone:** (314)935-5105.

EARLY, JAMES COUNTS
Government official. **Personal:** Born Jan 12, 1947, Ocala, FL; son of James Tweetie and Altobelle Hampton Flanders; married Miriam Stewart Early; children: Jah-Mir, JaBen. **Educ:** Morehouse Col, Atlanta, GA, BA, 1969; Canal Zone Col, Panama Canal Zone, attended 1967; Howard Univ, Wash, DC, PhD, 1971; Georgetown Univ Advan Port Inst, Wash, DC, attended 1973. **Career:** Antioch Col, Wash, DC, assoc prof, 1976-77; Howard Univ, Wash, DC, WHUR Radio, producer, writer & host, 1978-83; Inst Arts & Humanities, Nat Endowment Humanities, Wash, DC, humanist adminr, 1978-83; Smithsonian Inst, Wash, DC, exec asst, asst secy pub serv, 1984-88, dep asst secy pub serv, 1989-90, actg asst secy pub serv, 1990-91, asst secy educ & pub serv, 1991-95, asst provost Educ & Cult Prog, 1995-, Anacostia Mus & Ctr African Am Hist & Cult, actg dir, Cult Studies & Commun Ctr Folklife Prog & Cult Studies, dir, 1995-. **Orgs:** Arena stage outreach bd, Arena Stage, 1988-; adv bd mem, Textile Mus, 1989; bd vis, Ctr Pub Policy, Union Inst, 1988; bd mem, Wash Moscow Citizens Exchange, 1988; bd, Fondo Del Sol Gallery, 1988; 651 Kings Majestic Theater, bd, 1991; Environ Proj, Wash, bd, 1992; Africa Policy Info Ctr, 1992; Crossroads Mag, ed adv comt, 1990. **Business Addr:** Director Cultural Studies, Communication, Smithsonian Institution, 955 Lenfant Plaza SW, Rm 1406 MRC 923, Washington, DC 20560.*

EARLY, QUINN REMAR
Football player, executive. **Personal:** Born Apr 13, 1965, West Hempstead, NY; married Casandra; children: Quinn Camer & Chance. **Educ:** Univ Iowa, BA, com art, 1988. **Career:** Football player (retired), exec; San Diego Chargers, wide receiver, 1988-90; New Orleans Saints, wide receiver, 1991-95; Buffalo Bills, wide receiver, 1996-98; New York Jets, 1999; White Dragon Schs, teacher, 1997; QPro Products, design dir & vpres, 2002-.

EARLY, ROBERT S.
Educator, college teacher. **Personal:** Born Nov 10, 1935, New York, Zimbabwe; son of Robert S Early Jr and Rose C Jarrett; married Elizabeth Graham, Jun 7, 1986; children: David & Matthew. **Educ:** Univ Hartford, BS, 1957; Morgan State Col, attended 1956. **Career:** Executive (retired); RCA Global Comn, personnel admin, 1958-68; ColtIndus, mgr personnel & pub affairs, 1968-72; Paper Tech Found Western Mich Univ, rep; AMA, instr, 1969-70; Speakman Co, dir personnel & indust rels, 1972-74; Champion Int Corp, dir personnel, 1974-78; Columbia Univ, vpres human resources, 1978-94; Nat Urban League's Black Exec Exchange Prog, visprof, 1978-81; Del Community Col, employee rels instr. **Orgs:** Co chair, Planned Parenthood NY City, 1987, chair, 1989-93; bd pres,Today's Stud Tomorrow's Teachers, 1999-; chmn bd, Intercommunity Camp,Westport, CT; bd dirs, Higher Educ Retirement Community Asn; bd mem, Manhattanville Community Ctr; Metlife Higher Educ Adv Bd; voting bd mem, Empire Blue Cross & Blue Shield. **Military Serv:** AUS, 1954-56. **Home Addr:** 6504 Grand Pt Ave, Bradenton, FL 34201. *

EARLY, SYBIL THERESA
Executive. **Personal:** Born Aug 25, 1952, Staunton, VA. **Educ:** Bradley Univ, MBA, 1972; Fashion Inst, commun, 1974. **Career:**

United Airlines, flight attendant; Winston Network TDI Inc, mgr, acct exec; ET Media Inc, owner, pres, currently. **Orgs:** Nat Asn Female Execs; DuSable Museum. **Honors/Awds:** Winston Network Outstanding Sales Performance, 1981-82 & 1986, Salesperson of the Year, 1983; Assoc Mem of the Year Award, Am Health & Beauty Aids Inst. **Special Achievements:** First female and african-owned independent outdoor advertising firm representing 93% of the out-of-home vendors in the United States. *

EARLY LAMBERT, VIOLET THERESA
School administrator. **Personal:** Born Sep 24, 1924, New Orleans, LA; daughter of William Sr (deceased) and Alphonsine Harris (deceased); married Sylvester Early, Jul 25, 1945 (deceased); married Joe R Lambert, Dec 16, 1991. **Educ:** Young Men's Christian Asn, Sch Com, dipl, 1945; Agr Mech & Normal Col, BS, 1964; Henderson State Univ, MS, Ed, 1977; Univ Ark, LLD, 1993. **Career:** School administrator (retired); Univ Ark, Pine Bluff, asst registrar, 1961-85, foreign stud advisor, 1965-83, registrar/dir admis, 1983-90. **Orgs:** Ark Am Asn Col Registrars & Admis Officers, 1960-; advisor, Alpha Rho Chap, Alpha Kappa Alpha Sorority, 1960-71; advisor, Alpha Kappa Mu Honor Soc, 1970-89; Phi Delta Kappa Fraternity, 1977-; secy, Pine Bluff Boys Club, 1981-83; Kappa Delta Pi Educ Fraternity, 1983-; secy, Am Red Cross Chap, 1985-; secy, Phi Delta Kappa Educ Fraternity, 1985-; Phi Beta Lampda Bus Fraternity; lector, St Peter Catholic Church; vice chmn, Econs Opport Comn, 1975-00; PB Social & Art Civic Club, 1960-; EOC, 1975-; Golden Lion Found; life mem, AMEN/UAPB Alumni Asn; UAPB Found; perpetuator Sylvester Early Endowment Scholar Fund, UAPB, 1980-; volunteer, Am Red Cross; AR RSVP, 1990-; financial sponsor, UAPB Cheerleaders, 1999-; 25 Years Am Red Cross, 2002. **Honors/Awds:** This is Your Life Plaque, Univ Ark, PB, 1983; Alpha Kappa Mu Plaque, 1982-84; Alumni Service Award, AM&N/UAPB Alumni Assoc; Plaque Kappan of Month, Phi Delta Kappa, 1986; Hall of Fame, Leadership Pine Bluff, 1988; Appreciation Award, Royal Knight Soc, 1988; Keepers of the Spirit Hall of Fame, Univ Ark, PB, 1994. **Home Addr:** 706 W 14th St, Pine Bluff, AR 71601. *

EARVIN, LARRY L.
College administrator, chief executive officer. **Personal:** Born Feb 23, 1949, Chattanooga, TN; son of William and Clara Ware; married Valerie Johnson Earvin, Dec 8, 1974 (deceased); children: William Jarrett, Allyson Valeria. **Educ:** Clark Col, BA, 1971; Ga State Univ, MS, 1973; Emory Univ, PhD, 1982. **Career:** City of Atlanta & Clark Col, Atlanta Housing Policy Study, asst dir, 1973-75; Clark Col, Southern Ctr Studies Pub Policy, asst dir, 1975-81, assoc dir, 1981-84; Clark Col, Dept Social Sci, chair & tenured prof polit sci, 1981-87, interim dean fac & instr, 1987-88, Clark Atlanta Univ, dean col, 1988-89, dean Undergraduate Studies, 1989-90, assoc provost & dean stud affairs, 1990-92, assoc provost & acting dean, Sch Arts & Sci, 1992-93, dean, 1993-00; Houston-Tillotson Col, pres, 2000-, chief exec officer, currently. **Orgs:** adv bd mem, Austin Convention & Visitors Bur, 2000-; bd mem, Tex Campus Compact, 2001-; bd mem, Capital Area United Way, 2001-; bd mem, Austin Area Urban League, 2001-; bd mem, Nat Asn Equal Opportunity Higher Educ, 2002-; Univ Senate, United Methodist Church, senator, 2002-; bd mem, Independent Cols & Univ Tex, 2002-; bd mem, Coun Independent Col, 2003-. **Honors/Awds:** NAFEO, Distinguished Alumni, 1998; Clark Atlanta Univ, Distinguished Alumni, 2000; Black Caucus, Texas, Leadership in Education, 2001; Austin Links, Leadership Int Affairs, 2002; Texan of the Year in Higher Educ. **Business Addr:** President, Chief Executive Officer, Huston Tillotson Coll, 900 Chicon St, Austin, TX 78702, **Business Phone:** (512)505-3001.*

EASLER, MICHAEL ANTHONY
Baseball player, basketball coach. **Personal:** Born Nov 29, 1950, Cleveland, OH; married Brenda Jackson; children: Misty, Shandi & Khyla. **Educ:** Cleveland State Univ. **Career:** Baseball player-(Retired), baseball coach: Houston Astros, 1973-75; California Angels, 1976; Pittsburgh Pirates, 1977; Pittsburgh Pirates, 1979-83; Boston Red Sox, outfielder 1984; New York Yankees, outfielder, 1986; Philadelphia Phillies, outfielder, 1987; New York Yankees, outfielder, 1987; Nippon Ham Fighters, prof baseball coach, 1988-89; Milwaukee Brewers, hitting coach, 1992; Boston Red Sox, hitting coach, 1993; St. Louis Cardinals, hitting coach, 1999-2001; Jacksonville Suns, hitting coach, 2006; Las Vegas 51s, hitting coach, 2007; Los Angeles Dodgers, hitting Coach, 2008. **Honors/Awds:** Bo Sox Club's Man of the Year; Roberto Clemente Award, Pittsburgh Pirates, 1980. **Special Achievements:** National League All-Star Team, 1981. *

EASLEY, BILLY HARLEY
Photojournalist. **Personal:** Born Oct 10, 1925, St Louis, MO; son of William Harley and Myrtle Easley Edmondson Johnson; married Gladys Brown Easley, Jan 29, 1958; children: Cassandra V. **Educ:** Tenn State Univ, Nashville, cert, 1944; Nashville Sch Photography, cert, 1949; Nashville Tech Sch, cert, 1975. **Career:** Photojournalist (retired); The Tennessean, Nashville, TN, photojournalist, 1966-00. **Orgs:** National Press Asn, 1967-; Nat Asn Black Journalist, 1985-. **Honors/Awds:** Carter Goodwin Woodson Award-Negro History, 1969; Metro Firefighters Association Award, 1977; National Press Association Award, 1979; Gannett Award, Gannett Publishing, 1984; Gannett Award, Special Olympics Photo Competition, 1987. **Military Serv:** AUS, Corporal, 1943-45. **Home Addr:** 1906 15th Ave S, Nashville, TN 37212. *

EASLEY, BRENDA VIETTA
Association executive. **Personal:** Born Jun 28, 1951, Buffalo, NY; daughter of James T and Lacetta Dixon; children: Cynthia Duncan, Bryon Duncan & Robert Webb. **Career:** Buffalo & Erie County Public Library, Buffalo, NY, prin library clerk, 1968-88; Catholic Diocese Buffalo, Buffalo, NY, dir, off black ministry, 1988-. **Orgs:** Mem & chairperson, Nat Asn Black Catholic Admin, 1989-; reg coord, Nat Black Catholic Congress, 1989-; chair, mem, commun comt, Buffalo Area Metropolitan Ministers Bd Trustees, 1989-. **Business Addr:** Director, Office of Black Ministry, Catholic Diocese of Buffalo, 795 Main St, Buffalo, NY 14203.

EASLEY, CHARLES F., SR.
School administrator, consultant, vice president (organization). **Personal:** Born May 3, 1935, Dalton, GA; son of Oscar Sr and Bertha Kenyon; married Helen Saxton Easley, Jun 19, 1960 (deceased); children: Charles Jr, Tania Patrice. **Educ:** Knoxville Col, AB, 1956; Teachers Col, Columbia Univ, teacher cert, 1960; Atlanta Univ, Clark Atlanta Univ, MA, 1965; Ga State Univ, 1978. **Career:** School administrator (retired); Stephens Sch, counr social studies, asst prin, 1958-65; Morris Brown Col, dean stud & asst prof, 1965-74; Nat Urban League, fel prog, consult, 1967-73; Atlanta Jr Metrop Col, vpres stud affairs, 1974-97; Easley & Assoc, consult, 1997. **Orgs:** Phi Delta Kappa Educ Fraternity, 1972-; Warren Memorial Boys Club, 1980-86; bd trustees, secy, personnel comt chair, Trinity Sch, 1980-; Leadership Atlanta, 1982-; pres & secy, West Fulton Rotary Club, 1985-94; nat pres, Nat Coun Presbyterian Men, 1992-94; consult, Southwest Atlanta Youth Acad & Athletic Asn, 1992; West End Rotary Club, 1994-; vice moderator, 215th Gen Assembly, Presbyterian Church, USA, 2003. **Honors/Awds:** State Teacher of the Year, Ga Teachers & Educ Asn, 1963; Distinguished Alumni Award, NAFEO, 1992; Family of the Year, Nat Coun Negro Women, 1992; Churchman of the Year, Nat Coun Presbyterian Men, 1994. **Special Achievements:** "Personnel Selection & Placement in Selected Industries," master's thesis, 1964. **Military Serv:** AUS, sp-5, 1958-60; Res Comn, 1962-68. **Home Addr:** 787 Duffield Dr NW, Atlanta, GA 30318, **Home Phone:** (404)792-2024. *

EASLEY, DAMION (JACINTO DAMION EASLEY)
Baseball player. **Personal:** Born Nov 11, 1969, New York, NY; married Dawn; children: Rocky, Jazmin, Nathaniel & Jayce Derrick. **Educ:** Long Beach City Col, attended 1988. **Career:** Calif Angels, infielder, 1992-96; Detroit Tigers, 1996-2002; Tampa Bay Devil Rays, 2003; Fla Marlins, 2004-05; Ariz Diamondbacks, 2006; New York Mets, 2007-. **Honors/Awds:** AL All Star Team, 1998. **Business Phone:** (718)507-6387.*

EASLEY, DR. EDDIE V.
Educator. **Personal:** Born Nov 16, 1928, Lynchburg, VA; son of George Easley and Berta Easley; married Ruth Burton; children: Jacqueline, Michael & Todd. **Educ:** Va State Univ, BS, 1948; Iowa State Univ, MS, 1951, PhD, 1957. **Career:** Drake Univ, chmn prof, 1957-65 & 1966-84; Univ Wis Milwaukee, prof, 1965-66; Kimberly Clark Corp, mkt specialist, 1969-70; Wake Forest Univ, prof bus, 1984-99, prof emer, currently. **Orgs:** Alpha Phi Alpha Frat, 1946-; Am Mkt Asn, 1957-; Bd Zoning Adj, 1971-73; Nat Asn Advan Colored People, 1985; Sigma Pi Phi, 1985; Bd YMCA, Winston-Salem, 1990-94. **Honors/Awds:** Outstanding Teacher Award, Drake Univ, 1968; Outstanding Educator of America, 1970. **Special Achievements:** Author Contemporary Business: Challenges and Opportunities, 1978. **Military Serv:** AUS, sp3, 1954-56; Honorable discharge 1956. **Home Addr:** 4121 Winchester Rd, Winston-Salem, NC 27106. **Business Addr:** Professor Emeritus of Business, Wake Forest University, School of Business and Accountancy, 1834 Wake Forest Rd, Kirby Hall, Winston-Salem, NC 27106, **Business Phone:** (336)758-5304.

EASLEY, JACINTO DAMION. See EASLEY, DAMION.

EASLEY, JACQUELINE RUTH
Executive. **Personal:** Born Oct 21, 1957, Ames, IA; daughter of Dr Eddie V and Ruth Burton; married Odell McGhee; children: Carey Lucia, Ty Ellington. **Educ:** Carleton Col, BA, 1980. **Career:** Am Repub Ins Co, personnel assoc, 1980, asst vpres personnel, 1984. **Orgs:** Board trustees, Drake Univ; bd trustees, Blank Hosp; bd dir, YWCA Des Moines, 1983, pres, 1987; United Way Central IA, 1984; Minority Ed Braintrust, 1985; exec comt, NAACP, 1987; chairperson, Metropolitan Transit Authority, 1990. **Honors/Awds:** Woman Achievement, 1984; YWCA of Des Moines, 1984; Des Moines Register, Up & Coming Business Leader, 1986; Excellence in Leadership, 1990; Outstanding Young Citizen, Des Moines Jaycess, 1990; bd educ, Des Moines Independent Sch Dist, 1990-00, pres, 1994; Outstanding Young Iowan, Iowa Jaycees; Am Best and Brightest Bus Prof, 1992. *

EASLEY, KENNY MASON, JR.
Football player, businessperson. **Personal:** Born Jan 15, 1959, Chesapeake, VA; married Gail. **Educ:** Univ Calif, Los Angeles, BA, polit sci. **Career:** Football player (retired), Business person; Seattle Seahawks, safety, 1981-87; Makena Sport, owner; Foster-Easley Sports Mgt Group, owner; Roller Wheels Inc, owner; Alderwood Olds-Cadillac, owner; Sherm's BBQ Inc, owner; Norfolk Nighthawks, part-owner; bus entrepreneur, currently. **Orgs:** United Cerebral Palsy. **Honors/Awds:** Pro Bowl Selection, 1982-85 & 1987; AFC Defensive Player of the Year, 1983; Defensive Player of the Year, Nat Football League, 1984; Defensive Back of the Year, Nat Football League Alumni Asn; Virginia Sports Hall of Fame, 1998; First-team All-Nat Football League; Seagram Sports Award; First-team, All Asian Football Consideration; Seahawks Most Valuable Player; AFC Defensive Player of the Week; AFC Defensive Rookie of the Year; First-team All-Rookie; AFC Defensive Player of the Year; Football Hall of Fame, 1994; Seahawks Ring of Honor, 2002. **Special Achievements:** A four time All-Pacific 10 Conference selection, 1977, 1978, 1979 & 1980; Finished ninth in the Heisman Trophy balloting, 1980.

EASLEY, REV. PAUL HOWARD
Clergy. **Personal:** Born Sep 7, 1930, Charleston, WV; son of Alexander Pamplin Sr and Estella Allen; married Sarita (deceased); children: Paul Jr, Verita Green & David Allen. **Educ:** WV State Col, BS, 1956; Gammon Theol Sem, BD, 1959; Iliff Sch Theo, MTS, 1972; Interdenominational Theol Sem, MDiv, 1974. **Career:** John Wesley United Methodist Church, 1955-56; Seebert Charge, 1956; Fairmont Trinity Methodist Church, pastor, 1959-61; Roncevert-White Sulpher Charge, pastor, 1961; AUS, chaplain, 1961-80; Clark Col, chaplain, 1980-81; Clark Atlanta Univ, Atlanta, GA, univ chaplain; Ben Hill United Methodist Church, assoc pastor, currently. **Orgs:** Military Chaplains Asn, 1962-; Am Correctional Chaplains, 1964-; Correctional Chaplains Asn, 1964-; Clinical Pastoral Asn, 1977-; Nat Campus Ministers Asn, 1980-; charter pres, Optimist Int, 1984-; pres, PTA Therral HS, 1984-85; Omega Psi Phi Fraternity; Free & Accepted Masons; Nat Asn Advan Colored People; WV Conf, United Methodist Ch; Am Legion. **Honors/Awds:** Correctional Chaplain of Year, 1974; Year Book Dedication of the Year, Clark Col, 1981; Hall of Fame, ROTC WV State Col, 1986; Garnet High Hall of Fame, Charleston, WVA, 1996. **Special Achievements:** AUS, First Afro-American Colonel of the Regiment of the Chaplains Corps, 1993-96. **Military Serv:** AUScol 23 yrs; Legion of Merit, Bronze Star (2), Meritorious Serv Medal, Army Commendation (2). **Business Addr:** Associate Pastor, Ben Hill United Methodist Church, Kresge Hall 2099 Fairburn SW Rd Suite 201, Atlanta, GA 30331, **Business Phone:** (404)344-0618.

EASON, REV. GREGORY V
Clergy. **Personal:** Born Dec 24, 1960, Metter, GA. **Educ:** E Ga Col, Swainsboro, AA, 1981; Morris Brown Col, Atlanta, GA, BA, polit sci, 1983; Interdenominational Theol Ctr, Atlanta, GA, MDiv, 1986; Columbia Theol Sem, Decatur, GA, ThM, 1988. **Career:** St Mark & Hickman Tabernacle African Methodist Episcopal Church, Wadley & Augusta, GA, sr pastor, 1984-86; St James African Episcopal Church, Thomsom, GA, sr pastor, 1986-88; St James African Methodist Episcopal Church, Monticello, GA, sr pastor, 1988-90; St Phillip African Methodist Church, Savannah, GA, sr pastor, 1990-2004; Flipper Temple African Methodist Episcopal Church, Atlanta, GA, sr pastor, 2004-05; Big Bethen African Methodist Episcopal Church, Atlanta, GA, sr pastor, 2005-. **Orgs:** Bd trustees, Morris Brown Col, Atlanta, GA; bd trustees, Turner Theol Sem, Atlanta, GA; bd mem, Sicke Cell Asn, Savannah, GA; bd mem, Family Independence Adv Bd, Chatham County Dept Family & C Servs; vchmn & chair person, Savannah Dist Comt Preachers Annual Conf & Preachers Orders, 1990-2004; chairperson, Ga Annual Conf Bd Examiners, 1991-2004; chair person, Finance comt, Atlanta N Ga Annual Conf, 1991-2004; chair person, Ministerial Efficiency Comt Ga Annual Conf, 1991-2004; vpres, Connectioanl Coun African Methodist Episcopal Church, 2005-. **Special Achievements:** Auth: Looking at Aids Through the Eyes of God, 1991; Dreams and Nightmares, 1995; Article: "A Small Boy with a Big Fish". **Business Phone:** (404)827-9707.

EASON, OSCAR, JR.
Government official, civil rights activist. **Personal:** Born Jun 30, 1930, San Antonio, TX; son of Oscar and Doris Lucille; married Lois Anne Eason, Feb 3, 1961; children: Angela Green, Oscar Eason III. **Educ:** Prairie View A&M Col, BS, mech engineering, 1956; St Mary's Univ, MS, engineering, 1970. **Career:** Pac Architects & Engrs Inc, sup gen engr, 1970-72; Environ Protection Agency, gen engr, 1973-74; US Navy, Trident Missile Syst, proj mgr, 1974-81; AUS, Corps Engrs, sup mech engr, 1981-91, Chief Engineering Div, asst, 1991-. **Orgs:** Nat Soc Prof Engrs, 1972-; vpres, Northwest Coalition Against Malicious Harrassment, 1983-87; vpres, Seattle King City Dispute Resolution Ctr, 1983-92; bd mem, pres, NAACP, Seattle, 1983-; Nat pres, Blacks Govt Inc, 1994; Black Leadership Forum, 1995-; chair, Comn African-Am Affairs, 2006. **Honors/Awds:** Appreciation for Contrib, US Navy, Trident Weapon Syst Prog, 1981; Employee of the Year, Seattle Federationeral Exec Bd, 1990; Community Serv Award, Nordstorm Dept Stores, Outstanding Citizen Northwest, 1990; Achievement Medal Civilian Serv, US Army, Kuwait Emergency Recovery Off, 1991; Community Serv Award, Seattle Dist, Corps Engrs, 1992; Black Engr Award, Affirmative Action,

1996. **Special Achievements:** Newspaper articles: Trying to Liberate Whites from Prison of Prejudice, Seattle Times Newspaper; Halt the Cycle of Despair for Young Black Men; Analyzing Remarks By Nakasone; A Look At Changing White Attitudes Toward Black Americans; Nike Needs Push to Change Its Policies, Seattle Post Intelligencer; Total School Integration Remains the Only Answer, Seattle Post Intelligencer. **Military Serv:** AUS, spec-4, 1950-52. **Home Addr:** 5507 S Leo St, Seattle, WA 98178, **Home Phone:** (206)725-5303. **Business Addr:** Assistant to Chief, US Army Corps of Engineers, Engineering Div, 4735 E Marginal Way S PO Box 3755, Washington, DC 98134-2385, **Business Phone:** (206)764-3742.*

EASON-STEELE, ELAINE
Television producer, social worker. **Career:** The Rosa & Raymond Parks Inst, co-founder, 1987-; TV series: "Signs & Wonders", 1995; "Intimate Portrait", 2001; "The Rosa Parks Story", 2002. **Business Addr:** Co-Founder, Rosa & Raymond Parks Institute for Self Development, 65 Cadillac Sq Suite 2200, Detroit, MI 48226, **Business Phone:** (313)965-0606.

EASTER, ERIC KEVIN
Publisher, media executive, executive. **Personal:** Born Jan 19, 1961, Baltimore, MD; married Tina Tamara Hamilton. **Educ:** Howard Univ, BA, jour, 1983. **Career:** DC Coalition for the Homeless, exec dir, 1984; Easter & Assocs, pres, 1985-88; Jackson PRS, press ast, 1988; Nat Rainbow Coalition, press secy, 1988-90; Wilder PRS, press secy, 1991-92; New African Visions, pres, 1989-; One Media Inc, chair/chief exec officer, 1992-; Akin & Randolph Agency, creative consult, literary agent; Wash Area Lawyers Arts, exec dir, currently. **Orgs:** Nat Asn Black Journalists, 1984-; Howard Univ Commun Alumni Asn, 1985-86; secy, WritersCorps. **Honors/Awds:** Mayor's Special Recognition, City NY, 1992; Sojourner Truth Award, Links, 1993. **Special Achievements:** Co-creator, "Songs of My People" book and exhibit, 1992; co-producer, Taste of DC Annual Festival, 1991-. **Business Phone:** (202)289-4440.*

EASTER, HEZEKIAH H.
State government official. **Personal:** Born Oct 16, 1921, Suffolk, VA; son of Jamie Elnora Woodruff and Hezekiah; married Ruth D Lowe; children: Gregory Paul, Michael Curtis & Scott Anthony. **Educ:** Juilliard Sch Music; Metro Music Sch; NY S Indust & Labor Rels Sch;Cornell Univ. **Career:** Government official (retired); Nyack Village, trustee, 1965, 1967, 1969;Metro Area Apprentice Training, supvr, 1968-72; Rockland Co Legis,1969-89, republican legis emer; NY Dept Labor, job training specialist,1972-84; pub work wage investor, 1984-90. **Orgs:** Rockland Acacia Lodge No 59; trustee, Pilgrim Baptist Church; life mem, Nyack br NAACP; adv coun, BSA Rockland Co Coun, 1965; Nyack Rotary, 1965-77; Nyack Hosp Corp, 1966; sec bd vis, Letchworth Village, 1969,1974; pres, Mt Moor Cemetery Assn, 1977; pres, Hudson Valley Regional Coun, 1981-82; bd dirs, Welfare League, Letchworth Village, 1984-90; vpres,African-Am Hist Soc Rockland County, 1987; bd dirs, Abbott House, 1990. **Honors/Awds:** Distinguished Service Award, Rockland Coun BSA, 1962; Citizen of the Year,VFW, 1967; Rep of the Year, Orange town Rep Club, 1973; Service Award,Nyack Village Bd, 1971; Dr Martin Luther King Brotherhood Award, Human Rights Comn, LVDC, 1975; Capitals of the Age of Enlightment Award, AFSCI,1976; Outstanding Achievement, Kappa Alpha Psi Fraternity, 1988; 20 Years Service Award, Rockland Co Legis, 1989; Lifetime Achievement Award,Chamber Com Nyacks, 1990; Desert Storm for World Peace Medal, 1991; Gov's Medal for Conspicuous Public Service, 1992; inducted into the Rockland County Civil Rights Hall of Fame, 2004. **Special Achievements:** First Black elected to public office Rockland County. **Military Serv:** AUS, corporal, 1942-45. **Home Addr:** 100 N Franklin St, Nyack, NY 10960.

EASTER, DR. MARILYN
Educator. **Personal:** Born Jan 6, 1957, Oklahoma City, OK; daughter of William L Pettigrew and Delois Ann Pettigrew; married Dr Walter. **Educ:** Univ Colo, BA, 1979; Denver Univ, MA&MSW, 1981; Univ San Francisco, EdD, 1992. **Career:** General Dentistry, mkt mgr, 1982; Amador Adult Sch, instr, 1983-89; Chabot Col, instr, 1985-87; Nat Univ, Oakland, CA, adj prof, 1985-89; Chabot Comm Col, instr, 1987-89; Calif St Univ, lectr, 1987-99; St Mary's Col, mkt chair assoc prof, 1994-96; Col Notre Dame, from assoc prof to prof, 1994-99; Univ Calif, consult & actg dir, 2000; San Jose St Univ, Dept Mkt & Decisions Sci, lectr, 2000-02, assoc prof, 2002-. **Orgs:** Phi Delta Kappa Fraternity, 1991-; Nat Asn Girl Scouts Am, 1991-95; Am Soc Training & Develop, 1993-97; Calif St Teachers Asn, 1994-; NAACP, 1997-; chmn, College Notre Dame, SAFE, 1997-; co-chmn, steering comt, Col Notre Dame, 1997-; Asn Bus Commun; Int Acad Bus Commun; Asn Prof Commun Consult; Nat Asn African Am Studies. **Honors/Awds:** Outstanding Student Council Leadership Award, 1992; Outstanding Dissertation Award, 1993. **Special Achievements:** Publications: The ABCs of Marketing a Successful Business, 1986; Stress & Coping Mechanism Among Female Dentists, 1991; Evaluation of Higher Education, A Case Study, 1992; Picking the Perfect School, 1993; A Triangulated Reseaarch Design for Studying Stress, 1993; Emmy Nominee, Affirmative Action Pro 209, 1997. **Business Phone:** (408)924-3530.

EASTER, RUFUS BENJAMIN, JR.
School administrator, executive director, technician. **Personal:** Born Oct 5, 1928, Hampton, VA; married Evelyn Wills. **Educ:** NY Univ, Hampton Inst; Temple Univ; Piano Tech Schs. **Career:** Hampton Univ, admin, 1950, Music Dept, instr, Auxiliary Enterprises, dir, Sch Lib Arts Educ, Dept Music, piano technician, currently; Va State Sch Deaf & Blind, curric developer, consult to supt, 1954; Hampton Asn Arts & Humanities, founder, exec dir, 1967; WVEC, consult community affairs radio & TV stas, 1970; Whittaker Memorial Hosp, veteran; Newport News Gen Hosp, veteran. **Orgs:** Bd dirs, Asn Col & Univ Concert Managers; Peninsula Symphony Orchestra; Peninsula Community Theatre; Asn Coun Arts; Asn State & Local Hist; Asn Preserv Va Antiq; Bachelor Benedict Club; Eastern State Hosps Human Rights Comt & Hosp Adv Bd; Hampton-Newport News Community Serv Adv Bd; pres, Nat Alliance Ment Ill; chmn, Insight Enterprises Peninsula Ctr Independent Living. **Honors/Awds:** Man of the Year Award, Peninsula Vol Serv Bur, 1969. **Business Addr:** Piano Technician, Hampton University, Dept Music Sch Lib Arts Educ, Armstrong Hall Rm 137, Hampton, VA 23668.*

EASTER, WILFRED OTIS, JR.
School administrator. **Personal:** Born May 26, 1941, New York, NY; son of Wilfred Otis Sr and Mae Smith; married Mary Moore (divorced 1986); children: Allison Garner & Mallory; married Donna Maxey, Nov 25, 1990. **Educ:** Harvard Col, Cambridge, MA, BA, hist, 1964, Univ Minn, Minneapolis, MN, 1974-79. **Career:** Sports Illus Mag, New York, NY, advert prom, 1964-66; Windsor Mountain Sch, Lenox, MA, teacher & coach, 1966-68; Carleton Col, Northfield, MN, assoc dean studs, 1968-76; Control Data Corp, Minneapolis, MN, opers mgr, 1979-86; Univ Calif, Berkeley, CA, exec dir, 1986-. **Orgs:** Nat Asn PreCol Dirs, 1986-; Nat Asn Minority Eng Prog Adminrs, 1986-; Northern Calif Coun Black Prof Engrs,1986-; East Bay GO Club, 1986-; World Wildlife Fund, 1987-. **Honors/Awds:** Public Speaking Prize, Harvard College, 1964. **Home Addr:** 266 Adams St, Oakland, CA 94610. **Business Addr:** Executive Director, University California Berkeley, Lawrence Hall Sci, Berkeley, CA 94720, **Business Phone:** (510)642-5064.

EASTER, WILLIAM H, III
Executive. **Personal:** Born Jan 1, 1949?, Denver, CO; married Barbara; children: 2. **Educ:** Univ Houston, Bauer Col Bus, BBA, 1971; Stanford Univ, Grad Sch Bus, MS. **Career:** Conoco Inc, Gulf Coast Refining, Mkt & Transp Bus, gen mgr, 1998-2002; Conoco Phillips, vpres state Govt Affairs, 2002-04; DCP Midstream, LLC, chmn bd, pres & chief exec officer, 2004-08; TEPPCO GP, LLC, dir, 2004-05; DCP Midstream GP, LLC, dir, 2005-08; DCP Midstream Partners, LP, dir, 2008-. **Orgs:** Junior Achievement Rocky Mountain Inc; Univ Colo Denver Bus Sch Adv Bd; Exec Leadership Coun; La Mid-Continent Oil & Gas Asn; Chamber Com SW La; vice chmn, Am Chamber Com. **Honors/Awds:** Eagle Leadership Award, Nat Eagle Leadership Inst; DuPont Marketing Excellence Award; Conoco Distinguished Community Service Award. **Special Achievements:** One of the 75 Most Powerful African Americans in Corporate America by Black Enterprise magazine in 2005. **Business Addr:** Director, DCP Midstream Partners, LP, 370 17th St Suite 2775, Denver, CO 80202, **Business Phone:** (303)633-2900.*

EASTMOND, ARLINGTON LEON, JR.
President (organization). **Personal:** Son of Arlington Leon Sr; married; children: 3. **Career:** A L Eastmond & Sons Inc, chief exec officer; EASCO Boiler Corp pres & owner, 1981-. **Orgs:** NAACP; Urban League; Am Boiler Manufacturers Assn; Oil Heat Assn; Minority Students Business Club. **Honors/Awds:** Ernest & Young, Minority Regional Manufacturer of the Year, 1977; MBDA, Minority Manufacturer of the Year, 1996; NYS Governor's Award, 1995; Star Lite, Little League Award. **Special Achievements:** Company is ranked 77 on Black Enterprise magazine's list of top 100industrial service companies. Nation's only African-American manufacturer of boilers and steel storage tanks. **Business Addr:** Owner, EASCO Boiler Corp, 1175 Legett Ave, Bronx, NY 10474, **Business Phone:** (718)378-3000.*

EASTMOND, JOAN MARCELLA
Educator, president (organization). **Personal:** Born May 10, 1940, Brooklyn, NY; daughter of Evans E and Lerta Taylor; children: Brian S Malone. **Educ:** W Va State Col, BS, home econ, 1963; Cornell Univ, summer instr Afro Am Studies, cert, 1969; Lincoln Univ, Master Human Services, 1988; Union Experimental Cols/ Univ, PhD, 1988. **Career:** NY City Bd Educ, teacher, 1963-70; State Educ Opportunity Ctr, instr; Afram Asn, asst to pres, 1971-78; Bedford Study Restoration Corp, dir youth employment, 1978-85; Ft Green Sr Citizens Ctr, dir youth workers, sr ctr, 1985-; Lincoln Univ, adj prof, field study coord, 1988-. **Orgs:** Pres, Soc Unlimited, 1964-; chmn, Cotilion Found Comm, Nat Asn Bus Prof Women's Clubs, 1980-; Fund Raising Comt, NY Coun UNCF, 1980-84; chmn, Teens Found Comm, Jack & Jill Am, 1983-88; bd mem, Afram Assoc, 1987-, Health Watch, 1988-. **Honors/Awds:** Crisco Award, Home Economic Dept WVSC, 1963; Trophy, Lil' Sisters Soc Unlimited, 1966; Essence Women, 1971; Afrikan Liberation Day Bibliography (15pp), 1973; Devel Activities (12pp), 1973; Citation, Nat Coun Black Child Devel, 1974; Citation, Greater NY Coun, Exploring Div, 1981; Cert, 88 Precinct Coun, 1987; Key Women of America Award; Proclamation NYS Senate. **Home Addr:** 342 Macon St, Brooklyn, NY 11233. *

EASTON, EARNEST LEE
School administrator. **Educ:** Chicago City Col, AA, 1968; Univ Ill, Chicago, polit sci & german, 1970; Syracuse Univ, Maxwell Sch Citizenship & Affairs, masters, pub admin, 1971; Cornell Univ, MA, Am politics, 1975, PhD, Am politics, 1978. **Career:** Cornell Univ, Dept Govt, teaching asst, 1973-76, judicial admin, CT, 1976, prof philos, 1996-97; Entertainment related employment, 1978-; independent scholar, 1983-; writer, 1983-; Univ Pres Positions, presidency caliber cand, 1999; Foreign policy/ licensing, consult; Countries World, regist consult, 1999. **Orgs:** Creative Living Ctr; Writer's Guild, Los Angeles, 1983-; Bd UN Asn Am, Los Angeles, 1983, S Bend, Ind, 1993; Songwriters Guild, 1985; Artist Embassy; Am Polit Sci Asn, 2007-. **Honors/ Awds:** Numerous awards & commendations for heroic deeds. **Special Achievements:** Entertained Am soldiers in Germ, 1964-65; written screenplays: The Nightrider; The Hitchhiker; The Knightrider & the Helicopter Pirates; The Favorite One. **Business Addr:** Writer, 407 Lincoln Way W, PO Box 533, South Bend, IN 46624, **Business Phone:** (219)239-3185.

EASTON, RICHARD JAMES
Executive. **Personal:** Born Jul 30, 1934, Chicago, IL; married Iris A Walker; children: Michael, Danitra, Richard Jr, Shawn, Ricarda, Erika. **Educ:** Chicago State Univ, BS, 1962. **Career:** NYC, teacher, 1963-67; Bedford & Stuyvesant Restoration Corp, mgr, 1967-70; Recruitment & Training Prog, dir, 1970-75; NY State Spec Dept Controllers Off, chief analyst, 1976-77; Munic Credit Union NYC, controller. **Orgs:** Asn Accts; Nat Bus Teachrs Asn; Alpha Phi Alpha. **Military Serv:** USN, 1952-55. *

EATMAN, JANICE A
Manager, counselor. **Personal:** Born Mar 3, 1959, Cleveland, OH. **Educ:** Northwestern Univ, BS, Commun, 1981; Cleveland State Univ, Post Grad Work, 1983-86; Case Western Reserve Univ, MNO, 2001. **Career:** Welfare Rights Org, community rel specialist, 1984; Ohio Works, recruiter, 1985; Voc Guid Servs, employ & training specialist, 1985-88; Case Western Reserve Univ, intervention asst, 1987-90; HE Davis Intermediate Sch, coordr youth resource ctr, 1989-96, prog coordr Proj, STEP-UP, 1996-98, asst dir Edu Serv Learning Progs, 1998. **Orgs:** Northwestern Alumni Assoc Cleveland Chapter, 1981-; public relations consult, Group Dynamics Inc 1982-83; vol, UNCF 1983-; Messengers Joy Gospel Ensemble, 1984-86; planning comm, Martin Luther King Jr Day Celebration 1984-85; Urban League Greater Cleveland Fund Develop Comm, 1984-85; grad adv, Alpha Kappa Alpha Sor Inc, 1985-88; publicity co-chair, Ways & Mean Comm AKA Prog Years, 1985, 1986; Northwestern Black Alumni Assoc, 1986; presenter, Carver Connection Adopt-A-School Prog, 1987-88; presenter, Career Days Cleveland Public Sch, 1987-88; League Park Ctr Bd Mgrs, 1995-98, 2000-, treas, 2001; trainer, Tutoring & Mentoring Programs, 1996-; adv, Black Greek, Case W Reserve Univ, 2000-. **Honors/Awds:** Vol Serv Award, HARAMBEE Serv Black Families, 1983; Vol Award, Cleveland Pub Sch, Carver Connection Adopt-A-Sch, 1988; Workshop presenter, Pittsburgh Civic Garden Ctr, 1988. **Home Phone:** (216)481-7806.

EATMAN, JOSEPH W
Executive. **Career:** Corp Off Syst Inc, pres; Workplace Integrators, owner, dealer prin, currently; Off Concepts Inc, prin & pres. **Business Addr:** Dealer Principal, WorkPlace Integrators, 965 W Chicago Ave, Chicago, IL 60622, **Business Phone:** (312)942-1100.*

EATMAN, DR. TIMOTHY K
Educator. **Personal:** Born Dec 28, 1968, New York, NY; son of Charles and Lorraine; married Janet Quinones-Eatman, Aug 20, 1994; children: Jasmin Africali & Jamila Grace. **Educ:** Pace Univ, BS, 1991; Howard Univ, MED, 1993; Univ Ill, Urbana-Champaign, PhD, 2001. **Career:** Univ Ill, Comt Inst Coop, prog coordr, 1997-2000; Univ Ill, proj coordr & researcher, 2000-; Univ Mich, Ctr Study Higher & Postsecondary Educ, postdoctoral scholar, 2001-, Imagining Am, proj dir res & policy, currently, Imagining Am, co-prin investr, currently. **Orgs:** Alpha Phi Alpha, 1987-; bd dir, Mt Pleasant Christian Asn, 1992-; Am Ed Res Asn, 1993-; Phi Delta Kappa, 1994-; Brothers Acad, Leadership Team, 2000-; budget dir, Bros Acad Res Inst. **Special Achievements:** Numerous publications. **Business Addr:** Postdoctoral Scholar, Co-Principal Investigator, University of Michigan, Imagining America, 1210 Buhr Bldg 3213 837 Greene St, Ann Arbor, MI 48104-3213, **Business Phone:** (734)615-7287.

EATON, MINETTA GAYLOR
Educator. **Personal:** Born Oct 1, 1912, Whitakers, NC; married James W; children: Jeanne Phillips & Faye Yvonne. **Educ:** Morgan State Univ, BA, 1936; NY Univ, MA, 1942; NY Univ, Chicago, additional study tour Europe. **Career:** Raleigh City Schs NC, prin, 1959-73, teacher, 1944-59; Spaulding High Sch NC, teacher, librn, 1938-44; Brick Sch NC, teacher, 1936-38. **Orgs:** St 2nd vpres, exec bd, NC Admin Women Educ; NC Nat Coun Admin Women Educn; co-chairperson mem comn, St Dist & Raleigh-Wake Unit NC Retired Personnel; NC Asn Educrs; Nat Educ Asn;

Nat Elem Prins Asn; bd dir, Downtown Housing Improv Corp, 1974-77; bd dir, Res Triangle Lung Asn; bd dir, Wake Co Ment Health Asn; NC bd dir, Ment Health Asn; adv coun, Inner City Satellite Ment Health Ctr; St Steering Com; chairperson com state's, 1975 fall forum NC Coun Women's Orgn Inc; Nat Coun Negro Women; Com Admin & Mgt YWCA; Am Asn Univ Women; Alpha Kappa Alpha Sorrity Inc; Women Action Prev Violence & Its Causes; Task Force S Cent Comn; RSVP Adv Coun Bd, 1975-77; Wake Black Dem Cauces; NAACP; Raleigh-Wake Cit Asn; Dem Women Wake Co; Alphabettes Raleigh; Prestige Club; First Bapt Chap; Notable Am Era. **Honors/Awds:** Honored Radio Sta WPTF NC comn leader Am Award, 1969; Appointed State co-chairperson, Women Action Prev Violence's State Chap Meeting; Nat Publicity Com Moles Inc; Mid-Altantic Reg Nominating Com Alpha Kappa Alpha Sorority; Several Awards Alpha Theta Omega Chap of Alpha Kappa Alpha Sorority 1975; honored, Alpha Kappa Alpha Sorority Inc; Ilpah Thega Omega Chap; cert, Nat Caucus Black Aged Inc, 1974-75. *

EATON, THELMA LUCILE
Educator, elementary school teacher, college teacher. **Personal:** Born Dec 17, 1928, New Orleans, LA; daughter of T R W Harris and Inez Porter; married William; children: Maurice & Allison. **Educ:** Fisk Univ, BA, 1949; Xavier Univ, attended 1951; NY Univ, attended 1952; Univ Southern Calif, MSW, 1965, DSW, 1973. **Career:** Whittier Col, prof, 1970-94, prof emer, currently; Univ Southern Calif, Mini-Col, Admin Off Soc Work Prog; Dept Social Serv, staff develop officer training & supv; Suicide Prevent Ctr, psychiat soc worker; Orleans Parish Sch Bd, teacher nursery sch & elem sch. **Orgs:** Am Asn Univ Prof; State Leason Comn Human Serv; Nat Asn Soc Work; Geront Soc; Soc Stud Social Prob; Coun Social Work Educ; Nat Coun Negro Women; adv bd, Rio Hondo United Way; Univ Southern Calif, Geront Ctr Serv Black Aged; Nat Caucus Black Aged; Greater LA Community Action Agency; bd dirs, YWCA; Foster Grandparent Prog; Retired Sr Vol Prog; Rio Hondo Vol Ctr; pres, Awar Women Calif; Calif Demo State Ctr Comn, LA County Cent Comn; Alpha Kappa Delta; Calif State Comn; dir, Nat Coalition 100 Black Women. **Honors/Awds:** Outstanding Educator of America, 1974; Notable American Award, 1976-77; Key to Whittier College, 1976; Outstanding Women of the Year, Success Ltd Gov Calif; Community Service Award, Assembly Black Women's Lawyers. **Home Addr:** 1644 Wellington Rd, Los Angeles, CA 90019. **Business Addr:** Professor Emeritus, Whittier College, 13406 Philadelphia, PO Box 634, Whittier, CA 90608-0634.*

EAVES, DR. EUGENE
College administrator, educator. **Educ:** NC Cent Univ, PhD, 1958. **Career:** NC Cent Univ, interim provost & vice chancellor acad affairs, Off Int Affairs, dir, dean, prof, Dept Int Rels, prof emer, currently. **Business Addr:** Professor Emeritus, North Carolina Central University, Office of International Affairs, 104 Old Sr Bldg, Durham, NC 27701, **Business Phone:** (919)530-7912.

EAVES, DR. JOHN H.
College administrator, county government official. **Personal:** Born in Jacksonville, FL; married Lisa; children: Isaac & Keturah. **Educ:** Morehouse Col, BS, math, 1984; Yale Univ, MS, relig, 1987; Univ SC, PhD, educ admin, 1999. **Career:** Southern Educ Found, prog officer; Kennesaw State Univ, GA, asst prof educ leadership; NCCA Vols Youth Prog, nat dir; Johnson C Smith Univ, Charlotte, NC, adj instr; Davidson Col, asst dean; Clayton State Univ, Morrow, GA, asst dean; US Peace Corps, reg mgr; First Tabernacle, assoc minister; Am Marshall Memorial Fel, Ger Marshall Fund, 2001; Fulton County Comn, GA, Dist 1, chmn, 2006-. **Orgs:** Chmn, Atlanta Sister Cities Comn; Atlanta Coun Int Rels; Nat Urban League Black Exec Exchange Prog. **Honors/Awds:** Top volunteer, Atlanta Pub Sch Syst; Volunteer of the Year, Atlanta Univ Chap Phi Delta Kappa; Outstanding Young Man of America, Nat Sch Vol Prog. **Special Achievements:** Author: Speakers of the House: 25 Morehouse Men Reflect on their Journey to Manhood, 2006; The Morehouse Mystique: Lessons to Develop Black Men, 2009. *

EBBE, DR. OBI N I
Educator. **Personal:** Born Jul 8, 1949, Umuobom, Nigeria; son of Virginia Uduola and Ebbe Muoneke Ilonuma; married; children: Nneka I. **Educ:** Univ London, London, UK, GCE, A/level, 1967; Western Mich Univ, Kalamazoo, MI, BA, 1976, MA, 1977; Southern Ill Univ, Carbondale, Ill, PhD, 1981. **Career:** Western Illinois Univ, Macomb, IL, asst prof, 1981; Univ Tenn, Chattanooga, TN, asst prof, 1981-82, prof, currently; Ohio Northern Univ, Ada, OH, asst prof, 1982-84; Valparaiso Univ Sch Law, Valparaiso, IN, fel, 1984-85; Delta State Univ, Cleveland, MS, assoc prof, 1985-87; State Univ NY, Brockport, NY, prof, 1987. **Orgs:** Alpha Kappa Delta, Nat Sociol Honor Soc, 1975; Acad Criminal Justice Sci, 1981-; Am Soc Criminol, 1981-; Int Asn Organized Crime, 1985-; Acad Security Educr & Trainers, 1990-; Am Soc Indust Security, 1990-. **Honors/Awds:** Hussel H Seibert Honors Research Award, Western Mich Univ, Kalamazoo, MI, 1975-76. **Special Achievements:** Published numerous articles. **Business Addr:** Professor, University of Tennesse, Sociology Anthropology & Geography, 308E Brock Hall Dept 2102 615 McCallie Ave, Chattanooga, TN 37403, **Business Phone:** (423)425-4437.

EBO, ANTONA (ELIZABETH LOUISE EBO)
Clergy. **Personal:** Born Apr 10, 1924, Bloomington, IL; daughter of Daniel Ebo and Louise Teal Ebo. **Educ:** St Louis Univ, St Louis MO, BS, Med Records Admin, 1962, MHA Hosp Exec Develop, 1970; Aquinas Inst Theol, Dubuque, MA; MTh Health Care Ministry, 1978. **Career:** Franciscan Sister Mary, 1946-; St Clare Hosp, Baraboo, WI, exec dir, 1967-71; St Marys Hosp Med Ctr, Madison WI, asst exec dir, 1970-74, chaplain, 1978-81; Wis Cath Health Asn, Madison WI, exec dir, 1974-76; St Marys Hosp Med Ctr, chaplain, 1978-81; Univ Miss Med Ctr, Jackson MS, chaplain, 1981-87; Franciscan Sisters Mary, St Louis MO, counor, 1987-91; St Nicholas Church, pastoral assoc, 1992-; St. Clare Hosp, adminr. **Orgs:** First group sisters participating March Selma, St Louis Archdiocese, 1965; St Louis Archdiocesan Human Rights Comn, 1965-67, 1989-99; mem, Nat Black Sisters' Conf, 1968-, pres, 1979-81, secy, 1997-2001; vchmn, Madison Urban League Bd Dirs, 1972-76; comnr, Madison Housing Authority, 1974-76; vchmn, Wis Health Facilities Authority, 1976; Nat Asn Cath Chaplains, 1979-; Comn Cath Health Care Ministry, 1987-88; Leadership Conf Women Relig, 1987-91; bd dir, SSM Health Care Syst, 1987-91; Leadership Conf Women Relig Task Force Women's Concerns, 1989-90; planning comt, St Louis Archdiocesan Nat Black Cath Congress, 1988-; bd dir, 1991-2002, exec comn, secy, 1997-2002, Cardinal Ritter Inst; St Louis Archdiocesan Human Rights Comn, 1991-99; Miss Cath Conf Soc Concerns Dept, 1991-94; Archbishop's Pastoral Coun, St Louis Archdiocese, 2003-. **Honors/Awds:** Certificate of Commendation, Madison Urban League, Madison WI, 1976; Certificate of Commendation, Governor Patrick Lucey, Wis Health Facilities Authority, 1976; Delegate, Nat Black Catholic Congress, Jackson Diocese, St Louis Archdiocese, St Louis Archdiocesan Human Rights Comm, 1994; 1987, 1992, 1997, 2002; Harriet Tubman Award, Nat Black Sisters' Conf, 1989; Martin Luther King Jr Award, St Louis Archdiocese Human Rights Comn, 1994; Honorary Doctorate of Humane Letters, Loyola Univ, 1995; Living Legend Award, Nat Voting Rights Mus, 2000; Martin Luther King Jr Award, 2002; Distinguished Humanitarian, State Celebration Comn MO, 2002; Distinguished Citizen 2005, St Louis Argus; Spiritual Leadership Award, Xavier Univ Inst Black Catholic Studies, 2005; Rabbi Heschel & Rev Martin Luther King Jr Award, Jews United Justice, 2005. **Special Achievements:** First black woman religious to head a hospital. **Home Addr:** 8053 Hafner Ct, St Louis, MO 63130-1533, **Home Phone:** (314)567-0628. **Business Addr:** Pastoral Associate, St Nicholas Roman Catholic Church, 701 N 18th St, St Louis, MO 63103, **Business Phone:** (314)231-2860.

EBO, ELIZABETH LOUISE. See EBO, ANTONA.

EBONG, REGINA U
Accountant. **Personal:** Born Dec 9, 1953, Jos, Nigeria; daughter of Janet Chinweze and Francis Chinweze; married Ben Ebong, Mar 3, 1973; children: Nne, Ben, Victor & Francis. **Educ:** Univ Nebr, BSBA, 1981, MBA, 1983. **Career:** Enron Corp, sr EDP auditor, 1981-86; cert pub acct, 1986-; Hayes & Assoc, partner, 1986-88; Regina Ebong CPA, owner, 1988-; InterSecurities Inc, investment adv rep. **Orgs:** CISA, 1982; AICPA, 1983-; NE Soc CPA's; Inst Int Auditors, 1985-; vice chmn, Girls Inc, finance comn, 1988-90; State & Local Govt Acct comn, 1989-; bd mem, Voices C, 1992-. **Honors/Awds:** Leadership Omaha, Omaha Chamber Com, 1991. **Special Achievements:** nine months intensive leadership training prog, Omaha Chamber Com, Class 13, 1991. **Home Addr:** 804 S 131 Ave, Omaha, NE 68154, **Home Phone:** (402)333-2549. **Business Phone:** (402)346-1526.

ECHOLS, ALVIN E
Lawyer. **Personal:** Born Dec 5, 1930, Philadelphia, PA; son of Alvin and Rhydine; married Gwendolyn G; children: Donna G Echols-Kearse & Alison D. **Educ:** VA Union Univ, BS, 1955; Howard Univ, LLB, 1957. **Career:** Pvt Law Pract, 1957-63; N City Cong, exec dir, 1963-. **Orgs:** Comn Leadership Sem Prog, 1962; comnr, Human Rel Community, 1969; dep chmn, State Republican Party, 1971-75; PA chap, Nat Coun Crime & Delinquency, 1971-75; Friends Free Libr, 1972-75; Health & Welfare Coun, 1974. **Honors/Awds:** Achievement Award Industrialization Center, 1966; Distinguished Merit Citation, Nat Conf Christian & Jews, 1967; Certificate of Appreciation, Personnel Dept, Philadelphia Med Col, PA, 1972-; Greater Philadelphia Partnership, 1974; Philadelphia Asn Community Develop Corp. **Home Addr:** 1429 Dondill Pl, Philadelphia, PA 19122, **Home Phone:** (215)763-2346. **Business Addr:** Executive Director, North City Congress, 1438 N Broad St, Philadelphia, PA 19121-4326, **Business Phone:** (215)978-1300.

ECHOLS, DORIS BROWN
Educator, accountant, teacher. **Personal:** Born Oct 8, 1928, Oakwood, TX; daughter of William P Brown and Tinnie Viola Davis; married James Jerome Echols, Oct 12, 1950 (died 1974); children: Jennifer Diane Echols; married Richard Alexander, Dec 27, 1975 (divorced). **Educ:** Hughes Bus Col, bus cert, 1947; Tex Southern Univ, BA, 1954; Berkeley Police Dept Acad, attended 1998. **Career:** Educator (retired); Hughes Bus Col, teacher, 1948; Berkeley Unified Sch Dist, teacher, 1965-84; World Savings & Loans, acct specialist auditor, 1984, teacher, 1995-98, bd dirs. **Orgs:** Vol asst, Sr Citizen Ctr, 1985-; nominating comt mem, Nat Asn Adv Colored People, Berkeley, 1985-; tutor & planning comm, Adult Lit Prog, Oakland, 1986-; vol, How Berkeley Can You Be Parade, 1997, 1998; choir mem, treas, class leader, Downs United Methodist Church. **Honors/Awds:** Outstanding Work, Adult Lit Prog, 1986-95; Life Mem Award, Nat Asn Adv Colored People, 1989. **Home Addr:** 1514 Lincoln St, Berkeley, CA 94703-1222. *

ECHOLS, JAMES ALBERT
Marketing executive, public relations executive, military pilot. **Personal:** Born Sep 14, 1950, Memphis, TN; son of Joseph Echols, Jr and Vellar C McCraven Echols; married Dorothy Mae Mithcell, Jun 8, 1978; children: Justin Fitzgerald. **Educ:** Cent State Univ, Edmond OK, BA, 1981. **Career:** Office of the Governor, state affirmative action office, staff, 1979-; Nigh Gov Campaign, admin asst minority affairs, 1978; Reserve Life Insurance Co, ins agt, 1977-78; AUS, sr race rels instr, 1976-77; E & C Trades LTD, pres & chmn bd, 1980; Honor Enterprises Inc, chmn bd; US Army Reserve, career counr, 1986-. **Orgs:** Urban League of OK City, 1977; Nat Asn Advan Colored People, 1978; vpres, OK Human Rels Asn, 1978; Veterans Foreign Wars; Econ Develop Task Force, OK City Urban League. **Honors/Awds:** Member for excellent scholarship, Phi Eta Sigma, 1978. **Military Serv:** AUS, sgt 1st class, 1969-, Commendation medal Bronze Star, 1971. **Business Phone:** (405)524-8580.

ECHOLS, MARY ANN
School administrator. **Personal:** Born Jan 17, 1950, Youngstown, OH; daughter of Otis A Snipes (deceased) and Mable Ross Snipes; married Robert L, Oct 25, 1969; children: Robert Jr, Cheri, Michael & Anthony. **Educ:** Youngstown State Univ, Youngstown, OH, BA, Sociol, 1972, MS, Educ, 1977; Kent State Univ, Kent, OH, Couns Psychol. **Career:** Youngstown Metrop Housing Authority, Youngstown, OH, leasing aide, 1973; Youngstown Area Urban League, Youngstown, OH, dir educ & employ, 1973-76; Northeastern Ohio Employ & Training Consortium, Youngstown, OH, personnel, equal employ opportunity officer, 1977-80; Youngstown State Univ, Youngstown, OH, asst minority stud serv, 1980-84, dir spec stud serv. **Orgs:** Exec comt mem, chair review comt, Youngstown Area United Way; vpres, Associated Neighborhood Ctrs, 1984-89; bd dirs, Help Hotline, 1977-80; bias review panel mem, Ohio State Dept Educ; cultural pluralism task force mem, Lake River Girl Scout Coun, 1983-85; bd dir, Burdman Group. **Honors/Awds:** Resolution for Outstanding Community Service, Youngstown Area Urban League, 1976; Outstanding Black Faculty & Staff Award, Black United Stud, 1982, 1987; Luke N. Zaccaro Memorial Award, Exceptional Serv Stud Body, Youngstown State Univ, 1987; Distinguished Service Award, Youngstown State Univ, 1988. **Business Addr:** Director, Youngstown State University, 410 Wick Ave Kilcawley Ctr, Youngstown, OH 44555, **Business Phone:** (216)742-3538.*

ECHOLS, RUBY LOIS
Nurse, funeral director, chef. **Personal:** Born Oct 21, 1938, Atlanta, GA; daughter of George Clements (deceased) and Flora M Powell; married Lamar Echols, Sep 5, 1955; children: Ricky, Sheila D, Dexter B, Kenneth W. **Educ:** Atlanta Col Practical Nursing, LPN, 1968; Gupton Jones Col Funeral Serv, Funeral Dirs & Embalmers Lic, 1978. **Career:** Echols Weddings, Flowers & Catering Serv, owner, 1983-; Echols Mortuary, owner, 1985-; Grady Mem Hosp, registered nurse. **Orgs:** Ga Funeral Serv & Practitioners Asn, 1978-; Nat Funeral Dirs & Morticians Asn, 1978-; Epsilon Nu Delta Mortuary Fraternity, Alpha Omega Chap; Eastern Star; Black Women's Asn; Mother's March Dimes; US Negro Col Fund; Black Women Atlanta; EOA; Meals on Wheels. **Honors/Awds:** Mortician of the Year, 1993. *

ECKSTINE, ED
Executive. **Personal:** Son of Billy. **Career:** Mercury Recs, pres, currently. **Special Achievements:** "The Way Love Goes". **Business Phone:** (212)603-7648.*

ECTON, VIRGIL E.
Association executive. **Personal:** Born Jul 7, 1940, Paris, KY; married Harriette Morgan-Ecton; children: Virgil, Brian Keith, Blair Christina. **Educ:** Ind Univ, BS, 1962; Xavier Univ, MEd, 1966; Harvard Univ, advan mgt prog, 1989. **Career:** Ohio Civil Rights Comn, asst dir educ & community rels, 1968-70; United Negro Col Fund Inc, area develop dir, 1970-75, eatern reg supvr, 1975-76, deputy nat campaign dir, 1976-77, nat campaign dir, 1977-79, deputy exec dir fund-raising, 1979-82, exec vpres & chief oper officer 1982-90, acting pres & chief exec officer, 1990-91, sr exec vpres & chief oper officer, 1991-; sr exec vpres Develop; Howard Univ, vpres, 2001-. **Orgs:** Nat Soc Fund-raising Exec Found, bd mem; Nat Philanthropy Day Steering Comt, founding mem; Boy Scouts Am, Bergen Coun, exec bd, vpres; Community Access, bd mem; Int Parenting Asn, adv bd mem, Outward Bound, USA & SAfrica, adv bd mem; Bede Sch, adv bd mem; Dwight Englewood Sch, trustee; Japan S,oc adv bd. **Honors/Awds:** Nat Alliance Bus Men Serv Award, 1972-74; Merit Serv Award, Nat Alliance Businessmen, 1973; Tech Assoc Serv Award, 1974; Blacks Mgt Comn Serv Award, 1975; Nat UNCF Leadership Award, 1978. **Business Addr:** Vice President, Howard University Advancement, 2225 Georgia Avenue NW, Rm 901, Washington, DC 20059.*

EDA, JOAN. See BYRD, JOAN EDA.

EDDINGS, JOHN R
Government official. **Personal:** Born Feb 23, 1943, Corinth, MS; son of Rufus L and Malgline J; married Patricia J, May 25, 1968;

children: Carla J. **Educ:** Univ Hampton, BS, 1965; Wayne State Univ, 1976. **Career:** Daimler Chrysler Corp, personnel rep, 1972-74; Detroit Pub Sch, substitute teacher, 1974-75; City Detroit, transp personnel officer, 1975-80, recreatoin personnel officer, 1980-82, Civic Ctr, deputy dir, 1982-93, dep dir, human resources, 1993-94, city ombudsman, 1995-2004; Macomb County, ombudsman, currently. **Orgs:** Int Ombudsman Inst; pres, US Asn, 1999-2001; bd dir, US Ombudsman Asn; Nat Forum Black Pub Adminr; Soc Human Res Mgt; Am Soc Pub Adminr; Nat Hampton alumni Asn, Inc; Nat Asn Advan Colored People. **Business Addr:** Ombudsman, Macomb County, 5th Fl 10 N Main St, Mount Clemens, MI 48043-5668, **Business Phone:** (586)469-5275.

EDDY, DR. EDWARD A.
Educator. **Personal:** Born Feb 27, 1938, Kansas City, KS; married Joyce B Carter; children: Darrell, Duane & Aaron. **Educ:** Pittsburg State Univ, BS, 1962; Univ KS, MA, 1966; KS State Univ, PhD,1981. **Career:** Pub Schs KCK, instr, 1962-69; Univ KS, instr, 1969-73; Rockhurst, dir specprog, 1973-77; Rockhurst Col, dean, 1977-84; Chicago State Univ, dean; Chevy Chase Nursing Ctr, adminr. **Orgs:** OE regl steering comt, TRIO Prog, 1973-75; field reader, OE Title III, Proposals, 1982-83; consult educ, MLK Jr Hosp KCMO, 1975-77; Aacd mem, Am Assn Coun Dir, 1985; Nat youth conv staff Church of God, 1985; guestsoloist, Oper PUSH Chicago, 1985; Higher Educ Comn Col, 1986-88. **Honors/Awds:** Founder & dir, Black Ethos Performing Arts Troupe, 1971; Key to City Kansas City, KS, 1984. **Business Addr:** Administrator, Chevy Chase Nursing Center, 3400 S Indiana, Chicago, IL 60616.

EDELER, PHYLLIS
Executive. **Personal:** Born in Gary, IN. **Educ:** N Central Col, BA; Loyola Univ Chicago, MS, Ind Rels. **Career:** RH Edelen Assoc, prin, 1986-97; Disability Servs Southwest, state dir human resources, 1998-99; Tree Life/Gourmet Award Foods, region vpres human resources, 1999-. **Orgs:** Soc Human Resources Mgmt; Dallas Human Resources Mgmt Asn; Nat Asn African Am Human Resources; adv bd, Dallas Chap, Nat Asn African Am Human Resources; trustee, bd mem, Wheatland Community Learning Ctr. **Honors/Awds:** Volunteer of the Year, Wheatland Community Learning Ctr, 2001. **Business Addr:** Region Vice President-Human Resources, Tree Life & Gourmet Award Foods, 5101 Highland Place Dr, Dallas, TX 75236, **Business Phone:** (972)708-5503.

EDELIN, KENNETH C
Physician. **Personal:** Born Mar 31, 1939, Washington, DC; son of Benedict F and Ruby Goodwin; married Barbara Evans; children: Kenneth Jr, Kimberley, Joseph & Corinne. **Educ:** Columbia Univ, BA, 1961; Meharry Med Col, MD, 1967; Boston City Hosp, residency ob/gyn, 1974, chief resident 1973. **Career:** Boston City Hosp, chief resident, obstet & gynec, 1973-74; Ambulatory Care Boston City Hosp, coord, 1974-, instr, obstet & gynec, 1974-, assoc dir, obstet & gynec, 1974-;assoc prof, 1974-; Boston Univ Sch Med, assist prof obstet & gynec, 1976, chmn, prof obstet & gynec, 1979-89, gyn-in-chief, 1979-89, dir obstet & gynec, 1979-, assoc dean stud & minority affairs, obstet & gynec, 1989-2006; emer prof obstet & gynec, currently. **Orgs:** Bd trustees NARAL; physic adv Planned Parenthood Leag Am; Am Asn Gynecol Laparoscopists; chmn New England Comm Nat Asn Advan Colored People Legal Defense Fund; chmn bd, Planned Parenthood Fedn Am, 1989-91; Alpha Omega Alpha; Honor Med Soc. **Honors/Awds:** Columbia Univ, 1960-61; Dean's List Meharry Med Col, 1963-67; Alpha Omega Alpha, Honorary Med Soc, 1991; Good Guy Award, Nat Womens Political Caucus; Lifetime Achievement Award, Nat Medical Asn. **Military Serv:** USAF, capt, 1968-71; Commendation Medal USAF, 1971; Commendation Medal Army, 1971.

EDELMAN, MARIAN WRIGHT
Educator, lawyer, president (organization). **Personal:** Born Jun 6, 1939, Bennettsville, SC; daughter of Arthur J Wright and Maggie Bowen Wright; married Peter, Jul 14, 1968; children: Joshua, Jonah & Ezra. **Educ:** Univ Geneva, Switzerland, 1959; Spelman Col, BA, 1960; Yale Law Sch, LLB, 1963. **Career:** NAACP Legal Defense & Educ Fund, staff atty, 1963-64, dir 1964-68; Washington Res Proj Southern Ctr Public Policy, partner, 1968-73; Ctr Law & Educ Harvard Univ, dir 1971-73; C's Defense Fund, founder & pres, 1973-. **Orgs:** DC, MS, Commonwealth Asns; bd trustees The King Ctr; adv coun M L King Memorial Library; Coun Foreign Relations; Aetna Life & Casualty Found; Yale Univ Corp; chair, bd trustees Spelman Col; bd dir March Dimes; bd mem, Ctr Budget & Policy Priorities; bd mem, Citizens Constitutional Concerns; bd mem, Joint Ctr Polit & Econ Studies; bd mem, NAACP Legal Defense & Educ Fund Inc; bd mem, US Comt UNICEF; bd mem, Robin Hood Found; bd mem, Aaron Diamond Found; Howard Univ Comn; Nat Comn C. **Honors/Awds:** Albert Schweitzer Humanitarian Prize, 1988; the Heinz Award; MacArthur Foundation Prize Fellowship, 1985; Presidential Medal of Freedom, 2000; Robert F. Kennedy Lifetime Achievement Award; Community of Christ International Peace Award, 1995. **Special Achievements:** Author: Families in Peril: An Agenda for Social Change, 1987; The Measure of Our Success: A Letter to My Children & Yours, 1992; Guide My Feet: Prayers & Meditations on Loving & Working for Children, 1995; I'm Your Child, God: Prayers for Children & Teenagers, 2002; First African Am woman admitted to the Miss state bar. **Business Phone:** (202)628-8787.

EDGAR, JACQUELINE L.
Automotive executive. **Personal:** Born Nov 27, 1948, Lafayette, LA; daughter of Antoine LeBlanc and Effie Matthews; married Allen L Edgar Sr, Apr 20, 1968 (divorced); children: Rachael Marie, Allen L Jr, Lawrence (deceased). **Career:** Auto Mart Linc-Merc, salesperson, 1973-76; J P Thibodeaux Olds, salesperson, 1976-80; Broussard Pontiac, salesperson, 1980-83; Edgar Chevrolet Inc, pres, 1983-87; Edgar Ford Inc, pres. **Orgs:** Performance Inc, 1989-92; treas, Breaux Bridge Chamber Com, 1992; Lafayette Catholic Serv Ctr, 1992; Rehabilitaion Ctr Acadiana, 1992; St Jude C Res Hosp Dream Home Comt. *

EDGERTON, BRENDA EVANS
Executive, financial manager. **Personal:** Born Jun 15, 1949, Halifax, VA; daughter of Elmer Keith and Bernice; married Raymond Edgerton (divorced 1989); children: Lauren, Eric. **Educ:** Pa State Univ, State Col, 1969; Rutgers Univ, NJ, BA, 1970; Temple Univ, Philadelphia, MBA, 1976. **Career:** Scott Paper Co, Philadelphia, PA, mgr money & banking, 1976-84; Campbell Soup Co, Camden, NJ, dir finance, 1984-86, asst treas, 1986-88, dep treas, 1988-89, vpres, treas, 1989-94; US Soup, vpres finance, 1994-. **Orgs:** Philadelphia Treas Club, 1985-; Financial Exec Inst, 1989-; Nat Asn Corpe Treas, 1989; YWCA, 1989-; bd mem, Frontier Corp. **Honors/Awds:** Acad Women Achievers, YWCA, 1989. *

EDISON, JOANNE
Business owner. **Career:** Jo's UpClose & Personal Clothing, owner, currently. **Orgs:** Nat Asn Women Bus Owners, Greater Detroit Chap. **Business Addr:** Owner, Jo?s UpClose & Personal Clothing, 511 Beaubian St, Detroit, MI 48226, **Business Phone:** (313)965-4915.*

EDLEY, CHRISTOPHER F.
Educator, government official. **Personal:** Born Jan 13, 1953, Boston, MA; son of Christopher Sr and Zaida Coles; married Tana Pesso, Sep 23, 1983 (divorced); children: Christopher Edley III; married Maria Echaveste; children: Zara & Elias. **Educ:** Swartmore Col, Swartmore, PA, BA, 1973; Harvard Law Sch, Cambride, MA, JD,1978; Harvard Kennedy Sch, Cambridge, MA, MPP, 1978. **Career:** White House Domestic Policy Staff, asst dir, 1978-80; US Govt, Secy Housing, Educ & Welfare, spec asst, 1980; Harvard Law Sch, prof, 1981-2004; Washington Post, part-time ed page staff, 1982-84; Dukakis for Pres, nat issues dir, 1987-88; Off Mgt & Budget, assoc dir econ & govt, 1993-95; Pres US, spec coun, 1995; Harvard Law Review, ed & officer; Univ Calif, Berkeley, Boalt Hall Sch Law, dean & prof, 2004-; Russell Sage Found, trustee, currently; Century Found, trustee, currently. **Orgs:** Bd managers, Swarthmore Col, 1980-; bd dir, Am Coun Ger, 1981-84; founding trustee, Working Assets Money Fund, 1982-84; steering comt mem, Boston Lawyers Comt Civil Rights, 1984-87; Comt Policy Racial Justice, 1984-; consult, Joint Ctr Polit Studies, 1988-; bd dir, Ctr Social Welfare Policy & Law, 1989-; Am Bar Asn; Nat Bar Asn; Coun Foreign Rels; exec comt bd, People Am Way; adj scholar, Urban Inst; Nat Acad Pub Admin; bd testing & assessment, Nat Res Coun; fel, Nat Acad Pub Admin; fel, Coun Foreign Rel; fel, Am Acad Arts & Sci; fel, Am Law Inst; adv bd, Obama-Biden Transition Project. **Special Achievements:** Publications include Not All Black and White: Affirmative Action, Race and American Values and Administrative Law: Rethinking Judicial Control of Bureaucracy. **Business Phone:** (510)642-6483.

EDMOND, ALFRED ADAM
Editor, journalist, educator. **Personal:** Born Mar 8, 1960, Long Branch, NJ; son of Alfred Adam and Virginia E Monroe; married Topaza L Watkins, May 19, 2002; children: Monique Marie Brown, Christine Lorraine, David Adam Robeson & Allyson E Watkins. **Educ:** Rutgers Col, Rutgers Univ, New Brunswick, NJ, BA, 1983. **Career:** Big Red News, Brooklyn, NY, managing ed, 1984-86; Modern Black Men (MBM) Mag, New York, NY, sr ed, 1986-87; Earl G Graves Publ Co, New York, assoc ed, 1987, sr ed, 1987-89, bus ed, 1989-90, sr ed & admin, 1990-92, managing ed 1992-95, vpres, exec ed, 1995-2000, sr vpres, Black Enterprise Mag, ed-in-chief, 2000-; Rutgers Univ, Dept Jour, vis prof, 1994-95; Rutgers Univ, adj prof. **Orgs:** NY Asn Black Journalists, 1985-; Nat Asn Black Journalists, 1987-; Am Soc Mag Ed, 1988-; bd mem, Rutgers Alumni Fedn, 1990; founding life mem, Rutgers African-Am Alumni Alliance, 1990-; Rutgers Alumni Mag, ed bd mem, 1991-; Soc Am Bus Ed & Writers Inc, 1994-95; life mem, Rutgers Alumni Asn, 1996-; bd mem, Leadership Enterprise Diverse Am. **Honors/Awds:** Unity Award for Excellence in Media, Lincoln Univ, MO, 1989-90; Recognition of Excellence, Paul Robeson Cult Ctr, Rutgers Univ, 1990; Unity Award for Excellence in Media, 1991, 1992; NYABJ Journalism Award, Bus Reporting Magazines, 1992, 1994; Long Branch High School Alumni, Acad Hall of Fame, 1996; The Nation's 100 Most Influential Business Journalist, TJFR Bus News Reporter, 1998; Chapter Service Award, NY Asn Black Journalists, 2000. **Home Addr:** 919 Pk Pl Apt 6E, Brooklyn, NY 11213-1808. **Business Addr:** Senior Vice President, Editor-in-Chief, Earl G Graves Publishing Company Inc, Black Enterprise Magazine, Ed Dept, 130 5th Ave, New York, NY 10011-4399, **Business Phone:** (212)242-8000.

EDMOND, PAUL EDWARD
Manager. **Personal:** Born May 29, 1944, Shreveport, LA; son of Clarence Lee Edmond and Juanita Brown Allen; divorced; children: Neeve E Samuels, Doran & Oran. **Educ:** Southern Univ, Baton Rouge LA, BS, 1968; Ind Univ, Bloomington IN, MS, 1973; Univ Mich, Ann Arbor MI, 1976. **Career:** State Ind, Ft Wayne IN, hosp admin, 1969-71; Lincoln Nat Ins, Ft Wayne IN, personnel mgr, 1971-76; Miller Brewing Co, Milwaukee WI, corp indust rels mgr, 1976-. **Orgs:** Am Soc Personnel Asn, 1973-; Indust Rels Mgr Asn, 1979-; Personnel & Labor Rels Asn, 1980-; bd mem, OIC Am, 1986-; chairperson, United Way Allocation Community, 1986-; comn mem, Milwaukee Urban League, Long Range Planning, 1987-; Grambling Univ Accreditation Comn, 1987-; bd mem, Milwaukee Desegregation Community, 1988-; State Wis Educ Coun, 1988-. **Honors/Awds:** Outstanding Young Men, Ft Wayne Jaycees, 1973; Professional Achiever, Nat Career Ctr, 1974; Black Achiever, New York YMCA, 1982; President's Award, Miller Brewing, 1984. **Military Serv:** AUS, 1st lt, 1968-70. **Business Addr:** Manager, Miller Brewing Co, 3939 W Highland Blvd, Milwaukee, WI 53201, **Business Phone:** (414)931-2000.

EDMONDS, BEVELYN
Educator, writer. **Personal:** Born Feb 17, 1951, Chicago, IL; daughter of Walter D Edmonds and Ann Clotee Hecek (deceased). **Educ:** Tuskegee Univ, BSN, 1973; Med Col, MSN, 1975; St Xavier, MA, 1990. **Career:** Ill Cent County Hosp, staff, 1979-86; St Xavier Univ, asst prof, 1981-90; St Xavier Univ, grant adolescent study, 1982; St Frances Hosp, instr, 1990-94; Doctor's Hosp, educr, 1994-95; Jackson Park Med Ctr, staff, 1986-95; Health Staff, in-house, 1990-; Dimensions Int, staff writer, 1995-. **Orgs:** Asn Black Nursing Fac, 1987-; Delta Sigma Theta Sorority, 1969-; Sigma Theta Tau, 1986-; People United Save Humanity, 1979-; County Serv Block Club. **Special Achievements:** Mental Health School in System, Need for Laison Service, 1975; RN Working with Chemicals, Dependent Individuals in a Mental Health Setting, 1990. **Home Addr:** 3316A S Cobb Dr Box 322, Smyrna, GA 30080.

EDMONDS, BOBBIE
Lawyer. **Educ:** Southern Univ A&M, Baton Rouge, La, BA, arts; Southern Univ Sch Law, Baton Rouge, LA, JD. **Career:** McNeese State Univ, Lake Charles, LA, adj prof; Tex Wesleyan Univ, Fort Worth, adj prof; Reginald Heber Smith Fel, Wash, DC, staff atty, 1980; N La Legal Serv Corp, staff atty; Southwest La Legal Serv Corp, exec dir & gen coun, 1983; pvt pract, atty, 1987-; Tarrant County Civil Serv Comn, hearing officer, 2002-; City Forest Hill, alt munic judge, 2003-; Urban Am Network, talk show host, 2004-06. **Orgs:** Tarrant County Bar Asn; Tarrant County Family Bar Asn; Nat Asn Advan Colored People; Nat Asn Black Journalists. **Honors/Awds:** Lawyer of the Year, Tarrant County Black Bar Asn, 1996; Justice Award, Arlington Br, Nat Asn Advan Colored People, 1998; KKDA African Am Hero; Outstanding Director of the Year Award; received numerous awards. **Special Achievements:** Appeared on NBC Dateline, ABC 20/20, ABC Sunday Morning, CNN, ABC-WFAA-Channel 8, NBC-KXAS-Channel 5; record as the youngest executive director in the State of Louisiana. **Business Addr:** Attorney, 209 S Jennings Ave, Forth Worth, TX 76104, **Business Phone:** (817)332-6501.

EDMONDS, CAMPBELL RAY
Government official. **Personal:** Born Jun 9, 1930, Hopewell, VA; married Louise Smith. **Educ:** Va State Univ, Trade Sch, 1954, bus & mgt, 1956; Chase Inc Cost & Anal, 1961. **Career:** Traffic Bd Hopewell, co-chair, 1966-76; Blue Ribbon Crime Task Force, chmn, 1981; City Council, councilman, 1982; Hopewell Va, vice-mayor, 1984. **Orgs:** Adjuant gen, Albert Mills Post No 1387, VFW, 1975; bd dirs, C C, 1977-; Home Builder's Asn, 1980; comnr, Veterans Affairs Va, 1981; bd mem, Hopewell/Prince George Chamber Com; bd dirs, Prince George County Heritage Fair; Hopewell Voters League; trustee bd, Friendship Baptist Church, 1964-; aide, Va State Assoc Pres, IBPOE W. **Honors/Awds:** Outstanding Service, Sunlight Eld Lodge Hopewell, 1969; Achievement Award, Va State Asn, Health Dept, 1982; Community Service, Hopewell Action Coun, 1985; Certificate of Merit, City Hopewell, 1986; Outstanding Citizenship Award, United Fund, 1987. **Military Serv:** AUS, E-5, 1951-53; Korean Conflict. **Home Addr:** 1105 Winston Churchill Dr, Hopewell, VA 23860. **Business Addr:** Vice Mayor, City of Hopewell, Municipal Bldg, Hopewell, VA 23860.*

EDMONDS, CURTIS
Government official. **Career:** Government official (Retired); Detroit Fire Dept, chief, 1994.

EDMONDS, JOSEPHINE E.
Artist, art consultant. **Personal:** Born Oct 5, 1921, Cambridge, MA; daughter of Alexander M Mapp (deceased) and Zylpha O Johnson (deceased); married Howard L Edmonds; children: Joel V Bolden Jr. **Educ:** NY City Col; Am Art Sch; Springfield Col;

Univ Hartford. **Career:** Art consultant (retired), artist; YWCA, art instr, 1965-69; Johnson Publ, stringer, 1957-97; Afro-Am Cult Ctr, Am Int Col, art coordr, 1969-81. **Orgs:** Springfield Chap Girl Friends, 1958-; Women's Golf Asn, 1960-95; Springfield Art League, 1962-; co-founder, Afro-Art Alliance, 1968; Urban League; cultural comt, Springfield Bicentennial Comm, 1973; Nat Conf Artists, 1973-; Springfield Libr & Mus Asn; Studion Mus Harlem, 1974-; Nat Asn Advan Colored People; nat vpres, Girl Friends Inc, 1979-80; trustees comt, Springfield Mus Fine Arts; George Walter Vincent Smith Mus, 1980-; Springfield Arts Lottery Comn, 1986-91. **Honors/Awds:** President's Cup, 1965-82; Champion, Women's Golf Asn, 1973, 1986; Honor Willia, Hardgrow Ment Health Clin, 1974; Honoree, Alumni Asn Am Int Col, 1977; Golden Deed Award, Exchange Club Springfields, 1983; Josephine Edmonds Day, Springfield, MA, named in honor; Honoree, PRIDE, Black Stud Orgn Am Int Col; The Ubora Award, African Hall Steering Comm, 1998. **Home Addr:** 439 Union St Apt 7, Springfield, MA 01105, **Home Phone:** (413)739-7603. *

EDMONDS, KENNETH
Singer, music producer, composer. **Personal:** Born Apr 10, 1958, Indianapolis, IN; son of Marvin and Barbara; married Tracey McQuarn, 1992 (divorced 2007); children: Brandon & Dylan Michael; married Denise (divorced). **Career:** Edmonds Entertainment, co-founder; La Face Records, owner, 1998; singer & producer, currently; albums: Tender Lover, 1989; A Closer Look, 1991; For the Cool in You, 1993; The Day, 1996; Christmas with Baby face, 1998; Face2Face, 2001; Grown & Sexy, 2005; Playlist, 2007; Josie & the Pussycats, exec producer & music producer, 2001; The Spirit of Christmas, 2002; films: Soul Food, co-producer, 1997;Hav Plenty, co-producer, 1998; Light It Up, exec producer, 1999; Punks, exec producer, 2000; Josie & the Pussycats, exec producer, 2001; God Part II, 2005; TV: Soul Food, exec producer, 1997-; The Tonight Show with Jay Leno, 2005. **Honors/Awds:** Songwriter of the year, Broadcast Music Inc, 1989, 1990, 1991, 1995;Platinum Award, 1990; Trumpet Award, Turner Broadcasting Syst, 1998; Image Award, Recording Male Artist, Nat Advan Am Colored People, 1998; Grammy Award, 1998; Image Award, Outstanding Drama Series, Nat Advan Am Colored People, 2002. **Special Achievements:** Had a Federal highway named in his honor. **Business Addr:** Owner, Edmonds Entertainment, 1635 N Cahuenga Blvd, Los Angeles, CA 90028, **Business Phone:** (323)860-1550.

EDMONDS, LISA I.
Lawyer. **Career:** Abbott Labs Co, Domestic Legal Opers, atty, 2004. *

EDMONDS, TERRY
Writer, government official, advertising executive. **Personal:** Born Jan 1, 1949, Baltimore, MD; son of Naomi Parker; married Antoinette; children: Maya. **Educ:** Morgan State Univ, Baltimore, BA, 1973. **Career:** Md Mass Transit Admin, pub rels specialist, 1978-82; Trahan, Burden & Charles Advert, dir pub rels, 1982-87; Joint Ctr Polit Studies Inc, dir commun, 1985-87; Off Kweisi Mfume, press secy, 1987-88; Macro Systs, consult, 1987-89; Blue Cross Blue Shield, MD, mgr media rels, 1989-90; Univ Res Corp, subcontract mgr pub rels work, 1990-91; ROW Sci, task mgr pub rels proj, 1991-93; Off Donna Shalala, US Sec Health & Human Serv, sr speechwriter & dir speechwriting, 1993-95; Pres Bill Clinton, dep asst, pres speechwriter, 1995-97, dep dir speechwriting, 1997-99, asst pres & dir speechwriting; AARP, dir ed mgt, 2002-05; Time Warner Inc, exec speechwriter & sr mem corp commun team, 2005-. **Special Achievements:** First African American speechwriter to work in the White House for a President. **Business Addr:** Executive Speechwriter, Time Warner Inc, 1 Time Warner Ctr, New York, NY 10019-8016, **Business Phone:** (212)484-8000.*

EDMONDS, TRACEY E.
Executive. **Personal:** Born Feb 18, 1967, Los Angeles, CA; daughter of Jacqueline and George McQuarn; married Kenneth "Babyface" Edmonds, 1992 (divorced 2007); children: Brandon, Dylan; married Eddie Murphy, Jan 1, 2008. **Career:** Yab Yum Entertainment, owner & pres, currently; Edmonds Entertainment Inc, pres & chief exec officer, currently; Our Stories Films, pres & chief operating officer, currently; films: co-producer, Soul Food, 1997; HavPlenty, co-producer, 1998; producer, Light It Up, 1999; producer, Josie & the Pussycats, 2001; producer, The Lamb, 2001; Who's Your Caddy, 2007; Good Luck Chuck, 2007; TV series: "Soul Food", exec producer, 2000; "College Hill", 2004-07; "Lil Kim: Countdown to Lockdown", 2006; "Blackstage"; Schoolin, co-creator. **Orgs:** RIAA; Do Something; MAP; Mr Holland's Opus. **Honors/Awds:** Black Oscar Awards, three; NAACP Awards, five. **Special Achievements:** First African American to head a film studio. **Business Addr:** President, Owner, Yab Yum Entertainment, 1635 N Cahuenga Blvd 6th Fl, Los Angeles, CA 90028, **Business Phone:** (323)860-1520.*

EDMONDSON, JEROME
Business owner, writer, consultant. **Personal:** Married Alena; children: Cherita, Aaron & William. **Educ:** Ark State Univ, AA, criminal justice; Cleary Col, BA, bus finance. **Career:** KFC, staff, 1987, mkt mgr & dir opers, 1994; A&W Foods, owner, 1996; CBN Entrepreneur Training Inst, founder, 1998; Urban Hope Community Develop Corp, co-founder; Edmondson Assocs, sr partner & founder, currently. **Orgs:** Bd dir, The Resource Inst Atlanta; exec bd mem, Intl Third World Leadership Asn; UN rep, UN Headquarters, Geneva; tech assistance provider, US Small Bus Admin. **Honors/Awds:** Minority Entrepreneur of the Year Award, Minority Bus Develop Agency, 2005; Local Minority Advocate of the Year Award, US Dept Com, 2005. **Special Achievements:** Author: "Maximizing Misfortune". **Military Serv:** USAF, law enforcement officer, 4yrs. **Business Addr:** Founder, Senior Partner, Edmondson Associates, Entrepreneur Development Network, 1777 NE Expressway Suite 275, Lithonia, GA 30329, **Business Phone:** (770)879-0902.

EDMUNDS, ALLAN L.
Teacher, president (organization). **Personal:** Born Jan 1, 1949, Philadelphia, PA. **Career:** Philadelphia sch syst, art teacher; Tyler Sch art; Brandywine GraphicWorkshop, founder & pres, 1972-.

EDMUNDS, DAVID L., JR.
Lawyer. **Personal:** Born Mar 30, 1953. **Educ:** Univ Rochester, Col Arts & Sci, BA, 1975; Case Western Reserve Univ, Franklin Thomas Backus Sch Law, JD, 1978. **Career:** US Ct Appeals, Second Circuit; US Dist Ct, Western Dist, NY; US Supreme Ct; Neighborhood Legal Services Inc, Reginald Herber Smith Community Law fel, staff atty, 1978-81; Charles Drew Sci Magnet Sch, tutor; NY State Dept Law, Prison Litigation Bur, asst atty gen, 1981-83, Claims & Litigation Bur, 1983-86; Buffalo Regional Off, dep asst atty general-in-charge, 1986-; NY State Supreme Ct, Appellate Div, Fourth Judicial Dept, chief coun; Damon & Morey, partner; Phillips Lytle LLP, Buffalo, NY, spec coun, currently. **Orgs:** Pres, Minority Bar Asn Wyo, 1987-91; dir, Erie County Bar Asn; co-chair, Spec Task Force Minorities Legal Prof; chair, Civil Rights Comn, NY State Bar Asn; bd dir, Leadership Buffalo, class, 1989; bd trustees, First Shiloh Baptist Church; vpres, Geneva Scruggs Health Ctr; vpres, Erie County Col, Citizens Adv Coun; life mem, NAACP; bd gov, Case Western Reserve Univ Law Sch; trustee, Medaille Col; trustee, C Found; Buffalo Econ Renaissance Corp; Leadership Buffalo; pres, Shiloh Housing Develop Corp; Sigma Pi Phi Frat. **Honors/Awds:** Buffalo Business First & Buffalo Law Journal Who's Who in Law; Lawyer Service Award, Minority Bar Asn Western New York; Trailblazer Award, Minority Bar Asn Western New York; The National Conference for Community and Justice Legal Service Award. **Special Achievements:** First African American to be elected President of the Bar Association of Erie County in the 120 year history of the professional organization. **Business Phone:** (716)847-8400.*

EDMUNDS, FERRELL
Football player. **Personal:** Born Apr 16, 1965, South Boston, VA. **Educ:** Univ Md. **Career:** Football player (retired); Miami Dolphins, tight end, 1988-92; Seattle Seahawks, 1993-94. **Honors/Awds:** Pro Bowl, 1989.

EDMUNDS, DR. WALTER RICHARD
Oral surgeon, educator. **Personal:** Born Mar 25, 1928, Philadelphia, PA; son of Waltha and McKinley. **Educ:** Pa State Univ, BS; Howard Univ, Col Dent, DDS; Univ Pa, Grad Sch Med. **Career:** Pa Hosp oral surgeon; Univ Pa Sch Dent Med, assoc prof oral path;Jefferson Med Col, Thomas Jefferson Univ, clin asst prof otolaryngol; Univ Penn, clin asst prof pathol; pvt pract, oral & maxillofacial surgeon, currently. **Orgs:** Bd mem, Eagleville Hosp; fel, Am Col Oral & Maxillofacial Surgeons Soc Hill Club; Am Bd Oral Surgeons; Alpha Phi Alpha; Sigma Pi Phi; Chi Delta Mu; bd mem, Philadelphia City Dental Soc. **Military Serv:** AUS, lt. **Home Addr:** 257 S 4th St, Philadelphia, PA 19106, **Home Phone:** (215)925-8586. **Business Addr:** Surgeon, 257 S 4th St, Philadelphia, PA 19106, **Business Phone:** (215)925-8586.

EDNEY, NORRIS ALLEN, I
Association executive, college teacher, executive director. **Personal:** Born Jul 17, 1936, Natchez, MS; son of Willie Albert and Elizabeth Grayer; married Lillian Clark Edney, Jun 5, 1959; children: Norris Allen II, Albert DeFrance, Alvin Darcell. **Educ:** Natchez Jr Col, AA, 1955; Tougaloo Col, BS, 1957; Antioch Col, MST, 1962; Mich Stae Univ, PhD, 1969. **Career:** Alcorn State Univ, Lorman, MS, instr & asst prof biol, 1963-66, prof biol, 1969, chmn biol, 1972-79, USDA proj dir, 1972, dir grad studies, 1975, dir arts & sci, 1973; Ft Braden Sch, sch bd mem, currently. **Orgs:** Mycological Soc Am; AAAS; Am Asn Univ Profs; Miss Acad Sci; Alpha Phi Alpha Fraternity. **Honors/Awds:** First Annual White House Initiative Fac Award, 1988; Award, Nat Asn Equal Opportunity Higher Educ Res Achievement, 1988; Alumni Award, Natchez Jr Col, 1990. **Home Addr:** 302 Eastmoor Dr, Natchez, MS 39120. **Business Addr:** Board Member, Ft Braden School, 15100 Blountstown Highway, Tallahassee, FL 32310.*

EDNEY, TYUS DWAYNE
Basketball player. **Personal:** Born Feb 14, 1973, Gardena, CA; married. **Educ:** Univ Calif, Los Angeles, attended 1995. **Career:** Sacramento Kings, guard, 1995-97; Boston Celtics, 1997-98; BC Zalgiris Kaunas, 1999-2000; Benetton Basket Treviso, 2000-01; Ind Pacers, guard, 2000-01; Benetton Basket Treviso, 2003-04; Virtus Roma, 2005-06; Olympiacos Piraeus, guard; Climamio Bologna, 2006-07; Euroleague Basketball, Azovmash Mariupol, guard, 2007-. **Honors/Awds:** NCAA Division I Championship, 1995; Frances Pomeroy Naismith Award, 1995; Import Player of the Year, 2002.

EDUOK, DR. ETIM EFFIONG
Educator. **Personal:** Born Jul 10, 1949, Uyo, Nigeria; son of Ekanem and Ima E; married Victoria; children: Oto-Obong, Uyuho, Ekemini & Etim Jr. **Educ:** Univ Nigeria, Nsukka, BS, 1975; Univ Ala, MS, 1980; Tex Christian Univ, PhD, 1991. **Career:** Univ Ariz, asst prof, 1991; Concordia Col, assoc prof, 1992-93; Xavier Univ, assoc prof chem, 1994-96. **Orgs:** Am Chem Soc, 1977; Am Inst Chemists, 1986, Pkal, 1994. **Special Achievements:** Co-author of college textbook, Basic Calculations for Chemical & Biological Analysis, 2000, author of Chemistry of Diaminomaleonitrile: Synthesis & Structure of Two Unexpected Products from Its Condensation With 2, 5 Hexanedione, 2000, listed in Who's Who Among America's Teachers, Madison Who's Who (Lifetime), Empire Who's Who (Lifetime).

EDWARDS, DR. ABIYAH, JR. (ED EDWARDS)
Clergy. **Personal:** Born Dec 23, 1927, Princeton, KY; son of Ivory Bumpass (deceased) and Marcles (deceased); children: Ed III, Delesa, Carla, Cornell, Yahis, Edwina, Charise, Iva, Philip, SchaKerra, Leonard, Mark, Renita, Dontina, Jai & Sonya Sanford. **Educ:** Inst Divine Metaphysical Res Inc, DD, 1971. **Career:** Ford Motor Co, Dearborn, MI, 1949-65; UAW Local 600-Ford, cio, 1965-92; Kaiser Jeep; Enjoy Restaurant/Palace, creative consult, mgr, 1988-89; Third Baptist Church, assoc pastor; Inst Divine Metaphysical Res Inc, recruiter, lectr; Universal Sch Spiritual Awareness, dean, currently. **Orgs:** Inst Divine Metaphysical Res Inc. **Honors/Awds:** Vol Serv Award, Project Head Start, 1992. **Special Achievements:** Foundation of Universal School of Spiritual Awareness; Author, The Beauty of it All, 1995. **Military Serv:** AAF, pfc, 1946-48. **Business Addr:** Dean, Universal School Spiritual Awareness, 5300 Newport Ave, Detroit, MI 48213, **Business Phone:** (313)822-8415.

EDWARDS, HON. AL E.
State government official, real estate executive. **Personal:** Born Mar 19, 1937, Houston, TX; son of Josephine and E L Edwards Sr; married Lana Kay Cloth; children: Albert Ely II, Jason Kiamba & Alana Catherine Raquel. **Educ:** Tex Southern Univ, BS, 1966; Tuskegee Inst, Ala, cert corrective therapy. **Career:** Gen Foods Corp, acct mgr, 1958-80; Al Edwards Pub Rels Advertisement, pres, 1968-; NAACP, pub rels, 1976-78; Al Edwards Real Estate & Mortgage Co, 1979-; State Tex, state rep, dist 85, 1979-82, dist 146, 1983-. **Orgs:** Houston Bus & Prof Men; Dean Pledges Alpha Phi Alpha; founder, pres bd, Houston Team Tennis Asn, 1976-78; founder, Tex Emancipation Cult Asn; chmn, Jesse Jackson Pres Campaign, Tex, 1984; chmn, Tex Senatorial Dist 13Conv, 1984; Dem Nat Comn, 1984, chmn, 1995; nat vice chmn, Mondale Pres Campaign, 1984; Alpha Phi Alpha Fraternity. **Honors/Awds:** Outstanding Service Award, 66th Legis, Tex Railroad Passenger Asn, 1980; Al Edwards Freedom Heritage Pk, Dedicated San Antonio, Tex Emancipation Comn, 1980; hon doctorate, Univ Belize, 1983; Who's Who in America, 1989; Hall of Fame, African Am Biographic Asn, 1994; Who's Who of Global Decision Makers, 2006. **Special Achievements:** Authored House Bill 1015 Emancipation Day, Texas Legal State Holiday, 1979. **Business Addr:** State Representative, Texas House of Representatives, 4913 Griggs Road, Houston, TX 77054-4608, **Business Phone:** (713)741-8800.

EDWARDS, ANTHONY (ANTHONY QUINN EDWARDS)
Football player, football executive. **Personal:** Born May 26, 1966, Casa Grande, AZ; married Mary Ann; children: Tony, Torrey & Tynette. **Educ:** NMex Highlands Univ. **Career:** Football player (retired), Football executive; Philadelphia Eagles, wide receiver, 1989-90; Phoenix Cardinals, 1991-93; Ariz Cardinals, 1995-97, dir player develop, sr dir player develop, currently. **Business Addr:** Senior Director of Player Development, Arizona Cardinals, PO Box 888, Phoneix, AZ 85001, **Business Phone:** (602)379-0101.

EDWARDS, ANTHONY QUINN. **See EDWARDS, ANTHONY.**

EDWARDS, ANTONIO
Football player, football coach. **Personal:** Born Mar 10, 1970, Moultrie, NC; married Regina; children: Ashanti & Amahn. **Educ:** Valdosta State Univ. **Career:** Player (retired); Coach: Seattle Sea hawks, def end, 1993-97; NY Giants, 1997; Atlanta Falcons, 1998; Carolina Panthers, defensive end, 1999-2001; Philadelphia eagles, def line coach; Collegiate Sch, defensive line coach, currently. **Honors/Awds:** Rookie of the Year, 1993; Gulf South Defensive Player of the Year 1991& 1992; Inducted into VSU Hall Of Fame, 2000. **Business Addr:** Defensive Line Coach, Collegiate School, 103 N Mooreland Rd, Richmond, VA 23229, **Business Phone:** (804)740-7077.

EDWARDS, ANTUAN
Football player. **Personal:** Born May 26, 1977, Starkville, MS. **Educ:** Clemson, sports mkt. **Career:** Football player(retired);

Green Bay Packers, defensive back, 1999-03; Miami Dolphins, 2004; St Louis Rams, prof football player, 2004; New Eng Patriots, 2004; Atlanta Falcons, safety, 2005; Washington Redskins, 2006. **Orgs:** Make-A-Wish Children's Hosp, WI; Bornemann's Nursing Home; Geraldine Zuber Edwards Found, 2003-. **Honors/Awds:** Jim Thorpe Award. *

EDWARDS, AUDREY MARIE
Publishing executive. **Personal:** Born Apr 21, 1947, Tacoma, WA; daughter of Cyrill and Bertie; married Benjamin Williams. **Educ:** Univ Wash, BA, 1969; Columbia Univ, MA, 1974. **Career:** Coretta Scott King fel, Am Asn Univ Women, 1969; Fairchild Publ, prom news ed, 1977-79; Black Enterprise Mag, assoc ed, 1978-79, exec ed, vpres ed oper, 1990-; Family Circle Mag, sr ed, 1979-81; NY Univ, adj prof, 1982-; Essence Mag, sr ed, currently. **Orgs:** Regional dir, Nat Asn Black Journalists, 1981-83; prog chair, NY Asn Black Journalists, 1983-. **Honors/Awds:** Unity Award, Media Lincoln Univ, 1985. **Special Achievements:** Auth: The Picture Life of Muhammad Ali, F Watts, 1976; The Picture Life of Bobby Orr, F Watts, 1976; The Picture Life of Stevie Wonder, F Watts, 1977; Children of the Dream: The Psychology of Black Success, 1992. **Home Addr:** 426 Eastern Pkwy, Brooklyn, NY 11225. *

EDWARDS, BESSIE REGINA
Manager, real estate agent. **Personal:** Born Mar 14, 1942, Gates County, NC. **Educ:** Brooklyn Col, Special Bacculaurate Degree Prog, 1979; New Sch Soc Rsch, BA & MA, 1981. **Career:** Opportunity Industrialization, counselor & teacher, 1975-80; Manhattan Cable TV, affirmative action officer, 1980-86; Paragon Cable, mgr training & develop; BR Edwards Assoc Real Estate, broker & owner, currently. **Orgs:** Bd mem, NY Chap Coalition 100 Black Women; sec, Minorities Cable; sec, Women Cable; bd mem, EDGES; Women's City Club; Brooklyn Chamber Com, 1989-90. **Honors/Awds:** Black Achiever, Time Inc The Parent Co, 1987.

EDWARDS, CARL RAY, II
Lawyer. **Personal:** Born Jul 14, 1947, Detroit, MI; son of Carl R and Alice; married Alice Jennings Edwards; children: Patrick Phillips, Kwameena, Tonya Jennings, Ronald G Watters, Saraun, Carl Ray. **Educ:** Mich Lutheran Col, BA, 1970; Univ Detroit, MA, 1972; Wayne State Univ, JD, 1974. **Career:** Philo, Atkinson, Darling, Steinberg, Edwards and Jennings, partner, 1973-82; Edwards & Jennings PC, pres, 1982-. **Orgs:** Asn Trial Lawyers Am, 1976-; Nat Bar Asn, 1985-; Mich Bar Asn, 1975-; Mich Trial Lawyers Asn, exec bd mem, 1976-, treas, secy, vpres, pres, 1987-88; Nat Conf Black Lawyers, Mich Chap, co-founder. **Honors/Awds:** Praisal Citation, Nat Asn Equal Opport Higher Educ, 1981; Founder's Award, Mich Trial Lawyers Asn, Peoples Law Sch, 1989. **Special Achievements:** State Bar of Michigan delegation member of judges and attorneys on legal and constitutional fact-finding mission to USSR and People's Republic of China, 1988; Co-founder of the Michigan Trial Lawyers' Peoples Law School, operating across Michigan and established by the Association of Trial Lawyers of America and operating in over 18 states nationwide. *

EDWARDS, CLAUDIA L.
Association executive. **Personal:** Born in Bronx, NY; daughter of Mable and Joshua; divorced; children: Damon, Andre. **Educ:** Bronx Community Col, ASO, 1980; SUNY Purchase, BA, 1983; New York Univ, MA, 1988. **Career:** United Way, vp, 1989-92; Reader's Digest Fund, assoc dir, 1992-93, exec dir, 1993-03. **Orgs:** trustee, Westchester Medical Ctr; Westchester fund Women & Girls; exec, asn Black found; Women Commun; Women Philanthropy. **Honors/Awds:** Academy of Women Achievers, YWCA, 1996; Distinguished Service Award, County Westchester, 1996; Meritorious Award, Links Inc, 1997; Distinguished Alumna, Bronx Community Col, 1997; National Library Week Award, Westchester Library System, 1999; NY State Assembly for her work in corporate philanthropy. *

EDWARDS, CLAYBON JEROME
Funeral director. **Personal:** Born Jul 15, 1929, Peach County, GA; married Mary Nevel; children: Deneise. **Educ:** Morris Brown Col; Worsham Col; Ft Valley State NW. **Career:** Super Life Ins Co, home off rep, reg supr, inspector & dist mgr cons; C J Edwards Funeral Home Inc, dir & owner, currently. **Orgs:** Ga Funeral Serv Practioners Asn; vpres, Upsilon Nu Delta Morticians Fraternit; mem bd dir, Wabash YMCA; mem & pres, Alpha Phi Alpha Fraternity; mem bd, GA Area Planning & Develop Comn; treas, Citizenship Educ Comt; mem trustee bd, Trinity Baptist Church; mem trustee bd, Morris Brown Col; State Bd Dept Human Resources; Nat Asn Advan Colored People. **Honors/Awds:** Honored Mort of the Year, 1974. **Special Achievements:** First black elected official City Councilman of GA. **Business Addr:** Director, Owner, C J Edwards Funeral Home Inc, 409 Preston St, Fort Valley, GA 31030.

EDWARDS, DANIEL
Business owner, executive. **Personal:** Married Monica. **Career:** Morehead Manor Bed & Breakfast, inn keeper & owner, currently. **Orgs:** African Am Asn Inkeepers Int. **Business Addr:** Owner, Morehead Manor Bed & Breakfast, 914 Vickers Ave, Durham, NC 27701, **Business Phone:** (919)687-4366.

EDWARDS, DELORES A.
Journalist, television producer. **Personal:** Born Sep 22, 1965, New York, NY; daughter of Nathaniel and Lucy Miller. **Educ:** Northeastern Univ, Boston, MA, BS, 1988; Columbia Univ Graduate Sch Journalism, MS, 2000. **Career:** Columbia Univ Grad Sch Arts & Scu, grad adv, 1988-89; ABC News, Nightline, 20/20, prod assoc, 1989-92, assoc producer ABC Children's Special "Prejudice," 1992, "Kids in the Crossfire," 1994, "Live at the White House, pres Clinton: Answering Children's Questions," 1994; All Am TV, segment producer, 1992-93; TV Prog Enterprises, segment producer, 1992-93; Pacific Rim LTD, res consult, 1993; Arts & Entertainment Network, assoc producer "Biography," producer; WGBH/GR Productions, associate producer "Surviving the Odds: To Be a Young Black Male in America," 1994; Kelly Films, assoc producer "Fighting Destroyer Escorts," "Proudly We Served: The Men of the USS Mason," 1994; Barwall Productions, producer "Barbara Walters Interviews of a Lifetime," 1994; ABC News, Murder in Beverly Hills: The Menendez Trial, researcher, 1994; PBS, Imaging Am, assoc producer, 1997; FOX5, Good Day New York, producer; Freelance Television Segment Producer, New York, NY, currently. **Orgs:** Nat Asn Broadcasters , 1988-; NY Asn Black Journalist, 1988-; Nat Asn Broadcast Employees & Technicians, 1989-; Soc Professional Journalists, 1990-. *

EDWARDS, DENNIS, JR.
Judge. **Personal:** Born Aug 19, 1922, New York, NY; son of Dennis Sr and Gladys Wilson; married Dorothy Fairclough; children: Lynne Mosley & Denise Young. **Educ:** NY Univ, BA, 1941; Harvard Law Sch, JD, 1944. **Career:** NY Supreme Ct, law clerk, 1948-65; New York City Criminal Ct, judge, 1965-. **Orgs:** Dir, New York Co Lawyers Asn, 1961-65; Harlem Lawyers Asn, 1952; Am Judicature Soc, Am Bar Asn; dir, Speedwell Soc C; Omega Fraternity; Elks; Masons; Nat Asn Advan Colored People; Urban League; YMCA. **Home Addr:** 409 Edgecombe Ave, New York, NY 10032, **Home Phone:** (212)283-7737. **Business Addr:** Judge, New York Criminal Court, 100 Center St, New York, NY 10013, **Business Phone:** (646)386-4500.

EDWARDS, DIXON VOLDEAN, III
Football player. **Personal:** Born Mar 25, 1968, Cincinnati, OH; son of Dixon Jr; married Secola; children: Dixon IV & Taylor. **Educ:** Mich State Univ. **Career:** Dallas Cowboys, linebacker, 1991-95; Minn Vikings, prof football player, 1996-98. *

EDWARDS, DONALD PHILIP
Lawyer. **Personal:** Born Aug 27, 1947, Buffalo, NY; son of Robert D and Lorraine V Jarrett; married Jo Roberson. **Educ:** Morehouse Col, Atlanta, GA, BA, 1969; Boston Univ Sch Law, JD, 1973. **Career:** Nat Asn Advan Colored People Legal Defense Fund, fel, 1973-76; Thomas Kennedy Sampson Edwards & Patterson, partner, 1974-92; Law Off Donald P Edwards, sole practr, 1992-; Clef Prod Inc, co-owner & chmn bd dir, 1993-97. **Orgs:** State Bar GA, 1973-; chmn bd, Hillside Int Truth Ctr, 1980-83; bd adv, Atlanta Legal Aid Soc, 1981-85; bd mem, Atlanta Volunteer Lawyers Inc, 1983-84; pres, Northern Dist Litigation Fund, 1984-87; bd mem, Nat Bar Asn, 1984, 1985; pres, Gate City Bar Asn, 1984; chmn, Fulton County Dept Family & C Serv, 1990; dir, Nat Bar Asn, Region XI, 1986-87; pres, Christ Coun Metro Atlanta, 1998; bd mem, Am Cancer Society, Atlanta Unit, 1988-89; trustee, Southwest Hosp & Med Ctr, 1990-; pres, Southwest Hosp Found Inc, 1992-95; 100 Black Men Atlanta Inc; pres, Asn Metro Atlanta DFCS Bds, 1992-94; chair, S Atlanta District, Boy Scouts Am; bd mem, exec comm, Atlanta Area Coun, Boy Scouts Am, 1998-. **Honors/Awds:** Outstanding Community Service Award, Col Pk Neighborhood Voters League, 1980; Presidential Award, Nat Black Am Law Stud Asn, 1983; Civil Rights Award, Gate City Bar Asn, 1983; Lawyer of the Yr, DeKalb Cty Nat Asn Advan Colored People, 1984; Thurgood Marshall Award Award, Nat Asn Advan Colored People, Atlanta Br, 1985; Leadership Atlanta, 1985; Black Pages Prof Achievement Award, 1992; Chief Justice Robert Benham Community Service Award, State Bar GA, 2000; Silver Beaver Award, S Atlanta Dist, Boy Scouts of Ame, 2000; The Donald P. Edwards Humanitarian Award, South Atlanta Sankofa Dist, 2003; Blessed Are The Peacemakers Award, World Council of Churches, 2004; Allen Award, 2004; Gate City Bar Assn. "Hall of Fame", 2004. **Special Achievements:** Top 100 Atlantans under 40 Atlanta Mag 1984; Father of the Year; "100 Most Influential African Americans in Atlanta". **Home Addr:** 954 Willis Mill Rd SW, Atlanta, GA 30311. **Business Addr:** Practioner, The Law Office of Donald P Edwards, 170 Mitchell St SW, Atlanta, GA 30303-3424.

EDWARDS, DONNA
Congressperson (U.S. federal government). **Personal:** Children: Jared. **Educ:** Wake Forest University, Bachelors Degree; Franklin Pierce Law Center, JD. **Career:** Arca Foundation, Executive Director; Congressperson. **Orgs:** Co-Founder and Executive Director, National Network to End Domestic Violence. **Business Addr:** 434 Cannon House Office Building, Washington, DC 20515, **Business Phone:** (202)225-8699.*

EDWARDS, DONNA M. **See EDWARDS O, DONNA M.**

EDWARDS, DONNIE
Football player. **Personal:** Born Apr 6, 1973, San Diego, CA. **Educ:** Univ Calif, LA, BA, polit sci. **Career:** Kansas City Chiefs, linebacker, 1996-01, 2007-09; San Diego Chargers, linebacker, 2002-06. **Orgs:** Alpha Rho chapter of Zeta Beta Tau. *

EDWARDS, DOROTHY WRIGHT
Educator. **Personal:** Born Jan 13, 1914, Jacksonville, FL; daughter of John and Julia Peterson; married Oscar J, Jun 8, 1938 (deceased); children: Oscar J Jr. **Educ:** Fla A&M Univ, BS, 1935; NY Univ, MA, 1952. **Career:** Educator (retired); Phys educ instr, 1935-40; BTW, bus instr, 1940; Miami Housing Authority, cashier-booker, 1940-41; Dorsey Jr-Sr High, sec & phys instr, 1941-47, dean girls, 1947-55; Miami Northwestern Sr High, asst prin guid, 1955-70; Miami Spgs, asst prin guid, 1970-71; Edward Waters Col,dean women, 1971-72; Proj Upward Bound, counr, 1972-76; Fla Mem Col, counr women, 1976-78; Miami Northwestern Sr High Sch, jr col assistance prog adv. **Orgs:** Bd dir, OIC; bd dir, Dade Mt Zion Fed Credit Union, Am Asn Univ Women, Coun Int Visitors; life mem, YWCA, Alpha Kappa Alpha Sorority; Kappa Delta Pi; 100 Women Fla Mem Col; church clerk, Mt Zion Baptist Church; Docent, Jackson Mem Hosp Alamo; bd dir, Family Health Ctr Inc. **Honors/Awds:** Outstanding Service to Youth Award, Phi Delta Kappa; Star Teacher, Miami NW Sr HS, 1966-67; Certificate of Appreciation, YWCA, 1975; Outstanding Citizen Award, 1984; Outstanding Service Award, Econ Opportunity Family Health Ctr Inc, 1994; Act of Kindness Award, Miami Dade Community Col, 1996; Outstanding Service Award, Commitment & Leadership Educ Excellence, Algonguin Club, 1999; Certificate of Merit, Eta Phi Beta Sorority Inc, 1999; Special Recognition Award, Fla A & M Univ, 2002; Book of Life Certificate of Appreciation by the Black Archives, History & Res Found SFla, 2002; Florida A & M Sports Hall of Fame, 2004. **Home Addr:** 3200 NW 49th St, Miami, FL 33142.

EDWARDS, ED. **See EDWARDS, DR. ABIYAH, JR.**

EDWARDS, ELLA RAINO
Actor, storyteller. **Personal:** Born Oct 7, 1938, Kilgore, TX; daughter of John Henry Raino (deceased) and Lola B Taylor Raino (deceased); divorced; children: Bernard Otis Wright. **Educ:** Los Angeles Metropolitan Col, AA; John Robert Powers Sch Modeling, grad. **Career:** Films: Young Doctors in Love, 1982; Who Is Julia?, 1986; Bad Dreams, 1988; House Party, 1990; Vital Signs, 1990; Sneakers, 1992; On Hope, 1994; Fire Down Below, 1997; TV series: Dead Men Tell No Tales, 1971; "The White Shadow", 1979-80; Thursday's Child, 1983; "Doogie Howser, M.D.", 1991; "Wanda at Large", 2003; "ER.", 2008; consult & performance artist, Los Angeles Int House Blues Found Educ Tours Prog; Metrop Water Dist Southern Calif Educ Div, res, develop, perform water stories, 1998-99; story teller, currently. **Orgs:** Griot Soc Southern Calif; Tellers & Talkers; Nat Storytelling Asn; Nat Asn Black Storytellers; Screen Actors Guild; Am Fed TV & Radio Artists; Founding & charter mem, Fin Sec Kwanza Found; former mem & secy, Black Women Theatre W, 1984-86. **Honors/Awds:** Ohio Close School Boys Award, 1972-74; Community Service Award, Alpha Gamma Omega Chap, Alpha Kappa Alpha Award; Certificate Commendation, City Los Angeles, 1988 & 1995; Certificate of Recognition, Jenesse Ctr; Performance Bicentennial US, Shreveport Regional Bicentennial Comn, 1976; Bicentennial Minute Man Award. **Special Achievements:** Official storyteller of Allensworth State Historic Park, California's first town founded by African Am; Co-author: "Another Kind of Treasure: A Story of Dreams Fulfilled". **Home Addr:** 8722 Skyline Dr, Los Angeles, CA 90046. **Business Addr:** Storyteller, PO Box 1420, Studio City, CA 90001, **Business Phone:** (323)654-1922.

EDWARDS, ESTHER GORDY
Arts administrator. **Personal:** Born Apr 25, 1920, Oconee, GA; married George H; children: Robert Bullock. **Educ:** Howard Univ; Wayne State Univ. **Career:** Gordy Printing Co Detroit, co-owner & gen mgr, 1947-59; Motown Rec Corp, secy, Artists Personal Mgt Div, dir, sr vpres & chief exec officer, 1959-88; Motown Indust, Hollywood, corp secy, sr vpres, 1973-88; Motown Hist Mus, Detroit, founder, chmn & chief exec officer, 1985-. **Orgs:** Chmn, Wayne Co Dem Women's Comt, 1956; Detroit Recorders Ct Jury Comn, 1960-62; chmn bd, Am Develop Corp; exec dir, Gordy Found, 1968-; founder & chmn, African-Am Heritage Asn, 1976-; Mich del-at-large, Dem Nat Conv, 1960; interim asst dep auditor gen, MI, 1960; bd dir, Bank Commonwealth, 1973-79; Booker T Wash Bus Asn; Howard Univ Alumni Asn; vpres, Metro Detroit Conv & Visitors Bur; Wayne State Fund; adv bd sch mgt, Univ Mich; Alpha Kappa Alpha; bd trustees, Interlochen Ctr Arts. **Business Addr:** Director, Motown Historical Museum, 2648 W Grand Blvd, Detroit, MI 48208.*

EDWARDS, GENYNE
Secretary (Government), executive. **Educ:** Purdue Univ, BA, orgn leadership & supv; Marquette Univ Law Sch, law degree. **Career:** Secretary (retired), Director; YWCA, Greater Milwaukee, pub policy dir; Lanier Law Offs Ltd, atty; Chicago Lawyers for the Arts, staff; Milwaukee Art Museum, staff; Strive Media Inst, staff; Wisc Dept Tourism, dep secy, 2003-07; WYMS-Radio for Milwaukee, 88Nine Radio Milwaukee, community rels dir, currently. **Orgs:** Community bd, Marquette Univ Law Alumni Asn; community bd, Milwaukee World Festivals Inc; community bd, Ko-Thi Dance Co; community bd, Cult Alliance Greater

Milwaukee; community bd, Milwaukee chap, Black Pub Rels Soc. **Honors/Awds:** Volunteer of the Year, Volunteer Ctr of Greater Milwaukee, 2003; Most Influential African-Americans in the Tourism Industry, Nat Publ-Black Meetings & Tourism, 2004. **Special Achievements:** Featured in Milwaukee Mag as a "Top 35 under 35", 2003. **Business Addr:** Community Relations Director, Radio Milwaukee, 88Nine Radio Milwaukee, 5312 W Vliet St, Milwaukee, WI 53208, **Business Phone:** (414)475-8330.

EDWARDS, GEORGE R
Executive. **Personal:** Born Feb 1, 1938, New York, NY; son of John and Olga; divorced; children: Lisa, Veronica & George Drew. **Educ:** City Col New York, BA, eng, 1959. **Career:** British Airways New York, sales mgr, 1959-63; Pepsi-Cola, Brooklyn, New York, gen sales mgr, 1964-65, gen mgr, 1968-70; Venture Mkt Co, Heublein Inc, vpres mkt; Heublein Spirits Div, vpres, group mkt dir, 1974-78; Hartford Grad Ctr, vis prof mkt, 1975-78; Nat Black Network, pres & chief operating officer, 1983-. **Orgs:** Chmn, Mkt Community, Greater Hartford Arts Coun, 1976-78. **Business Addr:** President, Chief Operating Officer, National Black Network, 10 Columbus Circle, New York, NY 10019, **Business Phone:** (212)586-0610.

EDWARDS, GERALD DOUGLAS
Executive. **Personal:** Born Jul 13, 1950, Chicago, IL; son of William Kenneth and Lucille Elizabeth; married Jada Denise Brooks, Nov 18, 1972; children: Candice Rae, Gerald Douglas. **Educ:** Heidelberg Col, BA, 1972. **Career:** Ford Motor Co, gen supvr, 1983-86; Detroit Plastic Molding, asst plant mgr, 1986-87; Engineered Plastic Prod Inc, chief exec officer, 1987-, pres, 2004; Clear Stone LLC, Namibia, Africa, founder. **Orgs:** Minority input comt, Mich Minority Bus Develop Coun, 1989-; bd dir, 1989-, bldg fund campaign chmn, 1990-, Sumpter Community Church God; dir, Minority Technol Coun Mich, 1992-. **Honors/Awds:** Outstanding Young Men of America, 1989; Supplier of the Year awd, General Motors, 1999; Entrepreneur of the Year, Bus Owners Asn, Washtenaw Co; Outstanding Service Award, Nat Asn Advan Colored People; Coleman A. Young Business & Community Involvement Award, Mich Dem Party Black Caucus; Michiganian of the Year, Detroit News, 1999. **Special Achievements:** CORP! Magazine selected Gerald as one of Michigan's extraordinary African-American achievers. **Business Addr:** Chief Executive Officer, President, Engineered Plastic Products Inc, 699 James L Hart Pkwy, Ypsilanti, MI 48197, **Business Phone:** (734)483-2500.*

EDWARDS, GROVER LEWIS, SR.
Consultant, school administrator, president (organization). **Personal:** Born Feb 21, 1944, Henrico, NC; son of Grover C Edwards; married Lucy Priscilla Moody; children: Reggie Lamont, Telsha Nicole, Kelsey Daneen & Grover Lewis Jr. **Educ:** Elizabeth City State Univ, Assoc, attended 1965; Shaw Univ, BS, 1976. **Career:** RCA Training Prog, electronics instr, 1969-73, supvr instrs, 1973-79; Edwards & Assocs Bldg Contractors, owner & pres, 1979; Norfax Real Estate Corp, pres, 1983-; Northampton County Sch Bd, chmn. **Orgs:** Past youth adv, Nat Asn Advan Colored People, 1969; pres, Gaston Religious Civic Orgn, 1971; pres, Northampton Housing Asst Prog, 1972; NC Home Builders Asn, 1980; bd mem, Northampton Co Sch, 1972-, chmn, 1984-; Prince Hall Masonic Lodge, 1975-; bd dirs, NC Sch Bd, 1984-. **Honors/Awds:** Service Award, Northampton HS W, 1980; Service Award, Athlete Asn, Tri-City Chums, 1981; Outstanding Business Award, Northampton Co Nat Asn Advan Colored People, 1985. **Military Serv:** USN, E4, 1965-69; Nat Defense Award.

EDWARDS, DR. HARRY
Educator. **Personal:** Born Nov 22, 1942, St Louis, MO; married Sandra Y Boze; children: Tazamisha Heshima Imara, Fatima Malene Imara & Changa Demany Imara. **Educ:** San Jose State, BA, 1964; Cornell Univ, MA, 1966, PhD, 1967. **Career:** San Jose State, instr Sociol, 1966-68; Univ Santa Clara, instr Sociol,1967-68; Univ Calif, Berkeley, asst prof Sociol, 1970-77, assoc prof Sociol, prof sociol, 2004. **Orgs:** Nat Sports Inst Oslo Norway; Nat Sports Inst Moscow USSR; consult, San Francisco 49ers; Golden State Warriors. **Honors/Awds:** Man of the Year Award, San Francisco Sun Reporter, 1968; Russwurm Award, Nat Newspaper Publishers Assoc, 1968; fellowship, Cornell Univ, 1968; Dist Scholar, Ore State Univ, 1980; Hon Doctorate, Columbia Col, 1981; Miller Scholar, Univ Ill, 1982; Dist Scholar, Norwegian Col Physical Educ & Sports Oslow Norway, 1983; Dist Scholar, Univ Charleston, 1984; Dist Visiting Scholar, Ind State Univ, 1984. **Special Achievements:** Author; Revolt of the Black Athlete, Free Press, 1970. **Business Addr:** Professor of Sociology, University of California, 101 Zellerbach Hall, Berkeley, CA 94720, **Business Phone:** (510)642-9988.*

EDWARDS, HARRY THOMAS
Judge. **Personal:** Born Nov 3, 1940, New York, NY; son of George H and Arline Lyle; married Pamela Carrington; children: Brent & Michelle. **Educ:** Cornell Univ, BS, 1962; Univ Mich Law Sch, JD, 1965. **Career:** Seyfarth, Shaw Fairweather & Geraldson, Chicago, atty, 1965-70; Univ Mich Law Sch, prof, 1970-75, 1977-80; Harvard Univ Law Sch, prof, 1975-77; Harvard Inst Educ Mgt, 1976-82; Amtrak, bd dir, 1978-80, chmn bd, 1979-80; US Ct Appeals, Washington, DC, judge, 1980-94, chief judge, 1994-2001, sr judge, 2005-; NY Univ Sch Law, vis prof, 1990-. **Orgs:** Am Law Inst; Am Bar Asn; Am Acad Arts & Sci; Am Judicature Soc; bd dir, Unique Learning Ctr; Alpha Phi Alpha. **Honors/Awds:** LLD, Williams Col; LLD, Univ Detroit; LLD, Georgetown Univ; LLD, Brooklyn Col, LLD, State Univ NY; LLD, John Jay Col Criminal Justice; LLD, Lewis & Clark Col; LLD, St Lawrence Univ; Soc Am Law Teachers Award, 1982; Whitney North Seymour Medal, Am Arbitration Asn, 1988. **Special Achievements:** Co-author: Labor Relations Law in the Pub Sector, 1985; The Lawyer as a Negotiator, 1977; Collective Bargaining & Labor Arbitration, 1979; Higher Educ & the Law, 1980; author of more than 75 scholarly articles. **Business Phone:** (202)216-7000.

EDWARDS, HERMAN LEE
Football coach, football player. **Personal:** Born Apr 27, 1954, Eatontown, NJ; son of Sergeant (deceased) and Martha; married Lia; children: Marcus, Gabrielle & Vivian. **Educ:** San Diego State Univ, BA, criminal justice, 1977. **Career:** Football player (retired), Football coach; San Diego State, defensive back, 1975-76; Philadelphia Eagles, defensive back, 1977-85; AtlantaFalcons, defensive back, 1986; Los Angeles Rams, defensive back, 1986; SanJose St Univ, defensive backs coach, 1987-89; Kansas City Chiefs, scout, 1990-91, defensive backs coach, 1992-95, pro personnel scout, 1995, head coach, 2006-08; Tampa Bay Buccaneers, asst head coach, 1996-2000; NewYork Jets, head coach, 2001-05. **Orgs:** Founder, Herm Edwards Youth Found, 1985. *

EDWARDS, HORACE BURTON
Executive, consulting engineer, social worker. **Personal:** Born May 20, 1925, Tuscaloosa, AL; divorced; children: Adrienne, Paul, David & Michael. **Educ:** Marquette Univ, BS, Naval Sci, Mech Engr, 1947, 1948; Iona Col, MBA, 1972; Tex Southern Univ, LHD (Hon), 1982; Stillman Col, LLD (Hon) 1984. **Career:** Politician, Consultant, Corporate Executive (retired): Atlantic Richfield Co, controller mkt, 1968-72, mgr finance & opeartion analysis, 1973-76, mgr planning & control transp div, 1976-79; ARCO Transp Co, vpres planning & control, 1978-80; ARCO Pipe Line Co, pres, chief exec officer & chmn; Edwards & Assocs Inc, consult engr & owner, currently. **Orgs:** Trustee Leadership Independence, 1984-85, Kans Chamber Com Leadership, Kans 1985-86; dir, pres Independence Ind, 1985; Assoc Oil Pipe Lines Exec Comn, Am Petrol Inst & Cent Comn Pipe Line Transp; pres, bd dir, Jr Achievement Montgomery County Independence Kans; bd dir, Kans Chamber Com & Indust, Independence Community Col Endowment Bd; trustee, Inst Logopedics, Wichita, Kans; Kans Independent Col Fund; Kans Coun Econ Educ; Tex Southern Univ Bus Sch Found; Nat Bar Assoc Adv Comn Energy & Environ Law Sect; bd dir, Am Assoc Blacks Energy; participant Nat Urban League's Black Exec Exchange Prog; NAACP; Fla A&M Sch Bus; Indust Ctr Entrepreneurial Develop Roundtable. **Honors/Awds:** Distinguished Engr Alumnus Award, Marquette Univ, 1984. **Military Serv:** USN, lt jg, 1943-48. **Business Addr:** Consulting Engineer, Owner, Edwards & Associates Inc, 5800 SW Turnbery Ct, Topeka, KS 66114, **Business Phone:** (785)273-9561.

EDWARDS, JOHN L.
Educator. **Personal:** Born Oct 18, 1930, Muncie, IN; married Mavis J Jones; children: John & Robert. **Educ:** Ball State Univ, BS, 1953; Ariz State Univ, MA, 1959, EdD, 1965. **Career:** Julian Elem Sch, Phoenix, teacher, 1955-62; Ariz State Univ, grad asst, 1962-63, fac assoc, 1963-64, instr, 1964-66, asst prof, 1966-69, exten & prof Col, asst dean, 1973-, assoc prof, 1969-75, prof emer, 1996-. **Orgs:** Int Reading Assn, 1963; NEA, 1956; Ariz Educ Assn; Am Assn Univ Profs, 1964; Phi Delta Kappa, 1966; Kappa Delta Pi, 1962; fac Adv, Kappa Alpha Psi; Ariz State Univ, 1962-72 & 1975; bd mem, Southwestern Coop End Lab; brd dir, Jane Wayland Child Guidance Ctr, 1969-75; Ariz Right Read Comn, 1971;Phoenix Citizens Bond Comt, 1975; past chmn, Ariz Educ Assn Instr & Prof Develop Comn; brd dir, Assn Higher Educ, 1964; Desert Area reading coun, 1966. **Honors/Awds:** Outstanding Achievement, Western Provincial Alumni Award, Kappa Alpha Psi,1962; Phoenix Alumni Award, Kappa Alpha Psi, 1965, 1963 & 1960; Award for Outstanding Achievement, Adult Basic Educ Inst, 1970. **Special Achievements:** Has written many articles in his field. **Home Addr:** 5721 E Calle Camelia, Phoenix, AZ 85018, **Home Phone:** (480)949-7035. **Business Addr:** Professor Emeritus, Arizona State University, Univ Ex Acad Serv Bldg Room 110, Tempe, AZ 85281.

EDWARDS, JOHN LOYD, III
Foundation executive. **Personal:** Born Feb 18, 1948, Nashville, TN; children: Adrian Joel, Nikita Michelle, Derek Traimain. **Educ:** Tenn State Univ, attended 1968; Univ Tenn, Chattanooga, BFA, 1980. **Career:** Chattanooga Northstar Newspaper, writer & dir advert, 1981-83; Mary Walker Hist & Educ Found, exec dir, 1983-; pres, Visual Media Productions, 1985-; bd dirs, Joseph Johnson Ment Health Ctr, 1988-. **Orgs:** hon life mem, US Jaycees, 1987-; Asn Study Afro-American Life & Hist, 1985-; vpres, Lakeside Parent Teachers Asn, 1986-. **Honors/Awds:** Outstanding Community Achievement, Vietnam Era Veteran City Chattanooga, 1979; Public Relations Directo of the Year, Tenn Jaycees, 1983-84. **Military Serv:** AUS, sgt, 2 yrs; Bronze Star, Army Commendation Medal, Purple Heart, Vietnam Service Cross & Combat Infantry Badge, 1968-70. **Business Addr:** Executive Director, Mary Walker Hist & Educ Found, 3031 Wilcox Blvd, Chattanooga, TN 37411, **Business Phone:** (615)622-3217.*

EDWARDS, JOHN W., JR.
Physician. **Personal:** Born Apr 9, 1933, Ferndale, MI; son of John W (deceased) and Josephine Wood (deceased); married Ella Marie Law; children: Joella Marie, John W III. **Educ:** Alma Col, 1950; Univ Mich, Ann Arbor, BS, 1954; Wayne State Univ, attended 1956; Howard Univ Col Med, MD, 1960. **Career:** Walter Reed Gen Hosp, internship, 1960-61, surg resident, 1962-63, urological resident, 1963-66; Straub Clinic Inc, urologist, 1970-74, chief dept surgery, 1973; pvt pract, urologist, 1974-; asst chief dept surgery, Queen's Med Ctr, 1977-79; chief dept clinical serv, active staff, Kapiolani Women's & Children's Med Ctr, 1981-83; active staff, Kuakini Hosp; consulting staff, Rehab Hosp Pac; consult urol, Tripler Army Med Ctr; John Burns Sch Med, Univ Hawaii, assoc clinical prof, chief surg; Queen's Medical Ctr, Honolulu, vpres, med staff servs, 1993-94; The Queens Health Sys, Physician Rels, vpres, 1994-96; Diag Lab Servs, acting admin, 1995-96, pres, 1996-. **Orgs:** Am Bd Urol; fel, Am Col Surgeons; Am Urological Asn, Western Sec Am Urol Asn; Hawaii Urol Asn; Am Med Asn; Honolulu County Med Soc; Hawaii Med Asn; Nat Med Asn; Alpha Phi Alpha; Chi Delta Mu; Waialae Country Club; life mem, Nat Asn Advan Colored People; fel, Am Col Surgeons; comnr, chmn, City County Honolulu Liquor Commn, 1987-89; gov Hawaii, Am Col Surgeons, 1987-93; pres, Western Section Am Urol Asn, 1989-90. **Honors/Awds:** Alpha Omega Alpha Honor Medical Soc, 1959; The Links Inc, Hawaii Chap, Hawaii African Am Humanitarian of the Year, 1991; Howard Gray Award, Urology Section, Nat Med Asn, 1988; citation, City Honolulu, 1992; Outstanding Physician Award, Queen's Med Ctr, 1992. **Special Achievements:** Co-author: "Anuria Secondary to Bilateral Ureteropelvic Fungus Balls," Urology, 1974; "Representive Causes of Ambiguous Genitalia," Journal of Urology, 1967; "Herpes Zoster with Neurogenic Bladder Dysfunction," Archives of Dermatology, 1974, Journal of AMA, 1973, 1974; co-author, "Anuria Secondary to Bilateral Ureteropelvic Fungus Balls," Urology, Feb, 1980. **Military Serv:** AUS, capt, 1959-63; AUS, lt col, 1963-70; Bronze Star. **Business Addr:** President, Diagnostic Laboratory Services Inc, 650 Iwilei Rd Suite 300, Honolulu, HI 96817.*

EDWARDS, JOHN WILSON
Administrator. **Personal:** Born Feb 17, 1942, Durham County, NC; married Eloise Freeman; children: Brian, Robin. **Educ:** Durham Col, 1961; NC Fund, Comm Action Tech Training Pgm, 1965. **Career:** NAACP, student field worker, 1960-61; NAACP Youth Workers, field supr, student, 1961-62; NAACP Durham, field sec-at-large, 1962-65; Winston-salem Boys Club, dir, 1965-66; Operation Breakthrough Inc Durham, leadership devel coordr, 1966-67; State Econ Opp Office NC, dir Present; Institutional Devel Soul City Co, mgr; Alumni Affairs Durham Col, dir; Voter Educ Proj Atlanta, area coord; NC Voter & Educ Prgm Durham, organizer. **Orgs:** Soul City Found Inc; UOCI Fed Credit Union; Durham Con on Affairs of Black People; Durham Opp Found Inc; Durham Coll; Durham Bus & Professional Chain; NC Voter Educ Proj Inc; NC Fed of Child Care Ctrs ; Econ Devel Corp; Durham Coll Alumni Assn pres Pan African Early Educ Ctr; Lincoln Comm Health Ctr; past-chmn adv United Black Officers of Durham, NC consumer credit counseling serv of Wake Co Union Bapt Ct; Sr Usher Bd; mem Bd of Trustees. **Business Addr:** PO Box 27687, Raleigh, NC 27611.*

EDWARDS, KENNETH J.
Executive. **Personal:** Born Apr 5, 1947, Beaumont, TX; married Gloria J Holmes; children: Melissa R, Kenitha J, Kenneth J. **Educ:** Lamar Univ, BS 1970. **Career:** Executive (retired). US Govt, reliablty engr, 1970-71; John Deere Co, serv rep, 1971-72, sales prom supr, 1972-73, territory mgr, 1973-76, div serv mgr, 1976-77, serv mgr consumer prod, 1977-79, div sales mgr, 1979. **Business Addr:** East Moline, IL 61244.*

EDWARDS, KEVIN DURELL
Basketball player. **Personal:** Born Oct 30, 1965, Cleveland Heights, OH; married; children: 3. **Educ:** Lakeland Community Col, Mentor, OH, 1984; DePaul Univ, Chicago, IL, 1986. **Career:** Basketball player (retired); Miami Heat, guard, 1988-93; NJ Nets, 1994-98; Orlando Magic, 1998-2000; Vancouver Grizzlies, 2000-01. **Honors/Awds:** NBA All-Rookie Second Team, 1989. **Special Achievements:** Produced movies.

EDWARDS, LEO DEREK
Composer, educator. **Personal:** Born Jan 31, 1937, Cincinnati, OH. **Educ:** Mannes Col Music, BS, 1966; Brooklyn Col, MA, 1969. **Career:** Shumiatcher Sch Music, chmn theory dept, 1965; Brooklyn Col, teaching fel, 1966-68; Mannes Col Music, fac, 1968-; City Univ NY, fac, 1969-75. **Orgs:** Soc Black Composers; Phi Mu Alpha Sinfonia; Music Teachers Nat Asn. **Honors/Awds:** Phi Mu Alpha composition contest winner, 1960; Joseph Dillon Memorial Award Pedagogy, 1966; Citation Music Teachers National Association, 1975; National Endowment for the Arts grant, 1976. **Special Achievements:** Compositions in a wide variety of genres performed throughout the US, Central and South America; works published by Willis Music Co. **Home Addr:** Park W Finance Sta, PO Box 20037, New York, NY 10025. **Business**

Addr: Faculty, Mannes College The New School for Music, 150 W 85th St, New York, NY 10024.*

EDWARDS, LEWIS
Administrator, vice president (organization). **Personal:** Born May 16, 1953, Philadelphia, PA; son of Robert Norman and Margaret Norman; married Joan Southerland, May 1979; children: Amber G, Ariel D. **Educ:** Penn State Univ, State Col, PA, BS, acct, 1974. **Career:** Fidelity Bank, Philadelphia, PA, sr auditor, 1974-78; Chrysler First, Inc, Allentown, PA, vpres acquisitions, 1978-94; Nations Credit Corp, vpres & dir, govt affairs, 1994. **Orgs:** Bd mem, Big Brothers/Big Sisters, 1986-. **Home Addr:** 308 E Mosser St, Allentown, PA 18109. *

EDWARDS, LONNIE
Physician. **Personal:** Born in Asheville, NC; son of Lonnie Sr and Corrie Thomas; married Carrie Glover Edwards, Dec 1950; children: Lonnette, Lonnie III. **Educ:** Morehouse Col, attended 1945; Howard Univ Sch Med, MD, 1948; Roosevelt Univ, MPA, 1974; Nova Univ, MPA, 1977-. **Career:** Pvt Pract, gen surg, 1955-70, family pract, 1960; Fantus Health Ctr, assoc med dir, 1970-71, dir 1970-71; Cook County Hosp, dir div ambulatory serv, 1971-73, assoc med dir 1974-83; Fantus Health Ctr, dir employee health serv hosp coordr home health care prog, 1974-83; Roosevelt Univ, pub admin prog; Abraham Lincoln Sch Med, clinical asst prof family pract; Chicago Med Sch, clinical asst prof dept family, 1974-83; City Chicago, comnr health, 1984-89; Cook County Hosp, dep med dir, 1989 (retired); Bd Dir Eng speaking Grand Lodge Am, vpres, currently. **Orgs:** Am Hosp Asn; Health Serv Develop Grants Study Sect, Dept of Health Educ & Welfare; Nat Asn Neighborhood Health Ctrs; Prairie State Med Soc; Am Med Asn; Ill State Med Soc; Chicago Med Soc; Indust Med Asn; Cent States Soc Indust Med & Surg; AAAS; Asn Admin Ambulatory Serv; Am Acad Family Physicians; Nat Med Asn; Cook Co Physicians Asn; Am Pub Health Asn; Am Hosp Asn; Nat Asn Health Serv Exec. **Honors/Awds:** Distinguished Service, Hisp Health Alliance, 1985; Community Service Award, Nat Asn Health Serv Exec, 1986; Community Service Award, Truman Col, 1976; Pres Award, Ill Pub Health Asn, 1988; Human Service Award, Pilsen Neighbors Community Coun, 1988. **Special Achievements:** Numerous papers presented to various professional orgns and publications including, Ambulatory Care in a Large Urban Hospital Governors State Univ Seminar March 1978; Oral Cavity Evaluation-A Part of Prenatal Care IL Medical Journal Lonnie C Edwards MD Pedro A Poma MD et al Feb 1979 Vol 155 No 2; Selection of an Organizational Model for Maximizing the Effectiveness of Coordination of the Components of Outpatient Services 1977. **Military Serv:** AUS, Med Corp capt gen surgeon, 1953-55. *

EDWARDS, LUTHER HOWARD
Government official. **Personal:** Born Jan 6, 1954, Butler, AL; son of Lee J Edwards Sr and Alma Jackson; married Geraldine Palmer; children: Ashley Letitia. **Educ:** Livingston Univ, BS, 1972, ME, 1976. **Career:** James River Corp, Comp Info Serv; Town Lisman, coun man, vice-mayor. **Orgs:** Pres, Afro-Am Soc; vpres, Owen Love Bus Assn; Stud Govt Assn; Collegiate Civilian; Men's Housing Coun; Intramural Sports Asn; Yearbook Staff; Host& Hostess Comn; Phi Mu Alpha Sinfonia Frat; sec Lisman Vol Fire Dept1980-; secy, Pleasant Hill Lodge 950 1980-; secy, Edwards Pride Royal Arch Masons 1982-. **Honors/Awds:** Outstanding Man of the Yr. **Military Serv:** USY, reserves, master sgt, 19 yrs; Army Commendation Medal; Desert Storm veteran. *

EDWARDS, DR. MARVIN E
School administrator. **Personal:** Born Oct 2, 1943, Memphis, TN; son of Rev Simeon and Edna Henderson; married Carolyn Johnson, Jul 30, 1966; children: Belinda, Melissa, Craig, Eric & Derick. **Educ:** Eastern Ill Univ, Charleston, IL, BS, 1967; Chicago State Univ, Chicago, IL, MS, 1969; Northern Ill Univ, DeKalb, IL, EdD, educ leadership, 1973. **Career:** Proviso High Sch, Maywood, IL, teacher, 1967-72; Lockport High Sch, Lockport, IL, prin, 1972-75; Lockport Fairmont Elem Schs, Lockport, IL, supt, 1975-76; Joliet Township High Schs, Joliet, IL, asst supt, 1976-78; Richmond Pub Schs, Richmond, VA, asst supt, 1978-80; Joliet Township High Schs, Joliet, IL, supt, 1980-85; Topeka Pub Schs, Topeka, KS, supt, 1985-88; Dallas Independent Sch Dist, Dallas, TX, gen supt, 1988-93; Elgin Area Sch Dist U-46, IL, supt, 1993-2002; Aurora Univ, founding dir, 2002, assoc prof educ, currently. **Honors/Awds:** Distinguished Alumnus Award, Northern Ill Univ, 1987; Distinguished Alumnus Award, Eastern Ill Univ, 1989; Outstanding Tex Award, Tex Legis Black Caucus, 1991; The Executive Educator 100 List, Exec Educ Mag, 1986, 1992; Superintendent of the Year, Ill Asn Sch Adminr, 1998; Elgin Image Award, Elgin, IL, 1998; Ambassador of the Year Award, Ill Pub Rels Asn, 1998; Ill Senate & House Resolutions citing successes, 1998; Bob Grossman Leadership in School Committee Award, 2000; Superintendents Commission of NABSE Award, 2000. **Business Addr:** Associate Professor of Education, Aurora University, 1877 W Downer Rm 117 Inst Bldg Rm 219, Aurora, IL 60506.

EDWARDS, MATTIE SMITH
Educator. **Personal:** Born Apr 16, 1931, Roxboro, NC; married E Zeno MD; children: Zenia Colette MD & Tanise Indra MD. **Educ:** Elizabeth City State Univ NC, BS, 1949; NC Ctr Univ, MA, 1953; Duke Univ, EdD, 1970. **Career:** Newbold Sch Fayetteville St Univ, supr, teacher, 1953-58; Cleveland CoSch NC, gen supervisor, 1965-69, reading coord, 1965-69; Springfield ColMA, prof educ, 1969-85; faculty emer, currently. **Orgs:** Bd trustees, Bay Path Col Mass, 1974-89; adv commn, Educ Personnel StMass, 1978-81; Nat Advan Asn Colored People; vpres, Auxiliary Greensboro Med Soc, 1990-92; Links Inc. **Honors/Awds:** Award Appreciation, Elizabeth City St Univ, 1980. **Business Addr:** Faculty Emeritus, Springfield College, 263 Alden St, Springfield, MA 01109-3797, **Business Phone:** (413)748-3000.*

EDWARDS, MICHELLE
Basketball player, basketball coach. **Personal:** Born Mar 6, 1966, Boston, MA. **Educ:** Iowa, attended 1989. **Career:** Basketball player (retired), basketball coach: Cleveland Rockers, guard, 1997-00; Seattle Storm, guard, 2000-01; The State Univ NJ, coor dr opers,2003-04, Scarlet Knights, asst coach, 2004-05, Assoc Dir Opers, 2005-. **Honors/Awds:** University of Iowa, Athlete of the Year, 1988; Champion Product Player ofthe Year, 1988; WBCA, Player of the Year, 1988; Big 10 Conference Playerof the Year, 1988; mem, Iowa Hall of Fame; Three-time Big Ten Player of the Week, 1998. **Special Achievements:** First female athlete at the University of Iowa to have her number retired. **Business Addr:** Assistant Coach, The State University NJ, Scarlet Knights, Louis Brown Athletic Ctr, 83 Rockafeller Rd, Piscataway, NJ 08854, **Business Phone:** (732)445-4251.*

EDWARDS, DR. MILES STANLEY
Educator, school administrator. **Personal:** Born Mar 21, 1951, Fort Wayne, IN; son of William Howard Sr and Wanda L Woods. **Educ:** Ball State Univ, BS, 1973, admin cert, 1983; Ind Univ, MSEd, 1978; Univ Akron, PhD, 1994. **Career:** Educator, Administrator (retired): DeKalb Ga County Sch Dist, math teacher, 1975-76; Ohio State Univ, GE fel, 1980; Oper Breadbasket Learning Acad, teacher, 1985-86; Univ Akron, instr multicultural educ, 1992-93; Ft Wayne Community Schs, teacher spec educ, 1973-75, competency resource teacher, 1976-87, chap I resource teacher, 1988-90, coordr multicultural resource ctr, 1990-92, chap I specialist, 1993-94; Wash Elem Sch, asst prin, 1994-99. **Orgs:** Exec Bd, Old Fort YMCA, 1973-75; life mem, Nat Alliance Black Sch Educators; Ind Black Expo-Ft Wayne Chap, 1982-; bd mem, Ministerial Alliance Scholarship Found, 1983-2002; Asn Black Communicators, 1982-85; bd member-at-large, Ft Wayne Alliance Black Sch Educators, 1983-92; Phi Delta Kappa, 1985-; Bd Minority Affairs, Ind State Teachers Asn, 1985-86; Nat Educ Asn, 1985-94; dist rep, Int Reading Asn, 1986; MLK Living Memorial Inc, 1986-90; bd dirs, Martin Luther King Montessori Schs, 1986-98; Urban League; life mem, NAACP; pres, Ind Black Expo-Ft Wayne Chap, 1988-90; Pi Lambda Theta Nat Honor & Prof Asn Educ, 1988-; Asn Supv & Curriculum Develop, 1989-2000; Nat Coun Teachers Eng, 1990-96; bd dirs, Ft Wayne Cinema Ctr, 1991-97; vice pres, Ft Wayne Cinema Ctr, 1994-95; Allen County-Fort Wayne Hist Soc, 1994-2000; pres, Martin Luther King Montessori Schs, 1994-98; Alpha Phi Alpha, 1995-2002; founding mem, African & African Am Hist Soc & Mus, Ft Wayne, 1998; bd dir, Heartland Chamber Chorale, 2001; treas, African & African Am Hist Soc & Mus, 2002; vpres, Pi Lambda Theta, 2004-06; pres, Heartland Chamber Chorale. **Honors/Awds:** Outstanding Young Men of America, US Jaycees, 1984. **Special Achievements:** Leadership Fort Wayne, First Vice President, 1996. **Home Addr:** 4921 Indiana Ave, Fort Wayne, IN 46807.

EDWARDS, MONICA
Executive, business owner. **Career:** Morehead Manor Bed & Breakfast, co-owner & treas, currently. **Orgs:** NC Bed & Breakfasts & Inns; African Am Asn Inkeepers Int. **Business Phone:** (919)687-4366.

EDWARDS, MONIQUE MARIE
Lawyer, consultant. **Personal:** Born Aug 13, 1961, New Orleans, LA; daughter of Lloyd C Edwards and Mary Ann B Edwards. **Educ:** St Mary's Dominican Col, BS, 1982; Southern Univ Law Ctr, JD, 1986. **Career:** Hon Bernette J Johnson, law clerk, 1986-87; Travelers Co, supvr, 1987-94; Maher, Gibson & Guiley PA, 1994-99; Edwards, Valdez & Ellis LLC, managing partner, currently. **Orgs:** Moot Ct Bd, Southern Univ Law Ctr, 1985; La State Bar Asn, 1986-; Nat Bar Asn, 1990-; secy, 1990-91, Paul C Perkins Bar Asn, vpres, 1991-92; exec bd, Orange Co Br, Nat Asn Advan Colored People, 1991-, Acad FL Trial Lawyers; banquet chairwoman, Southern Christian Leadership Conf Greater Orlando, 1991-; Fla Bar Asn, 1992; pres, Fla Chap Nat Bar Asn, 1995-96; La House Rep, Natural Resources Comt, atty; pvt pract atty, currently. **Honors/Awds:** Merchandising Student of the Year, St Mary's Dominican Col, 1981; Orlando Bus Journal, 40 under 40 Award, 1998.

EDWARDS, DR. NICOLE
Educator. **Personal:** Born Jan 1, 1974. **Educ:** Tougaloo Col, PhD. **Career:** Tougaloo Col, asst prof; Lane Col, Inst Res, dir, New Student Orientation, coordr, dir inst effectiveness, assoc vpres learning support, currently. **Orgs:** Brownie troop leader, Jim Hill High Sch Parent Teacher Asn, 2001-02; adv bd mem, Leadership Jackson Class, 2002; vol, Habitat Humanity. **Business Addr:** Associate Vice President, Lane College, 545 Lane Ave, Jackson, TN 38301-4598, **Business Phone:** (731)426-7599.

EDWARDS, OSCAR LEE
Consultant, president (organization). **Personal:** Born Dec 8, 1953, Long Beach, CA; son of Lewis Allen and Susie Belle; married Anita Grace Johnson; children: Ivan Lewis, Oscar Jr, Christine. **Educ:** Univ Calif Los Angeles, BA, 1978, MBA, 1981. **Career:** Crenshaw YMCA, prog dir, 1977-79; Czand Assocs, vpres admin, 1981-84; Pacific Serv Inc, consult, 1984-85; Central News WAVE Publs, dir mktg, 1985-87; Edwards Assoc, pres, 1987; TMG/SER, Inc, pres, 1987-90; Triaxial Mgt Serv, bd dirs, 1989-; Edwards Assocs/Media Mktg Network, pres, 1990-92; Visionary Mkt Inc, bd dirs, pres, currently; Econ opportunity Ctr, adv bd, currently. **Orgs:** Bank credit analyst, Bank Am, 1980; res asst, Mayor Bradley's Africa Task Force, 1981-82; chmn bd mgrs, Crenshaw YMCA, 1983-84; pres, LA Chap Nat Black MBA Asn,1985-86; bd dirs, UCLA Black Alumni Asn, 1986-90; adv bd, Drew Health Educ Proj, 1986-90; prog comt, UCLA Mgt Alumni Asn, 1987-; cert NFL Contract Adv, 1987-90; bd advs, So CA chap, UNF, 1989-91; prog comt, Am Mkg Asn, 1993-; Inst Mgt Consults, 1984-; master trainer, United Way, Kellogg Training Ctr, 1990-; pres, Site Coun, Intensive Learning Ctr, 1999; PR comt chair, Conf Minority Transp Officials, 1999. **Honors/Awds:** UCLA, Football All-Am, 1977; MBA of the Year, NBMBAA, Los Angeles, 1985; MBA of the Year, Nat Black MBA Asn, 1986; Very Spec Prof, Cong Augustus Hawkins, 1986; Hon Race Dir Comm, City of LA Marathon, 1986, 1987, 1988; producer of Outreach Videos, 1986, 1988-89; Community Serv Award, City of Long Beach, 1994; Community Serv Award, MLK Jr Mem Fund, 1997. **Business Addr:** President, Visionary Marketing Inc, 3811 Long Beach Blvd Suite A, Long Beach, CA 90807.*

EDWARDS, PRENTIS
Judge. **Educ:** Wayne State Univ, BA, 1960, JD, 1965. **Career:** Wayne Co, Mich, asst county prosecutor; Wayne County Juv Ct, chief referee; Ct Appeals & Wayne County Circuit Ct Register, vis judge; Criminal Div, 36th Dist Ct, presiding judge; Recorder's Ct, Circuit Ct, Criminal Div, judge; State Mich, circuit ct, 3rd circuit, judge, currently. **Orgs:** State Bar Mich; Wayne County Bar Asn; Asn Black Judges; Mich Judges Asn; chmn, Grant Schs Scholar Fund; bd, Sickle Cell Info Ctr; Isuthu Inst; Fel Chapel Church; Nat Asn Advan Colored People. **Business Addr:** Judge, State Mich Circuit Ct, 3rd Circuit, 711 Coleman A Young Munic Ctr Suite 1107, Detroit, MI 48226.*

EDWARDS, PRESTON JOSEPH
Publisher, chief executive officer. **Personal:** Born Jul 3, 1943, New Orleans, LA; married Rosa; children: Preston Jr & Scott. **Educ:** Dillard Univ, BA, 1965; Atlanta Univ, MBA, 1966. **Career:** Nat City Bank, asst cashier, 1966-69; Southern Univ, Baton Rouge, asst prof, 1969-71; Great Atlantic & Pac Tea Co, reg mgr, 1975-76; Interracial Coun Bus Opportunity, vpres, 1976-77; IMinority Inc, staff; Black Collegian Mag, publ, 1970-, chief exec officer, currently. **Orgs:** Bd mem, Jr Achievment; pres, J Inc; publ, J Nat Tech Asn; founder, Nat Asn Cols & Employers. **Honors/ Awds:** DHL, Livingstone Col. **Business Phone:** (504)523-0154.

EDWARDS, RAYMOND
Judge. **Career:** Judge (retired); State Calif, Superior Ct, San Diego County, judge.

EDWARDS, RENIA
Administrator. **Educ:** Shaw Univ, BS, bus mgt, 1995; Norther Ill Univ, MS. **Career:** Shaw Univ Lady Bears Softball Team, Raleigh, NC; Austin Peay State Univ, Clarksville, TN, acad advising intern; Va Tech, asst dir stud athelete acad support servs, 2004; Univ SC, div dir, student-athlete develop, dir internal operations, currently, athletics acad adv, swimming & diving, Track & Field, cross country, currently. **Orgs:** Career coordr & adv, Minority Focus Group Men; Blacksburg Alumnae Chap, Delta Sigma Theta Sorority; bd dir, N4A.

EDWARDS, ROBERT
Educator, school administrator. **Personal:** Born Jan 30, 1939, Slocomb, AL; children: Randel Keith & Robert Corey. **Educ:** Bethune-Cookman Col, BS, 1965; City Col NY, MS, 1973. **Career:** Youth Training Acad, dir, 1969; Progress Asn Econ Develop, dir, 1972; Opportunity Indus Ctr, br mgr, 1974; Dade Co Pub Schs, prin, 1987-90. **Orgs:** Exec Counr, Asn Study Afro-Amer Life & Hist, 1971; bd dir, Lexia Sch Young Adults, 1974; bd dir, OURS Inc, 1974; Urban League, Nat Asn Adv Colored People, Nat Alliance Black Sch Educrs, Kappa Alpha Psi, Bethune-Cookman Col Alumni Asn, Asn Study Afro-Amer Life & Hist. **Honors/Awds:** Distinguished Alumni Award, Bethune-Cookman Col; OIC NY Supreme Dedication Award, Alpha Phi Alpha, Alpha Kappa Alpha, City of Miami; OIC NY Distinguished Service Award; Men of Achievement, Kappa Alpha Psi. **Military Serv:** AUS, 1961-63.

EDWARDS, ROBERT LEE
Football player. **Personal:** Born Oct 2, 1974, Tennille, GA. **Educ:** Univ Ga. **Career:** New Eng Patriots, running back, 1998; miami dolphins, 2002; montreal Alouettes, runner back, 2005-07. Tor-

onto Argonauts, 2007-08; free agent, currently. **Honors/Awds:** Jim Thorpe Courage Award, 2003; Pro Football Writers Asn Halas Award; East Division All-Star, 2005, 2006. *

EDWARDS, DR. ROBERT VALENTINO
Educator. **Personal:** Born Dec 15, 1940, Baltimore, MD; son of Robert Franklin and Laura Mae Jackson; married Anne Lindsay. **Educ:** Johns Hopkins Univ, AB, math, 1962, MS, chem eng, 1964, PhD (chem eng), 1968. **Career:** Case Western Res Univ, from asst prof to assoc prof, 1970-79, prof, 1979-, chmn chem eng dept, 1984-90, assoc dean, 1990-94. **Orgs:** Am Chem Soc; Optical Soc Am; fel Am Inst Chem Eng; Sigma Xi. **Honors/Awds:** Over 100 scientific papers and talks 1968-85; Received more than $1,000,000 in research grants 1968-85. **Special Achievements:** Published numerous articles and books. **Business Addr:** Professor, Case Western Reserve University, Chem Eng Department, 10900 Euclid Ave AW Smith Bldg 124B, Cleveland, OH 44106-7217, **Business Phone:** (216)368-4151.

EDWARDS, RONALD WAYNE
Manager, president (organization), chief executive officer. **Personal:** Born Mar 25, 1958, Birmingham, AL; son of Carl and Dorothy Smith; married Barbara Wallace, Jun 19, 1982. **Educ:** Univ Ala, Sch Com & Bus Admin, BS, mkt mgt, 1990. **Career:** Ala Gas Corp, Birmingham, AL, mgr community affairs, 1991; SEZ Am Inc, Advert Firm, ceo; pres & chief exec officer, currently; O2Ideas, partner & exec vpres. **Orgs:** Vulcan Kiwanis Club; Nat Mgt Asn; Am Heart Asn; City Stages; pres, Energen Mgt Asn; pres, Am Asn Blacks Energy; bd mem, United Way C Aid Soc; bd dir scouting comt, All Am Bowl; bd dir, Birmingham Tip-Off Club; comnr, Summer Basketball League; Ala Kidney Found; Ala Sports Found; Monday Morning Quarterback Club; bd vis, Univ Ala; Birmingham Tip-Off Club; trustee, Birmingham Chamber Com; United Way C Aid Soc; Shoal Creek Golf Club. **Special Achievements:** Top Forty Under Forty Acheivement, Birmingham Bus J. **Business Phone:** (602)437-5050.*

EDWARDS, DR. RONDLE E.
Educator, school superintendent. **Personal:** Born Jul 19, 1934, Richmond, VA; son of Irene Taylor Edwards and Alfred M Edwards; married Gloria Twitty; children: Cassandra L, Lanee D Washington & Ronda D. **Educ:** Va Union Univ, AB; Va State Univ, MA; Ohio Univ, PhD; Ohio State Univ, Columbia Univ, Post-doctoral Study. **Career:** Richmond Pub Sch, asst supt gen admin & pupil personnel, 1972-75, asst supt support serv, 1975-76; E Cleveland City Sch, supt, 1976-84; Portsmouth Pub Sch, supt, 1984-87; Va Dept Educ, asst st supt, 1987-92; HarperCollins, vpres, Sch Rel Develop, 1992-; Portsmouth Pub Sch, supt; JSargeant Reynolds Community Col, bd mem, 2008-; Va Commonwealth Univ, adj fac mem; Univ Richmond, adj fac mem; Old Dominion Univ, adj fac mem. **Orgs:** Richmond Rotary Club; trustee, Cleveland Scholar Fund; United Negro Col Fund; Phi Delta Kappa Prof Frat; Am Asn Sch Personnel Adminr; Am Asn Sch Adminr, Ohio Sch Bd Asn; expert witness before US House Rep Comn Educ & Labor. **Honors/Awds:** Award for Excellence in Public Education, Delta Sigma Theta Sor; Outstanding Achievement Award, Kappa Alpha Psi Frat, Phi Delta Kappa; Man of the Year, Cleveland Club Nat Asn Negro Bus & Prof Women's Clubs; Exec Educator's Recognition One of North America's Top 100 Educators; Ohio Univ Alumni Medal of Merit for Notable Accomplishments in Education Administration, 1986; authored 4 books; numerous presentations. **Home Addr:** 3320 Carney Farm Lane, Portsmouth, VA 23703. **Business Phone:** (804)371-3000.

EDWARDS, RUTH MCCALLA
Lawyer, educator. **Personal:** Born Apr 23, 1949, Cleveland, OH; married Michael M; children: Ashaunda, Alanna & Kamala. **Educ:** Hiram Col, BA, 1971; Univ Cincinnati Col Law, JD, 1974. **Career:** Legal Aid Soc Cincinnati, atty & off mgr, 1974-77; Pvt Law Practice, atty, 1977-79; Hamilton County Pub Defender Comn, atty, 1979; Univ Cincinnati, atty, prog coord, paralegal prog, 1979-, assoc prof, currently. **Orgs:** Admitted Ohio State Bar, 1974; admitted Fed Bar So Dist of Ohio, 1974; bd trustees, Cincinnati Tech Col, 1977-; Am, Cincinnati Bar Asns; pres, Black Lawyers Asn Cincinnati; bd mem, Legal Aid Soc Cincinnati; bd mem, officer Winton Hills Med & Halth Ctr; bd mem & officer, Comprehensive Comn ChildCare; bd mem, Cincinnati Tech Col; Alpha Kappa Alpha Sor; arbitrator Better Bus Bur Arbitration Prog; Asn Comn Col Trustees; secy, Cent Reg Minority Affairs Assembly Asn Comn Col Trustees; Am Asn Paralegal Educ Inc; chairperson bd trustees, Cincinnati Tech Col, 1983-84; bd mem,officer Winton Hills Med & Health Ctr; arbitrator, Am Arbitration Asn; chair, Cent Region Minority Affairs Comn Asn Conity Col Trustees. **Honors/Awds:** Hon Deg Tech Letters, Cincinnati Tech Col, 1985; Black Achievers Award,YMCA, 1985. **Business Addr:** Associate Professor, University Cincinnati, 2600 Clifton Ave, Cincinnati, OH 45221.*

EDWARDS, SHIRLEY
Administrator. **Career:** Compton Community Col, exec vpres acad affairs, 2003, actg dir, currently. **Business Addr:** Director, Compton Community College, Child development Center, 1111 E Artesia Blvd, Compton, CA 90221.

EDWARDS, SHIRLEY JEAN
Government official. **Personal:** Born Oct 23, 1949, Doddsville, MS; married Thomas E; children: Darron, Thomas Jr & Cheryl. **Educ:** Miss Valley State Univ, BS, 1983. **Career:** Fannie Humer Day Care, secy book keeper, 1969-79; Sunflower/Humphrey Co Progress, career counr, 1979-83; Sunflower County Schs, sch attendance officer, 1983-; City Ruleville, alderwoman, mayor, 1993-. **Orgs:** Nat Conf Black Mayors. **Honors/Awds:** Community Service Award, Nat Association Advance Colored People, Sunflower County,1983. **Home Addr:** 318 Skeeter Robertson Rd, Ruleville, MS 38771-0653. **Business Addr:** Mayor, Sunflower County, 200 E Floyce, PO Box 428, Ruleville, MS 38771-0428.*

EDWARDS, DR. SOLOMON
Educator. **Personal:** Born Apr 2, 1932, Indianapolis, IN; married Claudia; children: Gregory D & Risa M. **Educ:** Ind Univ, BS, 1954, MS, 1969, EdD, 1984. **Career:** Arts Festival, coord, 1956; dir, NY City Dramatic Readers, 1957-58; Ind Pub Schs, teacher; Purdue Univ, assoc fac, 1971-79. **Orgs:** Omega Psi Phi; Nat Asn Advan Colored People; Phi Delta Kappa Ind Univ. **Honors/Awds:** Writers Conf Poetry Award, 1953. **Special Achievements:** Author of "What's Your Reading Attitude?" 1979; "This Day Father" 1979. Poems publ, 1959-77; Discussion moderator, Int Reading Asn Nat Conv,1979; educ game "Freedom & Martin Luther King", 1980. *

EDWARDS, DR. SYLVIA
Lawyer. **Personal:** Born May 9, 1947, Lackawanna, NY. **Educ:** State Univ Col Buffalo, BS, 1969; Howard Univ Sch Law WA, JD, 1973. **Career:** Employ Sect Dept Justice, trial atty, 1973-76; Off Spec Litigation Dept Justice WA DC, sr trial atty; Coun DC, legis coun, 1977-79; DC Law Revision Comn, sr atty, 1979-. **Orgs:** Adv Comn Codification Wash DC, 1977-79; legis consult Comt Pub Serv & Consumer Affairs Coun DC, 1979; NY Bar, 1974; PA Bar, 1974; Nat Asn Black Women Atty, 1978. **Honors/Awds:** Special Achievement Award, Howard Univ Sch Law, 1972; Intl Moot Court Award, Howard Univ Sch Law, 1973; Special Achievement Award, Dept Justice Wash DC, 1975; Resolution Special Achievement, Coun DC, 1979. *

EDWARDS, TAMRA
City council member, executive. **Personal:** Born May 4, 1959. **Educ:** Mott Community Col. **Career:** Econ Empowerment Inc, chief operating officer, currently; Mott Community Col, Presidential ambassador; mortgage financing; pub advocator; City Durham, councilwoman, 2003. **Orgs:** Vpres, YMCA; Salem Housing orgn.

EDWARDS, TERESA
Basketball player, athletic coach. **Personal:** Born Jul 19, 1964. **Educ:** Univ Ga, Leisure Studies, 1989. **Career:** Atlanta Glory, player & coach; Philadelphia Rage; Lynx, 2003-04, asst coach, 2006; USA Basketball Bd Dir, 2009-. **Honors/Awds:** Youngest gold medalist in women's basketball, 1984; Female Athlete of the Year, USA Basketball, 1996; Olympic gold medals; oldest gold medalist in women's basketball, 2000; women's basketball hall of fame, 2010. **Special Achievements:** First basketball player played in five Olympics. **Business Phone:** (612)673-1600.*

EDWARDS, THEODORE ALLEN
Executive, vice president (organization). **Personal:** Born Jan 16, 1954, Chicago, IL; son of Theodore and Mary; married Katheryn Edwards, May 19, 1984; children: Christopher, Cara, Rachael & Casey. **Educ:** Northwestern Univ, BS, 1975; Kellogg Grad Sch Mgt, MM, 1988. **Career:** Ameritech Info Indust Serv, staff, 1978-90, opers div mgr, 1990-91, mkt pub serv, gen mgr, 1992, Opers Carrier Serv, vpres, 1993-96, Local Exchange Carriers, vpres sales, 1996-. **Orgs:** Bd trustees, Hull House Asn, 1990-97; bd dirs, COT Investment Fund, 1996-97; bd dirs, Pioneer Clubs Am, 1997. **Honors/Awds:** Minority Achievement Award, Chicago YMCA, 1988. **Business Addr:** Vice President of Sales, Ameritech Information Industry Services, 350 N Orleans Fl 3, Chicago, IL 60654, **Business Phone:** (312)335-6595.

EDWARDS, THEODORE THOMAS
Government official. **Personal:** Born Sep 8, 1917, Bridgeport, CT; son of Theodore and Maude; married Vivian Blackmon, 1956 (died 1987). **Educ:** Quinnipac Col, New Haven, CT, AA, 1941; NY Univ, BS, 1946; Columbia Univ, MSW, 1947; US Pub Health Hosp, Lexington, attended 1956; Univ Chicago, grad work, 1959. **Career:** Government Official (retired); Goldwater Hosp, NY, med social worker, 1947-48; NJ Parole Bd, parole officer, 1949-55; US Probation-US Parole Comn, probation officer, 1955-77. **Orgs:** Youth worker, NY Youth Bd, 1947; Nat Coun Crime & Del, 1955-80; life mem, Fed Probation Off Asn, 1956-80; co-founder, Narcotic Treatment Ctr, 1956; Middle Atlantic St Conf Correction, 1956-80; Rotary Int, Paterson, NJ, 1975-77; Am Correction Asn, 1975-80. **Honors/Awds:** Certificate of Appreciation, Newark Boys Club, 1969; Crox De Geurre; 4 Battle Stars. **Special Achievements:** First Black Federal Probation Officer, Newark NJ, 1955, co-founder of first Private Narcotic Treatment Center, Newark, NJ, 1957, subject of "The Probation Officer," Newark Sunday News, 1957, first Black Federal Probation Director, Paterson, NJ, 1975-77. **Military Serv:** AUS, sgt, 1942-45.

EDWARDS, THEODORE UNALDO
Government official. **Personal:** Born Sep 18, 1934, New York, NY; son of Joseph Unaldo (deceased) and Mary A; married Ione L D; children: Donna M O. **Educ:** St Peter's Col, BS, 1955; Rutgers Univ, MSW, 1962; BARO Clin, Cert, 1967. **Career:** US Court/ Justice Dept, probation officer, 1962-69; Harlem Child Guid Clin, clin dir, 1969-78; Community Serv Soc New York, exec dir, 1973-76; City New Rochelle Dept Human Serv, dep comnr, 1977-; Col New Rochelle, NY, adj prof, 1979-. **Orgs:** Bd mem, Catholic Big Brothers New York, 1975-; comnr, Off Black Ministry Archdiocese New York, 1977-; bd mem, Salvation Army New Rochelle, 1985-; exec bd, NAACP, 1985-; Omega Omicron Iota Chap. **Honors/Awds:** Community Service Award, Col New Rochelle, NY, 1983-85; Spike Harris Service Award, New York Counselors, 1985. **Special Achievements:** Numerous publications including "Why Bartering", Voice Mag, 1981; "Budget Time", Voice Mag, 1981; "The City of New Rochelle Senior Population", 1986; Columnist for Tomorrow Newspaper, Westchester, NY. **Military Serv:** AUS, sgt, 2 yrs. **Business Addr:** Deputy Commissioner, City of New Rochelle, Department of Human Services, City Hall, New Rochelle, NY 10801, **Business Phone:** (914)654-2084.

EDWARDS, THOMAS OLIVER
School administrator, psychologist. **Personal:** Born Jan 4, 1943, Vanceboro, NC; son of Calvin and Blanche Ethel; married Loretta McFadden; children: Tomia, Kuturi, Loretta, Tiffany, Calvin. **Educ:** CCNY, BA, 1965; NY Univ, MA, 1968; CUNY, MPh, 1980, PhD, 1981. **Career:** Peace Corps Costa Rica, volunteer, 1965-67; Alexander Burger Jr High Sch, teacher, 1967-71; Medgar Evers Col instr & lect, 1971-81, asst prof, 1981-84, assoc prof, 1984-, assoc dean admin, 1986-88, acting chmn, Social Sci Division, 1988-89; Medgar Evers Col, affirmative action officer, assoc prof, Dept Social & Behavioral Sci, chairperson, currently. **Orgs:** Baseball coach Rochdale Village Little League, 1979-; consult, Urban Strategies Inc, 1980-; consult, Hale House Promotion Human Potential, 1983; bd dir, mem Medgar Evers Col Child Care Ctr, 1983-; adjunct prof, Col New Rochelle, 1984-85; bd dirs, New York Chapter, Asn Black Psychol, 1990-92; execu coun mem, United Partners Asn, 1990-92; New York Asn Black Psychol, past pres, 1983-; Nat Asn Black Psychol, Black Family Task Force, chair. **Honors/Awds:** Pamela Galiber Memorial Scholarship, CUNY Grad Div, 1977; Communication Skills in the Inner City, Effects Race & Dialect Decoding New England Ed Res Org Annual Best Papers Monograph, 1983; co-organizer, Int African-Am Cultural & Res Asn; organizer, Annual Conf Focusing Black Male, Medgar Evers Col CUNY. **Business Addr:** Chairperson, Medgar Evers College CUNY, Department of Social and Behavioral Sciences, 1150 Carroll St, Brooklyn, NY 11225, **Business Phone:** (718)270-4851.*

EDWARDS, TONYA
Basketball player, basketball coach. **Personal:** Born Mar 13, 1968, Flint, MI. **Educ:** Univ Tenn, educ, 1990. **Career:** Flint Northwestern High Sch, girl's basketball coach, 1991-94; played for Israel, 1995-96; Columbus Quest, guard, 1996-98; Minnesota Lynx, guard, 1999; Phoenix Mercury, guard, 2000-01; Charlotte Sting, guard, 2001-02; Phoenix Mercury games, radio commentator, 2004; Nat Women's Basketball League, asst coach, 2004; Detroit titans, asst coach. **Honors/Awds:** Michigan High School Coach of the Year, 1993; NCAA National Championships, 1986-87, 1988-89; NCAA Final Four, MVP, 1986-87; Jones Cup Team, gold medal, 1987; ABL, Championship, 1996-97, 1997-98; ABL, All-Star Team, 1996-97, 1997-98; inducted, Greater Flint Afro-American Hall of Fame, 2006. *

EDWARDS, VERBA L.
Executive. **Personal:** Born Jul 15, 1950, Boligee, AL; son of George and Bertha Barker; married Roberta Mackel Edwards, Aug 25, 1973; children: Keith, Christopher, Raquel. **Educ:** Alcorn State Univ, BS, Bus Admin, 1973; Cent Mich Univ, MA, Personnel Admin, 1977. **Career:** General Motors Corp Chevy Truck Assembly Plant, coordr equal employment opportunity, gen supvr mfg, supvr indust rels, supvr hourly personnel admin, 1973-81; Gen Motors Corp Chevrolet Cent Off, div salaried personnel admin, 1981-83; Gen Motors Corp Saginaw Div, asst dir personnel, 1984-87; Wing Tips & Pumps Inc, pres & ceo, 1987-. **Orgs:** Omega Psi Phi Frat, Nat Alliance Bus Col/Indust Rels Div, Nat Asn Equal Opportunity Higher Educ; Nat Black MBA Asn. **Honors/Awds:** Author of "Wing Tips and Pumps". **Business Addr:** President, Chief Executive Officer, Wing Tips and Pumps Inc, 2357 Belmont Ct, PO Box 99580, Troy, MI 48098, **Business Phone:** (248)641-0980.*

EDWARDS, WILBUR PATTERSON, JR.
Lawyer. **Personal:** Born Aug 28, 1949, Yokohama, Japan; son of Wilbur P Sr and Mary C; married Evelynne Swagerty, Jun 8, 1989; children: Arielle Belson & Marissa Avery. **Educ:** Harvard Col, BA, 1971; Boston Col Law Sch, JD, 1984. **Career:** Purity Supreme, real estate rep, 1971-73; Grand Union Co, real estate rep, 1973-74; Southland Corp, real estate mgr, 1974-79; Toys R Us, real estate mgr, 1979-81; Roche, Carens & DeGiacomo, atty, 1984-88; McKenzie & Edwards PC, atty, 1989-; Southeastern Housing Ct, assoc justice, 2002-. **Orgs:** Mass Bar Lawyers Asn, 1984-, secy, 1985; Property Sect Coun, chair, Mass Bar Asn, 1984-; Mass Conveyancers Asn, 1988-; pres, Boston Col Law Sch Bar Alumni Network, 1990-94. **Home Addr:** 23 Pine Rd, Sharon, MA 02067, **Home Phone:** (781)784-6784. **Business Addr:** As-

sociate Justice, Southeast Housing Court, 289 Rock St, Fall River, MA 02720-3246, **Business Phone:** (617)788-8485.*

EDWARDS-ASCHOFF, PATRICIA JOANN
Educator, executive director, teacher. **Personal:** Born Feb 23, 1940, Louisville, MS; married Peter Richard. **Educ:** Chadron State Col, BS, 1972; Univ Northern Iowa, MA, 1974. **Career:** Dr. William J Walker Chicago, dental asst, 1963-70; Black Hawk Co, juvenile probation officer, 1974-77; Univ Northern Iowa, Ethnic Minorities Cult & Educ Ctr, dir, 1977; Univ Northern Iowa, human rels instr, 1979-80, spec prog asst; Domestic Violence Proj Inc, exec dir; Oxford Sch Dist, spec educ teacher, currently. **Orgs:** Bd chmn, Minority Alcoholism Action Prog, 1976-78; Prof & Sci Coun, 1977; training consult, Jesse Cosby Neighborhood Ctr Parent Groups, 1978; exec bd mem, Family & C's Coun, 1978; bd mem & treas, Wesley Found, 1978; Antioch Baptist Church, Waterloo, IA; bd mem, Friends KHKE/KUNI Pub Radio, 1979; Alpha Chi ESA Int Sorority, Oxford, MS. **Honors/Awds:** Special Achievement Award, Educ Opportunity Prog, 1973-74; Outstanding Young Women in America, 1974; Professional Service Award, Juvenile Ct Serv, 1977; Certificate of Appreciation, Kiwanis Club Oxford, MS. **Business Addr:** Special Education Teacher, Oxford Elementary School, 109 Pontiac St, Oxford, MS 48371, **Business Phone:** (248)969-5075.

EDWARDS O, DONNA M (DONNA M EDWARDS)
Lawyer. **Personal:** Born Jun 26, 1957, New York, NY; daughter of Theodore U Edwards and Ione Edwards; married Don T O'Bannon Jr, Dec 11, 1982 (divorced); children: Danielle Salone & Dionne Teddie. **Educ:** Wellesley Col, BA, 1979; Univ Va Sch Law, JD, 1982. **Career:** Exxon Co USA, tax atty, 1982-85; Harris County DA, ast DA, 1985-87; Equal Employment Opportunity Comn, trial atty, 1987-88; sr trial atty, 1988-89; FDIC, trial atty, dept head, 1989-94; litigation senior atty, 1989-94; Equal Employment Opportunity Comn, admin judge, 1994-2003; EEO Technical Adv, US Dept Treas, Treas Complaint Ctr, Dallas, 2003-; pvt pract, currently. **Orgs:** Links Inc, Dallas Chap; Thurgood Marshall Recreation Ctr Adv Coun, vpres, 1994-96, pres, 1996-98; chair, Parish Coun, Holy Cross Cath Church. **Honors/Awds:** Freshman Honors, Wellesley Col, 1975-76; Wellesley Scholar, 1979. **Special Achievements:** Special Achievement Awards from FDIC, 1992-94, from EEOC, 1994-02. **Home Addr:** 2122 Elderoaks Lane, Dallas, TX 75232-3309, **Home Phone:** (214)339-0309. **Business Addr:** Lawyer, 2122 Elderoaks Lane, Dallas, TX 75232, **Business Phone:** (214)339-0309.

EFFORT, DR. EDMUND D
Dentist. **Personal:** Born Jun 20, 1949, Chicago, IL; son of Beverley and Exzene; married Elaine Leaphart; children: Edmundson David & April Elaine. **Educ:** Univ Ill, BS, 1972; Univ Mich, DDS, 1977; US Dent Inst, 1989; Air War Col, 1998. **Career:** Pvt pract, dentist. **Orgs:** Alpha Phi Alpha, 1969-89; Am Dental Assoc, 1977-89; Nat Asn Advan Colored People, 1981-89, chmn, Health Affairs, 1995; Urban League, 1981-89, Pa Dent Assoc, 1981-89; bd dir, Lemington Home Aged, 1984; Lions, 1985, Elks, 1986; Urban Youth Action, 1986-87, bd dir, United Cerebral Palsy, 1987, Connely Trade Sch, 1987, Eva P Mitchell Residense, 1987; coach little league baseball, Boys Club, 1989; bd dir, Boys & Girls Club, 1990-; Felix vs Casey, expert witness, 1992-93; chmn, Med Assistance Advi Comt, PDA; Reizenstein Middle Sch, PTO, pres, 1994. **Honors/Awds:** Black Achievers News in Print Magazine, 1984; Three articles written for Talk Magazine, 1985; PA Air Commendation Medal PA ANG, 1986; Community Service Award, Upward Bound Proj, 1987; Good Samaritan Award, Am Red Cross, 1988; Martin Luther King Award, Hand-In-Hand Inc, 1990. **Military Serv:** Pa Air Natl Guard, Lt Col, 23 yrs; Pa Air National Guard, 171st ARW Lt Col, 1981-; General Stewart Medal, 1985; Air Commendation Medal, 1986.

EFFORT, ELAINE
Journalist. **Career:** KQV Radios, host & reporter, currently. **Orgs:** co-founder, The Girl Scout troop. **Honors/Awds:** Won Numerous awards including: 2 Golden Quills; PA AP; Women In Communs; Pittsburgh Black Media Fedn awards. **Business Phone:** (412)562-5900.*

EGGLESTON, NEVERETT A
Association executive, executive. **Personal:** Born in Richmond, VA; married Jean Deloris; children: Neverett A III & Jayne. **Educ:** A&T Univ, BS 1955. **Career:** Mainstream Inc, pres; Golden Skillet, prin; Silas Lee & Assocs, prin; Eggleston's Motel, pres & chief exec officer, 1960-; Eggleston Auto Serv Ctr, pres & chief exec officer, 1979-; Eggleston Develop Corp, pres & chief exec officer, 1992-. **Orgs:** Bd mem, Nat Bus League, 1970-, secy, currently; chmn bd, Minority Supplier Develop, 1978-; E & R Janitorial Serv Inc, 1978-; bd mgt, Radiantherm Inc; bd dirs, Jefferson Sheraton Hotel; adv bd, Womensbank; Richmond Chamber Com; vpres, Capital Area Innkeepers Asn; bd dirs & pres, Metro Bus League; bd dirs, Richmond Urban League; bd dirs, Richmond Community Action Prog; bd dirs, Am Red Cross; chmn, People League Voters; bd dirs, Greater Richmond Transit Co; United Givers Fund. **Honors/Awds:** Spoke Award and Spark Plug Award, Jr Chamber Com; Businessman of the Year Award, Metro Bus League; Martin Luther King Community Learning Week Business Recognition, 1982. **Business Addr:** President, Chief Executive Officer, The Eggleston Corporation, 2712 Seminary Ave, Richmond, VA 23220, **Business Phone:** (804)321-7159.

EGIEBOR, SHARON E.
Journalist. **Personal:** Born Jun 11, 1959, Kansas City, KS; daughter of William David Patterson Sr and Lester Alois Wilborn; divorced; children: Marcus Iyobosa. **Educ:** Dallas County Community Col Dist, Mountain View Campus, AA, lib arts, 1979; Univ Tex Arlington, Arlington, BA, jour, 1983. **Career:** Tex mag, managing ed; Dallas Times Herald, Dallas, TX, reporter, 1983-87, copy ed, 1987, asst reg ed, 1987-88, asst city ed, 1988-90, ed writer, 1990, exec ed; Egiebor Expressions, owner, 1993-; The Dallas Examiner, exec ed, 2002-05. **Orgs:** Dallas-Fort Worth Asn Black Communicators, 1985-; Nat Asn Black Journalists, 1986-. **Honors/Awds:** Times Mirror Scholar, Times Mirror Corp, 1982; Jack Butler Award, UTA-Sch Jour, 1983; Sch Bell Award, Tex State Teachers Asn, 1985; Inst Jour Educ Fel, Minority Journalists, 1987; Community Serv Award, Black State Employees Asn, 1990; Kaiser Family FoundHIV-Mini Media Health Fel, 2004. **Business Phone:** (972)291-8452.*

EGINS, PAUL CARTER
Manager. **Personal:** Born Sep 22, 1963, Columbus, GA; son of Paul C Egins, Jr and Jacquelyn Joy. **Educ:** Univ Ga, BS, biol, 1986; Fla A&M Univ, attended 1987. **Career:** Atlanta Braves, Class A, athletic trainer, 1988-89, minor league admin, 1990, asst dir, scouting/player dev, 1991; Colo Rockies, asst dir scouting, 1992, player dev, 1993-94, asst dir player personnel, 1995-97, dir player develop, 1997-2000, dir minor league opers, dir maj league opers, currently. **Orgs:** Kappa Alpha Psi Fraternity, 1989-; RBI Prog, 1995-; bd dirs, Bichette Baseball World, 1996-. **Honors/Awds:** Denver's Fifty Finest, Cystic Fibrosis Found, 1997. **Business Addr:** Director Major League Operations, Colo Rockies Baseball Club Ltd, Coors Field 2001 Blake St, Denver, CO 80205-2000, **Business Phone:** (303)292-0200.

EICHELBERGER, BRENDA
Executive director. **Personal:** Born Oct 21, 1939, Washington, DC. **Educ:** Govs St Univ, extens grad work in women's std 1976-; Chicago St Univ, MS, 1973; Eng & Bus Educ, BS; DC Teachers Col, 1963. **Career:** Wash DC Pub Sch Syst, teacher, 1964-65; Muscatine Community Sch Dist, teacher, 1966-67; Chicago Pub Sch Syst, teacher, librn, counr, 1967-77; Nat Allian Black Feminists, div exec dir, 1976; Nat Col Educ, m equiv sch admin & supvr. **Orgs:** bd mem, Pro & Con Screening 1976; bd mem, Chicagoland Women's Fed Credit Union, 1976-; found, Black Womens's Ctr 1976-; bd mem, treas, Chicago Consort Women Educ Prog, 1976; Chicago Chap Nat Black Feminist Org, 1974-76; bd mem, Citz Comt, 1975-76; adv bd mem, Blue Gargoyle Group 1975; Dist Ten Teacher Coun, 1974-75. **Honors/Awds:** Writer of artic 1977; Bicent Excellent Award, for Black Womanhood, Elite Soc Am 1976; Outstndng Elem Sch & Teacher Award, Fuller & Dees 1975; Internat Year of the Woman Award, Love Memorial Mission Bapt Church, 1975; Outstndng Young Woman, Am Award, Fuller & Dees, 1975. **Business Addr:** 202 S State St, Ste 1024, Chicago, IL 60604.*

EIKERENKOETTER, REV. DR. FREDERICK J. **See Obituaries section.**

EILAND, MIKE
Television director. **Career:** Clear Channel Inc, recruiting mgr, pub serv dir & air personality, currently. **Business Addr:** Recruiting Manager, Public Service Director, Air Personality, Clear Channel Inc, 1301 Dublin Rd, Columbus, OH 43215-7009, **Business Phone:** (614)487-2512.

EISLEY, HOWARD JONATHAN
Basketball player. **Personal:** Born Dec 4, 1972, Detroit, MI; children: Kennedy & Howard. **Educ:** Boston Col, BS, commun. **Career:** Minn Timberwolves, guard, 1994-95; San Antonio Spurs, 1995; Utah Jazz, 1995-2000, 2004-05; NY Knicks, 2001-04; Phoenix Suns, 2003-04; Los Angeles Clippers, guard, 2005-06; Denver Nuggets, guard, 2006; Chicago Bulls, 2006. **Honors/Awds:** Jazz nominee, 1997-98; NBA Sportsmanship Award, 1998-99.

EKE, KENOYE KELVIN
Educator, vice president (organization). **Personal:** Born Sep 1, 1956, Otari, Abua, Rivers State, Nigeria; son of Joseph and Nancy Owen; married Joy Grimes Eke, Jun 24, 1989; children: Kenoye Kelvin Joseph, Kebbin Henry Joseph. **Educ:** Ala A&M Univ, BA, polit sci, 1980; Atlanta Univ, MA, polit sci, 1982, PhD, polit sci, 1985; Harvard Univ, MA, 1988, 1990; Univ Wis-Madison, 1989. **Career:** Bethune-Cookman Col, Daytona Beach, FL, asst prof, 1985-89; Savannah State Col, assoc prof & coordr polit sci, 1989-93, dir int progs, 1991-93, Sch Humanities & Soc Sci, dean & prof, 1993-98; Univ Fla, Ctr African Studies, res fel, 1991; Cheyney Univ, Acad & Stud Affairs, provost & vpres, 2002-; Calif State Univ, Monterey Bay, interim asst vpres acad progs; Ky State Univ, assoc vpres acad affairs & chief acad admin, Col Prof Studies, assoc vpres acad affairs & actg dean, vpres acad affairs & summer session chief operating officer. **Orgs:** Exec bd, African Asn Polit Sci, N Am Chap, 1987-; pres, Pan-African Awareness Asn, Volusia County, FL, 1988-89; benefits adv bd, Chatham County, Dept Family & C Serv, 1989-; Pew fac fel int affairs, Harvard Univ, 1992-93; fel Am Coun Educ, 1994-95. **Honors/Awds:** Ja-Flo Davis Fac Mem of the Year Award, Admin & Fac Bethune-Cookman Col, 1988-89; Distinguished Serv Award, Nat Coun Black Polit Scientists, 1996. **Special Achievements:** Nigerian Foreign Policy under Two Military Governments, 1966-79, The Edwin Mellen Press, 1990; Co-editor, Media Coverage of Terrorism, Sage Publications, 1991. **Business Addr:** Provost, Vice President, Cheyney University, Acad Stud Affairs, 1837 Univ Cir PO Box 200, Cheyney, PA 19319-0200.*

EKECHI, FELIX K.
Educator. **Personal:** Born Oct 30, 1934, Owerri, Nigeria; son of Ekechi Egekeze; married Regina; children: Kemakolam, Chidi, Okechukwu & Chinyere. **Educ:** Holy Ghost Col, Umuahia, Nigeria, Gd 2 Teachers Cert, 1955; Univ Minn, BA, 1963; Kans State Univ, MA, 1964; Univ Wis-Madison, PhD, 1969. **Career:** St Dominics Sch Afara-Mbieri, Nigeria, headmaster, 1955-58; Mt St Marys Col, Azaraegbelu, Owerri, tutor, 1959-60; Alcorn A &M Col Lorman, MS,instr, 1964-65; KS State Univ, grad asst, 1964-65; Univ Wis-Madison, grad teaching asst, 1965-69; Kent State Univ, from asst prof to assoc prof, 1969-77, prof, 1978, African Studies Prog, dir, prof emer, currently; Univ Port Harcourt, Alvan Ikoku Col Educ, Univ Nigeria, vis prof, 1983; Alvan/Ikoku Col Educ, vis prof, 1994. **Orgs:** Pres, Black Faculty & Staff Assn, Kent State Univ, 1974; Am Bicentennial Comn, Kent, OH, 1976-77; cord, African Studies Prog Kent State Univ, 1985-; African Studies Assn; Igbo Studies Assn; Third World Studies Assn; Am Historical Assn; Am Missons & Educ Nigeria; Am Philosophical Soc, 1979-83. **Honors/Awds:** Citation for Meritorious Service, Kent City Coun, 1977; Distinguished Contribution Award, Kent State Univ, 1997; Distinguished Contribution Award, African Studies & Res Forum Inc, 2001. **Special Achievements:** Published numerous articles & reviews scholarly journals; Published his book "In Power & nationalism in Modern africa: Essays ion Honor Of Don Ohadaike", 2008; "in Emergent Themees in African Studies", 2009; "Religion & Politis in Igboland; ast & Present'. **Business Addr:** Professor Emeritus, Kent State University, Department of History, 321 Bowman Hall, Kent, OH 44242, **Business Phone:** (330)672-8921.

ELAINE, LOLETHA. **See FALANA, LOLA.**

ELAM, DONNA
Educator. **Personal:** Born Nov 5, 1951, Brooklyn, NY; daughter of Alfred Elam and Patricia; married Ernest Kennedy, Apr 11, 1998; children: Dana Martin Hazel, Jaimee & Helen Hazel. **Educ:** York Col, BS, 1976; NY Univ, MS, educ, 1980, PhD, educ, 1995. **Career:** NY City Pub Schs, spec ed teacher, 1979-81; Hemstead, NY, teacher,learning disabilities, 1981-85; NY Univ, Equity Assistance Ctr, asst dir,1987-91, dir, 1991-97; Southeastern Equity Ctr, assoc dir, 1997; Proact Search Inc, consult, currently; Training, Eval, Assessment & Mgt Consult, founder & chief exec officer, currently. **Orgs:** Co-founder, Northeast Consortium Multicultural Education (NECME), 1993-97;ed bd, Nat Asn Multicultural Educ, 1994-95; founder, Eastside Multicultural Community School, 1997-; hon bd mem, Fla Inst Peace Edu &Res, 1998-; charter pres, Fla Asn Multultural Educ (FAME), 1998-99; comnr educ, Fla State Charter Sch Review Panel, 1999-; State Comnr, 2000-04;City Tuskegee, Mayor's Office, adv bd develop & tech, 2000-; US Atty General's Working Comt Hate Crimes, 2001-; exec bd mem, FL Martin Luther King Jr Inst. **Honors/Awds:** Service Award, Nat Comt Sch Desegregation, 1995; Certificate of Appreciation, US Dept of Education, 1995; Certificate of Appreciation,Hills borough County Public Schools, 1997; Ikeda Inter Nat Award, More house Col; FBI Director's Award. **Special Achievements:** Author: Why They Marched: The Struggle for the Right to Vote; Contributing author, "A Dictionary of Multicultural Education" 1997; contributor,"Multicultural Education Moving From Theory to Practice", 1995;contributor, "Steps to Practice", 1994; "From the Schoolhouse to theJail house: Can We Stop It?," 2002. **Business Addr:** Consultant, Proact Search Inc, 126 N Jefferson St Suite 360, Milwaukee, WI 53202, **Business Phone:** (414)347-0200.

ELAM, DOROTHY R.
Educator, teacher. **Personal:** Born Jul 23, 1904, Philadelphia, PA; divorced; children: 2. **Educ:** Glassboro State Col, BS, 1956, MA; Univ Rutgers. **Career:** Educator (retired); Adult Eve Class Black Studies, teacher; Camden City Bd Educ, res progs; Berlin Township Schs, teacher, 1964. **Orgs:** Camden County Intercultural Coun, 1947; exec bd, Asn Study Negro Life & Hist, 1972; rep, Asn Negro Life & Hist; guest speaker, PTA Negro Hist; founder & dir, Conlam Enterprises. **Honors/Awds:** Cert of Appreciation, Mt Zion AME Church Albion, 1966; Woman of Year, Local Eta Chap; Cert of Merit, NJ Orgn Teachers; Plaque NJ State Fed Colored Women's Club Inc; Plaque Asn Bus Prof Woman Camden & Vicinity. **Special Achievements:** Wrote scripts for closed circuit Glassboro Bd Educ Harriet Tubman Dr G W Carver; assisted in writing radio progs celeb of Negro Hist Week; edited published poetry book "A Slice of Black Living" 1970, 1971 added color sound filmstrip w/record & cassette; res & produced record album-The Hist Interpretations of Negro Spirituals & Lift Every Voice &

Sing; among first of two blacks to receive Distinguished Alumnus Award Outstanding Achievement & Service; Fellowman, Glassboro State Col.

ELAM, HARRIET (HARRIET L ELAM-THOMAS)
Government official, ambassador. **Personal:** Born in Boston, MA; married Wilfred Thomas. **Educ:** Simmons Col, BS, int bus; Tufts Univ, Fletcher Sch Law & Diplomacy, MA, pub diplomacy. **Career:** USIA Foreign Serv, minister counr, 1997; US Ambassador, Senegal, 1999-2002; Chief Mission, Guinea-Bissau, 2001-; Univ Cent Fla, dipl residence, 2003-. **Honors/Awds:** Numerous award & honors including US Government's Superior Honor Award; Alumnae Achievement Award, Simmons Col, 1988; USIA's Lois Roth Award, 1991; special Achievement Award, 1991; Hon Doctorate of Law, Am Int Univ, 2001. **Special Achievements:** Highest ranking American woman in all three of the US diplomatic missions in Belgium. **Business Phone:** (407)823-0688.

ELAM, HARRY JUSTIN
Judge. **Personal:** Born Apr 29, 1922, Boston, MA; son of Robert and Blanche Lee; married Barbara Clarke; children: Patricia, Harry Jr, Keith, Jocelyn. **Educ:** VA State Col, attended 1942; Boston Univ Col Liberal Arts, AB, 1948; Boston Univ Law Sch, LLB, 1951. **Career:** Judge (retired); City Boston, lawyer, 1952-71; Gov's Coun MA, exec secy, 1960-62; Off Atty Gen MA, asst atty gen, 1964-66; Boston Municipal Ct, assoc justice, 1971, chief justice, 1978; MA Super Ct, assoc justice, 1983-88. **Orgs:** Chmn bd dir, Roxbury Multi Serv Ctr, 1967-70; chmn bd dir, The Advent Sch, 1973-77; chmn bd dir, The Elma Lewis Sch Fine Arts, 1974-78; chmn, Com EEO & Affirmative Action Trial Ct MA, 1978-; MA Judicial Coun, 1978-; pres, MA Black Judges Conf, 1979-83. **Honors/Awds:** Civil Rights Award, Boston Nat Asn Advan Colored People, 1968; Community Serv Award, Freedom House, 1969; Outstanding Citizen Award, Roxbury Multi Serv Ctr, 1974; Citizen of the Yr, Omega Psi Phi Frat, 1978; Distinguished Public Serv, Boston Univ Law Sch Alumni, 1979; Outstanding Public Serv, MA Asn Afro-Am Police, 1979; Alumnus of the Year, VA State Univ, 1986. **Special Achievements:** The first African American appointed to the Boston Municipal Court of Massachusetts. **Military Serv:** USAF, sergeant, 1942-46. *

ELAM, DR. HARRY PENOY
Physician, educator. **Personal:** Born Jul 31, 1919, Little Rock, AR; married Sallyann; children: Regina, Bernadette, Joanne, Susanne, Bernard & Christopher. **Educ:** Loyola Univ, BS, 1949, MD, 1953. Cook County Hosp. **Career:** Cook Co Hosp, intern, 1953-54, resident, 1954-56, res fel pediatric neurol, 1957-59, attending physician, 1956-61; Neurol Serv Children Div, assoc dir, 1956-57; St Vincent's Orphanage, attending staff, 1957; Mercy Hosp, jr attending staff, 1957; Stritch Sch Med Loyola Univ, instr, 1956-57, asst clin prof, 1957; Ment Health Clin, Dept Ment Health, med dir, 1962; Univ Ibadon Nigeria, sr lectr, 1962; Stritch Sch Med Loyola Univ, asst prof, 1965, assoc clin prof, 1967; Mile Sq Health Ctr, med dir, 1967; Rush-Presbytery-St Lukes Med Ctr, assoc clin prof, 1971; Rush Col Med, prof pediat, assoc prof med; pvt pract, physician, currently. **Orgs:** Adv bd, Good Samaritan Sch Mentally Retarded Children, 1963-65; adv bd,United Cerebral Palsy Greater Chicago, 1966-; Chicago Met Interagy Comn, Dept Ment Health, 1967; Am Acad Cerebral Palsy, 1970; Alpha Omega Alpha Hon Med Soc, 1971; Inst Med, Chicago, 1975; Am Soc Adlerian Psychologists; Chicago Pediatric Soc; Handicapped Children Coun; Am Acad Pediat. **Home Addr:** 924 Sheridan Rd, Evanston, IL 60202, **Home Phone:** (847)864-3137. **Business Addr:** Physician, 924 Sheridan Rd, Evanston, IL 60202, **Business Phone:** (847)864-3137.*

ELAM, DR. LLOYD C. See Obituaries section.

EL-AMIN, SA'AD (JEROYD X GREENE)
Lawyer. **Personal:** Born Feb 10, 1940, Manhattan, NY; married Carolyn Adams; children: Je Royd W III, Nicole, Anissa. **Educ:** Univ Southern Calif, BA, 1965; Yale Univ, JD, 1969, MA, 1969. **Career:** Sheffield & Greene, assoc law firm, 1969-71; Greene & Poindexter Inc, sr law practioner, 1971-75; Howard Univ, assit prof law, 1973-74; World Commun Islam W, nat bus mgr, 1975-76; City Councilman, 1998-03. **Orgs:** Nat Asn Criminal Defense Lawyer Bar US Supreme Ct, 1973; Nat Consult & Lectr Coun Legal Educ, 1974-75; pres, Adv Comt Am Muslims Propagation; Financial Asst Fund; Iman Consult Bd, Hon Elijah Muhammad Mosque 2; Am Bar Asn; Nat Bar Asn; Nat Donfer Black Lawyers; Old Dominion Bar Asn; Va State Bar; Va Trial Lawyers Asn; Richmond Criminal Bar Asn; fel Urban Ctr, Columbia Univ. **Honors/Awds:** Lawyer of the Yr, Nat Conf Black Lawyers, 1974.

ELAM-THOMAS, HARRIET L. See ELAM, HARRIET.

ELCOCK, DR. CLAUDIUS ADOLPHUS RUFUS
Physician. **Personal:** Born Jan 7, 1923; married Annie Bactowar; children: Julia & Claudia. **Educ:** Lincoln Univ, AB, 1954; Howard Univ Sch Med, MD, 1959. **Career:** Mercy Douglass Hosp, med rsd, chief med officer, 1960-70, med consult, 1973; Presby Hosp, staff mem, 1973-77; TeleCommuns tech British Guiana, 1941-43; Male nurse, 1944-50; Lincoln Univ, mgr; teleCommuns tech, 1941-43; Ft State Valley Col, Ga, instr chem & math, 1954-55; Howard Univ Med Col, instr, 1955-59; M.D Dougglas Hosp, 1959-73; Presby Hosp, 1973-77; pvt pract, currently. **Orgs:** Treas, Symposium, 1943-50; Chief Res M DH, 1966; emergency room dir, 1967-69; Chief Med Officer, chrmn URC; Qual Assurance Comn; Proj Outreach Comn; nurses adv Comn, Presby Hosp, 1977; AMA; PMS; PCMS; Elder Reeve Presby Church; Home & Sch Assoc Neighborhood Sch Hamilton, 1964-69; Grand Lodge Med dir, 1976-88; Worshipful Master lodge, 1979-80; Clin dir, HTH Ctr, Philadelphia, Clin, 1977-93. **Honors/Awds:** Chapel Four Chaplains, 1975. **Business Addr:** Physician, 4400 Haverford Ave, Philadelphia, PA 19104, **Business Phone:** (215)386-8901.

ELDER, GERALDINE H.
Administrator. **Personal:** Born Sep 13, 1937, Chicago, IL. **Educ:** Morris Brown Atlanta, attended 1957; Loyola Univ Chicago, attended 1959; Emory Univ Atlanta, attended 1969; Georgia State Univ, attended 1984. **Career:** Pope Ballard Uriell Kennedy Shepard & Foul, legal sec, 1964-65; Emory Comn Legal Serv Ctr, off mgr, 1967-70; Jackson Patterson Pks & Franklin, legal sec, 1970-73; Off Mayor City Atlanta, mayor's exec sec, 1974-76, chief staff, 1977-79; City Atlanta, dir, comm affairs, 1976-77, sec, vmayor, comnr parks & rec, 1985; RMC Inc, sr exec dir. **Orgs:** Alpha Kappa Alpha Sorority. **Honors/Awds:** Nominated for Outstanding Young Women of Am. *

ELDER, LARRY
Radio host, business owner, lawyer. **Personal:** Born Apr 27, 1952, Los Angeles, CA; son of Randolph and Viola; divorced. **Educ:** Brown Univ, BA, polit sci, 1974; Univ Mich Sch Law, JD, 1977. **Career:** Litigation law pract; Laurence A Elder & Assoc, founder & owner, currently; Warner Bros TV, Moral Court, host; PBS, Nat Desk, reporter; KABC, talk-show host, 1994-; ABC Radio Networks, talk show host, 2002-. **Honors/Awds:** AEGIS Award of Excellence, 1998; Telly award, 1998; Emerald City Gold Award of Excellence, 1999. **Special Achievements:** Auth: The Ten Things You Can't Say in Am, 2000; Showdown: Confronting Bias, Lies & the Spec Interests That Divide Am, 2002; "Stupid Black Men: How to Play the Race Card—and Lose", 2008. **Business Addr:** Owner, Laurence A Elder & Associates, 10061 Riverside Dr, Toluca Lake, CA 91602, **Business Phone:** 800-222-5222.

ELDERS, DR. M. JOYCELYN (MINNIE JOYCELYN LEE)
Physician, educator. **Personal:** Born Aug 13, 1933, Schaal, AR; daughter of Curtis L Jones and Haller Reed Jones; married Oliver B; children: Eric D & Kevin M. **Educ:** Philander Smith Col, BA, biol, 1952; Brooke Army Med Ctr, RPT, 1956; Univ Ark Med Sch, MD, 1960, MS, biochem, 1967. **Career:** Professor, health administrator (retired); Univ Minn Hosp, intern-pediatrics, 1960-61; Univ Ark Med Ctr, resident pediatrics, 1961-63, chief res & peds, 1963-64, res fel pediatrics, 1964-67, asst prof pediatrics, 1967-71, assoc prof peds, 1971-76, prof pediat, prof emer pediat, Col Pub Health, distinguished prof, 2002; USPHS fel, 1964; Ark Dept Health, dir, 1987-93; US Dept Health & Human Servs, surgeon gen, 1993-94. **Orgs:** Am Asn Adv Sci; Soc Pediat Res; Acad f Pediat; Cent Ark Acad Pediatrics; Am Diabetes Asn; Lawson Wilkins Endocrine Soc; Am Fed Clin Res; Ark Diabetes Asn; Endocrine Soc; assoc mem, FEBS Am Phys Soc; Am Bd Pediat, 1965; bd mem, N Little Rock Workman's Comp Comn, 1975-79; Ark Sci & Tech Comn, 1975-76; Human Growth Foundn 1974-78; chmn memship comn, Lawson Wilkins End Soc, 1976; Human Embryologoy & Develop Study Sect, 1976-80; Nat Adv Food & Drug Comn, 1977-80; pres, Sigma Xi, 1977-78; Nat Pituitary Agency, 1977-80; bd dir, Nat Bank Ark, 1979; Maternal & Child Health Res Comn, HHS, NIH, 1981-; Ed Bd J Ped, 1981-; secy, AR Sci & Tech Comn,1983-; bd mem, Noside YMCA, 1973-84; chair acad adv bd, Int Sex Worker Found Art, Culture, & Educ. **Honors/Awds:** Alumni Academic Scholar, Philander Smith Col, 1949-52; USPHS Career Develop Award, 1967-72; Distinguished Women in America, Alpha Kappa Alpha, 1973; Woman of the Year, Ark Democrat, 1989; Career Develop Award, NIH; DSc, Bates Col, 2002. **Special Achievements:** Author: "From Sharecropper's Daughter to Surgeon General of the United States of America," 1997; First African American and only the second woman to head the USPHS. **Military Serv:** AUS, 1st lt, 1953-56.

ELEAZER, GEORGE ROBERT, JR.
Psychologist. **Personal:** Born Oct 16, 1956, East Patchogue, NY; son of George Robert Eleazer Sr and Virginia Lee Conquest; children: George III. **Educ:** Choate Sch, attended 1974; Tufts Univ, BS, 1978; Hofstra Univ, MA, 1978, PhD, 1984. **Career:** Freeport Pub Schs, intern psychologist, 1980-81; United Cerebral Palsy of Suffolk, intern psychologist, 1981-82; Westbury Pub Schs, psychologist, 1982-84; William Floyd Pub Schs, psychologist, 1984; Middle Island Sch, psychologist; Longwood Cent Sch Dist, Middle Island, NY, psychologist, 1984-. **Orgs:** Pres bd, Bellport Local Action Ctr, 1980-81; South Country Sch Bd, 1982-; adv bd, Brookhaven Mem Hosp, 1984-; bd dirs, Bellport Rotary, 1985-86; pres, Bellport Rotary Club, 1991-92; S Country Sch Bd, 1982-; Brookhaven Mem Hosp Adv Coun, 1984-; co-chmn, S Country Sch Dist, pre kindergarten adv bd, 1997; S Country Sch Dist, budget adv comt, 1997; St Mary Church, pres lay coun, 1998. **Honors/Awds:** Am Legion Award, S Country Schs, 1970; David Bohn Mem Sch Award, S Country Schs, 1970; Daniel Hale Williams Award, Tufts Univ, 1978; Phi Delta Kappa, 1985; treas, Middle Island Rotary Sch, Middle Island WV. **Home Addr:** PO Box 255, Bellport, NY 11713. *

ELEWONIBI, MOHAMMED THOMAS DAVID
Football player, football coach. **Personal:** Born Dec 16, 1965, Lagos, Nigeria; married Sareh; children: Grace & Dylan. **Educ:** Snow Col, attended 1987; Brigham Young Univ, BA, bus mgt, 1989. **Career:** Football player (retired), football coach; Saanich Vampires, 1981-83; Saanich Hornets, 1983-84; Victoria Payless, 1984-86; Okanagan Sun, 1986-87; Brigham Young Univ, 1987-89; Wash Redskins, guard, 1992-93; Barcelona Dragons, 1995; Philadelphia Eagles, 1995-96; Canadian Football League, BC Lions, offensive line, 1997-2000; Winnipeg Blue Bombers, 2000-05; Winnipeg Rifles Jr Football, offensive line coach, 2003-04, currently; BC Lions, 2005-06. **Honors/Awds:** Outland Trophy, 1989; Cal Murphy Award, 2002.

ELEY, RANDALL ROBBI
Executive, chief executive officer, president (organization). **Personal:** Born Jan 29, 1952, Portsmouth, VA; son of Melvin and Florence Eley. **Educ:** Yale Univ, BA, polit sci, 1974; Univ Chicago Law Sch, JD, 1977. **Career:** Kutak Rock & Campbell, assoc atty & partner, 1977-86; The Edgar Lomax Co, pres, chief invest officer & portfolio mgr, 1986-. **Orgs:** DC Bar, 1986; bd of dirs, YMCA, 1992; adv coun mem, Norfolk State Univ, Bus Sch, 1996; trustee, William & Mary Coll Endowment Asn, 1997. **Honors/Awds:** "America's Best & Brightest Bus Prof Men", Dollars & Sense Mag, 1988; winner Wall Street Journal Dartboard Stock-Picking Contest, 1990. **Special Achievements:** Black Enterprise Top 100 Asset Mgrs Lists Co ranked No 10, 2000; TV appearances: "Nightly Business Report", CNN; CNBC. **Business Addr:** President, Founder, Edgar Lomax Co, 6564 Loisdale Ct Suite 310, Springfield, VA 22150, **Business Phone:** (703)719-0026.*

ELIE, MARIO ANTOINE
Basketball player. **Personal:** Born Nov 26, 1963, New York, NY; married Gina; children: Gaston, Glenn & Lauren. **Educ:** Am Int Univ. **Career:** Basketball player (retired), basketball coach; Milwaukee Bucks, 1985; CBA: Miami Tropics, 1987; Albany Patroons, 1989-91; Youngstown Pride, 1990; Los Angeles Lakers, 1990; Philadelphia 76ers, 1990; Golden State Warriors, 1991; Portland Trail Blazers, 1992; Houston Rockets, 1994-98; San Antonio Spurs, 1999-2000; Phoenix Suns; Golden State Warriors, asst coach, 2004-05. **Orgs:** Juvenile Diabetes Found. **Honors/Awds:** NBA Championship Team, 1994, 1995; All-CBA, First Team, 1991.

ELIZEY, CHRIS WILLIAM
Computer executive. **Personal:** Born Aug 3, 1947, Brooklyn, NY; son of Hollis and Dorris; married Georgia V Robinson, Dec 24, 1972; children: Christopher. **Educ:** Univ San Francisco, attended 1970; DePaul Univ, BS, 1976; Univ Okla, ME, 1989; Univ Va, PhD, 1990. **Career:** AT&T, syst engr, 1970-76; RCA Communications, vpres, 1976-80; Centurian Systs, vpres, 1980-. **Orgs:** Vpres, Nat bank Pages, 1985; vpres, Cleveland bus league, 1988; pres, Bank data Processors Asn, 1986-88; secy, 1990; pres, Outer City Golf, 1990. **Military Serv:** USN, e5, 1964-68. **Business Phone:** (212)881-3939.

EL-KATI, MAHMOUD (MILTON WILLIAMS)
Educator. **Personal:** Born Oct 30, 1936, Savannah, GA; married; children: Erick, Stokley & Kamali. **Educ:** Wilberforce Univ, BA, 1960; Univ Wis, attended 1965; Univ Ghana, attended 1969. **Career:** MacAlester Col Antioch-Minneapolis Col, instr; lectr, writer & community activist; Metrop State Univ, community fac mem; Macalester Col, prof hist, lectr hist, vis instr hist, currently, distinguished lectureship Am Studies, currently; black prison inmates, Educ Prog; Several Prison Inst, 1966-. **Orgs:** Vol, Urban League; Nat Asn Advan Colored People; SNCC; Cong Racial Equality; creative ed; dir, Way Community Ctr, 1967-71. **Honors/Awds:** Page One Award, Twin Cities Newspaper Guild, 1968; Urban League Award, 1969; EROS U-of-the-Streets, Merritt Col, 1969; Recognition Award, Univ Minn; Stillwater Black Inmate Pop, 1974; United Way's Award, Macalester Col, 1991. **Business Addr:** Visiting Instructor of History, Distinguished Lectureship in American Studies, Macalester College, History Department, Rm 311 Old Main 1600 Grand Ave, St Paul, MN 55105, **Business Phone:** (651)696-6292.

ELLARAINO
Entertainer, storyteller, actor. **Personal:** Born Oct 7, 1938, Washington, DC; daughter of Bernice Jefferson Ward and Myles Butler; married Ross Anderson (divorced 1982); children: Kawi Scott Anderson & Omar Hakam Anderson. **Educ:** Weist Barron Hill, Burbank, CA, attended 1988; Los Angeles Valley Col, North Hollywood, course in voice & diction, 1989. **Career:** Los Angeles Int House Blues Foundation's Educ Tours Prog, consult & performance artist; Allensworth State Historic Park, off storyteller;Compton Unified Sch Dist Consult, Theatre Arts & Drama, instr; Young People's Acting Workshop, Los Angeles, CA, voice & diction coach, 1988-89, producer & dir, 1989; storyteller, 1989-; "Wanda at Large", 2003; "ER", 2008. **Special Achievements:** Co-

author & publisher, Another Kind of Treasure. **Business Addr:** Storyteller, Los Angeles, CA 90001.

ELLER, CARL L.
Football player, executive. **Personal:** Born Jan 25, 1942, Winston-Salem, NC; son of Ernestine Eller and Clarence Eller; married Mahogany Jaclynne Fasnacht-Eller, Dec 21, 1979; children: Cinder, Regis, Holiday. **Educ:** Univ MN, Educ 1963, Certificate C D Counselor 1982; Metropolitan St Col, Inst Chemical Dependency, 19. **Career:** Football player (retired), executive; MN Vikings, defensive end 1964-78; Seattle Seahawks, 1979-80; Viking Personnel, employee consultant 1982; Nat Football League, health consultant; Nat Inst Sports & Hmnts, founder & dir 1981-; US Athletes Assoc, founder & exec dir 1983-; Triumph Serv, exec dir, currently. **Orgs:** SAG/AFTRA Actors Talent Asn, 1969-; Fel Christian Athletes; bd mem, MN Coun Chem Dependency, 1982-; MN Inst Black Chemical Abuse, 1982-; pres, NFL Alumni MN Chapter, 1982-85; Citizens Advisory Coun, State of MN, 1984-; bd mem, Univ MN 1984-; chair, Grants comn, 1983-86; Chem Dependency Div; State Dept Health Human Serv; Mayors Task Force Chem Dependency, 1985-; vice pres, NFL Alumni, Minn Chapter, 1986-; consult, Nat Football; pres, Univ Minn "M" Club, 1990. **Honors/Awds:** All American, Univ Minn, 1962-63; George Halas Award, Best Defensive Lineman, 1969; Defensive Player of the Year, NFLPA, 1971; Key Man Award, Miltiplecleros Soc, 1977; Minnesota Labor Award, Hubert H Humphrey, 1982; Good Neighbor Award, WCCO Radio, 1984; Minn Sports Hall of Fame, 1989; NC Sports Hall of Fame, 1991; Pro Football Hall of Fame, inductee, 2004. **Special Achievements:** Beating the Odds, author, 1985; Film: My 5th Super Bowl, producer, 1984. **Military Serv:** Nat Guard private, 1965-71. **Business Addr:** Executive Director, Triumph Service, 3735 Lakeland Ave N Suite 200, Robbinsdale, MN 55422, **Business Phone:** (612)522-5844.*

ELLERBE, BRIAN HERSHOLT
Basketball coach. **Personal:** Born Sep 1, 1963, Capitol Heights, MD; married Ingrid; children: Brian Jr & Morgan Ashleigh. **Educ:** Rutgers Univ, BA, urban planning, 1985. **Career:** Rutgers Univ, grad asst coach, 1985-86; Bowling Green State Univ, asst coach, 1986-88; George Mason Univ, asst coach, 1989-90; Univ SC, asst coach, 1989-90; Univ VA, asst coach, 1990-91, 1993-94; Loyola Col, MD, head coach, 1994-97; Univ Mich, interim head coach, 1997, head coach, 1997-2001. *

ELLERBY, WILLIAM MITCHELL
State government official. **Personal:** Born Sep 19, 1946, Manning, SC; married Sarah Croker; children: Clifford, Andre & Mitchell Jr. **Educ:** Benedict Col, Columbia, SC, BA, 1971. **Career:** Sears Roebuck, div mgr, 1971-73; Jackson Cty Head start, admin asst,1973-74; Chevron USA Refinery, refinery oper, 1974; State Miss, state rep,1984; LaFont Inn Pascagoula, sales & mkt. **Orgs:** Methodist Church, Omega Psi Phi; bd dir, Jackson Cty Area Chamber Com;VFW; Am Legion; Elks, Evening Lions Club; vpres, Moss Point Boxing Asn;pres, Eastside Voting Precinct; city dem exec comt, former comnr, Jackson Cty Port Authority; NAACP; chair, church Rels Sub comn. **Honors/Awds:** Host Awareness 1985 WHKS Moss Point. **Military Serv:** AUS, SP-4, 1966-68; Vietnam Campaign Medals, 1967-68. **Home Addr:** 3712 Baywood Dr, Moss Point, MS 39563.

ELLIGAN, REV. IRVIN, JR. See Obituaries section.

ELLINGTON, E DAVID
Media executive. **Personal:** Born Jul 10, 1960, New York, NY; married Wendy Marx (deceased). **Educ:** Adelphi Univ, BA, hist, 1981; Howard Univ, MA, comparative polit & govt, 1983; Georgetown Univ Law Ctr, JD; Cornell Univ, cert completion. **Career:** Served on the House Subcommittee on Africa, office of a U.S. congressman, early 1980s; Pub Interest Commun, telemarketing dept; McKenna & Cuneo, law clerk; practiced at law firms specializing entertainment law; E David Ellington Law Firm, founder, 1990; NetNoir Inc, co-founder, chief exec officer, chmn & pres, 1995-; 2i Capital Asset Mgt Co Ltd, adv brd, currently; Emory Capital Group LLC, managing dir, currently; Beverly Hills Bar Asn, chmn. **Orgs:** Co-founder & chmn, OpNet, 1997-2002; Telecommunications Comn City & County San Francisco, 1997-2002; bd dirs, San Francisco Jazz Orgn, 1999-2002; White House Fellowship regional rev panelist, 1999; US Fed Trade Comn Adv Comt Online Access & Security, 2000; Bus Execs Nat Security, 2000-02; bd governors, Commonwealth Club Calif, 2000-02; San Francisco Workforce Investment Bd, 2002- 08; charter mem, TiE-Silicon Valley, 2004-; bd dir, Temptation Foods, currently; State Bar Calif. **Honors/Awds:** Entrepreneurs Award: Business Innovator of the Year, 1996. UPSIDE magazine's Technology 'Elite 100', 1999 & 2000.

ELLINGTON, MERCEDES
Choreographer, television producer, educator. **Personal:** Born Jan 1, 1939?, New York, NY; daughter of Mercer and Ruth V Batts. **Educ:** Metropolitan Opera Sch Ballet; Juilliard Sch Music, BS, 1960. **Career:** June Taylor Dancers Jackie Gleason Show, dancer, 1963-70; Sophisticated Ladies, featured performer, 1980-83; Balletap America, USA, co-artistic dir, 1983-85; Blues in the Night, choreographer, 1984-85, Juba, choreographer, 1985-86; asst choreographer: No No Nanette; Hellzapoppin; Oh Kay; Happy New Year; The Grand Tour; Sophisticated Ladies; The Night That Made America Famous; DancEllington, artistic dir, 1985-93; Alvin Ailey Am Dance Cen, jazz tap teacher; Mercedes Ellington Enterprises, pres, currently. **Orgs:** Local 802, Songwriters' Guild Am; Actors Equity Coun, 1984-85; local bd & nat bd, Am Fedn TV & Radio Artists; bd mem, Career Transitions Dancers; Actors Equity Asn; Am Guild Musical Artists; Screen Actors Guild; Soc Stage Dir & Choreographers; Soc Singers; Friars Club; nominating comt, TONY. **Honors/Awds:** Generations Award, The Key to the City, Columbus Times; 52nd Street American Award; Duke Ellington Memorial Award; Mercedes Ellington Day, named in honor; Dramalogue Award, San Diego Old Globe; Black Theater Alliance Award, Chicago. **Special Achievements:** St Louis, 14 MUNY Productions including: Peter Pan; Wizard Of Oz; Meet Me In St Louis; Kiss Me Kate; Broadway: Play On!; Anything Goes; Symphony Space, "Wall to Wall Duke Ellington," with DancEllington; "Juba, "AMAS Production at the Vineyard Theatre; "No No Nanette," St Louis Muny; "Sophisticated Ladies," Birmingham Alabama, Columbus GA, Bring In The Morning-Apollo Theatre, NY; Twist-George St Playhouse; Indianapolis Yuletide Celebration, 9 years; Ain't Misbehavin-Mt Vernon, Columbus, GA, St Louis; Jeff Award Nomination Chicago for choreography Play on!. **Business Addr:** President, Mercedes Ellington Enterprises, 1560 Broadway Suite 1210, New York, NY 10036-1518, **Business Phone:** (212)724-5565.*

ELLIOTT, ANTHONY DANIEL
Conductor (Music), cellist, educator. **Personal:** Born Sep 3, 1948, Rome, NY; son of Charlie Mae White and Anthony Daniel; married Paula Sokol, Jun 9, 1975; children: Danielle, Michelle, Marie & Cecille. **Educ:** IN Univ Sch Music, Performer's Cert, 1969, BMus, 1970. **Career:** Aspen Chamber Symphony, principal cello, 1970; Toronto Symphony Orchestra, section cello, 1970-73; Univ MN, instr, 1973-76; Minnesota Orchestra, assoc prin cello, 1973-78; MacAlester Col, instr, 1974-76; Vancouver Symphony Orchestra, prin cello, 1978-82; Vancouver Youth Orchestra, 1982-83; Marrowstone Music Festival, asst music dir, 1986-87; Western MI Univ, assoc prof cello, 1983-87, music dir: univ opera, univ symphony orchestra; Johannessen Int Sch Arts, fac, 1985-93; Univ Houston, Sch Music, Houston, TX, assoc prof, 1987-91, prof, 1991-94; Houston Youth Symphony, Houston, TX, music dir, 1990-94; Eastman Sch Music, vis prof, 1994-95; Univ MI, prof cello, 1994-. **Orgs:** Adv bd, African-Am Musical Opportunities Asn, 1973-78; asst music dir, Marrowstone Music Festival, 1981-87; conductor, TX Music Festival, 1991-92; adv bd, Music Assistance Fund, NY Philharmonic, 1970-; Adv bd, Texaco-Sphinx Competition, 1998-. **Honors/Awds:** CBC Toronto Orch; CO Philharmonic; Indianapolis Philharmonic; Utica Symphony; Aspen Festival; Vancouver Symphony; Debut Recital-Town Hall; St Lawrence Ctr Perf Arts, Toronto CAN, 1973; recital appearances US & CAN; featuring & sponsoring compositions Black composers; supv, Inner-city Mus Proj, St Paul, 1974; string clinician; chamber & ensemble perf; Kraus Meml Prize, IN Univ, 1968; semi-finalist, CBC Radio CAN Talent Festival, 1973; World Premiere Perf Concerto Cello & Orch, Primous Fountain with Stanislav Skrowaczewski & MN Orch, 1977; First Black Musician Maintain Prin Position Maj Orchestra; only Am Semi-Finalist, Concours Cassado Florence Italy, 1979; Grand Prize, Feuermann Memorial Int Cello Solo Competition, 1987; Solo Appearances NY Philharmonic, Detroit Symphony, MN Orchestra; Spec Resolution Citation from Houston Mayor Kathryn Whitmire & Houston City Coun; guest soloist Am Cello Congress, 1986; recital Carnegie Hall, NY, 1988; compact disc recordings, Koch Intl Classics label, 1991; conducted Kent/Blossom Music Festival, Texas Music Festival, Guelph Spring Festival, Sphinx Symphony, Scott Joplin Chamber Orchestra, Plymouth Symphony, Kitchener-Waterloo Symphony, Vancouver Chamber Players, Houston Youth Symphony & Ballet, All Northwest Orchestra, All MI Honors Orchestra, Youth Arts Festival Orchestra, All State Orchestra of Alaska, Wash, ND, Tex, NC & MD. **Special Achievements:** Master Classes at most of America's leading conservatories including Oberlin, Eastman, Peabody, Rice Univ, Cleveland Inst of Music, IN Univ. **Home Addr:** 2020 Columbia Ave, Ann Arbor, MI 48104. **Business Addr:** Professor of Cello, University of Michigan, School of Music, 1100 Baits Dr, Ann Arbor, MI 48109-2085, **Business Phone:** (734)764-2523.

ELLIOTT, CATHY
Insurance executive. **Personal:** Born Jan 21, 1956, Holly Springs, MS; daughter of Mamon Jr and Magnolia Newsom (deceased). **Educ:** Univ Miss, Oxford, MS, BPA, 1973-77. **Career:** Hartford Ins Co, Memphis, casualty underwriter; Nationwide Ins Co, Memphis, commercial line underwriter; Cigna Corp, Dallas, prod underwriter, 1985-87; Wausau Ins Co, Dallas, reg casualty underwriter, 1987-. **Business Addr:** Regional Casualty Underwriter, Wausau Ins Company, 105 Decker Ct Suite 600, Irving, TX 75062-2211, **Business Phone:** (214)714-5342.

ELLIOTT, DARRELL STANLEY, SR.
Lawyer. **Personal:** Born May 11, 1953, Denver, CO; son of Frank and Mattie V; married Diane Elliott, Nov 10, 1991; children: Darrell S Jr, Clarke M. **Educ:** Univ Denver, BA, 1975; Univ Denver Col Law, JD, 1978. **Career:** Anaconda/Atlantic Richfield, landman, 1978-80; Goldfields Mining Corp, asst coun, 1980-81; Unocal, reg coun, mgr, 1981-83; Darrell S Elliott PC, atty, pres & gen mgr, 1984-. **Orgs:** Alfred A Arraj Am Inn Ct, vip, 1993-; Colorado Bar Asn; Am Bar Asn; Colo Trial Laywers Asn; Am Trial Lawyers Asn; Denver Bar Asn; Rocky Mountain Mineral Law Found. **Business Phone:** (303)863-1600.*

ELLIOTT, DR. DEREK WESLEY
Historian, educator. **Personal:** Born Oct 3, 1958, Nashville, TN; son of Irvin Wesley Jr and Joan Louise Curl. **Educ:** Harvard Univ, AB, 1980; Univ Calif, Berkeley, MA, 1985; George Wash Univ, PhD, 1992. **Career:** Smithsonian Inst, curator, 1982-92; Tenn State Univ, asst prof, hist,1992-98, assoc prof, 1998-. **Orgs:** Am Historical Asn, 1987-; Orgn Am Historians, 1987-; Soc Hist Technol,1987-. **Honors/Awds:** Phi Kappa Phi Hon Soc; Robinson Prize Comn, Soc Hist Technol, 1991-94. **Special Achievements:** Review: Technology and Culture, Vol 34, No 2, pp. 465-467, Apr 1993. **Home Addr:** PO Box 92335, Nashville, TN 37209. **Business Addr:** Associate Professor, Tennessee State University, 3500 John A Merritt Blvd, Nashville, TN 37209, **Business Phone:** (615)963-5505.

ELLIOTT, J. RUSSELL
Mechanical engineer, consultant, manager. **Personal:** Born in Chicago, IL; son of J Russell and Blanche Smith; married Sharon Lomax. **Educ:** Chicago Tech Col, BSME, 1968; Northwestern Univ, MBA, 1975. **Career:** Mechanical engineer, Consultant, Manager (retired); Johnson & Johnson Co,mech engr, supvr, 1966-75; Johnson & Johnson Baby Products Co, Group Engineering mgr, 1975-80; Ortho Pharmaceut Div of Johnson & Johnson, dir indust engineering, 1980-85, natl mgr package engineering, 1986-94; Bus Consult, Operations & Engineering, 1995. **Orgs:** Chicago Urban League, 1967-75; brd trustees, Sigma Phi Delta Engr Frat,1967-69; adv hs youth group, Good Shepherd Church, 1969-75; bd deacons,Good Shepherd Congregational Church, 1969-75; brd trustees Chicago Opportunity Industrialization Ctr, 1973-75; Int Orgn Packaging Professionals, 1986-; Alpha Phi Alpha; adv Soc Black Engrs, Princeton Univ; exec comn, brd dirs, Bucks County Pa, NAACP, 1992-94; brd dirs, Simon Found Pa, 1992-94. **Honors/Awds:** Certificate of Merit, Chicago Asn Com & Indust, 1973-75.

ELLIOTT, JOHN
Association executive, educator. **Educ:** Wayne State Univ, BA; Univ Mich, MA. **Career:** Educator, association executive (retired); Detroit Sch System, teacher; Detroit Fedn Teachers, admin asst, exec vpres, pres. **Orgs:** Am Fedn Teachers. **Special Achievements:** First African-American President of the Detroit Federation of Teachers.

ELLIOTT, JOY
Journalist. **Personal:** Born in St Ann, Jamaica. **Educ:** Univ WI, Mona, Jamaica, BS; New Sch Univ, MA, media studies; Univ Poitiers' Institut de Touraine, Tours, France, dipl; Univ Paris, Sorbonne, France, dipl. **Career:** Associated Press, cub reporter, 1970-72; Reuters News Serv, corresp, ed, 1972-92; Nat Endowment Humanities, fel, 1981; Univ Mich, fel; freelance journalist, writer, ed, vol tv producer, currently. **Orgs:** Nat Asn Black Journalists; Int Asn Mass Commun Res; Coalition 100 Black Women; Soc Prof J, NY Sponsoring Comn; Nat Advan Asn Colored People; Legal Defense Fund; interim bd dirs, NY Chap Univ WI Guild Gradmakers; bd mem, Carib News newspaper NY. **Special Achievements:** First black woman journalist; One among 100 "women of achievement" awarded Leadership America fellowships in 1989 for intensive professional development. **Business Addr:** Journalist, 220 E 63rd St, New York, NY 10021, **Business Phone:** (212)838-1550.

ELLIOTT, LARRY DOC. See WORTHY, LARRY ELLIOTT.

ELLIOTT, LORI KAREN
Lawyer. **Personal:** Born May 26, 1959, Patuxent River, MD; daughter of Winfred Anthony and Rhoda Graves. **Educ:** Ohio Univ, 1979; Univ Pittsburgh, BA, 1981, Sch Law, JD, 1984. **Career:** Legal Aid Soc Cincinnati, staff atty, 1984-89, sr atty, 1989-. **Orgs:** Womens City Club; Pa Bar Asn, 1984; Ohio Bar Asn, 1985; US Dist Ct Northern Dist Ohio, 1987; US Ct Appeals 6th Circuit, 1988. **Business Addr:** Senior Attorney, Legal Aid Society of Cincinnati, 901 Elm St, Cincinnati, OH 45202-1084, **Business Phone:** (513)241-9400.*

ELLIOTT, MELISSA ARNETTE. See ELLIOTT, MISSY.

ELLIOTT, MISSY (MELISSA ARNETTE ELLIOTT)
Rap musician, music producer, singer. **Personal:** Born Jul 1, 1971, Portsmouth, VA. **Career:** Albums: Diary of a Mad Band, 1993; The Show; The After Party; The Hotel, 1995; Supa Dupa Fly, 1997; Da Real World, 1999; Miss E So Addictive, 2001; Under Construction, 2002; This Is Not a Test!, 2003; The Cookbook, 2005; Respect M.E., 2006; The Countdown, 2007; Block Party, 2009; Films: Family Matters, 1997; TheWayans Bros, 1997; Pooty Tang, 2001; Honey, 2003; Shark Tale, 2004; Just for Kicks, 2005; TBA, 2007; Songs: "The Rain", 1997; "Beep Me 911", 1998; "All

N My Grill",1999; "Get Ur Freak On", 2001; "Take Away", 2001; "Pussycat", 2003; "I'm Really Hot", 2004; "Teary Eyed", 2005; "We Run This", 2006; "Ching-a-Ling", 2006; "Shake Your Pom Pom", 2009; "Best Best", 2009. **Honors/Awds:** Grammy Award for Rap Solo, 2001; ASCAP Award for Most Performed Songs from Motion Pictures, 2002; MTV Video Music Awards, Best Hip-Hop Video; American Music Award, Favorite Rap & Hip-hop Female, 2003, 2005; Grammy Award, Female Rap Solo, 2003; Grammy Award, Best Female Solo Rap Performance, 2004; Grammy Award, Best Rap Solo Performance, 2006; appeared on a ABC's Extreme Makeover, 2007. **Special Achievements:** Nominated for Grammy Award, 1998, 2000, 2002, 2003, 2004, 2006; two of hersingles ranked in the top five of the 2000s decade on Acclaimed music.net. **Business Addr:** Artist, c/o E & W Records, Elektra Entertainment Group, 75 Rockefeller Plz, New York, NY 10019-6917, **Business Phone:** (212)275-4000.*

ELLIOTT, MONTE RAY
Association executive. **Personal:** Born Dec 17, 1952, Fort Worth, TX; married Vernal, 1973; children: Makala, Monica. **Educ:** Tarrant County Col, AA, 1978; Tex Wesleyan Univ, BA, 1983. **Career:** Southwestern Bell, installer, 1971-73, test desk tech, 1973-75, PBX installer, 1975-78, mgr installation, 1978-88, mgr external affairs, 1988-92, area mgr external affairs, 1992-98, dir external affairs, 1998-00; Fort Worth Metropolitan Black Chamber Com, bd chmn, currently. **Orgs:** Co-chair, Tarrant County, United Negro College Fund, 1992-93; bd mem, Nat Asn Advan Colored People, Ft Worth, 1992-99; Aviation Adv Bd, 1993-95; chair, Ft Worth Human Rels Comm, 1997-99; bd mem, Sr Citizens of Tarrant County, 1997-00; chair, adv bd, Tex Asn African Am Chambers, 1999-; John Peter Smith Hosp Bd, 2000-. **Honors/Awds:** Father of the Yr, Fort Worth Star Telegram, 1993; Distinguished Alumni, IM Terrell Alumni Asn, 1996; Trailblazer Award, Business News, 2000. **Business Addr:** Board Chairman, Fort Worth Metropolitan Black Chamber of Commerce, 1150 S Freeway Suite 211, Fort Worth, TX 76104, **Business Phone:** (817)871-6538.

ELLIOTT, SEAN MICHAEL
Basketball player. **Personal:** Born Feb 2, 1968, Tucson, AZ. **Educ:** Univ Ariz, Tucson, AZ, 1989. **Career:** Basketball player (retired), basketball analyst; San Antonio Spurs, forward, 1989-93; Detroit Pistons, 1993-94; San Antonio Spurs, 1994-2001, ABC Sports, basketball analyst, 2004; ESPN, basketball analyst, 2004-05; Spurs Broadcasting, basketball analyst, currently. **Honors/Awds:** John Wooden Award, 1989; NBA All-Rookie Second Team, 1990; Western Conference All-Star, 1993, 1996. **Special Achievements:** NBA Draft, First round pick, #3, 1989; Joe Lapchik Trophy, 1989; NBA, All-Star game, 1993, 1996.

ELLIOTT, SHARON LOMAX
Executive. **Educ:** Northwestern Univ, BA, MA. **Career:** Bristol-Myers Squibb Inc, human resources mgr; AlliedSignal, human resources mgr; Starbucks Coffee Co, human resources mgr; Eastman Kodak Co, Rochester, NY, vpres human resources; Ingersoll-Rand Co Ltd, sr vpres human resources, 2003-. *

ELLIS, BENJAMIN F., JR.
Insurance executive. **Personal:** Born Sep 17, 1939, Philadelphia, PA; son of Benjamin H and Tinner F; married Sylvia Ann Simmons; children: Letitia A, Wendy S, Benjamin III, Melanie R. **Educ:** Temple Univ, Asn Electronics, 1967, BS, Bus Admin (cum laude), 1974. **Career:** Naval Air Eng Ctr, Philadelphia, proj admin, 1966-73; Penn Mutual Life Ins Co, bldg supt, 1973-76, bldg mgr 1976-79, asst vpres, 1979-81 & second vpres, 1981-88; City of Philadelphia, comnr pub property, 1988-90; Penn Mutual Life Ins Co, second vpres, Govt & Commun Rel, 1990-. **Orgs:** Toastmasters Int, 1967-73; Corp Financial Comt mem, BOMA Int, 1974-; dir, BOMA Philadelphia, 1978-; allocations comt, United Way of Southeastern Penn, 1978-; dir, Citizens Coalition Energy Efficiency, 1983-; dir, Philadelphia Ctr Older People, 1981-. **Honors/Awds:** Outstanding Apprentice of Year, Naval Air Engr Ctr, 1965. **Special Achievements:** First Black Vice President of Penn Mutual Life Insurance Co, 1979. **Military Serv:** USN, 3rd class petty officer, 2 yrs. **Home Addr:** 6702 Wayne Ave, Philadelphia, PA 19119. **Business Addr:** Second Vice President, The Penn Mutual Life Insurance Co, Govt & Community Relations, Independence Sq Suite 2G, Philadelphia, PA 19172.*

ELLIS, BENJAMIN F., JR.
Military leader. **Personal:** Born Dec 7, 1941, East Palatka, FL; son of Benjamin F and Edna Pinkston; married Aaron Robinson Ellis, Sep 8, 1963; children: Eric B, Traci A. **Educ:** Fla A&M Univ, Tallahassee, FL, BS, 1963; Ariz State Univ, Tempe, AZ, MA, 1972. **Career:** Military leader (retired); AUS, Ft Levenworth, KS, intelligence officer, 1973-75, Hawaii, battalion opers officer, 1975-78, Jackson State Univ, Jackson, MS, sr asst prof mil sci, 1978-81, Ft McPherson, GA, asst inspector gen, 1981-85, Norfolk State Univ, Norfolk, VA, cmdr Army/ROTC, prof mil sci, 1985-89; Norfolk State Univ, Norfolk, VA, asst dir/auxiliary enterprises, 1990-91; Norfolk State Univ, dir, placement & career servs, 1992. **Orgs:** Nat Asn Employers & Cols. **Military Serv:** AUS, Lt Colonel, 1963-89; Legion of Merit, 1989, Meritorious Service Medal, 1985, Silver Star, 1968, Bronze Star for Valor, 1966. *

ELLIS, CALVIN H., III
Educator. **Personal:** Born Jun 9, 1941, Whitesboro, NJ. **Educ:** Glassboro St Col, BA, 1970, MA, 1972. **Career:** Atlantic Human Res, training officer, 1968-69; Glassboro State Col, Univ Yr Action, dir, 1969-. **Orgs:** Pres, bd trustees, Atlantic Human Res, 1975; Nat Asn Community Develop,1975; Glassboro St Col Community Human & Res, 1975. **Business Addr:** Director, University Yr Action, Glassboro, NJ 08208.*

ELLIS, CLARENCE A
Educator, computer scientist. **Personal:** Born Jan 1, 1943, Chicago, IL. **Educ:** Beloit Col, BS, math & Physics 1964; Univ Ill, Urbana-Champaign, PhD, 1969. **Career:** AT & T Bell Telephone Lab, super comput researcher; Xerox, res scientist; IBM, comput res & develop; Microelectronics & Comput Tech Corp, computer r & d; Las Alamos Sci Labs, comput r & d; Argonne Nat Lab, comput r & d; Xerox Palo Alto Res Ctr, res scientist; Groupware Res Group, Software Technol Prog, MCC, head; Bull S A, chief architect, 1991; Stanford Univ; Univ Tex; MIT; Univ Colo Boulder, Prof comput Sci & dir Collaboration Technol Res Group, currently. **Orgs:** Comput sci adv bd, computer sci educ committee, Nat Sci Found; Univ Singapore, ISS int adv bd; special interest group info systems, Asn Computing Machinery; chair, NSF Comput Sci Educ Comt. **Special Achievements:** numerous publications. **Business Addr:** Professor, University of Colorado at Boulder, Department of Computer Science, ECOT 747 430 UCB, Boulder, CO 80309-0430, **Business Phone:** (303)492-5984.

ELLIS, CLARENCE JACK
Mayor. **Personal:** Born Jan 6, 1946, Macon, GA. **Educ:** St Leo Col, FL, BA. **Career:** US Census Bur; Pub access TV, host; producer; cable tv exec; US Census Bur, exec; City Macon, mayor, 2000-. **Special Achievements:** First African-American to become a Mayor. **Military Serv:** AUS, sr non-commn ocr; three Bronze Stars, Army Commendation Medal. *

ELLIS, DALE
Basketball player. **Personal:** Born Aug 6, 1960, Marietta, GA; married Monique; children: Ashley. **Educ:** Univ Tenn, attended 1983. **Career:** Basketball player (retired); Dallas Mavericks, guard-forward, 1983-86; Seattle Super Sonics, 1986-91, 1997-99; Milwaukee Bucks, 1990-92, 1999-2000; San Antonio Spurs, 1992-94; Denver Nuggets, 1994-97; Charlotte Hornets, 1999-2000. **Honors/Awds:** NBA Most Improved Player Award, 1987.

ELLIS, DOUGLAS, JR.
Executive, consultant. **Personal:** Born Jul 9, 1947, Chicago, IL; son of Douglas Sr and Dorothy Mae Rummage; divorced; children (previous marriage): Anthony Marcus, Chad Dominick & Jonathan Thomas (divorced); children: Aaron Christopher. **Educ:** Univ Ill, Chicago, Ill, BS, 1976; Roosevelt Univ, Chicago, Ill, MS, 1979; Cert Pub Acct, Ill Lic, 1995. **Career:** Chicago Police Dept, Chicago, Ill, sgt, 1972-86; City-Wide Cols, Chicago, Ill, instr, 1984-86; City Chicago, Bur Parking, Chicago Ill, dir, 1986-91; Carr & Assocs, Pub Acct Firm, managing partner, 1992; Dept Justice (ICITAP), tech adv Albanian Nat Police & Ministry Pub Order, currently; D Ellis Acct & Bus Serv, consult, currently. **Orgs:** Cert instr, Chicago Police Acad, 1976-78; Ill CPA Soc, 1985-; bd adv delegate, Inst Munic Parking Cong, 1986-; mem dir, Nat Asn Black Acct, 1987-88; Nat Asn Cert Fraud Examrs, 1995-. **Honors/Awds:** Dept Commendation, Chicago Police Dept, 1981; First Degree Black Belt, Tae Kwon Do, 1995. **Military Serv:** USMC Reserves (retired), E8 Master Sgt, 1964-68, active duty, 1974- reserve duty, 1974-96; Vietnam Combat Ribbons (various), 1966-68, activated for Persian Gulf War, 1991. **Business Addr:** Consultant, D Ellis Accounting & Business Services, 2838 Alexander Cress, Flossmoor, IL 60422, **Business Phone:** (708)799-4337.

ELLIS, DR. EDWARD V.
Educator. **Personal:** Born Feb 9, 1924, Louisburg, NC; married Elizabeth Gill; children: Ednetta K, Bruce E & Gary D. **Educ:** Shaw Univ, BS, 1949; NC Col, MSPH, 1950; Univ NC, PhD, 1964. **Career:** Educator (retired); Raleigh Pub Schs, Wake Co Health Dept, health educ, 1950-51; NC Col, instr, 1951-52; Wash DC TB Asn, assoc health educ, 1952-55; Ind St Col, fac mem, sch comn & health educ workshop, 1963; Pa Dept Health, consult, 1955-63, secy chief, 1955-63; Pa St Univ, fac mem, 1964-65; Div Pub Health Educ, dir, 1964-67; Univ Minnesota, asst prof, 1967-69; Pa St Univ, spec asst pres, 1970-71, ctr head, 1971-72, acting div dir, 1972-74, assoc prof, assoc dean, 1969-82; Univ Md Eastern Shore, vpres acad affairs, 1983-94, prof emer, currently. **Orgs:** Am Adult Educ Asn; Am Asn Univ Profs; Am Pub Health Asn; Prog Develop Bd; Soc Pub Health Educ; Nat Univ Exten Asn; Soc Pub Health Educ; Coalition Nat Health Educ Orgn; Pa Pub Health; Cent Pa Health Coun; Ctr Comn Health Coun; Comn Higher Educ; Adv Comn, Pa & Dept Pub Health; Pa Community Nat Health Security; Nat Black Alliance; Am Cancer Soc; Coun Serv Inc Ctr Co; Family Planning Coun Cent Pa; Family Serv Asn Am; Human Rel Comm; Pa Lung Asn. **Military Serv:** USN, 1943-46. *

ELLIS, ELIZABETH G.
Librarian. **Personal:** Born in Raleigh, NC; married Dr Edward V; children: Ednetta, Bruce, Gary. **Educ:** NC Cent Univ, BA, 1947, BSLS, 1949, MSLS, 1962. **Career:** Penn State Univ, head, undergrad libs, 1969, Librn Emerita, currently; Drexel Univ Grad Sch Lib Sci, adj prof, 1965-67; Pa St Lib, lib, 1956-67, lib, 1947-56, univ sen, 1975-76. **Orgs:** Chairmanships & Offs, Am Lib Asn; Pa Lib Asn; Asn Univ Women; League Women Voters; Am Asn Pub Admin Pubs, Lectures. **Honors/Awds:** Librarian Of the Year, NC Lib Asn. **Business Phone:** (814)865-6481.*

ELLIS, ERNEST W. (AKBAR KHAN)
Banker, musician. **Personal:** Born Dec 4, 1940, New York, NY; son of Edmund and Mabel; married Judy (deceased); children: Anthony, Darius Kenyatta & Edmund Kip. **Educ:** Hartman Inst Criminol, BS, 1963; Am Inst Banking, advanced degree, 1977; Inst Far Eastern Affairs, Cert, 1981. **Career:** Banker (retired), musician; United Nations, reporter gen assembly, 1962-64; Harmelin Agency, admin asst ins, 1964-66; Prudential, consultins, 1966-69; St Dept CIA, 1967-70; intelligence off; Chase, 2nd vpres; Galactic Int Ltd, chief exec off & pres, 1982-. **Orgs:** Contrib ed, Assets Protection Mag, 1976-; vis prof, Wagner Col, 1976; vice chmn, Area Policy Bd 7, New York, 1979-81; vis prof, Upsala Col, 1981; Asst treas, Western Hem Life Ins Co, 1982-. **Honors/Awds:** New Star Vibist, Sound of Music, 1970; Outstanding Citizen Award, Chase Bank, New York 1972; Clifford Brown Memorial Music Award, New York, 1976; Certificate of Merit, The Assembly State NY, 1981. **Home Addr:** 14055 Burden Cres, Jamaica, NY 11435. *

ELLIS, DR. GEORGE WASHINGTON
Educator. **Personal:** Born Jan 1, 1925, Arcadia, FL; son of George Edward Ellis and Gussie Staley Ellis; married Alvalia G Jones; children: George, Ruth, Cheryl & Jean. **Educ:** Fla A& M Univ, BS, 1947; Univ Pittsburgh, EdM, 1954; Columbia Univ, 1961; Univ Pittsburgh, attended 1960; Univ Fla, attended 1971; Univ Miami, attended 1969; Fla Atlantic Univ, attended 1970; Fla Int Univ, EdD, 1980; Dade Jr Col, attended 1977, CUT, 1952; MsD. **Career:** Educator (retired); Alcorn A & M Col, teacher & coach, 1947-48; Fla Mem Col, teacher, 1948, 1969-70; Carver High Sch, asst prin & coach, 1948-50; Bayview-Bonifay, prin, 1950-53; Shadeville High Sch, prin, 1953-56; Richardson High Sch, prin, 1953-56; Monitor High Sch, prin, 1956-57; Westside High Sch, prin, 1960-62; Williston Voc High Sch, 1962-63; Ctr High Sch, Waycross, 1963-67; Dade County Schs, from asst prin to prin, 1967-90. **Orgs:** Pres, Alpha Eta Chap, Phi Beta Sigma Frat, 1946-; pres, Rho Sigma Chap, 1970-72; officer, Nat Asn Advan Colored People, 1972-75; Orange Blossom Classic Comt, 1973-91; pres, Miami Chap, Kappa Delta Pi, 1977-78; vpres, Miami Chap Fla A & M Alumni, 1977-79; Fla State treas, Phi Beta Sigma, 1977-80; Fla State Chaplain, Fla A & M Alumni, 1979-80; pres, Miami Chap & FAMU Alumni, 1980; Affirm Act Comt, Minist & Laymen Asn Miami; chmn, Metro Dade Co Mayor's Advis Bd Animals; teacher, Sun Sch, Church of the Open Door; int historian & dir southern region, Third World Assembly Inc; Dade County Comt Rel, 1994-98; vpres, Former Stud Asn Reunion, 1996-99. **Honors/Awds:** Outstanding Principal, Ctr High Sch; Florida Sigma Man of the Year, 1972, 1977; Phi Beta Sigma's National Editorial Award; Regional Director Award, Phi Beta Sigma, 1977; Black Liberation Award, 1978, 1981, 1983; Commendation Award, Metro Dade County, Fla, 1978, 1987; Certificate of Appreciation, City of Miami Fla, 1978, 1979, 1984; Goodwill Industrial Awards, 1982, 1983; Martin Luther King Brotherhood Award, 1983, 1984,1986; Presidential Award, Nat Alumni Fla A & M Univ, 1984; The Third World Assembly Inc Award, 1990; Florida State Coordinator Council Service Award, 1990-96; Republican Presidential Legion of Merit, Order of Merit, 1994; Alternative Programming Inc Award, 1995; Florida State Reunion Association Award, 1996; Certificate of Appreciation, Metropolitan Dade County, 1997. **Home Addr:** PO Box 510072 Edison Sta, Miami, FL 33152.

ELLIS, GREG (GREGORY LEMONT ELLIS)
Football player. **Personal:** Born Aug 14, 1975, Wendell, NC. **Educ:** NC. **Career:** Dallas Cowboys, defensive end, 1998-2008; Oakland Raiders, 2009-. **Honors/Awds:** Pro Bowler, 2007. **Business Addr:** Professional Football Player, Dallas Cowboys, Cowboys Center, 1 Cowboys Pkwy, Irving, TX 75063, **Business Phone:** (972)556-9900.*

ELLIS, GREGORY LEMONT. See ELLIS, GREG.

ELLIS, J DELANO, II
Clergy. **Personal:** Born Dec 11, 1944, Philadelphia, PA; son of Jesse Sr and Lucy Mae-Harris; married Sabrina Joyce Clinkscale, Jan 8, 1982; children: Jesse III, David Demetrius, Lillian Marion, Jessica Delana & Jasmine Delana. **Educ:** Birmingham Univ, Doctor Humanities, 1968; Pillar Fire Sem, Doctor Canon Law, 1970; Mason Col, Doctor Divinity, 1984. **Career:** St James COGIC, pastor, 1976-78; Pentecostal Church Christ, sr pastor, 1989-; Col Bishops, pres. **Honors/Awds:** Birmingham Univ Award. **Special Achievements:** Author, "The Mother Church," 1984; author, "Judicial Administration," 1979; creator and author, The Dress Code for Clergy Church of God in Christ, 1972; founder, the Adjutancy, COGIC, 1970. **Military Serv:** USF, airman fc, 1960-62; US Civil Air Patrol, Lt Col, 1999-. **Business Addr:** Senior Pastor, Pentecostal Church of Christ, 10515 Chester Ave, Cleveland, OH 44106, **Business Phone:** (216)721-5934.

ELLIS, JOHNELL A.
Engineer. **Personal:** Born Sep 28, 1945, New Orleans, LA; married Audrey Baker; children: Kimberly & Sonja. **Educ:** Calif State

Univ, BS, Eng, 1968; Univ S Calif, MBA, 1972. **Career:** Getty Oil Co, staff engr, 1985; Rockwell Int, financial analyst, 1974; Dart Ind, acquisitions spec, 1972-74; TRW Sys, Redondo Bch, admin asst, 1969-72; Bunker-ramo & Westlake, engr, 1968; Bambini Stores, Beverly Hills, acct; Calif State Univ, instr. **Orgs:** Soc Petro Engr; Inst Elec & Electronics Engrs; Kappa Alpha Psi; Tau Beta Pi; Eta Kappa Nu. **Honors/Awds:** Award of Appreciation, Improvement Act Comn. **Business Addr:** 3810 Wilshire Blvd Suite 410, Los Angeles, CA 90010.

ELLIS, KENNETH K
Executive. **Career:** Morgan State Univ, Phys Plant Dept, assoc dir, dir, currently. **Business Addr:** Director, Physical Plant, Morgan State University, Wash Serv Ctr Rm 311, Baltimore, MD 21251, **Business Phone:** (443)885-3734.

ELLIS, LADD
Government official. **Personal:** Born Dec 23, 1946, Winnsboro, LA; son of Ladd and Christine; married Maryetta; children: Kimberlyn, Angela, Stanley, Chris & Sierra. **Educ:** NE La Univ, BBA, acct, 1972; N Tex State Univ, attended 1975; Syracuse Univ, MPA, 1983; CPA Colo, attended 1983; Harvard Univ, attended 1992. **Career:** USAF, air traffic controller, 1965-69; Internal Revenue Serv, from revenue agent to dir, 1972-, comnr, currently, dist dir, currently. **Orgs:** Asn Improv Minorities, AIM-IRS, exec comt, 1983-; exec comt, Fed Exec Bd, Kans City, 1993-; Internal Revenue Serv, Nat Educ Adv Bd, 1994-. **Honors/Awds:** Meritorious Award, AIM-IRS, 1992; Outstanding Performance Award, Internal Revenue Serv, 1992 & 1994; President of the United States Rank Award, 1996. **Military Serv:** USAF, sgt, 1965-69; Nat Defense Serv Medal, AFLSA, AFGCM, 1969. **Business Addr:** District Director, Commissioner, Internal Revenue Service, 1100 Com St, Dallas, TX 75242, **Business Phone:** (214)767-1092.

ELLIS, LAPHONSO DARNELL
Basketball player, broadcaster. **Personal:** Born May 5, 1970, East St Louis, IL; married Jennifer; children: Elexis & LaPhonso Jr. **Educ:** Univ Notre Dame, acct. **Career:** Basketball player (retired), broadcaster; Denver Nuggets, forward, 1992-98; Atlanta Hawks, 1999-2000; Minn Timberwolves, 2000-01; Miami Heat, forward, 2001-03; Notre Dame Men's Basketball team, radio sports announcer, currently.

ELLIS, DR. LEANDER THEODORE, JR.
Psychiatrist. **Personal:** Born May 30, 1929, Summerland, MS; son of Leander Theodore Ellis Sr and Regina Jackson; married Gettie Thigpen, Apr 27, 1957; children: Leonard, Lawrence, Lauram & Lowell. **Educ:** Hampton Inst, BS, 1950; Howard Univ, MD, 1954. **Career:** Philadelphia Gen Hosp, psychiat residency, 1957-60, staff psychiatrist, 1960-67; Philadelphia Psychiat Ctr, attending staff, 1962-; Woodhaven Southeastern State Sch & Hosp, staff psychiatrist, 1975-77; pvt practice, gen psychiat, 1960-. **Orgs:** Dipl Am Bd Psychiatry & Neurol; psychiatric consult, N Central & Comprehensive MH/MR, 1981, 1982; psychiatric consult, Sleighton Sch, 1981-90. **Honors/Awds:** Publication, "Stress, A Non-Specific Factor in Emotionality", Journal of Orthomolecular Psychiatry, Vol 6, No 4, 1977. **Military Serv:** USNR, Lt, Med Corps, 1954-57. **Home Addr:** 801 Yale Ave Suite 1128, Swarthmore, PA 19081, **Home Phone:** (610)544-2908. **Business Addr:** Psychiatrist, 2746 Belmont Ave, Philadelphia, PA 19131, **Business Phone:** (215)477-6444.

ELLIS, MARILYN POPE
Educator. **Personal:** Born Jun 24, 1938, Newark, NJ; daughter of James Albert and Gladys Hillman; children: Kristina Pope. **Educ:** Calif State Univ, Hayward, BA, 1969; Univ Calif, Berkeley, MA, 1972. **Career:** Peralta Community Col, prof hist, 1973-76; Skyline Col, prof, hist, 1973. **Honors/Awds:** Third World Artist in US, 1983-84; Crossroads Africa & Parsons African Artists Sch Design Ivory Coast & Crafts people, 1984. **Home Addr:** 67 Werner Ave, Daly City, CA 94014, **Home Phone:** (415)994-4649.

ELLIS, MICHAEL G.
Industrial designer, educator. **Personal:** Born Oct 31, 1962, Detroit, MI; son of Dave C and Cumire Roberston; married Marietta Kearney Ellis, May 25, 1991. **Educ:** Ctr Creative Studies, Detroit, MI, BFA, 1984; Wayne State Univ, MBA program. **Career:** Ctr Creative Studies, Detroit, MI, instr, 1989-91; Wayne State Univ, Detroit, MI, instr, 1990; Ford Motor Co, Dearborn, MI, desinger, design dir, currently; Ford Motor Co, GHIA, Turin, Italy, designer; Ford Ger, Cologne, Ger, designer. **Orgs:** Porsche Club Am, 1989-; Founder's Soc, Detroit Inst Arts, 1990-. **Honors/Awds:** Concept Showcar Interior, Probe V, 1985; Concept Showcar, Aerostar exterior, 1986; Grand Marquis Exterior, 1991; holds FAA airplane and helicopter pilot license. *

ELLIS, O. HERBERT, SR.
Educator. **Personal:** Born Mar 23, 1916, Chandler, OK; married Virginia Wilson; children: O Herbert Jr & Jeffrey W. **Educ:** Langston Univ, AB, AM, MPH, 1940; Univ Mich, attended 1949. **Career:** TB & Health Soc, Detroit MI, sr health educ, 1950-56; Mich Health Coun, vice chmn, 1954-56; Wayne Co Inter-Agency Coun, chmn, 1955; Washtenaw Co TB & Health Asn, pres, 1959-61; Ann Arbor Pub Schs, teacher, 1985. **Orgs:** United Ment Ch, 1956-; Wash Co Bd Comnr, 1959; Ann Arbor Rotary Club, 1964-; Wash Co Comn-Ment Health Bd, 1966-; chmn, Wash Co Bd Comnr, 1970; pres, Sr Cit Guild, 1974-75. **Honors/Awds:** Recipient, Ann Arbor Teacher of the Yr Award, 1969; vice chmn, chmn bd, & various com, Wash Co Bd Comnr. **Special Achievements:** Selected as one of five person to plan alternate HS in Ann Arbor 1971. First Black to serve chair Washtenaw County Board Commissioner. *

ELLIS, P. J.
Clergy. **Personal:** Born Sep 13, 1911, Alabama; widowed. **Career:** Morning Missionary Baptist Church, minister, 1985. **Orgs:** Bd dir, 28th St YMCA, 1957-; pres, Bapt Ministers Conf LA & So CA, 1959-62; moderator, LA Dist Asn, 1959-68; life mem, NAACP; parliamentarian, CA St Baptist Conv; Nat Baptist Conv USA, Inc.

ELLIS, RODNEY
State government official, lawyer, banker. **Personal:** Born Apr 7, 1954, Houston, TX; son of Eligha and O Theresa. **Educ:** Tex Southern Univ, BA, 1975; Univ Tex, MPA, 1977, JD, 1979. **Career:** Lt Govr Tex, admin asst, 1976-80; US Cong, admin asst, 1981-83; Apex Securities Inc, pres & chmn, 1987-; Houston City Coun; US Congressman Mickey Leland, chief staff; State Tex, sen, 1990-, chmn, Sen Comt, currently; McGlinchey Stafford Lang Coun, 1995-01. **Orgs:** State Bar Tex; Nat Bar Asn; Am Leadership Forum; Tex Lyceum; bd dir, ARC; Houston Int Univ; Soc Performing Arts; Houston READ Comn; Mickey Leland Ctr World Hunger & Peace; NAACP; Nat Coun Energy Policy; US Secy Energy Adv Bd; Univ Tex Found Bd; bd dir, Ctr Policy Alternatives; Nat Comn Energy Policy, Univ Tex Law Sch Found Bd; bd dir, Ctr Policy Alternatives, Innocence Project Inc; Coun Foreign Rels, Utley Found. **Honors/Awds:** Des Porres Scholarship, 1972-73; Athletic Scholarship, 1973-75; Lyndon B Johnson Sch Pub Affairs Fels, 1975-77; Earl Warren Legal Training Fels, 1977-79. **Business Addr:** Senator, Texas State Senate, 440 La Suite 575, Houston, TX 77002.*

ELLIS, TELLIS B., III
Physician, founder (originator), college teacher. **Personal:** Born Dec 15, 1943, Jackson, MS; son of Tellis B Jr and Lucinda Jenkins; children: Tellis B Ellis IV. **Educ:** Jim Hill High Sch, attended 1961; Jackson State Univ, BS, 1965; Meharry Med Col, MD, 1970. **Career:** Tufts Delta Health Ctr, med externship, 1969; Meharry Med Col, med internship, 1970-71, internal med residency, 1971-74; Univ Miss Med Ctr, cardiol fel, 1975-77; Jackson Cardiol Assocs, founding partner & physician, 1978-; Univ Miss Med Ctr, asst clin prof med, 1982-; Jackson Mem Hosp, staff physician; Central Miss Med Ctr, staff physician; Miss Baptist Med Ctr, staff physician; Madison County Med Ctr, staff physician. **Orgs:** Jackson Med Soc; Nat Med Asn; Asn Black Cardiologists; Kappa Alpha Psi Fraternity; pres, Miss Med & Surgical Asn; fel Am Col Cardiol; Cent Tex Med Found; Am Bd Internal Med; Jackson State Univ Alumni Asn; Pearl Street AME Church. **Honors/Awds:** Black Bd Cert Internist MS Award, Nat Alumni Asn, Jackson State Univ, 1975; Hall of Fame, Jackson State Univ, 1987. **Special Achievements:** Recruited by the NFL to play professional football for the Green Bay Packers in Green Bay Wisconsin. **Business Addr:** Physician, Professor, Jackson Cardiol Associates, 971 Lakeland Dr Suite 850, Jackson, MS 39216-4609.*

ELLIS, TERRY LYNN
Singer. **Personal:** Born Sep 5, 1966, Houston, TX. **Educ:** Prairie View A&M Univ, mkt. **Career:** Envogue, r& b singer, 1988-; Albums with Envogue: Born to Sing, 1990; Remix to Sing, 1991; Funky Divas, 1992; Run away Love EP, 1993; EV3, 1997; Masterpiece Theater, 2000; The Gift of Christmas. 2002; Soul Flower, 2004; Solo Album: Southern Gale, 1995; Films: Batman Forever, 1995; TV: "Saturday Night Live", 1992-97; Roc, 1993; "Sparks", 1997; Singles; Hold On, Lies, You Don't Have to Worry, Don't Go, Strange, My Lovin' (You're Never Gonna Get It), Giving Him Something He Can Feel, Yesterday, Free Your Mind, Give It Up, Turn It Loose, Love Don't Love You, Runaway Love, Don't Let Go (Love), Whatever, Too Gone Too Long, No Fool No More, Riddle, Losin' My Mind, Ooh Boy. **Special Achievements:** She contributed a track called "Call on me" for the HBO Film "Disappearing Acts" with Wesley Snipes. **Business Phone:** (212)707-2000.*

ELLIS, ZACHARY L
Executive. **Career:** Ellis Enterprises, Kenner, pres, currently. **Orgs:** Better Bus Bur. **Business Addr:** Owner, President, The Ellis Company Inc, 2201 Richland St, PO Box 1009, Kenner, LA 70063, **Business Phone:** (504)469-3295.

ELLISON, BOB
Association executive. **Personal:** Married Pam. **Educ:** St. John's Univ, BA. **Career:** White House, corresp; Walls Commun Inc, sr acct exec, pres media rels, 2000-, sr vpres, currently. **Orgs:** Head, Presidential Broadcast Asn; past pres, White House Corresp Asn. **Special Achievements:** First black head of the Presidential Broadcast Assn; US Radio with African American Listeners Guide, copublisher with wife. **Business Phone:** (301)588-1993.

ELLISON, DAVID LEE
Government official. **Personal:** Born Oct 11, 1955, Houston, TX; son of L T Sr and Alma L Shelton; married Lethia Fanuiel, Oct 4, 1977; children: Dayna Leigh, Lyndsay Dalethia, Drew Leslye & Landon David Oran. **Educ:** North Tex State Univ, BS, sec educ, 1980; Univ N Tex, MA, pub admin, 1988. **Career:** City Denton, TX, urban planner, 1980-83, sr planner, 1983-87, asst city mgr, 1987-89; City Mankato, MN, asst city mgr, 1989; City Scottsdale, AR, asst city mgr; City Sugar Land, asst city mgr, 2002-. **Orgs:** Nat Forum Black Pub Adminrs; Int City Mgt Asn; Nat Trust Hist Preservation; pres, N Tex Chap Conf Minority Pub Admin, 1988; exec dir,City Mankato & Blue Earth County Housing & Redevelop Authorities, 1989-;Minnesota City Mgt Asn; bd dictectors, Nat Community Develop Asn; bd dirs,Greater Mankato Area United Way; bd dirs, Mankato Area Young Men's Christian Asn; Innovations group. **Honors/Awds:** Distinguished Service in Historical Preservation, City Level Tex Hist Comn, 1981. **Business Addr:** Assistant City Manager, City Sugar Land, PO Box 110, Sugar Land, TX 77487-0110, **Business Phone:** (281)275-2489.

ELLISON, JERRY ERNEST
Football player. **Personal:** Born Dec 20, 1971, Augusta, GA; married Loretta. **Educ:** Univ Tenn, Chattanooga. **Career:** Tampa Bay Buccaneers, running back, 1995-98; New Eng Patriots, running-back, 1999. *

ELLISON, KEITH
Lawyer, legislator. **Personal:** Born Aug 4, 1963, Detroit, MI; married Kim; children: Amirah, Jeremiah, Elijah & Isaiah. **Educ:** Wayne State Univ, BA, econ, 1987; Univ Minnesota Law Sch, JD, 1990. **Career:** Pract atty, 1990-2006; US House Representatives, Fifth Cong Dist Minn, rep, 2007-. **Orgs:** House Fin Serv Comt; House Judiciary Comt. **Special Achievements:** First African American elected to the Congress from Minnesota, as well as the first Muslim American to be elected to the U.S. Congress. **Home Addr:** 1629 Bryant Ave N, Minneapolis, MN 55411, **Home Phone:** (612)529-1412. **Business Addr:** Representative, US House of Representatives, Fifth Congressional District of Minnesota, 2100 Plymouth Ave, Minneapolis, MN 55411, **Business Phone:** (612)522-1212.*

ELLISON, KEITH
Editor, farmer. **Personal:** Born Jan 1, 1968. **Educ:** Carnegie Mellon, BS, elec engineering & math, 1987; Univ Pa, Wharton Sch Bus, MBA, mkt & entrepreneurial mgt, 1995. **Career:** IBM, mkt rep, 1987-93; Next Step Mag, founder, ed & co publ, 1995-; Wharton Small Bus Develop Ctr, dir consult, 1998-00; Wharton Sch Bus, Univ Pa, lectr; Ellison Group, owner, currently; farmer. **Honors/Awds:** Golden Circle Award, 100% Club. **Special Achievements:** Taught Bus Develop to Renewable-Energy Firms, Beijing, China, 2002. **Business Addr:** Owner, The Ellison Group, 3226 W Cheltenham Ave, Philadelphia, PA 19150, **Business Phone:** (215)635-5572.*

ELLISON, NOLEN M
Educator. **Personal:** Born Jan 26, 1941, Kansas City, KS; married Carole; children: Marc & Steven. **Educ:** Kans Univ, BS, 1963; Hampton Inst, MA, 1966; Mich State Univ, PhD, 1971. **Career:** Cuyahoga Community Col Dist, chancellor; Seattle Cent Community Col, Wash, pres, 1972-74; Metrop Jr Col Dist, Kans City, MO, asst chancellor, 1971-72; Mich State Univ, E Lansing Mich, asst pres, 1970-71; Kellogg Found Project, Mich State Univ, admin intern; Urban Affairs, Mich State Univ, assoc dir ctr, 1968-70; Univ Mo, Kans City, dir & prof urban affairs, Pub Admin, prof emer, 2004, NME Assoc LLC, prin, currently. **Orgs:** Carnegie Coun Policy Studies Higher Educ, NY City, 1973-; bd overseers, Morehouse Med Prog, 1975; advy bd, ERIC Clearinghouse Jr Col, Univ Calif, Los Angeles, 1973-; bd dir, Am Asn Community & Jr Cols Asn; Gov Bds, Univ & Col, pres, adv com, 1974-; exec bd, N Cent Assoc Col & Schs, 1977; Phi Delta Kappa, 1968-. **Honors/Awds:** Recipient Nat Jaycees Award; Ten Outstanding Young Men of America, 1974. **Business Addr:** Professor Emeritus, University of Missouri, Henry W Bloch School of Business & Public Administration, 5100 Rockhill Rd, Kansas City, MO 64110-2499.

ELLISON, PAULINE ALLEN
Government official, executive. **Personal:** Born in Iron Gate, VA; married Oscar Ellison Jr; children: Oscar III, Michele, Karla. **Educ:** Am Univ, MPA; Wilberforce Univ, Dr, humanities, 1976; Livingstone Col, Dr, humane letters, 1979; Howard Univ; Georgetown Univ; Fed Exec Inst. **Career:** NOVA Chap Jack & Jill Am, founder & pres, 1963-69; Housing & Urban Develop, 1965; Dept Housing & Community Develop, dir personnel DC redevelop land agency; Links Inc, nat prog dir, 1970-74, pres, 1974-; Arling Chap Links Inc, vpres, adminr, consult, nat pres, 1974-78; Arlington Civil Serv Commn, commr, 1983-87; Cent Fidelity Banks Inc, dir, 1989-; Real Estate Ctr, mgt consult & realtor, 1994; Consult, fed & munic mgt, 1994; Drs Johnson & Ellison Ltd, consult; Arlington Hosp, adv. **Orgs:** Beta Kappa Chi Nat Honor Sci Soc; bd dirs, Nat Conf; chmn & bd dir, Fed Exec Inst Alumni Asn, 1972-76; bd dirs, Nat Conf Christians & Jews, 1978-87; vpres, Arlington Community TV, 1986-87; pres, Int Serv Club Coun, 1986-87; pres, Northern VA Chap Minority Polit Women, 1986-87; chmn, Ethics Community & Outreach Community; secy, bd dir, Burgundy Farm Country Day Sch; Drafting Comt Black Econ Summit Meeting; chmn, Personnel Policy Comn Burgundy Farm Country Day Sch;

pres, Girls 4-H Club; pres, Debating & Literary Club; pres, Sr Class; youth leader, Baptist Young Peoples Union & Baptist Training Union; Am Soc Public Admin; Nat Asn Housing & Redevelop Officials; Nat Asn Suggestion Sys; life mem, Nat Asn Advancement Colored People; adv, Northern VA Junior League; Public Policy Comt; vpres, Hubert Humphrey's Comt. **Honors/Awds:** Outstanding Group Performance Award, 1972; Outstanding Performance Award Personnel Administration, 1972-76; Distinguished Achievement Award, Fed Exec Inst, 1974; Distinguished Youth Service Award, 1974; Distinguished Service Award, Fed Exec Inst 1974; Outstanding Service Award, Mayor Wash, 1975; Key to City of Roanoke, 1975; Seal to City of Washington, 1976; Distinguished Service Award, Mayor Wash, 1976; Disting Leadership Awd The Links Inc 1978; Leadership Award, Alpha Phi Alpha Frat, 1978; Readers Digest Award; Danforth Foundation Award; Jack and Jill Award for Outstanding Service, 1981; Woman of the Year Arlington, 1986. **Special Achievements:** First Black woman to be named employee relation's officer at the Department of Housing and Urban Development; First Black Woman Employee Re & Mgt Specialist Housing & Urban Devel 1965; First Black Woman Dir of Personnel for Fed Agency 1968; 100 Most Influential Blacks Ebony Mag 1976-78; ; commendation Pres of US 1977; elected Pi Alpha Alpha Hon Somer Univ; One of Eight Civil Rights Leaders to Advise Pres of US; winner State Oratorical Contest; numerous scholastic & civic awards. **Business Addr:** President, The Links Inc, 1200 Ma Ave, Washington, VA 20005.*

ELLISON, PERVIS
Basketball player. **Personal:** Born Apr 3, 1967, Savannah, GA; son of Arthur Ashe; married Timi; children: Seattle, Aja & Malik. **Educ:** Univ Louisville, BA, criminal justice. **Career:** Basketball player (retired), coach; Sacramento Kings, forward-center, 1989-90; Washington Bullets, 1990-94; Boston Celtics, 1994-2000; Seattle Supersonics, 2000-01; football coach, Lawnside Jaguars, currently. **Honors/Awds:** Outstanding Player, NCAA Div I Tournament, 1986; NBA Most Improved Player, 1992.

ELLISON, ROSALIND
College administrator. **Career:** S Bend Community Sch Corp, dir stud servs, 2004. *

ELLISS, LUTHER
Football player. **Personal:** Born Mar 22, 1973, Mancos, CO. **Educ:** Univ Utah. **Career:** Football player (retired); Detroit Lions, defensive tackle, 1995-2003; Denver Broncos, 2004. **Honors/Awds:** Selected Western Athletic Conference Defensive Player of the Year, 1994. *

ELLSWORTH, PERCY DANIEL, III
Football player. **Personal:** Born Oct 19, 1974, Drewryville, VA. **Educ:** Univ Va. **Career:** New York Giants, defensive back, 1996-99; Cleveland Browns, 2000-01. *

ELLY, ANDREW JACKIE
Manager. **Personal:** Born Jul 24, 1949, Pascagoula, MS; son of Andrew Thomas and Augustine Rita Martin; married Faye Olivia Meggs Elly, May 30, 1987; children: Christopher, Naturio, Shawn, Orin, Jacketta. **Educ:** Jackson County Junior Col, 1967; Savannah State Col, 1970. **Career:** Refinery, mechanic, 1975-87; Chevron USA, maintenance supvr, 1987-. **Orgs:** comnr, Gulf Coast Regional Waste Water, 1977-; pres, Jackson County Sickle Cell, 1982-; natl sec, 1988-94, supreme knight, 1994-, Knights of Peter Claver; bd mem, Jackson County Mentorship Prog, 1990-. **Honors/Awds:** Silver Medal, Knights of Peter Claver, 1978; Male Role Model of the Year, City Moss Point, 1998. **Home Addr:** 5912 Meadow Dr, Moss Point, MS 39563. *

ELMORE, ERNEST ERIC
Lawyer. **Personal:** Born Aug 21, 1964, Jamaica, NY; son of Sheila Elmore. **Educ:** Cornell Univ, BA, 1986; Cornell Law Sch, JD, 1989. **Career:** Federal Trade Comn, atty, 1990-. **Orgs:** Alpha Phi Alpha Fraternity Inc, 1983-; Nat Bar Asn, 1988-. **Business Addr:** General Attorney, Federal Trade Comn, Premerger & Notification Off, 600 Pennsylvania Ave NW, Washington, DC 20580, **Business Phone:** (202)326-3109.

ELMORE, DR. RONN
Counselor, actor. **Personal:** Born Apr 27, 1957, Louisville, KY; married Aladrian; children: Corinn, Christina & Cory. **Educ:** Antioch Univ, BA, pub rels & jour, 1981; Fuller Theol Sem, MA, theol & marriage & family coun, 1989; Ryokan Col, Doctorate, clin psychol, 1992. **Career:** Actor, dancer, model, currently; Faithful Cent Church, asst pastor, dir coun ministries, 1984-94; Relationship Enrichment Progs, founder & dir, 1989-; Ronn Elmore Ministries Inc, Therapist, minister, auth, currently; Author: How to Love a Black Man & How to Love a Black Woman. **Orgs:** Exec bd, One Church, One Child; charter mem, Am Asn Christian Counrs. **Honors/Awds:** Chrysalis Award, Minority AIDS Proj, 1988. **Business Addr:** Minister, Author, Ronn Elmore Ministries Inc, 5050 Laguna Blvd Suite 112-423, Elk Grove, CA 95758, **Business Phone:** (916)760-0401.

ELMORE, STEPHEN A, SR.
Auditor. **Personal:** Born Feb 24, 1952, Montgomery, AL; son of Clinton R Sr and Margaret L; married Linda J Pryor, Jun 9, 1973; children: Stephen Jr, Dana Pryor & Jonathan Clinton. **Educ:** Morehouse Col, BA, 1973. **Career:** Arthur Andersen & Co, staff auditor, 1973-75, from sr auditor to audit mgr, 1975-80; Wachovia Corp, asst dir audit, 1980-83, gen auditor, 1983, dep gen auditor, 1987; Citizens Trust Bank, bd dirs, 2003-. **Orgs:** Am Inst Certified Pub Accounts, 1977; GA Soc Certified Pub Accounts, 1978; Nat Asn Black Acct, 1978; finance comm, Atlanta-Fulton Co Zoo Inc, 1985-91; Inst Internal Auditors, 1985; 100 Black Men Atlanta, 1991; dir, Univ Community Develop Corp, 1991-; dir, Am Diabetes Asn, 1992-96; treas, Nat Black Arts Festival Mem Guild, 1997; Morehouse Col Bus Dept Exec Mentorship Prog. **Business Addr:** Director, Citizen Trust Bank, 75 Piedmont Ave, Atlanta, GA 30303, **Business Phone:** (404)653-2815.

ELMORE ARCHER, DR. JOYCE A.
Nurse, educator. **Personal:** Born Dec 18, 1937, Newton Falls, OH; married Robert A Archer Sr. **Educ:** Howard Univ, attended 1956; Freedmen's Hosp, Sch Nursing, dipl, 1958; Santa Monica City Col, attended 1960; Cath Univ Am, BSN, 1962, MSN, 1965, PhD, 1974. **Career:** Dept Health & Human Serv Off Family Planning, dir training, 1978-; Col Nursing, Chicago St Univ, dean; Am Nurses Asn, Dept Nursing Educ, dir; Nat Health Serv Corp, sr prog mgt officer. **Orgs:** Pres, Elmore Enterprises Inc, 1984-; bd chair, Pearl Investors Inc, 1986-87; pres, bd chair, NorBrooke Knolls Ctr Inc, 1996-; ANA; NLN; Howard Univ Alumni Asn; Freedmen's Hosp Sch Nursing Alumni Asn Inc; Cath Univ Sch Nursing Alumni Asn; Asn Educ Commun & Technol; pres, Nurses Exam Bd DC; Commd Officers Asn; Ebenezer AME Church. **Honors/Awds:** Community Serv Award, 1973; Chief Nurse Badge, USAFR, 1978; Outstanding Alumni Achievement Award, Howard Univ, 1978; Commendation Medal, US PHS Comd Corps, 1980; Cert of Appreciation, US Dept Transp, US Coast Guard, 1983; Plaque of Appreciation, Major Gen Nat Guard, 1991; Plaque, Va St Univ, Trojan Warrior Battalion Res Officer's Training Corps, 1991; Outstanding Nursing Res, Freedmen's Hosp Nurses Alumni Clubs Inc, 1991; PHS Citation Award, OASH Awards Prog, 1991; Scholar & Outstanding Dedicated Award, McKendree United Methodist Church, 1991; Community Action Award, DC Nurses Asn, 1991; Pub Citation, Howard Univ Col Med Alumni Asn, 1992; Outstanding Serv Award, Senegal Friendship Comn, 1992; Except Sensitivity & Resourcefulness Award, Howard Univ, 1992; Outstanding Achievements, Alpha Kappa Alpha, 1992; 1st African American Youth Award, NAAYI, 1992; Recognition Plaque, Bur Primary Health Care, 1993-94; Outstanding Community Serv Award, Alpha Kappa Alpha, 1994; Cert of Recognition, Howard Univ, Col Med, 1994; DHHS/PHS Unit Commendation, 1994; Cert of Appreciation, US Public Health Serv, 1994; Crisis Response Serv Award, Actg Surgeon Gen Audrey F Manley, DHHS, PHS, 1996. **Special Achievements:** Author of various professional articles & publications; recipient of many scholarships for higher edn; "Miss Mecca Temple No 10", 1957; "Miss Capitol Classic", 1957; One of 100 Extra Ordinary Nurses, Sigma Theta TauInt Hon Soc, 1992. **Military Serv:** USAFR, flight nurse, capt-maj, 1971-78; US PHS, Comd Corps, capt, nurse dir0-6, 1986-. *

EL WILSON, BARBARA
Entrepreneur. **Personal:** Born Feb 17, 1959, Charlotte, NC; daughter of Joseph Robinson, Sr (deceased) and Doreather Robinson; married Alex Wilson, Sep 5, 1992; children: Parker Destino Wilson. **Educ:** Howard Univ, BFA, 1981. **Career:** Duke Ellington Sch Performing Arts, instr, 1981-82; Every Man Theatre, prod stage mgr, 1983-84; Sugarfoots, owner & creator, currently. **Orgs:** Women's Pres's Educ Org; Sistermoms. **Business Addr:** Owner, Creator, Sugarfoots, 5738 7th St NW, Washington, DC 20011, **Business Phone:** (202)723-8890.*

ELZEY, THOMAS J
College administrator. **Personal:** Married Monedia; children: Briana & Tommi. **Educ:** Bradley Univ, BS, econ; Carnegie Mellon Univ, MS, pub mgt & policy, 1977. **Career:** Drexel Univ, sr vpres, treas & chief financial officer, 2001-, Drexel Univ Col Med (formerly MCP Hahnemann Univ), sr vpres, treas & chief financial officer, 2001-. **Orgs:** Treas, Drexel Res Found; EDUCAUSE; Ford Found Fel, Carnegie Mellon Univ. **Honors/Awds:** Alumni Merit Award, Carnegie Mellon Univ. **Business Phone:** (215)895-2803.

EMANUEL, BERT TYRONE
Football player. **Personal:** Born Oct 26, 1970, Kansas City, MO; son of Ervin and Marilyn; married Teri; children: Sydni Brook, Cortni & Brittni. **Educ:** Rice Univ, BA. **Career:** Football player (retired); Atlanta Falcons, wide receiver, 1994-97; Tampa Bay Buccaneers, prof football player, 1998-99; miami dolphins, 2000; detroit lions, wide receiver, 2001; new england patriots, wide receiver, 2001. *

EMBRY, WAYNE RICHARD
Executive, administrator, basketball player. **Personal:** Born Mar 26, 1937, Springfield, OH; married Terri; children: Debbi, Jill & Wayne Jr. **Educ:** Miami Univ Oxford, OH, BS, educ, 1958. **Career:** Basketball player (retired), executive; Cincinnati Royals, prof basket ballplayer, 1958-66; Boston Celtics, prof basketball player, 1966-68; Milwaukee Bucks, prof basketball player, 1968-69, vpres & gen mgr, vpres & consult, 1977-85; Ind Pacers, vpres & basketball consult, 1985-86; Cleveland Cavaliers, vpres & gen mgr basketball opers, 1985-92; Michael Alan Lewis Co, chief exec; Toronto Raptors, sr adv, 2004-, interim gen mgr, 2006. **Orgs:** Alpha Phi Alpha; ABU-USA Olympic Basketball Player Selection Comm for US Olympic Team. **Honors/Awds:** Miami Univ Hall of Fame; Sporting News, NBA Executive of the Year, 1992, 1998; NBA Executive of the Year, Sports Illustrated, 1998; Naismith Memorial Basketball Hall of Fame. **Special Achievements:** First black named to a top front-office position in the NBA and one of the first in professional sports. **Business Phone:** (216)420-2100.

EMEAGWALI, DALE BROWN
Research scientist. **Personal:** Born Dec 24, 1954, Baltimore, MD; daughter of Johnnie Doris and Leon Robert; married Philip Emeagwali, Aug 15, 1981; children: Ijeoma. **Educ:** Coppin State Col, BA, biol, 1976; Georgetown Univ, PhD, microbiol, 1981. **Career:** Nat Insts Health, postdoctoral fel, 1981-84; Uniformed Servs Univ Health Sci, postdoctoral fel, 1985-86; Univ Wyoming, res assoc, 1986-87; Univ Mich, sr res fel, 1987-88, asst res scientist, 1989-91; Univ Minn, res assoc, 1992-95; Morgan State Univ, prof, 1996-; Morgan Dept Biol, State Univ, lectr, currently. **Orgs:** Sigma Xi, 1983-; AAAS, 1985-; Damon Runyon Walter Winchell Cancer Fund; Am Cancer Soc; Nat Sci Found. **Honors/Awds:** Biomedical Fellowship Award, Meharry Med Col, 1974; 3rd Place Award, Best Presentation, Beta Kappa Chi & Nat Inst Sci, 1976; Biomedical Research Award, Coppin State Col, 1976; Postdoctoral Fellowship Award, Nat Sci Found, 1981; Postdoctoral Fellowship Award, Am Cancer Soc, 1981; Scientist of the Year Award, Nat Tech Asn, 1996. **Special Achievements:** Co-author: "Evidence of a Constitutive and Inducible Form of Kynurenine Formamidase," Archives of Biochem Biophysics, 1980; "Sequence Homology Between the Structural Proteins of Kilham Rat Virus," Journal of Virol, 1984; "Purification and Characterization of Kynurenine Formamidase Activity from S Paravulus," Canadian Journal of Microbiology, 1986; "Modulation of Ras Expression by Antisense Non-ionic Deoxyoligonucleotide Analogues," Journal of Gene Research, 1989; "Amplified Expression of Three Jun Family Members Inhibits Erytholeukemia Differentiation Blood," 1990; National Technical Society, Scientist of the Year, 1996. **Home Addr:** 3713 Sylvan Dr, Baltimore, MD 21207-6364. **Business Addr:** Lecturer, Morgan State University, Department Biology, 1700 E Coldspring Lane, Baltimore, MD 21251, **Business Phone:** (443)885-3715.

EMEAGWALI, PHILIP
Computer scientist, educator, mathematician. **Personal:** Born Aug 23, 1954, Akure, Nigeria; son of James N and Agatha I; married Dale Brown, Aug 15, 1981; children: Ijeoma. **Educ:** Univ London, gen cert educ, 1973; Oregon State Univ, BS, Math, 1977; George Wash Univ, MS, civil Engineering, 1981, Engr degree, ocean, costal & marine, 1986; Univ Md, MA, appl Math, 1986; Univ Mich, Ann Arbor, PhD, sci comput, 1993. **Career:** Md State Highway Admini, various hwy Engineering duties, 1977-78; George Wash Univ, res, 1979-82; US Nat Weather Serv & Univ MD, researcher, 1984-86; US Bur Reclamation, civil Engineering & res Math duties, 1986-87; Univ Mich, Ann Arbor, researcher, 1987-91; Univ Minn, Army High Performance Comput Res Ctr, res fellow, 1991-93; Independent Consult, 1993-. **Orgs:** Inst Elec & Electronic Engrs' Comput Soc; Asn Comput Mach; Soc Indust & Appl Math; adv bd, Nat Tech Asn; Am Phys Soc; Inst Elect & Electronics Engrs; Geo Sci & Remote Sensing Soc; Am meteorol Soc; Nat Soc Black Engrs; Nat Soc Prof Engrs; Prof Commun Soc; Soc Res Tech Commun; Aircraft Owners & Pilots Asn; US Parachute Asn; Balloon Fedn Am; Nat Aeronaut Asn; Am Inst Aeronaut & Astronaut; Aerospace & Electronic Systs Soc; Nat Air & Space Mus; Underwater Explorers Soc. **Honors/Awds:** Gordon Bell Prize, Inst Elect & Electronics Engrs Soc, 1989; Distinguished Scientist Award, Nat Soc Black Engrs, 1991; Certificate of Recognition Award, Mobil Corp & US Black Engr Mag, 1991, 1992; Distinguished Visitor, IEEE Comput Soc, 1993-96; Computer Scientist of the Year Award, Nat Tech Asn, 1993; Eminent Engineer, Tau Beta Pi Nat Engineering Hon Soc, 1994; InterNat Man of the Year Award, Minority Technol Coun Mich, 1994; Certificate of Appreciation Award, Sci Mus Minn, 1994; Distinguished Scientist Award of the World Bank, 1998; Best Scientist in Africa Award of the Pan African Broadcasting, Heritage and Achievement Awards, 2001; History's Greatest Scientist of African Descent, New African magazine, 2004. **Special Achievements:** Extolled by the then U.S. President Bill Clinton as "one of the great minds of the Information Age? and described by CNN as "a Father of the Internet". **Business Addr:** Independent Consultant, 1101 30th St NW Suite 500, Washington, DC 20007.

EMEKA, MAURIS L P
Executive. **Personal:** Born Apr 4, 1941, Fargo, AR; married Sunday A Bacon; children: Amon, Gabriel & Justin. **Educ:** Univ Kans, BA, 1961; Univ Wash, MBA, 1970. **Career:** Bike Master Inc, pres; Bicycle Store, owner; Black Econ Union Kansas City, asst dir; Black Econ Research Ctr NY, asst dir. **Honors/Awds:**

Author of book and articles on Black & Banks. **Military Serv:** USAF, capt, 1962-67. **Business Addr:** 11 Bennett Rd, Englewood, NJ 07631.

EMERSON, MELINDA
Chief executive officer. **Career:** Quintessence Entertainment Inc, founder, pres & exec officer, 1999-. **Special Achievements:** Finalist for the 2003 Black Enterprise Small Business Awards in the "Rising Star of the Year" category. *

EMMANUEL, ANTHONY
President (Organization), executive. **Educ:** Rutgers Univ, BS, elec eng & BA, Math, 1996. **Career:** Lucent Technol Inc, syst engr; AlphaOne Comput Solutions Inc, multimedia developer & comput instr; Rutgers Col Eng, Dean's Off, develop specialist, currently; Rutgers Univ, Digital Media Lab, mgr, currently; Emmanuel Media Group Inc, chmn, chief tech officer, chief tech officer, content designer, video producer, currently. **Business Addr:** Chairman & Chief Executive Officer, Chief Technical Officer, Emmanuel Media Group Inc, 211 Warren St, Newark, NJ 07103, **Business Phone:** (973)242-0495.

EMMANUEL, DR. TSEGAI
College teacher. **Personal:** Born Mar 27, 1940; son of G Hiwet and Ghebray Leteyesus; married Karen; children: Sarah & Ribka. **Educ:** Okla State Univ, BS, 1968, MBA 1970; Univ Mo, PhD 1978; Univ Minn, dipl, 1986. **Career:** United Nations Econ Comm Africa, African Statist Anal Dept, Addis Ababa,Ethiopia, head, 1960-63; Lincoln Univ, Jefferson City, asst prof, 1970-79,dir, Int Stud Affairs, 1974-76; Eastern Wash State Univ, Cheyney, from asst prof to assoc prof, 1976-80; Wash State Univ, adj prof, 1979-80; Grambling State Univ, Col Bus, dean, 1980, prof, 1980-. **Orgs:** Am Assembly Collegiate Sch Bus; Southwest Bus Admin Asn; Southwest Fedn Admin Disciplines; secy, State Comm Corp, La; La Coun Black Econ Develop; Grambling Chamber Com; Grambling Econ Develop Coun. **Home Addr:** 708 Hundred Oaks Dr, Ruston, LA 71270. **Business Addr:** Professor, Grambling State University, Jacob T Stewart Bldg Room 255, PO Box 848, Grambling, LA 71245, **Business Phone:** (318)274-6196.

EMMONS, CARLOS
Football player. **Personal:** Born Sep 3, 1973, Greenwood, MS. **Educ:** Ark State Univ. **Career:** Football player (retired); Pittsburgh Steelers, linebacker, 1996-99; Philadelphia Eagles, 2000-03; NY Giants, 2004-06; NY Giants, Free Agt, 2004-07; NFL, Free Agt, currently. **Honors/Awds:** Teams Ed Block Courage Award, 2007. *

EMMONS, RAYFORD E.
Clergy. **Personal:** Born Jun 25, 1948, Philadelphia, PA. **Educ:** St Charles Sem, BA, 1970; Interdenom Theol. **Career:** Field work experience parochial schs, hosps, comm & parish church activ; Atlanta Univ, asst Cath chaplain, 1972; St Patrics Church Norristown, asst pastor, 1974-; Most Blessed Sanament Church, asst pastor, 1978-80; St Elizabeth Church Philadelphia, asst pastor, 1980; St Agatha, priest; St James Church, priest; Saint Cyril Of Alexandria, assoc pastor, currently. **Orgs:** Nat Black Seminarians Asn, 1970-73; Nat Black Cath Clergy Caucus, 1974-; affil, Nat Black Cath Lay Caucus. **Honors/Awds:** Several appearances on local & natl TV progs; speaker at civic & religious group affairs; featured in local newspapers; formerly involved in prison, hosp & youth work. **Special Achievements:** First black priest ordained for Archdiocese of Philadelphia, 1974. **Business Addr:** Associate Pastor, Saint Cyril Of Alexandria, Roman Cath Church, 153 Penn Blvd, East Lansdowne, PA 19050.*

ENDERS, MURVIN S
Executive. **Personal:** Born May 19, 1942; son of Murvin Enders Sr and Ruth King; married Linda; children: Murvin III, Kevin & Erik. **Educ:** Fisk Univ, Nashville, TN, BA, 1962; Univ Indianapolis, IN, MBA, 1981. **Career:** Executive (retired); Chrysler Corp, Indianapolis, IN, various positions, 1962-77, personnel mgr, 1977-81, prod facilities engr mgr, 1981-83, shift supt, 1983-84, mgr mfg engr, 1984-86, prod mgr, 1986-89, plant mgr, 1989-95; IWC Resources, vpres admin affairs, 1995-98, vpres human resources, 1998-2003. **Orgs:** Bd dir, Christal House Academy; Econ Develop Comn; bd dirs, Methodist Hosp Found; bd dirs, Christian Theol Sem; bd dirs, Bowen Found; bd dir, Univ Indianapolis; lifetime mem, Nat Asn Advan Colored People; Circle City Frontiers Serv Club; Alpha Phi Alpha Fraternity; Sigma Pi Phi Fraternity; bd dir, Conner Prairie Mus. **Honors/Awds:** Outstanding Achievement Recognition, LWCC, 1988; Business Achievement Award, Ctr Leadership Develop, 1989; Frontiers Drum Major Recognition, 1990; Outstanding Alumni Award for Community Service, Fisk Univ, 1991; inductee, Foundry Mgt & Technol Hall of Honor, 1992; Living Legend in Black Honoree, 1993; Urban League Family of the Year, 1993; inductee, Ind Acad, 1997. **Special Achievements:** 100 Black Men of Indianapolis, Indianapois Star Newspaper Family Album Feature, 1989, Children's Museum Generations Exhibit Family Feature, 1990.

ENGLAND, ERIC JEVON
Football player. **Personal:** Born Apr 25, 1971, Fort Wayne, IN. **Educ:** Tex A&M univ, sports mgt. **Career:** Phoenix Cardinals, defensive end, 1994-96; British Columbia Lions, canada, 2000; San Francisco Demons, 2001; Detroit Fury, 2002; New York Dragons, 2003; Toronto Argonauts, 2003, 2006. **Honors/Awds:** Grey Cup champion, 2004; CFL's Lineman of the Month, 2004; Lineman of the Week award, 2005, 2006.

ENGLAND, DR. RODNEY WAYNE
Physician. **Personal:** Born Jun 24, 1932, Mounds, IL; son of Lois and Katie; married Patricia R Shipp; children: Rodney, Michael, Stephen, John & Sarah. **Educ:** Univ Ill, BS, 1954, MD, 1956. **Career:** Univ Minn, clin assoc prof internal med, beginning 1978; Pvt practice, physician, beginning 1962; Health East Clinic-Internal Medicine, St Paul, beginning, 1993; Pvt pratice, currently. **Orgs:** Diplomate Am Bd Internal Med, 1964; bd dirs, Health East Corp. **Military Serv:** USAF, capt, 1957-59. **Home Addr:** 10367 Lancaster Cove, Woodbury, MN 55129. **Business Addr:** Physician, 10367 Lancaster Cove, Woodbury, MN 55129, **Business Phone:** (651)731-7708.

ENGLISH, ALBERT J.
Basketball coach, basketball player. **Personal:** Born Jul 11, 1967, Wilmington, DE. **Educ:** Va Union Univ, Richmond, VA, 1990. **Career:** Basketball player (retired); Wash Bullets, 1990; Prof Basketball Leagues, coach, 1991-2001; Salem Community Col, head coach, 2004. **Honors/Awds:** Player of the Year, Del High Sch, 1986; Nat Player of the Year. Inducted in to Delaware Sports Museum and Hall of Fame, 2004.

ENGLISH, ALEX
Basketball player. **Personal:** Born Jan 5, 1954, Columbia, SC. **Educ:** Univ SC. **Career:** Basketball player(retired); coach; Milwaukee Bucks, 1976-78; Indiana Pacers,1978-79; Denver Nuggets, 1980-90; Dallas Mavericks, 1990; Italian League,1991; NBA Players Assn, dir player progs & v pres; Nat Basketball Players Asn, Dir Player Prog; NBA & NBPA, interim exec dir, 1995; Flick2 Ltd, co-founder; Hoop life.com, Chmn Bd, vpres; tv series: Midnight Caller,actor, 1989; Eddie, actor, 1996; film: The Definite Maybe, actor, 1997;FOX Sports Network & FOX Rocky Mountain, color commentator Denver Nuggets,1997-98; NBA. com TV, analyst, coach, Philadelphia 76ers, 2008, Raptors as an asst coach, 2009-. **Honors/Awds:** NBA All-Star Game 1982, 1983; Naismith Hall of Fame, 1997. *

ENGLISH, HENRY L
Association executive, president (organization), chief executive officer. **Personal:** Born May 27, 1942, West Point, MS; son of Julie Pearl Smith and Flozell; married Denise Tulloch, Sep 11, 1989; children: Nkrumah, Kenya, Jumanne & Kamilah. **Educ:** Malcolm X Col; Univ NH, Durban, BA, 1972; Cornell Univ, Graduate Sch Mgt, Ithaca, NY, MPA, 1974. **Career:** Kittrell Col, Kittrell, NC, asst dir, develop dir admis, 1974-75; Jackson Pk Hosp, Chicago, IL, asst admin, 1975-77; S Chicago Community Hosp, Chicago, IL, dir planning & mkt, 1977-85; Black United Fund Ill Inc, Chicago, IL, pres & chief exec officer, 1985-. **Orgs:** Fel Woodrow Wilson Nat Fel Found, 1972-74; Co-Chmn, United Black Voters, IL, 1977-79; pres, COMPRAND Inc, 1981-85; pres, Coalition Save S Shore Country Club, 1980-84; Calumet Dist Comr, Boy Scouts Am, 1982-84; vpres, S Shore Comn, 1989-. **Honors/Awds:** Award for Service to the Community of Retarded Children, Mau-Glo Day Ctr, 1982; Governor's Service Award, State Ill, 1982; Leadership Service Award, Boy Scouts Am, 1983; Leadership Service Award, Coalition Save S Shore Country Club, 1983. **Military Serv:** US Marine Corps, CPL, 1961-66; Good Conduct Medal. **Business Addr:** President, Chief Executive Officer, Black United Fund Illinois Inc, 1809 E 71st St, Chicago, IL 60649, **Business Phone:** (773)324-0494.

ENGLISH, KENNETH
Government official. **Personal:** Born Jul 29, 1947, Waycross, GA; children: Crystal Denise, Constance MaryAlice & Kenneth II. **Educ:** Morehouse Col, Atlanta; GA State Univ, Atlanta. **Career:** US Dept of Labor, Off Intergovernmental Rel, regional rep region IV, 1978-. **Orgs:** Pres, United Rubber Workers Union Local, 1969-78; vpres, GA State AFL-CIO, 1972-78; Asn Fed Exec, 1978-; Indust Rel Res Asn, 1979-; bd mem, Southern Labor Hist Asn, 1979-; bd Dir, Urban League Albany Chap, 1970-78; del, Mini-Conv Nat Dem Party, 1974; secy, State Charter Comn, GA Dem Party, 1974-75; chmn, Second cong dist Affirmative Action Comt, GA Dem Party, 1975-77; GA State Employment & Training Coun, 1975-77; secy, Albany-Dougherty Comn, NAACP Branch, 1976-78; Dougherty County Dem Comt, 1976-78; Philip Randolph Inst Albany Chap, 1976-; chmn, Auditing Comt, GA Dem Party, 1977-7 8; chmn, Albany Urban League, 1977-78; GA State Crime Comn, 1977-78; Nat & Honor Soc; Alpha Lambda Delta, GSU, 1979; Select Comn Revision GA State, 1979; vpres, Labor Studies Student Asn, GSU, 1979-. **Honors/Awds:** Nominated for Who's Who in Am Nat Jaycees 1976. **Business Phone:** (404)657-8239.

ENGLISH, LEONTENE ROBERSON
Educator. **Personal:** Born Dec 20, 1930, Lexington, TX; daughter of Timothy and Willie L Smith Roberson; married George E, May 26, 1953; children: Byron D. **Educ:** Paul Quinn Coll, BS, 1952; Hoston Tillotson Coll, elem cert, 1953; TX Southern Univ, MEd, 1962, Univ Houston, doctoral work, 1966; Prairie View Univ, adm cert, 1982. **Career:** Educator (retired); Lee County CSD, teacher, 1953-62; Temple ISD, teacher, 1962-78, principal, 1978-92. **Orgs:** Trustee, Wayman Chapel AME, 1984-; ed chair, Nat Asn Advan Colored People, 1988-; chairperson, Bell Co Retired Teachers Scholarship, 1992-; TISD Grow Your Own Teacher Prog, 1996-; Homeless Aliance, Core Group, 1999-; chair, TISD Blue Ribbon Task Force Subgroup, 1999-; Ebony Culture Club, 1999-; mentor, TISD Volunteer Prog, 2000-01. **Honors/Awds:** Outstanding Leader, Outstanding Leaders in Educ, 1976; Golden Apple Award, Temple Daily Telegram; Educator of the Month, Rotary Club; Booker T Washington Educ Award, St John Regular Baptist, 1991; Dedicated Service, TISD, 1992.

ENGLISH, DR. PERRY T., JR.
Publisher. **Personal:** Born Aug 12, 1933, Blountstown, FL; son of Perry Sr; divorced; children: Sharilynn & Lori Laverne. **Educ:** Cent State Univ, BS, 1956; Faculte de Med Univ de Paris, MD, 1965. **Career:** Publisher (retired); Sainte Antoine Hosp, house physician, 1965-71; Friendship Med Ctr Ltd, asst exec dir, 1971-75, admin, 1975-77; St Lukes Family Health Ctr Inc, pres, 1977; Englewood Med Ctr Inc, pres, 1978-83; Beverly Hills Convalescent Ctr Inc, pres; Cook Co, phys assoc; Lopere Pub Co Inc, pres; Blair & Cole, Attorneys Law, adminr. **Orgs:** Am Pub Health Asn; treas, Chicago Investment Corp; vpres, Lake Vista CtrInc; pres, Lope Redevelop Corp; treas, Am Leasing Corp; secy, LET Develop Corp; pres, Lope Re Int Inc; treas, Madison Mgt Corp; pres, Lorgen Investment & Develop Corp; Med Group Mgt Asn; exec dir, AESULAPIUS Soc; Chicago Asn Com & Indust; Chicago Coun Foreign Affairs; treas, The Consortium. **Honors/Awds:** Award from 3rd Ward Democratic Party, 1976. **Military Serv:** AUS, 1953-55.

ENGLISH, REGINALD
Computer executive. **Career:** Intellisys Technology Corp, chief exec officer.

ENGLISH, DR. RICHARD ALLYN
Educator. **Personal:** Born Aug 29, 1936, Winter Park, FL; son of Wentworth and Mary; married Ireita G W. **Educ:** Talladega Col, AB, 1958; Univ Mich, MA, 1959, MSW, 1964, PhD, 1970. **Career:** Univ Oslo Norway, summer fel, 1956; Univ Mich, Woodrow Wilson fel, 1958-59; Flint Urban League, voc youth serv dir, 1959-61, acting dir, 1961-62; Neighborhood Serv Org Detroit, soc group worker, 1963-66; Wayne State Univ, lectr, 1965-67; Univ Mich, lectr, 1967-70, asst prof, 1970-72, Sch Soc Work, asst dean, 1971-74, assoc prof social work, assoc vpres acad affairs, 1974-; Hebrew Univ, Paul Baerwald Sch Social Work, vis scholar & lectr, 1975; Univ Tex, Austin, RL Sutherland chair ment health & social policy; Howard Univ, dean & prof sch soc work, 1985-2003, provost & chief acad officer, currently. **Orgs:** Coun Social Work Educ; Nat Asn Soc Workers; Nat Asn Black Social Workers; Ann Prog Meeting Coun Social Work Educ; Coun Soc Work Educ, Re-accreditation Teams Grad Sch Social Work, 1973-; elec & mem, House Dels Coun Soc Work Educ, 1974-77; Ann Prog Planning Comn Coun Social Work Educ, 1975-78; chmn, Am Soc Asn, 1977; elec pres, Coun Soc Work Educ, 1981-84; Prog Comt Sem Social Work Educ & Human Settlements; Int Asn Sch Social Work; Operation Crossroads Africa Ghana; bd, Am Civil Liberties Union; adv panel, Refugee Policy Group; Spaulding C Emer Found, 1987-; bd mem, Nat Assembly Nat Voluntary Health Orgn, 1988-; bd mem, Int Asiation Social Welfare, 1988-; int comt, Coun Social Work Educ, 1989-. **Honors/Awds:** Co-ed, Human Serv Org; Beyond Path Res & Theoretical Perspectives Black Families; Distinguished Service Award, Nat Asn Black Social Workers, 1983, Presidential Award for Excellence in Social Work Education, 1997; Certificate of Appreciation, Coun Social Work, 1984; Distinguished Alumni Award, 1985; Whitney Young Jr Scholar Award, Western Mich Univ, 1987. **Business Addr:** Provost, Chief Academic Officer, Howard University, School of Social Work, 601 Howard Pl NW, Washington, DC 20059, **Business Phone:** (202)806-7311.

ENGLISH, STEPHEN
Basketball player. **Personal:** Born Feb 4, 1970, Frankfurt, Germany. **Educ:** Univ SC. **Career:** Chicago Bulls, 1992-93, 1993-94, 1994-95; Tri-City Chinook, 1992-94; LaCrosse Catbirds, 1993-94; Minn Timberwolves, 1993; Adelaide 36ers, Australian National Basketball, 1995.

ENGLISH, WILLIAM E
Executive. **Personal:** Born May 18, 1936, Marianna, AR; son of Dan and Lorraine; divorced; children: William Jr, Romona, Cheryl & Amber. **Educ:** Univ MICH, BS, 1955. **Career:** Executive (retired); Group Health Mutual, underwriter, 1959-63; 3M Co, sales mgr, 1963-68; Ceridian, Bus Ventures, vpres, 1968-95. **Orgs:** Chair, Minnesota African Am Polit Caucus, 1993-; Men Are Responsible Cultivating Hope, 1994-; Chair, Minneapolis Model Cities Prog, 1969-71; chair & bd trustees, Minneapolis Urban League, 1975-78; trustee, Livingstone Col, 1986-90; chair, Howard Univ Cluster Prog, 1988-90; chair, Minnesota African Am Polit Caucus, 1993-; Men Responsible Cultivating Hope, 1994-; Nat Urban League. **Honors/Awds:** President's Award, Minneapolis Urban League, 1984; Good Guy Award, MN Women's Political Caucus, 1991; Outstanding Contribution, Howard Univ Cluster, 1992.

ENGRAM, BOBBY (SIMON ENGRAM III)
Football player. **Personal:** Born Jan 7, 1973, Camden, SC; married Deanna; children: Bobbi,Dean & Trey. **Educ:** Pa State, BS, exercise sci 1995. **Career:** Chicago Bears, wide receiver, 1996-00; Seattle Seahawks, 2001-.08; Kansas City Chiefs, 2009-. **Honors/Awds:** Three time AP All American; Biletnikoff Award, 1994; Ed Block Courage Award, 2005. **Business Addr:** Professional Football Player, Seattle Seahawks, 800 Occidental Ave South Suite 500, Seattle, WA 98134, **Business Phone:** 888-635-4295.*

ENGRAM III, SIMON. See ENGRAM, BOBBY.

ENGS, ROBERT FRANCIS
Educator. **Personal:** Born Nov 10, 1943, Colorado Springs, CO; son of Robert Engs and Myrtle Coger Engs; married Jean Oliver, Dec 20, 1969; children: Robert N. **Educ:** Princeton Univ, AB, (cum laude) 1965; Yale Univ, PhD, Hist 1972. **Career:** Univ Penn, Dept Hist, from asst prof to assoc prof, 1972-79, prof currently, undergrad chair hist, 1986, Afro-Am Studies Prog, co-chair, prof hist, currently; Princeton Univ, instr hist, 1970-72; NJ Black Hist Inst NJ Dept Educ, dir, 1969-72; Col William & Mary, commonwealth vis prof, 1984-85; Guggenheim Fel, 1982-83; . **Orgs:** Fac, cons Nat Humanities Fac, 1972-80; Orgn Am Historians, 1975-; Am Hist Asn, 1975; adv, Nat Humanities Ctr, 1978-80; Asn Study Afro-Am Life Hist, 1975; chmn, Presidents Forum Univ Penn, 1985-87; Exec Comt Alumni Coun Princeton Univ, 1989-91. **Honors/Awds:** Short Term Am Grantee, US Dept State, 1971; William Penn Fel, Moton Ctr Ind Studies, 1976-77; Freedom's First Generation, Univ Penn Press, 1979; Lindback Award, Univ Penn, 1988. **Special Achievements:** Books like: Freedom's First Generation: Black Hampton, Va., 1861-1890 & Educating the Disfranchised and Disinherited; Samuel Chapman Armstrong and Hampton Institute, 1839-1893. Also edited with Randall Miller, The Rise of the Grand Old Party, treats the early years of the Republican Party. **Business Phone:** (215)898-4956.

ENIS, CURTIS
Football player. **Personal:** Born Jun 15, 1976, Union City, OH; married Tiffanie; children: Samson. **Educ:** Pa State, Recreational Mgt . **Career:** Chicago Bears, running back, 1998-00; Cleveland Browns, running back,2001; Clopay, russia, currently. *

ENIS, SHALONDA (SHALONDA MOCHEA ENIS)
Basketball player. **Personal:** Born Dec 3, 1974. **Educ:** Univ Ala. **Career:** Seattle Reign, ctr, 1997-99; Wash Mystics, 1999; Charlotte Sting, ctr & forward, 2000-03; Charlotte Sting, 2005-. **Honors/Awds:** MVP honors, US Olympic Festival, 1994; Rookie of the Year, 1997-98; All-Star, ABL, 1997-98. **Business Phone:** (704)688-8600.*

ENIS, SHALONDA MOCHEA. See ENIS, SHALONDA.

ENNIX, DR. COYNESS LOYAL, JR.
Physician, educator. **Personal:** Born Feb 12, 1942, Nashville, TN; married Katharine; children: Nicole & Kristina. **Educ:** Fisk Univ, BS, 1963; Meharry Med Col, MD, 1967. **Career:** Baylor Col Med, asst prof, surg; Baylor Col Med, postdoctoral fel, 1976-77; Cleveland Clinic Educ Found, fel, 1974-76; Cardiovascular Disease Baylor Col Med, researcher; Methodist Hosp, staff surg; Inst Rehab & Res,St Joseph Hosp; Va Hosp; St Lukes Hosp; Alta Bates Med Ctr, Ctr Cardiac Surg, med dir & chief cardiac surg, 1993-2002; E Bay Cardiac Surg Ctr, cardiac surgeon, 2001-05; E Bay Cardiac Surg Ctr, bus mgr, 2003; CtrCardiac Surg, cardiac surgeon, 2005-. **Orgs:** Am Col Surg; Michael E DeBakey Int Cardiovascular Soc; Houston Med Forum;Harris Co Med Soc; Tex Med Asn; Houston Acad Med; AMA; Am Trauma Soc;Houston Surg Soc; Nat Med Asn; San Francisco Surgical Soc; Pan Pacific Surg Asn; Denton A Cooley Cardiovascular Surg Soc; dipl, Am Bd Surg; dipl,Am Bd Thoracic Surg; Soc Thoracic Surgeons; Am Heart Asn; pres, Bay Area soc Thoracic Surg; hon nat fel, Robert Wood Johnson Found, 1998. **Honors/Awds:** Most Outstanding Fellow Cardiovascular Surgery, Cleveland Clinic EducFound, 1976. **Military Serv:** USN, 1969-71. **Business Phone:** (510)704-8050.

ENOCH, HOLLACE J.
Federal government official. **Personal:** Born Jul 9, 1950, Mathews, VA; daughter of William Jackson and Gladys Jackson; married Hurley Enoch, Oct 10, 1981 (divorced 1991). **Educ:** Va Union Univ, Richmond, VA, BA, 1972. **Career:** Nat Labor Rels Bd, Baltimore MD, field examiner, 1972-78; US Patent & Trademark Off, Arlington, VA, labor & employee rels specialist, 1978-81; Nat Labor Rels Bd, Wash, DC, labor rels officer, 1981-89, assoc exec secy. **Orgs:** various leadership positions, Delta Sigma Theta Sorority, 1969-; Soc Fed Labor Rels Profs, 1978-89. **Honors/Awds:** Wall Street Journal Achievement Award, 1972; numerous Outstanding Performance Awards, during Govt career. *

ENOCH, JOHN D.
Executive, president (organization). **Career:** Minority & Women Bus, publ, chmn & ed; Indust Paper Prod Inc, pres, 2002-. **Orgs:** Adv bd mem, Randolph Bank; adv bd, Morris Plan Bank. **Business Addr:** President, Industrial Paper Products Inc, 530 Chapel Hill Rd, PO Box 210, Burlington, NC 27216, **Business Phone:** (336)226-2457.

ENSLEY, ANNETTE
Executive director. **Career:** Am Assoc Retired Persons, travel consult; Inverness Travel, exec vpres; Nat Conf Black Lawyers, assoc dir; Nathan Cummings Found, dir, admin & human res, 1989-, off mgr asst pres, currently. **Orgs:** Bd dir, Nat Conference Black Lawyers. **Business Addr:** Director of Administration & Resources, Nathan Cummings Foundation, 475 10th Ave 14th Fl, New York, NY 10018-9715, **Business Phone:** (212)787-7300.

EPHRAIM, DR. CHARLESWORTH W.
Educator. **Educ:** USAF Tech Sch, radio opers honors, 1964; USAF Instr Training Sch, 1964; State Univ NY, BA, honors purchase valedictorian, 1973; Nat Fel Ford Found, 1973-78; Yale Univ, MA, MPhil, PhD, philos, 1979. **Career:** USAF, tech instr, sgt, radio op US & overseas, 1964-68; Bankers Trust Co NY, supvr, 1968-73; State Univ NY, instr, Empire State Col, fac; Yale Univ, instr; Mercy Col, Dept Philos, assoc prof philos, currently; Univ Without Walls, Skidmore Col, fac, currently; Antigua State Col, sr lectr, currently. **Orgs:** Com Vets Affairs; NY Metrop Asn Develop Educ; Am Philos Asn; Nat Asn Advan Colored People; Urban League; founder, Free Comm Sch Mt Vernon, 1980. **Honors/Awds:** Summer Research Grant, Logic of Black Protest, NY African Am Inst study,1988. **Special Achievements:** Completed USAF morse-code course in half time, first person in USAF history to receive 24 GPM while in training, Keesler AFB MS 1964,graduated college in 2 1/2 years, research being done in Philosophy of theBlack Experience, is a radio talk show host whose program, "Let's Talk,"is a popular feature on ZDK radio. **Military Serv:** USF, sgt, 1964-68, res, 1968-70. **Business Addr:** Faculty, University Without Walls, Skidmore College, 815 N Broadway, Saratoga Springs, NY 12866, **Business Phone:** (518)580-5450.

EPHRIAM, MABLEAN
Television show host, judge. **Personal:** Born Apr 23, 1939, Hazlehurst, MS; divorced; children: 4. **Educ:** Pitzer Col, BA; Whittier Col Law, JD, 1978; Harvard Univ, eng, 1981; Juris doctorate, Univ Penn Law Sch, 1984. **Career:** Judge (retired), host: TV show host, currently; Dep city atty, Los Angeles, 1978-82; founded law pract, 1982; Divorce Ct, judge, 1999-2006; pvt pract, currently. **Orgs:** Co-founder, Harriet Buhia Ctr for Family Law, 1982; past pres, Los Angeles Black Women Lawyers group; former mem, Exec Comt, Los Angeles Co Bar & State Bar Calif Family Law Sects. **Honors/Awds:** Distinguished Service Award, Women Lawyers Asn Los Angeles, 1993; Calif Woman of the Year Award, 1995; Alumnus of the Year, Whittier Col of Law, 1997. **Special Achievements:** film appearance: Diary of a Mad Black Woman; Madea's Family Reunion. **Business Addr:** Host, Monet Lane Productions, Divorce Court, PO Box 3510, Hollywood, CA 90078.

EPPERSON, DAVID E.
School administrator, dean (education), college teacher. **Personal:** Born Mar 14, 1935, Pittsburgh, PA; son of Robert N and Bessie Lee Tibbs; married Cecelia Trower; children: Sharon & Lia. **Educ:** Univ Pittsburgh, BA, 1961, MSW, 1964, MA, 1970, PhD, 1975; Univ Bosporous & Chinese Univ. **Career:** Dean (retired); Univ Pittsburgh, Equal Opportunities Prog, co ordr, 1964-65, Dept Polit Sci, Urban Affairs, consult, 1969-72, Sch Social Work, dean & prof, 1972-2000; Community Action Pittsburgh Inc, exec dir, 1967-69, dep, 1965-67; Dean Emer & prof emer, Sch Social Work, Univ Pittsburgh, currently. **Orgs:** Vice chmn, Urban Redevelop Authority Pittsburgh; vice chmn, YMCA,Pittsburgh; bd dirs, YMCA, USA. **Honors/Awds:** David E & Cecilia Trower Epperson Scholar Fund. **Special Achievements:** Participated in Educ & Social Welfare Study Missions to Africa, Asia, Latin Am & Western Europe. **Military Serv:** USAF, staff sgt, 1954-58. *

EPPS, ANNA CHERRIE
School administrator. **Personal:** Born Jul 8, 1930, New Orleans, LA; daughter of Ernest Cherrie Sr and Anna J Cherrie; married Joseph M Sr, Nov 28, 1968 (died 1984). **Educ:** Howard Univ, BS, 1951; Loyola Univ, MS, 1956; Howard Univ, PhD, 1966. **Career:** Xavier Univ, asst prof & actg chair med tech, 1954-60; Howard Univ, asst prof microbiol, 1960-69; Tulane Univ Sch Med, assoc dean students serv & prof med, 1969-97; Meharry Med Col, dean & vpres acad affairs, 1997-2002, dean emer, 2002-, sr adv pres, 2002-, interim pres, 2006-07. **Orgs:** AAMC; NAMME; Am Soc Clin Pathologists; Am Soc Med Technologists; Am Asn Blood Banks; Am Asn Univ Profs; Sigma Xi; Am Asn Univ Women; AOA mem; Bd of Regents, Georgetown Univ; Nat Bd Med Examiners. **Honors/Awds:** Recognition Award, NAMME; Award for Meritorious Research, Interstate Post grad Med Asn Am; hon doctorate, Meharry Med Col, 1996; Herbert WNickens MD Award, AAMC, 2003; Harold Delaney Educ Achievement Award, Am Asn Blacks Higher Educ, 2008. **Special Achievements:** Published numerous articles and books. **Home Addr:** 769 Sinlcair Circle, Brentwood, TN 37027. **Business Addr:** Senior Advisor, Dean Emerita, School of Medicine, Professor, Internal Medicine, 1005 Dr DB Todd Jr Blvd, Nashville, TN 37208, **Business Phone:** (615)327-5935.

EPPS, C ROY
Association executive. **Personal:** Born Jun 6, 1941, Bronx, NY; son of Clarence and Alice; children: Leah, Roy III, Leslye Renee & Camara Rose. **Educ:** Wilberforce Univ, BS, 1963; Rutgers Univ, MS, 1970; MA Inst Tech, fel 1982; Upsala Col, Hon Doctorate, 1994. **Career:** Civic/Urban League Greater NB, community social worker, 1967-68, asst dir, 1968-70, exec dir & pres 1970-, pres & chief exec officer, currently. **Orgs:** NB Tomorrow, 1975-; chmn & hsng com, NB Develop Corp, 1976-94; former pres & mem NB Bd Ed, 1976-85; Greater Raritan Workforce Investment Bd, 1983-99; co-chair Black Leadership Conf, 1986-; chmn, Eric B. Chandler Health Ctr, 1998-; Middlesex County Workforce Investment Bd, 1999-; bd trustees, citizens campaign; founder, bd NB Tomorrow. **Honors/Awds:** Pres Award, Eastern Reg Coun Urban League Exec, 1977-81, President Award, Nat Coun Urban League Exec, 1978-80; comm fellows prog, MA Inst Tech, 1981-82. **Military Serv:** AUS pfc 2 yrs. **Business Addr:** President, Chief Executive Officer, Civic League Greater New Brunswick, 47-49 Throop Ave, New Brunswick, NJ 08901.

EPPS, CHARLES HARRY, JR.
Physician. **Personal:** Born Jul 24, 1930, Baltimore, MD; son of Charles Harry Epps Sr (deceased) and Marjorie Sue Jackson (deceased); married Roselyn Payne; children: Charles Harry III, Kenneth Carter, Roselyn Elizabeth, Howard Robert. **Educ:** Howard Univ, BS 1951, MD 1955. **Career:** Physician (retired); Howard Univ, prof & chief div orthop surg; Johns Hopkins Hosp, assoc prof orthop surg; Howard Univ Orthop Residency Training Prog, prog dir; ABOS, dipl, 1964; ABOS, examiner, 1974-92; Am Bd Orthotics & Prosthet, examiner, 1970-76; Howard Univ, CLG Med, dean, 1988-94; Howard Univ, Health Affairs, vp, 1994-96, special asst pres Health affairs, 1996-01. **Orgs:** Am Orthop Asn; Gov Health Legisl & Vet Affairs Comt; Am Acad Orthop Surg; Kappa Alpha Psi Frat Bd Trustees; Sidwell Friends Sch Wash DC; Nat Asn Advan Colored People; bd dir Boys Club Metro Police; gov Am Col Surgeon; Ethical & Judical Coun, Am Med Asn 1982-87; ABOS. **Special Achievements:** Has contributed more than seventy publications and thirty book chapters. First African Am member of the Am Orthop Asn. **Military Serv:** USAR, capt med corps, 1956-61; active duty 1961-62; inactive reserv 1962-65. *

EPPS, CONSTANCE ARNETTRES
Dentist. **Personal:** Born Feb 8, 1950, Port Chester, NY; daughter of Robert Gooden and Geneva Colbert Gooden; married Charles Ray Epps; children: Charles R II, Menika Elyse. **Educ:** Bennett Col, BS, biol, 1971; Howard Univ Col Dent, DDS, 1979; Univ NC, Chapel Hill, MPH, 1990. **Career:** Blood Res Inst Harvard Univ, coagulation technician, 1971-72; US Govt Torrejon Air Base Madrid, teacher, 1973-74; St Elizabeth Hosp, dent officer, 1979-80; NC Dept Human Resources, pub health dentist, 1980-86; Univ NC, Chapel Hill, adj assoc prof, 1986-; Guilford Co, Dept Health , Greensboro, NC, pub health dentist, 1986-, dent dir, 1990-, clinical supvr, 2003; Perry L Jeffries Assocs, Greensboro, NC, dentist, currently. **Orgs:** Am Dent Asn; Nat Dent Asn; Acad Gen Dent, NC Dent Asn, 1979; Old N State & Guilford County Dent Asn, 1984-; treas, 1986-87, vice chmn, 1987-88, NC Pub Health Asn; High Point Orgn Polit Educ; Delta Sigma Theta; Guilford County Headstart Adv Comn; chmn dent sect, NC Pub Health Asn, 1988-; choir dir, trustee, 1988-, chmn, trustee bd, 1990-95, First United Baptist Church; dent dir, Greensboro Urban Ministry Med & Dent Clinic, 1989-95. **Honors/Awds:** Dr Raymond L Hayes Scholarship Award, Howard Univ Dent Sch, 1979; Outstanding Young Women of America, 1982; Young Dentist of the Year, NC Dental Society 3rd District Nominee, 1988; Nal Assn of County Health Officials Recognition of Achievement, Homebound Dental Prog, 1988; Outstanding Coll Students of Amer, Delta Omega, Nat Public Health Honor Soc, 1990; A Consortium of Doctors, 1991; Belle Ringer Image Award, Bennett Col, 1997. **Business Addr:** Adjunct Associate Professor, University of North Carolina School of Dentistry, Manning Dr Columbia St, Chapel Hill, NC 27599-7450, **Business Phone:** (919)966-2788.*

EPPS, DOLZIE C. B.
Educator. **Personal:** Born Jan 1, 1907, Shreveport, LA. **Educ:** Dillard Univ, 1929; Wiley Col, Marshall, TX, AB, 1945; Columbia Univ, NY, MA, 1950. **Career:** Caddo Parish Sch Syst, teacher Health & Phys Educ, 1935-73; Nat Asn Advan Colored People & La St Univ, Sch Med, bd dir, 1976-. **Orgs:** Inst Review Comn Human Exp, Shreveport, LA; bd dir, Caddo-Bossier Ct Observers, 1976-; first vpres, Family Coun & C Serv, 1976-; bd dir, Shreveport Negro C C, 1976-; bd dir, Phi Delta Kappa Sorority (Beta Alpha Chap) 1976-. **Honors/Awds:** Community Service Award, Nat Coun Negro Women, 1976; Ann Brewster Community Service, Nat Asn Advan Colored People, 1978; Vacation Bible School Award, Galilee Bapt Church, 1979; Branch Service Award, Nat Asn Advan Colored People, 1980. **Business Addr:** Board of Director, Louisiana State University School of Medicine, 1501 Kings Hwy, Shreveport, LA 71103.

EPPS, EDGAR G.
Educator. **Personal:** Born Aug 30, 1929, Little Rock, AR; son of Odelle Epps and Clifford Epps; married Marilyn Miller, Dec 18, 1958; children: Carolyn & Raymond. **Educ:** Talladega Col, BA, 1951; Atlanta Univ, MA, 1955; Wash State Univ, PhD, 1959. **Career:** Tenn State Univ, asst, assoc prof, 1958-61; Fla A&M Univ, prof, 1961-64; Univ Mich, res assoc, assoc prof, 1964-67; Tuskegee Inst, assoc dir Carver Res Found, chmn div soc sci, prof sociol, 1967-70; Harvard Univ, vis prof, 1969; Univ Chicago,

Marshall Field IV prof Urban Educ, Marshall Field IV prof emer Urban Educ, currently, Consortium Chicago Sch Res, sr res assoc, currently; Univ Wis-Milwaukee, Sch Educ, Dept Educ Policy & Community Studies, prof, currently. **Orgs:** Chicago Bd Educ, 1974-80; fac mem, Salzburg Sem Am Studies Salzburg Austria, 1975; bd dirs, Southern Educ Found, 1976-88; consult, Chicago Pub Schs; co-chair, Nat Adv Comt, currently. **Honors/Awds:** Frazier, Du Bois & Johnson Award, Am Sociol Asn; W E B Du Bois Distinguished Lecture Award, Am Educ Res Asn; Giant in Science Award, Quality Educ Minorities Math, Science & Engineering Network. **Special Achievements:** Editor: "Black Students in White Schools", 1972; "Race Relations, Current Perspectives" 1973; "Cultural Pluralism", 1974; co-author "Black Consciousness, Identity & Achievement" 1975; co-editor: College in Black and White: African-American Students in Predominantly White and in Historically Black Public Universities, State University of New York Press, 1991; Restructuring the Schools: Problems and Prospects, McCutchan Publishing Co, 1992; "Affirmative Action and Minority Access to Faculty Positions," Ohio State Law Journal, 1998; "The Black Academic: Faculty Status Among African Americans in U.S. Higher Education", 2000. **Home Addr:** 5825 S Dorchester Ave, Chicago, IL 60637, **Home Phone:** (773)643-5715. **Business Addr:** Senior Professor, University of Wisconsin-Milwaukee, Department of Educational Policy and Community Studies, 2400 E Hartford Ave Enderis Hall 549, PO Box 413, Milwaukee, WI 53201-0413, **Business Phone:** (414)229-6547.

EPPS, EVERN COOPER
Executive, vice president (organization), president (organization). **Personal:** Born in Detroit, MI. **Educ:** Mich State Univ, BA, eng & jour; Emory Univ, grad studies; Harvard Sch Bus, grad studies. **Career:** High Sch, teacher, 1970; United Parcel Serv Found, strategic planning, delivery info, training, bus develop, assoc dir, 1974-98; United Parcel Serv Found, Corp Rel, vpres, 1998-; United Parcel Serv Found, pres & vice chair, 1998-2007. **Orgs:** Nat Urban League, Black Exec Exchange Prog; adv coun, Coalition of 100 Black Women; bd mem, Atlanta Partners Educ; NW Ga Girl Scouts Coun; corp adv, United Way Am; Nat Black Arts Festival; Close-Up Found; Points Light Found; Links-Dogwood Chap; bd dir, Ctr Corp Citizenship; chair, Bd Atlanta Partners Educ. **Honors/Awds:** Woman of Acheivement, YWCA of Greater Atlanta; Ordinary Women Extraordinary Talents Awd, Women Looking Ahead News Mag, 2000; mem coun, Pres Coun Serv & Civic Participation; Atlanta Bus League Women's Hall of Fame, 2006; Donald H. McGannon Award, Nat Urban League. **Special Achievements:** listed in Ga's 100 Most Powerful & Influential Women in Corporate America; First woman and the first African American to become president of the United Parcel Service Foundation. **Business Addr:** Vice President, United Parcel Serv, 55 Glenlake Pkwy NE Bldg, Atlanta, GA 30328.*

EPPS, GEORGE ALLEN, JR.
Executive. **Personal:** Born Jul 3, 1940, Fallis, OK; son of George Allen Sr and George Ellen Doak; married Linda Edwards, May 26, 1979; children: Gregory Allen & Michael Conrad. **Educ:** Kans City Jr Col, Kans City, Kans, 1957-58; Rockhurst Col, Kans City Mo, 1968-71. **Career:** Executive (Retired); Bendix Mfg Co, electronic technician, 1962-65; Southwestern Bell, Kans City, Mo, lineman, 1965-68, facil engr, 1968-71, installation supvr, 1971-76, St Louis, Mo, plant mechanization supvr, 1976-79, dist mgr-I&M, 1979-85, dist mgr, admin serv, 1985-; Gundacker Realty, sales, 1985. **Honors/Awds:** Black Achiever in Indusry, Southern Christian Leadership Conf, 1976; Optimist of the Year, Optimist Int, 1987. **Military Serv:** USN, E3, 1958-61.

EPPS, OMAR HASHIM
Actor, movie producer. **Personal:** Born Jul 23, 1973, Brooklyn, NY; married Keisha Spivey, Jan 1, 2004; children: 2. **Career:** Wolf pak, co-founder, 1991-; Films: Juice, 1992; Daybreak, 1993; The Program, 1993; Major League II, 1994; Higher Learning, 1995; Deadly Voyage, 1996; Don't Be a Menace to South Central While You're Drinking Your Juice in the Hood, 1996; Scream 2, 1997; Blossoms and Veils, 1997;Breakfast of Champions, 1999; The Mod Squad, 1999; The Wood, 1999; In Too Deep, 1999; Love and Basketball, 2000, Brother, 2000; Dracula 2000, 2000;Absolute Zero, 2000; Perfume, 2001; Big Trouble, 2002; Against the Ropes, 2004; Alfie, 2004; A Day in the Life, 2009. TV series: "Daybreak", 1993; "Conviction", 2002; "House M.D.", 2004-09. **Honors/Awds:** Silver Nymph, Best Actor, 1997; Image Award, Outstanding Supporting Actor in a Drama Series, 2007, 2008. **Special Achievements:** Has been nominated for Black Reel Awards, Image Awards, Teen Choice Award sand MTV Movie Awards. **Business Addr:** Actor, c/o Endeavor Agency, 9701 Wilshire Blvd 10th Fl, Beverly Hills, CA 90212, **Business Phone:** (310)248-2000.*

EPPS, PHILLIP EARL
Football player, advocate. **Personal:** Born Nov 11, 1958, Atlanta, TX; married Janice; children: Rachael Renee, Phillip Jordan, Alexis Jonae & LaShaunta Nicole. **Educ:** Tex Christian Univ, BS, criminal justice. **Career:** Football player (retired), Advocate; Green Bay Packers, wide receiver, 1982-88; New York Jets, wide receiver, 1989-90; Scott D Moore Juv Justice Ctr, juv probation officer, currently. **Honors/Awds:** Rookie of the Year, 1982. **Business Addr:** Juvenile Probation Officer, Scott D Moore Juvenile Justice Center, 2701 Kimbo Rd, Fort Worth, TX 76111-3099, **Business Phone:** (817)838-4600.

EPPS, DR. ROSELYN PAYNE
Pediatrician, physician. **Personal:** Born in Little Rock, AR; daughter of Mattie Beverly and Dr William Kenneth Payne Sr; married Dr Charles H Epps Jr; children: Charles H III (deceased), Kenneth C, Roselyn E & Howard R. **Educ:** Howard Univ, BS, 1951, MD, 1955; Johns Hopkins Univ, MPH, 1973; Am Univ, MA, 1981. **Career:** Sickle Cell Res, pvt pract, 1960-61; DC Govt, med officer, dir ment retardation clinic, c&y proj, infant & presch, maternal & child health, clin prog, actg comnr pub health, 1961-80; Howard Univ, Col Med, prof pediat & dir child devel ctr, 1981-88, prof emer, currently, Womens Health Inst, sr prog adv, currently; Nat Inst Health, expert, 1989-97, med off, 1997-98; Girls Inc, pres, 1990-92; med & pub health consult, pvt pract, pediat, 1998-. **Orgs:** Consult, US Dept Health & Human Serv, 1965-; bd dirs, Wash Performing Arts, 1971-; consult, PSI Inc Govt Liberia, 1984; consult, UN Fund Pop Activ, 1984; pres bd dir, Hosp Sick C, 1986-89; pres, DC Chap, Am Acad Pediat, 1988-91; pres, Am Med Women's Asn, 1991; Med Soc DC, 1992. **Honors/Awds:** Distinguished Public Service Award, Dist Columbia Govt, 1981; Recognition Resolution & Day Council District Columbia, 1983; DC Women's Hall Fame, DC Comn Women, 1990; Community Service Award, DC Am Med Women's Asn, 1990; Community Service Award, DC Hosp Asn, 1990; Elizabeth Blackwell Award, Am Med Women's Asn, 1992. **Special Achievements:** The Coun of the DC declared February 14 1981 Dr Roselyn Payne Epps Day in Wash DC. **Business Addr:** Professor Emerita, Howard University, 2400 6th St, Washington, DC 20012-1014, **Business Phone:** (202)806-6100.

EPTING, MARION
Artist, educator. **Personal:** Born in Forrest, MS. **Educ:** Los Angeles City Col, assoc arts, 1965; Otis Art Inst LA Co, MFA, 1969. **Career:** Otis Art Inst, rep permanent collections; Univ Calif, fac; San Jose State Col, fac; Denison Univ, fac; Seattle Art Mus, fac; pvt collections Bernie Casey, Dorothy Chandler, Claude Booker, Ruth Stoehr, James Bates; Calif State Univ, Chicago, Otis Art Inst, prof, prof emer, currently. **Honors/Awds:** Recipient Numerous Awards. **Military Serv:** USN. **Business Addr:** Professor Emeritus, California State University, Otis Art Institute, Kendall Hall 114 400 W First St, Chico, CA 95926, **Business Phone:** (530)898-5504.

ERICSSON, DR. APRILLE JOY
Educator, engineer. **Personal:** Born Apr 1, 1963, Brooklyn, NY; daughter of Henry and Corrinne; married Mark Jackson, Oct 11, 1992 (divorced 2001). **Educ:** City Col NY, 1984; Mich Inst Technol, BS, 1986; Howard Univ, ME, 1990, PhD, mech eng aerospace option, 1995. **Career:** Howard Univ, grad researcher, 1990-95; NASA Goddard Space Flight Ctr, altitude control systems analyst, 1992-2001, & aerospace engr, 1992-; Bowie St Univ, adj prof, math, 1997-99; Howard Univ, adj prof, mech eng, 1999; NASA HQ, prog mgr & prog exec, 2001-. **Orgs:** Am Inst Aeronautics Astronautics, 1985-; Nat Soc Black Engineers, alumni mem, 1986-; Am Astronaut Soc, 1995; Women Aerospace, 1996, 2002; pres Goddard Chapter, Nat Tech asn, 1998-; Blacks Govt, 2000; Howard Univ, GSAS, Responsive PhD Initiative Task Force, 2000-02. **Honors/Awds:** Women in Science & Engineering, Top Female Engineer in Fed Govt, 1997; NASA Goddard Honor Award for Excellence in Outreach, 1998; Center of Excellence Award for the TRMM Project, 1998; Customer Service Excellence Award for MAP Flight Software, 1999; Federal Career Award, The Federal Exec Bd Excellence Md, 1999; Giant in Science Award, The Quality Edu Minorities Network, 2000; Medgar Evers Col, Honorary Doctor Sci, 2001; Innovator in Internet Technology, Marketing, Opportunities in Business & Entertainment Conference, 2001; honorary Doctor of Science, Medgar Evers Col, Brooklyn, 2001; HU Col of Engineering, Architecture, & Computer Science Alumni Excellence Award, 2002; NASA Exceptional Achievement Award, 2002; Topp's Africa-Centered Award, Bowie State Univ; Centurion of Technology Award, Women Color Techno Awards Conference. **Special Achievements:** NASA representative to the White House; Top 50 minority women in Scienceand Engineering, National Technical Association; First (African American) female to receive a Ph.D. in Mechanical Engineering from HU; first African American female to receive a Ph.D. in Engineering at NASA GSFC. **Business Addr:** Aerospace Engineer, NASA, Goddard Space Flight Center, 300 E St NW Room 5P50, Washington, DC 20059, **Business Phone:** (202)358-0832.

ERVIN, DEBORAH GREEN
School administrator. **Personal:** Born Apr 4, 1956, Greenville, SC; daughter of David Green Jr and Annie V Williams-Green; married Larry Don (divorced); children: Sean Deon & Elanda Deliece. **Educ:** Berea Col, BA, 1977; Clemson Univ, MEd, 1986. **Career:** Clemson Child Develop Ctr, head teacher, 1978-81; Clemson Univ, admis counr, 1981-86, asst dir admis, 1986; Winthrop Univ, asst dir admis, 1987-92, assoc dir admis, 1992-. **Orgs:** Secy, 1989-90, vpres, 1991-93, Carolina's Asn Col Registr & Admis Officers; Southern Asn Col Admis Officers; Home Econs Adv Comn D W Daniel High Sch; Clemson Univ, Day Care Comn, Col Educ Fac Selection Comt; Cent City Optimists, 1990-. **Business Addr:** Associate Director, Winthrop University, 505 Eden Terr, Rock Hill, SC 29733, **Business Phone:** (803)323-2191.

ERVIN, KATHRYN
Executive, educator. **Career:** Cal State Univ, San Bernardino, Theatre Arts Dept, consult & chmn, currently. **Orgs:** Numerous theatre orgn including, Black Theatre Network; Int Asn Theatre C & Young People. **Special Achievements:** Auth & Ed: African American Scenebook. **Business Addr:** Chair, California State University, Theatre Arts Department, 5500 Univ Pkwy, San Bernardino, CA 92407, **Business Phone:** (909)880-5876.

ERVING, JOHN
Publisher, business owner. **Personal:** Born Jan 28, 1949, Philadelphia, PA; son of John and Juanita; married Margaret, Jun 8, 1991; children: Rena, Saeed, Brandon & Deborah. **Educ:** Temple Univ, bus law, 1979. **Career:** Wal-Mart Stores, part time staff; Am Greeting Corp, sales mgr, 1982-84; Kraft Food Serv, territory mgr, 1984-96; JonMar Creations Inc, pres, 1996-. **Orgs:** Cofounder, Asn Black Bus Students, 1973-; lifetime mem, NAACP, 1990-; Greeting Card Asn. **Military Serv:** USAF. **Business Addr:** President, JonMar Creations Inc, PO Box 702, Lawnside, NJ 08045.

ERVING, JULIUS WINFIELD
Basketball player, basketball executive, businessperson. **Personal:** Born Feb 22, 1950, Roosevelt, NY; son of Julius and Callie Mae Lindsay; married Turquoise, Jan 1, 1972 (divorced 2003); children: Cheo, Julius III, Jazmin & Cory; children: Alexandra Stevenson. **Educ:** Univ Mass, attended 1972. **Career:** Virginia Squires, 1971-73, New York Nets, 1973-76, Philadelphia 76ers, 1976-87; Film: The Fish That Saved Pittsburgh, actor, 1979; DJ Enterprises, dir; Orlando Magic, exec v pres; RDV Sports, v pres; The Erving Group Inc, pres, currently; Saks Inc, bd dirs; Williams Commun, bd dirs; Converse Inc, bd dirs; Darden Restaurants, Inc, bd dirs; The Sports Authority, bd dirs; Gold Stars Speakers Bureau, speaker, currently. **Orgs:** Trustee, Clark Atlanta Univ; bd dirs, Meridian Bancorp. **Honors/Awds:** Rookie of the Yr 1972; Lupus Found Award; NBA All Star Game 1977-80; MVP American Basketball Assn, 3 times, NBA 1980-81; J. Walter Kennedy Citizenship Award, 1983; Father Flanagan Award; scored 25,000 career point & became the 9th player in NBA-ABA history to do so, 1983; twice winner of Sea grams Seven Crown of Sports Award as the most productive player in the NBA; NBA Hall of Fame, 1993; One of 50 Greatest Players in NBA History, 1996; Special Achievement in Sports Trumpet Award, 2003; Horatio Alger Award. **Special Achievements:** One of the games' first players to have a shoe marketed under his name. **Home Addr:** PO Box 25040 SW Sta, Philadelphia, PA 19147. **Business Addr:** Speaker, Gold Stars Speakers Bureau, 7478 N La Cholla Blvd, Tucson, AZ 85741, **Business Phone:** (520)742-4384.

ESCO, FRED, JR.
Government official, insurance executive, mayor. **Personal:** Born Sep 13, 1954, Canton, MS; son of Fred Lee and Ida M Hudson; married Fleta Marie Jones, Aug 7, 1982; children: Tamaria, Amaya, Freda, Kristie & Ariel. **Educ:** Miss Valley State Univ, BA, bus admin, accounting, 1978; MS Baptist Seminary, Christianity. **Career:** Esco's Insurance co, owner & pres; City of Canton, alderman, 1979-97; City of Canton, mayor, 2002-. **Orgs:** Thirty Two Degree Mason Prince Hall Affiliation, 1979-85; Elk Club of Canton,1979-85; Nat Bus League, 1979-85; Mason; Elks; vpres NAACP Canton,1983-84; secretary & treasurer, Optimist Club Canton, 1984-85; Boys &Girls Club; Hispanic Outreach of Canton, Mt. Zion Missionary BaptistChurch. **Business Addr:** Mayor, City of Canton, 226 E Peace St, PO Box 1605, Canton, MS 39046, **Business Phone:** (601)859-4331.*

ESEONU, DR. DOROTHY N.
Educator. **Personal:** Born Sep 23, 1955, Obowo Imo, Nigeria; daughter of Benson and Iheomagwu Ogbonna; married Dr Maxwell, Jul 25, 1981; children: Ihuoma, Chijioke, Chikezie & Amarachi. **Educ:** E Strouds burg State Col, BS, 1977; Howard Univ, MS, 1981; Va Common wealth Univ, PhD, 1989. **Career:** Va State Univ, asst prof, 1990-93; J Sargent Reynolds Community Col, adj prof, 1990-93; Va Union Univ, chem prog coordr, assoc prof chem, 1993-; chairing the Section, 2006; Va State Univ, adj prof, currently. **Orgs:** Bd mem, Advocates Inter cultural Richmond, 1994-96; pres, IBO Women's Cultural Asn, 1996-99; chair, Am Chem Soc-Va Sect, Minority Affairs, 1999-; vchair, Va Sect Exec Comt, secy, treas, co-chair. **Honors/Awds:** Certificate of Recognition, Dept Minority Affairs, Am Chem Soc, 1998-99. **Home Addr:** 14002 Bridgetown Circle, Chester, VA 23831, **Home Phone:** (804)768-0784. **Business Addr:** Associate Professor, Virginia Union University, Department Natural Science & Mathematics, Rm 322 Ellison Hall 1500 N Lombardy St, Richmond, VA 23220, **Business Phone:** (804)257-5615.

ESKRIDGE, REV. JOHN CLARENCE
School administrator, educator. **Personal:** Born Jun 6, 1943, Pittsburgh, PA; son of John William and Constance Mary Rideout; children: Aziza & Mark. **Educ:** Duquesne Univ Pittsburgh, BA, 1966, MA, 1971; Pacific Southern Univ Calif, PhD, philos, 1978. **Career:** Community Col Allegheny County, philos fac, 1969;

Pittsburgh Child Guidance Clin, prog dir, creative recreational arts prog, 1969-70; Community Col Allegheny County Campus, dir black studies, 1969-71, Colspeakers bur, 1978-88; "Le Sacre Corps" Dance Co, artistic dir, 1969-79; First Baptist Church Pittsburgh, bd deacons, 1970-73; Carlow Col, dir,1973-74; Community Col, prof philos, 1978-; Hot Lix Concert Jazz Band, leader/producer, 1978-89; Pittsburgh High Sch Creative & Performing Arts, adv bd, 1979-90; Community Col Allegheny County, Dept Lang & Philos, chmn,1983-; Orpheo Concert Latin Band, leader/producer, 1989-. **Orgs:** Pittsburgh Musicians Soc, 1967-; Soc Phenomenology & Existential Philos,1967-80; Am Philos Asn, 1969-80; founding chmn, Hermeneutic Circle, 1977-80; bd dirs, Inst Collective Behav & Memory, 1980-87; vpres, African Am Fedn Am, 1983-89. **Honors/Awds:** NDEA study fel Duquesne Univ, 1967-70; Fac Spl Serv Award, Community Col Allegheny Co Stud Union, 1978; Col Blue Ribbon Fac Award, Comn Col Allegheny County, 1981-82. **Business Addr:** Chairman, Professor, Community College of Allegheny County, Deparment Phil & Foreign Lang, 808 Ridge Ave, Pittsburgh, PA 15212.

ESOGBUE, AUGUSTINE O.
Educator, engineer. **Personal:** Born Dec 25, 1940, Kaduna, Nigeria. **Educ:** Univ Calif LA, BS, elec eng, 1964; Columbia Univ, MS, indust eng & oper res,1965; Univ So CA LA, PhD, systs eng & oper res, 1968. **Career:** Com Minority Career Advs; Indust & Systs Eng, Sch Health Systs, GA Inst Tech Atlanta, prof; Morehouse Col Atlanta, adj prof community med; Atlanta Univ GA, adjuct prof math sci; Opers Res & Mem Syst Res Ctr, Case Western Res Univ Cleveland, asst prof, 1968-72; engr & Med, Univ Southern CA, res assoc, 1965-68; Water Resources Res Ctr, Univ CA Los Angeles, develop engr, 1966-67; Univ Assoc Inc & Environ Dynamics, consult, 1968-72; Ga Inst Tech, chmn, 1975, Sch Indust & Systs Eng, assoc prof, 1972-77, prof, 1977-. **Orgs:** Environ Adv Group; exec comt, Atlanta Regional Comt, 1974-89; comr & vicechair, Atlanta Sister Cities Comn, 1975; Atlanta-Lagos Sister Cities Comn, chair, 1975-; New Cities Development comn, chair; Atlanta Sister Cities comn, 1993-; Leadership Atlanta, Atlanta Leadership Develop Corp, (Class1979); bd mem, United Way's External Funding Admiss comn, 1987-89; chmn, Coalition 100 BLK Youth, Atlanta Chap, 1990-96; 100 BLK Men AME, Atlanta Chap, 1990-; co-chair, Retention & Academic Excellence, Project Success; Col 100 Mentorship Prog, chair; bd dir, Nigerian- Am, 1993-98; chair, bd dirs, Am Nigerian int Comn, 1998-; adv bd, Task Force GANGS, City Atlanta, 1993-; USA-AFRICA int comn on Manufacturing Tech, adv bd, 1996-; US Summiton Africa, steering comn, 1998-99; S Eastern Deleg US Nat Summit Africa, Wash DC, 1998-2000; coord, Worldwide Network Nigerian Prof & Intellectual, BrainDrain-Brain Gain, Inc, 1999-; Nigerians Diaspora Orgs Ams, bdtrustees, 2001-; GA Coun int Visitors, bd trustees, 2003-. **Honors/Awds:** Distinguished Faculty Adv Award, Univ CA, Berkley, 1988; Outstanding & Dedicated Service Award, Office MNY educ, GA Inst Technol, 1989; GA EngrFound, and the Col of Engr, GA IST Technol, 1991; Faculty Advanced Appreciation Award, outstanding Sr Design Project, 1991; (First Winner for ISYE); Most Outstanding Advisory Award; Recognition of Outstanding Contributions to the Nat Society of Black Engineers; Nat Conv Houston, TX,1993; Distinguished Serv Leadership Award, Operations Research SocietyAME, HTH Applications Technical Section, 1993; Certificate of Appreciation for Outstanding Serv on the Board, Operations Research Society of AME, Technical Applications Section, 1993; Certificate of Appreciation for Dedication & Service to the City of Atlanta, Mayor Bill Campbell, 1995;Upward Thrust Award, GA Inst Technology, 1996; Mentor of the Decade Award, Off educ, GA Inst of Technology, 1996; Certificate of Recognition forLoyal & Meritorious Serv, Bd Comnr, The Gov Fulton County, GA, 1996; Certificate of Appreciation on Behalf of the People of Atlanta for Outstanding Contributions and Commitment to Atlanta Sister Cities Commission, Mayor Bill Campbell, 1997; Golden Torch Award, Lifetime Achievement in education, Nat Soc of Black Engr, 1999; Andrew P Sage Bes tTransactions Paper of the Year Award, Institute of Electrical & Electronics Engineers-SMC, 1999; Distinguished Service Award in Int Cooperation, US Partnerships and USAID for Facilitating the Energy Partnerships Between the GA Power Co & the Nat Electric Power Authority of Nigeria, 2001; NASA Public Service Medal, 2006. **Special Achievements:** Co-author, Mathematical Aspects of Scheduling and Applications, Decision Criteria and Optimal Inventory Management. **Business Addr:** Professor, Georgia Institute of Technology, Groseclose 0205 Room 442, 765 Ferst Dr NW, Atlanta, GA 30332, **Business Phone:** (404)894-2323.

ESPOSITO, GIANCARLO
Actor. **Personal:** Born Apr 26, 1958, Copenhagen, Denmark; children: 4. **Career:** Television experience includes: Go Tell It on the Mountain; The Exchange Student; Finnegan Begin Again; Miami Vice, 1985; Rock a bye, 1986; Spenser: For Hire, 1987; Relentless: Mind of a Killer, 1993; Bakers field PD, 1993;The Tomorrow Man, 1993; Homicide: Life on the Street, 1998-99; The Street, 2000; Girls Club, 2002; theater experience includes: Maggie Flynn; Miss Moffet, 1974; The Me Nobody Knows; See saw; Zooman and the Sign, 1980; Keyboard, 1982; Do Lord Remember Me, 1984; Balm in Gilead, 1984; Don't Get God Started, 1987; One for Dexter, 1991; Distant Fires, 1992; films include: Trading Places, 1983; Cotton Club, 1984; Sweet Lorraine, 1987; School Daze, 1988; Do the Right Thing, 1989; Mo' Better Blues, 1990; Night on Earth, 1992; Bob Roberts, 1992; Amos and Andrew, 1993; Fresh, 1994; Benders, 1994; The Usual Suspects, 1995; Smoke, 1995; Reckless, 1995; The Keeper, 1995; Blue in the Face, 1995; Waiting to Exhale, 1995; Loose Women, 1996; California, 1996; Trouble on the Corner, 1997; The People, 1997; The Maze, 1997; Twilight, 1998; Phoenix, 1998; Lulu on the Bridge, 1998; Stardust, 1998; Where's Marlowe?, 1999; Big City Blues, 1999; Speak Truth to Power, 2000; Josephine, 2001; Monkey bone, 2001; Pinero, 2001; Ali, 2001; Blind Horizon, 2003; Ash Tuesday, 2003. **Orgs:** Screen Actors Guild. **Honors/Awds:** OBIE Award, for Zooman and the Sign, 1981; Theatre World Award, for Zooman and the Sign, 1981; Obie award for Distant Fires, 1993. **Home Addr:** c/o 40 Acres & A Mule Filmworks Inc, 124 Dekalb Ave, Brooklyn, NY 11217, **Home Phone:** (718)624-3703. *

ESPREE, ALLEN JAMES
College administrator, educator. **Personal:** Born May 4, 1941, Lake Charles, LA; married Clara G; children: Glenn Aldric, Gary Allen & Bernice Jeanine. **Educ:** Univ Nebr, BS, 1970; Command & Gen Staff Col, Master Military Sci, 1979; Univ MO, MPA, 1980. **Career:** RCPAC Enlisted Personnel Directorate, dep dir, 1980-83; A&C Carpet Co, Consult, 1984-85; Bishop Col, prof mil sci; La Tech Col, assoc dean, 2004-. **Orgs:** Supern Sunday Sch; Faith Comt Lutheran Church, 1984-85; Mil Affairs Comt; Dallas Chamber Com, 1984-85; policy Coun, Dallas Head Start Prog, 1985. **Military Serv:** AUS lt col, 23 yrs; Bronze Star; Purple Heart; Army Commendation; Vietnam Serv CIB. **Business Addr:** Campus Dean, Louisiana Technical College, TH Harris Campus 332 E South St, Opelousas, TX 70570-6114, **Business Phone:** (337)948-0239.

ESPY, BEN E.
State government official, u.s. attorney. **Educ:** Ohio State Univ, BA, polit sci, 1956; Howard Univ Law Sch, JD, 1968. **Career:** Allegheny Airlines, corp atty, 1968; State Atty Gen Off, Dep Chief Civil Rights Div, 1972-74, Div Criminal Activities, 1974; Pvt pract, atty, 1977-; Columbus City Coun, pres, 1982-92; Ohio state, sen, 1991-94, from asst minority leader to minority leader, 1994-00. **Orgs:** Columbus Bar Asn; Ohio Bar Asn; Am Bar Asn; Sigma Delta Tau Legal Fraternity; Cath Diocese Found Adv Bd; Kappa Alpha Psi Fraternity; co-founder, Urban Christian Leadership Asn; founder, Columbus Youth Corps; vpres Bd Dir, Ohio State Univ Alumni Asn, 2001. **Honors/Awds:** Ohio Dem Party Meryl Shoemaker Award; Legislator of the Year, Ohio Hunger Task Force; Legislator of the Year, Franklin County Trial Lawyers Association; Neighborhood House Volunteer Service Award; the Outstanding Community Leader Award, McDonald?s Restaurant; Distinguished Service Award, Ohio State University, 2001. **Special Achievements:** Founder of Columbus Youth Corps a summer employment and job readiness program for inner city youth. This program was designated a "Point of Light" by President George Bush in 1991; Espy created "The Job Show," a cable TV prog produced by the City Columbus, which helps people find jobs. He established the annual City of Columbus-Martin Luther King, Jr. Holiday Celebration. **Military Serv:** USAF, asst staff judge advocate, 1969-1972. *

ESPY, HENRY
Mayor, president (organization). **Career:** Clarksdale, MS, mayor, 1990-. **Orgs:** Pres, Nat Conf Black Mayors. **Business Addr:** Mayor, City of Clarksdale, 125 Hwy 322, Clarksdale, MS 38614, **Business Phone:** (662)624-2976.*

ESPY, MICHAEL
Lawyer, government official. **Personal:** Born Nov 30, 1953, Yazoo City, MS; son of Thomas J Huddleston Jr; married Sheila Bell (divorced); children: 2. **Educ:** Howard Univ, BA, 1975; Univ Santa Clara Law Sch, JD, 1978. **Career:** Law Practice Yazoo City, atty; Cent MS Legal Servs, mgr; State Secy Off, dir pub lands & elections div, 1980-84; State Atty Gen Off, chief consumer protection div, 1984-85; US House Reps, staff mem, 1986-93; US Dept Agr, secy, 1993-94; Dept Energy, sr adv; Butler, Snow, O'Mara, Stevens & Cannada, PLLC, lawyer, currently; Mike Espy, PLLC, owner & lawyer, currently. **Orgs:** Farm Found. **Special Achievements:** First African-American secretary of agriculture, 1993-94. **Business Addr:** Owner, Lawyer, Mike Espy PLLC, 317 E Capitol St Suite 101, PO Box 24205, Jackson, MS 39201, **Business Phone:** (601)355-9101.

ESQUERRE, JEAN ROLAND
Consultant, airline executive. **Personal:** Born Dec 28, 1923, Yonkers, NY; son of Jean B and Marie Bates; married Maria Elisabet Edman; children: Johanna Maria & Malin Elisabet. **Educ:** Col City NY, attended; NYU, attended; Republic Aviation Corps Staff Engr Sch, attended; Gruman Aerospace Corp, Training & Devel Ctr; Empire State Col SUNY, attended. **Career:** Airline executive, consultant (Retired); Specialty Assembling & Packing Co, draftsman, 1949-52; New York Transit Authority, mechanical engr draftsman, 1952-53; Repub Aviation Corp, prin designer, 1953-63; Lunar Modular, engineering supvr, test dir, cognizant engr, 1963-69; Grumman Aerospace Corp, engineering supvr & test dir, 1973-79, asst corp pres, 1979-87. **Orgs:** CCNY Boxing Alumni Club, 1948; ETA Chap Alpha Phi Alpha Frat, 1949-, pres 1951; CCNY Varsity Club, 1952; secy, LI Br NY Karate Asn, 1961-; Huntington Township Comn Human Rels, 1961-; Huntington Freedom Ctr, 1963-; chmn, Labor & Ind Comn, 1970; N Atlantic Karate Asn, 1976; pres, Planned United Devel Task Force Huntington; pres & instr, Grumman Martial Arts Club; Huntington Br Nat Asn Advan Colored Peopel; chmn, Sub-Comt feasibility Minority Enterprise Small Bus Invest Corp; vice chmn, Nathan Hall Dist BSA; pres, Urban League Long Island; bd dir, Grumman Aerospace Corps, Grumman Ecosystem Corp; bd dir, YMCA; Family Serv Asn; Girl Scouts Suffolk Co; pres, Citizens Adv Comn Capital But Huntington, former mem; former mem, Planned United Develop Task Force Huntington; Huntington C l C Human Develop Comn; Soc Automotive Engrs. **Special Achievements:** First African American elected to the Board of Directors of the Grumman Aerospace Company in 1973. **Military Serv:** USAF, sgt, WW II.

ESSIEN, DR. FRANCINE
Educator, administrator. **Personal:** Born in Philadelphia, PA. **Educ:** Temple Univ, BA, biol; Yeshiva Univ, Albert Einstein Col Med, PhD, genetics; Univ Conn. **Career:** Rutgers Univ, Off Minority Undergrad Sci Progs, dir, 1988, dir emer, currently, Dept Biol Sci, biol prof, Off Diversity & Acad Success Sci, dir emer, currently. **Orgs:** NIH Black Scientists Asn. **Honors/Awds:** US Professor of the Year, Carnegie Found Advan Teaching, 1994-95; CASE's Nat Professor of the Year award, 2006. **Special Achievements:** First African-American to receive the 14-year old award of US Prof of the Year. **Business Addr:** Director Emeritus, Rutgers University, Office for Diversity and Academic Success in the Sciences, Nelson Lab, Rm A 201 604 Allison Rd, Piscataway, NJ 08854, **Business Phone:** (732)445-6878.

ESSIET, DR. EVALEEN JOHNSON
Educator, nurse. **Personal:** Born Jun 21, 1933, Roxboro, NC; children: Aja & Bodie. **Educ:** Monte fiore Hosp Sch Nurs, Dipl, 1955; Univ Pgh, BS, nursing, 1965, MSW,1971, PhD Higher Educ, 1983. **Career:** George Wash Univ Hosp, Wash, DC, staff nurse psychol, 1955-58; Allegheny County Health Dept, supvr pub health nurses, 1958-63; Mone fine Hosp Sch Nursing, nursing fac, 1963-66; Home wd Bruston Ctr, St Francis Hosp CMHC,dir, 1968-69; Clinic Hempsted Hosp CMHC, dir out-patient, 1971-73;Community Col, Allegheny County, prof nursing, 1973-. **Orgs:** Pres, coun, E Johnson Essiet Corp, 1983-84; elder, Presby Church USA,1985-; pub chair, Chi Sta Phi Nursing Sorority, 1981-85. **Honors/Awds:** Inter pation of Nursing, 1983; Nat Study Pub, 1983; International Book of Honour, 1983. **Special Achievements:** Book: "Rev of Nursing for NLN", 1980; "The integrated curriculum in accredited baccalaureate nursing programs in the United States", 1983;Poems publ, Am Poetry Asn, 1981-84. **Military Serv:** USAFR, capt, 1962-68; Flight Nrs Wings, Sch Aerospace Med, 1963. **Home Addr:** 827 Bell Ave, Braddock, PA 15104. **Business Addr:** Professor of Nursing, Community College AC, 1850 Old Chairton Rd Rte 885, West Mifflin, PA 15122.

ESSOKA, GLORIA CORZEN
College teacher, nurse. **Personal:** Born May 25, 1938, Philadelphia, PA; daughter of William B and Thelma S; married Modi, Sep 11, 1965; children: Jonathan Dumbe & Ndome Lynette. **Educ:** Jefferson Hosp Sch Nursing, dipl, 1959; Univ Pa, BSN, 1962; Univ Pa, MSN, 1964; NY Univ, PhD, nursing, 1981; Hunter Col, post masters practr paediatric nurse cert prog, 1996. **Career:** Va State Col, instr, 1964-65; Hunter Col, instr, 1971-73; Seton Hall Univ, assoc prof, 1973-82, distinguished vis prof, Chair, currently; Hunter Col, assoc prof, 1982-; Univ Malawi, vis prof, 1991-93; certified paediat nurse practr, 1997. **Orgs:** Univ Pa Alumnae Asn, 1962-; Sigma Theta Tau, 1967-; Am Nurses Asn, 1973-; NY Univ Alumnae Asn, 1981-; Nat League Nursing, 1982-; St Mary's Hosp, bd trustees, 1981-89; Asn Black Nursing Fac Higher Educ, 1988-; Thomas Jefferson Univ Alumnae Asn, 1993; NCP, 1997; NONPF, 1997. **Honors/Awds:** Sigma Theta Tau, Research Grant, 1980; Young Publisher's Award, Asn Black Nursing Fac Higher Educ, 1990; Research Award, Concerned Black Nurses, Newark, 1991; Patient Care Award, 2008. **Special Achievements:** Author: "Homeless Families," 1990; "Disorders of Pregnancy", 1990; "Family Planning and Contraception," 1990; "Nursing Care of the Infant and Neonate", 1991; author: "Children's Ideas of Health", 1998; "Pain Perceptions of Korean-American & Euro-American Women". **Military Serv:** USY, Res, Army Nurse Corps, major, 1983-93. **Business Addr:** Chairman, Family Health Nursing, Seton Hall University, Schwartz Bldg Room 236, South Orange, NJ 07079, **Business Phone:** (973)761-9742.

ESTES, ELAINE ROSE GRAHAM
Librarian. **Personal:** Born Nov 24, 1931, Springfield, MO; daughter of James McKinley Graham and Zelma Mae Smith Graham; married John M Jr, Dec 29, 1953. **Educ:** Drake Univ, BS, 1953, Teaching Cert, 1956; Univ Ill, MS, 1960. **Career:** Librarian (retired); Pub Libr Des Moines, dir libr system, 1956-95. **Orgs:** Past pres, Iowa Libr Asn; past pres, Des Moines Metro Libr Asn; Am Libr Asn; past bd mem, Iowa Soc Preserv Hist Landmarks; past bd trustees, Des Moines Art Ctr; past bd mem, Des Moines Community Playhouse; past adv coun, Dept Adult Ed; past bd adv, Nat Trust Hist Preserv; past mem, Mayors Sister City Comn; past bd mem, Des Moines Civic Ctr; Polk City Hist Soc; past state vpres, The Questers; past pres, Terrace Hill Soc, Gov Comn

Restoration Gov Mansion; past pres, charter mem, DM Chap Links Inc; past basilius Sorority Beta Phi Mu Hon Libr Scholastic Soc; past chap City Des Moines Hist Dist Comn; Rotary 1987-; Nat Comn Future Dr Unake Univ, Task Force on Libraries & Learning Resources, 1987-88; pres, Willson Alexander Scott, Chap Questers, 1988-98; past bd, Wallace House Found, 1989-95; pres, IUPLA, 1991; Des Moines Sesquicentennial Comn, chair, hist comn, 1992-94; State Iowa Questers, vpres, 1999-; pres, 2001-03, Proteus, Iowa Antique Asn, 2000-02; Drake Univ Nat Adv Comn Cowles Libr; Iowa Governor's Centennial Found; chair, Tour Comn Int Quester Convention, 1999; Terrace Hill Comn, 2001-; Salisbury House Acquisition Comn; Drake Univ, 50-year Alumni Comn, 2003. **Honors/Awds:** Des Moines Leadership Award, 1975; Distinguished Alumni Award, Drake Univ, 1979; Outstanding Contribution to the Quality of the Built Environment, Des Moines Architects Coun Community Reward, 1981; Award of Merit for Historical Preservation, Iowa State Hist Soc, 1984; Women of Achievement Award, YWCA 1989; Historic Preservation Award, City Des Moines, 1993; Connect Foundation Achievement Award, 1995; Certificate of Appreciation, Midcity Vision Coalition, 1998; Friend of Literacy Award, Pub Libr Des Moines Found, 2003.

ESTES, JOHN M., JR.
Funeral director. **Personal:** Born Dec 6, 1928, Joplin, MO; married Elaine Graham. **Educ:** Univ Iowa, 1948; Drake Community Col, 1950, 1951, 1953; Kans City Col Mortuary Sci, 1952; Chicago Resorative Art, Post Grad Work, 1952. **Career:** Funeral director (retired); John Estes & Son Funeral Home, pres & owner, 1952-97. **Orgs:** Bd mem, BSA; Kappa Alpha Psi; Nat Asn Advan Colored People; March of Dimes; Des Moines Sch Bd; United Community Serv; Greater Des Moines United Way; Community Action Coun; Greater Opportunity Bd Chamber Com; Greater United Way; Community Survey Inc; Simpson Col Trustee; Des Moines Pub Housing Authority; Wilkie House Inc; Des Moines Symphony; Tiny Tots Inc; Iowa Civil Liberties. **Honors/Awds:** Black Athlete Award, 25 yrs; Des Moines Human Rights Comn Recognition; 3 Awards, March of Dimes; Univ Iowa Alumni Award; Iowa Employ Security Commission Award; Des Moines Adult Education Council Award; Polk City Rep Party Award; KSO Great City Award; Des Moines Pub Sch Award; Little All Am League Award; Nat Black Merit Academy Award; Nat Coun Christians & Jews Award. *

ESTES, SIMON LAMONT
Opera singer. **Personal:** Born Feb 2, 1938, Centerville, IA; son of Simon and Ruth Jeter; married Yvonne Baer (divorced); children: Jennifer, Lynn & Tiffany; married Ovida Stong. **Educ:** Univ Iowa; Juilliard Sch Music. **Career:** L-Beck Opera Co, singer; Hamburg Opera Co, singer; opera singer & bass baritone; Juilliard Sch Music, prof; Wartburg Col, distinguished prof & artist-in-residence, 2002-. **Orgs:** Old Gold Singers, Univ Iowa; Am Opera Soc; Simon Estes Int Fund Children; Simon Estes Educ Fund; Simon & Westella Estes Educ Fund. **Honors/Awds:** Numerous awards & honors including First prize, Int Tchaikovsky Vocal Competition, Moscow; grant, Martha Bard Rockefeller Found; Tchaikovsky Medal, 1985; honoree, Fine Arts Award, career achievements; acclaimed appearance, Porgy, Metropolitan Opera's first prod Porgy & Bess; Honorary doctorates from Siena Col, Drake Univ, Univ Tulsa, Luther Col; Honorary Colonel, Iowa Nat Guard; Distinguished Alumni Award, Univ Iowa Alumni Asn; The Simon Estes Music High School and choir, near Cape Town, South Africa, stress musical pursuits and are named in his honor. **Special Achievements:** First black member of the Old Gold Singers, became the first male African-American to sing a major role on the stage at Bayreuth, San Francisco Opera, San Sebastian Festival, Spain, performed all four of the Hoffman roles in Offenbach's Tales of Hoffman, Macbeth's Banquo, The Magic Flute, The Marriage of Figaro. **Business Addr:** Distinguished Professor, Artist-in-Residence, Wartburg College, 100 Wartburg Blvd, Waverly, IA 50677, **Business Phone:** 800-772-2085.*

ESTES-SUMPTER, SIDMEL KAREN
Executive. **Personal:** Born Nov 27, 1954, Marysville, CA; daughter of Emellen Mitchell and Sidney Harrison; married B Garnett, Aug 27, 1983; children: Joshua Khalid & Sidney Rashid. **Educ:** Northwestern Univ, BSJ, 1976, MSJ, 1977. **Career:** Chicago Daily Defender, reporter, 1974; Chicago Daily News, desk asst, 1975; Gram Cable TV, reporter & anchor, 1977-79; WAGA-TV, FOX 5 News, news producer, planning mgr, asst ed, exec producer, currently. **Orgs:** Pres youth coun, Atlanta Chap NAACP, 1970-72; pres, Atlanta Asn Black Journalists, 1985-87; comn mem, Leadership Atlanta, 1988-; bd mem, Atlanta Exchange, 1987-89; Ben Hill United Methodist Ch, sect leader, 1989-91; bd mem, Soc Prof Journalists, 1991; bd vis, Northwestern Univ, 1998-; immediate past pres, 1991-93, pres, 1993-95, regional dir, 1987-91, Nat Asn Black Journalists. **Honors/Awds:** Excellence in Community Science in Television Award, AABJ, 1983; Chair Award, Atlanta Asn Black Journalists, 1985; Producer of the Year, Am Women Radio & TV, 1986; Media Woman of the Year, Nat Asn Media Women, 1988; YWCA Award for Women of Achievement, 1988; Proclamation of Sidmel Estes-Sumpter Day, Atlanta, 1989; Community Award, Nat Asn Prof & Bus Women, 1989; Bronze Woman of the Year, Iota Phi Lombdo, 1989; Pioneer Black Journalist Award, Atlanta Asn Black Journalists, 1990; Top Young People of Atlanta, Outstanding Atlanta, 1991; Lifetime Achievement Award, Crisis Mag, 1992; Silver Circle Award, Nat Tv Acad SE Chap, 2003; Women's Hall of Fame, Atlanta Bus League, 2003; Alumni Service Award, Northwestern Univ, 2004; 5 Emmy Awards. **Special Achievements:** First woman president of the National Association of Black Journalists. **Business Addr:** Executive Producer, WAGA-TV, 1551 Briarcliff Rd NE, Atlanta, GA 30306, **Business Phone:** (404)875-5555.

ESTILL, DR. ANN H M
Singer, violinist, educator. **Personal:** Born in Washington, DC; daughter of Don V Estill and T Christine Smith-Estill. **Educ:** Western Mich Univ, B.Mus; Columbia Univ, Teachers Col, MA; New York Univ,DA, voice performance. **Career:** Kalamazoo Jr Symphony, violinist; Jersey City State Col, researcher & developer African & Afro-Am Classical music, prof music; actor, currently. **Orgs:** Am Inst Music Studies Graz Austria; pres, Sigma Alpha Iota Prof Hon Frat Women Music, NY Alumnae Chap; province officer, Al-Past Phi C; educ hon,Phi Delta Kappa; Kappa Phi Methodist Women; Nat Asn Teachers Singing. **Business Addr:** Actor, 1 Holly St, Jersey City, NJ 07305.

ETHEREDGE, JAMES W.
Government official. **Personal:** Born Jun 6, 1941, Leesville, SC; married Vanetta Bing; children: Lorna V, William Craig. **Educ:** SC State Col, BS, 1963; Ind State Univ, Soc, attended 1966; Winthrop Col, polit sci, attended 1973; Univ SC, MPA, 1973. **Career:** City Rock Hill, social prog spec, 1969-70; Winthrop Col, part time instr, 1973-79; City Rock Hill, dir admin serv, 1971-80; City Charleston, dir admin serv, 1980-. **Orgs:** SC City & Cty Mgt Asn; SC Municipal Asn; Am Soc Pub Admin; Omega Psi Phi Frat; Charleston United Way Agency; Charleston Bus & Prof Asn; Avery Inst. **Business Addr:** Director, City of Charleston, Dept Admin Serv, PO Box 304, Charleston, SC 29402.*

ETHRIDGE, JOHN E., JR.
Chief executive officer. **Career:** J E Ethridge Construction Inc, Fresno CA, chief exec officer. **Business Phone:** (559)435-2391.*

ETHRIDGE, RAY. **See ETHRIDGE, RAYMOND ARTHUR, JR.**

ETHRIDGE, RAYMOND ARTHUR, JR. (RAY ETHRIDGE)
Football player. **Personal:** Born Dec 12, 1968, San Diego, CA; son of Vernolia Walker; married Wanda Yvette; children: Rayven. **Educ:** Pasadena City Col, attended. **Career:** Football player (retired); Baltimore Ravens, wide receiver, 1996-97.

ETHRIDGE, DR. ROBERT WYLIE
School administrator. **Personal:** Born Nov 12, 1940, Monroe, MI; son of Claude Sr and Hazel Johnson; married Elizabeth Sneed; children: Stephan, Tracy & Michael. **Educ:** Western Mich Univ, AB, 1962, AM, 1970; Univ Mich, Ann Arbor, PhD, 1979. **Career:** Detroit Pub Sch, teacher, 1962-69; Western Mich Univ, area coordr housing,1969-72, from admin asst to pres, 1972-79, sec bd trustees, 1979-81; Emory Univ, coordr equal opportunity prog, 1981, from asst vpres to assoc vpres,1982-2000, adj asst prof, 1982-, Off Equal Opportunities Prog, vpres, 2000-; chairperson emer, Emory Federal Credit Union. **Orgs:** CUPA, NACUBO 1981-, Nat Asn Advan Colored People, 1981-; vpres, Am AsnAffirmative Action, 1981-84, pres, 1984-88, 1990-92; bd mem, Nat Conf Planner, 1982-84; bd, Nat Assault Illiteracy Prog, 1983-; financial subcomt mem, United Way, 1984-; United Way-Health Services Coun, 1984-85;United Way-Admissions Panel, 1984-85; Ga Pub Rels Asn, 1985; Nat Inst Employment Equity, 1986-; chmn bd, Am Contract Compliance Asn, 1987-89;pres, Onyx Soc Western Mich Univ, 1989, 1997-99; bd dirs, Western MichUniv Alumni Asn, 1989-91, vpres, 1993-94, pres, 1994-96; bd dirs,Community Friendship Inc, 1994-99, treas, 1996-98, vpres, 1998-2001; bddir, Ga Nursing Found, 1994-95; pres, WMU Onyx Soc, 1994-97, 1997-94; bddir, 100 Black Men Dekalb, 1997-98; bership comt mem, Leadership Atlanta,1997-99; Race Rels Comn, 1997-2001; bd mem, Am Contract Compliance Asn; bdmem, Leadership Conf Civil Rights; Asn Off Human Rights Agencies; bd dir, Emory Federal Credit Union; Rachel B. Noel Distinguished Faculty Mem, Metro State College in Denver, Colorado, 2006. **Honors/Awds:** Achievement Award, Northern Province KAY, 1961-62; Community BuildingAward, Black Monitor, 1985; Citation for Public Service, Kalamazoo, 1979;2nd Annual Civil & Human Rights Award, 1988; Delta Torch Award, DeltaSigma Theta Sorority, 1996; President's Award, Am Asn Affirmative Action,1992. **Special Achievements:** Several articles and made numerous local, regional and national presentations on management, personnel, supervision, law, leadership, civil rights, affirmative action, diversity, cross-cultural communication, preventing sexual harassment, recruitment and retention of black faculty, staff and students, and human relations. **Business Addr:** Vice President, Emory University, Office of Equal Opportunities Program, 110 Admin Bldg, Atlanta, GA 30322, **Business Phone:** (404)727-6016.

EUBANKS, DAYNA C
Journalist. **Personal:** Born Jun 7, 1957, Wichita, KS; married. **Educ:** Univ Kans, BS, journ, 1979. **Career:** KAKE-TV Wichita, KS, psa actress, 1975; KJHK Radio News, Univ Kans, reporter, vpres, Mondale trip, 1977; KJHK Radio, Univ Kans, newscaster, news ed, 1977-78; Audio-Reader Univ Kans, newscaster, broadcaster, reader, 1977-78; WREN-AM Topeka, KS, legislative reporter, 1978; WIBW-TV-AM-FM Topeka Kans, newscaster, reporter, photographer, weekend news anchor,TV & radio, 1978-79; KOOL-TV Phoenix, AZ, weekend news anchor, gen assignment reporter, 1979-81; WXYZ-TV ABC Detroit, MI, weekend-news anchor, field anchor, Good Afternoon Detroit, gen assignment reporter 1981; WJBK-TV, Detroit, MI, anchor, host of weekday talk show Dayna, until 1992; WKRC-TV, Cincinnati, 1994-. **Orgs:** Am Women in Radio & TV, Nat Asn TV Arts & Sci, Nat Asn Black Journalists, Sigma Delta Chi, Women in Commun, SAG, Am Fed TV & Radio Artists, Delta Sigma Theta; lifetime mem, NAACP; co-chair & co-org, Detroit Black-Jewish Leaders Forum; volunteer teacher & counr, "Who Said I Can't" Program; nat convention chairperson, nat exec bd mem, IAWS, 1979; adv, Judicial Bd GSP-Corbin Hall, Acad Success KU Studs; ku rep IAWS Nat Conv; rep, Asn Univ Residence Halls. **Honors/Awds:** Appreciation Award, NAACP for Generosity to People & Community; Appreciation Award, Black History Week, 82nd Flying Training Wing Williams AFB, 1981; Award for Contributions to Broadcasting Hartford; Baptist Church; Outstanding Achievement in Commun, Alpha Kappa Alpha, 1981; Award for Outstanding Achievement as an Anchorwoman Journalist Public-Minded Citizen & Patron of the Arts, 1982; Outstanding Woman in Broadcast News, Am Women in Radio & TV, 1982; Golden Heritage Award for Outstanding Achievment in Commun, Little Rock Missionary Baptist Church; Robert L Powell Lectr, NAACP, Oakland Univ; Outstanding Minority Ind, YMCA, 1984; Detroit Emmy Award, Nominee Behind the Best, 1985; Ebony Mag, Thirty Future Black Leaders, 1985. **Business Addr:** Anchor, WKRC-TV, 1906 Highland Ave, Cincinnati, OH 45219, **Business Phone:** (513)763-5500.*

EUBANKS, EUGENE E.
Educator, college administrator. **Personal:** Born Jun 6, 1939, Meadville, PA; married Audrey J Hunter; children: Brian K & Regina A. **Educ:** Edinboro State Univ, BA 1963; Mich State Univ, PhD 1972. **Career:** Cleveland Pub Schs, teacher & adminr, 1963-70; Univ DE, prof educ admin, 1972-74; Univ Mo, Kans City, Sch Educ, prof, 1974, dean, 1979-89, dean emer & prof emer, 2004, Ctr Study Metrop Issues Educ, dir, currently. **Orgs:** Consult Cleveland Found; consult, KC Pub Schs; consult, Miss State Dept Educ; consult, Nat Asn Advan Colored People; Nat Alliance Black Sch Educators; Nat Conf Profs Educ Admin; Phi Delta Kappa; Am Asn Univ Profs; PUSH; Urban League; pres, Am Asn Col Teacher Educ, 1988; admin, Nat Policy Bd Educ, 1988. **Honors/Awds:** Articles published: A Study of Teacher Perception of Essential Teacher Attributes, 1974; Big-City Desegregation since Detroit, 1975; Rev Jesee LJackson & PUSH Prog for Excellence in Big-City Schools, 1977. **Special Achievements:** First African American elected as President of the American Association of Colleges for Teacher Education. **Military Serv:** USAF, sec serv, 1956-60. **Business Addr:** Director, University of Missouri, Centre for the Study of Metropolitan Issues in Education, 5100 Rockhill Rd, Kansas City, MO 64110, **Business Phone:** (816)235-2448.

EUBANKS, KEVIN
Jazz musician, guitarist. **Personal:** Born Nov 15, 1957, Philadelphia, PA; son of William and Vera. **Educ:** Univ Berklee Col Music, 1979. **Career:** Composer: Psalms from the Underground, 1996; Rebound: The Legend of Earl 'The Goat' Manigault, 1996; The Dinner, 1997; The Week That Girl Died, 1998; Films: Longshot, 2000; TV: "V.I.P.", 2000; "The Tonight Show with Jay Leno", 2000; "Girlfriends", 2003; Auth, Creative Guitarist, Hal Leonard; recs include: "Turning Point"; "Spirit Talk"; "Spirit Talk 2; Revelations"; NBC-TV, The Tonight Show, musical dir, currently. **Orgs:** Kappa Alpha Psi Fraternity Inc. **Honors/Awds:** Hon doctorate degree, Berklee Col Music, 2005. **Special Achievements:** Auth, Creative Guitarist, Hal Leonard; recs include: "Turning Point," "Spirit Talk," "Spirit Talk 2, Revelations". **Business Addr:** Musical Director, NBC-TV, 3000 W Alameda Ave, Burbank, CA 91523, **Business Phone:** (818)840-4444.

EUBANKS, LEMELVA
Executive. **Career:** KLM Financial, pres. *

EUBANKS, DR. RACHEL AMELIA
Educator, musician, composer. **Personal:** Born in San Jose, CA; daughter of Joseph and Amelia; divorced. **Educ:** Univ Calif, BA, 1945; Columbia Univ, MA, 1947; Pacific Western Univ, DMA, 1980; Eastman Sch Music; Univ Southern Calif; Westminster Choir Col; Am Conserv, France, 1977. **Career:** Albany State Col, head Music Dept, 1947; Wilberforce Univ, chmn Music Dept, 1949-50; Eubanks Conser Music, pres, founder, 1951-; songs: Cantata for Chorus and Orchestra; Symphonic Requiem; books: Five Interludes for Piano, Vivace Press, 1995; The First & Fifth Interludes on CD, Leonarda Records; Kiep Nao Co Yeu Nhau for Piano & Violin, Hildequard/Theodore Presser Co, 2003. **Orgs:** SE Sym Asn; La Co Art Music; Nat Asn Negro Musicians; Musicians Union, Local 47, 1951; comn, Afro-Am Museum, 1984; Crenshaw Chamber Com; Int Congr Women Music. **Honors/Awds:** Composition Award, Nat Asn Negro Musicians, 1948. **Business**

Addr: Founder, Director, Eubanks Conservatory Music & Arts, 4928 S Crenshaw Blvd, Los Angeles, CA 90010, **Business Phone:** (323)291-7821.*

EUBANKS, W RALPH
Editor, publisher. **Personal:** Born Jun 25, 1957, Collins, MS; son of Warren R and Lucille; married Colleen Delaney Eubanks, Apr 22, 1989; children: Patrick Warren, Aidan Joseph & Delaney Marie. **Educ:** Univ Miss, BA, 1978; Univ Mich, MA, 1979. **Career:** Am Geophysical Union, copy ed, 1979-84; Univ Va Publ, adj fac; Am Psychol Asn, journals mgr, 1984-89; Taylor & Francis, managing ed, 1989-90; Am Psychol Asn, APA books, dir, 1990-95; Lib Cong, dir publ, 1995-; Books: Ever Is a Long Time: A Journey Into Mississippi's Dark Past; Mississippi Yearning; Still Learning From Dad; DNA is Only One Way to Spell Identity; Separate But Unequal; Before He Had His Dream, King Wrote a Letter; A Trip Back Home for a Lesson in Justice; Are We Putting Reading & Democracy at Risk?; I Know What He Means. **Orgs:** Wash Ed Press, 1979-; stud adv, Howard Univ Book Publ Inst, 1992-93; pres, Wash Book Publ, 1996-97. **Honors/Awds:** Guggenheim Fellowship, John Simon Guggenheim Found, 2007. **Home Addr:** 3135 Quesada St NW, Washington, DC 20015, **Home Phone:** (202)537-9536. **Business Addr:** Director Publishing, The Library of Congress, 101 Independence Ave SE, Washington, DC 20540-3000, **Business Phone:** (202)707-5000.

EUGERE, EDWARD J.
Pharmacologist, educator. **Personal:** Born May 26, 1930, New Orleans, LA; married Yolanda Rousseve; children: Edward, Jan, Gail & Lisa. **Educ:** Xavier Univ, BS, 1951; Wayne State Univ, MS, 1953; Univ Conn, PhD, 1956. **Career:** Numerous Co, pharmacist, 1951-57; Wayne St Univ, grad teacher asst, 1951-53; Univ Conn, 1953-56; Highland Pk Jr Col, lectr; Detroit Inst Technol, asst prof, 1956-57; Baylor Col Med, Postdoctoral Study Myocardial Biol, 1973; Tex Southern Univ, prof, 1957-; Sch Pharm, dean, 1968-70. **Orgs:** Harris County Pharm Asn; pres, Houston Pharm Asn; Am Heart Asn; Lone Star St Pharm Asn; pres, Houston Area Chi Delta Mu Prof Frat; Am Assn Col Pharm; Am Tex Pharm Asn; Houston Pharmcologists; Sigma Xi Soc; pres, Rho Chi Pharm Hon Soc; 1977; bd Educ, Diocess Galveston Houston, 1974-77; pres, Grand Jury Asn Houston-harris Co; pres, Cath Interracial Coun, Houston; Gulf Coast Area Child Develop Ctr; Am Asn Cols Pharm Chi. **Honors/Awds:** Fesler Research Award, Univ Conn, 1954-56; Travel Award, Detroit Inst Technol, 1957; Guide & Leadership Award, Sr Class Tex Southern Univ, 1968; Leadership Award, Houston Pharm Asn, 1971; Faculty Development Award, Tex Southern Univ, 1973; Consult Nat inst health adv group serv cert, NIH HEW, 1973; researcher, Fungal Toxins Pharmacol. **Business Addr:** Professor, Texas Southern University, 3100 Cleburne St, Houston, TX 77004.*

EURE, DEXTER D, SR.
Executive. **Personal:** Born Nov 20, 1923, Suffolk, VA; son of Luke and Sarah; married Marjorie A; children: Dexter Jr & David, Philip. **Educ:** WV State Col, BSME, 1946. **Career:** Executive (Retired); PRAC Assoc, vpres, 1960-61; Boston Globe, asst circulation mgr, 1963-68, asst ed, 1968-70, dir community rels, 1972-88; Bradlee Div Stop & Shop, advert prod mgr. **Orgs:** Boston Globe Found, 1980-90; first act dir, Boston Comm Media Comm; Pub Affairs Coun Greater Boston Chamber Com; former mem, Large United Way MA Bay; Cong Black Caucus Comm Braintrust Comm; adv com, Nat Asn Advan Colored People; panelist Nieman Found, Journalism Harvard Univ, Media Racism. **Honors/Awds:** Distinguished Serv Award, Union United Methodist Church, 1984; President's Award, 1986; MA Black Legislative Caucus Eight Annual Award, 1986. **Special Achievements:** First undergraduate elected to Omega Psi Phi Fraternity Supreme Council. **Military Serv:** AUS sgt 1st class 1948-50.

EURE, HERMAN EDWARD
Scientist, educator. **Personal:** Born Jan 7, 1947, Corapeake, IL; son of Grover T and Sarah Goodman; children: Lauren Angela & Jared Anthony. **Educ:** Md State Col, BS, 1969; Wake Forest Univ, PhD, 1974. **Career:** Wake Forest Univ, Dept Biol, prof biol & chmn, 1974-, from asst prof to prof, chair dept, 2006-08; dean, 2006-; Ford Found, fel; NSF, fel. **Orgs:** Inst Ecol Univ Ga; Sigma Xi; Nat Asn Advan Colored People; Alpha Phi Alpha Frat Inc; Am Soc Parasitol; SE Soc Parasitol; Beta Nat Biol Honor Soc; Beta Kappa Chi Nat Hon Soc. **Honors/Awds:** Man of the Year Award, Md State Col, 1968; Outstanding Alumnus, Md State Col, 1980; Featured Scientist, Distinguished African American Scientist of the 20th Century; Hall of Fame, Md State Col. **Special Achievements:** First African-American to receive PhD, Wake Forest Univ; One of Two, First Full-Time African-American Faculty Member, Wake Forest Univ; First African-American Tenured, Wake Forest Univ; Published several books. **Business Addr:** Professor, Associate Dean of the College, Wake Forest University, Department of Biology, 226 Winston Hall, PO Box 7325, Winston-Salem, NC 27109, **Business Phone:** (336)758-5322.

EURE, JERRY HOLTON, SR.
Administrator. **Personal:** Born Mar 4, 1923, Burdette, VA; son of Russie Bell Williams and Rev Alexander Holton; married Anna Blackwell Eure, Jun 6, 1948; children: Dianna, Geraldine, Jerry Jr, Sherri. **Educ:** West VA State Col Inst, WV, pre-eng, 1942; Rutgers Univ, New Brunswick, NJ, BS, 1951; Univ Penn, Philadelphia, MGA, 1970. **Career:** Administrator (retired); State NJ, US Govt, RCA, NAF Inc, Trenton, NJ, staff, 1949-72; State NJ, Trenton, NJ, supv planner, 1972-80; US Govt, NY & Newark, NJ, community planner, 1980-81; State NJ, Trenton, NJ, supv prog develop specialist, 1981-85; Coalition Nuclear Disarmament, Trenton, NJ, educ coordr, 1985-90. **Orgs:** bd mem, NJ Black Issues Convention, 1982; bd mem, Mercer St Friends, 1994; chair, Mercer County Off Aging Comn, 1994; Human Civil Rights Asn; bd trustees, Mercer County United Way. **Honors/Awds:** Appreciation Award, Boy Scouts Am, 1978; Father of the Year, Bronzettes Inc, 1984; Assembly Resolution, NJ Gen Assembly, 1987; Certificate of Honor, Mercer County Board of Chosen Freeholders, 1988; Serv & Community Outreach, Trenton Ecumenical Area Ministry, 1988; Certificate of Merit, Trenton Public School, 1989; Meritorious Award, Kappa Alpha Psi Fraternity, 1990; Life Memorial Award, NAACP, 1992; State & National Award, Nat Fed Colored Women's Club; Family of the Year Award, 1992. **Military Serv:** USAAF, Aviation Cadet, 1941-45. **Home Addr:** 924 Edgewood Ave, Trenton, NJ 08618, **Home Phone:** (609)396-3279. *

EVAIGE, WANDA JO
Educator, mayor. **Personal:** Born Jul 9, 1935, Frederick, OK; daughter of Sam and Lenora Oliver (deceased). **Educ:** Huston-Tillotson Col, BA, music, 1955; Univ Okla, current. **Career:** O.E. Kennedy Elementary Sch, Fredrick, 1956-68; Prather Brown Elementary, teacher; NCC USA, gov bd dir, 1973-76; Frederick City Council, rep, 1982; NEA, congressional contact, 1983; City of Frederick, vice-mayor, 1986, mayor, 1987-, coun mem; Frederick Economic Dev Authority, vice chmn, 1987; Frederick Pub Schs, music specialist; City Frederick, coun mem. **Orgs:** Pres, TUO Chap Alpha Kappa Alpha Sor, 1969-76; Boyd Alumni Asn, nat pres, 1973-75; Tillman County Classroom Teachers, pres, 1973; pres, Frederick Classroom Teachers, 1973-74/1979-81; City Coun mem, Ward III Frederick, Ok, 1983; legislative comn Okla Municipal League, 1984; lobbyist Okla Educ Asn, 1978-86; Okla Constitution & Revision Comn, State Okla, 1988-; Okla Judicial Nominating Comt, 1993-99; Fed Judicial Nominating Comn, 1997; Asn S Cent Okla Govts, vpres; pres, Asn S Cent Okla Govt, 2000-02; mem, Nat Judicial Comn; pres, Huston Univ Int Alumni Asn. **Honors/Awds:** Okla Human Rights Award; Teacher of the Year, Tillman County Teachers, 1981. **Special Achievements:** Was named 1981 Teacher of the Year for Fredrick and Tillman County; The first black Teacher of the Year in Fredrick and Southwest Oklahoma; first woman elected to the Fredrick City Council and the first woman to serve as a mayor in any Southwest Oklahoma community. **Home Addr:** 400 S 3rd St, Frederick, OK 73542. *

EVANS, ADA B.
Mayor, educator. **Personal:** Born Jun 9, 1932, Langley, SC; married Ray Allen; children: Cheri & Rachelle. **Educ:** Benedict Col, BS, 1955. **Career:** Aiken Co Schs, teacher, 1955-60; Park Co Schs, teacher, 1966-; IDS Mkt & Life Ins, registered rep. **Orgs:** Co Educ Asn NEA; Co Comn Status Women, 1974-77; Nat Asn Advan Colored People; S eastern Co Health Systs Agency; Pikes Peaks Coun Govt.

EVANS, AKWASI ROZELLE
Publisher, editor. **Personal:** Born Oct 17, 1948, Dayton, OH; son of Garfield and Geraline Dale; divorced; children: Sherilyn Ronetta Scott. **Educ:** Univ Kentucky, BA, 1978; Tex Southern Univ Grad Sch, attended 1982. **Career:** Austin Area Urban League, job developer & instr, 1983-84; Capitol City Argus Newspaper, reporter, 1983-85; The Villager Newspaper, reporter, 1985-87; NOKOA-The Observer, publ & ed, 1987-. **Orgs:** Nat Newspaper Publ Asn, 1986-; mem, Tex Publ Asn, 1986-, vpres, 1991-; pres bd dirs, Nat Bus League, 1986-91; pres, founder, African-Am Improvement Corp, 1986-; Multicultured Action Proj, bd dirs, 1990-; Black Arts Alliance, 1984-87, vpres, 1986-87; bd dirs, Save Austin's Neighborhoods & Environs, 1984-87; Capital City African-Am Chamber Com, 1999-; Coun Community Reconciliation, 1998-. **Honors/Awds:** Dewitty Overton Human Rights Award, Nat Asn Advan Colored People, 1990; Media Award, Tex Ment Health Ment Retardation, 1991; Sankhore Holistic Health Inst, Hon Doctorate, 1982; Abbie Hoffman Memorial Award, 1990; Leadership in Human Rights, Delta Sigma Theta, 1990; Phoenix Award, Friends of the Phoenix, 1990; A. Phillip Randolph Messenger Awardd, 1999, 2000. **Special Achievements:** Poetry Anthology: "Periplum Austin," 1990; "Seem Southern to Me," 1977; "Perfect Circle," 1974. **Business Addr:** Publisher, Editor, NOKOA-The Observer Newspaper, 1154 B Angelina St, PO Box 1131, Austin, TX 78767-1131, **Business Phone:** (512)499-8713.*

EVANS, ALBERT
Ballet dancer. **Personal:** Born in Atlanta, GA. **Educ:** Sch Am Ballet; Terpsichore Expressions. **Career:** NY City Ballet, corps mem, soloist, 1991-, prin, 1995-; ballet performances include: Phlegmatic in Four Temperaments; Episodes; Ash; Behind the China Dogs; The Unanswered Question; One Body. **Honors/Awds:** full scholarship, Sch of Am Ballet. **Business Addr:** Dancer, NY City Ballet, 20 Lincoln Ctr Plz, New York, NY 10023, **Business Phone:** (212)870-5656.*

EVANS, ALICIA
Public relations executive. **Personal:** Born May 28, 1960, Brooklyn, NY; daughter of Simon Levan and Magnolia Ballard. **Educ:** Hofstra Univ, Hempstead, NY, BA, comun, 1982; NY Univ, bus mgmt cert, 1984. **Career:** Fortunoffs, Westbury NY, promotional sales asst, 1977-84; CBS News, NY, prog transcriber, 1981; Lockhart & Pettus Advert Agency, NY, acct exec, 1982-87; Dark & Lovely; Always Nat Hair Care, NY, dir pub rels, 1987; Total Image Commun, founder & pres, 1993-. **Orgs:** Nat Asn Female Exec, 1988, Pub Rel Soc Am, 1988; NY Black Pub Rel Soc, 1990-; charter mem, Gotham Network's Diversity Group. **Honors/Awds:** African-American Achievement, NY Million Dollar Boys Club, 1988; 1000 Notable Business & Professional Women, Am Biographical Inst, 1990. **Special Achievements:** News & Feature Editor, "The Satellite," Hofstra Univ, 1981, 1982; producer/copywriter, Con Edison, NY Utility Co (radio commercial), 1984; copywriter brochure, Minority & Women's Div, New York Chamber of Commerce, 1984; senior editor, "Homecoming," Army ROTC Publication, 1984-87; producer/copywriter, Dark & Lovely Hair Care Products (radio commercial), 1987; Auth: The Mosaica Guide for Cultural Communicators. **Home Addr:** 41 Ave, Westbury, NY 11590. *

EVANS, AMOS JAMES
Association executive. **Personal:** Born May 11, 1922, Rayne, LA; married Carolyn S; children: Winnfred, Adrian J, Wendell P, Donald R. **Educ:** Lasalle Bus Col, 1946. **Career:** Gulf Oil Corp, operator no 1, 1946-80; Ch Sch, couns, 1964-80; 7th St Br YMCA, pres, 1973-77; Port Arthur Br NAACP TX, pres, currently. **Honors/Awds:** Recipient service award & membership 7th Br YMCA, 1970; outstanding service youth award, St Paul United Meth Ch, 1971; community service award, Negro BPW Port Arthur TX, 1976; meritorious award, Port Arthur Br NAACP, 1977; cong community award, Golden Gate Civic ZOB Sorority Man, 1977. **Military Serv:** USN, petty officer, 1944-46. **Business Addr:** President, Port Arthur Br NAACP, 1001 Texas Ave, PO Box 1583, Port Arthur, TX 77640, **Business Phone:** (409)982-8040.*

EVANS, ARTHUR L.
Educator. **Personal:** Born Jul 26, 1931, Macon, GA; married Hattie Fears; children: Ivan Hugh. **Educ:** Morehouse Col, AB, 1953; Columbia Univ, MA, 1957; Univ Miami, PhD, 1972; Union Theol Sem Sch Soc Music. **Career:** Educator (retired); Ballard-Hudson High Sch Macon, 1953-54; Miami Northwestern Sr High Sch,1957-69; Miami-Dade Jr Col, prof humanities, 1967-69; Hialeah-Miami Lakes Sr High Sch, chmn, choral dir, 1970-72; Vohelweh Chapel, Kaiserslautern, Ger, Organist-Choir dir; SC State Col, Orangeburg, dir concert choir, Dept visual & performing arts, chmn. **Orgs:** Chmn, Fine Arts Lyceum Comn, 1973; conductor Col Concert Choir, 1974-75; Kappa Delta; Phi Mu Alpha Sinfonia; Nat Mus Eds Conf; Am Choral Dir Asn; SC Music Ed Asn; Phi Beta Sigma; chmn, vice chmn, Col Div SC Music Educrs Asn; pres, SC State Am Choral Dirs Asn; chmn, Multi-Cultural Comt Southern Div Am Choral Dirs Asn; mem bd dirs, SC Philharmonic Orchestra. **Honors/Awds:** Ed Award, Phi Beta Sigma, 1972; Outstanding Achievement Award, Phi BetaSigma 1987. **Military Serv:** AUS, pfc, 1954-56. **Home Addr:** 449 Meadowlark Dr, Orangeburg, SC 29118, **Home Phone:** (803)534-3269. *

EVANS, DR. BILLY JOE
Educator, research scientist. **Personal:** Born Aug 18, 1942, Macon, GA; married Adye Bel; children: William & Carole. **Educ:** Morehouse Col, BS, summa cum laude, 1963; Univ Chicago, PhD, 1968. **Career:** Woodrow Wilson fel, 1963-; Univ Chicago, res assoc, 1968; Univ Manitoba, Dept Physics, fel, 1968-69; Howard Univ, asst prof chem, 1969-70; Univ Mich, asst prof, 1970-73, Dept Geol & Mineral, assoc prof, 1973-75, from assoc prof chem to prof chem, 1975-2003, prof emer chem, currently; Nat Res Coun Can fel, Univ Manitoba, 1968-69; Nat Bur Stand Alloy Phys Sect, consult, 1971-78; Alfred P Sloan res fel, 1972-75; BASF Wyandotte, consult, 1976-78; Danforth assoc, 1977-83; Humboldt sr fel, 1977-78; US Geol Surv, consult, 1980-84; Naval Res Lab, consult, 1986-; Atlanta Univ, Dept Chem, prof & chair, 1986-87; Am Soc Eng Educ, distinguished fac fel, 1988; Morehouse Col, Rauner prof chem & dir mat sci, 1998-99; Gallery Inventors, Tubman Mus, inductee; assoc, Chem Mfrs Asn, Danforth Found. **Orgs:** Sigma Xi, 1968-; Am Phys Soc; Mineral Soc Am; Can Mineral Asn; Am Geophys Union; Minorities Am Geophys Union; adv comt, Los Alamos, Nat Lab; Am Chem Soc, Comt Prof Training, 1999-; math & phys sci directorate, Nat Sci Found, Adv Comn, 1999-, chair, 2001-02; Am Soc Eng Educ; Phi Beta Kappa; Phi Kappa Phi, 1991; Nat Res Coun Can. **Honors/Awds:** Early Admis Col, Merrill Scholar Morehouse Col, 1959-63; Catalyst Medalist, Am Chem Soc, 1995; ACS Award Encouraging Disadvantaged Studs into Careers in Chemical Science, Am Chem Soc, 1996; Presidential Award for Excellence in Science, Mathematics, & Engineering Mentoring; LN Ferguson distinguished lect, Calif State Univ, 1998; HK Hall Mem lect, Univ Louisville, 1999; P Julian Mem lect, De Pauw Univ, 1999; Sigma Xi Col Distinguished Lectrs, 1999-2001; James Flack Norris Award, Am Chem Soc, 2000; Camille & Henry Dreyfus Award; Woodrow Wilson Fellow. **Business Addr:** Professor Emeritus of Chemistry, University of Michigan, 930 N Univ Ave, Ann Arbor, MI 48109-1055, **Business Phone:** (734)763-4228.

EVANS, CAROLE YVONNE MIMS
Judge. **Personal:** Born Oct 1, 1951, Hendersonville, NC; daughter of Evans King and Mary Louise Valentine; married Michael Duaine, Sep 5, 1991; children: Tracey Renee, Michael Thomas & Karen Michelle. **Educ:** Wellesley Col, BA, 1973; Duke Univ Sch Law, JD, 1976. **Career:** Chambers Stein Ferguson & Becton, atty, 1976-88; Children's Law Ctr, 1989-92; NC Resident Super Ct Judge, Judicial Dist 26th, NC, 1992-; Mecklenburg County Dist Judge, 1992-2003; Mecklenburg County Super Judge, 2003-. **Orgs:** Bd dirs, Charlotte Asn, Young Women's Christian Asn, 1978-80; bd dirs, Planned Parenthood Charlotte Affil, 1979-80; bd dirs, Charlotte Mecklenburg Urban League Orgn, 1979-81; Charlotte Mecklenburg Planning Comn, 1980-83; Charlotte Speech & Hearing Ctr, 1983-89; NC Bar Asn Bd Gov, 1986-89; mem bd, Bio-Ethics Resources Group, 1988-; mem bd, Leadership Charlotte, 1988-; bd dirs, Found Carolinas, 1992-. **Business Addr:** NC Resident Superior Court Judge, Superior Court (26A), 832 E 4th St, Charlotte, NC 28202.

EVANS, CHARLOTTE A.
Executive. **Personal:** Born in Providence, RI. **Educ:** NY Inst Credit. **Career:** First Nat City Bank, switchboard operator, platform customer rep, official asst, asst mgr. **Orgs:** Nat Asn Bank Women; Urban Banders Coalition; former bd mem, Hamilton Day Care Ctr; former mem, Manhattanville Com & Ctr; former mem, Scitarnard Players Providence RI; Black Achievers YMCA; original mem, Am Negro Theatre NY; hon mem, Iota Phi Lambda Sorority; vpres & secy, NY Rinkeydinks. **Honors/Awds:** Luncheon Award, Iota Phi Lambda Sorority, 1970. **Special Achievements:** First black women officer of any bank in NY.

EVANS, CHERYL LYNN
Banker. **Personal:** Born May 24, 1950, Gary, IN; daughter of William Henry and Charleston Fullerton; married Eldridge Anthony, 1990 (divorced); children: Jeffrey W Anthony, Shonda Y Anthony. **Educ:** Omega The Bank Training Co, San Francisco, CA, cert, 1982; Dun & Bradstreet Bus Educ Servs, NY, cert, 1984. **Career:** Crocker Bank, San Francisco, CA, consumer loan prod mgr, 1972-80; Sumitomo Bank, San Francisco, CA, vpres compliance officer loan admin, 1980; Citibank N Am Western Region, dir, community rels, 2003. **Orgs:** Bd mem, San Francisco Housing Develop; Corp & Reniassance Entrepreneurship Ctr bd; adv bd mem, AnewAmerica Community Corp. **Honors/Awds:** Community Involvement Award, Ella Hill Hutch Community Center, 1984. **Home Addr:** 3 Mabrey Ct, San Francisco, CA 94124-2485. **Business Addr:** Director Community Relations, Citibank North America Western Region, 1 Sansome St, San Francisco, CA 94104, **Business Phone:** (415)658-4354.*

EVANS, CHUCK. See Obituaries section.

EVANS, CLAY
Clergy. **Personal:** Born Jun 23, 1925, Tennessee; son of A Henry and Estanuly; married Lutha Mae; children: Diane (deceased), Michael, Ralph, Claudette, Faith. **Educ:** Chicago Baptist Inst; Northern Baptist Theol Sem; Univ Chicago Sch Div; AR Baptist Col, DD. **Career:** WCFL AM Radio & TV, ministry; Fellowship Baptist Church, pastor, founder, 1958-00; Bapt Ministers Conf, pres, 1964-66. **Orgs:** African Am Religious Connection, founder & pres, currently; , chair emer, Oper PUSH, found nat bd chair, 1971-76; founding pres, Broadcast Misiters Alliance Chicago; trustee bd chair, Chicago Baptist Inst; bd mem, Nat baptist Conention, USA Inc. **Special Achievements:** From Plough Handle to Pulpit, autobiography, 1992, 1997; Featured soloist, Voice Choir Fellowship Missionary Baptist Church; Stellar Award, 1996; numerous honorary doctor of divinity degrees. **Business Addr:** Founder, Fellowship Missionary Baptist Church, 4543 S Princeton Ave, Chicago, IL 60609, **Business Phone:** (773)924-3232.*

EVANS, DAVID LAWRENCE
Educator. **Personal:** Born Dec 27, 1939, Wabash, AR; married Mercedes L Sherrod; children: Daniel & Christine. **Educ:** Tenn State Univ, BS, electrical engineering, 1962; Princeton Univ, MS, electrical engineering, 1966. **Career:** Boeing Com, elec eng, 1962-64; Lockheed, elec eng, 1964; Princeton Univ, teaching asst, 1964-66; IBM Corp, elec eng, 1966-70; Harvard Univ, admin officer, asst dean, 1970, sr admis officer, currently. **Orgs:** Bd trustees, St Georges Sch; Gov Bd, Princeton Grad Alum Asn; Inst Elec & Electronic Engrs; Am Audlgy Soc; Nat Asn Col Admis Couns; Alpha Phi Alpha Fraternity; Harvard Club Boston; Asn Black Princeton Alumni; Princeton Alumni Asn New Eng; Nat Merit Corp; adviser, Harvard Found. **Honors/Awds:** Outstanding Young Men of America, 1971; Tennessee State University Alumni of the Year, 1972; FAS Administrative Prize, 2002; Hon name, David L. Evans Scholarship Fund, 2003. **Special Achievements:** Publ "Making It as a Black at Harvard/Radcliffe" NY Times, 1976; "On Criticism of Black Student", Ebony, 1977; "School Merit Pay System Gone Awry" LA Times, 1984; "An Appeal to Black Alumni", Newsweek, 1984. **Home Addr:** 8 Garden St, Cambridge, MA 02138. **Business Addr:** Senior Admissions Officer, Harvard College, 8 Garden St, Cambridge, MA 02138, **Business Phone:** (617)495-5375.

EVANS, DONALD LEE
Football player. **Personal:** Born Mar 14, 1964, Raleigh, NC; son of Novella Scott and Rhuben; married Debra Jeffers, Mar 27, 1988; children: Donald Lee II, Novella Leeann & Jessica Nicole. **Educ:** Winston-Salem State Univ, BS, health & physic edu, 1993. **Career:** Los Angeles Rams, 1987; Philadelphia Edges, 1988; Pittsburgh Steelers, 1990-93; NY Jets, 1994-95. **Orgs:** Project Bundle Up, 1987-; United Way, 1987-; Life of Life Mission, 1987-; Share the Warmth, The Hunger Project, Donald Evans Schlorship Fund, Black Arts Supporter. **Honors/Awds:** All CIAA Football Champions, Winston-Salem St Univ, 1986; Black andGold Barae Player of the Month, Pittsburgh Steeler Fan Club, 1992. **Special Achievements:** Winston-Salem State Univ, Dean's List, 1992; LA Rams, Number One DraftPick, 1987. *

EVANS, DR. DONNA BROWDER
Educator, school administrator. **Personal:** Born in Columbus, OH; daughter of Clarke and Margaret; divorced; children: Jocelyn Michelle Brown-Smith. **Educ:** Ohio State Univ, BS, Elementary Educ, 1958, MA, Counselor Educ, 1964, PhD, Counselor Educ, 1970. **Career:** Professor (retired); Univ Cincinnati, asst prof, 1969-73; Univ Maine, prof& grad dean, 1973-83; Skidmore Col, prof, chair dept educ, 1983-87, Wayne State Univ, prof, dean educ, 1987-91; Univ N Fla, prof & dean, 1991-95;Old Dominion Univ, Darden Col Educ, Va, dean, 1995-2000; Ohio State UnivCol Educ, Ctr Learning Excellence, co-dir, prof & dean, 2000-05, prof emer educ admin, currently; John Glenn Scholar Urban Educ Policy; John GlennInst Pub Serv & Pub Policy, currently. **Orgs:** Alpha Kappa Alpha Sorority Detroit Chap; Coalition 100 Black Women Albany,1984-87; Am Asn Univ Women Saratoga Springs, 1984-87; ed bd, J Reality Therapy, 1984-; bd dirs, Asn Black Educr Profs, 1985-87; bd dirs, Soroptomist Int, 1985-87; Links Inc Jacksonville Chap 1987-; bd dir, Lake George Opera Festival; bd dir, Task Force Against Domestic Violence Saratoga Springs; Sophisticates Savannah Chap, 1988-, Carrousels, DetroitChap, 1988-; bd dirs, Jr Achievement, Jacksonville, 1991-. **Special Achievements:** Reviewer Brooks Cole Publishing Co, 1980-; publications "Success Oriented Schools in Action", 1981, "A Conversation with William Glasser", 1982,"Opening Doors to the Future Through Education", 1984, "Reality Therapy, A Model for Physicians Managing Alcoholic Patients", 1984, "Curriculum Not Either-Or", 1991. **Business Addr:** Professor Emeritus Education Administration, Ohio State University, College of Education, 350 Page Hall 1810 Col Rd, Columbus, IA 43210-1172, **Business Phone:** (614)292-2461.

EVANS, DORSEY
Lawyer. **Personal:** Born Dec 7, 1930, Kansas City, KS; married Ruth Wilson; children: Dorsey Delwin, Velma, Elizabeth, Gary C. **Educ:** Univ KS, BA, 1952; Howard Univ, JD, 1958. **Career:** Howard Univ, legal aid soc; Turner Mem AME Church, consult; Local Funeral Home, consult; Pride Econ Devel Inc, consult; Storage Co, consult; Westinghouse ElectCorp, consult; Congressman Walter E Fauntroy's Camp Comn, former treas, 1972-; Delco Settlement Co, pres; Delwin Realty Co, pres; Pvt pract,attny; Howard Univ, legal coun. **Orgs:** Nat Bar Asn; WA DC Bar Asn; Am Bar Asn; Am Judicature Soc; Am Arbitration Asn; Supreme Ct US; Supreme & State Ct KS; adv comn, Super Ct Rules Civil Procedure DC; Info Ctr Handicapped C, Turner Meth Church; vpres, pres, Homemaker Serv; pres, Young Dem Clubs; Woodridge Civic Asn Young Adult Club; vpres, Fed Civic Asn; chmn, 12 Precinct Police Crime Coun. **Honors/Awds:** Outstanding Trial Counsel Chief Judge Bazelon. **Military Serv:** AUS, 1953-55. **Business Addr:** Attorney, Howard University, 1301 Pennsylvania Ave N W, Washington, DC 20004.

EVANS, DOUGLAS EDWARDS
Football player. **Personal:** Born May 13, 1970, Shreveport, LA; married Myria; children: Aymara & Doug. **Educ:** La Tech Univ, finance. **Career:** Football Player (retired); Green Bay Packers, defensive back, 1993-97; Carolina Panthers, defensive back, 1998-2001; Seattle Sea hawks, defensive back, 2002-03; Detroit Lions,defensive back, 2003. **Orgs:** Make Wish Found. **Honors/Awds:** Super Bowl Award XXXI.

EVANS, DWIGHT
State government official. **Personal:** Born May 16, 1954, Philadelphia, PA; son of Henry and Jean Odoms. **Educ:** Philadelphia Community Col, attended 1973; La Salle Col, attended 1975;Temple Univ, attended 1978. **Career:** State Pa, Dist 203, state rep, 1981-; Dem Appropriations Comt, chmn, currently. **Orgs:** Tutorial prog, Admiss Procedure Comt, La Salle Col; chmn, Black Stud League; 10th Ward Dem Exec Comt; City-Wide Polit Alliance; NW Polit Coalition; Philadelphia Coun Neighborhoods; consult, N Cent Community Mental Health Ctr, House Umoja, Coun Labor & Indust; Stenton Food Co-Op Prog; Public Sch Employees Retirement System; Black Alliance Educ Options; bd mem, Visitors Bureau and Presbyterian Foundation, Philadelphia; mem, NatGoverning Assessment Board; founder,ennsylvania Legislative Comnon Restructuring Urban Schools. **Honors/Awds:** Citizen of the Year, Philadelphia Tribune, Pepsi Cola, 1979; Community Service Award, La Salle Col, Urban Studies Ctr, 1981. **Business Addr:** State Representative, Pennsylvania House of Representatives, District 203, 512 E3 Main Capitol, PO Box 202203, Philadelphia, PA 17120-2203, **Business Phone:** (717)783-1540.

EVANS, ELINOR ELIZABETH
Marketing executive. **Personal:** Born Mar 6, 1948, Detroit, MI; daughter of Harold and Evelyn; divorced; children: Tracey D, Candace D &, Kevin D. **Educ:** Wayne County Conn Col, AA, 1989; Wayne State Univ, BS, 1997. **Career:** City Detroit, Transportation Dept, auto mechanic, 1974-77, sr clerk, 1977-83, prin clerk, 1983-84; City Detroit, COBO Conf/Exhib Ctr, event coordr, 1984-87, asst sales mgr, 1987-93, sales mgr, 1993-96, asst dir mkt, 1996-99, dir mkt, 1999-. **Orgs:** Prof Convention Mgmt Asn, 1999-; Nat Coalition Black Meeting Planners, 1993-; Int Asn Exhibit Mgrs, 1995-; Religious Conference Mgt Asn, 1993-; Am Soc Asn Execs, 1987-; Optimist Club Central Detroit, 1995-; Nat Asn Advan Colored People, 1965-; Asn Convention Mkt Execs, 1997. **Honors/Awds:** Connecticut Service Award, High Sch Com & Bus Admin, 1996; Certificate of Appreciation, Distributive Educ Clubs Am, 1994; Otto Finestein Writing Excellence Award, Wayne State Univ, 1997. **Business Addr:** Director Marketing, COBO Conference/Exhibition Center, 1 Wash Blvd, Detroit, MI 48226-4499, **Business Phone:** (313)877-8777.

EVANS, ERNEST (CHUBBY CHECKER)
Singer, actor, dancer. **Personal:** Born Oct 3, 1941, Spring Gulley, SC; married Rina Lodder, 1964; children: 3. **Career:** Cameo-Parkway Rec, rec artist; TV appearances: "Midnight Special"; "American Bandstand"; "Mike Douglas"; "Disco mania"; "Ally McBeal"; Recordings: The Class, 1959; Dancing Dinosaur, 1959; The Twist, 1959; Let's Twist Again, 1962; Pony Time, Dance the Mess Around, The Fly, 1961; Slow Twist in, 1962; Popeye the Hitchhiker, 1962; Dancin Party, 1962; Limbo Rock, 1962; Bird land, 1963; Twist It Up, 1963; Loddy Lo, 1963; 40 Twist, 1988; Jingle Bells; Peppermint Twist; Twist & Shout; Twist in the Night Away; Dances: The Jerk; The Hully Gully; The Boogaloo; The Shake; The Fly; The Pony; The Huckle buck; Films: Dont Knock The Twist; Twist Around The Clock. **Orgs:** Am Soc Composers, Authors & Publishers; BMI; Screen Actors Guld. **Honors/Awds:** Grammy Award, 1961. **Special Achievements:** Pony Time ranked No. 1, 1961; The Twist ranked No. 1, 1962; the only artist to have 5 albums in the Top 12 all at once; the only artist to havea song to be No. 1 twice; the only artist to have 9 Double-Sided Hits. **Business Addr:** Singer, Paradise Artists, 108 E Matilija St, Ojai, CA 93023.*

EVANS, ETU
Executive. **Personal:** Born Feb 2, 1969, Orangeburg, CA. **Educ:** SC State Univ, attended 1992; Parsons Sch Design, Shoe Design, 1994; Columbia Univ, MS, Appl Behav Psychol, 1996; Fashion Inst Technol, Footwear & Accessories Design 2000. **Career:** Medgar Evers Col, adj prof; The Inst Youth Entrepreneurship, asst dir; Berkeley Col, Fashion Dept, adj prof; Etu Evans LLC, chief shoemaker, pres & founder, 1993-. **Orgs:** Founder, The Etu Evans Found, Solesville, 1998-; Omega Psi Phi Fraternity. **Honors/Awds:** Crains Small Business of the Year, 2004; Proj Enterprise; New York Entrepreneur of the Year, 2005; Nat Urban League; Man of Influence; New face of the Martell Cognac Rise Above ad campaign saluting visionary men; Citizen of the Year, Omega Psi Phi Fraternity Inc; TONY Shopping Award, Time Out NY. **Special Achievements:** Burger King Everyday Heroes National Campaign Honor, 2005; adorned the feet of many high profile celebrities, including Halle Berry, Beyonce, Erykah Badu, Lil Kim & supermodels Ana Hickman, Tyra Banks, Iman & Roshumba Futher; first African-American to successfully compete in the high-end shoe design market; featured in a number of publications including Jet, Essence & Black Enterprise. **Business Addr:** Founder & President, Chief Shoemaker, Etu Evans LLC, 138 W 127th St, Harlem, NY 10027, **Business Phone:** (212)662-7787.*

EVANS, DR. EVA L
School administrator. **Educ:** Wayne State Univ; Mich State Univ, MA, 1970, PhD, 1977. **Career:** Sch Administrator (retired); teacher; asst prin; elem educ dir; asst supt-personnel; instr dep supt; E Lansing Pub Schs, dep supt. **Orgs:** Bd dir, Alpha Kappa Alpha, nat comt chmn, chap officer, vpres, int pres, 1994-98. **Honors/Awds:** Crystal Apple Award, E Sharon Banks & Lansing Sch Dist.

EVANS, FAITH RENEE
Singer, actor. **Personal:** Born Jun 10, 1973, Newark, NJ; daughter of Richard Swain and Helene Evans; children (previous marriage): Chyna; married Christopher Wallace, 1995 (died 1997); children: Christopher Jr; married Todd Russaw; children: Joshua. **Career:** Singer, songwriter, record producer & actress; Albums: Faith, 1995; Keep the Faith, 1998; Faithfully, 2001; Faithfully (Japan Bonus Track), 2002; The First Lady, 2005; A Faithful Christmas, 2005; Faith: Remixed, Unreleased & Featured, 2006; Film: Turn It Up, 2000; The Fighting Temptations, 2003; TV series: Orange Bowl Parade, 1997; Half&Half, 2004. **Honors/Awds:** Lady of Soul Award, 1996; MTV Video Music Award, 1997 & 1999; Soul Train Award, 1998. Best Rap Performance by a Duo or Group, 1998. **Business Addr:** Singer, c/o Capitol Records Inc, 1750 N Vine St, Hollywood, CA 90028, **Business Phone:** (323)462-6252.*

EVANS, GREGORY JAMES
Manager. **Personal:** Born Feb 15, 1954, Chicago, IL; son of Johnnie and Willie. **Educ:** Wilbur Wright Jr Col, AA, 1975; Southern IL Univ, BA, Philos, 1977; Southern Ill Univ, MS Health Ed, 1979; De Paul Univ, Chicago, Ill, PhD, cand, philos, 1986-.

Career: Am Cancer Soc, pub ed, coord, 1980-82; Oak Park YMCA, phys ed instr, 1982-84; Am Cancer Soc, publ ed dir, 1982; Health & Sports Prod, dir, 1982-84; Randolph Tower Fitness Ctr, mgr, 1983-84; Village Oak Park, mgr adult educ, 1986-; Spec Event Entertainment Group, pres, 1989-; Park Dist Oak Pk, mgr adult & leisure serv, currently; Frank Lloyd Wright Races, race dir, currently. **Orgs:** Ahn's Tae Kwon Do Asn, 1978; ice hockey coach vol, Oak Park Hockey Asn, 1980-81; gen mem, Ill Interagency Coun Smoking & Disease, 1980-83; Nat Pub Ed Ctr; Am Cancer Soc, 1980; vpres, Ill Soc Pub Health Ed, 1981-82; Oak Park Area Jaycees, 1984-; Ill Park & Recreation Asn, 1984-; Nat Youth Sport Coach Asn, 1987; Am Asn Physical, Health & Recreation, 1989; Chicago Conv Bur & Tourism, 1990; TAC Ill, Long Distance Running Comn, 1990; bd regents, Sch Sports Mgt, NC State Univ, 1992-95; regent, Sch Sports Mgt 1991-; coordr, Road Race Directions Conf; USA Track & Field Ill, 1992-. **Honors/Awds:** Semi-Pro Football Champs, Cook County Cowboys, 1981; Cultural Arts Award, Jack & Jill Asn Am W Suburban Chap, 1986. **Home Addr:** 18 Woodsorrel, Woodridge, IL 60517. **Business Addr:** Manager, Adult, Senior Leisure Services, Park Dist Oak Park, 218 W Madison, Oak Park, IL 60302, **Business Phone:** (708)725-2200.

EVANS, DR. GROVER MILTON
Government official, public speaker, consultant. **Personal:** Born Mar 6, 1952, Jonesboro, AR; son of William Evans and Georgia Lee Evans; married Pamela, Jun 7, 1981; children: Grover Evans Jr. **Educ:** Ark State Univ, BA, 1992; LaSalle Univ, PhD, nutrit coun, 1995. **Career:** Motivational speaker, educator, business consultant; Jonesboro Sun, journalist, 1974-77; KXRQ, news dir, 1982-83; City Jonesboro, city councilman, 1984; vice mayor, City Jonesboro, 1984-96; Self employed, consult & motivational speaker, 1992-; Ark Rehab Serv & Dept Human Serv, spec consult syst design, 2004-. **Orgs:** Chmn, Ark State Spinal Cord Comn, 1989-99; comnr, Ark Martin Luther King Jr Comn, comner, 1993; comnr, Early Childhood Comn, 1989-93; Ark Child Placement Adv Comt, 1987-; Consumer Adv Coun Rehab Serv, 1986-92; liaison, Nat Orgn Disabilities, 1986-; Jonesboro Chamber Com Educ Comt, 1995; US Water Fitness Asn Inc, vice chmn, 1993-. **Honors/Awds:** Outstanding Black Citizen Award, US Postal Serv, 1989; Paralympics, US Disabled Swim Team, 1992; Ambassador of Goodwill for the State of Arkansas, 1992; Swimmer of the Year, Nat Wheel chair Championships, 1993; Volunteer of the Year, Methodist Hosp, Jonesboro, 1993. **Special Achievements:** First Black American to swim in any Olympic Event, 1992; First Black American to swim in a World Championship, 1994; keynote speaker at 7th Annual I Have a Dream, Nat Youth Assembly, 1994; hold 10 American records in swimming, sponsored by Martin Luther King Jr Federal Holiday Commission, 1991-95; First African-American to be elected to the Jonesboro City Council. **Home Addr:** 1616 Brookwood Dr, Little Rock, AR 72202, **Home Phone:** (501)296-1615. **Business Addr:** Special Consultant, Arkansas Department of Human Services, 2201 Brookwood Dr Suite 117, PO Box 3781, Little Rock, AR 72202, **Business Phone:** (501)666-8868.

EVANS, GWENDOLYN
Executive, president (organization), chief executive officer. **Personal:** Born Jan 1, 1943?, North Carolina; daughter of James L and Talmadge Whitley. **Educ:** Essex Col Bus, Cert, 1965; Rutgers Univ, BS, 1973; New Sch Social Res, Post Grad Work, 1975-77. **Career:** Prudential Ins Co, vpres, agency career develop, var admin, tech & clerical assignments, 1962-74; Col Rels, assoc mgr, 1974-75; Equal Opportunity specialist, 1975-76; assoc mgr, corp personnel admin, 1976; mgr, field serv personnel, 1978-89; Calif & Idaho Locally Deployed Agents Proj, dir, 1989-90, vpres, career develop, 1990-93, vpres, sales support, 1993-95, vpres, urban mkt initiative, 1995-97; Strategy Plus Results Inc, chief exec officer & pres, currently. **Orgs:** Instr, Col Co Prud Essex Co Col, 1973-75; Hampton Inst Cluster Prog, Va, 1975-77; dir, serv personnel 1978-, dir, field off planning, 1982-, Prudential Ins CO; exec comt, bd mem, Nat Community Prev Child Abuse NJ Chap, 1983-88; Am Soc Develop NJ Chap, 1984-85; charter mem, Educ Ctr Youth Newark; Women Unlimited; adv bd, Prevent Child Abuse; bd mem, Community Day Nursery. **Honors/Awds:** YWCA Black Achiever Award, Newark, NJ, 1981; Certificate of Appreciation, Am Soc Training Develop, 1984. **Business Addr:** Chief Executive Officer, President, Strategy Plus Results Inc, 784 Morris Tpke Suite 339, Short Hills, NJ 07078, **Business Phone:** (973)762-2143.

EVANS, HUGH
Manager. **Personal:** Born Jan 1, 1943?. **Career:** Nat Basketball Asn, referee, currently. **Business Addr:** NBA Official, 645 5th Ave 15th Fl, New York, NY 10022-5986, **Business Phone:** (212)826-7000.*

EVANS, DR. JACK
College president. **Personal:** Born Jan 1, 1938?, Houston, TX; children: Jack Jr, Herbert Raye & David Paul. **Educ:** Southwestern Christian Col, grad, 1959; Eastern New Mex Univ, hist & relig, 1961; Univ Tex, MA, 1963. **Career:** Col Church Christ, assoc minister, 1959; SW Christian Col, Terrell, TX, dean & instr hist, 1963-67, pres, 1967-. **Orgs:** Bd birs, David Lipscomb Univ. **Honors/Awds:** LLD, Harding Univ; LLD, Pepperdine Univ; LLD, Abilene Christian Univ. **Special Achievements:** First Afro-America President of the only predominantly black Christian College; author/editor of the Evans-Barr Debate, the Curing of Ham, the Cross or the Crescent, Sermons that Save, Sinai or Zion, The Two Covenants; and co-author with Dr James Maxell, of Divorce and Remarriage and with G P Holt, of Sermons of the Crusades. **Business Addr:** President, Southwestern Christian College, PO Box 10, Terrell, TX 75160, **Business Phone:** (972)524-3341.

EVANS, JAMES L.
Administrator. **Personal:** Born Nov 11, 1954, Columbus, OH; son of Darlene; children: Erika Briana, Alonzo James. **Educ:** Univ Ky, BS, 1976. **Career:** Ohio Secy State, press secy, 1983-87; Franklin County Dem Party, exec dir, 1987-90; WSMZ-FM, news dir, 1990-. **Orgs:** Sigma Delta Chi; Ohio Asn Broadcasters; Nab, Central Ohio Chap. **Honors/Awds:** Assoc Press, Best Enterprise Reporting, 1991-92. **Business Addr:** News Director, WSMZ-FM, 510 E Mound St, Columbus, OH 43215-5571, **Business Phone:** (614)469-1930.*

EVANS, JOE B.
Government official. **Personal:** Born Dec 28, 1928, Fair Bluff, NC; son of Henry Perry Sr and Cora; married Mary Hammond, 2000; children: Joe Bardin Jr, Deborah Julia Epps, Rocky, Anthony & Natalie. **Career:** Addis Cates Co Inc; Fair Bluff City, mayor, 1993-. **Orgs:** Adv coun, Fair Bluff Sch, 1967-; worthy patron, Pleasant Plain Chap 275, 1969-; Evans Sub div Fair Bluff; Columbus Co Civic League; NAACP; City Counman, 1973-93-; master, Oak Grove Lodge 775, 1971-72; dir, United Carolina Bank; dir, Tel & Data Systs; pres, Int Govt Comn; bd dir, Carver Community Ctr; bd dir, TDS Tel Co Fair Bluff; adv bd, BB&T; Columbus CityBlack Mayors Asn; NC Criminal Justice Info Network Bd. **Honors/Awds:** Twenty-fourth Dist Award, United Masonic Comm Columbus Co, 1972; Tri-County UNCF Award, Barden Brunswick & Columbus Counties, 1998. **Military Serv:** AUS, sgt, 1950-56; Good Conduct Medal. **Business Addr:** Mayor, City Fair Bluff, Barden St, Fair Bluff, NC 28439.

EVANS, JOSH (MIJOSHKI ANTWON EVANS)
Football player. **Personal:** Born Sep 6, 1972, Langdale, AL. **Educ:** Ala-Birmingham. **Career:** Football player (retired); Houston Oilers, defensive tackle, 1995-96; Tennessee Oilers, 1997-98; Tennesse Titans, 1999-2001; NY Jets, 2002-04. *

EVANS, KAMIEL DENISE
School administrator. **Personal:** Born Jan 22, 1971, Wichita, KS; daughter of M D Fisher and Lois J Kempson; married Mario Evans, Nov 16, 1996; children: Kamerin Lydell & Marissa Lee. **Educ:** Butler County Comm Col, 1990; Friends Univ, BA, sci, 1993; Wichita State Univ, MA, educ admin, 1999. **Career:** Wichita Pub Sch, teacher, 1993-97, admin intern, 1997-99, asst prin, 1999-2000; Adams Elem Sch, prin, currently. **Orgs:** Pres, 1993-95, vpres, 1998-99, Zeta Phi Beta Sorority, Sigma Zeta; St Mark UMC, Strengthening the Black Church for 21st Century, 1998; Wichita Asn Black Sch Educr, 1998-; Kans Women Educ Leadership, 1999; Am Cancer Soc Breast Cancer Awareness Comt, 1999; Grow Your Own Teacher Speaker's Bur, 1999; KS Asn Elem Schs Principals, 1999-2000. **Honors/Awds:** Delta Sigma Theta Scholarship, 1989; Presidents Honor Roll, Friends Univ, 1990, Dean's Honor Roll, 1991-93; Kansas Minority Scholarship, 1990-93. **Home Addr:** 841 N Bristol Ct, Wichita, KS 67206-4319.

EVANS, LEE
Athlete, athletic coach. **Personal:** Born Feb 25, 1947, Madera, CA. **Educ:** San Jose State, 1970. **Career:** Nigeria & Saudi Arabia, coach, 1975-97; Nigerian Nat Team, phys fitness couns, coach, 1975-80; All-African team, sprint coach, 1977; wash Univ, sprint coach, 2002; Univ Ala, head coach. **Orgs:** Olympic Track Team, 1968, 1972. **Honors/Awds:** AAU champion, 1966- 69, 1972; Olympic Gold Medals Mexico, 1968; AAU 440 yrd, 1966-67, 1969-70; gold medal, Pan-Amer Games 1967; world 400m dash & 1600m relay records Olympics 1968; coach of the year, 1979; Fulbright Scholar award, 1986, 1987; Coach of the United States at the World Indoor Track & Field Championships, 2004.

EVANS, LEOMONT DOZIER
Football player. **Personal:** Born Jul 12, 1974, Abbeville, SC; married Felicia; children: Kamyia & Leomont Jr. **Educ:** Clemson Univ. **Career:** Football player (retired); Wash Redskins, defensive end, 1996-99; Houston Texans, safety, 2001-04.

EVANS, LEON, JR.
Insurance executive, consultant. **Personal:** Born Jan 8, 1953, Union Springs, AL; son of Leon Evans Sr. and Annie Ruth Beasley; married Nyle Denise Hallback; children: Andrea Lactrice, Carlos LaRoy. **Educ:** Tuskegee Univ, BS, 1977; Samford Univ, MBA, 1985. **Career:** New Eng Bankcard Assoc, mgr trainee, 1973-75; John Hancock Ins Co, life underwriter, 1977-80; BlueCross & BlueShield Ala, consult & mgr, 1980-; Ren Advan Off Controls, certified instr, 1986. **Orgs:** Team leader, Big Brothers Big Sisters Fund Dr, 1985; vpres, Groove Phi Groove Grad Chap, 1985; consult, Jr Achievement Birmingham, 1985-86; mem Nat Black MBA Asn, 1986-; fel Life Office Mgt Asn, 1987; Leadership Development Asn, 1988-; Birmingham Urban League, 1988-; bd trustee, Gateway. **Honors/Awds:** Award for Outstanding Leadership Junior Achievement, 1986. **Business Addr:** Manager, BlueCross & BlueShield of Alabama, 450 River Chase Pkwy E, Birmingham, AL 35298, **Business Phone:** (205)988-2580.*

EVANS, LEON EDWARD, JR.
Banker. **Personal:** Born Dec 28, 1942, Chicago, IL; married Doris J Davis; children: Aaron Gerard & Sheila Rene. **Educ:** Wilson Jr Col, Park Col, attended. **Career:** Continental Ill Nat Bank Chicago, bookkeeping clerk, 1963-67; Independence Bank Chicago, asst cashier, 1967-69; Exchange Nat Bank Chicago, asst cashier, 1969-70; Gateway Nat Bank Chicago, vpres cashier, 1970-72; Douglas State Bank, vpres, cashier, 1972-75; Comm Bank NE, pres, ceo, 1975-88; City Omaha, Off Mayor, econ develop aide, 1988-89; Bus Consult Specialists, consult, 1989-90; Am State Bank, exec vpres, 1990-92, pres, ceo, 1992-. **Orgs:** Am Bankers Asn, Community Bankers Coun; bd mem, Boys Town; bd mem, Metropolitian Tulsa Chamber Comm; bd mem, Oklahoma Bankers Asn; bd mem, Am State Bank; bd mem, Conn Grad Sch Community Banking, Okla City Univ. **Business Addr:** President, Chief Executive Officer, American State Bank, 3816 N Peoria Ave, Tulsa, OK 74106, **Business Phone:** (918)428-2211.

EVANS, DR. LEROY W.
Lawyer. **Personal:** Born Dec 15, 1946, Houston, TX; married Robbie Moore; children: Anana Salisha. **Educ:** Univ Houston, BA, 1969; Boalt Hall Sch Law, Berkeley, JD, 1972. **Career:** EE Worthing Scholar, 1965; Martin Luther King fel, 1969; Shear man & Steal, assoc, 1972-74; Emergency Land Fund, atty, gen couns, 1974-; Consortium Develop Rural, Southern E, exec dir, 1977-79; Small Farm Develop Corp, admin dir, 1979-. **Orgs:** Asst secy, treas, bd mem, Riverfront Enterprises Inc; Nat Conf Black Lawyers; LABA; bd mem, Southern E YMCA; Dekalb County Young Dem; Dekalb County Nat Asn Advan Colored People; Calif Bar Asn; NY Bar Asn; Practicing Law Inst; Sigma Iota Epsilon. **Honors/Awds:** Distinguished Mil Grad, 1969.

EVANS, LIZ
Executive. **Personal:** Born Jun 6, 1941, Augusta, GA; daughter of Robert D Sherard and Geraldine Payne; divorced; children: Tina, Emmet & Ida. **Educ:** Capital Univ, attended. **Career:** WTVN-AM, WBUK-FM, from asst to pub affairs dir, 1970; WTVN-TV, WTVN-AM, WBUK-FM, community rels dir, 1973; WTVN-AM, Q FM 96, dir pub affairs; Clear Channel Columbus, dir pub affairs. **Orgs:** Chair, Black Family Connections Adoption Adv Bd, 1987; Women's Health Month Adv Comt, 1988; founder, Mothers Against Crack Inc, 1989; Cols Aids Task Force Coalition, Media, 1989; founder, African Am Cancer Support Group, 1992; volunteer, Am Cancer Soc Reach to Recovery, 1992; Direction Youth Serv Bd, 1992; Ohio Breast & Cervical Cancer Coalition; Columbus Breast & Cervical Cancer Proj; Nat Black Leadership Initiative Against Cancer, Ohio Chap; bd mem, Am Cancer Soc; bd mem, Race for the Cure; ML King Arts Complex, Women's Serv Bd; founder, African Am Cancer Support Group, Mothers Against Crack; Ohio Dept Health Cancer Epidemiol Prevention & Control Prog Bur; Grant Med Ctr Cancer Libr Adv Bd; Columbus Open Shelter; United Way Proj Diversity Bd; Columbus Women's Roundtable. **Honors/Awds:** Ohio Governor's Citation, 1989; Media Awardee, Comin Home Community Found, 1992; Volunteer Service, Black Family Connections, 1992; Volunteer Service, Am Cancer Soc, 1992; Ohio Commission on Minority Health Award, 1992; YWCA Woman Achievement, 1996; inductee, Ohio Women Hall of Fame, 1996. **Business Addr:** Director of Public Affairs, Clear Channel Columbus, 1301 Dublin Rd, Columbus, OH 43215, **Business Phone:** (614)487-2519.

EVANS, MARI
Educator, writer. **Personal:** Born Jul 16, 1923, Toledo, OH; divorced; children: William Evan & Derek Reed. **Educ:** Univ Toledo; Marian Col, LHD, 1975. **Career:** Ind Univ-Purdue Univ Indianapolis, instr black lit & writer-in-residence,1969-70; Ind Univ Bloomington, asst prof black lit & writer-in-residence,1970-78; Northwestern Univ, vis asst prof, 1972-73; Nightstar, 1973-78; Purdue Univ, W Lafayette, vis asst prof, 1978-80; Wash Univ, St Louis, visasst prof, 1980; Cornell Univ, vis asst prof, 1981-83, asst prof, distinguished writer, 1983-85; State Univ NY-Albany, assoc prof, 1985-86; Miami Univ, Coral Gables, vis distinguished writer, 1989; Spelman Col, Atlanta, writer-in-residence, 1989-90; Books: Dear Corinne, Tell Somebody!, Singing Black Alternative Nursery Rhymes C, Dark& Splendid Mass, 1992; How We Speak; Poems: The Gospel Singers, Where HaveYou Gone, "I Am a Black Woman"; Producer, dir & writer television prog"The Black Experience," WTTV, Indianapolis, 1968-73; Author of poetry: Nightstar, 1980; author of books forjuveniles, including J.D., Doubleday, 1973, I Look at Me, Third WorldPress, 1974, Singing Black, Reed Visuals, 1976, Jim Flying High, Doubleday, 1979 & The Day They Made Beriani; playwright of "River of MySong," 1977, "Eyes" (musical), 1979, 1989, 1995; "Boochie," 1979,"Portrait of a Man," & "Glide & Sons" (musical); editor of Black Women Writers, 1950-80: A Critical Evaluation, Doubleday-Anchor, 1984. **Orgs:** Consult, Discovery Grant Prog, Nat Endowment Arts, 1969-70; consult ethnic studies, Bobbs-Merrill Co, 1970-73; chmn lit adv panel, Ind State Arts Comn, 1976-77; chmn, Statewide Comt Penal Reform; bd mgt, Fall Creek PkwyYMCA, 1975-81; bd dirs, 1st World Found; Ind Corrections

Code Comn; African Heritage Studies Asn; Authors Guild; Authors League Am. **Honors/Awds:** Contrib poetry textbooks, anthologies & periodicals; John Hay Whitney fel, 1965-66; Woodrow Won Found grantee, 1968; Ind Univ Writers Conf Award,1970; 1st Annual Poetry Award, Black Acad Arts & Letters, 1970; MacDowell Fel, 1975; Copeland Fel, Amherst Col, 1980; Nat Endowment Arts Grantee, 1981-82; Gwen Brooks Award, 1989, 1996; Du Sable Mus Award, 1989; Hazel J Bryant Award, Midwest African-Am Theatre Alliance; Zora Neale Hurston Soc Award, 1993; Alainhocke-Gwen Brooks Award, US Inc, 1995; Zora Nealst Hurston-Paul Robeson Award, Nat Coun Black Studies Inc, 1996. **Special Achievements:** Int Literary Hall Fame Writers African Descent. *

EVANS, MARY ADETTA
Educator. **Personal:** Born Jun 13, 1909, Coldwater, VA; married Warren A; children: James W, Warren & David. **Educ:** Va State Col, BS, 1948; Columbia Univ, MA, 1958. **Career:** King & Queen Pub Schs, teacher, 1931-39; Nottoway Training Sch, 1941-48; Baker Elem Sch, 1948-50; Albert V Norrell Elem Sch, 1950-74. **Orgs:** Bldg rep, Va Teachers Asn; Richmond Teachers Asn; Nat Educ Asn; Richmond Retired Teachers Asn; Va Nat Retired Teachers Asn; Richmond Nat Asn Univ Women; past pres, secy, Nat Coun Negro Women; past supt jr dept, Rapahannock River South side Bapt Asn; vpres, Area C Woman's Aux; Baptist Gen Conv Va; vpres, Baptist Woman's Aux, Rappahannock River South side Asn;Delver Woman's Club; YWCA; Crusade Voters; Va Mus Fine Arts; Jr Red Cross sponsor, 1972-73; Alpha Kappa Alpha Sor; chap pres, secy exec bd, Va Minister's Wives Asn; Baptist Church.

EVANS, MIJOSHKI ANTWON. See EVANS, JOSH.

EVANS, MIKE (MICHAEL EVANS)
Basketball coach, basketball player. **Personal:** Born Apr 19, 1955, Goldsboro, NC; married Kim; children: Michael, Rachelle & D'Ambra. **Educ:** Kans State Univ. **Career:** Basketball player (retired), basketball coach; San Antonio Spurs, profbasketball player, 1979-80; Milwaukee Bucks, 1981-82; Cleveland Cavaliers,1982; Denver Nuggets, prof basketball player, 1982-88, asst coach,1993-94, 1997, dir player personnel, TV anal, 1994-97, interim head coach,2001; scout, Toronto Raptors, 2006-07; Raptors, coaching staff, 2007-08. **Honors/Awds:** Big Eight, Player of the Year.

EVANS, MILTON L.
Chief executive officer. **Personal:** Born Oct 9, 1936, Snowhill, NC; son of Herbert Evans Jr and Lola Vines; married Alice Corella Brown; children: Milton Jr, Alan, Glenn, Warren & Kenneth. **Educ:** Shaw Univ, BS, Chem, 1960; Tuskegee Inst, MS, Chem, 1964. **Career:** General Electric, r&d mktg mgt, 1964-73, sect mgr compacts, 1974-78, sect mgr strategic planning, gen mgr, specialty elastomers, 1980-82; High Tech Systems Inc, pres & ceo, 1983-. **Orgs:** Dir, Siena Col Bus Coun; Outreach Inc; Schenectady Pvt Industry Coun; New York Head Injury Assn. **Honors/Awds:** Gold & Silver Medallions GE Inventors Awards. **Special Achievements:** Author: My Sentiments Exactly. **Business Addr:** President, Chief Executive Officer, High Technology Systems Inc., PO Box 751, Clifton Park, NY 12065, **Business Phone:** (518)877-8027.*

EVANS, PATRICIA P
Educator. **Personal:** Born in Topeka, KS; daughter of Lucille Mallory Phelps and C Kermit Phelps; divorced 1981; children: Langston Phelps, Kimberly Dawn & Kristina Ann. **Educ:** Avila Col, Kansas City, MO, BSCh, 1961; Columbia Univ, attended 1972. **Career:** St Mary's Hos, Kansas City, MO, med technologist, 1962-68; Univ Ill Med Center, Chicago, IL, clin teaching asst & asst supvr hematol, 1968-71; Mount Sinai Hosp, New York, NY, asst supvr abnormal hematol, 1971-72; Veterans Admin Hosp, Madison WI, med technologist, 1974-75; St Mary's Hosp, Madison,WI, med technologist, 1977-81; Methodist Hosp, Madison, WI, med technologist, 1981-82; Univ Hosp & Clin, Madison,WI, proj specialist oncol res 1982-86; Univ Wis, Dept Pathol & Lab Med, sr lectr, 1986; Univ Wis, Dept Pathol & Lab Med, emer prof, currently. **Orgs:** Am Soc Clin Lab Sci, 1961-; Am Asn Blood Banks, 1962-; Am Soc Clin Pathologists, 1962-; AAAS, 1968-; Wis Asn Clin Lab Sci, 1972-; Madison Soc Clin Lab Sci, 1977-; Shorewood League Bd, 1977-94; chairperson & bd mem, Jack & Jill Am Inc, 1979-84; girl scout leader, Girl Scouts Am, 1982-88; parent mem, Boy Scouts Am, 1983-90; Center for Health Sci Minority Affairs Comt, 1988-94; co-chair, Membership Comt, Wis Soc Clin Lab Sci, 1988-90; bd mem, West High Sch PTSO 1989-93; Parent Adv Comt, West High Sch, 1989-93; publicity chmn, Wis Soc Clin Lab Sci State Convention, 1990; Biol/Med Sci Area Review Comt, 1990-93; vpres bd, Shorewood League Bd, 1990-91; pres, Shorewood League Bd, 1991-92; Center Health Scis Comn Women's Issues, 1992-98; Women Sci, Engineering & Math Comt, 1994-; nom-chair, Shorewood League Bd, 1994; Am Asn Univ Women, 1995-; Univ Wis-Madison Acad Advan Selection Comt, 1995-; Stud Appeals Comt Undergraduate Prog Med Sch, 1997-; bd trustees, Am Soc Clin Lab Sci Educ & Res Fund Inc, 1998; mentor, Univ Wis-Madison Acad Staff Prog, 1998-; Am Soc Clin Lab Sci Comt Prof Affairs, 1999-2003. **Honors/Awds:** Faith Dravis Award, Wis Soc Clin Lab Sci, 1989; Omicron Sigma Recognition, Wis Soc Clin Lab Sci, 1989, 1990, 2001 & 2003. **Home Addr:** 3223 Topping Rd, Madison, WI 53705, **Home Phone:** (608)238-7380. **Business Phone:** (608)262-2468.

EVANS, PAUL F.
Police officer. **Educ:** Boston State Col, BS; Suffolk Univ Law Sch, JD, 1978; Mass Inst Technol. **Career:** Boston Police Dept, 28-year veteran, comnr, 1994-03; Police & Crime Stand Directorate, Brit, dir, 2003-. **Orgs:** Bd Dir, YMCA; Boston Police Athletic League; Police Exec Res Forum; Mass Bar Asn; Int Chiefs Police. **Military Serv:** US Marine Corps, 1967-69. **Business Phone:** (020)7035-4848.*

EVANS, ROBERT ORAN
Basketball coach. **Personal:** Born Sep 7, 1946, Hobbs, NM; son of Oscar and Gladys; married Carolyn Ann Marshall, Jul 25, 1970; children: Damon LaMont & Amber ShaRon. **Educ:** Lubbock Christian Col, AA, 1966; N Mex State Univ, BS, english, 1968. **Career:** Houston Colt 45s, baseball player; Dallas Chaparrals; Oakland Raiders, wide receiver, 1968; NMex State Univ, asst basketball coach, 1968-75; Tex Tech Univ, asst basketball coach, 1975-90; National Association of asst Basketball Coaches, pres, 1991; Okla State Univ, asst basketball coach; Univ Miss, head basketball coach, 1992-98; Ariz State Univ, Men's Basketball, head coach, 1999-2006; Ark, asst coach, 2008-. **Honors/Awds:** Valley Forge Hon Cert, Lubbock Christian Univ; Outstanding Achievement Award, Tex Tech Univ, 1986-87; Inducted, Lubbock Christian Univ Hall of Fame, 1990; inducted, N Mex State Univ Hall of Fame, 1993; N Mex State Univ's Sch of Educ Alumnus of the Yr, 1994; South eastern Conf Coach of the Year, Asn Press, 1996; Natl Coach of the Yr, 1996-97; Southeastern Conf Coach of the Year, Asn Press, 1997; All-South Coach of the Yr, Basketball Times; Nat Coach of the Yr, Hoop Insiders, 1997; AZ March of Dimes Sports Leadership Award, 2000; Man of Valor Award, S western Christian Col, 2000. **Special Achievements:** Hundred and one(101) Most Influential Minorities in Sports in 2003. **Home Addr:** 3426 E Cherokee St, Phoenix, AZ 85044.

EVANS, ROXANNE J
Journalist. **Personal:** Born Jun 6, 1952, Omaha, NE; daughter of James W Martin and Margaret L Steele; married Kelly Randolph, Apr 4; children: James, Imani, Askia & Joshua. **Educ:** Howard Univ, Wash, DC, 1975-76; Drake Univ, Des Moines, IA, BA, 1982. **Career:** Nat Urban League, Wash, DC, res asst, 1975-76; Des Moines Register, Des Moines, IA, reporter, 1978-83; Austin American-Statesman, Austin, TX, reporter, 1983-88, chief ed writer, 1988-. **Orgs:** Pres, Austin Asn Black Communicators, 1989-. **Honors/Awds:** 'Texas School Bell Award', Tex State Teachers Asn, 1985-88; 'Phoenix Award', Friends of Phoenix, 1984. **Business Addr:** Editorial Writer, Austin American-Statesman, 166 E Riverside Dr, PO Box 670, Austin, TX 78767, **Business Phone:** (512)445-3655.

EVANS, RUTHANA WILSON
Educator, consultant. **Personal:** Born Mar 26, 1932, Roxie, MS; daughter of James (deceased) and Lueberta (deceased); married Lit Parker Evans Jr, Mar 22, 1957; children: Cedric Glenn & Valerie Denise. **Educ:** Tougaloo Col, BS, 1955; Univ Ill, postgrad, 1965; NC Col, 1967; DeltaState Col, MS, 1971; Delta State Univ, MS, psychometrist, 1977, AAA Coun,1981; Admin Coursework, AA. **Career:** Educator (retired). Shaw Sch, elem teacher, 1955-57; Nailor Elem Sch,teacher, curriculum chmn, 1957-60, teacher, librn, 1960-62, librn,1963-64; Pre-sch Story Hour, librn, 1964-66; Bolivar County Dist 4; libr supvr, 1965-67; Ed, TV Jackson, curriculum resources teacher, 1968-70;Parks & Pearman Elem Schs, librn, 1968-70, org elem sch libr prog, 1969; Greenville Elem Sch, consult, 1970; MS Head Start, educ dir, 1970-79; Bolivar County Dist 4 Schs Titles I, counr, 1979-94; Bolivar County Headstart, psychometrist, 1985-94; Bolivar Schs, psychometrist; Cleveland Schs testing cord, 1986, consult, 1995; St Paul Baptist Church, Grant Writing Networker; Bolivar County Action Prog, consult, currently. **Orgs:** PTA, 1955; secy, Negro's Citizens Community Cleveland, 1957-61; job trainer, Neighborhood Youth Corps Cleveland, 1969; Nat Assn Advan ColoredPeople; Phi Delta Kappan; Tougaloo Alumni Delta State Alumni; Consult IndPre-sch Activities, 1971; org inventory, classification systs, Head Start,1970; MS Personnel & Guid Assoc, MS Libr Asn; trainer manpower prog, STEP,1970-, CETA, 1977; active, BSA; Baptist Training Union Cleveland, 1972-, Negro Voters League; treas, E Side HS Band Booster, 1972, treas, 1971, pres, 1973 Athena Soc Club; secy, Womens Club, 1970; Nat Coun Black Child Develop, 1975-78; MS Counsrs Assoc; Nat Educ Assoc; secy, St Paul Baptist Church; lay bd mem, Jake Ayers Case; Am Couns Assn; Delta Sigma Theta Sorority Inc. **Honors/Awds:** First runner-up to Miss, Tougaloo Col, 1955. **Home Addr:** 816 Cross St, Cleveland, MS 38732. *

EVANS, SAMUEL LONDON
School administrator. **Personal:** Born Nov 11, 1902, Leon County, FL; married Edna Hoye; children: Retha EB Kelly. **Educ:** Columbia Univ, attended 1948; NY Univ, integrated concepts sci philos & educ, 1953; Combs Col, MusD, 1968. **Career:** US Div Phys Fitness, coordr, 1941-45; Philadelphia Chamber Orchestra, impressario, 1961-71; S London Publ Co, publ; Pa State Athletic Comn, secy; Bicentennial Corp, exec vpres, 1971-; Am Found Negro Affairs, Nat Educ & Res Fund, pres & chmn bd, currently. **Orgs:** Columbia Univ, World Study Tour, 1948; founder, pres, nat chmn, Am Found Negro Affairs, 1968-; founder, African Am Hall of Fame Sculpture Garden, 1984; Mayors Comn Munic Serv; bd dir, Am Trauma Soc; Am Heart Asn; bd dir, prod gen mgr, Philadelphia Coffee Concerts Comt; Nat Trust Hist Preserv, Am Pub Health Asn; comt mem, US Const 200 year Anniversary. **Honors/Awds:** Black Expo Award, 1972; Serv Award, 3rd World 76' Inc, 1972; Achievement Award, Philadelphia Cotillion Soc, 1972; Community Serv Award, Philadelphia Oppertunity Indust Ctrs, 1972; Achievement Award, Nat Asn Adv Colored People Reg II, 1972; USN Award, 1976; Charles R Drew Award, 1978; Philadelphia Acad Sci Award, 1981; Sister Clara Muhammad Sch Annual Educ Award, 1983; Philadelphia Miniversity Citizens Award, 1985. **Special Achievements:** Auth: The AFNA Plan, A Projection for the Year 200 and Now in Medicine, Law, Business & Commerce, Science Tech, 1974; Nothing to Fear, Second Phase of Democracy An Amer Manifesto. **Business Addr:** President, Chairman, American Found Negro Affairs, 117 S 17th St Suite 1200, Philadelphia, PA 19103-5025.*

EVANS, STACEY LYN. See MORGAN, STACEY EVANS.

EVANS, THERMAN E.
Physician, health services administrator. **Personal:** Born Aug 20, 1944, Henderson, NC; son of Irvin Sr and Constine; married Bernetta Jones, Jul 30, 1966; children: Thomas E Evans Jr, Clayton Evans. **Educ:** Howard Univ, BS, 1966, MD, 1971; United Christian Col, PhD, 1999. **Career:** Oper PUSH, nat health dir; East River Health Ctr Wash, physician; CT Gen Ins Co, 2nd vpres & corp med dir; CIGNA, asst med dir, 1979-83, corp med dir, 1983-87, vpres & corp med dir, 1987; Wholelife Assocs Inc, founder & chief exec officer, 2004-. **Orgs:** Nat bd dirs, Oper PUSH, 1983, review & adv comt, var agencies Fed Govt; pres, Wash DC Bd Educ; clin fac Howard Univ; pres, Oper PUSH, Philadelphia Chap, 1983-86; bd dirs, Southeastern PA Wellness Coun, 1987-88, Philadelphia Health Mgt Corp, 1988-; pastor, morning star community christian ctr. **Honors/Awds:** Vis Regent's Scholar Lect Univ CA; published over 25 articles var health related subj jour & mag; guest expert numerous nat & local radio & TV health oriented progs; Alumnae of the Yr, Howard Univ Alumnae Asn, Philadelphia Chapter, 1988; Stress & the Col Stud, The Black Collegian Mag, 1989; Being Black in Am Hazardous to Your Health, J the Nat Med Asn, 1989; Outstanding Alumnus of the Year, Howard Univ Col Med, 2003. **Special Achievements:** For 10 years he hosted a 2-hour radio show called "Lifeline" on WHAT 1340 AM in Philadelphia, PA. **Business Addr:** Founder, Chief Executive Officer, Wholelife Associates Inc, 906 Rock Lane, Elkins Park, PA 19207, **Business Phone:** (215)576-8319.*

EVANS, TIMOTHY C.
Judge. **Personal:** Born Jun 1, 1943. **Educ:** Univ IL, BA, 1985; John Marshall Law Sch, JD, 1965. **Career:** Chicago Dept Investigations, former dep comnr; Secy State Off, Cook County, IL, chief hearing officer, 1973; Chicago, IL, city alderman, 4th ward, 1973-91; atty, pvt pract, 1991-; Cook City Circuit Ct, chief judge, 2001-. **Honors/Awds:** 4Unsuccessful bid for mayor, Chicago, IL, gen election, Harold Washington Party, 1989; first black chief judge, Cook County Cir Ct, 2001. **Business Addr:** Chief Judge, Circuit County of Cook County, 2600 Richard J Daley Ctr, Chicago, IL 60602, **Business Phone:** (312)603-6000.*

EVANS, VERNON D.
Auditor, accountant. **Personal:** Born Mar 7, 1950, Ft Worth, TX; son of Rev Dellie (deceased) and Thelma; married Viola Ruth Cross (divorced); children: Victor, Vinikka, Vernessa. **Educ:** N Tex State Univ, BBA, MBA, 1972. **Career:** Ernst & Ernst Cert Pub Acct, staff acct, sr acct, 1972-76; Cert Public Acct, 1973; Cert Mgt Acct, 1980; Ernst & Whinney, audit mgr & supvr, 1972-82; Evans McAfee & Co, managing partner, 1976-78; Fort Worth Int Airport Bd, Dallas, TX, dir audit serv, 1986-94, dep exec dir admin serv, exec vpres & chief financial officer; Fort Worth Independent Sch Dist, chief internal auditor, 1982-86; Cert Internal Auditor, 1985; Cert Fraud Examiner, 1989; San Diego County Regional Airport Authority, vpres, treas & chief financial officer, 2003-. **Orgs:** Nat Asn Accountants, 1974-80; chair, United Way Allocation Com III, 1979-80; chmn, McDonald YMCA, 1980; treas, Metro Econ Develop Corp, 1980; vpres, 1979-81, pres, 1981-83, Nat Asn Black Accountants; state dir, Tex Soc Cert Pub Accountants, 1988-90; founder & past pres, Asn Airport Internal Auditors, 1989-91; dir-at-large, chmn, Southern Regional Dir, 1987-90, N Am Regional Dirs Comt, 1991-94; Tex State Bd Pub Accountancy, vice chmn, 1991-98; adv bd, TCU, 1992-; bd trustees, Prof Develop Inst, 1992-; Inst Internal Auditors; Asn Govt Accountants; Govt Finance Officers Asn; Nat Forum Black Public Administrators; accounting dept ad bd, N Tex State Univ; bd dir, Ft Worth Black Chamber Com; bd dir, Day Care Asn; Jackie Robinson, YMCA, San Diego, CA. **Honors/Awds:** Outstanding Achievement Award, Sickle Cell Anemia Asn Tex, 1979; Outstanding Achievement Award, Nat Asn Black Accountants 1979, 1987; Greek Image Award, Pan-Hellenic Coun, 1983; Henry A Meadows Volunteer of the Year Award, YMCA-

MFW, 1983; Outstanding Service Awards, McDonald YMCA, 1985; Outstanding Service Awards, United Negro Col Fund, 1986; Chi Rho Award, YMCA-MFW, 1988; F M Miller Award, McDonald YMCA, 1989; National Achievement Award, Nat Asn Black Accountants, 1989; Outstanding Regional Director Award, Inst Internal Auditors Inc, 1990; CPA of the Year Award, Fort Worth Chap Tex Soc CPA, 1990; Outstanding Professional Achievement, Fort Worth Chap Nat Asn Black Accountants, 1992; Outstanding Leadership, United Negro Col Fund, 1994; Earnest Anderson Award, McDonald YMCA, 1994. **Business Addr:** Vice President & Treasurer, Chief Executive Officer, San Diego County Regional Airport Authority, PO Box 82776, San Diego, CA 92138-2776.*

EVANS, WANDA. **See COLEMAN, WANDA.**

EVANS, WARREN CLEAGE
Educator, lawyer, sheriff. **Personal:** Born Dec 30, 1948, Detroit, MI; son of E Warren and Gladys H Cleage; divorced; children: Erikka N & Nikki Lynn. **Educ:** Madonna Univ, Livonia, MI, BA, social sci, 1975; Univ Detroit, MI, MA, criminal justice, 1980; Detroit Col Law, Detroit, MI, JD, 1986. **Career:** Wayne Co Sheriff's Dept, dep, 1970, undersheriff, 1987-91; Univ Detroit Mercy, asst prof, 1988; Wayne County Comn, dir admin, 1991-92; Wayne County Prosecutor's Off, chief spec oper; Wayne County, sheriff, 2003-. **Orgs:** Pres, Detroit Bd Water Comners, 1989-. **Honors/Awds:** Chief Advocacy Award; Spirit of Detroit Award, Detroit City Coun, 1987; Distinguished Corrections Service Award, 1988. **Business Addr:** Sheriff, Wayne County, 1231 St Antoine, Detroit, MI 48226.

EVANS, WEBB
Association executive. **Personal:** Born Nov 20, 1913, Greensboro, AL; married Cora Golightly. **Educ:** Tenn State Col, 1937; Cortez Peters Bus Sch, 1943. **Career:** Wells Consumers Coop Inc, Chicago, mgr, 1945-47; Evans Food Mart Chicago, owner, 1949-74; House of Saunders Chicago, mgr, 1974-. **Orgs:** Bd dir, Southside Comm Com for Juv Delinq Prevention, 1949-65; pres, United Am Progress Asn, 1961-; bd dir, Cosmo C of C, 1961-65; treas, Forrestville Civic Improve League, 1963-74; trustee, Cathedral Bapt Church, 1964-; pres, Layman Dept Prog Bapt State Convention IL,1966-68; treas, Fellowship Bapt Dist Asn, 1971-73; pres, 41st & 42nd Wells St Block Club; mem, Chatham Avalon Park Community Coun. **Honors/Awds:** Recipient Top Male Volunteer Award, Vol Bur of Met Chicago, 1961; Award Outstanding Serv Civil Rights Movement, Christian Religious Builders,1964; Civil Progress Award, Inter-Denom Min Civ League IL, 1964; Citizen of Week, WBEE Radio, 1969; Hon Citizen State of TN, Gov Frank Clement, 1966; citation, United Am Prog Asn 1972. **Business Addr:** President, United American Progress Association, 701 E 79th St, Chicago, IL 60619, **Business Phone:** (773)268-1873.

EVANS, DR. WILLIAM E.
Educational consultant, educator, school administrator. **Personal:** Born Nov 28, 1931, Mebane, NC; son of Mozelle; married Gloria Battle. **Educ:** Hampton Inst, BS, 1954; Southern Conn St Col, MS, 1961; Bridgeport Univ, attended 1964; Southern Conn St Col; Yale Univ, Drug Educ, 1971; Univ Conn, PhD, 1985. **Career:** Educational consultant (retired); Laurel Ledge Sch, Beacon Falls Conn, teacher, 1957-58; Barnard Sch, Waterbury Conn, teacher, 1958; elem physical educ instr, 1958-59; Wilby High Sch, Waterbury Conn, phys ed &biol instr, 1958-67; Project Upward Bound, Univ Hartford, reading instr, 1966-67, curriculum coordr & reading instr, 1967-68, asst project dir, 1968-72; Community Action Agency, Waterbury, 1967; Waterbury Sch System, supvr health & physical educ, 1967-72; Waterbury Pub Sch, drug coordr, 1971; Mattatuck Community Col, Psychol Dept, 1971-72; Waterbury Dept Educ, dir educ grants, 1972-90; Waterbury Tercentennial Inc, stud coordr; New Opportunities Waterbury, Conn, educ consult; Univ Conn, educ consult. **Orgs:** Nat Advan Asn Colored People; bd incorporators, Boy's Club Am; First United Bapt Church, White Marsh, Va, deacon. **Honors/Awds:** Hampton Alumni Fellowship 1967; Outstanding Alumnus Award, Hampton Inst, 1974; Univ Conn Found Fellowship, 1984. **Military Serv:** AUS, artillery officer, 2nd lt, 1954-56, 1st lt, 1956-57. **Home Addr:** Hayes, VA 23072. *

EVANS-TRANUMN, SHELIA
School administrator. **Personal:** Born Aug 19, 1951, Durham, NC; daughter of George Watts Sr and Eunice Allen; married Howard James Tranumn Jr, Sep 3, 1988; children: DeAnna. **Educ:** NC Cent Univ, Durham, NC, BA, 1973; Long Island Univ, Brooklyn, NY, MS, 1977; NY Univ, New York, NY, currently. **Career:** New York Bd Educ, Auxiliary Servs High Schs, dir, 1973-; New York Sch & Community Servs, assoc comnr, currently. **Orgs:** Pres, New York Alliance Black Sch Educr, 1986-; Chancellor's Adv Comt Promote Equal Opportunity, 1987-; founder & dir, Educr Christ, AME Church, 1988-; chairperson, Multicultural Adv Bd, New York Bd Educ, 1988-; minister educ, Bridge St AME Church, 1988-. **Honors/Awds:** High Prof Achievement, Key Women Am, 1985; Risk Taker Award, New York Alliance Black Sch Educ, 1988; Richard Green Educ Leadership Award, Nat Asn Advan Colored People, 1989; Mary McLeod Bethune Award, 1989; African Heritage Award, Asn Black Educrs, 1989; Trailblazer Award, Admin Women Educ, 1990; Distinguished Service Award, 2005. **Home Addr:** 316 E 57th St, Brooklyn, NY 11203. **Business Addr:** Associate Commissioner, State Education Department, Office New York School & Community Services, 55 Hanson Pl, Brooklyn, NY 11217, **Business Phone:** (718)722-2796.

EVANZZ, KARL ANDERSON (KARL EVAN ANDERSON)
Editor, writer, journalist. **Personal:** Born Jan 16, 1953, St Louis, MO; son of Adolphus Anderson and Bernice; married Alexandra Jane Hamilton Evanzz, Jan 1, 1977; children: Aqila, Aaron, Kanaan, Arianna, Adrian. **Educ:** Westminster Col, BA, 1975; Am Univ, Wash Col Law, 1977. **Career:** St Louis Argus, nat correspondent, 1974-80; Law Offs Lowe, Mark & Moffitt, law clerk, 1975-76; Harry T Alexander, law clerk, 1977-80; The Wash Post, news aide, 1980-86, on-line ed, 1986-. **Orgs:** Nat Newspaper Guild, 1980-; Nat Asn Black Journalists, 1992-95. **Honors/Awds:** Grant, Fund for Investigative Journalism, 1991. **Special Achievements:** Poetry published in "Crevice of Illusion," 1975; "The Judas Factor: The Plot to Kill Malcolm X," 1992; "Elijah Muhammad: A Biography," Pantheon, 1997; Poetry published in Southern Exposure Mag, 1971; 1st Place Prize, for poetry, Proud Mag, St Louis, MO, 1970, 1971; Author books like: The Messenger: The Rise & Fall Elijah Muhammad. **Business Addr:** On-Line Editor, Washington Post, 1150 15th St NW 4th Fl News, Washington, DC 20071, **Business Phone:** (202)334-6000.*

EVE, ARTHUR O.
Government official. **Personal:** Born Jan 1, 1933?, New York, NY; married Constance Bowles; children: Arthur Jr, Leecia Roberta, Eric Vincent, Martin King & Malcolm X. **Educ:** Erie Comm Col, Assoc; WVa State Univ, BS. **Career:** Government official (retired); NY State Assembly, assemblyman, 1966-79, dep speaker, 1979-03; New York State Black & Puerto Rican Legislative Caucus, chmn, 1975-76; Western New York Legislative Del, dean; State wide Leadership Summit, architect, 1993. **Orgs:** Chmn, NY State Black & Puerto Rican Leg Caucus, 1975-76; Dep Speaker, Assembly, 1979; founder, Black Develop Found & Black Bus Develop Corp; formed, Minority Coalition; Roswell Park Inst; life mem, Nat Advan Asn Colored People; founder, former chmn, Northern Region Black Political Caucus; founder, chmn, Buffalo Youth Planning Coun; Comt Aging, Comt Rules& Ways; chmn, New York State Chap Nat Rainbow Coalition. **Honors/Awds:** Adam Clayton Powell Award, 2000; Distinguished Leadership in Arts-in-Education Awards, Kennedy Ctr, 1988; Achievement Award, NY State Minorities Corrections Inc, 1992; Leadership Legislative Award, New York Asn Sch Psychol, 1992; Malcolm X Leadership Award, African People's Christian Orgn, 1991; leadership Award, ET Marshall Scholarship Foundation, 1986; Legislator of the Decade Award, Hunters Col, 1984; President's Distinguished Service Award, State Univ New York, Buffalo, 1982. **Military Serv:** AUS, 1953-55. *

EVE, CHRISTINA M.
Educator. **Personal:** Born Mar 18, 1917, Gainesville, FL. **Educ:** Shaw Univ Raleigh NC, AB, 1940; NY Univ, MA, 1958; Univ Miami, Post grad. **Career:** Educator (retired); Treasure Island Elementary Sch, Miami Beach, FL, prin; Dade Co, dist reading teacher, owner-operator, pub steno serv, 1st black prin, white sch; 1969; Egelloc Civic & Soc Club, founder, press; Solar Energy Sch; Pine Villa Elem, prin; Gloria Floyd Elem, prin; Christina M Eve Elem sch, founder. **Orgs:** Sigma Gamma Rho; anti basileus Am Asn Univ Women; Meth Ch; Fla Adminr & Supr Asn; Asn Supr & Curric Dev; Dade Co Sch Adminrs Asn; Fla prins, Fla Elem Sch; Dept Elem Sch Prins, Citizen Day Local Radio Sta, 1969; chmn, Reading Mobile Unit; chmn, Illiteracy Comt Retired Teachers Asn. **Honors/Awds:** Outstanding serv awards, Egolloc Club & Sigma Gamma Rho, 1970; Award, Univ Miami TTT Proj, 1971; Award, dept elem prins dedicated serv, 1973; Citizen of the Day, local papers & radio stations; Lifetime Achievement Award, King Clubs Greater Miami; Soror of the Year Award, Gamma Delta Chap, 1990.

EVE, CONSTANCE B.
Chairperson. **Educ:** WVa State Col, BA, eng & drama; NY Univ, MA. **Career:** New York Univ, asst libr, res div; Bennett Col Women, prof eng & Drama, dir little theater; Erie Community Col, prof eng; Buffalo Pub Schs, instr; Women Human Rights & Dignity Inc, chmn & founder, currently. **Honors/Awds:** Martin Luther King Award, Alpha Kappa Alpha; Outstanding Citizen of NY State Award; Citizen of the Year, Buffalo Evening News; Western NY Leader Award, YMCA, 1997; Outstanding Women in Ministry Award, Westchester Black Women's Caucus, 1997; the Western New York Women's Hall of Fame Award; National United Way Alexis de Tocqueville Society Award, 1998. **Business Addr:** Founder, Chairperson, Women for Human Rights and Dignity Inc, 2278 Main St, Buffalo, NY 14211, **Business Phone:** (716)831-9821.*

EVE, ERIC V.
Public relations executive. **Career:** Citigroup, Head of Community Relations; Citigroup, Executive Director; Citigroup, Senior VP of Community Relations; Citi, Director of Community Relations; Citi, Senior VP of Community Relations. **Orgs:** Member, Congressional Black Caucus Foundation, Inc.; Board of Trustees Member, Brooklyn Public Library. *

EVEGE, WALTER L
Educator, college administrator. **Personal:** Born Jan 13, 1943, Jackson, MS; son of Walter L Sr and Cletora Carter; married Dorthy Ruffin Evege, Mar 1, 1974; children: Daryl, Dietrich & Daphine. **Educ:** Tougallo Col, Tougaloo BS, 1964, MS; Atlanta Univ, Atlanta Ga, MBA, 1969. **Career:** Jackson Pub Sch, Jackson MS, math teacher, 1964-66; Tougaloo Col, Tougaloo MS, dir financial aids, 1966-69; Univ Akron, Ohio, asst dir, 1970-80, dir, aa & eeo, 1987-; Community Action Agency, Akron Ohio, assoc dir, 1980-82; Allstate Ins Co, Akron OH, sales agt, 1982-87. **Orgs:** Bd dir, Alpha Phi Alpha Homes Inc, 1974-85; adv bd, Cuyahoga St Area Block Club, 1983-; Music Boosters, Copley-Fairlawn Sch, 1987-, chmn, Levey Comn, 1988-, Ohio Consortium Blacks Higher Educ, 1989-. **Honors/Awds:** Outstanding Young Men of America, Nat Jaycees, 1978; Youth Motivational Task, Akron Jaycees, 1979; Top New Sales Agent, Allstate Ins Co, 1983; Service Award, Alpha Phi Alpha Frat, 1980; Black History Brochure, Univ Akron, 1988; Stud Risk Workshops, 1988-89; Vol Serv, Crosby Elem Sch, 1989. **Business Addr:** Director AA, EEO, University of Akron, Department of Human Resources, Stud & Admin Serv, Bldg 138B, Akron, OH 44325-4709, **Business Phone:** (330)972-7300.

EVERETT, CARL EDWARD, III
Baseball player. **Personal:** Born Jun 3, 1971, Tampa, FL. **Educ:** Hillsborough High Sch, Tampa, FL, 1990. **Career:** Baseball Player (Retired); Florida Marlins, outfielder, 1993-94; NY Mets, designated Hitter, 1995-97; Houston Astros, designated Hitter, 1998-99; Boston Red Sox, designated Hitter, 2000-01; Tex Rangers, designated Hitter, 2002-03; Chicago WhiteSox, outfielder, 2003-05; Montreal Expos, designated Hitter, 2004; Seattle Mariners, designated Hitter, 2006. **Honors/Awds:** All Star Selection 2000, 2003; World Series Champion, 2005. *

EVERETT, CHARLES ROOSEVELT
Manager. **Personal:** Born Dec 2, 1962, Philadelphia, PA; son of Charles R Everett Sr and Precola C Aldrich; married Jean S; children: Christian C & Adrian F. **Educ:** Univ Pa, BA, transp planning, 1984. **Career:** Gannett Fleming Transp Engrs, trans planning engr, 1985-88; Woolpert Consults, proj mgr, trans planning, 1989-91; Syracuse Metro Transp Coun, dir, 1991-93; Syracuse Hancock Int Airport, NY, Dept Aviation, aviation comnr, 1994-2002, dir city opers, 2002-; Everett & Assocs LLC, pres & prin; Fed Aviation Admin, Dept Transp, Planning & Environ Div, Off Assoc Admin Airports, mgr, currently. **Orgs:** Transp Res Bd, 1987-; treas, 1993-94, secy, 1995, vpres, 1996, pres, 1997, NY Upstate Sect, Inst Transp Engrs; Am Asn Airport Execs, 1994-; mem, 1996-, vpres, 1997, pres, 1998-99, NY Aviation Mgt Asn; pres, Aviation Aerospace Educ Found, 1997-. **Special Achievements:** "Planning, Development & Operation of a Deicing Fluid Collection & Treatment System," Deicing Int Conf, UK, 1997, "Winter Operations, Regulators and Water Quality," "Terminal Expansion and Renovation: Discover The Airport," FAA Airports Conference, 1997, Syracuse Intl Airshow, USAF Thunderbirds, 1997, Syracuse Intl Airshow, Canadian Forces Snowbirds, 1998. **Military Serv:** USSAFR; New York Air Nat Guard (NYANG), major, 1984 (USSAFR) NYANG, 1992; Air Force Commendation Medal. **Business Addr:** Manager, Federal Aviation Administration, Office of the Associate Administrator for Airports, National Planning and Environmental Division, 800 Independence Ave, Washington, DC 20591, **Business Phone:** (866)835-5322.

EVERETT, CYNTHIA A
Lawyer, district attorney, government official. **Personal:** Born Jan 1, 1958?, Manchester, CT. **Educ:** Fla State Univ, BA, govt, 1978; George Wash Univ, Nat Law Ctr, JD, 1982. **Career:** Dade Co State Atty's Off, supv atty; Miami Dist, asst US atty; City Opa Locka City Atty, atty, currently. **Orgs:** Women Lawyers Div, 1989-91; Fla Bar Asn, 1992-95; treas, Fla Chap Nat Bar Asn, 1993-; bd govs, Fla Bar Asn, 1994-; bd trustees, United Way Dade Co, 1994-; Nat Asn Advan Colored People; Miami Partners Progress; pres, Black Lawyers Asn Dade Co; Fla Asn Women Lawyers; chair, Rules Community; past pres, Nat Bar Asn; Dade Co Chap; Community Stud Educ & Admis Bar. **Business Addr:** Attorney, City of Opa-locka City Attorney, City Hall 777 Sharazad Blvd, Opa Locka, FL 33054-3596, **Business Phone:** (305)688-4611.

EVERETT, J RICHARD
Lawyer. **Personal:** Born Oct 2, 1936, Montezuma, GA; married Bernice Knowings; children: Jocelyn & Jeannenn. **Educ:** Morehouse Col, BS, 1960; St John's Univ, Law Sch, LLB 1967; Patent Off Patent Acad, US, 1968. **Career:** Lawyer (retired); Food & Drug Admin, anal chemist, 1961-66; Food & Legal Officer, 1966-77; Eastman Kodak Co, admin asst, 1974-76; US Patent Off, patent exam, 1967-69, patent atty, 1969-79, sr patent atty, 1980-90; patent coun, 1990-99. **Orgs:** Am Intellectual Property Asn; Monroe Co Bar Asn; Rochester Patent Law Asn; Nat Bar Asn; vol, Nat Patent Law Asn, Vol Legal Proj; NY City Bar Asn; Monroe Co Bar Asn. **Honors/Awds:** Wiley A Branton Award, Nat Bar Asn. **Military Serv:** USN, E-5, 1954-57. **Home Addr:** 1 Circle Wood Rd, Rochester, NY 14625.

EVERETT, PERCIVAL L.
Dentist. **Personal:** Born Aug 1, 1933, Columbia, SC; married Dorothy L; children: Percival II, Vivian. **Educ:** Allen Univ, BS,

1955; Meharry Med Col, DDS, 1962. **Career:** State Park Health Ctr Columbia, staff dentist, 1962-68; Self Employed, dentist. **Orgs:** Am Dent Asn; SC Dent Asn; Cent Dist Dent Soc; Congaree Med Dent & Phar Soc; Palmetto Med Dent & Pharm Soc, City Columbia Bd Health; Greater Columbia Chamber Com; mem trustee, Civilian Military Liason Comt, Capital City Develop Found; SC Community Human Affairs; United Way Agency Rels bd; SC Chamber Com; Alpha Phi Alpha Fraternity. **Military Serv:** AUS, spec 1st class, 1956-58. **Business Addr:** Dentist, 2124 Washington St, Columbia, SC 29204.

EVERETT, RALPH B
Lawyer. **Personal:** Born Jun 23, 1951, Orangeburg, SC; son of Alethia Hilton and Francis G S Jr; married Gwendolyn Harris, Jun 22, 1974; children: Jason G. **Educ:** Morehouse Col, BA, 1973; Duke Univ Law Sch, JD, 1976. **Career:** NC Dept Justice, assoc atty gen, 1976; NC Dept Labor, admin asst legal affairs, 1976-77; Sen Fritz Hollings, spec asst, 1977-78, legislative asst, 1978-83; US Senate, Comn on Com, Sci & Transp, attny, dem chief coun, staff dir, 1983-86; US Senate, Comm on Com, sci & transp chief coun & staff dir, 1987-89; Paul Hastings, Janofsky & Walker LLP, partner, 1989-. **Orgs:** NC & DC Bars; US Ct Appeals DC Ct; US Tax Court; US Ct Claims; US Supreme Ct; bd dir, Cumulus Media Inc; bd dir, Shenandoah Life Ins Co; Am Bar Asn; Alpha Phi Alpha; Alumni Bd Visitors, Duke Unv Law Sch; trustee, Nat Urban League; Ctr Nat Policy; Econ Club Wash; Phi Beta Kappa; Phi Alpha Theta Int Hon Soc Hist. **Honors/Awds:** Earl Warren Legal Scholar. **Business Addr:** Attorney, Paul Hastings, Janofsky & Walker LLP, 875 15th St NW, Washington, DC 20005, **Business Phone:** (202)551-1700.

EVERETT, THOMAS GREGORY
Football player, athletic coach. **Personal:** Born Nov 21, 1964, Daingerfield, TX. **Educ:** Baylor Univ, BSc, educ; Cooper Inst, biomechanics strength training. **Career:** Football player (retired), athletic coach; Safety: Pittsburgh Steelers, 1987-91, Dallas Cowboys, 1992-93; Tampa Bay Buccaneers, 1994-95; Thomas Everett Athletics, performance dir & athletic coach, currently. **Honors/Awds:** Male Athlete of the Year, Southwest Conf, 1986; Jim Thorpe Award, 1986; Pro Bowl, 1993; Tex High Sch Football Hall Of Fame, 1998; Baylor Hall of Fame, 1998; Col Football Hall of Fame, 2006. **Business Addr:** Athletic Coach, Thomas Everett Athletics, Dallas, TX, **Business Phone:** (214)803-2727.

EVERS, JAMES CHARLES
Mayor. **Personal:** Born Sep 11, 1922, Decatur, MS; son of Jesse Wright and James Evers; married Nannie Laurie, Jan 1, 1951 (divorced 1974); children: Pat, Carolyn, Eunice, Sheila & Charlene. **Educ:** Alcorn State Univ, BS, 1951. **Career:** Fayette, MS, mayor, 1969-89; MS State Senate, candidate, 1975; MS, candidate, gov, 1971; US House Reps, candidate, 1968; MS Nat Asn Advan Colored People, field secy, 1963-69; Medgar Evers Fund, pres, 1969-, founder. **Orgs:** Dem Nat Com; adv bd, Black Enterprise Mag; exec comt, MS Municipal Asn; bd dirs, SW MS Planning & Devel Dist; Govs Manpower Conf, 1974-; Social Sci; Philosophy Jurisprudence. **Honors/Awds:** Nat Asn Advan Colored People Recipient Nine Hon Degrees Humanities; EVERS Author, 1970; Man of yr award, Nat Asn Advan Colored People 1969; MS Lectr Cols Univs, Sociology & Humanities, 1964-. **Special Achievements:** Author, Have No Fear: The Charles Evers Story, Wiley & sons, 1997; First black mayor of Fayette. **Military Serv:** AUS, sgt maj, 1946. **Business Addr:** President, Medgar Evers Funds Inc, PO Box 158, Fayette, MS 39069.

EVERS, WILLIAM PRESTON
Executive, executive director. **Personal:** Born Apr 12, 1952, Trenton, NJ; married Patricia, Nov 28, 1981; children: Kelsey A Evers & Justin A Evers. **Educ:** Montclair State Col, BA, 1975; Fairleigh Dickinson Univ, MBA, 1981. **Career:** Chicopee Mills, sales rep, 1976-78; Ford Motor Co, regional mgr, mkt rep, 1978-95; Harley-Davidson Motor Co, dir dealer develop, 1995-99, dir field opers, 1999-. **Orgs:** Kappa Alpha Psi Fraternity Inc; pres, Newark Alumni; Sigma Gamma Rho. **Honors/Awds:** Community Service Award, Sigma Gamma Rho, Gamma Nu Chapter, 1984; Achievement Award, Kappa Alpha Psi, Newark Alumni Chapter, 1985; Meritorious Service Award, 1987; Certificate of Appreciation, Northeastern Province, 1987; Polemarch's Recognition Certificate, Northern Province, 1990; Outstanding Leadership Award, Southfield Alumni Chapter, 1990; Polemarch's Recognition Award, East Central Province, 1994; Black Excellence Award, Milwaukee Times, 1998. **Business Addr:** Director of Field Operations, Harley-Davidson Motor Company, 3700 W Juneau Ave, PO Box 653, Milwaukee, WI 53201, **Business Phone:** (414)342-4680.

EVERS-WILLIAMS, MYRLIE
Association executive, social worker. **Personal:** Born Mar 17, 1933, Vicksburg, MS; married Medgar Evers (died 1963); children: three; married Walter Edward Williams, 1975 (died 1995). **Educ:** Pomona col, BA, sociol, 1968. **Career:** Claremont Col, asst dir educ opportunity, 1967; Seligman & Latz, vpres; Atlantic Richfield Co, nat dir community affairs; Los Angeles Bd Pub Works, comnr; MEW Assocs Inc, pres, 2000. **Orgs:** chairwoman, NAACP, 1995-98; first Field Secy, NAACP, Miss. **Honors/Awds:** Author, For Us the Living, 1967; Tribute To A Black America Award, Conference Black Mayors, 2002. **Special Achievements:** First female to chair the NAACP, 1995. **Business Addr:** President, MEW Associates Inc., 15 SW Colorado Ave Suite 310, Bend, OR 97702.*

EWELL, RAYMOND W.
Legislator. **Personal:** Born Dec 29, 1928, Chicago, IL; married Joyce Marie; children: David, Marc, Raymond. **Educ:** Univ Ill, BA, 1949, MA, 1950; Univ Chicago, LLB, 1954. **Career:** Ill Gen Assembly 29th Dist, legislator, 1966-; Williams Miller & Ferguson, atty, currently; teacher pub sch. **Orgs:** Cook Co Bar Asn; bd Chicago Conf to Fulfill These Rights; Fed Pub & Defender Prog; Nat Asn Advan Colored People; YMCA. **Business Addr:** Attorney, Williams Miller & Ferguson, 9415 S State St, Chicago, IL 60619.

EWERS, DR. JAMES BENJAMIN
Educator, school administrator. **Personal:** Born Sep 29, 1948, Winston-Salem, NC; son of Mildred Jane Holland and Dr James B; married Deborah Leu Froy; children: Christopher, Aaron & Courtney. **Educ:** Johnson C Smith Univ, BA, 1970; Catholic Univ Am, MA, 1971; Univ Mass, EdD, 1980; Harvard Univ, Mgt Develop Prog, Cert, 1996. **Career:** Wash DC Pub Schs, teacher, 1971-75; Stockton State Col, asst dir admis, 1976-78; Univ Md Eastern Shore, dir admin & registr, 1978-84; Livingstone Col, vpres stud affairs, 1984-87; Dillard Univ, vpres stud affairs, 1987-90; Savannah State Col, vpres stud affairs, 1990-94; Liberty County Sch Dist, Hinesville, Ga, fac mem; Miami Univ, Middletown, Ohio, assoc dean stud affairs, 1995-. **Orgs:** Alpha Phi Alpha, 1967-; Nat Asn Foreign Stud Affairs, 1981-; Am Asn Coun Develop 1982-; Miami Univ Community Fed Credit Union; Phi Kappa Phi, 1983-; life mem, NAACP 1983-; Salisbury/Rowan Human Rel Coun, 1985-87; Am Asn Higher Educ, 1987; Middletown Civil Serv Comn, 1996-; bd dirs, Middletown YMCA, 1996-2003; bd dirs, Middletown Red Cross, 1996-2003; bddirs, Middletown Regional Hosp, 1998-; bd dirs, Middletown Rotary Club, 1998-2001. **Honors/Awds:** Sports Hall of Fame, Winston-Salem High Sch, 1990; Image Award NAACP, Middletown Chap, Image Award, 1998. **Special Achievements:** Recognized by The Ohio House of Representatives for work in the areas of children & diversity. Publ: Perspectives from Where I Sit: Essays on Education, Parenting & Teen Issues. **Home Addr:** 4504 Rosewood Ct, Middletown, OH 45042-3862. **Business Addr:** Associate Dean for Student Affairs, Miami University, Office of Johnston Hall Suite 135B, Middletown, OH 45042.

EWING, MAMIE HANS
Government official, administrator. **Personal:** Born Aug 15, 1939, Houston, TX; married Robert; children: Steve, Perry. **Educ:** Univ Tex Austin, BA, 1960; Prairie View A&M Univ, MEd, 1974. **Career:** Tex Dept Human Resources, supvr child welfare div, 1969-71, dir & EEO, 1973-75, dir, Civil Rights, 1975-77, feild liason officer, 1977-78, regional admin, 1978-; Austin Neighborhood Youth Corps, div exec dir, 1972-73; Tex Dept Aging & Disability Serv, adminr, 2004. **Orgs:** Bd dir, Tarrant Co United Way, 1979-80; Nat Asn Soc Workers; Asn Black Soc Workers; Alpha Kappa Alpha Sorority; Jack & Jill; Nat Asn Advan Colored People; pres, Beta Psi Omega; Missouri City Links, 1985-. **Honors/Awds:** Recipient Meritorious Serv Award, Travis Co Child Welfare bd, 1971; Trailbazer of the Yr award, Bus & Professional Womens Asn Tarrant Co, 1979; Achievement Award, Asn Black Social Workers, 1979; Outstanding Women, TX Govt, Governor's Comn Women Govt, 1987; Outstanding African Am Alumnus, Univ Tex Austin, Ex-Studs Asn, 1990; Houston Works Member of the Year, 1994; Mayor's Public Private Partnership Award, 1996. **Business Addr:** Regional Administrator, Tex Dept Aging & Disability Serv, 5425 Polk Ave, PO Box 16017, Houston, TX 77222-6017, **Business Phone:** (713)767-2404.*

EWING, PATRICK ALOYSIUS
Basketball player, basketball coach. **Personal:** Born Aug 5, 1962, Kingston, Jamaica; son of Carl and Dorothy; married Rita; children: Randi, Corey & Patrick Jr. **Educ:** Georgetown Univ, BA, 1985. **Career:** Basketball player (retired), basketball coach; NY Knicks, ctr, 1985-2000;Seattle Supersonics, 2000-01; Orlando Magic, 2001-02, asst coach, 2007-; Wash Wizards, asst coach; Houston Rockets, asst coach. **Orgs:** NY City Bd Educ, Drop Out Prevention Prog, 1985; pres, NBA Players Asn, 1997. **Honors/Awds:** Olympic Gold Medal, 1984, 1992; NCAA Most Valuable Player, 1984; Big East Conf Co-player of the Year, 1984-85; Naismith Col Player of the Year,1985; Kodak Award, 1985; Adolph Rupp Trophy, 1985; "Met Life" Knick of the Year; DHL, Shaw Univ, 1991; Basketball Hall of Fame, 2008. **Special Achievements:** Selected as one of the 50 Greatest Basketball Players of All Time. **Business Addr:** Assistant Coach, Orlando Magic, 8701 Maitland Summit Blvd, Orlando, FL 32810.

EWING, SAMUEL DANIEL
Executive, investment banker, consultant. **Personal:** Born in Topeka, KS; son of Samuel Daniel Sr and Jane Elizabeth Smith; married Brenda Jean Arnold, Jul 29, 1985. **Educ:** Univ Cincinnati, BSEE, 1961; Univ Conn, MSEE, 1964; Harvard Univ, MBA, 1968. **Career:** Gruss & Co, investment mgr, 1968-69; Salomon Brothers, New York, NY, sr assoc, 1969-75; Bankers Trust Co, New York, NY, v pres, dir, 1975-78; Fed Savings & Loan Ins Corp, Wash, DC, dir, 1978-80; Ewing Capital Inc, Wash, DC, pres & founder, 1981-. **Orgs:** Fel, Fin Analyst Fed; DC Securities Adv Comn; trustee, Annuity Fund Ministers & Retirement Fund Lay Workers; trustee, Pension Bds, United Church Christ, Inc; trustee, United Church Bd Pension Assets Mgt; trustee, Peoples Congregational United Church Christ; chair, Diversity Comt, United Bd Pension Assets Mgt; chair, Investment Comt, Immigration & Refugee Serv Am; dir, United Church Bd Ministerial Assistance Inc; Comt Corp Social Responsibility; Investment Comt Pension Bd, United Church Christ; Exec Finance Comn, Juv Diabetes Found Int; Finance & Develop Comn; Harvard Club Wash, DC; Harvard Bus Sch Club Wash, DC; Harvard Bus Sch African-Am Alumni Asn; Nat Asn Investments Prof; bd mem, Shaw Heritage Trust Fund; bd mem; Juv Diabetes Found Int; trustee, Huston-Tillotson Col, Investment Comn; pres, Broadcast Capital Fund Inc, Wash, DC, 1980-81; adv bd, UConn Sch Engineering, currently; bd dir, Univ Conn Found, currently. **Honors/Awds:** Numerous awards & honors. **Business Addr:** President, Founder, Ewing Capital Inc, 727 15th St NW Suite 700, Washington, DC 20005, **Business Phone:** (202)737-1500.

EWING, STEVEN R
Chief executive officer, executive. **Career:** Wade Ford Inc, chief exec & owner, currently. **Business Addr:** Chief Executive Officer, Owner, Wade Ford Inc, 3860 S Cobb Dr, Smyrna, GA 30080-5537, **Business Phone:** (770)436-1200.*

EWING, WILLIAM JAMES
Lawyer. **Personal:** Born Sep 10, 1936, New York. **Educ:** Seton Hall Law Sch, BA, 1963, JD. **Career:** NJ & US Dist Ct, Dist NJ, admitted to bar, 1972; US Ct Appeals, Third Circuit, 1980; US Supreme Ct, 1981; NY & US Dist Ct, Southern, Northern & Western Dist NY, 1983; Essex County Prosecutors Off, dir spec invests; CBS Aspen Systs Corp, legal comput corp exec; Montclair, NJ, munic prosecutor & asst town atty; NJ Ct, arbitrator; Superior Ct, Annexed Arbitration Proj; Law Firm, NJ, pvt pract, atty, currently. **Orgs:** NJ State Am Nat Bar Asn; Concerned Legal Asn NJ; reg dir, Young Lawyers Sect Nat Bar Asn; Attys Montclair; Nat Asn Advan Colored People; exec bd, Montclair Urban Coalition. **Honors/Awds:** Outstanding Man Of Yr, 1973; Distinguished Serv Award, Garden State Bar Asn. **Business Addr:** Attorney, Law Firm, 70 Park St Suite 200, Montclair, NJ 07042.

EXUM, THURMAN MCCOY
Executive, educator. **Personal:** Born Mar 29, 1947, Seven Springs, NC; married Wanda R Edwards; children: Thurman Jr & Jermaine. **Educ:** NC A&T State Univ, BS, Auto Tech, 1969, MS; Colo State Univ, attended 1984; NIASE, Auto Serv Excellence, 1985, MS, Indust Ed, 1987. **Career:** Buick Div GM, dist serv mgr, 1971-78; GM Training Ctr, instr, 1978-79; Pat Mullery Buick, dir serv, 1979; No VA Community Col, instr & auto, 1980-81; Metro Auto Emission Serv Inc, pres, 1981-85; A&T State Univ, Sch Technol, instr, 1985, dean & dir motor sports technol, adj instr, currently. **Orgs:** Consult, Nat Home Study Coun, 1981-82; consult, NJ Comm Col, 1981; consult, Texaco Oil Co, 1981; vpres, Coun Auto Apprent Coordr, 1982-83; consult, Colo State Univ, 1983-84; coordr, Nat Auto Dev Assoc, 1983; MD Quality Assurance Moratorium, 1984; consult, DC Dept Transp, 1981-; consult, State Va, 1982-; N Am Emissions Control Conf, 1982-; coordr St MD Vehicle Admin, 1984-; Soc Automotive Engrs, 1986-. **Honors/Awds:** Instr Cert Dept State Police, VA, 1981; Cert Achievement MD State & EPA, 1983; Making It article Black Enterprise Mag, 1984; NASA HL20 PLS Proj, 1990-91. **Business Addr:** Adjunct Instructor, North Carolina Agricultural and Technical State University, 1601 E Market St, Greensboro, NC 27411, **Business Phone:** (336)334-7500.*

EXUM, WADE F
Health services administrator. **Personal:** Born Jan 31, 1949, Clayton, NC; son of Alfred D and Lucille E; married Carolyn Jan, Aug 1, 1970; children: Daniel E, Adam B & Cord H. **Educ:** Ottawa Univ, BS, biology, 1971; Univ Colo Med Ctr, MD, 1977; Univ Colo Grad Sch Bus Admin, MBA, 1986. **Career:** Reynolds Elect & Eng Co, indust hygenist, 1971-73; US Pub Health Servs, gen med off, 1977-80; Colo State Univ, stud health physician, 1980-81; IMB Corp, sr managing physician, 1982-90; US Olympic Comt, usoc dir, DCA, 1991-2000; Office Hearing & Appeal, pres, currently. **Orgs:** Am Med Asn, 1980-; Nat Med Asn, 1980-; Am Occup Med Asn, 1982-90; bd dirs, Athletes Against Drugs, 1992-; NCAA Sports Scis Subcomt, 1992-94; USA Olympic Team Delegation, 1992, 1996; bd dirs, Colo Springs Downtown YMCA, 1993-; bd dirs, Colo Springs Chamber Com, 1996; bd dirs, Shaka Found, 1997. **Special Achievements:** Editor: Athletic Drug Reference Book, annual, 1993-96; Author: USOC Drug Education Handbook, annual, 1991-96; USA Pan American Games Team Delegation, 1991, 1995;Alumni Hall of Fame Inductee, W J Palmer HS, 1993; Goodwill Games Anti-Doping Commission, 1994, 1998. **Military Serv:** US Pub Health Svcs, comdr, 1977-80. **Home Addr:** 807 Fontmore Rd, Colorado Springs, CO 80904-1603, **Home Phone:** (719)634-2258. **Business Phone:** (719)634-2258.

EZOZO, AGRIPPA O.
President (Organization), association executive. **Personal:** Born in Niger. **Educ:** Wudil Teachers Col, Kano State, Nigeria, pub

educ; Calif State Univ, Dominguez Hills, BS, comput info syst; Univ Calif, Los Angles, MA. **Career:** Kundila Primary Sch, Kano, Nigeria, teacher; African Diaspora Found, pres & founder, 2001-; Black Church Rev mag, publ; League of Patriotic Nigerians, Los Angeles, CA, exec dir. **Orgs:** Pres, Univ Calif Los Angles Black Fac & Staff Asn, 1991; co-chair, Calif delegation to the Nat Summit Africa, Wash, DC. **Special Achievements:** Hosted the Nigerian Women's Soccer Team, The Nigerian Falcons, during the Federal International Football Association games in Los Angeles; organized the African Diaspora Conference event with special guest Father Carlos Matsinhi of Mozambique, 1995. **Business Addr:** President, Founder, African Diaspora Foundation, 36914 Jenna Lane, Palmdale, CA 93550, **Business Phone:** (661)285-7513.*

F

FADULU, SUNDAY O.
Educator. **Personal:** Born Nov 11, 1940, Ibadan, Nigeria; married Jacqueline F; children: Sunday Jr & Tony. **Educ:** Okla Baptist Univ, BS, 1964, MS; Univ Okla, PhD, 1969. **Career:** Univ Nigeria, lectr pharmaceut microbiol, 1969-70; Univ Ife Nigeria, resdrug unit, 1969-70; Univ Okla Sch Med, res assoc hemat, 1970-71; Tex Southern Univ, asst prof, 1972, prof micro biol, currently, chmn dept biol, 2000. **Orgs:** Sigma Xi, 1968; Beta Beta Beta Biol Hon Soc, 1973; Nat Geog Soc, 1973; MedMycological Soc Am, 1974; Int Soc Human & Animal Mycol, 1975; Friends Youth Houston TX, 1975; Nat Inst Sci Beta Kappa Chi; Smithsonian Inst Recip Fac Res Grant Urban Resources Ctr Sickle Cell Res; Minority Bio med Res Nat Inst Health; bd Trustees, Riverside Gen Hosp. **Honors/Awds:** Hon DSc, Oklahoma Baptist Univ, 2000; Alumni Award 1986. **Business Addr:** Professor, Texas Southern University, Department of Biology, 3100 Cleburne St, Houston, TX 77004, **Business Phone:** (713)313-7219.

FAGBAYI, MUTIU OLUTOYIN
President (Organization), chief executive officer, executive. **Personal:** Born Jan 9, 1953, Lagos, Nigeria; married Patricia Ann Russell; children: Jumoke & Yinka. **Educ:** Univ Dayton, BS, 1976; Pa State Univ, MS, 1978. **Career:** Eastman Kodak Co, res scientist, 1978-85, sr bus res analyst; Nat Ctr Educ & Econ, chief operating officer, 1992-95; Performance Fact Inc, Oakland, CA, founder, pres & chief exec officer, 1997-. **Orgs:** Webster Rotary Club, 1982-; secy, Webster Rotary Club, 1983-84; pres, Rochester Chap Nat Orgn Prof Advan Black Chemists & Chem Engrs, 1983-; bd trustees, Webster Montessori Sch, 1984-86; exec bd, NOBCChE, 1986-; Tau Beta Pi Eng Nat Hon Soc; admin, NOBCCHE Long-Range Strategic Plan, 1987-92; bd advs, MicroSociety. **Honors/Awds:** United Way Volunteer Service Excellence Award, NOBCChE, 1986. **Business Addr:** President, Founder & Chief Executive Officer, Performance Fact Inc, 333 Hegenberger Rd Suite 707, Oakland, CA 94621, **Business Phone:** (916)979-7832.

FAGIN, DARRYL HALL
Manager, legislator (u.s. state government). **Personal:** Born May 18, 1942, Washington, DC; married Susan; children: Elizabeth Peggy & Adam Vincent. **Educ:** Olivet Col, BA, 1968; GWU Nat Law Ctr, JD, 1971. **Career:** Black Studs Union Olive t Col, charter pres, 1968; Indust Bank Wash, loan officer & asst cashier, 1973-74; Judge Sorrell, Superior Ct DC, law clerk, 1974-75; Am Security Bank, legal researcher assoc coun, 1975-77; Equal Employ Opportunity Comn, law clerk, 1977-78; US House of Representatives, leg asst, 1978-79; US Treas, Dept Treas, asst; Americans Dem Action, legis dir, currently. **Orgs:** Lawyers Com DC Arts Comn, 1971; Pub Protection Com Met Bd Trade, 1976. **Honors/Awds:** Legal fellowship award; Regional Huber Smith community law fellowship Washington DC, 1971. **Business Addr:** Legislative Director, Americans for Democratic Action, 1625 K St NW Suite 210, Washington, DC 20006, **Business Phone:** (202)785-5980.

FAIN, CONSTANCE FRISBY
Educator. **Personal:** Born Feb 11, 1949, Philadelphia, PA; daughter of William and Dorothy; married Herbert, Feb 4, 1972; children: Kimberly K. **Educ:** Cheyney Univ, Cheyney, Pa, BS, educ, 1970; Tex Southern Univ, Houston, Tex, JD, 1974; Univ Pa, Philadelphia, Pa, LLM, 1981. **Career:** US Atty, Dept Justice, law clerk, 1972-74; Funchess, Charles, Long & Hannah Law Firm, atty, 1975-76; Tex Southern Univ, Thurgood Marshall Sch Law, instr, asst prof, assoc prof, prof law, 1977-, Legal Skills Program, dir, 1978-90, CLEO Prog, instr, 1976, 1978, assoc prof, 1982, asst prof, 1979, prof, 1988-2005, Earl Carl prof law, 2005-; Glanville Publs, consult, reviewer law books, 1987. **Orgs:** State Bar Tex, 1975-; State Bar Pa, 1981-; fel Tex Bar Found, 1995-2000; US Dist Ct, Southern Dist Tex; US Ct Appeals, fifth Circuit; US Ct Appeals, Eleventh Circuit; Am Soc Writers Legal Subj; Phi Alpha Delta Law Fraternity; Black Women's Lawyers Asn. **Honors/Awds:** Recognition and Service Award, Moot Ct Bd, 1988; Professor of the Year, Stud Bar Asn, 1988; Professor of the Year, Women's Legal Soc, 1989; Dedicated Service, 1991; Outstanding Service, 1992. **Special Achievements:** Author: Wrongful Life: Legal & Medical Aspects, Kentucky Law Journal, vol 75, no 2, pp 585-631, 1986-87; Assault & Battery, Matthew Bender & Co Inc, vol 1a, pp 1-206, 1990; Conjugal Violence, Michie Co, Second ed, pp 121-122, 1991; Professional Liability, Matthew Bender & Co, Inc, vol 5a, pp 1-247, 1991; Clergy Malpractice, Mississippi Col Law Rev, vol 12, pp 97-141, 1991. **Business Addr:** Earl Carl Professor of Law, Texas Southern University, Thurgood Marshall School Law, 3100 Cleburne Ave, Houston, TX 77004, **Business Phone:** (713)313-7393.

FAIR, FRANK T.
Clergy, executive director. **Personal:** Born Oct 19, 1929, Clinton, SC; son of Vetda Thomas Bell (deceased) and Leo Fair (deceased); married Thelma Belton, Dec 22, 1956; children: Frank Thomas II, Tamera Lee, Donna Machelle Conn, Selwyn Tyrelle. **Educ:** Benedict Col, attended 1950; Crozer Sem, MDiv, 1955; Gammon Sem, STM, 1959; Eastern Baptist Sem, Philadelphia, DMin, 1979. **Career:** SC Area Trade Sch, chaplain & teacher, 1951-52; Royal Baptist Church, pastor, 1955-61; Benedict Ext Serv Ministry, teacher, 1957-61; JJ Starks Sch Theol, teacher, 1957-61; Farrow-Croft Ment Hosp, chaplain, 1959-61; New Hope Baptist Church, pastor, 1961-, pastor emer, currently; Am Baptist Conv, minister, 1961-; Montgomery County Opportunities Indust Ctr, exec dir, 1991; Gethsemane Asn Nat Baptist Conv Inc, ordained to minister. **Orgs:** Pres, Norristown Area Coun Churches, 1970-72; bd dir, Dept Pub Asst, 1971-; lay adv, Cent Montgomery Tech Sch, 1972; Norristown Area Sch & Discipline Comn, 1973-; Dep dir, Montgomery County Opportunities Indsut Ctr Inc, 1973-80; Norristown Area Manpower Coun, 1974-; exec dir, Montgomery County Opportunities Indst Ctr, 1980-; chairperson, bd dirs, Selective Serv Syst 107, 1982-89; chairperson, Interdenominational Clergy Energy Coun, 1985-; bd dirs, Habitat Humanities, Norristown, PA, 1988-. **Special Achievements:** Author Orita for Black Youth: An initiation into Christian Adulthood, Judson Press, 1977; Author "Orita for Black Youth" 1977. **Business Addr:** Pastor Emeritus, New Hope Baptist Church, 204 East Oak St, Norristown, PA 19401.*

FAIR, TALMADGE WILLARD
Association executive. **Personal:** Born Jan 15, 1939, Winston-Salem, NC. **Educ:** Johnson C Smith Univ, BA, sociol, 1961; Atlanta Univ Sch Social Work, MSW, 1963. **Career:** Urban League Greater Miami Inc, assoc dir, 1963, pres & chief exec officer, 1964-; Atlanta Univ Sch Social Work, Nat Urban League's Whitney M Young Jr, Ctr Urban Leadership, Fla Int Univ & Bethune Cookman Col, adj prof. **Orgs:** Pres, Miami Varsity Club, 1978-; Miami Citizens Against Crime Exec Comt, 1980-; pres, Community Blacks in Org Labor, 1981-; mem, Fla Reg Coord Coun Voc Educ, 1984-88, Beacon Coun Orgn Task Force, 1985; bd trustees, Fla Int Univ; chmn bd dir, Bayside Found; chmn, bd dir, Vis Indust; bd gov & exec comt, Greater Miami Conv & Visitor's Bur; mem, City of Miami Civil Serv Bd; Dade/Monroe WAGES Coalition's Eval Comt; bd gov & exec comt, Miami Coalition for a Safe & Drug-Free Community; co-founder, Liberty City Charter Sch; Gov Equity in Educ Task Force; chair bd dir, Miami-Bayside Found & Miami-Dade Empowerment Trust. **Honors/Awds:** Outstanding Dedicated Service, Troop 40 Boy Scouts Am, 1984; Appreciation Award, Martin Luther King Develop Corp, 1984; Gratitude Valuable Contrib Econ Opportunity Family Health Ctr, 1984; Appreciation Award, Progressive Firefighters Asn, 1985; Certificate of Appreciation Outstanding Service, City of Miami; Outstanding Citizen Service Award, State of Fla; Presidential Excalibur Award, Family Christian Agency Am; Community Service Award, Greater Miami Region Nat Conf Christians & Jews, 1995; Community Service Award, Phillip Morris Co Inc, 1992; Award, Nat Network Social Work Managers Inc, 1989; Leadership Award, Greater Miami Chamber Com. **Special Achievements:** Author of numerous published articles in the Miami Herald, Miami Magazine, Tropic Magazine; host of both radio and television programs; interviewed by 60 Minutes, Tom Brokaw, Ebony Magazine and National Geographic. **Business Addr:** President, Chief Executive Officer, Urban League of Greater Miami Inc, 8500 NW 25th Ave, Miami, FL 33147.*

FAIR, TERRANCE DELON. **See FAIR, TERRY.**

FAIR, TERRY (TERRANCE DELON FAIR)
Football player. **Personal:** Born Jul 20, 1976, Phoenix, AZ. **Educ:** Tenn State Univ, psychol. **Career:** Detroit Lions, defensive back, 1998-01; Carolina Panthers, 2002-04; Pittsburgh Steelers, 2005; St Louis Rams, defensive back, 2005-. **Honors/Awds:** All-Rookie hons, Pro Football Weekly, 1998; Spec Team Player of the Week, Nat Football League, 1998, 1999; Spec Team Player of the Month, Nat Football League, 1998; All-Sec, Assoc Press & Football News; All-Am hon mention. **Special Achievements:** Pro Bowl alternate, 1998; Returned punt 82 yards for touchdown to set state record, 1993. **Business Phone:** (314)982-7267.*

FAIRLEY, JULIETTE S
Writer. **Personal:** Born Jun 21, 1969, Chateauroux, France; daughter of James and Sophie Fairley. **Educ:** Univ Houston, BA, 1988; Columbia Univ Jour Sch, MA, 1991; Univ Wisconsin grad sch banking. **Career:** Money Talks: Black Financial Experts Talk to You About Money, 1998; Cliff's Notes on Investing in Mutual Funds, 1999; Money Rules: Personal Finance in Your 20s & 30's, 2002; Cash in the City: Affording Martinis, Manolos & Manicures on a Working Girl's Salary, 2002; TV show Cha Ching Money Makers, host, 2005; translator, Paris, France; Bergen Record, reporter; Bloomberg Bus News, producer; Am West In-Flight Media, prog host, 2001; seminar producer; author, currently. **Orgs:** NY New Media Asn; Author's Guild; Am Soc Journalists & Authors; NY nancial Writers Asn. **Business Addr:** Author, John Wiley & Sons, 111 River St, Hoboken, NJ 07030.

FAIRMAN, J. W., JR.
Administrator. **Personal:** Born May 20, 1948, Cleveland, MS; married Jeanne Arthur Hester; children: Bridgette, Darrin, Victor. **Educ:** Hardin-Simmons Univ, BS, 1970; Chicago State Univ, MS, 1975; Harvard Univ, Cambridge, John F Kennedy Sch Govt, prog sr execs state & local govt, 1994; Harper & Row Publishing Company, Hostage Negotiations, 1980; Am Abritration Asn, labor mgt, 1977; State IL, Dept Personnel, admin & org behavior, 1974. **Career:** Chicago DART Work Release, coun, 1971-72, ctr supvr, 1972-77; IL Dept Corr Work Release, dep supt, 1977-79, comn corr ctr supvr, 1972-77, correctional coun, 1971-72; Stateville Correct Ctr, asst supt, 1979; Pontiac Correct Ctr, warden, 1979-82; Joliet Correct Ctr, warden, 1982-91; IL Dept Corrections, Sheridan Correctional Ctr, warden, 1991; Cook Cty Dept Corrections, Chicago IL, exec dir, 1991, Juvenile Temp Detention Ctr, acct supt, Bur Pub Safety & Judicial Coordrn, chief, currently. **Orgs:** IL Correct Asn, 1979-; Am Correct Asn, 1980-; Nat Asn Blacks Criminal Justice, 1976-; Circuit Court Cook County Principal's Comt, 1991-; IL Attorney Gen Comn Af-Am Males, 1992-94; Chicago Salvation Army Corr Servs, adv bd, 1993-; Office Cook Cty State's Attorney Gay & Lesbian Task Force, 1993-; Will Cty Police Chiefs Asn; City Joliet, IL Task Force Gangs; Nat Asn Blacks Criminal Justice; Asn State Correctional Admins; IL Correctional Asn; Am Correctional Asn; Am Jail Asn. **Business Phone:** (312)603-1160.*

FAISON, DEREK E.
Executive. **Personal:** Born Jul 14, 1948, Newport News, VA; son of Edgar and Carmena Gantt; married Wilma A Faison (divorced 1990); children: Natalye, Marcus. **Educ:** Univ Colo, Denver, CO, BS, bus admin, 1970; Colo State Univ, Fort Colins, CO, attended 1972. **Career:** Penn Mutual Life Ins Co, Denver, CO, sales rep, 1970-72; IBM, Boulder, CO, copier planning mfg, 1972-81; Faison Off Prod Co, Aurora, CO, pres, 1981-00. **Orgs:** bd mem, Big Brother, 1988-; bd mem, Colo Black Chamber Com, 1990-; bd mem, Greater Denver Chamber Com, 1990-; bd mem, Dean's Adv Bd Columbia Bus Sch, 1990-; bd mem, Denver Broncos Active Rooster, 1990-; bd mem, Univ Colo Found; vice chair, Mile High United Way. **Honors/Awds:** Business of the Year, Minority Enterprise Inc, 1990; Cert Spec Cong Recognition Dan Schefer, 1991. *

FAISON, DONALD ADEOSUN
Actor. **Personal:** Born Jun 22, 1974, New York, NY; married Lisa Askey, Feb 27, 2001 (divorced 2005); children: 3. **Career:** TV series: "Clueless", 1996-99; "Felicity", 1999-01; "Scrubs", 2001-;"Clone High", 2002-; TV movies: "Supreme Sanction", 1999; Films: Juice, 1992; Sugar Hill, 1994; New Jersey Drive, 1995; Clueless, 1995; Waiting to Exhale, 1995; Can't Hardly Wait, 1998; Butter, 1998; Trippin', 1999; Remember ther Titans, 2000; Double Whammy, 2001; Josie and the Pussycats, 2001; Academy Boyz, 2001; Big Fat Liar, 2002; Molly Gun, 2003; Good Boy, 2003; Uptown Girls, 2003; King's Ransom, 2005; Something New; 2006; Bachelor Party Vegas, 2006; Next Day Air, 2009; Venus & Vegas, 2009. **Honors/Awds:** Won, BET Comedy Award, 2004, 2005. **Business Addr:** Actor, c/o Gold Marshak Liedtke & Associates, 3500 W Olive Ave, Burbank, CA 91505.*

FAISON, EUGENE M
Chairperson, chief executive officer. **Educ:** Hampton Univ, BS; Dartmouth Univ, Minority Bus Exec Prog, grad. **Career:** Nutrit Labs Int, co-founder, chmn & dir; Equals Three Communs Inc, chmn & chief exec officer, currently. **Orgs:** Chair, Agency Mgt Comt, Am Asn Advert Agencies; chair, Am Asn Advert Agencies Oper Success Diversity Adv Bd; Govt Rels Comt, Am Asn Advert Agencies; chmn, Empowerment Network Found; vice chmn & dir, Women Community Serv; bd mem, Friends Zambia; Pub Rel Soc Am. **Business Phone:** (301)656-3100.*

FAISON, FRANKIE R.
Actor. **Personal:** Born Jun 10, 1949, Newport News, VA; son of Edgar and Carmena Gantt; married Jane Mandel, Nov 26, 1988; children: Blake, Amanda & Rachel. **Educ:** Ill Wesleyan Univ, Bloomington, IL, BFA, 1971; NY Univ, MFA, 1974. **Career:** Films: Ragtime, 1981; CHUD, 1984; Coming to America, 1988; Mississippi Burning, 1988; Do the Right Thing, 1989; The Silence of the Lambs, 1991; City of Hope, 1991; Freejack, 1992; Sommersby, 1993; The Rich Man's Wife, 1996; The Thomas Crown Affair, 1999; Where the Money Is, 2000; Thirteen Conversations About One Thing, 2001; Hannibal, 2001; The Sleepy Time Gal, 2001; Red Dragon, 2002; Show time, 2002; Gods & Generals, 2003; In Good Company, 2004; Crutch, 2004; The Cookout, 2004; Messengers, 2004; White Chicks, 2004; Premium, 2006; My Blueberry Nights, 2007; Nick and Norah's Infinite Playlist, 2008;

Adam, 2009; # Cirque du Freak: The Vampire's Assistant; For Sale by Owner; Splinter heads, 2009. TV movies: The Spider and the Fly, 1994; The Langoliers, 1995; Call Me Claus, 2001; TV series: "True Colors," 1990; "Prey," 1997-98; "The Wire," 2002; "Law & Order: Special Victims Unit", 2007. **Orgs:** Actors Equity Asn, 1972-; Screen Actors Guide, 1974-; Am Fedn TV & Radio, 1974-; Local spokesperson, Orgn Prev Child Abuse, 1991. **Honors/ Awds:** Tony Nomination, 1988; Drama Desk Nomination, 1988; Audelco Award, 1989; Hon Doctorate Degree, Ill Weslyan Univ, 2002; FFCC Award, 2003. **Business Addr:** Actor, c/o Innovative Artists, 235 Park Ave S, New York, NY 10003.*

FAISON, DR. HELEN SMITH
Educator. **Personal:** Born Jul 13, 1924, Pittsburgh, PA; married George. **Educ:** Univ Pittsburgh, AB, 1946, M.Ed, 1955, PhD, 1975. **Career:** Allegheny Co, bd asst, social caseworker, teacher, girls adv, activites dir, counr, vice prin, prin; Pittsburgh Pub Sch, asst supt, actg supt, interim supt; Pittsburgh Teachers Inst, founder & dir, emerits trustee; Chatham Col, vis prof, educ dept chair. **Orgs:** Nat Coun Negro Women; bd mem, YWCA; Pi Lambda Theta; Admin Women Educ; Am Asn Univ Women; chmn, State Implementation; bd mem, Univ Pittsburgh; Educ TV Sta WQED; Negro Educ Emergency Dr; Harriet Tubman Guild Inc. **Honors/ Awds:** Award of Helping Women for Advancement, AASA/FORD Found, 1977; Helen S Faison Chair in Urban Education, Univ Pittsburgh, 2006; Baptist Temple Church Receptionist Courier Top Hat Award; Educator of the Year Award Guardians; Distinguished Alumnae Award, Univ Pittsburgh; Nat Asn Advan Colored People Homer Brown Award; Women of Spirit Award, Carlow Col; "Strong Men & Women: Excellence in Leadership", Dominion, 2009. **Special Achievements:** One of the First African-American Teachers; First Female and African-American High School Principal; First Woman Superintendent in Pittsburgh. **Business Addr:** Founder, Director, Pittsburgh Teachers Institute, Chatham Coll Braun Hall, Woodland Rd, Pittsburgh, PA 15232.

FAISON, SHARON GAIL
Marketing executive. **Personal:** Born Nov 21, 1955, Newport News, VA; daughter of Edgar and Carmena Gantt; married Melvin E Bryant (divorced 1985); children: Sharonda M, Jai R. **Educ:** Norfolk State Univ, BA, math, 1982. **Career:** Int Bus Mach Support Ctr, PSR, 1983-86; Faison Off Prod Co, Co, vpres, 1986-00. **Orgs:** Nat Off Prod Asn, 1982; Zeta Phi Beta, 1984-; Minority Enterprise Inc, 1986-; Greater Denver Black Chamber Com, 1986-. **Honors/Awds:** Grad Fast Track Prog, Minority Enterprise Inc, 1990; Cert Appreciation, Total Quality Mgt, 1990; Colo Bus of the Year, Minority Enterprise Inc, 1990. *

FAKHRID-DEEN, NASHID ABDULLAH
Educator. **Personal:** Born Feb 24, 1949, Monticello, AR; son of N T Thompson and Mary Thompson; married Pauline Rashidah Williamson; children: Jashed, Ayesha & Yasmeen. **Educ:** Grand Valley State Univ, BA, 1978; Western Mich Univ, grad work, 1979; Univ Baltimore, Sch Law, JD, 1988. **Career:** Nat Islam, minister, 1975-79; Grand Valley State Univ, asst dir talent search, 1980-83, asst dir admis, 1979-83; Bowie State Univ, coordr recruitment, assoc dir admis, 1988-90; Ky State Univ, Frankfort, Ky, exec asst pres, 1990-91; Ohio Univ, coordr minority stud affairs, 1992-94; State Ky, Ky Community & Tech Col System, coordr minority affairs, 1994, coordr cult diversity progs, prin investr, currently. **Orgs:** Gen bus mgr, Nat Islam, 1972-76; bd dirs, Climbing Tree Sch, 1977-78; bd dirs, Family Serv Outreach, 1982-83; Mid-Am Asn Educ Opportunity Prog Personnel; exec coun, Black Law Students, Univ Baltimore; Admis/Retention Comt; Moot Ct Bd, 1986-88; Developer/presentator, CARE (motivational workshop), Baltimore/Wash Metro Area; pres, Black Law Students Asn, Univ Baltimore Sch Law, 1987-88. **Honors/Awds:** Outstanding Community Service, 1980-82; Outstanding Community Service, World Community Islam, 1981 & 1982; Grand Valley St Univ, Outstanding Serv Talent Search Prog, 1983; Outstanding Service Award, Off Admis, 1983; Charles Hamilton Houston Award, Univ Baltimore Black Law Students Asn, 1988; Freedom Fighter Award, NAACP, Bowie State Univ Chap, 1991; Asante Award, Ohio Univ, 1993; Romeo Award, 1993; Significant Contribution Award to Project PARADE, Hopeville Community Col, 1995. **Military Serv:** USAF, E-4 sgt, 3 1/2 yrs. **Home Addr:** 4344 Calavares Dr, Lexington, KY 40514. **Business Addr:** Principal Investigator, Kentucky Community & Technical College System, 300 N Main St, Versailles, KY 40383, **Business Phone:** (859)256-3260.

FALANA, LOLA (LOLETHA ELAINE)
Religious reformer, singer, entertainer. **Personal:** Born Sep 11, 1942, Philadelphia, PA; daughter of Bennett and Cleo; married Feliciano Tavares, 1970 (divorced 1975). **Career:** Dancing jobs on the East Coast; Frank Sinatra's Reprise Label & Motown Records; Sammy Davis Jr's broadway musical Golden Boy, dancer; Films: A Man Called Adam, actress, 1966; Dr Jazz, actress & dancer, 1975; Las Vegas, singer, 1976-89; Mad About You, actress, 1990; Faberge, spokesperson; Album: My Baby, 1965; TV Prog: Lady Cocoa, 1975; "Ben Vereen.. Comin' at Ya", 1975; "The Joey Bishop Show"; " The Hollywood Palace"; "The Love Boat", 1978; Marooned, 1978; "Liberace: A Valentine Special, 1979; "The Big Show", 1980; "Capitol," actress, 1982; Hotel", 1986; Practice of religion & faith, currently. **Honors/Awds:** Nominated for a Tony Award, 1975; Female Performer of the Year, Am Guild Variety Artists. **Special Achievements:** Smashed nearly every Las Vegas nightclub attendance & box office record; First Lady of Las Vegas.

FALES, SUSAN
Television producer, writer. **Personal:** Born in Rome, Italy; daughter of Timothy Fales and Josephine Premice (deceased); married Aaron Christopher Hill, 1998; children: one. **Educ:** Harvard Univ, BA (with honors), hist, literature, 1985. **Career:** "The Cosby Show," apprentice writer, 1985-86; "A Different World," story editor, 1986-87, co-producer, writer, 1987-93; "Central Park West," tv series, writer, 1995; "Linc's," exec producer, head writer, 1998-00; For Real, feature film, actress, 2001; "Suddenly Susan," writer; "Vogue," "Town & Country," and "Travel & Leisure," writer. **Orgs:** Board of Trustees, American Ballet Theatre; Studio Museum in Harlem; East Side House Settlement. **Honors/Awds:** Nominated for the Humanitas Award. **Special Achievements:** Author Always Wear Joy, Harper Collins, 2003. **Business Phone:** (212)664-4444.*

FALKNER, BOBBIE E.
Automotive executive. **Career:** Harvey Chrysler Plymouth, Harvey, IL, chief exec officer, currently. *

FANAKA, JAMAA (WALTER GORDON)
Writer, artistic director. **Personal:** Born Sep 6, 1942, Jackson, MS; son of Robert L and Beatrice; children: Tracey L, Michael, Katina A, Twyla M. **Educ:** Compton Jr Col, AA, 1971; Univ Calif, Los Angeles, BA, 1973, MFA, 1978. **Career:** Jamaa Fanaka Prod Inc, writer, producer & dir; Bethlehem Steel, engineering clerk, 1964-68; IBM Corp, customer engr, 1968-70; Films: Welcome Home Brother Charles. 1975; Emma Mae, 1976; Penitentiary, 1980; Penitentiary II, 1982; Penitentiary III, 1987; Street Wars, 1992; TV series: "Mr. T", 1999; "E! True Hollywood Story", 1999. **Orgs:** Pres, Black Filmmakers Alliance, 1975-79; Big Brothers Am, 1980. **Honors/Awds:** Ford Found Grant, Ford Found, 1972; Rockefeller Grant, Rockefeller Found, 1973; Univ Calif Los Angeles Chancellor's Grant, Univ Calif, Los Angeles, 1973; Am Film Inst Grant, Am Film Inst, 1976. **Military Serv:** USAF, a/1c, 1960-64. **Business Addr:** MGM Studios, Culver City, CA 90230.*

FANCHER, DR. EVELYN PITTS
Librarian. **Personal:** Born in Marion, AL; daughter of D C Pitts and Nell Pitts; married Charles B; children: Charles Jr, Mark & Adrienne. **Educ:** Ala State Univ, BS; Atlanta Univ, MSLS, 1961; Peabody Vanderbilt Univ, EdS, 1969, PhD, 1975. **Career:** Librarian (retired); Lincoln High Sch, librn, 1951-56; Ala Agri & Mech Univ, librn, 1956; Tenn State Univ, librn, 1962-75, prof libr Sci, 1975, dir libr, 1976-89; Vanderbilt Univ, Kelly M Smith Res Collection, librn, 1991-96. **Orgs:** Bd dir, Girl Scout, Cumberland Valley, 1980-84; Libr consult, USAID, Swaziland, 1982; bd mem, Tenn Adv Coun Librarians, 1983-89; pres, Tenn Libr Asn, 1984-85; SE Libr Asn; Am Libr Asn; Tenn Libr Asn; Tenn Higher Educ Comn Libry Tech Coun; Tenn Long Range Planning Comn, five year plan for libraries; reviewer, Southern Asn Cols & Schs. **Honors/Awds:** One of the first women inducted into Phi Delta Kappa Ed Fraternity; recognitions received from Society of State & Mayor; Outstanding Service, Congregational Church, 1991; Outstanding Service, Numerous Churches, 1991; Nashville Volunteer of the Year, 1992; Good Neighbor Award, 1992; Tenn Historical Commission Merit Award, 1994; Historical Merit Award, 1994; Centennial Award, Tenn Libr Asn, 2002; mary Catherine Award. **Special Achievements:** Author: College Administrative Practices & the Negro Student, Negro Ed Rev XXII, 1971; Editing Ethnic Minorities, Negro Ed Rev, XXV, 1974; Merger of Ten State Univ & the University of Tennessee Libraries, TN Librarian Vol 32, Winter, 1980; Educational Technology A Black Perspective, Eric, 1984; A Study Guide for Discovering & Preserving Arican Church History Documents, 1991; A Directory of African Churches in Nashville, TN, 1991; Tennessee Vocational Sch for Colored Girls, TN Encyclopedia of History & Culture, 1998. *

FANN, ALBERT LOUIS
Educator, actor. **Personal:** Born Feb 21, 1925, Cleveland, OH; son of Albert Louis and Beulah; married Barbara (divorced); children: Tracy King, Shelley Peterson, Melanie, Albert, Kacie & Scott (divorced). **Educ:** Cleveland Inst Music, 1959; Living Ministries Int, DD, 1981. **Career:** Actor, 1950-; Al Fann Theatrical Ensemble, exec dir, 1965-; movies: Cotton Comes to Harlem, 1970; The French Connection, 1971; Come Back Charleston Blue, 1972; The Super Cops, 1974; God Told Me To, 1976; The Lady killers, 2004; Tv series: "Any Day Now", 1999; "Hefner: Unauthorized", 1999; "The Michael Richards Show- The Consultant", 2000; "Greetings from Tucson- Home Sweet Home", 2003; "The Lady killers", 2004. **Orgs:** Screen Actors Guild, 1965-; Am Fedn Tv & Radio Artists, 1965-; life-time hon mem, NAACP, 1979; founder, Inst Artistic Develop, Higher Mind Training, 1986; blue ribbon panel judge, Acad Artists & Sci, 1987. **Honors/Awds:** Best Play of the Year, 14 Awards, Nat Cable TV Asn, 1971; Emmy Award Nomination, 1989. **Special Achievements:** King Heroin, 1967, The World's No 1 Performing Unit, 1967, Drama as a Therapeutic Tool, 1978. **Military Serv:** AUS, aircorp pvt. **Business Addr:** Actor, Associate Producer, Al Fann Theatrical Ensemble, 6051 Hollywood Blvd Suite 207, Hollywood, CA 90028, **Business Phone:** (323)464-0187.

FANN, CHAD FITZGERALD
Football player. **Personal:** Born Jun 7, 1970, Jacksonville, FL. **Educ:** Fla A&M Univ, BA, criminal justice. **Career:** Football player (retired); Phoenix Cardinals, 1993; Ariz Cardinals, tight end, 1994-95; San Francisco 49ers, 1997-99; Minnesota Vikings, 2000.

FAREED, KAMAAL IBN JOHN
Rap musician, actor. **Personal:** Born Apr 10, 1970, Brooklyn, NY; married Michele Daves, Nov 10, 1990. **Career:** A Tribe Called Quest, co-founder, 1988-; Albums with A Tribe Called Quest including: People's Instinctive Travels & the Paths of Rhythm, 1990; The Low End Theory, 1991; Midnight Marauders, 1993; Beats, Rhymes, & Life,1996; The Love Movement, 1998; Solo Albums: Description of a Fool, 1989;Poetic Justice, 1993; Rhyme & Reason, 1997; Love Goggles, 1999; Amplified,1999; Open The Mix tape: Abstract Innovations, 2008; The Renaissance, 2008; "Kamaal/ The Abstract", 2009; Singles: "Vivrant Thing", 1999; "High Rollers (feat. Consequence)", 1999; "Breathe & Stop", 1999; "For The Nasty (feat. Busta Rhymes & Pharrell)", 2005; "Work It Out", 2007; Films: Poetic Justice, 1993; Disappearing Acts, 2000: Prison Song, producer & writer, 2001; Brown Sugar, 2002; Death of a Dynasty, 2003; She Hate Me, 2004; Cadillac Record, 2008; TV series: Disappearing Acts, 2000; The Hip Hop Project,assoc producer, 2006. **Business Addr:** Singer, Rapper & Actor, Hip Hop producer, c/o BMG Entertainment Inc, 1540 Broadway Fl 44, New York, NY 10036, **Business Phone:** (212)930-4000.*

FARLEY, DR. JONATHAN DAVID
College teacher, educator. **Educ:** Harvard Univ, AB, 1991; Oxford Univ, PhD, math, 1995. **Career:** Math Sci Res Inst, fel, 1995-97; Harvard Univ, vis scholar, 2005-, math prof, currently; Stanford Univ Ctr Int Security, sci fel, 2005; Mass Inst Technol, prof, vis assoc prof appl math, MIT affiliate. **Honors/Awds:** Johnson Prize, 1994; Sr Math Prize, 1994; Fulbright Distinguished Scholar, 2001-02; Distinguished Scientist Award, Harvard Found, 2004; Dr Jonathan David Farley Day, named in honor, 2004. **Special Achievements:** Published more than 10 articles. **Business Addr:** Mathematics Professor, Harvard University, Department of Mathematics, 1 Oxford St, Cambridge, MA 02138, **Business Phone:** (617)495-8477.*

FARLEY, WILLIAM HORACE, JR.
Lawyer. **Personal:** Born Feb 20, 1950, Skowhegan, ME; son of Laura C and William H Sr; married Gale Foster, Nov 27, 1982; children: William Foster & Royal Chase. **Educ:** Yale Univ, BA (cum laude) 1972; Oxford Univ England, Hons BA, 1974; Yale Law Sch JD 1977. **Career:** McDermott, Will & Emery, atty, 1977-86; City Chicago, First Asst, corp coun, 1987-89; Chicago Transit Authority, gen coun, 1989-92; Jenner & Block, partner, 1992-2000; Attorney's Liability Assurance Soc, sr claims atty, 2000-; Gonzalez Saggio & Harlan LLP, corp coun, currently. **Orgs:** Bd mem, Const Rights Found; Pub Interest Law Initiative; Lawyers' Trust Fund ILL; Urban Gateways; Chicago Bar Asn; Am Bar Asn; Cook County Bar Asn; Markey Inns Ct; trans pres bd, Comt Transit & Inst Transp Law; chmn, Legal Affairs Comt, Am Pub Transit Asn; Affirmative Action Cook County Bd Comnrs. **Honors/Awds:** Rhodes Scholarship, 1972. **Home Addr:** 1023 Oak Pk Ave, Oak Park, IL 60302. **Business Addr:** Corporate Counseling, Gonzalez Saggio & Harlan LLP, 225 E Mich St 4th Fl, Milwaukee, IL 53202, **Business Phone:** (414)277-8500.

FARMER, CLARENCE
Executive. **Personal:** Born Jun 19, 1920, Rochester, PA; son of Frank and Margaret Artope; married Marjorie Nichols, Apr 17, 1943; children: Clarence Jr (deceased) & Franklin. **Educ:** Geneva Col, PA, AB, 1940. **Career:** Philadelphia Police Adv Bd, exec secy, 1965-67; Comn Human Rels, chmn, 1967-82; Comn on Human Rels, exec dir & chmn, 1967-82; Self-employed, bus consult, Clarence Farmer & Assocs Inc, pres, owner, 1984-; Stadium Enterprise Inc, pres; Ctr Adult Training, pres; Farmer Commun Inc, pres; First Loan Co & Farmer Press Inc, pres. **Orgs:** Bd, Philadelphia Urban Coalition Inc; bd dir, Wissahick on Boys Club; bd dir, Founders Club; Greater Philadelphia Chamber Com; United Fund; Phila Housing Develop Corp; pres, Options Women Inc; Philadelphia Civic Ballet Co; Cape May Tennis Club; St Paul Epis Chap; NAACP; Urban League of Phila; Geneva Col Alumni Asn; Alpha Phi Alpha; Benjamin Lodge F & A M; bd trustees Geneva Col, Beaver Falls, PA; chmn emer, bd dirs, Afro-Am Hist & Cultural Museum; chmn, Phila Housing Develop Corp; chmn & founder, Greater Philadelphia Enterprise Develop Corp. **Honors/ Awds:** USAAF, 1943-45; North City Congr Award, 1965; Bapt Ministers Conf, 1965; Travelers' Club Award, 1967; Gardian Civic Leag Award, 1967; Legion Cornelius, 1967; Distinguished Serv Award, Geneva Col, 1969; Achievement Award, Philadelphia Bar Asn, 1969; Coun of Clergy Award, 1972; 100000 Pennsylvanians Award Community Serv, 1972; Cardinal's Comn Human Rel Award, 1972; Distinguished Serv Award, Alpha Phi Alpha, 1971; Richard Allen Award; Mother Bethel Am Chap, 1974; DHL, Tex Col, 1989; Chamber Com Award, 1991. **Military Serv:** USAAF, Sgt, 1943-45. **Business Phone:** (215)985-0505.*

FARMER, FOREST JACKSON, SR.
Executive. **Personal:** Born Jan 15, 1941, Zanesville, OH; son of William J and Leatha D Randolph; married Rosalyn Farmer McPherson, Dec 1966; children: Forest Jr & Christopher M. **Educ:** Purdue Univ, Lafayette, IN, BS, biol & phys educ 1965. **Career:** Chrysler Motors Corp, Jefferson Assembly Plant, plant mgr, 1981, Newark, DE, assembly plant mgr, 1983, Sterling Heights, MI, plant mgr, 1984, dir advance mfg planning, 1986-87, Highland Park, MI, gen plant mgr, 1987-88; Acustar Inc, Troy, MI, pres, 1988-95; Bing Manufacturing Inc, pres & chief exec officer, 1995-98; Regal Plastics Co, chief exec officer; Trillium Teamologies, chmn, chief exec officer & pres, 1995-; Farmer Group, chmn, pres & chief exec officer, 1998-; Enerflex Solutions LLC, chmn, chief exec officer & pres. **Honors/Awds:** Outstanding Businessman, 1989; 100 Black Men of America, 1989. **Business Phone:** (248)322-7079.

FARMER, HARVEY RAY. See FARMER, RAY.

FARMER, HILDA WOOTEN
Banker. **Personal:** Born Apr 25, 1950, La Grange, NC; daughter of Elbert Wooten and Janie Wooten (deceased); married William E, Aug 11, 1972; children: William Jr & Courtney. **Educ:** NC Cent Univ, Durham, NC, BS, 1972. **Career:** Wachovia Bank, Goldsboro, NC, dealer credit mgr, asst vpres, 1973-. **Orgs:** Treas, Am Cancer Soc, 1986-91. **Honors/Awds:** Service Awards, American Cancer Society, 1988-89. **Home Addr:** 494 Hare Rd Rte 4, PO Box 90, Goldsboro, NC 27534. **Business Addr:** Assistant Vice President, Sales Finance Department, Wachovia Bank & Trust Co, 301 E Ash St, Goldsboro, NC 27530, **Business Phone:** (919)735-0211.*

FARMER, JUDGE NANCY. See FARMER, NANCY.

FARMER, NANCY (JUDGE NANCY FARMER)
Judge. **Educ:** Eastern Mich Univ; Detroit Col Law, law. **Career:** Thirty sixth Dist Ct, Detroit, chief judge & ct adminr, currently. **Orgs:** Workers Compensation Bd & Chairperson Mich Employ Bd Rev; trustee, Detroit Metrop Bar Asn; bd dirs, St Francis Family Serv; Links Inc. **Business Addr:** Chief Judge, Court Administrator, 36th District Court, 421 Madison Ave, Detroit, MI 48226, **Business Phone:** (313)965-8720.

FARMER, RAY (HARVEY RAY FARMER)
Football executive, football player. **Personal:** Born Jul 1, 1972, White Plains, NY; married Vernet; children: Boyd & Kennedy. **Educ:** Duke Univ, BA, sociol, 1996. **Career:** Philadelphia Eagles, linebacker, 1996-98; Carolina Panthers; Duke Univ, acad coordr; Comcast Sports Network, tv sports analyst; Atlanta Falcons, 2002-05; Kans City Chiefs, dir pro personnel, 2006-. **Honors/Awds:** Inductee, Chiefs Hall of Fame, 1992; Pro Football Hall of Fame, 2008; Holds a Cheif Record with 58 Career INT's. **Special Achievements:** Was a two-time All-Atlantic Coast Conference selection for the BlueDevils; was named to the conference All-Academic Team in 1994. **Business Addr:** Director of Pro Personnel, Kansas City Chiefs, 1 Arrowhead Dr, Kansas City, MO 64129, **Business Phone:** (816)920-9400.*

FARMER, DR. ROBERT CLARENCE
Physician. **Personal:** Born Jan 1, 1941, Rochester, PA; son of Francis Alexander and Ora Juanita McClain; married Linda Kay Hill, Aug 4, 1983; children: Saundra, Robert, James & Wendy. **Educ:** Howard Univ, BS, 1963, MD, 1967. **Career:** Univ Pittsburgh, instr pediat radiol, 1973-74; Howard Univ, asst prof radiol, 1974-75, asst prof pediat, 1974-77; St Anthony Hosp, dir radiol, 1977-81; Fayette Co Hosp, dir radiol, 1978-83; Ft Stewart Hosp, dir radiol, 1980-81; Connellsville State Gen Hosp, dir radiol, 1982-85; Highlands Hosp & Health Ctr, dir radiol, 1985-2000; Farmer Diag Imaging Serv Inc, pres, health radiol, 1992-; HUA, pres, 1992-; African Am Chamber Com. **Orgs:** Life mem, Nat Asn Advan Colored People, 1953-; life mem, Alpha Phi Alpha Frat; Radiol Soc N Am, 1973-; Am Col Radiol, 1973-; Nat Med Asn, 1977-; Am Cancer Soc, 1983-; bd dirs, Am Lung Asn, 1985-; bd dirs, Comm Housing Resource, Bd Fayette City, PA; FROGS Club, Pittsburgh; pres, Fayette County, Nat Asn Advan Colored People, 1989-92; vpres, Pa State Conf Nat Asn Advan Colored People Branches, 1989-91; pres, Rotary Club Connellsville; vpres, Pittsburgh Lay Conf Am Methodist Episcopal Church; pres, Gateway Med Soc Nat Med Asn, 1994-96; pres, Chi Delta Mu Fraternity Pi Chap, 1995-97; bd mem, Blue Cross Western Pa, 1996; bd mem, HighMark Corp, 1996-. **Honors/Awds:** Black Achiever of SW Pennsylvania 11th dist Debora Grand Chapter OES, 1988; Physician of the Year, Gateway Med Soc, 1999. **Special Achievements:** Publications "Carcinoma of the Breast; A Clinical Study," NMA Journal 1969; "Immunological Responses in Infantile Cortical Hyperostosis," Pediatric Rsch Vol 10 1976; "Immunological Studies in Caffey's Cortical Hyperostosis," Pediatrics 1977. **Military Serv:** AUS, capt, 1966-68. **Business Addr:** President, Farmer Diagnostic Imaging Service, 210 N Pittsburgh St, Connellsville, PA 15425, **Business Phone:** (724)366-0535.

FARMER, SHARON
Photographer, government official. **Career:** The White House, Chief, White House Photography, 1993-98, dir, 1999-01; Assoc Press, photo ed, photo supvr, currently. **Honors/Awds:** Photographer of the Year, 2004. **Special Achievements:** First Black person & first woman to become the Chief White House Photographer. **Business Addr:** Photo Superviser, Associated Press, 1150 18th St NW, Washington, DC 20036, **Business Phone:** (202)466-3973.*

FARR, D'MARCO MARCELLUS
Football player, radio host. **Personal:** Born Jun 9, 1971, San Pablo, CA; married Cynthia; children: Grant Marcellus. **Educ:** Univ Wash, BA, soc & justice. **Career:** Football player (retired), host: St Louis Rams, defensive tackle, 1994-2000; San Francisco 49ers, 2003-04; KSPN radio, D'Marco Farr Show, host, 2005-07; KTVI FOX 2, TV color commentary, 2008; 103.3 KLOU, 2008; 101.1 WXOS, 2008; 101 ESPN, color commentary, 2009; FSN, The Best Damn Sports Show Period, co-host, 2009. *

FARR, HERMAN
Clergy, president (organization). **Personal:** Married Bruetta Dupre; children: 4. **Educ:** Detroit Bible Col. **Career:** Clien Air Bacteria Service, proprieter; Ford Motor Co, former employee; Lien Chemical Co, former salesman; Oak Hill Bapt Ch Chmn of Equal Employment Com, presently pastor; Interdenominational Ministerial Alliance, corresponding sec; Mt Herman Bapt & Dist Asn, treas; Bapt Ministers Fel, pres; Shreveport Chap Nat Asn Advan Colored People, publicity chmn 1-74; Nat Asn Advan Colored People, exec secy, 1968-71. **Orgs:** YMCA; coordinator Weekly Radio Broadcast for Ministerial Alliance. **Honors/Awds:** Appreciation Award, Nat Asn Advan Colored People, 1972; Community service award, AKA Sorority during 41st Central Regional Conf, 1973; Cert Appreciation for Serv, Kiwanis Club, 1973; Community Serv award, Negro C of C, 1973. **Business Addr:** 1900 Milan St, Shreveport, LA 71103.*

FARR, MELVIN, SR.
Automotive executive, football player. **Personal:** Born Nov 3, 1944, Beaumont, TX; son of Miller Sr and Dorthea; married Mae R Forbes; children: Mel Jr, Michael A, Monet A; married Linda Johnson Rice, 2004. **Educ:** UCLA, 1967; Univ Detroit, BS, 1970. **Career:** football player (retired), entrepreneur; Detroit Lions, prof football player, 1967-73; Mel Farr Ford Inc, co-owner, 1968-75, pres, 1978-; Mel Farr Lincoln Mercury, pres, 1986-; Mel Farr Imports, pres, 1986-; Mel Farr Ford, Ohio, pres, 1991-; Mel Farr Ford Grand Blanc, pres, 1993-; Mel Farr Lincoln Mercury, Ohio, pres, 1995-; Mel Farr Ford-Houston, pres, 1996-; Flint, MI 7-Up franchise, co-owner, 1985-87; Mel Farr Automotive Group, pres, currently. **Orgs:** co-founder, Minority Ford-Lincoln Mercury Dealers Asn; dir, Nat Asn Minority Auto Dealers; board mem, Sinai Hosp Health Care Found; bd dir, Better Bus Bureau Detroit & SE Mich; Public Advisory Committee Judicial Candidates; life mem, NAACP; db dir, Metropolitan Detroit YMCA; Oak Park, Mich Chamber Com. **Honors/Awds:** NFL Rookie of the Yr, 1967; UCLA Sports Hall of Fame, 1988; Entrepreneur of the Year, Michigan Black MBA Assn, 1992; Meg Mallon Sportsmanship Achievement Award, Mercy High School, 1992; Auto Dealer of the Year, Black Enterprise Magazine, 1992 ; Executive of the Year, Oakland County, 1993. **Special Achievements:** 1st 100% Black-owned major soft drink franchise. **Business Addr:** President, Chief Executive Officer, Mel Farr Automotive Group, 10550 W 8 Mile Rd, Ferndale, MI 48220-2152, **Business Phone:** (248)584-0370.*

FARRAKHAN, LOUIS (LOUIS EUGENE WALCOTT)
Clergy. **Personal:** Born May 11, 1933, Bronx, NY; son of Percival Clarke and Sarah Mae Manning; married Khadijah; children: Mustapha. **Educ:** Winston-Salem Teachers Col. **Career:** The Final Call, founder, 1979; Nation Islam, minister & acting head, currently. **Honors/Awds:** Named to the list of the Greatest Chicagoans of the Century; Rev Dr Jeremiah A Wright Jr Lifetime Achievement Trumpeteer Award, 2007. **Special Achievements:** Independent Black Leadership in America, 1991; organized Million Man March, 1995; organized Million Family March, 2000; achieved fame in Bostonas a vocalist, calypso singer, dancer & violinist; book: A Torchlight for Am, 1993. **Business Addr:** Minister, The Nation of Islam, c/o Mosque Maryam, 7351 S Stony Island Ave, Chicago, IL 60649, **Business Phone:** (773)324-6000.

FARRAR, MOSES
Business owner, writer. **Personal:** Born Dec 28, 1929, Richmond, VA; son of Lavinia and Percy B; married Naomi Boekhoudt, 2000; children: Muriel Locke, Regina Dyson, Valerie Dews, Miriam, Benjamin, Monique Marshall, Lisa Eaves. **Career:** Business owner (Retired); Norfolk J & Guide, 1951-60; Philadelphia Inquirer, typesetter, 1961-63; Wescott Thomson, Philadelphia, PA, typesetter, 1963-69; self-employed, 1969-92. **Orgs:** Temple Beth El's Fifth Tabernacle, 1973-76; Ninth Tabernacle, 1976-93; minister, Fifteenth Tabernacle, 1993-98; assoc minister, Seventh Tabernacle, 1998-00; First Tabernacle, 2002. **Special Achievements:** Published: The Deceiving of the Black Race, 1995; A Non-Christian's Response to Christianity, 2000; The Hebrew Heritage of Black Africa, 2002. **Home Addr:** 437 E 22nd St, PO Box 100065, Brooklyn, NY 11210-0065. *

FARRELL, CHERYL LAYNE
Banker. **Personal:** Born Sep 10, 1955, Los Angeles, CA; married Wendell Charles, May 19, 1985; children: Nia Grace & Alexander Layne. **Educ:** Univ Calif, Los Angeles, Calif, BA, 1987; Univ SC, Los Angeles, CA, MA, 2000. **Career:** Bullocks Dept Store, Los Angeles, CA, dept mgr, asst buyer, 1977-79; Union Bank, Los Angeles, CA, credit mgr, 1979-81, col recruiter, ops trainee, 1981-82; Bank Am, Los Angeles, CA, asst vpres, 1982-84, vpres, Cash Mgt & Govt Serv, mgr, 1984-95, commun vpres, 1995-96; M&I Electronic Banking, Glendale, CA, nat account mgr, 1997; Bank Am, Los Angeles, Calif, Global Payment Services Div, vpres, currently. **Orgs:** Dir pub rel, Los Angeles Urban Bankers, 1986-89; moderator, Morningside United Church Christ; mem, Bank Am Speaking Club; volunteer, Big Sisters, Los Angeles. **Honors/Awds:** CINDY Award, Faces Diversity Video, 1996; Suggestion Award, Union Bank. **Special Achievements:** "100 Most Promising Black Women in Corporate America," Ebony Magazine. **Home Phone:** (818)242-3124. **Business Addr:** Vice President, Bank of America, 333 S Hope St No 100, Los Angeles, CA 90071, **Business Phone:** (213)312-9000.

FARRELL, HERMAN DENNY
State government official. **Personal:** Born Feb 4, 1932, White Plains, NY; son of Herman Sr and Gladys; married Theresa, Jan 1, 1958; children: Monique, Herman III & Sopia Llene; married 1958. **Educ:** NY Univ, 1955. **Career:** Sup Ct Judge Confidential Aid, 1966-72; Mayor John Lindsay, asst dir local neighbor Govt, 1972-74; NY St Assembly, Ways & Means Comm, chmn, 1979-94, assembly man, 1974-, Currently. **Orgs:** Honorary mem, Tioga Carver Comm Found, 1989-95. **Honors/Awds:** Distinguished Legislator Award, St Parole Officers; NY Affirmative Action Coun's Award; Appreciation Award, Boricua Col; Childs Mem Church Award; NY St Ct Clerks Asn Award; Am Legion Cert Appreciation; Tioga Carver Comm Found. **Military Serv:** AUS, sgt, 1952-54. **Business Addr:** Assemblyman, New York State Assembly, 2541-55 Adam Clayton Powell Jr Blvd, New York, NY 10039, **Business Phone:** (212)234-1430.

FARRELL, ROBERT C.
Government official. **Personal:** Born Oct 1, 1936, Natchez, MS. **Educ:** UCLA, BA, 1961, Grad Sch Jour. **Career:** Calif Eagle Newspaper, reporter; Los Angeles Sentinel Newspaper, reporter; Jet Mag, corresp; Star Review News Watts, publ; State Assembly man Mervyn Dymally, consult, currently. **Orgs:** Dep city Counman, Billy C Mills, 1963-71; admin co ordr, S Los Angeles Mayor Bradley's & Staff, 1969-73; Los Angeles City Coun man, 8th Dist, 1974-91; Radio & TV News Asn So, CA; Pub Rels Soc Am; Nat Asn Advan Colored People; Sigma Delta Chi; Legal Defense & Educ Fund; UCLA Alumni Asn; Urban League; pres, Baptist Ministers Conf Los Angeles & vicinity; pres, San Pedro Sect Nat Conf Negro Women. **Military Serv:** USN, 1954-59. **Business Addr:** Consultant, Capitol Office, State Capitol, PO Box 942849, Sacramento, CA 94249-0052, **Business Phone:** (916)319-2052.

FARRELL, SAMUEL D.
Executive. **Personal:** Born Oct 7, 1941, New York, NY; children: Samuel Jr, Ronette. **Career:** DNR Asn, chmn & ceo, currently. **Orgs:** Pres, Alumni Varsity Asn, 1982-83; mem bd dir, CCNY Alumni Asn Dem. *

FARRINGTON, THOMAS ALEX
Executive. **Personal:** Born Nov 12, 1943, Chapel Hill, NC; son of O T Farrington and Mary; married Juarez Harrell; children: Christopher, Trevor, Tomeeka. **Educ:** NC A&T State Univ, BS, elec eng, 1966; Northeastern Univ, Grad Sch Eng. **Career:** RCA Corp, 1966-69; IOCS Inc, pres, 1969-; Input Output Comput Servs, pres, chief exec officer, 1969-94; Farrington Associates Inc, pres & chief exec Officer, 1994-. **Orgs:** Coun Foreign Rels, 1989-; dir, Boston Pvt Indust Coun; dir, Minority Bus Enterprise Legal Defense Fund; founder, Intelligent Transp Syst Consortium Inc; bd dir, Bankblackwell. **Honors/Awds:** Minority Contractor Yr, Dept Transp, 1984; Nat Minority Serv Indust Firm Yr, US Dept Com, 1986. **Special Achievements:** Top 100 Businesses, Black Enterprise; Special Achievement, Black Corporate Presidents of New England, 1988. **Business Addr:** President, Chief Executive Officer, Farrington Associates Inc, 1 Adams Pl, 859 Willard St Suite 400, Quincy, MA 02169.*

FARRIOR, JAMES
Football player. **Personal:** Born Jan 6, 1975, Ettrick, VA; son of James and Rebecca. **Educ:** Va Univ, psychol. **Career:** NY Jets, linebacker, 1997-01; Pittsburgh Steelers, 2002-. **Honors/Awds:** ACC Newcomer of the Week honors; Group AA co-Offensive Player of the Yr;All-Metro & All-State hons; ACC0 second team hons; Most Valuable Player,Pittsburgh Steelers, 2004; Pro Bowl, 2005; co-Player of the Year, The Richmond Times-Dispatch's. **Business Addr:** Professional Football Player, Pittsburgh Steelers, 3400 S Water St, Pittsburgh, PA 15203-2349, **Business Phone:** (412)432-7800.*

FARRIS, DR. ALICIA RENEE
Executive director. **Career:** Univ Detroit Mercy, Mich Inst Nonviolence Educ, exec dir, currently. **Orgs:** Mich Coalition for Human Rights.

FARRIS, DEBORAH ELLISON
Lawyer. **Personal:** Born Dec 29, 1950, Williamsburg, VA; daughter of John M Jr and Ethel C; married J Randolph Farris, Sep

15, 1978; children: James R II. **Educ:** Del State Col, BA, 1972; Antioch Grad Sch, MAT, 1973; Howard Univ Sch Law, JD, 1976. **Career:** Off Gov Rick Perry, one-call bd, 2003; pvt pract, atty, currently. **Orgs:** Black Women Atty Asn; local financial secy, Jack & Jill Am Inc; Nat Coalition of 100 Black Women; nat pres, Nat Carrousels, Inc, 1990-92; Gov Task Force Tuberc; Dallas Youth Orchestra Bd; NBA; Girl Friends Inc; J L Turner Legal Soc; Dallas Youth Orchestra Bd; State Bar Tex; Nat Bar Asn; Tex Criminal Defense Lawyers Asn. **Business Addr:** Attorney, Private Practice, 4136 High Summit Dr, Dallas, TX 75244, **Business Phone:** (972)484-2895.*

FARRIS, HON. JEROME
Judge. **Personal:** Born Mar 4, 1930, Birmingham, AL; son of Willie Joe and Elizabeth; widowed; children: Juli Elizabeth, Janelle Marie. **Educ:** Morehouse Col, BS, 1951, LLD, 1978; Atlanta Univ, MSW, 1955; Univ WA, JD, 1958. **Career:** Weyer Roderick Schroeter & Sterne, assoc, 1958-59; Weyer Schroeter Sterne & Farris, partner, 1959-61; Schroeter & Farris, partner, 1961-63; Schroeter Farris Bangs & Horowitz, partner, 1963-65; Farris Bangs & Horowitz, partner, 1965-69; WA State Court of Appeals, judge, 1969-79; US Ct Appeals 9th Circuit, circuit judge, 1979-. **Orgs:** Pres, Wash State Jr Community Col, 1965-66; trustee, Pacific NW Ballet, 1978-83; chmn, ABA Appellate Judges' Conf, 1982-83; chmn, State Fed Judicial Council of Wash, 1983-87; adv bd, Nat Ctr for State Courts Appellate Justice Proj, 1978-81; founder, Univ Wash Law Sch, 1978-84; adv bd, Tyee Bd of Adv, 1984-; regent, Univ Wash, 1985-97; bd, Am Bar Found, 1987-, exec comt, 1989-; vis comt, Harvard Law Sch, 1996-; US Supreme Ct, judicial fel comm, 1997-; Int Judicial Rels, judicial conf comm, 1997-. **Honors/Awds:** Clayton Frost Award Jaycees, 1966; Order of Coif Univ Wash Law Sch. **Military Serv:** USY, Signal Corps, 1952-53. **Business Addr:** Circuit Judge, United States Court of Appeals for the Ninth Circuit, 1200 6th Ave Suite 1805, Seattle, WA 98104, **Business Phone:** (206)553-2672.*

FARRIS, DR. VERA KING
College president, educator. **Personal:** Born Jul 18, 1940, Atlantic City, NJ; widowed; children: King. **Educ:** Tuskegee Inst, BS, biol, 1959; Univ Mass, MS, zoology, 1962, PhD, zool & parasitol, 1965. **Career:** Pres (retired), dir; Oak Ridge Nat Lab, res asst, 1958-59; Univ Mass, resasst, 1963-64; Univ Mich, res assoc, 1965-66, instr, 1967-68; Univ Mich, post-doctoral fel, 1965-68; State Univ New York, Stony Brook, lectr biol, 1968-71, asst prof, 1970-72, dean spec progs, 1970-72, assoc prof, 1972-73, asst vpres acad affairs, 1969-70, dir inst innovative teaching & couns, 1968-73; State Univ New York, Brockport, prof biol sci, 1973-80, admin fac, 1973-80, chairperson dept women's studies, 1975, actg dean lib studies, 1976, actg dean social progs, 1977, actg vpres acad affairs,1977-79, vice provost acad affairs, 1979-80; Kean Col NJ, vpres acad affairs, 1980-83, prof biol sci, 1980-83; Richard Stockton Col NJ, profbiol sci, 1983, pres, 1983-2003, pres emerita & distinguished prof, currently; Flagstar Corp, dir; Advantica Restaurant Group, dir; Dennys Corp, dir, currently. **Orgs:** Comn Adv Coun Holocaust ED, NJ, 1982-; Am Asn State Cols & Univs, 1984-; NJ State Bd Examiners, 1984-; Martin Luther King Jr Commemorative Comn, NJ, 1984-; Woodson Found Bd, 1986-; Bd Governor's Award Academy, 1986-; chair, Legal Comt, 1988; Overseers, Governor's Sch NJ, 1988-; bd dirs, Am Coun Educ, 1988-91; Exec Comt, Nat Conf, S Jersey Chap; NJ-Israel Comn, 1989-; pres, Bd Trustees, Middle States Asn Cols & Sec Schs, 1991-, 1994; Nat Adv Group Learning Matters, 1992-; Regents Comn Higher Ed, NY State Bd Regents, 1992-93; Flagstar Companies Inc, chair public affairs comt, 1993-; pres, Coun Post-secondary Accreditation, 1993; Nat Utility Investors Corp, 1994-; Comn Recognition Post-secondary Accreditation, 1994-; Nat Utility Investors Corp Exec Compensation Comt; chair, Comt Excellence & Accountability NJ Coun Col Pres, 1995-99. **Honors/Awds:** People of the Year Award, Galloway Township Educ Found, 1988; Father Thom Schiavo Brotherhood Award, Religious Community Greater Atlantic City, 1990; Charles D Moody Certificate of Appreciation, NJ Alliance Black Sch Educators, 1990; Woman of Distinction Award, Soroptimist Int Am, 1990; Certificate of Appreciation, Bermuda High Sch Girls, 1991; Outstanding Leadership Award, Am Asn Minority Veterans Prog Admin, 1991; Janicz Karazak Award, Nat Asn Holocaust Educ, 1991; Myrtle Wreath Award, Camden Co NJ Chap Hadassah Hosp Israel, 1992; NJ Woman of the Year Award, NJ Woman Mag, 1992; Education Award, Washington Ctr Internships & Acad Sems, 1992; Myrtle Wreath Award, Southern NJ Region Hadassah, 1993; Recognition Award, US Holocaust Mem Coun, 1993; Recognition of Appreciation, Richard Stockton Col NJ Bd Trustees, 1993; Woman of the Year Achievement Award, B'Nai B'rith Women's Reg Conf, 1993; NJ Assembly Commendation Outstanding Achievement in Education, Women of the 205th State Legis, 1993; Outstanding Community Service Award, Jewish War Veterans, Carr-Greenstein Post No 39, 1994; NJ Women Policymaker of the Year, Exec Women NJ, 1994; Dr Mary McLeod Bethund Achievement Award, Nat Coun Negro Women, 1994, Women of Achievement Award, Dr Ellen Carter-Watson Section, 1994; NewJersey's Best Recognition Award, NJ Woman Mag, 1994; numerous others; The Lifetime Achievement Award for Excellence in Higher Educ, Nat United Cultural Convention, 2005; Am Hall Fame, ABI Inc, 2006. **Special Achievements:** First African-Am pres of a NJ pub coll; holds seven honorary doctorate degrees; first African Am named to the Bd Dirs of Flagstar Corp; first African-American woman on the Board of Directors of Denny's Restaurants. **Business Phone:** (864)597-8000.

FARROW, HAROLD FRANK
Dentist. **Personal:** Born May 10, 1936, Pensacola, FL; married Virginia; children: Heather, Vance. **Educ:** TN State Univ, BS, 1959; Howard Univ, DDS, 1970. **Career:** C's Hosp, Detroit, staff mem, 1970-71; Wayne Co Health Dept, proj prescad, 1971-72; Dentist, pvt prac, 1972-. **Orgs:** Secy, Wolverine Dent Soc, 1974; pres, Wolverine Dent Soc, 1976; Wolverine Dent Soc, 1977; Am Dent Asn; Mich Dent Asn; DDDA; Nat Dent Asn; Chi Delta Mu Fraternity; noble Marracci Temple no 13, Mystic Shrine, 1974; Nat Asn Advan Colored People, 1976; New Prospect Baptist Church; Howard Univ; N15 Metabolism Edsel Ford Inst. **Honors/Awds:** Achievement hon award, Wolverine Dent Soc, 1974. **Military Serv:** AUS, 1960-62. **Home Addr:** 334 Livernois St, Ferndale, MI 48220, **Home Phone:** (248)547-2040. **Business Addr:** Dentist, Pvt Pract, 334 Livernois St, Ferndale, MI 48220, **Business Phone:** (248)547-2040.*

FARROW, SALLIE A
Lawyer. **Personal:** Born Dec 31, 1942, Plainfield, NJ; daughter of James R Rivera and Sallie Mitchell Rivera; divorced; children: Richard H Staton Jr. **Educ:** Denver Univ, Denver, Colo, BA, 1974; Univ Nebr, Lincoln, Nebr, JD, 1976. **Career:** Mutual Omaha, Omaha, Nebr, asst gen coun, 1977-87; NY Life Ins Co, New York, NY, assoc counr, 1987-. **Orgs:** Kappa Delta Pi, 1973-; consult, ACE Counr SBA, Omaha, 1980-85; panelist, US Off Educ, Wash, DC, 1981; chairperson, Boys Scouts Am, Omaha, 1982; organizer, adv, Metro Sci & Eng Fair Inc, 1982-87; moot ct judge, Creighton Univ, 1983-87; consult, Omaha Pub Schs, Career Awareness, 1983-87; dir, Girls Club Omaha, 1985-87; ed, bar-jour, Nat Bar Asn, 1986-; comt mem, Omaha Bar Asn, 1986-87; Nat Bar Asn Memoirs & Legal Jour, 1986 & 1988; mentor, Legal Outreach, 1992-; vol, gen coun, Nat Coun Negro Women Greater NY, 1993. **Honors/Awds:** Outstanding Achievement, Girls Club Omaha, 1987. **Home Addr:** 1 Rockwell Pl Apt 1D, Brooklyn, NY 11217, **Home Phone:** (718)852-6131. **Business Phone:** (212)576-7000.

FARROW, WILLIAM MCKNIGHT, III
Executive. **Personal:** Born Feb 23, 1955, Chicago, IL; son of William McKnight Jr and Ruth Katherine Haven; married Sandra High, Feb 7, 1981; children: Ashley Marie, William McKnight IV & Justin Matthew. **Educ:** Augustana Col, Rock Island, BA, 1977; Northwestern Univ, Evanston, MBA, 1979. **Career:** Northwestern Mem Hosp, mgt fel, 1978; Arthur Andersen & Co, Chicago, sr consult, 1979-83; GD Searle & Co, Skokie, mgr acquisitions, 1983-85; Dart & Kraft Inc, Northbrook, dir strategy, 1985-86; First Nat Bank Chicago, vpres, head mkt, 1986-88; First Chicago Capital Markets, Chicago, managing dir, 1988-92; NOW, sr vpres, 1992; First Chicago CRE & Inst Bank, head mkt, 1992-96; First Chicago NBD Corp, sr vpres, prog exec, 1996-99; Bank One Corp, sr vpres, Head Treas Mgt, 1999-2000, sr vpres, Head E-Bus, 2000-01; Chicago Bd Trade, exec vpres & chief info officer, 2001-. **Orgs:** Reg facilitator, LEAD, 1979-91; bd dirs, Ancilla Hosp Syst Inc, 1985-89; bd dir, Community Ment Health Coun, 1986-88; Chicago Bond Club, 1989-; bd dirs, Inroads Inc, 1992-; chmn, United Way/Crusade Mercy, West Region, 1993-; Leadership Greater Chicago, 1994; bd dir, Cabrini Green Tutoring, 1995-; Life Directions Inc, 1995-; Court Theatre, 1996-. **Honors/Awds:** Best & Brightest Young Businessman, Dollars & Sense Mag, 1988; Most Significant Marketing Achievement, GD Searle & Co, 1984. **Business Addr:** Chief Information Officer, Executive Vice President, Chicago Board of Trade, 141 W Jackson Blvd No 1101, Chicago, IL 60604, **Business Phone:** (312)435-3758.

FARROW, WILLIE LEWIS
Military leader, pilot. **Personal:** Born Nov 26, 1941, Wetumpka, AL; married Oneita Boyd; children: Stephen Michael. **Educ:** Knoxville Col, BS, 1965; Central MI Univ, MA, 1979. **Career:** Military leader, Pilot (retired); Dover AFB, squadron training mgr, 1974-75, opers exec officer, 1975-76, aircraft maintainence officer, 1976-77, pilot resource mgr, 1977-79, wing flying training mgr, 1979-81; Lt Col, C-5 pilot & air opers staff officer; Budget & Financial Adv, 1981-87; St Jude High Sch, asst prin, 1992-00. **Orgs:** Omega Psi Phi Frat; master mason Prince Hall; Sigma Iota Epsilon Hon Mgt Frat; Chi Gamma Iota Hon Mgt Frat. **Honors/Awds:** Recipient, Distinguished Flying Cross USAF, 1967; USAF Meritorious Service Medal; USAF Commendation Medal; USAF Air Medal; featured, Ebony Mag, 1979. *

FATTAH, CHAKA (ARTHUR DAVENPORT)
Congressperson (u.s. federal government). **Personal:** Born Nov 21, 1956, Philadelphia, PA; son of Russell Davenport and Frances Brown; married Renee Chenault, 2001; children: Francis,Cameron & chandler; married Michelle, 2001; children: Chaka Jr. **Educ:** Philadelphia Community Col, attended; Univ Pa, Wharton Sch, Fels Ctr Govt,master's, 1986; Harvard Univ, JFK Sch Govt. **Career:** State Pa, state rep, dist 192, 1982-88, state senator, dist 7, 1988-94; US House Reps, Second Cong Dist Penn, congressman, 1995-. **Orgs:** Democratic Congressional Campaign Comt; Cong Black Caucus. **Honors/Awds:** One of 50 Future Leaders, Ebony Mag, 1984; State Legislator of the Year Award, Pa Pub Interest Coalition; One of the country's 50 most promising leaders, Time Mag, 1994. **Special Achievements:** Created the Jobs Project which links employers with the unemployed; founded the Graduate Opportunities Conference which offers guidance, resources and scholarships to hundreds of Pennsylvania minority students; founded the American Cities Conference and Foundation which examines the fiscal, infrastructure and social problems of the nation's cities. **Business Addr:** Congressman, US House of Representatives, Second District of Pennsylvania, 4104 Walnut St, Philadelphia, PA 19104, **Business Phone:** (215)387-6404.

FATTAH, FALAKA
Writer, association executive, founder (originator). **Personal:** Born Dec 28, 1931, Philadelphia, PA; daughter of Percy Brown and Louise C Somers West; married David, Jan 26, 1969; children: Stefan, Robin, Kenneth, Chaka, Nasser & David. **Educ:** Course Whitern New Sch Mse, Course Completed 1949; Fleischers Art Sch, course completed, 1949; Temple Univ, English for Writers, course completed 1953; Junto Evening Sch, course completed, 1956. **Career:** Self employed free lance writer, 1950-91; Philadelphia Bull Tribune Afro-Am Newspaper Pittsburgh Courier, journalist, 1952-68; Umoja Mag, ed 1968-; Arthur A Little Assoc Off Jrvl Justice, consult, 1982-83; Eisenhower Found, Control Data, consult, 1982-83; self employed urban consult, 1970-91; House Umoja, chief exec officer, pres & founder, currently. **Orgs:** Exctr comm Urban Affair Partnership, 1980-91; vice chmn, West Philadelphia Youth Counsel Ctr, 1981-91; comm, Mayor's Drug Alcohol Comn, 1982-83; sec, Nat Ctr Neighborhood Enterprise, 1982-; bd dir, Exec Com Eisenhower Found, 1983-; bd dir, Mayonb Comn Women; Historical Soc PA 1983-; consult, Wilmington House UMOJA, 1987-91; consult Portland House UMOJA, 1989-91. **Honors/Awds:** Reduction of Gang Deaths in Philadelphia via vol; coordinator of "IV Gang War in 1974 Campaign"; Presidential Recognition, Temple Award for Creative Altruism, Inst Noetic Scis, 1990; Secretary's Award, US Dept Health & Human Serv, 1989; Grace B Flandnau Award, Nat Coun Crime & Delinquency, 1981. **Special Achievements:** Book: World Without Violence. **Home Phone:** (215)473-5893. **Business Addr:** Founder, Chief Executive Officer, House Umoja Inc, 5625 Master St, Philadelphia, PA 19131, **Business Phone:** (215)473-5893.

FAUCETT, BARBARA J.
School administrator, educator. **Personal:** Daughter of Wesley Murphy and Reonia Armstead Murphy; married Michael; children: Cynthia Mock & James Mock. **Educ:** Univ Wis, Milwaukee, BS, soc welfare, 1968, MS, ed, 1973. **Career:** School administrator, educator (retired); Univ Wis, Milwaukee, acad adv rels, 1971-72, dir, 1972-76, asst dean ed, 1976-79, dep asst chancellor,1979-80, dir human resources, sr spec asst chancellor, 1998; bd dir, Malaika Early Learning Center, 2009- . **Orgs:** Phi Kappa Phi, 1985-; Am Red Cross, Milwaukee; Nat Forum Black Pub Adminr; TEMPO, 1981-; bd, YWCA, Milwaukee; bd mem, Girl Scouts, Milwaukee; Harabee Sch Develop Bd; bd dirs, Penfield Children's Ctr. **Honors/Awds:** Black Achievement Award, YMCA, 1988; Academic Staff Outstanding Performance Award, Univ Wis, 1989. *

FAULCON, DR. CLARENCE AUGUSTUS, II
Educator. **Personal:** Born Aug 8, 1928, Philadelphia, PA; son of Leroy C and Addie Robinson; married Jacqueline Beach; children: David Clarence. **Educ:** Lincoln Univ, 1948; Univ Pa, BMus, 1950, MMus Ed 1952; Philadelphia Conserv Music, MusD, Musicolgy. **Career:** Educator (retried); Chairperson Sulzberger Jr Hi, Philadelphia, music teacher, chmn, 1951-63; Cazenovia Col, Cazenovia, NY, asst prof, chmn, 1963-68; Morgan St Univ, Baltimore, prof, chmn, 1968-79. **Orgs:** Del, Int Biographical Ctr Arts & Commun Congresses; Afro Am Music Health Promotion Disease Prevention & Therapy, Montreal, Canada; Conf Nat Med Asn, 1984. **Honors/Awds:** Faculty Award, Morgan St Univ Promethan Soc, 1983; Int Biographical Cong Medal, Budapest, Hungary, 1985; IBC Silver Medal, Queen of England. *

FAULCON, DR. GADDIS J.
Educator. **Personal:** Born Nov 29, 1950, Oxford, NC; son of Jack and Lucille; married Jeanette, Feb 12, 1972; children: Tina & Rukel. **Educ:** St Augustine's Col, BS, 1974; NC State Univ, MRR/MPA, 1981, EdD, 1994. **Career:** Garner Rd YMCA, physical dir, 1975-83; Elizabeth City St Univ, NNCT, asst dir, 1984-85; St Augustine's Col, from asst vpres stud affairs to vpres stud affairs, 1985-96; Christian Faith Ct, acad dean; Shaw Univ, asst prof, Dept Allied Health Professions, assoc prof & chair, currently, fac athletic rep, currently. **Orgs:** Adv bd, vpres, Wilton Elem Sch; adv bd, Nat Youth Sport, 1987-92; bd dirs, NC St Univ, 1990-92; Boy Scouts Am, Occoneechee Coun, 1992-94; adv bd, St Augustine's Col, Still Going On; Family First Granville County, 1990-95. **Honors/Awds:** Golden Consultant Award, Carlson Learning Co, 1997; Guest Presenter, African Am Male Conf, 2006. **Home Addr:** 4019 Eaton Rd, Kittrell, NC 27544, **Home Phone:** (919)693-3265. **Business Addr:** Associate Professor & Chair, Faculty Athletic Representative, Shaw University, Department of Allied Health Professions, 118 E South St, Raleigh, NC 27601, **Business Phone:** (919)546-8373.

FAULDING, JULIETTE J.
Financial manager. **Personal:** Born Aug 2, 1952, Jackson, MS; daughter of Vannette Johnson and Luella B Tapo. **Educ:** Tougaloo

Col, BA, 1974; Columbia Univ, MBA, 1976. **Career:** Mobil Oil Corp, banking analyst, 1976-77, financial analyst, 1977-79, short term investr, 1979-81, sr financial analyst, 1981-88, financial advisor, sales & supply treasr, 1989-; consult. **Orgs:** Comt mem, Boy Scout Troop 75, 1982-87; assoc adv, Explorer Post 75 Queens, NY, 1982-87; Black MBA Asn; CPMSACS Minority Achievement Representatives. **Honors/Awds:** Distinguished Graduate Award, Nat Asn For Equal Oppurtunity, 1984. **Special Achievements:** Participant Black Exec Exchange Prog; 100 of the most promising Black women in corporate America. **Home Addr:** 6168 Hidden Canyon Rd, Centreville, VA 20120.

FAULK, ESTELLE A.
Educator. **Personal:** Born in Chicago, IL; divorced; children: Lalita & Gina. **Educ:** Chicago State Univ, BE; De Paul Univ, MA; Univ Ill Chicago, PhD. **Career:** Malcolm X Col, instr part-time; Gladstone Sch, prin. **Orgs:** Samuel B Stratton Asn; Chicago Prin Asn; Nat Asn Elem Sch Prin; Nat Asn Supv & Curric Develop; Nat Alliance Black Sch Educr; Phi Delta Kappa; Am Asn Sch Admins; Near W Side Coun Chicago; Chicago Area Alliance Black Sch Educr; pres, De Paul Univ Educ Alumni Bd. **Honors/Awds:** Outstanding Leadership, Chicago Area Alliance Black Sch Educr, 1983; Commendation Award, Univ Ill Col Educ, 1984. *

FAULK, MARSHALL WILLIAM
Football player, foundation executive. **Personal:** Born Feb 26, 1973, New Orleans, LA; son of Roosevelt and Cecile; children: 3. **Educ:** San Diego State Univ, attended 1993. **Career:** Football player (retired), Foundation executive; Indianapolis Colts,running back, 1994-98; St Louis Rams, 1999-06; analyst, NFL Network, currently. **Orgs:** Founder, Marshall Faulk Found, 1994-. **Honors/Awds:** NFL Offensive Rookie of the Yr, 1994; Pro Bowl, 1994-95, 1999-00; Miller Lite Player of the Week, 1995; NFL Offensive Player of the Yr, 2000, 2001; NFL Player of the Yr, 2001; Bert Bell Award, 2001; San Diego Hall of Champions, Breitbard Hall of Fame, 2009. **Business Addr:** Founder, Marshall Faulk Foundation, 1116 E Market St, Indianapolis, IN 46202, **Business Phone:** 888-205-2800.*

FAULKNER, CAROLYN D. (CAROLYN D DIXON)
Manager, consultant. **Personal:** Born Aug 30, 1938, Mullins, SC; daughter of Rembert Gerald and Ollie Mae Smith; married Melvin Faulkner, Sep 15, 1962; children: Lenora, Leonard, Tasheba. **Career:** Shirlon Indust, bookkeeper, 1958-63; J H Taylor Mgt, bookkeeper, 1964-75; Wedding Plan Plus, pres & consult, 1966-; Oak Hill Indust, bookkeeper, 1976-80; Harry Zelenko, bookkeeper, 1981-91. **Orgs:** H & R Block, 1984-86; Block Asn, pres, 1987-; Asn Bridal Consults, 1989-; Brooklyn Chamber Com, 1990-93. **Honors/Awds:** Brooklyn Borough Pres, Proclamation, 1984; Edward Griffith Award, State Assemblyman, 1985; Cert of Achievement, Asn Bridal Consults, 1990-91. **Special Achievements:** Cert travel agt, Sobelsohn Sch Travel, 1985; accredited cruise counsr, Cruise Line Intl Asn, 1990; profiency, Congressman Ed Towns, 1990; Performance, Brides Mag, 1993. *

FAULKNER, GEANIE. See Obituaries section.

FAUNTROY, REV. WALTER EDWARD
Clergy, congressperson (u.s. federal government). **Personal:** Born Feb 6, 1933, Washington, DC; son of William T and Ethel Vine; married Dorothy Simms, Aug 3, 1957; children: Marvin Keith. **Educ:** Va Union Univ, BA, cum laude, 1955; Yale Univ Divinity Sch, BD, 1958. **Career:** New Bethel Bapt Church, pastor, 1958-2009, pastor emer, 2009-; Wash Bur Southern Christian Leadership Conf, dir, 1961-71, coordr hist, 1963-65; White House Conf Fulfill These Rights, vice chmn, 1966; DC City Coun, vice chmn, 1967-69; Poor People's Campaign, natl dir, 1969; House Reps, DC deleg, 1971-90; Walter E Fauntroy & Assoc, pres. **Orgs:** Pres, Nat Black Leadership Round table; chmn & bd dir, Southern Christian Leadership Conf; vpres, Govt Affairs, Martin Luther King Jr Ctr Soc Change; chmn, DC Coalition Conscience, 1965; pres & founder, Model Inner City Community Org Inc, Wash, 1966-72; co-chmn, Free S Africa Movement;chair, Bipartisan & Bicameral Task Force Haiti; chmn, Cong Black Caucus, 1981-83; nat dir, 20th Aniv March Wash Jobs Peace & Freedom 1983. **Honors/Awds:** Hubert H Humphrey Humanitarian Award, Nat Urban Coalition 1984; LLD, Georgetown Univ Law Sch, Yale Univ & VA Union Univ. **Business Addr:** Pastor, New Bethel Baptist Church, 6340 Ridge Rd, PO Box 8, Tobaccoville, NC 27050, **Business Phone:** (336)922-6320.

FAUST, NAOMI FLOWE
Educator, writer, poet. **Personal:** Born in Salisbury, NC; daughter of Christopher Leroy and Ada Luella Graham; married Roy Malcolm Faust. **Educ:** Bennett Col, AB; Univ Mich, Ann Arbor, MA; New York Univ, PhD. **Career:** Pub Sch Syst, Gaffney SC, elem teacher; Atkins High Sch, Winston-Salem NC, Eng teacher; Bennett Col & Southern Univ, Scotlandville LA, instr Eng; Morgan State Univ Baltimore, MD, prof Eng; Greensboro Pub Sch, teacher; New York City Pub Sch, teacher; Queens Col, City Univ New York, prof eng & educ; Books: "Speaking in Verse," a book of poems 1974; "Discipline and the Classroom Teacher," 1977; "All Beautiful Things," poems 1983; "And I Travel by Rhythms and Words," 1990. **Orgs:** Am Asn Univ Profs; Nat Coun Teachers Eng; Nat Women's Book Asn; World Poetry Soc Intercontinental; NY Poetry Forum, NAACP; Acad Am Poets; Am Asn Univ Women; Poetry Soc Am. **Honors/Awds:** Teacher-Author, Teacher-Writer, 1979; Govt Merit, Cooper Hill Writers Conf; Cert Merit, Poems by Blacks; Honored by Long Island Nat Asn Univ Women for High Achievement;Int Eminent Poet, Int Poets Acad; Poet of the Millennium Award, Int Poets Acad; Excellence in World Poetry Award, Intl Poets Acad. **Home Addr:** 112 01 175th St, Jamaica, NY 11433. *

FAVORS, STEVE ALEXANDER
School administrator. **Personal:** Born Dec 30, 1948, Texarkana, TX; son of Irma and Clarence Favors; married Charlotte Edwards Favors, Feb 18, 1977; children: Steve Jr & Jonathan. **Educ:** Tex A&M Univ, BS, pre-law, 1971, MS, stud personnel & guidance, 1973, EdD, 1978. **Career:** Wiley Col, vpres stud affairs, 1977-81; Prairie View A&M Univ, asst prof educ, 1979-81; Dillard Univ, vpres stud affairs, 1981-85; Univ New Orleans, vice chancellor stud affairs, 1985-90; Howard Univ, actg athletic dir, vpres stud affairs, 1990-98; Grambling State Univ, pres, 1998-2001. **Orgs:** Bd mem, Mid-South Delta Consortium, 1998-; SWAC President's Coun, 1998-; exec comm mem, Mid-Eastern Athletic Conf, 1990-98; bd trustees mem, Nat Order Omega, 1991-94; Nat Asn Student Personnel Administrators, Task Force, 1989-90; Nat Asn Col Univ Personnel Adminr, task force mem, 1989; Omega Psi Phi Fraternity Inc, 1970; charter mem, Tex Asn Blacks in Higher Educ, 1974-78; Nat Col Athletic Asn. **Honors/Awds:** Special Achievement Award, Howard Univ, 1991-96, Adminr of the Year Award, 1995; President's Award, Nat Asn Stud Personnel Adminr, 1992; Appreciation Award, New Orleans Black Caucus, 1990; Spec Achievement Award, Tex A&M Univ, 1995.

FAW, BARBARA ANN
School administrator. **Personal:** Born Jul 27, 1936, Cullen, VA; daughter of Bernard and Edna Wilkes; married Joseph A. **Educ:** Morgan State Univ, Baltimore, BA, 1965; Howard Univ, Wash DC, MA, 1966. **Career:** School administrator (retired); Baltimore Community Col, First Chancellor, 1986-; Community Col Baltimore, vpres admin, 1988-90, dean col, 1977-2000, dean stud activities, 1973-77, admin asst to pres 1971-73, chmn dept bus admin, 1970-71, prof bus admin, 1965-71; coord & sponsor small bus inst, 1967-70, chair woman Conf "Know your Rights" 1973; Baltimore City Community Col, dir rels, 1990-2000; Science is For Everyone, proj dir, 1992-2000. **Orgs:** Nat Coun Black Am Affairs Am Asn Community & Jr Cols, 1985-; presidential search comn, Community College Baltimore, 1985-86; panelist, Conf Women's Career Paths Univ Baltimore, 1986; bd review, Comn Mid States, 1987-; Nat Econ Asn; Sales & Mkt Asn; Am Asn Univ Prof; W Arlington Community Orgn; Mayor's Vol Cadre Educ; Task Force Role Scope & Commitment. **Honors/Awds:** Outstanding Educator of America, 1975; Senate of MD Resolution as First Chancellor of Community College of Baltimore, 1986; The City Council of Baltimore Resolution as the Chancellor of Community Col of Baltimore, 1986; Maryland Asn Higher Educ, Distinguished Program Award, Science Is for Everyone, 1997; Valued Hours Award, Fullwood Found, Inc, 2000 Sign of Hope Award, Payne Memorial America Church; Outstanding Achievement/Contribution, Science is for Everyone Baltimore City CommunityCol; Mentor Project Award, Lemmel Mid Sch, Baltimore City Pub Schs; MotherLange Service Award, Office Afro-Am Catholic Ministries.

FAY, TONI GEORGETTE
Media executive, consultant. **Personal:** Born Apr 25, 1947, New York, NY; daughter of Allie Smith and George. **Educ:** Duquesne Univ, BA, 1968; Univ Pittsburgh, MSW, 1972, MEd, 1973. **Career:** New York City Dept Social Serv, caseworker, 1968-70; Pittsburgh Drug Abuse Ctr Inc, dir, 1972-74; Gov Coun Drug & Alcohol Abuse, comnr, 1974-77; Nat Coun Negro Women, dir planning & develop, 1977-81; D Parke Gibson Assoc, exec vpres, 1981-82; AOL / Time Warner Inc, dir, 1981-92, vpres & officer, 1992-2000; TGF Associates Inc, pres, currently. **Orgs:** Corp Nat & Community Serv, 2000-01; US Comn, UNICEF; Cong Black Caucus Found; Franklin & Eleanor Roosevelt Inst; New York Coalition 100 Black Women; Exec Leadership Coun Found; vpres, Nat Coun Negro Women; Links Inc; Alpha Kappa Alpha Sorority; bd mem, secy, Appollo Theatre Found; bd mem, Nat Asn Advan Colored People Legal Defense Fund; bd mem, United Way Bergen Co; bd mem, vpres, Apollo Theater Found; bd mem, Franklin & Eleanor Roosevelt Inst; bd mem, Nat Hospice Found; bd mem, Nat Inst Literacy; bd mem, Nat Hospice Found, 2009; bd dir, NAACP Legal Defense Fund. **Honors/Awds:** Dollars & Sense-100 Black Women Bus, 1986; American Twin Award, YWCA, 1987; Nat Asn Advan Colored People Corp Award, 1989; New York Women's Foundation Award, 1991; New York Women's Award, 1996; President Award, Cong Black Caucus Found, 1996. **Home Addr:** 233 W Hudson Ave, Englewood, NJ 07631. **Business Phone:** (201)816-9050.

FEARN, JAMES E., JR.
Lawyer. **Personal:** Born Feb 2, 1945, Chattanooga, TN; son of James E and Kayte Marsh; married Karen Edmunds, Jul 29, 1968; children: Jeremy Kahlil, Jonathan Kyle. **Educ:** Antioch Col, BA, 1968; Univ Chicago Law Sch, JD, 1971. **Career:** Seattle Legal Serv, staff atty, 1971-76; Dept Housing & Urban Develop, aso regional coun, 1976-78; Seattle City Atty Off, asst city atty, 1978-85, Land Use Div, dir, 1985-89; Tousley Brain, Land Use Section, head, 1989-93; Seattle Commons, special coun, 1993-94; Inst Local Govt & Pub Serv, dep dir, exec dir, 1994-97; Ogden Murphy Wallace, coun; Housing & Urban Develop, atty; Seattle Housing Authority, gen coun, currently; pvt atty, currently. **Orgs:** Seattle Pks Bd; bd dir, Port Jobs; trust bd trustees, Mountains Sound Greenway; Sand Pt Blue Ribbon Comt; King County Conservation Futures Citizens Comt; Seattle Citizens Open Space Oversight Comt; Seattle Comprehensive Plan Adv Comt; Governor's Growth Mgt Task Force; Building Indust Legal Trust Fund Adv Comt; Historic Seattle Pub Develop Authority Coun. **Special Achievements:** Book: Preserving Seattle's Rental Housing; Greater Northwest Law Use Review, 1985; Transfer of Development Rights, Wash Asn Municipal Atty's Legal Notes, 1979; Tenants Rights: A Guide for Wash State, 1976, 3rd edition, 1991. **Business Addr:** General Counsel, Seattle Housing Authority, 120 6th Ave N, PO Box 19028, Seattle, WA 98109-1028, **Business Phone:** (206)615-3506.*

FEARN-BANKS, KATHLEEN
Publicist, writer, educator. **Personal:** Born Nov 21, 1941, Chattanooga, TN; daughter of Dr James E and Dr Kayte M; divorced. **Educ:** Wayne State Univ, BA, jour, 1964; Univ Calif, Los Angeles, MS, jour, 1965; Univ Southern Calif, Los Angeles, CA, ABD PhD, 1981. **Career:** NBC Publicity Dept, mgr, media rels, 1969-90; KNXT-TV News LA, newswriter, producer, 1968-69; Los Angeles Ctn Col, instructor, journ, english, creative writing, 1965-; Los Angeles Times, feature writer, 1968; Univ Wash, Sch Commun, Seattle, WA, tenured assoc prof, 1990-; freelance motion picture publicist, currently; co-ed, People to People, An Introduction to Mass Communications; Historical Dictionary, African Am TV, 2005. **Orgs:** Public Rel Soc Am, 1989-; Writers Guild Am; Publicists Guild; Acad TV & Sci; bd dir, vice pres, Neighbors Watts; Delta Sigma Theta Sorority, chapter vp; Asn Edu Journ & Mass Comm, 1990-; chair, Prof Freedom & Repsonsibility Ctr, 1998. **Honors/Awds:** Will Rogers Fel, Univ Calif, Los Angeles, 1964-65; CA Sun Magazine writers Award, Univ Calif, Los Angeles, 1965; Numerous freelance magazine & journal articles; 3 Textbooks, The Story of Western Man, co-authored w/David Burleigh; Woman of the Year, Los Angeles Sentinel (newspaper) 1986; Author: Crisis Communications; A Case Book Approach, 1996, 2nd edition, 2001; Teacher of the Year, Sch Commun, Univ Wash, 1993, 1995. **Business Addr:** Tenured Associate Professor, University Washington, Department Communication, Rm CMU 133 PO Box 353740, Seattle, WA 98195, **Business Phone:** (206)543-7646.

FEARS, EMERY LEWIS, JR.
Educator. **Personal:** Born Jul 23, 1925, Tuskegee Institute, AL; son of Emery and Evadne Angers; married Jeanette Johnson Fears, Aug 11, 1951 (died 1979); children: Cheryl; married Cheryl Perry Fears, Jul 31, 1981; children: Jason, Ashlyn. **Educ:** Howard Univ, BMusED, 1951; Univ MI at Ann Arbor, MMUS, 1962; Old Dominion Univ, attended 1974. **Career:** Educator (retired); J S Clarke High Sch, New Orleans, LA, band dir, 1951-52; I C Norcom High Sch, Portsmouth, VA, band dir, 1952-72; Manor High Sch, Portsmouth, VA, band dir & curriculum specialist, 1972-74; Norfolk State Univ, Music DEPT, assoc prof music, dir bands, 1974-91, prof emeritus music, 1992. **Orgs:** Charter mem, 1960-, bd dirs, 1978-82, 1984-86, Nat Band Asn; pres, southern div, 1980-82, Col Band Dirs Nat Asn; Am Bandmasters Asn, 1981-; Phi Beta Mus Nat Sch Bandmaster Frat, 1985-. **Honors/Awds:** Citation Excellence, Nat Band Asn, 1970; Proclamation, City Portsmouth, VA, 1987, 1991; Roy A Woods Outstand Teacher Award, Norfolk State Univ, 1989; Great Citizen Hampton Roads, Cox Cable TV, 1990; Proclamation, City Chesapeake, VA, 1991; Certificate Recognition, Commonwealth VA, 1991; Distinguished Service Music Medal, Kappa Kappa Psi Band Fraternity; Sudler Order Merit; John Philip Sousa found. **Military Serv:** USN, musician, 2nd class, 1944-46. *

FEARS, HARDING, JR.
Automotive executive. **Personal:** Born Apr 19, 1964, Detroit, MI; son of Harding Sr and Katherine; married Diane, Jun 23, 1990; children: Harding III. **Educ:** Tex Southern Univ, BA, 1987; Oakland Univ, attended 1992; Mich State Univ, MBA, 1997. **Career:** Bozell, Jacobs, Kenyon & Eckart, intern, 1987; ITT Teves N Am, mkt analyst, 1988-90; ITT Automotive, marketing analyst, 1990-95, mgr, bus develop, 1995-97; Intermet Corp, dir mkt, 1997-. **Orgs:** Am Mkt Asn; Soc Auto Analysts; Auto Mkt Res Coun; Soc Competitive Intelligence Professionals; Nat Black MBA Asn; Soc Auto Engineers; Nat Black Media Coalition; Alpha Pi Alpha Fraternity Inc. **Home Addr:** 14942 Stahelin Ave, Detroit, MI 48223, **Home Phone:** (313)493-0955. *

FEASTER, ALLISON
Basketball player. **Personal:** Born Feb 11, 1976, Chester, SC; married Danny Strong. **Educ:** Harvard Univ, econ, 1998. **Career:** Anadia Sanitana, portugal, 1998-99; Los Angeles Sparks, guard, 1998-00; ASPTT Aix-en-Provence, france, 1999-01; US Valenciennes Olympic, france, 2001-05; Charlotte Sting, guard & forward, 2001-07; Ros Casares Valencia, spain, 2006-07; C.B. San Jose Leon, 2007-08; Indiana Fever, currently. **Honors/Awds:** Player of the Yr, Eastern Col Athletic Conf, 1997-98; All-Am hon

mention, Assoc Press; 1997-98; Ivy League Player of the Yr; Most Improved Player Award, WNBA, 2001. *

FEASTER, BRUCE SULLIVAN
Lawyer, executive director. **Personal:** Born Jul 13, 1961, Flint, MI; son of John Alfred and Lillian Battle; married Deborah Mallory Feaster, Aug 21, 1993; children: Montez & Dante. **Educ:** Mich State Univ, BA, 1983; Univ Tex, Law Sch, JD, 1986. **Career:** WCNLS Children's Ctr for Justice & Peace, founder, exec dir, currently; Detroit City Council, atty, currently. **Orgs:** Alpha Phi Alpha; Metro Detroit Optimists; Nat Asn Advan Colored People; Detroit Urban League; Umoja-Nia; East Village Asn; Great New Mt Moraih Baptist Church; Conant United Methodist Church; True Rock Missionary Bapatist Church; Charles H Wright Maah; United Negro Col Fund; Mich Comt Juvenile Justice, 2000. **Honors/Awds:** Nat Mens Scholar; Turman Scholar; Optimist Club Scholar; Alpha Phi Alpha Scholar.

FEASTER, LAVERNE WILLIAMS
Educator. **Personal:** Born Oct 14, 1926, Cotton Plant, AR; daughter of James Waldred Williams Sr and Alma Dorthea Chism; married William Douglas Feaster, Jun 9, 1953; children: Sammie Lee Hart. **Educ:** Swift Meml Jr Col, Rogersville, dipl, 1947; Tenn State Univ, Nashville, BSE, 1949; Univ Ark, Fayetteville, MEd, 1966. **Career:** Educator (retired); Swift Jr Col, Rogersville, home econ teacher, 1949-50; Carver High Sch, Augusta, home econ teacher, 1950-53; Dermott High Sch, teacher, 1953-61; Univ Ark Ext, Arkadelphia, county ext agent, home econ, 1961-71; Univ Ark Ext, Little Rock, state 4-H specialist, 1971-77, dist prog leader, 1977-86, state leader, 4-H, 1986-90; Univ Ark, emer prof, 1991. **Orgs:** Ark Home Economists Asn, 1950-; Ark Asn, Ext 4-H Agents, 1975-; Ext Comn Org Policy, 1975-79; pres, Epsilon Sigma Phi, 1979-80; Comn Ark Future, 1989-; Gamma Sigma Delta, 1988; bd mem, SFP, currently. **Honors/Awds:** Distinguished Serv, Ark Asn; Ext 4-H Agents, 1976; Distinguised Serv, Epsilon Sigma Phi, 1983; 25-Year Award, Ark Asn; Ext 4-H Agents, 1987; State Serv Award, Ark Home Econ Asn, 1984; Delta of the Yr, Delta Sigma Theta, 1990; First Black Female State 4-H leader, Ark; Nat Asn Ext 4-H Agents, Am Spirit Award, 1992; Top 100 Women in Ark, 1995; Nat Spirit Award, 4-H & USAF, 1995; Distinguished Serv Award, Retired Sr Volunteer Prog (RSVP), 1996; Martin Luther King Jr Award, 2000; Alumnae of the Year Award, 4-H, 2000; Father Joseph Bilty Award, NH Conf Community & Justice, 2002; Volunteer Fundraiser of the Yr, Asn Fundraiser Prof, 2003. **Special Achievements:** AR Writer's Project, named as one of the top 100 Women in AR, 1995. **Home Addr:** One Fay Ct, Little Rock, AR 72204. *

FEATHERSTONE, KARL RAMON
Law enforcement officer, football coach. **Personal:** Born Oct 13, 1964, Indianola, MS; son of Charles Edward and Jessie Mae; married Lorie; children: Kadin. **Educ:** Tex Southern Univ, BS comput sci, 1985. **Career:** St Louis Cardinals, football player; US Marine Corps, spec forces; St Clair Shores Police Dept, police officer; Lake view High Sch, varsity football asst coach, 1997-98; Royal Oak Kimball High Sch, varsity football asst coach, 1998-2001; Royal Oak Dondero HS, varsity football asst coach, 2001; Port Huron Pirates Football Club LLC, head coach; Saginaw Sting, head coach, 2009. **Orgs:** Alpha Phi Alpha Fraternity Inc. **Honors/Awds:** Championship, 2006. **Military Serv:** USMC, sgt, 1985-95; Army Forces Expeditionary Medal, 1986; Marine Expeditionary Force Medal, 1986; Navy Achievement Medal, 1987.

FEEMSTER, JOHN ARTHUR
Physician. **Personal:** Born Sep 9, 1939, Winston-Salem, NC. **Educ:** Knox Col, BS, 1959; Meharry Med Col, MD, 1963. **Career:** Univ Minn, gen surg resd, 1970; bd cert, gen surg, 1971; Wayne State Univ, 1974-75; Thorocic Cardiovasc Surg, bd cert, 1975; Am Col Surgeons, physician self fel, 1977; Am Col Angiol; Kirwood Gen Hosp, chf dept surg; pvt pract, thoracic & cardiovasc surg. **Orgs:** Nat Med Soc; Am Col Emergency Physicians; vpres, Detroit Med Soc; Detroit Surg Soc; Detroit Surg Asn; Omega Psi Phi Frat; Alpha Omega Alpha Hon Med Soc; Nat Asn Advan Colored People; Founders Soc Detroit Inst Arts. **Honors/Awds:** Founders Soc Detroit Symphony Orch Young Investigator's Award, Am Coll Cardiology 1969; Fel, Oak Ridge Inst Nuclear Studies; Michigan Distinguished Citizen, Michigan House of Representatives; Doctor Recognition Award, Mercy Hosp, Detroit, 1993. **Special Achievements:** Written more than 30 articles for medical journals. **Military Serv:** AUS, col, 1970-72; Bronze Star Medal; Certificate of Merit, Saudi Arabia. **Business Addr:** 15266 Grand River Ave, Detroit, MI 48202-4119.

FELDER, CAIN HOPE
Educator, clergy. **Personal:** Born Jun 9, 1943, Aiken, SC; son of James (deceased) and Lula Mae Landy (deceased); married Annette Hutchins, Nov 15, 1973 (divorced 1982); children: Akidah H; married Jewell Richardson Smith, May 30, 1998. **Educ:** Howard Univ, Wash, DC, BA, 1966; Oxford Univ, Oxford, Eng, dipl, theol, 1968; Union Theol Seminary, New York, NY, MDiv, 1969; Columbia Univ, New York, NY, MPhil, 1978, PhD, Bibl Lang & Lit, 1982. **Career:** Black Methodists Church Renewal, Atlanta, GA, nat exec dir, 1969-72; Morgan State Univ, Baltimore, MD, dir fed rels & assoc prof philos, 1972-74; Grace United Methodist Church, New York, NY, pastor, 1975-78; Princeton Theol Sem, Princeton, NJ, instr, 1978-81; United Methodist Black Caucus; nat dir; Howard Univ Sch Divinity, prof, 1981-. **Orgs:** Soc Bibl Lit; Soc Study Black Religion; Am Acad Religion; Middle E Studies Asn; bd dirs, exec comt, chmn, Nat Convocation Planning Comt, Black Theol Project; bd mem, Interreligious Found Comn Orgn, 1970-72; founder, Enterprises Now; founder, Narco House, drug rehab ctr, Atlanta, GA; Coun Univ Senate, Howard Univ, 1985-98; chmn, Theol Search Comt, Howard Univ Sch Divinity, 1987; founder, chmn, the Bibl Inst Social Chg, Wash, DC. **Honors/Awds:** Fellowships award, Nat Fellowship Fund; Fellowships award, The Crusade; Fellowships award, Union Theological Seminary Graduate, Fellowships award, The Rockefeller Bro Fund-Protestant; Doctoral Fellowships, Columbia Univ Faculty Fellowship; Outstanding Leadership Citation, Black Methodists Church Renewal; Martin Luther King, Jr Scholar Service Award, Providence & Vicinity Coun Churches; Martin Luther King Jr Freedom Award, Progressive Nat Baptist Convention; Excellence Scholarship Award, African Methodist Episcopal, 1995. **Special Achievements:** publ numerous books. **Business Addr:** Professor, Howard University School of Divinity, Dept New Testament Lang & Lit, 1400 Shepherd St NE, Washington, DC 20017, **Business Phone:** (202)806-0760.*

FELDER, HARVEY
Conductor (music), educator. **Personal:** Born Nov 2, 1955, Milwaukee, WI; son of Emma Bell Felder and Harvey Felder Jr. **Educ:** Univ Wis-Madison, WI, BS, 1977; Univ Mich, Ann Arbor, MI, MA, 1982. **Career:** Eastern Mich Univ, Ypsilanti, MI, vis lectr, 1983-84; Haverford Col, Haverford, PA, Col lectr, 1984-88; Johns Hopkins Univ, Baltimore, MD, univ symphony conductor, 1987-90; Milwaukee Symphony Orchestra, asst conductor, 1988-95; St. Louis Symphony Orchestra, resident conductor, 1995-96; Tacoma Symphony Orchestra, music dir, 1995-. **Honors/Awds:** Citation for Excellence, Wis State Assembly; Distinguished Citizen Award, Wis Civic Music Asn; Distinguished Alumni Award, Univ Wis-Madison; Outstanding Achievement in the Arts Award, Tacoma's Arts Fund. **Business Addr:** Music Director, Tacoma Symphony Orchestra, 738 Broadway Suite 301, Tacoma, WA 98402, **Business Phone:** (253)272-7264.*

FELDER, JACK
Scientist, educator. **Personal:** Born Jan 1, 1939?, Columbia, SC. **Educ:** NY State Univ. **Career:** Natich Labs, Boston, MA, germ warfare specialist, 1964-66; Siemens Firm, Berlin, Ger, res scientist, translator, 1966-70; Harlem Prep, NY, fac; New York City Pub Sch. **Special Achievements:** Auth: From the Statue of Liberty to the Statue of Bigotry, 1986; AIDS-U.S. Germ Warfare at its Best with Documents and Proof, 1986; Who Really Assassinated Dr. Martin Luther King, 1987; Who Really Was Behind the Assassination of Malcolm X, 1988. **Military Serv:** AUS, germ warfare specialist, 1962-1964. *

FELDER, LORETTA KAY (DR FELDER MCKELVEY)
Dentist. **Personal:** Born Apr 19, 1956, Sumter, SC; daughter of Daniel DeLeon Felder Sr and Lorraine Perry. **Educ:** Old Dominion Univ, BS, 1978; Howard Univ, DDS, 1982. **Career:** US Pub Health Servs, lt, 1982-85; Ruskin Migrant Health Care Inc, Hillsborough Co, FL, dentist, 1982-84; Midlands Primary Health Care Inc, dental dir, 1984-87; pvt pract dentist, 1988-; Carolina Tribune Newspaper, Minority Health, assoc publ, 1992-. **Orgs:** Consult, SC Richland Co Governors Primary Health Task Force, 1984; Nat Dental Asn, 1985-87; bd dirs, YWCA of Sumter Area, 1986-88; Nat Coun Negro Women, Nat Asn Advan Colored People; bd dirs, Big Brothers & Big Sisters Inc, Greater Columbia; SC Dental Asn; Am Dental Asn; bd dirs, SC Women's Consortium, 1996; vol, C Dental Clinic; Conagree Med, Dental & Pharmaceut Asn; Central District Dental Soc; Palmetto Dental Study Club. **Honors/Awds:** Living the Legacy Award, Columbia NCNW, 1993; prestigious Fel Award, Acad Gen Dentistry. **Business Addr:** Dentist, Private Practice, 2329 Devine St, PO Box 50664, Columbia, SC 29205, **Business Phone:** (803)252-8101.*

FELDER, RONALD E.
Association executive. **Career:** Queen City Found, pres, 2002. **Orgs:** Achievement Found, Hamden, Conn, bd dir; Educ Rec Bur. **Honors/Awds:** Education Initiatives Award, Amistad Res Ctr. **Special Achievements:** First African American president of the Queen City Foundation. **Business Addr:** President, Queen City Foundation, 1 W 4th St Suite 300, Cincinnati, OH 45202, **Business Phone:** (513)241-1322.*

FELDER-HOEHNE, FELICIA HARRIS
Educator, librarian. **Personal:** Born in Knoxville, TN; daughter of Boyd S Ivey and Geraldine Celestine Harris; married Paul Arthur, 1979. **Educ:** Knoxville Col, BS, Atlanta Univ, MSLS, 1966; Univ Tenn, 1978. **Career:** SCLC, secy to Septima Poinsette Clark; McMinn County Schs, Eng teacher; Knoxville Col, admin asst, office pres & admin offices, 1960-63, asst to dir pub rel, 1963-65; Atlanta Univ, Trevor Arnett Libr, grad libr asst, 1965-66; United Presby Church, Bd Nat Missions, teacher/librn, summer study skills prog, 1968; Knoxville Col, Alumni Libr, head circulation servs, 1966-69; Univ Tenn, prof & ref librn, 1969-. **Orgs:** Am Libr Asn; Alpha Kappa Alpha Sorority; Tenn Libr Asn; E Tenn Libr Asn; Int Womens Year Decade, 1974-75; NAACP; YWCA; YMCA; Knoxville Col Alumni Asn; Knoxville Black Officials Coalition, 1976-79; Beck Cultural Exchange Ctr, charter mem, 1976-; Knoxville Nativity Pageant Choir, 1975-95;Inter denomi Nat Concert Choir; Payne Ave Baptist Church; bd dirs, Knoxville Community Chorus; pres, Spring Place Neighborhood Asn, 1980-; religious task force, 1982 World's Fair; bd dirs, UT Fed Credit Union, 1984-89; charter mem, Nat Museum Women Arts, 1985-; dir pub rels, Concerned Asn Residents E, 1988-90; Tenn Valley Energy Coalition, 1988-90; Mentoring Acad Boys, bd dir, 1996-; Knoxville Opera Guild, 1996-; Ctr Neighborhood Develop, bd dir, 1998-2001; Common Ground, 1998-; Payne Ave Bapt Church Media Libr, asst lib dir, 1998-2001; Knoxville Opera Co, bd dir, 1999-; Knoxville's Promise: Alliance for Youth, 1999-; Wall Tolerance, 2003-. **Honors/Awds:** Univ Tenn, Chancellor's Citation for Extraordinary Community Serv, 1978; Citizen of the Year Award, Order of the Eastern Star Prince Hall Masons, 1979; Pub Serv Award, Univ Tenn, Nat Alumni Asn, 1984; Religious Serv Award, Nat Conference Christians & Jews, 1976; Knoxville's Int Energy Exposition/The 1982 World's Fair, certificate of appreciation, 1982; Dictionary Int Biography, certificate of merit for distinguished serv to the community, 1985; UT Federal Credit Union, Cert of Appreciation, 1989; Habitat for Humanity, Plaque, 1992; Knoxville Mayor, Merit Award, 1994; Humanitarian Award, Univ Tenn Libraries, 1994; African American Hall of Fame, Univ Tenn, 1994; City Knoxville, Merit Award for Outstanding Achievements, 1994; Knoxville News-Sentinel Cornerstone Award, 1998; citation of serv, Knoxville Police Dept, 1998; The Miles 500 Library Spirit Award, 1999; Recipient, The Harold B Love, Sr, Outstanding Community Involvement Award, 2003; Volunteer Spirit Award, Univ Tenn, 2003. **Special Achievements:** First African American librarian, Univ Tenn; prin researcher, George Wash Carver Project, 2003; co-author, "The African American Collection at the Univ Tenn, Does It Measure Up?—An Overlap Study", pub in Behavioral & Social Sci Librn, 1993; Silence of Yesterday, 1996, The Ebbing Tide, 1995; Dance Upon the Shore, 1997; author of poems published in anthologies Winds of Freedom, 1998; contributor to numerous publications. **Home Addr:** 5413 Spring Place Circle NE, Knoxville, TN 37924-2174. **Business Addr:** Professor, Research Librarian, The University of Tennessee, 145 John C Hodges Library, Knoxville, TN 37996-1000, **Business Phone:** (865)974-0018.

FELICIANA, DR. JERRYE BROWN
School administrator. **Personal:** Born Aug 20, 1951, Bethesda, MD; daughter of James Dudley Brown and Katie Glean McNair Brown; married Albert; children: Wayne, Jaison & Kyanna. **Educ:** George Washington Univ, BA, 1974; Trinity Col, MA, 1976; Maple Springs Baptist Seminary, attended 1994. **Career:** Georgetown Univ, asst dir upward bound 1977-78; US Dept Agr, consult, 1981; Trinity Col, asst dir for minority affairs 1983-84, dir, upward bound, 1978-89; Maple Springs Baptist Bible Col & Seminary, vpres admin, 1991; Howard Univ, asst dir, stud support serv, 1989-2005. **Orgs:** Chairwoman, DC Consolidation Educ serv, 1983-89; Mid-Eastern Asn Educ Opportunity Prog, 1983-; mem bd dirs, Ethel J Williams Scholarship Comt, 1989-; Am Asn Christian Counselors; Am CounAsn. **Honors/Awds:** Nat Dean's List, 1992; Graduated Summa Cum Laude, 1994. **Home Addr:** 5200 Vienna Dr, Clinton, MD 20735.

FELIOUS, ODETTA. See HOLMES, ODETTA in the Obituaries section.

FELIX, DUDLEY E.
Educator. **Educ:** London Univ, London, Eng; Royal Fac Physicians & Surgeons, Scotland; Howard Univ, Wash, DC; Univ Pea, Med & Dent Cols; Philadelphia Gen Hosp. **Career:** Univ Pa Gen Hosp, Otorhinolaryngology & Temporo-Mandibular Joint Clinic, resident & attending physician; Philadelphia Gen Hosp, Dept Oral/Internal Med, resident; Howard Univ, clinical instr oral & maxillofacial surg, 1969-73; Howard Univ, Div Dist Columbia Gen Hosp, dir sr studs, 1974; Meharry Med Col, fac mem sch dent, dir didactic prog oral diagnosis & oral med, head sect oral med; assoc prof, dept Endodontics & Oral Diagnostic Scis, currently. **Orgs:** Acad Fel, Am Acad Oral Med; Attending consult, Hubbard Hosp; lectr & attending consult, Dept Pediat Med, Meharry Med Col; guest lectr & attending consult, Tenn State Univ; fel, Royal Soc Health, UK; Am Acad Gen Dent Surg, 1979; dipl, Am Specialty Bd Oral Med, 1981; Int Acad Prev Med, 1982; fel, Int Acad Med Preventics, 1983; Am Cancer Soc; Am Soc Regional Anesthesia; Int Asn Pain Study; Am Asn Pain Study; Int Soc Adv Educ; co-chmn, fac eval comn, 1987, grievance comn, 1987, fac rep fac senate, 1988, fac coun, 1988, curriculum comn, 1988, Meharry Med Col; Am Asn Study Headache. **Honors/Awds:** Outstanding Teacher Award, Howard Univ and Meharry Med Col; Outstanding and Dedicated Service Award of Oral/Maxillofacial Surgery, Howard Univ; Clinical Professor of the Year, Meharry Med Col; Expertise in Medical Lectures, Meharry Med Col; guest of Dr Siaka Stevens, pres Sierra Leone, 1983; guest lecturer in West Africa, Canada and USA; Instructor of the Year, Meharry Med Col, 1988. **Special Achievements:** Publs include, "Oral Symptoms as a Chief Sign of Acute Monoblastic Leukemia, Report of Case," JADA, 1986. **Business Addr:** Associate Professor, Meharry Medical College, Department of Endodontics and Oral Diagnostic Sciences, 1005 D B Todd Blvd, Nashville, TN 37208.*

FELKER, JOSEPH B.
Clergy, president (organization). **Personal:** Born Nov 25, 1926, Chicago, IL; married Ruthie Crockrom; children: Cordelia, Jacquelyn. **Educ:** Univ Chicago, CBI, 1953; Ill Barber Col, MA, 1952; No Bapt Theol Sem, BTH, 1956; McKennley Theol Sem. **Career:** Mt Carmel Baptist Church, pastor, 1957, Vet Barber Shop, pres, 1957-; Reverend, 2004; Mt Carmel Baptist Church, baptist, currently. **Orgs:** Moderator, Greater New Era Dist Asn Chicago, 1968-; treas, JH Jackson Libr; Nat Asn Advan Colored People; The Urban League; treas, MI Towers S; chmn, moderators, Bapt Gen State Conv, 1973-. **Honors/Awds:** CBI Cert of Achievment, 1971; Outstanding Leadership as Moderator, Chs, Greater New Era Dist Asn, 1973; Most Outstanding & Prog Moderator Yr, Midwestern Bapt Layman Fel Inc, 1974; Civic & Rel Work Hon, Fgn Mission Bd MB Conv, 1976; cert of recognition, Gen State Conv IL 25 Yrs of Denominational Christian Serv, 1977. **Military Serv:** USN, petty officer 3rd class. **Business Addr:** Baptist, Mt Carmel Baptist Church, 2978 S Wabash Ave, Chicago, IL 60616.*

FELTON, DENNIS
Basketball coach. **Personal:** Born Jun 21, 1963, Tokyo, Japan; married Melanie Smith; children: Jazz & Nile. **Educ:** Prince George Community Col, AA, 1983; Howard Univ, BA, radio, television& film production, 1985. **Career:** Oxon Hill High Sch, asst coach, 1984-85; Charles Co Community Coll, asst coach, 1985-86; Univ Del, asst coach, 1986-90; Tulane Univ, asst coach, 1990-91; St Josephs Univ, asst coach, 1991-92; Providence Col, asst coach, 1992-94; Clemson Univ, from asst coach to assoc coach, 1994-98; Western Ky Univ, head coach, 1998-2003; Univ Ga, head coach, 2003-09. **Honors/Awds:** Two year letterman, Prince George's Community Col, 1981-83; one year letterman, Howard Univ, 1983-84; Sun Belt Tournament Championship, 2001, 2002, 2003; SEC Tournament Championship, 2008. **Special Achievements:** First coach in Western Kentucky history to take three straight teams to the NCAA Tournament in 2003.

FELTON, JAMES A.
Educator, administrator, art museum director. **Personal:** Born Jun 20, 1945, New York, NY. **Educ:** Bradley Univ, BA, 1967; Tufts Univ, MA, 1969. **Career:** Univ Mass, asst dir financial aid & dir financial aid; Metro Mus Art NY, intern treas dept. **Orgs:** Foreign Affairs & Scholar, Phi Mu Alpha Sinfonia; Mass Asn Col Minority Adminr.

FELTON, JAMES EDWARD, JR. (JIM FELTON)
Executive. **Personal:** Born Dec 1, 1932, New York, NY; married Elizabeth Madison; children: Robin Felton Leadbetter, James E III, Cynthia, Corey. **Educ:** Robert Louis Stevenson Inst & NY Sch Tech, 1956; Rutgers Univ, courses principles supervision, 1974. **Career:** Gen Serv Admin grade level WC-l0, 1957-72; US Post Office, 1972-77; United Custodial Serv Armed Forces, 2 yrs; Ebon Serv Intl Inc, sr vpres, Chmn, 1972-94; Nobe Construction Co; Sierra finishing sevs, Vpres sales, currently. **Orgs:** Founder, United Custodial Serv, 1969; founder, EBON Servs Intl, 1973; Bldg Serv Contractors Asn Intl, Essex County Private Industry Coun, Human & Civil Rights Assoc NJ; vpres & Chmn, Bd EBON Serv Intl, 1985; Bethany Baptist Ch Newark, NJ; co-founder, NJ United Minority Bus Brain Trust; One Hundred Black Men NJ; Newark Chamber Com; Lions Club; New Jersey Minority Coun; the United Way. **Honors/Awds:** Dedicated services award, Young Man's Christian Asn, 1983; appreciation award, Area 9 Essex County Spec Olympics, 1983; certificate of appreciation, Muslums United Soc & Polit Change Award, 1984; advocacy award, Nwk Minority Bus Develop Ctr, 1984. **Military Serv:** AUS, pvt first class, 2 yrs; Honorable Discharge, 1955. **Business Addr:** Vice President, Sierra Finishing Sevices, 48 Wall St Suite 1100, New York, NY 10005, **Business Phone:** (212)918-4521.*

FELTON, JIM. See FELTON, JAMES EDWARD, JR.

FELTON, ZORA MARTIN
Educator, museum director. **Personal:** Born Jun 22, 1930, Allentown, PA; daughter of James William and Josephine Elizabeth Cobbs; married Edward P Felton Jr, Jul 12, 1975; children: stepchildren: Erica, Eric, Edward. **Educ:** Moravian Col, Bethlehem, PA, BA, 1952; Howard Univ, WA, DC, MEd, 1980. **Career:** Educator (retired); Sleighton Farm Sch Girls, Media, Pa, field counr, 1952; Dayton YWCA, Dayton, Ohio, dir teenage dept, 1952-58; SE Neighborhood House, WA, DC, dir educ & group work, 1958-67; Anacostia Mus, Smithsonian Inst, WA, DC, chief educ & outreach servs dept, emerita, 1967-94. **Orgs:** African-Am Mus Asn; bd mem, Anacostia Coordinating Coun; Delta Sigma Theta Sorority; secy, Ethel James Williams Scholar Fund; ed bd, Fort Stevens Sr Ctr Newsletter. **Honors/Awds:** Outstanding Graduating Sr Award, Moravian Col, 1952; First Annual Raymond S Haupert Humanitarian Award, Moravian Col, 1970; Cert Appreciation serv mus country, Inst Mus Servs, 1988; Cert Appreciation serv Ethel James Williams Scholar Fund, 1989; Prof Award Outstanding Accomplishments, Nat Asn Negro Bus & Prof Women's Clubs Inc, 1990; Margaret T Burroughs Award, African-Am Mus Asn, 1989; Educator of Excellence Award, Am Asn Mus, 1991; Moravian Col, Comenius Alumni Award, 1991; Mary McLeod Bethune Educ Award, Union Temple Baptist Church, 1992; Named to DC Com Women, Hall of Fame, 1994; Katherine Coffey Award, 1999; Recognized Pub Serv Contrib Anacostia Community, Anacostia-Cong Heights Partnership, 2003. **Special Achievements:** Auth, A Walk Through 'Old' Anacostia, 1991; numerous articles: mus educ mat & learning packages; Co-auth, A Different Drummer: John R Kinard and The Anacostia Mus, 1967-89, 1994. *

FELTUS, JAMES, JR.
Clergy. **Personal:** Born Apr 16, 1921, Gloster, MS; son of James Sr and Lillie Packnette; married Hazel Luter; children: James III, Elliott, Percy, Erasmus, Riley (deceased), Joan F, Wilson, Gerald, Eunice F Little, Michael. **Educ:** Xavier Univ, PhB, 1946; Southern Univ, EdM, 1963; Campbell Col, BD, 1954, DD, 1955; New Orleans Baptist Theol Sem, MRE, 1973, UBS, PhD, 1998. **Career:** British Honduras, dist supt dist 8, 1953-65, overseer, 1955; Orleans Parish Sch Bd, substitute teacher, 1954-74; First Church God Christ, pastor, 53 yrs; The Churches God Christ United US, London, Jamaica, South Africa, founder, sr bishop, 1974; Jurisdiction 2 Church God Christ, bishop. **Orgs:** pres, Interdenominational Ministerial Alliance, 1987-; District Attorney's Comt Against Drugs, 1988-89; Am Asn Christian Couns. **Honors/Awds:** Honorary Civil Sheriff Orleans Parish, Paul Valteau, 1983; Awarded by Mayor Moreal, 1983; Long career performing good works daily benefit City New Orleans, adopted City Coun New Orleans, 1986; Civil Sheriff Deputy, Paul Valteau; Colonel Staff to Gov Edwin Edwards State Louisiana, 1987; Certificate Appreciation, Contribuiton City New Orleans, Mayor S Bartholomew, 1987; Commended & cited City Coun contrib community & leadership exhibited, 1987; proclaimed Bishop James Feltus Jr's Day New Orleans; adopted Mayor S Bartholomew & City Coun New Orleans, 1987; Accomplishments Religion, The National Sorority Phi Delta Kappa, Inc, Alpha Theta Chapter, 1990. **Business Addr:** Bishop, Churches God Christ United, 2453 Josephine St, New Orleans, LA 70113, **Business Phone:** (504)523-6232.*

FENTRESS, SHIRLEY B.
Administrator. **Personal:** Born Nov 16, 1937, Bolivar, TN; daughter of John Lester McKinnie and Mammie Bernice Pankey McKinnie; married Ernest Fentress, Aug 3, 1957 (divorced); children: Sherral Fentress Mitchell. **Educ:** Tenn State Univ, attended 1957; Cortez Bus Col, attended 1968. **Career:** Administrator (retired); Frank Thrifty Grocery, owner, 1980-81; Frank Thrifty Liquor Corp, owner, 1981-84; City Col Chicago, dir payroll, 1989-95. **Orgs:** Sec New Philadelphia Baptist Courtesy Comn, 1972; co-chmn, 1st Union Baptist Church Pastor Anniversary, 1985, chairperson, Pastors Anniversary, 1986-87; capt, 1st Union Baptist Church Anniversary, 1985; Coordr, Crusade Mercy City Col Chicago, 1986-87, financial secy, Victory Christian Church Baptist, 1986. **Honors/Awds:** Woman of the Week, WBEE Radio Sta Chicago, 1974; Citation Merit WAIT 820 Radio Sta Chicago, 1974; Great Gal Award, WJPC Radio Sta Chicago, 1974. **Home Addr:** 308 S Hickory St, Glenwood, IL 60425, **Home Phone:** (708)758-3862. *

FERDINAND, DR. KEITH C
Cardiologist. **Personal:** Born Dec 5, 1950, New Orleans, LA; son of Vallery Jr and Inola Copelin; married Daphne Pajeaud, Feb 16, 1973; children: Kamau, Rashida, Aminisha & Jua. **Educ:** Cornel Univ, Telluride Scholar, 1969; Univ New Orleans, BA, 1972; Howard Univ, Col Med, MD, 1976. **Career:** US Pub Health Hosp, New Orleans, LA, intern, 1976-77; LSU Med Ctr, New Orleans, LA, internal med resident, 1977-79, cardiol fel, 1979-80; Howard Univ Hosp, Wash, DC, cardiol fel, 1981; Flint Goodridge Hosp, New Orleans, LA, chief cardiol, 1981-85; Med Assocs, New Orleans, LA, pvt practice, 1981-83; Xavier Univ, New Orleans, LA, vis prof, 1981-82, assoc prof, 1982, prof, currently; Health Corp, New Orleans, LA, consult, 1982-85; La State Univ, Med Ctr, New Orleans, LA, clinic instr, 1986-; United Med Ctr, New Orleans, LA, chief cardiol, 1985-, chief med staff, 1987-88; Heartbeats Life Ctr, New Orleans, LA, pvt pract, 1983-, med dir, currently. **Orgs:** Chm bd, 1990-, bd mem, 1987-, ed newsletter, 1988-90, dir, ABC Hurricane Relief Fund, currently, Asn Black Cardiologists; fel, Am Col Cardiol; bd mem, Am Lung Asn, LA, 1987-; vpres, La Med Asn, 1988-; Am Heart Asn; Trilateral Comt, End Violence Black Community; bd mem, Greater New Orleans Mental Health Asn, 1985-87; bd mem, Urban League Greater New Orleans, 1985-; Alpha Omega Alpha; bd mem several community serv groups; pres, Orleans Div Am Heart Asn, 1989-; La State Bd Med Examiners, 1990-; New Orleans Charity Hosp Bd, 1990-; pres, Physicians Asn La Inc, 1992-; Nat High Blood Pressure Edu Prog Coordinating Comt; chair, Section Four the Sixth Report Joint Nat Comt. **Honors/Awds:** First Place, Unity Awards in Media, Lincoln Univ, MO, 1982; Outstanding Service Award, LP Nurses, LA, 1983; Black Man of the Year, New Orleans Asn Black Social Workers, 1985; distinguished service award, Greater Liberty BC, 1987; Frederick Douglass Award, Nat Asn Negro Bus & Prof Womens Club New Orleans, 1988; recognized as one of the top 100 Best Black Physicians in the United States, mag, Black Enterprise; Louis B. Russell, Jr Memorial Award, AHA; Walter M Booker Community Service Award, ABC. **Business Addr:** Director, ABC Hurricane Relief Fund, Association of Black Cardiologists Inc, 5355 Hunter Rd, Atlanta, GA 30349, **Business Phone:** (404)201-6632.

FERERE, DR. GERARD ALPHONSE
Educator, college teacher. **Personal:** Born Jul 21, 1930, Cap Haitien, Haiti; son of Alphonse M and Marie Leroy; married Nancy; children: Magali & Rachel. **Educ:** Naval Acad, Venezuela, Ensign, 1953; Villanova Univ, MA, 1967; Univ PA, PhD, 1974. **Career:** Haitian Navy, naval officer, 1953-58; Haiti, lang teacher, 1958-63; SELF, transl/interpreter, 1964; St Joseph's Univ, prof, 1964-98; prof emer lang & lingustics, 1998-. **Orgs:** Founder, Coalition Haitian Concerns, 1982-; comnr, Haitian Am Pa Heritage Affairs Comn, 1991-95. **Special Achievements:** Publ: Haitian Creole: Sound-System, Form-Classes, Texts, 1974; Haitian Voodoo: its True Face, 1976; What is Haitian Voodoo (1979); Haitian VodouiUmlsme Vodouism, 1989; 1492: The Rape of the New World, collective test,1996. **Home Addr:** 20136 Ocean Key Dr, Boca Raton, FL 33498. **Business Addr:** Professor Emeritus, St Joseph's University, 5600 City Ave, Philadelphia, PA 19131, **Business Phone:** (610)660-1000.*

FERGERSON, MIRIAM N
Salesperson. **Personal:** Born Sep 15, 1941, Homestead, PA; daughter of James A Watson and Miriam King Watson; married Cecil; children: Melanie, John & Kinte. **Educ:** Va State Univ, BA, french ed, 1964; Azusa Pacific Univ, MA, Marriage, Family & Child Coun, 1975. **Career:** Calif Super Ct Conciliation Ct, family counr, 1977-78; Youth Training Sch, youth counr, 1978-83; San-Mar Group Homes, substance abuse social worker, 1983-; Art Educ Consult Serv, founder, admin consult, 1974-. **Orgs:** Youth counr, Missionary Dept Messiah Bapt Church, 1982-86; mem bd, Christian Educ Messiah Bapt Church, 1983-; bd chmn, Friends Wm Grant Still Arts Ctr, 1983-; vpres, Arts & Cult 10th Councilmanic Dist Women's Steering Comn, 1984-85; consult, Dr Chas R Drew Hist Exhibit Drew Med Sch, 1984-85; researcher City Watts, Watts Towers Art Ctr, 1984-85; Calif Drug Free Youth, 1984; Rev Jesse Jackson Pres, 1984; vpres, Parent Adv Coun Fairfax High, 1984-85; ed consult, Watts Towers Jazz Festival Publ, 1986; liason 10th Dist Arts Adv Coun, 1986-87; founder, Friends Los Angeles SW Col Art Gallery, 1991; Friends Kerman Maddox City Coun, 1991; Friends Geneva Cox City Coun; pres, Trinity Mission Circle Messiah Church. **Honors/Awds:** Community Coun Serv Award, Westminster Presby Church, 1984-85; West Angeles Christian Acad Outstanding Volunteer Serv Award, 1986; Nat Conf Artists Outstanding Serv Award, 1987. **Special Achievements:** Article Golden State Life Ins Travel & Art mag, 1978; publ, "Artaculture: Masud Kordofan," Los Angeles SW Col, 1990; publ, "Tribute of Carter G Woodson," Cal State Dominguez Hills, 1991; publ, "Listen Rap Movement," Los Angeles SW Col, 1991; Hon co-chair, Watts Summer Festival Inc, 2004; TV Doc Watts Festival Recounted Univ Jenkins Prod, 1980. **Home Addr:** 1417 So Ogden Dr, Los Angeles, CA 90019, **Home Phone:** (213)936-7779. **Business Addr:** Administrative Consultant, Art Education Consultant Services, 1417 So Ogden Dr, Los Angeles, CA 90019.

FERGUS, JOSEPH E
Chief executive officer, president (organization), founder (originator). **Educ:** Norfolk State Univ, BS, elec engineering, 1982; Univ Ill, MS, elec engineering, 1984. **Career:** AT&T Labs, sr scientist; Commun Technologies Inc, founder, pres & chief exec officer, 1990-. **Honors/Awds:** Entrepreneur of the Year, Va Minority Supplier Develop Coun; hon doctorate humane letters, Norfolk State Univ. **Military Serv:** AUS, veteran. **Business Addr:** Founder, President, Chief Executive Officer, Communication Technologies Inc, 14151 Newbrook Dr Suite 400, Chantilly, VA 20151, **Business Phone:** (703)961-9080.*

FERGUSON, CECIL
Graphic artist. **Personal:** Born Mar 13, 1931, Chicago, IL; married Irene; children: Mark. **Educ:** Art Inst Chicago; Inst Design, Ill Inst Technol; Am Acad Art. **Career:** Ebony Mag, asst art dir; The Ebony Success Libr, designer; Johnson Publ, promotional illustrations & layouts; Los Angeles County Art Mus, curator. **Business Addr:** 820 S Michigan Ave, Chicago, IL 60605.

FERGUSON, DEREK TALMAR
Publishing executive. **Personal:** Born Apr 20, 1965, Yonkers, NY; son of James Ferguson and Roberta Lewis Pieck; married Regina Bullock, Apr 2, 1988; children: Reginald James. **Educ:** Univ PA, Philadelphia, BS, econ, 1985; Harvard Bus Sch, Cambridge, MBA, 1990. **Career:** Coopers & Lybrand, New York, sr acct, 1985-88; Bain & Co, Cambridge, summer assoc, 1989; Urban Profile Commun, Baltimore, coo, assoc publ, beginning 1988; Bad Boy Worldwide Entertainment Group, cfo, currently. **Orgs:** Black Wharton, 1984; vpres, AASO-Harvard Bus Sch, 1989-90; corresponding secy. **Honors/Awds:** Maggie L Walker Award, Emma L Higgombothum Award, Black Fac & Admin, Univ Penn, 1985; Onyx Sr Hon Soc, Univ Penn, 1985; Cert Pub Acct, AICPA, 1988; Int Mar Corp Entrepreneurs Comp-Hon Mention, Univ Tex, Austin, 1990. **Home Addr:** 1900 Patterson Ave, Bronx, NY 10473. **Business Addr:** Chief Financial Officer, Bad Boy Worldwide Entertainment Group, 1440 Broadway 16th Fl, New York, NY 21208, **Business Phone:** (212)381-1540.

FERGUSON, ELLIOTT LAROY
Sales manager, vice president (organization). **Personal:** Born Nov 26, 1965, Spokane, WA; son of Gwendolyn Cooper Williams and

Elliott L Ferguson Sr. **Educ:** Savannah State Col, BA, mkt, 1988. **Career:** Savannah, Econ Develop, Authority, dir res, 1988-91; Savannah Conv & Visitors Bur, dir sales, 1991-92; Atlanta Conv & Visitors Bur, sales mgr, 1992-, vpres; Conv & Tourism Corp, Conv Sales & Serv, Washington, DC, Membership Dept, interim head, sr vpres, currently. **Orgs:** Alpha Phi Alpha, 1988-; bd mem, Rape Crisis Ctr, 1991-92; S Atlantic 2000 Club, 1991-92. **Home Addr:** 3920 Dogwood Farm Rd, Decatur, GA 30034-6435. **Business Addr:** Senior Vice President, Convention & Tourism Corporation, Convention Sales & Service, 801 Mount Vernon Pl NW, Washington, DC 20001, **Business Phone:** (202)789-7014.

FERGUSON, FAY
Executive. **Career:** Burrell Commun Group, managing partner, 1971-, co-chief exec officer, 2004-. **Orgs:** Chicago Advert Fedn; Perspectives Charter Sch; bd gov, Chicago Coun, The Am Asn Advert Agencies Inc. **Honors/Awds:** Most Influential Woman Award, Women's Leadership Fedn; Advertising Agency Award; Advertising Working Mother of the Year, Working Mother mag; Trailblazer Mom Award, Advert Women of NY; Advertising Woman of the Year, Women's Advert Club AChicago & Chicago dvert Fedn, 2006. **Business Addr:** Co-Chief Executive Officer, Managing Partner, Burrell Communications Group, 233 N Michigan Ave Suite 2900, Chicago, IL 60601, **Business Phone:** (312)297-9600.*

FERGUSON, IDELL
Real estate agent. **Personal:** Born in Montgomery, AL; daughter of Frank Lawson (deceased) and Mary I Harris Lawson (deceased); divorced; children: Ronald E, Mary K, Robertson & Dennis E. **Educ:** Actual Bus Col Mich; Univ Akron Ohio, Real Estate Courses; Cert, Hammel-19Actual Bus Col Akron, Ohio, Cert, Akron Univ; Mount Union Col, Alliance, Ohio, 1978, 1981. **Career:** Real estate agent (retired); License Real Estate Broker Akron, Ohio, 1960-87; Advan Realty, owner & broker, 1960-65; Corp Advan Realty, staff, 1961-66; Nat Asn Real Estate Brokers Inc, instr, real estate classes, 1965-71; pre-kindergarten, teacher, 1965; Idell Ferguson Realty, owner, broker, 1965; FHA, appraiser 1969-72; Lawyers Title Ins Corp, title plant mgr, 1966-82; Oasis Orgn, prog dir, 1987-88; Idell Ferguson Realty, Akron, Ohio, broker. **Orgs:** Wesley Serv Guild 1953; Ohio Civil Rights Comt 1961-65; State Bd, 1965-71; dist gov, NANBPW, 1972-74; bd mem Fair Housing Contact Serv, 1979; co-chairperson, admin bd Centenary United Methodist Church, 1979; coordr, Jesse Jackson Pres Comt Summit County, 1984; St Phillip Episcopal Ch, volunteer tutor, 1991-92; Ohio Asn Real Estate Brokers; Columbus Asn Realty Brokers; Akron Assoc Realty Brokers; State Conv; Women's Coun Akron Area; Human Rels Comt Akron Bd Realtors; Fair Housing Contact Serv; Urban League; Nat Asn Advan Colored People; YMCA; YWCA; Young Bus & Prof Womens Club; Akron Bus & Prof Womens League; Akron Club Nat Asn Negro Bus & Prof Womens Clubs; Centenary United Methodist Church; Nordic Environ Finance Corp; Womens Coun Realtors Nat Asn Realtors; United Church Women Columbus; Akron; Program Negro Hist; org, sponsored Akron Young Adult Club Nat Asn Negro Bus & Prof Womens Clubs; Akron Canton Reg Food Bank; Stan Hywet Hall & Gardens; Akron Urban League. **Honors/Awds:** Listed in Ohio State Newspaper; Achievement Award 1970; Recognition Award 1972; Leadership Citation 1973; Safari Excellence 1974; Outstanding Service Award for Leadership & Serv Re-Org, Akron Assoc Realty Brokers Ohio Asn Realty Brokers; Outstanding Service Award, Nat Asn Negro Bus & Prof Women's Club Kent Area Chap Links Inc 1980; Realtist Pioneer Award, Nat Asn Realty Brokers Inc, Akron, 1982. **Home Addr:** 1100 Bellevue Ave, Akron, OH 44320. *

FERGUSON, JASON
Football player. **Personal:** Born Nov 28, 1974, Nettleton, MA. **Educ:** Univ Ga. **Career:** NY Jets, defensive tackle, 1997-04; Dallas Cowboys, defensive tackle,2005-07; Miami Dolphins, defensive tackle, 2008-. **Honors/Awds:** AFC Defensive Player of the Week, 2003. **Business Addr:** Professional Football Player, Miami Dolphins, 7500 SW 30 St, Davie, FL 33314, **Business Phone:** (856)638-6843.*

FERGUSON, JASON
Football player. **Personal:** Born Nov 28, 1974, Nettleton, MS; married Gena; children: Jason II & Geno. **Educ:** Ga Univ. **Career:** New York Jets, defensive tackle, 1997-04; Dallas Cowboys, defensive tackle, 2005-07; Miami Dolphins, 2008-. **Orgs:** Founder, Jason Ferguson Found, 2007. **Honors/Awds:** First-team, All S eastern Conf, The Football News.

FERGUSON, JOEL I
Executive, real estate executive. **Personal:** Married Erma; children: 5. **Educ:** Mich State Univ, BA, elem educ, 1959. **Career:** WLAJ-TV, pres, owner & founder, 1990-; F&S Develop Co, co-founder & partner, currently. **Orgs:** Trustee, Mich State Univ; dir, Greater Lansing Urban League OJT prog. **Special Achievements:** First African American elected to the Lansing City Coun, 1967. **Business Addr:** Co-founder, Partner, F&S Develop Co, 1223 Turner St Suite 300, Lansing, MI 48906, **Business Phone:** (517)371-2515.*

FERGUSON, JOHNNIE NATHANIEL
Banker, manager. **Personal:** Born Jan 17, 1943, Washington, DC; son of James H and Viola Cooper (deceased); married Delphine David, Oct 31, 1964; children: Michelle D. **Educ:** Univ Dist Columbia, AAS, comput sci, 1973; Harcourt Learning Direct, PC repair, 2000; Prof Develop Inst, real estate cert, 2003. **Career:** FBI, fingerprint tech, 1964-67; Riggs Nat Corp, Washington, DC, programmer, 1967-79, data processing supvr, 1979-90, banking officer & asst mgr, 1990-93, banking officer & mgr, 1993-98, asst vpres, sales mgr, 1998-01, vpres, bus develop officer, 2001-. **Orgs:** Pres, Orr Elem Sch PTA, 1976-84; Wash DC Asn Urban Bankers, 1977-83; pres, Riggs Nat Bank Club, 1979; treas, DC Cong Parents & Teachers, 1982-84; treas, Adv Neighborhood Comm 6C, 1982-; DC Fed Farmers & Consumers Markets, 1983-; DC Cong PTA, 1986; Nat Cong Parents & Teachers, 1987; treas, Kiwanis Club Eastern Br, 1988-92; chmn, Local Board 1 Selective Serv Syst, 1988-01; vpres, DC Cong PTA, 1989-92; vpres, Kiwanis Club Eastern Br, 1990-91; secy, DC Comn Human Rights, 1990-91; bd mem, Anacostia/Cong Heights Partnership, controller, 1993-; Anacostia Bus & Prof Asn, 1994-01; Area D Community Mental Health Asn, 1995-99; Hadley Mem Hosp Community Bd, 1996-99; deacon bd, church treas, St Matthews Baptist Church,1999-01; Far SE Family Strengthing Collab, Finance Comt, 2000-. **Honors/Awds:** Cert Appreciation, Am Cancer Soc, 1980; Cert Appreciation, DC Adv Coun Voc Educ, 1980; Cert Award, Benjamin G Orr Elem Sch, 1980-84; Meritorious Pub Serv Award, 1997. **Military Serv:** AUS, sgt, 3 yrs; Army Commendation Medal; Good Conduct Medal. *

FERGUSON, LLOYD NOEL
Educator. **Personal:** Born Feb 9, 1918, Oakland, CA; son of Noel and Gwendolyn; married Charlotte Welch Ferguson, Jan 2, 1944; children: Lloyd Jr, Stephen Bruce, Lisa Ferguson Walker. **Educ:** Univ Calif, Berkeley, BS, 1940; PhD, 1943. **Career:** Educator (retired); Southern Pac Rwy Co, porter; Univ Calif, Berkeley, Nat Defense Proj, res asst, 1941-44; A&T Col, asst prof, 1944-45; Howard Univ, fac mem, 1945-65, chem dept head, 1958-65; Calif State Univ, prof, 1965-86, chem dept chmn, 1968-71. **Orgs:** Am Chem Soc; Am Asn Univ Prof; Sigma Xi; Phi Kappa Phi Nat Honor Soc; fel, AAAS; fel, Chem Soc London; founder, Nat Orgn Black Chemists & Chem Engrs; chair, ACS Div Chem Educ, 1980. **Honors/Awds:** Oakland Museum Asn Award, 1973; Award for Excellence in Teaching, Mfg Chemists Asn, 1974; Outstanding Professor Award, Calif State Univ, 1974; Distinguished American Medallion, Am Found Negro Affairs, 1976; Award in Chem Educ, Am Chem Soc, 1978; Outstanding Teaching Award, Nat Orgn Black Chemists & Chemic Engrs, 1979; Outstanding Professor Award, Calif State Univ & Col Trustees, 1981; Hon degrees: D.Sc, Howard Univ, 1970, Coe Col, 1979. **Special Achievements:** Author: Electron Structures of Org Molecules, Prentice-Hall, 1952; Textbook Org Chem, D Van Norstrand, 1958; The Modern Struct Theory Org Chem, Prentice-Hall, 1963; Org Chem, Prentice-Hall, 1972; Highlights of Alicyclic Chem, Franklin Publishing, 1973; Struct Org Chem, Willard Grant Press, 1975; Lloyd N. Ferguson Young Scientist Award; CibaGeigy Corp "Exceptional Black Scientists" Poster; birthdate in "Milestones in Chemistry" calendar. **Military Serv:** First African Am to earn a doctoral degree in chem. **Home Addr:** 4477 Wilshire Blvd, Los Angeles, CA 90010, **Home Phone:** (323)934-5568. *

FERGUSON, RALPH
Automotive executive. **Personal:** Born Feb 23, 1955, Warner Robins, GA; son of Jordan Georgia and Jesse. **Educ:** Citadel Col, Charleston, SC, 1973-77; Georgia Col, Milledgeville, GA, 1982-85. **Career:** Houston Bd Educ, Warner Robins, GA, teacher, 1977-83; 20th Century Realty, Warner Robins, GA, sales, 1981-84; J-Mac Olds, Warner Robins, GA, sales, 1984-85; Eddie Wiggins F-L-M, Warner Robins, GA, sales, 1985-86; Sumter Ford-L-M, Americus, GA, co-owner & vpres 1986-. **Orgs:** Citadel Alumni Asn, 1977-91; Alumni Football Asn, 1977-91; Black Ford Lincoln Mercury, 1986-91; pres, Ferguson Family Found, 1990-. **Honors/Awds:** Honorable Mention All-American, UPI, 1976; Entrepreneurship Award, Ferguson Family, 1988; Jerome Hartwell Holland Award, United Holiness Church, 1991. **Business Addr:** Co-owner, Vice President, Sumter Ford Lincoln Mercury, PO Box 1204, Americus, GA 31709, **Business Phone:** (912)924-2702.

FERGUSON, RENEE
Journalist. **Personal:** Born Aug 22, 1949, Oklahoma City, OK; daughter of Eugene and Mary; married Ken Smikle; children: Jason. **Educ:** Ind Univ, BS, jour, 1971; Ind Univ, MA, 1972; Jackson State Univ; Kent State Univ. **Career:** Indianapolis Star newspaper, writer, 1971-72; WLWI-TV Indianapolis, news reporter, 1972-76; WBBM-TV Chicago, news reporter, 1977-82; CBS News, news reporter, NY, corresp, 1980; NBC 5 Chicago, WMAQ-TV, investigative reporter, 1987-. **Orgs:** Bd dir, The Asn C, 1975-78; bd mem, Big Sisters Am, Indianapolis, 1975-78; Alpha Kappa Alpha Sorority; Nat Orgn Women; Am Civil Liberties Union; Chicago Black Women's Lawyers Asn; bd dir, Investigative Reporters & Ed Inc. **Honors/Awds:** DuPont Award, Columbia Univ; Goldsmith Award, Kennedy Sch Govt Harvard; Gracie Award, Am Women Radio & TV, NY; Asniated Press Award for Best Investigative Reporting; seven Chicago Emmys, Nat Asn Black Journalists; Studs Terkel Lifetime Achievement Award; Journalism Fellowship, Harvard Univ Nieman Found, 2006-07. **Special Achievements:** First African American woman to work as an investigative reporter in Chicago. **Business Addr:** Investigative Reporter, NBC 5 Chicago WMAQ, 454 N Columbus Dr, Chicago, IL 60611, **Business Phone:** (312)836-5703.

FERGUSON, DR. ROBERT LEE, SR.
Consultant. **Personal:** Born Feb 18, 1932, Rascon, San Luis Potoci, Mexico; son of Booker T (deceased) and Corillea Jackson (deceased); married Ruby Evelyn Brewer, Nov 1, 1953 (deceased); children: Robert Jr & Duane; married Raymonde Bateau Polk, Oct 2, 1993; children: Raymonde Polk-Wilson, Samuel Polk, Pierre Polk & Reginal Polk, Carmel Polk. **Educ:** Bakersfield Col, attended 1951; Naval Aviation Preflight, Pensacola, FL, 1964; South western Col, AA, 1969; Naval Postgraduate Sch, BA, 1973; Univ N Colo, MA, 1975; Pacific Western Univ Los Angeles CA, PhD, 1986. **Career:** USN Hawaii, captain's steward, 1951-52; Heavy Attack Squadron, aircraft maintenance chief; USN, Bombardier Navigator, adv human minority rels psychol counseling, 1967-77; Naval Flight Officer INFO, flighter squadron213, asst maintenance officer; NAS Miramar CA, asst dept head aircraft maintenance, 1973-75; USS Enterprise, asst dept head aircraft maintenance,1975-78; NAS, Lemoore CA, officer charge aircraft maintenance, 1978-80; Fighter Squadron 124, dept head aircraft maintenance, 1980; Rail Co,sr logistics analyst; syst acquisition mgt consult; self-employed, 1988-. **Orgs:** Fleet Res Asn, 1963-65; mgr, Park view Little League, Chula Vista, CA,1969-77; Veterans Foreign Wars, 1974-; Naval Aviation Tail hook Asn, 1972-;alumni, Naval Post grad Sch, 1973-; alumni, Univ N Colo, 1975-; Nat Naval Officer Asn, 1977-; San Diego Mus Art; corresp chmn, African Arts Comm; Naval Aviation Mus, Pensacola, FL. **Honors/Awds:** Author: The Four-O (4.0) Sailor, self-publish, 1990. **Military Serv:** USN comdr 30 yrs served; Naval Gallantry Cross; Vietnam Service; Korea; Secnav Medal 1967, 1971; Air Medal, 1971; Bronze Star; Navy Commendation,1980; Good Conduct Medal 3 Stars. **Business Addr:** Consultant & Publisher, Author, Left Brain Press, 604 Mariposa Cir, Chula Vista, CA 91911-2511.*

FERGUSON, ROGER W, JR.
Banker. **Personal:** Born Oct 28, 1951, Washington, DC. **Educ:** Harvard Univ, BA, econ, 1973, JD, 1979, PhD, econ, 1981. **Career:** NY Off Davis Polk & Wardwell, atty, 1981-84; Bd Gov Fed Res Syst, bd mem, 1997-2001, vice chmn, 2001-06; Swiss Re Am Holding Corp, chmn, head financial serv & exec comt mem, 2006-08; TIAA-CREF, pres & chief exec officer, 2008-; McKinsey & Co Inc, partner; Res & Info Syst, dir; Fed Res Bd, vice chmn; Pembroke Col, Frank Knox fel. **Orgs:** Bd Overseers Harvard Univ; bd trustees, Inst Advan Study; Coun Foreign Rels & Group Thirty; bd dirs, Harvard Alumni Asn; treas, Friends Educ; trustee, Comm Mus Mod Art, New York; chmn, Comt Global Fin Syst; chmn, Joint Year 2000 Coun, 1998-00; chmn, Group Ten Working Party Fin Sector Consol. **Honors/Awds:** Hon fel, Cambridge Univ, 2004; Distinguished Service Award, Bond Mkt Asn; hon deg, Lincoln Co; hon deg, Webster Univ. **Special Achievements:** First African American vice chairman of Federal Reserve Board. **Business Addr:** President, Chief Executive Officer, TIAA-CREF, PO Box 1259, Charlotte, NC 28201, **Business Phone:** 800-842-2252.

FERGUSON, ROSETTA A.
Government official. **Personal:** Born Jul 1, 1920, Florence, MS; daughter of Gaberil Sexton and Earnie; married; children: 4. **Educ:** Detroit Inst Tech. **Career:** Mich St House Res, mem 9th Dist, 1965-72, mem 20th dist, 1972-78; Loyalty Invest Community, mgr real estate firm. **Orgs:** Dem State Cent; exec bd & precinct Delegate for 10 Years; rec sect, 13th Cong Dist; Wayne Co Dem Rep Human Rels Coun Civil Rights; Gray Lady Red Cross; PTA; Nat Asn Advan Colroed People; TULC; Women's Pub Affairs Comm1000 Inc; Orgn Youth Civic Eagles; founder & fin, Sec Peoples Community Civil League; Missionary Soc Peoples Bapt Ch; Mich Right Life Community & People Taking Action Against Abortion Community. **Special Achievements:** Featured in Ebony Magazine as one of the Black Women Leaders in State of Michigan, Alpha Kappa Alpha Sorority's Heritage Series No 1, Black Women in Politics, was in Michigan House of Rep, 1970.

FERGUSON, SHERLON LEE
Executive. **Personal:** Born Mar 2, 1949, Richmond, VA; son of William Sr and Grace Brown; married Brenda Russell, 1972; children: Mia & Meaghan. **Educ:** Morgan State Univ, Baltimore, BS, math, 1971. **Career:** Blue Cross & Blue Shield, Baltimore, actuarial asst, 1971-73; Honeywell Inc, Baltimore, sr sales engr, 1973-83; FSCO Inc, Baltimore, pres & chief exec officer, 1983-. **Orgs:** Bldg Cong & Exchange Baltimore, 1973-; Am Soc Heating, Refrig & Air Conditioning Engs, 1973-; US Chamber Com, 1988-89; Better Bus Bur, 1988-; Minority Bus Develop Coun, 1988-; Asn Builders & Contractors, 1988-; Minority Supplier Develop Coun, 1988-. **Honors/Awds:** Outstanding Transp Project of the Yr, COMTO, 1987-88; STEP Award, Nat Safety Comn Asn Builders & Contractors, 1990. **Business Phone:** (410)668-3611.

FERGUSON, ST JULIAN
Musician, educator, salesperson. **Personal:** Born Apr 13, 1935, South Carolina; son of Irene and Alonzo; married Albertha Simmons; children: Darian, Gerald & Bernard. **Educ:** SC State Univ, BS, 1957; Loyola Univ, MEd, 1971. **Career:** Lower N Youth Ctr, music dir; Tilden Tech High Sch, inst music teacher, 1965-69; Madison Elem, teacher, 1969-71; Chicago Bd Educ, teacher early remediation, 1971; Bryn Mawr Elem Sch, teacher, 1971; Coldwell

Banker, sales assoc, 1993-. **Orgs:** Nat Educ Asn; Ill Teachers Asn; Chicago Fed Musicians. **Military Serv:** USMC, pfc, 1953-57. **Business Addr:** Sales Associate, Coldwell Banker, 11113 S Wern Ave, Chicago, IL 60643, **Business Phone:** (312)779-5400.

FERGUSON, VALERIE C
Hotel executive, vice president (organization). **Educ:** Univ San Francisco, BA, govt. **Career:** Hyatt Hotel, Atlanta, clerk, gen mgr, 1985-95; Ritz-Carlton, Atlanta, gen mgr; Loews Philadelphia Hotel, reg vpres & managing dir, 1998-. **Orgs:** Pa Travel Coun; Philadelphia Conv & Visitors Bur; Hist Philadelphia Inc; Urban League Philadelphia; Philadelphia Workforce Investment Corp; Sch Dist Philadelphia's Communities Schools & Widener Univ; chmn, Am Hotel & Lodging Asn; adv bd mem, Univ Del. **Honors/ Awds:** Pioneer Award, Atlanta Bus League, 1991; Women of the Year, Network Exec Women Hospitality, 1993; Trumpet Award, Turner Broadcasting, 1994; Lodging Leader of the Year, Ga Hospitality & Trade Asn, 1998; Drum Major for Justice Award, Southern Christian Leadership Conference; Honorary Doctorate, Food Manufacturing Asn; Hospitality Leader of the Year, Diversity Institute, 2000; Hospitality Hotelier of the Year, Multicultural Black Culinary Alliance Food Serv & Hospitality. **Special Achievements:** First African American to hold the position of vice chairwoman American Hotel and Motel Association; Named to the Atlanta Business League's list of Top 100 Black Women of Influence; Named one of the 100 Most Influential Women in Travel for 1998 and 1999 by Travel Agent magazine; Selected as one of the Top 100 Women in Corporate America by Ebony Magazine. **Business Addr:** Regional Vice President, Managing Director, Loews Philadelphia Hotel, 1234 Market St Suite 1812, Philadelphia, PA 19107, **Business Phone:** (215)231-7200.

FERNANDES, JULIE A
Government official. **Educ:** Univ Chicago Law Sch, AB, JD. **Career:** Justice Dept, voting expert; White House Domestic Policy Coun, from spec asst to pres Domestic Policy; Leadership Conf Civil Rights, sr policy analyst, spec coun; US Dept Justice, trl atty, Civil Rights Div & assoc coun asst atty gen civil rights; The Raben Group?s, prin health & educ & constitution & justice prac groups, currently. **Business Phone:** (202)466-8585.

FERNANDES, MARY A
Government official. **Career:** Mass Bay Transp Authority, Exec Office Transp & Construct, dep secy Civil Rights & Prog Develop, currently; Silver Line Communs & Community Develop, asst gen mgr, currently. **Orgs:** Pres, Boston Chap Conf Minority Transp Officials.

FERNANDEZ, DENISE BURSE
Actor. **Personal:** Born Jan 1, 1952, Atlanta, GA. **Career:** Film: Basquiat, 1996; On the One, 2005; The Juror, 1996; TV Series: "The American Experience", 1993; "New York Undercover", 1995; "Law & Order", 1999; Funny Valentines, 1999; "The Sopranos", 2000; "Cosby", 2000; "Third Watch", 2001; "100 Centre Street", 2001; "Law & Order: Special Victims Unit", 2001; "Law & Order: Criminal Intent", 2005; "House of Payne", 2006-08. **Business Addr:** Actress, Screen Actors Guild, 180 St Nicholas Ave Suite 21, New York, NY 10026, **Business Phone:** (212)663-5440.*

FERNANDEZ, JOHN PETER
Manager. **Personal:** Born Oct 22, 1941, Boston, MA; divorced; children: Michele, Eleni, Sevgi. **Educ:** Harvard Univ, AB, govt , 1969; Univ CA, Berkeley, MA, sociol, 1971; Univ CA, Berkeley, Sociol, PhD, 1973. **Career:** Bell PA, div mgr customer serv, 1978; AT&T Basking Rioge NJ, mgr mgt educ & develop, 1975-78; Yale Univ, asst prof, 1974-75; AT&T NYC, personnel supvr res, 1973-74; YMCA Dorchester MA, prog dir, 1965-69; Advan Res Mgt Consults, pres, currently. **Orgs:** Am Sociol Asn, 1973; Coun Concerned Black Exec, 1975-. **Honors/Awds:** Outstanding sophomore Govt Maj, Northeastern Univ, 1967; special careers fellow, Univ CA, Berkeley, 1969-73. **Special Achievements:** Author of 9 books. **Military Serv:** USN, elec tech E-5, 1960-64. **Business Addr:** President, Advanced Research Management Consultants Inc, PO Box 4076, Philadelphia, PA 19118-8076, **Business Phone:** (215)247-4546.*

FERNANDEZ, PETER JAY
Actor. **Personal:** Born Aug 15, 1953, Brockton, MA; son of Barbara Julio; married Densie Burse, Apr 9, 1994. **Educ:** Boston Univ Sch Arts, BA, 1975. **Career:** TV Serials: "The Prosecutors", 1996; "Funny Valentines", 1999; "Hack", 2001; "Deep Vote", 2001; "Law & Order: Criminal Intent", 2003; "Great Performances", 2008; "Fringe", 2009. Performed on stage with: Black & Hispanic Shakespeare Company, 1997; Classic Stage Co, New York, 1998; New York Stage & Film, 1998; Joseph Papp Public Theatre, 1997; Cincinnati Playhouse/Arena Stage, 1999; Via com Pictures, Adventures of Superboy, series regular, 1991-92; Jelly's Last Jam, Broadway, 1994; BET Movies & Starz USA Films, 1999; Fal Short, 2002; "The Egoists", 2003; "On the One", 2005; Deception, 2008. **Orgs:** Actor's Equity Asn, 1975-; Screen Actors Guild, 1978-; Am Fedn TV & Radio Artists, 1978-; Non Traditional Casting Proj, 1990-; 52nd Street Proj, 1989-. **Honors/ Awds:** Helen Hayes Award, Best Actor in a Musical, nominee, 1999; Cincinnati Theatre Awards, Best Actor in a Musical, nominee, 1999. *

FERNANDEZ, TONY (OCTAVIO ANTONIO CASTRO)
Association executive, baseball player. **Personal:** Born Jun 30, 1962, San Pedro de Macoris, Dominican Republic; married Clara; children: Joel, Jonathan, Abraham, Andy & Jazmin. **Career:** Baseball player (retired); Toronto Blue Jays, infielder, 1983-90; San Diego Padres, infielder, 1991-92; NY Mets, infielder, 1993; Toronto Blue Jays, infielder, 1993; Cincinnati Reds, 1994; NY Yankees, 1995-96; Cleveland Indians, 1997; Toronto Blue Jays, 1998-99, 2001; Milwaukee Brewers, infielder, 2001. **Orgs:** Founder, Tony Fernandez Found, 2002-. **Honors/Awds:** R Howard Webster Award as Syracuses Most Valuable Player, 1982-83; Rookie of the Year, Baseball Writers' Asn Am, 1984; Labatts Blue Player of the Month, 1986; Gold Glove Awards, 1986-89. **Special Achievements:** Tony took on an invitation to play with the Seibu Lions in Japan. **Business Phone:** (954)384-6345.

FERNANDEZ-SMITH, WILHELMENIA
Singer. **Career:** Someone to Watch Over Me, 1987; Motown 30: What's Goin' On!, 1990; Opera & Concert singer, currently. **Home Addr:** 3280 Brighton Place Dr, Lexington, KY 40509. **Business Addr:** Opera & Concert Singer, 3280 Brighton Place Dr, Lexington, KY 40509.

FERREBEE, THOMAS G.
Police officer, vice president (organization). **Personal:** Born Jan 24, 1937, Detroit, MI; married Irma; children: Gregory G, Debra L, Angela M. **Educ:** Iowa State Univ, BS, 1960; Eastern Mich Univ, MA, guidance & coun, 1963. **Career:** Detroit Police Dept, comdr recruiting div; Ford Motor Co; Hamtramck HS, teacher; Chrysler Corp; Wayne County, dir human relations; Wayne County Community Col, mgr labor relations, dir cert; CFS, vpres mktg, 2004. **Orgs:** Bd trustees personnel com, Childrens Hosp MI; Ctr Criminal Justice & Minority Employment Law Enforcement; consult, Minority Police Recruiting; Optimist Club Detroit; area activity chmn, BSA; Mich Pub Personnel Asn; Concerned Police Off Equal Justice. **Business Addr:** Vice President of Marketing, 8045 2nd Ave, Detroit, MI 48202.

FERRELL, DUANE
Basketball player, basketball executive. **Personal:** Born Feb 28, 1965, Baltimore, MD; married Tina; children: 3. **Educ:** Ga Tech Univ, BS, indust mgt. **Career:** Basketball player (retired), basketball executive; Atlanta Hawks, forward, 1988-89, 1990-94; CBA, Topeka Sizzlers, 1989-90; Ind Pacers, 1995-97; Golden State Warriors, 1998-99; Vidya Media Ventures Inc, mgr; Wash Wizards, dir player prog & asst coach, currently. **Business Phone:** (202)661-5000.

FERRELL, ROSIE E.
Executive. **Personal:** Born May 26, 1915, Clarksdale, MS; daughter of Andrew Carter and Catherine Weatherspoon; married Charlie; children: Henry (deceased), Joyce, Wilma, Lois, Joseph, Rose & Nathaniel. **Educ:** Delta Community Col, AA, 1974; SaginaWVAl State Col, BA, 1976. **Career:** Saginaw MI, city directory enumerator, 1946-71; Field Enterprises Inc, sales rep, 1964-66; Saginaw, sch census taker city & state, 1965-67; Saginaw Gen Hosp, ward clk, 1967; Dept Model Cities, team capt; Saginaw Multi-Purpose Serv Ctr, info referral specialist, 1971-76; Our Image Inc, founder, pres; Tri City Serv Employer Redevelop, Jobs Progress, career resources asst, career resources admin. **Orgs:** Greater Williams Temple Ch God Christ, 1934-; Nat Asn Advan Colored People, 1935-; chairlady, Muscular Dyst, 1961-75; personal evangelist, 1963; chairlady chap mem dr, 1965-75; Comn Action Comt, comt aide, 1967-69; bd mem, CAC, 1967; vpres, Police Comn Rels, 1973-76; bd mem, coordr, E Side MD Dr, 1974-75; Bd Saginaw Co Soc Serv Club, 1974-75; chairlady, Human Resources League Women Voters, 1974-75; pres, Saginaw City Coun PTA, 1975-76. **Honors/Awds:** Child Evangelism Teachers Cert, 1963; Sailors Regional Award, Week, 1964; Comt Serv Award, Prof & Bus Women, 1972; Woman of the Yr, Zeta Omega Phi Beta Sor Inc, 1975; Hon, Dinner Greater Williams Temple Ch God Christ, 1975; Humanitarian Award, Am Legion Post 500, 1975; treas, 8th Dist Co Rep Comn; candidate Saginaw City Coun, 1975-77. **Special Achievements:** Wrote book of Poetry, title prolonged copyright, 1982; Religous Tracks, printed, 1984. *

FERRELL, TYRA
Actor. **Personal:** Born Jan 28, 1962, Houston, TX; daughter of Rachel Johnson; married Don Carlos Johnson, Apr 9, 1992. **Educ:** Univ Tex, Austin, actg. **Career:** Broadway: The Lady and Her Music; Dreamgirls; TV Series: "Reaching for the Stars", 1985; "HIll Street Blues", 1985; "Moonlight", 1985; "The Twilight Zone", 1985; "ABC After school Specials", 1986; "Hunter", 1986; "Mathnet",1987; "The Bronx Zoo", 1987-88; "Side by Side", 1988; "Mr Belvedere",1988; "The Neon Empire", 1989; "Quantum Leap", 1989; "Thirty something",1989-90; "City", 1990; "Full house", 1990; "The Trials of Rosie O'Neill",1990; "You Must Remember This", 1992; "Better Off Dead", 1993; "The Cape",1993; "ER", 1994; "The Cape", 1996-97; "Early Edition", 1997; "The Corner", 2000; "Soul Food", 2000; "The Shield", 2002; "Futility", 2003;"Law & Order: Special Victims Unit", 2003; "NTSB: The Crash of Flight 323", 2004; Films: So Fine, 1981; Gimme an 'F', 1984; Lady Beware, 1987; School Daze, 1988; Tapeheads, 1988; The Mighty Quinn, 1989; The Exorcist III, 1990; Jungle Fever, 1991; Boyz n the Hood, 1991; Ulterior Motives,1992; White Men Can't Jump, 1992; Equinox, 1992; Poetic Justice, 1993; The Perfect Score, 2004; Coochie, 2004. **Special Achievements:** She was listed as one of twelve "Promising New Actors of 1991" in John Willis' Screen World, 2005; nominated for an image award as an outstanding actress in a Television Movie, 2005. **Business Addr:** Actor, Gersh Agency, 232 N Canon Dr, Beverly Hills, CA 90210, **Business Phone:** (310)274-6611.*

FERRER, JOSE
Executive. **Career:** Kwanzaa Fest Found, founder & chmn, currently.

FEWELL, RICHARD
Playwright. **Personal:** Born Feb 2, 1937, Rock Hill, SC; son of Thomas and Laura Steele; married Geraldine Whitted (died 1996); children: Renee Lorraine & Ritchard Gerald. **Educ:** Univ Bridgeport, BA (Magna Cum Laude) 1976, MA, 1980. **Career:** US Postal Serv, mail classification & reqs & postal servs, 1992; Univ Bridgeport, part-time Eng instr, 1994; Sacred Heart Univ, Fairfield, CT, adj instr; Housatonic Community Col, lectr, eng, 1996, part time fac, currently. **Orgs:** Pres, 1975-76, Alpha Sigma Lambda; bd mem, NAACP 1976-; Frank Silvera Writer's Workshop (Harlem), 1978-90; bur chief Fairfield County; INNER CITY Newspaper (New Haven & Statewide CT), 1990-2001; freelance writer, Fairfield County Advocate, contrib ed, Conn Update, 1982-83; bd dirs, Bridgeport Arts Coun, 1982-85; community mem, Action Bridgeport community Develop, 1984-86; found mem, New Bridge Ensemble, 1986-; ed Nat Alliance Postal & Federal Employees Newsletter & Local 808; African Am Family Forum, 1990-91; New Eng Found Arts, Adv Comt, 1992; adv comt, Artists Trust, Cambridge MA, 1992-96. **Honors/Awds:** Bert & Katya Gilden Memorial Short Story Award, 1975; First prize article, Writer's Digest Creative Writing Contest, 1977; Literature Award, Conn Comt Arts, 1984; publ Black Scholar, The Greenfield Review, Callaloo, Obsidian, Anthology Magazine Verse & Yearbook of American Poetry, The South Carolina Review, Okike (Nigeria), others; author "A Casualty of the Peace;" Heritage Award, Arts & Humanities, Alpha Kappa Alpha Sorority, 1987; actor, Dot Playhouse, played role of "Rev Sykes" in To Kill a Mockingbird, 1988; poetry readings Stan Nishimura Performance Arts/New Haven, CT 1988-89; excerpts from unpublished novel published Mwendo (Iowa), Obsidian (NC) & Beanfeast (CT); Grant, Conn Comn Arts, 1990; Nguzo Saba Award, Kwanzaa Seven Prod, 1996; Fairfield Review & On-Line Literary Mag, 1998; Poetry Readings: WPKN.FM, 1998; New Haven Free Pub Libr, 1998; Playwright Award, CT Comn Arts, 1999; Played role of "Luke" in Baldwin's "Amen Corner" HCC Performing Arts Ctr, 2000; Keeper of the Flame Award, Calvery SDA Church, 2000; Distinguished Advocate for the Arts Award, 2001; Distinguised Alumni, Univ Bridgeport, 2002. **Special Achievements:** Played Lead Role in Independent Film, Good Morning, premiered at Yale University, 1991; play Coon Dog, was a finalist in Theodore Ward prize for playwriting, 1991; play Hats was in five finalist in Theodore Ward prize, 1997-98; play, Skyy Piece, premiere reading, 2000, dramatic concert reading, Stamford Ctr for the Creative Arts, 2004; play, Juggie Bones, Rich Forum, 2003. **Military Serv:** USAF, 1955-61. **Business Addr:** Part Time Faculty, Housatonic Community College, 900 Lafayette Blvd, Bridgeport, CT 06604, **Business Phone:** (203)332-5200.

FIELDER, CECIL GRANT
Baseball manager, baseball player. **Personal:** Born Sep 21, 1963, Los Angeles, CA; son of Tina; married Stacey; children: Prince & Ceclyn. **Educ:** Univ Nev, Las Vegas, attended. **Career:** Baseball player (retired), baseball manager; Toronto Blue Jays, infielder, 1985-88; Detroit Tigers, infielder, 1990-96; NY Yankees, 1996-97; Anaheim Angels, 1997-98; Cleveland Indians, 1998; Atlantic City Surf, field mgr,2008-. **Honors/Awds:** Am League All-Star Team, 1990; Am League Home Run Champion, 1990-91; Babe Ruth Award, 1996. **Special Achievements:** Third American League player (6th overall) in the modern era to lead the league in RBIs in three consecutive seasons.

FIELDER, DR. FRED CHARLES
School administrator. **Personal:** Born Jun 16, 1933, Hattiesburg, MS; son of Ben Fielder and Quinnie Fielder White; married Vivian Johnson; children: Fred Charles Jr. **Educ:** Tougaloo Col, BS (magna cum laude), 1956; Meharry Med Col, DDS, 1960. **Career:** Hubbard Hosp, intern, 1960-61; Univ Mich, MS, oper dent, 1964; Mich Inst Tech, fel, 1966; Meharry Med Col, Dept Oper Dent, instr, 1961-63, from asst prof to assoc prof, 1964-74; Meharry Med Col Dent Clin, supt, 1971; Meharry Med Col Sch Dent, asst dean, exec assoc dean, interim dean, 1992-93, dean, 1993-97, deam emer, 1997-; Meharry Med Col, Dept Oper Dent, prof & chmn. **Orgs:** Acad Oper Dent; fel, United Health Found, 1963; Am Bd Oper Dent; fel, Col Dentists; Am Asn Dent Schs; comm mem Manpower & Aux Am Asn Dent Schsn 1969-70; coun Int Asn Dent Res, 1969-73; consul NC St, Bd Dent Exam, 1970; vpres, Capital City Dent Soc, 1972-74, pres, 1974-76; vpres, Omicron-Omicron Chap Omicron Kappa Upsilon Honor Dent Soc, 1970-72, past pres, 1972-74; past pres, Kappa Sigma Pi Honor Soc, 1961-62; past zone vpres, Pan TN Dent Asn, 1968-75, st vpres, 1979; clin consult comn, AmDent Asn, 1979-; consult,

Quarterly J Nat Dent Asn; Nat Dent Asn; Nashville Dent Soc; TN State Dent Soc; Asn Dent Res; Conf Oper Dentistry Educators; Clark Mem United Methodist Church. **Honors/Awds:** Most Outstanding Soph Dent Student, Meharry Med Col, 1958; Chi Delta Mu Awards, 1958; Meth Scholarship Award; Mosby Schol Bk Award; Caulk Prize, 1959; United Meth Scholar Award, High Sch Aver, 1959; Acad Dent Med Award, 1960; Acad Gold Foil Award 1960; Donley H Turpin Mem Award, 1960; Mizzy Award Crown & Bridge, 1960; Pan TN Dent Asn Award, 1960; Jos Frank Dent Award, 1960; Mosby Book Award, 1960; Caulk Prize, 1960; Nashville Dent Supply Prize, 1960; Snyder Dent Prize, 1960; Alpha Omega Award, 1960; Valedictorian Royal St HS, 1952; Recog & plaque one of 100 most valuable employees, Meharry Med Col, 1975; Dedication Recip Meharrian yearbook, 1964; Recog plaque Growth & Develop Meharry Col, 1971; Outstanding Faculty of the Year, Nat Alumni Asn, 1988; Student Appreciation Award, class of 1993; Fred C. Fielder, DDS Distinguished Dentist Award, Clark Mem United Methodist Church, named in honor, 2007. **Home Addr:** 4219 Drakes Hill Dr, Nashville, TN 37218, **Home Phone:** (615)876-1938.

FIELDING, HERBERT ULYSSES
State government official, funeral director. **Personal:** Born Jul 6, 1923, Charleston, SC; son of Julius P L and Sadie E Gaillard; married Thelma Erenne Stent; children: Julius PL II, Herbert Stent & Frederick Augustus. **Educ:** WVa State Col, BS, 1948. **Career:** Fielding Funeral Home, dir & owner, vpres, currently; SC House Representatives, rep, 1971-74, 1983-84; SC State Senate, sen, 1985. **Orgs:** SC Comt Voc Rehab; Trident Chamber Com; Univ SC Budget Bd; Bd McClennan Banks Hosp; SC Human Affairs Comt; SC Coastal Coun, 1987; chair, Charleston County Sen Deleg, 1989; pres, Robert Gould Shaw Boys Club; bdmem, McClennan Banks Hosp; Trident Coun Alcoholism; Omega Psi Phi Frat; founder & past co chmn, Charleston County Polit Action Comt; Nat Funeral Dir & Morticians Asn Inc. **Honors/Awds:** Man of Year Award, Chas Bus & Prof Mens Asn, 1966; Silver Beaver Award, Boy Scouts Am, 1971; Man of Year Award, Mu Alpha Chap, 1972; SC Legislative Black Caucus Award, 1975; Harvey Gantt Triumph Award, 1985; Citizens Comt Charleston County Award, 1985; Outstanding Legislator Award, 1987; Royal Arch Masons Award, 1988; SC Farm Cooperatives Award, 1988. **Special Achievements:** First African American elected to the South Carolina House of Representatives. **Military Serv:** AUS, Am & European Theaters, 1943-46; 500th QM Co. **Business Addr:** Owner, Vice President, Fielding Funeral Home, 7173 Hwy 162, Yonges Island, SC 29449-5603, **Business Phone:** (843)889-9181.

FIELDS, ALVA DOTSON
School administrator, teacher. **Personal:** Born May 29, 1929, Athens, TN; daughter of Walter E Dotson and Estella Vaught; married James Henry Fields III; children: Gordon, James & Sherri. **Educ:** Knoxville Col, TN, BA, 1958; Univ TN, MSW, 1966. **Career:** School administrator (retired); Tenn Dept Human Serv, asst dir, 1968-73, caseworker & field supv, 1958-68, dir, 1973-75; Florence Ala City Sch, sch soc worker, 1976-78; Univ N Ala, instr, 1976-78; Chattanooga State Tech Community Col, dept head, 1978-94, coordr minority affairs, counr. **Orgs:** Title XX Regional Adv Comt, 1979-82; Comn Serv Greater Chattanooga Inc, 1979-82; panelist, Tenn Gov Conf Families, 1980; bd mem, Metro Coun Comn Serv, 1980-91; pres, Tenn Conf Soc Welfare, 1984; vpres, Chatt Links Inc, 1989-91; adv bd, Univ Chattanooga SE Inst Educ Theatre, 1989-; pres, Metrop Coun Community Serv, 1991-; pres, Chattanooga Links Inc, 1991-; curric consult ethnic content, Univ N Ala; bd mem, Chattanooga Area Urban League Inc, Family & C Serv Inc, Presby Homes Chattanooga, VENTURE, Friends Black C; chmn, Consortium Adolescent Pregnancy, Venture Task Force Adolescent Pregnancy; Gov Task Force Healthy C, Infant Mortality Sub-Comt; Tenn Child Welfare Serv Comn; Delta Sigma Theta; Tenn Conf Soc Welfare; Nat Asn Soc Workers. **Honors/Awds:** Nominated Soc Worker of the Year, Muscle Shoals NASW, 1974; Big Brothers-Big Sisters Int, Chattanooga Chap, 1975; Tenn NASW Soc Worker of the Year, 1984; Hall of Fame, Delta Sigma Theta, 1985; Knoxville's Black Achievers, 1986; Outstanding AA Woman of Influence, Girls Club Chattanooga, 1996; Chattanooga Woman Distinction, 1996. *

FIELDS, BRENDA JOYCE
School administrator. **Personal:** Born in Tacoma, WA; daughter of Betty Mewborn. **Educ:** Ohio State Univ, BA, psychol, 1981; Columbus Chamber Com, Leadership Columbus, leadership cert, 1989; United Way, Proj Diversity, bd develop cert, 1989; Col Bus, Ohio State Univ, Sch Pub Policy & Mgt, MA, 1994. **Career:** Columbus Recreation & Parks Dept, dance instr, choreographer, 1980-90; Ohio State Univ, pub inquiries asst, 1983-93, asst dir stud progs, 1993; Sphinx Senior Honoraries, Ohio Union, asst dir, 1994. **Orgs:** Leadership Columbus, Chamber Com; Ohio State Univ, Women Color Consortium, 1984-; Delta Sigma Theta Sorority Inc; bd trustees, Nat Assault Prevent Ctr; Truth-Douglass Soc, 1992; United Negro Col Fund, Ohio State Univ, 1992-. **Honors/Awds:** Employee of the Quarter, Ohio Unions, 1990; Council of Honor, Ohio State Univ, African Am Stud Servs, 1994. **Special Achievements:** Featured in Blue Chip Profile.

FIELDS, C. VIRGINIA
Government official. **Personal:** Born Jan 1, 1946?, Birmingham, AL. **Educ:** Knoxville Col, TN, BA; Ind Univ, MSW. **Career:** NY, social worker, 1971-88; City NY, coun mem, 1989-97; Manhattan Bor, pres, 1998-06. **Orgs:** C's Aid Soc. **Honors/Awds:** Dr. Martin Luther King Jr. Leadership Award, 2003. **Special Achievements:** First African American woman elected to City Council from Manhattan; second black female borough president of Manhattan. *

FIELDS, C. VIRGINIA
Government official. **Personal:** Born Jan 1, 1946?, Birmingham, AL. **Educ:** Knoxville Col, BA; Ind Univ, MSW. **Career:** NY, social worker, 1971; NY City Coun, 1989-; NY City, dem cand Mayor; Manhattan Borough, pres, 1997-2006. *

FIELDS, CLEO
Lawyer, congressperson (u.s. federal government). **Personal:** Born Nov 22, 1962, Baton Rouge, LA; son of Isidore and Alice; married Debra Horton; children: Brandon & Christopher. **Educ:** Southern Univ, BA, 1984; Southern Univ Sch Law, JD, 1987. **Career:** State of Louisiana, senator, 1986-92; US House of Representatives,Louisiana's 4th Cong Dist, congressman, 1993-97; Clinton-Gore presidential campaign, volunteer sr advisor, 1996; 14th Senatorial Dist LA, state senator, 1998; The Fields Law Firm LLC, founder & owner, 1998-. **Orgs:** LA Leadership Inst; chair, LA Legis Black Caucus, 2000-01; co-chair,Rainbow/Push Bd Trustees; Mt Pilgrim Baptist Church. **Special Achievements:** The first African Am to became the democratic nominee; Youngest State Senator in Louisiana; Youngest person to serve as a member of the 103rdCong. **Business Addr:** Owner, Lawyer, The Fields Law Firm LLC, 2147 Govt St, Baton Rouge, LA 70806, **Business Phone:** (225)343-5377.

FIELDS, DR. DEXTER L.
Psychiatrist, educator. **Personal:** Born Oct 12, 1944, Detroit, MI; married Margaret L Betts. **Educ:** Wayne State Univ, BA, 1967; Wayne State Univ, Col Med, MD, 1972. **Career:** Kirwood Gen Hosp & Hutzel Hosp, staff physician; Boston City Hosp, psychiatric resident, 1972-73; Harvard Col, clinical fellow psychiatry, 1972-74; Detroit Psychiatric Inst, psychiatric resident, 1973-75; NE Guidance Substance Abuse Ctr, consult psychiatrist, 1974-76; Kirwood Mental Health Ctr, consult psychiatrist, 1976-80; Operation Hope, Community Mental Health Ctr, internal med resident, consult psychiatrist, 1976-77, 1980; Detroit Bd Educ, consult; Recorder's Ct Psychiatric Clinic, consult, chief psychiat, 2002. **Orgs:** Black Psychiat Forum Boston, 1972-73; Black Psychiat Am, 1973; fellow, Solomon Fuller, 1974; chmn, Bal Africain, 2004; mem, Friends Modern Art; adv bd, Found Jr Coun DIA; chmn, Nat Conf Artists Mich Chap; bd mem, Detroit Inst Arts, currently. **Business Addr:** Board Memeber, The Detroit Institute of Arts, Friends of African and African-American Art, 5200 Woodward Ave, Detroit, MI 48202, **Business Phone:** (313)833-7900.*

FIELDS, EARL GRAYSON
Consultant, housing developer. **Personal:** Born Jun 18, 1935, Brooklyn, NY; son of Ralph Allen and Queena Rachel Grayson; married Pauline Hay; children: Cheryl, Mark, Leslie. **Educ:** CCNY, BA, 1968. **Career:** US Bur Customs, customs inspector, 1963-68; US Dept Housing & Urban Devel, multi family & Col housing rep, 1968-72, model city rep, 1972-74, prog mgr, 1974-78; US Dept Housing & Urban Devel, Santa Ana CA, mgr, 1978-94; Housing & Community Devel, consult, currently. **Orgs:** Vchmn Orange County Urban League, 1981-82; treas & co chmn, Bowers Mus Black Cultural Coun, 1982-; Orange County Master Chorale, 1983-; chmn policy bd, Los Angeles Fed Exec Bd, 1988-92; Nat Asn Black County Offcals. **Honors/Awds:** Cert Assoc, Minority Real Estate Devel, 1980; Integrity Knowledge Serv Inland Empire Mortgage Bankers Asn, 1981; Vol Award United Way Orange City, 1982; Patriotic Serv US Dept Treas, 1984; US Dept Housing & Urban Devel, Region IX, Mgr of the Year, 1989-90. *

FIELDS, DR. EDWARD E.
Clergy. **Personal:** Born Jun 24, 1918, Kirkwood, MO; married Marshan; children: Marshan & Edward. **Educ:** Lincoln Univ, BS, 1940; KS State Teachers Col, MS, 1947; Univ Kansas City, Univ MO, NYU; Univ KS, D.Ed, 1959. **Career:** Indus arts teacher, 1945; Lincoln High Sch & RT Coles Vocational High Sch, coordr Co-op Occupational Educ, 1946-47; MO Public Sch, elem prin, 1947-56; Col St Teresa, instr, 1959-65; Central Jr High Sch, prin, 1962-71; Dept Career & Continued Educ, dir, 1971-72; Div Urban Edn, asst supt, 1972-74; assoc supt instr, 1974-75; Sch Dist Kansas City, act supt, 1975-78; ret sch dist, 1979; 5th Dist NW MO Annual Conf AME Church, minister. **Orgs:** MO State Teachers Asn; bd dir, Kansas City Teachers Credit Union; nat, state local Elem Prin Asns; past chmn Kansas City Teachers Ins Com; life mem NEA; Phi Delta Kappa; Nat Asn Supervision & Curriculum Develop; MO Asn Supervision & Curriculum Develop; Nat & State Asn Sec Sch Prin; Intl Reading Asn; Intl Indus Arts & Voc Educ Asn; Am Asn Sch Adminr; exec bd Kansas City Sch Admin Asn Nat Alliance Black Educators; Conf Minority Pub Admins; KCMO-TV Minority Rels Bd. **Honors/Awds:** Lecturer; Various Citations contributions educator & contributions BSA; Ordained, Am Methodist Episcopal Minister. **Military Serv:** USN. *

FIELDS, REAR ADM. EVELYN JUANITA
Government official. **Personal:** Born Jan 29, 1949, Norfolk, VA; daughter of Richard T Sr and Jerlean W. **Educ:** Norfolk State Univ, BS, math, 1971. **Career:** Government official (retired); NOAA, Atlantic Marine Ctr, Norfolk, Va, cartogr, 1972; NOAA/Ship McArthur, comndg officer, 1989-90; NOAA/Comn Personnel Ctr, Sci & Technol Fel, 1990-91; NOAA/Nat Ocean Serv/NGS, admin officer, 1991-94; NOAA/Nat Ocean Serv/C&GS, br chief, 1994-95; NOAA/Commissioned, Personnel Ctr Dir, 1995-97; NOAA/Nat Ocean Serv, dep asst admin, 1997-99; NOAA Off Marine & Aviation Opers, dir, 1999-, dir, comn personnel, 1999-2002. **Orgs:** NOAA Asn Comned Officers, 1975-; life mem, The Retired Officers Asn, 1980-; life mem, The Reserve Officers Asn, 1997-; Nat Military Family Asn, 1999-; hon mem, Zeta Phi Beta Sorority, 2000-; bd dirs, Mariners' Mus. **Honors/Awds:** Woman of the Year, MD Fedn Bus & Prof Women's Club, 1999; Ralph M Metcalfe Health Education & Science Award, Congressional Black Caucus, 1999; Lowell Thomas Award, Explorers Club, 2000; Strong Men & Women Award, Dominion Resources Inc, 2001. **Special Achievements:** First woman and the first African-American to head the NOAA Corps of Commissioned Officers. **Military Serv:** NOAA Corp, Rear Admiral, 1973-; Dept Com Gold Medal, 2000; NOAA Spec Achievement Award, 1998; NOAA Corps Commendation Medal, 1997; NOAA Corps Director's Ribbon, 1991.

FIELDS, DR. EWAUGH FINNEY
College administrator. **Personal:** Children: Jamie Benjamin (Deceased). **Educ:** Ky State Col, Frankfort, KY, BS, math; WVa Univ, Morgantown, WV, MA, sec educ; Temple Univ, Philadelphia, PA, EdD, math educ. **Career:** US Armed Forces Inst, Yokohama, Japan, algebra instr, 1956-57; Radio CorpAm, Camden, NJ, class C engr, 1959-63; Franklin Inst Lab, Philadelphia, PA, res mathematician, 1963; Cinnaminson Jr & Sr High Sch, teacher & mathdept head, 1963-69; Rutgers Univ, Camden, NJ, adjunct instr, 1967; Temple Univ, Philadelphia, PA, staff asst, 1967; Gloucester County Col, Sewell, NJ, adjunct lecturer, 1968-69; Drexel Univ, Philadelphia, PA, asst prof math, 1969-72, assoc prof math, 1972-76, asst vpres acad affairs, 1973-76, prof math, dean, evening & Univ Col, 1986-92, Outreach & Access, vprovost, 1992-96, prof emer & dean emer, currently; Univ Wash, Seattle, WA, vpresminority affairs, 1976-77, assoc prof math educ, 1976-77; Univ Dist Columbia, Wash, DC, dean, the Univ Col, 1978-86, prof math, 1981-86, interim coordr acad affairs, 1983-84, acting provost & vpres acad affairs, 1984-85; Univ Nairobi, Nairobi, Kenya, exchange prof, 1985. **Orgs:** Nat Coun Teachers Math; Nat Inst Sci; Am Soc Engineering Educ; AAAS; Am Coun Educ; Am Asn Higher Educ; Nat Asn Remedial & Develop Educ; bd dir, Philadelphia Bus Corp. **Honors/Awds:** Cost Reduction Incentive Award, Drexel Univ, 1988; Pioneer Award, Nat Action Coun Minorities Engineering, 1985; Black Faculty & Staff Award for Outstanding Service, Drexel Univ, 1985; Meritorious Service Award, Nat Sci Found, 1982. **Military Serv:** AUS, Women's Army Corps, lt, 1954-57. **Business Addr:** Professor Emeritus, Dean Emeritus, Drexel University, Mathematics education, 3141 Chestnut St, Philadelphia, PA 19104, **Business Phone:** (215)895-2000.

FIELDS, FAYE F
Executive. **Educ:** Univ Cincinnati, BS, MS, PhD, bus admin. **Career:** Integrated Resource Technologies Inc, founder, pres & ceo, 1986-; Wash Nat Baseball Club, founding partner, currently. **Honors/Awds:** Emerging Business of the Year Award, Black Enterprise Mag, 2004; DC Chamber of Commerce Small Business of the Year Award, 2004. **Business Addr:** Founder, President & Chief Executive Officer, Integrated Resource Technologies Inc, 5205 Leesburg Pke Suite 1115, Falls Church, VA 22041, **Business Phone:** (703)931-3330.*

FIELDS, FELICIA J
Executive, vice president (organization), executive director. **Educ:** Univ Mich, BA, psychol; Cent Mich Univ, MS, admin. **Career:** Ford Motor Co, exec dir hr, vpres hr, 2005-08, group vpres human resources & corp servs, 2008-. **Orgs:** Ford Exec Coun Diversity; bd mem, Prof Women's Network; founding mem, Ford Multi Cult Alliance; bd dir, Nat Action Coun Minorities Eng. **Honors/Awds:** Leading Woman in the North American Automotive Industry, Automotive News, 2005. **Business Addr:** Vice President of Human Resources, Ford Motor Company, 1 American Rd, Dearborn, MI 48121, **Business Phone:** (313)429-0009.

FIELDS, INEZ C.
Lawyer. **Personal:** Born in Hampton, VA; married F C Scott; children: Fred G Scott. **Educ:** Boston Univ Law Sch, LLD, 1921. **Career:** Atty. **Orgs:** Life mem, Nat Asn Advan Colored People; hon mem, Hampton Woman's Serv League; Am Asn Univ Women; Catherine Fields Lit Club; Women's Forum; Old Dominion Bar Asn; Va State Bar; Mt Olive Tent Lodge; Third Bapt Chap; Harry T Burleigh Comn Chorus; Delta Sigma Theta Sor. **Honors/Awds:** Appreciation Outstanding Comn Service Award, Plaque King St Comn Ctr; plaque significant comn serv. **Special Achievements:** Became the states first African American female lawyer.

FIELDS, KENNETH HENRY
Basketball player. **Personal:** Born Feb 9, 1962, Iowa City, IA. **Educ:** Univ Calif Los Angeles, BA, 1984. **Career:** Basketball

player (retired); Milwaukee Bucks, 1984-87; Los Angeles Clippers, 1987-88; CBA, Grand Rapids, Tulsa. **Honors/Awds:** Ranked sixth among UCLA's all-time scoring leaders; started first 16 games of his freshman season at UCLA; led the Bruins in field goal percentage.

FIELDS, KIM VICTORIA
Actor. **Personal:** Born May 12, 1969, New York, NY; daughter of Chip Fields; married Johnathon Franklin Freeman, Jan 1, 1995 (divorced 1998); married Christopher Morgan, Jul 23, 2007; children: Sebastian Alexander Morgan. **Educ:** Pepperdine Univ, BA, 1990. **Career:** TV Series: "Baby, I'm Back", 1978; "The Comeback Kid" 1980; "Children of Divorce", 1980; "Diff'rent Strokes" 1979-81; "The Facts of Life"1979-88; "Living Single", 1993-97; "Cupid", 1998; "Kenan & Kel", 1997-99; "Strong Medicine", 2000; "The Drew Carey Show", 2001; "The Facts of Life Reunion", 2001; "The Steve Harvey Show", 2001; "The Division", 2004; "One on One", 2004; "Bow", 2005; "The Comeback", 2005; "Eve", 2006; Victory Entertainment, pres & chief exec officer, currently. **Orgs:** W Angeles Church God in Christ; Am Fedn TV & Radio Artists; Screen Actors Guild; Delta Sigma Theta Sorority. **Honors/Awds:** Young Artist Award for Best Young Comedienne, 1981; Young Artist Award for Best Young Comedienne-Motion Picture or Television, 1982; Youth In Film Award, Best Actress; NAACP Image Award, Best Actress, 1985; Justice Dept Role Model of the Year Award, 1987. **Business Addr:** Actress, Endeavor Talent Agency, 9701 Wilshire Blvd Fl 10, Beverly Hills, CA 90212.

FIELDS, LYNN M
Executive. **Personal:** Born Jul 11, 1950, Philadelphia, PA; daughter of Barton A and Violet W. **Educ:** St Joseph's Univ, Philadelphia, BS, 1975; Harvard Univ, John F Kennedy Sch Govt, Cambridge, Mass, MPA, 1981. **Career:** Commonwealth Consultants, Inc, pres, former dir, 1988-91; Philadelphia Gas Works, vpres, govt & community affairs, 1991-95, dir, communicationist pub rels, 1995-97; United Way SE Pa, loaned exec, 1997-98; Philadelphia Int Airport, deputy dir aviation mkt & public affairs, 1998-. **Orgs:** Bd trustees, parlimentarian, chair external affairs, 1978-96, Lincoln Univ; bd mem, Delta Sigma Theta Sorority Inc; chair pun rels comt, Dist Scholar Endowment Found; League Women Voters; Women Commun; Pub Rels Soc Am. **Honors/Awds:** Wm J Walsh Medal for Excellence In Education, St Joseph's Univ, 1975. **Business Addr:** Deputy Director of Aviation Marketing & Public Affairs, Philadelphia International Airport, 8800 Essington Ave, Philadelphia, PA 19153, **Business Phone:** (215)937-6937.

FIELDS, MARK LEE
Football player. **Personal:** Born Nov 9, 1972, Los Angeles, CA; children: Mark Field Jr. **Educ:** Los Angeles S W Col,attended; Wash Univ, attended. **Career:** New Orleans Saints, linebacker, 1995-00; St. Louis Rams, 2001; Carolina Panthers, 2002-04. **Orgs:** A Child Wish. **Honors/Awds:** Pac 10 Defensive Player of the Year; winner of the ESPY come back Award. *

FIELDS, NATE
President (Organization). **Career:** US African Develop Found, vpres, pres, 1995, Africa Opers, chief exec officer, currently. **Business Addr:** Chief Executive Officer, United States African Development Foundation, 1400 I St NW Suite 1000, Washington, DC 20005-2248, **Business Phone:** (202)673-3916.*

FIELDS, DR. RICHARD A., SR.
Consultant, executive. **Personal:** Born Apr 18, 1950, Washington, DC; married Sylvia Crisp; children: Kirstyn & Richard Jr. **Educ:** Hampton Inst, BA, 1971; Duke Univ, Sch Med, MD, 1975; Duke Univ, resident Psychiat, 1878. **Career:** Dept Psychiat & Neurology AUS, chief, 1979-80; Neuse Mental Health Ctr,clinical dir, 1980-82; GA Regional Hosp Atlanta, supt, 1982-96; Fields &Assoc Inc, chief exec officer,1996; sr psychiat consult, currently. **Orgs:** Vice chair, APA Coun Psychiat Serv, 1994-96; pres, Black Psychiat Am,1984-88; pres, GA Psychiatric Assoc, 1992-93; pres, GA Chap Am Assoc Admin Psychiat, 1987-88; Omega Psi Phi Fraternity; NAACP; AME Church; fellow Am Psychiatric Asns, 1991; Nat coun community behavioral Healcare. **Honors/Awds:** Psychiatrist of the Year, Georgia Psychiatric Physician Asn, 1994-95. **Military Serv:** AUS, capt 2 yrs; Army Commendation Medal, 1980. **Business Addr:** Senior Consultant, Fields & Associates Inc, 150 St Marks Dr Suite 202, Stockbridge, GA 30281-1091, **Business Phone:** (770)389-3800.*

FIELDS, SAMUEL BENNIE
Executive. **Personal:** Born Dec 24, 1925, St Louis, MO; married Helen Lucille Brown; children: Sharon Hall. **Educ:** St Louis Music & Arts Univ, BA, Music Instrumental, 1949; Weaver Sch Real Estate, Diploma, 1950; Mensh Sch Real Estate, Cert, 1970. **Career:** Model Cities Comn DC, planning chmn, 1969-75; New Model Cities Housing Develop Corp, pres, chmn, 1971-73; DC Develop Co, vpres, 1974-77; DC Government, comn, 1976-; Sam Fields & Assoc, pres. **Orgs:** Planning chmn, Shaw Project Comt DC, 1975-79; chmn bd, Neighborhood Develop Ctr UPO, 1975-77; E Central Civic Assoc DC. **Military Serv:** USN, musician 3/c 1944-46; Am Theater Med & Pres Commendations, 1946.

FIELDS, SAVOYNNE MORGAN
Counselor, school administrator. **Personal:** Born May 26, 1950, Rocky Mount, NC; daughter of Charlie and Hazel C Brown; divorced. **Educ:** NC A&T State Univ, BS psych, 1972, MS guid, 1979. **Career:** Pub Libr High Pt NC, libr asst III, 1975-79; La State Univ Eunice, counsr, coord, 1979-82, minority recruiter, 1982-88, career placement coord, 1988-. **Orgs:** ASAP, 1979-, LAHSRP 1982-; coord, LSUE's Black History Activities, 1982-; founding mem, LADE, 1982-; NAUW 1983-; ACPA 1984-, AACD 1984; NAUW Historian, 1986-; past recording & corresponding sec, Chat-A-While Inc. **Honors/Awds:** First Black Recruiter, Louisiana State Univ, Eunice, 1982-; Matron of the Year, Little Zion Baptist Church, 1984; Little Zion BC Matrons President's Award, 1985; LADE Developmental Educ, LSUE, 1986; Outstanding Educator, Chat-A-While Club, 1987; Outstanding Developmental Educator, LSUE, LADE, 1988; Woman of the Year, NAUW, 1988. **Business Addr:** Coordinator, La State Univ Eunice, Career & Placement Ctr, PO Box 1129, Eunice, LA 70535, **Business Phone:** (318)457-7311.

FIELDS, STANLEY
Insurance agent. **Personal:** Born Sep 12, 1930, Detroit, MI; married Mamie Joan Grant; children: Veta Gabrielle & Scott Grant. **Educ:** Wayne State Univ, BA, 1956, MA, 1960. **Career:** Detroit Bd Educ, art instr, 1956-83; EIT, liaison person, 1974; Mayor's Comn Human Resources Develop, project FAST, 1967; Am Mutual Life Ins Co, ins agent, 1972-; Alexander Hamilton Life Ins Co, agent, registered rep, 1970-74; Multivest Investment Co, rep, 1974-75; N Am Life & Casualty Co, agent, 1975; World Wide Cycling Asn, Detroit area, dir, 1974-75; independent auctioneer, 1974-; direct sales, distributorship & world trade, 1970-; subcontractor, hardwood fls, 1942-75; Long Term Care Ins, consult, 1997; Water Systs Develop Corp, int corp rep; Conseco, ins rep, 1998; Am Travellers Life Ins, ins rep, 1998; TransAmerica Occidental Life, ins rep, 1998; Nat Group Underwriters, ins rep, 1998; GE Capital Assurance, insu rep, 1998; Real Estate One, real estate salesperson; Pre-Paid Legal Serv, independent rep. **Orgs:** Consult, Model Cities Educ Component, 1972-; bd dirs, Uplift-Harper House, 1970-71; Metro Distributors, 1972-; bd dirs, Detroit Pub Schs Art Teachers Club, 1972-73; vp, bd dirs, Wayne State Univ Art Educ Alumni, 1973-74; treasurer, First Nighter, 1970-; Friends Belle Isle, 1974-; Chequemates, 1970-73; Set Inc, 1955-75; Motor City Yacht Club, 1974-; Family Motor Coach Asn, Detroit chap, 1974-; judge, Detroit Edison Mich Chronicle Lighting Contest, 1972, Block Club Beautification Contest, 1975; US-Arab Chamber Com, 1976-98; Alpha Phi Alpha, Gamma Lambda Chap, 1986-98; Booker T Wash Bus Asn; Alpha Develop Corp, pres; bd dir, Brush Park Citizen's Dist Coun, 1987-93. **Honors/Awds:** X-Country Team, Wayne, 1948; hon lectr, Univ Detroit, 1969-70; individual record holder, Champion X-Country Run, Detroit Pub Schs, 1974; Dirty Dozen Award, Alpha Phi Alpha, 1991, Man of the Year; Positive Image Award, Brush Park Cultural Comn, 1994; US-Arab Chamber Com; Washington DC Award, 1996; Outstanding Service and Dedication to the Detroit West Siders, Detroit West Siders, 1996. **Military Serv:** AUS, 1952-54. **Home Addr:** 4290 Fullerton St, Detroit, MI 48238.

FIELDS, VALERIE K
Chief executive officer. **Personal:** Born in Raleigh, NC. **Educ:** Univ NC, Chapel Hill, BA, jour & mass commun; Covenant Bible Inst, Raleigh, NC, BTh, Mth, 2007. **Career:** Onyx Greeting Cards, owner; VK Fields & Co, chief exec officer, 1997-; Sch Jour & Mass Commn, Univ NC-Chapel Hill, adj prof, currently. **Orgs:** Bd mem, Literacy Coun Wake County; vpres mkt, Nat Black MBA Asn; bd mem, Greater Raleigh Chamber Commerce; founder, Miracle Ministries Inc; bd dir, Christian Career & Bus Women Am. **Honors/Awds:** Women in Business Award, Triangle Business Journal, 2006; Women in Business Award & Excellence in Mentoring Award, RBC Centura Bank, 2007; Outstanding Volunteer Award, Southeast Raleigh Assembly, 2007; Organization's '40 Under 40' Leadership Award; Young Adult Leadership Award, Womens Forum of NC; Lamplighter Award, McDonald's Corp & Radio One. **Special Achievements:** Christian novel: Forbidden Fruit. **Business Addr:** Chief Executive Officer, VK Fields & Co, 5 West Hargett St Suite 308, Raleigh, NC 27601, **Business Phone:** (919)829-5951.

FIELDS, WILLIAM I, JR.
Association executive, vice president (organization). **Personal:** Born May 4, 1944, Frankfort, KY; son of William I Fields, Sr and Kathryn Fields; married Faye Ford, Mar 29, 1974. **Educ:** Ky State Col, Frankfort KY, BS, 1966; Univ Louisville, Louisville, KY, MS, 1971. **Career:** Community Action Comn, Cincinnati, OH, coord field serv, 1971-72; Community Coun, Cincinnati, OH, planning assoc, 1972-74; Community Chest, Cincinnati, OH, assoc dir planning, 1974-77; United Community Planning Corp, Boston, MA, assoc exec vpres, 1978-81; ATE Mgt, Ridayh, Saudi Arabia, dir admin & personnel, 1981-83; United Way Am, Washington, DC, vpres & dir, 1983-90, regional vpres, 1990; Am Soc Training & Develop, Currently. **Orgs:** Vpres, Health Planning Coun Greater Boston, 1979-81; Nat Forum Black Pub Admin, 1984-86; Big Bros Greater Wash, 1985-86; Orgn New Equality, 1985-; Literacy Vol Ill, 1990-. **Honors/Awds:** Outstanding Young Men in America, US Jaycees, 1980; Henry M Smith Award, 1990; Quest for Excellence Award, United Way Am, 1992. **Military Serv:** AUS, spec-4, 1967-69. **Business Addr:** Vice President Membership & Client Service, American Society for Training and Development, 1640 King St, Alexandria, VA 22313-2043, **Business Phone:** (703)683-8100.

FIERCE, HUGHLYN F.
Banker, president (organization). **Personal:** Born in Brooklyn, NY; son of Millus and Helen; married Jewel; children: Holly, Heather, Brooke. **Educ:** Morgan State Univ, BA, econ; NY Univ, MBA, finance, APC, finance. **Career:** Banker (retired), President; Chase Manhattan Bank, asst br mgr trainee, com loan officer, vpres, sr vpres, 1984-94; Freedom Nat Bank, NY, pres, 1974-77; NY Univ, adj prof finance; Pace Univ Lubin Sch Bus; Jazz Lincoln Ctr, pres & chief exec officer, currently. **Orgs:** Bd Scudder Charitable Found; hon trustee, Am Mus Natural Hist, NY; Bd Marymount Manhattan Col; NY State Comptroller's Invest Adv Comn, NY State Common Retirement Fund; Baltic Am Enterprise Fund; bd dirs, Parsons Brinkerhoff Inc. **Honors/Awds:** Hon Doctor of Laws, Morgan State Univ; Banker of the Yr, Urban Bankers Coalition Inc; Black Enterprise Achievement Award. **Business Phone:** (212)258-9800.*

FIERCE, MILFRED C.
Educator. **Personal:** Born Jul 6, 1937, Brooklyn, NY. **Educ:** Wagner Col, BA, bus econ, 1960, MS, sec educ, 1967; Columbia Univ, MA, MPhil, PhD. **Career:** Curtis High Sch; Vassar Col, dir Black Studies, 1969-71; Hunter Col, prof,1973-81; Brooklyn Col, City Univ NY, Dept African Studies, chair(retired), 1982-88. **Orgs:** Exec dir, Asn Black Found Exec Inc, 1976; NY St Col Proficiency Exam Comt African & Afro-Am Hist, fall, 1976; res dir, Study Comn US Policy toward SAfrica, 1979; African-Am Teachers Asn; African Heritage Studies Asn; Asn Study Afro- Am Life & Hist; Am Hist Asn; Orgn Am Historians; consult, Ford Found supported study group Southern Africa; Coun Foreign Rels, 1995. **Honors/Awds:** Southern Historical Association Award, NDEA, 1965; EPDA, 1969; delegate,Int Congress Africanists, 1973; recipient Nat Endowment for the Humanities Fellowship, City Univ NY, 1976; Wagneroco's Athletic Hall of Fame inductee, 1997. **Special Achievements:** First dir, Black Studies, Vassar col. **Military Serv:** AUS, 1960-63. **Home Addr:** 835 Herkimer St, Brooklyn, NY 11233, **Home Phone:** (718)735-5932. *

FIFTY CENT (CURTIS JAMES JACKSON, III)
Singer, actor. **Personal:** Born Jul 6, 1976, Queens, NY; son of Sabrina Jackson; children: Marquise. **Career:** Albums: Get Rich or Die Tryin', 2003, 2005; The New Breed; In da Club, 2003; 21 Questions, 2003; P.I.M.P, 2003; The Massacre, 2005; Window Shopper, 2005; Hustler's Ambition, 2006; Date Movie, 2006; Little Man, 2006; Films: 50 Cent: Bulletproof, 2005; Get Rich or Die Tryin', 2005; Home of the Brave, 2006; The Ski Mask Way, 2006; Righteous Kill, 2006; The Ski Mask Way, writer, 2008. **Honors/Awds:** MTV Video Music Awards, Best Rap Video, Best New Artist in a Video, 2003; five World Music Awards, 2003; American Music Awards, Favorite Male Artist, Favorite Album, 2003. **Special Achievements:** Voted 8 on VH1's 100 Hottest Hotties. **Business Addr:** Rap Musician, c/o Shady & Interscope Records, 2220 Colorado Ave, Santa Monica, CA 90404, **Business Phone:** (310)865-1000.

FIGURES, DEON JUNIEL
Football player. **Personal:** Born Jan 10, 1970, Bellflower, CA. **Educ:** Univ Colo, sociology & criminol, 1993. **Career:** Pittsburgh Steelers, defensive back, 1993-96; Jacksonville Jaguars, 1997-98.

FIGURES, THOMAS H
Lawyer. **Personal:** Born Aug 6, 1944, Mobile, AL; son of Coleman and Augusta Mitchell; married Janice; children: Nora & Thomas Anthony. **Educ:** Bishop State Jr Col, Assoc Sci, 1964; AL State Univ, BS, bus admin, 1966; IND Univ, MBA, 1968; Univ Ill, JD, 1971. **Career:** Exxon Corp, atty & asst secy, 1971-75; Westchester City, NY, asst dist atty, 1975-76; Mobile Co, AL, asst dist atty, 1976-78; temp probate judge, 1999-; Southern Dist AL, asst US atty, 1978-85; Figures, Ludgood & Figures, partner, 1985-88; Thomas H. Figures, atty law, 1988-; munic, judge, 1988; Mobile Co Circuit Ct, referee, 1988-89; Sate AL, spec asst atty gen, 1992. **Orgs:** State Bars AL & NY, Fed Bars; US Supreme Ct; US Ct Appeals; US Dist C; Bar Asns AL State Bar; Nat Bar Asn Mobile Co AL; vice chmn, Mobile Co Dem Conf, 1976-78, chmn, 1989-; Mobile Comm Action Inc, 1976-80; grad, Leadership Mobile, 1978; NAACP; Omega Psi Phi; Nat Asn Bond Attys 1985-; Am Judges Asn, 1995-; mem, bd trustees, AL State Univ, 1998-. **Honors/Awds:** Outstanding Young Men Am, 1973; Community Leaders & Noteworthy Am, 1977; Outstanding Community Service Award, 1977; Christian Community Award, 1984; Citizen of the Year, Omega Psi Phi Fraterity, 1990. **Home Addr:** 6120 Palomino Dr N, Mobile, AL 36693. **Business Addr:** Attorney, Thomas H Figures, 212 S Lawrence St, Mobile, AL 36602, **Business Phone:** (251)433-0416.

FIGURES, VIVIAN DAVIS
State government official. **Personal:** Born Jan 24, 1957, Mobile, AL; married Michael A (deceased); children: Akil Michael, Shomari Coleman & Jelani Anthony. **Educ:** Univ New Haven, Conn, BS; Jones Sch Law, Montgomery. **Career:** Perfect Print, Inc, pres, owner; Mobile, AL, city councilwoman, 1993-97; Ala State Senate, senator, 1997-; Figures Legacy Educ Found, pres & chief exec officer, currently. **Orgs:** Member-at-large, Dem Nat Comt; del, Dem Nat Conv, 1984, 1988; elected mem, Ala State Dem Exec Comt, 1986-; Ala New S Coalition; State Ala Hwy Safety Comn; adv bd, Ala Alcoholic Beverage Control Bd; several

Senate Comts; Ala Women's Comn; Metrop Mobile Young Men Christian Asn; bd mem, Big Brothers & Big Sisters Prog; bd mem, Homeless Coalition Mobile Inc; bd mem, Drug Ed Coun; Green Grove Missionary Baptist Church; vchmn, Senate's Local del & Vet Mil Affairs comt; bd mem, Mobile Area Chamber Com; Mobile Area Educ Found; bd mem, Habitat Humanity; bd mem, Salvation Army; adv bd, Ala Alcoholic Beverage Control Bd; Ala New S Coalition; bd mem, Mobile Area Educ Found, currently. **Honors/Awds:** Business Woman of the Year, Minority Bus Develop Ctr, 1986. **Business Phone:** (334)242-7871.

FILER, KELVIN DEAN
Superior court judge. **Personal:** Born Nov 25, 1955, Compton, CA; son of Maxcy and Blondell; divorced; children: Brynne Ashley, Kree Donalyn. **Educ:** Univ Calif, Santa Cruz, BA, 1977; Univ Calif, Berkeley, JD, 1980. **Career:** Dep state pub defender, 1980-82; pvt pract, atty, 1982-; Super Ct, comnr, 2000-02; Munic Ct Compton, CA, comnr; Super Ct, Compton, judge, currently. **Orgs:** bd trustees, Compton Unified Sch Dist, 1981-93; bd dirs, Compton Chamber Com, 1984-; pres, Compton Chamber Com, 1988-89; vpres, Compton Chamber Com; S Cent Bar Asn; Compton Br, Nat Asn Advan Colored People; Calif State Bar; Am Bar Asn; Nat Bar Asn; Calif Asn Black Lawyers. **Honors/Awds:** Outstanding Comm Support, Compton Police Dept, 1985; Black Family of the Yr, Coca-Cola Bottling Co, Los Angeles, 1988; Award of Honor, Los Angeles City Bd Supv, 1989; Martin Luther King Drum Major Award, Compton Youth Action Ctr, 1990; Spec Serv Mem, S Cent Bar Asn, 1993. **Special Achievements:** Successfully argued case before CA Supreme Court resulting in a unanimous opinion (People vs Taylor 1982 31 Cal 3d 483). **Business Addr:** Judge, Superior Court, 200 W Compton Blvd, Compton, CA 90220.*

FILES, LOLITA
Writer, manager. **Personal:** Born Jan 1, 1964?, Fort Lauderdale, FL. **Educ:** Univ Fla, broadcast jour. **Career:** KinderCare Learning Ctrs, nat property mgr, 1991; Books: Scenes from a Sistah, 1997; Getting to the Good Part, 1999; Blind Ambitions, 2000; Child of God, 2001; Tastes Like Chicken, 2004; Sex.lies.murder. fame, 2006. **Business Addr:** Writer, c/o Simon & Schuster, 1230 Ave of the Americas, New York, NY 10020.*

FILLYAW, LEONARD DAVID
Educator, law enforcement officer. **Personal:** Born Jun 25, 1939, Brooklyn, NY; son of John David and Rose Rosalind; married Willie M Tate Fillyaw, Jan 26, 1964; children: Sharon, Denise, Tyrone David, MD. **Educ:** JohnJay Col Criminal Justice, AA, 1972, BA, 1973; Dowling Col, MEd, 1980; Liquid Oxygen Missile Sch. **Career:** Educator (retired); Brooklyn Union Gas Co, co rep, 1962-64; NY City Transit Police, police officer, 1966-97; NY City Police Acad, police instr, Social Sci Dept; Cent Islip Sch Dist, teacher, 1979. **Orgs:** Guardians Police Asn, 1964-; NCP, 1984-; UNCF, 1986-; Southern Poverty Law Ctr, 1984-; bd trustees, Cent Islip Libr; bd trustees, Cent Suffolk Libr; trustee, Suffolk County Coop Libr Syst. **Honors/Awds:** Robert Gaffney African Heritage Award, Suffolk County; 4 Meritorious Medals, 2 Hon Mentions, Unit Citation Award, 14 Outstanding Serv Awards, NY City Transit Police. **Special Achievements:** Essay, "Juvenile Deliquency: A Sociological Approach for a Cure," NY City Police Academy Social Science Department; Ran for Suffolk County Legislature, polled 32 percent; founded the first delegation of the Nat Asn Advan Colored People Islip Town Youth Council; first Afr American to serve on Cent Islip Library Board of Trustees; traveled to France, Germany, Britain, Italy, Belgium, Greece, Caribbean, Venezuela, China; instrumental in electing Phil Ramas 1st Hispanic assemblyman in Suffolk County. **Military Serv:** USY, sp-4c, 1959-63. **Home Addr:** 203 Leaf Ave, Central Islip, NY 11722, **Home Phone:** (516)234-0872. *

FINCH, GREGORY MARTIN
Lawyer. **Personal:** Born Sep 14, 1951, Madera, CA; son of Isaac and Deloma Dillard; married; children: Damon, Megan, Christopher. **Educ:** Univ CA, BA Soc & Art, 1974; McGeorge Sch Law, JD, 1979. **Career:** atty, currently. **Orgs:** Deleg, State Bar Conv, 1983; pres, Wiley Manuel Law Asn, 1994; Active 20 & 30 Club 1; pres, 1989; secy, Natomas Planning Adv Coun; chmn, Small Bus Advocacy Comn, Sacramento Chamber Com; bd mem, Child & Family Inst, 1989-99; pres, Active 20 & 30, United States & Canada, 1990; AME Regional chmn, World Coun Serv Clubs, 1993; Sutter Hosp, found bd; Rotary Club Sacramento; Rotary Club Sacramento, bd dirs, 2000-; YMCA Greater Sacramento, bd mem, 1996-; bd pres, YMCA, 1999-; bd dirs, Sierra Adoption Servs, 1999-; Suiter Hosp Community Benifil comts; Suiter Hosp Med Affairs comt. **Honors/Awds:** Rookie of the Year, Active 20 & 30 Chapter 1, 1985. **Military Serv:** USAF, Reserve staff sgt, 6 years. **Business Phone:** (916)924-0309.*

FINCH, DR. JANET M
Educator, chairperson. **Personal:** Born Jun 4, 1950, Nashville, TN; daughter of James W and Helen Ardis; married Harold William Finch; children: Harold & Toria. **Educ:** Tenn State Univ, BA, math, 1972, MAEd, 1978; Vanderbilt Univ, EdD, 1985. **Career:** Nashville State Tech, educ specialist 1977-80, proj dir, 1980-81, dept head develop studies, 1981-85, asst dean, 1981-86; Middle Tenn State Univ, actg vpres, 1985-87; Univ Ky, asst vice chancellor, 1986; Am Coun Educ fel, 1986-87; Motlow State Community Col, Tullahoma TN, dean acad affairs 1988-91; exec asst pres, 1991; Belmont Univ, dir, opportunities admis, 1992-94; State Community Col, pres, 1994-96; Metropolitan Community Col, 1996-98; Metro Schs, maths teacher, 1998-2000; Tenn State Univ, Dept Educ Admin, assoc prof & dept head, 2000-. **Orgs:** Secy, Temple Child Care Develop Ctr, 1984-85; youth choir dir & pianist 15th Ave Baptist Church, 1985-; Youth Comt YWCA; hon mem, Phi Delta Kappa; Nat Educ Asn; Tn Educ Asn; Nat Asn Sec Sch Prin; Am Coun Educ; Am Coun Fel. **Honors/Awds:** Leader of the 80's Fund for Improving Post Secondary Educ, 1984; selected to participate in exec leadership institute-sponsored by League for Innovation 1989. **Home Addr:** 221 Rising Sun Terr, Old Hickory, TN 37138.

FINGAZ, STICKY (KIRK JONES)
Rap musician, actor. **Personal:** Born Apr 3, 1970, Queens, NY. **Career:** Actor, singer, producer; Rap group ONYX, mem; Albums: Bacdafu cup, 1993; All We Got Iz Us, 1995; Shut 'Em Down, 1998; Black trash: The Auto biography of Kirk Jones, 2000; Bacdafu cup Part II, 2002; Triggernometry, 2003; Cold Case Files, 2003; Decade, 2003; Films: Clockers, 1995; Dead Presidents, 1995; Ride, 1998; New Yorker, Le, 1998; Game Day, 1999; In Too Deep, 1999; Love Goggles, 1999; In Too Deep, 1999; Black & White, 1999; Next Friday, 2000; Boricua's Bond, 2000; The Price of Air, 2000; Lock down, 2000; TrueVinyl, 2000; The Playaz Court, 2000; Lift, 2001; MacArthur Park, 2001; Flossin, 2001; LAX, 2002; Reality Check, 2002; Hot Parts (voice), 2003; Leprechaun: Back 2 Tha Hood (voice), 2003; Ride Or Die, 2003; Malibooty, 2003; Flight of the Phoenix, 2004; Gas, 2004; Over There, 2005; A Day in the Life, actor & producer, 2007; Karma, Confessions & Holi, 2008; Dough Boys, 2009; Order of Redemption, 2009; Steppin: The Movie, 2009; A Day in the Life, 2009. TV series: "New York Undercover", 1995-97; "413 Hope St", 1997; "Nash Bridges", 1999; "The Parkers", 1999; "18 Wheels of Justice", 2000; "The Twilight Zone", 2002; Just Cause, 2002; "The Shield", 2002-06; "Carnivores", 2002; Platinum, 2003; "Inferno", 2003; "Blood & Water", 2004; "Over There", 2005; House of the Dead 2, 2005; CSI: Miami, 2005; "Orphans", 2005; "Conclave", 2006; "Monsters", 2006; "Blade: The Series", 2006; "Law & Order: Criminal Intent", 2007; "Tell Me You Love Me", 2007; "The Beast", 2009; "Burn Notice", 2009. **Business Phone:** (310)859-4000.*

FINLAYSON, ARNOLD ROBERT
Lawyer, administrator. **Personal:** Born Jun 30, 1963, Washington, DC; son of Joseph Arnold Jr and Patricia Glenn. **Educ:** Bowie State Col, BS, 1985; Howard Univ Sch Law, JD, 1989. **Career:** US Dept State, procurement analyst, 1987-90; Hon George W Mitchell, assoc judge, DC Super Ct; judicial law clerk; 1990-92; Shaw, Pittman, Potts & Trowbridge, govt contracts assoc, 1992; Freedom Info Act, Off Documents & Admin Issuances, adminr, dir, currently. **Orgs:** DC Bar; Bar Commonwealth PA; US Ct Appeals Fed Circuit; Am Bar Asn; Kappa Alpha Psi Fraternity Inc. **Honors/Awds:** Wiley A Branton Leadership Award, Howard Univ Sch Law, 1989; American Jurisprudence Award, Prof Responsibility, 1989; American Jurisprudence Award, Nat Moot Ct, 1989. **Special Achievements:** Co-Author, Financing Govt Contracts, 1993. **Home Addr:** 701 Pa Ave NW Suite 1209, Washington, DC 20004, **Home Phone:** (202)737-1787. **Business Phone:** (202)727-7882.

FINLAYSON, WILLIAM E.
Physician. **Personal:** Born Sep 1, 1924, Manatee, FL; married Edith; children: Reginald, James. **Educ:** Morehouse Col, BS, 1948; Meharry Med Col, MD, 1953. **Career:** Physician (retired); Milwaukee Med Complex, teacher; pvt pract; Aurora Med Group, obstet & gynec. **Orgs:** Milwaukee Med Soc; House Del Wis Med Soc; past pres, Milwaukee Gynec Soc; St Joseph's Hosp; Mt Sinai Med Ctr; Deaconess Hosp; Cream City Med Soc; Am Col Surgery; fel Am Col Obstet & Gynec; Med Col Wis; bd dirs, chmn, N Milwaukee State Bank; bd dirs, Southeastern Wis Health Syst Agency; past pres, Alpha Phi Alpha; Frontiers Int; life mem, Nat Asn Advan Colored Poeple; Urban League; We-Milwaukeeans; past pres, YMCA local br; Greater Galilee Baptist Church. **Military Serv:** AUS, lt, 1943-46. *

FINLEY, BETTY M
Educator. **Personal:** Born Aug 3, 1941, Edison, GA; married Isaac T Jr; children: Michael. **Educ:** Tuskegee Inst, BS, 1962; Framingham State Col, MEd, 1977; Simmons Col Boston, MA, 1986. **Career:** E St Louis Sch Bd, eng teacher, 1967-68; Pemberton Township Sch Bd, NJ, eng teacher, 1968-70; Dept Pub Welfare Div Child Guardianship Boston, social worker, 1970-72; Metrop Educ Training Dover, Mass, coordr minority stud, 1973-74; Dover Sherbon Sch Bd, teacher, 1974-; Simmons Col, Ellen Raskin fel, 1985. **Orgs:** Comt mem, Headmaster's Adv Comn, 1981-82; Evaluation Team New England Assoc Schs & Cols, 1982, 1986; Nat Coun Teachers Eng, 1984-87; organizer, Operation Foodbasket, 1984; bd mem, C Lit Found, 1987-88. **Business Addr:** Teacher, Dover Sherborn School Board, Department of English, 137 Farm St, Dover, MA 02030, **Business Phone:** (617)785-1085.

FINLEY, DR. D. LINELL, SR.
Educator. **Personal:** Born Mar 27, 1948, Gunnison, MS; son of Celestine Hayes Finley and George Finley Sr (deceased); married Janet D Duff, Jun 11, 1983; children: Sharriette & D. **Educ:** Jackson State Univ, Jackson, MS, BA, 1972; Atlanta Univ, Atlanta, Ga, MA, 1974, PhD, 1981. **Career:** Atlanta Univ, Ford Found fel, 1972-75, asst prof, coordr polit sci prog, 1975-88, coordr, 1985-88; Auburn Univ Montgomery, Montgomery, Ala, adj assoc prof polit sci, 1988; Univ Ala, Grade Prog, Maxwell AFB, adj fac, 1991, asst prof, currently; South lawn Baptist Church, pastor. **Orgs:** Pi Gamma Mu Int Hon Soc Social Sci, 1978; Kappa Delta Pi Edu Hon Soc, 1982; Ala Polit Sci Asn, 1980-; Phi Delta Kappa Prof Educ Hon Fraternity,1986; pres, post sec div, Ala Educ Asn, 1990-91; bd dir, Ala Educ Asn, 1990-91; bd dir, Cent Ala Laubach Literacy Coun, 1990-93; Nat Conf Black Polit Scientists, 1977-;; pres, Capitol City Civitan, Montgomery, Ala,1990-91; Thirty Second Deg Mason, Phi Beta Sigma Fraternity Inc. **Home Phone:** (334)279-5518. **Business Addr:** Assistant Professor, Auburn University Montgomery, Political Science and Public Administration, 210L Goodwyn Hall, Montgomery, AL 36117-3596, **Business Phone:** (334)244-3741.

FINLEY, MICHAEL H
Basketball player. **Personal:** Born Mar 6, 1973, Melrose Park, IL; married Rebekah, Jan 1, 2006; children: Micah. **Educ:** Wis State Univ, attended 1995. **Career:** Phoenix Suns, forward, 1995-97; Dallas Mavericks, forward, 1997-2005; San Antonio Spurs, forward, currenlty; Finley & Friends, founder. **Orgs:** Make-A-Wish Found. **Honors/Awds:** NBA All-Rookie First Team, 1995-96; 2-Time NBA All-Star. **Business Addr:** Professional Basketball Player, San Antonio Spurs, 1 AT&T Ctr 777 Sports St, San Antonio, TX 78219, **Business Phone:** (210)444-5000.

FINLEY, SKIP
Executive. **Personal:** Born Jul 23, 1948, Ann Arbor, MI; son of Mildred V. Johnson Finley and Ewell W. Finley; married Karen M. Woolard, May 6, 1971; children: Kharma Isis, R. Kristin. **Educ:** Northeastern Univ, Boston MA, 1971. **Career:** Skifin Gallery, Boston MA, owner, 1970-71; WHDH-TV, Boston MA, floor dir, 1971; WSBK-TV, Boston MA, floor mgr, asst dir, producer, 1971-72; WRKO-Radio, Boston MA, acct exec, 1972-73; Humphrey, Browning, MacDougall Advert, Boston MA, acct mgr, 1973-74; Sheridan Broadcasting Corp, sales mgr WAMO AM/FM, 1974-75, gen mgr WAMO AM/FM, 1975-76, vpres/gen mgr SBC Radio Div, 1976-77, vpres, corp off, 1976-82, eastern sales mgr, 1977-79, exec vpres/gen mgr, 1979-81, pres, 1981-82; Albimar Omaha Ltd Partnership/Albimar Mgt Inc, Boston MA, pres & gen partner, 1982-95; KEZO AM-FM, Omaha, NE, gen partner, 1983-88; KDAB-FM, Ogden/Salt Lake City, UT, gen partner, 1985-90; WKYS-FM, Wash, DC, pres/gen mgr, 1988-95; AMR Urban Radio Networks, chief exec officer /chief Operating Officer, 1995-98; Answers & Solutions, pres, 1999-03; Inner City Broadcasting Corp, vice chmn, 2003-. **Orgs:** Nat Thespian Society; bd overseers, Vineyard Open Land Found; Martha's Vineyard Rod and Gun Club; Wash Area Broadcasters Asn; Nat Asn Broadcasters, 1990-94, vice chair 1993-94; bd, Radio Advert Bur; dir, Nat Asn Black Owned Broadcasters; 1977-95; bd, The Advertising CNL, 1998-99. **Honors/Awds:** Excellence in Media Award, Natl Assn of Media Women, 1981; Communicator of the Year Award, Wash Area Media Orgn, 1982; New Horizons Award, DC Gen Hosp, 1990; Advocacy in Education Award, DC Pub Sch, 1990; Outstanding Performance/Executive of the year, Radio Bus Report, 1990; Men & Their Children Award, Wash Urban League, 1993; author of numerous articles on media related subjects; Best Overall Broadcaster/ Radio, Ink Mag, 1994. **Special Achievements:** One of Top 25 African Americans in Radio, Radio Ink magazine, 1999. *

FINN, JOHN WILLIAM
School administrator. **Personal:** Born Apr 30, 1942, Lexington, KY; married Joan Washington; children: Jarell Wendell & Janelle Wynice. **Educ:** BS, 1966; MBA, 1971; taking courses toward PhD in higher educ. **Career:** Gary Ind Schs, teacher, coach, recreation leader, 1967-69; Anderson Boys Club, activity dir, 1968-69; Univ Mich, asst dir housing, 1969-71, assoc dir housing, 1977-86; Diversified Educ Products, Gary, IN, pres, 1986-, admin asst supt, 1991-. **Orgs:** Mich Housing & Food Serv Officers; Mich Col Personnel Asn; Nat Asn Stud Personnel Admins; Asn Col & Univ Housing Officials; Am Asn Higher Educ; Am Asn Jr Col; United Fund; Boys Club Am; Nat Asn Advan Colored People; Kappa Alpha Psi Frat Inc; pres, Ann Arbor Sportsmen; Black Faculty & Staff Asn. **Honors/Awds:** All City-All State Football, 1968-69; Outstanding Young Men of Amer. **Special Achievements:** First Black in Administrative position in Housing Office Univ of Michigan. **Business Addr:** School Administrator, 620 E 10 Pl, Gary, IN 46402.*

FINN, MICHELLE
Athlete. **Personal:** Married Leroy Russel Burrell; children: 2. **Educ:** Oak Ridge High Sch. **Career:** Track & field athlete. **Honors/Awds:** Gold medal, Barcelona Olympics, 400 Meter Relay, 1992. **Business Phone:** (317)261-0500.

FINN, ROBERT GREEN, JR.
Engineer. **Personal:** Born Jan 24, 1941, Lexington, KY; married Mary E Johson; children: Leatrice, Lezelle, Lechrista. **Educ:** Morehead State Univ, BS, 1963. **Career:** IBM, spec engineering

request coord. **Orgs:** Coun secound Dist; past pres, PTA; vpres, Nat Advan Asn Colored People; Mason; Shriner; Jaycee; mem exec bd, Blue Grass Boy Scouts; mem exec coun, Morehead Alumnus; mem, Nat Honor Soc, 1959; agent, DADS, currently. **Honors/Awds:** DAR Award, 1959. **Home Addr:** 655 Georgetown St, Lexington, KY 40511, **Home Phone:** (859)254-3618. **Business Addr:** Agent, DADS Inc, 655 Georgetown St, Lexington, KY 40511, **Business Phone:** (859)254-3618.*

FINNEY, ERNEST A., JR.
Judge. **Personal:** Born Mar 23, 1931, Smithfield, VA; son of Ernet A Finney Sr and Collen Godwin; married Frances Davenport; children: Ernest III, Lynn, Jerry. **Educ:** Claflin Col, BA (cum Laude), 1952; SC State Col Sch Law, JD, 1954; Nat Col State Judiciary Reno NV, Grad, 1977; NY Univ Sch Law, sr appellate judges sem, 1985. **Career:** Judge (retired); Sumter County Courthouse 3rd Judicial Circuit SC, resident judge, 1976-85; SC Supreme Ct, assoc justice, 1985-94, chief justice, 1994-00; SC State Univ, interim pres, 2002. **Orgs:** Chmn bd, Buena Vista Devel Corp; Am Bar Asn; SC Bar Asn; Nat Bar Asn; Sumter County Bar Ass; Am Judicature Soc; Nat Asn Advan Colored People; Alpha Phi Alpha; United Meth Church Gen Coun Fin & Admin Legal Responsibilities Comn; chmn bd trustees, Claflin Col; adv comt, Univ SC Sch Law. **Honors/Awds:** Distinguished Serv, City Sumter, 1970; SC Coun Human Rights, 1972; Alumnus Award, SC State Col, 1973; Civil Libertarian of the Year, ACLU, 1973; Citizen of the Year, Omega Psi Phi, 1973; Bedford-Stuyvesant NY Jaycee Award, 1974; Claflin Col Politic & Alumni Award, 1974; SC Council Human Rights James M Dabbs Award, 1974; Selected to rep SC at Am Bar Asn Criminal Code Revision Conf, San Diego, 1975; Wateree Comn Action Inc Serv, 1975; SC Nat Asn Advan Colored People Native Son, 1976; Delta Sigma Leadership Serv, 1976; Serv of Mankind Award, Emmanuel Meth Church, 1977; HHD, Claflin Col, 1977; LLD, Citadel; LLD, Johnson C. Smith Univ; LLD, Morris College; DHL, Col Charleston; DHL, SC State Univ; Nat Asn Equal Oppt Higher Educ, 1986; Distinguished Alumni of the Year Award, Claflin Col, SC State Col; Alpha Phi Alpha Award of Achievement, 1986; SC Order of the Palmetto, 1994; National Black College Hall of Fame, 1998. **Special Achievements:** The first African-American Supreme Court Justice appointed to the South Carolina Supreme Court. **Business Addr:** Attorney, Finney Law Firm, 2117 Park St, Sumter, SC 29201.*

FINNEY, DR. ESSEX EUGENE, JR.
Government official. **Personal:** Born May 16, 1937, Michaux, VA; son of Essex Eugene Sr and Etta Francis Burton; married Rosa Ellen Bradley; children: Essex E III & Karen Finney Shelton. **Educ:** VA Polytech Inst, BS, 1959; PA State Univ, MS, 1960; MI State Univ, PhD, 1963. **Career:** Government official (retired); Rocky Mt Arsenal Denver County, br chief, 1963-65; Agr Res Serv USDA, res scientist, 1965-77; Agr Mkt Res Inst, inst chmn, 1972-75; Beltsville Agr Res Ctr, asst dir, 1977-83, assoc dir, 1983-87; North Atlantic Area Asn, Dir, 1987-89; Beltsville Agr Res Ctr, USDA, dir, 1989-92; Agr Res Serv, USDA, assoc admin, 1992-95. **Orgs:** Counman Town Glenarden MD, 1975; sr policy analyst, Off Sci Adv to Pres, 1980-81; bd dirs, Prince George's Chamber Com, 1983-87; pres, Beltsville Org Prof Employees US Dept Agr, 1984-85; Bd Agr, Nat Res Coun, 1997-99. **Honors/Awds:** CRC Press Handbook Transportation & Mkt Agr, 1981; Fellow, Am Soc AgrEngrs, 1983; Award Administration, Gamma Sigma Delta Univ MD, 1985; Outstanding Engineering Alumni Award, Penn St Univ, 1985; Elected, Nat Acad Engr, 1994. **Military Serv:** AUS, Transportation Corps Capt, 1963-65. *

FINNEY, KAREN
Government official. **Career:** Press Off First Lady, dep press secy; Dem Nat Commun Press Off, dir, currently. **Business Phone:** (202)863-8000.*

FINNEY, LEON D., JR.
Association executive. **Personal:** Born Jul 7, 1938, Louise, MS; married Sharon; children: Kristin, Leon III. **Educ:** McCormick Theol Sem, doctor theol, MA, theol studies; Goddard Col, MS, 1974; Nova Univ, PhD, 1978. **Career:** vis Sch Theol, vis prof, 1968-70; chair, Luth Sch Theol, 1969; Univ Chicago, fac lectr, fld instr, 1970-; Fisk Univ, vis lectr, 1970-71; LA State Univ, cons; McCormick Theol Sem, prof, African Am Leadership Studies, 1993-; African Am Leadership Partnership, exec dir, 1993; The Woodlawn Orgn, pres, beginning 2002, chmn & ceo, currently; Univ IL, chair, Biochemical & Infectious Disease Comm, 2002-; Christ Apostolic Church, founder & pastor. **Orgs:** Chicago United; vice chmn, bd dirs, Guaranty Bank & Trust Co; mem, Chicago Assn Com & Ind; mem, Black IL Legis Lobby, 1976-; Chicago Urban League, 1970-; Natl Urban Coalition; deleg, White House Conf Balanced Growth & Small Bus; consult, mem, Urban Develop, Chicago Econ Develop Comm; pres, Chicago Planning Comm; chair, comm adv community, Chicago Transit Auth. **Honors/Awds:** Ford Found Grant, 1970; Cert Merit, Cent State Univ Alumni Assn, 1971; Outstanding Alumni Awd, Hyde Park HS, 1972; Distinguished Educr Award, 1972; Affirmative Action Merit Awd, Breadbasket Commercial Assn, 1973; PACE Award, Pervis Staples, 1973. **Special Achievements:** Chicago Jr Chamber Com, 10 Most Outstanding Young Men, 1970; One of four African Am invited to Israel to study Israeli-Arab Rel, Israeli govt, 1973; Auth, "Neighborhood Econ Develop-Myth or Fact," 1979; co-auth, "Comm Develop Policy Paper Struct Disinvestment: A Prob in Search of a Policy". **Military Serv:** USMC, 1959-63. **Business Addr:** Chairman, Chief Executive Officer, The Woodlawn Orgn, 6040 S Harper Ave, Chicago, IL 60637.*

FINNEY, MICHAEL ANTHONY
Accountant. **Personal:** Born Oct 2, 1956, Flint, MI; married Gina Michelle Mickels. **Educ:** Saginaw Valley State Col, BBA, 1979; Cent Mich Univ, MA. **Career:** Deloitte Haskins & Sells CPA, admin asst, 1978-79; Student Govt Saginaw Valley State Col, pres, 1978-79; J C Penney Co, merchandise mgr, 1979-81; Saginaw Valley State Col, admin rep, 1981-84; Mich Econ Develop Corp Emerging Bus Sectors, vpres, 2000; City Saginaw, asst city mgr; Greater Rochester Enterprise, chief exec officer, pres; Ann Arbor SPARK, pres & chief exec officer, currently. **Orgs:** State dir, Mich Phi Beta Sigma Fraternity, 1979-80; bd dirs, Saginaw Valley State Col Alumni Asn, 1981-; bd dirs, Big Brothers, Big Sisters Saginaw Inc, 1982-83; Saginaw Jaycees, 1984-; Int City Mgrs Asn, Mich City Mgrs Asn. **Honors/Awds:** Outstanding Young Men, Am US Jaycees, 1979; Outstanding Achievement in Black Affairs, SVSC Black Stud Asn, 1983. **Business Addr:** President, Chief Executive Officer, Ann Arbor SPARK, 201 S Div Suite 430, Ann Arbor, MI 48104, **Business Phone:** (734)761-9317.

FINNEY, SARA VERNETTA
Television producer. **Personal:** Born Jan 25, 1957. **Career:** United Paramount Network, Parkers, exec producer, 2004; TV series: "What's Happening Now", 1985; "227", 1985; "Married with Children", 1987; "Moesha", 1996; "The Parkers", 1999-2004; "Mo's House", 2006; "The Game", 2006-07. **Orgs:** Delta Sigma Theta Sorority. **Business Addr:** Executive Producer, c/o United Paramount Network, 11800 Wilshire Blvd, Los Angeles, CA 90025, **Business Phone:** (310)575-7000.*

FINNIE, ROGER L., SR.
Football player. **Personal:** Born Nov 6, 1945, Winder, GA; married Debbie; children: Shannon Monique & Rogers Lewis Jr. **Educ:** Fla A&M Univ, attended 1969. **Career:** New York Jets, offensive tackle, guard, defensive end, tight end, 1969-72; St Louis Cardinals, 1973-78; New Orleans Saints, 1979. **Orgs:** Youth orgn; NFLPA. **Honors/Awds:** Defensive Lineman of Yr; Ebony All-Am, Defensive Lineman; trophy, best offensive line NFL fewer quarterback sacks. **Special Achievements:** Named Pittsburg All-Am, 1968; received game balls, NY Jets, 1969 & 1971.

FISCHER, LISA
Singer. **Personal:** Born in Brooklyn, NY. **Career:** Luther Vandross, back-up singer; Albums: So Intense, Elektra Recs, 1991; Singles: "Glad To Be Alive," 1990; "How Can I Ease the Pain," 1991; "Save Me," 1991; "So Intense," 1992; "Colors of Love," 1993; solo artist, currently. **Honors/Awds:** Soul Train Music Award for Best R&B/Urban Contemporary Single - Female for "How Can I Ease the Pain", 1991; Grammy Award nomination for Best R&B Song for "How Can I Ease the Pain", 1991; Grammy Award for Best Female R&B Vocal Performance for "How Can I Ease the Pain", 1992. **Business Addr:** Vocalist, c/o Atlantic Records, 1290 Ave of the Americas, New York, NY 10104, **Business Phone:** (212)707-2000.

FISCHER, WILLIAM S.
Musician, educator, publisher. **Personal:** Born Mar 5, 1935, Shelby, MS; son of R A Fisher and Willye; married Dolores Labrie; children: Darius, Marc, Bryan & Paul. **Educ:** Xavier Univ, New Orleans, BS; Colo Col, MA; Univ Vienna, Akademie Fur Musik und Darstellende; N western Univ, Cyprus, PhD, meta physics, 1999. **Career:** Xavier Univ, assoc prof, 1962-66; Atlantic Rec, arranger & conductor, 1965-, music dir, 1968-70, rec producer, 1973-74; Newport Col & Cardiff Col, lectr, 1966; NY Pub Sch, 1967-75; NY, publ, 1967-; Arcana Rec, owner, 1971-; Album: Circles, 1971. **Orgs:** Am Fedn Musicians, 1953; Am Soc Composers Authors & Publishers, 1964; Nat Asn Music Educ, 1964; exec dir, Soc Black Composers, 1971-. **Honors/Awds:** Grants: Edger Stern Family Fund Comn, 1963-65; Akademischer Austausdienst W Ger, 1964; Orgn Am States; Pan Am Grant, 1964; New Orleans Phil harmonic Comt, 1964-65; Fulbright Grant, 1965-66; Austrian Govt Grant, 1965; NY Coun Arts, 1971; Nat Endowment Arts, 1971. **Special Achievements:** Commissioned Film Score Elliott, A Feature Film, Back roads of Jackson, WO, 1987; commissioned to write Mass for a Saint, SBS of Bensalem, Pennsylvania, 1988; meditation on Mt St Helens for Orch, Ready Productions, 1990-91; Commission to write MASS, Parish Le Beau Louisiana, First Established, by People of Color, Founded, 1897; New Music for Violin/Saxophone Concertos using computer assimilated orchestra, "The Cross Bronx Concerto" and other CD's, 1995-96; Gazelle for Alvin Ailey Co12 yrs performance feature films for United Artists Inc and Born to Win; Emi: Studios London "Boardwalk". **Military Serv:** USMC, 1956-57. *

FISHBURNE, LAURENCE JOHN
Actor. **Personal:** Born Jul 30, 1961, Augusta, GA; son of Laurence John Jr and Hattie Bell Crawford; married Hajna Moss, Jul 1, 1985 (divorced); children: Langston Issa & Montana Isis; married Gina Torres, Sep 29, 2002; children: Delilah. **Educ:** Lincoln Sq Acad. **Career:** Films include: Apocalyse Now, 1979; Fast Break, 1979; Death Wish II, 1982; Rumble Fish, 1983; The Cotton Club, 1984; The Color Purple, 1985; Quicksilver, 1986; Nightmare on Elm Street III, 1987; Sch Daze, 1988; Red Heat, 1988; King of New York, 1990; Boyz in the Hood, 1991; Cadence, 1991; Deep Cover, 1992; Searching for Bobby Fischer, 1993; What's Love Got To Do With It, 1993; Higher Learning, 1995; Bad Company, 1995; Just Cause, 1995; Othello, 1995; Fled, 1996; Event Horizon, 1997; Hoodlum, 1997, The Matrix, 1999; Osmosis Jones, 2001; Biker Boyz, 2003; The Matrix Reloaded, 2003; Mystic River, 2003; The Matrix Revolutions, 2003; Five Fingers, 2005; Bobby, 2006; The Death & Life of Bobby Z, 2006; TV movies: "Decoration Day," 1990; "Choices," 1992; "The Tuskegee Airmen," 1995; "Before Your Eyes," 1996; "Miss Evers' Boys," 1997; "Always Outnumbered," 1998; "Sex &the Matrix," 2000; TV series: "Pee-Wee's Playhouse," 1986; plays include: August Wilson's Two Train Running; The Lion in Winter, 1999; Assault on Precinct 13, 2005; Akeelah & the Bee, 2006. Producer: TriBeCa, 1993;Hoodlum, 1997; Once in the Life, 2000; Akeelah & the Bee, Mission: Impossible III, 2006; The Death and Life of Bobby Z, TMNT, Fantastic Four: Rise of the Silver Surfer, 2007; Tortured, Days of Wrath, 2008. **Honors/Awds:** Image Award, NAACP, Television Movie, Miniseries or Dramatic SpecialActor, 1998; PGA Golden Laurel Awards; Television Producer of the YearAward in Longform, 1998; Blockbuster Entertainment Award for FavoriteSupporting Actor - Action/Science-Fiction, 2000; MTV Movie Award for Best Fight, 2000; Boston Society of Film Critics Awards for Best Ensemble Cast, 2003; Outstanding Performance by an Actor in a Supporting Role, 2006. **Special Achievements:** First Black to portray Shakespeare's Othello on silver screen. **Business Addr:** Actor, c/o Paradigm, 10100 Santa Monica Blvd Fl 25, Los Angeles, CA 90067.

FISHER, ALMA M
Librarian. **Personal:** Born Dec 22, 1945, Learned, MI; married Eugene. **Educ:** Tougaloo Col, BA, eng, 1967; Dominican Univ; MALS, 1970. **Career:** Chicago Public Sch Syst, teacher, 1967-69; Chicago Pub Libr Sys librn, staff, 1970-72; Tougaloo Col, archivist; Tougaloo Col, sr archivist, 2004. **Orgs:** Am Libr Asn; Mich Libr Asn; Mich Teachers Asn; Black Caucus ALA; Urban League; Nat Asn Advan Colored People; Utica Jr Col Alumni Asn; Soc Am Archivists. **Honors/Awds:** HBCU Arch Internship, 2001. **Business Addr:** Senior Archivist, Tougaloo College, Library, 400 W Co Line Rd, PO Box 39174, Tougaloo, MS 39174.

FISHER, ANTWONE QUENTON
Writer. **Personal:** Born Aug 3, 1959, Ohio; son of Edward Eklins and Eva Mae Fisher; married; children: 2. **Career:** Terminal Island Fed Prison, guard; Sony Pictures Entertainment, security guard; author; Co-author: Finding Fish: A Memoir, 2001; Author: The Antwone Fisher Story (screenplay), 2002; Who Will Cry for the Little Boy?: Poems, 2003; Films: The Antwone Fisher Story, auth & screenwriter, 2004. **Military Serv:** USN, 11 yrs. **Business Addr:** Author, Screenwriter, c/o Author Mail William Morrow, 10 E 53rd St 7th Fl, New York, NY 10022.

FISHER, REV. DAVID ANDREW
Educator, clergy. **Personal:** Born Sep 12, 1958, Columbus, OH; son of Morgan Cecil and Jean Otis Peck. **Educ:** Ohio Dominican Col, Columbus, OH, BA, philos, 1980; Pontifical Gregorian Univ, Rome, Italy, STB, theol, 1983, STL, theol, 1985, STD, 2004. **Career:** St Paul Church, Westerville, OH, assoc pastor, 1985-87; SS Augustine & Gabriel, Columbus, OH, pastor, 1987-90; Ohio Dominican Col, Columbus, OH, prof philos, 1989-; St Joseph Cathedral, Columbus, OH, assoc pastor, 1990-; Columbus State Community Col, Dept Humanities, prof, currently. **Orgs:** Bd trustees, Alzhiemer Asn, 1986-89; bd trustees, St Stephen Comt House, 1988-90. **Honors/Awds:** Pastoral work in Sweden, Diocese of Stockholm, 1988; Seminar Member, The Intl Inst Cult, 1989; Vicar Forane, Northland Vicariate Diocese of Columbus, 1989-90. **Special Achievements:** First African-American to be ordained a priest by a Pope, May 31, 1984; Commendation from Ohio General Assembly, 1989. **Home Addr:** 1945 Ardenrun Way, Columbus, OH 43219, **Home Phone:** (614)253-1039. **Business Addr:** Professor, Columbus State Community College, Humanities Department, 550 E Spring St, PO Box 1609, Columbus, OH 43216-1609, **Business Phone:** (614)287-5056.

FISHER, DEREK LAMAR
Basketball player. **Personal:** Born Aug 9, 1974, Little Rock, AR. **Educ:** Univ Ark-Little Rock, attended 1996. **Career:** Los Angeles Lakers, guard, 1996-2004, 2007-; Golden State Warriors, 2004-06; Utah Jazz, 2006-07. **Orgs:** Ame Cancer Soc; Big Bros Big Sisters. **Honors/Awds:** NBA Sportsmanship Award, 2006-07. **Business Phone:** (310)426-6000.

FISHER, E CARLETON
College teacher. **Personal:** Born Nov 3, 1934, St Louis, MO; children: Victor, Bruce & Vernon. **Educ:** Howard Univ, BS, MS, 1957; Am Univ; Morgan State Univ, EdD, 1986. **Career:** Univ Chicago, numerical analyst, 1957-66; IBM, personnel mgr, 1966-72; Univ Md, exec asst chancellor affirmative action, 1973-77; Notre Dame, exec dir minorities engr, 1977-78; Prudential Ins, dir,

col rels, 1978-80; Affirmative Action, prof math, asst pres. **Orgs:** Kappa Alpha Psi; Am Guild Organists; pres & founder, Md Asn Affirmative Action Officers, 1975-77, 1983-85; goldseker fellow, Morgan State Univ, 1983-85. **Business Addr:** Professor, Anne Arundel Community College, Department of mathematics, 101 College Parkway, Arnold, MD 21012.

FISHER, EDITH MAUREEN
Entrepreneur, librarian, athletic coach. **Personal:** Born Jul 29, 1944, Houston, TX; daughter of Freeman and Ruby Jase. **Educ:** Univ Ill, Urbana IL, MLS, 1972; Queens Col CUNY, Cert Ethnicity & Librarianship, 1975; Univ Pittsburgh, PhD, 1991. **Career:** Univ Calif, San Diego, La Jolla, cent univ libr, 1972-90; Contemporary Black Arts Prog, adj lectr, 1981-90; Univ Calif, Los Angeles, Sch Libr &Info Sci, lectr, 1989; Eval & Training Inst, Los Angeles, CA, consult &tech adv, 1991; Tenge Enterprises, Encinitas, CA, pres, 1991-2001; UC San Diego, librn. **Orgs:** Pres, Black Caucus Am Libr Asn; CLBC-GLA. **Honors/Awds:** President Award, Black Caucus Am Libr Asn, 1990. **Special Achievements:** Author of "What Do I Read Next? Multicultural Literature".

FISHER, DR. EDWARD G
Surgeon. **Personal:** Born Apr 22, 1932, Jamaica; son of Guy O D and Elisa Howell Fisher Dawes; married Judy Ann; children: Yvonne & Ronald. **Educ:** Brooklyn Col, BS, 1956; Howard Univ, MD, 1961. **Career:** Howard Univ, med officer, 1966-68; Operating Rm, Com Hadley Hosp, chmn; Howard Univ Hosp; Freedmens Hosp, instr, 1966-68; Greater SE Comn, active staff privileges; Inst Urban Living Wash, DC, med dir; Hadley Mem Hosp, active attending physician; Full Gospel Church Lord's Missions Int Inc, pastor, currently; pvt prac, currently. **Orgs:** Med Care Evaluation Comn; DC Med Soc; DC Medico-chirugical Soc; Nat Med Asn; AMA & Interns & Residents Asn Freedmens Hosp; Nat Asn Interns & Residents; Political Action Com; Urban League; Hon Med Soc, 1961; Dipl Am Bd Surg; Joint Conf Hadley Hosp; Med Staff Hadley Mem Hosp; bd trustees, Hadley Mem Hosp; Alpha Omega Alpha; co-pastor, Full Gospel Church Lord's Missions Int Inc; chaplain, bd govrs, Med-Chi Society Wash, DC. **Honors/Awds:** Author of numerous publications; co-author with wife, Human Sexuality Christian Perspective, 1984. **Home Addr:** 11705 Bishops Content Rd, Mitchellville, MD 20721, **Home Phone:** (301)390-0024. **Business Addr:** Private Physician, 3536 Minn Ave SE, Washington, DC 20019, **Business Phone:** (202)581-0200.

FISHER, GEORGE CARVER
Accountant. **Personal:** Born Dec 12, 1939, Texarkana, AR; son of Thomas (deceased) and Naomi Johnson; married Annie Kate Carter; children: Anthony Karl. **Educ:** Univ Ariz, Pine Bluff, BS, 1969; Univ Ariz, Fayetteville, MBA, 1974. **Career:** Ark Best Corp, acct, 1969-73, supv carrier acctg, 1973-84, dir carrier acctg, 1984-. **Orgs:** Treas, EO Trent Consistory, 1973-79; dir, Ark Best Fed Credit Union, 1983-; chmn, Fort Smith Civil Serv Comn, 1983-; Am Inst Cert Pub Accountants; vpres, Fort Smith Girls Club; adv trustee, Sparks Reg Med Ctr; treas, Sunnymede Elem Sch, Parent Teachers Asn; Cert Pub Accountants, Ark; Nat Asn Advan Colored People; life mem, Kappa Alpha Psi; past master, Widow Son Lodge; bd dir, Leadership Fort Smith, 1989-92; bd dir, United Way Fort Smith, 1988-91. **Honors/Awds:** Distinguished Service, Arthritis Foundation, 1986. **Military Serv:** USN, storekeeper second class petty officer, 1957-60. **Home Addr:** 2007 N 48th Cir, Fort Smith, AR 72904. **Business Addr:** Director Carrier Accounting, Ark Best Corp, 1000 S 21st St, Fort Smith, AR 72902.*

FISHER, JOSEPH
Labor activist. **Personal:** Born Feb 7, 1933, Lawnside, NJ; son of Horace J and Vera Ann Arthur; married Barbara Bryant, Apr 1952; children: Joseph Jr, Darlene Still, Barbara Arthur & James. **Educ:** Temple Univ, Pa, BS, 1955. **Career:** Liberty Knitting Mills, Pa, office mgr, 1956-58; Int Ladies Garment Workers Union, Pa, vpres, dir, Eastern Pa Region; Union Needle trades Industrial & Textile Employees, trustee. **Orgs:** CHP, Pa Adv Comt, US Civil Rights Comn; bd mem, Pa Job Training Coordinating Counc; bd mem, Pa Urban Coalition; bd mem, Variety Club-Children's Charity; United Way, Camden County, bd mem; Red Cross, Camden County, bd mem. **Home Addr:** 234 Heaney Ave, Lawnside, NJ 08045.

FISHER, DR. JUDITH DANELLE
Consultant, physician. **Personal:** Born Feb 17, 1951, Sanford, NC. **Educ:** Howard Univ, Col Lib Arts, BS, 1974, Col Med, MD 1975. **Career:** Howard Univ Hosp, psychiat, 1975-77; Hahnemann Med Col, psyciatric resident, 1977-78, fel, 1978-79; CMHC Hahnemann, med dir, 1979-80; Hahnemann Hosp Philadelphia, asst dir in-patient unit, psychol unit, 1980-81; pvt pract, 1980-; CamCare Health Corp, psychol actg med dir, 1981-83; Eagleville Hosp, Women's In-Patient Unit, dir, 1983-84; Wake Co MHC, staff psychiat, 1984-85; NC Disability Determination Svcs, psychiat consult 1985-; Jacobi Med Ctr, Community Psychiat, currently. **Orgs:** Am Psychiat Asn, 1981-; bd dirs, Women Transition Philadelphia, 1982-84; Smithsonian Asn, 1984-; Nat Asn Disability Examrs, 1985-; Am Film Inst, 1986-; State NC Employees Asn, 1986-; Livingston Col Alumni Asn. **Honors/Awds:** NIMH Minority Fellowship, Am Psychiat Asn, 1976-78; Certificate of Recognition, Alpha Kappa Alpha Sorority Raleigh, 1985. **Home Addr:** 836 Boykin Ave, PO Box 822, Sanford, NC 27330. **Business Addr:** Community Psychiatric, Jacobi Medical Center, 1400 Pelham Pkwy S, Bronx, NY 10461, **Business Phone:** (718)918-5000.

FISHER, LLOYD B.
Lawyer. **Personal:** Born Jan 13, 1942, Marthaville, LA; married Shirley T Little; children: Jawara M J. **Educ:** Purdue Univ, BS; Valparaiso Univ Sch Law, JD, 1973. **Career:** B002 Allen & Hamiltol, consult, 1969-70; City Gary, asst city atty, 1973-76; Gary & Opportunities Industrialization Ctr, vpres, bd dirs, 1975; Lake Co Govt, pub defender, 1977-79; Lloyd B Fisher Atty Law, pvt pract, atty, 1979-. **Orgs:** Basileus Omega, Psi Phi Fraternity, Alpha Chi Chap, Gary, IN, 1974-76; Am Bar Asn, 1974-; Nat Bar Asn, 1974-; pres, Lake County Opportunities Develop Found Inc, 1975-; Nat Asn Advan Colored People, 1976-; bd mem, Purdue Club, Club Lake County, 1976-; TMLA, 1979-80; asst to chmn, Criminal Law Sect, Nat Bar Asn, 1980; Bar Asn 7th Fed Cir; Ill State Bar Asn; pub rels chmn, Comn Pack 23 of 23 Cub Scouts Am Gary; bd mem, Thurgood Marshall Law Asn. **Honors/Awds:** Cert of Appreciation, Tolleston Community Coun, 1977; Cert of Appreciation, Nat Asn Advan Colored People, 1977; Dedicated Serv Award, Gary Opportunities Industrialtization Ctr, 1980. **Military Serv:** AUS, 1st lt, 1966-68. **Business Addr:** Lawyer, Private Practice, 734 N Newton St, Gary, IN 46403.*

FISHER, RASHIYA. See DIGGA, RAH.

FISHER, RONALD L, SR.
Banker, vice president (organization). **Personal:** Born May 19, 1951, Hamlet, NC; son of William and Elizabeth; married Del Johnson, May 12, 1973; children: Ron Jr & Lacy. **Educ:** NC Cent Univ, BSBA, 1973; Univ Wis-Madison, MBA, 1976. **Career:** Cameron Brown Mortgage Co, acting vpres, commerical real estate, 1977-80; First Union Nat Bank, vpres, employee relations, 1980-89, vpres, cot lending, sr vp, currently. **Orgs:** Charlotte Urban League, 1991-; 100 Black Men of Charlotte, 1991-; Bus Adv Bd, JC Smith Univ, 1986-. **Business Phone:** (704)374-6558.

FISHER, RUBIN IVAN
College administrator. **Personal:** Born Sep 25, 1948, Baltimore, MD. **Educ:** Univ Conn, BA, 1971; Univ New Haven, MS, 1993. **Career:** Travelers Ins Co, asst dir personnel; adminr Personnel, 1977-78; employ coun, 1974-77; Aetna Life & Casualty Ins Co, supr field controllers dept, 1972-74; The Travelers, Hartford, CT, ast dir, 1974-88; Black Col Serv, New Orleans, LA, asst vpres, 1988-90; Saab Cars USA Inc, Orange, CT, mgr, employ & training, 1990-93; Univ Pa, dir human resources-Univ Libr, 1993-98; Capital Community Col, dir human resources, 1998-. **Orgs:** Soc Human Resources Mgt; Res Officer Asn Am; Urban League; Nat Asn Advan Colored People; Strategic Planning Community; accredited personnel specialist designation, Am Soc Personnel Admin-accreditation Inst, 1978; accredited prof, Human Resources designation Personnel Accreditiation Inst, 1987. **Honors/Awds:** Accredited Professional in Human Resources (PHR), Personnel Accreditation Inst, 1987. **Military Serv:** AUS capt 1971-72. **Business Addr:** Director of Human Resources, Affirmative Action Officer, Capital Community College, Human Resource Department, 950 Main St, Hartford, CT 06103.

FISHER, SHELLEY MARIE
Educator. **Personal:** Born Jul 2, 1942, Gary, IN; daughter of Wendell Brumfield; married Alfred J Fisher; children: Tiffiny, Eric. **Educ:** Indiana Univ, BS, 1964, MS, 1969. **Career:** Gary Community Sch Corp, educator, 1964-, prin, Ernie Pyle Elem Sch, prin, currently. **Orgs:** Past bd dirs, Self-Marketing Inc, 1981-84; past franchiser, Nat Employment Transmittal Inc, 1981-84; nat secy, Nat Tots & Teens Inc, 1981-85; 3rd vpres, Drifting Dunes Girl Scout Coun, 1986-; Alpha Kappa Alpha Inc; past facilitator, Learning Indiana Dept educ. **Honors/Awds:** Reading Fellowship, Indiana ST Univ, 1976; Short fiction published Indiana Univ & Literary magazine, 1979; authored "Resume Writing Slanting Skills in New Direction," 1981. **Business Addr:** Principal, Ernie Pyle Elementary School, 2545 W 19th Pl, Gary, IN 46404, **Business Phone:** (219)977-2142.*

FITCH, HARRISON ARNOLD
Lawyer. **Personal:** Born Jul 4, 1943, Elizabeth, NJ; married Ruth Mckinney; children: Harrison A Jr & Robin L. **Educ:** Columbia Col, AB, 1965; Columbia Univ, LLB, 1968. **Career:** Boston Legal Assistance Project, atty, 1968-69; Boston Univ, Sch Law, lectr, 1969; Goodwin Procter & Hoar Trustee Boston Five Cents Savs Bank, atty; Fitch, Wiley, Richlin & Tourse, partner; Fitch & Tourse, partner, currently. **Orgs:** Babson & Col; dir, Boston Legal Aid Soc Steering Com Lawyers Com Civil Rights Under Law; dir, MA Law Reform Inst; Boston Legal Assistance Proj; Governor's Ad Hoc Adv Com Judicial Appointments, 1972. **Business Phone:** (617)557-3700.

FITCH, MILTON F
State government official. **Personal:** Born in Wilson, NC; son of Milton F and Cora Whitted; married; children: Melanie Fitch & Milton Fitch III. **Educ:** NC Central Univ, BS, 1969; NC Central Univ Sch Law, JD, 1972. **Career:** NC House Rep, rep, 1985; Dist 7B, Super Court Judge, 2001; Most Worshipful Prince Hall Grand Lodge Free & Accepted Masons NC, most worshipful grand master, currently. **Honors/Awds:** North Carolina AFL-CIO; Youth for Social Change Award; Community Service Award, NC Asn Black Lawyers; Albert L. Turner Award, NC Central Univ; Legislator of the year Award, NC Asn Educ Office Personnel. **Special Achievements:** First African American in the State of North Carolina to preside over the House; First Majority Whip and the first African American to be elected House Majority Leader. **Business Addr:** Most Worshipful Grand Master, The Most Worshipful Prince Hall Grand Lodge Free and Accepted Masons of North Carolina Inc, 101 E Main St, Durham, NC 27701.

FITCHUE, M. ANTHONY
Educator, writer, dean (education). **Personal:** Born Dec 13, 1943, Kansas City, MO; son of Robert Anthony and Carrie Wilma Witherspoon; married Leah Doretha White (divorced 1978); children: Ebony Joy Fitchue. **Educ:** Hampton Univ, BS, 1967; Columbia Univ, MS, 1971; Harvard Univ, EdM, 1974; Columbia Univ-Teachers Col, EdD, 1990. **Career:** Dept Labor, Off Fed Contract Comphance, Wash, DC, spec asst to dir, 1979-81; US Info Agency, US Embassy, Banako, Mali, attache cult, 1981-82; US Info Agency, US Consulate, Madras, India, vice consult, 1982-85; Pratt Inst, Brooklyn, NY, asst dean, 1987-88; Col New Rochelle City, Univ NY, Iona Col, NY, adj prof, 1987-90; Chancellor, NY, consult, 1988; Le Moyne Col, Multicultural Affairs, dir, 1992-97; Suny Cortland, lectr, 1995-97; Southhampton Col, Multicultural Prog, dir, 1997-98; NYC, Bd Ed, Div Funded Prog, res assoc, 1999; Morgan State Univ, Educ & Urban Studies, transfer coordr, asst dean, currently. **Orgs:** Int Fel, Grad Sch Journ, Columbia Univ, 1970-71; Policy fel, Leadership Insts Educ, George Wash Univ, 1974-75; Harvard-Radcliffe Alumni Against Apartheid. **Special Achievements:** Author: Armageddon Bogeyman, Essence Mag, 1991; Of Choral Chants & Drum Cadences, The Hindu, 1985. **Business Addr:** Assistant Dean, Transfer Coordinator, Morgan State University, Sch Educ Urban Studies, Baltimore, MD 21251.*

FITTS, LEROY
Clergy, educator. **Personal:** Born Jul 6, 1944, Norlina, NC; son of Johnnie and Louise; married Alice Louise Alston, Aug 18, 1963; children: Timothy, Leroy, Dietrich E, Angelique L, Leticia A. **Educ:** Shaw Univ, BA, 1967; Southeastern Baptist Theol Sem, MDiv, 1970; Va Sem, DDiv, 1975, DHL, 1990; Princeton Univ, attended 1984; Baltimore Hebrew Univ, MA, 1985. **Career:** First Baptist Church, Jacksonville, NC, pastor, 1968-72; First Baptist Church, Baltimore, MD, pastor, 1972-; Community Col, Baltimore, adj prof, 1978-80; Va Sem & Col, pres, 1981; Black Church Hist, St Mary's Sem & Univ, Baltimore, MD, prof. **Orgs:** Ed, Loft Carey Baptist Conv, 1975-90; Nat Asn Advan Colored People, Asn Study Negro Hist, 1978-; bd mgr, Va Sem & Col, 1980; bd mgr, St Marys Sem & Univ. **Special Achievements:** Author, Lott Carey First Black Missionary to Africa 1978, A History of Black Baptists, 1985; article "The Church in the South & Social Issues", Faith & Mission vol II, No I, Fall 1984. **Home Addr:** 3912 The Alameda, Baltimore, MD 21218. **Business Addr:** Pastor, First Baptist Church, 525 N Caroline St, Baltimore, MD 21205.*

FITTZ, SENGA NENGUDI. See NENGUDI, SENGA.

FITZGERALD, HERBERT H.
Detective. **Personal:** Born Jul 17, 1928, Trenton, NJ; divorced; children: Darrel A & Denise A. **Educ:** Howard Univ Rider Col, bus admin & police admin, 1974. **Career:** Detective Mercer Co, prosecutor; Police Dept, Trenton, NJ, officer & detective. **Orgs:** Co Detectives Asn, NJ; pres, Bro Officers Law Enforcement Soc; NJ Narcotic & Enforcement Officers Asn; Int Narcotic Enforcement Officers Asn; Alpha Phi Alpha Zeta Iota Lambda Chap; Nat Asn Advan Colored People; comnr, Trenton Housing Authority, 1971; bd mem, Model Cities Policy Comn, 1972; Mercer County Alcoholism Prog, 1972; master mason, King David Lodge, Trenton, NJ; 32nd Degree Mason Ophir Consisteory 48, Trenton, NJ; adv bd mem, Union Indust Home Boys, Trenton, NJ; Frontiers Int Bd Gov Police Athletic League. **Honors/Awds:** Many certificates of commendation for meritorious service Trenton Police Dept; Drew Pearson Cultural Achievement Award. **Military Serv:** USN.

FITZGERALD, HOWARD DAVID
Government official, president (organization). **Personal:** Born Sep 24, 1938, Trenton, NJ; son of Mollie and Charles; divorced; children: Howard D Jr & Wayne. **Educ:** Antioch Univ, BA, human serv, 1976, MA, admin & supv, 1978. **Career:** NJ Dept Educ, migrant coordr, 1970-; Middlesex County Schs, dir CETA proj,1980; NJ Dept Educ, coordr prog mgt, 1982; We Inc, pres, 1983-; Trenton City Coun, coun mem-at-large, currently. **Orgs:** Chmn comt educ, Trenton Sch Bd, 1979; bd educ, Trenton Sch Bd, 1979-82;Trenton Housing Authority, 1982-; bd dirs, Henry Austin Health Ctr, 1982-; chmn, Carver YMCA 1982-. **Honors/Awds:** Outstanding Board Member Award, Trenton Sch Bd, 1980; Ed Excellence, African Peoples Movement, 1980; Up & Coming

Politician, Candlehight Sports Club, 1981; Recognition, World Hungry Prince Haile Salassie II, 1984. **Military Serv:** AUS, squad leader, 1957-59. **Business Addr:** President, WE Inc, PO Box 22136, Trenton, NJ 08607.

FITZGERALD, LARRY
Football player. **Personal:** Born Aug 31, 1983, Minneapolis, MN; son of Larry Sr and Carol (deceased). **Educ:** Univ Pittsburgh, attended 2002; Valley Forge Mil Acad, Wayne, Pa, attended 2002. **Career:** Ariz Cardinals, wide receiver, 2004-. **Honors/Awds:** Fred Biletnik off Award, 2003; Walter Camp Player of the Year Award, 2003; First Team All-Pro selection, 2008, Pro Bowl MVP, 2008. **Business Addr:** Wide receiver, Arizona Cardinals, 8701 S Hardy Dr, PO Box 888, Tempe, AZ 85284, **Business Phone:** (602)379-0101.*

FITZGERALD-MOSELY, BENITA
Athletic director, chief executive officer. **Career:** US Olympic Comt, dir; Women in Cable Telecommun, pres, & chief exec officer, currently. **Business Addr:** President, Chief Executive Officer, Women in Cable Telecommunications, 14555 Avion Pkwy Suite 250, Chantilly, VA 20151, **Business Phone:** (703)234-9810.*

FITZHUGH, B. DEWEY
Lawyer. **Career:** O'Neil & Fitzhugh, atty, 2003; B Dewey Fitzhugh, atty, currently. **Business Addr:** Attorney, B Dewey Fitzhugh, 1423 Main St, Little Rock, AR 72114-4128.*

FITZHUGH, KATHRYN CORROTHERS
Librarian. **Personal:** Born Feb 4, 1950, Warren, AR; daughter of Charles Edward and Billie Jean Burns; children: Erica Janine. **Educ:** Univ Ark, Fayetteville, AR, BA, 1971; Univ Ill, Urbana-Champaign, Champaign, IL, MS, 1976; Univ Ark, Little Rock, AR, JD, 1983. **Career:** Univ Ark, Grad Inst Technol, Little Rock, technol librn, 1977-79; US Ct Appeals, Little Rock, AR, br librn, 1980-83, 1989-92; Fitzhugh & Fitzhugh, Little Rock, AR, partner, 1985-87; Univ Ark-Little Rock, Pulaski Co Law Libr, ref, circulation libr, 1987-89, ref & spec collections libr, prof, 2003, William H Bowen Sch Law, prof, currently. **Orgs:** Am Asn Law Librs, 1982-; Ark Bar Asn, 1983-; Ouachita Girl Scout Coun, 1986-88; Delta Sigma Theta Sorority, 1991-; Am Bar Asn, 1992-; Am Libr Asn, 1993-; Soc Southwest Archivists, 1994-; Soc Am Archivists; Mid-Am Asn Law Librs; Southwestern Asn Law Librs; Ark Historical Asn; pres, South Western Asn Law Librs, 2002-03; Delta Sigma Theta. **Special Achievements:** Author: "Arkansas Practice Materials II: a Selective Annotated Bibliography," UALR Law Review 21, 1999, pp. 363-412; "Federal Income Taxation" in, Specialized Legal Research, Aspen Publishers, Boston, 1999, 2003. **Business Addr:** Professor, University of Arkansas at Little Rock, William H Bowen School of Law, 1201 McMath Ave, Little Rock, AR 72204, **Business Phone:** (501)324-9974.

FITZPATRICK, ALBERT E.
Publishing executive, management consultant, dean (education). **Personal:** Born Dec 30, 1928, Elyria, OH; son of Ben and Mary; married Derien Lucas; children: Sharon, Karyle & Albert II. **Educ:** Kent State Univ, BA, jour & sociol, 1956. **Career:** Sports reporter, Elyria Chronicle Telegram; Akron Beacon J, reporter, 1956-58; Pulitzer Prize-Winning Coverage, Kent State Disturbance, dir, 1970; Akron Beakon J, farm ed, asst state ed, copy ed news desk, asst news ed, news ed, asst managing ed, managing ed, 1973-77; Pulitzer Jury, 1975-76, 1983; Akron Beacon J, exec ed, 1977-84; ed, Year-Freedom J, Cuyahoga Community Col, Cleveland, 1978; assoc prof, Medill Sch Jour, NW Univ, 1979-80; Knight Ridder, dir minority affairs, 1985; Knight Ridder, asst vpres minority affairs, 1985-94; founding chair, Nat Asn Minority Media Execs; Leadership Develop Inst, dean, currently; Fitzpatrick Consults, chmn & chief exec officer, currently; Sch Journ & Mass Commun, adj prof, currently. **Orgs:** Chmn bd, Wesley Temple, AME Church, 1965-84; pres, Buckeye Chap, Sigma Delta Chi, 1971; pres, Akron Press Club, 1981-83; pres, Nat Asn Black Journalists, 1985-87; chmn & minorities bd mem, Am Cancer Soc, Boy Scouts, Ctr Econ Educ; chmn, UNCF adv bd, 1989; chmn, Nat Asn Minority Media Exercise, 1990-; Am Soc Newspaper Ed; prof adv bd, Kent State Univ Sch Commun. **Honors/Awds:** Outstanding Alumnus Award, Kent State Univ, 1973; John S Knight Award, Sigma Del Ta Chi, Akron, OH, 1980; Frederick Douglass Award Lifetime Achievement, Nat Asn Black Journalists, 1984; Ida B Wells Award, Nat Asn Black Journalists, Nat Conf Ed Writers, Nat Broadcast Ed Asn, 1989; Community Serv Award, Kent State Univ, 1991; Chairmans Citation, Nat Press Found, 2005; Robert G McGruder Award, 2005; Pulitzer Prize, Akron Beacon J. **Military Serv:** AUS, sgt, 2 yrs; USAF, staff sgt, 4 yrs; Sharpshooters Medal,1946. **Business Addr:** Dean, Leadership Development Institute, PO Box 19900, Detroit, MI 48219-0900.*

FITZPATRICK, B EDWARD
Executive. **Career:** Puget Sound Chrysler-Plymouth Inc, Renton, Wash, chief exec, 1986-. **Business Addr:** Chief Executive, Puget Sound Chrysler-Plymouth, 4622 W View Dr, PO Box 1510, Everett, WA 98203-2417, **Business Phone:** (206)226-0066.

FLACK, DR. JOHN M.
Physician, educator. **Personal:** Born Jan 23, 1957, Hill AFT, UT; son of John and Bernezetta Littles; married Jennifer Schoats, 1978; children: Courtney, Christen, Cathryn, Catelyn & Carey. **Educ:** Langston Univ, BS, 1978; Univ Okla, Sch Med, MD, 1982, Health Scie, chief med resident, 1986; Univ Minn, Sch Pub Health, MPH, 1990. **Career:** Univ Okla, Chief Med Resident, 1982-86, instr med, 1986-88; Univ Minn, asst prof, 1990-94; Bowman Gray Sch Med, assoc prof surg, 1994-97; Wayne St Univ, assoc chmn & prof, 1997-, Cardiovasc Epidemiol & Clin Appln Prog, dir, currently; ECEA dir & assoc chmn, clin res & urban healthoutcomes, 2002-. **Orgs:** Res Ctr Minority, 1992-96; bd trustees, Int Soc Hypertension Blacks, 1995-; Nebr Dept Health, 1999; 100 Black Men, 2000-; Am Black Cardiologist; chair, Nat Kidney Found, KEEP comt, 2000-. **Honors/Awds:** Distinguished Alumni, 1993; Positive Image Award, Pee Dee Newspaper Group, 1995; Dr Daniel D Savage Scientific Award, 1998; One Best Doctors in Am, 1998; Distinguished Research Award, Int Soc Hypertension in Blacks. **Special Achievements:** Authored more than 103 peer-reviewed manusacripts and book chapters; manuscript reviewer for several prominent medical journals; special consultant to the metabolic and endocrinologic drug products FDA Advisor. **Home Phone:** (248)681-5910. **Business Addr:** CECA Director, Associate Chairman, Wayne State University School Medicine, Department internal Medicine, 4201 St Antoine Suite 2E, Detroit, MI 48201, **Business Phone:** (313)745-8244.

FLACK, ROBERTA
Singer, songwriter. **Personal:** Born Feb 10, 1937, Black Mountain, NC; daughter of Laron and Irene; married Stephen Novosel, 1966 (divorced 1972). **Educ:** Howard Univ, BA, music educ, 1958. **Career:** Farmville, NC, 1959-60; Wash DC pub schs, teacher, 1960-67; singer & songwriter, 1968-; ABC TV spec, The First Time Ever, star, 1973; OCL Songs From the Neighborhood", 2005; Magic Lady Inc, singer & song writer, currently; TV theme song, Valerie, writer; Albums: First Take, 1969; Chapter Two, 1970; Quiet Fire, 1971; Killing Me Softly, 1973; Feel LikeMakin' Love, 1975; Blue Lights in the Basement, 1977; Roberta Flack, 1978; The Best of Roberta Flack, 1981; I'm The One, 1982; Born To Love, 1983; Hits & History, 1984; Roberta Flack, 1985; Oasis, 1989; Roberta, 1995; The Christmas Album, 1997; Holiday, 2003; The Very Best of Roberta Flack, 2006. **Orgs:** Sigma Delta Chi; trustee, Atlanta Univ; Delta Sigma Theta. **Honors/Awds:** Two Grammy Awards, Best Song & Best Record for The First Time Ever I Saw Your Face, 1972-73; Best Pop Duo for Where is the Love, 1972; Roberta Flack Human Kindness Day, City of Washington, DC, named in honor, 1972; 2 Grammy Awards, Best Record & Best Female Vocalist for Killing Me Soflty With His Song, 1973; STAR, Hollywood's legendary Walk of Fame, 1999. **Business Addr:** Singer, Songwriter, Magic Lady Inc., 21 W 58th St Suite 2E, New York, NY 10019, **Business Phone:** (212)644-7218.

FLACK, WILLIAM PATRICK
Executive. **Personal:** Born Mar 19, 1927, Anderson, SC; son of Alma Burris and Pinder; married Thomasenia Mattison. **Educ:** Tuskegee Inst, 1947; Rutgers Univ, attended 1973; Harvard Univ, attended 1975. **Career:** Government official (retired); RTP Inc, manpower coordr, 1970-83; Anderson Co Human Resources Comn, exec dir, 1983-84; William Ross & Assocs, consult, 1984; SC Dept Consumer Affairs, comnr. **Orgs:** Del, Nat Dem Party, 1972; elder & trustee, Salem Presby Church; comnr, Anderson Co Election Comn, 1973-77. **Military Serv:** AUS, 1945-47. *

FLAGG, DR. ELOISE ALMA WILLIAM
Consultant, educator. **Personal:** Born Sep 16, 1918, City Point, VA; daughter of Caroline E Moody Williams (deceased) and Hannibal G (deceased); married J Thomas (deceased); children: Thomas L & Luisa Flagg Foley. **Educ:** Newark State Col, BA, 1940; Montclair State Col, MA, 1943; Columbia Univ, EdD, 1955; Newark State Col, LittD (hon), 1968. **Career:** Teacher, asst supt (retired), consult; Wash, grade teacher, 1941-43; Elem Sch, grade teacher, 1943-57, remedial reading teacher, 1957-63, from vice prin to prin, 1963-67; Newark State Col, adj instr eng, 1964; Hawkins St Sch, prin; Sch Bd Educ Newark, asst supt, 1967-83; Montclair State Col, Rutgers Univ, adj instr, 1982; Educ & Ed, consult, 1983-; Newark Pub Libr, John Cotton Dana lectr, 2004; E. Alma Flagg Scholarship Fund Inc, consult. **Orgs:** NCTM; NCTE; NSSE; Am Asn Univ Women; Kappa Delta Pi Hon Soc Educ, 1954; dir, YMWCA, 1964-73; Alpha Kappa Alpha; Soroptimist Int Newark; Urban League Essex Co; life mem, Nat Asn Advan Colored People; educ chair, Proj Pride, 1980-; pres, League Women Voters Newark, 1982-84; Governor's Comm C Serv Planning, 1983-87; vpres, Newark Youth Art Exhib, 1988; Newark Sr Citizens Comn; vol, NJ Performing Arts Ctr, 1994; charter mem, Newark Preserv & Landmarks Comm; vpres, Share, NJ, 1996. **Honors/Awds:** Distinguished Service to Education, NSC Alumni, 1966; Citizenship Award, Weequahic Comm Coun, 1967; Roster Super Merit, E Side HS Alumni, 1969; Distinguished Service Award, Cosmopolitan, 1970; Adam Clayton Powell Education Award, NJ Alliance Black Sch Educr, 1981; E Alma Flagg Sch Newark, dedicated, 1985; Sojourner Truth Award, Negro Bus & Prof Women, 1985; ESHS Distinguished Alumni Award, 75th Anniversary, 1986; Education Law Center Award, 1986; Distinguished Alumna Award, Teachers Col Columbia Univ, 1986; Dr E Alma Flagg School, Newark, NJ, named in honor. **Special Achievements:** First African-American female principal in Newark, 1964; Published books like: Lines and Colors (poetry), 1979; Feelings, Lines, Colors (poetry), 1980; Twenty More with Thought & Feeling, 1981. **Home Addr:** 67 Vaughan Dr, Newark, NJ 07103. **Business Addr:** Educational Consultant, Owner, E. Alma Flagg Scholarship Fund Inc, 67 Vaughan Dr, Newark, NJ 07103.

FLAGG, THOMAS
College teacher. **Career:** Col teacher (retired); Howard Univ, assoc prof music, 1999-2003, prof music.

FLAKE, REV. FLOYD H.
Educator, clergy, government official. **Personal:** Born Jan 30, 1945, Los Angeles, CA; son of Robert Booker Sr and Rosie Lee Johnson; married Margaret Elaine McCollins; children: Aliya, Nailah, Rasheed & Hasan. **Educ:** Wilberforce Univ, BA, 1967; United Theo Sem, DMin, 1994. **Career:** Miami Valley Child Develop Centers, social worker, 1967-68; Bethel AME Church, pastor, 1968-70; Xerox Corp, mkt analyst, 1969-70; Sec Presby Church, pastor, 1971-73; Lincoln Univ, assoc dean students, 1970-73; Martin Luther King Jr Afro Am Ctr, Boston Univ, univ chaplain marsh chapel & dean students, 1973-76; Mt Zion AME Ch, pastor, 1974-75; Allen Sr Citizen Complex, developer; Allen Christian Sch, founder; Allen AME Church, Jamaica, NY, pastor, 1976; US House Representatives, congressman, 1986-97; Edison Charter Schs, pres, 2000; Wilberforce Univ, pres, 2002-; New York Post, columnist; Greater Allen A M E Cathedral New York, sr pastor, currently. **Orgs:** Life mem, NAACP; ordained minister, African Methodist Episcopal Church;life mem, SCLC; bd mem, Fannie Mae Found; adv bd, FDIC; bd mem, NYC Olympics, 2012; President's Comn Excellence Spec Educ; Princeton Rev; NewYork City Investment Fund Civic Capital Corp; Federal Deposit Ins Corp Adv Comt Banking Policy; Bank Am Nat Adv Bd; sr fel Manhattan Inst Social &Econ Policy; adj fel, Adv Bd, Brookings Inst Ctr Urban & Metrop Policy; New York 2012 Olympic Comt. **Honors/Awds:** Gilbert Jones Philos Scholar, Wilberforce Univ, 1964-66; Richard Allen Fel, Payne Theol Sem, 1967-68; Outstanding Administrator Award, Lincoln Univ, 1972; Alfred P Sloan Scholar, Northeastern Univ, 1974; DoctorDivinity, Monrovia Col, 1984; Ebony's Religion Award; Ebony magazine Black Achievement Award in Religion, 1986; Doctor of Humanities Degree, Wilberforce Univ 1987; DHL, Morris Brown Col, 1989. **Special Achievements:** Co-author, The Way of the Bootstrapper: Nine Action Steps for Achieving Your Dreams, Harper San Francisco, 1999; co-author, Practical Virtues:Everyday Values and Devotions for African-American Families; African American Church Management Handbook, 2005. **Business Addr:** Senior Pastor, The Greater Allen A.M.E. Cathedral of New York, 110-31 Merrick Blvd, Jamaica, NY 11433, **Business Phone:** (718)206-4600.

FLAKE, NANCY ALINE
Television producer, educator, artistic director. **Personal:** Born Jul 23, 1956, Detroit, MI; daughter of Thomas M and Margaret E. **Educ:** Howard Univ, BBA, acct, 1977; DePaul Univ, MS, taxation, 1981. **Career:** Arthur Andersen & Co, sr tax acct, 1977-80; pub acct, 1979-; Laventhol & Horwath, tax acct supvr, 1980-81; Coopers & Lybrand, tax acct mgr, 1981-84; Howard Univ, assoc prof taxation; Howard Univ, Small Bus Develop Ctr, dir, 1984-; "Small Bus Mag", exec producer & co-host, 1987-. **Orgs:** Adv, Jr Achievement, 1979-86; nat conf treas, Nat Black MBA Asn, 1983; pres, Nat Asn Black Accts, 1984-85; bd mem, Nat Asn Negro Bus & Prof Womens Clubs; Econ Develop Corp, 1984-87; bd mem, DC Chamber Com, 1987-; chairwoman, Bus Comm DC Chamber Com, 1986-87; coun mem, Mayor Barry's Coord Coun Self Sufficiency, 1985-; comnr, DC Comn Women, 1987-90; Nat Asn Black Accts; Delta Sigma Pi Frat, 1988-; chair, Alternatives Welfare Comt, 1989-. **Honors/Awds:** Outstanding Business Leader, Bus Exchange Network, Washington, DC, 1986; Advocate of the Year, US Small Bus Admin, Washington, DC, 1987; Certificate of Appreciation, Grad Sch Bus & Pub Admin, 1987. **Business Addr:** Director, Howard University, Small Business Development Center, 6th Fairmont St NW Rm 128, PO Box 748, Washington, DC 20059, **Business Phone:** (202)806-1550.*

FLAKES, GARLAND KAZELL, I
Clergy, business owner, law enforcement officer. **Personal:** Born Jun 12, 1963, Temple, TX; son of Myrtle L Captain; married Delena K Johnson, Dec 22, 1984; children: Brittany Alyse, Chaundra Dellouise, M'Kenzie Kay, Garland KaZell. **Educ:** Huston-Tillotson Col, Austin, TX, BA, govt & hist, 1985; Sam Houston State Univ, Huntsville, TX; Tex Lutheran Col, Seguin. **Career:** Tex Dept Criminal Justice/ID, Community Educ Prog, asst admin, 1980-90, Terrell Unit, chief classification, 1993-94, asst warden, 1994-97, sr warden, 1997-99; Flakes Family Serv, owner, 1997-; Pleasure Island, TX, comnr. **Orgs:** Comt Adv Panel, Indust Park, 1998; assoc minister, Greater Good Hope, 1998-; bd dirs, Nelson Credit Corp, 1998; counsr, Nat Inst Corrections, Therapeut Comt, Exec Training New Wardens, 1998; vol, Tex Youth Comn, 1999; vol, Prison Ministry, 1999; vol, Ct Appoint Spec Advocate, 2000. **Honors/Awds:** Cert License Ministry, Greater Good Hope Baptist Church, 1999. **Home Addr:** 5140 Linda Ln, PO Box 13058, Beaumont, TX 77726, **Home Phone:** (409)892-0085. *

FLAMER, JOHN H
School administrator, association executive. **Personal:** Born Oct 13, 1938, Philadelphia, PA; married Mary E Holder; children:

Crystal, Dawn, Melanie, Tedd, Todd, Tamiko, Timothy, John, III & Christopher. **Educ:** Southern Ill Univ, BS, 1964, MS, 1975. **Career:** Job Corps SIU, teacher, coach, 1965; Ill Youth, prin, 1967; Bus Affairs SIU, asst vpres, 1968; Affirmative Action Minority Affairs SIU, asst pres; EEO US Civil Serv, consult; Nat Affirmative Action Officers, pres, 1973. **Orgs:** State Ill; bd mem, Madison St Clair Co Urban League; pres, Metro Sickle Cell Anemia; Employ Adv Com Inland Steel; Alpha Phi Alpha; vpres, Ill Track & Field Coaches Asn; treas, Nat Black Alliance Grad & Prof Educ; Asn Health Recreation & Physical Educ; Ethnic Adv Comn; Nat Black Staff Network.

FLANAGAN, BETTY. See FLANAGAN, ELIZABETH.

FLANAGAN, ELIZABETH (BETTY FLANAGAN)
Activist, association executive, president (organization). **Career:** Retiree Coun Am Fed State, County & Munic Employees, Dist 47 Retiree Chap, pres, vice chair, 2004-. **Special Achievements:** First Black female Retiree Council officer. **Business Addr:** Vice Chair, National Retiree Council of the American Federation of State, County & Municipal Employees, 1625 L St NW, Washington, DC 20036-5687, **Business Phone:** (202)429-1000.*

FLANAGAN, T EARL, JR.
Dentist. **Personal:** Born Jan 20, 1937, Baltimore, MD; son of Thomas Earl Sr (deceased) and Marjorie B (deceased); married LaVerne; children: Thomas III, Shelley, Brian. **Educ:** Howard Univ, BS, 1959, DDS, 1966. **Career:** Retired; pvt pract, dentist, 1966; St Elizabeths Hosp, instr intern prog, chief dent officer, 1969. **Orgs:** Nat Dent Asn; Am Dent Asn; Acad Gen Dentists; Am Dent Soc Anesthesiol; Am Asn Hosp Dentists State; RT Freeman Dent Soc; Md Dent Soc Anesthesiol; Nat Asn Advan Colored People; Urban League; Kappa Alpha Psi; Chi Delta Mu; fel Am Dent Soc Anesthesiol. **Honors/Awds:** Am Cancer Soc, Harold Krogh Award. **Military Serv:** AUS, 1st lt, 1959-62. **Business Addr:** Dentist, 905 Sheridan St, Hyattsville, MD 20783.*

FLATEAU, DR. JOHN
Executive director, dean (education). **Personal:** Born Feb 24, 1950, Brooklyn, NY; married Lorraine Witherspoon. **Educ:** Wash Sq Col NY Univ, BA, 1972; Baruch Col, Masters Adm Baruch, 1977; US Off Educ, Pub Serv Educ, fel, 1976; City Of Univ New York Grad Centre, PhD, American studies. **Career:** NYS Comn Health Educ & Illness Prev, prin res analyst; Adult Educ Dist Coun 37 AFSCME & Hunter Col, City Univ NY, teacher, 1968-74; Prog Admin, BED-STUY Summer Prog, supvr, 1968-72; Harlem Youth Develop Ctr, past comnwckr, 1976; NY State Assembly Albet Vann NY State Legis, past admin asst; Black & Puerto Rican Caucus Inc NY State Legis, exec dir, 1977-78; Nat Black Lay Cath Caucus, past youth chmns natl off black caths, bd dir; Bedford Stuyvesant Pastoral Planning Prog, vpres; Bed-stuyvesant Laymen's Convocation, pres; DuBois Bunche Ctr Pub Policy, co found & exec dir; Medgar Evers Col, prof pub admin & dean external relations, currently. **Orgs:** Urban Voter Educ Assn; Comm Educ Task Force; founding mem, Vanguard &Independent Dem Asn Inc 56th AD; Kings Co Dem Comn, 1972-; del, NY Judicial Conv 2nd Dist, 1972-; Nat Assn Advan Colored People; Alumni Asns NY Univ/Baruch Col; MLK Jr Alumn Assn; pres, JARM Res Assocs Ltd, 1979-; political action chmn, Convention Planner Black Agenda Conv Brooklyn, NY,1980; Black United Front NY Met Chap; Macon-macdonough-lewis-stuyvesant Block Assn; former 592 Prospect Pl Tenants Assn; Chair, Economic Empowerment Committee for the NAACP Brooklyn Branch. **Honors/ Awds:** Life Membership Award, Vannguard Civic Assn; Listed Community Leaders &Noteworthy Americans, 1978; Listed, Outstanding Young Men of America, 1979. **Special Achievements:** Author: Young Lives, Am Dreams; The Prison Indust Complex; Blackout. **Business Addr:** Professor, Dean External Relations, Medgar Evers College, Department of Public Administration, 1650 Bedford Ave Room 2032C, Brooklyn, NY 11201, **Business Phone:** (718)270-5122.

FLATTS, BARBARA ANN
Lawyer. **Personal:** Born Sep 27, 1951, New York, NY; daughter of Albert Sr and Amy Morris; children: Albert Paul Peoples, Amy Christina Peoples. **Educ:** Hampton Inst, BA, 1972; Am Univ Wash Col Law, JD, 1974. **Career:** Laborer's Dist & Coun Wash DC, law clerk, 1973-74; US Dept Labor Benefits Rev Bd, atty adv, 1975-76; Off Corp Coun DC Govt, asst corp coun, 1976-80; US Dept Justice Environmental Enforcement Section Land & Natural Resources Div, trial atty, 1980; New York City Housing Auth Contracts Real Estate & Fin div, atty, 1984; Employ Security Bur, asst atty gen, 1986-87; New York State Dept Law, Harlem Regional Off, asst atty gen charge, 1988-. **Orgs:** exec comt bd dir, Coun Legal Educ Opportunity, 1973-75; pres, Am Univ Chap Black Am Law Stud Asn, 1974; Am Bar Asn, 1975-; bd dir, Wash Urban League, 1977-80; Bd dir, Girl Scout Coun Nation's Capital, 1977-81; Juvenile Justice Adv Comt DC, 1979-80; Alpha Kappa Alpha Sor; Wa bar Asn; past secy, Kappa Beta Phi Legal Asn, 1976; Alpha Kappa Alpha, Epsilon Pi Omega; connection community coordr Alpha Kappa Alpha; bd mem, Harlem Legal Servs, 1990-; United Negro Col Fund. **Business Addr:** Assistant Attorney General in Charge, State of New York Law Department, Harlem Office, 163 W 125th St 25th Fl, State Office Bldg, New York, NY 10271-0332, **Business Phone:** (212)961-4408.*

FLEETWOOD, THEREZ
Costume designer, business owner. **Educ:** Fashion Inst Technol, NY. **Career:** Designer, 1990-; Therez Fleetwood, owner & designer, currently. **Honors/Awds:** "From Whence We Came, African-American Women of Triumph" Award, Allstate Insurance Co; named the "New Day Designer of the Year"; selected as one of the New York Museum's Top Designers for their "New York Gets Married'' exhibit. **Special Achievements:** She designed the only Afrocentric costumes to be worn by Mickey and Minnie Mouse at Walt Disney World in Orlando; Books:The AfroCentric Bride, A Style Guide, Amber Books; featured in an array of publications, including Elle, Italian Glamour, Women's Wear Daily, & The New York Times. designed the first Afrocentric costumes to be worn by Mickey and Minnie Mouse at Walt Disney World in Orlando, Florida. **Business Addr:** Owner, Therez Fleetwood, 34 Pk Ave Suite 1, Bloomfield, NJ 07003, **Business Phone:** (212)714-8058.

FLEMING, ALICIA DELAMOTHE
Executive, labor relations manager. **Personal:** Born in New York, NY; married John A Fleming. **Educ:** NY Univ, BS, 1972, MS, 1980. **Career:** NY Univ Med Ctr, office mgr admin, 1966-79; Booz Allen & Hamilton, mgr non exempt personnel, 1979-81; Time Inc, employ counr, 1981-85; Non-Exempt Recruiting & Develop, mgr, 1985-; A D Fleming Group Inc, pres, currently. **Orgs:** EDGES 1985; Women Human Resources Mgt, 1983. **Business Addr:** President, A D Fleming Group Inc, 139 Fulton St, Room 720, New York, NY 10038, **Business Phone:** (212)227-0909.*

FLEMING, ARTHUR WALLACE
Surgeon. **Personal:** Born Oct 1, 1935, Johnson City, TN; son of Smith George Sr (deceased) and Vivian Cecile Richardson; married Dolores Caffey-Fleming, Apr 8, 1978; children: Arthur Jr, Robyn, Jon, Mark, Robert, Bernadette, Erik. **Educ:** Ill State Normal Univ, attended 1954; Wayne State Univ, BA, 1961; Univ Mich Med Sch, MD 1965. **Career:** Detroit Inst of Cancer Res, res asst, 1958-61; Walter Reed Army Med Ctr, thoracic & cardiovasc surgeon serv staff, 1972-83; Walter Reed Army Inst Res, dept surgery staff, 1974-76, div experimental surg chief, 1976-77, dir dept surg, 1977-83; Uniformed Serv Univ Health Sci, assoc prof surg, 1978-83; King-Drew Med Ctr, dir trauma ctr, 1983-, prog dir gen surg & chief surg, 1983-; Charles R Drew Univ Med & Sci, prof & chmn, Dept Surg, 1983-; MLK Gen Hosp, chief surg, 1983; La County Martin L King Jr Drew Med Ctr, chief of surgery, 1983-. **Orgs:** Chmn, Dept Surg Charles R Drew Univ Med & Sci, 1983-; Trauma dirs comt, Los Angeles Co, 1984-; bd dir, Am Col Surgeons Soc Calif Chap, 1986-; pres, Soc Black Acad Surgeons, 1986-91. **Honors/Awds:** Hoff Medal for Research, 1974; Gold Medal paper, Forum on Progress in Surgery Southeastern Surgical Congress, 1977; The Surgeon General's "A" prefix Highest Military Medical Professional Attainment, 1981; The Legion Merit Investigative projects combat casualty care pioneering of autologous blood transfusions US Army, 1983; William Sinkler Award, Surgical Sect Nat Medical Asn, 1990; Friend of the Nurses Award, King-Dew Med Ctr Nursing Dept, 1990; Commendation, Dir Trauma Ctr, 1989. **Military Serv:** AUS col 17 1/2 yrs; Meritorious Serv Awd USAF 1984. **Business Addr:** Chairman, Charles R Drew University Medical & Science, 12021 S Wilmington Ave, Los Angeles, CA 90059.*

FLEMING, DAVID AARON
Architect, engineer, government official. **Personal:** Born Aug 21, 1963, Washington, DC; son of Alton Leonard and Charlotte Ann Long. **Educ:** Stanford Univ, BSEE, 1986, MSME, 1988; Ill Inst Technol, MAr, 1992; Northwestern Univ, PhD, 1991-. **Career:** Cong Black Caucus, cong intern, 1982; IBM, engr, 1983; Johns Hopkins Applied Physics Lab, engr, 1985-87; Veteran's ADM Hosp, product designer, 1988; General Electric, product designer, 1989; Amoco Oil, engr, 1989-92; Walt Disney Imagineering, designer imagineer, 1992-; Tek Designs Int, engr, 1996-; US Patent & Trademark Office, patent examiner, 1998-99. **Orgs:** Nat Soc Black Engrs, nat chap, 1989-91, nat publs chair, 1987-89; Nat Stud Support Coun Africa, nat co-chap, 1991-95; Alpha Phi Alpha Fraternity Inc. **Honors/Awds:** Gen Electric, Latimer Scholar; Consortium for Degrees for Minorities Eng, Fel, 1985; Nat Org Minority Architects, Scholar, 1989; Am Inst Architects, Roche Traveling Scholar, 1990; Walt Disney Imagineering, Imaginations Design Contest, firsst Place, 1992. **Special Achievements:** Co-designed robotic sign language machine "Dexter, The Finger-spelling Robotic Hand," 1988; 4 patents in US. **Business Addr:** Engineer, Tek Designs International, 506 12th St NE, Washington, DC 20002, **Business Phone:** (202)543-7297.

FLEMING, ELLIS T.
Executive. **Personal:** Born Mar 26, 1933, Baltimore, MD; son of Lewis and Lavanna; married Subenia Mae Pettie, Jun 14, 1953. **Educ:** Brooklyn Col, Graduated Indust Rels, 1957; CCNY, attended 1959; La SalleLaw Corresp United Laundry & Dry Cleaners Baltimore Course, 1963. **Career:** NY Proc Dist, adminr dir mil personnel prog, 1957-62; Haryou-Act, asst exec dir prog, 1963-66; New Breed Ent, part-owner, 1966-70; ETF Assoc BusCons, pres; Org & Prog Consult, Bed Stuy Lawyers Asn, Gov Nelson-Rockefeller, White House, 1972-73, Jackie Robinson Mgt Corp, 1972; ETF Financial Serv, pres; consult exec dir, Nat Bankers Asn, CUNY Hostos Col, Bd Educ Health & Physical Educ Dept; Spanish Am Merchants Asn; Congressman Edolphus Towns eleventh CD New York, spec asst; United Laundry & DryCleaners Baltimore Inc, pres, 1998. **Orgs:** Co-found & exec dir, Marcus Garvey Health Facility; dir, E Flatbush Urban Planning Study, 1978-79; chair, EF Comn Corp; found & pres, Comn EF Pres; Oper Breadbasket; Congr Black Caucus Round table; co-found EF Church AVMerch Asn; Fed Block Asn; contrib writer, Consequences Powerlessness, Youth Ghetto; consult, clothing mfg & retailers; lect bus comt; Planning Bd Regional Planning Asn NY, NJ, CT; White House Consult prog Black Am; gen adv, Nat Youth Movement; adv, Opportunity Ind Ctrs NY; field coordr, Brooklyn Boro Pres, 1985. **Honors/Awds:** Man of the Year Award; Brooklyn Jaycees, 1964. **Special Achievements:** Writer & contribr "Consequences of Powerlessness" authored Dr Kenneth-Clark; author "The Great Deluge". **Military Serv:** Korean Conflict, 1950-52. *

FLEMING, GEORGE
School administrator. **Personal:** Born Jun 29, 1938, Dallas, TX; married Tina Bradley, Mar 2; children: Sonja & Yemi. **Educ:** Univ Wash, Seattle, WA, BA, bus admin. **Career:** Football player, Oakland Raiders, 1961, Winnipeg Blue Bombers, 1963-65; Wash Sec of State, Olympia, WA, examiner foreign corps, 1965-66; Wash-Idaho area Pacific Northwest Bell US West Commun, Seattle, WA, employment asst, 1966-70, commun cons, Seattle area, 1970-73, personnel sup, Wash-Idaho area, 1973-75, mgr econ develop, Wash-Idaho area, 1975; community develop mgr; State Wash, state rep, 1969-71, state sen, dist 37, 1971-91; US W Communs, Seattle, employee; Seattle Pub Schs, exec dir external rels, 1991-94, dir govt rels, 1995; Kings county, dept transp, dir gov rels (retired). **Orgs:** Am Indust Develop Coun; past pres, Pacific Northwest Indust Develop Coun; Econ Develop Coun Puget Sound; bd dirs, Randolph Carter; adv bd, Urban, Racial, Rural & Disadvantaged Educ; past pres, Econ Develop Coun Wash; NAACP; Rainer Valley Enterprise Ctr; fiscal adv comt, Nat Conf State Legislators; bus adv comm, Puget Sound Chamber Com; dir, Econ Devel Execs Wash; Mason; bd dir, Seattle Sports Comn. **Honors/Awds:** LLD, honorary, City Univ, Seattle; Community Service Award, US Justice Dept; UN Human Rights Asn Award; Univ Wash Husky Hall of Fame, 1980; Democratic Leader of the Year, 1980; Silvers cup MVP, Helms Athletic Found; Silvers cup, Touchdown Club of Columbus. **Special Achievements:** Mr. Fleming also was the first African American member of the Washington State Senate.

FLEMING, JOHN EMORY
Museum director. **Personal:** Born Aug 3, 1944, Morganton, NC; son of James E and Mary E; married Barbara Durr; children: Tuliza, Diara. **Educ:** Berea Col, BA, 1966; Univ Ky, 1967; Howard Univ, MA, PhD, 1974; Univ Calif-19Berkeley, Mus Mgt Inst. **Career:** Ky Civil Rights Comn, community serv & educ specialist, 1966-67; Peace Corps, Malawi, Africa, visual aids specialist & adminr, 1967-69; Youth Pride Inc, Dept Training & Educ, Wash, DC, supvr, 1970-71; US Civil Rights Comn, Fed Eval Div Prog Analyst, 1971-72; Inst Study Educ Policy, Howard Univ, sr fel, 1974-80; Dept Hist, Howard Univ, asst prof hist, 1974-78; Ohio Hist Soc, Columbus, OH, afro-am mus project dir, 1980-88; Nat Afro-Am Mus & Cult Ctr, dir, 1988-98; Nat Underground Railroad Freedom Ctr, dir & chief operating officer, 1998-00; Cincinnati Mus Ctr, Union Terminal, Cincinnati, OH, vpres mus, 2001-; Dept Hist, Univ Cincinnati, Cincinnati, OH, adj prof, 2005-. **Orgs:** Nat Asn Advan Colored People, 1974-87; bd, Assoc Study Afro-Am Life & Hist, 1978-93; bd, J Negro Hist, 1982-96; vpres bd, Art Community Expression, 1984-87; panel, Columbus Found, 1986-87; vpres, Ohio Mus Asn, 1989-90; bd mem, Am Asn Mus, 1990-95; bd mem, Museum Trustee Asn, 1989-95; pres & bd mem, African-Am Mus Asn, 1991-96; White House Conf Travel & Tourism, 1995; chair, Ohio Arts Coun; Ohio Becentennial Comn, 1996-03; Yellow Springs Hist Soc; nat pres, Asn Study African Am Life & Hist, 2007-. **Honors/Awds:** Distinguished Alumni Award, Berea Col; The Franklin H. Williams Award for Outstanding Community Service, Nat Peace Corps; Lifetime Achievement Award, African Am Mus Asn; Carter G Woodson Award, Berea Col; Outstanding Professional Achievement Award, Ohio Mus Asn; Martin Luther King Award; Ohioana Outstanding Humanities Award for Distinguished Service to Ohio in African American History, Ohiano Libr. **Special Achievements:** Author: The Lengthening Shadow of Slavery: Historical Justification for Affirmative Action for Blacks in Higher Education, Howard Univ Press, 1976; Affirmative Action for Blacks in Higher Education, A Report, Howard Univ Press, 1978; A Summer Remembered: A Memoir, Silver Maple Publ, 2005. **Business Addr:** President, The Association for the Study of African American Life and History, CB Powell Building, 525 Bryant St Suite C142, Washington, DC 20059, **Business Phone:** (202)865-0053.*

FLEMING, DR. JUANITA W.
Educator. **Personal:** Born in Lincolnton, NC; daughter of Joseph and Bertha; married William; children: Billy & Bobby. **Educ:** Hampton Univ, BSN, 1957; Univ Chicago, MA, nursing educ, 1959; Univ Md,Jour & Human Develop; Catholic Univ Am, PhD, educ except children & psychol, 1969. **Career:** DC Genl Hosp, head nurse, 1957-58; DC Bur PH, PH nurse, 1959-60; Freedman's Hosp Sch Nursing, instr, 1962-65; Howard Univ Dept Ped, PH

nursing consult, 1965-66; Univ KY, Col Nursing, prof nursing assoc dean dir grad studies, assoc vice chancellor acad affairs, special asst pres, acad affairs & prof nursing & educ, 1991-2001, prof emer, 2003-; Ky State Univ, interim vpres acad affairs, 2003-06; prof emer, 2006-. **Orgs:** Sigma Theta Tau, Am Nurses Asn Sec, 1986-89; mem, Coun Nurse Res, 1976-; exec comm, MCH Coun, 1982-85; inducted Am Acad Nursing, 1975, governing coun, 1982-84; mem, Inst Med, 1990; Nat Acad Sci Inst Med, 1991-. **Honors/Awds:** Mary Roberts Fel, 1963; Pre-Doctoral Fel, 1967-69; Great Teacher Award, Alumni Assn Univ KY, 1973; Outstanding Woman Frankfort Lexington Links Inc, 1976; ANA Comm Nursing Res, 1976-80; Fel Admin Am Coun Educ, 1977-78; Outstanding Alumni Award, Hampton Inst, 1977; Outstanding Educ Award, KY League Nursing, 1978; KY Health Servcs Adv Coun, Gov KY, 1979-83, 1983-85; Maternal Child Health Res Grants Review Comm Sec HEW, 1979-84; Cert Need & Licensure Bd, 1980-84; Omicron Delta Honr Frat, 1983; Women Achievement Award, YWCA, 1984; Alpha Kappa Mu Hon Soc; Hall of Fame Hampton Univ, 1987; Marion McKenna Leadership Award, Delta Psi Chapter Sigma Theta Tau,1988; Inducted, Inst Med, 1990; Lifetime Achievement Award from the Asn of Black Nursing Faculty, 1991; Distinguished Membership Award, Am Nurses Assn, 1994; Mary Elizabeth Carnegie Endowed Visiting Prof, Howard Univ, 1995; vis minority Scholar, West Chester Univ, 1997; Favill Lecture, Wayne State Univ, 1998; Houston Endowment Minority Health & Res distinguished prof, Prairie View Univ, 1998; Olhson Scholar lectures Univ Ill, 1999; Zumwinkle Award, Univ KY, Student Govt, 2001; honorary doctorate, Berea Col, 1994. **Home Addr:** 316 Exum Ct, Frankfort, KY 40601. **Business Addr:** Professor Emeritus, Kentucky State University, 400 E Main St, Frankfort, KY 40601, **Business Phone:** (502)597-6442.

FLEMING, JUNE H.
Government official, manager. **Personal:** Born Jun 24, 1938, Little Rock, AR; daughter of Ethel Thompson Dwellingham and Herman Dwellingham; married Roscoe L, Mar 11, 1966; children: Ethel & Roscoe Lee III. **Educ:** Talladega Col, BA, 1953; Drexel Univ, MLS, 1954; Stanford Univ, cert, 1974. **Career:** Government Official (retired); Brooklyn Pub Libr, br librn, 1954-55; Little Rock Sch Syst, librn, 1955-56; Phil Smith Col, assoc prof, 1960-66; Palo Alto Calif, dir librn, 1967-81; Palo Alto Calif, city mgr, 1992-2000; City Franklin, city mgr, currently. **Orgs:** Soroptimsit Club, 1980-82; adv bd, YWCA, 1983-; Peninsula Links, 1986-; Delta Sigma Theta Rotary, 1988-. **Honors/Awds:** Woman of Vision Award, 1997. **Home Addr:** 200 Sheridan Ave Suite 303, Palo Alto, CA 94306.

FLEMING, PATRICIA STUBBS
Federal government official. **Personal:** Born Mar 17, 1937, Philadelphia, PA; daughter of Fredrick D Stubbs and Marion Turner Stubbs; married Harold S (divorced); children: Douglass, Craig & Gordon. **Educ:** Vassar Col, BA, 1957, grad studies; Univ PA; Cranbrook Acad Fine Arts; PA Acad Fine Arts, NY Univ. **Career:** Legis asst to Rep Augustus Hawkins, 1971-73, Rep Shirley Chisholm, 1973-75, Rep Andrew Young, Comm on Rules, US House Rep, 1975-77; spec asst to secy Health, Educ & Welfare, 1977-79; Legis US Dept Educ, dep asst sec, 1980-81; Rep Ted Weiss, admin asst, 1983-86; Subcomt on Human Resources & Inter-Govt Rels, US House Rep, prof staff mem, 1986-93; Dept Health & Human Servs, spec asst to secy, 1993-94; Interim Nat Aids Policy, coordr, 1994; White House, Nat AIDS Policy, dir, 1994-97; artist, Patricia S Fleming Assocs, HIV & AIDS consult, currently. **Orgs:** Pres, Prev Works Needle Exchange Nation's Capitol; Foundry Gallery. **Honors/Awds:** Education Policy Fel Prog, 1971-72. **Special Achievements:** Speeches, panels, related to education for disadvantaged or minority persons, the AIDS epidemic; Articles on same topics in a variety of Publishing; has shown work in juried and solo shows in NYC & Wash, DC. **Home Addr:** 6009 Mass Ave, Bethesda, MD 20816.

FLEMING, QUINCE D., SR.
School administrator. **Personal:** Born Dec 7, 1915, Mt Hope, WV; married Vivian; children: Quince D. **Educ:** Tuskegee Inst, BS, 1939; Pa St; Univ Wis, River Fall. **Career:** Jefferson County Bd Educ, teacher, 1940-67, admin, 1967-72. **Orgs:** Pres, Charles Town City Coun; pres, Jefferson Co Parks & Recreation; Jeff Co Bd Educ. **Honors/Awds:** Achievement Award, Nat Asn Advan Colored People; Service Award, Selective Serv, USA; 5-10-15 & 20 Years Agriculture Service, Future Farmers Am.

FLEMING, PROF. RAYMOND RICHARD
Educator. **Personal:** Born Feb 27, 1945, Cleveland, OH; son of Theodore Robert and Ethel Dorsey; married Nancy Runge, Nov 15, 1969; children: John, Peter & Stephen. **Educ:** Univ Notre Dame, Ind, BA, 1967; Univ Florence, Italy, attended 1968; Harvard Univ, Cambridge, MA, 1969, PhD, 1976. **Career:** Univ Notre Dame, Notre Dame Ind, instr, 1969-72; Univ Calif, San Diego Calif, asst prof, 1973-80; Miami Univ, Oxford Ohio, assoc prof Italian, asst dean grad sch, assoc dean grad sch, 1985-87; Penn State Univ, Univ Park, Pa, prof com lit & Italian; Fla State Univ, Dept Interdisciplinary Humanities, prof, John Francis Dugan prof Modern Lang & Humanities, currently. **Orgs:** Dante Soc Am; Am Coun Learned Soc; Pac & Ancient Modern Lang Asn; pres, Am Conf Romanticism, 1998-2000; exec bd, Int Asn Study Italian Lang & Lit, 1998-2002. **Honors/Awds:** Fulbright Grant to Florence Italy, 1967; Woodrow Wilson Fel, Harvard Univ, 1968; Ingram-Merrill Poetry Award, 1971; Alexander Von Humboldt Fel Ger, 1978; Am Philos Soc Res Grant, 1979; Nat Endowment Humanities; Teaching Excellence Award, Fla State Univ, 1998-99; Fla Poetry Award, 2000; Britsh Lecturship, 2002; Djerassi artist residence, Woodside, Calif, 2003. **Business Addr:** John Francis Dugan Professor of Modern Languages & Humanities, Florida State University, Department of Interdisciplinary Humanities, 432 Diffenbaugh Bldg Suite 1549, Tallahassee, FL 32306, **Business Phone:** (850)644-1758.

FLEMING, THOMAS A.
Educator, teacher. **Personal:** Born Jan 1, 1933?, Reading, PA; married Diane Rosinski; children: Malcolm; children: Thomas & Sharon. **Educ:** William Tyndale Col, BA, 1964; Eastern Mich Univ, MA, spec educ, 1968; Col Misericordia, Dallas, PA, DHL, 1994; Detroit Bible Col, relig educ. **Career:** W J Maxey Boys Training Sch, social studies teacher, 1968; First Baptist Church, assoc minister, currently; Washtenaw County Juv Detention Ctr, head teacher; Acad Affairs, Eastern Mich Univ, spec asst provost, currently; Washtenaw Intermediate Sch Dist, teacher spec educ. **Orgs:** Vol, W J Maxey Boys Training Sch. **Honors/Awds:** Teacher of the Year, State Bd Educ, 1991-92; Nat Teacher of the Year, Coun Chief State Sch Officers, Encyclopaedia Brittanica, 1992; Hon Doctorate, Eastern Mich Univ, Education, 1994. **Military Serv:** AUS, Nat Guard, overseas France & Ger. **Business Addr:** Special Assistant Provost, Eastern Michigan University, 1349 S Huron St, Ypsilanti, MI 48197-7021.

FLEMING, VERN
Basketball player, basketball coach. **Personal:** Born Feb 4, 1962, New York, NY; married Michelle Clarke; children: Vern Jr. **Educ:** Ga Univ, attended 1984. **Career:** Basketball player (retired), basketball coach; Ind Pacers, guard, 1984-95; NJ Nets, guard, 1995-96; Ind Pacers, asst coach, 1999. **Orgs:** US Olympic gold medal winning basketball team, 1984; US Select Team. **Honors/Awds:** Kodak All-Am team, 1983-84; AP & UPI first team All-SEC; All-Amer hon, Most Valuable Player of SEC tourney, All-Tournament Selection.

FLEMING, VERNON CORNELIUS
Manager. **Personal:** Born Dec 19, 1952, Louisa County, VA; son of William E and Josephine Robinson; married Gloria A Murray (divorced 1994); children: Gino & Sean; married Gloria A Murray; children: Gino, Sean. **Educ:** Hampton Univ, BA, 1974; Col William & Mary, MBA, 1980; AUS Command & Gen Staff Col, dipl, 1987. **Career:** Col William & Mary, asst prof mil sci, 1980-83; US Army Res, instr, 1985-95; Procter & Gamble, purchasing mgr, 1983-84, sr purchasing mgr, 1984-95, purchasing group mgr, 1995, second vice chair, currently. **Orgs:** Chmn bd dirs, Williamsburg Head Start, 1982-83; Res Officers Asn, 1983-; Prime Mover, Purchases Support Group, 1989-94; Kappa Alpha Psi Frat; cochmn, prog comt, Nat Black MBA Asn; Nat Hampton Alumni Asn; pres coun, Boy Scouts Am; bd dirs, Kappa Alpha Psi Frat; chmn, Cert Comt, vice chmn, bd dir, Maryland, DC, Minority Supplier Develop Coun. **Honors/Awds:** Service Award, Peninsula League Youth, 1982; Officer of the Year, Cincinnati Chap Kappa Alpha Psi, 1985; Polemarch's Award, Cincinnati Chap Kappa Alpha Psi, 1987; Silver Beaver, Boy Scouts Am, 1996; Alumni of the Year, Hampton Univ Alumni Asn, 1995; MD/DC MSDC Chairman Award, 2001; Supplier Diversity Advocate of The Year, 2001. **Military Serv:** Air Defense Artillery, Ltcol (retired); Meritorious Service Medal; Army Commendation Medal with 3 Oak Leaf Clusters, Army Achievement Medal with Oak Leaf Cluster, Overseas Ribbon. **Business Addr:** Second Vice Chairperson, Procter & Gamble, 11103 Pepper Rd, Hunt Valley, MD 21030, **Business Phone:** (410)785-5549.

FLEMMING, CAROLYN
Editor. **Personal:** Born Jan 11, 1946, Orange, NY; daughter of James Ralph and Helen McCrary; married Ronald Howard Flemming I, Aug 17, 1968; children: Ronald H II, Solomon N J, Jasmin A K, Nimrod M, Jade C, Jewell C, Joy C, Janicka J, Jafrica & Jamaica B. **Educ:** Drake Col Bus, 1965; Va Union Univ, 1966. **Career:** Fine Print News, ed; Testing Dept, Va Union, 1966; Astara Inc, Mystery Sch, 1976; The Rosicurican Order AMORC; Glendale Public Libr, ed & libr administrator, currently. **Orgs:** Dir, Fashion Show Blacks Arts Festival, 1970; dir, Art & Show Black Arts Festival, 1970; NRA; Nu-Buff Sportsman Club; Regent Sportsman Club. **Home Addr:** 806 Fillmore Ave, Buffalo, NY 14212. **Business Addr:** Editor, Glendale Public Library, 222 E Harvard St, Glendale, CA 91205, **Business Phone:** (818)548-3999.

FLEMMING, DR. CHARLES STEPHEN
Diplomat. **Personal:** Born Oct 30, 1948, Saint Lucia, West Indies; son of James and Mary Magdalene Whitney; married; children: Albert, Charles, Alika, Nadine & Sean. **Educ:** City Col NY, New York, NY, BA, 1977; New York Univ, New York, NY, MA, 1979, M.Phil, 1984, PhD, 1985. **Career:** Malcolm-King Col, New York, NY, instr, 1979-81; New York Univ, adj instr,1981-84; Bronx Community Col, New York, NY, adj instr, 1981-; Mission St. Lucia UN, New York, NY, ambassador, 1980-94; Bronx Community Col, City Univ NY, adj asst prof polit sci, 1996-; Bronx Borough Pres's Off, direcon res & real estate, 1998-; Ashlin Realty, prin broker, 2003; BrizaTechnologies Sr Exec Team, cfo, currently; Ashlin Capital, pres, currently. **Orgs:** Am Polit Sci Asn, 1980-; Caribbean Studies Asn, 1987-; Int Polit Sci Asn,1988-; Int Studies Asn, 1988-; Int Asn Permanent Rep, 1989-. **Honors/Awds:** Commendation, City Govt New York, 1979; Pi Sigma Alpha, Nat Polit Sci Hon Soc, 1980; Taraknath Das Prize, New York Univ, 1983. **Special Achievements:** Author: The Zone of Peace Declamation, 1985. **Home Addr:** Grand Central St, PO Box 4254, New York, NY 10163-4254. **Business Addr:** President, Ashlin Capital LLC, 44 Wall St 12th Fl, New York, NY 10005, **Business Phone:** (212)208-4685.

FLEMMING, CLENTE
Banker. **Educ:** Univ SC, BA. **Career:** Bank Am, sr vpres, personal exec; The Flemming Group, Inc, founder; SC Community Bank, pres & chief exec officer, currently. **Orgs:** Chmn & bd mem, City Year, Inc; vpres, SC Diversity Coun; bd chmn, SC Am Red Cross; First Steps Ad bd; Zion Baptist Church Bd Trustees; exec dir, Columbia Chap 100 Black Men Am; chmn & bd mem, Columbia Soc Human Resource Mgt; Agency Head Salary Comn; bd mem, United Way midlands; comnr, SC State Housing Finance Authority; bd dirs, SC Chamber Com. **Honors/Awds:** Distinguished Black Alumnus, Univ SC Black Alumni Coun; Professional of the Year Award, Columbia Soc Human Resource Mgt, 1995; Order of Palmetto, Gov SC, 1999; Lifetime Service and Achievement Award, Rudolph Canzater Scholarship Fund, Inc. **Special Achievements:** One of South Carolina's top 25 African-American influences by South Carolina Business, Vision magazine; Mayor and City of Columbia proclaimed December 8, 1999, as "Clente Flemming Day,? and presented him with a Key to the City. **Business Addr:** President, Chief Executing Officer, South Carolina Community Bank, 1545 Sumter St Suite 200, Columbia, SC 29201, **Business Phone:** (803)733-8100.

FLEMMING, LILLIAN BROCK
Government official, educator. **Personal:** Born Jul 27, 1949, Greenville, SC; daughter of James Dennis Brock and Lila Mae; married Rev J M, Jan 2, 1980; children: Davit, M II & Emanuel. **Educ:** Furman Univ, BA, 1971, MEd, math, 1975. **Career:** Southside High Sch, math teacher, 1971; Greenville City Coun, pres, 1981-, vice mayor pro-tem, 1983-89; Donaldson Ctr, comnr; Greenville County Schs, Prof Employ recruiter, currently; mayor pro-tem, city coun mem, currently; Bergamo, Italy, rep. **Orgs:** Vpres, 1978-79, pres, 1979-80, Greenville County Educ Asn, 1978-79; bd dir, Sunbelt Human Advan Resource Ent, 1981-88; Dem Nat Conv, 1984, 1988; Nat Coun Negro Women; Nat Asn Advan Colored People; dir, Ronald McDonald House; Greenville Dem Women; Phyllis Wheatley Post Fels; Nat Edu Asn; Greenville Coun Teachers Math; Greenville Cent Area Partnership; founder, Conf Black Munic Elected Officials SC; Munic Asn SC; trustee, Furman Univ; bd dirs, Brockwood Sr Housing. **Honors/Awds:** Teacher of the Year, Southside High Sch, 1974, 1976, 1993, 1994; Outstanding Secondary Educator America, 1976; Outstanding Woman of America, 1977; Community Service Client Council of Western Carolina, 1981; Citizen of the Year, Client Coun Western Carolina, 1982; Outstanding Black American, 1982; Human Rel Greenville County Educ Asn, 1984; Cooper White Humanitarian Award, Greenville County Educ Human Rel Comn, 1984; Outstanding Community Service, Epsilon Iota Zeta Chap Sor, 1984; Distinguished Service Award, Mt View Baptist Church, 1988; Political Service Award, SC Baptist Educ & Missionary Conv, 1988; Outstanding Phyllis Wheatley Post Fellow Award, 1989; William F Gibson Service Award, Greenville, Nat Asn Advan Colored People, 1990; Martin Luther King Leadership Award, Phyllis Wheatley Leadership Orgn, 1991; Community Service Award, Azah Temple, 1991; Sch Dist Greenville County, Third Runner-Up for Teacher of the Year, 1993-94; Woman of Distinction Award, Girl Scouts Blue Ridge Coun, 1994; Lillian Brock Flemming Leadership Award, Furman Univ; Women's Triumph Award for State & Local Govt, SC Gov Comn; 2000; Richard Furman Baptist Heritage Award, 2002. **Special Achievements:** First Black to be elected vice mayor pro tempore in City of Greenville; First black to be elected mayor pro tempore in City of Greenville; First black female to be elected to Greenville City Council; First city council member to be elected to five consecutive terms since the 1960's; One ofthe first three African American women to attend Furman University in Greenville, South Carolina. **Business Addr:** Mayor Pro Tem, District 2 Representative, Greenville City Council, 398 Oscar St, Greenville, SC 29601.

FLETCHER, DR. ANTHONY M
Cardiologist. **Personal:** Son of Lawrence and Dr Patricia. **Educ:** Xavier Univ; Univ Cincinnati, Coll Of Med, MD, 1980. **Career:** George Wash Med Ctr, residency; Georgetown Univ Hosp, fel cardiol; St Vincent Infirmary Med Ctr, cardiologist; pvt pract, currently. **Orgs:** Exec coun, Heart Ball, 2002; Heart Walk; treas, Heartland Affil Bd; pres, Little Rock Am Heart Asn Bd, currently. **Honors/Awds:** Worthen-Cornett Award, Am Heart Asn's Cent Ark Heart Ball, 2003. **Business Addr:** Physician, 5315 W 12th St, Little Rock, AR 72204, **Business Phone:** (501)664-0941.

FLETCHER, DR. BETTYE WARD
Management consultant, educator, administrator. **Educ:** Tougaloo Col, BA, 1970; Atlanta Univ, MS, 1972; Univ Ala, DSW, 1986.

Career: Center for Substance Abuse Prevention, Comm Chr; Jackson State Univ, grad dean, vpres res & develop, interim pres, prof social, Jake Ayers Inst Res, fac, currently; Prof Assoc Inc, founder, pres & chief exec officer, currently. **Orgs:** Bd dir, Community Matters Inc; exec dir, Miss Dept Human Serv. **Honors/Awds:** Honor doctorate, alma mater. **Special Achievements:** First woman & first sitting campus administrator to be named president at Jackson State University. **Business Addr:** President, Chief Executive Officer, Professional Associates Inc, 1900 Dunbarton Dr Suite G, PO Box 5711, Brandon, MS 39047, **Business Phone:** (601)982-1593.

FLETCHER, CLIFF
Executive. **Career:** WWWZ-FM, pres; WAZS-AM, gen mgr, currently. **Orgs:** SC Broadcasters Asn. **Business Phone:** (843)277-1200.*

FLETCHER, GLEN EDWARD
Automotive executive. **Personal:** Born Aug 6, 1951, Auburn, NY; son of Merritt W and Naomi P; married Donna M Mattes, Jul 21, 1979; children: Kasha B, Garrison A. **Career:** NY State Electric & Gas, labourer, 1970-77; Motorla Commun, 1977-78; Fox Ford Co Inc, sales & sales mgr, 1978-, partner, gen mgr, currently. **Orgs:** Minority Ford Lincoln Mercury Dealers Asn. **Honors/Awds:** Businessman of the Year, Kappa Alpha Psi, 1992. **Home Addr:** 6 Cherry St Rd, Auburn, NY 13021. **Business Addr:** President, General Manager, Fox Ford Company Inc, 1068 Arsenal St, Watertown, NY 13601, **Business Phone:** (315)782-7200.*

FLETCHER, HOWARD R.
Government official. **Personal:** Born Dec 24, 1924, Washington, DC; married Eva Irene; children: Carolyn & Howard Jr. **Educ:** Howard Univ, BS, 1949, addn studies, 1950. **Career:** Bur Census, Wash, DC, comp mgt, 1951-80; UN, comp tech adv, 1980-81; Wash DC, data processing consult, 1981-82; Mt Vernon Col, Wash DC, comp sci fac, 1983; Towson State Univ, comput sci fac, 1984; MCES, Univ Md, Col Pk, comp & info sys officer, 1984. **Orgs:** Fin mem, Silver Spring (MD) Alumni Chap, 1947; Sr warden, 1975; vestry person, 1971-73; 1983-85, convenor convocation 10, 1971-73; lay reader, 1970-80; Transfiguration Episcopal Church; past pres, DC Chap Prometheans Inc, 1972-73; Kappa Alpha Psi Pole march, 1975-76; ACM; Am Nat Stardards Inst; ANSI SIG Programming Lang. **Honors/Awds:** Silver Medal Award for Computer Programming Techniques, US Dept Com, 1967; Episcopal, Wash Diocesan Review Brd, 1972-75; Achievement Award, Kappa Alpha Psi Eastern Province, 1974. **Military Serv:** AUS, 1943-46. *

FLETCHER, JAMES ANDREW
Chancellor (education), executive. **Personal:** Born May 8, 1945, Tulsa, OK; son of Howard Bruce and Edna Katherine; married Karen Kite (divorced); children: Howard Bruce, Jamie Katherine & Lancelot Lansing; married Maria Merissa; children: Jemila Pujadas & Aisha Pujadas. **Educ:** Mass Inst Technol, BS, aeronaut & astronaut, 1967; Harvard Grad Sch Bus Admin, MBA, 1972; Fairleigh Dickinson Univ, MS, mech eng, 1973; LaSalle Univ, Chicago, LLB, 1975. **Career:** Gen Elec Corp, Syst Simulation Eng, engr, 1967-70; Gen Res Corp, systs analyst, 1969; Int Bus Mach Corp, mkt rep, 1972-73, fin prog adminr,1974-76, lab controller, 1976-78, fin prog mgr, 1979-81, planning consolidation mgr, 1981-83, pricing mgr IPD, 1983, dir plans & controls, 1983-85, Syst Printing Bus Unit, chief financial officer; White House fel,Off Mgt & Budget, 1973-74, exec asst to dep dir; Burroughs Corp; Unisys Corp, staff vpres, pricing & bus anal, 1985-89, Communs Line Bus Mkt Div, vpres finance, 1989-90, Corp Fin Planning & Anal, vpres, 1990-91, vpres bus opers, 1991; Howard Univ, vpres bus & fiscal affairs, chief financial officer & treas, 1991-95; Univ Colo, Boulder, vice chancellor admin & finance, 1995-96; Morehouse Col, vpres bus & finance, 1997-2000; Entertainment Develop Corp, vpres & chief financial officer, 2000-01; Tex & M Univ Syst, vice chancellor admin, 2001; vpres. Finance and Admin, 2009-. **Orgs:** Bd mem, Am Friends Serv Comn, 1980-88, 1995-, mem exec comt, mem fin comn,2001-; Gen Comt, Friends Community Nat Legis; White House Fels Asn, Nat Asn Advan Colored People; 100 Black Men Atlanta. **Honors/Awds:** George F Baker Scholar, Harvard Grad Sch Bus Admin, 1972; AFSC South Africa Trip Deleg, 1979, FWCC South Africa Trip Deleg, 1989; elected mem,Harvard Bus Sch Century Club. **Special Achievements:** Author: "A Quaker Speaks from the Black Experience, The Life and Collected Works of Barrington Dunbar," 1980; co-author Friends Face the World, 1987. **Business Addr:** vice president for Finance and Administration, The Texas A&M University System, 200 Technology Way, College Station, TX 77845-3424, **Business Phone:** (979)458-6036.

FLETCHER, LONDON LEVI (BAKER)
Football player. **Personal:** Born May 19, 1975, Cleveland, OH. **Educ:** John Carroll univ, sociology. **Career:** St Louis Rams, linebacker, 1998-01; Buffalo Bills, 2002-06; wash redskins, linebacker, 2007- . **Honors/Awds:** Carroll Rosenbloom Memorial Award, 1998; Rams roy award, 1998. **Business Addr:** Professional Football Player, Washington Redskins, 21300 Redskin Park Dr, Ashburn, VA 20147, **Business Phone:** (703)478-8900.*

FLETCHER, LOUISA ADALINE
State government official. **Personal:** Born Jan 3, 1919, Independence, KS; daughter of Charles L Wesley and Anna T Wilson Wesley; married Allen T Fletcher, Mar 24, 1938 (deceased); children: Jerold V Fletcher. **Educ:** Am Tech Soc, Chicago IL, Cert, Bus Admin, 1938. **Career:** State government official (retired); US Navy Dept, Bremerton, WA, clerk typist, 1944-45; Campbell Grocery Store, Bonner Spring, KS, clerk, 1945-52; US Treasury, Kansas City MO, graphotype operator, 1952-53; Dept Health, Educ & Welfare, Social Security Admin, Kansas City, MO, clerk typist, 1954-65, reviewer, 1965-67, comput claims clerk supvr, 1965-75; Fletcher's Rentals, mgr; Kansas Pub Employ, Rel Bd, 1977-85. **Orgs:** Pres, Nat Asn Advan Colored People KS State Conf; Nat Asn Retired Fed Employ; Nat Asn Advan Colored People Nat bd dir; Nat Comn preserve Social Security & Medicare; pres, PTA Bonner Springs, KS Sch, 1940-42. **Honors/Awds:** Outstanding Performance, SSA, 1964-67; Outstanding service Award, Nat Asn Advan Colored People, 1964, 1977, 1984; Service Award, Nat Asn Advan Colored People, 1976, 1986, 1989; Louisa A Fletcher Day, Kansas City, KS, 1978; Mother of the Year, Church Award, 1979, 1986; Government First Martin Luther King Award, 1985; Plaque, Special Leader for Community, Bonner Springs, 1986. **Special Achievements:** Book: Kansas City Call & Globe papers, 1987-88; Speeches printed for Tabor Col, 1987-88. *

FLETCHER, MILTON ERIC
Executive. **Personal:** Born Feb 20, 1949, New Orleans, LA; son of Mertis Whittaker and Ervin Fletcher Jr. **Educ:** Southeastern La, BA, mkt, 1971; Univ Detroit, MBA, 1991. **Career:** Detroit Diesel Allison, EEO rep, 1976-79; Gen Motors Bldg Div, staff asst, 1979-81; Gen Motors Tech Staffs, supvr, human resources mgt, 1981-85, supvr, recruiting, 1985-87, mgr, personnel placement, 1987-92; Saturn Corp, mgr, human resources, 1992-; Great Minds Inc, chief success officer, currently. **Orgs:** Cot Case Mgt Serv Inc, pres bd dir, 1976-92; Alpha Phi Alpha, Gamma Lambda Chap, Educ Fund, 1988-; Southern Univ Bus & IDS Cluster, co-chmn, 1985-; Hartford Memorial Baptist Church, deacon, 1987-92; Spruce St Bapt Church, deacon, 1992-. **Honors/Awds:** CHR's Award For Excellence in Comm Services, Gen Motors Corp, 1987; Hon Alumni, Southern Univ, 1989; Black Enr of the Year for Affirmative Act Indust, HBCU Coun Deans, 1992; Commencement Speaker, Southeastern La Univ, 1992. **Home Phone:** (615)321-5237. **Business Addr:** Chief Success Officer, Great Minds Inc, 16500 N Pk Dr Suite 1811, Southfield, MI 48075, **Business Phone:** (248)569-9383.

FLETCHER, PATRICIA LOUISE
Educator. **Personal:** Born Jun 20, 1938, Stuebenville, OH; daughter of Clifford Mayo; married Lawrence Fletcher, Jan 24, 1960; children: Dr Anthony Fletcher. **Educ:** Steubenville Sch Cosmetology, 1964; Franciscan Univ, attended 1969; WVa Univ, MA, 1972; Dayton Univ, attended 1979. **Career:** Steubenville City Sch, 1967-72, high sch supt, 1972-80; Garfield Elem Sch, prin, 1991-97. **Orgs:** Pres, Fair Housing, 1980-92; pres, Alpha Kappa Alpha Sorority, 1990; UN Asn USA, 1994; pres, bd adv, Franciscan Univ, 1995; pres, Asn Colored Women's Clubs & Youth Affiliates, 1996-98; pres, United Way Jefferson City, 1996; vpres, Jefferson Community Col, 1997; pres, Asn Childhood Develop; Nat Asn Advan Colored People. **Honors/Awds:** Outstanding Educator Award, Cameo Women's Ctr, 1991; Honorary Doc Degree, Franciscan Univ, 1993; African-American Community Award, 1994; Ohio Women's Hall of Fame, 1994; Path Finders, Steubenville City School, 1996. **Special Achievements:** Develop curriculum for Steubenville City Sch, 1973. *

FLETCHER, ROBERT E.
Movie director, writer, lawyer. **Personal:** Born Dec 12, 1938, Detroit, MI; son of Robert and Rose Lillian; married; children: Kabenga. **Educ:** Fisk Univ, attended 1959; Wayne State Univ, BA, 1961; Nat Educ TV Film Training Sch, attended 1970; Com Film Workshop Coun, TV News Cinematography Prog, attended 1971; Nat Acad TV Arts & Sci/Third World Cinema Prod Inc, attended 1977; New York Univ Sch Law, JD, 1990. **Career:** No Student Movement Harlem, field organizer, 1963-64; Nat Stud Asn, Tutorial Prog, photographer & adminr, 1963; Harlem Educ Proj; SNCC, MS, photojournalist, 1964-68; Miss Freedom School; freelance photographer, journalist & film maker, 1968-; Rod Rodgers Dance Co, chmn & bd dir, 1973-; Brooklyn Col, Dept Film Studies, adj prof, 1975-76; Cravath, Swaine & Moore, atty, 1991-; Films: A Luta Continua, cinematographer & co-dir, 1971; O Povo Organizado, cinematographer, 1975; Vote for Your Life, producer & dir, 1977; Weatherization, What's It all About?; Voices of the Civil Rights Movement, panelist, 1980; TV series: "A Nation in View", co-producer; Author: "We're Gonna Rule!" The Movement, 1967; Co-author: Quiet War in Mozambique, 1973. **Orgs:** Int Photographers Motion Picture Indust. **Business Addr:** Attorney, Cravath, Swaine & Moore, Worldwide Plaza, 825 8th Ave, New York, NY 10019-7415.*

FLETCHER, SYLVESTER JAMES
Executive. **Personal:** Born Apr 24, 1934, Ebony, VA; son of Saint Luke Sr. and Christeal Bishop; married Catherine Moore, Sep 10, 1955; children: Karen Darlene, Keith Errol. **Educ:** VA State Univ, BA, agronomy & soil sci, 1956. **Career:** US dept of Agriculture, Soil Conservation Serv, suvy soil scientist, 1956-76; Natural Resource Dynamics, pres & mgr, certified professional soil scientist, 1976-; Mother Flercher's Inc, pres, 1983-; Energenesis Develop Corp, pres, 1986-90. **Orgs:** US & NJ Jaycees, nat dir, 1967-68; Newton Rotary, head various coms, 1976-; Soil Conservation SOC of AME, 1956-83; NJ Soil Conservation SOC of AME, pres, 1971-72; NJ ASN of Professional Soil Scientists, charter pres, 1974-76; Soil Sci SOC of AME, Agronomy SOC AME, 1956-; AMR Registry of Certified Professionals in Agronomy, Crops, Soils, 1980-; Nature Conservancy, NJ chp, bd trustees, 1994-03. **Special Achievements:** Outstanding Performance Rating, USDA, Soil Conservation Service, 1963; author, Soil Survey Report of Sussex County, NJ, publisher, USDA, SCS, 1975; author, Soil Survey Report of Warren Co, NJ, publisher, USDA, SCS, 1979; co-found, pres, Fast Food BUS: Mother Fletcher's Inc, 1983; inventor, modular-stackable front loading container, patent D 310.744, 1990. **Business Addr:** President, Natural Resource Dynamics, 9B Barrett Ave, Newton, NJ 07860, **Business Phone:** (973)383-5668.*

FLETCHER, TERRELL ANTOINE
Football player, founder (originator). **Personal:** Born Sep 14, 1973, St Louis, MO; married Sheree; children: Trey. **Educ:** Univ Wis, eng; San diego seminary, religious studies, attended. **Career:** San Diego Chargers, running back, 1995-2002. **Orgs:** Pastor & founder, city of hope interNatchurch. *

FLETCHER, WILLIAM G, JR.
Activist, president (organization). **Personal:** Born Jun 21, 1954, New York, NY; son of William G Fletcher Sr and Joan Carter; married Candace S Carson; children: Tasmin Jwahir Fletcher. **Educ:** Harvard Univ, AB, 1976. **Career:** Gen Mechanics shipyard, welder, 1977-80; Boston Jobs Coalition, organizer, 1980-81; Greater Boston Legal Servs, paralegal, 1982-86; Univ Mass Boston, adj fac, 1982-90; UAW, Dist 65, organizer, 1986-90; Nat Postal Mail Handlers' Union, org secy, admin dir, 1990-91; E & S, SEIU, asst educ dir, educ dir, field servs dir, pub sector div dir, asst to pres, 1991-96; AFL-CIO, educ dir, 1996-99, asst to pres, 1999-01; George Meany Ctr for Labor Studies, vpres, Intl trade union devel progs, 2001-02; vis prof Brooklyn Col, currently; TransAfrica Forum, pres, 2002-, chief exec officer, currently. **Orgs:** Maine & Shipbuiling Workers Union, 1977-80; Boston Black United Front, 1980-81; Black Radical Cong, nat coord comt, 1998-, nat co-chair, 2001-; Monthly Review Found, dir, 2001-; United for Peace & Justice, co-chair, 2002-, nat steering comt, 2003-. **Business Addr:** President, Chief Executive Officer, TransAfrica Forum, 1629 K St NW Suite 1100, Washington, DC 20006.*

FLETCHER, WINONA LEE
Educator. **Personal:** Born Nov 25, 1926, Hamlet, NC; daughter of Henry F Lee and Sarah Lownes Lee; married Joseph G Fletcher, Mar 28, 1952 (died 1994); children: Betty Ann Fletcher. **Educ:** Johnson C Smith Univ, Charlotte, NC, AB, 1947; Univ Iowa, Iowa City, MA, 1951; Ind Univ, Bloomington, PhD, 1968; attended Univ West Africa, Toga, Dahomey, Ghana, Nigeria, 1974. **Career:** Delwatts Radio, Electronics Inst, Winston-Salem NC, sec teacher, 1947-51; Ky State Univ, Frankfort, prof area coordr, 1951-78; Lincoln Univ, Jefferson City, MO, dir costumer instr, summers, 1952-60; consult, John F Kennedy Ctr, 1978-; Ind Univ, Bloomington, prof theatre & afro-am studies, 1978-94, asoc dean col arts & sci, 1981-84, prof emeritus, currently. **Orgs:** Costumer, Michiana Summer Theatre, summer 1956; dir cult affairs, Upward Bound, Ky State Univ, 1966-67; adjudicator, Am Col Theatre Festival, 1973-; Ky Arts Comn, 1976-79; nat pres, Univ Col Theatre Asn, 1979-80; Nat Comn Theatre Educ, 1980-85; Am Theatre Asn; US Nat Comn, UNESCO, 1981-85; coordr, Kennedy Ctr Black Col Proj, 1981-84; adv bd mem, First Int Women Playwrights Conf, 1987-88. **Honors/Awds:** Elected Col Fellows, Am Theatre Asn, 1979; co-author, Offshoots: The H F Lee Family Book, 1979; Graduate Nat Service Award, Alpha Kappa Alpha, 1980; US Delegate to 5th World Congress on Drama, Villach, Austria, 1981; Distinguished Alumna, Johnson C Smith Univ, 1986; Elected to Nat Theatre Conference, NTC, New York City, 1988; Career Achievement Award, ATHE, 1993; BTN Award Named in Honor, 1994; sr editor, Community Memories: A Glimpse of African American Life in Frankfort, KY, 2003. **Home Addr:** 317 Cold Harbor Dr, Frankfort, KY 40601. **Business Addr:** Professor Emerita, Indiana University, Department of Theatre & Drama, 275 N Jordan, Bloomington, IN 47405-1101.

FLEURANT, GERDES
Educator. **Personal:** Born Jul 7, 1939, Port-au-Prince, Haiti; son of Jacques Fabien Pradel and Fanie Jn-Charles; married Florienne Saintil; children: Herve & Maimouna. **Educ:** New Eng Conserv Music, BA, Social Sci, 1964; New Eng Conserv Music, BMus Organ, 1968; Northeastern Univ, MA, Sociol, 1971; Tufts Univ, MMus Compos, 1980, Caribbean Cult & Music, PhD, 1987. **Career:** Educator (retired); Ecole Ste Trinite Haiti, dir gen music, 1959-64; Col St Pierre Haiti, social studies teacher, 1962-64; Brockton Schs, gen music teacher, 1968-70; Brandeis Univ, lectr black music, 1973-74; Assumption Col, visiting prof, sociol, 1976-77; Wellesley Col, visiting prof, blackmusic, 1985, assoc prof, currently; Salem State Col, assoc prof sociol, 1971-89; prof sociol, 1989-; dir, African Am studies; Brown Univ, visiting prof, 1992. **Orgs:** Consult City Boston Bilingual & Bicultural Phase II, 1976, RI BlackHeritage Soc Desegregation Prog, 1980-81; bd mem, Advocacy Comn Changes, 1980-83; editorial bd New England Jour Black Studies, 1982-; bd mem, Cambridge Haitian Am As-

soc, 1984-85; Cambridge Peace Comt, 1984-85; pres, Nat Coun Black Studies NE Reg, 1984-86; consult, Humanities Inst Belmont, MA, 1987; Patriotic Coumbite Haitian Diaspora, 1987-91; bd chmn, CPDH, 1991-. **Honors/Awds:** Article "Class Conflict in Haiti" Ethnic Conflict & Power, 1973; Disting Service, Salem State Col, 1980, 1985; Prof Develop Grant, Salem State Col, 1981, 1985; Article "Ethnomusicology of the Rada Rite of Haiti" Perfiles Tufts Univ, 1984; Introductory Readings African Am Culture Ginn Press, 1988; Dancing Spirits; Rhythms & Rituals Haitian Vodun, Greenwood, pres, 1996. *

FLINT, DR. CHARLEY
Educator. **Educ:** NC A&T Univ, BS; Rutgers Univ, MA, PhD. **Career:** NC A&T Univ, fac, 1972-74; William Patterson Univ, Criminal Justice,coordr, currrently, Sociol Dept, prof & chair, currently, Grad Prog Sociol, dir; ALANA, founding coord. **Orgs:** Pres bd trustees, NJ Asn Corrections; secy bd dirs, pres bd dirs, YWCA Eastern Union County; mem bd dirs, NJ Chap, Am Correctional Asn; vpres, NJAsn Criminal Justice Educrs; Eastern Sociol Soc; Am Sociol Asn; Int Community Corrections Asn; Asn Black Women Higher Educ. **Special Achievements:** Numerous publications including, "Black Women in Higher Education: Forging Ties With Other Women of Color", The Black Scholar: Jour Black Studies &Res, 1995; "A book review of White Nation: Fantasies of White Supremacy ina Multiracial Society", Jour Int Migration & Integration, 2004; "Women and Reentry", NJ Inst Social Justice, 2004. **Business Addr:** Professor, William Patterson University, Department of Sociology, Sci 328 300 Pompton Rd, Wayne, NJ 07470, **Business Phone:** (973)720-2368.

FLINT, MARY FRANCES
Manager. **Personal:** Born Jan 28, 1950, Rustburg, VA; daughter of Cleveland James and Virginia James; married William B, Jun 29, 1974; children: JeVonda & RaShonda. **Educ:** Florida A&M Univ, BS, 1974; Xavier Univ, MBA, 1979. **Career:** Am Elec Power Co, acct, 1974-77, supvr, planning & budgeting, 1977-86, admin asst, off pres, 1986-89, customer serv mgr, 1989-93, community serv mgr, 1993-; Cert public acct, 1985. **Orgs:** Treas, PowerCo Credit Union, recording secy, 1992-; Ohio Soc CPA's, 1985-. **Business Addr:** Community Service Manager, American Electric Power Co, 850 Tech Center Dr, Gahanna, OH 43230, **Business Phone:** (614)883-6790.

FLIPPINS, GREGORY L.
Mayor. **Personal:** Born Jul 2, 1950, Shaw, MS. **Educ:** Delta State Univ, Grad, 1972; Valley State Univ, attended. **Career:** Shaw MS, mayor; Internal Revenue, 2 1/2 yrs; Bolivar Co Neighborhood Youth Corp, counr; Chenault Chevrolet Co, car salesman; Housing Authority City Greenwood, exec dir, currently. **Orgs:** Fel, Inst Polit. **Business Phone:** (662)453-4822.

FLONO, FANNIE
Journalist. **Personal:** Born May 4, 1952, Augusta, GA; daughter of Prudence King Flono and Adam Flono. **Educ:** Clark Col, Atlanta, GA, BA, Jour, 1974. **Career:** Greenville (SC) News, asst city ed, 1983-84; Charlotte (NC) Observer Newspaper, asst, state ed, 1984-86, asst Polit ed, 1986-88, Polit ed, 1988-90, night metro ed, 1990-91, city ed, 1991-93, edial writer & columnist, 1993-96, assoc ed, 1996-. **Orgs:** Charlotte Bus League, 1987-90; past pres, Charlotte Area Asn Black Journalists, 1988, recording secy, 1990; prog comt, Nat Asn Black Journalists, 1990; dep regional dir, Region IV Nat Asn Black Journalists, 1990; Nat Asn Black Journalists, Nat Scholar co-chairperson, 1992-93. **Honors/Awds:** Investigative Reporting, reporter, First Place, United Press Inter-Nat (GA), 1980; Georgia School Bell Award, Ga Asn Educr 1978; Investigative Reporting Editor 1st Place, NC Press Asn, 1988, 2nd Place, Column Writing, 1994; Fellow, Atlantic Bridge Found; Nieman Fellow, Harvard Univ, 1998-99; Fellow, Inst Educ Inquiry, 2003-04; Region III Hall of Fame, Nat Asn Black Journalists, 2007. **Business Addr:** Associate Editor, Charlotte Observer, 600 S Tryon St, PO Box 32188, Charlotte, NC 28202.

FLOOD, EUGENE, JR.
Executive, trader. **Educ:** Harvard Col, BA, econs, 1978; Mass Inst Technol, PhD, econs, 1983. **Career:** Stanford Univ, Graduate Sch Bus, instr, finance, five yrs; Morgan Stanley Asset Mgt, portfolio mgr, 1987-; Mas Inst Technol, dean; Nomura Sch Advanced Mgt; Int Mgt Inst,Tokyo; Geneva, lectr; Morgan Stanley & Co, res & develop group, mgr; Derivative Trading Group, mgr, 1990-91; mortgage-backed securities area, trader, 1991-95; Smith Breeden Assocs, pres & cheif exec officer, 1994-. **Honors/Awds:** Nat Sci Found, Minority Fels in Econs; Soc Quantitative Analysts; trustee, Col Retirement Equities Fund; bd mem, Mass Inst Technol. **Special Achievements:** Area of specialization: asset-backed securities. **Business Phone:** (919)933-5473.*

FLOOD, SHEARLENE DAVIS
School administrator. **Personal:** Born May 13, 1938, Jefferson County, AL; married Ralph; children: Angela Harris & Clinton Harris Jr. **Educ:** Ala State Univ, BS, 1958; Univ Ala Guidance Inst, EDPA, 1969; Educ Adminr & Higher Educ Univ Ala, Tuscaloosa, EdD, 1976. **Career:** Opelika Pub Sch Syst Music instr, 1958-60; Jefferson Co Pub Sch Syst, Eng & Music, instr, 1960-63; Birmingham Pub Sch Syst, instr, Speech Art & Music, 1963-68; Jefferson State Jr Col, dir coun, career lab, spec serv, 1969-. **Orgs:** Am Asn Community & Jr Col; Coun Black Am Affairs; exec mem, Stud Personnel Div Ala Jr & Comm Col Asn; Ala Personnel & Guidance Asn; Nat Asn Mental Health; community develop off, City Birmingham. **Honors/Awds:** Citizens Award, Merit Field Psychol Serv; Outstanding Faculty Member, Jefferson State & Jr Col; Service Award, Jefferson State Jr Col, 1980. **Business Addr:** Director, Jefferson State Junior College, 2601 Carson Rd, Birmingham, AL 35215.

FLORES, JOSEPH R
Artist, educator. **Personal:** Born Oct 22, 1935, New York, NY; son of Joseph L and Margaret Saunders Gray; children: Sam, Monique, Grace & Joe & Sean. **Career:** Model Cities Prog, Rochester, NY, dir commun, 1968-72; Action Better Community, Rochester, NY, artist, 1972-74; Rochester, NY, artist self-employed, 1974-86; Rochester City Sch Dist, Rochester, NY, instr aide, 1986-; artist, currently. **Honors/Awds:** First place, Mother Earth, Joseph Ave Art Show, 1987; First place, Martin Luther King Jr, Black Am Artists Inc, 1987; Second place, Tired, Letchworth State Park, 1988; first place, Roots & Wings, Waterfront Art Show, 1989; First place, Whole World in His Hands, St John Fisher Col, 1990. **Special Achievements:** Paintings in the White House, Oval Office during President Carter Administration, previous shows and Awards, street fair, Ann Arbor MI, Detroit Festival of Arts, 1996, Cornhill Arts Festival, Allentown Festival, Buffalo NY, Commissioned Portraits of Rochester Mayor & Executive Director Monroe County. **Home Addr:** 67 Rosalind St, Rochester, NY 14619, **Home Phone:** (585)436-4319. **Business Addr:** Artist, PO Box 19558, Rochester, NY 14619, **Business Phone:** 800-376-3087.*

FLORES, LEO
Banker. **Career:** Falcon Nat Bank, pres, currently.

FLOURNOY, VALERIE ROSE
Writer, consultant. **Personal:** Born Apr 17, 1952, Camden, NJ; daughter of Payton I Flournoy Sr (deceased) and Ivie Mae Buchanan; divorced. **Educ:** William Smith Col, Geneva, NY, BA, social studies, teaching cert, 1974. **Career:** Dial Books Young Readers, asst ed, 1977-79; Silhouette Books/Pocket Books, sr ed, 1979-82; Berkley Publ Group/Second Chance at Love, consult ed, 1982-83; Vis A Vis Publ Co, 1985-; Books: The Best Time of Day, 1978; The Twins Strike Back, 1980; The Patchwork Quilt, 1985; Tanya's Reunion. **Orgs:** Bd pres, Palmyra Bd Educ; Burlington County Prof Develop Bd. **Honors/Awds:** Christopher Award, Christophers Inc, 1985; Coretta Scott King Award, Am Libr Asn, Chicago, 1985; Ezra Jack Keats New Writer Award, Ezra Jack Keats Found & NY Pub Libr, 1986. **Special Achievements:** First recipient of Ezra Jack Keats New Writer Award in 1986 sponsored by Ezra Jack Keats Found and The NY Public Library. **Home Addr:** 505 Arch St, Palmyra, NJ 08065. *

FLOWERS, D. MICHELLE
Public relations executive. **Personal:** Born in Greensboro, NC; daughter of Thomas and Catherine. **Educ:** Winston Salem State Univ, MA, English, 1976; Northwestern Univ, MS, Advertising, 1982. **Career:** Integon Insurance Co, commun specialist, 1976-78; Chicago Urban League, commun spec & media rel mgr, 1978, dir pub rel, 1983; Golin & Harris, account supvr, 1984; Burrell Pub Rel, asst vpres, 1986, sr vpres, 1987; Flowers Commun Group Inc, pres & ceo, currently. **Orgs:** Museum SCI & Industry, Black Creativity Adv com; Alpha Kappa Alpha Sorority; Publicity Club Chicago; Pub Rels soc ame; Black Pub Rels soc; Life Directions bd trustees. **Honors/Awds:** Media Award, Cystic Fibrosis Found; Business Communicators Award, Carolinas asn; Pub Rels soc hall of fame, Two Silver Anvils; Three Gold & Four Silver Trumpets Award of Merit, Publicity Club Chicago; Founders Award, Nat Black Pub Rels, 2003; Society Platinum Trumpet award, Publicity Club Chicago, 2006. **Business Addr:** President, Chief Executive Officer, Flowers Communication Group, 542 S Dearborn Suite 1150, Chicago, IL 60605, **Business Phone:** (312)986-1254.*

FLOWERS, LEE. See FLOWERS, LETHON, III.

FLOWERS, LETHON, III (LEE FLOWERS)
Football player. **Personal:** Born Jan 14, 1973, Columbia, SC. **Educ:** Ga Tech Univ. **Career:** Football palyer (Retired); Pittsburgh Steelers, defensive back, 1995-02; Denver Broncos, safety, 2003. *

FLOWERS, DR. LOMA KAYE
Psychiatrist. **Personal:** Born Feb 27, 1944, Ohio; daughter of Elsie and Dr George W; married Edgar Flowers Jr; children: George & Brandon. **Educ:** Western Reserve Univ, AB (magna cum laude), biol, 1965; Case Western Reserve Univ, MD, 1968. **Career:** San Francisco Gen Hosp, internship, 1968-69; Stanford Univ Med Ctr, residency in psychiatry, 1969-72; E Palo Alto Comm Health Ctr, dir mental health, 1971-73; Va Hosp San Francisco, chief mental hygiene clinic 1973-77; Various Sch Health Business Org, consult, 1970-; Delaney & Flowers Dream Center, dir, 1983-; Univ Calif, clinical prof psychiatry; Host, BET Cable TV, "Dr Flowers on Call" 1985-86; Personal & Prof develop consult, currently. **Orgs:** Vpres 1983-85, chmn bd dirs Asn Study Dreams, 1984-85; Distinguished Fel Am Psychiatric Asn, 1987; pres, Northern Calif Psychiatric asn, 1998-99; Negro Bus & Prof Women's asn; NAACP, Black Psychiat Am; SFUSD, PTSA; AMA; Am Psychiat asn; Asn Study Dreams; Calif Med Soc; John Hale Med Soc; Nat Med Asn. **Honors/Awds:** Motar bd, 1963; Francis Hobart Herrick Prize,1964; Phi Beta Kappa 1964; Med Sch Faculty Award Reserch, 1968; Univ Calif San Francisco Henry J Kaiser Teaching Award, 1996; Special Recognition Award, Univ Calif San Francisco Clinical Faculty Assn, 1994; NCPS Presidents? Distinguished Service Award, Emotional Educ consult, 2002. **Special Achievements:** Author, "The Morning After: A Pragmatists Approach to Dreams," Psychiatric Journal, Univ Ottawa, 1988; author, "Psychotherapy Black & White," Journal Nat Med Assn, 1972; "The Dream Interview Method in a Private Outpatient Psychotherapy Practice," New Directions in Dream Interpretation, Suny Press, 1993; "The Use of Presleep Instructions and Dreams in Psyhcosomatic Disorders." Psychotherapy & Psychosomatics 1995; "The Dream Interview Method in Addiction Recovery, A Treatment Guide." Journal of Substance Abuse, Treatment, 1996; "The Changing Role of 'Using' Dreams in Addiction Recovery." Journal of Substance Abuse, Treatment, 1998. **Home Addr:** 1670 Plymouth Ave, PO Box 27173, San Francisco, CA 94127, **Home Phone:** (415)333-8631.

FLOWERS, MICHAEL E
Entrepreneur, lawyer. **Educ:** Bucknell Univ, BS, 1976; The Ohio State Univ Col Law, JD, 1979. **Career:** Porter, Wright, Morris & Arthur, assoc, 1979-86, partner, 1987-95; Bricker & Eckler LLP, partner, 1995-; The Bus Lawyer, ed, 1997-98; Community Capital Develop Corp, dir, 1998-2002; Columbus Urban Growth Corp, dir, 2000-04; Krieger Automobile Dealerships, asst secy & dir; Keith B Key Enterprises LLC, chief legal coun, currently. **Orgs:** Ohio Small Bus & Entrepreneurship Coun, 1991-92; gov coun, ABA Sect Bus Law, 1994-2001; deleg, The White House Conf Small Bus; secy, Columbus Bd Trustees, 1998-2002; chair, Bus Law Sect Am Bar Asn, 1999-2000; Entrepreneurship Steering Comt, Greater Columbus Chamber Com, 1999-2002; bd mem, Columbus Bar Serv Inc, 1999-2003; ABA Journal Bd Ed, 2005-; trustee, Columbus State Community Col; fel, Am Bar Found; appointee, Gov Taft's Minority Bus Coun; Nat Bar Asn; Negotiated Acquisitions Comt, ABA Sect Bus Law; founding mem, ed bd, Bus Law Today; Am Bar Asn Comt Continuing Prof Educ; founding mem, ABA Africa Law Initiatives Coun; chair & bd secy, Mount Carmel Health Found Bd Trustees; trustee & bd secy, Mount Carmel Health Syst; chair, Capital Park Health Ctr Bd Trustees; deacon, Genessee Avenue Church Christ; bd secy, Optimer Photonics Inc; exec, Capital Club; Am Law Inst. **Honors/Awds:** Columbus Jaycees Outstanding Young Citizen Award, 1988; Minority Small Bus Advocate of the Yr, US Small Bus Admin, 1993; Bus First Forty Under 40 Award, 1993; Business Law Chair's Award, Am Bar Asn Sect, 1995; Distinguished Alumnus, Col Law, Ohio State Univ, 2001; Ritter Award for Professionalism, Ohio State Bar Found, 2005; Prof Achievement Award, The Ohio State Univ Alumni Asn, 2005. **Special Achievements:** Author: Basic Legal Issues Associated with Internet Start-Ups, Ohio Assembly of Councils Business Trade Journal, June, 2000; Updated ABA Diversity Plan Forges Ahead, The National Law Journal, July, 2000; Leading US Corporation Files Amicus Brief Favoring Diversity, The Metropolitan Corporate Counsel, March, 2001; US Lawyers Can Promote Democracy In Distant Places, Business Law Today, November/December, 2002; List of Nation's Top Lawyers, Black Enterprise Mag, 2003; Listed in Best Lawyers in Am, 2005-06. Published Numerous Books & Articles. **Business Addr:** Partner, Bricker & Eckler LLP, 100 S 3rd St, Columbus, OH 43215.

FLOWERS, MICHAEL E
Lawyer. **Educ:** Bucknell Univ, B.S, 1976; Ohio State Univ, JD, 1979; Tuck Sch Bus Dartmouth Minority, bus exec prog, 2001. **Career:** Bricker & Eckler LLP, partner, currently. **Orgs:** Gov coun, ABA Section Bus Law, 1994-2001; Secy, COSI Columbus bd Trustees, 1998-2002; Entrepreneurship Steering Comt, Greater Columbus Chamber Com, 1999-2002;dir, Columbus Urban Growth Corp, 2000-04; Am Law Inst; ABA Jl bd Edit, 2005-. Nat Bar Asn; chair, Founding Mem, Ed Bd, Bus Law Today; Bus law, Am Bar Asn; Trustee & bd Secy, Mt Carmel Health Syst; dir, Community Capital Develop Corp; bd mem, Columbus Bar Servs; Exec mem, Capital Club;bus law group; Fells Am Bar Found. **Honors/Awds:** Distinguished Alumnus Col Law, Ohio State Univ, 2000; Am Law Inst, 2002; List Nations Top Lawyers, Black Enterprise Mag, 2003; Ohio Super Lawyers Listing, 2004-06; Professional Achievement Award, Ohio State Univ Alumni Asn, 2005; Ritter Award for Professionalism, Ohio State Bar Found, Listed Best Lawyers Am, 2005-06. **Special Achievements:** First African American elected chair of Bus Law section of the Amer Bar Assn. Author of U.S. Lawyers Can Promote Democracy In Distant Places," Business Law Today, November/December 2002 ."Leading U.S. Corporation Files Amicus Brief Favoring Diversity," The Metropolitan Corporate Counsel, March 2001 ."Updated ABA Diversity Plan Forges Ahead," The National Law Journal, July 2000. **Home Addr:** 1351 Camelot Dr, Columbus, OH 43220. **Business Addr:** Partner, Attorney, Bricker & Eckler LLP, 100 S 3rd St, Columbus, OH 43215-4291, **Business Phone:** (614)227-2340.

FLOWERS, RALPH L.
Lawyer. **Personal:** Born Jan 23, 1936, Palatka, FL; married. **Educ:** FL A&M Univ, BS, 1957, EdM, 1968, JD, 1968. **Career:**

Pvt Law Pract; Lincoln Pk Acad, band dir, 1959-65; Riviera Beach, prosecutor ad litem, 1971-73; City Fort Pierce, judge, prosecutor, 1972-73; atty, 1968-. **Orgs:** Bd dir & legal adv, Indian Rvr Investment Corp Pioneer Investment Capital Corp; bd dir, FL Rural Legal Serv; chmn, Judicial Coun FL Chap Nat Bar Asn; Exalted Ruler, Pride St Lucie Lodge IBPOE W, 1970; Alpha Phi Alpha; Am Bar Asn; FL Asn Trial Lawyers. **Honors/Awds:** St Lucie County C C Flowers for the living award, Radio Station WIRA, 1973; public safety award, St Lucie County Safety Coun, 1974; Alpha Phi Alpha man of the yr, 1976. **Military Serv:** AUS, 1st lt, 1957-59. **Business Addr:** Attorney, Private Practitioner, Sunrise Theatre Bldg, PO Box 3668, Fort Pierce, FL 34948-3668, **Business Phone:** (561)489-2785.

FLOWERS, RUNETTE
Physician. **Personal:** Born Apr 2, 1945, Donaldsonville, GA; married W Alphonso. **Educ:** Dillard Univ, BA, biol, New Orleans, 1967; Tuskegee Inst, MS, 1969; Meharry Med Col, Nashville, MD, 1973. **Career:** Dekalb Grady Clin, staff pediatrician, 1976-; Dept Preventive Med Emory Univ & Sch Med, asst prof, 1976-; Emory Univ, residency, 1973-76; Edwood-parent-child Ctr, consult, 1977-; Sch Nursing GA Baptist Hosp, lectr, 1978-79; Nurse Practritioner Prog Emory, preceptor 1978-79; S Dekalb Pediatrics, obstet & gynec, 2004-. **Orgs:** Greater Atlanta Pediatric Asn, 1978-; Health Syst Agency, GA, 1980; Delta Sigma Theta Sorority Beta Kappa Chi Sci Honor Soc; Composite State Bd Med Examiners, 1983-; Fedn State Med Bd US, 1992-; Nat Bd Med Examiners. **Honors/Awds:** Most Outstanding Student, Pediatrics Meharry Med Col, 1973; Grace M James Award, Pediatrics Meharry Med Col, 1973. **Business Addr:** Obstetrics & Gynecology Physician, South Dekalb Pediatrics Inc, 2855 Candler Rd suite 9, Decatur, GA 30034-1415, **Business Phone:** (404)243-9630.*

FLOWERS, SALLY A.
Dentist. **Personal:** Born Jun 18, 1954, Detroit, MI; daughter of Willie Oscar and Mary Jane Perry James; children: Krystle Maria, Dawn Amber. **Educ:** Eastern Mich Univ, attended 1974; Howard Univ Sch Dent, DDS, 1978; Johns Hopkins Univ, MPH, 1980. **Career:** Pimlico Dent Clin, Baltimore, MD, assoc dentist, 1979-; Dr Roy Baptiste, Silver Springs, MD, assoc dentist, 1980-82; Dr Barbara Johnson, Wash, DC, assoc dentist, 1981-82; Capital Hill Dent Ctr, Wash, DC, assoc dentist, 1981-82; pvt pract, gen dentist, 1982-. **Orgs:** Am Dent Asn, 1982-; Acad Gen Dent, 1982-; DC Dent Soc, 1982-; pres, Pin Pro High Golf Club, 1987-88; Rec secy, Kennedy St Asn Merchants Prof, 1989-91; Johns Hopkins Alumni; Howard Univ Alumni. **Business Addr:** Dentist, Private Practice, Dist Dent Ctr, 250 Kennedy St NW, Washington, DC 20011.*

FLOWERS, SONNY. See FLOWERS, WILLIAM HAROLD, JR.

FLOWERS, VONETTA
Athlete. **Personal:** Born Oct 29, 1973, Birmingham, AL. **Educ:** Univ Ala, Birmingham. **Career:** US Olympic Comt, bobsledder, currently. **Honors/Awds:** Gold medal, women's bobsled, Winter Olympics, 2002; Recipient of the USOC Team of the Year, 2002; Dodge Nat Athletic Olympian Award, 2003; Winter Olympics, sixth, 2006; US Olympic Spirit Award; 50 Most Beautiful People; 5th at World Championships with partner Jean Prahm (Racine), 2005; Annie Glenn Award, 2006; Hearing Hear-O Award, 2006. **Special Achievements:** First black athlete (male or female) from any country to ever win an Olympic Winter Games gold medal; first person from Alabama to win a medal in the Winter Olympics; named one of Essence Magazines 50 of the Most Inspiring African-Americans; named one of Ebony Magazine's 57 of the Most Intriguing Blacks; listed in People Magazine's 50 Most Beautiful People; Author: Running on Ice: The Overcoming Faith of Vonetta Flowers. **Home Addr:** 1609 Jody Ct, Jacksonville, FL 32259. **Business Addr:** Bobsledder, United States Olympic Committee, 1 Olympic Plz, Colorado Springs, CO 80909, **Business Phone:** (719)632-5551.

FLOWERS, WILLIAM HAROLD, JR. (SONNY FLOWERS)
Lawyer. **Personal:** Born Mar 22, 1946, Chicago, IL; son of Ruth C and W Harold; married Pamela Mays Flowers. **Educ:** Univ Colo, BA, 1967, Law School, JD, 1971. **Career:** Adams County, dep dist atty, 1977-78; pvt pract, 1979-; Holland & Hart, Denver, Colo, partner, 1989-97; Hurth, Yeager, Sisk & Blakemore LLP, partner, 1997-. **Orgs:** Bd dirs, KGNU Radio Sta, 1981-84; bd dirs, Colo Criminal Defense Bar, 1982-83; regional dir, Nat Bar Asn, 1984-85; vpres, Nat Bar Asn, 1990-91; bd govs, Nat Bar Asn, 1985-95; exec bd, Boy Scouts Am, 1983-99; pres, Sam Cary Bar Asn; Comt Corrections Bd, 1984-90; Judicial Nominating Comt, 1988-94; bd dir, Colo ACLU, 1990; pres, Colorado Trial Lawyers Asn, 1999-00; Asn of Trial Lawyers Am, exec comt, 2001-03; bd gov, Asn of Trial Lawyers Am, 2002-03; bd dirs, Coloradons Against the Death Penalty, 2001-; Colo Am Civil Liberties Union; pres, Univ Colo Alumni Asn, 1994-95; bd dir, Univ Colo Found, 1996-02; vpres, Colo Bar Asn, 2002-03; bd dir, Boulder County Bar Asn, 2003-04. **Honors/Awds:** Community Service Award, Univ Co Alumni Asn, 1998; Outstanding Alumnus, Univ Colo Black Students Alliance, 1990; Award in Bus Community Action, Boulder County, CO, 1990; Presidential Award, Nat Bar Asn, 1987. **Business Addr:** Partner, Hurth Yeager Sisk & Blakemore LLP, 4860 Riverbend Rd, PO Box 17850, Boulder, CO 80308.*

FLOYD, CHRIS (CHRISTOPHER MICHAEL FLOYD)
Football player. **Personal:** Born Jun 23, 1975, Detroit, MI. **Educ:** Univ Mich. **Career:** New Eng Patriots, running back, 1998-2000; Cleveland Browns, 2000. *

FLOYD, CHRISTOPHER MICHAEL. See FLOYD, CHRIS.

FLOYD, CLIFF, JR. (CORNELIUS CLIFFORD FLOYD)
Baseball player. **Personal:** Born Dec 5, 1972, Chicago, IL. **Career:** Montreal Expos, infielder, 1993-96; Fla Marlins, 1997-2002; Montreal Epos, 2002; Boston Red Sox, 2002; NY Mets, infielder, 2003-06; Chicago Cubs, Outfielders, 2007; Tampa Bay Rays, 2008; San Diego Padres, Not Active, 2009. **Honors/Awds:** World Series Champion, 1997; All Star Selection, 2001. **Business Addr:** Professional Baseball Player, San Diego Padres, Petco Pk, PO Box 122000, San Diego, CA 92112-2000.*

FLOYD, CORNELIUS CLIFFORD. See FLOYD, CLIFF, JR.

FLOYD, DR. DEAN ALLEN
Physician. **Personal:** Born Mar 10, 1951, Loris, SC; son of Stephen J Sr and Ernestine; married Gail Payton; children: Anissa Deanne, Dean Allen II & Allycia Summer. **Educ:** Clemson Univ, BS, 1972; Med Univ SC, MD, 1976. **Career:** Richmond Memorial Hosp, residency, 1977-80; Family Health Centers Inc, med dir, 1980-85; pvt pract, 1985-; SC State Health & Human Serv, health consult, 1985-; Richland Community Health Care Asn Inc, Columbia, SC, physician, currently.

FLOYD, DR. ELSON S.
College president, dean (education). **Personal:** Born Mar 1, 1956, Henderson, NC; son of Elson and Dorothy Garrett; married Carmento; children: 2. **Educ:** Univ NC, Chapel Hill, BA, polit sci & speech, 1978, Med, adult educ, 1982, PhD higher & adult educ, 1984. **Career:** Univ NC, Chapel Hill, asst dean stud life, 1978-81, dean stud affairs, 1981-84; exec vice chancellor & clin prof educ, 1995-98; Eastern Wash Univ, vpres Student servs, 1990-91, vpres Admin, 1991-92, exec vpres, 1992-93; Washington State Higher Educ Coordinating Bd, exec dir, 1993-95; Truman Scholarship Reviewer, 1999; Western Mich Univ, Pres & Prof Educ, 1998-2003; Univ Mo, pres, 2003-07. **Orgs:** Midwestern Higher Educ Comn; United Way Am Alexis de Tocqueville Soc; Am Coun Educ Comn Leadership & Inst Effectiveness; Knight Comn on Intercollegiate Athletics; bd dirs, Nat Merit Scholarship Corp; Edu Comn States, 1993; The Darling Sch Bd Trustees, 1997-2000. **Honors/Awds:** Outstanding Alumni Award, C Knox Massey Award, Univ NC; James C Kirk patrick Award, NW Mo Press Asn; Distinguished Alumnus Award, Univ NC, 2004; Communicator of the Year Award, Mid-Missouri Chapter Public Relations Soc Am, 2005. **Home Addr:** 1900 S Providence Rd, Columbia, MO 65203.

FLOYD, ERIC AUGUSTUS
Basketball player. **Personal:** Born Mar 6, 1960, Gastonia, NC. **Educ:** Georgetown Univ, polit sci & pub admin, 1982. **Career:** Basketball player (retired); NJ Nets, 1982-83, 1994-95; Golden State Warriors, 1982-88; Houston Rockets, 1987-93; San Antonio Spurs, 1993-94. **Honors/Awds:** Most Valuable Player, NCAA W Region Tourney.

FLOYD, JAMES T.
Association executive. **Personal:** Son of Willie J; married Dr Barbara Floyd; children: James T Jr, Norman V, Kimberly U, Javonda A, Brittaine Nakkole. **Educ:** Allen Univ, BS, 1957; Tuskegee Univ, MS, 1965. **Career:** Sanders High Sch, teacher, 1957-58, head football coach, 1960-64; Beck High Sch, chmn sci dept, 1965-69; Union Carbide Corp, process engr, 1969-72; WR Grace & Co, process engr, 1972-75, qual assurance mgr, 1976-82, group leader eng, 1983; F & M Development Enterprises Inc, chief exec officer, currently. **Orgs:** Bd dir, Phillis Wheatly Asn; adv bd, USCG Col; adv bd, Dept Mental Health. **Honors/Awds:** Selected to Ebony's 100 Most Influential Blacks in Am, 1985-87; Entrepreneur of the Year, 1990. **Military Serv:** AUS 2 yrs. **Home Addr:** 106 Brandon Way, Simpsonville, SC 29681. *

FLOYD, JANET. See LANGHART COHEN, JANET.

FLOYD, DR. JEREMIAH
Association executive. **Personal:** Born Jan 8, 1932, Laurens, SC; son of Willie James and Clairender; married Clara Brown; children: Camille & Edgar. **Educ:** Allen Univ, BS, 1956; NW Univ, MA, 1960, PhD, 1973. **Career:** Natl Sch Bds Asn, retired assoc dir; Evanston Pub Sch, prin, 1970-73; Nat Sch Bd Asn, dir urban & minority rel, 1973-76, form asst exec dir to assoc exec dir, 1976-78; Hands Sci Outreach, bd pres, currently; Floyd Consulting, sr partner & chief exec officer, currently. **Orgs:** Bd dir, United Way Evanston, 1971-76; pres, NU Chap, Phi Delta Kappa, 1972-74; vpres, Northwestern Univ Alumni Educ, 1973-76; vice chmn, Montgomery Community Servs Partnership, 1986-95; State Adv Comt Adult Educ & Community Service, 1986-88; Montgomery Col Gen Educ Adv Comt, 1988-. **Honors/Awds:** NSF fel, Nat Sci Found, Northwestern Univ, 1959-62; IDEA fel, Rockford Col, 1969; pres, Wilmette Sch Dist 39 Bd Educ, 1976; Montgomery County Bd Educ, MD, 1984; vpres, Montgomery County Bd Educ MD, 1985-86. **Military Serv:** AUS, Nat Defense Medal, Good Conduct Medal, 1955. **Home Addr:** 5909 Aberdeen Rd, Bethesda, MD 20817. **Business Addr:** Board President, Hands On Science Outreach, 12118 Heritage Pk Circle, Silver Spring, MD 20906, **Business Phone:** (301)929-2330.

FLOYD, MALCOLM
Football player. **Personal:** Born Dec 19, 1972, San Francisco, CA. **Educ:** Calif State Univ, Fresno. **Career:** Football player (retired); Houston Oilers, wide receiver, 1994-96; Tennessee Oilers, 1997; St. Louis Rams, 1997; San Diego Chargers, 2006-08. *

FLOYD, MARK STEPHEN
Lawyer, association executive. **Personal:** Born Nov 30, 1958, El Paso, TX; son of Columbus and Vardrene Bailey; married Lauren Generette, Sep 2, 1990. **Educ:** Stanford Univ, AB, music & polit sci, 1980; Columbia Law Sch, JD, 1983. **Career:** Sq Sanders & Dempsey, Cleveland, OH, partner, 1983-; Thompson Hine LLP, Labor & Employ Pract Group, vice chair, patner, Diversity Comt, chair, 2000-; Columbia J Art & Law, ed. **Orgs:** Exec comt mem, Cleveland Ballet, 1989-93; exec comt, legal coun, Cleveland Baroque Orchestra, 1992-96; steering comt mem, Cleveland Orchestra; tenor soloist, asst conductor, Mt Zion Congregational Church; bd trustees, Crains Cleveland Bus Top 40 Young Bus Leaders Under 40; bd trustees, Cleveland Bar Asn; bd trustees, Cleveland Inst; Am Bar Asn; Ohio State Bar Asn; Am Immigration Lawyers Asn; bd trustees, Urban League Greater Cleveland; chair, Cleveland Inst Music; parliamentarian, Coun Deleg, Ohio State Bar Asn; chmn, Club at Key Ctr. **Honors/Awds:** Ohio Super Lawyers Award, 2006-07. **Special Achievements:** 40 Under 40 Outstanding Young Business Leaders, Crain's Cleveland Business. **Business Addr:** Partner, Attorney, Thompson Hine LLP, 3900 Key Ctr 127 Public Sq, Cleveland, OH 44114-1291, **Business Phone:** (216)566-5836.

FLOYD, MARQUETTE L.
Judge. **Personal:** Born Oct 14, 1928, Winnsboro, SC; son of Mary Brown; married Mildred L Floyd. **Educ:** NYU, BS 1958; Brooklyn Law Sch, LLB 1960. **Career:** Judge (retired); Suffolk County, dist ct judge; Pvt Prac NY, atty; Ronek Park Civic Asn, pres; Dist Ct Suffolk County, county ct, 1986; New York State, Riverhead, NY, supreme court, presiding justice, 1990-03. **Orgs:** Pres, N Amityville Rep Club; dir, chmn ACE Ctr; dir, Legal Aid Soc; dir, Sunrise Psychia Clinic; dir & Key, Amityville Youth Orgn; secy, Eta Theta Lambda Chapter; Alpha Phi Alpha Frat Inc; Suffolk Co Bar Asn; NY State Bar Asn; Dist Ct bd Judges Suffold County; Dist Ct bd Judges Nassau & Suffolk Co; Supreme Ct Justices; Suffolk County Charter Revision Comt; NY State Jury Syst Mgt Adv Comt. **Honors/Awds:** Community Service Award, 100 Black Men Nassau & Suffolk, 1982; Schroll Honor Award, Nat Asn Bus & Prof Women, 1983; Achievement Award, Babylon Coun Black Republicans, 1985; County Court Judge of the Year, Suffolk County Court Officers Asn, 1986; Judge of the Year, Suffolk County Bar Asn, 1987; Man of the Year, Suffolk County Police Conf, 1990. **Special Achievements:** first African Am to be elected to the Dist Ct in Suffolk Co. **Military Serv:** USAF, t & sgt, 1948-54; National Service Award. *

FLOYD, DR. SAMUEL A.
Educator, college administrator, consultant. **Personal:** Born Feb 1, 1937, Tallahassee, FL; son of Samuel A Floyd and Theora Combs; married Barbara, Feb 1, 1956; children: Wanda LaVerne Green, Cecilia Ann Carruthers & Samuel A III. **Educ:** Fla A&M Univ, BS, 1957; Southern Ill Univ, Carbondale, MME, 1965, PhD, 1969. **Career:** Smith-Brown High Sch, Arcadia, Fla, band dir, 1957-62; Fla A&M Univ, Dept Music, instr, asst dir bands, 1962-64; Southern Ill Univ, Carbondale, assoc prof, 1964-78; Fisk Univ, Inst Res Black Am Music, dir, 1978-83; Columbia Col, Chicago, Ctr Black Music Res, dir, 1983-90, 1993-2002, acaddean, 1990-93, interim vpres acad affairs & provost, 1999-2001, dir emer &consult, 2002-. **Orgs:** Am Musiological Soc; nat Coun mem, Col Music Soc, 1978-80; Pi Kappa Lambda; bd trustees, Soc Am Music, Sonneck Soc, 1990-93; vis comt, Vanderbilt Univ, Blair Sch Music, 1990-; vis comt, Univ Chicago, deptmusic, 1992-. **Honors/Awds:** Young Execs Politics Award, Chicago, Ill, Outstanding Achievement Fine Arts, 1989; Ruth Allen Fouche Heritage Black Music Award, Chicago Park Dist, 1989; Irving Lowens Award Distinguished Scholar Am Music, SonneckSoc Am Music, 1991; Irving Lowens Award Distinguished Scholar Am Music, Sonneck Soc Am Music, 1991; Bellagio Study & Conf Ctr, Bellagio, Italy, scholar-in-residence, 1995. **Special Achievements:** Written: Black Music in the Harlem Renaissance: A Collection of Essays, Westport, Conn, Greenwood Press, 1990; The Power of Black Music, NY, Oxford Univ Press, 1995; Int Dict Black Composers, 2 vols, Chicago, Fitzroy Dearborn Publ, 1999; "Ring Shout Literary Studies, Historical Studies & Black Music Inquiry", BMBJ, pgs 267-288, Fall 1991; "Black Music Circum-Caribbean", Am Music 17, no. 1, pgs 1-37, Spring 1999. **Business Addr:** Director Emeritus, Columbia College Chicago, Center for Black Music Research, 600 S Michigan Ave, Chicago, IL 60605-1996, **Business Phone:** (312)344-7559.

FLOYD, VERNON CLINTON
Executive, engineer, educator. **Personal:** Born Nov 20, 1927, Chickasaw Terrace, AL; son of Nathan D and Ora A Ellis;

children: Marjorie A, Victor C. **Educ:** Dunbar Trade Sch, Chicago IL, 1946; Indust Training Inst, Chicago IL, 1946; Tuskegee Inst, AL, 1952. **Career:** Station WMOZ, Mobile, AL, chief engr, 1953-65; Carver Tech Trade Sch, Mobile, AL, electronics instr, 1966-68; Community Educ Prog, Hattiesburg, MS, 1988; Circuit Broadcasting Co, Hattiesburg, MS, founder/owner, 1969-; Elec Contractor, Hattiesburg, MS, 1972-. **Orgs:** Adv chmn, Boy Scouts Am, 1971-73; BOAZ Lodge No 4, 1980; elec bd mem, City Hattiesburg, 1981-83. **Honors/Awds:** One of 10 Most Outstanding Men, Hattiesburg Ministerial Group, 1971; designed, built & made total technical instillation, WJMG-FM, 1982. **Special Achievements:** Pioneered & developed station WORV-AM, 1969; designed, built & made total tech installation, WJMG-FM, 1982; owner and operator of the first African American radio station. **Military Serv:** One-hundred fifty-ninth Artillery Batt, T5, 1946-48. **Business Addr:** President, Circuit Broadcasting Company, Worv-Am & Wjmg-Fm, 1204 Graveline St, Hattiesburg, MS 39401.*

FLOYD, VIRCHER B.
Educator. **Personal:** Born Apr 3, 1928; married. **Educ:** Earlham Col, BA, 1952, MA, 1954; Univ Pittsburgh, MSW, 1962. **Career:** Educator (retired); Pittsburgh Regional Off Penn Dept Pub Welfare, statesocial worker, 1961-63; Rural Community Develop Unit Tlaxcala Mex AFSC, dir, 1963-65; Peace Corps Bogota, Colombia, urban prog rep & staff, dir, 1968-70; Career Serv Off Earlham Col, asst prof & dir, 1970-75; Bogota Field Off Columbia, field dir corresp, 1975-77; Child Reach Plan Int, Columbia, Nicaragua, Brazil, Liberia, Ecuador & Honduras, field dir, 1975-92; Foryth Tech Community Col Spanish, teacher, tutor. **Orgs:** Exec dir, Sewickley Community Ctr, 1956-60; Townsend Community Ctr, Richmond, IN, 1965-68; vpres, Allegheny Co Fed Settlements; nat bd mem, Am Friends Serv Community, 1972-75; Acad Cert Social Workers. **Special Achievements:** Author of several publications. **Military Serv:** AUS, 1954-56.

FLOYD, WILLIAM ALI
Football player. **Personal:** Born Feb 17, 1972, St Petersburg, FL; married Bonita; children: William Andrew & Thai. **Educ:** Fla State. **Career:** Football player (retired); San Francisco 49ers, running back, 1994-97; Carolina Panthers, 1998-00; color-commentator, Florida State football. **Orgs:** Benefit foundation; Able Body Labor, public relations liasion; William Floyd's Bar None Found. **Honors/Awds:** All-Sun Coast & All-Pinellas County honor. *

FLOYD, WINSTON CORDELL
Physician. **Personal:** Born Nov 13, 1948, Edgefield, SC; married Francena Pinckney. **Educ:** Tuskegee Inst, BS, 1969; MD 1973. **Career:** Cook County Hosp, intern, 1973-74; Meharry Med Col, resd 1974-77; Meharry Med Col, instr internal med, 1976-77; pvt pract, internal med, currently; Anderson Meml Hosp, attending staff; Palmetto Health Baptist Easley Hosp; Hart County Hosp; Oconee Memorial Hosp; Cannon Memorial Hosp. **Orgs:** Diplomate, Nat Bd of Med Exmnrs, 1974; Am Bd Internal Med; AMA; mem Alpha Phi Alpha Frat; Cent Tex Med Found. **Honors/Awds:** Cert, Am Bd Internal Med. **Business Addr:** 400 N Fant St Suite G, Anderson, SC 29621.*

FLUELLEN, VELDA SPAULDING
Executive, business owner. **Personal:** Born Feb 5, 1942, Durham, NC; daughter of John Lee White and Sarah Badie Spaulding White McEachin; married Arthur L, Jun 18, 1972; children: Randall, Tanya & Bryan. **Educ:** Hampton IST, BS, 1963, MS, 1969; NCA Cent UNIV, BUS ADM Cert, 1974. **Career:** Phoenix High Sch, sci dept chmn, 1963-70; Hampton Inst, grad asst, 1969-70; NC Cent Univ, prof biol, 1970-75; Fluellen's Seafood House, owner, 1975-78; Tucson Jobs Corps, educ curriculum, 1979-80; IBM Corp, staff position purchasing, 1981-89; A&B Trading Co, Inc, pres & chief exec officer, 1988-96; Art's BBQ & Vel's Catering Serv, owner, currently. **Orgs:** Alpha Kappa Alpha Sorority, 1967-; Natl Coun Negro Women, 1970-92; Nat Asn Advan Colored People, 1981-88; Links Inc, 1981-; Resources for Women, 1988-; golden life mem, Nat Asn Advan Colored People, 1988-; Chamber Com, 1988-; Tucson Metropolitan Conv Ctr & Viss Bur, 1988-; bd mem, Ariz Restaurant Asn, Tucson Chapter, 1991-; bd mem, Pima Early Rising Execs, 1992-. **Special Achievements:** Selected as an executive on loan from IBM to teach at Arizona State University, 1988-89; received several distinctions for this service. **Home Addr:** 2802 W Magee Rd, Tucson, AZ 85742-1500. **Business Phone:** (520)388-9295.*

FLUKER, ELAYNE M
Editor, executive. **Personal:** Born in Queens, NY. **Educ:** Hampton Univ, BA, Eng, 1995. **Career:** Essence Mag, ed asst, 1997-99, asst ed, 1999-2000, arts & entertainment ed, 2000-02; Essence Commun, ed-in-chief, 2002; Elite PA Serv, chief exec officer, currently.

FLUKER, PHILIP A.
Association executive. **Personal:** Born Nov 10, 1920, Birmingham, AL; son of Eunice Stanford and Ernest Herman; married Jeanette Robinson; children: Billy Ray, Samuel Fuston Andrew, Douglas Allen, Winfred, Willie Ernest,Tracy Lynn, Phyllis Gale Christian Johnson, Eunice Patricia Hicks, Barbara& James. **Career:** Association executive (retired); community serv vol. **Orgs:** Secy & treas, 1990-91, chmn, weatherization, 1990-91; pres, London District Asn Sunday Sch & tist Training Union Cong, 1990-; TCR Sunday sch, Supt, adult Sunday sch; bd trustees, Chmn, usher bd, First Bapt Church;r;Boy Scout Troop 104; del, Off Interior, State KY; SE Ky rep, Negro Leadership Conf; pres, Harlan Chapter Rosen wald Heritage Orgn; bd dir, Rosenwald Harlanite's Inc; chmn, Housing Comt, Harlan County Fair Housing Affirmative Action Community; Gov Breathitt Adv Comn, Hon Order Ky Colonel; chmn, Scholar Preserv Roserwald Heritage; chair, Scholar London Dist Missionary & Educ Asn; treas, Christian Outreach Appalachian People Inc; chmn, Harlan County Community Action Agency.

FLUKER, DR. WALTER EARL
Educator, clergy, administrator. **Personal:** Born Aug 26, 1951, Vaiden, MS; son of Clinton and Zettie; married Sharon, Jun 20, 1981; children: Wendy D, Tiffany M, Clinton & Hampton. **Educ:** Trinity Col, BA, 1977; Garrett Evangelical Theol Sem, MDiv, 1980; Boston Univ, PhD, 1988. **Career:** Boston Univ, Whitney M Young fel, 1981-82; Harvard Univ, Andrew W Mellon fac fel, 1990-91; Vanderbilt Univ Res Coun, univ fel, 1990-91; Colgate Rochester Divinity Sch, dean black studies, 1991-97; Christian Friendship MB Church, assoc pastor, 1992-97; Morehouse Col, Colgate Rochester Divinity Sch, Howard Thurman Papers Proj, ed & dir, 1992-97; VisionQuest Inc, pres & chief exec officer, 1997; Morehouse Col, Dept Philos & Relig & Leadership Stud, exec dir, prof, Leadership Stud, chair, 1998, Leadership Ctr, exec dir, currently, Coca-Cola prof leadership studies, currently; Harvard Divinity Sch, AA Relig Studies, vis prof, 2001-02. **Orgs:** Bd mem, Trinity Press Int; bd mem, Howard Thurman Educ Trust; bd mem, Toni Morrison Soc; Soc Christian Ethics; Soc Study Black Relig; Am Acad Relig; Nat Asn Advan Colored People; fac adv, Omicron Delta Kappa Soc. **Special Achievements:** Author: Recognition, Respectability, and Loyalty: The Quest for Civilty Among Black Churches; New Day Begun: Black Churches Public Influences and American Civic Culture, Duke Univ Press, 2002; Editor, Bread Upon the Waters: Essays on Ethical Leadership from the Black Church Tradition, Volume II, Trinity Press International, 2002. **Military Serv:** AUS, spec 4, 1971-73; Meritorious Award as Chaplains Asst, 1971-73. **Business Addr:** Executive Director, Coca-Cola Professor of Leadership Studies, Morehouse College, The Leadership Center, 830 Westview Dr SW, Atlanta, GA 30314, **Business Phone:** (404)614-8565.

FLYNN, H WELTON
Accountant. **Personal:** Born Dec 22, 1921, Blackville, SC; son of Inez M and Welton; married Dec 4, 1942 (widowed); children: Welton C & Gerald A. **Educ:** Golden Gate Univ, BA, 1951. **Career:** Accountant (retired); self-employed, pub acct, 1949-2004. **Orgs:** Alpha Phi Alpha Fraternity Inc, 1960; Nat Asn Advan Colored People, 1984; San Francisco Pub Utilities Comn, 1970-91; San Francisco Convention & Visitors Bur, chmn bd, 1992-; San Francisco Soc Acct, 1977, bd dir, Munic Transp Agency. **Honors/Awds:** City's First African-American on any commission, 1970; Alpha Phi Alpha, Man of the Year, 1985, 1995, Humanitarian Medal, 1988; Nat Asn Advan Colored People Legal Defense Fund, Man of the Year, 1989; San Francisco Bus & Prof Women, Man of the Year, 1983; State Calif, State Bd Accountancy, 1949; American Public Transportation Asn Hall of Fame, 2006. **Military Serv:** AUS, master sgt, 1942-46; Good Conduct Medal.

FOARD, FREDERICK CARTER
Publisher, executive. **Personal:** Born Mar 10, 1945, Philadelphia, PA; son of Howard A Sr and Adele; married Georgeanne Garrett; children: Nicole, Justin. **Educ:** Lincoln Univ PA, BA, psychol, 1967; Capital Univ Columbus, MBA, finance & mkt, 1976. **Career:** HRB-Singer Div Singer Co, behave scientist, 1967-69; Schering Labs/Schering-Plough, mkt res analyst, 1969-71; Bristol Labs/Bristol-Myers Co, sr mkt res, 1971-73; Warren-Teed Pharm/Rohm & Haas Co, mgr mkt res, 1973-74, prod mgr, 1974-77; Smith Kline & French Labs/Smith Kline Beckman Corp, sr prod mgr, 1977-83, prod dir, 1983-86, dir mkt, 1986-88, vpres, Diuretic Prod, 1988-91; Advan Commun Strategies Inc, Cherry Hill, NJ, pres & chief exec officer, 1991-; Commun Media Inc, exec vpres, currently. **Orgs:** Omega Psi Phi Fraternity, 1963-; Am Mgt Asn, 1977-89; Nat Black MBA Asn, 1983-; Pharmaceut Adv Coun, 1986-93; corp mkt rep, Pharmaceut Manufacturer's Asn, 1986-91; bd vice chmn, Nat Minority Health Asn, 1989-94; bd mem, Am Health Asn, Philadelphia Affil, 1990-94; bd mem, Health Policy Int, 1991-. **Honors/Awds:** Legion of Honor Chapel of Four Chaplains, 1981; MBA of the Year, 1990; Omega Man of the Year, 1992. **Home Addr:** 807 Manmouth Dr, Cherry Hill, NJ 08002. **Business Addr:** Executive Vice President, Communications Media Inc, 2200 Renaissance Blvd, King Of Prussia, PA 19406.*

FOBBS, KEVIN
Executive, public relations executive, consultant. **Personal:** Born Jan 11, 1954, River Rouge, MI; son of Geraldine Jenna and Booker Terry; married Patricia Marie Strunck, Apr 3, 1982; children: Katherine Marie Strunck. **Educ:** Eastern Mich Univ, BS, 1978; Wayne State Univ Law Sch, 1978-80. **Career:** Wayne Co Neighborhood Legal Serv, community outreach coordr, 1986-90; Fobbs & Strunck Communs, pres, 1989; Mich Repub State Comt, vice chmn; Soul Source, dir govt & civic affairs; Nat Urban Policy Action Coun, pres, currently, Kevin Fobbs Show, owner, currently. **Orgs:** Exec bd mem, Detroit Asn Black Orgn, 1984-; Mich Gov John Engler's Action Team, 1992-; Nat Asn Advan Colored People, ACT-BE Comn Jobs, Detroit Br, 1991-; Mich Enterprise Zone Authority, 1992-; bd mem, Wayne Co Dept Social Serv, 1992-; bd pres, Habitat Humanity, Metro Detroit Br; bd mem, Int Br, 1992-; co-chair and co-founder, Am-Can Cons Coalition. **Home Addr:** 20418 Lichfield, Detroit, MI 48221, **Home Phone:** (313)342-8568. **Business Addr:** Owner, National Urban Policy Action Council, The Kevin Fobbs Show, 12948 Farmington Rd, Livonia, MI 48150, **Business Phone:** (313)749-1659.

FOGAM, MARGARET HANORAH
Secretary (Office), educator. **Personal:** Born in Bali, Cameroon; daughter of Simon and Freida. **Educ:** Georgetown Univ, Wash, DC, BA, 1979; Clark-Atlanta Univ, GA, MA, 1985, ABD, 1985. **Career:** Clark-Atlanta Univ, GA, admin asst, 1989-; Morris Brown Col, prof, 1999. **Orgs:** Am Asn Sociologists, 1985-; Nat Conf Black Polit Scientists, 1987-; Nat Asn Social Scientists, 1988-; Am Asn Polit Scientists, 1987-. **Honors/Awds:** Key to City, Community Service, Tuskegee, Mayor Ford, 1980; Certificate of Appreciation, Teaching Foreign Lang Geog, Ogelthorpe Elem Sch, 1986-87. **Business Addr:** Administrative Assistant, Atlanta University, Internstional Affairs & Development, 223 James P Brawley Dr SE, Atlanta, GA 30314.*

FOGGS, EDWARD L.
Clergy, executive director, minister (clergy). **Personal:** Born Jul 11, 1934, Kansas City, KS; son of Eddie and Inez Lewis; married Joyce; children: Lynette, Iris, Edward Elliot, Joy, Alycia. **Educ:** Anderson Col & Ball State Univ, AB, 1958; Anderson Univ, DDiv, 1984; Anderson Sch Theol & Christian Theol Sem. **Career:** Sherman State Church God, Anderson, IN, pastor, 1959-69; Anderson Col, Afro-Am Studies Dept, adj fac, 1968-; Anderson Univ, adj fac, 1968-82; Urban Ministers Bd Ch Ext & Home Missions Church God, dir, 1970-75; Exec Coun Church God, assoc exec secy, 1975-88, exec secy & chief exec officer, 1988-; Church God Ministries, Anderson, gen dir, Leadership Coun, exec secy, minister at large, currently. **Orgs:** Pres, Inspirational Youth Conv, Nat Asn Church God, 1964-72; Family Serv Madison County, 1964-66; chmn, Ill Gen Assembly Church God, 1967-68; Contrib Nat Church Pub Bldg Bridges Racial Understanding, 1967; pres, Urban League Madison County, 1969-71; bd mem, Nat Conf Black Churchmen, 1971-72; key speaker, 5th World Conf Church God, Oaxlepec, Mexico, 1971; Oper PUSH, 1974-75; alt bd mem, Urban Training Ctr Christian Mission, 1974-75; Am Mgt Asn, 1976-; Black Exec Denominations Related Orgn & Communions, 1977-78; Nat Relig Adv Coun, Nat Urban League, 1978-; Planning Conf, Sixth World Conf Church God, Nairobi, Kenya, E Africa, 1978; Martin Luther King Jr Memorial Comt, 1987-88; bd mem, Community Hosp Ison County, 1988-; Inner City Found Excellence Educ, Los Angeles, CA, 1988-; Anderson Area Chamber Com, 1988-; United Way Madison County, 1989-; convener, World Conf Church God, Wiesbaden, West Ger, 1991; Conv Speaker/Conf & Leader/Consult Church Work; Nat Asn Evangelicals. **Special Achievements:** Co-authored Study Guide Andrew Billingsleys Book "Black Families & the Struggle for Survival" 1974. **Business Addr:** Minister at Large, Church of God Ministries, 1303 W 5th St, PO Box 2420, Anderson, IN 46018.*

FOGGS, JOYCE D.
Educator, teacher, school principal. **Personal:** Born Feb 13, 1930, Indianapolis, IN; daughter of Wilbur Stone (deceased) and Marry Elizabeth Stone (deceased); married Edward L, Jan 1, 1955; children: Lynette, Iris, Edward Elliot, Joy & Alycia. **Educ:** Anderson Col, BS, 1954; Ball State Univ, MA, 1967. **Career:** Educator, principal, School Administrator (retired); Park Place Sch, Anderson, IN, teacher; Dunbal Elem Sch, Kans City, teacher, 1954-55; Westvale Sch, Anderson, IN, teacher, 1959-60; Hazelwood Sch, Anderson, IN, teacher, 1963-70; Anderson Community Sch, asst prin; Robinson Elem Sch, 1988-89. **Orgs:** Am Asn Univ Women, 1959-65; vpres bd trustees, Anderson-Anderson Stoney Creek Lib bd, 1967-; Delta Kappa Gamma Honor Soc Women Educ, 1973-; Kappa Delta Pi, 1973-; comnr, Gruenwald Home Hist Preserv, 1977; Nat Spiritual Life; dir, Women Church God; exec bd, Women Church God 1978-; Urban League Madison Co, 1982-; comnr, Anderson Housing Authority, 1984-; Community Hosp Found, 1988-. **Honors/Awds:** Contributor Religious Devotional Books; Contributor to National Church Publication "Building Bridges to Racial Understanding".

FOLEY, BASIL A., SR.
Clergy, founder (originator). **Personal:** Born Jan 22, 1931, Indianapolis, IN; son of Lee and Alberta; married Loesther, Nov 17, 1977; children: Basil A Jr, Katrina R, Yvonne A, Brian, Kenneth G. **Educ:** McCormick Theol Sem, MDiv, 1982. **Career:** Newman AME Church & Youth Found, founder & pastor, 1953-. **Military Serv:** AUS, Cpl, 1951-53. **Business Addr:** Pastor, Founder, Newman AME Church Youth Foundation, 233 Bagley St, Pontiac, MI 48341-2202.*

FOLEY, STEVE
Football player. **Personal:** Born Sep 11, 1975, Little Rock, AR; son of Robert. **Educ:** Northeast La Univ, BS, sociol. **Career:**

Cincinnati Bengals, linebacker, 1998-2002; Houston Texans, 2003; San Diego Chargers, 2004-06. **Honors/Awds:** Chargers Alumni Player of Week, 2004.

FOLK, DR. FRANK STEWART
Physician. **Personal:** Born Oct 2, 1932, Varnville, SC; divorced; children: 3. **Educ:** Hampton Inst, 1954; Brooklyn Col, BS, 1957; Howard Univ, Col Med, MD, 1961. **Career:** Freedman Hosp, New York, NY, res gen surgery, 1962-66, med officer, 1969-70; Howard Univ, Wash DC, res gen surgery, 1962-66, instr surgery, 1969, res fel, 1969-70; US Pub Health Serv, Staten Island NY, asst resident, 1964-65, chief resident, 1967-68; DC Gen Hosp, Wash DC, chief resident, 1965-66, med officer, 1969-70; St Barnabas Hosp, Bronx NY, asst resident, 1966-67, assoc atnd, 1970-, assoc dir of surgery, 1980-82; IBM, Brooklyn, med dir, 1971-75; Downstate Med Coll, asst instr, 1973-76, clin instr, 1976-86; Hosp for Joint Diseases Med Ctr, NY, asst atnd, 1973-79; Brooklyn Jewish Hosp, Brooklyn NY, asst atnd surgeon, 1973-81; NY State Athletic Comn, NY, asst med dir, 1980, acting med dir, 1986; NY Med Coll, asst prof of surgery, 1987; Health & Hosp Corp, dir, 2004; Clin Surg Health Science Ctr, asst prof, 2004; pvt pract, currently. **Orgs:** Cert Nat bd med Examiners, 1966; NY State Med bd, 1967; Am bd Surgery, 1977; Am Col Cardiol; candidate, Am Col Surgeons; Nat Med Asn; NY Cardiological Soc; Asn Acad Surgery; Manhattan Control Med Soc; Provident Clin Soc Brooklyn; AMA; founding mem, Am Trauma Soc; Bronx Co Med Soc; Howard Univ Med Alumni Asn; Empire State Med Soc; NY State Med Soc; Unity Dem Club; asst former State Senotor Basil Paterson, 1970; bd dir NY City Hlth Hosp Corp Legis Med & Prof Capital; bd Dir Charles A Drew Health Clin, beginning 1974; Goldberg-paterson Election Fin Com, 1970; chmn, Reg 1 Nat Med Asn,1971-74; vchmn, United Dem Mens Club, 1971-75; mem exec, Com Unity Dem Club, 1972-; exec bd, Provident Clin Soc, beginning 1971; Kings Co Hosp comm bd for Mr Thomas RFortune, 1971-74; Num OthOrgns NG, 1962-66. **Military Serv:** DC Nat Guard, 115th Med Bn, 1962-66, OIC Troop & Med Clin, 1964-66; NY State Nat Guard, 42nd Infantry Div, div surgeon, col, beginning 1973. **Home Addr:** 490 New York Ave, Brooklyn, NY 11225, **Home Phone:** (718)363-6600. **Business Phone:** (718)270-1442.

FOLKS, BYRON ALLEN. **See ALLEN, BYRON.**

FOLLMER, PAUL L
Banker. **Career:** El Pueblo State Bank, pres & chief exec officer, currently. *

FOLSTON, JAMES EDWARD
Football player. **Personal:** Born Aug 14, 1971, Cocoa, FL. **Educ:** Northeast La Univ. **Career:** Los Angeles Raiders, 1994; Oakland Raiders, linebacker, 1995-99; Arizona Cardinals, 1999-2001. *

FOMUFOD, DR. ANTOINE KOFI
Physician, educator. **Personal:** Born Oct 16, 1940, Ngen-Mbo, Cameroon; son of Ngwabi; married Angelina Hirku; children: Antoine, Ngwabi & Nina B. **Educ:** Univ Ibadan Nigeria, MD, 1967, Residency Pediat, attended 1970; Johns Hopkins Univ Sch Med, Fel Pediat, 1973; Johns Hopkins Univ Sch Hygiene, MPH, 1974. **Career:** Howard Univ, from asst prof pediat to assoc prof pediat, 1974-92, dir, neonatology, 1986-, prof pediat, 1992-. **Orgs:** Affil Fel Franklin Square Hosp, 1971-73; Johns Hopkins Med-Surg Soc, 1974-; med staff, Hosp Sick C, 1975-77; DC Med Soc, 1975-; Am Acad Pediat, 1975-; secy bd, Assoc African Physicians N Am, 1980-; Sect Perinatal & Neonatal Pediat Am Acad Pediat; Southern Med Assoc, 1985-90; AAAS, 1985-90; Southern Perinatal Assoc, 1985-90; World Cong Martial Arts, 1986-. Fel, Am Acad Pediats; past adv trustee, Mt Wash Pediat Hospl Inc. **Honors/Awds:** Merit Award, Howard Univ Med Stud Coun, 1981; Outstanding Physician Residents, Dept Pediat Howard Univ Hosp, 1982; Med Productivity Award, Howard Univ Hosp, 1994. **Special Achievements:** Over 50 papers published in peer reviewed medical journals as of Dec 1994. **Business Addr:** Director, Professor, Howard University Hospital, 2041 Ga Ave NW, Washington, DC 20060.*

FONROSE, DR. HAROLD ANTHONY
Physician. **Personal:** Born Aug 31, 1925, Brooklyn, NY; married Mary Elizabeth; children: Wayne, Mark, Drew, Ward. **Educ:** Adelphi Univ, BA, 1952; Cornell Univ, MS, 1954; Howard Univ, MD, 1958. **Career:** Internist, 1962-; A Holly Patterson Home, consult, 1962-70; Am Bd Internal Med, diplomate, 1968; A Holly Patterson Home, med dir, 1970; Mt Sinai med Faculty Elmhurst Campus, attending staff physician. **Orgs:** NY State & Nassau Co Med Soc; Sigma Pi Phi Frat; Alpha Sigma Boule; Alphi Phi Alpha Frat; Am Col Geriatrics, 1971; past bd dir, Vanguard Nat Bank, 1972-76; Fellow, Am Col Physicians, 1977. **Special Achievements:** Publ "Digitalis Withdrawal in Aged" J Geriatrics; "Role of Med Dir in Skilled Nursing Facility". **Business Addr:** Physician, Old Cedar Swamp Rd, Jericho, NY 11753.*

FONTAINE, JOHN M.
Physician, educator. **Personal:** Born Apr 6, 1954, Haiti; son of Antoine and Gisele. **Educ:** Med Sch, Col Med & Dent NJ & Rutgers Med Sch, 1979; Internal Med Internship-19Nassau Co Med Ctr, 1980; Internal Med Residency-19Nassau Co Med Ctr, 1982; Cardiol Fel, clin educ, 1985. **Career:** Veterans Admin Med Ctr, dir, pacemaker clin, 1985-90, dir, cardiac arrhythmia clin, 1985-90, dir, electrophysiol lab, 1985-90; State Univ NY, Health Sci, asst prof med, 1985-90; Med Col Pa, dir cardiac, electro physiol serv, 1990-96, asst prof med, 1990-96; Allegheny Univ, Hosp-Med Division, dir cardiac arrhythmia serv, 1996-, assoc prof med, 1996-; pvt pract, currently; Drexel Univ Col Med, assoc prof, currently. **Orgs:** manuscript reviewer, J Pacing & Clin Electrophysiol, 1994; manuscript reviewer, J Am Col Cardiol, 1996; bd gov, AHA Southeastern PA Affiliate, 1996-99; mentors prog, Asn Black Cardiologists, 1992; mentors prog, Nat Med Asn, 1996; bd dirs, Asn Black Cardiololgists, 1990; Cardiac Electrophysiol Soc, 1987. **Honors/Awds:** Outstanding Young Doctor, Dollars & Sense Mag, 1993; Distinguished Service Award, Asn Black Cardiologists Inc, 1992; Certificate Achievement Award, Mentorship Minority Col Stud, 1996. **Special Achievements:** Co-auth: "The Optimal Use of Isopruterenol," Pace; "Double Potentials During Ventricular Tachycardia," Pace; "The Effects of Transcoronary Ethanol," J of Invasive Card; "Double Potentials in Ventricular Tachycardia;" "The Optimal Use of Isopruterenol". **Business Addr:** Physician, Private Pactitioner, Medical College of Pennsylvania Hospital, 3300 Henry Ave, Heritage Bldg Ste 803, Philadelphia, PA 19129, **Business Phone:** (215)842-7455.*

FONTAYNE, K. NICOLE (K NICOLE FONTAYNE-MACK)
Financial manager, executive. **Personal:** Born in Chicago, IL; daughter of James and Carole Youngblood; married James L Mack, May 20, 1990; children: Cameron J Underwood. **Educ:** Univ Chicago, AS, 1976; Roosevelt Univ, BA, 1978. **Career:** Int Harvester Credit, Albany, credit analyst, 1979-80; Farmers Ins Group, Santa Ana, supvr, 1980-81; Amerisure/MI Mutual, Detroit, jula mgr, 1987; Amerisure Companies, resource productivity mgr, 1991-94; City Detroit, dir info technol serv, 1994; Detroit Waldorf Sch, bd trustees; Broward Co Off, Ft Lauderdale, Off Info Technol, interim chief; Broward County Off, Off Info Technol, chief info officer, 1999-. **Orgs:** Word of Faith, 1985-; co-chairperson, Amerisure, United Way Campaign, 1990. **Honors/Awds:** Minority Achievement Award, YMCA, 1990. **Business Addr:** Chief Information Officer, Broward County, Off Info Technol, 540 SE Third Ave Suite 300, Ft Lauderdale, FL 33303-2922, **Business Phone:** (954)357-8500.*

FONTENOT, REV. ALBERT E., JR.
President (organization), chief executive officer, clergy. **Personal:** Born Oct 23, 1946, Alexandria, LA; son of Albert E Fontenot Sr and Fay Scott; married Beverly, Nov 20, 1967; children: Kimberly, Michelle & Albert III. **Educ:** DePaul Univ, BA, 1979, MBA, 1985; Bethany Theol Sem, DMinistry, 1993. **Career:** Wieboldt Inc, buyer, 1967-75; Playskool Toy Co, vpres res & develop,1976-81; Wilson Jones Co, vpres mkt, 1981-85; Eldon Off Prods, vpres mkt,1985-91; Antioch Bapt Ch, Long Beach, CA, deacon, 1986-89, assoc pastor,1989-92; Eldon-Rubbermaid Off Prod, vpres sales, 1991-93; Mt Calvary BaptCh, Knoxville, Tenn, assoc pastor, 1992-94; Atapco Off Prod, vpres mkt,1993-94, sr vpres sales & mkt, 1994-95, pres & chief exec officer, 1995;1st Bapt Ch Baldwin MO, assoc pastor, 1994-2002; Eagle OPG Inc, pres & chief exec officer, 1995-2001; Fellows Inc, vpres & gen mgr technol accessories Group, 2001-05; 2nd Baptist Ch, Elgin, IL, assoc minister,2002-06; Rhinotek Comput Prods Inc, chmn, pres, & chief exec officer,2006-; Mt Moriah Baptist Church, Los Angeles, assoc minister, 2006-. **Orgs:** Bd trustees, Bethel Bapt Ch, 1982-85, brd dirs, United Way Greater St Louis, 1995-2001. **Military Serv:** AUS, major, 1968-89; Bronze Star, Army Commendation Medal, Vietnam Serv Award, Res Serv Award. **Business Addr:** Chairman President, Chief Executive Officer, Rhinotek Computer Products Inc, 2301 E Del Amo Blvd, Carson, CA 90220.

FONTENOT, ALBERT PAUL
Football player. **Personal:** Born Sep 17, 1970, Houston, TX; married Stephanie. **Educ:** Baylor univ, commun. **Career:** Chicago Bears, defensive end, 1993-96; Indianapolis Colts, 1997-98; San Diego Chargers, 2000-02. *

FONTENOT-JAMERSON, BERLINDA
Manager. **Personal:** Born Jul 5, 1947, San Fernando, CA; daughter of Leroy and Velma Kyle; married Michael Jamerson, Jun 16, 1984. **Educ:** LA CA Trade Technological Col, AA, 1972; CA State Univ, LA, BA, 1978; Pepperdine Univ, LA CA, MBA, 1984. **Career:** Southern CA Gas Co LA CA, sr prof recruiter, consumer affairs mgr, 1984-87, community rels mgr, 1987-92, personnel rels & diversity mgr, 1992-95, Pacific Enterprises, Corp Diversity mgr, 1995; Sempra Energy, Dir Corp Diversity Affairs, currently. **Orgs:** Nat bd mem, Amer Asn Blacks Energy; bd mem, Women Color, 1987-; bd mem, Careers Older Ams, 1987-; bd mem, Museum African Am Art, 1988-; vpres, admin, DATACOM, 1988-; comt chair, NAACP-LDF Black Women Achievement, 1989; bd mem, Coalition Women's Econ Develop; UNCF Blue Ribbon COM; Diversity & EEO Mgr's Network. **Honors/Awds:** Leadership Award, YWCA, 1985; Gold Award, United Way, 1986; Black Women of Achievement Merit Award, NAACP-LDF, 1986; Merit Award, Am Asn Blacks Energy, 1986, 1988; Certificate of Support, LA Urban League, 1988-94; Women in NAALR Merit Award; Coalition Women Economic Development Award, 1992. **Business Addr:** Director Corporate Diversity Affairs, Sempra Energy, 101 Ash St, San Diego, CA 92101-3017, **Business Phone:** (619)696-2000.*

FONVIELLE, WILLIAM HAROLD
Executive. **Personal:** Born Dec 18, 1943, Chicago, IL; son of William B and Elizabeth Brown; married Carole Lynn Sharoff; children: Michelle R Williams, Deanne V & Jonathan W. **Educ:** Shimer Col, AB, 1963; Northwestern Univ, postgrad philos, 1964; Yale Sch Orgn & Mgt, MBA, 1981. **Career:** J Walter Thompson Co, media buyer, 1966-68; Vince Cullers Adv Inc, media dir, 1968-70; Communicon Inc, pres, 1970-75; State Ill, dir motion picture/TV prodn/publ info officer, 1975-77; Denver Regional Coun Govt, dir pub affairs, 1977-79; Goodmeasure Inc, vpres/dir consult, 1981-86; Forum Corp, vpres, 1987-94, sr vpres performance measurement, 1995-97; Performance Measurement Assocs Inc, founder & chief exec officer, 1997-; Harvard Bus Sch, prof; Mass Prod Develop Corp, chmn. **Orgs:** Dir, Apartment Store Inc, 1968-70; dir, Lovespace Inc, 1972-75; elec trustee, Village Carol Stream, Ill, 1973-77; dir, Northeastern Ill Planning Comn, 1973-77; dir, Homes Pvt Enterprise, 1973-77; trustee, Garrett-Evang Theol Sem, 1974-76; secy, Ill-Ind Bi-State Comn, 1976-77; Accrediation comt Colo Pub Rels Soc Am, 1978-80; founder, Coun City & Co Communicators, 1978-79; chmn, Mass Prod Develop Corp, 1986-; MENSA 1987-; founding mem, Greater Boston Chap Int Customer Serv Asn 1987-; Orgn Develop Network, 1988-; dir, Horizons Fund, 1990-94; Handel & Haydn Soc, overseer, 1992-; Nat Black MBA Asn, 1998-; dir, Atlantic Vacation Homes Inc, 1998-; chmn, Career Collaborative, 2001-05; chmn, City Glovester Plan Implementation Rev Comn, 2002-; Am Mgt Asn; Pub Rels Soc Am. **Honors/Awds:** Distinguished Alumni Award, Shimer Col, 1975; Best Public Service Commercial, Special Citation, 1975; SCLC MLK Jr Award, Chicago Suburban Chap, 1977. **Special Achievements:** Published dozens of business-related articles and is the author of From Manager to Innovator: Using Information to Become an Idea Entrepreneur, Administrative Management Society, 1988; co-author, The Changing American Workplace: Work Alternatives in the '80s, American Management Association. **Home Addr:** 27 Old Salem Rd, Gloucester, MA 01930. **Business Addr:** Chief Executive Officer, Founder, Performance Measurement Associates Inc, 115 Prospect St, Gloucester, MA 01930, **Business Phone:** (978)283-5408.

FONVILLE, CHAD EVERETTE
Baseball player. **Personal:** Born Mar 5, 1971, Jacksonville, NC. **Educ:** Louisburg Jr Col. **Career:** Player (retired); Coach; Montreal Expos, infielder, 1995; Los Angeles Dodgers, 1995-97; Chicago White Sox, 1997; Cleveland Indians, infielder, 1998; Boston Red sox, infielder, 1999; New York Yankees, infielder; Le Juene High Sch, head coach, currently. **Business Phone:** (910)451-2451.*

FONVILLE, DANNY D
Government official. **Career:** Calif Dept Corrections, corrections officer, 1981-; Becton Dickinson Pub Safety, NIT Narcotics Identification, master trainer; Folsom State Prison, conflict mgt trainer, trainer trainers; Equal Employment Opportunity Affirmation Action, counr & trainer; Folsom State Prison Youth Diversion Prog, Dept Corrections State Calif, recruiter. **Orgs:** Blacks Govt; Correctional Peace Officer Found. **Honors/Awds:** Correctional Officer of the Year, State Calif, 1995; Correctional Officer of the Year, City Folsom, 1995; Meritorious Servica Award, Int Asn Correctional Officers, 1995; Officer of the Year, Correctional Peace Officer Found, 1996. **Business Addr:** Corrections Officer, California Department of Corrections, PO Box W, Represa, CA 95671.

FOOTE, YVONNE
School administrator. **Personal:** Born Dec 24, 1949, Philadelphia, PA; daughter of Lorenzo L Alleyne and Alma Jenkens Alleyne; married Nathaniel A; children: Omar Y. **Career:** Del Valley Reg Planning Comm, cost acct, 1975-81; Thomas & Muller Co Inc, bookkeeper, 1982-84; Laborers Dist Coun Legal Fund, secy & bookkeeper, 1984-; Lawnside Bd Educ, pres; Rawle & Henderson, Philadelphia, PA, bookkeeper, 1987-. *

FOOTMAN, DAN ELLIS, JR.
Football player. **Personal:** Born Jan 13, 1969, Tampa, FL; children: Dantavian Hicks. **Educ:** Fla State univ. **Career:** Cleveland Browns, defensive end, 1993-95; Baltimore Ravens, 1996; Indianapolis Colts, 1997-98. *

FORBES, CALVIN
College teacher, educator. **Personal:** Born May 6, 1945, Newark, NJ; son of Jacob and Mary Short. **Educ:** New Sch Social Res; Rutgers Univ; Brown Univ, MFA, 1978. **Career:** Emerson Col, Boston, MA, asst prof eng, 1969-73; Tufts Univ, Medford, MA, asst prof Eng, 1973-74, 1975-77; Denmark, France, & England, fulbright lectr, 1974-75; Univ W Indies, guest lectr, 1982-83; Howard Univ, Wash, DC, writer residence; Wash Col, Chestertown, MD, asst prof creative writing, 1988-89; Sch Art Inst Chicago, chair writing, prof lib arts, currently. **Orgs:** Modern Lang Asn; fel, Nat Endowment Arts Grant, 1982-83; fel, DC Comn Arts, 1984; Col Lang Asn; Fulbright Teaching fel; fel, NJ State Coun

Arts. **Honors/Awds:** Ill Arts Coun Grant. **Special Achievements:** author: Blue Monday, Wesleyan Univ Press, 1974; From the Book of Shine, Burning Deck Press, 1979; The Shine Poems; Publ: Yale Review; Am Scholar; Poetry Mag; Black World; IA Review; Prairie Schooner; Chicago Review; Ploughshares; New Black Voices; The Poetry Anthology; Contemporary Am Poetry; The Jazz Poetry Anthology. **Business Addr:** Professor Liberal Arts, School of Arts Institute of Chicago, 37 S Wabash Ave, Chicago, IL 60603, **Business Phone:** (312)899-5100.*

FORBES, GEORGE L
Lawyer. **Personal:** Born Apr 4, 1931, Memphis, TN; son of Cleveland and Elnora; married Mary Fleming; children: Helen, Mildred & Lauren. **Educ:** Baldwin-Wallace Col, BA, 1957; Cleveland Marshall Law Sch, JD, 1962. **Career:** City Cleveland, teacher, 1958-62, housing insp, 1959-63; radio talk show host, 1972-75; Cuyahoga Co Dem Party, co-chmn, 1972-78; Cleveland City Coun, 1964-89, coun majority leader, 1972-73, pres, 1973-89; Baldwin-Wallace Col, guest lectr, 1990-; Forbes, Fields & Assoc Co, founding partner & prin officer, 1971-. **Orgs:** Nat Asn Def Lawyers; Cuyahoga, Ohio & Cleveland Bar Asns; Gtr Cleveland Growth Corp & Asn; Coun Econ Opportunity; Legal Aid Soc; pres, NAACP, Cleveland Chap 1992-, grand jury foreman, 1994; Urban League; John Harlan Law Club; Greater Cleveland Safety Coun; NAT League Cities; UNF; Oversight Bd Bur Worker's Compensation. **Honors/Awds:** Citation Merit, 1967; Distinguished Merit Award, 1976; Ohio Gov Award, 1977; Police Athletic League Outstanding Service Award, 1978; Outstanding Community Leadership Award, Black Affairs Coun, 1983; Honorary Doctorate Degree, Baldwin-Wallace Col, 1990; Honorary Doctorate Degree, Cent State Univ, 1989; Martin Luther King Jr Crusader Of the Year Award, 1989; Cleveland State Univ, Distinguished Alumni Award, 1990; In Tribute to Pub Service Award, Cleveland State Univ Maxine Goodman Levin Col Urban Affairs, 1994. **Special Achievements:** Humanitarian Of the Year, 1968; Man Of the Year, 1969; Outstanding Polit & Civic Efforts, 1971; Ohio Asn Commodores, 1973; Black Prof Of the Year, 1987. **Military Serv:** USMC, corpl, 1951-53. **Business Addr:** Founding Partner, Forbes Fields & Associates Co LPA, 700 Rockefeller Bldg, 614 W Superior Ave, Cleveland, OH 44113-1318, **Business Phone:** (216)696-7170.

FORBES, MARLON
Football player. **Personal:** Born Dec 25, 1971, Brooklyn, NY. **Educ:** Pa State Univ, BA, 1995. **Career:** Chicago Bears, defensive back, 1995-98; Cleveland Browns, 1999.

FORD, AILEEN W.
School administrator. **Personal:** Born Apr 28, 1934, Shelby, NC; daughter of John Watson and Rosa Watson; married Charles, Jun 8, 1967; children: Valerie Journeane & Regina Antoinette. **Educ:** Fayetteville State Univ, BS, 1954; Howard Univ, Western Carolina Univ, Appalachian Univ; Univ NC Charlotte, MA, 1978, CAS, 1982. **Career:** School administrator (retired); Shelby City Sch, Shelby, NC, teacher, 1954-80, elementary prin, 1980-89, dir testing & chapter I, supvr, 1989-96; Shelby City Coun, Ward six. **Orgs:** Pres, local chap NCAE; dist dir, NCAE; dist pres, NC All City Times; pres, Gastonia Chap Delta; organizer & sec Cleveland Co Civic League; YMCA; Girl Scouts; youth adv ch; Delta Sigma Theta Sorority; NC Asn Educ; NC Asn Classroom Teacher; Nat Educ Asn; Am Asn Univ Women; Int Reading Asn; bd dir, Cleveland Co Orgn Drug Abuse Prevention, 1974; bd dir, Cleveland Co Comn Concert Asn; Shelby Human Rels Coun; pres, PTA Shelby Jr HS, 1974; treas, Shelby Negro Woman's Club; pres, Audacian Club, 1974; Nat Advan Asn Colored People; Nat Coun Negro Women; Sunday sch tchr, Mount Calvary Bapt Ch; pres, Shelby Alumnae Chap; Delta Sigma Theta Soroity, Inc; pres, NC Fed Negro Women Inc; Shelby City Coun. **Honors/Awds:** Citizen of the Year, 1984; Elected Official Award, 1987; Outstanding Service Award, 1989; Woman of the Year, 1998. *

FORD, DR. ALBERT S.
Educator, dentist. **Personal:** Born Dec 31, 1929, Elizabeth, NJ; son of William H and Bessie M Lewis; married Mary Victoria Burkett; children: Albert S Jr MD, Stephen D MD, Teresa D esq, Kevin M, MD, Richard E. **Educ:** WVa St Col, Seton Hall Univ; Meharry Med Col, DDS, 1958; Rutgers, Grad Sch Mgt, Newark, NJ, attended 1982; New Sch Social Res, New York, NY, attended 1981; Nat Bd Dent Examiners, dipl. **Career:** Newark Comn Health Serv Group Dent Serv, dir; pvt practice, Roselle, NJ, 1962-; Fairleigh Dickinson Col Dent Med, Hackensack, NJ, assoc prof, 1980-90; Univ Med & Dent, Newark, NJ, assoc prof. **Orgs:** Bd mgt, Meharry Med Col; Am Dent Asn; vpres, Common wealth Dent Soc; int Assoc Begg Study Groups; Am Endodontic Soc; Acad Gen Dent; bd mem, NJ State Bd Dent Examiners NE Regional Bd Dent Examiners, 1979; past pres, Nat Advan Asn Colored People; mem exec bd, Urban League; vpres, Sr Cit Housing Corp; adv bd, First Nat Bank Cent Jersey; Sigma Pi Phi Mu Boule; Omega Psi Phi; past mem, NJ State Bd Dent Examiners; Fellow, Am Col Dentists; Fellow, Royal Soc Health; past vpres, assoc prof & chmn, Treatment Planning Fairleigh Dickinson Univ Sch Dent. **Military Serv:** AUS, Sgt, 1947-50. **Business Addr:** Dentist, 1003 Chestnut St, Roselle, NJ 07203-1934, **Business Phone:** (908)241-3175.*

FORD, ANTOINETTE
Executive. **Personal:** Born Dec 14, 1941, Philadelphia, PA; married Melvin W Ford. **Educ:** Laval Univ Quebec, attended 1960; Chestnut Hill Col, BS, 1963; Am Univ, MS, 1966; Stanford Univ, attended 1967. **Career:** Nat Oceanog Data Ctr, oceanogr, 1966-69; Ogden Corp, oceanogr, 1969-71; White House fel, 1971-72; Inst Serv Educ, develop dir, 1972-73; Telspan Int Inc, pres. **Orgs:** NSF fel, 1967; mem, DC City Co, 1973-75; exec vpres, B & C Asn Inc; Harvard Univ Fel Inst Polit, 1975; numerous prof & bus orgn; bd dirs, several orgn; mem, Pres Clemency Bd, 1975. **Honors/Awds:** Outstanding Serv Award, Presidential Classroom, 1972. **Special Achievements:** Most Successful Under-30 Woman, New Woman Mag, 1971. *

FORD, AUSBRA
Educator, sculptor. **Personal:** Born Feb 28, 1935, Chicago, IL; son of Thomas and Carrie; married Thelma Wakefield; children: Rangi & Maji. **Educ:** Ray Vogue Art Sch, attended 1977; Chicago Art Inst, BA, 1964, MFA, 1966. **Career:** Chicago Pub Sch, art instr, 1964-66; Gary Pub Sch, art instr, 1966-68; Southern Univ, Baton Rouge, La, asst prof art, 1968-69; Chicago State Univ, prof Art, 1969, emer fac, currently. **Orgs:** Nat Conf Artists, 1975-; chmn, Visual Artists Round table, 1983-; Smithsonian Nat Mus African Art; Chicago Field Mus; pres & founder, African Am Visual Arts Round table; Kemetic Inst Northeastern Ill Univ; Asn Study Classical African Civilizations. **Honors/Awds:** Fel Young scholars, Nat Endowment Humanities, 1971-72; Int Studies Award, Black Studies Dept, Chicago State Univ, 1973; Creative Service Award, Kemetic Inst Chicago, 1985. **Military Serv:** USAF, a/bc, 1954-56. **Business Addr:** Emeritus Faculty, Chicago State University, Department of Art & Design, 9501 S King Dr, Chicago, IL 60628-1598.

FORD, BARRY W.
Lawyer. **Personal:** Born Dec 23, 1946, Pontotoc, MS. **Educ:** Miss Valley State Col, Ba, 1964; Thurgood Marshall Sch Law, JD, 1977; Nat Judicial Col, attended 1991. **Career:** Municipal Ct judge, 1979-90; Ford & Ford, Tupelo, MS, atty, 1979-91; Prentiss & Tishomingo Counties, state Itawamba, Lee, Monroe, Pontotoc, MS, ct trial judge, serving Alcorn, 1990-01; First Circuit Court District, circuit ct judge; Baker, Donelson, Bearman, Caldwell & Berkowitz, PC, shareholder, currently. **Orgs:** Magnolia Bar Asn; Miss Bar Asn; Litigation Coun Am; Am Inns Ct; Baker Donelson Diversity Comt. **Honors/Awds:** Drum Major for Justice Award, 1998. **Business Addr:** Shareholder, Baker, Donelson, Bearman, Caldwell & Berkowitz, PC, Meadowbrook Off Pk 4268 I 55 N, PO Box 14167, Jackson, MS 39236, **Business Phone:** (601)351-8925.*

FORD, CHERYL
Basketball player. **Personal:** Born Jun 6, 1981, Homer, LA; daughter of Karl Malone and Bonita. **Educ:** La Tech Univ, health & educ, 2003. **Career:** Detroit Shock, forward, 2003-. **Honors/Awds:** Player of the Year, WAC; Most Valuable Player, WAC Tournament; State Player of the Year, LA Sports Writers Assn; Rookie of the Year, WNBA, 2003; Associated Press All-America Honorable Mention team, 2003; WNBA All-Star, 2004, 2005; MVP Award, WNBA All-Star, 2007. **Business Addr:** Professional Basketball Player, Detroit Shock, Palace of Auburn Hills 2 Championship Dr, Auburn Hills, MI 48326, **Business Phone:** (248)377-0100.

FORD, CLYDE W
Writer, chiropractor. **Personal:** Born Jan 1, 1951, New York, NY; son of John and Vivian. **Educ:** Wesleyan Univ, BA, 1971; Western States Chiropractic Col, Portland, Ore, PhD, 1980. **Career:** IBM Corp, systs engr, 1977; Chiropractor, 1980s-; Inst Somatosynthesis Training & Res, founder, 1987-; Leading Edge, ed; writer, lectr, 1989-; Inst African Mythology, dir & founder, currently. Author: Where Healing Waters Meet: Touching Mind & Emotion Through the Body, 1989; Compassionate Touch: The Body's Role in Healing & Recovery, 1993; We Can All Get Along: 50 Steps You Can Take to Help End Racism, 1994; The Hero with an African Face: Mythic Wisdom of Traditional Africa, 2000; Columbia Univ, fac; Wash Univ, fac. **Orgs:** Founder, NAACP, Northern Puget Sound region; founder, Inst Black World; past pres, Found Advancement Chiropractic Res. **Honors/Awds:** 2006 Hurston/Wright Legacy Award in Contemporary Fiction, Zora Neale Hurston/Richard Wright Found, 2006. **Business Addr:** Director, Founder, The Institute for Somatosynthesis Training and Research, PO Box 3056, Bellingham, WA 98227-3056, **Business Phone:** (206)398-9355.

FORD, DARRYL
Writer, radio host. **Personal:** Born Dec 27, 1953, Detroit, MI; married Cozette; children: Darryl II, Rhonda, Brandon, Chris, Rodney, Brionne. **Career:** Blue Cross Blue Shield, sr writer, 1977-96; WMUZ Christian Radio, station mgr, radio host, WEXL, gen mgr.

FORD, DR. DAVID LEON
Educator, president (organization). **Personal:** Born Sep 25, 1944, Fort Worth, TX; son of David Leon Ford and Vernita V Williams; married Joan Sessoms (divorced); children: David III. **Educ:** IA State Univ, BS, 1967; Univ Wis, Madison, MS, 1969, PhD, 1972. **Career:** Aerospace firm, indust engineer; Purdue Univ, asst prof mgt, 1972-75; Yale Sch Orgn & Mgt, visiting assoc prof, 1980-81; Univ Tex Dallas, Dept Orgn Stud Strategy & Int Mgt, prof, currently; DL Ford & Assocs, pres, currently. **Orgs:** Asn Social & Behavioral Scientists, 1978-79; Leadership Dallas Alumni Assoc; Leadership Dallas Adv Coun, 1978-80; bd dir, Greater Dallas Housing Opportunity Ctr, 1978-80; budget comn, United Way Metro Dallas, 1979; dir Pro Line Corp, 1981-84; chmn, bd dir, NTL Inst Applied Behavioral Sci, 1985-86; Nat Black MBA Asn; dean, Exec Develop Inst; Acad Mgt; former chair, Comt People Color; Asn Social & Behavioral Scientists; former pres & life mem, Orgn Develop Network, SYMLOG Consult Network; former chair, Inst Cert Prof Mgrs; faculty mem, Cent Eurasian Leadership Alliance; Leadership Dallas Alumni Asn; Soc Int Bus Fels. **Honors/Awds:** Leadership Award, KNOK AM-FM Radio, 1966; Outstanding Young Alumnus, IA State Univ, 1977; Scholarship Achievement, Asn Social & Behavioral Scientists, 1983; Distinguished Service Citation, Univ Wis Madison, 1988; Trailblazer Award, PhD Proj Mgt Doctoral Students Asn, 1997. **Military Serv:** AUS, Reserve capt, 1967-76. **Business Addr:** Professor, University Texas Dallas, School Management, PO Box 830688, Richardson, TX 75083-0688, **Business Phone:** (972)883-2015.

FORD, DEBORAH LEE
Educator, counselor. **Personal:** Born Sep 22, 1945, Decatur, IL; married David Franklin Ford; children: Alisa, Bryan, Laquitta. **Educ:** Millikin Univ, music; Richland Community Col, bus. **Career:** AE Staley Mfg Co, messenger & off pool sec, 1964; Day Care Licensed Family Serv, suprv, owned, operated, 1972-78; US Dept Com, res crew leader, 1980; Decatur Sch Dist 61, noon suprv, 1983, sch bd mem. **Orgs:** Dist secy, Title I, 1980; dist chairperson, Title I, 1981, 1982; task force mem, Comn Strategic Planning Group, 1984; asst leader, Pre-Sch Prog, Dove Inc, 1984; dir, Wedding Coord, 1984; bd mem, Mental Health Asn Macon Co Inc, 1985; bd mem, Family Serv, 1985; chmn, Educ Comt, Nat Asn Adv Colored People. **Honors/Awds:** Award Recognition, Title I, 1982; Award Appreciation, Vol Decatur Pub Sch, 1982; Cert Appreciation, Meritorious Asst Conduct 1970 Census, US Dept Com Bur Census. **Home Addr:** 846 S Webster St, Decatur, IL 62521.

FORD, DEBRA HOLLY
Physician. **Personal:** Married Dr Kevin Michael Ford Sr; children: 2. **Educ:** Howard Univ, BS, zool; Howard Univ Sch Med, MD. **Career:** Howard Univ Hosp, assoc prof, currently, vice chmn, currently, chief gen surg div, pres, head, section colon & rectal surg, currently; dir surg residency prog. **Orgs:** Am Col Surgeons; Am Soc Colon & Rectal Surg; surg Sect, Nat Med Asn. **Honors/Awds:** Kaiser-Permanente Teaching Excellence Award. **Special Achievements:** First African American female to become board certified in the field of colon and rectal surgery; first African American female to become a diplomate of the Board of Colon and Rectal Surgery. **Business Addr:** Associate Professor & Vice-Chairman, Director, Howard Univ Hospital, Department of Surgery, 2041 Georgia Ave NW Suite 4000, Washington, DC 20060, **Business Phone:** (202)865-3785.

FORD, DONALD A.
Executive. **Personal:** Born May 15, 1928, Philadelphia, PA; married Christina K; children: Donald A, Douglas E, Christel A. **Educ:** Shaw Univ, BA, 1950; Am Int Col. **Career:** Urban Educ Adv Third World, Westfield State Col, asst dir, 1971-74; Westfield State Col, asst dir students union. **Orgs:** Kappa Alpha Psi Frat, 1946-; church decon, St John's Congreational Church, 1964-; bd dir, Mass Heart Asn Western Chap, 1971-73; Asn Col Unions Int, 1971-; Asn Prof Admin, 1973-; chmn, Affirmative Action Comt, Westfield State Col, 1975; St John's Congregational Church Choir; Admis Comt, Westfield State Col. **Military Serv:** USAF, SMSgt, 1950-71; Air Force Commendation Award; 2nd Oak Leaf Cluster, 1970. *

FORD, EVERN D.
Consultant. **Personal:** Born Apr 28, 1952, Salem, NJ; son of Daniel Ford Sr. **Educ:** Goldey Beacom Col, BS. **Career:** EI DuPont Co, human resources consult, diversity consult, sexual harassment facilitator. **Orgs:** Bd dir, New Jersey Sch BD ASN; vpres, Salem County Vocational Tech Sch; United Way Salem County, bd dir, Fund Distrib Comt chair; Dale Carnegie Graduate Asst. **Honors/Awds:** Big Brother of the Year Award. **Business Addr:** Human Resources Consultant, E I DuPont, Barley Mill Plz Rt 141 148, Wilmington, DE 19805.*

FORD, FLORIDA MOREHEAD
Clergy. **Personal:** Born Feb 22, 1948, Altheimer, AR; daughter of Henry Thomas (deceased) and Ossie Morris Thomas; married Rev Fred Ford; children: Eurika, Sonya. **Educ:** Univ Ark, Pine Bluff, AR, BS, 1969; Univ Ark, Fayetteville, MS, chem, 1972; Howard Univ Divinity Sch, Wash, DC, MDiv, 1991. **Career:** The Dow Chem Co, Midland, MI, mgr minority recruiting, 1972-87; Nat Soc Black Engineers, Alexandria, VA, exec dir, 1987-93; Ebenezer African Methodist Episcopal Church, assoc minister; US Dept Energy, consult, 1993-96; Shalom Enterprises Inc, chief exec officer, 1996-98; Shalom Ministries Worship Ctr, pastor, 1998-. **Orgs:** Alpha Kappa Alpha Sor; dir, Christian Educ New Jerusalem Church; adv comn, Nat Assoc Minority Engineering Prog Admis, 1982; Nat Orgn Black Chemists & Chem Engineering; indust

adv bd, Nat Soc Black Engineering; bd mem, Woman Woman Ministries; chaplain, Nat Asn Black Seminarians; Wash Urban League; Nat Asn Black Meeting Planners. **Honors/Awds:** Special Service Award, New Jerusalem Church, 1974, 86; Teacher of the Year, New Jerusalem Church, 1982; Special Recognition, Univ Mich, 1985; Outstanding Service, Dow Chem, 1985; Ford Foundation Fellow, Howard Univ, 1989-90; Scholarship, Howard Univ Divinity Sch, 1988-90. **Business Addr:** Pastor, Shalom Ministries Worship Center, 515 Kerby Hill Rd, Fort Washington, MD 20744, **Business Phone:** (301)567-5505.*

FORD, GEORGE WASHINGTON, III
Funeral director, executive. **Personal:** Born Jan 14, 1924, Columbus, GA; son of George Washington Jr and Evergreen Thweatt; married Josephine Adele Bozman Ford, Jan 14, 1948; children: Evergreen Adele Ford-Reeves. **Educ:** Atlanta Col Mortuary Sci, GA, dipl, 1949. **Career:** Progressive Funeral Home Inc, Columbus, GA, pres, 1952-. **Orgs:** Ga Funeral Serv Practitioners Asn; Nat Funeral Dirs Asn; 837 Club; Modern Club; Men's Progressive Club; Pathseekers Civic & Social Club; A J Br, YMCA; Prince Hall Masons; Modernistic Club; Spencerian Club; Losers & Liars Sport Club; adv Controllers Civic & Social Club; bd dirs, Am Family Life Assurance Co, 1986-; bd dirs, Columbus Bank & Trust Co, 1986-. **Honors/Awds:** Thomas A Brewer Award, Columbus Br, Nat Asn Advan Colored People, 1971; Citizenship Award, Al Faruk Temple 145, Prince Hall Masons, 1971; Distinguished Service Award, Columbus Chamber Com, 1972; Outstanding Services Award, Ga State Beauty Culturist League, 1973; Outstanding Services & Dedicated Leadership in Politics & Community Affairs, Pathseekers Civic & Social Club, 1975; Community Services Award, Columbus-Phoenix City Negro Bus & Prof Women's Club, 1975; National Trend Award, LINKS, 1983; Distinguished Service Award, Bishop Frederick Talbot Retreat Ctr AME Church Ga, 1984; Appreciation Award, Controllettes Civic & Social Club, 1984, The Black Community Columbus, GA, 1985; Mortician of the Yr, State & Local Funeral Serv Practitioners Asn, 1985. **Military Serv:** USMC. **Business Addr:** President, Progressive Funeral Home Inc, 4235 St Mary Rd, PO Box 5624, Columbus, GA 31907.

FORD, HAROLD EUGENE
Congressperson (u.s. federal government), politician. **Personal:** Born May 20, 1945, Memphis, TN; son of Newton Jackson and Vera Davis; married Dorothy Jean Bowles, Feb 10, 1969; children: Harold Eugene Jr, Newton Jake & Sir Isaac. **Educ:** Tenn State Univ, BS, 1967; John Gupton Col, AA, mortuary sci, 1968; Howard Univ, MBA, 1982. **Career:** Politician, executive (retired-);Ford & Sons Funeral Home, vpres & mgr, 1969; TN House Rep, 1970-74; US House Rep, congressman, TN, Nineth Dist, 1975-96; Harold Ford Group, consult, 2004. **Orgs:** Nat Adv Bd, St Jude C Res Hosp; bd mem, Metro Memphis YMCA, Alpha Phi Alpha; chmn, Black Tenn Polit Conv; trustee, Fisk Univ; Rust Univ; Alpha Phi Alpha. **Honors/Awds:** Outstanding Young Man of the Year, Memphis Jaycees, 1976; Outstanding Young Man of the Year, TN Jaycees, 1977; Child Advocate of the Year, Child Welfare League Am, 1987. **Special Achievements:** First African-American to represent Tennessee in Congress. **Business Addr:** Member, Democratic Party, 430 S Capitol St SE, Washington, DC 20003, **Business Phone:** (202)737-4443.

FORD, HAROLD EUGENE
Congressperson (U.S. federal government). **Personal:** Born May 11, 1970, Memphis, TN. **Educ:** Univ Pa, BA, 1992; Univ Mich, JD, 1996. **Career:** Senate Budget Comt, staff, 1992; US Dept Com, spec asst, 1993; US House Rep, congressman, 1997-2006; Democratic Leadership Coun, chmn, currently. **Orgs:** Dem Party. **Honors/Awds:** Trumpet Young Star Award, 2002. **Special Achievements:** Youngest member of the 105th Congress. **Business Addr:** Chairman, Democratic Leadership Council, 600 Penn Ave SE Suite 400, Washington, DC 20003, **Business Phone:** (202)546-0007.

FORD, HENRY
Administrator, athletic director. **Educ:** Univ MD Eastern Shore, attended, 1969. **Career:** Univ Md-Eastem Shore, instr, basketball & swimming coach, 1972-73; Tuskegee Univ, asst prof & head basketball coach, 1973-75; Hampton Univ, head basketball coach, 1975-87; Alfred Univ, athletic dir; Howard Univ, athletic dir, begining 1996-2000; Savannah State Univ, athletic dir, 2001. **Orgs:** Nat Asn Collegiate Dirs Athletics; Nat Asn Collegiate Mkg Adminr; Nat Asn Athletics Develop Dirs; Nat Asn Div I-AA Athletics Directors; MEAC baseball championships, 1997-99; chair, MEAC Athletic Dirs Orgn, 1998-2000; MEAC men's & women's Outdoor Track Championships, 2000. **Business Addr:** Athletic Director, Savannah State UNiversity, 3219 College St, Savannah, GA 31404, **Business Phone:** (912)356-2186.

FORD, HENRY
Football player. **Personal:** Born Oct 30, 1971, Fort Worth, TX. **Educ:** Univ Ark. **Career:** Football player (retired); Houston Oilers, defensive tackle, 1994-96; Tennessee Oilers, 1997-98;Tennessee Titans, 1999-02; New Orleans Saints, 2003.

FORD, HILDA EILEEN
Executive. **Personal:** Born Apr 19, 1924, New York, NY. **Educ:** Brooklyn Col; Col St Rose. **Career:** Retired: City Baltimore, dir personnel; NY St Off Employ Rels, chief negotiator; NY St Dept Civil Serv, asst div dir; Youth Opportunities Ctr, dir. **Orgs:** Urban Services Commission, Baltimore City. **Honors/Awds:** Award, Outstanding Contrib Status & Welfare Women, Nat Org Women; Distinguished Women, 1986; Charles H Cushman Award. *

FORD, JACK (JOHN MARSHALL FORD)
Mayor, politician. **Personal:** Born May 18, 1947, Springfield, OH; son of Stanton Ford and Edna; married Claudia Worthy, 1990 (divorced); children: Jessica; married Cynthia Hall, 1992; children: Jacqueline. **Educ:** Ohio State Univ, BA, social work, 1969; Univ Toledo, JD, 1975, MA, pub admin. **Career:** Ohio Youth Comn, counr, 1959-80; Univ Toledo, adj prof polit sci, 1979-2001; Lucas County Substance Abuse Serv, dir, 1980-94; City Toledo, counselorman, 1987-94, mayor, 2001; Ohio State House Representatives, rep, 1994-2001; Bowling Green State Univ, Col Arts & Sci, practicioner in residence, currently. **Business Addr:** Practicioner in Residence, Bowling Green State University, College of Arts & Science, 205 Admin Bldg, Bowling Green, OH 43403, **Business Phone:** (419)372-9539.

FORD, JOHN MARSHALL. **See FORD, JACK.**

FORD, JOHN NEWTON
Government official, insurance agent, consultant. **Personal:** Born May 3, 1942, Memphis, TN; son of Newton Jackson and Vera Davis; married Tamara Mitchell; children: Michelle, Sean, Kemba, Autumn, Theo & Victoria. **Educ:** Tenn State Univ, BS, Bus Admin, 1964; Memphis State Univ, MS, Pub Admin Fin, 1978. **Career:** Memphis, TN, city councilman, 1971-79; Tenn Gen Assembly, Tenn state sen, 1974-2005; TN State Senate, Dist 29, state sen, speaker pro tempore, 1987-2005; JF Assocs, pres. **Orgs:** Chmn, Senate Gen Welfare, Health & Human Resources Comn; Finance, Ways & Means Comn; pres, NJ Ford & Sons Funeral Parlors; pres, Ford & Assocs; life mem, NAACP; Nat League Cities; Nat Black Caucus; bd mem, Regional Sickle Cell Anemia Coun; State & Local Govt Comn; Alpha Phi Alpha. **Honors/Awds:** Outstand Citizens Award, Mallory Knights Charitable, 1974; Outstanding Accomplishment Award, Civil Liberty League, 1975; Community Achievement Award, Lutheran Baptist Church, 1976; Distinguished Graduate Award, Memphis State Univ, 1978. **Home Addr:** 981 Villiage Pk Cove, Memphis, TN 38120.

FORD, JOHNNY
State government official. **Personal:** Born Aug 23, 1942, Tuskegee, AL; children: Johnny, Christopher & Tiffany. **Educ:** Knoxville Col, BA, 1964; Nat Exec Inst, postgrad, 1965; Auburn Univ, MPA, 1977. **Career:** Multi-Man Dist, exec Bronx, 1967-68; Sen Robt Kennedy, polit campaign strategist 1968; Tuskegee Model Cities Prog, exec coord, 1969-70; Atty Fred Gray, campaign mgr 1970; Multi Racial Corp, asst dir, 1970-72; US Justice Dept Montgomery, state supr comn rel serv, 1971-72; City Tuskegee, mayor, 1972-96; Ala House Rep, state rep, 1997; Johnny Ford & Assoc Inc, pres; City Tuskegee, mayor, currently; Macon County, 82nd Dist, State Rep, 1998-2004. **Orgs:** Founder & dir gen, World Conf Mayors Inc; Nat Asn Advan Colored People; Kappa Alpha Psi; past pres, Ala League Municipalities; pres, Johnny Ford & Assoc Inc; pres-emer & founder, Nat Conf Black Mayors; Ala Foreign Trade Comn; chmn, Nat Utility Alliance; Ala Municipal Electric Authority; past pres, Ala League Municipalities; Kappa Alpha Psi; founding pres, Tuskegee Optimist Club; Mount Olive Missionary Baptist Church. **Honors/Awds:** Top Campaigner Award BSA, 1967; Young Man of the Year, Women's Reserve 1967; Youngest Multi-Dist Exec in Nation BSA, 1967; Awarded the key to more than 100 Am foreign cities; Received 4 honorary doctorate degrees. **Special Achievements:** First black mayor in Alabama.

FORD, JUDITH DONNA
Judge. **Personal:** Born Aug 30, 1935, Eureka, CA. **Educ:** Univ Calif, Berkeley, BS, 1957; Boalt Hall Sch Law, JD, 1974. **Career:** Petty Andrews Tufts & Jackson, assoc atty, 1974-79; Consumer Fraud Crime Div, SF Dist Atty's Off, dir, 1977-79; Fed Trade Comn, dir, 1980-82; Alameda County Munic Ct, judge, 1982-98; State Calif Munic Ct Oakland-Piedmont- Emeryville Dist, judge, 1983-. **Orgs:** Chas Houston Bar Asn, 1974-; San Francisco Bar Asn, Lawyer Referral Serv Comt, 1976; NSF Software Auditing Workshop, 1976; Comn Admin Justice, 1976-79; deleg, San Francisco Bar Asn Lawyer Referral Serv Comn, 1976; chair, E Oakland Planned Parenthood Adv Comn, 1977-80; speaker, Bank Admin Inst, 1977; speaker, EDP Audit Controls Workshop, 1977; speaker, CPA Soc, 1977; speaker, Joint meeting IIA & EDPA, 1978; dir, Planned Parenthood, 1978-80; Calif Asn Black Lawyers, 1978-; chair, Black Women Lawyers, NCA Finance Comn, 1979-80; San Francisco Lawyers Comn, Urban Affairs, 1979-80; chair, San Francisco Bar Asn Comn, Legal Educ Comt, 1979-80; bd mem, Consumer Union, 1979-82; ref, St Bar Ct, 1979-82; consr, Law Ctr Bd Consr, 1979-83; radio & TV speaker, FTrade Comn, 1980-82; San Francisco Bar Asn Judiciary Comn, 1981-82; bd mem, judicial coun, Peralta Serv Corp, 1983-, 1991-94; chair, CTC Privacy & Access Subcommittee, 1995-96; adv comt, Judicial Coun Ct Technol, 1995-98; bd mem, Calif Judges Asn, 1996-98; CA Judges Asn; Alameda County Trauma Rev Comn; US Magistrate Merit Selection Comn; trustee, Alameda County Law Libr. **Special Achievements:** Calif Criminal Law Procedure & Practice, co-author, chapters 4 & 6; various TV & Radio appearances. **Business Addr:** Judge, Oakland-Piedmont Emeryville Municipal Court, 661 Washington St, Oakland, CA 94607.*

FORD, KENNETH A.
Association executive. **Personal:** Born Aug 10, 1949, Washington, DC; married Shirley Payne; children: Travelle. **Educ:** Howard Univ, BSCE, 1972, MCE, 1977. **Career:** Limbach Co, proj engr, 1972-75; Potomac Elec Power Co, env engr, 1975-77; Parametric Inc, prog dir, 1977-82; Wash Suburban Sanitary Comn, planning mgr, 1982-84; Nat Asn Home Builders, mgr civil eng. **Orgs:** Nat Soc Prof Engrs, 1977; adv bd, Utility Location & Coordr Coun, 1984; Building Seismic Safety Coun, 1984; bd dirs, BlackSci Inc, 1984-85; Am Soc Civil Engrs. *

FORD, KISHA (KISHA ANGELINE FORD)
Basketball player. **Personal:** Born Apr 4, 1975. **Educ:** Ga Tech, BA, 1997; Baker Col, MBA, 2001. **Career:** NY Liberty, guard & forward, 1997-98; Orlando Miracle, 1998-99; Satila, Sweden, 1998-99; Miami Sol, guard & forward, 2000-01; Nat Women's Basketball League, Alanta Justice, guard & forward, 2001-02. **Honors/Awds:** All-ACC, First Team; AP Honorable Mention All-Am; Kodak District III, All-Am. **Special Achievements:** First Georgia Tech player to be drafted by the WNBA. *

FORD, KISHA ANGELINE. **See FORD, KISHA.**

FORD, LISA DENISE
Chemist, educator. **Personal:** Born Aug 3, 1965, Memphis, TN; daughter of Samuel L. **Educ:** Fisk Univ, BS, chem, 1987, MA, chem, 1990. **Career:** Barrow-Agee Anal Lab, anal chemist, 1987-88; Cargill Corn Milling Div, qual control chemist, 1988; Fisk Univ, grad lab teacher's asst, 1988-89; MMES, Oak Ridge Nat Lab, grad res intern, 1989-90; MMES, Nuclear & Environ Plant, qual control chemist, supv chemist, tech support chemist, staff chemist, 1990-96; MMES, Gaseous Diffusion & Waste Mgt Plant, chemist, 1993-94; Millington Cent High Sch, teacher, chemist, 1996-98; Austin-E Magnet High Sch, teacher, chemist, 1998-. **Orgs:** Am Chem Soc, 1987; Nat Teachers Asn; Tenn Teachers Asn. **Honors/Awds:** MMES Certificate of Appreciation; Tennessee Quality Achievement Award; Environmental, Restoration & Waste Mgt Mission Success Award; Second Runner-up to Miss Fisk, Fisk Univ Libr, 1986-87; International Hall of Fame, Inventors Club of America; Advanced Technology Award, 1993; Y-12 Pathfinder Award, 1994. **Home Addr:** 7205 John Norton Rd, Knoxville, TN 37920, **Home Phone:** (865)579-3165. **Business Phone:** (865)594-1911.*

FORD, DR. LUTHER L. **See Obituaries section.**

FORD, DR. MARCELLA WOODS
Educator. **Personal:** Born in Athens, GA; daughter of Clem (deceased) and Lucy Smith (deceased); married Jesse W (deceased). **Educ:** Shaw Univ, AB, LHD, 1982; Am Bapt Sem, MA. **Career:** Mather Sch, teacher; Shaw Univ, asst prof, dir; Oakland, CA, dir release time classes; Berkeley Unified Sch Dist, teacher; Berkeley Adult Ed, teacher 1962-64; Black Hist. **Orgs:** Chair Women United; pres, Bus & Prof Women; N Calif Am Baptist Church; pres, Interfaith Intercultural fel E Bay; pres, Am Baptist Women Oakland Area Asn; bd dir, Intertribal Friendship House; Budget United Crusade Panel & Speakers Bur; Hist Docent Oakland Mus; Dedication Comn Oakland Mus; Am Baptist Church W Campus Ministry Stud Found; Nat Coun Negro Women; Steering Comn, Shaw Univ Alumni, 1968-69; gov mem, Allensworth State HistPark Adv Comn, 1969; Hist Landmarks Preserv Bd, Mayor & City Coun, 1973; Rel Ed Beth Eden Baptist Church; Alpha Nu Omega Chap Alpha Kappa Alpha Sorority; Am Asn Univ Women, YWCA; co-org, E Bay Negro Hist Soc; Oakland Mus Asn; Asn Study Afro, Am Life & Hist; Nat Asn Advan Colored People; Nat Retired Teachers Asn. **Honors/Awds:** Woman of the Year, Eden Bapt Church, Marcella Ford Circle Women's Soc McGee Ave Bapt Church 1959, 1969; The Post Newspaper, "Faces Around theBay", 1970; Woman of the Year, Comn Serv, Am Asn Univ Women; Leadership Award, Far Western Reg Conf Ark Sorority, 1976; Dedication of Allensworth State Hist Park Commission Service Awards, 1976; Christian Womanhood Award, Shaw Divinity Sch Raleigh NC, 1976; Recognition & MW Ford Scholarship, Shaw Univ, Beth Eden Bapt Church, 1977; Scholarship Honor of Memorial Ford, Oakland Piedmont Chap, AAUW, 1977; Community Service Award, Cult & Ethnic Affairs Gd Oakland Mus, 1977; Pre-Kwanza Award, Asn Africans & African Am Oakland; National Sojourner Truth Award, Nat Asn Negro Bus & Prof Womens Clubs Inc, East Bay Area Club, 1981; Woman of Achievement; Women Helping Women Award, Soroptimist Int Oakland, 1982; Resolution of Honor, Calif Legislature Assembly, 1989; Oakland Legacy Awards, Trailblazer, 1997; African-American Matriarch Honoree, Berkley RepertoryTheatre & African Am Advocate, 1997. **Special Achievements:** Num articles publ; Wee Pals, 1995; Black Women Stirring the Water, 1998. **Business Addr:** Founder, African American Museum & Library at Oakland, 659 14th St, Oakland, CA 94612, **Business Phone:** (510)637-0200.

FORD, NANCY HOWARD
School administrator. **Personal:** Born Jul 29, 1942, Wilmington, DE; children: Sergio Howard & Charis. **Educ:** Cent State Univ,

BS, 1964; Univ DE, MEd, 1972. **Career:** CT State Welfare Dept, welfare home economist, 1968; Seattle Pub Sch, teacher-home arts, 1968-70; Wilmington Pub Sch, teacher corps int, 1970-72; Cheyney State Col, assoc dean res life, 1972-76; Dept Pub Instruction DE, educ specialist, nutrit, educ & training summer food serv prog. **Orgs:** Vol, US Peace Corps in Brazil, 1964-66; vol, Teacher DE Adolescent Prog Inc, 1971. **Honors/Awds:** Received numerous awards including: National Honor Soc Wilmington High Sch, 1960; Highest Ranking Student, Central State Univ, 1964; Certificate of Recognition, US Peace Corps Serv, White House, 1966; Am Can Society; National Gold Award, Pub Educ, 1992. **Special Achievements:** TV Show appearance "Keeping Kid's Out of Harm's Way" Tom Brokaws nightly news, 1994; Participated in national news conf, C Defense Fund, Am Sch Food Serv Asn, 1994.

FORD, NATHANIEL P
Executive director. **Personal:** Born Jul 31, 1961, South Carolina; son of Phillip and Thomasina; married Crystal; children: Phillip, Whitney, Brittany & Taylor. **Educ:** Mercer Univ, BA, appl studies orgn leadership. **Career:** New York City Transit Authority, train conductor, 1983-86, train dispatcher, 1986-88, dep line supt, 1988-90, supt district night opers, 1990-92; San Francisco Bay Area Rapid Transit Authority, asst chief transp officer, 1992-97; Metrop Atlanta Rapid Transit Authority, sr vp opers, 1997-99, exec vp opers & develop, 1999-2000, gen mgr & chief exec officer, 2000-06; San Francisco Municipal Transp Agency, exec dir & chief exec officer, 2006-. **Orgs:** Vice chair, business management & finance, Am Pub Transp Asn; 2nd vice chair, Conf Minority Transp Officials; bd mem, Atlanta Neighborhood Develop Partnership; bd mem, Ga Chamber Com; bd mem, Metro Atlanta Chamber Com; Oversight & Proj Selection Com, Transp Coop Res Proj; APTREX Inst Int Transit Cert Review Bd; United Way Metrop Atlanta Alexis de Tocqueville Soc. **Honors/Awds:** Executive of the Year, Nat COMTO, 2000. **Special Achievements:** Transit Industry "Rising Star", Bus Ride Magazine, 1998; Panelist, United Nations Town Hall Mtg on Terrorism with UN Sec General Kofi Annan (nationally simulcast in 10 cities), 2001; Hosted first Bus Rapid Transit Conference in SE Region, 2002; A-1 Moody Bond Rating, 2002; APTA Top 10 Job Access Award Winner, 2002; 25 Most Interesting People in Transit, Metro Magazine, 2002. **Business Addr:** Executive Director, Chief Executive Officer, San Francisco Municipal Transportation Agency (SFMTA), 1 S Van Ness Ave 7th Fl, San Francisco, CA 94103, **Business Phone:** (415)701-4720.

FORD, ROBERT BLACKMAN
Dentist. **Personal:** Born Nov 22, 1924, Montgomery, AL; married Katherine Brosby; children: Teri, Wendy, Sondra. **Educ:** Morehouse Col, BS, 1948; Howard Univ, DDS, 1952; Veteran's Hosp Tuskegee, 1953. **Career:** Pvt prac, currently. **Orgs:** Am Dent Asn; Ohio State Dent Asn; Dayton Dent Asn coun, 1970-73; treas, Buckeye State Dent Soc; Acad Gen Dent; elected, Jefferson Twp Bd Educ, past pres, 1968-72; bd mgt, Young Men's Christian Asn; bd mem, Community Res Inc; Kappa Alpha Psi. **Special Achievements:** First Black in Ohio who is appointed to the State Dental Board in 1974. **Military Serv:** USMC, 1944-46. **Business Addr:** 3807 W 3rd St, Dayton, OH 45417.

FORD, DR. ROBERT L
Educator. **Educ:** Southern Univ & A&M Col, BS, chem, 1967; Purdue Univ, PhD, 1972. **Career:** Xerox Corp, assoc scientist, 1967-95; Southern Univ & A&M Col, assoc prof chem, 1975-81, 1985-87, prof chem, 1987-, Ctr Energy & Environ Studies, dir, 1989-96, Res & Strategic Initiatives, vice chancellor, 1996-98; LA Dept Urban & Comm Affairs, Off Comm Serv, asst secy, 1982-84; Dillard Univ, asst prof chem, 1984-85; Neo-Tech South Inc, pres & chief exec officer, 1985-; LA Bd Regents, asst assoc comnr sponsored prog. **Orgs:** Am Chem Soc; Nat Teaching Asn; Sigma Xi Scientific Res Soc; Nat Coun Univ Res Adminrs; Am Soc Trainers & Developers; Phi Delta Kappa Int; Tech Transfer Soc; Nat Org Prof Advan Black Chemists & Chem Engrs. **Honors/Awds:** Certificate of Service, US Comm Civil Rights, 1999; Certificate of Appreciation, LA Corpe Recycling Coun, 1999; Certificate of Appreciation, NAFEO, 2000; Powell Reznikoff Humanitarian Award, Baton Rouge Coun Human Rels, 2000; Advanced Certification, GLOBE prog, 2000; Certificate of Appreciation, Stud Teachers Orgn, SUBR Col Educ, 2000; Outstanding Contributor Award, Sci & Eng Alliance, 2001; Certificate of Appreciation, LA State Univ Stud NOBCChE Chapter, 2002. **Special Achievements:** Numerous publications & presentations.

FORD, SAM
Journalist. **Personal:** Born May 29, 1953, Coffeyville, KS; son of Kathleen Owens and Sammie Ford; married Gloria Murry, Nov 28, 1981; children: Murry & Gina. **Educ:** Univ Kans, BS, jour, 1974; Univ Minn, attended 1976. **Career:** KMSP-TV, reporter, 1974-75; WCCO-TV, reporter, 1975-77; CBS News, correspondent, 1977-87; ABC7/WJLA-TV, news reporter, 1987-. **Orgs:** Nat Asn Black Journalists, founding mem, 1975-; Lincoln Park United Methodist Church, 1997-. **Home Phone:** (202)544-0633. **Business Addr:** News Reporter, ABC7/WJLA-TV, Newschannel 8, 1100 Wilson Blvd, Arlington, VA 22209.

FORD, REV. SAMUEL LEE
Clergy. **Personal:** Born Jan 26, 1942, Leland, MS; son of Van and Lena B Ford; married Jul 26, 2000; children: Lisa F Davidson, Samuel Leon & Monica F Stokes. **Educ:** Masters degree, 1989. **Career:** W Canaan Baptist Church, sr pastor, 1976-. **Orgs:** Dir, Millington Action & Involvement, 1987-98; trustee, Tenn Sch Religion, 1989-92; pres, Friendship Dist Asn, 1990-; dir, Home Mission, TN Regular Bapt Missionary Ed, 1998-; adv bd, Tenn State Rep Barbara Cooper. **Home Addr:** 3033 Spring Hill Cove, Memphis, TN 38127. **Business Addr:** Senior Pastor, West Canaan Baptist Church, 8715 Wilkinsville Rd, Millington, TN 38053, **Business Phone:** (901)872-2426.

FORD, STACEY
Basketball player. **Personal:** Born Jan 14, 1969. **Educ:** Univ Ga, BA, 1991. **Career:** Columbus Quest, forward, 1996-98; New York Liberty, 2001; Sacramento Monarchs, forward, 2001-02. *

FORD, VERNON N.
Executive, vice president (organization). **Personal:** Born Feb 15, 1945, Eupora, MS; son of Robert N and Nancy E Jones; married Angela Graves Ford, Oct 10, 1970; children: Tatia L, Erin K. **Educ:** Cent State Univ, Wilberforce, OH, BS, 1970. **Career:** Alcoa, Los Angeles, CA, sales rep, 1973-77; Alcoa, Indianapolis, IN, br sales mgr, 1977-79; Alcoa, San Francisco, CA, sales mgr, 1979-84; Alcoa, Houston, TX, sales mgr, 1984-87; Separations Technol Inc, Warrendales, PA, mgr sales & distributor, 1987-90; Vancouver Extension Co, Vancouver WA, pres, 1990; Alcoa, Halethorpe Extrusions Inc, pres. **Orgs:** Exec Leadership Coun, 1986-; chairperson, MESO Adv Bd, 1990-; vpres, Cent State Univ Found, 1989-; chairperson, Col Bus, Adv Coun, Cent State Univ, 1990-; Rotary, 1990-. **Honors/Awds:** Achievement Hall Fame, Cent State Univ, 1990. **Military Serv:** USAF, E-5, 1962-66. *

FORD, WALLACE L
Educator, government official, legal secretary. **Personal:** Born Jan 13, 1950, New York, NY; son of Wallace and Carmen Ford; divorced; married Rikki E Langston, May 2, 1981. **Educ:** Dartmouth Col, BA, 1970; Harvard Law Sch, JD, 1973. **Career:** Wall St, investment banker; WDCR radio, disc jockey; State Supreme Ct, NY, law secy; State Assembly Comm Banking, NY, coun; Amistad DOT Venture Capital Inc, exec vpres & gen coun; State Dept Com Div Minority Bus Develop, NY, dep comnr; State New York Mortgage Agency, exec officer & chief exec officer; Int Bus Sch Bus Metrop Col, New York; Kaye Scholer law firm, atty; New York City, comnr bus; Drexel Burnham Lambert Inc, vpres; City NY, dept ports & trade, comnr; Columbia Univ, Sch Int & Pub Affairs, adj prof, currently; Fordworks Associates Inc, prin & founder, currently. **Orgs:** Dartmouth Alumni Coun; Dartmouth Black Alumni Asn; bd trustee, Malcolm King Col; Nat Asn Securities Prof; bd dir, Urban League, Harlem Br, NY; mem faculty, Sch Int & Pub Affairs, Columbia Univ; mem bd adv, Ctr Jazz Studies, Columbia Univ; mem bd adv, United Way Int; mem bd dirs, Haitel. **Honors/Awds:** Annual award, Nat Housing Conf, 1984. **Special Achievements:** Listed Ebony Mag 100 Leaders the Future, 1978; listed Time Mag Fifty Faces of the Future 1979. **Business Addr:** Adjunct Professor, School of International and Public Affairs, Int Affairs Bldg 13th Fl, 420 W 118th St, New York, NY 10027, **Business Phone:** (212)854-3213.

FORD, WILLIAM L., JR.
Executive. **Personal:** Born Jul 31, 1941, Kayford, WV; married Eleanor Holmes; children: Karen, Valerie. **Educ:** Russell Sage Evening Col, 1966; State Univ Albany, NY, 1968. **Career:** Mayfair Inc Albany, off mgr, 1968-70; WROW-WTEN Albany, chief acct, 1970-71; WROW Radio Albany, bus mgr, 1971; WKBW-TV & Radio Buffalo, bus mgr, 1971-76; WFSB-TV Hartford, vpres bus & admin affairs, 1976-78; Post-Newsweek Sta Mich Inc WDIV, vpres, sta mgr, 1978-83; Cellular Telecommun, vpres. **Orgs:** Bd dir, Better Bus Bur Met Detroit, 1979; Jr Achievement Southeastern MI, 1979; Broadcast Fin Mgt Assoc, 1979; Comnr, Detroit Black United Fund 1979; bd gov, Detroit Chap Nat Acad TV Arts & Sci 1980; bd dir, Mich Asn Broadcasters, 1980. *

FORDE, FRASER PHILIP, JR.
Executive. **Personal:** Born Nov 24, 1943, Tuskegee, AL; son of Fraser Philip Sr and Joyce Nourse; married LaVerne; children: Tracey, Fraser III, Erika. **Educ:** Hofstra Univ, BBA, 1965; Pace Univ, MBA, 1980. **Career:** Dun & Bradstreet Inc, credit analyst, 1967-69; Bank & Opers Dept, educ trainee, 1969-70; Money Transfer Dept, asst group head, 1970-71; asst officer personnel rep, 1971-73; Morgan Guaranty Trust Co, asst treas, 1973-87, asst vpres, 1987-89, vpres. **Orgs:** Treas, Milford Civic Asn Central Islip Inc, 1980-; delegate, Central Islip Sch Dist Budget Adv Comt, 1981. **Honors/Awds:** Black Achievers In Industry, YMCA Greater NY, Harlem Branch, 1974; Award, Outstanding Trainee; Basic Training; Scout Dog Training; CIB O & S Bar; Vietnam Service Award; Vietnamese Service Award. **Military Serv:** AUS, sp & 4, 1965-67. *

FORDE, JAMES ALBERT (JIM FORDE)
Health services administrator. **Personal:** Born Jan 23, 1927, Brooklyn, NY; married Gaille Faulkner Forde; children: Janice Ross & Jacqueline Sullivan. **Educ:** Brooklyn Col, BA, eng, 1949; City Col NY, MPA, 1955; NY State Univ, doctoral courses, 1960; Ithaca Col, nursing home admin, 1975. **Career:** Serv Dept Ment Hyg, dir bur mgt, 1963-67; Bur Budget Serv, dir, 1967-68; NY State Dept Mental Hyg, Local Serv Div, asst comnr, 1968-71; Off Prog Planning & Coord, NY State Dept Ment Hyg, assoc comnr, 1971-74; Willowbrook Devel Ctr, actg dir, 1974-75; Mid-Hudson Reg Dept Ment Hyg, reg dir, 1975-76; Health Care Agency Cty San Diego, dep admin, 1976-79; San Diego City Dept Health Serv, dir, 1979-86; SD Urban League, exec dir; Calif Black Health Network, exec dir, 1987-; San Diego Black Health Assoc, proj dir, admin dir, currently. **Orgs:** Am Pub Health Assoc, Calif Black Health Network, State Calif, Hypertension Adv Coun; consult, Fed Off Health Affairs, 1973; Willowbrook Review Panel, 1975-78; bd mem, CD Reg Ctr Devlopmentally Disabled, 1979-86. **Honors/Awds:** JCC Distinguished Service Award, 1963; Paper Unified Service A Shift from Who to How "The Bulletin," 1973; Aid Award for Medicine, 1980; Award for Health, Nat Asn Advan Colored People, 1981; Statewide Black Health Individual Achievement Award, 1982; Award for Excellence, Am Pub Health Asn, 1993; Hildrus Poindexter Award, 1995. **Military Serv:** AUS, sgt, 2 yrs. **Business Addr:** Administrative Director, San Diego Black Health Associates, 7851 Mission Ctr Ct Suite 260, San Diego, CA 92108, **Business Phone:** (619)299-0411.

FORDE, JIM. See FORDE, JAMES ALBERT.

FORDHAM, CYNTHIA WILLIAMS
Lawyer, administrative court judge. **Personal:** Born Dec 6, 1954, Philadelphia, PA; daughter of Paul and Ola N; married Rev Jerome Fordham. **Educ:** Pa State Univ, BA, 1975; Univ Pa Law Sch, JD, 1979. **Career:** Philadelphia Bd Educ, substitute teacher, 1976; Comn Legal Serv, law clerk, 1977-78; Pa Dept State, asst gen coun, 1980-84; Pa Human Rels Comn, asst coun, 1984-91; Pa Pub Utility Comn, spec agt, 1991-93, admin law judge, 1993-. **Orgs:** Am Bar Asn, 1976-; Pa Bar Asn, 1979-; Nat Bar Asn, 1983-; chairperson, Greater Philadelphia Health Action, 1984-; pres, bd dir, TSB Church Community Outreach Corp, 1986-. **Honors/Awds:** Chapel of Four Chaplains Award, 1967, 1981; Outstanding Young Women of Am Award, 1980. **Business Addr:** Administrative Law Judge, Pennsylvania Public Utility Commission, Broad Spring Garden St, 1302 State Off Bldg, Philadelphia, PA 19130.*

FORDHAM, MONROE
Educator. **Personal:** Born Oct 11, 1939, Parrott, GA; son of James and Arie Deloris Oxford; married Freddie; children: Cynthia, Barry & Pamela. **Educ:** Emporia State Univ, BS, 1957; Emporia State Univ, MS, 1962; State Univ NY, PhD, 1973. **Career:** Wichita Pub Sch, social studies teacher, 1962-69; Wichita St Univ, coord black studies, 1969-70; Buffalo State Col, hist teacher, Dept Hist & Soc Sci Educ, chmn, 1970-98, Dept Hist & Social Studies Educ, prof hist, 2000, prof emer hist & social studies educ, 2002-; Oxford Family Newsletter, co-ed. **Orgs:** Pres, Afro Am Hist Asn Niagara Frontier. **Honors/Awds:** Outstanding Alumni Award, Emporia State Univ; Inducted to Emporia State University Athletic Hall of Fame, 1995; DHL, State Univ New York, 2000; Carter G Woodson Scholars Medallion, ASALH, 2005; Named in honor, Monroe Fordham Regional Hist Ctr. **Special Achievements:** Author: Major Themes in Northern Black Religious Thought, 1800-1860, 1975; A History of Bethel AME. Church, Buffalo, New York, 1977; Carnegie Foundation & Change Magazine selected Fordham as a professor who made a difference in higher education. **Home Addr:** 4363 Chestnut Ridge Rd, Buffalo, NY 14228, **Home Phone:** (716)691-4257. **Business Addr:** Professor Emeritus of History and Social Studies Education, Buffalo State College, 1300 Elmwood Ave, Buffalo, NY 14222-1004, **Business Phone:** (716)878-4078.

FOREE, JACK CLIFFORD
Business owner, educator. **Personal:** Born Mar 29, 1935, New Castle, KY; son of Etta and Jesse; married Daisy Spencer; children: Julia Foree Burton, Stacey & Etta. **Educ:** Ky State Univ, BA, 1959; Catherine Spalding Univ, BA, 1966; Indiana Univ, MA, 1971; Grace Theol Sem, PhD. **Career:** Math teacher; Franklin Square W, pres; Sky brite Louisville Inc; Grace Bible Col Ky, Pres. **Orgs:** Pres, Breakfast Optimist; Jefferson Co Educators Asn; Ky Educators Asn; Nat Educators Asn; Nat Bldg Contractors Asn; Nat Asn Math Educators; St Asn Math & Sci Educators; chmn, Ky & Tenn Sunday Sch Asn, 1972-85. **Honors/Awds:** Ky Colonel. **Military Serv:** AUS, sgt, 2 yrs. *

FOREMAN, DOYLE
Sculptor, educator. **Personal:** Born Jun 17, 1933, Ardmore, OK; married Selma J; children: Doyle Jr & Maia. **Educ:** Ariz State Univ; Calif Col Arts & Crafts, BFA, 1960. **Career:** Sculptor & Educator (retired). Oakland Recreation Dept, arts & crafts specialist, 1957-60, landscape, gardening & land mgt, 1961-65; Univ Calif, Col V Santa Cruz, prof art & sculptor, 1968-01; Calif Col Arts & Crafts, 1969; Yard bird Publ Co, art ed, art dir, bd dir, 1971; art ed, Yard bird Reader. **Orgs:** Santa Cruz County Art Comn, 1972-74; City Santa Cruz Bicentennial Comn, 1975; comt chmn, Kaiser Ctr Gallery Oakland, 1968; Int Sculpture Ctr,1968; Comn Inter-Campus Art, Univ Calif, 1984, 1991-94; City Santa Cruz Pub Arts Comn, 1999-. **Honors/Awds:** The Josie King Humanatarian Award; Outstanding Community Service Award from Mayor; MEXUS grant for Pecked Rock drawing site, San Ignacio, Baja, Calif, Univ Calif, Santa Cruz; Best in Show, Kaiser Ctr Gallery, Oakland Museum, Oakland, CA; Mini-Grant for Ethnographic

Artist Series Totem, Univ Calif,Santa Cruz; Instructional Improvement Grant to complete film on African sculpture. **Special Achievements:** Most Imaginative Sculpture, Bechtel Int Ctr Show, Palo Alto Times; art work has been published in Song of Andoumboulou by Nathaniel Mackey, African American Art and Artists by Samella Lewis, and Art in the San Francisco Bay Area by Thomas All bright. **Military Serv:** AUS, 1953-55. *

FOREMAN, GEORGE EDWARD
Clergy, boxer. **Personal:** Born Jan 10, 1949, Marshall, TX; son of J D and Nancy Foreman; married Joan; children: Michi, Freeda, Georgetta, Natalie, Leola, George Jr & George III, GeorgeIV, George V, George VI & George Travis Walls. **Career:** Professional boxer (retired), preacher, pastor, business owner; Job Corps-,boxer, 1960; professional boxer, 1969-77, 1987-99; The Church of Lord Jesus Christ, pastor, preacher, proprietor & ordained minister, 1977-; Big George's ranch, owner, currently. **Orgs:** Founder, The George Foreman Youth & Community Ctr; Knock-Out Pediatric Cancer. **Honors/Awds:** Heavy weight Olympic Gold Medal, Mexico City, 1968; World Heavy weight Championship, 1973; Boxer of the Year, World Boxing Assn, 1974; Heavy weight Champion of the World, Int Boxing Fedn, World Boxing Assn, 1994; International Boxing Hall Of Fame, 2003. **Special Achievements:** Number one challenger, WBA & WBC, 1971; co-author: By George, Villard Books, 1995; Nineth greatest puncher of all time by Ring Magazine; Oldest man ever to win a major heavy weight title. **Business Addr:** Preacher, Ordained Minister, The Church of Lord Jesus Christ, 2501 Lone Oak Rd, Houston, TX 77093, **Business Phone:** (281)590-7480.

FOREMAN, JOYCE BLACKNALL
Entrepreneur. **Personal:** Born Jul 6, 1948, Thelma, TX; daughter of Roy and Betty Lockhart; divorced. **Educ:** Univ Tex Dallas, sociol; El Centro Col, AA; Paul Quinn Col, BS, mgt. **Career:** Foreman Off Prod, Dallas, TX, pres, currently. **Orgs:** Mem bd dirs, Tex Com Bank; mem bd mgt, Urban League; chairperson, Dallas Independent Sch Dists Minority Bus Adv Comm; Nat Asn Female Execs; NAACP; Womens Bus Connection; mem bd dirs, Channel 13; Dallas Assembly; Dallas Citizens Coun; Comn Educ Excellence; vice chmn, bd dirs, DART, currently. **Honors/Awds:** Vendor of the Year, Dallas, Ft Worth Minority Bus Develop Coun, 1984; Quest for Success Award, Miller Brewing Co, Dallas Morning News, Dallas Black Chamber Com, 1985; Dreammaker Award, Southeast Dallas Bus & Prof Women's Club, 1985; Business Recognition Award, Iota Phi Lambda, 1987; Spotlighting Your Success for Women Business Owner, 1986; Champion 100 Gran Award, 1984; Up and Comer to Watch, Dallas Times Herald, 1987; Community Service Award, Sigma Gamma Rho Sorority, 1987; Trailblazer Award, S Dallas Bus & Prof Women's Club, 1989; Minority Business Advocate of the Year for State of Texas, Small Bus Admin, 1989; Doers Award, 1989; Women who make a difference, Minority & Women Bus Mag, 1990; Certificate of Recognition, Congresswomen Eddie Bernice Johnson, 1993; Entrepreneur of the Year, Dallas Weekly, 1994; African American Hero Award, KKDA Radio & Coca-Cola, 1994; Fort Worth Black Chamber Excellence Award, 1997; Outstanding Business Award, Tex Black Women Conf, 1998; Community Service Award, KRLD & Guaranty Bank, 2001; Business of the month, Dallas Post Tribune, 2003.

FOREMAN, PEGGY E
Lawyer, executive. **Personal:** Born Feb 18, 1958, Houston, TX; daughter of Dave and Ella. **Educ:** Univ Penn, attended 1978; Univ Houston, BBA, 1981; Tex Southern Univ, Thurgood Marshall Sch Law, JD, 1985. **Career:** Peggy Foreman, atty, 1985-89; Burney & Foreman, partner, 1990-. **Orgs:** Am Bar Asn; Nat Bar Asn; State Bar Tex; Tex Young Lawyers Asn; Harris Co Young Asn; Houston Lawyers Asn; Houston Bar Asn; Young Lawyers Asn; Nat Asn Bond Lawyers; Tex Trial Lawyers Asn; Gulf Coast Black Women Lawyers Asn; Phi Delta Phi Legal Fraternity Alumni Chap; Thurgood Marshall Sch Law Alumni Asn. **Honors/Awds:** Special Recognition, Houston Bus & Prof Men's Club; Woman of the Year, Iota Phi Lambda Sorority Inc, Beta Delta Chap. **Special Achievements:** Author, Wills and Trusts in Texas, Harris County Young Lawyers Asn & Texas Lawyers Asn, 1989, Client Satisfaction, How to Thrive, Not Just Survive in a Solo/Small Firm Practice, State Bar of Texas, December 1993; numerous others. **Business Addr:** Partner, Burney & Foreman, 5445 Almeda Suite 400, Houston, TX 77004, **Business Phone:** (713)526-6404.

FOREMAN, S BEATRICE (SALLIE BEATRICE FOREMAN)
Teacher. **Personal:** Born Sep 23, 1917, Garysburg, NC; daughter of Douglas Ransom and Susie Ransom; married James W; married Charles. **Educ:** Hampton Inst, BS, 1939; Western Reserve Univ, MS, 1956. **Career:** Educator (retired); Murfreesboro Tenn, pub sch teacher, 1939-41; Cleveland OH, pub sch teacher, 1942-61; Stamford CT, pub sch teacher, 1961-82, bd educ mem. **Orgs:** Past pres, Westchester Co Chap Delta Sigma Theta Sor; League Women Voters; Retired Teachers Asn; Democratic Womens Club; Hampton Alumnae Asn; Urban League; Yerwood Ctr; Girlfriends Inc; Interfaith Coun Stamford; Cath Interracial Coun; St Bridgets RC Church; Heart Fund Chmn; Am Red Cross Bloodmobile Aide; Fairfield Co Alumnae Chap Delta Sigma Theta Sor Inc; first vpres, New Neighborhoods Inc, 1969-; bd trustees first black female Stamford Hosp, 1972-83; first vpres, NAACP, 1979-84; CT Justice Comn, 1981-82; pres, Bus & Educ Alliance, l988-89; bd educ, first black female, 1981-; bd dir, Wright Tech Sch, 1981-; Mayor's Comn Drugs & Alcohol; SNET adv, Southern New Eng Tel; adv bd, Salvation Army Stamford; bd dir, secy, CTE Anti Poverty Agency; bd dir, secy, Salvation Army; Urban League Guild Stanford. **Honors/Awds:** Service Award, Interfaith Coun, 1972; Educ Awd, Stamford Black Educators, 1978; Westhill HS, 1978; Stamford Educ Asn Outstanding, 1978; Outstanding Educr, Stamford Educ Asn, 1978; top vote getter city primary & regular election, 1981 & 1984; Serv Awd, CT Justice Comn, 1982; Outstanding Educator, CT State Ministers Wives & Widows Asn, 1983; Serv Awd, Stamford Hosp, 1984; Outstanding Sor Awd, Fairfield Co Alumnae Chap Delta Sigma Theta Sor Inc, 1984; Comn Serv Awd, Yerwood Womens Club, 1984; Ed Awd, NAACP, 1985; African American History Class Award, Stamford High Sch, 1988; Citizen of Year, 1987; Senior Employment Service Award, 1989; Kawanza Nguzo Saba Award for Community Service, 1999. **Home Addr:** 132 Oaklawn Ave, Stamford, CT 06905.

FOREMAN, SALLIE BEATRICE. See FOREMAN, S BEATRICE.

FORMEY, SYLVESTER C
Executive. **Career:** Airport Comn, vice chair, currently; Vanguard Distributors Inc, pres, currently. **Business Addr:** President, Vanguard Distributors Inc, 107 NE Lathrop Ave, PO Box 608, Savannah, GA 31402, **Business Phone:** (912)236-1766.*

FORNAY, ALFRED R, JR.
Editor, writer. **Personal:** Born in Cincinnati, OH; son of Alfred Fornay Sr and Marguerite Weatherford. **Educ:** Wilfred Acad Beauty & Hair Design, 1966; City Col NY, AAS, 1968; State Univ NY, Fashion Inst Technol, AAS, 1971. **Career:** Fashion Fair Cosmetics, beauty/training dir, 1973-78; Revlon Inc, polished ambers collection, creative dir, 1978-80; Elan Mag, elan beauty ed, 1980-82; Ebony Mag, beauty & fashion ed, 1982-85; EM Magazine, ed, 1985-88; Essence Mag, assoc beauty ed, 1972-73; Clairol Inc, asst ethnic mkt mgr, 1971-72, mkt mgr; Am Visions Mag, fashion & beauty contributing writer, 1989-; Johnson Publ Co Inc, Fashion Fair Div, beauty/training, 1988-; Business Week Careers Mag, contributing fashion & beauty writer, 1987-88; Procter & Gamble, Cover Girl cosmetic div, consult, 1992; New Rochelle HS Continuing Edu, tcr, cosmetics & color theory, 2003; Books: Fornay's Guide to Skin & Makeup for Women of Color, Simon & Schuster Publishers 1989; Amalgamated Publishers Special Beauty Edition, 1996; BE Magazine Article, 1997; BET Weekend Magazine Article, 1997; The African American Woman's Guide to Success Makeup & Skincare, 1999; Born Beautiful: The African American Teenager's Complete Beauty Guide, 2002. **Orgs:** NAB, NY Chapter, 1984, 1991-93; Nat Beauty Culturist League, 1983; friend/former bd mem, Boys Choir Harlem; NY Asn Black Journalist, 1991-92; The Authors Guild Inc, 1991-93; personal grooming & development consult, Girls Choir of Harlem, 1994-95. **Honors/Awds:** Alumni of the Yr Award, Fashion Inst Tech, 1976; Mortimer C Ritter Award, 1976; Judge, Miss World Beauty Pageant London, Eng, 1982; contrib., McGraw Hill Book Co Encyclopedia of Black Am, 1981; BBW articles, 1984; Award in Excellence Black Women in Publishing NY, 1986; contrib., Black State of the Arts, Love Child Publishing 1991; East NY Club of Brooklyn Nat Asn Negro Bus & Prof Women's Club Inc, 1981; Black Women in Publishing Connections III, 1986. **Home Addr:** PO Box 1321 Grand Central Sta, New York, NY 10163-1321, **Home Phone:** (914)576-5010.

FORNEY, MARY JANE
Social worker. **Personal:** Born May 23, 1949, Galesburg, IL; children: James LaMour. **Educ:** Sangamon State Univ, BA, Child Family Community Serv, 1977. **Career:** Springfield & Sangamon County, Community Action, admin asst, 1968-74; Ill Dept C & Family Serv, child welfare worker & soc serv planner, 1974-78; Child Care Serv, Family Serv Ctr, Sangamon County, dir, 1982-; Ill Dept Human Serv, Child Care & Develop Outreach, coord. **Orgs:** Coun mem, Head Start Policy Coun, 1974-76; Nat Asn Educ Young C, vpres, 1981-83; chmn, Mother's March-March Dimes, 1984 & 1985; Nat Asn Black Social Worker, 1974-; secy, Streetside Boosters Neighborhood Adv Bd, 1976-; comt mem, Springfield Reg Adv Bd, Dept C & Family Serv, 1981-; spec projs chmn, Delta Sigma Theta, 1983-; adv bd Chair, Sangamon County, Dept Pub Aid, 1985-; DPA Adv Bd, 1982-; vpres, exec bd, March Dimes; Ill Interagency Nutrit Coun; adv bd, Ctr Early Childhood Leadership. **Honors/Awds:** Founders Day Award, St John AME Church, 1979; Social Worker of the Year, Nat Asn Black Soc Workers, 1979; Vol Award, Am Lung Asn, 1981; Hall of Fame Award, Springfield Sangamon County Action Comt, 1981; Outstanding Young Women of Am, 1982; Mother's March Chairperson March of Dimes Award, 1985; YWCA Woman of the Year Award; March of Dimes 5 Year Service Award, 1987. **Home Addr:** 2033 Randall Ct, Springfield, IL 62703. **Business Addr:** Co Ordinator, Illinois Department of Human Services, Child Care & Development Outreach, 400 W Lawrence 2 W, Springfield, IL 62762.

FORREST, VERNON
Boxer. **Personal:** Born Jan 12, 1971, Augusta, GA. **Educ:** Northern MI Univ, bus admin. **Career:** Amateur boxer, 1980-92; pro boxer, 1992-; Champions Limo Service, owner, 2002-. **Orgs:** Destiny's Child, Inc. **Honors/Awds:** US jr welterweight nat champ, 1991; jr welterweight world amateur champ, 1992; IBF welterweight champ, 2001-02; USA Today Fight of the Yr, 2002; WBA, welterweight champ, 2002-03; Phoenix Awd, City of Atlanta, 2002; fighter of the yr award, Ring Magazine, 2002; few minor title belts. **Business Addr:** Director, Destinys Child Foundation Incoporation, 3915 Cascade rd, SW St 255, Atlanta, GA 30331-8523.*

FORREST-CARTER, DR. AUDREY FAYE
College teacher, educator. **Personal:** Born Apr 1, 1956, Greenwood, SC; daughter of Willie Forrest Sr and Ruth B Forrest; married Ewing Carter III, Sep 6, 1986; children: Channing Kamille & Ewing IV. **Educ:** Bennett Col, BA, 1978; NC A&T State Univ, MA, 1979; Miami Univ, PhD, 1990. **Career:** A&T State Univ, teaching asst, 1978-79; Winston-Salem State Univ, instr,1979-84, asst prof, 1990-91; Miami Univ, doctoral assoc, 1984-88; NC A&TState Univ, asst prof eng, 1992-96; Courtesy Kids, owner, currently; Winston-Salem State Univ, assoc prof, dept eng & foreign lang, currently. **Orgs:** Nat Coun Teachers Eng; NC Teacher Eng Asn. **Honors/Awds:** DAP Award, Miami Univ, 1984-88; Silver Poet Award, World Poetry, 1986; John Fountain Teacher's Award, Winston-Salem State Univ; Editor's Choice Award, Poetry.com. **Special Achievements:** Author, published poems and 2 novels: The Wages of Sin and Judge Not!. **Business Addr:** Associate Professor of English, Winston-Salem State University, Department of English and Foreign Languages, Hall-Patterson Room 308, 601 Martin Luther King Jr Dr, Winston-Salem, NC 27110.

FORSTER, CECIL R., JR.
Executive. **Personal:** Born Nov 11, 1943, New York. **Educ:** Middlebury Col, BA, 1964; St John's Univ, JD, 1967. **Career:** Retired; Irving Trust Co, lender officers training prog, 1967-68; Pepsico Inc, vpres & secy, coun, 1971-74; Westinghouse Broadcasting Co Inc, vpres, 1977-81; Unity Broadcasting Network Inc, vpres, 1981-85; Legal Bus Advisor, 1985-89; Pace Univ Sch Law, prof law, 1985-89; Nutrit & Syst Inc, sr vpres & interim admin corp opers, 1989, sr vpres law & human resources, 1989-90, sr vpres law & govt affairs, 1990-91; Patton Boggs & Blow, coun, 1991-93; Infinity Broadcasting Corp, vpres & gen mgr, 1993; SportsRadio WIP 610, vpres & gen mgr. **Orgs:** AFTRA Health & Retirement Funds, bd trustees, 1975-; Howard Mem Fund, bd dir, 1976-; Black Exec Exchange Prog, Nat Urban League, exec adv comt, 1977-; Fund Improv Postsecondary Educ, 1989; 100 Black Men; Amer Bar Asn; NY Bar Asn; Phi Alpha Delta Law Fraternity; Sigma Pi Phi Fraternity;bd dir, Found Excellent Sch, currently. **Honors/Awds:** YMCA, Black Achievers Award, 1972; Coun Concerned Black Execs, Corp Achievement Award, 1978; Commandant Marine Corps, Meritorious Public Serv Citation, 1981. **Special Achievements:** Admitted to the New York State Bar, 1968; Admitted to United States Court of Military Appeals, 1971; Admitted to Pennsylvania State Bar, 1992. **Military Serv:** USMC, capt, 1968-71. *

FORSTER, JACQUELINE GAIL
Insurance executive, management consultant. **Personal:** Born Jan 29, 1970, Queens, NY; daughter of Charles and Gloria; married Brian Michael Cooper, 1998. **Educ:** Cornell Univ, BA, 1991; Univ PA Law Sch, JD, 1995. **Career:** EG Bowman Co Inc, vp & sales mgr, Bowman Specialty Serv, sr vpres, currently. **Orgs:** Bd dirs, Nat Asn Ins Women, 1998-; planning comn, Harlem Bus Alliance. **Honors/Awds:** Harriet Tubman Leadership Award, 1998; 40 Under 40 Award, Network Jour, 2000. **Business Addr:** Senior Vice President, EG Bowman & Company Inc, 97 Wall St, New York, NY 10005-4302, **Business Phone:** (212)425-8150.

FORSYTHE, HAZEL
College teacher. **Personal:** Born in Georgetown, Guyana; daughter of Rupert and Isolene; married Vibert Forsythe, Jul 3, 1982; children: Vibh & Vahl. **Educ:** Bristol Univ, UK, BEd, Nutrition, 1977; Oklahoma State Univ, MS, 1984, PhD, 1987. **Career:** Oklahoma State Univ, Grad Asst, 1983-85, Grad Assoc, 1985-87; Inst Human Develop, fac assoc, 1992-95; Univ Ky, assoc prof nutrition & food sci, 1994-, dir, coord prog dietetics, 1997-2000, dir, dietetics internship, 1997-, chair, dept nutrition & food sci, 1999-2006, Grad Ctr Nutrit Sci, adj assoc prof, currently. **Orgs:** Am Dietetic Asn, 1989-; Int Fed Home Econs, Prog Affiliate Comt; Autism Soc Am, Bluegrass Chap Prog Coordr, 1999-; Asn Family & Consumer Scis, Awards Comt, 2000, accreditation review; Ky Dietetic Asn, pres, 2001-02; Am Asn Ment Retardation; Am Asn Family & Consumer Sci; Caribbean Asn Home Econ; Int Federation Home Econ; Kentucky Asn Family & Consumer Sci; Kentucky Early Childhood Asn; Res Asn Minority Prof; Soc Int Nutrt Educr; Soc Nutrt Educ; Southern Early Childhood Asn. **Honors/Awds:** Col Human Environ Scis, Dept Nutrition & Food Sci, Outstanding Educr, 1999; Ky Asn Family & Consumer Sci, Outstanding Dietitian, 2001; Ky Dietetic Asn, Outstanding Educr, 2003; Multi-cultural & Global Sensitivity Award, Fayette Coun Sch Bd; Text Writers Award, Caribbean Asn Home Economists; Minority Achievers Gold Award, Okla State Univ; Teacher of the Year, Cyril Potter Col Educ. **Special Achievements:** Co-author: "Dietetics Curriculum Integrates Virtual jnl Club to Enhance Communication at Geographically

Remote Supervised Practice Site," pub in Best Practices in Dietetics, 2000; numerous refereed publications, papers, and book reviews. **Business Addr:** Associate Professor, University of Kentucky, Department of Nutrition and Food Science, 102 Erikson Hall, Lexington, KY 40506-0050, **Business Phone:** (859)257-3800.

FORT, DR. EDWARD B.
Administrator, educator. **Personal:** Born in Detroit, MI; son of Edward Clark and Inez Corrine; married Lessie Covington; children: Clarke & Lezlie. **Educ:** Wayne State Univ, BS, 1954, MS, 1958; Univ Calif, Berkeley, PhD, 1964. **Career:** Detroit Pub Schs, curric coordr, 1964-67; Univ Mich, Ann Arbor, vis prof educ admin, 1965-66; Univ Mich, Dearborn, adj prof urban educ, 1968-71; Mich State Univ, vis prof, 1974; Inkster Mich Pub Schs, supt 1967-71; Sacramento Calif City Schs, supt, dep supt 1971-74; Univ Wis Ctr Syst, chancellor, 1974-81; NC A&T State Univ, chancellor, 1981-99, Dept Hum Develop & Serv, chancellor emer & prof, 1999-. **Orgs:** Bd adv, Fund Improvement Post Sec Educ, 1979-81; NASA Adv Coun, 1991-; bd dirs, NIEH, 1988-92; pres comn, NCAA, 1984-86; bd dirs, Nat Asn Equal Opportunity Higher Educ, 1984-; Greensboro NC Chamber Com Exec Bd. **Honors/Awds:** Press Award, Ed Press Asn Am, 1969; Chosen Symposium Participant, Dept Sociol Univ Pretoria S Africa, 1977; Eighty for the 80's, Milwaukee Jour Award, 1979; LLD, Wayne State Univ, 1986; Edward B. Fort Interdisciplinary Research Center, 1999. **Military Serv:** AUS, corpl, 2 yrs; Good Conduct Medal, 1955-56. **Business Addr:** Chancellor Emeritus, Professor, NC A&T State University, Dowdy Admin Bldg, 1601 E Market St, Greensboro, NC 27411, **Business Phone:** (910)334-7940.

FORT, DR. JANE GERALDINE
School administrator. **Personal:** Born Aug 27, 1938, Nashville, TN; daughter of William Henry Fort and Geraldine Bennett Fort; divorced; children: Sekou Fort Morrison. **Educ:** Fisk Univ, BA, 1958; Univ Mass, MS, 1960, PhD, 1962. **Career:** City NY, JOIN, dir res, psychologist, 1964; City Col & William Alanson White Inst, NY, res assoc, 1965; Harvard Univ Grad Sch Educ, res assoc, 1965-69; Newton MA Schs, Reading Prog, consult & psychologist, 1974-75; Brookline Pub Schs, Brookline, MA, consult & sr res assoc, 1977-81; Roxbury Comm Col, Roxbury, MA, staff assoc, prog develop, 1979-81; Univ Calif-Davis, lectr, researcher, 1981-83; Clark Col, prog mgr eval & dir, 1984-87; Morehouse Sch Med, Dept Comm Health & Prev Med, 1987-92; Meharry Med Col, Cancer Control Res Unit, Cancer Prev Awareness Prog, assoc dir &co-prin investr, 1995-97, asst dean stud affairs, 1998; Meharry Med Col, asst prof clin skills & competency, 1998-. **Orgs:** Numerous bds dirs; lect sem & conf coordr & chair; alumni clubs; Alpha Kappa Alpha Sorority; Asn Black Psychologists; Am Psychol Asn. **Honors/Awds:** Ford Found Fisk Univ, early entrant, 1953; Founder Award, Asn Black Psychologist, 1987. **Special Achievements:** Journal : REACH-Meharry Community-Campus Partnership: Developing Culturally Competent Health Care Providers, 2006. **Business Addr:** Assistant Professor, Meharry Medical College, 1005 Dr DB Todd Jr Blvd, Nashville, TN 37208-3599.

FORT, WILLIAM H. See Obituaries section.

FORTE, LINDA DIANE
Banker. **Personal:** Born Dec 25, 1952, Cleveland, OH; daughter of Delvin L and Bertha l; married Tyrone M Davenport, Nov 7, 1992; children: Lynette Davenport & Simone Perry. **Educ:** Bowling Green State Univ, BS, 1974; Univ Mich, MBA, 1982. **Career:** Comerica Bank, compensation analyst, 1977-80, loan analyst, 1980-83, asst vpres & mgr credit admin, 1983-87, asst vpres & lender, 1987-88, vpres & sr lender, 1988-92, vpres & alt group mgr, 1992-95, vpres & mgr, 1995-2004, sr vpres, 2004-. **Orgs:** Pres, Urban bankers Forum, 1975-; Nat Black MBA Asn, 1982-; bd dir, Black Family Develop Inc, 1987-93; Detroit Youth Found; Michigan's Women Found; dir, Econ Develop Corp, Detroit; dir, Neighborhood Develop Corp, Detroit; Detroit Symphony Orchestra; Henry Ford Health System Found. **Honors/Awds:** Banker of the Year Award, 1990; H Naylor Fitzhugh Award, Nat Black MBA, 1995; Minority Achiever Award, YWCA, 1984; Banker of the Year, Urban bankers Forum, 1988; Crain's Detroit Business Black Business Leaders, 1998; Michigan's Most Powerful African Americans, Corp Mag, 2003; John Copeland Community Leadership Legacy Award, YMCA, 2005; Best Corporate Executive Award, Black Women's Contracting Asn, 2005; Most Influential African-American Women in Michigan Award, Women's Informal Network's 2005; Aubrey W Lee Award, Urban Financial Services Coalition, 2005. **Business Addr:** Senior Vice President of Business Affairs, Comerica Bank, 500 Woodward Ave, PO Box 3409, Detroit, MI 48226, **Business Phone:** (313)222-5076.

FORTE, MINNIE T.
Educator. **Personal:** Born Jan 1, 1916?, Goldsboro, NC; children: William, Lonnie & Minnie Mae. **Educ:** Fayetteville State Univ, BS, 1939; NC Cent Univ, MA, 1951; NC Cent Univ, PhD, 1960. **Career:** Durham City Sch Syst, teacher, 1944-60; Fayetteville St Univ, 1960-62, prof elem educ, 1974-83; Shaw Univ, 1962-65; Operation Break Ctr C, dir, 1965-66; St Augustines Col, assoc prof coordr; Early Childhood Educ, 1966-74. **Orgs:** Chmn, Christian Educ; White Rock Baptist Church; vpres, New Hope Baptist Asn; life mem, Nat Educ Asn; adv stud, NEA CAE; spec asst, coordr, Early Childhood Educ, 1970-74; Nat Coun Accreditation Teacher Educ Evaluate, 1975; Fayetteville St Univ, 1975. *

FORTE, PATRICK
Sports manager. **Personal:** Born Mar 17, 1950, Flint, MI; married Christine; children: Brandi & Jade. **Educ:** Lincoln Univ. **Career:** General Motors, public relations exec; Honeywell Corp, public relations exec; Philadelphia Eagles, ceo, pres, chief contract negotiator, 1986-90; New England Patriots, vpres admin, 1991, exec vpres. *

FORTIER, THEODORE T., SR.
Dentist, association executive. **Personal:** Born Aug 15, 1926, San Diego, CA; married. **Educ:** Univ Calif, Los Angeles; Univ PA; Howard Univ Col Dent, DDS, 1957; Acad Gen Dent, DDS. **Career:** USPHS, fel; Los Angeles, dentist pvt practice; Continuing Dent Educ Univ SC Sch Dent, instr, 1968; chief, Dent Dept Hollywood Pres Med Ctr, 1972-74; Dent Asst Sch, instr, 1986-93; The Dent Co Calif Dent Asn, bd dir, currently; VSC Sch Dent, teaching staff; S Calif, Health Newsletter, app ed; pvt pract, dent, currently. **Orgs:** Los Angeles Coun; Univ SC Med Ctr, Compton; PTA Sch Dentist, 1959-61; pres, Angel City Dent Soc, 1968-69; vpres, Dental Found Calif, 1971; bd dir, Los Angeles Dental Soc; Fel Exam Comt, 1986-91; Acad Gen Dent; House Delegates Calif Dent Asn; pres, Kiwanis Club Angeles Mesa, 1976; gen chmn, Fund raising Dr Crenshaw YMCA, 1975, 1993; Omicron Kappa Upsilon; pres, SC Acad Gen Dent, 1987; trustee, Calif Dent Asn, 1986-89; pres, Crenshaw Chamber Com, 1993-94; Community Police Adv Comt Bd, currently; Parlimentarian, Tuskegee airmen Los Angeles Chap, currently; angel, Aviation Angel Tuskegee Airmen, 2007-; bd mem, Vector Control Bd. **Honors/Awds:** Dental Alumni of the Year, Howard Univ Col Dent, 1987; Dentist of the Year, Southern Calif Acad Gen Dent, 1992; Speaker of the Year Award, Recycling Black Dollars Inc; Honoree, The Sch Dent, 2002; Humanitarian Award, Acad Gen Dent, 2004. **Special Achievements:** Established a dental seminar course to be given in selected areas on selected subjects in dentistry. **Military Serv:** AUS, Med Corps, 1945. **Business Addr:** Dentist, 3701 Stocker St Suite 408, Los Angeles, CA 90008, **Business Phone:** (323)295-6883.*

FORTSON, DANIEL ANTHONY. See FORTSON, DANNY.

FORTSON, DANNY (DANIEL ANTHONY FORTSON)
Basketball player. **Personal:** Born Mar 27, 1976, Philadelphia, PA. **Educ:** Univ Cincinnati, attended 1998. **Career:** Denver Nuggets, forward, 1997-99; Boston Celtics, 1999-2000; Golden State Warriors, 2000-03; Dallas Mavericks, forward, 2003-04; Seattle SuperSonics, forward, 2004-. *

FORTSON, ELNORA AGNES
Poet, composer. **Personal:** Born May 7, 1943, Pittsburgh, PA; married Walter Lamarr; children: Akilah, Ayanna & Anika. **Educ:** Grace Martin Bus Sch, cert com, 1961; Univ Pittsburgh Deliverance Bible Inst, attended 1977-81 & 1992. **Career:** Univ Pittsburgh, Sch Social Work, secy, 1961-62; Westinghouse Elec Corp, data maintenance & accounting, capital stock clerk, 1962-77; Fuller Ins Agency, staff, 1983-84; ACT II Jewelry Inc, jewelry adv, 1984-86; Watkins Productions, staff, 1985; Temple Christian Acad, secy, librn, 1990-94; Greater Pittsburgh Christian Temple, songwriter & composer, 1992-; TOD Inc, 1994-; TALK Mag, ed & reporter; poet, currently; Poem: "Ridin' On a Good Wind" 1975; "Love from Black Women to Black Men", 1976; "Pre-Natal/Post-Natal", 1977; "Jesus Walks the Waters of My Soul", 1981; Voices froptlfortson7****mail.comm the Real World", 1991; "Nana's Song", 1996; "Singing Prayers, 2005; Noon Child; Women of the Bible, poetry book, 1993; Pittsburgh, Sought Out. A City Not Forsaken, play, 1992. **Orgs:** Int Platform Asn, 1980; Chicago Int Black Writers, 1976; publicity dir, Homewood Poetry Forum, 1973-75; publicity dir, Greater Pittsburgh Christian Temple, 1980-; publicity dir, Temple Christian Acad, 1981-93; Kuntu Writer's Workshop, 1980-; Wind's Writers, 1993; Bloomfield-Garl field, Neighborhood Reading Ctr, poeting inst, 1992-93; founder & dir, Praise Poets, 1984; Poet's & Writer's Club; founder & dir, Crossing Limits. **Honors/Awds:** Danae Award & Pub Clover Int Poetry Cont, 1974; Poet of the Year, Homewood Poetry Forum, 1975; Literary Fellowship, Pa Coun Arts, 1981; Golden Poet Award, World Poetry, 1990 & 1991; August Wilson Poetry Award, Adult Poetry Category, 1992; Pa Ave Arts Grant; Editor's Choice Award for Outstanding Achievement in Poetry, poetry.com & Int Lib Poetry. **Special Achievements:** Directed a recording of students poems ?Poetry Is Fun!". **Home Addr:** 5208 Broad St, Pittsburgh, PA 15224, **Home Phone:** (412)362-8218. **Business Addr:** Poet, 5208 Broad St, Pittsburgh, PA 15224, **Business Phone:** (412)362-8218.

FORTSON, HENRY DAVID, JR.
Dentist. **Personal:** Born Sep 11, 1946, Haines City, FL; son of Henry and Nancy; married Wilnita Yvette Varner; children: Henry D III, Dennis Gregory, William Christopher. **Educ:** Daytona Beach Jr Col, AA, 1966; Knoxville Col, BS, 1968; Meharry Med Col, DDS, 1984. **Career:** Holston Army Ammunition Plant, chemist; Pvt Pract, dentist. **Orgs:** Shriner 32 degree, 1976; Omega Psi Phi Fraternity, 1967-; Nat Asn Advan Colored People, 1985-; Thomasville Dent Study Group, 1986; GA Dent Soc, 1986; Thomasville Thomas Co, Community Club; bd mem, Recreation Thomasville. **Business Addr:** Dentist, Private Practice, 1205 E Jackson St, Thomasville, GA 31792.*

FORTSON, WALTER LEWIS
Lawyer. **Personal:** Born Jul 16, 1951, Hatchechubbee, AL; son of Oscar and Sallie; children: Walter Lewis II, Clara Alexis. **Educ:** Ala A&M Univ, BS, 1973; Atlanta Law Sch, JD, 1979. **Career:** Fortson & Secret, partner, 1991; Fortson & Assocs, atty, 2003-. **Orgs:** State Bar Ga; past regional dir, Nat Bar Asn; Gate City Bar Asn; Fountain City Bar Asn, 1995. **Business Phone:** (404)289-7650.*

FORTUNE, DR. GWENDOLINE Y.
Writer, educator. **Personal:** Born in Houston, TX; daughter of W Hermon Young and Mittie McCain; divorced; children: Frederic, Phillip & Roger. **Educ:** JC Smith Univ, BS, 1948; SC State Col, MS, 1951; Roosevelt Univ, MPh,1972; Nova Univ, EdD, 1979. **Career:** Chicago Pub Schs, teacher, 1954-66; Dist 68 Skokie Ill, team coord,1964-70; Oakton Community Col, prof ethnic studies cord, 1970-84; Consultant "Discovery", dir 1984-; poems & articles: "Dancing as Fast as We Can"; "Inner Scan"; Novels: Growing Up Nigger Rich, 2002; Family Lines, 2003. **Orgs:** Exec brd, Ill Coun Black Studies, 1980-83; exec comt, Ill Consult Ethnicity Educ, 1980-84; manuscript chair, Off-Campus Writers Workshop, 1990-. **Honors/Awds:** Outstanding teaching effectiveness, Oakton Community Col, 1981-82; Intl Black Writers Conf First Place Non-Fiction, 1986; Honor poem "Tom Cats "Korone, 1988.

FORTUNE-MAGINLEY, LOIS J.
Television producer. **Personal:** Born Mar 16, 1946, New York, NY; daughter of Roland K and Hilda O; married George H Maginley, Nov 25, 1978. **Educ:** Monteith Col, Wayne State Univ, PhB, 1968; NY Univ, MAT, 1969. **Career:** C's TV Workshop, assoc producer int dept, 1978-79, Philippines, resident producer, 1983, exec producer int dept, 1985-87, exec producer, 1988-90; Nickelodeon, Pinwheel series, exec producer, 1979-82; UNESCO, United Nations Develop Prog, ETV, producer & consult, New Delhi, India, 1987-88; Galaxy Classroom, exec producer, 1990-96. **Orgs:** Adv panel, Nat Endowment Arts, 1983; bd mem, Int Film & TV Festival, 1986-; judge, Nat Acad Cable Programming, 1987-88; Acad TV Arts & Sci, 1990-; Women in Film, 1993-; roundtable producer, Nat Acad TV Arts & Sci; coun mem, Dirs Guild Am; Am Film Inst. **Honors/Awds:** Certificate, Nat Acad TV Arts & Sci, 1976-77; Certificate of Merit, Nat Cath Asn Broadcasters & Allied Commun, 1981; 2 Ace Awards, Nat Cable TV Asn, 1982; Philippine Catholic Mass Media Award, 1983; Silver Medal, Baghdad Int TV Festival, 1988. **Home Addr:** 515 N Gertruda Ave, Redondo Beach, CA 90277, **Home Phone:** (310)374-5356. *

FOSKEY, CARNELL T.
District court judge. **Personal:** Born Dec 7, 1956, Darlington, SC; son of Thomas and Sadie; married Francina Little, Jul 4, 1987. **Educ:** State Univ NY, BA, polit sci & hist, 1977; Calif Western Sch Law, JD, 1980; Boston Univ Sch Law, LLM Taxation, 1982. **Career:** Nassau County Dept Social Serv, staff atty, 1982-83; Nassau County Off County Atty, dep county atty, 1983-89; Off Presiding Supvr, exec asst, 1989-90; Dept Planning & Econ Develop, interim comnr, 1990-91; Nassau Co Dist Ct, dist ct judge, 1992-, 9th Judicial Dist, Supv Judge,2005-. **Orgs:** Bar Asn Nassau County; 100 Black Men Nassau/Suffolk; Am Inns Ct; Nat Asn Advan Colored People Lakeview Br; Union Baptist Church; Union Sr Citizen Plaza; Nassau County Bar Asn. **Honors/Awds:** Nassau Black Hist Comt, Man of the Year, 1992; Dollars & Sense Mag, 100 Top Black Prof, 1992; Man of the Year, Nassau Black Hist Comt, 1992-. **Special Achievements:** The first African American to be named Supervising Judge. The youngest person to be elected to the Nassau County District Court in 1991. **Business Addr:** Supervising Judge, State NY District Court Nassau County, 9th Judicial Dist, 435 Middle Neck, Great Neck, NY 11023-1412, **Business Phone:** (516)566-2200.*

FOSTER, ALVIN GARFIELD
Veterinarian. **Personal:** Born Apr 7, 1934, Preston, MD; married Gertrude Dallis; children: Alvin Garfield Jr, Kerwin, Kelsie. **Educ:** Md State Col, BS, 1956; Tuskegee Inst, DVM, 1960; Wash State Univ, MS, 1967, PhD, 1969. **Career:** Veterinarian (retired). US Dept of Agr, Meat Inspec Div Spokane, vet meat insp, 1963-64; WA State Univ, NIH postdoctoral fel, 1965-69; Merck Inst for Therapeutic Res, Rahway, NJ, sr micro-biologist, beginning 1969; Merck & Co Inc Rsch, dir animal sci, until 1994. **Orgs:** Am Vet Med Assn; Alpha Kappa Mu; Phi Zeta; Sigma Xi; Alpha Phi Alpha; Monmouth Co Mens Club; fel, Am Sci Inst. **Honors/Awds:** Black Achiever in Industry, Young Men's Christian Asn, NY, 1974. **Military Serv:** USAF, capt, 1960-62. **Home Addr:** 27 Old Mill Rd, Tinton Falls, NJ 07724. *

FOSTER, BEA MOTEN
Executive, publisher. **Career:** Ind Ambassador; Ind Gov; Muncie Times Newspaper, owner & publ, currently. **Orgs:** Founder, Mun-

cie Coalition 100 women. **Special Achievements:** First African American television announcer in Indianapolis. **Business Addr:** Owner, Publisher, Muncie Times Newspaper, 1304 N Broadway, Muncie, IN 47303.

FOSTER, DR. BELLANDRA B.
President (organization). **Personal:** Daughter of Dr George and Ella Pearl Benefield; married Michael, Jan 1, 1984. **Educ:** Mich State Univ, BS, civil engineering, 1983; Wayne State Univ, MS, civil engineering, 1989; Mich State Univ, PhD, civil & environ engineering. **Career:** BBF Engineering Services PC, pres & prin engr, currently. **Orgs:** Family Victory Fellowship Church. **Honors/Awds:** USDOT Minority Bus Enterprise of the Year, Fed Highway Admin, 1998; Wayne State University Headliner Award. **Special Achievements:** Book : For Love And Money: Seven Guidelines for Achieving Success in Your Home and Business. **Business Addr:** President, BBF Engineering Services PC, 719 Griswold St Suite 820, Detroit, MI 48226-3311, **Business Phone:** (313)967-9652.*

FOSTER, CARL OSCAR, JR.
Administrator. **Personal:** Born Oct 23, 1926, Greensboro, NC; son of Carl Oscar Sr and Louise Slade; married Lola Alexander Foster, Aug 16, 1965; children: Angela Cheryl Foster. **Educ:** A&T State Univ, Greensboro, NC, BS, 1948, MS, 1956; Univ NC, Chapel Hill, NC, 1970; De Sales Sch Theol, Wash, DC, 1990. **Career:** Concord City Schs, Concord, NC, music teacher, 1948-55; Guilford County Schs, Greensboro, NC, classroom teacher, 1955-56; Greensboro City Schs, Greensboro, NC, classroom teacher, 1956-68, prin, 1968-74, dir cultural arts, 1974-86; Catholic Diocese Charlotte, Charlotte, NC, coordr African Am affairs, 1989-. **Orgs:** Basileus, Tau Omega Chapter, Omega Psi Phi Fraternity, 1971-73; chmn, Parish Coun, 1980-82; grand knight, Knights Columbus, 1985-87. **Honors/Awds:** Band Teachers Appreciation Award, Band Teachers, 1972; Omega Man of the Year, Omega Psi Phi Fraternity, 1973; Cultural Arts Award, Cultural Arts Teachers, 1984; Certificate, African-American Black Congress, 1990; Service to the Mentally Handicapped, State Coun, Knights Columbus, 1991. **Military Serv:** USN, Musician 2nd Class, 1945-46; Victory Ribbon, American Theater Ribbon, 1946. *

FOSTER, CLYDE
Executive. **Personal:** Born Nov 21, 1931; married Dorothy M Harri; children: Anitra, Edith, Clydis, Byron, Carla. **Educ:** Ala A&M Univ, BS, 1954. **Career:** Army Ballistic Missile Agency, Redstone Arsenal, 1957; Marshall Space Flight Ctr, mathematician, instr Comput Lab, 1960; Ala A&M Univ, dir, Comput Sci Dept, est Data Processing Lab & undegrad degree prog Comput Sci, first State Ala Educ Syst Higher Learning, 1968-70; Dallas Co Sch Syst, Selma, sci teacher; Marshall Space Flight Ctr, chief, EEO Civil Serv Employees, 1972, instr, training courses; Triana Indus Inc, founder, pres. **Orgs:** Petitioned Probate Judge, gained rejuvenation Triana, 1964; org Data Processing Assoc Inc, 1970. **Honors/Awds:** NASA apollo achievement award & MSFC award of achievement 1969; NASA fifteen Yr Serv Award, 1970; Dedicated Pub Serv & Outstanding Leadership Award, Alpha Kappa Sor, 1971; Merit Serv Award, Omega Psi Phi Frat, 1971; Appreciation & Serv Rendered, Delta Sigma Theta Sorority, 1972; TARCOG Appreciation Outstanding Contribution Toward Grown & Develop, 1972; MSFC Commen Achievement Award, 1972; Outstanding & Dedicated Serv Award, Citizens Triana Comn, 1972; Distinguish Serv Award, Ala A&M Univ, 1973; Comn Serv Award, African Meth Epis Chap, Burningham, 1973; Man Yr Award, Omega Psi Phi Fratenity Seventh Dist, 1974. **Military Serv:** AUS, pfc, 1954-56. *

FOSTER, DEBORAH
Executive. **Career:** Street Law Inc, prog dir, 2004, sr prog dir, currently. **Business Addr:** Senior Program Director, Street Law Inc, 1010 Wayne Ave Suite 870, Silver Spring, MD 20910, **Business Phone:** (301)589-1130.

FOSTER, DELORES JACKSON
School administrator. **Personal:** Born Jan 24, 1938, Halltown, WV; daughter of Daniel David Jackson and Mary Frances Taylor; married James Hadlei, Sep 25, 1982; children: James Jr & Arthur; married Robert L Bailey, Aug 24, 1957 (divorced 1968); children: Mark D. **Educ:** Shepherd Col, BA, 1960; Jersey City State Col, MA, 1974. **Career:** School Administrator (Retired); Page-Jackson High Sch, teacher, 1960-61; Dickinson High Sch, teacher, 1961-71, teacher coordr, 1971-73, guide counr, 1973-84, actg vice prin, 1982-83, vice prin, 1985-91, actg prin, 1986, guid counr, vice prin, 1987; PS No 34, prin, 1991-2000; educ consult commun sch, 2001. **Orgs:** Corresp sec, Black Educr United, 1975; adv bd, Upward Bound Proj, St Peter's Col, Jersey City, New Jersey, 1975-79; Empowerment for Change; leadership training United Church Christ, 1979; First vpres, Col Women Inc, 1979-81; pres, Col Women Inc, 1981-83, 1995-; vice chmn, cong Pk Ave Christ Church Disciples Christ, 1982-84; workshop leader, New Jersey Alliance Black Educ conf, 1983; pres, Cent Atlantic Conf United Church Christ, 1984-87; elected lay del, 15th Gen Synod OCC Am IA, 1985; lay delegate 16th Gen Synod, Cleveland, Ohio, 1987; adv bd, prin ctr Garden State, 1994-01; Emanuel AME Church, 1998; asst dir, bd Christian Ed; New Jersey, prin & Supvr Asn; Nat Alliance Black Sch Educr; Delta Sigma Theta Sorority. **Honors/Awds:** Honored as a lay woman in the United Church of Christ at 15th Gen Synod in Am IA, 1985; Summer Inst Prin, Geraldine R Dodge Foundation Award, 1993. **Special Achievements:** Co-author, Integrating the Classroom with the World of Work, 1980; Featured in doc, "Quicksand and Banana Peels", Dodge Found, 1998.

FOSTER, DR. E. C.
Educator, government official. **Personal:** Born Jan 4, 1939, Canton, MS; son of Hugh D (deceased) and Minnie L Pugh; married Velvelyn Blackwell; children: Garnet A & Sunyetta M. **Educ:** Jackson State Univ, BS, 1964; Carnegie-Mellon Univ, MA, 1967, DA, 1970. **Career:** Educator, Government official (retired); Natchez Pub Sch, teacher, 1964-65; Brushton Inner City Proj, community organizer, 1965-66; Pittsburgh Pub Sch, teacher, 1967-68; Jackson MS City Coun, pres, 1985-94; Jackson State Univ, prof hist, 1969. **Orgs:** Pres, Fac Senate, JSU, 1974-79; bd mem, Farish St YMCA 1976-79; assoc ed, J Negro Hist, 1978-; pres, Asn Soc & Behav Scientists, 1982; legislative comm chmn, Local PTA, 1984; city Counman Jackson MS; Chamber Com; Vicksburg/Jackson Trade Zone Comn, 1987; bd dirs, MS Munic Asn, 1994-; vice chair, Nat League Cities Leadership Training Coun, 1994. **Honors/Awds:** Jackson State Univ Alumni Service Award, 1985; Man of the Year Award, Omega Psi Phi 1985; NAEFO Presidential Citation Award, 1986; Dr Martin Luther King Service Award, JSU/SGA, 1986. **Special Achievements:** Author of approx 30 publications, 1969-85. **Military Serv:** AUS Specialist 4 1961-63; Good Conduct Medal 1963. *

FOSTER, EDWARD, SR.
Manager. **Personal:** Born Sep 27, 1945, Maplesville, AL; son of Mamie; married Jacqulyn E Grant; children: Edward & Forrest Cedric. **Educ:** Selma Univ, AS 1967; AL A&M Univ, BS, 1971. **Career:** Xerox Corp, prod supv, 1972-82; GTE Corp, sr quality supv, 1983-86; NCR Corp, prod mgr, 1986; Ingersoll Rand, supv, currently. **Orgs:** Pres, AL A&M ALumni Assoc, 1981-82; vpres Rochester Chap, AL A&M Alumni Assoc, 1982-83; Am Mgt Assoc, 1984; Am Soc Quality Control 1985; 32 degree Lodge 107 Masonic Temple, 1985; Surface Mount Tech, 1986. **Honors/Awds:** Outstanding Work Higher Ed NAFEO, 1983. **Business Addr:** Supervisor, Ingersoll Rand, 155 Chestnut Ridge Rd, Montvale, NJ 07675, **Business Phone:** (201)573-0123.

FOSTER, EZOLA BROUSSARD
Politician, educator. **Personal:** Born Aug 9, 1938, Louisiana, LA; married Chuck; children: 3. **Educ:** Tex Southern Univ, BS, bus educ, 1960; Pepperdine Univ, MS, sch mgt & admin, 1973. **Career:** Educator (retired), Politician; Watts, Los Angeles, high sch teacher, 1963-85; City Bell, high sch teacher, 1985-96; Black Am Family Values, founder, 1987, pres, 1987-; conservative polit activist, currently. **Orgs:** John Birch Soc. **Special Achievements:** Author: What's Right for All Americans, 1995; Named vice presidential candidate for Reform Party, 2000; first Black Woman to run on major party ticket. **Business Addr:** Founder, Black Americans for Family Values, Los Angeles, CA 90066, **Business Phone:** (310)313-2637.

FOSTER, DR. FRANCES SMITH
Executive director, educator. **Personal:** Born Feb 8, 1944, Dayton, OH; daughter of Quinton and Mabel; married Warren R; children: Lisa Ramirez, Krishna & Quinton. **Educ:** Miami Univ, BS, 1964; Univ S Calif, MA, 1971, PhD, 1976. **Career:** Cin Pub Schs, teacher, 1964-66; Detroit Pub Schs, teacher, 1966-68; San Fernando Valley State Col, instr, 1970-71; San Diego State Univ, lectr, 1971-72, asst prof afro am studies, 1972-76; asst prof, 1976-79, asst dean & dir, 1976-79, assoc prof, 1979-82, prof, 1982-88; Univ Southern Calif, teaching asst, 1969-70; Calif State Univ, lectr, 1970-71, admin fel,1983-84; Univ Calif, San Diego, instr, 1971-72, prof, 1988-94; Afro AmStudies Dept, chair, 1975-76, fac coordr, 1972-74; Emory Univ, Inst Womens Studies, prof, 1994-96, Charles Howard Candler prof, 1996-, dir, 1999-2002, chmn, 2005-; NEH Res Fel; CSU Fac Res Fel. **Orgs:** Exec dir, Philological Asn Pac Coast, 1981-84; Humanities Adv Coun; KPBS; San Diego State Univ, Career Plan & Placement Ctr, Adv Comm; NAACP, Col Lang Asn; Modern Lang Asn; W Coast Women's Hist Asn; Phi Beta Kappa; PhiKappa Pi; Althenoi Phi Kappa Delta; Alpha Kappa Alpha; Childrens Literature Asn; MELUS; Am Lit Asn; Am Studies Asn; Soc Study Am Women Writers. **Honors/Awds:** California State University Meritorious Performance and Professional Promise Award, 1987; San Diego State University Outstanding Contributions to Women's Studies Award, 1988; UCSD African American Student Union Outstanding Faculty Award, 1989; Col Language Asn Scholarly Discovery Award, 1995; Col Arts & Sci Distinguished Alumni Lectr, 2002; Gen Motors Scholar; Teacher of the Year, Emory Univ, 2006; SDSU Outstanding Faculty Award. **Special Achievements:** Articles published: "Changing Concepts of the Black Woman," "Charles Wright, Black Black Humorist," "The Black & White Masks of Franz Fanon & Ralph Ellison," "Witnessing Slavery, The Develop of the Ante-Bellum Slave Narrative," Greenwood Press, 1979; Voices Unheard Stories Untold, Teaching Womens Literature from a Regional Perspective; The Norton Anthology of African American Literature; itnessing Slavery: The Development of the Ante-Bellum Slave Narrative; Numerous articles and reviews on Afro-Amer literature. **Business Phone:** (404)727-6420.

FOSTER, DR. FRANK B., III
Musician, educator. **Personal:** Born Sep 23, 1928, Cincinnati, OH; married Vivian Wilson (divorced); children: Anthony & Donald; married Cecilia Jones; children: Frank IV & Andrea. **Educ:** Cent State Col, attended 1949. **Career:** Count Basie Orchestra, musician, composer & arranger, 1953-64; freelance composer, arranger, performer & instr, 1964-71; New York Pub Schs, music consult, 1971-72; Rutgers Univ, Livingston Col, Music Dept, asst prof; Swing That Music Inc, pres, currently; Ensemb Jazzmobile Inc, Jazz mobileWorkshop, instr; Albums: Here Comes Frank Foster, 1954; Two Franks Please, 1957; Fearless Frank Foster, 1965; Manhattan Fever, 1968; Shiny Stockings,1978; Frankly Speaking, 1984; Leo Rising, 1997; Swing, 1998. **Orgs:** Am Soc Composers Auth & Publ; Songwriters Guild Am; Mus Union Local 802; hon mem, Hartford Jazz Soc. **Honors/Awds:** Outstanding Contribution to Jazz Award, 1971; National Endowment for the Arts grant for Jazz/Folk/Ethnic Composition Fellowships; honorary doctorates: Central State Univ, 1983; Best Arrangement Accompanying Vocal, Grammy, 1987; Best Instrumental Arrangement, Jazz Category, Grammy, 1988; Col State Rose, 1997; Great American Fellowships Award, Nat Endowment Arts, 2002. **Special Achievements:** Author of innumerable published compositions and albums; currently performing with own 18-pc band in US & abroad; author of saxophone exercise book & stage band arrangements; monetary recognition by Popular Awards Panel of Am Soc Composers Authors & Publishers for past 10 years. **Military Serv:** AUS, pfc, 1951-53. *

FOSTER, GEORGE ARTHUR
Baseball player. **Personal:** Born Dec 1, 1948, Tuscaloosa, AL. **Educ:** El Camino Col, Torrance, CA. **Career:** Baseball Player (retired); San Francisco Giants, outfielder 1969-71; Cincinnati Reds, outfielder 1971-81; New York Mets, outfielder, 1982-86; Chicago White Sox, outfielder, 1986. **Orgs:** Founder, George Foster Home for Disadvantaged Children, Upper Dayton OH. **Honors/Awds:** World Series champion, 1975 & 1976; Most Valuable Player All-Star Game, 1976; Most Valuable Player, Nat League, 1977; All-Star Team, Nat League, 1976 & 1979, 1981; National League Home Run Champion, 1977-78; Silver Slugger Award winner, 1981.

FOSTER, GLADYS M.
Lawyer. **Personal:** Born Jul 12, 1927, Brooklyn, NY; married John Skidmore. **Educ:** Barnard Col Columbia Univ, AB, 1949; Columbia Law Sch, JD, 1953. **Career:** Lawyer (retired); Workmen's Compensation & Unemployment Ins Appeal Bd, atty; NY State Div Human Rights, sr atty. **Orgs:** Brooklyn Bar Asn; Brooklyn Women's Bar Asn; Vocational Adv Law Barnard Col; Nat Asn Advan Colored People; Barnard Col Alumni By-Laws Com; Crown Heights Asn; vpres, Nat Asn Col Women. *

FOSTER, GREGORY
Track and field athlete. **Personal:** Born Apr 4, 1958, Chicago, IL; married Karen Marie Houlemard. **Educ:** Univ Calif, Los Angeles, attended 1981. **Career:** Track & field athlete (retired); hurdler, 1981-92. **Orgs:** Asn Athletics Mgrs. **Honors/Awds:** Gold Medal, IAAF World Cup, 1981; Gold Medal, World Championships, 1983; Silver Medal, Summer Olympics, 1984; Gold Medal, Goodwill Games, 1986; Gold Medal, World Championships, 1987; Gold Medal, World Championships in Athletics, 1991; Gold Medal, IAAF World Indoor Championships, 1991; US Track & Field Athlete Hall of Fame, 1998. **Special Achievements:** Nominee, Jesse Owens Award, 1987; Foster won 11 national titles and broke the indoor world record twice.

FOSTER, GREGORY CLINTON
Basketball player. **Personal:** Born Oct 3, 1968, Oakland, CA; married Victoria; children: Victoria & Collette. **Educ:** Univ Calif Los Angeles; Univ Tex, El Paso,1990. **Career:** Basketball player (retired); Wash Bullets, ctr, 1990-92; Atlanta Hawks, 1992-93; Milwaukee Bucks, 1993-94, 2001; Chicago Bulls, 1994; Minn Timberwolves, 1995; Utah Jazz, 1995-99; Seattle Supersonics, 1999; Los Angeles Lakers, 2000; Toronto Raptors, 2002-03. **Orgs:** Nat Basketball Asn.

FOSTER, DR. HENRY WENDELL, JR.
School administrator, physician. **Personal:** Born Sep 8, 1933, Pine Bluff, AR; son of Ivie Hill Watson and Henry W; married St Clair Anderson; children: Myrna & Wendell. **Educ:** Morehouse Col, BS, 1954; Univ Ark, MD, 1958. **Career:** Receiving Hosp, Detroit, Intern, 1959; Malden Hosp, residency, surg, 1962; George W Hubbard Hosp, residency, Ob Gyn, 1962-65; Tuskegee Inst, obstet and gynec chief, 1965-70; John A Andrews Mem Hosp, chief obstet and gynec, 1970-73; Meharry Med Col, Dept Obstet and Gynec, prof, chmn, 1973-90, dean, vpres, health affairs, 1990-93, actg pres, 1993-94, prof emer obstet and gynec, currently; Pres Clinton Sr adv, Teen Pregnancy Reduction and Youth Issues, 1996-2001; Asn Acad Health Ctr, health policy fel, 1994-. **Orgs:** Macon Co Med Soc; AMA; Nat Med asn; Nat Acad Sci Inst Med; dipl, Am Bd Obstet & Gynec. **Honors/Awds:** Fel Am Col Obstet & Gynec; Alpha Omega Alpha. **Special Achievements:** Served as Senior Advisor to President Clinton on Teen Pregnancy & Youth Issues, 1996; Author of more than 250 publications including auto biography Make a Difference; Author:Make A Difference. **Military Serv:** USAF, capt, 1959-61; USAF, med officer, 1959-

61. **Business Addr:** Professor Emeritus, Meharry Medical College, Department of Obstetrics and Gynecology, 1005 Dr DB Todd Blvd, Nashville, TN 37208, **Business Phone:** (615)327-6284.

FOSTER, JAMES H.
Educator, association executive. **Personal:** Born Jul 20, 1931, Roanoke, AL; married Sallye Maryland Burton; children: James H. **Educ:** Bethune Cookman Col, BS, 1957; Atlanta Univ, MA, 1963. **Career:** Woodville Elem Sch, prin, 1957-59; Randolph Co Training Sch, head coach, 1959-61; Wedowee High Sch, head coach, 1961-62; Frederick Douglas High Sch, prin, 1962-63; Titusville High Sch, coun, 1964-72; Gen Electric Co & Bendix Corp, staff, 1967-71; Fla Theater, mgr, 1968-69; The Boeing Co, supvr indust rels, 1973-74; Duval Teachers United, Jacksonville FL, asst exec dir; Sears Roebuck & Co, sales person. **Orgs:** NAACP, 1957-; Titusville Negro Civic & Voters League, 1964-67; exec bd, Titusville Centennial Inc, 1966; exec bd dir, employ officer Classroom Teachers Asn; Human Rel Comn, 1969-72; bd dir, YMCA, 1969-73; bd dir, Brevard Co United Way, 1969-74; Nat Urban League, 1971-; pres, United Black Front, Brevard Co, 1972-74; A Phillip Randolph Inst, 1973-74; chair, Titusville Hum Rel Comn, 1973-74. **Honors/Awds:** Leadership award, United Black Front, Brevard Co, 1973. **Military Serv:** AUS, sgt, first class, 1950-53. *

FOSTER, JAMES HADLEI
Educator, clergy. **Personal:** Born Apr 29, 1938, Valdosta, GA; son of Arthur Sr and Willie Mae Wright; married Delores Jackson, Sep 25, 1982; children: Mark Darnell, Arthur. **Educ:** Morris Brown Col, BA, Atlanta, GA, 1960; Pittsburgh Theol Sem, 1970; United Theol Sem, MDIV, Dayton, OH, 1973; Vanderbilt Univ, DMIN, Nashville, TN, 1981. **Career:** Mass Coun Churches, dept pastoral serv, Boston, MA, 1962-63; Albany State Col, dean chapel & instr, Albany GA, 1962-66; Alcorn State Univ, chaplain & asst prof, Lorman, MS, 1966-68; Christian Assoc Metro Erie, assoc dir, Erie, PA, 1970-73; Wilberforce Univ, chaplain & assoc prof, Wilberforce, OH, 1973-80; Dartmouth Col, assoc chaplain & lectr, Hanover, NH, 1980-84; A Better Chance, Northern New Eng regional dir, Boston, MA, 1980-82; Mercy Col, prof religious, Dobbs Ferry, NY, 1984-; St Marks AME Church, assoc pastor, East Orange, NJ, 1985; Quinn Chapel AME Church, pastor, currently. **Orgs:** Optimist Club, 1975-; Community Rels Comn, NJ Coun Churches, 1985-88; Spec Task Force, E Orange Bd Educ, 1985-86; pres, Jersey Chapter, Morris Brown Col Alumni Asn, 1988-. **Honors/Awds:** Union Col, LHD, 1971. **Business Addr:** Pastor, Quinn Chapel Ame Church, 107 Prospect Ave, Atlantic Highlands, NY 07716, **Business Phone:** (732)291-1078.*

FOSTER, JANICE MARTIN
Lawyer. **Personal:** Born Jun 14, 1946, New Orleans, LA; married John P. **Educ:** Chestnut Hill Col, AB, 1967; Tulane Law Sch, JD, 1970. **Career:** Jones Walker Waechter Poitevent Carrere & Denegre LLP, partner & atty, currently. **Orgs:** Bd Dirs, Metrop Area Safety Coun, 1990; Govs Task Force Higher Educ, 1990; La Bar Asn; Am Bar Asn; bd dir, New Orleans Legal Aid Corp; bd trustees, Xavier Univ; bd trustees, Baptist Community Ministries; bd trustees, Greater New Orleans Found; La Univ Bd Supvrs; vpres, Bd Liquidation, City Debt; bd trustees, Mercy Hosp; bd trustees, Baptist Med Ctr; Nat Bar Asn. **Honors/Awds:** Monte M Lemann Award, 1984; Michaelle Pitard Wynne Professionalism Award, 1996; New Orleans City Business Leadership in Law Award, 2007; Young Leadership Council Role Model, 2007. **Business Addr:** Attorney, Partner, Jones Walker Waechter Poitevent Carrere & Denegre LLP, 201 St Charles Ave, New Orleans, LA 70170, **Business Phone:** (504)582-8168.

FOSTER, JENNIFER K
Executive. **Career:** Ill Community Col Bd, Adult Educ & Family Literacy, sr dir, currently, GED Testing, interim dir, currently.

FOSTER, JYLLA MOORE
Association executive, manager. **Personal:** Born Jan 1, 1954?, Salisbury, NC. **Educ:** Livingstone Col, BS, mathematics; Indiana Univ, MBA. **Career:** IBM, systs engr, 1978-83, syst eng mgr, 1983-96, vpres opers, 1996-97, vpres sales small & medium bus Midwest, 1997, vpres global channels, 1998 vpres & client exec, 1998-00; Crystal Stairs Inc, Hinsdale, IL, founder & chief exec officer, 2000-. **Orgs:** Zeta Phi Beta Sorority, 1973-; Int Asn Coaches; Am Soc Training & Develop; Nat Black MBA Asn; Info Technol Sr Mgt Forum; Nat Coun Negro Women. **Honors/Awds:** Most Influential African-Americans, Ebony mag; hon doctorate, Livingstone Col, 1999; Distinguished Alumna Award, Nat Asn Equal Opportunity Higher Educ, 2000. **Special Achievements:** Auth: DUE NORTH! Strengthen Your Leadership Assets. **Business Phone:** (630)734-1481.*

FOSTER, KEVIN CHRISTOPHER. See Obituaries section.

FOSTER, LLOYD L
Scientist. **Personal:** Born Jul 3, 1930, Austin, TX; married Leatrice Norman; children: Lloyd Jr, Lionel Laird & Lyle Lerone. **Educ:** Huston-Tillotson Col, BS 1951; Incarnate World Col, MS, 1966; Baylor Sch Med, cert physiol & mod instrumentation, 1967. **Career:** Scientist (retired); Brooks, AFB, med tech, 1963-64, biologist, 1964-70, res chemist, 1970-74, educ tech, 1974-76, res chemist, 1976-91; St Philips Col, biol instr, 1966-2001; Sch Aerospace Med, Brooks AFB; Brooks AFB, chief, equal employ counr, collateral duty, 1981-91. **Orgs:** Nat Asn Equal Opportunity Higher Educ; Am Chem Soc; Nat Asn Advan Colored People; Phyllis Wheatley Area Optismist Club; Houston Tillotson Col Alumni Asn. **Honors/Awds:** Academic Achievement Award, Huston-Tillotson Col, 1974; Alumni Chapter Award, Nat Asn Black Cols, 1976. **Special Achievements:** First African-American Male to receive a master's degree from Incarnate Word Col, San Antonio, Tex, 1966. **Home Addr:** 147 Morningview Dr, San Antonio, TX 78220. *

FOSTER, PARRAN L., III
Association executive, executive. **Educ:** Johnson C Smith Univ, BS, biol. **Career:** Phoenix Pharmaceut Inc, pres & chief exec officer, founder. **Orgs:** Chmn, Alma Mater Trustees Bd; Phoenix Scholar Found, founder & dir; Nat Kidney Found Womens Healthcare Comt; mem adv bd, Howard Univ Cancer Ctrs Community; bd trustees, Johnson C Smith Univ, 2000-. *

FOSTER, PORTIA L.
Educator. **Personal:** Born in Gadsden, AL; daughter of Porter and Myrtle Davenport. **Educ:** Sanford Univ, Birmingham, AL, BSN, 1979; Univ Ala Birmingham, Birmingham, AL, MSN, 1980, DSN, 1989. **Career:** Baptist Hosp, Gasden, AL, nurse, 1974-77; Univ Ala Hosp, Birmingham, AL, nurse, 1977-80; Jacksonville State Univ, Jacksonville, AL, educator, 1980-99; Gadsden State Community Col, Practical Nursing Prog, coordr. **Orgs:** Am Nurses' Asn, 1980-; Nat League Nursing, 1980-; Numerous positions held, Etowah County Nurses Soc, 1980-; pres, Dist 4, Alabama State Nurses' Asn; bd dirs, Alabama State Nurses' Asn; bd dirs, Alabama, League Nursing, 1989-; Phi Kappa Phi, 1989. **Honors/Awds:** Medical Center Fellow, WAB, 1988; Faculty Research Award, Jacksonville State Univ, 1990. *

FOSTER, ROBERT LEON
Executive. **Personal:** Born Mar 11, 1939, Atlanta, GA; married Ethel Doris Bolden. **Educ:** Morris Brown Col, BA, 1961. **Career:** Equal Employ Opportunity, officer, 1972-75, Asst dir, 1975-78; Ctr Dis Control HEW, asst exec officer; LMI Analyst. **Orgs:** Phi Beta Sigma Frat; Nat Asn Advan Colored People. **Honors/Awds:** MBC Athletic Hall Fame. **Military Serv:** AUS, prc, 1962-64. *

FOSTER, DR. ROSEBUD LIGHTBOURN
School administrator, educator. **Personal:** Born Nov 13, 1934, Miami, FL; daughter of Carol Allenmore and Dorothy Bernell; married Harris E; children: Harris Emilio II, Sheila Rosebud, Byron Edward & Lorna Lightbourn. **Educ:** Fisk Univ, Chem & Pre-Nursing, 1953; Meharry Med Col, Nashville, BS,nursing, 1956; Wayne State Univ, MS, nursing ed, 1960; Univ Miami, Ed-D,higher educ admin, 1976; Bryn Mawr Col, cert post grad Residency Inst 1981. **Career:** Detroit Gen Hosp, head nurse, 1956-58, 1969-72; Henry Ford Hosp Sch Nursing, Detroit, instr, 1960-62; Holy Cross Hosp, asst admin, 1960-72; Providence Hosp, Southfield, MI, asst dir, 1962-65; Kirkwood Gen Hosp, dirnursing, 1967-69; Olivia & Bancroft Extended Care Facil, consult, 1969-72; Univ Miami, prof nursing, 1972-73; Sch Health & Social Serv, assoc dean, 1973-77, dean 1977-78; Fla Int Univ, vice provost Bay Vista Campus, prof, health serv admin, 1978-90, proj dir, area health educ ctr, 1990-, prof nursing, 1982-; Nova S eastern Univ, Col Osteop Med, prof pub health,2001-, spec asst to chancellor, asst dir, currently. **Orgs:** Bd mem, exec bd secy, Fair Havens Nursing & Retirement Ctr, 1974; bd mem &exec bd officer, Health Systs Agency Southern Fla, 1976; Am Pub HealthAsn, 1976; Pub Health Trust Dade City Citizens Adv Coun, 1977; Health Educ& Qual Life Comn N Miami, 1980; bd dir mem, Young Men's Christian AsnGreater Miami; bd mem New Horizons Community Mental Health Ctr, 1981;Mayor's Econ Task Force N Miami, 1981; bd dir, Ruth Foreman Theatre, 1981;bd dir, N Dade Chamber Com, 1982; N Miami Chamber Com, 1982; chairperson,Delta Sigma Theta Task Force Econ Develop Bulk Community, 1983; adv bdmem, Health Planning Coun Dade & Monroe Counties, 1983; dir, Culture Fest,1983; Art Music, Drama N D Proj, 1983; bd mem, Concerned Citizens NE DadeInc 1983; Am Pub Health Asn, 1983; adv coun, Delta Int; The AfricanDiaspora; Nat Planning Comt & Adv Coun, 1984; Metro Dade County Coun Arts& Sci, 1984; bd dir, United Home Care Serv; vpres, Alliance for Aging,Area Agency on Aging for Dade and Monroe Counties, 1990-. **Honors/Awds:** JC Holman Microbiology Award, Meharry Med Col Sch Nursing, 1955; Recognition of Outstanding Service Certificate, Meharry Med Col; President Award, 25 Years, Outstanding Service to Mankind, 1956-81; Outstanding Nurse Alumni Award, Col Med Dent Nursing, Meharry Col, 1972; Certificate of Appreciation, Health Syst Agency S Fla, 1979; Certificate of Appreciation, Am Hosp Miami Inc, 1980; Certificate of Appreciation, Lutheran Service for the Elderly, 1982; Outstanding Professional Achievement Award, Miami Alumnae Chap, Delta Sigma Theta, 1983; Person of the Year Award, N Miami Chamber Com, 1984; Public Service Award, Outstanding Professional Achievement; Outstanding Women 12 honors, 1986; Miami Ballet Soc; Am Coun Educ; Outstanding Person for Quarter, North Dade Chamber Com, 1987; Lifetime Achievement Award, AXA Advisors, 2001; Sherman Winn "I Care" Award, 2004. **Home Addr:** 11041 SW 128th Ave, Miami, FL 33186. **Business Addr:** Assistant Director, Nova Southeastern University, College of Osteopathic Medicine, 3200 S University Dr, Fort Lauderdale, FL 33328.*

FOSTER, T. ELOISE
Secretary (office). **Personal:** Born in Richmond, VA. **Educ:** Howard Univ, BA; Am Univ, MBA; Harvard Univ, prog sr exec state & local govt, 1994. **Career:** Md Dept Fiscal Serv, fiscal analyst, 1978-84; Md Higher Educ Suppl Loan Authority, exec dir, 1984-87; Gov's Legis Off, Legislative officer, 1987-91; Md Dept Budget & Fiscal Planning, asst secy, 1991-95; Md Dept Budget & Mgt, dep secy, 1996-2000, secy budget & mgt, 2000-03, actg secy budget & mgt, 2007, secy budget & mgt, 2007-; Univ Md Baltimore, Sch Med, asst dean prog develop & bus affairs, 2003-07; T. Eloise Foster & Associates, LLC, founder, 2005-. **Orgs:** Natl Assn State Budget Officers; Nat Forum Black pub Adminr Adv Bd; Howard Univ Cancer Ctr; Breast Cancer Adv Coun, Magic Johnson Found; vpres, Wash Women's Investment Club; Seton Keough Sch Bd, 1987-91; Brd, Nat Chronic Pain Assn, 1988-91; Gov's Exec Coun, 2007-; Base Realignment & Closure Sub cabinet, 2007-; C's Cabinet, 2007-; Smart Growth Sub cabinet, 2007-;chair, State Employees' Health Ins Adv Coun, 2007-; chair, brd trustees, Md Teachers & State Employees Suppl Retirement Plans, 2007-; Asbestos Oversight Comt, 2007-; brd dirs, Assistive Technol Guaranteed Loan Prog,2007-; Bay Restoration Fund Adv Comt, 2007-; Capital Debt AffordabilityComt, 2007-; Climate Change Comn, 2007-; Comn Correctional Stand, 2007-;Comn State Debt, 2007-; Task Force Study Develop Disabilities Admin Rate-Payment Syst, 2007-; Interagency Disabilities Brd, 2007-; Md StateDrug & Alcohol Abuse Coun, 2007-; Md Green Bldg Coun, 2007-; Task Force Study Group-Home Educ & Placement Practs, 2007-; Task Force Health Care Access & Reimbursement, 2007-; brd dirs, Md Health Ins Plan, 2007-; Comn Develop Md Model Funding Higher Educ, 2007-; Md Pandemic Influenza Cord Comt, 2007-; Cord Coun Juvenile Serv Educ Progs, 2007-; Inter departmental Comt Minority Affairs, 2007-; Procurement Adv Coun, 2007-; Blue Ribbon Comn Study Retiree Health Care Funding Options, 2007-; brd trustees, St Retirement & Pension Syst, 2007-; Brd Revenue Estimates, 2007-; MdS ch-Based Health Ctr Policy Adv Coun, 2007-; Md War 1812 Bicentennial Comn, 2007; arts & Humanities counc Montgomery County; mem, Washington women's Investment Club. **Honors/Awds:** Hon lifetime membership for National Assn of Budget Officers. **Special Achievements:** First African American woman to serve as chief budget officer of a state; named one of Maryland's Top 100 Women in 2002 and 2007.

FOSTER, TONI
Basketball player. **Personal:** Born Oct 16, 1971. **Educ:** Univ Iowa, BA, 1993. **Career:** Phoenix Mercury, forward & ctr, 1997-04. **Honors/Awds:** Player of the week, 1990-93; Big Ten Player of the Year, 1993; Sports Channel Player of the Year, 1993; First Team all-Big Ten honors; Champion Player of the Year award. **Special Achievements:** Nominee for the prestigious Broderick Award. *

FOSTER, WILLIAM K.
Executive. **Personal:** Born Jun 10, 1933, Pittsburgh, PA; married Dolores J Porter; children: Kimberly Anne & William K. **Educ:** Duquesne Univ Pittsburgh, BA, 1963; Univ WI-MADISON Grad Sch Banking, 1977; Univ WI-MADISON Post Grad Sch Banking, 1978. **Career:** Nat Biscuit Co, sales rep, 1963-67; Pittsburgh Nat Bank, com banking officer, 1967-77; New & World Nat Bank, pres & Chief Exec Officer, 1977-79; Franklin Fed Savings & Loan Assn, vpres, 1979-. **Orgs:** Treas, Home wood-Brushton Med Ctr, 1975-76; bd mem, Governor's Coun Small Bus, 1977; treas, Prog Aide Citizens Enterprise, 1978-. **Honors/Awds:** Athlete of the year, Pittsburgh Optimist Club, 1948; airman of the month, USAF, 1955; good conduct National Service, USAF 1956. **Military Serv:** USAF, air 1st class, 1952-56.

FOSTER, DR. WILLIAM PATRICK
Educator, bandleader. **Personal:** Born Aug 25, 1919, Kansas City, KS; son of Frederick and Venetia Highwarden; married Mary Ann Duncan, Aug 8, 1939; children: William Patrick Jr & Anthony Frederick. **Educ:** Univ Kans, BMus, 1941; Wayne State Univ, MA, 1950; Columbia Univ, PhD, 1955. **Career:** Bandleader, educator (retired); Lincoln High Sch, dir bands, 1941-43; Ft Valley St Col, dir music, 1943-44; Tuskegee Inst, dir bands & orchestra, 1944-46; Fla Agr & Music Univ, dir bands, 1946-98, Dept Music, chmn, 1998, dir bands emer, 1998-2001; G Leblanc Corp, adv bd, 1966; Int Music Festivals, adv bd, 1970; McDonald's All Am High Sch Band, dir, 1980-91. **Orgs:** Bd dir, Am Bandmasters Asn, 1977-79; pres, Fla Music Educr Asn, 1977-79; pres, Col Band Dir Nat Asn, 1981-83; bd dirs, Rotary Club, Tallahassee, 1989-91; bd dirs, John Philip Sousa Found, 1989; pres elect, Am Bandmasters Asn, 1993; former mem, Nat Coun Arts. **Honors/Awds:** Director of Bands, 50th Anniversary, Florida A&M Univ, 1950; Distinguished Service Award, Kappa Kappa Psi, 1972; Distinguished Service Award, Kans Univ, 1973; Fel, Gen Educ Bd, 1953-55; joint resolution Fla House & Senate, 1977; FAMU Marching Band, Sudler Nat Inter collegiate Asn, 1985; Celebrity Roast, Fla A&M Univ Booster Club, 1987; Tallahassee National Achievement Award, Easter Seal Soc, 1988;

Distinguished Alumni Award, Wayne St Univ, 1988; Great Floridian, Fla Hist Assocs; Hall of Fame, Nat Band Asn; Leadership Tallahassee, Tallahassee Chamber Com; Distinguished Leadership of the Year Award, Tallahassee Chamber Com, 1998; Nat Asn Study & Performance African-American Music, Nat Award, 1999; one of 100 Most Influential FAMUANS of the Century, FL A&M Univ, 1999; Music Ed Hal of Fame, 2000; Arts Achievement Award, Wayne St Univ, 2000; Lifetime Leadership Award, Tallahassee Chamber of Com, 2000; Diploma of Chevalier of the Order of Arts & Letters, French Minister of Culture & Comm, 2000; Alpha Phi Alpha. **Special Achievements:** Auth: Band Pageantry, 1968; The Man Behind the Baton; Conducted AUS Band, USN Band, USAF Band, Marine Band; combined in-ter svc bands, Const Hall, Wash, DC; Guest conductor of bands throughout the country. **Home Addr:** 1003 Tanner Dr, Tallahassee, FL 32305. *

FOSTER-GREAR, PAMELA
Executive. **Personal:** Born Feb 20, 1957, Cleveland, OH; daughter of Curtis and Margaret; married Lance Grear, Sep 21, 1991; children: Yejide Hadassah-Noni Grear. **Educ:** Cuyahoga Community Col, attended 1979; Columbus State Community Col, attended 1983; Fashion Inst Technol, cert, 1987; Minority Bus Exec Prog, Amos Tuck Sch, Dartmouth Col, cert, 1990. **Career:** Univ Property Devel, mgr, 1973-83; Ohio Dept Youth Servs, comput literacy instr, 1983-86; Foster Corp, pres & chief exec officer, 1986-. **Orgs:** adv bd chairperson, Columbus Area Chamber Com, 1992-; bd mem, Light Ctr, 1989-; Jr Achievement, Ohio State Univ, Student Devel Prog, mentorship prog, 1992-; bd mem, Martin Luther King Jr Ctr Performing Arts, 1989-90; supporter, Afrikan Ctr, 1987-; supporter & guest speaker, NE Career Ctr, 1992; supporter, "I Know I Can" Prog, 1990-91; supporter, Southern Christian Leadership Conf, 1991-92. **Honors/Awds:** Small Bus Asn, finalist; Small Bus Person of the Year, 1992; Ohio Assembly Couns, Corp Hall of Fame, 1991; Borden, Inc, Minority Bus Entrepreneur Prog Scholarship, 1990. **Business Addr:** President, Chief Executive Officer, Foster Corporation, PO Box 09191, Columbus, OH 43209, **Business Phone:** (614)774-4536.*

FOULKS, CARL ALVIN
Physician. **Personal:** Born Jun 10, 1947, Greensboro, NC; married Deborah Casandra Smith; children: Carl Jr, Dion, Cory. **Educ:** Howard Univ Col Pharm, Washi, DC, RPh; Howard Univ Med Sch, MD. **Career:** Providence Hosp, chief resident; Cumberland County Med Clinic, dir; pvt pract, physician; Piedmont Health Ctr, Statesville, NC, physician currently. **Orgs:** Nat Med Asn; Am Gastroenterol Asn; Am Soc Gastrointestinal Endoscopy; Am Col Physicians. **Business Addr:** Physician, Piedmont Healthcare, 208 Old Mocksville Rd, Statesville, NC 28677.

FOULKS FOSTER, IVADALE MARIE
Government official, association executive. **Personal:** Born Mar 30, 1922, Sidney, IL; daughter of Warren T and Edwarda C Martin; married Wardell Foster, Oct 19, 1942 (deceased); children: Wardella Marie Rouse, Christina Jo. **Educ:** Danville Area Community Col, BS, elem educ, 1966. **Career:** Laura Lee Fel House, jr activities super, 1958-66; City Danville, Recreation Dept, Lincoln Park, recreation dir, 1968-73; Vermilion County, Health Dept, homemaker/home health aide, 1970-73; Sch Dist 118, teachers aide, 1973-74; Herb Crawford Multi Agency Inc, sr citizens dir & asst dir, 1974-78; E Cent Ill Area Agency, trainee, 1976-77; Vermilion County, bd mem dist 8, 1980-89, chmn, 1988-91; E Cent Ill Area Agency, sr citizen employ specialist, 1981-82; Vermilion County, Health & Educ Chaplain Comn, bd chair, 1994-, Pct 26 Comn Woman, 1996, dist 8 bd rep, currently; Health Dept, bd rep, 1996. **Orgs:** Pres, secy, Bradley-Maberry Am Legion Auxiliary 736, 1962-; pres, Vermilion County Coun Am Legion Auxiliary, 1972-90; secy, bd mem, Pioneer Ctr Substance Abuse, 1973-; secy, Neighborhood House Inc, 1975-; precinct comt woman, Precinct 26, 1978-; pres, Sr Citizens Adv Group, Neighborhood House Inc, 1980-90; bd rep, Vermelion County, E Cent Ill, Area Agency Aging, 1988-94; bd rep, Vermilion County Health Dept Bd, 1991-94; chaplain, Vermilion County Bd; Union Missionary Baptist Church. **Honors/Awds:** Most Outstanding Church Pianist, Faithful Worker & Pianist, 30 Yrs Allen Chapel AME Church, Union Missionary Baptist Church, 1976 & 1984; Hon Banquet, Letter Writers Ed Page Ed, Danville Com News, 1979 & 1980; Outstanding Community Contrib, Danville Br, Nat Asn Advan Colored People, 1981; Athena Award, Women Distinction, Girl Scouts Am, 2002; Hall of Fame, Danville High Sch, 2002. **Special Achievements:** One of 3 of Danville's Outstanding Women nominated by readers & sel by comm of Danville Commercial News 1964; First Black woman elected to serve on the Vermilion Co Bd, 1980; 10 Most Outstanding Leaders Danville, Danville Com News Ser & Pictures, 1981. **Home Addr:** 516 Anderson St, Danville, IL 61832. **Business Addr:** Board Representative, Vermilion County District 8, 6 N Vermilion St, Danville, IL 61832.*

FOUNTAIN, W. FRANK
President (Organization), vice president (organization). **Personal:** Born Jan 1, 1944?, Brewton, AL. **Educ:** Va Hampton Univ, BA, history & political sci, 1966; Univ Pa Wharton Sch, MBA, 1973. **Career:** Peace Corps, West Bengal, India, volunteer, 1966-68; Daimler Chrysler Corp Fund, pres; Daimler Chrysler Group, investment analyst, 1973, Corp Controller's Off, Treasurer's Off, Chrysler's Govt Affairs Off, vpres govt affairs, 1995-98, sr vpres external affairs & pub policy, 1998-; Wharton Sch, Univ Pa, overseer. **Orgs:** bd dir, Detroit Pub Schs, 1999-03; vice chair, Detroit Regional Chamber Com; Mus African Am Hist; Hudson-Webber Found; Mich Mfrs Asn; Community Found Southeast Mich; WTVS-Channel 56, Pub TV; Music Hall; Wharton Sch Bd Overseers; chair, Hampton Univ Bd Trustees; chair, Metro Detroit Conv & Visitors Bur; chair, Citizens Res Coun Mich; Int Visitors Coun Metro Detroit; Detroit Investment Fund; vice chair, New Detroit; Dennis W Archer Found; Econ Club Detroit; vice chair, Corp Coun Africa; Detroit Metro Sports Comn; Focus Hope Adv Bd; chair, Metropolitan Affairs Coalition; Mackinac Ctr Pub Policy Adv Bd; vice chair, Joint Ctr Political & Econ Studies; Bus Coun Ala; bd, Corp Coun Africa & Africare. **Honors/Awds:** Honorary Dr Pub Serv, Cent Mich Univ. **Special Achievements:** Region's number-one "most connected" person, Crain's Detroit, 2006. **Business Addr:** President, Daimler Chrysler Corporation Group, 1000 Chrysler Dr, Auburn Hills, MI 48326-2766, **Business Phone:** (248)576-5741.*

FOUNTLEORY, MILLICENT
Editor. **Career:** The News & Observer Publishing Company, slot ed, currently. **Business Addr:** Slot Editor, The News & Observer Publishing Company, 215 S McDowell St, PO Box 191, Raleigh, NC 27602.*

FOURNIER, COLLETTE V.
Educator, photojournalist. **Personal:** Born Jul 21, 1952, New York, NY; daughter of Alexander and Cynthia Hubbard Mann. **Educ:** Rochester Inst Technol, Rochester, NY, AAS, photographic illustration, 1973, BS, biomed commun, 1979; Union Inst & Univ Vt Col, Montpelier, VT, MFA, visual arts prog, 2003. **Career:** RA-ETA TV21 WXXI, Rochester, NY, prod asst, engr trainee, 1979-81; Malrite Communs, TV 31, WUHF, Rochester, NY, sr film ed, 1981-82, TV 21, WXXI, prod asst, 1981-82; Community Darkroom, Rochester, NY, photog instr, 1982-88; About Time Mag, Rochester, NY, photojournalist, 1982-88; J, News Gannett, West Nyack, NY, photojournalist, 1988-89; Bergen Record, Hackensack, NJ, photojournalist, 1989-91, freelance photogr, 2002; Art Dept, State Univ NY, Rockland Community Col, Suffern, NY, adj fac, 1992-, spec events coordr, Educ Asst Off Pres, 1992-94, Campus Communs & Photogr, 1994-; freelance photogr, NY Post, 1994-95. **Orgs:** Nat Asn Black Journalists, 1984-; Nat Press Photogr Asn, 1988-; Women's Caucus for Arts, 1984-; NJ Press Photogr Asn, 1989-; mem, Kamoinge Inc; mem, Univ Photographers Asn Am. **Honors/Awds:** Woman of Year Achievement, Arts, Am Asn, Univ Women, 1988; Photography Panelist, NY Found Arts Inc, 1989; A Ripple of Thunder, Multi-media, Art in Am, review exhibition, 1988; photography works published, Black Photogr: An Illustrated Bio-Bibliography, by Willis, Thomas, Schomburg, 1988; Community Service Award, Rockland County Legislature for the Arts, 2004; The Medallion Awards, Nat Coun Mkt & Pub Rels, 2005, 2001, 1999; Empire State, Women In Photography Series Lecture, 2007. **Special Achievements:** Published numerous publications which include "The Sweet Breath of Life", Atria Books, Simon and Schuster, Kamoinge Inc, 2004.

FOUSHEE, PREVOST VEST
Marketing executive. **Personal:** Born Apr 26, 1952, Pittsburg, NC; son of Prevex and Cora Cotton; married Trudi McCollum, Oct 1985; children: Prevost Jr & Ashlei. **Educ:** Fayetteville State Univ, BS, bus admin, 1977. **Career:** Pillsbury Corp, sales rep, 1978; Anheuser-Busch, Inc, sales rep, 1978-79, area sales mgr, 1979-81, dist sales mgr, 1981-83, proj mgr, mgt develop, 1983-84, special markets mgr, 1984-91, geog mkt mgr, 1991-92, prod mgr, Budweiser, 1992-94; National Light/Ice/King Cobra, brand mgr, 1994-97; Michelob Family & Specialty, dir, 1997, sr brand mgr. **Orgs:** Mkt comt, UNF, 1992. **Honors/Awds:** Black Achievers Award, Harlem YMCA, 1980; Yes I Can Award, Am Sentinel Newspaper, St Louis, 1990. **Military Serv:** AUS, sargent, 1972-75.

FOUTZ, SAMUEL THEODORE
Lawyer. **Personal:** Born May 3, 1945, Beaumont, TX; son of Freddie James and Mamie Ballard; married DeVonne Desmerries Draughn; children: Dietra Michelle & Fredrick William. **Educ:** Lamar State Col Tech, BS, 1967; Howard Univ Sch Law, JD, 1972. **Career:** Dallas Legal Serv Found Inc, atty, 1972-74, chief coun, 1974-76, exec dir, 1976-77; Pvt Pract, atty & coun law, 1978-. **Orgs:** Delta Theta Phi Legal Frat, 1967-; law clerk, Dept HEW, Off Gen Coun, 1971; Nat Bar Asn, 1972-; J L Turner Legal Soc, 1972-. **Honors/Awds:** Am Juris prudence Acad Award-property, 1972; Smith Fellow, Reginald Heber Smith Fel Fund, Inc 1972-75. **Military Serv:** AUS, spec-5, 1967-69; NDSM; VCM; VSM; GCMDL; SPS (M-14); 2 O/S Bars, 1967-69. **Business Addr:** Attorney, Pvt Pract, 401 Wynnwood Prof Bldg Suite 224, Dallas, TX 75224, **Business Phone:** (214)941-0568.*

FOWLER, BENNIE W
Executive, vice president (organization). **Personal:** Born Jan 1, 1956, Augusta, GA. **Educ:** Cent State Univ, Wilberforce, OH, BS, bus mgt; Ind Univ, MBA, opers mgt. **Career:** Gen Motors Corp, 1978-86; Chrysler Corp, var mfg mgt positions; Ford Motor Co, St Thomas Assembly Plant, supt, 1990, N Am Prod Develop, exec dir, 2002-03, Jaguar & Land Rover, vpres & coo, 2003-05, Advanced & Mfg Eng, vpres, 2005, vpres global qual, 2006-08, group vpres global qual, 2008-. **Orgs:** Founder, Powerstroke Athletic Club. **Special Achievements:** Listed Corporate Yellow Book & The Leadership Library on the Internet. **Business Addr:** Vice President of Advanced & Manufacturing Engineering & Quality, Ford Motor Company, One American Rd, Dearborn, MI 48126-0685, **Business Phone:** (313)322-3000.

FOWLER, JAMES DANIEL, JR.
Executive. **Personal:** Born Apr 24, 1944, Washington, DC; son of James D and Romay Lucas; married Linda Marie Raiford Fowler, May 24, 1968; children: Scott, Kimberly. **Educ:** Howard Univ, Washington DC, 1963; US Military Acad, West Point NY, BS, 1967; Rochester Inst Tech, Rochester NY, MBA, 1975. **Career:** Xerox Corp, rochester NY, coord of graduate relations, 1971-74, mgr personnel admin, 1974-75; DP Parker & Assoc Inc, Wellesley Ma, sr consul, 1975-76; ITT World Headquarters, new York MY, mgr of Staffing, 1976-78; ITT Aetna, Denver Co, vip dir of admin 1978; ITT Consumer Financial Corp, Minneapolis MN, svp, dir of admin 1978-84, svp, dir admin & mktg, 1984-87; evp, dir of admin & marketing, 1987-90, evp, drr of product mgt, marketing & adm, 1990-92, evp, dir of adm, 1992. **Orgs:** US Military Acad West Point, trustee, 1978-86, 1987-90; ASN of MBA EXEs, EXE Leadership CNL, charter mbr, bod; MR Financial Services ASN; AMR SOC for Personnel ADM. **Honors/Awds:** Black Achiever Awd, ITT, 1979. **Military Serv:** AUS, capt, 1967-71; Bronze Star w/Oak Leaf Cluster; Army Comm Medal with 2 Oak Leaf Clusters. *

FOWLER, JOHN D.
Educator. **Personal:** Born Mar 22, 1931, Clinton, NC; son of John D and Sallie L Howard; married Wilma J Butler, Apr 22, 1984; children: Ronald M, Valerie D Fowler Wall & Christopher E. **Educ:** Winston-Salem Cent Univ, attended 1954; State Univ New Paltz, MA, 1974; Northeastern Univ, educ studies; NC Cent Univ; Univ VT. **Career:** Mt Pleasant Elem Sch, prin 1955-58; CE Perry High Sch, teacher 1958-63; WPender Sch, 1963-64; Dunbar Elem Sch, 1964-65; Hudson City Sch Dist, asst prin, coordr; City Sch Dist, Rochester NY, vprin, 1985-. **Orgs:** NY State Reg Plan Asn; bd dirs, Columbia County Exten Serv; Omega Psi Phi;life mem, Nat Educ Asn; Nat Advan Asn Colored People; vpres, Kiwanis Greater Hudson; chmn, Const By-Laws Com Van Rennselear Div Kiwanis Int; city Counman, 1980-85; County Supvr, 1985; Lt Governor, Kiwanis Int,1981-82; bd dir, Anthony L Jordan Health Ctr; Maplewood YMCA; Kiwanis Club Eastridge Irondequoit. **Honors/Awds:** Alumni scholarship Winston-Salem Central Univ 1950; First black chosen from Columbia County to represent Northeast Synod; chairperson of many committees while on city council in Hudson NY, 1980-85; Administrator. ofthe Year, PTO of #6 School, 1988-89; Administrator of the Year Dag HammarskjoldSchool No 6 1989-90; C E Perry High School, valedictorian, graduated withhonors. **Home Addr:** 247 Maplewood Ave, Rochester, NY 14613. *

FOWLER, DR. QUEEN DUNLAP
School administrator. **Personal:** Born in St Louis, MO; children: Darnell Keith. **Educ:** Harris Teachers Col, BA, 1960; St Louis Univ, MEd, 1965, PhD, 1974, attended 1979. **Career:** WA Univ, St Louis, MO, asst dir adm coord of rec & pub relations, 1969-79, lectr & instr, 1975-79, coord field studies, 1977-78; Sch Dist Wellston, MO, supt, 1979-84; Pupil Personnel Serv, exec dir; educ consult; Fowler & Assocs Consult Servs, pres, currently. **Orgs:** Urban League Metrop St Louis, 1965-; bd dir exec bd, Girl Scouts Greater St Louis 1978-; bd dir, United Way Greater St Louis, 1979-; nat nominating comt & nat prog plan comt, Am Asn Sch Admin, 1980-94; nat adv bd, Am Psych Asn, 1982-86; bd curators, Lincoln Univ, Jefferson City, MO, 1983-87; vpres, bd dirs, Metro YWCA, 1984-; bd dirs, Nat Asn Christians & Jews, 1984-88; exec bd, Alpha Pi Chi Bus & Prof Sor, 1984-; regional counr, Delta Sigma Theta Sorority, 1986-; YWCA, nat task force retirement, 1990-94; gov coun rep, Am Coun Asn; rep, Asn Multicultural Coun Develop, 2006-. **Honors/Awds:** King Fanon Community Mental Health Award, 1980; Volunteer Service, Girl Scout Coun Greater St Louis, 1982; Alpha Phi Alpha Outstanding Educator Award, 1982; Distinguish Leadership, United Negro Col Fund, St Louis, MO, 1983; Community Service City of Wellston, MO, 1983; Distinguished Alumni Harris-Stowe State Col, St Louis, 1983; Excellence in Special Education Award, 1991; Kitty Cole Human Rights Award; America's Top 100 Black Business & Professional Women Award, Dollars & Sense Mag, 1988; Freeman-Kortkamp Award. **Special Achievements:** First African-American female superintendent in the state of Missouri. **Home Addr:** 14 Nob Hill Lane, St Louis, MO 63130-2038.

FOWLER, REGGIE
Executive, business owner. **Educ:** Univ Wyoming, soc work; Ariz State Univ, MBA. **Career:** Spiral Inc, founder & owner, 1987-; Kyrene OEM, owner; Minn Vikings, owner, currently. **Honors/Awds:** Rookie of the Year. **Business Addr:** Owner, Minnesota Vikings, 9520 Viking Dr, Eden Prairie, MN 55344, **Business Phone:** (952)828-6500.

FOWLER, RONALD J.
Clergy. **Personal:** Son of Robert L and Susie Bell. **Educ:** Kent State Univ, BS, educ, 1959, MS; Anderson Col Sch Theol, Mdiv,

1966; Pittsburgh Theol Sem, ThD; Jungian Inst, Zurich, Switz. **Career:** Detroit Pub Schs, teacher; Robert St Church God, assoc pastor; Arlington Church God, Akron, OH, sr pastor, currently. **Orgs:** Bd mem, Akron Pub Schs, 1988-00; chmn, Anderson Univ Trustee Bd; bd mem, Anderson Univ Exec Comt; bd mem, Knight Found; mem bd dirs, Nat City Bank. **Military Serv:** AUS, vet food instr, 2 yrs. **Business Addr:** Senior Pastor, Arlington Church of God, 539 S Arlington St, Akron, OH 44306-1797.

FOWLER, WILLIAM E
Judge. **Personal:** Born Nov 4, 1921, Akron, OH; son of William E Fowler Sr and Maude; married Norma June; children: Claude, John & Diane. **Educ:** Fordham Law Sch, AB, LLB. **Career:** US Nat Transp Safety Bd, chief adminstrv law judge; Bd Appeals & Review, US cvl serv comm, 1966-69; US Dept Labor, trial exam, 1964-66; US Dept Justice, spl asst atty gen, 1961-64; State OH, asst atty gen, 1959-61; Social Security Comn, admin law judge; US Dept Labor, admin law judge; Akron OH, city prosecutor, 1956-59; Ohio Atty Gen Off, chief hwy div; Nat Transp Safety Bd, chief admin law judge, 1969-, chief judge, 1977-. **Orgs:** Pres, Federal Adminstrn Law Judges Conference, 1974-75; DC Mental Health asn, 1972-74; Federal Bar Asn; Toastmasters Club, 1970-75; dir, Fed Bar Asn 1972-74; Housing Opportunities Coun, 1970-74; Am Bar Asn; Nat Bar Asn; Wash Bar Asn. **Honors/Awds:** Distinguished Serv Award, DC Public Sch, 1985. **Military Serv:** First black pres Judges Conference. **Business Addr:** Chief Administrative Law Judge, National Transportation Safety Board, 490 L Enfant Plz E SW Rm 4704, Washington, DC 20594, **Business Phone:** (202)314-6150.

FOWLKES, DORETHA P
Real estate executive. **Personal:** Born Apr 2, 1944, Meherrin, VA; children: Tracey. **Educ:** Va Commonwealth Univ, J Sargeant Reynolds, attended 1982. **Career:** RL Williams, sales assoc & off mgr, 1975-79; Robinson Harris, sales assoc, 1979-81; Fowlkes & Co Realtors, agent & pres, 1981-. **Orgs:** Pres, Ebony Ladies, 1975-77; pres, Richmond Bd Realtists, 1981-84; bd mem, N Richmond YMCA, 1983; bd mem, Zoning Appeals Bd, 1984; bd mem, Metro Bus League, 1985; pres, Va Assoc Realtist, 1985-; bd dirs, Consol Bank & Trust. **Honors/Awds:** Business of Year, Metro Business League, 1982; Business Asn of Year, Am Bus Women, 1984; business person Youth, Nat Asn Advan Colored People, 1984. **Business Addr:** President, Agent, Fowlkes & Co Realtors, 2519 Chamberlayne Ave, Richmond, VA 23222, **Business Phone:** (804)321-8000.

FOWLKES, NANCY P
Social worker. **Personal:** Born in Athens, GA; married Vester Guy (deceased); children: Wendy Denise. **Educ:** Bennett Col Women, AB, 1946; Syracuse Univ, MA, 1952; Smith Col Sch Social Work, MSW, 1963; Pace Univ, MPA, 1983. **Career:** Social worker (retired); Bennett Col, dir publ rels, 1946-47, 1949-50; Va Ed Bulletin, asst ed, 1950-52; Com Serv Soc, NY, asst off mgr, 1952-55; W City Dept Soc Serv, social caseworker, asst supvr div childrens serv, 1959-67; Adoption Serv, supvr, 1967-74; Homefinding, supvr, 1974-89. **Orgs:** Pres, zeta nu omega chapter, Alpha Kappa Alpha Sorority Inc, 1958-62; Urban League Women, 1960-; bd mem, Family Serv Women, 1961-71; pres, Regency Bridge Club, 1963-65; Acad Cert Soc Workers, 1964-; pres, W Chap Jack & Jill Am, 1965-67; vpres, Regency Bridge Club, 1965-67; secy & treas, Eastern Reg Jack & Jill Am, 1967-71; treas, United Meth Women, 1969-72; chmn, admin bd, Trinity United Methodist Church; pres, Womens Soc Christian Serv, 1970-72; adv coun, Adult Educ Ctr White Plains Pub Sch, 1970-74; vpres, E View Jr High Sch, 1970-71; Int Platform Asn, 1971; pres, Inter Faith Coun White Plains, 1971-74; pres, United Meth Women, 1972-75; lay speaker, Trinity United Methodist Church, 1972-; trustee, Trinity United Methodist Church, 1973-79; pres, 1983-86, United Methodist Women, NY Conf United Methodist Church; bd trust, NY Conf United Methodist Church, 1982-90; chmn, Program Div NY Conf, United Methodist Church, 1989-94; bd dir, Gen bd Global Ministries, United Methodist Church, 1988-96; pres, Northeastern Jurisdiction, United Methodist Church, 1988-92; bd dir, Women Div United Methodist Church, 1988-96; vpres, sec finance, Women's Div, 1992-96; assoc lay leader, Trinity United Methodist Church, 1990-; bd dir, Ordained Ministry, NY Annual Conf, United Methodist Church, 1999-; chmn, Metro N Dist Coun Ministries, 2003. **Honors/Awds:** Schaefer Award, 1963; Recognition Plaque Jack & Jill Am Inc, 1976; Distinguished Service Award, Church Women United, 1994; Visionary Award, Leadership Award, Zeta Nu Omega Chapter, 2000. **Home Addr:** 107 Valley Rd, White Plains, NY 10604-2316.

FOWLKES, NELSON J
Executive. **Personal:** Born Dec 26, 1934, Chattanooga, TN; son of Edward B Fowlkes Sr and Dorothy F Johnson (deceased); married Peggy Jackson, Sep 25, 1957; children: Errol A, Janet Fowlkes-Allen & Nelson Joseph. **Educ:** Central State Univ, BS, Chem, 1957; Univ Tenn, MS, Biochem, 1970; Pac Lutheran Univ, attended 1971-74; Consortium Calif Univ & Col, MPA, 1982. **Career:** Letterman Army Med Ctr, chief clinl chem., 1974-75; Mich Biomed Lab, admin asst, 1976-78; St Agnes Med Ctr, lab mgr, 1978-80, planning asst, 1980-82, asst dir planning, 1982-84, dir res & planning, 1984-86, dir corp rel, 1986-; St Francis Hosp, staff, currently. **Orgs:** Bus Adv Coun Sch Bus, 1980-89; treas, Alumni Trust Coun FSU, 1984-89; pres, Twentieth Century Golf Club, 1985-88; bd dir, Community Health Coun Inc, 2002; exec dir, Harrison Bryant Kearney Blvd Plaza, Inc; vice chmn, Valley Small Bus Develop Corp. **Special Achievements:** "Corporate Health Risk Mgmt: An Employer's Journal of Health Care Newest Tool to Reduce Health Care Costs" Mkt, 1989. **Military Serv:** AUS, Med Serv Corps, lt, 20 yrs; first Oak Leaf Cluster to Army Commendation Medal. **Home Addr:** 2935 Juniper Dr, Corona, CA 92882-3656, **Home Phone:** (209)439-7731. **Business Addr:** Staff, St. Francis Hospital, 333 Laidley St, PO Box 471, Charleston, WV 25322, **Business Phone:** (304)347-6500.

FOX, CHARLES WASHINGTON
Television producer, administrator. **Personal:** Born Jun 14, 1945, Clarksburg, WV; son of Charles W Fox Jr and Lucille Eleanor Penister; married Judy Delores; children: Charles W Fox IV, Renee Ann & Lori Michelle. **Educ:** Johns Hopkins Univ, MA, 1973. **Career:** MPTV, Owings Mills, PBS, writer, 1972-75; WCVB-TV, producer, 1975-79; Quick Brown Fox Prod, owner & producer, 1979-90; WNEV-TV, CBS, producer, 1981-85; WRC-TV, NBC, producer, 1985-86; Am Univ, assoc prof, 1987-89; Morgan State Univ, fac; Baltimore Community Col, fac; Md Film Comn, dir, 1990-93; Worldnet TV & Film Serv, dir, 1993-97; Ohio Univ Sch Flim, dir, 2002-. **Orgs:** Mgr, Commun & Outreach, Pres Off Diversity, Ohio Univ. **Honors/Awds:** Acad TV, Arts & Scis, Emmy, 1973, 1976, 1977, 1979, 1986; Iris Award, Look Show, Nat Asn TV Prog Execs, 1982-; Angel Award, Religion Media, 1981. **Special Achievements:** Established Mid-Atlantic Warner Bros Writers Workshop, 1990; established Multicultural Filmmakers Think Tank, 1990; Developed the Roc Dutton Youth Leadership Summit, 1993. **Military Serv:** US Air Force, staff sgt, 1963-67. **Business Phone:** (740)593-9433.

FOX, JEANNE JONES
Educator. **Personal:** Born Aug 17, 1929, Chicago, IL; daughter of John Jones and Helen Duckett Robinson; married Richard K Jr; children: Jeanne A, Jane E & Helen K. **Educ:** Rosary Col, 1949; Roosevelt Col, 1950; Univ Minn, BS, 1961; Fgn Serv Inst, lang training, 1968. **Career:** Buchanan Elem Sch, teacher, 1961-62; Wash DC Pub Sch, substitute teacher, 1962; Petworth Pub Libr, supvr & libr asst, 1962-64; US Info Agency, foreign serv & limited res officer, 1964-65; Radnor Elem Sch, teacher, 1970-71; Mark Battle Assos Mgt Cons, sr assoc, 1971-73; Joint Ctr Polit Studies, assoc dir res, 1973-77; Funders Comm Voter Regist, Wash, DC, staff consult, 1983-87; Comn Study Am Electorate, Wash, DC, proj mgr, 1987-89; Food Res & Action Coun, Wash, DC, dir develop, 1989-91. **Orgs:** Unit leader, League Women Voters, 1956-60; Pi Lambda Theta Hon Educ Asn; Scholarship Comt, Am Women's Club Madrid, 1965-66; bd dirs, Am Sch Madrid; sec scholar chmn, Madrid, Spain, 1968-70; Am chmn, Spanish Red Cross DrMadrid, 1969; bd mem, Meridian Ho Intl, 1973; Urban Mass Transit Adv Panel Cong US; off tech Assessment, 1974.

FOX, PAULETTE
Executive director. **Career:** Opportunities Industrialization Ctr New Brit, Inc., exec dir, currently. **Business Addr:** Executive Director, Opportunities Industrialization Center of New Britain, Inc., 1 Grove St, New Britain, CT 06053, **Business Phone:** (860)224-7151.

FOX, RICHARD K., JR.
Ambassador. **Personal:** Born Oct 22, 1925, Cincinnati, OH; son of Richard K Sr and Kathryn Lynch; married Jeanne Jones-(deseased); Catherine Mastny-Fox; children: Jeanne Fox Alston, Jane Fox-Johnson, Helen Fox-Fields. **Educ:** Ind Univ, AB, 1950; Ind Univ Grad Sch, 1950. **Career:** Ambassador (retired);Urban Leagues St Louis, St Paul, 1950-56; Minn Comm Against Discrimination St Paul, asst dir, 1956-61; Dept State, spec asst to dep asst secy personnel, 1961-63, spec asst to dep under secy admin, 1963-65; US Embassy Madrid, counr admin affairs, 1965-70; Bur Ed Cult Affairs, dep asst secy 1973-74, dep dir personnel, 1974-76, dep inspector gen, 1979-83; Sr Semnr Foreign Policy, mem, 1976-77; US Ambassador Trinidad & Tobago, 1977-79; Meridian Int Ctr, sr vpres, 1983-97. **Orgs:** Bd mem, past pres, Luth Human Rels Assoc Am, 1971-76; vice chmn, DC Bd Higher Educ, 1972-76; bd trustees, Univ DC, 1976-77; chmn, bd dir, Wheat Ridge Found Chicago, 1979-88; pres, Am Foreign Serv Protective Asn, WA 1979-92; bd mem, Vesper Society, CA; Bd mem, Luther Institute, 1999-; Wash Inst Foreign Affairs; Am Acad Diplomacy; bd govs, Diplomatic & Consular Officers Retired, Bacon House; Nat Coun Int Vistors, 1998-. **Honors/Awds:** Alpha Kappa Delta Hon Soc Indiana Univ, 1950; Superior Honor Awd Dept of State, 1964, 1983; Meritorious Honor Awd Embassy Madrid, 1970; Doctor of Laws, Valparaiso Univ, 1983; Wilbur Carr Award, Dept of State. **Military Serv:** USN, 1944-46. **Home Addr:** 5124 Waukesha Rd, Bethesda, MD 20816. *

FOX, RICK (ULRICH ALEXANDER FOX)
Basketball player, actor. **Personal:** Born Jul 24, 1969, Ontario-;children (previous marriage): Sasha; married Vanessa Willams, 1999; children: Kyle & Sasha Gabriella. **Educ:** Univ NC, attended 1991. **Career:** Basketball player (retired), actor; Boston Celtics, forward, 1991-97; Los Angeles Lakers, 1997-2004; Films: Blue Chips, 1994; Eddie, 1996; He Got Game, 1998; The Collectors, 1999; Resurrection, 1999; The Four Faces of God, 1999, Holes, 2003; Mini's First Time, 2006; Hysteria, 2007; Tv: "Oz", 1997-2003; "1-800-Missing", 1998; "Arti$$", 2001; "Street Time", 2003'; "Kevin Hill", 2005; "Love Inc", 2005-06; "One Tree Hill", 2006; "Dirt", 2006. **Honors/Awds:** NBA, All-Rookie second team, 1992; NBA Finals Championship ring, 2000. **Business Phone:** (310)859-4000.

FOX, THOMAS E, JR.
Lawyer. **Personal:** Born Jul 22, 1963, Brooklyn, NY; son of Thomas and Juanita Aquart. **Educ:** Jackson State Univ, Jackson MS, BA, 1988; Harvard Law Sch, Cambridge MA, JD, 1988. **Career:** Nat City Bd Correction, NY, asst coun, 1985; Harvard Prison Legal Assistance Proj, Cambridge MA, stud atty, 1986; Brown & Wood Law Firm, New York NY, summer assoc, 1987; Honorable Clifford Scott Green, Philadelphia PA, law clerk, 1988-89; White & Case Law Firm, NY, assoc, 1989-. **Orgs:** Nat Conf Black Lawyers; pres/chmn, Nat Black Law Stud Asn, 1987-88; NY State Bar. **Honors/Awds:** Allan Locke Scholar, Educ Found Phi Beta Sigma, 1984; Rhodes Scholar Finalist, State Miss 1984; Agnes fel Nat Asn Advan Colored People, 1985-86; Earl Warren fel, Legal Defense Fund, Nat Asn Advan Colored People, 1985-88. **Home Addr:** 17825 Leslie Rd, Jamaica, NY 11434. **Business Addr:** Associate, White & Case Law Firm, 1155 Ave of the Americas, New York, NY 10036, **Business Phone:** (212)819-8200.*

FOX, ULRICH ALEXANDER. See FOX, RICK.

FOX, VIVICA A
Actor. **Personal:** Born Jul 30, 1964, Southbend, IN; daughter of William and Everlyena; married Christopher Harvest, 1998 (divorced 2002). **Educ:** Golden West Col. **Career:** Foxy Brown Productions, owners, currently. Tv appearances: Generations, 1989; Beverly Hills 90210, 1991; In the House, 1991; The Fresh Prince of Bel Air, 1991; Out All Night, 1992; The Young & the Restless, 1994; The Tuskegee Airmen, 1995; Living Single, 1996; Arsenio, 1997; City of Angels, 2000; Kim Possible: A Sitch in Time (voice), 2003; films: Born on the Fourth of July, 1989; Independence Day, 1996; Set It Off, 1996; Booty Call, 1997; Batman & Robin, 1997; Soul Food, 1997; Solomon; Why Do Fools Fall in Love, 1998; Teaching Mrs Tingle, 1999; Idle Hands, 1999; Double Take, 2001; Kingdom Come, 2001; Two Can Play That Game, 2001; Little Secrets, 2001; Juwanna Mann, 2002; Boat Trip, 2002; Ride or Die, 2003; Motives, 2004; Ella Enchanted, 2004; Blast, 2004; Getting Played, 2005; The Salon, 2005; The Hard Corps, 2006; Citizen Duane, 2006; Kicking It Old Skool, 2007; Caught On Tape, 2008. **Honors/Awds:** Universe Reader's Choice Award for Best Supporting Actress in a Genre Motion Picture, 1996; MTV Movie Award for Best Kiss, 1997; Black Film Award for Best Actress, 1998; Chosen by People magazine as one of the 50 Most Beautiful People in the World, 1997. **Business Addr:** Actress, Foxy Brown Productions Inc, PO Box 3538, Granada Hills, CA 91394, **Business Phone:** (310)288-8000.

FOXALL, DR. MARTHA JEAN
Educator, nurse. **Personal:** Born Mar 17, 1931, Omaha, NE; married Pitmon. **Educ:** Bryan Mem Hosp Sch Nursing, RN 1952; Univ Nebr, Omaha, BSN, 1954; MA, 1961; Univ Nebr Med Ctr, MSN, 1976; Univ NE Lincoln, PhD, 1979. **Career:** Immanuel Med Ctr, Omaha NE, teaching fac maternity nursing, 1953-68, assoc dir nursing educ, 1968-75; Div Nurs Midland & Luth Col Fremont NE, assoc dir, 1975-80; Univ Nebr Med Ctr, Col Nursing, Omaha, asso prof, 1980, Parent & Child Admin Educ & Sci Dept, prof, chmn, emer prof nursing, currently. **Orgs:** Immunization prog, Midland Luth Col, 1977; diabetic screening Omaha Area Chap, 1978; Lect "Aging & Sexuality" Midland Lutheran Col, 1979-80; chmn CEU com NE League Nursing, 1979-80; res proj dir, Univ Nebr Med Ctr, 1979; chairperson, Com Ment Health Delta Sigma Theta Sorority, 1980. **Honors/Awds:** Sigma Theta Tau; Nat Hon Soc Nursing 1979; Am Acad Nursing (FANN), fel; Annual Alumni Award, Bryan Sch Nursing, 1997; Midland Lutheran Col, hon doctorate, 2000; Distinguished Alumnus Award, Col Nursing, Univ NE, 2002. **Business Addr:** Emeritus Professor, University Nebraska Medical Center, 985330 Nebr Med Ctr Rm 5041, Omaha, NE 68198-5330.

FOXWORTH, DERRICK
Police chief, government official. **Personal:** Married Linda; children: Teela & Derrick Jr. **Educ:** Univ Portland, BS, 1980. **Career:** Portland Police Bur, officer & uniform patrol, 1981-90, sgt, 1990-94, lt, 1994-96, capt, 1996-97, comdr, 1997-2002, asst chief, opers br, 2002-03, chief police, 2003-. **Business Phone:** (503)823-0000.*

FOXX, JAMIE (ERIC MARLON BISHOP)
Actor. **Personal:** Born Dec 13, 1967, Terrell, TX; son of Louise. **Educ:** US Int Univ, San Diego, classical music. **Career:** TV series: "In Living Color", 1994; "The Jamie Foxx Show", 1994; "Straight From the Foxx hole", 1994; Films: The Truth About Cats and Dogs, 1996;Booty Call, 1997; The Player's Club, 1998; Any Given Sunday, 1999; Bait, 2000; Ali, 2001; Shade, 2003; Breakin' All the Rules, 2004; Collateral Ray, 2004; Stealth, Jarhead, 2005; Album: Peep This, 1994; Miami Vice, Dreamgirls, 2007, The

Soloist, Law Abiding Citizen, 2009. **Honors/Awds:** Image Award, TV Comedy Actor, Nat Asn Advan Colored People, 1998; FFCC Award, 2004; Hollywood Breakthrough Award, 2004; BSFC Award, 2004; Academy Award, Best Actor, 2005; Oscar Award, 2005; BAFTA Film Award, 2005; BET Award, 2005; Black Reel Award, 2005; Critics Choice Award, 2005; Golden Globe, 2005; KCFCC Award, 2005; Sierra Award, 2005; Grace Award, 2005. Best Collaboration, BET Award, 2009. **Special Achievements:** TV sitcom No. 1 among African American viewers on WB network; fourth person in history who scored a No 1 album & won an Academy Award; first man of the millennium to host "Saturday Night Live" 1975; Is the first person to have been nominated for three acting awards at the Golden Globes in the same year; became one of the elite ten thespians to have been nominated for both a Supporting and Lead Acting Academy Award in the same year for their achievements in two different movies; Is only the second male in history to receive two acting Oscar nominations in the same year for two different movies; first African American to be nominated for two Oscars in the same year; second actor to win an Academy Award for "Best Actor" and to have had a No 1 billboard single; named one of People Magazine's "Hottest Bachelors" in 2006; amie Foxx hosted the 2009 BET Awards ceremony, 2009. **Business Phone:** (818)501-2800.*

FOXX, LAURA R.
College administrator. **Personal:** Children: 1. **Educ:** Univ NC, Charlotte, BA, eng; Univ NC, Chapel Hill, MA, educ. **Career:** Nations Bank Found, pres, 1997; Bank Am Corp, exec dir, sr vpres; LR Foxx & Co, pres; Univ NC, Univ Affairs Div, dir advan, 2003; interim vice chancellor, 2007-09. **Orgs:** Coun Advan Support Educ, Comn Philanthropy; trustee, Pub Libr Charlotte Mecklenburg County. **Special Achievements:** First African American president of Nations Bank Found.

FOXX, NINA
Writer. **Personal:** Born in Jamaica, NY; married. **Educ:** Hunter Col; Baruch Col; City Univ NY, PhD, Indust & Orgn Psychol; Univ Wash, grad literary fiction cert; Dickinson Univer, MFA Farleigh. **Career:** Books: Dippin' My Soul, 2000; Do The Write Thing, 2002; Get Some Love, 2003; Going Buck Wild, 2004; Marrying Up, 2005; Mama:Gone, 2005; Just Short of Crazy, 2006; NO Girl Needs A Husband Seven Days a Week 2007, Marrying UP: The Stage Play 2008, BlackWords Online, "In Search of Color", columnist; Black Issues Book Review, reviewer; Dell Comput Corp, designer; Brown Sugar IV, anthology, 2005; FoxxTale Productions, LLC Producer, 2007. **Orgs:** Bd mem, Austin Children's Museum; Austin Writer's League & Girls Scouts; mem, Jack & Jill Am; Alpha Kappa Alpha Sorority; Capital Area Food Bank; El Buen Samaritano Episcopal Mission. **Honors/Awds:** Open Book Award Comedy Fiction Nominee 2006, 2007. **Military Serv:** Retired capt, US Army Reserve Med Ser Corp. **Business Addr:** Author, writer, Foxx/Tale Productions, San Antonio, TX 78746.*

FOYLE, ADONAL DAVID
Entrepreneur, basketball player. **Personal:** Born Mar 19, 1975, Canouan, St. Vincent and the Grenadines; son of Jay Mandle and Joan. **Educ:** Colgate Univ,BA, 1998; Orinda Univ, MS, sports psychol, currently. **Career:** Golden State Warriors, ctr, 1997-2007; Memphis Grizzlies, 2009; Orlando Magic, 2009-; Adonal Foyle Enterprises, pres, currently. **Orgs:** Founder, Democracy Matters; founder, Kerosene Lamp Foundation Inc. **Honors/Awds:** Most Outstanding Player, Five-Star Camp, 1992; Rookie of the Year, Patriot League, 1995; Player of the Year, Patriot League, 1997; NBA Community Assist Award, Nat Basketball Asn, 2006; NBA Good Guys, Sporting News, 2006.

FRAME, GEORGE J
Executive. **Career:** Ford Motor Co, Minority Dealer Opers, Dealer Develop, exec dir, currently. **Orgs:** SCORE Asn. **Business Addr:** Executive Director of Dealer Development, Ford Motor Company, 1 Am Rd, Dearborn, MI 48121, **Business Phone:** (313)322-3000.

FRANCE, FREDERICK DOUG, JR.
Financial manager, football player, executive. **Personal:** Born Apr 26, 1953, Dayton, OH; son of Fred France Sr and Waldine M France Sr; married Lawrene Susan Hind, May 14, 1988; children: Kristin Renee, Jason Kenneth & Kari Lynn. **Educ:** Ohio State Univ, elem educ, 1975. **Career:** Football player (retired), actor; Prof football player, Los Angeles Rams, Houston Oilers; real estate agent; actor; A Plus Off Prod, pres. **Orgs:** Marathon runner; Stain Glass Artist. **Honors/Awds:** Hon mention All-Am Tight End Time Mag; 2nd team NEA; 1st team All-Bag TenAP; NFC Championship Game 1975-76, 1978-79; Pro Bowl 1977-78; SportingNews NFC All-Stars 1978; Superbowl XIV, 1980. *

FRANCIS, CHARLES K.
Executive, educator, physician. **Personal:** Born in Newark, NJ. **Educ:** Dartmouth Col, attended; Jefferson Med Col, Philadelphia; Philadelphia Gen Hosp, internship. **Career:** Martin Luther King Jr Gen Hosp, chief cardiol; Col Physicians & Surgeons Columbia Univ, Prof Clin Med; Harlem Hosp Ctr, chmn, dept med; assoc prof,Yale Univ; Cardiac Catherization Lab, Yale-New Haven Hosp, dir; Univ Southern Calif Med Sch; Am Col Physicians, pres, 2004-05, bd regents, currently; Charles R Drew Univ Med & Sci, asst prof med, pres; NY Med Col, Ctr Health Disparities, dir, currently; NY Acad Med, Off Health Disparities, adj investr, currently. **Orgs:** Inst Med Nat Acad Sci; adv comm dir, Nat Inst Health (NIH); pres, Am HeartAsn Western States Affil; chair, Coun Clin Cardiology Am Heart Asn; bddir, Am Bd Internal Med; bd dir, NY Acad Med; past chair, Bd Asn BlackCardiologists; cochair, Working Group Coronary Artery Dis Blacks; pres,Am Col Physicians. **Honors/Awds:** Louis B Russell Memorial Award, Am Heart Asn; Daniel D Savage MD Memorial Award, Asn Black Cardiologists; Distinguished Alumni Faculty Award, Cardiology Div, Yale Univ Sch Med; Jefferson Alumni Achievement Award, Jefferson Med Col. **Special Achievements:** Research Publications: Annals of Internal Medicine, 2004. **Military Serv:** USAF, gen med officer. **Business Addr:** Adjunct Investigator, New York Academy of Medicinne, 1216 5th Ave, New York, NY 10029, **Business Phone:** (212)822-7288.

FRANCIS, CHARLES S L
Government official. **Personal:** Born Sep 13, 1943, Kingston, Jamaica; son of Barbara and Claude; married Wilma Smith; children: Charles II, Michael, Erica & Aaron. **Educ:** Calif State Univ, BS, 1970; MCRP, 1977. **Career:** Fresno Model Cities Prog, proj develop specialist; Calif State Univ Fresno, adj prof; City Fresno, budget analyst, Fresno Pvt Indus Coun, exec dir & chief exec officer, currently; Fresno City Col, dir grant funded educ prog; County Brd Educ, pres, Training inst, dir, currently. **Orgs:** Regional chmn, Natl & Assn Planners, 1972-75; full mem, Am Soc Planning Officials, 1972-; bd dir, Cent Valley YMCA, 1973-; coordr, State Fed Liason Black Polit Coun, 1975-; chmn, Lincoln Elem Sch PTA; Affirmative Action Comm Fresno Co Bd Educ; pres, Alpha Phi Alpha Frat Iota Nu Lambda Chap, 1973-75; chmn, Sr Vol Prog, 1972-; exec officer, secy, currently,Fresno Br, NAACP; bd mem, Nat Assn County Training & Employ Prof, 1988-90;Leadership Fresno Alumni Asn; bus advisory coun, CSUF-Sch Bus & Admin Sci; brd dirs, Nat Assn Workforce Develop Prof; adv coun, Women to Women. **Honors/Awds:** Assn Students service & leadership award, 1970. **Military Serv:** USN, second class petty officer, 1960-64. **Home Addr:** 190 S Valentine Ave, Fresno, CA 93706, **Home Phone:** (559)485-5572. **Business Phone:** (559)256-0188.

FRANCIS, CHERYL MARGARET
Association executive. **Personal:** Born Sep 7, 1949, New Orleans, LA; daughter of Albert Francis Jr; married F Daniel Cantrell. **Educ:** Loyola Univ, BS, 1971; Univ Chicago, PhD, educ admin, 1975. **Career:** Upward Bound Proj, New Orleans, prog dir, 1968-70; Headstart, recruiter, 1970; Scope Prog, teacher, 1970; Coll Urban Sci, Univ Ill, prof; Nat Com Cits Educ, midwest staff; MW Admin Ctr, res asst, 1971-74, dir, studs serv, 1972-73; Midwest Admin Ctr, Univ Chicago, res asst; Supt Schs, Skokie Ill, admin asst, 1974; Niles Twp Demographic Study, consult, 1974; Contracting Corp Am Educ Admin & Counr, dir, 1979-; City Chicago, Dept Human Servs, proj mgr, 1981-88, Title XX Prog, mgr, 1985-88; United Way Chicago, mgr non profit consult unit, 1988-; Safer Found, vpres core progs, 2002-; Nonprofit Financial Ctr, exec dir, currently. **Orgs:** Bd secy, Chicago Opps Industrialization Ctr Inc, bd dirs; Nat Alliance Black Sch Educ; Chicago Focus; Am Asn Sch Adminr; League Black Women; S Shore Comn; Asn for Supv & Curric; adv panel, Nat Inst for Educ Women's Aux Mary Bartelme Home for Girls; Am Educ Res Asn, Ford Fel Urban Adminr, 1971; Nat Felowships Fund Fel, 1974. **Honors/Awds:** Louis J Twomney award, Humanitarian Concern, 1971; Cardinal Key Hon Soc. **Business Addr:** Executive Director, Nonprofit Financial Center, 29 E Madison St Suite 1005, Chicago, IL 60602-4415, **Business Phone:** (312)252-0420.

FRANCIS, DELMA J
Journalist. **Personal:** Born Dec 16, 1953, Lancaster, KY; daughter of George Jr and Marie Terry. **Educ:** Eastern Kentucky Univ, Richmond KY, BA, Jour, 1975; Univ Louisville, Louisville, KY, MS, community develop, 1978. **Career:** Lexington Herald, Lexington, KY, reporter, 1975-76; Louisville Times, Louisville, KY, reporter, 1976-86; Hartford Courant, Hartford, CT, asst bur chief, 1986-89; Richmond Times-Dispatch, Richmond, VA, asst city ed, 1989-94; Star Tribune, Minneapolis, MN, asst features ed, currently. **Orgs:** Louisville Asn Black Communicators, 1977-86; former alternate dir, Nat Asn Black Journalists, 1979-; Choral Club Louisville, 1981-86; vpres, Conn Asn Black Communicators, 1987-89; Big Brothers & Big Sisters, 1990-91; dir, Ebenezer Baptist Church Orchestra, 1990-94; Ebenezer Baptist Church Sanctuary choir, 1990-94; Richmond Festival Chorus, 1992-; Leigh Morris Chorale, 1994-; vpres, Twin Cities Black Journalists, 1995-. **Honors/Awds:** Investigative News Award, Ky Press Asn, 1976; Outstanding Communications Alumnus, Eastern Ky Univ, 1994. **Home Addr:** 7401 79th Ave N, Brooklyn Park, MN 55445-2608, **Home Phone:** (612)898-3274. **Business Addr:** Assistant Features Editor, Star Tribune, 425 Portland Ave N, Minneapolis, MN 55488, **Business Phone:** (612)673-1717.

FRANCIS, DR. E. ARACELIS
Educator, social worker. **Personal:** Born Dec 2, 1939, St Thomas, Virgin Islands of the United States; daughter of Amadeo I and Ethanie Maria Smith. **Educ:** Inter-Am Univ, BA (magna cum laude), 1960; Univ Chicago, Sch SS Admin, MA, 1964; Columbia Univ, Sch Social Work, DSW, 1979. **Career:** Adelphi Univ, Sch Soc Work, asst prof, 1971-75; Dept Social Welfare, exec dir, 1975-80; US Dept Health & Human Servs, HHS fel, 1980-81; Univ Md, Sch Social Work & CP, asst prof, 1982-85; Coun Social Work Educ, Minority Fel Prog, dir, 1986-; Howard Univ, Sch Social Work, adj assoc prof, 1995-96, assoc asst prof, 1997-; Coun Social Work Educ, Off Soc Work Educ, dir, 2004-, Minority Res Fellowship Prog, res dir, 2004-. **Orgs:** Am Public Welfare Assoc, 1962-, Acad Cert Soc Workers, 1965-; vice chmn, State Manpower Serv Coun, 1976-80; bd dir, League Women Voters VI, 1977-80, Caribbean Studies Assoc, 1981-85; pres, Nat Assoc Social Workers VI Chap, 1978-80; chmn, Comm Minority Groups, Coun Soc Work Ed, 1982-85; chmn, Comm Inquiry Nat Assoc Social Workers Metro DC Chap, 1984-86; chairperson, Planning Comn, Nat Assoc Social Workers, 1987; rec secy, Union Black Episcopalians, DC chap, 1990-92; Minority Issues Conf; nominations comn, Virgin Islands Asn, 1991-92; 1992 World Assembly Planning Sub comt, 1991-92; bd dir, Metrop Wash Chap Nat Assoc Social Workers, 1992-94; pres, Metrop Chap Nat Assoc Social Workers, 1994-96; bd, Columbia Univ Sch Social Work Alumni, 1998-. **Honors/Awds:** NIMH Scholarship, Columbia Univ, Sch Social Work, 1967-69, CWS Scholarship, 1969-70. **Special Achievements:** Author: Ed Black Task Force Report; Foreign Labor in the US VI; Two Outstanding Black Women in Social Welfare History: Mary Church Terrell andIda B Wells-Barnett; Wilma Peebles-Wilkins & E Arcelis Francis AFFILIA, vol 5, no 4, winter 1990; Black Americans in Ethnic Minority Soc Wk Mental Health Clinical Training Programs: Assessing the Past-Planning for the Future-NIHM survey 1989; Keynote Speaker: Expectations of Migration, Conference on Caribbean American Family, Brooklyn, NY, 1990; African Descent Immigrants, Chapter Public in Social Work With Immigrants, 2001; "The Status of former CSWE Ethnic Minority Doctoral Fellows in Social Work," Academic Journal of Social Work, Ed Vol 32, No Winter 96; chapter on African Descent Immigrants, in Social Work Practice with Immigrants and Refugees. **Home Addr:** 7836 Shepherd Hills Ct, Lorton, VA 22079-4325, **Home Phone:** (703)550-2750. **Business Phone:** (703)683-8080.

FRANCIS, DR. EDITH V.
School administrator. **Personal:** Born in Harlem, NY; daughter of James Audain and Iris; married Dr Gilbert H; children: Deborah Ann Scott-Martin, Denise Tolbert & Dwayne H. **Educ:** Hunter Col, BA, MA, childhood educ, MS, guidance; NYU, EdD, admin; Honorary degrees: Amer Bible Univ, PhD, Humanity Art, 1969, World Univ, PhD, Arts Phil, 1973. **Career:** Ed Dept Media Ctr-Audio Visual Proj Ph I Stud Teacher Imp, adj pr, 1959-61; Stud Teaching, instr suprv, 1962-63; Elem Sch, teacher, 1963-66; Stud Teaching Prog, critic teacher, 1963-66; Jr/Sr HS, suprv, 1967-68; Campus Schs, asst dir, 1968-69; Hunter Col Elem Sch, princ, 1968-69; NY City Bd Ed, consult, 1969-70; Except Gifted Children Proj PS, coord, 1970-71; Princeton Reg Schs, prin, 1970-76, act spt schs, 1976-77; Hunter Col Dept Curr & Teaching; adj prof, 1971-72; US Dept HEW, consult, 1973-; Ed Testing Serv, tech asst consult 1975-; Ewing Township Pub Schs, supt schs, 1977-87; Columbia Univ, Teachers Col, prof, practitioner, scholar, 1987-91; Irvington Public Schs, supt schs, 1991-92; East Orange Pub Sch,dir, community & adult education, 1992-2002, prin adult high sch, 2002. **Orgs:** Pres, Princeton Reg Admin Asn, 1974-75; chairperson ed comm Princeton Bicentennial Comm, 1974-77; bd dir, Pub Lib, 1976-77; Witherspoon Devel Corp, 1976-82; legislative comm NJ; Am Asn Sch Admin, 1977-; bd dir, YWCA Trenton NJ, 1977-89; int pres Grand Basileus Zeta Phi Beta, 1980-86; bd examrs, NJ Ed Dept, 1980-86; bd trustee Nat Assault Illiteracy, 1982-86; bd dir, Helene Fuld Hosp, 1982-86; governors task force Trenton NJ 1982-86; bd dir, Nat Merit Scholar Corp 1982-87; Nat Asn Suprv & Curriculum Devel, Nat Coun Admin Women Ed, NJ Coun Admin Women Ed, CUNY Black Profs & Admin Women Ed, Am Asn Sch Admin, Am Asn Univ Profs, Zeta Phi Beta Bd Dirs, School masters NJ, NJ Asn School Admin, NJ Ed Asn, NJ Coun Ed, Phi Beta Kappa; The Links Inc, 1986-, pres, Cent NJ chap, 1997-. **Honors/Awds:** Inter Nat Women's Achievement Award, Global News Synd, 1970; Woman of the Year, Zeta of the Year, 1971; Nat Asn Advan Colored People Award, 1978; Outstanding Woman Award, 1980; Life Membership Award, 1982; Honor Awards: NJ Dept of Ed, Rider Col, Ewing Cmmty & NJ State Fed Colored Womens Club, 1979; Prof Dev Award Mercer Cty CC 1980; Award Trenton St Col 1980; One of Most Infuential Black Amer, Commendation by Hamilton Twp Mayor, Mansfield M Finney Achievement Award, Ed Award Gamma Rho Sigma, 1981-84; Black Media Inc citation, 1982; Nat Black Monitor Hall of Fame Award 1982; Alpha Kappa Alpha Award for dedicated service 1982; Friends of United Negro Col Fund Award for Outstanding Ldrshp & Commitment to Furthering Higher Education, 1982; Natl Cncl of Women, The US Inc Woman of Conscience Award, 1982; Distinguised African-American Woman's Award, 1995; Leadership America Completion Award, 1998; East Orange Superintendent's Award for Excellence, 1998. **Special Achievements:** Speaking engagements include: Rider Col, Mercer Cty Com Col, Trenton St Col, Leadership Conf, Cleveland OH; Publications: "Booker T Washington, Temporizer

& Compromiser", "Educating Gifted Children," "Gifted Children As We See Them". **Home Addr:** 4116 Melrose Ct, Melbourne, FL 32940.

FRANCIS, GILBERT H.
Executive, educator. **Personal:** Born May 27, 1930, Brooklyn, NY; married Dr Edith V Francis; children: Dr Deborah Scott Martin, Denise Tolbert, Dwayne H Francis. **Educ:** St John's Univ, BBA, LLD; City Col; Hunter Col; City Univ. **Career:** Educator, Executive (retired); US Dept Health Educ & Welfare Off Civil Rights, asst chief elem & sec educ branch, 1967-73; NJ Div Civil Rights Dept Law & Pub Safety, dir civil rights, 1973-74; Supermarkets Gen Corp, dir equal employ opportunity, 1974-76; Comprehensive Compliance Servs, consult & pres, 1976; US Dept Educ, asst chief tech assistance, 1976-86; NJ State Dept Educ, educ prog specialist, 1986-97; NJ State Dept Treas, sr mgt specialist, 1997-02; lectr, Niagara Univ; lectr, Hunter Col; lectr, Trenton State Col; lectr, Lehman Col; lectr, Sweet Briar Col; Nat Pan Hellenic Coun, pres. **Orgs:** EDGES Group; nat comn co-chair, Assault Illiteracy Prog; bd dirs, chair higher educ prog NJ Conf Branches NAACP; Nat Alliance Black Sch Educrs; life mem, NAACP; Lions Intl, Frontiers Intl; legal comn Intl Asn Off Human Rights Agencies; Nat Asn Human Rights Workers, Comn One Hundred; comn affairs adv, Hunter Col Campus Schs, NYC; Phi Beta Sigma Frat Inc; pres, Nat Pan-Hellenic Coun Inc. **Honors/Awds:** Service Award, NJ Div Civil Rights; Distinguished Service Award, Nat Pan-Hellenic Coun; Distinguished Service Key Award, Phi Beta Sigma Fraternity; Man of the Year Award, Phi Beta Sigma Frat Inc; Distinguished Service Award, Zeta Phi Beta Sor; Hon Doctorates, World Univ L' Universite Libre, Boys H S Dist Alumnus Award; Man of the Yr Award, Zeta Phi Beta Sor Inc, Central NJ; Distinguished Humanitarian Award, Phi Beta Sigma Frat Inc; Key to the City Newark NJ; Dr Alvin J McNeil Outstanding Service Award, Phi Beta Sigma Frat Inc. **Military Serv:** AUS, corpl, 2 yrs; Army Service Medal. *

FRANCIS, HENRY MINTON
Consultant. **Personal:** Born Dec 23, 1922, Washington, DC; son of John Richard Francis Jr and Alice King Wormley; married Doris Elizabeth Hall, 1944; children: Marsha, Henry, Peter, M Kim Ferris & John. **Educ:** Univ Pa, 1941; US Mil Acad West Point, BS, eng, 1944; Syracuse Univ, MBA,honors, 1960. **Career:** Dept Housing & Urban Develop, 1965-67, exec asst to first secy, Office Postmaster Gen, Office Planning & System Analysis, dep plans, Richmond Orgn, 1967-70, exec vpres; AVCO Corp, Printing & Publishing, vpres, 1970-73; Dept Defense, dep asst secy, Defense Human Goals Prog, 1973-77; Howard Univ, 1979-81; Univ Planning Dir, Univ-Wide Self-Study Task Force, exec dir, Presidential Search Comt, exec secy, 1981-89, special asst to pres, Govt Affairs Dir; Secy Army, civilian aide, 1984-92; Black Revolutionary War Patriots Found, pres, 1992-96; Howard Univ, dir univ res & planning; Francis & Francis Inc, pres & chief exec officer, currently. **Orgs:** Volunteer, Catholic Charities, Archdiocese Wash; dir, Share; dir, Christ Child Soc; life mem, Disabled Am Veterans; Veterans Foreign Wars; Asn Grad US Mil Acad, trustee emeritus; Wash Inst Foreign Affairs; bd mgrs, Wash Historical Soc; dir, USO-Metro in Wash; Nat Press Club; Army & Navy Club Wash. **Honors/Awds:** Distinguished Civilian Service Medal, Dept Defense; Cert Appreciation Patriotic Civilian Service, Dept Army; Cert Appreciation, Urban League; Cert Appreciation, Distinguished Service Award, NAACP; Cert Appreciation, LDF; Beta Gamma Sigma; Knight Soverign Military Order Malta, 1996. **Military Serv:** AUS, lt col, 1944-65; Army Concept Team, Vietnam; comdr artillery troops, Korean Conflict, WWII; staff officer, Comptroller Army, Secy Defense.

FRANCIS, JAMES L.
Government official. **Personal:** Born Dec 30, 1943, Cincinnati, OH; son of James L and Marjorie L Murphy; married Melanie Hall Francis, Aug 6, 1966; children: Renee L Francis, Darryl L Francis. **Educ:** Ohio Univ, Athens, OH, BA, polit sci, 1965; Howard Univ, Wa DC, grad studies, 1967; Wright State Univ, Dayton, OH, 1976; Central Mich Univ, Mt Pleasant, MPA, 1978. **Career:** Govt Employs Ins Co, Wa DC, claims examiner; City Dayton, OH, field rep, human rels coun, 1970-71, asst to exec dir, human rels coun, 1971-72, supt, div property mgt, 1972-78, dir pub works, 1978-85, asst city mgr, administrative servs, 1985-90, exec asst, clerk city comn, 1990. **Orgs:** Alpha Pi Phi Fraternity, 1963-; Westmont Optimist Club, 1984-; Intl City Mgrs Asn, 1985-; Sigma Pi Phi Fraternity, 1986-; bd mem, Nat Forum Black Pub Admin, 1987-96; bd trustees, OH Municipal League, 1990-97; OH Adv Coun mem, US Civil Rights Comn. **Honors/Awds:** Readers Digest Found, Sister City Tech Asst Prog Monrovia, Liberia, 1986; Certificate of Merit, Louisville KY, Bd Aldermen, 1988; Marks Excellence Award, Nat Forum Black Pub Adminr, 1998. *

FRANCIS, REV. DR. JAMES N
Clergy. **Personal:** Born Mar 25, 1951, Kingston, Jamaica; son of David and Esther; married Edna Mc Intosh, Aug 14, 1976; children: Sharice, Crystal, James Jr & Justin. **Educ:** New York Univ & Pace Univ, BA, 1976; Merrill Lynch Sch Econ, MBA, 1983; Trinity Evangelical, MA, Biblical Studies, 1991; Jacksonville Theol Sem, DMin, 1996. **Career:** Merrill Lynch, stockbroker; Wall-Street, vpres finance; Merrill Lynch & Co; Monument Faith, pastor, sr paster & founder, currently, chmn, currently. **Orgs:** Chmn, Operation Reach Out Across Miami. **Honors/Awds:** Pastor of the Year, Church of God, 1996; Metro Miami Dade County, Key to the City, 1998; MIP Supervising Pastor Award, 2002. **Business Addr:** Chairman, Monument of Faith, 1956 NW 183rd St, North Miami Beach, FL 33179-5044, **Business Phone:** (305)621-1354.

FRANCIS, LIVINGSTON S
Management consultant, educator. **Personal:** Born Dec 2, 1929, Brooklyn, NY; son of James R and Ethel Price; married Helen Owensby; children: Brian, Ronald & Gary. **Educ:** Adelphi Univ, Garden City, NY, BS, MSW; Columbia Univ, New York, NY, Management Cert. **Career:** NYC Parks, Recreation & Cultural Affairs, New York, NY, asst comnr, 1960-69; Community Cou Greater New York, NY, assoc exec dir, 1970-77; YMCA Greater NY-Harlem Br, New York, NY, exec dir, 1977-80; Greater NY Fund/United Way, NY, dep exec dir, 1980-86; NY State Univ, Farmingdale, assoc adjunct prof, 1974-76; Adelphi Univ, Garden City NY, adjunct prof, 1976-80; Fordham Univ, New York NY, adjunct prof, 1980-2000; Livingston S Francis Assoc, pres & chief exec officer, currently. **Orgs:** Reveille Club; Omega Psi Phi; chair emer, bd dirs, North General Hosp; dir, United Hosp Fund; trustee, Helene Fuld Col Nursing; pres, Livingston S Francis Asn, Roosevelt NY, 1986-; exec dir, Asn Black Charities, NY, 1988-. **Honors/Awds:** Governor's Award for African Americans of Distinction, NY, 1994; Honorary Doctorate of Humane Letters, St John's Univ. **Business Addr:** President, Cheif Executive Officer, Livingston S Francis Associates, 65 Bauer Ave, Roosevelt, NY 11575, **Business Phone:** (516)546-8455.

FRANCIS, DR. NORMAN C
College administrator. **Personal:** Born Mar 20, 1931, Lafayette, LA. **Educ:** Xavier Univ, BS, 1952; Loyola Univ Law Sch, JD, 1955. **Career:** Xavier Univ, dean men, 1957, dir stud personnel serv, 1963, asst to pres, 1964, exec vpres, 1967, pres, 1968-. **Orgs:** Bd dir, WLAE-TV; Carnegie Found Advan Teaching; Am Asn Higher Educ; chmn bd, Col Entrance Exam Bd, 1976-. **Honors/Awds:** The Presidential Medal of Freedom, 2007. **Military Serv:** AUS, Third Armored Div, 1956-57. **Business Addr:** President, Xavier Uniiversity Louisiana, 1 Drexel Dr, New Orleans, LA 70125.

FRANCIS, PATRICK JOHN
Chancellor (Education), association executive. **Personal:** Born Sep 4, 1964, New Orleans, LA; son of Norman C and Blanche Macdonald; married Kristi; children: 3. **Educ:** Univ Notre Dame, South Bend, BA, am studies, 1986; LBJ Sch Pub Affairs Univ Tex, Austin, MPA, pub affairs, 1988. **Career:** Sloan Fel Grad Study Pub Affairs, 1986-87; US Senate Com Labor & Human Resources, Washington, DC, intern, 1987; Tex Dept Agr, proj consult, 1988; House Res Orgn Tex House Representatives, researcher & writer, 1989; Tex State Auditor's Off, performance auditor, 1990; Tex Asn Sch Bd, asst dir govt rels; Off Gov Tex, special asst to lieutenent gov, 1998; Univ Tex Syst, asst vice chancellor health affairs, currently. **Orgs:** Ed staff, quart publ, Profiling Minority Alumni LBJ Sch Pub Affairs, 1990.

FRANCIS, DR. RICHARD L.
Psychiatrist. **Personal:** Born Oct 10, 1919, Millerton, NY; son of Champ Carter and Irene Virginia Harris; married De Wreathe Valores Green (deceased); children: DeWreathe V & Irene D. **Educ:** Howard Univ, BS, 1941; Howard Univ Med Sch, MD, 1944; Sydenham Hosp, NY, Internship, 1945; VA Hosp Tuskegee, AL, psychiatric Residency, 1949; Harlem Valley psychiatric Ctr, Wingdale, NY, psychiatric Residency, 1957; Vanderbilt Clinic Columbia Presbyterian Med Ctr, psychiatric Residency,1959; NY State psychiatric Inst, Post Grad psychiatric & Neurol, 1960; Syracuse Univ, Advanced Mgt Training or Admin Pub Health Facilities, 1971. **Career:** Psychiatrist (retired); NY City Farm Colony Staten Island, resident physician, 1945-47; VA Hosp, Tuskegee, AL, neuro psychiatrist, 1947-53; Harlem Valley Psychiatric Ctr, Wingdale, NY, sr physician, 1955; Harlem Valley Psychiatric Ctr, supvr psychiatrist, 1955-61; Harlem Valley Psychiatric Ctr, asst dir, 1961-67; Sunmont Develop Ctr, Tupper Lake, NY, dir, 1968-81, chief med Serv, 1981-88, Psychiatric consul, 1988-99. **Orgs:** Asst dir & dir, NY State Dept Mental Hygiene Facility, asst dir, Harlem Valley Psychiatric Ctr, 1961-67, secy, Mid-Hudson Dist Br Am Psychiatric Assoc, 1963-67; dir, Sunmount Develop Ctr, 1968-81; adv, comn N Cty Comn Col, 1968-77; chmn, ethics comn Am Assoc Mental Deficiency, 1971-72; chmn, Narcotic Guidance Coun Tupper Lake, NY 1971-76; vpres, Rotary Tupper Lake NY, 1973; Nat Med Assoc; Am Assoc Psychiatric Admin; NY State Med Soc Franklin Cty Med Soc; Am Col Forensic Examiners, 1998. **Honors/Awds:** NY State Qualified Psychiatrist, 1959; Cert by Am Bd psych & Neurolo Psych, 1970; Community Leaders of America Award, 1973; Dipl, The Am Bd Forensic Med, 1998. **Special Achievements:** Publ "Further Studies in EKG Changes in Old Age", 1947. **Military Serv:** AUS, Med Corp capt, 1953-55; Nat Defense Service Medal, Army OccupationMed Germany. *

FRANCISCO, ANTHONY M.
Government official. **Personal:** Born Jun 30, 1960, Nashville, TN; son of Maurine E Moore and Anceo M; married Kimberly Statum, Oct 3, 1987; children: Alexandria Morgan. **Educ:** Univ Okla, Norman, BA, 1981; Univ Tex, Austin, SPPS, 1981; Syracuse Univ, Syracuse, NY, MPA, 1983. **Career:** Syracuse Housing Authority, NY, admin aide, 1983; City Kans, MO, mgt intern, 1983-84; City Okla, OK, mgt, budget analyst, 1984-86; financial enterprise budget officer, 1986-88, dir st maintenance, 1988-90, investment officer, 1990-; City Norman, OK, treas, 2002, finance dir, currently. **Orgs:** Christian Church, 1962-; local pres, Kappa Alpha Psi Fraternity, 1979-; Int City Mgt Asn, 1983-88; Ambassadors' Concert Choir, 1985-; local pres, Nat Forum for Black Public Admin, 1987-. **Business Addr:** Treasurer, Finance Director, City of Norman, 201 W Gray Bldg C, PO Box 370, Norman, OK 73069, **Business Phone:** (405)366-5413.

FRANCISCO, JOSEPH SALVADORE
Educator, physical chemist. **Personal:** Born Mar 26, 1955, New Orleans, LA; son of Joseph Salvadore Francisco Sr and Lucinda Baker; married. **Educ:** Univ Tex, Austin, Tex, BS, hons, 1977; Mass Inst Tech, Cambridge, Mass, PhD, 1983. **Career:** Univ Tex, Robert Welch Undergraduate Res fel, 1973-76; Univ Tex, jr fel, 1977; MIT, HEW fel, 1978-81; Univ Sydney, Sydney, Australia, vis lectr, 1981; St Edmund's Col, Cambridge Univ, res fel, 1983-85; Cambridge Univ, Cambridge, Eng, res fel, 1983-85; Mass Inst Tech, Cambridge, Mass, provost post doctoral fel, 1985-86; Wayne St Univ, Detroit, Mich, asst prof chem, 1986-90, assoc prof, 1990-94; Alfred P Sloan Found, res fel, 1990-92; Calif Inst Technol, res assoc, 1991; John Simon Guggenheim fel, 1993-94; Calif Inst Technol, Jet Propulsion Lab, vis scientist, 1993-94; Purdue Univ, prof phys chem & earth & atmosphere sci, 1995; Sterling Brownvis prof, Williams Col, 1998; Purdue Univ, William E Moore distinguished prof earth & atmospheric sci & chem, currently. **Orgs:** Fac adv, WSU, Nobcche Student Chapter, 1986-; vol, Inst Res Appreticeship Minority High Sch Students, 1987-; MIT Corp Visit Comn, 1987-; NASA HBCURes Panel, 1987-; consult, Inst Defense Analysis, 1988-; Am Physical Soc; AAAS; Nat Org Black Chemists & Chem Engrs; Sigma Xi, 1990-; Naval Research Adv Comt, Dept Navy, 1994-96; Army Sci Bd, 1996-. **Honors/Awds:** Wayne State Faculty Award, Wayne State Univ, 1986; Presidential YoungInvestigator Award, Nat Sci Found, 1988; Camille & Henry DreyfusTeacher-Scholar Award, Dreyfus Found, 1990-95; Outstanding Teacher Award,Nat Org Black Chemists & Chem Engrs, 1992; Percy Julian Research Award,1995; Mentor Award, AAAS, 1994; Alexander van Humbolt US Senior Scientist Award, 2001; McCoy Award, Purdue University, 2007. **Special Achievements:** Co-author book, Chemical Kinetics & Dynamics, 1989. **Business Addr:** William E Moore Distinguished Professor, Department of Earth & Atmospheric Sciences, Purdue University, Department of Chemistry, 1393 H C Brown Bldg, 560 Oval Dr, West Lafayette, IN 47907-1393, **Business Phone:** (765)494-7851.

FRANCO, JULIO CESAR
Baseball player. **Personal:** Born Aug 23, 1958, Hato Mayor, Dominican Republic. **Career:** Philadelphia Phillies, infielder, 1982; Cleveland Indians, infielder, 1983-88, 1996-97; Tex Rangers, infielder, 1989-93; Chicago White Sox, 1994; Chiba Lotte Marines, 1995, 1998; Milwaukee Brewers, 1997; Tampa Bay Devil Rays, 1999; Samsung Lions, 2000; Atlanta Braves, 2001-05, 2007; New York Mets, infielder, 2006-; free agent, currently. **Honors/Awds:** Most Valuable Person, Carolina League Peninsula Pilots, 1980; Topps All-Star Rookie Team, 1983; Silver Slugger Award, Am League, 1988, 1989,1990, 1991 & 1994; American League All-Star Team, 1989, 1990 & 1991; Most Valuable Person, All-Star Game, 1990; Milton Richman You Gotta Have Heart Award, 2007. **Special Achievements:** The oldest man to hit a home run in the big leagues, 2005.

FRANCOIS, EMMANUEL SATURNIN
Surgeon. **Personal:** Born Dec 23, 1938, Port-au-Prince, Haiti; son of Saturnin F Ceau and Fausta Lauren Ceau; married Edda Gibbs, Jun 19, 1965; children: Randolph Emmanuel, Herve Daniel, Chantal Claire. **Educ:** Col St Louis De Gonzague, attended 1958; Univ Haiti, attended 1964. **Career:** Surgeon (retired); Harlem Hosp Ctr Columbia Univ, 1966-72; Provident Hosp, 1972-73; pvt pract, surgeon, 1973. **Orgs:** Baltimore City Med Soc; Med Chi Soc MD; Am Med Asn; Nat Med Asn; Asn Haitian Physician Abroad; Am Asn Automotive Med; Trauma Soc; Smithsonian Inst. **Military Serv:** AUS, maj, 1969-71. *

FRANK, TELLIS JOSEPH
Basketball player. **Personal:** Born Apr 26, 1965, Gary, IN. **Educ:** Western Ky Univ. **Career:** Basketball player(retired); Golden State Warriors, 1987-89; Miami Heat, 1989-90; Phonola Caserta, 1990-93; Minnesota Timberwolves, 1991-92; Scandone Avellino, 1998-99, Basket Livorno, 1999-2000; Longobardi Scafati, 2000-01; Los Angeles City, asst mens basketball coach; Hampton Univ, asst mens basketball coach, 2002.

FRANKLIN, ALLEN D.
Educator. **Personal:** Born May 25, 1945, Berkeley, CA. **Educ:** Merritt Col, AA, 1966; San Francisco State Univ, BA, 1969; Univ Calif, Berkeley, MBA, 1971, PhD, 1974. **Career:** Math & Computing Dept, Lawrence Berkeley Lab, math programmer, 1969-71; Far West Lab, consult, 1972-73; Planning Dept City Hayward, consult, 1973-; Grad Sch Bus Admin, Univ Calif,

Berkeley, instr, 1973-74; Calif St Univ, Hayward Sch Bus & Econ, pres, assoc dean & asst. **Orgs:** Caucus of Black Economists/Nat Econ Asn; bd dir, Minority Bus Assistance Stud Develop Found; Asn computing Mach. **Honors/Awds:** Certificate of Honor, Bus Majors Asn, Calif St Univ, Hayward, 1974; Outstanding Young Man Am, 1975; Certificate of Appreciation, The Exchange Club Oakland, 1975. **Military Serv:** USNR, petty officer 3c, 1967-69. **Business Addr:** Associate Dean, California State University, Hayward, CA 95380.

FRANKLIN, ARETHA LOUISE
Singer, actor. **Personal:** Born Mar 25, 1942, Memphis, TN; daughter of Clarence L and Barbara Siggers; married Glynn Turman, 1978 (divorced); married Ted White, 1961 (divorced 1984); children: Clarence, Edward, Teddy & Kecalf. **Educ:** Julliard Sch, piano. **Career:** Gospel singer, 1952-61; Rhythm & Blues & Soul vocalist, 1960-84; Pop Music vocalist, 1985-; Albums include: Aretha, 1961; Electrifying, 1962; Tender Moving & Swinging, 1962; Laughing on the Outside, 1962; Unforgettable,1964; Songs of Faith, 1964; Running Out of Fools, 1964; Yeah, 1965; Soul Sister, 1966; Queen of Soul, 1967; I Never Loved a Man, 1967; Once in a Lifetime, 1967; Aretha Arrives, 1967; Lady Soul, 1968; Live at Paris,Olympia, 1968; Aretha Now, 1968; Soul 69, 1969; Today I Sing the Blues,1969; Aretha Gold, 1969; I Say a Little Prayer, 1969; This Girl's in Love with You, 1970; Spirit in the Dark, 1970; Don't Play That Song, 1970; Live at the Filmore West, 1971; Young, Gifted, & Black, 1971; Amazing Grace, 1972; Hey Hey Now, 1973; Let Me Into Your Life, 1974; With Everything I Feel in Me, 1975; You, 1975; Sparkle, 1976; Sweet Passion, 1977; Almighty Fire, 1978; Diva, 1979; Aretha, 1980; Who's Zoom in Who, 1985; Aretha After Hours, 1987; Love All the Hurt Away, 1987; One Lord, One Faith, 1988; Through the Storm, 1989; A Rose Is Still A Rose, 1998; One Lord, One Faith, One Baptism, 2003; So Damn Happy, 2003; Jewels In The Crown: All-Star Duets With The Queen, 2007; Soundtrack including: In Good Company, 2004; "Entourage", 2005; Larry the Cable Guy: Health Inspector, 2006; Bobby, 2006; Gracie, 2007; Eye See Me, 2007; Films, Blue Brothers2000, 1998; The Blue Brothers, 1980. **Orgs:** Delta Sigma Theta Sorority Inc. **Honors/Awds:** Grammy Award, Best Female R & B Performance, 1967-74 (every year), 1982, 1986, 1988, 1989, 2004, 2006 & 2008; Grammy Living Legend Award, 1991; Grammy Lifetime Achievement Award, 1994; Lifetime Achievement Award, R & B Found, 1992; Nat Medal for the Arts, 1999; honored by and appeared on "Divas Live," VH1, 2001; Damon J Keith Soul & Spirit Humanitarian Award, 2003; Presidential Medal of Freedom, 2005; MusiCares Person of the Year, 2008. **Special Achievements:** Author: Aretha: From These Roots; first woman to be admitted to the Rock and Roll Hall Of Fame; performed at President Bill Clinton's presidential inauguration in 1992; song "R-E-S-P-E-C-T" ranked no 4 on Natl Endowment for the Arts & Recording Indust Asn of Am list of The 365 Songs of the Century, 2001; Nineth Greatest Rock 'n' Roll Artist of all time, Rolling Stone. **Business Phone:** (310)859-4000.

FRANKLIN, AUDREY DEMPS
School administrator. **Personal:** Born Mar 20, 1950, Ft Meade, FL; daughter of John and Garnell Demps; married James, Jul 29, 1972; children: Wesley James. **Educ:** Benette Col, BS, 1972; NC A & T State Univ, MA, 1978. **Career:** Bennett Col, mgt info, 1973-90, employee benefits specialist, pres, 1990-. **Orgs:** Financial secy, Bennett Col, NAA, 1991-98; pres, Alpha Kappa Alpha Sorority, 1998-; assoc mem, Jack & Jill Am, 1998; pres, Nat Alumnae Asn. **Honors/Awds:** Alpha Kappa Alpha, Silver Award, 1997; Bennett Col, Susie W Jones, 1998. **Home Addr:** 404 W Meadowview Rd, Greensboro, NC 27406, **Home Phone:** (336)379-9613. **Business Phone:** (336)370-8669.

FRANKLIN, BERNARD W.
School administrator. **Educ:** Simpson Col, BA, relig, 1974; Western Md Col, MEd; Columbia Univ Teachers Col, PhD. **Career:** Livingstone Col, pres; St Augustines Col, chief exec officer; Johnson C Smith Univ, asst vpres stud affairs; Miami Univ, asst prof, 1983; Va Union Univ, pres, 1999-2003; Nat Col Athletic Asn, sr vpres governance, 2003, exec vpres mem servs & student-athlete affairs, currently. **Orgs:** Exec Comt, Nat Col Athletic Asn; vice chair, Division II Presidents Coun, Nat Col Athletic Assn. **Special Achievements:** One of 28 American Council on Education (ACE) Fellows for the 1988-89. **Business Phone:** (317)917-6222.

FRANKLIN, CLARENCE FREDERICK
Educator. **Personal:** Born Jan 30, 1945, Knoxville, TN; son of Geraldine Franklin Waller and Clarence David Shell; divorced; children: Carissa Racquel. **Educ:** Tuskegee Inst, attended 1963; Univ TN, attended 1964; Cooper Inst, BS, bus mgt, 1978. **Career:** Union Carbide Corp, machinist, 1968-79; Martin Marietta Inc, foreman, training admin. **Orgs:** VFW, 1962; alumni assoc, Tuskegee Inst; Optimist Club Mechanicsville; past pres & mem, Optimist Club Mechanicsville, Lonsdale; CC Russell Masonic Lodge 262; Payne Ave Baptist Church; secy, 100 Black Men Inc, Knoxville, TN. **Honors/Awds:** Hon Student, Campbell High, 1962; Hon Student, Cooper Inst, 1975-78; Optimist Int, Outstanding & Distinguished Lt-Governor, 1996-97; Unsung Hero Award, NAACP, 2000; Bronze Man, Iota Phi Lambda sorority, 2001; Male of The Year, Optimist Club Mechanicsville, Lonsdale, 2001. **Special Achievements:** First African American to enter the Univ Tennessee's school of Agriculture in 1964. **Military Serv:** AUS, spec-4, 2 yrs; Vietnam Serv Medals. **Home Addr:** 4258 St Lucia Lane, Knoxville, TN 37921, **Home Phone:** (865)909-0110.

FRANKLIN, COSTELLA M.
Nurse. **Personal:** Born Mar 14, 1932, Durham, NC; divorced; children: Saadia Ardisa, Kevin Leonard, Michale Bernard. **Educ:** Hampton Sch Nursing, attended 1953; Univ Calif. **Career:** Nurse (retired); Childrens Hosp, WA, nurse, 1955-56; Childrens Hosp Los Angeles, asst head nurse, 1956-60; Daniel Freeman Hosp, asst head nurse, 1960-65; Coronary Care Memorial Hosp Long Beach, nurse, 1968-71. **Orgs:** Life mem, Blue Angels Social & Charity Club, 1968-; chair, Banneker Alumni Parent Asn Developmentally Disabled Adults, 1977; Calif Prof Nurses Asn; Calif Coun Retarded; Nat Asn Retarded C; SW Asn Retarded C; Except Children's Found Women's Aux; Except Adult Parent Guild. **Honors/Awds:** Los Angeles Press Club Award, 1967; Lane Bryant Vol Citizens Community Award, 1967; Calif state Senate Award, Senator James Wedworth, 1968; Merit Award, Long Beach Memorial Hosp Qual control, 1969; Citation award for outstanding achievement in community, 1971; Angel of the year Award, 1972; Distinguished Award, 1977; Sweetheart of the Year, New Decade, 1980. **Home Addr:** 1351 E Bankers Dr, Carson, CA 90746. *

FRANKLIN, CURTIS U., JR.
Psychiatrist. **Personal:** Born Oct 30, 1929, Commerce, TX; married Rose Marie Henry; children: Curtis, III, Vicki, Lisa, William, Valerie, Rose Marie, Jr. **Educ:** Prairie View A&M Col; Fisk Univ, AB, 1949; Howard Univ, Col Med, MD, 1953. **Career:** Pvt Prac, psychiat, 1967-; Psychiat Receiving Ctr KC, residency psychiat, 1964-67; Doctor's Clinic KC, prac internal med, 1960-64; Homer G Phillips Hosp, internship residency. **Orgs:** Psychiatric consult, Swope Pkwy Health Ctr; Catholic Family & Community Serv; Vocational Rehab; Social Security Admin; asst clinical prof, Univ Miss-KC Med Sch; diplo, Am Bd Psychiatry & Neurol fel, Am Psychiatric Asn; Am Med Asn; Nat Med Asn; Miss Med Asn; Jackson Co Med Soc; KC Med Soc; Alpha Phi Alpha. **Military Serv:** USAR, med corp capt, 1955-58. **Business Addr:** Psychiatrist, 4301 Main Suite 14, Kansas City, MO 64111.

FRANKLIN, DAVID M. See Obituaries section.

FRANKLIN, DON
Actor. **Personal:** Born Dec 14, 1960, Chicago, IL; son of Donald and Dorothy Jean; married Sheila Burke (divorced 1997); married Kristine, May 5, 2002; children: 2. **Educ:** Studied acting under Soren Kirk, Zephyr Theatre; Dan LaMarte, Training Ctr Working Actor; studied voice under Robert Berthold, Joel Ewing. **Career:** NK & Co, head out-trade clerk; Films: Somewhere in Time, 1980; Fast Forward, 1985; The Big Picture, 1989; Moving, 1988; Nasty Boys, 1989; Killor Be Killed, 1990; Fight for Justice: The Nancy Conn Story, 1995; BlackDawn, 2005; tv series: Nightwatch, 1988; Young Riders, 1990-92; SeaQuestDSV, 1993-95; Seven Days, 1998-01; The Bernie Mac Show, 2004; CSI: Miami,2005; Frame Up, 2005; tv movies: Asteroid, 1997; Seven Days, 1998; tvguest appearances: The Cosby Show, 1987; The Outer Limits, 1997; LivingSingle, 1997; Moesha, 1998; Girlfriends, 2000; The Dist, 2000; She Spies,2002; Wild Card, 2003; theatre: Playboy of the West Indies, The Tempest,Dealing, West Memphis Mojo, The Middle of Nowhere in the Middle of the Night, A Chorus Line, One Shining Moment, Kismet, Life of Bessie Smith,Pippin, Amen Corner; TV episode: Smoked, 2006; Shalom, 2006; Pilot, 2006;What If They Run?, 2006; Day Break, 2007; What If She's Lying?, 2007; Double Down, 2007; Blowback, 2007; "Journeyman", 2007; Half Load, 2009; "The Closer", 2009. **Orgs:** Screen Actors Guild; Am Fed Television & Radio Artists; Actors Equity Asn. **Honors/Awds:** Joseph Jefferson Nomination, Best Actor, The Middle of Nowhere in the Middle of the Night. **Business Addr:** Actor, c/o Abrams Artists Agency, 275 Seventh Ave 26th Fl, New York, NY 10001, **Business Phone:** (646)486-4600.*

FRANKLIN, EUGENE T., JR.
Association executive, educator. **Personal:** Born Jun 8, 1945, Detroit, MI; married Beverkly King. **Educ:** KY State Col, BA, 1972; Univ Louisville, MEd, EPDA Grad, 1972. **Career:** KY State Univ, dir Title III proj teacher educ instr, 1972-74; Detroit Urban League, dir educ serv; Detroit Pub Sch, Facilitator; Detroit Pub Sch, asst prin Ford Henry High, currently. **Orgs:** Nat Educ Asn; KY Ctr Bio-Psychosynthesis; Asn Teacher Educ; Am Inst Econ Res; Detroits Coalition Peaceful Integration; Com Desegregation; Frankfort-Franklin Co Comn Human Rights. **Honors/Awds:** KY Sickle Cell Anemia Found, 1971; Receipient grad fel, Univ Louisville; butzel scholarship Detroit Urban League, 1970; deans list KY State Univ. **Special Achievements:** First black houseparents researchers KYC Child Welfare Research Found. **Military Serv:** AUSR 1966-72. **Business Addr:** Facilitator, The Detroit Public School, Sch Ctr Bldg, 3031 W Grand Blvd, Detroit, MI 48202, **Business Phone:** (313)494-7567.

FRANKLIN, GAYLE JESSUP. See JESSUP, GAYLE LOUISE.

FRANKLIN, DR. GRANT L
Physician. **Personal:** Born Jun 21, 1918, Pauls Valley, OK; married Rita Bruckschlogl; children: Monique, Julie, Grant Jr & Dr Carol Susan. **Educ:** Langston Univ, BS, 1941; Atlanta Univ, MS, 1947; Meharry Med Col, MD, 1951. **Career:** Hubbard Hosp, intern, 1951-52; Cleveland Veterans Admin & Case Western Res Univ Hosps, gen surg residency, 1952-56; Polyclinic Hosp, chief surg; Woman's Hosp, chief surg; Case Western Res Med Sch, sr clin instr surg; Cleveland Wade Veterans Admin Hosp, surg consult; Pvt Pract, surgeon; Huron Road Hosp, assoc chief surg. **Orgs:** Cert Am Bd Surg, 1957; Am Col Surgeons; 1959-; Cleveland Acad Med; Cleveland Surg Soc; Pan Am Surg Soc; Soc Abdominal Surgeons; AMA; Ohio Med Asn; Cleveland & Nat Med Asns; Nat Alumni Asn, Meharry Med Col; surgical staffs Lutheran Med Ctr; St Vincent's Med Ctr; St Luke's Hosp; adv bd, Cleveland Found; bd trustees, Summer Music Exp; life mem, Nat Asn Advan Colored People; PUSH. **Honors/Awds:** Physician of the Year, Polyclinic Hosp Reunion. **Special Achievements:** Ohio 21st Dist US Congressman Louis Stokes, Cuyahoga Co Commissioners Office, Virgil Brown, City of Cleveland Council, President George Forbes. **Military Serv:** USAF, 1st lt.

FRANKLIN, HAROLD A.
Educator, college teacher, manager. **Personal:** Married Lilla M Sherman. **Educ:** Ala State Univ, BA, History; Auburn Univ, MA, attended; Tufts Univ, attended; Bradeis Univ, attended; Univ Denver, MA, int studies. **Career:** Educator (retired); manager; Ala State Univ, teacher, 1965; Tuskegee Inst, 1965-68; NC A & T Univ, instr, 1969, visiting prof, 1970; Ala Serv Ctr Black Elected Off, dir, 1969-70; Talladega Col, asst prof, 1968-92; Terry's Metrop Mortuary, mgr, currently. **Orgs:** Pres, NAACP; E AL Planning Comn; Talladega County Overall Econ Comn; Black Coalition Talladega; Ala Dem Conf Boy Scouts Am; Citizen's Conf Pub Affairs; Ala Hist Comn Bd Adv; Ala League Adv Educ; treas, Star Zion AMEZion Ch; bd adv, Community Life Inst; Ala Crt Higher Edn; Ala Coun Human Relations. **Honors/Awds:** Sigma Rho Sigma Honor Soc; Community Leadership & service Award; Phi Alpha Theta Int Honor Soc Hist. **Special Achievements:** First African-American to enroll at Auburn University. **Military Serv:** USAF, 1951-58. **Business Addr:** Manager, Terry, 1702 Battle St W, PO Box 162, Talladega, AL 35160, **Business Phone:** (256)362-1041.

FRANKLIN, DR. HERMAN
School administrator. **Personal:** Born May 1, 1935, Mays Lick, KY; son of Arthur (deceased) and Margaret Taber (deceased); married LaRaeu Ingram; children: Stephen LaMonte. **Educ:** Ky State Univ, BS, 1960; Tuskegee Univ, MS, 1964; Ohio State Univ, PhD, 1973. **Career:** School Administrator (retired): Ala Coop Extension Serv, asst agent, 1963-64; Tuskegee Inst, dir adult educ res project, 1964-66; Ala State Off Econ Opportunity, Ala tech asst corp, dir, 1966-70; City Tuskegee, AL, ex dir model cities, 1970-71; Ohio State Univ, Off Minority Affairs, admin assoc, 1971-73; Tenn State Univ, asst prof ext cont educ, 1973-74; Tuskegee Inst, dean studs, 1974-77; Southern Assoc Cols & Schs, consult, 1976-81; Gene Carter & Assoc, consult/evaluator, 1981-83; Middle States Asn Cols & Schs, consult, 1981-99; US Dept Educ, consult, 1982-83; Univ Md, vpres stud affairs, 1977-99, sr vpres, 1999-01. **Orgs:** Charter mem & bd dirs, chair, Pub Comn, Optimist Int; Lions Int, 1968-70; vice chair bd, JJ Ashburn Jr Youth Ctr, 1970-73; chair comn, Chamber Com, Tuskegee, 1970, 1974-77; bd dir-exec bd-vpres, Chamber Com, 1975-77, 1976; presenter, Stud Servs Inst, 1979-80; presenter, Nat Asn Equal Opport Higher Educ, 1979-80; exec bd, Boy Scouts Am, 1984-. **Honors/Awds:** Graduate Fellowship, Tuskegee Inst, 1962-63; grad assistantship, Ohio State Univ, 1971-73; Patriotic Civilian Award, Tuskegee Inst ROTC, 1976; century mem, Boy Scouts Am, 1976, 1977; Outstanding Service Award, Lower Shore Asn Coun & Develop, 1983-84; Honorary Trustee Del-Mar-Va Council, Boy Scouts Am, 1985 & 1995; Boss of the Year, Bay Shore Chap, 1991; Distinguished Black Marylanders Award, 1999; Northeast Alumni Achiever, Tuskee Univ, 2001. **Military Serv:** AUS, E-4. **Home Addr:** 4743 Stratford Ct, Salisbury, MD 21804-2701. *

FRANKLIN, J E
Writer. **Personal:** Born Aug 10, 1937, Houston, TX; daughter of Robert and Mathie Randle; children: Olff & Malika. **Educ:** Univ Tex, Austin, BA, 1960; Union Theol Seminary, 1972-73. **Career:** City Univ New York, New York, lectr, 1969-75; Skidmore Col, Saratoga Springs, dir, 1979-80; Brown Univ, Providence, resident playwright, 1983-89; Harlem Sch of the Arts, fac mem, 1990-; Blackgirl Ensemble Theatre, founder & artistic dir, 1990-. **Orgs:** Dramatists Guild, 1971-. **Honors/Awds:** Drama Desk Award, The Drama Desk, 1971; Dramatic Arts Award, Howard Univ, 1974; NEA Award, Nat Endowment, for the Arts, 1979; Rockefeller Award, Rockefeller Found, 1980; Writers Guild Award, Writers Guild Am, E, 1981. **Special Achievements:** Author : Black Girl (play and film,) 1971; The Prodigal Sister, 1974; Where Dewdrops of Mercy Shine Bright, 1983; Borderline Fool, 1988; Christchild, 1989. **Business Phone:** (212)489-8008.

FRANKLIN, DR. JOHN HOPE. See Obituaries section.

FRANKLIN, KIRK
Singer, actor. **Personal:** Born Jan 26, 1970, Fort Worth, TX; married Tammy Renee Collins, Jan 20, 1996; children: Kerrion, Carrington, Kennedy & Caziah. **Career:** Mt Rose Baptist Church,

minister music, 1981; Greater, Stronger Rest MBC, minister music, 1988; Grace Temple SDA Church, musician, 1988; wrote material & performed on I Will Let Nothing Separate Me, DFW Mass Choir, 1991, Live in Indianapolis, GMWA Nat Mass Choir, 1993; Albums: Gospo-Centric, 1993; He Say, She Say But What Does God Say?, 1995; R Kelly album, 1995; Kirk Franklin & The Family Christmas; Whatcha Lookin' 4, 1996; Produced album by gospel group, God's Property, God's Property from Kirk Franklin's Nu Nation, 1997; Any Given Sunday, 1999; Get on the Bus, 1999; Tour of Life; The Rebirth of Kirk Franklin, 2002; Hero, 2005; Kirk Franklin Presents: Songs for the Storm, Vol 1, 2006; Norbit, 2007; Singles: "Looking For You"; "Imagine Me"; Films: Kirk Franklin: The Nu Nation Tour, 1999; Sweating in the Spirit, 2005; TV: "Sister, Sister", 1998; "Something to Sing About", 2000; "Boycott", 2001; "The Proud Family", 2003; "Access Hollywood", 2007; "Sunday Best", 2007; 22nd Annual Stellar Gospel Music Awards, 2007; Fo Yo Soul Prods Inc, founder, 1996-. **Honors/Awds:** Five Stellar Gospel Music Awards, 2002; Grammy Award, 2006. **Special Achievements:** Appeared on "The Oprah Winfrey Show". **Business Addr:** Gospel Vocalist, c/o Gospo-Centric Records, 421 E Beach St, Inglewood, CA 90302, **Business Phone:** (310)677-5603.

FRANKLIN, DR. LANCE STONESTREET
School administrator, executive director. **Personal:** Born Jul 3, 1962, Chicago, IL; son of Lawrence and Carrene Stonestreet; married Anita Valentina Martin, Mar 7, 1986; children: Lance Jabraan & Ian Jamaal. **Educ:** Wayne State Univ, BA, 1986, MS, 1988; MSCE, 1996, PhD, 2005. **Career:** Wayne State Univ, lab stud asst, 1984-86, mgr environ health & safety, 1988-92, interim dir, 1992-94, dir biosafety officer, 1994, Off Environ Health & Safety, dir & radiation safety officer, currently, adj prof civil & environ eng, currently; Detroit Edison, asst indust hyg technician, 1986-87; Wayne Co Med Examr, chemist, 1987-88; Chrysler Corp, res assoc, 1988; KCP Found, fel, 1989. **Orgs:** ACGIH, 1989; Freemason, F&AM, PHA, 1990; Nat Asn Advan Colored People, 1992; AIHA Toxicol Community, 1992; bd mem, Samaritan Non-Profit Housing Asn, 1993; bd mem, Univ Dist Asn, 1995; Wayne Co Interview Bd, 1995; Omega Psi Phi, Fraternity; C Ctr, Black Family Develop. **Honors/Awds:** Omega Phi Psi Scholar, 1985; Quality of Service Award, Wayne State Univ, 1993; Certificate of Congratulations, Off Govt, MI, 1993; Spirit of Detroit Award, City Detroit, 1993. **Special Achievements:** Author: "Maudsley Reactive & Nonreactive Rats: Performance in an Operant Conflict Paradigm", Physiology & Behavior, Vol 72, 1992. **Home Phone:** (313)862-3865. **Business Phone:** (313)577-2559.

FRANKLIN, MARTHA LOIS
Computer scientist. **Personal:** Born Nov 14, 1956, Nacogdoches, TX; daughter of William Sanders Jr and Ida Smith Sanders; divorced. **Educ:** Prairie View A&M Univ, Prairie View, TX, BS, 1980; Am Inst Banking, Houston, TX, 1987. **Career:** Texaco USA, Houston, TX, programmer analyst, 1980-83; Gulf Oil Corp, Houston, TX, sr bus analyst, 1983-85; City Houston, Houston, TX, sr programmer analyst, 1985-86; Pennzoil Co, Houston, TX, sr syst analyst, 1988-; Tex Commerce Bank, Houston, TX, sr programmer analyst, Software Design, vpres, 1989-. **Orgs:** Ski Jammers, 1985-89; pres, Black Data Processing Assoc, Houston, TX, 1985-89; Houston Educ Asn Reading & Training, 1987-89; 1987-89, fin secy, 1990, Alpha Kappa Alpha, Omicron Tau Omega; Prairie View A&M Univ, 1988-89; Toastmasters, 1989; vpres, Software Design, 1989; bd dir, United Negro Col Fund, Houston, TX, 1989-90. **Honors/Awds:** Nat Outstanding Sr, 1975; Member of the Year, Black Data Processing, Black Data Processing Assocs, 1990. **Business Addr:** Senior System Analyst, Pennzoil Co, 700 Milam Pennzoil Pl 9th Fl, Houston, TX 77002, **Business Phone:** (713)546-4178.

FRANKLIN, OLIVER ST CLAIR, JR.
Financial manager. **Personal:** Born Oct 30, 1945, Washington, DC; son of Rev Oliver St Clair Sr and Hyla Turner; married Patricia E Mikols, Jul 7, 1977; children: Julien K. **Educ:** Lincoln Univ, BA, 1966; Edinburgh Univ, dipl, 1967; Oxford Univ, Balliol Col, Eng Wilson fel, 1967-70. **Career:** Univ Penn, Annenberg Ctr, Philadelphia, dir, 1972-77; independent film producer & critic, 1977-84; City Philadelphia, dep city rep, 1984-89; independent publ, 1989-; Pilgrim, Baxter, Greig & Assocs, Wayne, PA, vpres; Right Mgt Consult Inc, dir; Intl House, pres. **Orgs:** Pres, Philadelphia Chap, Oxford & Cambridge Soc, 1985-; bd mem, Opera Co Philadelphia, 1985-; bd mem, Afro-Am Hist & Cult Mus, 1985-; bd mem, Inst Contemporary Art, 1986-; vpres, Int Protocol Assn, 1987-; brd adv, First Com Bank Philadelphia, 1989-; Franklin Inn, 1989; planning comt mem, Natl Assn Security Prof, 1990-; trustee, Philadelphia Found; trustee, RosenbachMus & Libr; trustee, Global Interdependence Ctr; trustee, S AfricanEnviron Trust; trustee, Sir Hans Koopler Trust, NY; pres & chief execofficer, Int House, currently; dep dir pub affairs, Gov's Comn, Md; trustee, Phil Foundn. **Honors/Awds:** Volunteer of the Year, Vol Action Coun, 1988; Distinguished Alumni, Nat Assn Equal Opportunity Higher Educ, 1989. **Home Addr:** 525 S 41st St, Philadelphia, PA 19104, **Home Phone:** (215)387-8468. **Business Phone:** (215)387-5125.

FRANKLIN, PRESTONIA D. (ANU PRESTONIA)
Business owner. **Personal:** Born Mar 26, 1957, Portsmouth, VA; daughter of Preston and Barbara; married Joseph Franklin II, Aug 24, 2003. **Career:** Khamit Kinks Inc, pres & founder, 1977-. **Orgs:** Curriculum comt mem, Int Braiders Network. **Honors/Awds:** Recognition Award, Nat Braiders Guild, 1989; Best Conrows Award, Uhuru Sasa, 1979; Best Creation Award, Robert Fiance Beauty Sch, 1986; Bronner Bros, trend setters, 1990-91; Nat Braiders Guild Recognition Award, Wash, DC, 1995; Bronner Brothers Braiders Competition 1st & 2nd place, Atlanta GA, 1996; Bronner Brothers Braiders Competition 1st place, FL, 1998; Natural Hair Stylist Hall of Fame Award, 2002; Women in the Black WIB nBus 2002 Award, 2002. **Special Achievements:** Cover of Essence Magazine, Angela Bassett's hair, Dec 1992; Conver sesneaker commercial, En Vogue's hair, 1993; Clairol styling for black market, 1992; Hype Hair, September cover, 1994; and Daring Dos: A History of Extraordinary Hair, 1994; celebrity makeup artist's Sam Fine's Fine Beauty: Beauty Basics and Beyond for African-American Women 1999; Miki Taylor's Self-Seduction: Your Ultimate Path to Inner and Outer Beauty, 2003; The International Hairstyle Index, 2003. **Business Addr:** Founder, President, Khamit Kinks Inc, 327 Gold St, Brooklyn, NY 11201.*

FRANKLIN, DR. RENTY BENJAMIN
Educator. **Personal:** Born Sep 2, 1945, Birmingham, AL; son of George and Pinkie; married Theresa C Langston; children: LaTania & Omari. **Educ:** Morehouse Col, BS 1966; Atlanta Univ, MS, 1967; Howard Univ, PhD, 1972; Harvard Sch Med, Porter Found Res Fel, 1974. **Career:** NSF, med educ prog grant reviewer; Morehouse Col, consult admis com; Atlanta Univ Ctr, pre-baccalaureate; Robert Wood Johnson Found, cons; NIH cons St Augustine's Col, instr, 1967-69; Howard Univ Col Med, asst prof, 1972-77; Univ MD Dent Sch, Dept Biomed Sci, assoc prof, 1980-86, prof, 1986-, Molecular & Cell Biol Track, dir, currently. **Orgs:** Sigma Xi Soc; Am Physiol Soc; AAAS; NY Acad Scis; Endocrinal Soc; chmn, NIH Scientific Review Group. **Honors/Awds:** Outstanding Faculty Research Award, Howard Univ Col Med, 1976; Porter Found Fellowship Award, 1974; Howard Hughes-Morehouse Distinguished Scientist Award, 1994. **Special Achievements:** Author of over 100 science articles & abstracts. **Business Addr:** Professor, Director, University Maryalnd, Dental School, Rm 7209 666 West Baltimore st, Baltimore, MD 21201.

FRANKLIN, DR. ROBERT MICHAEL
School administrator. **Personal:** Born Feb 22, 1954, Chicago, IL; son of Robert Michael and Lee Ethel; married Cheryl Diane Goffney; children: Imani Renee & Robert Michael III. **Educ:** Morehouse Col, BA, 1975; Univ Durham, Eng, post grad studies; Harvard Univ Divinity Sch, MDiv, 1978; Univ Chicago, PhD, 1985. **Career:** FTE BE Mays fel, 1975-78; St Paul Church God In Christ, asst pastor, 1978-84; St Bernards Hosp, prot chaplain, 1979-81; Prairie St Col, instr psychol, 1981; Univ Chicago, instr rels & psychol, field ed dir, 1981-83; Harvard Univ, Divinity Sch, assoc dir ministerial studies, 1984-85, vis lectr ministry & Afro-Am religion, 1986-88; Colgate Rochester Divinity Sch, dean & prof black church studies, 1985-89; Emory Univ, Candler Sch Theol, asst prof, 1989-91, dir black church studies, 1989-, assoc prof ethics & soc, 1991, presidential distinguished prof social ethics, currently; Ford Found, Rights & Social Justice, prog dir, 1995-; Interdenominational Theol Ctr, pres. **Orgs:** Phi Beta Kappa, Morehouse Col, 1975; Am Acad Religion; Soc Sci Study Rels; Asn Sociol Rels; Soc Study Black Rels. **Special Achievements:** Publications: Criterion 1984; The Iliff Review 1985, Union Seminary Qtrly Review, 1986, Liberating Visions: Human Fulfillment and Social Justice in African-American Thought, Augsburg Fortress Press, 1990. **Business Addr:** Presidential Distinguished Professor of Social Ethics, Emory University, Candler School of Theology, Bishops Hall, Atlanta, GA 30322, **Business Phone:** (404)727-0756.

FRANKLIN, ROBERT VERNON, JR.
Judge. **Personal:** Born Jan 6, 1926, Toledo, OH; married Kathryn Harris; children: Jeffery, Gary. **Educ:** Morehouse, BA, 1947; Univ Toledo, JD, 1950; Nat Col State Trial Judges; Traffic Inst Northwestern, Univ Denver, Fordham. **Career:** Judge (retired); Pvt pract, atty, 1950-60; Toledo Ohio, prosecuting atty, 1953-59, asst law dir, 1959-60; Toledo Munic Ct, judge, 1960-69; Lucas County, Comn Please Ct, admin judge, 1973-75, judge, 1969; pvt pract. **Orgs:** Exec comt mem, Ohio Common Pleas Judges Asn; Toledo Bar Asn; Nat Bar Asn; Lucas County Bar Asn; Ohio Bar Asn; bd mgr, Ill Ave YMCA; vpres, Boys Club Toledo; pres, Ohio State Conf, Nat Asn Advan Colored People; Toledo Nat Asn Advan Colored People; bd trustees, Morehouse Col; Defiance Col; Toledo Auto Club; Toledo Zool Soc; St Lukes Hosp; emer pub mem, Asn US Foreign Serv, Torch Club; pres, Scholar Fund Inc; 3rd Babtist Church; Phi Beta Kappa; Phi Kappa Phi Nat Honor Soc. **Honors/Awds:** Outstanding Super & Excellent Judicial Serv, Supreme Ct, State Ohio, 1972-76; Gold "T" Award, Univ Toledo, 1981; 1st BALSA Award, 1983. **Military Serv:** AUS, 1st sgt, 1950-52. **Home Addr:** 5018 Chatham Valley Dr, Toledo, OH 43615, **Home Phone:** (419)841-4666. *

FRANKLIN, SHIRLEY CLARKE (SHIRLEY CLARKE)
Mayor. **Personal:** Born May 10, 1945, Philadelphia, PA; daughter of Eugene Haywood Clarke and Ruth Lyons White; married David McCoy, Feb 5, 1972 (divorced 1986); children: Kai Ayanna, Cabral Holsey & Kali Jamilla. **Educ:** Howard Univ, Wash DC, BA, Sociol, 1968; Univ Pa, Philadelphia PA, MA, Sociol, 1969. **Career:** US Dept Labor, Wash DC, contract officer, 1966-68; Talladega Col, Talladega AL, instr, 1969-71; City Atlanta, Atlanta, dir, comnr cult affairs, 1978-81, chief admin officer, 1982-90, exec officer operations, 1990-91, Atlanta Comt Olympic Games, sr vpres external rels, 1991-97; A Brown Olmstead & Assoc, partner, 1996-; Shirley Clarke Franklin & Assoc, founder & chief exec officer, 1997-98; Urban Environ Solutions LLC, partner, 1998; GA Regional Trans Auth, vice-chair, 1999-2000; City Atlanta, mayor, 2001-. **Orgs:** Trustee, Atlanta Symphony Orchestra, 1977-81; Atlanta Found, 1980; GA Coun Arts, Atlanta, 1979-82; adv bd, GA Women's Polit Caucus, Atlanta, 1982-84; chmn, Expansion Arts Panel, Nat Endowment for Arts, Wash, DC, 1980-82; bd dir, Nat Urban Coalition, Wash, DC, 1980-83; Nat Black Arts Festival, Spelman Col, bd trustees; Atlanta Life Ins Co, bd dirs; United Way Atlanta, bd dirs; Atlanta Chamber Com, bd dirs; Carter Ctr, bd dirs; has also served on bds East Lake Comm Found, Charles Drew Charter Sch, King Baudouin, US Found, Paideia Sch, & Comm Found; Nat Forum Black Pub Adminrs; Delta Sigma Theta Sorority Inc. **Honors/Awds:** Distinguished alumni award, Nat Asn Equal Opportunity in Higher Educ, 1983; leadership award, Atlanta chap NAACP, 1987; Abercrombie Lamp Learning Award, Abercrombie Scholarship Fund, 1988; Woman Year, Atlanta YWCA, 1996; Community Service Award, Atlanta Boys & Girls Club, 1995; Profile in Courage Award, John F. Kennedy Library Found, 2005; Ethics Advocate Award, Southern Inst Bus & Prof Ethics, 2006. **Special Achievements:** First female mayor of Atlanta and the first African American woman to serve as mayor of a major southern city. **Business Addr:** Mayor, City Atlanta, 55 Trinity Ave, Atlanta, GA 30303.

FRANKLIN, WILLIAM B.
Consultant. **Personal:** Born May 2, 1948, Brooklyn, NY; married Barbara J Burton; children: Gerald R & Alyce M. **Educ:** NY City Community Col, AAS, acct, 1971. **Career:** Bache & Co Inc, supvr, 1966-71; Daniels & Bell Inc, opers mgr, 1971-75; WB Franklin & Assoc, owner, 1975-80; Davis & Franklin Planning Group, vpres, 1980-83; Franklin Planning Group, pres, 1983-. **Orgs:** NAACP, 1975; coun mem, South Belmar, 1982-; Intl Assoc Finan Planners,1982-; bd dir, Monmouth County Black United Fund, 1983, Monmouth Co Check Mate Inc Comn Action Agency, 1984; pres, Kiwanis Club Belmar, 1984; arbitrator, New York Stock Exchange, 1988; dir, Japan Am Soc, 2006. **Honors/Awds:** Professional Achievement Award, The Central Jersey Club NANB & PW ClubsInc, 1985; Outstanding President Award, Belmar Kiwanis Club, 1984; Professional Award Bus, Excellence nat Asn Negro Bus & Prof Women's Club Central NJ. *

FRANKS, CREE SUMMER
Actor. **Personal:** Born Jul 7, 1969, Los Angeles, CA; daughter of Don Francks and Lili Red Eagle. **Career:** Albums: Womb Amnesia, w/Subject to Change, 1993; Street Faerie, 1999; TVseries, actor: Inspector Gadget, 1983-84; Bay Cove, 1987; A Different World, 1988-93; Sweet Justice, 1994; Camp Lazlo, 2004; TV series, voice: Ewoks, 1985; Tiny Toon Adventures, 1990-92; Rugrats, 1991; Gargoyles,1994; Problem Child, 1993; Freakazoid!, 1995; The Twisted Adventures of Felix the Cat, 1995; Mortal Kombat: The Animated Series, 1995; Jungle Cubs, 1996; Project GeeKeR, 1996; The Incredible Hulk, 1996; 101 Dalmatians: The Series, 1997; Pepper Ann, 1997; Mummies Alive!, 1997; Pinky, Elmyra & the Brain, 1998; Histeria!, 1998; Batman Beyond, 1999; Sabrina the Animated Series, 1999; The Weekenders, 2000; Teachers Pet, 2000; Clifford the Big Red Dog, 2000; As Told by Ginger, 2000; Codename: Kids Next Door, 2002; My Life as a Teenage Robot, 2003; All Grown Up, 2003; Star Wars: Clone Wars, 2003; TV movies, voice: The Rugrats: All Growed Up, 2001; A Rugrats Kwanzaa Special, 2001; Elise: Mere Mortal, 2002; Film, actor: Wild Thing, 1987; Tuesday Morning Ride, 1995; Film voice: The Care Bears Movie, 1985; Care Bears II, 1986; Rugrats in Paris, 2000; Atlantis, 2001; Final Fantasy X, 2001; The Wild Thornberrys Movie, 2002; Rugrats Meet the Wild Thornberrys, 2003; Rugrats Go Wild, 2003; Final Fantasy X-2, 2003; Clifford's Really Big Movie, 2004. **Special Achievements:** Nominated for Emmy award. **Business Addr:** Actress, c/o William Morris Agency, 1 William Morris Pl, Beverly Hills, CA 90212.*

FRANKS, EVERLEE GORDON
Physician. **Personal:** Born May 11, 1931, Washington, DC; married Ruby H; children: Everlee G Jr, Philip W, Karen J. **Educ:** Howard Univ Col Pharm, BS, 1953; Howard Univ Col Med, MD, 1961. **Career:** Pvt Pract, physician internal med, currently. **Orgs:** Nat Med Asn, 1965-, treas, 1980-84; vpres, Medico Chirargical Soc DC, 1965-; DC Med Soc, 1965-; Am Soc Internal Med, 1968-; Gordon's Corner Citizens Asn, 1970-; grand pres, Chi Delta Mu Fraternity, 1984-86. **Military Serv:** AUS, Sp3, 2 yrs. **Business Addr:** Physician, 3230 Pennsylvania Ave SE Suite 204, Washington, DC 20020-3722.*

FRANKS, GARY A.
Congressperson (u.s. federal government). **Personal:** Born Feb 9, 1953, Waterbury, CT; son of Richard and Janery Petteway; married Donna Williams, Mar 10, 1990; children: Azia Williams. **Educ:** Yale Univ, BA, 1975. **Career:** GAF Realty, Waterbury, CT, pres; Conn Bd Alderman, mem, 1986-90; US Rep CT, Fifth Dist, mem, 1991-97. **Orgs:** Dir, Waterbury Chamber Comm; dir,

Waterbury YMCA; dir, Waterbury Am Red Cross; dir, Waterbury Found; dir, Waterbury Opportunities & Indust Ctr. **Honors/Awds:** Outstanding Young Man, Boy's Club; Man of the Year, Prof Women's Assn,Waterbury. **Special Achievements:** First black Republican to be elected to the US House of Representatives; featured in New York Times, Wall Str Jour, Wash Post Style Section, LA Times, Boston Globe, Newsweek, Time Mag & USA Weekend Mag; appeared Meet the Press, Face the Nation, 20/20, Larry King Live, Night line, Today Show, BET, Crossfire & Eye to Eye with Connie Chung.

FRANKS, DR. JULIUS, JR. See Obituaries section.

FRASER, GEORGE C.
Entrepreneur, chief executive officer, writer. **Personal:** Born May 1, 1945, Brooklyn, NY; son of Walter and Ida Mae Baldwin; married Nora Jean Spencer, Sep 7, 1973; children: Kyle & Scott. **Educ:** Dartmouth Col, Amos Tuck Sch Bus, MBEP. **Career:** Procter & Gamble, mkt mgr, 1972-84; United Way, Cleveland, OH, dir mkt communs, 1984-87; Ford Motor Co, Detroit, MI, minority dealer develop prog, 1987-89; Success Source Inc, Cleveland, OH, pres, 1988-; FraserNet Inc, Cleveland, OH, pres, chmn & chief exec officer, 1988-; Author: Success Runs In Our Race; The Complete Guide to Effective Networking in the African American Community; Race For Success: The Ten Best Business Opportunities for Blacks In America. **Orgs:** Bd trustee, Ohio Bldg Authority. **Honors/Awds:** Nat Volunteer of the Year, UNCF, 1982, 1983; Commendation for Outstanding Community Service, Ohio Senate & House Rep, 1985; First Place Award of Achievement for Community Events, Success Net, 1989; Communicator of the Year Award, Black Media Workers Cleveland, 1990; Communicator of the Year Award, Cleveland Chapter, Nat Asn Black Journalists, 1990; Communication Excellence to Black Audiences Award, 1991; City of Cleveland, Minority Business Advocate of the Year, 1991; Black Achiever of the Year, Voices of Cleveland, 1992; Black Professional of the Year, Black Professionals Asn of Cleveland, 1992; DHL, Jarvis Christian Col, 1999; Architects of the Village Award, Allstate Insurance, 2000; Manager of the Year, Procter & Gamble; Honorary Doctorate Degree of Humane Letters, Jarvis Christian Col. **Special Achievements:** City Cleveland, George C Fraser Day, Feb 29, 1992; First National speaker to have 4 speeches selected (over 10 yrs) by Vital Speeches to be published worldwide; One of the Top 50 Power Brokers in Black America, Upscale Mag. **Business Addr:** Chairman, Chief Executive Officer, FraserNet Inc, 2940 Noble Rd Suite 1, Cleveland Heights, OH 44121-2242, **Business Phone:** (216)691-6686.

FRASER, DR. LEON ALLISON
Physician. **Personal:** Born Nov 15, 1921, Winchester, TN; son of Phil E Sr and Dora L Seward; married Elizabeth Louise Smith; children: Leon Jr & Keith. **Educ:** Fisk Univ, BA, 1948; Howard Univ Sch Med, MD, 1952. **Career:** Physician (retired); Homer G Phillips Hosp St Louis, intern, 1952-53, resident, 1953-56; NJ State Dept Health, pub health physician, 1958-72, dir chronic dis, 1972-75; Trenton NJ Pub Sch, Med dir, 1982-94; Pvt Pract, internal Med, 1956-93. **Orgs:** Mercer Med Ctr Hosp Staff, 1956-; Mercer Co & NJ Med Socs, 1958-; Nat Med Asn, 1965-; Am Pub Health Asn, 1970-; Harvard-Radcliffe Parent's Asn, 1971-; life mem, NAACP; life member, Kappa Alpha Psi; trustee, Father's Asn Lawrenceville Prep Sch, 1972-75; Grand Boule Sigma Pi Phi Frat, 1986-; life mem, AMA. **Honors/Awds:** Alumni Achievement Award, Kappa Alpha Psi, 1968; published article: "Huntington's Chorea, Case Study", 1966; singles tennis champion, Mercer County Med Soc, 1982; golden merit award, Med Soc NJ, 2002. **Military Serv:** USN, SK 1c, 3 yrs. **Home Addr:** 217 Huff Ave, Trenton, NJ 08618, **Home Phone:** (609)393-7866.

FRASER, THOMAS EDWARDS
Lawyer. **Personal:** Born Sep 16, 1944, New York, NY; son of Thomas Augustus Fraser (deceased) and Vera Edwina Fraser; married Regina Stewart, Jul 24, 1982; children: Helena, Steven, David. **Educ:** Univ Wis, BS, 1969, MS, 1973; Univ Wis Law Sch, JD, 1979. **Career:** Pub Serv Comn Wis, legal clerk, 1977-79; United Airlines, sr coun, 1979-; Stewart Collection Mkt, sr vpres, 1996-; Staridea Inc, coun, 1999-. **Orgs:** State Bar Wis, 1979-; State Bar Ill, 1979-; Ill Coun Col Attendance, 1984. **Honors/Awds:** Am Best and Brightest, Dollar and Sense Mag, 1992. **Military Serv:** USF, lt col, 1964-76, active duty, 1978-91, reserve duty; Meritorious Service Medal, 1991. **Business Addr:** Senior Counsel, United Airlines Inc, PO Box 66100, Chicago, IL 60666, **Business Phone:** (708)952-4000.*

FRASIER, RALPH KENNEDY
Banker, lawyer. **Personal:** Born Sep 16, 1938, Winston-Salem, NC; son of Leroy B and Kathryn Kennedy; married Jeannine Marie Quick; children: Karen Denise F Alston, Gail S F Cox, Ralph K Jr, Keith L, Marie K & Rochelle D. **Educ:** Univ NC, 1958; NC Cent Univ, BS, com, 1962; NC Cent Univ, Sch Law, JD, 1965. **Career:** Wachovia Bank & Trust Co, Winston-Salem, NC, legal asst, 1965-66, asst secy, 1966-68; asst vpres, 1968-69; vpres, counsel, 1969-70; The Wachovia, vpres, counsel, 1970-75; The Huntington Nat Bank, Columbus, OH, exec vpres, gen coun, 1975-76, sr vpres, gen counsel, 1976-83, secy, 1981-98, exec vpres, gen counsel, secy, cashier, 1983-98, dir, 1998-2004; Huntington Bancshares Inc, gen coun, 1975-98, secy, 1981-98; Porter Wright Morris & Arthur LLP, atty, 1998-; Adatom.com Inc, dir, 1999-2001; Fraiser & Alston, Pa, Durham, NC, atty, 2001-. **Orgs:** NCA State Bar, 1965-; Nat Bar Asn, 1965-; trustee, Am Bar Asn, 1965-; Winston-Salem Transit Authority, vice-chmn, 1968-74, chair, 1974-75; OH Bar asn, 1976-; Columbus Bar Asn, 1976-; Columbus Urban League Inc, 1987-94, Greater Columbus Arts Coun, trustee, 1986-94; Riverside Methodist Hosps Found Inc, trustee, 1989-90; trustee, Grant Med Ctr; trustee, Grant/Riverside Methodist Hosp, 1996-97; vice chmn, 1995, chmn, 1996, treas, 1998-; Ohio Bd Regents; trustee, NC Cent Univ, 1994-2001; trustee, Nat Judicial col, Reno, Nev, 1996-; dir, Ohio HTH Corp, 1997; treas, 1998-2004; trustee OCLC Online Computer Libr Ctr Inc, Dublin OH, 1999; Nat Coun Col Law, The Ohio State Univ. **Honors/Awds:** Ritter Award, Ohio State Bar Found, 2002. **Military Serv:** AUS, 1958-60, Reserves, 1960-64. **Business Addr:** Attorney, Porter Wright Morris & Arthur LLP, 3100 Huntington Ctr 41 S High St, Columbus, OH 43215-6194, **Business Phone:** (614)227-2125.

FRAZER, DR. EVA LOUISE
Physician. **Personal:** Born Jun 30, 1957, St Louis, MO; daughter of Charles Rivers Frazer, Jr and Louise J Richardson Forrest; married Steven Craig Roberts, Nov 24, 1984; children: Steven Craig Roberts II, Christian Frazer Roberts & Darci Roberts. **Educ:** Univ Mo, BA, MD, 1981; Mayo Grad Sch Med, internship, residency 1981-84. **Career:** Physician (retired); St Mary's Health Ctr, physician, 1984-89; Barnes Care, physician, 1990, dir. **Orgs:** Nat Med Asn, 1984-; Univ Mo, Bd Curators, 1984-90. **Honors/Awds:** Kaiser Merit Award; Univ Mo Alumni Award, 1985; Univ Mo, Alumni Service Award, 1994.

FRAZER, VICTOR O
Lawyer, congressperson (u.s. federal government). **Personal:** Born May 24, 1943, St Thomas, Virgin Islands of the United States; son of Albert and Amanda Frazer; children: Kaaren Frazer-Crawford & Aileene. **Educ:** Fisk Univ, BA, 1964; Howard Univ Law Sch, JD, 1971. **Career:** Virgin Islands Water & Power Authority, gen coun, 1987-89; Congressman Mervyn Dymally, admin asst, 1989-91; Pvt Law Pract, 1991-; Manufacturer's Hanover Trust Co, staff; Comt Dist Columbia US House Rep, coun; One Hundred Fourth Congress, congressman, 1995-97. **Orgs:** Nat Bar Asn; Am Bar Asn; Virgin Islands Bar; State Md Bar; State NY Bar; Dist Columbia Bar; Omega Psi Phi.

FRAZIER, ADOLPHUS CORNELIOUS
Personal: Born in Jacksonville, FL; married Mary Charlene; children: Pamela & Eric. **Educ:** Fla A&M Univ, BS, 1968; Columbia Univ, MA, 1975. **Career:** Denver Broncos Football Team, prof athlete, 1961-63; Lookout Mtn Sch Boys,Denver, CO, prin supvr, 1964-67; York Col, City Univ NY, prof, 1969-, dir financial aid, asst dean stud develop, asst dean, div inst advan,2006; former chmn, Reach Into Cultural Heights Inc. **Orgs:** Nat Asn Advan Colored People, 1979; bd dir, Community Bd 12, 1979-; Rochdale Village, 1981; Jamaica Arts Ctr, 1982. **Honors/Awds:** Delegate Queens City Judicial Conv, 1976-84; Sports Hall of Fame, Fla A&M Univ, 1979; Campaign Aide Pres Carter, 1980; Community Service Award, SO zone Park Women Asn, 1981; elected Dist Leader 32nd Assembly Dist Queens Co NYC. **Military Serv:** AUS, pfc. **Home Addr:** 17240 133rd Ave, Jamaica, NY 11434.

FRAZIER, CHARLES DOUGLAS
Educator, athletic coach. **Personal:** Born Aug 12, 1939, Houston, TX; son of Rebecca Brown; married Betty Alridge. **Educ:** Tex Southern Univ, BS 1964, MS 1975. **Career:** Football Player (retired), Coach; Tex Christian Univ, receivers coach, 1976; Univ Tulsa, receivers coach, 1976; Rice Univ, receivers coach, 1975; Houston Oilers & New Eng Patriots, prof football player, 1962-70; Houston Independent Sch Dist, asst football coach, reciever, currently. **Orgs:** Football Coaching Asn; Hiram Clark Civic Club; Houston Coaches Asn. **Honors/Awds:** Mem Record-Setting US 400-meter Relay Team, 1962; AFL All-Star Team AFL, 1966; Helms NAIA Hall of Fame Track & Field LA, 1969. **Business Addr:** Assistant Football Coach, Houston Independent School District, 413 E 13th St, Houston, TX 77008.*

FRAZIER, CLIFF
Writer, television producer, executive director. **Personal:** Born Aug 27, 1934, Detroit, MI; son of Larney and Willie Mae; divorced; children: Marcus & Aliya Noel. **Educ:** Wayne State Univ, BA, theatre, 1957. **Career:** Community Film Workshop Coun, exec dir, 1968-74; Third World Cinema, admin, 1972-78; Inst New Cinema Artists, exec dir/pres, 1976-86; Commun Indust Skills Ctr, dir, 1987-91; Owens Commun's, vpres, 1991-94; NY Metrop Martin Luther King Jr Ctr Nonviolence, exec dir, 1994-; Author: Talking Cinematically, 20th Century Fox, 1974; Co-author: Arts Educ & the Urban Subculture, US Dept of HEW, 1967; Discovery in Drama, Paulist Press, 1969. **Orgs:** Comnr, Black Leadership comn on AIDS, 1996-; secy, African-Am Legal Defense & Educ Fund, 1997-; bd, Cable TV's Manhattan Neighborhood Network, 1998-; pres, Int Communs Asn, 1990-; chair, New Fed Theatre, 2001-; bd, Habitat for Humanity, 2002-; chair, Harriet Tubman Charter Sch, 2002. **Honors/Awds:** Man Borough Pres, Cliff Frazier Day Proclamation, 1976; Distinguished Serv Award, Am Film Inst, 1978; Emmy Award, NY Acad TV Arts & Sci, 1984; Outstanding Service, Int Radio & Television Soc, 1986; Special Commemoration New York City Comptroller, 1995; Special Citation, New York State Assembly, 1998; InterNat Peace Award, Kobe, Japan, 2007.

FRAZIER, CLYDE. See FRAZIER, WALT, JR.

FRAZIER, DAN E., SR.
Government official, clergy. **Personal:** Born Dec 23, 1949, Ypsilanti, MI; son of Horace and Mattie; married Evelyn Westbrook; children: Dennis, Sharron, Evelyn, Daniel Jr. **Educ:** Linfield Col; LaVerne Univ; Portland State Univ. **Career:** NY Life Ins Co, field underwriter, 1976-78; Dorite Gen Contractors, owner-operator, 1978-80; Carter Mem Church, assoc pastor, 1981-84; Abundant Life Ministries, pastor & founder, 1984-; City San Bernardino, city councilman. **Orgs:** Bd mem, San Bernardino Redevel Agency, 1983-; Nat Asn Advan Colored People San Bernardino; corp bd mem, San Bernardino Community Hosp; polit affairs chair, Inland Empire Interdenominational Ministrial Alliance. **Honors/Awds:** Million Dollar Round Table Club, NY Life Insurance Co; brought first communtiy-based police station to the city of San Bernardino, 1983; comn achiever, A Phillip Randolph Inst, San Bernardino Chapt; chosen Most Influential Black Metropolitan Precinct Reporter in the Inland Empire, 1984. **Business Addr:** City Councilman, City of San Bernardino, 300 N D St, San Bernardino, CA 92418.*

FRAZIER, EUFAULA SMITH
Executive director. **Personal:** Born Oct 16, 1924, Dodge County, GA; married Arthur Lee; children: Maurice, Noland, Edwin & Michelle. **Educ:** Fla Int Univ, BS, 1977. **Career:** Dade County Public Schs, teacher, 1982-95; Tenant Educ Asn, Miami, exec dir; community organizer, 1967-77; Little Nook Beauty Parlor, owner, 1956-67; Atlanta Life Ins Co, underwriter, 1951-53; Michelles Grocery, owner, 1962-. **Orgs:** Dir, Fla Tenant's Org; consult, S FL Hlth Task Force 1973-; Model Cities Task Force 1971; consult, Nat Welafare Rights Org, 1969-; exec com mem, Metro-Dade Co Dem Comt, 1974; co-host, Dem Nat Conv, 1972; People's Coalition, 1972-; planning adv, Coun for Countinuing educ for Women, 1971-74; Brownsville CAA, 1964-74; facilitator, Radical Relat Inst, 1973-74; dir, Tenant Educ Info Ctr, 1974; comm organizer, Family Health Ctr, 1969-72; NAACP, 1972-77; Legal Serv Miami, 1974-77; Mental Health, 1975-77; alternate Nat Dem Party Conv, 1976; chief exec officer, Beulah A G Smith Scholar Found, 2003. **Honors/Awds:** Women of year, Miami Time Newspaper, 1974; woman of yr, Achiever Civil Club, 1976. **Special Achievements:** Co-author, Fla Tenant's Bill of Right. **Business Addr:** Owner, Michelles Grocery, 4929 NW 17th Ave, Miami, FL 33142.

FRAZIER, FRANCES CURTIS
State government official. **Personal:** Born May 19, 1948, Philadelphia, PA; daughter of William Henry and Letiticia Patsy Thompson. **Educ:** Norfolk State Univ, BS, 1972; Ohio State Univ, MA, 1973. **Career:** Ohio State Univ, grad sch, 1974-75; The Ohio Asn Retarded Citizens Inc, project coordr, 1976-79; Columbus Community Col, behav sci, 1981-85; County Arts Project Inc, exec dir, 1982-84; Ohio Dept Mental Retardation & Develop Disabilities, develop disabilities consult, 1983-87; Nat Assault Prev Ctr, spec needs consult, 1985-87; Ohio Dept Human Servs, prog admin cultural initiatives; City Colombus, Comnr, currently. **Orgs:** A Quality Sharing Inc, founder, spokesperson, 1979-84; Greater Columbus YWCA, co-chair, racial justice co policy, 1987-95; Women Color Sexual Assault Community Ohio, core group, 1989-94; Gov's Interagency Coun Women's Issues, steering comt, 1989-91; self-help developer, Nat Black Women's Health Project, 1989-, bd dirs, 1993-; Riverside Hosp, black women's health prog steering comt, 1990-95; Women's Work as a Ministry, spokesperson, 1990-; Grailville/Nat Women's Task Force, 1992-96; US Civil Rights Comn, Ohio Adv Civil Rights Comn, 1992-97. **Honors/Awds:** Ruth Winstead Diggs Alumni Lectr, Norfolk State Univ, 1978; Salute to Black Women Recognition Award, Alpha Kappa Alpha Sorority Inc, 1983; Women of Achievement, Greater Columbus YMCA, 1991; Outstanding Community Serv, The Ohio State Univ, 1992; Women's Equality Day Award, Ohio Women Inc, 1992; Woman of the Year Award, Eldon W Ward YMCA, 1995; Woman Making A Difference (WMAD) Award, 2001. **Special Achievements:** Author, Sparkle Anyway, a self-talk book for women, 1982, 1990; delegate to the NGO World Conference on Women, United Nations, Kenya, East Africa, 1985; US delegate to World Congress of Women, Moscow, Russia, 1987. **Home Addr:** 3466 Bolton Ave, Columbus, OH 43227. **Business Addr:** Commissioner, City of Columbus, 109 N Front St, Columbus, OH 43215, **Business Phone:** (614)645-3111.

FRAZIER, GREG
Executive. **Educ:** Univ Cincinnati, BBA, 1979; Walsh Col, MS, prof acct, 1985. **Career:** Gen Motors, 1979-81; Unisys, 1981-83; Greg Frazier CPA, PLLC, founder & pres, 1989-. **Business Addr:** President, Founder, Greg Frazier CPA PLLC, 4245 Leslie St, Detroit, MI 48238, **Business Phone:** (313)867-7729.

FRAZIER, HERMAN RONALD
Athletic director. **Personal:** Born Oct 29, 1954, Philadelphia, PA; son of Frances and Nathaniel; married Katie Nance (divorced

1982). **Educ:** Ariz State Univ, Tempe, AZ, BS, polit sci, 1977. **Career:** Ariz State Univ, Tempe, AZ, asst dir events & facilities, dir athletics facilities, asst dir opers, assoc athletics dir, sr assoc athletics dirbus & opers, 1977-00; Univ Ala Birmingham, athletics dir, 2000-02; Univ Hawaii, athletics dir, 2002-08; Temple Univ, assoc athletic dir sports admin, 2008-. **Orgs:** Bd dirs, US Olympic Comt, 1984-; bd dirs, Athletics Cong, 1984-; adv bd, Dept Econ Security, 1985-; Bd dirs, Fiesta Bowl, 1988-; NCAA/USOC Task Force; Div I NCAA Football Issues Comt. **Honors/Awds:** Gold Medal, Olympic Games, 1976; Bronze Medal, Olympic Games, 1976. **Special Achievements:** Served as Chef de Mission of Team USA for the 2004 Summer Olympics in Athens, Greece. *

FRAZIER, DR. JIMMY LEON
Physician. **Personal:** Born Aug 29, 1939, Beaumont, TX; son of E Leon and Thelma Cooper; married Shirley Jolley; children: Andrea, Daveed & Keith. **Educ:** Tex Southern Univ, BS, 1960; Meharry Med Col, MD, 1967. **Career:** Beaumont Tex, teacher, 1960-63; NASA, engr, 1964; Family practician, physician, 1971-; Wright State Univ Sch med, admis com, 1977-81. **Orgs:** Alpha Phi Alpha, Am Acad Family Prac, Nat Med Asn, AMA, Ohio State Med Asn, Shriners-Prince Hall Mason; selectman Dayton Ohio Montgomery Co Med Asn; Gem City Med Soc; dipl Am Bd Family Practice; fel Am Acad Family Physicians; Dayton Racquet Club; NAACP. **Honors/Awds:** Achievement Award, Gem City Med Soc, 1999. **Military Serv:** AUS, major, 1969-71. **Home Addr:** 543 valewood lane, Dayton, OH 45405. **Business Addr:** Physician, 1401 Salem Ave, Dayton, OH 45406.

FRAZIER, JOE
Boxer, businessperson. **Personal:** Born Jan 12, 1944, Beaufort, SC; son of Rubin and Dolly; married Florence; children: Marvis, Weatta, Jo-Netta, Natasha, Jacqui, Hector, Marcus, Reene, Brandon,Joseph, Joye & Derrick. **Career:** Boxer (retired), trainer, business owner; prof boxer, 1965-76, 1981; Rock-Blues Group Knockouts, mem; Smokin Joe's Corner, owner; Joe Frazier & Sons Limousine Serv, owner & pres, 1974-; Joe Frazier's Gymnasium, owner, mgr & trainer, 1974-; Marvis Frazier, mgr & prize fighter; Smoking Joe Frazier Inc, owner & pres, currently; Smokin Joe Frazier Clothing Line, 1995. **Orgs:** Int Boxing Hall Fame; Cap Atlantic Juv Diabetes Found; Alzheimer's Disease Found; Arms Across Harlem; Police Benevolent Asn; Frazier's Father's Day Picnic; founder, Smokin' Joe Frazier Found. **Honors/Awds:** Heavyweight Champion, NY, MA, IL, ME, 1968; Olympic Gold Medal, 1964; Heavyweight Champion, World Boxing Asn, 1970-73; Ring Boxing Hall of Fame, 1980; Int Boxing Hall of Fame, 1990; New York Hall of Fame, 1992; Honoree, SC African-Am Hist Online, 1992; Phila Boxing Hall of Fame, 1993; New York Police Dept Award of Honor, 1995; WBA Living Legend Award, 1995; Rocky Marciano Award. **Business Addr:** Owner, Manager & Trainer, Joe Frazier's Gymnasium, 2917 N Broad St, Philadelphia, PA 19132, **Business Phone:** (215)221-5303.

FRAZIER, JORDAN
Automotive executive, business owner. **Personal:** Born in Screven, GA; married Cora; children: Edward, Shayla. **Educ:** Cert automobile dealer, Las Vegas, NV. **Career:** Afro-Am Life Ins Co; Seaboard Coastline Railroad; Roebuck Chrylser Plymouth, sales, ending 1975, used car mgr, 1979; Jim Bailey City Car Sales, finance mgr; Jim Burke Buick, finance mgr, 1980; Midfield Dodge, pres, owner, gen mgr, 1990-. **Orgs:** Vulcan Kiwanis Club; bd mem, Boys Scouts of Am; trustee, Miles Col. **Honors/Awds:** Small Bus Person of the Yr, Birmingham Chamber Com, 1996. **Special Achievements:** Listed 63 of 100 top auto dealers, Black Enterprise, 1992. **Military Serv:** AUS. **Business Addr:** Owner, President, Midfield Dodge, 549 Bessemer Super Hwy, Midfield, AL 35228, **Business Phone:** (205)365-3511.*

FRAZIER, JOSEPH NORRIS, JR. See Obituaries section.

FRAZIER, JULIE A
Engineer. **Personal:** Born Dec 9, 1962, Cleveland, OH; daughter of Gerald N. **Educ:** Tuskegee Univ, BS, 1986. **Career:** Sherwin Williams Tech Lab, lab technician, 1984-85; AT&T Bell Labs, Atlanta, GA, chem engineering asst, 1987-89. **Orgs:** Am Inst Chem Engrs, 1985-86; volunteer Greater Cleveland Literacy Coalition, 1986-87; Assault on Illiteracy Prog, 1986-87. **Home Phone:** (404)449-7352.

FRAZIER, LEON
Educator, dean (education), vice president (organization). **Personal:** Born May 16, 1932, Orangeburg, SC; married Irlene Janet Sharperson; children: Angela, Chris & Celeste. **Educ:** SC State Col, BS, 1954, 1955; Univ Okla, attended 1967; Ala A&M Univ, MS, 1969; Okla State Univ, DEd, 1970. **Career:** Aiken County Pub Schs, SC, teacher, 1954-56; USAF Electronics Training Ctr, Keesler AFB, MS, training instr, 1956-58; AUS Missile Sch RedstoneArsenal, instr, 1958-61, training admin, 1961-68, educ specialist, 1968-69; Ala A&M Univ, vpres acad affairs, dir, 1971-73, assoc prof, asst dean grad studies, 1971-73, prof psychol, vpres stud affairs, exec vpres,vpres admin serv, currently; State Ala, licensed psychologist. **Orgs:** AAAS; Am Psychol Asn; Nat Educ Asn; Nat Rehab Asn; chmn, Nat Asn CollDeans Registrars & Admis Comn; Coun Acad Deans Southern States; Phi Delta Kappa Int Educ Fraternity; Ala Educ Asn; Ala Psychol Asn; adv comt mem, Madison County Mental Health Bd Prof; dir, Huntsville-Madison County Community Action Comn; vpres, Madison County Mental Health Asn; Madison County Community Coun Orgn; trustee, Huntsville Art League & Mus Asn; Madison County Dem Exec Comt; Nat Asn Advan Colored People; state dir pubrels, Church God Christ; trustee, deacon & dir finance, Gov Div Church God Christ. **Honors/Awds:** Numerous community service awards. **Special Achievements:** Publ: Journals such as The Journal of Research and Development in Education, and the Journal of the Medical Association of the State of Alabama. **Military Serv:** Army. **Business Addr:** Vice President Administrative Service, Alabama Agricultural and Mechanical University, PO Box 1357, Normal, AL 35762.*

FRAZIER, RAMONA YANCEY
Executive. **Personal:** Born Jun 27, 1941, Boston, MA; daughter of Raymond E Yancey, Sr and Gladys E Springer Yancey; divorced; children: Pamela Rae Frazier. **Educ:** Howard Univ, attended 1960; Simmons Col, 1962; Pace Univ, BA, 1984. **Career:** Brown Bros Harriman & Co, employ mgr, 1969-73; Anchor Savings Bank, dir personnel, 1973-74; Boston Univ, personnel officer, 1974-77; Raytheon Co, eeo mgr, 1977; Anchor Savings Bank, asst vice pres personnel officer, 1977-79; GAF Corp, dir eeo, 1979-84; Venator Group, dir of personnel, 1984-87, corporate mgr, 1987-98, dir, 1998-. **Orgs:** Former pres, The EDGES Group Inc; Friend Mayor's Comn status Women NYC, Human Resources Planning Soc; Delta Sigma Theta; bd, Brookwood Childcare; JHRM. **Honors/Awds:** Mary McLeod Bethune Recognition Award, Nat Coun Negro Women, 1989; Corp Recognition, NAACP; Achievement, NYS Senator Velmanette Montgomery, 1998. **Business Addr:** Director, Employee Relations, Venator Group, 233 Broadway, New York, NY 10279, **Business Phone:** (212)553-2365.*

FRAZIER, RAY JERRELL
Government official. **Personal:** Born Jun 27, 1943, Lake Providence, LA. **Educ:** Grambling Univ. **Career:** KLPL Radio, announcer; Town Lake Providence, councilman, 1974, state comnr, currently. **Orgs:** MW Prince Hall Grand Lodge F & AM LA Sunrise Lodge No 109; Nat Asn Advan Colored People. **Business Addr:** State Commissioner, Town of Lake Providence, 201 Sparrow St, PO box 625, Lake Providence, LA 71254, **Business Phone:** (318)559-2288.

FRAZIER, REGINA JOLLIVETTE
Manager. **Personal:** Born Sep 30, 1943, Miami, FL; married Ronald E Frazier; children: Ron II, Robert Christopher, Rozalynn Suzanne. **Educ:** Howard Univ, BS, Pharm, 1966; Univ Miami, MBA, 1983. **Career:** Comn Drug Store Inc Miami, pharm intern, 1966; Peoples Drug Stores Inc Wash, pharm intern, 1967-68, staff pharmacist, 1968-69; Nat Assoc Retired Teachers & Am Assoc Retired Persons Drug Serv Wash, staff pharmacist, 1969-70; Econ Oppor Prog, volunteer coordr, 1970; Univ Miami Hosps & Clins, sr pharmacists, 1970-73, dir pharmacy. **Orgs:** Nat parliamentarian Assoc Black Hosp Pharmacists; Am Soc Hosp Pharmacists, Nat Pharmaceutical Assoc, Pharm Adv Comt Shared Purchasing Prog Hosp Consortium Inc, FL Pharmaceutical Assoc; adv comt FL & GA Cancer Info Servs; Women's Chamber Com So FL Inc, Miami Forum; Metro Dade County Zoning Appeals Bd, 1977-; pres, The Links Found Inc; League Women Voters, Am Assoc Univ Women; bd dirs, United Negro Col Fund, Nat Coalition Black Voter Participation; Alpha Kappa Alpha Sor Inc Gamma Zeta Omega Chapt; Carats Inc, Zonta Intl Greater Miami I Club. **Honors/Awds:** Devoted Service Award, Links Inc, 1980; Community Headliner Award, Women Commun, 1984; Trail Blazer Award, Women's Community 100, 1984; Salute to Leadership Award, Agri Invest Fund Inc, 1986.

FRAZIER, SHIRLEY GEORGE
President (Organization). **Personal:** Born in Brooklyn, NY; daughter of Albert Jr and Joan Branch; married John Beasley Jr, Jun 28, 1980; children: Genesis A. **Educ:** Essex County Col, AS, 1990; NY Univ, BA, jour, 1999. **Career:** Pres, Sweet Survival, 1989-. **Orgs:** Bd mem, Gift Asn Am, 1992-99; assoc mem, Gift Basket Profs Network, 1996-2001. **Honors/Awds:** Business Award, Carnie P Bragg Sr, Passaic County Comm Col, 1997. **Special Achievements:** Gift Baskets & Beyond, 1995; The Complete Gift Basket Industry Reference Directory, 1996; How To Start a Home-Based Gift Basket Business, 1998, 2000, 2004, 2007; Gift Basket Products Guide, 1998-2001; The Gift Basket Design Book, 2004, 2008; Marketing Strategies for the Home-Based Business: Solutions You Can Use Today, 2008. **Business Addr:** President, Sweet Survival LLC, River St Station, PO Box 31, Paterson, NJ 07544-0031, **Business Phone:** (973)279-2799.

FRAZIER, WALT, JR. (CLYDE FRAZIER)
Basketball player, broadcaster. **Personal:** Born Mar 29, 1945, Atlanta, GA; son of Walter and Eula; divorced; children: Walt III. **Educ:** Southern Ill Univ, attended 1967. **Career:** Basketball player (retired), commentator; NY Knicks, 1967-77; Cleveland Cavaliers, 1978-80; US Basketball League franchise, investor; US Virgin Islands Boat firm, boat capt, 1989; NY Knicks, TV anal & broadcaster; All Am Speakers, motivational speaker, currently; Walt Frazier Enterprises, pres; Just for Men, New York City, co-owner; Basketball Camp, Pawling, operator; Madison Square Garden Network, commentator, currently. **Honors/Awds:** NBA champion, 1970, 1973; NBA All-Star, 1970-73; All-Star MVP, 1975; Naismith Memorial Basketball Hall of Fame, 1987. **Special Achievements:** One of 50 Greatest Players in NBA History, 1996. **Business Addr:** Commentator, Madison Square Garden Network, Two Pa Plz, New York, NY 10121-0091, **Business Phone:** (212)465-6741.

FRAZIER, WILLIAM JAMES
Physician. **Personal:** Born Aug 20, 1942, Gary, IN; married Veronica; children: Kevin, Monica, Nicole. **Educ:** Fisk Univ, 1964; Ind Univ Sch Med, 1968; Baylor Univ Med Ctr, 1970; Barnes Jewish Hosp, S Campus, Wash Univ, 1975. **Career:** Pvt Pratice, currently. **Orgs:** Am Med Asn; Dallas Co Med Soc; Am Col Surgeon; dipl, Am Bd Urol; Am Col Emergency Physicians; CV Roman Med Soc; Nat Med Asn. **Honors/Awds:** Publ: "Use of Phenylephrine in the Detection of the Opening Snap of Mitral Stenosis", Am Heart J, 1969; "Early Manipulation & Torsion of the Testicle", Jour Urol, 1975; bronze star for Meritorious Service. **Military Serv:** USAF, maj, 1970-72. **Business Phone:** (214)552-6660.

FRAZIER, WYNETTA ARTRICIA
Association executive. **Personal:** Born Jul 21, 1942, Mounds, IL; daughter of Willie J Williams and Annie L Fite Williams; married Sterling R; children: Renee, Tommie, Clifford. **Educ:** Gov St Univ, BS & MA, 1975; Univ Ill, CDA; Columbia-Pacific, San Rafael, CA, PhD, 1989. **Career:** Gov Health Affairs, asst; Health Serv Adminr, sr health planner; Comp Health Planning Sub Area, exec dir; Lloyd Ferguson Health Ctr, asst adminr; Health Occup, dir; Nat Asn Health Serv Exec, vpres; Univ Ill, asst dir, 1985; Nat Hook Up Black Women Inc, Nat pres, 2007. **Orgs:** Am Pub Health Asn; Nat Asn Neighborhood Health Ctrs; Auxiliary Cook Co Hosp; Kozminski Sch PTA; Sch Com Hyde Park Kenwood Community Conf; Independent voters Ill; Health Comt; League Black Women; Afro Am Family & Community Serv; mem, Chicago Forum. **Honors/Awds:** Ten Outstanding Young People Award Chicago Jaycees; Grant Chas Gavin Scholar; Clin Awards Chicago Med Soc, 1972-74; Citizen of the Week WJPC & WAIT radio stations. **Business Addr:** National President, Nat Hook Up Black Women Inc, 1809 E 71st St Suite 205, Chicago, IL 60649.*

FRAZIER-ELLISON, VICKI L
State government official. **Personal:** Born Oct 24, 1963, New York, NY; daughter of Thomas Gerald and Lurine; married Alvin, Jul 3, 1992. **Educ:** Cornell Univ, BS, 1985. **Career:** Bank NY, acct adminr, 1985-86; Mellon Bank, sales, serv supvr, 1986-88; AT&T Communs, acct exec, 1988-89; GTE Mobile Communs, opers, serv mgr, 1989-91; Md Lottery Agency, dep dir, 1991-. **Orgs:** Nat Asn Female Execs, 1991; First Baptist Church Guilford, chap, men & women's day, 1992, deaconess, 1996; Md Pub Fin Officers Asn; Govt Fin Officers Asn. **Honors/Awds:** Premier Achievement Award, Mellon Bank, 1987; Sales Achievement Award, AT&T Communs, 1988; Premier Serv Quality Award, GTE Mobile Communs, 1990. **Business Addr:** Deputy Director, Maryland Lottery Agency, 6776 Reistertown Rd Suite 204, Baltimore, MD 21215, **Business Phone:** (410)764-4390.

FRAZIER-LYDE, JACQUI
Business owner, boxer, lawyer. **Personal:** Born Dec 2, 1961, Beaufort, SC; daughter of Joe and Florence; married Peter Lyde; children: PeterJr, Sable & John-Joseph. **Educ:** Am Univ, BA, Justice; Villanova Univ, law degree, 1989. **Career:** Lawyer, boxer; prof boxer, 2000-; Frazier-Lyde & Assocs LLC, owner, currently. **Honors/Awds:** WIBA Light Heavyweight Title, 2001. **Business Addr:** Owner, Frazier-Lyde & Associates LLC, 2917 N Broad St, Philadelphia, PA 19132, **Business Phone:** (215)229-1193.

FREDERICKS, HENRY SAINT CLAIRE. See MAHAL, TAJ.

FREDRICK, DR. EARL E
Physician. **Personal:** Born Aug 13, 1929, Chicago, IL; son of Earl Eugene Sr and Lucille Ray; married Barbara Cartman, Mar 21, 1987; children: Earl E III & Erica E. **Educ:** Univ Ill, BS, 1951; Howard Univ, MD, 1958. **Career:** Univ Chicago, Food Res Inst, 1953; Ill Dept Pub Health, bacteriologist, 1953-55; Freedmans Hosp, med lab technician, 1956-58; Cook County Hosp, rotating intern, 1958-59; residency, 1959-61; Va Res Hosp, hematology fel, 1961-62; Physician Cook County Hosp, attended, 1963-73; Fredrick Ashley Clinic, physician internal med & hemat; St Francis Hosp, Dept Med, chmn, 1974-76, pres med staff, 1978-79; Anchor Org Health Maintenance, physician internal med, 1974-97, Anchor-Park Forest Off, clinic dir, 1982-85; pvt practice, physician, currently; Roseland Community Hosp, consult staff; Provident Hosp; Louise Burg Hosp; Christian Community Health Ctr, physician, currently. **Orgs:** Alt deleg, AMA, 1987-95, deleg, 1997-2002; bd trustees, Ill State Med Soc, 1997-2000; Nat Med Asn; Cook County Physicians Asn; Clinic Asn Internal Med Chicago Med Sch, 1963-73; Am Col Physicians, 1975-; bd mem,

Chicago Found Med Care, 1977-83; bd trustees, Chicago Med Soc, 1977-85, vice chmn, bd trustees, 1983-85, Credentials & Elections Comn, Ethical Rels Comn, 2005-06, vice chair, Resolutions Reference Comn, 2005-06; chmn bd, Wash Park YMCA, 1977-80; S Suburban Soc Internal Med; Crescent County Found Med Care; Am Col Physicians; Am Soc Internal Med. **Honors/Awds:** Glucose 6-Phosphate Dehydrogenase Deficiency, A Review J, Nat Med Asn, 1962; honoree, Rotary Chicago SE; honoree, Sickle Cell Dis Asn, 2000; Pride in Profession Award, AMA, 2001. **Military Serv:** AUS, 1951-53. **Business Addr:** Physician, Christian Community Health Center, 9718 S Halsted St, PO Box 288080, Chicago, IL 60628, **Business Phone:** (773)233-4100.

FREE, KENNETH A.

Administrator, consultant. **Personal:** Born Jun 8, 1936, Greensboro, NC; son of Lee W and Margaret McMurray; married Carolyn Carter Free, Jun 3, 1967; children: Delana, Kenneth Jr, Benjamin. **Educ:** NC A&T State Univ, BS, 1970. **Career:** NY Mets Prof Baseball, minor leagues, 1960-64; Cent Motor Lines, Greensboro, NC, 1964-67; Greensboro Parks & Recreation, 1967-70; NC Dept Natural & Econ Resources, park & rec consult, 1970-78; Mid-Eastern Athletic Conf, Greensboro, NC, comnr, 1978-; Eastern Intercollegiate Athletic Conf, comnr, 1995-. **Orgs:** Pres, NC Recreation Parks Soc, 1978; pres, Fayetteville Alumni Kappa Alpha Psi Fraternity, 1972-77; NCAA Div I Basketball E Regional Advisory Comt, 1982-84; Nat Collegiate Athletic Asn Comt Committees, 1984-86; Collegiate Commissioners Asn; Univ Commissioners Asn; secy & treasurer, vpresident, Univ Commissioners Asn; NCAA Div I Basketball Comt; Comt Basketball Issues; Mason/Morning Star Lodge 691; Exec comt, Nat Asn Collegiate Dirs Athletics. **Honors/Awds:** Cert Recreator, State NC, 1968; Man of the Year, Fayetteville Alumni Kappa Alpha Psi Fraternity, 1976; Fel Award, NC Recreation Parks Soc, 1986; Jostens Distinguished Serv Award, 1992. **Military Serv:** AUS, Sp-4, 1955-58. *

FREE, LLOYD B. See FREE, WORLD B.

FREE, VICKY L

Executive. **Educ:** Univ SC, BS, jour & mass communications; Kellog Sch Mgt, Northwestern Univ, MBA. **Career:** Sunrise Enterprise, Columbia, SC; McDonald's Corp, head, 2000-03, mkt dir, vpres, dir women's initiatives, 2004-05; Turner Broadcasting Syst Inc, vpres entertainment mkt, 2005-. **Honors/Awds:** Ebony Outstanding Women in Marketing & Communications Award, Ebony Mag, 2005. **Business Addr:** Vice President Entertainment Marketing, Turner Broadcasting System Inc, One CNN Ctr, Atlanta, GA 30303, **Business Phone:** (404)827-1700.*

FREE, WORLD B. (LLOYD B FREE)

Basketball coach, basketball player. **Personal:** Born Dec 9, 1953, Savannah, GA. **Educ:** Guilford Col, NC, 1976. **Career:** Basketball player (retired), basketball coach; Philadelphia 76er's, 1975-78, 1986-87, strengthing & conditioning coach, 1994, ambassador basketball, dir player develop, currently; San Diego Clippers, 1978-79; Golden State Warriors, 1980-82; Cleveland Cavaliers, 1983-85; Houston Rockets, 1986-87; Oklahoma City Calvary, 1991. **Honors/Awds:** Inducted, New York City Basketball Hall-of-Fame, 1997; Cleveland Cavaliers Legend, 2005. **Special Achievements:** Ranks 44 th all-time on the NBA scoring list. **Business Addr:** Director of Player Development, Philadelphia 76ers, 3601 S Broad St, PO Box 25040, Philadelphia, PA 19148, **Business Phone:** (215)339-7600.*

FREELAND, ROBERT LENWARD, JR.

Executive, singer. **Personal:** Born May 5, 1939, Gary, IN; married Carolyn J Woolridge; children: Robin, Brandon. **Educ:** Ind Inst Real Estate, Cert, 1962; Ind Univ; Calumet Col, Whiting, IN, 1980, 1981. **Career:** Devaney Realtors, salesman, 1961-63; Mobil Oil Corp, sales engr, 1963-66; Len Pollak Buick, salesman, 1966-68; Four Roses Distillers Co, mkt rep, 1968-71; Black Horsemen Liquor Stores, owner, 1969-81; Ind state rep, 1973-74; Gary Common Coun, city councilman, 1975-79, vpres, 1976, pres, 1977-79; Gary, police comnr, 1979-83; Calumet Twp Trustee, Gary, IN, chief dep trustee, 1988; Lake Co Govt Ctr, Lake Co Recorder. **Orgs:** Nat Asn Advan Colored People; Urban League; Frontiers Int; bd mem, Northwest Ind Regional Plan Comn, 1975-78. **Honors/Awds:** Special Recognition & Commendation, Ind Dept Civil Defense, 1961; Patriotic Service Award, 1964; Meritorious Service Award, Club Carpetbaggers, 1972; Friendship Award, Frat Order Police, 1973; Legislative Award, Nat Asn Advan Colored People, 1973; Recognition Award, Precinct Orgn, 1973; Distinction Award, Ind Div Asn Study Afro-Am Life & Hist, 1973. **Special Achievements:** First Black from Gary elected as state representative; first Black to serve on House Ways & Means Com; elected delegate to First Nat Black Assembly, 1972; elected delegate to Democratic State Convention 4 Times; served on state democratic platform committee twice; Black History Commemorative Service, WTLC 105FM, Indianapolis, IN, 1988. **Home Addr:** 3877 Madison St, Gary, IN 46408, **Home Phone:** (219)884-4765. *

FREELAND, RUSSELL L

Consultant, administrator. **Personal:** Born Jul 13, 1929, Lawrenceburg, IN; son of John H Freeland (deceased) and Hulda M Ear-

ley (deceased); married Joan M; children: Deborah, Mark & Douglas. **Educ:** DePauw Univ, BA, 1951; Butler Univ, MS, 1960. **Career:** Administrator, Consult (retired): Indianapolis Plant Int Harvester Co, mgr indus engineering 1974-76, mgr production operations 1976-77, mgr mfg opers, 1977-78; Engine Opers Int Harvester, plant mgr, 1978-80; Int Harvester Co, mgr direct labor syst, 1978, mgr mfg oper, 1980-82, gen plants mgr, 1982-83, dir, renew opers, 1983; Navistar, dir tech admin, 1983-86, consult, 1987-92. **Orgs:** Am Inst Indust Engrs, 1974-82; Allocations Comm United Way Metro Chicago 1979-80; bd visitors DePauw Univ, 1979-85; Lions Club, 1986-; mem adv coun, Comn Dept Corrections; Nat Asn Basketball Coaches. **Honors/Awds:** Silver Anniversary Team, Indiana High School Basketball, 1972; Silver Anniversary Team All-Am, Nat Asn Basketball Coaches, 1976; Civic Award, Int Harvester, 1976; DePauw Univ, All Sports Hall of Fame, 1989; Lion of the Year, 1992; Elected to Indiana Basketball Hall of Fame, 1998. **Special Achievements:** Host TV talk show "Opportunity Knocks" WFBM-TV 1971-76; first black student to play varsity football at DePauw; first black to officiate in an Indiana high school basketball sectional tournament. **Military Serv:** USAF s/sgt 1951-55. **Home Addr:** 1569 Vest St, Naperville, IL 60563.

FREELAND, SHAWN ERICKA

Manager. **Personal:** Born Sep 10, 1968, Jacksonville, FL; daughter of Leonard Harris Freeland Sr and Sharon Conley Freeland. **Educ:** Fla Community Col, Jacksonville, Assoc Degree. **Career:** Gospel TV Video, exec producer, pub rels; Streetball Partners Int, event dir; UNC Media Jacksonville, prom dir; KJMS/KWAM, Clear Channel Commun, prom dir; NTR Enterprises, opers mgr, currently; Promotions Unlimited 2000 Inc, dir, currently. **Orgs:** Jacksonville Together; NCP. **Honors/Awds:** Community Service Award, Jacksonville Sheriff's Office. **Special Achievements:** Come Together Day, Metropolitan Park, 1992; Martin Luther King Jr Birthday Celebration, Jax Landing, 1992; Support First Coast First, 1992; Come Together Day, Jam 4 Peace, 1994; City of Jacksonville, Mayor's Office, Proclamation. **Business Addr:** Director, Promotions Unlimited 2000 Inc, KJMS/KWAM, 19111 W 10 Mile Rd Suite 205, Southfield, MI 48075, **Business Phone:** (248)372-7072.*

FREELON, NNENNA

Jazz singer. **Personal:** Born Jul 28, 1954, Cambridge, MS; married Phil, Jan 1, 1979; children: Deen, Maya & Pierce. **Educ:** Simmons Col, MA. **Career:** Jazz singer, currently; Albums: Nnenna Freelon, 1992; Heritage, 1993; Listen, 1994; Shaking Free, 1996; Maiden Voyage, 1998; Soulcall, 2000; Tales of Wonder: Celebrating Stevie Wonder, 2002; Live, 2003; Blueprint of a Lady, 2005; Better Than Anything, 2008; Films: "What Women Want", 2000. **Orgs:** Spokeswoman, Nat Asn Partners Educ; Women Jazz Asn Inc. **Honors/Awds:** Eubie Blake Award & Billie Holiday Award, Academie du Jazz (France), 1995. **Special Achievements:** Six Grammy Award nominations. **Business Addr:** Recording Artist, c/o Ed Keane Assocs, 573 Pleasant St, Winthrop, MA 02152, **Business Phone:** (617)846-0067.

FREEMAN, ALBERT CORNELIUS, JR.

Actor, college administrator. **Personal:** Born Mar 21, 1934, San Antonio, TX; son of Albert and Lottie Brisette; married Sevara E Clemon, Jan 1, 1960. **Educ:** Los Angeles City Col, attended 1957; Amherst Univ, MA. **Career:** Theatre performances: The Long Dream, 1960; Kicks & Co, 1961; Tiger Tiger Burning Bright, 1962; The Living Premise, 1963; Trumpets of the Lord, 1963; Blues for Mister Charlie, 1964; Conversations at Midnight, 1964; The Slave, 1964; Dutchman, 1965; Measure for Measure, 1966; Camino Real, 1968; The Dozens, 1969; Look to the Lilies, 1970; Are You Now Or Have You Ever Been, 1972; Medea, 1973; The Poison Tree, 1973; The Great Macdaddy, 1974; Soldier's Play; Movies: Torpedo Run, 1958; Dutchman, 1967; Finian's Rainbow, 1968; The Detective, 1968; Castle Keep, 1969; The Lost Man, 1969; My Sweet Charlie, 1970, Malcolm X, 1992; One Life to Live; TV series: "The Cosby Show", 1985; "Law & Order", 1990-2004; "Homicide: Life on the Street", 1995-96; Howard Univ, Col Fine Arts, Dept Drama, instr & chmn. **Honors/Awds:** Image Award, Malcolm X, Won, 1995; Emmy Award, "Roots: The Next Generation", 1979, My Sweet Charlie, 1970, Nominated; Day Time Emmy Award, "One life to Live", Won, 1979; Day Time Emmy, "One Life to Live, 1983, 1986, 1987, Nominated; Russwurm Award; Golden Gate Award; Emmy Award, 1979; AU-DELCO Award, Conflict Interest, 2001 . **Military Serv:** USAF. *

FREEMAN, ALGEANIA WARREN

College administrator. **Personal:** Born Jan 24, 1949, Dunn, NC; married Ernest Freeman, Aug 19, 1972; children: Ernest III. **Educ:** Fayetteville State Univ, BS, 1970; Southern Illinois Univ, Carbondale, MS, 1972; Ohio State Univ, PhD, 1977. **Career:** Americana Nursing Center, Decatur, IL, speech pathologist, 1972-73; Norfolk State Col, Norfolk VA, eng instr, 1973-75; Ohio State Univ, Columbus, teaching assoc, 1975-76; NC A & T State Univ, Greensboro, asst prof, 1977; Norfolk State Univ, from asst prof to prof, 1978-01; E Tenn State Univ, prof, 1987-90; Morgan State Univ, prof, 1990-92; Livingstone Col, pres, 2001-. **Orgs:** State dir, Theta Phi Beta, VA, 1980-82; exec dir, Nat Black Asn Speech Language Hearing, 1982-84; pres, Nat Allied Health, 1985-86; Allied Health Study Comt, 1987-88; pres, Coalition of 100 Black

Women, San Diego chap, 1994; bd dir, CIAA, 2001-; bd mem, Found Carolinas, 2002-; int consult, WK Kellogg Found, SAfrica; Nat Acad Scis; Statewide Task Force, VA; Calif Asn Instructional Adminr; Kids Voting Va; Montebello Rehab Hosp, Univ Md Hosp Syst; Md Easter Seals; Friends Norfolk Juvenile Ct; Girl Scouts Eastern Tenn. **Honors/Awds:** Teaching Associateship Award, Ohio State Univ, Columbus, OH; Internship Award, Southern Ill Univ; Outstanding Graduate Awards Citation, NAFEO; National Finalist, White House Fel, 1984; Fel, Am Soc Allied Health Professionals, 1998; Guardian of Our Legacy Awards, Harlem Renaissance, 2002. **Special Achievements:** First female President of Livingstone College; First African American female to be appointed as a dean at one of the majority institutions; in the State of TennesseeAuthor: Recipe for Grant Writing, 1997; Cultural Studies and Standards of Learning, 1999. **Business Addr:** President, Livingstone College, 701 W Monroe St, Salisbury, NC 28144, **Business Phone:** (704)216-6151.*

FREEMAN, DR. ANTOINETTE Y.

College teacher. **Educ:** PhD, 2002. **Career:** Huston Tillotson Col, asst prof; Boston Univ Sch Med. *

FREEMAN, ANTONIO MICHAEL

Football player. **Personal:** Born May 27, 1972, Baltimore, MD. **Educ:** Va Tech Univ. **Career:** Football player (retired); Green Bay Packers, wide receiver, 1995-2001, 2003, 2007; Philadelphia Eagles, wide receiver, 2002; Miami Dolphins, wide receiver, 2004. **Honors/Awds:** Super Bowl XXXI Champion, 1996; Pro Bowl selection, 1998; All-Pro selection, 1998. **Special Achievements:** Greatest play in the history of Monday Night Football, ESPN.

FREEMAN, BRIAN M.

Executive. **Personal:** Born Apr 25, 1957, Hartford, CT; son of Walter and Shirley; married Constance, Dec 28, 1985; children: Brian Mark Jr, Corey Cose. **Educ:** Calif Inst Technol, BS, 1979. **Career:** Menasco Aerosystems, sr metallurgist, 1981-87, dir engineering, 1987-97; Curtiss-Wright Flight Systs, Tech Serv, vpres, 1997; Curtiss-Wright Controls Inc, vpres, technol & mkt develop, 2006-. **Orgs:** Am Soc Metals, 1981-; Soc Automotive Engrs, 1990-. **Honors/Awds:** Engineer of the Year, SAE, San Fernando Valley, chapter, 1992. **Business Addr:** Vice President of Technology, Market Development, Curtiss-Wright Controls Inc, 15800 John J Delaney Dr Suite 200, Charlotte, NC 28277.*

FREEMAN, CLAIRE E.

Government official, executive director, chief executive officer. **Personal:** Born Sep 24, 1943, Cleveland, OH; children: Whitney Blair Morgan-Woods & Shani T'Nai. **Educ:** Univ Calif, Riverside, BA, sociol & hist; Univ Southern Calif, MS, urban &regional planning. **Career:** City Inglewood, Housing Community & Develop Div, human affairs supvr, 1973-77; Calif Asn Realtors, housing & community develop mgr, 1978-80; Dept Housing & Urban Devlop, Community Planning & Develop, dep asst secy, 1981-84; Cuyahoga Metrop Housing Authority, chief exec officer, 1999, dir, 1995-; Off Secy Defense & Civilian Personnel Policy, dep asst secy; Dept Housing & Urban Develop, asst secy for admin. **Orgs:** Chairwoman, bd trustees, Urban League Greater Cleveland, 1996; Housing Authority Ins Co, Coun Large Pub Housing Authorities, Dept Defense Qual Life Task Force. **Honors/Awds:** Outstanding Alumni, African Am Support Group, Univ Southern Calif, 1983; Distinguished Serv Medal, Housing & Urban Develop, 1984; Meritorious Serv Award, Nat Asn Advan Colored People, 1987; Medal Outstanding Pub Serv Award, Secy Defense, 1987, 1989; State & Local Small Bus Advocate Award,US Small Bus Admin, 1992; Social Justice Crusader of the Yr Award, Southern Christian Leadership Conf, 4th Annual Martin Luther King Jr, 1992; Black Prof of the Yr, Greater Cleveland, 1996. *

FREEMAN, DARNELL. See KEMP, LEROY PERCY.

FREEMAN, DENISE

School administrator. **Personal:** Married Barry; children: 4. **Educ:** Piedmont Col, BA; Inter-denominational Theol Ctr, Atlanta, GA. **Career:** Lincoln County Sch Bd, bd mem, 1992-96, chmn bd educ, 2006-; baptist minister, currently. **Special Achievements:** Only African American school board member in Lincoln County, GA. **Home Phone:** (706)359-2232. **Business Addr:** Chairman, Lincoln County Board of Education, Lincolnton, GA 30817, **Business Phone:** (706)359-3742.

FREEMAN, DIANE S.

School administrator, educator. **Personal:** Born in Springfield, MA; divorced; children: Urraca Jorge, Joaquin Arturo & Javier Akin. **Educ:** Cent Conn State Univ, BA, anthrop, 1970; Univ Conn, MSW, casework, 1977; Wellesley Col, cert mgt, 1983. **Career:** Univ Hartford, social work consult, 1977, dir, sociol & multi cultural studies prog, 1977-78, asst dir admin, 1978-80; New Hampshire Col, Conn, instr, 1979-82; Eastern Conn State Univ, instr, 1981; Hartford Brd Educ, therapist, spec educ, 1989-91; Trinity Col, asst dir, career coun,1981-84; Greater Hartford Community Col, dir, spec serv/ASTRA, 1984-87; Manchester Community & Tech Col, Social Div, asst prof, social serv prog, cord, 1987, dept chair & assoc prof, prog cord, currently. **Orgs:** New

Eng Minority Women Admin Higher Educ, 1984-86. **Business Addr:** Associate Professor, Manchester Community & Technical College, Department of Social Service, PO Box 1046, Manchester, CT 06045-1046, **Business Phone:** (860)512-2781.

FREEMAN, FRANKIE M.
Lawyer. **Personal:** Born Nov 24, 1916, Danville, VA; married Shelby; children: Shelbe Freeman Bullock. **Educ:** Howard Univ, LLB, 1947; Hampton Inst, 1936. **Career:** US Treas Dept, clerk, 1942-44; Off Price Admin, statistician, 1944-45; Col Finger lakes, instr bus law, 1947-49; atty law, 1949-56; St. Louis Land Clearance & Housing Authorities, from assoc gen coun to gen coun, 1957-70; US Comn Civil Rights, comnr, 1964-80; Community Serv Admin, inspector gen; Freeman Whitfield Montgomery Staples & White, partner & atty; Montgomery Hollie & Assocs LLC, atty, currently. **Orgs:** Am Bar Asn; Nat Bar Asn; Mound City Bar Asn; Lawyers Asn St Louis; Nat Asn Housing & Redevelopment Officials; Nat Housing Conf; League Women Voters; former pres, Delta Sigma Theta Sorority; bd dir, Nat Coun Negro Women; bd mem, St Louis Br; Nat Asn Advan Colored People, United Way, St Louis; bd trustees, Howard Univ, Laclede Sch Law; first vpres, Nat Coun Aging; bd mem, St Louis Region Nat Conf Christians & Jews; Am Red Cross; St Louis Bi-State Chapt, St Louis Urban League; Gateway Chap Links Inc; trustee bd, Wash Tabernacle Baptist Church. **Honors/Awds:** Recipient of numerous honors including Outstanding Citizen Award, Mound City Press Club, 1953. **Special Achievements:** Honored by Dollars and Sense Magazine as one of America's Top 100 Women 1985; author, A Song of Faith and Hope: The Life of Frankie Muse Freeman. **Business Addr:** Attorney, Montgomery Hollie & Associates LLC, 3920 Lindell Blvd Suite 100, Saint Louis, MO 63108-3254.*

FREEMAN, HAROLD P.
Surgeon. **Personal:** Born Mar 2, 1933, Washington, DC; son of Clyde and Lucille; married Artholian C; children: Harold Paul, Neale Palmer. **Educ:** Catholic Univ Am, AB, 1954; Howard Med Sch, MD, 1958. **Career:** Howard Univ Hosp, intern, 1958-59, resident, gen surg, 1959-64; Sloane Kettering Cancer Ctr, 1964-67; Columbia Presbyterian Hosp, assoc attending surgeon, 1974-89; Harlem Hosp Ctr, attending surgeon, dir surg; Columbia UNIV, pro clinical surg, 1989-; North General Hosp, dir surgery, 1999-, pres & Chief Exec Officer, 1999-. **Orgs:** Soc Surg Oncology, 1975-; bd dir, Am Cancer Soc, 1978-; med dir, Breast Examination Ctr Harlem, 1979; chmn, Nat Adv Comt Cancer Socio-Econ Disadvantaged Am Cancer Soc, 1986-88; Exec Coun Soc Surg Oncology, 1987-89; Governor Am Col Surgeons, 1988; nat pres, Am Cancer Soc, 1988-89; elected Alpha Omega Alpha, 1989; Exec Comt Am Col Surgeons, 1990; PRS's Cancer Panel, chair, 1991-94; past Chmn, US Pres's Cancer Panel. **Honors/Awds:** Harris Award, Outstanding Gentlemen Cath Univ, 1954; Prize in Psychaitry, Howard Univ, 1958; Daniel Hal Williams Award, Outstanding Achievement Chief Resident Howard Univ Hosp, 1964; National Boys Singles Tennis Champion, Am Tennis Asn, 1948; Honorary Doctor Sci: Albany Sch Med, 1989, Niagara Univ, 1989, Adelphi Univ, 1989; Catholic UNIV, Honorary Doctor Sci, 1989; Mary Lasker Award; Health Lifetime Achievement Award; American Cancer Society Medal Honor; Jill Rose Award; American Society Clinical Oncology Special Recognition Award. **Special Achievements:** "Harold P. Freeman Award" was established by the American Cancer Society in 1990. **Business Addr:** Associate Director, National Cancer Institute, NIH Bldg 31 Rm 10A16, Bethesda, MD 20892-2520, **Business Phone:** 800-422-6237.*

FREEMAN, KERLIN
Educator. **Personal:** Born Sep 24, 1930, Chelsea, MA; son of Lucille and Kerlin; married E Juanita Maybin; children: Leslie R, Beverly F & Alan K. **Educ:** Metro State Col, Denver Co, BA, elem ed, 1975; Lesley Col, cambridge, Mass, MA, computers ed, 1985. **Career:** Educator (retired); NAACP, human relations com, 1976-82, pres, 1977-82; Xi Pi Chapter Omega Psi Phi, recorder, 1977-81; Colo Springs Dist no 11, elementary sch teacher, NEA dir, 1990-92; XI Chapter Omega Psi Phi, vice baselius, 1986-90. **Orgs:** Chmn human rel comm., City CO Springs, 1983-85; chmn mny caucus CO Ed Assoc, 1982-; United Teaching Prof CO Football Officials Assoc, Black Ed Dist 11; del Dem Nat Conv, 1976; mem, Int Assoc Approved Basketball Officials, 1973-92; Opp, Xi Pi Chapter, basileus, 1991-94; bd dir, NEA, 1990-91; bd dir, CEA, 1990-91; bd dir, CO Springs Edu Asn, 1985-91; regional dir, CSEA, 1991-92; at-large dir, CEA, Ethnic Mny Adv Coun, 1991-92; Pikes Peak Lodge No. 5, F&A Masons Precinct Committeman, Precinct 125. **Honors/Awds:** Voted One of Ten Most Influential Blacks in CO Springs. **Military Serv:** USAF, msgt, 1950-71; Non-Commd Officer of the Year USAF-ADC, 1970; Meritorious Serv Medal AF, 1971. **Home Addr:** 3003 Greenwood Circle, Colorado Springs, CO 80910, **Home Phone:** (719)633-7193.

FREEMAN, KIMBERLEY EDELIN
School administrator, educator. **Personal:** Born Jun 11, 1970, Laken Heath, England; daughter of Kenneth and Ramona Edelin; married Clyde Freeman III, Sep 26, 1998; children: Clyde IV & Czleb. **Educ:** Spelman Col, BA, 1992; Univ Mich, MA, 1995, PhD, 1998. **Career:** Rackham Grad Sch, Merit fel, 1992-97; Rackham Grad Sch, Dissertation/Thesis Grant, 1995; Spencer Found, Dissertation fel, 1996-97; Frederick D Patterson Res Inst & UNCF, res scientist, 1997-99, exec dir, 1999; George Wash Univ, Columbian Col Arts & Sci, vis asst prof orgn sci & indust psychol; Brown Univ, fel; Howard Univ, Dept Human Develop & Psychoeducational studies, asst prof, currently. **Orgs:** AERA Spec Interest Group, Res Focus Black Educ, 1993-2001; Am Educ Res Asn, 1994-2002; Am Psychol Asn, 1996-2001; Nat Alliance Black Sch Educ, 1998-2004; comer, AERA Comm Res Black Educ, 1999; assoc ed, Rev African Am Educ, 1999; NPEC, 2000; adv coun, Nat Ctr Educ Stats, 2001; Nat Black Grad Stud Asn, adv bd, 2001-04; Soc Res Child Develop, 2001. **Honors/Awds:** Sandra Johnson Memorial Award, 1994-95; Barbara Oleshansky Research Prize, 1995; Diamond Best Dissertation Award, Univ Mich Sch Educ, 1999. **Special Achievements:** Numerous publications.

FREEMAN, LAURETTA
Basketball player, basketball coach. **Personal:** Born Mar 17, 1971, Mobile, AL; children: Jamie. **Educ:** Auburn Univ, MBA, 1993, MEd. **Career:** Basketball player (retired), basketball coach; Atlanta Glory, forward,1996-99; Auburn Tigers, admin asst, 1999, asst coach. **Special Achievements:** Became the first Auburn women's basketball player to earn her degree in four years; Member of the 1994 USA Goodwill Games team which won gold in St. Petersburg, Russia. *

FREEMAN, DR. LELABELLE CHRISTINE
Physician. **Personal:** Born Oct 27, 1923, Chicago, IL; daughter of Henry C and Ella Washington; children: Christine Crearym & James E Robinson Jr. **Educ:** Spelman Col, BA, 1944; Howard Univ Med Sch, MD, 1949. **Career:** Cook Co Sch Nursing, pediat instr, 1952; Howard Univ Med Sch, pediat instr, 1952-53; pvt pract pediatrician, 1953-77; City Cleveland Well Baby Clin, clin physician, 1953-57; E 35th St Clin, clin physician, 1953-63; Univ Hosp Cleveland, med staff, 1953-; Metropo Gen Hosp Cleveland, med staff, 1953-63; Health Resources Cleveland, clin physician, 1975-77; Cuyahoga Co Bd Health, contracting physician, beginning 1977. **Orgs:** Acad Med Cleveland, Family Pract Liaison Comm, 1964-65; bd trustees, Mt Pleasant Community Ctr; Cuyahoga Co Bd Mental Retardation, 1967-73; PTA, Health & Safety, 1961-70; child consult, Cedar Br YMCA, 1954-61; charter mem, Northern Ohio Pediat Soc. **Honors/Awds:** Numerous awards & citations including: 'Consortium of Doctors', 'Seminole Humanitarian Award', 1993, 'Relationships Award', 1994. **Special Achievements:** Articles: "Erythromycin in Treatment of Pyoderma in Children," Journal of Pediatrics, vol 42, no 6, pp 669-672, June 1953; "Influenzal Meningitis Treated Successfully with Polymyxin B," Illinois Medical Journal, vol 102, no 3, pp 205-207, Sept 1952; "Incidence of 'Subclinical' Trichinosis in Children," AMA American Journal of Diseases of Children, vol 87, no 4, pp 464-467, April 1954; "Gastric Suction in Infants Delivered by Cesarean Sections; Role in Prevention of Respiratory Complaints," AMA American Journal of Diseases of Children, vol 87, pp 570-574, May 1954; "Studies in Sickle Cell Anemia: Effect of Age (Maturation) on Incidence of the Sickling Phenomenom," Pediatrics, vol 14, no 3, pp 209-214, Sept 1954; "Observations on Trichinosis: Report of Community Outbreak," AMA American Journal of Diseases of Children, vol 89, no 2, pp 194-198, Feb 1955. **Business Addr:** Clinical Instructor, Case W Research College of Medicine, Cleveland, OH 44106.

FREEMAN, LOUIS LAWRENCE
Pilot. **Personal:** Born Jun 12, 1952, Austin, TX. **Educ:** E Tex State Univ, BS, sociol & psychol, 1974; Reese Air Force Base, Texas, USAF Pilot Training, 1975. **Career:** Flight Training Squadron, Mather Air Force Base, CA, Co-Pilot, pilot, instr pilot, 1975-80; Southwest Airlines, AZ, IL, first officer, capt, asst chief pilot, chief pilot, 1980- . **Honors/Awds:** Squadron Pilot of the Year, 454th Flight Training Squadron, USAF; Winning Spirit Award; President's Award, Southwest Airlines; Corporate Trailblazer Award, Dollars & Sense Mag, 1993; Keynote speaker, Black Hist Month Celebration, Miami Int Airport, 1996. **Special Achievements:** The first black pilot to be hired by Southwest Airlines. His professional skills enabled him to become Southwest's first African American captain as well, and later, chief pilot for the Chicago pilot base of the airline; The first African American cadet corps commander in the school's ROTC (Reserve Officers Training Corps). **Business Addr:** Chief Pilot, Southwest Airlines, Attn: Personnel, 5333 S Laramie Ave, Chicago, IL 60638, **Business Phone:** (773)284-5900.*

FREEMAN, MARIANNA
Basketball coach. **Personal:** Born Jul 30, 1957, Wilmington, DE; daughter of Marion L Freeman. **Educ:** Cheyney Univ, BS, 1979; Slippery Rock Univ, MS. **Career:** Del state Col, head coach, 1981-83; Univ Iowa, asst coach, 1983-93;Syracuse Univ, head coach, 1993-96; USA Jr World Championship Team, asstcoach, 1998; USA World Championship Team, asst coach, 2002; Syracuse, head caoch. **Orgs:** Black Coaches Assn; Women's Basketball Coaches Assn; Nat Coun Negro Women; chair, NCAA Rules Comm. **Honors/Awds:** Hall of Fame, Cheyney Univ, 1993; Spirit of American Women Award, GirlsInc. of Central. *

FREEMAN, MELINDA LYONS
Educator. **Personal:** Born Apr 22, 1956, Chapel Hill, NC; daughter of Eugene Lyons and Mary; divorced; children: Tyler Mason. **Educ:** NC Cent Univ, BSHE, 1982; Univ NC, Greensboro, MEd, 1985. **Career:** Univ NC Hosp, cardiology tech; Alamance County Health Dept, nutritionist, outreach coordr health educr, & technician, currently. **Orgs:** Int Childbirth Educators Assoc, 1993-97; local chap pres, Delta Sigma Theta Sorority, 1986-; NAACP, 1997-; trainer, NC Family Resource Coalition, 1997-; trainer & volunteer, NC Volunteer Families Children, 1997-; Alamance Juvenile Crime Prev Coun, 1995; comt chair, Alamance Child Abuse Prev Task Force, 1997-. **Honors/Awds:** Benita R Kearney Service Award, Delta Sigma Theta, 1995. **Home Addr:** 908 Stone St, Burlington, NC 27215, **Home Phone:** (336)570-0373. **Business Addr:** Health Educator, Alamance County Health Department, 316 N Graham Hopedale Rd Suite B, Burlington, NC 27215, **Business Phone:** (336)227-0101.

FREEMAN, MORGAN PORTERFIELD, JR.
Actor. **Personal:** Born Jun 1, 1937, Memphis, TN; son of Morgan Porterfield Freeman and Mayme Edna Revere Freeman; married Jeanette Adair Bradshow, Oct 22, 1967 (divorced 1979); children: Alphonse, Saifoulaye, Deena & Morgana; married Myrna Colley-Lee, Jun 16, 1984. **Educ:** Los Angeles City Col, theater arts, 1960. **Career:** Stage appearances include: The Nigger-Lovers, 1967; Hello Dolly, 1967;Jungle of the Cities, 1969; The Recruiting Officer, 1969; Scuba Duba,1969; Purlie, 1970; Black Visions, 1972; Sisyphus & the Blue-Eyed Cyclops, 1975; Cockfight, 1977; The Last Street Play, 1977; The Mighty Gents, 1978; White Pelicans, 1978; Coriolanus, 1979; Julius Caesar, 1979; Mother Courage & Her Children, 1980; Othello, 1982; All's Well That Ends Well,1982; Buck, 1982; The World of Ben Caldwell, 1982; The Gospel at Colonus, 1983; Medea & the Doll, 1984; Driving Miss Daisy, 1987; The Taming of the Shrew, 1990; Films: Who Says I Can't Ride a Rainbow?, 1971; Brubaker,1980; Eyewitness, 1980; Harry & Son, 1983; Teachers, 1984; Marie, 1985;That Was Then, This Is Now, 1985; Street art, 1987; Clean & Sober, 1988;Glory, 1989; Lean on Me, 1989; Driving Miss Daisy, 1989; Johnny Handsome, 1989; Robin Hood: Prince of Thieves, 1991; Unforgiven, 1992; Bopha, dir,1993; The Shawshank Redemption, 1994; Outbreak, 1995; Seven, 1995; Kiss the Girls, 1997; Chain Reaction, 1997; Deep Impact, 1998; Hard Rain, 1998;Nurse Betty, 2000; Under Suspicion, 2000; Along Came a Spider, 2001; High Crimes, 2002; The Sum of All Fears, 2002; Dream catcher, 2003; Levity,2003; Bruce Almighty, 2003; The Big Bounce, 2004; Danny the Dog, Edison,2005; The Code, 2006; The Contract, 2006; 10 Items or Less, 2006; The Bucket List, 2007; Feast of Love, 2007; Gone Baby Gone, 2007; Evan lmighty, 2007; The Dark Knight, 2008; Thick as Thieves, 2008; Wanted, 2008; The Maiden Heist, 2009; TV Series: "Electric Company", 1971-76; "Another World, 1982; "Hollow Image", 1979; "Attica", 1980; "The Marva Collins Story", 1981; "The Atlanta Child Murders", 1985; "Resting Place", 1986; "Flight for Life", 1987; "Clinton & Nadine", 1988; "Mutiny",1999; "Million Dollar Baby", 2004; "The Downward Spiral", 2005; "Slavery &the Making of America", 2005; "A Raisin in the Sun", 2008; "Stephen Fry in America", 2008; "Smithsonian Channel's Sound Revolution", 2008. **Orgs:** Actor's Equity Asn; Screen Actors Guild; Am Fedn Television & Radio Artists. **Honors/Awds:** Clarence Derwent Award; Drama Desk Award; Outstanding Featured Actor in aPlay; Tony Award nomination; The Mighty Gents, 1978; Obie Award, Driving Miss Daisy, 1987; New York Film Critics Circle Award; Los Angeles Film Critics Award; Nat Soc Films Critics Award; Obie Awards, Mother Courage &Her C, Coriolanus, The Gospel at Colonus; Best Actor, Driving Miss Daisy,1991; NAACP Image Award, Motion Picture Supporting Actor, 1998; CrystalIris Award, 1998; Joseph Plateau Life Achievement Award, 2000; Hollywood Discovery Award for Outstanding Achievement in Acting, 2000; Philadelphia festival of World Cinema Lifetime Achievement Award, 2001; Special Prize for Outstanding Contribution to World Cinema, 2003; Nat Board of Review Career Achievement Award, 2003; Crystal Globe Award, 2003; Lifetime Achievement Award, Miss Inst Arts & Letters, 2007; Kennedy Ctr Honors, 2008. **Military Serv:** USAF, 1955-59. **Business Addr:** Actor, c/o William Morris Agency, 1325 Ave of Americas, New York, NY 10019, **Business Phone:** (212)586-5100.

FREEMAN, DR. PAUL D.
Conductor (music). **Personal:** Born Jan 2, 1936, Richmond, VA; son of L H Freeman; married Cornelia Perry; children: Douglas Cornelia. **Educ:** Eastman Sch Music, BMus, 1956, MMus, 1957, PhD Theory, 1963; Hochschule Fur Musik Berlin, addn studies. **Career:** Hochstein Music Sch, Rochester NY, dir 1960-66; Opera Theatre Rochester, music dir, 1961-66; San Francisco Community Music Ctr, dir, 1966-68; San Francisco Little Sym, music dir, 1967-68; Dallas Sym Orchestra, assoc conductor, 1968-70; Detroit Sym, conductor-in-residence, 1970-79; Saginaw Sym, music dir; Helsinki Philharmonic Orchestra, prin guest conductor; Columbia Black Composers Series, artistic dir; numerous recs; Chicago Sinfonietta, music dir & conductor, 1987-; Victoria, BC, Canada Symphony, conductor, 1979-89; Victoria Sym Orchestra, music dir emer, 1988-; Czech Nat Sym Orchestra, music dir & cheif conductor, 1996; Chicago Sinfonietta, founder & dir music, currently. **Honors/Awds:** Winner, Dimitri Mitropolous Int Conductors Competition, 1967; Special Spoleto Award, Festival Two Worlds, 1968; Distinguished Alumni Citation, Univ Rochester, 1975; Distinguished Citation Award, United Negro Col Fund; Koussevitzky International Recording Award, 1974; Nominee, Ebony Arts Award, 1989; LHD, Dominican Univ, 1994; LHD, Loyola Univ,

1998; Jubilate Award; Mahler Award, Europ Union Arts. **Special Achievements:** Numerous guest appearances in the US, Austria, England, Germany, Denmark, Norway, Sweden, Poland, Italy, Russia, Mexico, Israel, Finland/Yugoslavia, included in Time magazine's Top Five Classical Records Listing, 1974, has approximately 200 releases to his credit, was designated a History Maker, having been nominated by the DuSable Museum of African American History for his outstanding contributions to African American life, history & culture. On January 25, 2005 the Detroit Free Press published a story by music writer Mark Stryker entitled: A BLACK KEY: Conductor Paul Freeman, in town for the Sphinx Competition, adds color to the national classical music scene. **Business Addr:** Founder, Music Director, Chicago Sinfonietta, 70 E Lake St Suite 226, Chicago, IL 60601, **Business Phone:** (312)236-3681.

FREEMAN, PRESTON GARRISON
School administrator. **Personal:** Born Apr 12, 1933, Washington, DC; married Jean Marie Hall; children: Jacqueline, Michelle, Nicole & Monica. **Educ:** Morgan State Col, BS, 1955; George Wash Univ, MA, 1961; Catholic Univ Am, PhD, 1974. **Career:** Educator (retired); Wash DC Pub Sch, teacher, 1955-63, couns, 1963-66, dir, 1966-69, exec asst, 1969-72, asst supt, 1972-91. **Orgs:** Am Asn Sch Admin; Asn Supv & Curric Develop; Phi Delta Kappa; Kappa Alpha Psi Fraternity; vice chmn, Health & Welfare Coun, 1965-70; vice chmn,Prince Georges Comm Action Com, 1967-70; Child Day Care Asn, 1968-70; fel, Coun Great Cities, 1970-71; Exec Internship. **Military Serv:** AASA, Arlington, VA, 1973-74.

FREEMAN, ROBERT, JR.
Government official, business owner. **Personal:** Born in Milledgeville, GA. **Educ:** Ga Southern Univ, BS, MS. **Career:** Freeman's Barber Shop, founder & owner, 1993-; Fed Govt, asst chief staff, currently. **Honors/Awds:** Barbershop of the Yr, 1999 & 2000; Community Bus of the Yr, Prince George's County, NAACP; Nat Asn Advan Colored People, 2003. **Business Phone:** (301)350-5399.

FREEMAN, RONALD J.
Judge. **Personal:** Born Aug 17, 1947, Winslow, NJ; married Carmen Martinez. **Educ:** Lincoln Univ, BA, 1969; Rutgers Law Sch, JD, 1972; State Univ NJ Sch Law. **Career:** Rutgers State Univ Col Ctr, staff asst, 1970; NJ Dept Law & Pub Safety, Div Civil Rights, Rutgers State Univ Sch Law Clinical Prog, 1971; Camden Reg Legal Serv Inc, legal coun, 1972-73; NJ Dept Law & Pub Safety & Div Civil Rights, Rutgers Law Sch Clinic Prog, sr field rep aide, 1972; Legal coun, comt legal serv phil, 1973; Glassboro State Col, adj fac, 1973; Freeman, Zeller & Bryant, gen partner, 1974-97; NJ Supreme Ct, state bd bar examr, 1989-97; Super Ct, 4th Vicinage, NJ, judge, currently. **Orgs:** Bar Supreme Ct, PA, 1973; Bar US Dist Ct, E Dist, PA, 1973; Bar US Ct, Appeals Third Ciruit, 1974; Bar Supreme Ct, NJ, 1974; Bar US Dist Ct, Dist NJ, 1974; chair, NJ Bd Bar Examr, 1989-97; chair, NJ Supreme Ct Comn Minority Concerns, 1999-01; Pa Bar Asn; Am Bar Asn; Nat Bar Asn; Phil Bar Asn; Nat Conf, Black Lawyers; Phi Alpha Delta; NJ Bar Asn; Camden County Correctional Facil Adv Bd Comn; bd dir, Haddon Field Sch Creative & Performing Arts; Sigma Psi Phi, Delta Epsilon Boule; NCP; Nat Coun Juv & Family Ct Judges. **Business Addr:** Judge, Superior Court 4th Vicinage, Hall Justice, 101 S 5th St, Camden, NJ 08103-4001, **Business Phone:** (856)379-2364.*

FREEMAN, DR. RUGES R.
Educator. **Personal:** Born Feb 25, 1917, St Louis, MO; son of Ruges R and Willie C Barr; married Maxine Carter; children: Wilatrel. **Educ:** S Ill Univ, BE, 1935; Univ Ill, MA, 1936; Wash Univ, PhD, 1972. **Career:** Dunbar High Sch, teacher, 1936-38; Chicago Relief Admin, caseworker,1938-40; Vashon High Sch, teacher, 1940-47, boys counr & admin asst, 1947-50; Dunbar Elem, asst & prin, 1950-51; Carver Elem, Dumas Elem, Cote Brilliante Elem, prin, 1951-64; Sumner High Sch, asst prin, 1964-68; Beaumont High Sch, prin, 1965-66; Harrison Elem, prin, 1968-73; Teacher Corps, from asst dir to dir, 1977-82; Sec Stud Teaching Southern Ill Univ, from assoc prof & co-ord to prof, 1973-82, prof emer, 1983-. **Orgs:** Bd dir, United Church Men, 1972; vpres, Social Health Asn Greater St Louis, 1972; dir teacher corps, Prog Dev Specialist, 1977-79; Dean's Adv Coun, 1978-81; bd dir, Nursery Found, 1978-81; Southwest Ill Supt Conf, 1979-81, chmn, 1981-82; Presidential Scholars; dir, Teacher Corps, 1979-82; Nat Soc Study Educ; Am Educ Res Asn; Nat Educ Asn; Asn Supv & Curric Develop; Phi Delta Kappa; Alpha Phi Alpha; Gaylords; Gnashers; St James AME Church. **Military Serv:** AUS, 1944.

FREEMAN, SHIRLEY WALKER
Librarian. **Personal:** Born Jun 7, 1951, Jackson, MS; daughter of Leroy Walker Sr and Louise Luster; married N Trent Freeman, Aug 15, 1992; children: Jerry, Lamont, Courtney, Nate, Trevor, Kelli & Darwin. **Educ:** Livingston Col, 1970; Tougaloo Col, BS, 1973; Univ Ill, Urbana-19Champaign, MLS, 1978. **Career:** Rowland Med Libr, ass librn, 1972-76; Univ Ill, grad teaching asst, 1976-78; Champaign Pub Libr, br mgr, librn, 1977-83; Columbus Metrop Libr, br mgr, librn, 1983-, Freeman Construct Servs Inc, co-owner, currently. **Orgs:** Delta Sigma Theta Sorority, 1969-; Am Libr Asn; United Methodist Church; Black Caucus Am Libr Asn. **Home Addr:** 2881 Castlewood Rd, Columbus, OH 43209, **Home Phone:** (614)231-6386. **Business Addr:** Branch Manager, Librarian, Columbus Metropolitan Library, Livingston Branch, 3434 E Livingston Ave, Columbus, OH 43227, **Business Phone:** (614)645-2275.

FREEMAN, THOMAS F.
Clergy, educator. **Personal:** Born Jun 27, 1920, Richmond, VA; married; children: Thomas Jr, Carter & Carlotta. **Educ:** Univ Nigeria, Lagos; Univ Ghana, Ghana E Africa; VA Union Univ, BA, 1939; Andover Newton Theol Sch, BD, 1942; Univ Chicago, PhD, 1948; Howard Univ, further study; Boston Univ, further study; Univ Vienna, Austria, further study; African Univ. **Career:** Rice Univ, vis prof; Concord Baptist Church, Boston MA, asst minister, 1939-40; Pleasant St Baptist Church, Westerly RI, minister, 1940-44; Monumental Baptist Church Chicago, assoc minister, 1942-44; VA Union Univ, prof pract theol, 1944-49; Carmel Baptist Church, minister, 1944-50; Mt Horem Baptist Church, pasto, 1951; Col Arts & Sci Tex Southern Univ, dept head philos, 1950-67, asst dean, 1968-70; Model Cities Training Ctr Tex Southern Univ, dir, 1970-74; Tex Southern Univ, dir continuing educ; Weekend Col, dean. **Orgs:** Pres, Alpha Kappa Mu Nat Honor Soc, 1962-66; alumni dir, Alpha Kappa Mu Nat Honor Soc, 1966; bd dir, Andover Newton Alumni Asn; bd dir, Asn Churches; Nat Asn Advan Colored People; Boy Scouts; Urban League. **Honors/Awds:** Clarke Scholarship, VA Union Univ, 1939; Turner fellowship, Andover Newton, 1939-42; fellowship, Univ of C, 1942-46; Univ Faculty Mem of Yr, Univ Divinity, 1950-51; book Choices of The Pew, 1963; Tex Southern Univ-PI CC Award, Tex Southern Univ, 1974; DHL, Eastern Mass Univ; Faculty Member International Recognition Award, Tex Southern Univ, 1992; Margaret Ross Barnett Leadership Award, Houston Urban League, 1992. **Special Achievements:** Am Press co-author "From Separation to Special Designation", 1975. *

FREEMAN, V DIANE
Manager. **Personal:** Children: Dione & Kenisha. **Career:** AT&T, operator; Gen Motors Corp, sr mgr supplier diversity prog, currently. **Orgs:** Native Am Bus Alliance; exec & finance comt mem, Mich Minority Bus Develop Coun; bd dir, Ctr Empowerment & Econ Develop, Ann Arbour, MI. **Honors/Awds:** Corporate Amiga Award, 2005; Corporate Champion of the Year Award, Mich Women's Bus Coun, 2005; Advocate of the Year Award, Mich Minority Bus Develop Coun, 2007. **Business Addr:** Senior Program Manager of Supplier Diversity, General Motors Corp, 300 Renaissance Ctr, Detroit, MI 48243, **Business Phone:** (586)575-4100.

FREEMAN, WALTER EUGENE
Computer executive, manager. **Personal:** Born May 25, 1955, Hartford, CT; son of Walter and Shirley; married Marsha, Jun 22, 1985; children: Walter & Taylor. **Educ:** Boston Univ, BS, 1978; Cambridge Col, MS, mgt, 1991. **Career:** Pratt & Whitney Aircraft, buyer, 1979-84, sr buyer, 1984-87; Digital Equipment Corp, purchasing specialist, 1987-90, purchasing consult, 1990-93; TM Industs, sales engr, 1993-94; Compaq Computer Corp, commodity mgr, 1994-97, procurement mgr, 1997-2000; Dell Inc, Worldwide Procurement, sr mgr, 2000-04, fed bid, contracts & proposals mgr, 2004-06; Apple, Applecare procurement mgr, 2006-. **Orgs:** Bd dirs, Springfield Day Nursery, 1992-94; Nat Soc Black Engrs. **Home Addr:** 12811 Justin Trail, Houston, TX 77070, **Home Phone:** (281)807-4463. **Business Addr:** Applecare Procurement Manager, Apple Inc, 12545 Riata Vista Circle, Austin, TX 78727, **Business Phone:** (512)674-2000.

FREEMAN, WARREN L.
Military leader. **Personal:** Born in Jackson, GA; son of Sara; married Barbara Ann; children: Kevin, Brandon. **Educ:** Pac Western Univ, BBA, mgt, 1982; US Army War Col, 1990; Nat Louis Univ, MS, Mgt, 1993; Sr Reserve Component Officer Course, 1993; Harvard Univ, Nat & Int Security Mgt Seminar, 1996. **Career:** Reserve Forces Policy Bd, army nat guard mem; DC Army Nat Guard, dep brigade Commander, 260th MP Brigade, DCARNG & chief staff, 1996-91; US Army, Comndg Gen DC Nat Guard, 1995-02. **Orgs:** Kappa Alpha Psi; US Army War Col Alumni Asn; Nat Guard Asn US; Asn United States Army. **Honors/Awds:** Outstanding Young Men of America; honary doctorate of humane letters, Nat Louis Univ; Air Force Commendation Medal; Army Achievement Medal; Army Reserve Components Achievement Medal; National Defense Service Medal; Humanitarian Service Medal; Armed Forces Reserve Medal; Meritorious Service Medal; Army Commendation Medal; Distinguished Service Medal; US Meritorious Service Medal; Army Commendation Medal. **Military Serv:** AUS Nat Guard, major gen. *

FREEMAN, YAUSMENDA
Fashion model, actor, president (organization). **Personal:** Born in Los Angeles, CA. **Educ:** Univ Calif, Berkeley, BA, archit; Van Mar Acad, camera tech, bus actg, Improv & Comedy; WLAC, voice coach. **Career:** Film: Still Bout It, 2004; Black Love; Forget Paris; TV Show: The George Lopez Show; The Martin Lawrence Show; Theatre Performance: A Woman's Worth; Diary of a Catholic Sch Dropout; The Wiz; The Grass Ainocot Greener; In-dust: Women Talking; Mech of Life; African-Aerobics & Exotica; Knock Out Base Inc, pres & ceo, 1996. *

FREEMAN-WILSON, KAREN MARIE
Judge, lawyer. **Personal:** Born Oct 24, 1960, Gary, IN; daughter of Travis Lee and Myrlin Delores Patterson; married Carmen Wilson Jr, Feb 17, 1991. **Educ:** Harvard Col, Cambridge, MA, BA, 1982; Harvard Law Sch, Cambridge, MA, JD, 1985. **Career:** Lake Co Prosecutor's Off, Crown Point, IN, dep prosecutor, 1985-89; Lake Co Defender's Off, Crown Point, IN, pub defender, 1989; Ind Civil Rights Comn, Indianapolis, IN, dir, 1989-92; pvt pract, atty, civil & criminal litigation; Gary City Judge; atty gen, IN, currently. **Orgs:** Vpres, Delta Sigma Theta Sorority, 1980-; Nat Coun Negro Women; chair, Israel CME Steward Bd, 1985-; Coalition of 100 Black Women, 1990-. **Honors/Awds:** Fifty Leaders of the Future, Ebony Mag, 1990; Bethune Award, Nat Coun Negro Women, 1990. **Home Addr:** 475 Garfield St, Gary, IN 46404, **Home Phone:** (219)882-4700. **Business Addr:** Attorney General, Indiana County, Office of the Attorney General, 302 W Wash St 5th Fl, Indianapolis, IN 46204, **Business Phone:** (317)232-6255.

FREEMONT, JAMES MCKINLEY
Physician. **Personal:** Born Dec 2, 1942, Monroe, LA; married Erma Turner; children: James Jr, Joi Michelle, Jonathan Marcus. **Educ:** Southern Univ, BS, 1966; Emory Univ Sch Med, MD, 1973. **Career:** Women Health Ctr, med dir, 1980-; HMO, secy/treas, 1980-82; Southwest Community Hosp, Dept Obstet & Gynec, chief, 1985-86; pvt pract, currently. **Orgs:** Omega Psi Phi Fraternity, 1962-; pres, Atlanta Chap Southern Alumni Asn, 1983-; bd mem, United Community Corp, 1985-. **Honors/Awds:** Outstanding Alumni, Nat Asn for Equal Opportunity Higher Educ, 1986. **Military Serv:** AUS, sergeant, 1966-68. **Business Addr:** Obstetrician, Gynecologist, 777 Cleveland Ave SW Suite 210, Atlanta, GA 30315.*

FREGIA, DARRELL LEON
Administrator. **Personal:** Born Sep 8, 1949, San Francisco, CA; married Deborah Brooks; children: Marque, Akil, Shani. **Educ:** City Col San Francisco, AA, Gen Educ, 1969; Stanford Univ, BA, Sociol, 1972; Univ Wash, MHA, 1977. **Career:** San Mateo Co Probation Dept, Redwood City, Ca, adult probation officer, 1973-75; scholar grad sch, VPres Health Affairs Univ Wash, 1975-77; Va Hosp Seattle, adminr, intern, 1976; Group Health Coop East-side Hosp & Med Ctr, adminr, 1977-78; Group Health Coop Fed Way Med Ctr, adminr, 1978-79; Group Health Coop Puget Sound Ctl Hosp & Med Ctr, asst hosp adminr, 1979-; asst comptroller, 1988-90; State Wash Employ Security Depat, risk mgr, 1990-97, fiscal mgr & policy coordr, 1997-. **Orgs:** Guiding Light Youth Mentorship Prog; Stanford Univ Buck Club, 1972-; Stanford Univ Alumni Asn, 1972-; life mem Alpha Phi Alpha Frat Inc 1977; Seattle Comn Col Curriculum Task Force, 1978; sec bd dirs, Ctr Addiction Servs Seattle, 1978-; cons/analyst Pioneer Mgmt Inc Seattle 1978-; vpres bd dir, Paul Robeson Theatre Prod, 1980; Univ Wash Mentorship Prog, 1995-. **Honors/Awds:** Recipient Player Yr Award, San Francisco HS AAA Basketball, 1967; buck club athletic scholar, Stanford Univ Basketball, 1970-72; traineeship, US Dept Pub Health, 1975-77; Outstanding Young Man Am Award, US Jaycees, 1979. **Business Addr:** Fiscal Manager, Policy Coordinator, Dept Employ Security, W Region, 8815 S Tacoma Way SW Suite 122, Tacoma, WA 98499, **Business Phone:** (253)589-7278.*

FREGIA, RAY, SR.
Executive. **Personal:** Born Nov 22, 1948, Beaumont, TX; son of Betty Thomas; married Jewell M Perkins, Apr 17, 1971; children: Ray Jr, Rik. **Educ:** Lamar Univ, BBA, 1971. **Career:** Ford Motor Corp, regional opers mgr; River View Ford Inc, co-owner & pres, currently. **Honors/Awds:** Ford Motor Credit Partners Quality Award, Blue Oval Cert. **Business Addr:** President, Co-Owner, Riverview Ford Inc, 2200 Rte 30, Oswego, IL 60543, **Business Phone:** (630)897-8900.*

FREISEN, GIL
Association executive, movie producer, founder (originator). **Career:** Kapp Rec, pres; A&M Rec, pres; Classic Sports, founding partner; Digital Entertainment Network, dir; Painted Turtle, founder, currently; Films: Love It or Leave It, 1971; The Breakfast Club, 1985; Better Off Dead, 1985; One Crazy Summer, 1986; The Beast of War, 1988; Worth Winning, 1989; Blaze, 1989; Crooked Hearts, 1991. **Orgs:** Pres, Mus Contemporary Art; adv bd, Akamai. **Business Phone:** (310)451-1353.

FRELOW, ROBERT DEAN
Educator. **Personal:** Born Aug 1, 1932, Seminole, OK; divorced; children: Robert, Fred, Michael. **Educ:** San Francisco State Col, BA, 1954; San Francisco State Univ, MA, 1964; Univ Calif-Berkeley, PhD, 1970. **Career:** Oakland Unified Schs, teacher, 1960-66; Berkeley Unified Schs, from asst to supt, 1966-70; Greenburgh Dist 7, asst supt, 1970-74, supt 1974-. **Orgs:** Am Asn Sch Admin, 1970; adj assoc prof, Pace Univ, 1973; bd dirs, Westchester Arts Coun, 1982-87; Am Red Crss, 1985-86. **Honors/Awds:** Omega Citizen of the Yr, Beta Alpha Chap Omega Psi Phi, 1984; Proclamation Robert D Frelow Day, Westchester Bd of Legislators, 1985. **Military Serv:** USAF, capt, 3 yrs. **Home Addr:** 25A Hillside Terr, White Plains, NY 10601.

FRENCH, GEORGE WESLEY, JR. See Obituaries section.

FRENCH, HOWARD W
Journalist, editor. **Personal:** Born Oct 14, 1957, Washington, DC; son of David Marshall and Carolyn Alverda; married Agnes Koffi, Oct 5, 1987; children: William Howard & Henry Nelson. **Educ:** Univ Mass, Amherst, MA, BA, 1979. **Career:** Self-employed, Abidjan, Ivory Coast, conf translator, 1979-80; Univ Ivory Coast, Abidjan, Ivory Coast, asst prof Eng, 1980-82; Wash Post, Abidjan, Ivory Coast, W Africa stringer, 1982-86; NY Times, New York, NY, metrop reporter, 1986-90, NY Times, Miami, FL, Caribbean corresp, 1990, bur chief, 1990-94; NY Times, W african bur chief, Abidjan Ivory Coast, 1994, sr writer & shanghai bur chief, 2003-. **Orgs:** Nat Asn Broadcasters; Inst AMEs; African Studies Asn. **Business Addr:** Shanghai Bureau Chief, Senior Writer, The New York Times, 229 W 43rd St, New York, NY 10036.

FRENCH, MARYANN
Journalist. **Personal:** Born Aug 12, 1952, Washington, DC; daughter of David M and Carolyn Howard; married Dennis M Marshall, Nov 5, 1988 (divorced 1995); children: French Scott. **Educ:** Boston Univ, attended 1970; Johns Hopkins Univ, 1979; Johns Hopkins Sch Advanced Intl Studies, MA, 1982. **Career:** Black Women's Comm Develop Found, dir prog admin, 1977-78; The Washington Post, researcher, 1981-82; Time Magazine, reporter/researcher, 1982-84; The Louisville Courier Journal, reporter, 1984-86; St Petersburg Times, Washington corres, 1986-; St Petersburg Florida Times, Washington correspondent, 1986-88; Baltimore Sun, Washington correspondent, 1988; The Daily News, St Thomas, Virgin Islands, ed, 1989-90; The Washington Post, Washington, DC, staff writer, 1990-; books: 40 Ways to Raise a Nonracist Child, 1996. **Orgs:** Louisville Assoc Black Communicators, 1984-86, Nat Assoc Black Journalists, 1984-, Wash Assoc Black Journalists, 1986-. **Honors/Awds:** Fel Modern Media (Poynter) Inst, 1982; Metro Louisville Sigma Delta Chi Award continuing coverage of the artificial heart experiment, 1984; Journalism Award, Outstanding Coverage of the Black Condition, First Place, Features Natl Assn Black Journalist, 1996; Fel, Duke Univ Ctr Public Policy, 1993. **Home Phone:** (202)265-1180. **Business Addr:** Reporter, The Washington Post, 1150 15th St NW, Washington, DC 20071, **Business Phone:** (202)334-7350.

FRESH, EDITH MCCULLOUGH
Educator, counselor. **Personal:** Born Sep 23, 1942, Quincy, FL; daughter of Harry M McCullough (deceased) and Edith Anderson; married Frederick Anthony Fresh; children: Kevin W, Bradford, Carla, Eric. **Educ:** Ind Univ, AB, 1970; Univ Mich, MSW, 1972; Gestalt Inst Cleveland, Dipl, 1977; Ga State Univ, MA, 1988, PhD, clin child & family psychol, 1993. **Career:** Project Headline, Detroit MI, dir outpatient treat, 1972-73; Pub Tech Inc, human resources spec, 1973-77; FL A&M Univ, asst prof, 1977-83; EM Fresh & Assoc, FL, sr assoc, 1977-83; Morehouse Sch Med, clin social worker, 1983-88; Spelman Col, clin social worker, 1988-90; Georgia Mental Health Inst, Atlanta, GA, psychol intern, 1990-91; The New Found, marriage & family therapist, 1990-; DeKalb Col, North Campus, asst prof, 1991-94; Morehouse Sch Med Div dir, Biopsychosocial Med, 1994-, Dept Psychiat & Behav Sci, assoc prof, currently. **Orgs:** Acad Cert Social Workers, 1976-; Nat Asn Social Workers, 1976-; Nat Hook-Up Black Women, 1980-84; clin mem, Am Asn Marriage & Family Therapists, 1980-; site visitor, Comn Accreditation Marriage & Ther Educ, 1982-; vis staff, Gestalt Inst Cleveland, 1981-; bd mem, Mental Health Dist Bd II-B Leon City, FL, 1982-83; Am Asn Univ Women, 1983-85; chairperson, Ga Asn Marriage & Family Therapists Minority Affairs Task Force, 1991-94; ethics community, 1993-96, approved supvr, 2001, chair, 2003, Am Asn Marriage & Family Therapists. **Honors/Awds:** Gwen Cherry Memorial Award Outstanding Contribution Women's Rights, State of Florida Southern Reg Journalists Asn, 1980; Woman of the Year, Zeta Phi Beta, 1982. **Business Addr:** Associate Professors, Morehouse School of Medicine, Department of Psychiatry & Behavioral Sciences, 720 Westview Dr SW, Atlanta, GA 30310-1495.*

FRETT, LA KESHIA
Basketball player. **Personal:** Born Jun 12, 1975, Carmel, CA; daughter of Raymond and Linda. **Educ:** Univ Ga, Consumer Econs, 1997; Md Univ Col, MBA. **Career:** Basketball player (retired), basketball coach; Philadelphia Rage, forward, 1997; Los Angeles Sparks, 1999-00; Sacramento Monarchs, 2001-03; NY Liberty, forward, 2004-05; Lady Bulldog, asst coach, 2005-. **Honors/Awds:** Parade All-Am, 1991, 1992, 1993; Nat Prep Player of the Yr by Parade, USA Today, Boost & Naismith, Gatorade, 1993. **Special Achievements:** Film appearance: Love and Basketball, 2000. **Business Addr:** Assistant Coach, University of Georgia Athletic Association, PO Box 1472, Athens, GA 30602, **Business Phone:** (706)542-3000.*

FRETWELL, CARL QUENTION, II
Law enforcement officer, government official. **Personal:** Born May 5, 1951, Fort Worth, TX; son of Carl Q Fretwell Sr and Georgetta Enge; married Constance Barron (divorced 1989). **Educ:** Tarrant County Jr Col, Fort Worth, AA, 1972; Tex Wesleyan Univ, Fort Worth, BBA, 1975; Univ N Tex, Denton, TX. **Career:** Tex Youth Coun, Crockett, caseworker I, 1975-76; Tex Youth Coun, Gainesville, caseworker II, sr dorm dir, 1976-82; Bd Pardons & Parole, Ft Worth, parole officer I, unit supvr, 1982-88; Tex Youth Comn, Ft Worth, parole officer II, parole officer III, off mgr, 1988-, court liasons off, 1990, parole supvr, 1996-. **Orgs:** Prof mem, Tex Corrections Asn, 1976-97; Nat Asn Advan Colored People, 1978-; founder, Fort Worth Chap, NABCJ, 1986; Nat bd dirs, 1988-; asst treas, 1989; Nat Asn Blacks Criminal Justice; bd dirs, Boy Scouts, Fort Worth, 1990; Nat treas, 1994. **Honors/Awds:** Gang Unit Award, Fort Worth Mayor's Off, 1984; Mgt Cert, Govr Tex, 1986; Outstanding Supvr Award, Bd Pardons & Parole, 1988; Eminent Man Award, Phi Delta Kappa, Inc, 1997; Spirit Award, Tex Youth Comn, 2003. **Business Addr:** Parole Supervisor, Texas Youth Commission, 4900 N Lamar Blvd, PO Box 4260, Fort Worth, TX 78765.*

FRIDAY, JEFF
Movie producer, entrepreneur, executive. **Personal:** Born Jan 1, 1964, New York, NY; married Nicole. **Educ:** Howard Univ, BA, finance; Leonard Stern Sch Bus, NY Univ, MBA. **Career:** Bristol Myers Int, mkt, 1987; Schiefflin & Sommerset, mkt, 1989; Mingo Group, vpres, prom & event mkt directing new product initiatives for Tyco Toys, 1990; UniWorld Films, pres, 1996; Acapulco Black Film Festival, founder, exec dir & producer, 1997-; Am Black Film Festival, founder; One Week, co-exec producer, 2000; Film Life Inc, founder & chief exec officer, 2002-; Black Movie Awards, creator & exec producer, 2005-. **Honors/Awds:** Outstanding New Jerseyans Award, Kean Univ, 2003. **Special Achievements:** featured in numerous publications included: Variety, Hollywood Reporter, Crains, Black Enterprise, Essence, The New York Times, The Los Angeles Times, NV magazine, VIBE & he has been profiled on WNBC-TV in New York. *

FRIERSON, MICHAEL ANTHONY
Surgeon. **Personal:** Born Mar 2, 1961, Detroit, MI; son of Benjamin and Hattie Marie Chandler; married Jo'crisshawn Gardner-Frierson, Feb 14, 1988 (divorced); children: Michael A Frierson II, Ashley Ryan Frierson. **Educ:** Univ MI, attended 1983; Univ MI Med Sch, MD, 1987; Loyola Univ Med Ctr, orthopaedic residency, 1992; Shriners Hosp, pediatric fellowship, 1993. **Career:** Ochsner Clinic, partner, 1993-00; Baton Rouge Gen Med Ctr, chief orthopaedic, 1999-01; Bone & Joint Clinic, 2000-, partner, 2001-. **Orgs:** Alpha Phi Alpha, 1980-; East Baton Rouge Parish Med Asn. **Honors/Awds:** Blounts Award, Pediatric Ortho Soc N Am, 1990. **Military Serv:** AUS, Capt, reservist, 1990-97. **Business Addr:** Partner, Bone & Joint Clinic, 7301 Hennessey Blvd, Ste 7000, Baton Rouge, LA 70808, **Business Phone:** (225)766-0050.*

FRIES, SHARON LAVONNE (SHARON FRIES BRITT)
Educator. **Personal:** Born Jul 26, 1959, Chattahoochee, GA. **Educ:** Univ Md, Col Park, BS, 1981, PhD, 1995; Ohio State Univ, MA, 1983. **Career:** Ohio State Univ, asst dir, 1981-82, stud develop grad asst, 1982-83; Towson State Univ, area coordr, 1983-85; Univ Md, from asst to vpres stud affairs, chancellor, 1985-95, Dept Educ Policy & Leadership, asst prof, 1995-2003, assoc prof, 2004-; Harvard Grad Sch Educ, vis prof, 1998-99. **Orgs:** Am Col & Personnel Asn, 1981-; res bd, ACPA, 1985; directorate comn IX assessment stud develop mem, ACPA, 1986; Omicron Delta Kappa, 1989; chair, assoc staff rep, Black Fac, Staff Asn; Full Gospel AME Zion; Media & Ed Bd ACPA; Am Asn Affirmative Action Officers; Black Women's Coun Univ Md, College Park; consult, Univ MD Campus Prog & Off Campus Presentations; Am Asn Univ Prof; Asn Study Higher Educ; Am Asn Higher Educ. **Honors/Awds:** New Presenters Award, MACUHO, 1985; Human Relations Service Award, State Md, 1986; Outstanding Service Award, Black Fac & Staff, 1986-88; Asn Staff Outstanding Contibution Award, Univ Md, 1988; Presidents Award Outstanding Contribution Asniate Staff Member, Univ Md, 1988; Outstanding Minority Staff Member of the Year, Presidents Comn Ethnic Minority Issues, 1991; Woman of Color Award, Univ Md, President's Comn Women's Affairs, 1992. **Special Achievements:** Numerous presentations. **Business Addr:** Associate Professor, University of Maryland, Department of Education Policy & Leadership, 2203 Benjamin Bldg, College Park, MD 20742-1165, **Business Phone:** (301)405-0186.

FRINK, SAMUEL H.
Business owner, executive, government official. **Personal:** Born Mar 20, 1944, La Grange, NC; son of E B Frink and O W Frink; married Juanita Vereen, Jun 8, 1968; children: Ivan & Chaun. **Educ:** NC Cent Univ, Durham, NC, BS, chem, 1966; Ford Motor Dealer Training, Virginia Beach, VA, 1986. **Career:** Ford Motor Co, Fairfax, VA, sales rep, 1970-80; Major Lincoln-Mercury, Virginia Beach, VA, sales mgr, 1980-86; Bobby Gerald Ford-Lincoln-Mercury, partnership, 1991; Grand Strand Nissan, partnership, 1994; Lay-Fisher Chevrolet/Olds Inc, partnership, 1995; Conway Ford Inc, Conway, SC, pres, 1986, partner; Grand Strand Nissan, partner; Gubernatorial designee, currently. **Orgs:** Exec bd mem, Boy Scouts Am; mem, bd visitors, Coastal Carolina Col, 1989-90; pres, Conway Area Chamber Com, 1990; adv coun mem, Horry County Youth 2000, 1988-90; adv bd, Myrtle Beach Br Nat Bank SC, 1991; bd mem, Coastal Educ Found, 2003-; bd visitors, E. Craig Wall Sr Col Bus Admin; secy/treas, exec comm, vchair, acad stud affair comm, vchair, gov affair comm, Coastal Carolina Univ, currently. **Honors/Awds:** Minority Small Businessman of the Year, 7 States of Southeast Region, 1990; Elks Americanism Award, Scouts Am, 1989; Businessman of the Year, Phi Beta Sigma Fraternity, 1988; Man of the Year, Cherry Hill Baptist Church, 1988. **Military Serv:** AUS, capt, 1966-70; Commendation Medal, 1970. *

FRINK REED, CAROLIESE INGRID
Educator, librarian. **Personal:** Born Dec 24, 1949, Jacksonville, FL; daughter of Neal and Catherine Danberg; married Dwight D Reed Sr (died 1988); children: Kasimu Clark, Kali Reed. **Educ:** Temple Univ, BS, 1976; Drexel Univ, MS, 1980; Univ Ghana, attended 1993. **Career:** Free Libr Philadelphia, c librn, 1980-81; Prince William County Libr, Woodbridge, VA, librn, 1982-84; Nassau County Sch Bd, Fernandina Beach, FL, librn, 1985-87; Sch Dist Philadelphia, librn, 1987-96; Fitzsimons Mid Sch, librn, 1996-. **Orgs:** Media selection & rev comt mem, Pa Sch Librns Asn, 1990-91; pres, admin assist, Nat Asn Black Storytellers, 1994-96, 1986-92; Black Caucus Am Libr Asn; dir, Nat Festival Black Storytelling; Nat Asn Preserv & Perpetuation Storytelling. **Honors/Awds:** L Valeria Richmond Serv Award, Nat African Am Storytellers Retreat, Pine Bluff, NC, 1995. **Home Addr:** 859 N 29th St, Philadelphia, PA 19130. **Business Addr:** Librarian, Fitzsimons Middle School, 26 Cumberland St, Philadelphia, PA 19102.*

FRISBY, H. RUSSELL, JR.
Executive. **Personal:** Born Dec 28, 1950, Baltimore, MD; son of H Russell Sr and Kathryn T; married June J Frisby, Jul 15, 1978; children: H Russell III, James. **Educ:** Swarthmore Col, BA, 1972; Yale Law Sch, JD, 1975. **Career:** Cable, McDaniel, Bowie & Bond, assoc, 1975-77; MD Atty Gen's Off, asst atty gen, 1977-79; Fed Communs Comn, atty, 1979-83; Weil, Gotshal & Manges, assoc, 1983-86; Melnicove, Kaufman, Weiner & Smouse, partner, 1986-89; Venable, Baetjer & Howard, LLP, partner, 1989-95; MD Pub Serv Comn, chmn, 1995-98; Competitive Telecommun Asn, pres; CompTel/ASCENT, chief exec officer, 1998-05; Fleischman & Walsh LLP, partner, currently. **Orgs:** Fel Am Bar Found, 1992; fel MD Bar Found, 1992; Am Bar Asn; vice chair communs comm, Nat Asn Regulatory Comnrs, 1997-98; Fed-State Joint Bd Universal Serv, 1997-98; bd dirs, PAETEC Holding Corp. **Honors/Awds:** Charles Hamilton Houston Award, Minority Bus Enterprise Legal Defense & Educ Fund Inc, 1989. **Business Phone:** (202)939-7900.*

FROHMAN, ROLAND H.
Dentist. **Personal:** Born Aug 18, 1928, Detroit; married Alice F Hibbett; children: Roland, Jr, Shelley, Jill. **Educ:** Wayne State Univ, BA, 1951; Howard Univ, DDS, 1955. **Career:** Dr Robert L Moseley, assoc, 1957-61; Dent, pvt prac, 1961-; Harper Hosp Detroit, staff, 1968-. **Orgs:** Am Dent Asn; Wolverine Dent Asn; Mich State Dent Asn; Detroit Dist Dent Asn; Moors Club. **Honors/Awds:** Certificate Recognition by Mayor of Detroit for service in Mayors Youth Employment Program, 1968. **Military Serv:** AUS, capt, 1955-57. **Business Addr:** Dentist, Private Practice, 13026 W McNichols, Detroit, MI 48235.*

FROST, DR. OLIVIA PLEASANTS
Educator, research scientist, business owner. **Personal:** Born Jan 1, 1915, Asbury Park, NJ; daughter of William Henry and Theresa Mitchell; married Charles (deceased); children: Carolyn Olivia Frost Downes, James William & Charles S Jr. **Educ:** Hunter Col, BA; Columbia Univ, MA, 1951; NY Univ, Dept Human Rels, Sch Educ, PhD, 1972. **Career:** Haryou-Contrib Youth Ghetto, res assoc, 1963-66; NY Urban League, res dir, 1965-66; NY Univ, Dept Human Rels, Sch Educ, Warburg fel, 1968; Haryou-ACT, res assoc, 1969-70; Columbia Univ, MARC Demonstration Proj Adolescent Minority Females, res consult, 1971-75; City Univ NY, assoc prof, 1972-77; Dept Labor, Washington DC, doctoral dissertation grant; NY City Youth Bd Comn, Coun NY, res assoc; Olivia Frost Res Assocs, owner. **Orgs:** Nat Asn Social Workers; Afro-Amer Hist & Geneal Soc Inc; dir, Comt Study, Harlem A Neglected Investment Opportunity; Nat Asn Adv Colored People, NY Urban League; trustee, Schomburg Corp; trustee, Schomburg Corp; chmn, Genealogy Comt Schomburg Ctr Res Black Cult, NY Pub Libr; founder, Asn Black Women Higher Educ. **Home Addr:** 1540 York Ave Apt 2L, New York, NY 10028-5979, **Home Phone:** (212)570-1556. *

FROST, WILLIAM HENRY
Mayor. **Personal:** Born Apr 17, 1930, Maysville, NC; son of Philanders and Gracie Parlen Perry; married Ari Mae Jones; children: Warren, Leddia Frost Chapman, Aletha & Elroy. **Career:** US Civil Serv, Camp Lejeune, NC, warehouseman, 1955-65, chauffeur, 1965-68, radio dispatcher, 1968-77, bus driver, 1977-85; Town Maysville, NC, alderman, 1972-85, mayor, 1985-99. **Orgs:** Maysville Develop Corp, 1967-; bd, 1969-, Costal County Develop Bd, Sr Citizen Bd, pres, currently; chmn, Jone County, Dem Party; Meals Wheels. **Honors/Awds:** Three Civil Service Awards for Outstanding work, 1981 & 1983-84. **Military Serv:** AUS, E4, 1950-55; 2 Good Conduct Medal, Combat Ribbon with 3 stars, United Nation Ribbon, Koran Ribbon. **Home Addr:** 86 Main St, PO Box 191, Maysville, NC 28555.

FRY, DARRELL
Journalist, writer. **Personal:** Born Apr 16, 1963, Oklahoma City, OK; son of Jay D and Helen M Holmes Gray. **Educ:** Fla State

Univ, Tallahassee, FL, BS, 1986. **Career:** St Petersburg Times, St Petersburg, FL, staff writer, 1986-, sports columnist & reporter, currently. **Orgs:** Phi Beta Sigma Fraternity, 1984-; Nat Asn Black Journalists, 1986-. **Honors/Awds:** First Place, Fla Sports Writers Asn, 1987; Honorable Mention, AP Sports Ed, 1988, 1990. **Home Addr:** 8904 Hannigan Ct, Tampa, FL 33626, **Home Phone:** (813)920-3379. **Business Addr:** Sports Columnist, Reporter, St Petersburg Times, 490 1st Ave S, St Petersburg, FL 33701, **Business Phone:** (727)893-8111.

FRY, SIMON. See AGURS, DONALD STEELE.

FRYAR, REV. IRVING DALE, SR.
Clergy, football player. **Personal:** Born Sep 28, 1962, Mount Holly, NJ; married Jacqueline; children: Londen, Irving Jr, Adrianne & Jacqueline. **Educ:** Univ NE; The S Fla Bible Coll & Theol Sem, bible study. **Career:** Football player (retired), Pastor, Speaker; New Eng Patriots, wide receiver, 1984-92; Miami Dolphins, 1993-95; Philadelphia Eagles, 1996-98; Wash Redskins, wide receiver, 1999-2000; CNN & Sports Illustrated, football analyst; New Jerusalem House God, pentecostal minister, founder & pastor, currently. **Orgs:** Bd dir, Christian Quarterly; partner, Kingdom Network; Stop Child Abuse Now; founder, Irving Fryar Found, 1996-. **Honors/Awds:** Community Service Award, New Eng Patriots 1776 Quarterback Club, 1988; True Value & NFL Man of the Year, Philadelphia Eagles, 1996; Emmy Award. **Special Achievements:** first player selected, NFL draft, 1984; had featured in the Oliver Stone movie, On Any Given Sunday; author of the book, Sunday Is My Day. **Business Addr:** Founder, Pastor, New Jerusalem House of God, 400 Washington St, PO Box 129, Jobstown, NJ 08060, **Business Phone:** (609)267-7600.

FRYE, HENRY E.
Chief justice. **Personal:** Born Aug 1, 1932, Richmond County, NC; son of Walter A Frye (deceased) and Pearl A Frye (deceased); married Shirely Taylor; children: Henry E & Harlan E. **Educ:** A&T State Univ, BS, 1953; Univ NC Law Sch, JD, 1959; Syracuse Univ Law Sch, attended 1958. **Career:** US atty, NC, pract, 1959-63, asst, 1963-65; NCC Univ Law Sch, prof, 1965-67; Frye & Johnson, atty; NC House Rep, mem, 1969-80; NC Senate, mem, 1981-82; Supreme Ct NC, assoc justice, 1983-99, chief judge, 1999-2001; Brooks, Pierce, McLendon, Hunphrey & Leonard, LLP, counr, 2001-; NC A&T State Univ, vis prof, currently. **Orgs:** Greensboro Bar Asn; Am Bar Asn; NC Bar Asn; NC Asn Black Lawyers; Ame Bar Assoc; Am Judicature Soc; life mem, Nat Bar Asn; Kappa Alpha Psi Frat; former mem, secy bd mgt, Hayes Taylor YMCA; deacon, Providence Bapt Church; life mem, NAACP. **Honors/Awds:** Hon doctorate, Shaw Univ, 1971; Alumni Excellence Award, A&T State Univ, 1972; R R Wright Award, Nat Bankers Asn, 1983; Charles D. McIver Medal, UNC-Greensboro, 1986; Distinguished Alumnus Award, UNC-Chapel Hill, 1986; Lawyer of the Year, Asn Black Lawyers, 1988; Appellate Judges Award, NC Acad Trial Lawyers, 1989; Brotherhood Award, Nat Conf Christians & Jews, 1991; Greensboro Business Leaders Hall of Fame, 1991; North Carolina Award for Public Service, 2007. **Special Achievements:** First African-American to be elected to the North Carolina House of Representatives in the Twentieth Century; First African-American to serveon the Supreme Court of NC; Elected one of Guilford Co 6 repin NC House, 1968. **Military Serv:** USAF, capt, 1953-55; USAFR. **Business Addr:** Of Counsel, Brooks Pierce McLendon Humphrey & Leonard LLP, 2000 Renaissance Plz, PO Box 26000, Greensboro, NC 27420, **Business Phone:** (336)373-8850.

FRYE, NADINE GRACE
Nurse. **Personal:** Born in Greensburg, PA; daughter of Charles Frye and Virgie Middles Frye Grasty (Adopted). **Educ:** Univ Pittsburgh, BSN, 1947, M Lit, 1951, PhD, 1987. **Career:** Nurse (retired); Western Psych Inst & Clinic, Pgh PA, staff nurse/head nurse, 1948-50; Detroit Dept Health, Detroit MI, pub health nurse, 1951-53; Northville State Hosp, Nursing Educ Dept, instr/dir, 1953-56; Lafayette Clinic, Detroit MI, dir nursing educ, 1956-57; Wayne State Univ, Detroit MI, instr, nursing, 1957-59; Mercywood Hosp, Ann Arbor MI, dir nursing educ 1959-61; Univ Mich Sch Nursing, asst prof/dir nursing, 1961-66; Western Psych Inst & Clinic, Pittsburgh Pa, assoc dir cmh/mr nursing, 1969-73; Univ Pittsburgh Sch Nursing, prof Nursing, 1969-90. **Orgs:** Bd dir 3 Rivers Youth Pittsburgh, 1971-77; consult St Agnes Cath Sch Pittsburgh 1971-73; consult Univ S MS Sch Nursing 1976; consult Univ Pittsburgh Sch Nursing 1980-81; Am Nurses Asn, 1947; Alpha Kappa Alpha; Pittsburgh Club Nat Asn Negro Bus & Prof Women; Adv Community, Youth Ministry, Pittsburgh, PA, 1988-91; Int Sigma Theta Tau Honorary Nursing Sorority; pres, Congress Bridge Clubs, 1996-99; secy & treas, Am Bridge Asn. **Honors/Awds:** Honor Award Kappa Alpha Psi, Pgh, PA, 1943; Robert L Vann Mem Scholar, 1943; Alumni Award Univ Pittsburgh, 1980; Alumni Serv Award, Univ Pittsburgh, 1986. **Home Addr:** 6352 Aurelia St, Pittsburgh, PA 15206-4319. *

FRYE, REGINALD STANLEY
Executive. **Personal:** Born May 18, 1936, Yakima, WA; son of Elise Garrett and Virgil O; married Mikki Goree, Jun 24, 1956; children: Gregory, Martin, Trana. **Educ:** Los Angeles Community Col, Los Angeles, CA, 1956. **Career:** V O Frye Mfg, Seattle WA, salesman, 1959-64; Wash Natural Gas, Seattle, WA, salesman, 1964-72; 3A Industs Inc, Seattle, WA, pres & owner, 1972-. **Orgs:** Pres, Cent Contractors Asn, 1976-85; vice-chair, State Wash Off Minority & Women's Bus Enterprises Adv Bd, 1983-87. **Honors/Awds:** Martin Luther King Jr Humanitarian Award, The Medium Newspaper, 1974; Community Service Award, United Inner City Develop Found, 1974, 1976; Special Recognition, Port of Seattle, 1983; Special Recognition, Nat Asn Minority Contractors, 1983. **Business Addr:** President, Owner, 3A Industries Inc, PO Box 14029, Seattle, WA 98114.*

FRYE, ROBERT EDWARD
Association executive. **Personal:** Born Oct 11, 1936, Washington, DC; son of James E Frye Jr and Alberta Edwards; married Deloris Ann Smith, Nov 17, 1963 (divorced 1986); children: Robert Jr & Amanda; married Rotha Isabel Holbert, May 30, 1987. **Educ:** Howard Univ, BSc, 1958; Am Univ, MPA, 1970; Fed Exec Inst, attended 1975. **Career:** AUS, Map Serv, cartographer, 1958-65; Wolf R&D Corp, proj mgr, 1965-69; Nat Bur Stand, comput syst analyst, 1969-73; US Consumer Prod Safety Comn, dir injury surveillance div, 1973-77, dir, hazard analysis div, 1977-96, Off Planning & Eval, dir, 1997-99; Nat Sch Bd Asn, consult, 1985-89; Fairfax Co Sch Bd, mem-at-large, 1978-85, 1989-93, 1996-2003, vice chmn, 1998-99, chmn, 1999-2000. **Orgs:** Founding mem, Reston Black Focus, 1969-; Kappa Alpha Psi, Nat Fire Reporting Comt, NFPA, 1972-85; Nat Caucus Black Sch Bd Mem, 1983-85, 1989; finance comt, 1982-85, VA Sch Bd Asn, 1989-93; Fairfax County Comt 100, 1985-89; Fairfax Co Civil Service Comt, 2005-; bd Visitors, Longwood Univ, 2006-. **Honors/Awds:** Community Service Award, Urban League Nova Chap, 1981; Community Service Award, Nat Coun Negro Women, 1985; CPSC EEO Achievement Award, 1986; CPSC Chairman's Award, 1988, 1996; Community Service Award, Northern VA Alumni Chap, Omega Psi Phi, 1990, 2000; CPSC Distinguished Service Award, 1993; Chairman's Commendation, 1995; Fairfax County Community Service Award, 1992; Nova Alumni Award, Howard Univ, 1999; Community Hero Award, A & E Biography, 2002. **Military Serv:** USY, lt, 1959-61. **Home Addr:** 5514 Ivor St, Springfield, VA 22151.

FRYE, THOMAS JOHN
Entrepreneur, chief executive officer. **Personal:** Born Jan 17, 1945, New York, NY; son of Thomas and Gloria; married Linda, May 9, 1987; children: Thomas Jr. **Educ:** Lincoln Univ, BA, 1969; John Marshall Law Sch, LLB, 1974. **Career:** Belranie Ins Co, claim adjuster & claim mgr, 1967-73; US Dept of Labor, br chief, dep comnr, asst reg adminr, 1973-84; State Ill, dir, 1984-85; Zenith Ins Co, claim mgr, 1985-90; prof liability independent adjusting co, vpres; Frye Claims Consul & Admin, founder & chief exec officer, 1990-. **Orgs:** Pres, San Francisco Indust Claim Asn, 1994-95; Minority Claim Assoc, exec dir, 1990-92. **Special Achievements:** Wrote a column, "Managers Corner," California Worker Conspector Enquirer, 3 years. **Military Serv:** US Air Force, sgt, 1963-67; supply man of the month. **Business Phone:** (510)782-9882.

FRYSON, SIM E.
Chief executive officer, automotive executive. **Educ:** WVa State Univ, BA, educ; Gen Motors Inst, assoc degree mktg & bus. **Career:** IBM Corp; Kanawha County car dealership, sales exec, sales mgr; C & O Motors; Joe Holland Chevrolet, bus mgr; Sim Fryson Motor Co Inc, ceo & pres, 1995-. **Orgs:** Ashland Rotary-Nissan Dealer Adv Bd; bd dirs, Paramont Arts Theather; bd mem, Ashland Alliance. **Honors/Awds:** Nissan Pres Circle. **Special Achievements:** Company ranked 72 on Black Enterprise magazine, 1997; He is named among the top 100 black businessmen by Black Enterprise Magazine; Kentucky's NAACP Man of the Year, 2002. **Military Serv:** USAF, sgt. **Business Addr:** President, Chief Executive Officer, Sim Fryson Motor Co Inc, 2565 Winchester Ave, Ashland, KY 41105, **Business Phone:** (606)329-2288.*

FUDGE, ANN MARIE
Executive. **Personal:** Born Apr 23, 1951, Washington, DC; married Richard Fudge Sr; children: Richard Jr, Kevin. **Educ:** Simmons Col, BA, 1973; Harvard Bus Sch, MBA, 1977. **Career:** Gen Elec, manpower spec, 1973-75; Gen Mills, mkt asst, 1977-78, asst prod mgr, 1978-80, prod mgr, 1980-83, mkt dir, 1983-94; Kraft Foods, exec vpres; Maxwell House Coffee Co, pres, 1994-01; Young & Rubicam Brands, Young & Rubicam Advertising, chmn, ceo, 2003-. **Orgs:** Nat Black MBA Asn, 1981-; Jr League, 1981-; Exec Leadership Coun, pres, 1994-96; Links; Comt 200; bd dirs, Allied Signal, Inc; bd dir, Liz Claiborne; bd dir, Fed Res Bank New York; bd dir, Marriott Intl; bd dir, Honeywell; bd dir, Gen Electric; Coun Foreign Rels. **Honors/Awds:** COGME Fellow, 1975-76; YWCA Leadership Award, 1979; Candace Award, 1992; Glamour Mag, Woman of the Year, 1995; Advert Woman of the Year, 1995; Alumni Achievement Award, Harvard Bus Sch, 1998; Achievement Award, Exec Leadership Coun, 2000; named by Fortune mag, one of 50 Most Powerful Women in American Business; Matrix Award, 2004. **Special Achievements:** First African Am woman to head major ad agency. **Business Addr:** Chairman, Chief Executive Officer, Young & Rubicam Brands, 285 Madison Ave, New York, NY 10017, **Business Phone:** (212)210-3000.*

FUDGE, MARCIA L
Lawyer, association executive, mayor. **Educ:** Ohio State Univ, BS, bus admin, 1975; Cleveland Marshall Col Law, Cleveland State Univ, JD, 1983. **Career:** Pvt indust; Cuyahoga County; Cong USA; Cuyahoga County Prosecutor's Office, dir budget & finance & office admin; Warrensville Heights City, mayor, currently. **Orgs:** Pres, Delta Sigma Theta Sorority, 1996-98. **Business Addr:** Mayor, Mayors Office, 4301 Warrensville Ctr Rd, Warrensville Heights, OH 44128, **Business Phone:** (216)587-6505.

FUERST, JEAN STERN
Educator. **Personal:** Born Sep 29, 1919, New York, NY; son of Charles F and Rose S; married Dorothy Braude, Jun 1944. **Career:** Educator (retired); Chicago Housing, dir res, 1943-52; Loyola Univ, prof social welfare policy. **Special Achievements:** Author: When Public Housing Was Paradise: Building Community in Chicago. **Home Addr:** 5401 S Hyde Pk Blvd, Chicago, IL 60615, **Home Phone:** (773)324-3285. *

FUFUKA, TIKA NY
Entrepreneur. **Personal:** Born Feb 21, 1952, Cleveland, OH; daughter of Mindoro Reed and Russell Reed. **Educ:** Cuyahoga Community Col, AA, AAB, 1973; Mich State Univ, BA, 1975; Cleveland State Univ, int bus. **Career:** May Co, asst personnel dir, 1975-78; JC Penny, merchandiser, 1978-80; Joseph Horne, sports mgr, 1980-81; Higbee, fashion buyer, 1981-86; Mindoro & Assocs, exec vpres, 1982-; Fashion Bug, merchandise exec, 1986-92; Mindys Return Fashion, pres & ceo, 1993-; Exec & Prof Protection Serv Inc, exec vpres, 1996. **Orgs:** Chair, Bus Women Comt, 21st Cong Dist Caucus, 1984; Urban League Greater Cleveland, 1984-90; Operation Push, 1987-90; Ohio Youth Adv, 1987-90; chmn bd, Black Focus, 1989-; Cleveland State Univ, BLK Aspiration Week Celebration Comn, 1990; Cleveland Opera, MAP Prog, 1990; Cleveland Female Bus Enterprise; Mayor's Census Task Force; 100 Bulk Women Coalition; Bulk Congressional Caucus Braintrust; Asn MBA Exec; Black Prof Asn; Nat Asn Negro Bus & Prof Women; Nat Asn Female Execs; United Bulk Fund; Greater E Cleveland Democratic Club; League Women Voters; Ohio Rainbow Coalition; Black Elected Democratic Off Ohio; Cuyahoga Hills Boys Adv Coun; Nat Coun Negro Women; Nat Polit Cong Bulk Women; Career Beginning Prog, 1991-93; United Way Leadership Dev Prog Comt, 1992; vice chmn, Joint Comt Med Provider Impact State OH, 1992-; chmn, United Way Centralized Resource & Referral Serv, 1993; United Way Gen Assembly, 1993-96; Women Community Fed, 1993; Women App Off Proj, 1994; WCPN Radio, 1994; Planned Parenthood Greater Cleveland, 1995; Citizen League Cleveland, 1995; Friends Fed Libr, 1995; United Way Appeal Comt, 1996; Cleveland Mus Art, 1996; Pub Affairs Comt, Greater Cleveland Growth Asn, 1996; United Way Public Policy Comt, 1997; Outstanding Young Am Nomination Comt, 1997; assoc, Nat Non-Profit Bd, 1997; Outstanding Young Woman Am, Nat Nomination Comt, 1997. **Honors/Awds:** Committee Award, Cleveland State Univ, 1991; United Way Leadership Award, 1991; Outstanding Young Man of America, Nat Nomination Comt, 1998; United Way Service Appreciation, 1998 & 2001; Community Relation Council Service Award, Cleveland Job Corps, 1998.

FUGET, DR. CHARLES ROBERT
School administrator. **Personal:** Born Dec 15, 1929, Rochester, PA; son of Clinton H Fuget and Mary Harris Fuget; married Enid Deane (deceased); children: Craig D; married Audra Blanding. **Educ:** Geneva Col, BS, 1951; Pa State Univ, MS, 1953, PhD, 1956. **Career:** Educator (retired); Esso Res & Eng, Linden, NJ, res chemist, 1955-56; Callery Chem Corp, Callery, PA, res chemist, 1957-63; State Univ NY, Col, Buffalo, prof chem, 1963-64; Geneva Col, Beaver Falls PA, chmn, prof physics, 1964-71; AUS, Ballistic Res Labs, Aberdeen, MD, consult, 1968-69; Ind Univ Pa, Sch Arts & Sci, assoc dean, 1971-76, Col Natural Sci & Math, dean, 1977-84, Student Univ Affairs, acting vpres, 1984-85, Col Natural Sci & Math, dean, 1985-88; Pa Dept Educ, Harrisburg, PA, dep secy, 1988-91; Ind Univ, PA, interim pres, 1991-92; Pa Dept Educ, Harrisburg, PA, deputy secy, comnr, post-sec & higher educ, 1992-94; Bennett Col, interim pres, 2002, special asst to pres Johnetta B Cole, 2002; Fisk Univ, interim pres, 2003-04. **Orgs:** Ind Hosp Corp, 1978-83; chmn, Pa Comn United Ministries Higher Educ, 1978-80; bd govs, Gen Bd Higher Educ & Ministry, 1980-88, 1992-2000; bd dir, Ind Rotary Club, 1982-88; vpres, Univ Senate United Methodist Church, 1989-92; Nat Collegiate Athletic Asn. **Honors/Awds:** Distinguished Service Award, Upper Beaver Valley Jaycees, 1969; Distinguished Service Award, Alumni Asn, Geneva Col, 1976; Presidents Medal of Distinction, Ind Univ, PA, 1988; Hahnemann Univ, LHD, 1988; Geneva Col, DSc, hon, 1990; Ind Univ Pa, Hon Doctor Pub Serv, 1995.

FUGETT, JEAN SCHLOSS, JR.
Football player, executive, lawyer. **Personal:** Born Dec 16, 1951, Baltimore, MD; son of J R Fugett and Carolyn Fugett. **Educ:** Amherst Col, attended (hons); George Wash Law Sch, JD. **Career:** Football player (retired), exec, lawyer; Dallas Cowboys, tight end, 1972-75; Wash Redskins, tight end, 1976-79; Wash Post, intern; CBS Sports, football color commentator; TLC Beatrice Int Holdings Co, chief exec officer & chmn; Jean S Fugett Jr Firm, atty, currently; Baltimore lawfirm, founding partner; TLC Beatrice International Food, mgr. **Orgs:** Pres, Nat Football League Players

Asn, 2005-. **Honors/Awds:** Pro Bowl, 1977. **Special Achievements:** Participated in Super Bowl X with Dallas Cowboys; first African Am to be inducted into the Md Soc of the Sons of the Am Revolution.

FUHR, GRANT SCOTT
Hockey player, hockey coach. **Personal:** Born Sep 28, 1962, Alberta;son of Robert and Betty; married Corrine (divorced); children: 2; married Jill; children: Robert. **Career:** Hockey player (retired), hockey coach; Edmunton Oilers, goalie, 1981-90; Toronto Maple Leafs, goalie, 1991-92; Buffalo Sabres, goalie, 1992-95; St Louis Blues, 1995-99; Saint John Flames, 1999-2000; Calgary Flames, goalkeper, 1999-2000, goalkeeping consult, 2000-04; Phoenix Coyotes, goaltending coach, 2004-. **Honors/Awds:** Hockey Hall of Fame, 2003; Alberta Sports Hall of Fame, 2004. **Business Addr:** Goaltending Coach, Phoenix Coyotes, 5800 W Glenn Dr Suite 350, Glendale, AZ 85301, **Business Phone:** (623)463-8800.

FULGHAM, ROIETTA GOODWIN
Educator. **Personal:** Born Jan 28, 1948, Oakland, CA; daughter of Roy Alexander and Dovie Juanita Miles; divorced; children: Kendall Young Blood & Keia Syreeta. **Educ:** Utah State Univ, Logan, BS, 1971, MS, 1977. **Career:** Area Voc Ctr Ogden UT, off occups supvr, 1971-75; Yosemite Jr Col Dist Modesto, instr, 1975-76; Los Rios Comm Col Dist ARC, bus technol prof, 1976-; Am River Col, prof; support analyst, Wang Labs Inc, 1986; consult, Westroots Bus Writing Syst, 1986-2000. **Orgs:** Nat Western Calif Bus Educ Asn, 1976-; Nat Educ Asn, Calif Teachers Asn, 1976-; secy, NAACP Cent Area Conf, 1976-87; vpres, NAACP Calif St Conf, 1988-93; treas, NCP Sacramento Br, 1991-94; St coun rep, Calif Teachers Asn, 1979-85; nat teller, NAACP, 1980-81; secy, Utah St Univ Black Alumni Asn, 1980-; chairperson, NAACP W Coast Region, 1982-83, NAACPACT-SO Prog Sacramento Br, 1982-85; chairperson, Outstanding Bus Stud ProgCalif Bus Educ Asn, 1983; off mgr, IDS Financial Serv, 1985-86; DeltaSigma Theta Inc, 1991-; pres, Growing Alternatives Foster Family Agency, 1995-2007; NAACP Nat Youth Work Comn, 2000-02; pres-elect, Calif Bus Educ Asn, currently. **Honors/Awds:** Cert Bus Educr, Bus Educ Cert Coun, 1976; Cert Prof Secy, Prof Secy Int, 1982; Outstanding Young Woman Am, 1982; NAACP Golden Gavel Award, NAACP Northern Area Conf, 1984; Outstanding Instr Year, Am River Col, 1986;NAACP DD Mattocks Award, Community Serv, Sacramento, 1999. **Home Addr:** 6600 Branchwater Way, Citrus Heights, CA 95621. **Business Addr:** Chairperson, American River College, Business Technology Department, 4700 Col Oak Dr, Sacramento, CA 95841, **Business Phone:** (916)484-8258.

FULLER, ALMYRA OVETA
Scientist, college teacher. **Personal:** Born Aug 31, 1955, Mebone, NC; daughter of Herbert R and Deborah Evelyn Woods; married Jerry Caldwell, Jun 16, 1984; children: Brian Randolph Caldwell. **Educ:** Univ NC, Chapel Hill, BA, 1977, PhD, 1983; Univ Chicago, IL, postdoctoral Study, 1988. **Career:** Univ NC, res asst, 1977-83; Univ Chicago, IL, instr & fel, 1983-87, res assoc, 1987-88; Univ Mich, Ann Arbor, asst prof, assoc prof, currently. **Orgs:** Alpha Kappa Alpha, Basileus Alumni Chap, 1977-78; co-founder Res Triangle, Nat Tech Asn, 1980-; asst dir, Summer Apprentice Res Prog, Univ NC, Chappel Hill, 1981-82; Sigma Xi, 1983-; AAAS, 1984-; Am Soc Microbiol, 1984-; Adv Comy Fel Prog, Line berger Cancer Res Ctr, 1989-; La bd regents, Ad Hoc Reviewer, 1989; Howard Hughes Doctoral Fel Panel, 1991. **Honors/Awds:** NTA Service Award, Res Triangle Chap NTA, 1983; Anna Fuller Fund Postdoctoral Award, 1983-84; Thornton Professional Achievement Award, Chicago chap, NTA, 1984; NIH Postdoctoral Research Award, Nat Inst Sci, 1984-86; Postdoctoral Research Award, Ford Found, 1986-87. **Special Achievements:** Author of scientific publications, 1983-. **Business Addr:** Associate Professor, University of Michigan, Department of Microbiology & Immunology, 5641 Med Sci Bldg II, 1150 W Med Ctr Dr, Ann Arbor, MI 48109-0620.

FULLER, CHARLES
Playwright, writer. **Personal:** Born Mar 5, 1939, Philadelphia, PA; son of Charles Henry and Lillian Anderson; married Miriam A Nesbitt, Aug 4, 1962; children: Charles III, David. **Educ:** Villanova Univ, attended 1958; La Salle Univ, DFA, 1967. **Career:** Afro-American Arts Theatre, co-founder & co-dir, 1967-71; Playwriting Creative Artist Pub Serv, CAPS fel, 1975; Nat Endowment Arts, fel playwriting, 1976-77; Radio work: The Black Experience, dir, 1970-71; Stage writings: The Perfect Party, 1969; In My Many Names and Days, 1972; The Candidate, 1974; In the Deepest Part of Sleep, 1974; First Love, 1974; The Lay Out Letter, 1975; The Brownsville Raid, 1976; Sparrow in Flight, 1978; Zooman and the Sign, 1980; A Soldier's Play, 1981, 1982, 1983; Sally, 1988; Prince, 1988; We, 1989; Films: A Soldier's Story, adaptation of play, 1984; Miles, 1994; TV series: "Roots, Resistance, and Renaissance", 1967; "The Sky Is Gray, American Short Story", 1980; "A Gathering of Old Men", 1987; "Sonnyboy", 1993; "Zooman", 1995; "The Badge", 1995; "Love Songs", 1997; "The Slave Dancer", 1998; Soldier's Story, author, currently; Chadama Ltd & Chadama II, pres & chief exec officer. **Orgs:** Guggenheim fel playwriting, 1977-78; Writers Guild Am E. **Honors/Awds:** Rockefeller Grant Playwriting, 1976-77; Obie Award, Best Playwright, 1981; Audelco Awards, Best Playwright & Best Play, 1981, 1982; Theatre Club Award, Best Play; Pulitzer Prize for Drama, 1982; Best American Play Award, New York Critics, 1982; Outer Circle Critics Award, Best Play, 1982; Hazelett Award, Distinguished Artist, Pa Coun Arts. **Special Achievements:** Nominee, Academy Award, screenwriting, Soldier's Story. **Military Serv:** AUS, 1959-62; Good Conduct Medal. *

FULLER, COREY
Football player. **Personal:** Born May 11, 1971, Tallahassee, FL. **Educ:** Fla State Univ, criminol & child develop. **Career:** Football player (retired); Minnesota Vikings, defensive back, 1995-98; Cleveland Browns, 1999-2003; Baltimore Ravens, corner back, 2003-04. **Honors/Awds:** All-ACC First Team Defensive Back in 1994.

FULLER, CURTIS D.
Musician, composer, music arranger or orchestrator. **Personal:** Born Dec 15, 1934, Detroit, MI; married Judith Patterson; children: Ronald, Darryl, Gerald, Dellaney & Wellington. **Educ:** Univ Detroit, Detroit Inst Arts; Wayne State Univ, BA; Bronx Comm Col, music theory; Henry St Settlement Inst, jazzmobile prog. **Career:** Yusef Lateef's Quintet; Dizzy Gillispie Orchestra; Quincy Jones Orchestra; Art Blakey "Jazz Messengers" Count Basie Orchestra; LITU, Long Island, NY, counr & Instr; Compositions: Smokin; Jacque's Groove; Sop City; People Places & Things; Crankin; Kwanza; Love & Understanding; A Caddy for daddy; Albums: New Trombone, 1957; Curtis Fuller with Red Garland, 1957; The Opener, 1957; Bone & Bari, 1957; Sliding Easy, 1959; Blues-ette, 1959; Meet The Jazztet, 1960; Blues-ette, Part 2, 1993; Up Jumped Spring, 2004; Keep It Simple, 2005. **Orgs:** Local 802 Musicians Union; Broadcast Music writers. **Honors/Awds:** Downbeat Award; Pittsburg Courier Award. **Special Achievements:** Recorded World Award Shaefer Beer Award, recorded musical Cabin In Sky by Vernon Duke with the NY Phil Strings & Brass on ABC Paramount; performed at NY Radio City Jam Session 1973; performed at Tribute to Charlie Parker, 1975; performed at Newport Jazz Fest. **Military Serv:** AUS band. **Business Addr:** Musician, 1864 7 Ave Suite 52, New York, NY 10026.*

FULLER, DORIS J
Association executive. **Personal:** Born May 26, 1945, Houston County, GA; daughter of Sim Clinton Jr and Bertha Mae Clark. **Educ:** Morris Brown Col, BS, 1966; Univ San Francisco, attended 1969; Ga State Univ, MEd, 1975. **Career:** Atlanta Bd Educ, teacher, 1966-78, 1996; Southern Bell, asst mgr, 1978-94; Atlanta Metrop Col, adj instr & math, 1994; Benjamin Elijah Mays High Sch, teacher. **Orgs:** Second vpres, Atlanta Alumnae Chap, DST Sorority, 1977-79; nominating comt chairperson, Southern Region DST Sorority Inc, 1978-80; pres, Magic Toastmasters TI, 1979, 1983, 1986; Southern Bell Speaker's Bur, 1980-94; State Youth Leadership Coord Dist 14 TI, 1981; recording sect mem, MBC Nat Alumni Asn, 1984-88; pres, Atlanta Chap MBC Alumni Asn, 1985-87; co-chairperson, Men's & Women's Unity Day Beulah Bapt Church, 1985; vpres, MBC Nat Alumni Asn, 1988-95. **Honors/Awds:** President's Award, Toastmasters Int, 1980; Outstanding Corp Alumni, NAFEO Wash DC, 1983; Presidential Citation, MBC Alumni Asn, Atlanta Chap, 1985; Outstanding Alumni MBC Student Govt Asn, 1985; Southern Bell Speakers Bureau Achievement Award, 1986; Southern Bell Best-of-the-Best Winner, 1988; Alumna of the Year, MBC Nat Alumni Asn, 1989; Woman of the Year, Beulah Baptist Church, 1997; Trustee of the Year, 1998.

FULLER, GLORIA A
Librarian. **Personal:** Born May 28, 1952, Brunswick, GA; daughter of Calvin Sinclair Atkinson Sr and Rosetta Frazier Atkinson; married Jimmy Lee, Aug 23, 1986; children: Gabrielle Amanda Fuller. **Educ:** South Carolina State Univ, Orangeburg, SC, BS, 1974; Prince George's Community Col, Largo, MD, AA, 1980; Univ Maryland, Col Park, MD, MLS, 1982. **Career:** Florence Sch Dist, Florence, SC, media specialist, 1974-75; Fedl Law Enforcement Training Ctr, Brunswick, GA, libr tech, 1975-76; Smithsonian Inst, Wash, DC, libr tech, 1976-83, libr, 1983-85; Defense Intelligence Agency, Wash, DC, info serv specialist, 1985-92; DIA Classified Libr, Database Servs Div, chief, 1992-. **Orgs:** Am Asn Law Libr, 1983-89; Am Libr Asn, 1981-; ALA Black Caucus, 1988-89; treasurer, fin secy, chair audit, chair reg his, Delta Sigma Theta Sorority, Inc, 1971-; DC Online Users Group, 1984-; mem, FEDLINK Executive Advisory coun, 1991-93; Fed Libr & Info ctr Comt, 1992-, Budget & Finance Working Group, 1994-95; Fed Libr Round Table, 1985-; Armed Forces Libr Round Table, 1991; Intelligence Community Librarians' Committee (ICLC); Community Open Source Prog Off (COSPO) Research Secretariat, 1993-96; Emmanuel Baptist Church; Delta Sigma Theta Sorority Inc, MD jour, 1997-. **Honors/Awds:** Letters of Appreciation, 1986, 1987, 1988, 1989, 1994-95, Service Award, 1985, 1990, 1995-00, Defense Intelligence Agency; Certification of Award for Exceptional Service, Smithsonian Inst, 1979-80, 1984-85; Certificate of Recognition, Oper Desert Shield & Desert Storm, 1991; Community Open Source Prog Off, Certificate of Apppreciation, 1995; Defense Intelligence Agency, Special Achievement Award, 1995-02; Exceptional Performance Award, Central Intelligence Agency, 1995; Delta Sigma Theta Sorority Inc, 25 Years of Membership, 1996; Certificate of Appreciation in recognition of support to DIA & family mem employees who lost their lives as result ot the Sept 11, 2001 terrorist attack on the Pentagon. **Home Addr:** 10715 Tyrone Dr, Upper Marlboro, MD 20772-4630. **Business Addr:** Defense Intelligence Agency, Database Servs Div, Attn: SVI-4 Rm E4-250, Washington, DC 20340-5100, **Business Phone:** (202)231-3231.

FULLER, HAROLD DAVID
Educator. **Personal:** Born Sep 1, 1937, Oklahoma City, OK; son of Andrew and Tisha Mae; married Annie Laurie Blood, Aug 26, 1961; children: April Beth Fuller, Jeremy David Fuller. **Educ:** Okla Univ, Norman, OK, BA, 1959; Ariz State Univ, Tempe, AZ, MA, 1968; EdD, 1992. **Career:** Educator (retired); USAF, Luke Air Force Base, airman, 1960-66; Roosevelt Sch Dist, Phoenix, AZ, teacher, 1964-68, community sch dir, 1968-71, asst prin, 1971-73; Mesa Pub Schs, Mesa, AZ, prin, 1973; Preside Sirrins Adult Day Health Care Bd. **Orgs:** Champaign chmn, Mesa United Way, 1990-91; pres bd, Mesa ARC, 1987-89; vice chair bd, Mesa United Way, 1987-89; pres bd, Mesa Family Young Men's Christian Asn, 1986-87; chmn bd, HEATS Found, 1990-; Preside Sirrino Adult Day Health Care. **Honors/Awds:** Spirit of America, USAF, 1960; Boss of the Year, Jonas Salk Sch, 1980; Leadership Award, Mesa Young Men's Christian Asn, 1986-87; Presidential Award, Mesa ARC, 1987-89; Human Service Award, Mesa Community Coun, 1988; Achievement Award, Mesa Pub Schs, 1988; Citizen of the Year, Mesa Tribune Newspaper, 1988; Leadership Award, Mesa United Way, 1990-91. **Military Serv:** USAF, Airman First Class, 1960-66; received Spirit Am Award. **Home Addr:** 1724 E Hope St, Mesa, AZ 85203. *

FULLER, DR. HOWARD L.
Educator. **Personal:** Born Jan 14, 1941, Shreveport, LA; divorced. **Educ:** Carroll Col, BA, 1962; Western Reserve Univ, MSA, 1964; Marquette Univ, PhD, 1985. **Career:** Urban League, Chicago, Ill, staff, 1964; Oper Breakthrough, Durham, NC, staff, 1965-70; Malcolm X Liberation Univ, staff, 1970-74; labor organizer, 1974-76; Marquette Univ, Office Edu Opp, dir spec servs, 1976-83, Inst Transformation Learning, founder, dir & distinguished prof educ, 1995-; Wis Dept Employment Rels, secy, 1983-86; Milwaukee Area Tech Col, dean, 1986-88; Milwaukee Dept Health & Human Servs, dir, 1988-91; Milwaukee Pub Sch, supt, 1991-95; Black Alliance Edu Options, co-founder, 2000-. **Orgs:** Bd mem, Tran center for Youth; Greater Milwaukee Edu Trust; Crusade to Save Our Children; Johnson Found; Pew Forum Standards-based Reform; chair, Quest-Milwaukee; bd dirs, Transcenter for Youth; Johnson Foundation; Joyce Foundation; School Choice Wisconsin; Advocates for School Choice. **Honors/Awds:** Hon doctorates, Marion Col; Hon doctorates, Milwaukee School Engr; Hon doctorates, Caroll Col; Hon doctorates, Edgewood Col; Fordham Prize for Excellence in Education, Thomas B Fordham Found, 2004. **Business Addr:** Director & Distinguished Professor of Education, Marquette University, Institute for the Transformation of Learning, 750 N 18th St, Milwaukee, WI 53233, **Business Phone:** (414)288-5774.

FULLER, JACK LEWIS
Fashion designer. **Personal:** Born Dec 30, 1945, Toombs County, GA; son of Mell and Elvera Gillis. **Educ:** Parsons Sch Design, BFA, 1965. **Career:** Kasper Joan Leslie, asst designer; Elliott Bass, Jardine Ltd, designer; Bleyle-By Jack Fuller, designer; Harlem Pub Schs, NY City Bd Educ, consult. **Orgs:** NY City Bd Educ. **Honors/Awds:** Key to City Cincinnati, 1975-76; Rising Stars Fashion Show, Press Week, Plz Hotel, 1975; Urban League Designer of the Yr, 1975; Pres Award, Univ Cincinnati, 1976. *

FULLER, JAMES J.
School administrator, association executive. **Personal:** Born Nov 11, 1946, Eutawville, SC; married Ruth Smothers; children: Julian, Mark. **Educ:** Morgan State Univ, BA, hist & polit sci, 1972; Howard Univ Sch Divinity, MDiv, 1982, Doctorate Ministry, 1990. **Career:** Univ Md, Baltimore Co, Off Minority Recruitment, asst dir, 1972-74, Campus activ, dir, 1974-80, Upward Bound Prog, counr, 1990; New Hope Baptist Church, pastor, 1977; Ctr Integration of Spirituality & Mental Health Inc, bd dirs, currently. **Orgs:** Nat Coun Educ Opportunity Asn; Mid-Eastern Asn Opportunity Personnel Prog; Md Exec Coun Educ Opportunity; Nat Asn Advan Colored People; Nat Urban League; vice chmn, Gov Comn Afro-Am Hist & Cult; Baltimore Mental Health Syst Inc; Baltimore Bd Ed, African & African-Am Curric Task Force; vpres, Baltimore Baptist Ministers Conf; holds memberships in numerous organizations. **Honors/Awds:** Man of Yr, Prudential Life Ins, 1971; Richard H Hunt mem Fund Resolution, 1975; Sons of Prophet Cert, 1975; City of Baltimore, Citizen's Citation; Baltimore Junior Academy Natl Alumni Assn, Humanitarian Award; Mayor's Citation for outstanding contributions to church and community; White House invitation from former President Jimmy Carter; received numerous awards, special honors and citations. **Military Serv:** AUS, spec-Four, 1966-68; Am Legion Serv Award, 1963; AUS Good Conduct Medal 1968. **Business Phone:** (410)752-7940.*

FULLER, RANDY LAMAR
Football player, football coach. **Personal:** Born Jun 2, 1970, Columbus, GA; married Gussie Carr; children: Ellington & Eden

Haylee; married Gussie. **Educ:** Tenn State Univ, BS, criminal justice, 1994. **Career:** Football player (retired), football coach; Detroit Tigers, letterman, 1990-93; Denver Broncos, defensive back, 1994-95; Pittsburgh Steelers, 1995-98; Atlanta Falcons, 1998-99; Seattle Seahawks, 1999-2000; Sw De Kalb, defensive consult; Grace Heritage Christian Sch, Stone Mountain, head football coach, athletics dir, currently; motivational speaker, Fulton. **Orgs:** Co-found, Hometown Heroes Found; bd mem, Project Destiny DeKalb County, Planning comt, Western Penn Sch Deaf. **Special Achievements:** Georgia state record with a long jump. **Business Phone:** (615)963-5918.

FULLER, THOMAS S.
County government official, president (organization). **Personal:** Born Oct 18, 1934, Abbeville, SC; children: Hazel Jenkins & Toni. **Educ:** Allen Univ, B Psy; Roosevelt Univ, MPA. **Career:** Pres (retired); Am Hosp Assn, dir div community relations, 1969-74; State IL Equal Employment Opp Off, dir, 1975-77; Cook Co Sheriff, asst, 1977-78; Metro Water Reclamation Dist Gr Chicago, pres brd of comnrs, 1978. **Orgs:** Am Public Works Assn; bd mem, Community & Econ Devel Assn Cook Co; Natl Assn Advan Colored People; Oper PUSH Chicago Urban League. **Honors/Awds:** Adjunct professorship, Chicago State Univ. **Military Serv:** AUS, 2 yrs. *

FULLER, DR. VIVIAN L
Athletic director. **Personal:** Born Oct 17, 1954, Chapel Hill, NC. **Educ:** Fayetteville State Univ, BS, phys educ, 1977; Univ Idaho, MEd, 1978; Iowa State Univ, PhD, higher educ, 1985. **Career:** Bennett Col, 1978-84; NC A&T Univ, asst athletic dir, 1984-87; Ind Univ Pa, prof & assoc athletic dir, 1987-92; Northeastern Ill Univ, dir intercollegiate athletics, 1992-97; Tenn State Univ, athletics dir, 1997-99; Univ Md-Eastern Shore, dir athletics, 2000-03. **Orgs:** Nat Collegiate Athletic Asn; Black Women's Sports Found; Nat Asn Collegiate Dirs Athletics; Delta Sigma Theta; Nat Asn Collegiate Women Athletic Adminrs; Am Alliance Health, Phys Educ & Dance. **Honors/Awds:** Atalanta Award, Athletic Mgt, 1995. **Special Achievements:** First black woman to run a Division I athletics department with a football program.

FULLER, WILLIAM HENRY, JR.
Football player, president (organization). **Personal:** Born Mar 8, 1962, Norfolk, VA; married Precilla; children: Karen, Kalisa, Krystal & Kimberly. **Educ:** NC State Univ, BA, psychol, 1986. **Career:** Football player (retired), President; Philadelphia Stars, USFL, 1984; Baltimore Stars, USFL, 1985; Houston Oilers, 1986-93; Philadelphia Eagles,1994-96; San Diego Chargers, 1997-98; Fulco Development Inc, chief exec officer & pres, currently; Frank W. Cox High Sch, asst coach. **Orgs:** UNC Educational Found; Juvenile Diabetes Found; Int & Norfolk Convention & Visitors Bureau. **Honors/Awds:** Pro-Bowl, 4; UNC's sports hall of fame; mem, ACC's 50th Anniversary Football Team, 2002. **Business Addr:** President, Chief Executive Officer, Fulco Development Inc, 500 E Main St, Norfolk, VA 23510.

FULLWOOD, EMERSON U
Executive, philanthropist. **Personal:** Born Jan 1, 1947?; married Vernita; children: 2. **Educ:** NC State Univ, Bachelor's Degree, econ; Columbia Univ, MBA, mkt. **Career:** Xerox Corp, acct rep, beginning 1972, corp vpres, Xerox Worldwide's Customer Serv Group, pres, Xerox Regional Opers, Latin Am, pres, Develop Markets Opers, corp vpres, exec chief staff officer & mkt officer, 2004-; Gen Signal Corp, dir; SPX Corp, dir, 1998-. **Orgs:** Dir, Threshold, the United Way Greater Rochester; Rochester Urban League; Rochester Boy Scouts of Am; Xerox Found; Fullwood-Johnson Scholarship Fund. **Home Phone:** (585)248-3313. **Business Addr:** Executive Chief Staff, Marketing Officer, Xerox Corp, 800 Long Ridge Rd, Stamford, CT 06902, **Business Phone:** (203)968-3000.*

FULWOOD, SAM
Journalist. **Personal:** Born Aug 28, 1956, Monroe, NC; son of Samuel L Jr and Hallie Bernice Massey; married Cynthia Marie Bell, Sep 1, 1984; children: Katherine Amanda. **Educ:** Univ NC, Chapel Hill, BA, jour, 1978. **Career:** Charlotte Observer, NC, bus reporter, sports writer, police reporter, 1978-83; Baltimore Sun, MD, asst city ed, bus reporter, Africa corresp, ed writer, 1983-87; Atlanta Jour-Const, Atlanta, GA, state polit ed, asst bus ed, 1987-89; Los Angeles Times, Wash, DC, corresp, 1989-2000; Emerge Mag, columnist, 1990-92; Nieman fel, Harvard Univ, 1993-94; Inst Polit fel, John F Kennedy Sch Govt, Harvard Univ, 2000; The Plain Dealer, metro columnist, 2000-; Case Western Reserve Univ. **Orgs:** Alpha Phi Alpha Fraternity, 1976-; Parliamentational bd mem, 1989-90; Nat Asn Black Journalists. **Honors/Awds:** Unity Awards in Media, 1st Political Reporting Lincoln Univ, 1988; Break Through Award, Women, Men and Media, 1992. **Special Achievements:** Author: "Walking From the Dream: My Life in the Black Middle Class," Anchor Books, 1996. **Business Addr:** Metro Columnist, The Plain Dealer, 1801 Super Ave, Cleveland, OH 44114-2198, **Business Phone:** (216)999-4084.

FUNDERBURK, DR. WILLIAM WATSON
Physician. **Personal:** Born Aug 26, 1931, South Carolina; son of William L and Florence; married Marilyn; children: William, Julie & Christina. **Educ:** Johnson C Smith Univ, BS, 1952; Howard Univ, MD, 1956. **Career:** Howard Med Sch & Hosp, intern, 1957; residency, 1961, fel, 1962; staff, 1956-74; Howard Univ, assoc dean stud affairs, 1970-72; Howard Univ, assoc prof surg, 1971-77; Ctr Ambulatory Surg med dir, 1977-84; Schmn, Dept Surg, Providence Hosp, DC, 2001-02; self Employed, physician, currently. **Orgs:** AOA, 1956-, NMA 1956-99; Med Chi Soc, 1956-; Dist Columbia Med Soc, 1989-. **Honors/Awds:** Certificate of Humanitarian Service, AMA, 1967; Distinguished Surgeon, Howard Dept Surg, 2000. **Home Addr:** 1160 Varnum St NE, Washington, DC 20017. **Business Addr:** Physician, 1160 Varnum St NE Suite 211, Washington, DC 20017, **Business Phone:** (202)877-3627.

FUNDERBURKE, LAWRENCE DAMON
Basketball player, writer. **Personal:** Born Dec 15, 1970; son of Laura; married Monya Fairrow, Jan 1, 1998. **Educ:** Ohio State, bus fin, 1994. **Career:** PAOK BC, 1995-96; Pau-Orthez, 1996-97; Sacramento Kings, forward, 1997-2003; Chicago Bulls, 2005. **Orgs:** Founder & pres, Lawrence Funderburke Youth Organ, 2000-. **Honors/Awds:** Hometown Hero of the Month, 2001; Good Guys Honor Roll. **Special Achievements:** Author: Hook Me Up, Playa!. **Business Addr:** President, Owner, Lawrence Funderburke Youth Organization, 1255 N Hamilton Rd Suite 135, Gahanna, OH 43230, **Business Phone:** (614)751-1541.

FUNN, CARLTON A., SR.
Educator. **Personal:** Born Jan 29, 1932, Alexandria, VA; married Joan Berry; children: Carlton Jr, Tracye & Marc. **Educ:** Storer Col Harpers Ferry, WV, BA, 1953; Va State Univ, Petersburg, VA, MEd, 1972. **Career:** Fairfax Co Pub Sch Syst, teacher, minority rels cons; VA Sch Syst, teacher; Washington DC Pub Sch Syst, teacher; Wash, DC, teacher; The Hist& Cult Minorities, dir, cult educ prog, currently. **Orgs:** Nat Educ Asn; Alexandria Dem Committeeman, 1967-69; trustee, Alfred St Baptist Church, 1967-68; Alexandria Chamber Com, 1967-68; vpres, Alexandria Coun Human Rels, 1972-73; vpres, Hopkins House Asn, 1972; bd mem, Alexandria Human Rels Coun,1973-; Va Educ Asn; Fairfax Educ Asn; Wash Urban League; Nat Asn Advan Colored People; Alexandria Bicentennial Comt, Parent Teachers Asn, 1974; Omega Psi Phi Fraternity Inc, 1977-; The Soc For the Preserve Black Heritage, 1996; Alexandria VA city comnr 250th city anniversary, 1997-98. **Honors/Awds:** American College Student Leaders Award, 1953; Human Civil Award, VA Ed Assoc, VA Min Caucus, 1976; Human Relation Award, Fairfax VA Ed Assoc,1976; Citizen of the Year Award, No VA Psi Nu Chap Omega Psi Phi Frat. Inc,1976; Carter G Woodson Award, Nat Educ Assoc, 1976; Appreciation Award,Fairfax Ed Assoc Black Caucus, 1977; Citizen of the Year Award, Recog Commof 3rd Dist Omega Psi Phi Frat Inc, 1977; Service Awards, Storer Col;Robert F Kennedy Scroll Cincinnati Teachers, 1972; Certificate ofAppreciation, Hopkins House Assoc, 1973; DOD sponsored showing at PentagonBldg, 1975; State Dept Rec Assoc sponsored exhibit, 1975; National DefenseService Medal, Good Conduct Medal & Marksman Badge, AUS; Human RelationsExhibit, 1979; National Trends Award, Arlington VA Chap of the Links Inc,1979; NAACP Award of Appreciation, The Alexandria VA Br, 1979; Certificateof Appreciation, Nat Assoc of Human Rights Workers, 1979; Omega Man of theYear, Omega Psi Phi Frat Inc, 1979; Meritorious Serv Awards, 3rd DistOmega Psi Phi Frat Inc, 1979-80; History & Culture of Minorities Exhibit,Nat Shown 169 Times, 1980. **Military Serv:** AUS, pfc, 1953-55. *

FURLOUGH, JOYCE LYNN
Administrator, executive. **Personal:** Born Mar 4, 1961, San Francisco, CA; daughter of Eddie Thompson and Geraldine; married Durrell Furlough, Feb 15, 1986; children: Durrell Jay Jr. **Educ:** Calif State Univ, Northridge, BS, health care admin, 1983. **Career:** Norrell, staff coordr; Pacificare Health Systs, sales rep, mkt mgr, proj mgr, mkt analysis mgr, Serv & Develop, dir, Prod Develop, corp vpres mkt & prod develop, 1995-00; Expedient Solutions, managing partner, 2000-04; Medicare Prod, Kaiser Permanente, nat dir, Secure Horizons Corp Mkt, vpres; Care More, vpres mkt & prod planning, currently. **Orgs:** Am Mkt Asn; Calif Asn Health Maintenance Orgn; Nat Female Exec Asn; Nat Coun Aging. **Business Addr:** Vice President of Market, Product Planning, Care More, 12900 Park Plaza Dr Suite 150, Cerritos, CA 90703, **Business Phone:** 877-211-6614.

FUSE, BOBBY LEANDREW, JR.
Educator, high school teacher. **Personal:** Born Feb 17, 1952, Americus, GA; married Angela Michelle Lamar. **Educ:** Morehouse Col, BA, 1974; Mich State Univ, MA, 1975. **Career:** Col Urban Develop, grad asst to the dean, 1974-75; Martin Luther King Jr Ctr, dir youth component, 1974-76; Fulton Co Dem Party, exec dir, 1977-78; Atlanta Pub Sch, Atlanta Bd Educ, Frederick Douglass High Sch, teacher, 1976-. **Orgs:** Jr Deacon Friendship Baptist Church-Americus, 1970-; Ga Baptist Conv, 1970-74; adv, Douglass HS Student Govt 1977-85; Century Club Butler St, YMCA, 1981; fac mem, Martin Luther King Ctr Inst Nonviolence, 1987; bd trustees, Martin Luther King Jr Ctr Nonviolent Social Change Inc; youth coun adv, Nat Asn Adv Colored People; St John Lodge 17 F&AM; Holy Royal Arch Lodge 4 Americus; Nat Educ Asn; Nat Asn Sec Sch Principals; Asn Supv & Curric Develop; State Comn Life Hist Black Georgians; Mich State Univ Alumni Asn; Morehouse Col Alumni Asn. **Honors/Awds:** John Wesley Dobbs Scholar, Prince Hall Masons Ga, 1970; Scholar, Alberta Williams King Fund, 1977. *

FUTRELL, DR. MARY ALICE HATWOOD
Educator. **Personal:** Born May 24, 1940, Altavista, VA; daughter of Josephine Austin; married Donald Futrell. **Educ:** Va State Univ, BA, 1962; George Wash Univ, MA, 1968, EdD, 1992; MD Univ. **Career:** Alexandria's George Wash High Sch, headed bus educ dept; Ed Assoc Alexandria, pres, 1973-75; NEA Va Educ Assocs, pres, 1976-78; NEA, bd dir, 1978-80, secy-treas, 1980-83, pres, 1983-89; World Confederation Org Teaching Prof, bd dir, 1984-89, pres, 1989-93; Educ Int, pres, 1993-2004; George Wash Univ, Dept Educ Leadership, sr fel, 1989-92, Grad Sch Educ & Human Develop, dean, 1995-, prof educ, currently. **Orgs:** Bd adv, Esquire Regist, 1985; Task Force Teaching Carnegie Forum Educ & Econ, 1985; Nat Comn Role & Future State Cols & Univs; ed bd, Pro Educ Mag; Educ Adv Coun Metrop Life Ins Co; bd trustees, Joint Coun Econ Educ; NEA's Spec Comn Attacks Pub Educ; Select Comt Educ Black Youth; US Nat Comn United Nat Educ Sci & Cult Orgn; bd mem, Carnegie Found Improv Teaching; Kettering Found; Nat Comn Teaching & Am 's Future; chair, bd dirs, Holmes Partnership; bd dirs, Inst Educ Leadership; bd dirs, Soc Study Educ; chap sponsor, Phi Delta Kappa, currently; bd dir, Nat Soc Study educ; Bethlehem Baptist Church. **Honors/Awds:** Human Relation Awards, Nat Conf Christians & Jews, 1976 & 1986; Anne & Leon Schull Award, Am Dem Action, 1986; Friend of Educ Award, Nat Educ Asn, 1989; Cert Appreciation, UN Asn/Capital Area Div; NAACP President's Award; David Imig Award, Am Asn & Col Teacher Educ, 2002; 20 honorary doctoral degrees; UNESCO Comenius Award 2004; Am Asn Col Teacher Educr Award, 2006; NEA Found Award, 2007; Va Woman of the Year Award. **Special Achievements:** Outstanding Black Business & Prof Person, Ebony Mag, 1984; One of the Country's 100 Top Women, Ladies Home Jour, 1984; One of 12 Women of the Year, Miss Mag, 1985; One of the Most Influential Blacks in America, Ebony Mag, 1985 & 1986. **Business Addr:** Dean, Professor, George Washington University, Graduate School Education & Human Development, 2134 G St NW, Washington, DC 20052, **Business Phone:** (202)994-6161.

G

G, WARREN (WARREN GRIFFIN, III)
Rap musician, television producer. **Personal:** Born Nov 10, 1970, Long Beach, CA; son of Ola Mae; children: 4. **Career:** Albums: "Regulate. . . G Funk Era", 1994; "Take a Look Over Your Shoulder," 1997; "I Want it All," 2000; Top 10 song: "Regulate"; Contributed songs to the movie soundtracks of "Poetic Justice" and "Above the Rim"; TV shows: "Parenthood" and "Clueless,"; Barbershop 2: Back in Business, 2004; "All of Us", 2005; Secret of Life, 2009; G-Funk Millennium 2000, rap artist, producer, currently. **Honors/Awds:** Grammy nomination; Nominated for MTV Movie Award for Best Song Regulate (Above the Rim), 1995. **Business Addr:** Rap artist, G-Funk Millennium 2000, Los Angeles, CA 90024.*

GABBIN, DR. ALEXANDER LEE
Educator. **Personal:** Born Sep 6, 1945, Baltimore, MD; son of John and Dorothy Johns; married Joanne Veal; children: Jessea Nayo. **Educ:** Howard Univ, BA, 1967; Univ Chicago, MBA, 1970; Temple Univ, PhD, 1986. **Career:** Tech Construct Co, asst pres, 1968-70; Touche Ross & Co, staff auditor, 1970-72; Chicago Urban League, dep exec dir, 1972-74; Price Waterhouse & Co, auditor, 1974-75; Lincoln Univ, assoc prof, 1975-85; James Madison Univ, Sch Acct, assoc prof, 1986, KPMG LLP prof acct, currently. **Orgs:** Ill Soc CPA's, 1978; Chicago Urban League; Kappa Alpha Psi; Am Acct Asn; Am Inst Cert Pub Accountants; Nat Asn Accountants, 1990-. **Honors/Awds:** Grad Fel, Humble Oil & Refining Co, 1968-69; Builder's Award, Third World Press, 1978; Accounting Educators Award, Nat Asn Minority CPA Firms, 1979; Lindback Distinguished Teaching Award, 1982; Outstanding Teacher, Sch Acct, 1986, 1988 & 1990; Distinguished Teacher Award, 2005. **Special Achievements:** Published many articles including, "Skills Versus Apprehension: Empirical Euidence on Oral Communication". **Business Addr:** Professor, James Madison University, School of Accounting, 423 Zane Showker Hall, Harrisonburg, VA 22807.

GABBIN, DR. JOANNE VEAL
Educator. **Personal:** Born Feb 2, 1946, Baltimore, MD; daughter of Joseph and Jessie Smallwood; married Alexander L, Jul 2, 1967; children: Jessea Nayo. **Educ:** Morgan State Univ, Baltimore, MD, BA, 1967; Univ Chicago, Chicago, IL, MA, 1970, PhD, 1980. **Career:** Catalyst Youth Inc, Chicago, IL, prog dir & instr, 1973-75; Lincoln Univ, Univ Pa, asst prof eng, 1977-82, assoc prof eng, 1982-85; James Madison Univ, Harrisonburg, VA, assoc prof eng, 1985-86, Honors Prog, dir, 1986-, prof eng, 1988-2005, Furious Flower Poetry Ctr, founder & exec dir, 1999-2009. **Orgs:** Chairperson, Toni Morrison & The Supernatural, panel at the Middle Atlantic Writers Asn, 1988; Speaker, Creating a Masterpiece, Freshman Convocation James Madison Univ, 1988;

Langston Hughes Soc, Zora Neale Hurston Soc; Mid Atlantic Writer Asn Inc, MAWA Jour; Col Lang Asn; chairperson, Stud Emergency Fund, First Baptist Church, 1989-; chairperson, Bd Va Found Humanities & Pub Policy. **Honors/Awds:** Outstanding Achievement Award, Black Conf Higher Educ, 1982; Distinguished Teaching Award, Christian R & Mary F Lindback Found, 1983; Creative Scholarship Award, Col Language Asn, 1986; Women of Color Award, James Madison Univ, 1988; hon mem, Golden Key Nat Honor Soc, 1988; Outstanding Faculty Award, Va State Coun Higher Educ, 1993; George Kent Award, Gwendolyn Brooks Ctr, Chicago State Univ, 1994; Provost's Award; JMU Alumni Distinguished Faculty Award. **Special Achievements:** Publications: Sonia Sanchez: A Soft Reflection of Strength, Zora Neale Hurston Forum, 1987, A Laying on of Hands: Black Women Writers Exploring the Roots of their Folk & Cultural Tradition, Walk Together Children: Color and the Cultural Legacy of Sterling A Brown, 1988, Sterling A Brown: Building the Black Aesthetic Tradition, 1985 "A Laying on of Hands" Wild Women in the Whirlwind, Rutgers Univ Press, 1990, reprinted by Univ Press in VA, 1994, The Furious Flowering of African American Poetry, Univ Press of VA, 1999. Furious Flower: African American Poetry from the Black Arts Movement to the Present, Univ Press of VA,2004; Mourning Katrina: A Poetic Response to Tragedy, Mariner Press, 2009; Shaping Memories: Reflections of African American Women Writers, univ Press of Mississippi, 2009. **Military Serv:** Board Member, Cave Canem, 1999-2007. **Business Addr:** Executive Director, James Madison University, Furious Flower Poetry Center, MSC 3802, Harrisonburg, VA 22807, **Business Phone:** (540)568-6310.

GABRIEL, BENJAMIN MOSES
Executive. **Personal:** Born Sep 17, 1931, Brooklyn, NY; married Rebecca; children: Shirley Ann, Janice, Brenda & Benjamin Jr. **Educ:** Cornell Univ; Empire State Univ, BS. **Career:** NY Transit Authority, reporter, 1957, supvr, 1968, mgr training ctr, 1971, contract compliance officer, 1973, supt, 1976. **Orgs:** Training coord, Asso Transit, 1971; campaign mgr, Local Sch Bd Elections, 1973, 1975; bd dir, Brooklyn Tuberc & Lung Asn, 1975; candidate, dist leader 40th AD Dem Party, 1976; mem, 100 Black Men; trustee, Lutheran Hosp, 1976; chmn, Labor & Indust, ENY NAACP, 1976; vice chmn, bd dir, Asso Transit Guild. **Honors/Awds:** Comm Serv Award, Grace Bapt Church, 1974; Comm Serv & Transit Accomplishments, Elite Benevolent Soc, 1975; Doswell Mem Award, Asn Transit Guild, 1977. **Military Serv:** USAF, 1949-53. **Business Addr:** Superindent, NYCTA, 370 Jay St, Brooklyn, NY 11201.*

GADIKIAN, RANDOLPH L
Librarian, administrator. **Educ:** State Univ NY, Buffalo, MLS, 1981. **Career:** Buffalo State Col, E H Butler Libr, staff, 1981-99, coordr syst & technol, coordr comput assisted reference serv, coordr circulation serv, Emerging Technologies librn, Computing Services liaison; State Univ NY, Fredonia Col, lib dir, 2000-. **Orgs:** Chair, State Univ NY Connect Adv Coun. **Business Phone:** (716)673-3181.

GADSDEN, REV. DR. NATHANIEL J
School administrator, association executive. **Personal:** Born Oct 3, 1950, Harrisburg, PA; son of Rosetta Robinson and Nathaniel; married Carol L, Aug 3; children: David L & Nathaniel J III. **Educ:** West Chester Univ, BS, 1973; Columbia Pac Univ, MA, 1984; NJ Bible Inst; Hershey Med Ctr, clin pastoral educ; Harrisburg Hosp, clin pastoral educ; Columbia Pac Univ, PhD, 1986. **Career:** Pastor, Poet, Columnist, TV & Radio Show Host; Western Carolina Univ, resident hall dir, 1973-77; Child Abuse Hotline, case worker, 1977-80; Pa Dept Educ, equity coordr, 1980; planner alternative sentencing Pa, 1985; HelpHouse Inc, Harrisburg, Pa, counr, 1989; Writer's Wordshop Inc, dir, currently; United Way Capital Region, community bldg assoc, community impact mgr, currently. **Orgs:** Bd dirs, Multi-Disciplinary Team Dauphin Co C & Youth; bd dirs, Multi-Disciplinary Team Pa Dept C & Youth; bd mem, Comn Home Care Serv Inc; dir, Writers Wordshop 1978-; host, WMSP-FM radio, 1979-; Nat Alliance Third World Journalists, 1980-; pres, Cent Pa Black Social Workers, 1982-84; host, WHP TV Channel 21, 1982-; bd dirs, Metro Arts, 1982-; bd dirs, Susquhanna Arts Coun, 1982; black adv bd, WITF-TV; bus assoc, Cent Pa Guid Assoc, 1984-; columnist, City News Harrisburg Pa, 1984-; Int Orgn Journalists; Harrisburg dir, Pa Black United Fund; bd dir, C Playroom Inc; minister, Community Chapel Church God Christ, Harrisburg, Pa. **Honors/Awds:** Interviewed Yasser Arafat; Prime Minister Maurice Bishop of Grenada; Community Worker of the Year, Conf Black Basic Educ; Harrisburg Chap, Frontiers Int. **Special Achievements:** Author, "Stomop the Dust: The Million Man March". **Home Addr:** 123 Forster St, Harrisburg, PA 17102. **Business Addr:** Community Impact Manager, United Way of the Capital Region, 2235 Millennium Way, Enola, PA 17025, **Business Phone:** (717)732-0700 Ext 4056.

GADSDEN, ORONDE BENJAMIN
Football player, entrepreneur. **Personal:** Born Aug 20, 1971, Charleston, SC; married Bianke. **Educ:** Winston-Salem state Univ. **Career:** Drew Pearson Companies, intern; Dallas Cowboys, 1995-96, 1997; Pittsburgh Steelers, 1996; Portland Forest Dragons, 1998; Arena Football League; Miami Dolphins, wide receiver, 1998-03; Original Gear Inc, founder, 1999-. **Orgs:** Volunteer, Habitat for Humanity, 1999; volunteer, Big Brothers and Big Sisters of Broward County. **Honors/Awds:** AFL Rookie of the Year, 1998. **Business Addr:** Founder, Original Gear Incorporated, 500 Fashion Ave, New York, NY 10018-4502, **Business Phone:** (646)312-8982.*

GAFFNEY, DERRICK TYRONE
Football player. **Personal:** Born May 24, 1955, Jacksonville, FL; children: Jabar. **Educ:** Univ Fla. **Career:** Football player (retired); New York Jets, wide receiver, 1978-84, 1987. **Orgs:** Alpha phi alpha fraternity. *

GAFFNEY, LESLIE GALE
Executive. **Personal:** Born Feb 21, 1951, Cleveland, OH; daughter of George Douglas and Lucille Miller; married Kenneth Wilson Sr, May 19, 1989. **Educ:** Ky State Univ, BS, 1972. **Career:** R H Macy's, vendor inquiry mgr, 1979-84; Sony Corp Am, Corp Controllers, A/R project mgr, 1984-85; Components Prod Co, oper mgr, 1985-86, accts payable mgr, 1986-87; Consumer Co Mid-Atlantic, oper mgr, 1987-88; Peripheral Products Co, admin mgr, 1988-89, dir community affairs, 1989-02; Broad Inst Mass Inst Technol & Harvard, dir commun, 2005-. **Orgs:** Exec comt, EDGES Group, 1988-; chair, adv bd, Nat Sci Found, Southern Calif Access Ctr, 1989-97; pre-col adv bd, NJ Inst Technol, 1992-; pres, Greater Montvale Bus Assn, 1992-; Ky State Univ Alumni bd dir, 1993-96; bd of dir, Com & Indust Asn NJ, 1996-. **Honors/Awds:** Special Achievement Award, Ky State Univ Alumni Asn, 1992, Diversity Award, 1996; Most Valuable Player Award, Congressional Black Caucus, 1998. **Business Addr:** Director Of Communications, Broad Institute of MIT and Harvard, 320 Charles St, Cambridge, MA 02141-2023, **Business Phone:** (617)258-0900.*

GAFFNEY, MICHELE ELIZABETH
Zoologist, zoo keeper, zoo keeper. **Personal:** Born Nov 13, 1960, Long Island, NY; daughter of Dr Floyd and Yvonne. **Educ:** Univ Calif-Davis, BS, 1982; Calif Polytech Univ, MS. **Career:** Zool Soc San Diego, Wild Animal Park, sr mammal keeper, 1983-. **Orgs:** Comparative Nutrit Soc, 1998-. **Business Addr:** Senior Mammal Keeper, Zoological Society of San Diego, Wild Animal Park, 15500 San Pasqual Valley Rd, Escondido, CA 92027, **Business Phone:** (760)747-8702.*

GAFFNEY, THOMAS DANIEL
Government official. **Personal:** Born Jun 19, 1933, Laredo, TX. **Career:** San Antonio Independent Sch Dist Sch Bd, vpres; US Govt, 23 yrs. **Orgs:** AFRES; San Antonio Mus Asn; Ruth Taylor Theater; Nat Asn Advan Colored People; 433 TAW & EEOC; 2851 ABGP & WELFARE Fund; LCL Adv Coun; Exec Comt UNCF; pres, Poverty Agency Bd; vpres, sch bd, 1973-77; San Antonio River Comn; Black Unity Coordination Coun; life mem, BT Wash PTA; AFA; ACLU; Nat Caucus Black Sch Bds; NCOA. **Military Serv:** USAF, 4 yrs. *

GAINER, FRANK EDWARD
Manager. **Personal:** Born Jun 18, 1938, Waynesboro, GA; son of Walter and Edith; married Alice M Ingram; children: Edward, Ervin & Todd. **Educ:** Morehouse Col, BS, 1960; Tuskegee Inst, MS, 1962; Iowa State Univ, MS, 1964, PhD, 1967. **Career:** Antibiotic Anal & Qual Control, mgr, 1978; Eli Lilly & Co, sec treas; JCG&M; M-MED, founder, 2000-; Fundamental Baptist Fel Asn, CFO; Christian Heritage Ministries, founder, currently. **Orgs:** Asn chmn, Am Chem Soc, 1975; chancellor, Am Chem Soc, 1977; Sigma Xi; Beta Kappa Chi Hon Sci Soc; NAACP; Urban League; secy, Mary Riggs Neighborhood Ctr, 1976, treas, 1977, bd dir, beginning 1975. **Special Achievements:** publ sci j. **Business Addr:** Founder, M-MED, 3140 N Ill St, Indianapolis, IN 46208, **Business Phone:** (317)283-1454.

GAINER, PROF. JOHN F
Choral conductor, educator, composer. **Personal:** Born Aug 8, 1954, East Orange, NJ; son of Benjamin Franklin and Stella Wynn. **Educ:** Ariz State Univ, BA, 1980; Univ Oregon, Sch Archit & Allied Arts, 1987. **Career:** Various church & comm choirs, dir & musician, 1968-; Ariz State Univ Gospel Ensemble, founder & dir, 1975-80; Lane Comm Col, music instr, 1984-85; Univ Ore, adj asst prof, 1983-99; Inspirational Sounds Community Choir, founder & dir, 1983-2000; Ore Sym Orchestra & NW Community Gospel Chorus Gospel Christmas Concerts, 1999-; Northern Calif Mass Choir Gospel Music Workshop Am, staff music dir & soloist, 2001-; Federated Stores Inc, selling specialist, 2001-04; Almac Clin Technologies, admini asst, 2004-06; Fair Housing Council Ore, admin asst & office adminr, 2007-. **Orgs:** Am Soc Composers Auth & Publ, 1972-; minister, Church God Christ Inc, 1979-; Ore Lane County Rainbow Coalition, 1983-88; precinct comm person, Cent Dem Comm, 1984-88; Edwin Hawkins Music & Arts Sem, 1984-; chap rep & nat mass choir music comm, Gospel Music Workshop Am, 1986-. **Honors/Awds:** Honorary DD, Church God, 1986; Martin Luther King Junior Award, Martin Luther King Jr Celebration Comm, 1998; Leadership Recognition Award, Univ Ore, Sch Music, 1998. **Special Achievements:** First African-American gospel artist to perform at the Hult Center for the Performing Arts 1983, invited to teach original compositions in the New Song Seminar at the National Conventions of the Gospel Music Workshop of America Inc, Inspirational Sounds one of 4 gospel choirs nationwide which performed at the Great American Gospel Gala at Alice Tully Hall of the renown Lincoln Center for the Performing Arts, 1987, invited to perform at World's Fair 1992, invited to conduct master class and perform, Central Europe, 1992-93. **Home Addr:** 4101 Lincoln Way, San Francisco, CA 94122-1200, **Home Phone:** (415)731-1594. **Business Addr:** Administrative Assistant, Office Administrator, Fair Housing Council of Oregon, 1020 S W Taylor St Suite 700, Portland, OR 97205, **Business Phone:** (503)223-8295.*

GAINES, ADRIANE THERESA
Executive. **Personal:** Born Aug 27, 1947, Mt Vernon, NY; daughter of James McCoy and Dorothy McCoy. **Educ:** Fordham Univ, BA, 1978. **Career:** Marine Midland Bank, secy & safekeeping deputy, 1965-68; State Nat Bank El Paso, investment & sec deputy, 1968-71; Rochester Inst Tech, asst info spec, 1971-72; Culinary Inst Am, asst librarian, 1972-73; Unity Broadcasting Network, dir of corp admin, 1973-82, corp vpres NBN Broadcasting Inc, 1995; WWRL-AM, pres & gen mgr, 1995-. **Orgs:** Co-founder, bd mem, The World Inst Black Comt CEBA Awards, 1978-; acting gen mgr KATZ AM WZEN FM Radio 1982; comt bd dir, Coalition 100 Black Women, 1984-85; Women Cable, 1985; Adv Women Radio & TV, 1982-; bd trustees, Apollo Theater Hall Fame, 1986-; adv comt mem, Schomburg Ctr Res Black Culture; bd mem, Aaron Davis Hall; bd mem, The Joan Mitchell Found. **Honors/Awds:** Media Woman of the Year, Nat Asn Media Women, 1985; Leadership Award, NAACP, 1995. **Business Addr:** President, General Manager, WWRL AM, 333 7th Ave 14th Fl, New York, NY 10001, **Business Phone:** (212)631-0800.*

GAINES, AVA CANDA
Clergy. **Personal:** Born Feb 19, 1963, Madison, WI; daughter of George and Zelma Hamilton. **Educ:** Univ Dist Columbia, WA, DC, 1982-83; Univ Tex, Dallas, TX, BA, 1991; Perkins Sch Theol, MA, Theol Studies, 2000. **Career:** St Paul CME Church, Chester, PA, sr pastor; Mt. Pleasant Christian Methodist Episcopal Church, sr pastor, currently. **Orgs:** Recruiting comt, Nat Asn Advan Colored People, 1984-l Black Polit Scientist Asn, 1986-. **Honors/Awds:** Author, Anybody Can Get the Holy Ghost, CME Church, 1986; Ordained Elder, CME Church, 1989. **Home Addr:** 2601 W 9th St, Chester, PA 19013. **Business Addr:** Senior Pastor, Mt. Pleasant Christian Methodist Episcopal Church, Hwy 360 W, Halifax, VA 24558, **Business Phone:** (804)476-6513.*

GAINES, BRENDA J.
Executive. **Personal:** Daughter of DeLouise and Clarence. **Educ:** Univ Ill Urbana-Champaign, BA, 1970; Roosevelt Univ, MA, 1976. **Career:** U.S Dept Housing, dep regional admin, 1980-81; Commissioner Housing, Chicago, 1983-85; Deputy Chief Staff, 1985-87; Diners Club, N Am, pres & chief exec officer, 1999-04; Tenet Healthcare Corp, bd dir; NICOR Inc, dir; Fannie Mae, dir, 2006-. **Honors/Awds:** Woman of Achievement Award, Anti-Defamation League; Black Achievers Industry Award, 1995; Pioneer Award, Urban Bankers Forum, 1996; Volunteer of the Yr, Boys & Girls Club of Chicago, 1999; Otto Wirth Award, Roosevelt Univ, 2000. **Business Addr:** Director, Fannie Mae, 3900 Wisconsin Ave, NW Washington, DC 20016, **Business Phone:** (202)752-7000.*

GAINES, CASSANDRA JEAN
Executive, founder (originator). **Personal:** Born Feb 21, 1953, Oakland, CA; children: Annje Linaii Wilkerson. **Educ:** Connors State Col, 1979; Northeastern State Univ, 1989. **Career:** City Muskogee, multicult events coordr, 1996-; Black Town Tours, founder, 1997-. **Orgs:** Muskogee COC; Nat Asn Advan Colored People; Women Who Care; Nat Coalition Black Meeting Planners; Okla Human Rights, 2000; Travel Indust Asn, 2000; ed & mkt consult, Black Meeting & Tourism Mag; Muskogee Chamber Com. **Honors/Awds:** Listed in Top Fifty Women of Oklahama, 1999; Maxine Cissel Horner Spirit of Community Excellence Award, 2002. **Business Addr:** Multicultural Events Coordinator, Muskogee Convention and Tourism, PO Box 2361, Muskogee, OK 74401, **Business Phone:** (918)684-6363.*

GAINES, CLARENCE L.
Judge. **Personal:** Born Mar 9, 1914, Dallas, TX; married Pearl; children: Pearl, Delaney, Clarence III & George. **Educ:** Western Res Univ, BBA, 1950; Cleveland Marshall Law Sch, LLB, 1955. **Career:** City Coun, elected, 1963, 1965; City Cleveland, dir health & welfare, 1966-68; Gaines Rogers Horton & Forbes, sr partner; Cleveland Munic Ct, judge. **Orgs:** Coun Human Rels; Nat Asn Advan Colored People; Boy Scouts; Urban League; Welfare Fedn; Alcoholic Control Ctr; Cleveland Pub Libr. **Military Serv:** WW II, officer.

GAINES, COREY YASUTO
Basketball player, basketball coach. **Personal:** Born Jun 1, 1965, Los Angeles, CA. **Educ:** Univ Calif, Los Angeles, 1986; Loyola Mary mount Univ, 1988. **Career:** Basketball player (retired), basketball coach; Quad City Thunder, 1988-89; NJ Nets, 1988-89; Omaha Racers, 1989-90; Philadelphia 76ers, 1989-90, 1994-95; Denver Nuggets, 1990-91; NY Knicks, 1993-94; Long Beach Jam,

Am Basketball Asn, guard, asst coach, 2003-04, head coach, 2005-07; Calif Buzz, asst coach, 2004; Phoenix Mercury, asst coach, 2006-07; head coach, 2007-. **Special Achievements:** ABA Champions, 2003-04. **Business Addr:** Head Coach, Phoenix Mercury, 201 E Jefferson St, Phoenix, AZ 85004, **Business Phone:** (602)514-8333.

GAINES, CRYSTAL MONIQUE
Executive. **Personal:** Born Oct 14, 1972, Brooklyn, NY; daughter of J Kendall Flowers and LaVerne S; married Ludwig P Gaines, Sep 5, 1998. **Educ:** Hampton Univ, BS, mkt, 1994; George Wash Univ, MSPM, 2000. **Career:** Soza & Co, mgt analyst, 1994-96, dep proj mgr, 1996-98, prog mgr, 1998-99, bus mgr & sr vpres, CIO, 1999-2003. **Orgs:** Proj Mgt Inst, 1998-; Tucker Plus Adv Bd, 2000-. **Honors/Awds:** Outstanding Performance, Soza & Co Ltd, 2000.

GAINES, ERNEST J.
Educator, writer. **Personal:** Born Jan 15, 1933, Pointe Coupee Parish, LA. **Educ:** Vallejo Jr Col; San Francisco St Col, attended 1957; Denison Univ, DLitt. **Career:** Books: Catherine Carmier, 1964; Catherine Carmier, 1966; Of Love & Dust, 1967; Bloodline, 1968; Of Love & Dust, 1968; The Autobiography of Miss Jane Pittman, 1971; A Long Day in November, 1971; In My Father's House, 1978; A Gathering of Old Men, 1983; A Lesson Before Dying, 1993; National Book Critics Circle Award for fiction, 1993; Oprah's Book Club, 1997;Mozart & Leadbelly: Stories & Essays, 2005; Univ La, Lafayette, Dept Eng, prof & writer-in-residence, prof emer, currently. **Orgs:** Am Acad Arts & Letters. **Honors/Awds:** Wallace Stegner fellow, 1957; Solomon R. Guggenheim Foundation fellow, 1971; Gold Medal, Commonwealth Club CA, 1972, 1984; LA Libr Asn Award, 1972; Black Acad Arts & Letters Award, 1972; Award for Excellence of Achievement, San Francisco Arts Comt, 1983; Mac Arthur Fel, 1993; Louisiana Humanist of the Year, 1993; Nat Book Critics Circle Award, 1993; John D.and Catherine T. MacArthur Foundation fellow, 1993; Dos Passos Prize, 1993; Chevalier in the Order of Art & Letters, Govt France; Emmy Award for Best Television Movie, 1999; Nat Governor's Arts Award, 2000; Nat Humanities Medal, 2000; Louisiana Writer of the Year Award, 2000; Nat Humanities Medal, 2000. **Special Achievements:** Published numerous articles. **Business Addr:** Professor Emeritus of English, University of Louisiana, English Department, PO Box 44691, Lafayette, LA 70504-4691.

GAINES, GRADY
Saxophonist. **Personal:** Born May 14, 1934, Waskorn, TX. **Career:** Albums: Full Gain, 1987; Down and Dirty, Live At Tipitina's; House of Plenty, 1992; Jump Start, 2002; Songs: "Baby Work Out"; "The Night Time Is The Right Time"; "So In Love With You"; "I Can't Turn You Loose"; "Harlem Shuffle". **Honors/Awds:** Blues Heritage Award, Tex Blues Preserv Soc; Blues Artist of the Year, Juneteenth Festival, 1993; Best Blues, Best Horn Section, Best Funk/R&B, Houston Press, 2001; Local Musician of the Year, Houston Press, 2001. **Special Achievements:** Honored by Texas Blues Preservation Society with its first annual Blues Heritage Award, citing him as being a Texas Blues Ambassador Around the World and a Pioneer in the Creation of Rock & Roll; in 1993, he played at one of President Clinton's inaugural parties. **Business Addr:** Saxophonist, Recording Bandleader, Gulf Coast Entertainment, PO Box 130026, Houston, TX 77219, **Business Phone:** (713)523-7004.*

GAINES, HERSCHEL DAVIS
School administrator. **Personal:** Born Oct 7, 1942, Parkin, AR; married Wilbert; children: Jacquelyn LaRue, Michelle LaRue & Genee La Rue. **Educ:** Univ Ariz, Pine Bluff, BSE, 1962; AR State Univ, MSE, 1979. **Career:** Phelix High Sch, eng teacher, 1962-69; Marion Sr High Sch, eng teacher, 1969-71; Mc Arthur Middle Sch, chmn eng dept, 1971-81; Jonesboro High Sch, asst prin, 1981-94; Ark State Univ, eng instr, supvr elem educ stud teachers, 1994; Williams Baptist Col, adj instr eng, currently. **Orgs:** Bd dirs, Jonesboro Classroom Teachers Asn, 1972-; bd dir, Ariz Educ Asn, 1976-79; basileus anti-basileus & grammateus Kappa Nu Omega Alpha Kappa Alpha Sor, 1976-80; affiliate rels comt, Nat Educ Asn, 1977-79; corr secy, Alpha Delta Kappa, 1979-; appointed by Gov Bill Clinton to Employment Sec Div Adv Coun, 1981; nom comt, Crowley's Ridge Girl Scout Coun, 1981-83; educ comn, Crowley's Ridge Girl Scouts, 1981-83; bd dir, United Way Greater Jonesboro, 1985-86; Adv Coun Upward Bound, Ariz State Univ, 1980-; pres, Ariz State Univ Faculty Women's Club, 1985-87. **Honors/Awds:** Educ Award, Alpha Kappa Alpha Sor Jonesboro AR & AR Coun of AKA, 1976,1978; Outstanding Young Educator Award, Jaycees Jonesboro, 1977; Silver Soror, Alpha Kappa Alpha, 1985; pres Nu Chap, Alpha Delta Kappa, 1994-96. **Business Addr:** Adjunct Instructor of English, Williams Baptist College, 60 W Fulbright Ave, Walnut Ridge, AR 72476, **Business Phone:** (870)886-6741.*

GAINES, JO EVA
Association executive. **Career:** City Newport, vice chmn; Newport Sch Comt; RI Asn Sch Comt, pres, currently. **Business Addr:** President, Rhode Island Association of School Committees, RIC Campus Bldg Suite 6, 600 Mt Pleasant Ave, Providence, RI 02908, **Business Phone:** (401)272-9811.*

GAINES, JOHN A., SR.
Lawyer. **Personal:** Born May 23, 1941, Rock Hill, SC; son of John and Ernestine Moore; divorced; children: John A Jr, Janee Latrice. **Educ:** Benedict Col, BA, 1964; Howard Univ Law Sch, JD, 1968. **Career:** Rock Hill Model Cities Prog, adv & citizen; participation specialist, 1969-70; Nat Asn Advan Colored People Legal Defense Fund Inc, intern, 1970-71; self-employed atty, 1971-. **Orgs:** SCA State Bar; Nat Bar Asn; Nat Asn Advan Colored People Florence; APA Fraternity, 1963-; trustee, legal coun church & prayer coordr, New Life Assembly God, ; Small Bus Mgt Asn, 1976. **Honors/Awds:** American Jurisprudence Award, Bancroft-Whitney Co, 1968; Personalities of the South Award, Am Biographical Inst, 1970-71; Best Lawyers in America, Reveal Publ, 1979; Pineville AME Zion Church Award, 1995; awarded internship, Nat Asn Advan Colored People Legal Defense Fund Inc, 1970-71; Award recognizing membership Friendship 9, Friendship Jr College, 1979; award recognizing membership in Friendship 9, Alpha Kappa Alpha Sorority, 1990; Pagel Award, York County Coun, Nat Asn Advan Colored People, 1999. **Business Addr:** Attorney, 200 W Evans St Suite 211, Florence, SC 29501, **Business Phone:** (803)679-3035.*

GAINES, LADONNA ANDREA. See SUMMER, DONNA.

GAINES, MARY E
Publicist, administrator. **Personal:** Born in Boligee, AL; daughter of Mattie L Hamilton and Willie. **Educ:** Loop City Col, Chicago, Ill, AA, 1970; Midwestern Broadcasting, Chicago, Ill, diploma, 1972; Brewer State Junior Col, Fayette, Ala, 1975; Univ Ala, Tuscaloosa, Ala, BA, 1982. **Career:** WCBI-Television, Columbus, Miss, anchor producer & reporter, 1975-77; WNPT-Radio, Tuscaloosa, Ala, announcer, 1976-79; Fed Sothern Co-ops, Epes, Ala, admin asst, 1977-79; Arrington Mayor, Birmingham, Ala, office coordr, 1982-83; WBRC-TV, Birmingham, Ala, reporter/editor, 1978-82; Ala Public TV, Montgomery, Ala, TV producer, 1983-93; USDA Forest Serv Nat Forests Ala, pub affairs officer, currently. **Orgs:** Faithful Navigator, KPC, Ladies Grace, 2002-; Grand lady, Knights Peter Claver, Ladies Aux, 1990-; state coordr, Nat Asn Black Journalists, 1983-; founder, Central Ala Black Media Asn, 1988; Youth Develop & Birmingham Urban League Bds, 1981-82; SCLC & NAACP, 1972-75; vpres, Knights Peter Claver Ladies Auxiliary, Gulf Coast Dist; Emancipation Proclamation Comt; secy, auditor, Archdiocesan Coun Catholic Women; treas, Knights Peter Claver Ladies Auxiliary; co-chair, Nat Black Catholic Cong. **Honors/Awds:** President & Distinguished SVC, Ala Poultry/Egg Asn, 1988-86; Media Awards: Ala Farmers Fed, Humane Soc, 1985-82; Media Awards, Emancipation Asn, Alpha Eta Chap, Iota Phi Lambda, 1982; Fight for Freedom Award, MS, NAACP, 1977. **Business Addr:** Public Affairs Officer, USDA Forest Service, National Forests in Alabama, Supvr Off, 2946 Chestnut St, Montgomery, AL 36107, **Business Phone:** (334)241-8173.

GAINES, DR. OSCAR CORNELL
Physician. **Personal:** Born May 21, 1954, Memphis, TN; divorced. **Educ:** Lambuth Col, BS, 1976; Meharry Med Col, MD, 1982. **Career:** AUS, capt & physician, 1983-87. **Orgs:** Prince Hall Mason Lodge, 1986; Alpha Phi Alpha. **Military Serv:** AUS, capt, 3 yrs.

GAINES, PATRICIA
Journalist, writer. **Career:** The Wash Post, reporter; Laughing in the Dark: From Colored Girl to Woman of Color, author; A Journey from Prison to Power and the inspirational Moments of Grace: Meeting the Challenge to Change, author. **Orgs:** Joseph's House; Nat Asn Black Journalists. **Honors/Awds:** Excellence Award, Nat Asn Black Journalists. **Business Addr:** Reporter, Author, The Washington Post, 1150 15th St NW, Washington, DC 20071, **Business Phone:** (202)334-6000.*

GAINES, PAUL LAURENCE
Educator, government official. **Personal:** Born Apr 20, 1932, Newport, RI; son of Albert P Sr and Pauline P Jackson; married Jo Eva Johnson, Jul 18, 1959; children: Jena, Patricia, Paulajo & Paul Jr. **Educ:** Xavier Univ LA, BEd, 1955; Bridgewater State Col, MEd, Coun, 1968. **Career:** Educator (retired); Newport RI Pub Sch, sch teacher, 1959-68; Newport RI Rogers HS, basketball coach, 1959-68; Newport RI Youth Corps, counr,1960-66; Bridgewater State Col Mass, admin, 1968-96, asst to pres, 1983-96; Bridgewater State Grad Sch, Col prof, 1970-94. **Orgs:** Newport Br Nat Advan Asn Colored People; Newport Lions Club; Coun, 256 Knights Columbus; Urban League RI; comnr, RI Ethics Comn, 1987-93; RI Black Heritage Soc; bd trustees, St. Michael's Country Day Sch; bd, Newport Historical Soc; chair, Canvassing Authority, Newport, RI; chair, Black Regt (Patriots Park) Enhancement Memorial Proj, 1997; chair, bd dirs, Newport county mental health Ctr. **Honors/Awds:** Citizen of the Year, Omega Psi Phi Frat (Sigma Nu Chapt), 1981; George T Downing Award, RI, 1982; inductee, Newport Sports Hall Fame, 2002. **Special Achievements:** First Black Mayor in New England, 1981; All-AM (Catholic) Basketball(District 3) Team, 1952-2000; First Black Sch Committee man Since, 1900; First Black City Council man, Newport City Council, 1977-81; First Black Mayor State RI, 1981-83. **Military Serv:** AUS, 82nd recon div sp 3, 1955-57; 2nd Armored Div. *

GAINES, DR. RAY D.
Surgeon, educator, college teacher. **Personal:** Born Aug 4, 1932, Minneapolis, MN; married Frances Hunter. **Educ:** Creighton Univ, BS 1954, MD, 1958. **Career:** Wayne Co Gen Hosp, internship, 1958-59; Santa Cruz Co Hosp CA, gen pract residency, 1959-60; Wayne Co Gen Hosp, residency surg, 1960-64; Wayne County Gen Hosp, staff, 1964-73; Univ Mich Ctr, clin instr, 1965-73; Pub Health Serv Bur Health Manpower, consult, 1967-70; Creighton Univ, asst prof, 1973-92, CUMC Trauma Ctr, dir, 2003, prof surg, currently; Douglas Co Hosp, NE, chief surg serv, 1974-76; St Joseph Hosp, assoc chief emergency serv, 1975-78; Va Med Ctr, Omaha, NE, assoc chief surg serv. **Orgs:** Fel Am Col Surgeons, 1966; guest examr, Am Bd Surg, Omaha, 1974; bd dirs, Dougals/Sarpy Div, Am Cancer Soc, 1975-; adv coun, Med Am Coun BSA, 1975-76; med officer, Gen Daniel James Ct Squad CAP, 1976-77; Am Burn Asn; Creighton Univ Surg Soc; Asn Va Surgeons; Asn Acad Surg; Omaha Midwest Clin Soc; Asn Emergency Med; Detroit Surg Asn; Kappa Alpha Psi; Phi BetaPi; NAACP; bd dir, NE Heart Asn; Joslyn Art Mus; Nat Med Asn; Metrop Omaha Med Soc; NE Med Soc; bd mem, NE Div, Am Cancer Soc; fel Southwestern Surg Cong. **Business Addr:** Professor, Creighton University School of Medicine, Department Surg, 601 N 30th St 3700, Omaha, NE 68131.*

GAINES, RICHARD KENDALL
Insurance executive, consultant. **Personal:** Born Apr 11, 1947, St Louis, MO; son of Richard Harris and Jewell Gaines Harris; married Anne-Marie Clarke, Apr 3, 1979; children: Kimberly & Yvette. **Educ:** Coe Col, BA, sociol, 1969; St Louis Univ, urban affairs. **Career:** City Des Moines, dep dir, 1969-70; St Louis Bd Educ, dir comn educ, 1970-73, pres, 1987-88; St Louis Univ, dir upward bound, 1973-76; Urban League Metropolitan St Louis, dir educ, 1976-77; state MO statewide Task force, 1984; St Louis Pub Sch, pres, 1987-88; Daniel & Henry Ins Brokers, vpres, dir; Richard K Gaines & Assocs, pres, ceo, currently. **Orgs:** Jaycees St Louis 1972-75; Am Personnel & Guidance Asn, 1973-76; past pres, YMCA Men's Club City N, 1979-83; Nat Asn Life Underwriters; registered rep, Nat Asn Security Dealers; Independent Ins Agents MO; St Louis Bd Educ, 1983-89; bd dir, YMCA; past pres, St Louis Bd Educ 1987-88; grand pharoah, pres, Royal Order Vagabonds Inc, 1992-96; bd dir, Tower Village Nursing Home, 1989; mem bd dir, Olympic festival comt, 1994; st Louis area boys scout, 1994; past chmn, black leadership roundtable, 1998-99, NAACP; mem, SAB, St. Louis Public School, 2009. **Honors/Awds:** Sales Award, Lincoln Nat Life Ins, 1977; Community service award, 1999. **Business Phone:** (314)444-1969.*

GAINES, ROBERT
Executive, educator. **Personal:** Born Jul 19, 1942, Manhattan, NY; son of Richard D Gaines and Lillian; married Jinko A Gaines, Aug 16, 1967; children: Robert Jr & Barrone. **Educ:** Eastern Wash Univ, BS, 1976; Victor Valley Col, MS, 1987; Southern Ill Univ, attended. **Career:** Gaines Mobil Servs, owner & operator, 1980-81; Boeing Serv Int, security supvr, 1981-82; Boeing Military Airplane, Avionices Lab supvr, 1982-92; Victor Valley African Am Chamber Com, Chief Exec Officer, chair, currently. **Orgs:** Past pres, US Military Retiree's Social Club, 1976-; High Desert Lodge 107, Masonic Lodge Tyler, 1977-; exec comt, Victor Valley NAACP, 1978-; comnr, past chair, County Ment Health Comn, 1991-; founding dir, CA Black Chamber Com, 1994-; adj, Calif Cadet Corps, Second Region. **Honors/Awds:** Certificate of appreciation, Boeing Military Airplane Co, 1988; Employee of the Month, 1987; 2 certificates of merit, 1988, 1989; certificate of recognition, County San Bernardino, 1995; Optimist, Citizen of the Month, 1997. **Special Achievements:** Mental Health in African American Communities, High Desert Gold Magazine; founding board mem CA Black Chamber Com and first honorary lifetime. **Military Serv:** USN, cpt, 1958-60, USAF, cpt, 1960-81. **Business Addr:** Chairperson, California Black Chamber of Commerce, 2951 Sunrise Blvd Suite 175, Rancho Cordova, CA 95742, **Business Phone:** (916)463-0177.

GAINES, SAMUEL STONE
Executive. **Personal:** Born Jan 25, 1938, Fort Pierce, FL; married Theressa Ann Dillard; children: Andre, Arnold, Alwyn. **Educ:** Talladega Col, BA, 1960; McAllister Sch Embalming, attended 1961. **Career:** Fla Mortician Asn, pres, 1979-81; Epsilon Nu Delta Mortuary Fraternity, nat pres, 1982-84; Nat Funeral Dir & Morticians, nat pres, 1985-86; St Lucie Co Sch Bd, bd mem & chmn, currently. **Orgs:** Treas, Omicron Tau Chap Omega; treas, Fla Mortician Asn; St Lucie Co Sch Bd, 1972-; life mem, Omega Psi Phi Frat; golden hertigage mem, Nat Asn Adv Colored People ; Grand Inspector Gen, 33rd degree Ancient & Accepted Scottish Rite Free Masonry Southern Jurisdiction; Asn Independent Funeral Dirs Fla. **Honors/Awds:** Community Service Award, Club Entre Nous, 1980; Ft Pierce Chap Links, 1981; Fla Mortician Asn, 1982; Man of The Year, Alpha Gamma Chap Epsilon Nu Delta, 1983; Hon Doctor of Laws, Faith Grant Col, 1994. **Home Addr:** 1505 Ave Q, PO Box 831, Fort Pierce, FL 34950, **Home Phone:** (561)466-1025. **Business Addr:** Chairman, School Board of St Lucie County, 4204 Okeechobee Rd, Fort Pierce, FL 34947, **Business Phone:** (772)461-1800.*

GAINES, THURSTON LENWOOD, JR.
Physician. **Personal:** Born Mar 20, 1922, Freeport, NY; son of Thurston Lenwood Gaines and Albertha Reubena Robinson; mar-

ried Jacqueline Eleanor Kelly; children: Beverly Doreen, Terrell Lance, William Wesley. **Educ:** Howard Univ, 1943; NY Univ, BA 1948; Meharry Med Col, MD 1953. **Career:** Hempstead, NY, pvt pract surg, 1959-76; Assoc attending surgeon Nassau County Med Ctr, East Meadow, Long Island, NY 1959-77; South Nassau Community Hosp, Oceanside, NY, dir prof educ & training, 1964-69; Mercy Hosp, Rockville Ctr, NY, dir surg educ, 1969-74; Western Mass Hosp, Westfield, MA, chief prof serv, 1977-78; Soldiers Home Holyoke, med dir, 1979-88; pvt pract. **Orgs:** Kiwanis Club Hempstead, NY 1963-67; deputy county med examr Nassau County, Long Island, NY, 1964-77; Hempstead Community Chest, Hempstead, NY 1965; bd trustees Cath Hosp Asn, St Louis, MO 1973-76; asst clinical prof surg State Univ NY Stonybrook Med Sch, 1976-77; fel Am Col Surgeons; fel Int Col Surgeons; Fel, Am Col Utilization Review Physicians, 1987. **Honors/Awds:** Diplomate, Am Bd Surg, 1963; Diplomate, Am Bd Qual Assurance Utilization Review Physicians, 1987. **Military Serv:** USAAF 1st lt fighter pilot instructor pilot; 332nd Fighter Group Air Medal; 2 Oak Leaf Clusters; Purple Heart 1943-47. *

GAINEY, LEONARD DENNIS, II
Association executive, consultant, president (organization). **Personal:** Born Aug 23, 1927, Jacksonville, FL; divorced; children: Leonard III, Derek & Kassandra. **Educ:** Morehouse Col, BA, 1949. **Career:** US Post Office Dept, Ft Lauderdale, FL, carrier, 1953-66; Gaineys Bus Affairs, owner, 1953-66; Econ Opportunity Coord Group Inc, dep dir, controller, 1966-73; State Fla Ed Dept, fiscal officer, 1973-76; Urban League Broward City, pres, ceo, 1976-81; Ken Thurston & Assoc Inc, bd mem, 1979-80; The Omega Group Inc, mgr mgt consult br office; N Broward Hosp Dist, dir minority bus affairs, mgt consult, currently. **Orgs:** Nat Asn Health Servs Execs; Omega Psi Phi, 1957; Ed Community Ft Lauderdale Broward C of C, 1980, Human Affairs Coun; Nat Coun Christians & Jews, 1980; chmn, Broward Co Human Rels Adv; Am Mgt Asn; Nat Soc Pub Acct; Nat Soc Tax Prof; Am Asn Prof Consult; Fla Asn Minority Bus Off; Nat Forum for Black Adminrs; Omega Psi Phi Fraternity Inc; zoning bd mem, City Lauderdale Lakes, FL. **Honors/Awds:** Omega Man of the Yr, Omega Psi Phi Fraternity; Citation Broward Co Human Rels Div, 1979. **Military Serv:** AUS, corpl, 1950-52. **Business Addr:** Management Consultant, North Broward Hospital District, 303 SE 17TH ST, Fort Lauderdale, FL 33316, **Business Phone:** (954)831-2792.

GAINOUS, FRED J.
College administrator, educator. **Personal:** Born Jul 6, 1947, Tallahassee, FL; son of Eddie Gainous and Lucy Gainous; married Dr Madie, Nov 6, 1988; children: Tamara, Nikki Meeks & Kelli. **Educ:** Fla A&M Univ, BS, Agr Educ, 1969; Univ Fla, Ms, Agr Educ, 1972, Educ Specialist, 1974, Doctorate, 1975. **Career:** Fla A&M Univ, assoc prof educ, 1977-78, pres, 2002-04; Fla State Dept Educ, pro dir, 1978-79, coord, 1979-85; Kans State Dept Educ, asst comnr, 1985-87; St Peters burg Jr Col, assoc vpres, 1987-88; Dept Post secondary Educ, chancellor, 1988-2002. **Orgs:** Leadership Montgomery, 1993; Ala Comn Higher Educ Adv Coun; Pres &Chancellors, Ala Coun Col & Univ; Asn Community Col Trustees; Jr Col & Trade Sch Authority; pres Acad, Am Asn Community Col, 1994; pres, Nat Coun State Dir Community Col, 1995; Leadership Ala, 1996. **Honors/Awds:** Kermit Mathison Outstanding Jr Col Admin Award, Univ Montevallo, 1989; Shirley B Gordon Award Distinction, Phi Theta Kappa Honor Society, 1997; Black Issues Higher Education, 1999; Bellwether Award, Univ Fla.

GAITAN, FERNANDO J., JR.
Lawyer, judge. **Personal:** Born Aug 22, 1948, Kansas City, KS. **Educ:** Pittsburgh State Univ, BS, 1970; Univ Mo, Kans City, JD, 1974. **Career:** Southwestern Bell Tel Co, atty, 1974-80; Sixteenth Judicial Circuit Ct, MO, judge, 1980-86; Mo Ct Appeals, Western Dist, judge, 1986-91; Bur Prisons; US Justice Dept; pub defender; Legal Aid Soc; Sixteenth Judicial Circuit, Jackson City Ct House, judge; US Dist Ct, Western Dist Mo, judge, currently. **Orgs:** Mo Bar Asn; Kans City Bar Asn; Jackson County Bar Asn; Am Bar Asn; Nat Bar Asn; State & Nat Judicial Conf; St Lukes Hosp; De La Salle Educ Ctr; Ozanam Home Boys; Nat Asn Advan Colored People; Vol Corrections, Nat Conf Christians & Jews. **Special Achievements:** The first African-Am to serve as a Judge of the United States District Court for the Western District of Missouri; The youngest person ever app an Appellate Judge of the Missouri Court of Appeals-Western Dist. **Business Addr:** Judge, US District Court Western District, Charles Evans Whittaker Ct House, Rm 7552 400 E 9th St, Kansas City, MO 64108, **Business Phone:** (816)512-5630.*

GAITER, TONY (TONY BERNARD GAITER, JR.)
Football player. **Personal:** Born Jul 15, 1974?, Miami, FL; son of Tony Sr and Mary Gaiter. **Educ:** Univ Miami, BA, Criminal Justice. **Career:** New Eng Patriots, wide receiver, 1997; Nat Football League-Europe, Amsterdam Admirals; San Diego Chargers, 1998; Xtreme Football League, Orlando Rage, wide receiver. **Honors/Awds:** Dade County Athlete of the Year; State Champion Thrice.

GAITER, TONY BERNARD, JR. See GAITER, TONY.

GAITHER, BARRY (EDMUND BARRY GAITHER)
Arts administrator. **Educ:** Morehouse Col; Ga State Univ; Brown Univ. **Career:** Spelman Col, lectr, 1968-69; Nat Ctr Afro-Am Artists, Mus, dir & cur, 1969-; Mass Col Art, lectr, 1970-71; Wellesley Col, lectr, 1971-74; Boston Univ, Afro-Am Studies, fac, 1971-83; Harvard Col, lectr, 1972-75; Univ Minn, Arts Leadership Inst, summer fac, 1989; Mus Fine Arts, Boston, cur, spec consult, currently. **Orgs:** Am Asn Mus, 1984, 1986, 2000; Pres George W Bushs Adv Bd; Historically Black Cols & Universities; dir & cur, Mus Nat Ctr Afro-Am Artists, currently; panel chmn, Nat Endowment Arts . **Honors/Awds:** Outstanding Contributions, WGBH Community Adv Bd, 1979-83; Honorary Doctorate of Humane Letters, Northeastern Univ, 1984; Mass Art Award, Mass Col Art, 1988; The J Eugene Grigsby Award, Comt Minority Concerns, Nat Art Educrs Assn, 1989; Men of Vision Award, Mus Afro-Am History, 1992; 20th Anniversary Award, Fondo del Sol, Wash, 1993; Honorary Doctorate of Humane Letters, Framingham State Col, 1993; Honorary Doctorate of Fine Arts, Rhode Island Col, 1994; Commonwealth Award, Organizational Leadership, state Mass, 1997; Unity Award, John D O Bryant African Am Studies Inst, Northeastern Univ, 1998. **Special Achievements:** He has published many articles & essays including: Robert Blackburn: Millennial Portrait, American Visions, 2000; Toward a Truer History of American Art: The Contributions of Black Colleges & Universities; Revisiting American Art: Works from the Collections of Historically Black Colleges & Universities, Katonah Museum of Art, Katonah, NY, 1997. **Business Addr:** Director, Curator, The National Center of Afro-American Artists, 300 Walnut Ave, Boston, MA 02119, **Business Phone:** (617)442-8614.

GAITHER, CORNELIUS E.
Dentist. **Personal:** Born Feb 28, 1928, Philadelphia, PA; son of Cornelius Hopson and Edith Albertha Robinson; married Anna Louise Whittaker Gaither, Dec 23, 1952; children: Cornelius, Carmen, Carol, John, Reginald. **Educ:** Meharry Med Col, DDS, 1953; Lincoln Univ, AB, 1949. **Career:** Salem Memorial Hosp, chief dent servs; USAF, reserves dent corps, 1957-87, Lt Col, 1987. **Orgs:** Rho Chap, Alpha Phi Alpha Fraternity; Chi Delta Mu, Med Dent Pharmaceut Fraternity; Salvation Army Serv Comt, 1958-; Aerospace Med Asn; S Jersey Med Dent Asn; Kiwanis Int: Christ Presb Church, 1970-; Sigma Pi Phi Fraternity. **Honors/Awds:** Others Award, Salvation Army; honoree, NJ State Colored Women's Federated Clubs. **Military Serv:** USAF, 1954-57; USAFR, lt col, 1957-87. **Business Addr:** Dentist, 505 Auburn Ave, Swedesboro, NJ 08085.*

GAITHER, EDMUND BARRY. See GAITHER, BARRY.

GAITHER, ISRAEL L
Association executive. **Personal:** Born Oct 27, 1944; son of Israel L Sr and Lillian; married Eva D Shue, Jul 1, 1967. **Career:** USA Eastern Territory, Corps, 1964, DHQ, 1965, Corps, 1966, DHQ, 1975, div comdr, 1986, field secy, secy personnel, 1993, chief secy, 1997; S Africa Territory, territorial comdr, 1999; USA Eastern Territory, territorial comdr, 2002; Int HQ, chief staff, 2002-06, nat comdr comnr, currently. **Special Achievements:** First African American and youngest officer appointed as chief secretary for Salvation Army; first African to serve as territorial leader for the Salvation Army in South Africa; First African to receive the rank of Commissioner. **Business Addr:** National Commander Commissioner, The Salvation Army Southern Africa Territory, 119-121 Rissik St Wanderers, Johannesburg 2001, Republic of South Africa.

GAITHER, JAMES W., JR.
Engineer. **Personal:** Born Dec 16, 1954, Battle Creek, MI; son of James W Sr and Marie Elizabeth Stubbs; married Susan Lynn Bryant-Gaither, Jun 19, 1982; children: Anika Marie, James Bryant. **Educ:** Mich State Univ, E Lansing, MI, BS, packaging eng, 1981. **Career:** Revlon Prof Prod, Cincinnati, OH, tech packaging eng, 1982-84; Avon Prods, Inc, New York, NY, package develop engr, 1984-89; Revlon, Inc, NY, group leader, package develop, 1989-. **Orgs:** Packaging coun, Am Mgt Asn, 1990-; Inst Packaging Profs, 1989-; MSU Packaging Soc, Alumni, 1987-. **Special Achievements:** America's Best and Brightest Young Business & Professional Men, Dollars & Sense Mag, 1989. **Business Addr:** Group Leader, Revlon Inc, Package Development Department, 625 Madison Ave, New York, NY 10022.*

GAITHER, KATRYNA
Basketball player. **Personal:** Born Aug 13, 1975, Bronx, NY. **Educ:** Notre Dame Univ, 1997. **Career:** San Jose Lasers, ctr, 1997; Utah Starzz, 2000; Brisaspor Izmit, 2001; Tarbes GB, 2003-06; Dexia Namur, Belgian League, 2006-07.

GAITHER, MAGALENE DULIN
Educator. **Personal:** Born Jul 13, 1928, Mocksville, NC; daughter of Leroy Robertson and Edith Hazel Britton (deceased); married Troy Baxter Hudson (divorced 1960); children: Eric Lynn Hudson Sr & Hazel Shanlon Hudson; married William Eugene, Nov 17, 1969. **Educ:** Bennett Col, Greensboro, NC, BA; NC A&T State Univ, Greensboro, NC, MS, adult educ. **Career:** Educator (retired); Buckingham Co Training Sch, Dillwyn, Va, eng, reading, 1950-51; Cent Davie High Sch, Mocksville, NC, eng, hist, 1951-61; Unity High Sch, Statesville, NC, eng teacher, 1961-70; N Iredell High Sch, Olin, NC, eng teacher, 1970-71; Davie High Sch, Mocksville, NC, eng teacher, 1971-83; Davidson Co Community Col, Lexington, NC, instr, 1983-87. **Orgs:** Shiloh Baptist Church, 1938-; Nat Asn Advan Colored People, 1950-; Nat Educrs Asn, 1950-; chairperson, bd Nursing Home Advocacy, 1980-83; bd advs, Milling Manor Home Handicapped Women, 1985-; bd dirs, Davie Co Arts Coun, 1979-81; co chairperson, Democratic Party, 1991-; Zeta Phi Beta Sorority Inc; pres, NC Asn Educrs, Davie Co Unit. **Honors/Awds:** Valedictorian, Cent Davie High Sch, 1945; Honorary Graduate, Bennett Col, 1949; delegate, Dist & NC State Libr Confs, 1990-91; Service Award, Nat Asn Advan Colored People; Zeta Minority Women of the Year.

GAITHER, RICHARD A
Lawyer. **Personal:** Born Oct 28, 1939, Washington, DC; son of John and Miriam; married Deanna Dixon; children: Jamala & Marisa. **Educ:** Univ Dayton, BS, chem, 1962; Univ Baltimore, JD, 1970; NY Univ, LLM, trade regulation, 1981. **Career:** AUS, officer, 1963-65; FDA, res chemist, 1963 & 1965-67; US Patent & Trademark Off, patent examinerm, 1967-72; Lever Brothers Co, atty, 1972-74; Hoffmann La Roche Inc, asst gen coun, 1974-. **Orgs:** Nat Bar Asn, 1970-; Am Bar Asn, 1970-; Nat Patent Law Asn, 1970-; Alpha Phi Alpha Fraternity. **Honors/Awds:** Black Achiever Newark, NJ Young Men Christian Asn, 1980. **Military Serv:** AUS, first lt, 1963-65; numerous letters of commendation. **Business Addr:** Assistant General Counsel, Hoffmann La Roche Inc, 340 Kingsland St, Nutley, NJ 07110-1199.

GAITHER, DR. THOMAS W
Educator. **Personal:** Born Nov 12, 1938, Great Falls, SC; married. **Educ:** Claflin Col, BS, 1960; Atlanta Univ, MS, 1964; Univ Iowa, PhD, 1968. **Career:** Cong Racial Equality CORE, field secy, 1960-62; Iowa City, forester, 1968; Slippery Rock State Univ, assoc prof, prof biol, currently. **Orgs:** Bot Soc Am; Mycol Soc Am; AAAS; Soc Sigma Xi. **Honors/Awds:** Outstanding Young Member, Am Alpha Kappa Mu Nat Scholastic Hon Soc, 1972. **Business Addr:** Professor, Slippery Rock University, Department Biology, 1 Morrow Way, Slippery Rock, PA 16057, **Business Phone:** (724)738-2477.

GALBRAITH, SCOTT
Football player. **Personal:** Born Jan 7, 1967, Sacramento, CA. **Educ:** Univ Southern Calif. **Career:** Football player (retired); Cleveland Browns, tight end, 1990-92; Dallas Cowboys, 1993-94, 1997; Wash Redskins, 1995-96; Green Bay Packers, 1998.

GALBREATH, HARRY CURTIS
Football coach, football player. **Personal:** Born Jan 1, 1965, Clarksville, TN. **Educ:** Univ Tenn, BA, human serv, 1988. **Career:** Football player (retired), football coach; Miami Dolphins, offensive guard, 1988-92; Green Bay Packers, offensive guard, 1993-95; NY Jets,1996; Austin Peay State Univ, offensive line coach, 1997-99; Tenn State Univ, offensive line coach, 1999-2004; Hampton Univ, offensive line coach, 2005; Assoc volunteer, 2007. **Orgs:** Nat Incarcerated Parents & Families Network. **Honors/Awds:** Jacobs Award. **Business Phone:** (757)727-5328.

GALE HICKS, AUGUSTA M.
Nurse. **Personal:** Born Feb 14, 1941, Ruston, LA; daughter of Perry; children: Byron Barrington Berry. **Educ:** Provident Hosp & Training Sch, attended 1963; Gov State Univ, BSN, 1979; Univ Ill Med Ctr, MPH, 1981. **Career:** Vis Nurse Asn Greater Lynn, dir staff develop, 1991-92; REW Home Health, dir clinical serv, 1992-93; Prof Med Enterprises, clinical dir, 1993-95; Blue Cross/Blue Shield MA, case mgr, 1996. **Orgs:** Am Cancer Soc. **Honors/Awds:** Women of Distinction Award, 1995; She Knows Where She's Going Award, Girls, Inc, 1997; Women of Hope Award, Am Cancer Asn, 1997; Community Service Award, Blue Cross/Blue Shield MA, 1998; Continous Service & The Fight Against Breast Cancer, Am Cancer Society, 1998. **Special Achievements:** Author, "How I Coped With the Number One Killer of Black Women," Ebony, June 1979; published book, Older Than My Mother. *

GALES, JAMES. See Obituaries section.

GALL, LENORE ROSALIE
School administrator. **Personal:** Born Aug 9, 1943, Brooklyn, NY; daughter of George Whitfield and Olive Rosalie Weekes. **Educ:** New York Univ, AAS, 1970; New York Univ, Tisch Sch Bus & Pub Admin, BS, 1973, training & develop cert, 1975; New York Univ SEHNAP, MA, counr educ, 1977; Teachers Col, Columbia Univ, EdM, 1988; EdD, 1988. **Career:** Sch administrator (retired); Ford Found, 1967-76; New York Univ, Grad Sch Bus, dep dir, 1976-79; Pace Univ Lubin Sch Bus, dir career develop, 1979-82; LaGuardia Community Col, City Univ New York, asst prof, 1981-95; Yale Univ Sch Orgn & Mgt, dir career develop, 1982-85; Brooklyn Col, City Univ New York, asst to the assoc provost, 1985-88, asst to the provost, 1988-91; Fashion Inst Technol, asst to vpres acad affairs, 1991-94; New York, City Tech Col, City Univ New York, asst provost, 1994-2000; City Col Technol, New York, dean studs & acad serv (retired), 2000; Audience Develop Task Force, Dance Theatre Harlem, co-chair. **Orgs:** Chairperson bd dirs, Langston Hughes Comm Libr, 1975-79, 1982-91; vpres, awards comn chairperson, 1976-99, 1999-, Dollars Scholars pres; dir, Placement Secretarial Develop Workshops, Col Placement

Serv, 1978-81; prog chairperson, New Haven Chamber Com, 1984; bd dirs, 1985, pres, 1989-93; Asn Black Women Higher Educ Inc; Am Asn Univ Women, northeast sectional dir, 1993-96, nat vpres, 1996-2002, nat pres, 2003-; Educ Hon Orgn, Kappa Delta Pi, 1986; Columbia Univ Chap, Phi Delta Kappa, 1986; vpres, Nat Asn Univ Women, 1986, pres, 2003; Am Asn Univ Adminr, 1986; Nat Asn Women Educ; Nat Urban League; vpres, 1987-89, pres, 1989-93, Nat Coun Negro Women N Queens Sec. **Honors/Awds:** Grant/scholarship, Jewish Found Educ Women, 1986-87; Sojourner Truth Award, Nat Asn Negro Bus & Prof Women's Club Inc, Laurelton Club, 1991; Dollars for Scholars Award, Nat Honor Roll, Citizen Scholar Found Am; Community Service Award, Concerned Women Brooklyn Inc; Distinguished Service Award; Nat Asn Univ Women; Education Award, Stuyvesant Heights Lions Club.

GALLAGHER, DR. ABISOLA HELEN
Psychologist, educator. **Personal:** Born Oct 13, 1950, Chicago, IL; daughter of Lee Roy Gallagher and Lulla Mae. **Educ:** Northeastern Ill Univ, BA (w/Honors), 1972; Univ WI-Whitewater, MS, 1974; Rutgers Univ, EdD, 1983. **Career:** Univ Wisconsin Systm Cent Admin, educ admin intern, 1974-75; Univ Winconsin-Parkside, counr-prog coordr, 1975-78; Douglass Col Rutgers Univ, asst dean student life, 1981-85; Unlimited Potential, mgt consultant, 1985-87; Rutgers Col, Rutgers Univ, residence dir, 1978-81, asst dean off acad serv, 1987-90; Jersey State Col, coun psycholgist, 1990-, NJ City Univ, Coun & Psychol Serv Ctr, dir, currently. **Orgs:** Vpres, Asn Black Psychologists New Jersey Chap, 1983-87,1989-; exec bd mem, Coalition 100 Black Women New Jersey, 1985; Asn Black Psychologists, 1985-87; Am Psychological Asn, 1987; NJ Psychological Asn, 1987; NJ Chap, Asn Black Psychologists, 1989-91; exec bd mem, Women's Resource Ctr, 1991-92; dir, Coun& Psychological Serv Ctr. **Honors/Awds:** Martin L King Scholarship, Rutgers Univ, 1979-80, 1980-81; Outstanding Young Women Am, 1982, 1984; Outstanding Service Award, Kappa Alpha Psi Frat, 1984; Distinguished Service Award, Paul Robeson Cult Ctr Rutgers Univ,1985. **Special Achievements:** Publication: Black Women in Group Psychotherapy, Women in Groups Springer Press, 1986. **Home Addr:** 175 Slocum Ave, Englewood, NJ 07631-2221. **Business Addr:** Director of Health and Wellness, New Jersey City University, Counseling & Psychol Service Center, 54 Col St, Jersey City, NJ 07305-1597.

GALLAGHER, MIKE JOHN
Media executive. **Personal:** Born Jan 19, 1945, Toledo, OH; married Mary. **Educ:** John Carroll Univ, bus, 1967. **Career:** Reams Broadcasting Corp, sr vpres, 1977-80; WABQ Inc, pres, 1980-87. **Orgs:** Alpha Kappa Psi, 1968. **Military Serv:** AUS, capt.

GALLON, DR. DENNIS P.
Educator. **Personal:** Born in Monticello, FL. **Educ:** Edward Waters Col, BS, 1964; Ind Univ, Bloomington, MS, 1969; Univ FL, PhD, 1975. **Career:** Florida Community Col, prof, 1972-79, bus mgr, 1979-81, dean voc ed, 1981-84, dean instr, 1984-85, dean, Col Liberal Arts & Sci, 1985-; Palm Beach Community Col, pres, currently. **Orgs:** Am Soc Training & Develop; Jax Chamber Com; FL Asn Community Col; Jax Urban League. **Honors/Awds:** Whitney M Young Jr Nat Service Award, Gulf Stream Coun Boy Scouts Am, 2005; Martin Luther King Jr Distinguished Leader Award, NAACP-South Palm Beach Branch, 2004; Silver Medallion Award, Nat Conf Community & Justice, 2007; Life Time Achievement Award, Urban League Palm Beach County, 2007. **Business Addr:** President, Palm Beach Community College, 4200 Congress Ave, Lake Worth, FL 33461.*

GALLOT, RICHARD JOSEPH
Government official. **Personal:** Born Jan 31, 1936, Swords, LA; son of Freddie and Loretta; married Mildred Bernice Gauthier Gallot; children: Daphne, Loretta & Richard Jr. **Educ:** Tyler Barber Col, 1961; Grambling State Univ, BS, acct, 1975. **Career:** Gallo's Barbershop, barber 1961; Gallo's Grocer & Liquor & Serv, owner, 1969-; Town Grambling, mayor, 1981; Lincoln Parish, justice Peace Ward 2, currently. **Orgs:** Pres, Grambling Chamber Com, 1967; dir, Grambling Fed Credit Union, 1973, Parish Coun, St Benedict Church, 1975; Lion's Club, 1983; La Bd Ethics. **Honors/Awds:** Businessman of Year, Bus Dept, Grambling State Univ, 1981; Outstanding Black in Louisiana, Teal Enterprise, 1982; Appointed to Governor's Commission on Community Development, 1985. **Military Serv:** AUS, spec 4, 1958-62. **Home Addr:** 1604 Martin Luther King A, PO Box 148, Grambling, LA 71245. **Business Addr:** Owner, Gallot, 102 S Grand Ave, Grambling, LA 71245.

GALLOWAY, JOEY
Football player, executive. **Personal:** Born Nov 20, 1971, Bellaire, OH. **Educ:** Ohio State Univ, bus & mkt, attended. **Career:** Seattle Seahawks, wide receiver, 1995-99; Dallas Cowboys, 2000-03; Tampa Bay Buccaneers, wide receiver, 2004-; Arena Football League, Columbus Destroyers, co-partner, currently; Smoothie Junction, onwer, 2007-; NBC Sports, studio analyst. **Orgs:** Make-A-Wish Found; founder, Joey Galloway Family Found, 2003-. **Honors/Awds:** NFL Offensive Rookie of the Year, Col Pro Football Weekly, 1995. **Special Achievements:** First round, 8th overall NFL draft pick, 1995; studio analyst, NBC Sports. **Business Addr:** Wide Receiver, Tampa Bay Buccaneers, 1 W Buccaneer Pl, Tampa, FL 33607, **Business Phone:** (813)870-2700.

GALLOWAY, LULA BRIGGS
Lawyer, association executive, president (organization). **Personal:** Born Jul 8, 1945, San Bernardino, CA; daughter of David R and Lillie Chatham; married Charles E Galloway, Sr; children: Kimberlyne M. **Educ:** San Jose State Univ, attended 1987. **Career:** Paralegal Serv Co, owner, 1992-; Nat Asn Juneteenth Lineage Inc, founder, pres & chief exec officer, 1995-; Mayor, City Galveston, TX, Special Tribute, 1997; Flint, MI, Bd Comnr Resolution, 1997; State MI, House Reps, 1997. **Orgs:** Nat Independent Paralegal Asn; Nat Parliamentarians Asn. **Honors/Awds:** PRS Bill Clinton, Contribution of Nat Juneteenth, 1997; US Congressional Recognition, First Nat Juneteenth Convention. **Special Achievements:** First art exhibition on Juneteenth/Slavery at Rotunda of the Russell Senate Office Bldg, Wash, DC; Nat Juneteenth Independence Day; Juneteenth Calendar with collectable Black Art; Chair for all festivals & parades, city of San Jose, CA; helped bring recognition of Juneteenth Day in State of Michigan; author, Ring the Bell of Freedom; opened the first Juneteenth creative Cultural Ctr & Museum, Saginaw County, Grand Opening, 2003. **Business Addr:** President & Chief Executive Officer, Founder, National Association Juneteenth Lineage Inc, 1104 Janes Ave, Saginaw, MI 48607, **Business Phone:** (989)752-0576.*

GALVIN, DR. EMMA CORINNE
Educator. **Personal:** Born May 2, 1909, Richmond, VA; married Alx Galvin MD. **Educ:** Shaw Univ, BA 1929; Univ Pa, MA, 1931; Cornell Univ, PhD, 1943. **Career:** Educator (retired); Ithaca Col, prof; Ithaca Sch Dist, acad counsult; South side Ctr, teacher; Tompkins Co Med Aux, lectr, writer, pres. **Orgs:** Nat Comt Am Asn Univ Women; pres, Pi Lambda Theta & Phi Gamma Delta; Alpha Kappa Alpha; Citizens Adv Comn Environ Quality, State of NY; del Nat Conv League Women Voters; chairperson, Tompkins County Comm Chirst; pres, Ithaca PTA; Ithaca B & P W Club; bd chmn & bd trustees, Southside Community Ctr; organizer, Ithaca Wmn's Comm Bldg. **Honors/Awds:** Women of yr, Shaw Univ, 1924; Women of yr, Ithca B & PW 1959; Comm serv Award, Black Mem of Ithaca, 1974; achievement comm for a better Am black pub Eisenhower Admin.

GAMBLE, G. ARLIVIA BABBAGE
Vice president (organization). **Personal:** Married Raymond; children: Angelique. **Educ:** Murray State Univ, BA; Austin Peay State Univ, MA, 1979. **Career:** Limra Leadership Inst Fel, 2004; State Farm Ins Cos, vpres agency & sales resources, currently. **Orgs:** Nat Asn Ins Women's Leadership Prog; Nat African-Am Womens Leadership Inst; Hopkinsville-Christian County Chamber Com; bd trustee, Murray State Univ. **Honors/Awds:** Innovative Award, Ky Chamber Com, 1991; Outstanding Young Alumna Award, APSUNAA, 1998; Athena Award, Hopkinsville-Christian County Chamber Com. *

GAMBLE, KENNETH
Executive, musician. **Personal:** Born Aug 11, 1943, Philadelphia, PA; married Dione La Rue. **Career:** Kenny Gamble & Romeos, lead vocal; Columbia Recs, rec artist, 1963; Philadelphia Music Found, bd dir; Philadelphia Int Recs, co-owner; Raising Horizons Quest Charter Sch, instr, currently; Albums: Gonna Take a Miracle, 1971; Back Stabbers, 1972; 360 Degrees Of Billy Paul, 1972; Ship Ahoy, 1973; The Sound of Philadelphia, 1973; Black & Blue, 1973; Philadelphia Freedom, 1975; We Got The Rhythm, 1976; Goin' Places, 1977; Expressway To Your Heart; Cowboys To Girls; I Can't Stop Dancing; Only The Strong Survive; I'm Gonna Make You Love Me; One Night Affair; We'll Be United; Silly, Silly Fool; Don't Let The Green Grass Fool You; Slow Motion. **Orgs:** Asn Music; Broadcast Music; Am Fed Musicians; Nat Asn Rec Merchandiser; Rec Indust Asn Am; T. J. Martell Leukemia Found; AMC Cancer Res Ctr & Hosp. **Honors/Awds:** Decade award Top 100 Black Enterprises Rec World, 1973; Producer of the Year, NATRA, 1968-69; Top Pub Award, Broadcast Music; Songwriter of the Year, Broadcast Music; Essence Award, 2002; co-recipient Grammy Award, 1990; co-recipient Grammy Trustees Award, 1999; Dance Music Hall of Fame, New York. **Business Addr:** Co-Founder, Philadelphia International Records, 309 S Broad St, Philadelphia, PA 19107.*

GAMBLE, KENNETH L.
Government official. **Personal:** Born Apr 24, 1941, Marshall, MO; son of Rev Ira J Sr(deceased) and Elizabeth Lane (deceased); married Shiela M Greene, Apr 19, 1969; children: Jerry L Swain, Andrew J Swain, Kendra L E Gamble. **Educ:** Morgan State Col, Baltimore, MD, attended 1962; Youngstown State Univ, Youngstown OH, BA, 1971; Univ Akron, Akron OH, MA, Urban Studies, 1975. **Career:** Univ Akron, Ctr Urban Studies, Akron OH, res asst, 1972-73; Trans Century Corp, Wash DC, consult, Public Housing, 1973; Canton Urban League, Canton, OH, assoc dir, housing & community serv, 1973-77; Toledo NHS, Toledo, OH, exec dir, 1977-80; City Saginaw, Saginaw, MI, dir, dept neighborhood serv; Saginaw Housing Cms, dir, 1991-92, ade asst asst city mgr, 1993, dep city mgr. **Honors/Awds:** Dean's List, Youngstown State Univ, 1969-71; Dean's List, Univ of Akron, 1972-73; HUD Fellowship Recipient, 1972-73. **Military Serv:** USAF, staff sergeant, 1962-65. **Business Addr:** Administrative Assistant, Deputy General Service, City Saginaw, 1315 S Wash, Saginaw, MI 48601.*

GAMBLE, OSCAR CHARLES
Baseball player. **Personal:** Born Dec 20, 1949, Ramer, AL. **Career:** Baseball player (retired); Contributor; Chicago Cubs, outfielder, 1969; Philadelphia Phillies, 1970-72; Cleveland Indians, 1973-75; New York Yankees, 1976, 1980-84; Chicago White Sox, 1977, outfielder, 1985; San Diego Padres, 1978; Tex Rangers, 1979;The Baseball page, contributor, currently. **Home Addr:** 2129 Edinburgh Dr, Montgomery, AL 36116-1313.

GAMBLE, ROBERT LEWIS
Government official. **Personal:** Born Apr 27, 1947, Carroll County, GA; married Lucy Ann Dixon; children: Venus Marie & Athenia Marie. **Career:** USMC, printing press oper, 1966; United Parcel Serv, feeder driver, 1970; Whitesburg City, mayor. **Orgs:** Chmn, Carroll Co Pre-health Clin, 1981; vice-chmn, Carroll Co Voc Sch, 1984. **Military Serv:** USMC, sgt, 3 yrs; two Purple Hearts Vietnam Service Medal, National Defense Good Conduct Medal. **Business Addr:** Mayor, City of Whitesburg, PO Box 151, Whitesburg, GA 30185.

GAMBLE, DR. WILBERT
Educator. **Personal:** Born Jun 19, 1932, Greenville, AL; married Zeferene Tucker; children: Priscilla Ann. **Educ:** Wayne State Univ, BS, 1955, PhD, 1960. **Career:** Educator(retired); Ore State Univ, asst prof, 1962-67, prof, biochem, prof emer; Johnson Res Found, Univ Pa, vis prof, 1967-76; Univ Sci & Tech Kumasi Ghana, Ful bright prof, 1971-72; NIH, vis res worker, 1976-77, 1983-84, IPA, invest, 1990-91. **Orgs:** Lehn & Fink Medal Advan Pharm Sci, 1955; NIH Predoctoral Fel, 1959; NIH Post doctoral Fel, 1960 & 1968; Phi Lambda Upsilon Hon Soc, 1957; Sigma Chi Honor Soc, 1960; Am Soc Bio chem & Molecular Biol; NIH Post doctoral Fel, Cornell Univ, 1960-62; Danforth Asn Danforth Found, 1969-. **Business Addr:** Professor Emeritus, Oregon State University, Department Biochemistry & Biophysics, Corvallis, OR 97331.*

GAMBRELL, DONNA J
Executive. **Personal:** Born Nov 26, 1954, Washington, DC; daughter of Louis and Betty Snowden; divorced. **Educ:** Towson State Univ, BS, 1977; NY Univ, MS, 2000. **Career:** Gen Acct Off, positions, 1979-87; Fed Savings & Loan Ins Corp, chief, policy devel, 1987-89; Resolution Trust Corp, sr claims specialist, 1989-91; Fed Deposit Ins Corp, community affairs off, NY region, 1991-96, dep reg dir, NY region, 1996-97, assoc dir, consumer community affairs, 1997-2000, deputy dir, consumer community affairs, 2000-02, dep dir, compliance & consumer protection, 2002-. **Orgs:** Women in Housing and Finance, 2003-. **Honors/Awds:** Excellence Award, FDIC, Financial Education, 2001; Excellence Award, 2002. **Home Addr:** 532 F St Terr SE, Washington, DC 20003, **Home Phone:** (202)547-5155. **Business Addr:** Deputy Director Compliance & Consumer Affairs, Fedral Deposit Insurance Corp, 550 17th St NW, Washington, DC 20429-9990, **Business Phone:** 877-275-3342.

GANDY, WAYNE LAMAR
Football player. **Personal:** Born Feb 10, 1971, Haines City, FL. **Educ:** Auburn Univ. **Career:** St Louis Rams, tackle, 1995-98; Pittsburgh Steelers, tackle, 1999-2002; New Orleans Saints, tackle, 2003-05; Atlanta Falcons, tackle, 2006-. **Orgs:** Nat Honor Soc.

GANEY, JAMES HOBSON
Dentist. **Personal:** Born Apr 29, 1944, Plainfield, NJ; married Peggy; children: Jayme, Christopher. **Educ:** Howard Univ Col Pharm, BS, 1969; NJ Col Dent, DMD, 1974. **Career:** Fac, Farleigh Dickinson Univ Dent Sch, 1979; Bronx-Lebanon Hosp Ctr, Div Restorative Dent, dir, Gen Pract Residency Prog, Co-Dir, currently; pvt practice dent, currently. **Orgs:** Am pharmaceut Asn; NJ Pharmaceut Asn; Nat Pharmaceut Asn; Am Dent Asn; NJ Dent Asn; Nat Dent Asn; Acad Gen Dent; Union Co Dent Soc; Plainfield Dent Soc; Commonwealth Dent Soc; Health Prof Educ Adv Counc State NJ, 1979; mem bd dir, Planfield Camp Crusade; Nat Asn Advan Colored People; Psi Omega Dent Frat; Chi Delta Mu Frat. **Honors/Awds:** Certificate of Merit, Howard Univ Col Pharm. **Home Addr:** 1094 Kenyon Ave, Plainfield, NJ 07060-280, **Home Phone:** (908)757-1190. **Business Addr:** Dentist, 1094 Kenyon Ave, Plainfield, NJ 07060-280, **Business Phone:** (908)757-1190.*

GANT, CRYSTAL M.
Educator, business owner. **Personal:** Born Jan 13, 1972, Detroit, MI; daughter of Marshall and Jewell. **Educ:** Univ Detroit, BA, 1993, teacher cert, 1995; Univ Mich, attended 1998. **Career:** Detroit Bd Educ, educ, 1993-03; Crystal Clear Images, pres & chief exec officer, 1996-. **Business Phone:** (313)272-8433.*

GANT, PHILLIP M, III
Executive, vice president (organization). **Personal:** Born Aug 21, 1949, Chicago, IL; son of Phillip M II and Naurice; married La-

Jule Steele Gant; children: Kimberli & Lyndsay. **Educ:** Linbloor Tech, Chicago, IL; Univ Ill, Chicago, IL. **Career:** Foote Cone & Belding, Chicago, IL, copywriter to vpres & creative dir, 1971-79; Young & Rubican Adv, New York, NY, sr copy writer, 1979-81; J Walter Thompson Adv, Chicago, IL, vpres & creative dir, 1982-84; BBDO Chicago, Chicago, IL, exec vpres & exec creative dir, 1984-87, chief creative officer, 1987-2004. **Orgs:** Bd mem, Evanston, IL, Community Daycare Ctr; bd mem, Evanston, IL, Sch Little C. **Honors/Awds:** Honoree, Dollars & Sense Mag-Chicago, 1989; Black Achievers in Industry-New York, 1991; Black Achievers Indust-Chicago, 1988. **Business Addr:** Chief Creative Officer, BBDO Chicago, 410 N Michigan Ave, Chicago, IL 60611, **Business Phone:** (312)337-7860.

GANT, RAYMOND LEROY
School administrator. **Personal:** Born Jul 7, 1961, Paw Paw, MI. **Educ:** Ferris State Univ, BS, bus admin, 1984; Cent Mich Univ, MA, 1998. **Career:** Ferris State Univ, mgt intern, off Planning & develop, 1984-86, dir minority stud affairs, 1986-, spec asst to pres, currently. **Orgs:** Ferris State Col, mem, alumni bd dir, minority stud scholar selection comt; Phi Beta Sigma. **Honors/Awds:** Distinguished Service Key Award, Phi Beta Sigma; Distinguished Staff Award, Ferris State Univ, 2002. **Business Addr:** Special Assistant to the President, Ferris State University, Ferris State Col, Rankin Center, Big Rapids, MI 49307.*

GANT, RICHARD E.
Actor. **Personal:** Born Mar 10, 1944, San Francisco, CA. **Career:** TV appearances: "Attica", 1980; "Internal Affairs", 1988; "The Cosby Show", 1989; "Miami Vice", 1989; "MacGyver", 1991; "False Arrest", 1991;"Reasonable Doubts", 1991, 1992; "Beverly Hills, 90210", 1992; "Roc",1992; "Murphy Brown", 1992; "Condition: Critical", 1992; "L.A. Law"; "MenDon't Tell"; "Empty Nest"; "Seinfeld"; "The Tower"; TV Series: "Trade Winds", 1993; "Wings", 1993; "Lois & Clark: The New Adventures of Superman"; "Martin"; "MacShayne: The Final Roll of the Dice"; "Living Single"; "Picket Fences", 1994; "Trial by Fire"; "The Bonnie Hunt Show",1995; "The Client", 1996; "Touched by an Angel", 1996; "Yes, Dear", 2004;"Eve", 2005; "Deadwood", 2005; "In Justice", 2006; "How I Met Your Mother", 2006; "The Bill Engvall Show", 2007; "Boston Legal", 2008; "General Hospital", 2007-08; "General Hospital: Night Shift", 2007-08; "Cold Case", 2009. Films: Night of the Juggler, 1980; Death of a Prophet, 1981; Krush Groove, 1985; Suspect,1987; Collision Course, 1989; The Freshman, 1990; Rocky V, 1990; Love or Money, 1990; Stone Cold, 1991; Last Breeze of Summer, 1991; CB4, 1993;Posse, 1993; Jason Goes to Hell: The Final Friday, 1993; City Hall, 1996;Ed, 1996; The Glimmer Man, 1996; Raven, 1997; Bean, 1997; The Big Lebowski, 1998; Sour Grapes, 1998; Godzilla, 1998; Divorcing Jack, 1998;Johnny B Good, 1998; Nutty prof II, 1998; Kingdom Come, 2001; Built to Last, 1997; The Job, 2001; Smallville, 2002; The Partners, 2003; Lesser of Three Evils, 2005; Hood of Horror, 2006; Ezra, 2007; Norbit, 2007; Cover, 2007. **Business Addr:** Actor, c/o Pakula King, 9229 Sunset Blvd Suite 315, Los Angeles, CA 90069.*

GANT, RONALD EDWIN
Baseball player, baseball executive. **Personal:** Born Mar 2, 1965, Victoria, TX; married Heather Campbell; children: Ryan Edwin & Alexus. **Career:** Baseball player (retired), Baseball executive; Atlanta Braves, outfielder & infielder, 1987-93; Cincinnati Reds, 1995; St Louis Cardinals, 1996-98; Philadelphia Phillies, 1999-2000; Anaheim Angels, 2000; Colorado Rockies, 2001; Oakland Athletics, 2001; San Diego Padres, 2002; Oakland Athletics, 2003; TBS, baseball analyst, 2005; FSN South & Sport South Braves, baseball Analyst, currently. **Honors/Awds:** Comeback Player of the Year, Sports Illus & USA Today, 1990; Silver Slugger Award, Sporting News, 1991; Sporting News Comeback Player of the Year, 1995. **Business Addr:** Baseball Analyst, FSN South, 1175 Peachtree St NE Suite 408, 100 Colony Sq, Atlanta, GA 30361, **Business Phone:** (404)230-7300.

GANT, TRAVESA
Basketball player. **Personal:** Born Oct 10, 1971. **Educ:** Lamar Univ, BA, kinesiology. **Career:** Nanya Formosa Plastic (Taiwan), center, 1994-95; Olympiakos Volos(Greece), 1996-97; Los Angeles Sparks. **Honors/Awds:** Orange County Athletes of the Year, 1989. *

GANT, WANDA ADELE
Administrator. **Personal:** Born Oct 4, 1949, Washington, DC; daughter of Monore E Banks (deceased) and Adela Mills Banks; married Ronald Gary Owens, Jun 24, 1989; children: Richard W Gant V & Ronald Gary Owens II. **Educ:** Cent State Univ, Wilberforce, OH, BS, 1971; Southeastern Univ Wash, DC, MBPA, 1982. **Career:** Gen Servs Admin, equal opportunity specialist, 1971-78; US Dept Labor, equal opportunity specialist, 1978-84; US Info Agency, fed women's prog mgr, 1984-89; UISA, int visitors exchange specialist, 1989-93; US Dept Justice, equal employ opporunity specialist, 1993-. **Orgs:** Outstanding Young Women Am, 1981; Nat Coun Negro Women, 1983-; Alpha Kappa Alpha, 1983; Fed Women's Interagency Bd, 1984; DC-Dakar Sister Cities Friendship Coun, 1985-; Am Asn Univ Women, 1986; Bus & Prof Women, 1986. **Honors/Awds:** Super Performance Duty, 1971; Outstanding Young Women Am, 1983. **Home Addr:** 7811 Harder Ct, Clinton, MD 20735. **Business Addr:** Specialist, US Dept Justice, 10th Pa Ave NW Rm 1246, Washington, DC 20530, **Business Phone:** (202)616-4800.

GANTT, HARVEY BERNARD
Architect, politician. **Personal:** Born Jan 14, 1943, Charleston, SC; son of Christopher and Wilhelmenia; married Cindy; children: Sonja, Erika, Angela & Adam. **Educ:** Iowa State Univ, attended 1962; Clemson Univ, BArch, 1965; Mass Inst Technol, MA, city planning, 1970. **Career:** Odell Assocs, intern; architect, 1965-70; Soul City, experimental city, planner, 1970-71; Univ NC, Chapel Hill, lectr, 1970-72; Gantt Huberman Architects, prin partner, 1971-; Clemson Univ, vis critic, 1972-73; City Charlotte, city council mem, 1974-79, mayor pro tem, 1981-83, mayor, 1983-87; US Senate, dem cand, 1990. **Orgs:** AIA; Am Planning Asn; Charlotte Chap, Nat Asn Advan Colored People; NC Design Found; US Coun Mayors, uncommitted deleg, 1984 Dem Conv. **Honors/Awds:** Citizen of the Year, Charlotte Nat Asn Advan Colored People, 1975, 1984; Legacy Award, Leadership Charlotte, 2006; hon degrees: Belmont Abbey Col, Johnson C Smith Univ, Clemson Univ. **Special Achievements:** First black student to enter the previously all-white Clemson University in 1963; First African-American mayor of Charlotte. **Home Addr:** 517 N Poplar St, Charlotte, NC 28202. **Business Addr:** Principal Partner, Gantt Huberman Architects PLLC, 500 N Tryon St, Charlotte, NC 28202, **Business Phone:** (704)334-6436.

GARBA, BABA
Executive, founder (originator). **Personal:** Married Gloria. **Career:** Infonit LLC, founder, 2000-. **Business Addr:** Founder, Infonit LLC, 210 E Main St Fl 3, Niles, MI 49120, **Business Phone:** (269)687-8180.*

GARBEY, BARBARO
Baseball player, athletic coach. **Personal:** Born Dec 4, 1956, Santiago De Cuba, Cuba. **Career:** Baseball player (retired), Athletic coach; Detroit Tigers, amateur free agent, 1980, outfielder & infielder, 1984-85; Tex Rangers, outfielder & infielder, 1988; Tenn smokies, hitting coach, 2006; Peoria Cheifs, Batting Coach, Currently. **Honors/Awds:** Tiger Rookie of the Year, Detroit Sports Broadcasters Asn, 1984; World Series Champion, 1984. **Business Phone:** (309)680-4000.

GARCIA, KWAME N
School administrator. **Personal:** Born Apr 4, 1946, St Croix, Virgin Islands of the United States; married Grete James; children: Kenny, Sharifa, Khalfani, Gustavo, Luanda & Kwame Jr. **Educ:** Col Virgin Islands, AA, 1967; NY Univ, BS, 1969; Univ Mass, MBA, 1973. **Career:** VI Bd Ed, elected mem, 1978-; Univ VI, state dir coop ext serv, 1979-. **Orgs:** Nat Sch Bd Asn, 1978-; bd trustees VI Pub TV Syst, 1982-84, Col Virgin Islands, 1982-84; bd dir, Caribbean Food Crops Soc; bd dir, Caribbean Coun Higher Educ Agr. **Home Addr:** PO Box 1307, Kingshill, Virgin Islands of the United States 00851. **Business Addr:** State Director, University of the Virgin Islands, Virgin Islands Extension Serv, RR 02, PO Box 10000, Kingshill, Virgin Islands of the United States 00850.

GARCIA, DR. WILLIAM BURRES
Educator. **Personal:** Born Jul 16, 1940, Dallas, TX; son of Eural Clinton and Willie Mae Jefferson. **Educ:** Prairie View A&M Univ, music courses, 1961; N Tex State Univ, BMus 1962, MMus Ed, 1965; Univ IA, PhD, 1973; Howard Univ, NEH, Fel 1974; Carnegie-Mellon Univ, Col Mgt Prog, 1984; Inst Learning Assistance Prof, Calif State Univ, Long Beach, 1988. **Career:** Philander Smith Col, instr music, 1963-64; Langston Univ, asst prof music, 1965-69; Miles Col, assoc prof music, 1974-77; Talladega Col, actg acad vpres, 1982-83, prof music, 1977-, chmn music dept, 1977-, chmn humanities div, 1981-85; Selma Univ, acad dean, 1986-87; Lane Col, prof music, 1987-93, chair div humanities, 1989-93, choir dir, 1987-93, dir Ctr Acad Skills Develop, 1987-92; Langston Univ, prof music & chair music dept, conductor choirs, 1993-99; Fort Valley State Univ, prof Music & chair dept fine arts, 1999-2001; Lincoln Univ, prof Music, 2001-, chair music dept, 2001-03, chair visual & performing arts dept, 2003-06, artistic dir & conductor Lincoln Univ concert choir 2001-07. **Orgs:** Phi Mu Alpha Sinfonia, 1965; Am Choral Dirs Asn, 1967-; bd mem, Div Higher Educ Disciples Christ, 1978-81; bd mem, Talladega Arts Coun, 1981-85; Nat Asn Teachers Singing; Nat Asn Music Educ. **Honors/Awds:** Doctoral Fellowship Grants S Fellowships Fund Inc, 1969-73; Ford Found Fellowship Grant for Dissertations in Ethnic Studies, 1971-72; Ethnic Music Workshop Col Fine Arts, 1974; Outstanding Educators of America, 1975. **Home Phone:** (410)620-5623. **Business Addr:** Professor of Voice & Choral Music, Lincoln University Commonwealth Pennsylvania, 1570 Baltimore Pke Ware Ctr 104, Lincoln University, PA 19352-0204, **Business Phone:** (484)365-8000.

GARDENER, DARYL RONALD
Football player. **Personal:** Born Feb 25, 1973, Baltimore, MD; married Tarnesia, Dec 2, 1995; children: Da'vante and De'Andre& Sha'nice. **Educ:** Baylor Univ. **Career:** Football player (retired); Miami Dolphins, defensive tackle, 1996-2001; Wash Redskins, 2002; Denver Broncos, 2003-04. **Special Achievements:** NFL Draft, First round pick, No 20, 1996.

GARDINER, GEORGE L.
School administrator. **Personal:** Born May 3, 1933, Cambridge, MA; married Reida B Dykes; children: Jesse B, Veronica, Lynne & George DeWitt. **Educ:** Fisk Univ Nashville, BA, 1963; Univ Chicago, MA, 1967, CAS, 1969. **Career:** Am Libr Asn Chicago, asst exec sec, libr admin div, 1967; IL State Univ,Normal Ill, refrence libr, 1967-70; Cent State Univ, Wilber force OH, dir libr, 1970-72; Oakland Univ, Rochester, MI, prof, dean libr sci, 1972-; Univ Mich Sch Libr Sci, Ann Arbor MI, vis prof, 1975; Univ Libr, profemer, currently. **Orgs:** Am Lib Asn, 1967-; Am Soc Info Sci, 1979-; Nat Lib Asn, 1978-; bd mem, Normal Pub Lib Normal, IL, 1968-70; Afro-Am Hist Comm Ill C Supt Pub Instr, 1969-70; Bd Black Col Prog Pontiac, 1974-; chmn bd, Mich Lib Consortium, 1978-79; chmn, Mich Coun State Libr Dir, 1979-80. **Honors/Awds:** First prize, Nat Essay Contest Am Missionary Asn, 1961. **Special Achievements:** Mem Lect Harvard Univ, 2005. **Military Serv:** AUS, corpl, 1953-55. **Business Addr:** Professor Emeritus, Oakland University Library, 2200 N Squirrel Rd, Rochester, MI 48309, **Business Phone:** (248)370-4426.

GARDNER, AVA MARIA
Manager. **Personal:** Born Jun 1, 1962, Fort Sill, OK; daughter of John M. and Essie W. **Educ:** Cameron Univ, Lawton, OK, BS, 1985. **Career:** Okla City Conv & Visitors Bur, conv sales mgr, 1987-93; Denver Metro Conv & Visitors Bur, sr sales mgr, 1993-2003; Kans City Conv & Entertainment Ctrs, dir Sales & Mkt, currently. **Orgs:** Nat Coalition Black Meeting Planners, 1988-. **Business Addr:** Director, Kansas City Convention & Entertainment Centers, 414 E 12th St, Denver, CO 64106.*

GARDNER, BARRY ALLAN
Football player, executive. **Personal:** Born Dec 13, 1976, Harvey, IL; son of Jerry and Brenda. **Educ:** Northwestern Univ, BS, commun. **Career:** Philadelphia Eagles, linebacker, 1999-2002; Cleveland Browns, 2003-04; New York Jets, 2005; New England Patriots, 2006; Contrado Partners, partner; free agent, currently. **Honors/Awds:** NFL All-Rookie Team honors, Football Digest, 1999.

GARDNER, DR. BETTYE J.
Educator. **Personal:** Born in Vicksburg, MS; daughter of Janie Foote and Glover C. **Educ:** Howard Univ, BA, Hist, 1962, MA, Hist, 1964; George Wash Univ, PhD, 1974. **Career:** Howard Univ, instr, 1964-69; Social Sys Intervention Inc, sr res assoc, 1969; Wash DC Bd Educ, consult, 1969; Black History Calvert Ct, consult; Wash Tech Inst, asst prof, 1969-71; Coppin State Col, dean arts & sci, 1981-87, Dept History, prof, 1982-, chmn, 1988-90. **Orgs:** Nat Asn Advan Colored People; Org Am Historians; Assoc Black Women Historians; Assoc Study Afro-Am Life & History; Nat Educ Asn; Nat Coun Negro Women, 1980; assoc, Danforth Found, 1980-86; ed bd, J Negro History; exec counc, Asn Study Afro-Am Life & Hist; vpres, Asn Afro-Am Life & History, 1993-95, nat pres, 1995-97; chmn, Educ Licensure Comn; Bethune House Fed Com; nat bd, Special Congressional Task Force. **Honors/Awds:** Moton Fel, Moton Inst, 1978-79; Fel, Smithsonian, 1988; Blassingame Award, 2004; Outstanding Educator Award, 2005; Bethune Service Award, 2006. **Special Achievements:** Published numerous articles. **Home Addr:** 6101 16th St NW, Washington, DC 20011. **Business Addr:** Professor, Coppin State University, Department History, Rm GJ 408 2500 W N Ave, Baltimore, MD 21216, **Business Phone:** (410)951-3439.

GARDNER, CEDRIC BOYER
Lawyer. **Personal:** Born Jul 22, 1946, San Antonio, TX; son of Tommie L and Willie Mae; married Sylvia Irene Breckenridge, May 7, 1972; children: Zayani Aisha, Bilal Amin, Cedric Ahmed & Saida Ujima. **Educ:** Calif State Univ, Los Angeles, BA, 1975; Univ Kans, JD, 1983. **Career:** Urban League Wichita, assoc dir, 1977-80; Shawnee Co Dist Atty, asst dist atty, 1983-84; Univ Kans, training mgr, 1984-85; Kans Dept Health & Environ, atty, 1985-. **Orgs:** Douglas Co, Nat Asn Advan Colored People, 1978-81, Urban League Wichita, 1980-87; Douglas Co Amateur Radio Club, 1984-87; Douglas Co Asn Retarded Citizens. **Honors/Awds:** Outstanding Service, Wichita Nat Asn Advan Colored People, 1980. **Military Serv:** USAF, airman 1st class, 4 yrs; Outstanding Airman of the Year, 1966. **Home Phone:** (913)842-7461. **Business Addr:** Special Assistant Attorney General, Kansas Department of Health and Environment, Curtis State Off Bldg 1000 SW Jackson, Topeka, KS 66612, **Business Phone:** (785)296-1500.

GARDNER, EDWARD GEORGE
Executive, business owner. **Personal:** Born Mar 25, 1925, Chicago, IL; married Betty Ann; children: Gary, Guy, Tracy & Terri. **Educ:** Chicago Teachers Col, BA; Univ Chicago, MA. **Career:** Beauty supply salesman, part time, late 1950; Chicago Sch Syst, elem sch & asst prin, 1945-64; Soft Sheen Prod Inc, founder & pres, 1964-85; Garden Investment Partners, pres; E G GardnerBeauty Prod Co, owner; House of Kicks, owner, currently.

Orgs: Founder, Regal Theater. **Military Serv:** AUS, s/sgt. **Business Addr:** Owner, House of Kicks, 9535 S Cottage Grove Ave, Chicago, IL 60628, **Business Phone:** (773)721-4351.

GARDNER, DR. FRANK W.
Educator. **Personal:** Born Jun 12, 1923, Chicago, IL; married Elaine St Avide; children: Craig M, Glenn P & Susan M. **Educ:** Chicago Teachers Col, BA, 1948; De Paul Univ, MEd, 1953; Univ Chicago, attended 1958; Northwestern Univ, PhD, 1975. **Career:** Educator (retired); Chicago Pub Sch, teacher, 1948-54; asst sec, 1968; dist supt, 1974-83; Betsy Ross Elem Sch Chicago, asst prin, 1955-65; Ray Elem Sch Chicago, prin, 1965-68; Loyola Univ Chicago, lectr. **Orgs:** Dir, writing Title III Proposal Established Independent Learning Center Ray Elem Sch; Chicago Urban League; Phi Delta Kappa; Am Asn Sch PersonnelAdmin; chmn St Clotilde Elem Sch Bd, 1966-69; Sch Study Comn Archdiocese Chicago, 1970-71; bd dir, Faulkner Sch Chicago, 1971-72; bd ed pres, City of Chicago, 1984-89; dir emer, Golden Apple Found. **Honors/Awds:** Leadership Award, Harold Washington; Boys & Girls Club of Chicago;Outstanding Alumnus, De Paul Univ. **Military Serv:** WWII, sgt, 1943-46. **Home Addr:** 8426 S Indiana Ave, Chicago, IL 60619.

GARDNER, HAROLD
Vice president (Organization). **Educ:** Mich State Univ, BA, indust mgt; Harvard Bus Sch, MBA. **Career:** Ford Motor Credit Co, sr fin anal; Detroit Sci Ctr, dir finance; MCN Energy Group, mgr corp develop,1989; Mich Consol Gas Co, sr vpres, mkt, sales & regulatory affairs; DTE Energy, sr vp corp serv; Mich Consol Gas Co, vpres gas opers; DTE Energy, sr vpres & asst chmn, currently. **Orgs:** Bd trustees, Leader Dogs Blind; bd trustees, Heat & Warmth Fund; Am Red Cross Southeastern MI Chap, Matrix Human Servs; Adult Well-Being Servs; Mich Higher Edu Fac Authority; bd mem, The Heat & Warmth Fund; bd mem, Loyola High Sch. **Business Addr:** Senior Vice President, Assistant to the Chairman, DTE Energy, 2000 2nd Ave, Detroit, MI 48226-1279.

GARDNER, HENRY L.
Government official. **Personal:** Born Oct 29, 1944, Jacksonville, FL; son of Annie B. **Educ:** Univ Ill, Urbana-Champaign, IL, AB, 1967; Southern Ill Univ, Carbondale, MA, 1969. **Career:** City Oakland, Oakland, CA, asst personnel analyst, 1971-73, admin asst, 1973-76, asst to city mgr, 1976-78, asst city mgr, 1978-81, city mgr, 1981; Asn Bay Area Govts, exec dir & secy, treas, currently. **Orgs:** Am Soc for Pub Admin; Int City Mgt Asn; Alameda City & Co Mgt Asn; pres, Nat Forum Black Pub Admin, 1987-89; bd, Alliance Redesigning Govt; Nat Asn Local Arts Agencies. **Honors/Awds:** Investment Leadership, Coro Found, 1985; Most Valuable Pub Off, City & State Mag, 1990; Pub Off of the Yr, 1990; Marks of Excellence Award, Nat Forum for Black Pub Admin, 1991. **Business Addr:** Executive Director, Secretary, Association of Bay Area Governments, 101 Eigth St, Oakland, CA 94607.*

GARDNER, JACKIE RANDOLPH
Physician. **Personal:** Born Apr 7, 1930, Tampa, FL; son of Isaac and Georgette Mattox; children: Adrian Randolph, Pia JoAnna. **Educ:** Fisk Univ, BA, 1948; Univ Mich, Grad Sch Pub Health, 1950; Meharry Med Col, MD, 1955. **Career:** Mercy Hosp Buffalo, internship, 1955-56; Sydenham Hosp NY, residency, 1958; Kingsbrook Med Ctr, Brooklyn, residency, 1958-59; Brooklyn, pvt pract physician gen med & family pract, 1961-. **Orgs:** Chmn, The Source, Brooklyn, NY 1980; Alpha Phi Alpha Fratertnity. **Military Serv:** USN, lt, 1956-58. **Business Addr:** Physician, 678 Saint Marks Ave, Brooklyn, NY 11216, **Business Phone:** (718)363-8000.*

GARDNER, LOMAN RONALD
Educator, business owner. **Personal:** Born Feb 9, 1938, Detroit, MI; son of Loman Sr (deceased) and Lillian; married Aug 6, 1958 (divorced); children (previous marriage): Hansel, Loman III, Toi & Troy; married Kay, Jun 25, 1995. **Educ:** Eastern Mich Univ, BFAE, 1964; Mich State Univ, MA, 1970, MS, 1976, PhD,1985. **Career:** Mich Sch Syst, instr & counr; Boys Republic Training Sch, instr; Detroit Pub Sch, instr, Battle Creek Pub Sch, sch adv; FBI, spec agent; Detroit Police dept, dep & acting chief investr; Tots & Toys Pre Sch, owner, dir; Detroit Pub Sch, instr, Learning Disabled, spec educr; Loman Investigations, owner & investr. **Orgs:** Kappa Alpha Psi, 1960-; Mason, Prince Hall, 1972-; Mich Asn Learning Disabilities Educr, 1990-; life mem, NCP, 1992. **Special Achievements:** Book: Reflections in Black & Blues, 1999. **Military Serv:** USN, sn, 1956-60. **Home Addr:** 2046 Cleo Lane, Deltona, FL 32738, **Home Phone:** (386)574-1820.

GARDNER, WALTER
Government official. **Career:** Civil Rights activist; Newton County, MS, bd supvr, 1991-. **Special Achievements:** First African American member of Newton County, Missisipi board of supervisors since Reconstruction. **Business Phone:** (601)683-2011.

GARIBALDI, DR. ANTOINE MICHAEL
College president, college teacher, educational psychologist. **Personal:** Born Sep 26, 1950, New Orleans, LA; son of Augustin and Marie Brule; married. **Educ:** Howard Univ, BA, 1973; Univ Minn, PhD, Educ Psychol, 1976. **Career:** Holy Comforter-St. Cyprian, elem teacher, 1972-73; Univ Minn, Col Educ, res asst, 1973-75; St. Paul Urban League St Acad, prin, 1975-77; Inst Educ Leadership, educ policy fel, 1977-78; Nat Comn Excellence Educ, staff, 1981-82; Nat Inst Educ, res assoc, 1977-82; Xavier Univ LA, Dept Educ, chmn, prof educ, 1982-89, dean, Col Arts & Sci, 1989-91, vp acad affairs, 1991-96; Howard Univ, provost & chief acad officer, 1996-2000; Educ Testing Serv, sr fel, 2000-01; Gannon Univ, pres, 2001-. **Orgs:** Am Educ Res Asn; fel Am Psychol Asn; Asn Black Psychologists; Alpha Phi Alpha; Phi Delta Kappa; Phi Kappa Phi; Sigma Pi Phi, Chair, SAC 2006-08; pres, Univ Minnesota Black Stud Psychol Asn, 1974-75; US Army Sci Bd,1979-83; assoc ed Am Educ Res J, 1982-84; consult US Dept Educ, 1983-85;New Orleans Libr Bd 1984-93, chmn, 1991-93; bd dirs, J Negro Educ; co-chmn, Mayor's Found Educ, 1987-90; co-chmn, educ comm, Urban League Greater New Orleans, 1984-90; Metrop Area Committee, 1992-96, educ fund bd, 1991-96; bd dir, Am Libr Asn; Alpha Kappa Mu, Psi Chi; bd dir, Ctr Educ African-Am Males 1991-92; bd dir, AAHE bd dirs, 1995-2003, chair2001-02, past chair 2002-03; AACTE committee mem 1988-98; ACE bd dirs2006-08, committee on LIE 2004-07; bd dir, Sr Thea Bowman Black Catholic Educ Found; bd dir, chair 2002-, Coun Independent Col, chair 2006-08, vice chair prog, 2003-05; Asn Independent Col Univ PA, bd dir, 2008-; NACUBO, bd dir, 2006-12; chair, NCAA Exec Comm subcomt Gender and Diversity, 2008-09, NCAA Div II Pres Coun, 2005-09; Univ of St. Thomas (MN), bd trustees 2004-; bd of regents, Seton Hall, 2007-10; bd dir, Academic Search, 2008-; USCCB Nat Review Bd, 2009-; Asn Governing Bds Coun Pres, 2009-. **Honors/Awds:** Nat Service Award, Dr. Martin Luther King Jr, 2001; Hon Doctorate, Our Lady Holy Cross Col, 2001; Distinguished Alumni Award, Howard Univ, 2004; Outstanding Achievement Award, Univ Minn, 2006; Papal Honor of Knight of St. Gregory the Great, 2006; Hon Doctorate, Seton Hall Univ, 2007. **Special Achievements:** Author; The Decline of Teacher Production in Louisiana, 1976-83: Attitudes Toward the Profession, 1986; Southern Education Foundation monograph, 1986; Educating Black Male Youth: A Moral and Civic Imperative, 1988; Ed: Black Colleges and Universities: Challenges for the Future, 1984; "Teacher Recruitment and Retention: With a Special Focus on Minority Teachers", National Education Association, 1989; co-ed: The Education of African-Americans; more than 80 chap & articles in prof journals & books. **Home Addr:** 204 Bay Mist Dr, Erie, PA 16505, **Home Phone:** (814)835-7403. **Business Addr:** President, Gannon University, Office of the President, 109 Univ Sq, Erie, PA 16541-0001, **Business Phone:** (814)871-7609.

GARLAND, JOHN WILLIAM
School administrator. **Personal:** Born Oct 24, 1944, Harlem, NY; son of John W and Amy; married Carolyn Farrow, Jan 1975; children: Amy, Jabari. **Educ:** Cent State Univ, BA, 1971; Ohio State Univ Col Law, JD, 1974. **Career:** Coastal Plains, dir legal servs, 1979-83; Hayes & White, PC, sr atty, 1983-84; Law Off John W Garland, atty, 1984-88; Univ DC, gen coun, 1988-91; Univ Va, assoc gen coun, 1991-93, exec asst pres, 1993-96, assoc vpres intellectual property, 1996-97; Cent State Univ, pres, 1997-. **Orgs:** Bd dirs, Nat Asn Col & Univ Atty; Nat Conf Black Lawyers; Asn Univ Technol Mgr; bd dirs, Wash Lawyers Comm Civil Rights Under Law; bd dirs, Nat Veterans Legal Servs Proj; ed bd, J Col & Univ Law; US Supreme Ct; Supreme Ct NC: Supreme Ct Va; Ct Appeals, DC; pres, US Ct Mil Appeals; LeDroit Park Civic Asn, 1974-76; life mem, Disabled Veterans Am; trustee, Miami Valley Res Pk Found; trustee, Greater Dayton Pub TV; trustee, Southwestern Ohio Coun Higher Educ; chair, Am Coun Educ Ctr Advan Racial & Ethnic Equity; bd mem, Edison Materials Technol Ctr, Dayton, OH; bd dir, Fifth Third Bank; Nat Afro Am Mus & Cult Ctr; Nat Coun Col Law Alumni Asn, Ohio State Univ; founding dir, Tawawa Community Develop Corp. **Honors/Awds:** Father of the Year, Fed Civic Asn, 1978; TransAfrica Award, 1987; Alumni Certificate of Achievement, Ohio State Univ Col Law, 1997; Top Ten African-American Males in the Miami Valley, Parity 2000 prog, 1998; Path to Excellence Black Achiever Award, Calvary Missionary Baptist Church, 1999; Alumnus of the Year, Ohio State Univ Moritz Col Law, 1999; Educational Leadership Award, Marshall Scholarship Fund, 2004. **Special Achievements:** Legal Servs of the Coastal Plains, founding dir. **Military Serv:** USMC, cpl E-4, 1967-92; Purple Heart, Vietnam Serv Medal, Good Conduct Medal. **Business Addr:** President, Central State University, PO Box 1004, Wilberforce, OH 45384-1004, **Business Phone:** (937)376-6011.*

GARNER, CHARLES
Musician, educator. **Personal:** Born Jul 27, 1931, Toledo, OH; married Judith Marie Bonner; children: Kevin & Darchelle. **Educ:** Cleveland Inst Mus, Bmus, 1953; Boston Univ, MA, 1957; Yale Univ, adv stud; Columbia Univ, New York, NY, PhD, 1991. **Career:** Univ Hartford, Hartt Sch Music, instr, 1961-65; East & Midwest, numerous piano & ensemble recitals; Southern Conn State Univ, composer, arranger, prof of music, 1968-96, prof emer, currently. **Orgs:** Am Asn Univ Prof; Phi Delta Kappa; Kappa Gamma Psi; Kappa Alpha Psi; Am Soc of Composers Authors & Pub. **Honors/Awds:** Recipient Am Fed of Mus; Mu Phi Epsilon Scholar, 1948; Friends of Mus Award, 1949; First place OH Mus Teacher Auditions; Ranney Scholar of Cleveland, 1949-52; Charles H Ditson Award, Yale Univ, 1968; Frances Osbourn Kellogg prize in counterpoint, Yale Univ, 1969; Charles Garner Recital Hall, Southern Conn State Univ, named in honor. **Military Serv:** AUS, radio operator, 1953-55. **Business Addr:** Professor Emeritus of Music, Southern Connecticut State University, 501 Crescent St, New Haven, CT 06515, **Business Phone:** (203)392-5841.*

GARNER, CHARLIE, III
Football player. **Personal:** Born Feb 13, 1972, Falls Church, VA. **Educ:** Univ Tenn. **Career:** Football player (retired); Philadelphia Eagles, running back, 1994-98; San Francisco 49ers, 1999-2000; Oakland Raiders, 2001-03; Tampa Bay Buccaneers, 2004-05. **Honors/Awds:** Pro Bowl, 2000.

GARNER, CHRIS (CHRISTOPHER WINSLOW GARNER)
Basketball player. **Personal:** Born Feb 23, 1975, Memphis, TN. **Educ:** Memphis Univ. **Career:** Toronto Raptors, guard, 1997-98; Detroit Pistons, guard, 2003-04; MaccabiGivat Shmuel, 2004-05; GS Larissa, Greece, 2005-06; Cholet Basket, FranceProA, 2006-07; Apollon, Greece, 2007; Achilleas K, Cyprus, 2007-08; Polpak Swiecie, 2008; Banks BPS Basket Kwidzyn, Poland, 2008-09; Achilleas K, Cyprus, 2009-.

GARNER, CHRISTOPHER WINSLOW. **See GARNER, CHRIS.**

GARNER, EDWARD, JR.
Executive. **Personal:** Born Dec 4, 1942, Skippers, VA; married Betty J; children: Erica P, Edward P, Elizabeth P. **Educ:** NC A&T State Univ, BS, 1967; Squadron Off Sch, USAF, 1972; Univ NC Law Sch Chapel Hill, JD, 1975; Air Command & Staff Col, 1983; Air War Col, 1994. **Career:** Executive (retired); Akzo Am Inc, corp attny, 1976-85; NC Dept Crime Control & Pub Safety, asst secy, 1985-89; NC Indust Comn, dep comnr, 1989-04; Garner Mediation, owner, currently. **Orgs:** NC Bar, Am Bar Asn, Air Force Asn, NC Asn Black Laywers, Aircraft Owners & Pilots Asn, Negro Airmen Intl Inc, Asn Trial Lawyers Am, NC Acad Trial Lawyers, US Air Force Reserve & NC Air Nat Guard; chmn, bd dir, Asheville Buncombe Community Rels Coun; mem bd, YMI Cultural Ctr Inc; Asheville City Personnel Comn; Govs adv comn Military Affairs; comt, NC bar asn. **Military Serv:** USAF, pilot, 1968-73; NC Air Nat Guard, 1979-; Disting Flying Cross; Flew C-123 Transport, B-52 Bomber & C-130 Transport; 2 yrs combat duty Southeast Asia. **Business Addr:** Owner, Garner Mediation, P O Box 690104, Mint Hill Station, Charlotte, NC 28227-7001, **Business Phone:** (704)621-6167.*

GARNER, JAMES
Politician, president (organization), mayor. **Educ:** Adelphi Univ, BS. **Career:** Republican Mayor Hempstead, New York, 1984-2005; US Conf Mayors, pres, 2003-04. **Orgs:** Nat Asn Advan Colored People; Town of Hempstead Minority Adv Coun; Local Am Legion. **Honors/Awds:** First African-American to be elected a mayor on Long Island.

GARNER, JOHN W.
Manager. **Personal:** Born Dec 29, 1924, Franklin, TN; married Leslie Olga Abernathy; children: Reginald J, Paul L. **Educ:** Fisk Univ, BA, Chem, 1950, MS, 1952; Ill Inst Tech, MS, phys chem, 1955. **Career:** Manager (retired); Percy L Julian Labs, chemist, 1952-53; Ill Inst Tech Res Inst, res chemist, 1954-66; 3M Co Dent Prod Lab, sr res chemist, 1966-70; 3M Co Med Prods Div, sr clin res coordr, 1974-75; 3M Health Care Group, acad rels mgr, 1976-85; Riker Labs Int & 3M Co, mgr licensing adm, 1985-89. **Orgs:** Bd dir, Big Bros Sis Greater St Paul, 1972-87; life mem, Alpha Phi Alpha Fraternity, 1976-; bd trustees, Fisk Univ, 1977-89; human rel adv comt, 3m Co, 1978-86; adv bd, Biomed Eng Dept Tulane Univ, 1979-; mem, Omicron Boule Sigma Pi Phi Fraternity Inc, 1979-; MN Metro Golf League, 1980; mem, Am Chem Soc, AAMI Nat Tech Asn, 1985; vpres, Sterling Club, 1985; bd dir, City Walk Condo Assoc, 1985-87; mem, Nat Org Black Chemist & Chem Engrs; Urban League; Nat Asn Advan Colored People. **Honors/Awds:** Christian Father of Year Award, Trinity United Church, Chicago, IL 1966; Think Higher Award, 3M Health Care Group, 1972; Nat Life Mem Prog Award, Alpha Phi Alpha Fraternity, 1978; Distiguished Black Col Alumnus Award, Fisk Univ, 1983. **Military Serv:** AUS, staff sergeant, 1943-46; 4 Bronze Battle Stars, 2 Invasion Arrow Heads, Europe, Purple Heart, 1943-46. **Home Addr:** 66 9th St E, St Paul, MN 55101, **Home Phone:** (651)224-1499. *

GARNER, JUNE BROWN
Columnist. **Personal:** Born Jul 19, 1923, Detroit, MI; daughter of Simpson Malone and Vela Malone; married Warren C Garner; children: Sylvia Mustonen. **Educ:** Wayne State Univ. **Career:** Columnist (retired); Detroit News, columnist; Mich Chronicle, classified adv mgr, 1974; Warren Garner Realty; vol teacher, N Tazewell Elem Sch, VA. **Orgs:** Founder, Let's Read Summer Sch, 1980; Comput Programming. **Honors/Awds:** Best columnist, Nat Asn Newspaper Publ, 1967, 1968; Best columnist, Detroit Press Club, 1972, 1973. **Special Achievements:** Books: Let's Read'nd ed. **Home Addr:** 107 Vernon Ave, Tazewell, VA 24651, **Home Phone:** (276)988-0031. *

GARNER, DR. LA FORREST DEAN
School administrator. **Personal:** Born Aug 20, 1933, Muskogee, OK; son of Fannie M Thompson and Sanford G; married Alfreida

Thomas; children: Deana Y, Thomas L & Sanford E. **Educ:** Ind Univ Sch Dentistry, DDS, 1957, MSD, 1959, Cert, Orthodontics, 1961. **Career:** Ind Univ, Sch Dent, assoc prof, 1967-70, prof & chmn, 1970, assoc dean, minority stud serv, 1987, Grad & Post Grad Dent Educ IUSD, dir, 1994-, IUPUI, ombudsman, prof emer orthod, currently; Va Hosp Dental Div, consult, 1979-; James Whitcomb Riley Hosp, orthod coordr, 1979-. **Orgs:** Bd dir, Vis Nurses Asn, Indianapolis, 1973-77; local pres, Omicron Kappa Upsilon Local Chap, 1974-75; fel Am Col Dent, 1974; bd dirs, Am Cleft Palate Educ Found, 1975-79; Boys Clubs, 1976-; Sigma Xi, 1976; chmn, Coun Res, Am Asn Orthodontists, 1976-77; Boule, 1978-; bd dirs, Park Tudor Sch, Indianapolis, Ind, 1980-; life mem, NAACP, 1980-; chmn, United Way Ancillary Serv, 1984-85; pres, Am Asn Dent Res, 1984-85; bd dirs, Indianapolis Zoo, 1987-; bd dirs, Fall Creek Pkwy YMCA, 1989. **Honors/Awds:** Nat Pres Omicron Kappa Upsilon Nat Dent Scholastic, 1974-75; Garner Minority Student Scholarship, named in honor, Ind Univ, 2006; DSc, Ind Univ, 2007. **Business Addr:** Professor Emeritus of Orthodontics, Indiana University, 107 S Indiana Ave, Bloomington, IN 47405-7000.

GARNER, LON L.
Funeral director, politician. **Personal:** Born Jul 17, 1927, San Augustine County, TX; married Vonzella Jones; children: David, Conchita, Alex. **Career:** Percy Garner & Son, mortician; San Augustine, city alderman; San Augustine Fed Credit Union, dir; Alberta King Day Care Ctr, dir, 1974; Percy Garner & Son Mortuary, mgr, currently. **Orgs:** Patron McPhearson Lodge Order Eastern Star 150 San Augustine, 1967; Nat Funeral Dirs Asn, 1953; Masonic Lodge; Order Knight Pythian; serv chmn, bd mem, Am Red Cross Dr & Chap; San Augustine C C; chmn, deacon bd True Vine Bapt Ch, 1969. **Honors/Awds:** cert award, C C, 1972; outstanding ambul serv, 1969. **Special Achievements:** 1st black elected official & 1st elected official, San Augustine Co. **Business Addr:** Manager, Percy Garner & Son Mortuary, 304 Ironosa St, PO Box 491, San Augustine, TX 75972, **Business Phone:** (936)275-2511.*

GARNER, DR. MARY E.
Psychologist, chief executive officer. **Personal:** Born in Paterson, NJ; children: Floyd Jr & Steven. **Educ:** William Paterson Col, BA Psycol, 1973; Fairleigh Dickinson Univ, MA Clinical Psycol, 1976; CUNY, PhD, 1983. **Career:** Passaic City Community, prof psycol, 1983; Fairleigh Dickinson Univ, prof psycol summers, 1982-84; William Paterson Col, prof psycol, 1982-; Paterson Dept Human Resources, spec asst to dir, 1982-83, dir, 1983-; Paterson Community Health Ctr Inc, chief exec officer, currently. **Orgs:** Pres, preakness Hosp Bd Mgrs, 1982-84; chairwoman, Riverview Towers Tenants Asn, 1973-; Coalition Pub Acct, 1982-; Zonta Intl, 1983-; Black Bus & Prof Assoc, 1983-; NJ Amer Psychol Asn. **Honors/Awds:** Community serv Social & Economic Change for All Inc, 1983, Modern Beautician's Asn, 1983, Black History Month Comt, 1984 & 1985; President Award, Preakness Hosp Bd Mgrs, 1984. **Business Addr:** Chief Executive Officer, Paterson Community Health Center Inc, 32 Clinton St, Paterson, NJ 07505, **Business Phone:** (973)790-6594.*

GARNER, MELVIN C
Lawyer. **Personal:** Born Feb 9, 1941, Philadelphia, PA; son of George L and Freida White; married R Patricia Grant. **Educ:** Drexel Univ, BS, 1964; NY Univ, MS 1968; Brooklyn Law Sch, JD, 1973. **Career:** IBM Poughkeepsie NY, jr engr, 1964-66; CBS Labs, Stamford, CT, engr, 1966-69; Sequential Inf Sys Dobbs Ferry, NY, proj engr, 1969-70; Bell Tel Labs Holmdel, NY, patent staff, 1970-73; Brumbaugh Graves Donohue & Raymond, attny, 1973-82; Darby & Darby, atty, 1982-; New York State Bar, atty; United Supreme Ct, atty; Ct Appeals Second & Fed Circuits, atty; Dist Ct Eastern & Southern Dist NY; Darby & Darby, prin, currently. **Orgs:** NY Intellectual Property Law Asn, Nat Patent Law Asn, Eta Kappa Nu(Hon Elect Engrs Soc), Brooklyn Law Review. **Honors/Awds:** Award, Drexel Univ, 2005. **Business Addr:** Principal, Darby & Darby, 7 World Trade Ctr 250 Greenwich St, New York, NY 10007, **Business Phone:** (212)527-7717.

GARNER, NATHAN WARREN
Executive. **Personal:** Born Dec 25, 1944, Detroit, MI; married Indira S Licht; children: Mark C, Erica D, Vincent C & Warren C. **Educ:** Wayne State Univ, BS, 1966; Wayne State Univ, Grad Sch Educ, MS, MEd, 1971; Columbia Univ, Grad Sch Bus, MBA, 1975; Stanford Grad Sch Bus, finance mgt prog, 1984. **Career:** Scholastic Inc, dir mkt, 1969-78; Time Distribution Serv Inc, dir mkt, 1978-80; US Dept Educ, spec asst secy educ, 1980-81; Time-Life Films Inc, vpres, 1981-82; Preview Subs TV Inc, pres, 1982-83; Manhattan Cable TV Inc, vpres; Paragon Cable TV Manhattan, pres; USA Networks, vpres, 1986-94; Scholastic Inc, pres, 1995-. **Orgs:** Adv bd, Fla A&M Univ Entrepreneurial Develop Ctr, 1983-85; Cable TV Admin & Mkt Soc 1983-85; Asn Better New York, 1984-85; bd dirs, E Mid Manhattan Chamber Com, 1984-85; chmn, Nat Asn Minorities Cable, 1987-88; steering community, 21st Century Fund; Friends Alvin Ailey Dance Theatre Alumni Asn; pres, Exec Exchange Prog; adv group, Columbia Univ Bus Sch Telecommunications Policy Res & Infor Studies Prog. **Honors/Awds:** Black Achievers Award, Harlem YMCA Greater New York, 1983; Andrew Heiskell Award, Time Inc, 1986; Excellence in Communications, E Manhattan Chamber Com, 1987. **Military Serv:** AUS, spec 5th class, 2 yrs. **Home Addr:** 442 Pac St, Brooklyn, NY 11217, **Home Phone:** (718)624-2014. **Business Addr:** President, Scholastic Inc, 555 Broadway, New York, NY 10012, **Business Phone:** (212)343-6734.

GARNER, THOMAS L.
Executive director. **Personal:** Born Sep 13, 1930, Cincinnati, OH; married Joann Calmeise; children: Stuart, Geoffrey. **Educ:** Cincinnati Univ, BSE, 1952, Grad Work, 1975; Mich State Univ; Ohio State Univ. **Career:** Cincinnati Human Rels Comm, exec dir; Model Cities Bd, chair; Better Housing League, neighborhood coor, 1966-68; Southwestern Reg Coun Alcoholism, assoc dir. **Orgs:** Cent Psychiat Clinic; YMCA; Cincinnati Firearms Comn; Nat Asn Human Rights Workers; Int Asn Off Human Rights Agencies; Housing Opportunities Made Equal Bd; bd mem, Cincinnati Pub Dent Asn; bd mem, Union Col Univ Without Walls; bd mem, Seven Hills Schs; founder, Prog Unlimited; Comm Ctr Bd. **Military Serv:** USAF, res, 1948-68. *

GARNER, VELVIA M
State government official, chairperson. **Personal:** Born Nov 21, 1941, Halsted, TX; daughter of Edgar and Mary Elizabeth McKenzie; married Edward J, Mar 9, 1964; children: Angela, Tonia & Edward. **Educ:** Prairie View A&M Univ, BS, 1963; Univ Colo, Denver, CO, 1974; DPA, in progress. **Career:** Associate director, chairperson (retired); Ben Taub Gen Hosp, Houston, TX, team leader, 1963-64; Madigan Gen Hosp, Tacoma, WA, team leader, 1964-65; St Joseph Hosp, Denver, CO, clinic supvr, 1965-73; Univ Colo, Denver, CO, asst prof, 1974-80; Mental Health Ctr Denver, State Colo, Div Youth Servs, dir med & psychological servs, 1980-87, assoc dir; Colo State Parole Bd, vchair, 1987-92; Lookout Mountain Youth Servs Ctr, asst dir, until 1992; Gilliam Detention Ctr, dir, 1993, assoc dir, 2001-05. **Orgs:** Chair, Mental Health Corp Denver, 1985-; Colo Community Corrections Adv Coun, 1987-; Rocky Mt Ctr for Health Promotion & Educ, 1987-; NURSES Colo Corp, 1984-, pres, 1988-90. **Honors/Awds:** Community Corrections Adv Coun, 1989; Adv Coun Adolescent Health, 1982-87; Colo Black Women Polit Action, 1986-; Teacher of the Year Award, Studs, Univ Colo, 1975-76; Community Service Award, CBWPA, 1983; Certificate for Recognition for Outstanding Community Service, Joint Effort Found, 1983. **Home Addr:** 13095 E Elk Pl, Denver, CO 80239.

GARNES, SAM AARON
Football player. **Personal:** Born Jul 12, 1974, Bronx, NY. **Educ:** Univ Cincinnati. **Career:** Football player (retired); New York Giants, safety, 1997-2001; New York Jets, 2002-03.

GARNETT, KEVIN
Basketball player. **Personal:** Born May 19, 1976, Mauldin, SC; son of O'Lewis McCullough and Shirley. **Career:** Minnesota Timberwolves, forward, 1996-. **Honors/Awds:** Most Outstanding Player, McDonald's All Am Game; Mr. Basketball of thestate of Ill, 1994; Nat Basketball Assn, All-Star, 1997, 1998; Olympicgold medal, 2000; Most Valuable Player, 2003, 2004; NBA All-Star Game MVP,2003; Nat Player of the Yr, USA Today Mag; NBA Most Valuable Player, 2004;J. Walter Kennedy Citizenship Award, 2006 . **Business Addr:** Professional Basketball Player, Minnesota Timberwolves, 600 1st Ave N, Minneapolis, MN 55403, **Business Phone:** (612)673-1600.*

GARNETT, RONALD LEON
Lawyer. **Personal:** Born May 27, 1945, Louisville, KY. **Educ:** Cent State Univ, BS, 1967; Columbia Univ, JD, 1970. **Career:** US Dist Judge Robert McRae, law clerk 1971-72; Winthrop Stimpson Putnam & Robts, Atty 1972-73; Am Express Co, atty 1973-74; US Atty's Off, asst US atty 1974-77; GTE Corp, sr coun, 1977-82; New York City, criminal ct judge, 1984-86; pvt pract, atty, currently. **Orgs:** Am Bar Asn; New York State Bar Asn, 1973; New York Co Lawyers Asn; Kappa Alpha Psi; Nat Basketball Asn, 1981; Nat Asn Criminal Defense Lawyers, 1986. **Business Addr:** Attorney, 299 Broadway Suite 1601, New York, NY 10007-1901, **Business Phone:** (212)587-5159.*

GARNETTE, DR. BOOKER THOMAS
Dentist. **Personal:** Born Apr 28, 1930, Norfolk, VA; son of Willie Mae Davidson Wiley (deceased) and Booker S (deceased); divorced; children: Barbetta Breathwaite, Donna Yvonne Garnette Alexander & Carla Riddick. **Educ:** Howard Univ, BS, 1951, DDS, 1955. **Career:** Dentist (retired); Norfolk Gen Hosp; St Vincent DePaul Hosp; Norfolk Comm, staff; Va Tidewater Dental Assoc, comm on dental health; VA Dental Assoc, alt house of del; pvt pract, dentist, 1957-95. **Orgs:** Tidewater Dental Assoc; Amer Dental Assoc; John McGriff Dental Soc; Old Dominion Dental Soc; Campbell Lodge no 67 F&A Masons Prince Hall; Tux Club; Bachelor Benedict Club; past 3rd dist rep Omega Psi Phi; housing auth Omega Psi Phi, Nat Soc Action Comm, Nat Publ Rel Comm; life mem, Omega Psi Phi; chmn Nat Recommendations Commt Omega Psi Phi; commt mem, Nat Assault Illiteracy, Omega Psi Phi, 1990-. **Honors/Awds:** Omega Man Award, Pi Gamma Chap, 1977; Omega Man of the Year, Lambda Omega Chap Omega Psi Phi, 1977; 3rd Dist Omega Man of the Year, Omega Psi Phi, 1977; 25 Year Cert Omega Psi Phi; Forty Year Plaque, Omega Psi Phi, 1988; Founders Award, Third District, Omega Psi Phi, 1990; Founders Award, Lambda Omega Chapter, Omega Psi Phi, 1990. **Special Achievements:** First black dentist, Norfolk Gen Hosp, St Vincent DePaul Hosp; First black naval officer from Norfolk, Va. **Military Serv:** USNR, comrd, 1955-75; Naval Reserve medal, USNR. **Home Addr:** 5435 Sandpiper Lane, PO Box 1823, Norfolk, VA 23501-1823.

GARNIER, THOMAS JOSEPH
Auditor. **Personal:** Born Apr 7, 1942, New Orleans, LA; son of Thomas and Louisa; married Grace L Garnier, Apr 21, 1984; children: Thomas J Garnier III & Joshua DeJalma Garnier. **Educ:** Dillard Univ, BA, 1966; Oklahoma Univ, attended 1970. **Career:** Chevron Oil Co, acct anal, 1966-68; Shell Oil Co, acct anal, 1968-69; Off Econ Opportunity TCA, acct supvr, 1969-70; Model Cities, City New Orleans, chief fiscal off, 1970-71; La State Dept Educ, dir auditing, 1972-76; Garniers & Garniers Inc, pres, 1976-88; Bur Alcohol Tobacco & Firearms, US Treas Dept, sr auditor, currently. **Orgs:** Asn Govt Acct, 1989-; Asn Cert Fraud Examiners, 1990-; High Technol Crime Invest Asn, 2000-; Int Asn Law Enforcement Intelligence Analysts, 2001-; Nat Org Black Law Enforcement Execs, 2001-; Nat Asn Blacks Criminal Justice, 2001-; The Acad Acct Historians, 2002-; Inst Internal Auditors, 2002-. **Honors/Awds:** Scientific Prof, Employee of the Year, Fed Exec Bd, 1997; Cert Appreciation, ATF FBI, 1998; Letter of Commendation, ATF, 1999; Special Act Award, ATF, 2000; Letter of Recognition, FBI, 2002. **Special Achievements:** Author: Audit Manual-Policies & Procedures, 1973; Ten Most Wanted Audit Discrepancies, 1974; Financial Expert Witness (State & Federal Courts), 1993-. **Military Serv:** US Air Force, A/3C, 1961-62. **Business Addr:** Senior Forensic Auditor, Bureau of Alcohol, Tobacco, Firearms & Explosives (ATF), 2600 Century Pkwy Suite 330, Atlanta, GA 30345, **Business Phone:** (404)417-2653.

GARRETT, ALINE M.
Educator. **Personal:** Born Aug 28, 1944, Martinville, LA. **Educ:** Univ Southwestern La, BA, 1966; Oberlin OH, AM, 1968; Univ MA, PhD, 1971. **Career:** Educator (Retired); Univ Southwestern La, Lafayette, assoc prof psychol, 1971; Univ Mass, Amherst, grad res asst; Summer Sch Fac, Univ Southwestern La, teacher, 1969 & 1970; Psychometrist Lafayette Parish Schs, summer, 1967; Project Head Start, Lafayette LA, teacher, 1966; Univ LA, Lafayette, Psychol, full prof, 2001. **Orgs:** Am Psychol Asn; Nat Asn Black Psychol; Soc Res Child Develop; Psi Chi; SE Psychol Asn; LA Psychol Asn; bd dir Nat Coun Black Child Develop; comn Acad Affairs & Standards, 1972; Fac Senate, 1973-; Grad Fac, 1971-; Equal Employment Opportunity Comn, 1972; coun teacher educ col educ Univ Southwestern La, 1974-; adv bd SGA- Univ Southwestern La, Child Care Ctr; adv bd, Cath Soc Serv, 1973; Health Adv Bd, Tri-Parish Progress Inc, 1974; candidate, St Martin Parish Sch Bd, 1974; Agency Parent Coun, SMILE Inc, USL Rep, 1974; by appointment Mayor Willis Soc & Econ Com St Martinville, 1974; bd dir, Lafayette Chap Epilepsy Found; Alpha Lambda Delta. **Honors/Awds:** Research grant to do family res, HEW Office Child Develop, 1974-75; SEPA Visiting Women Program, 1974-; Faculty advisor, Nat Honor Soc; outstanding black citizen award, Southern Consumers Educ Found Field Educ, 1975. **Home Addr:** 615 N Theatre St, St Martinville, LA 70582, **Home Phone:** (337)394-4106. *

GARRETT, CAIN, JR.
Military leader, commander. **Personal:** Born May 11, 1942, Kilgore, TX; son of Cain Garrett Jr (deceased) and Everett V Woods Henry. **Educ:** Univ CO Boulder, BSEE, 1968; Naval Post Grad Sch Monterey, MSEE, 1973; Naval Post Grad Sch Monterey, elec engr deg, 1974. **Career:** Commander (retired); USN, elec engr, 1974, communs officer, 1968-70, opers dept head, 1970-72, lt comdr flag secy, 1974-77, oper analyst & admin officer, Navy Oper Test Facility, 1977-80. **Orgs:** Inst Elec & Electronics Engrs; Big Brothers Steering Com Boulder, 1964-68; tournament dir, US Chess Federation 1989-; Sacramento Chess Club. **Military Serv:** USN, Lt comdr, 1959-80; Commendation Medal; Achievement Medal, Vietnam; 4 unit awards, Vietnam; Sea of Japan, S China Seas Operations; Spirit of Honor Award, Kiwinas 1968; Meritorious Serv Medal, 1980. **Home Addr:** 618 Lake Front Dr, Sacramento, CA 95831. *

GARRETT, CHERYL ANN
Government official, educator. **Personal:** Born Aug 31, 1946, Bethel Springs, TN; daughter of Robert Eugene Smith and Jewel Perkins King Smith; married Larry Eugene; children: Larry Eugene II, David Conrad & Cheryl Lynn. **Educ:** Grambling Univ, BS, 1969. **Career:** Memphis Park Comn, community ctr dir, 1970-72; Central State Hosp, coordr adj therapy, 1972-74; Memphis City Schs, sub teacher, 1974-; CJH Resources Inc, pres, 1983-; Nat Black Republican Coun, southern reg, vpres; Fixit Home Repair, admin asst, 1985; City Memphis, Memphis, TN, Cunningham Community Ctr dir, currently. **Orgs:** Comn Shelby Cty Civil Serv Bd, 1979-; vice chmn, TN Comn Status Women, 1980; state pres, TN Republican Assembly, 1980-; treas, South Shelby Republican Club, 1982-. **Honors/Awds:** Merit Award, Shelby County Republican Party, 1979; Key to City, Chattanooga, TN, 1981; Family Award, Shelby County Republican Party, 1983; State Coordr, Black Vote Div Regan & Bush, 1984 Campaign, 1984; Key to the City Memphis, City Government, Mayor Hackett, 1990;

Best Program Award, TN Rec & Parks Asn, Ethnic Minority Soc, 1991. **Business Addr:** Director, City Memphis, Cunningham Community Center, 3373 Old Allen Rd, Memphis, TN 38128, **Business Phone:** (901)377-3037.*

GARRETT, DARRELL W
Executive. **Personal:** Born Nov 16, 1966, New York, NY; daughter of Daniel and Lucy. **Educ:** Univ Calif, Berkeley, BA, archit, 1989; SJ State Univ, MS, civil eng, 1992. **Career:** O'Brien Kriteberg, proj mgr, 1990-94; Combass, pres, chief exec officer, 1994-98; ViaNovus, founder, chief developer, sr vpres, 1998-. **Business Addr:** Senior Vice President, ViaNovus, 1001 Marina Village Pkwy Suite 401, Alameda, CA 94501, **Business Phone:** (510)337-1930.

GARRETT, DEAN
Entrepreneur, basketball player. **Personal:** Born Nov 27, 1966, Los Angeles, CA; married Natasha Denise Taylor, Jan 1, 2001. **Educ:** Indiana Univ; San Francisco City Col. **Career:** Basketball player (retired), business owner; Minn Timberwolves, free agent, 1996-97, 1999-2001; Denver Nuggets, free agent, 1997-98; Golden State Warriors, 2002; Escape nightclub & Bellanote restaurant, co-owner, currently. **Business Addr:** Co-Owner, Bellanotte, 600 Hennepin Ave S Suite 170, Minneapolis, MN 55403, **Business Phone:** (612)339-7200.

GARRETT, DENISE EILEEN (DEE DEE BRIDGEWATER)
Singer. **Personal:** Born May 27, 1950, Memphis, TN; daughter of Matthew; married Gilbert Moses (divorced); children: China; married Jean-Marie Durand; children: Gabriel; married Cecil Bridgewater (divorced); children: Tulani. **Educ:** Mich State Univ; Univ Ill, Urbana-Champaign. **Career:** Thad Jones/Mel Lewis Orchestra, lead vocalist; Albums: Afro Blue, 1974; Dee Dee Bridgewater, 1976; Just Family, 1978; Bad for Me, 1979; Keeping Tradition, 1992; Love & Peace: A Tribute to Horace Silver, 1995; Dear Ella, 1997; Victim of Love, 1998; Live at Yoshi's, 2000; This is New, 2002; Jai Deux Amours, 2005. **Honors/Awds:** Tony Award, Best Supporting Actress, 1975; Grammy Award for Best Musical Show Album, 1976; Grammy Award, Best Jazz Vocal Performance, 1998; Commandeur de L'Ordre des Artes et des Lettres, 2007. **Special Achievements:** Played Glinda the Good Witch in The Wiz, on Broadway, 1975; named Ambassador to the United Nations Food and Agriculture Organization; First American to be inducted to the Haut Conseil de la Francophonie. **Business Addr:** Vocalist, c/o Verve Music Group, 1755 Broadway 3rd Fl, New York, NY 10019-3743, **Business Phone:** (212)331-2000.*

GARRETT, E. WYMAN
Obstetrician, gynecologist. **Personal:** Born May 25, 1933, Newark, NJ. **Educ:** Morgan State Col, Balto, BS, 1955; Howard Univ Col Med, MD, 1961. **Career:** Newark Mini-Surgi-Site, owner & med dir; Freemdmen's Hosp, internship, 1961-62; Harlem Hosp NY City, resident obstet/gynecol; Newark City Hosp, resident; Obstet/Gynecol NJ Col Med & Dent, asso prof. **Orgs:** Newark Bd Educ, 1967-70; All-Am Basketball Morgan State; Beta Kappa Chi; Nat Sci Soc; Alpha Kappa Mu; dir, Drive Increase Black & Puerto Rican Enrollment, NJ Col Med & Dent; Orgn Black Prof & Bus Women; Nat Hon Soc Morgan State. **Honors/Awds:** Man of the Year Award, 1972. **Military Serv:** AUS, 1st lt chem corps, 1955-57.

GARRETT, EUFAULA
Manager. **Career:** Magic Johnson Theaters Corp Off, mkt dir. *

GARRETT, JACQUELYN BREWER
Physician, dermatologist. **Personal:** Born Apr 28, 1961, Washington, DC; daughter of Marlene H Brewer; divorced; children: Jacquelyn Marie, Duane Jr. **Educ:** Howard Univ, BS, 1983; Howard Univ Col Med, MD, 1985. **Career:** Barnes Hosp, internal med intern, 1985-86, dermat resident, 1986-89; pvt pract, dermat, currently. **Orgs:** Mound City Med Forum; St Louis Dermat Soc; Nat Med Asn, Dermat Sect. **Business Addr:** Dermatologist, Private Practice, 11125 Dunn Rd Suite 206, Saint Louis, MO 63136, **Business Phone:** (314)355-7111.*

GARRETT, JAMES EDWARD, JR.
State government official. **Personal:** Born Feb 26, 1959, Shelbyville, IN; son of James Edward Sr and Patricia Joan. **Educ:** Ind State Univ, BA, 1981; Ind Univ Purdue Univ, 1990. **Career:** Ind State Univ, resident asst, 1979-80; Ind Gen Assembly, house staff intern, 1981; Dayton Hudson Corp, Target Store, sales & floor mgr, warehouse mgr, 1981-85; Ind Dept Com, Div Energy, prog asst, 1985-89; US Senator Dan Coats, ast state dir, 1989-98; city councilman at large, City Shelbyville, IN, 1995-99; Shelby County Bank, Community reinvestment act dir, 1999-02; Shelby City Lifelong Learning Corp, exec dir, 2002-. **Orgs:** Phi Beta Sigma Fraternity Inc, 1978-, past chapter pres & IN state dir; Ind State Univ, Quality Life Study Comn, 1979; Coun Black Execs, 1990-; Shelbyville Central Schs, bd trustees, pres, 1985-93; Second Baptist Church, trustee, 1986-; Shelby County Cot Corrections Bd, 1985-; bd mem, Bears Blue River Festival, 1984-02. **Honors/Awds:** Youngest School Board Member, Ind Sch Bd Asn, 1985; Ed Simcox, Honorary Ind Soc State, 1981; Rhoads Hall Scholar, Ind State Univ Rhoads Hall, 1980; Hoosier Scholar, Ind State Dept Educ, 1977; voice of "Scuffy," Shelby County, 1970; AFA Service Award, Second Baptist Church, 2000. **Special Achievements:** Minority Bus & Prof achiever Ctr Leadership Develop, 1990. **Business Addr:** Executive Director, Shelby County Life Long Learning Corporation, 54 W Broadway Suite 11, Shelbyville, IN 46176, **Business Phone:** (317)398-1332.*

GARRETT, JAMES F.
Executive. **Personal:** Born in Greensboro, NC. **Career:** Naval Sea Systs Command, Systs Electromagnetic Div, dir; NATO US Rep, chief tech spokesman; Sentel Corp, founder, cheif exec officer & pres, 1987-; Bd Nat Coalition Minority Bus, pres & chmn. **Orgs:** NASA Minority Bus Adv Coun; bd dirs, Eastern Choral Soc. **Honors/Awds:** Inductee, Natl Black Col Alumni Hall of Fame, 2003; The Northern Va Urban League's Corp & Community Service Award; Ernst & Young Technological Entrepreneur of the Year, 1999. **Special Achievements:** Co has ranked No 75 on Black Enterprise magazine's list of Top 100 Black businesses, 1997. **Military Serv:** US Navy; Super Civilian Service Award. **Business Addr:** President & Founder, Chief Executive Officer, Sentel Corp, 225 Reinekers Lane Suite 500, Alexandria, VA 22314, **Business Phone:** (703)739-0084.*

GARRETT, KATHRYN
Radiologist. **Personal:** Born Mar 26, 1955, Cincinnati, OH; daughter of Leonard and Naomi Garrett; married Audley Murphy, Jan 1, 1986; children: Hamadi & Mehari. **Educ:** Brown Univ, BA, 1976; Univ Cincinnati Med Sch, MD, 1981, cert pediat radiol. **Career:** Med Ctr Radiol Group, partner, 1989-. **Orgs:** Fla Bd Med, 1991-, chair, 1996; United Cerebral Palsy Cent Fla Inc, 1997; chair by laws com, Fedn State Med Bds, 1996-97. **Honors/Awds:** Dr James R Smith Award, African American Physician of the Year, NAACP, Orlando Chapter, 1993, 1997; Summit Award, Cent Fla Women's Resource Ctr, 2004. **Business Addr:** Radiologist, Medical Center Radiology Group, 20 W Kaley St, Orlando, FL 32806, **Business Phone:** (407)423-2581.

GARRETT, LOUIS HENRY
Manager. **Personal:** Born Jul 16, 1960, Monroe, LA; son of Mattie M. **Educ:** La Tech Univ, 1983; Moody Bible Inst; US Army, New Orleans, LA, legal course, second MLC, 1990-91. **Career:** Public sch teacher; Miss La Pageant, Inc, dir advert; Grambling State Univ, McCall Dining Hall, mgr, facilities mgt, planning & opers; Ouachita Parish Ct, dep clerk, currently. **Orgs:** Phi Beta Sigma Frat Inc; Phi Beta Sigma Frat; La State Educ dir, Phi Beta Sigma Frat Inc; Ouachita Parish Election Comn; Comnr-in-Charge Ward 10, Precinct 8; Nat Asn Miss Am State Pageants, 1986-87; Monroe City Planning & Zoning Comn, 1990-96; Ouachita Regional Bd of Adjustments, 1996-; Fac adv, GSU chapter of Gamma Beta Phi Honor Soc, 1998-00; Nat Baptist Sunday Sch; Voc Bible Sch. **Honors/Awds:** Sigma Tau Delta Honor, Soc English, 1981-83; Phi Alpha Theta Honor, Soc History, 1982-83; La State Brother of the Year; Phi Beta Sigma Fraternity. **Special Achievements:** First African American member of the LA Pageant Board of Dir, 1986-87; Monroe Jaycee of the Quarter, Springboard of the Yr. **Military Serv:** USAF Reserves 1979-87; US Army Reserves, 1987-00; LA Army National Guard 2000-03; Cert Outstanding military performance 1988 at Fort Benning Georgia Infantry Training Center, 1987; Army Achievement Medal; Army Commendation Medal. **Home Addr:** 1605 Booth St, Monroe, LA 71201-8210. **Business Addr:** Ouachita Parish Clerk Court, Parish Court House, Ouachita Parish Clerk of Court, 4th Judicial Dist, 300 St John, PO Box 1862, Monroe, LA 71210-1862.

GARRETT, MELVIN ALBOY
Marketing executive. **Personal:** Born Jun 1, 1936, Montclair, NJ; married Maryann Harris. **Educ:** Upsala Col Eng, Orange, NJ, attended 1964. **Career:** Eisle King Libaire Stout & Co, NYSE, mgr, 1957-60; Halevy H Simons Archit, pub rel coordr, 1962-63; Nat St Bank Newark, banking clerk, 1963; United Airlines, mktg mgr; Becker Construct Co, acct, 1964-65; United Airlines, ticket agent, sales rep, acct exec, mktg mgr, 1965-. **Orgs:** Dist Comt Man, Montclair, NJ; Nat Asn Advan Colored People; Urban League; United Airlines Black Employees Asn; Black Prof Orgn; Alpha Kappa Psi Frat. **Honors/Awds:** Interliner of the year, 1977; Detroit Interline Club, 1977; hon mem, Detroit Interline Club, 1978; Ambassador of Goodwill, Detroit-WindsorInterline Club Inc; Salesman of the Year Award, United Airlines; Community Service Award, United Airlines; Leadership Award, United Airlines; Black Achiever Award, NY Harlem YMCA, 1980; Black Acheivers Indust, 1980. **Military Serv:** AUS, 1960-62; soldier-of-the-month, Good Conduct Medal, 1962.

GARRETT, NATHAN TAYLOR
Executive, accountant, lawyer. **Personal:** Born Aug 8, 1931, Tarboro, NC; son of York and Julia; married Wanda June Jones; children: Andrea Mausi, Devron & Nathan Jr. **Educ:** Yale Univ, BA Psychol, 1952; Wayne State Univ, post grad Acct & Bus 1960; NC Cent Sch Law, JD, 1986. **Career:** Accountant, Lawer (retired), Executive; Richard H Austin & Co Detroit, acct, 1958-62; Nathan T Garrett, CPA Durham, proprietor, 1962-75; NC Fund Durham, dep dir, 1964-67; Found Community Develop Durham, founder & exec dir, 1967-72; Garrett, Sullivan, Davenport, Bowie & Grant; Garrett & Davenport, Cherry Beraert & Holland, partner, 1975-98; NCCU Sch Bus, tenured fac; NC Mutual Life Ins Co, chmn emer, currently. **Orgs:** Bd exec comn, Mech & Farmers Bank Durham, 1965-78; chmn investment comm chair Coop Asst Fund NY, 1970-88; bd exec comm, Opportunity Funding Corp DC, 1970-77; bd chair & exec comn, NC Mutual Life Ins Co Durham, 1977-; bd vice chr Acad Affairs Comm Duke Univ 1978-90; corp mem Triangle Res Inst Found, 1980-91; chmn, People Panel NC 2000 Comn the Future 1983; NC State Bd CPA Examr, 1986-92; pres, NC Asn Minority Bus; bd pres, Scarboro Nursery Sch, 1989-91; pres, Nat Asn State Bds Accountancy, 1992-93. **Honors/Awds:** Served as elect official 25 Civic Groups in Durham & State of NC 1975; Served as president, Nat Asn Minority CPA Firms, 1978. **Military Serv:** AUS, corpl, 1952-54. **Home Addr:** 3923 Northampton Rd, Durham, NC 27707, **Home Phone:** (919)489-4889. **Business Addr:** Chairman Emeritus, North Carolina Mutual Life Insurance Co, 411 W Chapel Hill St, Durham, NC 27701, **Business Phone:** (919)682-9201.

GARRETT, PAUL C
Government official. **Personal:** Born Feb 8, 1946, Charlottesville, VA; son of Pauline H and Dr Marshall T; married Louise Lawson; children: Matthew L. **Educ:** Brown Univ, AB, 1968; Univ Va Sch Law, JD, 1971. **Career:** USAF, asst staff judge advocate, 1972-76; City Charlottesville, Va, asst city atty, 1976-80; Charlottesville Circuit Ct, clerk, 1981-. **Orgs:** Charlottesville Albemarle Bar Asn. **Military Serv:** USAF, capt, 1972-76; USAFR, lt col, 1976-96. **Business Addr:** Clerk of the Court, Charlottesville Circuit Court, 16th Circuit, 315 E High St, Charlottesville, VA 22902, **Business Phone:** (434)970-3766.

GARRETT, RUBY GRANT
Executive. **Personal:** Born May 13, 1941, Covington, GA; daughter of Robert L and Lola Price; married William H; children: Victoria, Laran. **Educ:** Carver Voc Sch Practical Nursing, LPN, 1960; Atlanta Col Art, BFA, 1971; Ga State Univ, attended 1973. **Career:** Ruby G Graphics Design, owner, 1969-72; Eric Hill & Assoc Planning, art dir design consult, 1971-72; G Designs Inc Adv & PR, pres & owner, 1972-79; Garrett Comun, pres, 1979-; Grant-Garrett Comun Inc, pres, currently. **Orgs:** Pres, Nat Alliance Market Developers, Atlanta Chap, 1982-83; bd mem, Enterprise Atlanta, 1983-85; comt chmn, Nat Alliance Market Developers, Atlanta Chap, 1983-87; bd & comt chmn, Atlanta Bus League, 1983-87; consult, speaker Univ Ga Exten Serv, 1984; consult, Atlanta Jr Coll, 1984. **Honors/Awds:** Recognition The Collaborative Inc, 1974; recognition Broadcast Enterprise Nat Inc, 1984; Pres Award, Nat Assoc Mkt Developers ATC Chap, 1984. **Home Addr:** 2121 Beecher Rd SW, Atlanta, GA 30311, **Home Phone:** (404)758-6660. **Business Addr:** President, Grant-Garrett Communication Inc, PO Box 53, Atlanta, GA 30301, **Business Phone:** (404)755-2513.*

GARRETT HARSHAW, KARLA
Newspaper editor. **Personal:** Born Jan 23, 1955, Cleveland, OH; daughter of Morgan Garrett and Bertha C Johnson Garrett; married Timothy C; children: Jason D Milton, Vincent V Harshaw & Alexander M Harshaw. **Educ:** Wright State Univ, Dayton, OH, BS, sec educ. **Career:** Dayton Daily News, Dayton, OH, various positions, 1971-90; Springfield News-Sun, Springfield, OH, ed, 1990-; Cox Newspapers Inc, ed & sr ed, currently; Cox Enhancement Seminar, consult. **Orgs:** Chair, Am soc Newspaper Eds Educ Jour Comt; Maynard Inst Jour Educ; Ohio State Univ, Sch Jour Adv Coun; founder, Dayton Asn Black Journalists, 1984; Nat Asn Black Journalists; Nat Asn Minority Media execs; Ohio Newspaper Womens Asn; keynote speaker, Inland Press Asn Convention, 1994; Pulitzer Prize Nominating Juries Jour, 1995-96; John S & James L Knight Found Newspaper Residence Prog, 1997; vchair, Am soc Newspaper Eds, pres, 1998-99, 2004-05; founder, Dayton Asn Black Journalists. **Honors/Awds:** Media Award, Montgomery County Ment Health Asn, 1980; Community Service Award, Miami Valley Health Systs, 1982; Daytons Up & Comers Award, Price Waterhouse & the Muse Mach, 1989; Honor Religon Writing, Ohio Newspaper Womens Asn, 1981-82; Springfield Urban Leagues Equal Opportunity Day Award, Career Achievement, 1990; second Place Award, Ohio Asniated Press, Column Writing, 1995; Third-Place Award, Ohio Asniated Press, Editorial Writing, 1997; Hall of Fame, Nat Asn Black Journalists Region VI, 1997; Best of Cox. **Business Addr:** Editor, Senior Editor, Cox Newspapers Inc, 6205 Peachtree Dunwoody Rd, Atlanta, GA 30328, **Business Phone:** (678)645-0000.

GARRISON, ESTHER F.
College administrator. **Personal:** Born Jul 16, 1922, Ocilla, GA; divorced. **Educ:** Savannah State Col. **Career:** Sub teacher; sec real estate firms int firms; AUS; Int Longshoreman's, gen mgr; Sunday Sch, teacher, pres & sr choir. **Orgs:** Chatham-Savannah Bd Educ, 1964-; vpres & temp life mem, Nat Asn Advan Colored People sec local Br; mem, Zion Baptist Church; dir, Youth Fel; schbd mem, The eighth dist, 1964-84; secy, Savannah chapter Nat Asn Advan Colored People, 1954. **Honors/Awds:** Outstanding serv to commn Adult Educ Prog, 1965; woman of year, Savannah State Col Chap Nat Asn Advan Colored People, 1966; Award Prince Hall Mason & Eastern Stars 1975; hon tribute to a black woman, Mutual Benevolent Soc 1974; Richard R Wright Award

Savannah State Col, 1974. **Special Achievements:** First black woman elected Bd educ S of Mason-Dixon Line; The Am Assn of Univ Women named her one of the five most influential women in Savannah, 1978; First woman hon in history of 98 yr of Soc. **Business Addr:** 221 NE Lathrope Ave, PO Box 1262, Savannah, GA 31402.

GARRISON, JEWELL K.
Educator. **Personal:** Born Nov 6, 1946, Dayton, OH; children: Brandon. **Educ:** Cent State Univ, BA, social work, 1969; Atlanta Univ, Grad Sch Social Work, MSW, 1972. **Career:** Montgomery Co Juv Ct, probation counr, 1969-70; Cath Social Serv, sch social worker, 1970-71; Atlanta Pub Sch Syst, sch social worker, 1971-72; Montgomery Co Children Serv Bd, dir staff develop, 1972-77; Wright State Univ Dayton, asst prof, 1977-84, Dept Social Work & Med Soc, asn prof &practicum coord, 1984-89; Community Connections, exec dir, 1989-92; New Futures Dayton Area Youth, dep dir, 1992-93; Columbus Med Asn Found, sr prog officer, 1993, dir progs, currently. **Orgs:** Secy, 1976-78, pres, 1977-80 Dayton Chap Nat Asn Black Social Workers; First vpres, OH State Chap, Nat Asn Black Social Workers, 1978-81; bd dir, Dayton Urban League, 1977-83, 1984-93, bd dirs chair person, 1989-92; reg trustee, Nat Urban League, 1988-91; vpres bd dirs, Community Connections, 1988-89; exec comt bd dirs, New Futures Dayton Area Youth, 1988-89; bd mem, Dayton Area Coun Youth, 1988-90; Human Serv Collab, 1993-; bd dirs, Prevent Inst, 1994-96; United Way Franklin City-Vision Coun, 1996-; chair& dir prog, Columbus Med Asn Found, currently. **Honors/Awds:** Leadership Dayton, 1986; The Altursa Soc, 1986-89; Zeta Phi Beta, Community Service Award, 1989; Nat Inst Ment Health; Alpha Kappa Delta Award, Nat Sociol Hon Soc Alpha Chap. **Business Addr:** Chair, Director of Programs, Columbus Medical Association Foundation, 1234 E Broad St, Columbus, OH 43205.

GARRISON, DR. JORDAN MUHAMMAD, JR.
Physician. **Personal:** Born Nov 1, 1956, Montclair, NJ; son of Jordan Muhammad Garrison Sr and Kathleen Wallace; married Fitrah Muhammad, Jan 24, 1992; children: Khadijah & Naimah. **Educ:** Lehigh Univ, BS, chem, 1978; Rutgers Med Sch, MD, 1982. **Career:** Univ Hosp, UMDNJ, Dept Surg, surgical intern, 1982-83, chief surgical resident, 1985-89, clinic prof surg, 1989-90; Danbury Fed Corrections Inst, U.S. Dept Justice, Fed Bureau Prisons, chief med officer, 1983-85; Northern Surgical Asn, surgeon, 1990-; pvt pract, currently. **Honors/Awds:** Surgical Residents Teaching Award, 1983, 1988. **Business Phone:** (804)644-0141.

GARRISON-CORBIN, PATRICIA ANN
Management consultant, founder (originator). **Personal:** Born Jun 18, 1947, Louisville, KY; married Dr James D Corbin. **Educ:** Western Ky Univ, BS, 1969; Univ Louisville, MS, urban studies & community develop, 1971; Mass Inst Technol, MS, mgt, 1979. **Career:** Mass Inst Technol, asst vpres, 1971-78; S Fla State Hosp, dir human resources, 1979-81; City Philadelphia, 1981-83; Greater Philadelphia First Corp, dep exec dir & treas, 1983-85; Drexel Burnham Lambert Inc, vpres munic finance, 1985-86; PG Corbin Asset Mgt Inc, pres & chief exec officer; PG Corbin & Co Inc, pres, currently; PG Corbin Group Inc, pres, currently; PG Corbin Asset Mgt Inc, pres & chief info officer. **Orgs:** First dep city mgt, City Philadelphia, 1982-84; dep exec dir, Greater Philadelphia First Corp, 1984-; bd dir, Nat Asn Black Pub Admin; vpres, Pa Coalition 100 Black Women; chair, Nat Asn Securities Professionals, 1996-97; vis comt, Univ Louisville Bus Sch, 1998; co-chair, United Way SE Pa, 1998; bd dirs, chair, Nominating & Governance Comt, Erie Ins Co; chmn & bd dir, Delancey Capital Group LP. **Honors/Awds:** Urban Ed Fel, Louisville Bd Educ, 1971; Revlon Business Woman of the Year, 1995; Woman of Achievement Award, Girl Scouts Am, 1996; inducted, Distinguished Hall of Alumni, W KY Univ, 1996. **Special Achievements:** First Black Female Sloan Fellow at Massachusetts Institute of Technology, 1979.

GARRISON-JACKSON, ZINA LYNNA
Tennis player, association executive, manager. **Personal:** Born Nov 16, 1963, Houston, TX; married Willard Jackson, Sep 21, 1989 (divorced 1997). **Career:** Tennis player (retired), tennis coach, manager; Prof tennis player, 1982-97; The Zina Garrison All Ct Tennis Acad, founder & chmn, pres & player develop coach, 1993-; Adult Training Camps & Clins, 1997-; USA Nat Team, head coach, 1999; Minority Excellence Training Camps, 1999-; Ace Player Develop Prog, co-founder; Womens Sports Legend, partner; Fed Cup, asst coach, 1999-; Womens Tennis Coach US Olympic Team Fed Cup, head coach, 2004-06. **Orgs:** USTA Tennis & Educ Fed Founding Bd; USTA; USTA Olympic Comt; Womens Tennis Asn; Alpha Kappa Alpha Sorority Inc; US Pres Coun Phys Fitness Sports; Zina Garrison Found; Presidents Coun on Physical Fitness & Sports, 1994. **Honors/Awds:** ITF Junior of the Year Award, 1981; Olympics, Doubles, gold medal, Singles, bronze medal, 1988; Wimbledon, runner-up, 1990; Family Circle Community Service Award, 1992; Family Circle Community Service Award,1992; Tennis Educational Merit Award, 1993; USTA Bowl Service Award For Community Service, 1998; Texas Tennis Hall Of Fame, 1998; African-American Ethnic Hall of Fame, 2004; Texas Professional Athletes of All Time, 2004. **Business Phone:** (713)857-3167.

GARRITY, MONIQUE P.
Educator. **Personal:** Born Mar 26, 1941; divorced. **Educ:** Mary grove Col, BA, 1963; Boston Col, PhD, 1970. **Career:** Educator (retired); Metro Area Planning Coun, Boston, state analyst, 1965; Univ Mass, from asst prof to assoc prof; Wellesley Col, asst prof, 1970-71; Econ Res Unit, instr; OECD Paris, cons. **Orgs:** Regional chmn, Caucus of Black Econ, 1971-72; dir, Black Econ Res Ctr; Am Scholar Coun; Fulbright Hayes Sr Lectureship Ave, Univ Dakar, 1974-75; consult, Guinea-Bissau, 1978. **Honors/Awds:** Research Grant to Haiti, Yale Univ, 1972-73.

GARTIN, CLAUDIA L.
Judge. **Career:** Judge (retired); 36th Dist Ct, Detroit, judge, 1987-00. *

GARTRELL, BERNADETTE A
Lawyer. **Personal:** Born Jun 21, 1945, Plainfield, NJ; daughter of Barnett (deceased) and Doryse Laws. **Educ:** Howard Univ, BA, 1967, Sch Law, JD, 1970. **Career:** US Dept Housing & Urban Develop, atty-adv, 1970-71; DC Corp Coun, asst corp coun, 1971-73; Mitchell, Shorter & Gartrell, managing partner, 1973-85; Leftwich Moore & Douglas, coun, 1985-87; Gartrell, Alexander & Gebhardt, managing partner, 1987-92; Gartrell & Assoc, managing partner, 1992-. **Orgs:** Bd dirs, Trial Lawyers Asn Metrop, WA, DC; Am Trial Lawyers Asn; Md Trial Lawyers Asn; Nat Asn Black Women Atty; Nat Bar Asn, Greater Wash Area Chap, Women Lawyers Div; Wash Bar Asn; J Franklyn Bourne Bar Asn; Alpha Kappa Alpha; Md Bar Asn. **Home Addr:** 8016 Ellingson Dr, Chevy Chase, MD 20815, **Home Phone:** (301)776-9078. **Business Addr:** Managing Partner, Gartrell & Associates, 8401 Colesville Rd Suite 620, Silver Spring, MD 20910, **Business Phone:** (301)589-8855.

GARTRELL, LUTHER R.
Engineer. **Personal:** Born Aug 20, 1940, Washington, GA. **Educ:** NC A&T State Univ, BSEE, 1964; Old Dominion Univ, MEEE. **Career:** NASA Langley Res Ctr, res engr, currently. **Orgs:** Nat Asn Advan Colored People; Inst Elec & Electronics Engrs; Am Inst Aeronaut & Astronaut; Va Acad Sci NASA publ. **Honors/Awds:** Special Achievement Award, NASA. **Business Addr:** Research Engineer, NASA, Langley Research Center, 100 NASA Rd, Hampton, VA 23681.*

GARVIN-LESLIE, PENOLA M
Physician. **Educ:** Wayne State Univ, attended; MD. **Career:** Oakwood Hosp &Med Ctr, Wayne State Univ, residency; Barbara Ann Ctr Family Med, med dir, currently; pvt pract, currently. **Business Addr:** Physician, 15565 Northland Dr Suite 1080 E, Southfield, MI 48075, **Business Phone:** (248)905-5470.*

GARY, HOWARD V
Executive. **Career:** Howard Gary & Co, pres, prin & chief exec officer; Hvg Investment Corp, pres, prin & chief exec officer, currently. **Business Addr:** President, Principal & Chief Executive Officer, HVG Investment Corporation, 4141 N Miami Ave, Miami, FL 33127, **Business Phone:** (305)571-1380.

GARY, KATHYE J.
Opera singer. **Personal:** Born in Anderson, SC; daughter of Colletha Lee Richardson; divorced; children: Russell Alexander, William Rodney & Charles Reginald. **Educ:** Forrest Bus Col, secretarial sci, 1971; Morris Brown Col, elec engineering, 1988. **Career:** Morris Brown Col, admin asst, 1990-00, dir alumni affairs, 2000; NY Harlem Opera Theatre, Actor, "Madame C.J.,"; cast mem/understudy, 1994-; Mt Carmel Baptist Church, soloist, 1998-. **Orgs:** Advisor, Delta Omicron Int Music Fraternity, 1993-96; Spec performer, Alpha Kappa Alpha, 1998-02. **Honors/Awds:** Outstanding Young Women of America, 1981. **Home Addr:** 5112 Hantcrest Dr SW, Mableton, GA 30126, **Home Phone:** (770)948-2480. *

GARY, DR. LAWRENCE EDWARD
Educator. **Personal:** Born May 26, 1939, Union Springs, AL; son of Ed and Henrietta Mays; married Dr Robenia Baker, Aug 8, 1969; children: Lisa Che, Lawrence Charles Andre & Jason Edward. **Educ:** Tuskegee Inst, BS, 1963; Univ Mich, MPA 1964, MSW, 1967, PhD, 1970. **Career:** Mich Econ Opportunity Prog, staff asst, 1964; Univ Mich, lectr, asst prof, 1968-71; Howard Univ, asst vpres acad affairs, 1971-72, dir prof, Inst Urban Affairs & Res, 1972-90, prof social work, 1985-; Va Commonwealth Univ, the Samuel S Wurtzel prof, 1990-92. **Orgs:** Action bd Am Public Health Asn, 1973-74; bd dir, DC Inst Ment Hygiene, 1976-84; ed bd, Jour Social Work, 1977-81; Health Brain Trust Black Congressional Caucus, 1977-87; publ bd Coun Social Work Educ, 1982-87; consult ed Jour Social Work, 1985-90; social welfare adv bd, Nat Urban League, 1985-89; bd mgt, Howard Univ Press, 1987-; youth adv bd, Lilly Endowment Inc, 1987-; bd mem, Child Welfare Inst, 1988-91; ed bd, Jour Teaching Social Work, 1987-; bd trustees, St Paul Am Church, 1984-; adv bd, DC Comm Pub Health, 1984-87; vis comm, Sch Social Work, Univ Mich, 1991-; Alpha Phi Alpha Fraternity Inc; Coun Social Work Educ, 1992-95; chair, Fac Develop Comt, Howard Univ. **Honors/Awds:** Distinguished Alumni Award, Nat Asn Equal Opportunity Higher Educ, 1979; Eminent Scholar, Va State Univ, 1982; Outstanding Publication, Nat Asn of Black Social Workers, 1983; Labor of Love Award, Nat Head Start Asn, 1984; Eminent Scholar, Norfolk State Univ, 1986; Henry & Lucy Moses Distinguished Visiting Professor, Hunter Col NY 1986-87; Coun Social Work Educ, 1988-89; Founder's Medallion, Nat Asn Social Workers, 1988; Distinguished Alumni Award, Nat Asn Equal Opportunity Higher Educ, 1988; Merit Award, Tuskegee Univ Alumni, 1991; Galt Visiting Scholar, VA Dept Ment Health, 1994; Distinguished Scholar Social Work, Albany State Col, GA, 1994; Distinguished Research Award, Howard Univ, 1995; Distinguished Recent Contributions to Social Work Award, Coun Social Work Educ, 1996; Distinguished Alumni Award, Univ Mich, Ann Arbor, 2001. **Special Achievements:** Author: Mental HTH: A Challenge to Black Community, 1978; Black Men, 1981. **Business Addr:** Professor, Howard University, School of Social Work, 601 Howard Pl NW, Washington, DC 20059, **Business Phone:** (202)806-7300.

GARY, MELVIN L
Psychologist. **Personal:** Born Apr 12, 1938, Brownsville, PA; son of Joseph Gary and Marie Hood; married Juneau Gloria Mahan; married Lanetta Jean Scott (divorced 1981); children: Joseph Tyler. **Educ:** Haverford Col, BA, 1961; OH State Univ, MA, 1964, PhD, 1967. **Career:** Veterans Admin Hosp, psychol trainee, 1964-65; Ohio State Univ, res assoc, Dept Psych & Ctr Voc & Tech Educ, 1965-66; Temple Univ, asst prof, 1968-69; Rutgers State Univ, assoc dean stud affairs, 1971-72, assoc prof, dept psychol, 1973-, assoc dir, off budget & planning, assoc dean & dean acad affairs, Livingston Col, 1977-80, fac senator. **Orgs:** AAAS; Am Asn Univ Professors, Am Psychol Asn; Asn Black Psychologists; Soc Psychol Study Social Issues. **Honors/Awds:** Hon men Woodrow Fels, 1961; Soc of Sigma Xi, 1968; fel, Am Coun on Educ Fel UCLA, 1974. **Home Addr:** 32 Bowsprit Dr, Bayville, NJ 08721.

GARY, SEKOU
Lawyer. **Personal:** Son of Willie and Gloria. **Educ:** NC Central Univ, BA, 1995; Quinnipiac Univ Sch Law, JD, 1999. **Career:** Gary, Williams, Parenti, Finney, Lewis, McManus, Watson, & Sperando, PL, partner & atty, 1999-; private practice, currently. **Orgs:** Kappa Alpha Psi Fraternity Inc; Nat Bar Asn; Fla Bar. **Business Phone:** (772)283-8260.

GARY, TANISHA
Lawyer. **Personal:** Daughter of Willie. **Educ:** Spelman Col, BA, political sci, 1996; Quinnipiac Univ Sch Law, JD, 1999. **Career:** Gary, Williams, Parenti, Finney, Lewis, McManus, Watson, & Sperando, PL, assoc atty, 1999-. **Orgs:** Am Bar Asn; Nat Bar Asn; St Lucie Co Bar Asn; Alpha Kappa Alpha Sorority Inc; S FL Chap; Nat Alumnae Asn Spellman Col; Florida Bar, 2000; Fla Bar Asn; exec dir, Gary Found. **Honors/Awds:** Magna Cum Laude, Spelman Col, 1996; Earl Warren Legal Educ Opportunity Fel, 1997-99. **Business Addr:** Associate Attorney, Gary, Williams, Parenti, Finney, Lewis, McManus, Watson, & Sperando, PL, 221 E Osceola St, Stuart, FL 34994, **Business Phone:** (772)283-8260.

GARY, TIM
Manager. **Career:** Nordstrom Inc, gen mgr, regional vpres, currently. **Business Addr:** General Manager, Mountain Region Nordstrom Inc, 8465 Park Meadows Ctr Dr, Lone Tree, CO 80124, **Business Phone:** (303)799-3400.*

GARY, WILLIE E.
Lawyer, chairperson, chief executive officer. **Personal:** Born in Eastman, GA; son of Turner and Mary; married Gloria Royal Gary; children: Kenneth, Sekou, Ali, Kobie. **Educ:** Shaw Univ, bus admin, 1971; NC Cent Univ Law Sch, JD, 1974; Shaw Univ, LLD, 1992. **Career:** Gary, Williams, Parenti, Finney & Taylor, atty, sr partner; Gary Enterprises, pres; Black Family Channel, Major Broadcasting Cable Network, chmn & chief exec officer, currently. **Orgs:** Bd trustees, chmn, Shaw Univ, 1987-. **Honors/Awds:** Trumpet Award, 1997. **Special Achievements:** Donated 10 million dollars to Shaw University, the largest cash donation given to an African American university, 1992. **Business Addr:** Chief Executive Officer, Chairman, Black Family Channel, 800 Forrest St NW, Atlanta, GA 30318, **Business Phone:** (404)350-2509.*

GASH, SAMUEL LEE, JR.
Football player, football coach. **Personal:** Born Mar 7, 1969, Hendersonville, NC; married Kate; children: Samantha Leigh & Samuel Kolby. **Educ:** Pa State Univ, liberal arts. **Career:** Football player (retired), Football coach; New England Patriots, running back, 1992-97; Buffalo Bills, running back, 1998-99, 2003; Baltimore Ravens, running back, 2000-02; Detroit Lions, asst spl coach, 2007, running backs coach, 2008-. **Honors/Awds:** Pro Bowl selection. 1998, 1999; Ed Block Courage Award, 1996. **Business Addr:** Running Backs Coach, Detroit Lions, 222 Republic Dr, Allen Park, MI 48101, **Business Phone:** (313)216-4000.

GASKIN, DR. FRANCES CHRISTIAN
Business owner, nurse. **Personal:** Born Feb 7, 1936, New York, NY; daughter of Therese Farrelly Christian and Clement J Christian; married Conrad A, Sep 14, 1957; children: Conrad II, Tracy & Troy. **Educ:** Fordham Hosp Sch Nursing, Bronx, NY,

diploma, 1957; Hunter Col, City Univ New York, New York, NY, BS, 1962; A delphi Univ, Garden City, New York, NY, MS, 1970; Fordham Univ, New York, NY, PhD, 1982. **Career:** New York Univ, New York, NY, adj lectr, 1978-79; Long Island Univ,Brooklyn, NY, asst prof, 1979-81; Regents Col Prog Albany, NY, prof, 1981-82; Hostos Community Col, Bronx, NY, prof, dir, 1983-85; Melanin Plus, hair care & skin products, 1986-; New York Tech Col, Brooklyn, NY, adj prof, 1991-; Univ New York, New Patty, asst prof, 1992-95; Brook haven Nat Lab, res scientist, 1993-; Frances Christian Gaskin Inc, founder & pres, currently. **Orgs:** Hunter Alumni Asn, 1962-; A delphi Alumni Asn, 1970-; Fordham Alumni Asn, 1982-; Phi Delta Kappa Frat, 1982-; Sigma Theta Tau, Int Hon Soc, 1984-; Soc Cosmetic Chemists, 1988-; Black Nurses Asn Capital Dist; Nat Black Nurses Asn, 1991-. **Honors/Awds:** Drum Major for Peace, Justice Our Lady Charity RC Church, 1979; Mabel K Staupers (Nursing), Omicron Chap, Chi Eta Phi Soc, 1984; US Patent, protectant composition & method, US Patent and Trademark Office, 1989; presented personal experience as an inventor, State of NY Legislative Resolution, Senator Farlee, 1991. **Business Addr:** President, Frances Christian Gaskin Inc, 298 State St Suite 2a, Albany, NY 12210-2033.

GASKIN, JEANINE
Manager. **Personal:** Born Dec 11, 1945, Detroit, MI; married Harry Thomas Gaskinn III. **Educ:** Univ Mich, BA, 1971. **Career:** Manager (retired); Detroit News, personal asst, 1966-69; Detroit Bd Educ, teacher, 1970-71; Detroit Med Hosp, personal asst, 1971-74; Harper-Grace Hosp, human resource rep, 1976. **Orgs:** Univ Mich Alumni Asn; ed com, Coleman Young Cent Conf Com; secy, Blenheim Forest Comt Coun; Northwest Orgn Detroit; Am Personal Guide Asn; Nat Employ Coun Asn; Asn Non white Concerns Personal & Guide; Fed Soc Detroit Inst Arts; Nat Hist Soc, 1975. **Honors/Awds:** National Honorary Society Award, 1964; Citzenship Award, 1964; Scholarship Award, 1964; Archdiocesan Development Fund Writing Award, 1964. *

GASKINS, DR. HENRY JESSE
School administrator. **Personal:** Born Feb 27, 1935, Washington, DC; son of William Gaskins; married Mary Ann Brown, Apr 14, 1961; children: Phyllis, Gregory, Henry J II, Derek J & Kendra L. **Educ:** Int Univ, BA; Nova Col, PhD, educ, 1978. **Career:** Libr Cong, supvr, 1957-97; Freedom Youth Acad, pres, chief exec officer, founder, 1980-. **Orgs:** Intl Acad & Professional Soc. **Honors/Awds:** President of the US, Honored for After School Program, 1987; Southeast Neighbors Community Award, Outstanding Community Service, 1989; President of the US, Volunteer Action Award, 1990; Mayor Marion Barry, Certificate of Commendation, 1990; Education Award, Washington Space Business Round table, 1994; Sister Clara Mohammed Education Award; Delta Sigma Theta Educational Development Award; Lambda Kappa Mu Community Service Award;Kimberly Clark's, "Kleenex Says Bless You" Award; Dossier Magazine's Philanthropy Award; Newsweek Magazine,'s "Good Neighbor" and "Unsung Hero"Awards; Nat Asn of Blacks in Criminal Justice Award; The Questers, Inc.Distinguished Service Award; The Washington Space Business Round table Education Award; United Planning Organization's Martin Luther King, Jr.Community Service Award; Volunteer Action Award. **Business Addr:** President, Founder, Freedom Youth Academy Inc, 1600 Morris Rd SE, Washington, DC 20020, **Business Phone:** (202)584-3012.

GASKINS, LOUISE ELIZABETH
Educator. **Personal:** Born Jun 2, 1930, Raleigh, NC; daughter of Joseph B F Cutchin (deceased) and Claytae V Hall Watson (deceased); children: Pamela, Donna Gaskins-Wetherbee & Eric. **Educ:** NC Cent Univ, BS, 1951; Fitchburg State, MEd, 1972. **Career:** Educator (retired); Atkins High Sch, math teacher, 1951-54; AEC Germ, teacher, 1957-58; Ger, teacher, 1959; Wash State, teacher, 1960-61; Ligon High Sch, teacher, 1961-62; Army Educ Ctr Ger, teacher, 1964; Ayer High Sch, teacher math, 1965-72; Ayer Jr High Sch, guid counr, 1972-75, prin, 1975-91; Ayer Pub Schs, admin & prin, 1975-91. **Orgs:** Ayers Tchr Asn, 1965-91; Nat Educ Asn, 1965-; Mass Teachers Asn, 1965-; past fac rep, Professional Asn, 1966-70; past advr, Afro Am Cult Club, 1967-74; N Cent Mass Guide Asn, 1968-75; Mass Sch Couns Asn, 1968-75; past mem, Adm Selec Team, 1970-73; past mem, Prof Negot Team, 1970-75; past chmn, Supt Sel Comt, 1971-72; past mem, bd dir, Adven House, 1973-75; Mass Jr H Middle Sch Prin Asn, 1975-91; state delegate, Nat Educ Asn Conv, 1975-; dir, Mass Nat Educ Asn, 1976-85; Nat Sec Sch Prin Asn; New Eng Asn Black Educr; Black Polit Task Force; Mass Dept Educ Study Com Jr High & Middle Sch; Mass Dept Educ Evaluation Strategy Group Handicapped Students; vpres Montachusett Region Nat Asn Advan Colored People, 1977-78; bd mem, Ctr Well Being Inc, 1980-; MTAR, 1991-. **Honors/Awds:** National Science Found Grant, 1966; Human and Civil Rights Award, Massachusetts Teachers Assn, 1988, 1998; Teachers Make the Difference, Christa Corrigan McAuliffe Ctr for Educ & Teaching Excellence, 1991; Louise E Gaskins Achievement Award, MA Teachers Assn, 1999. **Home Addr:** 35 Boston Rd, Groton, MA 01450. *

GASKINS, MARY ANN
School administrator. **Personal:** Born May 18, 1940, Washington, DC; daughter of Paul F Brown; married Henry J, Apr 14, 1961; children: Henry J II, Derek J & Kendra L. **Educ:** Nova Col, BA, educ, 1989. **Career:** NASA Hq Adv, comm specialist, 1964-95; Freedom Youth Acad, co-founder & exec dir, 1980-. **Honors/Awds:** Martin Luther King Jr Community Service Award, United Planning Orgn, 1996; Educational Award, Questors, Inc, 1995; Hall of Fame, DC Comn Women, 1993; Volunteer Action Award, Pres US, 1990; Honored for After School Program, Pres US, 1987. **Business Addr:** Executive Director, Freedom Youth Academy Inc, 1600 Morris Rd SE, Washington, DC 20020, **Business Phone:** (202)889-1682.

GASKINS, PERCELL (PERCELL MCGAHEE GASKINS)
Football player. **Personal:** Born Apr 25, 1972, Daytona Beach, FL. **Educ:** Kans State Univ. **Career:** Football palyer (Retired); St Louis Rams, linebacker, 1996; Carolina Panthers, linebacker, 1997. *

GASKINS, PERCELL MCGAHEE. **See GASKINS, PERCELL.**

GASPARD, DR. PATRICE T
Pediatrician. **Personal:** Born Jun 30, 1954, New Orleans, LA; daughter of Octave and Shirley; married LeRoy Maxwell Graham; children: Arianne Marie & LeRoy M III. **Educ:** Tulane Univ, BS, 1976, Sch Med, MD, 1980. **Career:** Fitzsimmons Army Med Ctr, pediat residency; Ft Knox Ky, chief inpatient servs; Fitzsimmons Army Med Ctr, fel adolescent med; Adolescence Med Clin, FAMC, chief; Morehouse Sch Med, Adjunct Clinic Asst Prof, pediats, 1997-; Kaiser Permanente, pediats & adolescent med, physician, currently; pvt pract, currently. **Orgs:** Certified Am Bd Pediats, 1984; Am Acad Pediats; Am Med Asn, Nat Med Asn, Soc Adolescent Med; Mary Hall Freedom House Inc, adv coun chair, currently. **Special Achievements:** First black elected to Alpha Omega Alpha Honor Medical Soc at Tulane Univ. **Military Serv:** AUS, 1980-; Army Commendation Medal, 1st Oak Leaf Cluster. **Business Addr:** Physician Pediatrics, Adolescent Medicine, Kaiser Permanente, 20 Glenlake Pkwy, Atlanta, GA 30328, **Business Phone:** (770)677-6032.

GASTON, DR. ARNETT W
Clinical psychologist, educator. **Personal:** Born Apr 1, 1938, New York, NY; married Sandra; children: Robyn & Brett. **Educ:** AA, 1970; John Jay Col Criminal Justice, BA, 1971; City Univ NY, MA, 1976, MPh, 1979, PhD, 1981. **Career:** Prince Georges County, Md, dir corrections; Mayor's Crisis Task Force, exec asst comnr; Minimum Stand, bd rev; NY State Stand & Goals Criminal Justice Planning Comn; Honolulu Symphony Orchestra, 1957; composer; author; musician; conductor; City Univ NY, John Jay Col Criminal Justice, prof psychol & forensic studies; New York Dept Corrections, first dep comnr, chief mgt planning, chief ricers island, comndg officer training acad, clin psychologist; Am Univ, Wash, DC, fac; West Point Military Acad; Univ Md, Dept Criminol & Criminal Justice, adj assoc prof, currently, fac adv, currently; West Point Mil Acad, John Jay Satellite Prog, fac; Int Criminal Justice, consult, currently. **Orgs:** Nat Asn Black Psychologists; 100 Black Men; Nat Asn Black Criminal Justice; Am Psychol Asn; Am Correctional Asn. **Military Serv:** USAF, 1956-59. **Business Addr:** Adjunct Associate Professor, University of Maryland College Park, Department of Criminology & Criminal Justice, New York City Dept Corrections, 2220 LeFrak Hall, College Park, MD 20742-8235.

GASTON, REV. DR. JOSEPH ALEXANDER
School administrator, clergy. **Personal:** Born Jan 3, 1928, Winnsboro, SC; son of John N and Lilla R; married Theresa Dutch, Oct 5, 1974. **Educ:** Johnson C Smith Univ, BS, 1949; Johnson C Smith Seminary, Mdiv, 1952; Univ Denver, MA, 1960; Mich State Univ, PhD, 1970. **Career:** School administrator, clergy (Retired); Booneville Edward Webb Presbyterian Church, stud pastor, pastor, 1951-52; Bd Nat Missions (UPCUSA), Sunday sch missionary, 1953-56; Johnson C Smith Univ, dir, promotions univ, asst dean men, vip, stud affairs, exec pres, 1956-85; Catawba Inter-Presbyterian Prog Agency, exec presbyter, 1985-88; Johnson C Smith Seminary, admin dean, 1988-93. **Orgs:** Catawba Inter-Presbytery Prog Agency, chair, personnel div, 1972-77; Div, Voc & Prof Develop, Piedmont Synod, chair, 1978-80; Presbytery Catawba, stated clerk, 1983, chair, personnel div, 1972-77; Career & Personal Counseling Serv Bb, Synod NC, 1986-88; Urban Mission Support Team Metro/Urban Ministry, 1986-87; Bd Pensions (PCUSA), 1987-89; Church Voc Ministry Unit Com, 1987-92; Comn Theol Educ, 1988-93; Presbyterian Church, Comn Mission responsibility through investment, 1989-94. **Honors/Awds:** Distinguished Alumnus, Johnson C Smith Theol Seminary, 2006.

GASTON, LINDA SAULSBY (LINDA E SAULSBY)
Association executive. **Personal:** Born Jun 15, 1947, San Francisco, CA; daughter of Arvis Dixon Harris and Harvey Harris; married James, Sep 27, 1985; children: Loren Saulsby & Leslie Saulsby. **Educ:** City Col San Francisco, San Francisco, Calif, AA; State Univ New York, Albany, New York, BA; St Mary?s Col Calif, MA, lib studies. **Career:** Morris Davis & Co, mgr admin, 1978-80; Linda Saulsby Mgt Consult, Oakland, Calif, staff, owner, 1981-83; Coopers & Lybrand, Wash, DC, Tucson Ariz, dir personnel & admin, 1983-86; Nat Asn Black Acct, Wash, DC, nat exec dir, 1986-1989; Gen Elec Co, mgr, gen mgr, pres, sr vpres; Exploratorium, dir human resources & orgn develop, 1997-99; Les Consult Group, orgn develop, strategic planning & human resources consult, 1999-; Univ Calif, Haas Sch Bus, lectr, 2005-; Univ San Francisco, Sch Prof Studies, lectr, 2005-; St Mary?s Col Calif, actg prog dir, 2006-07, thesis adv, 2007-08; Commun Dept & Col Sem Dept, adj assoc prof, currently, adj assoc prof & thesis advisor, Sch Extended Educ, reg dir corp & community rels, currently; Univ Ariz, Eller Col Mgt, adj lectr, 2007-. **Orgs:** Bd dirs, YWCA, Oakland, Calif, 1981-83, Tucson, Ariz, 1985-86; Howard Univ, Sch Bus Adv Bd, 1987-; pres, Longmead Crossing Homeowners Asn, 1988-; Nat Community Asn Inst, 1988-; Price Waterhouse & Co Minority Recruiting Task Force, 1989-; bd mem & chair, Finance Comt, E Bay Agency C, Oakland, Calif. **Honors/Awds:** President's Membership Council Award, Greater Wash DC Bd Trade, 1985. **Special Achievements:** Article Published: Spectrum (Jour Nat Asn Black Acct), 1987 & 1988. **Home Phone:** (202)598-0065. **Business Phone:** (925)631-4000.

GASTON, MACK CHARLES
Military leader, association executive. **Personal:** Born Jul 17, 1940, Dalton, GA; son of John and Felicia Gilliard; married Lillian Bonds, Aug 15, 1965 (deceased); children: Sonja Marie. **Educ:** Tuskegee Inst, BS, Electronics, 1964; US Naval War Col, grad level cert, 1977; US Indust Col Armed Forces, dipl, 1983; Marymount Col, MBA, 1984. **Career:** Military leader (retired); USN, electronic officer/combat info officer USS Buck, 1965-67, eng officer USS O'Brien, 1967-69, mat officer/squad engr destroyer sqd five staff, 1969-71, personal aide/aide asst navy dir res & develop test & eval office cno, 1971-73, exec officer USS Conyngham, 1974-76, commanding officer USS Cochrane, 1977-79; br head jr off assignment Navy mil pers command, 1979-81, commanding officer USS Cone, 1981-82, head surface warfare tra br off cno, 1983-84; USN, dir equal opportunity div; commanding officer battle cruiser, USS Josephus Daniels, CG 27, 1986-88; chief naval opers strategic studies group, CNO Fel, 1988-89; surface warfare manpower & training dir, 1989-90; Defense Nuclear Agency, comdr, field command, 1990-92; Naval Training Ctr, Great Lakes, IL, comdr, 1992-95. **Orgs:** Jr Deacon & Sunday Sch Teacher Hopewell Baptist Church, 1953-64; counr & career planner, Nat Naval Off Asn, Wash, DC, 1977-; Sunday Sch Teacher Greater Zion Baptist Church, 1981-85; US Naval Inst, 1987-; Flag & Gen Officer's Mess, 1991-; pres, Great Lakes Navy/Marine Corps Relief Soc, 1992-; chmn, Great Lakes Combined Fed Campaign, 1992-; chmn, Drug Education Youth, DEFY, 1992-; exec bd, United Way Lake County, 1992-; Northern Ill Coun Alcoholism & Substance Abuse, 1992-; bd dir, USO Ill, 1992-; exec comt, Lake County Econ Develop Comn, 1992-; Rotary One, 1992-; exec comt, Fed Exec Bd, 1992-; Naval Order US, 1992-; Surface Navy Asn; Nat Military Family Asn, 1992-; bd dirs, Am Red Cross, 1992-; Retired Officer's Asn, 1992-; Am Legion, 1993-; Tin Can Sailors, 1993-; Navy Club US, 1993-; Nat Strategy Forum; Navy Memorial Found; N Chicago Citizens Against Drugs & Alcohol Abuse; N Chicago C Future; Tuskegee Alumni Asn; Lake County Learns; trustee, Benedictine Univ; chair, Military Officers Asn Am. **Honors/Awds:** Ga Educ Hall of Fame, Dalton, 1990; Dalton Baugh Award, Mass Bay Area Navy League, 1992; Ga State renamed portion of N Dalton Bypass Hwy, Admiral Mack Gaston Parkway, 1992; Nat Image Inc President's Award, 1992; Nat Asn Advan Colored People Wilkins Meritorious Service Award, 1994; James Kemper Humanitarian Service Award, Northern Ill Coun Alcoholism & Substance Abuse, 1994. **Military Serv:** USN, rear admiral, 28 yrs; Defense Superior Serv Medal; Meritorious Serv Medal, two awards; Navy Commendation Medal, two awards, one with Combat "V"; Navy Achievement Medal; Nat Defense Serv Medal, two medals; Vietnamese Gallantry Cross; Vietnamese Serv Medal with 4 Campaign Stars; Republic Vietnam Campaign Medal; Sea Serv Ribbon. **Business Addr:** Chair, Military Officers Association of America, 201 N Wash St, Alexandria, VA 22314.

GASTON, DR. MARILYN HUGHES
Physician, educator, administrator. **Personal:** Born Jan 31, 1939, Cincinnati, OH; daughter of Myron Hughes and Dorothy Hughes; married Alonzo; children: Amy & Damon. **Educ:** Miami Univ, AB, zool, 1960; Univ Cincinnati, MD 1964. **Career:** Physician, educator (retired), administrator; Philadelphia Gen Hosp, intern 1965; C Hosp Med Ctr, resident, 1967; Community Pediats, assoc prof, 1968-70; C Hosp Med Ctr, asst dir, 1968, assoc prof pediats, 1972;Cincinnati Comprehensive Sickle Cell Ctr, dir, 1972; Lincoln Heights Health Ctr, med dir, 1973; Inst Med, inductee, 1997; Howard Univ, asst clin prof pediats; NIH Sickle Cell Dis Br Nat Heart Lung & Blood Inst, depbr chief; US Pub Health Serv, asst surgeon gen, rear admiral, Bur Primary Health Care, dir; Gaston & Porter Health Improv Ctr, co-dir, currently. **Orgs:** Am Acad Pediat; United Black Fac Asn; Am Pub Health Asn; med adv bd, State Crippled C Serv; bd trustees, C Health Asn; Pi Kappa Epsilon; med dir, Comn Corps US Pub Health Serv; Nat Med Asn; Inst Med; 9 Tampa Leadership Meeting for Prime Time Sister Circles, Inc, 2008. **Honors/Awds:** Outstanding Black Women Cincinnati, 1974; City's Young Leader of Health, 1974; Harriet Tubman Woman of the Year, 1976; Gaston H et al-Proph Penicillin in Sickle Cell Anemia, New Eng J, 1986; Gaston Scholars, Univ Cincinnati, 1999; Nathan Davis Award, Am Med Asn; Commendation Medal, Pub Health Serv, Dept Health & Human Serv; Outstanding Service Medal, Univ Cincinnati; Distinguished

Alumnae Award; NIH Directors Award; Univ Pa, hon doctorates; Dartmouth Univ, hon doctorates. **Special Achievements:** Marilyn Hughes Gaston Day, City Cincinnati, OH; First African American Woman to Direct a Public Health Service Bureau. **Home Addr:** 8612 Timber Hill Lane, Potomac, MD 20854, **Home Phone:** (301)983-9586. **Business Addr:** Co-Director, The Gaston & Porter Health Improvement Center, 8612 Timber Hill Lane, Potomac, MD 20854, **Business Phone:** (301)765-1942.

GASTON, PATRICIA ELAINE
Journalist. **Personal:** Born Mar 26, 1959, Kansas City, MO; daughter of Charles and Camille Weems; married Keith A Gaston, Aug 29, 1981; children: Erin Michelle, Jonathan. **Educ:** Kans City Community Jr Col, AA, 1979; Univ Kans, BA, journ, 1981. **Career:** Boston Globe, copy ed, 1981; Rochester Ny Democrat & Chronicle, copy ed, 1981-86; Dallas Morning News, asst int ed, 1986; The Wash Post, reporter, 2000. **Orgs:** Journ & Women Symp, 1993-95; Coun Foreign Rels, 2004. **Honors/Awds:** Pulitzer Prize, Int Reporting, 1994. *

GASTON, PATRICK REGINALD
President (Organization). **Personal:** Born Aug 5, 1957, Port Au Prince, Haiti. **Educ:** Univ Mass, BA, mgt, 1984; Northeastern Univ, MBA, 1992; Ecole Superieure de Com, int cert bus. **Career:** Bell Atlantic Commun Inc, asst vpres; Verizon Found, Strategic Alliances, exec dir, pres, 2003-. **Orgs:** Nat Am Adavan Colored People; Found Univ W Indies; Nat Coalition Cancer Survivorship; World Inst Disability; pres & chmn, Am Cancer Soc; William B Price Unit; vol, St Jude C Res Hosp; Nat Children's Latino Inst; Nat Found Women Legislators; Nat Governors Asn. **Business Addr:** President, Verizon Foundation, 1095 Ave Americas Rm 3200, New York, NY 10036, **Business Phone:** 800-360-7955.*

GATERS, DOROTHY L.
Athletic coach. **Personal:** Born Jan 4, 1946, Beulah, MS; daughter of Charlie and Ethel. **Educ:** Crane Community Col, AA, 1966; DePaul Univ, BA, 1969; Gov State Univ, MA,1975. **Career:** John Marshall High Sch, teacher, coach, head coach, currently. **Orgs:** Ill Basketball Coaches Asn; Women's Basketball Coaches Asn; Chicago Basketball Coaches Asn. **Honors/Awds:** Coach of the Yr, Ill Basketball Coaches Asn, Dist 22; Coach of the Yr, Chicago Pub League Basketball Coaches Asn; Women's Basketball Hall of Fame, 2000. **Special Achievements:** Coach National Team US Youth Develop. **Business Addr:** Head Coach, John Marshall High School, Girls Basketball, 3250 W Adams, Chicago, IL 60624.

GATES, AUDREY CASTINE. See Obituaries section.

GATES, CLIFTON W.
Executive. **Personal:** Born Aug 13, 1923, Moscow, AR; son of Lance and Mattie; married Harriet; children: Mark, Lisa. **Educ:** Harris Stowe Col. **Career:** CW Gates Realty, owner & pres, 1959-; Gateway Nat Bank, chmn, 1964-; Lismark Distributing, pres, 1975-. **Orgs:** Bd dirs, Munic Opera; bd dirs, Cardinal Glennon Hosp C; bd dirs, Blue Cross; bd dirs, Boy Scouts Am; bd dirs, Boys Town MO; bd dirs, Conv & Visitors Bur; bd dirs, Press Coun St Louis Univ; bd dirs, Gateway Nat Bank; bd dirs, Local Develop Co; bd dirs, St Louis Comprehensive Health Ctr; Nat Asn Advancement Colored People; bd dirs, Civic Entrepreneurs; Urban League; chmn, St Louis Housing Authority. **Honors/Awds:** Management Award, City Hope Beta Gamma Sigma, Univ MO Chap; St Louis Argus Public Service Award; Hall Of Fame, St Louis, 2001. **Military Serv:** AUS, 1943-45. **Home Addr:** 5855 Lindell Blvd, St Louis, MO 63112. **Business Addr:** President, Gates Realty Investment Company, St Louis, MO 63110.*

GATES, DR. HENRY LOUIS
Editor, writer, educator. **Personal:** Born Sep 16, 1950, Keyser, WV; son of Henry-Louis Gates Sr and Pauline Augusta Coleman; married Sharon Lynn Adams, Sep 1, 1979; children: Maude Augusta & Elizabeth Helen-Claire. **Educ:** Yale Univ, BA (summa cum laude), 1973; Clare Col, Cambridge, England, MA, Eng Lang Lit, 1979, PhD, Eng Lang Lit, 1979. **Career:** Time, London Bur, London, England, staff correspondent, 1973-75; Am Cyanamid Co, Wayne, NJ, pub rels rep, 1975; Yale Univ, New Haven, CT, lectr, Eng & Afro-Am Studies, 1976-79, from asst prof to assoc prof, Eng & Afro-Am Studies, 1979-85; Cornell Univ, Ithaca, NY, prof Eng, Comparative Lit & Africana Studies, 1985-88, WEB Du Bois Prof Lit, 1988-90; Woodrow Wilson National Fel, 1988-90; Duke Univ, Durham, NC, John Spencer Bassett Prof Eng & Lit, 1990; Harvard Univ, WEB Du Bois prof humanities, chmn, African-Am Studies, dir, WEB Du Bois Inst African-Am Res, dir, 1991-, Dept African & African Am Studies, chair, WEB Du Bois Prof Humanities, currently; Author: Figures in Black: Words, Signs & the Racial Self, 1987; The Signifying Monkey: Towards a Theory Afro-Amer Literary Criticism, 1988; Loose Canons: Notes on the Culture Wars, 1991; Colored People: A Memoir, 1994; The Future of the Race, 1996; Thirteen Ways of Looking At A Black Man, 1997; America Behind the Color Line: Dialogues with African Americans, 2004. Editor: Our Nig, 1983; Black Literature & Literary Theory, 1984; "Race," Writing & Difference, 1986; The Classic Slave Narratives, 1987; The Norton Anthology of African-American Literature, 1996; Series Editor: The Schomburg Library of Nineteenth-Century Black Women Writers, 1988; Co-Editor: Transition: An International Review; Co-Compiler, Wole Soyinka: A Bibliography of Primary & Secondary Sources, 1986; The Trials of Phillis Wheatley: America's First Poet & Her Encounters with the Founding Fathers, 2003; In Search of Hannah Crafts: Critical Essays on the Bondwoman's Narrative, 2004; Civil Rights : An A-to-Z Reference of the Movement that Changed America, 2005; Race & Reason: Black Letters in the Enlightenment, 2007. **Orgs:** Coun Foreign Rels; bd dirs, Lincoln Ctr Theater & Whitney Museum; bd dirs, European Inst Literary & Cultural Studies, 1990-; bd dirs, Am Coun Learned Socs, 1990-; Am Antiquarian Society; Union Writers African Peoples; Asn Documentary Ed; African Roundtable; African Lit Asn; Afro-Am Acad; Am Studies Asn; Asn Study Afro-Am Life & Hist; Caribbean Studies Asn; Col Lang Asn; Modern Language Asn; The Stone Trust; Zora Neale Hurston Soc; Pulitzer Prize Bd; Am Civil Liberties Union Nat Advisory Coun; TransAfrica Forum Scholars Coun; German Am Studies Asn; New England Historic Geneal Soc; Am Philos Soc. **Honors/Awds:** Carnegie Found fel Africa, 1970-71; Phelps fel, Yale Univ, 1970-71; Mellon fel, Yale Univ, 1973-75, 1983-; A Whitney Griswold fel, Yale Univ, 1980; Nat Endowment for the Humanities grants, 1980-84, 1981-82; Rockefeller Found fel, 1980-81; MacArthur Prize fel, MacArthur Found, 1981-86; Whitney Humanities Center fel, 1982-84; Afro-Am Cultural Center Faculty Prize, 1983; Ford Found grant, 1984-85; Zora Neale Hurston Soc Award for Creative Scholar, 1986; Honorable Mention, John Hope Franklin Prize, Am Studies Asn, 1988; Am Book Award, 1989; Anisfield Book Award for Race Rels, 1989; Candle Award, Morehouse Col, 1989; George Polk Award, 1993; Lilliam Smith Award, Southern Lit, 1994; Chicago Tribune Heartland Award, 1994; 22 Honorary Degrees; Distinguished Editorial Achievement, Critical Inquiry, 1996; Tikkun Nat Ethics Award, 1996; The Richard Ellman Lectures, Emory Univ, 1996; Alternative Press Award for Transition, An Int Review, 1995; Natl Medal of Arts, presented by President Clinton, 1998; Bologna New Media Prize, 1999; Multiculturalism Award, Fairleigh Dickinson Univ, 1999; Healthy Lifestyle Award, 2001; Josiah Willard Gibbs Award, 2002; Carl Sandburg Literary Award, 2004; William C. Nell Living Legend Award, Afro-American Museum, 2004; Henry James Award, 2004; PBS Channel Thirteen Annual Award, 2006; Graduate of Distinction, 2006; The Parents' Choice Awards-Gold Award. **Business Addr:** Professor of the Humanities, Harvard University, Department of African & African American Studies, Barker Ctr, 12 Quincy St, Cambridge, MA 02138, **Business Phone:** (617)496-5468.

GATES, JACQUELYN BURCH
Executive. **Personal:** Born Jul 12, 1951, Brooklyn, NY; daughter of Herman Knight and Blanca Knight; children: Antoinette, Anthony & Jacquelyn Tiffany. **Educ:** Univ Ill; Brooklyn Col, BA, 1973; New Sch Univ, Trinity Theol Sem. **Career:** Agency Child Develop, family coun, 1973-76; NY State Supreme Ct, secy to supreme ct justice, 1976-77; JC Penny Corp Hq, employ placement rep, 1977-79; Revlon Inc, personnel admin & recruiter, 1979-81; Paramount Pictures Corp, mgr indust rels, NY, 1981-82; Pepsi Cola Co, mgr prof placement, 1982-83; PepsiCo Inc Purchase, NY, mgr of corp rels; Nynex Mobile Communicators Co, Orangeburg, vpres, Qual & Ethics, 1990-93; Corp Cult Initiatives, dir, 1994-95; NYNEX Corp, vpres ethics; Bell Atlantic, vpres, Ethics Compliance & Diversity; Oakwood Univ, vpres advance & develop; Dukes Energy, vpres div & ethics; World Bank, ethics officer; SOARing LLC, pres & chief exec officer, currently. **Orgs:** Past pres, Nat Asn Negro Bus & Prof Women Club, 1987-91; bd dirs, Oper Reachback; Ethics Officer Asn; vis prof, Black Exec Exchange Prog, Nat Urban League; past pres, Spelman Corp Womens Roundtable; NYNEX Multicultural Asn; bd dirs, Martin Luther King Sr, Citizen Ctr; past pres, Edges Group, 1993-96; adv bd, Bentley Univ; Nat Asn Black Telecommunications ProfS; Black Women Film Preserv Proj., Junior Achievement's Blue Ribbon Ethics Panel. **Honors/Awds:** Student Achievement Award, Brooklyn Young Adults NANBPW, 1965; Achievement Award, Alpha Cosmetologists of Brooklyn, 1979; Nat Youth Achievement Award, Nat Asn Negro Buss & Prof Women Clubs, 1980; Black Achiever, Indust Harlem YMCA, 1984; Sojourner Truth Award, E NY Club Brooklyn NANBPW, 1984; Business Award, Kings Co Club Nat Asn Negro Buss & Prof Women Clubs, 1986; Young Achiever Award, Natl Coun of Women of USA, 1986; NY YWCA, Acad Women Achievers, 1996, Frasernet- Woman of Grace, 2003, Levine Museum of the New South-Women's Hall of Fame, 2004. **Special Achievements:** 100 Young Women of Promise in 21st Century, Good Housekeeping Mag, 1985; Top 100 Black Business & Professional Women in America, Dollars & Sense Mag, 1986; 100 Most Influential Black American, Ebony Mag, 1988-91; amed as one of the "Top 50? companies for Asians, Blacks, Hispanics and Native Americans by Fortune Magazine and named to Latina Style magazine's "Top 50? for professional Hispanic women. Bell Atlantic was also named as one of "America's Top 15? companies for women-owned businesses by the Women's Enterprise Business National Council and was recognized as a "Promising Practice? company by the President's Initiative on Race for its work with employee resource groups, EBONY-Women at the Top of Corporate America, 2001. **Business Addr:** President, Chief Executive Officer, SOARing LLC, PO Box 353, Harvest, AL 35749-0353, **Business Phone:** (704)562-3941.

GATES, JIMMIE EARL
Journalist. **Personal:** Born Jun 3, 1956, Jackson, MS; son of Allen and Birdie Lee; married Pattie Denise Kendrick, Jun 20, 1987; children: April Jimel. **Educ:** Jackson State Univ, BS, 1981, MS. **Career:** Jackson Daily News, staff writer, 1983-86; USA Today, Rosslyn, VA, travel & health update line ed, 1986-87; The Clarion-Ledger, Jackson, MS, staff writer, 1987-. **Orgs:** Jackson Br NAACP, 1985-; pres, Jackson Asn Black Journalists, 1990-91; Soc Prof Journalists, 1990-. **Honors/Awds:** Merit Award, Southern Inst Jour, 1985; AP Community Award, Asniate Press, 1985; AP Community Award SE Region, Asniate Press, 1985; Best of Gannett, The Gannett Corp, 1987. **Business Addr:** Staff Writer, The Clarion Ledger, 311 E Pearl St, Jackson, MS 39205, **Business Phone:** (601)961-7212.

GATES, LEE
Judge. **Educ:** Univ Nevada, Las Vegas, BA, 1974; Univ Colo, JD, 1977. **Career:** Dep dist atty, 1978-81; pvt pract, 1982-86, 1987-91; dep pub defender, 1986-87; chief dist ct judge, 1998-00; Eighth Dist Ct judge, 1991-. **Orgs:** Am Judges Asn; Nat Conf Metrop Courts. **Business Addr:** Judge, Eighth Judicial District Court, 200 S Third St, Las Vegas, NV 89155, **Business Phone:** (702)455-4681.*

GATES, NINA JANE
Manager. **Personal:** Born Jul 27, 1947, Beckley, WV; married Charles W Gates Sr; children: Charles Jr, Stephanie Lee-Ann. **Educ:** Applachian Reg Hosp Sch Nursing, nursing dipl, 1968; Cent State Univ, BS, 1978; Cent Mich Univ, MA, 1983. **Career:** Dayton Sch Pract Nursing, instr, 1975-78; Good Samaritan Hosp & Health Ctr, continuing educ coordr, 1978-80, supr, 1980-86, asst dir clinics, 1986-. **Orgs:** Montgomery County Joint Voc Adv Bd, 1978-; safety serv instr, Am Red Cross, 1978-; leader, Buckeye Girl Scouts, 1983-; reg recording secy, Iota phi Lambda Sorority, 1985-; financial secy, Jack & Jill Am, 1986-; Ambulatory Nurses Asn, 1986-; Delta Sigma Theta Sorority Dayton Alumnae Chap. **Honors/Awds:** Outstanding Young Women of America, 1983.

GATES, OTIS A., III
Executive. **Personal:** Born Feb 26, 1935, Chattanooga, TN; married Barbara L; children: George, Theresa, Todd, Khari. **Educ:** Harvard Col, AB; Harvard Grad Sch Bus Admin, MBA. **Career:** Kaufman & Boad Homes Inc, asst to gen mgr, 1963-64; MI Blue Shield, mgr comput systs & opers, 1964-66; Zayre Corp, mgr comput systs develop, 1966-68; Arthur Andersen & Co, 1969-76, partner 1976-85; Long Bay Mgt Co, chief financial officer, currently. **Orgs:** Youth Serv comt, Mass Bay United Way Fund, 1974-80; bd trustees, Univ Hosp, 1983-90; chmn, Jobs Youth Boston; bd dirs, Danforth Mus; Harvard Bus Sch African Am Alumni Asn. **Military Serv:** USAF, capt reserve. **Business Addr:** Chief Financial Officer, Long Bay Management Company, 351 Mass Ave, Boston, MA 02115.*

GATES, DR. PAUL EDWARD
Oral surgeon. **Personal:** Born Aug 16, 1945, Keyser, WV; son of Henry Louis Sr and Pauline Coleman; married Gemina; children: Eboni, Jennifer & Aaron Pierce. **Educ:** Potomac State Jr Col, AA, 1964; WVa Univ, BA, 1966 WVa Univ Sch Dentistry, DDS, 1970; NY Univ Sch Dentistry, 1971; Harlem Hosp Ctr, Resd, 1970-73; Fairleigh Dickinson, MBA, 1992. **Career:** Fairleigh Dickinson Dent Sch, oral surgeon, 1973, asst clin prof, 1973-76, dir, minority affairs, 1979-86, prof, 1986, asst vpres acad admin, 1986-87; acting dean Col Dent Med, l988-89; from asst to pres, health planning & policy, l988-89; Bronx-Lebanon Hosp, Bronx, NY, dir, oral & maxillofacial surg & dept dentistry, 1990, chmn, currently; Albert Einstein Col Med, assoc prof med, 1994-. **Orgs:** ADA Stud, 1966-70, 73-77; Xi Psi Phi Frat; WVa Univ Alumni Asn; stud Am Dent Asn; Passaic Co Dent Soc, 1973-77; NJ Dept Dentistry, 1973-77; bd dir, INCAA, 1973-74; NJ Dent Soc, 1973; Am Bd Oral Surg Dipl, 1975; Am Soc Oral Surg, 1977; Am Soc Dent Anesthesiol; Am Asn Hosp Dentistry, 1977; NJ Soc Dent Anesthesia; Harlem Hosp Soc Oral Surg; attg oral surgeon St Joseph's Hosp; NJ Dept Dentistry, 1973-77; bd dir, INCAA, 1973-74; ed, Jour Passaic Co Dent Soc; chief, oral & maxillacial surg & assoc chmn, Dept Dent St Joseph's Hosp & Med Ctr; bd trustees, St Joseph's Hops & Med Ctr, 1984-87; N Dent Asn Commonwealth Dent Soc; dir, mny scholarship program, Nat Dent Asn Found, 1990-92; bd Governors, WVa Univ, 2000-; bd trustees, Bronx AIOs Soc, 2001; bd dirs, NY AHEC, 2001-; MAN Etc, Inc. **Honors/Awds:** OKU Nat Dent Honor Soc, 1980; Am Coun Educ Fellow, 1984-85; "Minority Recruitment and Retention at FDU" Journal Nat Dent Asn 1988; Fellow Am Col, Dentist 1989; Outstanding Young Men in Amica, 1970, 1980; Outstanding Oral Surgery Faculty Award, 1977-81; Outstanding Achievement, Bronx-Lebanon Hosp, Employees African Descent, 1992-93; Distinguished Practitioner Dentisty, Nat Acad Practice, 1997; Sixth Annual Achievement Award, Nat Pro-Am Inc, 1997. **Special Achievements:** Published "Meningitis as a Result Post Extraction Infection Report a Case". Journal Oral Surgery 1972; "Visceral Kaposis's Sarcoma presenting with Gingival Lesions" Oral Surgery Oral Med & Oral Pathology 1980, "Oral Lesions in Crohn's Disease, Report a Case" NY

State Dent Jrnl, "The Dent Cartridge-Its Contents & Clinical Implications" DMD 1980, "Calcium Nutrition & the Aging Process, A Review" Journal Gerodontology, 1985, "The Dent Cartridge It's Contents & Clinical Implications" DMD 1985. **Home Phone:** (973)835-0593. **Business Phone:** (718)901-8115 Ext 8110.

GATES, REGINALD
President (Organization). **Career:** Bishop Col, admin, United Negro Col Fund, fundraiser & mkt specialist; Dallas County Community Col, sr acct exec; Fort Worth Metrop Black Chamber Com, pres & chief exec officer; Dallas Black Chamber Com, pres & coo, currently. **Business Addr:** President, Dallas Black Chamber of Commerce, 2838 Martin Luther King Jr Blvd, Dallas, TX 75215, **Business Phone:** (214)421-5200.

GATES, PROF. THOMAS MICHAEL
Educator. **Personal:** Born Jan 9, 1943, St Louis, MO; married Doris Atwater; children: Steven A & Genice Arnold. **Educ:** Howard Univ, BFA, 1970; Calif State Univ, Sacramento, MA, 1972. **Career:** Econ Opportunity Coun, instr, drama workshop, 1971-72; Calif St Univ, dir, black theatre prog, 1972, Sacramento, assoc prof, theatre, prof theatre; Film: South by Northwest, 1975. **Orgs:** Am Theatre Assoc; Calif Black Staff & Faculty Assoc; Sacramento Kwanza Comn; guest dir, Black Arts & W Theatre Seattle Wash, 1975; dir, The River Nigger, 1976; dir, five black-one-act plays, 1979. **Honors/Awds:** National Finalist and Award of Excellence, Am Col Theatre Festival, 1973. **Military Serv:** USAF, E-4, 4 years.

GATES, YVONNE ATKINSON
Government official. **Personal:** Married Lee; children: 4. **Educ:** Univ Nev, BS, Polit Sci & Jour, 1978, MS, 1982. **Career:** Clark County, Las Vegas, comnr, 2004-07. **Orgs:** Nev Asn Counties; bd dirs, Inner City Games; Debt Mgt Comn; Las Vegas Conv & Visitors Authority; Clark County Sch Bd Trustees. **Special Achievements:** First African American female commissioner, Clark County, Las Vegas.

GATEWOOD, DR. ALGIE C.
School administrator. **Personal:** Born Dec 17, 1951, Wadesboro, NC; son of Bessie M and Haywood J; married Elaine Thornton, Oct 1973; children: Wendolyn Charmaine, Andrea Marzina & Algie Carver Jr. **Educ:** Livingstone Col, BA, social sci/hist, 1974; Appalachian State Univ, MA,higher educ/col admin, 1977; Univ NC, Charlotte, cert guid & coun, 1982; NC State Univ, EdD; Winthrop Univ, sch admin lic, 1994. **Career:** Anson Community Col, dir human resources develop, 1974-81, dir inst res,1980-81, from acting dean students to dean students, 1981-97; Univ NC, gen admin, asst dir, 1997; Portland Community Col, Cascade Campus, pres, currently. **Orgs:** Phi Beta Sigma Frat; trustee, Ebenezer Baptist Church; vpres, NC Found Advan Health Progs; bd mem emer, Anson Regional Med Serv; past mem, Anson County Bd Educ; NC Contract Progs Dentistry, Med & Optometry, comn mem; past mem, NC Allied Health Coun; past mem, NC Trustees Asn; bd dir, Urban League Portland. **Honors/Awds:** Bd mem emeritus, Anson Regional Medical Services, 1997; bd mem of the year, Anson Regional Medical Services, 1996; nominated John B. Grenzebach Award, CASE, 1996; Martin Luther King Jr. Education Award from Asn of Univ. Women of Anson. **Special Achievements:** Dr. AC Gatewood Scholarship, named in honor, Alpha Pi Chi Sorority & Women Action Club. **Military Serv:** Published numerous articles including, "A Model for Assessing the Fund-Raising Effectiveness of Community College Non-profit Foundations in NC"; "A Comparative Analysis & Evaluation of Community College non-profit Foundations in NC"; "The Student Recruitment and Retention Manual". **Business Addr:** President, Portland Community College, Cascade Campus, 705 N Killingsworth St, Portland, OR 97217, **Business Phone:** (503)244-6111.

GATEWOOD, DR. WALLACE LAVELL
Economist, educator. **Personal:** Born May 31, 1946, West Bend, KY; son of Cecil and Minnie Lucas; married Sharon JM Oliver, Sep 29, 1985; children: Eboni, Shannon & Ashley. **Educ:** Berea Col, BS, Berea, KY, 1968; Oberlin Col, Post-Baccalaureate Cert, Oberlin, OH, 1969; Wash Univ, MBA, St Louis, 1971; Univ Ill, Champaign-Urbana, PhD, Labor & Ind Rels, 1975. **Career:** WL Gatewood & Assoc Consulting Firm, pres, 1979-; FMCS, labor arbitrator, 1980; independent certified fin planner, 1980-; Fla A&M Univ, Tallahassee, asst prof econs, 1974; Fla State Univ Tallahassee, asst prof mgmt labor rels, 1974-77; Morgan State Univ, Baltimore, assoc prof bus & econs, 1977-79; Univ Baltimore, assoc prof mgmt & labor, 1980-82; Baruch Col NYC, asst prof, 1982-84; Coppin State Col, Baltimore, assoc prof mgmt sci, 1984-86; Morgan State Univ, prof bus admin & mgmt, 1986-, chair, 1988-; Long & Foster Real Estate Inc, real estate agent, 1987-89; Century 21 Associated Inc, real estate agent 1989-; Morgan State Univ, prof; Villa Julie, fac, currently; Lavell Consul & Performance Syst, founder & sr consult; Strayer Univ, prof mgt. **Orgs:** Am Soc Productivity Improvement; Am Soc Training & Develop; Ind Rels Res Asn; Nat Black MBA Asn; Nat Econs Asn; employment adv comt, Baltimore Urban League, 1968-; Nat Asn Advan Colored People, Baltimore, 1980; acad mgmt, Asn Human Resources Mgt & Org Behavior; exec bd, pres Maryland Chap, Asn Human Resources Mgt & Organisational Behavior; Baltimore Mkt Asn; coordr, Nat Asn Advan Colored People Lecture Series, 1981-82; Howard County Comn Women, 1981-84; coordr, Mgt Sci Serv Coppin State Col, 1984-86; secy, Patapsco Valley Regional Coun Episcopalian Diocese 1987-88; dir, Ctr Fin Success, 1986-; bd, Women Virtue Inc. **Honors/Awds:** Scholar, Berea Col, 1964-68; Post-Baccalaureate Fel, Oberlin Col, 1968-69; Consortium Fellowship, Washington Univ, 1969-71; Fellowship, Univ Ill, 1971-73; Res Intern, Congressional Budget Off, 1978; Fac Fel, Social Security Admin, 1979; Man of the Year, Soc for Advancement Mgt, Morgan State Univ, 1980; Advisor of the Year, Univ Baltimore, 1981. **Home Addr:** 12 Devlon Ct, Owings Mills, MD 21117, **Home Phone:** (410)581-7033. **Business Phone:** 877-468-6852.

GATLING, CHRIS RAYMOND
Basketball player, business owner. **Personal:** Born Sep 3, 1967, Elizabeth City, NJ. **Educ:** Old Dominion Univ, attended 1991. **Career:** Basketball player (retired); Golden State Warriors, forward, 1991-96; Miami Heat, 1995-96, 2001-02; Dallas Mavericks, 1997; NJ Nets, 1996-99; Milwaukee Bucks, 1998-99; Orlando Magic, 1999-2000; Denver Nuggets, 1999-2000; Cleveland Cavaliers, 2000-01; Chris Gatling Recreation Ctr, owner, currently; Cut Me Twice Barbershop, Oakland, owner, currently. **Honors/Awds:** Jack McMahon Award, Golden State Warriors, 1993. **Business Addr:** Owner, Chris Gatling Recreation Center, 285 Union Ave, Irvington, NJ 07111, **Business Phone:** (973)399-6597.

GATLING, JOSEPH THEODORE
Lawyer. **Personal:** Born Mar 11, 1947, Washington, DC; son of Arphelius and Inez Gatling Sr. **Educ:** Federal City Col, pol sci, 1974; Prince Georges Community Col, paralegal studies, 1987; Univ Md, law, 1988; Disabled Am Veterans Nat Serv Officer Training Prog, 1992; Col Southern Md, 2004-. **Career:** Off Personnel Mgt, info specialist, 1980-83; Coun DC, admin asst, 1984; Arts Comn DC, arts info coord, 1985; DC Off Human Rights, prog specialist, 1985-86; Bd Veterans Appeals, legal technician 1987, asst chief hearing sect, 1988-89, chief, 1990-; Disabled Am Vet, nat serv officer, 1990-95; Pvt Pract, atty, currently. **Orgs:** Chap comdr, Disabled Am Veterans, 1968, dept comdr, DAV DC, 1997-99, dept serv officer, 2000-02; chmn, Peoples Govt Assoc Inc, 1974-78; Nat Asn Advan Colored People, 1980-; master, Redemption Lodge No 24, PHA, 1997; staff vol, Wash Very Spec Arts, 1995; legal ministry, First Baptist Church Glenarden, 1997-, card ministry, 2004-; selection bd adv, Help Disabled War Veterans, 1999-2001; acad scholar chmn, Redemption Lodge No 24, F& AM, PHA, DC Jurisdiction, 2000-; thrice illustrious grand master, Prince Hall Grand Coun, Royal & Select Masters, 2000-02; W Grand asst dir pub rels, Most Worshipful Prince Hall Grand Lodge DC, F& AM, PHA, 2000-02, Emer W Grand Asst Dir Community Affairs. **Honors/Awds:** Charles Coleman Award, Fed City Col, 1973; Outstanding Service, Exec Off Mayor, 1985; Community Service Award, United Black Fund, 1986; Outstanding Service, Combined Fed Campaign, 1988-90; Outstanding Membership Achievement, Disabled Am Veterans, 1991; Certificate of Appreciation, US Marines Corp Reserve, Toys Tots Found, 1993; Certificate of Appreciation, Shiloh Baptist Church, 1993, 1995, 1996; Certificates of Merit, United Supreme Coun, Ancient & Accepted Scottish Rite Freemasonry, Southern Jurisdiction, PHA, 1994 & 1997; Lodge of the Year, Redemption Lodge No. 24, F& AM, PHA, 1997; Community Service Award, US Dept Veterans Affairs Med Ctr, 1998; Certificate of Appreciation, Metro Police Boys & Girls Clubs, 1997 & 1998; Director's Recognition Award, Dept Vet Affairs Med Ctr, 2000. **Special Achievements:** Created Geographic Development Art Program in DC, 1985; Honors Graduate, Prince Georges, Community Col, 1987; Combined Federal Campaign Fundraising, 1988; Dept Vet Affairs, Office of General Counsel, Legal Rep, 1990; Shiloh Bapt Church, superintendent of Primary Dept Church School, 1985-96; R.E.P.A. Inc., Type I & Type II Technician, 2005. **Military Serv:** US Marine Corp, LCpl, Vietnam Era; Good Conduct Medal, 1966. **Business Addr:** Legal Consultant, PO Box 10127, Washington, DC 20018, **Business Phone:** (202)716-3212.

GATLING, PATRICIA LYNN
Lawyer. **Personal:** Born Jan 16, 1960, Annapolis, MD; daughter of Virginia D and Luther C. **Educ:** Johns Hopkins Univ, BA, int studies, 1979; Univ Md, Sch Law, JD, 1982. **Career:** Kings Co Dist Atty, asst dist atty, 1983-86, Major Narcotics Bur, exec asst, dist atty, 1992-96, dep dist atty, 1996; Spec Narcotics Ct, Sterling Johnson Jr, spec narcotics asst, 1986-87; Spec State Prosecutor, New York City Criminal Justice Syst, spec asst atty gen, 1987-90; New York City Comn Human Rights, comnr & chair, 2002-; US State Dept Int Law Enforcement Acad, John Jay Col Criminal Justice, sr trainer, currently. **Orgs:** Nat Black Prosecutors Asn, vice pres, 1992-, pres, 1993-94. **Home Addr:** 1175 York Ave Apt 2T, New York, NY 10021, **Home Phone:** (212)355-6035. **Business Addr:** Commissioner, Chair, New York City Commission on Human Rights, 40 Rector St 10th Fl, New York, NY 10006, **Business Phone:** (212)306-5070.

GATSON, WILINA IONE
Secretary (Office). **Personal:** Born Apr 17, 1925, Galveston, TX; daughter of Willie Lee and Ina Ivory Sibley; divorced; children: Natalie & Kenneth. **Educ:** Univ Tex Med Br, Sch Voc Nursing, 1954, BS, 1960; Tex So Univ, 1957. **Career:** Lecturer (retired); Moody State Sch Cerebral Palsied C, Univ Tex Med Br, first black nursing supr, guest lectr; John Sealy Hosp, LVN psychiat; St Mary's Hosp, US Pub Health Hosp, asst night supvr; Galveston Col, guest lectr; Jack & Jill Am Inc. **Orgs:** Nat Asn Advan Colored People-TNA; Am Nurses Asn; Nat Coun Negro Women Inc; Delta Signa Theta Sorority Inc; Ladies Aux Am Leg; bd mem, Univ Tex Med Br Alumni Asn, 2006-08; Versatile Dames; Sickle Cell Anemia Found; Officer First Union Baptist; Officer Courts Calanthes Chap; Heroines Jericho. **Honors/Awds:** Outstanding student of Year Award, Univ Tex Med Br, 1958; Distinguished Alumnus Award, Univ Tex Sch Nursing, 1989, Distinguished Alumnus Award, 1989, Hall of Fame, 1992; Only Black in Hall of Fame, Only Black Distinguished Alumnus. **Special Achievements:** First black to grad from University Texas Medical Branch Degree Nursing School, 1960; first black to serve as Off in University Texas Nursing Alumni Asn, 1961-62. **Home Addr:** 1317 Ave L, Galveston, TX 77550, **Home Phone:** (409)762-3411.

GAULT, WILLIE JAMES
Football player, athlete, actor. **Personal:** Born Sep 5, 1960, Griffin, GA; son of James Gault Jr and Willie Mae Roberts; married Dainnese Mathis, Jun 11, 1983; children: Shakari Denise & Gabriel James. **Educ:** Univ Tenn, Knoxville, TN, mkt, 1983. **Career:** Football player (retired), athlete (retired), actor; US Olympic Team, track & field, 1980; US Nat Team, track & field, 1980-83; Chicago Bears, wide receiver, 1983-87; Los Angeles Raiders, wide receiver, 1988-93; Winter Olympics Bobsleigh, 1988; US Olympic Bobsled Team, pusher, 1990-91; Films: "Street of Dreams," 1988; Room 302, 2001; Grounded for Life, 2002; SWAT, 2003; Cellular, 2004; Deuce Bigalow: European Gigolo, 2005; Shut Up & Shoot!, 2006. **Orgs:** Chmn, Ministry Lay Witnesses Christ, 1983-; pub speaker, Schs & Churches; Lou Garrett commercial, 1983; Distonia Commercial, 1985; Fair Housing Commerical, City Chicago; nat spokesperson, AIDS & Diabetes Asn; spokesperson, Long Beach Ballet Dance Camp, 1990-91; Willie Gault's Youth Enrichment Prog. **Honors/Awds:** Most Valuable Player, Univ Tenn Track & Football Team, 1983; Athlete of the Year, SE Conf, 1983; NFL All Rookie Team, Chicago Bears, 1983. **Special Achievements:** First man in history of NCAA to win both 60 yards & 60 yard hurdles, 1982; World record in 4 x 100 relay track & field, 1983; World record 4 x 110hurdlers track & field, 1982; First Place, Super Stars Competitions, 1989, 1990. **Home Addr:** 7700 Sunset Blvd Suite 205, Los Angeles, CA 90046. **Business Phone:** (310)859-4000.

GAVIN, JAMES RAPHAEL, III
Physician, executive. **Personal:** Born Nov 23, 1945, Mobile, AL; son of James R Gavin II and Bessie S; married Dr Annie Ruth Jackson Gavin, Jun 19, 1971; children: Raphael Hakkim, Lamar Kenyon. **Educ:** Livingstone Col, BS, chem, 1966; Emory Univ, PhD, biochem, 1970; Duke Univ Med Sch, MD, 1975. **Career:** Nat Inst Health, staff assoc, 1971-73; Duke Univ Hosp, pathologist, 1975-76; US Pub Health Serv, comdr, 2 1/2 yrs active, 11 1/2 yrs reserves; Wash Univ Sch Med, assoc prof med, 1979-86; Univ Okla Med Ctr, prof med, chief diabetes sect; Okla Univ Health Sci Ctr, William K Warren prof Diabetes Studies, 1989-91; Howard Hughes Med Inst, sr sci officer, 1991-02; Morehouse Sch Med, pres, 2002-05; Baxter, dir, 2003-; Emory Univ, clin prof med & sr adv health affairs, 2005-; Healing Our Village LLC, exec vpres, 2005-. **Orgs:** Life mem, Alpha Phi Alpha; bd dirs, Am Diabetes Asn, 1983-87; bd dirs, Alpha Educ Found, 1986-; nat prog dir & sr prog consult, Robert Wood Johnson Found, 1987-; Nat Diabetes Adv Bd, 1988-92; trustee, Okla Sch Sci, Math Found, 1992-; pres, Am Diabetes Asn, 1993-94; Nat Inst Diabetes & Digestive & Kidney Adv Coun, 1995-; trustee, Robert Wood Johnson Found, 1996-; Alpha Omega Alpha; Am Asn Acad Minority Physicians; Am Asn Physicians; Am Soc Clin Invest; Endocrine Soc; Omicron Delta Kappa Honorary Soc; Sigma Xi Sci Hon Soc. **Honors/Awds:** Clinical Teacher of the Year, Barnes Hosp Dept Med, 1981-82; William Alexander Leadership Award, Epsilon Lambda Alpha Phi Alpha, 1982; Special Achiever, St Louis Sentinel, 1982; Distinguished Alumnus of HBI, Nat Asn For Equal Opportunity, 1987; ed bd, Acad Med, 1994-; Outstanding Clinician in Field of Diabetes, Am Diabetes Asn, 1990; Banting Medal for Distinguished Service, Am Diabetes Asn, 1994; Internist of Year, Nat Med Asn, 1997. **Business Addr:** Director, Baxter, 1 Baxter Pkwy, Deerfield, IL 60015-4625.*

GAVIN, L. KATHERINE
School administrator, college administrator. **Personal:** Born in Chicago Heights, IL. **Educ:** Chicago State Univ, BA, 1952; Columbia Univ, MA, 1963; Nova Univ, EdD, 1976. **Career:** School administrator (retired); Lincoln Sch, Chicago Heights Sch Dist No170, prin, 1966; Prairie State Col, child develop prog, 1968, dir personalized learning prog, 1970; Chicago Heights Sch Dist No 170, dean stud, classroom instr. **Orgs:** S Suburban Chicago Chap Links Inc; chair bd dirs, Dr Charles E Gavin Mem Found; Nat Asn Advan Colored People, PUSH. **Honors/Awds:** Outstanding Citizens Award, PUSH; Outstanding Civic & Service, S Suburb Chicago Chap of Links Inc; Scholar Image Award, Fred Hampton Found; lifetime hon, ALUMNI Asn Gov State Univ; Hall of Fame Bloom Township High Sch, 1980; Recognition Award Outstanding Service, Prairie State Col.

GAVIN, MARY ANN
Government official. **Personal:** Born Aug 8, 1945, Elmhurst, IL; daughter of Vernus (deceased) and Evelyn Thomas-Wilford (deceased); married Joeneather, May 23, 1966; children: Charles A & Darrell E. **Educ:** Col St Francis, Il BA, 1973. **Career:** Social Security Admin, serv rep, 1973-76, claims rep, 1976-79, supvr, 1979-85, mgt info specialist, 1985-86, labor rels mgt analyst, 1986-89, section chief labor rels, 1989-99, dir, Ctr Human Resources, 1999-2000; Civil Rights & Equal Opp, actg dir, 2000-. **Orgs:** Black Adv Coun, 1994-96; Woman's Adv Coun, 1995-; Social Security Black Caucus, 1996. **Honors/Awds:** Excellence In Service Award, 1994; Fed Employee Year Nominee, Chicago Fed Exec Bd, 1995, 1996; Quality Service Award, Social Security Admin, 1998, Commissioners Citation, 1996, Regional Comners Citation, 1995; Soc Gov Meeting Profs, 1999-; Black Affairs Adv Coun, 1999; Am Indian/Alaskan Native Adv Coun, 1999-; Hispanic Affairs Comm, 1999-; Cultural Diversity Coun, 1999-. Fed Employee Year, nominee, 2000. **Home Addr:** 1920 Tawny Ct, Joliet, IL 60435. **Business Addr:** Director, Civil Rights and Equal Opportunity, 600 W Madison St 10th Fl, Chicago, IL 60601, **Business Phone:** (312)575-6394.

GAY, ALVIN
Businessperson, executive. **Career:** UniWorld, exec; Footsteps LLC, founder & managing partner, 2000-. **Business Addr:** Founder, Managing Partner, Footsteps LLC, 200 Varrick St Suite 610, New York, NY 10014, **Business Phone:** (212)924-6432.

GAY, BIRDIE SPIVEY
Library administrator. **Personal:** Born Mar 13, 1918, Atlanta, GA; married Howard Donald. **Educ:** Morris Brown Col, attended 1939; Atlanta Univ Sch Libr Serv, attended 1962. **Career:** Brooks County, teacher, 1939-41; Eatonton, GA, 1941-42; Moutlrie, GA, teacher & librarian, 1942-45; ER Carter Elem Sch, Atlanta, 1946-59, librarian & media specialist. **Orgs:** Nat Educ Asn; Ga Am Libr Asn; com adminr, YWCA; solicitor, Cancer Drive, Easter, Retarded C, Muscular Dystrophy; Nat Advan Asn Colored People; United Negro Col Fund; Morris Brown Alumni Asn. **Honors/ Awds:** Teacher of the year, ER Carter Sch, 1960-61; Outstanding Service plaque, Sigma Gamma Rho Sorority, 1970.

GAY, EDDIE C.
Chemical engineer. **Personal:** Born May 13, 1940, Starkville, MS; married Sylvia J; children: Steven E, Richard C. **Educ:** BS, 1962; DSc, 1967. **Career:** Chemical engineer (retired); Argonne Nat Lab Battery Prog, group leader, 1941-75;Lithium & Chalcogen Cell Develop Argonne Nat Lab, asst engr, 1968-69; Lithium-chalcogen Cell Develop Argonne Nat Lab, problem leader, 1969-71; Argonne Nat Lab Battery Prog, mgr, 1975. **Orgs:** Electrochem Soc; Am Inst Chem Engr; sigma xi; Nat Orgn Prof Advanc Black Chemists & Chem Engr; Faith United Protestant Church. **Honors/ Awds:** Thesis Award, Argonne Nat Lab; Technical Achiever of the Year, 2002. **Military Serv:** AUS, capt, 1967-68. *

GAY, HELEN PARKER
Government official, chef. **Personal:** Born Mar 14, 1920, Rocky Mount, NC; daughter of Dillie Virginia Shaw Parker and Frank Leslie Parker Sr (deceased); divorced; children: Leslie Claudius Gay (deceased). **Educ:** Barber-Scotia Col; NC State col. **Career:** Employ Security Comn NC, interviewer II; Rocky Mount City Coun, council mem, 1987-, mayor pro term, 1993; caterer. **Orgs:** Hon Mem, Sigma Gamma Rho Sor Inc, 1986; mem, Rocky Mount Moles Inc, 1988; hon life mem, Presby Women Rocky Mt, 1989; Region IV chair, 1991, pres, 1993-, NC Black Elected Munic Officials; bd mem, NC League of Cities, 1990-91; elder, clerk session, Mt Pisgah Presby Church, Rocky Mt, 1990-91, 1993-; bd mem, Community Shelter Homeless. **Honors/Awds:** Merit Award, Employ Security Comn NC, 1950, 1960. **Special Achievements:** First African American female elected, Rocky Mount City council, mayor pro tem, 1985. **Home Addr:** 1629 King Cir, Rocky Mount, NC 27801. *

GAYLE, CRUISE
Advertising executive, manager. **Educ:** Fla A&M Univ; Harvard Bus Sch. **Career:** McKinsey & Co; Microsoft Corp, sr public relations mgr diversity mkt, mgr diversity mkt & commun, currently. **Business Addr:** Manager of Diversity Marketing, Communications, Microsoft Corporation, 1 Microsoft Way, Redmond, WA 98052-6399.

GAYLE, HELENE DORIS
Physician, executive. **Personal:** Born Aug 16, 1955, Buffalo, NY; daughter of Jacob A and Marietta D. **Educ:** Barnard Col, New York, NY, BA, 1976; Univ Pa, Philadelphia, PA, MD, 1981; Johns Hopkins Univ, Baltimore, MD, MPH, 1981. **Career:** Children's Hosp Nat Med Ctr, Wash, DC, pediat resident, 1981-84; Centers Dis Control, Epidemic Intelligence Serv, 1984-86; Atlanta, GA, med epidemiologist, 1986-87; Centers Disease Control, Ped & Family Studies Sect, med epidemiologist, 1987-89, Div HIV/ AIDS, asst chief sci, 1989-90, chief, int activ, 1990-92, agency AIDS coordr & chief, 1992-94; Wash Centers Dis Control & Prev, assoc dir, 1994-95; Bill & Melinda Gates Found, Centers Dis Control & Prev, HIV, TB, & Reproductive Health , dir, 1995-02; Centers Dis Control, Atlanta, GA, researcher & epidemiologist; Care USA, pres & chief exec officer, currently. **Orgs:** Am Pub Health Asn; Am Acad Pediat; Nat Med Asn; Int AIDS Soc; bd mem, Inst Med & Coun Foreign Rels. **Honors/Awds:** National Merit Scholar Fellowship Award, 1981; Henrietta & Jacob Lowenburg Prize, 1981; Joel Gordon Miller Award, 1981; Administrators and Black Faculty Merit Award, Univ of PA, 1981; Outstanding Unit Citation, 1989, 1990; US Pub Health Service Achievement Medal, 1989; Celebration of Public Service Award, 1990; Colgate-Palmolive Co, Model of Excellence, 1992; US Public Health Service, Outstanding Service Medal, 1992, Unit Commendation Medal, 1992; Serwa Award, Nat Coalition 100 Black Women, 1995; Poindexter Award, US Pub Health Serv, 1996; Medal of Excellence, Columbia Univ, 1996. **Business Addr:** President, Chief Executive Officer, Care USA, 151 Ellis St NE, Atlanta, GA 30303.*

GAYLES, FRANKLIN JOHNSON
Government official. **Personal:** Born in Marshallville, GA; son of Franklin Johnson Sr and Marian Richardson; married Ruth Teele; children: Michael Perry. **Educ:** Univ Ill, AB, 1942, AM, 1947; New York Univ, PhD, 1960. **Career:** Government official (retired); Va Union Univ, prof polit sci, div dir, acad dean, 1948-80; City Richmond, treasurer, 1979-93. **Orgs:** Treasurers' Asn Va; Asn Constitutional Officers Va; life mem, Alpha Phi Alpha; life mem, Sigma Pi Phi; life mem, Crusade of Voters; life mem, Nat Asn Advan Colored People; bd friends, Housing Opportunities Made Equal. **Honors/Awds:** Founders Day Award, New York Univ, 1976; Moton Scholar, Univ Pa, 1976; Civic Award, Alpha Phi Alpha, 1983; Civic Award, Delta Sigma Theta, 1983. **Special Achievements:** First John Hancock Distinguished Chair, 1977. **Military Serv:** USN, 1942-46. *

GAYLES, DR. JONATHAN
College teacher. **Educ:** Morehouse Col, BA, pshycol, 1991; Winthrop Univ, MS, pshycol, 1993; Univ S Fla, PhD, appl anthrop, 2002. **Career:** Tougaloo Col, adj prof dept pshycol, 1993-94; Univ South Florida, grad teach asst dept anthrop, 1999-2002, grad teach asst, dept africana studies, 2000-02; Indiana Univ Pennsylvania, teach fellow dept anthrop, 2002; Georgia St Univ, asst prof dept african-american studies, 2002-09, assoc prof, currently. **Orgs:** KMT Asen. **Special Achievements:** Has published a number of articles in scholarly journals.

GAYLES, DR. JOSEPH NATHAN WEBSTER
Scientist, educator, school administrator. **Personal:** Born in Birmingham, AL; son of Joseph N Gayles Sr and Earnestine Gayles; children: Jonathan & Monica. **Educ:** Dillard Univ, AB (summa cum laude) 1958; Brown Univ, PhD, 1963. **Career:** Brown Univ, res assoc, 1958-62; OR State Univ, post doc res assoc, 1962-63, asst prof; Morehouse Col, Woodrow Wilson teaching assoc, 1963-66, prof (tenured) 1969-77, assoc prof chem 1969-71, dir med educ prog, founder & dir 1972-75, off health professions adv, founder, 1969-77; IBM, staff sci & proj dir, 1966-69; Talladega Col, pres, 1977-83; Jon-Mon & Assoc, fundraising chmn, chief exec officer, 1983-; Morehouse Sch Med, vpres, 1983-97, res prof med, 1983-97; Sojourner Douglass Col, vpres, 2002-. **Orgs:** Bd dir, Morehouse Col, 1973-77; consult, Whitney Found, Ford Found, Woodrow Wilson Found; bd dir, Woodrow Wilson Found, 1977-97; nat bd dir, NSFRE Found; consult, Nat Inst Health & DHHS; bd visitors MIT; Alpha Phi Alpha, Reg III charter bd; Coun Admin & support edu; Am Chem Soc; Am Physical Soc; Phi Beta Kappa; Asn Fund raising Profs; fel, Rohm & Haas; Kiwanis Talladega. **Honors/Awds:** Andover Full Support Scholarship, Phillips Acad, 1953; Exchange Cup Scholar B'ham, 1954; Brawley Writing Award, 1955; Davage Award; Brown Univ Fel; Summer European Travel Fellowship, 1965; Rohm & Haas Fel; Woodrow Wilson Teaching Fellow; Dreyfus Teacher Scholar, Powers Travel Fellow, 1975; Teacher of the Year, Morehouse Col, 1976; Distinguishing Alumnus Award, Dillard, 1977; Omega Psi Phi Ed Achievement Award; Community Service Award, Elks; Ed Achievement Award, Emancipation Day Comm Birmingham, 1980; Kiwanis Talladega; Morehouse School of Medicine Award, Trustees, 1985; Honorary Degrees: (LLD), Dillard Univ, 1983; (DSC) Morehouse School of Med, 2000; Atlanta Rotary Club, 1992-. **Business Addr:** Chairman, Gayles Associates, 1515 Austin Rd SW, Atlanta, GA 30331-2205, **Business Phone:** (404)344-2483.

GAYLES-FELTON, DR. ANNE RICHARDSON
Educator, college teacher. **Personal:** Born Jun 4, 1923, Marshallville, GA; daughter of Franklin J and Marion R; married Ambrose M Felton (died 1994). **Educ:** Fort Valley State Col, BS, 1943; Columbia Univ, MA, 1949, prof dipl, 1953; Ill Univ, EdD, 1961. **Career:** Lamson Richardson High Sch, teacher; Ark Baptist Col, Dept Sociol, head, 1947-50; Fort Valley State Col, instr, social sci, 1950-54; Stillman Col, dir stud teaching, 1951-52; Albany State Col, assoc prof social sci & educ, 1954-57; Fla A&M Univ, dir stud teaching, 1957-62, Dept Sec Educ, head, 1962-82, supvr interns, prof sec educ, 1982-03, prof emer, 2003-; Rust Col, assoc prof social sci; Ga Pub Schs, teacher. **Orgs:** First vpres, Asn Social & Behavioral Serv, 1961-62; exec comt, Soc Prof Educ,1969-70; comt mem, Am Asn Teacher Educ Col, 1970-80; comt master teacher, Asn Teacher Educrs, 1982-85; USS/China Joint Conf Educ, Beijing, China,1992; USS Mil Acad Appointments Bd; Citizen Ambassador Prog, People to People Int, 1992; Gov Bush's Task Force, Equity Educ Opportunity; DST; Pi Lambda Theta; Phi Delta Kappa; Kappa Delta Pi; Alpha Kappa Mu; Pi Gamma Mu; Nat Republican Party, Presidential Task Force; State Fla Gov Commemorative Celebration Comn Dr Martin Luther King Jr; Gov Bd Independent Col & Univ, State Fla; Gov Comn Qual Educ; Urban League; Republican Party Fla; Delta Sigma Theta Sorority. **Honors/Awds:** Alumni Hall of Fame, Inductee, Fort Valley State Col, 1984; Teacher of the Year, Fla A&M Univ, 1989; Distinguished Teacher Educr, Asn Teacher Educrs,1990; Teacher of the Year, Col Educ, 1991; Banquet Honoree, 1991; Living Legend, Fla A&M Univ, 1997; Dean's Distinguished Acad & Serv Award, Fla A&M Univ, 1999; FAMU Teacher Incentive Award; Distinguished Alumni Award, Div Social Sci; Distinguished Alumni Citation of the Year Award, Nat Asn Equal Opportunities Higher Educ. **Special Achievements:** One of most influential Famuans of the Century, Fla A&M Univ, 1999; Author: two books; four monographs, (co-author of one book and three monographs:)63 articles; 5 research studies; 5 bibliographies; dissertation; editor, writer, reader for first book devoted solely to Multicultural Education; Delivered paper at the 43rd World Assembly of the Intl Council on Edu for Teaching in Amman Jordan; chmn of the Lamson Richardson Scholarship Fedn, founded in 1886. **Home Addr:** 4425 Meandering Way Apt 226, Tallahassee, FL 32308-5746. **Business Addr:** Professor Emeritus, Florida A&M University, 1500 Wahnish Way, Tallahassee, FL 32307.

GAYLE-THOMPSON, DELORES J.
Physician. **Personal:** Born Feb 28, 1938, Portland, Jamaica; daughter of William Ellison and Lucilda Rebecca; married Amos F Thompson, Aug 28, 1965; children: Colin, Allison. **Educ:** Howard Univ, Col Liberal Arts, BS, 1963, Col Med, MD, 1967; Columbia Univ Sch Pub Health, MPH, 1984. **Career:** Freedmen's Hosp Wash, intern, 1967-68; Harlem Hosp, resident pediatrics, 1968-70, physician pediatric clinic, 1970-83, assoc dir; Col Physicians & Surgeons, Columbia Univ, asst prof pediatrics, 1990-. **Orgs:** Nat Med Asn; Ambulatory Pediatric Asn; Am Pub Health Asn; Susan Smith McKinney Steward Med Soc; bd mem, White Plains Cot Fair Inc; exec bd, Fund For Greater Harlem. **Honors/ Awds:** Citation, Howard Univ Century Club, 1986; Civic Award, Friends E Portland Jamaica W Indies, 1986. **Business Addr:** 506 Lenox Ave, New York, NY 10037.*

GAYNOR, GLORIA
Singer. **Personal:** Born Sep 7, 1949, Newark, NJ; daughter of Daniel Fowles and Queenie May Proctor. **Career:** Albums: Never Can Say Goodbye, 1975; I've Got You, 1976; Glorious, 1977; Park Ave Sound, 1978; I Have A Right, 1979; Stories, 1980; I Kinda Like Me, 1981; I Am Gloria Gaynor, 1984; The Power of Gloria Gaynor, 1986; I Will Survive, 1990; I Am What I Am, 1996; I Wish You Love, 2002; I Will Survive (Go), 2003; Christmas Presence, 2007; The Answer, 2006; TV: "The Keith Harris Show", 1983; "Entertainment Express", 1983; "Prom Night", 1999; "The 2002 World Music Awards", 2002; "Pyramid", 2003; "Good Morning Australia", 2004; "When Disco Ruled the World", 2005; "Gray Matters", 2006. **Honors/Awds:** Grammy Award for Best Disco Recording for "I Will Survive", 1979; Radio Regenbogen for Lifetime Disco, 1999; Inducted into the Dance Music Hall of Fame, 2005; Honorary Spokesperson, American Diabetes Association, 2008; 30th anniversary of "I Will Survive.", 2009. *

GAYTON, GARY D.
Lawyer. **Personal:** Born Feb 25, 1933, Seattle, WA. **Educ:** Univ Wa, BA, 1955; Gonzaga Univ, JD, 1962. **Career:** Western Dist Wash, asst US atty, 1962-65; Stern, Gayton, Neubauer & Brucker, atty PS, 1965; US Secy Transp, spec asst, 1977-79; Urban Mass Trasp Admin, acting admin, 1979; Smothers, Douple, Grayton & Long, partner, 1979-81, Diamond & Sylvester, coun, 1981-93; Grigsby Branford Co, sr vpres, 1985-96; Gaitan & Cusack, coun, 1994-95; Siebert Branford Shank & Co, sr vpres, 1996-, regional mgr, Cusack Knowles Ferguson, PLLC, coun, 1996-01; pvt pract, 2001. **Orgs:** Am Bar Asn; Am Trial Lawyers Asn; King Co Bar Asn; Wash State Bar Asn; Bar-Pac comt, chair, Resolution comn, admin comn, legis comn, civil rights comn; Nat Bar Asn; bd memn Universal Security Life Ins Co; SeattlePark Comn; Seattle Repertory Bd; Seattle Ethics & Fair Camp Comn; Seattle King Co Bicentennial Comn; bd mem, Salvation Army; bd mem, NW Civic Cultural & Char Orgns; bd mem Nat Asn Advan Colored People; bd mem, Inst Black Am Music Inc; pres, Loren Miller Bar Asn; chair, sr adv bd, 9th Circuit Judicial Conf, 2000-01; DC Bar Asn; charter mem, Nat Conf Black Lawyers; chair, bd, YMCA E Madison; asst secy, bd, Wash Children's Home Soc; Nat Comn Support Pub Schs; vice chair, Boy Scouts Am; Bd, Metrop Dem Club; Seattle Urban League. **Honors/Awds:** Outstanding Community Service Awd, Loren Miller Bar Asn; Ethic Award, Cultural Ctr, Univ Wash, 1977; Humanitarian Award, Sigma Delta Tau. **Military Serv:** AUS 1955-57. **Business Addr:** Senior Vice President, Regional Manager, Siebert Brandford Shank & Co LLC, 601 Union St 42nd Fl, Seattle, WA 98101.*

GEARY, REGGIE (REGINALD ELLIOT GEARY)
Basketball player, basketball coach. **Personal:** Born Aug 31, 1973, Trenton, NJ. **Educ:** Univ Ariz. **Career:** Basketball player (retired), basketball coach; Cleveland Cavaliers, guard, 1996-97; San Antonio Spurs, 1997-98; CBA, 1998-2000; Univ Ariz, asst

coach, 2005; Flowing Wells High Sch, head coach; Anaheim Arsenal, asst coach & dir opers, currently. **Business Phone:** (714)635-2255.

GEARY, REGINALD ELLIOT. See GEARY, REGGIE.

GECAU, DR. KIMANI J
Educator. **Personal:** Born Jul 17, 1947; married. **Educ:** Univ E Africa, BA, 1969; McMaster Univ, MA, 1970; State Univ NY, PhD, 1975. **Career:** McMaster Univ, teaching asst, 1969-70; State Univ NY Buffalo, teaching asst, 1970-72; State Univ Col, Buffalo, instr, 1970-71; Geneseo, instr, 1972-75; Univ Nairobi, lectr, 1975; Univ Zimbabwe, Harare, lectr. **Business Addr:** Lecturer, University of Zimbabwe, Mt Pleasant, PO Box 167, Harare, Zimbabwe, **Business Phone:** (263)430-3211.

GEE, AL. See GERMANY, ALBERT.

GEE, CAMMIE. See GIST, CAROLE ANNE-MARIE.

GEE, WILLIAM ROWLAND, JR.
Engineer. **Personal:** Born Oct 4, 1940, Washington, DC; son of William Rowland and Marietta L Brittain; married Sadie H Phillips; children: Moira G Travis, Morris B, Cathy P Kearney, Julia E & W Rowland III. **Educ:** Howard Univ, BSME (cum laude), 1962; Oak Ridge Sch Reactor Tech, Nuclear Engineering, 1963; Stanford Univ, MS, Applied Mech, 1971; Loyola Col Baltimore, MBA, 1981. **Career:** US Atomic Energy Comn, project engr, 1962-66; GE Breeder Reactor Develop, engr, 1966-73; Potomac Electric Power Co, mgr nuclear engineering, 1975-77, mgr generating engineering, 1981-89, vpres system engineering, 1989-. **Orgs:** Omega Psi Phi; ASME; ANS; Edison Electric Inst. **Home Addr:** 1006 Coral Berry Ct, Great Falls, VA 22066. **Business Addr:** Vice President, System Engineering, Potomac Electric Power Company, 1900 Pa Ave NW, Washington, DC 20068, **Business Phone:** (202)872-2000.

GELLINEAU, VICTOR MARCEL
Marketing executive, business owner, entrepreneur. **Personal:** Born Nov 3, 1942, New York, NY; son of Victor M Gellineau and Marcella Gonzalez; married Carole Joy Johnston, Jun 5, 1965; children: Victor M III, Maria M & Carmen E. **Educ:** Howard Univ, BA, 1967; Baruch Col Bus & Pub Admin, MBA, 1974. **Career:** Burlington Industs, salesman, 1967-69; Lever Bros, asst prod mgr, 1969-71; Am Home Prod, prod mgr, 1971-73; Zebra Assoc, vpres & dir acct mgt, 1973-76; Heublein Inc, mkt mgr, 1976-83; Ponderosa Inc, dir mkt, 1983-85; Gen Foods Corp, sr prod mgr, 1985-89; Carole Joy Creations Inc, pres & owner, 1985-. **Orgs:** Omega Psi Phi Fraternity, Inc, 1967-; Am Mgt Asn, 1970-; vis prof, Nat Urban League Beep Prog, 1974-; bd mem & pres, Artists Collective, 1978-83; bd mem & pres, Jr Achievement, 1978-; Nat Black MBA Asn, 1983-; facilitator Inroads; bd mem, The Hord Found Inc., 1988-; bd mem, United Way, 1989-98; pres, Minority Bus Asn, bd mem, 1990-2000; bd mem & treas, Hispanic Asn greater Danbury, 2000-06. **Honors/Awds:** Black Achiever Award, Hartford, YMCA, 1980; Minority Bus Development Award, State Conn, 1992; Community Service Award, Danbury, Nat Asn Advan Colored People, 1993; Minority Supplier Award, JC Penney, 1994; Div 2000 Community Award, 2001. **Business Addr:** President, Owner, Carole Joy Creations Inc, 1087 Fed Rd Suite 8, Brookfield, CT 06804-1156, **Business Phone:** (203)740-4490.

GEMEDA, DR. GULUMA
Educator, college teacher. **Educ:** Addis Ababa Univ, Ethiopia, BA, 1980, MA, 1984; Mich State Univ, PhD 1996. **Career:** Addis Ababa Univ, lectr & asst prof, 1984-87, lectr & researcher, 1990-92; Mich State Univ, teaching asst, 1987-90 & 1992-95; N Mich Univ, vis asst prof, 1996-97; Univ Mich-Flint, Dept Africana Studies, adj asst prof, 1998-2001, assoc prof, currently. **Orgs:** African Studies Asn; Int Conf Ethiopian Studies; Oromo Studies Asn; secy, Oromo Studies Asn. **Special Achievements:** Published numerous articles & books including "Political Domination & Exploitation of Mineral Resources in Oromia (Ethiopia)"; From Menilek toMeles," Journal of Oromo Studies; Subsistence, Slavery & Violence in the Lower Omo Valley. **Business Addr:** Associate Professor, University of Michigan-Flint, Department of Africana Studies, 303 E Kearsley St, 346 David M French Hall, Flint, MI 48502-1950, **Business Phone:** (810)762-3353.

GENET, MICHAEL
Actor, writer. **Personal:** Born Aug 25, 1958, Washington, DC; son of Dewey Hughes and Jeanette Butler Adams; married Karen Charles Hughes, Feb 1, 1986; children: Jasmin G & Michael C Hughes. **Educ:** Julliard Sch Drama, 1977; Calif Inst Arts, BFA, 1980. **Career:** Off-Broadway: Pvt. Wilkie in Charles Fuller's A Soldier's Play; August Wilson's Joe Turner's Come & Gone; The Colored Museum; Ma Rainey's Black Bottom; Earth & Sky; Creon in The Oedipus Plays; Broadway: Marius in Elton John & Ann Rice's "Lestat"; A Few Good Men; Hamlet; Northeast Local; Television: "As the World Turns", 1956; "All My Children"; "Happy End"; "New York Undercover", 1997; "The Equalizer", 1988; "Janick"; "Hallelujah", 1993; "Law & Order", 1992-2008; "Law & Order CI", 2003; "Hindsight" 2007; "Guiding Light"; "One Life to Live"; "Another World"; Film: Simple Justice, 1990; Presumed Innocent, 1990; Close to Eden; Stranger Among Us; It Only Happens With You; One Fine Day, 1996; Booty Call; 25th Hour, 2002; She Hate Me, 2004; Dream Street, 2005; The Verdict, 2008; Writer: "Hallelujah", 1993; She Hate Me, 2004; Talk to Me, 2007. **Honors/Awds:** John F Kennedy Ctr Award, New American Plays, 2000; Nominee, Essence Award Nominee Outstanding Writing Motion Picture, 2004; NAACP Image Award for Outstanding Writing in a Motion Picture, 2008. **Home Addr:** 400 W 43rd St Suite 5D, New York, NY 10036.

GENTRY, ALVIN
Basketball coach. **Personal:** Born Nov 5, 1954, Shelby, NC; son of B H Gentry and Bulah; married Pat Sue DeLuca, Jan 1, 1981 (divorced 1986); children: Alexis; married Suzanne Harris; children: Ryan & Jack. **Educ:** Appalachian State Univ, Mgt, 1977. **Career:** Colo Univ, asst coach, 1977-78, 1981-85; Baylor Univ, asst coach, 1980; Kans Univ, asst coach, 1985-88; San Antonio Spurs, asst coach & scout, 1988-90; Los Angeles Clippers, asst coach, 1990-91, 1999-2000, head coach, 2000-03; Miami Heat, head coach, 1991-95; Detroit Pistons, asst coach, head coach, 1998-2000; Phoenix Suns, asst coach, 2004-. **Business Addr:** Assistant Coach, Phoenix Suns, 201 E Jefferson St, Phoenix, AZ 85004, **Business Phone:** (602)379-7900.

GENTRY, DR. ATRON A.
Educator. **Personal:** Born Jan 1, 1938?, El Centro, CA; son of Hannah Gentry and Horace. **Educ:** Pasadena City Col, AA, 1958; Calif State Polytech Col, 1959; Calif State Univ, Los Angeles, BA, 1966; Univ MA, EdD, 1970. **Career:** Ctr Urban Educ Prog, dir, 1968-71; Univ Mass, Sch Educ, assoc dean,1971-75; Apple Creek State Inst Oh, asst supt, 1975-76; Cleveland State Hosp Oh, supt, 1976-78; dir, Univ Mass, Boston Secondary Schs; Hull Col Higher Educ Hull Eng, vis prof, 1981; Beijing Teachers Col, vis prof, 1986; Univ Mass, prof educ, prof emer, 1999-. **Orgs:** Phi Delta Kappa, 1971; staff mem, Olympic Games LA Olympic Org Comm, 1984. **Honors/Awds:** Citizen of the Year, Omega Psi Frat, 1967; Urban Service Award, Off Econ Apport US Govt, 1966; Urban Educ The Hope Factor Philadelphia Sounder,1972; Dedication & Service, Boston Secondary Sch Proj, 1987; Dr. Carter G.Woodson Memorial Uplift Award, Tau Iota Chapter, Omega Psi Fraternity,1988; Crispus Attucks Award, Nat Comt Commemoration Am Revolutionary War Black Patriot, 1991. **Special Achievements:** Author for Learning to Survive: Black Youth Look for Education and Hope; Co-editor, Equity and Excellence in Education; Voice-over in an animation TV series "Fat Albert and the Cosby Kids", 1972. **Military Serv:** AUS, sgt, 1954-56; Kentucky col, 1974. **Business Addr:** Professor Emeritus, University of Massachusetts, School of Education, 300 Massachusetts Ave, Amherst, MA 01003, **Business Phone:** (413)545-0111.

GENTRY, LAMAR DUANE
Government official. **Personal:** Born Dec 19, 1946, Chicago, IL; children: Mark J, LaMar P & Carlos D. **Educ:** Southern Ill Univ, BA, polit sci, 1970; Univ Ill, JD, 1979. **Career:** Gov Ill, model cities specialist, 1970-72, dir, model cities, 1972-74, dir, prog planning & develop, 1974-75; Capital Develop Bd Ill, regional sch dist anal, 1975-76; City E St Louis, IL, comnr community develop, 1981, acting comptroller, 1983, dep mayor, dir admin, 1979-, city mgr, 2001; Pub & Govt Rels Consult, currently. **Orgs:** Bd dir, E St Louis Community Develop Credit Union; bd dir, Boy's Club Springfield, IN, 1973-75; bd dir, Springfield Urban League, 1973-75; pres, Kappa Alpha Psi Springfield Alumni, 1974-76; bd dirs, N Cent Province, currently; bd dirs, E St Louis Alumni Chap.

GENTRY, NOLDEN L., JR.
Lawyer. **Personal:** Born Aug 30, 1937, Rockford, IL; son of Nolden L and Omega; married Barbara Lewis, Apr 24, 1965; children: Adrienne, Natalie, Brian. **Educ:** Univ Iowa, BS, 1960; Iowa Col Law, JD, 1964. **Career:** FBI, spec agt, 1964-65; Iowa, asst atty gen, 1965-66; Brick, Gentry, Bowers, Swartz, Stoltze, Schuling & Levis, PC, atty, 1967-. **Orgs:** State Bd Pub Instr, 1968-70; Delta Dent Plan Iowa, 1971-; Firstar Bank Des Moines, 1978-; Des Moines Independent Sch Dist, 1970-83; Polk County Bar Asn; Iowa State Bar Asn; Bd mem, Des Moinse Independent Comn Sch Bd; bd mem, Greater Des Moines Comn Found; Drake Relays Comn; bd mem, Delta Dent Plan, IA; bd mem, Mid-Iowa Health Found; bd mem, Bankers Trust Co. **Home Addr:** 1517 SW Pleasantview Dr, Des Moines, IA 50315, **Home Phone:** (515)282-0831. **Business Addr:** Attorney, Brick Gentry Bowers Swartz Stoltze Schuling Levis PC, 550 39th St Suite 200, Des Moines, IA 50312, **Business Phone:** (515)274-1450.*

GEORGE, ALLEN
Lawyer. **Personal:** Born Oct 13, 1935, New York, NY; married Valerie Daring; children: Gerald, Kenneth & Johnathan. **Educ:** NYH Univ, BS, 1964; NY Univ Grad Sch Bus, attended 1965-68; Howard Univ, attended 1973; Cleveland State Univ, LLM, 1980. **Career:** Bur Credit Unions, credit union examr, 1965-66; IRS, revenue agt, 1966-69; Lucas, & Tucker & Co, tax acct, 1969-70; Stand Oil Co, atty, 1973-77; Pittman George & Copeland Co LPA, pvt pract, 1978; Allen George & Assoc, atty, currently. **Orgs:** Treas, Phi Alpha Delta Law Fraternity, 1972-73; Nat Bar Asn; Am Bar Asn; Ohio Bar Asn; Bar Asn Greater Cleveland; Cleveland Lawyers Asn; Cuyahoga Co Bar Asn Bd; Glenville YMCA, 1976; bd mem, Cath Interracial Coun; Caribbean Comt Cult Club; Knights Columbus. **Honors/Awds:** Published "The Tax Treatment of The-cost of Class C Stock Purchases", Farmers' Coop, 1971; Cleveland State Univ Col Law, 1975-76. **Military Serv:** USAF, a/1c, 1956-59. **Business Addr:** Attorney, Allen George & Associates, 12200 Fairhill Rd, Cleveland, OH 44120, **Business Phone:** (216)432-1880.

GEORGE, ALMA ROSE
Physician, surgeon, association executive. **Personal:** Born in Mound Bayou, MS; daughter of Phillip M; married Frederick Finch; children: Franklin. **Career:** Detroit Gen Hosp, internship, 1960; Wayne County: operates three surgical outpatient centers & a patient care mgt system, currently; med practitioner, currently. **Orgs:** Pres, Detroit Med Soc; secy, pres, Wolverine State Med Soc; bd delegates, elected, 1966, bd trustees, treeas, pres-elect, 1990, pres, Nat Med Asn; pres, Wolverine State Med Soc. **Honors/Awds:** The 100 Most Influential Black Americans, Ebony Mag, May, 1992. **Business Addr:** President, Wolverine State Medical Society, 10730 W 7 Mile Rd, PO Box 21489, Detroit, MI 48221, **Business Phone:** (313)342-5189.*

GEORGE, CONSTANCE P.
Clergy. **Personal:** Born May 1, 1931, Farmsville, VA; widowed; children: Otis Jr, Gary, Randall, Lisa George Hamilton, Kirby. **Educ:** Col New Rochelle, BA, 1984; NYK Theological Seminary, MDiv, 1988; United Theological Seminary, DMin, 1994. **Career:** Grace Baptist Church, minister missions; Westchester Med Ctr, chaplin consult; Grace Baptist Church, exec minister, assoc pastor congregational care, currently. **Orgs:** YMCA, Mount Vernon, bd; Westchester Childcare; United Black Clergy, Westchester; pres, Mount Vernon Coun Churches; Mount Vernon Human Rights Comn; spiritual life cmnr, Nat Baptist Convention USA; Alpha Kappa Alpha Sorority; Zeta Nu Omega Chap, Westchester County; NCP. **Honors/Awds:** Minister of the Year Award, Black Women's Health, Project, Westchester Chap, 1990; Wall of Honor Citation, Grace Baptist Church, 1991; Recognition Dedicated & Untiring Serv, United Black Clergy, Westchester, 1992; Cert Appreciation, Off County Exec, Westchester, County Women's Adv Bd, 1988; Service Award, Westchester County Bd Legislators, Proclamation, 1992. **Special Achievements:** Sermon printed, "Those Preaching Women," Ella P Mitchell, editor, 1985; first African Baptist ordained clergywoman raised in Mount Vernon, 1986. **Business Addr:** Associate Pastor, Grace Baptist Church, 1 Grace Plz 52 S 6th Ave, Mount Vernon, NY 10550, **Business Phone:** (914)664-2676.*

GEORGE, EDDIE
Football player, television broadcaster. **Personal:** Born Sep 24, 1973, Philadelphia, PA; married Tamara; children: Eriq Michael. **Educ:** Ohio State Univ, Kellogg Scol of Mgt MBA, 2009-. **Career:** Football player (retired), television broadcaster; Houston Oilers, running back, 1996; Tenn Oilers, 1997-2003; Dallas Cowboys, running back, 2004; G4Network, G4 Sports, Training Camp host. **Honors/Awds:** Heisman Trophy, 1995; Maxwell Award, 1995; Walter Camp Award Winner, 1995; Doak Walker Award Winner, 1995; NFL Rookie of the Year Award, 1996; Pro Bowl alternate, 1996; Super Bowl XXXIV, 2000; Ohio State Buckeyes. **Special Achievements:** First round pick, NFL Draft, 1996. **Home Addr:** PO Box 150283, Nashville, TN 37215.

GEORGE, EDWARD
Executive. **Personal:** Married Cutie Bell; children: 5. **Career:** Amalgamated Transit Union, pres & bus agt, 1970-72. **Orgs:** Bd mem, Legal Aid Soc San Joaguin Co, 1969-73; dir, Southeast Comm Asn, 1972-73; bd mem, A Phillip Randolph Ins, 1972-73; bd mem, KUOP FM Radio Sta Univ Pacific Stockton CA; pres, Nat Asn Advan Colored People Stockton; bd Mem, Cit Adv Com San Joaquin Co Planning Asn; adv bd, San Joaquin Co Manpower Prog; adv bd mem, Child Health Disability Prev Prog San Joaquin Co. **Honors/Awds:** Achievement Award, SE Community Ctr, 1971. *

GEORGE, FRANKIE
Association executive. **Career:** Gardere Lane Kids Activ Group, bd pres; La Leadership Inst, Baton Rouge, LA, exec dir, currently. **Honors/Awds:** Where Service Matters Award, WAFB-TV, 2001. **Special Achievements:** Listed in Young Leaders of the Future in 2003 by EBONY Mag. **Business Addr:** Executive Director, Louisianna Leadership Institute, 1206 Florida Blvd, Baton Rouge, LA 70802, **Business Phone:** (225)387-8000.

GEORGE, DR. GARY RAYMOND
State government official, senator (u.s. federal government). **Personal:** Born Mar 8, 1954, Milwaukee, WI; children: Grace Chevalier. **Educ:** Univ Wis, Madison, BBA, acct, 1976; Univ Mich, Ann Arbor, JD, 1979. **Career:** Arthur Young & Co, tax atty, 1979-80; self-employed, atty, 1982-; State Wis, sen 6th dist. **Orgs:** Uniform State Laws Comt, 1981; Ed Block Grant Adv Comt, 1981; Ed Comt Bd,1981; chmn, Pk W Redevel Task Force, 1981; co-chair, Joint Audit Comt,1981-85; mem, Milwaukee City Zoo Bd, 1981; Neighborhood Improve Develop Corp, 1982; bd

trustee, Family Hosp Inc & Family Hosp Nursing Home Inc,1983; chmn, Joint Finance Comt Ed Sub comt, 1983; co-chair, Joint Comt Finance, 1983-; Comt Develop Finance Authority, 1983; Alcohol & Drug Abuse Study Comt, 1983; State Supported Prog Adv Comt, 1983; Mayor's Anti-Gang Initiative Task Force, 1984; Performing Arts Ctr Bd Dir, 1985; Wis State Bar; Dem Party Wis; Nat Caucus State Legislators; Coun State Govts; Milwaukee Forum; Nat Black Caucus State Legislators; Nat Asn Advan Colored People; Wis Spec Olympics; Sexual Assault & Child Abuse Study Comt. **Honors/Awds:** Image Award, Career Youth Develop, 1990; Legislator of the Year, WisFraternal Cong; Human Services Award, Gaylord Nelson; Community Service Award, Harambee Ombudsman Proj Inc; Minority Business Development Award,Minority Bus Enterprise Legal Defense & Educ Found; Distinguished Service Award, Wis Asn Educ Opportunities Personnel; Outstanding Community Advisor Award, Wis Chap Nat Black Alcoholism Coun; Distinguished Service Award,Wis YMCA; Community Service Award, Waukesha Br Nat Asn Advan Colored People. **Special Achievements:** Co-produced films: Adam Clayton Powell, The Milwaukee-Rebirth of a River;author, "Winning is a Habit".

GEORGE, HERMON, JR.
Educator. **Personal:** Born Nov 22, 1945, Tampa, FL; son of Hermon Sr and Henrene Smith; divorced; children: Dahren Malcolm, Melissa Niani. **Educ:** Wilkes Col, Wilkes-Barre, PA, BA, 1967; Middlebury Col, Middlebury, VT, MA, 1968; Univ Calif, Irvine, CA, PhD, 1979. **Career:** Wartburg Col, Waverly, IA, instr Spanish, 1968-70; Fisk Univ, Nashville, TN, instr Spanish, 1970-71; Spelman Col, Atlanta, GA, instr Spanish, 1971-73; Calif State Univ, Fresno, CA, asst prof ethnic studies, 1978-81; SUNY Col, New Paltz, NY, asst prof, Black Studies, 1981-85; Univ Northern Colo, Greeley, CO, assoc prof & coordr, 1985-91; prof, 1991-. **Orgs:** Member-at-large, exec bd, Nat Coun Black Studies, 1980-87; reviewer, Social Sci Jour, 1980-81, 1985-; reviewer, Sci & Soc, 1987-; regional editor, Western Jour Black Studies, 1991-96; Nat Conference Black Polit Scientists, 1988-89. **Honors/Awds:** American Race Relations Theory, Lanham MD, Univ Press Am, 1984; "Black Power in Office: The Limits of Electoral Reform", reprinted in Talmadge Anderson Ed, Black Studies: Theory, Method & Critical Perspectives, 1990; Fellowship, NEH, Summer Inst African-Am Culture, 1987; Faculty Excellence Award, Univ Northern Colorado, 1987; "Clarence Thomas: 'Loyal Foot Soldier' Reaganism"; Court Appeal: The Black Community Speaks Out Racial & Sexual Politics Thomas vs Hill, 1992. **Special Achievements:** The Black Scholar, advising & contributing editor, 1994; Western Social Science Assn, exec council, 1993-96; The Social Science Journal, assoc editor, 1994-95; Contemporary Authors, V 126, 1989. **Business Addr:** Professor, University of Northern Colorado, Department of African Studies, Campus Box 159, Greeley, CO 80639, **Business Phone:** (970)351-1743.*

GEORGE, JASON WINSTON
Actor. **Personal:** Born Feb 9, 1972, Virginia Beach, VA; married Vandana Khanna, Jul 10, 1999; children: 1. **Educ:** Univ Va, BA; Temple Univ, MFA. **Career:** Films: Fallen, 1998; Barbershop, 2002; The Climb, 2002; Clock stoppers, 2002; Straighten Up America, 2003; Sledge: The Untold Story, 2005; Bewitched, 2005; Good Vibrations, 2005; You Did What?, 2006; Coffee, Tea,or Milk?, 2006; The Box, 2007; Three Can Play That Game, 2007; Race, 2008; Broken Windows, 2008; TV Series:"Sunset Beach", 1997-99; "Moesha", 1998-99; "Roswell", 2000; "Arli$$",2000; "Girlfriends", 2000; "Titans", 2000-01; "Friends", 2001; "OffCentre", 2001-02; "Jeremiah", 2002; "She Spies", 2003; Abby, 2003; "Half &Half", 2002-03; "Boomtown", 2003; "Platinum", 2003; Eve, 2003-06; "She Spies," 2003; "Without a Trace," 2005; "Stargate SG-1," 2005-06; "What About Brian", 2006-07; "House M.D.", 2007; Shark, 2007; ER, 2007-08; "Eli Stone", 2008. **Business Addr:** Actor, c/o Writers & Artists Agency Inc, 8383 Wilshire Blvd, Beverly Hills, CA 90211, **Business Phone:** (323)866-0900.*

GEORGE, DR. LUVENIA A
Musicologist, educator. **Personal:** Born Feb 26, 1934, Chicago, IL; daughter of Rev Floyd D and Sweetie; married Henry H, Jun 26, 1953; children: Karen Marsha & Adrianne Rose. **Educ:** Howard Univ, BMEd, 1952; Univ Md, MEd, 1969, PhD, 1995. **Career:** DC Pub Schs, music teacher, 1954-92; Smithsonian Inst, res scholar, 1993-94, Duke Ellington Youth Proj, coordr, 1994-. **Orgs:** Organist, Sargent Presbyterian Church, 1960-, elder, 1991-; pres, DC Music Educrs Asn, 1970-72; pres, DC Chap Am Choral Dirs Asn, 1978-80; Int Asn Jazz Educrs Resource Team. **Honors/Awds:** Hall of Fame Inductee, Africa Am Museum, 1997. **Special Achievements:** Author: "Teaching the Music of Six Different Cultures," 2nd ed, 1987; Lucie Campbell in "We'll Understand It Better Bye & Bye," 1992; Duke Ellington: "Composer Beyond Category," 1993; "The Source of African-American Music," 1991; co-author, Louis Armstrong Education Kit, Smithsonian Inst, Nat Museum Am Hist, 2005. **Business Addr:** Coordinator, Smithsonian Institute, Duke Ellington Youth Project, 301 7th St SW, Washington, DC 20407, **Business Phone:** (202)633-8998.

GEORGE, PAULINE L
Executive. **Personal:** Born Apr 9, 1963, Cleveland, OH. **Educ:** Eastern Mich Univ, BA, 1985; Mich State Univ, MA, 1990. **Career:** WKYC TV-3 News, desk asst, weekend assoc producer, 1986; Continental Cablevision, telemarketing & sales, 1988-89; CNBC, affil rels acct exec, Midwest, 1989-90, affil rels regional mgr, Midwest, 1990-92, affil rels regional mgr, NE, 1992-93; CNBC/America's Talking, reg dir Midwest & Can; NBC Cable Networks, regional dir, Midwest & Can, currently. **Orgs:** Founding pres, Detroit chap, Nat Asn Minorities Cable; dir, nat bd dirs, exec comt, 1997, Women Cable & Telecommunications, 1995-96; Cable Tv Admin & Mkt (CTAM); Nat Asn Female Exec; Alpha Kappa Alpha Sorority. **Honors/Awds:** Carla Laufer Achievement Recognition, Women Cable, Detroit & NW, Ohio Chaps, 1991; Pres Leadership, Nat Asn Minorities Cable, Detroit Chap, 1992; Gerald L Phillipe Award Community Serv Nominee, Gen Elec, 1994. **Special Achievements:** The Effects of Race & Gender on Newscaster Believability, Thesis, MSU, 1990; Proficient in French. **Business Addr:** Regional Director, NBC Cable Networks, 2855 Coolidge Hwy Suite 201A, Troy, MI 48084, **Business Phone:** (810)643-9033.

GEORGE, RON. See GEORGE, RONALD.

GEORGE, RONALD (RON GEORGE)
Football player. **Personal:** Born Mar 20, 1970, Heidelberg, Germany; married Julie. **Educ:** Stanford, econ, 1992. **Career:** Atlanta Falcons, linebacker, 1993-96; Minnesota Vikings, 1997; Kansas City Chiefs, 1998-2000. *

GEORGE, TATE CLAUDE
Basketball player, executive. **Personal:** Born May 29, 1968, Newark, NJ. **Educ:** Univ Conn, attended 1990. **Career:** Basketball player (retired), executive; NJ Nets, 1990-93; Milwaukee Bucks, 1994-95; The George Group, pres, chief exec officer, chmn bd dirs, currently.

GEORGE, DR. THEODORE ROOSEVELT
Physician. **Personal:** Born Dec 27, 1934, Cincinnati, OH; son of Theodore R and Christine Tatum; married Jeanne Sharpe; children: Theodore III & Blair. **Educ:** Howard Univ, BS, 1956, MD, 1960; Freedman's Hosp, intern, 1961, resident, 1967. **Career:** DC Gen Hosp, Howard Univ Hosp, WA Hosp Ctr, physician; Howard Univ Col Med, asst prof; DC Gen Hosp, sr med officer; physician, currently. **Orgs:** Nat Med Asn, Med Soc DC, Chi Delta Mu Med Soc; Former Interns & Resd Freedmen's Hosp, Am Asn Gynec Laparoscopists, Alpha Phi Alpha Frat; WA GynEC Soc, Medico-Chirurgical Soc, Pan AMA, Urban League, Jr Citizens Corps, NAACP, Police Boy's Club, MD Med Lic, 1960; DC Med Lic, 1965; Cert, Am Bd Ob & Gynec, 1969; trustee bd, St Paul Am Ch; Daniel Hale Williams Reading Club, 1972-; Southern Med Asn, 1980-; Howard Univ Med Alumni Assoc. **Honors/Awds:** Natioanlional Competitive Scholarship, 1952-56; Representative Aviation Award, 1954; Dean's list, 1952-56; Dean's Cup, 1955; Presidents Cup, 1956; AFROTC Award, 1956; Outstanding Male Gradugate Student Counsel, 1956; Graduate Cum Laude, 1956; Natioanlional Medical Asn Scholarship, 1957; Psychiatric Award, 1960; Natioanl Medical Asn Award, 1967; American Physicians Recognition Award, 1972; American Academy of Family Physicians Award, 1974; Howard Univ Med Alumni Asn Award, 1974; American Cancer Soc Cert of Merit, 1975; Natioanl Fraternal Order of Police, 1976; Delivery in Elderly Primagravida Following Myomectomy, 1964; Vascular Systems Recovery of Red Blood Cells from the Peritonial Cavity, 1965; Concomittant Use of Stomaseptin & Metronidazole in the Treatment of Trichomonas Vaginalis Complicated by Moniliasis, 1966; Pelvic Exenteration, 1967; The Changing Role of Crean Section, 1969; Wyeth Teaching Award, 1993. **Military Serv:** USAF, capt, 1961-63; Commendation Medal; DC Coun Recognition Resolution, 2001. **Home Addr:** 1840 Primrose Rd NW, Washington, DC 20012, **Home Phone:** (202)726-7534. **Business Addr:** Physician, General and Family Practice, 5505 5th St NW, Washington, DC 20011, **Business Phone:** (202)726-4847.

GEORGE-BOWDEN, DR. REGINA
Educator. **Personal:** Born Mar 14, 1947, Durham, NC; daughter of Johnetta Holloway George and Reginald C George; divorced; children: Morris LaSalle. **Educ:** Tenn State Univ, BS, 1968; NC Cent Univ, MA, 1971; NC A&T Univ, MEd, 1977; NC State Univ, EdD, 1989. **Career:** NC A&T State Univ, asst prof sociol, 1972-77; Shaw Univ, prof sociol & educ, 1990-2000; Durham Tech Community Col, laison teacher educ prog; NC Cent Univ, Teacher Liaison, dir campus ministries, currently. **Orgs:** Durham Pub Schs, sch bd mem, 1998, vice chmn, currently; sr bd mem, NC Cent Univ. **Honors/Awds:** Faculty Research Award, Mobil Fel, 1998; Teaching Int Res Grant, NIH HBCU's, 1996 & 1997. **Special Achievements:** Co-published Character Education for Shared Democracy, 1996; Evaluation & Community Service Programs, NCCU, 1997; Women In Costa Rica, 1997. **Business Addr:** Director of Campus Ministries, North Carolina Central University, 1801 Fayetteville St, Durham, NC 27707, **Business Phone:** (919)530-6100.

GERALD, ARTHUR THOMAS, JR.
School administrator. **Personal:** Born Oct 13, 1947, Boston, MA; married Henrietta; children: Arthur Michael & Alama Michelle. **Educ:** Lincoln Univ, attended 1967; Berkshire Christian Col, AB, Theology, 1970;Gordon-19 Conwell Seminary, MA, 1972. **Career:** Salem State Col, advisor to afro-american soc 1972-73, dir minority affairs 1973-81; assoc dean acad affairs, 1981-. **Orgs:** Associate minister 12th Baptist Ch. **Business Addr:** Associate Dean Academy Affairs, Salem State College, 352 Lafayette St, Salem, MA 01970, **Business Phone:** (978)542-6000.*

GERALD, DR. MELVIN DOUGLAS
Association executive, physician. **Personal:** Born Jul 17, 1942, Cerro Gordo, NC; son of Paul Sr and Mattie Vann; married Lenora Graham Gerald, Dec 24, 1965 (died 2003); children: Sonja Z & Melvin D Jr. **Educ:** Morehouse Col, Atlanta, BS, 1964; Howard Univ, MD, 1970; Johns Hopkins Univ, Sch Pub Health, MPH, 1974. **Career:** Shaw Community Health Ctr, med dir, 1973-75; Howard Univ, asst prof, 1974-, dir, family practice, 1976-78; Gerald Family Care Assoc, physician 1978-, pres & chief exec officer, currently; Providence Hosp, chmn, Dept Family Practice, 1989-93; Howard Univ Hosp Med, pres, 1996-98. **Orgs:** Bd dirs, Md State Cancer Soc, 1979-85; DC Acad Family Physicians, pres, 1992-94; chair, Dept FP, Prince Georges Hosp Ctr, 1994-98; pres, Howard Univ Med Alumni Asn, 1996-98; pres medical staff, Howard Univ Hosp, 1996-98; bd dirs, Am Acad Family Physicians, 1996-99. **Home Addr:** 11403 Dundee Dr, Mitchellville, MD 20721, **Home Phone:** (301)262-6674. **Business Addr:** President, Chief Executive Officer, Gerald Family Care Associates, 1160 Varnum St NE Suite 117, Washington, DC 20017, **Business Phone:** (202)832-7007.

GERALDO, MANUEL ROBERT
Lawyer. **Personal:** Born Dec 20, 1950, Newark, NJ; son of Iria Gouveia and Joaquim dos Santos; married Cynthia Hart, Jun 9, 1984; children: Manuel R II & Alexander Joaquim. **Educ:** Seton Hall Univ, BS, 1972; Rutgers Univ, Sch Law, JD, 1977; Georgetown Univ, Sch Law, LLM, 1984. **Career:** Newark Munic Coun, exec asst, 1974-77; Dep Housing & Urban Develop, trial atty, 1977-79; Robinson & Geraldo, atty, 1979-. **Orgs:** Comnr, Wash Suburban Sanitary Commn; Greater Wash Ibero Am Coc, 1988-; dir, Leadership Wash, Portuguese Heritage Scholarship Found, 1990-; dir, Portuguese Am Leadership coun US; Prince Hall Free & Accepted Mason, 1984-; Prince Hall Shriner, 1985-; usher, First Baptist Church Suitland, 1990-. **Military Serv:** NJ Nat Guard, e-4, 1970-76. **Business Addr:** Attorney, Robinson & Geraldo, 1316 Pennsylvania Ave SE, Washington, DC 20003, **Business Phone:** (202)544-2888.

GERMAN, JAMMI (JAMMI DARNELL GERMAN)
Football player. **Personal:** Born Jul 4, 1974, Ft Myers, FL. **Educ:** Miami Univ. **Career:** Football player (retired); Atlanta Falcons, wide receiver, 1998-2000; Cleveland Browns, 2001. **Honors/Awds:** Mr Football Award, 1992.

GERMAN, JAMMI DARNELL. See GERMAN, JAMMI.

GERMANY, ALBERT (AL GEE)
Disc jockey, administrator. **Personal:** Born Oct 23, 1942, Leeds, AL; married Jessica Khan; children: Mark, Shawn. **Educ:** Univ Pittsburgh, Geo Heide Sch Announcing, attended 1964. **Career:** WAMO, 1964-66; WZUM, Pittsburgh, 1966-68; WWRL, 1968-72; Washington Radio, 1968; WPIX, 1972; WLIB, NY, prog dir, 1973; Syndicated Radio Show Rap & Rythm; Radio Station ZDK, co-owner; Nat Asn Radio & TV Announcers, exec dir, 1976-77; St Johns Antiqua Prof Black Announcers NY, West Indies pres. **Business Addr:** 801 2nd Ave, New York, NY.

GERMANY, SYLVIA MARIE ARMSTRONG
College administrator. **Personal:** Born Jan 10, 1950, New Orleans, LA; married Plenty Morgan Jr; children: Jobyna Joidella & Adam Nathan. **Educ:** Southern Univ, New Orleans, BS, 1980. **Career:** Orleans Parish Sch Bd, admin exec secy, 1977-80; Pre-Employ Prog, bus instr, 1980-81; Sidney N Collier Vo-Tech, bus instr, 1981-85; Oakwood Col, personnel assist, 1985, human resource dir, currently. **Orgs:** La Vo-Tech Asn, 1981-85; Am Soc Personnel Administrators, 1985-. **Business Addr:** Director, Oakwood College, Human Resource Department, 7000 Adventist Blvd, Huntsville, AL 35896, **Business Phone:** (256)726-7274.

GERVIN, GEORGE
Basketball coach, association executive. **Personal:** Born Apr 27, 1952, Detroit, MI; married Joyce; children: George Jr, Jared & Tia Monique. **Educ:** Eastern Mich Univ, attended 1973. **Career:** Basketball player (retired), coach, association executive; ABA Va Squires,1972-74; Phoenix Suns, 1974; San Antonio Spurs, 1974-85, Chicago Bulls,1985-86; Italian League Banco Roma, 1986-87; Quad City Thunder (CBA),1989; San Antonio Spurs, community rels rep, 1992, asst coach, 1993, community rels dept, 1994; George Gervin Youth Ctr, founder, currently. **Orgs:** Continental Basketball Asn Quad City Thunder, 1989-90; NBA Hall Fame. **Honors/Awds:** NBA All Star Game, 1977, 1979, 1980; NBA Scoring Champion; All Star, 8times; League's Leading Scorer 4 times; All-Star Game MVP, 1980; Seagram's Crown, 1978, 1979; inducted into Naismith Memorial Basketball Hall of Fame, 1996. **Special Achievements:** One of 50 Greatest Players in NBA Hist, 1996; Top 75 NBA Players, SLAMMag, 2003. **Business Addr:**

Founder, George Gervin Youth Center, 6903 S Sunbelt Dr, San Antonio, TX 78218, **Business Phone:** (210)804-1786.

GEYER, EDWARD B, JR.
Clergy. **Personal:** Born Aug 23, 1929, New York, NY; married Laura E Williams; children: Edward Blaine III & Ruth Anne. **Educ:** Wash Sq Col; STB Magna Cum Laude, Div Sch, Episcopal Ch Phila; Sch Educ New York Univ, post grad Work. **Career:** St Peter's, New York, curate, 1958-60; St Luke's, New Haven, CT, rector, 1960-68; St Peter's, Bennington, VT, 1968-72; Good Shepherd, Hartford, CT, 1972; Greater Hartford Coun Churches, vpres 1973-78; Provincial Synod, 1974; Martin Luther King Jr Housing Develop, Hartford, pres, 1974; Capitol Region Conf Church, 1978-79. **Orgs:** Supvr, Gen Theol Sem, 1958-60; bd dirs, New Haven Community Coun, 1964-68; Educ Comn, 1964-68; Exec Coun Diocese Conn, 1965-68; Dept Christ Educ, 1965-68; Steering Comt NH Young Mother's Prog, 1965-68; bd mem, Ctr Mental Retardation 1965-68; Clergyman's Adv Com Conn Planned Parenthood, 1965-68; chaplain, New Haven State Jail, 1966-68; Children Ctr, Hamden, CT, 1967-68; mem bd trustees, Philadelphia Div Sch, 1968-73; Urban Task Force New Haven C of C, 1968; Civil Serv comnr, New Haven, 1698; Christ Church Cathedral Chap Hartford, 1968-73; Bennington Ministerial Asn, 1968-72; bd mem, Bennington-Rutland Opp Coun, 1968-72; vpres, Bennington Coun Churchs, 1969-72; Gen Theol Sem 1970; Bennington Housing Authority, 1970-72; exec coun, Diocese Vermont, 1970-72; New Eng Provincial Synod, 1971-72; treas, BROC 1971-72; Comm on Ministry, 1971-72; Church Diocesan Liturgical Comn, 1971-72; mem bd, Phoenix House, 1971-72; New Eng Prov Synod Coun, 1973; Comn On State Church 1975.

GHENT, HENRI HERMANN
Writer, museum director, critic. **Personal:** Born Jun 23, 1926, Birmingham, AL; son of Reuben Gantt and Jennie Gantt. **Educ:** New Eng Conserv, Boston, MA, attended 1951; Mus Sch Fine Arts, Boston, MA, attended 1952; Longy Sch Music, Cambridge, MA, attended 1953; Univ Paris, France, attended 1960. **Career:** Martha Baird Rockefeller fel Music, 1957-58; Elegant Mag, New York, cult news ed, 1964-68; Inst Arts & Sci, Brooklyn, asst dir, 1968-69; Brooklyn Mus, Com Gallery, dir, 1968-72; Le Monde de la Musique, Paris, New York corres; Danser Mag, Paris; Ford Found Travel & Study fel, 1974-75. **Orgs:** Consult, Nat Endowment Arts, Wash, DC, 1973-74; chief juror, Dayton Art Inst, All-Ohio Painting Sculpture Biennial, 1972; chief juror, Grad Stud Art & Design, Pratt Inst, Brooklyn, NY, 1972; Nat Asn Advan Colored People. **Honors/Awds:** Marian Anderson Scholarship Award, 1951, 1952; Art Critics Award, Nat Endowment Arts, Wash, DC, 1973-74; Samuel H Kress Found Award in Arts Research; Achievement in the Arts Award, Nat Asn Advan Colored People, 1973. **Special Achievements:** Hon degree humanities, Allen Univ, Columbia, SC, 1966; Contributed significant articles on visual & performing arts to Le Monde de la Musique Paris, New York Times, Los Angeles Times, Cleveland Plain Dealer, Art Int, Lugano, Switz, Artforum, New York, Art in America, New York, Boston Globe, Village Voice, New York. **Military Serv:** AUS, technician, 1945-46; Good Marksmanship, 1946. **Home Addr:** 310 E 75th St, New York, NY 10021. *

GHOLSON, DR. GENERAL JAMES
Musician, educator. **Personal:** Born Oct 15, 1944, Norfolk, VA; son of G James and Elsie; children: Christopher James. **Educ:** Mich State Univ, BM, 1966; Cath Univ, MM, 1970, DMA, 1975. **Career:** USN Band, Wash, DC, sect clarinetist & solist, 1966-70; Cath Univ, Wash, DC, grad asst, 1970-72; Opera Memphis, solo clarinet, 1972; Memphis State Univ, instr, asst prof, assoc prof clarinet, 1972-99, prof, 1999-; Memphis Woodwind Quintet, 1972-99, prof, 1999-; Memphis Sym, solo clarinet, 1975, prin clarinet. **Orgs:** Vol, SMART House; Promise Acad, bd dirs, Memphis, 2004-08; mem, Memphis Woodwind Quintet. **Honors/Awds:** FLAME Award, Univ Memphis, 2007. **Special Achievements:** Author: The Seasonal Clarinetist; The Seasoned Clarinetist; videos: How to Make All West, Jamus, 1985; Kards in the Key of Kroepsch, Jamus, 1986; How to Make All Region a Breeze, Jamus, 1986; Project Solo, Jamus, 1987. **Military Serv:** USN Band, Wash, DC, 1966-70; sect clarinetist & soloist. **Business Addr:** Professor of Clarinet, University of Memphis, Music Department, Suite 293 Music, Memphis, TN 38152, **Business Phone:** (901)678-3793.

GHOLSON, ROBERT L
Executive, president (organization). **Educ:** Tenn State Univ, BS, bus admin; Univ Memphis, MBA; Life Off Mgt Asn, educ & mgt credits. **Career:** Universal Life Ins Co, pres, 1995-. **Orgs:** Bd mem, Memphis Boys Club; bd mem, Jr Achievement. **Business Addr:** President, Universal Life Insurance Co, 480 Linden Ave, Memphis, TN 38106, **Business Phone:** (901)775-0930.

GHOLSTON, BETTY J.
School administrator, vice president (organization). **Personal:** Born Feb 1, 1942, Wagram, NC; married Willie Gunter; children: Lisa Regina, Betty Cornelia, Saranarda & Willie G Jr. **Educ:** NC Cent Univ, BS, Com, 1963; NC A&T State Univ, MS, admin, 1979; Univ NC, further study, 1978. **Career:** Richmond County Sch, media specialist, 1968; Cameron Morrison Sch, media specialist, 1968-77; Cameron Morrison Youth Ctr, project dir & media specialist, 1977-83; Richmond County Schs, job placement coordr, 1984; NC Dept Correction, dir fed proj & educ spec; Scotland Spring Hill Township, Vice Chair, currently. **Orgs:** Vpres, Cameron Morrison NCAE, 1982-83; bd dirs, Black Elected Municipal Officials, 1983-84; Bd Comnrs, Mayor Pro Tem Wagram, 1974-; rep, NC Coun Govt-Region N, 1982-; vice chair, Scotland Co Bd of Educ, 1986-98. **Honors/Awds:** Founder, Wagram Br Libr, 1975; Teacher of the Year, NC Dept of Youth Serv, 1977. **Business Addr:** Vice Chair, Scotland County Government, SpringHill TownShip, 21681 Ctr St, PO Box 135, Wagram, NC 28396.*

GIBBONS, DEVERON M
Vice president (Organization), lobbyist. **Educ:** Univ Fla, BA, polit sci, 1995; Univ S Fla, MS, pub admin, 2006. **Career:** Mayor St Petersburg, spec asst; Holland & Knight, sr pub affairs adv; Amscot Financial Corp, vpres, pub affairs, currently. **Orgs:** Bd Gov, St Petersburg Area Chamber Com; past chair, Chambers S Cent Coun; former bd mem, local Nat Asn Advan Colored People; mem, Water Leadership Adv Bd, Univ S Fla; bd mem, Worknet Pinellas; Bd trustees, St Petersburg Col, 2006-. **Special Achievements:** First African-American appointed to Pinellas County Parks Board of Directors, 2000. **Business Addr:** Vice President of Public Affairs, Amscot Financial Corp, 8430 N Armenia Ave, Tampa, FL 33604, **Business Phone:** (813)932-4339.*

GIBBS, JACK GILBERT, JR.
Lawyer. **Personal:** Born Aug 11, 1953, Columbus, OH; son of Jack Gilbert Sr and Ruth Ann; married Aloma, Jul 27, 1992; children: Jack Gilbert III & Anna Louise. **Educ:** Mich State Univ, BA, 1975; Capital Univ Law Sch, JD, 1981. **Career:** Columbus Pub Schs, teacher, 1976-78; Ohio Atty Gen, legal intern, 1980-81; Ben Espy, law clerk, 1982; Self Employed, atty, 1982-. **Orgs:** Columbus Bar Asn, 1982-; Ohio State Bar Asn, 1982-; Am Bar Asn, 1982-; bd mem, pres, Hilltop Civic Coun Inc, 1987-93; chmn admin bd, Centenary United Methodist Church, 1987-95; Capital Law Sch Black Alumni, pres, 1990-; UNCF Star Panelist, star panelist, 1993-; Am Inns Ct, 1994-; bd counr, Capital Univ Law Sch, 2006-07. **Honors/Awds:** Community Service Award, Columbus Dispatch, 1988; Community Service Award, Ohio State Univ Bus Sch, 1989; Service Award, Capital Law Sch, 1990; Service Award, Hilltop Civic Coun Inc, 1994; David D White Award, African Am Law Alumni Asn, 2004. **Special Achievements:** Lecture to community groups; Teach one seminar to attorneys a year; testified as an expert witness on Probate Law; Written serveral articles on Probate Law & Estate Planning. **Home Addr:** 3855 McDannald Dr, Columbus, OH 43230, **Home Phone:** (614)475-0569. **Business Addr:** Attorney, 233 S High St Suite 208, Columbus, OH 43215, **Business Phone:** (614)224-3191.

GIBBS, DR. JEWELLE TAYLOR
Educator. **Personal:** Born Nov 4, 1933, Stratford, CT; daughter of Margaret P Morris and Julian A; married James Lowell Jr; children: Geoffrey Taylor & Lowell Dabney. **Educ:** Radcliffe Col, AB, 1955, Cert Bus Admin, 1959; Univ Calif, MSW, 1970, MA, psychol, 1976, PhD, psychol, 1980. **Career:** US Labor Dept, Wash, jr mgt asst, 1955-56; Pillsbury Co, Minneapolis, MN, mkt res analyst, 1959-61; Stanford Univ, psychiatric social worker, 1970-74, 1978-79; Univ Calif, Berkeley, prof, 1979-2000; ed, Young, Black & Male Am: An Endangered Species, 1988; Zellerbach Family Fund Chair Social Policy, Community Change & Pract. **Orgs:** John Hay Whitney Opport Fel, Radcliffe Col, 1958-59; task force specp opulations, Pres Comn Ment Health, 1976-78; NIMH Pre-Doctoral Fel, Univ Calif, 1979-80; bd publs, Nat Asn Social Workers, 1980-82; bd regents, Univ Santa Clara, 1980-85; ed bd, Am J Orthopsychiatry, 1980-84; clinicalpsychol, pvt pract consult, 1983-90; consult, Carnegie Corp, 1983-87; fel, Bunting Inst, Radcliffe Col, 1985; bd dir, Am Orthopsychiatric Asn, 1985-88; Adv Bd, Nat Ctr C Poverty, 1987-95; fel, Am Psychol Asn, 1990; vpres, bd trustees, Radcliffe Col, 1991-95; vpres, bd trustees, Van LobenSells Found, 1999-; bd dir, Theatre Works, 1999-2002; ed bd, Int J SocialWelfare, 1998-2002. **Honors/Awds:** McCormick Award, Am Asn Suicidology, 1987; Alumnae Achievement Award, Radcliffe Col, 1990; Berkeley Citation, Univ Calif, 2000; Hewlett Fel, Res Inst Comparative Study Race & Ethnicity, Stanford Univ, 2001-02; Lamplighter Award, Black Leadership Forum, 2001; vis scholar, Wash Univ, St Louis, spring, 2003; alumna hon mem, Harvard Univ Chapter Phi BetaKappa Soc, 2005. **Special Achievements:** Author: Young, Black and Male in America: An Endangered Species. AuburnHouse, 1989; "Race and Justice: Rodney King and O J Simpson in a House Divided", 1996 & co-author, Preserving Privilege: Californian Politics, Propositions, and People of Color, 2000, co-author, Children of Color, with Larke N Huang PhD, 1989, 2003 (3rd ed).

GIBBS, KAREN PATRICIA
Television news anchorperson. **Personal:** Born May 9, 1952, Boston, MA; daughter of James and Bertha Gibbs. **Educ:** Roosevelt Univ Chicago, BSBA, 1976; Univ Chicago Grad Sch Business, MBA, 1978. **Career:** Cont Commodity Serv Inc, interest rate specialist 1978-82; Harris Trust & Savings Bank, govt securities rep 1982-83; Dean Witter Reynolds, hedging & trading strategist 1983-85, sr financial futures analyst 1985-, vpres, 1985-92; CNBC, specialist, anchor, 1992-97; FOX News Channel, sr bus corresp; Wall Street Week, co-anchor, currently. **Orgs:** bd dirs, Henry Booth House 1981-85; bd dirs, Chicago Lung Asn 1983-86; pres, Dorchester Condo Asn, 1984-89; Chicago Chap Nat Black MBA Asn, 1985-86; Nat Asn Security Prof; Chicago Pvt Indust Coun, 1990-92; Univ Ill Chicago, Col Med Corp Adv Bd. **Special Achievements:** Quoted frequently in NY Times and Wall St Journal; Articles published in CBOT's Financial Exchange; selected by pres of Dean Witter's Capital Mkts Group for Nat Ad Campaign to recruit minority employees; Featured Guest on Wall Street Week, 1991. **Business Addr:** Co-Anchor, Wall Street Week, Md Pub TV, 11767 Owings Mills Blvd, Owings Mills, MD 21117.*

GIBBS, KEVIN CASEY
Baseball player. **Personal:** Born Apr 3, 1974, Washington, DC. **Educ:** Old Dominion Univ. **Career:** Director; Yakima Bears, 1995; San Bernardino, 1995-97, 2000; Vero Beach Dodgers, 1995-96, 2000; San Antonio Missions, 1997, 2000; Albuquerque Isotopes, 1998-99, 2000; Los Angeles Dodgers, 1996, 1999-01; Carolina, 2000; Colo Rockies, left field, 2001; Tampa Bay Devil Rays, 2002; Norwich Navigators, 2002; Camdan, 2003; Philadelphia Phillies, outfielder, 2004; Diamond Skills Baseball, Currently. **Orgs:** Director, Diamond Skills Baseball. **Honors/Awds:** Fastest Baserunner, Baseball Am, 1996. **Business Addr:** Director, Diamond Skills Baseball, PO BOX 1452, Olney, MD 20830, **Business Phone:** (301)570-2833.*

GIBBS, MARLA
Actor. **Personal:** Born Jun 14, 1931, Chicago, IL; daughter of Douglas Bradley and Ophelia Birdie Kemp; divorced 1969; children: Angela Elayne, Jordan Joseph Jr & Dorian Demetrius. **Educ:** Cortez Peters Bus Col, 1950-52. **Career:** Serv Bindery, receptionist, 1951-56; Kelly Girls, 1956; Gotham Hotel,switchboard operator, 1957; United Airlines, travel consult, 1963-74;Marla Gibbs Enterprises, pres, 1978; Hormar Inc, vpres, 1978; Marla's Memory Lanes, restaurant owner; actress, currently; Films: Sweet Jesus,Preacherman, 1973; Black Belt Jones, 1974; Passing Through, 1977; NobodysChild, 1986; Menu for Murder, 1990; Florence; 1990; Up Against the Wall,1991; Last Breeze of Summer, 1991; The Meteor Man, 1993; Lily in Winter,1994; Border to Border, 1998; Foolish, 1999; Lost & Found, 1999; The-Visit, 2000; Stanley's Gig, 2000; The Brothers, 2001; The Ties That Bind,2006; TV series: "The Jeffersons", 1975-85; The Missing Are Deadly, 1975;"Barney Miller", 1975; "Arthur Hailey's the Moneychangers", 1976; YouCan't Take It with You, 1979; "Checking In", 1981; The Love Boat, 1981;"Pryor's Place", 1984; "227", 1985-90; Menu for Murder, 1990; "A DifferentWorld", 1993; "In the Heat of the Night", 1993; "Empty Nest", 1993; Lilyin Winter, 1994; "Burke's Law", 1995; "Martin", 1995; "The Fresh Prince of Bel-Air", 1996; "101 Dalmatians: The Series", 1997-98; "The Hughleys",1998-2002; "Martial Law", 1999; "Happily Ever After: Fairy Tales for EveryChild", 1999; "Dawson's Creek", 1999; "Touched by an Angel", 2000;"Judging Amy", 2001; "Mother's Day", 2001; "The King of Queens", 2002;"The Rerun Show", 2002; "Arli$$", 2002; "Profiles in Agenting", 2002;"Passions", 2004; "Listen Up", 2004; "ER", 2005; "Only Connect", 2005;"Cold Case", 2005; "It's Never Too Late", co-writer, 227's theme song 2006. **Orgs:** Treas, UGMAA Found; Sci Mind Church; Am Fedn Tv & Radio Artists; hon mem, Alpha Kappa Alpha Sorority. **Honors/Awds:** Numerous honors & awards including Award, Nat Acad Arts & Sci, 1976; Award, Miss Black Culture Pageant, 1977; Award, United Negro Col Fund, 1977; Appreciation Award, La Sch Dist, 1978; Award, Women Involved, 1979; Tribute to the Black Woman Award, WISE, 1979; Community Service Award, Crenshaw High Sch, 1980; Award, Paul Robeson Players, 1980; Image Award for Best Performance, Actress Comedy Series Spec, 1982; Emmy Award, nominations, Outstanding Performance, supporting actress, 1981-85; Golden Globe Nominee for Best Performance, 1985. **Home Phone:** (310)275-6028. **Business Addr:** Actress, c/o Buzz Halliday & Associates, 144 S Doheny Dr Suite 206, Los Angeles, CA 90048, **Business Phone:** (310)275-6028.*

GIBBS, NATHANIEL K.
Artist. **Personal:** Born Jun 15, 1948, Baltimore, MD; son of John W and Rosie M. **Educ:** MD Inst Col Art, BFA, Fine Arts, 1975; Am Univ, MFA, Fine Arts, Painting, 1980. **Career:** Baltimore City Mural Prog, 1981; Sch 33 Art Ctr, workshop instr, 1982-84; self-employed painter, currently. **Orgs:** Baltimore Charcoal Club of Fine Arts, 1994. **Special Achievements:** Works include: mural at Trinity Episcopal Church, Baltimore; 12 works appearing in Jame Melton Collection; painting appeared in film Runaway Bride; two portraits at John Hopkins Univ; mural at Frederick Douglass; exhibitions: Monticello's Kenwood House, 2000, 2003. **Business Addr:** Artist, Privately, 2432 W Coldspring Lane, Baltimore, MD 21215, **Business Phone:** (410)664-7249.*

GIBBS, ROBERT LEWIS
Circuit court judge, lawyer. **Personal:** Born Jul 26, 1954, Jackson, MS; son of William and Mary; married Debra, Aug 29, 1987; children: Ariana & Justis. **Educ:** Tougaloo Col, BA, 1976; Univ Miss, JD, 1979. **Career:** Southeast Miss Legal Services, staff atty, 1979-80; Seventh Circuit District, asst dist atty, 1980; Miss Atty Gen, deputy atty gen, 1980-90; Hinds County Circuit Ct, judge; Brunini, Grantham, Grower & Hewes LLC, partner, currently.

Orgs: MS Bar, 1979-; Magnolia Bar Asn, 1979-; Charles Clark Inns Ct, 1989-; Am Trial Nat Bar Asn, 1992-; Lawyers Asn, 1993-; Hinds County Bar Asn; Nat Bar Asn; Tougaloo Col Alumni Asn; Miss Bar Found; pres, 100 Black Men Jackson. **Honors/Awds:** Award of Distinction, Univ Miss, 1988; Government Service Award, Magnolia Bar Assn, 1989; Award of Appreciation, Tougaloo Col, 1991; Community Service Award, Alpha Kappa Alpha, 1992. **Business Addr:** Partner, Brunini, Grantham, Grower & Hewes LLC, 1400 Trustmark Bldg 248 E Capitol St Suite 1400, PO Box 119, Jackson, MS 39201, **Business Phone:** (601)960-6861.

GIBBS, DR. SANDRA E
Educator, association executive. **Personal:** Born Aug 16, 1942, Chicago, IL; daughter of Willa Marie Hurd and Louis Shelby. **Educ:** AM & N Col, Pine Bluff, Ark, AB, AM, Eng, 1964; Univ IL, Urbana, IL, AM, Eng, 1971, PhD Eng, 1974. **Career:** Little Rock Ark Pub Sch, high sch Eng teacher, 1964-70; Univ IL, teacher fresh rhtrc, 1970-71; Nat Coun Teacher Eng, dir min affairs spec proj, 1973-77, dir spec progs, assoc exec dir, currently; Enterprise Human Resources, proj dir. **Orgs:** Con AR Dept Educ Little Rock Ark, 1969; mem, adv bd Prime Time Sch TV, 1975; consult, HEW Women's Proj Benedict Col, 1978-80; prop reviewer, Nat Endowment Humanities, 1979; mem, Delta Sigma Theta Soc; mem, Alpha Kappa Mu Hon Soc. **Honors/Awds:** Teachers Chairs of English Fellow, 1971; Crest Co Scholar, 1960-64; NDEA Fel, 1966-67; Distinguished Alumni Citation, Nat Asn Equal Opportunity Higher Educ, 1986. **Special Achievements:** Publications: co-editor, A Celebration of Teachers, 1986, National Council of Teachers of English; "Black Novels Revisited," New Directions For Women, 1987; "Maria Stewart: Heroic Role Model," New Directions for Women, 1988; "A Symphony of Voices," Maryand English Journal, 1989; "Considering Diversity in Teaching Language and Literature," Michigan English Teacher, 1990; Zelma Watson George biographical sketch, Notable Black American Women. **Home Addr:** 1812 Braodmoor Dr, Champaign, IL 61821. **Business Addr:** Associate Executive Director, National Council of Teachers of Engineering, 1111 W Kenyon Rd, Urbana, IL 61801-1096, **Business Phone:** (217)278-3635.

GIBBS, WILLIAM LEE
Banker, chief executive officer. **Personal:** Born Apr 11, 1945, Hinton, WV; son of William McKinley and Louise A; married Amporn Mankong, May 25, 1991; children: Vince Visuti (stepson). **Educ:** WVA State Col, BS, 1972. **Career:** Am Fletcher Nat Bank, vpres, 1972-82; Am Bankers Asn, assoc dir, 1982-83; Stonier Graduate Sch Banking, fac, 1984-; BankSouth Corp, sr vpres, 1983-92; Citizens Trust Bank, pres & chief exec officer, 1993-. **Orgs:** bd mem, United Way Metropolitan Atlanta, 1992-; Atlanta Action Forum, 1993-; bd & exec mem, Cent Atlanta Prog Comt, 1993-; bd dirs, Atlanta Life Ins Co; Atlanta Chamber Com; Am Bankers Asn Community Bank Coun; bd councilors, Carter Ctr. **Honors/Awds:** The Pioneer Award, Atlanta Urban Bankers Asn; Honorary Commissioner of Agriculture, State of Ind. **Business Addr:** President, Chief Executive Officer, Citizens Trust Bank, 75 Piedmont Ave, Atlanta, GA 30303, **Business Phone:** (404)653-2800.*

GIBEL, RONALD L
Executive. **Career:** Urban Off Prod, pres, ceo, currently. **Home Addr:** 55 Washington St, Brooklyn, NY 11201. **Business Addr:** President, Chief Executive Officer, Urban Office Products, 55 Washington Str Suite 501-502, New York, NY 11201, **Business Phone:** 800-340-7870.*

GIBEL MEVORACH, KATYA (KATYA GIBEL AZOULAY)
Educator. **Educ:** Hebrew Univ Jerusalem, BA, 1982, MA, 1988; Women's Studies, Duke Univ,cert, 1992; Duke Univ, PhD, Cult Anthrop, 1995. **Career:** Duke Univ, Univy Writing Prog, instr, 1994, Inst Asian & African Lang,1995; Grinnell Col, chmn, Africana Studies Concentration Minority Scholar-In-Residence, 1996-2006, chmn, Am Studies Concentration, 2004-05, assoc prof, Dept Anthrop & Am Studies Concentration, 1996-. **Orgs:** Am Studies Asn; Am Anthrop Asn; Asn Black Anthropologists; consult & coordr, South Africa, Int Affairs Comt, Civil Rights & Peace Movement Party, Israel; ed bd, Iton Aher, Israel, 1989-91; ed bd, New Outlook,Israel, 1990-91; chair, Africana Studies Concentration, 1996-2000; Grinnell Col Diversity Steering Comm, 2002-05; Presidential Diversity Comm Task Force. **Special Achievements:** Author: "It's Not the Color of Your Skin but the Race of Your Kin, and Other Myths of Identity", 1997; Articles: "Kol Ha'ir, 1988; "Elitism in the Women's Peace Camp", 1989; "Inaccurate Equations: Racism vs. Nationalism", 1989; "South Africa: Reflections and Lessons", 1990; "Injustice, Prejudice, and Peace", 1991; "Jewish After Mount Sinai: Jews, Blacks and the (Multi) racial Category", 2001; "Not An Innocent Pursuit: The Politics of a 'Jewish' Genetic Signature", 2003; "Greater DesMoines Jewish Press", 2006. **Business Addr:** Associate Professor, Grinnell College, ARH 121, Grinnell, IA 50112, **Business Phone:** (641)269-4324.*

GIBSON, BENJAMIN F.
Judge, government official. **Personal:** Born Jul 13, 1931, Safford, AL; son of Eddie and Pearl; married Lucille Nelson; children: Charlotte, Linda, Gerald, Gail, Carol, Laura. **Educ:** Wayne State Univ, BS, 1955, LLM, 1980; Detroit Col Law, JD, 1960. **Career:** Judge (retired); City Detroit, acct, 1955-56; Detroit Edison Co, acct, 1956-61; State Mich, asst atty gen, 1961-63; Ingham County MI, asst pros atty, 1963-64; Lansing MI, pvt practice law, 1964-78; Thomas Cooley Law Sch , prof, 1979; US Dist Ct Western Dist Grand Rapids, judge, 1979, chief judge, 1991-95, sr judge, 1996-99. **Orgs:** Grand Rapids Bar Asn; Mich Bar Asn; Black Judges Mich; Fedl Bar Asn; bd dir, Cooley Law Sch; United Way, Project Blueprint; Floyd H Skinner Bar Asn; Fed Judges Asn; bd dir, Metropolitan YMCA; Peninsular Club; Beta Gamma fraternity, Sigma Pi Phi fraternity, Delta Theta Phi Law Fraternity. **Honors/Awds:** Hon LLD, Detroit Col Law; Award Recog, Harvard Law Sch, Prog Instn Lawyers; Outstanding Leadership Award, Sigma Pi Phi; Distinguished Volunteer Serv Award; Outstanding Serv Award, Community Western Dist Mich. *

GIBSON, BETTY M.
College administrator, government official. **Personal:** Born May 15, 1938, New Orleans, LA; daughter of Jerome G Greene Sr and Irene L Hannibal Greene; married Kenneth D Gibson, Aug 22, 1960; children: Tracy Jerome, Tamara Angelique. **Educ:** Ky State Univ, Frankfort, KY, BS, 1961; Eastern Ky Univ, Richmond, KY, MA, 1974. **Career:** College administrator (retired), government official; Fayette County Bd Educ; Lincoln Parish Bd Educ, Ruston, LA, music teacher, 1966-67; Franklin County Bd Educ, Frankfort, KY, music teacher, 1967-79; Va Beach Bd Educ, Va Beach, VA, music teacher, 1979-84; Ky State Univ, Frankfort, KY, asst vpres stud affairs, 1984-88; actg vpres stud affairs, 1988, vpres stud affairs, 1991-00; Ky State, personnel bd mem, 2006-. **Orgs:** Frankfort Alumni Chap Alpha Kappa Alpha Sorority, 1967-; bd mem, Frankfort Arts Found, 1985-; Good Shepherd Church Parish Coun, 1986-; Top Ladies of Distinction Inc; pres, Frankfort Lexington The Links Inc, 1990-; dir, Lexington Diocese Comn Black Cath Concerns Comt, 1990-; pres, Beta Upsilon Omega Chap; bd dir, Salvation Army. **Home Addr:** 5400 Louisville Rd, Frankfort, KY 40601. **Business Addr:** Personnel Board Member, Kentuky State, 28 Fountain Pl, Frankfort, KY 40601, **Business Phone:** (502)564-7830.*

GIBSON, CHERYL DIANNE
Physician. **Personal:** Born Oct 10, 1955, Detroit, MI; daughter of Dr George and Peggy; married Renzo Fountain, Dec 27, 1996; children: Anne Marie Frances Damron. **Educ:** Univ Mich, 1977; Wayne State Univ, MD, 1987. **Career:** Mercy Hosp, attending physician, obstetrics & gynec, 1992-93; Detroit Riverview Hosp, attending physician, obstetrics & gynec, 1993-; Charles C Vincent Continuing Educ Ctr, med dir, obstetrics & gynec clinic, 1994-; Macomb Hosp Ctr, attending physician obstetrics & gynec, 1996-; pvt pract, obstet & gynec, currently. **Orgs:** Nat Asn Advan Colored People , 1970-; Oak Grove Am Church, 1978-; Nat Med Asn, 1984-; Am Med Asn, 1984-; Am Col Obstetrics & Gynecol, 1984-; Mich State Med Soc, 1984-; Wayne County Med Soc, 1984-; Detroit Med Soc, 1984-; Int Corresp Soc Obstetricians & GynecologistS, 1988-; Southeastern mich Surg Soc, 1989. **Honors/Awds:** Community Serv Award, Am Bus Women's Asn, 1995; Community Speaker for Women's Health Issues. **Special Achievements:** Mich Chronicle Newspaper, articles; Established Obstetrics & Gynecology Clinic in Detroit Public Schools for pregnant teens, 1994. **Business Addr:** Obstetrics & Gynecology Physician, Private practice, 15201 W Mcnichols Rd, Detroit, MI 48235, **Business Phone:** (313)837-0560.*

GIBSON, DAMON
Football player. **Personal:** Born Feb 25, 1975, Houston, TX; married Ruqayya; children: Damon Jr. **Educ:** Iowa Univ, BS, sociol. **Career:** Football player (retired); Cincinnati Bengals, wide receiver, 1998; Cleveland Browns, 1999; Jacksonville Jaguars, 2001-02; Atlanta Falcons,wide receiver, 2002; Scottish Clay-Mores, wide receiver, 2002.

GIBSON, DERRICK LAMONT
Baseball player. **Personal:** Born Feb 5, 1975, Winter Haven, FL. **Career:** Minor Leagues : Rockies, 1993; Bend Rockies, 1994; Asheville Tourists, 1995; New Haven Ravens, 1996-97; Colorado Springs Sky Sox, 1997-99; Calgary Cannons, 2000; El Paso Diablos, 2001; Tucson Sidewinders, 2001; Duluth-Superior Dukes, 2002; Long Island Ducks, 2003; Arkansas Travelers, 2004; Salt Lake Stingers, outfielder. 2004;; Mississippi Braves, 2005; Richmond Braves, 2005; New Haven County Cutters, 2005-06; Major League, Colorado Rockies, outfielder, 1998-99. **Honors/Awds:** Rockies Minor League Player Yr. *

GIBSON, DONALD B.
Educator. **Personal:** Born Jul 2, 1933, Kansas City, MO; son of Florine Myers and Oscar J; married Jo Anne Ivory, Dec 14, 1963; children: David, Douglas. **Educ:** Univ Kansas City, Kansas City, MO, BA, 1955, MA, 1957; Brown Univ, Providence RI, PhD, 1962. **Career:** Brown Univ, instr, 1960-61; Wayne State Univ, asst prof, 1961-67; Univ Conn, assoc prof, 1967-69, prof, 1969-74; Nat Endowment Humanities, study grant, 1970; Am Coun Learned Soc, res grant, 1970; consult, Educ Testing Serv, 1976-; Rutgers Univ, distinguished prof, 1974-01, emer prof, 2001-. **Orgs:** Col Lang Asn; Modern Lang Asn, 1964-; African Am Rev, 1972-; Nat Coun Teachers Eng, 1987-. **Special Achievements:** Author, The Fiction of Stephen Crane, 1968; editor, Five Black Writers, 1970; editor, Twentieth-Century Interpretations of Modern Black Poets, 1973; author, The Politics of Literary Expression: A Study of Major Black Writers, 1981; author, The Red Bridge of Courage: Redefining The Hero, 1988; editor, W E B Du Bois, The Souls of Black Folk, 1989; Stephen Crane, The Red Badge of Courage, Editor, 1996. **Business Addr:** Emeritus Professor, Rutgers University, Dept Eng, 520 George St, New Brunswick, NJ 08903-5054.*

GIBSON, EDWARD LEWIS
Physician. **Personal:** Born Jun 6, 1932, Chicago, IL; married Nannette; children: Joan, Edward Jr, Paula. **Educ:** Roosevelt UL, BS, 1953; Howard Univ Col Med, MD, 1957. **Career:** Columbia Univ, physician, self, asst prof ,anesthesiol, Col physicians & surgeons; Bellevue Med Ctr, vis fel, 1962-64; Columbia-presbyn Med & Ctr, asst resid, 1958-62; Michael Reese Hosp, intern, 1957-58; Princeton Med Ctr, dir anesthesiol, 1967-74; Robert R Moton Memorial Inst Inc, Test; physician, pvt pract, currently. **Orgs:** Am Med Asn; Am Soc Anesthesiologists. **Military Serv:** USAF, capt, 1958-62. **Business Addr:** Physician, Private Practice, 47 Locust Lane, Princeton, NJ 08540.*

GIBSON, ELVIS SONNY
Consultant. **Personal:** Born Jul 15, 1937, Calvert, TX; married Sylvia M; children: Patricia Elaine. **Educ:** Park Col, BA, social work, 1973. **Career:** US Dept HUD, Fair Housing Enforcement, chief; author & lectr; social eng consult, currently. **Orgs:** Chmn, Forum Social Expression Inc, 1980; bd gov, Bruce Watkins Cult Ctr, 1989-; pres, Black United Fund, Kansas City, MO, 1976-; bd dir, Nat Black United Fund, 1978; chair, Charlie Parker Acad Arts, 1980; vpres, Black Hist & Geneal, 1980-. **Honors/Awds:** Jefferson Award, Taft Broadcasting Corp, 1986; Dr Martin Luther King Distinguished Community Service Award, Gov Mo, 1988. **Special Achievements:** Books Published: Mecca of the New Negro. **Military Serv:** USAF, staff sgt, 1955-58. **Home Addr:** 3605 Prospect Ave, Kansas City, MO 64128, **Home Phone:** (816)861-9107. **Business Addr:** Social Engineering Consultant, Black United Appeal of Kansas City, 3338 Benton Blvd, Kansas City, MO 64128, **Business Phone:** (816)861-1222.

GIBSON, HARRIS, JR.
Surgeon, administrator. **Personal:** Born Nov 19, 1936, Mobile, AL; son of Harris Sr and Maude Richardson; married Marva A Boone; children: Michael, Michelle. **Educ:** AL State Univ, BS, 1956; Northwestern Univ, MS, 1957; Meharry Medical Col, MD, 1961. **Career:** USPHS Hosp NY, internship, 1961-62; USPHS Hosp Boston, surg residency, 1962-66; USPHS, asst chief surg; Boston City Hosp Boston Univ, thoracic surg residency, 1966-68; Cardio-Thoracic Assocs Inc, surgeon, 1969-; Winchester Hosp, chief thoracic surg; Boston Univ Med Sch, asst clinical prof surg; Pvt Pract, Cardiothoracic Surg, currently. **Orgs:** Pres New Eng Med Soc Nat Med Asn, 1981-82; Middlesex East Dist Med Soc, Am Med Asn 1983-84; Am Med Asn, Soc Thoracic Surg. **Honors/Awds:** Alpha Omega Alpha; fel Am Col Surgeons, Am Col Chest Physicians; Sigma Xi. **Business Addr:** Surgeon, 101 George P Hassett Dr, Medford, MA 02155.*

GIBSON, JOANN
Business owner. **Personal:** Born Jul 2, 1946, Detroit, MI; daughter of Frederick E and Loretta; married Ronnie L, Mar 23, 1985; children: Drew Allen & Dayna C Harris. **Educ:** Wayne County Community Col, attended 1977; Marygrove Col, attended 1984. **Career:** Bendix Corp, staff, 1965-84; Dyna Path Systems, customer serv, 1984-91;Non-Stop Customer Serv, pres, 1992-; Wayne State Univ, Detroit Employ Proj, bus consult, 1995-96; Girlbiz Prog, exec dir. **Orgs:** Nat Women's Hist Project, 1990-; Northwest Area Bus Asn, 1991-; Nat Asn Women Bus Owners, 1992-; Women on Bd Comt, Detroit Women's Forum, 1995; Victory Village Ctr for Community Youth, bd mem, 1996-; adv bd, SBA-Women's Bus Develop Ctr, 1999-. **Honors/Awds:** Business Person of the Month, Northwest Area Bus Asn, 1992, 1994; Jewels of Area D, Detroit Pub Schs, 1992; Mich Women's Historical Ctr & Hall of Fame, Michigan Women: Firsts and Founders; Nat Asn Women Bus Owners, Community Service Award, 1997; National Association of Women Business Owners Leadership Award, 1998. **Special Achievements:** Listed as one of the Most Influential Black Women in Met Detroit, Women's Informal Network, 1999; Selected as Top 10 Michigan Women in Business by the Greater Detroit Chapter of The National Association of Women Business Owners, 2006. **Business Addr:** President, Non-Stop Customer Service, 16634 Greenlawn St, Detroit, MI 48221-4912, **Business Phone:** (313)863-3901.

GIBSON, JOHN A
Law enforcement officer, clergy. **Personal:** Born in Philadelphia, PA; married Eleanor Simmons; children: Sean Edward. **Educ:** Camden Co Col, AS, 1979; Glassboro State Col, BA, 1981; Eastern Baptist, MA, 1984; Temple Univ, Philadelphia, PA, PhD. **Career:** Rutgers Univ, mgr, 1964-75; Lawnside Police Dept, police lt, 1975-; Borough Somerdale, NJ, councilman & chief police, 1987-93. **Orgs:** Minister, Calvary Baptist Church, Chester, PA, 1987-. **Honors/Awds:** Outstanding Law Enforcement Profes-

sional of America. **Military Serv:** AUS, reserves comndg officer. **Home Addr:** 200 Gloucester Ave, Somerdale, NJ 08083.

GIBSON, DR. JOHN THOMAS
Educator. **Personal:** Born Sep 19, 1948, Montgomery, AL; son of Herman F Gibson and L P Gibson; married Mayme Voncile Pierce; children: John Thomas Jr, Jerard Trenton, Justin Tarrance & Shayla Voncile. **Educ:** Tuskegee Inst, BS, EdM, Distinguished Mil Grad, 1971; Univ Colo, Boulder, EdS, PhD, 1973; Harvard Univ, cert mgt, 1982. **Career:** Tuskegee Inst, instr physical educ, 1971-72; Smiley Jr High Sch Denver, admin asst, 1971-73; Ala St Univ, dir lab exp, 1973-75, coordr fedrels, 1975-76, coordr, 1976-83, exec asst pres, 1983-86, vpres bus & finance, 1986, Admin & Finance Higher Educ, pres & prof (tenured), currently; Affirmative Action Comm Mont Elmore & Autauga Co, chmn, 1976-; Montgomery Alumni Chap, Kappa Alpha Psi Inc, vice polemarch & polemarch, 1978-; Sci & Eng Alliance Inc, pres, 1999-2000; Ala A&M Univ, Pres, 2000-05. **Orgs:** Bd mem, Bellingrath Exec Coun, 1976-; treas, mem, bd trustees, First Congregational Chap, 1977-; secy, IBPOE The Elks Southern Pride No 431, 1978; Shaaban Temple No 103, 330 Mason, Optimist Int. **Honors/Awds:** Publs, Public Sch Finance; 56 publs subj educ finance & admin FA; Outstanding Educational Leader, Phi Delta Kappa, 1981. **Military Serv:** AUS, capt, 1970-78.

GIBSON, JOHNNIE M. M.
Executive. **Personal:** Born Mar 1, 1949, Caryville, FL; daughter of Alphonso Maldon and Rosa Lee Maldon; children: Tiffany Michele. **Educ:** Chipola Junior Col, FL, AA Nursing, 1968; Albany State Col, GA, BS Health Physical Educ, 1971; Georgia State Univ, GA, Med, 1976. **Career:** Retired: Marianna HS, FL, high school tchr, 1971-72; Albany, GA Police Dept, policewoman, 1972-76; FBI, FL, special agent, 1976-79; FBI, Washington, special agent 1979-82; FBI, White Collar Crime Div, supervisory special agent 1981-82; Office of Congressional and Public Affairs, supervisory special agent 1982-87; Criminal Investigative Division FBI-Detroit, supervisory spec agent, 1988-93; Unit Chief Bur, applicant invest unit, FBI Head. **Orgs:** NOBLE, 1981-; mem, Capital Press Club, 1982-; guest lecturer Historical Black Colleges Univs, 1982-; visiting lect, Urban League Black Exec Exchange Pgm, 1982-; FBI spokeswoman FBI Public Affairs Office, 1982-; IAWP, 1984; large Nat Assoc of Media Women, 1985-. **Honors/Awds:** Several letters of commendation from Dir of FBI, 1978, 1980, 1981, 1989; Key to City of Louisville, KY, 1982; Honorary Kentucky Colonel, City of Louisville, 1982; Community Service Award, United Black Fund, Greater National Chapter, 1984; Law Enforcement Pioneer Award, North State Law Enforcement Officers Association, 1988; Outstanding Support of Men & Women of the Air Force, The Air Force District of Washington, DC; CBS movie, Johnnie Mae Gibson: FBI, 1986; Exceptional Performance Award, 1992-98. **Special Achievements:** The First Black Woman F.B.I. Agent. *

GIBSON, KALA
Executive. **Career:** Comerica Bank, vpres & mgr, sr vpres. **Orgs:** Dir, Urban Fin Serv Coalition, Detroit Chap, 2006-, sr advisor, currently. **Business Addr:** Director, Senior Advisor, Urban Financial Services Coalition, Detroit Chapter, PO Box 310722, Detroit, MI 48231.*

GIBSON, KENNETH ALLEN
Mayor. **Personal:** Born May 15, 1932, Enterprise, AL; widowed; children: Cheryl, JoAnn & Joyce. **Educ:** Newark Col, BS, civil eng, 1960. **Career:** NJ Hwy Dept, engr, 1950-60; Newark Housing Authority, chief engr, 1960-66; City Newark, chief structural engr, 1966-70; City Newark, 34th mayor, 1970-86; Gibson Assoc Inc, construction mgt firm, pres, currently. **Orgs:** Past pres, US Conf Mayors, 1976-77; bd dirs, Newark Urban Coalition; cochmn, Bus & Indust Coord Coun; bd dirs, Newark Young Men's Christian Asn-Young Women's Christian Asn; Am Soc CE; Frontiers Int. **Honors/Awds:** Jaycee's Man of the Year Newark, 1964. **Special Achievements:** First African American president of the U.S. Conference of Mayors, 1976. **Military Serv:** CE, AUS, 1956-58. **Business Addr:** President, Gibson Associates Inc, Renaissance Towers, 111 Mulberry St Suite 1G, Newark, NJ 07102, **Business Phone:** (201)624-2001.*

GIBSON, NELL BRAXTON
Executive, administrator. **Personal:** Born Apr 9, 1942, Cordele, GA; daughter of John Thomas Braxton and Anne Thomas Braxton; married Bertram M Gibson II, Apr 10, 1966; children: Erika Anne. **Educ:** Tougaloo Col, attended 1961; Spelman Col, attended 1962; Calif State Univ Sacramento, attended 1964; Empire State Col, BA, 1982. **Career:** Gen Theol Sem, pastoral assoc, 1982-85; Episcopal Diocese New York, exec asst Bishop, 1983-89; Episcopal Mission Soc, Parish Based Serv, dir, 1989-95; Nat Coun Churches, prog dir, 1995-96, assoc gen secy inclusiveness & justice, 1996-2000; mgt consult, 2000-; Episcopal Urban Caucus, co-ordr, currently. **Orgs:** Transafrica, 1984-; Black Diocesan Exec, 1986-; Metro-Manhattan Chap, Links, 1990-; New York Chap, Union Black Episcopalians, pres, 1991-96, 2000-03; St Mary's Episcopal AIDS Ctr. **Honors/Awds:** Black Ministries Service Award, 1982; Hon Doctor Divinity, Berkeley Divinity Sch, Yale Univ, 1985; Gen Conv Cert Appreciation, 1991; President's Award, Outstanding Serv & Nat Union Black Episcopalians, 1992, 2003. **Special Achievements:** Publ, articles: Journey to Johannesburg, 1987, Namibia, Ground of Hope, 1988, Karibu, 1985, Racism, The Church's Spiritual Death, 1984, Is This Ministry?, 1983; First Woman Elected Berkeley Divinity Sch Yale Univ, Bd Trustees, 1970. **Home Addr:** 100 W 94th St Apt 21-G, New York, NY 10025, **Home Phone:** (212)865-4596. **Business Addr:** Coordinator, Episcopal Urban Caucus, Park W Station, PO Box 21182, New York, NY 10025, **Business Phone:** (212)699-2998.

GIBSON, OLIVER DONNOVAN
Football player, football coach. **Personal:** Born Mar 15, 1972, Chicago, IL; son of Dave and Barbara. **Educ:** Univ Notre Dame, econ. **Career:** Football player (retired); football coach; Pittsburgh Steelers, defensive tackle, 1995-98; Cincinnati Bengals,defensive tackle, 1999-2003; Tampa Bay Buccaneers, defensive tackle, 2004; Buffalo Bills, defensive tackle, 2004; Proviso West High sch, defensive line coach. **Honors/Awds:** USA Today High School Defensive player of the year, 1989; Linemen of the Year Award, Nat Football Found; Nick Piet-rosante Award; Unsung Hero Award, Nat Football League, 2001. *

GIBSON, PAUL, JR.
Executive. **Personal:** Born Aug 5, 1927, New York, NY; married Marcia A Johnson. **Educ:** City Col NY, BA, 1953; NY Univ Sch Law, JD, 1952. **Career:** City NY, dep mayor plan; NY City Bd Educ; Fleary Gibson & Thompson, atty, 1954; NY City Housing Authority, comt coordr, 1955-59; NY City Coun, leg coun, 1966; NY State Supreme Ct, law secy, 1969; Am Airlines, gen mgr, dir urban affairs, 1969; Urban & Environ Affairs, asst vpres, 1971; Davidoff Malito & Hutcher LLP, atty, 2002. **Orgs:** Gen coun, Nat Asn Advan Colored People, NY, 1962-69; housing chmn, Nat Asn Advan Colored People; pres, NAACP, Jamaica NY; chmn, bd dir, Jamaica Nat Asn Advan Colored People Day Care Ctr; dir, Nat Aerospace Educ Assn; vpres, Jamaica C C;Urban & Reg Affairs Com US C C; Urban Affairs Comt Nat Asn Mfr; corp adv comt, Nat Urban Coalition; bd dir, Flagship Int Inc; pres, City Coun, 1966-69; chmn, Pragmetic Indust, NY; chmn, Int Trav Indust Exec Comt & St John's Episcopal Church; Queens Co Bar Asn; bd trust, Niagara Univ; NY State Bar. **Military Serv:** AUS, 1946-47. *

GIBSON, REGINALD WALKER
Judge. **Personal:** Born Jul 31, 1927, Lynchburg, VA; son of McCoy and Julia Ann Butler; children: Reginald S Jr. **Educ:** Va Union Univ, BS, 1952; Univ Pa, Wharton Grad Sch Bus Admin, attended 1953; Howard Univ Sch Law, LLB, 1956. **Career:** Judge (retired); Dept Treas, Internal Revenue Serv, agent, 1957-61; Dept Justice Tax Div, trial atty, 1961-71; Int Harvester Co, sr tax atty, 1971-76, gen tax atty, 1976-82; US Ct Fed Claims, judge, 1982-95. **Orgs:** DC Bar Asn; Fed Bar Asn; Ill Bar Asn; Nat Bar Asn; Claims Ct Bar Asn; emer mem J Edgar Murdock Am Inn Ct Taxation; Chicago Bar Asn; Ct Fed Claims Bar Asn; Am Judicature Soc. **Honors/Awds:** Wall Street Journal Award, Ranking Student in Business Admin, 1952; American Juris prudence Award, Excellence in Taxation & Trusts, 1956; Certificate of Award, US Atty Generals, 1969; Special Commendation for Outstanding Service in Tax Division, US Dept Justice, 1970; Distinguished Alumni of the Year, Howard Univ Sch Law, 1984. **Military Serv:** AUS, cpl, 1946-47.

GIBSON, ROBERT
Baseball player. **Personal:** Born Nov 9, 1935, Omaha, NE; son of Pack and Victoria; married Wendy Nelson (divorced); children: Annette & Renee; married; children: Chris. **Educ:** Creighton Univ. **Career:** Baseball player (retired), coach, speaker; St Louis Cardinals, pitcher, 1959-75, announcer, 1985-94, asst coach, 1995-97; NY Mets, coach, 1981-82; Atlanta Braves, asst coach, 1982-84; Am League, spec adv pres, 1998; Playing Field Promotions, Speakers Bur, sports speaker, currently. **Honors/Awds:** World Series MVP Award, 1964, 1967; Gold Glove Awards, 1965-73; City Young Award, Nat League, 1968, 1970; Most Valuable Player, Nat League, 1968; Baseball Hall of Fame 1981; St. Louis Walk of Fame. **Special Achievements:** Ranked Number 31 on The Sporting News' list of the 100 Greatest Baseball Players, 1999; named as the most intimidating pitcher of all time from the Fox Sports Net series The Sports List, 2004; street on the north side of Rosenblatt Stadium, home of the College World Series in his home town of Omaha, is named Bob Gibson Boulevard. **Business Addr:** Sports Speaker, Playing Field Promotions, Speakers Bureau, 960 Syracuse Ct, Denver, CO 80230, **Business Phone:** (303)377-1109.

GIBSON, ROGER ALLAN
Airline executive, vice president (organization). **Personal:** Born Jun 9, 1946, Oakland, CA; son of Betty J.; married Patrice Gibson, Oct 21, 1995; children: Terrence, Kai, Jennifer. **Educ:** Merrit Col, attended 1973; Chabot Col, attened 1976; Saint Mary's Col, BA, 1986. **Career:** United Airlines, mgr inventory planning & control, 1979-86; MOC supply & syst dist, dir, 1986-87, dir inventory planning & control, 1987-89, dir, resource planning & control, 1989, dir, total qual, 1990-91, Oakland Aircraft Mod Ctr, gen mgr, 1991-92; N AME Mountain, vpres, 1992-; United Cargo, vpres & chmn, 2001. **Orgs:** Bd mem, Colo Nat Bank, 1995-; bd mem, Colo Ocean Journey, 1996-; bd mem, Colo Uplife, 1993-; bd mem, Denver Area Coun Boy Scouts, 1993-; bd mem, Denver Found 1996-; bd mem, Denver Zool Found, 1996-; bd mem, Metropolitan State Col Denver, 1996-; bd mem, Nat Jewish Ctr, 1996-. **Military Serv:** US Navy, 1965-70. *

GIBSON, DR. SARAH L
Educator, consultant, college teacher. **Personal:** Born May 8, 1927, Princeton, KY; daughter of Earl N Gray Sr and Fiercie E Edmonds; children: Piper E Fakir & Kyle C. **Educ:** Wayne State Univ, BS, 1948, MEd, PhD, 1972. **Career:** Bur Social Aid, social worker, 1949-53; Pontiac Sch Syst, teacher, 1955-60; Detroit Pub Sch, teacher, 1960-68, sch admin, 1968-84; Univ Detroit, assoc prof, 1965-67; Harper Hosp, consult nurse, 1969-72; Marygrove Col, consult, 1970-71; Gibson Educ Consult Serv, educ consult, 1974; Oakland Univ, Sch Educ & Human Serv, assoc prof, currently. **Orgs:** Mich Asn Middle Sch Educr, 1963; consult, Trade Leadership Coun, 1967-; secy, Metrop Detroit Asn Black Admin, 1969-72; Asn Supv & Curric Develop; Nat Asn Advan Colored People. **Home Addr:** 2139 Bryanston Crescent St, Detroit, MI 48207. **Business Addr:** Associate Professor, Oakland University, School of Education & Human Services, 475D Pawley Hall, Detroit, MI 48207, **Business Phone:** (248)370-3056.

GIBSON, TYRESE (TYRESE DARNELL GIBSON)
Fashion model, actor, singer. **Personal:** Born Dec 30, 1978, Los Angeles, CA; son of Pricilla Murray; children: Shayla Somer Gibson. **Career:** Albums include: Tyrese, 1998; 2000 Watts, 2001; I Wanna Go There, 2002; Alter Ego, 2006; Films: Baby Boy, 2001; Fast & Furious 2, 2003; Guess, model, 1999; Flight of the Phoenix, 2004; Four Brothers, 2005; Annapolis, 2006; Waist Deep, 2006; Transformers, 2006; The Take, 2007; HQ Pictures, owner. **Honors/Awds:** Grammy Award, Best R&B Male Vocal Performance, for "Sweet Lady," 2000. **Business Addr:** Actor, Singer, BMG Records, 1540 Broadway, New York, NY 10036, **Business Phone:** (212)930-4000.

GIBSON, TYRESE DARNELL. **See GIBSON, TYRESE.**

GIBSON, WARREN ARNOLD
Lawyer. **Personal:** Born Jul 16, 1941, Gary, IN. **Educ:** Ill Univ, BS, 1965, attended 1972, attended 1973. **Career:** Montgomery Wards, supvr, 1966-67; Exxon Corp, employ rels rep, 1967-70; Dow Chem Co, atty. **Orgs:** Am Bar Asn; Nat Bar Asn; Mich Bar Asn; Midland Bar Asn; Alpha Phi Alpha; Urban League Black Exec Exchange Prog. **Honors/Awds:** Midland Jr Achievement, 1976-78.

GIBSON, WAYNE CARLTON
Executive. **Personal:** Born Oct 20, 1958, Fordyce, AR; son of Odis and Gertrude Thrower; married Ruthie N Gibson, Jul 26, 1980; children: Carla Roschelle. **Educ:** Henderson State Univ, BSBA, 1980; Northwestern Univ, J L Kellogg Sch Bus, 1989, cert, Petrol/Energy Econs & Mgt. **Career:** Murphy Oil USA Inc, acct, 1980-84, sr div order analyst, 1984-86, supvr, Lease Rec & Div Orders, 1986-92, gen mgr corp purchasing, 1992, spec proj & permitting mgr, currently; Coldwell Banker Robinson Real Estate, referral agent, currently. **Orgs:** Bd mem, El Dorado Sch Bd, 1990-; bd dirs, Barton Libr, 1989-93; bd dirs, S Ark Symphony, 1990-; bd dirs, Salvation Army, 1985-; Nat Asn Purchasing Managers, 1992-; Am Mgt Asn, 1986-; Ark & El Dorado Bd Realtors, 1983-; bd dirs, Union County Literacy Coun, 1991-94; Nat Asn REALTORS; Ark REALTORS; El Dorado Sch bd. **Honors/Awds:** Community Volunteerism, Ark Dept Parks & Tourism, 1990. **Home Addr:** 710 White Oak Dr, El Dorado, AR 71730. **Business Addr:** Referral Agent, Coldwell Banker Robinson Real Estate, 542 N Wash Ave, El Dorado, AR 71730, **Business Phone:** (870)862-9292.

GIBSON, WILLIAM M.
Clergy. **Personal:** Born Sep 11, 1934, Hackensack, NJ; son of James and Evelyn Scott; married Jean J Gibson, May 2, 1989; children: Monica, Wayne, Wesley, Gibson, Cayce, Jerrell Johnson. **Educ:** Rutgers, BA, 1956; Law Review Boston Univ Law, JD, 1959; Boston Col, MSW, 1966; Harvard Bus Sch, AMP Cert, 1973; Valordictorian MDiv Virginia Magna Cum Laude, 1989. **Career:** US Dept Justice, asst US Atty, 1961-64; Boston Univ Law, dir law & poverty project, 1966-70; Boston Univ Sch Afro Am Studies, Assoc Prof, 1968-71; Off Econ Opportunity, regional coun, 1970-72; FTC, regional dir, 1972-78; Fuller Mental Health Ctr, supt area dir; Boston, Metro Dist, deputy dist mgr; St Paul's Baptist Church, minister educ & singles; Med Col VA Hosp, Richmond, staff chaplain, 1990-91; VA Union Univ, Criminology & Criminal Justice Dept, instr, 1993-; Police Acad, recruit class chaplain, 1998; Saint Stephen's Baptist Church, pastor, currently. **Orgs:** Nat Asn Social Work, 1966; Academy Cert Social Worker, 1968; MA Bar Asn, 1984; Sports Anglers Club, VA; Blue Waters Club Bermuda; Henrico County Community Criminal Justice Bd; Richmond Police Citizens Acad Bd. **Honors/Awds:** 10 Outstanding Young Men Award, Boston Jr CC, 1968; Young Lawyers Chair, Boston Univ Law Sch, 1969; Community Service Award, Roxbury YMCA, 1969; Outstanding Performance Award, FTC, 1972; Outstanding Government Service Award, NAACP Boston,

1975; Outstanding Service Award, Salvation Army, 1980; Samuel H James, Sr Theological Award, VA Union Sch Theol, 1989; Man of the Year, St Stephens Bapt Church, 1996. **Military Serv:** USAF, Med Corps staff sgt, 1959-64. **Business Addr:** Pastor, St Stephen's Baptist Church, P O Box 689, Bowling Green, VA 22427, **Business Phone:** (804)633-9353.*

GIDDINGS, HELEN
State government official. **Personal:** Born Apr 21, 1943, Dallas, TX; daughter of Arthur and Catherine Warren Ferguson; married Donald; children: Lizette, Lisa & Stanley. **Educ:** Univ Tex, BA, bus, 1968. **Career:** Sears & Roebuck, training dir, 1975-77, personnel mgr, 1977-81, dir community affairs, 1979-81; Select Personnel, pres, 1981-86; Dallas Assembly, elected mem, 1981-; Tex state rep, dist 109, 1993-; Small bus owner, currently; Multiplex Inc, founder. **Orgs:** Dallas Symphony, 1980-; trustee, Dallas Alliance, 1981-, exec dir, 1987; pres, Dallas Black Chamber Com, 1981-92; secy, Dallas Hist Soc, 1983-; bd dirs, Dallas Theatre Ctr, 1984-; exec dir, Leadership Dallas, 1985-86; Dist Six State Bar Grievance Comt; pres, Nat Order Women Legislatures, 2000-. **Special Achievements:** First African American pres of National Order of Women Legislatures. **Business Addr:** State Representative, Texas House of Representatives, 1510 N Hampton Suite 220, PO Box 2910, DeSoto, TX 75115, **Business Phone:** (972)224-6795.

GIDDINGS, PAULA JANE
Writer, educator, historian. **Personal:** Born Nov 16, 1947, Yonkers, NY; daughter of Curtis Gulliver and Virginia Stokes. **Educ:** Howard Univ, WA, DC, BA, 1969; Bennett Col, DHL, 1990; Wesleyan Univ CT, hon degree, 1995. **Career:** Random House, ed asst, 1969-70, copy ed, 1970-72; Howard Univ Press, assoc book ed, 1972-75; Spelman Col, Atlanta, GA, distinguished UNCF scholar, 1986-87; Rutgers Univ, chair women's studies, 1989-91; Princeton Univ, 1992-93; Duke Univ, res prof, 1996-2000; Smith Col, African Am Studies, prof, 2001-; Books: "When & Where I Enter: The Impact of Black Women on Race & Sex in America, 1984; In Search of Sisterhood, 1988; ed: Burning All Illusions. **Orgs:** Delta Sigma Theta Inc, 1967-; bd mem, Nat Coalition 100 Black Women, 1985-; Am Hist Asn, 1990; PEN, 1990-; Auth Guild Am, 1991; Asn Black Women Historians; Nat Women's Studies Asn. **Honors/Awds:** United Negro Fund Distinguished Scholar, Spelman Col, 1986-87; Guggenheim Found Fel, 1993; fel, Nat Humanitics Ctr, 1993-95; Phi Beta Kappa Vis Scholar, 1996-97; Candace Award, Nat Coalition 100 Black Women. **Business Addr:** Professor, African American Studies, Smith College, 17 New South St, Northampton, MA 01063, **Business Phone:** (413)584-2700.

GIFFORD, DR. BERNARD R.
Educator. **Personal:** Born May 18, 1943, Brooklyn, NY; married Ursula M Jean; children: Antoinette & Bernard. **Educ:** Long Island Univ, BS, 1965; Univ Rochester Med Sch, MS, 1968, PhD, 1972. **Career:** Russell Sage Found, resident scholar, 1977; New York City Pub Sch System, dep chancellor & chief bus affairs off, 1973-77; New York City Rand Inst, pres, 1972-73; Univ Calif, Berkeley, chancellors prof & dean grad scheduc, 1983-89, Div Educ Math, Sci, Engineering & Technol, prof, currently; The Distributed Learning Workshop, pres, ceo & instructional officer, currently. **Orgs:** US Atomic Energy Comn, Fel Nuclear Sci, 1965-71; appointed adj prof, pub admin, Columbia Univ, 1975-77; appointed adj lectr, Pub Policy, John F Kennedy Sch Govt, Harvard Univ, 1977-78; adv Comt, John F Kennedy Inst Polit, Harvard Univ; bd visitors, City Col New York; bd trustees, New York Univ; acad adv com, US Naval Acad; consult, Calif Supreme Ct, 1978-79; consult, Asst Secy Comn Planning & Develop, Dept Housing & Urban Develop, 1979; consult, Nat Acad Pub Admin, 1979-80; consult, Nat Inst Educ; bd dirs, New York Urban Coalition; bd trustees, German Marshall Fund US; ed bd, Urban Affairs Quarterly; bd ed adv New York Affairs; ed bd, New York Educ Quarterly; ed bd, policy Analysis; appointed adj & vis prof, Dept Urban Studies & Planning, Hunter Col, City Univ New York, Mass Inst Technol; founding fac chair, Calif State Univ Joint Doctoral Prog, currently. **Honors/Awds:** Mem, Phi Beta Kappa. **Special Achievements:** Co-author, "Revenue Sharing & the Planning Process", 1974; author, "The Urbanization of Poverty: A Preliminary Investigation of Shifts in the Distribution of the Poverty Population by Race Residence & Family Structure", 1980; numerous other publications. **Business Addr:** Professor, University of California, Graduate School of Education, Berkeley, CA 94720, **Business Phone:** (510)643-4733.

GIGGER, HELEN C.
Lawyer. **Personal:** Born Dec 24, 1944, Houston, TX; married Nathan J Gigger. **Educ:** Tex South Univ, BA, polit sci, 1965, JD, 1968. **Career:** State OK, OK crime comn, legal coun, planner; Dean Law Sch, res asst; Houston Leg Found, legal intern; Okla City & Co Comm Act Prog Inc, prog analyst. **Orgs:** Am Nat & Okla Bar Asns; secy, JJ & Bruce Law Soc; Am Judiccature Soc; EEOC off Okla Crime Comn; Nat Spa Courts Plan Org; lect, Crim Just OK City U; YWCA; Urban League; League Women Voters Georgia Brown's Demo Women's Club; OK Black Pol Cau; pres, Delta Sigma Theta Sor Inc; secy, Local & State Nat Asn Advan Colored People; elected Nat Scholarship & Standards Com 4 yr term; policy making com Delta Sigma Theta Inc, 1975. **Honors/Awds:** Grad with Hons, 1961, 1965 & at top of Law Class, 1968; chairperson of Reg VI Nat Asn Advan Colored People Conf, 1974; Parliament; Nat Delta Conv, 1973; Delta Cen Reg Parliament, 1974; Mem of Greater Cleves CME Church; Church Prog Chairperson. **Business Addr:** Attorney, Oklahoma City Municipal Counselor, 200 N Walker, Oklahoma City, OK 73102-2232.*

GIGGER, NATHANIEL JAY
Lawyer. **Personal:** Born Jan 1, 1944, Elmore City, OK; son of Ernest and Katie Wyatt; married Helen Coleman Gigger, Oct 25, 1968; children: Nikolle Janelle. **Educ:** Langston Univ, Langston, OK, BA, 1963; Tex Southern Univ, Houston, TX, JD, 1967. **Career:** State Okla, Oklahoma City OK, asst state atty gen, 1970-79, dep atty, Dept Human Resources, 1979; Derryberry, Duncan & Nance Law Firm, Oklahoma City, OK, mem, 1979-82; Self-Employed, Okla City OK, atty, 1982-. **Orgs:** Prince Hall Masons, 1967-; vpres, State Conf Br Nat Asn Advan Colored People, 1972-77; state legal chmn, Int Benevolent Protective Order Elks, 1975-80; Mayor's Comn Bus Develop, 1976-79; exec bd mem, Community Action Agency, 1976-81; Asn Black Trial Lawyers, 1982-; bd mem, Okla Bus & Develop Coun, 1984-86; Northeast Okla City Chamber Com, 1987-, J J Bruce Law Soc. **Honors/Awds:** Roscoe Dunjee Humanitarian Award, Okla Nat Asn Advan Colored People, 1975; Outstanding Citizenship Award, Alpha Phi Alpha Fraternity, 1976; Outstanding Citizen Award, Okla City Set Club, 1981; Outstanding Lawyer Award, Nat Asn Advan Colored People Youth Coun, 1986. **Business Addr:** Attorney, Private Practice, 732 NE 36th St, Oklahoma City, OK 73105.*

GILBERT, ALBERT C
Executive. **Personal:** Born Oct 19, 1924, Carlisle, PA; married Iris Boswell; children: Brenda, Richard, Walda Ann, Albert C III & Charles. **Educ:** Morgan State Univ, Baltimore, MD, BS, 1950; St John Col, Cleveland, Ohio, 1966; Cambridge Ctr, New York, NY, 1967. **Career:** Executive (retired); Continental Can Co, Cleveland, Ohio, hourly employee, finance secy, pres union, 1950, supvr, 1958, supt, 1964, mgr, 1969-74, special sales rep, 1974-83; Congressman Louis Stokes, Wash, DC, sr intern, 1985. **Orgs:** Vice chmn, Fibre Box Asn; bd mem, E Cleveland Sch, 1971-83; Nat Black Sch Bd; Nat Safety Coun; Citizens League Greater Cleveland; El Hasa Masonic Shrine 32 Degree Mason; Cleveland Chamber Com; Ohio Manufacturer Asn; bd dirs, Rainey Inst Music; spec sales rep, Continental Group; pres, E Cleveland Kiwanis, 1987; Cuyahoga Co, Ohio, Western Res Agency Sr Citizens, 1987-93; bd mgrs, YMCA, 1988-94; gov, Ohio Dist Kiwanis Int, 1994-95; pres, E Cleveland (FOPA) Fraternal Order Police Asn, 1996-99; E Cleveland Parks Inc. **Honors/Awds:** Hall of Fame Outstanding Football Player & Wrestler, Morgan State Col, 1974. **Special Achievements:** First Black Manager of Continental Can Company. **Military Serv:** AUS, WW II sgt; Awarded 4 Bronze Stars. **Home Addr:** 2100 N Taylor Rd, Cleveland Heights, OH 44112-3002.

GILBERT, CHRISTOPHER
Psychologist, poet, college teacher. **Personal:** Born Aug 1, 1949, Birmingham, AL; son of Floyd and Rosie. **Educ:** Univ Mich, BA, 1972; Clark Univ, MA, 1975, PhD, 1987. **Career:** Judge Baker Guidance Ctr, psychologist, 1979-84; Univ Mass Med Sch, psychologist, 1979-84; Cambridge Family & Childrens Serv, psychologist, 1983-85; Univ Pittsburgh, Eng Dept, vis poet, 1986; Bristol Community Col, psychol prof, 1990; poem: "Across the Mutual Landscape"; "Pushing"; "Muriel Rukeyser as Energy"; "Time with Stevie Wonder in It"; "Fire Gotten Brighter"; "Pitch". **Orgs:** Bd dirs, Elm Park Ctr Early Educ, 1980-84, Worcester Chap Civil Liberties Union Mass, 1983-85, Worcester Children's Friend, 1983-86. **Honors/Awds:** Fel Mass Artists Found, 1981; Walt Whitman Awd Acad Am Poets, 1983; Fel Nat Educ Asn, 1986; Robert Frost Award, 1986.

GILBERT, DR. FRED D.
College administrator. **Personal:** Born Dec 2, 1947, New Orleans, LA. **Educ:** Dillard Univ, BA, bus admin, 1970; Loyola Univ, MEd, educ admin, 1972; IA State Univ Higher Educ, PhD, 1978. **Career:** Upward Bound Proj, admin dir, 1971-73; Upward Bound & Special Serv Proj Univ, proj dir, 1973-75; IA State Univ, res asst, 1975-76, univ married housing area adv, 1976-77, TRIO dir, asst prof, 1978-; IA State Univ ColEd, asst dean, 1987-; Des Moines Area Comm Col, dean urban campus,1987-90, exec dir dist admin, 1990-92, exec dir res, found, grants &contracts, 1992-94, vpres res & develop, 1994-, exec dean, currently. **Orgs:** Bd dirs, Ames Sch Dist Found; C & Families Iowa, Family Enrichment Ctr, IA Comprehensive Manpower Serv & Nat Coun Res & Develop. **Special Achievements:** Book Review of Black Coll in Amer Publishing in Educ Studies 1979; A Study of Power & Authority unpublished PhD Dissertation 1978; Dissertion ranked tenth in nation by Amer Assoc of Higher Educ. **Business Addr:** Executive Dean, Des Moines Area Community College, 1100 7th St, Des Moines, IA 50314-2597, **Business Phone:** (515)248-7206.

GILBERT, JEAN P.
Educator. **Personal:** Born Aug 6, 1928, McDonald, PA; married Aug 1, 1940. **Educ:** Univ Buffalo, EdM, 1955, EdD, 1962; Bluefield St Col, BS (cum laude), 1947. **Career:** Clergy (retired); AL A&M Col, counr & lectr, 1956-57; Hampton Inst, dir testing, 1957-60; Univ IL, counr & educator, 1962-63; Brooklyn Col, counr & educator, prof emer; SC St Col, counr & educator, 1964-65. **Orgs:** Mem bd dir, DST Telecommunications Inc; Delta Sigma Theta; Pi Lambda Theta; Kappa Delta Pi; Am Psychol Asn; Am Personnel & Guid Asn; Nat Voc Guid Asn; Asn Non-White Concerns; Psychomet Dir Educ Prog Eval & Res JPG Consults Inc; JOB'S Prog; bd grdns bd dir, NY City Protestant; GS Coun Greater NY; mem Bd, Gov NY St Personal & Guid Asn. **Honors/Awds:** James Foundation Grant, 1957; John Hay Whitney Foundation Grant, 1960; Women of Achievement Award, 1966; Outstanding Editors of America, 1974; Grant, Ford Foundation. **Special Achievements:** Author of "Counseling Black Inner City Children in Groups".

GILBERT, SEAN
Football player. **Personal:** Born Apr 10, 1970, Aliquippa, PA; married Nicole; children: Deshaun, Sean Zacchaeus & Alexus. **Educ:** Pittsburgh Univ. **Career:** Football player (retired); Los Angeles Rams, defensive end, 1992-94; St Louis Rams, 1995; Wash Redskins, 1996; Carolina Panthers, 1998-2002; Oakland Raiders, defensive line, 2003. **Honors/Awds:** Carroll Rosenbloom Memorial Award, 1992; Rams Rookie of the Year Award, 1992; Pro Bowl, 1993.

GILBERT, SHEDRICK EDWARD
Clergy. **Personal:** Born Jun 21, 1922, Miami, FL; married Wilma Wake, Jan 22, 1947; children: Janelle Gilbert Hall, Stephen, Jeffrey. **Educ:** Hampton Univ, BS, 1954. **Career:** US Post Off, lett carrier, 1956-78, supvr, 1978-84; St Agnes Episcopal Church, treasurer, 1967-94, asst deacon, 1984-. **Orgs:** Vpres, head prog, Algonquin Civic Club, 1989-; OPP, 1952-; Overtown Adv bd, 1991-; Diocese SE Fla, stewardship cms, 1983-85; pres, BTW Class 1938, 1988-; dir, St Agnes & Rainbow Village Corp, 1990-; dir, eight week summer recreation prog, 1992; stewardship, chmn, Every Mem Canvas Campaign, 1990; comt credentials, chmn, Diocese SE Fla, 1974-84; Jefferson Reaves Sr Health Ctr Comt; pres, dir, Algonquin Club, currently. **Honors/Awds:** Post Office Superior Achievement Award, 1970-84. **Military Serv:** USY, sergeant t-4, 1943-46. *

GILBERT, SHIRL E
President (Government), school administrator. **Career:** Ind Pub Schs, supt, 1994; Tacoma Urban League, pres & chief exec officer; Sch Dist Pa, regional supt, currently. **Orgs:** Nat Adv Bd; Nat Ctr Res Evaluation, Standards Studs Testing. **Business Addr:** Regional Superintendent, School District of Philadelphia, 4909 Chestnut St 1st Fl, Philadelphia, PA 19139, **Business Phone:** (215)471-2271.

GILCHRIEST, LORENZO
Educator, college teacher. **Personal:** Born Mar 21, 1938, Thomasville, GA; married Judith Graffman; children: Lorenzo David & Lorena. **Educ:** Newark State Col, BS, 1962; Pratt Inst, MS, 1967; Md Inst Col Art, MFA, 1975. **Career:** Senator Robert Kennedy Proj, Bedford Stuyvesant Youth Action, asst dir, 1965-67; Cornell Univ, guest prof, 1972-73; Baltimore Mus Art, art teacher adult prog, 1973-74; Morgan State Univ, guest artist print workshop summer, 1977; prof emer, 1997-; Towson State Univ, asst prof art dept. **Orgs:** Fel Int Artists Sem, 1962; Afro Am Slide Depository Samuel Kress Found, 1971; Gen Class Amateur Radio Lisc, 1976; Advan Class Amateur Radio Lisc, 1980; Am Radio Relay League. **Honors/Awds:** Protege of Elaine De Kooning, 1963; Samuel Kress Award, 1971. **Military Serv:** AUS, 1956-57. *

GILCHRIST, ROBERTSON
Government official, businessperson. **Personal:** Born Aug 24, 1926, Parksville, SC; married Evelyn Landise Searles; children: Gezetta. **Educ:** Mims High Sch, dipl, 1945. **Career:** Construct Co, owner; council mem. **Orgs:** Nat Asn Advan Colored People; Masonic Lodge. **Honors/Awds:** Public Service & Private Business Award, Community Black History, 1980; Appreciation Service & Leadership Award, 4-H Club, 1983. **Military Serv:** AUS, corpl, 18 months. **Home Addr:** 442 William Self Rd, Plum Branch, SC 29845. **Business Addr:** Councilmember, PO Box 1147, McCormick, SC 29835-1147.*

GILDON, JASON LARUE
Football player. **Personal:** Born Jul 31, 1972, Altus, OK; married Joy; children: Jason Jr. **Educ:** Okla State Univ. **Career:** Pittsburgh Steelers, linebacker, 1994-2003; Jacksonville Jaguars, 2004. **Honors/Awds:** Pro Bowl, 2000, 2001, 2002; All-Pro selection, 2001; Pro Bowl AFC Starters, 2002. *

GILES, ALTHEA B
Advertising executive. **Personal:** Born Mar 10, 1926, East Orange, NJ; daughter of Russell Banks and Beatrice Smith; married William R, Jun 15, 1947; children: William R, Sharon Giles-Alexander & Kevin E. **Educ:** Kean Col, Union, NJ, BS, 1951. **Career:** East Orange Bd Educ, teacher, 1952-82; Extra Personal Care Inc, East Orange, NJ, vpres, 1983, pres, currently; New Day Promotions, consult, currently. **Orgs:** Consult, Selig Assoc Inc; consult, Nancy Wilson Cosmetics; secy, Enterprising Twenty Inc; Arts & Culture Comt, Coalition 100 Black Women; NAACP; Nat

Urban League; United Negro Col Fund; Specialty Advertising Int Inc; Links Inc; bd dir, Coalition 100 Black Women; co-chmn, NJ Lou Rawls Parade Stars Telethon; bd trustees, Newark Mus; Found Bd, Kean Col. **Honors/Awds:** Community Service Award, East Orange Mayor Hatcher; Black Heritage Award, City East Orange; Meritorious Service Award, United Negro Col Fund; Outstanding Volunteer Award, United Negro Coll Fund; Citiation, Newark Munic Coun, Newark, NJ; Achievement Award, UMD, NJ; Outstanding Service Award, East Orange Bd Educ; Community Service Award, Nat Coun Negro Women; Certificate of Appreciation, Essex County, Chap, Links Inc; Woman of the Year Award, Zeta Phi Beta Sorority Eta Omicron Zeta Chap. **Home Addr:** 43 Edgemont Rd, West Orange, NJ 07052. **Business Addr:** President, Extra Personal Care Inc, PO Box 832, East Orange, NJ 07019, **Business Phone:** (201)678-6068.

GILES, CHARLOTTE EMMA
Educator. **Personal:** Born Mar 29, 1937, Baltimore, MD; daughter of Samuel Hopkins and Phozie Dawson. **Educ:** Fisk Univ, BA, 1958; Ind Univ, MM, 1960, DM, 1970. **Career:** Tuskegee Inst, instr, 1958-59; Fla A&M Univ, asst prof music, 1960-65; Knoxville Col, assoc prof music, 1968-71; WVa State Col, Dept Music, fac, 1971-, interim chmn, 1971, prof & chair, currently, cultural activities coord. **Orgs:** Asn Performing Arts Presenters, 1978-; fel, Nat Endowment Humanities,1979-80; bd mem, Asn Performing Arts Presenters, 1985-87; Governor's Comt Arts Educ, 1992. **Honors/Awds:** Sara Maloney Scholarship Award in Music, 1956; Louis Gottschak Music Prize, 4th place, 1970. **Special Achievements:** Concert pianist, 1960-92; pianist with Charleston Symphony Orchestra, 1971-82; pianist for WVA Opera Theatre, 1972-85. **Business Addr:** Professor, Chair, West Virginia State College, Department of Music, John W Davis Fine Arts Bldg Suite 203, PO Box 1000, Institute, WV 25112-1000, **Business Phone:** (304)766-3194.

GILES, HENRIETTA
Television producer. **Personal:** Born Feb 23, 1962, Stanton, TN; daughter of Geraldine Maxwell and Jesse Cornelius. **Educ:** Univ Tenn Martin, Martin, Tenn, BS, 1984. **Career:** WTVF-TV, Nashville, Tenn, assoc producer, 1984-85, producer, 1988; WSOC-Radio, Charlotte, NC, copy writer, 1985-88; Odyssey Channel, Locked Out, host. **Orgs:** Nashville Asn Minority Communicators, 1989-; Nat Asn Black Journalists, 1990-. **Honors/Awds:** Award, Nat Asn Black Journalists, 2001. **Home Addr:** 317 Village Green Dr, Nashville, TN 37217.

GILES, JAMES T.
Judge. **Personal:** Born Jan 31, 1943, Charlottesville, VA. **Educ:** Amherst Col, BA, 1964; Yale Univ, LLB, 1967. **Career:** Nat Labor Rels Bd, mem, 1967-68; Pepper Hamilton & Scheetz, assoc atty, 1968-79; US Dist Ct, Eastern Dist, Philadelphia, PA, judge, 1979-99, chief judge, 1999-2006, United States District Court Eastern Pennsylvania; dist judge, 2005-08; Pepper Hamilton LLP, coun, 2008- . **Orgs:** Fed Bar Asn; Philadelphia Bar Asn; Hist Dist Ct Rec Comt. **Special Achievements:** First African-American hired as an associate by the Philadelphia law firm of Pepper, Hamilton & Scheetz. **Business Addr:** Counsel, Pepper Hamilton LLP, 3000 Two Logan Square, Eighteenth and Arch Streets, Philadelphia, PA 19103-2799, **Business Phone:** (215)981-4131.

GILES, JOE L
Executive. **Personal:** Born Dec 6, 1943, Elrod, AL; son of Pinkie and Jessie; married Sarah Fisher, Dec 29, 1969; children: Alycia, Fredrick & Jolanda. **Educ:** Stillman Col, Tuscalusa, Ala, BA, 1966; Univ Detroit, Detroit, Mich, MA, 1976. **Career:** Joe L Giles & Assocs, owner & pres, 1980-. **Orgs:** Bd dirs, MYFO, 1981-83; dir placement, Kappa Alpha Psi, 1985-87; pres, Stillman Col Alumni Asn, 1988-90. **Honors/Awds:** Top Biller, MAPC, 1988; Top Trainer, NAPC, 1988; Man of the Year, Church New Convenant, 1990. **Home Addr:** 18105 Parkside, Detroit, MI 48221, **Home Phone:** (313)863-2046. **Business Addr:** Owner/President, Joe L Giles and Associates, 18105 Parkside St Suite 14, Detroit, MI 48221, **Business Phone:** (313)864-0022.

GILES, NANCY
Actor, comedian, writer. **Personal:** Born Jul 17, 1960, New York, NY; daughter of Thomas Jefferson and Dorothy Aileen Dove. **Educ:** Oberlin Col, Oberlin, OH, BA, 1981. **Career:** Theatre performance: Hey, Stay A While; The Best Of Second City; A Raisin the Sun; Mayor; Urban Blight; Police Boys; The Wacky Side Of Racism; Notes Of A Negro Neurotic; TV series: "China Beach", 1988-91; "Delta", 1992; "FOX After Breakfast", 1996; "PB&J Otter", 1998; "Dream On; Fresh Prince"; "LA Law; Spin City"; Films: Off Beat, 1986; Ich und Er, 1987; Big, 1988; Working Girl, 1988; True Crime; Everything's Jake; Angie, 1994; Loverboy; Me & Him; New York Stories; Fear of a Black Hat, 1994; I'm Not Rappaport, 1996; True Crime, 1999; States of Control, 2001; Pop Life, 2002; Joshua; Superheroes; Before the Music Dies; True Crime, Angie, Working Girl. **Orgs:** Actors Equity Asn, 1983; Screen Actors Guild, 1984; Am Fedn TV & Radio Artists, 1984; hon mem, Alliance Women Veterans, 1989. **Honors/Awds:** Theatre World Award, Outstanding New Talent, Theatre World, 1985. **Special Achievements:** Writer and contributor to the Emmy award-winning "CBS News Sunday Morning", was the announcer and co-host of the alternative morning show "Fox After Breakfast"; Black Comedy: The Wacky Side of Racism (solo show), Mill Hill Playhouse, Trenton, NJ, 1999. **Business Addr:** Actress, c/o Bret Adams Ltd, 448 W 44th St, New York, NY 10036.

GILES, TERRI LYNNETTE
Executive. **Personal:** Born in Miami, FL. **Educ:** Grambling State Univ, BS, mkt. **Career:** Burger King World Hq, supvr, consumer response line, dept supvr, consumer response line, mgr, consumer relations; Herman Electronics, customer serv mgr; Qual Solutions Personnel Servs, pres, founder, currently. **Orgs:** Soc Consumer Affairs Professionals, 1989-; Alpha Kappa Alpha Sorority, Inc, 1990-; Nat Asn Female Execs, 1990-. **Honors/Awds:** Dollars & Sense Magazine, A Salute to America's Best & Brightest Business Professionals, 1992.

GILES, WILLIE ANTHONY, JR.
School administrator. **Personal:** Born Mar 8, 1941, Conway, AR; married Carolyn Joan Williams; children: Dwayne, Keenon & Dana. **Educ:** Ark AM & N Col, BS, 1964; Univ Mich, MA, 1967; Univ Mo, Kansas City, 1986. **Career:** Detroit Mich Sch Syst, teacher, 1964-67; Kansas City MO Sch Syst, teacher,1968-69; Humboldt High Sch. Kansas City, MO, Sch Syst, prin, 1969-70;Paseo High Sch, Kansas City, MO, Sch Syst, prin, 1971-75; NE High Sch,Kansas City, MO Sch Syst, prin, 1976-78; Kansas City MO Sch Dist, assoc supt, 1986-, dir, desegregation monitoring, 1985-86, dir sec educ, 1981-85, dir admin servs, 1978-81. **Orgs:** Bd mem, Whatsoever Cir Comm House; bd mem, Urban Serv Kansas City, MO; bd mem, Paseo Day care Serv; trustee secy, Paseo Baptist Church;Citizens Crusade Against Crime; Phi Delta Kappa. **Honors/Awds:** Boss of the Year Award, Bus & Prof Women Starlight Chap, KS City MO, 1978;Outstanding Educator Award, Alpha Phi Alpha Fraternity 1980. *

GILES-ALEXANDER, SHARON
Executive, entrepreneur. **Personal:** Born Sep 12, 1951, East Orange, NJ; daughter of William R and Althea B; married Willie L Alexander II, Jun 20, 1982; children: Willie L Alexander III, Jayson A Alexander. **Educ:** Morgan State Univ, BS, 1973; Rutgers Univ, MEd, 1975. **Career:** Newark Bd Educ, 1973-75; East Orange Bd Educ, teacher, 1975-77; EPC Int Inc, pres. **Orgs:** Am Mkt Asn; Advert Specialty, IST; Specialty Advertising Asn; Federal Credit Union; New Hope Baptist Church; Coalition 100 Black Women, vpres, econ develop; Nat Asn Female Exec; Nat Bus Coun; NCP; White House Conf Small Bus, delegate; Greater Newark Coc; E Orange COC. **Honors/Awds:** WBE, Distinguished Achievement Award, 1989; NBDA, Regional Minority Bus Woman of the Year, 1989; Congressional Black Caucus Chr's Award, 1982; Kappa Delta Pi, Honor Soc Educ; Kizzy Award, 1980; Sharon A Giles Day, West Orange, NJ, Mayor Samuel A Spira City Proclamation, 1981; Outstanding Minority Bus Develop Award, 1984; Role Model of the Year, 1985. **Special Achievements:** One of the Top 100 Black Business Professionals. **Business Addr:** President, EPC Int Inc, 34 Woodland Rd, Roseland, NJ 07068, **Business Phone:** (201)403-2900.

GILES-GEE, DR. HELEN FOSTER
Educator, college president. **Personal:** Born Oct 21, 1950, Fairfield, AL; daughter of Foster and Nannette Young; married Gilford Gee. **Educ:** Univ Pa, Philadelphia, PA, BA, 1972, MS, 1973, PhD, 1983; Rutgers Univ, New Brunswick, NJ, MS, 1977. **Career:** Rutgers Univ, New Brunswick, NJ, teaching fellow, 1973-75; Stevens Inst Technol, Hoboken, NJ, sci teacher, Summer, 1974; Cheyney State Univ, Cheyney, PA, assoc prof, 1975-86, chair biol, 1983-85; Univ, Towson, MD, exec asst pres & prof biol, 1986-92; Univ System Md, Aldelphi, MD, assoc vchancellor acad affairs, dir articulation, 1991-98; Towson State univ NY, Cortland, NY, Sch Prof Stud, Dean, 1998-04; Keene State Col, pres, 2005-. **Orgs:** Pres, Cortland YWCA; vpres, pres Bd dirs, Soc Col & Univ Planning, 1993-94; Leadership Md; Am Coun Educ & Planning Bd; pres, Am Asn Higher Educ, 1989-90; Am Assoc Inst Res; Nat Coun Measurement Educ; Omicro Delta Kappa, leadership honor soc; Phi Delta Kappa, honor fraternity; Pi Lambda Theta, honor soc, 1982-89; Sigma Xi, scientific honor; steering comt, treasurer, Univ Am System Women's Forum, 1990-91; Fund Raising Comn, 1990-91; Am Asn Higher Educ. **Honors/Awds:** Nat Achievement Scholarship, Nat Merit Corp, 1968-72; Biology Club Award & Outstanding Faculty Service, Cheyney Univ, 1979; Faculty Fellowship, Nat Inst Ment Health, 1979-82; Research Award, Md Asn Higher Educ, 1987; Distinguished Program Award, 1992. **Business Addr:** President, Keene State College, 229 Main St, Keene, NH 13045-0900.*

GILFORD, VERA E
Executive, consultant. **Personal:** Born Dec 20, 1953, Detroit, MI; daughter of James and Ruby; divorced. **Educ:** Mich State Univ, BA, bus, 1975; Tex Southern Univ, JD, 1978; Mediation Int Am, circuit civil mediator, 1995. **Career:** Off Chief Coun, atty, 1978-82; Dept Justice, spec prosecutor, 1983; Off Dist Coun, sr atty, 1983-87; Pete's Fountain & Bar, pres, 1987-; Gilford Broadcasting Co, ceo, 1990-; Women Wisdom Inc, atty consult, currently. **Orgs:** Tax sect, Fla Bar, 1982-; Nat Asn Broadcasters, 1993-; Authors Guild, 1984-; Brickell Ave Literary Soc, 1993-; Exec Women's Golf League, 1994; bd mem, Fla Int Univ, 1995; bd pres, Miami Civic Chorale, 1995; Conflict Resolution Ctr Int, 1995; co chmn, United Way Endowment, 2001. **Honors/Awds:** Outstanding Business Person, St John Cot Develop Corp, 1988; Most Significant Contribution to the Law Review Award, Tex Southern Univ, 1978. **Special Achievements:** Accumulated Earnings Tax, 1977; The Constitutionality of No-Fault Auto Ins, 1978; Proclamation, Vera E Gilford Day, Miami Fla, 1987. **Business Phone:** 877-947-3667.

GILKEY, BERNARD
Baseball player. **Personal:** Born Sep 24, 1966, St Louis, MO; married Patrice; children: Jaelen & Dawson. **Career:** St Louis Cardinals, outfielder, 1990-95; New York Mets, 1996-98; Ariz Diamondbacks, 1998-2000; Boston Red Sox, 2000; Atlanta Braves, 2001; St. Louis Cardinals, free agt, 2001; Atlanta Braves, free agt, 2001-. **Special Achievements:** Made a cameo appearance in the movie Men in Black, 1997.

GILL, GLENDA ELOISE
Educator. **Personal:** Born Jun 26, 1939, Clarksville, TN; daughter of Melvin Leo and Olivia Dunlop. **Educ:** Ala A&M Univ, BS, 1960; Univ Wis-Madison, MA, 1964; Univ Iowa, PhD, 1981. **Career:** Ala A&M Univ, asst prof eng, 1963-69; Univ Tex, El Paso, instr eng,1970-75; Simpson Col, asst prof eng, 1981-82; Tuskegee Univ, assoc profdept head, 1982-83; Winston-Salem State Univ, assoc prof eng, 1984-90;Mich Technol Univ, assoc prof drama, 1990-2000, prof drama, 2000-06, profemer drama, 2006-. **Orgs:** Eugene O'Neill Soc, 1998; Am Soc theatre Res, 1984-; Assn theatre Higher Educ, 1987-; World Congress Theatre, 1989-; Delta Sigma Theta, 1958-; Natl Coun Teachers Eng, 1963-83; Conf Col Composition Comm, 1963-83; Amer Soc for Theater Research. **Honors/Awds:** Natl Portrait Gallery, Smithsonian, summer fellow, 1990; Nat Endowment for the Humanities, Summer Institute, Duke, 1991, Summer Institute, Univ NC-Chapel Hill, 1989, Summer Seminar, Yale, 1985, Summer Institute, Iowa,1974; Rockefeller Foundation Grant, 1976, 1977. **Special Achievements:** White Grease Paint on Black Performers, New York: Peter Lang, 1988; "The African-American Student: At Risk," CCC, Vol 43, No 2, May 1992; "Canada Lee: Black Actor in Non-Traditional Roles," JPC, Winter, 1991; "View From My Window," Obsidian II, p 41-42, Winter 1990; "White Dresses, Sweet Chariots," Southern Literary Journal, Spring 1990; "Rosamond Gilder:Influential Talisman for African-American Performers," Theatre Survey,1996; "The Alabama A & M Thespians, 1944-63: Triumph of the Human Spirit, "The Drama Review, 1994; "Her Voice Was Ever Soft, Gentle and Low, AnExcellent Thing in Ruby Dee," Journal of Popular Culture, 1994; "Love In Black and White: Miscegenation on the Stage, " Journal of Amer Drama andTheater, fall, 1998; "Morgan Freeman's Resistance and Non-TraditionalRoles," Popular Culture Review, vol 9, no 2, 45-58, August, 1998; "No Surrender! No Retreat-African-American Pioneer Performers of 20th Century American Theater," St Martin's Press, 2000; "The Triumphs and Struggles of Earle Hyman in Traditional and Non-Traditional Roles," JADT, Winter, 2001;"Nothing But A Man,: Leonard de Paur's Legacy of Subtle Activism in Theatre and Music," JADT, Fall, 2003. **Home Addr:** 7584 Old Madison Pike NW Apt 13, Huntsville, AL 35806, **Home Phone:** (256)971-9399. **Business Addr:** Professor Emerita, Michigan Technological University, Department of Humanities, 1400 Townsend Dr, Houghton, MI 49931.

GILL, PROF. JACQUELINE A.
Librarian, educator. **Personal:** Born Jun 4, 1950, New York, NY; daughter of Maude L Flanagan and Nathan S; children: Christopher B Aden. **Educ:** Borough Manhattan Community Col, New York, NY, AA, libr tech, 1976; QueensCol, Flushing, NY, BA, sociol, 1979; Pratt Inst, Brooklyn, NY, MLS, libr Sci, 1988; City Col, New York, NY, MS, Educ Supervision Admin, 1989. **Career:** Maritime Col, Bronx, NY, serials asst, 1976-79; City Col, NY, res asst,1979-83, libn instr, 1983-90, asst prof, 1990-98, assoc prof, 1998-,Acquisitions Division, chief, 1996-2000, ref librn & bibliographic coordr, 2000-; Borough Manhattan Community Col, adj assoc prof, 1995-. **Orgs:** Cognotes reporter, Am Libr Asn, 1989-91; recording secretary, New York Black Librns Caucus, 1989-90; personnel admin secy, liaison for JMRT, Am Libr Asn, 1989-91; Systs & serv secy, acquisition Syst comm mem, AmLibr Asn, 1990-91; CCNY Fac Senate Elections Comt, 1995-98; CCNY Fac Senate Affairs Comt, secy, 1995-98; N Am Serials Users Group, 1995-2000; NY Libr Asn, 1996-; Libr Asn City Univ NY, 1983-. **Honors/Awds:** PSC-City Univ New York Research Award Recipient, 1995-96; City Col City Women, 1999. **Business Addr:** Associate Professor, Reference Librarian, City College New York, W 138th St Convent Ave, New York, NY 10031.

GILL, JOHNNY
Singer. **Personal:** Born May 22, 1966, Washington, DC; son of Johnny Gill Sr and Annie. **Career:** New Edition, mem; Solo Albums: Johnny Gill, 1983; Chemistry, 1985; Johnny Gill, 1990; Provacative, 1993; Let's Get the Mood Right, 1996; Favorites, 1997; Ultimate Collection, 2002; Singles: "Super Love," "Tiger Beat," "Rub You the Right Way," "When Something is Wrong with My Baby", "Slow & Sexy "(with Shabba Ranks)", "My, My, My"; motion picture soundtrack contributor:Boomerang, Mo' Money, New Jack City; Filmography: Saturday Night Live; The

Best of Keith Sweat, 2005; One on One, 2005; Behind the Music, 2005; R Uthe Gir, 2005; Cuts, 2005; movie: The Ballad of Walter Holmes, 2006. **Business Phone:** (310)865-5000.

GILL, KENDALL CEDRIC
Basketball player. **Personal:** Born May 25, 1968, Chicago, IL. **Educ:** Univ Ill, Urbana-Champaign, BA, speech commun, 1989. **Career:** Basketball player (retired), boxer; Charlotte Hornets, guard, 1990-93, 1995; Seattle Super Sonics, 1993-95; NJ Nets, 1995-2001; Miami Heat, 2001-02; Minn Timber wolves, 2002-03; Chicago Bulls, 2003-04; Milwaukee Bucks, 2004-05; Comcast Sports Net, analyst, 2006-07; boxer, currently. **Orgs:** Founder, Kendall Gill House; Mem; NBA Pacific Division Champion Seattle Supersonics team, 1993-94. **Honors/Awds:** All Rookie first team, NBA, 1991; winner, cruiser weight four-rounder. **Special Achievements:** First round pick, No 5, NBA Draft, 1990; TV appearance: "My Brother and Me".

GILL, REV. LAVERNE MCCAIN
Clergy, executive, writer. **Personal:** Born Oct 13, 1947, Washington, DC; daughter of Paul McCain and Mary McCain Williams; married Tepper, Feb 11, 1977; children: Dylan McDuffie & Tepper M. **Educ:** Howard Univ, BA, 1969; Am Univ, grad studies, commun, 1973; Rutgers Univ, MBA, 1977; Princeton Theol Sem, MDiv, 1997, MTh, 1998. **Career:** US Senate, Senator Alan Cranston, legis aide, 1970-72; Lassiter & Co, vpres, 1973-77; Univ DC, assoc prof, 1979-82; Fed Res Bd Govs, budget analyst, 1983-86; Metro Chronicle Newspaper, ed, co-founder, 1986-94; McCain Media Inc, pres; Women's Radical Discipleship Ministries, founder, currently; Author: African American Women in Congress: Forming & Transforming History, Rutgers Univ Press, 1997; Wash Post Article, Princeton Packet, July 8 1997; article, Lectionary Preaching for Women Abingdon Press 2000; books: My Mother Prayed for Me: Faith Journaling for African American Women Pilgrim, 2000; Daughter's of Dignity: African Biblical Women, Virtues of Women, Pilgrim Press, Cleveland, OH, 2000; Vashti's Victory, Pilgrim Press, 2003; Webster Church, United Church Christ, MI, pastor, currently. **Orgs:** Nat Newspaper Publishers Asn; Capital Area Chap, Acad Arts & Sci; Am Film TV Radio Asn; Friends Rankin Chapel; Congional Press Gallery, 1986-94; African-Am Media Coalition. **Honors/Awds:** Montgomery NAACP Award, 1987; Emmy Nomination, Nat Acad Arts & Sci, 1992; Borscht Found Fel, 1992; Mayor's Community Service Award, 1991; commendation, chmn, Fed Res Bd Governors, 1985; Jagow Preaching Award; Excellence in Homiletics Award, Princeton; ordained pastor, 1999; Antoinette Brown Award for Excellence in Ministry. **Special Achievements:** First African American to pastor the Webster United Church of Christ. **Business Addr:** Pastor, Webster United Church Christ, 5484 Webster Church Rd, Dexter, MI 48130-9635, **Business Phone:** (734)426-5115.

GILL, NIA H
Senator (U.S. federal government), lawyer, politician. **Personal:** Born Mar 15, 1948, Glen Ridge, NJ; married; children: 1. **Educ:** Upsala Col, BA, hist & polit hist; Rutgers Univ Sch Law, JD; Foreign Policy Inst, Ctr Women Policy Studies, grad, 2006. **Career:** NJ State Senate, state sen, 2002-; Gill & Cohen PC, atty, partner, currently; Am Dem Party, politician, currently. **Orgs:** NJ State Bar Asn; Million Dollar Advocates Forum. **Honors/Awds:** Distinguished InterNat Award, Int Affairs Div United Nations, 2005; Women of the Year, NJ Bus & Indust Asn. **Special Achievements:** Honored in Selma, Alabama as one of "100 Women in the 20th Century? who contributed to the struggle for civil rights; New Jersey Monthly magazine "Profiles in Courage?. **Business Addr:** State Senator, New Jersey State Senate, Gill for Senate, 19 Elm St PO Box 8041, Montclair, NJ 07042, **Business Phone:** (973)509-2379.

GILL, ROBERTA L.
Lawyer. **Personal:** Born Jun 25, 1947, Baltimore, MD; daughter of Robert and Rubye; children: Tara Maraj. **Educ:** Univ Chicago Law Sch, 1971; Univ Md Law Sch, JD, 1972; Johns Hopkins Sch Hyg & Pub Health, MPH, 1976. **Career:** Atty, pvt pract, 1972-88; E Baltimore Community Corp, coun, admin, 1979-83; Sickle Cell Dis Asn Md, admin, 1985-88; Off Atty Gen, asst atty gen, 1988-. **Orgs:** Delta Sigma Theta Sorority, 1967-; Cooley's Anemia Found, secy, 1988-; Baltimore Cable Access Corp, 1986-; Nat Gill Family Reunion, pres, 1996-. **Honors/Awds:** Outstanding Contributions, Sickle Cell Disease Asn Md, 1996. **Special Achievements:** Member of Rafiki Na Dada, an all female acapella singing group, 1987-. **Home Addr:** 3415 Callaway Ave, Baltimore, MD 21215. **Business Phone:** (410)576-6300.*

GILL, ROSA UNDERWOOD
Accountant, association executive. **Personal:** Born May 14, 1944, Wake County, NC; married Jimmie; children: Angie Rosharon, Natalie Denise. **Educ:** Shaw Univ Raleigh NC, BS, Math, 1968; NC Cent Univ Durham, attended 1978; NC State Univ Raleigh, attended 1979. **Career:** Nationwide Ins, Raleigh, NC, acct clerk, 1965-68; Johnson Co, Smithfield, NC, math instr 1968-70; Wake Co Raleigh NC, mat instr, 1971-80; State Govt Raleigh NC, acct I, 1980-; Wake Comt Pub Sch Syst, sch bd mem, vice chair, currently. **Orgs:** Secy, Dem Party Wake Co, 1974-78; girl scout leader Girl Scouts of Am, 1974-78; adv Student Coun, 1975-80; trnd girl scout leader, 1976-78; dem vice chmn, Dem Party Wake Co, 1978. **Special Achievements:** First black female chairperson in Wake Community Board Elections. **Business Addr:** Vice Chair, Wake County Public School System, District 4, 3600 Wake Forest Rd, PO Box 28041, Raleigh, NC 27611-8041, **Business Phone:** (919)850-1600.*

GILL, SAMUEL A.
Violinist. **Personal:** Born Nov 30, 1932, Brooklyn, NY; son of Everton and Clarendon; divorced. **Educ:** Juilliard Sch Music; Manhattan Sch Music, BA, music, MD, music educ, 1960; Univ Colo, DMus, 1989. **Career:** Denver Symphony Orchestra, bass violin; Colo Symphony Orchestra, bassist, currently. **Orgs:** Denver Symphony Soc. **Honors/Awds:** Shriner Syrian Temple Sym Social Award, Tilden High, 1950; Win of Down Beat International Crit Award, 1955. **Special Achievements:** Played with Max Roach; Coleman Hawkins; J J Johnson; Harry Belafonte Singers; Randy Weston Trio Master Mason Mt Evans Lodge; 32 Degree Mason Mountain & Plains Consis; among first of race to be engaged by major symphony 1960. **Business Addr:** Bassist, Colorado Symphony Orchestra, Boettcher Concert Hall, Denver Performing Arts Complex, 1000 14th St Suite 15, Denver, CO 80202.*

GILL, DR. TROY D.
Physician. **Personal:** Born Aug 7, 1937, Chicago, IL; son of Troy and Mary; divorced; children: Eunice, Donald, Mary, Omari. **Educ:** Dillard Univ, BA, 1959; Howard Univ Col Med, MD, 1963. **Career:** Little Co Mary Hosp Ill, med intern, 1963-64; Maricopa City Gen Hosp Ari, ped res, 1964-65; Good Samaritan Hosp Ari, chief ped res, 1965-66; Univ Utah Med Ctr, adult & child psych fel, 1968-72; Rubicon Int, phys, pub speaker, bus owner; Utah State hosp, clinic dir youth ctr. **Orgs:** Bd governors, Salt Lake Area Chamber Com, 1975-78; bd mem, Nat Alliance Bus, 1977-80; int Platform Asn; World Med Asn; chmn, Utah State Bd Mental Health, 1976-83; Univ Utah Col Nursing Adv Bd; mental health consult, US Job Corp Clearfield Utah, 1972-73; staff mem & consult, Raleigh Hills Hosp, 1972-82; Salt Lake Exec Asn, 1972-76; Utah Med Asn; Am Sco Training & Develop; White House Conf C, 1970. **Military Serv:** USN, lt comm, 1966-68. *

GILL, WALTER HARRIS (WALI HAKEEM)
Educator. **Personal:** Born Aug 16, 1937, Greenville, MS; son of Robert and Rubye C; married Frances Nichols, Dec 21, 1961; children: Valerie Palmer, Michelle Queen, Stacey Palmer, Danell Gill & Daren Gill. **Educ:** Morgan State Col, BS, 1960; Syracuse Univ, MEd, 1971, PhD, 1977. **Career:** Sec sch art teacher, 1962-64, 1966-70, 1992-93, 1997-2002; Bowie State Col, asst prof, 1973-78; Morgan State Univ, asst prof, 1978-84; Univ Nebr, Omaha, asst prof, 1985-91; Millerville Univ, asst prof, 1994-96; Hickey Sch, art teacher, 1998-2001; Woodbourne Sch, art teacher, 2001-; Dual Image Consult, vpres, currently. **Honors/Awds:** Best Supporting Actor, Center Stage, Omaha, NE, 1986; Best Actor, Omaha Community Playhouse, 1991; Hall of Fame, Baltimore City Col, 1997. **Special Achievements:** Author of books: Issues in African American Education, 1991; Common Sense Guide to Non-Traditional Urban Education, 1998; Essential Teaching Strategies for Urban Educators, 2002; Walter was the first Black to graduate from the city college. **Military Serv:** AUS, lt, 1960-62. **Home Phone:** (410)366-7160. **Business Addr:** Vice President, Dual Image Consultants, 4228 Evans Chapel Rd, PO Box 4618, Baltimore, MD 21211, **Business Phone:** (410)889-9100.

GILL, DR. WANDA EILEEN
Executive. **Personal:** Born Feb 7, 1945, Burlington, NJ; daughter of Thomas G Waples Jr and Marian J Waples; married Bruce L, Dec 24, 1968; children: Candace & Kimberly. **Educ:** Va State Univ, BS, 1967; Univ Cincinnati, MA, 1968; Bowie State Univ, MEd, 1982; George Wash Univ, EdD, 1987. **Career:** Georgetown Univ Sch Med, coordr, 1977-79; Bowie State Univ, Dir, coordr & learning skills specialist, 1979-92; Middle States Asn Comn Higher Educ, assoc dir, 1993-94; Diverse Ed Solutions Inc, pres, 1994-98; US Dept Ed, consult, 1998-2000; Inst Prof Develop, dir, 2000-01; OESE, sr adv & dir SIP, 2001-02; Office Innovation & Improvement, prog mgt analyst, 2002-; IPA Prog Bowie State Univ, 2004-06; IPA Prog Sojourner-Douglass Col, 2006-08. **Orgs:** Conf chair, Mid-Eastern Asn Educ Opportunity Prog Personnel, 1987-89; pres, MD Exec Coun Educ Opportunity, 1989-92; Am Educ Res Asn, 2005-; life mem, Blacks In Govt, 2005-, gold mem, 2007; regional rep, US Dept Educ BIG Chapter, 2006-. **Honors/Awds:** Operation Crossroads Africa, Spelman Col, 1964; Danforth Found Fel, Univ Cincinnati, 1967-68. **Special Achievements:** 32 publications. **Business Addr:** Management Analyst, Technology in Education Programs, US Department of Education, Office of Innovation and Improvement, 400 Maryland Ave SW, Washington, DC 20003.

GILLESPIE, BONITA
Business owner, educator. **Personal:** Born Jan 20, 1951, Knoxville, TN; daughter of James Edward and Hildritn Doris Johnson. **Educ:** Knoxville Col, Knoxville, TN, BS, 1973; E Tenn State Univ, Johnson City, TN, MA, 1976. **Career:** Martin-Maretta Energy Syst, Oak Ridge, TN, acct, 1978-86; Knoxville Col, Knoxville, TN, asst prof acct & mgt, 1986-; BG Acct, Knoxville, TN, owner & acct, 1987-; Gillespie Financial & Tax Serv, owner, currently. **Orgs:** Charter mem, Nat Asn Black Acct, Knoxville Chap, 1980-; dir, S Cent Region, Zeta Phi Beta Sorority Inc, 1986-90; trainer & site coordr, Internal Rev Serv, Knoxville Off. **Honors/Awds:** Distinguished Service Award, Knoxville Col Alumni Asn, 1983; Silver Service Award, IRS, 1990; Community Service Award, Knoxville Community Action Community, 1990, 1994. **Home Addr:** 2518 Chillicothe St, Knoxville, TN 37921. **Business Addr:** Owner, Accountant, Gillespie Financial & Tax Service, 3611 Western Ave, Knoxville, TN 37921-1637, **Business Phone:** (865)974-9674.

GILLESPIE, MARCIA A.
Editor, writer, consultant. **Personal:** Born Jul 10, 1944, Rockville Centre, NY; daughter of Charles M and Ethel Young. **Educ:** Lake Forest Col, BA, am studies, 1966. **Career:** Time-Life Books, Time Inc, NY, 1966-70; Essence Mag, ed-in-chief, 1971-80; Ms Mag, New York, NY, exec ed, ed-in-chief, commun consult, ed & writer, 1980-93; Ms Found Educ & Commun, Times Sq, consult, 1990-92; Mothers Mag,ed-in-chief, ed emer, currently. exec ed, 1992-93; Johnnetta B. Cole Inst, prof diversity in residence, currently; Author; "Maya Angelou:A Glorious Celebration. **Orgs:** Nat Coun Negro Women; Am Soc Mag Ed; bd dirs, Rod Rodgers Dance Co; Arthur Ashe Inst Urban Health; Black & Jewish Women, New York; guest lectr, Univ W Indies Sch Commun; adv to the vice chancellor, Univ W Indies, Outreachto N Am; Studio Mus, Harlem; Educ Equity Concepts, EEC; adv comt, Take Our Daughters to Work Day; adv brd, Feminist Press; brd dirs, Violence Policy Ctr, Washington, DC; adv brd, Girls, Re-Cast TV; adv brd, Feminists Animals Rights, FAR; adv brd, ISMN; Aspen fel, Aspen Inst; brd dir, New Federal Theater New York City. **Honors/Awds:** Outstanding Alumni Award, Lake Forest Col, 1973; Matrix Award, NY Women Commun, 1978; Mary MacLeod Bethune Award, Nat Coun Negro Women; March of Dimes Award; NYABJ Life Achievement Award, Print Jour; Matrix Awd from New York Women In Commn; Mary MacLeod Bethune award from the National Council of Negro Women. **Special Achievements:** Named one of the fifty faces for American Future Time Magazine, 1979; one of ten outstanding women in mag publ, 1982. *

GILLESPIE, DR. RENA HARRELL
Educational consultant. **Personal:** Born Oct 26, 1949, Starkville, MS; widowed. **Educ:** Miss State Univ, BS, 1972, PhD, 1981; Univ Cincinnati, ME, 1974. **Career:** Cincinnati Pub Schs, resident counr, 1972-74; Miss Univ Women, minority stud counr, 1974-78; Miss State Univ, residence hall dir, 1979-82; Univ NC Chapel Hill, assoc dir health careers prog, 1983-86; Benjamin Eiijah Mays High Sch, counr, currently; self-employed, educ consult, currently. **Orgs:** United Methodist Local Bd Ministries, 1975-; Southern Col Personnel Asn, 1979-; Am Personnel & Guid Asn, 1980-; Asn Col Stud Personnel, 1980-; Nat Minority Health Affairs, 1984-; vol, Outreach Counr Econ Opportunities Atlanta Proj Delay, Teenage Pregnancy Prev Prog, 1987-; vol, Helpline Counr Ga Coun Child Abuse, 1987-. **Honors/Awds:** Minority Doctoral Fel, Miss Univ Women, 1978-81; Outstanding Young Woman of America, 1984. **Home Addr:** 1735 Flintwood Dr, Atlanta, GA 30316. **Business Addr:** Educational Consultant, 2895 Benjamin E Mays Dr S, Atlanta, GA 30311, **Business Phone:** (404)758-6724.

GILLESPIE, WILLIAM G.
Clergy, educator. **Personal:** Born May 12, 1931, Knoxville, TN; married Martha Cox; children: Vendetta Lambert, William, Harry. **Educ:** Knoxville Col, BS, 1952; Johnson C Smith, BD, 1955; Tarkio Col, DD, 1969; Eden Sem, STM & D Min, 1970; Univ MO, LLD, 1987. **Career:** Davie St Presb Ch Raleigh, pastor, 1955-56; Cote Brilliante Presby Church, pastor, 1956-; Linwood Col St Chas, asst prof, 1971-73; Eden Sem Webster Groves, lectr, MO, 1972-74; Maryville Col, lectr, St Louis, 1972-74. **Orgs:** pres, bd dirs, Mathews-Dickey Boys Club, St Louis, 1970-; pres, bd trustees, Johnson C Smith Sem Atlanta, 1976-; pres, bd regents, Harris-Stowe State Col, St Louis, 1978-; bd mem, Family & Children Serv, St Louis, 1978-; bd trustees, Interdenom Theol Ctr, Atlanta, 1979-; bd mem, United Way Greater, St Louis, 1980. **Honors/Awds:** Citizen of the Year Award, Sigma Gamma Rho Sor, 1975; Distinguished Citizen Award, Mathews-Dickey Boys Club, 1977; Distinguished Service Award, St Louis Argus Newspaper, 1979; Martin L King Jr Humanitarian Award, St Louis Alliance Against Racial Repression, 1980. **Home Addr:** 7328 Ravinia Dr, St Louis, MO 63121. **Business Addr:** Pastor, Cote Brilliante Presbyterian Church, 4673 Labadie Ave, St Louis, MO 63115, **Business Phone:** (314)381-2770.*

GILLETTE, FRANKIE JACOBS
Consultant. **Personal:** Born Apr 1, 1925, Norfolk, VA; daughter of Frank and Natalie Taylor; married Maxwell Claude, 1976. **Educ:** Hampton Inst, BS, 1946; Howard Univ, MSW, 1948. **Career:** Ada S McKinley Comm House Chicago, supvr, 1950-53; Sophie Wright Settlement, Detroit, prog dir, 1953-64; Concerted Serv Proj, dir, 1964-65; Univ Calif Soc Welfare Exten, prog coordr, 1965-68; US Comm Serv Admin, spec prog coordr, 1968-81; G & G Enterprises, pres, 1978-. **Orgs:** San Francisco Bus & Prof Women, Inc, 1970-; dir, Time Savings & Loan Asn, 1980-90; vpres, San Francisco Handicapped Access Appeals Bd, 1982-87;

chairperson, bd dirs, NANBPWC Inc, 1983-87; pres, Nat Asn Negro Bus & Prof Women's Clubs Inc, 1983-87; life mem, Delta Sigma Theta Sorority; chairperson, San Francisco-Abidjan, Cote d'Ivoire Sister Cities Comm; vpres, Urban Econ Develop Corp, San Francisco, 1987-91; bd, San Francisco Conv & Visitors Bur, 1987-94, 1997-; comnr, San Francisco Human Rights Comn, 1988-92; trustee, Fine Arts Museums San Francisco, 1993-; Links Inc; bd dirs, Museum African Diaspora, 2006, trustee, currently. **Honors/Awds:** Alumnus of the Year, Hampton Inst, 1966; Sojourner Truth NANBPWC Inc, 1980; publications The Organizer; The Governor NANBPWC Inc, 1978, 1981;"Lives of Accomplishment," San Francisco Sr Ctr, 2003; Woman of the Year, Delta Delta Zeta Chapter, Zeta Phi Beta Sorority, 1991. **Special Achievements:** Women Who Make It Happen" Frito-Lay and National Council of Negro Women,1987. **Business Addr:** President, G & G Enterprises, 85 Cleary Ct Suite 4, San Francisco, CA 94109, **Business Phone:** (415)563-8299.

GILLETTE, DR. LYRA STEPHANIE
Physician. **Personal:** Born Mar 1, 1930; children: 1. **Educ:** Barnard Col, AB, 1960; Howard Univ, MD, 1964; Columbia Univ, MPH, 1968. **Career:** Harlem Hosp, visiting clinician & consult, 1969; Univ Vienna, guest physician, 1969; US PUSH, dept chief obstet & gynec, 1970; Martin Luther King Jr Hop, dir ambulatory serv obstet & gynec, 1971; Watts Health Found, chief obstet & gynec; Univ S Calif, clinical prof obstet & gynec, 1990; Los Angeles County, Dept Health Servs, md specialist; pvt pract, currently. **Orgs:** Chmn, Pub Health Comn, Am Med Women's Asn, 1977; consult, obstet & gynec, Device Panel FDA, 1976; dip, Nat Bd Med Examiners, 1965; Am Bd obstet & gynec, 1972; Am Col obstet & gynec, 1974; Los Angeles obstet & gynec Soc 1973; Am Pub Health Asn, 1971; Asn Pub Health obstet & gynec, 1974. **Honors/Awds:** PHS grant, 1968; AMA Physician Rec Award, 1969. **Special Achievements:** Publication, "Mgmt of Adenomatous Hyperplasia", OB World, 1977. **Military Serv:** USAF, Med Corps maj, 1980-83. **Home Addr:** 4483 Don Milagro Dr, Los Angeles, CA 90008. **Business Addr:** Physician Specialist, 2611 N Dinuba Blvd, Visalia, CA 93291, **Business Phone:** (559)733-6342.

GILLIAM, ARLEEN FAIN
Labor activist. **Personal:** Born Jan 2, 1949, Huntington, WV; daughter of Cicero and Lorraine; married Reginald E Gilliam Jr. **Educ:** Skidmore Col, BS, 1970; Mass Inst Tech, MBA, 1976. **Career:** Cong Budget Off, budget analyst, 1976-77; Labor US Dept Labor, exec asst, 1977-81; Am Fedn Labor & Cong Indust Orgn, asst dir dept soc sec, 1981-84, dir budget & planning, 1984-91, Planning & Personnel Policy, dir budget, 1991-96; Clinton-Gore transition team, 1992-; Am Fedn Labor & Cong Indust Orgn, asst pres, 1996, sr asst, currently. **Orgs:** Reston Chapter of Links, 1977-87; Sloan Sch Bd Govs, 1989-95; Fairfax County Park Authority Bd, 1991-93. **Home Addr:** 2413 Black Cap Lane, Reston, VA 20191. **Business Addr:** Senior Assistant, American Federation of Labor & Congress of Industrial Organizations, 815 16th St NW, Washington, DC 20006.*

GILLIAM, ARMEN LOUIS
Basketball player. **Personal:** Born May 28, 1964, Pittsburgh, PA. **Educ:** Independence Jr Col, Independence, attended 1983; Univ Nev-19 Las Vegas, BS. **Career:** Basketball Player (retired), Coach; Phoenix Suns, forward, 1987-89; Charlotte Hornets, forward, 1989-91; Philadelphia 76ers, forward, 1991-93; New Jersey Nets, forward, 1993-96; Milwaukee Bucks, forward, 1996-99; Utah Jazz, free agent, 1999-2000; Mount Lebanon High Sch, vol asst coach; head coach, 2001; head coach, Pa State-Altoona, 2002-05; Pittsburgh Xplosion, free agent, 2005-06. **Honors/Awds:** NBA All-Rookie Team, 1988; Met Life Net of the Year, 1995; Bethel Park Hall of Fame, 1997; UNLV Hall of Fame, 1998.

GILLIAM, DOROTHY BUTLER
Editor. **Personal:** Born in Memphis, TN; married Sam; children: Stephanie, Melissa, Leah. **Educ:** Sch Jour, attended 1961; Lincoln Univ, BA; Columbia Grad Sch Jour & grad, attended 1961. **Career:** Ebony Mag; Johnson Publ; Jet, ed; The Post, gen assignment reporter, 1961-65, asst ed, 1972-79; Panorama WTTG TV, broadcaster, 1967-72; Am Univ & Howard Univ, lectr, 1967-68, writer, 1967-72; The Post, reporter, 1961-66, asst ed 1979; Va Commonwealth Univ Sch Mass Commun, distinguished Prof, 2000; Robert C Maynard Inst Journ Educ, bd dirs, currently. **Orgs:** dir, Young Jour Develop Prog; Nat Asn Black Woman; Am Soc Newspaper Editors. **Honors/Awds:** grant, African-Am Inst, 1961; Anne O'Hare McCormick Award, NY Newspaper Womens Club; Jour of Year, Capital Press Clubs, 1967; Emmy award for Panorama; outstanding alumni, Lincoln Univ, 1973; Journalist of the Year award, Capital Press Club; Honor Medal, Univ Mo; Journalism Alumni of the Year Award, Columbia Grad Sch. **Special Achievements:** First black woman hired as a full-time reporter The Post; Publ: Paul Robeson All Am, 1976. **Business Addr:** Board of Director, Robert C. Maynard Institute for Journalism Education, 1211 Preservation Pkwy, Oakland, CA 94612.*

GILLIAM, FRANK DELANO
Football executive. **Personal:** Born Jan 1, 1934?, Steubenville, OH; son of Ed and Viola; married Velma, Jan 1, 1954; children: Frank Jr, Gayle & Michelle. **Educ:** Iowa Univ, BA, 1957. **Career:** Football player personnel, "retired"; Winnipeg and Vancouver CanadianFootball League, pro football player, 1957- 63; Iowa Univ, asst coach1966-70; Minnesota Vikings, scouting dir, 1971-75, dir of player personnel1975- 94, vp, sr consult & player personnel, 1994- 02. **Orgs:** Nat Assn Advancement of Colored People; Univ Iowa Alumni Assn, Univ Iowa Black Alumni Assn, Univ Iowa Lettermans Club. **Honors/Awds:** National Education Association All-American, 1953, All Big Ten, 1956, All-American, 1956. *

GILLIAM, HERMAN ARTHUR, JR. (ART GILLIAM)
Executive. **Personal:** Born Mar 6, 1943, Nashville, TN; son of Herman Arthur Gilliam Sr and Leola Hortense Caruthers. **Educ:** Yale Univ, BA, 1963; Univ Mich, MBA, 1967. **Career:** Universal Life Ins Co, 1967-75; US HouseRepresentatives, 1975-76; Gilliam Commun Inc, chmn & pres, 1977-; 1340 WLOK, owner, currently. **Orgs:** Pres, Memphis Area Radio Stas; chmn bd, Black Bus Asn Memphis; chmn, Tenn Humanities Coun; bd mem, Nat Fedn State Humanities Coun; mem, Soc Entrepreneurs. **Special Achievements:** First African-American owner of an electronic news media in Memphis. **Business Addr:** Chairman, President, Gilliam Communications Inc, 363 S 2nd St, Memphis, TN 38103, **Business Phone:** (901)527-9565.*

GILLIAM, JAMES H., SR.
Executive, consultant. **Personal:** Born Aug 6, 1920, Baltimore, MD; son of James E and Pocahontas; married Louise Hayley; children: James Jr & Patrice. **Educ:** Morgan State Univ, BA, sociol, 1948; Howard Univ Sch, MSW, 1950; Yale Univ Summer Sch Alcohol Studies. **Career:** Director (retired); Greater Wilmington Dev Council Inc, dir neighborhood & housing serv, 1965-67; Greater Wilmington Housing Corp, chmn, pres, 1967-70; Greater Wilmington Housing Corp, founder, exec dir; Leon N Weiner & Assoc Inc, vpres, 1970-71; Family Court of the State of Del, admin/dir treatment serv, 1971-72; Leon N Weiner & Assoc Inc, vpres, 1972-74; Del Community Housing Inc, pres, chmn, 1974-90; mgt consult; Newcastle county, chmn, currently. **Orgs:** Dir, Med Ctr, Del; bd parole, Del State; NAACP; Sigma Pi Phi Fraternity; exec comn, Grand Opera House, Del; chmn, Metro Wilm Urban League; Kappa Alpha Psi Fraternity; pres, trustee, Nat Asn Housing Orgn; Wesley Col; dir, Nat Tuberculosis Asn. **Honors/Awds:** Alumni Award, Howard Univ Sch Soc Work, 1952; Social Worker of the Year, Nat Asn Social Workers Del Chap, 1969; Distinguished Delawarean Award, 1982; NAHRON Ambassador Award, 1985; Regional Ambassador Award, MARC/NAHRO, 1985; BPA Achievers Award, 1985; State Ambassador Award, Del NAHRO, 1985; Conf Christian & Jews-Del Region Wallace M Johnson Award, 1986; Hon Doctorate, Bus Admin Goldey Beacom Col, l989; Community Service Award, Kiwanis Club, Wilmington, Del, 1990; Brotherhood Award, 1992; Josiah Marvel Cup Award, Del State Chamber of Com, 1994; Liberty Bell Award, 1997; hon doctorate, Univ Del, 1999; J. Caleb Boggs Comn Serv Award, Order of the First State, 1999; James H Gilliam Community Services Building, named in honor. **Military Serv:** USY, capt; Bronze Star with cluster, 1945. **Home Addr:** 900 N Broom St Apt 35, Wilmington, DE 19806-4545, **Home Phone:** (302)656-1066. **Business Addr:** Chairman, New Castle County, 87 Reads Way, New Castle, DE 19720-1648, **Business Phone:** (302)395-8383.*

GILLIAM, JOEL
Law enforcement officer. **Personal:** Born in Tuscumbia, AL. **Educ:** FBI Nat Acad, grad; Wayne State Univ, BA, police admin; Univ Detroit Mercy, MA, pub admin. **Career:** Law enforcement officer (retired); Von Braun Civic Ctr, AL, pub servs supvr; Detroit Police Dept, cmdr, 1987-97; Decatur Police, chief, 1997-2007. **Orgs:** Ala Asn Chiefs Police; Rotary Club Decatur; Kiwanis Club Decatur. **Special Achievements:** First African American police chief in Decatur, AL; Guest on ABC's "20/20" TV news show and was quoted in "Newsweek" magazine. **Military Serv:** AUS, air force veteran. **Home Addr:** PO Box 488, Decatur, AL 35602.

GILLIAM, ROBERT M., SR.
Lawyer. **Personal:** Born Jul 12, 1926, Cleveland, OH; married Elva Ann Hickerson; children: Georgia & Robert Jr. **Educ:** BBA, 1950; LLB, 1958; JD, 1961. **Career:** Pvt Prac, 1958-61; City Cleve, asst law dir, 1961-68; Legal Aid Soc Cleveland, atty, 1968-; Civic Dir, 1971-73; Senate Staff, atty, 1973-. **Orgs:** Cleveland Bar Asn; Ohio Bar Asn; Cleveland Lawyers Asn; John Harlen Law Club; NAACP; Urban League; NLADA; Kappa Alpha Psi Frat; P Omega P; Hon Bus Frat; bd dir Margie Home Retarded Adults; bd dir, Broadway YMCA, 1945-46.

GILLIAM, ROOSEVELT SANDY, JR.
School administrator. **Personal:** Born Sep 9, 1932, Union, SC; son of Roosevelt and Lillia Trapp; married Bety Davis Gilliam, Dec 24, 1955; children: Roosevelt, Wayne, Sonja Patrice. **Educ:** Allen Univ, Columbia, SC, BS, phys educ; Indiana Univ, Bloomington, IN, MS, phys educ. **Career:** Sims High Sch, Union, SC, athletic dir, head football & basketball coach, 1952-53, 1955-58; Barr St High Sch, Lancaster, SC, athletic dir, 1960-64; Maryland State Col, Princess Anne, MD, head football coach, 1964-69; Empire Sports Co, Denver, CO, prof scout, 1967-75; Springs Indust, Fort Mill, SC, mgr, employ rels, 1975-87; State South Carolina, Dept Social Servs, Columbia, SC, execu asst to comnr, 1987-88; South Carolina State Col, Orangesburg, SC, vpres develop & indust rels, 1988, exec secy, special asst to pres, 1996. **Orgs:** South Carolina Comn Higher Educ; South Carolina State Develop Bd; New Horizons Comn Lancaster, SC; adv bd, Lancaster City Develop Bd; pres, Palmetto Area Coun Boy Scouts Am; bd mem, Lancaster Children's Home; bd mem, Adam Walsh Child Resource Ctr; Clinton Junior Col Bd Trustees; pres, Allen Univ Yellow Jacket Club; vpres, Lancaster Chamber Com; pres, Lancaster East Precinct, 1976-; pres, Lancaster Colt League; pres, Lancaster Democratic Party; chmn, bd trustees, Mt. Zion A.M.E.Z. Church; chmn, Lancaster County Democratic Party; pres, WAS Baptist Church Men Fellowship; Omega Psi Phi Fraternity; chmn, bd dirs, Lancaster Community Ctr. **Honors/Awds:** Omega Man of the Year, Omega Psi Phi, 1977; Silver Beaver, Distinguished Eagle, Boy Scouts Am; Inductee, The South Carolina Athletic Hall Fame, 1989; The Order of the Palmetto, Governor South Carolina; Inductee, Allen University Hall of Fame; has also hosted several televsion shows & been play by play & color analyst several sports progs. **Military Serv:** AUS, 1953-55. *

GILLIAM, SAM, JR.
Artist, arts administrator. **Personal:** Born Nov 30, 1933, Tupelo, MS. **Educ:** Univ Louisville, BA, 1955, MA, 1961, LHD, 1980; Northwestern Univ, LHD, 1990. **Career:** Wash Gallery Modern Art, 1964; Inst Contemp Art, 1965; 1st World Festival Negro Arts, 1966; Embassies, Wash Gallery Modern Art, artist, 1967; Corcoran Gallery, 1969; Martin Luther King Mem, exhib mus modern art, 1969; Harlem, exhibited studio mus, 1969; Venice Biennale, Italy, 1970; Whitney Mus Annual, painter, educr & artist, 1970; Art Inst Chicago, 1970; Pacy Gallery, NY, 1972; Maison de la Culture Rennes, France, 1973; Phoenix Gallery, San Francisco, 1974; Philadelphia Mus Art, 1975; Galerie Darthea Speyer Paris, 1976; Dart Gallery Chicago, 1977. **Honors/Awds:** Norman Walt Harris prize; Doctor of Humane Letters, Univ Dist Columbia, 2006. **Business Addr:** Artist, 1900 Quincy St NW, Washington, DC 20011.

GILLIS, SHIRLEY J BARFIELD
Educator. **Personal:** Born Oct 2, 1943, Kinston, NC; daughter of George and Sarah Daughety; married Harvey; children: LaChale R. **Educ:** Elizabeth City State Univ, Elizabeth City, NC, BS, 1970; Eastern Conn State Univ, Willimantic, CT, MS, 1975; Southern Conn State Univ, New Haven, CT, attended 1990. **Career:** New London Bd Educ, New London, CT, kindergarten teacher, 1970; Harbor Elem Sch, New London, CT, teacher, currently. **Orgs:** Chairperson, New London Educ Asn, 1975; pres, New London Educ Asn,1980-81; Phi Delta Kappa, 1988-; corresondancy secy, Delta Kappa Gamma,1989-; African Am Latino Coalition, 1989-; pres, New London Nat Asn Advan Colored People; Hist Black Col Alumni; pres, New London Alumni Chap, Delta Sigma Theta; founder & bd dir, Kente Cult Ctr; auxillary bd dirs & vpres, Lawrence & Mem Hosp; corresponding secy, New London Dem Party. **Honors/Awds:** Alumni Award, Eastern Connecticut State Univ, 1970; Connecticut Teacher of the Year, State Dept Educ, 1981; Connecticut Educator Award, State Dept Educ & Milken Family Found, 1989; Martin Luther King Community Award, NAACP; Community Service Award, Nat Coun Negro Women, 1990; Celebration of Excellence Award, Net & Conn State Dept Educ, 1995. **Special Achievements:** National Teacher of the Year Finalist. **Home Addr:** 340 Bayonet St, New London, CT 06320, **Home Phone:** (860)447-9536. **Business Addr:** Teacher, Harbor Elementary School, Kindergarten, 432 Montauk Ave, New London, CT 06320, **Business Phone:** (860)447-6040.

GILLIS, THERESA MCKINZY
Government official. **Personal:** Born Sep 16, 1945, Fort Meade, FL; daughter of Arthur McKinzy and Dezola Williams; married Eugene Talmadge, Dec 23, 1973; children: Reginald, Jarett & Jeraemy. **Educ:** Talladega Col, BA, 1967; Barry Univ, Miami, FL, MS, 1993. **Career:** Broward Employ & Training Admin, counr, mgr SYEP dir, 1976-82; Broward County Community Develop Div, citizen participation coordr, 1982-84, from asst dir to dir, 1984-94; Proj & Community Coord, Pub Works Dept, Off Environ Serv, dir, 1994-. **Orgs:** SSO'S Mem past officer, Delta Sigma Theta Sorority, 1968-; Fla Community Develop Asn, 1984-; Nat Asn Counties, 1986-; Home Econs Adv Bd, Broward Sch Bd, 1987-89; comt mem, Mt Hermon AME Church Credit Union, 1988-; bd mem, Code Enforcement City Lauderdale Lakes, 1988-; Minority Recruitment Broward County Sch Bd, 1989; bd mem, City Lauderhill, Econ Develop Agency, 1996-; charter mem, Coalition 100 Black Women, Broward County Chap; adv bd mem, Lauderhill Pub Safety. **Business Addr:** Director, Public Works Department, Office of Environmental Services, 2555 W Copans Rd, Pompano Beach, FL 33069, **Business Phone:** (954)831-0704.

GILLISPIE, WILLIAM HENRY
Aerospace engineer, consultant. **Personal:** Born Jan 8, 1927, Hanna, WY; son of Nathan and Susie Anderson; married Laura, Dec 21, 1977; children: Vincent, Shiela & Richard. **Educ:** Lincoln Univ, BSME, 1950; Wash Univ, Univ Missouri Rolla & St Louis, grad study. **Career:** A/C Proj Off USA, ch test, 1953-61; USA Aviation Syst Comn, oper res anal, 1961-62, spec asst res & develop, 1962-63, dep chief observation helicopter field off, 1963-70, spec asst comndg gen prog mgt, 1970-73, mgr aircraft div,

1973; WHG Inc, prin, aerospace & mgt consult, 1989-. **Orgs:** Mgt trans Aviation Res & Develop resp, 1960; command work act, AUS Mobility Comm, 1963; chmn, CFC camp USA Aviation Syst Comn, 1974; pres, Lincoln Univ Mo State chap, 1975-76; Chmn, St Louis Sect, Am Inst Aeronaut & Astronaut, 1977; pres Lincoln Univ Alumni Asn, 1979-85. **Honors/Awds:** Army Civilian Merit Award, 1971; Section Leadership Award, Am Inst Aeronaut & Astronaut, 1977; Distinguished Alumni Award, Lincoln Univ. Mo, 1977; Army Commanders Award for Civil Service, 1980; Service Award, Am Inst Aeronaut & Astronaut, 1980; Presidential Award, Nat Asn Equal Opportunity Higher, 1985; Outstanding Service Award, Lincoln Univ, 1985; Commanders Award for Meritorious Achievment, 1988-89; Outstanding Service Award, Kinloch, Mo, 1998; Outstanding Service Award, Kirkwood, Mo Sch Bd, 1999. **Military Serv:** AUS, air corps, 1945. **Home Phone:** (636)532-5171. **Business Addr:** Principal, Consultant, WHG Inc, 1915 Claymills Dr, Chesterfield, MO 63017, **Business Phone:** (636)532-5171.*

GILLOM, JENNIFER
Basketball player. **Personal:** Born Jun 13, 1964; daughter of Ella Gillom. **Educ:** Univ Miss, attended 1986. **Career:** Italian League, Italy, 1987-91; Ancona, 1991-94, Messina, 1995-96, Phoenix Mercury, ctr, 1997-02; Taronto, 2002; Los Angeles Sparks, forward, 2003; Xavier Col Preparatory, head coach, 2006-. **Orgs:** Mercury Community Relations Department, 2001-02. **Honors/Awds:** Basketball Sportswoman of the Yr, Olympian mag, 1985; Basketball Sportswoman of the Yr, US Olympic Comm, 1985; Miss Sportswoman of the Yr,1986; Gold Medal, US Olympic Basketball Team, 1988; Nat Distinction Award,Univ Miss, 1998; Univ Miss Sports Hall of Fame, 1999; Kim Perrot Sportsmanship award; Women's Basketball Hall of Fame, 2009. **Home Addr:** PO Box 1921, Phoenix, AZ 85001, **Home Phone:** (602)332-7544. **Business Addr:** Professional Basketball coach, Xavier College Preparatory High School, 4710 North Fifth St, Phoenix, AZ 85012-1738, **Business Phone:** (602)277-3772.*

GILLUM, ANDREW D
Commissioner. **Personal:** Born Jul 26, 1979, Miami, FL; son of Charles and Frances. **Educ:** Fla A&M Univ, polit sci. **Career:** Fla Dem Party, dep polit dir; Tallahassee City Comn, comnr, 2003-, mayor pro tem, 2004-05. **Orgs:** Bd dir, Mary Brogan Mus; bd dir, Keep Tallahassee-Leon County Beautiful; bd dir, Kids Inc; bd dir, Whole Child Leon Leadership Coun; Riley House Bd Dirs; Tiger Bay Club; Capital City Chamber; Leadership Tallahassee Class XXII; Capital City Child Care Consortium; nat dir, People For Am Way Found Young Elected Officials Network; Black Youth Vote Coalition; Nat Asn Adv Colored People; Nat Coalition Black Civic Participation. **Honors/Awds:** Emerging Leaders Award, Cong Black Caucus Found Inc, 2003. **Special Achievements:** listed in "The Fast Track 30 Leaders Who are 30 and Under " by Ebony, 2004. **Business Addr:** Commissioner, Tallahassee City Commission, Commission Office, 300 S Adams St, Tallahassee, FL 32301, **Business Phone:** (850)891-8181.

GILLUM, RODERICK D.
Public relations executive. **Personal:** Born in Detroit, MI. **Educ:** Michigan State University, BA, 1972; Northeastern University School of Law, JD, 1975; MIT, Masters Degree in Management, 1985. **Career:** Saturn Corp., Manager of Strategic Planning, 1985-1986; General Motors, Board of Directors Secretary and Asst. General Counsel, 1986-1988; Saturn Corp., VP, General Counsel and Secretary, 1988-1993; General Motors, VP of Corporate Relations and Diversity; Motor Enterprises Incorporated, Chairman of the Board and President. **Orgs:** Member, Congressional Black Caucus Foundation; Chairman, General Motors Foundation; Chairman of the Board, Charles H. Wright Museum of African American History; Co-Chair, American Bar Association Section of Labor and Employment Law on Opportunities for Minorities in the Profession. **Special Achievements:** Was elected and serves as a Fellow for American Bar Association's College of Labor and Employment Lawyers. **Home Addr:** 004850. *

GILLUM, DR. RONALD M.
School administrator. **Personal:** Born May 21, 1939, Gates, PA; son of Roger O and Edna R; married Harriette A Coleman, Dec 21, 1963; children: Ronald Jr, Rhonda & Robin. **Educ:** Western Mich Univ, BS, 1963; Wayne State Univ, MEd, 1972, EdD, 1975. **Career:** Detroit Pub Sch, instr, 1963-69, teacher, 1963-70, admin, 1969-71; Wayne County Community Col, instr, 1969-71; Mich Dept St, dir prog develop, 1978-80; Boy's Club Am, recreation dir; Mich Dept Educ, Adult Educ, deputy dir, Lansing, MI, 1980-83, dir, off Adult Exten Learning, currently; Detroit Col Bus, exec dir, 1996-. **Orgs:** Mich Alliance Black Sch Educr; Mich Asn Pub Adult Community Educ; Nat Alliance Black Sch Educr; co-founder, Black Teacher Workshops, Detroit; Urban League, Lansing; NAACP; PTA Lansing; bd dirs, Am Asn Adult & Continuing Educ, 1987-; policy fel, Educ Policy Fel Prog, Nat Inst Educ Leadership. **Honors/Awds:** Outstanding Leadership Award in Literacy, US Dept Educ 1985; hon mem, Sheet Metal Workers Int Asn; Focus & Impact Award, Cotillion Club Inc, Detroit; Distinguished Service Award, Mich St Bd Educ, 1987; President Award, Mich Asn Adult & Continuing Educ, 1989. **Special Achievements:** Published articles, "Michigan is Learning How to Close Its Literacy Gap", Detroit Free Press, 1987; "Adult Literacy-Can We Handle the Problem", OPTIONS 1987.

GILMORE, DR. AL TONY
Educator. **Personal:** Born Jun 29, 1946, Spartanburg, SC; married Beryl Sansom; children: Jack S & Genevieve M. **Educ:** NC Cent Univ, BA, 1968, MA, 1969; Univ Toledo, Ohio, PhD, 1972. **Career:** Howard Univ, prof hist, 1972-78; Inst Serv Educ, prog assoc; Univ MD, prof hist, 1978-84; Nat Educ Asn, Nat Afro-Am Mus Proj, consult, dir; ASALH, researcher; Nat Educ Asn, instr & prof develop specialist, 1985-89, Human& Civil Rights div, sr prof assoc, 1989-2000, mgr, Leadership Training & Develop; Calif Comn on the Status of African-Am Males, consult. **Orgs:** Bd dirs, Asn Study Afro Am Life & Hist, 1977-88; Org Am Historians; Am Hist Asn; Asn Study African-Am Life & Hist; pres, The Forum Study Educ Excellence; bd dirs, Quality Educ Minorities Proj; Nat Coun on Educ Black. **Special Achievements:** Author: Revisiting the Slave Community Revisited, The Natl Impact of Jack Johnson & The Life, Times of Amos n Andy: A Social Hist; book reviews &articles have appeared in Wash Post, NY Times, New Repub, Am Scholar. **Home Addr:** 6108 Clearwood Rd, Bethesda, MD 20817-6002. **Business Addr:** Manager of Leadership Training & Development, Nat Educ Asn, 1201 16th St NW, Washington, DC 20036, **Business Phone:** (202)822-7395.*

GILMORE, EDWIN C. See Obituaries section.

GILMORE, JOHN T
Educator. **Personal:** Born Aug 1, 1935, Prescott, AR; married Curley Usher. **Educ:** BS, 1957; MSIE, 1970; PhD, 1971. **Career:** Univ Ark, Dept Math Sci, prof, chair, 1982-96; Boeing Air Co, assoc engineer, 1958-60, statistical consult, computer prog consult; Gilmore Appraisal Serv, real estate appraiser, currently; Trinity Church, admin asst; Univ Ark Pine Bluff, dir engineering; Diversified Unlimited Corp Inc, sec bd trustees. **Orgs:** Am Inst Indust Engr Inc; Pine Bluff Planning Comn; bd chmn, Trinity Church God Christ; mem, Alpha Kappa Mu Univ Nat Honor Soc; Beta Kappa Chi Sci Hon Soc; Alpha Pi Mu Indsust Eng Hon Soc. **Honors/Awds:** Outstanding Math Student. **Military Serv:** AUS, e3 staff, 1962. **Home Addr:** 902 Rosswood Colony Dr, Pine Bluff, AR 71603, **Home Phone:** (870)536-2896. **Business Addr:** Real Estate Appraiser, Gilmore Appraisal Service, 1116 State St, Pine Bluff, AR 71603.

GILMORE, MARSHALL
Clergy. **Personal:** Born Jan 4, 1931, Hoffman, NC; married Yvonne Dukes; children: John M & Joan M. **Educ:** Paine Col, Augusta, GA, BA, 1957; Drew Theol Sem Madison, NJ, MDiv, 1960; United Theol Sem, Dayton, OH, DMin, 1974. **Career:** Clergy (retired); Bray Temple CME Chicago, IL, pastor, 1960-62; W Mitchell St CME Church, Atlanta, 1962; Allen Temple CME Church, Detroit, 1962-64; Phillips Temple CME Church, Dayton, 1964-; Payne Theol Sem Wilberforce, OH, instr, 1972-73; Christian Methodist Episcopal Church, eight episcopal dist, sr bishop. **Orgs:** Pres, Dayton NAACP, 1971-72; mem bd, Phillips Sch Theol, 1966-; Paine Col, 1969-; Gen Conn Bd CME Church, 1966-. **Military Serv:** USAF, airman 1-C, 1950-54.

GILMORE, DR. ROBERT MCKINLEY, SR.
Educator, president (organization). **Personal:** Born May 14, 1952, Houston, TX; son of Marvin and Olan; children: Robert Jr & Reshun. **Educ:** Tex Southern Univ, BA, 1980, MA, 1981, MA, 1984; Univ Houston, EdD, 1985; Houston Grad Sch Theol, MDiv, 1989. **Career:** KTSU & KPVU, radio producer & host, 1980-85; Tex Southern Univ, instr, 1981-83; City Houston, asst dir, 1982-84; Univ Houston, grad asst, 1982-85; Prairie View A&M Univ, asst prof, 1985-89; Houston Grad Sch Theol, urban ministry prog dir; Real Urban Ministry Inc, pres & ceo, 2002-. **Orgs:** Asst to pastor, Barbers Mem Bapt Church, 1979-89; pres, Real Prods, 1980-; consult, Baptist Ministers Asn, 1985-95; Phi Delta Kappa, Univ Houston, 1985-89; Prairie View A&M Univ, 1986-89; dir, Drug Training Prog Independent Missionary Baptist Asn; pres, Real Educ Alternatives Leadership & Learning, 1989-91; pres, One Church/One Child, 1988-90; drug educ consult, City Houston. **Honors/Awds:** PV Choice Award, Prairie View A&M Univ, 1989. **Special Achievements:** Publication "Effective Communication a Drug Education Solution," 1986. **Military Serv:** USAF, sgt, 1971-75; National Security Award, 1971. **Business Addr:** President, Chief Executive Officer, Real Urban Ministry Inc., 3253 Winbern, Houston, TX 77004, **Business Phone:** (713)741-6642.*

GILMORE, VANESSA D
Judge. **Personal:** Born Oct 26, 1956, St Albans, NY; daughter of Clifton and Laura. **Educ:** Hampton Univ, BS, clothing & textile mkt, 1977; Univ Houston Col Law, JD, 1981. **Career:** Foleys Dept Store, fashion buyer, 1977-79; Univ Houston Col Law, adj prof, 1984; Sue Schecter & Assoc, atty, 1985-86; Vickery, Kilbride, Gilmore & Vickery, atty, 1981-94; pvt pract, Houston, Tex, 1981-94; US Courts, US dist Judge, 1994-. **Orgs:** Houston Bar Asn; chairperson church comm, Nat Asn Advan Colored People, 1989-93; pres & bd dirs, YWCA, 1990-92; chairperson, LEAD, Links Inc, 1990-91; chairperson, Tex Dept Com, 1992-94; Univ Houston Alumni Bd, 1993-; chairperson, Texans N Am Free Trade Agreement . **Honors/Awds:** Houston's Young Black Achiever, Human Enrichment Life, 1989; Citizen of the Month, Houston Defender Newspaper, 1990; Distinguished Service Award, Nat Black MBA Asn, 1994; Community Service Award, Holman Street Baptist Church, 1994. **Special Achievements:** Using Expert Help, 1991, Motions In Limine, 1993, Am Bar Asn, How to Ethically Dev an Environmental & Toxic Torts Practice, Am Trial Lawyers Asn, 1990. **Business Addr:** Judge, US Courts, Rm 9513 515 Rusk Ave, Houston, TX 77002, **Business Phone:** (713)250-5512.

GILOTH-DAVID, KING R.
Clergy, editor. **Personal:** Born Dec 23, 1940, White Plains, NY; son of Henry and Frances Cook; married Mary Lou; children: Laura Lee, Daniel Louis, Matthew David, Jonathan Henry, King David. **Educ:** Univ Notre Dame, BA, polit sci, 1963, MA, teaching, 1965. **Career:** Reformer Newspaper Inc, ed, publ, 1967-96; Northeast Africa Zion Media, ed, 1995-; Ethiopian Christian Spiritualist Church, founder, pastor, 1997-. **Orgs:** Dir, Christian Dem Ctr, S Bend, IN, 1964-87; chmn, Christian Dem Movement, 1968-; bd dir, St Joseph Col Comt Fed Credit Union, 1980-82; dir, Reg Fed Anti-Poverty Agency, 1980-82; dir, Ctr Christian Dem Socialism, 1987-; coord, Christian Dem Socialist Party, 1987-; secy, Tolton Soc, 1987-; mgr, secy, St Augustine Church Gospel Choir, 1988-; Volkswagen Remanufacturing Coop, 1988-; bd dirs, Wash-Chapin African-Am Learning Prog, 1989-94; master mason, St Peter's Lodge 31, F&AM, Prince Hall, 1995-; bd dirs, S Bend Br NAACP, 1996-97; S Bend Chap Ind Black Expo, 1997-98. **Honors/Awds:** US Deleg Christian Dem World Union, Rome, Italy. **Home Addr:** 1036 W Jefferson Blvd, South Bend, IN 46601, **Home Phone:** (574)289-8127. *

GILPIN, CLEMMIE EDWARD
Educator. **Personal:** Born Aug 12, 1942, Beaverdam, VA. **Educ:** VA State Col, BA, 1966; OH Univ, MA, 1970; PA State Univ, PhD, 1998. **Career:** Nigeria Peace Corps, vol, 1966-68; Vista, recruit, 1969-71; PA State Univ Harrisburg, instr, 1971-; PA State Univ, Harrisburg, asst prof, social sci Prog coordr, currently. **Orgs:** PA Sociol Soc; PA Prostate Cancer Coalition; UN Asn South central PA. **Honors/Awds:** James A Jordan Memorial Award for Teaching Excellence, 1978; Provost's Community Service Award, 1987; Faculty Senate Outstanding Service Award, 1995; World Citizenship Award, NJ YMCA/Model United Nations, 1999; Penn State Harrisburg Faculty Service Award; President's Award, Penn State Univ, 2003. **Business Addr:** Assistant Professor, Coordinator, Penn State University Harrisburg, 777 W Harrisburg Pke, W 311 Olmsted, Middletown, PA 17057-4898, **Business Phone:** (717)948-6066.

GILTON, DR. DONNA L.
Educator, librarian. **Personal:** Born Jul 9, 1950, Lynn, MA; daughter of Charles W Sr and Hattie Franklin. **Educ:** Simmons Col, Boston, MA, BA, 1972, MS, 1975; Univ Pittsburgh, PA, PhD, 1988. **Career:** Boston Pub Libr, Boston, MA, asst, 1972-75; Codman Square Br, librn I,1975-78, Uphams Corner Br, librn II, 1978-79; Belize Teachers Col, Belize City, Belize, head librn, 1979-81; Univ Pittsburgh, Title IIB fel,1981-82; Western Ky Univ, Bowling Green, KY, bus ref librn, 1984-88; Pa State Univ, Univ Park, PA, bus ref librn & Pattee Libr, coordr, 1988-91;Univ RI, Grad Sch Libr & Infor Studies, asst prof, 1992-98, assoc prof,1998-. **Orgs:** Belize Libr Asn, 1979-81; Spec Libr Asn, 1982-83, Pittsburgh Chap,1982-83; Bus & Finance Div, 1982-83; Am Soc Info Sci, 1982-83; Am LibrAsn, 1987-; Asn Res & Col Libr, 1987-, Instr Sect, 1988-, Continuing Educ Comt, 1989-91, Instr Diverse Pop Comt, 1991-95; Asn Libr & Info Sci Educ,1990-; RI Libr Asn, 1998-; Mass Black Librn Network, 1998-. **Honors/Awds:** The Provost Fund, Univ Pittsburgh, 1983-84; Harold Lancour Award, Univ Pittsburgh, 1983; The Unsung Heroine Award, African Methodist Episcopal Church, 2007; Education Award, Newport Womens League, 2007; Service Award, Bethel A.M.E. Church, 2007. **Business Addr:** Associate Professor, University Rhode Island, Graduate School of Library and Information Studies, Rm 9 Rodman Hall 94 W Alumni Ave, Kingston, RI 02881-0815.

GILYARD, DR. GERALINE
Educator. **Personal:** Born Nov 24, 1938, Miami, FL; daughter of Robert and Rosabelle; widowed; children: Vanessa Henelle. **Educ:** Bethune-Cookman Col, BS, 1962; Fla Atlantic Univ, MS, 1967; Univ Miami, EdD, 1975. **Career:** Greenville Training Sch, 1962-63; Dade County Schs, 5th grade teacher, 1963-67; guidance counr, 1967-70, human rels specialist, 1970-72, dir, admin servs, 1976-78, dir non-inst training, 1978-86, dir inst staffing, 1987-95; NOVA Southeastern Univ, adj prof, 1996-. **Orgs:** Negro Bus & Prof Women's Club; Top Ladies Distinction, United Methodist Women, coordr, Educ & Interpretation; Gamma Zeta Omega, Alpha Kappa Alpha, first vpres, 1985-; United Methodist Women, coordr, Ed & Interp, 1997-2001; Col Gardens Homeowner's Asn, Historian, 1999-2003; Wesley Found, Univ Miami, chair personnel com, 1999-; Dania Beach Airport Adv Com, 2001-. **Honors/Awds:** Sojourner Truth Award, Negro Bus & Prof Women's Club, 1993; GilyardIngraham Day, City Miami, FL, Proclamation, 1995. **Special Achievements:** Dissertation: "Coping Behaviors and Self-Concepts of Black Girls in All Black and Integrated Secondary School Settings," 1975. **Business Addr:** Past-President, United Methodist Women-Ebenezer United Methodist Church-Miami, PO Box 914, Dania Beach, FL 33004, **Business Phone:** (954)925-7403.

GINUWINE (ELGIN LUMPKIN)
Actor, singer. **Personal:** Born Oct 15, 1970, Washington, DC; son of James and Sandra Lumpkin; children: Elgin Jr & Story. **Educ:**

Prince George Community Col. **Career:** Albums: Booty Call, 1997; The Best Man, 1999; Down to Earth, 2001; Barbershop, 2002; Juwanna Mann, 2002; Love Don't Cost a Thing, 2003; Honey, 2003; Deliver Us from Eva, 2003; Wild Hogs, 2007; TV guest appearances: "Moesha," 1996; "Martial Law," 1998; Films: Juwanna Man, 2002; Platinum, 2003; Half & Half, 2004; Da Jammies, voice, 2006; Single: "When We Make Love," 2005. **Business Phone:** (212)833-7442.

GIOVANNI, NIKKI (YOLANDE CORNELIA GIOVANNI)
Poet, educator. **Personal:** Born Jun 7, 1943, Knoxville, TN; daughter of Jones and Yolande Watson; children: Thomas Watson. **Educ:** Fisk Univ, BA, hist, 1967; Univ Pa, Sch Soc Work, attended 1967; Worcester Univ, LHD, 1972; Ripon Univ, DLitt, 1974; Smith Col, D Litt, 1975; Columbia Univ Sch Arts. **Career:** Poet, writer, commentator, activist & educator, currently; Queens Col, asst prof black studies, 1968; Livingston Col, Rutgers Univ, assoc prof eng, 1968-72; Niktom, founder, 1970; Ohio State Univ, vis prof eng, 1984; Mt St Joseph, OH, prof creative writing, 1985; Va Tech, vis prof eng, 1987-89, prof eng, 1989-, Gloria D Smith prof, 1997-99, distinguished prof Eng, 1999-; Warm Hearth Writer's Workshop, dir, 1988-, Books: Black Feeling, Black Talk, 1970; Ego Tripping & Other Poems for Young People,1973; Those Who Ride the Night Winds, 1983; Sacred Cows & Other Edibles, 1988; Poetry: Black Feeling, Black Talk, 1968, 1970; Black Judgement, 1969; Re: Creation, 1970; Spin a Soft Black Song: Poems for Children,1971; My House, 1972; Ego Tripping & Other Poems for Young People, 1973; The Women & the Men, 1975; Cotton C & Y on a Rainy Day, 1978; Those Who Ride the Night Winds, 1983; The Genie in the Jar, 1996; The Sun Is So Quiet, 1996; Love Poems, 1997; Blues: For All the Changes: New Poems, 1999; Quilting the Black-Eyed Pea: Poems & Not Quite Poems, 2002; Recordings: Truth Is On Its Way, 1971; Like a Ripple on a Pond, 1973; The Way I Feel, 1975; Legacies: The Poetry of Nikki Giovanni, 1976; The Reason I Like Chocolate, 1976; Cotton C&y on a Rainy Day, 1978; Nonfiction: Gemini: An Extended Biographical Statement on My First Twenty-five Years of Being a Black Poet, 1971; Sacred Cows & Other Edibles, 1991; Racism 101, 1993; Editor: Night Comes Softly: An Anthology of Black Female Voices, 1970; Gr & Mothers: A Multicultural Anthology of Poems, Reminiscences, & Short Stories About the Keepers of Our Tradition, 1994. **Orgs:** Nat Coun Negro Women; co-chair, Lit Arts Festival, State Tenn, 1986; bddir, Va Found Humanities & Pub Policy, 1990-93; Soc Mag Writers; Nat Black-Heroines PUSH; Winnie Mandela C's Fund Comt; Delta Sigma Theta Sorority;Omega Psi Phi. **Honors/Awds:** Woman of the Year, Ebony Mag, 1970; Woman of the Year, Mademoiselle Mag, 1971; Woman of the Year, Ladies Home Jour, 1972; Woman of the Year, Cincinnati Chapter YWCA, 1983; Inducted to Ohio Women's Hall of Fame, 1985; Distinguished Recognition Award, Detroit City Council, 1986; Silver Apple Award, Oakland Museum Film Festival, 1988; Community Volunteer of the Year Award, Warm Hearth Village, 1992; Black Women's Honor Society Award, Univ Southern Calif, 1994; Tennessee Writers Award, Nashville Banner, 1994; Jeanine Rae Award, National Womens Music Festival, 1995; Tennessee Governor's Award, 1996; Langston Hughes Award, City Col NY, 1996; Parents' Choice Award, 1996; Appalachian Medallion Award, Univ Charleston, 1998; Image Award, NAACP, 2000; Distinguished Member Recognition Award, Delta Sigma Theta, Wilberforce, Ohio, 2000; City Council Resolution Honoring and Welcoming, Youngstown City, Ohio, 2000; Rosa Parks Women of Courage Award, 2002; Black Caucus Award, Am Libr Asn, 2003; Image Award for Outstanding Literary Work, NAACP, 2003; Honorary Citizen of Louisville Award, 2003; Honored in a Proclamation from the Mayor of Hartford which proclaimed that 10 April 2003 Nikki Giovanni Day, 2003; Atlanta Daily World 2nd Atlanta Choice Award, 2004; East Tennessee Writers Hall of Fame Award, 2004; Certificate of Appreciation, Delta Sigma Theta Sorority, 2005; Fourth Humanitarian Award, 2005; Lifetime Achievement Award, ALC, 2005; Certificate of Appreciation, Delta Sigma Theta Sorority, 2006; Women of Color Award, Va Univ Women Ctr, 2006; Honorary degrees:LHD, Wilberforce Univ, 1972; LittD, Ripon Univ, 1972; LittD, Univ Md, 1974; LittD, Smith Col, 1975; LHD, Col Mt St Joseph, 1983; LHD, Fish Univ, 1987; LHD, Mt St Mary Col, 1988; LHD, Ind Univ, 1991; LHD. Otterbein Col, 1992; Dr, Rockhurst Col, 1993; LHD, Widener Univ, 1993; LHD, Albright Col, 1995; LHD, Cabrini Col, 1995; LHD, Allegheny Col, 1997; LHD, Del State Univ, 1998; LHD, Martin Univ, 1999; LHD, Wilmington Univ, 1999; LHD, State Univ W Ga, 2000; LHD, Manhattanville Col, 2000; LHD, Cent State Univ, 2001; LHD, Pace Univ, 2002; LHD, WVa Uni, 2003. **Special Achievements:** Recorded six albums, including Truth Is On Its Way, 1972; Cotton Candy ona Rainy Day, 1978; tv appearances: Soul!, Natl Educ TV network, the Tonight Show; particip Soul at the Center, Lincoln Center Performing Arts New York City, 1972; contributor to numerous anthologies. **Business Addr:** Distinguished Professor of English, Virginia Tech University, English Department, 323 Shanks Hall, Blacksburg, VA 24061, **Business Phone:** (540)231-6501.

GIOVANNI, YOLANDE CORNELIA. See GIOVANNI, NIKKI.

GIPSON, BERNARD FRANKLIN, SR.
Surgeon. **Personal:** Born Sep 28, 1921, Bivins, TX; son of John Tom; married Ernestine Wallace; children: Bernard F Jr, Bruce Edward. **Educ:** Morehouse Col, BS, 1944; Howard Univ Col Med, MD, 1947; Diplomat Am Bd Surg, 1954. **Career:** Surgeon (retired); Private Pract Surg, 1956-95. **Orgs:** Clinical assoc prof, surg Univ CO Sch Med, 1985; chmn, Dept Surg Mercy Med Ctr, 1968; life mem, NAACP, 1980; chmn, Emancipation Proclamation Scholarship Fund Newhope Baptist Church, 1974; New Hope Baptist Church; Bd Deacons; Am Col Surgeons, Denver Acad Surg, Nat Med Assoc & Am Med Asn. **Honors/Awds:** Community service award, Methodist Conf Western States, 1984; article Denver Post, 1984; Story my Life Denver Post Newspaper, 1984; Frederick Douglass Award, Esquire Club, 1985. **Military Serv:** USAF, capt, 1954-56. *

GIPSON, CHARLES, JR.
Baseball player. **Personal:** Born Dec 16, 1972, Orange, CA. **Career:** Seattle Mariners, 1998-02; NY Yankees, outfielder, 2003; Tampa Bay Devil, 2004; Houston Astros, outfielder, 2005. **Honors/Awds:** All-Star OF, Calif League, 1994. *

GIPSON, FRANCIS E., SR.
Administrator. **Personal:** Born Apr 25, 1923, Huntington, WV; married Clara; children: Francis, Jr, Linda, Pamela, Teresa, Constance. **Educ:** Kent State Col, BS, 1950. **Career:** Administrator (retired). Dept Interior, Nat Park Serv, sr br chief, youth activites;E Cleveland City, Ohio, former city official, dir, Parks & Recreation, mgr, 1973. **Orgs:** Former mem, E Cleveland Bd Educ; Lake Erie Asn; Amateur Athletic Union; former asst dist mgr, Equitable Life Assurance Soc US. **Military Serv:** AUS, Combat Veteran, WW II, 1943-45. *

GIPSON, HAYWARD R., JR.
Executive. **Educ:** Princeton Univ. **Career:** Playtex Inc, mktg exec; Corning, Vitro Intl, vpres & gen mgr, 1989; Playtex Apparel Inc, pres, 1994-. **Business Addr:** President, Playtex Apparel Inc, 700 Fairfield Ave, PO Box 10064, Stamford, CT 06904, **Business Phone:** (203)356-8000.*

GIPSON, DR. LOVELACE PRESTON, II
Dentist. **Personal:** Born Jan 9, 1942, Clarksdale, MS; married Amanda; children: Lovelace III, Tamitha, Teresa & Tinile. **Educ:** AM&N Col Dd, BS, 1963; St Louis Univ, attended 1965; Univ MO, attended 1966; Atlanta Univ, attended 1967; Univ TN Sch Dent, DDS, 1973. **Career:** Nashville, AR, bd Educ, 1963-64; St Louis & E St Louis Bd Educ, teacher, 1965-70; Hamilton Co Chattanooga Health Dept, staff dentist, 1974; Pvt Pract, dentist; Firestone Dental Group PLLC, owner, currently. **Orgs:** Nat Bus League; pres, Prof Corp, 1977; PK Miller Youth Orgn, 1955; Nat Den Asn; Am Dent Asn; Memphis Shelby Co Dent Soc; NAACP; UAPB Alumni Asn; Elks Lodge; Chickasaw Coun BSA; Urban League; hon del, TN Const Conv; Am Endodontic Soc; Fndrs Club The Memphis Goodwill Boy's Club. **Honors/Awds:** Recipient, Ford Found Fel, St Louis Univ, 1965; NSF Grant, Univ MO & Atlanta Univ, 1966-67. **Business Addr:** Dentist, Owner, Firestone Dental Group LLC, 1216 Thomas St, Memphis, TN 38107, **Business Phone:** (901)525-3266.

GIPSON, REVE
Consultant, county commissioner. **Educ:** Los Angeles Valley Col, Van Nuys, CA; Univ Calif Los Angeles, Exten/Workshops, Westwood, CA. **Career:** Freelance writer & ed; KNBC News, Burbank, CA, personal asst & news res, 1974-78; Capitol Recs, Los Angeles, CA, publicist, 1978-87; Maze Featuring Frankie Beverly, Los Angeles, CA, pub rels consult, 1987-; Los Angeles County, Dept Parks & Recreation Comn, comnr; County Pub Libr Comn, comnr, currently. **Orgs:** Nat Acad Recording Arts & Scis; Alpha Theta Chap, Beta Phi Gamma. **Honors/Awds:** Distinctive Women of Southern California, City Los Angeles; Dr. Mary McLeod Bethune Award, County Los Angeles, Bd Supvrs; Bill of Rights Speaker's Award, Bill Rights Commendation Comt; County Awards, Los Angeles City Coun; organized M C Hammer Day in the City of Los Angeles; founder of the annual "Youth on Parade" program. **Business Addr:** Commissioner, County Public Library Commission, 7400 E Imperial Highway, Downey, CA 90242, **Business Phone:** (562)940-8418.*

GISSENDANNER, DR. JOHN M.
Educator. **Personal:** Born Aug 13, 1939; son of Roy L and Plessie M Matthews; married Pamela Morgan (divorced 1976); married Cindy L Hines. **Educ:** San Francisco State Univ, San Francisco, BA, 1971, MA, 1972; Univ Calif, San Diego, PhD, 1982. **Career:** Calif State Univ, San Diego, CA, asst prof, 1972-75; Towson State Univ, Towson, MD, asst prof, 1975, assoc prof, 1991-98, prof, 1998-, prof emer, currently. **Orgs:** Am Asn Univ Prof, 1972-; Nat Asn Advancement Colored People, 1982-; Middle-Atlantic Writers' Asn, 1978-; Nat Collegiate Honors Coun, 1980-; Md Writers Coun, 1980-. **Honors/Awds:** Univ Merit Award, Towson State Univ, 1989; San Diego Fel Award, Univ Calif, San Diego, 1971-74; Ford Found Fel Award, Univ Calif, San Diego, 1973-74. **Special Achievements:** Memorial and Honorary Employee Scholarships named after him as "John Gissendanner Fund for African-American Study". **Business Addr:** Professor Emeritus, Towson University, Department of Engineering, Linthicum Hall 201J, Towson, MD 21252-7097, **Business Phone:** (410)830-2863.

GIST, CAROLE ANNE-MARIE (CAMMIE GEE)
Fashion model, singer. **Personal:** Born Jan 1, 1970, Detroit, MI; daughter of David Turner and Joan. **Educ:** Northwood Univ, Midland, MI, mkt & mgt. **Career:** Midland, MI, club singer, currently; WORD network, co-host gospel show, currently. **Honors/Awds:** Miss Michigan Pageant, winner, 1989; Miss USA Pageant, winner, 1990; Miss Universe Pageant, first runner-up, 1990. **Special Achievements:** First African American woman to be crowned Miss USA, 1990; first Miss Michigan to be crowned Miss USA, 1990. **Business Phone:** (213)965-0800.*

GIST, DIANE
Executive. **Career:** JAN-PRO, Charlotte, NC, franchise owner, currently. **Business Addr:** Franchise Owner, JAN-PRO, 5950 Fairview Rd Suite 650, Charlotte, NC 28210, **Business Phone:** (704)553-8007.

GIST, KAREN WINGFIELD
Educator. **Personal:** Born May 14, 1950, Harrisburg, PA; daughter of Raleigh Wingfield and Mary Gooden Wingfield; divorced; children: Maya Jemelle. **Educ:** Clarion State Univ, BS, 1972; Univ Pittsburgh, Med, 1974; Calif State Univ, attended 1983. **Career:** NHS Fel, 1993; Pittsburgh Bd Educ, sec teacher, lit coach, Currently. **Orgs:** Instr, Community Col Allegheny County, 1974-84; fel, Western Penn Writing Proj, 1983-; Lambda Kappa Mu Sorority Inc Zeta Chapter; Pittsburgh Fedn Teachers; Nat Coun Teachers Eng; Urban League; fel, Carnegie Mellon Univ, Making Thinking Visible Proj, 1990-91; instr, Carlow Col, 1994-95. **Honors/Awds:** Golden Apple Award for School Service, 1990, 1992. **Business Addr:** Teacher, Pittsburgh Board Education, 341 S Bellefield, Pittsburgh, PA 15213.

GITE, LLOYD ANTHONY
Journalist. **Personal:** Born Oct 16, 1951, Houston, TX. **Educ:** N Tex State Univ, Denton, attended 1974; Southern Methodist Univ Dallas, attended 1977; Univ Mich, Ann Arbor, attended 1980. **Career:** KNOK AM/FM, Dallas, news dir, 1977-78; Black Forum Dallas, host, producer, ABC prog, 1977-78; Sheridan Broadcasting Network, corresp, 1980-83; Nat Black Network, corresp, 1975-83; WTVS TV, Detroit, reporter, producer, 1981-83; Essence Mag, writer; Black Enterprise, writer; USA Today, writer; Gentlemen's Quarterly, writer; Working Woman, writer; Monthly Detroit, writer, 1981-00; KRIV TV, reporter, producer, 1983-01. **Honors/Awds:** Essence Man, Essence Mag, 1976; Media Award, Press Club of Dallas, 1977; one of the Most Outstanding Young Men in America, US Jaycees, 1978; one of the Fifty Leaders of the Future, Ebony Mag, 1978; Mentor of Year Award, Nat Asn Black Women Entrepreneurs, 1982; UNITY Award in Media, Lincoln Univ, 1982, 1983; Houston Press Club Awd for Media 1984.

GITHIGA, JOHN GATUNGU
Chaplain. **Personal:** Born Jul 27, 1942, Muranga, Kenya; son of Isaac Gitogo and Joyce Njeri; married Mary N Githiga, Dec 7, 1968; children: Rehema, Isaac Cyprian, June. **Educ:** Makerere Univ, theol dipl, 1974; Univ South, MDiv, 1979, DMin, 1981; Int Bible Inst & Sem, DREd, 1980. **Career:** Diocese Nakuru, dir St Nicholars C Ctrs; St Paul's United Theol Col, dept head, pastoral theol, 1980-86; African Asn Pastoral Studies & Couns, fed pres, 1985-88; St Cyprian Church, vice chair, 1986-91; Ecumencial Christian Fel, founder, pres, 1992-; Lakeview Ctr, tel crisis counr, Kairos spiritual dir, voluntary, 1992-; Extended Arms Outreach Ctr, field counr juvenile offenders & their parents, 1992-96; Grambling State Univ, vice chair, chaplain; W Tex A&M Univ, chaplain, 1996-02; West Tex A&M Univ, adj fac, currently. **Orgs:** Secy, Nat Christian Coun Kenya Youth Dept, Nakuru, 1966-68; Capt, First Nakuru Comp Boys Brigade, 1967-68; secy, Diocese Nakuru Youth Dept, 1968-71; pres, United Campus Ministry, Cursillo Secretarial, Diocese NW Tex; Univ W Fla Select Comt Minority Affairs, 1987-92; Martin Luther King Jr Celebration Comt, 1989; Ecumenical & Interfaith Comt, 1987-91; Greater Kiwanis Pensacola, 1988-92; Asn Theol Insts Eastern Africa, 1980-85; St Cyprian's Episcopal Church, 2002, vice chair, 2003-. **Honors/Awds:** Certificate of Appreciation for Presentation, Pensacola Jr Col, 1987; Certificate of Appreciation for Presentation, Kiwanis Club Greater Pensacola, 1988; Certificate of Appreciation for Planning, Martin Luther King Commemorative Comt, 1989; Kiwanis Certificate of Appreciation for Spiritual leadership and Service to Community, 1989. **Special Achievements:** Author, "The Use of Psychology in Pastoral Counseling in Africa," Theological Journal, 1982; The Spirit in the Black Soul, 1984; "Family in Transition," Beyond, July 1987; Initiation & Pastoral Psychology; Christ & Roots, 1988; co-author, Ewe Ki Jana (Oh Young Man), 1971. **Business Addr:** Vice Chair, Chaplain, W Texas A & M University, 2516 4th Ave, Canyon, TX 79015.*

GITTENS, ANTHONY EDGAR (TONY GITTENS)
Executive director, educator. **Personal:** Born Dec 25, 1944, Brooklyn, NY; son of Henry Edgar and Rita; married Jennifer, May 29, 1982; children: Kai & Zachary. **Educ:** Howard Univ, BA, 1968; Union Grad Sch, PhD, 1976. **Career:** Univ DC, prof, 1971-96, prof emer, currently; Black Film Inst, dir, 1976-; DC Comn Arts & Humanities, exec dir, 1996-. **Orgs:** Wash DC Int Film Festival, 1986; DC Comn Arts & Humanities. **Honors/Awds:** Mayor's Award for Excellence in Service to The Arts, 1987, 1993; Public Humanist of The Year, 1991; Knight in the Order of Arts & Letters, French Govt. **Business Addr:** Executive Director, District of Columbia Commission of Arts & Humanities, 1371 Harvard St NW, Washington, DC 20009, **Business Phone:** (202)724-5613.

GITTENS, TONY. See GITTENS, ANTHONY EDGAR.

GIVENS, CLEMENTINA M
Administrator. **Personal:** Born Nov 15, 1921, Baltimore, MD; daughter of James and Lavinia Nicholson. **Educ:** Webster Grove Col, Webster Grove, MO, BS; Cath Univ, WA, DC, MA, 1975. **Career:** Archdiocese Wash, DC, WA, DC, elem teacher, 1956-62; Archdiocese Miami, Miami, FL, elem teacher, 1962-73; Archdiocese Wash, WA, DC, elem adminr, 1973-77; Archdiocese Baltimore, Baltimore, MD, 1977-79; Archdiocese Wash, DC, WA, DC, DC teacher, 1979-81; Archdiocese of Miami, Miami, FL, sch adminr, 1981-88; St Patrick Church, dir religious educ, currently; Office Black Cath Ministry, Rockford, IL, dir. **Orgs:** Sch bd mem, Archdiocese Wash, DC, 1958-62; bd mem, sec, Archdiocese Wash, DC, 1973-77; black pastorial coun, Archdiocese Miami, 1981-88. **Business Addr:** Director Religious Education, St Patrick Church, 3716 Garden Ave, Miami Beach, FL 33140, **Business Phone:** (305)531-1124.

GIVENS, DR. DONOVAHN HESTON
Physician, educator. **Personal:** Born Dec 31, 1930, Chicago, IL; married Shirley; children: Linda, Rachel, Donna & Elizabeth. **Educ:** Univ Pa; Wayne State Univ; Univ Mich Med Sch, MD, 1961. **Career:** St Joseph Mercy Hosp, intern, 1961-62; Wayne State Univ, clinical asst prof, 1965-; St Joseph's, resident, 1962-65; Oakland Internist Assoc, owner. **Orgs:** Nat Med Asn; Detroit Med Soc; Wayne Co Med Soc; Mich Med Soc; Am Med Asn; Am Soc Internal Med; Am Col Phys; Adv Plann Com Univ Out patient Clinic, 1971-72. **Special Achievements:** Author: Urinary Salt Wasting in Chronic Renal Failure, Grace Hosp Billiton, 1970. **Military Serv:** USAF, 1951-55.

GIVENS, E. TERRIAN
Executive. **Personal:** Born Mar 8, 1930, Spartanburg, SC; daughter of Josephine Porter Smith (deceased) and Howard Porter; married Howard; children: Darrick H & Dermot D. **Educ:** Univ Detroit, BS 1970, MS, 1972. **Career:** Executive (retired); Mayors Comt Human Resources Develop, staff coordr, 1965-71; Detroit Youth Bd, coordr summer activ, 1971-73; Detroit Mayor Roman S Gribbs, exec asst, 1973-74, admin asst Detroit Bicent, 1974; City Detroit, prin soc planning & develop asst; City Detroit, admin asst gradeIV. **Orgs:** Pres, Detroit Jet Setters; vpres, pres, Nat Drifters Inc, 1967-68, 1968-70; Nat Asn Community Developers; vpres, Soc Workers Metro Detroit, 1972; pres, Soc Workers Metro Detroit, 1973-75; Detroit Black Coalition; vpres, Tri-City Bus & Prof Womens Club; Citizens Adv Coun, Southeastern Mich Transit Authority; Metro Summer Community Detroit, 1972-73; Womens Econ Club; chairperson, Asn Munic Prof Women; bd dir, St Peter's Home Boys, 1973-88; secy, treas & bd dir, Hancock Residential Care Ctr, 1975-88; Nat Round Table Christians & Jews; Nat Asn Advan Colored People; Nat Drifters Inc; Int Afro-Am Mus; Marion Park Civic Club; YMCA; bd dir, Detroit Asn Retarded C. **Honors/Awds:** WJLB Radios Citizen Day, 1967; Toppers Club Citation, Boy Scouts Am, 1970; Optimist Club, 1971; Black Woman of the Year, Nat Drifters Inc, 1974-75; Medal Dedicated Public Service & Proclamation, City Detroit, 1975; Woman of the Year, Am Bus Women's Asn, 1976-77; Certificate of Apppreciation, Detroit Asn Retarded Citizens, 1976; Appreciation Award, Conastoga Col Kitchner, Ontario, Can, 1979; Service Award, Detroit Pub Sch, 1981; Certificate of Apppreciation, Detroit Black United Fund, 1984-87; Proclamation, Mayor City Detroit, 1988; Resolution, City Coun Detroit, 1988; Letter of Congratulations from White House, Pres Ronald Reagan, 1988. **Special Achievements:** First female executive assistant to any mayor in the history of Detroit; Established first Sub-Center in US under Poverty Program, Nat Asn Community Developers. *

GIVENS, DR. HENRY, JR.
College president. **Personal:** Born Jan 1, 1933?. **Educ:** Lincoln Univ, BA; Univ Ill, MA; St Louis Univ, PhD. **Career:** Laclede Group, dir, currently; Peabody Energy Corp, dir, currently; Harris-Stowe State Univ, St Louis, MO, pres, currently. **Orgs:** Bd dir, Am Asn State Cols & Univs; Asn Gov Bds, Mo Coord Bd Higher Educ; Nat Alliance Black Sch Educrs. **Honors/Awds:** Hon DHL, Lincoln Univ & St Louis Univ. **Business Addr:** President, Harris-Stowe State University, 3026 Laclede Ave, St Louis, MO 63103, **Business Phone:** (314)340-3366.

GIVENS, JOSHUA EDMOND
Marketing executive. **Personal:** Born in Norfolk, VA. **Educ:** Northwestern Univ, BS, Speech, 1975, MS, jour advert, 1977. **Career:** WGN-TV, promotional writer & news writer, 1974-75; Benton & Bowles Advert, acct exec, 1977-79; Nat Black Network Radio, acct exec, 1979-80; Ebony Magazine, acct exec, 1980-81; Caldwell Reingold Advert, acct supvr, 1981; Revlon, Inc, dir mkt, 1981-86, vpres, dir mkt ethnic retail mkt, 1987-93; Lou Roppolo & Assoc, ethnic mkt spec, mkt consult, 1993. **Orgs:** Nat Black MBA Asn NY Chap, 100 Black Men, NY Chap, Nat Asn Mkt Develop; NAACP. **Honors/Awds:** Acad Scholar Northwestern Univ, 1971-77. *

GIVENS, LARRY
Vice president (Organization), executive director. **Educ:** Wayne State Univ, BS, educ, 1962, MBA, 1968. **Career:** Vice president (retired), Executive director; Chrysler Corp, vpres pub rel; Detroit Pub Sch, asst gen supt; AAA Mich, spokesperson, asst vpres human resources, dir corp rels, asst vpres corp rels & vpres corp rels; Detroit Empowerment Zone, exec dir, currently. **Orgs:** Bd dir, City Year Detroit; mem bd dir, Covenant House Mich Corp; bd mem, Detroit Neighborhood Housing Serv Inc; bd mem, Starr Commonwealth C; vice chmn, Southfield Community Found; mem, New Detroit Inc; mem, The Youth Connection; vice chmn, Horizon Health Syst; 100 Black Men of Greater Detroit. **Honors/Awds:** Manager of the Year Award, Chrysler Corp, 1968; Outstanding Leadership Award, United Negro Col Fund, 1989; Pioneer Support Award, Mich Legis Black Caucus Found, 1996; Legacy Award Community Serv, Mays Acad, 2000. *

GIVENS, LAWRENCE
Insurance executive, executive director, president (organization). **Personal:** Born Nov 30, 1938, Detroit, MI; son of Timothy and Senia Smith McClain; married Delores Clark Givens, May 2, 1959; children: Kimberly, David, Lisa, Stefanie. **Educ:** Wayne State Univ, BS, educ, 1962, MBA, 1968. **Career:** Detroit Bd Educ, teacher, 1962-64; Chrysler Corp, vpres pub rels, 1964-82; Detroit Pub Schs, asst to the gen supt, 1982-84; AAA Mich, dir corp rels, 1984-87, asst vpres corp rels, 1987-89, asst vpres human resources, 1989-91, asst vpres corp rels, 1991-92, vpres corp rels, 1992; Blackmond Givens Group, pres; Detroit Empowerment Zone Develop Corp, exec dir, currently. **Orgs:** Pres, Bus Educ Alliance, 1989-91; secy, bd trustees, Horizon Health Systs, 1985-91; chmn, telethon, United Negro Col Fund, 1987-89; secy, bd dir, Efficacy Detroit, 1985-91; bd mem, Centrum Insurance Co, 1983-91; bd dir, Henry Ford Village; Sloan Fel, Chrysler Corp, 1968; pres, Covenant House Mich Life Skills Ctr-E; secy, Starr Commonwealth C; New Detroit Inc; bd mem, Henry Ford Bi-C Hosp; Gilda's Club; 100 Black Men Greater Detroit. **Honors/Awds:** Manager of the Year Award, Chrysler Corp, 1968; Outstanding Leadership Award, United Negro Col Fund, 1989; Pioneer Support Award, Mich Legis Black Caucus Found, 1996; Legacy Award, Mays Acad, 2000. **Special Achievements:** Minority Achiever of the Year, Detroit YMCA, 1985. **Business Addr:** Executive Director, Detroit Empowerment Zone Development Corporation, 1 Ford Pl Suite 1F, Dearborn, MI 48202.*

GIVENS, LEONARD DAVID
Lawyer. **Personal:** Born Sep 10, 1943, Elmira, NY; married Patricia. **Educ:** Mansfield State Col, BS, 1965; Howard Law Sch, JD, 1971. **Career:** IBM, Owego, NY, admin asst, 1965-68; AFSCME, Wash, law clerk, 1968-69; NLRB, Wash, law clerk, 1970-71; Miller Canfield Paddock & Stone PLC, assoc, 1971-77, prin, 1978-, chief exec officer, 1991-94, Labor & Employ Law Pract Group, former co-leader, dep leader, 2006-. **Orgs:** Am Bar Asn; Nat Bar Asn; Detroit Bar Asn; Oakland Co Bar Asn; labor coun, MI State Bar Asn; Am Judicature Soc; bd dir, Homes Black C; Greater Detroit Chamber Com; Metrop Affairs Corp; Mich Biotechnological Inst; Fedn Girls Home; Law Jour Invitee Moot Ct Team. **Special Achievements:** Maintaining a Union Free Environment. 9th Annual Society for Human Resource Management Michigan Conference, Kalamazoo, Michigan, 9/18-19/97. **Business Addr:** Principal, Miller Canfield Paddock & Stone PLC, 150 W Jefferson Suite 2500, Detroit, MI 48226-4415, **Business Phone:** (313)496-7505.

GIVENS, REGINALD ALONZO
Football player. **Personal:** Born Oct 3, 1971, Emporia, VA. **Educ:** Pa State Univ. **Career:** Football Player (retired); San Francisco 49ers, linebacker, 1998-99; Wash Redskins, 2000.

GIVENS, ROBIN (ROBIN SIMONE GIVENS)
Actor. **Personal:** Born Nov 27, 1964, New York, NY; daughter of Reuben Givens and Ruth Roper; children (previous marriage): Michael; married Mike Tyson, Feb 7, 1988 (divorced 1988); married Svetozar Marinkovic, Aug 22, 1997 (divorced 1999); children: William. **Educ:** Sarah Lawrence Col, attended. **Career:** Actress, Entrepreneur; films: A Rage in Harlem, 1991, Boomerang, 1992, Foreign Student, 1994; Blankman, 1994; Smoke, 1995; Blue in the Face, 1995; Secrets, 1997; Ride, 1998; Everything's Jake, 2000; Elite, 2000; Book of Love, 2000; Antibody, 2002; Head of State, 2003; A Cold Day in August, 2003; Flip the Script, 2005; Little Hercules in 3-D, 2006; Restraining Order, 2006; Flip the Script, 2006. TV mini-series: The Women of Brewster Place, 1989; TV movies: Beverly Hills Madam, 1986; Dangerous Intentions, 1995; A Face to Die For, 1996; The Expendables, 2000; Spinning Out of Control, 2001; Hollywood Wives: The New Generation, 2003; television series: Head of the Class, 1987-91; Angel Street, 1992; Courthouse; Sparks, 1997-98; host, Forgive or Forget, 2000; founder & dir, Never Blue Productions, 1990; Head of State, 2003; Spy Games Reloaded, 2004; Captive Hearts, 2005. **Business Addr:** Actress, Twentieth TV, 2121 Ave of the Stars 21st Fl, Los Angeles, CA 90067, **Business Phone:** (310)369-1000.

GIVENS, ROBIN SIMONE. See GIVENS, ROBIN.

GIVENS-LITTLE, AURELIO DUPRIEST
Clergy, manager. **Personal:** Born Nov 16, 1966, Charleston, SC. **Educ:** Francis Marion Univ, BS, sociol, 1990; Interdenominational Theol Ctr, MDiv, 1995. **Career:** Abundant Life PPW Ctr Inc, pastor & exec dir, 1998-; Project MEN Inc, chief exec officer, 2001-; Francis Marion Univ, coordr multicultural affairs, 2000-. **Orgs:** Life mem, Alpha Pi Alpha Fraternity Inc; Suburban Lodge #213 F&A Masons, PHA; life mem, Nat Asn Advan Colored People; Nat Conv Gospel Choirs & Choruses Inc; adv, treas, Greater Columbia Choral Union; Qual Unlimited Inc. **Honors/Awds:** Outstanding Leadership Award, 2003. **Home Addr:** 50 Teaberry Lane, Elgin, SC 29020. **Business Addr:** Coordinator, Francis Marion University, PO Box 100547, Florence, SC 29501, **Business Phone:** (843)661-1188.

GIVHAN, ROBIN DENEEN
Journalist, fashion editor. **Personal:** Born Sep 11, 1964, Detroit, MI; daughter of Robert and Stella Thompson. **Educ:** Princeton Univ, NJ, BA, 1986; Univ Mich, Ann Arbor, MI, MA, 1988. **Career:** Detroit Free Press, staff writer, 1988-92, fashion ed, 1993-; San Francisco Chronicle, staff writer, 1992-93; Wash Post, fashion ed, currently. **Orgs:** Detroit Hist Soc, Costume Exhib Comt, 1990-91; Detroit Inst Arts, Founders Soc, 1989-91. **Honors/Awds:** Atrium Award, excellence in fashion writing, Univ Ga, 1990; Pulitzer Prize Winner, 2006. *

GIVINS, ABE, JR.
Government official, consultant. **Personal:** Born Apr 22, 1951, Columbus, MS; son of Abe Sr and Corine; married Linda Sue Robinson; children: Abe III, Ryan Eugene & Christel C. **Educ:** Cent State Univ, BS, educ, 1977. **Career:** Normandy Sch Dist, teacher 1980-82; City Pine Lawn MO, alderman 1982-; Ins Agency, ins broker 1982-; City Pine Lawn, alderman; St Louis Pub Schs,teacher biol, 1989-91, spec educ, 1989-91; Mo Dept Ment Health, St Louis, MO, residental therapist, 1991-. **Orgs:** Normandy Munic League, 1982-, MS Munic League, 1982-, Normandy Democ Club,1982-, Candidate Mayor, City Pine Lawn, MO, 1989. *

GLADDEN, BRENDA WINCKLER
Lawyer. **Personal:** Born May 29, 1943, Baltimore, MD; daughter of Raymond McDonald Winckler and Grace Lucille Morton Dixon; married Major Paul; children: Miriam P & Paul B. **Educ:** Cedar Crest Col, Allentown Pa, BA, 1965; Howard Univ Sch Law, WA, DC, JD, 1973. **Career:** NY Hosp NY, chemist, 1965-67; US Dept HUD, Wash, DC, atty, 1974-99; Housing & Urban Develop Dept, DC Field Off, atty, currently. **Orgs:** Phi Alpha Delta Law Fraternity, 1971-; Law Rev Invitee Howard, 1972; DC Bar Asn; Pa Bar Asn; Am Bar Asn, 1974-; Delta Sigma Theta; Jack & Jill of Am Inc; Aux Medico-Chirurgical Soc DC; Aux Nat Med Asn; Nat Bar Asn; Links Inc. **Honors/Awds:** DC Ct Appeals, 1974; Supreme Ct Pa, 1974; US Dist Ct DC, 1974; US Ct Appeals DC Circuit, 1980; US Supreme Ct, 1980. **Home Addr:** 7315 Westminster Ct, University Park, FL 34201. **Business Addr:** Attorney, Housing & Urban Development Department, District of Columbia Field Office, 451 7th St SW, Washington, DC 20410-0001, **Business Phone:** (202)708-0290.

GLADDEN, DR. MAJOR P.
Orthopedic surgeon. **Personal:** Born Dec 8, 1935, Chester, SC; son of Joseph and Isabelle Woodward; married Brenda Winckler; children: Miriam P, Paul B. **Educ:** Morgan State Univ, BS, 1957; Howard Univ, MD, 1961; Am Bd Orthopaedic Surg, cert 1969, recertified, 1983. **Career:** DC Gen Hosp, internship, 1961-62; Mt Alto Va Hosp, res training, gen surgeon, 1962-63; DC Gen Hosp, res ortho, 1963-64; Bronx Municipal Hosp, residency ortho, 1964-66; Albert Einstein Col Med Bronx, instr, 1966-68; Howard Univ Col Med, asst prof, 1969-80; DC Gen Hosp, chief orthopaedic surg, 1968-80; Howard Univ Col Med, assoc prof ortho surg, 1980; pvt pratice, currently. **Orgs:** Alpha Phi Alpha Frat; team physician & ortho consul Howard Univ; volunteer Orthopaedics Medico Prog Dominican Rep, 1978; examiner, Am Bd Ortho Surg Chicago, 1979; vol ortho surg Olympic Training Ctr Colorado Springs, 1984; bd dirs, Morgan State Univ Found, 1984; chief physician DC Boxing & Wrestling Comn, 1984. **Military Serv:** AUS, maj, 1957-71. *

GLADMAN, CHARLES R
Government official. **Educ:** Univ Akron, assoc degree fire sci, 1977; Nat Fire Acad, Exec Fire Officer Prog, 1995. **Career:** City Akron Fire Dept, firefighter, 1973-79, lt/co officer, 1979-85, capt, 1986-89, dist fire chief, 1990-91, dep chief, 1992-96, fire chief, 1997-. **Special Achievements:** First African American Fire Chief in Akron, Ohio; One of seven African American to integrate Akron's Fire Department, 1973. **Business Addr:** Fire Chief, Akron Fire Department, 146 S High St, Akron, OH 44308, **Business Phone:** (330)375-2410.

GLADNEY, DR. MARCELLIOUS
Dentist, consultant. **Personal:** Born May 14, 1949, West Point, MS; son of Robert and Annie; married Elizabeth F Jones; children: Scott, Tarik M & Tonia M. **Educ:** St Johns Univ, BS, pharm, 1972; Univ Med & Dent, NJ, DMD, 1977; Univ Nebr,MS, 1993. **Career:** Eli Lilly & Co, pharm sales rep, 1972-74; US Pub Health Serv, asst dent surgeon, 1977-80; Mercer McDowel Dent Group, pres & founder, 1980-86; US Pub Health Serv, UNIT chief dent officer, 1991; PHS Indian Hosp, Indian Health Serv, pediat dent

consult, currently. **Orgs:** Am Dent Asn, 1979-; Princeton WV Civitans, 1982-85; pres, Southern W Va Roadrunners Club, 1983-86; fel Am Acad Pediat Dent, 1995; Omega Psi Phi; Sigma Pi Phi; Nat Dent Asn; Am Acad Pediat Dent; vpres, NMex Asn Pediat Dent. **Honors/Awds:** PHS Citation Award, 1980 & 1991; PHS Achievement Medal, 1988 & 1994; PHS Commendation Medal, 1997; Indian Health Service Area Directorss Award, 2001. **Home Addr:** 1905 Blue Spruce Dr, Grants, NM 87020. **Business Addr:** Pediatric Dentistry Consultant, PHS Indian Hospital, PO Box 649, Fort Defiance, AZ 86504, **Business Phone:** (928)729-8000.

GLADNEY, RUFUS D
Executive. **Personal:** Born Dec 12, 1955, Kosciusko, MS; married Evelyn, Jun 2, 1979; children: Joshua & Jamila. **Educ:** Miss Col, BA, 1977. **Career:** Consumers Energy, Region Mat Dist, supt, 1988, Region OPS Support, supt, 1992, electric field mgr, 1995-97, mgr, 1997-, bus serv mgr, 2001-; exec mgr elec serv, currently. **Orgs:** Chair, asst treas, Am Asn Blacks Energy; Int Develop Res Ctr, 1997-; Construct Specif Inst, 1998-; Nat Asn Fleet Managers, 1998-; comt mem, Edison Elec Inst Fleet Mgt & Policy, 1998-; bd mem, Parkside YMCA, 1999-; Nat Petrol Coun. **Honors/Awds:** Chairman's Cup, AABE, 1999. **Business Addr:** Executive Manager of Electric Services, Consumers Energy, 1945 W Parnall, Jackson, MI 49201.

GLADWELL, MALCOLM
Writer, Journalist. **Personal:** Born Sep 3, 1963, Canada; son of Joyce Gladwell and Graham Gladwell. **Educ:** Univ of Toronto, BA, 1984. **Career:** Science and medicine writer, The Washington Post, 1987-96; Staff writer for The New Yorker, 1996-. **Honors/Awds:** Natl Magazine Award; received the first Award for Excellence in Reporting of Social Issues from the Am sociological Assoc, 2007; honorary Doctor of Letters degree from the Univ of Waterloo, 2007. **Special Achievements:** Won the 1500m Midget Boys title, Ontario High School championships, 1978; Author, The Tipping Point (2000), New York Times number one bestseller; author, Blink (2005), New York Times number one bestseller; author, Outlier (2008); "100 Most Influential People", Time Magazine, 2005; Outliers debuted as the number one bestseller for The New York Times, The Wall Street Journal, The San Francisco Chronicle, Barnes & Nobel, and Publishers Weekly;. **Business Addr:** Leigh Bureau, 92 East Main St., Ste. 200, Somerville, NJ 08876, **Business Phone:** (908)253-8600.*

GLANVILLE, DOUGLAS METUNWA
Baseball player, manager. **Personal:** Born Aug 25, 1970, Hackensack, NJ. **Educ:** Univ Pa, BS, sci & eng, 1988. **Career:** Baseball player (retired), mgr; Chicago Cubs, outfielder, 1996-97; Philadelphia Phillies, outfielder, 1998-02; Texas Rangers, 2003; Chicago Cubs, 2003; Philadelphia Phillies, outfielder, 2004; NY Yankee, outfielder, 2005; Metrop Develop group, mgr & lead designer, currently. **Orgs:** President, co-founder, Glanville-Koshul Homes; Exec Sub com, Major League Baseball Players Asn; Players Trust for Children, Boys & Girls Club of Am; sponsor, Am Diabetes Asn, Philadelphia Phillies; founding mem, Philadelphia Futures Mentoring Program; bd overseers, Penn Engineering. **Business Addr:** Manager, Lead Designer, Metrop Development Group, 63 E Pk Blvd, Villa Park, IL 60181, **Business Phone:** (630)834-1806.*

GLAPION, MICHAEL J
Insurance executive, executive. **Personal:** Born May 15, 1947, New Orleans, LA; son of Armand P Glapion Jr and Alma Broussard; married Angeler Robert Glapion, Sep 27, 1969; children: Nicholas, Stacie Rose, Nina Simonne & Christopher. **Educ:** Xavier Univ La, BFA, 1969. **Career:** St Paul Fire & Marine Ins Co, com property underwriter, 1971-75; Medtronic Inc, mgr, risk mgt, 1975-78; Graco Inc, mgr risk mgt & ins, 1978-83; Harvest States Coop, dir risk mgt, 1983-88; Ins & Surety Specialist Inc, pres & chief exec officer, 1988; Gillis, Ellis & Baker Inc, dir risk mgt serv, currently. **Orgs:** Chmn, MN African Am Chamber Com, 1990-95; co-founder & vice chair, MN Cultural Diversity Ctr, 1991-97; bd member & chair, Turning Point Inc, 1990-97; exec bd, Nat Asn Minority Contractors MN, 1993-95; bd member & chair, N Community Br YMCA, 1979-84; bd mem, Children's Home Soc MN, 1981-84; comnr, Richfield Human Rights Comn, 1971-74; bd mem & pres, Risk & Ins Mgt Soc MN, 1978-81; bd mem & pres, Prof Ins Agt MN; New Orleans Blighted Housing Citizens Task Force; Ins Mgt Soc. **Honors/Awds:** President's Award, Nat Asn Minority Contractors MN, 1994. **Business Addr:** Director Risk Management Services, Gillis, Ellis & Baker Inc, 1615 Poydras St Suite 600, New Orleans, LA 70112-1238, **Business Phone:** (504)581-3334.

GLASCO, DR. ANITA L.
Educator. **Personal:** Born Oct 24, 1942, Kansas City, KS. **Educ:** Univ Southern Calif, AB, 1964; Harvard Univ, Law Sch, JD, 1967; Univ Chicago, MCL, 1970; Univ Chicag, Ford Foundation Fellow. **Career:** Univ Chicago Law Sch, master comparative law, 1970; Southwestern Univ Sch Law, prof law, 1975, prof emer, 2002-; SW, Asso prof law, 1972-75; Smith & Glascod partner, 1971-72; Lewis & Clark Col, vis prof law, 1975; Univ Wash, vis prof law 1974; Univ Tenn knoxville, vis prof law, 1980. **Orgs:** Calif State Bar Asn, 1968-; Black Women Lawyers Asn; Calif Asn Black Lawyers; chmn, Elect Minority Groups Sect Asn Am Law Sch, 1977; chmn, Minority Groups Sect Asn Law Sch, 1978; fel Inst French Lang & Civil Univ Geneva, 1968; fel Inst French Lang & Civil Univ Pau, 1969; fel Inst French Lang & Civil, Univ Paris 1969; comparative law fel Univ Aix-Marseilles,1969-74. **Honors/Awds:** Outstanding Young Woman of America honoree 1971; Langston Bar Association, Los Angeles Hall of Fame, 2004. **Home Addr:** 14108 Tahiti Way Suite 622, Marina Del Rey, CA 90291. **Business Addr:** Professor Emeritus, SW University School Law, 675 S Westmoreland Ave, Los Angeles, CA 90005, **Business Phone:** (213)738-6717.

GLASGOW, DOUGLAS G.
Educator, government official. **Educ:** Brooklyn Col, BA, 1959; Columbia Univ, MSW, 1961; Univ Southern Calif, DSW, 1968. **Career:** HEW Off Juv Delinq Youth Develop, LA, prin investr, 1968-69; Univ Calif Los Aageles, Ctr Study Afro-Am Hist Cult, interim dir, 1969-70; Coun Soc Work Educ, LA, Juv Delinq Comn, 1969-70; Univ Calif Los Angeles, Sch Soc Welfare, assoc prof, 1970-71; Howard Univ, Sch Soc Work, prof, dean emer, 1972-75; Nat Urban League Inc, wash oper, 1983; Frazier Ctr for Social Res Howard Univ, Washington, DC, Scholar Residence, Currently. **Orgs:** Co-chmn, Black Fac Staff Univ Calif Los Angeles, 1969; Gls Comn Juv Delinq Adult Crime, 1969-70; bd dir, adv comt, Community Cols Guid, 1969, 1972-74; ed bd, NASW J Soc Worker, 1970-73; CSWE Struct Rev Comn, 1971-72; Rev Design Comn, 1972; vice chmn, Div Prog NCSW Cent Conf, 1973; US Prog Comt, ICSW, 1973; adv comt, Howard Univ, Inst Drug Abuse & Addiction, 1973; bd dir, United Black Fund Inc, Wash; Nat Asn Soc Workers; Int Coun Soc Welfare Inc; Acad Cert Soc Workers; Am Acad Polit & Social Sci; Nat Asn Black Soc Workers; Nat Asn Soc Workers; bd mem, Coun Soc Worker Educ. **Honors/Awds:** Award, M J Palevsky Found, 1970; fel Award, Danforth Found, 1971; Sr Stipend Award, NIMH, 1975. **Business Addr:** Washington Operation, National Urban League Inc, 1101 Connecticut Ave NW, Washington, DC 20036, **Business Phone:** (202)898-1604.*

GLASS, ERECKA TIFFANY
Law enforcement officer. **Personal:** Born Dec 8, 1965, Chicago, IL; daughter of Harry and Ruby. **Career:** Dept Corrections, dep sheriff, 1988-; Joel Hall Dance Ctr, jazz instr, 1997-98; Chicago Multi Cultural Dance Ctr, jazz instr, 1995-98. **Orgs:** Apostolic Church of God, 1995-. **Honors/Awds:** Pretty Girl USA, Miss Black Chiago, 1989. **Special Achievements:** Jump for Joy, theatre, dancer/principal, 1993; Dukes Place, dancer/principal, 1996; Hoodlum, motion oicture, dancer/principal, 1996; Gospel Music Then & Now, actor/principal, 1997; Rhythm the Soul of Life, dnacer/principal, 1997. **Business Phone:** (773)869-6518.

GLASS, GERALD DAMON
Basketball player. **Personal:** Born Nov 12, 1967, Greenwood, MS. **Educ:** Delta State Univ, Cleveland, MS, attended 1987; Univ Miss, attended 1990. **Career:** Basketball player (retired); Minn Timber wolves, 1990-92; Detroit Pistons,1992-93; NJ Nets, 1995-96; Charlotte Hornets, 1996; FIBA, Europe, 1997.

GLASS, JAMES
Administrator. **Personal:** Born Jan 27, 1928, Birmingham, AL; married. **Educ:** Miles Col, Birmingham AL, attended 1951; Detroit Inst Technol, Detroit MI, BA, Sociol, 1976; Wayne State Univ, Labor Sch, Detroit MI. **Career:** Chrysler Assembly Plant, 1952-54; Detroit Gen Hosp, 1952-55; Wayne County Juvenile Court, 1955-81; Todd Phillips C Home, 1965-78; AFSCME Coun 25, int vpres, elected 1981, pres, 1982-. **Orgs:** United Found; chmn, Council 25 Exec Bd; exec bd mem, Mich AFL-CIO; vpres, int exec bd, AFSCME; Coalition Black Trade Unionists; governor's appointee, Michi Job Training Coord Coun; bd dir, Nat Asn Advan Colored People; exec bd mem, Mich Trade Union Coun Histadrut. **Honors/Awds:** Dedicated Committeeman, AFSCME Local 409, 1981; Distinguished Service, CoalitionBlack Trade Unionists, 1981; testimonial dinner honoree, AFSCME, 1985; Outstanding Leadership, AFSCME Local, 1985. **Military Serv:** US Navy, honorable discharge, 1947. **Business Addr:** International Vice President, Michigan AFSCME Council #25, 1625 L St NW, Washington, DC 20036-5687, **Business Phone:** (202)429-1000.*

GLASS, RONALD E.
Actor. **Personal:** Born Jul 10, 1945, Evansville, IN; son of Crump and Lethia. **Educ:** Univ Evansville, BA, drama & lit, 1968. **Career:** Tyrone Guthrie Theater, co mem, 1968-72; TV Series: "Day of Absence", 1970; "Slow Dance on the Killing Ground", 1972; Beg, Borrow, or Steal, 1973; "Barney Miller", 1975-82; "Shirts & Skins", 1973; The Streets of San Francisco, 1974-76; Change at 125th Street, 1974; Let's Switch!, 1975; Foster & Laurie, 1975; "Crash", 1978; "The New Odd Couple", 1982-83; "Amen", 1989-91; "Rhythm & Blues", 1992; "Teen Angel", 1997; "Incognito", 1999; "Fire fly", 2002; "Sanford & Son", 1972; "Good Times"; All in the Family"; "The Streets of San Francisco", 1972; "The $10000 Pyramid", 1973; "When Things Were Rotten", 1975; "Hart to Hart", 1979; "The New Odd Couple", 1982-83; "Murder, She Wrote", 1984; Gus Brown & Midnight Brewster, 1985; "The Twilight Zone", 1985; "Amen", 1986; "Designing Women", 1986; Perry Mason: The Case of the Shooting Star, 1986; "227", 1987; "Family Matters", 1989; "Rugrats", 1992-2004; "Rhythm & Blues", 1992; "Mr. Rhodes", 1996; "The Practice", 1997; Teen Angel, 1997-98; Incognito, 1999; "Friends", 1999; "Twice In a Lifetime", 1999; "Yes, Dear", 2000; "Zoe, Duncan, Jack & Jane", 2000; Too Much Pressure, 2000; "Jack & Jill", 2000; "The Education of Max Bickford", 2001; "The Proud Family", 2001; "Fire fly", 2002-03; Secret History of Religion: Knights Templar, 2006; Secret History of Religion: Doomsday - Book of Revelation, 2006; "Shark", 2006-07; Films: The Crazy World of Julius Vrooder, 1974; Deep Space, 1988; House guest, 1995; It's My Party, 1996; Back in Business, 1997; Unbowed, 1999; Deal of a Lifetime, 1999; Recess: School's Out, 2001; Serenity, 2005; Lakeview Terrace, 2008; Fable II, voice for Garth, 2008. **Orgs:** Screen Actors Guild; Hollywood Acad TV Arts & Sci; Actors Equity Asn; Alpha Psi Omega; Am Fedn TV & Radio Artists; Alpha Psi Omega Fraternity Inc; Al Wooten Jr. Heritage Ctr, chmn bd. **Honors/Awds:** Blue Key Scholastic Honor Society; Alumni Certificate of Excellence, Univ Evansville, 1975; Dionysus Award, Hollywood Club Forum Int, 1977; Communtiy Award, La Sentinel Entertainment Writer Gertrude Gibson, 1975; Community Award, Phil Wilkes, Freddie Jett, 1976; William A Gumbertz Award, 1968; Medal of Honor, Univ Evansville; Pearl Le Compte Award. **Business Phone:** (310)838-1200.*

GLASS, VIRGINIA M.
Consultant. **Personal:** Born Dec 14, 1927, Manila, Philippines; daughter of Maria Moreto and Tomas N McKinney; divorced; children: Sidney & Luis. **Educ:** Fordham Univ; Columbia Univ, BA; Columbia Univ Sch Libr Sci; Hunter Col; Queens Col Sch, attended 1977. **Career:** Self-employed consult, Prom, Publicity, Community Devel & Educ; head librn, LaJolla Country Day Sch, 1980-81; founder/past pres, Mt. View Tennis Club; editor, Black Tennis Magazine; dir, community serv, City Col, 1978-80; educ coordr, San Diego Human Rels Comn, 1974-78; dir, pub rels, San Diego Urban League; consult, Univ Calif, San Diego, 1972-74; consult, San Diego City Sch, 1970-72; High Sch Admin, NY City Sch Dist, 1952-70; librn, Brooklyn Pub Libr, 1949-52; Community Tennis Serv, pres & dir. **Orgs:** Exec comm US Tennis Assn; San Diego Dist Tennis Assn; Contemp Black Arts,Univ Calif San Diego; Chrysler LeBaron Series; cord, Jr Olympic Tennis;Nat Jr Tennis League, Cord, San Diego; past pres, Am Tennis Assn; Phoenix Challenge; Manila Liberation, Southern California Tennis Asn; Nat Conf Christians & Jews; Nat Assn Female Execs; Pac Womens Sports Found;Multicultural Participation Comt. **Honors/Awds:** S E Community Theatre Award; US Tennis Assn Community Serv Award, 1977; Mildred Pierce Award; San Diego City Col Citizens Coun Award; Honor Roll,Nat Conf Community & Justice; San Diego Dist Tennis Award; Calif Fedn, Black Leadership Serv Award; Leadership Award, Community Serv, 1985; Outstanding Community Service to San Diego, 1990; Captain Allhea Gibson Cup. **Special Achievements:** Ranked first in the World, Womens 60s, 1989; Ranked 4 in the US Sr Women's Tennis & 2 in Southern California, 1989; Elected to Tennis Hall of Fame. *

GLAUDE, STEPHEN A (STEPHEN ANTHONY GLAUDE)
Executive. **Personal:** Born Jul 25, 1954, Washington, DC; son of William Criss and Phyllis Taylor; married Rhonda Roland, Aug 10, 1980; children: Koya, Shani & Khary. **Educ:** Morgan State Univ, BS, 1977. **Career:** Capitol E Children's Ctr, asst dir, 1977-79; DC Asn Retarded Citizens, voc evaluator, 1979-80; Nat Cong Community Econ Develop, pres & chief exec officer; Men's Ctr, Wash, DC, health educr, 1980-82. **Orgs:** Founder & pres, Inst Life Studies, 1970-; chair & bd dirs, Capitol E Children's Ctr, 1979; bd mem, Montgomery Mental Health Asn, 1980; exec dir, Nat Asn Neighborhoods, Wash, 1980-; Pres Task Force Privaate Sector Initiatives, 1981; chair & fundraising mem develop comt, Black Child Develop Inst, 1984; Coun Black Econ Agenda, 1985; Nat Asn Advan Colored People; Neighborhood Coalition; Inst Life Studies; Natural Living Res Com Republican; exec dir, Men Can Stop Rape, pres & chief exec officer, currently. **Honors/Awds:** President's Second Mild Award, 1977; Mental Health Community Service Award, 1977. **Special Achievements:** First African American to serve as President of the National Congress for Community Economic Development and to serve as Executive Director of the National Association of Neighborhoods. **Home Addr:** 7200 16th Ave, Silver Spring, MD 20912-7046. **Business Addr:** President, Chief Executive Officer, Men Can Stop Rape, PO Box 57144, Washington, DC 20037, **Business Phone:** (202)265-6530 Ext 15.

GLAUDE, STEPHEN ANTHONY. **See GLAUDE, STEPHEN A.**

GLEASON, DR. ELIZA VELERIA ATKINS
Librarian, educator. **Personal:** Born Dec 15, 1909, Winston-Salem, NC; daughter of Simon G Atkins and Oliona P; married Maurice F; children: Joy Carew. **Educ:** Fisk Univ, BA, 1926-30; Univ Ill, BS, 1930-31; Univ Calif, MA, 1935-36;Univ Chicago, PhD, 1937-40. **Career:** Louisville Munic Col, from asst librn to librn, 1931-36; Fisk Univ, asst prof, 1936-37; Talladega Col, dir libr, 1940-41; Atlanta Univ, prof, 1941-46, sch dean; Univ Chicago, guest lectr, 1953; Chicago Techers Col, assoc prof, 1954-

65; Ill Teachers Col, assoc prof, 1965-67; Ill Inst Tech, prof, 1967-70; John Crerar Libr, asst librn, 1967-70; Chicago Pub Libr, asst chief librn, 1970-73; Northern Ill Univ, prof, 1974-75; Self Employed, prof consult, 1975-. **Orgs:** Women's Aux Cook Co Physicians Asn, 1940-; Women's Aux Meharry Med Col Alumni Asn, 1940-; Hyde Park-Kenwood Comn Conf, 1950-; SE Chicago Comn,1952-; Ind Voters Ill, 1952-; Women's Aux Int Col Surgeons, 1961-;co-chmn, Fisk Univ Centennial Campaign, 1963-65; exec comn, Fisk Univ Alumni Asn, 1964-; Phi Beta Kappa; Beta Phi Mu Nat Hon Soc Libr Sci; AmLibr Asn. **Honors/Awds:** Fisk Univ Alumni Award, 1964. **Special Achievements:** Frst Afro-American awarded the PhD in librarian ship.

GLEN, RODNEY. See WARD, RONNIE.

GLEN, ULYSSES, JR.
Government official. **Personal:** Born Aug 11, 1970, Cleveland, OH; son of Ulysses Sr and Janis W. **Educ:** Univ Cincinnati, BA, 1993. **Career:** Blue Cross/Blue Shield, sales coordr, 1994-96; Total HTH Care Plan, mktg mgr, 1996; Wash DC Lottery & Charitable Games, chief staff, 1996; Wash DC, Off Chief Financial Officer, gen coun, currently. **Orgs:** Nat Asn Advan Colored People, 1993; Kappa Alpha Psi Fraternity Inc, vice polemarch, 1996. **Business Addr:** Chief of Staff, Administrative Officer, DC Lottery & Charitable Games Control Bd, 2101 Martin Luther King Jr Ave SE, Exec Off 5th Fl, Washington, DC 20020-5731, **Business Phone:** (202)645-8010.*

GLENN, AARON DEVON
Football player. **Personal:** Born Jul 16, 1972, Humble, TX; married Devaney; children: Aaron II, Tristen & Rheagan. **Educ:** Tex A&M Univ. **Career:** New York Jets, conerback, 1994-2001; Houston Texans, conerback, 2002-04; Dallas Cowboys, conerback, 2005-06; Jacksonville Jaguars, 2007; New Orleans Saints, cornerback, 2008-09; Free agent, currently. **Honors/Awds:** Texans Player of the Year, 2002; Ed Block Courage Award, 2003; Houston Quarterback Club Awards; Foleys Texans Player of the Year; Pete Rozelle Awards; Most Valuable Player, XXXVI & XXXVIII; Pro Bowl selection, 1997-98 & 2002.

GLENN, CECIL E.
Educator, sociologist. **Personal:** Born Dec 18, 1938, Nashville, TN; married; children: Cecil LaVel & Gerald. **Educ:** Tenn A&I State Univ, BS, attended; Northeastern Ill St Col, MA, attended; Univ Colo, EdD, 1975. **Career:** Chicago Dept Educ, Pub Health Serv Civil Rights Envolvement; Teacher; Higher Educ, area urban sociologist; Ment Health Inc, serv mental health, field chmn; Univ Colo, prof Soc Sci, head Ethnic Studies, assoc prof emer social. **Orgs:** Chmn, Malcolm X Mental Inc; Nat Asn Advan Colored People. **Honors/Awds:** Recipient awards, Nat Alliance Bus, 1975; Mt Plains Comm Col Leadership, 1974; Partners corrective progs, 1974. **Home Addr:** 2560 Krameria St, Denver, CO 80207, **Home Phone:** (303)377-1922.

GLENN, DIANE
Banker, president (organization), chief executive officer. **Career:** Community Bank Lawndale, exec dir, pres & ceo, currently. **Orgs:** bd dir & bd adv, MidAmerica Leadership Found; bd mem & chair, ACCESS Community Health Ctr; Nat Bankers Asn; bd mem, Ill State Univ. **Business Phone:** (773)533-6900.

GLENN, PATRICIA CAMPBELL
Manager. **Personal:** Born Dec 15, 1942, Brandon, MS; daughter of James Alvin and Ewnice Agnes Finch; divorced; children: Allison, Jennifer & Lee. **Educ:** Ohio State Univ, Columbus, BS, educ, 1970; Montclair State Univ, MS, communs, 1999. **Career:** E High Sch, Columbus, teacher, 1971-74; Ohio Civil Rights Comn, Columbus, supvr, investr, 1974-78; US Dept Justice, regional dir, 1989-2000, sr mediator, 2001; Nat Arson Task Force, coord, 1995; Univ Conflictology, Moscow & Komi, Russia, instr, 1996; US Dept Justice, regional dir, NY Region, 1989-2001; US Dept Justice, dep regional dir, Chicago Region, 2001-. **Orgs:** Nat Coun Negro Women, 1980-; pres, Major Charles L Hunt VFW Post, 1984-85; dist comnr, Boy Scouts, 1987-89. **Honors/Awds:** Humanitarian Award, Columbus Metropolitan Community Action Org, 1980; Outstanding Performance Award, 1984; Human Relations Service Award, 1985; Kiwanis Award, Cert Appreciation, 1987; Silver Beaver, Chicago Area Coun, 1989; Outstanding Effort Hurricane Hugo, Fed Emergency Mgt Agency, 1990; 50 Outstanding Women in Justice, 1994; Outstanding Regional Dir, 1998; Award from NJ Assembly, 2000; Commendation, US Cong, 2001; Distinguished Service Award, US Dept Justice, 2003.

GLENN, TARIK
Football player, social worker. **Personal:** Born May 25, 1976, Cleveland, OH. **Educ:** Univ Calif, Berkeley, BA, social welfare, 1999. **Career:** Football player (retired); Indianapolis Colts, guard & offensive tackle, 1997-06. **Orgs:** Founder, DREAM Alive Found, 2001-. **Honors/Awds:** Unsung Hero Award, Indianapolis Colts, 2000.

GLENN, TERRY TYREE
Football player. **Personal:** Born Jul 23, 1974, Columbus, OH; children: Terry Jr. **Educ:** Ohio State Univ, hist. **Career:** New England Patriots, wide receiver, 1996-2001; Green Bay Packers, wide receiver, 2002; Dallas Cowboys, wide receiver, 2003-07; free agent,currently. **Orgs:** DARE prog. **Honors/Awds:** Fred Biletnikoff Award, 1995; Rookie of the Year, Sports Illustrated, 1996; AFC Rookie of the Year, United Press Intl, 1996; Super Bowl champion. **Special Achievements:** First-team All-Big Ten, 1995; First-team AP All-American, 1995; Pro Bowl selection, 1999. *

GLOSTER, JESSE E.
Educator, executive. **Personal:** Born Apr 15, 1915, Ocala, FL; son of Lorin and Mattie; married Norma Robinson. **Educ:** Lincoln Univ, AB, 1941; Univ Pittsburgh, MA, 1947, PhD, 1955. **Career:** Educator (retired); Tex Southern Univ, prof econs, 1948; NC Mutual Life Ins Co; Afro-Am Life Ins Co, ins rep. **Orgs:** Organizer, Tex So Univ, Fed Credit Unoin; organizer, chmn, bd Tex So Financer Corp; co-organizer, Riverside Nat Bank. **Honors/Awds:** Recipient ins res grant, 1956, 1f, grant Tex So Univ, 1957; case inst fellow Econ-in-Action, 1960; fac research grants TX So Univ, 1964, 67; Ford Found Grant, 1968-69. **Special Achievements:** Auth: Economy of Minority Groups; publ, NC Mutual Life Ins Co Arno Press NY Times subs, 1976; Minority Economic Policy & Social Development, Univ Press of Am, 1978; also numerous publs for prof jour; auth: The Black Presence in the Tex Sesqui centennial, 1987; Am Must Lift Its Cloud of Debt; Houston Post, 1988; Breaking the Chain of Poverty; Alpha Publ Co, Houston, TX, 1995. **Military Serv:** AUS, lt, 1942-46. **Home Addr:** 3219 Milburn St, Houston, TX 77021, **Home Phone:** (713)747-9249. *

GLOVER, AGNES W.
School administrator. **Personal:** Born Mar 6, 1925, Orangeburg, SC; daughter of Benjamin I Williams and Victoria Glover; married Freddie V. **Educ:** SC State Col, BS, educ, 1956; Hunter Col, MS, 1973; Queens Col, MA, Supr & Admin, 1983. **Career:** School administrator (retired); Nat Sor of Phi Delta Kappa Inc Beta Omicron Chap, third Anti Basileus, 1965-67, tamias, 1967-69, basileus, 1969-71, chmn bd of dir Big Sister Educ Action & Serv Ctr, 1972; Hallet Cove Child Dev Ctr, dir. **Orgs:** Dir, Grosvenor DC, 1968-72; vpres, Flushing Br Nat Asn Advan Colored People, 1982, pres 1974-78; Basileus Nat Sor Phi Delta Kappa Div Beta Omicron Chap, 1969-71, chmn bd dir, Big Sister 1972-; life mem, Nat Asn Advan Colored People, 1987; SC St Col Chap Phi Delta Kappa, 1988. **Honors/Awds:** Serv & dedication Big Sister Educ Action Serv Ctr, 1978; Cert Appreciation La Guardia Community Col, 1981, Flushing Br Nat Asn Advan Colored People, 1984; Outstanding Serv, Flushing Br Nat Asn Advan Colored People, 1984; Outstanding Serv, Coun Supvrs & Admin of New York City, 1987; Dedicated Serv, The Nat Sorority of Phi Delta Kappa Inc, Beta Omicrom Chapter BigSister Educ Action & Serv Ctr, 1987. *

GLOVER, ANDREW LEE
Football player. **Personal:** Born Aug 12, 1967, New Orleans, LA; married Mary Harris; children: Andrew Keith & Christon Dion. **Educ:** Grambling State Univ. **Career:** Football player (retired); Los Angeles Raiders, tight end, 1991-94;Oakland Raiders, 1995-96; Minn Vikings, 1997-99; New Orleans Saints, 2000.

GLOVER, DR. BERNARD ELLSWORTH
Dentist. **Personal:** Born Apr 9, 1933, Suffolk, VA; married Juanita Cross; children: Cheryl, Kevin. **Educ:** Morgan State Col, BS, 1959; Meharry Med Col, DDS, 1963; St Elizabeth Hosp, internship, 1964. **Career:** Pvt Pract, 1964-. **Orgs:** Bd mem, dir, Obici Hosp; bd mem & dir, Nansemon Credit Union; Suffolk City Forum; John L McGriff Dent Soc; Am Nat & Old Dominion Dent Asn; Am Endodontic Soc; C of C; Bi-racial Coun; Obia Hosp Staff. **Honors/Awds:** E end bapt ch Schorlship award, Morgan State Col, 1955-59; Mosby Schorlship Award, 1962; Man of the yr, Kappa Alpha Si, 1974; Elks award en, 1975. **Military Serv:** AUS, Pvt first class , 1963-65. **Business Addr:** Dentist, Private Practice, 811 E Washington St, Suffolk, VA 23434, **Business Phone:** (757)539-7244.*

GLOVER, CHESTER ARTIS
Journalist. **Personal:** Born Sep 3, 1954, Detroit, MI; son of Artis O and Leona Johnson; married Mae Vaughn Glover, May 31, 1977. **Educ:** Valencia Community Col, Orlando, FL, AA, 1977; Rollins Col, Winter Park, FL, BS, 1982. **Career:** WCPX-TV Channel 6, Orlando, FL, weekend assignment ed, 1980-83; Gov Press Off, Tallahassee, FL, press aide, 1982; Stetson Univ, Deland, FL, asst sports info, 1982-84; LAOOC-1984, Los Angeles, CA, asst press chief, 1984; Orlando Sentinel, Orlando, FL, staff writer, 1984-92; Allen & Assocs, Orlando, FL, proofreader & copy ed, 1995-96; Orange Co Dem Exec Comt, comt man, 2004-. **Orgs:** Assoc dir, Multicultural Resources, Orlando, FL, 1989-; pres, Cent Fla Press Club, 1990-92; charter mem, Cent Fla Asn Black Journalists & Broadcasters, 1988-; educ chmn, Sentinel Commun Employees Fed Credit Union, 1990-91; Nat Asn Black Journalists, 1990-. **Home Addr:** 5807 Elon Dr, Orlando, FL 32808-1809, **Home Phone:** (407)290-0193. *

GLOVER, CLARENCE ERNEST, JR.
Educator, school administrator. **Personal:** Born Apr 19, 1956, Shreveport, LA; son of Clarence E Sr and Elizabeth Bradford. **Educ:** Grambling State Univ, BA, 1978; Southern Methodist Univ, Master Theology, 1982; Harvard Univ, post grad, 1985. **Career:** St Duty CME Church, pastor, 1974-75; Wash Temple CME Church, pastor, 1978-80; Caddo Bossier Asn Retarded Citizens, instr & supvr, 1978-79; El Centro Col, campus minister, 1979-80; Clarence Glover Ministries, Inc, pres, 1981-; Southern Methodist Univ, asst to chaplain, 1980-81, coordr intercultural educ African-Am student serv, 1980-89; adjunct prof, African-Am Studies, 1987; Clarence Glover & Asn, prof lecturing & consul agency, 1987; Intercultural Educ & minority affairs, dir, 1989-94; Multicultural Educ Dallas Pub Schs, exec dir, currently. **Orgs:** African-Am cultural consult Dallas Independent Sch Dist, 1980-; TX Asn Col & Univ Student Personnel Adminrs, 1980-; nat coordr Nat Black Christian Student Leadership Consultation, 1985-; third vpres TX Asn Black Personnel Higher Educ, 1985-; NAACP; Christian Leadership Conf; Nat Asn Student Personel Admin; Am Cancer African-Am Task Force; co-host Cable TV Show Religion Focus; lectr & consult African-Am Religion & Culture; Black Male-Female Rels; The Life & Time Dr King Civil Rights Movement & Inter-Cultural Rels & Racism. **Honors/Awds:** Outstanding Young Men America, US Jaycees, 1982-83, 1986; WE DuBois Award, 1980; Advisor of the Year Award, Nat Christian Student Leadership Consult, 1983; consult & interviewer "In Remembrance of Martin" the First Nat Martin Luther King Jr PBS Nat Documentary, 1986; Humanitarian Service Award, El Centro Col & Street Acad, 1986; Spirituality: An African View, Interview Essence Magazine, 1987; On Being African-Am: The Challenge New Generation, Nat Soc Black Engrs Journ, 1988; Honorary Mayor San Antonio, TX, 1988. **Business Addr:** Executive Director, Dallas Public Schools, 3700 Ross Ave, Dallas, TX 75204-5491, **Business Phone:** (972)925-3700.*

GLOVER, DANNY LEBERN
Movie producer, actor. **Personal:** Born Jul 22, 1946, San Francisco, CA; son of James and Carrie; married Asake Bomani (divorced 1999); children: Mandisa. **Educ:** San Francisco State Univ; Am Conserv Theatre; Black Box Theatre Co. **Career:** San Francisco Mayor's Office, researcher; actor; Stage: Master Harold &the Boys, 1982; The Island; Sizwe Bansi Is Dead; The Blood Knot; Suicide in B Flat; Macbeth; Nevis Mountain Dew; A Lesson From Alloes; Master Harold & the boys, 1982-83; Master Harold & the boys, 2003; TV: "Chiefs",1978; "Lonesome Dove", 1988; "A Raisin in the Sun", 1989; "A Place at the Table", 1988; "John Henry", 1987; "How the Leopard Got His Spots",audio-visual, 1989; "Dead Man Out", HBO, 1989; "Hill Street Blues", guest appearance; "Lou Grant", guest appearance; "Many Mansions" Paris, guest appearance; "BJ & the Bear", guest appearance; American Heroes & Legends, 1992; "Civil War Journal", 1993; "Queen", 1993; "America's Dream", actor & exec producer, 1996; "Freedom Song", actor & exec producer, 2000; "Life by the Numbers", 1998; "Buffalo Soldiers", actor & exec producer, 1997; "The Henry Lee Project", 2003; "Henry Lee Good Fences", actor & producer, 2003; "Brothers & Sisters", 2007-08; Films: Escape from Alcatraz, 1979; Chu Chu& the Philly Fh, 1981; Iceman, 1984; Birdy, 1984; Places in the Heart, 1984; Witness, 1985; Silverado, 1985; The Color Purple, 1986; Lethal Weapon, 1987; Mandela, 1987; Bat 21, 1988; Lethal Weapon 2, 1989; To Sleep with Anger, 1990; Predator 2, 1991; Flight of the Intruder, 1991; A Ragein Harlem, 1991; Pure Luck, 1992; Lethal Weapon 3, 1992; Grand Canyon, 1992; Bopha, 1993; Angels in the Outfield, 1994; Gone Fishin, 1997; Buffalo Soldiers, TNT, 1997; Switchback, 1997; Lethal Weapon 4, 1998; Antz, 1998; Beloved, 1998; Prince of Egypt, 1998; Battu, 2000; Boesman &Lena, 2000; 3 AM, actor & exec producer, 2001; The Royal Tenen baums, 2001; Saw, 2004; The Cookout, 2004; Missing in America, 2005; Manderlay, 2005; The Adventures of Brer Rabbit, 2006; The Shaggy Dog, 2006; Dream girls,2006; Barnyard, 2006; Bamako, actor & exec producer, 2006; Honey dripper, 2007; Terra, 2007; Shooter, 2007; Poor Boy's Game, 2007; Africa Unite, exec producer, 2008; Trouble the Water, exec producer, 2008; Gospel Hill, 2008; Be Kind Rewind, 2008. **Honors/Awds:** Image Award, NAACP; Black Filmmakers Hall of Fame; Theatre World Award, Master Harold & the Boys, 1982; hon degree, Paine Col, 1990; Lifetime Achievement Theatre Award, Nat Asn Advan Colored People, 2001; Humanitarian Of The Year, 2006. **Special Achievements:** PBS, host, Celebrate Storytelling; United Nations Development Programme, Goodwill Ambassador, 1998-99. **Business Addr:** Actor, International Creative Management Inc, 8942 Wilshire Blvd, Beverly Hills, CA 90211-1934, **Business Phone:** (310)550-4198.

GLOVER, DIANA M.
Labor relations manager. **Personal:** Born Apr 19, 1948, Buffalo, NY. **Educ:** Cornell Univ, BA, sociol, 1971; Gen Motors Inst, liberal arts cert, 1973. **Career:** Gen Motors Co Chev Div Tonawanda Motor, employ interviewer, 1973-74; Gen Motors Co Chev Div Tonawanda Motor, ast supv employ, 1974-75; Gen Motors Co Chev Div Tonawanda Motor, EEO rep, 1975-76; Gen Motors Co Chev Div Tonawanda Motor, supr employee benefits, 1976; Gen Motors Co Che Div Tonawanda Motor, supr salaried pers admin, 1976-78; Gen Motors Co Chev Div, Tonawanda Motor, supr labor rel, 1978-. **Orgs:** Indust Rel Asn Western NY, 1976-80; dir, Ctr Women Mgt, 1978-80; adv coord Jr Achievement, 1975-78; Buffalo Urban League, 1976-; Nat Asn Adv Colored People, 1978-. **Honors/Awds:** Black achievement award, 1970; Jefferson Enterprises Inc, 1976. **Business Addr:** Assistant Personnel Director, General Motors, CPC Tonawanda Engineering Plant, PO Box 21, Buffalo, NY 14240.

GLOVER, DON EDWARD
Judge. **Personal:** Born Jan 1, 1944?, Dermott, AR; son of Silas Sr and Lucinda; married Dorothy Glover, Aug 17, 1974; children: Dorcedar, Doven. **Educ:** Howard Univ, Sch Law, JD, 1973; Univ Ark Pine Bluff, BS, bus admin, 1965. **Career:** Tulsa County Legal Aid, Baton Rouge Legal Aid, staff atty, 1973-78; N La Legal Aid, managing atty, 1978-80; Jamison & Glover Law Off, atty, 1981-83; Law Off Don Glover, atty, 1983-92; Elected Municipal Judge, Dermott, 1986-88, 1989-92; Elected Circuit Judge, 10th judicial dist, 1993-96, 1997-00, 2001-04, 2004-. **Orgs:** Peace Corps, volunteer Venezula, 1965-67; treasurer, St Paul Baptist Church; Dermott Area C C; bd chair, Morris Boaker Day Care Ctr; Ark Judicial Coun. **Honors/Awds:** Man of the Year, Dermott Area Chamber Com, 1989. **Military Serv:** Army, sgt, 1967-70. **Business Phone:** (870)222-6885.*

GLOVER, DR. GLENDA B.
Dean (education). **Educ:** Georgetown Univ Law Ctr, JD; George Wash Univ, PhD. **Career:** Potomac Elec Power Co, proj mgr, 1979-84; Metters Indust, chief financial officer & sr vpres, 1985-90; Howard Univ, Dept Acct, chairperson & asst prof, 1990-94; Jackson State Univ, Sch Bus, dean, 1994-. **Orgs:** Founder, Nat Ctr Enterprise Zone Res, 1987; adv bd, Union Planters Bank Miss; bd examr, Am Inst Cert Pub Acct.

GLOVER, HAMILTON
Manager. **Personal:** Born Feb 24, 1937, Atlanta, GA; son of Thomas R Sr and Lucile C. **Educ:** Morehouse Col, BA, 1957; Atlanta Univ, MBA, 1958. **Career:** Manager (Retired); Mutual Fed Savings & Loans, trainee, asst treas, 1958-60, asst treas, 1963, secy, treas, vpres-treas, sr vpres-treas, pres, 1994. **Military Serv:** AUS, SP4, 1960-63. **Home Addr:** 994 Willis Mill Rd SW, Atlanta, GA 30311, **Home Phone:** (404)753-0827.

GLOVER, JONATHAN A
Executive. **Personal:** Born in Asheville, NC. **Career:** Merrill Lynch & Co inc, financial adv, 2004-. **Orgs:** Asheville Housing Authority; Asheville Bd Adjusts, Asheville City Coun; dir, chair Fundraising Comm Kid's Voting Asheville, 2001-04; exec bd mem, Asheville-Buncombe Vision; chair, Diversity Adv Coun Carolina Day Sch; Univ of NC, Asheville diversity efforts; vol, YWCA Women's Adv Bd & Caring C; NC Arboretum Soc. **Business Addr:** Financial Advisor, Merrill Lynch & Company Inc., 4 World Financial Ctr 250 Vesey St, New York, NY 10080, **Business Phone:** (212)449-1000.*

GLOVER, KEVIN BERNARD
Football player, executive. **Personal:** Born Jun 17, 1963, Washington, DC; married Cestaine; children: Maya Nikkole & Matthew Robert Romeo. **Educ:** Univ MD, 1984. **Career:** Football player (retired), executive; Detroit Lions, ctr & guard, 1985-97; Seattle Seahawks, ctr & guard, 1998-99; Univ MD, dir character educ, currently. **Honors/Awds:** Athletic Hall Of Fame, Univ MD, 2000. **Business Phone:** (301)314-9289.

GLOVER, LA
Football player. **Personal:** Born Jul 4, 1974, San Diego, CA; married Spring; children: La'Roi Jr, Neomie & Sophia. **Educ:** San Diego State Univ, pub admin & sociol. **Career:** Football player-(retired), Oakland Raiders, defensive tackle, 1996; New Orleans Saints, 1997-2002;Dallas Cowboys, defensive tackle, 2003-05; St. Louis Rams, quarterback,2006-08. **Orgs:** Founder, The LaRoi Glover Found, 1999. **Honors/Awds:** San Diego Co-Player of the Year; Lineman of the Year, Los Angeles Times; CIF Player of the Year; NFC Defensive Player of the Week Award; Unsung Hero Awards, 1999; Man of the Year, St. Louise Saints, 1999. **Business Phone:** (310)649-5222.

GLOVER, LINDA F. See BAILEY, LINDA F.

GLOVER, NAT, JR. (NATHANIEL GLOVER)
Law enforcement officer. **Personal:** Born Mar 29, 1943; married Doris J Bailey; children: 2. **Educ:** Univ N Fla, Edward Waters Col, MS; FBI Nat Acad, grad. **Career:** Law enforcement officer (retired); Jacksonville Sheriff's Off, 1966, Detective Div, investr, 1969; sgt, 1974; dir police servs, 1991; polit democrat; police officer; Duval Co, Fla, sheriff; Jacksonville, Fla, sheriff, 1995-2003. **Special Achievements:** Florida's first African American elected sheriff.

GLOVER, NATHANIEL. See GLOVER, NAT, JR.

GLOVER, ROBERT G
Chemist, president (organization). **Personal:** Born Jul 4, 1931, Bradley, AR; married Mary; children: Mary, Andrew, Alvin, Shirley, Dedra & Robert. **Educ:** Univ Philadelphia, Printing Ink Inst LeHigh, attended. **Career:** St Clair & Valentine Co; Printing Ink Inst LeHigh Univ, lab, staff; Qual Printing Ink Co, Houston, pres. **Orgs:** Litho Club, Craftsman Club, PTA Houston. **Special Achievements:** Only black owner of a firm which manufactures printing inks of all types for distribution throughout the world. **Business Addr:** President, Quality Color Printing Inks, 1803 Cleburne St, Houston, TX 77004-4129, **Business Phone:** (713)528-6976.

GLOVER, SAVION
Dancer. **Personal:** Born Nov 19, 1973, Newark, NJ; son of Yvette Glover. **Educ:** Rye Country Day Sch, grad. **Career:** Broadway prods, "The Tap Dance Kid" 1985, "Black & Blue" 1989, "Jelly's Last Jam" 1992, "Bring in 'Da Noise, Bring in 'Da Funk" 1995; film, "Taps" 1988; "Bamboozled", 2000; "Happy Feet", choreographer, 2006; TV, Sesame St, 1991-95, "Dance in Am:Tap," "Black Filmmakers Hall of Fame," "The Kennedy Ctr Honors"; "Cedric the Entertainer Presents", 2003; Not Your Ordinary Tappers, founder, 1997; Ti Dii, Dance Co, founder, currently. **Honors/Awds:** Martin Luther King Jr Outstanding Youth Award, 1991; Tony Award, best choreography, 1996; Dance Mag Award, 1996; Nat Endowment for the Arts grant, 1996; Best New Theater Star, Ent Weekly, 1996; Capezeo Award, 2004. **Home Addr:** 000100.

GODBEE, THOMASINA D.
Research scientist. **Personal:** Born Apr 10, 1946, Waynesboro, GA; married Cornelius; children: William Jr, Cornelius Tremayne II. **Educ:** Paine Col, BS, 1966. **Career:** Butts Co Bd Educ, Jackson, GA, chem instr, 1966-67; EI du Pont de Nemours & Co, lab tech, 1967-69; Grady Mem Hosp, lab tech, 1970-71; Univ Calif, Irvine, staff res assoc, nuclear physics, 1971-. **Orgs:** Nat Asn Advan Colored People; Paine Col Alumni Club; United Presby Women; Nat Asn Univ Women; Westminster United Presby Church, Soloist Paine Col Concert Choir, 1966; second vpres, scrapbook co-chmn, first vpres, comm chmn, Nat Asn Univ Women. **Honors/Awds:** Eng & Soc Sci Awards, 1960, 1962; Natural Sci Award, 1961; Outstanding Serv to the Community Award, Nat Asn Univ Women, 1977; Spec Performance Award, Univ Calif, 1984. **Home Addr:** 3501 Stafford St, Hephzibah, GA 30815, **Home Phone:** (706)790-6189. **Business Addr:** 3501 Stafford, Hephzibah, GA 30815.*

GODBOLD, DONALD HORACE
School administrator. **Personal:** Born Oct 3, 1928, Detroit, MI; son of Eugene Quemado (deceased) and Alice Virginia Kinney (deceased); married Delores Roxanna Cofer; children: Michelle Roxanne, Donald Terrence Juan, Monique Toi, Darwyn Eugene. **Educ:** Wayne State Univ, BS, 1950, MEd, 1956; Univ Mich Ann Arbor, PhD, 1967. **Career:** Wayne State Univ, teacher spec educ & supv teacher, 1953-67; Oakland Community Col, Orchard Ridge Campus, dean stud serv, 1967-68, provost & chief exec, 1968-70; Community Col Denver Auraria Campus, dean campus & founding chief exec, 1970-71, campus dir & chief exec, 1971-72, vpres & chief exec, 1972-73; Univ Northern Colo, guest prof sociol black hist & cult, counr, 1971-74; Merritt Col, pres, 1973-77; Peralta Community Col Dist, vice chancellor educ serv, 1977-80, chancellor, 1980-88; independent consult, 1988-; Alameda Co Youth Develop Inc, George P Scotlan Youth & Family Ctr, exec dir, currently. **Orgs:** bd mem, Comn Urban Community Col, 1972-75; Am Asn Community & Jr Col; Adv Comt, Am Coun Educ, 1984-87; bd dir, Goodwill Indust Greater East Bay, 1975-86; bd dirs, vpres & secy, New Oakland Comn, 1975-87; bd dirs, Oakland Soc Prev Cruelty Animals, 1978-86; comt mem, Am Coun Educ Comn Col Athletics, 1977-80; City Oakland Pvt Indus Coun, 1978-88; chmn, Accreditation Team, Western Asn Sch & Col, 1979; bd dir, Cs Hosp Med Ctr, 1980-; Am Col Personnel Asn; Am Personnel & Guid Asn; Colorado Asn Comunity Jr Col; Coun Exceptional C; Nat Asn Stud Personnel Adminr; Mich Acad Sci Arts & Letters; Nat Voc Guid Asn; dir, Univ Mich Chap; Phi Delta Kappa; Wayne State Univ Col Educ Alumni Asn; Wayne State Univ Alumni Asn; Univ Mich Alumni Asn; Asn Calif Community Col Admin; bd mem, Urban League CO Inc; bd dir, League Innovation Community Col, 1980-87; bd dir, Bay Area Black United Fund, 1981-87; Conv Adv Comn Calif Asn Community Col, 1983. **Honors/Awds:** Clifford Woody Mem Scholar Award, Univ Mich, 1966; Faculty Award, Community Col, Denver, 1971; Distinguished Service Award, Western Region Coun Black Am Affairs, 1976; Meritorious & Unselfish Leadership & Service, Nat Chair Founding Orgn Coun Black Am Affairs Nat Chair, 1980-85; Leonard F Saine Award; Esteemed Black Alumni Award; Univ Mich, 1982; Leadership & Supportive Service Award, N Cent Region Coun Black Am Affairs, 1986; Recognition, Exxon Educ Found, 1986. **Military Serv:** AUS, 2 yrs. **Home Addr:** 75 Mission Hills St, Oakland, CA 94605-4612. **Business Addr:** Education Consultant, 6201 Clive Ave, Oakland, CA 94611, **Business Phone:** (510)832-4544.

GODBOLT, RICKY CHARLES
Military engineer. **Personal:** Born Mar 7, 1959, Buckner, AR; son of Eddie B and Beatrice; children: LaKelya, LaChelya, Candice & Marcus. **Educ:** Univ Phoenix, AA, MA; Cent Texas Col, AA, 1989; Park Univ, BS (magna cum laude), social psychol, 1993. **Career:** AUS, track mech, 1978-80, electrician, 1981-86, mechanic, 1986-90, instr, 1990-93, chief eng, 1994-99; mech training instr, 2000-; Prince George's Community Col, part-time fac, prog dir, basic elec instr, 2001-, Construct & Develop Inst, dir, 2006-, assoc prof, 2006-; Army Family Team Builder instr, 2002-. **Orgs:** Prince Hall Masons, Samuel T Daniels Chap No107, 1991-93, Mount Moriah Commandry No1, 1991-93; Shadrach Jackson Consistory No156, 1992-94; Magnus Temple No3, 1992-94; Phylaxis Soc, 1992-, dir, military affairs, 1996-; Eastern Stars, Majorie T Lancaster No 84, 1992-95; African Lodge, No 459, 1992-; Asn AUS, 1992-94; Retired Officers Asn, 1993-; Park Col, Pinnacle mem, 1994; Fraternal Order Police, 1994-96; Prince Hall Masons, Zedekiah No167, 1994-; charter mem, Citizen's Flag Alliance, 1995-; AUS Warrant Officer's ASN, 1995-; Veterans Foreign Wars Post 6002, 1996-; first class operator, Nat Inst Uniform Licensing Power Engrs, 1996-; Nat Soc Black Engrs, 1996-; charter mem, Howard Bailey McAfee Heritage Soc Park Col, 1997-; Lord Fairfax Silver chap, US Warrant Officer's Asn, 1997-; Am Legion Post No 0259, 1999-; Nat Black Social Workers; Asn Black Psychologists; Nat Asn Advan Colored People; Mt Vernon Lodge Odd fel; Disabled Am Veterans Chap No17, 2000-; Fraternal Order Police, Lodge No119, 2000-; Int Toast Masters, Ft Belvoir, VA chp, 2001-; Ft Belvoir Speakers Bur, 2001-; Military Order World Wars, 2001-; Retiree Coun, 2001-; Ft George G Meade, MD chap, Retired Officers Asn, 2001-; Soc Am Military Engrs, 2001-; Nat Asn Black Veterans, 2001-; Blacks Govt, 2001-; Oxon Hill Lions Club, 2002-; assoc mem, Fraternal Order Police Fed Lodge, 2002-; life mem, Disabled Am Veterans; Howard Bailey McAfee Heritage Soc. **Honors/Awds:** Honor Roll, Educ Ctr ANFB, 1991-92; Acad Scholarship, Asn AUS, 1992; Certificate Meritorious Service, Phylaxis Soc, 1993; Best Table Topic Award, Ft Belvoir, VA Toast Masters, 2001; 249th Engrs Commander's Coin Excellence, 2002. **Special Achievements:** NCO Quarter, 1983; First mechanic in history to win instructor year, 1992; First African-Am to win instructor year, 1992; First graduate sch for extended learning to become a member Howard Bailey McAfee Heritage Soc Park Col; first Afr Am mem Howard Bailey McAfee Heritage Soc, Park Col. **Military Serv:** AUS, CW2, 1978-99; AUS Mechanic's Badge, 1979; Air Assault Badge, 1985; AUS Driver's Badge-Special Equipment, 1991; Certificate Achievement, 7th Award, 1992; Army Achievement Medal, 9th Award, 1992; Army Good Conduct Medal, 5th Award, 1992; Humanitarian Service Medal, 2nd Award, 1992; AUS Driver Badge-Wheel Vehicle, 1992; Nat Defense Service Medal, 1992; Army Commendation Medal, 4th Award, 1993; AUS Superior Unit Award, 1993; Meritorious Serv Medal. **Business Addr:** Associate Professor, Director Construction and Development Institute, Prince George's Community College, 301 Largo Rd, Largo, MD 20774-2199, **Business Phone:** (301)336-6000.

GODDARD, ROSALIND KENT
Librarian. **Personal:** Born Mar 7, 1944, Gadsden, AL; daughter of George and Nettye George Kent. **Educ:** San Francisco State Col, BA, 1965; Univ Calif, Los Angeles, MLS, 1982. **Career:** Los Angeles Pub Libr, Los Angeles, CA, sr librn, 1967-92; Los Angeles Community Col, exec asst to chancellor, 1992-94, opers div, Human Resources, assoc dir, recruitment & training; Los Angeles Southwest Col, Los Angeles Comm Col, actg assoc dean, 1994; Los Angeles Trade Tech Col, actg assoc dean, 1996-97; Los Angeles City Col, Col Libr, ref librn, Learning Skills Ctr, instr, 1998-. **Orgs:** Calif Librarians Black Caucus, 1980-; Am Libr Asn, 1980-; Women Color, 1989-97; Nat Asn Advan Colored People, 1989-; comn mem, Calif Postsecondary Educ Comn, 1990-92; pres bd, Friends Watts Towers, 1997-; Asn Calif Community Col Adminr, 1997-98. **Honors/Awds:** Staff Commendation, Los Angeles Pub Libr, 1969; Exceptional Leadership Award, Los Angeles Brotherhood Crusade, 1973; Outstanding Black Leader, LA Communit Cols, 1993. **Home Addr:** 5268 Village Green, Los Angeles, CA 90016. **Business Addr:** Librarian, Los Angeles City College, 855 N Vermont Ave, Los Angeles, CA 90029, **Business Phone:** (323)953-4000.

GODETTE, FRANKLIN DELANO ROOSEVELT
Lawyer. **Personal:** Born Nov 3, 1932, North Harlowe, NC; son of Henderson and Lucinda; married Eunice Godette, Mar 10, 1959; children: Flondezi, Arturo, Felicia. **Educ:** Howard Univ, BA, 1955, JD, 1958. **Career:** Atty, 1958-. **Orgs:** NC State Bar, 1958. **Honors/Awds:** Cert Appreciation assoc ed, Howard Univ Law Sch, 1958; Cert Outstanding Accomplishments Criminal Justice Syst, Ebenezer Presby Church, 1984. **Special Achievements:** Publ articles as assoc editor, Howard Law J, 1957-58. **Home Addr:** 1140 Adams Creek Rd, Havelock, NC 28532. **Business Addr:** Attorney, 821 Queen St, New Bern, NC 28560.*

GODFREY, DR. FRANK EDEN
School administrator. **Personal:** Born Dec 23, 1944, Charleston, SC; married Andrea Ollivierra; children: Frank Jr, Marlin & Shannon. **Educ:** St Augustines, BS, Bus, 1967; Tex Southern, MBA, 1971; Harvard Univ, MPA, 1979, EdD, 1983. **Career:** Ford fel, Tex Southern Univ, 1969-71; Hampton Inst, instr, 1971-75; assoc dir, Ctr Minority Bus Develop, 1972; St Leo Col, adj fac, 1975-78; NASA, contracting officer, 1974-80; EPM fel, NASA/Harvard Univ, 1978-79; Harvard Univ, res asst, 1980-82; tutor, Elliott Congregational Church, 1983; StAugustines Col, dir alumni affairs, 1984, Div Bus, chmn, currently. **Orgs:** Nat Scholar, Alpha Kappa Mu, 1966; bd adv, Martin Luther King Open Sch, 1982-83. **Honors/Awds:** Whitney Young Fel, 1983. **Military Serv:** AUS, spec 5th Class, 2 yrs; Army Commendation Oak Leaf Cluster, 1968.

GODFREY, RANDALL EURALENTRIS
Football player, business owner. **Personal:** Born Apr 6, 1973, Valdosta, GA. **Educ:** Univ Ga. **Career:** Dallas Cowboys, linebacker, 1996-99; Tenn Titans, linebacker, 2000-02; Seattle Seahawks, linebacker, 2003; San Diego Chargers, linebacker, 2004-06; Wash Redskins, 2007; Godfrey Funeral Home, owner, currently; free agent, currently. **Business Phone:** (229)242-9500.

GODFREY, WILLIAM R.
Financial manager. **Personal:** Born May 18, 1948, Gay, GA; son of John W and Iula; married Joyce Lincoln; children: Runako,

Kenan & Nyasha. **Educ:** Clark Col, BBA, 1970; State Univ New York, MBA, 1973. **Career:** US Gen Acct Off, sr auditor, 1973-80; US Gen Serv Admin Off of the Inspector Gen, sr auditor, 1980; Fulton Co, asst finance dir; William R Godfrey & Assocs Inc, currently. **Orgs:** Treas, Mental Health Asn Metro Atlanta, 1984-89. **Home Addr:** 3401 Prince George Dr, East Point, GA 30344. **Business Phone:** (404)588-2254.

GOFF, WILHELMINA DELORES
Association executive, counselor. **Personal:** Born Jun 18, 1940, Columbia, SC; daughter of William Earl Goff and Katie Mae Goff. **Educ:** Morgan State Col, BS, 1962; John Carroll Univ, MA, 1971; New York Univ; Cleveland State Univ, EdSD. **Career:** Hillcrest Ctr C Bedford Hills, counr, 1962-64; Cleveland Pub Sch, music teacher, 1964-78, guidance counr, 1971-78; Cuyahoga Community Col, coordr, counr job corps, 1978-, assoc dir access & job corps act, 1979-80; Cleveland, asst dean stud personnel serv; Nat Coun Negro Women, dir prog & develop; Delta Sigma Theta Sorority, Wash, DC, dep exec dir, 1990-. **Orgs:** Newsletter ed, Phi Delta Kappa Reg dir Delta Sigma Theta Sor, 1976-; pres, OH Asn Non-White Concerns Personnel & Guid, 1978-80; corresp secy & mem, large NE OH Personnel & Guid, 1978-80; bd mem & chmn, ed com Cleveland NAACP, 1979-80; coordr speakers bur, Gr Cleveland Com IYC, 1979; pres, Delta Sigma Theta Tutoring & Nutrit Prog, 1986-. **Honors/Awds:** Award for Congressman Stokes Cleve, 1974; Pan-Hellenic Award, Cleveland, 1976; Outstanding Service, Delta New Orleans LA convention, 1979; Key to the City, Indianapolis Ind, 1980; Higher Educ Counr Yr NEOPGA, 1980; Outstanding Serv, Teen Father Prog, 1984; Proclamation, City Cincinnati, 1982; Outstanding Serv, OH Personnel & Guid Asn; Outstanding Serv, Dyke Col Stud Body, 1986; Outstanding Serv Youth & Educ, Cleveland Chap Negro Bus & Prof Women's Club, 1986. **Home Phone:** (202)328-0474. **Business Addr:** Director, Delta Sigma Theta Sorority Inc, 1707 New Hampshire Ave NW, Washington, DC 20009, **Business Phone:** (202)986-2509.

GOGGINS, HORACE
Dentist. **Personal:** Born May 14, 1929, Hodges, SC; son of Mattie Butler and Ulysses; divorced; children: Horace W. **Educ:** SC State Col, BS, 1950; Howard Univ, DDS, 1954. **Career:** Self-Employed, Rock Hill, SC, dent surgeon, currently. **Orgs:** Nat Dent Asn; past pres, Palmetto Med & Dent Asn, 1973; SE Analgesia Soc; Tri County Dent Soc; Piedmont Dent Soc; Beta Kappa Chi Sci Soc; Rock Hill Planning Comn; Nat Asn Advan Colored People; Coun Human Rels; Mt Prospect Baptist Church deacon; Alpha Phi Alpha Fraternity; Sigma Pi Phi Fraternity; SC Dem Party; Am Legion Elks. **Honors/Awds:** Doctor of the Year, Palmetto Dent Asn, 1983-84; Certificate of Appreciation, Delta Sigma Theta, 1992; Minority Business Person of the Year, 1994; Outstanding Service & Leadership Award, Rock Hill Br Nat Asn Advan Colored People, 1995. **Military Serv:** AUS, capt dent corps, 1954-56; USAR, maj. **Business Addr:** Dentist, 427 Dave Lyle Blvd, Rock Hill, SC 29730.*

GOINES, DR. LEONARD
Educator. **Personal:** Born Apr 22, 1934, Jacksonville, FL; son of Willie Mae LaMar Goines and Buford Goines; married Margaretta Bobo (divorced); children: Lisan Lynette. **Educ:** Manhattan Sch Music, BMus, 1955, MMus, 1956; Fontain bleu Sch Music France, Cert, 1959; Columbus Univ, MA, 1960, Prof Dipl, 1961, EdD, 1963; New Sch Soc Res, BA, 1980; New York Univ, MA, 1980; Harvard Univ, CAS, 1984. **Career:** Educator (retired); New York City Bd Educ, teacher music, 1959-65; Leonard Goines Quintet, trumpeter-leader 1960-; Symphony New World, trumpeter, 1965-76; Bedford Stuyvesant Youth Action, dir music, 1965-66; Morgan State Col, assoc prof music, 1966-68; York Col City Univ NY, lectr, 1969; Manhattan Community Col, prof music, 1969-92; City Univ New York, Queens Col, lectr; Howard Univ, assoc prof music, 1970-72; NY Univ, lectr, 1970-88; WEB DuBois Inst Harvard Univ fel, 1982-85; Shepard & Goines, partner org & educ arts consultants, 1984-; Williams Col, vis prof music, 1984; Vassar Col, vis prof music, 1985; Lafayette Col Easton PA, distinguished vis prof music, 1986; NY Univ, jazz hist. **Orgs:** Folklore consult, Smithsonian Inst, 1974-76; jazz consult, Creative Artists Pub Serv Prog,1980; bd trustees, Nat Asn Community Sch & The Arts, 1982-85; chmn, special arts sect panel New York State Coun Arts, 1982-85; jazz res consult, Nat Endowment for the Arts, 1983; music consult, US Info Agency, 1984; co-exec producer, BAM Majestic Theater, Brooklyn, NY, 1988-96; adv bd mem, Universal Jazz Coalition Inc; adv bd mem, Afro-Am Music Bicentennial Hall of Fame & Museum Inc. **Honors/Awds:** Citizenship Winnipeg Canada, 1958; fac res grants, Howard Univ, State Univ NY, City Univ NY, 1971-73; first Annual NY Brass Conf for Scholar Award, 1973; develop series of music filmstrips for Educ Audio Visuals Inc, 1975; Public Service Award, US Dept of Labor, 1980; Col Teachers Fel, Nat Endowment for the Humanities, 1982-83; Scholar Incentive Award, City Univ NY, 1983-84; Hon writer & contrib articles to Groves Dict of Music & Musicians, Black Books Bulletin, first World, The Black Perspective in Music, Journ of African & Asian Studies, Black World, Downbeat, Music Educ Journ, Allegro. **Special Achievements:** Appointed To Preservation of Jazz Adv Comn by Secy of Smithsonian Inst, 1991-93. **Military Serv:** AUS, 1958. *

GOINS, MARY G.
Educator. **Personal:** Born Sep 8, 1929, Orange, TX; married Lee A Randle. **Educ:** BA, MA. **Career:** Instr, prin, 1961; Enterprise Jr High Sch, Compton CA, prin. **Orgs:** Vpres, Compton Educ Asn, 1969-70; pres, Asn of Compton Sch Cours, 1970-71; secy, Asn Compton Unified Sch Adminrs, 1971-72; Asn of CA Sch Adminrs; Calif Pers & Guid Asn; PTA; officer Exec PTA. **Honors/Awds:** Recip finer womanhood Award, Xavier Univ, 1948; life hon Award, PTA, 1972.

GOINS, RICHARD ANTHONY
Educator, lawyer. **Personal:** Born Mar 1, 1950, New Orleans, LA; son of James Milton and Vivian Wiltz; married Nannette, Mar 3, 1990. **Educ:** Yale Univ, BA, hist, 1972; Stanford Univ & Law Sch, JD, 1975. **Career:** Stanford Univ, Sch Law, Reginald Heber Smith fel, 1975; New Orleans Legal Asst Corp, mgr & staff atty, 1975-77, dep dir, 1977-78, exec dir, 1978-81; Loyola Univ, Sch Law, asst prof, 1981-84; Hon Adrian G Duplantier, law clerk, 1982; Adams & Reese, asst atty, 1984-87; Loyola Univ, Law Sch, adj prof, 1984-; atty, partner, 1987; Thomas More Inn Ct, barrister, 1988-; Goins Aaron PC, atty, currently. **Orgs:** La State Bar Asn, 1975-; Calif State Bar, 1977-; Am Bar Asn Conf Minority Partners Majority/Corp Law Firm, 1990-; bd dirs local chap, Fed Bar Asn, 1992-; Merit Selection Panel, Selection & Appointment US Magistrate, 1992-96. **Special Achievements:** Leadership Louisiana 1992 Participant; Practical Issues in Class Action Litigation, The Practical Litigator, Vol 6,# 1, Jan 1995, Author; Seminar Presenter, LA Public Retirement Seminar, Baton Rouge, LA 1989, 1990, topic: "Fiduciary Responsibilities of Trustees of Pension Plans;" Seminar Presenter, Recent Dev Seminar, Tulane Univ, New Orleans, LA, 1994, topic: "Recent Dev in Labor & Employment Law". **Home Addr:** 1010 Common St Suite 2600, New Orleans, LA 70112, **Home Phone:** (504)569-1805. **Business Phone:** (504)569-1800.

GOLDBERG, WHOOPI (CARYN ELAINE JOHNSON)
Comedian, actor. **Personal:** Born Nov 13, 1955, New York, NY; daughter of Emma Johnson; married Alvin Martin, Jan 1, 1973 (divorced 1979); children: Alexandrea Martin; married David Edward Claessen, Sep 1, 1986 (divorced 1988); married Lyle Trachtenberg, Oct 1, 1994 (divorced 1995). **Career:** Stand-up comedian, Los Angeles, CA; Films: The Color Purple, 1985; Jumpin' Jack Flash, 1986; Burglar, 1987; Fatal Beauty, 1987; Clara's Heart, 1988; Homer & Eddie, 1989; Ghost, 1990; The Long Walk Home, 1990; Soap Dish, 1991; Sarafina, 1992; Sister Act, 1992; Made in America, 1993; Sister Act 2, 1993; Corrina, Corrina, 1994; Bogus, 1996; Eddie, 1996; The Associate, 1996; Ghosts of Mississippi, 1996; How Stella Got Her Groove Back, 1998; Girl Interrupted, 1999; Kingdom Come, 2001; Monkey bone, 2001; Rat Race, 2001; Blizzard, 2003; Pinocchio 3000, 2004; Super Babies: Baby Geniuses 2, 2004; Jiminy Glick in Lalawood, 2004; Racing Stripes, 2005; Whoopi: Backto Broadway - The 20th Anniversary, 2005; Doogal, 2006; Farce of the Penguins, 2006; Everyone's Hero, 2006; Homie Spumoni, 2006; It's Under My Skin, 2006; The Lasy Guy on Earth, 2006; Saturday Night Live: The Best of Saturday TV Fun house, 2006; If I Had Known I Was a Genius, 2007; Stream, 2008; Snow Buddies, 2008; TV Series: "Star Trek: The Next Generation", 1987; "Baghdad Cafe", 1990; "Hollywood Squares", producer, 1998; "Whose Line Is It Anyway?", 2000; "What Makes a Family", 2001; "Call Me Claus", 2001; "Madeline: My Fair Madeline", voice, 2002; "It's a Very Merry Muppet Christmas Movie", 2002; "Absolutely Fabulous", 2002; "Good Fences", producer, 2003; "Whoopi", producer, 2003; "Little burg", 2004; "Bear in the Big Blue House", 2005; "Just for Kicks", develop & exec producer, 2006; "Dawn French's Girls Who Do Comedy", 2006; "Everybody Hates Chris ", 2006; "Comic Relief seven times"; Academy Awards, host; Appearances on Moonlighting; "Scared Straight: 10 Years Later"; "Carol, Carl, Whoopi &Robin"; "An All-Star Celebration: The '88 Vote"; "Funny, You Don't Look 200"; "My Past Is My Own"; "Broadway: A Funny Thing Happened On the Way To The Forum"; "Cinderella"; Untitled IDT Entertainment Proj, 2006; "Sonotorious", 2006; "Law & Order: Criminal Intent", 2006; "If I Had Known I Was a Genius", 2006; "Everybody Hates Chris", 2006; HBO specials; Whoopi Goldberg Show. **Orgs:** Screen Actors Guild; Am Federation Television and Radio Artists. **Honors/Awds:** Golden Globe Award, Performance by an Actress in a Dramatic Motion Picture, 1985; Academy Award Best Actress, 1985; Image Award, NAACP, 1985; Grammy Award for Best Comedy Recording of the Year, 1985; Kid's Choice Award Favorite Movie Actress, Nickelodeon; Humanitarian of the Year, Starlight Found, 1989; Image Award, Best Supporting Actress Motion Picture, NAACP, 1990; Image Award for Entertainer of the Year, NAACP, 1990; Oscar Award, 1991; BAFTA Film Award, 1991; Saturn Award, 1991; Academy Award for Best Supporting Actress, 1991; American Comedy Award, 1991, 1993; TV Prize, 1992; Am Cinema Award, 1992; University of Vermont, hon degree, 1997; Hosted two Academy Awards; First African-American female to host the Academy Awards; American Comedy Award, 1993; Star on Hollywood Walk of Fame, 2001; BAFTA Film Award, 2002; Tony Award, 2002; Gracie Allen Awards, 2003; MVP of the Kinko's Celebrity Softball Game, 2003; Image Award, 2004. **Special Achievements:** ABC's A Gala for the President, Ford's Theatre; Emmy Award nomination for hosting The 66th Annual Academy Awards; Broadway, A Funny Thing Happened on the Way to the Forum, 1997; Book: Alice, 1992; book 1997.

GOLDEN, ARTHUR IVANHOE
Lawyer, insurance executive. **Personal:** Born Jan 14, 1926, New York, NY; married Thelma O Eastmond; children: Thelma Ann, Arthur E. **Educ:** NYU, BS, 1959; Brooklyn Law School, JD, 1973. **Career:** Golden & Golden Ins, pres, 1957-; Harlem Branch New York County Dist Atty's Off, mem legal staff, 1973-; Mayor's Off Develop, proj dir, 1969-70; Jackson High Sch, instr, 1966-69; Dept Licensing, NY, 1963-66; Dept Social Serv, Harlem, 1960-63; First Presbytarian Church in Jamaica, Lay Pastor, NY, Currently. **Orgs:** Past pres, United Ins Brokers Asn; Moot court honor soc Brooklyn Law Sch; Iota Nu Sigma ins hon soc NYU; neighborhood sponsor Queens DA Comn Crime Prevention Bureau; Black Am Law Students Asn; Mayor's High Sch Career Guidance Conf, 1966-72; mem adv coun, SBA; One Hundred Black Men; past pres, bd dir, Prof Ins Agents NY State; vpres, bd dir, Coun Ins Brokers Greater NY; state appointed pub mem, governing comt; Automobile Underwriting Asn; chmn, Anti-Arson Comt; chmn, Property Mgt Div, Presbyterian NY; ruling elder, First Presbyterian Church Jamaica, clerk session; Producer Liaison Comt, Ins Serv Office. **Honors/Awds:** Brooklyn Law Sch, 50 yr alumni, 1999-; Distinguished Serv & Lifetime achievement, CIB-GNY, 1996. **Military Serv:** AUS major 1950-54. **Home Addr:** 18936 Lewiston Ave, St Albans, NY 11412, **Home Phone:** (718)454-4111. **Business Phone:** (718)526-4775.*

GOLDEN, DONALD LEON
College teacher, lawyer. **Personal:** Born Jan 3, 1940, Walnut Cove, NC; married; children: Donna & Amber. **Educ:** Howard Univ, BA, 1972; Howard Univ Law Sch, JD, 1972. **Career:** US Attorney's Off, law clerk, 1971; Judicial Panel Multi-Dist Litigation, temp researcher asst, 1971; Howard Law Sch Libr, 1971-72; US Dist Ct, law clerk, 1972-73; Covington & Burling, assoc, 1973-77; Howard Univ Law Sch, adjunct prof, 1974-81, prof, 1981-; Asst US Attorney's Off, attorney, 1977-81. *

GOLDEN, JOYCE MARIE
Executive. **Personal:** Born in Berkeley, CA; married William Paul; children: Shawn Patrick. **Educ:** Calif State Univ, Hayward, BA, psychol, MBA, acct & fin. **Career:** Arthur Andersen & Co, sr acct, 1977-81; Bank Am, vpres & financial mgr, vpres & planning mgr, vpres & financial controller, asst vp & acct mgr, 1981-86; Citi Corp Savings, dir acct, 1986-87; San Francisco Newspaper Agency, vpres & chief financial officer, 1987-93. **Orgs:** Newspaper Asn Am; Am Womens Soc CPAs; vpres, Oakland Ensemble Theatre, 1986-89; Nat Asn Urban Bankers; vpres, Bus Vol Arts, 1990-93; treas, Bay Area Adoption Placement & Res Ctr, 1992-; vpres, Nat Geog Soc.

GOLDEN, LOUIE
Educator. **Personal:** Born May 2, 1940, Matthews, SC; married Batty Washington. **Educ:** Claflin Col, BS, 1963; Southern Ill Univ, MS, 1971. **Career:** Sterling High Sch Greenville, coach, teacher, 1963-65; Beck High Sch, coach, teacher, 1965-70; Carolina High Sch, coach, teacher, 1970-72; Riverside High Sch Greer, athletic dir, 1973; Greenville Co Sch Dist, athletic dir, currently. **Orgs:** Coack Clin SC Basketball; SC Educ Asn; Greenville Co Educ Asn; NEA Coun Math; SC HS League; master Mason; polemarch Kappa Alpha Psi Frat; Comn, Citizen week Co Coun; Park & Tourist Comn Appalachian Coun Govt Park & Recreation Comn Greenville C C; vice chmn, trustee bd, vice chmn fin com church treas, St Matthew United Meth Church. **Honors/Awds:** First black head coach prodominent white school; First black athletic dir Greenville Co Sch Dist; 750 winning percent basketball for ten yrs; one season 23 wins & no losses. **Business Addr:** Athletic Director, Greenville County Schools, 100 Blassingame Rd, Greenville, SC 29651.

GOLDEN, MARITA
Novelist, college teacher. **Personal:** Born Apr 28, 1950, Washington, DC; daughter of Fancis Sherman and Beatrice Reid; children: Michael Kayode. **Educ:** Am Univ, BA, 1972; Columbia Univ, MS, 1973. **Career:** WNET Channel 13, NY, assoc producer, 1974-75; Univ Lagos, Nigeria, asst prof, 1975-79; Roxbury Community Col, Boston, MA, asst prof, 1979-81; Emerson Col, Boston, MA, asst prof, 1981-83; author; George Mason Univ, senior writer Creative Writing Prog, currently; Roxbury Community Col, fac; Va Commonwealth Univ, prof MFA creative writing prog, 1994-; Words Power LLC, novelist, currently; Univ Dist Columbia, writer in residence, currently. **Orgs:** exec dir, Inst Preserv & Study of African-Am Writing, 1986-87; pres emer, African-Am Writers Guild; pres, Zora Neale Hurston/Richard Wright Found; pres emer, African Am Writers Guild. **Honors/Awds:** Woman of the Year, Zeta Phi Beta, 1997; hon doctorate, Univ Richmond, 1998; Literary Hall of Fame for Writers of African Descent, Chicago State Univ; Writers for Writers Award, Poets & Writers mag, 2001; Distinguished Service Award, Authors Guild, 2002; Fiction Award, Black Caucus Am Libr Asn, 2007. **Special Achievements:** Novels: Migrations of the Heart, 1983; A Woman's Place, 1986; Long Distance Life, 1989; And Do

Remember Me, 1992; Saving Our Sons, Doubleday, 1994; The Edge of Heaven, Doubleday, 1998; Skin Deep: Black and White Women on Race, edited by Marita Golden and Susan Shreve (Anchor Press); A Miracle Everyday: Triumph & Transformation in the Lives of Single Mothers, Anchor Press, 1999. **Business Addr:** Novelist, Words of Power LLC, PO Box 4853, Largo, MD 20775.*

GOLDEN, MARVIN DARNELL
College teacher. **Personal:** Born Dec 9, 1955, Chicago, IL; son of Catherine L. **Educ:** DePaul Univ, Chicago, BA, 1978; Univ Ill, Chicago, MPA, 1985. **Career:** Independent pub policy consult & orgr, 1955-97; Greenpeace, midwest reg energy campaigner, 1991-94; dir vol serv, 1998-2000; Career Col Chicago, instr, 1999-. **Orgs:** APA, 1977-; Souvenir Prog Comt Chicago Sinfonietta Ann Benefit, 1991; Energy Justice Campaign, 1995-96; bd dir, Citizen Utility Bd, 1997-2001. **Honors/Awds:** Certificate of Appreciation, DST, 1994; Certificate of Achievement, Organizing Award, Lakeview Action Coalition, 1995. **Special Achievements:** Author of : An Analysis Documenting the Legislative History of The Reauthorization of the Community Development Block Grant Programs of 1977; An Analysis of the Judicial System as Compared to Contemporary Organization Theory, Graduate Research Project, University of Illinois, Chicago, 1984. **Home Addr:** 3550 N Lake Shore Dr, Chicago, IL 60657. **Business Phone:** (312)895-6300.

GOLDEN, RONALD ALLEN
Insurance executive. **Personal:** Born Feb 6, 1944, St Louis, MO; married Clementina Joyce Thompson; children: Stephanie, Lisa, Ronald. **Educ:** Southwest Mo State Univ, BS, 1970; Am Educ Inst, Cert, casualty claim law assoc, 1979. **Career:** McDonnell & Douglas Corp, tool & parts control specialist, 1966-68; St Louis Bd Educ, teacher, 1968; The Travelers Ins Co, supvr casualty prog claims, 1968-, sr claim law assoc, currently; Third World Band, bus mgr, 1973-; Simply US Bank, bus mgr, 1977-. **Orgs:** Am Fed Musicians Local, 1973-. **Honors/Awds:** Outstanding Freshman Award, Southwest Mo State Univ. **Special Achievements:** First black athlete to win track & field scholarship SMSU, 1962-66; first black in CP Claim St Louis Office Travellers Ins Co. **Business Addr:** Senior Claim Law Associate, The Travelers Companies, 701 Market St, Saint Louis, MO 63101.*

GOLDEN, WILLIE L
Law enforcement officer. **Personal:** Born Aug 16, 1952, Miami, FL; son of Louise Smith and Willie S; married Myra E Jones, Dec 19, 1979; children: Bryan, Kyle, Christopher & William Justin. **Educ:** Southeast Fla Inst Criminal Justice, Miami Fla, Cert Completion, 1974; Miami-Dade Community Col, Miami Fla, AA, 1978; Biscayne Col, Miami Fla, BA, 1980; St Thomas Univ, Miami Fla, MS, 1981. **Career:** Police officer (retire); Metro-Dade Police Dept, Miami Fla, police officer lt; Dade County Sch Syst, Miami Fla, teacher, 1977-84; Dade County Citizen Safety Coun, Miami Fla, instr, consult, 1984-; Fla Mem Col, Miami Fla, assoc prof, 1986-; Alexander & Alexander, Miami, FL, pub rel consult, 1986-88; Metrop Police Inst, Miami Fla, instr, 1987; Metro Dade Police Dept, first lt. **Orgs:** Jr warden, Prince Hall Masons, 1974-; pres, Progressive Officers, 1975-; Dade County Police Ben Asn, 1975-; parliamentarian, Nat Black Police Asn, 1977-; chaplain, Phi Beta Sigma Fraternity, 1984-; Nat Asn Advan Colored People, 1984-; bd dir, South Fla Inst Traffic Safety Unlimited, 1985-; Prince Hall Shriner, temple, 149; Police Benevolent Asn; Univ Miami Med Adv Bd; Nat Orgn Black Law Enforcement Exec. **Honors/Awds:** Planned, Organized & Developed, Community Oriented Police Unit Metro-Dade Police Dept, 1982; Outstanding POC, Progressive Officers Club, 1985; Outstanding Young Man of America, Young Am, 1986; Distinguished Service Commendation, Metro-Dade Police, 1988; WD Cameron Leadership Award, Nat Black Police Asn, 1994; Law Enforcement Award, Nat Black Police Asn, 1995; Proclamation, Dade County Comn, 1995; Venerable Order of Michael the Archangel, Am Police Hall Fame, 2001. **Home Addr:** 18910 NW 29th Pl, Miami, FL 33056, **Home Phone:** (305)621-0537.

GOLDSBERRY, RONALD EUGENE
Automotive executive, chairperson, association executive. **Personal:** Born Sep 12, 1942, Wilmington, DE; children: Ryan, Renee. **Educ:** Central State Univ, BS, chem, 1964; Mich State Univ, PhD, inorganic chem, 1969; Stanford Univ, MBA, fin & mkt, 1973. **Career:** Univ Calif, San Jose, asst prof chem, 1969-71; NASA Am Res Ctr, res chemist, 1969-72; Hewlett Packard Co, prod mgr, 1972-73; Boston Consult Group, mgt consult, 1973-75; Gulf Oil Corp, dir corp planning, 1975-78; Occidental Chem Corp, vpres bus develop, 1978-81, vpres & gen mgr surface treatment prods, 1981-83; Parker Chem Co, pres, 1983-87; Ford Motor Co, Plastic Products Div, gen mgr, 1987-90, North Am Automotive Opers, exec dir sales & serv strategies, 1990-93, vpres, customer serv, 1993; OnStation Corp, chmn bd, 2000-. **Orgs:** Nat Acad Engrs; bd mem, Cranbrook Educ Inst; bd mem, Mich State Univ Alumni Asn; bd mem, Black Exec Exchange Prog; Am Chem Soc; Nat Black MBA Asn; Nat Org Black Chemists & Chem Engrs; Asn Consumer Growth; Comn Devlop Asn; Am Mgt Asn; Econ Club; Greater Detroit Chamber Com; Omega Psi Phi Frat; bd trustees, WTVS Channel 56 Detroit; bd mem, Am Can Co; bd mem, Rockefeller Found; bd mem, Adrian Col; bd mem, William Beaumont Hosp; bd mem, Boy Scouts Am; bd mem, Mich State Univ Develop Fund; bd mem, ExPrimerica Corp. **Honors/Awds:** Beta Kappa Chi Hon Soc, 1962; Alpha Kappa Mu Hon Soc, 1963; Omega Psi Phi Man of the Year, 1971; Outstanding Alumnus MI State Univ, 1983; Outstanding Alumnus NAFEO, 1983; patent Ultraviolet & Thermally Stable Polymer Compositions, 1974; Top 50 Black Execs, Black Enterprise; Excellence Mgt Award, Indust Week. **Special Achievements:** only the 2nd African-American vice president at Ford Motor Company, 1994. **Military Serv:** AUS, capt, 1969-71. **Business Addr:** Chairman Of the Board, On-Station Corporation, 720 Bay Rd Suite 200, Redwood City, CA 94063, **Business Phone:** (650)292-0200.*

GOLDSON, AMY ROBERTSON
Lawyer. **Personal:** Born Jan 16, 1953, Boston, MA; daughter of Irving E Robertson and E Emily Robertson; married Alfred L Goldson, Jun 24, 1974; children: Erin, Ava. **Educ:** Smith Col, BA, 1974; Cath Univ Law Sch, JD, 1976. **Career:** Internal Revenue Serv, Off Chief Coun, Tax Ct Litigation Div, atty, 1976-77; Smothers, Douple, Gayton & Long, atty, 1977-83; Law Off Amy Goldson, atty, 1983-. **Orgs:** Cong Black Caucus Found, gen coun, 1978-; Black Entertainment & Sports Lawyers Asn, bd dirs, 1986-; Nat Bar Asn, 1976-; Am Bar Asn, 1976-; Mayor's Comt Entertainment, chairperson, 1994; Wash Area Lawyers Arts, 1992-; Wash Performing Arts Soc, bd dir, 1987-, SE Tennis & Learning Ctr and Recreation Wish List. **Honors/Awds:** First Group Scholar, Phi Beta Kappa, Smith Col, 1973. **Special Achievements:** Ct Admis: US Supreme Ct, 1980; DC Ct Appeals; US Ct Appeals, 1980; US Tax Ct, 1978; US Ct Mil Appeals, 1978; US Dist Ct, DC, 1978; US Ct Appeals 4th Circuit. **Business Addr:** Attorney, Law Off Amy Goldson, 4015 28th Pl NW, Washington, DC 20008, **Business Phone:** (202)966-7531.*

GOLDSTON, BOBBY F
Chief executive officer. **Career:** Family Ford Sales Inc, chief exec officer, currently. **Business Addr:** Chief Executive Officer, Family Ford Sales Inc, 1602 Florence Blvd, Florence, AL 35630, **Business Phone:** (256)764-3351.*

GOLDSTON, NATHANIEL R., III
Executive. **Personal:** Born Oct 20, 1938, Omaha, NE; son of Nathaniel II and Mary Burden; married A Darleen; children: Nathaniel IV, Steven, Kimberly. **Educ:** Univ Denver, BA, 1962. **Career:** Catering Mgt Inc, food serv dir, dist mgr & regional vpres, 1963-74; Gourmet Serv Inc, pres & chmn bd, 1975, chmn & ceo, currently. **Orgs:** chmn bd, Tuskegee Inst Food Serv Task Force; bd dirs, Atlanta Regional Comn; nat bd dirs, Am Bus Coun; Atlanta Chamber of Com, Am Mgt Asn, Pvt Indust Coun, Nat Restaurant Asn, GA Hospitality & Travel Asn; bd mem, Sch Hospitality & Mgt Wiley Col; Univ Denver Alumni Asn; bd trustees, Univ Denver, 1990-. **Honors/Awds:** Minority Bus Person of the Yr, Urban Bus Develop Ctr; Catalyst Award Most Outstanding New Bus, Interracial Coun Bus Opportunity, 1976; Black Enterprise Mag Ann Achievement Award in the Area of Serv, 1977; Columbia MO Restaurateur of the Yr, 1978; Leadership Atlanta, 1980; Minority Bus of the Yr, Interracial Coun for Bus Opportunity, 1981; Nat Urban League Cert of Appreciation, 1981. *

GOLDSTON, RALPH PETER
Scout, football coach. **Personal:** Born Feb 25, 1929, Campbell, OH; son of Richard and Alice; married Sarah Sloan; children: Ralph Jr, Ursula, Beverley & Monica. **Educ:** Youngstown Univ, BS, Educ, 1952. **Career:** Scout (retired), football coach; Burlington Cent High Sch, Burlington Ontario; Penguins, 1950-51; City Youngstown & Mahoning Co, surveyor during off-season; City Philadelphia, rec dir, 1952; Philadelphia Eagles, 1952-55; Hamilton Tiger-Cats, 1956-64; Burlington Ontario, teacher, 1962-67; Montreal Alouettes, 1965; Montreal Alouettes, 1966-69; Canadian Football League, pro coach, 1966; NY Giants, scout, 1970; Harvard Univ, 1971-72; Harvard Univ, coach, 1971-72; Univ Colo, coach 1973; Chicago Bears Club, asst football coach, 1974-75; Seattle Seahawks, scout, 1975-89; New England Patriots, scout, 1989-95. **Orgs:** All-Co HS Mahoning Co Ohio, 1945-46; Youngstown Univ, 1950-51, All-Pro defback CFL, 1956-63. **Honors/Awds:** Athletic scholarship, Ind Univ. *

GOLDWIRE, ANTHONY
Basketball player. **Personal:** Born Sep 6, 1971, West Palm Beach, FL; son of Willie and Betty. **Educ:** Univ Houston, sports mgt. **Career:** Yakima Sun Kings, CBA, 1994-96; Charlotte Hornets, guard, 1996; Denver Nuggets, 1997-98, 2001; San Antonio Spurs, 2002-03; Wash Wizards, 2002-03; Minn Timberwolves, 2003-04; NJ Nets, 2003-04; Detroit Pistons, 2005; Milwaukee Bucks, 2005; Los Angeles Clippers, guard, 2005-06; Panellinios Gymnastikos Syllogos, 2007; Lokomotiv Rostov, 2007-. **Honors/Awds:** All-Rookie second team, CBA, 1994-05; Second All-Rookie Team, CBA, 1994-95. **Special Achievements:** CBA, Championship, 1995.

GOLIDAY, WILLIE V.
Executive, chief executive officer, president (organization). **Personal:** Born Feb 22, 1956, Oxford, MS; married Mary Ann Cration. **Educ:** Jackson State Univ, BS, 1978, MBA, 1980. **Career:** Delta Capital Corp, investment analyst, 1980-82; Action Commun Co Inc, pres; Moeller Manufacturing, Inc, pres. **Orgs:** Advisor Jr Achievement, 1981; JSU Alumni Asn. **Honors/Awds:** Outstanding Young Man of America, 1985. **Home Addr:** 64 Milhem, Greenville, MS 38701. **Business Addr:** President, Chief Executive Officer, Action Communications Company Inc, PO Box 588, Greenville, MS 38701, **Business Phone:** (601)335-5291.

GOLIGHTLY, LENA MILLS
Composer, radio producer, writer. **Personal:** Born in Horse Cave, KY. **Educ:** Ky State Col, attended 1936. **Career:** Composer: "I Don't Worry", 1955; "Sugarpie Tears Easy Now", 1955; "Jack is Back", 1957; "Miss Bronzeville", 1961; "Eternal Flame", 1964; "Resurrection City USA", 1968; "Do Your Thing & I'll Do Mine", 1969; "King Dr", 1969; "I Had Too Much To Dream Last Night", 1970; Poems: Golden Chain of Friendship, 1967; Am You're Dying, 1969; WXFM-Radio, Chicago, IL, producer, 1966-; WBEE-Radio, Chicago, IL, producer, 1967; Ada S McKinley Comn Serv, active pub rels, 1967; Author: Premonition of Last Christmas, 1947, Top of the Mountain, 1967, The Seventh Child, 1967. **Orgs:** Nat Asn Media Women; Chicago Mus Asn; dir, Civic Liberty League IL; Nat Asn Advan Colored People; Urban League, AME Church; dir, Am Friendship Club; Chicago Mus Asn, 1965. **Honors/Awds:** Am Friendship Club Award, 1962-65; Award Merit, WVON, 1965, 1969; Awards Chicago, No Dist Asn Federated Clubs, 1966; WXFM, 1966; Carey Temple, 1966; WGRT Chicago, 1970; Nat Acad Best Dressed Churchwomen, 1972, 1973; Humanitarian Award, Baptist Foreign Mission Bur, 1973; Dr Martin Luther King Jr Humanitarian Award, Love Mem Missionary Baptist Church, 1974.

GOLLADAY, MAMIE HOWARD. **See HOWARD, DR. MAMIE R.**

GOLSON, BENNY
Musician, composer. **Personal:** Born Jan 25, 1929, Philadelphia, PA. **Educ:** Howard Univ, attended 1950; Honorary doctorates: William Paterson Col;Wayne, NJ; Berklee Sch Music, Boston, MA. **Career:** Tenor Saxaphonist, Composer & Arranger; Tv, film & ad scores, composer; albums: New York Scene, 1957; Gone With Golson, 1959; Gettin' With It, 1959; Meet the Jazz tet, 1960; Free, 1962; Stockholm Sojourn, 1964; Tune In, Turn On to the Hippest Commercials, 1967; Killer Joe, 1977; Benny Golson Quartet, 1990; Up Jumped Spring, 1990; I Remember Miles, 1992; Up Jumped Benny, 1997; Tenor Legacy, 1998; That's Funky, 2000; One Day Forever, 2001; Terminal 1, 2004; Free, 2004; Turning point, 2005; The Masquerade is Over, 2005; The Many Moods Of Benny Golson, 2007; Take A Number From 1 to 10, 2007; Three Little Words, 2007; New Time, New 'Tet, 2007; Carribean drifting; Park Avenue Petite. **Honors/Awds:** Grant, Guggenheim Found, 1995; American Jazz Masters Award, Nat Endowment Arts, 1996; BMI Music Award, 1998; William Paterson College, Wayne, NJ, hon doc. **Business Addr:** Musician, Klose & Klose, 6399 Wilshire Blvd Suite 1002, Los Angeles, CA 90048, **Business Phone:** (323)653-7826.

GOLSON, LEON
Executive director. **Career:** Midwest AIDS Prev Proj, prog dir; HIV/AIDS Resource Ctr, Ypsilanti, dir prev prog, currently. **Business Addr:** Director of Prevention Programs, HIV/AIDS Resource Center, 3075 Clark Rd Suite 203, Ypsilanti, MI 48197, **Business Phone:** 800-578-2300.

GOMES, REV. PETER JOHN
Clergy, college administrator. **Personal:** Born May 22, 1942, Boston, MA. **Educ:** Bates Col, Lewiston, AB, 1965; Harvard Divinity Sch, 1968; New England Col, DD, 1974; Waynesburg Col, LHD, 1978; Gordon Col, HumD, 1985. **Career:** Am Baptist Church, ordained ministry, 1968; Tuskegee Inst, AL, instr hist, dir fresmen expert prog 1968-70; The WEB Du Bois Inst Afro-Am Res, Harvard Univ, former acting dir; Harvard Univ, Memorial Church, asst minister, acting minister, 1970-74, minister, 1974-; Christian Morals & Pusey Minister, Plummer prof, 1974-. **Orgs:** Fellow, Royal Soc Arts; Royal Soc Church Music, Colonial Soc, MA; Farmington Inst Christian Studies; Am Bapt Hist Soc; Unitarian Hist Soc; pres, Signet Soc; Harvard Musical Asn; dir, English-Speaking Union; Phi Beta Kappa; trustee, Pilgrim Soc; Donation Liberia; Bates Col, 1973-78, 1980-; Charity Edward Hopkins; Boston Freedom Trail, 1976-; Plimoth Plantation; Rosbury Latin Sch; Wellesley Col; Boston Found; Jordon Hosp; Plymouth Pub Libr; pres, trustee, Int Fund Def & Aid S Africa; Nat chaplain, Am Guild Organists, 1978-82; Mass Hist Soc, currently; trustee, Nat Cathedral Sch, Wash, DC; trustee, Harvard Univ; trustee, The Roxbury Latin Sch; The Colonial Soc Mass; The Royal Soc Arts, London & England; past pres, The Signet Soc; Harvard's oldest literary soc; former trustee, Wellesley Col. **Special Achievements:** Books: Books of the Pilgrims; editor Parnassus, Co-auth, 1970; History of the Pilgrim Soc, Co-auth, 1970. **Business Addr:** Professor, Harvard University, Memorial Church, Harvard Yard, Cambridge, MA 02138.*

GOMES, WAYNE MAURICE
Baseball player. **Personal:** Born Jan 15, 1973, Hampton, VA; married Melissa Marie Gilbert, Nov 7, 1997. **Educ:** Old Dom Univ,

recreation & leisure studies. **Career:** Baseball player (retired); Philadelphia Phillies, pitcher, 1997-2001; San Francisco Giants, 2001; Boston Red Sox, pitcher, 2002; Oakland Athletics, pitcher, 2004. *

GOMEZ, DENNIS CRAIG
Labor relations manager. **Personal:** Born May 14, 1948, Suffern, NY; son of Carlos and Elizabeth; married Henrietta McAlister; children: Camille, Mark, Brian. **Educ:** S IL Univ, BA, 1971. **Career:** Chase Manhattan Bank, credit corres, 1971-72; Allstate Life Ins Co, office oper super, 1972-73, claim super, 1973, div supvr, 1973-74, personnel asst, 1974-76, personnel div mgr, 1976-79, human resources mgr, 1979-80, personnel serv mgr, 1980-82, regional personnel mgr, 1982-86, human resource dir, customer rels dir, 1987-88, field human resources dir, 1989-97, asst vp, 1997-01, vpres human resource, 2002. **Orgs:** ASPA; Urban League Phila; NAACP N Philadelphia br; chmn, OIC Fund Raising Montgomery Co, PA, 1985; CASA Lake County; Parent Coun Wake Forest Univ. *

GOMEZ, JEWELLE L
Writer. **Personal:** Born Sep 11, 1948, Boston, MA; daughter of John Gomez and Dolores LeClaire. **Educ:** Northeastern Univ, BA, 1971; Columbia Univ, Ford Found Fel, MS, jour, 1973. **Career:** Hunter Col lectr, 1989-91; NY State Coun Arts, prog assoc, 1983-90, dir lit, 1990-93; New Col, lectr, 1993-94; Menlo Col, vis writer, 1993; Poetry Ctr & Am Poetry Archives San Francisco State Univ, exec dir, 1996-99; Cult Equity Grants Prog, San Francisco Arts Comn, dir, 2001-06; Horizons Found, prog off, 2006-. **Orgs:** Founding bd mem, Gay & Lesbian Alliance Against Defamation, 1988-90; bd mem, Open Meadows Found, 1989-; ed adv bd, Belle Lettres, 1990-96; ed adv bd, Multi-Cult Rev, 1991-95; adv bd, Cornell Univ Human Sexuality Archives, 1992-; bd mem, Coalition Against Censorship, 1993-; Astraea Nat Lesbian Found; Open Meadows Found. **Honors/Awds:** Lambda Lit Awards, Fiction & Sci Fiction, 1991; Barbara Deming, Money for Women Fund, fiction, 1987; Bead's Fund Award for Fiction, 1985; Calif Arts Coun, Artist in Residence, 1994, 1995; fel, Nat Endowment for Arts, 1997. **Special Achievements:** Author: The Lipstick Papers, Grace Publs, 1980; Flamingoes & Bears, Grace Publs, 1986; The Gilda Stories, Firebrand Books, 1991; Forty Three Septembers, Firebrand Books, 1993; Oral Tradition: Poems Selected & New, Firebrand Books, 1995; Playwright "Bones & Ash: A Gilda Story" US tour, 1995-96; Don't Explain: Short Fiction, Firebrand Books, 1998. **Business Addr:** Program Officer, Horizons Foundation, 870 Market St Suite 728, San Francisco, CA 94102, **Business Phone:** (415)398-2333.

GOMEZ, DR. MICHAEL A
Writer, college teacher. **Educ:** Univ Chicago, BA, african hist, 1981, MA, african hist, 1982; PhD, african hist, 1985. **Career:** Wash Univ, St Louis, MO, Dept Hist/African & Afro-Am Studies, asst prof, 1985-88; Spelman Col, GA, Dept Hist, from asst prof to assoc prof, 1988-97; Spelman Col, dept Hist, chair, 1989-92, 1993-97, dir African Diaspora & World Core Curri Course, 1992-97; Univ Ga, Athens, Dept Hist/African Am Studies, prof, 1997-99; NY Univ, Dept Hist & Dept Middle Eastern & Islamic Studies, prof, 1999-, chair, Dept Hist, 2004-07. **Orgs:** Dir, Asn Study Worldwide African Diaspora (ASWAD), 2000-07. **Business Addr:** Professor, Chair, New York University, Department of History, 53 Wash Sq S 7th Fl Rm 511, New York, NY 10012-1098, **Business Phone:** (212)998-8618.*

GONA, DR. OPHELIA DELAINE
Research scientist, educator. **Personal:** Born Jul 4, 1936, South Carolina; daughter of Joseph Armstrong and Mattie; married Amos; children: Shantha & Raj. **Educ:** Johnson C Smith Univ, BS, 1957; Yeshiva Univ, MS, 1965; City Col NY, MA, 1967; City Univ NY, PhD (biol), 1971. **Career:** Research scientist (retired); City Col NY, res asst, teacher asst,1966-70; Peace Corps Volunteer Ghana, 1961-63; Eastern Dist High Sch Brooklyn, biol teacher, 1958-61; Cornell Univ Med Sch, lab tech 1957-58;Montclair State Col, asst prof biol, 1970-77; NJ Col Med & Dent, asst prof anat; UMD-NJ Med Sch, assoc prof Anat, 1986, dir, 2001; NIH grant. **Orgs:** Educ consult, Hoffman LaRoche Pharms, 1972-73; AIBS, AAAS, Am Asn Anatomists, ARVO, NY Acad Sci. **Honors/Awds:** Distinguished Alumnus, Johnson Smith Univ, 2004; Golden Apple Award. **Special Achievements:** Author of scientific publications concerning comparative endocrinology ofprolactin cataracts of the lens of the eye; developer of computer-based instructional materials for Gross Anatomy, 1972-77.

GONGA, DAWILLI. See DUKE, GEORGE M.

GONZALEZ, ANITA LOUISE
Artist, educator. **Personal:** Born Feb 20, 1957, Newark, NJ; daughter of Cambell and Juanita Nash; married Feb 20, 2002 (divorced); children: Xochina Cora El Hilali; married Feb 20, 2002. **Educ:** NY Univ, attended 1976; Fla State Univ, BA, 1977; Am Univ, MA, 1979; Univ Wis, PhD, 1997. **Career:** Viacom, asst dir, 1983-86; NYPL Lincoln Ctr, film video activist, 1987-92; Urban Bush Women, performer, 1984-89; Bandana Women, artistic dir, 1985-95; Beloit Col, scholar in residence, 1995-96; Conn Col, asst prof, 1997-99; Fla State Univ, asst prof; State Univ NY, Dept Theatre Arts, assoc prof, currently; dir, writer & choreographer. **Orgs:** Bd dir, Mad Alex Arts Found, 1984-86; resident artist, Thompkins Square Libr, 1986-90; artistic dir, Stack Motion Prod, 1987-92; resident artist, Tribeca Performing Arts Ctr, 1993-96; bd dir, Soc Dance Hist Scholars, 1998-2004; artist comt, Performance Studies Int, 1999-; Am Soc Theatre, 2000-; founder, Art Boundaries Unlimited. **Honors/Awds:** Fulbright Senior Scholar, 1987, 1992. **Special Achievements:** Author: Hola Ola, 1996; Yanga, 1996; Conjure Women, PBS film, 1997-99; Migrant Imaginations, 1999; "Directory As Cultural Exchange," Latinas Onstage, 2000; The Mother Courage Project, 2001; Cigar Memories, 2002. **Home Addr:** 187 Beechwood Dr, Crawfordville, FL 32327, **Home Phone:** (850)926-7168. **Business Addr:** Associate Professor, State University of New York, Department of Theatre Arts, CT 110 1 Hawk Dr, New Paltz, NY 12561, **Business Phone:** (845)380-1499.

GONZALEZ, CAMBELL
Engineer, financial manager. **Personal:** Born Aug 26, 1918, Tampa, FL; married Juanita Nash; children: Amelia, Anita & John. **Educ:** Howard Univ, BSEE, 1949; Stevens Inst, grad courses; Brooklyn Polytech, Newark Col Engineering. **Career:** Engineer, financial manager (retired); RCA, engr training, 1949, applied engr, 1950-55; design devel engr, 1955-70; proj engr, 1970-82; Col Financial Planning, Denver, CO, CFP, 1983-86. **Orgs:** Inst Elec & Electronics Engineers; bd dir, YMCA, Orange, NJ; Alpha Phi Alpha Fraternity; planning bd, adv gr, Reading Township; Sewer Adv Commn; teacher elder, Flemington Presby Church; pres, Inv Club Alumni; Rotary Club Flemington, NJ, 1990. **Honors/Awds:** Achievement Award, Howard Univ, 1957; tech art pub, RCA Engr IRE Trans Electronics; Pat disclosure, RCA. **Military Serv:** AUS, commanding officer, 1942-52. **Home Addr:** 158 W Woodschurch Rd, Flemington, NJ 08822. *

GONZALEZ, TONY
Football player, businessperson. **Personal:** Born Feb 27, 1976, Huntington Beach, CA; children: Nikko. **Educ:** California. **Career:** Oliver Stone Prod, consult; Kans City Chiefs, tight end, 1997-; Sutra Restaurant, partner, currently. **Honors/Awds:** Role Model of the Yr; 2004 Natl Football League Good Guy; Presidential Volunteer Award, 2004; "NFL Good Guy", The Sporting News. **Special Achievements:** NFL Draft, First round pick, 1997; Formed the 'Tony Gonzalez Found'; The second-longest active string on the roster; Film & TV appearances: Spike TV, "Super gents"; "ABC, Extreme Makeover: Wedding Edition"; Shock Wave; "ABC, Married With the Kellys"; HBO, "Arliss"; Introduced "Books and Buddies" prog, 2003; featured on MTVs 'Cribs' in 2005; Tony Gonzalez Football Camp, 2005; Authored a book for adolescents in 2005 entitled 'Catch & Connect'; Spokesman for various Oper: Oper Shadow Buddies; Chiefs United Way; Susan G. Komen Race for the Cure for Breast Cancer; Midwest Donor Organ Bank; US Dept Transp Safety Campaign; state of Kans Sch Safety Hotline; Becoming the youngest individual ever named to "40 Under 40" list. **Business Addr:** Professional Football Player, Kansas City Chiefs, 1 Arrowhead Dr, Kansas City, MO 64129, **Business Phone:** (816)924-9300.

GONZAQUE, OZIE BELL
City commissioner. **Personal:** Born Jun 8, 1925, Thornton, AR; daughter of John Henry Woods and Wilie Lee Brown; married Roy Sylvester Gonzaque, Mar 15, 1955; children: Frieda Elaine, Barbara Jean, Bernadette, Roy Jr, Janet, Mary Nadene, Joseph Gregory. **Educ:** Southwest Col, cert; Univ Southern Calif, cert. **Career:** Fradelis Frozen Foods, Los Angeles, CA, prod supvr, 1951-63; Dist Attys Evelle Younger, Joseph Busch & John Von DeCamp, adv coun mem, 1969-84; Atty Gen Evelle Younger, adv coun mem, 1971-83; Bur Consumer Affairs, advert & promotional policy vol, 1972-84; Juv Justice Ctr, vol, 1977-79; Los Angeles Housing Authority, comnr, 1985-. **Orgs:** Chmn bd, HACLA, 2003; Dir bd, S Cent Social Serv Corp; Community Develop Comn, County Los Angeles; pres, Southeast Businessmen's Booster Asn; bd dirs, LA Community Develop Bank. **Honors/Awds:** Public Serv Award, ABLE, 1985; People's Choice Award, People's Choice Inc, 1985; Woman of the Yr, State Calif Legis Body, 1989; Achievement Award, NOBLE, 1990; Commissioner of teh Yr, Nat Asn Housing & Redevelopment Officials, 1998; Woman of the Yr Award, Assemblywoman Maxine Waters; Meritorious Award, LAPD. **Business Addr:** Commissioner, Los Angeles Housing Authority Department, 515 Columbia Ave, Los Angeles, CA 90017, **Business Phone:** (213)484-6772.*

GOOCH, JEFFREY LANCE
Football player. **Personal:** Born Oct 31, 1974, Nashville, TN; married Tonya. **Educ:** Austin Peay State Univ. **Career:** Tampa Bay Buccaneers, linebacker, 1996-2001, 2004-05; Detroit Lions, linebacker, 2002-03; free agent, currently. **Honors/Awds:** Most Valuable Player Award, Yale Lary Special Teams.

GOOD, MEGAN MONIQUE
Actor. **Personal:** Born Aug 8, 1981, Panorama City, CA. **Career:** Films: House Party 3, 1994; Friday, 1995; Make a Wish, Molly, 1995; Eve's Bayou, 1997; The Secret Life of Girls, 1999; 3 Strikes, 2000; House Party 4: Down to the Last Minute, 2001; Awakenings 1, 2001; Awakenings 2, 2001; Ride Or Die, 2003; Deliver Us from Eva, 2003; Biker Boyz, 2003; DEBS, 2004; The Cookout, 2004; You Got Served, 2004; Roll Bounce, 2005; Venom, 2005; Waist Deep, 2006; Scarface: The World Is Yours, 2006; Miles from Home, 2006; Stomp the Yard, 2007; One Missed Call, 2008; The Love Guru, 2008; Saw V, 2008; The Unborn, 2009; TV Series: "Just One of the Girls", 1997; "The Famous Jett Jackson", 1998-2001; "Don't Stand Too Close to Me", 2000; "He Doth Protest Too Much", 2000; "Raising Dad", 2001; "My Wife & Kids", 2001; "The Parent Trap", 2001; "The Division", 2001-04; "Graduation: Part 1", 2003; "Graduation: Part 2", 2003; "Here Comes Da Judge", 2003; "Jr.'s Risky Business: Part 1", 2003; "Jr's Risky Business: Part 2", 2003; "Kevin Hill", 2004-05; "Losing Isn't Everything", 2005; "Sacrificial Lambs", 2005; "Cardiac Episode", 2005; "Occupational Hazard", 2005; "Brick", 2005; Sundays in Fort Greene, producer, 2008; Miles from Home, producer, 2006; "House M.D.", 2007; "All of Us", 2007; "Cold Case", 2009. **Honors/Awds:** Nominee, Image Award for Outstanding Youth Actor/Actress, 1998; nominee, Young Star Award, 1998; nominee, Black Movie Award, 2005; Independent Black Film Festival Award, 2006; nominee, Teen Choice Award, 2006. **Business Addr:** Actress, c/o Agency Performing Arts, 9200 W Sunset Blvd Suite 900, Los Angeles, CA 90069, **Business Phone:** (310)273-0744.*

GOODALL, HURLEY CHARLES
State government official, politician. **Personal:** Born May 23, 1927, Muncie, IN; son of Hurley Charles and Dorene Mukes; married Fredine Wynn, May 1, 1948; children: Hurley E Jr & Fredrick. **Educ:** Ind Bus Col, attended 1949; Purdue Univ, time & motion courses, 1952. **Career:** Firefighter (retired), government official (retired), politician; Muncie Malleable Foundry Co, 1944-50, time & motion steward, 1950-58; Muncie Fire Dept, fire fighter, 1958-78; Hur Co Inc, owner; Muncie Bd Educ, mem, 1970-78, pres, 1974-75; Del Co, IN, asst co engr, 1978-80; Ind House of Reps, St rep, 1978-92, asst fl leader, 1989-92; Middletown Ctr Ball St Univ, vis fel & vis scholar. **Orgs:** Pres, Whitely Community Coun, 1966-69; chair, Cent Reg, Nat Black Caucus Sch, 1972-78; bd trustee, Muncie Sch Bd Trustee, 1974-75; bd mem, WIPB-TV Chan 49 Muncie PBS Sta, 1974-80; chmn, Ind Black Leg Caucus, 1979-92; In Jobs Training Coord Coun; Gov Comn Minority Bus Develop; Muncie Human Rights Comn; coun mem, United Way Community Serv; comt mem, Ind Sch Bd Asn. **Honors/Awds:** Muncie Black Hall of Fame, Multi-Serv Ctr Muncie, 1979; Government Service Award, OIC DE County, 1980; Horatio Alger Award, Muncie Boys Club, 1984; President's Medal, Ball St Univ, 1992; Nation Builder Award, NBCSL,1992; Service Award, IN chap NAACP, 1999; Distinguished Hoosier Award, Ind Arts Comn, 2000; hon doctorate, Ball St Univ, 2007. **Special Achievements:** He was one of the first two African-Americans selected to work for the fire department; He also was the first African-American selected to serve on the Muncie Community Schools Board of Education; co-author, History of Negroes in Muncie, Ball St Press, 1974; Inside the House, Ball St Press, 1995. **Military Serv:** AUS, pfc, 1945-47. **Home Addr:** 1905 E Carver Dr, Muncie, IN 47303.

GOODE, BRUCE T
President (Organization), chief executive officer. **Educ:** Univ Toledo, BS. **Career:** EB Magic Fund, sub-adv, currently; Goode Investment Mgt Inc, pres & chief exec officer, currently. **Orgs:** Bd trustees, Cleveland Restoration Soc. **Business Addr:** President, Chief Executive Officer, Goode Investment Management Inc, 1700 Terminal Tower 50 Pub Sq Suite 904, Cleveland, OH 44113-2207, **Business Phone:** (216)771-9000.*

GOODE, CALVIN C.
Government official. **Personal:** Born Jan 27, 1927, Depew, OK; married Georgie M; children: Vernon, Jerald & Randolph. **Educ:** Phoenix Col, AA, 1947; AZ State Col, BS, 1949; AZ State Univ, MA, 1972. **Career:** Goode & Asso Tax & Acct Srev, owner & oper, 1950-; Phoenix Union HS Dist, sch community worker, 1969, sch bus mgr, asst property control dir, asst budget dir, 1949-69; Phoenix City Councilman, 1972-94; Phoenix City V Mayor, 1974, 1984. **Orgs:** Bd mem, Community Coun; dir, Investment Opportunities Inc; CTA, AEA, NEA; United Fund Budget Com; Phoenix Urban Leag; Nat Asn Advan Colored People; bd chmn, BT Wash Child Develop Ctr Inc; co-chmn, Child Care Proj Comm Coun; Omega Psi Phi Frat; Downtown Breakfast Optimist Club; bd mem, George Wash Carver Mus & Cult Ctr,2008. **Honors/Awds:** Hon Kachina Volunteer Award, 2004; Lifetime Achievement award, named in honor, 2006. **Home Addr:** 1508 E Jefferson, Phoenix, AZ 85034, **Home Phone:** (602)253-5845. *

GOODE, GEORGE RAY
Government official. **Personal:** Born Feb 8, 1930, Clifton Forge, VA; married Doris Hatcher (deceased); children: Cassandra White, George Jr, Ava, Stanley, Kim Rickten, Carren, Stacey & Dana. **Educ:** Va Seminary Ext, attended 1976. **Career:** City Clifton Forge, city councilman, 1974, mayor. **Orgs:** Chmn, Greater Allegheny United Fund, 1984. **Home Addr:** 700 Pine St, Clifton Forge, VA 24422, **Home Phone:** (540)862-2736. **Business Addr:** Mayor, City Clifton Forge, 600 Main St, Clifton Forge, VA 24422.*

GOODE, JAMES EDWARD
Clergy. **Personal:** Born Nov 18, 1943, Roanoke, VA. **Educ:** Immaculate Conceptn Col, BA, 1969; Col St Rose, MA, 1971; St

Anthony Theol Sem, MDiv, 1972, MTh, 1974; PhD; Univ Louvain Belgium, post-doctoral studies, 1980. **Career:** Our Lady Charity, pastor, 1974-; City Univ NY, adj prof, 1975-, chaplain, 1975-; Ctr Positive Directn, dir, 1976-; Black Religious Experne Inst, co-dir; Directions A Jour of Black Ch/Comm Studies, ed; Nat Black Cath Apostolate Life, founder & pres, currently; Survival & Faith Inst of NY, cons; Juvenile Justice Task Force of Ctrl Brooklyn, cons; Off Black Ministry Diocese Brooklyn, bd dirs; Bldg a Better Brooklyn, bd dirs; lectr, psychol & theol; Solid Ground Franciscan Ministry, Pastoral dir; Solid Ground Ministry, founder. **Orgs:** NY City Comn Sch Bd; Cent Brooklyn Youth & Family Servs; Juvenile Prev Progs Brooklyn; NY City Comn Planning Bd; Culture & Worship Adv Bd Nat Offc for Black Cath; Coalition of Concerned Black Educrs NY; Black Ministers Coun; Nat Black Cath Clergy; Nat Asn Black Social Workers; Educ Task Force for Positive Direction of NY Urban Comn; hon mem, Catholic Social Workers Asn. **Honors/Awds:** DHL, VA Theol Sem; Preacher of First Black Cath Revival in US Chicago, 1974; Martin Luther King Scholrship, NY Univ, 1975-76; Black Cath Leadership Award; proclmtn declaring Nov 18 1978 Father James E Goode Day NY City, 1978; proclmtn declaring Nov 16 1979 Father James E Goode Day Mayor of Brooklyn, 1979; Nat Black Cath Clergy Tribute Award, 1979; proclmtn, NY State Assembly; lead, Nat Protest Prayer Serv Against Budget Cuts in Human Servs. **Special Achievements:** Numerous publs, "Catholicsm & Slavery in US" Labor Press, 1975; "Ministry in the 80's in the Black Comm" Liberation Press, 1980; The first Black Catholic Pastor in the Archdiocese of San Francisco. **Business Addr:** Pastoral Director, Solid Ground Ministries, 440 W 36th St, New York, NY 10018-6326.*

GOODE, REV. W. WILSON
Executive. **Personal:** Born Aug 19, 1938, Seaboard, NC; son of Albert and Rozelar; married Velma Helen Williams, 1960; children: Muriel, W Wilson Jr & Natasha. **Educ:** Morgan State Univ, BA, hist & polit sci, 1961; Univ Pa, Wharton Sch, MPA, 1968; Eastern Baptist Theol Sem, DMin, 2000. **Career:** Philadelphia Coun Community Advan, pres & chief exec officer, 1966-78; Pa Pub Utilities Comn, chmn 1978-80; City Philadelphia, managing dir, 1980-82; City Philadelphia, mayor, 1984-92; Goode Group, pres & chief exec officer, 1992-; US Dept Educ, secy regional rep, region III; probation officer; bldg maintenance supr; insurance claims adjuster; Faith Based Initiatives Pub & Pvt Ventures, sr adv, currently. **Orgs:** Founder, Goode Cause Inc; Eastern Univ; chair, Free Libr Philadelphia; chair, Cornerstone Christian Acad; chair, Self Inc; chair, Philadelphia Leadership Found; vice-chair, Coun Leadership Found. **Honors/Awds:** Numerous honorary degrees in US Universities; Purpose Prize. **Special Achievements:** First black mayor of Philadelphia, PA; Author, In Goode Faith, autobiography, 1992. **Military Serv:** AUS, Mil police, CPT, 1961-63; Commendation Medal, meritorious service. **Business Addr:** Senior Advisor, Faith Based Initiatives for Public & Private Ventures, 2000 Market St Suite 600, Philadelphia, PA 19103, **Business Phone:** (215)557-4400.

GOODE, WILLIE K.
President (Organization). **Career:** Amco Disposal; Garbage Collection Enterprise, pres, 1991-. **Business Phone:** (301)779-4208.*

GOODE, HON. WILSON
Government official. **Personal:** Born Aug 9, 1965, Philadelphia, PA; son of W Wilson and Velma W. **Educ:** Univ Pa, BA, 1986. **Career:** Philadelphia Com Develop Corp, vpres, 1991-99; Philadelphia City Coun, city councilman at-Large, currently. **Orgs:** Alpha Phi Alpha Fraternity Inc, 1984-; Young Am Polit Comt, 1997-. **Honors/Awds:** 100 People to Watch, Business Philadelphia Magazine, 1993; Minority Executive Award, 40 under 40, 2001. **Special Achievements:** Author: New Leadership for a Community Development Agenda, 1998. **Business Addr:** City Councilman At-Large, Philadelphia City Council, City Hall Rm 316, Philadelphia, PA 19107, **Business Phone:** (215)686-3414.

GOODEN, C. MICHAEL
Executive. **Career:** Integrated Systs Analysts Inc, chmn & chief exec officer, currently. **Special Achievements:** Company ranked #34 on Black Enterprise's list of Top 100 Industrial/Service Companies, 1992. **Military Serv:** USN, eng duty officer & comdr, 25 yrs. **Business Addr:** Chairman, Chief Executive officer, Integrated Systems Analysts Inc, 2800 Shirlington Rd Suite 1100, Arlington, VA 22202, **Business Phone:** (703)824-0100.*

GOODEN, CHERRY ROSS
Educator. **Personal:** Born Nov 7, 1942, Calvert, TX; daughter of John R and Ludia Beavers; children: Deron LeJohn & DeShaunda Lorraine. **Educ:** Tex Southern Univ, BS, elem educ, 1964, MEd, elem educ, 1972; Univ Houston, EdD, 1991. **Career:** Houston Independent Sch Dist, teacher, 1964-76; NAME board, President Elect, 2007-09; Tex Southern Univ, asst prof, assoc prof & interim chair, currently. **Orgs:** Consult, Sch Dists State, 1981-; bo mem, Lockhart Tech Acad, 1984-86; Texas Southern Chapter Phi Delta Kappa; former treas, Houston Chapter Jack& Jill Amer, chaplain 1st vpres & pres; Humble-Intercontinental ChapterTop Ladies Distinction; Houston Chapter Nat Women Achievement; mem, AlphaKappa Alpha Sorority; mem, Nat Alliance Black Sch Educrs, 1988-; mem, Asn Teacher Educrs, 1986-; mem, Asn Supv & Curriculum Develop, 1987-; Nat Asn Multicultural Educ; Tex Asn Black Personnel Higher Educ; Int Reading Asn. **Honors/Awds:** Publication in Texas Tech Journal of Educ, 1984; publication in Journal of Educational Equity 1985; appeared in Black History in the Making, Vol 1Published by Riverside Hospital Houston, TX; Learning Styles of Urban Children, Texas Southern Univ, 1990. **Special Achievements:** Listed in Who's Who Among Black Americans and Who's Who in American Education. **Business Addr:** Associate Professor, Interim Chairman, Texas Southern University Department of Curriculum & Instruction, ED 204 3100 Cleburne St, Houston, TX 77004, **Business Phone:** (713)313-1922.

GOODEN, DOC. See GOODEN, DWIGHT EUGENE.

GOODEN, DWIGHT EUGENE (DOC GOODEN)
Actor, baseball player. **Personal:** Born Nov 16, 1964, Tampa, FL; son of Dan Gooden and Ella May Gooden; married Monica Harris, Nov 21, 1987 (divorced 2004); children: Devin, Darren, Ariel & Ashley. **Career:** Baseball player (retired); NY Mets, pitcher, 1984-94; NY Yankees, 1996-97, 2000; Cleveland Indians, 1998-99; Houston Astros, 2000; Tampa Bay Devil Rays, 2000. Film: Batman Begins, 2005. **Honors/Awds:** Nat League Rookie of the Year, Baseball Writers Asn of Am, 1984; NL Player of the Week; Topps Major League Rookie All-Star Team; Honoree Jackie Robinson Award for Athletics; Cy Young Award winner, 1985; Sporting News NL Pitcher of the Year; Male Athlete of the Year, Asniated Press, 1985; New York Athlete of the Year, Sports Channel, 1985; Silver Slugger Award, Nat league, 1992. **Special Achievements:** Books: Heat (memoir), 1999; First pitcher in major league history to strike out 200 batters in each of his first three seasons.

GOODEN, LINDA
Executive. **Educ:** Youngstown State Univ, BS; San Diego State Univ; Univ Md, BS bus admin; Univ Md Univ Col, hon dr pub serv. **Career:** Lockheed Martin's Info & Technol Servs, vpres, 1994-2006, dep exec vpres & pres, currently; Gen Dynamics San Diego, engr. **Orgs:** Armed Forces Communs & Electronics Asn Int; Info Technol Asn Am; Univ Md, A. James Clark Sch Engr & Robert H. Smith Sch Bus Ctr Electronic Markets & Enterprises; Univ Md, Baltimore County; & Prince George's Community Col Found; Md Bus Roundtable Educ; Exec Leadership Coun. **Honors/Awds:** Annual Peat Marwick High Tech Entrepreneur Award, 1994; Corporate Leadership Award, Women Technol, 2002; Black Engr Year, US Black Engr & IT Mag, 2006; Eagle Award, Fed Comput Week. **Business Addr:** President, Executive Vice President, Lockheed Martin Information Technology, 6801 Rockledge Dr, Bethesda, MD 20817-1836, **Business Phone:** (301)897-6000.

GOODEN, WINSTON EARL
Educator, dean (education), clinical psychologist. **Educ:** Muskingum Col, BA; Yale Univ Divinity Sch, MDiv, MS, PhD. **Career:** Pvt pract, clin psychol, 1984-; Fuller Theol Sem, asst prof, assoc prof psychol, dean, 2000-; Two Churches Conn, pastored; Unoja Juv Prog, co-founder & dir; Univ Ill, Chicago, asst prof. **Orgs:** Am Psychol Asn; Nat Coun Schs & Progs Prof Psychol. **Special Achievements:** Published many articles; presented papers across the nation. **Business Addr:** Associate Professor, Dean, Fuller Theological Seminary, Sch Psychol, 135 N Oakland Ave, Pasadena, CA 91182.*

GOODING, CUBA
Actor. **Personal:** Born Jan 2, 1968, Bronx, NY; son of Cuba Gooding Sr and Shirley; married Sara Kapfer, 1994; children: Spencer, Mason & Piper. **Career:** Films: Boyz N the Hood, 1991; Gladiator, 1992; A Few Good Men, 1992; Lightning Jack, 1994; Outbreak, 1995; Losing Isaiah, 1995; Jerry Maguire, 1996; As Good As It Gets, 1997; What Dreams May Come, 1998; A Murder of Crows, producer, 1999; Chill Factor, 1999; Instinct, 1999; Men of Honor, 2000; Pearl Harbor, 2001; Rat Race, 2001; Snow Dogs, 2002; Boat Trip, 2003; Psychic, 2003; The Fighting Tempations, 2003; Radio, 2003; Shadowboxer, 2005; Dirty, 2005; End Game, 2005; Norbit, 2006; What LKove Is, 2006; Daddy Day Camp, 2006; American Gangster, 2007; Hero Wanted, 2007; The Land Before Time XIII: The Wisdom of Friends, 2007; TV: "Murder Without Motive: The Edmund Perry Story," 1992; "Daybreak," HBO special, 1993; "The Tuskegee Airmen," HBO Movie, 1995; "Home on the Range," 2004; "The 2006 Black Movie Awards," 2006. **Honors/Awds:** Academy Award, Best Supporting Actor, 1997; American Comedy Award for Funniest Supporting Actor in a Motion Picture, 1997; Blockbuster Entertainment Award for Favorite Supporting Actor - Comedy/Romance, 1997; BFCA Award for Best Supporting Actor, 1997; CFCA Award for Best Supporting Actor, 1997; Nominee for Golden Globe Best Performance by an Actor in a Supporting Role in a Motion Picture, 1997; Golden Satellite Award for Best Performance by an Actor in a Supporting Role in a Motion Picture, Comedy or Musical, 1997; Screen Actors Guild Award for Outstanding Performance by a Male Actor in a Supporting Role, 1997; Blockbuster Entertainment Award Favorite Supporting Actor, Drama/Romance, 1999; Hollywood Walk of Fame, 2002; Image Award, 2004; CAmie Award, 2005. **Special Achievements:** Listed as one of twelve "Promising New Actors of 1991" in John Willis' Screen World, 1991; one of the 50 most beautiful people in the world, People Mag, 1997. **Business Phone:** (310)859-4000.

GOODING, OMAR
Actor. **Personal:** Born Oct 19, 1976, Bronx, NY; son of Cuba Sr and Shirley. **Career:** Tv series: "Just the Ten of Us", 1990; "Wild & Crazy Kids", 1990; "Hangin'with Mr. Cooper", 1992; "Blossom", 1992; "Thea", 1994; "Smart Guy", 1997; "Batman Beyond", 2000; "Static Shock", 2000; "Touched by an Angel", 2001; "The Division", 2002; "One on One", 2003; "Play makers", 2003-06; "Barbershop", 2005; "Mysterious Island", 2005; "Deadwood", 2006; "CSI:Miami", 2006; "Miami Trauma"; films: Ghost Dad, 1990; The Ernest Green Story, 1993; Freedom Song, 2000; Baby Boy, 2001; Verbal Communications, 2002; The Gospel, 2005; The Candy Shop, 2006; Lord Help Us, 2007; The Candy Shop, 2008; Knuckle Draggers, 2009. **Honors/Awds:** Young Artist Award, 1992; Special Mention, 2001; nomination, Image Award, 2006. **Business Addr:** Actor, c/o Talentworks, 3500 W Olive Ave Suite 1400, Burbank, CA 91505, **Business Phone:** (818)972-4300.*

GOODLOE, CELESTINE WILSON
School administrator. **Personal:** Born May 7, 1954, Brooklyn, NY; married John W Goodloe Jr; children: Jasmine R & Courtney M. **Educ:** Bennett Col, BS, 1976; Miami Univ, MS, 1982. **Career:** Bennett Col, admin counr, 1979-81; Miami Univ, grad asst, 1981-82; Col Wooster, asst dir, coord minority, 1982-84; Xavier Univ, assoc dir admin, 1984-, dir transfer recruitment & dir undergrad transfer admission, 2000-, Currently. **Orgs:** Ohio Asn Col Admin Counrs, 1980-; panel participant, NACAC, 1982, 1985; Am Personnel & Guid Asn, 1981-82; local arrangement comt mem, OACAC Spring Conf, 1994; Nat Asn Foreign Stud Advs, 1994; local arrangements comt mem, Region VI, NAFSA Conf, 1996; Southern Ohio Transfer Coun, 1999; pres, Southern, Ohio Transfer Coun, 2000-; vpres, Greater Cincinnati Alliance Black Sch Educrs; Nat Alliance Black Sch Educrs. **Honors/Awds:** Marie Clapp Moffitt Scholarship, Bennett Col, 1975; Advisor of the Year, Xavier Univ, 1993-94. **Business Addr:** Director, Undergraduate Transfer Admission, Xavier University, Off Admis 3800 Victory Pkwy, Cincinnati, OH 45207-5311, **Business Phone:** (513)745-3163.

GOODMAN, GEORGE D
Association executive. **Personal:** Born Sep 13, 1940, Saginaw, MI; son of George V and Thelma Kaigler; married Judith A Mansfield; children: George & Mark. **Educ:** BA, 1963; MA, 1970. **Career:** Association executive (retired); Eastern Mich Univ, instr, 1967-68; Univ Mich, asst dir admis, 1968-73, Opportunity Prog, dir, 1973-82; City Ypsilanti, mayor, 1972-82; Mich Munic League, exec dir, 1983, gov bd, 1990-93, pres, chief exec officer, 2005-08; Nat Acad Pub Admin, fel, 1998. **Orgs:** Life mem, Alpha Phi Alpha Frat; Emanon Club, 1967-; trustee, Starr Commonwealth Schs, 1983-92; United Way Mich Bd Dir, 1987-; Ann Arbor Summer Festival Bd, 1988-96; Nat Governing Bd, Common Cause, 1990-94; pres, Mich Munic League Found, 1991; chmn, United Way Mich Bd, 1994-96; Nat League Cities, gov bd, Pub Technol Inc, 1996; Nat Asn Co. **Honors/Awds:** Distinguished Service Award, Ypsilanti Area Jaycees, 1973; Public Service Achievement Award, Common Cause, 1987. **Military Serv:** AUS, capt, 1963-67.

GOODMAN, HAROLD
Executive. **Personal:** Born Jun 3, 1954, Beaumont, TX; son of Harold C Sr and Gloria Lee; married Jean, Jun 7, 1980; children: Harold P, Winston E. **Educ:** Prairie View A&M Univ, BA, mgt, 1976, MBA, 1978. **Career:** Fed Express Corp, mgr station ops, 1982-84, sr ramp mgr, Houston Metro Dist, 1985-89, sr dist mgr, IAH Dist, 1989-91, managing dir, 1991-. **Orgs:** bd dir, Oakland PIC, 1991-93; bd dir, Oakland Conv & Visitor's Bur, 1991-93; bd dir, Oakland Chamber Com, 1994-. **Business Addr:** Managing Director, Federal Express Corporation, 1 Sally Ride Way, Oakland, CA 94621.*

GOODMAN, DR. JAMES ARTHUR
School administrator, consultant. **Personal:** Born Apr 22, 1933, Portsmouth, VA; son of Accie and Viola James; married Gwendolyn Jones, Apr 12, 1956; children: James A Jr & Rhonda. **Educ:** Morehouse Col, AB, 1956; Atlanta Univ, MSW, 1958; Univ Minn, PhD, 1967. **Career:** Nat Acad Sci, Inst Med, Wash, DC, sr prof assoc, 1973-75; Univ Minn, Sch Social Work, Minneapolis, MN, prof & dir, 1975-77; State Dept, Off Int Training, Wash, DC, dir, 1977-79; Inst Pub Mgt, Wash, DC, exec vpres, 1979-83; Morehouse Sch Med, Atlanta, GA, assoc dean admin, 1980, vpres admin & policy, exec vpres, 1985-89, pres, 1989-91; Managed Healthcare Syst, chief exec officer; prof consult; Rivera, Sierra & Co Inc, assoc consult, currently. **Orgs:** Ed adv bd mem, Ment Health Digest, 1971-73; bd dir, Atlanta Urban League, 1981-88; HealthSouth Inc, 1982-88; DeKalb County Hosp Authority, 1984-88; Nat Adv Coun Educ Health Prof, 1985-89; Rotary Int; Nat Accreditation Comt, Coun Social Work Educ; Nat Asn Social Workers; Acad Certified Social Workers; Coun Social Work Educ; Am Sociol Asn. **Honors/Awds:** Oustanding Achievement, Atlanta Med Asn, 1985; Dean Brailsford Brazeal Lect, Morehouse Col,

1986; Outstanding Contribution to Medical Education, Nat Asn Med Minority Educ, 1988; Frankie V Adams Award for Excellence, Atlanta Univ, 1988; Fanon Scholar, Charles Drew Postgrad Med Sch. **Special Achievements:** Author of "The Health Community: Perspective for the Future," 1973; author of The Dynamics of Racism in Social Work Practice, 1973; author of "The Social Health of Disadvantaged Black Coll Students," Amer Journal of Col Health, 1974; author of "Race and Reason in the 1980's," Social Work, 1975. **Business Phone:** (718)858-0066.

GOODMAN, ROBERT O
Military leader. **Personal:** Born Nov 30, 1956, San Juan, Puerto Rico; son of Robert Oliver Goodman Sr and Marylyn Joan Dykers Goodman; married Terry L Bryant, Jun 2, 1979; children: Tina & Morgan. **Educ:** US Naval Acad, Annapolis MD, Bachelors Opers Analysis, 1978; US Nava l Post Grad Sch, Monterey, CA, Masters Systs Technol (Space), 1987. **Career:** USN, A6E Intruder Bombadier/Navigator (retired); Booz Allen Hamilton, sr assoc, currently. **Orgs:** US Naval Acad Alumni Asn. **Military Serv:** USN, lt comdr, 1978-. **Business Phone:** (703)902-5000.

GOODMAN, RUBY LENE
Educator. **Personal:** Born Oct 15, 1957, Pinehurst, NC; daughter of James Leland and Magdaline Hough. **Educ:** Univ NC, Charlotte, BA, 1979; Fayetteville State Univ, cert, mid level educ, 1980; Univ NC, Pembroke, MA, 1992. **Career:** US Census, off asst; Sandhills Community Col, adult edur; Hoke Community Schs, educr, currently. **Orgs:** Nat Coalition Aviation Educ; Nat Acad Educ. **Honors/Awds:** Master Teacher, Sandhills Education Consortium, 1997; Teacher of the Year, Hoke County, 2000-01. **Home Addr:** 2850 N Shannon Rd, Shannon, NC 28386. *

GOODNIGHT, PAUL
Artist, founder (originator). **Personal:** Born Dec 31, 1946, Chicago, IL; son of James Lockett and Esie Lockett; children: Aziza. **Educ:** Vesper George Col Art, 1971; Roxbury Community Col, 1972; Mass Col Art, BA & MFA, 1976. **Career:** Color Circle Art Pub Inc, founder & artistic dir, 1991-. **Honors/Awds:** Nat Conf Artists Award, 1979; Unsung Heroes Award, Mus Afro-Am Hist, Boston, 1988; Sports Artist of the Year Award, US Sports Acad, 1997; 21st Century Award, Urban League of Eastern Mass, 2000. **Special Achievements:** "Ten Artists at Their Best," Martin Luther King Libr, 1984; Work featured on tv shows, including: The Cosby Show, ER, Seinfeld; founded Color Circle Art Publishing, Boston MA, 1991; designed the World Cup poster, 1998. **Business Addr:** Founder, Artistic Director, Color Circle Art Publishing Inc, 791 Tremont St Suite N104, PO Box 190763, Boston, MA 02118, **Business Phone:** (617)437-1260.

GOODRICH, HAROLD THOMAS
Educator. **Personal:** Born Aug 1, 1931, Memphis, TN; married Verastine; children: Ivan DeWayne & Michael Rene. **Educ:** Le Moyne-Owen Col, BS, 1956; Memphis State Univ, MA, 1969; addn studies, 1974. **Career:** Educator (retired); Mitchell High Sch, Memphis, eng teacher, 1956-65, coordr 1965-67; Adult Basic Ed, teacher 1966; supvr of instrs, 1967-74; Title I Consult, 1967-70; Adult Basic Educ, supvr, 1967-69; Consult AV, 1971; Nat Teacher Corps, team leader, 1972-74; Capleville Elem, teacher, 1974-76; Ross Elem, teacher, 1976-80; Crump Elem, teacher, 1980-85; Shelby County Schs. **Orgs:** Deleg, Nat Educ Asn, 1971, 1974; Chmn, Vis Com of Southern Asn Col & Schs, 1974-76; Tex Educ Agency; Wis Technol Educ Asn; SCEA; TASCD; Asn Educ Commun & Technol, Asn Supv & Curriculum Develop, Dem, Omega Psi Phi; vpres, GAIA Invest Club; deacon, finance com, housing com Mt Vernon Bapt Chruch. **Honors/Awds:** Phi Delta Kappa Award, 1969; Outstanding Educator in America for 70's. **Military Serv:** AUS, pfc, hon gd, 1953-55. *

GOODRICH, LINDA S
Educator, choreographer. **Personal:** Born in Columbus, OH. **Educ:** Ohio State Univ, MA & PhD; Mills Col, MFA. **Career:** Dancing at Lugnasa, choreographer; The Colored Museum, choreographer; Jar the Floor, choreographer; Cabin in the Sky, choreographer; Raisin, choreographer; A Thousand Cranes, choreographer; Viva Carnival show, producer; Venus, dir, 2002; Calif State Univ, chair & dance coordr, currently; Sacramento/Black Art Dance, founder, currently. **Business Addr:** Chair, Dance Coordinator, California State University, 6000 J St, Sacramento, CA 95819-6069, **Business Phone:** (916)278-4784.

GOODRICH, THELMA E.
Insurance executive. **Personal:** Born Apr 19, 1933, New York, NY; daughter of James Goodrich and Evelyn; married Lawrence Hill, Jan 24, 1960. **Educ:** Baruch City Col, New York NY, attended 1952; Col Ins, New York, cert, 1960; Col New Rochelle, New York, attended 1985; Empire State Col, New York. **Career:** Fay Weintraub-Sterenbuck, New York, NY, secy, 1953; Thelma E Goodrich Inc, New York, owner & mgr, 1959; Goodrich & Johnson Brokerage, New York, pres & chief exec officer, 1980-. **Orgs:** Iota Phi Lambda Sorority, 1975; New York Club Negro Bus & Prof Women, 1978; Bd chair, United Mutual Life Ins Co, 1983-86; bd mem, New York Property Fire Ins Orgn, 1983-; NY Auto Plan treas, East Harlem Renewal Agency, 1985-; dir, Aron Davis Hall, 1987-; dir, 100 Black Women, 1987-; pres, Harlem Bus Alliance, 1989; dir, Prof Ins Agents, 1989; pres, Coun Ins Brokers, 1989; chair, Greater Harlem Real Estate Bd, 1989; pres, Bus & Prof Women Club Inc, 1992. **Honors/Awds:** Community Service Award, Ins Women of New York State; Community Service Award, New York City Bus & Prof Women, 1988; Community Service Award, New York State Black & Pub Rel Caucus, 1989. **Special Achievements:** First vice president of New York Club, National Association of Negro. **Business Addr:** President, Chief Executive Officer, Goodrich & Johnson Brokerage, 271 W 125th St Suite 208, New York, NY 10037.*

GOODSON, ADRIENNE M.
Basketball player. **Personal:** Born Oct 19, 1966, Bayonne, NJ; daughter of Ralph Feuker and Margo. **Educ:** Old Dom Univ, BA, sec educ, mkt, 1989. **Career:** Basketball player(retired); Banco de Credito (Brazil), forward, 1991-92; Unimed (Brazil), 1992-94; Ponte Preta (Brazil), 1994-95; Seara (Brazil), 1995-96; Atlanta Glory, 1996-98; Philadelphia Rage, 1998-99; Utah Starzz, guard, 1999-02; San Antonio Silver Stars, guard, 2003-04; Houston rockets, unrestricted free agent, 2005; Charlotte bobcats, 2005. **Orgs:** NatChampionship squad. **Honors/Awds:** Most Valuable Player, Sun Belt Conference Tournament; Sun Belt Player of the Year, 1988. *

GOODSON, ANNIE JEAN
Government official, chairperson, president (organization). **Personal:** Born in Camp Hill, AL; married Adolph. **Educ:** Ala State Univ, BS (cum laude), 1954; Fisk Univ, grad study, 1956; Howard Univ Sch Soc Work, MSW, 1962; Univ Southern Calif, MPA, 1982. **Career:** Government Official (retired); E Highland HS Sylocauga AL, pub sch teacher, 1954-56; DC Children's Ctr, teacher, 1957-58; DC Dept Pub Welfare, caseworker, 1958-60; Med Eval & Rehab Serv, chief, 1967-71; DC Dept Human Serv, chief spec serv div, 1971-76; Group Ther St Elizabeths Hosp, Phelps-Stokes fel; DC Dept Human Resources, dep bur chief, 1976-80; Family Serv Admin, adminr, 1980-83; Comn Homelessness, Columbia, DC, exec dir, 1984-87, sr policy adv, 1987-95, acting comnr social serv, 1995-97; Links Inc, div social serv, acting comnr, human resources, chairperson, currently. **Orgs:** Nat Asn Social Workers; psychiatric soc worker, St Elizabeths Hosp, 1962-67; Acad Cert Social Workers; John Wesley Am Zion Ch; Delta Sigma Theta Inc Sor, chap pres, Montgomery Co Alumnae Chap, 1975-77; pres, Wash Carats, 1998-2000; pres, Capital City Links, 1999-. **Honors/Awds:** Nominee, Fed Woman's Award, 1975; Soror of Year Award, Delta Sigma Theta Sor, 1975; nominee, Zeta Phi Beta Community Volunteer Service Award, 1998. **Home Addr:** 7914 13th St NW, Washington, DC 20012. **Business Addr:** Chairperson, The Links, Inc, Division of Human Resources, 609 H St NE 5th Fl, Washington, DC 20002.

GOODSON, DR. ERNEST JEROME
Dentist. **Personal:** Born Dec 16, 1953, Concord, NC; married Patricia Timmons, Nov 17, 1984; children: Ernest Jerome Jr (Sonny) & Aaron Timmons. **Educ:** Univ NC, Chapel Hill, BSD, 1976, Sch Dent, DDS, 1979; Univ Calif-San Francisco, MS, 1984. **Career:** Cent Piedmont Comm Col, fac, 1980; Univ London Royal Dent Hosp, fel dent surg, 1980; Pasquotank-Perquimans- Cander-Chowan Dist Health Dept, dir dent serv; Univ NC Sch Dent, adj fac, 1981-82; Elizabeth City State Univ, lectr math, 1981-82; Nash-Edgecombe-Halifak Counties, dir dent serv, 1984-85; Fayetteville State Univ, lectr math, 1985-86; Pvt Practice, orthodontist, currently. **Orgs:** Tutor, First Baptist Math-Sci Tutorial Prog, 1986-; vpres, Minority Health Profs; bd mem, Cumberland Co ABC, 1990-94; found bd mem, Fayetteville State Univ; adv bd mem, United Nat Bank; dentist rep, Comm Health Serv, 1993-; adv bd, Leap Community; bd dir, Fayetteville Museum Art, 1994-; NC Teaching Fel Bd, 1994-; bd visitors, Univ NC, currently. **Honors/Awds:** Dentist of the Year, Old N State Dent Soc, 1998. **Special Achievements:** Research and publications include "Detection and Measurement of Sensory Illusions" with Dr Barry Whitsell and Dr Duane Dryer, Dept of Physiology, Univ of NC, School of Medicine and School of Dentistry, "The London Experience" 1981, "Dental Education in England" The Dental Asst 1981, "Orthodontics for the Public Health Dentist" NC Dental Public Health 1986. **Business Addr:** Orthodontist, 950 S McPherson Church Rd, Fayetteville, NC 28303, **Business Phone:** (910)483-2633.

GOODSON, FRANCES ELIZABETH
School administrator. **Personal:** Born in Nashville, TN; married David; children: Shereen & David Hughes. **Educ:** Hofstra Univ, attended 1978; Negotiations Sem, attended 1979; Nat Asn Educ Negotiators, Negotiations Sem, attended 1980; Comput Educ, mgt sem, 1980; Nat Sch Bd Jour, Pub Rels Sem, attended 1983, Admin Eval Workshops, attended 1984. **Career:** Roosevelt Coun Parent Teachers Asn, pres, 1973-74; Legis Liaison Bd Educ, NYS, 1981-; Adv Coun Gov NYS, st human rights, 1984-, div women, 1995-; Roosevelt Pub Schs, bd educ, pres. **Orgs:** Bd mem, Adult Basic Educ, 1977-; Nat Caucus Black Sch Bd, 1978-; mem, bd dirs, 1978-80, chair elect comn, 1982, exec vpres, 1986-87, 1987-88, Nat Caucus Black Sch Bd Mem; Elem Educ Accrediation Comm, 1983; bd dirs, Nat Caucus Black Bd; NY St Liaison representing Roosevelt Bd Educ, 1982-; St Human Rights Adv Coun, 1983-84; vpres, Northeast Region Nat Caucus Black Sch Bd, 1983-84; vpres, 1983-84, pres, 1984-85, Roosevelt Bd Educ; Comn Child Care, 1984-; NY St Comn Child Care, 1985; Govt appointment NYS Comm on Child Care, 1985; campaign coordr, co exec republican party, 1989; mem, task force, NY St assembly, 1990; Nassau Cty Exec campaign reelection, 1990; res asst, Nassau City Off Women Servs, 1994; spec asst, Nassau City Off Minority Affairs, 1997-; local pres, Evangelical Lutheran Church Am, 1998. **Honors/Awds:** Black Faces in High Places, 1979; Outstanding Member Award, NCBSBM, 1982, President Award Appreciation, 1983; National President Award, Nat Black Caucus, 1983, 1984, 1985; Student Award, Frances E Goodson Award Est, 1980; Dem Club of Roosevelt Award, 1984; Northeast Region VPres's Award, NCBSBM, 1984; National Woman of the Year Award, 100 Black Men Inc, 1985; New York State Senate Commendation Resolution, 1985; equalization rate-Roosevelt Pub Schs, NYS Legis law passed, 1988; Nassau City proclamation, Republican Party, 1988; NYS Assembly proclamation educ, 1988. **Special Achievements:** Poetry, Our World's Most Beloved Poems, 1985. **Home Addr:** 236 Beechwood Ave, Roosevelt, NY 11575. *

GOODSON, JAMES ABNER, JR.
Advertising executive. **Personal:** Born Jul 11, 1921, Cuero, TX; married Emma E; children: James III, Theresa Jasper, Johnny L, Jerome K. **Educ:** Metropolitan Col Los Angeles, attended 1943; Harold Styles Sch Radio Announcers, attended 1952. **Career:** Tire salesman, 1940; BF Goodrich, 1944; Nat Record Newspaper, publ, pres. **Orgs:** pres, Cosmopolitan Rep Voters Club Inc; Nat Advan Asn Colored People; Urban League; Hollywood Community Police Coun, 1977,81, Southside C C Los Angeles; Happiness Project, Masonic Lodge, New Hope Baptist Ch; JAGME Found, pres-. **Honors/Awds:** Exceptional Achievement Award, Nat ass Advan colored People, 1971; Personal & Professional Achievement Award, Hon Mike Roos 46th Assembly Dist, Hon Maxine Waters 48th Assembly Dist, Hon David Roberts 23rd Senatorial Dist 1980; Cert Apprec County Los Angeles, 1980; Cert Commendation Republican Central Comn Los Angeles County, 1985; Plaque Appreciation Young Men's Christian Assoc, 1986. **Military Serv:** AUS, engr, 1945. **Business Addr:** President, Jagme Foundation, 1605 N Cahuenga Blvd, Los Angeles, CA 90028, **Business Phone:** (323)461-4196.

GOODSON, LEROY BEVERLY
Physician. **Personal:** Born Feb 11, 1933, Elyria, OH; son of Inez Louise Leach and Franklin Beverly; married Evelyn Wimmer Goodson, Aug 27, 1965; children: Earl, Kenneth, Parker. **Educ:** Univ Mich, BS, 1955; Univ Mich, MD, Med Sch, 1959; Kenyon Col, 1953. **Career:** St Rita's Hosp, intern, 1959-60; Carl S Jenkins, partner, 1960-61; Wilberforce Univ, med dir, 1960-62; Pvt Prac, physician, 1963-72; Wright Patterson AF Base, 1966-68; Clark Co Drug Control Coun, med dir, 1971-; pvt pract, physician, 1972-; Wright State Univ, consult, 1973-; HK Simpson Ctr Maternal Health, instr physical diag & anemia, 1973-; Wright State Univ, assoc clin prof; Alcohol Chem Detox Unit, med dir, 1975-83; family prac, 1975-. **Orgs:** Clark Co Med Soc, 1960-, secy, 1968-70, pres, 1971; Community Hosp Med Staff, 1960-, vpres, 1973; Ohio Acad Family Physicians, 1960-; Hosp Com, 1971-; dipl, Am Bd Family Prac, 1973-; Operation Big Sister, 1968-70, pres bd, 1970; Am Red Cross, 1968-71, exec comt mem, 1969-71; Community Hosp Bd, 1968-71, exec comt mem, 1969-71; chmn bd, Ronez Apt Inc, 1972-74; bd mem, St John's Nursing Home, 1980-; dipl, AMSADD, 1989. **Honors/Awds:** Outstanding Service to Community, Frontiers Int Inc, 1973; Service Award, Am Red Cross, 1971; Service Award, Community Hosp, 1971; 25 yrs Service Award, Alcohol, Drugs & Ment Health, 1993. **Military Serv:** AUSMC, capt, 1961-63. **Home Addr:** 2701 Moorefield Rd, Springfield, OH 45502, **Home Phone:** (937)399-6650. **Business Phone:** (937)399-6650.*

GOODSON, DR. MARTIN L
Educator. **Personal:** Born Feb 14, 1943, Boligee, AL; children: Monique. **Educ:** Stillman Col, BS, 1964; Ind State Univ, MS, 1970; Ind Univ, EdD, 1975. **Career:** Rochelle High Sch, Lakeland FL, biol teacher, 1964-65; Woodrow Wilson fel, 1964; Druid High Sch Tuscaloosa, physics teacher, 1965-66; Seagrams Distilling Inc, lab technician, 1967; Ind State Univ, instr, 1970-72; Ala State Univ, Huntsville, assoc prof, 1975-77; Delta Col MI, assoc prof, prof physics, 2004-. **Orgs:** Ala State pres, Nat Pres New Farmers Asn, 1959-60; keeper rec & seals, Omega Psi Phi Fraternity, 1963-64, secy, 1963-; adv, IN State Univ, 1968-75; pres, Nat Asn Advan Colored People Terre Haute, 1970-72; consult, Am Inst Physics, 1973-75; outside evaluator, Proj Impact State Ind, 1973-75; consult & evaluator, POT Modules, 1973-75; Phi Delta Kappa, 1974-; Outside Col Univ Ctr, MI, 1977-; bd mem, Amer Baptist Ol Sem, 1978-; mem, Nat Asn Res Sci Teaching. **Special Achievements:** Jour Col Sci Teaching, "The Effect of Objective-Based Diagnostic Test on Physical Science Students", 1978. **Military Serv:** ROTC Tuskegee Inst, 1959-62. **Business Addr:** Professor of Physics, Delta College, Department Physics, Rm D-156 1961 Delta Rd, University Center, MI 48710.

GOODWIN, CURTIS LAMAR
Baseball player. **Personal:** Born Sep 30, 1972, Oakland, CA. **Career:** Baltimore Orioles, outfielder, 1995; Cincinnati Reds, 1996-97; Colorado Rockies, 1998; Chicago Cubs, 1999; Toronto Blue Jays, outfielder, 1999. **Honors/Awds:** Carolina League All-Star OF, 1993; Eastern League All-Star OF, 1994. *

GOODWIN, DELLA MCGRAW
Nurse, administrator, dean (education). **Personal:** Born Nov 21, 1931, Claremore, OK; daughter of James Edward McGraw and Allie Mae Meadows. **Educ:** Paul Laurence Dunbar High Sch, attended 1950; Dunbar Jr Col, AA, 1952; Freedmen's Hosp Sch Nursing, Howard Univ, dipl nursing, 1955; Wayne State Univ, BSN, 1960, MSN, 1962. **Career:** Educator (retired); Detroit Receiving Hosp, hosp head nurse, 1958-60; Blvd Gen Hosp, Detroit, MI, dir nursing, 1963-69; Paramedical Serv, Detroit, MI, consult, 1969-70; Wayne County Community Col, Detroit, MI, chair nursing, 1970-82, dean, nursing & health, 1982-86. **Orgs:** Chair, Detroit Substance Abuse Coun, 1981; Cabinet Nursing Educ, Am Nurses Asn, 1984-88; pres, chief exec officer, Nat Ctr Advan Blacks Health Prof, 1988; Health Brain Trust, Mich Legis Black Caucus, 1988; bd dir, Southeast Mich Chap, Am Red Cross; pres, Comprehensive Health Planning Coun Southeastern Mich; Chi Eta Phi; Sigma Theta Tau Nursing Sororities; Detroit Dist Nurses Asn; Delta Sigma Theta Sorority. **Honors/Awds:** Headliners Award, Women of Wayne, 1974; Distinguished Educr Award, Col Alumni Wayne County Community Col, 1980; Bertha Lee Culp Human Rights Award, Mich Nurses Asn, 1985; Induction, Acad Black Women Health Professions, 1991; Nat African-Am Leadership Award, New Detroit Inc, 1992. **Home Addr:** 19214 Appoline, Detroit, MI 48235. *

GOODWIN, DONALD EDWARD
Engineer. **Personal:** Born May 5, 1949, Detroit, MI; son of James A and Thelma L; married Patricia Davis, Mar 25, 1972; children: Malik, Idris & Layla. **Educ:** Univ Mich, BS, mech eng, 1971, postgrad mgt, 1978; Duke Univ, Dynamic Magt Prog, 2005. **Career:** Cummins Engine Corp, prod engr, 1971-72; Chrysler Corp, prod engr, 1972-73; Ford Motor Co, prod engr, brakes & other, 1973-76; Pontiac DIV GM, proj engr, 1976-79; Ford Motor Co, suv, powertrain reliability & other, 1979-85; Chrysler Corp, mgr, eng quality & reliability assurance, 1985-89, mgr, restraints eng, 1989-92, exec engr, LCP interior eng, 1992-94; Proving Grounds & Durability Testing, exec eng, 1994-98; Daimler Chysler Develop System, dir, 1998-; Scientific Labs Providing Grounds, vpres, 1999; DaimlerChrysler Corp, vpres, 2007-. **Orgs:** Am Soc Quality Control, 1985-91; NCP, 1989-; Eng Soc Detroit, 1990-; bd mem, Washtenaw United Way, 1996-98; bd trustee, New Calvary Baptist Church; dir, Chrysler Develop Syst. **Honors/Awds:** MNY Achiever Award, Detroit YMCA, Chrysler Corp, 1989; Am's Best & Brightest Men, Dollars & Sense Magazine, 1996. **Business Addr:** Vice President, DaimlerChrysler Corp, CIMS 483-05-02, Chrysler Dr E, Auburn Hills, MI 48326-2757, **Business Phone:** (248)576-2521.

GOODWIN, JAMES OSBY
Lawyer. **Personal:** Born Nov 4, 1939, Tulsa, OK; married Vivian Palm; children: Jerry, Davey, Anna, Jeanne, Joey. **Educ:** Univ Notre Dame, BA, 1961; Univ Tulsa, JD, 1965. **Career:** pvt pract, atty; Okla Eagle Publ Co, publ, currently. **Orgs:** bd chmn, Tulsa Comprehensive Health Ctr, 1973; Tulsa City Co Bd Health; OK Bar Asn; Am Trial Lawyers; secy, vpres, OK Trial Lawyers; Tulsa Co Bar Asn; Tulsa Co Legal Aid; ACLU Award Serv Chmn Tulsa City Co Bd Health, 1975; chmn, Tulsa Human Serv Agency, 1978-80. **Honors/Awds:** Award for Service as member board chairman, Tulsa Comprehensive Health Ctr, 1973. **Business Addr:** Publisher, Oklahoma Eagle Publishing Company, 624 E Archer St, Tulsa, OK 74120, **Business Phone:** (918)582-7124.*

GOODWIN, DR. JESSE FRANCIS
Government official. **Personal:** Born Feb 7, 1929, Greenville, SC; son of Frances Byrd and Jesse; children: Gordon Francis, Paula Therese & Jesse Stephen. **Educ:** Xavier Univ, BS, Pharm, 1951; Wayne Univ, MS, 1953, PhD, 1957. **Career:** Wayne State Univ Col Med, res assoc, 1958-59; Wayne City Gen Hosp; clin bio chem, 1959-63; Gen Clin Res Ctr Childrens Hosp Wayne State Univ Sch Med, lab dir, 1963-73; Detroit Health Dept, dir labs. **Orgs:** Pres, Gamma Lambda Chap Alpha Phi Alpha Frat, 1972-76; bd trustees, Horizon Health Systs, 1982-, Detroit Osteopathic Hosp Corp, 1980-, Mary grove Col, 1977-93; 1st vpres, Det Branch NAACP, 1982-84, 2nd vpres, 1978-82; comnr, MI Toxic Substance Control Comn, 1986-89; bd dirs, MI Catholic Conf, 1986-89; bd dirs, Am Asn Clin Chem, 1987-90; bd, Nat Acad Clin Bio chem, 1987; Detroit Archdiocesan Educ, adv comt, 1993-; bd trustees, Loyola High Sch, 1993-. **Honors/Awds:** Chairman MI Section, AACC, 1964; author, 36 Sci Publ, 1958-; Distinguished Service Award, Detroit Branch NAACP, 1983. *

GOODWIN, MAC ARTHUR
Educator, consultant. **Personal:** Born Jan 31, 1942, Orangeburg, SC; son of Romie Goodwin; married Junita; children: Bobbie Theresa, Michael Anthony & Gerard Arthur. **Educ:** Claflin Univ, BA, 1963; Univ SC, MAT, 1976. **Career:** Greenville County Sch Dist, teacher, 1964-65; Comt St Elem Jr High, art teacher, 1965-66; Carver High Sch, art teacher, 1965-70; Spartanburg High Sch, visual arts dept chmn, 1970-85; SC Dept Educ, fine arts consult & educ assoc, 1985-2000; Goodwin's Arts Consult, exec dir, currently. **Orgs:** Nat Visual & Performance Arts, Stands Comt, 1990-93; co-chmn, Nat Bd Pro Teaching Standards, 1990-; Col Bd, Arts Advisory Comt, 1995-; pres-elect, 1999-2000, pres, 2000-03, pres, Nat Art Edu asn; dir, Nat Supv & Admin Div; Art Edu Stands Develop Task Force; chair, Consortium Nat Prof Arts asns; Nat Bd Prof Teaching Stds Early Adolescence through Young Adulthood/Art Stands; chair, SC African Am Monument Citizen Advisory Comm; SC Alliance Arts Edu; SC Governor's Sch Arts & Humanities; bd dir, State Dept Edu Representative; bd dir, Columbia Museum Art; bd dir, SC Arts Alliance. **Honors/Awds:** SC Governor's Award for Arts Education, 1990; Nat Art Educator of the Year, NAEA, 1991; Lifetime Achievement Award, SC Art Educ Asn, 1999; Lifetime Achievement Award, SC General Assembly, 2000; honorary degrees: doctorate, Columbia Col, 2000. **Special Achievements:** Published articles: "Student Achievement & Assessment: Existing Frameworks", US Dept Educ, 1991; "Design Standards for School Facilities", NAEA, 1992; "The NBPTS Standards: Implications for Art Teacher Prep", NAEA, 1997; "Achievements or Disasters", Arts Educ Policy Review, 2000; The first exhibit titled "A Journey of Imagery & A Tribute to the Quilt Makers of Gee's Bend", 2008. **Home Addr:** 136 Jefferson Pl, Columbia, SC 29212.

GOODWIN, MARIA ROSE
Historian. **Personal:** Born Aug 27, 1950, Washington, DC; daughter of Thomas Cephas and Sarajane Cohron. **Educ:** George Washington UNIV, MFA, 1974. **Career:** NAT Endowment Arts, prog specialist, 1974-89; US Mint, historian, 1989-; Smithsonian's Anacostia Mus. **Orgs:** NAT Genealogical SOC, counr, 1996-98; Treasury Historical ASN, vip, 1996-98; Orgn AMR Historians, 1990-; Smithsonian Inst, volunteer staff, 1974-; Daughters Dorcas, 1990-; SOC History Federal GOV, 1991-; AFA Hist & Genealogical SOC, guest speaker, 1996-. **Honors/Awds:** Smithsonian Inst, Volunteer Appreciation; Smithsonian & Anacostia, Ujim's Award. **Special Achievements:** Co-author, Guide to Black Washington, 1989-; FDR, Family Heritage Group, Anacostia Museum, 1988-95; Lecturer & Writer on conducting AFA Geneology RES; author of The Bones-Keeper's Journal, An African-American Geneology Sourcebook; Co-DRR "Hidden History Church Proj," Hist SOC WAS DC, 1990-92. **Business Addr:** Historian, US Mint, 801 9th St NW, Washington, DC 20220, **Business Phone:** (202)354-7724.*

GOODWIN, MARTIN DAVID
Journalist. **Personal:** Born May 1, 1964, Tulsa, OK; son of James Osby and Vivian Edwina Palm; married Angela Denise Davis Goodwin, Oct 27, 1990. **Educ:** Benedictine Col, Atchison, KS, BA, eng jour, 1986. **Career:** The Oklahoma Eagle, Tulsa, reporter, photogr, copy ed, 1983-86; The Ithaca Jour, NY, reporter, copy ed, 1986-88; The Courier-Jour, Louisville, KY, reporter, copy ed; USA Today, rewrite ed & ed page asst, 1995-96; The Courier Jour, asst metro ed, Ind state ed, reporter, bur chief, 1996; Star-Ledger, city ed; The Middletown Jour, ed; Cox Ohio Publishing, managing ed presentation, 2006-. **Orgs:** Scholar comt mem, Nat Asn Black Journalists, 1986-; pres, Louisville Asn Black Communicators, 1988-98;Am Soc Newspaper Ed, 2003-. **Honors/Awds:** Soc Prof Journalists Award; Best of Gannett Award. **Business Addr:** Managing Editor-Presentation, Dayton Daily News, 1611 S Main St, Dayton, OH 45409, **Business Phone:** (937)225-2397.

GOODWIN, NORMA J.
Physician, administrator. **Personal:** Born May 14, 1937, Norfolk, VA; daughter of Stephen and Helen. **Educ:** Virginia State Col, BS, 1956; Medical Col Virginia, MD, 1961. **Career:** Kings County Hosp Ctr Brooklyn, internship residency, 1961-65; Downstate Med Ctr, dir clinical asst, asst prof clinical, asst prof med, 1964-72; Nat Inst Health, postdoctoral & fellow nephrology, 1965-67; Kings County Hosp, Den & State Univ NY, Downstate Med Ctr Brooklyn, served; Kings County Hosp, clinical dir hemodialysis unit, 1967-69, 1969-71; Univ Hosp Downstate Ctr, attending physician, 1968-75; Health & Hosp Corp, vpres, sr vpres, 1971-75; Dept Family Pract, clinical asst prof, 1972-; Howard Univ Sch Bus & Pub Admin, adjunct prof, 1977-; AMRON Mgt Consult Inc, pres, 1976-; Columbia Univ Teachers Col, adjunct prof; Health Power, founder, pres & chief exec officer, currently. **Orgs:** staff Kings County Hosp Ctr, 1965-; charter mem, bd dir NY City Comp Health Planning Agency, 1970-72; 2nd vpres, Nat Med Asn; 1st vpres, Empire State Med Soc State Chapter Nat Med Asn, secy, v speaker & house del, 1972-74, exec comn, 1974; regional adv group NY Metro Regional Med Prog; past pres, Provident Clinical Soc Brooklyn Inc, 1969-72; consult, Dept Health Educ & Welfare; Health Serv Res Study Section Dept HEW; chmn, com comn med Kings Co Med Soc; 1st vice chmn, Bedford Stuyvesant Comp Health Plan Coun; NY Am & Intl Soc Nephrology Am Pub Health Asn; bd trust Atlanta Univ Ctr; NY Col Podiatric Med; bd dir, NY Asn Ambulatory Care; NY Heart Asn; Pub Health Asn NYC; bd dir Am Red Cross Greater NY; past mem, lth Sci Careers Advisory Comt; LaGuardia Comt Col City Univ NY; Nat Asn Comt Health Ctrs Inc; Med Adv Bd Hypertension New York City Health Dept; Leg Comn Med Soc Co Kings; subcom Hosp Emer Servs Med Soc Co Kings; task Force Emer Med Care NY St Health Plan Comn; founder & pres, Health Watch Information & Promotion Serv Inc, 1987-. **Honors/Awds:** Nat Found Fellow, 1958; Jesse Smith Noyes & Smith Douglas Scholarships; Alpha Kappa Mu Nat Honor Soc; Beta Kappa Chi Nat Science Honor Soc; Soc Sigma Xi; author or co-author more than 30 publications; Health Watch News, brochures cancer & AIDS; Videos AIDS. **Business Phone:** (718)434-8103.*

GOODWIN, ROBERT KERR
Association executive. **Personal:** Born Nov 15, 1948, Tulsa, OK; son of Edward L and Jeanne B Osby. **Educ:** Oral Roberts Univ, Tulsa, OK, BA, 1970; San Francisco Theol Sem, Marin, CA, MA, 1973. **Career:** Okla Eagle Publishing Co, publ, 1973-81; Nat Univ Soc, Houston, TX, regional sales mgr, 1985-87; Texas A&M Univ Syst, Col Station, TX, asst dep chancellor external affairs, 1987-89; US Dept Educ, White House Initiative on HBCU's, exec dir, 1989-92; Nat Points Light Found, exec vpres, 1992-95, pres & chief exec officer, 1995-. **Orgs:** Founding bd mem, Am's Promise Alliance Youth; bd mem, Generations United; bd mem, Nat Assembly; bd mem, PFLAG; bd dir, Salvation Army. **Honors/Awds:** Hon Doctorate Laws, Univ Md, Eastern Shore, 1990; Hon Doctorate Humane Lett, LeMoyne-Owens Col, 1990; Man of the Year, Nat Coun Christians & Jews. **Special Achievements:** one of the 50 most influential people in the nonprofit sector by the NonProfit Times. **Business Addr:** President, Chief Executive Officer, Points Light Found, 1400 I Eye St NW Suite 800, Washington, DC 20005-2208.*

GOODWIN, STEFAN CORNELIUS
Anthropologist, educator. **Personal:** Born Feb 13, 1941, Norfolk, VA; son of S Cornelius and Dr Helen J. **Educ:** Tenn State Univ, BA, French, 1960; NY Univ, MA, Int Rels, 1964; State Univ NY, 1971; Northwestern Univ, MA, Anthrop, 1972, PhD, Anthrop, 1974. **Career:** NYC, social worker, 1961-62; Prudential Ins, actuarial corresp, 1963-65; Ministry Educ, Peace Corps vol, Nigeria, 1966-67; Inst Mod Lang, lectr, Saudi Arabia, 1968-69; Wayne State Univ, anthropologist, 1974-76; Morgan State Univ, anthropologist, 1976-2003, assoc prof Sociol & Anthrop, 2003-. **Orgs:** Bd mem, Baltimore Crisis Response Inc, 1996-99; pres & vpres, Baltimore Neighborhoods Inc, 1998-2001; chair, Task Force Study Hist & Legacy Slavery Md, Md Comn African Am Cult & Hist, 1997-2005; chair, Comn Coordinate Study, Commemoration & Impact Slavery's Hist & Legacy Md, 2001-05; life mem, NAACP. **Honors/Awds:** Alpha Kappa Alpha; Alpha Kappa Mu; Pi Delta Phi; Sigma Rho Sigma; Alpha Kappa Delta. **Special Achievements:** Author: "Emergence of A Continent from Racial Dismemberment," Anthropologie Africaine, 1999; "Malta", Countries and Their Cultures, 2001; Malta, Mediterranean Bridge, 2002; African Legacies of Urbanization, 2004; Late Stone Age in the Nile Valley pub in Encyc of African History, 2004; Late Stone Age in the Nile Valley in Encyclopedia of African History, 2005; "Malta", Greenwood Encyclopedia of World Folklore and Folklife, 2006; African Legacies of Urbanization: Unfolding Saga of a Continent, 2006. **Business Addr:** Associate Professor of Sociology & Anthropology, Morgan State University, 1700 E Cold Spring Lane, Baltimore, MD 21251, **Business Phone:** (443)885-3333.

GOODWIN, THOMAS JONES
Baseball player. **Personal:** Born Jul 27, 1968, Fresno, CA. **Career:** Baseball Player (retired), baseball coach; Los Angeles Dodgers, outfielder, 1991-93, 2000-01; Kans City Royals, 1994-97; Tex Rangers, 1997-99; Col Rockies, 2000; San Francisco Giants, 2002; Chicago Cubs, 2003-04; Tampa Bay Devil Rays, 2005; Atlantic League, 2005; Lewisville Lizards, mgr; Lowell Spinners, coach, currently.

GOODWIN, VAUGHN ALLEN. **See ABDULLAH, SHARIF.**

GOODWIN, DR. WILLIAM PIERCE, JR.
Physician. **Personal:** Born Sep 18, 1949, Harrisburg, PA; son of William P Goodwin Sr and Joan L Robinson; married Gloria Baker, Sep 27, 1980. **Educ:** Dillard Univ New Orleans, BA (Magna Cum Laude), 1972; Meharry Med Col, MD, 1976. **Career:** Univ Okla, assoc prof, 1981-85; Martin Army Community Hosp, resident family practice prog, 1985-88; Reynolds Army Hosp, Ft Sill Okla (Flint River Rural Health Care), family practice; pvt pract, currently. **Orgs:** Nat, Am Med Asns; Am Asn Family Practice, 1985, Am Geriatrics Soc, 1986; Am Acad Family Physicians. **Honors/Awds:** Alpha Chi, 1971; Beta Kappa Chi Nat Hon Soc, 1971. **Military Serv:** AUS, Lt Col, 12 years; Overseas Ribbon, Serv Award, Army Commendation Medal. **Home Phone:** (912)937-2834. **Business Addr:** Physician, 7 S Broad St, Ellaville, GA 31806-0562, **Business Phone:** (912)937-5333.

GORDEN, GEN. FRED A.
Military leader. **Personal:** Born Feb 22, 1940, Anniston, AL; son of P J and Mary Ethel Johnson Harper; married Marcia Ann Stewart; children: Shawn Nicole & Michelle Elizabeth. **Educ:** US Mil Acad; Middlebury Col, MA, spanish lang & lit; Armed Forces Staff Col; Natl War Col; St Augustine Col, DHL, 1988. **Career:** Military leader (retired); Seventh Infantry Div, asst div comdr; Off Asst Sec Defense Intl Security Affairs, Wash DC, dir; Army Off Chief Legis Liaison, exec officer; Div Artillery Seventh Infantry Div, comdr; Eighth AUS Korea, artillery battalion exec officer; field artillery battalion comdr, 25th infantry div; 25th Infantry, div inspector gen; US Mil Acad,commandant cadets, 1987-89; maj gen, 1996. **Orgs:** Adv Comt Minority Veterans; bd dir, USAA Ins Co. **Honors/Awds:** Defense Distinguished Service Medal; Legion of Merit; Bronze Star Medal with V Device; Meritorious Serv Medal; Air Medal; Army Commendation Medal with one Oak Leaf Cluster; Alumnus of the Year, Am Asn Community & Jr Col, Middlebury Col, 1988; Candle in the Dark, Morehouse Col, 1989. **Military Serv:** AUS, brigadier gen.

GORDON, AARON Z., JR.
Educator. **Personal:** Born Oct 11, 1929, Port Gibson, MS; divorced; children: Aaron jr, Aaryce & Alyta. **Educ:** Univ Mich,

BS, 1952, PhD, 1974; Wayne State Univ, MA, 1956. **Career:** Ft Monmouth, Assoc Officers Signal Course, 1952; Commun Ctr Qualification Course, 1952; Teletype Operators Sch, asst officer in charge; Message Ctr Clk Sch, officer in charge; SW Signal Sch Training Ctr, Camp San Luis Obispo, CA; 3rd Infantry Div AFFE Korea, commun ctr officer, asst cryptographic officer, 1953-54; Br Officers Advan Signal Officers Course, 1963; Command & Gen Staff Col Ft Leven worth; Air War Col Maxwell AFB; personnel Officer, 1965; S1 5064 USAR Garr, 1967-69; 5032 USAR Sch, br officer advan course instr, 1969-71, dir, 1971-73; ICAF, 1974. **Orgs:** Asst dist leader, E Dist & Dist Leader, 1961-63; Health & Curric Workshop Detroit Pub Schs, 1963; Blue Star Mothers Detroit, 1963; comn chmn, Health& Phys Ed Teachers Inst Day E Dist, 1964; comt mem, Midwest Dist AAHPR Conv, Detroit, 1964; sch dist rep, Last Two Millage Campaigns Educ TV Teacher Channel 56 Detroit Pub Schs, 1964; bd dir, Troop 775 BSA, 1964; P gmd Educ Soc, Detroit, 1965; Detroit Orgn Sch Adminr & Suprs; Phi Delta Kappa; prog chmn, Detroit Sch Mem Club Metro; Detroit Sch Black Educ Admin; Nat All Black Ed; Mich Asn Elem Sch Admn Region 1; Carter Cath Methodist Episcopal Church, Detroit; coord, Annual Spelling Bee, 1967; participant, Maximizing Benefits from Testing Workp Test Admin, 1968; participant, Educ Admin Workshop, 1970-73; dir, Professional Skills Dev Workshop Metro Detroit Soc Black Educ Admin, Ann Arbor, 1973. **Honors/Awds:** Bronze Star Decoration; co-holder worlds record Outdoor Distance Medley Relay; co-holder world's record Indoor Distance Medley Relay; co-holder am record Indoor Two Mile & Relay, 1951. **Special Achievements:** Co-author: Guide to Implementation of Unit of Smoking & Health, 1963. **Military Serv:** USAR, col. *

GORDON, ALEXANDER H., II
Sports manager, athletic director. **Personal:** Born Jun 13, 1944, Phoenix, AZ; son of Alexander Houston Gordon I and Elizabeth DeLouis Davis; married Loretta Perry, Jan 28, 1967; children: David Anthony & Ellen Alicia. **Educ:** Marquette Univ, BA, speech & radio TV, 1967; LaSalle Corresp Sch, dipl,bus admin, 1967. **Career:** WTMJ AM FM TV, promotion intern & asst, sales promotion & merchandising dir, 1965-69; Avco Broadcasting Corp, corp advert writer, 1969-70; WLWITV, prom & publicity dir, 1970-71; WPVI TV, audience prom dir, 1971-72; WPVI TV, mgr advert, 1972-74; WIIC TV, dir advert, prom & publicity, 1974-77; WPXI TV, dir co mmunity rels, 1977-79; Church God Prophecy, asst pastor, 1978-79, pastor, 1979-93; WPXI TV, acct exec, 1979-87; Pittsburgh Pirates Baseball Club, dir, community service & sales, 1988; RobertoClemente Found, exec dir, 1997-. **Orgs:** Petra Ministries, elder, 1995-98; Mt Ararat Community Ctr, bd mem,1992-96; Allegheny Trails Coun, Boy Scouts of Am, bd mem, 1977-93,1997-; Urban Scouting comt, vice chmn-programming, 1990-93, Spring RoundupRecruitment Drive, chmn, 1990, 1991, 1992; Cub Scout Day Camp Comt,chmn, 1977-86; Kingsley Asn, treas/bd mem, 1990-92; Neighborhood Ctr-sAsn, bd mem/pres, 1977-83; Pittsburgh Advert Club, bd mem/vp, 1975-77;Rotary Club Pittsburgh, chaplain, 1977-80; Braod casters Promotion Asn, bd mem/treas, 1971-77; The Mews of Towne North Home Owners Asn, pres, 1975-83; United Way of Allegheny County, allocations review comt, 1977-81; Wilkinsburg comt Ministry, bd mem, 1983-87; Three Rivers Youth Inc, bdmem/ vp, 1988-92. **Honors/Awds:** Honorable Pastor Church of God of Prophecy PA 1980-81, 1983-84, 1987;Appreciation Award Allegheny Trails Council Boy Scouts of Am 1985; Clio Awards Comm for Advertising 1975; Golden Reel Award Pittsburgh Radio TV Club 1976; Whitney Young Award for work with minority scouts 1986; Silver Beaver Award, Boy Scouts of America, 1988; Salute to Negro League Baseball, The Homestead Grays and the Pittsburgh Crawfords, 1988;California State Coll Alumni Assn, Special Service Award, 1980; Greater Pittsburgh Council, Boy Scouts of America, Special Appreciation Award, 1993. **Military Serv:** AUS, spec-5, 1966-72; Sharpshooter. **Home Addr:** 133 Locust Ct, Pittsburgh, PA 15237. **Business Addr:** Executive Director, Roberto Clemente Found, 320 E N Ave, Pittsburgh, PA 15212, **Business Phone:** (412)231-2300.

GORDON, BERTHA COMER
Educator, government official, nurse. **Personal:** Born Feb 27, 1916, Louisville, GA; married Carlton. **Educ:** NY Univ, BS, 1945; Hunter Col, MA, 1955. **Career:** NY City Dept Hosp, regist nurse, 1937-50; Manhattan Sch, teacher, 1950-52; coun, 1952-62; Eli Whitney Voc High Sch, dept head, 1962-69; Bronx, NY, from asst supt to supt, 1972-78. **Orgs:** NY City Admin Women Educ, 1970; pres & life mem, Nat Asn Advan Colored People; NY City Supt Asn; Am Asn Sch Admin; Am Voc Educ Asn; Am NY State City Dist 14 Nurses Asn; Dr Asn NY City Educ; exec bd mem, Asn Study African Am Life & Hist Hunter Col & NY Univ Alumni Asn. **Honors/Awds:** Hall of Fame, Kappa Delta Pi.

GORDON, BRIDGETTE
Basketball player, basketball coach. **Personal:** Born Apr 27, 1967, DeLand, FL. **Educ:** Univ Tenn, polit sci, 1989. **Career:** Basketball player, "retired", 2000, coach; Pool Comense, Italian League,1990-96; Sacramento Monarchs, forward, 1997-98; Italy; Turkey; Fox SportsS, broadcaster; Stetson Univ, asst coach, 2006. **Honors/Awds:** Gold Medal, Olympics gold, 1988; Championship Most Valuable Player, NCAA,1989; Broderick Cup, 1990; Women's Basketball Hall of Fame, 2007. *

GORDON, BRUCE S.
Executive, chief executive officer. **Personal:** Born Feb 15, 1946, Camden, NJ; son of Walter and Violet; married Genie Alston, Feb 20, 1970 (divorced); children: Taurin S. **Educ:** Gettysburg Col, Gettysburg, PA, BA, 1968; Univ Illinois, Bell Advan Mgt, 1981; Univ PA, Wharton Exec Mgt; MIT Sloan Sch Mgt, Boston, MS, 1988. **Career:** Retired: Bell Atlantic Corp, Arlington, VA, init mgt develop, 1968-70, bus office mgr, 1970-72, sales mgr, mkt, 1972-74, personnel supvr, 1974-76, market mgt supvr, 1976-78, mkt mgr, 1978-80, div staff mgr, 1980-81, div opers mgr, 1981, div mgr, phone ctr, 1981-83, mkt mgr II, 1983-84, gen mgr, mktg & sales, 1985, vpres mkt, 1988; Bell Atlantic Network Serv, group pres retail, 1993; Verizon Commun, pres, retail markets group; NAACP board pres, 2005-07; Tyco Int Finance, dir, 2005-; CBS Corp, Dir & Mem Compensation Comm, 2006-; Northrop Grumman Corp, Dir, Mem Compensation Committee & Mem Policy Comm, 2008-. **Orgs:** Founder, past vpres, Alliance Black Mgrs; Toastmasters Intl; bd trustees, Gettysburg Col; dir, Urban League, 1984-86; bd dirs, Inroads Philadelphia, 1985-88; chair, United Negro Col Fund Telethon, 1985-86; volunteer, United Way, 1986-88; The Southern Company, bd dirs, 1994; Bar tech Personnel Servs, bd dirs, 1995; Bell Atlantic New Jersey, bd; EXE Leadership Coun; dir, Urban League; Alvin Ailey Dance Found, Lincoln Ctr; Advertising Coun Inc. **Honors/Awds:** Mass Inst Tech, Alfred P Sloan fellow, 1987; Black Enterprise Magazine, Executive of the Year, 1998; 50 Most Powerful Black Executives, Fortune magazine, 2002. *

GORDON, CHARLES D.
Housing developer. **Personal:** Born Aug 10, 1934, Memphis, TN; married Hazel D Mannings; children: Debra, Charles jr, Marshall, Kenneth, Derrick & Carlton. **Educ:** Univ Wyo; Tenn State Univ; Hampton Inst; Roosevelt Univ. **Career:** Chicago Hous Auth, clerk, mgt training prog, asst mgr, hous mgr I, housmgr II, 1961-. **Orgs:** NAHRO; Control Southside Community Workers; bd dir, Horizon House; lectr various schs; Dist Ill Educ Coun; Area A Berea Coun Dep comnr hit, basketball league, hous invitational tour; bd dir, Afro-Am touch football league; bd dir, housing bowling league. **Honors/Awds:** Won commnr flag beautification grounds CIIA, 1971-74; placed 3rd City Chicago beautiful grounds mgr Wentworth Gardens, 1974; achievement plaque for outstanding achievement as hous mgr Community Wentworth. **Military Serv:** USAF, s/sgt, 1955-61.

GORDON, DR. CHARLES EUGENE
Educator, teacher. **Personal:** Born May 31, 1938, Gallatin, TN; married Barbara Gibbs. **Educ:** Hist Western Mich Univ, BS, 1962; Wayne State Univ, M.Ed, spl educ emotion disturbed, 1970; Univ Mich, PhD, higher educ admin, 1976. **Career:** Wayne State Univ, dir off spec stud serv progs, 1970-; Project Upward Bound, dir, 1968-70; Detroit Youth Home, boys coun, supvr, 1965-67; Detroit Pub Schs, sec teacher social studies, spec educ, 1962-65. **Orgs:** ANWC bd dirs; pres, Region V Trio Adv Coun; pres, Mich Coun Educ opp progs; exec bd mem, Nat Alliance officer grad & prof Educ; exec bd mem, Nat Asn Minority Fin Aid Admin; numerous prof & bus orgns; Am Asn Higher Educ; Am Pers & Guid Asn; Nat Coord Coun Educ Opp Progs; Nat Vocat Guid Asn; Mid-West Asn Educ Opp Prog Personnel; Mich Coun Educ Opp Progs; Nat Alliance Grad & Prof Educ; Am Educ Res Asn. **Honors/Awds:** Region V citation merit US Off Educ; Distinguished Service Award, Mich Coun Educ Opp Progs; Outstanding Serv Award, Mich Inter-Asn Black Bus & Eng Studs; Three-yr Appointment Nat Adv Coun Finance Aid Stud, Hon Casper WWeinberger; pres exec dir, Cybernetic Res Systs Inc; auth Employer Attitudes in Hiring Culturally Different Youth, Career Educ Implications for Coun Minority Studs Career Educ; Short Steps on a Long Journey & The Devel Sys Model as a Tool of Prog Adminr & Eval, several art in prof jour. **Military Serv:** AUS, radio operator.

GORDON, CLAUDIA LORRAINE
Association executive, U.S. attoeney general. **Personal:** Born in Jamaica, West Indies. **Educ:** Howard Univ, BA, polit sci, 1995; Am Univ, Wash Col Law, attended, 2000. **Career:** Skadden fel; Nat Asn Deaf Law Ctr, advocacy leadership, 1989; The Civil Prac Clinic, Wash Col Law; DC Serv-Mental Health Div, pub defender; Nat Black Deaf Advocates Asn, vpres; Nat Coun Disability, independent consult; US Dept Homeland Security Off Civil Rights & Civil Liberties, atty adv, sr policy adv, currently; Lexington Sch Deaf & Ctr Deaf, bd trustee & secy, 2004-. **Orgs:** The Black Law Stud Asn; vpres, Nat Black Deaf Advocates Asn; Black Deaf Advocates. **Honors/Awds:** Paul G Hearne & AAPD Leadership Award, 2002; honor from Am Asn People with Disabilities, 2003; Secretarys Gold Medal Award, 2006. **Special Achievements:** First Black deaf female attorney in the US. **Business Addr:** Secretary, Member of the Board of Trustees, Lexington School for the Deaf & Center for the Deaf, 30th Ave & 75th St, Jackson Heights, NY 11370, **Business Phone:** (718)350-3056.

GORDON, DARRELL R.
Executive. **Personal:** Born May 18, 1926, Philadelphia, PA. **Educ:** Univ Pa, BS. **Career:** Gordon Chrysler-Plymouth-Dodge Inc, pres, bd chmn, 1989-. **Business Addr:** President, Board Chairman, Gordon Chrysler Plymouth Dodge Inc, 899 S Delsea Dr, Vineland, NJ 08360, **Business Phone:** (609)794-9700.

GORDON, DARRIEN X. JAMAL
Football player. **Personal:** Born Nov 14, 1970, Shawnee, OK; son of James Gordon and Goldia Gordon; children: Jalil Tanyu Gamnje & Najim Tariq Gamnje. **Educ:** Stanford Univ. **Career:** Football player (retired); San Diego Chargers, defensive back, 1993-96; Denver Broncos, 1997-98; Oakland Raiders, 1999-2000; Atlanta Falcons, 2001; Green Bay Packers, 2002. **Honors/Awds:** Four Times All Pro Selection, 1994, 1996, 1997, 2001.

GORDON, DEREK E.
Arts administrator. **Personal:** Born Dec 6, 1954, Baton Rouge, LA; son of Wilson and Deasry Jackson. **Educ:** Louisiana State Univ, Baton Rouge, LA, BM, Music, 1976; MM, Music, 1977. **Career:** Baton Rouge Arts & Humanities Coun, Baton Rouge, LA, community devt dir, 1976-78; Texas Community Arts, Austin, TX, prog assoc, 1978-80; Cultural Arts Coun Houston, Houston, TX, asst dir, 1980-85; LA Coun Arts, Baton Rouge, LA, exec dir, 1985-89; PA Coun Arts, Harrisburg, PA, exec dir, 1989; Jazz Lincoln Ctr, pres, chief exec officer & exec dir, currently. **Orgs:** 2nd vpres, Nat Assembly State Arts Agencies, 1989-; bd mem, Nat Assembly Local Arts Agencies, 1986-90; bd mem, Southern Arts Fed, 1980-88; bd mem, Mid Atlantic Arts Found, 1989-; panelist & consult, Nat Endowment Arts, 1980-. **Business Addr:** President, Chief Executive Officer, Jazz at Lincoln Center, 33 W 60th St 11th Fl, New York, NY 10023, **Business Phone:** (212)258-9829.*

GORDON, DWAYNE K.
Football player. **Personal:** Born Nov 2, 1969, White Plains, NY; married Melissa. **Educ:** Univ NH. **Career:** Football player (retired); Atlanta Falcons, linebacker, 1993-94; San Diego Chargers, 1995-96; New York Jets, 1997-2000.

GORDON, ED
Journalist. **Personal:** Born in Detroit, MI; married Karen; children: Taylor. **Educ:** Western MI Univ, BD, commun & political sci. **Career:** Black Entertainment TV, host, anchor, journalist; Dateline NBC, corresp; MSNBC, host, reporter, corresp; NPR, host, currently. **Honors/Awds:** Emmy NAACP Image Award; Journalist of the Yr Award, Nat Asn Black Journalists. **Business Addr:** Host, National Public Radio, Program Information, 635 Massachusetts Ave NW Suite 1, Washington, DC 20001, **Business Phone:** (202)513-3232.*

GORDON, DR. EDMUND W.
Educator, college teacher, executive director. **Personal:** Born Jun 13, 1921, Goldsboro, NC; married Susan Gitt; children: Edmund T, Christopher W, Jessica G & Johanna S. **Educ:** Howard Univ, BS, 1942, BD, 1945, DHL, 1998; Am Univ, MA, 1950; Columbia Univ Teachers Col, EdD, 1957; Yeshiva Univ, DHL, 1986; Brown Univ, DHL, 1988; Bank St Col, DHL, 1992; Mt Holyoke, DS, 1994. **Career:** Educator (retired), administrator; Yeshiva Univ, Ferkauf Grad Sch, Dept Spec Educ, chmn,1959-60, Albert Einstein Col Med, res assoc prof pediat, 1961-68; Proj Head Start, dir div res & eval, 1965-67; Ferkauf Univ, Dept Educ, Psychol & Guid, chmn, 1965-68; Columbia Univ, Dept Guid, chmn, 1968-73; Teachers Col, dir div health serv sci & educ, 1970-73; Am J Orthopsychiatry, ed, 1978-83; Rev Res Educ, ed, 1981-84; Yale Univ, John M Musser prof psychol, John M Musser prof psychol emer, 1991-; City Univ NY Grad Sch, distinguished prof, educ psychol, 1992-96, Col Bd, sr adv to pres, 1992-98, exec dir acad affairs, 1998-00; Teachers Col, Columbia Univ, vpres acad affairs & interim dean, 2000-01; Columbia Univ, Inst Urban &Minority Educ, Teachers Col, Richard March Hoe prof psychol & educ dir, 2001-, Richard March Hoe prof emer psychol & educ; Ctr Excellence Teaching & Learning, scholar-in residence, 2006-07. **Orgs:** Fel life mem AAAS; fel Am Psychol Asn; fel Am Psychol Soc; fel Orthopsychiatric Asn; Asn Black Psychologists; AERA; trustee, Pub Educ Asn; trustee, Savings Bank Rockland County Monsey; AERA Plaque Life. **Honors/Awds:** Outstanding Achievements Award, Howard Alumni, 1973; elected, Nat Acad Educ, 1978; Distinguished Serv Educ, Teachers Col Medal, 1993; Distinguished Career Contrib Award, Am Educ Res Asn, 1994. **Home Addr:** 3 Cooper Morris Dr, Pomona, NY 10970-3309. *

GORDON, FANNETTA NELSON
Educator. **Personal:** Born Nov 29, 1919, Hayneville, AL; daughter of Frank A Nelson Sr and Sophia Bailey Nelson; divorced; children: Kelso Jr. **Educ:** Univ Pittsburgh, BA, 1941, M.Ed, 1960; Univ Wash, MA, 1967; Franklin & Marshall Col, 1970. **Career:** Educator (retired); Cole Tutoring Serv, tutor French, Ger, eng, 1960-65; Fannetta Nelson Gordon Music & Dance Studio, owner & oper, 1941-69; City of Pittsburgh YWCA, youth adv, 1941-43; Dept Com, weather map plottng supvr 1943; State Dept Welfare Allegheny County Bd of Asst, social worker 1944-45, 1947-50; Pittsburgh Bd of Educ, teacher Ger, Eng Language background, Eng for foreigners 1955-69; Fillion Music Studios, teacher Piano, French & Ger, 1964-69; Penn Dept Educ, German educ adv 1969-73; Penn Dept Foreign Lang Educ, sr adv, st coordr of bilingual educ, 1973-82; Penn Hall Acad Pvt Sch, teacher summer sch. **Orgs:** Nat Asn Advan Colored People, 1936; Alpha Kappa Alpha 1938-; Sigma Kappa Phi, for lang hon, Univ of Pittsburgh, 1941; State youth adv Penn, Nat Asn Advan Colored People, 1942-44; Penn St Modern Lang Asn, 1960; Am Counc on the Teaching of Foreign Lang 1969-; Nat Counc of St Supr of Foregin Lang, 1969-; founder, Penn Black Conf on Higher Educ, 1971-; Teachers of Eng to Speakers of Other Lang, 1972-; Nat Asn on Bilingual

Educ, 1973-; Nat Asn Black Child Develop, 1976-; bd mem & vpres, Harrisburg, PA Branch Nat Asn Advan Colored People, 1983; Coalition for Coop between Harrisburg Nat Asn Advan Colored People Br & The Jewish Comn, 1994; liaison with Penn Dept of Educ Penn Black Conf on Higher Edn; fouder finan sec, vpres, mem govrning counc liaison with Penn Dept Educ, Penn Conf on Black Basic Educ; Steering com Nat Black Alliance on Grad Level Educ; Nat Counc of Negro Women; Univ Pittsburgh Alumna Asn; Univ Wash Alumna Asn; YWCA; Chruch of the Holy Cross; Choir Pgh, St Paul Epis Church, Harrisburg; st co-ordrIndo chinese Refugee Asst Educ. **Honors/Awds:** Gold Medal Award, Excellence in French, Univ Penn, 1941; 1 of 22 German teachers named as Fellows in the Experienced Teacher Fel Prog, Univ WA,1966-67; Nat Def Educ Act Fel, Univ, WA German; Nat Def Educ Act Fel, Stanford Univ Bad Boll Ger; citat serv to the commonwealth Gov Milton JShapp PA; scholar, Dawson MUS Studios, PA; scholar, Fillion Mus Studios,PA; Citation, Univ Pittsburgh Sch Educ Prof Contributions, 1985. **Special Achievements:** Articles: " Articulation in the Tchng of German" 1969; "The Status of Frgn Lang Educ & What Teachers Can Do to Improve It" 1973; "The Soc Purpose of Lang Learning" 1974; "Strategies for Improving the Status of Lang Techning Learning" 1976; "Is Foreign Lang Educ Necessary" 1977; "Foreign Lang Learning an open door to the world" 1976; "foreign language for the gifted& talented". **Home Addr:** 6160 Springford Dr, Harrisburg, PA 17111, **Home Phone:** (717)652-3581. *

GORDON, GARTH
Executive, president (organization), founder (originator). **Career:** Phones Etc, founder & pres, 1994-. **Business Addr:** Founder, President, Phones Etc, 8263 Causeway Blvd Suite E, Tampa, FL 33619, **Business Phone:** 877-888-7931.

GORDON, HELEN A.
Lawyer. **Personal:** Born Jul 20, 1923, New York; married Joseph A Bailey; children: Josette, Jonathan, Gordon. **Educ:** Hunter Col, NY, AB, 1947; Brooklyn Law Sch, LLB, JD, 1950. **Career:** Pvt Pract; AAA, arbitrator; City Col NY, lectr continuing educ; Gordon & Wilkins, atty, currently. **Orgs:** bd trustees, Grahan Sch Child Hastings Hudson, NY; bd dir, E Tremone Child Care Ctr; Bronx & Women's Bar Asn; Gothamettes Inc, NY. **Business Addr:** Attorney, Gordon & Wilkins, 304 W 138th St, New York, NY 10030, **Business Phone:** (212)690-2990.*

GORDON, DR. JOSEPH G
Scientist, administrator. **Personal:** Born Dec 25, 1945, Nashville, TN; son of Joseph G and Juanita T; married Ruth Maye Gordon; children: Perry. **Educ:** Harvard Col, AB, 1966; MIT, PhD, 1970. **Career:** Calif Inst Tech, asst prof, chem, 1970-75; IBM Almaden Res Ctr, res staff mem, 1975, New Directions Sci & Technol, mgr, currently; interfacial electrochem mgr 1978-84, interfacial sci mgr 1984-86, technical asst dir res, 1986-88; interfacial chem & structure mgr, 1988-90, materials sci & analysis mgr, 1990-94, batteries & displays mgr, 1994. **Orgs:** Am Chem Soc, Royal Soc Chem, Electrochemical Soc, Sigma Xi, Am Asn Advanc Sci; bd dir, 1973-75, chmn, 1975, Caltech Y; treas, 1982-84, pres, 1984-85, San Francisco Sect Electrochem Soc; secy, San Francisco Bay Area Chap Nat Org Prof Advan Black Chemists & Chem Engrs, 1983-86; chmn, Gordon Res Conf, Electrochemistry, 1987; Am Physical Soc; exec bd, Nat Org Prof Advan Black Chemists & Chem Engrs, 1986-92; treas, Soc Electroanalytical Chem, 1995-98. **Honors/Awds:** Outstanding Black Engineer for Technical Achievement Award, US Black Engineer & The Council of Engineering, Deans of Historically Black Cols & Universities, 1990; Percy Julian Award, Nat Org Prof Advan Black Chemists & Chem Engrs, 1993. **Special Achievements:** Published 10 patents & 26 articles in professional journals. **Business Addr:** Manager, New Directions for Science & Technology, IBM Research Division, Almaden Research Center, 650 Harry Rd, San Jose, CA 95120-6099, **Business Phone:** (408)927-1266.

GORDON, LANCASTER
Basketball player. **Personal:** Born Jun 24, 1962, Jackson, MS. **Educ:** Univ Louisville, attended 1984. **Career:** Basketball player (retired); Los Angeles Clippers, 1984-88; Pensacola Tornados, 1988-89. **Honors/Awds:** All-Am, The Sporting News; All-Am, Basketball Weekly; All-Metro Conf. **Home Addr:** Jackson, MS 39201, **Home Phone:** (601)922-7496.

GORDON, LEVAN
Judge. **Personal:** Born Apr 10, 1933, Philadelphia, PA; married Vivian J Goode; children: Shari-Lyn L. **Educ:** Lincoln Univ Pa, AB; Howard Univ Law Sch, LLB; Pa State Univ. **Career:** Judge (retired); Gov Comn Chester, Pa, assoc coun, 1964; Philadelphia Housing Info Serv, exec dir, 1966-68; Pa Labor Rel Bd, hearing examr, 1971-74; Munic Ct Philadelphia, judge, Ct Common Please Philadelphia, elected judge, 1979; Temple Univ Sch Criminal Justice, instr; Georgetown Univ, Intensive Session Trial Advocacy Skills, instr; Ct Common Pleas, judge. **Orgs:** Alpha Phi Alpha; Zeta Omicron Lambda; Lincoln Univ Alumni Asn; W Philadelphia HS Alumni Asn; Philadelphia Bar Asn; Pa Bar Asn; Lawyers Club Phila; Am Judicature Soc; Am Bar Asn; Nat Bar Asn, Pa Conf Trial Judges; Philadelphia Tribune Charities; Philadelphia Tribune Bowling League; Chris J Perry Lodge Elks IBPOE W; Nat Bowling Asn; Am Bowling Cong; AFNA Preceptor Prog; Nat Asn Blacks Criminal Justice; World Asn Judges; bd dir, Nat Kidney Found; Men Malvern; bd trustees, supvr jr ushers, Tindley Temple United Methodist Church; Black Methodist Church Renewal; bd dir, Combined Health Appeal Am; Nat Kidney Found, currently; bd trustees, alumni trustee, Lincoln Univ; Communities Sch Philadelphia Inc. **Honors/Awds:** Distinguished Service Award, Liberty Bell Dist Philadelphia Coun Boy Scouts Am; Community Service Award, Strawberry Mansion Civic Asn Puerto Rican; Lincoln Univ Alumni Achievement Award; Man of the Year, Zeta Omicron Lambda Chap, Alpha Phi Alpha, 1975; Man of the Year Award, Asn Bus & Prof Women Philadelphia & Vicinity, 1984; Distinguished Service Award, McMichael Home & Sch Asn; Award of Excellence, Methodist Men Tindley Temple United Methodist Church, 1986; Hall of Fame, W Philadelphia High Sch. **Military Serv:** AUS, 1953-55; USNR, res, 1958-61. **Home Addr:** 906 E Slocum St, Philadelphia, PA 19150.

GORDON, PATRICK HENRY
Detective. **Personal:** Born Oct 22, 1959, Kalamazoo, MI; son of Henry and Griselda Daniel. **Educ:** Kalamazoo Valley Community Col, AA, 1983; Western Mich Univ, BS, 1985; Univ Md, MS, 2002. **Career:** Correctional officer, 1985-87; probation officer, 1987-99; chief case mgr, 1994-95; Office Corp Coun, investr, 1999-. **Orgs:** Criminal Justice Student asn. **Special Achievements:** Certified Notary for the District of Columbia. **Business Addr:** Investigator, Office of the Corporation Counsel, 441 4th St NW Suite 600 S, Washington, DC 20001, **Business Phone:** (202)442-9887.

GORDON, ROBERT L. See Obituaries section.

GORDON, RONALD EUGENE
Executive. **Personal:** Born Feb 22, 1946, Springfield, OH; married Felicity Ralph; children: Mark, Rebecca & Ryan. **Educ:** Cent State Univ, BS, 1973; Xavier Univ, MBA, 1976. **Career:** Continental Can Co, prod supvr, 1971-77; Formica Corp, prod supvr, 1977-79; Miller Brewing Co, prod supvr, 1979-. **Honors/Awds:** The Olubandek Dada Award, Dept Bus Admin, Central State Univ, 1973. **Military Serv:** USAF, sgt, 4 yrs. **Business Addr:** Production Supervisor, Miller Brewing Company, PO Box 1170, Reidsville, NC 27320.

GORDON, RUFUS CARL, JR.
Actor. **Personal:** Born Jan 20, 1932, Richmond, VA. **Educ:** Brooklyn Col, 1959; Gene Frankel Theatre Workshop, 1969. **Career:** Theater : " Day of Absence/Happy Ending", 1966-67; "Kongi's Harvest", 1968; "Trials of Brother Jero", 1968; "Strong Breed", 1968; "One Last Look", 1968; "The Great White Hope", 1968; "Black Girl", 1971; "Ain't Supposedto Die a Natural Death", 1971; "The River Niger", 1973-74; "The Death of Boogie Woogie", 1979; "Zooman and the Sign", 1980; "In an Upstate Motel", 1981; "Do Lord Remember Me", 1983; "The Piano Lesson", 1987; "Master Harold & TheBoys"; "We"; "The Great Macdaddy"; "Nevis Mountain Dew"; "The Sixteenth Round"; "The Brownsville Raid"; "The Sty of the Blind Pig"; "Versus the IRS"; "Of Mice and Men"; "Checkmates", 1997; Ma Rainey's Black Bottom, 2003; Film : Gordon's War, 1973; The Bingo Long Traveling All-Stars and MotorKings, 1976; The Brother from Another Planet, 1984; Violated, 1984; No Mercy, 1986; TV: 'One Last Look", 1970; "Man in the Middle", 1970; "Ed Sullivan Show, with cast of Great White Hope", 1970; "Love Is a Many Splendored Thing", 1970; "Where the Heart Is"; "The Murder of Mary Phagan",;"Piano Lessons", "New York times",1988; "Roc"; "Malcolm & Eddie", 1997; Hanging with Mr Cooper, 1996; NYNews, 1995; Can't Hurry Love, CBS, 1994; The Piano Lesson, Hallmark Hallof Fame, 1995; Due South, 1994, Burke's Law, 1993; Crossroads, 1993;Disaster on the Coastliner; As the World Turns, 1991; The Practice, 1997;The Wedding, 1997; Nash Bridges, 1999; "Nash Bridges", "Felicity", "ER", 2000; "JAG", 2002; "Whoopi", 2003; "Law & Order", 2004. **Orgs:** AEA; Am Federation of Television & Radio Artists; Screen Actors Guild; Project 2000, advisory bd. **Honors/Awds:** NAACP Theatre Awards, Nomination for Best Supporting Actor, 1991; City of Inglewood, CA, Commendation for Commitment to Performing Arts, 1996; Inst of Musical Arts Award, 1996; City of Los Angeles, Certificate of Recognition, 1996; CA State Senate Award, Recognition of Time and Effort for Youth, 1997; County of Los Angeles Commendation, 1997; Living Legend Awd, 12th Natl Black Theatre Festival, 2001. **Special Achievements:** Appeared in "Love Songs" (Charles Fuller) TV movie produced for Showtime TV, 1999; Appeared in August Wilson's Pulitzer winning Play "The Piano Lesson". **Business Addr:** Actor, Krasny Agency, 1501 Broadway Suite 1510, New York, NY 10036.*

GORDON, SHERMAN A
Clergy. **Personal:** Born May 27, 1972, Greenwood, MS; son of Turner Jr and Malissie C Price; married Marina Renee, Aug 19, 1995; children: Exodus G. **Educ:** Univ Calif, Santa Barbara, BA, 1994; Claremont Sch Theol, MAR, 1999; United Theol Sem, DMin, 2001. **Career:** Marcus Garvey Elem sch, teacher, 1995; Brookins Comm AME Church, youth minister, 1995-97; New Philadelphia AME Church, sr pastor, 1997-. **Orgs:** Counr, Upward Bound, 1992-94; pres, NuPower Community Outreach, 2001-02; pres, NuPhilly Invest club, 2001-03; pres, Nat Asn Advan Colored People, 2002-. **Honors/Awds:** Going Beyond The Wall Award, Watts Health System, 2001; Outstanding Support Award, SCCLO, 2002; Cert Ecognition/Service, Carson City, 2003; Outstanding Leadership Award, Nat Asn Advan Colored People, Torrance, CA, 2003. **Special Achievements:** Empowering, Equipping & Employing Youth, 2001; Future Leader of America, Ebony Magazine, 2003. **Business Phone:** (310)537-8777.*

GORDON, THOMAS
Baseball player. **Personal:** Born Nov 18, 1967, Sebring, FL. **Career:** Kansas City Royals, pitcher, 1988-95; Boston Red Sox, 1996-99; Chicago Cubs, 2001-02; Houston Astros, 2002; Chicago White Sox, 2003; NY Yankees, pitcher, 2004-05; Philadelphia Phillies, pitcher, 2006-08; Arizona Diamondbacks, 2009-. **Honors/Awds:** Rolaids Relief Man of the Year Award, 1998; Steve Carlton Most Valuable Pitcher Award, 2006. **Business Addr:** Professional Baseball Player, Philadelphia Phillies, Veterans Stadium, 3501 S Broad St, Philadelphia, PA 19148, **Business Phone:** (215)463-6000.

GORDON, WALTER CARL, JR.
Hospital administrator, physician. **Personal:** Born Oct 25, 1927, Albany, GA; married Suzanne Patterson; children: Walter III, Tia. **Educ:** Hampton Inst, BS 1947; Tuskegee Inst, MS 1948; Meharry Med Col, MD 1955. **Career:** Physician (retired); Lincoln Univ, fac; Albany Univ, fac; Letterman Army Hosp, intern, 1956; Walter Reed Army Hosp, resident, 1961; Fitzsimmons Gen Hosp, chief gen surgeon, 1966-68; Phoebe Putney Mem Hosp, surgeon, past chief staff, past chmn bd, bd mem emer, 2005; Va Clin, physician, 2003-06. **Orgs:** AMA; Dougherty County Med Asn; GA State Med Asn; dipl Am Bd Surgery; Sigma Pi Phi; mem Alpha Phi Alpha Frat; bd dir, FL A&M; Criterion Club; Albany C of C; fel Am Col Surgeons. **Honors/Awds:** Recip 3 Commendation Med AUS; Legion of Merit. **Special Achievements:** He became the first African-American surgeon at Walter Reed, the Army's most distinguished medical center. **Military Serv:** AUS lt col, 1956-68, col, 1981-93; 3 Army Commendation Medals, 1 Legion of Merit award. *

GORDON, WALTER LEAR, III
Lawyer. **Personal:** Born Mar 6, 1942, Los Angeles, CA; married Teresa Sanchez; children: Maya Luz. **Educ:** Ohio State Univ, BA, 1963; Univ Calif Los Angeles, MPA, 1965, JD, 1973, PhD, 1981. **Career:** Univ Calif Los Angeles Law Sch, lectr, 1978-82; Gordon Law Firm, atty, currently. **Orgs:** bd mem, SCLC W, 1980-85; Langston Bar Asn, 1986. **Special Achievements:** publications: The Law & Pvt Police, Rand, 1971, Crime & Criminal Law; also published several articles. *

GORDON-DILLARD, JOAN YVONNE
Educator. **Personal:** Born Oct 4, 1955, Eglin AFB, FL; daughter of Charles Robert and Lois Jackson; married Marvin Clinton, Aug 29, 1992. **Educ:** Fisk Univ, BA, 1977; La Sorbonne, Paris, France, cert, 1976; Ohio State Univ, MA, 1978, PhD, 1982. **Career:** US Dept Labor, educ media specialist, 1979; Ohio State Univ, coordr res, develop & support, 1983-94; IBM, info developer, 1984-86, educ specialist, 1986-87, mkt rep, 1988-90, adv instr, developer, 1990-94; Lucent Technol, proj mgr distance learning, 1996. **Orgs:** Alpha Kappa Alpha Sorority Inc, 1978-; Asn Commun & Technol, 1982-85, 1993; Doug Williams Found, 1988-89; Minority Athletes Networking Inc, fundraising, 1990-; Crescent Moon Found, 1990-; Women Commun, 1991, 1993; team leader, IBM Aristotle Prog, 1992-. **Honors/Awds:** Travel Grant, Fisk Univ & Vanderbilt Univ, 1976; One-Year Minority Fellowship, Ohio State Univ, 1977. **Special Achievements:** Honored during high school graduation ceremony, Grace Dodge Vocational High School, Barbara Bush was keynote speaker, 1991. **Home Phone:** (201)945-6310. **Business Addr:** Project Manager, Lucent Technol Inc, 140 Centennial Ave, Piscataway, NJ 08854, **Business Phone:** (908)457-7301.

GORDY, BERRY, III
Executive, television producer, composer. **Personal:** Born Nov 28, 1929, Detroit, MI; son of Berry Sr and Bertha Fuller; married Grace Eaton, 1990 (divorced); children: Berry IV, Terry James, Hazel Joy, Kerry A, Kennedy W & Stefan K; married Thelma Coleman (divorced); married Raynona Singleton (divorced). **Career:** Featherweight boxer; auto worker; composer; 3-D Record Mart, owner; composer: You Made Me So Very Happy; Motown Rec Corp, founder & pres, 1959-88; Tamla Rec, founder; Motown Record Co, founder & owner; Films: Mahogany, dir, 1975; The Wiz, exec producer, 1978; The Last Dragon, producer, 1985; Soundtrack: Daddy Day Care, 2003; The Italian Job, 2003; Lord of War, 2005; Jarhead, 2005. **Orgs:** Dir Guild Am; chmn, Motown Ind entertainment complex. **Honors/Awds:** Bus Achievement Award, Interracial Coun Bus Opportunity, 1967; SecondAnnual American Music Award, 1975; Whitney M Young Jr Award, Los Angeles Urban League, 1980; exec producer film Berry Gordy's The Last Dragon, 1984; elected Gordon Grand Fel, Yale Univ, 1985; inducted into the Rockand Roll Hall of Fame, 1988; hon degree, Mich State Univ, 2006; hondegree, Occidental Col, 2007. **Special Achievements:** One of Five Leading Entrepreneurs of Nation, Babson Col, 1978; author, Berry Gordy: To Be Loved, 1994.

GORDY, DESIREE D'LAURA
Lawyer. **Personal:** Born Jul 14, 1956, Long Beach, CA; married Terry J Gordy Sr; children: Terry James Jr, Whitney Jade. **Educ:** San Diego State Univ, BA, 1978; Southwestern Univ Sch Law, JD, 1982. **Career:** Jobete Music Co Inc, in-house coun; Motown Productions Inc, in-house coun; Motown Rec Corp, in-house coun, 1983-88; WORK Rec, Div MCA Rec, outside coun & bus affairs, 1987-90; Ice Cube & Pat Charbonnet, in-house coun, 1990-92; pvt pract, entertainment law practr, currently. **Orgs:** Vol, Bradley Gov Campaign, 1986; vol, All Africa Games Kenya, 1987; Black Women Lawyers Asn; John Langston Bar Asn; Calif Women's Lawyers Asn; Women Lawyers Asn Los Angeles. **Special Achievements:** Top 100 Black Bus & Prof Women, 1986; sponsor c underdeveloped nations; concert promoter, artist management, songwriter.

GORDY, SONJA M.
School administrator. **Career:** St Anthony Catholic Sch, admin asst. *

GORE, CEDRIC J
Entrepreneur, software developer, musician. **Personal:** Born Jul 24, 1969, Brooklyn, NY; son of Roy and Lillian; married April-Leite Gore, 1998. **Educ:** Johnson & Wales Univ, AS, hospitality mgt; Fla Int Univ, BA, bus mgt. **Career:** Kapkin Communs, sr web developer, 1998-2000; Javakitty Media, pres, 1998-2002; CD Intelligence LLC, pres, chief technol officer, 2002-. **Business Addr:** Chief Technology Officer, CD Intelligence LLC, 1117 Peachtree Walk Suite 121, Atlanta, GA 30309, **Business Phone:** (404)817-8050.

GORE, DAVID L.
Lawyer. **Personal:** Born Dec 17, 1937, Horry County, SC; son of Samuel B and Sadie M Anderson; married Mary L Andrews; children: David Jr, Sheila. **Educ:** Allen Univ, BA, 1959; SC State Col, MEd, 1966; Howard Univ Sch Law, JD, 1969. **Career:** Nat Labor Rels Bd, legal asst to chmn, 1969-70; United Steelworkers Am, asst gen coun, 1970-81, dist coun, 1982-; Gore & Gore, 1999. **Orgs:** Ill & Pa Bar; 3rd 6th 7th & 10th & DC Ct Appeals, US Supreme Ct; Phi Alpha Delta Legal Fraternity. **Military Serv:** AUS, seargeant, 1960-63. **Business Addr:** District 7 Counsel, United Steelworkers of America, 155 N MI Suite 706, Chicago, IL 60601, **Business Phone:** (312)616-4224.

GORE, JAMES ANTHONY
Executive. **Personal:** Born Jul 25, 1971, Brooklyn, NY; son of Roy and Lillian. **Educ:** Cleveland State Univ, BA, bus admin & finance, 1998. **Career:** WW Grainger, Internet Com Div, sales, 1993-2000; Javakitty Media, co-founder & vpres, 1998-2002; CD Intelligence, vpres, sales, 2002-. **Orgs:** Bd Adv, Gruuve Inc. **Business Addr:** Vice President, CD Intelligence, 1117 Peachtree Walk Suite 121, Atlanta, GA 30309, **Business Phone:** (404)817-8050.

GORE, JOHN MICHEL
Government official. **Personal:** Born Aug 6, 1955, Columbus, OH; son of John L and Rose M; married Judith Ann Jackson, Jun 24, 1978; children: Johnel Marie & Janee Michelle. **Educ:** Bowling Green State Univ, bus admin, 1976. **Career:** Ohio State Auditor, welfare investr, 1976, asst auditor, 1978, asstauditor in charge, 1984, field audit supv, 1987, asst audit mgr, 1990, astdep auditor, 1992-; City Columbus, equal bus opportunity specialist, 1995-96, admin analyst II, 1996-97, exec asst dir, 1997-, regional execdir, currently; Alpha Midwestern, regional exec dir, 2004. **Orgs:** Nat Asn Black Acct; Nat Asn Cert Fraud Examiners, 1992-; deacon bd &finance com, Free & Accepted Masons; Sec Baptist Church; UNF; Alpha Phi Alpha Fraternity Inc. **Honors/Awds:** Exceptional Service Award, Alpha Phi Alpha, 1989, 1999; Man of the Year, Sec Baptist Church, 1990; Chapter Member of the Year, Nat Asn Black Accountants, Columbus, 1992-93. **Home Addr:** 183 Farmwood Pl, Gahanna, OH 43230-6261. **Business Addr:** Executive Assistant, Regional Executive Director, City of Columbus, Equal Business Opportunity Commmission Office, 4th Fl 90 W Broad St, Columbus, OH 43215, **Business Phone:** (614)645-4764.

GORE, JOSEPH A.
School administrator. **Personal:** Born in Supply, NC; married Gloria Gardner; children: Duane K. **Educ:** Livingstone Col, BS, 1952; Univ Mich, MS, 1960; Yale Univ, MPH, 1970; Univ Mass, EdD, 1977. **Career:** Mary Holmes Col, dean men & sci instr, 1956-58, dean students, 1959-62, acad dean, 1962-68, dir health servs, 1968-70, pres, 1972; Mary Holmes High Sch, prin, 1958-59; Tougaloo Col, acad dean, 1970-72; Brunswick Community Col, special asst to pres, currently. **Orgs:** FAFEO; Am Pub Asn; Nat Educ Asn; Clay City Chamber Com; bd dir, I M Hosp; bd trustee, Burnswick Community Hosp; Cape Fear Area United Way; Brunswick County Parks & Recreation; Brunswick Community Col Found; Supply NC Coastal Resources Comn. **Military Serv:** AUS, medic 82nd airborne div, 1953-55. **Business Addr:** Special Asssistate to President, Burnswick Community College, 50 College Rd, PO Box 30, Supply, NC 28462-0030.

GOREE, JANIE GLYMPH. See Obituaries section.

GORMAN, BERTHA GAFFNEY
Executive, association executive. **Personal:** Born in Greenville, TX; daughter of Vivian Shoals and Bernice; married Prentice (divorced); children: Gregory G & Glen G. **Educ:** Sacramento Community Col & Am River Col, attended 1969; Sacramento State Col, Sacramento, BA, 1972; Univ Uppsala, Sweden, attended 1973. **Career:** Sacramento Bee Newspaper, reporter, 1971-79; CA State Dept Mental Health, pub info officer, 1979-80; CA State Assembly, prin consult in-chg media, 1980-85; Lockheed Corp, Calabasas, dir, issues mgt, 1985-95; State & Local Govt Affairs, Lockheed Martin, dir, 1995; CA State, Asn Secy External Affairs, Health & Human Serv Agency, assoc secy, currently; Gaffney, Gorman & Assoc, dir, currently. **Orgs:** Bd chair, Sacramento Regional Asst Dist, 1981-85; secy, Black Pub Rels Soc CA, LA, 1986-90; Black Women's Forum, LA, 1987; vice chair, Great Beginning Black Babies Task Force, LA, 1990-91; bd dirs, Cares Clinic, 2002; Legis Advocate CA, Nat Asn Advan Colored People, currently; bd dir, Am Cancer Soc, CA Div; Am Cancer Soc Mkt & Commun Comt, CA Div. **Honors/Awds:** Black Public Relations Society Honoree, 1991; PRSA Prism Award, 1994; IABC Merit Award. **Business Addr:** Associate Secretary, California Department of Health, External Affairs, Health & Human Services Agency, PO Box 997413, Sacramento, CA 95899-7413, **Business Phone:** (916)654-3304.

GOSLEE, DR. LEONARD THOMAS
Physician. **Personal:** Born Aug 5, 1932, Salisbury, MD. **Educ:** Howard Univ, BS; Boston Univ, MS; Meharry Med Col, MD. **Career:** Detroit Gen Hosp, internship, 1958-59; Children's Hosp Mich, residency, 1959-62, chief residency, 1962-63; Laguardia Med Group Inc, physician, 1964-; pvt pract, currently. **Orgs:** Nat Med Asn; Am Acad Pediatrics; NY State Med Asn; Queens Col Med Asn; Am Asn Pediatrics; Sch Health Planning Prog. **Home Addr:** 639 W End Ave 11A, New York, NY 10025. **Business Addr:** Physician, 11218 Springfield Blvd, Jamaica, NY 11429, **Business Phone:** (718)479-6600.

GOSS, CLAYTON
Playwright. **Personal:** Born Jan 1, 1946, Philadelphia, PA. **Career:** Plays: "Homecookin"; "Of Being Hit"; "Space in Time"; "Bird of Paradise"; "Ornette"; "Oursides"; "Mars"; "Andrew"; Howard Univ, Washington, DC, playwright-in-residence. **Home Addr:** 6653 Sprague St, Philadelphia, PA 19119, **Home Phone:** (215)844-5017. *

GOSS, LINDA
Storyteller, folk artist, cultural historian. **Personal:** Born in Alcoa, TN; daughter of Willie Louise McNair and Willie Murphy McNair; married Clay Goss; children: Aisha, Uhuru & Jamal. **Educ:** Howard Univ, Wash, DC, BA, drama, 1969; Antioch Univ, Yellow Springs, OH, ME, educ, 1978. **Career:** Prof storyteller; Smithsonian Inst, several mus, performer; major mus, festivals, univs, performer; Nat Asn Black Storytellers Inc, co-founder, currently; Rosenbach Mus, artist-in-residence, currently; PFPs Local Knowledge proj, featured artist, currently. **Orgs:** Pres, Asn Black Storytelling, 1984-; pres, Hola Kumba Ya Cult Orgn, 1989-; founding mem, Keepers Cult. **Honors/Awds:** Linda Goss Day, City Wash, DC, named in honor, 1983; Official Storyteller of Philadelphia, City Philadelphia, PA, 1984; Lind Goss Day, City Alcoa, TN, named in honor, 1986; Talk That Talk, anthology African-American storytelling, Simon & Schuster, 1989, Best Paperback of 1989, Publ Weekly, selected by Book of the Month Club for their Quality Paperback Club; Oracle Lifetime Achievement Award in Storytelling, Nat Storytelling Network, 2003. **Special Achievements:** Co-author of The Baby Elopard book and cassette, Bantam/Doubleday/Dell, 1989. **Home Addr:** 6653 Sprague St, Philadelphia, PA 19119. **Business Addr:** Co-Founder, National Association Black Storytellers Inc, PO Box 67722, Baltimore, MD 21215, **Business Phone:** (410)947-1117.

GOSS, TOM
Vice president (Organization), athletic director, executive. **Personal:** Born Jul 6, 1946, Knoxville, TN; married Carol Goings; children: Anika, Fatima & Maloni. **Educ:** Univ Mich, BS, phys educ, 1968. **Career:** Procter & Gamble Corp, 1969; R. J. Reynolds Industs, Del Monte Corp, sales mgt staff; Faygo Beverage, Detroit, MI, sales exec; Nat Beverage, exec vpres; PIA Merchandising, Irvine, CA, pres & chief exec officer, 1993-97; Univ Mich, athletic dir, 1997-2000; Goss LLC, chmn, 2000-; The Goss Group, Inc., partner & advisor, chmn, 2000-; United Am Healthcare Corp, vice chmn bd, 2000-; Goss Steel & Processing LLC, chmn, 2003-; Bristol Logistics LLC., chmn, currently. **Honors/Awds:** All-Big Ten, Univ Mich, 1968. **Special Achievements:** First black athletic dir at University of Michigan.

GOSS, WILLIAM EPP
Executive. **Personal:** Born Feb 3, 1941, Baltimore, MD; married Charlotte; children: Maisha, Zuri & Malaika. **Educ:** Morgan State Univ, BA, 1968; Univ Chicago Grad Sch Bus, MBA, 1975, MA, soc serv admin, 1970. **Career:** Talent Asst Prog Inc, asso dir, 1975-76, exec dir, 1976-; Minority Bus, mgt consult; Henry Booth House Settlement-Hull House Asn, ctr dir; Univ IL, Jan Addams Sch Work, field instr; Hull House Asn, bd dir; Henry Booth House, pres & chief exec officer, currently. **Orgs:** Nat Asn Soc Workers; Asn Black MBA'S; Asn Black Soc Workers. **Honors/Awds:** Fel, Univ Chicago Grad Sch Soc Serv Admin, 1969-70; Outstanding Community Serv, Chicago Police Dept, 1973; Chicago Asn Com & Indust Bicentennial Award, Great Am Excellence Econ, 1976. **Home Addr:** 6108 S Dorchester Ave, Chicago, IL 60637, **Home Phone:** (773)363-0611. **Business Addr:** President, Chief Executive Officer, Henry Booth House, 2929 S Wabash, Chicago, IL 60628, **Business Phone:** (312)225-0800.

GOSSETT, LOUIS CAMERON, JR.
Actor. **Personal:** Born May 27, 1936, Brooklyn, NY; son of Louis Sr and Hellen Rebecca Wray; married Christina Mangosing (divorced 1975); children: Sate; married Cyndi James (divorced 1992). **Educ:** NY Univ, BA, drama. **Career:** Actor, made Broadway debut in Take A Giant Step; The Desk Set, Broadway; Lost in the Stars, Broadway; Raisin in the Sun, Broadway; The Blacks; My Sweet Charlie; Carry Me Back to Morning side Heights; The Charlatan; Tell Pharoah; Roots; Murderous Angels, 1971-72; Chicago, 1996; tv series: Resurrection Boulevard, 2002; tv movies: Inside, 1996; The Inspectors, 1998; Love Songs, 1999; Strange Justice, 1999; Dr Lucille, 2000; For Love of Olivia, 2001; What About Your Friends: Weekend Getaway, 2002; Jasper, Texas, 2003; Momentum, 2003; films: The Skin Game, 1971, The Laughing Policeman, 1974, It's Good to Be Alive, 1974, The White Dawn, 1975, Little Ladies of the Night, 1977, The Choirboys, 1977, The Deep, 1977, He Who Walks Alone, 1978, An Officer & a Gentleman, 1982, Jaws 3, 1983, The Guardian, 1984, Finders Keepers, 1984, Iron Eagle, 1985, Enemy Mine, 1985, Firewalker, 1986, The Principal, 1987, Iron Eagle II, 1988, Toy Soldiers, 1991; Diggstown, 1992; Monolith, 1993; Flashfire, 1993; Curse of the Starving Class, 1994; Iron Eagle IV, 1995; Managua, 1996; The Wall That Heals, 1997; Legend of the Mummy, 1997; The Highway man, 2000; Deceived, voice, 2002; Momentum, 2003; Solar Strike, Window, 2005; Club Soda, 2006; Daddy's Little Girls, 2007; Cover, 2007; Delgo, 2008; The BAMN Squad, 2008; The Perfect Game, 2008; The Least Among You, 2008; The Real Catch, 2008; Buttermilk Sky, 2008. **Orgs:** Motion Picture Arts & Sciences Acad; SAG; NAG; AEA; AFM; Alpha Phi Alpha; AGVA; Legal Defense Fund, Nat Asn Advan Colored People. **Honors/Awds:** Emmy Award for role of Fiddler in Roots; Oscar, Best Supporting Actor; Trumpet Award, 1997; NAACP, Image Award, TV Drama Supporting Actor, 1998; Daytime Emmy Award for Outstanding Children's Special, 1998; Black Reel Award for Best Director, 2000; Maverick Spirit Award, Ciniquest, 2009. **Business Addr:** Actor, Writers & Artists Agency Inc, 8383 Wilshire Blvd Suite 550, Beverly Hills, CA 90211-2404, **Business Phone:** (323)866-0900.

GOSS-SEEGER, DEBRA A
Manager. **Personal:** Born Apr 21, 1958, San Francisco, CA; daughter of Waymond and Mildred Wilson; married Willie Seeger (divorced 1982); children: Justin Seeger. **Educ:** Alameda Jr Col, AS, bus admin, 1986; Univ San Francisco, CA, BS, bus admin, 1988; Univ Calif, Berkeley, CA. **Career:** Xerox Corp, Sunnyvale, CA, exec acct rep, 1975-80; Clorox Corp, Oakland, CA, admin asst, 1980-85; Pacific Gas & Electric Co, Berkeley, CA, major acct rep; Hewlett-Packard Co, staff, currently. **Orgs:** Exec comt mem, Nat Black MBA Asn. **Business Addr:** Staff, Hewlett-Packard Company, 3000 Hanover St, PO Box 1048, Palo Alto, CA 94304.

GOTHARD, BARBARA WHEATLEY
Educator, school principal, government official. **Personal:** Born Nov 23, 1937, Springfield, IL; married Donald L; children: Donald Jr & Ann Marie. **Educ:** Mt Mary Col, Milwaukee, BA, 1959; Long Island Univ, Greenvale, NY, MS, 1972; Mich State Univ, PhD, 1977. **Career:** Milwaukee Pub Sch, art teacher, 1959-64; Union Free Sch Dist 4, Northport, NY, art teacher, 1966-71; Crimel Oakland Univ, Rochester, MI, free lance graphic artist, 1972-73; Cult Arts Events, Advisor Newspaper Utica, MI, ed, 1973-75; Utica Community Sch, art teacher, 1973-77; Utica High Sch, MI, assoc prin, 1977-; Mich State Univ, instr, 1980; Burger King Corp, Pub Affairs & Corp Social Responsibility Dept, 1983-89; Univ Calif, Sch Mgt, lectr & adj prof; Univ NC, Kenan-Flagler Bus Sch, lectr; Hill & Knowlton's Corp, Social Responsibility & Corp Sustainable Develop Groups, sr counr; Mid E & African Region, dir pub affairs; Dow Chem Co, global leader external affairs; Community Cols, bd gov, currently. **Orgs:** Bd dir, Meadow brook Art Gallery, Oakland Univ, 1973-76; bd dir, Xochipilli Gallery, 1974-76; Chairperson pub comn, Mich Asn Sec Sch Prin, 1977-; Nat Asn Sec Sch Prin, 1977-; Mich Coun Women Sch Admin, 1978-; vpres & gen mgr, Jackie Robinson Found. **Honors/Awds:** Outstanding Young Women of Am, 1973. **Special Achievements:** Utica Cultural Arts Council Exhibits Paintings include Main Streams "74"Marietta College, OH, Detroit Artists Market "Woman Works" Univ of Michigan, Midwest Artists Milwaukee Performing Arts Center, Macomb CoBi-Centennial Exchange Program, Coventry, England; solo shows at Delta College, Univ City, MI, Art Gallery Central Michigan University, Mt MaryCollege, Milwaukee, WI, Xochipilli Gallery, MI; newspaper reviews prev collections, 1972-80; publ: "Art Tchr, Admin" Secondary Educ Today Jour ofthe MI Assn of Second Sch Prin 1978. **Business Addr:** Board of Governors, Community Colleges, 1102 Q St, Sacramento, CA 95811-6549.

GOTHARD, DONALD L.
Automotive executive. **Personal:** Born Dec 2, 1934, Madison, WI; son of William H (deceased) and Lorraine M Williams (deceased); married Doris M Smith, May 27, 1990; children:

Donald Jr, Ann Marie. **Educ:** Univ Notre Dame, BSEE, 1956; Res Officers Training Corp, attended 1956; GMI Tech, staff mgt prog cert, 1974. **Career:** Automotive executive (retired); United Technologies, consult; GM AC, Sparkplug Div, jr engr, prod engineering, 1956, Electron Div, design syst engr, Mace Missile Guidance & Navig Equip, 1958-62; Apollo Ground Support Syst, engr, 1962-66; GM Delco, Electron Div, lab supvr; Apollo Guidance Sys Lab, 1966-71; GM Auto, Electron Control Syst Develop, 1971; GM Instrumentation Sect, Test Dept, supvr engineering staff, 1972; GM Engineering Staff, asst mgr, 1973-76; GM Chevrolet, Motor Div, sr design engr, 1976-77, from asst staff engineer to staff engineer, 1977-82; GM Truck & Bus Engineering Opers, chief engr, elec components, 1982-85, exec engr, adv vehicle engineering, 1985-90; GM Res Lab, dir res admin serv, 1990-92; GM Design Ctr, exec prototype & process engineering, 1992-93; GM Mfg Ctr, Prototype Shops, dir qual & mfg eng, 1993-95. **Orgs:** Adv comt, Utica Community Sch Citizens, 1975-76; secy, Shelby Township Cable TV Reg Comt, 1980-84; Soc Auto Engrs, 1976-00; citizens comt educ & Financial needs & resources, Macomb Co Community Col, 1976; vol, YMCA Youth Basketball Prog, 1971-87; Meadow Brook Art Gallery Asn, 1972-80; asst coach, Utica Eisenhower High Sch Girls Basketball, 1985-87; bd dirs, Black Alumni Notre Dame, 1988-94; adv coun, Univ Notre Dame, 1989-; bd dirs, Detroit Sci & Engineering Fair, 1992-99. **Honors/Awds:** NASA Apollo Achievement Award, 1969; Mass Inst Technol Cert Commend Apollo Program, 1969; Certificate of Appreciation Utica Community Schools, 1972-74; Distinguished Service Award, Utica Educ Asn, 1975-76; Certificate of Appreciation Macomb County Community Col, 1976; Society of Automotive Engineers Excellence in Oral Presentation, 1987; nominated, Black Engineer of the Year Award, 1991; Honor Award, Univ Notre Dame, Engineering Col, 1994; Rev Edward Williams Service Award, Black Alumni Notre Dame, 1994; Black Engineer of the Year Award For Lifetime Achievement-Industry, 1995. **Special Achievements:** Name carried to moon on first two lunar landings 1969. **Military Serv:** AUS Ordnance, lt, 1956-58; Distinguished Military Graduate Award, Notre Dame 1956. **Home Addr:** 5510 Brookside Lane, Washington, MI 48094. *

GOTTI, IRV (IRVING DOMINGO LORENZO, JR.)
Songwriter, actor, composer. **Personal:** Born Jun 26, 1970, Hollis, NY; married Debbie; children: Sonny & JJ. **Career:** Films: Rush Hour, 1998; Belly, 1998; Light It Up, 1999; Next Friday, 2000; Romeo Must Die, 2000; Bamboozled, 2000; Double Take, 2001; Down to Earth,2001; Exit Wounds, 2001; The Fast & the Furious, 2001; The Wire, 2002; Friday After Next, 2002; Barbershop 2: Back in Business, 2004; Bride & Prejudice, 2004; Shall We Dance, 2004; Animal 2005; Angel: One More Road to Cross, Composer, 2001; Mighty D-Block, composer, 2006; Albums: "Heroes and Thieves", 2007; "Gotti's Way", actor, 2007; Blunt/TVT Records, A&R rep, 1995; Def Jam Records, A&R rep, 1995-99; Top Dawg Prod, founder & ceo; Murder Inc Records, founder & ceo, 1999; The Inc Records, ceo. **Honors/Awds:** Two BMI Urban Awards; one BMI Pop Award, 2002. *

GOUDY, DR. ANDREW JAMES
Educator. **Personal:** Born Apr 15, 1943, Martins Ferry, OH; son of Bertha and Sidney. **Educ:** Ind Univ Pa, BS, 1967, MS, 1971; Univ Pittsburgh, PhD, phys chem, 1976. **Career:** Cameron City High Sch, teacher, 1968; Bald Eagle Nittany Hifh Sch, teacher, 1969; Canon Mcmillan High Sch, teacher, 1971; W Chester Univ, prof, 1977, chmn dept chem, 1983-87; Delaware State Univ, Dept Chem, prof & chairperson, currently; Hydrogen Storage Res Ctr, dir, currently. **Orgs:** Am Chem Soc, 1976-; Intl Asn Hydrogen Energy, 1982, Nat Asn Advan Colored People; Nat Org Prof Advan Black Chemists & Chem Eng; Nat Hydrogen Asn; vpres, Capital City Rotary Club. **Honors/Awds:** Article publ J Less Common Metals 99, 1984, J Less Common Metals 91, 1983; Research Grants: Petroleum Research Fund, 1982; NSF, 1986; Distinguished Teacher and Researcher, West Chester Univ, 1992. **Business Addr:** Professor, Chairperson, Delaware State University, Department of Chemistry College of Mathematics Natural Sciences andTechnology, Rm 301 Mishoe Sci Ctr S 1200 N DuPont Hwy, Dover, DE 19901, **Business Phone:** (302)857-6534.

GOUGH, DR. WALTER C
Physician. **Personal:** Born Apr 24, 1943, Pittsburgh, PA; son of Walter C Gough Sr and Kathryn Scott Grinage; married May Ella Bailey, Sep 24, 1974; children: Wanda, Marcus, Henry, Lynette, Kathryn & Nora. **Educ:** Tarkio Col, AB, 1965; Meharry Med Col, MD, 1970; Mercy Hosp Pittsburgh, intern resident, 1970-72; Meharry Med Col, pediatrics resident, 1973. **Career:** Mound Bayou, MS, med dir, 1974-; Black Belt Family Health Ctr, med dir, 1973; Taboman Hosp, dir, 1972-75; Delta Comm Hosp & Health Ctr, physician, 1974-; Choctaw Indian Hosp, med dir, 1976-78; Nat Health Serv, med dir, 1978-81; Spectrum ER Care, dir, 1981-84; Gough's Family & Pediats Clinic, owner, 1984-. **Orgs:** Allegheny County Med Co, 1971-72; AMA, NMA 1973-74; Omega Psi Phi 1967-; MS Heart Asn, 1974; bd trustees, Delta Health Ctr, 1986-89, WQSZ 1989-; ACEP, MS Chap, pres, 1999; MS State Bd of Health, 2000-. **Honors/Awds:** Man of the Year Award, Pittsburgh Jaycees, 1972; Outstanding Alumnus 15 yrs, Tarkio Col, 1974; Distinguished Alumni, Tarkio Col, 1974; Bronze Medal Tarkio Col, 1965; Best Scientific Article, Meharry Col, 1966; Stud Christian Med Soc, 1967; Jaycee's Man of the Year, 1970; Board Certified, Am Bd Physicians, 1977, 1983, 1989; Bd Certified, Am Bd Emergency Med, 1983, 1989; Man of the Year, Omega Psi Phi 1986; No 1 Award Iota Omicron Charter, 1986. **Special Achievements:** First black graduate at Tariko Col; first African-American physician in Sunflower County, MS; first black physician on the MS State bd of health. **Home Addr:** PO Box 107, Mound Bayou, MS 38762. **Business Addr:** Physician, Gough, 189 N Main St, PO Box 68, Drew, MS 38737, **Business Phone:** (662)745-6638.

GOULBOURNE, DONALD SAMUEL, JR.
Social worker, administrator, executive director. **Personal:** Born May 5, 1950, New Rochelle, NY; son of Donald Samuel Goulbourne Sr and Girthel Grayson; children: Antoine Donald. **Educ:** Columbia Union Col, Takoma Park, MD, BA, 1973; Columbia Univ Sch Social Work, NY, MS, 1977; Albert Einstein Col Med/ Yeshiva Univ, Post-Grad Cert, 1984. **Career:** New Rochelle Bd Educ, New Rochelle, NY, teachers asst, 1974-75; Washington Heights Community Ctr, NY, social work trainee, 1975-76; Family & C Serv, Stamford, CT, clin social worker, 1977-79; Nat Health Serv Corps, Einstein Med Col, NY, social work coord, 1979-84; Dept Social Serv, Albert Einstein Col Medicine, NY, 1984-89; Lincoln Ave Clinic, The Guidance Ctr, New Rochelle, NY, dir, 1989, exec dir, currently. **Orgs:** USR Officers Asn, 1989; US Commissioned Officers Asn, 1989; Nat Asn Social Workers, 1989; Soc Clinical Work Psychotherapists Inc, 1989; vol group leader, Minority Task Force AIDS, 1989; vpres, Westchester Townhouse Condominium Asn, 1989; prof coun, Community Adult Patients, 1989. **Honors/Awds:** Letter of Commendation, NY State Dept Health, 1981; Clin Asn Nomination, Dept Sociol, Herbert H Lehman Col City Univ NY, 1982; Serv Citation, NY City Dept Pub Health, 1983; Certificate of Appreciation, Yeshiva Univ, 1986, 1987. **Business Addr:** Executive Director, The Guidance Center, 70 Grand St, New Rochelle, NY 10802.*

GOULD, PROF. WILLIAM BENJAMIN
Lawyer, educator. **Personal:** Born Jul 16, 1936, Boston, MA; son of William Benjamin Gould III and Leah Felts; married Hilda; children: William, V, Timothy & Bartholomew. **Educ:** Univ RI, AB, 1958; Cornell Law Sch, LLB, 1961; London Sch Econ, grad study, 1963; Univ Cambridge, MA, 1975. **Career:** United Auto Workers, asst gen coun, 1961-62; Nat Labor Rels Bd, atty, 1963-65; Battle, Fowler, Stokes & Kheel, mgt, 1965-68; Wayne State Law Sch, Detroit, prof law, 1968-71; Harvard Law Sch, vis prof law, 1971-72; Churchill Col, Cambridge, vis fel & lectr, 1975; Stanford Law Sch, Overseas Fel Churchill Col Cambridge, prof law, 1975, Charles A Beardsley, prof law, 1984-94, Charles A Beardsley, emer prof law, currently; Univ Tokyo, law fac, 1975, 1978; East-West Ctr, Honolulu, vis prof, 1982-83; Australian Nat Univ, vis prof, 1985; European Univ Inst, vis prof, 1988; Howard Law Sch, vis prof law, 1989; Univ Witwatersrand, vis prof, 1991; Nat Labor Rels Bd, chair, 1994-98;Univ Hawaii Law Sch, vis prof law, 2005; Univ San Diego, Summer Law Study Abroad Prog, prof law, 2005. **Orgs:** Nat Acad Arbitrat; Labor Law Sect; Am Bar Asn atty; racial discrim class act involving Detroit Edison Co Int Bro Teamsters; Am Fed Mus; del Dem Party mid-term conv, 1974; chmn, Nat Labor Rels Bd. **Honors/Awds:** Cert Merit, Primer, Am Labor Law, 1983; Endowed Chair Holder, Charles A Beardsley Prof Law, 1984; LLD, Univ RI, 1986; LLD, Stetson Univ, 1996; LLD, DC Sch Law 1996; LLD, Capital Univ, 1997; LLD, Rutgers Univ, 1998. **Special Achievements:** Author articles lab law & unions Stanford, Yale, Duke, Cornell, Penn & other law jour. **Business Addr:** Charles A Beardsley Professor Emeritus, Stanford Law School, Crown Quadrangle 559 Nathan Abbott Way, Stanford, CA 94305, **Business Phone:** (650)723-2111.

GOURDINE, SIMON PETER
Lawyer. **Personal:** Born Jul 30, 1940, Jersey City, NJ; son of Simon Samuel and Laura Emily Rembert; married Patricia Campbell, Aug 1, 1964; children: David Laurence, Peter Christopher, Laura Allison. **Educ:** The City Col NY, BA, 1962; Fordham Univ Law Sch, JD, 1965; Harvard Univ Grad Sch Bus, Cert Prog Mgt Develop, 1979. **Career:** Southern Dist NY, asst US atty, 1967-69; Nat Basketball Asn, NY, asst comnr, 1970-72, vpres admin, 1973-74, dep comnr, 1974-81; NY Dept Consumer Affairs, comnr, 1982-84; The Rockefeller Found, secy, 1984-86; Metrop Transp Authority New York, NY, dir labor rels, 1986-90; TCS-TV, gen partner, 1990-93; Nat Basketball Players Asn, NY, gen coun, 1990-95, exec dir, 1995-96. **Orgs:** bd dirs, Police Athletic League, 1974-, Fresh Air Fund, 1985-, The Fund City NY, 1990-93; NY Civil Serv Comn, 1981-82, Gov Exec Adv Comn Admin Justice, 1981-82, Mayor's Community Taxi Regulatory Issues, 1981-82; NY State Banking Bd, 1979-90; NY Charter Rev Comn, 1988-89; NY State Bar, US Dist Ct Bar, US Supreme Ct Bar. **Military Serv:** AUS, capt, 1965-67; Army Commendation Medal, Vietnam. *

GOVAN, REGINALD C
Lawyer. **Personal:** Born Dec 2, 1953, New York, NY; son of Oswald Govan and Gwendolyn Minor. **Educ:** Carnegie-Mellon Univ, BA, 1975; Univ Penn Law Sch, JD, 1978. **Career:** Squire, Sanders & Dempsey, assoc, 1978-79; US Court Appeals, 6th Circuit, Judge Nathaniel R Jones, sr law clerk, 1979-81; Manhattan District Atty, asst dist atty, 1981-83; sole practitioner, federal civil rights & gen litigation, 1983-85, 1987-89; US Sen, Com Judiciary, coun, 1985-87; US House Rep, Edu Labor Com, coun, 1989-94; Orgn Resource Couns Inc, sr consult, 1995-98; Freddie Mae, assoc gen coun, 1998-; vice chair, Am Corporate Counsel Assn, currently. **Orgs:** Nat Bar Asn, 1984-; Wash Bar Asn, 1990-. chair, Dist Bar, Atty-Client Arbitration Bd, 1991-94, Disciplinary Rev Com, 1991-93, Task Force Continuing Legal Educ, 1992-94. **Honors/Awds:** co-chair, PLI Annual Institute on Employment Law. **Special Achievements:** One Nation, Indivisible: The Civil Rights Challenge for the 1990's, Wash, DC, Citizens' CMS on Civil Rights, 1989; "Framing Issues and Acquiring Codes: An Overview of the Legislative Sojourn of the Civil Rights Act of 1991," 41 The DePaul Law Review 1057, 1992; "Honorable Compromises and the Moral High Ground: The Conflict Between the Rhetoric and the Content of the Civil Rights Act of 1991," 46 The Rutgers Law Review 7, 1993; "The Politics of Principle: Why Employment-Law Reform is Floundering," Organizations & People, 1996; "Alcohol At Company-Hosted-Events-Worth the Risk?" AACA Docket, 2003; "Employment Law is a Fishbowl: Coping with Less Privilege and Confidentiality," Employee Relations LJ, Vol 23, No 3 (Winter 1997). **Business Addr:** Associate General Counsel, Freddie Mac, 8200 Jones Branch Dr, McLean, VA 22102, **Business Phone:** (703)903-2770.

GOVAN, RONALD M.
Physicist. **Personal:** Born Jan 20, 1931, Los Angeles, CA; married. **Educ:** Pacific State Univ, Col Elec Engr, BSEE, 1962. **Career:** Univ SC, physics dept res assoc; Ryan Aircraft, elec main & calibration tech; Hughes Aircraft, elec fabric tech & elec main tech; USN ET2, main radar, sonar & commun equip; Univ S Calif, Los Angeles, physics dept asst res, 1962-64, chem dept instrument design, 1964-66; Rockwell Int Sci Ctr, staff assoc physics, 1966-; Univ Calif, Santa Barbara Dept Urban Aff, conf coordr, 1969. **Orgs:** Educ Coun Col & Univ Ventura Co; chmn local bd 81 selec serv, Ventura Co; bd dir, S Calif Comprehen Health Plan Bd; vpres, S Area Conf, Nat Asn Advan Colored People; vpres, Ventura County Nat Asn Advan Colored People; lab chmn, Educ Chmn; Camarillo Jaycees; chmn, John C Montgomery Forum Welfare; bd dir, Camarillo Boys Club; chmn, United Fund Ventura County Budget & Com Task Force; chmn, Ventura County Community Action Comn; Ventura County Criminal Justice Planning Delegate Conf Crim Just Sci & Technol Wash, DC, 1972; found past pres, Camarillo Dem Club; Task Force On Excellence Educ Pomona, 1972; Calif State Dept Educ; lectr paid consult, Ventura Co Human Relat Comn; Task Force Housing Ventura Co Plann Dept; Equal Opport Comn; Calif State Personnel bd adv comt, Career Opport Develop; Gov's Conf Law Enforcement Standards Control Comt; Pub Spectroscopy Group; Atmospheric Sci Group. **Honors/Awds:** Recipient Of Outstanding Contribution Award, Nat Asn Advan Colored People S Area Conf; Community Service Award; Outstanding Community Interest Award, 1967; Jaycee of Month award; Distinguished Service Award; Commendation for High Service. **Military Serv:** USN, electronics tech, second class, 1949-54. **Business Addr:** 1049 Camino Dos Rios, Thousand Oaks, CA.

GOVAN, SANDRA YVONNE
Educator, college teacher. **Personal:** Born Jul 28, 1948, Chicago, IL; daughter of Tanzel Romero and Sarah D Wilson. **Educ:** Valparaiso Univ, BA, 1970; Bowling Green Univ, MA, 1972; Emory Univ, PhD, 1980. **Career:** Luther Col, Decorah, IA, instr, 1972-75; Univ Ky, asst prof, 1980-83; Univ NC, assoc prof eng, 1983, Dept Eng, prof eng, currently. **Orgs:** Asn Study African-Am Life & Hist; Mod Lang Asn, 1980-; Col Lang Asn, 1975-; Emory Univ Fel, 1975; Langston Hughes Soc; coordr, Ronald E McNair Postbaccalaureate Achievement Prog. **Honors/Awds:** Schomburg Scholar in Residence, NEH, Schomburg Ctr Res Black Cult, 1990-91; Outstanding Alumni Award, Valparaiso Univ, 1982; Nat Fel Fund Award, Ford Found, 1976-80. **Business Addr:** Professor, University North Carolina, Dept Eng, 9201 Univ City Blvd, Charlotte, NC 28223-0001, **Business Phone:** (704)687-2000.*

GRACE, BOBBIE H
Government official. **Personal:** Born Sep 29, 1945, Donaldsonville, GA; daughter of Willie Calvin Hutchins Sr and Helen Williams; married James Allen, Mar 2, 1962; children: Denise Renee Grace George & Cheryl Lynette. **Career:** Government official (Retired); City Dania Beach, mayor, comnr, vice mayor, 1989-97; Bell S, Info Technol, 1968-98. **Orgs:** Pres, Dania Beach Econ & Develop; vpres, Progress Democratic Club; pres, Cent Broward Kiwanis; pres, N W Byrd Pointe Asn; Col Garden Homeowners Asn; Broward County Planning Coun; comnr, Dania Beach Housing Authority; bd mem, Habitat for Humanity. **Honors/Awds:** Outstanding Community Leader Pride, 1981; Outstanding Citizen Award, NE Community, 1988; Bethel Woman of the Year, Baptist Church, 1986; Trail Blazers Award, TJ Reddick Bar Asn, 1990; Golden Star Award, Men United Positive Action, 1991; Women's Hall of Fame Award, Broward County; Black Hist Govt Award; Good Am Citizenship Award; Zeta Phi Beta Citizen of the Year Award.

GRACE, GEORGE H
Executive, association executive. **Personal:** Born May 20, 1948, Bartow, FL; son of DeeCee and Lillie Mae; married Barbara Milton, Jan 1, 1992; children: Jerhonda, Gregory & Keenyn; married Regina Mobley (divorced 1991). **Educ:** Tuskegee Univ, attended 1967. **Career:** Gen Motors, prod supvr, 1972; Omega Psi Phi,

grand keeper records & seals, 1998, grand basileus, immediate past grand basileus, currently. **Orgs:** Nat Asn Advan Colored People; Urban League; Hialeah Chamber Com. **Special Achievements:** One of the 100 Most Influential Black Americans, Ebony Mag, 2004. **Business Addr:** Immediate Past Grand Basileus, Omega Psi Phi Fraternity Inc., 3951 Snapfinger Pkwy, Decatur, GA 30035, **Business Phone:** (305)260-8083.

GRACE, HORACE R
President (Organization). **Personal:** Born Jan 13, 1943, Timpson, TX; son of Robert and Lena Roberts Williams; married Margaret Richardson (divorced 1979); children: April Grace. **Educ:** Prairie View Univ, Prairie View, Tex, BS, 1966; Va State Univ, Petersburg, Va, MS, 1975. **Career:** Federal Acquisition Consults, pres, 1982-; The Lawn Barber Landscaping, pres, 1982-; Grace Investments, pres, 1985-; AMG Enterprises Inc, owner & pres, currently. **Orgs:** Vice chmn, Texas Credit Union Comn, 1985-89; Christian Farm Bd, 1988-; Cent Tex Alliance Black Bus, 1988-; mem bd, Private Industry Coun, 1989-; United Way Bd, 1991. **Honors/Awds:** Businessman of the Year Award, CENTABB, 1989. **Military Serv:** AUS, major, 1970-83; Army Accomodation Medal, 1977; Bronze Star, 1978; Meritorious Medal, 1979. **Business Addr:** President, AMG Enterprises Inc, 180 Mighty Oak Ln, PO Box 10065, Killeen, TX 76542, **Business Phone:** (254)526-9200.

GRACE, DR. MARCELLUS
Pharmacist, educator. **Personal:** Born Oct 17, 1947, Selma, AL; son of Capp and Mary; married Laura Dunn; children: Syreeta Lynn, Marcellus Jr & K. **Educ:** Xavier Univ LA, BS Pharmm, 1971; Univ Minn, MS Hosp Pharm, 1975, PhD Pharm Admin, 1976. **Career:** Tulane Med Ctr Hosp & Clin, dir pharm serv, 1976-77; Xavier Univ LA, Col Pharm, asst prof, dir prof exp prof, 1976-78, dean prof, prof pharm admin; Howard Univ Col Pharm & Pharmacol Sci, asst dean serv ed, 1979-82, chmn dept pharm admin, 1982, Nursing & Allied Health Sci, prof pharm admin, Sch Pharm, assoc dean; Xechem, adv bd, currently. **Orgs:** New Orleans Hist Pharm Comn, 1983-98; pres, Asn Minority Health Prof Schs, 1987-89; pres, Minority Health Prof Found; Nat Heart, Lung & Blood Inst Adv Coun, 1991-93; bd dir, Am As Col Pharm, 1992-94; NY Acad Sci, 1991; bd dir, Ernest N Morial Asthma & Respiratory Dis Ctr, 1995-; bd dir, Alton Ochsner Med Found, 1996-; bd dirs, Urban League Greater New Orleans, 1996-98. **Honors/Awds:** Eli Lilly Achievement Award, Eli Lilly Co, Indianpolis, 1971; Recipient of Fellowship, Nat Fellowship Fund Grad Fellowship Black Am, 1975-76; Rho Chi Nat Pharm Honor Soc, 1977; Bowl of Hygeia Award, 1998; Wendell T Hill Award, Asn Black Hosp Pharmacists, 2000. **Military Serv:** USN Reserve, capt, 1976-. **Business Addr:** Advisory Board, Xechem Inc, New Brunswick Technology Center, Bldg B 100 Jersey Ave Suite 310, New Brunswick, NJ 08901, **Business Phone:** (732)247-3300.

GRACE, PRINCESTON
Automotive executive. **Career:** Montgomery Ford Lincoln Mercury Inc, exec; Advantage Ford-Lincoln-Mercury Inc, pres & cheif exec officer, 1990-. **Orgs:** Ford Motor Minority Dealers Asn. **Special Achievements:** Top 100 Black Business men in America. **Business Phone:** (317)825-0594.

GRACE, SHERRY
Founder (Originator), executive director, interior designer. **Career:** Mothers Incarcerated Sons Inc, founder, 1954-, exec dir, 2004; interior designer. **Orgs:** Keynote speaker, Hardee Correctional Facil, 2006; keynote speaker, Chap 5135, NAACP, 2005. **Honors/Awds:** Nominee Humanitarian Award, Black Hist Banquet & Celebration, 2006. **Business Addr:** Founder, Executive Director, Mothers of Incarcerated Sons Inc, 5029 N Lane Suite 8, Orlando, FL 32808, **Business Phone:** (407)389-1416.*

GRADY, GLENN G
Executive, president (organization), chief executive officer. **Career:** Stroh, staff; Cimarron Express Inc, pres & chief exec officer, currently. **Honors/Awds:** Ernst & Young Entrepreneur of the Year. **Business Addr:** President, Chief Executive Officer, Cimarron Express Inc, 21611 State Rte 51, Genoa, OH 43430, **Business Phone:** (419)855-7713.

GRADY, WALTER E.
President (organization), chief executive officer. **Career:** Seaway Nat Bank, Chicago, Ill, pres & ceo, 1980-. **Orgs:** Oakland African Am Chamber Com. **Business Addr:** President, Chief Executive Officer, Seaway National Bank, 645 E 87th St, Chicago, IL 60619, **Business Phone:** (773)487-4800.*

GRADY-SMITH, MATTIE D
Lawyer, government official. **Personal:** Born Apr 29, 1952, Blackstock, SC; married; married. **Educ:** Westchester Community Col, AAS, 1977; Mercy Col, BS, 1980; Pace Univ, MPA, 1982, Pace Univ Sch Law, JD, 1994. **Career:** Westchester County, Dept Social Serv, 1973-95; Westchester Med Ctr, 1995-99; Westchester County Off, EEO/AA, dir, 1999-. **Orgs:** Bus Coun Westchester, HR Coun; Westchester County Afr Am Adv Bd, Liaison; adv comt, City White Plains Youth Bur; mediator, Volunteer Coun Serv. **Honors/Awds:** Proclamation of Merit, Westchester County Exec, 2000; Proclamation, Westchester County Bd Legislators, 2000; Alumni Honor Roll, State Univ NY, 2000; Volunteer Recognition, City White Plains Youth Bureau, 2002-05; Voyager Award, Westchester Community Col Found, 2002. **Business Addr:** Director, County of Westchester, Office of Equal Employment Opportunity/Affirmative Action, 148 Martine Ave Suite 103, White Plains, NY 10601, **Business Phone:** (914)995-2141.

GRAGG, LAUREN ANDREA
Manager, educator. **Personal:** Born Dec 20, 1967, Detroit, MI; daughter of J Robert and LaBarbara A. **Educ:** Howard Univ, BA, 1989; Wayne State Univ, MA, commun pub rels. **Career:** Detroit Pistons, Palace Found, spec proj asst, 1990; EDS, serv rels analyst, 1990-93, pub rels rep, 1993-95, recruiter, 1995-98, prog mgr, 1998-99, sr mkt rep, 1999; pvt commun consult, currently; Oakland Univ, Dept Rhetoric, Commun & Jour, spec lectr/instr, currently. **Orgs:** Howard Univ Alumni Asn; Delta Sigma Theta; Nat Urban League. **Honors/Awds:** Women of Color in Technology Award. **Business Phone:** (248)370-4120.

GRAHAM, ALBERTHA L.
Educator. **Personal:** Born in Georgetown, SC; married Sam Ellison; children: Kezia Ellison. **Educ:** Morris Col, 1965; NY Univ, Cert Leadership Develop Training, 1968; Erikson Inst, MEd, 1971; Univ Pittsburgh, grad stud. **Career:** Educator (retired). Chopee High Sch, teacher, 1965-67, summer librn, 1966; Brook haven High Sch, head start teacher, 1967-68; Cent Brook haven Head Start Prog, dir, 1968-70; Suffolk County Summer Head Start Patchoque NY, dir, 1970; Kezia Enterprises, counr; Calif Univ, PA, state training officer, assoc prof, dir affirmative action & human rels, coun. **Orgs:** Nat Asn Educ Young Child; Nat Coun Black Child Develop; Pa Reg Adv Comn, Day Care Person Proj conduc EPI, 1973; Educ Com Pittsburgh Chap, Nat Asn Advan Colored People; nat pres, Black Women Asn Inc; vol & adv bd mem, Nat Coun Jewish Women Pittsburgh Sec Friends Indeed Proj, 1975-; African AmInst; bd mem, Inst Women Ent; Nat Asn Women Bus Owners; Greater Pittsburgh Comn Women. **Honors/Awds:** Business Woman of the Year Award, Alleghenians LTD Inc.

GRAHAM, CHARLENE
Firefighter. **Personal:** Divorced; children: Jessica & Jennelle. **Educ:** Ferris State Univ. **Career:** Detroit Fire Dept, div chief, currently. **Orgs:** Alpha Kappa Alpha Sorority Inc. **Honors/Awds:** Certificate of Special Recognition; Golden Heritage Award; Detroit City Coun Testimonial Resolution; Proclamation, City Detroit Off Mayor; Recognition of Excellence Award, Nobel/Woman. **Special Achievements:** First woman to hold the rank of division chief in the Detroit Fire Department. **Business Addr:** Division Head, Detroit Fire Department, 250 W Larned St, Detroit, MI 48226, **Business Phone:** (313)596-2900.

GRAHAM, DEMINGO
Football player. **Personal:** Born Sep 10, 1973, Newark, NJ. **Educ:** Hofstra Univ. **Career:** San Diego Chargers, tackle, 1998-2001; Houston Texans, 2002-03; Dallas Cowboys, 2004, free agent, currently.

GRAHAM, DONALD
Banker. **Personal:** Born Jan 28, 1947, Youngstown, OH; son of Morris and Katheryn; married Barbara, Sep 8, 1996; children: Anneke. **Educ:** Youngstown State UNIV, BS, bus admin, 1970; Xavier UNIV, MBA, 1979; COL Mt St Joseph, Acct Cert, 1988. **Career:** Pitney Bowes, Inc, sales, 1973; Ford Motor Co, zone mgr, 1973-80; Fifth Third Bank, banker, 1980-, exec vpres, currently; Akron Region, Market Pres. **Orgs:** Omega Psi Phi Fraternity Inc, 1968; pres, NAT BLACK MBA ASN Cleveland, 1990-92; bd mem, Cleveland Children's Mus, 1993-95; trustee, Urban League Cleveland, 1994-99; bd mem, AM Cancer SOC, 1995-; Urban Financial ASN, 1995-; trustee, Alumni Asn Youngstown State Univ, 1999; pres, Pepper Pike Civic League, 2000; visiting comt, James J Nance Col Bus Admin, Cleveland State Univ, 2000-; dir, Fifth Third Bank, 2000-; trustee, Better BUS BUR, Cleveland OH, 2000-; Faith Fellowship Church; Northeastern Neighborhood Develop Corp; Williamson Col Bus Youngstown State Univ. **Honors/Awds:** Cleveland Growth ASN, Leadership Cleveland, 1997; Outstanding Businessman, Dollar & Sense Magazine, 1993; BLACK Achiever, YMCA, 1984. **Military Serv:** AUS, 1971-73; Army Commendation Medal, Vietnam, 1972. **Business Addr:** Executive Vice President, Fifth Third Bank Northeastern Ohio, 1404 E 9th St, Cleveland, OH 44114, **Business Phone:** (216)274-5449.*

GRAHAM, GEORGE WASHINGTON
Government official. **Personal:** Born Feb 16, 1949, Kinston, NC; son of George W Graham Sr and Mattie L; married Marilyn, Jun 18, 1988; children: Marilyn, George III, Alicia & Brandi. **Educ:** Fayetteville State Univ, BS, 1971; NC State Univ, MS, 1975, doctoral prog, currently. **Career:** US Post Off, Fayetteville, NC, mail handler, 1967-71; Simone Jr High Sch, instr & athletic coach, 1971-72; Lenoir Community Col, Kinston, NC, adult basic educ dir, 1972-76, admin asst to the pres & resource develop officer, 1977-79, chmn, currently; Dobbs Sch, Kinston, NC, dir, 1979-. **Orgs:** Omega Psi Phi; NAACP; St Augustus AME Zion Church; Jaycees, Masons, Kinston Rotary Club; NC Asn Black Elected Officials, Lenoir County Black Artist Guild; bd comnrs, Lenoir County; bd dirs, Lenoir Mem Hosp; bd dirs, United Way; Lenoir County Comn 100; bd dirs, Lenoir County Health; NC Gen Assembly Spec Legis Comn Fairness Taxation; NC Asn County Comnrs Taxation & Finance Steering Comm; chmn, bldg comn, St Augustus AME Zion Church; bd dirs, NC Asn County Comnrs; jr chmn, bd dirs, Lenoir County, currently. **Honors/Awds:** Teacher of the Year, 1971; Jaycee of the Month, 1973; Outstanding Educator of the Year, 1974; Outstanding Educator of America, 1974-75; Outstanding Black Educator, 1976; Jaycee Boss of the Year, 1979; Man of the Year, Omega Psi Phi, 1979; Distinguished Service Award Nominee, Kinston, Lenoir County Chamber Com, 1980; Governor's Award for Excellence Nominee, 1987. **Business Addr:** Chairman, Lenoir County, Lenoir County Board Of Commissioners, 130 S Queen St, PO Box 3289, Kinston, NC 28502, **Business Phone:** (252)523-9552.

GRAHAM, GREGORY LAWRENCE
Basketball player, basketball coach. **Personal:** Born Nov 26, 1970, Indianapolis, IN. **Educ:** Ind Univ, attended 1993. **Career:** Basketball player (retired), basketball coach; Charlotte Hornets, guard, 1993; Philadelphia 76ers, 1993-95; NJ Nets, 1995-96; Seattle Supersonics, 1996-97; Cleveland Cavaliers, 1997; Ind Alley Cats, head coach, currently. **Orgs:** Am Basketball Asn.

GRAHAM, HELEN W
Educator. **Personal:** Born in New York, NY; daughter of Raymond and Pauline; married Fitzroy, Jun 26, 1949; children: Rosalyn & Shelle. **Educ:** Howard Univ, DC, BA, 1950; Hunter Col, New York, NY, MS, 1974. **Career:** Educator (retired); S Siegel Inc, New York, NY, off mgr, 1950-55; Brooklyn Bd Educ, Brooklyn, NY, teacher, 1962-89. **Orgs:** Treas, Nat Sorority Phi Delta Kappa Inc, Beta Omicron Chap, 1987-91; vpres, Key Women Am Inc, 1989-92; Protestant Teachers Asn; Nat Asn Univ Women. **Honors/Awds:** Teacher of the Year, PTA, PS 37Q, 1975; Appreciation of Service, PS 37Q, 1979-81; Appreciation of Outstanding Contribution, Key Women Am Inc, 1990; Appreciation Dedicated Community Service, Jamaica Hosp, 1987-90; Grace Episcopal Church, Jamaica, Soc Action Comm, Altar Guild.

GRAHAM, JAMES C, JR.
Association executive. **Personal:** Born Aug 1, 1945, Fort Wayne, IN; son of James C Sr and Marjorie Dickerson; married Cecelia; children: James C III, Joy, Angela, Margie & Audrey. **Educ:** Nat Urban League Whitney M Young Exec Prog, New York, NY, dipl, 1984; Univ Wis; IBM Exec Develop Prog; Hillsdale Col, Hillsdale, Mich, BS, psychol, 1972. **Career:** Metrop Human Rel Comn, Fort Wayne, Ind, dir, 1972-77; Madison Urban League, Madison, Wis, exec dir, 1977-83; Birmingham Urban League, Birmingham, Ala, pres & ceo, 1983-. **Orgs:** Chmn, PIC Nomination Comt, Pvt Indust Coun; pres, Nat Urban League, Southern Coun CEOs, 1990-; Inclusiveness Comt, Govt Rel Comt, United Way; Alpha Phi Alpha Fraternity; Boy Scouts Am, Leadership Birmingham; Chamber Com Community Rel Comt; Southern Inst C & Families; Birmingham Youth Task Force. **Honors/Awds:** Martin Luther King Humanitarian Award, Madison, Wis. **Home Addr:** 5404 Cornell Dr, Irondale, AL 35210, **Home Phone:** (205)956-5565. **Business Phone:** (205)326-0162.

GRAHAM, JEFF TODD
Football player, radio host. **Personal:** Born Feb 14, 1969, Dayton, OH. **Educ:** Ohio State Univ. **Career:** Football player (retired), Radio host; Pittsburgh Steelers, wide receiver, 1991-93; Chicago Bears, 1994-95; New York Jets, 1996-97; Philadelphia Eagles, wide receiver, 1998; San Diego Chargers, wide receiver, 1999-2001; KISS-FM, Ottawa, radio dj, currently. **Honors/Awds:** Rodney Culver Mem Award, 1999. **Business Addr:** Radio DJ, KISS FM, 2001 Thurston Dr, Ottawa, ON, Canada K1G 6C9, **Business Phone:** (613)736-2001.

GRAHAM, DR. JO-ANN CLARA
School administrator, college administrator. **Personal:** Daughter of James Harold and Clara Polhemus. **Educ:** NY Univ, BS, 1962, MA, 1968, PhD, 1982. **Career:** City Univ NY, Bronx Community Col, prof commun arts & sci, 1970, dept chairperson & head humanities, chmn commun, div coordr humanities, prof emer. **Orgs:** Exec bd, NY State TESOL, 1970-73; comn panel, Am Arbitration Asn, 1976; bd dir, Asn Black Charities, 1982; consult, Mayors Vol Action Ctr; NY City Bd Educ; Maj NY City Law Firm; McGraw-Hill; Addison Wesley; Macmillan; N Hudson Language Develop Ctr; Haryou-Act; vpres, G & S Assocs-Human Commun; bd mem, The Hammond Mus; Cinque Art Gallery; founded, Romare Bearde; Ernest Crichlow; Norman Lewis. **Honors/Awds:** Fel Univ Puerto Rico, NY Univ, 1966; co-auth, The Pub Forum, A Transactional Approach to Pub Commun, Alfred, 1979. **Special Achievements:** Chosen 1 of 100 top women in mgt nationwide to participate in Leaders for the 80s, 1983. *

GRAHAM, LADELL
Executive, president (organization). **Personal:** Born Oct 16, 1957, Shreveport, LA; son of Johnnie Lee and Corine Horton; married Gwendolyn Smith, Dec 14, 1985; children: Justin, Jonathan & Jasmine. **Educ:** Southern Univ, BBS, acct, 1981. **Career:** Assocs Corp, portfolio mgr, 1981-87; Dean Witter, investment mgr, 1987-

88; Am Capital, investment vpres, 1988-90; Smith, Graham & Co, pres & chief investment officer, 1990-. **Orgs:** Dist enrollment chmn, Boy Scouts Am, 1992; Nat Investment Mgrs Asn, 1995; Nat Asn Securities Professionals, 1995; Am Diabetes Asn, 1995; Tex Children's Hosp Develop Coun, 1995. **Honors/Awds:** Houston Black Achiever Award, 1990.

GRAHAM, LARRY, JR.
Musician. **Personal:** Born Aug 14, 1946, Beaumont, TX; married Tina. **Career:** Dell Graham Jazz Trio, 1951-67; Sly & The Family Stone, bass play, 1967-73; Graham Cent Sta Mavimus Prod, founder & pres, 1973-77; Albums: One in a Million You, 1980; Just Be My Lady, 1981; Sooner or Later, 1982; Victory, 1983; Fired Up, 1985; Songs: "One in a Million You", 1980; "When We Get Married", 1980; "Guess Who", 1981; "Just Be My Lady", 1981; "Sooneror Later", 1982; "Don't Stop When You're Hot", 1982; "I Never Forget Your Eyes", 1983. **Orgs:** Jehovah's Witness. **Honors/Awds:** Top Star Award; Best Dress, 1973; Best Dress, 1973-74; Entertainer of the Year, 1975.

GRAHAM, MARIAH
Executive, artist. **Personal:** Born Nov 3, 1946, South Carolina. **Educ:** Sch Visual Arts, cert grad, 1968. **Career:** Mariah Graham Studios, pres & owner, 1969-; NY Times, freelance artist, 1968-; Marymount Col, prof, 1977-; Fashion Inst Technol, instr, 1978-; Greenwich Art Soc, fac, currenlty. **Orgs:** Soc Illus; Graphic Art Guild; Drama & Guild Broadway. **Honors/Awds:** Certificate of Appreciation, Baruch Col, 1976; The One Show Merit Award, Art Direct Club, 1976; Certificate of Merit, Soc Illus, 1978; Certificate of Merit, New York Col, 1979. **Business Addr:** President, Owner, Mariah Graham Illustrations, PO Box 425, Jeffersonville, NY 12748, **Business Phone:** (845)482-4036.

GRAHAM, ODELL
Scientist. **Personal:** Born Mar 31, 1931, Chicago, IL; son of James Graham and Gertha Scott; married Loretta Harriet Lewis, Jul 17, 1960; children: Karyn, Cynthia & Jessica. **Educ:** Univ Calif Los Angeles, BS, physics, 1961, MS, elec engineering, 1967, PhD, elec engineering, 1976. **Career:** Scientist (retired): Hughes Aircraft Co, Culver City, CA, res & asst 1954-60, Canoga Park, CA, div chief scientist, 1961-92; Hycon Mfg Co, Monrovia, CA, elec engr, 1960-61; ATK Missile Systs Co, prin scientist, 1992. **Orgs:** Life sr mem, Inst Electronic & Elect Engr, 1972-; chmn, Los Angeles Chap Anten & Prop Soc Inst Elec & Electron Engr; NAACP; exec comt mem, engineering dean's coun, UCLA, 1987-; Tech Adv Comt, Hughes Univ. **Honors/Awds:** Fel, Inst Advan Engineering, 1981; Engineering Merit Award, San Fernando Valley Engineering Coun, 1986; Black Engineer of the Year, Outstanding Tech Achievement, 1991. **Military Serv:** USMC, corpl, 1952-54. **Home Addr:** 3152 W Cumberland Ct, Westlake Village, CA 91362.

GRAHAM, PATRICIA
Educator. **Personal:** Born Mar 9, 1949, Saluda, SC; daughter of Eddie Roy and Lillian Leo Wertz; widowed. **Educ:** Rutgers Univ, BA, 1972; Antioch Col, Med, 1974; Univ Mass, EdD, 1995. **Career:** Morrell Sch Girls, group leader, 1972-74; Widener Univ, coun, 1974-77; E Stroudsburg Univ, assoc prof, 1977, coun, 1977, Dept Acad Enrichment & Learning, prof, currently. **Orgs:** Pres, Pocono Chap, Phi Delta Kappa, 1994-95; Nat Asn Aadvan Colored People; Am Asn Coun & Develop; Am Asn Univ Prof; pres, PA Asn Multicultural Coun; div PA coun Asn; bd dirs, NE PA Region, United Negro Col Fund. **Honors/Awds:** Appreciation Award, Black Student Asn E Stroudsburg Univ, 1981; Chi Alpha Epsilon Honor Society Award, 1994. **Business Addr:** Professor, E Stroudsburg University, Department of Academic Enrichment & Learning, 200 Prospect St, East Stroudsburg, PA 18301-2999.*

GRAHAM, PAUL
Basketball player. **Personal:** Born Nov 28, 1967, Philadelphia, PA; married Rosa M Gonzales; children: Paul. **Educ:** Ohio Univ. **Career:** Basketball player (Retired), basketball coach; CBA: Albany Patroons, 1990-91; Philadelphia Spirit, 1991; Altanta Hawks, 1991-94.

GRAHAM, PROF. PRECIOUS JEWEL
Lawyer, social worker, educator. **Personal:** Born May 3, 1925, Springfield, OH; daughter of Robert Lee Freeman and Lulabelle Malone Freeman; married Paul Nathaniel; children: Robert & Nathan. **Educ:** Fisk Univ, BA, 1946; Case Western Reserve Univ, MSSA, 1953; Univ Dayton, JD, 1979. **Career:** YWCA, prog dir, 1946-53; Antioch, other positions, 1964-69; 1992-94;Antioch Col, prof soc welfare, 1969-92, fac lectr, 1979-80, Inst Human Develop, dir, 1984-89, social welfare & legal studies, emer prof, currently. **Orgs:** Pres, YWCA USA, 1979-85; pres, Yellow Springs Community Found, 1980; OHBar; Acad Cert Social Workers; dir, Yellow Springs Instrument Co, 1981-93;bd dir, Meadville Lombard Theological Sch, 1983-87; pres, World YWCA1987-91; bds, Unitarian Universalist Serv Comt; Vernay Found. **Honors/Awds:** Social Worker of the Year, Miami Valley NASW, 1975; Greene County Women's Hall Fame Greene City OH 1982; Ten Top Women Miami Valley, Dayton Daily News 1987; Ohio Women's Hall Fame, 1988; J.D. Dawson Award, 2006. **Business Addr:** Emeritus Professor, Antioch College, Social Welfare & Legal Studies, 795 Livermore St, Yellow Springs, OH 45387, **Business Phone:** (937)769-1332.

GRAHAM, RHEA L
Geologist. **Educ:** Bryn Mawr Col, BA, 1974; Ore State Univ, MA, 1977. **Career:** Sci Appln Int Corp, sr scientist; NMex Interstate Stream Comn, dir, currently. **Special Achievements:** First African American to be nominated as director for the US Bureau of Mines in its 84 year history, 1994. **Business Addr:** Director, New Mexico Interstate Stream Commission, Springer Square Bldg 121 Tijeres Ave NE Suite 2000, Albuquerque, NM 87102, **Business Phone:** (505)841-9494.

GRAHAM, SAUNDRA M.
State government official, activist. **Personal:** Born Sep 5, 1941, Cambridge, MA; daughter of Charles B Postell and Roberta Betts Postell; divorced; children: Carl Jr, Rhonda, Tina, Darryl & David. **Educ:** Univ Mass, attended 1973; Harvard Univ. **Career:** Harvard Univ, Loeb fel; Riverside Cambridgeport Community Develop Corp, pres, 1971; Cambridge City Coun, chairwoman Housing & Land Use Comt, 1972-88; State MA, vice mayor, 1976-77, counr, state rep, 1976-88; Multicultural Arts Ctr Comt, chairwomen, 1977-78; Graham & Parks Alternative Pub Sch, 1981; polit activist. **Orgs:** Bd dir, Cambridge Community Ctr, 1968; pres, Riverside Planning Team, 1970; Mass Legislators Asn; co-chair, Mass Coalition, 1983; Mass Black Legis Caucus; Mass Caucus Women Legislators. **Honors/Awds:** Distinguished Citizen Award, Mass Asn Afro-American Policeman, 1974; Award for Community Service, Boston Masons, 1974; Citations from Gov & Mass Secy State; Sojourner Truth Award; Distinguished Citizen Award, Nat Asn Negro Bus & Professional Women's Clubs, 1976; Recognition Award, Cent Sq Cambridge Businessmen Asn, 1980; Woman of the Year, Boston Chap, Nat Orgn Women, 1982; The Graham and Parks Alternative Public School was named in her honor. **Special Achievements:** First black woman representative from Cambridge to the State House.

GRAHAM, SCOTTIE
Football player, executive director. **Personal:** Born Mar 28, 1969, Long Beach, NY; married Mary; children: Dennis & Marika Skot. **Educ:** Ohio State Univ, BA, recreational educ, MA, black studies & Black community. **Career:** Football player (retired), Executive director; New York Jets, running back, 1992; Minnesota Vikings, running back, 1993-96; Cincinnati Bengals, running back, 1997. **Orgs:** Reg dir, Nat Football League Players Asn, currently. **Business Phone:** (202)463-2200.

GRAHAM, STEDMAN
Marketing executive, chairperson, chief executive officer. **Personal:** Son of Stedham and Mary; divorced; children: Wendy. **Educ:** Hardin-Simmons Univ, BA, 1974; Ball State Univ, MA, 1979. **Career:** European Leagues, basketball player; B&C Assocs; Graham Gregory Bozell Inc, chief exec officer, 1996-; Coker Col, distinguished vis prof, currently; S Graham & Assoc, chmn & chief exec officer, currently. **Orgs:** Dir, George Wash Univ, Forum Sport & Event Mgt & Mkt, 1994; founder & exec dir, Athletes Against Drugs; co-founder, Youth Opportunity Movement. **Special Achievements:** Author, The Ultimate Guide to Sport Event Mgt & Mkt, 1995; You Can Make It Happen: A Nine-Step Plan for Success, 1997; Build Your Own Life Brand; Move Without the Ball; Who Are You? A Success Process For Bldg Your Life's Found; Diversity: Leaders Not Labels. **Business Addr:** Chairman, Chief Executive Officer, S Graham & Associates, 455 N Cityfront Plz Dr 15th Fl, Chicago, IL 60611, **Business Phone:** (312)755-0234.

GRAMBY, SHIRLEY ANN
Manager. **Personal:** Born Jun 1954, Hartford, CT; daughter of Sarge McCall Jr. and Elizabeth McCall; married Charles E Gramby, Aug 16, 1975; children: Talib Eric, Shamar Terrell. **Educ:** BS, elementary, special educ, 1977; MA, human resource, mgt supervision, 1990. **Career:** OH BUR of Workers Compensation, public information asst, 1979-81; Indust CMS of OH, mgt analyst, 1981-86; OH DEPT Human Serv, prog planner, policy analyst, human serv specialist, 1986-; Sunrise Broadcasting, Power 106.3, WCKX Radio, Community events, 1992-. **Orgs:** bd mem, Neighborhood House, fundraising chair, 1989-; United Way, new program com, 1989-; Leadership Columbus, recruitment com, 1990-; DST, co-chair, arts & letters, 1988-90; I Know I Can, steering com, 1990-; Wilberforce UNIV Alumnae, Columbus cha, vip, 1991-92; AMR Cancer SOC, Franklin County Breast Cancer Task Force, 1990-91; North East Linden Athletic ASN, exe vip, 1989-90. **Honors/Awds:** Mayors Award, Outstanding COT Service, 1988; James Penney Cash Award Outstanding Volunteers, 1987; Jaycee of the Year, PRS's Award, Columbus Jaycees, 1989; Walter and Marian English COT Service Award, 1990; Distinguished Service Award, DST, 1989-90. **Special Achievements:** Showcasing Younth in the 90's, DST, Columbus Alumnae Proj, 1988-89; Afro Fair, 1990; Family Festival, Columbus Urban League, 1990, 1991; Greater Columbus Arts Festival, 1992; Celebrity Waiters, Comedy Night, 1991-92. **Business Addr:** Human Services Specialist, Ohio Department Human Service, 30 East Broad St 27th Fl, Columbus, OH 43266-0423, **Business Phone:** (614)466-6742.*

GRANDBERRY, NIKKI
Public relations executive. **Career:** WJBK-TV, gen assignment reporter, 1978-86; Detroit Pub Schs, substitute teacher; Simons Michelson Zieve Inc, pub rels, pub rel partner, currently; WXYZ-TV, cohost "Company", 1994. **Business Phone:** (248)362-4242.

GRANDMASTER FLASH (JOSEPH SADDLER)
Rap musician. **Personal:** Born Jan 1, 1958, Barbados, West Indies. **Career:** Grandmaster Flash & the Furious Five, mem; The Chris Rock Show, HBO, musical dir; Solo Albums: They Said It Couldn't Be Done, 1985; The Source, 1986; Ba Dap Boom Bang, 1987; On the Strength, 1988; Greatest Messages, 1983; Grandmaster Flash vs the Sugarhill Gang, 1997; Greatest Mixes, 1998; Adventures on teh Wheels of Steel, 1999; Official Adventures of Grandmaster Flash, 2002; Essential Mix: Classic Edition, 2002; Mixing Bullets & Firing Joints, 2005; Grandmaster Flash Enterprises, founder, currently. **Business Addr:** Founder, Grandmaster Flash Enterprises, 600 Johnson Ave Suite E7, Bohemia, NY 11716, **Business Phone:** (631)218-2942.

GRANGER, DR. CARL VICTOR
Personal: Born Nov 26, 1928, Brooklyn, NY; son of Carl Granger and Marie Granger; married Eloise M Walker, Jan 9, 1995; children: Glenn & Marilyn. **Educ:** Dartmouth Col, AB, 1948; New York Univ, MD, 1952. **Career:** Yale New Haven Hosp, fac, 1961-67; Tufts New Eng Med Ctr, fac, 1967-77; Brown Univ, fac, 1977-83; State Univ NY, Buffalo, Dept Rehab Med, chair, prof, 1983-, chair emer, currently; Uniform Data Syst Med Rehab, founder & dir; physician, pvt pract, currently. **Orgs:** Am Acad Phys Med & Rehab; Asn Acad Physiatrists; Int Soc Phys & Rehabiliation Med. **Honors/Awds:** Krusen Award, Zeiter Lectr, Asn Acad Physiatrists; Lifetime Achievement Award, Third Annual Health Care Heroes Breakfast, 2002. **Special Achievements:** Established the FIM instrument to measure level of severity of disability and outcomes for inpatient rehabilitation facilities. **Military Serv:** AUS, 1st lt to major, 1954-61. **Business Addr:** Director, Uniform Data System for Medical Rehabilitation, 270 Northpointe Pkwy Ste 300, Amherst, NY 14228-1897, **Business Phone:** (716)817-7828.

GRANGER, EDWINA C.
Artist. **Personal:** Born in Yonkers, NY; daughter of Paul Weldon and Christina White Weldon Small; widowed. **Educ:** NY Univ, courses & cert sculp ceramic, 1952; Caton Rose Inst Fine Arts, landscape anat, 1958; Art Stud League New York, portrait fig, 1962; N Mex Univ, compos abstract, 1965; Rutgers Univ, cert real estate, 1978. **Career:** Creative Arts McGuire AFB, teacher, 1963-64; exhibiting artist, 1964-69; Portugal & TTS Colonies People Exhibits, original pen & ink prints, 1973-80; Doll Shows Applehead, doll maker, 1976-80; Art work: The Spectators; African Market Place, 1990; Holiday Walk, 1990; Caribbean Dancer, 1990; Girl with Oranges; The Family; Lost in the Fog. **Orgs:** Festival art consultant, 1980, art judge, 1984, Garden State Art Center, 1980; Meadow Lands Race Track 3 Shows, 1979-84; mem, NAACP, 1985; mem, Nat Conf of Artists; mem, Nat League of Am Pen Women, 1965-81; mem, Southern Christian Leadership Conf Women, 1988-92. **Honors/Awds:** Alexander Medal of Honor, Walton High Sch; Outstanding Achievement Art Award, NBPW, Willingboro, NJ. **Special Achievements:** Martin Luther King Show/Prints/Oils/Pen/Ink; Women Artists, p 33, 1990; Publication: Artist of GA Vol III, cover resume pictures, p 37-38, 1994; first prize in many art shows, Illinois, New Mexico, New York, New Jersey, and Azores. **Home Addr:** 7145 Chestnut Lane, Riverdale, GA 30274. *

GRANT, ANDRE M.
Attorney general (U.S. federal government), lawyer. **Educ:** Univ Iowa Col Law. **Career:** Law Off Andre M Grant, prin & atty. **Orgs:** N'Digo Found Scholar Comt; Cook County Bar Asn. **Business Addr:** Principal, Attorney, Law Office of Andre M Grant, 25 E Washington Suite 1225, Chicago, IL 60602-1800, **Business Phone:** (312)236-8004.*

GRANT, ANTHONY T
Banker, president (organization), chief executive officer. **Personal:** Married Helen; children: Hamilton,Alexander, Kristina & Katherine. **Educ:** SC State Univ, BS, bus admin. **Career:** Bank of Am, mgt trainee, pres, prof African Am banking group; Grant Bus Strategies, Inc, chief exec officer, currently. **Orgs:** NCCBI; bd mem, BobbyPhillsFund. **Honors/Awds:** National Distinguished Alumnus Award, Alma Mater's; National Urban League's Volunteer Services Award; Randolph Canzater Lifetime Achievement Award; Donald H. McGarmon Award; Charlotte Post's People of Prominence Award, 2001; Eagle Award, Omega Psi Phi Fraternity. **Business Addr:** Chief Executive Officer, Grant Business Strategies Inc, PO Box 23527, Columbia, SC 29244-3527, **Business Phone:** (803)419-8500.

GRANT, ASHLEY
Business owner. **Career:** Artco Systems Inc, co-owner, currently. **Business Addr:** Co-owner, Artco Systems Inc, 1810 Forrest Pkwy, Lake City, GA 30260, **Business Phone:** (404)635-9001.*

GRANT, AUGUSTUS O
Physician, educator. **Personal:** Born in Jamaica, West Indies; married Stephanie; children: Siobhan Earlyn. **Educ:** Univ Edinburgh, Scotland, MBChB, 1971; Univ Calif San Francisco, attended

1975; Univ Manitoba, Can, attended 1977; Duke Univ Med Ctr, NC, attended 1980. **Career:** Duke Univ Med Ctr, prof med, vice dean fac enrichment, currently; J Cardiovasc Electrophysiology, dep ed, currently; Am Jour Physiol Heart & Circulation, consult ed, currently. **Orgs:** Am Heart Asn; fel Am Col Cardiol; Biophysical Soc; Am Soc Clin Invest; Asn Black Cardiologists. **Honors/Awds:** Gold Heart Award, Am Heart Asn. **Special Achievements:** First African-American physician-scientist in Duke's Division of Cardiology. **Home Addr:** 2562 Bittersweet Dr, Durham, NC 27705. **Business Addr:** Cardiologist, Duke Heart Center, PO Box 3504 DUMC, Durham, NC 27710, **Business Phone:** (919)684-3901.

GRANT, BRIAN WADE
Basketball player. **Personal:** Born Mar 5, 1972, Columbus, OH; married Gina; children: Elijah & Jaydon. **Educ:** Xavier Univ, orgn commun, 1994. **Career:** Basketball player (retired); Sacramento Kings, forward, 1994-97; Portland Trailblazers, 1997-2000; Miami Heat, 2000-04; Los Angeles Lakers, 2004-05; Phoenix Suns, forward, 2005-06; Boston Celtics, 2006. **Orgs:** Founder, Brian Grant Found. **Honors/Awds:** Rookie of the Year Award, 1994; NBA All-Rookie First Team, 1995; J Walter Kennedy Citizenship Award, 1999. **Special Achievements:** Film appearance: Eddie.

GRANT, C D. See GRANT, CLAUDE DEWITT.

GRANT, CHERYL DAYNE
Lawyer. **Personal:** Born Jan 3, 1944, Cincinnati, OH; married Daniel R (divorced); married Claude H. Audley. **Educ:** Univ Cincinnati, BA, 1966; Univ Cincinnati, Law Sch, attended 1973. **Career:** Memorial Community Ctr, social worker, 1966-68; Cincinnati, police officer, 1968-70; Nat Asn Advan Colored People scholar, 1970-73; Cincinnati Lawyers Housing, 1972; Legal Aid Soc, atty, 1973-74; Cong Thomas A Luken House Rep, admin aide, 1974-; Univ Cincinnati, asst prof, 1976-78; CD Grant & Assoc Co LPA, asst ohio atty gen, 1979-80; Off Munic Invest, chief invest; City Lincoln Heights, OH, dir legal serv; US Atty, asst; ABC'S Law WCIN-RADIO, co-mod; Hamilton County Munic Ct, judge, currently. **Orgs:** Ohio Youth Adv Bd, 1974-77; OH Juv Justice Adv Comt, OH, 1976-; Nat Asn Advan Colored People; bd dir, Womens City Club; bd mem, City Comn Justice & Corrections; pres bd, Community Ctr; Alpha Kappa Alpha; Cincinnati Bar Asn; Ohio Bar Asn; ABA; Cincinnati Lawyers Club; Black Lawyers Asn Cincinnati; Regin Heber Smith fel, Howard Univ. **Business Addr:** Judge, Municipal Court of Hamilton County, Hamilton County Courthouse, 1000 Main St PO BOX 9687, Cincinnati, OH 45209.*

GRANT, CHRISTINE S.
College teacher. **Educ:** Brown Univ, BS, chem engineering, 1984; Ga Inst Technol, MS, 1986, chem engineering, PhD, chem engineering, 1989. **Career:** NC State Univ, Fac Develop & Special Initiatives, prof & assoc dean, currently. **Honors/Awds:** Young Faculty Award, Dow Chemical Co; Distinguished Service Award, Am InstChem Engineers; Top Women in Science and Engineering Award, Nat Tech Asn;Exxon Engineering Foundation Research Award; Outstanding Alumni in Academia Award, GEM, 2003; Presidential Award, NSF, 2003. **Special Achievements:** One of only five African-American women faculty members in chemical engineering in the United States.

GRANT, CLAUDE DEWITT (C D GRANT)
School administrator, educator. **Personal:** Born Dec 20, 1944, New York, NY; son of Claude Allen Grant and Rose Levonia Nelson; married Gloriana B Waters, Aug 7, 1982; children: Tahra Lore. **Educ:** US Armed Forces Inst, Ger; Bronx Comm Col, (with Honors), 1972; Hunter Col, BA, social sci, 1974; IONA Col, MS, jour & electronic publ, 1997. **Career:** NY Psychiatric Inst, psych intern, 1973-74; Yonkers Youth Serv, adolescent counr, 1974-76; Jamaica Comm Adolescent Prog, assoc psychiatrist & sr social worker, 1976-79; Bronx Comm Col, coordr prog & cult affairs, 1979-86, Eng Dept, adj instr, 1991-, Bus & Prof Develop Inst, dir, coordrmkg & pub rels, dir col rels, currently; Consult Plus comp/bus consult pract proprietor, 1991-. **Orgs:** Admin ed & fiscal officer, Blind Beggar Press, 1977-; spec proj dir, Unity& Strength BCC, 1981-; Col Media Adv, 1982-, Assoc Ed Jour 1983-; exec bd& pres, Bronx Coun Arts, 1983-; Col Jour Asn, 1984; freelance contrib, Essence Mag; freelance contrib, Amsterdam News; exec bd & vpres, Mind Builders Creative Arts Ctr, 1990-99; pres, Bronx Coun Arts Develop Corp, 1996-2000; Int Freelance Photographers Orgn, 2001-; Nat News Photographers Asn, 2002-. **Honors/Awds:** Service Awards, Bronx, CT, 1972, 1980, 1981, 1983, 1984; BCC Meritorious Service Awards, 1972-86; Certificate of Appreciation, US Comn Minority Bus Develop, 1992; Bronx Community Col Found, Faculty Research Award, 1993; Citation of Merit, Bronx Borough Pres Off, 1998; Cert of Graduation in Professional Photography, NY Inst Photography, 2000; Certificate of Recognition, City Univ NY, 2002, 2003, 2004. **Special Achievements:** Presented papers "Jazz, Lost Legacy of A People", University of California at Berkeley, "Creativity, Imagination Help Preserve Quality Programs on a Limited Budget", Bulletin of Associates of College Unions International, papers presented at BCC, 1986, Pace University, 1985, Howard University, 1987, books published are Keeping Time, 1981, Images in a Shaded Light, 1986, Just a Little Love, 2004; Journals: African Voices, Black Mask Magazine, Essence, Suburban Styles. **Military Serv:** AUS, corporal, 3 yrs. **Home Addr:** 24 Bowbell Rd, White Plains, NY 10607-1106. **Business Addr:** Director of College Relations, Bronx Community College, City University of New York, W 181 St & Univ Ave Language Hall Room 16, Bronx, NY 10453, **Business Phone:** (718)289-5179.

GRANT, REV. DEBORA FELITA
Clergy. **Personal:** Born Jul 28, 1956, Georgetown, SC; daughter of Rev Joseph James and Lillie M Ward. **Educ:** Clark Col, Atlanta, GA, BA, mass commun, 1981; Interdenominational Theological Ctr, Atlanta, GA, Master Divinity Pastoral Care & Coun, 1987. **Career:** SALT ministries, co founder; DHR & Div Youth Serv, Atlanta, GA, court serv worker, 1977-85; Interdenominational Theological Center, presidential scholar; Flipper Temple African Methodist Episcopal Church, Atlanta GA, youth pastor, asst minister; Morris Brown Col, Atlanta, GA, chaplain; St John African Methodist Episcopal Church, pastor, currently. **Orgs:** Black Women Church & Soc, 1986-89; exec secy, Concerned Black Clergy Metro Atlanta, 1987-89; Nat Advan Asn Colored People, 1987-89; mentor & dir, African Methodist Episcopal Ministers Union, 1988-89; Nat Asn Col & Univ Chaplains, 1989; Nat Black Campus Ministers Asn, 1989; Southern Christian Leadership Conf Women, 1989; Turner Alumini Asn; Judicial Alternative, Ga; Black Women Church Soc; Women Ministry, Ga. **Special Achievements:** first women to serve as chaplain at Morris Brown College. **Home Addr:** 827 Lynn Cir SW SW, Atlanta, GA 30311-2354. **Business Addr:** Pastor, St John African Methodist Episcopal Church, 3980 Steam Mill Rd, Columbus, GA 31907.*

GRANT, DENISE
Lawyer. **Educ:** George Washington Univ, BA, 1986; Georgetown Univ Law Ctr, JD, 1989. **Career:** Shearman & Sterling, Co-Chairperson, currently, partner, currently. **Orgs:** Am Bar Asn. **Special Achievements:** First African Am partner in the history of Shearman & Sterling. **Business Addr:** Partner, Shearman & Sterling, 599 Lexington Ave Rm 1016, New York, NY 10022, **Business Phone:** (212)848-7959.

GRANT, DR. ELLSWORTH R
Physician. **Career:** Hemat & oncol, Los Angeles, pvt pract, currently; Elizabeth Ctr Cancer Detection, med dir, currently. **Home Addr:** 1245 Wilshire Blvd, Los Angeles, CA 90017, **Home Phone:** (213)481-3948. **Business Addr:** Physician, 1338 S Hope St Lowr Level, Los Angeles, CA 90015, **Business Phone:** (213)742-5634.*

GRANT, ERNEST J
Nurse. **Educ:** Univ NC, Greensboro, MSN, nursing educ; NC Cent Univ, BSN, nursing; AB Tech Col, Diploma, practical nurse educ. **Career:** Univ NC Hosps, NC Jaycee Burn Ctr, Chapel Hill, licensed practical nurse, 1967, nursing educ clinician II, 1987-. **Orgs:** Burn Ctr, QA Comt; The Am Nurses Asn Inc; NC Nurses Asn. **Honors/Awds:** Medical-Surgical Nurse of the Year, NC Nurses Asn, 1994; Prevention Award, Am Burn Asn, 1998; Governor's Award of Excellence, the highest honor bestowed on a state employee, 1998; Honorary Nursing Practice Award, Am Nurses Asn, 2002; Nurse of the Year, Nursing Spectrum Mag, 2002; 2004 Outstanding Alumni Award, Am Asn Community Cols, 2004. **Special Achievements:** named in The Great 100, a list of 100 outstanding nurses in North Carolina, 1997; featured in the newsmakers section in the February 17th issue of Jet Magazine, 2002; developed a National Burn Awareness Campaign. **Business Addr:** Nursing Education Clinician II, North Carolina Jaycee Burn Center, Univ NC Hosps, 101 Manning Dr, Chapel Hill, NC 27514, **Business Phone:** (919)966-4131.

GRANT, GARY
Basketball coach, basketball player, president (organization). **Personal:** Born Apr 21, 1965, Canton, OH; children: Taryn Bree & Mahogany Simone. **Educ:** Univ Mich, BS, kinesiol, 1988. **Career:** Basketball player (retired), basketball coach, pres; Los Angeles Clippers, guard, 1988-95; New York Knicks, 1995-96; Miami Heat, 1996-97; Portland Trailblazers, guard, 1997-2001, asst coach, 2002-03; San Diego State Univ,asst coach, 2003-04; So Cal Legends, pres & head coach, currently. **Honors/Awds:** Big Ten Defensive Player of the Year, 1987, 1988; All-Am, 1988.

GRANT, GARY RUDOLPH
Executive. **Personal:** Born Aug 19, 1943, Newport News, VA; son of Florneza M and Matthew; widowed. **Educ:** NC Cent Univ, BA, 1965; Shaw Univ, post grad, attended; NC Wesleyan Col, post grad; Eastern NC Theological Seminary, PhD, humanities, 1997. **Career:** Halifax Cty Sch, teacher, 1965-79; Tillery Casket Mfg Inc, gen mgr, 1979-; Flo-Matt United Inc, pres; Black Farmers & Agriculturalists Asn, pres, currently. **Orgs:** Bd mem, Concerned Citizens Tillery, 1979-85; NC Hunger Coalition, 1982-86; Halifax City Bd Ed, 1982-86; chairperson, Committee to Save Black Owned Land, 1983-; Environ Protection Agency's (EPA) Small Towns & Cities Advisory Coun, 1996-98; African Am Environ Action Justice Network; NC Environ Justice Network; planning comm mem, Who Owns Am Conference III, Land Tenure Ctr, Univ Wis-Madison. **Honors/Awds:** Gary Grant Day, Tillery Committe, 1978; 4-H Club Halifax City; Goverment Volunteer Award, Gov James B Hun,t 1982; Trail Blazer for Environmental Justice, 1996; Halifax County NAACP, Humanitarian Award, 1997. **Business Addr:** President, Black Farmers Association, Tillery, NC 27887, **Business Phone:** (252)826-2800.

GRANT, DR. GEORGE C
Library administrator. **Personal:** Born Oct 22, 1939, Memphis, TN; son of Willie L Sr and Clara Lawson; married Alice Morgan Grant, Mar 16, 1963; children: Genine M & Melanie C. **Educ:** Owen Jr Col, Memphis Tenn, AA, 1959; Morehouse Col, Atlanta Ga, BS, 1961; Atlanta Univ, Atlanta Ga, MSLS, 1962; Univ Pittsburgh, SLIS, Pittsburgh Pa, PhD, 1981. **Career:** Owen Jr Col, Memphis Tenn, head librn, 1962-65; Southern Ill Univ, Edwardsville Ill, E St Louis Campus, chief librn, 1965-67, assoc dir libr, 1967-76; Morgan State Univ, Baltimore Md, libr dir, 1976-81; Stockton State Col, Pomona NJ, libr dir, 1981-86; Rollins Col, Winter Park Fla, dir librs, 1986; Four-G Publ, pres, chief exec officer; Ark State Univ, Libr & Info Servs, dean, 2003-; GrantHouse Publ, chief exec officer currently. **Orgs:** Am Libr Asn, 1967-; mem, 1971-, exec bd, 1980-, ed, newsletter, 1980-, ed, mem diry, 1984-, Black Caucus ALA; chair, 1982-86, adv comn, 1982-88, ALA Off Libr Outreach Serv; Fla Libr Asn, 1986-; bd dir, Cent Fla Soc ARO Heritage, 1987-89; steering comn, Preserve Eatonville Fla Community, 1988-90; steering comn, Cent Fla Libr Network, 1988-; adv comn, Fla State Libr, LSCA, 1988-. **Honors/Awds:** Fel PhD Studies, Univ Pittsburgh, 1974-75; Coun Libr resources Acad, Libr Internship Yale Univ, 1975-76; Newsletter Black Caucus Ala, 1980-88; Mem Diry, Black Caucus ALA, 4th edition, 1984, 5th edition, 1986, 6th edition, 1988; Preserve Etonville Community Inc Serv Award, 1989. **Special Achievements:** Compiler: Diry Ethnic Profs in Libr & Information SCI, FOUR-G Publishers Inc, 1991. **Business Phone:** (870)934-0418.

GRANT, GWENDOLYN GOLDSBY
Counselor, writer. **Personal:** Daughter of Esters and Ethel Lee Goldsby; married Ralph T Grant, Jr; children: Ralph III, Sally-Ann, Rebecca. **Career:** Psychologist, sex educr, lectr; Essence, advice columnist, 21st Century Speakers Inc, currently. **Orgs:** Phi Delta Kappa; Phi Kappa Phi; Alpha Kappa Alpha Sorority; National Council of Negro Women; National Assc of Black Journalists. **Honors/Awds:** Assc of Black Psychologists, Bobby E. Wright Community Service Awrd. *

GRANT, HARVEY
Basketball coach, basketball player. **Personal:** Born Jul 4, 1965, Augusta, GA; married Beverly; children: Jerai, Jaren & Jeremy. **Educ:** Clemson Univ, Clemson, SC, 1985; Independence Jr Col, Independence, KS,1986; Univ Okla, Norman, OK, law enforcement. **Career:** Basketball player (retired), basketball coach; Washington Bullets, forward, 1988-93; Portland Trail Blazers, 1993-96; Washington Wizards, 1996-98; Philadelphia 76ers, 1998-99; Brevard Blue Ducks, head coach, 1999-2002. **Honors/Awds:** NBA Most Improved Player Award, 1991. **Special Achievements:** NBA Draft, First round pick, #12, 1988.

GRANT, HORACE JUNIOR
Basketball player. **Personal:** Born Jul 4, 1965, Augusta, GA; married Donna (divorced 1994); children: Horace Jr. **Educ:** Clemson Univ, Clemson, SC, 1987. **Career:** Basketball player (retired); Chicago Bulls, forward, 1987-94; Orlando Magic, forward, 1994-99, 2001-03; Seattle Supersonics, forward, 1999-2000; Los Angeles Lakers, forward, 2000-01, 2003-04. **Honors/Awds:** NBA All-Star, 1994; NBA All-Defensive Second Team, 1992-93, 1993-94, 1994-95, 1995-96.

GRANT, IAN
Executive, president (organization). **Career:** Umoja Fine Arts Inc, founder & pres, currently. **Business Addr:** President, Founder, Umoja Fine Arts Gallery, 16250 Northland Dr Suite 104, Crossroads Bldg, Southfield, MI 48075, **Business Phone:** (248)552-1070.*

GRANT, REV. DR. JACQUELYN
Educator. **Personal:** Born Dec 19, 1948, Georgetown, SC; daughter of Rev Joseph James and Lillie Mae; married John W P Collier Jr. **Educ:** Bennett Col, BA, 1970; Interdenominational Theol Ctr, MDiv, 1973; Union Theol Sem, MPhil, 1980, PhD, 1985. **Career:** Union Theol Sem, tutor & relief teacher 1975-77; Harvard Divinity Sch,assoc in res, 1977-79; Candler Sch Emory & Theol Univ, vis lectr, 1981; Princeton Theol Sem, vis lectr, 1985; Inter denominational Theol Ctr, prof1980, Fuller E Calla way prof Syst Theol, currently. **Orgs:** Assoc minister, Allen AME Church, 1973-80; itinerant elder, African Methodist Episcopal Church, 1976, asst minister, 1980-82; Disserta tionfel, Fund for Theol Educ, 1979-80; DuBois fel, Harvard Univ, 1979-80;assoc minister, Flipper Temple AME Church, 1980-93; founder & dir, BlackWomen in Church & Soc Ctr, InterdenomiNat Theol Ctr, 1981-; asst minister,Victory AME Church, 1993; bd dirs, Black Theology Proj in the Am. **Honors/Awds:** Woman of the Yr, Iota Phi Lambda Sorority, 1984; Martin Luther King Jr Ministry Award, 1986; Outstanding Alumni, Colgate & Rochester Theol Sem;Turner Theol Sem, Interdenomi Nat Theol Ctr; nominated as

the Woman of the Year in Religion by the Iota Phi Lambda Sorority. **Special Achievements:** Author: White Women's Christ & Black Women's Jesus, Feminist Christology &Womanist Response, Perspectives on Womanist Theol; Am Black Achievement Award nominee, 1982. **Business Addr:** Fuller E Callaway Professor of Systematic Theology, Interdenominational Theological Center, 700 Martin Luther King Jr Dr, Atlanta, GA 30314-4143, **Business Phone:** (404)527-7792.

GRANT, JAMES
School administrator, educator. **Personal:** Born Dec 28, 1932, Ruffin, SC; married Maggie Ruth Harrison; children: Christopher, Kevin & Karen. **Educ:** Adelphi Univ, BBA, 1959, MBA, 1973. **Career:** Adelphi Univ, asst controller, 1970-73, controller, 1973; City Univ NY, Medgar Evers Col, assoc dean admin, 1973-78, dean admin, 1978-79; SUNY Col, New Paltz, vpres admin. **Orgs:** Eastern Asn Univ & Col Bus Officers, 1970-; pres, Auxillary Compus Enterprises Inc, 1979-; pres, State Univ NY Bus Officers Asn, 1983-85; consult, MD State Higher Educ, 1984, 1985; consult, Mid States Asn, 1985. **Military Serv:** AUS, sp4, 2 yrs. **Business Addr:** Vice President, State University NY, Hab 905, New Paltz, NY 12561.*

GRANT, JOHN H., SR.
Manager. **Personal:** Born May 11, 1927, Philadelphia, PA; married Carolyn Sawyer; children: John Jr, Marsha L. **Educ:** Tuskegee Inst, BA, bus, diploma aerospace mechanic, qualified private pilot, 1949. **Career:** Manager (retired); Boeing Vertol, inspector, supvr, gen supvr, asst mgr contract maintenance mgr, qual assurance corrective action unit, qual assurance rep, qual control final assembly supvr, sr prod assurance analyst, coord qual control functions, supvr dynamic components. **Orgs:** Past pres, Boeing Mgt Assoc; dir emer, Northeastern Regional, Tuskegee Inst Alumni Asn; Am Helicopter Soc; past vice chmn, exec bd, Nat Tuskegee Alumni; chmn trustee bd, New Bethlehem Baptist Church, 1975-85; past pres, First Masonic Dist Coun; pres, Absalom Jones Found, 1999-. **Honors/Awds:** Deputy Lecture Award, Outstanding Worshipful Master First Dist Prince Hall Masons. **Military Serv:** AUS, motor sgt, 1946-50. **Home Addr:** 267 E Meehan Ave, Philadelphia, PA 19119. *

GRANT, DR. KINGSLEY B
Physician. **Personal:** Born Feb 13, 1931, Central America; son of Barrister E A and Mina Grant; married Margaret; children: Ward & Conrad Maxwell. **Educ:** Univ London, BA, 1948; Howard Univ, BS, 1955, MD, 1959; Am Bd Pathol, cert, 1964; Am Bd Pathol & Dermatopathol, cert, 1980. **Career:** La Co Harbor Gen Hosp, resident anatomic & clinical pathologist, 1962-64, chief resident, 1963-64; St Lukes Hosp, resident anatomic & clinical path, 1960-62, assoc path, co-dir path, 1970, dir dept pathol & lab serv, 1975-88; The Am Acad Neurological & Orthopaedic Surgeons, prof, currently. **Orgs:** Staff St Lukes Hosp, 1964-92; bd dir, United Way, 1966-71; Hawkeye Area Community Action Prog, 1968-69; CR chap, Nat Conference Christians & Jews, 1969; Am Soc Clin Path Chmn Cedar Rapids Community Human Rights, 1969; pres, PTA 1969; clin asst prof, Col Med Univ Iowa, 1973-78; exec comm mem, Iowa Asn Pathologists, 1974-89; pres, St Lukes methodist Hosp Med, Dental Staff, 1981; fel Am Col Pathologists; Comn Race & Religion Iowa United Meth Ch, Rotary Club, Educ Oppor Prog Comm Col Med Univ Iowa; AMA, NMA, Int Acad Pathologists; delegate Col Am Pathologists; sectytreasu/pres, Iowa Asn Pathologists, 1986-89. **Honors/Awds:** Phi Beta Kappa, 1955; Comm Bldr Awd B'nai B'rith 1970; Certificate of Appreciation, City of Cedar Rapids, 1974. **Business Addr:** Professor, The American Academy of Neurological & Orthopaedic Surgeons, 2300 S Rancho Dr Suite 202, Las Vegas, NV 89113, **Business Phone:** (702)388-7390.

GRANT, NATHANIEL
Executive. **Personal:** Born Sep 8, 1943, Washington, DC; married Patricia A; children: Monica D, Nathaniel D. **Educ:** Norfolk State Col, bus admin courses, 1966. **Career:** Communs Satellite, admin supvr, 1966-69; Am Assoc Univ Women, prod mgr, 1969-73; Nat Pub Radio, admin mgr, 1973-77; Neighborhood Reinvest Corp, dir human res, 1995. **Orgs:** Nat Forum Black Pub Admin, 1984-87. **Honors/Awds:** Board Resolution for Outstanding Service, Neighborhood Housing Serv Am, 1982; Bd Resolution and Monetary Award, Neighborhood Reinvest Corp, 1986, 1988. **Military Serv:** USN, yeoman 2nd class, 4 yrs. *

GRANT, STEPHEN MITCHELL
Football player. **Personal:** Born Dec 23, 1969, Miami, FL; married Leslie; children: Michael. **Educ:** WVa Univ. **Career:** Football player (retired); Indianapolis Colts, linebacker, 1992-97; Tampa-Bay Buccaneers, 1997. **Orgs:** Face To Face Inc.

GRANT, TIMOTHY JEROME
Social worker. **Personal:** Born Aug 6, 1965, Greenville, SC; son of John M Sr and Mamie J Rosemond. **Educ:** Univ SC, Columbia SC, BS, 1987. **Career:** SC House Rep, Cola SC, legis aide, 1987-89; Richland County Dept Social Serv, Cola SC, social serv specialist I, 1987-89, social serv specialist II, 1989-90, social serv specialist III, 1990-93, work support specialist, 1993-96, assessment specialist 1996-. **Orgs:** Phi Beta Sigma Frat; Notary Pub, SC Notary Pub; Outstanding Young Men of Am, 1987, 1989; Outstanding Col Stud Am; Phi Beta Sigma Fraternity, life mem, 2000; Indian Waters Coun, Boy Scouts Am, Explorers counr. **Honors/Awds:** Undergraduate Brother of the Year, Phi Beta Sigma, 1986; Order of Omega Honor Soc, USC Greeks, 1987; Serv Award, SC House Rep, 1987; Grad Brother of the Year for chapter, state & region, Phi Beta Sigma, 2000; Graduate Brother of the Yr for S.C. & Southeastern Region, 2002. **Home Addr:** 7 Sterling Ridge Ct, Columbia, SC 29229. **Business Addr:** Family Independence Prog, Richland Co, Dept Soc Serv, 3220 2 Notch Rd, Columbia, SC 29204.*

GRANT, DR. WILMER, JR.
Educator. **Personal:** Born Jul 29, 1940, Ahoskie, NC; married Ruth Dale Ford. **Educ:** Hampton Inst, BA, 1962; Ind Univ, MS, 1967, PhD, 1974. **Career:** Univ Toledo, asst prof, 1973-; Univ Mo, asst dean, 1972-73; Ind Mil Acad, instr, 1966; Ga Southern Col, prof emer. **Orgs:** Am Phys Soc; Am Inst Physics; cent Ohio Black Studies Consortium; Nat Coun Black Studies; consult, DHEW, 1976; Asn Study Afro-Am Life & Hist, 1976-; Alpha Phi Alpha, 1961-; Sigma Pi Phi, 1977-; Community Chest Budget Comn, 1975; bd trustees, Cordelia Martin Neighbourhood Health Ctr, 1974-76; Toledo Coun Bus, 1975-77. **Honors/Awds:** Omega Psi Phi, talent contest, State Va, 1958; commendation, AUS, 1961;developer, "Famous Black Symphomic Composers & Their Works", 1976; certificate of merit, Kappa League, 1977. **Military Serv:** AUS, first lt capt, 1962-64. **Business Addr:** Professor Emeritus, Georgia Southern College, Department of Physics, Landrum, PO Box 8031, Statesboro, GA 30460.*

GRANT BISHOP, ELLEN ELIZABETH
Government official. **Personal:** Born Mar 25, 1949, Buffalo, NY; daughter of Herman and Verba; married George M Bishop Jr, Mar 19, 1983; children: Justin Mason. **Educ:** State Univ NY, Buffalo, BA, 1972, MSW, 1974, PhD, 1979; Medaille Col, Humane Letters, Honis Causa, 1996. **Career:** Erie County Med Ctr, licensed practical nurse, 1968-74; Buffalo Gen Hosp, prog coord, dep dir, asst vpres, 1973-83; Buffalo Psychiat Ctr, social worker, actg team leader, 1975-80; Erie County, Dept Ment Health, comnr ment health, 1988-; County Ment Health Ctr, admin; Healthnow New York Inc, vpres, currently. **Orgs:** Acad Cert Social Workers, 1974-; NY State Cert Social Workers, 1974-; Am Col Ment Health Admin; Buffalo & Erie County Hist Soc. **Honors/Awds:** Nelson Mandela Community Service Award, NY State Black Psychologists, 1991; Social Workers Year, NY State, 1997; Health Award, NY State Women's Comns, 1997; Locam Parker Achievement Award, Iota Phi Lambda Sorority; Nat Outstanding Bus Woman Year Award. **Special Achievements:** Managing in Black & White: A Guide for Prof Woman Color, book; "Self-Mktg Skills for New ADM," in Comtemporary Directions in Human Resource Mgt, book chap. **Business Addr:** Vice President, HealthNow New York Inc., 1901 Main St, PO Box 80, Buffalo, NY 14240-0080, **Business Phone:** (716)887-6900.

GRANT-BRUCE, DARLENE CAMILLE
Lawyer. **Personal:** Born Apr 25, 1959, Jackson Heights, NY; daughter of Leonard and Lucille; married Raymond L, Nov 30, 1996. **Career:** VI Dept Justice, asst atty gen, 1989-94; Nat Coun Crime & Delinquency, gen coun, 1994-98; Coun DC, asst gen coun, 1994; US Dist Ct VI, spec master, 1996-99; Berkshire Farm Ctr & Serv Youth, gen coun, 1999-. **Orgs:** Delta Sigma Theta Sorority; US Supreme Ct; US Cts Appeals, 3rd circuit, DC; Appellate Div, NY State Supreme Ct; Am Bar Asn; Nat Bar Asn; NY State Bar Asn; Macon B Allen Bar Asn; DC Bar Asn; Phi Delta Phi; vpres, Delta Sigma Theta Inc, 1990-92, legal advisor, 1992-94; bd dirs, Metro Black Bar Asn, 1997-2003; Legal Affairs Com, Am Correctional Asn, 1997; VI Bar Asn. **Honors/Awds:** Certificate of Appreciation, VI Dept Justice, 1993; Certificate of Service, Narcotics Strike Force, 1993; Earl Warren Legal Scholar, 1981; Coun Legal Educ Opportunities, 1981. **Special Achievements:** Should Prison Litigation Be Curtailed?, May, 1996, Focus-NCCD; Congressional Study on the DC Department of Corrections, Jan, 1996; Prison Litigation Reform Act, Corrections Today, August, 1998. **Business Addr:** General Counsel, Special Master, US District Court for VI, Office of Special Master, 210 W 137 St Suite 1, East Elmhurst, NY 10030, **Business Phone:** (212)371-9150.*

GRANTE, JULLIAN IRVING
Consultant. **Personal:** Born Oct 18, 1950, Washington, DC; married Jo Draper, Jan 2, 1990; children: Jamil Patricia, Dusan Arthur & Blake Alexander. **Educ:** Univ Md, 1972; Southern Ill Univ, Carbondale, 1976. **Career:** Land'Or Internatl, vpres, sales & mkt, 1980-88; J Irving & Draper, sr partner, 1988-. **Orgs:** Comm advisor, Gov Commonwealth Va, 1986-; advisory bd, dept Minority Bus Enterprise, 1995; Criminal Justice Service Bd, 1994-00; Dept Juvenile Justice, release review comm, 1996-00; Am Wellness Alliance, sr partner & exec vpres, currently. **Honors/Awds:** Family Literacy Award, Barbara Bush Found, 1990; Recognition for Volunteerism in Ed, White House Points of Lights, 1992. **Military Serv:** USAF, 1968-80. **Business Addr:** Senior Partner, Executive Vice President, The American Wellness Alliance, 2103 E Parham Rd Suite 101, Richmond, VA 23228, **Business Phone:** 800-578-5010.

GRANTHAM, CHARLES
Educator, basketball player, chief executive officer. **Educ:** Cheyney State Univ, BS; Univ Pa Wharton Sch, MBA; Pa Sch Edu, Doctoral Course. **Career:** Nat Basketball Players Asn, exec dir, 1988-95; Univ Penn, Wharton Sport Bus Initiative, Dept Legal Studies, sr fel, currently; Univ Penn, adj prof, 2002-04; Seton Hall Univ, Stillman Sch Bus, adj prof, currently; Ceruzzi Sports & Entertainment Group Inc, pres & ceo, currently. **Orgs:** Bd dir selection comt, USA Basketballs Dream Teams I & II; bd dir, Womens Sports Foundation & Sports Career, Inc. **Honors/Awds:** K-Swiss Sports Executive of the Year Award, 1990, 1993; Success Guide Leadership Award; The Black Athletes in America Forum Spirit Award; The Wheelchair Classic Businessman of the Year Award; The Rainbow Coalition Leadership Award; Pro-Am Achievement Award; Cheyney State University Basketball Hall of Fame, 1992; 100 Most Powerful Sports People, Sports News, 1993-95. **Special Achievements:** Mr. Grantham has appeared frequently on local and national television programs including ABCs "Good Morning America," and PBSs The MacNeil-Lehrer Report. Mr. Grantham has authored several articles featuredin The New York Times, USA Today, Inside Sports and The New York Daily News and was executive producer and narrator for a 35-minute documentary video titled "Cocaine Drain," which featured NBA players speaking out against illegal drug use. As a Presidential Conferee in the Reagan Administration, he helped to develop public policy to combat drug use in America. In addition, Mr. Grantham has testified before Congress regarding drug policies in professional sports & about collegiate eligibility and professional sports issues. **Military Serv:** Bd dir selection comt, USA Basketballs Dream Teams I & II; bd dir, Womens Sports Foundation & Sports Career, Inc. **Business Phone:** (212)268-5757.*

GRANTHAM, PROF. REGINA
Educator, chairperson. **Personal:** Born Nov 12, 1947, Philadelphia, PA. **Educ:** Pa State Univ, BS, MEd. **Career:** State Univ NY, Col Cortland, Speech Pathol & Audiol Dept, assoc prof & chairperson, currently. **Orgs:** Am Speech-Lang-Hearing Asn. **Honors/Awds:** Chancellor's Award for Excellence in Faculty Service, 2004; fel, Am Speech-Lang-Hearing Asn, 2006. **Business Addr:** Associate Professor, Chairperson, State University of New York College at Cortland, Speech Pathology & Audiology Department, 60 Tompkins St, Cortland, NY 13045, **Business Phone:** (607)753-5423.

GRANTLEY, ROBERT CLARK
Executive, vice president (organization). **Personal:** Born Aug 30, 1948, Atlanta, GA; son of Robert Charles and Edith Clark; married Sandra Prophet Grantley, Nov 22, 1979; children: Michael, Robyn. **Educ:** Howard Univ, WA, DC, BSEE, 1971; Catholic Univ, WA, DC, JD, 1983. **Career:** Challenger Res Inc, Rockville MD, electronics engr, 1971-73; Potomac Elec Power Co, WA, DC, start-up engr, 1973-75, site mgr, 1975-78, construct coordr, 1978-84, mgr, Energy Use Mgt, 1974-87, vpres, Customer Serv, 1987-94, group vpres, 1994-. **Orgs:** Wash DC Bar Asn, 1983-, Md Bar Asn, 1983-; bd dirs, The Levine Sch Music; bd dirs, The Greater Wash Urban League; bd dirs, Leadership Wash. **Business Addr:** Group Vice President, Potomac Electric Power Company, Customer Service & Power Distribution, 1900 Pa Ave NW, Washington, DC 202872-297, **Business Phone:** (202)331-6366.*

GRANVILLE, BILLY (III)
Football player, entrepreneur. **Personal:** Born Mar 11, 1974, Lawrenceville, NJ. **Educ:** Duke Univ, BA, sociol. **Career:** Football player (retired), Entrepreneur; Cincinnati Bengals, linebacker, 1997-2000; Houston Texans, linebacker, 2002; Northwestern Mutual Financial Network, financial rep, 2004-. **Orgs:** Bd, Greater Houston Fel Christian Athletes; Soc Fin Serv Prof; Houston Estate & Fin Forum; NFL Alumni, Houston Chap. **Business Addr:** Financial Representative, The Northwestern Mutual Life Insurance Company, 720 E Wis Ave, Milwaukee, WI 53202-4797, **Business Phone:** (414)271-1444.

GRANVILLE, WILLIAM, JR.
Executive, school administrator, association executive. **Personal:** Born Dec 6, 1940, Warner Robins, GA; son of William Granville Sr and Marian Hicks; married Jessica Katherine Hilton; children: Cheryl Lynn, Michelle Marie, William Lamont. **Educ:** Delaware State Col, BS, Math, 1962, Doc Humane Letters, Honoris Causa, 1987. **Career:** Dept Army, mathematician, 1962-65; Mobil Res & Develop Corp, res math, 1965-69; Mobil Int Div, int planning anal, 1969-70, int rels exec, 1970-76; Mobil Oil Corp, mgr Middle East training oper, 1976-81, mgr tech transfer Middle E, 1981-; Mobil Int Consult Serv Inc, exec vpres, 1983; Granville Acad Nat, founder & chmn, 1983-. **Orgs:** Woodrow Wilson Fel; bd trustees, Rider Col; bd dir, US Black Engr & US Hispanic Engr mag. **Honors/Awds:** Community Service Award, NAACP, 1984; Distinguished Alumnus Award, DE State Col 1984; Award Nat Asn Equal Opportunity, Higher Educ Wash; Hon DHL Del State Col; mem, Omicron Delta Kappa Honorary Soc. **Business Phone:** (202)298-8226.*

GRATE, DR. ISAAC, JR.
Physician. **Personal:** Born Dec 20, 1952, Georgetown, SC; son of Isaac Grate Sr and Beulah Grate; married Frankie Lee Young; children: Chelsea. **Educ:** Howard Univ, attended 1971-74; Meharry Med Col, MD, 1978; UCLA, Sch Pub Health, Grad, Sch,

1979-80. **Career:** Martin Luther King Jr Gen Hosp, intern, 1978-79; Johns Hopkins Hosp, resident, 1980-82; Tex Tech Univ, instr surg/em, 1982-84; St Lukes Episcopal Hosp, dir emergency svcs, 1985-87; Southeast Tex Emergency Physicians, partner, 1987-92; La Emergency & Trauma, specialist, 1992; Univ Tex, Health Sci Ctr, Houston, Clinic Asst Prof, currently; pvt pract, currently. **Orgs:** Univ Asn Emergency Physicians,1992-97, Soc Teachers Emergency Med, 1992-97, Am Col Emergency Physicians, 1992-97; affiliate fac, instr ACLS, Am Heart Asn, 1984-87; Houston Med Forum, 1987-92; Southwest Tex Emergency Physicians, 1987-92, Nat Med Asn, 1987-91, NAACP, 1996. **Honors/Awds:** Dir Medical Educ Texas Tech Univ Sch of Medicine Div Emergency Medicine, 1982-85; Fellow Amer College Emergency Physicians, 1996-. **Military Serv:** USAF Reserves, major, 5 yrs, flight surgeon, 1987. **Home Addr:** 11811 Pepperdine Lane, Houston, TX 77071. **Business Addr:** Physician, 6411 Fannin St, Houston, TX 77030, **Business Phone:** (713)704-4000.

GRAUER, GLADYS BARKER
Artist, educator. **Personal:** Born Aug 15, 1923, Cincinnati, OH; daughter of Charles and Maude; married Solomon, Dec 27, 1947 (deceased); children: Antoinette Baskerville, Edith, Edward & Leon. **Educ:** Art Inst Chicago, Rutgers Univ, attended 1941-45, attended 1972-74. **Career:** Essex Co Votech High Sch, teacher, 1974-89; New Jersey State Coun Arts fel, 1985; Newark Mus, 1989-90; Essex Co Col, teacher, 1989-92; artist residence, Newark Mus, 1992; artist residence, Art Coun Essel Co; Rutgers Innovative Printmaking fel, 1993; artist, currently. **Orgs:** Alumni assoc, Art Inst Chicago, 1945-; Nat Educ Asn, 1974-; pres, Black Woman Visual Perspective, 1980-; bd mem, Newark Arts Coun, 1981-98; bd mem, City Without Walls Art Gallery, 1995-98. **Honors/Awds:** First Prize Watercolor, James St Commons, 1983. **Special Achievements:** Art works in permanent collections of the Newark Museum, Montclair Museum, Noyes Museum, Newark Public Library, Artist Library of the Victoria & Albert Museum, London, England, Museum of Modern Art, National Museum of American Art Library. **Business Addr:** Artist, 352 Seymour Ave, Newark, NJ 07112-2135, **Business Phone:** (973)923-7928.

GRAVENBERG, ERIC VON
Educator, school administrator, consultant. **Personal:** Born May 18, 1950, Oakland, CA; son of Allen and Myrtle LeBlanc; married Deborah Elaine; children: Roshan, Ashande. **Educ:** Calif State Univ, BA, black studies, 1972, MA, pub admin, 1974; Columbus Univ, PhD, educ admin. **Career:** Calif State Univ, Chico, dir educ opportunity prog, 1979-80; Calif State Univ Hayward, dir educ resource ctr, 1980-81; Off Chancellor Calif State Univ, asn dean educ progs, 1981-86; Univ Calif Riverside, dir undergrad admis, 1986-; Renaissance Enterprises Pvt Consult Co, pres 1989-; Inst Contemp Leadership, dean fac, 1989- 91; Univ Calif Riverside, supt, dir undergrad admis, 1990-93; Alliant Univ, assoc vp enrollment mgt, 1993-94, assoc vpres Enrollment Mgt & Stud Servs, vpres, ctr undergrad educ, currently. **Orgs:** Affirmative Action Comt Adv Bd Univ Calif Irvine, 1985-86; bdm Western Asn Educ Opportunity Personnel, 1985-86; Nat Coun Access Serv Col Bd, 1985-; orgn develop consult Calif State Univ-Chico, 1986; chmn minority affairs, Western Asn Col Admis Counr, 1988-; pres, Kevin Johnson's St. Hope Acad. **Honors/Awds:** Achievers Award WESTOP Long Beach, 1983; Presdent's Award, Nat Coun Educ Opportunity Assoc Wash DC, 1984; Univ Calif Riverside, Outstanding Staff Award, 1990; Human Rels Awards, 1990; The Island Consortium Articulation & Transfer, Ed of the Year, 1992. **Special Achievements:** Author, Learning Assistance Prog, 1986; exec producer, writer, dir theatrical prod: "On the Edge of a Dream," 1988; writer, producer, host of over 25 multicultural television prod, 1976-78. *

GRAVES, ALLENE
Executive, president (organization). **Personal:** Born Jan 5, 1952, Washington, DC; daughter of Allen R and Eula D; children: Kym R Murray, Daquan Murray, Rico Plesant & Jamea Murray. **Educ:** Univ DC. **Career:** United Plannning Orgn, secy, 1972-76; Shaw Proj Area Comt, admin asst, 1976-79; Am Coun Capital Formation, word processor, 1979-83; Acad Educ Develop, exec secy, 1983-84; Bergson, Borkland & Margolis, legal secy, 1984-85; Sherman & Lapidus, off mgr, 1984-86; Answer Staffing Serv Inc, pres, 1987-. **Orgs:** Metrop Wash Temp Asn, 1989; Better Bus Bur; DC Chamber Com. **Honors/Awds:** Minority Business Women of the Year, Wash DC Minority Develop Ctr, 1994. **Business Addr:** President, The Answer Staffing Services Inc, 1920 L St NW Suite 320, Washington, DC 20036, **Business Phone:** (202)835-0190.

GRAVES, CAROLE A.
Administrator, teacher. **Personal:** Born 0413, Newark, NJ; daughter of Jennie Valeria Stafford Anderson and Philip Burnett Anderson; married David Leon Graves, Nov 4, 1962. **Educ:** Kean Col, Newark, BA, 1960; Rutger Inst Labor & Mgt Rels, labor rels specialist cert, 1976. **Career:** Newark Sch Syst, Newark, NJ, spec educ teacher, 1960-69; Newark Teachers Union, Am Fedn Teachers, Newark, NJ, pres. **Orgs:** vpres, NJ State AFL-CIO; vpres, NJ State Indus Union Coun; vpres, Essex West/Hudson Central Labor Coun; vpres, NJ State Fedn Teachers; Rutgers Lacor Alumni Exec Bd; A Philip Randolph Inst; Coalition Labor Union Women. **Honors/Awds:** Martin Luther King Award, NJ Labor Press Coun, 1973; Labor Achievement Award, Women's Affirmative Action Comt, IUC/AFL-CIO, 1983. **Special Achievements:** Named one of Labor's Outstanding Black Women, Nat Orgn of Black Leaders, 1973; Inducted into NJ Labor Hall of Fame, Newark Community Action Team, 1977. *

GRAVES, CLIFFORD WAYNE
Investment banker. **Personal:** Born Mar 30, 1939, San Francisco, CA; son of Wilbur Earl and Ruth Louise; married Anasa Briggs, Sep 17, 1988; children: Sharon & Diane. **Educ:** Univ Calif, Berkeley, BA, 1961, M City Planning, 1964. **Career:** City Santa Rosa, asst city planner, 1961-62; E Sussex Co, town planner & civic designer, 1964-66; San Francisco Bay Consult & Dev Comn, assoc planner, 1966-69; Univ Calif, Berkeley, lectr, 1968-69; spec proj officer, 1969-70; Comprehensive Planning Asst Div, dir, 1970-71; Howard Univ, lectr, 1970-73; Off Planning & Mgt Asst, dir & asst dir, 1971-72; Sec Comn Planning & Mgt, dep asst, 1972-74; Off Mgt & Budget, dep assoc dir, eval & prog implem; Co San Diego, chief admin officer, 1978-85; San Diego State Univ, assoc prof, 1979-85; Int Technol Corp, Torrance, Calif, dir planning, 1986-88; Grigsby & Graves Environ, San Diego, Calif, pres, 1988-, managing dir, 1988-2002; Los Angeles Community Develop Dept, gen mgr, 2003-. **Orgs:** Am Inst Planners; Am Soc Planning Off; Am Soc Pub Admin; Nat Asn Planners; comnr, Port San Diego, 1990-. **Honors/Awds:** Distinguished Service Award, HUD, 1972; Wm A Jump Foundation Award, 1972; Student Award, Am Inst Planners, 1972. **Home Addr:** 110 Cresta Vista Dr, San Francisco, CA 94127-1635, **Home Phone:** (619)296-2538. **Business Addr:** General Manager, Los Angeles Community Development Department, Garland Bldg 1200 W 7th St, Los Angeles, CA 90017, **Business Phone:** (213)744-7300.

GRAVES, CURTIS M.
Manager. **Personal:** Born Aug 26, 1938, New Orleans, LA; son of Joseph F. and Mabel Haydel; married Joanne Gordon; children: Gretchen, Christopher, Gizelle. **Educ:** Xavier Univ; Tex Southern Univ, BBA, 1963; Princeton Univ, Woodrow Wilson Fel, 1985. **Career:** Standard Savs Asn Houston, mgr, 1962-66; Tex House Reps, elected, 1966-72; Educ & Comm Affairs Br NASA, chief, 1977-87, dept dir civil affairs; Leadership Inst Community Develop Wash, DC, training officer teaching state & local govt procedures; Nat Civil Serv League, managing assoc, dir continuing educ; NASA, dept dir civil affairs defense & inter govt rels div, dep dir acad serv pub affairs, chief community & educ serv, minority univ prog mgr. **Orgs:** Steering comt, Nat Congr Aerospace Educ; former pres, World Aerospace Educ Org; Wash Alumni Chap Kappa Alpha Psi Frat; pres, World Aerospace Educ Orgn, 1983-; bd mem, Ky Inst. **Honors/Awds:** Awards from the Coun Negro Women, Delta Sigma Theta Sorority, Nat Asn Col Women, City Los Angeles, Kappa Alpha Psi Fraternity, Tex Southern Univ, NY City Sch Syst, Nat Congr Aviation & Space Educ; two hon doctorate degrees, Union Baptist Bible Sem; Frank G Brewer Trophy, 1989. **Special Achievements:** Publ book: Famous Black Amers, vol I & II. *

GRAVES, DENIQUE
Basketball player. **Personal:** Born Sep 16, 1975, Philadelphia, PA. **Educ:** Howard Univ, BS, teacher educ, 1997. **Career:** Basketball player(retired); Sacramento Monarchs, ctr, 1997; San Benardo, Brazil; Istanbul, Turkey, basketball player, 1999; Orlando Miracle, 2001; Sofia Slavia, Bulgaria, 2001-02; Jiangsu, China, 2002; BC Power basket Wels, Austria, ctr, 2003; Binghamton Univ Bearcats, asst coach, currently. **Honors/Awds:** Howard Athletic Hall of Fame. **Business Addr:** Assistant Coach, Bearcats, Binghamton University, PO Box 6000, Binghamton, NY 13902-6000, **Business Phone:** (607)777-6339.

GRAVES, DENYCE ANTOINETTE
Opera singer. **Personal:** Born Mar 7, 1964, Washington, DC; daughter of Charles Graves and Dorothy Graves-Kenner. **Educ:** Oberlin Col Conserv, 1984; New Eng Conserv Music, B Music, AArst dipl, 1988. **Career:** Mezzo-soprano opera singer; Hansel & Gretel, 1989; Suzuki in Madame Butterfly, Houston Grand Opera, 1990; Maddalena in Rigoletto, DC, 1991; Carmen, Minn Opera, 1991; Concert For Planet Earth, Sony Classical, 1993; Hamlet, EMI, 1993; Recital Denyce Graves: Heroines de l'Opera romantique Francais, FNAC Music, 1993; Denyce Graves: A Cathedral Christmas, PBS Prod, 1998; Angels Watching Over Me, NPR Classics, 1998; Metro Opera, Dallas Opera, Opernhaus Zurich; Turk in Rake's Progress, Chatelet, Paris; XM Satellite Radio, Voce di Donna, host, 2005; Amn Idol Underground, indust panelist, currently. **Orgs:** Panel mem, Am Guild Musical Artists; Wash Opera Open Forum, 1991; active supporter, African Nat Cong, Boston, 1985. **Honors/Awds:** Northeast Metro Opera Regional Auditions, first place, 1987; Richard F Gold Career Grant, Houston Grand Opera, 1989; Grand Prix du Concours Intl de Chant de Paris, 1990; Jacobsooon Study Grant, Richard Tucker Music Found, 1990; Nat Endowment for Arts Grant, 1990; Metro Opera Grant, 1990; Grand Prix Lyrique, Asn des amis de l'opera de Monte-Carlo, 1991; Marion Anderson Award, 1991; hon doctorate, Oberlin Col Conserv, 1998; Wash Award in Lit & Arts, 2000. **Special Achievements:** "Women of the Year", Glamour Magazine, 1997; "Standard Bearers for the 21st Century", WQXR Radio, 1999; Played in NY's Metrop Opera prod of Samson et Dalila with Placido Domingo; "50 Leaders of Tomorrow" by Ebony Magazine. **Business Addr:** Opera Singer, Columbia Artists Management Inc, Columbia Artists, 165 W 57th St, New York, NY 10019, **Business Phone:** (212)397-6900.

GRAVES, EARL G.
Publisher. **Personal:** Born Jan 9, 1935, Brooklyn, NY; son of Earl Godwin and Winifred Sealy; married Barbara Kydd, Jul 2, 1960; children: Earl Jr, John Clifford & Michael Alan. **Educ:** Morgan State Col, BA, 1958. **Career:** Senator Robt F Kennedy, admin asst, 1965-68; Earl G Graves Ltd, founder;Earl G Graves Pub Co Inc, founder; Earl G Graves Assoc, founder; Black Enterprise Mag, founder & publ; Pepsi-Cola of Washington, chmn & chief-exec officer, 1990-98; Earl G Graves Ltd, chmn & chief exec officer, currently; Aetna Life & Casualty Co, dir; AMR Corp, dir; Chrysler Corp, dir; Federated Dept Stores Inc, dir, currently; Rohm & Haas Corp, dir, currently. **Orgs:** Bd dir, Rohm & Haas Corp; Mag Pubs Asn; Nat Minority Purchasing Coun Inc; Nat Bd Exec Comt, Interracial Coun Bus Oppor; Nat Bus League; NY State Econ Develop Bd; exec comt, Greater NY Coun BSA; bd selector, Am Inst Pub Serv; trustee, Am Mus Natural Hist; NAACP; SCLC Mag Publ Asn; Interracial Coun; Sigma Pi Phi; Statue Liberty Ellis Island Centennial Comt; visitingcomt, Harvard Univ, John F Kennedy Sch Govt; Pres's Coun Bus Admin, UnivVT; bd mem, New York City Partnership; trustee, NY Econ Club; bd dirs, NYUrban Develop Corp; chmn, Black Bus Coun; exec comt, Coun Competitiveness; Stroh's Adv Coun; nat comnr & mem exec bd, Nat Boy Scouts Am; Nat Minority Bus Coun; tree coun, Bus Econ Develop; bd mem, NY City Partnership; New Am Schls Develop Copr; TransAfrica Forum; Am Mus Natural Hist & lanetarium; Am Inst Pub Serv; Adv Coun, Character Educ Partnership; Steadman-Hawkins Sports Med Found; Nat Adv Bd, Nat Underground RR Freedom Ctr; trustee, Howard Univ. **Honors/Awds:** Silver Beaver, 1969; 45 honorary degrees, including: LLD, Morgan St Univ, 1973, VA Union Univ, 1976, FL Memorial Col, 1978, J C Smith Univ, 1979,Wesleyan Univ, 1982, Talladaga Col, 1983, Baruch Col, 1984, AL St Univ, 1985, Mercy Col, 1986, Iona Col, 1987, Elizabeth City St Univ, 1987, Brown Univ, 1987, Lincoln Univ, 1988, Central St Univ, 1988, Howard Univ, 1989, Livingstone Col, 1989; Rust Col, 1974, Hampton Inst, 1979, Dowling Col,1980, Bryant Col, 1983, St Josephs, NY, 1985, Morehouse Col, 1986, Suffolk Univ, 1987, Meharry Med Col, 1989; Scroll of Honor, Nat Med Asn; Black Achiever, Talk Mag; Broadcaster of the Year, Nat Asn Black Owned Broadcasters; Poynter Fel, Yale Univ; Boy Scouts Nat Awards, SilverBuffalo, 1988, Silver Antelope, 1986; Earl G Graves School of Business & Management, named in honor; Spingarn Medal, NAACP, 1999; Lifetime Achievement Award, Caribbean Tourism Org, 1999; fel, Acad Arts & Sci, 2000; Lifetime Achievement Award, Caribbean Tourism Org; Harvey C Russell Award, PepsiCo, 2005; Inducted into Junior Achievement U.S. Business Hall of Fame, 2007; Silver Anniversary Award, Nat Collegiate Athletic Asn, 2009. **Special Achievements:** Author, How to Succeed in Bussiness Without Being White, 1997; one of 100 Influential Blacks, Ebony Mag; one of 10 Most Outstanding Minority Businessmen in US, ex-Pres Nixon; one of 200 Future Leaders in US, Time Mag; one of Top 100 Business Lumanaries, TJFR, 1999; In 2002, Mr. Graveswas named by Fortune Magazine as one of the 50 most powerful and influential African Americans in corporate America. **Military Serv:** AUS, capt, US Army Commendation Award. **Business Addr:** Chairman, Chief Executive Officer, Earl G Graves Ltd, 130 Fifth Ave Fl 10, New York, NY 10011, **Business Phone:** (212)242-8000.

GRAVES, EARL G
Basketball player, publishing executive. **Personal:** Born Jan 5, 1962, Scarsdale, NY; son of Earl G Sr and Barbara; married Roberta; children: 4. **Educ:** Yale Univ, BA, econ, 1984; Harvard Univ, Grad Sch Bus Admin, MBA. **Career:** Basketball player (retired); Philadelphia 76ers, basketball player, 1984; Milwaukee Bucks; Cleveland Cavaliers, basketball player; Morgan Stanley, investment banker; Black Enterprise Mag, vpres advert & mkt, sr vpres advert & mkt, 1991, exec vpres & chief oper officer, 1995, pres & chief oper officer, 1998, publ, 2006-; Earl G Graves Publ Co, pres, chmn & chief exec officer, currently; AutoZone Inc, dir, 2002-. **Orgs:** Exec Comt, Nat Off Boy Scouts Am; bd dirs, Aetna Found, Inc. **Honors/Awds:** Editorial Excellence Award Bus/Finance, 1996; AAF Jack Averett Volunteer Spirit Award; Hall of Achievement, Am Advert Fedn, 2002; Nat Award of Excellence, Minority Bus Enterprise; received honorary degrees from 53 Cols & universities. **Special Achievements:** Listed in Who's Who in America, and in 1974, was named one of Time Magazine's 200 future leaders of the country. **Business Addr:** President, Chief Executive Officer, Earl G Graves Publishing Inc, 130 5th Ave Fl 10, New York, NY 10011, **Business Phone:** (212)242-8000.

GRAVES, DR. JERROD FRANKLIN
Dentist, army officer. **Personal:** Born Sep 25, 1930, Greensboro, NC; son of Everett and Lola; married Earnestine Ross; children: Jerrod M & Gwendolyn Graves Irowa. **Educ:** Johnson C Smith Univ, BS, 1951; A&T Univ, MS, 1955; Meharry Med Col, DDS, 1959. **Career:** Harlem Hosp, intern/resident, oral surg, 1959-61; self-employed, pvt pract, dent, currently. **Orgs:** Omega Psi Phi, 1949-; Nat Asn Advan Colored People; 32 Degree Mason; 369th Veterans Asn; Nat Dent Asn; Acad Gen Dent; Am Soc Anesthe-ologists; Am Endodontic Soc; Am Soc Military Surgeons. **Honors/Awds:** Mizzy Award, Best in Oral Surg. **Military Serv:**

Dent Corp, col, 15 years, 1952-; USAR, 1951-; Bronze Star, Army Achievement, Overseas Medal, Army Commendation Medal, Good Conduct Medal, United Nations Ribbon, 1 Oak Leaf Cluster. **Business Addr:** Dentist, 771 Woodland Ave, Plainfield, NJ 07062, **Business Phone:** (908)757-8244.*

GRAVES, JOHN CLIFFORD
Lawyer, chairperson. **Personal:** Born May 10, 1963, Brooklyn, NY; son of Earl Gilbert and Barbara Eliza Kydd; married Caroline Veronica Clarke Graves, Nov 10, 1990. **Educ:** Colgate Univ, Hamilton, NY, 1982; Brown Univ, Providence, RI, BA, 1986; Yale Law School, New Haven, CT, JD, 1989. **Career:** Cleary, Gottlieb, Steen & Hamilton, New York, NY, assoc; Catholic Big Brothers Inc, pres; Graves Ventures, pres & chief exec officer, currently; Earl G Graves Ltd, chief staff, currently. **Orgs:** Stud & Sponsor Partnership; Black Enterprise Entrepreneurs Conf, 1996; trustee, Meharry Med Col, Nashville; dir, Black Enterprise & Greenwich St Corp Growth Partners; Supvry Bd Daimler Chrysler AG; mem exec bd & exec comt, Nat Off Boy Scouts Am; bd dir, Aetna Found, currently. **Business Addr:** Chairman, Earl G Graves Ltd, 130 5th Ave 10th Fl, New York, NY 10011-4399, **Business Phone:** (212)242-8000.*

GRAVES, LESLIE THERESA
Lawyer. **Personal:** Born Mar 27, 1956, Detroit, MI; daughter of Louis and Nora Mallett. **Educ:** Smith Col, Northampton, Mass, BA, 1977; Catholic Univ, Wash, DC, JD, 1981. **Career:** State Mich, Detroit, Mich, workers compensation appeal bd mem, 1987-91; Wayne Co Community Col, gen coun; Wayne Co Circuit Ct, family div, dep juvenile regist, 1995, assoc ct adminr, currently. **Orgs:** State Bar Mich Comt Expansion Under-represented Groups Law, 1984-91; Women Lawyers Asn Mich, 1984-; exec bd, Wolverine Bar Asn, 1986, pres, 1990-91; bd dirs, Brazel Dennard Chorale, 1988-; Int Visitors Coun, 1990-; Links Inc. **Honors/Awds:** Member of the Year, Wolverine Bar Asn, 1985; Private Attorney Involvement Award, WBA, 1990. **Home Addr:** 2016 Hyde Pk Dr, Detroit, MI 48207, **Home Phone:** (313)962-0250. **Business Addr:** Associate Court Administrator, Wayne County Circuit Court, Family Division, 2 Woodward Ave, Detroit, MI 48226, **Business Phone:** (313)224-5261.

GRAVES, RAY REYNOLDS
Judge, administrator. **Personal:** Born Jan 10, 1946, Tuscumbia, AL; son of Olga Wilder and Isaac; divorced 1995; children: Claire Elise Glass & Reynolds Douglass. **Educ:** Trinity Col, BA, 1967; Wayne State Univ, JD, 1970. **Career:** Pvt law pract, atty, 1970-81; Lewis, White, Clay & Graves, PC, 1974-81; Univ Detroit Law Sch, adj prof, 1981-85; US Bankruptcy Ct, Eastern Dist, MI, judge, 1982-2002, chief judge, 1991-95; BBK Ltd, managing dir & prin, currently. **Orgs:** Trustee, Mich Cancer Found, 1979-83; bd govs, Nat Conf Bankruptcy Judges, 1985-88; fel, Am Col Bankruptcy, Wash DC, 1993; Christ Church Grosse Pointe, Mich, Vestry, 1993-96; Sigma Pi Phi Fraternity, Iota Boule, Sire Archon, 1999-2001; fel, Am Col Bankruptcy; Am Bankruptcy Inst. **Honors/Awds:** Esquire Mag Regist, Am Under 40 Leadership, 1986. **Business Addr:** Managing Director, Principal, BBK Ltd, 300 Galleria Officentre Suite 103, Southfield, MI 48034, **Business Phone:** (248)356-0800.

GRAVES, RAYMOND LEE
Clergy, teacher, minister (clergy). **Personal:** Born Jan 3, 1928, Yanceyville, NC; married Pauline H. **Educ:** Winston-Salem State Univ, BS, 1951; NC Cent Univ, MA, 1954; Colgate Rochester-Crozier-Bexley Hall Div Sch, MDiv, 1968. **Career:** Sch Bd, Danville, VA, teacher, 1954-62; States Va & Ga, NY, SC, minister, 1959-80; Rochester Econ Opportunities Ctr, instr, 1969-73; New Bethal CME Church, Rochester, NY, pastor, 1973-. **Orgs:** Orgn bd mem, Action Better Community, 1963-65; co-founder, Fight Orgn, 1964; founder, Rochester Affil OIC, 1978; bd mem, Push-Excel Rochester Chap, 1979-80; exec dir, Rochester OIC; pres, United Church Ministry. **Honors/Awds:** Martin Luther King Prof Chair Award, Colgate Rochester Div Sch, 1968; Serv Award, Urban League, Rochester, 1978; Achievement Award, Colgate Rochester-Crozier-Bexley Hall, Colgate Rochester Div Sch, 1980; Social Justice Award, UCM. **Military Serv:** USAF, 1951-53. **Business Addr:** Pastor, New Bethel CME Church, 270 Scio St, Rochester, NY 14606.

GRAVES, VALERIE JO
Executive, media executive. **Personal:** Born Feb 27, 1950, Pontiac, MI; daughter of Deloris and Spurgeon; married Alvin E Bessent; children: Brian. **Educ:** Wayne State Univ, attended, 1969-73; New York Univ, Filmmaking Prog, 1985-. **Career:** D'Arcy MacManus & Masius Ad Agency, copywriter, 1974-75; BBDO Inc Ad Agency, copywriter, 1975-76; Kenyon & Eckhardt Boston Ad Agency, copywriter, 1977-80; J Walter Thompson USA Ad Agency, sr copywriter, 1981-82; Ross Roy Inc, vpres & assoc creative dir, 1982-85; Uniworld Group Inc, vpres, assoc creative dir, sr vpres, creative dir, sr vpres & chief creative officer, currently; Clinton/Gore Campaign, creative/media consult, 1992; Motown Rec LP, sr vpres creative serv, 1996-99. **Orgs:** Mem bd, Harvard Univ Black Community & Stud Theater, 1979-80; Adcraft Club Detroit, 1982-; consult, Creative Network Inc, 1984-, dir, 1984-; Nat Asn Black Women Entrepreneurs, 1985; bd dirs, Advert Club New York, 1996-; Creative Rev Comt, Partnership Drug-Free Am. **Honors/Awds:** Corporate Ad Award, 1981; Boston Ad Club Francis Hatch Award, 1981; Merit Award, Art Dirs Club New York, 1982; CEBA Award of Excellence, Black Owned Community Asn NY, 1983; Graphic Excellence Merchandising Graphics Award Competition, 1984; Notable Midwest Adwoman, Adweek Mag, Chicago, 1984; Creative Excellence to Black Audiences Award, CEBA, 1987-92; YWCA Academy Women Achievers, YWCA New York, 1989; Creativity Magazine Award. **Special Achievements:** One of the 100 Best and Brightest. **Business Addr:** Senior Vice President, Chief Creative Officer, Uniworld Group Inc, 100 Ave of the Americas, New York, NY 10013-1699, **Business Phone:** (212)219-1600.

GRAY, ANDREW JACKSON
Executive. **Personal:** Born Jun 20, 1924, Charlotte, NC; married Lucille Jackson; children: Andrew Jr & Amizie. **Educ:** Morehouse Col, BA, 1946; NC State Univ, addl studies. **Career:** Andrew J Gray Acct Firm, acct, 1962-; NC Con NAACP Br, auditor. **Orgs:** Nat Soc Pub Acct; NC Soc Acct; Nat Asn Enrolled Agt; Nat Asn Black Acct; Kappa Alpha Psi; NAACP; St Paul Bapt Chi; YMCA. **Honors/Awds:** Hall of Fame Award, Charlotte Bus League, NAACP. **Business Addr:** Accountant, Andrew J Gray Acct Firm, 2202 Beatties Ford Rd, Charlotte, NC 28216, **Business Phone:** (704)394-0179.*

GRAY, BEVERLY A
Librarian. **Personal:** Born Aug 3, 1940, Boston, MA; daughter of Mark and Lula. **Educ:** Simmons Col, BS, 1962; Columbia Univ, MA, 1964, MLS, 1965. **Career:** Harvard Univ, Africana bibliographer, 1965-67; Boston Univ, librn, African Studies Libr, 1967-72, African section, area specist, 1972-78; Libr Cong, sr reference librarian, head, African section, 1978-94, African & Middle Eastern Div, chief, 2004-. **Orgs:** African Studies Asn; exec bd, Africana Librns Coun; Mid E Librns Asn; Asn Jewish Libr; exec bd, Coop Africana Microfirm Proj; Am Libr Asn; Asn Study & Life African Am Hist. **Special Achievements:** Author, Uganda: Subject Guide to Publications, 1977; Africana Library Resources, In: Ethnic Collections in Libraries, 1983; Liberia During the Tolbert Eval A Guide, 1983; Africana Acquisitions at the Library of Congress, In: Africana Resources & Collections, 1989. **Business Phone:** (202)707-2905.

GRAY, BRIAN ANTON
Business owner, president (organization), chief executive officer. **Personal:** Born Apr 13, 1939, Philadelphia, PA; son of Cecil Gray and Bertha; married Linda, Jun 3, 1967; children: Brian & Christian. **Educ:** Cheyney State Univ, BA, 1964; Howard Univ, MA, 1972. **Career:** Miller Brewing Co, mgr col rels, 1975-81; BG & Assocs Staffing Serv, pres & chief exec officer, 1981-; Howard Univ, dir personnel, 1982-91. **Orgs:** Omega Psi Phi Fraternity, 1962-; Employ Mgt Assn, 1982-; brd chmn, Bur Rehab, 1985-95; chmn & brd trustees, Nomination Comt, 1985-93; Soc Human Res Mgt, 1990-; Nation wide Interchange Serv, 1992-. **Honors/Awds:** Outstanding Volunteer, Montgomery County Gov, 1993; Outstanding Volunteer, Bur Rehab, 1993. **Home Addr:** 10112 Langhorne Ct, Bethesda, MD 20817-1250, **Home Phone:** (301)365-4138. **Business Addr:** President, Chief Executive Officer, BG & Associates Staffing Services, 10112 Langhorne Ct Suite B, PO Box 34162, Bethesda, MD 20827-0162, **Business Phone:** (301)365-4046.

GRAY, DR. C. VERNON
Government official, college teacher, school administrator. **Personal:** Born Jul 30, 1939, Sunderland, MD; son of Major and Virgina; married Sandra Lea Trice; children: Michael & Angela. **Educ:** Morgan State Univ, BA, 1961; Atlanta Univ, MA, 1962; Univ Mass, PhD, 1971. **Career:** Philander Smith Col, instr, 1961-66; Oakland Univ, instr, 1970-71; Joint Ctr Polit Studies, Wash DC, staff, 1971-72; Morgan State Univ, chmn Politsci, 1972-87, dir pub serv internship prog, 1972-87, assoc dean social sci, 1974-75, prof Polit sci, 1972-, chmn Polit sci & intl studies,1984-87, internship cord, off campus advisor, currently; Goucher Col, vis prof, 1974; Univ MD, vis prof, 1978-81. **Orgs:** Exec coun, Nat Capitol Area Polit Sci Assn, 1976-; pres elect, Nat Conf Black Polit Sci, 1976-77; chmn, Polit Action Comm MD State Conf, Nat AsnAdvan Colored People, 1976-77; brd dir Meals on Wheels Cent Md, 1976; chmn, Ad Hoc Contribs Community Meals Wheels, 1976-77; pres, Nat Conf Black Polit Sci, 1977-78; nominating comm, Southern Polit Sci Assn, 1977-78; chmn, Ethnic & Cultural Pluralism Award Comt, Am Polit Sci Asn, 1977-78;Polit analyst WJZ, WBAL, 1977-; host, producer Polit Power & People,1977-80; speakers bur, United Way Cent MD, 1977-78; allocations panelUnited Way Cent MD, 1977-78; adv comt, Ctr Urban Environment Studies,1977-80; resources brd, Minority Energy Tech Asst Prog, Ctr Urban EnvironStudies, 1978; bd dir, Nat Policy Studies Goucher Col, 1978; chmn progcomn, Alpha Phi Alpha, 1979-80; dir, Educ Activities Alpha Phi Alpha, 1979; Election Laws Revision Comm MD, 1979-80; Howard County, coun man, 1982-; chmn county coun, Howard County MD, 1985-87; brd dirs, Natl Assn Counties, 1986-, health adv comt, 1992-93, pres, 1999-2000; chmn, UnitedNegro Col Fund Howard County Campaign, 1990-91; bd dir, pres, Md Assn Counties, 1992; brd dir, African Art Mus MD; brd dir, Howard County Red Cross; brd dirs, Howard Health Found; brd dirs, NACO Financial Serv Ctr; NACO Taxation & Finance Steering Comt. **Honors/Awds:** WEAA-FM Award for Service, 1978; Community Service Award, United Way Cent MD, 1978; Appreciation Award, Calvert County, Natl Assn Advan Colored People, 1978; Community Service Admin Certificate of Training, 1979; Certificate of Merit Black Women's Consciousness Raising Assn, 1979; Community Service Award, Howard Community Action, 1980; Award for Distinguished Service, Natl Conf Black Polit Sci, 1980; Outstanding Faculty Award for Community Service, Morgan State Univ, 1980; Alpha Man of the Year, 1982; Ford Found Fellowship, Crusade Scholar, Southern Found Scholar; Citizen of the Year, Omega Psi Phi Fraternity 1987; Outstanding Service Award, Alpha Kappa Alpha Sorority 1989; Honorary 4-H member; Outstanding Achievement Award, Maryland State Teachers Assn; Jewish Natl Fund Tree of Life Award, Am Lung Assn; Lawmaker of the Year, 1993. **Special Achievements:** First black elected Howard County Council 1982. **Business Addr:** Professor, Morgan State University, Department of Political Science, Rm G-05 Holmes Hall 1700 E Cold Spring Lane, Baltimore, MD 21201, **Business Phone:** (443)885-3247.

GRAY, CARLTON PATRICK
Football player. **Personal:** Born Jun 26, 1971, Cincinnati, OH. **Educ:** Univ Calif, Los Angeles. **Career:** Football player(retired), Seattle Sea hawks, defensive back, 1993-96; Indianapolis Colts, 1997; New York Giants, 1998; Kans City Chiefs, 1999-2000; Cincinnati Bengals, 2001.

GRAY, CAROL COLEMAN
Pediatrician. **Personal:** Born Jun 22, 1946, Wharton, TX; married James Howard Gray MD; children: Nakia, James. **Educ:** Univ Tex, BS, 1967, Med Sch, MD, 1972. **Career:** Walter Reed Army Med Ctr, pediatric internship, 1972; Univ Md Hosp, pediatric residency, 1977; Dallas Independent Sch Dist Project Find, med coordr, 1979-83; Baylor Univ, Med Ctr, assoc attending, 1981-; Pvt Prac, pediatrician, 1981-. **Orgs:** Am Med Asn; Nat Med Asn; CV Roman Med Soc; Nat Asn Advan Colored People. **Honors/Awds:** Civilian Achievement Award, Walter Reed Army Med Ctr, 1978; Black Women Against the Odds Award, Dallas Independent School Dist; Dream Maker's Award, Southeast Dallas Bus & Prof Women. **Special Achievements:** Second Annual Salute to America's Top 100 Black Business & Professional Women, Dollars & Sense Mag, 1986; publication: "Wednesday's & Thursday's Children, Medical Assessment of the Child with a Handicap", Early Periodic Diagnosis & Treatment Programs. **Military Serv:** AUS, capt, 1972-73; Internship Cert, 1973. **Business Addr:** Pediatrician, Private Practice, 3600 Gaston Ave Suite 760, Dallas, TX 75246.

GRAY, CHRISTINE
Manager. **Personal:** Born in Hartford, CT; married Herman C, 1945 (deceased); children: Dianne Greene & Donna F White. **Educ:** Admin Sch WAAC, attended 1943; Sch Comptometer, attended 1944; Exxon, math keypunch, 1971. **Career:** Kolodney & Meyers Hartford, payroll clerk, 1940-46; Hop Equip, customer serv rep, 1970-71; Credit Union, secy, 1965-67; Thompson & Weinman Co, asst off mgr, 1967-70; Union Co OIC, keypunch instr, 1971-73, 1975; Union Co Dept Youth Serv, secy; Union Co OIC, mgr spec; Employ Resource Specialist, 1981-83; Companion Aide, prog dir, 1985-94. **Orgs:** Charter mem, NCNW Vauzhall Sect; pres, Burnet Jr High PTA; Jr Dgt Ruler Emma V Kelly Elks, 1940-42; inter club pres, YWCA 1942-45; jr clerk, Hopewell Bapt Church, 1941-46; secy, Concerned Citizens Vauxhall; secy, Citizens Coun Vauxhall; pres, Jefferson Sch PTA; pres, Nat Coun Negro Women Vauxhall Sect; chairlady, Consumer Educ NCNW; dist leader, Dist 8 Union Co Girl Scout Leader; bd mem, Union Co Anti-proverty bd; secy, Calvary Bapt Church, 1959-67, 1970-77; charter mem, Gary Family Asn; Cancer Soc; Comn Vacation Bible Sch; Calvary Bapt Sunday Sch; Census Bur, 1960-70; Calvary Bapt Ch, 1973; Historian Nat Coun Negro Women, Vauxhall Sect,1980-; Mentor Vauxhall & Brookside African-Am Youth Literary Club; Time Teens, sr adv, 1988-90; Togetherness Asn, sr adv, 1991-. **Honors/Awds:** Gold pin Girl Scouts; plaque, Nat Coun Negro Women Vauxhall Sect, 1972 & 1973; cert, NCNW; guest part, Esther Roll Theresa Merritt; Maude Johnson Cultural Award, 1976; Comn Serv Award, Nat Coun Negro Women, 1978; Comn Serv Award, Bethune Tradition, 1986; Comn Serv Award, Vauxhall Homecoming Asn, 1987; Study Comn Union Twp, Bd Educ, 1986. **Military Serv:** WAAC, 1943. **Home Addr:** 29 Maple Ave, Vauxhall, NJ 07088.

GRAY, DERWIN LAMONT
Television show host, football player, association executive. **Personal:** Born Apr 9, 1971, San Antonio, TX; married Vicki; children: Presley. **Educ:** Brigham Young Univ, BA, sports bus mgt. **Career:** Football player (retired); Indianapolis Colts, defensive back, 1993-97; Carolina Panthers, 1998; Fox TV Network, co-host, 2003; One Heart at a Time Ministries, co-founder, 1999-; Gathering, Pastoral leadership team. **Orgs:** Founder, Derwin Gray Found, 1996-99. **Honors/Awds:** Man of the Year, Indianapolis Colts, 1994; Count My Blessings Hall of Fame, 1998; Outreach Resource of the Year Award, 2006. **Special Achievements:** Nominated to Jim Thorpe Award, 1992. **Business Phone:** (704)543-9485.

GRAY, DONNEE L
Librarian, manager. **Personal:** Born Jul 4, 1951, Camp Springs, MD; son of Mattie; married Vedia Thompson, May 10, 1975;

children: Marcus D. **Educ:** St Marys Col Mar, BA, social sci, 1976. **Career:** US Sen Libr, adminr, head legis ref asst, currently; US Nat Champions, head coach; Int Tournament, Mozambique, Africa, head coach, 1985. **Orgs:** Chmn bd, US Senate FDL Employees Credit Union; bd mem, Cage Page Basketball Referee Publ; pres, Int Asn Approved Basketball Off Inc, 1991-; Nat Amateur Basketball Asn; Nat Col Athletic Asn. **Honors/Awds:** Basketball Official of the Year, CIAA, 1990, 1992. **Special Achievements:** Alantic Coast CNF, Alantic Ten CNF, Big East CNF, Colonial Athletic ASN, East Coast CNF, Mid-Eastern Athletic CNF, Southwest CNF, USA Basketball (FIBA); US Natl Champions, head coach, 1985. **Home Phone:** (301)292-0825. **Business Addr:** Head, Legislative Reference Assistant, US Senate Library, B15 Russell Bldg, Washington, DC 20510-7112, **Business Phone:** (202)224-7106.

GRAY, DR. E DELBERT
Association executive. **Educ:** Tennessee State Univ, BS, industrial educ & admin; Michigan State Univ, MA, guidance & personnel serv, PhD, admin, com, urban develop. **Career:** State Mich Depat Com, Minority Bus Enterprise, dir; Mich Minority Bus Develop Coun, pres & chief exec officer; Visionary Group Inc, pres & chief exec officer. **Orgs:** Vpres, exec finance com, pres bd dirs, Spaulding C; trustee, Marygrove col. **Home Addr:** 28776 W Kalong Circle, Southfield, MI 48034, **Home Phone:** (248)357-0254.

GRAY, EARL HADDON
Administrator. **Personal:** Born Apr 19, 1929, Richmond, VA; son of William Joseph(deceased) and Annie Baker Atkins (deceased); married Jane N Harris Gray, Dec 25, 1953; children: Adrienne Anne. **Educ:** Va State Univ, Petersburg, VA, BS, acct, 1970, MEd, 1974. **Career:** Administrator (retired); Assoc Dir Student Act, Petersburg, VA, assoc dir, 1966-70; VSC, Petersburg, VA, pers dir, 1970-71; Model Cities JTPA, Richmond, VA, dir, 1971-77; Planning & Eval, Bal State, asst dir, 1978-82; Res Div VEC, Richmond, VA, chief dir, 1982-85; Imp Coun, Detroit, MI, imp potentate, 1986-88. **Orgs:** Chair, labor & industry comt, Nat Asn Advan Colored People, 1966-70; mem, Comt Elderly, City of Richmond, 1971-74; bd mem, Gold Bowl Classic, City Richmond, 1975-; Nat Assault literacy, New York, NY, 1984-; pres, Community Motivators Inc, New York, NY, 1988-; pres, Beta Gamma Lambda, 1998-; Ancient Egyptian Arabic Order Nobles Mystic Shrine, imp conv dir, 2000-02. **Honors/Awds:** DHL, Va Union Univ, 1988; Seagrams Vangard Award, Seagrams Co, 1985. **Military Serv:** Navy, Chief Petty Officer, 1946-66; numerous. **Home Addr:** 2930 Seminary Ave, Richmond, VA 23220, **Home Phone:** (804)321-3733. *

GRAY, EARNEST
Football player. **Personal:** Born Mar 2, 1957, Greenwood, MS. **Educ:** Memphis State Univ. **Career:** Football player (retired); Wide receiver: New York Giants, 1979-84; St.Louis Cardinals, 1985. **Honors/Awds:** All Nat Football League Rookie Honors, UPI, Pro Football Weekly, Professional Football Writers Asn & Football Digest. **Home Addr:** 600 E Saguaro Dr, Benson, AZ 85602, **Home Phone:** (520)586-8771.

GRAY, ED (EDWARD GRAY, JR.)
Basketball player. **Personal:** Born Sep 27, 1975, Riverside, CA. **Educ:** Univ Tenn; Univ Calif, Berkley. **Career:** Atlanta Hawks, guard, 1997-99. **Honors/Awds:** Pac-10 Player of the Year, 1997.

GRAY, EDWARD, JR. See GRAY, ED.

GRAY, F GARY
Movie director, actor, movie producer. **Personal:** Born Jul 17, 1969, New York, NY. **Educ:** Los Angeles City Col; Golden State Col. **Career:** Video & film dir, 1990-; BET, Fox TV Networks, camera operator; W C & the Maad Circle, Coolio, TLC, Ice Cube, Dr Dre, music video; Films: Major League, 1989; Murder Was the Case: The Movie, 1995; Friday, 1995; Set It Off, 1996; The Negotiator, 1998; Ryan Caulfield: Year One, 1999; Cypress Hill: Still Smokin, 2001; Babyface: A Collection of Hit Videos, 2001; The Italian Job, 2003; A Man Apart, producer & dir, 2003; OutKast: The Videos, 2003; Be Cool, producer, 2005; The Brazilian Job, 2006; TV: "Ryan Caulfield: Year One", 1999; "enemies", 2006. **Honors/Awds:** Billboard Music Video Awards, Best Rap Video & Best New Artist Rap Video, 1995; MTV Music Video Awards, four awards including Video of the Year for TLC's "Waterfall" & Best Rap Video for Dr Dre's "Keep Their Heads Ringin'," 1995; Best Dir Award, Acapulco Black Film Festival, 1999.

GRAY, FRED DAVID
Lawyer, evangelist. **Personal:** Born Dec 14, 1930, Montgomery, AL; son of Abraham and Nancy; married Bernice Hill (died 1997); children: Deborah, Vanessa, Fred David Jr & Stanley. **Educ:** Nashville Christian Inst; Ala State Univ, BS, 1951; Case Western Res Univ, JD, 1954. **Career:** Rosa Parks, atty; Dr Martin Luther King Jr, first civil rights atty; NAACP Legal Defense Fund Inc, coop atty; Tuskegee Univ, local gen coun; Gray, Langford, Sapp, McGowan Gray & Nathanson law firm, sr mem, sr partner, currently; pvt pract, currently. **Orgs:** Rep, Ala State Legis, 1970-74; pres, Nat Asn Co Civil Attys, 1982-83; Bar comm 5th Judicial Circuit, 1983-86; pres elect, Nat Bar Asn, 1984-85; pres, Nat Bar Asn, 1985-86; Am Bar Asn; Omega Psi Phi Frat Inc; elder, Tuskegee Church Christ; chmn, bd trustees, Southwestern Christian Col; pres, Ala State Bar Asn. **Honors/Awds:** The Man in the News NY Times, 1966; First Annual Equal Justice Award, Nat Bar Asn, 1977; Drum Major's Award, MLK Jr Mem Southern Christian Leadership Conf, 1980; Presidential Award, Nat Bar Asn, 1982; Legal Award, World Conf Mayors, 1985; Graduate of the Year; Case Western Res Univ, 1985; Man of the Year Award, Women Work Los Angeles CA & Southwestern Christian Col, 1986; Charles Hamilton Houston Medallion of Merit, WA Bar Assn, 1986; C. Frances Stradford Award, Nat Bar Asn; World Conference of Mayors' Legal Award; Nat Bar Asn's Equal Justice Award; Southern Christian Leadership Conference's Drum Major's Award. **Special Achievements:** First African-American to hold the position of President in Alabama State Bar Association. Elected to the House of Representatives in 1970, he was one of the first African Americans to serve in the Alabama Legislature since Reconstruction. **Business Addr:** Senior Partner, Gray, Langford, Sapp, McGowan, Gray & Nathanson, 205 The Bailey Bldg 400 S Union St, PO Box 830239, Montgomery, AL 36104, **Business Phone:** (334)269-2563.

GRAY, FRIZZELL GERARD. See MFUME, KWEISI.

GRAY, HAROLD B.
Executive. **Career:** Hercules Inc; Andersen Consult; Enterprism Solutions LLC, pres, chief exec officer; TechniData Am, chief exec officer, bd dir, currently. **Orgs:** Del Environ Appeals Bd. *

GRAY, DR. JAMES E
School administrator. **Career:** Natchez Junior Col, Natchez, MS, pres, currently. **Business Phone:** (601)445-9702.

GRAY, JAMES HOWARD
Physician, consultant. **Personal:** Born May 20, 1943, Kaufman, TX; son of Wilmer Oscar and Ocie Bell Blakemore; married Carol Coleman; children: Nakia, James. **Educ:** North Tex State Univ, attended 1966, attended 1967; Univ Tex Med Sch, MD, 1971; Johns Hopkins Hosp, Wilmer Ophthal Inst, attended 1978. **Career:** Bexar Co Hosp, internal med intern, 1971-72; Wilmer Ophthal Inst, Johns Hopkins Hosp, resident, 1975-78; Khalili Hosp Ophthal, Dept Shiraz Iran, vis instr, 1978; Baylor Univ Med Ctr, assoc, 1978-; Southwestern Med Sch, clin fac, 1979-88; Tex Instrument & Terrell State Hosp, eye consult, 1979-81; pvt pract, ophthal, 1978-. **Orgs:** Fee review comt, Dallas County Med Soc, 1985-87; bd mem, Good St Baptist Church; NAACP; YMCA; Am Heart Asn; Soc Prevent Blindness; Dallas Black Chamber Com; Am Med Asn; Johns Hopkins Hosp Resident's Asn; Wilmer Resident's Asn; Am Acad Ophthal; Tex Ophthal Asn; fel Am Col Surg. **Honors/Awds:** Legis Merit Schol; Galaxy Starts Award, Dallas Independent Sch Dist; Social Serv Award; First Place & Best of Show Awards, Tex Med Asn; First Place Awards, SNMA Wyeth Nat Contest. **Military Serv:** AUS, MC, major, 1972-75. **Business Addr:** Ophthalmologist, Private Practice, 3600 Gaston Ave Suite 760, Dallas, TX 75246.*

GRAY, JERRY
Football player, football coach. **Personal:** Born Dec 16, 1962, Lubbock, TX; married Sherry; children: Jeremy & Jayden. **Educ:** Univ Tex, BS, commun. **Career:** Football player (retired), Football coach; Los Angeles Rams, corner back, 1985-91; Houston Oilers, corner back, 1992; Tampa Bay Buccaneers, corner back, 1993; Southern Methodist Univ, defensive back coach, 1995; Tenn Titans, defensive asst & quality control coach, 1997-98; Tenn Titans, defensive back coach, 1999-2000; Buffalo Bills, defensive co ordr, 2001-05; Wash Redskins, sec & corner backs coach, 2006-. **Orgs:** Univ Tx All-Time Team and All-Decade Team, 1980s. **Honors/Awds:** Most Valuable Player, Pro Bowl; Defensive Back of the Year, Nat Football Conf, 1989. **Business Phone:** (301)365-4785.

GRAY, JOANNE S
Educator, school administrator. **Personal:** Born Dec 19, 1943, Headland, AL; daughter of Charlie and Gussie Jones; married Kenneth Byron; children: Kina Carisse. **Educ:** Chicago City Col, AA, 1965; Chicago State Col, BS, 1970; Governor State Univ, MS, 1979. **Career:** Teacher, 1970-; Chicago Bd Educ, teacher rep, local sch coun, 1991-93, dist chairperson sci fair, 1983-, chairperson citywide acad Olympics, 1985-86, sci dept chairperson, 1984-, ECIA coord 1986; Fermi Nat Lab & Chicago State Univ, Summer Inst Sci & Math Teachers, admin dir, 1990; Chicago State Univ, Anthony Sch, prin, currently. **Orgs:** Bd dir, Pre-medical & Allied Health Prog, Chicago State Univ, 1978-81; secy, vpres, Rebecca Circle United Methodist Women, 1980-86; Phi Delta Kappa, 1984-86; prog chmn, Nat Asn Biol Teachers, 1984; coord & facilitator, Nat Sci Educ Comn, 1984; sci curric bd gov, State Univ, 1986; bd mem, Women's Div Global Ministries, 1987; area teen adv, Top Ladies Distinction Inc, 1987-89; exec secy, bd dirs, Chicago State Alumni Asn, 1989-; coord, Local Sch Improv Plan Sci, 1990-; chairperson, Vol Comt, Chicago Pub Sch Sci Fair, 1991-; co-chairperson, Judging Ill Jr Acad Sci State Exhib, 1991-; bd dirs, Chicago Orgn Autism, 1990-; chairperson, Outstanding logy Teachers Awards Subcomt; pres, Nat Asn Biol Teachers Sect Role and Status Women & Minorities Biol Educ, 1992-93. **Honors/Awds:** Celebrated Teacher, Beta Boule' Sigma Pi Phi, 1981; Ora Higgins Youth Foundation Award, 1981; Exceptional Service to Students, Blum-Kovler Found, 1981; Principal Scholars Program Service Award, 1982; Master Teacher Award, Gov Ill, 1984; Outstanding Biology Teacher, Nat Asn Biol Teachers, 1986; MidWest Region Excellence in Teaching Award, Nat Coun Negro Women, 1991. **Special Achievements:** Science curriculum writer, Chicago Bd of Educ, 1985-87; Outstanding Biology Teacher, Nat Asn Biol Teachers, 1986;author, "Motivating Females in Science, Mathematics, and Technolgy Related Careers," Zeta Phi Beta Sorority, 1989; curriculum writer, Illinois Institute of Technology SMILE Program, 1989; reader/editor, American Biology Teachers Journal, 1988-; writer of national curriculum standards for science education, with National Research Council/National Science Foundation, 1992-94. **Business Addr:** Principal, Chicago State University, Anthony School, 9800 S Torrence, Chicago, IL 60617, **Business Phone:** (773)535-6526.

GRAY, JOHNNIE LEE
Football player. **Personal:** Born Dec 18, 1953, Lake Charles, LA; married Barbara. **Educ:** Allan Hancock Col; Calif State Univ, Fullerton. **Career:** Football player (retired); Green Bay Packers, safety, 1975-83.

GRAY, JOSEPH WILLIAM, III
Physician. **Personal:** Born May 31, 1938, Memphis, TN; married Jacquelyn Cooper; children: Joseph IV, Jaylynn, Jeffrey, Jerron, Jerome. **Educ:** St Augustine's Col, BA; Meharry Med Col, MD, 1963. **Career:** Santa Monica Hosp, intern, 1963-64; GW Hubbard Hosp, resident, 1966-69; pvt pract, physician, 1985-. **Orgs:** Nat Med Asn; Am Med Asn; Toledo & Lucas Pediat Soc; Ohio Chap Am Acad Pediat; fel, Am Acad Pediat; Am Bd Pediat; life mem, Nat Asn Advan Colored People; Sigma Pi Phi; Alpha Phi Alpha; Alpha Kappa Mu. **Military Serv:** USN, 1964-66. **Home Addr:** 2109 Hughes Dr Suite 660, Toledo, OH 43606. *

GRAY, KAREN G (KAREN GRAY HOUSTON)
Journalist. **Personal:** Born in Montgomery, AL; daughter of Thomas W and Juanita Emanuel; married. **Educ:** Ohio Univ, Athens, OH, BA, psychol, 1972; Columbia Univ, New York, NY, MS, jour, 1973. **Career:** United Press Int, Boston, MA, reporter, ed, 1973-75; WHDH-AM, Boston, MA, reporter, anchor, 1975-76; ABC News, New York, NY, radio anchor, 1976-81; NBC News, Wash, DC, radio & tv corresp, 1981-83; WCBS-TV, New York, NY, writer, assoc producer, 1984-87; WTOP Newsradio, Wash, DC, reporter, anchor, beginning 1987; WTTG(FOX5), reporter, currently. **Orgs:** Nat Asn Black Journalists; Wash Asn Black Journalists; Capitol Press Club. **Business Addr:** Reporter, WTTG/FOX TV 5, 5151 Wis Ave NW, Washington, DC 20016, **Business Phone:** (202)244-5151.

GRAY, KEITH A, JR.
Government official. **Personal:** Born Nov 3, 1947, Camden, NJ. **Educ:** Career Educ Inst, Cert, 1975; Pierce Jr Col, attended 1977; Rutgers Univ, attended 1983. **Career:** Conrail, customer rep, 1982; Juv In Need Suprv, counr, 1984; Cumberland City Welfare, intake maintenance, 1985; Bayside State Prison, furlough coordr, currently; Fairfield Twp Comm, mayor. **Orgs:** Adb bd Fairfield Twp Schs, 1983; leg comm adv Comm Women, 1984; bd dir, NJ Citizen Action, 1985; Nat Conf Black Mayors, 1985, NJ Asn Mayors, 1985, NJ Conf Mayors, 1985. **Honors/Awds:** Certificate NJ State Assembly, 1984; Certificate, SCOPE, 1984; Placque Concerned Citizens of Fairfield, 1984; Cert Concerned Citizens of Fairfield, 1984. **Special Achievements:** First African Woman to become mayor of Cumberland County. **Military Serv:** USAF, E-4, 4 yrs.

GRAY, KENNETH D
College administrator, army officer. **Personal:** Born in Excelsior, WV; married Carolyn. **Educ:** West Virginia State, BA, polit sci, 1966; West Va Univ, Morgantown, JD, 1969; Univ V, law degree, 1975. **Career:** Army officer (retired), educational administrator; AUS: second lt, 1966, defense coun, legal assistance Officer, Ft Ord, Calif, 1969, Vietnam, 1969, Ft Meade, Md, 1971; Pentagon, Minority JAG Prog, Personnel, Plans, & Training Off, personnel mgt Offr; Actg Judge Advocate Gen, brigadier gen, spec asst to actg judge advocate gen; AUS Legal Serv Agency, comdr, 1991-93; AUS Ct Mil Review, chief judge; Trial Judiciary, chief; Secy Army, Procurement Fraud Matters, representative; WVa Univ, vpres stud affairs, 1997-. **Honors/Awds:** The Kenneth D Gray Award, name in honor by WVa Univ; Outstanding Alumnus, WVa Univ Alumni Asn; Justitia Officium Award, 1991. **Special Achievements:** At one time was only African-American attending West Virginia University's law school and third African-American to graduate, 1966-69; established Summer Intern Program for Judge Advocate General's corps; only commander in JAG; US Army Court of Military Review is the highest court in the Army. **Military Serv:** AUS, 1966-97; Legion Merit, Bronze Star Medal, Meritorious Serv Medal, Army Commendation Medal, Army Achievement Medal & Army Gen Staff Identification Badge. **Business Addr:** Vice President for Student Affairs, West Virginia University, 205 E Moore Hall, PO Box 6411, Morgantown, WV 26506, **Business Phone:** (304)293-5811.

GRAY, REV. MACEO
Manager. **Personal:** Born Dec 22, 1940, Dallas, TX; married Annie P Hatcher; children: Karen & Kathleen. **Educ:** Prairie View

Agr & Mech Univ, BS, elec engineering, 1963; Univ Mo; Dallas Theol Sem, ThM; Univ Miss, MSc, elec engineering; Rockhurst Col, MBA. **Career:** Bendix Corp, jr engr, 1963; Test Equip Design Dept, engineering supvr, 1969; Elec Prod, eng supr; Allied-Signal Aerospace Div, engineering prog mgr, environ restoration prog, MO; Marketplace Chaplains USA, region dir, 1998-, region vpres, currently. **Orgs:** Jr Achievement Co, 1970; dir comn proj, Bendix Mgt Club, 1973-74; vpres, Spec Events Bendix Mgt Club, 1975-76; vpres, Camp Fire Bowling League. **Honors/Awds:** Chaplain of the Year in 1997; Dallas Theological Seminary Lewis Sperry Chafer Award; W. E. Hawkins Jr Award; received numerous outstanding service awards. **Special Achievements:** Author of "The Christian Comfort Companion" and "Passing on Your Christian Heritage to Your Children, Grandchildren and Generations to Come". **Business Addr:** Region Vice President, Marketplace Chaplains USA, 13795 N Mur len Rd Suite 205, Olathe, KS 66062.

GRAY, MACY (NATALIE MCINTYRE)

Actor, singer. **Personal:** Born Sep 6, 1970, Canton, OH; married Tracy Hinds, Jan 1, 1996 (divorced 1998); children: 3. **Educ:** Univ Southern Calif. **Career:** M Gray Music Acad, owner, 2005-; Albums: On How Life Is, 1999; The Id, 2001; The Trouble With Being Myself, 2003; The Very Best of Macy Gray, 2004; Live in Las vegas, 2005; Big, 2007; Films: Training Day, 2001; Spiderman, 2002; Gang of Roses, 2003; Scary Movie 3, 2003; Lightning in a Bottle, 2004; Around the World in 80 Days, 2004; Domino, 2005; Shadowboxer, 2005; The Crow: Wicked Prayer, 2005; Idlewild, 2006; TV: "Ally McBeal", 2000; "American Dreams", 2004; "Blue's Clue", 2004; That's So Raven, 2004; "American Dragon: Jake Long", 2005. **Honors/Awds:** MTV Video Music Awards, Best New Artist & Best Cinematography, 2000; Grammy Award, Best Female Pop Vocal Performance, 2000; BRIT Awards, InterNat Breakthrough Act & InterNat Female, 2000. **Business Phone:** (310)278-9010.

GRAY, MARCUS J.

Government official. **Personal:** Born Sep 22, 1936, Kansas City, MO; son of Marcus and Christina; married Abbey Dowdy; children: Marcus, III, Sean & Yolanda. **Educ:** Kellogg Community Col, BBA. **Career:** County clerk, 1964-72; Eaton Mfg, prod insp chief clerk qual concommercial trans clerk; Kellogg Co, mach operator; Cahoun County, county clerk regist, 1972-; Paradigm Cash Flow Solutions, partner, currently. **Orgs:** Exec comt, Calhoun County Dem Party; Haber & Comn Polit Reform Elections; sub comt chmn, MI Non Partisan Election Comn; pres, MI Asn County Clerks; pres, Nat Asn County Recorders & Clerks, 1979; United County Officer's Asn; pres, Battle Creek Area Urban League; pres, Battle Creek Area County Church. **Honors/Awds:** Les Bon Amie Club award, outstanding serv; certificate merit, Dem Party MI & Calhoun County Dem Women's Club; clerk of the yr, MI Asn County Clerks. **Military Serv:** USAF, a & 2c.

GRAY, MARVIN W.

Lawyer. **Personal:** Born Aug 12, 1944, Chicago, IL; married Taffy; children: Derek, Jason, Meagan. **Educ:** Southern Ill Univ, attended 1966; Ill Inst Tech, attended 1972. **Career:** Chicago Pub Sch, teacher, 1966, 1970-72; Aetna Life & Casualty Ins, claims rep, 1967-70; Montgomery & Holland, assoc & self-employed, 1967-79; Cook Co, asst pub defender, 1972-74; Harth Vital Stroger Boarman & Williams, atty; Braud Warner & Neppl, atty; Firm of Ward & Gray, partner; Pvt Prac Chicago, atty, currently. **Orgs:** Consult, Opera PUSH, 1973-74; coun, 10 Dist Omega Psi Phi Frat; Ill Trial Lawyers Asn; Phi Delta Phi Int Legal Frat; Nat Cook Co Ill; Am Bar Asns. **Honors/Awds:** Moran fund scholar, 1968; Ill Inst Tech scholar, 1970. *

GRAY, MEL

Football player. **Personal:** Born Mar 16, 1961, Williamsburg, VA; children: Melanie & Devon. **Educ:** Coffeyville (Kan) Community Col. **Career:** Football player (retired); Los Angeles Express, 1984; New Orleans Saints, running back, 1986-88; Detroit Lions, 1989-94; Houston Oilers, 1995-96; Tenn Oilers, 1997; Philadelphia Eagles, wide receiver, 1997. **Honors/Awds:** All-Decade Team, Nat Football League, 1990; Special Teams Player of the Year, Nat Football League Players Asn, 1991.

GRAY, MOSES W.

Automotive executive. **Personal:** Born Apr 12, 1937, Rock Castle, VA; son of Moses Gray Jr and Ida Young; married Ann Marie Powell, Nov 22, 1962; children: Tamara Ann, William Bernard. **Educ:** IN Univ, BS, phys educ, 1961; Detroit Diesel Allison Apprentice Training Prog, 1967. **Career:** Automotive Executive (retired); Indianapolis Warriors, prof football player; Gen Motors, Detroit Diesel Allison, Indianapolis, inspector, 1962-63, apprentice tool & die maker, 1963-67, journeyman tool & die maker, 1967-68, prod supvr, 1968-69, supvr-tool room, 1969-73, genl supv tool room, 1973-76, asst supt master mech, 1976-79, dir community rel, 1979-83, mgr mfg serv, 1983-88, gen supt mfg eng, 1990-92. **Orgs:** Bds, Indianapolis Bus Develop Found; Black Adoption Comt; C Bur Indianapolis; Child Welfare League Am; Indianapolis Urban League; Community Serv Coun, Ind Voc Tech Col; United Way Greater Indianapolis; NAACP; Off Equal Opportunity, City Indianapolis; Channel 20 Pub Serv TV; Ind Black Expo; Black Child Develop Inst; United Way Agency Rel Adv Comt; Madame Walker Urban Life Ctr; Wilma Rudolph Found; pres, Indianapolis Chapter Sigma Xi; Ind Asn Rights C; Homes Black C, 1980; mem bd dir, Ind Univ Found. **Honors/Awds:** B'nai B'rith Man of the Yr 1974; Gold Medal Genl Motors Awd for Excellence in Comm Serv, 1978; Outstanding Achievement in Pub & Community Serv, 1982; Pub Citizen Year, Nat Asn Social Workers, 1986; Citizen Year, Omega Psi Phi frat, 1986; Moses Gray Awd (first recipient) Outstanding Serv Spec Adoptions, 1986; Chivas Regal Entreprenuer Award, 1990. **Special Achievements:** He was recognized in Who's Who in the Mid-West from 1978-1984. **Business Addr:** Indianapolis, IN 46206.*

GRAY, MYRTLE EDWARDS

School administrator. **Personal:** Born Nov 20, 1914, Tuscaloosa, AL; daughter of Alabama Bryant Edwards Melton and Burton Edwards; married Samuel Alfred Gray, Mar 13, 1938; children: Myrtle Imogene & Samuel A Jr. **Educ:** Alabama State Univ, BS, MEd, 1950; Univ Alabama, EdS, 1971. **Career:** School administrator (retired); Tuscaloosa City Sch Dist, elem teacher, 1935-36, 1936-54, prin elem schs, 1954-63, suprv prin, 1963-80. **Orgs:** Bd dir, YMCA, 1975-2000; Salvation Army, 1975-2000; chmn, Westside Cancer Dr, 1979; vpres, Alabama Baptist State Women's Conv; second vpres, Nat Asn Colored Women's Clubs, 1980-; pres, NW Dist, 1981-2000; Alabama Educ Asn; Elem Prins Asn; Univ Ala Alumni Asn; Nat Baptist USA Womens Auxiliary; Nightingale, Cosmos Study; pres, Tuscaloosa City Fed; pres, Ala Baptist State NW Dist Women's Convention, 1981; chairperson, Ala Asn Women's Clubs Bd; pres, Retired Teachers Tuscaloosa, 1989-90; dir music, New Antioch Bethlehem Dist Baptist Women's Convention & Congress Chirstian Educ; Ala Asn Women's Clubs; Ala Reading Asn. **Honors/Awds:** Honorary Doctorate, Selma Univ, 1986; Past President's Award, NACWC, 1990; Lifetime Distinguished Service Award, Ala Asn Women's Clubs; Teacher of the Year; Zeta Phi Beta Sorority's Woman of the Year; Tuscaloosa County Civic Hall of Fame, 2008. **Special Achievements:** Ebony Magazine's 100 Most Influential Black Women. **Home Addr:** 49 Washington Sq, Tuscaloosa, AL 35401, **Home Phone:** (205)752-7857. *

GRAY, ROBERT DEAN

Mayor, executive, chief executive officer. **Personal:** Born Jun 30, 1941, Clarksville, TN; son of R D Gray and Willa M Bush; married Gloria Enochs, Aug 19, 1967. **Educ:** Miss Valley State Univ, BS, 1964; Tex Southern Univ, MS, 1968; Chevron Oil Co Bus Sch. **Career:** Bolivar County Sch Dist 3, teacher, coach, 1964-67; Tex Southern Univ, asst coach, grad asst, 1967-68; Bolivar County Head start Prog, dir, 1968-70; Shelby Chevron Serv St, owner, operator, 1968-78; City Shelby, mayor, 1976-97; Griffin Lamp Co, pres, chief exec officer, 1987-. **Orgs:** Bd dir, Municipal Ass MS, 1978-92; chmn, Municipal Assn Serv Co Ins Pool; brd dir, MS Inst ST Small Town, 1979-; brd dir, MS Delta Coun, 1986-; vpres, Natl Conf Black Mayors, 1984-86; pres, MS Conf Black Mayors, 1979-86; brd dir, Nat Assn Mfrs, 1989-91. **Honors/Awds:** MS Valley State Univ, Sports Hall Fame Inductee, 1980. **Business Addr:** President, Chief Executive Officer, Griffin Lamp Co, US Hwy Suite 61 S, PO Box 66, Shelby, MS 38774.*

GRAY, RONALD A

Lawyer. **Personal:** Born Dec 15, 1952, Blackstone, VA; son of Archie and Mary Frances; married Doris, Aug 31, 1985; children: Avery & Lindsay. **Educ:** Ohio Univ, BA, econs, 1975; Case Western Res Univ, Col Law, JD, 1978. **Career:** Fed Trade Comn, atty, 1978-81; Am Express, atty, 1981-85, assoc coun, 1985-87, coun, 1987-91, sr coun, 1991-95, managing coun, 1995-. **Orgs:** Am Bar Asn, 1978-; bd mem, C Hope Found, 1991-94; bd mem, S African Legal Servs & Legal Assistance Proj, 1993-; vice chair, NY Bar Asn, Comt Minorities, 1994-97; bd mem, MFY Legal Servs, 1996-97; corp coun exec comt, NY State Bar Asn, 1997, Comn Multi-Discipline Pract, 1998-99; City Bar Arbit Com. **Honors/Awds:** Harlem Black Achievers in Industry Award, 1998; Ohio University, Gene Chapin Memorial Award, 1975. **Special Achievements:** Companies Aim for Diversity, New York Law Journal, 1993; Employees at Risk, New York Law Journal, 1994; Chairman, Succeeding in the Business Card Market, Credit Card Inst, Executive Enterprises, 1997. **Home Addr:** 630 Wellington Rd, Ridgewood, NJ 07450, **Home Phone:** (201)447-4205. **Business Addr:** Managing Counsel, American Express Company, 200 Vesey St 50th Fl, New York, NY 10285-4911, **Business Phone:** (212)640-2000.

GRAY, RUBEN L.

Lawyer. **Personal:** Born Nov 6, 1938, Georgetown, SC; married Jean Dozier; children: Ruben, Jr, Valencia, Valerie. **Educ:** SC State Col, BS, 1961; SC State Col, LLB, 1963; Nat Moot Ct Competitor, grad 1st class. **Career:** SC Econ Opp Bd Inc, exec dir, 1968-70; Morris Col, vpres develop, 1970-73; Finney & Gray, atty; State SC Family Court 3rd Judicial Circuit Sumter County, judge, currently. **Orgs:** SC State Elections Comn; bd trustee Sumter Sch Dist 17; ABA, NBA; SC Bar Asn; chmn, Sumter County Child Uplift Bd Inc; pres, Sumter Br NAACP; UMCA; Goodfellows; Sumter County Black Polit Caucus; Sumter County Dem Exec Comt. **Honors/Awds:** Recipient, Community Leader of Amrica Award, 1968. **Military Serv:** AUS, 1963-65. **Business Addr:** Judge, State of South Carolina Family Court 3rd Judicial Circuit Sumter County, PO Box 2636, Sumter, SC 29151-2636, **Business Phone:** (803)773-4914.*

GRAY, TORRIAN (TORRIAN DESHON GRAYBARTOW)

Football player, football coach. **Personal:** Born Mar 18, 1974, Bartow, FL; married; children: Tori. **Educ:** Va Tech, attended 1996. **Career:** Football player (retired), football player coach; Minn Vikings, defensive back, 1997-99; Univ Maine, defensive backs coach, 2000-02; Univ Conn, defensive backs coach, 2002-04; Chicago Bears, defensive backs coach, 2004-05; Va Tech, defensive backfield coach, 2006-. **Honors/Awds:** Three times all Big East free safety; 2 Big East Conference as a player, 1995, 1996; 2 ACC Championships as a coach, 2007,2008. **Business Addr:** Football Defensive Backs Coach, Virginia Tech, Virginia Tech Athletics, 901 Prices Fork Rd, PO Box 90001, Blacksburg, VA 24062-9001, **Business Phone:** (540)231-8000.

GRAY, VALERIE HAMILTON

Civil engineer. **Personal:** Born May 10, 1959, Houma, LA; daughter of Allen A and Lucia T Legaux; married Ian A Gray, Jun 11, 1983; children: Adrienne Theresa & Ian Alexander. **Educ:** Univ Notre Dame, Notre Dame, Ind, BS, 1981; Corpus Christi State Univ, Corpus Christi, Tex, Comput Sci, 1987. **Career:** Texaco, USA, Harvey, La, proj engr, 1980-85; City Corpus Christi, Corpus Christi, Tex, neighborhood improv div supvr, 1985-88, engr II, 1988-89, water construct supt, 1989-95, storm water supt, 1995-. **Orgs:** Am Soc Civil Engrs, 1981-; Am Water Works Asn, 1989-; Nat Soc Prof Engrs. **Honors/Awds:** Young Engineer of the Year, Nuects Chap Tex Soc Prof Engrs, 1994. **Business Addr:** Storm Water Superintendent, Storm Water Department, City Corpus Christi, 1201 Leopard St, PO Box 9277, Corpus Christi, TX 78469-9277, **Business Phone:** (361)857-1875.

GRAY, WILFRED DOUGLAS

Executive. **Personal:** Born Oct 1, 1937, Richmond, VA; son of Richard L and Lula B Duvall; married Shirley M Durant, Nov 23, 1957; children: Alden D, Kathleen Y. **Educ:** Dale Carnegie, Buffalo, NY, attended 1971; State Univ, NY, Buffalo, BA, 1974; Printing Industry Metropolitan Wash, Wash DC, attended 1981. **Career:** Republic Steel, Buffalo, NY, scarfer, inspector, 1962-76; Buffalo Envelope, Buffalo, NY, sales rep, 1976-80; Envelopes Unlimited, Rockville, MD, sales rep, 1980-81; Gray Paper Prod Inc, Washington DC, pres. **Orgs:** Chamber Commerce, DC, NAACP; bd dir, Boys & Girls Clubs Greater Wash; Am Asn Retired Persons; Nat Asn Black Public Officials; Upper Ga Ave Bus & Professional Asn; Nat Bus Forms Asn; Rotary Club Wash, DC. **Honors/Awds:** President's Award, Federal Envelope, 1979. **Military Serv:** US Navy, Airman, 1956-60; Honorable Discharge, 1960. **Business Addr:** President, Gray Paper Production Incorporation, 214 L St NE, Washington, DC 20002, **Business Phone:** (202)546-4919.*

GRAY, WILLIAM HERBERT, III

Association executive, clergy, educator. **Personal:** Born Aug 20, 1941, Baton Rouge, LA; married Andrea Dash; children: William H IV, Justin Yates & Andrew Dash. **Educ:** Franklin & Marshall Col, BA, 1963; Drew Theological Sem, MDiv, 1966; Princeton Theol Sem, MDiv, 1970; Univ Pa, Temple Univ, Mansfield Col Oxford Univ, England, grad work. **Career:** Union Baptist Church Montclair NJ, pastor, 1964-72; Bright Hope Baptist Church, Philadelphia, sr pastor, 1972-; US Cong, rep, Philadelphia, PA, 1978-91; United Negro Col Fund, pres, 1991-2004; Sec State Haiti Affairs, spl advisor; Buchanan Ingersoll, sr adv pub policy & bus diversity; Dell Inc, bd dirs; JP Morgan Chase, bd dirs; Pfizer, bd dirs; Prudential Financial, bd dirs; Visteon Corp, bd dirs; Pew Foster Care, vice chmn, currently. **Orgs:** Dem Steering Comt ninety sixth US Congress; secy, Cong Black Caucus; House Comn Foreign Affairs; Comt Budget; Comt DC; US Liberia Presidential Comn; vice chmn, Cong Black Caucus. **Honors/Awds:** Over 80 honorary degrees from US cols & univs; Desmond Tutu Award, Franklin Delano Roosevelt Freedom of Worship Medal; LHD, Bates Col, 1994. **Special Achievements:** First African Am to chair House Budget Committee, chmn of Democratic Caucus, Majority Whip; Named one of 100 Most Important Blacks in the World in the 20th Century, Ebony; Author, The House version of the Anti-Apartheid Acts of 1985, 86. **Business Addr:** Senior Policy Advisor, Buchanan Ingersoll, 1700 K St NW Suite 300, Washington, DC 20006-3807, **Business Phone:** (202)452-7900.

GRAYBARTOW, TORRIAN DESHON. See GRAY, TORRIAN.

GRAYDON, WASDON, JR.

School administrator, executive director. **Personal:** Born Sep 22, 1950, Fort Mammoth, NJ; son of Wasdon and Lenora; married Veronica Brooks; children: Tremayne, Jasmaine. **Educ:** Abraham Baldwin Agr Col, AS, sec educ, 1970; Ga Southern Col, BS, 1972; Valdosta State Col, 1974. **Career:** Spec Serv Prog, dir, 1973-76; Upward Bound Spec Serv Prog, dir, 1973-76, spec serv/min adv prog, 1983-87; Tift County, comnr dist 2, 1984-88; G&M Enterprises, partner, 1985-87; Abraham Baldwin Agr Col, dir minority advising/TRIO Progs, 1983-, Ctr Multicultural Awareness, dir, 1997, Col Serv External Progs, interim dir, 2000-01; CAMP/HEP Progs, interim dir, 2002-03. **Orgs:** Phi Delta Kappa, 1975-83; bd mem, SW Ga Health Syst Agency Inc, 1976-81; Treas, Ga Asn Spec Prog Inc, 1980-84; consult, Ga Statewide Health Coord Coun, 1980-83; Tift Co Nat Asn Adv Colored People, 1980-87; trustee, Everette Temple CME Church, 1980-87; PROMISE Club, 1983-84; trustee, Tifton Tift Co Pub Libr, 1984-88; Tift Co Arts Coun, 1984-87; bd mem, Tifton-Tift Co United Way, 1986-88; Tifton-Tift Co C of C, 1986-87; bd dir, Tifton-Tift Co Main State Prog, 1986-87. **Honors/Awds:** GASPP Outstanding Serv Award, 1983; SAEOPP Cert of Recognition, 1984; Mgr of the Year, 1989-90; Leadership Ga Found Inc, 1991; Arts Citizen of the Year, Tifton-Tift County Arts Coun, 1994; Outstanding Serv Award, Univ Syst Ga, 1994; Pres Appreciation Award, ABAC, 2000-01; E Lanier Carson Leadership Award, ABAC, 2000-01. **Home Addr:** 4504 Woodland Dr W, Tifton, GA 31794-6553. **Business Addr:** Director, Abraham Baldwin Agricutural College, 2802 Moore Hwy, PO Box 21, Tifton, GA 31793.*

GRAY-LITTLE, DR. BERNADETTE
Educator, psychologist. **Personal:** Born Oct 21, 1944, Washington, NC; daughter of James Gray and Rosalie Lanier Gray; married Shade Keys; children: Maura M & Mark G. **Educ:** Marywood Col, BA, 1966; St Louis Univ, MS, 1968, PhD, 1970. **Career:** Univ NC, from asst prof to assoc prof, 1971-82, prof 1982-, chair, 1993-98, assoc dean, 1999-2001, exec assoc provost, 2001-, dean, col arts & sci, 2004-06, execu vice chancellor & provost, 2006-09; Kansas Univ, Chancellor, Currently. **Orgs:** Fel Am Psychol Asn; Sigma Xi. **Honors/Awds:** Distinguished Alumna, Marywood Col, Scranton, Pa, 1996; Alumni Merit Award, St Louis Univ, 1997; Fulbright Fel Phi Beta Kappa. **Business Addr:** Chancellor, Kansas University, Lawrence, KS 66045, **Business Phone:** (785)864-2700.

GRAY-MORGAN, DR. LARUTH H.
College administrator. **Personal:** Born in Texarkana, TX; daughter of Hazel Johnson and Curtis Hackney; married Joseph Morgan; children: Diendra & Phillip; married Norris Gray, Aug 27, 1977 (deceased); children: Phillip Anthony & Dierdra Alyce Gray. **Educ:** Howard Univ, BA, 1954; Columbia Univ, MA, 1957; Nova Univ, EdD, 1975. **Career:** New Rochelle NY Public Sch, chmn English Dept, Educ Support Ctr, prin, dir instructional serv, asst supt, 1980-83; Abbott Univ Free Sch District, supt sch, 1983-89; NY Univ, Metrop Ctr Urban Educ, dep dir, 1989, prof, ed admin, 1990-, affil prof, 2003, dir external rels, 2003-. **Orgs:** Bd mem, comm White Plains, Young Women Christian Asn; Comt Aging City New Rochelle; past chair, Urban Affairs Comm NYS Asn Super & Curr Develop; past vpres, NY State Eng Coun; pres, emer, bd dirs Martin Luther King Child Care Ctr, 1980-; Coun Arts 1986-; pres, bd trustees, New Rochelle Pub Libr, 1986-90, pres, 1993-95; bd dir, NY State Alliance Art, 1989-91; Westchester Children's Asn, 1989-95; vpres, Westchester Coun Arts, 1987-94, exec vpres, 1996-99; Am Asn Sch Admin, Comt Minorities & Women, chair, 1990-; pres, Westchester Libr Syst, 1996-2000; pres, Methodist Art Coun, 2000-02. **Honors/Awds:** Outstanding Educator, New Rochelle Br, Nat Asn Advan Colored People & Leadership Adv Comt, 1973; Outstanding Educator, Nat Coun Negro Women, 1975; Outstanding Educator, Nat Asn Minority Bankers, 1976; Community Service Award, West Salute Comt, 1984; Cert Recognizing Unique Contribution to Educ US Congressional Black Caucus, 1984; 100 Top Educators US & N Am, 1986; Outstanding superintendent in the Arts, Kennedy Ctr DC Arts Alliance 1988; Leadership Award, Nat Alliance Black Sch Educs Serv, 1996. **Special Achievements:** Publ: White & Black Females in the Classroom, American Educational Journal, 1998; The Best For Our Children: The Sherburne-Earlville Story, Metro Center Press, New York University, 1993; Women of Color: In a Different Context, from An Action Plan for Equity in New York State Education Administration, New York State Congress of School Administrator Organizations Publications, 1994; The Twin Problems of Declining Enrollment & Fiscal Constraints; A Dissemination Model for Community-Based Decision-Making for the Experience of the City School District of New Rochelle; Monograph, City School District of New Rochelle, New York, 1983; Aspirations & Achievements of Italian and Black American Youths, New Rochelle Public Schools ERIC Document, 1978); Urban Education by Whom? For Whom? Impact, Vol. 13, No. 2, New York State Association of Curriculum and Development, 1971; a book, The Urban Nomad: A Study of the Abused & Neglected Paradigm for the African-American Teenager (in progress); & Charter Schools: An Answer to Closing the Achievement Gap for Urban Education?. **Business Addr:** Director, New York University, Metro Center Urban Education, 82 Wash Sq E Suite 72, New York, NY 10003-6644, **Business Phone:** (212)998-5137.

GRAYS, DR. MATTELIA BENNETT
School administrator. **Personal:** Born Jul 26, 1931, Houston, TX; daughter of A B Bennett; married Horace, Jan 1, 1952; children: Karen. **Educ:** Dilliard Univ, BA, 1952; Univ Mich, MA, spec educ; Pacific Univ, Sacramento, EdD, educ admin, 1985. **Career:** Educator (retired); consult, continuous Progress Learning Corp; prin, Rogers Educ Enrichment Ctr, 1970-87; Univ Houston, supvr lab experiences teachers; Houston Independent Sch Dist, Dist three supt, 1987. **Orgs:** Int Asn Childhood Educ; exec bd mem, Nat Pan Hellenic Coun Inc; 18th intpres, Alpha Kappa Alpha Sorority Inc, 1970-74. **Honors/Awds:** AKA Sorority S Cent Region scholarship fund, named in honor. **Special Achievements:** Youngest person ever elected National President of the Alpha Kappa Omega Chapter Sorority in 1968. **Business Addr:** Educator Administration Operator, Houston Independent School District, 3101 Weslayan, Houston, TX 77027.

GRAYSON, BYRON J., SR.
Manager. **Personal:** Born Sep 3, 1949, York, PA; son of Charles F Sr and Hurline V Bridgette; married Jennifer Gibson Grayson, Jan 1, 1985; children: Cortella Jones, Paul Jones, Byron Grayson Jr, Nicolle Grayson. **Educ:** Howard Univ, Wash, DC, BA, Finance, 1971, MBA, 1978, Sch Divinity, MDiv, 1995. **Career:** Bell Atlantic, Wash, DC, mgr, residence serv ctr, 1979-81, mgr, reg matters, 1981-97, sr specialist, Oper Serv, 1997; African Methodist Episcopal Church, ordained elder, 1997; St Jude AME Church, pastor, currently. **Orgs:** bd, Ed Partnership Technol Corp, 1991-96; elected comm, vice chmn, Adv Neighborhood Comm, 1988-95; elected mem, Wash, DC Ward 3 Dem Comt, 1988-95; Alpha Phi Alpha Fraternity; Brown Memorial AME Church, asst pastor, 1995-98. **Home Addr:** 1018 Eastbourne Ct, Frederick, MD 21702-5119, **Home Phone:** (301)353-9007. **Business Addr:** Pastor, St Jude AME Church, 19314 Archdale Rd, Germantown, MD 20904, **Business Phone:** (301)972-9400.*

GRAYSON, DEREK L., II
Executive. **Personal:** Born Feb 11, 1971, Sandusky, OH; son of Derek Sr. and Jill; married Carmen Felice Grayson, Sep 21, 1996. **Educ:** Morehouse Col, BA, Bus Admin, 1993. **Career:** Wachovia Bank, banking officer, 1993-97; Citizens Trust Bank, vpres, 1997-; Peachtree Nat Bank. **Orgs:** South DeKalb Bus Incubator, bd dirs, sec, 1998-; Stone Mountain Main St Comn; Habitate Humanity DeKalb, bd dirs, chair, 1998-; South DeKalb Bus Asn, 1998-; Nat Asn Gov Guaranteed Lenders, 1999-. **Business Addr:** Vice President, Citizens Trust Bank, 75 Piedmont Ave NE, Atlanta, GA 30303, **Business Phone:** (404)653-2840.*

GRAYSON, ELSIE MICHELLE
Counselor. **Personal:** Born May 5, 1962, Fairfield, AL. **Educ:** Univ Ala, Tuscaloosa, BS; Univ Ala, Birmingham, MA, Educ. **Career:** Child Mental Health Serv, teaching parent, 1983-84; Ala Dept Human Resources, social worker, 1984-. **Orgs:** Alpha Kappa Alpha Sor Inc; Omicron Omega Chapter; Eastern Star Corine Chap 257; choir dir, pres, asst teacher, New Mount Moriah Baptist Church. **Home Addr:** 322 Knight Ave, Hueytown, AL 35023. **Business Addr:** Social Worker, 1321 5th Ave S, Birmingham, AL 35202, **Business Phone:** (205)933-6045.

GRAYSON, GEORGE WELTON
State government official. **Personal:** Born Nov 1, 1938, Dixons Mills, AL; son of Aaron and Martha Harper; married Lucille Lampkin, Dec 20, 1963; children: Anthony, Reginald & Deirdre. **Educ:** Ala A&M Univ, BS, 1965, MS, 1968; Vanderbilt Univ, PhD, 1976. **Career:** Tenn Valley High Sch, Hillsboro, AL, teacher, 1966-67, guid counr & asst prin, 1967-68; Ala A&M Univ, biol instr, dept chmn, 1968-71; Ala House of Reps, rep, 1983-. **Orgs:** Ala New S Coalition; Synod Mid-South; Presbyterian Coun. **Honors/Awds:** Man of the Yr, Phi Beta Sigma, 1984; Resolution of Commendation, Mich State House Reps, 1984; Good Government Award, Jaycees, 1985; James Weldon Johnson Freedom Award, 1986. **Special Achievements:** First black candidate in modern history to seek state office from northern Alabama with the full endorsement & support of the Alabama Democratic Party, 1978. **Business Addr:** Representative, District 19, 3810 Melody Rd NE, Huntsville, AL 35811, **Business Phone:** (205)851-5329.

GRAYSON, JENNIFER A
Executive. **Personal:** Born Apr 26, 1949, Union, SC; daughter of Martha Gist Gibson and Cortelyou Gibson; married Byron Grayson, Jan 1, 1985; children: Cortella, Paul, Byron Jr & Nicolle. **Educ:** SC State Univ, Orangeburg, SC, BS, 1972; George Wash Univ, Wash, DC, 1978. **Career:** Food & Drug Admin, Brooklyn, NY, consumer safety off, 1972-74; Food & Drug Admin, East Orange, NJ, consumer safety off, 1974-77; Food & Drug Admin, Rockville, Md, consumer safety off, 1977-90, actg br chief, 1990, br chief, 1990, actg assoc div dir, 1993-95; Bio-Reg Assoc, sr regulatory affairs specialist, Laurel, MD, 1995-96; Oncor, Inc, sr regulatory affairs specialist, Gaithersburg, MD; Bio-Tech Imaging, vpres regulatory affairs, Frederick, MD, 1999-2003; Independent consult, currently. **Orgs:** Delta Sigma Theta Sorority, 1968-; first vpres, Alpha Wives Wash, DC, 1987-90; class leader, St Paul AME Ch, 1989-; mem, historian, Missionary Soc/St Paul Ch, 1990-; first vpres, Missionary Soc/St Paul AME Church, 1991-95; Wash Conf, Ministers Wives, Spouses & Widows Alliance, 1994. **Honors/Awds:** Various service awards from church, 1986-. **Business Addr:** Independent Consultant, 1018 Eastbourne Ct, Frederick, MD 21702, **Business Phone:** (301)846-7880.

GRAYSON, JOHN N.
Executive. **Personal:** Born Sep 4, 1932, Brooklyn, NY; married Dorothy Lane; children: Lois, Theresa (Wallace), Susan, April. **Educ:** BSEE, 1959. **Career:** Hughes Aircraft Co El Segundo CA, proj engr, 1955-62; Guidance & Nav Lab TWR Sys Redondo Beach CA, bus mgr, 1962-71; Electronics Harward Operations, sub-proj mgr; prod line mgr mgr-manu engr test sec; Unified Ind Alexandria VA, dir energy problems proj on minority bus enter, 1973; UNIVOX CA Co, pres. **Orgs:** Nat Assn Black Manu; Inst Elec & Electronics Engr Inc; chrtr pres, Consolidate Comn Action Assn; mem pres, Youth Motivation Task Force; Urban League; Nat Asn Advan Colored People; com sel-help group Mexican Am Comm E LA; Oriental-Am Caucus; ruling elder, Westminster Presb Ch LA; comnr, Gen Assembly United Presb Ch, 1969; past moderator, Synod So Bca UPCUSA; past chmn, com synod So CA; The Gen Assembly Mission Coun UPCUSA; chmn, The Section Eval UPCUSA. **Honors/Awds:** Man of the Year Award, Westminster Presb Ch, 1972; Outstanding Service Award National Association of Black Manufactures, 1974. **Military Serv:** AUS, sgt 1st class, 1950-55. *

GRAYSON, MEL
Fashion designer, educator. **Personal:** Born Dec 3, 1950, Dallas, TX; son of Coot and Ruby Lee; divorced; children: Damon, Shannon Grayson-Fields, Lillian Grayson-Holmes. **Educ:** Trade-Tech Col, AA, 1971. **Career:** TV Serials: "Pride & Prejudice", costume desginer, 1990; "A Different World", costume desginer, 1990; House Party 3, costume desginer, 1994; "Bringing Up BayBay", production designer, 2005; Freelance fashion designer, 1972-74; ARPEJA, fashion designer, 1971-75; Bullock's Dept Store, visual merchandiser, 1975-77; Aaron Brothers Art Marts, manager, 1977-86; fashion & costume designer, 1986-, Fashion Inst Design & Merchandising, fac, currently; Pinky Rose Boutique, visual dir, currently. **Orgs:** West Coast Fashion Alliance. **Special Achievements:** 5 Celebrity Covers for Ebony Magazine, 1996, 1997;Alpha Kappa Alpha Annual Mother's Day Fashion Shows; 1st Afr Amer Male Fashion Stylist featured in LA Times Mag; 1st Afr Amer Stylist featured in several national publications; 1st Afr Amer male costumed designer on an international TV series, A Different World. **Business Addr:** Faculty, The Fashion Inst Design & Merchandising, 919 S Grand Ave, Los Angeles, CA 90015-1421, **Business Phone:** 800-624-1200.*

GRAYSON, STANLEY EDWARD
Banker. **Personal:** Born Sep 11, 1950, Chicago, IL; son of George C Jr and L Elizabeth Smith; married Patricia Ann McKinnon Grayson, Jul 4, 1981; children: Lauren Ashley, Stephen Edward. **Educ:** Col Holy Cross, Worcester, BA, MA, 1972; Univ Mich Law Sch, Ann Arbor, MI, JD, 1975. **Career:** Metrop Life Ins Co, NY, atty, 1975-84; City New York, comnr financial servs, 1984-88, comnr finance, 1988-89, dep mayor finance & econ develop, 1989-90; Goldman Sachs & Co, NY, vpres, 1990-96; Prudential Securities Inc, managing dir, 1996; MR Beal & Co, pres & chief operating officer, currently. **Orgs:** NY State Bar Asn, 1977-; 100 Black Men, 1986-; bd dirs, Boys Choir Harlem, 1987-91; bd dirs, March Dimes NY, 1990-96; bd dirs, The Mus City NY, 1990-; bd dirs, Region Plan Asn, 1990-95; bd trustees, Mgt Col, Tarrytown, 1991-96; bd dirs, The NY Downtown Hosp, 1991-95; bd trustees, Col The Holy Cross, 1995-; bd dirs, NY Outward Bound, 1995-. **Honors/Awds:** Crusader of the Year, 1972; Coll Holy Cross, 1972; Man of the Year, Brooklyn Chamber Com, 1989; Hall of Fame, 1991. **Business Addr:** President, Chief Operating Officier, MR Beal & Co, 110 Wall St, New York, NY 10005-3801.*

GREAR, DR. EFFIE CARTER
School administrator. **Personal:** Born Aug 15, 1927, Huntington, WV; daughter of Harold J Carter and Margaret Tinsley Carter; married William A; children: Rhonda Kaye & William A Jr. **Educ:** WVa State Col, BS, Music, 1948; OH State Univ, MA, 1955; Nova Univ, Doctor Educ, 1976. **Career:** Educator (retired); Excelsior High WV, music & band teacher, 1948-49; FAMUHS Tallahassee Fla, band & chorus teacher, 1949-51; Smith-brown HS ArcadiaFla, band & chorus teacher, 1952-56; Lake Shore HS Belle Glade Fla, band &chorus teacher, 1956-63; dean, 1963-66; asst prin, 1966-70; Glades Cent HSBelle Glade Fla, asst prin, 1970-75; prin, 1975-2000. **Orgs:** Pres, Elite Comt Club Inc, Belle Glade, 1971-82; pres, Belle Glade Chamber Comt Beautification, 1974-80; bd dirs Ment Health Asn Palm Beach City, 1984-; pres, City Asn, Belle Glade, 1984-, bd dir, Palm Beach County Ment, Health Agency, 1984-; pres, Belle Glade City Asn Women's Clubs, 1985-; bdgov, Everglades Area Health Educ Ctr, 1986-; seyc, Fla Asn Women's Clubs, 1988-90; bd dir, Fla High Sch Activities Asn, 1987-88; bd dir, Glades ACTS, 1987-; secy, Palm Beach City Criminal Justice Comn, West Palm Beach,Fla, 1997. **Honors/Awds:** Outstanding Comt Ach, Fla Atlantic Univ, 1977; Woman of Year, Elite ComtClub, 1979 1982; Outstanding Achivement, Hon Mem Glades CorrectionalJaycees Unit, 1979; Special Recognition, Fla Sugar Cane League LobbyingSugar Indust, Wash DC, 1985; Srv Awd United Negro Col Fund Telethon, 1985;Zeta Phi Beta Educator of the Yr, 1984; Educator of the Yr, Phi DeltaKappa Palm Beach Co, Fla, 1986; Hon Chap Farmer of the Future, Farmers Amlocal chap, 1986; Hon Gov Bob Graham Fla, first celebration Martin LutherKing Jr Nat observance, 1986; Woman of the Yr, Fla Asn Women's Clubs,1986; Citizen of the Y,r Belle Glade Chamber Com, 1986; Community ServiceAward, El Dorado Civic Club, 1987; Martin L King, Jr Humanitarian Award-,West Palm Beach UrbanLeague, 1988; Community vice Award, Palm Beach CountyNat Asn Advan Colored People Br, 1989; Club Woman of the Year, Fla AsnWomen's Clubs, 1989; Citizen of the Year, Kappa Upsilon Chap, Omega PsiPhi Fraternity, 1990;

Principal of Excellence, Fla Asn Sec Sch Prin, 1992;finalist, da Baker Distinguised Black Educator, Fla Dept Educ, 1992;Outstanding Educator Award, Links Inc, West Palm Beach, Fla, 1996; Outstanding Col Svc Award, Alpha Kappa Alpha Sorority, Mu Rho Omega Chap,Belle Glade, Fla, 1996; Outstanding Educator Award, Zeta Phi Beta Sorority, Inc, Belle Glade, Fla, 1997. **Home Addr:** 661 4th St, Belle Glade, FL 33430.

GREAUX, CHERYL PREJEAN
Entrepreneur, consultant, government official. **Personal:** Born Jul 30, 1949, Houston, TX; daughter of Evelyn F Jones; married Robert Bruce. **Educ:** Tex Southern Univ, BA (Magna Cum Laude), 1967; Univ Tex, MA, 1973. **Career:** NASA Johnson Spacecraft Ctr, procurement specialist, 1968-71; Dept Labor, superior compliance officer, 1973-80; Allied Corp, corp mgr, EEO Progs, 1980-85; Dean Witter Reynolds Inc, exec recruiter, 1986-88; USDA, civil rights dir, rural housing, 1995, Alternative Dispute Resolution Prog, dir, civil rights dir; Greaux & Assoc, prin consult & partner, currently. **Orgs:** Delta Sigma Theta Sorority, 1965-; chmn, Fund Raising NJ Inst Tech, 1981-84; bd mem, Morris County Urban League, 1983-85; Coalition 100 Black Women, 1994; co-founder, Wash Edges Group Inc; Corp Womens Network. **Honors/Awds:** President's Leadership Award, Nat Asn Negro Bus & Prof Women's Clubs, 1993; Ford Found Scholar; Exec Loan; Mass Inst Technol, Presidential Classroom Vol Instr, 1994; Fed Exec Inst, 1995. **Business Addr:** Civil Rights Director, Greaux & Associates, Fairfax County, VA 22015, **Business Phone:** (703)323-7115.

GREAVES, MCLEAN (MCLEAN MASHINGAIDZE GREAVES)
Chief executive officer. **Personal:** Born Sep 27, 1966, St Thomas, Virgin Islands of the United States; son of Marion and Oswald (deceased). **Educ:** British Columbia Inst Technol, Jour, 1986. **Career:** Int Bus Mach, Delrina Softkey Software, consult, 1993-96; Paper Mag, new media ed, 1995-96; CBC TV, corresp, 1996-; Columbia Sch Bus, lectr, 1997-98; Pratt Institute, lectr, 1998; Virtual Melanin Inc, chief exec officer; The Nimble Co Inc, founder & chief exec officer, currently. **Orgs:** Panelist, Comn Concerned Journalists, 1998. **Honors/Awds:** AT&T Link Award, Web Design, 1997; Brooklyn Innovators Award, Friends Errol T Louis, 1997. **Special Achievements:** Articles published in : Essence; The Source; Vibe; BET Weekend; selected by Village Voice, One of Top 10 Silicon Alley Entrepreneurs, 1997; selected by New York Times/PC Expo, Top 10 NY Websites, 1996; selected as "Cyber Star," Virtual City Mag, 1996. **Business Phone:** (604)638-6789.

GREAVES, MCLEAN MASHINGAIDZE. See GREAVES, MCLEAN.

GREAVES, WILLIAM
Writer, movie producer, administrator. **Personal:** Born Oct 8, 1926, New York, NY; son of Garfield and Emily Muir; married Louise Archambault, Aug 23, 1959; children: David & Taiyi 7 Maiya. **Educ:** City Col New York, 1945; Film Inst City Col, 1952. **Career:** Nat Film Bd Canada, filmmaker, 1952-60; Canadian Drama Studio, artistic dir, 1952-63; UN TV, producer & dir, 1963-64; William Greaves Prods Inc, owner, 1964-, pres, currently; Black Jour, exec producer & co-host, 1968-70; Lee Strasberg Theatre Inst, instr, 1968-82; films: Symbiopsychotaxiplasm: Take One, 1968; Ali, the Fighter, 1973; From These Roots, 1974; Ida B Wells: A Passion for Justice, PBS, 1989; Ralph Bunche: An American Odyssey, 2001; Symbiopsychotaxiplasm: Take 2.5, 2003. **Orgs:** NY Actors Studio; AFTRA; Am Guild Auth & Composers; DGA; co-founder, Nat Asn Black Media Producers, 1970; WGA; Equity Asn; SAG. **Honors/Awds:** Inductee, Black Filmmakers Hall of Fame, 1980; Special Recognition, Black Am Independent Film Festival, Paris, 1980; Indy Spec Life Achievement Award, Asn Independent Video & Filmmakers; Dusa Award, Actors Studio, NY, 1980; Emmy Award, Nat Acad TV Arts & Sci; over 70 film festival awards. **Special Achievements:** Four Emmy nominations; Directed and co-produced a celebration of Paul Robeson's 90th birthday, Shubert Theater; has made over 200 documentary films, has conducted workshops for film directors and screen actors throughout the world, Ralph Bunche: An American Odyssey, selected for competition at Sundance Film Festival, 2001. **Business Addr:** President, William Greaves Productions Inc, Radio City Station, PO Box 2044, New York, NY 10101-2044.

GREELY, M GASBY (GASBY GREELY BROWN)
Entrepreneur, financial manager. **Personal:** Born Oct 23, 1946, Detroit, MI; daughter of Wesley and Stella Gasby; children: Janine. **Educ:** Wayne Co Community Col, AA, 1971; Wayne State Univ, BA, 1973; MIT, Advan Res, 1982; Harvard Univ, MPA, 1982. **Career:** WNET/Thirteen, mkt dir, 1983-87; Fox Tv, gen assignment reporter, 1987-89, financial corresp, 1989-93; Greenpeace, nat commun dir, 1993-95; Nat Urban League, vpres develop & commun, 1995-2000, sr vpres, 2001; Wash Opera Co, exec vpres & dir strategic res planning; Greenpeace, nat dir commun; Nat Urban League, sr vpres develop & commun; Gasby Group Inc, Chmn & Chief Exec Officer, currently. **Orgs:** Pub Rel Soc Am, 1983-; Brooklyn Tabernacle, 1991-; Nat Press Club, 1993-; bd dirs, Nat C Film Festival, 1996-; Nat Soc Fundraising Execs, 1997-. **Honors/Awds:** Alum of the Year, Nat Asn Community Col, 1989; Legacy Messenger, Black Career Women, 1997; Women of Industry Award, Nat Coun Negro Women.

GREELY BROWN, GASBY. See GREELY, M GASBY.

GREEN, A. C., JR.
Basketball player, president (organization). **Personal:** Born Oct 4, 1963, Portland, OR; married Veronique, Apr 20, 2002. **Educ:** Ore State Univ, BS, speech commun. **Career:** Basketball player (retired), pres; Los Angeles Lakers, forward, 1986-94,1999-2000; Phoenix Suns, 1994-96; Dallas Mavericks, 1996-99; Miami Heat, 2000-01; AC Green Youth Found, pres, currrently. **Orgs:** AC Green Youth Found; Athletes for Abstinence. **Honors/Awds:** NBA Iron Man title; All-Star, 1990; Oregon Sports Hall of Fame, 2003. **Business Addr:** President, AC Green Youth Foundation, 125 W McDowell Road, PO Box 1709, Phoenix, AZ 85003, **Business Phone:** (602)528-0790.*

GREEN, AHMAN (AHMAN RASHAD GREEN)
Football player. **Personal:** Born Feb 16, 1977, Omaha, NE; children: Ahmani & Myahni. **Educ:** Univ Nebr, geog. **Career:** Seattle Seahawks, running back, 1998-99; Green Bay Packers, 2000-06; Houston Texans, 2007-08. **Honors/Awds:** Four Times Pro Bowler Selection, 2001-04; All Pro Selection Twice, 2001, 2003. **Business Addr:** Running Back, Houston Texans, Two Reliant Pk, Houston, TX 77054, **Business Phone:** (832)667-1400.

GREEN, AHMAN RASHAD. See GREEN, AHMAN.

GREEN, AL
Singer, executive, clergy. **Personal:** Born Apr 13, 1946, Forrest City, AR. **Educ:** Lane Col, Hon, BA Music, 1976; Lemoyne Owen, Hon BA, Music 1977. **Career:** Green Enterprises Inc, owner, pres, 1970; Bell then Hi-Records, recording artist; Al Green Music Inc, owner, pres, recording artist 1970-; Full Gospel Tabernacle Church, pastor, 1976-; Songs include "Rhymes," "Lets Stay Together," "Tired of Being Alone," "How do You Mend a Broken Heart," "Back up Train," "Love & Happiness"; Broadway: Your Arms Too Short to Box with God, 1982; Albums: He is the Light, 1986; Love Is Reality, 1992; Gospel Soul, 1993; I Can't Stop, 2003; Everything's OK, 2005. **Orgs:** NARAS, 1970-; AGVA, 1970-; spec dep, Memphis Sheriffs Dept 1976-; hon capt, Bolling AFB, Wash DC, 1976-; pres, Lee County Pub Co, 1983-; Econ & Devel City Hall, 1984-. **Honors/Awds:** Tribute in the Music Ind Sullivan Award, 1982; Grammy Award for Precious Lord, NARAS, 1983; Grammy for I'll Rise Again, NARAS, 1984; Dove Award, Gospel Music Asn, 1984; Gospel Hall of Fame, inducted, 2004. **Special Achievements:** Autobiography, Take Me To The River, 2000, A Road in Memphis named Reverand Al Green Road.

GREEN, ALEXANDER N
Association executive, government official, judge. **Personal:** Born Sep 1, 1947, New Orleans, LA. **Educ:** Fla A&M Univ, attened 1971; Tuskegee Inst Technol, attened 1974; Thurgood Marshall Sch Law Tex Southern Univ, JD. **Career:** Harris Co, TX, judge, justice peace, precinct 7, position 2, 1977-2004; Tex House Reps, Dist 9, rep, 2005-; Tex Southern Univ, Thurgood Marshall Sch Law, instr; Green, Wilson, Dewberry & Fitch Law Firm, co founder. **Orgs:** Pres, Houston Br Nat Asn Advan Colored People; Alpha Phi Alpha. **Honors/Awds:** Distinguished Service Award, Houston Citizens Chamber Com, 1978; Outstanding Leadership Award, Black Heritage Soc, 1981; Courageous Defender of Due Process for Educators, Am Fed Teachers, 1983. **Business Phone:** (713)383-9234.

GREEN, ANITA LORRAINE
Banker, president (organization). **Personal:** Born Jul 18, 1948, Brooklyn, NY; daughter of Angus and Queen Esther; children: Corey James. **Educ:** Brooklyn Col City Univ, NY, BA, econs, 1980. **Career:** Nat Urban League, prog develop specialist, 1972-82; Citicorp Diners Club, mkt commun mgr, 1982-88; Citibank FSB, vpres, community rels & CRA officer, 1988; Foster Green Morgan LLC, vpres mkt, currently; Anita Green Relocation Mgmt, pres, currently. **Orgs:** Chairperson, Museum Sci & Ind, black creativity prog, 1992-; adv bd, DePaul Univ, Ctr Urban Educ, 1990-; bd mem, Ill Facilities Fund, 1993-; bd mem, Life Directions; bd, Univ Chicago; Friends Against Aids; Life Directions; Museum Sci; Ind Adv Comn. **Honors/Awds:** Dollars & Sense Mag, Ams Best & Brightest Bus, Prof Men & Women, 1991; Mahogany Found, Community Relations Award, 1993-; YMCA Black & Hispanic Achievers of Industry Award, 1993; Success Guide, Top Ten To Watch, 1995; Today's Chicago Women, 100 Women Making a Difference. **Business Addr:** Vice President, Marketing, Foster Green Morgan LLC, 3148 South King Dr, Chicago, IL 60616-3940, **Business Phone:** (312)225-7224.

GREEN, BARBARA MARIE
Publisher, journalist. **Personal:** Born Mar 21, 1928, New York, NY; daughter of James and Mae McCarter. **Educ:** Hunter Col, New York, NY, BA, 1951; Syracuse Univ, grad study, 1955; City Col NY, New York, NY, MA, 1955; NY Univ, New York, NY, PhD, 1965-80. **Career:** New York City Bd Educ, New York, NY, teacher, jr high sch & high sch eng, prin, 1952-82; Creative Record, Va Beach, Va, owner, publisher, 1985-. **Orgs:** Pub rel, Nat Sorority Phi Delta Kappa, 1953-56; NY Block Asn; Queens adv bd, NY Urban League, 1965-85; nat bd mem, 1985-89, Nat Asn Negro Musicians, eastern region dir, 1989-91; Queens Borough Wide publicity chair, UNCF, 1986; Harpers Ferry Hist Soc, Va Poetry Soc; Princess Anne Business & Prof Womens Club, 1992-; African Am Biographics Hall Fame, Atlanta Ga, 1994; pres, State Public Rels, first vpres, corres sec; chair, Va Fed Bus & Prof Women's Club Inc; Alpha Kappa Alpha Sorority; Am Bus Women's Asn; Am Acad Poets; First Lynnhaven Baptist Church; instnl head, Cub Pack 400, Boy Scouts Am. **Honors/Awds:** Citation of Appreciation, Dedicated Service as a Volunteer, Associated Black Charities, 1985; Poetry Books, 1990; Certificate of Appreciation, Outstanding & Dedicated Service in Our Community, Arlene, New York, 1990; Love Pain Hope, anthology, 1993; More Poetic Thoughts; Poet Laureate-in-Residence, First Lynnhaven Baptist Church, VA Baptist Church, VA; Hall of Fame inductee, Hunter College Alumni Asn, 1997; Ageless Hero Citation, Blue Cross Blue Shield, 1998; Citation, Black History Month speaker, US Nat Guard, 1998. **Special Achievements:** Author: poetry, Love Pain Hope, 1990; More Poetic Thoughts, 1993; Dreams and Memories 1996; Spirit, 1997; Keeper of the Flame, 1997; radio show, Keeping It Real, WPMH-AM, Chesapeake, VA; Keynote speaker, Natl Comm Coll Observance Day, Houston Comm Coll, Houston, TX, 1998. **Home Addr:** 814 Poquoson Crossing, Chesapeake, VA 23320, **Home Phone:** (757)547-7440. **Business Addr:** Publisher, The Creative Record, PO Box 15442, Chesapeake, VA 23328.

GREEN, BERTRUM SCARBOROUGH. See GREEN, SCARBOROUGH.

GREEN, BRENDA KAY
Educator. **Personal:** Born Dec 7, 1947, Baton Rouge, LA; daughter of Lillian White George and Jackson Willis. **Educ:** Southern Univ, Baton Rouge, La, BS, 1969; Northwestern Univ, Evanston IL,Mass, attended 1973. **Career:** E Baton Rouge Parish Schs, Baton Rouge, LA, dean stud, 1969-. **Orgs:** Pres, Beta Alpha Chap, Zeta Phi Beta, 1968; Nat Educ Asn, 1969-; La EducAsn, 1969-72; Phi Delta Kappa, 1974-89; 3rd vpres, Mu Zeta Chap, Zeta PhiBeta, 1976-80; Nat Coun Negro Women, 1980-; La State dir, Zeta Phi BetaSorority Inc, 1980-88; First vpres, Mu Zeta Chap, Zeta Phi Beta, 1984-88;Nat Second vpres, Zeta Phi Beta Sorority Inc, 1988-92; chmn scholar, NatEduc Found, ZOB, 1988-92. **Honors/Awds:** Teacher of the Year, La Educ Asn, 1973, 1974; Outstanding Young Educ,Scotlandville, La Jaycees, 1974; Hon Dist Atty, E Baton Rouge Parish DistAtty's Off, 1983. **Business Addr:** Dean of Students, Broadmoor High School, 10100 Goodwood Blvd, Baton Rouge, LA 70815, **Business Phone:** (225)926-7663.

GREEN, DR. CALVIN COOLIDGE
Educator, clergy. **Personal:** Born Jul 19, 1931, Laneview, VA; son of James Herman and Consula Levallia Deleaver; married Ella Mary Osbourne; children: Robert Caesar, Carroll Anthony & Charles Conrad. **Educ:** Va State Col, Petersburg, BS, biol, 1956; NC A&T Col, Greensboro, NC, MS, chem, 1965; Grad Sch Med Col, Va, physiol, 1971; Va Union Univ, Sch Theol, MDiv, theol, 1982; Int Bible Inst & Sem, Orlando, ThD, coun, 1983; Nova Univ, Ft Lauderdale, FL, Ed D, 1987; Int Sem, PhD, 1990. **Career:** Pastor (retired); Downingtown Indust Sch, PA, sci teacher, 1956-57; Med Col Va, Heart Lung Proj, surgical lab tech, 1957-59; Armstrong High Sch, Richmond, sci teacher, 1959-62, prof mil sci, commandant cadets, 1963-69; Thomas Jefferson High Sch, Dept Head Sci, staff, 1969-76; Jefferson-Hugeunot-Wythe High Sch, Dept Sci Head, staff, 1976-80, chmn sci dept, 1980-85; Lebanon Baptist Church, New Kent, VA, pastor, 1977-82; Calvary Baptist Chruch, Saluda, VA, pastor, 1979-91; Thomas Jefferson High Sch, sci dept chmn, 1985-91; Mt Carmel Baptist Church, Richmond, VA, interim pastor, 1997, 2002; Church Comput Workshops, self employed consult. **Orgs:** Va Acad Sci Comn, 1981-85, 1996-99; chaplain, Dept Va ROA, 1983-88; gen bd, Baptist Genral Conv, VA, 1985-89; Nat Soc Study Educ, 1986-90; Phi Delta Kappa, 1988-. **Honors/Awds:** ROTC Hall of Fame, Va State Col, 1969-; Chaplain of Virginia, Dept of Res Officers Asn, ROA, 1984-88, 1990; honorarium & banquet by New Kent, Nat Asn Advan Colored People, 1989; Plaque from Professional Business Women's Organization, Middlesex & Victoria, 1989. **Special Achievements:** Chief plantiff US Supreme Court Decision, "Green v New Kent" 1968; Author, "Counseling, With the Pastor and CPE Stdnt in Mind," Vantage, 1984. **Military Serv:** Armed Forces Reserve, 1951-; enlisted service, 1951-53; Command & Gen Staff Col, adj fac, 1986; AUS, Med Serv, col, 23 yrs; Chaplain Corps, col, 10 yrs; USAR, officer; Korean War; Two Meritorious Service Awards, 1990; Occupation Medal (Japan); Korean Serv; Armed Serv. **Home Addr:** 5135 New Kent Hwy, Quinton, VA 23141-2519.

GREEN, DARLENE
Government official. **Personal:** Born in St Louis, MO. **Educ:** Wash Univ, BS, bus admin. **Career:** City St Louis, budget dir, comptroller, 1995-, chief fiscal officer, currently. **Orgs:** Zeta Phi Beta Sorority Inc; Nat Asn Black Accts; Nat Asn Advan Colored People; Govt Finance Officers Asn; Antioch Baptist Church;

metrop st.louis bd dirs & finance comt, YWCA; bd dirs, Employ Connection; St Louis Community Educ Task Force; Airport Comn; trustee, City Retirement Systs; Bd Estimate and Apportionment. **Honors/Awds:** Political Leadership Award, Young Dem St Louis City; Distinguished ServiceAward, Dr. Martin Luther King Jr State Celebration Comn, Miss; NatAchievement Award, Nat Asn Black Accts Inc; Lifetime Achievement Award,Gateway Classic Sports Found; Shining Star Award, Nat Orgn Black ElectedLegis Women; Achievement Award, Sister to Sister Expo; DistinguishedCommunity Service Award, Mound City Bar Asn; Community Service Award, St.Louis Dist Christian Methodist Episcopal Church Ministerial Alliance, 2003. **Special Achievements:** First African American female comptroller of St. Louis. **Business Addr:** Comptroller, Chief Fiscal Officer, City of St Louis, City Hall 1200 Market St Room 212, St Louis, MO 63103-2875.

GREEN, DARRELL
Football player, business owner. **Personal:** Born Feb 15, 1960, Houston, TX; married Jewell Fenner; children: Jarrel, Jarod & Joi. **Educ:** Tex A&M Univ; St Pauls Col, Lawrenceville, VA, BS, gen studies & social sci, DHumLitt, 2002; Marymount Univ, DHumLitt, 1999; George Wash Univ,DHumLitt, 2002. **Career:** Football player (retired), Business owner; Wash Redskins, cornerback,1983-2002; Darrell Green Enterprises, owner, currently; Intekras Inc,owner, currently; Trusted Solutions Group, owner, currently; Darrell GreenMortgage & Score Title & Escrow, owner, currently. **Orgs:** Spokesperson, Big Bros Big Sisters Am, DC Chap; hon chmn, Am Red Cross, Northern Va Chap; founder, Darrell Green Youth Life Found; founder, Darrell Green Youth Life Learning Ctr, 1993-; Baltimore-Washington 2012 Olympic Bid; Nat Football League Players Asn September 11th Relief Fund; Loudoun Educ Found; Wolf Trap Found; Wash Bd Trade; Marymount Univ; chair, Coun Service & Civic Participation. **Honors/Awds:** Lone Star Conference Defensive Player of the Year; NFL Defensive Rookie of the Year, Associated Press, 1983; Worlds Fastest Athlete, 1991; winner ofthe NFLs Fastest Man; True Value Man of the Year, 1996; Bart Starr Award,1996; Ken Houston Humanitarian Award, 1996; Redskins Player of the Year, 1998; Good Guy Award, Sporting News, 1999; Pro Football Hall of Fame, 2008. **Special Achievements:** Top 100 Athletes of the Century, The Sporting News, 2000; selected to serve as the Chair of President Bushs Council on Service and Civic Participation in 2003. **Business Addr:** Founder, Owner, Darrell Green Enterprises, 21515 Ridgetop Circle Suite 290, Sterling, VA 20166, **Business Phone:** (703)547-7903.*

GREEN, DARRYL LYNN
Manager. **Personal:** Born Sep 29, 1958, Ypsilanti, MI; son of Clarence and Eleanor; children: Robert Green. **Educ:** Cent Mich Univ, attended 1978; Comput Learning Ctr, cert completion, 1988. **Career:** Alcoa Aluminum, inspector, 1979-91; Packard Bell, proj mgr, 1991-. **Business Addr:** Manager, Packard Bell Electronics Inc, 8285 W 3500 S, Magna, UT 84044, **Business Phone:** (801)579-3054.

GREEN, DEBORAH KENNON
Lawyer. **Personal:** Born Aug 14, 1951, Knoxville, TN; daughter of George and Florence Jones; children: Joshua. **Educ:** Knoxville Col, BA, 1973; Georgetown Law Ctr, JD, 1976. **Career:** David N Niblack Wash DC, law clerk, atty, 1976-77; DC Govt Rental Accommodations Off, hearing examiner, 1977-78; Govt Oper Arrington Dixon, DC City Coun, comn clerk, 1978-79; Coun DC Off Arrington Dixon, leg asst to chmn, 1979-80; US Dept Labor, coun, Arlington, VA; Pvt Pract, currently. **Orgs:** County chmn, 7th Annual Conv Nat Asn Black Women Atty, 1978-; WV Bar Asn, 1979, WA Bar Asn, 1980, Alfred St Baptist Church, 1989. **Honors/ Awds:** Tuition Scholarship, Georgetown Law Ctr Wash DC, 1973-76; Earl Warren Legal Training Scholarship, 1973-74; Special Award of Merit, DC Bar, 1979; Meritorious Achievement Award, 1985, Federal Women's Program Award, 1990, Dept Labor; Exceptional Secretary Achievement Award, 1993. *

GREEN, DENNIS
Football coach, football player, executive. **Personal:** Born Feb 17, 1949, Harrisburg, PA; married Margie; children: Patty & Jeremy. **Educ:** Iowa State Univ, BA (cum laude), finance, 1971. **Career:** Football player (retired), football coach; British Columbia Lions Canadian Football League, starting tailback; Iowa State, grad asst, 1972, quarterbacks/receivers coach, 1974-76; Dayton, offensive backs/receivers coach, 1973; Stanford Univ, offensive coord, 1980, football coach, 1989; North western Univ, head coach, 1980-85; San Francisco 49ers, receivers coach, 1986-88; Stanford Cardinals, coach, 1992; Minnesota Vikings, head coach, 1992-2001; NFL Competition Comt, chair, 2000; ESPN, NFL analyst, 2002; Ariz Cardinals, head coach, 2004-06; Dennis Green Sports Mkt, currently; head coach, San Francisco franchise, 2009-. **Honors/Awds:** Big 10 Coach of the Year, 1982; NFC Coach of the Year, Col & Pro Football News Weekly, 1992; NFC Coach of the Year, United Press Int, 1992; NFL Coach of the Year, Wash Touchdown Club, 1992; Pop Warner's Golden Football Award, 1993; Pro Coach of the Year, Upper Midwest, Midwest Sports Channel, 1998; Coach of the Year, Sports Illus, 1998; Coach of the Year, Maxwell Club, 1998; Community Coach of the Year, World Sports Humanitarian Hall Fame, 2001. **Special Achievements:** Autobiography: No Room For Crybabies.

GREEN, DENNIS O.
Auditor, executive director. **Personal:** Born Nov 14, 1940, Detroit, MI; son of Arthur Salvador and Olive May Dean McCaughan; married Katherine F, Aug 12, 1961; children: Damon, Leslie. **Educ:** Wayne State Univ, BS, bus admin/finance, 1967; State Mich, CPA. **Career:** Arthur Andersen & Co, staff sr acct, 1967-69, audit mgr, 1971-73; Wells & Green Prof Corp, pres, 1969-71; City Detroit, finance dir, 1974-76; Off Mgmt & Budget Wash DC, assoc dir exec of the pres, 1977-78; Ford Motor Co, gen auditor, 1978-90; Citicorp, chief auditor, 1990-97; Citibank NA, chief auditor, 1990-97; Keiretsu Investments Inc, pres; Celadon, founder & managing partner, currently; Coastal Banking Co, vice chmn, currently; Allete, dir; Adesa Inc, dir, currently. **Orgs:** Inst Internal Auditors, 1984-; bd dir audit comt, Allete Inc, 2003-; Am Inst CPA's; Nat Asn Black Accountants; dir & pres, Olive Tree Found; dir & vpres, Boys & Girls Club Lowcountry; trustee, Beaufort Acad; Bd United Way Beaufort. **Business Addr:** Director, Adesa Inc, 13085 Hamilton Crossing Blvd, Carmel, IL 46032.*

GREEN, DEREK
Fashion designer. **Educ:** Art Inst, Philadelphia, degree, fashion illus; Parsons Sch Design, BA, fashion design. **Career:** Am Eagle Outfitters, head designer; Tommy Hilfiger, head designer; Derek Green Designs, founder & head designer, currently. **Business Addr:** Head Designer, Derek Green Designs, 350 Fifth Ave Suite 6603, New York, NY 10118, **Business Phone:** (212)273-3300.*

GREEN, EDDIE L.
School administrator, school superintendent. **Personal:** Born Mar 7, 1942, Houston, TX; son of Matthew and Mary Rose; married Jacqueline, Apr 5, 1969; children: Shelley, Bryce. **Educ:** Grambling State Univ, BS, 1963; Wayne State Univ, MEd, 1970, EdD, 1993. **Career:** Detroit Pub Schs, bus educ dept head, 1979-81, dir, prin, 1981-85, asst dir, 1985-89, area asst supt, 1989, area supt, 1989-97, interim dep supt, 1997, interim gen supt & dep supt, 1997-; Murray-Wright, supt, currently. **Orgs:** Pres, Mich Bus Educ Asn, 1967-; pres, Delta Pi Epsilon, 1975-; newsletter ed, Phi Delta Kappa, Detroit, 1980-; consult, NAPE, 1984; AASA, 1989-; MASA, 1989-; MASSP, 1989-; Detroit Pub Schs Ninth Grade Restructuring Prog, 1992; ASCD, 1996-; bd dir, Horizons-Upward Bound Cranbrook Kingswood Schs. **Honors/Awds:** Distinguished Serv Award, Mich Bus Educ Asn, 1981; Spirit Detroit Award, Detroit Pub Schs, 1982; Outstanding Serv Award, Detroit Pub Schs, 1982; Outstanding Trainee Consult, Nat Sch Vol Prog, 1984; Educr of the Year, Phi Delta Kappa, 1992. **Special Achievements:** The Effects of Mentoring on Selected Detroit Public Schools Students, 1993. **Military Serv:** AUS, spec-4, 1964-66; US Quartermaster Sch, Hon Grad. **Home Addr:** 3200 Cambridge Rd, Detroit, MI 48221, **Home Phone:** (313)861-9282. *

GREEN, ERNEST G.
Investment banker. **Personal:** Born Sep 22, 1941, Little Rock, AR; son of Ernest G Green Sr and Lothaire S; married Phyllis; children: Adam, Jessica, McKenzie Ann. **Educ:** Mich State Univ, BA, 1962, MA, 1964. **Career:** Adolph Inst, apprenticeship, 1965; A Philip Randolph Educ Fund, dir, 1968-76; US Labor Dept, asst secy labor, 1977-81; Green & Herman, partner, 1981-85; E Green & Assocs, owner, 1985-86; Lehman Brothers, investment banker, 1987, managing dir pub finance, currently. **Orgs:** Bd mem, Winrock Int; Omega Psi Phi; chmn, AfriCare; chmn, African Devel Found; chair, Nat Asn Securities Profs; Sigma Pi Phi; Nat Asn Advan Colored People. **Honors/Awds:** Rockefeller Public Service, Princeton Univ, 1976; Spingarn Award, Nat Asn Advan Colored People; Hon Doctorates, Tougaloo Col, 1979, Mich State Univ, 1994, Cent State Univ, 1996; Congressional Gold Medal. **Special Achievements:** Member of the Little Rock Nine. **Business Addr:** Managing Director, Lehman Brothers, 800 Connecticut Ave NW Suite 1200, Washington, DC 20006.*

GREEN, FORREST F.
Government official, executive. **Personal:** Born Feb 2, 1915, East Point, GA; married Mamie E Logan; children: Forrest, Jr, Saul A & Darryl L. **Educ:** Morehouse Col, BA, 1937; Wayne State Univ, MA, 1967. **Career:** Government official (retired); social worker, 1938-46; City Detroit, cityombudsman, bus exec, 1947-74; Mich Barber Sch Inc, pres & chief exec officer. **Orgs:** Int Bar Asn; Ombudsman & Adv Comn; Am Arbitration Asn; Int Personnel Mgt Asn; Greater C of C; Detroit Rotary Club; Detroit's Charter Revisn Comn,1970-73. **Honors/Awds:** State cert of hon MI Acad of Voltr Leadership, 1964; outstanding Cit Award, Detroit Urban League, 1965; Cert for Serv to Youth, Wayne Univ,1968; Liberty Bell Award, Detroit Bar Assn, 1969. **Special Achievements:** First black member, Michigan Civil Service Commission, 1961-68; First black member, Detroit Parks & Recreation Commission, 1962-69. **Business Addr:** Founder, Michigan Barber School Inc, 8988 90 Grand River Ave, Detroit, MI 48204-2244.*

GREEN, DR. FREDERICK CHAPMAN
Physician, pediatrician. **Personal:** Born Oct 7, 1920, Fort Wayne, IN; son of Oliver (deceased) and Luretta M Rhodes (deceased); married Lucille Ingram, Jun 20, 1947; children: Frederick C & Sharman L. **Educ:** Ind Univ, BS, 1942; Ind Univ Sch Med, MD, 1944; Harlem Hosp New York City, internship & residency, 1947. **Career:** New York City, pvt practice pediatrician, 1947-67; AUS Hosp, Ft Devene, MA, chief pediatrician, 1951-53; Sydenham Hosp NY, dir pediatrics, 1961-71; Pediatric Ambulatory Care Roosevelt Hosp NY, dir, 1967-71; US CBureau DHEW, assoc chief, 1971-73; C Hosp Nat Med Ctr, assoc dir; Child Health Advocay C Hosp Nat Med Ctr, dir officer; Child Health & Develop George Wash Univ Sch Med & Health Sci, prof; US Nat Comn Int Yr Child, comnr, 1979; George Wash Univ Sch Med, asst dean prog planning, prof emer child health develop; pvt pract, physician, currently. **Orgs:** Chmn, Mayor Marion Barry's Interagncy & Interdepartmental Com Child Abuse & Neglect; chmn, Mayor Marion Barry's Blue Ribbon Com Infant Mortality Wash DC; bd dirs, UNICEF Am Humane Asn Nat Com Citizens Educ; pres, Nat Comn Prevention Child Abuse. **Honors/Awds:** Job Lewis Smith Award; Am Acad ped, 1975; distinguished black am fellow Phelps-Stokes Fund, 1975-76; guest ed, Ped Annuals, 1979; pres medal for distinguished comm serv The Catholic Univ of Am & Madison Nat Bank, 1979; Hildrus Poindexter Award, Am Pub Health Asn Black Caucus, 1983; Washingtonian of the Year, Washingtonian Mag, 1984; Martha M Elliot Award, Maternal & Child Health: Am Pub Health Asn, 1989. **Military Serv:** AUS, Capt. **Business Addr:** Physician, 10595 N Tatum Blvd Suite E1, Paradise Valley, AZ 85253, **Business Phone:** (602)954-7714.*

GREEN, GEORGIA MAE
Lawyer. **Personal:** Born Apr 15, 1950, Knoxville, TN; daughter of George Edward (deceased) and Florence Jones (deceased). **Educ:** Knoxville Col, BA, 1972; Howard Univ, Sch Law, Wash, DC, JD, 1976. **Career:** Dept Corrections, atty. **Orgs:** WVa Bar Asn, 1979-; conv co-chmn, Nat Asn Black Women Atty, 1980-; first vpres, Am Fed Govt Employees Local 1550, DC Dept Corrections Union, 1984; DC Bar Asn, 1985-. **Honors/Awds:** WVa Ambassador of Good Will Among All People, WVa Secy State, 1979. **Business Addr:** Attorney, District Of Columbia, 1923 Vermont Ave NW, Washington, DC 20001.*

GREEN, GERALDINE D.
Lawyer. **Personal:** Born Jul 14, 1938, New York, NY; daughter of Edward and Lula. **Educ:** City Col NY Baruch Sch Bus, BBA, 1964; St John's Univ Law Sch, JD, 1968. **Career:** Coopers & Lybrand CPA's, tax acct, 1966-68; IBM Corp, staff atty, 1968-72; Atlantic Richfield Co, sr atty asst corp secy, 1972-80; Calif State Bar Comn Corp, 1974-76; CA Corp Comnr, 1980-83; Rosenfeld Meyer & Susman, partner, 1983-85; Burke, Robinson & Pearman, atty coun, 1985-86; Law Off Geraldine D Green, 1987-99; LA Traffic Comn, comnr; Bus Law & Fin, Dillard Univ, Fla Mem Col, visiting prof; Green Mgt Consults, pres, 1999-01; Asn Advan Disabled Am, exec dir, 2001-03; Disabled Am Inc, exec dir, 2003-. **Orgs:** Pres, Beverly Hills/Hollywood Br Nat Asn Advan Colored People, 1979-82; spec coun, LA Urban League; Youth Motivation Task Force. **Honors/Awds:** Community Serv Award, LA Urban League, 1973; Freedom Award Cit, Nat Asn Advan Colored People, 1973; YWCA Cert of Achievement, 1976; Cert of Appreciation, City Los Angeles, 1981; Certificate of Appreciation, CA State Senate, 1984; Geraldine D Green Day in City of Los Angeles, 1984; Certificate of Achievement, CA State Legis, 1986. **Business Addr:** Attorney, Private Practice, 500 Shatto Pl Suite 630, Los Angeles, CA 90020-1707, **Business Phone:** (213)365-0559.*

GREEN, GLORIA J
Lawyer. **Personal:** Born Dec 8, 1954, Atlanta, GA; daughter of Alfred Sr and Mattie; divorced; children: Avery Dyan Kelley & Jennifer Green. **Educ:** Duke Univ, Durham, NC, BA, 1976; Georgetown Univ Law Ctr, Wash, DC, Juris Doctor, 1979. **Career:** Securities & Exchange Comn, Wash, DC, from atty to sr atty, 1979-86; Fed Home Loan Bank Atlanta, Atlanta, GA, vpres, dep gen coun, & dir legal servs, 1986-96; Atlanta Housing Authority, dep gen coun & chief legal off, 1998-. **Orgs:** Bd dirs, Wesley Community Ctrs, 1988-93; bd dirs, South DeKalb Young Men Christian Asn, 1990-; bd dirs, DC Express Track Club, 1990-; trustee, Kelley's Chapel United Methodist Church, 1990-; Nat Coalition 100 Black Women, 1989-93. **Honors/Awds:** Leadership Award, Partners With Youth, South Dakalb Young Men Christian Asn, 1992; Service Award, DC Express Track Club Inc, 1991-98. **Special Achievements:** PTSA President (two terms). **Business Addr:** General Counsel, Chief Legal Officer, Housing Authority of the City of Atlanta, 230 John Wesley Dobbs Ave NE, Atlanta, GA 30303, **Business Phone:** (404)817-7293.

GREEN, HAROLD
Football player, businessperson. **Personal:** Born Jan 29, 1968, Sacramento, CA; son of Harold Sr. **Educ:** SC Univ, retail sales, 1989. **Career:** Football player (retired), Businessperson; Cincinnati Bengals, running back, 1990-95; St Louis Rams, 1996; Atlanta Falcons, 1997-98; Pro Bowl Motors, partner, currently. **Honors/Awds:** Heisman Trophy winner; Athletic Hall of Fame, Univ SC, 2002. **Business Phone:** (803)251-0301.

GREEN, HUGH
Football player, business owner, football coach. **Personal:** Born Jul 27, 1959, Natchez, MS. **Educ:** Univ Pittsburgh, attended 1980. **Career:** Football player (retired), Football coach, Business owner; Tampa Bay Buccaneers, linebacker, 1981-85; Miami Dolphins, linebacker, 1985-91; Barcelona Dragons, Nat Football League

Europe, asst defensive coach, 2003; Luxury Car Rental Co, Las Vegas, owner, currently. **Honors/Awds:** Player of the Year, Touch down Clubs, Cleveland, Columbus, & Wash; first team All-Am, 1978; All-time All-Am team, Sporting News; Walter Camp Award; Lombardi Award, 1980; National Player of the Year Awards, 1980; Best Defensive Player, NY Times; Hula Bowl; Japan Bowl; first team All-Pro, The Sporting News, Sports Illustrated & Football Digest; Most Valuable Player, All-Pro & St Petersburg Times Buc; Pro Bowl, 1982, 1983; College Football Hall of Fame, 1996; Pro Football Hall of Fame, 1998.

GREEN, HYDIA LUTRICE
Banker. **Personal:** Born Dec 24, 1963, New Orleans, LA; daughter of Jimmie Lee and Mertis Marie Flanders; married. **Educ:** La State Univ, Baton Rouge, LA, BS, Mgt. **Career:** First Union Nat Bank, asst branch mgr; County Savings Bank, Columbus, Ohio, dir mkt; Corporate One Inc, staff, currently. **Orgs:** Chamber Com, 1988-; Civitan, 1989-, Sertoma, 1989-; third vpres, Zeta Phi Beta Sorority Inc, 1982-; Proj Bus Inst, jr achievement, 1989-. **Honors/Awds:** Outstanding Young Women Am, 1987; Nat Collegiate Greek Merit Award, 1987; Zeta of the Year, Zeta Phi Beta Sorority Inc, 1986. **Home Addr:** 6621 Pauline Dr, New Orleans, LA 70126-1040, **Home Phone:** (904)645-9053. **Business Addr:** Staff, Corporate One Inc, 12 Werville Sq Suite 352, Westerville, OH 43081-2919, **Business Phone:** (740)965-8225.

GREEN, JACQUEZ
Football player, football coach. **Personal:** Born Jan 15, 1976, Fort Valley, GA. **Educ:** Univ Fla. **Career:** Football player (retired), Football coach; Tampa Bay Buccaneers, punt hunter, 1998-2001; Wash Redskins, punt hunter, 2002; Detroit Lions, wide receiver, 2002; Gibbs High Sch, offensive coordr, currently. **Honors/Awds:** Rookie of the year, 1998. Knoxville News-Sentinel SEC All-Freshmen Team. **Special Achievements:** An avid video game player, who once won the annual Madden Bowl in back-to-back seasons. **Business Addr:** Offensive Coordinator, Gibbs Senior High School, 850 34th St S, St Petersburg, FL 33711-2297, **Business Phone:** (727)893-5452.

GREEN, JAMES
Basketball coach. **Career:** Univ Idaho, asst coach, 1988-90; Texas A&M Univ, Col Sta, asst coach, 1990-92; Alab Univ, asst coach, 1992-94; Iowa State Univ, asst coach, 1994-96; Univ Southern Miss, head basketball coach, 1996-2004; Miss Valley State Univ, head men's basketball coach, 2005-08; Jacksonville State Univ, head coach, 2008-. **Special Achievements:** First African American head basketball coach at University of Southern Mississippi; First African-American Head Coach of a Major Sport at Jacksonville State University. **Business Addr:** Head Basketball Coach, Jacksonville State University, 700 Pelham Rd N, Jacksonville, AL 36265, **Business Phone:** (256)782-5535.

GREEN, DR. JAMES L
Physician. **Personal:** Born Feb 2, 1945, Hampton, VA; son of James; children: Timothy B & Jenifer L. **Educ:** Hampton Inst, BA, 1967; Meharry Med Col, MD, 1973. **Career:** Hubbard Hosp, intern, 1973-74, resident, 1975-77; VA Hosp, Tuskegee, AL, chief retina sect, 1978-79; Univ Ill, asst prof clin ophthal, 1980-; Univ Ill, fel vitreous surg, 1979-81, asst prof ophthal, 1980-; Michael Reese Hosp & Med Ctr, attending surgeon, 1981-; Retinal Vitreal Consults; Mercy Hosp & Med Ctr, chief retina serv, 1986-; Univ Chicago, IL, clin assoc prof, currently. **Orgs:** Fel, Am Acad Opthal, 1979-; Am Bd Opthal, 1979-; NMA; Chicago Opthal Soc; Ill Asn Ophthal. **Honors/Awds:** Rowe Award in Ophthalmology, 1973; Merk Award 1973. **Special Achievements:** 8 publications. **Business Addr:** Clinical Associate professor, University of Chicago, Deparment of Ophthalmology & Visual Science, 2525 S Mich Ave, Chicago, IL 60637, **Business Phone:** (773)702-3937.

GREEN, JARVIS R
Executive, accountant. **Personal:** Born Feb 20, 1953, Tuskegee, AL; son of Jerry Green and Johnnie Lewis; married Desiree E; children: Kawanna. **Educ:** Ala A&M univ, BS, 1976. **Career:** Brandon, Smith & Jones CPA Firm, sr acct; Atlanta Minority Bus Develop, construct acct; Atlanta Housing Authority, progs mgr; AGE Indust, exec vpres; AGE Enterprises, Ltd, vpres, currently. **Orgs:** Fin secy, 100 Black Men Dekalb; finance & finance comn, Omega Psi Phi Fraternity; Dekalb Chamber Com; Geo Minority Supplier Div Coun; Better Bus Bur; US Chamber Com. **Honors/ Awds:** Certificate of Apppreciation, Christmas July Com; State Small Business of the Year Candidate, US Bus Acad.

GREEN, JOHN M.
Historian. **Personal:** Born May 11, 1932, Lawton, OK; son of Johnny M and Jannie McClanahan; married Melanie; children: John M, Tiffny E. **Educ:** Lincoln Univ, attended 1953; Wayne State Univ, BA, 1977. **Career:** Santa Fe Railroad, chair car, 1954-55; State of Mich, meter vehicle oper, 1956-64; Automobile Club of Mich, supvr-legal, 1964-80; Hist Res Repository Inc, exec dir, currently. **Orgs:** Alpha Phi Alpha, dean of pledges, 1953; Financial Forum, 1966; historian, Museum of African Am Hist, 1984-86; bd mem, AAA Housing & Transport Trust, 1985-; historian, African Am Sports Hall of Fame, 1992-94; Founding Comt & Retired Int Underground Railroad Monument Collaborative, 1999-. **Honors/Awds:** Senate Res, Mich Legis, 1968; House Res, 1987; Resolution, Wayne County, MI, 1988; Senate, Mich Legis, 1990. **Special Achievements:** Negroes in Michigan History, 1968, 3rd reprint, 1985; Black Nobel Prize Winners, poster, 1985; International Black Nobel Prize Winners, poster, 1994; African Historical Tins; Cake Walk, Come Join Us Bro, Henry O Flipper, 1993-94. **Military Serv:** AUS, spec-4, 1956-58, adjutant gen sect; Suggestion Award, 1957, 1960. **Business Addr:** Executive Director, Historical Research Repository Inc, PO Box 15364 Fox Creek Station, Detroit, MI 48215-0364, **Business Phone:** (313)822-9027.*

GREEN, JONATHAN
Artist. **Personal:** Born Aug 9, 1955, Gardens Corner, SC; son of Melvin and Ruth J. **Educ:** Sch Art Inst Chicago, BFA, 1982; Univ SC, hon doctoral degree, 1996. **Career:** Jonathan Green Art Collection LLC, pres & dir, 1985-; Works: Bathing, Norton Gallery, 1990; Silver Slipper Club, Morris Mus Art, 1990; Christening, Greenville Mus Art, 1991; Corene, Gibbes Mus Art, 1995; Vessels, McKissick Mus, 1998; Personal Treasures of Bernard & Shirley Kinsey, Calif African Am Mus, Los Angeles, CA, 2006. **Orgs:** Comn mem, Chicago Acad Arts, 1990-95; vpres, Colier County United Arts Coun, 1992-94; comm mem, Share Our Strength, 1993-95; chmn, Nat Adv Coun, Afr Am Res Libr & Cult Ctr, 2002-; Mus Am Folk Art, 2000-03; bd visitors, Col Arts & Sci, Howard Univ, 2003-. **Honors/Awds:** Martin Luther King Jr Humanitarian Award, City Beaufort, 1993; Alberta G Peacock Award, 1996; Clememte C Pickney Award, SC House Reps, 1997; Certificate of Honor, City Portland, 1998; Order of the Palmeto Award, Columbia, SC, 2002; History Makers Award, Chicago, IL, 2002; Century of Achievement Award, Mus Am, 2003; Man of Distinction Award, Educ Found Collier County, 2003; Honorary Chair, Sch Art Inst Bare Walls, 2003. **Business Addr:** Director, President, Jonathan Green Art Collection LLC, 470 Bayfront Pl, Naples, FL 34102-6454, **Business Phone:** (239)261-9994.

GREEN, LARRY A
Administrator, consultant. **Personal:** Born Jul 22, 1952, Canton, GA; son of Jimmie Edwards and Cornelius Green; married Doris, Nov 15, 1993. **Educ:** Georgia State Univ attended 1974. **Career:** A&M Records, nat prom dir, 1974-80; MCA Records, midwest regional mgr, 1980-85; Whilfield Assoc, consult, 1988-91; Chrysalis Records, midwest regional mgr, 1985-88; Winston & Green, vpres, 1991-. **Orgs:** Bd mem, Chicago Youth Ctrs, 1992-96; 100 Black Men Chicago, 1998-; bd mem, Chicago Area Coun Boy Scouts, 1995; bd mem, LaSalle Street Cycle, 1998-; bd mem, Goodman Theatre Discovery, 2000-; St Chrysostoms Church, euchartic minister. **Honors/Awds:** Promotion Man of the Year, Pop Music Survey, 1979; Appreciation Award, Chicago Youth Ctr, 1993. **Business Addr:** Vice President, Winston & Green, 111 W Washington St, Chicago, IL 60602, **Business Phone:** (312)201-9777.

GREEN, LEE
Planner. **Career:** Lee Green Fin Planning, fin planner, currently. **Business Addr:** Financial Planner, Lee Green Financial Planning, 3011 W Grand Blvd Suite 2402, Detroit, MI 48202, **Business Phone:** (313)870-1000.

GREEN, LESTER L.
Electrical engineer, executive. **Personal:** Born Jun 27, 1941, Lynchburg, VA; married Lucille Withers. **Educ:** Howard Univ Sch Archit & Engr, Wash, DC, attended 1966; BSEE, 1966. **Career:** Am Tel & Tel Co, Silver Spring, MD, transmsn man, 1964-65; Elect Switching Syst Western Elect Co, proj engr, 1966-; Comm Commun Res Inc, pres, 1973-. **Orgs:** Chmn bd dir, Community Commun Syst, Baltimore 1970-; chmn, Cablecommunication Task Force Develop Reg Learning Ctr, Morgan State Col, Baltimore, 1973-74; indust mem rep, WE Co Howard Univ Cluster; Soc Cable TV Engr; Inst Elect & Electronic Engrs; Alpha Phi Alpha Frat; Urban Reg Learning Ctr Policy Bd; exec bd, NW Baltimore Corp; charter mem, Pk Heights Comm Corp, Baltimore; charter mem & vpres, Beacon Hill Tenants Asn, Baltimore; charter mem, Oxford Manor Tenants Asn, Wash, DC. **Honors/Awds:** Citizenship & Leadership Award, Howard Univ, 1961; Cost Reduction Award, WE Co, 1974. **Special Achievements:** Author: The Design and Economics of an Urban Cable & Distrbution Systens, 1973. **Home Addr:** 737 Stoney Spring Dr, Baltimore, MD 21210.

GREEN, LILLER
School administrator. **Personal:** Born Dec 1, 1928, Atlanta, GA; daughter of Walter and Henrietta; married William Clarence; children: Pamela A & Jan A. **Educ:** Morgan State Univ, BA, 1951; Bryn Mawr Col, MSW, 1953. **Career:** C Adolescents, Psychiatric Clinic, dir social work, 1957-59; Child Study Ctr, dir social work, 1959-60; Bryn Mawr Col, field instr, consult, 1963-65; Ivy Leaf Sch, dir, founder, 1965-2008. **Orgs:** Grace Baptist Ch; golden life mem, Delta Sigma Theta; life mem, Nat Advan Asn Colored People; bd dir, YWCA, 1983-85; Elem Educ Study Group, 1985-86. **Honors/Awds:** Eliza Jane Cummings Award, Morgan State Univ, 1951; Richard Allen Award, Community Serv Mother Bethel AME, 1982; Zeta Outstanding Woman of the Year, Beta Delta Zeta, 1983; Citizen of the Year, Omega Psi Phi, 1985; Community Service Award, Nat Advan Asn Colored People, 1990; Minority Enterprise Special Achievement Award, 1991; Outstanding Alumna Award, Morgan State Univ, 1991; Sadie T Alexander Community Service Award, Delta Sigma Theta, 1991; Bryn Mawr College Community Service Award, Black Alumnae Coordinating Comn Grad Sch Social Work & Social Res, 1992; Education of the Year Award, Philadelphia Chap Nat MBA Asn, 1992; National Kwanzaa Award, Philadelphia area, Kujichagulia, 1994; Excellence in Education Award, Phila Coun Clergy, Presented MLK Memorial Serv, 1995. *

GREEN, LISA A
Law enforcement officer. **Personal:** Born in Charleston, SC; daughter of Edward Jr and Mary LM (deceased). **Educ:** Claflin Univ, BA, 1986. **Career:** Charleston City Sheriff's Off, training coordr sgt, 1997-99, Patrol Div, lt, 1999-. **Orgs:** Palmetto State Law Enforcement Officers Asn; SC Law Enforcement Officers Asn; Nat Orgn Black Law Enforcement Officers. **Honors/Awds:** Albert T Leppert Memorial Award, Civitan Int, 1997. **Special Achievements:** First African American Female Lieutenant in Charleston Cty Sheriff's Office, 1996. **Business Addr:** Lieutenant, Charleston County Sheriff, Training Division Coordinator, 3505 Pinehaven Dr, Charleston, SC 29405, **Business Phone:** (803)554-4700.*

GREEN, LISA R.
Journalist, vice president (organization). **Personal:** Born Nov 2, 1964, Evanston, IL; daughter of Rev Albert W (deceased) and Elease W. **Educ:** Eastern Ill Univ, jour, 1986. **Career:** Rockford Regist Star, reporter, 1986-90, asst city ed, 1990-91, city ed, 1991-93, asst bus ed, 1993, bus editor, currently; Zion Gazette, ed, 1997; NBC Int Ltd, NBC News Channel Inc, NY, sr producer broadcast stand, NBC broadcast stand exec; vpres stand & practices, currently; attorney, currently. **Orgs:** Nat Asn Black Journalists, 1988-; big sister, Big Brother/Big Sister Prog, 1992-97; YMCA-Booker, Wash Ctr, Black Achievers Steering Comt, 1993-98; New Zion Missionary Baptist Church; Salter Ensemble; Am Soc Newspaper Ed. **Honors/Awds:** Black Achievers, Black Achiever of the Year, 1994; Gannett Midwest Newspaper Group, 1994; ed mem, Unity 94 Journalist Conv, Atlanta. **Business Addr:** Vice President, NBC International Limited, NBC News, 30 Rockefeller Plaza, New York, NY 10112-0002.*

GREEN, LITTERIAL
Basketball player, basketball coach, basketball executive. **Personal:** Born Mar 7, 1970. **Educ:** Univ Ga. **Career:** Basketball player (retired), basketball coach, basketball executive; Orlando Magic, 1992-94; Detroit Pistons, 1997; Milwaukee Bucks, 1998; Cleveland Cavaliers, 1999; St Louis Steamers, head coach; Chattanooga Steamers, head coach, 2005; Comcast Sports, color analyst; Pract with Pros Basketball Camps, founder; St Basketball Asn, Junior SBA, Youth Basketball & Camps/Clinics, dir, currently. **Honors/Awds:** Coach of the Year, World Basketball Asn, 2004. **Business Addr:** Director of Junior SBA, Youth Basketball & Camps/Clinics, Street Basketball Association LLC, 12138 Cent Ave Suite 390, Mitchellville, MD 20721.

GREEN, OLIVER WINSLOW
Labor activist, vice president (organization), army officer. **Personal:** Born Aug 18, 1930, Baltimore, MD; son of William S and Ethel I Gray; married Loraine E Johnson, Sep 7, 1951; children: Oliver W Jr, Michael G. **Educ:** Morgan State Univ, Baltimore, MD. **Career:** Vice President (retired). Baltimore Tansit Co, Baltimore MD, operator, 1953-69; Mass Transit Admin, Baltimore MD, operator, 1969-70; Amalgamated Transit Union, Baltimore MD, financial sec, 1970-75, Wash DC, vpres. **Orgs:** Bd mem, United Way Cent Md, 1972-75, Pres's Comn Employment, 1985-; mem operating comn, A Philip Randolph Inst, 1985-; pres, 43/44 Dem Club, 1986-; founding mem, Nat Asn Black Accountants; steering comt, secy treas conf, AFL-CIO; chair, comt polit educ, ATU. **Military Serv:** AUS, staff sergeant, 1951-53. *

GREEN, PHA M
Business owner, entrepreneur. **Personal:** Born Feb 10, 1939, Monroe, LA; son of Marteal and Willie; married Joan Turner, Dec 21, 1990. **Educ:** Prairie View A & M Univ, indust arts, 1958. **Career:** Pha Green Printing Inc, pres & owner, currently. **Business Addr:** President, Owner, Pha Green Printing Inc, 4403 Akard St, Houston, TX 77047, **Business Phone:** (713)734-1251.

GREEN, REUBEN H.
Clergy, educator. **Personal:** Born Jun 14, 1934, Wright City, OK; son of Mack Crawford and Idella Clark (deceased); married Mildred Denby; children: Reuben H, Howard D. **Educ:** Bishop Col, BA, 1955; Oberlin Grad Sch Theo, BD, 1959; Iliff Sch Theol, STM, 1969; Vanderbilt Univ Div Sch, DMin, 1973. **Career:** Control Bapt Ch Inc, minister, 1968-; Lemoyne-Owen Col, assoc prof, 1968, prof, currently, chaplain, 1974-; Bells Chap Bapt Ch, pastor, 1964-68; OT OK Sch Religion, dean studs instr. **Orgs:** Omega Psi Frat; Knights Pythians; Prince Hall A F&M; past vpres, Memphis Br, Nat Asn Advan Colored People; dean, Memphis SS & BTU Cong; Tenn Leadership Educ Cong; dean, Tenn Bapt Sch Rel. **Business Addr:** Chaplain, Lemoyne-Owen College, Department Fine Arts & Humanities, 807 Walker Ave, Memphis, TN 38126.*

GREEN, RICHARD CARTER
Physician. **Personal:** Born Oct 28, 1947, Brooklyn, NY; married Florence Elayne Parson; children: Damani Saeed Tale, Taiesha

Tene Tale, Khalid Abdu Tale. **Educ:** Central State Univ, BA, 1969; Wright State Univ, MS, 1983. **Career:** Montgomery County Juvenile Court, probation officer, 1969-70; US Army 1st Lt Infantry, instructor of offensive tactics, 1970-72; Montgomery Co Juvenile Court, probation counselor, 1972-73; Tale Retail and Wholesale Co, owner, 1985-; Nicholas Residential Treatment Ctr, family resource counr, 1973-. **Orgs:** Omega Psi Phi Frat Inc, 1966-; Greater Dayton Jaycees, 1972; Nguzo Saba Family Educ and Unity Club, 1980-; master mason Prince Hall Free Masonry-Ancient Square Lodge 40, 1982-; lecturer Child Discipline and Residential Treatment, 1984-; fellow Menninger Foundation, 1985. **Honors/Awds:** Certificate of Participation, seminary Adolescence Menninger Found, 1978; Outstanding Young Men of Am, US Jaycees, 1980; Comput Today & comput Literacy Sinclair Comt Col & Comput Tech, 1983; Gerontological Counseling Wright State Univ, 1985; Licensed Professional Counselor, OH Counr and Social Worker Bd, 1985. **Military Serv:** AUS Infantry 1st lt 1970-71; Nat Defense Serv Medal 1970, Master Tactician AUS Infantry Sch, 1971. **Home Addr:** 811 Neal Ave, Dayton, OH 45406. **Business Addr:** Family Resource Counselor, nicholas residential treatment center, 5581 Dayton Liberty Rd, Dayton, OH 45418, **Business Phone:** (513)496-7109.*

GREEN, RICKEY
Basketball player. **Personal:** Born Aug 18, 1954, Chicago, IL; married; children: Kandyce. **Educ:** Vincennes Univ, Vincennes, attended 1973; Univ Mich, Ann Arbor, attended 1975. **Career:** Basketball Player (retired); Golden State Warriors, 1977-78; Detroit Pistons, 1978-79; Hawaii, 1979-80; Billings Volcanos, 1980-81; Utah Jazz, 1980-88; Charlotte Hornets, 1988-89; Milwaukee Bucks, 1988-89; Ind Pacers, 1989-90; Philadelphia 76ers, 1990-91; Boston Celtics, 1991-92. **Honors/Awds:** Leader in steels, NBA, 1984; NBA All-Star Game, 1984; inductee, Univ Mich Athletic Hall of Honor, 1984.

GREEN, ROBERT DAVID
Football player. **Personal:** Born Sep 10, 1970, Washington, DC. **Educ:** Col William & Mary. **Career:** Football player (retired); Washington Redskins, running back, 1992; Chicago Bears, 1993-96; Minnesota Vikings, 1997.

GREEN, ROBERT LEE
Association executive, educator. **Personal:** Born Nov 23, 1933, Detroit, MI; son of Thomas and Alberta; married Lettie Cornelius, Aug 10, 1956; children: Robert, Melvin & Kurt. **Educ:** San Francisco State Col, BA, 1958, MA, 1960; Mich State Univ, PhD, 1963. **Career:** Southern Christian Leadership Conf, educ dir, 1965-66; USOE Grant Chicago Adult Educ Proj, Southern Christian Leadership Conf, dir, 1967; Ctr Urban Affairs, dir; Mich State Univ, prof, 1968-73, Col Urban Develop, dean, 1973; NCJW Ctr Res Educ Disadvantages, Hebrew Univ, Jerusalem, vis lectr, 1971; Univ DC, former pres; Univ Nairobi, Kenya, 1971; Cuyahoga Community Col, Ctr Urban Educ, dir, currently; Mich State Univ, Urban Affairs Prog, prof & dean, prof emer & dean emer, currently. **Orgs:** Am Psychol Asn; Am Asn Black Psychologists; Am Res Asn; bd dirs, Martin Luther King Jr Ctr Nonviolent Social Change; Phi Kappa Phi Nat Hon Soc. **Honors/Awds:** InterNat Ghandi-King-Ikeda Award, Morehouse Col, Atlanta, Ga, 2002. **Special Achievements:** Author of several books, including The Urban Challenge: Poverty & Race & Metropolitan Desegregation; Expectations: How Teacher Expectations Can Increase Student Achievement, 2000. **Military Serv:** AUS, 1954-56. **Business Addr:** Professor Emeritus, Dean Emeritus, Michigan State University, University Outreach and Engagement, Kellogg Ctr Garden Level, East Lansing, MI 48824-1022, **Business Phone:** (517)353-8977.

GREEN, ROY
Football player, television show host. **Personal:** Born Jun 30, 1957, Magnolia, AR. **Educ:** Henderson State Univ. **Career:** Football player (retired); St Louis Cardinals, defensive back, 1979-80, wide receiver, 1981-87; Phoenix Cardinals, 1988-90; Cleveland Browns,1991; Philadelphia Eagles, wide receiver, 1991-92; KXAM, co-host, currently. **Honors/Awds:** Sporting News NFC All-Star Team, 1979, 1983, 1984; Pro Bowl, 1983, 1984; Hall of Honor, Henderson State Univ, 1997;Gold Ribbon Award for Best Community Service, Canadian Association of Broadcasters; Gold Ribbon Award for Best News, Public Affairs and Documentaries, Canadian Association of Broadcasters. **Special Achievements:** First NFL player to start both ways including wide receiver & defensive back in 21 years. **Business Phone:** (480)423-1310.

GREEN, RUTH A.
Administrator. **Personal:** Born Feb 2, 1917, Oklahoma; widowed. **Educ:** BS, 1936. **Career:** Social worker, Probation officer; Step Parent Adoption; Social Serv, dir; Sr Citizens Preventive Health Care Serv Elderly Minority, clin adminr. **Orgs:** Past coun Youth, Free Clinics Vol; appreciated bd dir, Pres Nixon to Small Bus Bur San Diego; past reg pres, Calig Probation & Parole Asn; bd supervisors charter, Rev Comt; past pres, Nat Asn Advan Colored People; second vpres, Urban League; past grand sec Charity; Order Eastern Star; orgn San Diego Chap, The Links Inc; founder, Civic Orgn Women Inc; Housing Adv Bd; All prof jobs San Diego Pres Comn Hosp San Diego Aux, 1973-74; Gov Calif intergovernmental Rels Coun & Calif St Community Aging, 1974-75. **Honors/Awds:** Service Awards, YMCA, NAACP, Bus & Prof Womens Clubs; Probation Officer of Year Award, 1971. **Home Addr:** 5415 Bonita Dr, San Diego, CA 92114.

GREEN, SAUL A.
Consultant, lawyer. **Personal:** Born 1947; married; children: 1. **Educ:** Univ Mich, BA, 1969; Univ Mich Law Sch, JD, 1972. **Career:** US Atty's Off, asst, 1973-76; Wayne County, corp coun, 1989; Atty Off, Eastern Dist Mich, US atty, 1994-; Minority Bus Group, former leader, 2001-04; Univ Mich Law Sch, adj prof, 2002-; Miller, Canfield, Paddock &Stone PLC, prin, 2001-, sr coun, currently. **Orgs:** Sixth Circuit Judicial Conf; NAACP; Am Bar Asn, 1973-; Open Justice Comn, 1998-; pres, Univ Mich Alumni Asn, 2001-03; Public Interest/Public Service Faculty Fellow, 2009-10. **Honors/Awds:** Champion of Justice Award, 1999; Wade Hampton McCree Jr Award, 2002; Name done of Michigan Most Powerful African-American Leaders, Corp Mag, 2003. Trailblazer Recipient, 2005. **Special Achievements:** First African American to hold post of US Attorney in Detroit; Top federal prosecutor in the Eastern district of Michigan; The Best Lawyers in America, Listed in the Criminal Defense Law Sect, 2005-06, 2006. **Business Phone:** (313)496-7535.

GREEN, SCARBOROUGH (BERTRUM SCARBOROUGH GREEN)
Baseball player. **Personal:** Born Jun 9, 1974, Creve Coeur, MO. **Career:** St Louis Cardinals, outfielder, 1997; Texas Rangers, 1999-2000; Kansas City Royals, outfielder; Howard Payne Univ, Wide receivers Coach, currently. *

GREEN, SEAN CURTIS
Basketball player, athletic trainer, executive. **Personal:** Born Feb 2, 1970, Santa Monica, CA. **Educ:** NC State Univ; Iona Col, BA, commun. **Career:** Ind Pacers, guard, 1992-93; Philadelphia 76ers, 1994; Utah Jazz, 1994; Puerto La Cruz, Venezuela, 1994, 1997; Jerusalem, israel, 1995; Milano, Italy, 1996; Napoli, Italy, 1997; Manila, Philippines, 1997, 2000; Turkey, Istanbul, 1998-2000; France, Dijon, 2001; Guanare, Venezuela, 2002; trainer, 2000-; Green Storm Fitness LLC, chief exec officer & trainer, currently. **Special Achievements:** Appeared in numerous television commercials, primetime TV shows and 2 off Broadway productions. **Business Addr:** Chief Executive Officer, Trainer, Green Storm Fitness LLC, 123 Green St Suite 2, Brooklyn, NJ 11222.

GREEN, SIDNEY
Basketball player, basketball coach. **Personal:** Born Jan 4, 1961, New York, NY; married Deidra; children: LaShawn & Taurean. **Educ:** Univ Nev, Las Vegas, 1983. **Career:** Basketball player (retired), Basketball coach; Chicago Bulls, Forward,1983-86; Detroit Pistons, 1986-87; New York Knicks, 1987-89; OrlandoMagic, 1989-90; San Antonio Spurs, 1990-92; Charlotte Hornets, 1992-93;Fla Atlantic Univ, head coach, 2001-02; Lonf Island Univ, coach; Ind Univ,asst coach; free agent, currently. **Honors/Awds:** Nat Spirit of Love Award, Nat Basketball Asn Players Asn, 1989; Atlantic Sun Conference Coach of the Year. **Special Achievements:** First player drafted in franchise history by the Orlando Magic, 1989.

GREEN, STERLING
Executive, real estate developer, government official. **Personal:** Born Oct 8, 1946, Washington, DC; married Sophie Ann Pinkney; children: Sterlicia Sophia, Tamika Tamara. **Educ:** Williams Col, MA, 1964; USASATC&S, Ft Devens MA, 1967. **Career:** Government official (retired), real estate; United House Prayer, ordained as elder, 1967, asst minister, 1971; DC Govt Adv Neighborhood Comm, vice chmn & comnr, 1978-85; United House Prayer, ordained as apostle, 1984, Bishop W McCollough, dir spec proj, 1991-01; Long & Foster Real Estate Inc, realtor, currently. **Orgs:** Elected adv neighborhood Comn, 1978; bd mem, SHAW Proj Area Comn, 1979; delegate DC Fed Civic Asn, 1979; Mayors Comn Coop Econ Develop, 1980; Nat comm mem McCollough Property Invest Comn, 1980; from asst exec dir to exec dir, McCollough Scholar Col Fund, 1984. **Honors/Awds:** Harvard Book Award, Wash, DC, 1964; Participant White House Briefing on the Cities 1980; Wash Post Article "Remap or Outmap" Census Mapping, 1981. **Military Serv:** AUS, 1967-69; Vietnam Campaign, Outstanding Trainee. **Business Addr:** Realtor, Long & Foster Real Estate Inc, 7301 Georgia Ave NW, Washington, DC 20012-1719, **Business Phone:** (202)882-2121.*

GREEN, THOMAS L
State government official. **Personal:** Born Sep 9, 1940, Bronxville, NY; son of Grace and Louis T; married Patricia S, Oct 13, 1963; children: Thomas II & Jennifer. **Educ:** State Univ, Winston-19Salem, NC, BS, 1963; AFL-19CIO Labor Studies Ctr, Silver Spring, MD, post grad work, 1972; Univ Utah, post grad work, 1976. **Career:** Manufacturer Traders Trust Co, asst mgr, 1966-69; Recruitment Training Prog, field rep, 1969-71; Westchester Affirmative Action Agency, White Plains, NY, exec dir, 1970-90; New York State Dept Labor, job training specialist, 1973-83, assoc employ consult, 1983-90, dep dir, 1990-, Off Community Serv, County Operations Div, asst dir, currently. **Orgs:** Relocation dir, Urban Renewal Agency, 1962-64; resource consult, US Dept HEW, 1964-69; proj dir, Pres, Community Juvenile Delinquent & Youth Develop, 1964-70; prog dir, Urban Educ Ctr, 1965-68; consult, Southern Ill Univ, 1966-67; consult/proj dir, Cent State Univ, 1967-68; prog dir, Urban League Westchester, 1969-70; Int Asn Personnel Employ Security, 1983-; exec bd mem, Nat Asn Pub Sector Equal Opportunity Officers, 1987-. **Honors/Awds:** 32 degree United Supreme Coun 33 AASR Free Masonry USA; Community Service Award, Westchester/Rockland Boy Scouts Am. **Special Achievements:** Author 2 years study Juvenile Delinquent & Youth Development Program, 1965-66. **Business Addr:** Assistant Director, Off Community Serv, Div Co Opers, Slot 1330, PO Box 1437, Little Rock, AR 72203.

GREEN, VERNA S
Executive. **Personal:** Born Oct 9, 1947, Columbus, GA; daughter of Evelyn Robinson Crouch and Oscar L Crouch; children: Grant Langston & Jason Wayne. **Educ:** Wayne State Univ, Detroit Mich, BS, bus admin, 1973; Mich State Univ, E Lansing Mich, MBA, 1976. **Career:** Gen Motors Corp, Detroit, Mich, orgn develop specialist, 1970-76; Vis Nurse Asn, Detroit, Mich, personnel dir, 1977-78; Detroit Med Ctr, Detroit Mich, assoc dir pub affairs, dir support serv, mgr training & develop, 1979-81; Booth Am Co, WJLB-FM, WMXD-FM, Detroit, vpres, gen mgr, pres, 1982-; Detroit Black Chamber Com, pres & chief exec officer, currently. **Orgs:** Nat Asn Advan Colored People, 1982-; Urban League, 1982-; alumni bd, Wayne State Univ Bus Sch; res comn, Nat Asn Broadcasters; Leadership Detroit, Grad Class No 7, 1986; bd mem, YWCA Metrop Detroit, 1986-87; Women's Advert Club, 1986-87; Mich Asn Broadcasters, 1987-; adv bd, Wayne State Univ Jour Inst Minorities, 1987-; bd mem, Detroit United Fund, 1987; Mich Women's Forum, 1987-; bd mem, C's Aid Soc, 1989; bd mem, YMCA Metrop Detroit, 1990; Detroit Sports Comn, 1992-; bd mem, Detroit Econ Growth Corp, 1994-; bd dir, MAB, currently; bd mem, Nat Asn Broadcasters, 1995-. **Honors/Awds:** Gen Man of the Year, Black Radio Exclusive, 1986; Most Outstanding Woman in Radio Management, Detroit Chap, Am Women Radio & TV, 1986; Woman of the 80's Award, J C Penney Co, 1987; Distinguished Alumnus Award, Wayne State Univ Bus Sch, 1988; General Manager of the Year, Young Black Programmer's Coalition, 1988; Corporate Leadership Award, Wayne State Univ, 1989; Manager of the Year, Gen Urban Network, 1992. **Business Addr:** President, Chief Executive Officer, Detroit Black Chamber of Commerce, 3011 W Grand Blvd Suite 1200, Detroit, MI 48226, **Business Phone:** (313)664-1093.

GREEN, VICTOR BERNARD
Football player. **Personal:** Born Dec 8, 1969, Americus, GA; married Esther, Jan 1, 1998; children: Victoria & Alexandria. **Educ:** Univ Akron, criminal justice, 1993. **Career:** Football player (retired); New York Jets, defensive back, 1993-2001, 2006; New Eng Patriots, defensive back, 2002; New Orleans Saints, safety, 2003.

GREEN, VINCENT
Government official. **Personal:** Born Aug 10, 1957, Brooklyn, NY; son of Robert and Ozzie; married Fannie, Jan 28, 1992; children: Franklin Hartzog, Donna Hartzog, Doris Hartzog, Erika J. **Educ:** John Jay Col Criminal Justice, BS, criminal justice, 1979; Brooklyn Col, MS, urban studies, 1998. **Career:** NY City, Dept Invest, dep comnr & supervising inspector, asst comnr, 1981-; Col New Rochelle, Sch New Resources, adj prof, 1992. **Orgs:** Dept Interior, Training Comn, co-chair, Recruitment & Retention Comn, chair, Advy Bd, Equal Employ Opport & Sexual Harassment, coun; Mayors Steering Comt Monitory, Woman Bus Enterprise Prog; pres, Toast Master Int; Nat Orgn Black Law Enforcement Execs; Nat Orgn Cert Fraud Examiners; Nat Inst Govt Purchasers; Fraternal Order Police; Soc Prof Investr. **Honors/Awds:** Outstanding Manager Award, 1993, 1996; Outstanding Achievement Award Major Investment, 1983, 1991, 1996; Perfect Attendance Award, 1981. **Special Achievements:** First African American assistant commissioner in the history of the Department of Interior to rise from investigator to executive management position; headed the largest invest in DOI history; lectured all over NYC; monitored 13 separate city agencies; lectured in Africa; auth, cert firearms instr, defensive tactics instr. **Business Addr:** Assistant Commissioner, Department of the Interior, 1849 C St NW, Washington, DC 20240.*

GREEN, WALTER
Business owner. **Personal:** Born Sep 5, 1924, Coconut Grove, FL. **Educ:** Miami-Dade Col Sch Continuing Educ, 1971-72. **Career:** Walt's Laundromat, owner, 1972-80; real estate investor, 1947-80. **Orgs:** Pres, fdr Black Grove Inc; New Frontiers Environ Understanding; Human Commun & Social Justice, 1970-80; pres, Grove Golfers Asn, 1960-70; mem, Proj Area Com HUD, 1967-70; dir, Black Grove Com Design Ctr, 1970-76; exec comt, Intl Optimist Club Coconut Grove, 1972-76; mem, Coconut Grove Plng Task Force, 1974-76; mem, Man Proj Comt, 1976. **Honors/Awds:** Conf partic in 1st Nat Seminar on Environmental Quality & Social Justice in Urban Am The Consrvtn Found, 1972; Voice of Am Intervw for W African Nats, 1976. **Special Achievements:** Co-author, Black Grove a plng model for am Miami Interactn, 1973. **Military Serv:** Pfc, WW II, 1943-46. **Business Addr:** Laundry Self Service, Walt's Laundromat, 3571 Grand Ave, Miami, FL 33133-4924, **Business Phone:** (305)443-0652.

GREEN, DR. WILLIAM EDWARD
Educator. **Personal:** Born May 17, 1930, Pittsburgh, PA; son of J Edward Green and Willa Lawson Stewart; married Betty Jayne Garrison, Nov 9, 1950; children: William Jr, Bobbi Brookins, Nancy Hill & Kenneth. **Educ:** Univ Pittsburgh, BS, 1953, MEd, 1958, EdD, 1969. **Career:** Retired: Herron Hill Jr HS, teacher, 1955-60; Westinghouse HS, counr, 1960-65, vice prin, 1965-68, exec asst to supt, 1968-69, asst supt, 1969-75; Carnegie Mellon Univ, lectr; Pittsburgh Pub Sch, asst supt middle schs, 1976-81, asst supt pupil serv, 1981-85; W PA Conf United Methodist Church, dir ethnic minority concerns, 1985-93; Pittsburgh Dist Lay Leader, UM Church, 1990-96. **Orgs:** Phi Eta Sigma, 1949-53; Prince Hall Mason (Boaz 65), 1959-; dissertation Sch Col Orientation Prog, 1969; bd dir Need, 1969-90; Univ Pittsburgh Alumni Coun, 1974-77; chmn, PACE, 1974-80, 1984-90; PA State Adv Coun Voc Educ, 1974-78; State ESEA Title IV Adv Coun, 1975-78; Alpha Phi Alpha; exec dir, Pittsburgh Upward Bound Prog; Omicron Delta Kappa; Phi Delta Kappa; treas, Warren United Methodist Church, 1980-94; chmn, Ethnic Minority Local Church; Coord, Comm Western PA Conf United Methodist Church, 1980-84; deleg, 1984, 1988, & 1994; United Methodist General/ Jurisdictional Conf, 1988. **Military Serv:** USAF, capt, 1953-55. **Home Addr:** 5456 Clarendon Pl, Pittsburgh, PA 15206, **Home Phone:** (412)661-1294.

GREEN, WILLIAM ERNEST
Lawyer, executive. **Personal:** Born Nov 19, 1936, Philadelphia, PA; married Loretta Martin; children: Billy, Roderic, Nicole. **Educ:** Univ Pittsburgh, BS, 1957; Duquesne Univ Sch Law, LLB, 1963. **Career:** NY & US Patent Off, admitted; Palo Alto Area Chapter Am Red Cross, dir; Palo Alto CA, atty pvt pract, CA; William green Assocs, founding partner, atty, currently; Williams Companies, Inc, dir, 1998-. **Orgs:** Palo Alto City Plann Comn; Charles Houston Bar Asn; Palo Alto Area Bar Asn; San Mateo Co Bar Asn; Bar Peninsula Patent Law Asn; SF Patent Law Asn; Am Bar Asn; asst gen couns Boise Cascade Corp, 1971-73; atty Sybron Corp, 1963-71; chemist, US Steel Corp; Applied Res Lab PA, 1957; past chmn, Rochester City Plann Comn five yrs; chmn bd trustees, World Inquiry Sch; rep, County & Regional Plann Couns; bd dir, Rochester Savngs Bank; Community Chest; Rochester Urban League; Rochester Health Serv Corp; Ind Training Sch; Rochester Monroe Co Chap Am Red Cross; Planned Parenthood League Rochester & Monroe Co; PTA Bd Sch 1; managing ed, Law Review Duquesne Univ Sch Law; dir, Philanthropic Ventures Fund; vpres, gen coun; secy, AIM Broadcasting, LLC. **Honors/Awds:** Record Folette Greeno Public Award, 1966; NY State Jaycees Distinguished Service Award, 1967; candidate for NY State Assembly, 1968. **Home Phone:** (650)321-9992. **Business Phone:** (650)321-9992.*

GREEN, WILLIE AARON
Football player, actor. **Personal:** Born Apr 22, 1966, Athens, GA. **Educ:** Univ Miss. **Career:** Football player(retired), actor; Detroit Lions, wide receiver, 1991-93; Tampa Bay Buccaneers, 1994; Carolina Panthers, 1995-96; Denver Broncos, 1997-98; Miami Dolphins. Films: Sheffey, 1977; Diggstown, 1992; "Lizzie McGuire", 2002; Terra Firma, 2008.

GREENBERG, REUBEN M.
Police chief. **Personal:** Born Jun 24, 1943, Houston, TX. **Educ:** San Francisco State Univ, BA, 1967; Univ CA, MPA, 1969, MCP, 1975, PhD,study; Fed Bur Invest, grad. **Career:** Government official, police chief (retired); City Berkeley, human re lofficer, 1967-69; Calif State Univ Hayward, asst prof sociol, 1969-73; San Francisco County, under sheriff, 1971-73; Opa Locka, Fla, chief police; Orange County, Fla, chief dep sheriff; Mobile, Ala, dir pub safety; Fla Dept Law Enforcement, dep dir; Univ NC Chapel Hill, asst prof polit sci; City Charleston, SC, chief police, 1982-05. **Orgs:** Nat Asn Black Law Enforcement Exec; Int Asn Chiefs Police; bd mem, SC Comn Racial Rels; bd mem, SC Crime Victims Compensation Bd; bd mem, SC Sentencing Comn; pres, SC Law Enforcement Officers Asn. **Honors/Awds:** LLD, Citadel Mil Col, 1987; Achievement Award, Found Improv Justice, 1989; Justice Professional of the Year, Southern Criminal Justice Asn, 1991; Free Spirit Award, Freedom Forum, 1994. **Special Achievements:** Authored several police-related articles; Book: Let's Take Back Our Streets, 1989.

GREEN-CAMPBELL, DEARDRA DELORES
Financial manager, association executive. **Personal:** Born Jan 21, 1959, Gary, IN; daughter of Herman W and Harriet L; married Thomas L, May 24, 1980; children: Evan T. **Educ:** Western Mich Univ, attended, 1977; Purdue Univ, attended, 1978. **Career:** Stuart James Corp, stock broker, 1983-84; Charles Schwab & Corp, vpres, 1984-91; D Campbell & Co, pres, 1991-. **Orgs:** Hundred Black Women, 1991-; Alanta Bus League, 1991-; Nat Asn Female Exec, 1991-; exec dir, Women's Econ Develop Agency Inc, currently. **Honors/Awds:** Chairman's Club, Charles Schwab & Corp, 1989, 1990. **Special Achievements:** Columnist, Financial Management Column, The Atlanta Tribune, 1991-. **Business Addr:** Executive Director, Women's Economic Development Agency Inc, 675 Metrop Pkwy Suite 2026, Atlanta, GA 30310, **Business Phone:** (678)904-2201.

GREENE, AURELIA
State government official. **Personal:** Born Oct 26, 1934, New York, NY; daughter of Edward Henry and Sybil Russell Holley; married Rev Jerome A, Apr 18, 1975 (deceased); children: Rhonda & Russell. **Educ:** Rutgers Univ, Livingston Col, BA, 1975. **Career:** Public agency administrator (retired), public official (retired),assemblywoman (retired); Bronx Area Policy Bd No 6, exec dir, 1980-82; NY State,asst majority leader, chair banking standing comn; NY State Assembly, 77thAssembly Dist, assemblywoman, 2003-09; Pres, Deputy Bronx Borough, 2009-. **Orgs:** Distinguished leader, 76th Assembly Dist, Bronx, 1979-82; Community Sch BdNo 9, 1985; exec officer, Bronx Unity Dem Club, 1986; educ adv, Morrisania Educ Coun, 1986; NAACP; Urban League. **Honors/Awds:** Numerous awards & honors including Woman of the Year, NAACP; Brotherhood Award, New York State Employees; Organization Impact Award, Alpha Kappa Alpha; Distinguished Community Leadership Award, Morrisania Educ Coun;Gold Helmet, NY State Head Injury Asn, 1994. **Special Achievements:** Author, Motor Vehicle Leasing Act; First Chairwoman of the Assembly Standing Committee on Banks.

GREENE, DR. BEVERLY A
Clinical psychologist, educator. **Personal:** Born Aug 14, 1950, New Jersey; daughter of Samuel and Thelma. **Educ:** NY Univ, BA, 1973; Adelphi Univ, Derner Inst Advan Psychology, MA, clin psychol, 1977, PhD, clinal psychol, 1983. **Career:** NY Bd Educ, sch psychologist, 1980-82; Kings County Hosp, Impatient Child & Adolescent Psychol Servs, dir, 1982-89; Univ Med & Dent NJ, Newark, supv psychologist, clin ast prof psychiat, 1989-91; St John's Univ, assoc clin prof psychol, 1991-93, assoc prof, 1993-95, prof, 1995-. **Orgs:** Int Neuropsychol Soc, 1979-87; NY Asn Black Psychologists, 1980-; NY Coalition Hosp & Inst Psychologists, 1982-91; Nat Asn Black Psychologists; Asn Women Psychol; NY State Psychol Asn, 1984-85; Am Psychol Asn, Task Force Ment Health Ethnic Minority Women, 1992-; Women Color Task Force, 1992-; Task Force Diversity Clin Psychol, 1991-92; co-chair, Continuing Educ, 1991-93; fel Acad Clin Psychol, 1998. **Honors/Awds:** Martin Luther King Jr Scholar, NYK Univ, 1968-72; Women Color Psychologies Publication Award, 1991; Distinguished Prof Contributions to Ethnic MNY Issues Award, 1992; St John's Univ Res Merit Awards, 1992-98; Distinguished Humanitarian Award, Am Asn Applied & Prev Psychol, 1994; Awarded Tenure, St John's Univ, 1995; Psychotherapy with Women Research Award, 1995, 1996; Distinguished Publication Award, 1995; Women Color Psychologies Pubation Award, Asn Women Psychol, 1995; Am Psychological Asn Award, Comm Lesbian, Gay & Bisexual Issues, 1996. **Special Achievements:** Author, works include: "Psychotherapy with AFA Women: Integrating Feminist & Psychodynamic Models," Journal Training & Pract in Prof Psychology, 1993; "Human Diversity in Clinal Psychology: Lesbian & Gay Sexual Orientations," Clinal Psychologist: Journal DIV Clinal Psychology, 1993; "Racism & Antisemitism: An AFA Feminist Perspective," Catalogue Black INT Cinema-Berlin, 1992; co-ed: Div 44 AMR Psychological Asn annual pubation series; Psychological Perspectives on Lesbian & Gay Issues, vols, 1-5; "Women Color: Integrating Ethnic & Gender Identities in Psychotherapy"; Guilford Press, co-ed, 1994; "Abnormal Psychology In a Changing World," Prentice Hall, co-author, 1994; assoc ed, Violence Against Women, 1994-99; ed, Ethnic & Cultural Diversity Among Lesbians & Gay Men, Sage Pubations, 1997. **Business Addr:** Professor, St John University, Department of Psychology, 8000 Utopia Pkwy Marillac Hall, Jamaica, NY 11439, **Business Phone:** (718)990-1538.

GREENE, CECIL M
Executive. **Personal:** Born Oct 10, 1932, Pass Christian, MS; married Joaquina Lizama; children: Joaquina Deborah & Cecil Gregory. **Educ:** Central State Univ, BS, 1952; Univ Chicago, grad work; Knoxville Col, chem. **Career:** Executive (retired); Argonne Nat Lab, res technician, 1956-66; Univ Chicago, adminr, 1966-71; Enroci Fermi Inst, admin asst, 1966-71; Montgomery Ward & Co, Corp EEO Prog, mgr, 1971; City Col Chicago, registr; Timmons Realty Co, property mgr, salesperson; Knoxville Col (TN), placement dir & dir admin serv. **Orgs:** Chicago Urban Affairs Coun, 1971-; Nat Urban Affairs Coun, 1971-; Nat Alliance Businessmen; Col Placement Asn; Chicago Ment Health Asn; Wabash YMCA; NAACP; Kappa Alpha Psi Frat; S Shore Comn, personnel comn. **Military Serv:** First lt, 1952-54.

GREENE, CHARLES ANDRE
Executive. **Personal:** Born May 17, 1939, Blockton Junction, AL; divorced. **Educ:** Tex So Univ, Sch Bus; Wayne State Univ, Sch Mortuary Sci. **Career:** dist gov, Dist 4 Nat Funeral Dirs & Mortcns Asn, 1973-74; vpres, Genesee Co Funeral Dir Asn; Greene Home Funerals, pres, 1998. **Orgs:** Nat Funeral Dir & Mortcns Asn; bd dir, Greater Flint Opport Indust Controls Inc; Vehicle City Lodge No 1036 IBPOE W; Tall Pine Counc BSA; Epsilon Nu Delta Mortuary Frat; elected fin chmn 5th Ward Charter Revision Comn, 1974; asst exec secy, Nat Funeral Dir & Mortcns Asn Inc 1974; Foss Ave Bapt Church; found dir, Foss Ave Fed Credit Union; Wayne State Univ Alumni Asn; Tex Southern Univ Alumni Asn; Urban League Urban Coalition; Cent Optimist Club; chmn, Educ Com Nat Funeral Dir & Mortcns Asn 1972-73. **Honors/Awds:** NAACP Achievement Award, 1913; Foss Ave Leadership Award, pres Credit Union, 1973-74; Big Bro & Distinguished Service Award 1973; award of merit, Flint Fire Dept, 1974. **Special Achievements:** Youth Specialist, Nat Funeral Dir & Embalmer Mag. *

GREENE, CHARLES EDWARD. See GREENE, JOE.

GREENE, DR. CHARLES EDWARD CLARENCE
Government official, actor. **Personal:** Born Apr 1, 1921, Philadelphia, PA; son of Raymond and Christine; married Julia Castenedes; children: Ruth Gumbs, Martin, Rene, Vincent Cocom & Gamel Bowen. **Educ:** LaSalle Ext, LLB, 1940; Univ Church Brotherhood, DD, 1955; TV Southwest Col, ref courses. **Career:** Actor, producer, writer, dir, 1937; Negro Cowboys Asn; Rodeo Champ, Natpres, 1945-49; Step Inc, chmn bd, 1970-71; Black Polit Asn, pres; Independent Prod Asn, pres, 1971-72; Casey Col, exec vp; Universal Brotherhood Churches, serge arch bishop; Lbr & Indus Comt, Nat Asn Advan Colored People, chmn; Trans-Oceanic Indus Inc, pres; Adelphi Bus Col, pubrels consult; Most Worshipful Prince Hall Grand Lodge F&AM CA & HI Inc, pub rels consult; St Calif, sr legisr & sr sen, currently. **Orgs:** Pres, Inglewood Southbay Br Nat Asn Advan Colored People, 1979-; comnr, Los Angeles County Obscenity & Pornography Comt, 1980-; pres, Sr Coalition Polit Action Comt, 1983-; very rev asst gr chaplin MW Prince Hall GrandLodge CA Inc, 1984-; sr deacon, James H Wilson Lodge 68 Pha, 1985; Independent Producer & Asn. **Honors/Awds:** Grad inspector gen 33rd Deg, Supreme Coun PHA, 1985. **Military Serv:** AUS, sgt. **Business Addr:** Senior Senator, California Senior Legislative, State Bldg, Los Angeles, CA 90018, **Business Phone:** (213)732-7890.

GREENE, CHARLES LAVANT
Educator. **Personal:** Born Feb 22, 1938, Headland, AL; married Delores Johnson; children: Charles L. **Educ:** Univ Akron, OH, BS, biol, 1962; Univ Pittsburgh, PA, MSW, 1967; Akron Law Sch, OH, JD, 1977. **Career:** CAC Prog, Syracuse NY, dep dir admin, 1968-70; E Akron Comm House, coord comm level, 1967-68; Kent State Univ, asst prof & asst dean stud life, 1972-, asst prof, 1970-, asst prof & coord vol & comm serv, 1971-72; Human Resources, vpres, 1989. **Orgs:** Vpres, Urban Affair Tomorrow's People Consult Firm, 1972-; bd mem, Urban League Akron, OH, 1977-; bd mem, Fair Housing Contact Serv, Akron, OH, 1977-; bd mem Mental Health Assn of Summit Co, Akron, OH, 1977-80; bd mem, Alpha Homes Inc, Akron, 1979-; bd secy, Ebony Blackstar Broadcast Corp, 1980. **Honors/Awds:** US Public Health Scholarship, Univ Pittsburgh, 1965-67; found Law Firm Davison Greene Holloway & Walker, 1977; Frat Award, KY State, 1979. **Military Serv:** AUS, capt, 1962-65; Commend medal. *

GREENE, CLIFTON S.
Executive. **Personal:** Born Oct 21, 1920, Georgetown, SC; son of Wally and Janie; married Irene (deceased). **Educ:** SC State Col, attended 1940. **Career:** Executive (retired); Cliff Greene's Wines & Liquors Brooklyn, owner, 1948-74; Wally-Thel Inc, pres, 1959-69; Greenoung Enterprises, pres, 1966; Green-Harris Enterprises, Inc, chmn, chief exec officer, 1966; Ebony Enterprises Inc, pres, 1972. **Orgs:** Pres, sole stock holder Nu-way Investors Corp; life mem, NAACP; Urban League; Prince Hall Mason 32nd Degree; Shriner; Widow's Son Lodge #11; Long Island Consistory #61; Imperial Coun; AEAONMS, Inc; Am Legion; 100 Black Men Inc; Retired Army Officer's Asn; Ft Hamilton Officer's Club. **Honors/Awds:** First Black in US to file with FCC for UHF TV station; First Black or white to build multi-million dollar housing for elderly in Bedford Stuyvesant, Brooklyn; published "Unique & Mae" magazine; various articles, Stock Market Fundamentals, 1966. **Military Serv:** AUS, Staff Sargent to Capt in 29 mo 1943-45; hon discharge Nov, 1946. **Home Addr:** 1333 President St, Brooklyn, NY 11213.

GREENE, DR. DENNIS
Educator. **Personal:** Born Jan 11, 1949, New York; son of Fred and Hortense. **Educ:** Columbia Univ, BA, 1972; Harvard Univ, MA, 1984; Yale Law Sch, JD, 1987. **Career:** Sha Na Na, cast mem, 1977-80; Columbia Pictures, vpres; Lenox & Greene Films, pres; City Col NY, instr; Fla A&M Univ, vis prof; Univ Ore, asst prof law, assoc prof law, currently; Ohio State Univ, vis prof; Seton Hall Univ, vis prof; Univ Conn, vis prof; Univ Dayton Sch Law, prof, 2004-; Columbia Univ, Sha Na Na, co-founder . **Orgs:** Alpha Phi Alpha; Screen Actors Guild; AFTRA; life mem, Nat Asn Advan Colored People; bd dir, Soc Am Law Teachers; Law Sch Admis Coun Serv & Prog Comt. **Honors/Awds:** Alumnus of the Year, Columbia Univ Club Southern Calif. **Special Achievements:** Author of the play, Harlem Exchange; contributed few publications. **Business Phone:** (937)229-2362.

GREENE, EDITH L
Government official. **Personal:** Born Oct 29, 1919, Darlington County, SC; daughter of Cohen Galloway Sr and Olivette Mazone Galloway; married Isaac Greene Jr, Apr 22, 1937 (died 1975); children: Doris, Robert Allen, Elouise, Isaac, Frank, Jean, Cohen, Mae, Fred & Gennette, Don. **Career:** Town Bolton, Bolton, NC, mayor. **Orgs:** County coun pres, Extension Homemakers Club, 1950-78; leader, 4-H Club, 1970-79. League Women Voters, 1976-80; VFW Ladies Auxilary, 1977-; Eta Phi Beta, 1980-. **Honors/Awds:** Service Award, NC Chap Cystic Fibrosis, 1976; Leadership Award, Columbus County Ext Homemakers, 1976; Meritorious Service Award, NC Joint Coun Health & Citizenship, 1978; Outstanding & Dedicated Service, Nat Conf Black Mayors, 1980; Outstanding Public Leadership, NC Against Racist &

Religious Violence, 1990. **Home Addr:** PO Box 129, Bolton, NC 28423, **Home Phone:** (919)655-8482.

GREENE, FRANK S
Executive, president (organization). **Personal:** Born Oct 19, 1938, Washington, DC; son of Frank S Sr and Irma O Swygert; married Carolyn W, Sep 1990; children: Angela, Frank III & Ronald. **Educ:** Washington Univ, BS, 1961; Purdue Univ, MS, 1962; Santa Clara Univ, PhD, elec eng, 1970. **Career:** Fairchild Semiconductor R&D Labs, mem tech staff; USAF, electronics officer; ZeroOne Systs Inc, pres & chmn bd, 1971-87; Technol Develop Corp, pres, bd mem, 1985-92; Sterling Software Inc, 1987-89; Networked Picture Systs, chmn bd, 1989-94; New Vista capital Fund, gen partner, 1993-. **Orgs:** Inst Elec & Electronic Engrs, 1960-85; asst chmn & lectr, Stanford Univ, 1972-74; IEEE Comput Soc Gov Bd, 1973-75; bd dir, Nat Conf Christians & Jews, 1978-; bd dir, Security Affairs Support Asn, 1980-83; bd regents Santa Clara Univ, 1983-89, trustee, 1990-2000; Am Electronics Asn; Bay Area Purchasing Coun; dir, Comsis Corp, 1984; mem Nat Cont Mgt Asn; Eta Kappa Nu, Sigma Xi; Nat Asn Advan Colored People; Northern Calif Coun Black Prof Engrs; bd mem, Compliance Coach; bd mem, ZNYX; bd mem, Res Comm; bd mem, Reach Communications; bd mem, Compliance Coach Inc; chmn bd, Am Musical Theatre San Jose; bd mem, Nat Conf Community & Justice; bd trustees, Santa Clara Univ. **Honors/Awds:** Marketing Opportunities in Business & Entertaiment Award, 2001. **Special Achievements:** Author of 10 tech articles 2 indl textbooks; 1 patent received. **Military Serv:** USAF, capt, 1961-65. **Home Addr:** 967 LA Mesa Ter, Sunnyvale, CA 94086. **Business Addr:** Partner, New Vista Capital, 161 E Evelyn Ave, Mountain View, CA 94041, **Business Phone:** (650)864-2553.

GREENE, FRANKLIN D
Automotive executive. **Personal:** Born Jan 23, 1950, Hot Springs, AR; son of John H and Jessie L Muldrow; married. **Educ:** The Col Ozarks Point Lookout, MO, BS, 1972. **Career:** Cit Financial Serv, customer serv rep, 1972-73; Ford Motor Co, Kansas City, MO, zone mgr, 1973-81; Indian Springs Ford, Kansas City, MO, pres, 1981-83; Repub Ford Inc, pres, 1983-; Columbus Ford, Mercury, Columbus, KS, pres, 1987-; Zodiac Lounge, Springfield, MO, pres 1988-90; Quality Ford, Inc, West Des Moines, IA, pres & owner, 1989-; B & G Automotive Group, partner. **Orgs:** Bd dir, Big Bros & Sisters Springfield, MO, 1985-; pres, Sch Ozarks Springfield Alumni Asn, 1986-87; bd mem, Metro Credit Union, 1987-; bd mem, Am Red Cross, 1987-; bd mem, Minority Breakfast Club, 1990-; past pres, Black Ford Lincoln Mercury Dealers Asn, 1991-; Kappa Alpha Psi Fraternity, 1994; adv bd, Bankers Trust Des Moines; athletic bd, Drake Univ; Partners Econ Progress (PEP); bd mem, West Des Moines Police Adv Bd. **Honors/Awds:** Athletic Hall of Fame, Col Ozarks, 1986; Meritorious Achievement Award, Col Ozarks, 1989. **Special Achievements:** Republic Ford listed as one of Black Enterprise's Top 100 Auto Dealers, 1984-91. **Business Addr:** President, Quality Ford Inc, 1271 8th St, PO Box 66040, West Des Moines, IA 50265, **Business Phone:** (515)273-4256.

GREENE, GABRIELLE ELISE
Businessperson. **Personal:** Born Jun 17, 1960, New York, NY; daughter of Gregory and Patricia Simms; married W Michael, Jun 12, 1988; children: Savannah Elise. **Educ:** Princeton Univ, BA, 1981; Harvard Bus, MBA, 1987; Harvard Law Sch, JD, 1987. **Career:** Bain & Co, consult, 1982-84; UNC partners, prin, 1987-91; Commonwealth Enterprise Fund, 1991-94; BE/Greenwich St Capital, partner, 1998-2000; Crown Servs, chief financial officer, 2000-02; Villanueva Co, chief financial officer, 2002; Whole foods mkt, dir, 2003-. Bright Horizons Family Solutions Inc, bd dir, 2006-; HPB Ventures, gen partner, currently; Celestial Seasonings Inc, found; Rustic Canyon/Fontis Partners, gen partner, currently. **Orgs:** Nat Black MBA Asn, 1988; treas, Social Justice Women, 1989-91; Boston Partnership Steering Comt, 1992-; Boston C Mus, 1993; Bright Horizons Family Solutions Inc; Milbank Memorial Fund; Massachusetts State Bar. **Honors/Awds:** First Annual Scholarship Recipient, Nat Black MBA Asn, 1985; 100 Most Infulential People in Boston, Roxbury Chamber Com, 1994-95. **Home Addr:** 80 Clifton St, Belmont, MA 02478-3363. **Business Addr:** Director, Bright Horizons Family Solutions Inc, 200 Talcott Ave S, Watertown, MA 02472, **Business Phone:** (617)673-8000.

GREENE, GRACE RANDOLPH
Government official. **Personal:** Born Oct 5, 1937, Washington, DC; divorced; children: Denise, Samuel, Michael, Annette, Wayne, Katerina, Grace E & Deloris. **Career:** Dept Housing & Community Develop, actg mgr-mgt aide, 1969-82; Adv Neighborhood Comn, comnr, 1982-84. **Orgs:** Co-chairperson, Libr Cent Baptist Church, Women's Dept Cent Baptist; vol, Friends & Anacostia Libr, 1984. **Honors/Awds:** Certificate, OES Chap, 5 Prince Hall, 1972; certificate, Women's Dept Cent Baptist Church, 1984. **Home Addr:** 1924 Naylor Rd SE, Washington, DC 20020.

GREENE, GREGORY A.
Financial manager, executive director. **Personal:** Born Aug 29, 1949, Boston, MA; son of Harry and Edna; married Pearline Booth Greene, Apr 13, 1974; children: Adria. **Educ:** Northeastern Univ, Boston, MA, BS, Bus Admin, 1972. **Career:** Arthur Andersen, Boston, MA, staff auditor, 1972-75; Arthur Andersen, Cincinnati, OH, sr auditor, 1976-77; Philip Morris Inc, New York, NY, mgr financial servs, 1977-; dir corp acct, 1994-. **Orgs:** Simon Found Pa. **Military Serv:** AUS, SSgt, 1972-78. **Home Addr:** 1582 Revere Rd, Yardley, PA 19067, **Home Phone:** (215)493-0906. **Business Addr:** Director of Corporate Accounting, Philip Morris Inc, 120 Park Ave 21st Fl, New York, NY 10017, **Business Phone:** (212)880-3239.*

GREENE, HORACE F.
Physician, administrator. **Personal:** Born May 5, 1939, Tuscaloosa, AL; married Stephanie Rodgers; children: Amanda, David, Jason. **Educ:** Fisk Univ, BA, 1960; Meharry Med Sch, MD, 1964. **Career:** Johns Hopkins Hosp; Rollman Psych Inst; Reynolds Memorial Hosp; Area Chamber Com Mental Health Ctr, dir adolescent serv, dir Youth serv, clin dir, part time staff psychiatrist, supvr, 1970-74; Georgetown Univ Sch Med, asst prof clin & psychiat, 1970; Va Hosp Wash, Drug Treat & Res Prog, consult, 1971; Howard Univ Sch Med, consult Residency Training Prog, 1973; Alexandria Community Mental Health Ctr, dir, 1971-74; Bur Mental Health Serv, NHA , DC, dep admin chief, 1974; Va Hosp, consult dept psychiat, 1974; N Va Prison Aftercare Prog, consult, 1974-75; pvt pract, physician, currently. **Orgs:** Adv Coun Eastern Area Alcohol Educ & Training Prog Inc; Beta Kappa Chi Hon Sci; Kappa Alpha Psi Fraternity Inc; pres, ALL Progress Psychiat; Wash Psychiat Soc; Am Psychiat Asn; Wash Soc & Adolescent Psychiat; Psychiat Adv Coun, Mental Health Admin Wash; chmn, Prof Adv Comt, Mental Health Asn Inc; Wash Coun Child Psychiat; APA Task Force Psychosurgery; nominating Comt, Wash Psychiat Soc, 1974; Peer Rev Comt, Wash Psychiat Soc; Nat Med Fedn; Wash Hosp Ctr, vice chmn clin affairs, Dept psychiat, 1987-. **Military Serv:** USNL, med officer, 1965-67. **Home Addr:** 4600 Conn Ave NW Suite 224, Washington, DC 20008. **Business Addr:** Physician, 4600 Conn Ave NW Suite 224, Washington, DC 20008.*

GREENE, JAMES R, III
Lawyer. **Personal:** Born Apr 2, 1959, Evreux, France; son of James Russell Jr and Laura Malvoney-Clay Calhoun. **Educ:** Wright State Univ, Dayton, OH, BA, communs, 1983, BA, polit sci, 1983; Ohio State Univ Col Law, Columbus, OH, JD, 1985. **Career:** Pub Defender's Off, Columbus, OH, law clerk, 1983-84; City Prosecutor's Off, Columbus, OH, law clerk, 1984; US Atty's Off, Columbus, OH, law clerk, 1985; Columbus, OH, asst atty gen, atty, 1986-88; Dayton Power & Light Co, Dayton, OH, atty, 1988-93; AT&T Global Info Solutions Law Dept, Litigation Sect, 1993; James R Greene III & Assocs, atty, currently. **Orgs:** Pres, Dayton Chap AABE, 1989-91; pres, Thurgood Marshall Law Soc, 1990-91; vice-chmn, Concerned Christian Men Inc, 1990-92; second vice-chmn, Am Asn Blacks Energy, 1990-92; bd dirs, Eastway Corp, 1990-92. **Honors/Awds:** Black Leadership Development, Dayton Urban League, 1988-89; Leadership Dayton, Class Pres, 1989-90. **Home Addr:** 1820 Ruskin Rd Upper Dayton View, Dayton, OH 45406-1820. **Business Phone:** (937)225-3991.

GREENE, JEHMU
Executive director. **Personal:** Born Jun 22, 1972, Wash, DC. **Educ:** Univ Tex. **Career:** Rock the Vote, dir, 2000, pres, 2003-05, exec dir, 2005-; Dem Nat Comt, dir women's outreach & southern polit dir; Ctr Policy Alternatives Youth Voices Proj & Nat Student Voter Educ Day, prog dir; Univ Tex Neighborhood Prog, exec dir tex young dem & vol coordr. **Orgs:** Exec Comt, Youth Vote Coalition; Bd Am Prospect; adv bd mem, Partnership Pub Serv; adv bd mem, Vote Am; adv bd mem, White House Proj Vote; adv bd mem, Run, Lead Proj & Freedom's Answer; co-founder & adv bd mem, Econ & Pub Policy Orgn Young Adults. **Honors/Awds:** Women Who Make a Difference Award, 2005. **Business Addr:** Executive Director, Rock the Vote, 10635 Santa Monica Blvd Suite 150, Los Angeles, CA 90025, **Business Phone:** (310)234-0665.*

GREENE, JEROYD X. See EL-AMIN, SA'AD.

GREENE, JERRY LOUIS
School administrator. **Personal:** Born Mar 30, 1957, Albany, GA; son of Ollie and Lucius; married Renee Green, Dec 23, 1987; children: Ashley Renee. **Educ:** Los Angeles Metrop Col, AA, 1981; Dekalb Community Col, attended 1981; Univ Md, AA, 1986. **Career:** Fort McPherson Ga Commun, comput operator, 1984-85; Camp Tango Korea, comput operator, 1984-85; US Training Mission, Soudi Arabia, comput operator, 1984-86; Defense Intelligence Agency, watch officer, 1986-89; White House Mil Off, oper officer, 1989-93; White House Commun Agency, opers officer, 1993-95; Defense Intelligence, supt, 1995-. **Honors/Awds:** Defense Meritorious Award, 1995. **Special Achievements:** Hand Selected by the White House Support the President; Recognized by VIP Al Gore for Superb Briefing; First NCO to be selected to work in the Presidents Operation Ctr; Top 5% of Army to be Nominated to work at the White House. **Military Serv:** AUS, master sgt, 1976-. *

GREENE, JOANN LAVINA
Educator, psychiatrist, nurse. **Personal:** Born in Columbus, OH; daughter of Lacy Davis and Lavina Allen Davis; divorced; children: David. **Educ:** San Jose State Univ, BS, 1969; Univ Calif San Francisco, MS, 1970; UnivSouthern Calif, PhD. **Career:** Psychiatrist (retired); VA Hosp Ment Hygiene Clin, head nurse, 1970-72; San Jose State Univ, instr psychiat nursing, 1972-74; W Valley Col, instr psychiat tech prog, 1974-76; W Valley Mission Col, dir psychiat tech prog, 1976-99. **Orgs:** Alpha Kappa Alpha Sor 1960-62; CNA, 1972-, ANA, 1972-, FACCC, Phi Kappa Phi, Sigma Theta Tau, pres, Calif Asn Psychiat Tech Educrs, 1980-83. **Honors/Awds:** Delta Sigma Theta Scholarship; NIMH Fellowship; Dean's List, President Scholar, Phi Kappa Phi; Florence Nightingale Award, 2 years; Sigma Theta Tau Nat Nursing Hon. *

GREENE, JOE (CHARLES EDWARD GREENE)
Football coach, actor. **Personal:** Born Sep 24, 1946, Temple, TX; son of Cleo Thomas; married Agnes; children: Major, Delon & JoQuel. **Educ:** N Tex State Univ, attended 1968. **Career:** Football player (retired), Football coach, motivational speaker; Pittsburgh Steelers, defensive tackle, 1969-81, spec asst player personnel, 2004-; CBS-NFL Today, color commentator, 1983; Pittsburgh Steelers, asst coach, 1987; Miami Dolphins, defensive line coach, 1992-96; Ariz Cardinals, asst coach, 1999; Films: The Black Six, actor, 1974; Horror High, actor, 1974; Lady Cocoa, actor, 1975; Fighting Back: The Story of Rocky Bleier, actor, 1980; Smokey & the Bandit II, actor, 1980. **Honors/Awds:** Col All Stars, Sporting News, 1968; NFL Eastern Conf All Stars, Sporting News, 1969; AFC All Stars, Sporting News, 1970-74, 1979; Pro Bowl, 1970-76, 1978, 1979, 1981; Super Bowl; Nat Football Hall of Fame, 1987. **Special Achievements:** Acted & appeared in numerous TV commercials. **Business Addr:** Special Assistant for Player Personnel, Pittsburgh Steelers, 100 Art Rooney Ave, PO Box 6763, Pittsburgh, PA 15212, **Business Phone:** (412)432-7800.

GREENE, DR. LIONEL OLIVER
Research scientist. **Personal:** Born Apr 28, 1948, Brooklyn, NY; son of Lionel Oliver Sr and Dollie Chapman; children: Tera Aun. **Educ:** Calif State Univ Los Angeles, BA, 1970; Stanford Univ, PhD 1978; MIT, Postdoctorate, 1980. **Career:** NASA, res scientist, 1973-77, 1979-81; Mass Inst Tech, res assoc, 1977-79; Lockheed Missiles & Space Co, res scientist, 1981-84; MacDonnell Douglas Astronaut, sr eng scientist, 1984-85; Univ Santa Clara, vis prof; AT&T Bell Labs, sr engr sci human factors, 1985-; lectr, Stanford Univ, 1979-84; adj prof, Fla A&M Univ; vis prof, San Jose State Univ; NIH, ROI Level Rev, 1995; Greene's Admin & Statist Servs, chief exec officer, 1995-; Nat Inst Clin Res, dir Biostatistics, 1998-; Boys & Girls Clubs, dir Technol, 1999-; Mt States Biomedical Res Inst, vpres, 2007-. **Orgs:** Soc Neuroscience 1978-; Mission Spec Astronaut candidate, 1978; Aerospace Med Asn, 1979-; Asn Black Psychologists; Am Defense Preparedness Asn, 1986-; FCC Radiotlphn License DJ, 6 Yrs; bd dirs, Goodwill Indus Am Inc, 1992-; bd dirs, Lafayette Prog, 2004-; bd dirs, got-COM, 2005-. **Honors/Awds:** Nat Acad Sci Bethesda MD; Honor Soc, Mensa Soc, 1980-; NASA Sci Achievement Award, Top secret Clearance, Defense Investigative Servs. **Special Achievements:** 12 research publications 1975-; Ebony Magazine Bachelor, Ebony Magazine, 1980; 20 publications, 1975-; recorded 2 jazz LP's; FAA Pilots License 1972; Reviewer of Papers, NIH, 1988-; Guest Panelist, Our Voices/BETV, 1991. **Military Serv:** AUS capt; Air Defense Artillery Co (Hawk Missiles), 1970-82; USN High Altitude Test Cert, 1975. **Home Addr:** 1937 W 95th St, Los Angeles, CA 90047.

GREENE, MARY ANN
Criminologist, president (organization). **Personal:** Born Aug 25, 1934, Los Angeles, CA; daughter of George Buford and Gladys Buford; widowed. **Educ:** Univ Calif, Los Angeles, BA, 1956; Pepperdime Univ, MA, 1979. **Career:** Los Angeles County, placement officer, 1961-73; community develop analyst, 1973-76; SW Community Col, prof, 1974-77; Los Angeles County Probation Dept, supvr, 1976-81, sr dir II, 1981-92; Baldwin Hills Conservancy, chair, 2002-03, pres gov bd, gov bd appointee, currently. **Orgs:** Chap chair, Calif Probation, 1978-81; Parole Correctional Asn; chair, Blair Hills Asn, 1997-. **Honors/Awds:** Resolution Honoring Service, Blair Hills Asn, Calif Park Serv, 2002; Resolution Honoring Service, Baldwin Hills Conservancy, 2003. **Special Achievements:** Led development of urban park in Los Angeles. **Business Addr:** Governor Appointee of the Board, Baldwin Hills Conservancy, 3578 C Eastham Dr, Culver City, CA 90232, **Business Phone:** (310)558-5593.

GREENE, MAURICE
Athlete, businessperson. **Personal:** Born Jul 23, 1974, Kansas City, KS. **Career:** Athlete, (retired), Businessperson; adidas, athelete, 2008; Race youth found, founder, 2001-; USA track & field inc, track & field athlete; Mo Greene Entertainment, owner, currently. **Orgs:** United Negro col fund. **Honors/Awds:** US 100m champ, 1997, 2000 & 2002; World 100m champion, 1997, 1999 & 2001;Jesse Owens Award, 1999; World 200m & 4 x 100m champion, 1999; WorldIndoor 60m champion, 1999; US 200m champion, 1999; Gold Medal, Olympic,2000; US Indoor 60m Champ, 2001; Visa Humanitarian of the Year Award, USA Track & Field inc, 2001; Bronze Medal, 100m, Olympic, 2004; Silver

Medal, 4x100m relay, Olympic, 2004. **Special Achievements:** Guest appearance in varient television programs.

GREENE, NATE. See GREENE, NATHANIEL D.

GREENE, NATHANIEL D (NATE GREENE)
Executive. **Personal:** Married Roberta. **Career:** Empire Ford Inc, Spokane, pres, owner, 1986-2007, vice chair. **Orgs:** Pres, Eastern Wash Univ, Bus Adv Coun; Northwest Ford Dealers Advert Asn; bd mem, Wash Econ Develop Funding Authority, 2007-; bd dir, Spokane Pub Facil, 2004-07. **Business Addr:** Board Member, Washington Economic Development Finance Authority, 1000 Second Ave Suite 2700, Seattle, WA 98104-1046.

GREENE, NELSON E., SR.
Educator, funeral director. **Personal:** Born May 20, 1914, Danville, VA; married Gloria Kay; children: Nelson Jr & Terry F. **Educ:** Shaw Univ, AB, 1941; Renourd Sch Embalming, NY, attended 1948. **Career:** Langston High Sch, Danville, teacher, 1941-42; Greene Funeral Home, Alexandria, Va, funeral dir, owner & pres, currently. **Orgs:** Comnr, Alexandria Redevelopment & Housing & Authority, 1966-69; sr warden, Meade Episcopal Church, 1969-72; bd dir, Alexandria Hosp, 1970; Va Bd Funeral Dirs & Embalmers, 1972; Va City Coun, Alexandria, 1979-82; Nat Funeral Dir Asn; bd dir, Va Mortician Asn; Nat Asn Advan Colored People; Urban League, Masons, Elks, Shrine; bd dirs, Alexandria Bd Trade; Omega Psi Phi Fraternity. **Military Serv:** AUS, major, 1942-46, 1951-53. **Business Addr:** Owner, President, Greene Funeral Home Inc, 814 Franklin St, Alexandria, VA 22314, **Business Phone:** (703)549-0089.*

GREENE, RONALD ALEXANDER
Executive. **Personal:** Born Nov 1, 1945, Greenwood, SC; married Margaret St Mark; children: Ronald Jr, Jennifer. **Educ:** SC State Col, BS, 1968. **Career:** Blue Cross Blue Shield, programmer analyst, 1975-76, mgr data entry, 1976-78, coordr, 1978-79, mgr telecommunications, 1979. **Military Serv:** AUS 1974-75; oak leaf cluster; AUS, capt, 7 yrs. *

GREENE, SARAH MOORE
Educator, politician. **Personal:** Born Feb 22, 1912, Madisonville, TN; daughter of Isaac and Mary Toomey; married William J Greene, Oct 3, 1939 (deceased). **Educ:** A & I State Col, Nashville Tenn, 1934. **Career:** Monroe County Sch Bd, Sweetwater Tenn, teacher, 1934-36; NC Mutual Ins Co, Knoxville, Tenn, special agent, 1936-46; Knoxville Tenn, pvt kindergarten proprietor, 1946-66; State Tenn, Nashville Tenn, pardon & parole bd mem, 1967-69; Knox County, Knoxville Tenn, sec finance comn, 1971-80; US Govt, Knoxville Tenn, staff aide, 1980-85; Nat Head Start Assoc, ceo, currently. **Orgs:** Chmn, bd dir, YWCA, 1956-62; KOIC, 1964-88; bd mem, Community Action Comm, 1965-71; Knoxville Bd Educ, 1969-85; secy, Nat Advan Asn Colored People. **Honors/Awds:** Cert Appointment, Pres Gerald Ford, 1975; Torch Bearer Award, Opportunity Indust Corp, 1976; Honorary Mem, Alpha Kappa Alpha Sorority Inc, 1976; Civic Service Award, Greater Knoxville Minority Bus Bureau, 1978; Honor Service Award, Knoxville Opportunity Indust Corp, 1988; Advocacy Award, 47th Annual NAHRW Conf, 1994; Nation Builder Award, Nat Black Caucus, 1994; Award for Contributions & Accomplishments, Tenn Lawyers Asn Women, 1996; Life Time Service Award, Nat Advan Asn Colored People, 1997; Ebony Service Award, 1997. **Special Achievements:** 1st black elected to Knoxville City Schools Board of Education, 1969-85; elementary school named Sarah Moore Greene Elementary School, 1972. *

GREENE, TALIB KWELI. See KWELI, TALIB.

GREENE, WILLIAM
Clergy, minister (clergy). **Personal:** Born Sep 13, 1933, Rowland, NC; son of Joe and Margaret Brunson; married Wilhelmenia O. Greene, Dec 28, 1953; children: Wanda Greene. **Educ:** Anchorage Community Col, AA, 1982; Alaska Pac Univ, BA, 1983. **Career:** Shiloh Missionary Baptist Church, Anchorage, AK, chmn, 1974-79, admin, 1979-85; Alaska, chaplain, 1980-; Eagle River Missionary Baptist Church, minister, pastor, 1985-. **Orgs:** Pres, Interdenominational Ministerial Alliance, 1987-90; pres, Chugiak Food Pantry, 1988-; chair, Black Educ Task Force, 1988-92; chair, Minority Community Rels Police Task Force, 1988-; pres, Chugiak & Eagle River Ministerial Alliance Asn, 1999. **Honors/Awds:** Man of the Yr Award, Alaska State Asn Colored Women, 1987; Outstanding Leadership Award, Alaska Black Caucus, 1988; Hon Doctor Divinity, Arkansas Baptist Col, 1997; Four Star Chaplain Award, US Chaplains Asn, 1999; Spec Appreciation Award, Minority Community Police Rels Task Force, Anchorage, AK, US Dept Justice Community Rels Serv, 1999. **Military Serv:** USAF, fuel supt, 1953-80; NonCommissioned Officer Acad Grad Ribbon; Army Good Conduct Medal Two Devices; Korean Serv Medal; AF Longevity Serv Award Ribbon Five Devices; Nat Defense Serv Medal One Device; AF Outstanding Unit Award Seven Devices; Korean Presidential Unit Citation; United Nations Serv Medal; AF Good Conduct Medal Five Oak Leaf Clusters; AF Commendation Medal; Meritorious Serv Medal One Oak Leaf Cluster. **Home Addr:** 7310 E 17th Ave, Anchorage, AK 99504. **Business Addr:** Pastor, Eagle River Missionary Baptist Church, 16050 Lesmer Ct, PO Box 773568, Eagle River, AK 99577-5188.*

GREENE, DR. WILLIAM HENRY L
School administrator. **Personal:** Born Jul 28, 1943, Richburg, SC; son of Malachi and Mattie Macon; married Ruth Lipscomb; children: Omari & Jamila. **Educ:** Johnson C Smith Univ, BA, 1966; Mich State Univ, MA, 1970, PhD, 1972. **Career:** Univ Mass, Amherst, asst prof, 1972-76, dir serv teacher educ, Ctr Urban Educ, 1974-76; Fayetteville State Univ, asst to chancellor, dir develop & univ rels, 1976-79; Johnson C Smith Univ, dir career coun & placement, 1979-83; Livingstone Col, pres, 1983-88; Gaston Coll, Dallas, NC, dean arts & sci, 1989-2000; dir develop, 2000-, coordr, reunion, currently. **Orgs:** NC Intern Coun, 1986; Mint Museum, Charlotte, NC, dir; NC Chap, Am Heart Asn; bd dirs, Salisbury-Rowan Chamber Com, 1986; Phi Delta Kappa; Omega Psi Phi; Sigma Pi Phi; Salisbury Rowan Symphony Soc; Gaston County, YMCA; Salisbury YMCA; First Union Nat Bank; exec bd, Fayetteville Bus League, 1986; dir, Gaston County Mus Art & Hist; dir, Gaston County Family Servs. **Honors/Awds:** Outstanding Black Educr, Black Caucus, 1976; Advisor of the Year, Fayetteville State, 1978-79; Achievement Recognition Award, Am Heart Asn,1984; Community Service Award, Charlotte, NC, Zeta Phi Beta, Delta Zeta Chap, 1984. **Home Addr:** 1000 Clifton St, Charlotte, NC 28216. **Business Addr:** Director of Development, Reunion Coordinator, Ohio State University, Enarson Hall 154 W 12th Ave, Columbus, OH 43210, **Business Phone:** (614)292-6446.

GREENE, WILLIE LOUIS
Baseball player. **Personal:** Born Sep 23, 1971, Milledgeville, GA. **Career:** Baseball player (retired), Cincinnati Reds, infielder, 1992-98; Baltimore Orioles, 1998; Toronto BlueJays, 1999; Chicago Cubs, infielder, 2000. **Honors/Awds:** The 26 homers and 91 RBIs, 1997. *

GREENE-THAPEDI, DR. LLWELLYN L.
Judge. **Personal:** Born in Guthrie, OK; daughter of Latimer Hamilton and Fannye M Gaines; divorced; children: Severn Latimer Deck, Letha Llwellyn Deck, Sheryl Renee Deck, Andre MartinThapedi & Anthony Isaac Thapedi. **Educ:** Langston Univ, Okla, BA; Univ Saskatchewan, MA; Loyola Univ, Chicago, Ill, JD. **Career:** Judge (retired); Univ Saskatchewan, Canada, instr, 1971-72; Amoco Oil Co, Chicago, IL, atty, 1976-81; Chicago State Univ, Chicago, IL, instr bus law, 1977-78; pvt pract, atty, 1981-92; State Ill, Circuit Ct Cook Co Judicial Circuit, judge. **Orgs:** Delivery Legal Serv Standing Comn, Ill State Bar Asn, 1976-85; pres, Cook County Bar Asn, 1988; bd dirs, Pub Interest Law Internship, 1982-83; bd dirs, Chicago Bar Asn, 1983-85; bd dirs, Ill Inst Continuing Legal Educ,1985-87; Citizen's Adv Comn Circuit Ct, 1987; Ill Trial Lawyers Asn, 1978-88; bd dirs, Nat Bar Asn, 1987-88; pres, Cook County Bar Asn, 1987-88; mem hearings comn, Atty Regist & Disciplinary Comn, 1989-90; Urban League; Nat Asn Advan Colored People; Delta Sigma Theta. **Honors/Awds:** Meritorious Service Award, 1983; Award, Nat Asn Equal Opportunity Educ,1984; Legal Assistance Found Award, 1984; Richard E Westbrook Award for legal excellence, 1986; Kizzie Award, 1987; Martin Luther King Teen Leadership Award, 1988.

GREENFIELD, ELOISE
Writer. **Personal:** Born May 17, 1929, Parmele, NC; married Robert J; children: Steven, Monica. **Educ:** Miner Teachers Col, 1949. **Career:** US Patent Off, clerk typist, 1949-56, supvr, 1956-60; DC Unemploy Compensation Bd, secy, 1963-64; Case Ctrl Tech Work & Training Opportunity Ctr, 1967-68; DC Dept Occup & Prof, adminr, 1968; DC Writers Workshop, staff mem, 1971-74; DC Comn Arts, writer in residence, 1973; freelance writer, currently; Books: Grandpa's Face, 1988; Night on Neighborhood Street, 1991. **Orgs:** African Am Writer's Guild; Authors Guild; Black Lit Umbrella; Inst Preserv & Study African Am Writing, 1984. **Honors/Awds:** Carter G Woodson Book Award, 1974; NY Times Outstanding Book; Irma Simonton Black Book Award, 1974; Jane Addams Children's Book Award, 1976; Coretta Scott King Award, 1978; American Library Association Notable Book; Award, Nat Black Child Develop Inst, 1981; Award, Black Women in Sisterhood for Action, 1983; Washington DC Mayor's Art Award for Literature, 1983; Grants, DC Comn Arts & Humanities. **Special Achievements:** Citation, Coun Interracial Books C; Citation, DC Asn Sch Librarians; Citation, Celebrations in Learning; short stories & articles for Negro Digest, Black World, Scholastic Scope, Ebony Jr, Negro Hist Bull, num children's Books; producer of children's recordings, 1982; works reviewed & dramatized on public TV (Reading Rainbow); was inducted into the National Literary Hall of Fame for Writers of African Descent. **Business Addr:** Author, PO Box 29077, Washington, DC 20017.*

GREENFIELD, MARK STEVEN
Executive director, artist. **Personal:** Born May 24, 1951, Los Angeles, CA; son of Russell E and M Geraldine; divorced. **Educ:** Calif State Univ, Long Beach, BA, 1973; Calif State Univ, Los Angeles, MFA, painting & drawing, 1987. **Career:** Ca State Univ, biology dept illus, 1971-73; May Co Dept Stores, asst dir, 1973-77; Los Angeles County Dept Parks & Recreation, park dir, 1973-79; Wing-foot prod, owner, 1975-; Rosey Grier's Giant Step, art instr, 1976-81; Brockman Gallery Prods, art coordr, 1977-78; Los Angeles Police Dept, artist, 1980-93; Watts Towers Arts Ctr, dir cult affairs, 1993-2002; Cult Affairs City Los Angles, art ctr dir, 1993-95; Los Angeles City Col, art instr, 1997-; Harbor Art Ctrs, LA, dir, 2002-04; LA Munic Art Gallery, exec dir, 2004-; Exhibitions: "Crenshaw Consciousness," 1987; "Iconography-The Banner Series," 1999; "Iconography," 2000; "Blackatcha," 2000. **Orgs:** Pres, Calif African Am Genealogical Soc, 1993-; bd mem, Los Angeles Art Asn, 1995-; bd mem, Watts Village Theater Co, 1997-; bd mem, Korean Am Mus, 1998-. **Honors/Awds:** Local Hero Award, Season Nonviolence, 1998; Golden State Mutual Life Insurance Company scholarship; House of Seagrams scholarship. **Home Addr:** 1250 Long Beach Ave Suite 206, Los Angeles, CA 90021, **Home Phone:** (213)623-3868. **Business Addr:** Director, Watts Towers Arts Center, Department of Cultural Affairs, 1765 E 107th St, Los Angeles, CA 90002, **Business Phone:** (213)847-4646.*

GREENFIELD, DR. ROBERT THOMAS
Physician. **Personal:** Born in Washington, DC; son of Robert T Sr and Avis; married Wilma Sue Robertson; children: Kimberly, Karyn, Robert III, Richard, Brian & Ashley. **Educ:** Howard Univ, BS, 1954, Col Med, MD, 1958. **Career:** Madigan Gen Hosp, intern, 1958-59; Freedmen's Hosp, res phys obstet/gynec, 1963-67; Howard Univ, Col Med, clinic instr, 1976-; Georgetown Univ, instr clinic, 1978-; Drs Greenfield, Booker Chartered, physician, pres, 1969-; Chartered Health Plan, med dir, founder, 1987-90. **Orgs:** Bd dir, Columbia Hosp Women, 1981-85; Joint Perinatal Site Visit Task Force, Wash, DC, 1982-85; chief staff, Columbia Hosp Women, 1983-85; chmn, bd dir, Colmesh Inc, 1985-86; adv bd, DC Maternal & Infant Health; Joint Venture Med Staff & Columbia Hosp; vchmn, Wash, DC, Sect Dist IV Am Col Obstet/Gynec; chmn, Wash, DC, Sect Dist IV, Am Co Obstet/Gynec; chmn, Perinatal Mortality Comn, Dist IV Amer Col Obstet/Gynec; Mayor's Comt Infant Mortality, 1990; founder, med dir, Chartered Health Plan, 1998-. **Honors/Awds:** Alpha Omega Alpha Med Scholastic Frat. **Military Serv:** AUS, capt, 5 yrs. **Home Addr:** 2010 Spruce Dr NW, Washington, DC 20012. **Business Addr:** Surgeon, Washington Hospital Center, 3300 Pa Ave, Washington, DC 20020, **Business Phone:** (202)877-3627.

GREENFIELD, DR. WILLIAM RUSSELL, JR. See Obituaries section.

GREENIDGE, KEVIN C.
Educator. **Personal:** Born Feb 5, 1952, New York, NY; married Dawn; children: Christopher, Ryan. **Educ:** Howard Univ, BS, 1973; Harvard Univ, pub health, health servs admin, 1977; State Univ NY, doctor med, 1977. **Career:** The New York Eye & Ear Infirmary, dir resident training, 1983-87, adj surgeon, 1985-91, assoc attend surgeon, 1991-; Metrop Hosp Ctr, chief, dept opthalmol, 1987-91, dir, glaucoma serv, 1987-96; Beth Israel Med Ctr, asst attend, 1987-; Long Island Col Hosp, chmn ophthalmol, 1996-; SUNY Brooklyn Health Sci Ctr; Kings Co Med Ctr, Dept Opthalmol, chmn, prof; Univ Hosp Brooklyn, Dept Opthalmol, dir; SUNY Brooklyn HSC Opthalmol Residency prog, Dept Opthalmol, dir, 1996-, State Univ New York Downstate Med Ctr, prof & chmn, currently. **Orgs:** The New York Co Med Soc, Legis Comm, 1985-89; adv bd dirs, Am Soc Contemp Ophthal, 1987-; pres, Int Glaucoma Congress, 1991; Am Bd Ophthal, assoc examiner, 1991-; deleg, Nat Med Asn, 1992-94; Manhattan Cent Med Soc, Managed Care Comt, chair, 1993-96; Skills Transfer Adv Comm, rep, Am Acad Ophthal, 1993, 1994-00; Med Soc State NY, alt deleg Am Med Asn. **Honors/Awds:** Honor Award, Am Acad of Ophthal, 1990; Hon Police Surgeon, New York City Police Dept, 1991; Leadership Award, Manhattan Cent Med Soc, 1994; Cert Achievement, One Hundred Black Men, 1994; Distinguished Alumni Award, Howard Univ, 1994; Richard C Troutman Distinguished Chair in Opthal & Opthalmic Microsurgery. **Special Achievements:** Featured in: Invest Ophthal supp, March 1985; Opthal, July, 1985; Glaucoma Associated With The Leaky Lens, Spaeth, GL, Katz J eds, Current Therapy in Opht Surgery, 1988; "Head Pain Assoc With The Eye, Cooper, BC, Lucente, FE, Mgt of Facial, Head, and Neck Pain, 1989; Angle Closure Glaucoma, Drake, M ed, Intl Ophthal Clin, 1990; Rainbow Yacht Club, commodore 1996, 1998. **Business Addr:** Chairman, Professor, State University of New York Downstate Medical Center, Department of Ophthalmology, 450 Clarkson Ave, PO Box 58, Brooklyn, NY 11203, **Business Phone:** (718)245-2165.*

GREENLEAF, LOUIS E
Government official. **Personal:** Born Apr 9, 1941, Newark, NJ; married Cynthia Robinson Conover; children: Bridget, Michael, Brectt & Towanna. **Educ:** Essex Co Col, AS, 1973; John Jay Col Criminal Justice, BS, 1975; Rutgers Sch Law, JD, 1978. **Career:** Pvt Law Pract, atty, 1983-86; Newark City, police dept, 1968-86, police dir, 1986-88; Essex County Prosecutors Off, chief investigators, 1988-94; Pvt Law Pract, 1994-97; Weights & Measures, supt, 1997-. **Orgs:** NJ Bar Asn, 1985-; Nat Orgn Black Law Enforcement Execs; bd trustees, Garden State Bar Asn; bd dir, Newark Emr Servs Families. **Military Serv:** AUS, E-4 2, yrs; Vietnam Serv, Good Conduct, 1964-66. **Business Addr:**

Superintendent, Office of Weights & Measures, 1261 Routes 1 & 9 South, Avenel, NJ 07001-1647, **Business Phone:** (732)815-4842.

GREENLEE, PETER ANTHONY
Lawyer. **Personal:** Born Feb 18, 1941, Des Moines, IA; son of Archie M and Donna O Graham; married Marcia McAdoo, Sep 5, 1965. **Educ:** Univ Wash, BA, 1965; Howard Univ Law Sch, JD, 1971. **Career:** Univ OR, instr; Job Corps, 1965-66; US Peace Corps Ethiopia, 1966-68; Reginald Heber Smith Fel Neighbourhood Legal Serv, atty, 1970-72; Redevelop Land Agency, 1972-74; Dept Energy, Wash, DC, atty & adv, 1974-90; Social Security Admin, Wash, DC, admin appeals judge. **Orgs:** Am Bar Asn; Nat Bar Asn; Delta Theta Phi; US Dist Ct Bar; US Supreme Ct Bar.

GREENLEE, SAM
Writer, television journalist, educator. **Personal:** Born Jul 13, 1930, Chicago, IL; married Nienke (divorced); children: 1. **Educ:** Univ Wis, BS, polit sci, 1952; Univ Chicago, attended 1957; Univ Thessalonikki, Greece, attended 1965; Community Film Workshop, attended 1974. **Career:** US Info Agency, foreign serv officer, 1957-65; LMOC, dep dir, 1965-69; Univ Djakarta, Indonesia, 1960-; WVON-AM, talk show host, 1988-; Ragdale Found fel, 1989; Ill Arts Coun fel, Blues for Little Prez, 1990; Columbia Col, screenwriting tutor, 1990-; Books: The Spook Who Sat by the Door, 1968; Blues for an African Princess, 1971; Baghdad Blues, 1976; Djakarta Blues, 2002. **Honors/Awds:** Meritorious Service Award, US Info Agency, 1958; Ill Poet Laureate Award, 1990. **Special Achievements:** Contributor of articles & short stories to magazines and journals. **Military Serv:** AUS, 1st lt, 1952-54.

GREENWOOD, DR. CHARLES H
Administrator. **Personal:** Born Jul 30, 1933, Anderson, IN; son of Lida M Lampkins and Huddie; married Theresa M Winfrey; children: Lisa Renee & Marc Charles. **Educ:** Ball State Teachers Col, BS, 1956; Colorado Col, attended 1958; Ball State Univ, MA, 1961; Indiana Univ, EdD, 1972. **Career:** Ball State Univ, grad asst, 1958-59, instr, 1961-63, assoc prof, 1973-, asst dean undergrad prog, 1974-84, Sch Continuing Educ, asst dean 1984-; E Chicago Pub Schs, teacher, 1959-61; N Ill Univ, vis prof 1973-74; pres, SHAC, 2005-. **Orgs:** Bd mem & vpres, pres, Family Coun Serv, 1961-71; bd mem, Col Ave Methodist Church, 1961-71, 1975-78; bd mem, secy, Muncie Housing Authority, 1968-78; bd trustees, All Am Family Inst, 1971-73; Am Asn Higher Educ, 1974-; Asn Supervision & Curric Develop, 1974-78; Asn Acad Affairs Admin, 1974-78; Phi Delta Kappa, 1976-; secy, YMCA Bd 1978; Adult Educ Asn Ind, 1978; vpres, Jr Achievement, 1979-81; vpres/pres, Kiwanis Club Muncie Ind, 1980-81; lt gov Wapahanal Div, 1982-83; evaluator, Am Coun Educ 1984; bd dirs, E Cent Ind Community Singers, 1985-86, 1998-99; gov elect, Sigma Iota Epsilon 1986; gov, Ind Dist Kiwanis Int, 1990-91; educ coord Acad Comn Leadership; liaison officer, Liason Adv Bd, Midwest rep; dir, Aerospace Educ USAF CAP Aux Ind Wing; bd dir, Ball Mem Hosp, 1996-2005; Int Chmn Coun & Conv Munic, Kiwanas, int bd mem, United Way, 1997; Ind Blacks Higher Educ; Am Asn Blacks Higher Educ; Sigma Iota Epilson; NUCEA; Loaned Exec United Way, 2001-04; diversity comt, Kiwanis Int, 2001-04; Kiwanis Adv Bd Riley Hosp. **Honors/Awds:** Nat Bronze Award Jr Achievement, 1980; Outstanding Minority Fac, Ball State Univ; Distinguished Lt Gov Kiwanis Int, 1983; Sagamore of the Wabash, 1991; Singing Hoosiers Outstanding Alumni Award, Ind Univ, 2001. **Military Serv:** AUS, sp4, 1956-58; Civil Air Patrol USAF Aux CAP Lt Col, 1989-, Col, 2002; Wing Comdr, USAF-CAP; Good Conduct Medal; Aerospace Educ Mem, 1956-83; Presidential Unit Citation. **Business Addr:** Associate professor and Assistant Dean School of Extended Education, Ball State University, School of Extended Education, 2000 Univ Ave WQ 403, Muncie, IN 47306, **Business Phone:** (765)285-5776.

GREENWOOD, DAVID KASIM
Basketball player. **Personal:** Born May 27, 1957, Lynwood, CA; married Joyce; children: Tiffany Crystal Marie. **Educ:** Univ Calif, LA, BA, Hist, 1979. **Career:** Basketball player (retired); Chicago Bulls, 1980-85; San Antonio Spurs,1986-89, 1990; Denver Nuggets, 1989; Detroit Pistons, 1990. **Orgs:** Taught basketball clinics Western US, 1980; Natl Basketball Retired Players Assn. **Honors/Awds:** Hall of Fame, Univ Calif Athletic. **Special Achievements:** NBA First Team All Rookie Team, 1978-79.

GREENWOOD, EDNA TURNER
Editor. **Personal:** Born in Shiner, TX; daughter of David Koontz and Mamie; married Wilbert (deceased); children: Ronald Vann Turner; married Norris Greenwood. **Educ:** Tucker Bus Col, St Louis, MO, 1953. **Career:** Editor (retired); Good Publ Co (magazines, Jive, Bronze Thrills, Hip, Soul Confessions, Sepia & Soul Teen) Ft Worth TX, ed dir; circulation mgr, ed, 25 yrs. **Orgs:** Baker Chapel Am Ch; Nat Asn Advan Colored People; Ft Worth C of C; bd mem, Neighborhood Action Comm, Tarrant Action on Aging; bd mem, United Ctrs. **Honors/Awds:** Award Margaret Caskey Women in Commun, Ft Worth Prof Chap Women Commun, 1977. **Home Addr:** 5950 Alexandria Sky Lane, Fort Worth, TX 76119, **Home Phone:** (817)478-9813. *

GREENWOOD, MONIQUE
Business owner, editor, writer. **Personal:** Born 1959, Washington, DC; married Glen Pogue, Jan 1, 1988; children: Glynn. **Educ:** Howard Univ, BA; Simmons Grad Sch Bus, MBA. **Career:** Fairchild Prods, staff, 1981-96; Essence Mag, lifestyle dir, 1996-98, execed, 1998-2000, chief ed, 2000-01; Akwaaba Bed & Breakfast, pres & chief exec officer, 1995-; Author: Go On Girl! Book Club Guide to Reading Groups, 1999; Having What Matters: The Black Woman's Guide to Creating the Life You Really Want, 2001; Life Under New Management: How to Fire Your Job & Become Your Own Boss. **Honors/Awds:** Points of Light Award, Pres George W Bush, 2001. **Business Addr:** Owner, Akwaaba Mansion Bed & Breakfast, 347 McDonough St, Brooklyn, NY 11233-1012, **Business Phone:** (718)455-5958.

GREENWOOD, DR. THERESA M WINFREY
Educator, musician. **Personal:** Born Dec 28, 1936, Cairo, IL; daughter of Hubert Augusta Winfrey and Lillian Theresa Williams Winfrey; married Dr Charles H Greenwood, Jun 1, 1960; children: Lisa Renee & Marc Charles. **Educ:** Millikin Univ, BA, music educ, 1959; Ball State Univ, EdM, 1963, EdD, 1976; Jewish Studies fel, Ball State Univ, 1998. **Career:** E Chicago Pub Sch, music teacher, 1959-61; Muncie Pub Schs, teacher, 1962-68; Ball State Univ, acad counr, 1971-72, Burris Lab Sch, asst prof educ, 1979, 1995-, teacher gifted/talented prog, 1986-, primary educ prof, currently. **Orgs:** Past pres, Sigma Alpha Iota, 1958; music adjudicator, NISBOVA, 1961-; bd dir, United Way, ARC, Huffer Day Care & WIPB-TV, 1969-75; Kappa Delta Pi, 1972-73; mem & state secy, Nat League Am Pa Women,1973-78; fel, Nat Fel Funds Emory Univ, 1973-76; testified, White House Conf Families, 1980; chiar, Eastern Ind Community; adv bd, Social Studies Coun Nat Pub, 1982; ed bd, White River State Park, 1983; judge, Social Study Hist Days; ed bd, Nat Soc Studies J; speaker, High Sch Young Writers Conf, 1986; media vol, Pan-Am Games, 1987; Nat League Am Pen Women; Pi Lambda Theta; Sigma Alpha Iota. **Honors/Awds:** Nat Asn Advan Colored People Award, 1980; Soc Studies Grant, 1982; Teacher of the Year, runner-up, Ind Dept Educ, 1982-83; Commendation Ind Gov Orr, 1982; Indiana All-American Family Award, Family Weekly Mag & Eastern Airlines, 1972; Ball State Univ Minority Achievement Award, Minority Stud Develop, 1989; Ford Fellowship Doctorate, Eli Lilly Found, 1989; Women of the Rainbow, Indianapolis Minority Chamber Com, 1992; The American Teacher Telecast, Disney, 1994; Geraldine R Dodge, 1994; Indiana Teacher of the Year Finalist, 1994; Unsung Heroes Award, 1998; Fulbright Memorial Scholar to Japan, 1998. **Special Achievements:** Feature Story, Ball State University Research Publication Bene Facta; Article: "Cross-Cultural Educ for Elementary School," The Social Studies Teacher, 1983; published poems in the Saturday Evening Post, 1974; students gained extensive publicity for "DearWorld" letters to Pres Reagan & Gen Sec Mikhail Gorbachev during Washington Summit (exhibited 10 months at World's Largest Children Museum), 1988; writing, "Open Letter to Miss Crawford, Diary of a Black Girl Growing Up in America," Madison County Magazine, March 1991; Published: Psalms of a Black Mother, Warner Press ,1970, "Break Thru (Upper Room Anthology)," 1972, "Black Like It Is/Was," 1974, "Crazy to be Alive in Such a Strange World," 1977, Gospel Graffiti, M Evans, NY, 1978, weekly newspaper column, Muncie Eve Press Poems; Bibliographic: Church Herald, 1972, Essence Mag, 1975, Ladies Home Journal, 1976; Technology Horizons Education Journal, "Let's Pop Some Corn and Watch Your Report Card" Principal Magazine (NAESP), 1995; frequent colomunist for The Muncie Star Press; Interviewed for Indianapolis Star and Ball State Information Bureau for national wire services for views on "The Status of Minorities in Teaching" and "Black Creativity and Education; "Created and Produced Educational television show, "What's In The Attic?"; Presented at state and national Gifted Conferences, Indianapolis and Salt Lake City, Utah (Young Entrepreneurs Project); Panal for local PBS telecast, "Parents, The Early Years," 1992; Developed a theoretical, Multiple Intelligence Model based on African Proverbs; "Wood, Paint and a Good Idea: Young Entrepreneurs," The Technology Teacher, 1998; "Traveling Teddy Bears Teach More Than Geography," Teddy Bear Review, 1999; Int Tech Ed Asn Conference, presenter, 1999. **Business Addr:** Assistant Professor, Primary Education Professor, Ball State University, Burris Laboratory School, 2000 W Univ Ave, Muncie, IN 47306, **Business Phone:** (765)285-1131.

GREER, BAUNITA
Executive. **Educ:** Am Univ, BSBA, acct. **Career:** Daniel & Bell Inc, treas & bd dir; New York Sch Continuing & Prof Studies, adj prof; Cromwell, Miller & Greer, Inc, ceo, currently; Wall Street Conferences Inc, pres, exec, currently; NY Stock Exchange, examiner; GRW Capital Corp, exec, currently. **Orgs:** Dir, New York Soc Security Analysis. **Honors/Awds:** Volunteer of the Year Award, NYSSA, 1998 & 2001. **Business Addr:** Executive, GRW Capital Corporation, 1010 Vermont Ave Suite 710 2nd Fl, Washington, DC 20005, **Business Phone:** (202)628-0880.

GREER, CHERIE
Athlete, executive. **Personal:** Born in Philadelphia, PA; daughter of Hal and Mayme. **Educ:** UVA, bachelors, communications, 1994. **Career:** Athlete (retired), Executive; Lacrosse player; exec asst; GranHco Enterprises, vpres, currently. **Honors/Awds:** World Cup Champions, Lacrosse, 1993, 1996 & 1997; most valuable player, 1997. **Special Achievements:** Became only the fourth woman in the history of Virginia athletics and the first women's lacrosse player to have her number retired. Greer's number 18 was officially retired at halftime of the Virginia vs. Florida Statemen's basketball game on Feb 4, 1995; first Black and the youngest player.

GREER, DONOVAN ORLANDO
Football player. **Personal:** Born Sep 11, 1974, Houston, TX. **Educ:** Tex A&M univ. **Career:** Football player (retired); New Orleans Saints, defensive back, 1997; Atlanta Falcons, 1997; Buffalo Bills, 1998-00; Wash Redskins, 2001; Detroit Lions, corner back, 2002.

GREER, EDWARD M
Real estate agent. **Personal:** Born Mar 8, 1924, Gary, WV; married Jewell Means; children: Gail Lyle, Michael & Kenneth. **Educ:** WVa State Col, BS, 1948; George Wash Univ, MS, 1967. **Career:** Greer & Assoc Realtors, broker & owner, currently. **Orgs:** Asn AUS Mil Order World Wars; Nat Asn Uniformed Serv, Disabled Am Veterans; Nat War Col Alumni Asn; Kappa Alpha Psi Fraternity Retired Officers Asn. **Honors/Awds:** Alumnus of the Year, WVa State Col, 1963. **Military Serv:** AUS, Major Gen; Distinguished Service Medal; Silver Star; Legion Merit Oak Leaf Cluster; Bronze Star Oak Leaf Cluster; Air Medal; Joint Services Commendation Medal; Army Commendation Medal. **Home Addr:** 3134 Mesa Verde Lane, El Paso, TX 79904, **Home Phone:** (915)755-2244. **Business Addr:** Owner, Broker, Greer & Associates Realtors, 3134 Mesa Verde Lane, El Paso, TX 79904, **Business Phone:** (915)751-4293.*

GREER, HAROLD EVERETT (HAL GREER)
Basketball coach, basketball player. **Personal:** Born Jun 26, 1936, Huntington, WV; married Mayme; children: 3. **Educ:** Marshall Univ, Huntington, WV, attended 1959. **Career:** Basketball player (retired), basketball coach; Syracuse Nationals, guard, 1959-63; Philadelphia 76ers, guard, 1964-73; CBA, Philadelphia Kings, coach, 1980-81. **Honors/Awds:** NBA All-Star Game MVP, 1968; Naismith Memorial Basketball Hall of Fame, 1982; Hal Greer Day, named in honor; Hal Greer Blvd, named in honor. **Special Achievements:** First African American to play for a major college team in the state; Only African-American athlete enshrined in a major sports hall of fame from West Virginia.

GREER, KARYN LYNETTE
Television journalist. **Personal:** Born Jun 20, 1962, Chicago, IL; daughter of Ronald Virgil and Jeanette Brenda Crossley; married. **Educ:** Univ Ill, Champaign, IL, BA, broadcast jour & speech commun, 1984. **Career:** WCIA-TV, Champaign, IL, asst dir newscasts, 1983-84; WICD-TV, Champaign, IL, weekend anchor & reporter, 1985-87; WCSC-TV, Charleston, SC, weekend anchor & reporter, 1987-89; WGNX-TV, Atlanta, GA, weeknight anchor & med reporter, 1989; Wxia Tv-11 Alive, anchor & reporter, 1999-. **Orgs:** Magnolia Chap, Links Inc; bd dirs, Arthritis Found; bd dirs, Volleyfest; bd dirs, Atlanta 2 Day Walk Breast Cancer; bd govs, Nat Acad TV Arts & Sci, currently; Alpha Kappa Alpha Sorority Inc, 1982-; pres, Atlanta Press Club; bd mem, Arthritis Found. **Honors/Awds:** Revlon Kizzy Award; Black Woman Hall of Fame, 1990; First Place Feature, Atlanta Asn Black Journalists, 1990; Emmy Award, Specialty Reporting, 1991, Best Newscast, Collab Writing, Nat Acad TV Arts & Sci; Best of Gannett, Best Newscast.

GREER, DR. ROBERT O, JR.
Pathologist, writer, educator. **Personal:** Born Mar 9, 1944, Columbus, OH; son of Robert O Sr and Mary A; married Phyllis Ann Harwell. **Educ:** Miami Univ, Oxford, OH, BA, 1965; Howard Univ, DDS, 1969; Boston Univ, ScD MD, 1974, MA, creative writing, 1988. **Career:** Univ Colo Health Sci Ctr, Dept Path, asst prof, 1974-77; UCHSC, Dept Path, assoc prof, 1977-80; Mile High Med Soc, secy, 1978-79, pres, 1983-85; Univ Colo Sch Dent, Div Oral Path & Oncol, prof & chmn, 1980-; UCHSC, Dept Path & Oncol, prof, chmn, 1984-; Western States Regional Path Lab, pres & chief pathologist; Books: Limited Time, 2000; Isolation & Other Stories, 2002; Heat Shock, 2003; The Devil's Hatband, 2004; The Fourth Perspective, 2004; The Devil's Red Nickel, 2005; Resurrecting Langston Blue, 2005; The Devil's Backbone, 2006; The Mongoose Deception, 2007; Blackbird, Farewell, 2008. **Orgs:** Miami Univ, Alumni Bd Dir, 1984-; Am Cancer Soc. **Military Serv:** USCG, lt & comdr. **Business Addr:** Professor, University of Colorado School of Dentistry, University of Colorado Health Science Center, 4200 E 9th St 1738C4, Denver, CO 80045, **Business Phone:** (303)315-5225.

GREER, THOMAS H.
Newspaper executive. **Personal:** Born Jul 24, 1942, Nashville, TN; son of Thomas H (deceased) and Eliza S (deceased); children: Kasey Lynn, Janna W. **Educ:** Dillard Univ, BA, 1963. **Career:** Chicago-Sun Times, sports reporter; Philadelphia Daily News, sports columnist, writer; New York Daily News, sports columnist; Plain Dealer, sports ed, managing ed, vpres, sr ed, 1992-99, sr vpres, 1999-. **Orgs:** Omega Psi Phi Fraternity Inc, 1959-; Am Soc Newspaper Eds, 1986-; bd dirs, Cleveland Chap Red Cross, 1990-; bd trustees, Int Serv Ctr; bd trustees, Greater Cleveland Roundtable, 1991-; Nat Asn Minority Media Execs, 1992-; bd trustees, Cuyahoga Plan; bd trustees, Metro Health Found, 1999-; Nat Asn

Black Journalists Associated Press Sports Ed Asn. **Honors/Awds:** Paul Miller Distinguished Journalism Lectr, Okla State Univ, 1993; Ed Writing Award, Judge, Scripps-Howard Found Walker Stone, 1993. **Special Achievements:** Twice served on the Pulitzer Prize Nominating Jury. **Business Addr:** Senior Vice President, Senior Editor, Plain Dealer, 1801 Super Ave, Cleveland, OH 44114, **Business Phone:** (216)999-4360.*

GREG, G-MONEY. See ANTHONY, GREGORY C.

GREGG, HARRISON M, JR.
Lawyer. **Personal:** Born Sep 24, 1942, Longview, TX; son of Harrison and Ola Timberlake; married Arizona Johnson, Jun 18, 1963; children: Sherri Kimberly. **Educ:** Tex Southern Univ, BA, 1968, JD, 1971; Master Barber, 1958. **Career:** State Tex, second admin region, 4D master judge, 1987-; Tex Paralegal Sch, instr, 1976-; Gregg Okehie & Cashin, atty, 1972-; Pvt Pract, currently; Harris County Attorney's Off, atty, currently. **Orgs:** Houston Bar Asn; Tex State Bar; Houston Lawyer Asn; Tex Crimnal Defense Lawyers; Harris Co Criminal Defense Lawyers; Nat Bar Asn; Am Bar Asn. **Honors/Awds:** Phi Alpha Delta; Free & Accepted Prince Hall Mason; vol UNCF. **Military Serv:** AUS. **Home Addr:** 3442 Eldorado Blvd, Missouri City, TX 77459. **Business Phone:** (713)755-5101.

GREGG, LUCIUS PERRY, JR.
Executive. **Personal:** Born Jan 16, 1933, Henderson, NC; married Doris Marie Jefferson. **Educ:** US Naval Acad, BS, 1955; MA Inst Tech, MS, 1961; Cath Univ, doctoral candidate, 1963; Grinnell Col, hon DSc, 1973; Aspen Inst Exec Prog, 1974; Adv Mgmt Prog Harvard Bus Sch, 1975. **Career:** USAF Office Scientific Research, proj dir in space tech, 1961-65; Northwestern U, assoc dean of Scis & dir research coordr, 1965-69; Alfred P Sloan Found, prog officer, 1969-71; 1st Chicago Univ Finance Corp, pres, 1972-74; 1st Nat Bank Chicago, vice pres, 1972. **Orgs:** Bd dirs, Corp for Pub Broadcasting, 1975-; acad bd US Naval Acad, 1971-; Harvard Univ Trsts Visiting Comm in physics, 1973-; Pres's Com on White HouseFellows Midwest Reg Selec Com, 1974-; Nat Acad of Sci Found Com on Human Resources, 1973-; bd mem, Fermi NatAccel Lab, 1967-77; Roosevelt Univ, 1976-; Garrett Theol Sem, 1974-; Tulane Univ Bd of Visitors, 1972-; Chicago Coun on Foreign Rel, 1975-; Harvard Bus Sch of Chicago, 1977; MIT Trsts Visiting Con in Aero & Astronautics; Harvard Club of Chicago, 1975-; Univ Club Chicago, 1972-; Econ Club Chicago, 1967-. **Honors/Awds:** Hon mem, Sigma Gamma Tau, 1969; 1 of 10 outstanding young men, Chicago Asn Commerce & Indus, 1966; outstanding young engr, Wash Acad Sci, 1964. **Military Serv:** USMC, pfc, 1950-51; USAF, 1955-62.

GREGORY, DICK. See GREGORY, RICHARD CLAXTON.

GREGORY, FREDERICK DREW
Military leader, astronaut. **Personal:** Born Jan 7, 1941, Washington, DC; son of Francis A and Nora Drew; married Barbara Ann Archer, Jun 3, 1964; children: Frederick D Jr & Heather Lynn Gregory Skeens. **Educ:** USAF Acad, BS, 1964; George Wash Univ, MSA, 1977; Univ DC, Hon Doctorate Sci. **Career:** Military service (retired), airforce Official, NASA Astronaut; USAF, helicopter & fighter pilot, 1965-70; USAF & NASA, res test pilot, 1971-78, astronaut, 1978-92; NASA, assoc adminr, 1992-2001, dep adminr, 2002-05, actg adminr, 2005. **Orgs:** Soc Exp Test Pilots; Order of Daedalians; Tuskegee Airmen Inc; Air Force Assoc; Am Helicopter Soc; Nat Tech Asn; USAF Acad Asn Graduates; Omega Psi Phi; Sigma Pi Phi; Air Force Acad Asn Grad; Order Daedalians; Asn Space Explorers; Photonics Lab Fisk Univ; Engineering Col, Howard Univ; bd trustees, Md Space Ctr; Nat Tech Asn; Tuskegee Airmen Inc; bd dir, Young Astronaut Coun; Va Air & Space Center-Hampton Roads History Ctr. **Honors/Awds:** Distinguished Nat Scientist Award, Nat Soc Black Engrs, 1979; Two NASA Distinguished Service Medals; Three NASA Space Flight Medals; NASA Outstanding Leadership Award, NASA; Distinguished Alumni Award, George Wash Univ; Top 20 Minority Engineers, 1990; IRA Eaker Fel, Air Force Asn; President Medal, Charles R Drew, Univ Med & Sci; Meritorious Service Medal; Recipient of numerous NASA group & individual achievement awards as well as civic & community awards. **Military Serv:** USAF, col; Defense Super Service Medal, 2 Distinguished Flying Crosses, Meritorious Service Medal, 16 Air Medals, Air Force Commendation Medal; Defense Meritorious Service Medal; Legion of Merit; National Intelligence Medal of Achievement.

GREGORY, KARL DWIGHT
Executive, consultant, educator. **Personal:** Born Mar 26, 1931, Detroit, MI; son of Bertram Gregory and Sybil Gregory; married Tenicia Ann Banks; children: Kurt David, Sheila Therese & Karin Diane. **Educ:** Wayne State Univ, BA, econ, 1951, MA, fin, 1957; Univ Mich, PhD, econ,1962; Brown Univ, Postdoctoral, micro econ, attended. **Career:** Detroit Housing Comn, tech aid-acct, 1951-53; Fed Res Bank St Louis, economist, 1959; Wayne State Univ, prof, 1960-61, 1964-67; Off Mgt & Budget, Wash DC, economist, 1961-64; Fed for Self-Determination, exec dir, 1968-69; Accord Inc Housing Rehabil Detroit, pres, chief exec officer, bd chmn, 1970-71; SUNY Buffalo, vis prof, 1974; Congressional Budget Office, exec staff, sr economist, 1974-75; 1st Independence Nat Bank, inter impres, 1980-81; Karl D Gregory & Assoc, managing dir; Oakland Univ, prof in & strategic planning, 1968-96, distinguished prof emer econs, 1996-. **Orgs:** Dir, Nat Econ Asn, Black Econ Res Ctr, 1968-75, Inner City Bus Improvement Forum, 1968-87; dir, chief org, chmn bd, 1st Independence Nat Bank, 1970-81; bd trustees Protestant Episcopal Diocese MI, 1972-74, 1984-86, 1989-92; dir Inner City Capital Formation, 1973-86; Detroit Capital Access Ctr, 1973-86; adv comm US Census Black Population, 1976-79; US Trade Negotiations Tokyo Round, 1978-81; dir, Detroit Br Fed Reserve Bank Chicago, 1981-86; Barden Cable vision Detroit, 1982-94; Detroit Metro Small Bus Investment Corp, 1982-85; Detroit Econ Growth Corp, 1982-94; bd trustees Oakland Cty Bus Attraction & Expansion Comn, 1983-84; Gov Blanchard's Entrepreneurs & Small Bus Comn, 1984-89; vpres, Econ Club Detroit, 1984-89; first vice chair, Mich Minority Technology Coun,1988-96; dir Detroit Urban League, 1989-92; Detroit Alliance for Fair Banking, 1989-; chmn bd, Greater BIDCO, 1990-96; Mich Gov Engler's Coun Econ Advisors, 1992-94; chair, Adult Well Being Services, 2007-. **Honors/ Awds:** Numerous community service & academic awards; numerous publications in academic journals; expert witness on econ matters; Nat Asn for the Advancement of Colored People Research Award, 1987; Michigan Minority Business Advocate of the Year, US Small Business Admin, 1989; Distinguished Professor, Oakland Univ, 1995. **Military Serv:** AUS, artillery 1st lt, 1953-56. **Business Addr:** Distinguished Professor Emeritus, Oakland University, School of Business Administration, 238J Elliott Hall, Rochester, MI 48309-4401, **Business Phone:** (248)370-3280.

GREGORY, MICHAEL SAMUEL
Administrator. **Personal:** Born Dec 25, 1949, Barbourville, KY; son of Royal and Dorothy; married Linda Joy McCowan, May 13, 1973; children: Arron K, DaNiel K & Brittany M. **Educ:** KEN State UNIV, BS, 1973, MPA, 1974; UNIV MIN, advan graduate study, 1981; Ohio State UNIV, advan graduate study, 1982. **Career:** KEN State UNIV, Coop EDUC, asst dir, 1973-74, dir, 1974-77; St John's UNIV, Career Planning, dir, 1977-81; Ohio State UNIV, Law Placement, dir, 1981-87; Columbus Urban League, Sr Prog, dir, 1987-. **Orgs:** Columbus Urban League; NCP; AM Soc Personnel ADRs; Columbus Children's Hosp Develop Bd; NAT Urban League; Ohio Soc Prevent Blindness Bd. **Honors/Awds:** KEN State UNIV, Alpha Mu Gamma Honor Soc, 1972; Big Ten Univs, CIC Fellowship, 1980; Ohio State UNIV, Black Law Students ASN, 1987; DPT Housing & Urban Develop Fellowship, 1973. **Special Achievements:** NAT Urban League, Senior Job Placement Leader, 1988, Affiliate, 1992. **Business Addr:** Chief Operations Officer, Creative Medical Personnel, PO Box 578, Brice, OH 43109-0452.*

GREGORY, RICHARD CLAXTON (DICK GREGORY)
Entrepreneur, lecturer, civil rights activist. **Personal:** Born Oct 12, 1932, St Louis, MO; son of Presley and Lucille Franklin; married Lillian Smith, Feb 2, 1959; children: Michele, Lynne, Paula, Pamela, Stephanie, Gregory, Christian, Ayanna, Miss& Yohance. **Educ:** Southern Ill Univ, Carbondale, attended 1953, 1956. **Career:** Esquire Club, Chicago, entertainer; night club Apex Robbins, IL, owner; MC Roberts Show Club, Chicago, 1959-60; appeared in night clubs in Milwaukee, Akron, San Francisco, Hollywood, numerous other cities, 1960-; TV guest appearances Jack Parr Show, others; rec include: Dick Gregory in Living Black & White; Dick Gregory; The Light Side-Dark Side; lectr; Am Prog Bur, lectr, 1967-; Peace & Freedom Party Presidential Candidate, 1968; Dick Gregory Health Enterprises, Chicago, founder, 1984-; Films: Sweet Love, Bitter, 1967; Panther, 1995; Children of the Struggle, 1999; The Hot Chick, 2002; One Bright Shining Momen, 2006; Albums: In Living Black and White, 1961; East & West, 1961; Dick Gregory Talks Turkey, 1962; The Two Sides of Dick Gregory, 1963; Dick Gregory Running for President, 1964; So You See.. We All Have Problems; Dick Gregory On, 1969; The Light Side: The Dark Side, 1969; Dick Gregory's Frankenstein, 1970; Live at the Village Gate, 1970; At Kent State, 1971; Caught in the Act, 1974; The Best of Dick Gregory (1997). **Orgs:** Alpha Phi Alpha. **Honors/Awds:** Winner No Mile Championship, 1951, 1952; Outstanding Athlete, So Ill Univ,1953; Ebony-Topaz Heritage & Freedom Award, 1978; Doctor of HumaneLetters, Southern Ill Univ, Carbondale, 1989; numerous other honorary-doctoral degrees; Smile of the Year Award, Angel City Dental Soc, 1999. **Special Achievements:** Books : From the Back of the Bus, 1962; Nigger, 1964; What's Happening, 1965; The Shadow That Scares Me, Write Me In, No More Lies, 1971; Dick Gregory's Political Primer, 1971; Dick Gregory's Natural Diet for Folks Who Eat Cookin, 1973; Dick Gregory's Bible & Tales with Commentary, 1974; Up From Nigger, 1976; The Murder of Martin Luther King Jr, 1977; Callus On My Soul, 2000. **Military Serv:** AUS, 1953-55. **Business Addr:** Founder, Dick Gregory Health Enterprises, 61 Russell St, Plymouth, MA 02360, **Business Phone:** (508)746-7427.

GREGORY, ROBERT ALPHONSO
Executive. **Personal:** Born Jun 21, 1935, Hertford, NC; married Barbara Ann White; children: Alan & Christopher. **Educ:** Elizabeth City State Univ NC, BS, 1956. **Career:** Rheingold Breweries Inc, acct sales rep, 1963-68; Faberge Inc, acct exec, 1968-72; 3M Duplicating Prod Div, area sales rep, 1972-74, nat mkt coordr, 1974-75; 3M Copying Prod Div, nat sales develop coordr, 1975-; Off Sys Div 3M, competitive anal supvr, 1980-82; Syst Bus Develop Unit, OSD 3M, mkt develop supvr, 1982-83; LES Ed Mkt OSD 3M, nat pub sector mkt coordr, 1983-2001; US Ct Appeals, 2001-. **Orgs:** Chap organizer Alpha Phi Alpha Frat Inc, 1955-56; presenter, St Paul C C, 1974; family mem, St Paul Urban League, 1975-76; nat coordr Copying Prod Div 3M, 1975-80; finance com spokesman, Guardian Angels Parish Coun, 1977-80. **Honors/Awds:** Author, mkt res bks, 1974-75, awareness bullet, 1975-80, competitive awareness bks, 1977-80, prod, VTR Ser Competition, 3M Copying Prod Div, 1979-80. **Military Serv:** AUS, corpl, 1957-60. **Business Phone:** (202)331-3967.

GREGORY, ROGER LEE
Lawyer. **Personal:** Born Jul 17, 1953, Philadelphia, PA; son of George L and Fannie Mae Washington; married Carla Eugenia Lewis Gregory, Sep 6, 1980; children: Adriene Leigh, Rachel Leigh, Christina Leigh. **Educ:** VA State Univ, Petersburg, VA, BA, 1975; Univ MI, Ann Arbor, MI, JD, 1978. **Career:** Butzel, Long, Gust, Klein & Van Zile, Detroit, MI, assoc atty, 1978-80; Hunton & Williams, Richmond, VA, assoc atty, 1980-82; Wilder & Gregory, Richmond, VA, managing partner, 1982-01; US Court Appeals Fourth Circuit, judge, 2001-. **Orgs:** Dir, Industrial Develop Authority, 1984-91; dir, Richmond Metro Chamber Com, 1989-91; Pres, Old Dominion Bar Asn, 1990-92; bd visitors, VA Commonwealth Univ, past rector, 1985-93; VA State univ Found Bd, 1993-; Richmond Renaissance, chair exec comt, 1993-; bd visitors, VA State Univ, 1993-; bd dirs, Richmond Bar Asn, 1989-93; dir, Richfood Holding Inc, 1994-; bd, Richfood Holding Inc, 1994-; bd visitors, Left VA State Univ, 1996; bd, Christian Children's Fund, 1997-; VA Asn Defense Attys bd dir, 1996-; Fourth Circuit Judicial Conf. **Honors/Awds:** Honor Society, Alpha Mu Gamma, 1973; Honor Society, Alpha Kappa Mu, 1974; Top 75 Black College Students America, Black Enterprise Mag, 1975; 100 Most Influential Richmonders, Richmond Surroundings Mag, 1990; Proclamation of Achievement, VA State Univ, 1991; Humanitarian Award, Nat Conf Christians & Jews, 1997; Virginia Law Foundation fellow. **Business Addr:** Judge, United States Department Justice, Office Legal Policy, 950 Pennsylvania Ave NW, Rm 4234 Main Justice Bldg, Washington, DC 20530-0001, **Business Phone:** (202)514-4601.*

GREGORY, MOST REV. WILTON DANIEL
Clergy, archbishop. **Personal:** Born Dec 7, 1947, Chicago, IL; son of Wilton D Gregory Sr and Ethel D Duncan. **Educ:** Niles Col Loyola Univ, BA, 1969; St Mary Lake Sem, STB, 1971, MDiv, 1973, STL, 1974; Pontifical Liturgical Inst Sant'Anselmo Rome, Italy, SLD, 1980; DHL, Spring Hill Col, Mobile, AL; DHL, Xavier Univ, Cincinnati, OH; DHL, McKendree Col, Lebanon, IL. **Career:** St Mary Lake Sem, teacher; Titular Bishop Oliva; Archdiocese of Chicago, auxiliary bishop, 1983-93; Catholic Diocese Belleville, bishop, 1994-05; archbishop, Atlanta, 2005-. **Orgs:** Catholic Theol Soc Am; N Am Acad Liturgy; Midwestern Asn Spiritual Dirs; Catholic Theol Soc Am, 1980; N Am Acad Liturgy, 1981; Midwestern Asn Spiritual Dirs, 1981; chair, 1990-93, educ, 1993, doctrine, 1994, Bishops Comm Liturgy; bd trustees, Archdiocese Chicago Seminaries; pres, US Conf Catholic Bishops, 2002. **Honors/Awds:** Sword of Loyola, St Louis Univ, 2004; Cardinal Bernardin Award, Catholic Common Ground Initiative, 2006; Doctorate of humanities, Lewis Univ, Romeoville, IL; Doctorate of humanities, St Louis Univ, MO. **Special Achievements:** Chicago's first black Bishop; first black pres, US Conf Chatholic Bishops, 2001-04. **Business Addr:** Archbishop, Catholic Diocese Belleville-Chancery Off, 222 S 3rd St, Belleville, IL 62220-1985.*

GRESHAM, DARRYL WAYNE
Manager. **Personal:** Born Feb 4, 1958, Pittsburgh, PA; son of James Gresham and Lillian; married Lydia R Woods (divorced); children: Avery. **Educ:** Carnegie-Mellon Univ, mechanical engineering, 1980. **Career:** Abbott Laboratories, diagnostics sales rep, clin chemistry specialist, field product mgr, sr product mgr, district sales mgr, mgr sales training, marketing mgr, dir, chemistry marketing, area dir, Great Lakes Region. **Orgs:** Nat Society Black Engineers; Black MBA Asn; Nat Sales Network; Black Bus Netwok. **Honors/Awds:** YMCA, Black Achievers Award, 2000. **Home Addr:** 1107 Whispering Oaks Dr, Keller, TX 76248.

GREY, MAURICE E.
Executive. **Career:** Edwards Sisters Realty, partner, currently. **Business Addr:** Partner, Edwards Sisters Realty, 740 St Nichols Ave, New York, NY 10031, **Business Phone:** (212)926-1200 Ext 16.

GRIER, ARTHUR E., JR.
Executive. **Personal:** Born Mar 21, 1943, Charlotte, NC; married Linda Clay; children: Anthony, Eugene Grier, III. **Educ:** Fla A&M Univ; Cent Piedmont Community Col; Cincinnati Col Mortuary Sci, 1969. **Career:** Arthur E Grier & Arthur Grier Jr. Trust, pres; Grier Funeral Serv, owner, currently. **Orgs:** Funeral Dirs & Mort Asn NC; Western Dist Funeral Dirs & Mortuary Asn NC Inc; Nat Funeral Dir p Mort Asn NC Inc; bd mem, Nat FD; chmn, Funeral Dirs & Mort Asn NC Inc; Black Caucus; Big Bros Asn; Epsilon

Nu Delta Mortuary Frat; Grier Heights Masonic Lodge No 752; Ambassadors Social Club; bd dir, Big Bros Asn; vpres, Western Dist Funeral Dirs; Eastside Coun. **Honors/Awds:** Ouststanding service award, funeral dirs & mort Asn NC, 1972; professional of the year, Western Dist Funeral Dirs & Mort Asn NC Inc, 1974. **Military Serv:** AUS sp/5-e5 1963-66. **Business Addr:** Owner, Grier Funeral Serv, 115 N Cloudman St, Charlotte, NC 28216.*

GRIER, BOBBY
Football coach, executive director. **Personal:** Born Nov 10, 1942, Detroit, MI; married Wendy; children: Chris & Michael. **Educ:** Univ Iowa, BS, phys educ. **Career:** Football coach (retired), Executive director; Northwestrn Univ, offensive coord; Pittsburgh Panthers, defender; Eastern Mich, running backs coach, 1974-77; Boston Col, running backs coach, 1978-80; New England Patriots, offensive backfield coach, 1981, col scout, 1982-84, offensive backfield coach, 1985-92, dir pro scouting, 1993-94, dir player personnel, 1995-96, vpres player personnel, 1997-99; Houston Texans, assoc dir pro scouting, 2000-. **Special Achievements:** First African-American to play in Sugar Bowl. **Military Serv:** USAF. **Business Addr:** Associate Director of Pro Scouting, Houston Texans, Two Reliant Pk, Houston, TX 77054, **Business Phone:** (832)667-2000.

GRIER, DAVID ALAN
Movie producer, actor, screenwriter. **Personal:** Born Jun 30, 1955, Detroit, MI; son of William Henry and Aretas Ruth Dudley; married Christine Y Kim; children: Luisa Danbi; married Maritza Rivera, Jul 17, 1991 (divorced 1995). **Educ:** Univ Mich, BA, 1978; Yale Univ Sch Drama, MFA, 1981. **Career:** Films: A Soldiers Story, 1982; Streamers, 1982; Beer, 1984; From the Hip,1986; I'm Gonna Git You Sucka, 1988; Boomerang, 1992; The Player, 1992;Blank man, 1992; In the Army Now, 1994; Jumanji, 1995; Tales from the Hood,1995; McHale's Navy, 1997; Stuart Little, 1999; The Adventures of Rocky &Bullwinkle, 2000; Damned If You Do, 2000; Return to Me, 2000; East of A,2000; 3 Strikes, 2000; 15 Minutes, 2001; I Shaved My Legs for This, 2001;How to Get the Man's Foot Outta Your Ass, 2003; Tiptoes, 2003; The Woodsman, 2004; Instant Karma; Bewitched, 2005; Little Man, 2006; Kissing Cousins, 2006; The Poker House, 2008; Theatre: "Jackie Robinson; A Soldier's Play" "Dream Girls; A Funny Thing Happened on the Way to the Forum", 1996-98; TV series: "In Living Color", 1990; "Preston Episodes",producer, 1995; "Premium Blend", writer, 1997; "Damon", 1998; "DAG", 2000;"Buzz Light year of Star Comm&", 2000; "Stress Test", 2000; "The X Files",2000; "Hollywood A.D.", 2000; "Angels in the Infield", 2000; "The X Files", 2000; "King of Texas", 2002; "Chapter Forty-Two", 2002; "SesameStreet", 2002; "Crank Yankers", 2002; "Boston Public", 2002; "Tough Crowd with Colin Quinn", 2002; "King of Texas", 2002; "The Sweet Hair after", 2003; "Life with Bonnie", 2003; "The Sweet Hair after", 2003; "Boomerang",2003; "Assaulted Nuts", 2003; "Rock Stars Do the Dumbest Things", 2003; "Cedric the Entertainer Presents", 2003; "The Truth True feld", 2004; " The Muppets Wizard of Oz", 2005; "The Muppets' Wizard of Oz", 2005; "My Wife &Kids", 2005; "The Bahamas: Part 2", 2005; "The Bahamas: Part 1", 2005;"The Davey Gee Show", producer, writer, & actor, 2005; "Crank Yankers",2002-05; "Thugaboo: Sneaker Madness", voice, 2006; "Thugaboo: A Miracle on D-Roc's Street", 2006. **Honors/Awds:** Theatre World Award for Musical, The First, 1981; The Golden Lion for Best Actor in a Film Venice Film Festival for Streamers, 1983; Western Heritage Bronze Wrangler Awards for Television Feature Film, 2003. **Special Achievements:** Tony Award Nomination for The First, 1982. **Business Addr:** Actor, United Talent Agency, 9650 Wilshire Blvd Suite 500, Beverly Hills, CA 90212-2401, **Business Phone:** (310)273-6700.

GRIER, JOHN K
Executive. **Personal:** Born May 15, 1950, Charlotte, NC; widowed. **Educ:** Andrews Univ, MA, 1976. **Career:** Lake Region Off Supply Inc, pres, currently. **Business Phone:** (313)963-2626.

GRIER, JOHNNY
Manager. **Personal:** Born Apr 16, 1947, Charlotte, NC; son of Walter and Ruth Minor; married Victoria Miller Grier, Feb 12, 1966 (divorced 1987); children: Lowell. **Educ:** Univ DC, Wash, DC, BA, 1987, MA, 1991. **Career:** Chesapeake & Potomac Telephone Co, Wash, DC, engr; Verizon Telephone Co, engr, until 2002; Nat Football League, New York, NY, referee, 1981-04; Mid-Eastern Athletic Conf, supvr, football officials, 1998; Nat Football League officiating office, supvr officials, currently. **Orgs:** Awards comt, Pigskin Club Wash, DC, 1980. **Honors/Awds:** Butch Lambert Award for officiating, Nat Football Found, 2000; First African-American referee in the history of the NFL with the start of the 1988 NFL season. **Military Serv:** Air Force, E-5, 1965-69. **Business Addr:** Supervisor, National Football League Officiating Office, 280 Park Ave, New York, NY 10017.*

GRIER, MARRIO DARNELL
Football player. **Personal:** Born Dec 5, 1971, Charlotte, NC. **Educ:** Clemson, Tenn-Chattanooga. **Career:** Football player (retired); New England Patriots, running back, 1996-97; Colorado Crush, running back, 2003.

GRIER, MIKE
Hockey player. **Personal:** Born Jan 5, 1975, Detroit, MI. **Educ:** Boston Univ. **Career:** Edmonton Oilers, right wing, 1996-2002; Washington Capitals, 2002-03; Buffalo Sabres, forward, 2003-05; San Jose Sharks, 2006-. **Honors/Awds:** Bronze Medal, Men's World Ice Hockey Championships, 2004. **Business Addr:** Professional Hockey Player, San Jose Sharks, 525 W Santa Clara St, San Jose, CA 95113, **Business Phone:** (408)287-7070.

GRIER, PAMELA S.
Actor. **Personal:** Born May 26, 1949, Winston-Salem, NC; daughter of Clarence Ransom and Gwendolyn S Samuels; married. **Career:** Films: The Big Doll House, actress, 1971; The Bird Cage, actress, 1972; Black Mama, actress, White Mama, actress, 1973; Coffy, actress, 1973; Foxy Brown, actress, 1974; Friday Foster, actress, 1975; Sheba Baby, actress, 1975; Greased Lightning, actress, 1977; Fort Apache: The Bronx, actress, 1981; Something Wicked This Way Comes, actress, 1983; Stand Alone, actress, 1986; Posse, actress, 1993; Escape From LA, actress, 1996; Jackie Brown, actress, 1997; In Too Deep, actress, 1999; Holy Smoke, actress,1999; Fortress 2, actress, 1999; Snow Day, actress, 2000; 3 AM, actress,2000; Ghosts of Mars, actress, 2001; Bones, actress, 2001; Love the Hard Way, actress, 2001; Pluto Nash, actress, 2002; The Adventures of Pluto Nash, 2002; Baby of the Family, actress, 2003; Back in the Day, 2005;Tv movies: Roots: The Next Generations, actress, 1979; Badge of the Assassin,actress, 1985; A Mother's Right: The Elizabeth Morgan Story, actress,1992; Family Blessings, actress, 1996; Hayley Wagner, actress, Star,actress, 1999; Feast of All Saints, actress, 2001; First to Die, actress,2003; Earthlings, actress, 2003; Tv guest appearances: "Miami Vice", 1985;"Crime Story", 1986; "The Cosby Show", 1987; "Fresh Prince of Bel Air",1994; "Martin", 1995; Plays: Fool for Love, 1986; Lincs, Show time, 1998. Ladies of the House, 2008. **Orgs:** Acad Motion Picture Arts & Scis; Screen Actors Guild; Am Fedn TV & Radio Artists; Actors Equity Asn. **Honors/Awds:** Image Award, Nat Asn Advan Colored People, 1986, 1998-2006; Satellite Awards, 1998; Career Achievement Award, Acapulco Black Film Festival, 1999; Golden Slate Award Best Female Performance, 2000; Daytime Emmy Awards, 2000; Black Reel Awards, 2002; Film Trumpet Award, 2003. **Special Achievements:** Golden Globe Nominee, 1998. **Business Phone:** (310)656-0400.

GRIER, ROSEY
Football player, actor, community activist. **Personal:** Born Jul 14, 1932, Cuthbert, GA; son of Joseph and Ruth; married Beatrice Lewis, Feb 2, 1962 (divorced 1970); children: 1; married Margie Hanson; children: Denise, Roosevelt Kennedy & Cheryl Tubbs. **Educ:** Pa State Univ, BS, 1955. **Career:** New York Giants, NY, prof football player, 1955-62; Los Angeles Rams, LosAngeles CA, prof football player, 1963-68; Nat Gen Corp, pub rels dir;Films: The Thing with Two Heads, actor, 1972; Skyjacked, actor, 1972;Rabbit Test, actor, 1978; The Glove, actor, 1979; Roots, actor, 1979; TheGong Show Movie, actor, 1980; Reggie's Prayer, actor, 1996; tv series: TheSeekers, 1979; Concrete Cowboys, 1981; The List, 1983. **Orgs:** Anti-Self-Destruction Program; Soulville Found; Direction Sports;Teammates; Giant Step; Kennedy Found Ment Retarded; Are You Committed?,founder, 1984. **Honors/Awds:** Member of Los Angeles Rams Fearsome Foursome, 1963-67. **Special Achievements:** Author: The Rosey Grier Needlepoint Book for Men, Walker, 1973; The GentleGiant: An Autobiography, 1986; Rosey Grier's All-American Heroes:Multicultural Success Stories, 1993. **Military Serv:** AUS, 1957-59. **Business Phone:** (310)859-4000.

GRIFFEY, DICK
Executive, president (organization), chief executive officer. **Personal:** Born Nov 16, 1943, Nashville, TN; son of Juanita Hines; married; children: 3. **Educ:** Tenn State Univ. **Career:** Dick Griffey Productions, pres & chief exec officer, 1977-; Guys & Dolls Night Club, co-owner; Soul Train Recs, partner; SOLAR Rec, chief exec officer & pres, currently. **Orgs:** Black Concert Promoters Asn. **Honors/Awds:** Industrial/Service 100, Dick Griffey Productions, Black Enterprise, 1991. **Special Achievements:** Black Enterprise List Top 100 Black Owned Businesses. **Business Addr:** President, Chief Executive Officer, Dick Griffey Productions, 1635 N Cahuenga Blvd, Los Angeles, CA 91411, **Business Phone:** (323)461-0390.

GRIFFEY, GEORGE KENNETH, JR. **See GRIFFEY, KEN, JR.**

GRIFFEY, KEN, SR.
Sports manager, consultant, baseball player. **Personal:** Born Apr 10, 1950, Donora, PA; married Alberta Littleton; children: George Jr & Craig. **Career:** Baseball player (retired), Consultant, sports Manager; Cincinnati Reds, outfielder, 1973-81; NY Yankees, outfielder/infielder, 1982-86; Atlanta Braves, outfielder/infielder, 1986-88; Cincinnati Reds, outfielder/infielder, 1988-90; Seattle Mariners, outfielder, 1990-92, special asst for player development, hitting coach, 1992; Cincinnati Reds, spec consult, currently. **Honors/Awds:** Most Valuable Player All-Star Game; 1980; Cincinnati Reds Hall of Fame, 2004. **Business Addr:** Special consultant, Cincinnati Reds, Cinergy Field 100 Cinergy Field, Cincinnati, OH 45202, **Business Phone:** (513)421-4510.*

GRIFFEY, KEN, JR. (GEORGE KENNETH GRIFFEY, JR.)
Baseball player. **Personal:** Born Nov 21, 1969, Donora, PA; son of Ken Griffey Sr and Alberta Littleton; married Melissa; children: Trey Kenneth & Taryn Kennedy. **Career:** Seattle Mariners, outfielder, 1989-2000, 2009-; Cincinnati Reds, 2000-08; Chicago White Sox, 2008. **Honors/Awds:** Prep league's Player of the Year in 1986, 1987; Sports Star of the Year, Seattle Sports Intelligencer, 1989; AL All-Star Team, 1990-99; AL Gold Glove, 1990-96, 1998-99; Silver Slugger Award, 1991, 1993-94, 1996-99; Celebrity Recognition Award, Make-a-Wish Foundation, 1994; A Bartlett Giamatti Award, Baseball Assistance Team, 1994; Seattle Mariners, Roberto Clemente Award, 1996, 1997, 1998; American League Most Valuable Player, Baseball Writers Asn Am, 1997; Player of the Year, BWAA, Seattle Chapter, 1999; World Baseball Classic (WBC), 2006. **Special Achievements:** Author, Junior: Griffey on Griffey, 1997; youngest Major League player in baseball history to hit 400 home runs, 2000; TV: "Love Hurts". **Business Addr:** Professional Baseball Player, Cincinnati Reds, Cinergy Field, 100 Cinergy Field, Cincinnati, OH 45202, **Business Phone:** (513)421-4510.

GRIFFIN, ANN WHITE
Government official. **Career:** City Columbus, Treasurer's Office, treas. *

GRIFFIN, ARCHIE
Football player, association executive, football coach. **Personal:** Born Aug 24, 1954, Columbus, OH; married Bonita; children: Anthony, Andre & Adam. **Educ:** Ohio State Univ, BS, indust mgt, 1976. **Career:** Football player (retired), football coach, association executive; Cincinnati Bengals, running back, 1976-82; US Football League, Jacksonville Bulls, 1983; OH State Univ, Columbus, OH, spec asst to athletic dir, 1985-87, asst dir athletics, 1987-94, assoc dir athletics, 1994; The OH State Univ Alumni Asn, pres & chief exec officer, 2004-; Wendy's High Sch Heisman, spokesman, currently. **Orgs:** Founder, Archie Griffin Scholarship Fund; co-founder, Archie & Bonita Griffin Found Fund; Columbus Found; Columbus Youth Found; Adv Bd ADA's Advocacy Leadership Coun, Am Diabetes Asn; James Cancer Hosp & Res Inst; hon chair, Children's Hunger Alliance Endowment Fund, 2006. **Honors/Awds:** The Big 10 Most Valuable Player Award, 1973-74; Heisman Trophy Winner, 1974, 1975; Player of the Year, United Press Int, 1974, 1975; Maxwell Award, 1975; Man of the Year, Sporting News, 1975; Varsity O Hall of Fame, 1981; Col Football Hall of Fame, 1986; Rose Bowl Hall of Fame, 1990. **Special Achievements:** Only player in NCAA history to start in four Rose Bowl games in a single career; Ranked No.21 on ESPN's Top 25 Players In College Football History list, 2007. **Business Addr:** President, Chief Executive Officer, The Ohio State University Alumni Association Inc, 2200 Olentangy River Rd, Columbus, OH 43210-1035, **Business Phone:** (614)292-2200.

GRIFFIN, BERTHA L.
Business owner, president (organization). **Personal:** Born Feb 8, 1930, Blythewood, SC; daughter of Lula Woodard Cunningham and Dock Cunningham; married James, Feb 1, 1947; children: Wayne, Denise E Bryant & Geoffrey L. **Educ:** Greystone State Hosp, NJ state psychiat technician training course, 1956; Riverton Bio-Anal Lab Sch, Newark, NJ, 1959. **Career:** Greystone State Hosp, Newark, NJ, psychiat technician, 1953-56; Drs. Burch& Williams, Newark, off mgr, 1957-63; Girl Friday Secretarial Sch, Newark, dir, 1963-71; Newark Manpower Training, Newark, dir, 1971-73; Porterhouse Cleaning, Edison, NJ, pres, 1973-. **Orgs:** Secy, Nat Asn Negro Bus & Prof Women, 1961-63; Nat Key Women Am, 1978-83;secy, Edison, NJ Bd Edn, 1978-84; delegate, White House Conf Small Bus,1980; Small Bus Unity Coun & NJ Braint Trust Comn Small Bus; Minority Bus Enterprise Legal Defense Educ Fund Inc. **Honors/Awds:** Minority Business Woman of the Year, Newark Minority Bus Develop Ctr,1984; Entrepreneur of the Year, YMCA NJ, 1987, NJ Black Achievers, 1987,Venture Magazine, 1988; recognition award, Nat Coun Negro Women, 1987. **Home Addr:** 1 Newburgh Dr, Edison, NJ 08817, **Home Phone:** (908)382-9160. **Business Phone:** (201)769-0997.

GRIFFIN, DR. BETTY SUE
Educator, executive. **Personal:** Born Mar 5, 1943, Danville, KY; daughter of Allen James and Elise Taylor; divorced. **Educ:** Fisk Univ, BS, 1965; Ore State Univ, MS, 1976, PhD, 1985. **Career:** Over brook High Sch, Philadelphia, teacher, 1968-70; Model Cities, Portland, OR, placement dir, 1970-72; Ore State Univ, dir, field prog, 1972-, prof educ psych, dir teacher training prog; Ky Dept Educ, dir teacher internship prog, 1986-89, exec advisor; Griffin Group, founder, pres & chief exec officer, currently. **Orgs:** Delta Sigma Theta; Phi Kappa Phi; Eastern Star; pres, Nat Forum Black Pub Adminr, Bluegrass Chapter; bd mem, Ore Gov Comn, 1978; pres, Nat Forum Black Pub Administrator; bd mem, Governor's Com Voc Educ; bd mem, Governor's Comn Black Affairs, Ore; bd dirs, Ky Long Term Policy Res Ctr. **Honors/Awds:** Outstanding Young Women of America, 1977; Danford Fellow, Ore State Univ; African-American Adult Achiever of the Year, Lexington YMCA.

GRIFFIN, BOBBY L.
Executive, accountant. **Personal:** Born Jan 28, 1938, Prospect, TN; son of Frank and Kathleen Hogan; married Betty Wilson Grif-

fin, Mar 15, 1961; children: Barbara, Lindonna, Bobbi. **Educ:** Tenn State Univ, BS, 1963; Cent Mich Univ, MA, 1985. **Career:** US Postal Serv, DC, sr acct, 1958-. **Orgs:** Master Mason, Charles Datcher Lodge 15, Prince Hall Affiliation, Washington, DC; Sigma Iota Epsilon Bus Mgt Fraternity; Tenn State Univ Alumni Asn; Cent Mich Univ Alumni Asn. *

GRIFFIN, EDDIE
Actor, movie director. **Personal:** Born Jul 15, 1968, Kansas City, MO; son of Eddie Griffin Sr and Doris Thomas; married Carla, Jan 1, 1983 (divorced 1984); children: Eddie Griffin jr; married Rochelle, Jan 1, 2002. **Career:** TV series: "Malcolm and Eddie", 1996-2000; "The Year Without a Santa Claus", 2006; Films: Metor Man, 1993; Foolish, 1999; Picking Up the Pieces, 2000; Double Take, 2001; John Q, 2002; Scary Movie 3, 2003; Prod, My Baby's Dadd, 2004; Who Made the Potatoe Salad?, 2005; Date Movie, 2006;Irish Jam, 2006; Norbit, 2007; Redline, 2007. **Special Achievements:** Was number 64 on Comedy Central's list of the 100 Greatest Stand-ups of All Time; Nominee, Image Award, 2000. **Business Addr:** Actor, c/o United Paramount Network, 11800 Wilshire Blvd, Los Angeles, CA 90025, **Business Phone:** (310)575-7000.*

GRIFFIN, DR. ERVIN V
President (Organization), executive. **Personal:** Born in Coawood, WV; divorced. **Educ:** Bluefield State Col, BS; Western Ill Univ, MS; Va Polytechnic Inst & State Univ, EdD. **Career:** SW Va Community Col, counr & dir; Patrick Henry Community Col, Stud Develop & Vocational Sex Equity Progs, prof & dir; WVa State Col, Student Affairs, vpres; WVa State Community & Tech Col, provost & coo, pres & chief exec officer, currently; Halifax Community Col, pres & chief exec officer, 2006-. **Orgs:** Bd dirs, Charleston Lions Club; Law Enforcement Training Comt, WV Div Criminal Justice; bd trustees, St. Francis Hosp; exec bd, Charleston Connecting People to Jobs Proj; Am Asn Community Cols; Halifax-Warren Smart Start Partnership C; Halifax Horizons; Sigma Pi Phi Fraternity; Alpha Phi Alpha Fraternity Inc. **Honors/Awds:** Outstanding Alumni Brother of the Year, Alpha Phi Alpha Fraternity Inc; Governors Living the Dream Award, WVa Martin Luther King Holiday Comn; Seven-time Administrator of the Year, WVa State Col Stud Govt Asn; Community Impact Award, WVa Minority Bus Develop Ctr; Sports Hall of Fame, WVa State Univ; Distinguished Service Award, London Missionary Baptist Church, 2008; Local African American Hero Award, Halifax Community Col, 2008. **Business Addr:** President, Halifax Community College, 100 Col Dr, PO Box 809, Weldon, NC 27890.*

GRIFFIN, DR. ERVIN VEROME
School administrator. **Personal:** Born May 15, 1949, Welch, WV; son of Roy and Martha; children: Ervin Jr. **Educ:** Bluefield St Col, BS, 1971; Western Ill Univ, MS, 1974; Va Polytechnic Inst & State Univ, Cert Advan Grad Study Higher Educ, 1979, Doctorate Educ, 1980. **Career:** McDowell Co, Bd Educ, spec educ teacher, 1971-72; Western Ill Univ, asst head resident adv, 1972-74; SW Va Community Col, dir stud financial aid, 1974-78; Va Polytech Inst & St Univ, counr, 1978-79; SW Va Community Col, coordr co-curricular activities, 1979-84; Patrick Henry Community Col, dir stud develop, 1984-89; WVa St Community & Tech Col, vpres stud affairs, 1989-, pres, sr pres, currently. **Orgs:** Am Col Personnel Asn; Am Asn Non-White Concerns; Am Personnel & Guid Asn; elected to Comm XI, Directorate Body Am Col Personnel Asn 1984-87; bd dirs Tazewell Co Helpline, 1984-86; Martinsville-Henry Co, Nat Asn Advan Colored People, 1985-86; Martinsville-Henry Co Men's Roundtable, 1985-86; OIC Inc Charleston, 1991; prs W Vir Asn, Stud Personnel Adminr, 1991-92; Nat Asn, Stud Personnel Adminr; Psi Chi Nat Hon Soc; Charleston OIC; WV SCRes & Develop Corp; bd adv, Southeastern Regional CMS Drug & Alcohol; exec bd, W Va, Asn Stud Personnel Adminr, 1992-93. **Honors/Awds:** Outstanding Young men of America, Jaycees SVCC, 1978; "The Pareto Optimality Problem", Minority Educ, 1981; "Adults Making the Commitment to Return to School" 1985; "Cocurricular Activities Programming, A Tool for Retention and Collaboration" 1985; Innovative Practs & Develop, Vocational Sex Equality, a monograph, 1988; The Alliance for Excellence: A Model Articulation Between the Community Coll and the Black Church, 1988; Award Excellence, Alliance for Excellence, 1989; Meritorious Serv Award, Patrick Harvey Community Col, 1989; W Va St, Col, Adminr of the Year, 1991-92; Innovative Prog Award, W Va Asn Stud Personnel Adminr, 1991-93; Retention Excellence Award, Noel Levitz Ctr Stud Retention, 1991; Excelsior High Sch Nat Alumni Award, 1991; Outstanding Serv Award, WVSC SGA, 1989-91. **Special Achievements:** Publications/presentations: Innovative Pract & Develop Stud Mentoring,1990; Bluefield St Col, A Time of Crisis and Reflection, 1991; keynote speaker: The Legacy of the Past & Challenges of the Future, Mingo County EOC, 1992; numerous others; First Black, adminr SW Va Community Col; First Black adminr, Patrick Henry Community Col. **Home Addr:** 807 Elvira Rd, Dunbar, WV 25064. **Business Addr:** Senior President, WVa State College, PO Box 1000, Charleston, WV 25112-1000.*

GRIFFIN, EURICH Z.
Lawyer. **Personal:** Born Nov 21, 1938, Washington, DC; son of Eurich and Lucille; divorced; children: Jennifer, Eurich III. **Educ:** Howard Univ, BA, econ, 1967; Harvard Law Sch, JD, 1970. **Career:** US Fifth Cir Court Appeals Judge Paul H Roneyd, law clerk, 1971; Carlton, Fields, Ward, Emmanueal, Smith, & Cutler, PA, atty; Joyner & Jordan-Holmes, PA, atty, currently. **Orgs:** Am Bar Asn; Nat Bar Asn; Hillsborough Co; Fla Bar Asn; pres, Harvard Club W Coast Fla; St Petersburgh Kiwanis Club, 1971-74. **Military Serv:** USAF, airman, 2nd class, 1959-63. **Business Addr:** Attorney, Joyner & Jordan-Holmes, 1112 E Kennedy Blvd, PO Box 172297, Tampa, FL 33672-0297.*

GRIFFIN, FLOYD LEE
State government official, executive, army officer. **Personal:** Born May 24, 1944, Milledgeville, GA; son of Floyd and Ruth Griffin Sr; married Nathalie E, Jun 15, 1966; children: Brian E & Eric B. **Educ:** Grupton Jones Col, AS; Tuskegee Inst, BS, 1967; FL Inst Tech, MS, 1974; Army Command & Gen Staff Col, 1979; Nat War Col, 1989. **Career:** Colonel (retired), State Govermental Off, Bus Owner; AUS, col, 1967-90; Slater's Funeral Home Inc, vpres, 1990-; Cent State Hosp Found Inc, vice chair, 1991-; Ga State Senate, sen, 1994-98; Milledgeville, mayor, 2001-03. **Orgs:** Am Legion, 1967-; life mem, Omega Psi Phi Fraternity, 1979-; Prince Hall Free & Accepted Masons, 1985-; Sigma Pi Phi Fraternity, 1995-; bd dirs, Nat Ctr Missing & Exploited C, 2006-. **Honors/Awds:** Community Service Award, Milledgeville-Baldwin County Chamber Com, 1993. **Military Serv:** AUS, col, 1967-90; Legion of Merit, 1990. **Business Addr:** Vice President, Slater's Funeral Home Inc, 244 N Wayne St, Milledgeville, GA 31061, **Business Phone:** (478)452-2412.

GRIFFIN, GREGORY O
Lawyer. **Personal:** Married Debra; children: Greg Jr, Alexis Ivana & Christopher Michael. **Educ:** Morehouse Col, Atlanta, GA, BA, polit sci, 1980; Univ Pittsburgh Sch Law, Pittsburgh, PA, JD, 1983; Boston Univ Sch Law, Boston, MA, LLM, taxation, 1984. **Career:** Judicial Syst, Pittsburgh, PA, chief prosecutor, 1981-83; AG Gaston Enterprises Inc, Birmingham, AL, assoc gen couns, 1984-85; pvt pract, atty, Birmingham, AL, 1985-86; Legal Servs Corp Ala Inc, Selma, AL, 1986-87; Off Atty Gen, Montgomery, AL, Civil Litigation Div, Utilities Litigation Div, asst atty gen, 1987-; Ala State Univ, Montgomery, AL, adj prof, income tax acct, 1989-; Ala Bd Pardons & Paroles, chief legal coun, 1995-, chief coun, currently, Legal Div, atty, currently. **Orgs:** State Pa Bar Asn; Dist Columbia Bar Asn; State Ala Bar Asn; Tax Law Review, Boston Univ Sch Law, 1983-84; 11th US Circuit Ct Appeals; US Dist Ct, Northern Dist Ala; Dist Columbia Bar. **Honors/Awds:** Martin Luther King Jr Scholarship to Europe, Student Body Pres, Morehouse Col, Atlanta, GA; Law Sch Scholastic Scholar, winner, First Year Oral Argument, received honors in Oral Advocacy, judge, First Year Arguments, Univ Pittsburgh Sch Law, Pittsburgh, PA. **Home Addr:** PO Box 250194, Montgomery, AL 36125, **Home Phone:** (334)318-5132. **Business Addr:** Chief Counsel, Attorney, Alabama Board of Pardons and Paroles, Legal Division, 301 S Ripley St, PO Box 302405, Montgomery, AL 36130-2405, **Business Phone:** (334)242-8710.

GRIFFIN, JEAN THOMAS
Educator, college teacher. **Personal:** Born Dec 26, 1937, Atlantic City, NJ; daughter of Clifton Washington and Alma Washington; married James A; children: Lillian Hasan, Tallie Thomas, Karen Brondidge, James A IV & Wayne. **Educ:** Temple Univ, BA, psychol, 1969, MEd, psychol, 1971, EdD Ed, psychol, 1973; Nat Training Lab, training internship, 1973; Yale Univ, clin internship, 1975; Univ PA, physicians Alcohol Educ Training Prog, 1976. **Career:** Educator, college teacher (retired); Yale Univ, asst prof dir, 1972-76; Solomon Canter Fuller MHC, clin dir, 1976-77; Union Grad Sch, core prof, 1976-; Univ Mass Boston, assoc prof to prof, 1979-93, Union Inst & Univ, Grad Col, prof, currently. **Orgs:** Comm on racism & sexism Nat Educ Asn, 1975; women's career devel Polaroid Corp, 1977; trainer, Nat Training Lab, 1977-83; pres bd, Women Inc. 1977-84; consult & ed, Univ Okla Col Nursing, 1978-81; fel Am Ortho psychiatric Asn, 1978-85; assoc, Black Psychiat Eastern Rep, 1979; consult & training Bank Boston, 1980-84; racism workshop Boston State Col, 1981; adv to dir, Roxbury Community Sch, 1981-82. **Honors/Awds:** Grant Prof Growth & Devel, 1974; Fellow Mellon Faculty Devel Award, 1982; article W African & Black Am Working Women published Journal Black Psychol, 1982; chapter in Contemporary Blk Marriage, 1984; numerous publications including Exploding the Popular Myths Review of Black Women in the Labor Force Equal Times, 1982; Fullbright Fellow to Barbados, 1994; Kelloge Foundation Award, 1993. **Home Addr:** 1927 Kuehnle Ave, Atlantic City, NJ 08401-1703. *

GRIFFIN, LEONARD JAMES, JR.
Football player, football coach. **Personal:** Born Sep 22, 1962, Lake Providence, LA. **Educ:** Grambling State Univ. **Career:** Football player (retired), football coach; Kansas City Chiefs, defensive end, 1986-93; Grambling State Univ, strength coach, currently.

GRIFFIN, LULA BERNICE
Educator. **Personal:** Born Oct 16, 1949, Saginaw, MI. **Educ:** Tuskegee Inst, BSN, 1971; Univ Mich, attended 1974; Med Col Ga, MS, nursing, 1977. **Career:** Univ Ala, Hosp B'Ham, staff psychiat, 1971-73; Lawson State Community Col, Birmingham, AL, nursing instr, level II coordr, 1974-85; Cooper Green Hosp, Birmingham, AL, staff high risk nursing, 1982-83; Community Hosp, Birmingham, AL, staff. **Orgs:** Chi Eta Phi Sorority, 1969; Help One Another Club Inc, 1981; secy, Tuskegee Inst Nurses Alumni, 1982; vol diaster serv, Am Red Cross, 1984-85; Am Nurses Asn; Ala State Nurse Asn; Sixth Ave Baptist Church. **Honors/Awds:** Cert Psychiat & Ment Health Nurse, Am Nurses Asn, Cert Bd Psychiat & Ment Health Pract, 1985-89. **Business Addr:** Nurse Instructor, Lawson State Community College, 526 Beacon Crest Cir, Birmingham, AL 35209.

GRIFFIN, MICHAEL D.
Automotive executive, engineer. **Personal:** Born May 11, 1958, McKeesport, PA; son of Wilbur and Thelma Webb Taborn; married Brenda Olive Griffin, Nov 24, 1990. **Educ:** Rensselaer Polytech Inst, Troy, NY, BS, mech eng, 1980; Univ Pa, Wharton Sch, Philadelphia, PA, MBA, finance & mkt, 1988. **Career:** Gen Motors-Rochester Products Div, Rochester, NY, sr design eng, 1980-88, sr analyst, N Am passenger cars, 1988-90; Gen Motors Automotive Div, Flint, MI, asst prog mgr, vehicle syst engr, 1990-. **Orgs:** Soc Automotive Engineers, 1980-86; co-chairperson, bus corp comt, Nat Black MBA Asn, Detroit Chap, 1990-. **Honors/Awds:** Fel General Motors, 1986-88; US Patents (3 total), US Patent Office, 1984, 1985, 1986. **Business Addr:** Assistant Program Manager, Vehicle Systems Engineer, General Motors, Flint Automotive Division, 4100 S Saginaw St, Flint, MI 48557.*

GRIFFIN, PERCY LEE
Administrator. **Personal:** Born Dec 10, 1945, Tougaloo, MS; son of Percy L and Mary F Perry Gray; married Andrealene Myles A Griffin, Jul 10, 1969 (divorced); children: Gregory T. **Educ:** Jackson St Univ, BS; Ind Univ, MS Recreation Admin. **Career:** Jackson State & Univ Alumni Asn Indianapolis, vpres; Detroit Lions, 1969; Indianapolis Capitols, football player, 1969-74; Indianapolis Caps Pro-Football Team, owner, pres, 1976-; City Indianapolis, admin Resource Recovery Coun. **Orgs:** Small Bus Asn. **Honors/Awds:** Small College All-Amer Pitts Courier. *

GRIFFIN, PLES ANDREW
Educator. **Personal:** Born Apr 5, 1929, Pasadena, CA; married Lora Lee Jones. **Educ:** Univ Calif, BA, 1956; Univ SC, MS, 1964. **Career:** Pasandena Settlement Asn, exec dir, 1953-59; Pasadena Sch Dist, educr, coun, 1960-66; Pasadena City Col, coun, 1964-66; US Off Educ, consult, 1969-; Calif Dept Educ, chief off intergroup rels. **Orgs:** Nat All Balck Sch Educrs; Asn Calif Sch Adminr; Asn Calif Intergroup Rel Educrs; Nat Asn Advan Colored People, Sacramento Urban League; Alpha Phi Alpha; Episc Church. **Military Serv:** UAS, mil intell, 1953-55. **Business Addr:** Chief, California Department of Education, Intergroup Relations, 721 Capitol Mal, Sacramento, CA 95814.*

GRIFFIN, RONALD CHARLES
Educator. **Personal:** Born Aug 17, 1943, Washington, DC; son of Gwendolyn Jones-Points and Roy John; married Vicky Lynn Tredway; children: David Ronald, Jason Roy & Meg Carrington. **Educ:** Hampton Inst, BS, 1965; Harvard Univ, 1965, JD, 1968; Univ VA, LLM, 1974. **Career:** Office Corp Counsel Dist Columbia Govt, legal intern, 1968-69, legal clerk, 1969-70, asst corp counsel, 1970; the JAG Sch AUS, instruct, 1970-74; Univ Ore, asst prof; Notre Dame Univ, vis prof, 1981-82; Washburn Univ, prof law, currently. **Orgs:** Legal Educ Com Young Lawyers Sect Am Bar Asn; Young Lawyers Liaison Legal Educ & Admission Bar Sect Am Bar Asn; Bankruptcy Com Fed Bar Asn; Ore Consumer League, 1974-75; grievance examiner Mid-West Region EEOC, 1984-85; pres, Central States Law Sch Asn, 1987-88; vice chairperson, Kans Continuing Legal Educ Commn, 1989-90; chmn bd, 1996-99, bd mem, The Brown Found, 1988-; chair bd, Mid-West People Color Legal Scholarship Conference Inc, 2001-05. **Honors/Awds:** Rockefeller Found Grant; Outstanding Young Men Am Award, 1971; Outstanding Educators Am Award, 1973; Int Men Achievement, 1976; Outstanding Young Man Am Award, 1979; William O Douglas Award Outstanding Prof, 1985-86, 1994-95; Phi Kappa Phi Honor Soc; Phi Beta Delta InterNat Honor Soc. **Military Serv:** AUS, capt, 1970-74. **Home Addr:** 3448 SW Birchwood Dr, Topeka, KS 66614-3214. **Business Addr:** Professor, Washburn University Law School, 1700 SW Coll Ave Rm 310, Topeka, KS 66621, **Business Phone:** (785)670-1678.

GRIFFIN, VIRGIL
Congressperson (U.S. federal government). **Educ:** Boston University; Johns Hopkins University, Carey Business School, MBA, 2003. **Career:** Freddie Mac, Director of Congressional Relations. **Orgs:** Secretary, Congressional Black Caucus Foundation, Inc. **Home Addr:** 000150. *

GRIFFIN, WARREN, III. **See G, WARREN.**

GRIFFIN, WILLIAM MICHAEL, JR. **See ALLAH, RAKIM.**

GRIFFIN GOLDEN, DR. CECILIA
Educator, president (organization). **Personal:** Married Ronald Golden; children: Chaton, Jeryn & Adam. **Educ:** State Univ Ge-

nesco, BA, spanish educ; State Univ Albany, MS, tesl; State Univ Buffalo, DPhil, social educ. **Career:** Rochester City Sch Dist, teacher, 1975-87, proj supvr reading, 1987-89;State Univ NY, Brockport, vis asst prof, urban ed specialist, 1989-91; Jefferson MS, HS, Edison Tech HS, vice prin, 1992-93; Andrew J Townson SchNo 39, prin, 1993-96; Rochester City Sch Dist, interim exec dir acad op, 1996-97, chief acad officer, 1997-; YWCA Greater Pittsburgh, chief exec officer; WQED Multimedia Inc, bd dir, 2003-; Vols Am Chesapeake, Lanham, MD, pres & chief exec officer, 2006-. **Orgs:** Delta Kappa Gamma; Nat Alliance Black Sch Educr; Am Ed Res Asn; Asn Supv & Curric Develop; Phi Delta Kappa; Sch Admin Asn NY State; Rochester Women's Network; Urban League Rocheser. **Business Addr:** President, Chief Executive Officer, Volunteers of America Chesapeake, 7901 Annapolis Rd, Lanham, MD 20706, **Business Phone:** (301)459-2020.

GRIFFITH, DARRELL STEVEN
Executive, basketball player. **Personal:** Born Jun 16, 1958, Louisville, KY. **Educ:** Univ Louisville, KY, commun, 1980. **Career:** Basketball player (retired); Utah Jazz, 1980-93; Metro Enterprises Inc, founder & pres, currently. **Honors/Awds:** Rookie of the Year, NBA, 1981; Led NBA in three-point field goal percentage, 1984, 1985. **Business Addr:** Founder, President, Metro Enterprises Inc, 8055 Nat Turnpike, Louisville, KY 40214-4803.

GRIFFITH, ELWIN JABEZ
Educator. **Personal:** Born Mar 2, 1938; married Norma Joyce Rollins; children: Traci. **Educ:** Long Island Univ, BA, 1960; Brooklyn Law Sch, JD, 1963; NYU, LLM, 1964. **Career:** Modern HS, teacher, 1955-56; Chase Manhattan Bank, asst couns, 1964-71;Cleveland Marshall Law Sch, asst prof, 1968; Teachers Inst & Annuity Asn,asst counsel, 1971-72; Drake Univ, asst dean & asst prof, 1972-73; Univ Cincinnati Col Law, assoc dean & prof, 1973-78; DePaul Law Sch, dean &prof, 1978-85; Fla State Univ Col Law, prof, 1986, alumni prof, currently, Caribbean Law Inst, dir, 1988. **Orgs:** Barbados Independent Com, 1966; Bedford-Stuyvesant Jr C C, 1970-72; Black Exec Exchang Prof, 1971; NY State Bar Asn; Am Bar Asn; Am Law Inst. **Special Achievements:** Author of many law journal articles on immigration law; Publ "Final Payment & Warranties Under the Uniform Commercial Code" 1973;"Truth-in-Lending & Real Estate Transactions" 1974; "Some Rights &Disabilities of Aliens" 1975; "Deportation of Aliens - Some Aspects" 1975;"The Creditor, Debtor & the Fourteenth Amendment Some Aspects" 1977. **Business Addr:** Tallahassee Alumni Professor, Florida State University, College Law, 425 W Jefferson Street BK Roberts Hall Room 336, Tallahassee, FL 32306, **Business Phone:** (850)644-7731.

GRIFFITH, DR. EZRA E H
Physician, educator. **Personal:** Born Feb 18, 1942; son of Vincent and Ermie; married Brigitte Jung. **Educ:** Harvard Univ, BA, 1963; Univ Strasbourg, MD, 1973; Albert Einstein Col Med, residency. **Career:** French Polyclinic Health Ctr, internship, 1973-74; Albert Einstein Col, chief res psychiat, 1974-77; Yale Univ, Sch Med, asst prof, 1977, assoc prof, 1982-91, Psychiat & African & African-Am Studies, prof, 1991-, med dir, 2003-, Clin Affairs, dep chmn, 1996-; Conn Mental Health Ctr, assoc dir, 1986-89, dir, 1989-96; Yale Psychiat Quarterly, editor-in-chief, Deputy Chair for Clinical Affairs, Currently. **Orgs:** Black psychiat Am; Am Psychiat Asn; Am Acad Psychiat & Law; FALK fel; traveling fel Solomon Fuller Inst, 1976; fel WK Kellogg Found, 1980; pres, Am Acad Psychiat & Law, 1996-97; mem & ed bd, Hosp & Community Psychiat. **Special Achievements:** Assoc ed, Diversity & Mental Health, 1995; ed, Journal of the American Academy of Psychiatry and Law; "Race and Excellence: My Dialogue with Chester Pierce", Univ IA Press. Ethics In Forensic Psychiatry, 1998; Race and Excellence: My Dialogue with Chester Pierce, 1998. **Home Addr:** 6 Marlborough Rd, North Haven, CT 06473. **Business Addr:** Deputy Chair for Clinical Affairs, Yale University, Department of Psychiatry, 300 George St Suite 901, New Haven, CT 06510, **Business Phone:** (203)785-2018.

GRIFFITH, HOWARD THOMAS
Football player, television show host. **Personal:** Born Nov 17, 1967, Chicago, IL; married Kim; children: Howard II. **Educ:** Univ Ill, BA, speech commn, 1991. **Career:** Football player (retired), Television show host; Los Angeles Rams, 1993-94; Carolina Panthers, 1995-96; Denver Broncos, 1997-2002; Big Ten Network, med rel mgr, other prim analyst & studio commentator, currently. **Orgs:** Bd dir, Natl Able Network Inc. **Honors/Awds:** Nat Football League championship rings in Super Bowl XXXII & Super Bow lXXXIII. **Special Achievements:** Third All time rusher in Illinois history. **Business Phone:** (312)665-0700.

GRIFFITH, JOHN A.
Educator, government official. **Personal:** Born Dec 14, 1936, Greensburg, PA; married Patricia Cuff; children: Pamela, Gail & Jennifer. **Educ:** Ind Univ, BS, Educ, 1960; Fairleigh Dickinson Univ, MBA, Mgt, 1985. **Career:** Counselor, teacher, manager (retired), Education board member; Asst Beaver Co, PA, social worker, 1960-62; Allen crest Juvenile Detention Ctr, Beaver, PA, counr, 1963-64; Nutley Pub Sch, NJ, teacher & football coach, 1964-68; Montclair Pub Sch, NJ, counr, 1968-69; Newark Boys Chorus Sch, trustee; Newark Day Care Ctr, pres; Kean Col, New Jersey, NJ, adj prof personnel mgt; Montclair Bd Educ, 1979-85; PSE & G, personal develop mgr, 1980-89, mgr employ develop progs, 1989-91, regional pub affairs mgr, 1991-2003; bd mem, NJ State Bd Educ. **Orgs:** Adv bd, Nat Bank, 1979-; Int Coun Bus Opportunities, 1985-; Edges Inc,1970-; Am Soc Training & Develop, 1980-; pres, Bd Ed Montclair, NJ, 1979-85; trustee, Urban League Essex Co, NJ, 1970-; pres, Bloom field Better Human Rels Coun; YMCA; Montclair Fund Educ Excellence. **Honors/Awds:** Seventy five Achievers Award, Black Media Inc. **Military Serv:** AUS. **Home Addr:** 23 Stephen St, Montclair, NJ 07042. **Business Addr:** Member of State Board of Education, NJ Department of Education, PO Box 500, Trenton, NJ 08625-0500, **Business Phone:** (609)292-4469.*

GRIFFITH, JOHN H.
Educator. **Personal:** Born Aug 28, 1931, Pittsburgh, PA; son of Cicero and Doris; married Euzelia Cooper; children: Nell & Ronald (dec). **Educ:** Lincoln Univ, PA, BA, 1954; Atlanta Univ, Atlanta, MA, 1964; US Int Univ, San Diego, PhD, 1979. **Career:** Coahoma Jr Col, Clarksdale MS, instr, basketball coach, 1955-63; AtlantaUniv, instr summer sch, 1964; City Sch Dist, Rochester, NY, counr,Manpower Develop & Training Prog, 1964-66, head counr, 1966-67, dir testing, 1967-68, planning & res dir, 1968-71; San Diego City Schs, asst dir planning & res dept, 1971-76, dir planning & res, 1976-84, dir res, 1984-. **Orgs:** Phi Delta Kappa Educ Fraternity, 1966-; San Diego Sch Admin Asn; Am Asn Sch Adminrs; Am Educ Res Asn; Asn Calif Sch Admin. **Honors/Awds:** Rockefeller Found Support Training Internship, 1970-71. **Special Achievements:** Academy Achievement Award, San Diego City Schs named in honor. *

GRIFFITH, MARK RICHARD. See Obituaries section.

GRIFFITH, REGINALD WILBERT
Architect. **Personal:** Born Aug 10, 1930, New York, NY; married Linden James; children: Courtney, Crystal, Cyrice. **Educ:** Mass Inst Technol, BA, 1960; Inst Int Educ, attended 1962. **Career:** Boston Redevelop Authority, architect, 1962-67; MICCO, dep exec dir, 1967-70; Howard Ud profl, 1970-; Howard Uni, chmn dept city reg planning, 1971-74; Nat Capital Planning Comn, commr vice chmn, exec dir, 1979-2000; Reg Griffith Asso, owner city planner architect; Am Inst Planners, vpres, 1977; Millennium Inst, treas, currently. **Orgs:** bd dir, Am Soc Planning Officials, 1974-76; bd dir, Am Planning Asn Found, 1971-; bd dir mem, Am Inst Architect; Georgetown Day Sch, 1972; chmn, Urban Trans Comn Consortium Univ, 1972-73; Mass Inst Technol Educ Coun, 1971; adv panel, City Baltimore, MD. **Military Serv:** AUS, lt, 1956-58. *

GRIFFITH, ROBERT OTIS
Football player, talk show host. **Personal:** Born Nov 30, 1970, Lonham, MD. **Educ:** San Diego State Univ, BS, Electrical Engineering, 1994. **Career:** Football player (retired); Minnesota Vikings, defensive back, 1994-2001, 2008; Cleveland Browns, defensive back, 2002-04; Ariz Cardinals, defensive back, 2005-06; CBS Channel 8, co-host, currently. **Orgs:** Founder, Robert Griffith Found, 1998. **Honors/Awds:** One time Pro Bowl selection, 2000; Two times All-Pro selection, 1998, 1999; Minnesota Vikings Community Man of the Year Award; NFLs Ed Block Courage Award. **Special Achievements:** Modeled for Bad Boy clothing in an ad that appeared in Rolling Stone. **Business Addr:** Co-host, CBS Channel 8, 204 Regent St, Missoula, MT 59801, **Business Phone:** (406)542-4400.

GRIFFITH, YOLANDA YVETTE
Basketball player. **Personal:** Born Mar 1, 1970, Chicago, IL; children: Candace. **Educ:** Palm Beach Community Col; Fla Atlantic Univ, 1993. **Career:** Long Beach Stingrays, forward, 1997; Chicago Condors, forward; Sacramento Monarchs, forward, 1999-2009. **Honors/Awds:** ABL All-Star, ABL Team, 1998; Defensive Player of the Year, 1998; Victor Award; WNBA Most Valuable Player Award, 1999, 2004; Defensive Player of the Year, 1999; New ABL All-Star, ABL Team, 1998; Defensive Player of the Year, 1998; Victor Award; WNBA Most Valuable Player Award, 1999, 2004; Defensive Player of the Year, 1999; New ABL All-Star, ABL Team, 1998; Defensive Player of the Year, 1998; Victor Award; WNBA Most Valuable Player Award, 1999, 2004; Defensive Player of the Year, 1999; New Comer of the Year, 1999; Defensive Player of the Year, ABL; WNBA title, Series MVP, 2005; Gold Medals, Summer Olympics, 2000 & 2004. Comer of the Year, 1999; Defensive Player of the Year, ABL; WNBA title, Series MVP, 2005; Gold Medals, Summer Olympics, 2000 & 2004. Comer of the Year, 1999; Defensive Player of the Year, ABL; WNBA title, Series MVP, 2005; Gold Medals, Summer Olympics, 2000 & 2004.ABL All-Star, ABL Team, 1998; Defensive Player of the Year, 1998; Victor Award; WNBA Most Valuable Player Award, 1999, 2004; Defensive Player of the Year, 1999; New Comer of the Year, 1999; Defensive Player of the Year, ABL; WNBA title, Series MVP, 2005; Gold Medals, Summer Olympics, 2000 & 2004. *

GRIFFITHS, ERROL D.
Advertising executive. **Personal:** Born Feb 5, 1956, Kingston, Jamaica; son of Canute U; married Joan M Nealon, Apr 23, 1988; children: Justin, Jason. **Educ:** Col City NY, BA, 1977; Fordham Univ, MBA, 1988. **Career:** Benton & Bowles Inc, media planner, 1977-80; Dancer Fitzgerald Sample, acct exec, 1980-82; HBO Inc, dir affil rels, 1982-85; Am Visions Mag, sales rep, 1985-86; Johnson Publ Co, vpres, advert dir, 1986-97; Disney Adventures, eastern ad sales mgr, 1997-2002; Disney Adventures & Disney Mag, dir ad sales, 2002-. **Business Addr:** Director of Ad Sales, Disney Adventures & Disney Magazine, 114 5th Ave, New York, NY 10011.*

GRIGGS, ANTHONY
Football player, social worker, football coach. **Personal:** Born Feb 12, 1960, Lawton, OK. **Educ:** Villanova Univ, BA, commun. **Career:** Football player, Football coach (retired), Social worker; Philadelphia Eagles, linebacker, 1982-86; Cleveland Browns, linebacker, 1986-89; KansCity Chiefs, linebacker, 1989; Pittsburgh Steelers, asst strength conditioning coach, coordr player develop, dir player develop; AG Found, founder & exec dir, currently. **Business Addr:** Founder, Executive Director, AG Foundation, PO Box 101261, Pittsburgh, PA 15237, **Business Phone:** (412)281-5146.

GRIGGS, HARRY KINDELL, SR.
School administrator. **Personal:** Born Mar 26, 1910, Reidsville, NC; son of Jessie P and Alica B; married Mary Swan; children: Harry Kindell Jr & Gary Maurice. **Educ:** Shaw Univ, BS, 1934; Univ Mich, MA, 1948, 1952. **Career:** School administrator (retired); Roanoke Inst, teacher, 1934-36; Yanceville Sch, teacher, 1936-40; Riedsville City Elem & High Schs, teacher, 1940-48, high sch prin, 1948-59, sr high sch prin, 1959-74. **Orgs:** Bd dir, United Fund, 1960-70; Reidsville C of C, 1968-87; Nat Lib Trustee Asn, 1968-87; NC Pub Lib Trustee, 1968-87; trust, County Pub Lib Prin Sect, 1987; Boy Scouts. **Honors/Awds:** The "Education of Blacks From Slavery to Covert Enforced Integration", 1987. **Home Addr:** 1713 Courtland Ave, Reidsville, NC 27320. *

GRIGGS, JAMES CLIFTON, JR. See Obituaries section.

GRIGGS, JOHN W.
Executive. **Personal:** Born Dec 20, 1924, Birmingham, AL; married Leola Griggs; children: Sylvia, Linda. **Career:** E Linwood Lawnview Dev Corp, pres. **Orgs:** Bd trustee, Cleveland Model Cities, 1967-73; chmn, Model Cities Housing Comt, 1967-73; United Steel Workers Am & Jone Laughlin Steel Corp, 1970-72; mem past, Jr Sr Warden Upper Lawnview St Club, 1971-72. **Honors/Awds:** Housing & Urban Develop Cert, Cuyahoga Community Col, 1969; Housing Spec Award, Cuyahoga Community Col, 1970; Bd Fundamental Educ Award, 1969; United Steel Workers Educ Award, 1971; Parents of Year Award, 1971. *

GRIGGS, JUDITH RALPH
Educator. **Personal:** Born May 2, 1946, Pittsburgh, PA; married Phillip L. **Educ:** Cheyney State Col, BS, 1968; Carnegie-Mellon Univ, MA, 1969; Univ Pgh, doc studies. **Career:** Westinghouse HS St & Kieran Elementary Sch Pittsburgh, teacher, 1968; Pittsburgh St Acad Prog, teacher, 1969-70, head teacher acting dir, 1971-72; Duquesne Univ, Coun & Learning Dept, asst dir, 1972-75, adv, currently, assoc dir, affirmative action officer, currently, dir,currently. **Orgs:** Founder, Together Inc, 1967-71; bd dir, Harambee Bookstore, 1969-71; An Psychol Guidance Asn; educ consult, Pittsburgh Model Cities; adv bd, sec adv bd WDUQ Radio Sta & TV Sta Duquesne Univ; adv bd, Action Prog Point Park Col; fac, adv, Blck Stud Unoin Duquesne Univ Gospel Choir; Alpha Kappa Alpha Sor. **Honors/Awds:** Richard Humphrey Scholarship Cheyney State Col; cert sch achievement Cheyney State Col; prospective teacher fellowship eng Carnegie-Mellon Univ, 1968; cert Pub Sch in PA area comp English; pvt acad schs, Penn area english reading educ Dir of pvt acad schs. **Business Addr:** Director, Affirmative Action Officer, Duquesne University, Learning Skills Ctr, 600 Forbes Ave, Pittsburgh, PA 15219, **Business Phone:** (421)396-6661.

GRIGGS, DR. MILDRED BARNES
Educator. **Personal:** Born Mar 11, 1942, Marianna, AR; married Alvin Scott; children: Scott & Paul. **Educ:** Ark A M & N Col, BS, 1963; Univ Ill, M.Ed, 1966; Univ Ill, Ed.D, 1971; Clinton Jr col, PhD. **Career:** Champaign Sch Dist, teacher, 1966-68; Univ Ill Col Educ, asst prof,1971-76, assoc prof, 1976, dean, 1995-2000, prof emer, currently. **Orgs:** Phi Delta Kappa, 1976-; consult, Nat Inst Educ, 1979-80; vpres, Am Home Econs Asn, 1979-81; Delta Sigma Theta Sorority, 1960-; Urban League; NAACP. **Honors/Awds:** Recipient outstanding undergraduate teaching award, Univ Ill, 1975. **Business Addr:** Professor Emeritus, University of Illinois, Col Educ, 38 Education Bldg, Champaign, IL 61820, **Business Phone:** (217)333-0960.*

GRIGSBY, ALICE BURNS
Librarian. **Personal:** Born in Monroe, LA; daughter of Alex A and Ollie Hamilton Burns; married John, Feb 12, 1977; children: Myron (step-son). **Educ:** Southern Univ, Baton Rouge, BS, 1961; Louisiana State Univ, MLS, 1964; Univ Southern CA (USC), MPA, 1972; Univ CA, Los Angeles (UCLA), attended 1984. **Career:** Carroll High Sch, teacher, librn, 1961-65; Fresno County Libr, bookmobile librn, 1965-67; Univ Southern CA, bus sch li-

brn, 1967-71; Santa Ana Col, ref librn, libr technol instr, 1971-84; El Camino Col, cataloging, systs develop libr, 1984-99; instrnl serv div, actg dean, 1999-2003; dir learning resources, currently. **Orgs:** Past chap pres, Alpha Kappa Alpha Sorority, 1959-; past trustee, finance comt, Holman United Methodist Church, 1971-; past nat vpres, past Nat Historian, past area VI dir, Top Ladies Distinction, Nat Standards Chmn, 1977-; Los Angeles City/CA demo cent comts, 1990-2000; past bd mem, CA Asn Libr Trustees & Comnrs, 1992; mem, vpres, pres, Inglewood Unified Schs Bd, 1997-; South State Systs Adv Bd, 1997-2003; pres, Southern Regional Occup Ctr Bd, 1999-2001, mem 2005-. **Honors/Awds:** Assembly Dist (female) Domocrat of the Year, 1988; Outstanding Member, Southern Univ, LA Chap, 1987; Women's Wall of Fame, El Camino Col, 1999; Service Award, Nat Women's Polit Caucus/South Bay, 1999; Southern Ca Chaps Education Award, Nat Coun Negro Women, 2005; Service Award, Inglewood, Compton & Los Angeles City Couns; Inglewood Educators Award, Phi Delta Kappa, 2005. **Business Addr:** Director of Learning Resources, El Camino Community College, East Wing Rm 110 16007 Crenshaw Blvd, Schauerman Libr Main Fl, Torrance, CA 90506, **Business Phone:** (310)660-3526.

GRIGSBY, CALVIN BURCHARD

Investment banker, lawyer, educator. **Personal:** Born Dec 24, 1946, Osceola, AR; son of Janever Burch and Uzziah P; married Cheryl, Feb 24, 1968; children: James, Janene & Calvin Jr. **Educ:** Univ Ariz, BA, econ, 1968; Univ CA, JD, 1972. **Career:** Pillsburg, Madison & Sutro, corp lawyer, 1972-75; Univ San Francisco, securities law prof, 1975-76; Itel Corp, nat mkt mgr, munic finance, 1975-79; Fiscal Funding, chief exec officer & gen coun; Grigsby & Assocs, chief exec officer & pres, 1981-. **Orgs:** Calif Bar Asn, 1972-; Fed Bar Asn; bd dirs, Bond Mkt Asn; Charles Houstion Bar Asn, 1973-; vice chair, Nat Asn Securities Prof, 1985-; Nat Bar Asn, 1987-; bd trustees, San Francisco Symphony, 1987-; bd dirs, Boalt Hall Alumni Asn, 1987-; bd trustees, UC Berkeley Found, 1990-; bd chmn, Fiscal Funding Co; chmn bd, Civic Improv Corp; Nat Asn Advan Colored People. **Special Achievements:** Author: "Fiduciary Duties of Bank Trustees," Calif Law Rev, 1972; "Buy, Borrow or Lease?" 1988; Speaker at Public Admin Conf, New Orleans, 1988. **Military Serv:** USN, res, 1968-71. **Home Addr:** 2406 Saddleback Dr, Danville, CA 94526, **Home Phone:** (510)838-1713. **Business Phone:** 800-392-4877.

GRIGSBY, DAVID P

Executive. **Personal:** Born Mar 6, 1949, Greenville, MS; divorced; children: Reginald, Kayla Ann & Jasohn. **Educ:** MS Valley State Univ, BS 1970; AMA Mgmt Acad Saranac Lake NY, Mgmt 1971; St Johns Univ Jamaica NY, MBA 1973; Donald T Regan Sch Advanced Fin Mgmt, 1984. **Career:** NBC TV NY City, coord, sales develop & prom, 1971-73; Metromedia TV Sales, NY City, dir, res & sales prom, 1973-75; Arbitron TV NY City, acct exec, easterntv sales, 1975-78; WENZ-AM Drum Commun Inc, pres, 1978-81; Merrill Lynch Pierce Fenner & Smith, investment broker, asst vpres, sr financial consult; Prudential Securities, first vpres investments, 1993; RSL Group, pres & chief executive officer; Baron Capital Partners, exec vpres, bus develop, currently; founding partner in MRI Pharmaceut. **Orgs:** Second vpres, bd dir, Nat Asn Black Owned Broadcasters, 1979-81; adv bd mem, US Small Bus Admin Reg III, 1979-81; TV for All Children/Viewer Prom Ctr, 1979-80; chmn media comn., Fed Arts Coun, 1979-80; Manhattan Stockbrokers Club, 1984-; adv bd mem, US Small Bus Admin Reg II, 1984-87; selection comt, Small Bus Person the Year Reg II, 1985-87; issues specialist White House Conf Small Bus, 1986; publ speaker, broadcasting, Temple Univ, Hunter Univ, Union Univ, Howard Univ. **Honors/Awds:** Outstanding Sales US Arbitron TV Sales, 1977; Outstanding Service to Youth Salvation Army Boys Club, 1979; March of Dimes Service Award, Nat Found March Dimes, 1979; Award of Appreciation "To Be Ambitious Gifted & Black", Hunter Col, 1979; Certificate of Appreciation, Small Bus Admin, 1979,81; Award of Appreciation, Asn Black Acct, 1984; Outstanding Officer, Governor Award NY Militia Award; President's Club Merrill Lynch. **Military Serv:** NYARNG, First lt Gov Awd; NY Militia Award. **Home Addr:** 360 W 22nd St, New York, NY 10011. **Business Addr:** Executive Vice President Business Development, Baron Capital Partners, 642 NW 38th Circle, Boca Raton, FL 33431, **Business Phone:** (561)417-7111.

GRIGSBY, JEFFERSON EUGENE

Artist. **Personal:** Born Oct 17, 1918, Greensboro, NC; son of Jefferson Eugene Grigsby Sr and Purry Leone Dixon; married Rosalyn Thomasena Marshall, Jun 12, 1943; children: J Eugene III & Marshall C. **Educ:** Morehouse Col, BA, 1938; Am Artists Sch, 1939; Johnson C Smith Univ, 1941; Ohio State Univ, MA, 1940; NY Univ, PhD, 1963. **Career:** Artist (retired); Johnson C Smith Univ, artist-in-residence, 1940-41; Bethune Cookman Col, art instr & dept head, 1941-42; Barber Scotia Col, art instr, 1945-46; Carver High Sch & Phoenix Union High Sch, art teacher & head dept, 1946-66; Ariz State Univ, prof art, 1966-88, prof emer, 1988-. **Orgs:** Consult ed, African Arts mag, 1968-80; bd mem, Phoenix Opportunity Ind Ctr, 1968-; vpres, Nat Art Educ Asn, 1972-74; chmn, contrib ed, Sch Arts Mag, 1978-83; Minority Concerns Comm NAEA, 1980-85; bd mem, Phoenix Arts Coming Together, BTW Child Develop Ctr; bd dir, Phoenix Urban League, Arizona Job Cols, OIC; bd chmn, Consortium Black Orgns & others for the Arts 1983-; contrib ed, Arts & Activ Mag, 1983-; pres, Ariz Art Educ Asn, 1988-; vpres, Garfield Neighborhood Orgn, 1989-; pres, Booker T Wash Child Develop Ctr, 1989-; chmn, Artists Black Community, AZ, 1990-; Delta Beta Omega Chapter AKA, 1990; charter mem, Ariz Hist Makers Hall Fame, Ariz Hist Museum, 1992; Herberger Col Fine Arts. **Honors/Awds:** DFA, Philadelphia Sch Art, 1965; Twenty Fifth Anniversary Medallion of Merit, Nat Gallery Art, 1966; Seventy Fifth Anniversay Medallion of Merit, Univ Ariz; Visual Arts Panelist, Nat Found Advan Arts, 1981-85; Distinguished Research Fellow, Ariz State Univ, 1983; Distinguished Fellow, 1985; Art Educator of the Year, 1988; Retired Art Educator of the Year, Nat Art Educ Asn, 1997 & 1998; Eigth annual Arizona Governor's Award, 1989; Bennie Trailblazer Award, Morehouse Col, 1995; The Art of Eugene Grigsby, Jr: a 65-year Retrospective, Phoenix Art Museum, 2001-02; NAACP's Man of the Year Award. **Special Achievements:** Contributions to State & Nation; Book publ: Art & Ethics: Background for Teaching Youth in a Pluralistic Society, the first book ever written for art teachers by an African Am artist & author. **Military Serv:** AUS, m/sgt, 1942-45. **Home Addr:** 1117 N 9th St, Phoenix, AZ 85006, **Home Phone:** (602)253-0668. **Business Addr:** Professor Emeritus, Arizona State University, 300 E Univ Dr, PO BOX 876505, Tempe, AZ 85281, **Business Phone:** (480)965-3391.

GRIGSBY, JEFFERSON EUGENE, III

Educator, city planner. **Personal:** Born May 30, 1944, Charlotte, NC; son of Jefferson Eugene Grigsby Jr and Rosalind; married Sharon; children: Jefferson Eugene IV, Jenna. **Educ:** Occidental Col, AB, sociol, 1966; Univ Calif Los Angeles, MA, sociol, 1968, PhD, sociol, 1971. **Career:** Los Angeles 2000, staff consult, 1986-88; 2000 Partnership, staff consult, 1989-91; Univ Calif Los Angeles, Grad Sch Archit & Urban Planning, prof, 1971-, Ctr Aro Studies, actg dir, 1991-92, dir, 1992-96; The Planning Group, pres, 1972-; Advan Policy Inst, dir, 1996; Nat Health Found, pres & chief exec officer, 2004. **Orgs:** Rebuild LA Task Force Land Use & Transp, co-chair, 1992; Am Col Sch Planning, exec comt, 1985-91, bd mem, 1988-91; bd mem, Am Gov Bd Cols & Univ; Occidental Col, bd trustees; J Am Planning Asn, bd ed, 1988-92; J Black Studies, bd ed, 1971-80; HUD Scholars, task force, exec comt, 1980-81; 1010 Develop Corp, bd dirs, 1991-. **Honors/Awds:** United Parcel Serv Vis Scholar Award, Stanford Univ, 1978; Occidental Col, Booker T Wash Outstanding Alumni Award, 1987; Outstanding Book, Residential Apartheid, 1996. **Special Achievements:** Speaker: Assembly Special Comt Los Angeles Crisis, Calif Legis, statement about urban planning and transit issues, 1992; House Comt Dis, statement about urban problems in Los Angeles since the Watts Riots, 1981. **Business Addr:** President, Chief Executive Officer, National Health Foundation, 1 Kaiser Plaza, Oakland, CA 94612.*

GRIGSBY, DR. MARGARET ELIZABETH. See Obituaries section.

GRIGSBY, DR. MARSHALL C

Clergy, school administrator, executive. **Personal:** Born Aug 18, 1946, Charlotte, NC; son of Eugene and Thomasina; married Germaine A Palmer; children: Rosalyn Kimberly & Michelle Alexandria. **Educ:** Morehouse Col, BA, 1968; Univ Chicago Div Sch, MTh, 1970, DMn, 1972. **Career:** Black Legis Clearing House, exec dir, 1970-72; First Unitarian Church Chicago, assoc minister, 1970-75; S Shore Community Planning Asn, proj dir, 1972; Asn Theol Sch, assoc dir, 1973-75; Howard Univ Sch Relig, asst dean & assoc prof, 1976-85; Benedict Col, Columbia, SC, pres, 1985-93; Grigsby & Assocs LLC, founder & owner, pres & chief exec officer, currently. **Orgs:** Ordained minister, Unitarian Universalist Church, 1970-; Soc Study Black Religion, 1973-; consult, Asn Theol Schs, 1975-; nat selection panel, Fund Theol Educ Inc, 1976; consult, Religion Div Lilly Endowment, 1977-; Nat Coun Negro Women, 1979-; Columbia City Bd SC Nat; Jr Achievement Greater Columbia; bd trustees, ETV Endowment SC; bd trustees, USA Funds; sr legis assoc, US House Comt Educ & Workforce; Am Soc Appraisers. **Honors/Awds:** Fel, Southern Fellowships Fund Inc, 1968-71; fel, Fund Theol Educ Inc, 1969-71; Regional Finalist White House Fel Prog, 1978. **Business Phone:** (301)598-2090.

GRIGSBY, TROY L

Federal government official. **Personal:** Born Oct 25, 1934, Holly Grove, AR; son of Velma May Ammons and Roy Vell Grigsby; children: Shari, Gloria, Alexis & Troy Jr. **Educ:** Wayne State Univ, BA, 1958, MUP, 1964. **Career:** Federal Government official (retired); State Mich Dept Pub Welfare, soc worker, 1959-62; Ypsilanti Mich Dept Urban Renewal, asst dir, 1962-64; Inkster Mich Dept Planning & Urban Renewal, asst dir & dir, 1964-68; Greater Cleveland Growth Asn, mgr community dev, 1968-71; State OH Dept Urban Affairs, dep dir, 1971-72; State OH Dept Econ & Community Develop, dep dir, 1972-75; Dept Community Develop Highland Park, MI, admin, 1976-79; US Dept HUD Omaha, NE, dep area mgr, 1979-82; US Dept HUD Milwaukee, WI, mgr, 1982-86; US Dept HUD Okla City OK, dep mgr, 1986-97. **Orgs:** Am Soc Planning Offs; Mayor's Comn Crisis Welfare, 1968; Mayor's Comn Urban Transp, 1968; Cleveland City Club, 1969-71; Cleveland Citizens League, 1969-71; bd dirs, Plan Action Tomorrow Housing, 1970-71; Cleveland Contractor's Asst Corp, 1970-71; Mayor's Comn Trans & Redevelop, 1970-71; secy, OH State Bd Housing, 1971-75; OH Dept Transp Adv Comt Highways, Terminals & Parking, 1971-72; Gov Housing & Community Develop Adv Comn, 1971-74, staff dir; OH Water & Sewer Rotary Comn, 1971-75; state rep, Appalachian Reg Comn, 1971-75; OH Comprehensive Health Planning Adv Coun 1972-74; Govs Conf Task Force Nat Regional Develop Policy, 1973; dir, Dayton State Farm Develop Bd, 1973-75; Coun State, Housing Finance Agencies Task Force Nat Housing Policy 1973-74; Coun, State Community Affairs Agencies, 1974; Fed Reg Coun Task Force Inter-Govt Rels 1974; Okla Gov's Small Bus Conf Community, 1987-90; chair, Okla City Weed & Seed Prog, 1996-97; Church Redeemer vestry, 1999-2002, 2005; Okla Episcopal Church Diocean coun, 2000-04; chair, NE Home Ownership Consortium, 2000-02. **Honors/Awds:** Plaque Recognizing Outstanding Service, Mil Fed Officials Asn, Wisconsin, 1986; Governors Certificate of Recognition, Okla, 1988; Certificate of Appreciation, Okla Civil Rights Comn, 1990; numerous others. **Home Addr:** 11600 Richaven Rd, Oklahoma City, OK 73162-2987.

GRILLO, LUIS

Manager, sports manager, basketball player. **Personal:** Born Oct 10, 1948. **Career:** Basketball player (retired), Referee (retired); Sports manager; Natl Basketball Referee Assn. *

GRIMES, CALVIN M., JR.

Executive. **Educ:** Boston pub sch syst. **Career:** Grimes Oil Co Inc, Boston, MA, pres & chief exec officer, 1999. **Orgs:** Nat Minority Supplier Develop Coun Inc. **Business Addr:** President, Chief Executive Officer, 50 Redfield St, Boston, MA 02122.*

GRIMES, DARLENE M C

Executive. **Personal:** Born Jul 23, 1960, Boston, MA; daughter of Calvin M Grimes and Leah E Christie. **Educ:** Lesley Col, Cambridge, BS, 1983. **Career:** Grimes Oil Co, Boston, vpres opers, currently. **Business Addr:** Vice President Operations, Grimes Oil Company, 50 Redfield St Suite 109, Boston, MA 02122-3630, **Business Phone:** (617)825-1200.

GRIMES, DOUGLAS M.

Lawyer. **Personal:** Born Aug 11, 1942, Marshall, TX; married Bernadette. **Educ:** Calif State Col, BA, 1965; Howard Univ Sch Law, JD, 1968. **Career:** Ill Nat Bank & Co, Chicago, admin asst, 1968-70; Univ Ill, Col Law, asst prof law & dir, Community Involvement, 1970-71; Grimes, Barnes & Gill, atty, 1971-; City Gary, asst city atty; Gary City Ct, pub defender, judge; Douglas M Grimes PC, atty, currently. **Orgs:** Deleg, Nat Black Assembly Conv, 1972-74; Police Civil Serv Comn; Gary Fire Comn; pres, Legal Aid Soc Gary; pres, Thurgood Marshall Law Asn; legal adv mem, Minority Businessmen's Steering Comt; legal adv, Lake County Corner; Gary Jaycees; adv bd mem, Urban League NW Ill Inc; Gary Frontiers Serv Club; secy, treas, bd mem, Gary Leased Housing Corp; Ill State Black Assembly; Gary chap, Ill State Black Assembly; bd dir, Gary Gus Resource Ctr; Chicago Jaycees, Southend Jaycees; legal & counsel, Ill Jaycees; corp coun mem, City Gary; Gary Sch Bd Trustees. **Home Addr:** 6941 Ironwood Ave, Gary, IN 46403, **Home Phone:** (219)938-5395. **Business Addr:** Attorney, Douglas M Grimes PC, 6941 Ironwood Ave, Gary, IN 46403-1216, **Business Phone:** (219)939-9511.*

GRIMES, NIKKI (NAOMI MCMILLAN)

Writer. **Personal:** Born Oct 20, 1950, New York, NY; daughter of James and Bernice McMillan. **Educ:** Rutgers Univ, Livingston Col, NB, NJ, BA, English, 1974. **Career:** Unique NY Mag, New York, NY, contributing ed, 1977-78; Cult Coun Found, New York, NY, lit consult, 1978-79; Swedish Educt Radio, Stockholm, Sweden, writer, co-host, 1979-80; AB Exportspaok, Stockholm, Sweden, proof reader, translr, 1980-84; freelance writer, 1984-88; Walt Disney Co, Burbank, CA, ed, 1988-90; Elizabeth Harding, writer, currently; Author: Essence, Todays Christian Woman, Book Links; Books: When Daddy Prays; Malcolm X: A Force for Change; Parents' Choice Honors for Is It Far to Zanzibar? Aneesa Lee & the Weaver's Gift; Book for the Teen Age; Quick Pick for Reluctant Young Adult Readers; 100 Books for Reading & Sharing; Horn Book Fanfare; Bank Street Children's Book; Poems, 1970; Growin', 1977; Something on My Mind, 1978; Disney Babies Bedtime Stories; Meet Danitra Brown, 1994; C is For City, 1995; Come Sunday, 1996; It's Raining Laughter, 1997; A Dime A Dozen, 1998; My Man Blue, 1999; Is It Far to Zanzibar, 2000; A Pocketful of Poems, 2001; Bronx Masquerade, 2002; Talkin' About Bessie, 2002; When Daddy Prays, 2002; Under the Christmas Tree, 2002; Danitra Brown Leaves Town, 2002; Co-producer & Host: The Kid Show, WBAI FM, New York. **Orgs:** Soc C's Book Writers & Illusrs; Authors Guild. **Honors/Awds:** Featured author, Nat Book Festival, 2003; 2003 Kerlan Award; Coretta Scott King Author Award for Bronx Masquerade; CSK Author Honor Awards, Talkin' About Bessie, Jazmin's Notebook; Children's Literature Council of California Award for Body of Work; ATB Best Children's Book Award; IMAGE Award Finalist; Best Book of the Year, New York Public Library; Coretta Scott King Author Award, 2003; Golden Dolphin Award, Southern Calif C's Book Asn, 2005; NCTE Award for Excellence in Poetry for Children, 2006. **Business Addr:** Writer, Curtis Brown Ltd, Ten Astor Pl, New York, NY 10003.

GRIMES, VONI B.

School administrator. **Personal:** Born Dec 23, 1922, Bamberg, SC; son of Mittie and McKinley; married Lorrayne; children:

Johnsie Silas, Edgar Gibson, Naomi Davis, Beverly Devan & Toni Gibson. **Educ:** Pa State Univ, attended 1951, cert, 1973; Univ Ky, cert, 1982, 1983 & 1985. **Career:** School administrator (retired); Philadelphia Ship Yard, sheet metal mechanic, 1942-44; York Hoover Corp, sheet metal worker/oper, 1947-49; Cole Steel Equip/ Litton Ind, supvr, 1949-70; Pa State Univ/York Campus, dir bus serv, 1970-88; Golden Personal Care Inc, pres. **Orgs:** Himyar Temple No. 9, PHA, 1951-; past master Soc Friendship No. 42, PHA, 1956-; Nimrod Consistory No. 9, PHA, 1956-; bd dirs, Indust Mgt Club, 1965-; budget chmn, York Co Red Cross, 1978-; secy, adv bd, White Rose MotorClub, AAA, 1980-; mgr, City York Bus Entrepreneur Resource Ctr, 1983-; adv, bd pres, York Co Voc-Tech Sch, 1985-88; pres, E York Lions Club, 1988-89; bd dir, 70001 (for drop-out students); lay leader Small Mem AMEZion Church. **Honors/Awds:** Voni B Grimes Day, named in honor, 1984; "Voni B Grimes Gym", named in honor, 1984. **Special Achievements:** Author, "Bridging Troubled Waters". **Military Serv:** AUS, Corpl 2 yrs, 4 months, Good Conduct Medal.

GRIMSLEY, ETHELYNE
Consultant. **Personal:** Born Jun 13, 1941, Clayton, AL; married Calvin H; children: Kelvin & Karen. **Educ:** NY Community Col, AS, 1975. **Career:** Staten Island Develop Ctr, social work, 1962-80; NJ Sch Assoc, 1980-; Roselle Sch Bd, mem bd; Lankmark Travel, travel consult; chmn, Zoning board, Borough of Roselle. **Orgs:** Pres, Union City Sch Bd Asn, 1983-85; Nat Advan Asn Colored People; Union City Negro Bus & Prof Women's Club. **Honors/Awds:** Women of Achievement Award, Leadership & Community Serv Phileman BaptistCh, 1983.

GRISHAM, ARNOLD T.
Banker, administrator. **Personal:** Born Dec 3, 1946, Chicago, IL; son of John and Gladys; married Jane, Jan 18, 1969; children: Kristine, Jonathan. **Educ:** De Paul Univ, BS, mgt, 1970; De Paul Univ, Grad Sch Bus, MBA, finance, 1972. **Career:** Continental Ill, second vpres, 1975-81; Wells Fargo Corp Serv, vpres & dep mgr, 1981-82, vpres & mgr, 1982-86; Wells Fargo Bank, Oakland, CA, vpres & loan team mgr, 1986-88, regional vpres, 1988-89, sr vpres & regional mgr, 1989-94, exec vpres, 1994; Civic Bank Com, pres, coord & chief lending officer; Civic Bancorp, bd mem; Korn & Ferry Int, partner; Grisham Group LLC, managing partner, currently. **Orgs:** Pres, Marcus Foster Educ Inst, 1989; chmn, Cult Diversity Comt, Wells Fargo Bank, 1990; bd mem, Wells Fargo Bank; bd regents, Holy Names Col, 1991-; United Negro Col Fund, East Bay Adv Comt, 1991-; chair, Finance Comt, Hanna Boys Ctr, 1992-; adv bd, E Oakland Youth Develop Ctr; mem, Exec Leadership Coun; co-chair, Parents Coun, Morehouse Col, Atlanta, GA; foundation bd, C Hosp Oakland; adv bd, Col Fund Northern Calif; adv coun, De Paul Univ Col Com, Exec Leadership Coun, Washington, DC. **Honors/Awds:** Frederick D Patterson Award, United Negro Col Fund, 1992; Bus Award, Watts Found Community Trust, 1996. **Military Serv:** Nat Guard, spec-5, 1967-73. **Business Phone:** (510)625-9040.*

GRISSOM, MARQUIS DEAN
Baseball player. **Personal:** Born Apr 17, 1967, Atlanta, GA; married Tia. **Career:** Baseball Player (retired), baseball executive; Montreal Expos, outfielder, 1989-94; Atlanta Braves, 1995-96; Cleveland Indians, 1997; Milwaukee Brewers, 1998-2000; Los Angeles Dodgers, 2001-02; San Francisco Giants, 2003-05; Chicago Cubs, 2006; Marquis Grissom Baseball Asn, founder, currently. **Honors/Awds:** Major League Baseball All-Star Game, 1993-94; Rawlings Gold Glove Award, 1993-96; American League Championship Series Most Valuable Player, 1997.

GRIST, ARTHUR L.
Educator. **Personal:** Born Apr 29, 1930, Tampa, FL; son of Edwin and Eleanor; married Nancy Jackson; children: Michelle, Arthur & Michael. **Educ:** Ohio State Univ, BS; Univ Mich, MPH. **Career:** Cleveland Div Health, pub health sanitarian, 1955-61; Southern Ill Univ, Carbondale, fac, 1961; Health Zoning & Housing, consult, 1961-65; Southern Ill Univ, Edwards ville, asst vpres, 1965-70, asst pres, 1970-76, spec asst vpres bus affairs, 1976-79, asst prof, 1968-82, assoc prof emer, 1982-. **Orgs:** Black Caucus Health Workers, 1969-71; treas, St Louis Health Syst Agency, 1970-78; vpres, St Clair City Health & Welfare Coun, 1974-80; Edwardsville City Planning Comn, Zoning Bd Appeals, 1975-81; pres, Metro E Health Serv Coun Inc, 1978-80; City Edwards ville Park & Recreation Bd, 1985-86; Alderman Ward 4 Edwardsville, IL, 1986-93; life mem, Kappa Alpha Psi; Am Pub Health Asn; Nat Environ Health Asn; Madison Co Red Cross; YMCA; United Fund; United Way; treas, Metro E Labor Coun; vpres, Alliance Reg Community Health MO, IL; Reg Adv Group, IL; Reg Med Prog. **Honors/Awds:** Service Award, Tri-City Health & Welfare Coun, 1972; Hildrus A Poindexter Distinguish Service Award, 1975. **Military Serv:** AUS, 1953-55; Res Med Serv Corps, environ sci officer, rank O-6 col,1961-90; Meritorious Service, 1983, 1988. **Home Addr:** 1912 McKendree Dr, Edwardsville, IL 62025. **Business Addr:** Associate Professor Emeritus, Southern Illinois University, PO Box 1122, Edwardsville, IL 62026-1653, **Business Phone:** (618)650-2000.

GRIST, RONALD
Executive. **Personal:** Born in New York, NY; son of Arthur and Ena; married Joyce. **Educ:** City Col NY, BBA. **Career:** Aetna Business Credit, New York, NY, vpres; Fidelity Bank, Philadelphia, PA, sr vpres; Fidelcorp Business Credit Corp, New York, NY, exec vpres; The CIT Group/Credit Finances Inc, exec vpres, chief fin officer. **Home Addr:** 1921 Lark Lane, Cherry Hill, NJ 08003.

GROCE, CLIF. See GROCE, CLIFTON ALLEN.

GROCE, CLIFTON ALLEN (CLIF GROCE)
Football player. **Personal:** Born Jul 30, 1972, College Station, TX. **Educ:** Tex A&M Univ. **Career:** Indianapolis Colts, running back, 1995-98; New England Patriots, 1998; Cincinnati Bengals, 1998-2000.

GROCE, REV. HERBERT MONROE, JR.
Clergy. **Personal:** Born Apr 17, 1929, Philadelphia, PA; son of Herbert M Groce Sr and Gertrude Elaine McMullin; married Linda Jane Rosenbaum; children: Eric H, Cheryl M, Karen D, Herbert M III & Lauren S; married Marcella, Jun 6, 1953 (divorced 1974). **Educ:** La Salle Col, Philadelphia, PA, 1960; Gen Theol Sem, New York, 1972-74; Inst Theol Cathedral, St John the Divine, New York, 1978. **Career:** Fairchild-Hiller Inc, Hagerston, MD, engineering planner, 1963-64; The Singer Co, Link Div, Binghamton, NY, admin, 1964-69; Delta Found, Greenville, MS, exec dir, 1970-71; Col Med & Dentistry, Newark, NJ, vpres human resources, 1971-78; Mutual Benefit Fund, Newark, dir, 1977; St Stephen's Pearl River, NY, episcopal priest asst, 1978; Lincoln Ctr Performing Arts Inc, dir opers, 1978; Trinity Cathedral, Trenton, asst, 1980-84; St Andrews Church, New York City Rector, 1984-93; Missionary Diocese of St Paul, bishop, 1994; St Luke's Anglician Church, pastor, currently. **Orgs:** Vpres, Unit Serv, Boy Scouts Am, NE Region, 1978; Mason 33 degree Ancient Accepted Scottish Rite, NY, 1979; shriner, Mecca Temple, AAONMS NY, 1980; dir, MBF-MBL Growth Fund Inc, 1982; dir, MBF-MAP-Govt Fund Inc, 1982; grand chaplain, Grand Lodge New York, 1984; grand chaplain, Grand Chapter Royal AR Masons, 1986; dir, Frances Federal Halfway House, 1986-89; Supreme Council 33 degree Ancient Accepted Scottish Rite Freemasonry, Assoc Grand Prior, 1991. **Honors/Awds:** Law Day Award, Broome/Tioga Bar Asn, 1968; Silver Beaver & Silver Antelope Awards, BSA, 1975; Serv Award, Whitney M Young Jr BSA, 1979; Hon Alumnus, Gen Theol Seminary 1983; Northern Masonic Jurisdiction, US Am, 1989. **Military Serv:** USAF, Good Conduct Medal, Korean War, 1951-55; USAF, Sargent, 1951-55. **Home Addr:** 875 Berkshire Valley Rd, Wharton, NJ 07885. **Business Addr:** Pastor, Saint Luke Anglician Church, 555 River Rd W, Manakin-Sabot, VA 23103-3103, **Business Phone:** (804)784-6190.

GROFF, PETER CHARLES
Government official. **Personal:** Born Apr 21, 1963, Chicago, IL; son of Regis and Ada; married Regina C, Jun 13, 1997; children: Malachi Charles & Moriah Cherie. **Educ:** Univ Redlands, BA, 1985; Univ Denver Law Sch, JD, 1992. **Career:** XM Satellite Radio, co host; Groff/Ellison Political Report, ed chief; City Denver, asst councilwoman A Haynes, 1991-94; Ray Romer Gov Campaign, political dir, 1994, City Denver, sr asst to the mayor, 1994-96; Univ Denver, exec dir & lectr, 1996-; Vadent Evans LLC, counsel, 2000-; State Colo, state rep, 2000-, State Sen, currently. **Orgs:** Founding fel, Future Focus, 1996-; exec bd, Urban League Denver, 1998-; Colo Unity, comt chair, 1998-; Shorter AME Church, sr steward, 2000-; founder & exec dir, Univ Denver, CO, ctr African Am Policy. **Honors/Awds:** Rising Star Award, 1997; Chairman's Award, Urban League Denver, 1999; person to watch in 2008, BlackAmericaWeb.com, 2008. **Special Achievements:** Co-auth: Standing at the Gap: Leadership for the 21st Century, 1998; ed: I Do Solumnly Swear: Chronology of African Amer Politics & Policy, 1999; Urban Spectrum Newspaper, monthly column; KDKO; host of Legal Brief; First African American in Colorado to serve as President of the Colorado Senate. **Business Addr:** Colorado State Senator, Colorado General Assembly, 200 E Colfax, Denver, CO 80203, **Business Phone:** (303)866-4864.

GROFF, REGINA COLEEN
Educator, clergy. **Personal:** Born Jul 17, 1971, Brooklyn, NY; daughter of John and Bonita Darby; married Peter C. Groff, Jun 13, 1998; children: Malachi Charles Groff, Moriah Cherie Groff. **Educ:** Duke Univ, BA, Philos, 1993; Duke Divinity Sch, MDiv, 1996; Univ Denver, PhD, Educ, 2004. **Career:** St Mary's Acad, religion teacher, comn service dir, 1996-98; Barney Ford Elem Sch, reading asst, 1998-99; Jr Achievement, ed mgr, 1999-00; Shorter Community African Methodist Episcopal Church, assoc minister christian educ, sr assoc minister; Campbell African Methodist Episcopal Church, pastor, 2004-. **Orgs:** Colorado Coalition Against Domestic Violence; Nat Coalition Against Domestic Violence; Women Ministry & Rocky Mountain Dist; Future Black Women Leaders Colo; Colo Black Women Political Action. **Honors/Awds:** Associate scholar, Rocky Mountain Women Inst, 1996-97; Mother & Daughter Ministry Team of the Yr, Daughters of Destiny, 2000; Tribute to Black Women Honoree in Religion, Colo Black Women Political Action, 2003; Dynamic Duo; Hall of Fame, 2005. **Business Addr:** Pastor, Campbell Chapel African Methodist Episcopal Curch, 1500 E 22nd Ave, Denver, CO 80205, **Business Phone:** (303)839-5058.*

GROFF, REGIS F.
State government official, association executive. **Personal:** Born Apr 8, 1935, Monmouth, IL; son of Eddie and Fenimore Thomas; married Ada Lucille Brooks, Jan 1, 1962 (divorced 1999); children: Traci Lucille & Peter Charles; married Silvia Wallace, Jan 1, 1955; children: James. **Educ:** Western Ill Univ, BS, 1962; Univ Denver, MA, 1972; Urban Affairs Inst,attended 1972; Harvard Univ, John F Kennedy Sch Govt, prog for sr exec in State & Local Govt, 1980. **Career:** Cook County Dept Pub Aid, case worker, 1962-63; Denver Pub Schs, teacher,1963-66; Rockford Pub Schs, teacher, 1966-67; Univ Denver, instr black hist, 1972-73; Metro State Col, instr black polit, 1972-73; Colo State Univ, instr black hist, 1972-73; Univ Colo, instr black hist, 1974-75; Colo State Senate, sen, 1974-94; Colo Dept Corrections, Youthful Offenders Syst, dir, 1994-98; Metro Denver Black Church Initiative, exec dir, 1998-. **Orgs:** Chmn, Nat Conf State Legislators Energy Comt, 1986-, Educ Comt, 1988-; bd mem, Am & Israel Friendship League, 1988-; pres, Nat Black Caucus State Legislators, 1990-94; co-founder, Nat Black Caucus State Legislators; Dem Planning Bd Gov Comn C & Families; Pvt Adv Coun, State Legis Leaders Found. **Honors/Awds:** Legislator of the Year Award, Asniated Press, 1981. **Military Serv:** USAF, airman first class, 1953-57. **Business Addr:** Executive Director, Metro Denver Black Church Initiative, 3601 Martin Luther King Blvd, Denver, CO 80205, **Business Phone:** (303)355-3423.

GROOMES, DR. FREDDIE LANG
School administrator, educator. **Personal:** Born in Jacksonville, FL; children: Linda & Derek. **Educ:** Fla A&M Univ, BS, 1962, MEd, 1963; Fla State Univ, PhD, 1972. **Career:** Proj Upward Bound, coordr, counr, 1965-68, assoc dir, 1968-70; Fla A & M Univ, dir inst res, 1970-72; Fla State Univ, exec asst pres, dir human affairs, assoc prof, Human Serv & Studies, exec asst & dir equal opportunity & Pluralism vpres acad affairs, Off Univ Human Resources, asst to pres, currently. **Orgs:** Consult, Hewitt Assoc Inc; Am Coun Educ; Col & Univ Pers Asn; chmn, Fla Gov Comn Status Women; Fla Human Rels Comn; Fla Coun Indian Affairs; exec bd, Am Asn Affirm Action. **Honors/Awds:** Rockefeller Fel, 1976; Outstanding Educators Am; Kappa Delta Pi Nat Hon Soc. **Business Addr:** Assistant to the President, Florida State University, Office of University Human Resources, Admin Bldg 301 Westcott Ave, Tallahassee, FL 32306-1049.

GROOMS, DR. HENRY RANDALL
Engineer. **Personal:** Born Feb 10, 1944, Cleveland, OH; son of Leonard D and Lois Pickell; married Tonie Marie Joseph; children: Catherine, Zayne, Nina, Ivan, Ian, Athesis, Shaneya, Yaphet, Rahsan, Dax, Jevay & Xava. **Educ:** Howard Univ, BSCE, 1965; Carnegie-Mellon Univ, MS, Civil Eng, 1967, PhD, Civil Eng, 1969. **Career:** DC Highway Dept Wash, DC, hwy engr, 1962; Peter F Loftus Corp Pittsgh, PA, struct Engr, 1966; Blaw-Knox Co Pittsgh, PA, struct engr, 1967-68; Rockwell Int Downey, CA, struct engr, 1969, engineering mgr; Boeing Integrated Defense Systs, engineering mgr, sr mgr, currently. **Orgs:** Kappa Alpha Psi, 1963-; Tau Beta Pi, 1964-; Am Soc Civil Engrs, 1965-; Sigma Xi, 1967-; scoutmaster, Boy Scouts Am, 1982-88; coach, Youth Basketball, 1984-; coach, Youth Soccer, 1985-; Watts Friendship Sports League, 1990-; co-founder, Proj Reach Scholar Found, 1994-; Watts Friendship Sports League. **Honors/Awds:** Col Recruiter of the Year, 1979-80; Engineer of the Year, Rockwell Int Space Div, 1980; Alumni Merit Award, Carnegie-Mellon Univ, 1985; Honoree, Western Res Hist Soc, Cleveland OH, Black Hist Arch Proj, 1989; Outstanding Engineering Volunteer Award, 1999; elected fellow of the African Scientific Institute, 2002; Golden Torch Awards, Nat Soc Black Engr, 2004. **Special Achievements:** Author & co-author of 19 technical papers. **Business Addr:** Senior Manager Strength, Boeing Integrated Defense Systems, 5301 Bolsa Ave, Huntington Beach, CA 92647.

GROOMS, LEJUANA HARDMON. See HARDMON, LADY.

GROOMS-CURINGTON, TALBERT LAWRENCE, SR.
Government official. **Personal:** Born Oct 21, 1956, Dayton, OH; son of James and Lucy M Grooms; divorced; children: Talbert L Jr. **Educ:** Sinclair Col, AS, lib arts, 1981; Wilberforce Univ, BS, mgt; Univ Dayton, MEd. **Career:** Wright Patterson AFB, acct, finance asst, 1975; Dayton Metrop Housing Authority, purchasing agent, 1977, purchasing assoc dir, 1987, asset mgt dir, currently; Miami Univ, Ohio, purchasing mgr, 1986; Wilberforce Univ, prof, currently. **Orgs:** Vice regional dir, Phi Beta Sigma; Beta Xi Sigma Chap; Citizens Fed Bank, CRA Bd; bd mem, United Way; Kiwanis Club; Nat Asn Housing & Redevelopment Officials; Nat Purchasing Coun; Nat Asn Black Accountants; Nat Asn Blacks Govt; Cong Adv Coun; Nat Asn Advan Colored People; vice regional dir, Phi Beta Sigma Fraternity. **Honors/Awds:** Community Service Award, Phi Beta Sigma; Black Leadership Recognition Award; Mayor's Proclamation for Outstanding Leadership, 1992; Visionary Award, Beta Xi Sigma Chap, 1992. **Special Achievements:** Elected into the Purchasing Manager Association; Top Ten African American Males, 1995. **Home Addr:** 5146 Weddington Dr, Dayton, OH 45426, **Home Phone:** (513)854-9913. **Business Addr:** Director, Contracts, 400 Wayne Ave, Dayton, OH 45410, **Business Phone:** (937)910-7600.

GROSVENOR, VERTAMAE
Writer, journalist. **Personal:** Born Apr 4, 1938, Fairfax, SC; married; children: Kali, Chandra. **Career:** Elan Mag, contrib ed; Es-

sence Mag, contrib ed; Plain Brown Rapper, 1975; SC Arts Comn, Lit Task Force; Penn Ctr, writer-in-residence; Amsterdam News, Chicago Courier, writer food column, currently; Nat Pub Radio's Cult Desk, corresp, "Seasonings", host, currently; Books: Vibration Cooking, 1970; Thursday and Every Other Sunday Off, 1970. **Orgs:** People United to Save Humanity. **Honors/Awds:** Robert F. Kennedy Award; Ohio State Award; Columbia Award; National Association of Black Journalists Award; Communications Excellence to Black America Award, 1991. **Special Achievements:** Has written for The New York Times, The Village Voice, The Washington Post, Life, Redbook, Ebony, and Viva; appeared on various TV programs including The Phil Donahue Show, The Today Show, ABC's Nightline, BET's Our Voices, and The Galloping Gourmet; had a featured role in Julie Dash's American Playhouse movie, Daughters of the Dust, for which she was also a language consultant. **Business Addr:** Correspondent, National Public Radio, Culture and Arts Information Unit, 635 Mass Ave NW, Washington, DC 20001, **Business Phone:** (202)513-2300.

GROTH, CHAD
Executive. **Personal:** Born Apr 25, 1970, Minneapolis, MN; son of Karl Groth; children: Chazz Marie Groth. **Educ:** Minneapolis Tech Col, 1992. **Career:** Minn Timberwolves, team attendant, 1989-92; Harlem Globetrotters, dir scouting & mgr basketball opers, 1993, vpres Stand & Player Personnel & chief scout, currently; Chad Groth Found, exec dir, currently. **Military Serv:** USN, basic training, summer, 1988. **Home Phone:** (602)753-5669. **Business Addr:** Vice President of Standards & Player Personnel, Harlem Globetrotters, 400 E Van Buren St Suite 300, Phoenix, AZ 85004-2257, **Business Phone:** (602)258-0000.

GROVES, DR. DELORES ELLIS
School administrator. **Personal:** Born Jan 29, 1940, Shelby County, KY; daughter of David Irvin and Mary Powell; married Clyde, Dec 20, 1969; children: Angela D Payden & Robin L Ham. **Educ:** Spalding Col, BS, educ, 1966; John Carroll Univ, MA, educ, 1972; Cleveland State Univ, admin cert, 1976-79; Univ Akron, EdD, 1996. **Career:** Shaker Heights City Sch Dist, elem prin, currently. **Orgs:** Pres & organizer, VIP's Social & Civic Club, 1973-75; dean pledges, Phi Delta Kappa Sorority, 1979-80; Phi Delta Kappa Fraternity, 1981-; consult, Cuy Sp Educ Serv Ctr, 1983-85; delegate & county rep, OAESA, 1984-87; health fair coordr, Shaker Heights Int Group, 1985; fund raiser & cochairperson, Delta Sigma Theta, 1985-87; NAESP, 1978-; delegate rep assembly, 1985-87, nat nominating chairperson, NABSE, 1986; Olivet Inst Bapt Church; pres, Shaker Heights Interest Group, 1991; bd mem, Cleveland Children's Museum, 1992-94; Links Inc, Cleveland Chap, 1993-, treas, 1994-97;bd mem & secy, Gt Clev Delta Fund Life Develop Ctr, 1997-. **Honors/Awds:** Professional of the Year, Nat Asn Negro Bus & Prof Women Inc, 1985;Ohio School of Excellence, 1991-92. **Special Achievements:** Led school to first "Hall of Fame" Award, OAESA, 1984-85; "Salute to Black Women Recognition," Call & Post newspaper, 1989. **Business Addr:** Elementary Principal, Woodbury Elementary, 15400 S Woodland, Shaker Heights, OH 44120, **Business Phone:** (216)295-4150.

GROVES, HARRY EDWARD
School administrator. **Personal:** Born Sep 4, 1921, Manitou Springs, CO; son of Harry (deceased) and Dorothy Cave (deceased); married Evelyn Frances Apperson; children: Sheridon Hale. **Educ:** Univ Colo, BA, 1943; Univ Chicago, JD, 1949; Harvard Univ, LLM, 1959. **Career:** School administrator (retired); Tex Southern Univ, dean sch law, 1956-60; Univ Singapore, dean fac law, 1960-64; Cent St Univ, pres, 1965-68; Sch Law Cincinnati, prof, 1968-70; NC Cent Univ, Durham, dean sch law, 1976-81; Univ NC, prof sch law, 1981-86; Memphis State Univ, Herbert Heff, vis prof law, 1989-90; Univ Minn, vis prof law, 1992; US Olympic Comt, Ethics Comt, Chair, 1993-96. **Orgs:** Elected mem, City Coun, Fayetteville, NC, 1951-52; chmn, Gov's Task Force Secy & Privacy, 1979-; bd dir, Mutual Savings & Loan Asn, 1979-80; pres, NC Prisoner Legal Serv Inc, 1979-81; pres, Legal Serv NC, 1983-85; SigmaPi Phi, Alpha Phi Alpha Frat; NC Bar Asn; Tex Bar Asn; Ohio Bar Asn; vpres bd gov, NC Bar Asn, 1986-87; bd dir, Am Bar Found, 1986-90; Am Bar AsnCoun Sec Legal Educ & Admis Bar, 1989-95; bd dir, Law Sch Admis Coun,1980-82. **Honors/Awds:** Judge John J Parker Award, North Carolina Bar Association, 1986; Robert L Kutak Award, American Bar Association, 1997. **Special Achievements:** Comparative Constitutional Law Cases & Materials Oceana Publs Inc, 1963; The Constitution of Malaysia, Malaysia Publs Ltd, 1964; pub more than 30 other books & articles; Phi Beta Kappa; Phi Delta Kappa; Kappa Delta Pi; prest, Wake County North Carolina Phi Beta Kappa 1989-90; sire archon, Alpha Tau Chapter of Sigma Pi Phi 1986-88; The Constitution of Malaysia, 4th ed (with Sheridan) 1979; Malayan Law Journal Ltd; Tun Abdul RazakMemorial Lecture, Kuala Lumpur Malaysia 1983. **Military Serv:** AUS, capt, 1943-46, 1951-52. **Home Addr:** 3050 Military Rd NW Apt 601, Washington, DC 20015. *

GRUNDY, CHESTER
Administrator. **Personal:** Born Aug 22, 1947, Louisville, KY; married; children: 2. **Career:** Ky State Univ, Frankfort, interim vpres student affairs; Univ Ky, UK African-Am Stud Affairs, dir, currently, Martin Luther King Jr Cultural Ctr, dir, currently. **Orgs:** Co-founder, Roots & Heritage Festival. **Honors/Awds:** Diversity Award, Univ Ky, 2007. **Business Addr:** Director of UK African-American Student Affairs, University of Kentucky, 557 Patterson Off Tower, Mathews Bldg, Lexington, KY 40506-0027, **Business Phone:** (859)257-5641.

GRUNDY, DALLAS A
Executive director, administrator. **Personal:** Born Oct 24, 1972, Philadelphia, PA; son of Donald and Yolande. **Educ:** Rutgers Univ, BS, civil eng, 1995, MBA, mgt info syst & mkt, 1998. **Career:** Taylor, Wiseman & Taylor, engineering-in-training, 1992-96; Hackensack Meadowlands Develop Comn, team leader, 1997-98; Mt Zion AME Ch, consult, 1887-; Lucent Tech, mkt strategy & staff oper mgr, 1997-98, staff oper mgr, 1998-2000; MBS Enterprises, vpres, 1995-99, exec vp, 2000-; BCT Partners, founder & partner, currently; Somerset Christian Col, dir bus affairs, 2004-06; Rutgers Grad Sch Educ, assoc dean, 2006-. **Orgs:** Pres, Rutgers Chapter Nat Soc Black Engineers, 1994; pres, Rutgers Nat Black MBA Asn, 1997-98; Renaissance Econ Develop Corp, 2000-; asst youth dir, First Baptist Ch Youth Ministry, 2000-; fel leadership prog, Partnership for NJ, 2005-. **Honors/Awds:** Outstanding Achievement Award, NJ Comn on Higher Educ; inducted into the 2006 class of the Rutgers University African-American Alumni Alliance Hall of Fame. **Business Addr:** Chief Operating Officer, BCT Partners Inc, 105 Lock St, Newark, NJ 07103, **Business Phone:** (973)622-0900.

GUDGER, ROBERT HARVEY
Executive, lawyer. **Personal:** Born Nov 17, 1927, Mamaroneck, NY; married Priscilla Kirby; children: Margo T, Gail T, Robin. **Educ:** Univ Redlands CA, BA Polit Sci, 1953; Columbia Univ NYC, MA Psychol 1958; NY Law Sch NYC, JD 1961. **Career:** Executive (retired), lawyer; NY State Dept Labor, employ coun, 1955-57; NY State Dept Educ, rehab couns, 1957-59; Urban League Westchester, assoc dir, 1959-62; Am Airlines Inc, mgr labor rels, 1962-65, 1967-71; Rochester Urban League, exec dir 1965-67; Xerox Corp, mgr higher educ progs, 1971-82; vpres, Xerox Found, 1982-93. **Orgs:** Bd mem, Comm Savings Bank, Rochester 1974-76; bd mem Girl Scouts Am, Rochester 1974-76; bd, Art Gallery Rochester, 1975-76; bd mem, Jr Achievement Stamford, 1979-; bd mem, Drug Liberation Inc, Stamford 1979-; bd mem, United Way Stamford, 1980; Int Legal Frat, Phi Delta Phi, 1961. **Honors/Awds:** Frederick Douglass Award, Comm Serv Rochester, 1966; Black Achievers Award, YMCA New York City 1971. **Business Addr:** Stamford, CT 06904.*

GUEST, WILLIAM, II
Singer. **Personal:** Born Jun 2, 1941, Atlanta, GA. **Career:** Gladys Knight and the Pips, mem; TV Series: "Toast of the Town", 1968-71; "Bandstand", 1970-85; "Soul Train", 1971-88; "Too Pooped to Pip", 1984; "Solid Gold", 1985; "When A. Lansing Loves a Woman", 1996; "Murphy Brown", 1996. **Honors/Awds:** Inductee, Rock and Roll Hall of Fames, 1996; Lifetime Achievement Award,Rhythm & Blues Found, 1998. **Business Phone:** (818)777-4500.*

GUFFEY, EDITH A
Statistician, executive. **Personal:** Married Jerry. **Career:** United Church Christ, secy, exec officer, assoc gen minister, currently. **Special Achievements:** First African Am female & lay person to hold the post of secy of the 1.5 million-mem group of United Church of Christ. **Business Addr:** Secretary, Associate General Minister, United Church Christ, Office Of General Ministries, 700 Prospect Ave, Cleveland, OH 44115-1000, **Business Phone:** (216)736-2110.

GUICE, REV. GREGORY CHARLES
Counselor, clergy. **Personal:** Born Nov 13, 1952, Detroit, MI; son of Rufus and Corrine Bowens; married Deena Dorsey, May 5, 1979 (divorced 1991); children: Merrin & Morgan; married Francine. **Educ:** Ky State Univ, Frankfort, KY, BA, hist & sociol, 1975; Ctr Humanistic Studies, Detroit, MI, MA, clin psychol, 1986. **Career:** St Theresa Sch, Detroit, MI, teacher, 1983-86; Black Family Devt Inc, social worker, 1986-88; Don Bosco Home for Boys, Detroit, MI, social worker, 1988-89; Gesu Sch, Detroit, MI, social worker, 1989; specialist/family counr, 1990-93; Detroit Unity Temple, rev, co-minister; Unity Christ Church, Ft Wayne, Ind, sr minister; Unity Church Lake Orion, unity minister, 2000-. **Orgs:** Co-founder, 'Be The Best That You Can Be', 1986-; jr deacon, Prince Hall Masonic Lodge, 1989-; bd mem, Unity Inst; bd mem, Unity Village. **Honors/Awds:** Mason of the Year, Prince Hall Lodge, 1990. **Special Achievements:** Selected as one of the 10 Best Educators, Ebony Magazine, 1989. **Home Phone:** (313)531-9137. **Business Addr:** Reverend, Unity Minister, Unity Church of Lake Orion, 3070 Baldwin Rd, Orion Township, MI 48359, **Business Phone:** (248)391-9211.

GUICE, LEROY
Judge. **Personal:** Born Dec 12, 1944, Fayette, MS; married Rosemary Thompson; children: Leroy, Cedric. **Educ:** Co-19Lin Jr Col, continuing educ, 1976; Miss Col, continuing educ, 1984; Univ Miss, 1984. **Career:** USAF, aircraft frame tech, 1964-68; Thomasville Furniture Co, plant production supvr, 1972-85; Jefferson County, justice ct judge, 1984-; Bus Owner. **Orgs:** Brother, United Methodist Church, 1972-; mason, brother Jefferson Lodge, 1984; judge, Justice Ct Judges Asn, 1984-. **Military Serv:** USAF, airman 1st class; Vietnam Veteran. **Home Addr:** 1011 Hwy 33 Rt 2, PO Box 35, Fayette, MS 39069. **Business Addr:** Judge Justice Court, Jefferson County District 1, PO Box 1047, Fayette, MS 39069.*

GUIDRY, DAVID
Executive. **Personal:** Born Aug 20, 1957, Palmetto, LA; son of Raphael and Agnes; married Ava Dejoie; children: Raphael, Amber, Bryce. **Educ:** La Tech Univ, attended 1977; TH Harris Voc Tech, assoc, 1978. **Career:** Bibbins & Rice Electronics, technician, 1979-82; Guico Mach Works, pres & chief exec officer, 1982-. **Orgs:** bd mem, Gulf S Minority Purchasing Coun, 1989; Chamber Com, 1989; La Regional Vo-Tech Board, 1990; app mem, Gov Task Force African Trade & Finance, 1992; Black Econ Develop Coun, 1990; bd mem, Harvey Canal Indust Asn, 1991; adv bd, W Jefferson Tech Col; gov app, La Workforce Develop Comn, La Econ Develop Coun, La Highway Safety Comn; vice chair, Jefferson Bus Coun; bd, Meadowcrest Hosp; bd dirs, Fed Res Bank Atlanta, New Orleans br. **Honors/Awds:** Charlet Bus Award, Jefferson Parish Econ Develop, 1994; State La, Mfgs; Lantern Award, 1994; Blue Chip Enterprise Initiative Award, US Chamber Com, 1993; State La, Minority Bus Person of the Yr, 1993; Minority Bus Advocate of the Yr, SBA, 1992; Small Bus Champion, Chamber Com, 1991; Minority Bus Enterprise Award, GSMPC, 1988; Employer of the Yr, Lincoln Career Ctr, 1987; Role Model Award, Young Leadership Coun, 1997; Joseph W Simon Jr Memorial Award, New Orleans Chamber. **Special Achievements:** Featured by CBS & NBC affiliates on Guico's business Kuwait, 1991; Featured in Times-Picayune Money Section profiling Guico, 1992. **Business Addr:** President, Chief Executive Officer, Guico Machines Works Inc, 1170 Destrehan Ave, Harvey, LA 70058, **Business Phone:** (504)340-7111.*

GUILFORD, DIANE PATTON
Librarian. **Personal:** Born Feb 15, 1949, Detroit, MI; daughter of Kathleen Droughn and Nesbitt B; married Samuel, Jun 2, 1973. **Educ:** Ky State Univ, Frankfort, KY, BA, 1970; Atlanta Univ, Atlanta, GA, MSLS, 1971. **Career:** Atlanta Public Libr, Atlanta, GA, asst br head, 1971-73; Frostproof Pub Libr, Frostproof, Fla, consult, 1972; Romulus Community Schs, Romulus, Mich, media specialist, 1973-77; Fairfax County Public Schs, Springfield, VA, head libr, 1978. **Orgs:** Vpres, Nat Coun Negro Women, Reston Chap, 1982-83; chairperson, Southeastern Library Asn, Outstanding Southeastern Authors Committee, 1987-89; vpres, Alpha Kappa Alpha/Lambda Kappa Omega Chapter, 1990-91; chairperson, Va Library Asn, Sch Library Section, 1991-92; charter mem, Old Dominion Chap, The Links Inc. **Honors/Awds:** Human Relations Award, 1986, Commendation for Prof Excellence, 1987, Fairfax County Schools; Am Library Assn Award for Programs for Youth in Sch & Public Libraries, 1994.

GUILLAUME, DR. ALFRED JOSEPH, JR.
Educator, chancellor (education). **Personal:** Born Apr 10, 1947, New Orleans, LA; married Bernice Forrest; children: Alfred III. **Educ:** Xavier Univ LA, BA, 1968; Brown Univ, AM, 1972, PhD, 1976. **Career:** Fulbright-Hays Teaching Asst, Int Inst Educ, 1974-75; Xavier Univ, coord admis, 1977-78, dean freshman studies, 1978-80, dean arts & sci, 1980-; Ind Univ, S Bend, Acad Affairs, vice chancellor, currently; Humbol dt St Univ, vpres acad affairs. **Orgs:** Bd, Coun Develop Fraternity LA, 1976-; Baudelaire & Nature, S Cent Mod Lang Asn Conv, 1977; asst treas, Col Lang Asn, 1978-81; sect chmn, S Cent Mod Lang Asn, 1978-79; pres, LA Col Hon Coun, 1980-81; gov appointee & mem acad adv coun, Develop Fr LA; pres, LA Col Hon Coun, 1980-81; La Athenee; assoc mem, Sociedad Nacional Hispanica; presentor & discussion leader, Competency Assessment Teacher Educ; panelist, Ed Testing Serv Workshop Testing, Dallas, TX; consult, Methods Improving Oral Commun Target Lang. Am Conf Acad Deans, Nat Asn Col Deans Registrars & Admis Officers, LA Coun Deans Arts & Sci, Asn Am Col; Am Asn Teachers Fr; Col Lang Asn. **Special Achievements:** Conversation with Leopold Sedar Senghor on His Poetry & Baudelaire's, French Review 1978; The Baudelairian Imagination, Positive Approaches to Nature", Coll Lang Assoc Jrnl 1979; To Spring (Au Printemps), New Laurel Review, 1980; Women and Love in the Poetry of the Free People of Color, South Central Modern Lang Assoc Conv, 1980; The Emotive Impulse & the Senghorian Response to Nature, Coll Lang Assoc Conv, 1980; Literature in Nineteenth Century LA, Poetry & the Free People of Color, Jambalaya Public Library Lecture Series, 1980; Jeanne Duval as the Cornerstone of the Baudelairian Imagination, South Central Modern Lang Assn Convention, 1982; Love Death & ith in the New Orleans Poets or Color, Southern Quarterly, 1982; Joanni Questi, Monsieur Paul, LA Literature 1984; Le Divin Mystere, Religious Fervor in the Literature of the Free People of Color, Southern Conf on Christianity in Literature 1984. **Military Serv:** AUS, sp4, 2 yrs; Commendation Medal, Bronze Star, 1970. *

GUILLAUME, ROBERT
Actor, television producer. **Personal:** Born Nov 30, 1927, St Louis, MO; married Donna Brown, Jan 1, 1984; children: Kevin & Rachel. **Educ:** St Louis Univ; Wash Univ. **Career:** Theater appearances: Fly Blackbird, 1962; No Place to Be Somebody, 1969-70; Fire in the Mindhouse, 1970-71; Purlie, 1971-72; Benito Cer-

eno, 1975-76; Guys & Dolls, 1976; Don Juan, 1977; The Phantom of the Opera, 1990; Films: Seems Like Old Times, 1980; The Kid with the 200 IQ, exec producer, 1983; Prince Jack, 1985; Wanted: Dead or Alive, 1987; Christmas, producer & dir, 1988; Lean On Me, 1989; The Land Before Time VIII: The Big Freeze, voice, 2001; 13th Child, 2002; The Adventures of Tom Thumb & Thumbelina, voice, 2002; Extreme Skate Adventure, voice, 2003; The Lion King 1 1/2, voice, 2004; Big Fish, 2003; Half-Life 2, voice, 2004; Kingdom Hearts II, voice, 2005; Jack Satin, 2005; Satin, 2008; TV Series: Soap, 1977-79; Benson, 1979-86; North & South, 1985; John Grins Christmas Special, exec producer & dir, 1986; Perry Mason: The Case of the Scandalous Scoundrel, 1987; Fire & Rain, 1989; The Robert Guillame Show, exec producer & actor, 1989; Sports Night, 1998; Sports Night, 1998-2000; His Body guard, 1998; The Happy Prince, 1999; Moesha,2000; Quo Vadimus, 2000; La Forza Del Destino, 2000; Bells & a Siren, 2000; April Is the Cruelest Month, 2000; Draft Day: Part 2 -The Fall of Ryan OBrian, 2000; All This, & Turkey Too, 2000; 8 Simple Rules for Dating My Teenage Daughter, 2003; Every Picture Tells a Story, 2003; Century City, 2004; To Know Her, 2004; Half-Life 2, voice, 2004, 2006-07. **Orgs:** Screen Actors Guild; Am Federation Television & Radio Artists. **Honors/Awds:** Emmy Award for Outstanding Supporting Actor in a Comedy, 1978-79; Emmy Award for Oustanding Lead Actor in a Comedy, 1984-85; Image Awards, Nat Asn Advan Colored People; Golden Nymph, Outstanding Male Actor, 2001; Interactive Achievement Award, 2005. **Special Achievements:** Only African American actor to win the Lead Comedy Actor award.

GUILLEBEAUX, TAMARA ELISE
Administrator, educator. **Personal:** Born in Philadelphia, PA. **Educ:** Butler Univ, BA; New York Univ, MA; PA Ballet Co Sch Dance; Judimar Sch Dance; Marion Cuyjet; Essie Marie Dorsey Sch Dance. **Career:** Metrop Opera, Lincoln Ctr, Develop Dept, admin, 1986-. **Orgs:** Alpha Kappa Alpha Sor Inc; bd dirs, Saraband Ltd; dir, Scholar Develop Saraband Ltd, 1985-; Nat Asn Female Exec; spec adv, bd dir, Robin Becker & Co; panelist, NY Found Arts, 1992-95; Nat Coalition 100 Black Women, 1994-96. **Honors/Awds:** Rosenblith Scholarship Award; soloist 51st Boule, Alpha Kappa Alpha Sor, 1984; partic, Int Olympics Black Dance Art Festival 1984. **Business Addr:** Admin, Metropolitan Opera Assoc, Develop Department, Lincoln Ctr, New York, NY 10023, **Business Phone:** (212)799-3100.

GUILLORY, KEVEN
Television news anchorperson, journalist. **Personal:** Born Feb 20, 1953, Berkeley, CA; son of Emma Crenshaw and Jesse Guillory; married Arleigh Prelow (divorced 1986); children: Alison, Kara; married Donna Barati-Guillory, Mar 24, 1990; children: Maiya. **Educ:** Col Alameda, 1972; Univ California, Berkeley, CA, 1974; Stanford Univ, Stanford, CA, fellowship 1991. **Career:** KSOL, San Mateo, CA, news/public affairs reporter, 1974-75; KBLX, Berkeley, CA, news director, 1976-79; KIOI, San Francisco, CA, public affairs director, 1979-80; Youth News, Oakland, CA, teacher, 1980-82; KQED Inc, San Francisco, CA, producer/reporter, 1985-. **Orgs:** Member, national Association of Black Journalists, 1981-; former president, current mem, Bay Area Black Journalists Association, 1983-; mem, RTNDA, Radio Television News Directors Association; Bass Anglers Sportsmen Society. **Honors/Awds:** Associated Press News Award for Feature News, Associated Press, 1989, 1990; John Knight Journalism Fellowship, Stanford University, 1990-91. **Business Addr:** Anchor, Reporter, KQED-FM, 2601 Mariposa St, San Francisco, CA 94110, **Business Phone:** (415)553-2368.*

GUILLORY, LINDA SEMIEN
Business owner. **Personal:** Born Oct 4, 1950, Lake Charles, LA; daughter of Leo Semien and Adeline Semien; divorced; children: Tina G & Ashley F. **Educ:** Univ Colo, BA, 1985. **Career:** Mountain Bell, mgr, 1970-85; Transformative mgt, Inc, pres, owner; Handz On Designs, owner, currently. **Orgs:** Bd mem, Coun Black Comt, 1988-91; vpres, Coun Black Prof, 1989-90; bd mem,Denver Victims Serv Ctr, 1989-; Mayor's Comt on Employ, 1992-. **Honors/Awds:** Continued Leadership in Pluralism Award, 1987; Dedication to Women of Color Project Award, US West, Inc, 1989. **Special Achievements:** Published manual, Myth and Methods for Managing a Multi-cultural Workforce, 1989.

GUILLORY, DR. WILLIAM A.
Educator. **Personal:** Born Dec 4, 1938, New Orleans, LA; children: William Jr & Daniel S. **Educ:** Dillard Univ, BS, 1960; Univ Calif, PhD, 1964. **Career:** Howard Univ, asst prof, 1965-69; Naval Ordnance Sta, consult, 1967-76; EPA, adv com, 1972-75; Prof Black Chemists & Chem Engrs, nat chmn, 1972; Nat Acad Sci, consult, 1973-74; Drexel Univ, assoc prof, 1969-74; Univ Utah, assoc prof, chem, 1974-76, prof & chmn, dep chem, 1976; Innovations Int Inc, founder & chief exec officer, currently; Ctr Creativity & Inquiry, exec dir, currently. **Orgs:** Fel, Nat Sci Found Post doctoral, Paris, 1964-65; fel, Alfred P Sloan Found, 1971-73; adv panel, NSF, 1974-77; Beta Kappa Chi; Sigma Xi; Alpha Chi Sigma; Am Phys Soc; AAAS; NY Acad Sci; Phi Kappa Phi; Am Chem Soc. **Honors/Awds:** Outstanding Educators America, 1972; Merit Award, City New Orleans, 1974; Danfort Found Asn, 1975. **Special Achievements:** Presented over 4,000 seminars, N & S Am, Gt Brit, Europe, Mex, Asia Pac &Can; facilitated seminars over 300 corps; author of numerous publications, including, "EMPOWERMENT" and "The Living Organization — Spirituality in the Workplace". **Business Addr:** Founder, Chief Executive Officer, Innovations International Inc, 310 E 4500 S Suite 420, Salt Lake City, UT 84107.*

GUILMENOT, RICHARD ARTHUR
President (Organization), executive. **Personal:** Born Mar 15, 1948, Detroit, MI; married Melanie Williams. **Educ:** Fisk Univ, BA, 1970; Northwestern Univ, MBA, 1972. **Career:** Ted Bater Adv, acct exec, 1972-74; BBDO Adv, acct supvr & vpres, 1974-77; Mingo Jones Guilmendt, vpres & dir client serv, 1977-79; Warner Am Satellite Ent Co, vpres mkg, 1980-82; GCI, pres, currently. **Orgs:** Adv, Amsterdam News, 1977-82; dir, Nat Urban League, 1978-81; barileur Omega Psi Phi. **Business Addr:** President, GCI, 92 Grandview Ave, Great Neck, NY 11020, **Business Phone:** (516)482-0152.

GUINIER, CAROL LANI. See GUINIER, LANI.

GUINIER, LANI (CAROL LANI GUINIER)
Educator, lawyer. **Personal:** Born Apr 19, 1950, New York, NY; daughter of Ewart and Genii; married Nolan A Bowie, Jan 1, 1986; children: Nikolas. **Educ:** Radcliffe Col, BA, 1971; Yale Law Sch, JD, 1974. **Career:** US Dist Judge, Damon Keith, clerk, 1974-76; Wayne County Juvenile Ct, referee, 1976-77; US Dept Justice, Civil Rights Div, 1977-81; NAACP Legal Defense Fund, 1981-88; New York Univ, adj law prof, 1985-89; Univ Pa, from assoc law prof to prof, 1988-92; Harvard Law Sch, law prof, 1998-2001; Bennett Boskey, law prof, 2001-. **Orgs:** Am Law Inst, 1996-; Penn Nat Comn Soc, Community and Culture, 1996-98; trustee, Open Soc Inst, 1996-; prin investr, RACETALKS; bd dirs, Juvenile Law Ctr, Philadelphia, PA, 1992-98; bd dir, Juvenile Law Ctr, 1992-98; Asn Am Law Sch, 1992-93; adv Comt, Southern Regional Coun, 1992-95; bd dir, NOW Legal Defense Fund, 1990-96. **Honors/Awds:** Harvey Levin Teaching Award, Univ Pa Law School, 1994; Congressional Black Caucus Chairman's Award, 1993; Rosa Park Award, Am Asn Affirmative Action, 1994; Margaret Brent Women Lawyers of Achievement Award, Am Bar Asn Comt on Women in the Profession, 1995; Champion of Democracy Award, Nat Women's Political Caucus, 1995; Big Sisters Award, 1999; Sacks Freund Award for Teaching Excellence, Harvard Law Sch, 2002. **Special Achievements:** Books: Tyranny of the Majority, 1994; Lift Every Voice, 1998; The Miner's Canary, 2002; First African-American woman member of the Harvard law faculty, 1998. **Business Addr:** Bennett Boskey Professor of Law, Harvard Law School, 1525 Mass Ave, Cambridge, MA 02138, **Business Phone:** (617)496-1913.

GUITANO, ANTON W.
Executive, president (organization), auditor. **Personal:** Born Jul 5, 1950, Brooklyn, NY; son of Whitney J and Blanche Epps; married Leslie Marie Ferguson, Jun 15, 1975; children: Jessica Lynn, Jennifer Whitney, Jason Anton. **Educ:** St Peters Col, Jersey City, BS, 1971; Cert Pub Acct, NY State Dept Educ, 1979. **Career:** Price Waterhouse, NY, sr auditor, 1971-78; CBS Inc, NY, sr dir auditing, 1978-83; CBS Tv Stations, NY, controller, 1983-86; CBS Tv Network, NY, controller, 1986-88; CBS Inc, NY, vpres finance, gen auditor, 1988; Viacom TV Stations Group, sr vpres & chief financial officer, currently. **Orgs:** Am Inst Cert Pub Acct, 1979, NYSSCPA, 1979; pres, Walden & Country Woods Homeowners Asn, 1980-84; Broadcast Financial Mgt Asn, 1983, Nat Asn Broadcasters, 1983; Inst Internal Auditors, NY State Chap, bd gov, 1995-98; Financial Exec Inst, 1995; NY, Internal Audit Industry Comn, 1995. **Business Addr:** Senior Vice President, Chief Financial Officer, Viacom Televison Station Group, 524 W 57th St, New York, NY 10019-2902, **Business Phone:** (212)975-3216.*

GUITON HILL, BONNIE
Foundation executive, president (organization). **Personal:** Born Oct 30, 1941, Springfield, IL; daughter of Zola Elizabeth Newman Brazelton and Henry Frank Brazelton; married Walter; children: three. **Educ:** Mills Col, BA, psychol, 1974; Calif State Univ, MS, educ psychol, 1975; Univ Calif, EdD, 1985. **Career:** Mills Col, asst dean studs, 1974-76; Marcus Foster Educ Inst, exec dir, 1976-79; Kaiser Ctr Inc, vpres & gen mgr, 1979-84; US Postal Rate Comn, comnr, 1984-87; US Dept Educ Wash, DC, asst secy, 1987-89; US Off Consumer Affairs, Wash, DC, spec adv to the pres & dir, 1989-90; Earth Conservation Corps, chief exec officer, 1990-91; State Calif, State and Consumer Servs Agency, secy, 1991; Univ Va, McIntire Sch Com, dean, prof; The Times Mirror Co, vpres; The Times Mirror Found, pres & chief exec officer; Los Angeles Times, Community Rels, sr vpres; Icon Blue, co-founder, 1998-; B Hill Enterprises LLC, pres, 2001-. **Orgs:** Nat Asn Advan Colored People Legal Defense Fund; Urban Land Inst; bd dirs, Conf of Christians & Jews Asn, 1983-86; Nat Urban Coalition; Nat Asn Regulatory Utility Comrs, 1984-87; Exec Women Govt 1985-; bd dirs, Nat Mus Women Arts, 1988-89; bd dirs, Niagara Mohawk Power Corp, 1991; RREEF; LA Pac Corp; Hershey Foods Corp; bd dir, AK Steel Holding Corp; Crestar Financial Corp; bd dir, Yum! Brands, 2003; bd dir, Home Depot. **Honors/Awds:** Tribute to Women in Int Indust, YWCA, 1981; Outstanding Community Leader & Humanitarian Award, Nat Asn Advan Colored People Legal Defense Fund, 1981; Candace Award, Nat Coalition 100 Black Women, 1982; Equal Rights Advocate Award, 1984; Distinguished Meritorious Award, DC Human Servs, 1987; Hon Doctorate Tougaloo Univ, 1988; Dirs Choice Award, Nat Women's Econ Alliance Coun, 1992. **Business Addr:** Director, Chief Operating Officer, Icon Blue, 5670 Wilshire Blvd Suite 600, Los Angeles, CA 90036, **Business Phone:** (323)634-5301.*

GULLATTEE, ALYCE C.
Physician, educator. **Personal:** Born Jun 28, 1928, Detroit, MI; married Latinee G; children: Jeanne, Audrey & Nat. **Educ:** Univ Calif, BA, 1956; Howard Univ Col Med, MD, 1964. **Career:** St Elizabeth's Hosp & DC Gen Hosp, rotating internship, 1964-65; St Elizabeth's Hosp, med officer, gen prac, 1965-66, Med Officer Psychiat, 1968-71; St Elizabeth's Hosp & George Wash Univ Hosp, residency psychiat,1965-68; Howard Univ Col Med, asst prof, psychiat, 1970-, clinical asst prof, Family Pract, 1970-, physician; Nat Inst Ment Health, career teacher, Addictive Substances Abuse, 1974-77. **Orgs:** Med bd, J Nat Med Asn, 1967-; consult, Juvenile & Domestic Rels Ct, Arlington County, 1968-; recording secy, All Psychiat Progress, 1967-70; chief consult, Drug Educ Prog, Juvenile Ct, Arlington, 1969, vchmn, 1969-70, chmn elect, 1970-71, chmn, 1971-72; Psychiat-Neurol Secy, Nat Med Asn; Hosp Dels, Nat Med Asn, 1968-75; observator consult, Coun Int Orgn, Am Psychiat Asn, 1969-73; consult, EEO, 1969-70; co-coordr, Drug Abuse Seminar, Nat Coun Juvenile Ct Judges, 1970; chmn ad hoc com, HEW, Poor C & Youth, 1969-; rep Am Psychiat Asn, Chicago, 1970; Com Psychiat & Law, Am Psychiat Asn, 1973-; chmn Prog Comt, Am Psychiat Asn, 1974-75; chmn, Grad Com Int Progs, Howard Univ, 1974-; chief consult, Arlington County Drug Abuse Treatment Prog, Prelude 1969-; Nat Psychiat Consult & Prog Develop; Nat Coun Negro Women, 1972-; chmn, Comt Int Med, Nat Med Asn, Medsurg Soc, 1974-78; sr adv, co-founder, Stud Nat Med Asn, Wash; Nat Inst Drug Abuse Task Force, 1975-. **Honors/Awds:** Outstanding Teacher Award, Howard Univ, Col Med, 1973; Career Teacher Award, Nat Inst Ment Health, 1974-; Academic Honors Zoology, Univ Calif, 1956; first award Clinical Acumen, Howard Univ, Col Med, 1964; Magna Cum Laude Internship Award, St Elizabeth Hosp, 1965; Citizens Award -Outstanding Contributions to Community, Santa Monica Nat Asn Advan Colored People, 1960; Outstanding Black Woman of 1970, Nat Med Asn; nominee TV Emmy award, Wash Chap Nat Acad TV Arts & Scis, NBC Spl The Disabled Mind; fel, Inst Soc, Ethics & Life Scis Hastings-on-Hudson 1975-77. **Special Achievements:** Selected as member by the President of US for Nat Adv Com Juvenile Justice & Delinquency Prevention, US Dept Justice, 1975-76. *

GULLEY, WILSON
Executive, state government official. **Personal:** Born Oct 6, 1937, Buckner, AR; married Katherine Richardson; children: Debbie Renee Collins, Wilson Jr, Bruce Edward & Keith Ramon. **Educ:** Everett Community Col, AA, 1966; Univ Wash, AA & BA, 1968; New York Univ, post grad, 1969. **Career:** Nat Bus League Seattle Chap, pres, 1970-79; United Inner City Develop Found, pres, 1971-75; F & G Construct Inc, pres, 1977-; Omni Homes Inc, pres, 1979-; Cent Contractors Asn, Wash State Dept Transp, OJT Supportive Serv, proj adminr, 1989-92; Dist I, Opers, contract compliance officer, 1992-94; Wash State Dept Transp, Northwest Region, eeo officer, 1994-. **Orgs:** Exec dir, Rotary Boys Club, Seattle, 1968-70; inst rep, Boy Scouts Am, 1968-70; credit comm chmn, Cent Area Fed Credit Union, 1968-73; Boys Club (Pres Nixon), Boys Club Am, 1969; comm develop, Seattle Police & Fire Depts, 1969; counsr & founder, Youth Bus Orgn, 1971-72; adv bd mem, Seattle Pub Schs; adv bd mem, Port Seattle; Contract Compliance Officers, Region 10; adv bd mem, Seattle Worker's Ctr; affirmative action comm, Wash Dept Labor & Indust. **Honors/Awds:** Special Recognition, Seattle Kiwanis Club, 1971; Outstanding Business Proposal, Roxbury Bus Inst, 1972; Community Development Award, SER, Seattle Chap, 1973; Recognition Award, On-the-Job Training Prog, Wash State Dept Transp, 1990; Committment to Civil Rights Award, Wash State Joint Apprenticeship Training Coun, 1991; Cert Performance, Wash State Employee Combined Fund Dr, 1992. **Military Serv:** US Air Force, airman second class, 1956-60.

GUMBEL, BRYANT CHARLES
Television broadcaster. **Personal:** Born Sep 29, 1948, New Orleans, LA; son of Richard Dunbar and Rhea Alice LeCesne; married June Carlyn Baranco, Dec 1, 1973 (divorced 2001); children: Bradley Christopher & Jillian Beth. **Educ:** Bates Col, BA, 1970. **Career:** Black Sports Mag, writer, 1971, ed-in-chief, 1972; KNBC-TV, weekend sportscaster, 1972-73, sportscaster, 1973-76, sports dir, 1976-81; NBC's Rose Bowl Parade & coverage, co-host, 1975; NBC, Grandstand Show, co-host, 1976; Super Bowl XI, co-host, 1977; 19-Inch Variety Show, 1977; KNBC, performer & co-host, 1977; NBC, co-host, 1982-97; Olympics, Seoul, South Korea, host, NBC, 1988; CBS, host, 1997-98; CBS, co-host, 1999-2002; PBS Show, co-host, 2002; HBO, host, currently; WABC-TV, guest host, 2006. **Orgs:** AFTRA, SCSBA, NATAS. **Honors/Awds:** Emmy Award, 1976, 1977; Golden Mike Award, Los Angeles Press Club 1978, 1979; Edward R Murrow Award, Overseas Press Club, 1984; Frederick D Patterson Award, United Negro Col Fund; Martin Luther King Award, Cong Racial Equality; NAACP Image Awards; Inter Nat Journal Award;

Africa's Future Award, US Comm United Nations C's Fund; Alfred I DuPont-Columbia University Award, 2005; Peabody Award; Leadership Award, African-Am Inst;Trumpet Award. **Special Achievements:** Guest appearances in various films including: The Weather Man. **Business Addr:** Host, Home Box Office Inc, 1100 Avenue of the Americas, New York, NY 10036, **Business Phone:** (212)512-1208.

GUMBEL, GREG
Television journalist. **Personal:** Born May 3, 1946, New Orleans, LA; son of Rhea Alice LeCesne and Richard Dunbar; married Marcy; children: Michelle. **Educ:** Loras Col, BA, eng, 1967. **Career:** Am Hosp Supply Co, sales rep, 1968-73; WMAQ-TV, Chicago, sports anchor, 1973-81; ESPN, SportsCenter, co-anchor, 1981-89; CBS TV, NFL Today show, co-host, 1990-94, NBC Sports, host & play-by-play announcer, 1994-98; NFL Preview, host, currently; NFL Live, Olympic Winter Games, host, 1994. **Honors/Awds:** 3-time Emmy Award winner. **Special Achievements:** Selected to host 1994 Winter Olympic Games in Lillehammer, Norway. **Business Phone:** (212)664-4444.*

GUMBY, DR. JOHN WESLEY
Educator. **Personal:** Born May 22, 1942, Harrisburgh, PA; son of William H and Anna E; children: John W Jr & Angela D. **Educ:** Cheyney State Univ, BS, 1968; Western Md Col, MEd, 1975; Columbia Univ, PhD, 1998. **Career:** Harrisburg City Schs, varsity football coach, head track coach, 1968-70, Spanish teacher, 1968-74, sec prin, 1975-97. **Orgs:** NAACP, 1960-; Chosen Friends Lodge No 43 (PHA), 1963-; former dir, Sibletown Reunion Comt, 1972-; Phi Delta Kappa, 1975-; basileus, Omega Psi Phi Frat Inc, 1978-82. **Honors/Awds:** Merit Award, Monroe St Workshop, 1973; Citizen of the Year, City Harrisburg, 1976; Omega Man of the Year, Omega Psi Phi, 1982; Merit Award, UNCF, 1985; Educator Award, Chosen Friends Lodge No 43, 1995. **Military Serv:** AUS, sp-4, 1966-71; Marksmen, 1966, Honorable Discharge 1971. **Home Addr:** 1110 N 14th St, Harrisburg, PA 17103-1202. *

GUNDY, ROY NATHANIEL, JR.
Computer scientist. **Personal:** Born Sep 26, 1967, Philadelphia, PA; son of Elizabeth. **Educ:** Drexel Univ, BS, com engineering operations mgt, 1991. **Career:** Channel 6, talk show panelist, 1983-85; Bonatsos, database analyst, 1987-; Devon Systems Int Inc, network analyst, 1988-89; Thomas Jefferson Univ Hosp, micro comput technician, 1987-88, ic analyst, 1992-; Johnson & Johnson, dir Stands Strategies & Emerging Technol, currently. **Orgs:** Region 2 programs chair, Nat Soc Black ENRs, 1986-; guide right chair, Kappa Alpha Psi, 1990-; Philadelphia Area Comput Soc, 1992-; Philadelphia Regional Introd Minorities Engineering, 1982-. **Honors/Awds:** scholarship, Club Cornucopia, 1988-90; scholarship, Kodak, 1987-88; Achievement in Communication Industry, Nat Black Media Coalition, 1983; Sales Achievement, Timberland Co, 1986. **Home Addr:** 1834 W 73rd Ave, Philadelphia, PA 19126. **Business Addr:** Analyst, Thomas Jefferson University Hospital, Info Syst, 130 S 9th St Edison Suite 104, Philadelphia, PA 19107, **Business Phone:** (215)955-8099.

GUNN, ARTHUR CLINTON
Educator. **Personal:** Born Apr 29, 1942, New Castle, PA; son of John O Sr and Magnolia Hill Murray. **Educ:** Wilberforce Univ, Wilberforce, OH, BS, educ, 1964; Atlanta Univ, Atlanta, GA, MS, libr sci, 1969; Univ Pittsburgh, Sch Libr & Info Sci, Pittsburgh, PA, PhD, 1986. **Career:** Educator (retired); City Univ NY, fac; Del State Col, Dover, DE, librn, 1969-71; Howard Univ, Wash, DC, librn, 1971-76; Univ Md, Col Park, MD, adj prof, 1972-76; Univ Pittsburgh, Pittsburgh, PA, librn, 1983-86; Wayne State Univ, Detroit, MI, prof, 1986-, Clark Atlanta Univ, Sch Libr & Info Studies, dean, 2004. **Orgs:** Am Libr Asn, 1969-, Am Libr & Info Sci Educ, 1986-; consult, Gen Motors Corp, 1988-; pres, Asn African-Am Librn, 1988-; chair, Govt Rels Comt, Asn Libr & Info Sci Educ. **Special Achievements:** Author of 30 scholarly publications & professional papers & specialized in African-American bibliography; "Early training for Black librarians in the U.S.—microform :—a history of the Hampton Institute Library School and the establishment of the Atlanta University School of Library Science", 1986. *

GUNN, GLADYS
School administrator. **Personal:** Born Apr 28, 1937, Columbus, GA; daughter of John R and Jessie. **Educ:** Cent State Univ, BS, elem educ, 1959; Miami Univ, Med, 1964; OH State Univ, attended 1972. **Career:** School administrator (retired); Dayton Pub Schs, teacher, 1959-66, federally funded prog, interviewer, 1966-69, assoc personnel, 1969-71; Ohio Youth Comn, asst supt, 1972-73; CSU W & CSU Training Ins, dir, 1973-77; Cent State Univ, training & employ prog, 1977-78, coordr, SDIP, 1978-80; Dept Health & Human Serv, spec asst, 1980-81; Dayton Pub Sch, coordr, 1982-86; Dayton Pub Schs, spec asst admin & ident of grants, 1986-92. **Orgs:** Officer, Alpha Kappa Alpha Sorority, Soroptimist Int, Asssoc Supvr & Currriculam Develop, Phi Delta Kappa, Subcomt Educ Ad Hoc Comt Civil Rights, City of Dayton Comm Ed; bd mem, Daymont Ment Health Prog; former elected mem Inner W Priority Bd; bd mem, Comprehensive Manpower Training Ctr; Am Asn Sch Admin, 1989-92; League Women Voters; life mem, Nat Asn Advan Colored People, 1990-, Educ comt chair, 1999-. **Honors/Awds:** Presidential appointment, Nat Adv Coun Women's Educ Prog, 1978-80; pres appt Spec Asst, Spec Grps, 1980-81; Miley O. Williamson Award of Distinction, 1999; The Ohio Dr. Martin Luther King, Jr. Holiday Comn, 1990-98, chair, 1996-98. **Home Addr:** 4237 Catalpa Dr, Dayton, OH 45405. *

GUNN, WILLIE COSDENA THOMAS
Educator, counselor. **Personal:** Born Dec 24, 1926, Seneca, SC; daughter of Fletcher Gideon and Mattie Riley Gideon; married Willie James Gunn, Dec 24, 1975; children: Dr John Henderson Thomas III. **Educ:** Benedict Col, BS, 1946; Univ MI, MA, Educ, 1967, MA Guidance 1970; Urban Bible Col, Detroit, MI, doctorate, 1987. **Career:** Emerson Jr HS, teacher common learnings & sci, 1956-64; Headstart Prog, supvr, 1965; Title I Oper Summer Prog, supvr, 1967-73; MI State Univ, teacher supvr, 1962-64; Emerson Jr HS, guidance counr, 1964-76; Mott Col, instr social sci, 1969-78; Flint Open Sch, guidance counr, 1976-82; Jordan Col, instr social sci dept, 1981; Southwestern HS, guidance counr, 1982-88; Southwestern Acad, guidance counr. **Orgs:** Flint City Adv Comt League Women Voters; Voter Educ Coalition Drug Abuse Task Force; bd dirs, WFBE Pub Radio Station; bd dirs, Nat Asn Media Women; life mem & past pres, Zeta Phi Beta Sor; life mem & past pres, Nat Sor Phi Delta Kappa; Am Asn Univ Women; life mem, Nat Asn Negro Bus & Prof Women; NAACP, Urban League, Africa Care, Nat Coun Negro Women; Genesee Area Asn Counseling Develop; United Teachers Flint; Nat Educ Asn; Michigan Educ Asn; Metropolitan Chamber Com, 1984-; 2nd vpres, Top Ladies Distinction, 1985-; pub rels dir, Black Panhellenic Coun, 1987-. **Honors/Awds:** Woman of the Year, Nat Asn Media Women, 1976; Sepia Award, Nat Asn Media Women, 1978; Zeta Phi Beta Sor Woman of the Year, 1982; Zeta Phi Beta Sor Zeta of the Year, 1969; Panhellenic Woman of the Year, 1972; Educational Award, Nat Sor of Phi Delta Kappa, 1974; Achievement Award, Res Alcoholism Univ WI, 1967; Community Service Award, March Dimes, 1971; author & counr consult Comt Educ Network Proj, 1983; Woman of the Year, Nat Asn Media Women, 1988; Bigger & Better Bus Award, Phi Beta Sigma Fraternity, 1989; Hall Fame, Zeta Phi Beta Sorority, 1989; Counselor of the Year, Genesee Area Asn Counseling Develop, 1989; author, Black Achievement Register; co-author, "Feelings" (poems), 1971; author, "Countdown to College," 1984; co-author, "Career Planning," 1988. *

GUNNINGS, DR. THOMAS S.
Educator, president (organization), college teacher. **Personal:** Born Feb 8, 1935, Gastonia, NC; married Barbara. **Educ:** Winston-Salem Teachers Col, BS, 1958; Ore State Univ, DMA, 1967, PhD,1969. **Career:** Mich State Univ, Col Human Med, adj prof psychol, prof psychol, prof emer,currently; G & P Properties, vpres; Meridian Prof Psychol Consult Inc,pres. **Orgs:** Kappa Delta Phi Hon Soc; Nat Inst Ment Health Training Grants; vis scientists, vis psychol, Am Psychol Asn, 1969-72; Am Psych Asn; bd dir, Asn Black Psych; Nat Asn Coun & Develop; fel APA; Coun Psychologist Asn. **Business Addr:** Professor Emeritus, Michigan State University, Col Educ, 134 Erickson Hall, East Lansing, MI 48824.*

GUNTER, LAURIE
Educator. **Personal:** Born Mar 5, 1922, Navarro County, TX; daughter of Lewis Marion Martin and Hollie Myrtle Carruthers; children: Margo Alyce Gunter Toner & Lara Elaine Bonow. **Educ:** Tenn A&I State Univ, BS, home Sci, 1948; Univ Toronto, Cert Nursing Ed, 1949; Fisk Univ, MA, 1952; Cath Univ Am, 1956; Univ Cailf, Berkeley, 1959; Univ Chicago, PhD, 1959. **Career:** George W Hubbard Hosp, staff nurse, 1943-44, head nurse, 1945-46, supvr, 1947-48; Meharry Med Col Sch Nursing, asst instr, 1948-50, instr, 1950-55, asst prof, 1955-57, acting dean, 1957-58, dean, 1958-61; Univ Calif, asst prof nursing, Los Angles, 1961-63, assoc prof 1963-65; Ind Univ Med Ctr, prof nursing, 1965-66; Univ Wash, prof, 1969-71; Pa State Univ, prof nursing human develop, 1971-75; Allegheny Hosp, prof nursing; Univ Park, prof nursing; Hershey Med Ctr, prof nursing; Pa State univ, interim dept head, 1984-85; prof emer, currently. **Orgs:** Am Nurses Asn, 1948-; fel, Rockefeller Found, 1948-49; Nat League Nursing, 1948-87; Am Asn Univ Profs, 1949-87; Gerontological Soc, 1959-91; res projgrants, 1965-; Am Asn Col Nursing 1971; Am Pub Health Asn, 1974-87; consult, HRA/Nat Ctr Health Serv Res, 1976-89; reviewer, HEW, 1976-89; steering comt, Pa Nurses Asn; Coun Nurse Res; Am Nurses Asn; ad hoc ed, adv comt, Div Geriatric Nursing Pract, Am Nurses Asn; proj dir, Composite Ed Prog Geriatric Nursing, 1976-77; Am Acad Nursing, 1979-, Inst Med Nat Acad Sci, 1980-. **Honors/Awds:** Charles Nelson Gold Medal, Meharry Med Col, Sch Nursing, 1943; Foster Memorial Prize, Meharry Med Col, Sch Nursing, 1943; Alpha Kappa Mu Hon Soc, Tenn A&I St Univ, 1948; Rockefeller Found, 1953-55; Training Inst Soc Geront, Univ Calif, 1959; Golden Annual Citation for Special Competence in Nursing, Tenn A&I Univ, 1963; invitee, White House Conf Food Nutrition & Health, 1969; guest lectr, Japanese Nurses First Res Conf, 1971. **Special Achievements:** The first black women to receive a Ph.D. in human development from the University of Chicago, 1959; author and co-author for numerous articles & audio visual productions, 1949-. **Home Addr:** Seattle, WA 98101. **Business Addr:** Professor Emeritus, Pennsylvania State University, School of Nursing, 201 Health Human Develop E, Univ park, PA 16802.*

GURLEY, ANNETTE DENISE
Administrator. **Personal:** Born Aug 24, 1955, Chicago, IL; daughter of C W Jackson and Rutha; married William Gurley Jr, Aug 16, 1980; children: Gregory Sheldon. **Educ:** Univ Ill, Chicago, BA, elem educ, 1977; Chicago State Univ, MS, reading, 1992; Concordia Univ, MA, admin & supv, 1995. **Career:** St Justin Martyr Sch, teacher, 1977-85; Chicago Public Schs, teacher, 1985-90, teacher facilitator, 1990-94, Elem Area Instr Officer, currently; Michele Clark Middle, asst prin, 1994; DePaul Univ, instr, 1998-99, Michele Clark Prep High Sch, prin. **Orgs:** Former treas, Progressive Community Church, 1983-; Jack & Jill Am, Chicago Chap, 1991-, teen sponsor, 1998-; presenter, Nat Middle Sch Asn, 1991-; chair, Gregory Scholarship Awards Comm, 1995-; Chicago Prin Asn, 1997-. **Honors/Awds:** Those Who Excel Award of Recognition, Ill State Bd Educ, 1989-90; Teacher of the Year, Michele Clark Sch, 1989; Outstanding Leadership Award, Depaul Univ, SAS Prog, 1995; Nat Educators Award, Milken Family Found, 1999. **Special Achievements:** NMSA, "More Than Talk: Practical Teaching Strategies", presenter, Orlando, 1999, Chicago, 2000. **Business Addr:** Elementary Area Instruction Officer, Chicago Public Schools, Central Office, 125 S Clark St, Chicago, IL 60644, **Business Phone:** (773)553-1000.

GURLEY, DR. HELEN RUTH
School administrator. **Personal:** Born Dec 5, 1939, Ogemaw, AR; daughter of Curtis Hildreth (deceased); married Archie Gurley Sr; children: Archie Jr, Thomas Jeffrey, Vallissia Lynn. **Educ:** Nat Univ San Diego, MBA, 1975; The Union Inst, PhD. **Career:** Univ Calif, counr, 1971-77; Nueces Co MHMR Community Ctr, serv dir, 1977-79; City Corpus Christi, admin human rels, 1979-83; Del Mar Col, EEO & affirmative action officer, 1985-95, dir human rels, 1995-00; Corpus Christi Independant Sch Dist, dir acad, dir auxiliary personnel, currently. **Orgs:** consult, Mary McLeod Bethune Day Nursery, 1983-85; pres, Littles-Martin House Fund Inc, 1984-89; pres, Corpus Christi Br, Nat Advan Asn Colored People, 1984-89; chmn, United Way Coastal Bend Agency Coun, 1984-86; chmn, Coastal Bend Coun Govt Health Adv Comn, 1985-95; bd mem, Nat Conf Christians & Jews; treas, Am Asn Affirmative Action, 1988-95. **Honors/Awds:** Woman of the Year, Corpus Christi Alumnae Chap, Delta Sigma Theta Sorority, 1983-84. **Military Serv:** USN, E-3 seaman, 3 yrs; USAR, E-8 MSG, 21 yrs; Army Commendation; Army Achievement; Humanitarian Serv Medal. **Business Addr:** Director for Auxiliary Personnel, Corpus Christi Independent School District, 801 Leopard St, PO Box 110, Corpus Christi, TX 78401, **Business Phone:** (361)886-9100.*

GUTHRIE, CARLTON LYONS
Automotive executive, executive. **Personal:** Born Sep 15, 1952, Atlanta, GA; married Danille K Taylor; children: Carille & Adam. **Educ:** Harvard Coll, BA(Hons), econs, 1974; Harvard Bus Sch, MBA, gen mgt, 1978. **Career:** Philadelphia Nat Bank; Procter & Gamble, Salesman; Jewel Co Chicago, internal consult, 1978-80; McKinsey & Co, Chicago, sr assoc, 1980-82; James H Lowry & Assoc Chicago, exec vpres, 1982-85; Trumark Inc, co-owner, pres, chief exec officer & chmn, 1985-; Guthrie Investment Group, vpres, currently. **Orgs:** Dir, Ctrs New Horizons Chicago, 1980-, Urban League Lansing MI, 1986-; dir, Gifted & Talented Educ Prog, Ingham County Church, 1986-; chmn bd, Single Parent Family Institute, Lansing, MI, 1987-; dir, Joyce Foundation, Chicago Ill, 1991-; Shorebank Corp; Joyce Found; Ctrs New Horizons; Initiative Competitive Inner City, Nat Asn Black Automotive Suppliers; Single Parent Family Inst; adv bd, Governor's State Univ Sch Bus; adv bd, Joint Ctr Polit & Econ Studies; bd dir, Trumark Inc. **Honors/Awds:** Extrepreneur of the Year, Chivas Regal/Seagrams, 1990; Mich Mfr of the Year,1991; Trumark Inc: Supplier of the Year, Nat Minority Supplier Develop Coun, 1992. **Business Addr:** President, Chief Executive Officer, Chairman, Co-Owner, Trumark Inc, 1820 Sunset Ave, Lansing, MI 48917, **Business Phone:** (517)482-0795.

GUTHRIE, MICHAEL J
Executive, u.s. attorney, president (organization). **Personal:** Born Sep 19, 1950, Lithonia, GA; son of Willie and Mary; married Valorie C Walker; children: Lauren & Kayla. **Educ:** Harvard Col, BA, 1972; Harvard Law Sch, JD 1975. **Career:** Sonnenschein, Carlin, Nath & Rosenthal, atty, 1975-79; Johnson Products Co Inc, sr atty, 1979-83, vpres corp planning, 1983-85; Trumark Inc, co-owner, exec vpres, 1985-; Guthrie Investment Corp, pres, currently. **Orgs:** Bus adv bd, found bd, nsing Comm Col; pres, Nat Asn Black Automotive Suppliers; Jr Achievement Mid-Michigan; Physicians Health Plan Mid-Michigan; Govs Task Force Entrepreneurship & Small Bus; Mich Coun Voc Educ; Single Parent Family Inst. **Business Addr:** President, Chief Executive Officer, Spectra LMP LLC, 6501 Lynch Rd, Detroit, MI 48234-4140, **Business Phone:** (313)571-2100.

GUY, BUDDY
Guitarist, business owner, songwriter. **Personal:** Born Jul 30, 1936, Lettsworth, LA; son of Sam and Isabell. **Career:** Blues guitarist; Albums: Crazy Music, 1965; A Man & the Blues, 1968; I Was Walking Through the Woods, 1974; Pleading the Blues, 1979; Stone Crazy!, 1981; Buddy Guy, 1983; Buddy Guy on Chess, Vol one, 1988; Damn Right, I've Got the Blues, 1991; Sweet Tea, 2001; Blues Singer, 2003; Jammin' Blues Electric & Acoustic, 2003; Chicago Blues Festival 1964, 2003; DJ Play My Blues,

2003; A Night of the Blues, 2005; Bring 'Em In, 2005; Everyday We Have the Blues, 2006; Can't Quit the Blues, 2006; Live: The Real Deal, 2006; Buddy Guy's Legends, owner, currently. **Honors/Awds:** Grammy Award for Best Blues Album of the Year, 1992; Billboard's Century Award for lifetime achievement, 1993; Nat Medal of Arts, 2003; Rock & Roll Hall of Fame, 2005. **Business Addr:** Owner, Buddy Guy, 754 S Wabash Ave, Chicago, IL 60605-2111, **Business Phone:** (312)427-0333.

GUY, JASMINE
Dancer, actor. **Personal:** Born Mar 10, 1964, Boston, MA; daughter of Dr William and Jaye Rudolph; married Terrence Duckette, Aug 22, 1998; children: Imani. **Educ:** Alvin Ailey Dance Theatre. **Career:** Alvin Ailey Am Dance Theater, dancer; Atlanta Ballet Junior Co, dancer; TV Series: "A Different World", 1987-93; "Dead Like Me", 2003-04; "Haunted", 2004; TV Miniseries: "Queen", 1993; "A Century of Women", 1994; "Feast of All Saints", 2001; TV Movies: "America's Dream", 1996; "Perfect Crime", 1997; "Call Me Claus", 2001; "Carrie", 2002; Films: School Daze, 1988; Harlem Nights, 1989; Boy Meets Girl, 1993; Kla$h, 1995; Cat's Don't Dance(voice), 1997; Madeline, 1998; Guinevere, 1999; Lillie, 1999; Diamond Men, 2000; Grease; Chicago, 2000; The Law of Enclosures, 2000; Dying on the Edge, 2001; The Violet Hour, 2003; video: I Was a Network Star, 2006; That's So Raven, 2006; Tru Loved, 2008; Dead Like Me, 2009. **Honors/Awds:** NAACP Image Award, Best Actress in a Comedy Series, for A Different World, 1990. **Business Addr:** Actress, Stone Manners Agency, 6500 Wilshire Blvd Suite 550, Los Angeles, CA 90048.

GUY, LYGIA BROWN
Executive. **Personal:** Born Apr 23, 1952, Charleston, SC; married Peter Steele; children: Aja Steele. **Educ:** Spelman Col, attended 1972; Fashion Inst Am, AA, merchandising & design, 1973; Pepperdine Univ, BA, sociol, 1974. **Career:** Chelsa Rec, promotional coordr, 1975; Greedy Rec, promotional coordr, 1976; ABC Rec, promotional coordr, 1977; Connections, dir & owner co-personnel agent, 1984; RCA Rec, merchandising mgr. **Orgs:** Nat Asn Advan Colored People, 1969; Acad Country Music, 1980; Am Fed TV & Radio Artists, 1980; Nat Acad Rec Arts & Sci, 1982; Black Music Asn. **Honors/Awds:** Promotional Manager of the Year Award, BRE Mag, 1984. **Home Addr:** 73 W Altadena Dr, Altadena, CA 91001.

GUY, ROSA CUTHBERT
Writer. **Personal:** Born Sep 1, 1925, Trinidad, West Indies; daughter of Henry Cuthbert (deceased) and Audrey Gonzalez (deceased); married Warner (deceased); children: Warner Jr. **Educ:** NY Univ. **Career:** Books: Bird at My Window 1966; Children of Longing, 1970; The Friends, 1973; Edith Jackson, 1979; The Disappearance, 1980; Ruby, 1981; Mother Crocodile, 1981; Mirror of Her Own, 1981; New Guys Around the Block, 1983; A Measure of Time, 1983; Black Women Writers at Work, 1983; Contemporary Literary Criticism, 1983; Paris, Pee Wee & Big Dog, 1984; Afro-American Fiction Writers, 1984; Dictionary of Literary Biography, 1984; My Love, My Love or The Peasant Girl, 1985; I Heard a Bird Sing, 1987; Children's Literature Review, 1987; Presenting Rosa Guy, 1988; Ups & Downs of Carl Davis III, 1989; Black Authors & Illustrators of Children's Books, 1992; The Sun, The Sea, A Touch of the Wind, 1995; St. James Guide to Young Adult Writers, 1999; Authors & Artists for Young Adults, 2001. **Orgs:** Comm mem, Negro in the Arts; Harlem Writers Guild. **Honors/Awds:** Notable Book Award, Am Library Asn; Coretta Scott King Award; Phyllis Wheatley Award, Harlem Book Fair, 2005. **Business Addr:** Author, Trident Media Group LLC, 41 Madison Ave 36th Fl, New York, NY 10010, **Business Phone:** (212)262-4849.

GUYNES, THOMAS V.
Football player. **Personal:** Born Sep 9, 1974, Marion, IN. **Educ:** Univ Mich. **Career:** Ariz Cardinals, tackle, 1997; Berlin Thunder, tackle, 2000-01; Detroit Seminoles, 2008. **Orgs:** Omega Psi Phi; Prince Hall mason. **Honors/Awds:** Ernie Siegler Award, M Club Chicago, 1995.

GUY-SHEFTALL, BEVERLY
Educator, writer. **Personal:** Born Jan 1, 1946?, Memphis, TN; daughter of Ernestine Varnado. **Educ:** Spelman Col, BA, 1966; Atlanta Univ, MA, 1968; Emory Univ, PhD. **Career:** AL State Univ, fac, 1968-71; Spelman Col, prof Eng & women's studies, 1971-; Women's Res & Resource Ctr, Anna Julia Cooper prof Eng, 1981; SAGE: A Scholarly Jour Black women, founding co-editor; speaker; Emory Univ Inst Women's Studies, adjunct prof, currently; Women's Res & Resource Ctr & Anna Julia Cooper Prof Women's Studies, dir, currently. **Honors/Awds:** Fellow, Kellogg; fellow, Woodrow Wilson; Presidential Faculty Award for Outstanding Scholarship, Spelman Col. **Special Achievements:** Author: Daughters of Sorrow: Attitudes Toward Black Women, 1880-1920, Carlson, 1991; Words of Fire: An Anthology of African-American Feminist Thought; Spelman: A Centennial Celebration, 1981; co-edited Sturdy Black Bridges: Visions of Black Women In Literature, Anchor Books, 1979; Double Stitch: Black Women Write About Mothers & Daughters, Beacon Press, 1992; African American Men on Gender and Sexuality, 2001; The Struggle for Women's Equality in African American Communities, 2003. **Business Addr:** Founding Director, Spelman College, Women's Research & Resource Center, 350 Spelman Ln S W, Atlanta, GA 30314-4399, **Business Phone:** (404)681-3643.*

GUYTON, BOOKER T.
Executive, school administrator. **Personal:** Born Dec 27, 1944, Clarksville, TX; married Mary Allen Guyton; children: Booker Jr, Roxann, Keisha, Katrina. **Educ:** Univ Pacific, BS, educ, 1971, MA Religion, 1972. **Career:** Facilities Mgt & Inst for Personnel Develop, dir; Humanities & Intercultural Ed Div, chmn; Mgt Serv, admin asst to vp; affirm action officer; Johnson & Johnson, supvr mfg; John F Kennedy Ctr, exec dir; Fed Teacher Corps prog, teacher intern; Parks Chapel AME Church, pastor; San Joaquin Delta Community Col, instr; Parks Chapel African Methodist Episcopal Church, presiding elder, currently. **Orgs:** North Stockton Rotary; Assoc Calif Community Col Admin; Calif Comm Serv Asn; Nat Ed Asn; CA Sch Bd Asn; Official Black Caucus Nat Ed Asn; Kappa Alpha Psi; bd dir, Dameron Hosp Found; pres, McKinley Improvement Asn; State Coun Oppurtunity Indust Ctr State Calif. **Honors/Awds:** New Educators Award, Calif Asn; Man of the Yr, Kappa Alpha Psi, 1979; Community Serv Award, City of Stockton; Community Serv Award, Black Teachers Alliance, Stockton, CA; Cert of Appreciation of Serv, CA Black Student Union Assoc; Community Serv Award, League of Black Voters Stockton, CA. **Military Serv:** USMC, staff, sgt 6 yrs. **Business Addr:** Presiding Elder, Parks Chapel African Methodist Episcopal Church, 476 34th St, Oakland, CA 94609, **Business Phone:** (510)654-8758.*

GUYTON, LOUISE GREEN
Banker, manager. **Personal:** Born Mar 4, 1948, Tyro, MS; daughter of Eldridge Green and Ruth; divorced; children: Curtis G & Patrice Y. **Educ:** Univ Memphis, attended 1967; Univ Detroit-Mercy, BS, 1986; Lewis Col Bus, Hon Doctor, bus admin. **Career:** Comerica Inc, staff, 1968-, vpres pub affairs, 1995-, compliance mgr, currently. **Orgs:** Financial adv, Southern Christian Leader Conf, 1982-; Delta Sigma Theta, 1995-; NAACP, 1995-; bd pres, New Hope Community Develop Corp, 1995-; vpres, Black Caucus Found, 1999-; Abayomi Community Develop Corp, 1999-; Mich Coalition Human Rights, 2001-; bd mem, Detroit Community Health Connection Inc, 2003-; vol, Detroit Convoy Hope, currently; trustee, Lewis Col Bus; life mem, Nat Am Advan Colored People. **Honors/Awds:** Minority Achievers Award, YMCA, 1996; Spirit of Detroit Awards, City Detroit, 1997, 2000; Most Influential African American Women in Metropolitan Detroit, Women's Informal Network, 2000; Community Builders Award. **Special Achievements:** Notable Speaker at Women's Religious Conferences & Leadership Seminars. **Home Addr:** 20255 Greenview, Detroit, MI 48219, **Home Phone:** (313)532-4432. **Business Addr:** Vice President Public Affairs, Comerica Inc, PO Box 75000, Detroit, MI 48275-3352, **Business Phone:** (313)222-8620.

GUYTON, SISTER PATSY
Educator, nun. **Personal:** Born Jun 16, 1949, Mobile, AL; daughter of Wes and Marie Johnson. **Educ:** Bishop State Jr Col, Mobile AL, Assoc Psychol, 1969; Alabama State Univ, Montgomery AL, BS, Hist, 1971; Springhill Col, TIPS, Mobile AL, attended 1983; Xavier Univ, New Orleans LA, Masters Theol, 1989. **Career:** Boca Raton Middle Sch, Boca Raton FL, teacher, 1971-75; Christian Benevolent Ins Co, Mobile AL, debit mgr, 1975-76; St Mary's Children Home, Mobile AL, child care worker, 1976-79; Marion Corp, Theodore AL, personnel specialist, 1979-82; Parish Social Ministry, Mobile AL, coordr, 1982-88; Most Pure Heart Mary Church, dir religious educ, coordr ministries, 1988-92, Religious Educ, assoc dir, 1992-. **Orgs:** Alpha Kappa Alpha Sorority, 1970-; bd mem, Valentine Award, Catholic Social Servs, 1982-; religious educ consult, Archdiocese Mobile AL, 1985-; bd mem, Nat Asn Lay Ministry, 1985-; interparish coun, Black Catholic Congress & Nat Asn Black Sisters; prog coordr, Cath Enrichment Ctr, 2003-; Sisters Christian Community religious order. **Honors/Awds:** Present Presidents Club, Christian Benevolent Ins Co, 1975; Outstanding Debit Manager, Christian Benevolent Ins Co, 1975; Catholic of the Year, Interparish Coun, 1991. **Business Addr:** Program Coordinator, Office of Multicultural Ministries, Catholic Enrichment Center, 3146 W Broadway, Louisville, KY 40211, **Business Phone:** (502)776-0262.*

GUYTON, TYREE
Artist. **Personal:** Born Aug 24, 1955, Detroit, MI; son of George (deceased) and Betty Solomon; divorced; children: Tyree Jr, Towan, Omar, Tylisa. **Educ:** Northern High Sch Adult Training; Franklin Adult Educ; Ctr Creative Studies, Detroit, MI. **Career:** Ford Motor Co, Dearborn, MI, inspector; Northern High Sch, Master Residence Art Prog, Detroit, MI, teacher; Heidelberg Proj, Detroit, MI, pres, 1987-, painter, sculptor, currently. **Honors/Awds:** Summer Youth Assistance Prog Award, Detroit, MI, 1989; Spirit of Detroit Award, Detroit City Coun, 1989; David A Harmond Awd, City of Detroit, 1989; Commission Resolution Award, Wayne County, 1990; Testimonial Resolution Award, City of Detroit, 1990; Michiganian of the Year, State Mich, 1991; Mich Artist of the Year, Governor John Engler, State Mich, 1992; Humanity in the Arts Award, Center for Peace & Conflict Studies, Wayne State Univ, 1992; Volunteer Community Service Award, Youth Volunteer Corps, 1995; House of Representatives Resolution No 117, State Mich, 1995. **Special Achievements:** Solo Exhibitions: The Heidelberg Project, Detroit, MI, 1986-; Alexa Lee Gallery, Ann Arbor, MI, 1994, 1995; The Front Room Gallery, Detroit, MI, 1988; Group Exhibitions: Minnesota Museum of American Art, St Paul, 1996; Center Galleries, Detroit, MI, 1995; Urban Institute of Contemporary Art, Grand Rapids, MI, 1994; numerous others; featured in various books. **Military Serv:** USY, pvt, 1972. **Business Phone:** (313)537-8037.*

GUYTON, WANDA (WANDA MARIE GUYTON)
Basketball player. **Personal:** Born Oct 14, 1968; daughter of Johnny Guyton Sr (deceased). **Educ:** Univ S Fla, attended 1989. **Career:** Player (retired); Coach; NEC, Japan, forward, 1989-90; Tenerife, Spain, 1990-92; NEC, Italy,1992-96; Houston Comets, 1997; Ger DBBL, Wasserburg, 2004-07; TSV Wasserburg Ger, asst coach, currently. **Honors/Awds:** Kodak All American Honorable Mention, 1989; NCAA National Rebounder Leader, 1988-89; Sunbelt Conference Player Of The Year, University Of South Florida, 1988-89; 2 Time WNBA Champion, Houston Comets, 1997-99. *

GUYTON, WANDA MARIE. **See GUYTON, WANDA.**

GUZMAN, JUAN ANDRES CORREA
Baseball player. **Personal:** Born Oct 28, 1966, Santo Domingo, Dominican Republic. **Career:** Baseball player (retired); Los Angeles Dodgers, 1985; Toronto Blue Jays, 1991-98; Baltimore Orioles, 1999; Cincinnati Reds, 1999; Tampa Bay Devil Rays, 2000.

GWYNN, FLORINE EVAYONNE
Physical therapist, counselor, administrator. **Personal:** Born Jan 16, 1944, Beckley, WV; daughter of Flauzell Calhoun and Jean Daisy Wright; married Herman L Gwynn, Aug 5, 1979; children: Towanna M, Catherine S, Alvin, Calvin, Robert. **Educ:** Beckley Col, AS, 1970; Bluefield State Col, BS, 1977; WVa Col Grad Studies, MS, 1982; WVa Union Col Law, Morgantown, attended 1989. **Career:** Raleigh County, youth/sr citizens dir, 1969-72; Fed Prison Women, fed correctional officer, 1972-75; Nutrit Elderly, proj dir, 1979-80; Raleigh County Comn Aging, exec dir, 1980-81; Social Security Admin, hearing asst, 1982-; Bluefield State Col, Criminal Justice Prog, asst prof, 1982-; NCWVCAA, Kingwood, WVa, counr/coordr; Floetta's Inc, pres; Another Way Inc, clin dir, lead therapist, currently. **Orgs:** Bluefield State Col Alumni, 1977-; WV Col Grad Studies, 1979-; bd dir, Domestic Violence Ctr, 1984-; treas, Raleigh County Rainbow Coalition, 1984-; Phi Alpha Delta Law Fraternity, 1986-; coordr, Tygart Valley Baptist Asn Sunday Sch Cong, 1988-, Youth Action Inc, 1989-; bd mem, Sex Equity-Teen Pregnacy Proj, 1989-; vpres, Florence Crittenton Home & Serv, Wheeling, WV; pres, Tygart Valley Dist Baptist Asn Women's Conv. **Honors/Awds:** Appreciation Serv, Am Legion Aux 70, 1969; Community Serv, Bluefield State Col, Beckly Chap Alumni, 1984; Teacher of the Year, Bluefield State Col, 1985; Serv Award, Bluefield State Col Alumni, 1986. **Home Addr:** 1401 Anderson Ave, Morgantown, WV 26505. **Business Addr:** Lead Therapist, Another Way Inc, 530 W Main St, Uniontown, PA 15409.*

GWYNN, TONY (ANTHONY KEITH GWYNN)
Baseball player, athletic coach. **Personal:** Born May 9, 1960, Los Angeles, CA; married Alicia Cureton; children: Anthony II & Anisha Nicole. **Educ:** San Diego State Univ. **Career:** Player(retired); Coach; Sports Analyst; San Diego Padres, outfielder, 1982-01; San Diego State Univ Aztecs, vol coach, 2001, coach, head coach, 2003-; Sports Analyst; Yahoo!, San Diego Channel 4; TBS. **Orgs:** Founder, Tony Gwynn Found. **Honors/Awds:** Most Valuable Player, Rookie NW League, 1981; NL All-Star Team, 1984-99; NL Batting Champion, 1984, 1987-89, 1994-97; Natl League Gold Glove,1986-87 1989-91; Silver Slugger Award, The Sporting News, 1984, 1986-87, 1989, 1994-95, 1997; Padres Most Valuable Player, Baseball Writers Assn of Am, 1984, 1986-88, 1994-95, 1997; Branch Rickey Award, 1995; Chairman's Award, 1995; Athlete Who Cares, USA Today Weekend Mag, 1997; Lou Gehrig Mem Award, Phi Delta Theta fraternity, 1999; Roberto Clemente Man of the Yr Award, 1999; Inducted, World Sports Humanitarian Hall of Fame, 1999. **Special Achievements:** San Diego Padres stadium named after him. **Business Addr:** Head Coach, Aztecs baseball team, San Diego State University, 5500 Campanile Dr, San Diego, CA 92182-4313, **Business Phone:** (619)594-5200.*

H

HABER, LOIS
Banker, executive. **Educ:** Arcadia Univ. **Career:** Delaware Valley Financial Servs LLC, co-founder, pres & chief exec officer, 1999. **Orgs:** Chair bd mem, Ctr Women's Bus Res; past chair, Nat Found Women Bus Owners; trustee, Arcadia Univ. **Honors/Awds:** Woman Business Owner of the Yr, Philadelphia Chap Nat Asn Women Business Owners; Penn Honor Roll of Women, 1996; Penn Top Women in Bus, 1997. *

HABERSHAM-PARNELL, JEANNE
Educator. **Personal:** Born May 20, 1936, New York, NY; daughter of Paul and Ethel; divorced; children: Richard Parnell Habersham.

Educ: Howard Univ, BA, 1958; Columbia Univ, MA, 1972. **Career:** Amsterdam News, Dawn Magazine, Black Am, syndicated columnist; Inner City Broadcasting, WLIB & WBLS & WHCR, producer & host City Lights; WNYE Bd Educ Radio & TV, educational programmer & producer; International Magnet Sch, admin asst, asst prin, dir, 1990-93; IMPACT II, Bd Educ citywide, dir. **Orgs:** NYC 100 Black Women; Metropolitan Jack & Jill Alumni; Harlem YWCA, bd mem; Opera Ebony, bd mem; Lincoln Ctr, adv educ comt; Am Fed TV & Radio Artists; Howard Univ Hall Restoration Comt; Nat Storytelling Asn. **Honors/Awds:** Esteem Teams Mentor Award, Nat Asn Female Execs, 2003; Success Guide, Named one the top 15 Educators NYC, 1991; Cultural Educational Curriculum Award, WNET-TV, PBS, 1989; WNYE Award Program Excellence Educational Programming, Images Black; Frank Silvera Writers Award, 1983; Edythe, NBC & TV, Writer & Producer, 1975. **Special Achievements:** Designed & developed the educational curriculum of The International Magnet School; Created & developed professional grant proposal prototype for Dist 2 Perf Arts; Designed & implemented a performing arts program, NYC Public Schools/Rensulli Method; Directed the NYC International Children's Chorus, which performed nationally; Syndicated Columnist/48 markets nationwide/Dawn Magazines. *

HACKETT, BARRY DEAN
Football player, president (organization). **Personal:** Born Jun 28, 1964, Greensboro, NC; married Cindy; children: Dustin Marie & Jax. **Educ:** Appalachian State Univ, criminal justice, 1986. **Career:** Football player (retired), pres; Kans City Chiefs, linebacker, 1986-91; Seattle Seahawks, 1993; Hackett Properties, pres, currently. **Business Addr:** President, Hackett Properties, 813 Granite St, Greensboro, NC 27403.

HACKETT, OBRA V.
Educator, school administrator. **Personal:** Born Sep 9, 1937, Osyka, MS; son of James Hackett and Letha T Williams; married A Carolyn Evans; children: Obra V Jr. **Educ:** Jackson State Univ, BS, 1960; Atlanta Univ, MA, 1967; Mississippi State Univ, attended 1968. **Career:** Henry Weathers HS, math teacher, 1960-62, asst prin, 1962-64; Carver HS,counr, 1965-66; Utica Jr Col, voc counr, 1966-69, dean studs, 1969-73;Jackson State Univ, dir pub info, 1973-77, dir develop, 1977-84; JSU Dev Found, exec secy, 1984-87; Jackson State Univ, asst dean career coun &placement, 1987-89, actg dir, career coun & placement, 1989-91, dir, 1991, pres, currently. **Orgs:** Charter mem, Col Pub Rels Asn MS, 1970; bd dir, Hinds Co Heart Asn,1974-79; secy bd dir, Goodwill Indus MS, 1979-; comnr, scouting Seminole Dist Andrew Jackson Coun BSA, 1979-83; pres, Callaway HS PTA, 1986-87;Third vpres, Jackson Coun PTA, 1986-88; key communicator JPS, 1986-; first vpres, Jackson Coun PTA, 1988-90; treas, Jackson State Univ, Nat Alumni Asn, 1996-98; pres, Jackson Coun PTA, 1990-91; bd mem, Miss PTA, 1990-, pres, 1997-99. **Business Addr:** Director, Jackson State University, Career Counseling & Placement, 1400 J R Lynch St, PO Box 17280, Jackson, MS 39217, **Business Phone:** (601)979-2477.

HACKETT, WILBUR L
Manager. **Personal:** Born Oct 21, 1949, Winchester, KY; married Brenda. **Educ:** Univ Kent, BA, 1973. **Career:** Louisville Reg Criminal Justice Comn, comn coordr; Gen Election Louisville, supvr, 1973; Black Baron Construct Inc, staff, currently. **Orgs:** Adv Comt, Russel Area Youth; adv bd, Urban League Youth Prog; vpres, Concerned Young Men Louisville; adv bd, Proj WayOut; Sickle Cell Anemia Found Kent; Comn Restoration Black Hist; bd dir, Erwin House. **Honors/Awds:** Hon mention All-SEC Linebacker. **Special Achievements:** First black captain in SFC University of Kentucky. **Business Addr:** Owner, Black Baron Construction Inc, 3020 Bardstown Rd, Louisville, KY 40205.

HACKEY, GEORGE EDWARD, JR.
Law enforcement officer. **Personal:** Born May 19, 1948, Bethesda, MD; son of George Edward Sr and Doris Plummer; married Dory Ann Gray Hackey, Jun 10, 1978; children: Derick, Cari, George III. **Educ:** Montgomery Col, Rockville, MD, AA, gen educ, 1969; Towson State Univ, Towson, MD, BS, sociol, 1971. **Career:** Montgomery County Dept Recreation, Rockville, MD, playground dir, 1962-70; Montgomery County Bd Educ, Rockville, MD, building monitor, 1971-73; Montgomery County Dept Police, Rockville, MD, community rels officer; The United Methodist Church, pastor, currently. **Orgs:** Treas & mem, Montgomery County African-Am Employees Asn, 1989-; Montgomery County Police Asn; chaplain, pres, Montgomery County Coalition Black Police Officers, 1974-; chaplain, pres, Great & Respectable Black Orgn, 1980-; mentor, Seneca Valley High Sch Models & Mentors Prog, 1990-; John Wesley United Methodist Church, exec officer. **Honors/Awds:** Member of the Year, Montgomery County Coalition Black Police Officers, 1978, 1985; Dedicated Service to the Community, Md House Deleg, 1985; Community Leadership-Youth Development, Montgomery County Nat Asn Advan Colored People, 1986; Dedicated Service, Montgomery County Bd Educ Headstart, 1987; Dedicated Service, Nat Black Police Asn, 1988; Dedicated Service, African-Am Employees Asn, 1989-91; Bernard D Crooke, Jr Community Service Award, Montgomery County Chamber Com, 2001; Athlete of the Year, Montgomery Col, Rockville Campus. **Military Serv:** AUS, Reserves, Sergeant First Class, 1971-77. **Business Addr:** Pastor, The United Methodist Church, 1310 Olney Sandy Spring Rd, Sandy Spring, MD 20860, **Business Phone:** (301)774-7047.*

HACKLEY, DR. LLOYD VINCENT
School administrator, executive, administrator. **Personal:** Born Jun 14, 1940, Roanoke, VA; son of David W Hackley Sr (deceased) and Ernestine Parker (deceased); married Brenda L Stewart, Jun 12, 1960; children: Dianna Hackley-Applin, Michael R. **Educ:** Mich State Univ Polit Sci, BA, 1965; Univ Colo, psychol, 1967; Univ NC, Polit Sci, PhD, 1976; Govt Exec Inst, Sch Bus Admin, Univ NC, Chapel Hill, 1980. **Career:** Univ NC, Gen Admin, assoc vpres acad affairs, 1979-81; Univ NC, Chapel Hill, fac govt execs inst sch bus admin, 1980-81; Univ Ariz, Pine Bluff, chancellor chief exec officer, 1981-85; Univ NC, Gen Admin, vpres stud serv & spec prog, 1985-88; USAF Acad, coach track & cross country, 1974-78, assoc prof, course dir polit sci, 1974-78; Fayetteville State Univ, Fayetteville NC, chancellor, 1988, chancellor emer, 2003-; NC Community Col Syst, pres; Tyson Foods Inc, dir, 1992-; Br Banking & Trust Co, dir, currently; Blue Cross & Blue Shield, NC, dir, 2003; Nat Character Counts! Coalition, chair, 1999, consult; Lloyd V Hackley & Assocs, Inc, chief exec officer & owner. **Orgs:** Exec comn Triangle World Affairs Ctr, 1978-79; bd dirs, United Fund Carrboro, Chapel Hill, 1978-80; bd trustees, The Village Company Found, 1980-81; exec comt NC Comn, Int Educ, 1980-81; mem adv bd, Nat Ctr Toxicological Res, 1983; adv comt, Univ Ariz, Grad Inst of Tech, 1983; chmn, subcomt curriculum & stud matters Ariz Quality Higher Educ Study Comn, 1984; chmn, subcomt middle & jr high schs Ariz Educ Stand Comn Elem & Sec Schs, 1983-84; vpres, United Way of Jefferson Co, 1985; vpres bd dirs, Ariz Endowment for the Humanities, 1985-86, 1984-85; chmn, Ariz Adv Comm to the US Comn Civil Rights 1985; Strategic Planning Team, Cumberland Co Bd of Educ 1989; Fayetteville Area Econ Develop Corp; chmn, Pres Clinton's Adv Bd Historically Black Col & Universities; chair, NC Child Advocacy Inst. **Honors/Awds:** Scholastic Achievement Award, Dean's List Award, Univ MD European Div, 1961; Outstanding Young Man Am, US Jaycees, 1977; Gov Ariz Traveler Award, 1982; Ariz Cert Merit, 1983; Key to City Flint Mich, 1984; Resolution of Tribute, Mich Legis, 1984; Community Serv Award, Pine Bluff & Jefferson County Ariz, 1984. **Special Achievements:** "Disadvantaged Students: Testing Education Not Cultural Deprivation, American Middle Sch Education," 1983; "The Agony of Orthodoxy in Education," Congressional Record, Vol 129, Number 161, Part III, 1983; Resolution of Commendation, Arkansas Legislature, 1985; also numerous papers and publications. **Military Serv:** USAF, major (retired), 1958-78; Aircraft Control & Warning School, Honor Grad 1958; Outstanding Airman Rosas Air Sta, Spain, 1961; Distinguished Military Grad Officer Training Sch, 1965; Vietnam Cross of Gallantry, 1968; Bronze Star, Meritorious Serv in Combat with Valor Vietnam, 1968; Man of the Hour, Headquarters Europe, 1970; Bronze Star & Meritorious Serv Medal, Europe, 1971. **Business Addr:** Director, Branch Banking & Trust Corporation, PO Box 580364, Charlotte, NC 28258-0364, **Business Phone:** 800-226-5228.*

HACKMAN, LUTHER GEAN
Baseball player. **Personal:** Born Oct 10, 1974, Columbus, MS. **Career:** Colo Rockies, 1994-99; St Louis Cardinals, 1999-02; San Diego Padres, pitcher, 2003; Cleveland Indians, 2003; Pittsburgh Pirates, 2004; Milwaukee Brewers; Uni-President 7-Eleven Lions, 2008-. *

HACKNEY, L. CAMILLE
Executive. **Educ:** Princeton Univ, BA, econs; Harvard Bus Sch, MBA, 1994. **Career:** Merrill Lynch & Co, financial analyst; HBO, mkt/mkt anal dept; independent consult; Warner Music Group, sr dir, new media mkt develop, Elektra Entertainment Group, sr dir, multimedia mkt & bus develop, vpres, multimedia, mkt & bus develop, vpres, strategic mkt & new media, currently. **Orgs:** Time To Read, tutor, mentor. **Business Addr:** Vice President of Strategic Marketing and New Media, Elektra Entertainment Group, 75 Rockefeller Plz 16th Fl, New York, NY 10019, **Business Phone:** (212)275-4000.*

HADDEN, EDDIE RAYNORD
Lawyer, pilot. **Personal:** Born May 25, 1943, Many, LA; son of Eddie and Emma Cross; married Kay Dupree; children: Eugene. **Educ:** Univ Tex El Paso, BA, jour, 1965; George Washington Univ, incomplete MBA, 1971; Hofstra Univ Sch Law, JD, 1979. **Career:** JF Small Adv, vpres, 1973-74; Eastern Airlines, pilot, 1972-89; pvt pract, lawyer, 1980-; Aircraft Owners & Pilots Asn, regional counl. **Orgs:** Vpres, Bergen Co NJ, Nat Asn Advan Colored People, 1980-83; pres, Bergen Co NJ Urban League Housing Auth, 1981-85; bd dir, Org of Black Airline Pilots Inc, 1981-85; city councilman, City Englewood NJ, 1983-86; bd govs, Englewood, Chamber Com, 1990; bd mgrs, Englewood Community Chest, 1990; chmn educ outreach, Alpha Phi Alpha fraternity, Kappa Theta Lambda Chap, 1990-; vice-chair, Community Resource Coun; NJ State Bar Asn; Bergen County Bar Ass; Rotary Intl; pres & chief exec officer, Nat Urban League. **Honors/Awds:** Elected official, Englewood NJ City Coun, 1983; Youth Serv Award, Tuskegee Airman Inc; Nat Conv, 1984; Rare Bird Award, Airline Pilots Asn, 1975. **Military Serv:** USN, officer & aviator, 1965-72, comdr, 21 yrs. **Business Addr:** Attorney At Law, Eddie Raynord Hadden LLC, 440 Sylvan Ave Ste 130, PO Box 5793, Englewood, NJ 07631.*

HADDOCK, MABLE J.
Consultant, educator. **Personal:** Born Jun 20, 1948, Clover, VA; daughter of Nephew R Staten; children: Kevin. **Educ:** Mercy Col, BA, 1974; NBC Fell Kent State Univ, MA, 1976; Wharton Bus Sch,Cert 1982. **Career:** HEOP Mercy Col, asst dir, 1974-76; NBC, writer, res, 1977-78; Canton Cult Ctr, urban arts dir, 1978-80; Nat Black Prog Consortium, founder, 1980-, pres & chief exec officer, currently; producer: The Fannie Lou Hamer Story; Mandela; State Black Am, 1984; Ohio State Univ, Columbus, lectr, 1988-; Dialogue Mag, Columbus, contributor; Nat Video Resources Rockefeller Found, consult, cur, 1990-91; Black Am Facing Millennium, 1997; Charles H Revson fel, 2005-06. **Orgs:** Women Commun, Ohio Arts Coun Minority Arts Task Force, 1980-82; consult, Ohio Arts Coun, 1980-82; bd dir, YWCA, 1982; bd, Columbus Cable Comm, 1982-83; Columbus Comm Cable Access, 1983-; founding dir, Nat Black Programming Consortium. **Honors/Awds:** Women of Achievement, YWCA, 1997; Participated conf on Media in Africa held in Senegal 1981; Minority Arts Award, Ohio Arts Council; Award of Excellence, Urban League; Kool Achiever Award, Unsung Heroes; Black Studies Heritage Award; NAMAC Media Award, 1998; Trailblazers Award,black film.com, 2002. **Special Achievements:** Selected by the UN as rep on "Seminar on the Intensification of Int Media Action for the Immediate Independence of Namibia" held in Brazzaville,Congo, 1985. **Business Phone:** (212)234-8200.

HADDON, JAMES FRANCIS
Investment banker. **Personal:** Born Aug 12, 1954, Columbia, SC; son of Wallace James and Ida Beatrice; married Sezelle Antoinette Gereau, Sep 25, 1988; children: Madeleine Louise, James Douglass. **Educ:** Wesleyan Univ, BA, 1976; Stanford Univ, MBA, 1980. **Career:** Mellon Nat Corp, real estate analyst, 1976-78; Blyth Eastman Paine-Webber, assoc, 1982-83; Paine-Webber, vpres, 1984-89, managing dir, 1989-. **Orgs:** Bd mem, Nat Asn Securities Prof, 1991-; Sponsors Econ Opportunity Mentor Prog, 1984-. **Business Phone:** (212)713-3304.*

HADLEY, ERMA JOHNSON. **See JOHNSON, ERMA CHANSLER.**

HADLEY, SYBIL CARTER
Lawyer. **Personal:** Born in Dallas, TX; married Roy E Hadley Jr; children: Lauren Elizabeth, Dustin Carter. **Educ:** Univ Houston, 1985; Univ Va, JD, 1988. **Career:** Swift, Currie, McGhee & Hiers, sr assoc atty, partner, 1997; Insley & Race, litigation partner; Fulton County Bd Elections & Registration, chair & chief registrar, 1996-; Home Depot, corp coun, 2002, dir litigation dept; home based bus. **Orgs:** Peachtree Presbyterian Church; Ed Bd, JB Moore Soc Int Law; Legal Assistance Prog; Post-Conviction Assistance Prog; Trial Advocacy Prog; Nat Legal Aid & Defender Asn; Leadership Acad Women Color Attys. **Special Achievements:** First woman chair and chief registrar of Fulton County Board of Elections and Registration. *

HADNOTT, BENNIE L
Consultant, executive, president (organization). **Personal:** Born Nov 23, 1944, Prattville, AL; son of James Hadnott and Flora Hadnott; children: Danielle & Johnathan. **Educ:** Bernard M Baruch Col, BBA, 1971; Iona Col, MBA, 1976; CPA. **Career:** Pace Grad Sch Bus, asst prof acct; Rutgers Univ, asst prof acct; Watson Rice LLP, managing partner & chief exec officer, 1981-2000; Watson Rice Consult Group Inc, pres; PIC Coun Bergen Co, treas; Watson Rice LLP, managing partner, sr consult, currently; Watson Rice Consult Group Inc, pres, currently; Watson Rice LLP, Exec Comt, chmn, currently. **Orgs:** Am Inst Certified Pub Acct; Asn Govt Accts; NY/NJ Intergovt Audit Forum; Munic Finance Officers Asn US & Can; NY State Soc Certified Pub Acct, State & Local Govt & Health Care Community, dir-at-large; Govt Acct & Auditing Educ Subcomt, Am Inst Certified Pub Acct, Fed Acquistion Comn, Wash, DC, Acct Future Issues Community; treas, Berger Co Br, Nat Asn Advan Colored People; NJ Bd Accountancy; Nat Asn Black Accts; pres, Hadnott Found. **Military Serv:** USAF, airman first class, 1962-67. **Business Addr:** Senior Consultant, Managing Partner, Watson Rice LLP, 5 Penn Plz, New York, NY 10001, **Business Phone:** (212)447-6162.

HAGAN, GWENAEL STEPHANE
Executive. **Personal:** Born Oct 9, 1960, Everux, France; son of Willie D and Suzanne J Boule; divorced; children: Gael Y. **Educ:** Colo Univ-Boulder, BS, Acct, 1982; Marquette Univ, MBA, 1988; Colo State Univ, MBA; CPA. **Career:** KMPG, auditor, 1982-83; Jones Intercable, sr auditor, 1983-85, bus mgr, 1985-86, cable TV syst mgr, 1986-88, dir new product develop, 1988-90; Mind Extension Univ, vpres, bus develop, 1990; Webb Interactive Serv, sr vpres strategic develop, vpres corp develop, 1999-2001; Jabber Inc, CFO, 2001-02, COO, 2002; Hagan Ventures LLP, prin, currently. **Orgs:** Com chmn, vpres, bd mem, Nat Asn Minorities Cable, 1984-. **Honors/Awds:** Colo Soc Accountancy, CPA, 1984. **Business Addr:** Principal, Hagan Ventures LLC, 500 Hagan Ave, New Orleans, LA 80202, **Business Phone:** (504)262-0400.

HAGAN, WILLIE JAMES
School administrator, educator. **Personal:** Born Dec 17, 1950, Montgomery, AL; son of Oliver and Dorothy Marie Wright; mar-

ried Constance Marie Diaz, Jul 4, 1979; children: Lynea Marie Diaz-Hagan. **Educ:** Mitchell Col, New London, CT, AS, 1971; Conn Univ, Storrs, CT, BA, 1973, MA, 1975, PhD. **Career:** Univ Conn, Storrs, CT, dir govt rels, 1986-90, acting vpres, 1990, assoc vpres, 1990; Dept Higher Educ, Hartford, CT, asst dir legis servs; Calif State Univ, Fullerton, vpres admin & finance & chief financial officer, currently. **Orgs:** Govt Rels & Commun Officers, 1982-87. **Home Addr:** 8850 E Foxhollow Dr, Anaheim, CA 92808-1671. **Business Addr:** Vice President Administration & Finance, Chief Financial Officer, California State University, Langsdorf Hall 805, Fullerton, CA 92834, **Business Phone:** (714)278-2115.

HAGEMAN, HANS ERIC
Educator, lawyer, executive. **Personal:** Born Jan 1, 1957, Chicago, IL; son of Rev Dr Lynn and Leola; married Bernadette Baptiste; children: Jamila & Viclar. **Educ:** Princeton Univ, BA, 1980; Columbia Univ Sch Law, JD, 1983. **Career:** Thacher Profitt & Wood, assoc, 1986-86; NY Co Dist Atty, asst DA, 1986-89;US Senate, minority chief coun & staff dir, 1989-90; Neighborhood Defender Serv Harlem, chief coun, 1990-91; E Harlem Sch Exodus House, founder & exec dir, 1992-2001; Boys & Girls Harbor, exec dir, 2002-; Sulaxmi Sch Girls, founder, 2002-; Off Special Narcotics Prosecution New York, asst dist atty; Neighborhood Defender Serv, chief counsel. **Orgs:** Trustee, Harlem Congregation Community Improvement, 2000-; trustee, Bill Traylor Found, 2001-; bd mem, Police Corps, 2001-; chair brd, Salus Found Inc; trustee, Harlem Episcopal Sch; adv mem, Bill Traylor Found. **Honors/Awds:** Hero Award, Robin Hood Found, 1998; 40 Under 40 Award, Network J, 1998;Community Service Award, Black Princeton Alumni, 2000; Community Service Award, NY Law Sch, 2000; Distinguished Alumni Award, Assn Black Princeton Alumni, 2000; Essence Award, Essence, 2001. **Special Achievements:** Founder, Sulaxmi Sch Girls, Lucknow, India, 2000. **Military Serv:** USA, First Lt, 1980-89. **Business Addr:** Executive Director, Boys and Girls Harbor, 1 E 104th St, New York, NY 10029, **Business Phone:** (212)427-2244.

HAGEMAN, IVAN
Educator. **Personal:** Son of Lynn L. **Educ:** Harvard Univ, BA, social Anthropol,; Harvard's Grad Sch Educ MEd. **Career:** Klingenstein fel, Columbia Univ; fel, Rockefeller Found; Martin Luther King High Sch; East Harlem Sch, Exodus House, co-founder & head, currently. **Orgs:** Charter Sch Inst, State Univ, Albany. **Honors/Awds:** Iscol prog, Cornell Univ; Essence Award; Robin Hood Found Hero Award. *

HAGER, JOSEPH C., JR.
Educator. **Personal:** Born Jun 11, 1944, Washington, DC. **Educ:** Marist Col Poughkeepsie, NY, BA 1967; Sherwood Sch Music Chicago, cert music, 1960; cand MA. **Career:** Am Univ, camp cour, 1960-61; Family & Child Servs; Marist House Formation St Joseph Novitiate, asst dir music; Marist Col, asst dir music, 1965-66; Marist Col, dir music, 1966-67; St Mary Parish, Poughkeepsie, instr, 1964-65; Mt St Michael Acad Bronx, sec educ teacher, 1967-70; EmmaculateConcoption, Bronx, teacher adult educ, 1968; Our Lady Perpetual Help, Pelham NY, teacher, 1968; New Rochelle High Sch, religion, sec teacher, 1968-70; New Rochelle High Sch religion, CCD training instr, 1968-69; NewRochelle High Sch religion, CCD curric developer, 1969-70. **Orgs:** Staff consult, Nat Office Black Cath, 1970-73; exec dir, Nat Black Cath Clergy Caucus, 1970-73; dir religious educ, St Benedict the Moor Wash DC, 1973-74; Alpha Kappa Psi Frat; DC bicentennial com; Nat Educ Asn; Nat Cath Educ Asn; Nat Black Cath Clergy Causus; bd mem camping programs, Family & Child Servs; Delta Psi Omega; Nat Off Black Caths; consult, DESIGN; CarterG Woodson Comn; Nat Black Churchmen Comt. **Business Addr:** Educator, Woodward Building Archdiocese, 733 15 St NW Suite 725, Washington, DC 20005.*

HAGGINS, JON
Fashion designer, writer, television show host. **Personal:** Born Sep 5, 1943, Tampa, FL; son of John and Willie Mae; divorced. **Educ:** Fashion Inst Tech, AAS, 1964. **Career:** Fashion designer, motivational speaker, host, producer, writer; Off the Avenue (first studio), designer, 1966; Jon Haggins Inc, pres & fashion designer; Procter & Gamble, Ultra Detergents, spokesperson; GlobeTrotter Jon Haggins TV, producer & host, currently; Books: The African American Travel Guide To Hot, Exotic & Fun filled Places, 2007; Yes I Can Jon Haggins Memoir, 2008; Jon Haggins Inspirational Book 2, 2008. **Honors/Awds:** Black Designer of the Year, 1981; Key to the City, Baltimore, MD, 1982; Artist-in-Residence, Cornell Univ, 1988. **Special Achievements:** First recognized black designer and one of the youngest designers nominated for The Coty American Fashion Critics Award; One of the designs named "The Dress of the Year" by Bill Cunningham; Honored for achievements with 9 other black designers by Harvey's Bristol Cream 1980, 1981, 1983; Numerous radio and television shows including CNN-Daybreak, Joan Hamburg-WOR Radio, Sunday Classics with Hal Jackson WBLS Radio, Sean Cort-Breakfast Cort and the Bob Law show on WWRL Radio, Geraldo, Regis & Kathie Lee, Saturday Morning Tribune, Midday Live, Evening Magazine & The McCreary Report; Clothes featured in magazines & newspapers including Cosmopolitan, Harper's Bazaar, Vogue, Town & Country, New York Times, Essence, Ebony, & many more. **Business Phone:** (212)319-2894.

HAGINS, OGBONNA
Entrepreneur, educator. **Personal:** Born Feb 22, 1966, Philadelphia, PA; son of Paul (deceased) and Anne (deceased); married Sheena Lester; children: Atamusi Kamau & Atamanu Zaki. **Educ:** Temple Univ, 1984; Community Col Philadelphia, 1987. **Career:** Educator (retired); Davis Poole & Sloan, jr draftsman, 1984-87; The Salkin Group, working drawing specialist, 1987-89; Murray Archit, archit designer draftman, 1987-94; Dobbins High Sch, Sch Dist Philadelphia, archit design & drafting teacher, 1991-96; Reconstruction Inc, mentor. **Orgs:** Philadelphia Fed Teachers, 1991-96. **Honors/Awds:** Dedication & Leadership, Dobbins & Randolph Alumni Asn, 1995. **Special Achievements:** Develop Manhood Develop & Rites of Passage at Murrell Dobbins High Sch, 1993; implementing a private, African-centered educ facility.

HAGLER, GRAYLAN S.
Clergy. **Career:** Plymouth Congregational United Church Christ, pastor, sr minister, currently. **Business Addr:** Pastor, Senior Minister, Plymouth Congregational United Church Christ, 5301 N Capitol St NE, Washington, DC 20011, **Business Phone:** (202)723-5330.*

HAGLER, MARVELOUS MARVIN
Actor, boxer. **Personal:** Born May 23, 1954, Newark, NJ; divorced; children: Gentry, James, Celeste, Marvin Jr & Charelle. **Career:** Boxer (retired), actor; boxer, 1980-87; World Boxing Asn, prof middleweight boxer, world boxing champion, 1980-88; Films: Indio, 1989; Indio 2-La rivolta, 1991; Cyber flic, 1997; Notti di paura, 1997; Night of Fear. **Orgs** World Boxing Asn; US Boxing Asn; World Boxing Coun. **Honors/Awds:** Won Nat Am Middleweight Championship 1973; Won AAU Championship 1973; Outstanding Fighter Award; Middle weight Champion 1980; Honed as Boxer Year, World Boxing Coun, 1984; first in middleweight div to earn a $1million purse; Honee Jackie Robinson Award, World Boxing Asn, World Boxing Coun & Int Boxing Fed middle weight div titles, 1985; Int Boxing Hall Fame, 1993. **Special Achievements:** Former undisputed middleweight champion of the world: WBA, WBC, IBF, 1980-87; television commercial appearances include: Pizza Hut, Diet Coke, Gillette Sport Stick; guest appearances include: "Saturday Night Live," "Punky Brewster," "Room 227"; film appearances include: Indio; Indio 2; established scholarship fund, Massasoit Community College, 1980.

HAGOOD, HENRY BARKSDALE
Real estate developer, executive. **Personal:** Born Aug 19, 1942, Wilson, NC; son of Emmett B Sr and Aurelia Muir; married Theresa, Nov 26, 1989; children: Gabrielle Toles. **Educ:** Mich State Univ, BA, 1965. **Career:** Millender Ctr Asn, developer; Signet Develop Co, develop mgr; Walbridge Aldinger, dir bus develop; Detroit Housing Dept, mayor's exec liaison; Detroit Water & Sewerage Dept, admin asst, Contract & Grant Division; City Detroit, Community & Econ Develop Dept, dir; City Detroit, Mayor's Off, exec asst to Mayor Young; The Farbman Group, vpres; Tecknowledge Group LCC, managing partner, currently; City Detroit, Dept Planning & Develop, dir, currently. **Orgs:** Detroit Econ Growth Corp Exec Comt; Econ Develop Corp; Downtown Develop Authority; Detroit Neighborhood Housing Serv; Highland Park YMCA, bd dirs; Franklin Wright Settlement, bd dirs; New Detroit Inc; Housing & Construction Comt, vice-chmn. **Honors/Awds:** Distinguished Service Award, Southeastern Michigan Builder's Asn, 1992; Board of Recognition, Univ Citizens District Coun; Outstanding Service Award, Detroit Neighborhood Non-Profit Housing Corp; Outstanding Service Award LeadershipArea Coun Citizens Dist Coun. **Business Addr:** Director Development Activities, Department of Planning & Develepement, City Detroit, 65 Cadillac Sq Suite 2300, Detroit, MI 48226, **Business Phone:** (313)224-6380.*

HAGOOD, JAY
Football player, football coach. **Personal:** Born Aug 9, 1973, South Carolina. **Educ:** Va Tech Univ, 1994-96. **Career:** Football player (retired), Football coach; New York Jets, tackle, 1997; Miami Dolphins; San Diego Chargers; New Orleans Saints; NFL Europe, Frankfurt Galaxy, 2000; Centurions, NFL Europe, 2001; NFL Europe, Cologne Centurions, offensive asst coach, 2005-.

HAILE, ANNETTE L
Executive. **Personal:** Born Oct 3, 1952, Latrobe, PA; daughter of Edith Hill. **Educ:** John Carroll Univ, Cleveland, BS, 1974; Baldwin Wallace Col, Berea, MBA, 1978. **Career:** IBM Corp, Bethesda, dir, vpres, 1974-; John Carroll Univ, bd dir, currently. **Orgs:** Bd trustees, Studio Theatre; bd mem, United Arts Orgn. **Honors/Awds:** Hall of Fame, Negro Bus & Prof Womens Clubs, 1990. **Business Addr:** Vice President, IBM Corp, 6710 Rockledge Dr, Bethesda, MD 20817, **Business Phone:** (301)803-1400.

HAILES, EDWARD A.
Clergy, association executive. **Personal:** Son of Walter and Maggie; married Nettie Drayton; children: Edward Jr, Gregory, Patricia. **Educ:** VA Union Univ, attended 1950; VA State Col, Cert; Harvard & Boston Univs, advan studies; Howard Univ, Cert. **Career:** Union Baptist Church New Bedford, pastor, 1951-63; Inter Church Coun Greater New Bedford, supvr religious educ, 1954-61, exec secy, 1963-66; MA Pub Sch Syst, substitute teacher, 1962-63; DC Branch NAACP, exec secy, 1963-66; Opportunity Industrialization Ctr, exec dir;, 19th St Baptist Church Washington, DC, assoc pastor, 1978-; Mt Moriah Baptist Church, asst pastor, currently. **Orgs:** Community Adv, Equal Employ, 1967-71; bd dir, vpres, 1980-, nat NAACP; pres, 1968-72, 1978-, DC Branch NAACP; bd dir Housing Develop Corp, 1969-74; Health & Welfare Coun, 1969-; Comn Criminal Justice Stand & Goals, 1970-71; vice chmn Project Build Inc, 1972; Mayor's Comn Project HOME Washington, 1973-; adv panel, Adult Educ Demonstration Proj 1974-; bd dir, DC Chamber Com, 1983-; pres, Charitable Found, United Supreme Coun Ancient & Accepted Scottish Rite Freemasonry Prince Hall Affiliation, 1984-; bd dir, United Givers Fund; DC chap US Civil Rights Comn. **Honors/Awds:** Chamber Commerce Award, role march Washington, 1963; Created Grand, Insp Gen 33rd Degree The United Supreme Coun Sovereign Grand Inspector Gen 33rd & Last Degree Ancient & Accept Scottish Rite Freemasonry Prince Hall Affiliation, 1974; Man Year Award, Shiloh Men's Club Shiloh Baptist Church, 1980; Citizen of the Year, Omega Psi Phi Chapters Washington DC, 1981; Distinguished Service Award, United Supreme Coun Ancient & Accept Scottish Rite Freemasonry Prince Hall Affiliate; Outstand Young Citizen of Year, Jr Chamber Com New Bedford. **Business Addr:** Assistant Pastor, Mt Moriah Baptist Church, 1636 E Capitol St SE, Washington, DC 20003, **Business Phone:** (202)547-5078.*

HAILEY, CEDRIC RENARD. See HAILEY, K-CI.

HAILEY, JOEL. See HAILEY, JOJO.

HAILEY, JOJO (JOEL HAILEY)
Singer, writer. **Personal:** Born Jun 10, 1971, Charlotte, NC; children: 1. **Career:** Jodeci, mem; Ki-C & JoJo, mem, 1997-; Albums: Money Man, 2007; Wadsyaname, 2007; films: Don't Be a Menace to South Central While Drinking Your Juice in the Hood, 1996; Soul Food, 1997; Shake, Rattle & Roll: An American Love Story, 1999; tv series: "Martin", 1993; "Malcom & Eddie", 1997; "The Jamie Foxx Show", 1998; "Live with Regis & Kathie Lee", 2004; "Cribs", 2005; "Karaoke Revolution Presents: American Idol", 2007; From Siberian Deeps, 2008. *

HAILEY, K-CI (CEDRIC RENARD HAILEY)
Singer. **Personal:** Born Sep 2, 1969, Tiny Grove, NC; children: 1. **Career:** Mem, Jodeci; mem duo, K-Ci & JoJo, 1997-; albums: Love Always, 1997; It's Real, 1999; X, 2000; Save the Last Dance, 2001; Films: Soul Food, 1997; Soundtrack: "Eddie", 1996; "Bulletproof", 1996; "Deliver Us from Eva", 2003; "Alpha Dog", 2006. **Business Phone:** (310)865-5000.

HAILEY, PRISCILLA W
Publisher. **Personal:** Born Oct 22, 1947, Georgia; married Howard L. **Educ:** Savannah State Col, BS, 1969. **Career:** Head Start, teacher, 1967-68; Dublin Ga Bd Educ, teacher, 1969-70; Kaiser Gypsum Co, credit secy, 1969; Medium Newspaper, Seattle, assoc publ, 1970-; Tiloben Publ, pres, currently. **Orgs:** Bd dir & treas, Tiloben Publ Co Inc; Nat Asn Advan Colored People; Black Educ & Economics Conf; team capt, Neighborhood Cancer Soc; Nat Educ Asn, 1969-70; Ga Educ Asn, 1969-70; vol acct inner city residents & vol trainer-typesetter, Garfield HS Messenger, 1970-71; trainer & supr, Seattle Univ Minority Stud Newspaper, 1971-73. **Honors/Awds:** Recipient Model Cities Citizen Participation Award; Black Community Unsung Hero Award. **Business Addr:** President, Tiloben Publishing Co Inc, 2600 S Jackson St, Seattle, WA 98144, **Business Phone:** (206)323-3070.

HAILSTOCK, SHIRLEY
Writer, association executive. **Personal:** Born in Newberry, SC; daughter of Eugene and Hattie Johnson. **Educ:** Howard Univ, Washington, DC, BS, chem; Fairleigh Dickinson Univ, MBA, chem mkt. **Career:** Rutgers State Univ, NJ, adj prof acct; Middlesex Co Col, prof novel writing; Women Writers Color, officer; Books: Whispers of Love, 1994; Clara's Promise, 1995; White Diamonds, 1996; Legacy, 1997; Mirror Image, 1998; Opposites Attract, 1999; More Than Gold, 2000; Her 1-800 Husband, 2001; A Family Affair, 2002; A Father's Fortune, 2003; Love on Call, 2004; You Made Me Love You, 2005; Secret, 2006; My Lover, My Friend, 2006. **Orgs:** Bd mem, Romance Writers Am. **Honors/Awds:** Heart of the West Award; Career Achievement Award, Romantic Times; Waldenbooks Award; Outstanding Achiever of the Year, 2002. **Special Achievements:** The first and only African-American board member of Romance Writers of America. **Business Phone:** (281)440-6885.*

HAINES, CHARLES EDWARD
Arts administrator, college teacher. **Personal:** Born Apr 20, 1925, Louisville, KY; son of William and Willie M Warfield; divorced; children: Charles Jr. **Educ:** Ind Univ, AB, 1950, MFA, 1953, MA, 1959. **Career:** Free lance adv art; WTHR TV, Indianapolis, IN, art dir, 1959-; Purdue Univ, Indianapolis, lectr, 1969-; Ind Univ, grad asst, lectr; Sarkes Tarzian Inc, art dir; Avco Broad, art dir; Crosley Broad, art dir; Marian Col, lectr. **Orgs:** Col Art Asn Am; Dean's Select Comn Search & Screen appt new dean; Herron Sch Art

Indianapolis. **Honors/Awds:** Black Expo Feat in "Ebony Mag" 1957; Exhibitions & Awds various state fairs; art work IN Basketball Hall of Fame; painting Atlanta Univ Collection. **Military Serv:** AUS, Corp of Engrg pfc, 1944-46; Bronze Star, Rhineland Campaign. **Business Addr:** Art Director, WTHR TV, 1000 N Meridian St, Indianapolis, IN 46204.*

HAIR, PRINCELL
Vice president (Organization). **Personal:** Born Jan 1, 1967?. **Educ:** Fla Intl Univ, BS, broadcast jour; Univ Baltimore's Merrick Sch Bus, MBA. **Career:** WPLG-TV Miami, producer, 1990-91; WSVN-TV Miami, producer, 1991-92; WDIV-TV Detroit, producer, 1992-93; WBBM-TV, exec producer news, 1993-95; WCPX-TV Orlando, Fla, asst news dir, 1995-97; WMAQ-TV, news dir, 1997-98; WBAL-TV Baltimore, news dir, 1998-02; Viacom TV Stas Group, news dir; KCBS-TV, news dir; CNN/US, exec vpres & gen mgr, 2003-04, sr vpres, prog & talent develop, 2004-. **Honors/Awds:** Emmy Award Chicago Exec Producer "Our Future Crisis", 1994; Best Newscast, Associated Press. **Special Achievements:** Best Newscast Mich, Asn Press. **Business Phone:** (404)827-2300.*

HAIRSTON, ABBEY GAIL
Lawyer. **Personal:** Born Oct 15, 1955, Chicago, IL; daughter of Horace W and Rosietta. **Educ:** Drake Univ, BA, 1976; Univ Iowa Col Law, JD, 1980. **Career:** Fla Rural Legal Serv, staff atty, 1980-82, supv atty, 1982-84; Palm Beach Co Fla Sch Bd, atty & gen counsel, 1988-93; Nova Univ, adj prof, 1984-92; Barry Univ, adj prof, 1991-93; Alexander, Bearden, Hairston & Marks, partner, 1994; Epstein, Becker & Green, PC, partner; DC Pub Sch, gen counsel, 2006- 07; Thatcher Law Firm LLC, atty, currently. **Orgs:** Am Bar Asn; Asn Trial Lawyers Am; Fed Bar Asn; Nat Bar Asn; Outstanding Lawyers Am; Steering Comt Litigation Sect, DC Bar Asn; chmn, Bd Gov, Fed Bar Asn; Md Bar Asn. **Honors/Awds:** One of Washington's 50 Best Lawyers, Washingtonian Mag, 1997; Outstanding Lawyer in America, 2003. **Special Achievements:** Book: The Leave and Disability Coordination Handbook, 1997. **Business Phone:** (301)441-1400.*

HAIRSTON, EDDISON R, JR.
Dentist. **Personal:** Born Apr 4, 1933, York Run, PA; married Audrey Barnes; children: Eddison jr & Robert Eugene. **Educ:** Lincoln Univ, AB, 1954; Howard Univ Dental Sch, DDS, 1962. **Career:** Pvt pract, dentist,1963-; Howard Univ Comm Dent Chronically Ill & Aged Prog, clin asst prof, 1967. **Orgs:** Consult, Armstrong Dental Asst Prog, 1973-74; mem, Robt T Freeman Dental Soc; Am & Nat Dental Asns; DC Dental Soc; Am Soc Dent C; Omega Psi Phi; Wash Urban League; NAACP. **Military Serv:** AUS, dental tech, 1954-57. **Home Addr:** 3417 Minnesota Ave SE, Washington, DC 20019, **Home Phone:** (202)584-3331. **Business Addr:** Dentist, 3417 Minnesota Ave SE, Washington, DC 20019, **Business Phone:** (202)584-3331.

HAIRSTON, HAROLD B.
Government official. **Personal:** Born Jan 1, 1940?. **Career:** Philadelphia Fire Dept, 1964, fire comnr (retired), 1992-04; CBS 3, KYW-TV, on-air consult, 2004-. **Orgs:** Int Asn Black Fire Fighters; Boca; Nat Fire Protectors Asn. **Special Achievements:** Philadelphia's first African American fire commissioner. **Home Addr:** 823 W Mount Airy Ave, Philadelphia, PA 19119, **Home Phone:** (215)248-0666. **Business Addr:** On Air Consultant, KYW-TV CBS, 101 S Independence Mall E, Philadelphia, PA 19106, **Business Phone:** (215)238-4700.*

HAIRSTON, JERRY WAYNE
Baseball player. **Personal:** Born Feb 16, 1952, Birmingham, AL; son of Sammy Hairston; married Esperanza Anellano; children: Jerry Jr, Justin, Scott & Stacey Lynn. **Educ:** Lawson St Jr Coll, Birmingham, AL. **Career:** Baseball player (retired); Chicago White Sox, outfielder, 1973-77, 1981-89; BristolWhite Sox, batting coach, currently. **Business Addr:** Batting Coach, Bristol White Sox, PO Box 1434, Bristol, VA 24203, **Business Phone:** (276)645-7364.

HAIRSTON, JERRY WAYNE, JR.
Baseball player. **Personal:** Born May 29, 1976, Naperville, IL; son of Jerry. **Educ:** Southern Ill Univ, Carbondale. **Career:** Baltimore Orioles, outfielder, 1998-2004; Chicago Cubs, outfielder, 2005-06; Tex Rangers, outfielder, 2006-07; Cincinnati Reds, 2008-09; New York Yankees, 2009-. **Special Achievements:** First African American to be a third-generation major-leaguer. **Business Addr:** Professional Baseball Player, New York Yankees, Yankee Stadium, 1 East 161 St, Bronx, NY 10451, **Business Phone:** (718)293-4300.*

HAIRSTON, JOSEPH HENRY
Lawyer. **Personal:** Born May 8, 1922, Axton, VA; son of James and Julia; married Anna L Allen; children: Nancy R, Naomi, JoAnn & Victoria M. **Educ:** Univ Md, BS, 1957; Am Univ, JD, 1960; Georgetown Univ, LLM, 1961. **Career:** Lawyer (retired); Office Solicitor Dept Labor Wash, atty, 1960-61; Operations Div IRS, dir, 1976-85. **Orgs:** DC Bar Asn; Am Bar Asn; treas, trustee, Baptist Sr Adult Ministries; Nat Lawyers Clubvpres, Neighbors Inc; past v chmn, moderator, Takoma Park Bapt Ch; founder & pres, Nat Neighbors, 1969, 1975; del, Shepherd Park Citizens Asn; exec com, DC Fed Citizens Asn, 1970-73; Shepherd PTA; Takoma PTA; Officers Club, Walter Reed Army Med Ctr; Nat Asn Uniformed Serv; Comner, District Columbia Advisory Neighborhood Comn; trustee, DC Bapt Found; ex-bd, exec comm, DC Bapt Convention; co-chair, DC Postal Advisory Comm; chmn, Wash Gas Co, Citizens Advisory Comm; treas, Coordinating Coun, Cooperative Bapt Fel; treas emer, Nat Bar Asn, 2007-; bd dir, Wash Bar Asn, currently; bd dir, Am Inst Parliamentarians, currently. **Honors/Awds:** First black attorney apptd sr exec, Office of Chief Counsel, IRS. **Military Serv:** AUS, 1940-60.

HAIRSTON, RALEIGH DANIEL
Social worker, clergy. **Personal:** Born Nov 15, 1934, Amonate, VA; son of Samuel Hardin and Elsie Wilson; married Helen Carol Covington, Dec 22, 1962 (divorced); children: John Lesley Daniel, Karen Nancy. **Educ:** Bluefield State Col, BS, 1959; Atlanta Univ, MSW, 1962; Bexley Hall Episcopal Sem, MA, 1969; Case Western Reserve Univ, MA, 1975; Colgate Rochester Divinity Sch, DMin, 1978. **Career:** Boston Univ Med Sch, Psychiatry Dept, adjunct asst prof, 1970-71; Cleveland Metro Gen Hosp, proj adr, 1972-77; St Simon Cyrene Episcopal Church, rector, 1977-81; Emmanuel Episcopal Church, interim rector, 1982; Cleveland Municipal Court, probation officer, 1982-85; Veterans Admin Hosp, med social worker, 1985-88; Calvary Episcopal Church, asst priest, 1989-91; City WA Child & Family Servs, social worker, 1989-94; Saint Augustine's Col, chaplain, 1995-98; St Marks Episcopal Church, rector, Priest Charge, 2001-. **Orgs:** NAACP, currently; Nat Asn Social Workers; Asn Black Social Workers; Union Black Episcopalians; former Am Fed State, Country & Municipal Employees; Interdenominational Ministerial Asn; Diocese Ohio CMS Ministry, 1975-77; Diocese Southern Ohio CMS Ecumenical Rels, 1979-81; life mem, Kappa Alpha Psi Fraternity. **Honors/Awds:** Sigma Rho Sigma Honor Fraternity Social Sciences, Bluefield State Col, 1959; Firestone Scholarship, Bexley Hall Episcopal Sem, 1965; Human Services Volunteer Award, City Lincoln Heights, Ohio, 1980; Distinguished Service Award, St Augustine's Col, 1998. **Special Achievements:** "A Study of Formal Training Provided, Employment, and the Availability of Jobs for Negro High School Graduates in Tampa, Florida," unpublished thesis, June 1962, Atlanta Univ, GEO; Author, "Blacks and the Episcopal Church in the Diocese of Ohio," unpublished dissertation, May 1978, Colgate Rochester Divinity School, NY. **Military Serv:** USY, Specialist 3, 1955-57, Good Conduct, 1957. **Business Addr:** Priest in Charge, St Mark's Episcopal Church, 601 Grace St, Wilmington, NC 28401, **Business Phone:** (910)763-3212.*

HAIRSTON, ROWENA L.
Manager, association executive. **Personal:** Born Mar 17, 1928, Mohawk, WV; daughter of Paul L Winfrey and Roewnia; married Charles B Hairston, Sep 26, 1946. **Educ:** Central Night Sch, Columbus, OH, 1958. **Career:** Manager (retired), association executive; Bur Employ Serv, Columbus, typist & clerk, 1961-70, examr data control, 1970-95; Nat Alliance Postal & Fed Employees, nat auxiliary pres, currently. **Orgs:** Nat rep, Leadership Conf Civil Rights; life mem, Nat Asn Advan Colored People. **Honors/Awds:** Recognition plaque Local No 605 Auxiliary Nat Alliance Postal & Fed Employees, Columbus, 1975; key to city Mayor of Kans, MO, 1977; Gold medal, Mayor Atlantic City, NJ, 1978. **Home Addr:** 2023 Maryland Ave, Columbus, OH 43219, **Home Phone:** (614)252-3227. **Business Addr:** President, National Alliance of Postal & Federal Employees, 1628 11th St, Washington, DC 20001, **Business Phone:** (202)939-6325.*

HAIRSTON, SANDRA W.
Physician. **Educ:** Univ NC, Chapel Hill, MD. **Career:** York Hospital, York, Pa, resident physician; Johns Hopkins Community Physicians, Wyman Pk Med Ctr, internal med physician, currently. *

HAIRSTON, WILLIAM
Artistic director, writer, administrator. **Personal:** Born Apr 1, 1928, Goldsboro, NC; son of William Russell and Malissa Carter; married Enid Carey; children: Ann Marie. **Educ:** Univ Northern Colo, Greeley, CO, BA, polit sci; Columbia Univ, New York, NY; New York Univ, New York, NY. **Career:** Greenwich Mews Theatre, New York, prod coordr, 1963, coproducer, 1963-64; New York Shakespeare Festival, theatre mgr & adminr, 1963-66; Ford Grant, Arena Stage, Washington, DC, asst to exec dir, 1965-66; Dem Nat Comt, radio news ed & corresp, 1968; DC, Exec Off Mayor, Off Personnel, exec mgr, 1970-90; DC Pipeline, Wash, DC, publ & ed, 1973-79; Books: The World of Carlos, 1968; Sex and Conflict, 1993; Ira Aldridge, 1998; Spaced Out: A Space Adventure, 1998; Showdown At Sundown, 1998; History of the National Capital Area Council, 1998; Passion And Politics, 2001; Playwright: Swan-Song of the 11th Dawn, 1962; Walk in Darkness, 1963; Curtain Call Mr Aldridge, Sir, 1964; Black Antigone, 1965; Ira Aldridge, 1988; Double Dare, 1995; Poems: Poetry and Prose of Passion & Compassion, 2002; Anthologies: Echoes of Yesterday; Best Poems of 1995; A Voyage to Remember; Forever and A Day; Fields of Gold; Essence of a Dream; Tracing Shadows; The Scenic Route; Journey Between Stars; Scriptwriting for US Info Agency: Apollo 11 - Man on the Moon; Media Hora; Festival of Heritage; Jules Verne vs Real Flight to the Moon; Operation Money-Wise; TV series: "Harlem Detective", 1953; Films: Take the High Ground; Jerico-Jim Crow, 1964; Curtain Call Mr Aldridge, Sir!, 1964. **Orgs:** Dramatists Guild; exec bd, Nat Capital Area Coun; Boy Scouts Am. **Honors/Awds:** Theatre Admininistration Grant, Ford Found, 1965-66; Literary Study Grant, Nat Endowment Arts, 1967; Playwrights Festival Award, Group Theatre, Seattle, WA, 1988; The Silver Beaver Award, Boy Scouts Am, Nat Capital Area, 1988; Multi Cultural Playwrights Festival Winner, 1988; Meritorious Public Service Award, DC, 1990; Creative Achievement Award, Univ Northern Colo, 2005. **Home Addr:** 5501 Seminary Rd, Falls Church, VA 22041. *

HAKEEM, WALI. **See GILL, WALTER HARRIS.**

HAKIM, AZ-ZAHIR
Football player. **Personal:** Born Jun 3, 1977, Los Angeles, CA. **Educ:** San Diego State Univ. **Career:** Football player (retired), St Louis Rams, wide receiver, 1998-2001; Detroit Lions, wide receiver,2002-04, 2006; New Orleans Saints, wide receiver, 2005; San Diego Chargers, wide receiver, 2006; Miami Dolphins, 2007. **Honors/Awds:** Second-team All-WAC, 2005; Super Bowl champion (XXXIV), All-Pro selection (2000).

HALE, CLEO INGRAM
Educational consultant. **Personal:** Born Nov 27, 1922, Atlanta, GA; daughter of John Y and Janist I Preston; married Phale Dophis Hale, Aug 16, 1943; children: Phale D Jr, Janice, Marna A Leaks, Hilton I. **Educ:** Spelman Col, BS, 1944; Ohio State Univ, MA, 1975. **Career:** Educational consultant (retired); Third Ave Child Care Ctr, dir, 1968-70; Franklin Co Head Start Prog, educ dir, 1970-76; S Side Child Develop Ctr, assoc dir, 1976-84. **Orgs:** Adv comt, Voc Home Econ Child; Nat Asn Educ Young C, 1970-90; Nat Asn Black Child Develop, 1976-90; bd mem, Action C, 1978-82; parent advisor, S Side Child Develop Ctr, 1980-84; Fort Hayes Career Ctr, Care Job Training Prog 1982-84; Ohio Asn Educ Young C, 1980-90; Proj Literacy US Task Force, 1986-87. **Honors/Awds:** Community Honoree, Metrop Dem Women Fr Co, 1986; Columbus Chapter of Coalition of 100 Black Women, 1992. **Special Achievements:** One of 27 extraordinary African Am Women, Black Silhouettes, 1992. **Home Addr:** 2480 Floribunda Dr, Columbus, OH 43209, **Home Phone:** (614)231-5722. *

HALE, REV. CYNTHIA LYNNETTE
Clergy. **Personal:** Born Oct 27, 1952, Roanoke, VA; daughter of Harrison and Janice Hylton. **Educ:** Hollins Col, Hollins, VA, BA, Music, 1975; Duke Divinity Sch, Durham NC, MDiv, 1979; United Theological Seminary, Dayton OH, Doctorate Ministry, 1991. **Career:** Fed Correctional facilities, Colorado & NC, Chaplain, 1979-85; Ray Hope Christian Church, Decatur GA, pastor, founder & sr pastor, currently. **Orgs:** Nat Coun Churches, New York, 1978-83; vpres, bd dir, Greenwood Cemetery Co, 1979-80; pres, Nat Convocation Christian Church, 1982-88; Gen Bd Christian Church, 1982-88; vpres, Concerned Black Clergy; bd dir, Christian Coun Metrop, Atlanta, 1989; Project Impact, DeKalb. **Honors/Awds:** Outstanding Young Woman Am, 1982, 1986-88; Liberation Award, Nat Convocation CCDC, 1984; The Religious Award, Ninety-Nine Breakfast Club, 1990; The Religion Award, DeKalb Br, Nat Advan Asn Colored People, 1990; inducted Martin Luther Kind Bd Preachers, Morehouse Col, 1993; Chosen Award, Atlanta Gospel Choice, 1998; inducted into the African Am Biographies Hall of Fame; Profiles of Prominence Award, Martin Luther King, 2000; Outstanding Religious Leader Award, Alpha Kappa Alpha; Outstanding Ga Citizen, Ga Secy State; Ga Goodwill Ambassador. **Special Achievements:** first female chaplain to serve in an all-male institution. **Business Addr:** Founder, Senior Pastor, Ray of Hope Christian Church, 2778 Snapfinger Rd, Decatur, GA 30034-2439.*

HALE, DERRICK F.
State government official. **Personal:** Born Sep 7, 1963, Detroit, MI; son of Thomas and Mildred Hall; married Cleo; children: Christina, Nicole & Derrick II. **Educ:** Wayne State Univ, BA, mass communs, 1995. **Career:** WDIV Channel 4, sports intern, 1987-88; Mich State Rep Michael J Bennane, legis aide, 1989-96; Fourteenth Dist, MI, State Rep, 1997-; Congressman Sander Levin, campaign coordr, 1998. **Orgs:** Wayne State Univ Alumni Asn; USA Boxing Asn; bd mem, Northwest Young Men's Christian Asn; Nat Black Caucus State Legislators; Nat Asn Advan Colored People; founder, pres, Derrick F Hale Found; Coun State Govs; Coalition Labor Union Women; Am Coun Young Political Leaders; Motor City Blight Busters; pres, Eighth Precinct Community Coun; pres, Eighth Precinct BUOY; vice chair, Michigan Family Forum; Old Redford Asn. **Honors/Awds:** Volunteer of the Year, Eight Precinct Community Rels, 1998; Murray-Wright Hall of Fame, inductee, 1998; Legislator of the Year, Mich Minority Women's Network, 2000; Certificate of Recognition, Detroit Bd Police Comnrs, 2005; Spirit of Detroit Award, Detroit City Coun, 2005. **Special Achievements:** American council of young political leaders, selected as ambassador to South Korea, 1999.

HALE, DR. FRANK WILBUR, JR.
College administrator. **Personal:** Born Mar 24, 1927, Kansas City, MO; son of Frank and Novella; married Mignon Scott, Jul 12,

2003; children: Ifeoma Kwesi, Frank W Hale & Sherilyn R Thomas. **Educ:** Univ Nebr, BA, commun, polit sci & eng, 1950, MA, commun, polit sci & eng, 1951; Ohio State Univ, PhD, commun & polit sci, 1955. **Career:** Oakwood Col, prof, 1951-59, pres, 1966-71; Potomac Univ, vis prof, 1957; Cent State Univ, chmn & prof, dept Eng, 1959-66; Univ London, postdoctoral fel, 1960; Ohio State Univ, assoc dean & chmn, grad sch, 1971-78, viceprovost minority affairs, 1978-88, vice provost, prof emer, distinguished univ rep & consult, 1999-05; Kenyon Col, from exec asst to pres, 1989-92; Univ Nebr, vis prof, commun, 1995. **Orgs:** Bd trustees, United Negro Col Fund, 1966-71; bd trustees, Loma Linda Univ, 1966-71; bd mem, Harding Hosp, 1975-; chmn, bldg comt, Ephesus SDA Church, 1978-88; Operation Reach Back, 1999-2000; bd trustees, Oakwood Col, 2000-; bd mem, Breath Live TV, 2002-. **Honors/Awds:** Patterson Award, UNCF; DHum, Wilberforce Univ; LHD, Shaw Univ; Dhum, Capital Univ, Dhum, Univ Nebr; LLD, La Sierra Univ; LLD, Andrews Univ. **Special Achievements:** Author: The Cry For Freedom, 1970; Angels Watching Over Me, 1996; A Letter to African American Males, 2000; What Makes Racial Diversity Work in Higher Education, 2003. **Business Addr:** Vice Provost, Professor Emeritus, Ohio State University, Black Cultural Center, 153 W 12th Ave, Columbus, OH 43210-1389, **Business Phone:** (614)292-0074.

HALE, GENE
Executive, founder (originator), president (organization). **Personal:** Born Apr 19, 1946, Birmingham, AL; son of Matt and Minnie; married Cecelia L. Davis Hale, Aug 29, 1978; children: Reginald, Kevin, Crystal. **Educ:** Calif State Univ, Dominguez Hills, Carson, BS, bus admin, 1980. **Career:** Co-founder, Fourth Annual Black Bus Day Luncheon; G&C Equip Corp, Gardena, CA, founder & pres, 1980-; Gence, pres, currently. **Orgs:** advisory bd, Historical Black Col, 2004; chmn, Congressional Task Force Minority Bus Set Asides Pvt Sector; chmn, Greater Los Angeles African Am Chamber Com; advisory coun chmn, Calif Dept Transp; chmn, Century Freeway Employ Advisory Comt; chmn, Fedn Minority Bus Asn; co-chmn, Calif Dept Transp Employ Comt; dir, Gardena Valley Chamber Com; advisory comt mem, Entrepreneurial Prog Disadvantaged Youth; advisory bd, Calif Pub Utilities; chair, Greater Los Angeles African Am; expert coun, Dept Com; advisory bd, AT&T Technol Bd; comnr, City Los Angeles; dir, Los Angeles Conv & Visitors Bur. **Honors/Awds:** Cert Appreciation, Century Freeway Advisory Comt, 1990; SBA Recognition Award, Support Los Angeles Minority Small Bus Community, 1990; Supplier of the Year, Nat Minority Supplier Develop Coun, 1990; Supplier of the Year, Southern Calif Purchasing Coun Inc, 1990; Community Architect Award, 49th Assembly Dist, 1989; Bridging the Gap Award, SBE, 1988; Cong Cert Appreciation, 1987; Cert Recognition, Los Angeles Area Coun, Boy Scouts Am, 1985; Outstanding Minority Bus, State Calif Minority Enterprise Develop Coun, 1986; Outstanding Minority Bus, State Calif, 1985; Black Bus of the Year Award, Black Bus Aciation Los Angeles, 1985. **Military Serv:** AUS, Sergeant. **Business Addr:** Founder, President, G&C Equipment Corporation, 1875 W Redondo Beach Blvd Suite 102, Gardena, CA 90249-0151.*

HALE, HILTON I
Insurance agent. **Personal:** Born May 17, 1956, Columbus, OH; son of Phale D Sr and Cleo I Hale. **Educ:** Northwestern Univ, attended; Atlanta Univ, attended; Morehouse Col, attended; San Diego State, BA, bus, econ & Commun, 1979; Chartered Life Underwriter designation Am Col, 2002. **Career:** United Parcel Serv, indust engr, 1979-81, revenue auditor, 1981-85; H & R Block, tax preparer, 1983-85; Hilton I Hale & Assoc LLC, chief exec officer, 1985-. **Orgs:** Columbus Life Underwriters Asn, 1986-; Ohio Asn Life Underwriters, 1986-; Nat Asn Underwriters, 1986-; King's Men, 1989-91; treas, Hilliard Democratic Club, 1997-98; pres, Linden Kiwanis, 1998-99; Life Underwriters, Polit Action Community, 1998-99; Rainbow/PUSH Coalition, 1998-99; Nat Asn Ins & Financial Advisors, 2000-; Thursday Club, 2000-; ambassador, Am Heart Asn, 2007-08; ambassador, Am Stroke Asn, 2007-08. **Honors/Awds:** The Nat Quality Award, The Nat Asn Life Underwriters & Life Ins Mkt & Res Asn, 1993, 1997, 1998; Executive Council Award, NY Ins Co, 1987, 1988; Centurion Award, 1988; Quality Award, 1997, 1998; Award of Excellence, Columbus East High Sch Class of 1974, 2004; Sr NYLIC Designation, NY Life Ins Co, 2005; Community Serv Award, Black Pages Ohio, 2006. **Special Achievements:** Columbus Corporate Challenge Basketball Champions, 1987. **Home Addr:** PO Box 9863, Columbus, OH 43209-0863, **Home Phone:** (614)238-3021. **Business Addr:** Chief Executive Officer, Hilton I Hale & Assoc LLC, 897 E 11th Ave, Columbus, OH 43211-2757, **Business Phone:** (614)291-4253.

HALE, KIMBERLY ANICE
Librarian, college administrator. **Personal:** Born Dec 6, 1962, Champaign, IL; daughter of Emery S White and Margaret I. **Educ:** Univ Ill, Urbana-Champaign, BS, sociol, 1985, MS, lib & info sci, 1989. **Career:** Columbia Col Libr, Chicago, acquistions librn, coordr collection develop, 1989-2002; head collection mgt, 2002-, actg dir, currently. **Orgs:** Alpha Phi Omega Serv Fraternity, 1983-; Asn Col & Res Libr, 1988-; Asn Libr Colections & Tech Servs Div, 1988-; Am Libr Asn, 1989-; Women Dir's Chair, 1998-; Ref & User Servs Asn, 2003-; Libr Admin & Mgt Asn, 2003-; Libr Fundraising Adv Comt; Ill Libr Asn Intellectual Freedom Comt. **Honors/Awds:** Diana V Braddom Scholarship, 2006. **Business Addr:** Head of Collection Management, Columbia College Library, 624 S Mich Ave 2nd Fl Rm 111, Chicago, IL 60605, **Business Phone:** (312)344-7355.

HALE, LORRAINE
Executive. **Personal:** Born Jan 1, 1926?, Philadelphia, PA; daughter of Thomas and Clara. **Educ:** Long Island Univ, BA, 1960; City Col NY, MS, 1964; Bank St Col Educ, attended 1967; Univ Ghana, Cert, african history, 1970; Western Univ, PhD, 1974; NY Univ, DEd, 1977. **Career:** NY City Pub Sch Syst, teacher, guidance counsr & sch psychologist, 1960-69; Hale House Ctr Promotion Human Potential Inc, NY City, exec dir, 1969-89, pres & chief exec officer, 1989-2002; City Univ NY, adj prof, 1972-78; Bronx Community Col, adj prof, 1985-89; Col New Rochelle, adj prof, 1987-88; Col Human Serv, adj prof, 1989-90; Harlem Urban Develop Ctr Inc, bd dirs, 1984-; Joint Inst Review Bd, 1985-. **Orgs:** Minority AIDS Comn, Nat Comn Drug-Free Sch, Mt St Ursuela Speech Ctr; NY Div Substance Abuse Servs, 1984-. *

HALE, MARNA AMORETTI (MARNA HALE LEAKS)
Educator. **Personal:** Born Jan 13, 1951, Columbus, OH; daughter of Rev Phale D Sr; married Emanuel, Oct 29, 1988 (divorced 2004); children: Richard W Hale Pace, Deante George & Deandre George. **Educ:** Spelman Col, BA, 1973; John Carroll Univ, MA, 1992; Case Western Res Univ, attended 1993. **Career:** AT&T Technologies, sect chief training, 1977-87; Allen-Bradley Co Inc, sr instrnl developer, 1987-92; Data Corp Bus Systs Inc, training consult, 1994-96; Ernst & Young LLP, Prof & Orgn Develop, consult, 1998-2000; Intellinex, opers load/prog leader, sr mgr progs; City Cleveland, Div Water, proj dir, currently. **Orgs:** Int Soc Performance Improv, 1977-; Am Soc Training & Develop, 1992-98; Nat Writer's Asn, 1992-; Nat Spelman Alumni Asn, 1997-; Mothers Against Drunk Drivers, 1997-. **Honors/Awds:** Achievement Award, SCLC, 1972; Citation for Publication of Take Refuge Under the Halo, Ohio State Legis, 1982. **Special Achievements:** Author: Take Refuge Under the Halo, 1982; Confessions of A Sister Out of Time, 1999; Princess Diana, After Life, 1999; The prequel to Confessions of A Sister Out of Time, 2001; How to Get Married: A Strategic and Literary Approach to Wedlock, 2002. **Home Addr:** 5455 N Marginal Rd Suite 345, Cleveland, OH 44114, **Home Phone:** (216)431-6172. **Business Addr:** Project Director, City of Cleveland, Division of Water, 1201 Lakeside Ave, Cleveland, OH 44114, **Business Phone:** (216)664-2444.

HALE, PHALE D. See Obituaries section.

HALE, PHALE DOPHIS
Educator. **Personal:** Born Jan 19, 1946, Fort Wayne, IN; son of Phale Sr and Cleo Hale; divorced. **Educ:** Howard Univ, BS, 1967; Colgate Rochester Divinity Sch, attended 1970; State Univ NY, Brockport, MS, 1974; Univ Rochester, attended 1976. **Career:** Univ Rochester, CAPP dir, 1968-70; City Sch Dist Rochester, NY, supervising dir, 1970-87; Juliana Group, pres, 1994-97; Phale D Hale Educ Consult Inc, pres, 1987-. **Orgs:** Past pres, bd mem, Magnet Schs Am, 1994-; vpres, Nat Asn Magnet Sch Develop, 1994-; secy bd, Nat Comn Sch Desegregation, 1975-82. **Honors/Awds:** Distinguished Service Award, Magnet Schs Am, 1994. **Special Achievements:** Published & created: Writing Grant Proposals That WIN, Capitol Publications, 1992, 1998; Grant Write, software, 1993; Budget Write, software, 1996; Winning Federal Grants, Capitol Publications, 1995; Kansas City MSR: A Comprehensive Plan, 1990. **Business Addr:** President, Phale D Hale Education Consulting Inc, 2300 M St NW Suite 750, Washington, DC 20037, **Business Phone:** (202)296-3500.

HALES, EDWARD EVERETTE
Lawyer. **Personal:** Born Feb 13, 1932, Leechburg, PA; son of Charles and Bertha. **Educ:** Baldwin-Wallace Col, attended 1955; Univ Wis, Madison Law Col, attended 1962. **Career:** Ford Motor Co-United Auto Workers, permanent umpire; Pacific Bell, arbitrator; State Ak Pub Employees, arbitrator; State Minn, legal asst, atty gen, 1962-63; City Racine, asst city atty, 1965-67; Goodman Hales & Costello, atty, 1965-73; Hales Harvey & Neu, atty, 1973-79; Hales Hartig, atty, 1979-; Int Fel, consult; VISTA, consult; State Mich OEO, consult; IA Urban Res Ctr, consult; AIM Jobs, bd, pvt consult; City San Diego, atty, currently. **Orgs:** Spec arbitrator, Bd Arbitration US Steel Corp United Steel Workers Am; spec arbitrator, Fed Mediation Serv; spec arbitrator, Wiss Employ Rel Comn; spec arbitrator, Bd Arbitration State Minn, Nat Asn Advan Colored People; Urban League; Nat Bar Asn; Am Bar Asn; WIS State Bar Asn; WIS Coun Criminal Justice; WIS Higher Educ Aids Bd; WIS Univ Merger Implementation Com; Alpha Phi Alpha; chmn, Finance Com Bd Regents Univ Wis System, 1975-77; pres, Bd Regents Univ Wis Syst, 1977-79; bd trustees Asn Gov, Bds Univ & Col, 1977-; selection com US 7th Circuit & Judicial Ct, 1978-79; bd dirs, Pub Broadcasting Serv, 1979-80; bd trustees, Asn Pub Broadcasting, 1979-; arbitrator, Am Arbitration Asn, 1980-; bd trustees, Ripon Col, Ripon, Wi, 1980-; State Wis, Investment Bd, 1987-90; State Wis, Racing Comn, 1988-90; Ford Motor Co & United Automobile Workers, permanent umpire. **Honors/Awds:** Urban Serv Award, 1967; Eeffort Award Kings Daughter Club, 1974. **Military Serv:** AUS, 1956-58. **Business Addr:** Attorney, City San Diego, 4089 Porte De Palmas Suite 118, San Diego, CA 92122-5120.*

HALES, MARY A.
Educator, bail bond agent. **Personal:** Born Jul 27, 1953, Fayetteville, NC; daughter of Jack E Melvin and Dorothy M Allen; divorced; children: Michelle, Mario, Dominique. **Educ:** Fayetteville State Univ, BS, Psychol, 1981, elem educ & math, 1989; Cert Educ Admini & Supvr, 1994. **Career:** Foxe's Surety Bail Bonding Co, admin chief, 1978-81; Fayetteville Tech Inst, adult basic educ instr, 1981-88; WFBS Radio, radio commun operator, 1982-83; HSA Cumberland Psychiat Hosp, mental health counr, 1985-87; All Am Bail Bonding Co, owner & agent, 1987-; Long Hill Elem Sch, sixth grade teacher, 1989-90; Montclair Elem Sch, Fayetteville, NC, fourth grade teacher, 1990; Coun Real Estate, sales agent, 1994-; Margaret Willis Elem Sch, Fayetteville, NC, asst prin, 1997-. **Orgs:** Vpres, Cumberland Co Chap Bail Bondsmen, 1978-81; notary pub State NC, 1980-; NC Asn Adult Educr, 1981-; NC Bail Bondsmen Asn, 1987; NC Asn Educr, 1989-; Nat Educ Asn, 1989-; NC Coun Teachers Mathematics, 1988-; Asn Teacher Educr, 1989-; Fayetteville Jaycees, 1990-; US Jaycees, 1990-; Fayetteville State Univ, athletic club, 1993-; NC Asn Realtors, 1994-; Fayetteville Area Bd Realtors, 1994-; NC Asn Sch Adminr, 1994-. **Honors/Awds:** Nat Dean's List, 1978-; Alpha Kappa Mu Nat Hon Soc, 1979; Kappa Delta Pi Int Hon Soc Educ, 1994; First Union Educr of the Yr Award, 1995. *

HALEY, CHARLES LEWIS
Football player, football executive. **Personal:** Born Jan 6, 1964, Gladys, VA; married Karen; children: Princess Kay, Charles Jr & Brianna. **Educ:** James Madison Univ. **Career:** Football player (retired), football exec; San Francisco 49ers, defensive end, 1986-91, 1999; Dallas Cowboys, 1992-96; Detroit Lions, defensive asst coach, 2001-02. **Orgs:** Alpha Phi Alpha; Xi Delta Chap. **Honors/Awds:** Pro Bowl, 1988, 1990-95; Football Digest, Defensive Player of the Year, 1990, 1994.

HALEY, DAMON L
Founder (Originator), executive. **Educ:** Univ Calif, BA; Univ Mich, MBA. **Career:** Reebok, marketer; Nike, mkt mgr; Chevron Corp, staff; Urban Mkt Corp Am, co-founder, 1999-, chief strategist, sr vpres & chief exec officer, currently. **Business Phone:** (323)934-8622.

HALEY, DAVID
State government official, lawyer. **Personal:** Married Michelle; children: 4. **Educ:** Moorehouse Col, BA, 1980; Howard Univ Law Sch, JD, 1984. **Career:** Kans Sen, 4th Dist, sen & pub affairs coun, currently. **Orgs:** Kans Vet Med Asn. **Business Addr:** State Senator, Kansas State Senate 4th Dist, 936 Cleveland Ave Rm 403N, Kansas City, KS 66101, **Business Phone:** (913)321-3210.

HALEY, GEORGE WILLIFORD BOYCE
Lawyer, ambassador. **Personal:** Born Aug 28, 1925, Henning, TN; son of Simon and Bertha Palmer; married Doris Elaine Moxley; children: David Barton, Anne Palmer. **Educ:** Morehouse Col, BA, high honors, 1949; Univ Ark, JD, 1952. **Career:** Kans City KS, dep city atty 1954-64; State KS, KS state senate, 1964-68; US Urban Mass Trans Admin, chief coun, 1969-73; US Info Agency, gen coun & cong liasion, 1975-76; George W Haley Prof Corp, pres; Postal Rate Comn, chmn, 1990-94, comnr, 1994-97, vice chmn, 1997-; Repub The Gambia,ambassador, 1998-01. **Orgs:** Lay-leader Methodist-KS-MO-CO Conference 1956-68; pres, Wyandotte Cty Kansas Young Republicans 1959-60; UNESCO monitoring panel US State Dept 1984; bd of directors Universal Bank 1985; bd of directors Antioch Sch of Law 1985; U S envoy to Gambia, chosen by president Clinton, 1998. **Honors/Awds:** Comments editor AR Law Review 1951-52; Outstanding Alumni Award, Univ Ark, 1988; Man of the Year, Morehouse Col, 1991; honorary chair, 2nd anniv Kunta Kinte Day, Annapolis, MD, 1988. **Special Achievements:** President Clinton named him Ambassador to the Republic of The Gambia in West Africa. **Military Serv:** USAF, sgt, 3 yrs. *

HALEY, PROF. JOHNETTA RANDOLPH
College administrator, educator, musician. **Personal:** Born Mar 19, 1923, Alton, IL; daughter of Rev John and Willye Smith; divorced; children: Karen Douglas & Michael. **Educ:** Lincoln Univ, BS, 1945; Southern Illinois Univ, Edwardsville, MM, 1972. **Career:** Educator, Col Administrator (retired); Lincoln HS, vocal & gen music teacher, 1945-48; Turner Jr HS, vocal music teacher & choral dir, 1950-55; Nipher Jr HS, vocal, gen music teacher & choral dir, 1955-71; Title I Prog Culturally Disadvantaged C, teacher black hist/music, 1966; Human Develop Corp, prog specialist, 1968; St Louis Coun Black People, interim exec dir, 1970; Sch Fine Arts, Southern Ill Univ, Edwardsville, grad res asst, 1971-72, asst prof music, 1972-77, prof music, 1982, prof emer, currently, dir, Emerita St Louis Br, chairperson, 1982-92, chairperson emerita, currently; Tex Southern Univ, visiting prof, 1977. **Orgs:** Am Asn Univ Prof; Col Music Soc; Music Educrs Nat Conf; Ill Music EducrsAsn; Nat Choral Dir Asn; Mu Phi Epsilon; Asn Teachers Educrs; Mid-WestKodaly Music Educrs; Orgn Am Kodaly Educrs; Artist Presentations Soc; PiKappa Lambda; Alpha Kappa Alpha, supreme parliamentarian; pres, Jack &Jill Inc, St Louis chap; pres, Las Amigas Social Club; Friends St LouisArt Museum; Top Ladies Distinction Inc; United Negro Col Fund Inc; UrbanLeague; co-founder, St Louis Coun Black People; St Louis Mayor's CommProtection Innocent; Pilot Counr Aide Prog St

Louis Pub Sch Delinq Stud;adv bd, Help Inc; chairperson, Ill Comm Black Concerns Her Educ; bdtrustees, Lincoln Univ, 1974-83; bd trustees, Stillman Col, 1984-; bd dir,Asn Governing bds Univs & Cols; bd dir, Links Inc; bd dir, Southern IllUniv Friends Music; bd dir, St. Louis area Red Cross. **Honors/Awds:** Woman of the Year, Greyhound Bus Corp, 1969; Distinguished Citizen Award, St Louis Argus Newspaper, 1970; Community Service Award, Las Amigas Club, 1970; Key to the City, Mayor R Hatcher, 1972; Service to Music Award, MoMusic Educrs, 1972; Service to Education Award, Kirkwood Sch Dist, 1972; Duchess of Paducah, Award Paducah, KY, 1974; Signel Hon Award for Outstand Community Service, St Louis Sentinel Newspaper, 1974; Pi Kappa Lambda Int Music Hon Soc, 1977; Distinguished Alumni Award, Lincoln Univ, 1977; Womanof Achievement/Education, KMOX radio & surburban newspaper, 1988; Urban League, Merit Award, 1994; Red Cross, Good Neighbor Award, Missouri State Cultural Diversity Award, 2001. **Special Achievements:** Initiated first Exhibit of Black-Artist at St Louis Art Museum. **Home Addr:** 1926 Bennington Common Dr, St Louis, MO 63146-2555. **Business Addr:** Chairperson Emerita, Southern Illinois University, Edwardsville, IL 62026.

HALFACRE, FRANK EDWARD
Association executive, executive director, president (organization). **Personal:** Born Jun 21, 1936, Youngstown, OH; son of Walter Melvin (Thompson) (deceased) and Consuelo Massey Stewart Velar (deceased); married Mary Tyson; children: Lyle Edward (deceased), Laura Maria Lewis, Keith Russell, Frank Earl II, Mary Consuelo, Madelyn Larue & Walter Allan. **Educ:** Youngstown State Univ, BA, telecommunications, speech, 1981. **Career:** Youngstown Park & Rec Comn, caretaker, 1955-65; Kings Rec, rec promoter, 1965; freelance Writing including Buckeye Review (Jazz & Sports); WWOW-WFIZ, disc jockey, 1965; WFAR, disc jockey, music & prog dir, 1966; WNIO & WJMO Radio, disc jockey, 1968; James Brown Prod, 1969; African Am Music Hall Fame & Museum Inc, exec dir, 1969; Starday King Rec, promotions; pub affairs & res positions, 1970-72; Stop 26/Riverbend Inc, vpres, 1992-; WRBP-FM Radio Station, operations mgr & prog dir, 1992-; Shup N Gubble Enterprises, co-founder; T BOB Inc, exec dir, 1995-; WSMZ Radio, prog dir & music dir, 1995-; Stop 26 Riverbend Inc, pres, 1998-, chmn, currently. **Orgs:** Nat Asn TV & Radio Announcers (NATRA); FORE; Black Indust & Econ Union; DAV; PTA; Lexington Players; co-founder, 7-11 Club; founder, Kleen Teens; vpres, Youngstown Sickle Cell Found; Emanon Jaguars Track Club; co-chmn & coach, Youngstown Rayen Girls Track; track coach, Rayen Boys Freshman St Edward Jr HS; Youngstown State Univ Track Club; Jack the Rapper Family; asst field dir, Goodwill Games, 1990; Disabled Am Veterans; Nat Asn Advan Colored People; Fraternal Order Record Exec; Youngstown Area Urban League. **Honors/Awds:** Man of the Year, Ohio Asn Beauticians, 1968; Disting Service Award, NATRA, 1969; Call and Post, The Voice, Jazz & Sports; Hit Kit, Jazz, Rhythm & Blues; Appreciation Day, oungstown/Hubbard Coalition; Award for Community Service, E/W Network Asn. **Military Serv:** AUS, 1951-53. **Home Addr:** 440 Tod Lane, Youngstown, OH 44504. **Business Addr:** Executive Director, African-American Music Hall of Fame & Museum Inc, PO Box 5921, Youngstown, OH 44504, **Business Phone:** (330)744-5115.

HALL, AARON
Singer. **Personal:** Born Aug 10, 1964, Bronx, NY. **Career:** Solo career, singer, 1990-; Albums: The Truth, 1993; Inside of You, 1998, Adults Only: The Final Album, 2005. **Orgs:** Part trio, Guy. **Honors/Awds:** The 3rd Annual Soul Train Music Awards, 1989-92; BET Awards 2009, 2009. **Special Achievements:** Appeared in movie, New Jack City, 1991. *

HALL, ADDIE JUNE
School administrator, educator, clergy. **Personal:** Born Apr 11, 1930, Houston, TX; daughter of Milton Gray and Aniece Clair Ware; divorced; children: Sharmane C, Dr LeRoy B Jr. **Educ:** Bethune Cookman, BS, 1955; Columbia Univ, MA, 1962; FL State Univ, PhD, 1975; Emory Univ, Cert, Theol, 1981; Candler Sch Theol, MDiv, 1999. **Career:** Agat Guam, instr, 1955-58; Escambia City Sch Bd, instr, 1959-69, curriculum coordr, 1969-71, instr coordr, 1971-73; United Methodist Church, minister, 1971-; FL State Univ, grad instr, 1973-74, instr, 1974-75; Pensacola Jr Col, asst prof, 1975-78, prof, 1980, dir adult educ & prof, 1978-90, dir Minority Recruitment & Retention, 1990-95, prof Behavioral Scis, 1991-95; evangelist, lect, auth, 1995-. **Orgs:** Kappa Delta Pi, 1972-; Phi Delta Kappa, 1974-; parliamentarian FL State Adv Coun, 1983-; adb bd Dept Corrections Reg, 1983-; NAACP; Tiger Bay Club; FL Admin, 1983; TV appearances Adult Educ, Black Hist, 1983, 1984; radio WBOP, 1983, 1984; journalist, Delta Sigma Theta, 1985-; marcher, March Dimes, Arthritis, Leukema Soc; lectr, counr, Churches Schs Inst; Nat Polit Congress Black-women, AACE, US Senate Educ Adv Coun; pres, Pensacola Chapter Links Inc, pres, chair, 1988-92; Waterfront Mission Bd, 1990; Societas Docta, Inc; Code Enforcement Bd, 1990-95; Solid Waste Environment Adv Bd, 1990-93; vpres, Bayside Optimist Club, 1991. **Honors/Awds:** Pensacola Women, 1978; Outstanding Educator, Delta Sigma Theta, 1982, 1986; Articles publ, The New Am, 1983, The Self-Concepts & Occupational Aspiration Level ABE Students, 1983; Pensacola Leadership Chamber Commerce, 1984-85; Nominee BIP Prog Chamber of Commerce, 1984-85; many certificates appreciation; certificate from Govt Graham, 1986; certificate from Senator Hawkins, serving the US Senate Educ Adv Coun, 1986; Supervisor of the Year, Col Asn Educ Off Personnel, Pensacola Junior Col, 1986; Lady Distinction, Pensacola Chapter Top Ladies Distinction, 1987; Community Service Award, & A Believer Under Achiever Award, Jordan Street SDA Church, 1987 & 1988; finalist Distinguished Black Educator Recognition Award, 1991; Resolution, State Florida; Deputy Marshall Martin Luther King Parade, 1990; Proclamation, Pensacola Junior Col, 1991; Black Women Move Award, Nat Coalition 100 Black Women Inc, 1994; Third Annual Crime Prevention Award, State Fla, Dept Corrections, 1994; Many other Awards & Certificates for Community Services, Religious & Political Services. **Special Achievements:** Author : The Wife & The Other Woman; appeared Nat TV religious programs discussing book. *

HALL, ALBERT
Baseball player. **Personal:** Born Mar 7, 1958, Birmingham, AL. **Career:** Baseball player (retired); Cleveland Indians, left fielder; Atlanta Braves, outfielder, 1981-88; Pittsburgh Pirates, outfielder, 1989.

HALL, ALFONZO LOUIS
President (Organization). **Personal:** Born Jun 20, 1954, Statesboro, GA; son of Collis and Beaulah Coleman; married Lori-Linell Hall MD, Jul 9, 1988; children: Lyndon, Jordan, Marjani. **Educ:** Indiana Wesleyan Univ, BS, sociology and psychology, 1976; General Motors Institute, advanced operation planning, 1984, manufacturing certificate, 1986, MS, 1988; Univ Pa School Bus, 1987; Univ Mich School Bus, 1989. **Career:** Gen Motors, general supv of press room and metal assembly, 1982-85, supt of manufacturing, 1985-88, engineer-in-charge of model systems, 1989-92, production mgr, Pontiac luxury car division, 1992, acting plant mgr, 1992-93, loaned exec, 1993-94, plant mgr, 1994; Int Agile Mfg LLC, pres & ceo, 2002-. **Orgs:** PNC Bank Urban Advisory Board; prog review bd, Agility Forum, Lehigh UNV; Urban League of Pittsburgh; Jr Achievement of SW Pa, Inc; exec advisory bd, Penn State McKeesport Campus; ENG SOC of Detroit; vip, Explorer Scouts of AME, Clinton Valley & Oakland County Councils; founding mem, Mission Inc; 32nd Degree Mason, Prince Hall Masonic Order. **Honors/Awds:** Man of the Year Award, Third World Black Caucus, 1978; Distinguished Citizen Award, Marion (IN) Chamber of Commerce, 1985; Outstanding Business and Professional Award, Dollars and Sense Magazine, 1992. **Business Phone:** (412)469-6501.*

HALL, ANTHONY W., JR.
Government official. **Personal:** Born Sep 16, 1944, Houston, TX; son of Anthony William Hall Sr and Quintanna William Hall Alliniece; married Carolyn Joyce Middleton; children: Anthony William & Ursula Antoinette. **Educ:** Howard Univ, BA, 1967; Thurgood Marshall Sch law, JD, 1982. **Career:** Harris County Comn Bray Houston, asst, 1971-72; Houston City Council, 1979; Metropolitan Transit Authorty, chmn, 1990; Williamson Gardner Hall & Wiensenthal, partner; Jackson Walker LLP, partner; State Tex, state rep; Coastal Corp, dir, 1999-01; City Houston, city coun mem & atty, 1998-04, chief administrative officer, 2004-; Houston Endowment Inc, dir,currently; El Paso Corp, dir, currently. **Orgs:** Rules Budget & Fin Coms, Tex Dem Party; state dem exec committee man Senatorial Dist 13; del, 1972, 1974, 1976, 1980; Dem Nat Conv; Kappa Alpha Psi, Sigma Pi Phi; Natl Municipal League; brd mgrs, YMCA Houston; Masons, Shriner, OES, Houston Bus & Prof Mens Club; brd dir, vpres, pres, Riverside Lions Club; exec bd mem, United Negro Col Fund, Gr Zion Baptist Church; Nat Bar Assn; Tex Bar Assn; Am Bar Assn; Houston Bar Assn; Houston Lawyers Assn; chmn, Boule Found. **Honors/Awds:** Fifth Wards Enrichment Prog Heart Houston; Black Achiever Award, YMCA, 1972; Citation for Outstanding Comn Serv, Natl Assn Advan Colored People, 1972; Cotton Hook of the Year Award, ILA Local872, 1973. **Special Achievements:** First Black & Minority Chairman of Metropolitan Transit Authority. **Military Serv:** AUS, capt, 1967-71. **Business Addr:** Chief Administrative Officer, Attorney, City Houston, PO Box 1562, Houston, TX 77251-1562.*

HALL, ARSENIO
Television talk show host, actor, comedian. **Personal:** Born Feb 2, 1955, Cleveland, OH; son of Annie Hall and Fred Hall; children: Arsenio Jr. **Educ:** Ohio Univ, Athens, OH; Kent State Univ, BA, gen speech, 1977. **Career:** Actor, currently; Stand-up comedian; films: Coming to Am, 1988, Harlem Nights, 1989; TV: "The Half Hour Comedy Hour, host", 1983; "Thicke of the Night", 1984; "The New Love, Am Style", 1985; "Motown Revue", 1985; "Solid Gold', 1987; "The Late Show', host, 1987; "The Arsenio Hall Show, host & exec producer", 1989-93; 'The Proud Family Movie", 2005; "Scooby-Doo! Pirates Ahoy!", 2006; "The Tonight Show with Johnny Carson"; Movie:"Amazon Women on the Moon". **Business Addr:** Actor, M L Management Associates Inc, 1740 Broadway, New York, NY 10019-4315, **Business Phone:** (212)333-5500.

HALL, BENJAMIN LEWIS
Lawyer, educator. **Personal:** Born Mar 13, 1956, Laurens, SC; son of Benjamin Lewis II and Lilease Rogers; married Saundra Turner, Apr 18, 1981; children: Benjamin Lewis IV & Zachary Bass. **Educ:** Univ Southern Calif, BA, cum laude, 1977; Duke Divinity Sch, MDiv, 1979; Rheinische Friedrich-19Wilheims Univ, Bonn, Fed Fulbright Rep Ger Scholar-19Deutscher Akademischer Austausch Dienst, 1982; Duke Univ Grad Sch, Phd, 1985; Harvard Law Sch, JD, 1986. **Career:** Vinson & Elkins LLP, trial lawyer, spec coun, 1986-92; Univ Houston Law Ctr, adj prof law, 1987-; S Tex CLG Law, adj prof law, 1991; City Houston, city atty, 1992-95; O'Quinn & Laminack, atty, 1995-2000; Hall Law Firm LLP, partner, currently; Bell Street Chapel, minister, currently. **Orgs:** Fel, Ger Res, Bonn Universitat, 1980; fel, James B Duke Grad, 1980-81; fel, Duke Black Grad, 1979-80; fel, Black Doctoral Dissertation, 1982-83. **Honors/Awds:** Rockefellar Scholar Award, 1977-78; Duke Merit Scholar Award, 1977-79; Benjamin E Mays Scholar Award, 1978-79; DADD Scholar to Germany, 1981-82;Shell Fellow to Lambarene, Gabon, Africa, 1982-83; Merrill Griswold Scholar, 1986; Outstanding Texan Award, 1993, 1995 & 1999. **Special Achievements:** Bar admissions: TEX, South District of TEX, Fifth Circuit Court ofAppeals, DIS, USS Supreme Court. **Business Addr:** Partner, The Hall Law Firm LLP, 4310 Yoakum Blvd, Houston, TX 77006, **Business Phone:** (713)942-9600.

HALL, BRIAN EDWARD
Executive. **Personal:** Born May 5, 1958, Cleveland, OH; son of William D and Virginia; married Susan Reed, Mar 14, 1987; children: 3. **Educ:** Univ Cincinnati, BBA, 1980; Baldwin-Wallace Col, MBA, 1987. **Career:** Industrial Inventory Solutions LLC, chmn, chief exec officer & owner, currently. **Orgs:** Founder, Tremont Elem Sch Adv Group; co-chmn, Comn Econ Inclusion; secy & governance chmn, Rock & Roll Hall Fame; Pres's Coun Found; Greater Cleveland Partnership; Cleveland-Cuyahoga County Port Authority. **Honors/Awds:** Outstanding Men of America, 1982, 1983; Kappa Alpha Psi Award Entrepreneurship, 1987, Outstanding Achievement Award, 1989; Minority Business Exec Prog scholarship, 1988; nominee for business excellence, Crain's Cleveland Bus, 1989; R H Adler Community Leadership Award, Am Jewish comt; Volunteer of the Year, Leadership Cleveland; Supplier of the Year Community Serv, Ford Motor Co. **Home Addr:** 16260 S Pk Blvd, Shaker Heights, OH 44120, **Home Phone:** (216)751-1023. **Business Addr:** Chairman, Chief Executive Officer, Industrial Transport Inc, 2330 E 79th St, Cleveland, OH 44104, **Business Phone:** (216)881-5052.

HALL, CHARLES HAROLD
Administrator. **Personal:** Born Mar 10, 1934, Sapelo Island, GA; son of Charles and Beulah; divorced; children (previous marriage): Ronald Charles, Reginald Harold; married Margaret, 1979; children: Chuckie, Lori, Reginald, Ronald. **Educ:** Morehouse Col, BS, 1955; DT Watson Sch Psychiat, Dipl, phys therapy, 1956; Air Univ, USAF, Cert, 1957. **Career:** VA Hosp, supvr phys therap, 1961-69; Therapeutic Serv Inc, pres & cheif exec officer, 1970-; Total Living Care Inc, adminr, 1976-; Dev Corp, Jefferson Twshp, OH, treas 1970-; Dayton Metropolitan Housing Authority, 1985-. **Orgs:** Nat Asn Advancement Colored People, 1960-; secy, Chap Am Phys Therap Asn, 1967-; bd dir, BS Am, 1972-. **Honors/Awds:** Super Performance Award, VA Hosp; Outstanding Service Award, Am Phys Therap Asn; Delta Sigma Theta Business Man of the Year Award, 1992; National Business League Award, 1992; Robert G Dicus Award, pvt prac phys therap, 1992. **Special Achievements:** First black Cheif & chmn OH Chapter Am Phys Therap Asn, 1967-69; first black treas pvt pract; first black pres pvt prac sect; First Black To Win most prestigious award for private practice physical therapist, 1992; inductee, Order of Military Medical Merit. **Military Serv:** USAF, first lt, 1957-61; USAFR, lt col, 1977-; AUS, med dept, currently; numerous serv medals & awards. **Business Addr:** President, Prof Therapeut Serv Inc, 45 Riverside Dr, Dayton, OH 45405.*

HALL, CHRISTINE C. IIJIMA
College administrator. **Personal:** Born Mar 31, 1953, Colorado Springs, CO; daughter of Roger Leroy and Fumiko. **Educ:** Los Angeles Harbor Community Col, Wilmington, CA, AA, 1972; Calif State Univ, Long Beach, CA, BA, 1974; Univ Calif, Los Angeles, Los Angeles, CA, MA, 1975, PhD, social psychology, 1980. **Career:** Univ Calif, Irvine, Irvine, CA, stud affairs officer, 1979-81, counseling psychologist, 1981-86, dir, stud develop, 1983-86; Am Psychol Asn, Wash, DC, dir, off ethnic minority affairs, 1989-96; Ariz State Univ W, Phoenix, AZ, assoc vprovost, 1989-96; Asian Am Psychol Asn, pres, 1995-97; Glendale Community Col, assoc dean, 1998-00; Maricopa Community Col, dir employee serv, 2000-. **Orgs:** Membership chair, bd dir, Asian Am Psychol Asn; Asn Black Psychologist; Am Psychol Asn; Japanese Am Citizens League; bd dirs, Am Cancer Society, Glendale Chap, 1990-; bd, Planned Parenthood of Northern & Cent Ari; bd, Ariz Humanities Coun; bd governors, State Bar Ariz; mem comt, Asian Pacific Am Studies prog. **Honors/Awds:** Outstanding Alumna, Calif State Univ Long Beach, 1987; Outstanding Black Staff, Univ Calif, Irvine, 1985. **Special Achievements:** first female pres Asian Am Psychol Asn, 1995-1997. **Business Phone:** (480)731-8000.*

HALL, DANA ERIC
Football player. **Personal:** Born Jul 8, 1969, Bellflower, CA; married Carrie; children: Johnathan & Dana Jr. **Educ:** Univ Wash, polit sci, 1992. **Career:** Football player(retired); San Francisco

49ers, defensive back, 1992-94; Cleveland Browns, 1995; Jacksonville Jaguars, safety, 1996-97.

HALL, DARNELL
Athlete. **Personal:** Born Sep 26, 1971, Detroit, MI; son of Nelson. **Career:** Athlete, 1991-; US Olympic Team, track & field, 1992. **Honors/Awds:** Olympic Games, Gold Medalist, 4X400 relay, Barcelona, 1992; Gold Medal, World Indoor Championships, 1995.

HALL, DAVID
School administrator, educator. **Personal:** Born May 26, 1950, Savannah, GA; son of Ethel Glover Hall and Levi Hall; married Marilyn Braithwaite, Jun 23, 1990; children: Rahsaan, Sakile & Kiamsha. **Educ:** Kans State Univ, BA, polit sci, 1972; Univ Okla, MA, human rels, 1975, JD,1978; Harvard Law Sch, LLM, 1985, SJD, 1988. **Career:** Fed Trade Commun, staff atty, 1978-80; Univ Miss Law Sch, asst prof law, 1980-83; Univ Okla Law Sch, assoc prof law, 1983-85; NE Univ Sch Law, assoc prof law, 1985-88, assoc dean & prof, 1988-98, provost & sr vpres, 1998-2002, prof law, 2003-; Sabbatical res, S Africa, 1992. **Orgs:** Nat Conf Black Lawyers, 1978-80; Okla Bar Asn, 1978-; atty, Fed Trade Commun, Chicago, IL, 1978-80; Am Bar Asn; bd dirs, Legal Serv Corp, 2003. **Honors/Awds:** Outstanding Senior Award, Okla Bar Asn, 1978; Professor of the Year, Oxford Miss Branch, Nat Asn Advan Colored People; Floyd Calvert Law Faculty Award, Univ Okla Law Sch 1984; Order of the Coif, Univ of Okla LawSch Chap, 1984; Robert D Klein, Northeastern Univ; Floyd Calvert Law Faculty, Univ Okla; Outstanding KS State Student; Massachusetts Black Lawyers Outstanding Contribution to the Legal Profession Award, 1993; Outstanding Dean of the Year, Nat Asn Pub Interest Lawyers, 1997; Nat Conference of Community and Justice Humanitarian Award, 1999. **Special Achievements:** Published numerous articles including Fed Trade Commun, staff atty, 1978-80; Univ Miss Law Sch, asst prof law,1980-83; Univ Okla Law Sch, assoc prof law, 1983-85; Northeastern Univ Sch Law, assoc prof law, 1985-88, assoc dean & prof, 1988-98, provost & sr vpres, 1998-2002, prof law, 2003-; Sabbatical res, S Africa, 1992.g "Legal Education & the Twenty-first Century: Our Calling to Fulfill", 1997; "The Law School's Role in Cultivating a Commitment to Pro Bono", 1998; "Raising the Bar: A Guide to Transform the Legal Profession," 1998; "The Challenge of Black Leadership in the Twenty-First Century", 1999; "Giving Birth to a Racially Just Society in the Twenty-first Century", 1999. **Business Addr:** Professor of Law, Northeastern University School of Law, 39 Cargill Hall, 400 Huntington Ave, Boston, MA 02072, **Business Phone:** (617)373-3668.

HALL, DAVID ANTHONY, JR.
Dentist. **Personal:** Born Sep 19, 1945, San Francisco, CA; married Pamela C Hall; children: David III & Darryl C. **Educ:** Sothern Univ, BS, 1967; Meharry Med Sch, DDS, 1972. **Career:** Pvt pract, dentist, 1973-; Health Power Assoc, dentist, 1972-73. **Orgs:** Louisiana State Bd of Dentistry, 1994-. **Honors/Awds:** ADA, NDA pres, Pelican State Dental Assn, 1980; LDA 6th Dist Dental Assn; Capital & City Dental Assn, Scottlandville Jaycees; Baton Rouge Alumni, Kappa Alpha Psi; Mt Zion 1st Bapt; Sothern Univ Alumni Assn; life mem Meharry Med Coll Alumni Assn. **Home Addr:** 1704 Convention St, Baton Rouge, LA 70802, **Home Phone:** (225)293-8434. **Business Addr:** Dentist, 1137 Brookhollow Dr, Baton Rouge, LA 70810, **Business Phone:** (225)752-6925.

HALL, DAVID MCKENZIE
Educator. **Personal:** Born Jun 21, 1928, Gary, IN; son of Alfred M and Grace Elizabeth Crimiel; married Jacqueline V Branch, Apr 30, 1960; children: Glen D & Gary D. **Educ:** Howard Univ, BA, bus, 1951, MSEd, soc, 1966; NC Agr & State Univ, Greensboro, NC; MIT, Cambridge MA, cert, 1976; Kennedy-19 Western Univ, PhD, bus, 2002. **Career:** Scott AFB IL USAF, deputy base cmd, 1974-75, base cmd, 1975-76; Air Force Logistics Cmd, USAF, deputy cmptrlr, 1976-77, cmptrlr, 1977-83; Delco-Remy Div Gen Motors, dir data processing, 1983-84; Electr Data Systems Corp, acct mgr, 1985-88; Electronic Data Systems, Saginaw, Mich, regional mgr, 1988-93; N wood Univ, prof, 1993-97; Saginaw Valley State Univ, Col Bus & Mgt, executivec-in-residence, currently. **Orgs:** Mem, Air Force asn, 1960-83; mem, Boy Scouts Am, 1942-; bd mem, Saginaw Community Found; Life mem, NAACP; Kapa Alpha Psi; mem, Community Affairs Comt, 1988-; exec bd mem, St. Mary's Hosp, 1989-93; St. Mary's Advisory Bd, 1997-2003. **Honors/Awds:** Key to city Gary, Ind, 1981; hon citizen city of E St Louis, 1976; crtfd systms prof Assn Systms Mgt, 1984; crtfd cost anlyst Assc Anal, 1983;Computers in Combat, AF Comptroller Magazine, 1967. **Military Serv:** USAF, brigadier gen; Distinguised Serv Medal, 1983; Legion of Merit, 1974; Meritorious Serv Medal, 1971, 1976. **Home Addr:** 49 W Hannum Blvd, Saginaw, MI 48602-1938, **Home Phone:** (989)791-1192. **Business Addr:** Executive in Residence, Saginaw Valley State University, 7400 Bay Rd, Saginaw, MI 48710-0001, **Business Phone:** (989)964-6076.

HALL, DELILAH RIDLEY
School administrator. **Personal:** Born Aug 23, 1953, Baton Rouge, LA; daughter of Samuel Sr and Mamie Jones; married Holmes G Hall Sr; children: Holmes, Byron, Marsha, Michael & Monica. **Educ:** Jarvis Christian Col, BS, 1975; E Tex State Univ, MS, 1977. **Career:** E Tex State Univ, coordr, 1975-77; Long view Independent Sch Dist, ind instr, 1978; Jarvis Christian Col, Hawkins, TX, upward bound prog counr, 1978, asst dean acad affairs, 1980, asst pres, 1981-, interim vpres, 1991-; Title III coordr & assist pres, pres, Church Finance Coun, currently. **Orgs:** JCC/SCI Nat Alumni & Ex-Stud Asn, 1975; secy, Hawkins Elem PTA, 1985-87; Zeta Phi Beta Sorority Inc. **Honors/Awds:** Award, Alpha Kappa Mu. **Home Addr:** PO Box 37, Hawkins, TX 75765. **Business Addr:** Title III Coordinator, Jarvis Christian College, PO Box 1470, Hawkins, TX 75765-1470.*

HALL, DELORES
Actor. **Personal:** Born in Kansas City, KS; married Michael Goodstone. **Educ:** Harbor Jr Col, LACC. **Career:** Actress & singer; Broadway Show: Your Arms Too Short To Box With God; Godspell; Hair; The Best Little Whorehouse in Texas, 1982; night club performer; TV Series: "Diagnosis Murder", 1993-95; Films: Scrooged, 1988; Leap of Faith, 1992; Lethal Weapon 3, 1992. **Honors/Awds:** Antoinette Perry Award, Best Supporting Actress in a Musical, 1977; Tony Award, Best Actress, 1977; Toro Award, Young Woman Am; nominated for Joseph Jefferson Award for Actress in a Revue for "Street Dreams", 1983. **Business Addr:** Actress, c/o William Morris Agency, 151 El Camino Dr, Beverly Hills, CA 90212, **Business Phone:** (310)859-4000.*

HALL, DR. DOLORES BROWN
School administrator, educator. **Personal:** Born in Brooklyn, NY; married Rev Kirkwood M; children: Alexander Chapman. **Educ:** Brooklyn Hosp Sch Nursing, RN, dipl, 1962; Long Island Univ, BS, 1966; Adelphi Univ, MS, 1969; NY Univ, PhD, 1977. **Career:** Medgar Evers Col NIMH Res Proj, proj dir, 1975-77; Del State Col, assocprof, 1977-79; Health & Human Serv, NIMH St Elizabeth Hosp, dir nursinged, 1979-84; Edison State Col, Nursing Prog, assoc dean & dir, 1984; Gerontological Soc Am, fel, 1985; Seton Hall Univ, asst prof, currently. **Orgs:** Workshop leader Delaware Home Aged, 1976; bd dir, Good Shepard Home Health Aide Prog, 1977-79; Mental Health Plan Task Force, 1978-79; USPHS Cont EdReview Comn, 1980-83; consult, Charles Drew Neighborhood Health Ctr. **Business Addr:** Assistant Professor, Seton Hall University, 400 S Orange Ave, South Orange, NJ 07079, **Business Phone:** (973)761-2152.

HALL, EDDIE, JR.
Automotive executive. **Career:** Briarwood Ford, owner & pres, currently. **Business Phone:** (734)429-5478.*

HALL, ELLIOTT SAWYER
Lawyer, automotive executive. **Personal:** Born Jan 1, 1938?, Detroit, MI; son of Odis and Ethel B; married Shirley Ann Robinson; children: Fred, Lannis & Tiffany. **Educ:** Wayne State Univ, Detroit, Mich, BA, polit sci, 1961, JD, 1963. **Career:** Govt Wayne Co, Mich, Detroit, Mich, chief asst prosecutor; Dykema Gossett Spencer Goodnow & Trigg, Detroit Mich, law partner; Ford Motor Co, Dearborn Mich, lawyer, lobbyist, vpres govt affairs, 1987; Georgetown Univ, bd mem; Clark Atlanta Univ, bd mem; Dykema Gossett PLLC, atty. **Orgs:** Pres, Detroit Metrop Bar Asn; pres, Wolverine Bar Asn; bd mem, Georgetown Univ; Clark Atlanta Univ; chmn, Joint Ctr Polit & Econ Studies, currently; bd mem, Cong Black Caucus Found; chmn bd dirs, Constituency Africa, 2006-. **Honors/Awds:** Distinguished Alumnus Award, Wayne State Univ. **Special Achievements:** First African American Chief Assistant Prosecutor for Wayne County, Michigan; First African American Corporation Counsel for the City of Detroit.

HALL, DR. ETHEL HARRIS
Educator, vice president (organization). **Personal:** Born Feb 23, 1928, Decatur, AL; daughter of Harry Harris; married Alfred James Hall Sr; children: Alfred Jr & Donna Hall Mitchell. **Educ:** Ala A&M Univ, BS, 1948; Univ Chicago, MA, 1953; Univ Ala, DSW, 1979. **Career:** Educator (retired), Administrator; Jefferson City Bd Educ, teacher, 1955-66; Neighborhood Youth Corps, dir, 1966-71; Univ Montevallo, assoc prof, 1971-78; Univ Ala, assoc prof, 1978-90, assoc prof emer, 1990-; Ala State Bd Educ, vpres, 1987-. **Orgs:** Pres, Ala Personnel & Guid Asn, 1972-73; fel Int Study Dept State Jamaica,W Indies, 1975; pres, Ala Conf Child Care, 1977; Ala Conf Soc Work, 1981-82; Ala Asn Womens's Clubs, 1984-88; Social Work Bd Examrs; Ala State Bd Educ, 1987-. **Honors/Awds:** Leadership Award, Ala Personnel & Guid Asn, 1974, 1976, 1977; Alumus of the Year, Ala A&M Univ, 1975; Serv Award, Ala Conf Social Work, 1982; Hall of Fame, Ala Social Work, 2005. **Business Addr:** Vice President, Alabama State Board of Education, PO Box 302101, Montgomery, AL 36130-2101.*

HALL, EVELYN ALICE (EVELYN MANNING)
Physician. **Personal:** Born Oct 31, 1945, Paterson, NJ; married Dr Macy G Hall Jr. **Educ:** Howard Univ, BS, 1967; Howard Univ Col Med, MD, 1973; Columbia Univ, MPH, 1977. **Career:** Roosevelt Hosp, 1974-75; Columbia Univ, fel pediatric ambulatory care, 1975-77; Rockville Ctr Group Health Assoc, physician chief, 1977-. **Orgs:** Cand Am Acad Pediatrics; Alpha Omega Alpha Med 1973; bd, Elgible Am Pediat Bds; DC Med Soc, 1977; Howard Univ Med Alumni. **Business Addr:** 6111 Executive Blvd, Rockville, MD.

HALL, EVERETT
Executive, fashion designer. **Educ:** Howard Univ. **Career:** Everett Hall Designs, founder, owner & designer, 1982-. **Special Achievements:** Nominated as a finalist for the Cutty Sark Award; Has been featured on CNN Style, E! Television, FOX Philadelphia & Main Floor. **Business Addr:** Designer, Owner, Everett Hall Designs, Chevy Chase Pavillion, 5345 Wisconsin Ave NW, Washington, DC 20015, **Business Phone:** (202)362-0191.*

HALL, FRANCES WHITE
Executive. **Career:** Hall Commun Inc, pres & chief exec officer, currently. **Orgs:** Knoxville Area Chamber Partnership; City Knoxville Equal Bus Opportunity Bd; HUD Minority Bus Coun; Univ Tenn Chancellor's Assocs. **Business Addr:** President, Chief Executive Officer, Hall Communications Inc, 1515 E Magnolia Ave Suite 301, Knoxville, TN 37917, **Business Phone:** (865)521-6500.

HALL, FRED, III
Financial manager, government official. **Personal:** Born Feb 9, 1945, St Louis, MO; married Pattie M Burdett; children: Fred IV & Rose M. **Educ:** Sinclair Col, AS Engg Tech, 1968; Univ Dayton, BS Engg Tech, 1976; Wright State Univ, MBA, 1992. **Career:** Delco Prod Div GMC, lab tech, 1968-73, sales coordr, 1973-78, sales engr,1978-85, mkt analyst, 1985-; Greene Co Brd Elections, chmn, currently. **Orgs:** Bd mem, Camp Fire Girls, 1975-77; city comnr, City of Xenia, 1977,81-; sec Xenia Wilber force Dem Club, 1979-82; pres, Wilberforce Xenia Optimist Club, 1981-82; chmn, brd zoning appeals City Xenia, 1982-83, 1985; vpres, Chi Lambda Chap Alpha Phi Alpha, 1984-85; pres, Chi Lambda Chapter, Alpha Phi Alpha, 1986-87; deputy mayor, City Xenia 1984-; plng comn, chmn, City of Xenia, 1984, 1992-93; pres, city comn, City of Xenia, 1989-90; bd mem, Boys and Girls Clubs, 1992-93. **Honors/Awds:** Award for Excellence in Community Activities, General Motors Corp, 1979;Citizen of the Year, Omega Psi Phi Fraternity, 1992. **Business Addr:** Chairman, Greene County Board Elections, 651 Dayton Xenia Rd, Xenia, OH 45385, **Business Phone:** (937)562-7470.*

HALL, HANSEL CRIMIEL
Executive. **Personal:** Born Mar 12, 1929, Gary, IN; son of Alfred M (deceased) and Grace Eliz (deceased); divorced; children: Grace Jean. **Educ:** Ind Univ, BS, 1953; Indust Col Armed Forces, nat security mgt cert, 1971; Blackstone Sch Law, B Laws, 1982. **Career:** US Dept Housing & Urban Develop, prog specialist, 1969-73, dir, FH & EO div Minn, 1973-75, div Ind, 1975-79; US Dept Interior, dir off human resources, 1979-88; Korean War Veterans Educ Grant Corp, chief financing officer; Crimiel Commun Inc, pres. **Orgs:** Pres, Crimiel Ltd Consult, 1979-; pres, MN-Dakota Conf; golden heritage mem, Nat Advan Asn Colored People, 1981-86; pres & bd dirs, Riverview Towers Homeowners Asn, 1985-87; life mem, Ind Univ Alumni Asn; Omega Psi Phi; life mem, Veterans Foreign Wars; elected bd, Korean War Veterans Asn, 1992-95; pres, Minn State Asn Parliamentarians, 1997-99; Reserve Officers Asn. **Honors/Awds:** Distinguished Toastmaster Award, Toastmasters Int, 1986; Outstanding Leadership Award, Nat Advan Asn Colored People Region IV, 1986. **Special Achievements:** US Parliamentary delegate to Russia & Czechoslovakia, 1992. **Military Serv:** USF Reserve, lt col, 25 yrs; United Nations Service Medal. **Business Addr:** President, Crimiel Communications Inc, PO Box 14648, Minneapolis, MN 55414-0648.*

HALL, HAROLD L
Executive. **Career:** Delta Enterprises Inc, Greenville MS, chief exec, chief operating officer. **Business Addr:** Chief Operating Officer, Delta Enterprises Inc, 819 Main St, Greenville, MS 38701, **Business Phone:** (601)335-5291.

HALL, HORATHEL
Educator, artist. **Personal:** Born Dec 3, 1926, Houston, TX; married Howard D; children: Kenneth A, Admerle J, Horace D. **Educ:** Prairie View A&M Univ, BA, 1948; NM Highlands, Las Vegas, MFA, 1962; W African States Art Res, fel, HISD, 1975. **Career:** Worthing High Sch, art teacher & dept chmn, 1951-80; Tes Southern Univ, art prof, 1964-79; Houston Comm Col, art prof, 1975-77; Adept New Am Folk Gallery, crafts consult, 1977-79; Eliza Johnson Home Elderly, crafts consult, 1977-79; Houston Independent Sch Dist, art teacher & artist, 1980-. **Orgs:** Affil mem, Nat Art Educrs Asn, 1951-80; VP Contemp Handweavers Houston, 1968-69; secy, E Sunny Side Civic Club Houston, 1970-80; secy, Orgn Black Artists, 1975-80; treas, Houston Art Educrs Asn, 1976-80; affil mem, Nat Conf Artists, 1976-80; spec publ, Black Artist Generation, 1977; The Arts & the Rural & Isolated Elderly Univ, KY, 1980. **Honors/Awds:** Outstanding Service Award, Tex Southern Univ; J. Eugene Grigsby Jr Award, Nat Art Educ Asn, 1984. **Special Achievements:** Published "Contemporary Concepts of the Liberian Rice Bag Weave", vol 27 no 2, Contemporary Handweavers of Tex Inc, 1975; Arrowmont Scholar, Pi Beta Alumnae Club, Gatlingburg, Tenn, 1980. **Business Addr:** Artist, Houston Independent School District West, 9215 Scott St, Houston, TX 77051.*

HALL, IRA D.
Executive director, president (organization), chief executive officer. **Educ:** Stanford Univ, BS, elec eng; Stanford Grad Sch Bus, MBA. **Career:** Executive director, President (Organization), Chief executive officer (retired); LF Rothschild, Unterberg, Tow-

bin Inc, sr vpres; IBM Corp, dir intl oper; IBM, treas, 1990-98; IBM World Trade Corp, controller; IBM WTC Ins Corp, chmn & chief exec officer; Texaco, Alliance Mgt, gen mgr, treasurer, 1998-01; Utendahl Capital Mgt LP, pres & chief exec officer, 2002-04; Pepsi Bottling Group Inc, bd dir; Reynolds & Reynolds Co, bd dir; Publishers Clearing House, bd dir; TECO Energy Inc, bd dir; Imagistics Int Inc, bd dir; Praxair Inc, dir, 2004-. **Orgs:** immediate past chmn, Exec Leadership Coun, 2000; bd dir, Jackie Robinson Found; governer, US Postal Serv Audit Comt; mem dean adv coun, Stanford Sch Bus. **Special Achievements:** Named as one of Black Enterprise's 25 Hottest Black Mgrs, 1988. *

HALL, JACK L.
Administrator. **Personal:** Born Feb 11, 1941, Cairo, IL; son of J K and Clemmie Lee; married Effie D, Jun 27, 1959; children: Marvin D, Marilyn R Goldwire. **Educ:** Lansing Community Col, assocs, criminal justice, 1961; Mich State Univ, BA, criminal justice, 1979; W Mich Univ, MPA, 1992. **Career:** Administrator (retired); Benton Township Police Dept, patrolman, 1962-67; Mich Dept State Police, capt, 1967-92; Mich Dept Corrections, internal affairs mgr, 1992-02. **Special Achievements:** The first African-American to become a Michigan state trooper in 1967. **Home Addr:** 11475 Upton Rd, Grand Ledge, MI 48837, **Home Phone:** (517)627-5355. *

HALL, LT. GEN. JAMES REGINALD
Military leader, administrator. **Personal:** Born Jul 15, 1936, Anniston, AL; son of James Reginald Sr and Evelyn Dodson; married Helen Kerr, Jun 25, 1960; children: Sheila A, James R III & Cheryl D. **Educ:** Morehouse Col, Atlanta, Ga, BA, 1957; Shippensburg State Univ, Shippensburg, Pa, MS, pub admin, 1975; Harvard Univ, Sr Managers Prgm, 1988. **Career:** Military leader (retired), trustee; AUS, lt gen; mem, Atlanta Committee for the Olympic Games, 1996; Morehouse Col, Campus Opers, vpres, Bd Trustees, asst secy, currently. **Orgs:** Alpha Phi Alpha Fraternity, 1954-; Prince Hall Mason, 1962-; pres, Nat Alumni Asn, Morehouse Col; bd trustee, Morehouse Col. **Honors/Awds:** Hon Degree, Morehouse Col, 1987; Outstanding Service Award, Drug Enforcement Agency, Anti-Drugs Dept. **Military Serv:** AUS, lt gen, 1957-; Distinguished Service Medal, Legion of Merit, Bronze Star, Meritorious Serv Medal, Combat Infantryman's Badge, Parachute Badge. **Home Addr:** 115 N Dr, Fairburn, GA 30213. **Business Addr:** Assistant Secretary, Board of Trustees, Morehouse College, 830 Westview Dr SW, Atlanta, GA 30314, **Business Phone:** (404)681-2800.

HALL, DR. JARVIS
Administrator. **Career:** NC Cent Univ, Dept Polit Sci, chmn & prof, currently. **Orgs:** Dir, Acad Community Serv Learning Pro.

HALL, JEFFREY MAURICE
Surgeon. **Personal:** Born Oct 31, 1958, Ypsilanti, MI; son of James and Maureen; married Janet R Hall, Aug 24, 1987; children: Elliott Joshua. **Educ:** Univ Mich, BS, 1981; Univ Mich Med Sch, MD, 1985. **Career:** Wayne State Univ fel; Hand Surgery Assocs Mich, PC, surgeon, currently; Providence Hosp; St John Hosp & Med Ctr; St John Macomb Hosp. **Orgs:** Am Med Asn, 1991; Am Asn Surg of the Hand, 1995; Am Col Surgeons fel, 1996; Am Bd Med Specialties Bd Surg. **Honors/Awds:** Candidate for Chevron Scholar, Univ Mich, 1979; Citizen of the Week, WWJ Radio, 1995. **Special Achievements:** Multiple talks on Cumulative Trauma disorders. **Business Addr:** Medical Doctor, Surgeon, Hand Surgery Associates of Michigan PC, 19701 Vernier Rd Suite 210, Harper Woods, MI 48225, **Business Phone:** (313)640-7999.*

HALL, DR. JESSE J.
Educator. **Personal:** Born Dec 16, 1938, Clover, SC; married Nancy Thorne; children: Nathaniel Craig & Yoland Yevette. **Educ:** State Teachers Col, Fayetteville, NC, BS, 1962; Univ NV, MEd, 1970; Univ San Francisco, attended 1984. **Career:** Educator(retired); Washoe Co Sch Dist, Orvis Ring & Sierra Vista Schs, prin, 1971-72, Glen Duncan Sch, prin, 1972-80, Lloyd Diedrichsen Sch, prin, 1981-84. **Orgs:** Int Reading Asn, 1962; Phi Delta Kappa, 1968; NV State Textbook Comn, 1969-79; Nat Asn Elem Sch Prin, 1971; NV Asn Sch Admn, 1972; Equal Opportunity Bd, UNR, 1980; bd dir, panel chmn, United Way NV, 1972-78; Nev Parents Teachers Asn. **Honors/Awds:** Man of the year, Second Bapt Church, Reno, 1978; Distinguished Service Award, NAACP, 1978; Dist Service Award, Negro Bus & Prof Women's Asn, 1980. **Special Achievements:** First black teacher in the district; first black administrator. **Business Addr:** Principal, Lloyd Diedrichsen School, 1735 Del Rosa Way, Sparks, NV 89431.*

HALL, JOEL
Artistic director. **Personal:** Born Apr 20, 1949, Chicago, IL; son of Louis and Emma Lee. **Educ:** Northeastern Ill Univ, BA, socio, 1972. **Career:** Dance: "Nightwalker", 1978; "Now You See It, Now You Don't", 1998; "El Gato Negro", 1992; "The Crossing", 1997; "Y-2 Day", 1999; Joel Hall Dancers & Center, artistic dir, currently, prin choreographer, chief instr, 1974-. **Honors/Awds:** City of Chicago Gay & Lesbian Hall of Fame, 1993; Katherine Dunham Award, 1997; Black Theatre Alliance Chicago Award of Merit, 1999, Best Choreography, 1997, 2000; YMCA Metropolitan Chicago, Black & Hispanic Achievers Award, 2001; Bailiwick Repertory, Larry Osburn Trailblazers Award, 2002. **Business Addr:** Artistic Director, Chief Instructor, Joel Hall Dancers & Center, 1511 W Berwyn Ave, Chicago, IL 60640, **Business Phone:** (773)293-0900.

HALL, DR. JULIA GLOVER
College teacher. **Personal:** Born in Philadelphia, PA; daughter of Harold Heywood and Isabel Dickson; married William Francis Jr; children: William Francis III (deceased) & Michael David. **Educ:** Temple Univ, Philadelphia, PA, BA, 1968; Wharton Sch, Univ Pa, Philadelphia, PA, MA, 1969; Univ Pa, Philadelphia, PA, PhD, 1973; Harvard Univ, attended 1978. **Career:** Dept Justice, Gov's Justice Comn, Harrisburg, PA, project evaluator, 1974-79; Drexel Univ, Philadelphia, PA, assoc prof, psychol & sociol, 1982-91, prof sociol, 1991-; State Correctional Inst, Graterford, PA, coordr Concerned Srs/Gray Panthers, 1986-; Pa Bd Probation & Parole, trainer, 1988-; Pa Family Caregiver Support Prog, Gerontological Soc Am, prin investigator & project dir, 1988; Nat Inst Corrections, consult, 1989-; US Dept Health & Human Servs, prin investigator & project dir, 1989-91. **Orgs:** Southern Home Servs; pres, Pa Asn Criminal Justice Educrs, 1990-93; convenor, Gray Panther chap, Graterford, PA, 1989-; pres, Pa Prison Soc, 1996-; chairperson, Victim Offender Reconcilation Prog Graterford; Pa Legis Adv Comt. **Honors/Awds:** Distinguished Service Award, Boy Scouts Am, 1964; Woodrow Wilson Fellow, 1968-; Nat Sci Found Fel, Univ Pa, 1968-73; Legion of Honor, Chapel of The Four Chaplains Award, 1976; Lindback Award for Distinguished Teaching, 1979; Drexel Univ Faculty Scholar Research Award, 1989. **Special Achievements:** Producer: TV prog Criminal Justice Today, Correcting our Elders, videotape documentary. **Business Addr:** Professor of Psychology, Sociology & Anthropology, Criminology, Drexel University, Department of Psychology/Sociology, 3141 Chestnut St PSA 220, Philadelphia, PA 19104-2816, **Business Phone:** (215)895-2472.

HALL, KATHRYN LOUISE (KATHRYN HALL-TRUJILLO)
Health services administrator, public speaker. **Personal:** Born Jul 19, 1948, Moscow, AR; daughter of Chester and Corrine Starks; children: Kennya Thornburg, Eddie Stokes & Tamu Green. **Educ:** Univ Calif, Los Angeles, BA, sociol, 1973, MPH, 1975; DDiv, metaphorum ministry, 1999. **Career:** Calif State dept Health, health prog adv, 1975-82; Calif State Dept Serv, regional oper mgr, 1982-83; Independent Consult, 1982-; Family Health Prog Inc, Long Beach, adv, 1983-84; Health Choice Inc, Portland OR, regional mgr, 1984-86; Calif State Dept Health Serv, health prog adv, 1986-90; The Ctr Community Health & Well-Being, founder & dir, 1988-; City Univ Los Angeles, Grad Sch Life, Health & Environ Sci, adj prof; Earth Mama Healing, speaker, currently. **Orgs:** Appointee, Calif Select Comn Perinatal Substance Abuse; Am Pub Health Asn; patic, Resources Person's Network, Off Minority Health; bd, Sacramento YWCA; chmn health comt, Black Advocates State Serv; Nat Coun Negro Women; Sacramento Black Infant Health Adv Comt; Bereaved Parents USA. **Honors/Awds:** HEW, HEW Traineeship Pub Health, 1973; Girl Scouts, Role Model of the Yr, 1989; Soroptomist, Women Helping Women Award, 1989; YWCA, Outstanding Woman of the Yr, Health Serv, 1989; Woman of the Yr, Calif State Legis, 1990; Prof of the Yr, Calif Child Abuse Prev, 1993; Outstanding Community Serv Award, Calif Pub Health Asn, 1993; Community Serv Award, Essence Mag, 1995; US Pub Health Serv, Woman's Health Leadership Award, 1997; Hero in Health Care, 1999; Annual Luminary Award, Nat Asn Women Bus Owners. **Special Achievements:** The Birthing Project, Founder, 1988. **Business Phone:** (916)442-2229.

HALL, KATIE BEATRICE
Educator, government official. **Personal:** Born Apr 3, 1938, Mount Bayou, MS; daughter of Jeff L Green and Bessie Mae Hooper; married John H, Aug 15, 1957; children: Jacqueline, Junifer & Michelle. **Educ:** Miss Valley State Univ, BS, 1960; Ind Univ, MS, 1968. **Career:** City Gary Schs, teacher, 1961-75; Ind Fifth Dist, state rep, 1974-76; Ind House Rep, teacher; 1974-76; Ind Third Dist, state sen, 1976-82; US Cong, rep, Ind first Dist, 1982-84; City Gary, city clerk, IN, 1985-93; Third Dist Ind, senator. **Orgs:** Pres, Gary Coun Soc Studs, 1972-74; mem, Ind house rep;1974-76; vicechair, Gary Housing Bd Comn, 1975; House Comm Affairs Lake & Marion Cos,1975-76; chairperson, Senate Educ Comm, 1977; life mem, Nat Asn AdvanColored People; Am Asn Univ Women; pres, Gary Ind br, Nat Coun NegroWomen; Nat Black Polit Caucus; Nat Orgn Women; Ind State Teachers Asn; NatEduc Asn; Am Fedn Teachers; US Cong Black Caucus; US Cong Caucus Women'sIssues; Alpha Kappa Alpha Natl Sor; exec bd & secr-treas, Cong SteelCaucus; Chair, House sub-comm census US pop; vice chair, Gary Housing BdComnr; chair, Lake Co Demo Comm; mem,Ind State Demo conv, 1980; mem,Cuyahoga Co Bd Health, 2006. **Honors/Awds:** Received more than 200 awards for serv to religion, educ, politics, civic& community groups; Outstanding Legislator Award, NAACP, 1975; Outstanding Women in Politics, Ind Black Polit Asn, 1975; Outstanding Woman in Politics Award, City of Gary, 1975; Outstanding Service to Community Award, Gary Comt on Status of Women, 1976; Mary White Irvington Award, NAACP, Gary, IN, 1984. **Special Achievements:** Wrote and served as chief sponsor of the Martin Luther King Jr National Holiday Law passed in 1983; First Black Congress woman in Indiana. *

HALL, KIM FELICIA
Educator. **Personal:** Born Dec 25, 1961, Baltimore, MD; daughter of Lawrence Harold and Vera Webb. **Educ:** Hood Col, Frederick, BA, 1983; Univ Pa, PhD, 1990. **Career:** Dem Nat Conv, commun coordr, 1984; Univ Pa, grad fel, 1985-86; Folger Inst, Wash, DC, fel, 1986; Comt Re-Elect Clarence Blount, campaign coordr, 1986; Friends Vera P Hall, publ rels dir, 1986-87; Woodrow Wilson Nat Fel Found, Mellon dissertation fel, 1988-89; Georgetown Univ, Wash, DC, lectr, 1989-90, asst prof, 1990-96, assoc prof eng, 1995-; secy, Ford Found, fel, 1991-92; Folger Shakespeare Libr, Folger Inst fel, 1991; NEH Newberry Libr, postdoctoral fel, 1996-97; Fordham Univ, Thomas F X Mullarkey chair lit, 2001-; Swarthmore Col, vis instr. **Orgs:** Vpres, Grad Eng Asn, Univ Pa, 1985-86; secy, Grad Eng Asn, 1984-85; Modern Lang Asn Shakespeare Div chair, 2000; Shakespeare Asn Am; Renaissance Soc Am; Mellon Fel Humanities, Woodrow Wilson Nat Fel Found; Soc Study Early Modern Women. **Honors/Awds:** Hood Scholar, 1983; Gov's Citation, Gov Harry Hughes Md, 1986; Paul Robeson Award, Univ Pa, 1989. **Special Achievements:** First holder of Thomas FX Mullarkey Chair in Literature at Fordham Univ. **Home Addr:** 90 LaSalle St Apt 9A, New York, NY 10027, **Home Phone:** (212)665-0774. **Business Addr:** Associate Professor of English, Georgetown University, Department of English, PO Box 571131, Washington, DC 20057-1131, **Business Phone:** (202)687-7455.

HALL, KIRKWOOD MARSHAL
Health services administrator. **Personal:** Born May 13, 1944, Montclair, NJ; son of Marshal Eugene and Alice Chapman; married Dolores Brown; children: Malaika Estelle, Dalili Talika & Alexander Chapman. **Educ:** Va Union Univ, BA, Sociol, 1967; Pittsburgh Theol Sem, MDiv, 1974; Univ Pittsburgh, Sch Pub Health, MPH, 1978. **Career:** Hill Mental Health Team, mental health clinician, 1970-74; Western Psychol Inst & Clinic, dir, 1974-75; NJ Dept Pub Advocate, Div Mental Health, supvr, field rep, 1975-77; Project SAIL, dir, 1977-79; Univ Med & Dentistry Newark, NJ, mental health clinician, 1980-82; Henry J Austin Health Ctr, clinic supvr, mental health. **Orgs:** Asst dir, Black Campus Ministries Inc, 1971-; chmn, Neighborhood Community on Health Care, 1974; elder, Unification Assoc Christian Sabbath, 1976-80; assoc pastor, Union Bapt Church Trenton, NJ, 1981-; vpres, Samuel DeWitt Proctor Greater NJ Alumni Chap, Va Union Univ, 1983-84; assoc pastor, St Paul AME Zion, Trenton NJ, 1987-. **Honors/Awds:** Service Award Neighborhood Adv Bd, Mercy Hosp, Pittsburgh, 1971-75; Cited in Black Am Writers Past & Present Ed Rush, 1975. **Special Achievements:** Pub, "Chapman New Black Voices", Davis Spectrum in Black, "Haynes Voices of the Revolution", Jones & Neal Black Fire, "Porter Connections", Univ Pittsburgh, J Black Poetry Periodical. **Home Addr:** 8 Belmont Cir, Trenton, NJ 08618, **Home Phone:** (609)989-9604. **Business Addr:** Clinic Supervisor, Henry J Austin Health Centre, 321 N Warren St, Trenton, NJ 08618.

HALL, L PRISCILLA
Judge, lawyer. **Personal:** Daughter of Shelvin Jerome Hall and Lucy Mae. **Educ:** Howard Univ, BA, 1968; Columbia Univ Sch Journ, MS, 1969; Columbia Univ Sch Law, JD, 1973. **Career:** Gen Electric, corp atty, 1973-74; NY County, asst dist atty, 1974-79; NY State Dept of Law, asst atty gen, 1982; NYC Human Resources Admin, inspector gen, 1982-86; Criminal Ct New York, judge, 1986-89; Ct Claims, judge, 1990-94; NY State Supreme Ct, judge, 1994-2007; Fordham Univ Sch Law, adj prof, 2001-04; NY Kings County, admin judge, 2008-. **Orgs:** NYS Asn Women Judges; Metropolitan Black Bar Asn; Asn Black Women Attys; Columbia Law Sch Asn. **Business Addr:** Administrative Judge, New York State Kings County, Supreme Court Bldg, 360 Adams St, Brooklyn, NY 11201, **Business Phone:** (347)296-1061.

HALL, LAMONT
Football player. **Personal:** Born Nov 16, 1974, York, SC. **Educ:** Clemson Univ, BA,history. **Career:** Green Bay Packers, tight end, 1999; New Orleans Saints, 2000-02, 2004-05; Atlanta Falcons, 2003. *

HALL, LEMANSKI
Football player, sports manager. **Personal:** Born Nov 24, 1970, Valley, AL. **Educ:** Univ Ala, criminal justice. **Career:** Football player (retired), Sports manager; Houston Oilers, linebacker, 1994-96; Tenn Oilers, 1997; Chicago Bears, 1998; Dallas Cowboys, 1999; Minn Vikings, 2000-02; D-1 Sports Training, dir opers, D1 Huntsville, recruiting coordr, currently. **Orgs:** Acting pres, Tenn NFL Alumni Asn; pres, Tenn Chap, Nat Football LeagueRetired Players Asn. **Honors/Awds:** All-Decade; Legend of Ala. **Business Addr:** Recruiting Coordinator, D1 Huntsville, 7242 Bailey Cove Rd, Huntsville, AL 35802, **Business Phone:** (256)880-1717.

HALL, LEWIS J.
Executive. **Career:** NY State Educ, coordr; Univ State NY, Scholar & Grants Admin, supvr, currently. **Business Addr:** Supervisor, University of the State of New York, Scholarships and

Grants Administration, 1400 Washington Ave, Rm 1078 EBA, Albany, NY 12234, **Business Phone:** (518)486-1319.*

HALL, MELVIN CURTIS
Lawyer. **Personal:** Born Jun 2, 1956, Tulsa, OK; son of Isiah and Eunice Jean Taylor; married Alicia Williams Hall, Jul 26, 1980; children: Natasha Marie, Tenia Shanta. **Educ:** Langston Univ, Langston, OK, BS, 1978; Univ Okla, Norman, OK, JD, 1981. **Career:** Cleveland County Dist Atty, Norman, OK, asst dist atty, 1980-83; Okla Human Rights Comn, Okla City, OK, exec dir, 1983-87; US Ct Appeals, Tenth Circuit; Chapel, Riggs, Abney, Neal, Turpen, Orbison & Lewis Inc, Okla City, OK, atty, 1988-. **Orgs:** Okla Bar Asn, 1982-; Okla City Asn Black Lawyers, 1986-; bd mem, Southwest Ctr Human Rels Studies, 1987-; bd mem, Progress Independence, 1988-; bd mem, Okla State Chamber Com & Indust, 1989-; Regent, Univ Okla, 1992-99. **Honors/Awds:** Blue Ribbon Award, Metropolitan Fair Housing Coun Okla City, 1985; Certificate Appreciation, US Dept Housing & Urban Develop, 1986; A C Hamlin Tribute, Okla Legislative Black Caucus, 1987; Certificate Appreciation, Marion Anderson Middle Sch, 1987; Plaque Appreciation, A Philip Randolph Okla, 1990. **Business Addr:** Attorney, Counselor, Riggs, Abney, Neal, Turpen, Orbison & Lewis Inc, Law, 5801 N Broadway Ext, Paragon Bldg Ste 101, Oklahoma City, OK 73118, **Business Phone:** (405)843-9909.*

HALL, MORRIS B
Lawyer. **Personal:** Born Oct 26, 1975, Port Huron, MI; son of Morris and Terry; children: Matea Kearns & Dontae Bassham. **Educ:** Univ Mich, BA, polit sci, 1997, BA, psychol, 1997; Wayne State Univ, JD, 2001. **Career:** N Am Lighting, QS 9000 standards engr, 1999-; H&L Develop Co LLC, pres & chief exec officer, 2000-. **Orgs:** Rules comt, Aggressive Diversified Investment Group, 1998-; Nat Asn Investors Corp, 1998-; Soc Automotive Engineering, 2000-; Am Trial Lawyers Asn, 2001-. **Honors/Awds:** Young Man of the Year, Port Huron Men's Club, 1990, 1993; Outstanding Student Athlete, Jim Wilhelm Scholarship, 1993; Distinguished Mediator, Straus Inst Dispute Resolution, 2001. **Home Phone:** (248)888-0639.

HALL, PAMELA VANESSA
Financial manager, consultant. **Personal:** Born Jul 2, 1954, Ann Arbor, MI; daughter of James D Hall and Maureen. **Educ:** MI State Univ, BA, 1976. **Career:** AJC Bus Consul, financial consult, 1980-98; Am Express, fin adv, 1998-2003; Charter One Securities, financial consult; New York Life, financial serv prof, currently. **Orgs:** Metro Women's Civic Coun, 1997-; NAACP, Ypsilanti/Willow Run Br, 1998-2001, 2nd vp, 2001-02; planning comnr, Wastenaw County Planning Comn, 2001-02. **Business Addr:** Financial Services Professional, Consultant, New York Life, 1330 Post Oak Blvd Suite 1900, Houston, TX 77056, **Business Phone:** (713)499-7605.

HALL, PERRY ALONZO
School administrator, executive director, executive director. **Personal:** Born Sep 15, 1947, Detroit, MI. **Educ:** Univ MI, BA, psychol, 1969; Harvard Univ, EdD, educ & soc policy, 1977. **Career:** Ford Found, doctoral fel, 1971; Northeastern Univ, instr, 1974; Wayne State Univ, prog coordr, 1974-76, asst prof, 1977-80, actg dir, dir, 1980-. **Orgs:** Substance Abuse Comn, New Detroit Inc, 1974-; Exec bd mem, Nat Coun Black Studies, 1978; consult, Chicago Ctr Afro-Am Studies & Res, 1982; consult, State Mich, Off Substance Abuse Serv, 1982; adv bd mem, Equal Opportunity Ctr, 1983-. **Honors/Awds:** Outstanding Young Men of Am, 1980. **Business Addr:** Director, Wayne State University, Ctr Black Stud, 5980 Cass Ave, Detroit, MI 48202.

HALL, REGINA
Actor. **Personal:** Born Dec 12, 1970, Washington, DC. **Educ:** NY Univ, MS, jour, 1997. **Career:** Films: The Best Man, 1999; Love & Basketball, 2000; Scary Movie, 2000; Scary Movie 2, 2001; The Other Brother 2002; Paid in Full, 2002; Malibu's Most Wanted, 2003; Scary Movie 3, 2003; Six Months Later, 2005; King's Ransom, 2005; The Honeymooners, 2005; Danika, 2006; Scary Movie 4, 2006; The Elder Son, 2006; First Sunday, 2008; Superhero Movie, 2008; Law Abiding Citizen, 2009; TV appearances: Loving,. 1992; "New York Undercover", 1997; "NYPD Blue",2000; "Disappearing Acts", 2000; "Ally McBeal", 2001-02; "Bygones", 2002, "What I'll Never Do for Love Again", 2002; Untitled Cedric the Entertainer Project, 2008. **Honors/Awds:** Nominated for Best Supporting Actress for Disappearing Acts (2000), 2001; Nomination for Image Award for Outstanding Supporting Actress in a Comedy Series "Ally McBeal", 2003; Festival Award for Best Actress in Danika, 2006. **Business Phone:** (323)866-0900.*

HALL, DR. REGINALD LAWRENCE
Physician, educator. **Personal:** Born Jun 19, 1957, Whiteville, NC; son of Lawrence and Vera; married Ranota Thomas, Jun 17, 1989. **Educ:** Baltimore Polytech Inst, 1975; St Vincent Col, summa cum laude, BS, chem, 1979; Duke Univ Sch Med, 1983. **Career:** Duke Univ Med Ctr, res, 1983, jr asst res, 1985, res orthopedic surg, 1989; fel Med Col Wis, Milwaukee, 1990; St Vincent Col, chem lab asst; Mayor's Coordr Coun Criminal Justice Baltimore, work & study alumni develop off intern; Res & Planning Dept Mass Transit Admin Baltimore, intern; Res & Planning Dept Mass Transit Admin, mayor's coordr coun criminal justice; St Vincent Col, chem lab asst, work & study alumni develop off; Duke Med Ctr, phlebotomist, res fel div ped cardiol, clin chem lab orthopedic surg resd, asst prof, cur; summer fel Cornell Med Col; Duke Univ Med Ctr & pvt pract, physician, currently. **Orgs:** Black Student Union, Freshman Orientation Comn, Dean's Col Sub comm, Res Adv Coun, Alumni Telethon, Duke Univ Med Sch Admis Comn, Davison Coun Stud Govt, Stud Nat Med Asn, Am Med Student Asn, Dean's Minority Affairs Subcomt; adv, Duke Univ Undergrad Premed Soc. **Honors/Awds:** CV Mosby Book Award; Analytic Chem Award. **Business Phone:** (919)575-3900.*

HALL, ROBERT JOHNSON
School administrator. **Personal:** Born Jun 5, 1937, Crumrod, AR; married Jerlean. **Educ:** N Col Pine Bluff, BS & MA, 1963; UCA Conway MA, 1972; UA Fayetteville adminstrv spec, AR, 1977. **Career:** Tucker Rosenwald High Sch, prin, 1966-67, teacher, 1963-66; JS Walker High Sch, teacher, 1967-68; AM & N Col, asst dean men, 1967-72; UAPB, assoc dean studs, 1972-75; Wabbaseka Sch Dist, supt, 1975-. **Orgs:** Phi Delta Kappa Educ Frat; NEA AR Adminstr Asn; Phi Beta Sigma Frat; Royal Knight Soc Deacon Pine Hill Baptist Church, 1969; pres, Gamma Psi Sigma Chap Phi Beta Sigma Frat 1974; bd mem, OIC, 1976. **Honors/Awds:** Outstanding Young Man America, 1976. **Business Addr:** PO Box 210, Wabbaseka, AR 72175.*

HALL, ROBERT L
Educator, curator. **Personal:** Born in Miami, FL. **Educ:** Fisk Univ, Nashville, Tenn, BS, arts, 1972; George Wash Univ, Wash, DC, MAT, mus educ, 1975. **Career:** Fisk Univ Mus Art, Nashville, Tenn, curator, 1973-84; Anacostia Community Mus, Smithsonian Inst, Anacostia Mus & Ctr African Am Hist & Cult, assoc dir educ, 1984-, cur new visions, 1990-. **Orgs:** Am Asn Mus; African Am Mus Asn; Commonwealth Asn Mus. **Honors/Awds:** Nat Juror, Pres Comt Arts & Humanities. **Special Achievements:** Exhibitions Curated: Anacostia Mus & Ctr for African Am Hist & Cult, Wash, DC, "In Arms Elders." 2002-03; "New Visions: Emerging Trends in African Am Art." 2004; "On Their Own: Selected Works by Self-taught African Am Artists." 2005; Pubations: Anacostia Mus & Ctr for African Am Hist & Cult, Wash, DC, Precious Memories: Family Hist Res for Intermediate-level Studs2002 (Stud res & study guide); New Visions: Emerging Trends in African Am Art 2003 (Exhibition catalog). **Business Addr:** Associate Director for Education, Curator New Visions, Anacostia Community Museum, Smithsonian Institution, 1901 Fort Pl SE, Washington, DC 20020, **Business Phone:** (202)633-4868.

HALL, ROBERT L.
Government official, mayor. **Personal:** Born Apr 1, 1937, Stuart, FL; married Rose Ann. **Career:** City Stuart, supt parks & cemetery; City Stuart, mayor, comnr. **Orgs:** Pres, Martin Co Dem Mens Club; potentate, FL St Nursing Home Investr; chmn, Ombudsment Comn nursing home; Stuart Vol Fire Dept; 32 degree Mason; Shriner; So Asn Cemeteries; Park Personnel Asn; Mason. **Honors/Awds:** Many awards from Civic & Church Organizations; Award for Serving as Commissioner & Mayor City Stuart; Award for Voters Registration Participation Super of Election. *

HALL, RONALD
Executive, president (organization), chief executive officer. **Educ:** Western Mich Univ, BS, math; Wayne State Univ, Masters Degree, bus. **Career:** New Detroit Inc, exec; New Ctr Stamping, chmn & ceo, 2003; Renaissance Capital Alliance, pres & ceo, currently; Bridgewater Interiors, pres & ceo, currently. **Orgs:** Pres, Mich Minority Bus Develop Coun, 1992-98; Casino Adv Comm; bd dir, St John Hosp & Med Ctr; chmn, Am Diabetes Assn of Mich; 100 Black Men; Native Am Bus Alliance; Detroit Empowerment Zone; chmn, Southeastern Mich Jr Achievement; Walsh Col Pres's Advs Coun; bd dir, United Am Healthcare Corp; Booker T Wash Bus Asn ; Bus Enterprise Develop Ctr; pres, Mich Amateur Athletic Assn; Metrop Growth & Develop Corp; Detroit Urban League; Va Pk Community Investment Asn; vice chmn, Family Serv of Detroit & Wayne Co; Rotary Club; Child Care Coord Coun Detroit/Wayne Co. **Honors/Awds:** Jeffery W Barry Award, Educ Excellence & Serv, Walsh Col, 2004. **Special Achievements:** Bridgewater Interiors LLC, 11th largest African-American owned business in the US. **Business Phone:** (313)842-3300.*

HALL, SARAH N.
Lawyer. **Career:** Nat Conf Bar Examiners, pres & chair; WVa Bd Law Examiners, vpres & staff; Atty Law, currently. **Business Phone:** (304)558-7815.*

HALL, SHARON
Manager, executive director. **Educ:** Morris Brown Col, Atlanta, BS; Univ Southern Calif, MBA. **Career:** Procter & Gamble, staff; Allen & Hamilton, mkt mgr; Avon Products, staff; Spencer Stuart, Atlanta, consult, 1997, Diversity Pract, co-founder, 1999, head off & partner, 2001-, office mgr, exec consult, bd dir, mgr, currently. **Orgs:** Bd mem, Urban League, Greater Kansas City. **Special Achievements:** First African American woman to run a major search firm. **Business Phone:** (404)504-4433.

HALL, SHELVIN LOUISE MARIE
State court judge, lawyer. **Personal:** Born Jun 15, 1948; daughter of Shelvin Jerome and Lucy M. **Educ:** Hampton Univ; Boston Univ Sch Law, JD. **Career:** Pvt practice atty; US Congressman Mickey Leland, legislative dir, 1980; Ill Dept Human Rights, gen coun, 1982, sr atty, 1984; Circuit Ct Judge Cook County, circuit ct judge, 1991; Ill Appellate Ct, Justice, 1999-. **Orgs:** Past chair, Ill Judicial Coun Nat Bar Asn, 1998-99; educ & exec comt, Supreme Ct Ill Judicial Conf; Nat Asn Advan Colored People Legal Defense Fund & Educ Fund; nat vpres, Nat Bar Asn; chair, Young Lawyers Div; chair, Admin Law Section; mem exec comt, Mem Bd Governors & Creator Interdenominational Prayer Breakfast, 1985; past chair, Ill Judicial Coun; Cook County Bar Asn; Nat Bar Asn; Lutheran Family Mission; Legal Asst Found Chicago; Judges Asn; Nat Asn Women Judges; Ill State Bar Asn; The Cook County Bar Asn; Women's Bar Asn Ill; Black Women Lawyer's Asn Greater Chicago; Chicago Bar Asn; Am Bar Asn; Delta Sigma Theta Sorority; Bars Supreme Ct Ill, Tex & US; Friendship Baptist Church; dir, Church Youth Dept; chair, Christian Care Dept; chair, Dept Christian Educ. **Business Phone:** (847)695-3750.*

HALL, SOPHIA H.
Judge. **Personal:** Born Jan 1, 1943?, Chicago, IL. **Educ:** Univ Wis, Madison, BS, hist, 1964; Northwestern Univ, Sch Law, JD, 1967. **Career:** McCoy, Ming & Black, assoc, 1967-76; Mitchell, Hall, Jones & Black, PC, shareholder, 1976-80; State Ill, Circuit Ct Cook County Judicial Circuit, Juv Justice & C Protection Dept, Chancery Div, 1986-, Criminal div, presiding judge, 1992, judge, 1995-; Loyola Univ Chicago Law Sch, adj fac, 1996. **Orgs:** US Dist Ct Northern Dist Ill Bar Asn, 1967; bd dirs, Nat Ctr State Cts, 1988-94; past pres, Nat Asn Women Judges, 1989-90; chair, Civil Damages Awards Comt, Ill Task Force; Bd State Justice Inst, 1998; chair, NAWJ Comt Task Force Family Violence; past pres, Ill Judges Asn, secy, treas & third vpres; Comt Circuit Ct Cook County; Judicial Admin Div, Am Bar Asn; Ill State Rep, Nat Conf State Trial Judges; Chicago Bar Asn; Nat Asn Advan Colored People; Zonta Club Southside Chicago; Chicago Network. **Honors/Awds:** Outstanding Jurist, John Marshall Law Sch, 1992; Distinguished Service Award, Nat Ctr State Cts, 1995. **Special Achievements:** First Women Presiding Judge Within the Circuit Court of Cook County, 1993; publ: Declaratory Judgments, Chicago Bar Record, November, 1991; Interlocutory Injunctions, Chicago Bar Record, Jul/Aug, 1992. *

HALL, STANLEY H.
Foundation executive, chief executive officer, president (organization). **Career:** Bay Area Urban League, pres & chief exec officer, currently. **Business Addr:** President, Chief Execuitve Officer, Bay Area Urban League, 2201 Broadway St, Oakland, CA 94612, **Business Phone:** (510)271-1846.*

HALL, SYDNEY JAY, III
Lawyer. **Personal:** Born Feb 27, 1959, Sumpter, SC; son of Sidney and Loretta. **Educ:** Howard Univ, BBA, 1982, JD, 1987. **Career:** Fireman's Fund/Am Express, para-legal, 1978-81; Am Express, spec asst vpres finance, 1982; Travelers Ins, claims adjuster, 1987; Freistat & Sandler, assoc, 1987; Hall Sydney J Law Off, atty, 1992-. **Orgs:** Nat Bar Asn; Am Bar Asn; Calif State Bar; Md State Bar; Penn State Bar. **Honors/Awds:** Int Youth in Achievement Award, Cambridge, Eng; Leadership, San Mateo, 1992. **Special Achievements:** Founder, Asa T Spaulding Ins Soc, 1990; ATSIS Bus J, Howard Univ. **Home Addr:** 251 Topsail Ct, Foster City, CA 94404, **Home Phone:** (415)345-2497. **Business Addr:** Attorney, Hall Sydney J Law Off, 1308 Bayshore Hwy Suite 220, Burlingame, CA 94010, **Business Phone:** (650)342-1830.*

HALL, TANYA EVETTE
Association executive. **Personal:** Born Aug 12, 1966, Stratford, NJ; married Jun 1993. **Educ:** Drexel Univ, BS, 1988. **Career:** Penn Tower Hotel, 1989-97; Philadelphia Conv & Visitors Bureau, Multicultural Affairs Congress, exec dir, 1997-. **Orgs:** Nat Coalition Black Mkt Planners, 1989-; bd mem, Hospitality Sales & Mkt Asn Int, 1995-97; womens ministry dir, Impacting Your World Christian Ctr. **Honors/Awds:** Emerging Leader, Ebony Mag, 1996. **Special Achievements:** Philadelphia Tribune, African Am Leader; 40 Under 40, Philadelphia Bus Jour; Mover & Shaker, Am Women's Heritage Soc. **Business Addr:** Executive Director, Philadelphia Multicultural Affairs Congress, A Division of the Philadelphia Convention & Visitors Bureau, 1700 Market St Suite 3000, Philadelphia, PA 19103, **Business Phone:** (215)636-4433.

HALL, TERRY
Administrator. **Personal:** Born Feb 23, 1957, Port Huron, MI; daughter of Richard and Audrey Pack; married Morris B Hall, Sr, Jun 26, 1976; children: Morris B, Antwan L. **Educ:** Northwood Univ, BBA; Baker Col, MBA, 1998. **Career:** DTE Energy, admin supvr, 1981-. **Orgs:** Nat Asn Advan Colored People, 1999-; United Way Citizen's Review Comt, 2000-; Port Huron Scholarship Asst Comt, 2001-; Mich Freedom Trail Comn, comnr, 2002-. **Home Addr:** 2690 Whitney Pl, Fort Gratiot, MI 48059, **Home Phone:** (810)385-7619. *

HALL, TRACEE K
Government official. **Educ:** Ariz State Univ, BA, social, 1995, MPA, 2000. **Career:** City Phoenix, asst, sr asst to mayor, currently. **Orgs:** Black Bd Dirs Proj; bd mem, Conf Minority

Transp Off Ariz; bd mem, Ariz Coalition Adolescent Pregnancy & Prev; mentor, Young Families CAN; community mem, Community Alliance Black Stud Support, Ariz State Univ; adv group mem, Sistas Planned Parenthood Cent & Northern Ariz; adv coun mem, Ariz State Univ. **Honors/Awds:** American's Finest Honour, Cystic Fibrosis Found, 2003. **Special Achievements:** One of the 30 young leaders in America, Ebony magazine. **Business Phone:** (602)534-9502.

HALL, DR. WILLIE GREEN
Dentist. **Personal:** Born May 23, 1947, Prattville, AL; son of Willie G Sr and Kattie R; married Cheryl F Wesley, Jan 30, 1971; children: Darius & Dashia. **Educ:** Howard Univ, BS, 1971, DDS, 1978. **Career:** People's Drug Store, pharmacist/asst mgr, 1969-72; Standard Drugs, pharmacist, 1972-74; Syracuse Community Health Ctr, dentist, 1979-80; Southeast Dent Asn, partner/pres, 1984-91; E River Health Asn, dent dir, 1980-88; Lake Arbor Dent Asn, partner, 1991; CW Funding, owner; Dentist, pvt pract, currently. **Orgs:** Nat Dent Asn, 1986-; Am Dent Asn, 1986-; Nat Pharm Asn, 1986-87; Alpha Omega Psi Phi Fraternity, 1986-; Robert T Freeman Dent Soc, 1986-; Howard Univ, Pharm & Dent Alumni Asns; DC Dent Soc, 1988-; Int Asn Orthodontics, 1988-; Acad Gen Dent, 1989-; Campbell AME Church, Wash, DC; Nat Asn Entrepreneurs, Cert Mortgage Investors. **Honors/Awds:** Volunteer Award, DC Dept Recreation Spec Act, 1984; Capital Head Start Community Award, 1984; Award for Volunteer Service, Wash Srs Wellness Ctr, 1986. **Home Addr:** 4513 Holmehurst Way, Bowie, MD 20720-3455. **Business Addr:** Dentist, Private Practice, 12164 Cent Ave Suite 221, Mitchellville, MD 20721.

HALLIBURTON, CHRISTOPHER
Executive. **Personal:** Born Apr 27, 1958, New York, NY; son of Norman Halliburton and Camille Simonette. **Educ:** Tufts Univ, BA, hist & polit sci, 1980. **Career:** Aetna Life Ins, EBR, 1980-84; Mayer & Meyer Assocs, acct exec, 1984-89; Tannenbaum-Harber, acct exec, 1982-84; Crossroads Films, sales rep, 1989-91; 900 Frames, exec producer, 1991-93; Relativity Records, dir video prod, currently. **Special Achievements:** Video Award Best Int Video, MTV, 1991. **Business Addr:** Director of Urban Product Marketing, Relativity Records, 79 Fifth Ave 16th Fl, New York, NY 10003, **Business Phone:** (212)337-5317.*

HALLIBURTON, WARREN J.
College teacher, writer, editor. **Personal:** Born Aug 2, 1924, New York, NY; son of Richard H and Blanche Watson; married Marion Jones, Dec 20, 1947; children: Cheryl, Stephanie, Warren, Jr, Jena; married Francis Fletcher, Feb 11, 1971. **Educ:** New York Univ, BS, 1949; Columbia Univ, MEd, 1975, DEd, 1977. **Career:** Prairie View Agricultural and Mechanical Col, Prairie View, Tex, Eng instr, 1949; Bishop Col, Dallas, Tex, Eng instr, 1951, assoc, Inst int Educ, 1952; Recorder, New York NY, reporter & columnist, 1953; Brooklyn NY, teacher & dean, high school, 1959-60; New York City Bd Educ & assoc New York State Dept Educ, coordr, 1960-65; McGraw Hill, New York NY, ed, 1967; Hamilton-Kirkland Cols, Clinton NY, visiting prof Eng, 1971-72; Columbia Univ, Teachers Col, New York NY, ed, res assoc & dir scholarly j, govt prog, & Ethnic Studies Ctr, 1972-77; Reader's Digest, New York, NY, ed & writer; freelance ed & writer; Books: Nomads of the Sahara, Africa Today Series, Crestwood, 1992; African Industries, Africa Today Series, Crestwood, 1993; African Landscapes, Africa Today Series, Crestwood, 1993; Africa's Struggle to Survive, Africa Today Series, Crestwood, 1993; City and Village Life, Africa Today Series, Crestwood, 1993; Clarence Thomas: Supreme Court Justice, Enslow, 1993; Historic Speeches of African Americans, F. Watts, 1993. **Military Serv:** AUS, Air Forces, 1943-46.

HALL-KEITH, JACQUELINE YVONNE
Judge. **Personal:** Born Jan 8, 1953, Detroit, MI; daughter of William H and Evelyn V Callaway; married Luther A, Sep 17, 1988; children: Erin Yvonne. **Educ:** Gen Motors Inst, Bus Indus Admin, 1971-76; Detroit Col Law, JD, 1976-80. **Career:** Gen Motors Corp, col co-op, 1971-76; Ford Motor Co, mgt trainee, 1976-78, personnel analyst, 1978-80, staff atty, 1980-84; State Mich, Dept Labor, admin law judge/magistrate, 1984-94; Mich Dept Civil Rights, atty-at-law, dir off legal affairs, 1994-. **Orgs:** State Bar Mich; Wolverine Bar Asn; GMI & DCL Alumni Asn; Asn Black Judges Mich; Nat Asn Advan Colored People; Delsprite Sponsor, Delta Sigma Theta Sorority, 1984-95; Top Ladies of Distinction; pres, 1993-94, bd dir, 1988-91; mentor, Nolan Middle Sch, 1993-94; coun mem, State Bar Mich, Alternative Dispute Resolution Sect; bible study instr, Fel Chapel; Mich State Bar Asn. **Honors/Awds:** Speaking of People, Ebony Magazine, 1984; Judicial Excellence Award, Top Ladies of Distinction, 1990. **Home Addr:** 19521 Burlington Dr, Detroit, MI 48203. **Business Addr:** Attorney-at-Law, Director, Michigan Department of Civil Rights, Office of Legal Affairs, 3038 W Grand Blvd Suite 7450 Cadillac Pl, Detroit, MI 48202, **Business Phone:** (313)456-1012.

HALL-TRUJILLO, KATHRYN. See HALL, KATHRYN LOUISE.

HALL-TURNER, DEBORAH
Health services administrator. **Personal:** Born Jun 6, 1951, Detroit, MI; daughter of Herbert and Haroline; married Michael G Sr, Jan 22, 1978; children: Michael G Turner. **Educ:** Mercy Col Detroit, BSN, 1973; Case Mgt Soc Am, Cert, 1994. **Career:** Wayne County Pt Care Mgmt, dir qual assurance, 1988-91; Mercy Health Servs, sr mgr qual mgmt, 1991-93, dir qual servs, 1993-94, dir accrediation, regulation, 1994-95; Mich Peer Review Orgn, dir state gov progs, 1995-96, dir behav health prog & managed care eval, 1996-. **Orgs:** Past pres, Asn Managed Care Nursing, bd mem, 1993-; treas, Thea Bowen Wellness Inst, 1995-; Black Nurses Asn; Mich Asn Health Plans. **Honors/Awds:** MaCauley Award, Mercy Col, Detroit, 1973. **Special Achievements:** Qual Mgmt Prog, System for Indigent Managed Care Program-County Care, 1988. **Home Addr:** 20515 Vernier Suite 4, Harper Woods, MI 48225. **Business Addr:** Director Behavioral Health Program, Michigan Peer Review Organisation, 22670 Haggerty Rd Suite 100, Farmington Hills, MI 48335-2611, **Business Phone:** (517)796-6469.

HALL TYLER, DELORA
Business owner. **Educ:** Univ Detroit, BA. **Career:** freelance media consult; Detroit News; WGPR; First Media Group, founder, pres, cheif exec officer, 1990-. **Honors/Awds:** Best Small Bus, Mich Small Bus Develop Ctr, 1999. **Business Addr:** President and Cheif Executive Officer, Founder, First Media Group, 29623 Northwestern Hwy, Southfield, MI 48034, **Business Phone:** (248)354-8705.*

HALLUMS, BENJAMIN F.
Educator. **Personal:** Born Mar 6, 1940, Easley, SC; married Phyllis; children: Jacqueline, Bernard & Maisha. **Educ:** BA, 1970. **Career:** Quinnipiac Col, coun, 1971-75; Allied Health Prog, coun, 1974; Sch Mentally Retarded, coun, 1972-73; Quinnipiac Col, asst prof Black Studies, 1973-75, asst prof Fine Arts, 1972-75. **Orgs:** Ass Black People Higher Educ, 1970-75; Conn Liason Prog, 1973; Minority Col Couns, 1973; Eastern Alliance Balck Couns, 1974-75; Nat Black Col Choir Annual Fest; rep, United Ministry Higher Edun; Nat Quinnipiac College of Choirs; secy, Coalliation Black Prin, 1975; vpres, Couples Inc. **Military Serv:** AUS e5 1961-64. **Business Addr:** College Counselor, Quinnipiac College, Mt Carmel Ave, Hamden, CT 06518.

HALYARD, DR. MICHELE YVETTE
Physician, educator. **Personal:** Born Apr 13, 1961, Buffalo, NY; married Paul Edward Leroy Richardson; children: Hamilton. **Educ:** Howard Univ, BS, 1982; Howard Univ Col Med, MD, 1984. **Career:** Howard Univ Hosp, resident radiation oncol, 1984-87; Mayo Clin, fel radiation oncol, 1987, asst prof oncol & chair radiation oncol, currently. **Orgs:** Nat & Am Med Assocs, Phi Beta Kappa Honor Soc, Alpha Omega Alpha Med Hon Soc, Alpha Kappa Alpha Sor Inc. **Honors/Awds:** Am Med Women's Asn Award Scholar Achievement; Grandy Award for Internal Med; Award for Clin Excellence in Psychiat; Frederick M Drew Award for Outstanding Performance in Radiation Ther; article "The Use of Intraoperative Radiotherapy and External Beam Therapy in the Mgt of Desmoid Tumors," w/JoAnn Collier-Manning MD, Ebrahim Ashayeri MD, Alfred Goldson MD, Frank Watkins MD, Ernest Myers MD in J Nat Med Asn, 1986. **Business Phone:** (480)301-8000.

HAM, DARVIN (DUNKIN DARVIN)
Basketball player. **Personal:** Born Jul 23, 1973, Saginaw, MI; son of Wilmer Jones. **Educ:** Tex Tech. **Career:** Denver Nuggets, 1996; Ind Pacers, forward, 1996-97; Wash Wizards, 1997-98; Milwaukee Bucks, 1999-2002; Atlanta Hawks, 2002; Detroit Pistons, forward-guard, 2003-05; Talk N Text Phone Pals, Philippine Basketball Assn, basketball player, 2006; Dallas Mavericks, forward, 2007; Albuquerque Thunderbirds, forward, 2007. **Business Addr:** Professional Basketball Player, Albuquerque Thunderbirds, 111 Lomas Blvd NW, Albuquerque, NM 87102.

HAM, DR. DEBRA NEWMAN
Educator, historian. **Personal:** Born Aug 27, 1948, York, PA; daughter of Earl F and Eva Mitchell Owens; married Lester James Sr, Apr 29, 1989; children: Lester James Jr & Leslyn Jaye. **Educ:** Howard Univ, BA, 1970, PhD, 1984; Boston Univ, MA, 1971. **Career:** Nat Archives, Wash, archivist, black hist specialist, 1970-86, NVA Comm Col, adj prof, 1986-88, Libr Congress, African-Am Manuscript Historian, 1986-95; Morgan State Univ, prof, hist, 1995-. **Orgs:** Founding mem, African-Am Hist & Geneal Soc, 1978-; publ dir, Asn Black Women Historians, 1987-90; exec coun, Asn Study Afro-Am Life & Hist, 1990-96; ed bd, Soc Am Archivists, 1990-92; Adv Comt African-Am Interpretation Monticello, 2003-. **Honors/Awds:** Coker Prize, Soc Am Archivists, 1985; Finding Aid Award, Mid-Atlantic Regional Archivists, 1985, 1995n Newsboy Award, Baltimore Afro-American newspapers, 2007. **Special Achievements:** Author, numerous articles on African-American history and guides to African-American American history; exhibit curator, "The African-American Mosaic: The Quest for Full Citizenship," Library of Congress, 1998; Black History: A Guide to Civilian Records in the National Archives, 1984; African-American Mosiac: A Library of Congress Resource; ed, Guide for the Study of Black History & Culture, 1993; ed, African-American Odyssey, 1998. **Business Addr:** Professor, Speaker, Morgan State University, Department Hist, 1700 E Cold Spring Lane, Baltimore, MD 21251, **Business Phone:** (443)885-3190.

HAMBERG, DR. MARCELLE R.
Physician. **Personal:** Born Jul 4, 1931, Anderson, SC; son of Robert Clark and Pauline Hamlin; married Cheryl Jones; children: Marcelle Jr, Gabrielle. **Educ:** Hampton Inst, BS, 1953; Meharry Med Col, MD, 1957; Internship, 1958, Hubbard Hosp Meharry Med Col, Surg Residency, attended 1959, Urolo Residency, attended 1962. **Career:** Physician (retired); Univ Louisville, instr urolo, 1967; Meharry Med Col, chief div urolo, 1976, assoc prof, 1974-82; physician, pvt practice, Currently. **Orgs:** Am Bd Urolo, 1968; Am Urolo Asn, SE, 1969; mem, Sloan-Kettering Cancer Ctr, fel cancer urolo, 1962-63; Newman Van High Spl; Fed Cancer Urolo; Hosp Cancer & Allied Diseases, NY, 1962-63. **Military Serv:** AUS, first lt, 1958-68. **Home Addr:** 4474 Clarksville Pike, Nashville, TN 37218. *

HAMBERLIN, DR. EMIEL
Educator. **Personal:** Born Nov 8, 1939, Fayette, MS; married Minnie; children: Emiel III & Mark. **Educ:** Alcorn State Univ, BA, biol, 1964; Univ Ill, MEd, voc educ, 1978, PhD, hort, 1982; Northwestern Univ, adv studies, 1993. **Career:** Chicago Pub Schs, Biol & Hort Environ Studies, prin, prof & teacher, 1964(Jean Baptiste Pointe De Sable High Sch, teacher). **Orgs:** Omega Psi Phi Fraternity, 1964-; Nat Geog Soc, 1970-; Oper PUSH, 1972; Nat Biol Asn, 1974-; Int Wild life Fedn, 1974-; Ill Teachers Asn, 1975-; Phi Delta Kappa 1976-; Ill Sci Teachers Asn, 1978-; hon mem, Kappa Delta Pi, 1979-; bd mem, Ada McKinley Highland Spec C, 1980; Acad Fel, Golden Apple Found, 1992. **Honors/Awds:** Teacher of the Year, City Chicago, 1971; The Governors Award, World Flower Show, 1972; Outstanding Secondary Educator of America, 1974; Professional Personnel in Environmental Education, Ill Environ Educ Asn, 1975; Omega Man of the Year, 1977; Those Who Excell Award, State Ill, 1977; Illinois Teacher of the Year, 1977; Outstanding Educator Award, Lewis Univ, 1980; Phi Delta Kappa Educator, 1981; Ill Master Teacher, Governor Ill, 1981; Ora Higgins Leadership Award, 1985; Distinguished Alumni of Black Universities, Nat Asn Equal Opport Higher Educ, 1986; Outstanding Achievements as an Educator in Horticulture, Mayor H Wash, 1986; One of the Heroes of Our Time Newsweek, Newsweek Mag, 1986; Who's Who Among Black Americans - Educators, 1988; Kohl Family Foundation International Educator, 1992; National Teachers Hall of Fame, 2001. **Home Addr:** 8500 S Winchester ave, Chicago, IL 60620. **Business Addr:** Teacher of Biology and Horticulture, Jean Baptiste Pointe DeSable High School, 4934 S Wabash Ave, Chicago, IL 60615.*

HAMBLIN, ANGELA
Basketball player, basketball coach. **Personal:** Born Sep 30, 1976, Gary, IN. **Educ:** Univ Iowa, BA, eng, 1998. **Career:** Basketball player (retired), basketball coach; Lew Wallace Hornets, 1994; Washington Mystics, 1998; Detroit Shock, guard, 1998-99; Lew Wallace High Sch, basketball coach, currently. **Honors/Awds:** Big Ten Conf Tournament, MVP, 1997. **Business Addr:** Basketball Head Coach, Lew Wallace High School, 415 W 45th Ave, Gary, IN 46408-3998, **Business Phone:** (219)980-6305.

HAMBRICK, DARREN
Football player. **Personal:** Born Aug 30, 1975, Lacoochee, FL. **Educ:** Univ SC. **Career:** Football Player (Retired); Dallas Cowboys, linebacker, 1998-2001; Carolina Panthers, 2001; Cleveland Browns, mid linebacker, 2002.

HAMBRICK, HAROLD E., JR.
Association executive. **Personal:** Born Feb 17, 1943, New Orleans, LA; married Margaret (divorced); children: Tyra, Jeffery, Sharon. **Educ:** Pepperdine Univ, BS, bus admin, 1974; Univ Santa Clara, Cert, organ mgt, 1980; Univ Calif, Prof Desig, pub rel, 1987. **Career:** Western Asn Community Health Ctrs Inc, exec dir, vpres, 1974-; Watts Health Found Inc, sr acct, 1969-75; New Communicators Inc, bus mgr, 1967-69; IBM Corp, office mgr, Trn, 1966-67; Los Angeles Black Bus Expo & Trade Show, exec dir, pres, currently. **Orgs:** Treas Nat Asn Community Health Ctrs Inc, 1974-76; founding pres, Western Asn Community Health Ctr Inc, 1973-75; vpres, Hambricks Mort Inc, 1975-; pres, Employees Serv Asn, 1972-74; bd mem, Watts United Credit Union Inc, 1974-75; Am Soc Asn Exec, 1976-; State Calif, Dept Health Adv Coun; Am Pub Health Asn, 1973-; Nat Notary Asn, 1972-; Nat Asn Tax Consult, 1972-; Calif Asn Tax Consult, 1972-; Greater La Press Club; Nat Press Club; Los Angeles World Affairs Coun; Chmn Bd Dir, Watts United Credit Union; vpres, Pres Community Adv Coun, Charles R Drew Univ Med & Sci; Past Pres, Calif Black Health Network Inc; Past Pres, Black Health Leadership Coun Inc, Los Angeles; Latino/Black Roundtable; Curator, co-founder, River Rd African-Am Museum & Gallery. **Honors/Awds:** Selected as one of the Young Men of America, 1978. **Business Addr:** President, Black Business Expo of San Antonio Inc, 305 E Euclid St Suite 101, San Antonio, TX 78212.

HAMBRICK-DIXON, PRISCILLA J
Psychologist. **Educ:** Univ Mich, MA, Develop Psychol, PhD, Educ & Psychol. **Career:** Hunter Col, Dept Educ Found & coun prog, assoc prof, currently. **Honors/Awds:** Spencer Found; Fel Program, Nat Inst Health & Postdoctoral; Nat Res Coun; Nat Acad Sci & Ford Found.

HAMELTON, LYNNE. See HAMILTON, LYNN.

HAMER, DR. JAQUATOR
Educator. **Personal:** Born May 16, 1968, Ashland, MS; daughter of Joseph Sr and Edith Mae. **Educ:** Miss State Univ, BBA, 1990,

MS, 1994; Univ AR-Fayetteville, EdD, 2000. **Career:** Univ AR-Fayetteville, asst dean, multicult stud serv, 1994-2000; Bradley Univ, dir multicult stud serv, 2000-02; Southern Univ & A&M Col, dirretention & transition servs, 2002-. **Orgs:** Zeta Phi Beta Sorority Inc, 1988-; Am Col Personnel Asn, 1995-; Asn Black Cult Ctrs, 1996-; NAACP, 2001-. **Honors/Awds:** Outstanding Leadership Award, Univ Ark, 2001; People with a Purpose award, Peoria Black Expo Inc, 2002. **Special Achievements:** Dissertation: University of Arkansas's African American Undergraduate Students Perceptions of the Campus Climate, 2000. **Home Addr:** 8001 Jefferson Hwy, Baton Rouge, LA 70809.

HAMER, DR. JUDITH ANN
Executive. **Personal:** Born Jan 3, 1939, Brooklyn, NY; daughter of Frank Leslie Thompson and Martha Louise Taylor Thompson; married Martin J; children: Kim T, Fern S & Jill T. **Educ:** Cornell Univ, BA, 1960; Smith Col, MAT, 1961; Columbia Univ, PhD, 1984. **Career:** CCNY, instr, 1971-76; Columbia Univ, adj instr, 1977-83; Learning Int, consult writer, 1984-86; Paine Webber Inc, dp trainer, 1986, training mgr, corp training dept, div vpres, currently. **Orgs:** Coalition 100 Black Women Stamford CT. **Honors/Awds:** Ford Found Fel Black Am, 1976-81. **Special Achievements:** Co-editor with Martin J Hamer, Centers of the Self: Short Stories by Black American Women from the Nineteenth Century to the Present, Hill & Wang, 1994. **Home Addr:** 19 Webb Rd, Westport, CT 06880, **Home Phone:** (203)226-9942. **Business Phone:** (201)902-8222.

HAMER, STEVE (STEVIE RAY HAMER)
Basketball player. **Personal:** Born Nov 13, 1973, Memphis, TN. **Educ:** Univ Tenn, attended 1996. **Career:** Basketball player (retired); Boston Celtics, ctr, 1996-97.

HAMER, STEVIE RAY. See HAMER, STEVE.

HAMILL, MARGARET HUDGENS
Educator. **Personal:** Born Mar 9, 1937, Laurens, SC; children: Beatrice Chauntea. **Educ:** Benedict Col, BA 1958; St Peter's Col, Ed diploma, 1962. **Career:** No 5 Pub Sch, educr, 1966-68; Frank R Conwell, educr, 1968-74; Joseph H Brensinger, educr, 1974-. **Orgs:** School rep NJ Educ Asn, 1985-; adv, Tauette Club, 1985-; bd dirs, Bayonne Chap Nat Conf Christians & Jews, 1985-; pres, Young Women's League Friendship Bapt Church, 1986-; First vpres Bayonne Youth Ctr Inc, 1986-; sgt-of-arms Tau Gamma Delta Sor Psi Chapt. **Honors/Awds:** Community Service Award Bayonne, Nat Asn Advan Colored People, 1979; Brotherhood Award Nat Conf, Christians & Jews, 1985; Mary McLeod Bethune Award, 1985. **Home Addr:** 42 W 18th St, Bayonne, NJ 07002. **Business Phone:** (201)547-5703.

HAMILTON, ART
State government official, lawyer. **Personal:** Born Jan 1, 1947?, Phoenix, AZ; married; children: 3. **Educ:** Phoenix Col. **Career:** Began as public affairs representative; Arizona State Legisl, Phoenix AZ, state rep, Dist 22, House Minority Leader, 1993-99; Hamilton, Gullett, Davis & Roman LLC, patner, pub affairs consult, currently. **Orgs:** Found State Legis, Nat Conf State Legis; founding mem, State Legis Leaders Found; Dem Nat Comt; Phoenix Sky Harbor Aviation Adv Bd; Ariz State Bar Bd Gov; Labor's Community Serv Agency Maricopa County; bd dir, Phoenix C Hosp; Int Brotherhood Elec Workers; life mem, NAACP Maricopa County br; mem, Phoenix C Hosp. **Honors/Awds:** Arthur M Hamilton School, named in honor, 1985. **Special Achievements:** He was the first African-American and only Arizonan to be elected President of the National Conference of State Legislatures. **Business Addr:** Partner, Public Affairs Consultant, Hamilton Gullett Davis & Roman LLC, 300 W Westwood Cir Suite 460, Phoenix, AZ 85013, **Business Phone:** (602)266-6565.

HAMILTON, ARTHUR LEE, JR.
Newspaper editor. **Personal:** Born Oct 19, 1957, Detroit, MI; son of Arthur Hamilton and Lucy; married Marilyn, Aug 27, 1992; children: Kyala, Omar, Arlinda, Chineca & Mike. **Educ:** S Western Mich, 1979; Northern Mich Univ, 1984; Jackson Community Col, assoc, 1987; Spring Arbor, 1988. **Career:** Oracle Newspaper, staff writer, 1979-81; Huron Valley-Monitor Newspaper, ed, 1985-87; Snow Bird Newspaper, staff writer, 1988-89; Lakeland Pen Newspaper, ed, 1993-. **Orgs:** Chmn & publicity, Nat Asn Advan Colored People, 1992-93; pres & founder, Fathers Behind Bars Inc, 1993-; Numens Masonic Lodge, 1993-. **Honors/Awds:** Southern Univ ill, Best Prison Paper Country, 1986-87; Member of the Year, Nat Asn Advan Colored People, 1993; Member of the Year, Fathers Behind Bars, 1994. **Special Achievements:** Learning to Die, 1981; Caged by the Wolverine, 1995; Rat Race, Poem. **Military Serv:** USN, seaman, 1975-77. **Home Addr:** 525 Superior, Niles, MI 49120, **Home Phone:** (269)684-5715.

HAMILTON, ARTHUR N.
Judge. **Personal:** Born Jan 21, 1917, New Orleans, LA; married Mary; children: Lisa. **Educ:** Kent Col Law, JD, 1950; Nat Col Juvenile Ct Judges Univ NV, grad, 1973. **Career:** Judge (retired); Cook County, asst states atty, 1955-56; Chicago Park Dist, first asst gen atty, Ill, spec asst atty gen, 1968-69; Cook County Circuit Ct, assoc judge, 1971; City Chicago, asst corp coun. **Orgs:** Mem bd, Augustana Hosp; bd mem, Inter Relig Conf Urban Affairs; bd mem, Church Fed Greater Chicago; bd mem, Pkwy Community House; deleg, Nat Conv Lutheran Church Am, 1970; pres, Ill Judges Asn; Chicago, Cook County; Am & Nat Bar Asns. **Honors/Awds:** Advocacy C Award, Lake Bluff Chicago Homes C, 1974.

HAMILTON, AUBREY J. See Obituaries section.

HAMILTON, DR. AWILDA
Educator, dean (education). **Educ:** Howard Univ, BA; Ohio Univ, MA, 1972; Univ Akron, PhD, 1980. **Career:** Univ Cent Fla, fel, 2004-05; Ohio Brd Regents, prin investr; Kent St Univ, fac mem, prog cord, spl asst to dean, assoc prof, Col & Grad Sch Educ, assoc dean, currently, Educ Found & Spec Serv, chair, currently. **Orgs:** Fel Am Coun Educ, 2004-05. **Business Addr:** Associate Dean, Department Chair, Kent State University, College & Graduate Shcool of Education, 409 White Hall, PO Box 5190, Kent, OH 44242-0001, **Business Phone:** (330)672-2294.

HAMILTON, BOBBY
Football player. **Personal:** Born Jul 1, 1971, Columbia, MS; son of Billy. **Educ:** Southern Miss Univ. **Career:** Football player (retired), Seattle Sea hawks, 1994-95; Amsterdam Admirals, 1996; New York Jets, defensive end, 1996-99, 2006; New Eng patriots, 2000-03; Oakland Raiders,2004-05; Cleveland Browns, defensive lineman, 2007. **Honors/Awds:** Super Bowl champion, XXXVI, XXXVIII.

HAMILTON, CHARLES VERNON
Educator. **Personal:** Born Oct 19, 1929, Muskogee, OK; son of Owen and Viola Haynes; married Dona Louise Cooper Hamilton, Oct 5, 1956; children: Valli, Carol. **Educ:** Roosevelt Univ, Chicago, IL, BA, 1951; Loyola Univ, Sch Law, Chicago, IL, JD, 1954; Univ Chicago, Chicago, IL, MA, 1957, PhD, 1964. **Career:** Retired, Tuskegee Univ, AL, asst prof, 1958-60; Rutgers Univ, Newark, NJ, asst prof, 1963-64; Lincoln Univ, Oxford, PA, prof, 1964-67; Roosevelt Univ, Chicago, IL, prof, 1967-69; Columbia Univ, NY, prof, 1969-97; Metrop Appl Res Ctr, dir; Ford Found, consult. **Orgs:** Bd trustees, Twentieth Century Found; bd Nat Asn Advan Colored People, 1975; bd eds, Polit Sc Quart, 1975; fel Am Acad Arts & Sci, 1993. **Honors/Awds:** Lindback Teaching Award, Lincoln Univ, 1965; Alumni Award, Univ Chicago, 1970; Roosevelt Univ Alumni Award, 1970; Named Wallace S. Sayre Professor, Government Columbia, 1971; Mark Van Doren Teaching Award, Columbia Univ, 1982; Great Teacher Award, Columbia Univ, 1985. **Special Achievements:** Adam Clayton Powell Jr, 1991; One of the first African Americans to hold an academic chair at an Ivy League university; Chicago Sun-Times listed in the leading scholars in America, one of four Columbia professors included in 1995. **Military Serv:** AUS, Pvt, 1948-49. **Business Addr:** Professor, Columbia University, 420 W 118th St Rm 727, New York, NY 10027.*

HAMILTON, DARRYL QUINN
Baseball player, baseball executive. **Personal:** Born Dec 3, 1964, Baton Rouge, LA; son of John C Sr and Geraldine Pitts; married Shaun Robinson. **Educ:** Nicholls State Univ, Thibodaux, LA, attended 1986. **Career:** Baseball player (retired), baseball executive; Milwaukee Brewers, outfielder, 1988, 1990-95; Tex Rangers, 1996; San Francisco Giants, 1997-98; Colo Rockies, 1998-99; NY Mets, 1999-2001; MLB Radio, on-airhost, 2004-06, MLB comnr off, sr specialist on-field opers, 2006-. **Honors/Awds:** Topps Minor League Player of the Month, Topps Baseball Card, 1987; Milwaukee Brewers Player of the Month, Milwaukee Minor League, 1986, 1987; Milwaukee Brewers Unsung Hero Award, Milwaukee Brewers, 1991; Nicholls State University Hall Fame, 1991; Milwaukee Brewers Good Guy Award, 1992. **Home Phone:** (713)864-6509.

HAMILTON, DEAN
Entrepreneur, founder (originator). **Career:** NetExpress Ventel Inc; LPCom Inc; Subspace Commun, co found & chief exec officer; Ascend Communs, gen mgr; CoSine Commun, founder, pres & chief exec officer, currently. **Business Addr:** Cheif Executive Officer, President, CoSine Communications Inc, 1200 Bridge Pkwy, Redwood City, CA 94065, **Business Phone:** 877-426-7463.*

HAMILTON, EDWARD N
Sculptor. **Personal:** Born Feb 14, 1947, Cincinnati, OH; married Bernadette S Chapman. **Educ:** Louisville Sch Art, attended 1969; Univ Louisville, attended 1971; Spalding Col, attended 1973. **Career:** Iroquois High Sch, teacher, 1969-72; Louisville Art Workshop, 1972; Louisville Speed Museum, lectr, 1974; self-employed sculptor; Ed Hamilton Studio, owner, currently. **Orgs:** Alpha Phi Alpha Fraternity; Nat Conf Artists, 1980; bd mem, Renaissance Develop Corp; Art Circle Asn; bd mem, St Frances High Sch, Louisville; bd mem, Ky Minority Businessmen; Speed Art Mus; bd mem, Ky Hist Ctr. **Honors/Awds:** Kentucky Black Achievers Award, 1980; Bronze St Frances of Row, St Frances of Row Ch Louisville; Bronze of Whitney M Young Jr, comn by Ky State Alumni, 1998; Bronze portrait bust of Medgar W. Evers, comn by Don Coleman Advert Co, Detroit, MI; Governors Awards in the Arts, 1991; DA Honorary Degree, Univ Louisville, 2004; DA Honorary Degree, Western Ky Univ, 2004. **Special Achievements:** Numerous exhibitions, group shows, pub comn works in pvt collections including, Owensboro Mus Fine Art; Memphis State Univ Gallery; Washington Design Ctr; JB Speed Art Mus; Gibellina Mus in Palermo Italy; Nat Comn Joe Louis, Cobo Hall in Detroit, MI; Booker T Wash, Hampton Univ; Amistad Memorial, New Haven, CT; The Spirit of Freedom Memorial, Wash, DC, 1998; Abraham Lincoln Memorial, 2009. **Business Addr:** Owner, Ed Hamilton Studio Inc, 543 S Shelby St, Louisville, KY 40202, **Business Phone:** (502)587-7709.

HAMILTON, DR. EDWIN. See Obituaries section.

HAMILTON, EUGENE NOLAN
Judge. **Personal:** Born Aug 24, 1933, Memphis, TN; son of Thomas E and Barbara Blakey; married Virginia, Jun 16, 1956; children: Alexandra, Steven, James, Eric, David, Rachael, Jeremiah, Michael & Marcus. **Educ:** Univ Ill, BA, 1955, JD, 1959. **Career:** Judge (retired), Educator; AUS, judge advocate officer, 1959-61; US Dept Justice, trial atty, 1961-70; Super Ct DC, judge, 1970; DC Super Ct, sr judge, chief judge; Am Univ Wash Col Law, adj prof, 1985-; Harvard Law Sch, lectr law, 1995-. **Orgs:** Am Bar Asn, 1970; Wash Bar Asn; Bar Asn DC; DC Bar Asn. **Honors/Awds:** Ollie Mae Cooper Award, Wash Bar Asn, 1993; Wiley A Branton Issues Symposium Award, Nat Bar Asn; Oldender Found Generous Heart Award; Medallion Merit, Charles Hamilton Houston; Humanitarian Award, Univ Ill Alumni Asn. **Military Serv:** AUS, capt, 1959-61. **Business Addr:** Lecturer, Havard Law School, 1563 Mass Ave, Cambridge, MA 02138, **Business Phone:** (617)495-3136.

HAMILTON, DR. FRANKLIN D.
Educator. **Personal:** Born Oct 30, 1942, Aucilla, FL; son of Verdell and Esther; children: Kayla, Ebony & Nikki. **Educ:** Fla A&M Univ, BS 1964; Univ Pittsburgh, PhD, 1969. **Career:** Univ Pittsburgh, USPHS fel, 1964-69; State Univ NY, USPHS fel, 1969-71; Univ Tenn, from asst prof to assoc prof, 1971-79; Atlanta Univ, assoc prof, 1979-88; Univ Calif, Berkeley, vis prof, 1986-87; Univ Calif, Berkeley, Dept Biochem, vis prof, 1986-89; Fla A&M Univ, Div Sponsored Res, dir, 1989, Environ Scis Inst, prof chem, currently, vpres res,currently. **Orgs:** Vice chair, Sci Adv Comn Nat Asn Equal Opprtunity Higher Educ; consult, Nat Inst Health; consult, Robert Wood Johnson Fund; consult, Premed, Rev Comn, United Negro Col Fund; AAAS; Am Soc Cell Biol; comn mem, MARC Rev Comn, NIGMS, NIH; comn mem, NSF Pre-doctoral Fel Rev Comn; coun mem, Am Soc Biochem & MSI Biol, 1988-91. **Special Achievements:** Published, "Minorities in Sci, A Challenge for Change in Bio medicine",1977; "Proceeding of the Conference on Health Professional Educational Programs", 1980; "Participation of Blacks in the Basic Sciences, An Assessment in Black Students in Higher Education in the 70's, Condition sand Experiences" edited by Gail Thomas, Greenwood Press, 1981. **Business Addr:** Professor of Chemistry, Vice President for Research, Florida A&M University, Environmental Sciences Institute, 1515 Martin Luther King Blvd, Tallahassee, FL 32307, **Business Phone:** (850)599-3554.

HAMILTON, H J BELTON
Judge. **Personal:** Born Jun 1, 1924, Columbus, MS; married Midori Minamoto; children: Konrad & Camille. **Educ:** Stanford Univ, AB, polit sci, 1949; Northwestern Sch Law, Lewis & Clark Col, JD, 1953; Univ Ore, postgrad studies pub affairs, 1960-61. **Career:** Gen Pract Law, atty, 1953-54; State Bur Labor, asst atty gen, state Ore & staff atty, 1955-58; Ford Found fel, 1960-61; US, admin law judge; Soc Security Dept, admin law judge. **Orgs:** Secy treas, Freedom Family Ltd; pres, Alpha Devel Invest Corp; Ore State, Am Bar Asns; Am Trial Lawyers Asn; World Asn Judges; chmn, Admin Law Secy, Nat Bar Asn; Nat Urban League Quarter Century Club; Ore State Adv Comt, US Comn Civic Rights; Ore State Adv Coun; co-founder, chmn, Legal Coun & Parliamentarian, Int Asn Off Human Rights Agencies; Nat Urban League New Thrust Task Force Instnl Reorientation; pres, Urban League Portland; Boltol-Cedar Oak PTA; Portland chap, Alpha Phi Alpha; TV host, PBL-Spin Off. **Honors/Awds:** Outstanding Civic Contributions to Community, Alpha Phi Alpha. **Special Achievements:** First confirmed African-Am grad, Stanford Alumni Asn, 1949; Author, 'legislation - attorney general opinion', scholarly articles on wide range of subjects; Book: '33 Years Inside An Interracial Family', 1994. **Military Serv:** AUS, s/sgt, 1943-46. **Home Addr:** 2622 S Marylhurst Dr, West Linn, OR 97068.

HAMILTON, HARRY EDWIN
Lawyer, football player. **Personal:** Born Nov 26, 1962, Jamaica, NY. **Educ:** Pa State Univ, BA, pre-law, lib arts, 1984. **Career:** Football player (retired), lawyer; NY Jets, 1984-87; Tampa Bay Buccaneers, defensive back, 1988-91; atty, currently. **Honors/Awds:** Sporting News NFL All-Star Team, 1989. **Business Addr:** Attorney, 307 Silo Ridge Ct Apt 301, Odenton, MD 21113-3271.

HAMILTON, HOWARD W
Executive. **Personal:** Born Jul 21, 1948, Chicago, IL; son of Etta Mae and Howard; divorced; children: Howard, Christina, James

& Olivia. **Educ:** Parsons Col, BA, 1971; Columbia Univ, MBA, 1979. **Career:** E R Squibb Pharmaceut, field sales, 1972-77; Lederle Labs, prod prom mgr, 1979-80; Schering Labs, prod mgr, 1980-83; Abbott Labs, sr prod mgr, 1984-93; Essilor Am, group mkt mgr, 1994-95; Essilor Thin Films, gen mgr, 1996-; Johnson & Johnson Vision Care Inc, Spectacle Lens Group, dir mkt, 1998-. **Orgs:** Parlimentarian, Action Alliance Black Prof, 1988-90; pres, bd trustees, 1989-92, Actor's Summer Theatre; pres, 1991-92, African Am Action Alliance. **Home Phone:** (704)366-8330. **Business Addr:** Director of Marketing, Johnson & Johnson Vision Care Inc, The Spectacle Lens Group, 5568 Airport Rd NW, Roanoke, VA 24012-1311, **Business Phone:** (540)362-2020.

HAMILTON, JOHN M
Executive. **Career:** Wash Shores Savings Bank, FSB, Orlando, Fla, chief exec. **Business Addr:** Chief Executive, Wash Shores Savings Bank FSB, 715 S Goldwyn Ave, Orlando, FL 32805.

HAMILTON, DR. JOHN MARK, JR.
Dentist. **Personal:** Born Oct 2, 1931, Washington, DC; son of John M; married Dorothy Wilson; children: John M III & Sheree R. **Educ:** US Mil Acad, West Point, NY, BS, 1955; AUS Command & Gen Staff Col, 1964; AUS War Col, 1977; Univ Med & Dentistry New Jersey, DMD, 1982. **Career:** Hundred & one Airborne Div, Vietnam, brigade dep commander, infantry battalion commander, 1970-71; AUS Command & Gen Staff Col, Fort Leavenworth KS, fac mem, 1971-74; US Military, Dist Wash, DC, chief human resources div, 1974-75; Office US Secy Defense, military advr, 1975-78; pvt practice, dentist, 1982-; JB Johnson Nursing Ctr, consulting dentist, 1985-; E River Health Ctr, consulting dentist, 1984-; John M Hamilton Jr, DMD, PC, dir, 1988-; Hamilton Prof Enterprises Inc, pres, 1988-. **Orgs:** Kappa Alpha Psi Fraternity, 1951-; vpres, Wee Care Youth Acad, 1974-; consult, Lawrence Johnson & Assoc, 1983; Robert T Freeman Dent Soc, 1984-; vpres, Investors Consolidated Asn Inc, 1985-87; bd dir, Ethel James Williams Scholar Found, 1986-; bd dir, La Mirage Beauty Enterprises, 1986-87. **Honors/Awds:** Harvard Prize Book Award, Harvard Club Wash, DC; Recruiting Award, USAF Recruiting Serv, 1982. **Military Serv:** AUS Infantry col, 23 yrs; Ranger Tab, Parachute Badge, Army Commendation Medal with Oak Leaf Cluster, Vietnam Gallantry Cross with Palm, Legion of Merit, Air Medal with 13th Oak Leaf Cluster, Bronze Star with 1st Oak Leaf Cluster, Vietnam Gallantry Cross with Silver Star, Combat Infantryman Badge. **Home Addr:** 10806 Braeburn Rd, Columbia, MD 21044, **Home Phone:** (301)596-9235. **Business Addr:** President, Hamilton Professional Enterprises Inc., 10806 Braeburn Rd, Columbia, MD 21044.

HAMILTON, JONNIE
Association executive, nurse. **Career:** Sch-based health ctr, St John Health Syst, Detroit, Mich, Pediatric Nurse Practr; Middlewest Region, dir, 2002-04; Chi Eta Phi Sorority Inc, regional dir; Napoleon B Jordan Ctr Health, clinic dir & Pediatric nurse parctr, currently. **Orgs:** Lambda Chi Chap; pres, Mich Nurses Asn; Am Nurses Asn; Nat Black Nurses Asn; Sigma Theta Tau Nursing Honor Soc; NAACP; Delta Sigma Theta Sorority Inc; Mich & Detroit Black Nurses Asn. **Honors/Awds:** Advanced Practice Nurse Excellence Award: Mich Nurses Asn, Nat Black Nurses Asn, Chi Eta Phi Sorority Inc. **Business Addr:** Clinic Director, Pediatric Nurse Practitioner, Napoleon B Jordan Center for Health Care, Butzel Elementary and Middle Sch, 2301 Van Dyke Rm 506, Detroit, MI 48214, **Business Phone:** (313)866-9973.

HAMILTON, LEONARD
Basketball coach. **Personal:** Born Aug 4, 1948, North Carolina; son of John and Bennie Ruth; married Claudette; children: 2. **Educ:** Univ Tenn-Martin, BA, phys educ, 1971; Austin Peay State Univ, MA, phys & health educ, 1973. **Career:** Austin Peay State Univ, grad asst, 1971-73, full-time asst, 1973-74; Univ Ky, asst coach, 1974-80, asst coach, 1980, asst head coach; Okla State Univ, Still water, OK, head coach, 1986-90; Univ Miami, Coral Gables FL,head coach, 1991-2000; Wash Wizards head coach, 2000-01; Fla State Univ, head coach, 2002-. **Orgs:** Kappa Alpha Psi Fraternity. **Honors/Awds:** Univ Tenn-Martin Hall of Fame; Coach of the Year, Big E Conf, 1994-95, 1998-99; National Coach of the Year, United Press Intl, 1995; BCA Coach of the Year, 2000; University Miami Hall of Fame, 2006; Coach of the Year, The Atlantic Coach Conf, 2009. **Special Achievements:** First Associate Head Basketball Coach in Kentucky history. **Business Addr:** Head Coach Basketball, Florida State University, Athletics Department, 525 Stadium Dr W, PO Box 2195, Tallahassee, TN 32306, **Business Phone:** (850)644-2525.

HAMILTON, LISA GAY
Actor. **Personal:** Born Mar 25, 1964, Los Angeles, CA; daughter of Ira and Tina. **Educ:** NY Univ, BA, theatre; Juilliard Sch Drama, MA. **Career:** Actress, producer, director; Films: Krush Groove, 1985; Reversal of Fortune, 1990; Naked in New York, 1993; Palookaville, 1995; Drunks, 1995; Twelve Monkeys, 1995; Nick & Jane, 1997; Drunks, 1997; Life Breath, 1997; Jackie Brown, 1997; Beloved, 1998; True Crime, 1999; Ten Tiny Love Stories, 2001; The Sum of All Fears, 2002; The Truth About Charlie, 2002; Beah: A Black Woman Speaks, dir & producer, 2003; Nine Lives, 2005; Conviction, 2005; Honeydripper, 2007; Deception, 2008; The Soloist, 2009; TV appearances: Way Cool, 1991; Law & Order, 1995; "Homicide: Life on the Street", 1993; "New York Undercover", 1994; All My Children, 1994; Clarissa, 1995; One Life to Live, 1996; The Practice, 1997-2003; "The Defenders: Choice of Evils", 1998; "Ally McBeal", 1998; Swing Vote, 1999; "A House Divided", 2000; "Hamlet", 2000; "Sex & the City", 2002; "The L Word", 2004; "ER", 2005; "Law & Order: Special Victims Unit", 2006-07; "Without a Trace", 2006; "Numb3rs", 2007; "Law & Order: Special Victims Unit", 2006-07; "Men of a Certain Age", 2008. **Honors/Awds:** Documentary Award, AFI Fest, 2003; Bronze Leopard Award, Locarno Int Film Festival, 2005. **Business Addr:** Actress, c/o Paradigm Agency, 10100 Santa Monica Blvd Suite 2500, Los Angeles, CA 90067, **Business Phone:** (310)277-4400.*

HAMILTON, LYNN (LYNNE HAMELTON)
Actor. **Personal:** Born Apr 25, 1930, Yazoo City, MS; daughter of Louis and Nancy; married Frank S Jenkins; children: 1. **Educ:** Goodman Theatre, BA, 1954. **Career:** TV appearances: "The Practice"; "Sanford & Son"; "Roots I"I; "The Waltons"; "227"; "Golden Girls"; "Amen"; "Generations"; "Oh, Mama!", 2002; "Sins of the Father", 2004; "Dangerous Women"; "Judging Amy", 2004; Films: Shadows, 1959; Lady Sings the Blues; Buck & the Preacher; Bro John; Leadbelly; Legal Eagles; The Vanishing; Baby's Breath, 2003; stage appearances: Only In America, 1959; The Face of a Hero, 1960; The Miracle Worker; The Skin of Our Teeth. **Honors/Awds:** NAACP Image Award; Trail Blazer Award, NAACP; Living Legend Award, Nat Black Theatre, 2003. **Business Phone:** (213)653-7073.

HAMILTON, MCKINLEY JOHN
Clergy. **Personal:** Born Nov 24, 1921, Lake Charles, LA; son of Lincoln (deceased) and Jennie Virginia Keys; married Mary H Stone, Oct 19, 1957. **Educ:** Butler Col, Tex, AA, 1943; Bishop Col, Tex, BA, 1945; Crozer Theol Sem, PA, 1946; Howard Univ, Wash, MD, 1958. **Career:** Clergy (retired); St James Baptist Church & New Hope Baptist Church, pastor, 1942-43; Shiloh Baptist Church, asst to pastor, 1947-58; Good Samaritan Baptist Church, pastor, 1955-57; First Baptist Church, pastor, 1958-91. **Orgs:** Bd mem, T & C Ministers; pres, Fr City Ministerial Asn; pres, Am Cancer Soc; moderator, Bapt Pigg River Asn; bd mem, Sheltered Workshop Comt Action Fr Co; Fr Co Hist Soc; Men Health; pres, local chap, Nat Asn Advan Colored People; bd mem, United Fund; bd mem, Cancer Soc; vol, Sr Nutrit Prog Sr Citizens. **Honors/Awds:** Plaque, Outstanding Contrib, Community Franklin Co; Plaque, Mem Centurion, Club Ferrum Col, 1975; Honorary Doctor Humanities, Ferrum Col, 1981. **Home Phone:** (540)483-9384. *

HAMILTON, MICHAEL ANTONIO
Football player. **Personal:** Born Dec 3, 1973, Greenville, SC. **Educ:** NC A&T Univ. **Career:** San Diego Chargers, linebacker, 1997-2000; Miami Dolphins, 2000.

HAMILTON, DR. PAUL L.
Educator. **Personal:** Born Apr 1, 1941, Pueblo, CO; divorced; children: Askia Toure. **Educ:** Univ Denver, BA, 1964, MA, 1972; Univ N Colo, Ed.D, 1975. **Career:** Educator (retired); York St Cafe, managing partner; Denver Pub Schs,teacher, 1964-91, prin, 1991-95; State Colo, rep, 1969-73; Univ Denver,instr, 1971, lectr & res asst, 1971-72; adj prof hist, 1982-96; Univ Colo,instr, 1995-96; Hamilton Educ Consults, pres, currently; Power Learning Systs, dist dir, 1995; R A Renaissance Publs, pres, 1993. **Orgs:** Asn Study Classical African Civilizations; Nat Alliance Black Sch Educrs; Univ Denver Nat Hon Soc; pres, Renaissance Publs. **Honors/Awds:** Educator of the Year, Denver Asn Retd Citizens, 1991; Black Alumni Award,Univ Colo, 1995; Citizen of the Year, Omega Psi Phi Fraternity, Chi Phi Chap, 1995. **Special Achievements:** Author: Teacher's Guide for Afro American History; African People's Contributions to World History: Shattering the Myths, Vol 1. *

HAMILTON, PHANUEL J.
Government official. **Personal:** Born Aug 3, 1929, Detroit, MI; married; children: Thieda, Deborah & Gregory. **Educ:** Eastern Mich Univ, BA, 1951; Northwester Univ, grad sch speech; DePaul Univ; Chicago State Univ; KY Christian Univ, MA, 1973. **Career:** Teacher, 1956-64; Community Youth Welfare, dir, 1964-66; Cook County OEO, dir, 1965-66; OEO, manpower, 1966-69; Human Motivation Inst, consult, 1969; Mayor's Off Sr Citizens Chicago, dir field servs, 1970-. **Orgs:** Am Asn Retarded Persons, 1973-75; Cerontological Soc, 1975; Nat Coun Aging, 1974-75; Nat Asn Soc Workers; Nat Asn Community Develop; Kappa Alpha Psi; Sigma Phi; Pi Kappa Delta; Urban League; NAACP; Shiloh Baptist Church Mgt Develop. **Honors/Awds:** Award, 1971; Community Efford Organization Certificate Merit; achievement award, Kappa Alpha Psi. **Military Serv:** USAF, first lt, 1951-56.

HAMILTON, RAINY, JR.
Architect, business owner. **Personal:** Born Sep 22, 1956, Detroit, MI; son of Rainy Hamilton Sr and Bernice Hodges. **Educ:** Univ Detroit, MI, BS, archit, 1978, bachelors architecture, 1979. **Career:** Schervish, Vogel and Merz, PC, Detroit, MI, partner, 1979-90; Smith, Hinchman, and Grylls Assocs Inc, assoc & proj mgr, 1990-93; Hamilton Anderson Assoc, owner, 1993-, pres. **Orgs:** Am Inst Architects, 1979-; liaison, Minority Resources Comt, Am Inst Architects, 1989-; Detroit chap, pres, 2001-; founding mem, Mich Nat Orgn Minority Architects; State Mich Bd Architects & Bd surveyors. **Honors/Awds:** Young Architect of the Year, Detroit chap, Am Inst Architects, 1988; Outstanding Achievement Award for Building Design & Construction, Eng Soc, 1999; Merit Award, Mich Chap Am Soc Landscape Architects, 2000-01; Spec Community Initiative Award, Mich Soc Planning, 2002; Environ Achievement Award, Mich Environ Mgt Asn, 2003. **Special Achievements:** Hamilton Anderson Associates as one of the "Future 50" companies in metropolitan Detroit from over 6,400 establishments. INC Magazine also named the firm as one of the nation's fastest growing companies for 1999. Hamilton Anderson Associates was featured in the list of the Twenty Largest Architectural Firms in Crain's Detroit 2000 at the 17th spot. **Business Addr:** President, Hamilton Anderson Associates, 1435 Randolph St Suite 200, Detroit, MI 48226, **Business Phone:** (313)964-0270.*

HAMILTON, ROY L.
Educator. **Personal:** Born Jul 11, 1958, Baton Rouge, LA; son of Shirley I Wilson; children: Johnny F. **Educ:** Morehouse Col, BA, hist; Univ Wis-Milwaukee, MA, am hist; Ind Univ, further study am hist. **Career:** CIC Minority fel; Ind Univ, Albert L Kohlmier fel; Univ Wis, Advan Opportunity Prog fel; Ind State Univ, asst dir upward bound prog, 1984-89; Purdue Univ Calumet, dir educ talent prog, 1989-90, McNair Prog, dir, 1990-; Calumet Col St Joseph, adj fac degree completion prog, 1994-2001; Purdue Univ Calumet, lectr ethnic stud prog, 1995, Educ Oppurtunity Progs, asst vice chancellor, 2003-. **Orgs:** Mid-Am Asn Educ Opportunity Progs; Kappa Alpha Psi; Ind Coalition Blacks Higher Educ; Northwest Ind Symphony Orchestra Chorus; Christ United Methodist Church; Black Methodist Church Renewal (BMCR); Phi Delta Kappa;bd dir, Rose S Child Day Care Ctr; Monarch Awards Found; Xi Nu Omega Chap. **Honors/Awds:** Recognition for Distinguished work in Education, Alpha Kappa Alpha Sorority.

HAMILTON, RUFFIN, III
Football player. **Personal:** Born Mar 2, 1971, Detroit, MI; married Dena; children: Whitney. **Educ:** Tulane Univ. **Career:** Football player (retired); Green Bay Packers, linebacker, 1994; Atlanta Falcons, linebacker, 1997-99.

HAMILTON, SAMUEL CARTENIUS
Lawyer. **Personal:** Born Mar 29, 1936, Hope, AR; married Flora Elizabeth; children: Leslie Terrell, Sydne Carrigan; Patrice Alexan. **Educ:** Philander Smith Col, BS, 1958; Howard Univ, JD, 1970. **Career:** Roy M Ellis & Louise Eighnie Turner Gen Prac Law, Silver Spring, MD, assoc; Montgomery Co MD, asst states pros atty; Lilver Spring MD, pvt pract law; Legal Aid Clin US Dist Attys Off DC; Off Chief Coun Fed Highway Admin Litigation Div, legal intern; Ft Detrick MD, res asst; Hamilton & Assocs, atty, currently. **Orgs:** MD State Bar Asn; Am Bar Asn; Nat Bar Asn; pres, Frederick Co Br Nat Asn Advan Colored People; vpres, MD State Conf Nat Asn Advan Colored People Br; co-chmn; Comm Uphold State Pub Accomodation law; Prince Hall Masons; Kappa Alpha Psi Soc Frat; Phi Alpha Delta Legal Frat; bd dir, Comn Action Agency. **Honors/Awds:** Frederick Co Award for Service & Leadership, Stud Bar Asn, Howard Univ Sch Law; Outstanding Citizen Award, Am Legion; Outstanding Serv Award, Nat Asn Advan Colored People; Serv Award, Prince Hall Masons. **Home Addr:** 14 Hilltop Rd, Silver Spring, MD 20910, **Home Phone:** (301)565-0432. **Business Addr:** Attroney, Hamilton & Assocs, 8401 Colesville Rd Suite 620, Silver Spring, MD 20910, **Business Phone:** (301)589-3000.*

HAMILTON, THEOPHILUS ELLIOTT
School administrator. **Personal:** Born Feb 6, 1923, Detroit, MI; married Fannie L; children: Millicent. **Educ:** Eastern Mich Col, MusB, 1955, MA, 1962; Eastern Mich Univ, Spec Arts Degree Leadership & Sch Admin, 1967. **Career:** School administrator (retired); Pickford Pub Schs, teacher, dir vocal & instumental music, 1955-62; Highland Pk Pub Sch, vocal music teacher, 1962-64, asst prin, 1964-67; Eastern Mich Univ, asst dir personnel, 1967, career planning & placement ctr, asst dir, 1969-2004. **Orgs:** Past secy, treas, Mich Col & Univ Placement Assoc; admin appt, mem, Eastern Mich Univ Judicial Bd, 1977-78; appointed mem, Soc Ministry Comm Mich Synod Luth Church Am, 1977-78; Washtenaw County Am Red Cross Chap, 1988-90; assoc mem, Mich Assoc Sch Admin; Great Lakes Asn Col & Univ Placement, Col & Univ Personnel Asn, Sch Admin & Prin Assoc, Kappa Alpha Psi, Black Fac & Staff Assoc, EMU; fac adv, Delta Nu Chap, EMU; Ypsilanti Twp Planning Comn; bd dir, Washtenaw City Black Caucus Comn, Washtenaw City Citizens Comn Econ Opport; chmn, Ypsilanti Citizens Advising Comn, OEO; affirm action comn, Ypsilanti Pub Sch; bd dirs, Ypsilanti Fed Credit Union, 1996. **Honors/Awds:** Alumni Achievement Award, Kappa Alpha Psi, 1974; Dedication & Service to Community Award, Kappa Alpha Phi; Best Teacher Award, EMU Personnel; Gold Medallion Award, Div Stud Affairs, 1988; Sustained Super Service, Black Fac & Staff Assoc, 1991; Chairman Award, Washtenaw County Metrop Planning Comn, 1991-92; International Award, Kappa Delta Pi, 1992; Silver Medallion Award, Div Mkt & Stud Affairs, 1993; Honored for 25 years of Service & 70years of Inspiration by

Career Services, 1993; Oper ABLE, Most ABLE Award, 1994; Hon Mem, Golden Key Nat Hon Soc, 1996; Chief's Civilian Award, 1996. **Military Serv:** AUS, 1943-46. *

HAMILTON, WILBUR WYATT
Executive, baptist clergy. **Personal:** Born Jan 28, 1931, San Antonio, TX; son of E E Hamilton; married Joy Coleman. **Educ:** Simpson Bible Col, BS, social sci, DD; San Francisco City Col, AA; Golden Gate Univ, MBA. **Career:** Am Pres Line, terminal chief, 1965-69; San Franciso Housing Authority, actg exec dir & pres; San Franciso Redevelop Agency, area dir, 1969-71, asst exec dir admin, 1971-74, dep exec dir, 1974-77, exec dir, 1977-; Greater Victory Temple, sr pastor; Northern Calif Church God Christ, dir youth serv; San Francisco Redevelopment Agency, exec dir; Hamilton Memorial COGIC, San Franciso, pastor; Church God Christ Inc, secy gen bd, currently; Northwest Ecclesiastical Jurisdiction Calif, Seaside, CA, prelate, currently. **Orgs:** Secy, San Francisco Interdenom Minstrial Alliance; judge field fac, CORO Found; pres, Northern Calif Region, Nat Asn Housing & Redevelopment Officials; pres, Pac Southwest Region, Nat Asn Housing & Redevelopment Officials; NAACP; St Mary's Hosp Comt Bd. **Honors/Awds:** Outstanding Graduate Academy Achivement, Church God Christ Int; Chruch Chairman of the Year, Nat Conf Church God Christ. **Business Addr:** Prelate, California Northwest Ecclesiastical Jurisdiction, 874 36th Ave, Oakland, CA 94601, **Business Phone:** (510)547-8315.*

HAMILTON-ROSE, LESSIE
Educator, administrator. **Career:** Flower City Sch No 54, prin, currently. **Honors/Awds:** Distiguished Alumni Award, Niagara County Community Col, 1994. **Business Addr:** Principal, Flower City School No 54, 311 Flower City Park 14615, Rochester, NY 14619-2255, **Business Phone:** (585)254-2080.*

HAMITER, UHURU
Football player. **Personal:** Born Mar 14, 1973, Kingstree, SC. **Educ:** Dellaware State Univ. **Career:** New Orleans Saints, def end, 1998-99; Philadelphia Eagles, def end, 2000-01; Houston Texans, def end, 2002. **Honors/Awds:** Rookie of the Year, 1998.

HAMLAR, DR. DAVID DUFFIELD, SR.
Dentist. **Personal:** Born Sep 27, 1924, Roanoke, VA; son of Maude Smith and Robert; married Maxine Harbour, Apr 16, 1945 (died 2004); children: Jocelyn Hamlar Clark, David Jr & Deidre Diane Hamlar. **Educ:** Hampton Inst, Hampton, VA, 1943; Toledo Univ, Toledo, OH, BE, 1948; Howard Univ, Wash, DC, DDS, 1952; Providence Hosp, Baltimore, MD, intern, 1952-53. **Career:** Columbus OH private prac, 1954-. **Orgs:** Chmn, Children's Dental Health Week, Columbus Dental Assoc, 1960; chmn, patient care, Children's Hosp, Columbus, OH, 1984-90; pres, Columbus Bd Educ, 1975-79; basileus, Omega Psi Fraternity, Columbus, OH, 1958; chrmn, Commi Remem the C, 1990; Columbus Chamber Comm Ed Commt, 1990; Sire Archon, Lambda lamdba Boule; 25 yr, Sigma Pi Phi; 50 yr, Omega Psi Phi. **Honors/Awds:** Martin Luther King Humanitarian, Columbus Education Assoc, 1980; Equal Opportunity Award, Urban League, 1976; Distinguished Service Award, Columbus Bd Educ, 1979; Citizen of the Year, Omega Psi Phi Fraternity, 1976; Varsity "T" Hall of Fame, Toledo Univ, 1985; Ohio State Univ, Distinguished Citizen Award; Alpha Kappa Alpha Sorority, Humanitarian Award; Junior League, Outstanding Personal Achievement Award; Franklin Lodge Elks, Outstanding Service to Community Award. **Military Serv:** USN, 1943-45. **Home Addr:** 705 Bryden Rd, Columbus, OH 43209, **Home Phone:** (614)224-4841. **Business Addr:** Dentist, 705 Bryden Rd, Columbus, OH 43209, **Business Phone:** (614)224-4841.

HAMLAR, JOCELYN B
Banker, executive. **Personal:** Born Jan 8, 1954, Columbus, OH; daughter of Maxine Eloise Harbour(deceased) and David Duffield; married Roy Clark, Aug 12, 1978 (divorced 1993); children: Morgan Allison & Sydney Erin; married Leighton J Toney, Aug 26, 2000. **Educ:** Boston Univ, MS, 1981, BLS, 1976. **Career:** Bank New Eng, asst mkt off, 1978-80; WNEV-TV, prod asst, 1979-81; United Community Planning Corp, commun dir, 1981-82; Am Hosp Assn, mkt commun specialist, 1982-83; WXRT-FM Radio Sta, dir adv & prom, 1983-86; LaSalle Nat Bank, vpres, dir public rel, 1986-91; WBEZ-FM, dir mkt, 1991-93; ABN Amro N Am Inc, dir corp communs, vpres, 1993-97; LaSalle Bank Corp, sr vpres corp commun & dir comms, 1997-. **Orgs:** Next Theatre, bd dir, 1989-91; Child Care Ctr Asn, bd dir, 1990-; Remains Theatre, bd dir, 1992-93; Pub Allies, bd dir, 1995-; Chicago Coun Urban Affairs, bd dir, 1999-; Hubbard St Dance Chicago, bd dir, 2000-; presidents adv coun, Harold Wash Col, Chicago, Ill, 1999-. **Honors/Awds:** Black Women Hall of Fame Found, Kizzy Award, 1987, 1990; Greater Boston YMCA, Black Achievement Award, 1979. **Business Addr:** Senior Vice President Corporate Communications, LaSalle Bank Corporation, 135 S LaSalle St, Chicago, IL 60603, **Business Phone:** (312)904-2171.

HAMLAR, PORTIA YVONNE TRENHOLM
Lawyer, college teacher, executive director. **Personal:** Born Apr 30, 1932, Montgomery, AL; daughter of Harper Councill (deceased) and Portia Lee (deceased); children: 1. **Educ:** Ala State Univ, BA, 1951; Mich State Univ, MA, 1953; Univ Detroit Sch Law, JD, 1972; Wayne State Univ, attended. **Career:** Lawyer (retired), Detroit Pub Schs, vocal music instr, 1953-71; Univ Mich; acad counr, 1957-58; Pontiac High Sch,vocal music instr, 1963-65; Hyman Gurwin Nachman & Friedman, legal secy, 1966-68; Univ Detroit, law rev staff, 1970-72; Mich Appellate Defender, Detroit, legal researcher, 1971-73; Am Bar Asn Lawyers Housing Prog, LA, admin asst, 1973; Gr Watts Model Cities Housing Corp, LA, legal coun, 1973; DE Law Sch Widener Univ, asst prof law, 1980-82; Mich State Bar Atty Grievence Comn, assoc coun, 1982-; Chrysler Corp, atty; Univ Wis, Stevens Point, WI, asst chancellor & dir equity & affirmative action, currently; Univ Detroit Sch Law, adj prof law; Hazardous Mat Mgt J, ed bd. **Orgs:** Organist, choir dir, St Andrews Presby Church, 1955-72; lit & res, Am Bar Asn Comn Real Property Law, 1971-72; ABA Comn OSHA Law, 1978-; Am Asn Affirmative Action; Resources Counr Occup Safety & Health Lawyers Group; Mich State Bar; Detroit Bar Asn; Delta Sigma Theta; Kappa Beta Pi; Alpha Kappa Mu; Mu Phi Epsilon. **Special Achievements:** Publ: "Landlord & Tenant", 1971; "HUD's Authority to Mandate EffectiveManagement of Public Housing", 1972; "Defending the Employer in OSHA Contests", 1977, "Minority Tokenism in American Law Schools", 1983. *

HAMLIN, ARTHUR HENRY
Educator. **Personal:** Born Jan 4, 1942, Bastrop, LA; son of Augustine and Elmore; married Deloris E; children: Eric & Erica. **Educ:** Grambling State Univ, BS, 1965; Northeast La Univ, MA, 1970. **Career:** CTA, bus oper, 1966-67; City Bastrop, gym super, 1973-76; City Bastrop, councilman, 1977-; Morehouse Parish Sch Bd, teacher-coach, 1966-; Morehouse Parish Drug Free Schs & Communities, coordr. **Orgs:** Oper Greenview Club, 1971-72; past pres, Morehouse Community Improvment Org, 1973; past pres, Morehouse Concerned Citizens, 1979; past secy, Club21, 1981; Gents Civic & Social Club. **Home Addr:** 2302 Bonnie Ave, Bastrop, LA 71220. *

HAMLIN, DAVID W.
Manager. **Personal:** Born Jan 1, 1989, Pittsburgh, PA. **Educ:** Carnegie Mellon, Master Pub mgt. **Career:** Hills Dept Store, hard lines merchandise mgr, 1976-80; Equitable Gas Co, buyer, 1980-90; Duquesne Light Co, dir minority bus develop, 1990-96; Carnegie Mellon Univ, dir purchasing, 1996-99; Rutgers Univ, exec dir univ procurement servs, 1999-2007; McCann-Erickson USA Inc, vpres & mgr supplier diversity, 2007-. **Orgs:** Nat Purchasing Mgt Asn, 1980-; chmn, Pittsburgh Regional Minority Purchasing Coun, 1980-. **Honors/Awds:** Man of the Year, Black Opinion Magazine, 1989; Excellence Award in Business, Minority Business Opportunity Comm, 1993. **Business Phone:** (646)865-2778.

HAMLIN, ERNEST LEE
Clergy. **Personal:** Born Dec 9, 1943, Sussex County, VA; son of Arish L and Elma R; married Pamela Diane Carter, May 6, 1978; children: Kevin, Rafael & Cherry. **Educ:** Va Union Univ, BA, 1970, Sch Theol, MDiv, 1974; Presby Sch Christian Educ, 1976; Va Commonwealth Univ, pastoral educ, 1976-77. **Career:** Bethesda Baptist Church, pastor, 1981-83; Richmond Va Sem, theol & christian educ, prof, 1982-89; Ebenezer Baptist Church, supply pastor, 1984; Union Hill United Church Christ, pastor, 1986-89; Christian Educ Ministries, pres, 1990-; Emmanuel-St Mark's United Church Christ, pastor, 1990-92; Tubman-King COT Church, sr pastor, 1992; Pembroke Manor United Church of Christ, interim pastor, currently. **Orgs:** Bd dirs, Richmond Chap, 1981-85; bd dirs, SCLC, Va State Unit, 1982-90; exec secy, East Side Ecumenical Fel, 1990-91, exec vpres, 1991-92; bd dirs, OIC Metro Saginaw, 1990-92, exec vpres, Northeast Ministerial Alliance, 1991-92; bd dirs, One Church One Child MIC, 1991-92;; bd dirs, Habitat for Humanity, 1992-. **Honors/Awds:** Hon CHP, UNF, 1983; Outstanding Service Award, Richmond Va Sem, 1986; Outstanding Leadership Award, Emmanuel-St Mark's UCC, 1992. **Special Achievements:** "A True Mother & Christ," published poem, 1990; SCLC, Richmond Chap, Mass Meeting, crd, 1984-85; Negro BUS & Prof Women's Sisterhood Sunday, preacher, 1991; Women's Hist Celebration, crd, 1991-; City-Wide Martin Luther King Jr Christian Unity Serv, preacher, 1992. **Home Addr:** 148 Springwood Dr, Daytona Beach, FL 32119-1425. **Business Addr:** Interim Pastor, Pembroke Manor United Church of Christ, 600 Independence Blvd, Virginia Beach, VA 23462, **Business Phone:** (757)490-8290.

HAMM, PAULA
Executive. **Career:** Symantec Corp, Security Prod Mgt, sr dir, 2003. **Business Phone:** (408)517-8000.*

HAMMER, M. C. (STANLEY KIRK BURRELL)
Singer. **Personal:** Born May 30, 1962, Oakland, CA; son of Louis Burrell Sr; married Stephanie; children: Akeiba Monique, Sarah Brooke, Stanley Kirk, Jeremiah & Samuel. **Career:** Oakland Athletics, bat boy; Holy Ghost Boys, rap group, singer; Bust It Records, founder; solo performer, currently; Albums: Feel My Power, 1987; Let's Get It Started, 1988; Please Hammer Don't Hurt 'Em, 1990; Too Legit to Quit, 1991; The Funky Headhunter, 1994; Inside Out, 1995; Family Affair, 1998; Active Duty, 2001; Full Blast, 2003; Look Look Look, 2006; Borat: Cultural Learnings of America for Make Benefit Glorious Nation of Kazakhstan, 2006; DanceJamtheMusic, 2008; TV: "The Surreal Life", 2002; "Dance Fever", 2003; "I Married", 2004; "Praise the Lord", 2006; "LOOK", 2006; "So Long", 2006. **Honors/Awds:** Grammy Award with Rick James & Alonzo Miller for Best Rhythm and Blues Song, U Can't Touch This, 1990; Grammy Award for Best Rap Solo, U Can't touch This, 1990; Grammy Award for Best Video Long Form, Please Hammer Don't Hurt 'Em the Movie, 1990; Image Award, NAACP; Billboard Diamond Award; Soul Train Music Award, 1991; Living Legends of Hip Hop Award, Hip Hop Intl, 2008. **Military Serv:** USN. **Business Addr:** Recording Artist, c/o Capitol Records Inc, 1750 Vine St, Los Angeles, CA 90028-5209.

HAMMETT, WILLIE ANDERSON
Educator. **Personal:** Born Apr 19, 1945, Sumerton, SC; children: Jamal. **Educ:** Hudson Valley Comm Col, AAS, 1966; WV St Col, BS, 1968; State Univ NY, Albany, MS, 1971, EdS, 1977. **Career:** Educator (retired); Troy Sch System, guidance coun, 1969-71, basketball coach, 1969-71; Hudson Valley Community Col, coun, 1971-72, asst basketball coach, 1971-72, dir educ opportunity prog, 1972, vpres stud affairs, 1972-03; Troy Savings Inc, trustee. **Orgs:** Bd dir, Camp Fire Girls, 1969-72; vpres, Troy Jaycees, 1969-72; bd trustees, Troy YWCA, 1972-; pres, NA-MAL Enterprises Inc, 1977-79; Coun Black Am Affairs, 1977-; bd dir, Samaritan Hosp, Troy, NY, 1978-; vchairperson, exec bd, NY State Spec Prog Personnel Assoc, 1979-; Troy Boys & Girls Club; St Anne's Inst, Albany. **Honors/Awds:** Listed in Outstanding Young Men of America, 1972. *

HAMMOCK, EDWARD R.
Government official, lawyer. **Personal:** Born Apr 20, 1938, Bronx, NY; married Jeanne Marshall; children: Erica, Rochelle & Regina. **Educ:** Brooklyn Col, BA, 1959; St John's Univ Law Sch, LLB, 1966. **Career:** Youth Coun Bur, caseworker, 1960-63; Supreme Ct Kings County, probation officer, 1963-66; NY Homicide Bur, asst dist atty, 1966-69; Daytop Village Inc, exec dir, 1969-72; Dept Law, NY State Criminal Invest, Attica Prison Riot, spec asst atty gen, 1971-73; NY City Dept Invest, dep comnr,1973-76; NY State Parole Bd, chief exec officer & chmn div parole, 1976; St John's Univ Sch Law, adj prof; Nat Inst Drug Abuse, spec consult; Proj Return Inc, bd dir; pvt prac, atty, currently. **Orgs:** The 100 Black Men; NY Lawyers Asn; NY State Bar Asn; pres, Stud Bar Asn, St. John's Univ, Sch Law. **Business Addr:** Attorney, Private Practice, 13030 31st Ave Suite 700, Flushing, NY 11354-2501.

HAMMOCK, JIMMY
Executive. **Career:** Phi Beta Sigma Fraternity Inc, Int Gen Bd, int treas, currently. **Orgs:** Beta Theta Boule. **Home Addr:** 1081 Hickory View Dr, Morristown, TN 37814. **Business Addr:** International Treasurer, Phi Beta Sigma Fraternity Inc, International General Board, 1081 Hickory View Dr, Morristown, TN 37814.

HAMMOND, DR. BENJAMIN FRANKLIN
School administrator, educator, microbiologist. **Personal:** Born Feb 28, 1934, Austin, TX; son of Virgil Thomas and Helen Marguerite Smith. **Educ:** Univ Kans, BA, 1954; Meharry Med Col, DDS, 1958; Univ PA, PhD, microbiol, 1962. **Career:** Oak Ridge Inst Nuclear Studies, postdoctoral fellowship, 1963; Univ Pa Sch Dent Med, Periodontal Microbiol Lab, Dept Microbiol, prof, 1970-91, chmn, 1972-85, dir, 1980-91, assoc dean acad affairs, 1984-91, prof emer microbiol, 1991-; R Metcalf Chair- Marquette Univ, distinguished vis prof, 1986; Hahnemann Univ Col Med, Med Col Pa, prof med & dent med, 1991-97; Oral Microbiol Testing Serv, dir, 1991-94; Temple Univ Sch Dent, Oral Microbiol Testing Serv Lab, dir emer, 1996-. **Orgs:** Bd mem, Hist Soc PA; Mus Art Philadelphia; Nat Adv Dent Res Coun, NIH, 1975-78; vpres, Am Asn Dent Res, 1977, pres, 1978-79; Racquet Club Philadelphia; Union League Philadelphia; Metropolitan Opera Guild; bd mem, Philadelphia Mus Art; Am Soc Microbiol; Philadelphia Club; bd dir, Arthur Ross Gallery; bd dir, Atwater Kent Mus Philadelphia; bd dir, Am Poetry Ctr. **Honors/Awds:** EH Hatton Int Asn Dental Res, 1959; Lindback Award Distinguished Teaching, Univ PA, 1969; Medaille D'Argent City Paris France, 1976; Dean's Lect, NW Univ Med Ctr, 1987; Hon Pres, Int Asn Dent Res, 1978; Hon Membership, Societe Francaise de Parodontologie. **Home Addr:** 560 N 23rd St, Philadelphia, PA 19130. **Business Addr:** Professor Emeritus, University of Pennsylvania, School Dental Medicine, 240 S 40th St, Philadelphia, PA 19104, **Business Phone:** (215)707-5857.

HAMMOND, BRANDON LA RON
Actor. **Personal:** Born Feb 6, 1984. **Career:** Films: Menace II Society, 1993; Strange Days, 1995; Waiting to Exhale,1995; What's Love Got to Do With It; The Fan, 1996; Space Jam, 1996; Mars Attacks, 1996; No Easy Way, 1996; Soul Food, 1997; Blue Hill Avenue, 2001; Summer Blame, 2006; TV Series: "The Gregory Hines Show", 1997-98; TV Films: "Love, Lies & Lullabies", 1993; Coach, 1994; Dr. Quinn, Medicine Woman, 1996-98, "Road to Galveston", 1996; "Our America", 2002. **Honors/Awds:** Image Award for Outstanding Youth Actor/ Actress, 1998. **Special Achievements:** Nominee, Young Artist Award, 1998, 2003; Nominee, Young Star Award, 1998. **Business Addr:** Actor, c/o William Morris Agency Inc, 151 S El Camino Dr, Beverly Hills, CA 90212, **Business Phone:** (310)274-7451.*

HAMMOND, CAROL H. (CAROL HOWARD)
Educational psychologist. **Personal:** Born Oct 14, 1935, Knoxville, TN; daughter of D N Howard; married James M, Dec 20, 1959; children: Endea Thibodeaux, Atty Renata Craig, Rona Smith & James M Hammond Jr. **Educ:** Oakwood Col, BA, 1957; Univ Md, MEd, 1981; Howard Univ, PhD, 2000. **Career:** Abney Chapel SDA Sch, prin, teacher, 1959-60; Bekwai Overseas Cs Sch,teacher, 1962-68; Columbia Union Col, loan supvr, 1974-77, adj prof, psychol, 1998-; Slingo Adventist Sch, teacher, 1977-98; Bowie State Univ,adj prof & counr psychol & educ, 2001-. **Orgs:** Bd Ed, K-12, 1986-88. **Special Achievements:** Conducted Family Life Seminars in US, Bermuda & Africa, 1980-, author; Precious Memories of Missionaries of Color, co-author of "The School & Community Resources: A Cooperative Venture," published in Journal of Adventist Education, 1985, Marriage, Family, & Singleness, Advent Press, 1986, "Motivation: the Key to Success," pub in Educamus, 1993, conducted Parenting Seminar, John Nevins Seventh-day Adventist School, 1999. **Home Addr:** 3200 Fullerton St, Beltsville, MD 20705. **Business Addr:** Adjunct Professor, Counsilor of Psychology & Education, Bowie State University, 14000 Jericho Pk Rd, Bowie, MD 20715-9465, **Business Phone:** (301)860-4000.

HAMMOND, FRED
Gospel singer. **Personal:** Born Jan 1, 1961?, Detroit, MI; married Kimberly; children: BreeAnn & Darius Sean. **Career:** Gospel vocalist; composer; producer; Face to Face Prod Co, owner, 1992-; FHammond Music, label founder; Albums: I'm Going On, 1985; Go Tell Somebody, 1986; On The Winning Side, 1987; Will You Be Ready?, 1988; Ordinary Just Won't Do, 1989; State of Mind, 1990; Number 7, 1991; I Am Persuaded, 1991; Deliverance, 1993; Matters of the Heart, 1994; The Inner Court, 1995; Gospel Greats, 1995; The Spirit of David, 1996; Pages of Life: Chapters 1&2, 1998; Purpose By Design, 2000; In Case You Missed It And Then Some, 2001; Christmas Just Remember, 2001; The Commissioned Reunion Live, 2002; Speak Those Things: POL Chapter 3, 2002; Hooked on the Hits, 2003; Somethin 'Bout Love, 2004; Praise & Worship, 2006; Free to Worship, 2006; Singles: "Let the Praise Begin", 1998; "Power", 1998; "King of Glory", 2001; "All Things Are Working", 2001; "We Have Not Forgotten", 2003; "Celebrate", 2004; "By Faith - with Sean Combs", 2005; "Better Than That' with The Singletons", 2007; Films: Zero Option, 2009. **Honors/Awds:** Numerous honors & awards including 6 Dove awards, 4 Stellar awards & a Grammy award. **Special Achievements:** His release Free To Worship bombarded Billboards No 1 position on the Gospel Charts, and was hailed as one of the years best selling gospel albums for 2006. **Business Addr:** Gospel Vocalist, Face to Face Productions, 21421 Hilltop St Suite 20, Southfield, MI 48034, **Business Phone:** (248)354-5151.

HAMMOND, JAMES A
Executive. **Personal:** Born Nov 11, 1929, Tampa, FL; son of William and Lucile V; married Evelyne L Murrell; children: Kevin, Gary & Lisa. **Educ:** Hampton Univ, BS, indust voc educ, 1951; US Command & Gen Staff Col, attended 1971; Indust Col Armed Forces, attended 1974. **Career:** Executive (retired); Hammond Elec Contracting Inc, pres, 1951-65; Community Rels City Tampa, admin dept head, 1965-70; Ala Nellum & Assocs Inc, vpres, 1969-73; Impact Asn Inc, pres, 1972-74; Walter Industs Inc, dir progs, 1974-89; Impac Commun Inc, pres & chief exec officer, 1983-86; Automation Res Systs Ltd, vpres, 1990-97. **Orgs:** Dir, Comn Fed Savings & Loan Asn, 1967-; Tampa Urban League, 1967; Am Asn Affirmative Action, 1977-81; chmn, City Civil Serv Bd, 1980-87; Comn Access Legal Syst, 1984; Kappa Alpha Psi Fraternity; Nat Asn Advan Colored People; comnr, Unemployment Appeals Comn, State Fla. **Honors/Awds:** Government Award, State Fla, 1967; Outstanding Alumnus Award, Hampton Inst, 1971; Whitney Young Award, Tampa Urban League, 1978. **Military Serv:** AUS, lt col. **Home Addr:** 2505 E 19th Ave, Tampa, FL 33605, **Home Phone:** (813)248-6225. *

HAMMOND, DR. JAMES MATTHEW
Military leader, educator. **Personal:** Born Jul 10, 1930, Kenansville, NC; married Carol Howard; children: Endea Renee, Renata Melleri, Rona Meiata & James Matthew Jr. **Educ:** Oakwood Col, BA, 1953; SC State Univ, MSc, 1960; Catholic Univ Am, MA,1975; Friendship Col, DDiv, 1963; S Ill Univ, PhD, 1973. **Career:** Atkins HS, guidance counselor, 1960-61; Sci Dept Bekwai Teachers Col, chair, 1961-68; Seventh Day Adventist Church of Sierra Leone, pres,1968-70; SDA Church of N Ghana, exec dir, 1972-74; Pan African Dev Coop, brd mem, 1981; Columbia Union Col, teaching fac, 1974-2006, chair, dept psychol, 1982-, emer prof, 2006-; Md Defense Force; Pa Mil Res, briggen, currently. **Orgs:** Psi Chi, 1989; bd mem, Pan African Develop Coop, 1981; Md Defence Force,1991; Am Psychol Assoc, 1986; chaplain, Ltc, Civil Air Patrol, 1983. **Honors/Awds:** UNESCO fel, United Nations Orgn, 1972; Phi Delta Kappa, SIU Chap, 1972; Distinguished Service Cross, Md Defense Force, 2003. **Special Achievements:** Missionary to Africa for SDA Church; supt, Sierra Leone mission. **Military Serv:** Md State Guard, Chief of Chaplains. **Home Addr:** 3200 Fullerton St, Beltsville, MD 20705. **Business Addr:** Department Chairman, Columbia Union College, Psychology Department, 7600 Flower Ave, Takoma Park, MD 20912, **Business Phone:** (301)891-4000.

HAMMOND, JOHN B., III
Activist. **Personal:** Married Yoko Hammond; children: Therese Morgan, John B., Yoji William. **Educ:** MIT, Bachelors Degree in Mechanical Engineering; Emory University, MBA. **Career:** Booz Allen Hamilton, Senior Manager on the Organization and Change Team; Independent Consultant in Organizational Change and Development; Associate Dean and Director of Emory University's Evening MBA Program. **Orgs:** Chief Operating Officer, Association of Black Cardiologists; Chairman and CEO, South African American Business Association of the United States; Member, Emory University's Presidential Commission on the Status of Minorities; Board Member, National Black Herstory Taskforce; President and CEO, 100 Black Men of America, Inc. **Home Addr:** 007830. *

HAMMOND, KENNETH RAY
Clergy. **Personal:** Born Jul 28, 1951, Winterville, NC; son of Hoyt Hammond; married Evelyn Patrick; children: Kennetta, Brandon. **Educ:** E Carolina Univ, BA, hist, 1973, MEd, coun educ, 1983, CAS, coun ed, 1985; Shaw Univ, M Div, 1978; NC State Univ, ABD, 1986. **Career:** Mendenhall Stud Ctr E Carolina Univ, asst prog dir, 1973-74, prog dir, 1974-85; Cedar Grove Baptist Church, pastor, 1974-79; Mt Shiloh Baptist Church, pastor, 1980-91; E Carolina Univ, asst dir, Univ Unions, 1985-88, assoc dir, Univ Unions & Stud Activities, 1988-91; Union Baptist Church, Durham, NC, sr pastor, currently; Shaw Divinity Sch, adj prof; United Christian Bible Inst, adj prof. **Orgs:** chmn, Pitt Co Adolescent Sexuality Task Force, 1979-81; Phi Alpha Theta, Honor Hist Soc, 1972; Asn Col Unions Int, 1973-91; Nat Asn Campus Activities, 1973-91; Nat Baptist Conv, 1975-91; bd dirs, Pitt Co Arts Coun, 1984-86; NC Asn Couns & Devel, 1985-91; Alpha Phi Alpha Fraternity, 1971; NC Col Personnel Asn, 1986; Am Asn Coun & Devel, 1987; Am Col Personnel Asn, 1987; Interdenominational Ministerial Alliance Durham; secy, Area III, Am Baptist the S; chair exec bd, E Cedar Grove Baptist Asn; pres, Shaw Univ, Divinity Sch bd of trustees; pres, Nat Theol Alumni Asn; bd dirs, 1st Citizens Bank, 1989-91; bd dirs, Greenville Utilities Comm, 1989-91; gen bd, Gen Bapt State Conv, NC; bd dirs, Habitat for Humanity; bd dirs, Downtown YMCA Durham; regional bd mem, Am Baptist Churches South; pres ministers coun, vice moderator, Area III, 1999; vchmn, Exec Comm, Gen Baptist State Conv, 1996; Mechanic & Farmer Bank City, adv bd, 1999. **Honors/Awds:** Coach of the Yr, Eastern Carolina Conf, 1973; Joint Coun on Health & Citizenship DSA, 1979; Phi Alpha Theta, Honor Hist Soc, 1972; Alpha Phi Alpha, ML King Jr Community Service Award, 1986; Phi Kappa Phi, 1988; One of America's Most Loved Pastors, Gospel Today Mag, 2001. **Home Addr:** 211 November Dr, Durham, NC 27712-2438. **Business Addr:** Senior Pastor, Union Baptist Church, 904 N Roxboro St, Durham, NC 27701.*

HAMMOND, LESLIE KING
Dean (Education), artist, educator. **Personal:** Born Aug 4, 1944; son of Oliver and Evelyne Alice Maxwell. **Educ:** Univ Minn, Queens Col, BFA, 1969; La State Univ, Shreveport, MLA; Univ Md, MFA; Johns Hopkins Univ, MA, 1973, PhD, 1975. **Career:** Queens Col, Dept Performing Arts Workshops, chmn art, 1969-71; Md Inst Col Art, lectr, 1973-76, dean grad studies, 1976-; Howard Univ, Dept African Studies, doctoral supvr, 1977-81; Nat Endowment Arts, panelist, 1980-82; Civic Design Comn, comnr, 1983-87; Phillip Morris Scholars Artists Color, proj dir, 1985-98; Afro-Am Hist & Cult Mus, art consult, 1990-96; Artscape, cur, 1992; Jacob Lawrence Catalog Raisonne Proj, vpres, 2000. **Orgs:** Fel, Cambridge Ctr Residency, GA, 1993 & 1994; pres, Col Art Asn, 1997-99; exec bd, Int Asn Art Critics; fel, Ragdale Found Artist Residency, 2000; fel, Va Ctr Creative Arts Residency, 1999 & 2000; chmn bd dirs, Reginald F Lewis Mus Md African Am Hist & Culture, 2007. **Honors/Awds:** Trustee Award, 1986; Nat Endowment for the Arts Award, 2001. **Special Achievements:** Author: Celebrations, 1982; The Intuitive Eye, 1985; Art As A Verb, 1989; Black Printmakers and the WPA, 1989; Three Generations of African American Women Sculptors, 1996; Artist Scholar-Finding a Balance, 1998; Mask and Mirrors, Abbeyville Press, 2005. Solo exhibitions include a show at the Delaware Center for Contemporary Art, Wilmington, DE, 2000; "Luminosity of Space," Rosenberg Gallery, Goucher College, Baltimore, 2000; "Accumulations," Turner Art Center Gallery, Centenary College of Louisiana, 1999. Group exhibitions include "Summer Exhibition" at Grounds for Sculpture, Hamilton, New Jersey, 2000; "Birth," 57 N. Street Gallery, Washington, DC, 2000; "RE:collect," Art Center of South Florida, Miami, 1999; "Elusive Source," Hemicycle Gallery, Corcoran Museum of Art, Washington, DC, 1995. Works were featured in The Art of 9/11, curated by Arthur Danto in New York City, and in the traveling exhibition, It's for the Birds, organized by the Bernice Steinbaum Gallery in Miami.

HAMMOND, MELVIN ALAN RAY, JR.
Dentist. **Personal:** Born Feb 6, 1949, Austin, TX; son of Melvin Alan Ray Hammond Sr and Helen Bernice Rucker; married Elloree Sanora Lawson; children: Melvin A R III. **Educ:** Huston-Tillotson Col, BS, 1971; Howard Univ Col Dent, DDS, (Honors) 1981. **Career:** Harris Co Hosp Dist, staff dentist, 1981-83; pvt pract, dentist, 1981-; Melvin A.R. Hammond DDS & Assocs, gen dentist, currently. **Orgs:** Omega Psi Phi Fraternity, Rho Beta Beta, 1976-; vpres, Charles A George Dent Soc, 1984 & 85; pres, Gulf States Dent Asn, 1989-90; Am Tex & Nat Dent Asns; Houston Dist Dent Soc; Gulf States Dent Asn; Charles A George Dent Soc. **Honors/Awds:** Outstanding Young Men of America, 1982; Estelle Coffey Young Mem Award; Robert Hardy Jr Mem Award. **Home Phone:** (713)747-3345. **Business Addr:** General Dentist, Melvin A.R. Hammond & Associates, 1213 Hermann Dr Suite 840, Houston, TX 77004, **Business Phone:** (713)523-1666.*

HAMMOND, DR. PAMELA V
Educator. **Educ:** PhD, RN, FAAN. **Career:** Hampton Univ, Sch Nursing, dean & prof, prof, currently. **Orgs:** Bd mem, Nat League Nursing; Veterans Admin. **Business Addr:** Professor, Hampton University, School of Nursing, E Tyler St & Emancipation Dr, 127-L Freeman Hall, Hampton, VA 23668, **Business Phone:** (757)727-5251.

HAMMOND, ULYSSES BERNARD
School administrator. **Personal:** Born Feb 18, 1951, Washington, DC; son of Eliza Jones Hammond and Cleveland Hammond; married Christine Pointer, May 26, 1979; children: Damon Moore & Shayna. **Educ:** Kenyon Col, Gambier, OH, BA, 1973; Wayne State Univ, Detroit, Mich, MPA, 1975; Wayne State Univ Law Sch, Detroit, Mich, JD, 1980. **Career:** Citizens Res Coun Mich, Detroit, Mich, res asst, 1974-75; Detroit City Coun, Detroit, Mich, spec proj asst, 1975-78; Wayne County Circuit Ct, Detroit, Mich, ct exec, 1978-83; Mich Supreme Ct, Lansing, Mich, assoc state ct adminr, 1983-90; DC Ct, Wash, DC, chief exec officer, 1990-2000; Connecticut Col, vpres admin, 2000-. **Orgs:** Pres, Optimist Club North Detroit Found, 1980-83; bd mem, Boys & Girls Club Lansing, 1988-90; Lansing Chap, 1989-90; mem, Conf State Ct Adminr, 1990-96, bd dir, 1996-, bd mem, 1995-; mem, Nat Asn Ct Mgt 1990-, bd dir, 1996-, bd mem, 1995; Nat Bar Asn, 1991-; vice polemarch, Kappa Alpha Psi; Bar Asn DC, 1991-; bd mem, Anthony Bowen YMCA, Wash, DC, 1994-; second vice polemarch, WAS chap, 1996-; bd trustees, Kenyon Col; SE CT Sci Ctr Bd, 2000; New London Rotary, 2000-; bd mem, SE CT COC, 2001-; vpres, NCP, New London Chap, 2001-; bd mem, United Way New London, 2001-. **Honors/Awds:** Distinguished Alumni Award, Wayne State Univ, 1989; Award Appreciation, Family Law Sect, Mich Bar Asn, 1988; Outstanding Leadership Award, United Negro Col Fund Mich, 1987, 1989; Certificate of Apppreciation, Bar Asn DC, 1990; Nat Asn Ct Mgr, 1992; Nat Asn Child Support Enforcement, 1992; Hon Doctor Laws Deg, Kenyon Col, 1995; Measure Man Award, United Negro Col Fund, 1996. **Special Achievements:** First person to be bd mem of nation's two leading court admin asn at the same time. **Business Addr:** Vice President for Administration, Connecticut College, 270 Mohegan Ave, New London, CT 06320, **Business Phone:** (860)439-2046.

HAMMOND, VERLE B
Executive. **Personal:** Born Mar 20, 1934, St Augustine, FL; son of Genevieve M and Elzer T; married Eleanor, Jun 11, 1955; children: Veronne Williams, Anthony & Pamela Holmes. **Educ:** Florida Agri & Mech Univ, BS, math & physics, 1956; Fla State Univ, MBA, 1971. **Career:** US Army Colonel, military officer, 1956-84; Innovative Technol Inc, army prog mgr, 1984-85, vpres & dir opers, 1985-88, sr vpres & gen mgr, opers group, 1988-89; Innovative Logistics Tech, Inc, pres & ceo, 1989-. **Orgs:** Info Technol Unit, 1984-; Retired Military Officers Asn; Contract Servs Asn Am, exec comt; advisory bd, Enterprise Federal Savings Bank, 1995; bd dir, Fairfax County Coc, 1998-; bd trustee, Univ DC, 2005-; founder, Verle & Eleanor Hammond Found, 2002. **Honors/Awds:** Clinton A West Minority Ent Award, Small Bus Admin, 1994; Black History Makers of Today, McDonald's Corporation, 1998; Corporate Award, Northern Va Urban League, 1998; keynote speaker, Minority Enterprise Development Week, 1998; 5-Star Award, Retired Military Officers Asn, 1999; Capital Leadership Award, Fla Agri & Mech Alum Asn, DC Chap, 2000. **Military Serv:** AUS, col, 1956-84; Legion of Merit Medal, Bronze Star with three Oak Leaf Clusters, Air Medal with two Oak Leaf Clusters, Army Commendation Medal with one Oak Leaf Cluster, Vietnamese Cross of Gallantry First Class. **Business Addr:** President, Chief Executive Officer, Innovative Logistics Techniques, Inc, 2010 Corporate Ridge 9th Fl, McLean, VA 22102-7838, **Business Phone:** (703)506-1555.

HAMMOND, DR. W RODNEY
Psychologist, administrator. **Personal:** Born Jan 12, 1946, Hampton, VA; son of William R, Sr and Mildred; married Andrita J Topps; children: William Rodney III. **Educ:** Univ Ill, Champaign & Urbana, BS, 1968; FL State Univ, MS 1970, PhD 1974; Harvard Univ, post-doctoral, 1990. **Career:** FL State Univ, instr 1973; Univ TN, asst prof Psychology, 1974-76; Meharry Med Col CMHC, asst prof psychiat, 1976-83, dir c serv, 1976-83; Wright State Univ, assoc prof & asst dean, Sch Prof Psychology 1983-96; Div Violence Prev, Ctr Dis Control & Prev, Atlanta, GA, dir, currently. **Orgs:** Fellow, Amer Psychological Assoc, 1975-; pres, bd trustee, Asn Advan Psychology, 1991; Ohio Develop Disabilities Planning Coun, 1986-88; bd dirs, Am Assoc Gifted C, 1986; bd prof affairs, Am Psychological Assoc, 1988-90; bd educ affairs, Am Psycology Asn, 1991-94; chmn, Montgomery County Bd Ment Retardation, 1989-; bd dirs, Prevent Child Abuse Am, 2001-. **Honors/Awds:** 100 Outstanding Seniors,Univ of IL Champaign & Urbana, 1968; President's Award for Outstanding Contribution in Teaching Research and Service, Wright State Univ, 1986; Fellow and Diplomate, American Board of Medical Psychotherapists, 1987; Fellow, InterNat Society for Research on Agression, 1992; Fellow, American Psychological Asn, 1994;

Outstanding Article interesting research and policy issues on adolescence, to research in adolescence, 1994; Outstanding Contributions to Health, OH Commission on Minority Health; Top Ten African American Male, Dayton Parity, 2000; US Dept of Health and Human Services Secretary Award for Distinguished Service, 2001. **Business Addr:** Director Division of Violence Prevention, Centers for Disease Control, National Center for Injury Prevention and Control, 4770 Buford Hwy NE MS K68, Atlanta, GA 30341-3724, **Business Phone:** (770)488-4362.

HAMMOND, DR. W RODNEY
Public health official. **Personal:** Born Jan 12, 1946, Virginia; married Andrita; children: William R Hammond III. **Educ:** Univ Ill, Champaign-Urbana, IL, BS; Harvard Univ, Cambridge, MA; Fla State Univ, PhD, psychol. **Career:** Wright State Univ, Sch Prof Psychol, asst dean, assoc prof; PACT prog, develop; Nat Ctr Injury Prev & Control, Div Violence Prev, dir, currently. **Orgs:** Am Psychol Asn. **Honors/Awds:** Inducted Nat Acad Practice. **Special Achievements:** Publications focused on violence as a pub health concern. **Business Addr:** Director Division of Violence Prevention, National Center for Injury Prevention & Control, Centers for Disease Control, 4770 Buford Hwy NE, Mailstop K68, Atlanta, GA 30341-3724, **Business Phone:** (770)488-4362.

HAMMONDS, ALFRED
Executive. **Personal:** Born Feb 6, 1937, Gary, IN; married Pearlena J Donaldson; children: Alfred, Jr, Danelle J. **Educ:** Bus Col, Hammond, IN, cert acct, 1963; Am Inst Banking, attended 1968. **Career:** Executive (retired). HC Lyttons & Co, salesman, 1961-63; Gary Nat Bank, baker asst vpres & br mgr; Gainer Bank, vpres & regional financial mgr. **Orgs:** Am Inst Banking; pres, Gary Frontiers Serv Club; vpres, Urban League; US Selective Serv Bd No 44. **Special Achievements:** First Black salesman HC Lyttons & Co Gary in 1961-63. **Military Serv:** USAF, 1955-59. *

HAMMONDS, DR. CLEVELAND, JR.
School administrator. **Personal:** Born Jan 8, 1936, Rayville, LA; son of Cleveland and Louise Buchanan; married Yvonne Parks, Sep 5, 1959; children: Deborah, Rhonda & Marsha. **Educ:** Southern Ill Univ, Carbondale, IL, BS, 1958; Southern Ill Univ,Edwardsville, IL, MS, 1963; Univ Ill, Urbana, IL, EdD, 1973. **Career:** Sch administrator (retired); Champaign Pub Sch, Champaign, IL, teacher & counr, 1964-68; Champaign Pub Sch, asst supt, 1968-75; Inkster Pub Schs, Inkster, MI, supt, 1975-79; Durham Pub Schs, Durham, NC, supt, 1979-88; Univ NC, Chapel Hill, part-time instr, 1984; Birmingham Pub Schs, Birmingham, AL, supt; St Louis Pub Schs, supt, 1996-2003. **Orgs:** Am Asn Sch Adminr; Phi Delta Kappa; Kappa Delta Pi Honor Soc; Nat Alliance Black Educr; Ala Asn Sch Adminr; life mem, Southern Ill Univ Alumni Asn. **Honors/Awds:** Superintendent of the Year Award, NC Pub Rels Asn, 1984-85; J E Shepard Sertoma Award, 1987; The Executive Educator 100 Award, Exec Educ Magazine, 1987 & 1990. **Military Serv:** AUS, Specialist 4, 1959-62.

HAMMONDS, GARFIELD
Law enforcement officer. **Career:** U.S. Drug Enforcement Agency, spec agt, 1969-94; Ga Dept Juvenile Servs, comnr, 1994-95; Dep C & Youth, head; Ga State Bd Pardons & Paroles, bd mem, 1995-96, 2002-, chmn, 1996-97. **Orgs:** Kappa Alpha Psi Fraternity; 100 Black Men, Atlanta; Int Asn Chiefs Police; Nat Orgn Black Law Enforcement Execs. **Honors/Awds:** Presidential Meritorius Service Award; Award for Excellence, U.S. State Dept. **Special Achievements:** First African American parole board chairman in Georgia; first African American to serve as US Drug Enforcement as Regional Director, SE Region. **Business Addr:** Board Member, Georgia State Board of Pardons and Paroles, 2 Martin Luther King Jr Dr SE Suite 458, Balcony Level East Tower, Atlanta, GA 30334-4909, **Business Phone:** (404)656-5651.

HAMMONDS, JEFFREY BRYAN
Baseball player. **Personal:** Born Mar 5, 1971, Scotch Plains, NJ. **Educ:** Univ Stanford. **Career:** Baseball player (retired); Baltimore Orioles, outfielder, 1993-98; Cincinnati Reds, 1998-99; Colorado Rockies, 2000; Milwaukee Brewers, outfielder, 2001-03; San Francisco Giants, outfielder, 2003-04; Wash Nationals, outfielder, 2004-05. **Honors/Awds:** All-Star, 2000; hit three home runs in a single game, 1999. *

HAMMONDS, TOM
Basketball player, race car driver. **Personal:** Born Mar 27, 1967, Crestview, FL; married Carolyn; children: Tommy Jr & Keelan. **Educ:** Ga Tech Univ, attended 1989. **Career:** Basketball player (retired), race car driver; Washington Wizards, forward,1989-92; Charlotte Hornets, 1992; Denver Nuggets, 1993-97; Minnesota Timberwolves, 1997; Tom Hammonds Chevrolet, Darlington SC, owner; Nat Hot Rod Asn, race car driver, 2003, 2007-. **Orgs:** Crestview Church God, deacon. **Honors/Awds:** FIBA World Championship, Gold medal, 1986. **Business Addr:** Race Car Driver, National Hot Rod Association, 2035 Financial Way, Glendora, CA 91741, **Business Phone:** (626)914-4761.*

HAMMONS, WILLIAM, II
Entrepreneur. **Career:** LoveLife Found, media producer, cofounder, currently. **Business Phone:** (510)663-5683.*

HAMPTON, CHERYL IMELDA
Journalist. **Personal:** Born in Portsmouth, VA; daughter of George Livingston and Helen Bowen; divorced; children: Reed Thomas Smith & Adrienne Hampton-Smith Brown. **Educ:** Syracuse Univ, BS, 1973. **Career:** Regional Learning Ctr, outreach coord, 1981-87; Syracuse Herald J/Herald Am, ed asst, 1987-88, staff writer, 1988-89, asst city ed, 1989-90, asst to managing ed, 1990-91, asst managing ed, 1991-92; The Orange County Register, asst managing ed, 1992-96, dep ed/nights, 1996-97; Nat Pub Radio, dir news staffing & admin, 1997-; Auth: Health & Wealth: Poverty & Disease in Onondage County, 1989. **Orgs:** Bd dir, Junior League Syracuse, 1981-82; pres, League Women Voters Central New York, 1983-87; New York State Fair Women's Exec Coun, 1986-92; bd dir, The Vol Ctr, Syracuse, NY, 1986-92; Nat Asn Black Journalists, 1989-; African Cult Arts Coun Bowers Mus Cult Art, 1993-97; Nat Asn Minority Media Exec, 1992; vice chair membership, Nat Press Club; pres, Jour & Women Symposium, 2000. **Honors/Awds:** Woman of Achievement, Syracuse Post Standard, 1986; Special Achievement Award, Urban League of Onondage County, 1989; Best Story Written Against Deadline, 1989; Syracuse Press Club, Best Investigative Story, Best Series, 1990; Prism Award, Rape Crisis Ctr, 1991. **Business Addr:** Director, National Public Radio, News Staffing & Administration, 635 Massachusetts Ave NW, Washington, DC 20001-3753, **Business Phone:** (202)513-2211.

HAMPTON, DR. DELON
Consulting engineer. **Personal:** Born Aug 23, 1933, Jefferson, TX; son of Uless Hampton (deceased) and Elizabeth Lewis (deceased). **Educ:** Univ Ill, Urbana IL, BSCE, 1954; Purdue Univ, West Lafayette IN, MSCE, 1958, PhD, 1961; Purdue Univ, Hon Doctor Engineering, 1994; NJ Inst Technol, Hon Doctor Sci, 1996. **Career:** Consult activities, 1961-; Kans State Univ, asst prof, 1961-64; Eric H Wang Civil Engineering Res Fac, assoc res engr, 1962-63; IIT Res Inst, sr res engr, 1964-68; Howard Univ, Wash, DC, prof civil engineering, 1968-85; Gnaedinger, Banker, Hampton & Assoc, pres, 1972-74; Delon Hampton & Assoc, Chartered, Wash, DC, chmn bd & chief exec officer, 1973-. **Orgs:** Vpres, Housing & Pub Facil, Montgomery County Chamber Com, 1983-85; pres, Nat Capital Sect, 1984-85; bd, Wash DC Chamber Com, 1985-86; chmn, exec comn, Am Soc Civil Engrs, Engr Mgt Div, 1985-89; vpres, Am Consult Engrs Coun, 1987-89; Pres Forum, Montgomery Col Found, 1987; bd, Dist 5 dir, Am Soc Civil Engrs, 1991-94, pres-elect, 1998-99, pres, 1999-2000; hon mem, Am Soc Civil Engrs, 1995; assoc mem bd govs, Am Pub Transit Asn; transp Coord, Community, Greater Wash Bd Trade. **Honors/Awds:** Nat Acad Engr; Edmund Friedman Professional Recognition Award, Am Soc Civil Engrs, 1988; Business Man of the Year, Govt DC, Office Human Rights, 1988; Distinguished Alumnus, Civil Engineering Alumni Asn, Univ ILL, 1990; Outstanding Journal Paper Award, Jour Mgt Engineering, Am Soc Civil Engrs, 1990; President Award, DC Coun Engr & Archit Soc, 1991; James Laurie Prize, Am Soc Civil Engrs, 1997; Alumni Award, Col Engineering, Univ Ill, 2000; Theodore R Hagans Jr Memorial Achievement Award, Outstanding Award, Los Angeles Coun Black Consult Engrs. **Special Achievements:** First African American president of American Society of Civil Engineers; featured in Philadelphia Electric Co's permanent exhibit of 24 outstanding black engrs from 1962-. **Military Serv:** AUS, sp2, 1955-57; US Naval Reserve, Lt, 1967-72. **Business Addr:** Chairman of the Board, Chief Executive Officer, Delon Hampton & Associates, 800 K St NW Suite 720, Washington, DC 20001, **Business Phone:** (202)898-1999.

HAMPTON, EDWIN HARRELL. See Obituaries section.

HAMPTON, FRANK, SR.
Executive, government official. **Personal:** Born Jan 2, 1923, Jacksonville, FL; married Willa D Wells; children: Frank, Jr. **Educ:** Edward Waters Col. **Career:** Hamptons Gulf Serv Stn, owner, oper; Hamptons Fuel Oil; Hampton Villa Apt; H & L Adv & Pub Rel; councilman 8th Dist. **Orgs:** chmn & trust bd Mt, Ararat Bapt Church; pres, Duval Co Citizens Bene Corp Char Org; first vpres, Donkey Club Jacksonville; chmn Youth Adv Com ARC; Gov Coun on Crim Just; Gator Bowl Asn; Nat Asn Adv Colored People; Young Men's Christian Asn; Jacksonville C C; Boy Scouts Am; comnr, Civil Liberites Elks Lodge IBPOE W. **Honors/Awds:** Number of awards for outstanding service to the community. **Special Achievements:** Lead the fight for 1st black police officers, 1950; Fla fist black beverage supvr, 1953; desegregated Jacksonvilles golf courses, 1958; filed Omnibus Suit in Fed Ct which desegregated all mun rec facil, 1960; placed blacks in city & state off, 1961; appointed by Gulf Oil to visit Africa Angola to investigate discrimination practice in jobs, salary & living conditions. **Military Serv:** AUS, WWII, 1943-45. *

HAMPTON, FREDERICK M.
College teacher. **Educ:** Winston-Salem State Univ, BS, elem educ, 1979; NC A&T State Univ, MS, educ admin, 1984; Appalachian State Univ, EdS, educ admin, 1988; Univ NC, Greensboro, EdD, educ admin, 1991. **Career:** Elem sch teacher; elem sch prin; dir community educ; Cleveland State Univ, Dept Coun, Admin, Supv & Adult Learning, assoc prof, 1991-. **Orgs:** Am Educ Res Asn; Am Asn Sch Adminr; Mid-Western Educ Res Asn; Cleveland State Univ, Black Fac & Staff Orgn, 2003-. **Honors/Awds:** Ohio's Best Practices, 1996; Planting the Seeds of Change, 1997. **Business Phone:** (216)687-3828.

HAMPTON, GRACE
Educator. **Personal:** Born Oct 23, 1937, Courtland, AL. **Educ:** Art Inst Chicago, BAE, 1961; Ill State Univ, MS, 1968; Ariz State Univ, PhD, 1976. **Career:** Ill State Univ, Art Educ, prof; Northern Ill Univ, fac; Sch Art Inst Chicago, fac; Calif State Univ, Sacramento, fac; Univ OR, fac; Pa State Univ, Art Educ & Integrative Arts, prof, currently, head african am studies, currently. **Orgs:** Nat Art Educ Asn; Nat Conf Black Artist; artist-in-residence, Hayden House Phoenix; presented papes local & nat confs; del, Festac, 1977. **Business Phone:** (814)863-4243.

HAMPTON, DR. JANET J
College teacher. **Educ:** Univ Kans, BA, 1958; Mexico City Col, MA, 1961; Cath Univ Am, PhD, 1985. **Career:** George Washington Univ, assoc prof Spanish, adj ast prof med, assoc prof emer spanish, 2006-. **Business Addr:** Emeritus Associate Professor, George Washington University, Department Spanish, 2121 Eye St NW, Washington, DC 20052, **Business Phone:** (202)994-1000.

HAMPTON, KYM
Singer, basketball player, actor. **Personal:** Born Nov 3, 1962, Noraville, KY. **Educ:** Ariz State, attended 1984. **Career:** Basketball player (retired), actor, singer; Vigo, basketball player,1985-87; Barcelona, 1987-89; Valencia, Spain, 1989-91; Bari, 1991-92; Chanson, Japan, 1992-93; Aix-en-Provence, France, 1993-94; Avellino, 1994-95; Sive Pavia, Italy, 1995-97; NY Liberty, basketball player, 1997-99; Films: She Hate Me. Leader, New york Liberty's fan Development, currently. **Orgs:** Women's Nat Basketball Asn. **Honors/Awds:** Sun Angel Athlete of the Year award, 1984; Ariz State Univ Hall of Fame,1989; Italian League, All-Star Team, 1992, 1995, 1996; Yolanda Jackson Giveback Award, 2002.

HAMPTON, LEROY
Pharmacist, executive director. **Personal:** Born Apr 20, 1927, Ingalls, AR; married Anne; children: Cedric, Candice. **Educ:** Univ CO, BS, pharmacy, 1950; Denver Univ, MS, chem, 1960. **Career:** Pharmacist (retired), executive director; Dow Chem Co, Colo, chemist, 1953-67, Midland, recruiting mgr, mgr minority employ rels, issues mgr health & environ sci res, 1967-86; Saginaw Valley State Univ, dir affirmative action; part time pharmacist, 1986-05. **Orgs:** Am Chem Soc; Midland Kiwanis Club; United Way; Dow's Community Action Panel. *

HAMPTON, OPAL JEWELL
Educator. **Personal:** Born Jul 4, 1942, Kansas City, KS; daughter of William A Blair and Mary Overton Blair; divorced; children: Kenton B. **Educ:** Emporia State Univ, BSE, 1966; Azusa Pac Univ, MA, 1974. **Career:** Educator (retired); Kans City United Sch Dist, teacher, 1964-66; Pasadena United Sch Dist, Pasadena, Calif, teacher, 1966-97, curric resource teacher & sci resource teacher, 1997; literacy coach, 2002. **Orgs:** Usher, First AME Church, 1966-; regional dir, 1987-91, Nat Sorority Phi Delta Kappa Inc; life mem, Nat Asn Advan Colored People. **Home Addr:** 1030 Chevron Ct, Pasadena, CA 91103.

HAMPTON, PHILLIP
Lawyer. **Educ:** Mass Inst Technol, BS, 1977, MS, 1977; Univ Chicago, JD, 1980. **Career:** US Patent & Trademark Office, asst comnr trademarks, 1993-98; Gardner Carton & Douglas LLP, atty & partner, 1998-2004; Dickstein Shapiro LLP, Intellectual Property Group, partner, 2004-. **Orgs:** Nat Bar asn, chair IP section, 1989-91, bd mem-at-large, 1991-94, mem exec committee, 1990-93; Am Intellectual Property Law asn, chair membership committee, 2004-07; co chairTrademark Legislation Comt; DePaul Univ Col Law. **Honors/Awds:** Diversity & the Bar, "Top Minority IP Partner," 2003; Black Enterprise Magazine, "America's Top Black Lawyers," 2003. **Business Addr:** Attorney, Partner, Dickstein Shapiro LLP, 1825 Eye St NW, Washington, DC 20006-5403, **Business Phone:** (202)420-2664.

HAMPTON, PHILLIP JEWEL
Educator. **Personal:** Born Apr 23, 1922, Kansas City, MO; son of Cordell Daniels and Goldie Kelley; married Dorothy Smith, Sep 29, 1946 (deceased); children: Harry J & Robert Keith. **Educ:** Kans State Col, attended 1948; Drake Univ, attended 1949; Kans City ArtIst, attended 1952; KS City Univ, attended 1952. **Career:** Savannah State Col, dir art, assoc prof, 1952-69; Southern Ill Univ, Edwardsville, prof painting, 1969, prof emer, currently; Collectors Choices: African Art, 1998, African Am Art Works, 1999. **Orgs:** Instr, painting Jewish Ed Alliance, Savannah, 1967-68; bd mem, Savannah Art Asn Savannah, GA, 1968-69; Citizens Adv Coun, Edwardsville, IL, 1973-74; Saint Louis Art Mus, workshop, 2001; St Louis Artists' Guild; St Louis Art Mus; Contemporary Art Mus, St Louis; Art St Louis. **Honors/Awds:** Certificate of Excellence, Savannah Chap Links, 1960; Danforth Association Danforth Found, 1980-86; Governors Purchase Award, IL State Fair, 1991; Retrospective Exhibition, King-Tisdell Cottage Found Inc, Savannah, GA, 1995; AKA Sorority, Inc; Salute to Black Men Awdars, Omicron Eta Omege Chapter Award, 2001. **Military Serv:** AUS s/sgt 3 yrs; ETO 5 Campaign Stars 1945. **Home Addr:** 832 Holyoake Rd, Edwardsville, IL 62025. *

HAMPTON, RANDALL C.
Banker, chief executive officer, president (organization). **Career:** ABN AMRO Asset Mgt, pres, ceo, 2000; LaSalle Bank Corp,

Trust Asset Mgt, exec vpres. **Orgs:** Centers for New Horizons;Chicago State Univ; trustee, Ill Inst of Technol. *

HAMPTON, DR. ROBERT L
Educator. **Personal:** Born Nov 18, 1947, Michigan City, IN; son of T L and Annie A Williams; married Cathy M Melson; children: Robyn & Conrad. **Educ:** Princeton Univ, BA, 1970; Univ Mich, MA, 1971, PhD, 1977. **Career:** Connecticut Col, asst prof, 1974-83, assoc prof, 1983-89, prof 1989-94, dean, 1987-94, Family Studies, prof, prof sociol, 1994; Univ Md, dean undergraduate studies, assoc provost acad affairs, prof sociol & family studies; Harvard Med Sch, lectr ped, 1981-93; City Univ NY, York Col, Dept Social Sci prof & pres; Tenn State Univ, provost & exec vpres, currently. **Orgs:** Consult, Urban Inst, 1975; consult, Women Crisis, 1979-82; consult, C Hosp, Boston, 1982; mem exec comt, Peguot Community Found, 1983-86; chmn, Oper Develop Corp, 1977-78; pres, Child & Family Agency, 1987-90; New London County Child Sexual Abuse Task Force; United Way Southeastern CT, 1992-95; Prince Georges County Supt Schs, Adv Comt; Inst Women's Policy Res, Adv Comt; founder, Inst Domestic Violence African Am Community. **Honors/Awds:** Danforth Asn, Danforth Found, 1979; NIMH Post Doc Fel, 1980; NRC Fel, Nat Res Coun, 1981; Rockfeller Fel, Rockefeller Found 1983; Hartman Mentoring Scholar. **Special Achievements:** Published extensively in the field of family violence including several edited books: Violence in the Black Family: Correlates & Consequences; Black Family Violence: Current Research & Theory; Family Violence: Prevention & Treatment; Preventing Violence in America & Substance Abuse, Family Violence; Child Welfare: Bridging Perspectives & Promoting Racial Ethnic & Religious Understanding in America; The Prevention & Treatment of Interpersonal Violence; Within the African American Community: Evidence-based Approaches. **Military Serv:** AUSR, ltc, 1972-96; Army Commendation Medal. **Business Addr:** Provost, Executive Vice President, Tennessee State University, Division of Academic Affairs, 3500 John A Merritt Blvd, Nashville, TN 37209, **Business Phone:** (615)963-5301.

HAMPTON, RODNEY
Football player. **Personal:** Born Apr 3, 1969, Houston, TX. **Educ:** Univ Ga. **Career:** Football player (retired); New York Giants, running back, 1990-97. **Honors/Awds:** Season Opener, Univ Ga, 1988; Natl Player of the Week, Sporting News; ESPN Player of the Game; SEC Player of the Week, 1989; Pro Bowl, 1992 & 1993.

HAMPTON, RONALD EVERETT
Law enforcement officer. **Personal:** Born Jan 5, 1945, Washington, DC; son of Memory J and Annie L Hunt; married Quintina M Hoban, Aug 27, 1982; children: Candace, Jasmine & Ronald Quinten. **Educ:** Am Univ, Wash, DC, BS, 1978. **Career:** US Air Force, Dover Air Force Base, staff sgt, 1968-72; Wash DC Metrop Police Dept, Wash DC, police officer, 1972-95; Nat Black Police Asn, Wash DC, chair, exec dir, 1987-. **Orgs:** Regional chmn, Eastern Region, Nat Black Police Asn, 1982-84, nat chmn, 1984-86, exec dir, 1987-; bd dir, Am Civil Liberties Union; Adv Comt, Capital Punishment Proj; bd mem, Amnesty Int; Fed Bd, Drug Policy Found Law Enforcement Comt. **Honors/Awds:** Police Officer of the Year, Eastern Region, Nat Black Police Asn, 1983; Extended Community Policing, 1989; Outstanding Community Relations Officer, Wash DC Police Dept, 1989. **Special Achievements:** Writings on Community/Police Relations, 1988. **Military Serv:** USAF, staff sgt, 1968-72, Vietnam Valor, 1969, US Air Force Good Conduct Medal, 1970. **Home Addr:** 303 Allison St NW, Washington, DC 20011, **Home Phone:** (202)882-3023. **Business Addr:** Executive Director, National Black Police Association Inc, 3251 Mt Pleasant St NW, Washington, DC 20010, **Business Phone:** (202)986-2070.

HAMPTON, THOMAS EARLE
Government official. **Personal:** Born Sep 28, 1950, Greenville, SC; married Sheila Dixon. **Educ:** Morgan State Univ, BA, polit sci & govt, 1973; Univ Baltimore, MPA, 1984. **Career:** Baltimore Mayor's Off, admin aide, 1974-83; Md Real Estate Comt, sales consult, 1981; Md Mass Transit Admin, Off Pub Affairs, community rels officer, 1983, sr govt rels off, lobbyist, currently. **Orgs:** Kappa Alpha Psi Fraternity, 1971-; Nat Forum Black Pub Adminr, Md Chap; chmn, Mayor's Cable TV Adv Conf; bd dirs, 10th Dist Dem Orgn; Conf Minority Trans Officials; Mayor's Cable Commun Adv Comt. **Honors/Awds:** Outstanding Young Man of the Year Award, 1978; Community Service Award, United Way, 1978, 1979, 1980 & 1981; Two Mayoral Citations, 1980 & 1983; Baltimore City Coun, Resolution, Recognizing Nine Years Community Service; Md State Employees Conf, 1988, 1989 & 1990; AdWheel Award, Am Pub Transp Asn, Pub Sch Safety Campaign, 1992. **Special Achievements:** Host, coordinator: "Inside the Criminal Justice System", public affairs radio show, 1979-83; provided technical assistants to federal grant recipients regarding Federal guidelines & regulations; guest speaker before various community & business groups. **Business Addr:** Lobbyist, Maryland Mass Transit Administration, 6 St Paul St, Baltimore, MD 21202-1614, **Business Phone:** (410)539-5000.

HAMPTON, WILLIE L.
Funeral director. **Personal:** Born May 9, 1933, Montgomery County, TN; son of G F Hampton and Geneva L. **Educ:** Ky Sch Mortuary Sci, MS, 1970. **Career:** Winston Funeral Home, licensed fun dir & embalmer, owner & oper, 1971-. **Orgs:** So Ky Econ Opportunity Coun; Russellville City Coun; Men's Welfare League; 32 Deg Mason; Am Legion; Ra Coun Exec Bd; mem bd dir, Elec Plant Bd. **Honors/Awds:** First Black appointed bd dir Elec Plant Bd; city park named honor. **Military Serv:** AUS, corpl, 1953-55. **Business Addr:** Owner, Winston Funeral Home, 162 S Morgan St, Russellville, KY 42276.*

HAM-YING, J. MICHAEL
Physician, educator. **Personal:** Born Mar 16, 1956, Gainesville, FL; son of John Russel and Dorothy McClellan; married Franeco Cheeks Ham-Ying, Jun 24, 1989. **Educ:** Oakwood Col, BA, biol, 1977; Meharry Med Col, MD, 1981. **Career:** King Drew Med Ctr, asst med dir, 1984-85; Los Angeles Doctors Hosp, exec staff secy, 1984-85; South Eastern Col Osteopath Med, asst clin prof, 1985-96; Hendry Gen Hosp, attend physician, 1985-96; Clewiston Community Health Ctr, asst med dir, 1985-87; Fla Community Health Centers Inc, med dir, 1987-89, chief med officer, 1989-96; Alpha Health Plan, chief med officer, currently; Bur Primary Health Care, clin consult; Pine Hills Family Health Ctr, physician, currently. **Orgs:** Am Med Asn; Am Acad Family Physicians, FL Chapter, 1983; charter mem, T Leroy Jefferson Med Soc, 1990-96; Fla Acad Family Physicians. **Honors/Awds:** Geriatric Fel, Dept Family Med, King-Drew Med Ctr, 1985; Regional Health Administrators Award, USPHS, 1987; Certificate of Merit, Everglades AHEC, 1988; Certification, Am Bd Family Pract, 1984; Outstanding Service Award, Fla Asn Community Health Centers, 1992. *

HANCOCK, DARRIN
Basketball player. **Personal:** Born Nov 3, 1971, Birmingham, AL. **Educ:** Garden City Community Col; Univ Kans. **Career:** Mauri-enne (France), 1993-94; Charlotte Hornets, 1994-96; San Antonio Spurs, 1996-97; Milwaukee Bucks, 1997; Atlanta Hawks, 1997; Dodge City Legend, 2000, 2002.

HANCOCK, HERBERT JEFFREY. **See HANCOCK, HERBIE.**

HANCOCK, HERBIE (HERBERT JEFFREY HANCOCK)
Musician. **Personal:** Born Apr 12, 1940, Chicago, IL; son of Wayman and Winnie Griffin; married Gudrun Meixner, Aug 31, 1986; children: Jessica. **Educ:** Grinnell Col, BA, music, 1960, BS, elec eng, 1960; Manhattan Sch Music, MA, music; Roosevelt Univ, attended. **Career:** Albums: Takin' Off, 1962; Inventions & Dimensions, 1963; My Point of View,1963; Maiden Voyage, 1965; Speak Like a Child, 1968; Herbie Hancock, 1968; The Prisoner, 1969; Mwandishi, 1970; Crossings, 1972; Sextant, 1973; Thrust, 1974; Death Wish, 1974; Dedications, 1974; Flood, 1975; Man-Child,1975; Secrets, 1976; The Herbie Hancock Trio, 1977; V.S. O.P.: The Quintet, 1977; Sunlight, 1977; Direct Step, 1978; The Piano, 1978; Live Under the Sky, 1979; Monster, 1980; Herbie Hancock Trio, 1981; Quartet, 1981; Double Rainbow, 1981; Lite Me Up, 1982; Future Shock, 1983; Sound System, 1984; Village Life, 1985; Jazz Africa, 1986; Third Plane, 1986; Songs for My Father, 1988; Perfect Machine, 1988; Dis Is Da Drum, 1994; Jamming, 1994; The New Standard, 1995; 11, 1997; Gershwin's World, 1998; Future 2 Future, 2001; Directions In Music: Live at Massey Hall, 2002; V.S.O.P.: Live Under the Sky, 2004; Possibilities, 2005; The Essential Herbie Hancock, 2006; River: The Joni Letters, 2007; Thelonious Monk Inst Jazz,chmn, currently. **Orgs:** Co found, Rhythm Life Orgn, 1996; co founder & brd dirs, Bayview Hunters Point Ctr Arts & Tech; chmn, Thelonious Monk Inst Jazz; Alzheimer's Found Am; Elizabeth Glaser Pediatric AIDS Found. **Honors/Awds:** GBMI Film Music Award, Colors, 1989; Grammy Award, Best Jazz Instr Perf, Gershwin's World, 1998; Grammy Award, Best Jazz Instrumental Album, Directions In Music, 2002; NEA Jazz Masters Award, 2004; Downbeat Magazine Readers Poll Hall of Fame, 2005; Album of the Year, 2007; Harvard Foundation Artist of the Year, 2008. **Special Achievements:** VH1's 100 Greatest Videos Rockit is 10th Greatest Video in 2001, was one of the first mainstream musicians to use an Apple computer in creating music in the early 1980s, author of The Buddha In Your Mirror. **Business Addr:** Chairman, Thelonious Monk Institute of Jazz, 5225 Wisconsin Ave NW Suite 605, Washington, DC 20015, **Business Phone:** (202)364-7272.*

HANCOCK, MICHAEL B
City council member, president (organization). **Personal:** Married Mary Louise Lee; children: three children. **Educ:** Hasting Col, BA, polit sci; Univ Colo, MA, pub admin. **Career:** Urban Leage Metrop Denver, pres & chief exec officer, 1999-2006; Denver City Coun, Dist 11, city coun pres, currently. **Orgs:** Chmn, Coun Econ Develop Comt; vchmn Technol Comt; Public Works; FasTracks Mass Transp; Blue Print Denver; Investment Comts; City's Public Safety Comn; co-chair, City's Airport Review Comn. **Business Addr:** City Council President, Denver City Council, District 11, 4730 Oakland St Suite 200, Denver, CO 80239, **Business Phone:** (303)331-3872.

HAND, JON THOMAS
Football player, president (organization). **Personal:** Born Nov 13, 1963, Sylacauga, AL; married Tanya. **Educ:** Univ Ala, attended. **Career:** Football player (retired), association founder; Indianapolis Colts, defensive end, 1986-94; 4J Enterprises LLC, owner, currently. **Orgs:** Founder, JT's Hand. **Business Phone:** (317)767-0586.

HAND, NORMAN
Football player. **Personal:** Born Sep 4, 1972, Queens, NY; married Tammy; children: Norman Derrell Jr & Alexis Ariel. **Educ:** Univ Miss, criminal justice. **Career:** Football player (retired); Miami Dolphins, defensive tackle, 1996; San Diego Chargers, 1997-99; New Orleans Saints, 2000-02; Seattle Seahawks, 2003; NY Giants, defensive tackle, 2004-05. *

HANDWERK, JANA D.
Insurance agent, financial manager. **Personal:** Born Nov 22, 1959, Kingston, Jamaica; daughter of Vera M; married A Bernard Wil-liams; children: 2. **Educ:** Brown Univ, BS; Univ PA, Wharton Sch, MBA. **Career:** Mass Mutual Life Ins Co, investment adv & agent; Cowan Financial, pres; Financial Educr Inc, prin, Currently.

HANDY, DELORES
Television news anchorperson. **Personal:** Born Apr 7, 1947, Little Rock, AR; daughter of Rev George G and Myrtle Carr; married James Lawrence Brown, Jun 24, 1989. **Educ:** Univ Arkansas, attneded 1970. **Career:** FKAAY Radio, Little Rock, reporter & announcer, 1970-72; WHBQ-TV, Memphis, reporter & anchorperson, 1972-73; KABC-TV, LA, reporter, 1973-74; CBS-KNXT-TV, reporter & anchorperson, 1974-76; WJLA-TV Channel 7, Six O'clock News, co-anchor, 1976-78; WTTG-TV Channel 5, Washington, DC, Ten O'clock News & Black Reflections, anchorperson & host; Channel 7, Boston, broadcast journalist; Channel 2, Boston, producer, news anchor & host; Channel 68, Boston, producer, news anchor & host; Monitor Channel, news anchor; CNN Headline News, news anchor; WBUR, anchor, World of Ideas, fill-in host, currently. **Orgs:** Hollywood-Beverly Hills Chap, Nat Asn Media Women; Am Women Radio & TV; Radio & TV News Asn Southern Calif; charter mem, Sigma Delta Chi AR Chap; bd dirs, Jr Citizens Corps; exec comt, Nat Capital Area March Dimes; vol, Big Sisters Am Washington DC Chap; Wash Chap Am Women Radio & TV. **Honors/Awds:** Journalist of the Year Award, Capitol Press Club, 1977; Awards, Nat Coun Negro Women; Awards, United Black Fund Excellence Community Service; Award for Journalistic Achievement, Univ DC; Emmy Award, America's Black Forum Special Jesse Jackson, 1985; Emmy Award, Channel 7-Boston, 1987; Journalist of the Year, Washington Press Club; New York InterNat Film Festivals Award. **Special Achievements:** Honored on 350th anniversary of Black Presence in Boston as one of 350 people who represented Black Presence in Boston 1988; induction in the "Silver Circle" of the National Academy of Television Arts and Sciences for 25-years of excellence in television. **Business Addr:** Anchor, Fill-In Host of World of Ideas, WBUR, 3rd Fl 890 Commonwealth Ave, Boston, MA 02215.

HANDY, JOHN RICHARD
Saxophonist, composer. **Personal:** Born Feb 3, 1933, Dallas, TX; divorced. **Educ:** City Col NY, 1960; San Francisco State Col, BA, 1963. **Career:** Saxaphonist, Composer, Educator: Modern Jazz Groups, Rhythm & Blues Bands, San Francisco-Oakland, CA,1948-58; Carnegie Recital Hall, concerts, 1962, 1967; Monterey Jazz Festival, 1964-66; Hollywood Bowl, CA, 1966; Santa Clara Calif Symphony,1967; Newport Jazz Festival, 1967; Antibes Jazz Festival, 1967; San Francisco prod Opera, head jazz band, 1967; part time fac mem in the Mus Dept San Francisco St Univ, 1968-80, Artist-in-Residence, 1998-02; La Red Hot Rec, 2000; SanFrancisco State Univ, fac; Stanford Univ, fac; Univ Calif, Berkeley, fac; San Francisco Conserv Music, fac; Albums: Projections, 1968; Two Originals: Karuna Supreme/Rainbow, 1975; Hard Work, 1976; Carnival, 1977; Where Go the Boats, 1978; Handy Dandy Man, 1978; Excursion in Blue, 1988;Centerpiece, 1989; Very First Recordings, 1994; Live at the Monterey Jazz Festival, 1996; John Handy's Musical Dreamland, 1996; Live at Yoshi's Nightspot, 2000; Side person: Charles Mingus Big Band: Alice's Wonderland, 1958; Mingus Ah Uhm, 1959; Blues & Roots, 1959; Various Artists: From Spirituals to Swing, 1967; Brass Fever, 1977; Mingus Dynasty Group: Epitaph & Char in the Sky, 1979-89; Jazz Mine (1980); Garland, 1981; Movie Sound tracks: All About the Benjamins, 2002; TV: The Bernie Mack Show, 2002; NPR, BBC, BET. **Orgs:** Music dir, Jazz Arts Soc, 1960-61; San Francisco Interim Arts Adv Comt, 1966-67. **Honors/Awds:** Downbeat Poll Award; 1st Place Award, Rec World All-star Band, 1968; Lifetime Achievement Award, San Jose Jazz Soc, 1995; Jazz Note Award, Russian River Jazz Festival, 1996; Bill Graham Life time Achievement Award, Bay Area Music, 1997. **Special Achievements:** Grammy nominations; inducted into the Alumni Hall of Fame San Francisco State University, 2006. **Military Serv:** Army, 1953-55. **Home Addr:** 410010 Redwood Rd Suite 251, Oakland, CA 94619, **Home Phone:** (510)638-8234. **Business Addr:** 618 Baker St, San Francisco, CA 94117.

HANDY, LILLIAN B.
Executive, chief executive officer. **Career:** Arthur Young & Co, mgt consultant; Electronic data systems inc, mgt consultant;

TRESP Assocs Inc, pres, ceo, 1981-. **Orgs:** Chair, Minority-Owned Bus Tech Transfer Consortium; bd trustees, Hosp Found, Alexandria, VA; bd visitors NC Agr & Tech State Unit, AT&T; Greensboro Delta Sigma Theta Sorority. **Honors/Awds:** Black Engineer of the Year Entrepreneur Award, 1994; Greater Washington Entrepreneur of the Year, Woman-Owned Businesses, 1994; Alumna of the Year, Morgan State Univ. **Special Achievements:** Black Enterprise (BE) magazine's annual list of 100 top black-owned companies.

HANDY, DR. NORMAN
Clergy, minister (clergy). **Personal:** Married Carolyn K; children: Angela, John, Nancy Murray & Norman Jr. **Educ:** Univ DC, BA; Howard Univ Divinity Sch, MDiv, 1989; Wesley Theol Sem. **Career:** Priv pract marriage & family therapist, Wash DC, Columbia, MD; City Coun, Baltimore, MD, 1995; Unity United Methodist Church, dir, sr minister, 2001-. **Orgs:** Pres, Black United Methodist Preachers; co-chmn, City-Wide Liquor Coalition; co-chmn, Coalition Beautiful Neighborhoods; past pres, Harlem Park Neighborhood Coun; Md State Adv Coun Alcohol & Drug Abuse; Prince George's County Task Force Group Living Facilities; Sykesville Town Home Asn; Strategic Planning Prog Baltimore-Wash Conf; Pan-Methodist Coalition. **Honors/Awds:** Whitney Young Jr Award for Community Serv, Baltimore Urban League, 1995. **Business Addr:** Senior Minister, Unity United Methodist Church, 1433 Edmondson Ave, Baltimore, MD 21223, **Business Phone:** (410)728-4826.*

HANES, WENDELL L
Television producer, entrepreneur. **Personal:** Born Jan 1, 1971; son of Odessa Hanes and Eugene Hanes; married Lesley Aisha Stephens, Jan 1, 2003. **Educ:** Brown Univ, summa cum laude. **Career:** Bang Music, composer, musician & sound designer, currently. **Business Addr:** Composer, Musician, Bang Music, 16 W 18th St Suite 2, New York, NY 10011, **Business Phone:** (212)242-2264.

HANEY, DON LEE
Television news anchorperson. **Personal:** Born Sep 30, 1934, Detroit, MI; married Shirley; children: Karen Lynn, Kimberly Joy. **Educ:** Wayne State Univ, Radio-TV Arts major, 1959, polit sci & law, 1974. **Career:** WSJM, staff announcer, 1956-57; CKCR, staff announcer, 1957-59; WQRS-FM; WLIN-FM; WGPR-FM, prog dir, 1959-60; WCHD-FM, 1960-63; WJR, staff announcer, 1963-68; CFPL-TV, host weekly pub affairs prog, 1967-68; WXYZ-TV, Haney's People, host, 1967-81. **Orgs:** New Detroit Inc Commun Comt; bd dir, Am Fedn TV & Radio Arts Union; bd dir, Sudden Infant Death; bd mem, Equity Justice Coun; chmn, Mus Dyst Asn Am; Detriot City Airport Comn. *

HANEY, NAPOLEON
Government official. **Personal:** Born Oct 1, 1926, Texas City, TX; married Sylvia C; children: Lorraine, Katherine, Angela, Lynette & Napoleon. **Career:** Village Park Forest, asst village mgr, currently. **Honors/Awds:** Award, Men Progress Kankakee, 1983; Awarded $3,500,000 Sewer Grant for Village, State Ill, 1984. **Home Addr:** Rte 4, PO Box 47Y, St Anne, IL 60964. **Business Addr:** Asssistant Village Manager, Village Park Forest, 350 Victory Dr, Park Forest, IL 60466, **Business Phone:** (708)748-7712.

HANKIN, NOEL NEWTON
Public relations executive, marketing executive. **Personal:** Born Apr 30, 1946, Kingston, Jamaica; son of Iris Penso Hankin and Ivanhoe Hankin; married Gwendolyn Diaz Hankin, Jun 2, 1974; children: Arana & Loren. **Educ:** Fordham Univ, New York, NY, attended 1969; Queens Col, Queens, NY, BS, 1968; New York Univ, attended 1970; Wharton Sch Bus, Mkt Cert, 1985. **Career:** Young & Rubicam, New York, NY, acct exec, 1970-72; Best Friends, New York, NY, prin, 1970-76; Benton & Bowles, New York, NY, acct exec, 1972-74; Hankin & Smith, New York, NY, prin, 1974-76; Ogilvy & Mather, New York, NY, vpres, acct supvr, 1976-86; Miller Brewing Co, Milwaukee, Wis, brand mgr, Miller Lite, 1986-88, dir mktg rel, 1988-94, dir ethnic mktg, 1994-96, dir, corp rel, 1996-97; Schieffelin & Somerset Co, vpres corp affairs, 1997-2001, vpres, multicultural mkt, 2001-03; Moet Hennessy USA, sr vpres, multicultural initiatives, 2003-. **Orgs:** Founder & bd dir, secy, Thurgood Marshall Scholarship Fund, 1987; sr vice chair, New York Urban League; 100 Black Men. **Honors/Awds:** Black Achievers Award, YMCA-NYC, 1984; CEBA Award, Word Inst Black Comm, 1985, 1989, 1990; Black Book Award Outstanding Bus Person, 1989; Fundraising Award, UNCF, 1989; Nat Am Advan Colored People Community Service Award, 1992; Men Who Dare Award The Family Acad; Top 100 Alumni, Queens Col, 1998; Support Network Corporate Award, 2001; Concord Family Serv; Community Serv Award, 2002; Community Service Award, Nat Am Advan Colored People Community Service Award, 2005; NatUrban League Guild Legacy Award, 2005; Hon Doctor Humane Letters, Medgar Evers Col, City Univ NY. **Special Achievements:** Appointed by President Clinton to Commission of Historically Black Colleges & Universities, 1994-01. **Business Addr:** Senior Vice President, Multicultural Initiatives, Moet Hennessy USA, 85 10th Ave 2nd Fl, New York, NY 10011, **Business Phone:** (212)251-8279.

HANKINS, DR. ANDREW JAY
Radiologist. **Personal:** Born Jul 15, 1942, Waukegan, IL; son of Andrew Sr and Julia Lampkins; married Margaret Roberts (deceased); children: Andrea Marie, Corbin Keith & Trent Allen. **Educ:** Univ Iowa, BA, 1964; Univ Mich, Med Sch, MD, 1968. **Career:** Michael Reese Hosp & Med Ctr, intern, 1968-69; Univ Chicago, resident, 1971-74; Dept Radiol, Univ Chicago, instr, 1974-75; Milton Community Hosp, staff radiol, 1975-84; Wayne State Univ, clinic asst prof, 1977-85; SW Detroit Hosp, radiologist, 1975-80, vchmn, dept radiol, 1980-83, chmn, radiol, 1984-90; Mich Health Ctr, radiologist, 1991; Southwest Detroit Hosp, vchief med staff, 1988-89; Goodwin Ervin Hankins & Assoc PC, pres, 1988-90; Henry Ford Hosp, sr staff physician, 1991-. **Orgs:** Consult, radio pharmaceut drug adv comn, FDA, 1982-84; pres, Equip Lsng Firm Hankins Ervin Goodwin & Assoc, 1984-89; vpres, Goodwin Ervin & Assoc PC, 1980-87; Hartford Mem Baptist Church, 1984-; Nat Asn Advan Colored People; Detroit Med Soc, Nat Med Asn & Wayne County Med Soc; RSNA, SNM, & AIUM; Iowa Black Alumni Asn; YMCA; Big Ten Conference, Adv Comn, 1988-94; Univ Iowa, alumni bd dir, 1994-; Downtown Detroit YMCA, bd govrs, 1991-96; Detroit Athletic Club, 1997-. **Honors/Awds:** Distinguished Young Alumni, Univ Iowa Alumni Asn, 1977; Phi Beta Kappa Alpha Chap Iowa, 1964; Omicron Delta Kappa Univ Iowa Cir, 1963; Big Ten Medal of Honor, Univ Iowa, 1964; Nile Kinnick Scholar, Univ Iowa, 1963; Sloan Found Scholar, Univ Mich Med Sch, 1964-68. **Military Serv:** USAF, capt, 1969-71. **Business Addr:** Senior Staff, Henry Ford Hospital, Diagnosis Radiology & Medical Imaging, 2799 W Grand Blvd, Detroit, MI 48202, **Business Phone:** (313)916-3471.

HANKINS, ANTHONY MARK
Fashion designer. **Personal:** Born Nov 10, 1968, Elizabeth, NJ; son of Willie and Mary Jane. **Educ:** Pratt Inst, attended 1988; Ecole de la chambre Syndicale de la Couture, 1989. **Career:** Yves Saint Laurent, design asst, 1989-90; Adrienne Vittadini, design asst, 1990-91; JC Penney Co, Los Angeles, qual control inspector, 1991-92, Dallas, first in-house designer, JC Penney, 1992-94; Ramone Moya Ltd, fashion dir, vpres, partner, owner, 1994; Univ NTex, exec in residence, 1995; Anthony Mark Hankins Inc, founder, sr vpres & design dir, 1998-. **Orgs:** SPCA Texas, 1995-; adv bd, Easter Seals, 1995-; bd dir, Attitudes & Attire, 1995-; Design Industs Found Fighting AIDS, 1996; South Dallas Bus & Prof Women's Youth Club, 1996; Good Morning Tex, Channel 8, 1996; MacDill Air Force Base, Black History Comt, 1996; Black Retail Action Group, 1996. **Honors/Awds:** Hon Citizen, Jackson, MS, 1996; Fabric Of Dreams Fashion Show, MacDill Air Force Base, 1996; Fashionetta, AKA Sorority, Inc, 1996; State of Oklahoma Citation, 1996; Turner Broadcasting Trumpet Award, 1996; Absolute Vodka Award, Dallas Design Intiative, 1996; Bus Achievement Award, Black Retail Action Group, 1996; Trailblazer Award, Nat Assn Negro Bus & Prof Women, 1995; Award of Excellence, New Jersey Education Asn, 1995; Trumpet Awards, Young Star Award, 1997; Bus Week Entrepreneur of the Year, 1998; Quest for Success Award, Black Chamber Com, 1998. **Special Achievements:** "The Fabric of Dreams," Motivational Biography, Dutton Books Publishing, 1998; First In-House Designer, JC Penney Co., 1992-94; Newsweek's top 100 People to Watch in 21st century, 1997. **Business Addr:** Design Director, Founder, Senior Vice President, Anthony Mark Hankins Inc, 5450 Gaston Ave, Dallas, TX 75214, **Business Phone:** (214)887-1777.

HANKINS, BENJAMIN B., JR.
Chief executive officer. **Career:** Axiom Resource Mgt Inc, pres & ceo, currently. **Honors/Awds:** Role Model of the Year, 2006; One of Fifty Influential Minorities. **Business Phone:** (703)998-0327.*

HANKINS, GROVER (GROVER GLENN HANKINS)
Lawyer. **Educ:** Augustana Col, BA, 1962; Univ Ill Col Law, Champaign, Ill, JD, 1972. **Career:** US Dept Justice, Criminal Div, Organized Crime & Racketeering Sect, prosecutor, 1975-79, Employment Sect, Civil Rights Div, trial atty, 1979-85; N Bryant & Hankins, Kans City, Mo, partner, 1985-89; Dept Health & Human Servs, prin dep gen coun, 1989-92; Tex Southern Univ, Thurgood Marshall Sch Law, Houston, Tex, distinguished vis prof, 1992-93, prof; The Hankins Law Firm, managing partner & prin, currrently. **Orgs:** Nat Asn Advan Colored People; Nat Gen Coun; Tex Bar Asn. **Business Addr:** Managing Partner, The Hankins Law Firm PLLC, 440 Louisiana St Suite 725, Houston, TX 77002, **Business Phone:** (713)292-2720.

HANKINS, GROVER GLENN. See HANKINS, GROVER.

HANKINS, HESTERLY G, III
Educator, computer scientist. **Personal:** Born Sep 5, 1950, Sallisaw, OK; son of Hesterly G Hankins II and Ruth Faye Jackson. **Educ:** Univ Calif, Santa Barbara, BA, sociol, 1972; Univ Calif, Los Angeles, MBA, mgt info systems, 1974; Golden Gate Univ, postgrad study, 1985-86; La Verne Univ, postgrad study, 1987. **Career:** Xerox Corp, appln programmer, 1979-80; Eng Div, comput programmer, 1981-84; Ventura Col, instr, 1983-84; Golden Gate Univ, instr, 1984; Naval Air Sta, spec asst, 1984-85; PMTC, comput scientist, 1985-88; Chapman Col, instr, 1985; De Anza Col, instr, 1985; West Coast Univ, fac, 1987-88; West Coast Univ, Dept Bus Mgt, fac, 1987-91; Defense Contract Mgt Dist, Mgt Info Systs, sr analyst, 1988-94; Nat Univ, writing instr, 1994-, DPT Comput Soc, fac, currently. **Orgs:** Sec, Alpha Kappa Psi, 1977-, life mem; Fed Mgr's Asn; ICTIP; IEEE Compu Soc; Int Platform Asn; YM/WCA Benefit Jr Rodeo Asn; City Oxnard United Methodist Church; Combined Fed Campaign Keyperson; Asn Compu Machinery; Fed Mgr's Asn; Nat Univ Alumni Asn; UCSB Alumni Asn; Grad Stud Mgmt Asn; bd dir, Int Who's Who and Who's Who Prof; Nat Asn Acct; Am Biographical Inst; Calif Asn Acct. **Honors/Awds:** Oustanding Young Man Am, Ala Jaycees, 1980; ENT of the Year, nomination, Arthur Young, 1987; Cert Merit, Intl Biographical Ctr, 1988; ENT of the Year, nomination, Ernst & Young, 1991; hon doctorate, NRI McGraw-Hill Sch Writing, 1993. **Special Achievements:** Chief academy credential, State Calif, 1988; US Appraisall Task Force, 1990; four patented inventions; author: Campus Computing's Accounting I.S. As A Measurment of Computer Performance, 1973; Campus Computer, 1986; Network Planning, 1986; Satellites & Teleconferencing, 1986; Quotable Expressions from Memorable Quotations of Notables, 1993; Idea Bank, 1993; Product Rating System, 1993; Training Base Model, 1993; Sound Seal/Shield, 1994. **Business Addr:** Faculty, National University, Department of Computer Science, 9920 La Cienega Blvd Suite 300, Inglewood, CA 90301, **Business Phone:** 800-628-8648.

HANKS, CAMILLE. See COSBY, CAMILLE OLIVIA HANKS.

HANLEY, J FRANK
Lawyer. **Personal:** Born Mar 11, 1943, Charlotte, NC; son of Robert D and Frank; divorced; children: Laura Elizabeth & Melinda Lee. **Educ:** Hampton Inst; NC Cent Univ Sch Law, LLB, 1968. **Career:** State Ind, dep atty gen, 1969-71; Standard Oil Div Am Oil Co, real estate atty, 1971-72; Marion Co, dep prosecutor, 1972-73; Ind Employment Security Div, mem review bd, 1974-78; pub defender, 1985-88; pvt pract atty, currently. **Orgs:** Marion Co Bar Asn; Indianapolis Bar Asn; Nat Org Social Security Representatives. **Special Achievements:** Tennis Doubles Champion, Cent Inter-Atlantic Asn, 1965; Tennis Doubles Champion, Nat Collegiate Athletic Asn Atlantic Coast, 1965. **Business Addr:** 4249 Lafayette Rd, Indianapolis, IN 46254.

HANLEY, JEROME HERMAN
Psychologist, educator. **Personal:** Born Feb 24, 1950, Detroit, MI; son of Ralph H and Ethel Shelton; divorced; children: Courtney E. **Educ:** Hillsdale Col, BS, 1973; St Louis Univ, MSR, 1975, PhD, 1977. **Career:** Wheeler Clinic, staff psychologist, 1977-78; Howard Univ, asst prof, 1978-79; Coustal Empire Mental Health Ctr, dir, 1979-80, asst dir, 1980-83; Gov Richard W Riley, dir, health affairs, 1983-85; SC Dept Mental Health, dir, children's services, 1985-2001; SC Ctr for Innovation Public Mental Health, dir, 2001-; Univ SC, DMH prof, currently. **Orgs:** Am Psychological Asn, 1977-; Alpha Phi Alpha, life mem, 1984-; Asn Study Classical African Civilizations, 1993-; Asn Study Afro-Amer Life & History, 1994-; Fed Families for Children's Mental Health, 1994-; Asn Black Psychologists, 1995-; Clinical Psych Ethnic Minorities, 1998-; Am Col Mental Health Admin, 1999-. **Honors/Awds:** Rape Crisis Network, Visionary Award, 1997; Wash Perry Middle School, Service Award, 1999; Morris College, Distinguished vis prof, 1999; Agogo Village, Ghana, Honorary Mem, 2001; Fed milies, presidents Award, 2001. **Special Achievements:** First African American clinical child psychologist licensed in SC, 1980. **Home Addr:** 208 Old Manor Rd, Columbia, SC 29210, **Home Phone:** (803)216-0083. **Business Addr:** DMH Professor, University South Carolina, 6311 Garners Ferry Rd, Columbia, SC 29209, **Business Phone:** (803)733-3200.

HANNA, CASSANDRA H.
Educator, musician. **Personal:** Born Jan 1, 1940, Miami, FL. **Educ:** St Augustines Col, BA, 1961; Univ Miami, MusM, 1971; Univ Miami, attended; Ind Univ, attended. **Career:** Episcopal Church St Agnes, organist, choir dir; Miami Dade Comm Choir; Concerts radio & TV, co-dir; Comm Col Fla;; pianist-lectr recitalist; Cassie's Cookies, pres; Miami Dade Community Col, assoc prof music, srprof music, currently. **Orgs:** MENC, NEA, FEA, FCME, NFHAS, FHEA, Alpha Kappa Alpha, Phi Kappa Alpha, AABWE, Nat Guild Organists; pres, Cardiney Corp/Diversified Investments; Music Teachers Nat Asn. **Honors/Awds:** Featured Performer, Nat Black Music Colloquim & Competition, Kennedy Ctr,1980. **Special Achievements:** Presented various lecture-recitals; Performed with Greater Miami Symphony Soc Orchestra: Grieg piano and concerto, Beethoven 3rd Piano Concerto. **Business Addr:** Senior Professor, Miami Dade Community College, 11380 NW 27th Ave, Miami, FL 33167-3418.

HANNAH, HUBERT H., SR.
Association executive. **Personal:** Born Jul 6, 1920, Hill Top, WV; married Edith C; children: Hubert, Jr, Dwayne, Judith, Marc & Don. **Educ:** Bluefield St Col, BS, 1942; OH State Univ, BS, 1949; OH State Univ, MBA, 1952; Depaul Univ, EDP comput acct, 1968. **Career:** J Cameron Wade & Assoc Chicago, mgt consult acct, 1969-72; Statistical Sect Gen Office Int Harvester Co, Chicago, supr & Acct, 1963-69; Steel Div Intl Harvester Co, div acct, 1952-63; Antioch Book plate Co, Yellow Springs, chief acct officer, 1949-51; Dept Budget & Finance Health & Hosps Governing Comn Cook Co Hosp Financial Mgt Asn, bus mgr, 1975. **Orgs:** Omega Psi Phi Frat; Trinity United Ch chmn bd trustees, 1973-75; Urban League; Beta Alpha Psi Hon Acct Frat, 1951. **Military Serv:** AUS, sgt, 1942-45. *

HANNAH, JOHNNIE, JR.
Computer executive, college teacher. **Personal:** Born Nov 20, 1970, Akron, OH; son of Johnnie and Joanne. **Educ:** Howard Univ, BBA, info systs, 1993; Heidelberg Col, MBA, 2001. **Career:** GeuCorp, syst analysis, 1993-96; United Way, Great Toledo, dir info syst, 1996-98; City Toledo, tech serv coordr, 1998-; Heidelberg Col, adj prof, 2002-. **Orgs:** Upward Bd Prog, 1989; InRoads Alumni Asn, 1993; chair, Black Data Processing Assoc, Toledo Chap, 1996; bd mem, African Am Christian Fel Asn, 1996; vpres mem serv, Black Data Processing Assoc, 1997; Nat Asn Advan Colored People, 1997; Greater Toledo Urban League, 1997; ONYX, 1997; Asn Info Technol Professionals, 1997; Presidents Summit Americas Future, delegate, 1997; bd mem, KEVIN; founding mem, City Toledo Found Future. **Honors/Awds:** Distinguished Leadership Award Finalist, Leadership Toledo, 1997; Twenty Under 40 Award Recipient, Toledo Jaycees, 1997; Mentor Award for Young Male Palever, Ghahanian Found, 1997; President Award, Black Data Processing Assoc, 1997. **Special Achievements:** 30 Leaders of the Future selected by Ebony Magazine, 1996. **Home Addr:** 2207 Rockspring Rd, Toledo, OH 43614, **Home Phone:** (419)865-3565. **Business Addr:** Adjunct Professor, Heidelberg College, Grad Studies Bussiness, 310 E Market St, Tiffin, OH 44883-2462, **Business Phone:** (419)448-2221.*

HANNAH, MARC REGIS
Electrical engineer, vice president (organization), scientist. **Personal:** Born Oct 13, 1956, Chicago, IL. **Educ:** Ill Inst Technol, BS, elec eng, 1977; Stanford Univ, MS, elec eng, 1978, PhD, elec eng, 1985. **Career:** Silicon Graphics, co-founder & mem tech staff, 1982-85, principal scientist, vpres & chief scientist, 1997; Omniverse Digital Solutions, vpre technol devel, currently. **Orgs:** Inst Elec & Electronics Engrs; ACM, Northern Calif Coun Black Prof Engrs, NTA. **Honors/Awds:** Recipient of 13 patents and numerous awards and honors, including the Prof Achievement Award from both Ill Inst Technol & Nat Tech Asn.

HANNAH, MOSIE R.
Banker. **Personal:** Born Jul 11, 1949, Lake City, SC; married Doris Horry; children: Michelle, Brandon. **Educ:** Voorhees Col, BS, 1970; Univ Mich, Grad Sch & Banking, 1981; Univ OK, Retail Banking Sch, 1983. **Career:** Fleet Financial Group, br mgr, 1973-75, asst vpres, 1975-79, vpres, 1979-84, sr vpres, 1984-. **Orgs:** Dir, United Neighbourhood Ctrs Am; Vstg Nurses Serv Monroe County; Rochester Bus Opporutnites Corp; allocaties Com United Way Greater Rochester. **Business Addr:** Senior Vice President, Fleet Bank, 1 E Ave, Rochester, NY 14604.*

HANNAHAM, FRED
Engineer. **Educ:** PE. **Career:** Pvt pract, engr, currently. *

HANNAH-JONES, BEVERLY K
Architect, chief executive officer. **Personal:** Married Carlton Jones. **Educ:** Mich State Univ; Lawrence Technol Univ; BS, archit, 1985; BArch, 1988. **Career:** Hanna Jones Group, chief exec officer, 1993-. **Orgs:** Delta Sigma Theta Sorority; Am Inst Architects; bd mem, Mich State Fire Safety Bd; Nat Asn Negro Bus & Prof Womens Club Inc. **Honors/Awds:** Honor, Nat Asn Negro Bus & Prof Womens Club Inc. **Special Achievements:** One of only ten licensed African American female architects in the country to head her own firm; Recognized as the first licensed African-American female to own & operate an architectural firm in Oakland County. **Business Phone:** (313)837-8457.

HANSBERRY-MOORE, VIRGINIA T
Educator. **Personal:** Born Jan 26, 1930, Ocala, FL; daughter of L T Thompson (deceased) and Beatrice Thompson (deceased); married Clarence (divorced 1977); children: Katrina Veronica; married James, Sep 5, 1981. **Educ:** Fla Mem Col, St Augustine, FL, BS, elem educ, 1947-51; Masters Admin Supv, Melbourne, FL, 1976-77. **Career:** Broward Co Sch Syst, Fort Lauderdale, FL, teacher, 1951-84; Zeta Dove Found Inc, bd dir, currently. **Orgs:** Zeta Phi Beta Sorority, 1948-; Youth worker, First Baptist Church Piney Grove, 1951-; bd dirs, Fla Endowment Fund Higher Educ, 1984-; dist dean, Christian Educ; supv dir, State Pageantry (CE); Nat First vpres, 1984-90. **Honors/Awds:** Harriet Dorrah Award, NW Federated Woman's Club, 1973; Mother of the Year, First Baptist Church Piney Grove, 1974; State Director Award, Zeta Phi Beta, State Fla, 1978; Regional Director's Award, 1980; Teacher of the Year, Sunland Park Elem Sch, 1984; Zeta of the Year, 1986. **Home Addr:** 3511 NW 23rd St, Fort Lauderdale, FL 33311. **Business Addr:** Board of Director, Zeta Dove Foundation Inc, PO Box 15811, Plantation, FL 33318.

HANSBURY, VIVIEN H
Educator. **Personal:** Born Feb 5, 1927, Richmond, VA; daughter of Arthur J Holmes and Mary Spain Holmes; widowed; children: Horace A Trent, Sandra Lewis & Vernard Trent. **Educ:** Va State Univ, BS, 1966; Temple Univ, MEd, 1970, prin cert, 1972. **Career:** Educator (retired); Delaware County Intermediate Unit, teacher, ment retarded/learning disability, 1966-68, supvr spec educ, 1968-69; Pa State Univ, counr, 1969-74; Sch Dist Philadelphia, educ advr, 1974-76, Pre-Sch Handicapped, prog mgr, 1976-78, instr advr, 1978-80, instr support teacher, 1980-92; NIA Psychol Asn, educ consult. **Orgs:** Nat rep, Civil Rights, Zeta Phi Beta Sorority, 1986-92, Black Family, dir, 1992-; pres, Sigma Pi Epsilon Delta, Philadelphia Chap, Grad Div, 1987-; pres, Top Ladies Distinction, Philadelphia Chap, 1988-93; pres, Phi Delta Kappa Fraternity, Univ Pa Chap, 1990-94; scholar comt mem, Phi Delta Kappa Nat Sorority, 1990-; nat mem-at-large, Nat Asn Colored Women's Clubs, 1992-; secy, Pinochle Bugs Social & Civic Club, Philadelphia Chap, 1992-; pres, Va State Univ Alumni Asn, Philadelphia Chap, 1993-; treas, Top Ladies Distinction, Area II, 1993-; Nat Coun Negro Woman, Philadelphia Local; chmn, Travel Educ & Cult Comt; Philadelphia Fedn Teachers; Am Fedn Teachers. **Honors/Awds:** Achievement & Recognition, Sch Dist Philadelphia, 1977, 1983-84; Recognition & Appreciation, Pan Hellenic Coun, Philadelphia Chap, 1981-82; Zeta of the Year, Zeta Phi Beta Sorority, 1981-82, Recognition & Appreciation, 1985-87, 1991-92; Outstanding Community Service, Am Red Cross, 1984 & 1986; Teacher of the Year, Sch Dist Philadelphia, 1988; Outstanding Achievement Award, Top Ladies Distinction, 1989, Appreciation Award, 1990-91, Recognition Award, 1992; Dedication to the Community & Outstanding Leadership Among African American Women, Nat Finalist. **Special Achievements:** Is Your Child Ready for First Grade, 1969; Identifying Preschool Handicapped Children, 1969; The Remediation Approach of Hortense Barry, 1970; Educ Assessment, 1978; Diagnostic Prescriptive Teaching, 1979. **Home Addr:** 2246 N 52nd St, Philadelphia, PA 19131-2313.

HANSEN, JOYCE VIOLA
Educator. **Personal:** Born Oct 18, 1942, Bronx, NY; daughter of Lillian Dancy Hansen and Austin Hansen; married Matthew Nelson, Dec 18, 1982. **Educ:** Pace Univ, New York, NY, BA, Eng, 1972; New York Univ, New York, NY, MA, Eng Educ, 1978. **Career:** Educator (retired); New York City Bd Educ, teacher, 1973-95; Empire State Col, teacher, 1987-95. **Orgs:** Soc C's Bk Writers, 1980-; Harlem Writer's Guild, 1982-. **Honors/Awds:** Parent's Choice Award, 1986; Coretta Scott King Honor Book Award, 1987, 1995; Children's Book Award, African Studies Asn, 1995; Coretta Scott King Honor Book Award, 1998, 1999; Nat Parenting Publications Award, 1998; Carter G Woodson Honor Book Award, 1999. **Special Achievements:** Author, The Gift-Giver, 1980; Home Boy, 1982; Yellow Bird and Me, 1986; Which Way Freedom?; 1986, Out From This Place, 1988; Between Two Fires: Black Soldiers in the Civil War, 1993; I Thought My Soul Would Rise and Fly, 1997; Breaking Ground, Breaking Silence, 1998; Women of Hope, 1998; The Heart Calls Home, 1999; Bury Me Not in a Land of Slaves, 2000; One True Friend, 2001; Freedom Roads, 2003; African Princess: The Amazing Lives of Africa's Royal Women, 2004.

HANSEN, STANLEY S., JR.
Educator. **Career:** NY State Educ Dept, Off Higher Educ, exec coordr, currently. **Business Addr:** Executive Coordinator, New York State Education Department, 89 Washington Ave, Rm 967 Education Bldg Addition, Albany, NY 12234, **Business Phone:** (518)474-3969.*

HANSFORD, LOUISE TODD
Publisher. **Personal:** Born Nov 6, 1944, Cincinnati, OH; daughter of James and Josephine; divorced; children: Eric. **Career:** The Andrew Jergens Co, secy, 1963-68; Procter & Gamble, org effectiveness consult, 1968-90; Fine Arts By Todd, owner & pres & Chief Exec Officer , 1990-. **Orgs:** Valley Forge Federated, 1967-69; NAT Coun Negro Women, 1984-86; founder, Black Aware & Concerned, 1973-78; Atlanta BUS League, 1997; NAT Conf Artists, 1997; NAT Black Arts Festival, 1996; co-chair, Mayor's Masked Ball, 1997; Atlanta COC. **Honors/Awds:** Atlanta BUS League, Outstanding Achievement BUS, 1997; Woman of Enterprise Awards, Avon Products, nominated, 1998. **Business Addr:** President, Chief Executive Officer, Fine Arts by Todd, 1240 Chattahoochee Ave NW, Atlanta, GA 30318, **Business Phone:** (404)351-5553.*

HANSON, JOHN L
Media executive, disc jockey. **Personal:** Born Aug 5, 1950, Detroit, MI; son of Lavinia Collins; children: Kacey. **Educ:** Huston-19Tillotson Col, attended 1972. **Career:** KHRB-AM Lockhart, disc jockey, 1970-71; KUT radio, Austin, disc jockey, 1974-80, producer In Black Am radio series, 1980-, exec producer, interim gen mgr, 1984-, admin serv officer, 2001-. **Orgs:** Pres, John Hanson & Assoc, 1970-; bd dir, Black Arts Alliance, 1985; bd dir, Camp Fire, 1985; pres, Austin Asn Black Communicators, 1986-87; bd dir, Nat Asn Black Journalists, 1987-89, adv, currently. **Honors/Awds:** Community Service Awards, Greater Austin Coun Alcoholism, Community Serv Award, Over the Hill Inc; Phoenix Award, Travis County. **Business Addr:** Administrative Services Officer, Senior Producer, Host & Reporter, KUT Radio, Campus Mail Code A0704, Austin, TX 78712, **Business Phone:** (512)471-8260.

HANSPARD, BYRON COURTENAY, SR.
Football player. **Personal:** Born Jan 23, 1976, Dallas, TX; married Yolanda. **Educ:** Tex Tech Univ. **Career:** Football player (retired); Atlanta Falcons, running back, 1997-99; Tampa Bay Buccaneers, 2002-05. **Honors/Awds:** Doak Walker Award, 1996; NFL All-Rookie Team, 1997.

HAQQ, KHALIDA ISMAIL
School administrator. **Personal:** Born Jul 11, 1946, Cape Charles, VA; married; children: Hassana, Majeeda, Thaky, Hussain, Jaleel & Jameel. **Educ:** Rutgers NCAS, BA Psychol, Black Studies, 1980; Rutgers GSE, MEd coun psychol, 1983. **Career:** Rutgers Univ, counr, 1976-80, res asst, 1981-82; Plainfield Brd Ed, sub teacher, 1980-81; New Brunswick HS, career ed intern, 1982;Caldwell Col,coun, 1982-84, cord of coun, tutor, 1984-; Rider Col, eop asst dir, counr 1985-; Mercer Co Community Col, dir, educ opportunity fund, currently. **Orgs:** Irvington Parent Teachers Assn, NJ Assn Black Ed 1980-, Assn Black Psychologists 1982-, NJ Ed Opportunity Fund Prof Assn 1982-, Am Assn for coun & Develop 1982-; NAACP 1985, Community Awareness Now 1986-, Mercer County Black Dem Caucus 1986; leadership adv brd Rutgers Minority Community. **Honors/Awds:** Soroptimist Scholarship Recipient 1978; Martin Luther King Jr Fellowship Recipient 1982. **Business Addr:** Director, Mercer County Community College, WWC Stud Ctr 238 JKC Room 324, 1200 Old Trenton Rd, Trenton, NJ 08550, **Business Phone:** (609)586-4800.

HARALSON, LARRY L
Government official, manager. **Personal:** Married Irene Williams; children: Kimberly & Ashley. **Educ:** Memphis State Univ, Memphis, TN, BBA, 1972. **Career:** Nat Bank Com, Memphis TN, main off br mgr, 1978-79; First Tenn Bank, Memphis TN, sales & br mgr, 1979-87; Memphis City Govt, Memphis, TN, city treas & dir, 1988. **Orgs:** Chmn, Tenn Jaycees Personal Growth Sweepstakes, 1986; bd mem, Shelby County Bd Equalizations, 1990-; bd mem, Whitehaven Community Develop Corp, currently; 100 Black Men Memphis Inc, currently. **Honors/Awds:** Volunteer of the Year, Memphis Hemophilia Found, 1983. **Military Serv:** AUS, SP5, 1966-68. *

HARBIN-FORTE, BRENDA F
Judge. **Personal:** Born Apr 19, 1954, Meridian, MS; daughter of Woodroc and Sophie; married Napolean, Sep 2, 1989; children: Ken M. **Educ:** Univ Calif, Berkeley, BA, 1976; Boalt Hall Sch Law, Univ California, Berkeley, JD, 1979. **Career:** Legal Aid Soc Alameda Co, law clerk, 1977-78; Alameda Co Pub Defender, law clerk, 1978; Moore & Bell, law clerk, 1978-79; Harris, Alexander, Burris, & Culver, assoc, 1982-84; Hastings Col Law, adj prof law, 1983-84; Thelen, Marrin, Johnson, & Bridges, assoc, 1984-89, partner, 1990-92; Munic Ct State Calif, Co Alameda, Oakland-Piedmont-Emeryville Judicial Dist, judge, 1992-; CJER?s B E Witkin Judicial Col, dean, 2000-02; Juv Court, Super Ct Calif, Co Alameda, presiding judge, currently. **Orgs:** Vpres, Calif Asn Black Lawyers, 1987-89, pres's spec asst judicial, 1992-; exec bd mem & newsletter ed, Charles Houston Bar Asn, 1988, adv bd, 1993-; master, Edward J McFetridge Am Inn Ct, 1993-, chairperson, 1994-95; fel, Am Bar Found, 1993-; assoc trustee, Alta Bates Med Ctr Community Mem, 1994-; Am Bar Asn. **Honors/Awds:** Honoree, Nat Black Law Stud Asn Tribute Black Women Legal Prof, 1988; Community Service Award, Charles Houston Bar Asn, 1991; Woman of the Year, Oakland Bus & Prof Women, 1992; Bernard S Jefferson Judge of the Year Award, Calif Asn Black Lawyers, 1994; President's Award, Charles Houston Bar Asn, 1994. **Special Achievements:** First African-American woman President of the Alameda County Bar Association, first African-American woman to clerk for the Central Staff of the Ninth Circuit, first African-American woman elected Boalt Hall Class President, "Unfair Media Coverage of Judicial Misconduct Investigations, or Taking Landmark Communications Too Far," The San Francisco Attorney, August/Sept, 1987, "Black Women Pioneers in the Law," The Historical Reporter, 1987, "350 Days to Trial, Strategies for Survival Under Trial Court Delay Reduction Programs", 1988. **Business Addr:** Presiding Judge, Superior Court of California, Juvenile Court County of Alameda, 400 Broadway, Oakland, CA 94605, **Business Phone:** (510)268-7373.

HARDAWAY, ANFERNEE DEON
Basketball player. **Personal:** Born Jul 18, 1971, Memphis, TN; son of Fae. **Educ:** Univ Memphis, BA, prof studies, 2003. **Career:** Orlando Magic, guard-forward, 1993-99; Phoenix Suns, 1999-2004; NY Knicks, forward, 2004-06; Miami Heat, 2007; free agent, currently. **Orgs:** Penny Hardaway Found; nat spokesman, UNICEF. **Honors/Awds:** Nat High School Player of the Year, Parade Mag, 1990; Schick Rookie Game, MVP, 1994; NBA All-Rookie Team, 1994; NBA All-Star, 1995, 1996, 1997, 1998; All-NBA First Team, 1995, 1996; All-NBA Third Team, 1996; Gold Medal, Men's Basketball, Olympics, Atlanta, 1996; Rich & Helen DeVos Community Enrichment Award, 1997. **Special Achievements:** First round, third pick, NBA Draft, 1993; Film appearance: Blue Chips, 1994; Gold medal, US Olympics Men's Basketball, 1996; featured on, "Cribs", MTV show, 2001.

HARDAWAY, DR. ERNEST, II
Oral surgeon, educator. **Personal:** Born Mar 3, 1938, Col, GA; son of Virginia L and Ernest. **Educ:** Howard Univ, BS, 1957, DDS, 1966, Oral Surg, 1972; Johns Hopkins Univ, MPH, 1973. **Career:** Bureau Med Serv, dep dir, 1980; Pub Health Wash DC, dep comnr, 1982; Pub Health Wash DC, comnr, 1983-84; Fed Employee Occup Health Prog HHS Region V, dir, 1985; Howard Univ, asst prof oral & maxillofacial surgery, 1970; Int Inst Bus Technol Inc, dir, enterprise govt; USPHS, 1977-80; dep comnr, comnr pub health,

City of Washington, 1982-84; Mile Sq Health Center Inc, actg vpres, finance & admin affairs, 1984; Federal Employee Occupational Health Program, asst regional health adminr, 1985, dir, 1986-89, Chicago and Kansas City, 1989-90; CFO coun comt entrepreneurial govt off Mgt & Budget, Wash, member, 1991-2001; Comt Acad affairs Col Bus Univ Illinois, chmn, 2001-. **Orgs:** Chief policy coord, Bur Med Serv 1978. **Honors/Awds:** Pub Health Serv Plaque, 1980; Commendation Medal, US Pub Health Serv, 1973; Meritorious Serv Medal; Outstanding Unit Citation Commendation Medal, US Pub Health Serv; Dentist of the Year, 1983; Distinguished Dentist of the Year, Nat Dent Asn, 1984; Fel, Am Col Dentists; Nat Dent Asn Found; Fel, Int Col Dentists; Fel, Am Asn Oral & Maxillofacial Surgeons; Fel, Acad Dentistry Int; Distinguished Serv Awards. **Military Serv:** US-PHS, col 16 yrs. *

HARDAWAY, JERRY DAVID
Scout. **Personal:** Born Oct 23, 1951, Memphis, TN; son of Jerry D and Bennie Louise Carter; married Lisa A Mills, Dec 31, 1986; children: Jason D, Jheri D. **Educ:** Southern Ill Univ, BS, speech edu, 1973; Grambling State Univ, MA, sports admin, 1973. **Career:** Memphis State Univ, asst football coach, 1975-77; Grambling State Univ, asst football coach, 1978-83; Univ Calif, Berkeley, asst football coach, 1984-86; Carolina Panthers, area scout, 1995; Ariz Cardinals, prof football team, area scout, 1996-. **Business Addr:** Scout, Arizona Cardinals, 8701 S Hardy Dr, Phoenix, AZ 85284, **Business Phone:** (602)379-0101.*

HARDAWAY, TIMOTHY DUANE
Basketball player, basketball coach, business owner. **Personal:** Born Sep 1, 1966, Chicago, IL; son of Donald; married Yolanda; children: Tim Jr & Nia. **Educ:** Univ Tex, El Paso, TX, 1989. **Career:** Basketball player (retired), basketball coach; Golden State Warriors, guard, 1989-96; Miami Heat, guard, 1996-2001; Dallas Mavericks, guard, 2001-02; Denver Nuggets, guard, 2002; Ind Pacers, guard, 2003; Waterloo Kings, guard, 2005; Fla Pit Bulls, pres, gen mgr, co-owner & head coach, 2005; Trinity Sports & Entertrainment Group, co-founder & chief basketball opers adv; business owner, currently. **Orgs:** The Support Group, co-founder. **Honors/Awds:** Jack McMahon Award, 1989-90; NBA All-Rookie First Team, 1990; NBA All-Star, 1991-93, 1997, 1998; Frances Pomeroy Naismith Award, 1989; Gold medal, Tournament of Americas, 1999; Gold medal, Olympic Games, 2000.

HARDEMAN, DR. CAROLE HALL
School administrator. **Personal:** Born in Muskogee, OK; daughter of Ira D Hall Sr and Rubye Hibler Hall; children: Paula Suzette. **Educ:** Fisk Univ, BA, music; Univ Okla, MA, 1975, PhD, sec ed admin, 1979; Harvard Univ, MLE Prog, 1988. **Career:** Okla State Regents Higher Ed, Regents doctoral fel, 1975-79; Univ Okla, Col Educ & Human Rels, vis prof, 1980-85; SW Ctr Human Rels Studies, exec dir, 1982-85; Adroit Publ Inc, pres; Twelve Inc, staff; LeMoyne-Owen Col, vpres acad affairs, 1990-92, vpres res & develop, 1992-97; Nat Alliance Black Sch Educr, Res Round table Monographs, ed; Langston Univ, assoc dean educ, grad prof educ & behavioral sci, 1997-; Carole Hardeman Assocs, owner, 2006-; Ind Univ, vis prof, 2007. **Orgs:** Founder, Okla Alliance Black Sch Educators, 1984; exec bd, Nat Alliance/Black Sch Ed, 1996-; Links Inc; Jack & Jill Inc; Nat Alliance Black Sch Educr; Urban League; Nat Asn Advan Colored People; NAMPW; Am Asn Sch Adminr; ASCD; AERA; Alpha Kappa Alpha; YWCA; Asn Women Math; Nat Task Force Multicultural Ed; Memphis Arts Coun Comt 100; bd dir, Planned Parenthood; bd dirs, Southern Region Planned Parenthood, exec bd, 1994-; Memphis May, Memphis Literacy Coun; Okla Urban League; Okla Philharmonic Soc; United Way Res & Convening Comt; Nat Coun Accreditation Teacher Educ; Bd Examiners Cent Okla; bd dirs, The Ambassadors' Concert Choir. **Honors/Awds:** Outstanding Faculty, Univ Okla, 1984; Roscoe Dungee Award Excellence in Print Journalism, Okla Black Media Asn, 1984; W.E.B. DuBois Higher Education Award, Nat Alliance Black Sch Educr, 1997. **Special Achievements:** She developed Inst "Effective Pedagogy for Urban Learners" under funding from Ford Found at LeMoyne-Owen Col, Univ Memphis, & Langston Univ; author math & Sci textbooks middle schs: MATHCO, & SOUNDS Sci. **Business Addr:** Associate Dean of Education, Graduate Professor, Langston University, 4001 Lincoln Blvd Page Hall Suite 312B, PO Box 1500, Oklahoma City, OK 73050, **Business Phone:** (405)466-3394.

HARDEMAN, JAMES ANTHONY
Social worker, administrator. **Personal:** Born Feb 2, 1943, Athens, GA; divorced; children: Maria & Brian. **Educ:** Howard Univ, BA, 1967; Boston Col, MSW, 1973; Harvard Univ, MPA, 1974; Brandeis Univ, PhD, 1995. **Career:** Dept Corrections, prison warden, 1975-78; Dept Ment Health, sr social worker, 1978-79; Ex-Off Human Serv State House Boston, dep dir planning, 1979-83; Polaroid Corp, mgr corp employee asst prog, 1983; Workplace Violence Interventions & Strategies, exec dir, currently. **Orgs:** Bd dirs, Boston Col, 1981-83; pres, Boston Col Grad Sch Social Work Alumni Asn, 1981-83; vpres, Nat Asn Social Work, Mass, 1982; bd mem, Mayflower Ment Health Asn, 1983-92; Catholic Charities, 1983-85; Crime & Justice Found Boston, 1985. **Honors/Awds:** Nat Asn Social Workers Mass Chap Nat Delegate Rep, 1981; Community Service Award, 1991 & 1992; Black Achiever Community Service, 1992; Independent Spirit Award, 1992; Greatest Contribution to Social Work Practice, 1997. **Military Serv:** USAF, capt, 1967-71. **Home Addr:** 128 Bettencourt Rd, Plymouth, MA 02360-4202. **Business Addr:** Executive Director, Workplace Violence Interventions & Strategies, PO Box 4066, Plymouth, MA 02361.

HARDEMAN, STROTHA E, JR.
Dentist. **Personal:** Born Oct 26, 1929, Ft Worth, TX; married Willie Mae; children: Sharon Kaye & Keith Dion. **Educ:** Va Union Univ, BS, 1950; Meharry Med Coll, DT, 1956; Meharry Med Sch, DDS, 1963. **Career:** Gulf State Dent Assn, pres; pvt pract, dentist, currently. **Orgs:** NT Wallis Dent Soc; Ft Worth Dent Soc; Tex Dent Asn; Am Dent Asn; Ambassadore Club; Jack & Jill Am Inc. **Military Serv:** AUS, med corp, 1950. **Home Addr:** 612 NW 25th St, Fort Worth, TX 76106-7095, **Home Phone:** (817)626-0481. **Business Addr:** Dentist, 612 Nw 25th St, Fort Worth, TX 76106-7095, **Business Phone:** (817)626-0481.

HARDEN, ALICE VARNADO
Senator (u.s. federal government), teacher. **Personal:** Born Apr 17, 1948, Pike County, PA; married Dennis Labert. **Educ:** Jackson State Univ, BS, MS. **Career:** Teacher; Miss St, senator, 1988-, currently; St James Baptist Church, mem; Hinds County Democratic Women, mem. **Orgs:** Miss Asn Educr; Alpha Kappa Alpha Sorority; Women's Polit Network; Nat Coun Negro Women; life mem, Nat Asn Advan Colored People; NOBEL women; NatConf St Legislators; Nat Black Caucus St Legislators; chairs, Southern Legis Conf Educ Comt; Miss Adv Coun; US Civil Rights Comn; Miss Educ Comn St; Nat Educ Asn. **Business Addr:** Senator, Mississippi State Senate, Rm 407, PO Box 1018, Jackson, MS 39215, **Business Phone:** (601)359-3232.

HARDEN, CEDRIC
Football player. **Personal:** Born Oct 19, 1974, Atlanta, GA. **Educ:** Fla A&M Univ, criminal justice. **Career:** Football player(retired), San Diego Chargers, defensive end, 1998-99. **Honors/Awds:** Rookie of the Year, 1999.

HARDEN, MARVIN
Artist, educator. **Personal:** Born in Austin, TX; son of Theodore Roosevelt and Ethel Sneed. **Educ:** Univ Calif, Los Angeles, BA, fine arts, 1959, MA, creative painting, 1963. **Career:** Univ Calif, Los Angeles, exten instr art, 1964-68; Los Angeles Harbor Col, evening div instr art, 1965-68; Univ High Adult Sch, instr art, 1965-68; Santa Monica City Col, evening div instr art, 1968; Calif State Univ, Northridge, prof art, 1967-97, prof emer, 1997-; One man shows: Whitney Museum of American Art; Irving Blum Gallery; Los Angeles Municipal Art Gallery; Newport Harbor Art Museum; Eugenia Butler Galleries; James Corcoran Gallery; David Stuart Galleries; Ceeje Galleries; Rath Museum, Geneva, Switz; Armory Center for Arts, Pasadena, CA; Brand Library Art Center; Group shows: Brooklyn Museum; Chicago Museum of Contemporary Art; Equitable Gallery, NY; Nagoya City Museum, Japan; Tel Aviv Museum of Art; Contemporary Art Asn, Houston; Philadelphia Civic Center Museum; San Francisco Museum of Art; High Museum of Art; Minneapolis Institute of Arts; Univ of California, Los Angeles; US State Dept tour of USSR; Franklin Furnace NY; San Diego F Art Gallery; Cheney Cowles Museum, Spokane, WA; Davis & Cline Gallery, Ashland, OR. **Orgs:** Fel Nat Endowment Arts, 1972; co-founder, Los Angeles Inst Contemp Art, 1973; bd dir, Images & Issues Mag, 1980-85; Los Angeles Munic Art Gallery Asn Artist's Adv Bd, 1983-87; fel John Simon Guggenheim Mem Found, 1983; Nat Endowment Arts Visual Arts Fel Painting Panel, 1985; chmn, Los Angeles Cult Affairs Dept, Peer Review Bd, Visual Arts Grants, 1990. **Honors/Awds:** Fellowship Awards in Visual Arts 1983; Distinguished Professor Award, 1984, Exceptional Meritorious Service Award, 1984, Calif State Univ, Northridge. **Home Addr:** PO Box 1793, Cambria, CA 93428. **Business Phone:** (818)677-2242.*

HARDEN, ROBERT JAMES
Physician. **Personal:** Born Jul 16, 1952, Washington, GA; married Margaret Ellanor Hemp; children: Robert Jr, John Phillip. **Educ:** Univ Ill Chicago, BS, 1975; Meharry Med Col, MD 1979. **Career:** Weiss Mem Hosp, med intern, 1980-81; US Pub Health Serv, asst surgeon gen, 1981-83; Timberlawn Psychiat Hosp, psychiat resident, 1984-87,child & adolescent fel, 1987-89; Pvt Pract, Physicain Psychiat, currently. **Orgs:** Resident mem exec coun, Tex Soc Psychiat Physicians, 1986-87. **Honors/Awds:** S01 W Ginsburg Fel Group for the Advancement of Psychiatry, 1987-89. **Business Addr:** Psychiatry Physician, 2222 W Spring Creek Pkwy, Plano, TX 75023.

HARDIE, ROBERT L., JR.
Executive. **Personal:** Born Oct 22, 1941, Portsmouth, VA; son of Robert L Sr and Janie Norman; married Marianne Lowry; children: Levon, Robin, F Gary Lee (stepson). **Educ:** Hampton Univ, BS, 1963; Univ MD, Southern IL, MBA. **Career:** AUS Security Agency Warrenton, chief elect engr, 1964-66; Bunker-Ramo Corp, Silver Spring, syst integration engr, 1966-69; Vitro Lab Automation Inc, Silver Spring, proj leader, 1969-72; Raytheon Serv Co, Hyattsville, sr systs engr, 1972-73; Systs Consult Inc, Wash, sr systs engr, 1973-75; Scientific Mgt Asn Inc, prog mgr, 1975-85; Evaluation Res Corp Int, sr systs engr, 1985-86; Fairfax, engr; Sentel Corp, Virginia, cheif exec officer & chmn, 1986-. **Orgs:** Am Soc Naval Engrs, 1974-; Navy League, 1974-87; Naval Inst; Inst Elec & Electronic Engrs, 1965-77; pres, Greenbelt Jaycees, 1973-74; chmn, Greenbelt Comn; Rels Adv Comt, 1974-76; vpres, Greenbelt Labor Day Festival Comt; bd dirs, Camp Springs Boys & Girls Club, 1979-80; Greenbelt Rep Transp Citizen Adv Comt; Met Wash Coun Govts, 1975; Nat Asn Minority Bus, 1984. **Honors/Awds:** Greenbelt Jaycees Keyman Award, 1973, 1975; Jaycee of the Month, 1971, 1972; Distinguished Military Grad; Gold Plaque Award, Letter of Appreciation, Naval Sea Systs, 1985. **Special Achievements:** Graduated with dept honors; co-authored & publ: "Let's Design Out EMI," 1981. **Military Serv:** AUS, first lt, 1964-66. **Business Addr:** Chairman, Chief Executive Officer, Sentel Corporation, 1735 Jefferson Davis Hwy Suite 407, Arlington, VA 22202, **Business Phone:** (703)685-7110.*

HARDIN, EUGENE
Educator, physician, executive director. **Personal:** Born Dec 6, 1941, Jacksonville, FL; widowed; children: Jeffrey, Gregory. **Educ:** Fla A&M Univ, BS, pharm, 1964; Univ S Fla, MD, 1977. **Career:** Walgreens, asst mgr, pharmacist, 1964-66; Va Hosp, staff pharmacist, 1966-74; King-Drew Med Ctr, Dept Emergency Med, physician specialist, 1980-, asst prof, emergency med, 1980-, vice chmn, 1990-93, Residence Training Prog, dir, 1990-, chmn, currently. **Orgs:** Med dir, Carson Med Group, 1981; Nat Med Asn, 1984-92; Am Med Asn, 1984-; Drew Med Soc, 1985-92; Carson Chamber Com, 1985; SCLC, 1986; Martin Luther King Hosp, Joint Prac Comt, chmn, 1987; Am Col Emergency Physicians, 1990; dir, Calif Coun Emergency Med Residency, 1991; med dir, King-Drew Med Ctr, Physicians Assistance Prog. **Honors/Awds:** Most Outstanding Residence Internal Med, Martin Luther King Hosp, 1980. **Special Achievements:** Auth paper: The Dynamics of Parental Abuse, 1987. **Military Serv:** AUS, sp-5, 2 yrs; Foreign Serv Medal, 1969. **Home Addr:** PO Box 901, Harbor City, CA 90710. **Business Addr:** Chaiman, Director, King-Drew Medical Center, Emergency Med Dept, 12021 S Wilmington Ave Rm 1034, Los Angeles, CA 90059-1744.*

HARDIN, HENRY E.
Educator, businessperson, clergy. **Personal:** Born Jan 1, 1912?, Ft Motte, SC; married Carrie; children: Isadora Wallace & Henrietta Butler. **Educ:** Benedict Col, BA, 1944; Benedict Col, BD, 1945; NY Univ, MA, 1947; NY Univ, Union Theol Sem City Col, NY, pursued addn grad studies. **Career:** St Paul Bapt Church, pastor; Morris Col, Sumter, SC, pres, prof, dean trustees head Col, 1970, dean & dir col financial aid prog, Centennial Celebration SC Bapt Conv, instr, chmn, currently. **Orgs:** Nat Humanities Fel, Duke Univ, 1971; mem on Staff, Colgate-Rochester Seminar on Black Ch Curric, 1969; pres, Comn on Equal Opp. **Business Addr:** Chairman, Morris College, Sumter, SC 29150.

HARDIN, DR. JOHN ARTHUR
Educator. **Personal:** Born Sep 18, 1948, Louisville, KY; son of Albert A and Elizabeth Hansbro(deceased); married Maxine Randle, Dec 22, 1973; children: Jonathan Rico. **Educ:** Bellarmine Univ, BA, hist, 1970; Fisk Univ, MA, hist, 1972; Univ Mich,PhD, hist, 1989. **Career:** Univ Louisville, adj fac, 1972-84; Spokane Community Col, instr, 1989; Three Univ Fel, Fisk Univ, 1970-72; Ky State Univ, asst prof,1976-84, area coordr, 1978-80, instr, 1972-74, 1976-78; Univ Ky, vis asst prof, 1980-81; Eastern Wash Univ, asst prof, 1984-90, assoc prof, 1990-91; Potter Col Arts, Humanities & Social Scis, asst dean, 1997-2002; Western KY Univ, instr, 1972-78, asst dean, 1997-2002, asst to provost diversity enhancement, 2002-05, assoc prof, 1991-. **Orgs:** Mem exec, community Ky Asn Teachers Hist, 1976-80, 1991-; state dir, Phi Beta Sigma Fraternity Inc, 1981-83; club pres, Frankt Kiwanis Club,1983-84; Ky Hist Preserv Review Bd, 1983-84, Publ Adv Community Ky Hist Soc, 1983-84, Nat Coun Black Studies, 1984-; NAACP,1984-; ed adv bd mem, Filson Club Hist Quarterly, 1989-92; life mem, Phi Beta Sigma, 1980-; Ky Oral Hist Comn, 1995-2003, comn chair, 2006-; Phi Alpha Theta Hist Honor Soc; Kentucky African Am Heritage Comn, 2007; chair, mem, Ky Hist Soc, 1984-. **Honors/Awds:** Lenihan Award, Bellarmine Univ, 1969; Graduate Opportunity Award, Univ Mich, 1974-76; J Pierce Scholarship, Univ Mich, Dept Hist, 1976;Distinguished Alumni Gallery, Bellarmine Col, 1979-80; President Award, Nat Coun For Black Studies-Region X, 1987. **Special Achievements:** Publisher of more books. Author: Onward and Upward: A Centennial History of Kentucky State University, 1886-1986, Fifty Years of Segregation: Black Higher Education in Kentucky, 1904-54. **Home Addr:** 2424 Tipperary, Bowling Green, KY 42104-4558, **Home Phone:** (270)781-6992. **Business Addr:** Associate Professor, Western Kentucky University, Department History, Cherry Hall 233, 1906 Col Heights Blvd Suite 21086, Bowling Green, KY 42101-1086, **Business Phone:** (270)745-2233.

HARDIN, MARIE D
Administrator. **Personal:** Daughter of Harrison Ridley and Emma; married Granville N (deceased); children: Oliver & Alyce Hardin-Cook. **Educ:** Wayne State Univ; Ind Univ; Capital Univ, attended 1984. **Career:** City Columbus, div mgt coordr, 1970-74, dep dir CDA, 1974-76, dir div CDA, 1975-77, equal employ opportunity adminr, 1977-; Ohio Sen, legal secy, 1977-78. **Orgs:** Am Asn Af-

firmative Action; bd dirs, Amethysts; Cent Ohio EEO Coun; Centenary United Methodist Church; Personnel Soc Columbus; Columbus Area Col Placement Consortium; Cent Ohio Personnel Asn; United Methodist Ministers Wives; Interdenominational Ministers' Wives Asn; Friend Action; Century Found; Nat Asn Advan Colored People; Nat Coun Negro Women; Columbus Urban League; St Paul Methodist Church; co-founder, Ebondy House; Bethune Ctr Governing Bd; Phillis Wheatley Club. **Honors/Awds:** Outstanding Youth Counr of the Yr; Exec of the Month, Nat Mgt Inst. **Special Achievements:** Development of an EEO training manual for supervisors & managers in city; First EEO administrator to be appointed to serve directly under the office of the mayor; First chosen to represent the city at World Conference Decade for Women; Instituted the first Women's Week in Government; Outstanding recognition advancing the cause of equality in employ & housing; recognition human rights serv. **Business Addr:** EEO Administrator, City of Columbus Ohio, Equal Employment Opportunity Off, 90 W Broad St, Columbus, OH 43215, **Business Phone:** (614)645-8292.

HARDING, JOHN EDWARD
Manager. **Personal:** Born May 28, 1938, Nashville, TN; son of James A and Helen E; married Delores Evon Kelly, Dec 18, 1960; children: Sheri Harding Daley. **Educ:** Tennessee A&I State Univ, Nashville TN, BS, Civil Eng, 1960. **Career:** AUS, dirate Civil Engr, Ohio, civil engr, 1960-67; Air Force Logistics Command, Ohio, civil engr, 1967-71; VI Dept Pub Works, St Thomas VI, comnr, 1971-75; VI Port Authority, St. Thomas VI, dir engr, 1975-77, exec dir, 1977-. **Orgs:** Am Soc Civil Engrs; Airport Operators Coun Int; Am Asn Port Authorities; Southeastern Airport Mgrs Asn; Southeastern & Caribbean Port Authorities; Am Asn Airport Execs. **Military Serv:** USAF, 1963-64. **Business Addr:** Executive Director, VI Port Authority, PO Box 1707, St Thomas, Virgin Islands of the United States 00801, **Business Phone:** (809)774-1629.

HARDING, MICHAEL S
Executive. **Personal:** Born Sep 5, 1951, St Louis, MO; son of Derwood and Katie; divorced; children: Lindsey, Michael & Morgan. **Educ:** Cent Mo State Univ, BS, 1973; Univ N Fla, attended 1975-82; Pepperdine Univ, MBA, 1987. **Career:** Anheuser-Busch, prod mgr trainee, 1973-74, prod supvr, 1974-80, asst supt, 1980-83, supt, 1983-85, pkg mgr, 1985-90, sr asst plant mgr, 1990-91, senior asst plant mgr, 1991-95, plant mgr, 1996-. **Orgs:** Kappa Alpha Psi Fraternity, 1973-; Nat Black MBA Asn, 1991-; bd trustees, Columbia East Houston Med Ctr; bd mem, Sam Houston Area Coun Boy Scouts Am; Nat Beverage Pkg Asn. **Honors/Awds:** Black Achiever of Business & Education Award, NJ YMCA, 1988. **Special Achievements:** Completed Production Management Training Program, Anheuser-Busch Inc, 1973. **Business Addr:** Sr Plant Manager, Anheuser-Busch Inc, 775 Gellhorn Dr, Houston, TX 77029-1405, **Business Phone:** (713)675-2311.

HARDING, ROBERTA
Educator, lawyer. **Educ:** Univ San Francisco, BS, 1981; Harvard Law Sch, JD, 1986. **Career:** Univ Ky, Col Law, from asst prof to assoc prof, 1991-99, prof law, Willbert D Ham prof law, currently; Capital Case consult, 1997-; Wake Forest Univ Sch Law, vis assoc prof, 1997; Univ Ga Sch Law, vis assoc prof law, 1999. **Orgs:** California Bar, 1986-; Am Bar Asn, 1986-; ABA Sect Individual Rights & Responsibilities, 1991-; Am Asn Law Schls, 1991-; AALS Sect Human Rights, 2001-; bd mem, Ky Chap Am Civil Liberties Union, 2003-. **Honors/Awds:** Wilburt D Ham Professor of Law, Univ Ky. **Special Achievements:** Numerous articles are in review at many cols & univs. **Business Addr:** Willburt D Ham Professor of Law, University of Kentucky, College of Law, 630 Col Law Rm 255, Lexington, KY 40506-0048, **Business Phone:** (859)257-1880.

HARDING, VINCENT
Historian, educator. **Personal:** Born Jul 25, 1931, New York, NY; son of Graham Augustine and Mabel Lydia Broome; married Rosemarie Freeney (deceased) (deceased); children: Rachel & Jonathan. **Educ:** City Col NY, BA, 1952; Columbia Univ, MS, 1953; Univ Chicago, MA, 1956, PhD, 1965. **Career:** Seventh Day Adventist Church Chicago, sply pastor 1955-57; Woodlawn Mennoite Church Chicago, lay assoc pastor, 1957-61; Mennonite Cent Com Atlanta, southern rep, 1961-64; Spelman Col Atlanta, asst prof Hist, dept chmn Hist Social Sci, 1965-69; Martin Luther King Jr Ctr, dir, 1968-70; Inst Black World, Atlanta, GA, dir 1969-74; Blackside Inc, Boston, acad adv "Eyes on the Prize" documentary, 1985-90; Iliff Sch Theol, prof, 1981-2004, prof emer, 2004-; Drew Univ, African-Am Religion, vis distinguished prof, currently. **Honors/Awds:** Hon Doctorate, Swarthmore Col, Lincoln Univ, 1987; Kent fel Soc Rel, Higher Educ; Howard Thurman Trust, 1990; Humanist of the Year, Colo Coun Humanities, 1991; Outstanding Achievement in Humanities, Colo Endowment Humanities. **Special Achievements:** Author of: must walls divide, 1965, There Is a River, 1981, Hope and History, 1990; ed bd concern Christianity & crisis christian country; others, also poems, short stories, articles, sermons to professional publications.

HARDISON, KADEEM
Actor. **Personal:** Born Jul 24, 1965, New York, NY; son of Donald McFadden and Bethann; married Chante Moore, Nov 17, 1997 (divorced 2000); children: Sophia Milan. **Career:** Model; actor, currently; TV series: "A Different World," 1987-93; "Between Brothers," 1997; "Static Shock," 2000; "Just Shoot Me!", 2000; "Livin' Large", 2002; "Abby," 2003; "One on One", 2005; "My Name Is Earl", 2006; "Born a Gamblin Man", 2006; "Just for Kicks", 2006; "House M.D", 2006-07; "Everybody Hates Chris", 2007; "Girlfriends", 2007; TV movies: "Fire & Ice", 2001; "Red Skies", 2002; Films: Sch Daze, 1988; Def By Temptation, 1990; White Men Can't Jump, 1992; Panther, 1995; Vampire in Brooklyn, 1995; The Sixth Man, 1997; Drive, 1997; Blind Faith, 1998; Dancing in September, 2000; Thank Heaven, 2001; Thirty Years to Life, 2001; Instinct to Kill, 2001; Who's Your Daddy?, 2001; Thank Heaven, 2001; Dunsmore, 2001; Red Skies, 2002; Showtime, 2002; Biker Boyz, 2003; Face of Terror, 2003; Who's Your Daddy?, 2003; Love Hollywood Style, 2006; The Cassidy Kids, 2006; Life Is Not a Fairytale: The Fantasia Barrino Story, 2006; Bratz, 2007; video recordings include: The Imagination Machines, 1992; CBS-TV Schbreak Special; Word's Up; coexec producer & actor: Showtime Special; Blind Faith; 1998; Dunsmore, 2003; I Was a Network Star, 2006. **Honors/Awds:** NAACP Image Award, 1989; Image Award for Outstanding Lead Actor, 1991; Image Award, Outstanding Lead Actor in a Comedy Series, 1992. **Special Achievements:** Has acted as director for A Different World. **Business Addr:** Actor, clo Bethann Management Company Inc, 36 N Moore St, New York, NY 10013, **Business Phone:** (212)925-2153.

HARDISON, RUTH INGE
Sculptor. **Personal:** Born Feb 3, 1904, Portsmouth, VA; daughter of William Lafayette and Evelyn Jordan; children: Yolande. **Educ:** Tenn State A&I, 1935; Art Stud League, 1935; Vassar Col, 1944. **Career:** Comn Sculptor By Old Taylor Whiskies, "Ingenious Am", 1966; New York City Bd of Educ, "New Generation", 1975; New York City Dept Cult Affairs, Jackie Robinson Portrait 1980; Black Alumni, Princeton Univ, Frederick Douglass Portrait, 1982; creator of on-going portrait series "Negro Giantsin History" began 1963 includes, Harriet Tubman, "The Slave Woman, "Frederick Douglass, Dr WEB DuBois, Dr Mary McLeod Bethune, 1965; Dr Geo Washin Carver, Sojourner Truth 1968, Dr Martin Luther King Jr 1968, 1976, Paul Robeson, 1979; Sojourner Truth head, 1976; Sojourner Truth Pin, 1980; Phillis Wheatley, 1989; new series "Our Folks" began in 1985, collectible sculptures of ordinary people doing ordinary things; Portrait of Al Diop, pres, Local 1549 NYC, commissioned by the Women's Comt, on his 20th yr serv; "Mother & Child," 1957, Klingenstein Pavillion, Mt Sinai Hosp, NY; Hardison Works, owner & sculptor, currently. **Orgs:** Presentation, "Sculpture and the Spoken Word" with associate Margaret McCaden; founding mem, Harlem Cult Coun, 1964; founding mem, Black Acad Arts & Letters, 1969. **Honors/Awds:** Self Discovery Workshops, Harlem Cult Coun, 1975; Sch C studio visits Cottonwood Found, 1980; Cultural Achievement Award, Riverside Club Nat Bus& Prof Women's Clubs, 1987; exhib of 26 photographs, "Views From Harlem, "Portsmouth Museum, Portsmouth, VA, 1988; Sojourner Truth figure presented by NY Gov, Cuomo to Nelson Mandela, 1990. **Special Achievements:** Included in "Call Them Heroes", a social studies textbook, published by the Board of Edication of NY; One Hundred Successful Blacks, Book 2, Ebony Success Libr. **Business Addr:** Sculptor, Owner, Hardison Works, 444 Central Pk W Suite 4B, New York, NY 10025, **Business Phone:** (866)243-7495.*

HARDMAN, ARTINA TINSLEY
Government official. **Personal:** Born Jul 13, 1951. **Career:** Saunders Memorial African Methodist Episcopal Church, officer; Detroit City Councilwoman Alta Tinsley Talabi, staff; Detroit Job Corps Ctr,health care supvr; Detroit Mich House Rep, Dist 3, state rep, currently. **Orgs:** Chmn, Mich Legislative Black Caucus; Coalition Against Bill Bd Advert Alcohol & Tobacco; Fedn Youth Servs; Nat Asn Advan Colored People;Empowerment Zone Community Prevention Coalition. **Business Addr:** State Representative, Michigan House Representatives, District 3, SO587 House Office Bldg, PO Box 30014, Lansing, MI 48909-7514, **Business Phone:** (517)373-1776.

HARDMAN-CROMWELL, DR. YOUTHA CORDELLA
Educator. **Personal:** Born Jan 10, 1941, Washington, DC; daughter of Esther Willis Jubilee; married Oliver W Cromwell, May 28, 1988; children: Darnell Whitten, Dwayne Whitten, Debra Whitten & Michael Cromwell. **Educ:** George Wash Univ, AA, 1960, BS, Math 1963; Troy State Univ, AL, MS, Educ, 1971; Univ Va, EdS, Math & Educ, 1984; Howard Univ, Mdiv, 1986; Am Univ, PhD, 1992. **Career:** Mountain Home Primary Sch, ID, second grade teacher, 1964-67; Garrison Elem, DC, second grade teacher, 1967-68; Fledgling Sch AL, first grade teacher, 1968-70; Misawe Dependents Sch Japan, chmn Math dept & teacher, 1972-75; Elmore County High Sch, AL, math teacher, 1975; Stafford Sr High Sch, VA, math teacher, 1976-79; Germanna Comm Col, assoc prof math, 1979-86; Woodlawn United Methodist Church, VA, pastor, 1986-89; Howard Univ Sch Divinity, coordr, Field Based Fel Prog, 1987-91, lectr practical theol, 1989-91; Am Univ Sch Educ, adj fac, 1989-95; Ford Fel Prog, dir, 1987-; Wesley Theol Sem, Dept Pract Ministry & Mission, dir, assoc prof, currently. **Orgs:** Chmn, Polit action Orange County, Nat Asn Advan Colored People, 1978-86; comm Planning, Nat Asn Advan Colored People, Dist Nine, VA, 1979-84; bd mem, Orange County Recreation Asn, 1979-80; Orange County Libr Bd, 1982-84; pres, Black Caucus, Va Conf UMC, 1986-88; consult, secy, Churches Transitional Communities, 1987-; Va Conf Comm Religion & Race, 1987-, chairperson, 1990-; vice chmn, SEJ Comm Religion & Race; bd dirs, Edna Frazier Cromwell Scholarship Fund, Inc; bd dirs, Hardman-Cromwell Ministries, Inc; bd dirs, U Street Theatre Found; bd dirs, Uplift; bd dirs, Reconciling Congregations Prog; bd dirs, ethics & prof adv comt, Vis Nurses Asn; Asn Theological Field Education; Acad Homiletics; bd mem, AMERC, 2002-; vice chmn, Asn Theol Field Educ, 2003-05; Trinity United Methodist Church, Alexandria, VA. **Honors/Awds:** Outstanding Teacher, Dept Defense Dependent Sch, Japan, 1974; Service Award, Nat Asn Advan Colored People, Orange County, 1982, 1983; Benjamin Mays Fel, Howard Univ Divinity Sch, 1984-86; Anderson Fel, 1985-86; Henry C Maynard Award; Staff Award, Am Univ, 1989-90; Women Color Doctoral Fel, 1989-90; Nat Methodist Fel, 1990-91; Distinguished Alumni, Howard Univ Sch Divinity, 2001. Graduation Speaker, Am Univ, 1993; Nat Methodist Fel, 1990-91; Distinguished Alumni, Howard Univ Sch Divinity, 2001. **Business Addr:** Director, Associate Professor, Wesley Theological Seminary, Department Practice Ministry & Mission, 4500 Mass Ave NW, Washington, DC 20016-5690, **Business Phone:** (202)885-8618.

HARDMON, LADY (LEJUANA HARDMON GROOMS)
Basketball player. **Personal:** Born Sep 12, 1970. **Educ:** Ga, attended 1992. **Career:** Player (retired); Deniz, Turkey, 1993-94; Bologna, Italy, 1994-95; Schio, Italy, 1996-97; DKSK, Hungary, 1995-96; Utah Starzz, guard, 1997; Sacramento Monarchs,guard, 1998-05, scout, 2005. **Honors/Awds:** Winner bronze medal, World Univ Games Buffalo, 1993; winner gold medal, Jones Cup Team, 1992; Honorable Mention Kodak All-Am. **Special Achievements:** Named league MVP in first professional season in Turkey for Deniz in1993-94. *

HARDNETT, CAROLYN JUDY
Librarian. **Personal:** Born Aug 12, 1947, Washington, DC; daughter of Freddie P and Ada West. **Educ:** Hampton Inst, Hampton, VA, 1969. **Career:** First & Merchants Nat Bank, Pentagon & Arlington, VA, 1968-70; Chicago Tribune, Wash, DC, libr asst, 1970-76, librn, 1976-85; Univ Dist Columbia, Sch Libr Sci, Lorton Col Prog: Profile of a Special Libr (Newspaper), guest lectr, 1982; lectr, Ky State Univ, Sch Libr Sci, News Media Libr Workshop, 1984; The Baltimore Sun, Baltimore, MD, chief librn, 1985; St Petersburg Times, news researcher; BET Publ, res dir; Newseum, sr researcher, currently. **Orgs:** SLA, 1977; Secy, treasurer, Spec Librs Asn, News Div, 1982-83, conference planner, 1983-84, chair, 1984-85, dir, Baltimore Chap, 1986-88, bd dirs, 1987-89; Nat Asn Black Journalists, 1985-; Asn Black Media Workers, Baltimore Chap, parliamentarian, 1985-86. **Honors/Awds:** Award of Merit, Spec Librs Asn, News Div, 1985; Certificate of Recognition, Black Enterprise Prof Exchange & Networking Forum, 1989; Joseph F Kwapil Memorial Award, 2007. **Special Achievements:** Reference and Information Gathering in a Special Library (Newspaper) 1983; Participated in several Regional Newspaper Workshops in 1983 and 1984. **Home Addr:** 1008 Dartmouthglen Way, Baltimore, MD 21212. **Business Addr:** Senior Researcher, Newseum, 1101 Wilson Blvd Suite 12, Arlington, VA 22209, **Business Phone:** (703)284-3544.

HARDWICK, CLIFFORD E., III
Educator. **Personal:** Born Sep 4, 1927, Savannah, GA; son of Clifford E Jr (deceased); married Beautine Williams; children: Clifford IV & Kenneth Allen (deceased). **Educ:** Savannah State Col, BS, 1950; Univ Pittsburgh, LittM, 1959; Howard Univ; NC Col; Atlanta Univ; Univ Ga; Mott Leadership Inst; Morris Brown Col, LLD, 1975. **Career:** Effingham City Training Sch, teacher; instr, physical sci lectr, geninorganic chem, 1951-52; Springfield Terrace Elem Sch, teacher, 1952-53; Alfred E Beach High Sch, Biol Dept, chmn, 1953-61; Sec Educ, supvr, 1961-68; Comm Educ Savannah, dir, 1968-70; Univ Ga Continuing Educ Prog, asst prof, dir, 1970-97, asst prof emer, 2003-; Coastal Ga Ctr Continuing Ed ASC& SSC, asst dean. **Orgs:** Am Methodist Episcopal Church, itinerate elder, 1980; Nat Univ Ext Asn; Nat Comt Sch Educ Asn; Ga Adult Educ Coun; adv comt, Adult Basic Ed; Alpha Phi Alpha; pres, Greenbriar C Ctr, Savannah Tribune; dir, Carver State Bank; exec bd, Savannah Chap, Nat Asn Advan Colored People; Comn Christian, Ed St Philip AME Church; Savannah State Col Alumni Asn; Cardiovasc Nutrit Comn; vchmn, bd dir, Am Red Cross Savannah Chap; Hospice Savannah Bd; Am Heart Asn; exec comt, Coastal Area Coun Boy Scouts Am; United Way Allocations Panel. **Honors/Awds:** Man of the Year, Alpha Phi Alpha, 1962; Model Cities Recognition Award,1971; Citizen of Day, WTOC, 1974; Cirus G Wiley Distinguished Alumnus Award, Savannah State Col, 1974; Community Service Award, Savannah Bus League, 1976; Honorary Doctor of Laws Degree, Morris Brown Col; Jefferson Award for Public Service Certificate of Excellence, 2009. **Special Achievements:** First black elected to serve as foreman on grand jury 1974. First African American to be appointed Supervisor of Secondary Education by the SavannahChatham County Board of Education. He was the highest ranking African American in the local public school system. *

HARDWICK, GARY C
Movie producer, screenwriter, movie director. **Personal:** Born in Detroit, MI. **Career:** U.S. Dept Justice, CA, atty. TV Serials:

"Hangin' with Mr. Cooper", 1992; "Where I Live", 1993; "South Central", 1994; "Me & the Boys", 1994; "In the House", 1995; "Matt Waters", 1996; "Trippin'", 1999; "The Brothers", 2001; "Deliver Us from Eva", 2003; "Universal Remote", 2007. Movie producer: "Me & the Boys", 1994; "In the House", 1995; "Matt Waters", 1996; "Universal Remote", 2007. Director: "Where I Live", 1993; "Thea", 1993; "South Central", 1994; "The Brothers", actor, 2001. **Special Achievements:** First African-American class president of Wayne State Law School.

HARDWICK, DR. LINDA T.
School administrator, administrator. **Career:** Cleveland Munic Sch, prin; Forest Hill Parkway Acad, prin, currently. **Business Addr:** Principal, Forest Hill Parkway Academy, 450 E 112th St, Cleveland, OH 44108, **Business Phone:** (216)268-6138.*

HARDY, CHARLIE EDWARD
Insurance executive. **Personal:** Born Jan 19, 1941, Montgomery, AL; son of William H and Sarah W; married Lillie Pearl Curry; children: Randall Charles, Christa Valencia. **Educ:** Ala State Univ, BS, sec educ, 1962; Ind State Univ, attended 1967; Life Underwriters Training, coun grad, 1972; Univ Phoenix, Orgn Mgt. **Career:** Brewton City Sch Syst, dir bands, 1962-66; Macon City Pub Sch, dir bands, 1966-69; MetLife, sr sales rep, assoc br mgr, 1988, sr acct exec; Financial Planning pract group, owner. **Orgs:** Nat Assoc Life Underwriters, 1969; NAACP; Tuskegee Civic Asn; 33 Degree Mason Shriner; life mem, Alpha Phi Alpha Frat Inc; deacon Greenwood Missionary Baptist Church; legis liason Tuskegee Civic Asn, 1989; Finance Comt, City Tuskegee, 1997; chmn, MetLife Multicultural Career Initiative Southern Territory, 1997; pres, Tuskegee Area Chamber Com, 1998; chmn & bd dir, Comt, 2001. **Honors/Awds:** Outstanding Alumnus Award, Ala State Univ, 1972; Alpha Man of the Year, Alpha Phi Alpha Frat Inc, 1975; Salesman of the Year, Metropolitan Life Montgomery Dist, 1979; Alpha Man of the Year, Alpha Phi Alpha Frat Tuskegee, 1984; Distinguished Alumnus Award, Ala State Univ, 1985; Inducted, Veteran for 20 Yrs Serv, Metropolitan Life & Affiliated Companies 1989. **Business Addr:** Owner, Financial Planning Practice Group, PO Box 830330, Tuskegee, AL 36083, **Business Phone:** (334)727-4198.*

HARDY, DARRYL GERROD
Football player. **Personal:** Born Nov 22, 1968, Cincinnati, OH. **Educ:** Univ Tenn. **Career:** Ariz Cardinals, linebacker, 1994-95; Dallas Cowboys, 1995-97; Seattle Seahawks, 1997; Free agt, currently.

HARDY, DOROTHY C.
School administrator, founder (originator), teacher. **Personal:** Born in Town Creek, AL; daughter of Odis Cal and Lorean Cal; children: Althea J Mootry (deceased). **Educ:** Ala State Univ, BS; Xavier Univ, MEd; Univ Cincinnati, EdD. **Career:** Univ Cincinnati, Groups & Univ Progs, asst dean stud, 1973-77; Cincinnati Life Adj Inst, pres, 1980-83; Ohio Dept Ment Health, community div bus admin, 1983-84; Southeast Mo State Univ, 1984-89; Hardy Residential Rentals, 1986-96; Single Parent Prog, Cape Girardeau Area Voc Tech Sch, coordr, 1991-95; Univ N Ala, adj prof eng, 1997; Northwest-Schs Community Col, eng teacher, 1997-98; Shoals Life Adjust Inst, founder, 1999; Intergenerational Writer's Guild, teacher, 1999-; Kans State Univ, asst prof & employ recuitment specialist; Univ Cincinnati, instr. **Orgs:** Human Involvement Prog, 1979; bus acct, Madisonville Job Training, 1982; consult, Archdiocese Greater Cincinnati, 1983; Prog Assoc Econ Develop; minority coordr, Issues 2 & 3 Citizens Gov Richard F Celeste, 1983-84; training dir, Mondale/Ferraro Camp, 1984. **Honors/Awds:** Brodie Researcher Award, 1000 Plus, 1975; Outstanding Community Serv, 1976; Outstanding Women, Nat Asn Adv Colored People, 1981; Cert of Merit, Pebble in the Pond, 1985; Golden Poet Award, 1986; Alumni of Distinction, Ala State Univ, 1997; Pub Exhib, Southeast Mo State Univ, 1999. **Special Achievements:** Background Player, "The Jesse Owens Story", Paramount Studio for ABC-TV, 1984; Fiction published in the Summerfield Journal Castalia Publishers & Ellipsis, Literary Journal; Poetry published in Essence Magazine, 1989, 1991-93; Southwest Missouri State Univ Museum Exhibit, Black Women: Against the Odds, 1996. **Home Addr:** 901 N Pine St, Florence, AL 35630-3342. *

HARDY, EURSLA DICKERSON
Teacher, educator. **Personal:** Born May 5, 1933, Thibodaux, LA; daughter of Albertha Lucas Dickerson and McNeil Dickerson; married McHenry Jr, Jul 23, 1955; children: Timothy Wayne. **Educ:** Grambling State Univ, BS, 1955; Northwestern Univ & Grambling State Univ Libr Sci, attended 1967; Prairie View A&M Univ, MA, lib sci. **Career:** Educator (retired); Corn Elementary School, teacher & basketball coach, 1955; W Baton Rouge Parish, Port Allen, teacher, 1956-58; Herndon High Sch, teacher, 1958; Newton Smith Elementary Sch, teacher & librarian, Caddo Parish Sch Brd, Shreveport, teacher, librn, 1958-85. **Orgs:** Founder, orgnr, 1990, Sigma Rho Omega Chap, Alpha Kappa Alpha Sorority,1990-92, anti basileus, 1990-92; bd mem, Allendale Bunch, YWCA, 1991-92;charter mem, Friends Lib; brd dirs, Northwest, La YWCA, 1992-96; vice grandlady, Lady Auxillary St Peter Claver; exec bd mem & corres secy, Shreveport Art Guild & Friends Meadows Mus Art, Centenary Col, 1994-95; steering comt mem, CWW; Volunteer Docent Meadows Mus Centenary Col; Mentorship Prog, Green Oaks Lab High Sch; Tutorial Prog Volunteer, George P Hendrix Elem Sch, Newton Smith Elem Sch; Esquirettes Social Club; brd dirs, Caddo Parish Career Ctr, 1997-99; pres, Green Oaks Teaching; brd,Prof Magnet Scholarship FND Inc; bd mem, CADDO Parish Sch, District 2; bd mem, Shreveport Art Guild, Friends of Meadows Museum of Ar; mem, Caddo Career and Technology Center; David Raines Community Health Center; pres, Theatre Of Performing Arts; pres, Newton Smith First Fac. **Honors/Awds:** Bookworm Reading Club Librn Award, 1977-78; PTA Service Award, Newton Smith Elem, 1985; Recognition of Faithful Serv Educr Award, Caddo AssnEducr, 1985; Area Retreat AKA Cert Award, Hostess Chap, 1993; Sigma RhoOmega Chap, Alpha Kappa Alpha Sorority Inc; Outstanding Grad Basileus Award, S Cent Reg, Alpha Kappa Alpha Sorority Inc, 1994; Outstanding Grad Prog Serv Award, 1994; AKA Educ Advan Fund, 4 Stars Chap Award, 1994;Outstanding Community Serv Recog, Shreveport past Mayor Hazel Beard, 1994; Woman of the Year Award, Zeta Phi Beta, 1997; Best Dressed Award, Times Newspaper, 1998. **Special Achievements:** You Are in The News, Outstanding Comm Service Recognition. **Home Addr:** 106 Holcomb Dr, Shreveport, LA 71103-2026.

HARDY, DR. FREEMAN
Educator, college teacher. **Personal:** Born May 22, 1942, Winona, MS; married Cozetta Hubbard; children: Tonya & Tasha. **Educ:** Ark AM & N Col, BS, 1964; Howard Univ, DDS, 1970; Georgetown Univ, MSc, 1974. **Career:** AR AM & N Col, lab instr, 1964; Howard Univ, instr, 1970-72; Howard Univ Col Dent, asst prof, 1974-77, assoc prof, 1977-83, prof, 1983-. **Orgs:** Diag & Treat Planning Rem Partial Dentures, 1976; Comparison Fluid Resin & Compression Molding Methods Processing Dimensional Changes, 1977; Consult, Howard Univ Hosp; Oral Cancer Soc, Chi Delta Mu; Omicron Kappa Upsilon; ADA; Robert T Freeman Dent Soc; NDA; Am Col Prosthodontics; AADR; IADR; Sigma Xi; DC Dent Soc; Alpha Phi Alpha. *

HARDY, KENNETH
Educator. **Educ:** Pa State Univ, BS, 1973; Mich State Univ, MS, 1974; Fla State Univ, PhD, 1980; Family Therapy Inst, Wash, DC, Cert, 1986; Ment Res Inst, Family Therapy Training Prog, 1989. **Career:** Comprehensive Youth Serv, prog dir, 1974-76; Appalachee Community Mental Health Serv, mental health therapist, 1978-80; Fla State Univ, Ment Health Ctr, coun psychologist, 1977-80; Appalachee Community Ment Health Serv, mental health therapist, 1978-80; Univ Del, asst prof, 1980-83; Va Polytech & State Univ, adj prof, 1985-88; Syracuse Univ, Dept Marriage & Family Therapy, prof, 1990-, Clin Training & Res, dir, 1990-95, Marriage & Family Therapy Summer Inst, dir, 1993-, Dept Child & Family Studies, chmn, 1995-96; Family Therapy Inst New Jerseym, vis fac, 1991-; Ackerman Inst Family, sr fac, 2000-04; Jour Marital & Family Therapy, ed bd; Jour Family Psychotherapy, ed bd; Jour Family Counseling, ed bd; Jour Divorce, ed bd. **Orgs:** Prog dir, Comprehensive Youth Serv, 1974-76; dir, Southeast Delco Family Young Men Christian Asn, 1981-83; dep dir, Comn Accreditation Marriage & Family Therapy, Am Asn Marriage & Family Therapy, 1983-84, exec dir, 1984-90, actg exec dir, 1985-88; Nat Coun Family Rels; Am Family Therapy Acad; Am Asn Marriage & Family Therapy Lic Bd; Ctr Res Women Wellesley Col. **Honors/Awds:** Leadership Award, Am Asn Marriage & Family Therapy, 1990; Outstanding Organizational Contribution Award, Am Asn Marriage & Family Therapy, 1991; Cultural Diversity Honors Award, New York Asn Marriage & Family Therapy, 1994; Virginia Simons Award for Outstanding Service, Col Human Develop, Syracuse Univ, 1994; Outstanding Contribution to the Field of Marriage and Family Therapy, Hofstra Univ, Hempstead, New York, 1995; Distinguished Contribution to Marriage and Family Counseling Award, Int Asn Marriage & Family Counselors, 1996; Outstanding Contribution to Marriage and Family Therapy Award, Am Asn Marriage & Family Therapy, 1998. **Special Achievements:** Co-author with Tracey Laszloffy, Dying to be Saved: Strategies for Addressing Adolescent Violence; Numerous publications including, Effective treatment of minority families. Family Therapy News, 21 (5), 1990;). Forward to 101 Family Therapy Intervention. In Nelson & Trepper (Eds). Haworth, 1991; For minorities only: Tips for becoming a GEMM family therapist. Family Therapy News, 22 (5), 2001. **Business Addr:** Professor, Syracuse University, Department of Marriage and Family Therapy, 008 Slocum Hall 119 Euclid Ave, Syracuse, NY 13244-1250, **Business Phone:** (315)443-9329.

HARDY, KEVIN LAMONT
Football player. **Personal:** Born Jul 24, 1973, Evansville, IN. **Educ:** Univ Ill. **Career:** Football player (retired); Jacksonville Jaguars, outside linebacker,1996-2001; Dallas Cowboys, outside linebacker, 2002; Cincinnati Bengals, linebacker, 2003-05; South Beach club venture, owner, currently. **Orgs:** Omega Psi Phi Fraternity Inc. **Honors/Awds:** Dick Butkus Award, 1995.

HARDY, MICHAEL LEANDER
Marketing executive. **Personal:** Born Feb 21, 1945, Petersburg, VA; married Jacqueline; children: Sheila Jacqueline, Michelle Lorraine. **Educ:** Columbia Univ New York City NY, BS, 1966; Rollins Col Winter Park FL, MCS, 1973. **Career:** Martin-Marietta Corp Orlando Div, assoc engr, 1966-67, prog planning analyst, 1967-71; The Carburundum Co Pangborn Div, mgr mkt planning & control, 1973-79; The Carborundum Co, mgt maint servs & repairs pangborn. **Orgs:** Bd mem, Bethel Corp; Citizens Adv Com Wash Co Bd Educ; bd mem, Big Bros Wash Co; past pres, Orange Co FL Br; Nat Advan Asn Colored People, 1971-73.

HARDY, TIMOTHY W
Lawyer, business owner. **Personal:** Born Feb 7, 1952, Shreveport, LA; married Stacia Saizon, Oct 5, 1985; children: Nicole Saizon & Amanda Victoria. **Educ:** Southern Univ, BS, Chem, 1978; Southern Univ Law Ctr, JD, 1981. **Career:** Pennzoil Res, 1977; Allied Chem, lab techinican, 1978; La Dept Justice, asst atty gen, lands & natural resources div, environ sect, 1981-88; La Dept Environ Quality, asst secy, Off Solid & Hazardous Waste, 1988-92; Gov Environ Affairs, exec asst, 1990-92; Gov Edwin Edwards' Dept Environ Quality Transition Team, chmn, 1991; La Dept Justice, dir pub protection div, 1992-94; Lemle & Kelleher, partner & chmn mgt comt, 2004-; Shaw E&I, exec vpres. **Orgs:** La State Bar Asn; Am Heart Asn; pres, E Baton Rouge Div; bd trustees, bd mem, The Nature Conservancy La; Baton Rouge C C; La Leadership Class, Coun Better La, 1994; Mid City Redevelopment Alliance; Nat Orgn Prof Advan Black Chemists Chemical Engrs; Phi Alpha Delta Law Fraternity; past bd mem, C Charter Sch; Exec leadership Coun; Sigma Pi Phi Fraternity. **Business Addr:** Partner, Lemle & Kelleher LLP, 1Am Pl 301 Main St Suite 1100, Baton Rouge, LA 70825, **Business Phone:** (225)387-5068.

HARDY-HILL, EDNA MAE
Psychologist. **Personal:** Born Feb 14, 1943, Thomasville, GA; daughter of Leroy and Hagar Harris; married Davis Vincent, Jun 22, 1974; children: Davis Vincent Jr (deceased), Michael A. **Educ:** Bennett Col, AB, 1965; Howard Univ, MS, 1968. **Career:** Psychologist (retired). Nat Inst Ment Health, res psychologist, 1967-74, health scientist adminr, 1974-83, Chief Behav & Appl Review Br, 1983-98; peer reviewer, Breast Cancer Res Prog, 2000. **Orgs:** Treas, Asn Black Psychologists, 1983 Nat Conv; Peoples Congregational Church; Bennett Coll Alumnea Asn; Lotts Read Book Club, 1999-01; Bethany Congregational Church, 2002-. **Honors/Awds:** Honor soc, Beta Kappa Chi; Pi Gamma Mu; Psi Chi; Howard Univ Fel, 1966-67; Bennett Col Scholar, 1961-65; Outstanding Work Performance, Nat Inst Ment Health, 1982, 1985, 1987, 1989-98, Director Award for Significant Achievement, Nat Inst Ment Health, 1989; Special Achievement Award, Nat Inst Ment Health, 1997; Award for Outstanding Accomplishments in Chosen Profession, Bennett Col, 1993; Staff Recognition Award, Nat Inst Ment Health, 1998. **Home Addr:** 64 Pebble Point Dr, Thomasville, GA 31792, **Home Phone:** (229)226-7595. *

HARDY-WOOLRIDGE, KAREN E
Public speaker. **Personal:** Born Oct 29, 1951, Chicopee, MA; daughter of Humphrey Christopher Hardy and Janet Elizabeth Chaffin Lee; married Victor, Jun 2, 1985; children: James, Matoaca, Kara Jean & Kendra. **Educ:** Springfield Tech Community Col, Springfield, MA, AS, 1971; Univ NC, Elizabeth City, NC, BS, bus admin, 1974; Western New England Col, 1978. **Career:** Martin Ins Agency, Springfield, MA, ins sales, 1974-81; Regency Cove Hotel, Barbados, West Indies, gen man, 1981-83; Mass Mutual Life Ins Co, Springfield, MA, sales div consult, recruiting mgr, 1983, assoc dir, IFM Sales, dist mgr, staff plans, 1991; Musical Ministry & Motivational speaker for youth & women groups, currently. **Orgs:** Participant, Pro-Motion, 1989, 1991-; parent adv, SDA Community Youth, Young Adult Choir, 1989-; prof develop bd vchair, Mass Mutual Life Ins, 1989-90, prof develop bd chairperson, 1990; vol, SDA Community Servs, 1990-; women's div coordr, Seventh-day Adventist, 1991; mentor, I Have a Dream Prog.

HARE, JULIA
Educational psychologist, executive director. **Personal:** Married Nathan Hare. **Educ:** Langston Univ, BA, music, 1960; Roosevelt Univ, Chicago, MEd, music, 1962; Calif Coast Univ, PhD, educ, 1987. **Career:** Oakland Mus, dir educ prog; Fed Housing Prog, pub rels dir, 1971-73; Black Think Tank, co-founder, 1979-, nat exec dir, currently; Chicago, IL, elem sch teacher. **Orgs:** Asn Black Social Workers; Asn African Historians; Int Black Writers & Artists. **Honors/Awds:** Educator of the Year, Washington, DC; Abe Lincoln Award; Carter G Woodson Educ Award; Harambee Award, Asn Black Social Workers; Scholar of the Year, Asn African Historians; Lifetime Achievement Award, Int Black Writers & Artists. **Special Achievements:** ABC TV, talk-show host; KSFO radio, talk-show host; Co-author: The Endangered Black Family; Bringing the Black Boy to Manhood: The Passage; How to Find and Keep a Black Man Working; Appeared in: CNN & Co, C-SPAN, Tony Brown's Journal & Inside Edition. *

HARE, JULIA REED
Journalist, administrator. **Personal:** Born Nov 7, 1942, Tulsa, OK; married Dr Nathan Hare. **Educ:** Langston Univ, BA, 1964; Roosevelt Univ Chicago, MA, 1966; Calif Coast Univ, Santa Ana, CA, PhD; DC Teachers Col, attended 1967. **Career:** Chicago Pub Sch, teacher, 1966; DC Teachers Col, supvr stud teachers, 1967-68; Nat Comt Against Discrimination Housing, pub rels dir, 1969-72; Univ San Francisco, instr, 1969-70; Golden W Broadcasters

KSFO radio, dir comm affairs, 1973-; Black Think Tank, exec dir, currently. **Orgs:** Northern Calif Broadcasters Asn, 1973-; hon bd, Sickle Cell Anemia Develop Res Found, 1976-; bd Afro-Am Cultural & Hist Soc, 1978-; bd dirs, Bay Area Black United Fund, 1979-. **Honors/Awds:** Outstanding Educator of the Year, World Book Ency & Am Univ, 1967; Abe Lincoln Award Broadcaster of the year, 1975; Cert of Appreciation Sickle Cell Anemia Res & Educ, 1976; Meritorious Community Service Award, 1979; Special Service Award, Calif Soc Cert Pub Accountants, 1980; Carter G. Woodson Education Award, The Association of Black Social Workers' Harambee Award. **Special Achievements:** The Hare Plan to Overhaul the Public Schools and Educate Every Black Man, Woman and Child, 1991. publ, Black Male/Female Relationships, 1979. **Business Addr:** Executive Director, Black Think Tank, 1801 Bush St Suite 127, San Francisco, CA 94109-5273.*

HARE, LINDA PASKETT
School administrator. **Personal:** Born Jun 10, 1948, Nashville, TN; daughter of Hulit (deceased) and Juanita Hicks (deceased); married Dr George C Hill; children: Nicole, Brian. **Educ:** Tenn State Univ, BA, 1969, EdD, 1984; Ind Univ, MS, 1974. **Career:** Gary IN Schs, eng teacher, 1969-80; Tenn State Univ, adj eng instr, 1985-88; Meharry Med Col, asst dir & corp & fed rels, 1983-84, spec asst & dep vpres, 1983-87, asst vpres instnl advan, 1987-90, exec asst pres & corp secy, 1990-92, vpres instnl advan, 1992-95; Mid Tenn State Univ, vpres develop & univ rel, 2002-. **Orgs:** Consult, Nat Baptist Publ Bd, 1983-84; Tenn Planning Comn Am Coun Educ, Nat Identification Prog, 1986-; partic, Leadership Nashville, 1990-91; bd mem, Cumberland Mus; bd mem, Coun Community Servs; Coun Advan & Support Educ Comn Philanthropy; Phi Kappa Phi, Nat Hon Soc; Leadership Nashville Alum Rotary Int; adv bd, Nashville Pub TV. **Honors/Awds:** Grad Fel, Tenn State Univ, 1980-81. **Business Addr:** Vice President, Mid Tenn State University, Develop & Univ Rel, 209 Cope Admin Bldg, Murfreesboro, TN 37132.*

HARE, DR. NATHAN
Sociologist, psychologist. **Personal:** Born Apr 9, 1933, Slick, OK; son of Tishia Lee Davis Hare Farmer and Seddie Henry Hare; married Julia Reed, Dec 27, 1956. **Educ:** Langston U, AB 1954; Univ Chicago, MA 1957; Univ Chicago, PhD Sociology 1962; CA Sch Professional Psychology, PhD Clinical Psychology 1975. **Career:** The Black Scholar The Black World Found, founding pub; Howard U, asst prof sociol 1964-67; Black Male-female Relationships, ed, 1979-82; pvt pract & clin psychol, 1977-; San Francisco State Col Dept of Black Studies, chmn 1968-69, instr, 1961-63 & 1957-58; San Francisco Stat, lectr part-time, 1984-88; The Black Think Tank, chmn bd, 1979-, chief exec officer, currently. **Orgs:** No Am Zone Second World Black & African Festival Arts & Culture; Black Speakers Club. **Honors/Awds:** Co-editor Contemporary Black Thought 1973; co-editor Pan-Africanism 1974; Author of The Black Anglo Saxons, The Endangered Black Family 1984, Bringing the Black Boy to Manhood 1985 & various articles in mag & journals; Distinguished Alumni Award Langston Univ 1975; presidential citation Natl Assn of Blacks in Higher Education 1981; Natl Awd Natl Council for Black Studies 1983; Crisis in Black Sexual Politics 1989; Fire on Mount Zion, 1990; The Hare Plan: To Educated Every Black Man, Woman and Child, 1991; shared Marcus and Amy Garvey Award, Institute of Pan African Studies, 1990; United Negro Col Fund Distinguished Scholar at Large, 1990. **Special Achievements:** first person hired to coordinate a black studies program in the United States. **Home Phone:** (415)929-0204. **Business Addr:** Chief Executive Officer, The Black Think Tank, 18001 Bush St Suite 118, San Francisco, CA 94109-5273, **Business Phone:** (415)474-1707.

HARGRAVE, CHARLES WILLIAM
Scientist. **Personal:** Born May 12, 1929, Dandridge, TN; son of Electa Tulip Snapp and Walter Clarence; married Iona Lear Taylor. **Educ:** Johnson C Smith Univ, BS, 1949; Washington Univ St Louis, MA, 1952. **Career:** Scientist (retired); Dept Navy, physicist 1954-55; US Atomic Energy Comn, sci analyst, 1955-62; Nat Aeronaut & Space Admin, tech info, 1962-89. **Orgs:** Adv neighborhood comnr DC Govt, 1979-84, 1991-96; pres, First Dist Police Adv Coun 1985-88; Mayor's Adv Comm Budget & Resources; SW Neighborhood Assembly; Omega Psi Phi. **Honors/ Awds:** Award of Merit, Johnson C Smith Univ Alumni Asn, 1979; Spaceship Earth NASA 1982, 1988; Alumni Award, Univ Wash, 1983. **Military Serv:** AUS 1952-54; USNR, capt, 1955-89; reserve unit co 1984-86. **Home Addr:** 600 3rd St SW, Washington, DC 20024. *

HARGRAVE, THOMAS BURKHARDT, JR.
Association executive. **Personal:** Born Oct 5, 1926, Washington, GA; married Meredith Higgins; children: Kenneth, Anna. **Educ:** Knoxville Col, AB, 1951; Springfield Col, grad study. **Career:** James Welden Johnson Br YMCA FL, exec dir, 1960-64; Pasadena YMCA, asst gen exec, 1964-68; YMCA LA, assoc gen exec, 1968-71; YMCA Metro Wash, pres, 1973, pres Emer, currently. **Orgs:** Rotary Club Intl; adv bd Studio Theatre; adv comt, Tom Sawyer Training Sch; YMCA Af Crisis Comn. **Honors/Awds:** Certificate of Civic Rights, FL NAACP, 1964. **Special Achievements:** author "Private Differences-General Good, A History of the YMCA of Metropolitan Washington," 1985. **Military Serv:** USAF sgt 1945-47; Good Conduct, 1947. **Business Phone:** (202)232-6700.*

HARGRAVES, COL. WILLIAM FREDERICK, II
Military pilot. **Personal:** Born Aug 18, 1932, Cincinnati, OH; son of William F and Annie L (deceased); married Maurine Collins; children: William III, Jock & Charles. **Educ:** Miami Univ, BS, Cum Laude, 1954, MA, 1961. **Career:** USAF, res physicist, 1961-65, aircraft comdr, 1965-70, air liaison officer, 1970-71; Miami Univ, asst prof air sci, 1971-74; Wright Patterson AFB, chief flight deck develop, 1974-78; Pentagon, Wash, DC, deputy div chief, 1978-82; Central State Univ, asst prof, currently. **Orgs:** Vice comdr, Veteran Foreign Wars, 1986; Founder, Alpha Phi Alpha, Miami Univ Chap; leader/founder, Pilgrim Baptist Men's Chorus; Phi Beta Kappa; Omicron Delta Kappa; Kappa Delta Pi; Pi Mu Epsilon; Sigma Pi Sigma, Phi Mu Alpha; charter mem, Phi Kappa Phi. **Special Achievements:** Rhodes Scholar Candidate, 1950; comput sci adv, N Cent Eval Team & US Dept Educ Wash, DC; 6 publ "Magnetic Susceptability of Manganese Compounds," "The Effect of Shock Waves on various Plastic Nose Cone Materials"; Length, Mass, Time, & Motion in One Dimension, software prog, 1986. **Military Serv:** USAF, col, 28 yrs; Air Force Commendation Medal with two Oak Leaf Clusters; Flying Cross & Air Medal for Meritorious Achievement, Vietnam Serv Medal with five Bronze Stars; Repub Vietnam Commendation Medal; Nat Defense Serv Medal. **Home Addr:** 123 W Walnut St, Oxford, OH 45056. **Business Addr:** Assistant Professor, Central State University, Department of Mathematics, 210 Banneker Hall, PO Box 1004, Wilberforce, OH 45384, **Business Phone:** (937)376-6357.

HARGRETT, JAMES T., JR.
State government official, executive. **Personal:** Born Jul 31, 1942, Tampa, FL; married Berlyn Chatard; children: Crystal Marie & James T III. **Educ:** Morehouse Col, BA, 1964; Atlanta Univ, MBA, 1965. **Career:** US Comptroller Currency, nat bank examr, 1965-67; Aetna Life & Casualty Co, ins underwriter, 1967-68; Leadership Develop Prog Tampa Urban League, dir, 1968-69; Community Fed Sav & Loan Asn, Tampa, FL, exec vpres & mgr, 1969-82; Fla State Rep, Dist 63, 1983-92; Fla State, sen, 1992; Bay Area Concessions Inc, chmn & pres, currently; Tampa Hillsborough County Expy Authority, bd chmn, currently. **Orgs:** Treas, Urban League, 1971-75; cit adv comn, Hillsborough County Sch Bd, 1974-; Dem Exec Comt, 1974; Greater Tampa Chamber Com; bd dir, United Way, Tampa; Fla Housing Adv Comt; Fla Sheriffs Asn; Tampa Bay Area Comt Foreign Rels; Fla Coun Crime & Delinquincy; Gulf Coast Epilepsy Found; Ybor City Chamber Commerce; Tampa Housing Authority; Fla Trust Historic Preservation. **Honors/Awds:** Dedicated Service & Commitment to Florida's Environment Award, Legal Environ Asst Found; Legislator of the Year, Fla Asn DUZ Prog, Manatee County Farm Bur, FL Chamber Com; Most Effective Legislator, Fla Legal Serv Inc; Outstanding Young Man of America; Martin Luther King Memorial Award; Recognition Award, Dist VI Transp Coalition Inc; Leadership Award, Fla Voter Leagues. **Business Phone:** (813)396-3908.

HARGROVE, DR. ANDREW. See Obituaries section.

HARGROVE, LIZ RILEY. See RILEY, LIZ.

HARGROVE, TRENT
Lawyer, government official. **Personal:** Born Aug 25, 1955, Harrisburg, PA; son of Odessa Daniels and Willie Clarence; married Eugenia Russell Hargrove, Sep 8, 1984; children: Channing Leah, Tyler Trent. **Educ:** Bucknell Univ, Lewisburg, Pa, BA, 1977; Dickinson Law Sch, Carlisle, Pa, JD, 1980. **Career:** Off Atty Gen, Harrisburg PA, dep atty, 1979-81; Pa Housing Finance Agency, Harrisburg Pa, asst coun, 1981-86; McNees Wallace & Nurick, assoc, 1987-90; Pa Dept Transp, asst coun charge utilities, 1990-92; Off Atty Gen, chief dep atty gen, Civil Rights Enforcement; Pa Dept Gen Serv, chief coun, 2003-. **Orgs:** Harrisburg Jaycees, 1984-; Dauphin County Bar Asn, 1986-; Omega Psi Phi Fraternity, 1986-; pres, Harrisburg Black Attys, 1986-87; bd mem, Vol Ctr, 1986-; external vpres, Harrisburg Jaycees, 1986-87; exec comt, NAACP, 1987-; chmn mgt comn, Vol Ctr, 1988-; bd mem, Harrisburg Sewer & Water Authority, 1988-; chmn, Harrisburg Authority, 1991-04; chair, Harrisburg City Sch Dist Bd Control, 2000-04 . **Special Achievements:** He was named one of the 50 most influential African American and minority lawyers in Pennsylvania by the Legal Intelligencer in 2002. **Home Addr:** 3018 Green St, Harrisburg, PA 17110. **Business Addr:** Chief Counsel, PA Dept Gen Serv, N Off Bldg Rm 507, Harrisburg, PA 17125, **Business Phone:** (717)787-6679.*

HARKEY, MICHAEL ANTHONY
Baseball player. **Personal:** Born Oct 25, 1966, San Diego, CA; married Nikki; children: Michael Jr, Cory & Miani. **Career:** Baseball player (retired), baseball player coach; Chicago Cubs, pitcher, 1988-93; Colorado Rockies, 1994; Oakland Athletics, 1995; California Angels, 1995; Los Angeles Dodgers, 1997; San Diego Padres, pitching coach, 2000-05; Rancho Cucamonga Quakes, pitching coach, 2000; Fort Wayne Wizards, pitching coach, 2001, 2003; Lake Elsinore Storm, pitching coach, 2002, 2004; Mobile BayBears, pitching coach, 2005; Florida Marlins, bullpen coach, 2006; Iowa Cubs, pitching coach, 2007; NY Yankees, bullpen coach, currently. **Orgs:** Minor League Baseball Alumni Asn. **Honors/Awds:** Rookie Pitcher of the Year, Nat League, Sporting News, 1990. **Business Phone:** (718)293-6000.

HARKINS-CARTER, DR. ROSEMARY KNIGHTON
School administrator. **Personal:** Born Aug 5, 1938, Amarillo, TX; daughter of Herbert Curtis and Pauline Cloteal; married Elmer Bud Carter, Nov 18, 1994; married Clarence, Nov 24, 1964 (divorced 1977). **Educ:** Amarillo Jr Col, AA, 1957; West Tex State Univ, BS, 1964; Univ Okla, MS,1971; Univ Okla, Health Sci Ctr, PhD, 1972; Cent State Univ, BS, 1976. **Career:** Veterans Admin Med Ctr, hemat supvr, 1968-70; Advan Studies Ford Found, fel, 1971-72; Univ Okla Col Allied Health, asst prof, 1972-77; Sch Allied Health Prof Univ Okla, dir & assoc prof, 1977-81; Univ Okla Col Allied Health, assoc dean & prof, 1981-88; Howard Univ, Col Allied Health Sci, dean; Langston Univ, dept bio, chairperson, fac emer, currently. **Orgs:** Consult, Petroleum Training & Tech Serv Workman Inc, 1978; bd dirs, Nat Adv Comm Accreditation & Inst Eligibility, 1981-83; nat secy bd dirs, Am Soc Allied Health Prof, 1982-84; chmn bd dirs, Okla Minority Bus Develop Ctr US Dept Com, 1982-88; consult Bd Regents, Fla St Univ Syst, 1983; consult, Am Phys Ther Asn, 1983; vice chairperson bd trustees, Okla Inst Child Advocacy, 1983-87; exec coun, Nat Inst Disability & Rehabilitation, US Dept Educ; fel, Am Soc Allied Health Prof Wash, DC, 1984. **Military Serv:** AUS Reserve, col, 1981-91. **Business Addr:** Faculty Emeritus, Langston University, Department of Biology, HAMH Room 219 Hwy 33, PO Box 1500, Langston, OK 73050, **Business Phone:** (405)466-3309.

HARKLESS-WEBB, MILDRED
Educator. **Personal:** Born Aug 17, 1935, Cedar Lane, TX; daughter of Cody Powell and Mayfield; married James E Webb, Jun 27, 1981. **Educ:** Prairie View A&M, BS, 1957; San Francisco State Univ, MA,1976. **Career:** Webb's Pest Control, vpres, 1979-; Everett Mid Sch, teacher, Currently. **Orgs:** Sponsor Scholar Soc, 1968-; NEA; CTA; ISBE; WBEA; CBEA; ABE; 1970-; NAACP 1974-; staff rep, ALC SFCTA, 1976-; facilitator, NBEA, 1976-; sponsor Black Stud Club 1983-; Commonwealth Club Calif, 1988-; co-chair, Self-Esteem/Stud Performance Comt; San Francisco Bus Chamber Com Leadership Class, presenter, 1988. **Home Addr:** 35 Camellia Pl, Oakland, CA 94602. **Business Addr:** Teacher, Everett Middle School, 450 Church St, San Francisco, CA 94114, **Business Phone:** (415)241-6344.

HARKNESS, JERRY
Association executive. **Personal:** Born May 7, 1940, New York, NY; son of Lucille and Lindsay; married Sarah; children: Jerald, Julie Lyn & Brandon. **Educ:** Loyola Univ, Chicago, IL, BS, sociol, 1963. **Career:** NY Knicks, Nat Basketball League, 1964; Ind Pacers, 1967-69; United Way, campaign assoc, 1969-95; WTHR TV-13, weekend sports caster, 1969-81; Morning sports anchor WTLC Radio; Indiana Pacers, Indianapolis, IN, basketball analyst, 1983; United Way Cent Ind, dir community affairs, beginning, 1985; Sports Channel, Chicago, IL, basketball analyst, 1988-; Athlete's Foot, co-owner, mgr, cur, currently. **Orgs:** Exec bd dirs, Hundred Blackmen Indianapolis Inc, 1986-, exec dir, 1997; bd dirs, Police Athletic League, Indianapolis, 1986-; Coun Black Execs, 1987-; Eastern Star Baptist Church. **Honors/Awds:** Silver Anniversary Basketball Team, NCAA, 1988; 20 Year Volunteer Award, Indiana Black Expo, 1990; Two time All-American; Boy Scouts This is your Life Award. **Home Phone:** (317)823-9688. **Business Addr:** Co-owner/Manager, Athlete's Foot, 49 W Maryland St Suite C5, Indianapolis, IN 46204-3522, **Business Phone:** (317)226-9596.

HARLAN, CARMEN
Television journalist. **Personal:** Born Nov 4, 1953, Detroit, MI; married Andrew Henry Jr. **Educ:** Univ Mich. **Career:** WDIV-TV, Channel 4, Detroit, MI, news anchor, 1978-, sr anchor, currently. **Honors/Awds:** Feted by Nat Coalition 100 Black Women, Detroit, MI; Detroit's top news anchor, Ladies Home Jour Mag, 1991. **Special Achievements:** Carried the Olympic Torch in the summer of 1996 and repeated the honor as the torch again passed through Detroit en route to the 2002 Winter Olympics. **Business Addr:** Senior Anchor, WDIV-TV Channel 4, 550 W Lafayette, Detroit, MI 48226, **Business Phone:** (313)222-0444.

HARLAN, EMERY KING
Lawyer. **Personal:** Born Jan 18, 1965, Gary, IN; son of Wilbert and Bertha. **Educ:** Siena Heights Col, BA, bus admin, 1986; Univ Wisc Law Sch, JD, 1989. **Career:** US Ct Appeals Sixth Circuit, Hon George Edwards, law clerk; US Dist Ct, Northern Dist, Ill, practr; US Ct Appeals Sixth & Seventh Circuits, practr; Ross & Hardies, labor & employ atty; Gonzalez Saggio & Harlan LLP, atty & partner, currently. **Orgs:** Vchmn, gen pract sec, Corp Coun Comm, Am Bar Asn; Chicago Bar Asn; Minority Coun Prog Steering Comm; Dem Leadership 21st Century, Steering Comm; Nat Asn Minority & Women Owned Law Firms. **Honors/Awds:** Ray & Ethel Brown fel, Univ Wisc Law Sch, 1988. **Home Addr:** 5337 S Cornell Suite 1, Chicago, IL 60615, **Home Phone:** (312)643-6887. **Business Addr:** Partner, Attorney, Gonzalez Saggio & Harlan LLP, 225 E Michigan St, Milwaukee, WI 53202-4900, **Business Phone:** (414)277-8500.

HARLESTON, BRIGADIER GEN. ROBERT ALONZO
Educator. **Personal:** Born Jan 28, 1936, Hempstead, NY; son of Henry M Harleston Sr and Anna Elizabeth Tobin Harleston; married Sheila C; children: Robert, Bernice & Paul. **Educ:** Howard Univ, Wash, DC, BA, 1958; Mich State Univ, East Lansing, MI, MS, 1965; Georgetown Law Ctr, Wash, DC, JD, 1984. **Career:** Univ Md, Eastern Shore, MD, Dept Criminal Justice, chmn & as-

soc prof, currently. **Orgs:** Omega Psi Phi, 1953-; bd dirs, Eastern Shore Red Cross, 1990-93, 2002-; bd dirs, Delmarva Boy Scouts, 1990-93; Rotary Club, 1990-93; Black Adv Comt Episcopal Bishop, 1990-93; interview comt, Humanity Habitat, 1995-; sire archon, Gamma Theta Boule, Sigma Pi Phi, 1996; Govenors Educ Coord Comt Correctional Insts, 1997-; Acad Criminal Justice Sci; Am Correctional Asn. **Honors/Awds:** Martin Luther King Jr Award, Maryland Classified Employees Asn, 1996. **Military Serv:** AUS, brigadier gen, 1959-89. **Home Addr:** 30420 Mallard Dr, Delmar, MD 21875.

HARLEY, DR. DEBRA A.
College teacher. **Personal:** Widowed; children: 4. **Educ:** SC State Univ, BS, 1981, MA, 1983; Southern Ill Univ, Carbondale, IL, PhD,1992. **Career:** SC Employ Security Comn, Beaufort, employ counr, 1984; SC Dept Voc Rehab, Hartsville, rehab counr, 1984-86; Southern Ill Univ, Carbondale, proj coordr, 1990-91, teaching asst, 1991-92, Dept Spec Educ, asst prof, 1992-93; Easter Ill Univ, Charleston, asst prof, 1992-93; Univ Ky, Lexington, Dept Spec Educ & Rehab Coun, from asst prof to assoc prof, 1993-2003, Grad Prog Rehab Coun, aast dir, 1996-98, Rehab Endorsement Curric, Grad Prog Rehab Coun, coordr, 1996-2003, Grad Prog Rehab Coun, coordr, 1998-2000, Col Arts & Sci, dir, 2002-03, assoc dir, 2003-04, prof, currently; Infants Young C, reviewer, 1997-; Rehab Psychol, reviewer, 2001-; Jour Counseling Psychol, reviewer, 2001-; Jour Rehab Admin, 2002-. **Orgs:** Kappa Delta Pi; Chi Sigma Iota. **Honors/Awds:** Educator of the Year, Nat Coun Rehab Educ, 2001, 2006; Mary E. Switzer Scholar in Rehabilitation Seminar, Nat Rehab Asn, 2001; Provosts Award for Outstanding Teaching for Tenured Faculty, Univ Ky, 2002. **Special Achievements:** Publisher: Planned happenstance in developing and managing career development for rehabilitation personnel; An analysis of competitive employment outcomes for VR customers with mild, moderate, and severe/profound mental retardation; Professional portfolio development for rehabilitation counselors and human service providers: A tool for professional development and leadership. **Business Addr:** Department Chair, Professor, University of Kentucky, Department Spec Educ & Rehab Counseling, 116 Taylor Education Bldg, Lexington, KY 40506-0001, **Business Phone:** (859)257-7199.

HARLEY, LEGRAND
Association executive. **Personal:** Born Jan 19, 1956, Florence, SC; son of Willie Harley. **Educ:** Francis Marion Col, Florence, SC, BS, polit sci, 1981. **Career:** Red Carpet Inn, Florence, SC, asst mgr, 1973-80; Florence Co Community on Alcohol & Drugs, residential mgr, 1981-84; SC Dept Youth Serv, Columbia, SC, youth counr, 1984-86; Lt Gov Mike Daniel, Columbia, SC, field coordr, 1986-87; SC Atty General Off, Columbia, SC, admin asst, 1987-92; Merchants Asn Florence, coordr, 1993-95; Florence Co, asst, 1995; Dem Party, activist; Florence Co, coordr. **Orgs:** Pres, chmn, emer, SC Young Democrats; Black Caucus, admin bd, lay leader, life mem, Salem United Methodist Church; legal redress comt, leader, Nat Asn Advan Colored People, 1982-; field rep, Florence Jaycees, 1980-82. **Honors/Awds:** Young Man of the Year, The Key Inc, 1980; Outstanding Young Men of America, US Jaycees, 1981; Young Democrats of Florence, Florence Young Democrats, 1982; Longest Serving Young Democrat in SC, SC Democratic Party, 1988; Outstanding & Most Loyal Young Democrat, SC Young Democrats, 1989. **Home Addr:** 209 Pearl Circle, Florence, SC 29506. *

HARLEY, PHILIP A.
Educator. **Personal:** Born in Philadelphia; married Ireleen I; children: Anthony, Antoinette, Richard, Michael, Bruce, Annette & Terri. **Educ:** Morgan State Col, BA, 1945; Temple Univ; Univ Cincinnati; Capital Univ Sch Theol; Garrett Theol Sem, M.Div, 1956. **Career:** Educator (retired). IL, IN, OH, SD, WI, pastor; Garrett Theol Sem, assoc prof; Practical Theol & Field Educ, assoc prof emer. **Orgs:** Chmn, Regional Consultative Com Race; Mayors Com Human Relations; dist dir, Res & Devel Ministries Educ, IN, SD; prog leadership develop Prog Coun, Northern Ill Conf; vchmn, Leadership Develop Com N Central Jurisdictron; regional vpres, Natl Com Black Churchmen; chmn, Chicago Coordinating Com Black Churchmen; vice chmn, Serv Review Panel Comm Fund; Ch Fed Met Chicago; Chicago Conf Religion & Race; mem bd dir, Welfare Coun Met Chicago. **Military Serv:** USNR, sp/x, 1944-46. *

HARMON, CLARENCE
Government official. **Personal:** Married Janet; children: 4. **Educ:** Northeast Mo State Univ, BS; Webster Univ, MPA, criminal justice & pub admin. **Career:** St Louis Police Dept, various positions, comdr area I, 1988-90, Bd Police Comnrs, secy, 1991, chief police, 1991-97; City St Louis, mayor, 1997-2001; Southern Ill Univ, Pub Policy Inst, part time lectr, currently. **Orgs:** Int Asn Chief Police; Am Mgt Asn; bd trustees, Webster Univ; bd trustees, St Louis Sci Ctr; bd dir, St Louis Symphony; vpres, Fair Found bd dirs; bd dirs, M Botanical Garden; bd dirs, United Way St. Louis. **Honors/Awds:** four Letters Commendation for outstanding performance duty, Metrop Police Dept, City St Louis; Police Chief of the Year, Mo Police Chiefs' Asn, 1995; Danforth Found Fel, JFK Sch Govt, Harvard Univ; Most Distinguished Alumnus Award, Phi Theta Kappa, 2000. **Special Achievements:** First African American chief of police in the St Louis Police Dept; developed Community Oriented Policing Service program as area commander at the St Louis Police Dept; implemented gun buyback program as chief of the St Louis Police Dept, 1991. **Business Phone:** (618)453-4009.

HARMON, JAMES F., SR. (JIM HARMON)
Executive. **Personal:** Born Apr 18, 1932, Savannah, GA; married Clarissa V Poindexter; children: James F Jr, Valerie H Seay, Laurence E, Wendell E. **Educ:** NC A&T Col, BS, 1954; Air Univ, Squad Officer Sch, 1961; Troy State Univ, MS, 1974. **Career:** Atlanta Marriott Hotels, personnel dir, 1975-80; Marriott Hotels, reg dir training, 1980-82; Atlanta Perimeter Ctr Marriott, res mgr, 1982; Courtyard Marriott Hotels, prop mgr, 1983. **Orgs:** Alpha Phi Alpha, 1952-; pres, Atlanta Falcon Club Inc, 1983-; chmn, Ed Comn Nat Hosp Ed Mgr Assoc, 1983. **Military Serv:** USAF, lt col, 1954-74; Command Pilot DFC, Air Medal, DSM, Vietnam Serv Medal. *

HARMON, JESSIE KATE. **See PORTIS, KATTIE HARMON.**

HARMON, JIM. **See HARMON, JAMES F., SR.**

HARMON, JOHN H.
Lawyer. **Personal:** Born Feb 10, 1942, Windsor, NC. **Educ:** BA, 1963; BL, 1965. **Career:** US Dept Labor, solictor's off, 1965-66; US House Rep Com Educ & Labor, asst coun, 1966-67; Harmon & Raynor, owner, 1967-. **Orgs:** Fed Bar Asn; Craven Co Bar Asn; Nat Conf Black Lawyers; NC Acad Trial Lawyers; Omega Psi Phi Frat; pres, NC Asn Black Lawyers; Nat Asn Advan Colored People; SCLC; Black Prog Businessmen Inc; pres, New Bern Chap NC Cent Univ Alumni Asn; pres, Craven County Bar Asn, 1985-86. **Honors/Awds:** Merit Award, NC Cent Univ Sch Law, 1974. **Military Serv:** USAR e-5 1966-72. **Business Addr:** Owner, Harmon & Raynor, 1017 Broad St Suite C, New Bern, NC 28560.*

HARMON, M LARRY
Executive. **Personal:** Born Nov 15, 1944, Kansas City, MO; son of Vivian N Berry and E Morris; married Myrna L (Hestle); children: Robert T, M Nathan & Dana E. **Educ:** Rockhurst Col, Kans City, MO, BA, indust rels, 1971; Univ Mass, Amherst, MBA, 1972. **Career:** Joseph Schlitz Brewing Co, Milwaukee, WI, corporate employment mgr, 1978, Syracuse, NY, indust rels mgr, 1978-80; Anheuser-Busch Inc, Syracuse, NY, indust rels mgr, 1980-85, St Louis, MO, sr exec asst, 1985-87, Baldwinsville, NY, employee rels mgr, 1987-. **Orgs:** Am Soc Personnel Admin, 1976-; Kappa Alpha Phi, 1982-; exec bd mem, Personnel Mgt Coun, 1987-; bd dir, Onondaga County Urban League, 1987-. **Honors/Awds:** Black Achievers in Indusry, YMCA Greater New York, 1979; Nat Asn Advan Colored People Image Award, Outstanding Men Achievers, 1989. **Military Serv:** USN, petty officer, 1962-66; Vietnam Serv Medal. **Home Addr:** 3478 Melvin Dr N, Baldwinsville, NY 13027. **Business Addr:** Employee Relations Manager, Anheuser-Busch Inc, 2885 Belgium Rd, Baldwinsville, NY 13027-2706, **Business Phone:** (315)635-4000.

HARPER, DR. ALPHONZA VEALVERT, III
Dentist. **Personal:** Born Feb 5, 1948, Alexander City, AL; son of Alphonza V and Barbara B; married Debra Sanders; children: Niaya A Harper. **Educ:** Tenn State Univ, BS, 1969; Meharry Med Col, DDS, 1975. **Career:** Beverly Hills Dent Off, Self employed dent, St Louis, MO, currently. **Orgs:** Am Dent Asn; Nat Dent Asn; Greater St Louis Dent Soc; Mound City Dental Soc, 1975-; NAACP, 1980-; vpres, Normandy Kiwanis Club, 1979-. **Home Addr:** 6910 Natural Bridge, St Louis, MO 63121, **Home Phone:** (314)387-7858. **Business Addr:** Dentist, Beverly Hills Dental Clinic, 6830 Natural Bridge Rd, St Louis, MO 63121, **Business Phone:** (314)383-8060.

HARPER, BEN. **See HARPER, BENJAMIN CHASE.**

HARPER, BENJAMIN CHASE (BEN HARPER)
Singer, songwriter. **Personal:** Born Oct 28, 1969, Claremont, CA; son of Leonard and Ellen; married Joanna (divorced 2001); children: CJ Harris. **Career:** Virgin Rec, rec artist, 1994-2001; Inland Emperor Rec, founder, 2001-; Albums : Pleasure and Pain, 1992; Welcome to the Cruel World, 1994; Fight for your Mind, 1995; The Will to Live, 1997; Burn to Shine, 1999; Live from Mars, 2001; Diamonds on the Inside, 2003; There will be a Light, 2004; Live at the Apollo, 2005; Both Sides of the Gun, 2006; Lifeline, 2007; Live at Twist & Shout, 2007; White Lies for Dark Times, 2009; Songs: "Burn to shine", 2000; "Forgiven", 2000; "Steal My Kisses", 2000; "With My Own Two Hands", 2003; "Diamonds on the Inside", 2004; "So High So Low", 2004; "Brown Eyed Blue", 2004; "Better Way", 2006; "Morning Yearning", 2006; "Fight Outta You", 2007; "In the Colors", 2007; "Fool For A Lonesome Train", 2008; "Shimmer & Shine", 2009; "Fly One Time", 2009. **Special Achievements:** Performed on tour with Taj Mahal, 1992; collaborated with Mahal on soundtrack for The Drinking Gourd, a bio of Harriet Tubman; toured US as both solo and warm-up act with his band The Innocent Criminals, 1994-95;toured US, Europe, and New Zealand, 1995-97; headlined at HORDE Festivaland Montreaux Jazz Festival. *

HARPER, BERNICE CATHERINE
Government official. **Personal:** Born in Covington, VA; widowed; children: Reginald. **Educ:** VA State Col, BS, 1945; Univ So CA, MSW, 1948; Harvard Univ, MSC, 1959; Faith Grant Col, LLD, 1994. **Career:** Childrens Hosp, social worker, 1947-57; City Hope Med Ctr, dir social work, 1960-74; Dept HEW, chief NH br, 1970-72, dir div ltc, 1973-77, spec asst to dir hsqb, 1977-79, med care adv. **Orgs:** Bd Intl Hospice Inst, Bd Intl Coun SW US Community; steering community NASW; pres, Found Hospices Sub-Saharan Africa, 1999-. **Honors/Awds:** Ida M Cannon Award, AHA, 1972; PHS Superior Service Award, 1977; Better Life Award, AHCA, 1978; HCFA Admin Award, 1982; Distinguished Member of Los Amigos Award, Univ Southern Calif, LA, 1993; Person of the Year Award, Nat Hospice Orgn, 1993; Francine F Douglas Award, Outstanding Contribs Women's Causes, 1993; Knee-Wittman Health & Mental Health Outstanding Achievement Award, Nat Asn Social Workers Inc, 1990; Faith Grant Col, LLD, 1994. **Business Addr:** Chairperson, Foundation For Hospices in Sub Saharan African, 1700 Diagonal Rd Suite 630, Alexandria, VA 22314, **Business Phone:** (703)647-5176.*

HARPER, CONRAD KENNETH
Lawyer. **Personal:** Born Dec 2, 1940, Detroit, MI; son of Archibald L and Georgia F Hall; married Marsha L Wilson; children: Warren & Adam. **Educ:** Howard Univ, BA, 1962; Harvard Law Sch, LLB, 1965. **Career:** Lawyer (retired); Nat Asn Advan Colored People, Legal Defense Fund, law clerk, 1965-66, staff lawyer, 1966-70; Rutgers Law Sch, lectr, 1969-70; Simpson Thacher & Bartlett, assoc, 1971-74, partner, 1974-93; US Dept State, legal adv, 1993-96. **Orgs:** Phi Beta Kappa, 1962; Yale Law Sch, 1977-81; US Dept HEW, consult, 1977; trustee, NY Pub Libr, 1978-93; bd eds, Am Bar Asn Jour, 1980-86; Vestryman St Barnabas Epis Church, Irvington, NY, 1982-85; Comn Admis & Grievances, US Ct Appeals (2nd Cir), 1983-93, chmn, 1987-93; fel Am Bar Found; Coun Foreign Rels; Coun Am Law Inst, 1985-, 2nd vp, 1998-00, 1st vp, 2000-; chancellor, Epis Diocese NY, 1987-92; bd dir, co-chair, Lawyers Comn Civil Rights under Law, 1987-89; trustee, William Nelson Cromwell Found, 1990-; pres, Asn Bar City New York, 1990-92; pres, NY City Bar, 1990-92; dir, Am Arbitration Asn, 1990-93, 1997-01; dir, NY Life Ins Co, 1992-93, 1996-; trustee, Metrop Mus Art, 1996-; dir, Pub Serv Enterprise Group, 1997-; Harvard Corp, 2000; fel Am Acad Arts & Scis; bd dir, Acad Am Poets; bd dir, Acad Polit Sci; fel Am Col Trial Lawyers; Am Law Inst Coun; Coun Foreign Rels; bd dir, Inst Int Educ; trustee, Lawyers' Comt Civil Rights Under Law; trustee, Metrop Mus Art; vice chmn, NY Pub Libr; Obama Am; Permanent Ct Arbitration. **Honors/Awds:** LLD, City Univ New York, 1990; LLD, Am Philosophical Soc; Bishop's Cross, Episcopal Diocese of New York, 1992; Alumni Achievement Award, Howard Univ, 1994; Whitney North Seymour Award, Fed Bar Coun, 1994; C Francis Stratford Award, Nat Bar Asn, 1999.

HARPER, CURTIS
Research scientist, educator. **Personal:** Born May 13, 1937, Auburn, AL. **Educ:** Tuskegee Inst, BS, 1959; Tuskegee Inst, MS, 1961; IA State Univ, MS, 1965; Univ Miss, PhD, 1969. **Career:** Univ NC Sch Med, Dept Biochem & Moleculr Biophysics, resrch assoc, 1970-71, instr, 1971-72, assoc prof, prof, prof emer, currently, co dir; Yale Univ, resch assoc, 1969-70; Nat Inst Environ Health Sci, sr staff fel, 1972-76. **Orgs:** Am Chem Soc; AAAS; Soc Sigma Xi; Soc Toxicol; Am Soc Pharmacol & Experimental Therapeut Human Rel Comn, 1970-74; Drug Act Comt, 1971-73; Interch Coun Soc Act Comt, 1971-74; bd mem, NC Civ Lib Union, 1976-; bd mem, Interch Coun Housing Auth 1977-. **Military Serv:** USAR capt, 1963-65. **Business Addr:** Professor Emeritus, University of North Carolina School of Medicine, Department of Pharmacology, 1106 Mary Ellen Jones Bldg CB 7365 98 Manning Dr, Chapel Hill, NC 27599-0001, **Business Phone:** (919)966-4495.

HARPER, DAVID B.
Executive, chief executive officer, president (organization). **Personal:** Born Dec 3, 1933, Indianapolis, IN; married Mae McGee; children: Vicki Clines, Sharon Chaney, Wanda Mosley, Lydia Restivo, Kathleen Bass,Carol, Kyra, David, Daniel & Ralph. **Educ:** Ariz State Univ, BS, 1963; Golden State Univ, MBA, 1968; Eastern Mich Univ, Doctor Law (Hons), 1970. **Career:** Bank of Am NT & SA, bank officer & magr, 1963; First Independence Nat Bank Detroit, pres & ceo, 1969-76; Gateway Nat Bank, pres & ceo, 1976-83; County Ford Inc, pres, 1983-88; David B Harper Mgt Inc, pres, 1988-; New Age Financial Bancorporation Inc, pres & ceo, 1989-. **Orgs:** Bd dirs, K-Mart Corp, 1975-; bd dirs, Stud Mkt Loan Asn, 1973-; bd dirs, Detroit Edison, 1975-83; bd dirs, Oper Food Search; bd dirs, Cystic Fibrosis Found; bd dirs, Cent Inst Deaf; bd dirs, St Louis Regional Med Ctr Found; vpres, Fair Found; bd dirs, Confluence St Louis. **Honors/Awds:** Distinguished Volunteer Award, Univ Missouri, 1990. **Military Serv:** USAF, acct supvr, 1954-58. **Business Addr:** President, Chief Executive Officer, New Age Financial Bancorporation Inc, 211 N Broadway Suite 2080, Saint Louis, MO 63121, **Business Phone:** (314)725-5445.

HARPER, DWAYNE ANTHONY
Football player, executive. **Personal:** Born Mar 29, 1966, Orangeburg, SC. **Educ:** SC State Coll, BA, mkt, 1988. **Career:** Football player (retired), exec; Seattle Seahawks, corner back, 1988-93; San Diego Chargers, 1994-98; Detroit Lions, 1999; ETL Associates Inc, vpres & dir player develop, currently. **Orgs:** Nat Asn Ad-

van Colored People; bd trustees, Claflin Univ. **Honors/Awds:** Sports Illustrated, All-NFL Team, 1991 & 1995; Unsung Hero Award, 1995; Most Valuable Person, 1995.

HARPER, EARL
Educator. **Personal:** Born Jul 7, 1929, Jackson, MS; married Clara Louise; children: Felicia, Denise, Julie, Earl Jr, Andre Robinson & Sharmeka Robinson. **Educ:** Western MICH Univ, BS ind supervision, 1968; MS Eng Tech, 1971, MBA mgt,1973, specialist arts mgt, 1979; TEX Tech Univ, PhD, 1988. **Career:** Doehler-Jarvis, training dir, asst to plant mgr, 1946-71; Grand Valley State UNIV, FE Siedman Sch BUS, chair, mgt dept, 1981-94, prof, 1994, prof emer, currently. **Orgs:** Developed Grand Rapids, Mich Model Cities Career & Acad CounCtr, 1971; developed Gen Acad Prog Grand Rapids & Muskegon Inner-City Col Ed Prog Grand Valley State Col, 1971; comt develop Higher Educ Prog Grand Rapids Model Cities, 1972-73; Personal Admin Soc; Delta Mu Delta Epsilon; Die Casting Soc; Indust Mgt Soc; Indust Eng Soc; bd mem, Indust Rel Res Asst; bd mem, Bus Opportunities Soc; Am Legion; NAACP. **Honors/Awds:** Certificate Appreciation, AM Legion; Management Scholarship Award, State TX; Outstanding EDRs Award, Grand Valley State Univ Alumni Asn, 1993; Excellence in Research Award, Grand Valley State Univ, 1994, Outstanding EDUCATION Award, 1994; Earl Harper Scholarship, named in honor. **Special Achievements:** Publications: "Management the Diversified Workforce: Current Efforts and Future Directions," Sam Advanced Management Journal, 1993; "An Empirical Examination of the Relationship Between Strategy and Scanning," The Mid Atlantic Journal of Business, 1993; Numerous others. **Military Serv:** AUS, corpl, 1951-53. *

HARPER, EUGENE, JR.
School administrator, executive director. **Personal:** Born Feb 1, 1943, Atlanta, GA; son of E Eugene and Sula Mae; married Maryetta, Sep 27, 1966; children: Angelia M Harper. **Educ:** Cameron State Col, AA, 1966; Ohio State Univ, BS, 1971; Cent Mich Univ, MS, 1980. **Career:** Cols Recreation Dept, dist supv & dir, 1967-72; Ohio State Univ, assoc dir intramurals, 1972-88; Columbus Pub Schs, dir athletics & stud activ, 1988-. **Orgs:** APA; bd dir, Ohio Spec Olympics; bd dir, Cols Parks & Recreation; consult, Ohio State Univ Nat Youth Sports Prog; chairperson, Ohio Asn Health, Phys Educ, Recreation & Dance; Nat Interscholastic Athletic Asn; Ohio Interscholastic Athletic Asn; Ohio High Sch Athletic Asn; Alpha Phi Alpha, Alpha RHO Lambda Chap; Recreation & Parks Comn. **Honors/Awds:** Sportsmanship, Ethics & Integrity Award, Ohio High Sch Athletic Asn, 1995-96. **Military Serv:** USF, 1961-64. *

HARPER, GERALDINE SEAY
Educator. **Personal:** Born Dec 7, 1933, Memphis, TN; daughter of James Edward Seay and Janie Lee Bolden Seay; married Charles N Harper, Mar 4, 1954; children: Dr Deborah Harper Brown, Elaine Harper Bell & Charles Terrence Harper. **Educ:** LeMoyne-Owen, Memphis, Tenn, BS, 1955; Chicago State Univ, Chicago, IL, MS, 1977. **Career:** Educator (retire): Chicago Bd Educ, Chicago, IL, teacher, 1958-76, teacher & librn, 1976. **Orgs:** Chicago Teacher Libr Asn, 1980-; Lilydale First Baptist Church Chicago, 1983-; rooms comt chair, Chicago Teacher Libr Asn, 1986-87; reservations secy, Chicago Teacher Libr Asn, 1987; Delta Sigma Theta Sorority; dir, Vacation Bible Sch; chair, Sr Citizens Comt, Top Ladies Distinction Inc Chicago Chap, 1987-89; corresponding secy, Chicago Teachers Libr Asn, 1988-89; correspondence secy, Chicago Teacher Libr Asn, 1988-; pres, Manassas High Sch Alumni Asn, Chicago Chap, 1995-; pres, LeMoyne-Owen Col Alumni Asn, Chicago Chap, 2000-. **Honors/Awds:** Lady of the Year, Top Ladies Distinction Inc, Chicago Chap, 1989; Certificates of Appreciation, City of Memphis. **Home Addr:** 515 W 97th St, Chicago, IL 60628.

HARPER, HILL
Actor. **Personal:** Born May 17, 1973, Iowa City, IA. **Educ:** Brown Univ, BA; Harvard Univ, JD; Harvard Univ, Kennedy Sch Gov, MPA. **Career:** Boston's Black Folks Theater Co, full time mem; Film appearances: Confessions of a Dog, 1993; Pumpkinhead II, 1994; One Red Rose, 1995; Drifting School, 1995; Get On The Bus, 1996; Steel, 1997; Hav Plenty, 1997; Hoover Park, 1997; He Got Game, 1998; Park Day, 1998; The Nephew, 1998; Beloved, 1998; Slaves of Hollywood, 1999; Loving Jezebel, 1999; In Too Deep, 1999; The Skulls, 2000; The Visit, 2000; Higher Ed, 2001; Crossthe Line, 2002; Love, Sex and Eating the Bones, 2003; Constellation, 2003; Lackawanna Blues, 2005; 30 Days, 2006; Premium, 2006; The Breed, 2006; This Is Not a Test, 2008; A Good Man is Hard To Find, 2008; Mama, I Want to Sing!, 2008, TV series: "Live Shot", 1995; "City of Angels", 2000; "The Court", 2002; "The Handler", 2003; TV movies: "Zooman", 1995; "Mama Flora's Family", 1998;"The Badge", 2002; writer: One Red Rose, 1995; The Game, 2009. **Honors/Awds:** Audience Award, Urban world Film Festival, 2000; Emerging Artist Award-,Chicago Int Film Festival; John Garfield Best Actor Award, 2001; Hon Doctorate, Westfield State Col, 2009. **Special Achievements:** First black practicing anesthesiologists in the United States. **Business Addr:** Actor, c/o Principato-Young Entertainment, 9465 Wilshire Blvd Suite 430, Beverly Hills, CA 90212, **Business Phone:** (310)274-2294.*

HARPER, JOSEPH W
Executive director, educator. **Personal:** Born Jan 10, 1931, Charlotte, NC; married Mary A Turner; children: Delcia Marie, Lisa Yvette & Jonette Michelle. **Educ:** Johnson C Smith Univ, BS, 1955; A&T State Univ, MS, 1963, NSF grants; Univ Calif, Berkeley, cert molecular biol, 1968; Western Mich Univ; Univ NC Charlotte; Univ NC, Chapel Hill, cert grad study educ, 1977. **Career:** E Mecklenburg Adult Educ Ctr Cent Piedmont Community Col, teacher, coach, 1955-74, biol teacher, 1969-73, dir, 1974-99; E Mecklenburg Sr High Sch, asst prin, 1974-91; Omega Psi Phi Fraternity Inc, exec dir sixth dist, currently. **Orgs:** Nat Educ Asn; NC Found Pub Sch C; NC Prins Asn; adv bd, Upward Bound Prog Johnson C Smith Univ; pres, NC Southwestern Dist Ath Asn, 1960-62 & 1964-65; dir, NC State Basketball Tourn Western Div AA Confs, 1966-68; Model Cities Task Force; YMCA; adv bd, Helping Hand Scholarship; Charlotte-Mecklenburg Rec Comn; Pan-Hellenic Coun; Omega Psi Phi Fraternity. **Honors/Awds:** Cert Merit, NC Sci Teachers Symposium, 1965; Coach of Year, NCHSAA Western Div football, 1966, basketball 1967; Outstanding Service Plaque, 1966; Outstanding Leadership Award Lincoln Co PTA, 1967; Most Understanding Teacher 2d Ward HS, 1969; Bell & Howell Schs Fellowship Award, 1973; Dem Omega Man of Year Award, Pi Phi Chap, 1974; sixth dist, 1975. **Military Serv:** AUS, pvt first class, 1952-54. **Home Addr:** 5925 Sierra Dr, Charlotte, NC 28216, **Home Phone:** (704)394-2276.

HARPER, LAYDELL WOOD
Marketing executive, president (organization). **Personal:** Daughter of R Wood and Felicia; divorced; children: Licia Lyn. **Educ:** Wayne State Univ, BA, 1980; Knight Ridder Inst, mgt. **Career:** Detroit Free Press, downtown advert mgr, 1987-89; Detroit Newspaper Agency, features advert gen mgr, 1989-90, co-op advert mgr, 1990-91, community affairs dir, 1991-; Wood & Assocs, pres & chief exec officer, 2004-. **Orgs:** Adv bd, BART, 1991-92; bd dirs, Sci & Eng, 1991-93; bd mem, Berat Human Servs, 1992-; mkt comt, co-chair, Nat Asn Advan Colored People, 1992-; co-chair, United Negro Col Fund, fashion fair, 1992; bd dirs, Project Pride Chamber, 1992. **Honors/Awds:** Woman of the Year, Friday Women's Club, 1988. **Home Addr:** 1751 Seminole St, Detroit, MI 48214. **Business Addr:** President & Chief Executive Officer, Wood & Associates, PO Box 14541, Detroit, MI 48214, **Business Phone:** (313)925-4067.

HARPER, MARY L.
Accountant. **Personal:** Born Feb 24, 1925, Emporia, KS; married Edward J. **Educ:** Lincoln Univ, Jeff City, MO; Emporia State Teacher Col, Emporia, KS; State Col, LA. **Career:** LA Co Prob Dept Juvenile Reim Sect, invest, girls coun, 1960-63; Self Employ, acct tax counsult, 1965-; Cong Dist Dem Union, special asst. **Orgs:** Treas, Dem Coal Pomona Valley; treas, Nat Asn Advan Colored People, So CA Area Conf, 1966-71; chmn, Pomona Valley, Nat Asn Advan Colored People; bd pres, Nat Asn Advan Colored People; Southern Calif Area Conf, 1971-73; comnr, City Pomona; vice chmn, Parks & Recreation Comn; bd dirs, YMCA Outreach. **Honors/Awds:** Service Award, So Area Conf Nat Asn Advan Colored People, 1969, 71; Elected Delegate Dem Charter Conf KC, MO 35th Cong Dist 1974. **Special Achievements:** Only black candidate in field of 12, one of two female during city council election. *

HARPER, MICHAEL STEVEN
Educator, poet. **Personal:** Born Mar 18, 1938, Brooklyn, NY; son of Walter Warren and Katherine Johnson; married Shirley Ann Buffington, Dec 24, 1965 (divorced 1998); children: Roland Warren, Patrice Cuchulain & Rachel Maria. **Educ:** Los Angeles City Col, AA, 1959; Los Angeles St Col, Los Angeles, BA, 1961, MA, 1963; Univ Iowa, MFA, 1963; Brown Univ, ad eundem, 1972. **Career:** Contra Costa Col, Engl instr, 1964-68; Lewis & Clark Col, poet in residence, 1968-69; Calif State Col (now CA St Univ), assoc prof Eng, 1970; Harvard Univ, vis prof, 1974-77; Yale Univ, vis prof, 1976; Carleton Col, Northfield, MN, benedict prof, 1979; Univ Cincinnati, Elliston poet, 1979; Brown Univ, prof Eng, 1970-, Israel J Kapstein prof Eng, 1983-90; Distinguished Minority prof, Univ Del, 1988; distinguished vis prof, Creative Writing, Macalester Col, MN, 1989; numerous vis profships. **Orgs:** Coun mem, Mass Coun Arts & Humanities, 1977-80; judge, Nat Book Award Poetry, 1978; Bicentennial poet Bicentennary Exchange, Britain & USA, 1976; Am spec ICA State Dept tour Africa, 1977; lectr Ger Univ ICA tour nine univ, 1978; ed special issue Carleton Miscellany, 1980 on Ralph Ellison; bd mem, Yaddo Artists Colony Saratoga Springs NY; ed bd TriQuarterly, the Ga Review, Obsidian; ed Collected Poems Sterling A Brown; publ Am Jour by Robert Hayden, 1978; Am Acad Arts & Lett; fel, Am Acad Arts & Sci. **Honors/Awds:** Ctr Advan Study fel, Univ Ill, 1970-71; Black Acad Arts & Lett award, History Is Your Own Heartbeat, 1972; Nat Inst Arts & Lett award & Am Acad award lit, both 1972; Guggenheim Fel, Poetry John Simon Guggenheim Found, 1976; NEA Creative Writing Award, 1977; Poetry Soc Am, Melville-Cane Award for Images of Kin New & Selected Poems, Univ Ill Press, 1978; Nat Book Award nomination for Images of Kin, 1978; Nat Humanities Distinguished Prof Colgate Univ, 1985; Black Academy of Arts & Letters Award, 1971; Carleton Miscellany, on Ralph Ellison, co-ed, 1980; Obsidian, special issue on Robert Hayden, guest ed, 1981; Healing Song of the Inner Ear, 1985; Hon Amendments, 1995; Collected Poems, 1996; Songlines in Michaeltree, 1998; Hon Doctorate Lett, Trinity Col, CT 1987; DHL, Coe Col, 1990; First Poet Laureate, State of RI, 1988-93; Robert Hayden Mem Poetry Award, UNCF, 1990; Phi Beta Kappa, vis scholar, 1991; George Kent Poetry Award, 1996; Claiborne Pell Award for excellence in the Arts, 1997. **Special Achievements:** Published first book of poetry, Dear John, Dear Coltrane, 1970; eight full-length Books of other poems and collections; edited stand collections of African-Am poetry; Books of poems: "Dear John, Dear Coltrane" 1970, History Is Your Own Heartbeat 1971, Song, I Want A Witness 1972, History As Apple Tree 1972, Debridement 1973, Nightmare Begins Responsibility 1975, Images of Kin 1977, Healing Song For The Inner Ear 1985, Chant of Saints 1979; Songlines: Mosaics, 1991; Every Shut Eye Aint Asleep, 1994. **Business Addr:** Professor, Brown University, Department of English, Rm 301 Wilbour Hall, Providence, RI 02912.

HARPER, ROBERT LEE
Dentist. **Personal:** Born Oct 3, 1920, Longview, TX; married Eldora; children: Robert Jr & Beverly. **Educ:** Jarvis Christian Col, 1942; Wiley Col, BA, 1948; Meharry Med Col, DDS, 1952. **Career:** Dent, pvt prac, 1952-77; Jarvis Christian Col, 1960-77. **Orgs:** Secy, E Tex Med Dent & Pharm Asn, 24 yrs; pres, Gulf St Dent Asn, 1962; E Tex Dist Dent Soc; Tex Dent Asn; Am Dent Asn; Nat Dent Asn; Gulf St Dent Asn; Am Soc Dent C; Am Acad Gen Dent; bd dir, Logview C C, 1977; bd, Parks & Rec Prog, 1969-75; Piney Woods Am Red Cross; chmn, adv bd, GoodSamaritan Nursing Home; bd mem, Ment Health Asn Gregg Co; E Tex Area Coun BSA; past mem, bd, Voc Tech Training Longview Ind Sch Dist Hon; Omega Psi Phi Frat; Kappa Sigma Pi Hon Dent Frat. **Honors/Awds:** Recipient Of Clinical of Dentistry, 1952; Silver Beaver Award, Boy Scouts Am, 1966; Omega Man Of the Year, 1967; candidate, City Comnr Longview, 1967. **Military Serv:** USN, yeoman first class, 1942-45. **Business Addr:** Dentist, Harper RL, 1002 S Martin Luther King Blvd, Longview, TX 75602.*

HARPER, RONALD
Basketball player, basketball coach. **Personal:** Born Jan 20, 1964, Dayton, OH. **Educ:** Miami Univ, Oxford, OH, attended 1986. **Career:** Basketball player (retired), basketball coach; Cleveland Cavaliers, guard, 1986-89; Los Angeles Clippers, 1989-94; Chicago Bulls, 1994-99; Los Angeles Lakers, 1999-2001; Detroit Pistons, asst coach, 2005-07. **Honors/Awds:** NBA All-Rookie Team, 1987. **Special Achievements:** Appeared in TV show Kenan and Kel.

HARPER, RONALD J
Lawyer, legal consultant. **Personal:** Born Dec 20, 1945, W Palm Beach, FL; married Betty Vance; children: Ronald Jr & Jennifer. **Educ:** Temple Univ, BA, econs, 1968; Temple Law Sch, JD, 1971. **Career:** Metro Life Ins Co, salesman, 1968; NY Life Ins Co, salesman, 1970; Comt Legal Serv Philadelphia, atty, 1971; OIC Am Inc, atty; Haper & Paul, atty, currently. **Orgs:** Pres, Barristers Asn, 1977; Nat Bar Asn; Philadelphia Bar Asn; Philadelphia Barristers Asn; Am Bar Asn; bd mgr, Temple Univ, 1974; Zion Bapt Church; bd mem, Community Legal Serv. **Business Addr:** Attorney, Harper & Paul, 140 W Maplewood Ave, Philadelphia, PA 19144, **Business Phone:** (215)844-4848.

HARPER, RUTH B.
State government official. **Personal:** Born Dec 24, 1927, Savannah, GA; daughter of Rev Thomas DeLoach and Sallie; married James (deceased); children: Catherine & Deloris (deceased). **Educ:** Beregan Inst Philadelphia, grad; Flamingo Modeling Sch, grad; LaSalle Univ, grad. **Career:** One Hundred & Ninety Sixth Legis Dist, state legislator, 1977-91; Gratz HS, instr; Strawberry Mansion Jr HS, instr; Miss Ebony Pa Scholar Pageant, producer; Ruth Harper's Modeling & Charm Sch, owner & dir, currently. **Orgs:** Nat Dem Comm; Pa Coun Arts; founder & pres, N Cent Philadelphia Women's Pol Caucus; bd mem, YMCA Columbia Br; bd mem, ARC SE Chap; pres, Zion BCCh Womens Serv Guild; life mem, Nat Asn Advan Colored People; Urban League; HOGA Civic League; bd mem, Philadelphia Univ; bd mem, Nat Polit Cong Black Women; Continental Socs Inc; bd dirs, Afro Am Museum; life mem, Nat Coun Negro Women. **Honors/Awds:** Recipient, Citation of Honor, Philadelphia Tribune Newspaper, 1963; Service Award, Nat Asn Advan Colored People, 1964; Bright Hope BC Ch Award, 1965; Cosmopolitan Club Award, 1969; Achievement Award, LaMode Mannequins Inc, 1969; Black Expo Award, 1972; Women in Politics, Cheynew State Univ, 1978; Freedom Award, Nat Asn Advan Colored People, 1978; Service Award, YMCA, 1979. **Business Addr:** Owner, Ruth Harper Modeling School, 1427 W Erie Ave, Philadelphia, PA 19140, **Business Phone:** (215)225-4268.

HARPER, SARA J.
Judge. **Personal:** Born Aug 10, 1926, Cleveland, OH; daughter of James Weldon and Leila Smith. **Educ:** Western Res Univ, BS; Franklin Thomas Backus Sch Law, Western Reserve Univ, LLB. **Career:** Judge (retired); Eighth Appellate Dist, Cuyahoga, OH, judge. **Orgs:** Judicial coun & historian, Nat Bar Asn; OH Vet Hall Fame; life mem, Mt Olive Baptist Church. **Honors/Awds:** Victims Award, OH Ct Claims, 1990; Ohio Women's Hall of Fame, 1991; OH Supreme Courts Excellent Judicial Service Award; Unsung Heroine Award; Raymond Pace Alexander Award; Hall of Fame,

Nat Bar Asn. **Special Achievements:** First African American woman to graduate from Case Western Reserve University Law School; first woman to serve on the judiciary of the USMCR; Ohio Supreme Ct first African American woman Judge. **Military Serv:** USMCR, Mil judge, lt col, 1986.

HARPER, SHARI BELAFONTE. See BELAFONTE, SHARI.

HARPER, T ERROL
President (Organization), automotive executive. **Personal:** Born Feb 12, 1947, Birmingham, AL; son of Rev Theophilus E and Callie O; married Elaine Betz, Mar 23, 1975; children: Rena Nicole & Zachary Jordan. **Educ:** Morris Brown Col, Atlanta, GA, BA, 1970. **Career:** Ernst & Ernst, Philadelphia PA, auditor, 1970-73; Philadelphia '76 Inc, Philadelphia, PA, controller, 1973-74; Dupont Co, Wilmington, DE, staff acct, 1974-76; Ford Motor Co, Dearborn MI, dealer trainee, 1977-78; Phillips Ford Inc, Conshohocken PA, bus mgr, 1978-79; Harper Pontiac Inc, Upper Darby PA, pres, 1979-82; Heritage Lincoln-Mercury, Hackensack NJ, pres, 1983; Queen City Lincoln-Mercury, pres, currently. **Orgs:** Dir, Com & Indust Asn NJ, 1985-; United Way Bergen Co, 1985-92; Hackensack Lions Club, 1987-; dir & former vpres, Black Ford & Lincoln-Mercury Minority Dealer Asn, 1989-91; Lincoln-Mercury Div Nat Dealer Coun; adv coun, Univ Okla; bd dir, Better Bus Bur, 2002; 100 Black Men in Charlotte; dir & secy, C Aid & Adoption Soc. **Honors/Awds:** Hon Doctor Humanities, Monrova Col, Monrovia, Liberia, 1986. **Military Serv:** USMCR, corporal, 1970-74. **Business Phone:** (704)553-8300.

HARPER, TERRY JOE
Baseball player. **Personal:** Born Aug 19, 1955, Douglasville, GA. **Career:** Baseball player (retired); Atlanta Braves, amateur draft, 1973,outfielder, 1980-86; Detroit Tigers, outfielder, 1987; Pittsburgh Pirates, outfielder, 1987; Yakult Swallows (Tokyo), 1988. **Honors/Awds:** Braves Minor League Player of the Month, 1982.

HARPER, THELMA MARIE
State government official. **Personal:** Born Dec 2, 1940, Williamson County, TN; daughter of William Claybrooks and Clora Thomas Claybrooks; married Paul Wilson Harper, 1957; children: Dylan Wayne & Linda Gail. **Educ:** Tenn State Univ, BS, business admin & acct, 1978. **Career:** Paul Harper's Convenience Markets, entrepreneur; financial analyst; city councilwoman; Tenn Senate, 19th dist, sen, 1991-. **Orgs:** Davidson Co Dem Womens' Club; Cable Inc; Nat Hook-up Black Women; Nashville Women's Polit Caucus; YWCA Advisory Comt Links Inc; Delta Sigma Theta Sorority Inc. **Honors/Awds:** First Black female ever elected to Tenn state senate. **Business Addr:** Senator, Tennessee State Senate, 8 Legislative Plz, Nashville, TN 37243-0219.

HARPER, TOMMY
Baseball player, consultant. **Personal:** Born Oct 14, 1940, Oak Grove, LA; son of Ulysses and Louetta Weir; married Bonnie Jean Williams, Oct 6, 1962. **Career:** Baseball player (retired), consultant; Cincinnati Reds, player, 1962-67; Cleveland Indians, player, 1968; Seattle Pilots, baseball player, 1969; Milwaukee Brewers, player, 1970-71; Boston Red Sox, 1972-74, spec asst to gen mgr, pub rels, minor league instr, 1978-79, asst dir, mkt & promotions, 1980, major league coach, 1981-84, spec asst to gen mgr, 1985-86; coach, 1980-84, 2000-02, player develop consult, 2003-; Calif Angels, 1975; Oakland Athletics, 1975; Baltimore Orioles, 1976; NY Yankees, minor league instr, 1977-78; Montreal Expos, minor league instr, 1988-89, major league coach, 1990, coach, 1990-99. **Honors/Awds:** Seattle Post Intelligtencer, Man of the Year, 1969; Milwaukee Brewers, Most Valuable Player, 1970; Boston Red Sox, Most Valuable Player, 1973. **Special Achievements:** First black coach in Boston Red Sox history. **Business Phone:** (617)267-9440.

HARPER, WALTER EDWARD
Educator. **Personal:** Born Jul 10, 1950, Chicago, IL; son of Walter Edward Harper Sr and Elizabeth Mercer. **Educ:** Loyola Univ, Chicago, IL, AB, hist, 1972, MA, coun psychol, 1978; Inst Psychoanal, Chicago, IL, cert, teacher educ prog, 1979; Loyola Univ, Chicago, IL, post grad studies, 1986; Brown Univ, AM, anthrop, 1996; Doctoral study, currently. **Career:** Precious Brood Grammar Sch, Chicago, IL, teacher, 1972-74; Loyola Univ,Chicago, IL, adminr, 1974-79; N Park Col, Chicago, IL, teacher & counr, 1979-86; Brown Univ, Providence RI, asst dir financial aid, 1986-, post doctrol fel, currently; Urban League RI, health consult, 1996-; Salveregina Univ, instr, Sociol dept, currently, asst prof, currently. **Orgs:** Bd mem, Eisenberg Chicago Boy & Girls Club, 1978, Loyola Univ, UpwardBound Prog, 1978; C G Jung Ctr, 1980; bd mem, Friendship House, Chicago, 1981; Ill Psychol Asn, 1982, Phi Delta Kappa, Loyola Univ Chap, 1982; fel, Soc Values Higher Educ, 1982; Asn Black Admis & Financial Aid Admin, IvyLeague & Sister Schs, 1986; workshop leader, High Sch Summer Intern Prog, Philadelphia Daily News, 1987; workshop leader, Atlanta Dream Jamboree, 1988, 1989; mgt develop prog, Brown Univ, 1988; Eastern Asn Financial Aid Admin; adv, NAACP Stud Chap, 1990, co-chairperson, Campus Ministry Affairs Comm, 1990; pres, Santore Soc, 1990-91, Brown Univ; bd mem, AIDs Proj RI; bd mem, Community Prep Sch; bd mem, Providence Black Repertory Co; bd mem, Stone Soup Found; vol, Providence Sch Dept. **Honors/Awds:** Certificate of Merit, Chicago, Youth Ctr, 1975; Most Eligible Bachelor/Promising Minority Professional, Ebony Mag, 1976; Citizen Citation, City Providence; Recognition Award, Keep Am Beautiful; Volunteer of the Year, Planned Parenthood RI. **Home Phone:** (401)751-0319. **Business Addr:** Teacher, College Adminstrator, Consultant, Salve Regina University, Sociology Department, 100 Ochre Point Ave, Newport, RI 02840-4192, **Business Phone:** (401)847-6650.

HARPER, WILLIAM THOMAS, III
Psychologist, educator. **Personal:** Born Sep 10, 1956, Newport News, VA; son of William T Jr and Queen V. **Educ:** Va State Col, Petersburg, BS, psychol, 1978, MEd, coun, 1980; Hampton Univ, VA, attended 1984; Col William & Mary, Williamsburg, VA, attended 1987; Old Dominion Univ, PhD, educ & psychol, 1991. **Career:** Hampton Univ, VA, dir stud support servs, 1980-88; USY, Arlington, VA, psychologist & educr, 1986; Olde Hampton Bus Educ Ctr, VA, asst prof, psychologist, vres, 1987-; Norfolk State Univ, VA, dir undeclared students, 1989-; Old Dominion Univ, Norfolk, VA, asst prof coun, 1990. **Orgs:** Undergrad adv, 1982-88, chmn youth guide right, alumni chap, 1987-89, Kappa Alpha Psi Fraternity; comt chmn, Va Asn Black Psychologists, 1987-; counr, Peninsula Literacy Coun, 1982-88; comt chmn, Va Asn Adminr Higher Educ; bd gov, International Platform Asn, 1990. **Honors/Awds:** Recognition for Achievement, Christopher Newport College, 1985, 1986; Certificate of Recognition, William & Mary Col, 1990, 1991; Black Student Retention Conference Recognition, 1989, 1990; Volunteer Program Achievement Award, Sarah Bonwell Hudgins Regional Center, 1989, 1990; Black American Doctoral Research Award, 1991, 1992; Armed Services Recognition, YMCA, 1990; Roads Recognition, Boys Club of Greater Hampton, 1990; Office of Human Affairs Achievement Award, 1990. **Home Addr:** 204 Dogwood Dr, Newport News, VA 23606. *

HARPS, WILLIAM S.
Real estate executive. **Personal:** Born Jul 3, 1916, Philadelphia, PA; son of Richard Harps and Blanche Hobbs Harps; married Justine McNeil, Nov 14, 1942; children: Richard & Eunice. **Educ:** Howard Univ, BS, 1943. **Career:** Real Estate Executive (retired); John R Pinkett Inc, first vpres, 1939-44; WA Bd Realtors, chmn; Am Inst Real Estate Appraisers, nat pres, 1981; Harps & Harps Inc Real Estate Appraisers & Counr, pres & chief exec officer, 1984. **Orgs:** Bd dir, Met Police Boys Club, 1963-; bd trustees, Fed City Coun, 1969-; vpres, bd trustees, Childrens Hosp, 1969-; bd mem, Tax Equalization & Rev,1970-74; Mayors Econ Develop Community, 1970-74; DC Comn Judicial Disabilities & Tenure, 1971-75; bd dirs, Columbia Title Ins Co; Nat Bank,WA, 1971-86; Pepertual Fed Sav & Loan Asn, 1971-87; pres, WA Chap 18 Am Inst Real Estate Appraisers, 1976; pres, WA Bd Realtors, 1977; consult,Dist Title Ins, 1984-; pres, Wash DC Asn Realtors, 1985; exec Comm, NAR, 1986-87; chmn, Housing Comm Legis Community NAR, 1989; int pres, Am Inst Real Estate Appraisers, 1968-81; Soc Real Estate Appraisers; nat past pres, Nat Soc Real Estate Appraisers; NY Real Estate Bd; Wash Real Estate Brokers Asn; Lambda Alpha On Land Econ; Investors 15 Inc; Soc Real Estate Counr. **Honors/Awds:** Metro Womens Democratic Club Award, 1971; Alumni Award, Howard Univ, 1972;Jos Allard Award, Am Inst Real Estate Appraisers, 1974; Realtor Year, 1980 & 1988; Awarded Martin Eisen Award, Wash DC Asn Realtors, 1986. **Home Addr:** 1111 14th St NW, Washington, DC 20005.

HARRELL, ADAM NELSON
Lawyer. **Educ:** Univ Va, BA; Univ Pa Sch Law, JD. **Career:** Harrell & Chambliss LLP, atty, currently, co-managing partner, currently. **Orgs:** Metrop Bus League, 2002-; Exec Comt, Old Dominion Bar Asn; Third Dist Comt, Va State Bar; Lawyers Helping Lawyers Comt, Va Bar Asn; Virginia Bd Asbestos Licensing & Lead Certification; bd dirs, Greater Richmond Chap, Am Red Cross; bd dirs, Richmond Chap, Nat Coun Community & Justice. **Business Addr:** Attorney, Co-Managing Partner, Harrell & Chambliss LLP, 707 E Main St Suite 1000, Richmond, VA 23219, **Business Phone:** (804)915-3237.

HARRELL, ANDRE
Executive, music producer. **Personal:** Born Sep 26, 1960, Harlem, NY; children: Gianni. **Educ:** Lehman Col, commmuns major, attended. **Career:** With Alonzo Brown, formed Dr. Jekyll & Mr. Hyde (rap duo); Rush Mgt, vpres & gen mgr, 1985; Uptown Records, founder & pres, 1987-92; Uptown Entertainment, pres, 1992-95; "New York Undercover", producer, 1994-96; Motown Records, pres & ceo, 1996-98; Bad Boy Entertainment, pres, 1999-2001; Nu Am Music, founder & chief executive officer, 2001-05; Bad Boy TV, producer, 2005-06; consult, currently. *

HARRELL, CHARLES H (CHUCK HARRELL)
Automotive executive. **Career:** Harrell Chevrolet-Oldsmobile Inc, Flat Rock, MI, chief exec officer, currently. **Orgs:** Gen Motors Minority Dealer Asn, pres, currently. **Business Phone:** (734)782-2421.

HARRELL, CHUCK. See HARRELL, CHARLES H.

HARRELL, ERNEST JAMES
Military leader. **Personal:** Born Oct 30, 1936, Selma, AL; son of William (deceased) and Arrilla Moorer (deceased); married Paola Boone Harrell, Jun 22, 1962; children: Ernest J II, Jolene. **Educ:** Tuskegee Inst, Tuskegee, AL, BS, 1960; Ariz State Univ, Tempe, AZ, MS, 1972. **Career:** Military leaderv (retired); AUS, various locations, gen officer, commissioned officer, 1960; EH & Assocs, consulting engr. **Orgs:** Dean pledges, Omega Psi Phi Fraternity, 1958-60; vice chair, discipline comt, Ariz State Univ, 1967-70; regional vpres, Soc Am Mil Engrs, 1986-91, fel, 1988. **Military Serv:** AUS, Major General; Distinguished Service Medal, 1995; Legion of Merit, 1986, Bronze Star Medal, 1967, Meritorious Service Medal (3), 1971, 1979, 1982, Army Commendation Medal, 1970, Combat Infantryman Badge, Airborne Badge. *

HARRELL, H STEVE
Automotive executive. **Personal:** Born Apr 25, 1948; son of James and Lula Bell Thomas; divorced; children: Shemanthe E Smith & H Steve II. **Career:** Shelby Dodge, Memphis, TN, pres, 1987-; H S Harrell Real Estate Invest, Atlanta, GA, pres, 1978-. **Orgs:** Dist chmn, Boy Scouts Am. **Business Addr:** President, Shelby Dodge Inc, 2691 Mt Moriah Rd, Memphis, TN 38115, **Business Phone:** (901)363-0006.

HARRELL, OSCAR W., II
Consultant. **Personal:** Born in Bristol, VA; son of Oscar Harrell Sr and Bernice W Harrell; married Sophia M; children: Oscar W III & Stafford B. **Educ:** Va Union Univ, BA, social sci, 1960; Assumption Col, Mass, CAGS, 1974; res fel Northeastern Univ, attended 1990; Brandeis Univ, PhD, 1994. **Career:** Leonard Training Sch NC Bd Corr, head counr, 1963-64; Gardner State Hosp, psych Soc Worker, 1964-67; Rutland Heights Hosp, coord rehab, 1967-72; Mt Wachusett Community Col, fac, 1968; Fitchburg State Col, asst dir admis, dir minority affairs/AID, 1974-81; Fitchburg State Col, fac, 1976-80; Tufts Univ, dir african am ctr, 1981-87; Mass Dept Ment Retardation, de passt comn, 1987-90; Assumption Col, Inst Social & Rehab Serv, consult & educr, 1996-2000; Harrell & Harrell Inc, consult, currently. **Orgs:** Mem & bd dir, Mass Ment Health Asn, 1969-89; Am Psychol Asn, 1976-78; Am Personnel Guid Asn, 1976-78; Am Rehab Coun Asn, 1976-78; sec & pres, Soc Organized Against Racism, 1982-; treas, Greater Boston Inter Univ Coun; Alpha Phi Alpha Fraternity; Mass Halfway House Asn; former pres, Mass Branch Nat Asn Advan Colored People; vpres Mass Asn Ment Health; comt mem, Racial Justice Comn; Nat YWCA; bd dirs, Community Change Inc, Boston MA; bd ordained ministry, United Methodist Church, New England Conf; bd mem, Deaconess Abundant Life Communities. **Honors/Awds:** City Representative, Gardner Massachusetts Opportunity Coun, 1970-72; Citation, Gov Mass, 1981; Citation, Mass Senate, 1987; Citation, Mass House of Rep, 1987; Plaque Appreciation as Dir African Am Ctr, Tufts Black Alumni. **Special Achievements:** Performer (non-professional) in the play "The Man Nobody Saw"; plaque, Outstanding Supporter of Education, Fitchburg Faculty, 1990. **Military Serv:** AUS E-5, 1960-62. **Home Addr:** 15 Bent Brook Rd, Sudbury, MA 01776. **Business Addr:** Board Member, Deaconess Abundant Life Communities, 80 Deaconess Rd, Concord, MA 01742, **Business Phone:** (978)369-5151.

HARRELL, DR. PAULA
Educator. **Career:** NC Cent Univ, Dept Music, chairwoman, currently. **Orgs:** Int Asn Jazz Educ. **Business Addr:** Chairwoman, North Carolina Central University, College of Ats and Science Department of Music, 204 1801 Fayetteville St, Durham, NC 27707, **Business Phone:** (919)530-7213.

HARRELL, WILLIAM EDWIN
Government official. **Personal:** Born Mar 16, 1962, Norfolk, VA; son of Adam Sr and Charity Nix; married Johnna Carson, Nov 19, 1988; children: Charity Majette. **Educ:** Univ Va, BS, 1984, MS, 1986, MPA, 1986. **Career:** City Suffolk, Suffolk, VA, aide analyst, 1986, sr admin analyst, 1986-87,dir mgt servs, 1987-90, dir pub utilities, 1990-95; City Greensboro, NC,asst city mgr; City Richmond, interim chief admin officer, 2005-07; Chesapeake City, VA, city mgr, 2007-. **Orgs:** Bd dirs, Suffolk Chamber Com, 1988-; fund distrib comt, United Way-SuffolkDiv, 1988-90; vpres, Great Bridge-Chesapeake Jaycees, 1989; Int City MgrAsn, 1986-89; Am Soc Pub Admin, 1986-88; vice chmn, Com Diversity, AmWaterworks Asn; Conf Minority Pub Adminr; trustee, St John's AME Church. **Honors/Awds:** G. Robert House Young Public Administrator Award, Virginia Chapter for the American Society for Public Administration. **Business Addr:** City Manager, Chesapeake City, 306 Cedar Rd 6th Fl, PO Box 15225, Chesapeake, VA 23219, **Business Phone:** (757)382-6166.

HARRIGAN, RODNEY EMILE
Administrator. **Personal:** Born Jul 23, 1945, New York City, NY; married Elaine Mims; children: Pamela & Sherrice. **Educ:** Paine Col, BS, math, 1967; IBM System Res Inst, attended 1969; Howard Univ, MS, comput sci, 1975. **Career:** Royal Globe Ins Co, programmer, 1968; Fed City Col, assoc prof, 1977; Howard Univ, assoc prof, 1977; IBM, systems engr, 1968-72, staff programmer, 1972-75, proj mgr, 1975-76, adv proj mgr, 1976-77, systems eng mgr, 1977-79; Post Col, instr, 1980-81; IBM, employee rels mgr, 1979-81, spec proj mgr, 1981-82, fac loan prof, 1982-92; NC A&T Univ, prof, comput sci, currently; NC A&T State Univ, Info Technol & Telecommunications, vice

chancellor, chief info officer, currently. **Orgs:** Asn Computing Machinery; Data Processing Mgt Asn; Inst Elec Electron Engrs; Compu Soc; Alpha Kappa Mu Honor Soc; Omega Psi Phi Fraternity. **Honors/Awds:** Scholar of the Year, Alpha Kappa Mu, 1966; Honor Graduate Award, 1967; President Award, Paine Col, 1967; Golden Circle Award, IBM, 1975; Symposium Award, IBM 1972, 1974-76; 100% Club Award, IBM, 1977-78 1981; Young Executive of Hartford Leadership Award, 1982; Operation Push Hartford Chapter Award, 1981-82; ACM Award, NCA&J State Univ, 1984. **Special Achievements:** 100 Most Important Blacks in Technol, US Black Engr & Info Technol Mag, 2006. **Business Addr:** Vice Chancellor, CIO, North Carolina A&T State University, Dowdy Bldg Rm 307, Greensboro, NC 27411-0002, **Business Phone:** (336)256-0544.

HARRINGTON, DENISE MARION
Consultant, executive. **Personal:** Born Apr 14, 1955, Washington, DC; daughter of Harold Greene and Alma; married Michael, Jan 14, 1989; children: Nia. **Educ:** Univ DC, music & voice; Dartmouth Col, Tuck Sch Exec Mgmt. **Career:** Harrington & Assocs, founder & chief exec officer, 1990-. **Orgs:** Bd, Classroom Law Pro; adv bd chair, Boys & Girls Club Portland, 1992-. **Special Achievements:** Worked with Tiger Woods, Ken Griffey Jr, Vlade Divac, Michael Johnson, Mia Hann, Sheryl Snoopes, among others. **Business Addr:** Founder, Chief Executive Officer, Harrington & Associates, 1500 NE Irving St Suite 410, Portland, OR 97232, **Business Phone:** (503)236-5336.

HARRINGTON, ELAINE CAROLYN
Educator. **Personal:** Born Aug 31, 1938, Philadelphia, PA. **Educ:** Tuskegee Inst, BS, elem educ, 1961; A&T State Univ, grad study, 1964; Univ Conn, Storrs, MA, supr admin, 1972; Fairleigh Dickinson Univ, develop educ, attended. **Career:** JC Price Sch, teacher, 1961-71; A&T State Univ, demonstration teacher, 1965; Shiloh Baptist Church, dir cultural prog, 1967; A&T State Univ, matls co-ord mus inst jr high students, 1968; Passaic Comm Col, prof & actg dean stud, 1972-80, prof acad founds, 1980-87, Eng & Math dept, prof, 1988-2005, prof emer, 2005-; Univ Pittsburgh, Seminar fel, 1980. **Orgs:** Soloist Radio City Music Hall NY City, 1958; pres, secy, NCEA & NJEA Educ Org, 1961-05; NEA, 1961-05; secy, Zeta Phi Beta Sorority Inc, 1963-; Nat Alliance Black Sch Educrs, 1973-; Am Personnel & Guidance Asn, 1976-; YWCA; Christ Ch United Method; Paterson Bd Educ; chairperson, Reg II, Nat Asn Advan Colored People, pres, Paterson Br, pres, NJ State, 1993-99; layleader, Admin Coun Chair-Christ Church United Methodist, Paterson, NJ; Nat Bd Dirs. **Honors/Awds:** Outstanding Young Educator Award, Greensboro Public Schs, NC, 1968; Participant Leadership Seminar Guilford Co Schs, NC, 1969; Gradute Scholarship, Zeta Phi Beta Sorority Inc, 1971; NEH, 1980. **Special Achievements:** Professor Elaine C Harrington Lecture Hall; Professor Elaine C Harrington Scholarship. **Business Addr:** Professor Emeritus, Passaic County Community College, One Col Blvd, Paterson, NJ 07505, **Business Phone:** (973)684-6868.*

HARRINGTON, GERALD E
Banker. **Personal:** Born Jan 1, 1945?, Detroit, MI. **Educ:** Tenn State Univ, attended 1967. **Career:** First Independence Nat Bank, sr vpres & cashier, ceo, 1974-90. **Orgs:** Am Inst Banking; Bank Admin Inst. **Business Phone:** (313)256-8200.

HARRINGTON, JOHN M.
Police chief. **Educ:** St Thomas, MA, pub safety, 1985. **Career:** St Paul Police Dept, chief, currently. **Military Serv:** AUS, sergeant, lt, sr comdr & comdr. *

HARRINGTON, OTHELLA
Basketball player. **Personal:** Born Jan 31, 1974, Jackson, MS; married Shannon. **Educ:** Georgetown univ, attended 1998. **Career:** Houston Rockets, forward-centre, 1996-99; Vancouver Grizzlies, 1999-2001; New York Knicks, forward-centre, 2001-04; Chicago Bulls, 2004-06; Charlotte Bobcats, power forward-center, 2006-08. **Business Addr:** Professional Basketball Player, Charlotte Bobcats, 333 East Trade St, Charlotte, NC 28202, **Business Phone:** (704)688-8600.*

HARRINGTON, PHILIP LEROY
Educator. **Personal:** Born Apr 27, 1946, Southern Pines, NC; son of Neville W and Blanche McNeil; married Chandra Salvi, Sep 15, 1968; children: Kafi Nakpangi, Kamala Nwena. **Educ:** NC Cent Univ, Durham, NC, BS, 1968. **Career:** Roxbury Multi-Serv Ctr, Boston, MA, educ prog dir, 1972-74; Lena Park Community Develop Corp, Boston, MA, prog dir, 1974-76; Action Boston Community Develop, Boston, MA, admin, 1976-81; Dover-Sherborn Regional Schs, Dover, MA, 1981-; Indeprep Sch, Boston, MA, founder, dir, 1985-88; Freedom House, Boston, MA, consult, 1988-. **Orgs:** Educator, Mass Dept Educ, 1974-77; Youth Motivation Task Force Nat Alliance Bus, 1975-78; bd mem, Inner City Coun C, 1976-80; dir, Boston Youth Develop Prog, 1978-80; Omega Psi Phi Fraternity, Iota Chi Chap, 1982-; pres, founder, Parents Black Studs Buckingham, Browne & Nichols, 1984-88; review comt, Mass Arts Coun, 1984-87; bd mem, Nat Alliance Black Sch Educrs, 1987-; vpres, Black Educators Alliance Mass, 1988-. **Honors/Awds:** Performed in Black Nativity, produced by Nat Ctr Afro-Am Artists, Boston, MA, 1984-89; Honoree, Mus Afro-Am Hist, Boston, MA, 1988; Certificate of Recognition, Mayor Boston, 1988. **Home Addr:** 27 Walden St, Cambridge, MA 02140. *

HARRINGTON, ZELLA MASON
Administrator, nurse. **Personal:** Born Jan 29, 1940, St Louis, MO; married Melvyn A; children: Melvyn A, Jr, Kevin Mason. **Educ:** Jewish Hosp Sch Nursing, dipl, 1960; Webster Col, BA, 1976; Webster Col, MA, 1977. **Career:** Vis Nurses Asn, sr staff nurse, 1960-65; Nursery Found St Louis, nurse consult, 1963-65; St Louis, Bd Educ, practical nursing instr, 1966; Cardinal Ritter Inst, chief nurse trainer, 1966-68; Vis Nurses Asn, sr staff nurse, 1960-65; Urban League St Louis, health specialist, 1968-69; Nursing & Health Servs ARC, dir, 1969-; St Louis Div Health, chief health prom & educ, 2001. **Orgs:** Pres, secy, treas, MO State Bd Nursing, 1974-; pres, vice pres, bd dirs, Family Planning Coun Inc, 1976-77; Health Adv Com Human Devel Corp, 1977-; bd dirs, Maternal & Child Health Coun Inc, 1978-; fac panel mem, St Louis Univ Sch Comm Med, 1976-79; comm consult, Maternal & ChildHealth Coun Inc, 1979-; ANA, 1961-80; Jack & Jill Am Inc, 1970-; Nat League Nursing, 1977-80. **Honors/Awds:** Assisted with pub "Handbook for Home Health Aides" Cardinal & Ritter Inst 1968; listed Outstanding Contributions of Blacks in Health Care Delta Sigma Theta Sorority 1977; George Washington Carver Award, Sigma Gamma Rho Sorority 1978. *

HARRIS, AL (ALSHINARD HARRIS)
Football player. **Personal:** Born Dec 7, 1974, Pompano Beach, FL; married Shyla, Mar 1, 2007; children: Alshinard Jr & Gavin. **Educ:** Tex A&M Univ, Kingsville, kinesiol. **Career:** Tampa Bay Buccaneers, Off season/squad member, 1997; Philadelphia Eagles, defensive back, 1998-2002; Green Bay Packers, corner back, 2003-. **Honors/Awds:** Pro Bowler Selection Twice, 2007-08; All Pro Selection, 2007. **Business Addr:** Conerback, Green Bay Packers, 1265 Lombardi Ave, PO Box 10628, Green Bay, WI 54304, **Business Phone:** (920)569-7500.

HARRIS, AL CARL
Football player, public speaker. **Personal:** Born Dec 31, 1956, Bangor, ME; son of Alfred C Jr and Gloria Smith; married Margaret D, Apr 7, 1990; children: Emily & Jason. **Educ:** Ariz State Univ, BS, 1982. **Career:** Football player (retired), Motivational speaker; Chicago Bears, linebacker1979-88; Philadelphia Eagles, 1989-90; Ambassador Speakers Bur & Lit Agency, speaker, currently. **Orgs:** Founder, Faith God Found; served churches, banquets, companies, corporations and charities, as well as doing chapels for professional baseball and football teams. **Special Achievements:** First unanimous all-American selection in Arizona State University history. **Business Addr:** Motivational Speaker, Ambassador Speakers Bureau & Literary Agency, 1107 Battlewood St, PO Box 50358, Franklin, TN 37069, **Business Phone:** (615)370-4700.

HARRIS, ALONZO
Judge. **Personal:** Born Jul 20, 1961, Opelousas, LA; son of Aaron and Rosa B; married Dawn W Harris, Dec 19, 1989; children: Ashley, Lanisha, Valenia, Alonzo Jr, Alexis. **Educ:** Southern Univ, BS, 1983, Law Ctr, JD, 1986. **Career:** Harris & Harris Law Firm, atty law, 1983-87; La Secy State 27th Judicial Dist, dist judge, 1993-. **Orgs:** La Bar Asn, 1987; SW Lawyers Asn, 1990-; La Judicial Col, 1993; Am Asn Juv Judges, 1994; Opelousas Rotary Club, 1994. *

HARRIS, ANTHONY
Executive. **Personal:** Born Jun 27, 1953, Chicago, IL; son of Roy and Alberta; married Angela C Harris; children: Anthony & Alexander. **Educ:** Purdue Univ, BS, mech engineering, 1975; Harvard Bus Sch, MBA, 1979. **Career:** Standard Oil Co, Indiana, proj engr & design engr, 1975-79; Ford Motor Co, quality & prod supvr, 1979-81; Eastern Mich Univ, vis lectr, 1980-81; Ford Aerospace & Communs, prog mgr, 1981-86; Anaheim Lincoln Mercury, gen mgr, 1986-87; Sonoma Ford Lincoln Mercury, pres & chief exec oficer, 1987-92; Pacific Gas & Electric Co, vpres sales & mktg, 1995-96, vpres nat acct servs & western region sales; Pacific Conserv Corp, chief exec officer, 1995-96, vpres bus customer serv, 1996-2001; Calpine Corp, vpres mkt, currently. **Orgs:** Founder & adv bd, Nat Soc Black Eng, 1975-; vice pres, 100 Black Men Am, 1990-92; bd dirs, OICW, 1994-; bd dirs, Oakland Museum, 1995-; bd dirs, Marcus Foster Found, 1996-; pres & adv bd, Sonoma State Col, Purdue Univ,; Am Soc Mech Engrs; Soc Automotive Engrs. **Honors/Awds:** Founders Plaque, NSBE, 1996; Eagle Award, Black Employees Asn, 1995; Purdue Outstanding Mechanical Engineer, 1999. **Business Addr:** Vice President of Marketing, Calpine Corporation, 50 W San Fernando St, San Jose, CA 95113, **Business Phone:** (408)995-5115.

HARRIS, ARCHIE JEROME
Executive. **Personal:** Born Dec 2, 1950, Atlanta, GA; son of Richard E Harris Sr and Essie Lee Brown; children: Ajeenah K Harris. **Educ:** Morehouse Col, BA, 1972; Univ GA, MA, Educ, 1978. **Career:** Atlanta Public Sch Syst, sub teacher, 1972-74; AP Jarrell Pre-Voc Ctr, work adjustment inst, 1974-75; Bobby Dodd Rehab & Industry Ctr, voc eval, 1975-77; Rehab-Exposure Inc, pres 1983-; GA Dept Human Resources, Div Rehab Serv, sr rehab counr, 1977-88; Rehab-Exposure Inc, Atlanta, GA, pres, dir, 1999. **Orgs:** Mental Health Asn Metro Atlanta, 1983-; Statewide Minority Advocacy Group against Alcohol & Drug Abuse, 1984-86; pres, Atlanta Chapt Asn Black Psychologists; pres, 1984-86, vice pres, 1990-, Atlanta Chapt Statewide Minority Advocacy Group for Alcohol & Drug Prevention, 1987-; bd mem, Mental Health Asn Metropolitan Atlanta, 1989-; chmn, Multicultural Resource Ctr, Mental Health Asn, 1989-. **Honors/Awds:** Awards for Outstanding Serv & Dedication, SMAGADAP, 1983-86; Outstanding Young Men Am, 1984-85; Outstanding Serv Awd, Nigerian Student Coun, 1985; Bobby E Wright Community Serv Award, Asn Black Psychologists, 1987, 1999; Mentor of the Year Award, Big Brothers Big Sisters Metrop Atlanta, 1988; Community Award, Chi Eta Phi, Gamma Chi chp, 1991; Cert Appreciation, GA Black United Fund, 1998; Partnership Award, Atlanta Black United Fund, 1999; Cert Appreciation, Nat Asn Black Social Workers, 2000. **Home Addr:** 1948 Creekside Ct, Decatur, GA 30032. **Business Addr:** President, Director, Rehab Exposure Inc, 1513 Cloveland Ave Suite 105 A, East Point, GA 30344.*

HARRIS, ARTHUR L
Association executive. **Personal:** Born Feb 14, 1935, Texarkana, AR; son of Charlie Harris and Dorthy Johnson; married Martha A, Dec 29, 1967; children: Lisa A, Alfred L & Arthur L Jr. **Educ:** San Diego City Col, assoc sci, 1981. **Career:** US Postal Serv, 1976-80; Defense Finance & Acct Serv, Dept Defense, acct tech, 1981-97; CA Veterans Bd, 1991-96. **Orgs:** Life mem, Disabled Am Veterans; life mem, Fleet Res Asn; post comdr, 1984-86, dist comdr, 1989-90, state comdr, 2000-01, Veterans Foreign Wars. **Special Achievements:** First African Am Triple Crown Comdr, Veterans Foreign Wars of the USA. **Military Serv:** USN, 1955-96; Navy Achievement Medal, Good Conduct. **Home Addr:** 8759 Dewsbury Ave, San Diego, CA 92126-2427. **Business Addr:** Past State Commander, Department of California, 1510 J St Suite 110, Sacramento, CA 95814, **Business Phone:** (916)449-8850.

HARRIS, DR. ARTHUR LEONARD
Educator. **Personal:** Born Jul 12, 1949, Pittsburgh, PA; married Wendy; children: Arthur L IV & Wesley P. **Educ:** Community Col Allegheny County, AS, 1971; Temple Univ, BA, 1973; Univ Mass, MEd, 1976, EdD, 1986. **Career:** Univ Mass, grad asst, 1973-74; Brd Educ Springfield, MA, classroom instr,1974-82; Pa State Schuylkill Campus, prog asst, 1982-84; Pa State Univ,Hazleton, dir continuing educ, 1984-, Dept African Am Studies, instr, currently. **Orgs:** Bd mem, Hazleton Leadership; past master, Mt Nebo 118 Prince Hall Affiliated; Nat Univ Continuing Educ Asn; mem, Hazleton Area Chamber Com;City Coun, Pottsville, PA, 1994-. **Home Addr:** 319 N 3rd St, Pottsville, PA 17901. **Business Addr:** Instructor, Pennsylvania State University, Department African American Studies, 76 Univ Dr 107 Mem Bldg, Hazleton, PA 18202, **Business Phone:** (570)450-3111.

HARRIS, BARBARA ANN
Judge. **Personal:** Born Jul 18, 1951, Atlanta, GA; daughter of Rev Thomas Harris Sr. **Educ:** Harvard Univ, AB, cum laude, 1973; Univ Mich Law Sch, JD, 1976. **Career:** Ga Supreme Ct, Justice Charles L Weltner, law clerk, 1976-77; Northern Dist Ga, asst US atty, 1977-82; Atlanta Munic Ct, assoc judge, 1982-92, chief judge, criminal Law, 1992-. **Orgs:** Bd dirs, Am Judicature Soc; Eta Phi Beta, 1980-; State Bar Ga; bd mem, Determine Fitness Bar Applicants Supreme Ct Ga; exec comn, Gate City Bar Asn, 1985-87; co-founder Ga Asn Black Women Attys; bd mem: Am Bar Asn, Nat Conf Spec Ct Judges; judicial coun, Nat Bar Asn; exec comn, Leadership Atlanta, 1987-88; Officer, Atlanta Womens Network; Drifters Inc, Nat parliamentarian, 1990-; bd mem, Lit Vol; Ga Supreme Ct, Comn Race & Ethnic Bias, 1993-95, Comn Equality, 1993-, Comn Substance Abuse, 1995-. **Honors/Awds:** One Ga 50 Most Influential Black Women; Ga Coaltion Black Women, 1984; NAACP Award, 1985; Recognized Amicus Curiae, Supreme Ct Ga, 1995; Torch Award, Delta Simga Theta, 1995; 2006 Georgia Association of Black Women Attorneys Award. **Special Achievements:** First woman to serve in such capacity. **Business Addr:** Chief Judge, Municipal Court of Atlanta, 150 Garnett St SW, Atlanta, GA 30303-3612, **Business Phone:** (404)658-6940.

HARRIS, BARBARA CLEMENTE
Clergy, executive. **Personal:** Born 1931. **Educ:** Charles Morris Price Sch Advert & Jour; Villanova Univ, attended; Urban Theol Unit, Sheffield, Eng, attended 1979; Pa Found Pastoral Coun, grad. **Career:** Joseph V Baker Assocs Inc, Philadelphia, pres, 1968; Sun Co, community rels consult, mgr community & urban affairs, pub rels mgr, 1973-77, sr staff consult; ordained Episcopal priest, 1980; St Augustine Hippo Episcopal Church, Norristown PA, priest-in-charge, 1980-84; Episcopal Church Pub Co, exec dir, 1984-89; Mass Diocese Episcopal Church, Boston, Mass, bishop, 1989-2002; Episcopal Diocese of Wash, assisting bishop, 2003-, currently. **Orgs:** Union Black Episcopalians; Episcopal Churchs Standing Comn; Int Peace; mem bd trustee, Episcopal Divinity Sch; past vpres, Episcopal City Mission; pres, Episcopal Urban Caucus. **Honors/Awds:** Consecrated first female Episcopal Bishop, 1989; received honorary degrees from numerous Cols, universities and theological schools, including Yale University and the Church Divinity School of the Pacific. **Special Achievements:** On February 11, 1989, Barbara C. Harris was the first woman to

be ordained to the episcopate in the worldwide Anglican Communion. **Business Addr:** Assisting Bishop, Episcopal Diocese of Washington, Episcopal Church House, Mt St Alban, Washington, DC 20016-5094, **Business Phone:** (202)537-6555.

HARRIS, DR. BERNARD A.
Astronaut, physician, association executive. **Personal:** Born Jun 26, 1956, Temple, TX; son of Bernard Sr and Gussie H Burgess; married Sandra Lewis; children: 1. **Educ:** Univ Houston, BS, biol, 1978; Tex Tech Univ Health Sci Ctr, MD, 1982; Univ Tex Med Br, MS, 1996; Univ Houston, MBA, 1999. **Career:** Univ Tex Speech & Hearing Inst, res asst, 1975-78; Spectrum Emergency Care, pvt pract, 1983-85; S Tex Primary Care Group, pvt pract, 1985-86; San Jose Med Group, pvt pract, 1986-87; NASA & Johnson Space Ctr, clin scientist & flight surgeon, 1987-90, proj mgr, 1988-90, astronaut cand,1990-91, astronaut, 1991-96; Univ Tex Sch Med, clin prof, 1988-96; Baylor Col Med, asst prof, 1989-; Univ Tex Sch Pub Health, adj prof, 1989-96; Univ Tex Med Br, clin assoc prof, 1993-98; Space lab Inc, chief scientist, vpres sci & health servs, 1996-2000; Space Media Inc, vpres bus develop, 2000; Harris Found, founder & pres, currently. **Orgs:** Bd regents, Tex Tech Univ; fel Am Col Physicians; Am Soc Bone & Mineral Res; Asn Space Explorers; Am Astronaut Soc; Aerospace Med Asn; Nat Med Asn; Tex Med Asn; Harris County Med Soc; bd dirs, Boys & Girls Club Houston; comt mem, Greater Houston Area Coun Phys Fitness & Sports; bd dirs, Manned Space Flight Found; Nat Space Club; chair, Space & Tech Adv Bd; Houston Tech Ctr Comn; Med Informatics & Tech Applications Consortium, NASA Life Sci Comn; NASA Life & Microgravity Sci & Appln Adv Comn; Aircraft Owners & Pilot Asn. **Honors/Awds:** University of Houston Achievement Award, 1978; Group Achievement Award, NASA Lyndon B Johnson Space Ctr, 1993; Flight Medal, 1993; NASA Space; Physician of the Year, Nat Tech Asn, 1993; Achiever of the Year, 1993; Achievement Award, Kappa Alpha Psi Fraternity, 1993; NASA Outstanding Performance Rating, 1993; Distinguished Alumnus, Univ Houston Alumni Orgn, 1994; Distinguished Scientist of the Year, ARCS Found, 1994; Space Act Tech Brief Award, 1995; DSc, Morehouse Sch Med, 1996; Medal of Excellence, Golden State Minority Found, 1996; Challenger Award, Ronald McNair Found, 1996; Award Achievement, Asn Black Cardiologist, 1996; Strong Men, Strong Women Award, VA Power, 1997; Civil & Humanitarian Award, Fiesta Inc, 1997; NASA Group Achievement Award, 1997; NASA Team Excellence Award, 1998; Savvy Award Comm Serv, 1999;Candle in Dark Award, Morehouse Col, 2000; Hall Fame, Tex Sci 2000; Horatio Alger Award, 2000; numerous other honors and awards. **Special Achievements:** First African-American to walk in space, 1995. **Military Serv:** Author & co-author of several scientific articles and papers. **Business Phone:** (713)877-1731.

HARRIS, BERNARDO JAMAINE
Football player. **Personal:** Born Oct 15, 1971, Chapel Hill, NC; married Kellie; children: Bradley. **Educ:** NC State Univ. **Career:** Football player (retired); Green Bay Packers, linebacker, 1995-2001; Baltimore Ravens, linebacker, 2002. **Honors/Awds:** Rookie of the Year, 1995. *

HARRIS, DR. BETTY WRIGHT
Administrator. **Personal:** Born Jul 29, 1940, Monroe, LA; daughter of Henry Jake and Legertha; married Alloyd Sr (divorced); children: Selita, Jeffrey (deceased) & Alloyd. **Educ:** Southern Univ Baton Rouge, BS, chem, 1961; Atlanta Univ, Atlanta, MS, chem, 1963; Univ NMex, PhD, 1975. **Career:** Miss Valley State Univ, math, physical sci & chem teacher, 1963; Southern Univ, New Orleans, chem instr, 1964-72; Univ Okla, res asst summer, 1966; Int Bus Machines, vis staff mem summer, 1969; Los Alamos Sci Lab, vis staff mem summers, 1970-72; Los Alamos Nat Lab, res chem, 1970-2002, Conn Col, chem teacher, 1974-75; Solar Turbines Inc, chief chem technol, 1982-84; Univ NMex, adj prof organic chem, 1999; US Dept Energy, sr document reviewer, 2000-. **Orgs:** Delta Sigma Theta Sorority, 1959-; Nat Consortium for Black Prof Develop, 1975-; nat mem, Nat Asn Advan Colored People, 1975; Planning Conf Status Women Sci, Wash, DC, 1977; US Dept Labor Women Community Serv, 1978-; Nat Tech Asn, 1979-; Sunday sch, catechism teacher, Lutheran Ch Coun; chmn, bd dirs, Self-Help Inc; chmn, Mission Outreach Bd, sec, Multicultural Comn, Rocky Mountain Synod Evangelical Lutheran Ch Am; Women United for Youth, Albuquerque Pub Sch; outreach prog, Los Alamos Nat Lab; Sigma Xi, 1980-; Nat Asn Parlimentarians, 1989-; past NMex State pres, Bus & Prof Women, Los Alamos, 1996-97; chair, Cent NM Section Am Chem Soc, 1993-94; bd dir, Lutheran Off Govt Ministry, 1998-; pres, Southern Christian Leadership Conf, Albuquerque, Metrop Chap Inc. **Honors/Awds:** Area Gov of Year Award, 1978; Able Toastmaster Award, 1979; Distinguished Toastmaster Award, 1980; Distinguished Dist, 1981; Toastmasters Hall Fame; awarded patent, 1986; NMex Comn Status Women, Trail Blazer Award, 1990; NMex Gov's Award for Outstanding Women, 1999. **Special Achievements:** Author of 26 articles published in professional journals & 8 internal reports for Los Alamos & Solar Turbines Inc. **Business Addr:** Senior Document Reviewer, US Department of Energy, HS-93 Off Document Review, 19901 Germantown Rd, Germantown, MD 20874, **Business Phone:** (301)903-1563.

HARRIS, BILL. See HARRIS, WILLIAM ANTHONY.

HARRIS, BILL
Educator, poet, writer. **Educ:** Wayne State Univ, BA, MA. **Career:** Poet; playwriter; Yardbird Suite, writer; "Every Goodby Ain't Gone,", 1989; Stories About The Old Days, 1990; Wayne State Univ, prof eng, currently. **Business Phone:** (313)871-2982.

HARRIS, BRUKLIN. See WRIGHT, N'BUSHE.

HARRIS, BURNELL
Educator, government official. **Personal:** Born Oct 19, 1954, Fayette, MS; son of Levi and Louiza; married Dyann Bell; children: Tomika Tantrice, Tineciaa & Tiaura Tichelle. **Educ:** Alcorn State Univ, BA, 1975, MS, 1976. **Career:** W Dist Jr High Sch, instr hist, 1976-77; AJFC Comn Action Agency, instr adult ed, 1977-78; Alcorn State Univ, instr hist, 1978-81; Grand Gulf Nuclear Station, bechtel security, 1981-83; Jefferson County, circuit clerk, 1984-03. **Orgs:** Jefferson Co Nat Advan Asn Colored People; Phi Beta Sigma Fraternity; secy, Mountain Valley Lodge 6; MS Circuit Clerks Asn; potentate Arabia Shrine Temple 29. **Honors/Awds:** Outstanding Leadership Award, Governors Off Job Develop & Training, 1978. *

HARRIS, CALVIN D.
School administrator, county government official. **Personal:** Born Aug 27, 1941, Clearwater, FL; son of Augustus and Alberta Beatrice; married Ruth H Owens, Dec 19, 1964; children: Randall, Cassandra & Eric. **Educ:** Gibbs Jr Col, St. Petersburg, FL, AA, 1965; Univ S Fla, BA, 1966; Truman State Univ, Kirksville, MA, 1970; Nova Univ, Ft Lauderdale, EdD, 1975. **Career:** Pinellas Co Sch Syst, instr, hist, 1966-70; Seminole High Sch, Social Studies Instr, 1968-70; St Petersburg Jr Col, dean, dir continuing educ, 1970-75, provost, open campus, 1979-94, dir spec prog, 1975-79, dir stud comn & serv, 1970-75; Pinellas Co Govt, comnr, 1998-. **Orgs:** Chmn, Pinellas Co Arts Coun, 1980; State Employ & Training Coun; Pinellas Co Coord Coun; Pinellas Manpower Planning Consortium; State Fla Standing Comn Continuing Educ; chmn, Ponce de Leon Elem Sch Adv Com; dep comnr Clearwater Babe Ruth Baseball; Deleg White House Conf Families; guest columnist, Eve Ind Newspaper; chmn, Juvenile Welfare Bd; mem bd dir, Am Red Cross, YMCA; mem adv bd, First Union Bank; mem bd dir, Upper Pinellas Asn Retarded C; Employ & Develop Coun; Fla Asn Counties; Fla Counties Found; Nat Asn Counties; mem, Pres cabinet. **Honors/Awds:** Past-Pres Award, Clearwater Am Little League, 1978; Certificate of Appreciation, Pinellas Co Sch Bd, 1978; David Bilgore Memorial Award, Clearwater Kiwanis Club 1989. **Military Serv:** AUS, sp/4th class, 1960-63. **Business Addr:** Commissioner, Pinellas County Government, Pinellas County Commissioner District, 315 Co St Fifth Fl, Clearwater, FL 33756, **Business Phone:** (727)464-3360.

HARRIS, DR. CARL GORDON
Educator. **Personal:** Born Jan 14, 1936, Fayette, MO; son of Carl Harris Sr and Frances. **Educ:** Philander Smith Col, AB, 1956; Univ Mo, Columbia, AM, 1964; Vienna State Acad Music, 1969; Univ Mo, Kans City Conserv Music, DMusA, 1972; Westminster Choir Col, attended 1979. **Career:** Philander Smith Col, choral dir asst prof music, 1959-68; Va State Univ,choral dir prof & chmn, 1971-84; Norfolk State Univ, Music Dept, choral dir, prof & head, 1984-97; Bank St Mem Baptist Church, minister music,1991-; Hampton Univ, Dept Music prof music & univ organist, 1997-. **Orgs:** Organist Centennial United Methodist Church, 1968-71; organist & dir, Gillfield Baptist Church, 1974-84; adv panel, Va Comn Arts, 1980-84,1992-; bd dirs, Choristers Guild, Dallas, Tex, 1981-87; organist & dir,Bank St Mem Baptist Church, 1984-; dean, Southside Va Chap, Am GuildOrganists, 1984-85; mem exec bd, Tidewater Chap, Am Guild Organists,1987-; mem, Am Choral Directors Asn, 1987-; adv panel mem, Va YouthSymphony, 1990; bd dir, I Sherman Greene Chorale, 1990; music advisorypanel, Southeastern Va Arts Asn, 1991-; Nat Asn Sch Music ComnAccreditation, 1992; Norfolk, Via Comn Arts & Humanities, 1992; NorfolkHost Lions Club Int; Va State chmn, Jazz & Show Choir; Phi Mu AlphaSinfonia; Omega Psi Phi Fraternity Inc; Nat Asn Negro Musicians, AlphaKappa Mu Nat Hon Soc; Phi Delta Kappa Educ Fraternity; Kappa Delta Pi HonSoc Educ; Kappa Kappa Psi; Tau Beta Sigma Band Fraternities. **Honors/Awds:** Distinguished Alumnus Award, Philander Smith Col, 1975; Outstanding Alumnus Achievement Award, Conservatory Music, Univ Mo, Kansas City, 1982; Ark Traveler Award, Gov Frank White State of Ark, 1982; Outstanding Teaching Award, Norfolk State Univ, 1987. **Special Achievements:** Published Article on "Negro Spiritual" Choristers Guild Letters, 1985,"Conversation with Undine Smith Moore," Black Perspective in Music 1985;Author of, The Future of Church Music, Proceedings of the National Association of School of Music, 1994, Guide My Feet, 1995; Guide My Feet,Wonder, Love & Praise Hymnal, 1997. **Home Addr:** 141 Atlantic Ave Apt A, Hampton, VA 23664-1092. **Business Addr:** Professor of Music, University Organist, Hampton University, Department Music, Armstrong Hall, Hampton, VA 23668, **Business Phone:** (757)637-2242.

HARRIS, CARLA ANN
Executive. **Personal:** Born Oct 28, 1962, Port Arthur, TX. **Educ:** Harvard Univ, AB, econ; Harvard Business Sch, MBA. **Career:** Practising Law Inst, fac; Morgan Stanley, managing dir global capital markets, currently. **Orgs:** Bd chair, NY City Food Bank Food for Survival; bd chair, Morgan Stanley Found; adv bd, Harvard Univ Bus Sch Alumni Asn; St Charles Borromeo Cath Church; bd coun, Manhattan Coun Boy Scouts Am; Exec Leadership Coun. **Honors/Awds:** Woman of the Year, Harvard Univ Blackmen forum, 2004; Bert King Award, Harvard Bus Sch African Am Alumni Asn, 2005; Women's Professional Achievement Award, Harvard Univ; , Blazing New Trials award, Robert A. Toigo Found; Bethune Award, Nat Coun Negro Women; the Ron Brown Trailblazer Award, St. John's Univ Sch Law; Women of Distinction Award, Girl Scouts Greater Essex and Hudson Counties; Frederick Douglass Award, NY Urban League. **Special Achievements:** Selected as the 50 Most Powerful Black Executives in Corporate America by Fortune Magazine; Selected Top 50 African Americans on Wall Street by Black Enterprise Magazine; Selected as the 50 Women Who are Shaping the World by Essence Magazine; Selected as 15 Corporate Women at The Top by Ebony Magazine; Singer: Carla's First Christmas. *

HARRIS, CAROL R (CAROL SUE HARRIS)
Sales manager. **Personal:** Born Jun 12, 1954, West Point, MS. **Educ:** Cornell Col, IA, BA, 1976; Keller Grad Sch Bus, MBA, 1978. **Career:** ADT Security Systs, sales mgr, 1977-. **Orgs:** Co-chmn, Nat Conv NBMBAA, 1981; Nat Black MBA Asn, 1981-; treas, 1986-89, vpres, 1991, Young Execs in Politics; co-chmn, Young Execs in Polit Awards Banquet, 1989. **Honors/Awds:** ADT Chicago Sales Rep of the Year, 1982, 1984, 1986; Youth Executive of the Year, Young Exec in Politics, 1986; ADT Career Develop Prog, valedictorian, 1992.

HARRIS, CAROL SUE. See HARRIS, CAROL R.

HARRIS, CASPA L, JR.
Association executive. **Personal:** Born May 20, 1928, Washington, DC. **Educ:** Amer Univ, BS, 1958; Am Univ Wash Col Law, JD, 1967. **Career:** Associate executive (Retired); Peat Marwick Mitchell & Co, sr auditor, 1958-62; Howard Univ, vpres bus & fiscal affairs, treas, comptroller, 1965-87, chief internal auditor, 1962-65, prof law sch, 1967-87. **Orgs:** Comnr, Fairfax Co Redevel & Housing Auth, 1970-73; bd, The Common Fund; bd, Connie Lee Insurance Co; State Va Debt Mgt Comn; Presidential Comn Historical Black Col & Univ; Columbian Harmony Soc; Nat Harmony Memorial Park; Supreme Court Bar; Am, DC, Va Bar Asn; Ar Inst CPA's; Va Soc CPA's; The Academy Mgt; Fin Exec Inst; Nat Asn Col & Univ Bus Officers; consult, NIH; bd dir, Morse Enterprises Inc. **Honors/Awds:** Distinguished Alumni Award, The Am Univ, Sch Bus Admin.

HARRIS, CHARLES CORNELIUS
Financial manager. **Personal:** Born Mar 2, 1951, Arkadelphia, AR; son of Benjamin Franklin and Lucy Lois; married Marva Lee Bradley (deceased); children: Charla Nicole. **Educ:** Stanford Univ, BCE, 1973, MCE, 1974. **Career:** Procter & Gamble Cincinnati, Ohio, cost engr 1974-75, Affirmative Action specialist, 1975-76, bldg design engr, 1976-81, proj engr, 1981-84, proj mgr, 1984-91, prog mgr, 1991-94, purchasing mgr, 1994. **Orgs:** Kappa Alpha Frat, 1969; Adv Jr Achievement, 1978-81; Sun Sch teacher, chmn deacon bd, Mt Zion Bapt Chap Woodlawn, OH, 1979, 1983-96; consult, Cincinnati Minorty Contractors Asst Corp, 1981; exec bd mem, Cincinnati Nat Asn Advan Colored People, 1994-96; Black Male Coalition, 1994. **Honors/Awds:** Scholar Stanford Univ, 1968-73; EIT St Ohio, 1976.

HARRIS, CHARLES F.
Manager. **Personal:** Born Jan 3, 1934, Portsmouth, VA; son of Ambrose Edward and Annie Eula Lawson; married Sammie Jackson; children: Francis, Charles. **Educ:** Va State Univ, BA 1955; NY Univ Grad Sch, attended 1963. **Career:** Doubleday & Co Inc, rsch analyst to editor, 1956-65; John Wiley & Sons Inc, vice pres gen mgr Portal Press, 1965-67; Random House Inc, managing editor & sr editor, 1967-71; Howard Univ Press, exec dir, 1971-1986; Amistad Press, dir, 1986-1999; vpres ed dir, HarperCollins Publishers, 1999-2003; adj prof, jour Howard Univ; Alpha Zenith Media, Owner, 2003-. **Orgs:** Nat Press Club; bd dirs, Reading Fundamental; Asn Am Publishers; Asn Int Scholarly Publishers; Wash Area Book Publishers; bd dir, Asn Am Univ Presses, 1984; dir, Laymen's Nat Bible Comt 1985. **Military Serv:** AUS 1st Lt 1956; Honorable Discharge.

HARRIS, CHARLES SOMERVILLE
Educator. **Personal:** Born Aug 22, 1950, Richmond, VA; married Lenora Billings. **Educ:** Hampton Inst, BA/BS, 1972; Univ Mich, 1973. **Career:** Hampton Inst, audio-vis specialist, 1972-73; Newsweek, staff writer, 1973; Univ Mich, asst athletic dir, 1973-79; Univ Pa, dir athletics, 1979-85; Ariz State Univ, dir athletics, 1985-96; Excel Develop Systs Inc, partner, 1987-; Mid-Eastern Athletic Conf, comnr, 1996-2002; Averett Univ, dir Atheltics, 2004-07, vpres student servs, 2007-09, exec vpres, currently. **Orgs:** Kappa Alpha Psi, 1971-; Valley Big Brother, 1985-96; Valley Sun YMCA, 1986-96; Sigma Pi Phi, 1987-; Greensboro Sports Comn, 1996-2004; Danville, Pittsylvania Habitat Humanity, 2004; numerous Natcollegiate athletic Asn. **Business Addr:** Vice President for Student Services, Averett University, 420 W Main St, Danville, VA 24541, **Business Phone:** (434)791-5701.

HARRIS, DR. CHARLES WESLEY
Educator. **Personal:** Born Sep 12, 1929, Auburn, AL; children: Neeka & Angela. **Educ:** Morehouse Col, BA, 1949; Univ Pa, MA,

1950; Univ Wis, PhD, 1959; Harvard Univ, attended 1964; Univ Mich, attended 1966. **Career:** Prof, dean (retired); Tex Col, asst prof polit sci, 1950-53; Tuskegee Inst, asst prof polit sci, 1954-56; Univ Wis, James Found fel, 1956-58; Grambling State Univ, assoc prof polit sci, 1959-61; Coppin State Col, assoc prof polit sci, 1961-70; res assoc, Xerox Corp, 1968; Ford Found,res grant, 1969; Smithsonian Inst, Woodrow Wilson fel, 1992-94; Howard Univ, assoc dean col arts & sci, prof polit sci. **Orgs:** Pi Gamma Mu Hon Soc, Univ Pa Chap, 1951; div chair & sr specialist, Govt Div Cong Res Serv, 1974-74; Alpha Phi Alpha Frat; Alpha Kappa Mu Hon Soc. **Honors/Awds:** Am Polit Sci Assn. **Special Achievements:** Author: "Regional Councils of Government and the Central City", Detroit: Metrop Fund, 1970; "Resolving the Legislative Veto Issue", Wash, DC, Natl Inst Pub Mgt, 1979; Perspectives of Political Power in the District of Columbia, Nat Inst Pub Mgt, 1981; "Congress & the Governance of the Nation's Capital", Georgetown Univ Press, 1995; "Foreign Capital City Governance", Georgetown Univ Pub Policy Inst, 1997. **Military Serv:** AUS t-4 1947-48. **Home Addr:** 13908 Turnmore Rd, Silver Spring, MD 20906.

HARRIS, CLIFTON L.
Businessperson, mayor, business owner. **Personal:** Born Feb 3, 1938, Leland, MS; son of Willie and Gertrude; married Maxine Robinson; children: La'Clitterfer Charisse. **Career:** Harris Construction Co, Arcola, MS, owner; C&M Realty Co, Arcola, MS,owner; Town Arcola, Arcola, MS, mayor, 1986; Miss Rural Water Asn, presdist I, currently. **Orgs:** Nat Asn Advan Colored People, 1969; Elk Lodge, 1984; Deercreek Nat Gas Dist, 1986-; Salvation Army, 1986; bd mem, Am Red Cross, 1988-; treas,Miss Conf Black Mayors, 1990; bd mem, Nat Asn Advan Colored People. **Honors/Awds:** Certificate of Achievement, Delta Jr Col, 1983-84; Certificate of Achievement, Howard Univ, 1988; Certificate of Accomplishment, Clark Atlanta Univ; Meritorious Serv Award, Nat Asn Advan Colored People. **Home Addr:** PO Box 383, Arcola, MS 38722. **Business Addr:** President District I, Mississippi Rural Water Association, 5400 North Midway Rd, Raymond, MS 39154.*

HARRIS, COREY
Singer, guitarist. **Personal:** Born Feb 21, 1969, Denver, CO. **Educ:** Bates Col, anthropol. **Career:** Albums: Between Midnight & Day, 1995; Fish Ain't Bitin', 1997; Greens from the Garden, 1999; Vu-Du Menz, 2000; Downhome Sophisticate, 2002; Didn't My Lord Deliver Daniel; Mississippi to Mali, 2003; Daily Bread, 2005; Winston fel. **Honors/Awds:** Honorary Doctorate, Bates Col, 2007. **Business Addr:** Rounder Records, 1 Camp St, Cambridge, MA 02140.*

HARRIS, COREY LAMONT
Football player, business owner. **Personal:** Born Oct 25, 1969, Indianapolis, IN; children: Lauren. **Educ:** Vanderbilt Univ, BS, human resources. **Career:** Football player (retired), Business owner; Houston Oilers, 1992; Green Bay Packers, defensive back, 1992-94; Seattle Seahawks, 1995-96; Miami Dolphins, 1997; Baltimore Ravens, 1998-2001; Detroit Lions, 2002-03; Somethin Live, R&B club owner, currently; SYBE Rec, prod & dir, currently. **Orgs:** Kappa Alpha Psi Fraternity Inc. **Honors/Awds:** Raven's Ed Block Courage Award, 2001; Joe Schmidt Leadership Award, 2002. **Business Addr:** Producer, Director, SYBE Rec, 209 Printers Alley, Nashville, TX 37201, **Business Phone:** (615)254-5483.

HARRIS, CORNELIA
Educator. **Personal:** Born Sep 30, 1963, Ennis, TX; daughter of Virgil L Sr and Cleo; married Douglas E, Jun 6, 1992. **Educ:** Texas Woman's Univ, BS, social work, 1985; Alternative Cert Prog, Dallas, TX, 1990; MS, educ admin, 1996. **Career:** Big Brothers & Sisters Metro Dallas, caseworker, 1986-90; Dallas Independent Sch Dist, Dallas, TX, teacher, kindergarten, 1990-. **Orgs:** Young Dem TWU campus, 1982-83; Nat Asn Advan Colored People TWU Campus, 1982-85; Alpha Omega Social Club TWU, 1983-84; Delta Sigma Theta Sorority Inc, 1983-; Social Sci Soc TWU Campus, 1985; Nat Asn Social Workers, 1985-88; Nat Asn Black Social Workers, 1985-90. **Honors/Awds:** Teacher of the Year, 1996-97; Outstanding Young Women of America, 1996. **Home Addr:** PO Box 2006, Red Oak, TX 75154-1570. **Business Addr:** Teacher, Nancy Cochran Elementary School, 6000 Keeneland Pkwy, Dallas, TX 75211, **Business Phone:** (972)794-4600.

HARRIS, CYNTHIA JULIAN
President (organization), business owner. **Personal:** Born Oct 11, 1953, Burlington, NC. **Educ:** Univ NC Chapel Hill, BA, psychol, 1975; Univ Va, Charlottesville, MA, counr educ, human Serv, 1977. **Career:** Project AID-SIR, Richmond, VA, rehab counr, 1977-78; NC St Univ, dir Upward Bound, 1978-98; CJH Educ Grant Servs Inc, owner & pres, 1998-. **Orgs:** Greater Raleigh Chamber Com: SAEOPP; Delta Sigma Theta Sorority; Mission tree, interim exec dir, pres; First Baptist Church in Raleigh. **Honors/Awds:** The 'Outstanding Contribution to Profession', NC State Univ; US Dept Educ, recognition for Model Prog components Upward Bound. **Business Addr:** Owner, President, CJH Educational Grant Services Inc, PO Box 14264, Raleigh, NC 27620-4264, **Business Phone:** (919)832-0306.

HARRIS, CYNTHIA M.
Educator. **Educ:** Univ Kans, BA, 1978, MA, 1981; Meharry Med Col, PhD, 1985; Am Bd Toxicol, DABT. **Career:** Agency Toxic Substances & Dis Registry, Div Health Assessment & Consult, staff toxicologist & br chief, 1990-96; Fla A&M Univ, Inst Pub Health, dir & assoc prof, currently. **Orgs:** Fla Pregnancy Associated Mortality Review Coun; Kid Care Outreach Spec Populations Task Force; Leon County Indigent Health Care Adv Coun; bd mem, NW Fla Chap March Dimes; bd mem, Trust America's Health; bd mem, Fla Pub Health Asn; Nat Acad Scis Inst Med Gulf War & Health Comt; Solvent Toxicity Panel; Congressional Black Caucus Homeland Security Adv Comt; Fla Disaster Preparedness Initiative, prin investr. **Business Addr:** Director, Associate Professor, Florida A&M University, Inst Pub Health, 207E Frederick S Humphries Sci Res Ctr, Tallahassee, FL 32307, **Business Phone:** (850)599-8655.

HARRIS, DAISY (DAISY GRIFFIN HARRIS WADE)
Disc jockey, activist. **Personal:** Born Apr 22, 1931, Hattiesburg, MS; daughter of Joseph and Annie B Griffin; married James Harrison, Apr 7, 1951 (divorced); children: James jr, Anthony & Harold; married Willie, Apr 8, 1978. **Educ:** Pearl River Jr Col, sec cluster course. **Career:** Disc jockey, activist (retired); WDAM-TV, secy & receptionist; WORV Radio, disk jockey & secy; Cong Racial Equality, off work; Stud Non-Violent Coord Comt, off work; activist. **Orgs:** Secy, Forrest Co Br, Nat Asn Advan Colored People; Forrest Co Action Comt; Fifth Dist Loyalist Dem Party; vol, Southern Christian Leadership Conf; Miss Freedom Dem Party. **Honors/Awds:** Vernon Dahmer Community Service Award, Hub City Bus & Prof Men's Club, 1978; Certificate of Special Recognition, Miss Community Found, 1994; Long Distance Runner Award, Forrest Co Br, Nat Asn Advan Colored People, 1996; A Voice & A Vote, Freedom's Foundation Award, Hattiesburg Pub Sch Dist, 1998; Achievement Award, Miss Homemakers Vol Inc & Miss State Univ Exten Serv; Most Popular Disc Jockey. **Home Addr:** 216 Fredna Ave, Hattiesburg, MS 39401.

HARRIS, DALE F.
Chief executive officer. **Career:** Bound Brook Ford Inc, chief exec officer, 1997-. **Business Addr:** Chief Executive Officer, Bound Brook Ford Inc, 427 W Union Ave, Bound Brook, NJ 08805, **Business Phone:** (732)356-2000.*

HARRIS, DAVID
Chief executive officer. **Career:** Beststaff Servs Inc, chief exec officer, currently. **Orgs:** Pinnacle Award, 1999. **Business Addr:** Chief Executive Officer, Beststaff Services Inc, 3730 Kirby Dr Suite 320, Houston, TX 77098-3986, **Business Phone:** (713)527-8233.*

HARRIS, DAVID ELLSWORTH
Pilot. **Personal:** Born Dec 22, 1934, Columbus, OH; son of Ruth A Estis Harris (deceased) and Wilbur R Harris (deceased); married Lynne Purdy, Feb 26, 1989 (died 2000); children: Camian & Leslie. **Educ:** Ohio State Univ, BS, 1957. **Career:** Pilot (retired); Amer Airlines, capt 1964-94. **Orgs:** Pres, Org Black Airline Pilots; NAI. **Honors/Awds:** Black Achievement in Industry Award, YMCA, 1971. **Military Serv:** USAF, cpt 1958-64.

HARRIS, DAVID L. **See Obituaries section.**

HARRIS, DERRICK
Football player. **Personal:** Born Sep 18, 1972, Angleton, TX. **Educ:** Miami, Fla. **Career:** St Louis Rams, running back, 1996-99; San Diego Chargers, 2000-01; Dallas Cowboys, running back, 2002; Sam Houston bearkats, defencive back. **Honors/Awds:** DEFENSIVE PLAYER OF THE WEEK, Southland Conference, 2006.

HARRIS, DEWITT O.
Government official. **Personal:** Born Aug 10, 1944, Washington, DC; son of DeWitt and Corinne Banks Thomas; married Brenda Bing Harris, Dec 31, 1968; children: Rhonda, Tanya. **Educ:** Johnson C Smith Univ, Charlotte, NC, BA, 1966; Southeastern Univ, Wa, DC, MBPA, 1979. **Career:** US Postal Serv, Wa, DC, contact compliance examiner, 1968-76, mgr, eeo complaints div, 1976-79, gen mgr affirmative action div, 1979-86, US Postal Serv, Green Bay, WI, msc & mgr postmaster, 1986-90; US Postal Serv, Milwaukee, WI, dir city oper, 1988-90; US Postal Serv, Dayton, OH, msc mgr & postmaser, 1990-92, Employee Resource Mgt, vpres, currently. **Orgs:** Nat Asn Advan Colored People, 1966-. **Honors/Awds:** PCES Special Achievement Award, US Postal Serv, 1988; Central Region Eagle Award, US Postal Serv, 1988. **Military Serv:** AUS, E5, 1968-70, Bronze Star, Commendation Medal, Air Medal, Vietnam Cross of Gallantry, Purple Heart. **Business Addr:** Vice President, United States Postal Service, Employee Resource Management, 2970 Market St Rm 316A, Philadelphia, PA 19104-9997, **Business Phone:** (215)895-8680.*

HARRIS, DR. DOLORES M.
School administrator. **Personal:** Born Aug 5, 1930, Camden, NJ; daughter of Roland H (deceased) and Frances Gatewood (deceased); married Morris E Harris Sr, 1948 (divorced 1987); children: Morris E Jr, Sheila D Davis & Gregory M. **Educ:** Glassboro State Col, BS, 1959, MA, 1966; Rutgers Univ, EdD, 1983. **Career:** School administrator (retired); Glassboro Bd Educ, teacher admin, 1959-70; Camden Welfare Bd, supvr adult ed ctr, 1968; SCOPE Glassboro Ctr, dir Headstart, 1969-70; Nat ESL Training Inst Jersey City State Col, assoc dir, 1971; Glassboro State Col, dir cont educ, 1970-, acting vpres acad affairs, 1989, dir continuing educ, 1990-91; Pierce Col, adjunct faculty,currently. **Orgs:** Bd dirs, Adult Educ Asn USA, 1973-79; consult, NJ Gov's Conf on Libraries & Info Serv 1979; examiner, NY Civil Serv 1976-; chair adv bd, Women's Educ Equity Comm Network Project, 1977-78, 1980; bd dirs, Glassboro State Col Mgt Inst, 1975-; consult, Temple Univ, 1978-79; consut, NY Model Cities Right to Read Nat Training Conf, 1973-81; comm, NJ Task Force on Thorough & Efficient Educ, 1976-78; legislative comm Amer Asn for Adult & Continuing Educ, 1982-; Gloucester Co Private Industry Counc, 1984-; first vpres, 1984-88, pres, 1988-92, Nat Asn Colored Women's Clubs Inc, 1984-; vpres at large N eastern Fedn of Colored Women's Clubs Inc, 1983-; pres & vpres other offices NJ State Fed Colored Women's Clubs Inc, 1972-80; pres, South Jersey Chap Links Inc, 1984-; pres vice pres other offices Gloucester Co United Way, 1968-; chair of bd Glassboro Child Develop Ctr, 1974-82; pres Glassboro State Col Alumni Asn, 1975-77; delegate Intl Women's Yr Nat Conf, 1978; vice chair, 1983-86, chair, 1986-, Commn on Status of Women Gloucester Co NJ; Nat Coun of Women, exec comm & educchair; founding mem, Societas Docta; bd of dir, Women for Greater Philadelphia; Zeta Phi Beta Sorority; Omicron Omicron Zeta Chapter; Anti-Basileus, Phylacter; EMC Score Chair, seminar program, 2001-. **Honors/Awds:** Distinguishing Service Award, Asn Adult Educ NJ, 1974; DistinguishingAlumna Award, Glassboro State Col NJ, 1971; Community Service Award, HollyShores Girl Scouts NJ, 1981; President's Award, United Way of Gloucester Co Woodbury NJ, 1985; Woman of the Year Award, Gloucester County Bus & Professional Women's Club, 1985; Citizen of the year award, Holly Shores Girl Scouts, 1987; Woman of the year Zeta Phi Beta, Gamma Nu Zeta, 1989; Women of Achievement Award, Douglas Col NJ; State Federation of Women'sClub, 1991. **Special Achievements:** Hundred Most Influential Black Americans, Ebony. **Home Addr:** 7439 Barclay Rd, Cheltenham, PA 19012-1302.

HARRIS, DR. DON NAVARRO
Biochemist. **Personal:** Born Jun 17, 1929, New York, NY; son of John Henry and Margaret Vivian Berkley; married Regina B (died 1993); children: Donna Harris-Wolfe, John Craig & Scott Anthony. **Educ:** Lincoln Univ Pa, AB, 1951; Rutgers Univ, MS, 1959, PhD, 1963. **Career:** Biochemist (retired); Colgate Palmolive Res Ctr, sr res, 1963-64; Rutgers Univ, asst res specialist, 1964-65, assoc prof, 1975-77; Bristol-Myers Squibb Pharmaceut Res Inst, res fel, 1965; Lincoln Univ, Pa, vis lectr, 1983-; Southern Univ Baton Rouge, LA, lectr, 1987; Temple Univ Sch Med, assoc prof. **Orgs:** AAAS, 1966-; mem, treas, bd dir, Frederick Douglass Liberation Libr, 1970-82; steering comm, 1975-, secy, 1986-, Biochem Pharmacol Discussion Group NY Acad Sci; Philadelphia Physiological Soc, 1978-; Am Soc for Pharmacol & Exp Therapeut, 1980-; consult, US Army Sci Bd, 1981-85; reviewer, NSF, 1981-; adv comm Biochem Sec, NY Acad Sci 1983-; mem, Bd Trustees, Lincoln Univ, Pa, 2005-; participant Nat Urban League Black Exec Prog; lecturer, Tex Southern Univ, 1984; ed bd mem, Jour Enzyme Inhibition 1985-; mem, Sigma Xi, NY Acad Sci, Am Heart Assoc, Amer Chem Soc, Theta Psi Lambda Chapter Alpha Phi Alpha, Mu Boule, Sigma Pi Phi. **Honors/Awds:** Recipient of Harlem YMCA Black Achievers Award, 1984. **Special Achievements:** Author or co-author of 40 scientific papers, 40 scientific abstracts and 4 patents. **Military Serv:** AUS, med corp specalist, 2 yrs.

HARRIS, PROF. DONALD J
Economist, educator. **Personal:** Born in Jamaica. **Educ:** Univ Col WI-London Univ, BA, 1961; Univ Calif, Berkeley, PhD, 1966. **Career:** Univ Ill, Urbana-Champaign, asst prof, 1965-67; Univ Wis, Madison, assoc prof, 1968-72; Stanford Univ, dept econs, prof, 1972-98, prof emer, 1998-; J Econ Lit, ed bd, 1979-84; Consult. **Orgs:** Am Econ Asn. **Honors/Awds:** Ford Found fel, Nat Res Coun, 1984-85; Fulbright Scholar, Brazil, 1990, 1991, Mexico, 1992. **Special Achievements:** Has published various books & numerous articles in professional journals. Has been a visiting researcher and has delivered lectures in numerous universities & institutions in various countries including: Mexico, Holland, England, Brazil, Italy, India, Africa, the Caribbean. **Business Addr:** Professor Emeritus, Stanford University, Department of Economics, Econ Bldg, 579 Serra Mall, Stanford, CA 94305-6072.

HARRIS, DOUGLAS ALLAN
Public relations executive, manager. **Personal:** Born Feb 7, 1942, Burlington, NJ; son of Milton and Marvel Clark; married Myrna L Hendricks. **Educ:** Trenton State Col, BA, Educ, 1964; Rutgers Univ Grad Sch Educ, MEd, 1973; Fordham Univ Grad Sch Bus, MBA, Mgt & Mkt, 1980. **Career:** NJ Bd Educ, teacher, 1964-69; Webster Div McGraw-Hill Book Co, dir mkt serv, 1969-76; RR Bowker, mgr Educ Admin book div, 1976-79; Scott, Foresman & Co, mkt mgr, 1980-86; Am Dental Asn, dir mkt, 1986-88; Silverman's Dental Supplies, mkt mgr; Portfolio Assoc Inc, project mgr, currently; Covenant House Church God, co-pastor, currently. **Orgs:** Coun Concerned Black Exec, 1975-78, Am Asn Adult Continuing Educ, 1980-; founding bd mem, Literacy Volunteers Chicago, 1982-; vpres bd, Simek Mem Coun Ctr, 1983-; dir,

Middle Atlantic Asn Temporary Servs, 1989. **Honors/Awds:** Volunteer of the Year, N Shore Mag, 1985; Gold Award/Mkt Training, Am Mkt Asn, 1987; Ordained Baptist Deacon, 1985; Licensed Minister, 1997. **Home Addr:** 10 Drummers Lane, Wayne, PA 19087. **Business Addr:** Project Manager, Portfolio Associates Inc, 510 Walnut St, Philadelphia, PA 19106, **Business Phone:** (215)627-3660.*

HARRIS, DUCHESS
Educator, chairperson. **Educ:** Univ Ibadan, Nigeria, Inst African Studies, 1989; Univ Oxford, Eng, Oxford Ctr African Studies, 1990; Univ PA, BA, Am hist, Afro-Am studies, 1991; Univ Mich, attended 1992; Yale Univ, 1994; Lund Univ, Sweden, 1996; Univ Minn, PhD, Am studies, 1997. **Career:** Univ Pa, instr, 1991; US Sen Paul David Wellstone, constituent advocate, issue liaison, 1993-94; Univ Minn, instr, 1993-95, teaching asst, 1993-94, reader, grader, 1995; Macalester Col, Women's & Gender Studies, instr, 1994-97, vis asst prof polit sci & women's & gender studies, 1997-98, Dept African Am Studies & Polit Sci, asst prof, 1998-2004, Dept Am Studies, chmn, 2003-05, assoc prof, 2004-; Univ Ga, fel, 1996; Woodrow Wilson Career Enhancement fel, 2001-02. **Orgs:** Mensa, 1983-; Onyx Senior Honor Soc, 1990-91; Mortar Bd Nat Honor Soc, 1990; bd, secy, Model Cities Family Develop Ctr, chair, Nominations & Planning, 1994-99; comnr, Minneapolis Comm Civil Rights, co-chair, Educ & Planning comt, 1996-98; Univ Minn Law Sch, Inst on Race & Poverty, res fel, co-dir, 1996-97; bd mem, vpres, Genesis II For Women Inc, 1996-99; Delta Sigma Theta Sorority; policy fel, Hubert Humphrey Inst Pub Affairs, 1998-99; Am Studies Asn. **Honors/Awds:** Minority Nat Merit Scholar, 1987; Alice Paul Award, 1991; Raymond Pace Alexander Award, 1991; Althea K Hottel Award, Univ Pa, 1991; GRI certificate, Minn State Realtor's License, 1995-98; 91; Ralph Henry Gabriel Dissertation Prize, Nat Am Studies Asn. **Special Achievements:** Writings include: "Spike Lee and the Black Agenda", Ctr for Afro-American and African Studies, UNV of MI, Dec 1992; Lectures include: "Pro Bono Projects Training", MN Justice Foundation, 1996; Book reviews include: "Colin Powell's American Journey: Not to the Capitol, but to Capital", The Journal of Intergroup Relations, Fall 1997; Nat Endowment for the Humanities Research Inst, Dartmouth Coll, 1998; moderator, advisor. Television/Radio Appearances. **Business Addr:** Associate Professor, Macalester College, Department of American Studies, Old Main 213 1600 Grand Ave, St Paul, MN 55105, **Business Phone:** (651)696-6478.

HARRIS, E. LYNN. See Obituaries section.

HARRIS, E. NIGEL (EON NIGEL HARRIS)
Physician, educator, college administrator. **Personal:** Born in Georgetown, Guyana; married Yvette; children: Zaman, Tamia, Sandhya. **Educ:** Howard Univ, BS, chem, 1968; Yale Univ, MPhil, Biochem, 1973; Univ PA, MD, 1977; Univ the West Indies, DM, 1981. **Career:** Univ Louisville, prof med, Div Rheumatology, chief, 1987-93; Morehouse Sch Med, dean & sr vpres, acad affairs, 1996; Univ W Indies, vice chancellor & prof, 2004-. **Orgs:** Am Med Asn; Nat Med Asn; GA State Med Asn; Asn Am Med Cols; Nat Ctr Res Resources; Asn Acad Health Ctrs. **Honors/Awds:** CIBA Geigy Prize, Int League Against Rheumatism, 1994; Alpha Omega Alpha, 1977; Phi Beta Kappa, 1968; fel, Am Col Rheumatology, 1989-; Centennial Award, 1995. **Special Achievements:** Over 150 publications in medical journals and medical textbooks on subjects of Anti-Phospholipid Antibodies and Anti-Phospholipid Syndrome. **Business Addr:** Professor, Vice Chancellor, The University of the West Indies, Mona Campus, Kingston 7, Jamaica, West Indies, **Business Phone:** (876)927-1660.*

HARRIS, EARL L.
Entrepreneur, state government official. **Personal:** Born Nov 5, 1941, Kerrville, TN; son of Collins and Magnolia Hall; married Donna Jean Lara, 1969. **Educ:** Indiana Univ, 1962; Purdue Univ, Calumet, IN, 1967; Ill Inst Technol. **Career:** Inland Steel Co; Am Maize Products Co, lab tester; Ky Liquors & Ky Snack Shop, owner & operator; Ind House Rep, 2nd Dist, legis rep, 1982-; City E Chicago Schs, fixed asset admin, currently. **Orgs:** Nat Asn Advan Colored People; pres, E Chicago Black Coalition, E Chicago Homeowners Asn; vice chmn, Ways & Means Comt, Ind House Rep; chmn, Ind House Statutory Comt Interstate & Int Coop; chmn, Indiana House Statutory Comt Ethics; Ind House Standing Comt; Ind House Rules & Legislative Procedures Comt; chair, African Am Leadership Forum; bd mem, Northwest Ind League; pres, Sunnyside Homeowners Asn. **Military Serv:** Naval Reserves, 2 yrs. **Business Addr:** Representative, Indiana House of Representatives, District 2, East Chicago, 200 W Wash St, Indianapolis, IN 46204-2786, **Business Phone:** (317)232-9600.

HARRIS, EDDY LOUIS
Writer. **Personal:** Born Jan 26, 1956, Indianapolis, IN; son of Samuel and Georgia Louise. **Educ:** Leland Stanford Jr Univ, BA, 1977. **Career:** Wash Univ, St. Louis, MO, writer-in-residence; Author of books: Mississippi Solo, 1988; Native Stranger, 1992; South of Haunted Dreams, 1993; Still Life in Harlem, 1996; Jupiter et Moi, 2005. **Honors/Awds:** MVP Award, A World of Difference, & Am Motorcyclist Assn; Missouri Governor's Humanities Award.

HARRIS, ELIHU MASON
Lawyer, legislator. **Personal:** Born Aug 15, 1947, Los Angeles, CA; son of Frances and Elihu Harris Sr; married Kathy Neal. **Educ:** Calif State Hayward, BA, 1968; Univ Calif, Berkeley, MA, 1969; Univ Calif, Davis, JD, 1975. **Career:** Congresswoman Yvonne Burke, legislative asst, 1974-75; Nat Bar Assn, exec dir, 1975-77; Alexander Millner & McGee, partner, 1979; Calif Uniform Law Comnr, 1981-; City Oakland, Mayor, 1991-99; Peralta Community Col Dist, interim chancellor, 2003-04, chancellor, 2004-. **Orgs:** Chair, Bay Area World Trade Ctr. **Honors/Awds:** Elihu M Harris State Building, named in honor, 1998. **Business Phone:** (510)466-7204.

HARRIS, EON NIGEL. See HARRIS, E. NIGEL.

HARRIS, EUGENE EDWARD
Labor relations manager. **Personal:** Born Feb 10, 1940, Pittsburgh, PA; married Marva Jo. **Educ:** PA State Univ, BA, Labor Econ; Univ Pittsburgh, MPA, Pub Admin, 1969; Duquesne Univ Law Sch, JD, 1980. **Career:** personnel serv analyst, 1964, labor contract adminr, Clairton Works, 1965; labor contract adminr, 1968, Gary Proj, prog coordr, 1969; asst mgr & mgr labor rels, 1973-78; US Steel, mgr employ, 1978; Harris Consult, principal, currently; Allegheny County Bar Asn. **Orgs:** chmn, Gary Concentrated Employ Pgm, 1969-73; chmn, Gary Econ Devel Corp, 1970-73; dir, Gary Urban League, 1970-72; treas, Community Partners Corp, 1975-. **Honors/Awds:** Capt, PA State Univ Basketball team, 1962; hon mention, All-Am, 1962. **Military Serv:** AUS, sp4, 1963-68. **Business Addr:** Principal, Harris Consulting, Dominion Tower Ctr, 625 Liberty Ave Suite 2800, Pittsburgh, PA 15230, **Business Phone:** (412)402-6674.

HARRIS, EVERETTE LYNN. See HARRIS, E. LYNN in the Obituaries section.

HARRIS, FRAN
Media executive, business owner, basketball player. **Personal:** Born Mar 12, 1965. **Educ:** Univ Tex, BA&MA, jour, PhD, bus admin. **Career:** Basketball player (retired), media executive, business owner; Houston Comets, guard, 1997; ESPN, Lifetime TV & FOX Sports, sports announcer;host; film & television producer; speaker; fitness expert; minister; busstrategist; Books: Dream Season; About My Sister's Business: The Black Woman's Road Map to Successful Entrepreneurship, 1996; Fran Harris Enterprises, exec dir, currently. **Special Achievements:** First woman to host her own sports talk radio show in Austin, Texas in2001. **Business Addr:** Executive Director, Fran Harris Enterprises, PO Box 3594, Culver City, CA 90231, **Business Phone:** (310)745-7762.

HARRIS, FRANCIS C
Writer, historian. **Personal:** Born Sep 25, 1957, Brooklyn, NY; son of Charles and Sammie. **Educ:** Cambridge Col, MEd, mgt, 1992. **Career:** Senior Researcher for A Hard Road To Glory, The History of the African-American Athlete, 1983-86, summer, 1987, 1992-93; Essay: Paul Robeson: An Athletes Legacy; co-author: The Amistad Pictorial History of the African American Athlete, Collegiate (1 & 2) & prof, 2003. **Orgs:** Nat Black MBA Asn; Soc Am Baseball Res (SABR).

HARRIS, FRANCO
Football player, executive, president (organization). **Personal:** Born Mar 7, 1950, Fort Dix, NJ; son of Cad and Gina Parenti; married Dana Dokmanovich; children: Franco Dokmanovich Harris. **Educ:** PA State Univ, BS, food serv & admin, 1972. **Career:** Football player (retired), President, Executive; Pittsburgh Steelers, running back, 1972-83; Seattle Seahawks, running back, 1984; Francos All Natural, pres; Pk Sausages Co, owner, currently; Super Bakery Inc, owner & chief exec officer, currently. **Honors/Awds:** Am Football Conf Championship Game, 1972, 1974-75, 1978-79; Pro Bowl, 1972-78; Rookie of the Year, Nat Football League, 1972; Rookie of the Year, United Press Int; won four Super Bowls with Pittsburgh Steelers; Most Valuable player, Super Bowl IX; Distinguished Alumnus, PA State Univ, 1982; Pro Football Hall of Fame, 1990; Man of the Year, Am Acad Achievement; 'Golden Plate Award; Whitney M Young Award, Nat Urban League; Volunteer of the Year, Nat Multiple Sclerosis, 2001; Alumnus of the Year, Penn State Sch Hotel, Restaurant, Recreation Mgt; Alumni Fellow, Penn State Alumni Asn, 2005 . **Business Addr:** Owner, President, Super Bakery Inc, 5700 Corp Dr Suite 455, Pittsburgh, PA 15237-5851, **Business Phone:** (412)367-2518.

HARRIS, DR. GARY LYNN
Educator. **Personal:** Born Jun 24, 1953, Denver, CO; son of Gladys Weeams and Norman; married Jennifer Dean, May 19, 1984; children: Jamie. **Educ:** Cornell Univ, Ithaca, NY, BS, EE, 1975, MS, EE, 1976, PhD, Elec Engineering, 1980. **Career:** Nat Research & Resource Facility Sumicron Structures, Ithaca, NY, asst, 1977-80; Naval Research Lab, Wash, DC, vis scientist, 1981-82; Lawrence Livermore Nat Lab, consult, 1984-; Howard Univ, Wash, DC, assoc prof, prof elec eng & Mat Sci Res Ctr, dir, currently. **Orgs:** Sigma Xi, Inst Electrical & Electronic Engineers; chmn, IEEE Electron Devices, Wash Sec, 1984-86; mem, selection comm, Black Engineer the year, 1989. **Special Achievements:** Author Origin Periodic Surface Structure Laser Annealed Semi conduct, 1978; Robert Earle Fel; 1980; author of SIMS Determinations on Ion Implanted Depth Distributions, 1980; author of An Experimental Study of Capless Annealing on Ion Implanted Ga As, 1983; author of Electronic States of Polycrystalline Ga As & Their Effects on Phtovoltaic Cells, 1983; author of Geltering of Semi-Insulation Liquid Incapsulated Ga As for Direct Ion Implanation, 1984. **Business Addr:** Director, Professor, Howard University, Department of Electrical & Computer Engineering, 2400 6th St NW, Washington, DC 20059, **Business Phone:** (202)806-6618.

HARRIS, GENE THOMAS
Educator. **Personal:** Born Apr 4, 1953, Columbus, OH; daughter of William Sr and Thelma Thomas; married Stanley E Harris, Jun 25, 1977; children: Wade Thomas Harris. **Educ:** Univ Notre Dame, BA, 1975; Ohio State Univ, MA, 1979, PhD, 1999. **Career:** Columbus City Schs, teacher, 1975-79, high school asst prin, 1980-85, prin, 1985-89, supvr principals, 1989-91, asst supt, curric, 1991-94; Ohio Dept Educ, state asst supt, 1995-98; Columbus City Schs, dep supt, 1999-2000, supt, 2000-. **Orgs:** Bd mem, United Way Cent Ohio, 2001-; bd mem, Columbus Symphony Orchestra, 2001-; bd mem, CAPA, 2003-; trustee bd, Mt Olivet Baptist Church, 2003-. **Honors/Awds:** Ingram Award, Principal Leadership, 1986, 1989; YWCA, Woman of Achievement, 1991; African American Role Model Award, Phi Beta Sigma, 2002; Master Achiever in Education Award, Who's Who in Black Columbus, 2002-03; Community Impact Award, CMACAO, 2003; Award for Oustanding Accomplishments, Cavalier's Club, 2003; Personal Achievement and Devoted Service Award, Nat Coun 100 Black Women, Columbus Chapter, 2003; Excellence in Educational Leadership Award, Univ Council for Educational Admin, 2003. **Special Achievements:** Author: The Communications Relationship between Urban Superintendents and Teachers Union Presidents in 21 School Districts in Ohio (dissertation), 1999. **Business Addr:** Superintendent, Columbus City Schools, 270 E State St, Columbus, OH 43215, **Business Phone:** (614)365-5888.

HARRIS, DR. GERALDINE E.
Scientist, microbiologist, college teacher. **Personal:** Born in Detroit, MI; divorced; children: Reginald & Karen. **Educ:** Wayne State Univ Med Tech, BS, 1956, MS, microbiol, 1969, PhD, microbiol, 1974. **Career:** Detroit Gen Hosp, med tech, 1956-60; Parke Davis & Co, asst res microbiol, 1961-66; Wayne St Univ, Dept Biol, res asst, 1967-68; Wayne St Univ, Col Med, tutor/adv post baccal prog, 1971-73; Drake Inst Sci, consult, 1971-73; Met Hosp Dt, microbiol, 1975; Winston-Salem St Univ, asst prof microbiol, 1975-77; Nat Caucus Black Aged, consult, 1976; Food & Drug Admin, Ctr Food Safety & Appl Nutrit, consumer safety officer, 1980-; Clin Microbiol Group Health Asn Inc, chief; Allied Health Prog Develop, Am Asn State Cols & Univ, Washington, assoc coord. **Orgs:** Reg Am Soc Clin Pathol MT 28926, 1956-; Am Soc Microbiol, 1967-; fel NIH, 1968-71; Asn Univ Prof, 1968-; Sigma Xi; Asn Advan Sci, 1975-; Educ ComputMinority Inst, 1977; Alpha Kappa Alpha Sorority; Urban League, Orphan Found; fel African Sci Inst. *

HARRIS, GIL W.
Educator. **Personal:** Born Dec 9, 1946, Lynchburg, VA; married Paula Bonita Gillespie; children: Deborah Nicole Gillespie & Paul Henry Gillespie. **Educ:** Nat Acad Broadcasting, dipl radio & TV, 1965; Winston-19, Salem Col, AS,1971; Shaw Univ, BA, 1980; NC A&T State Univ, MS, 1982; Pac Western Univ, PhD, 1986. **Career:** WEAL WQMG Radio Stations, oper dir, 1972-79; Shaw Univ, dir radio broadcasting, 1979-81; Col Telecommun, syst producer, sport dir, 1981-84;SC St Univ, asst prof broadcasting, 1984, instr, currently. **Orgs:** Omega Psi Phi; Prince Hall Mason; Nat Asn Advan Colored People. **Honors/Awds:** Citizen of the Week, WGHP TV High Point NC, 1977; Radio Announcer of the Year, Dudley HS, 1979; Outstanding Media Service, Triad Sickle Cell, 1979; Outstanding Media Service, Mid-Eastern Athletic Conf, 1983; Outstanding Media Service, Cent Intercol Athletic Asn. **Military Serv:** AUS, sp5-e5, 3 yrs; Army Commendation with "V" Device, 1965-68. **Home Addr:** 416 Robinson St NE, Orangeburg, SC 29115.

HARRIS, GLADYS BAILEY
Judge. **Personal:** Born Mar 23, 1947, Boykins, VA; daughter of William L and Dorothy R Ferguson; married Stanley Christian Harris Sr, Aug 3, 1968; children: Stanley Jr, Chad Gregory, Adrienne Michelle. **Educ:** Va State Univ, Petersburg, BS, biol, 1968; Univ Richmond, Richmond, JD, 1981. **Career:** Sch Bd City Richmond, Richmond, gen coun, 1981-83; Univ Richmond, Richmond, adj prof, 1983-84, 1991-; Law Off Gladys Bailey Harris, solo practicioner, Richmond, 1983-86; Supreme Ct Va, Richmond, hearing officer, ade law judge, 1983-; Clute & Shilling, Richmond, partner, atty, 1986-87; VIR Alcoholic Beverage Control Bd, Richmond, VA, agency head, cbd, 1987-90; VIR Alliance Minority Particip Sci & Eng, VAMPSE, Richmond, VA, exd, 1990-91; Law Off Gladys Bailey Harris, solo practitioner, Richmond, VA, 1990-92; Carpenter & Harris, Richmond, partner, 1992-; pvt pract, atty, currently. **Orgs:** Arbitrator, NY Stock Exchange, 1983-; Alumni bd mem, Univ Richmond, 1988-; bd

mem, Va Instr Law & Citizenship Studies, 1988-; bd mem, Commonwealth Girl Scout Coun Va, 1988-; bd mem, Local Community Cols Bd, 1991-; comnr, Circuit Ct City Richmond, 1991-; mbr, VIR State Bar Com Prof, 1991-. **Honors/Awds:** Hon Woodrow Wilson Fel, Woodrow Wilson Found, 1968; Distinguished Serv Award, Richmond Area Prog Minorities Eng, 1988; Citizen of the Year, NAFEO/Va State Univ, 1990; SERWA Award, Nat Coalition of 100 Black Women, 1990. **Home Addr:** 4210 Southaven Rd, Richmond, VA 23235-1029. **Business Addr:** Attorney, Private Practitioner, 4210 Southaven Rd, Richmond, VA 23235-1029.*

HARRIS, REV. H. FRANKLIN, II
Clergy. **Career:** Tried Stone Baptist Church, pastor, currently. **Business Addr:** Pastor, Tried Stone Baptist Church, 2434 E Houston St, San Antonio, TX 78202, **Business Phone:** (210)226-1162.*

HARRIS, HARCOURT GLENTIES
Physician. **Personal:** Born Apr 16, 1928, New York, NY; married Charlotte L Hill; children: Harcourt Jr, Michael, Brian, Andrea. **Educ:** Fordham Univ, BS, 1948; Howard Univ, MD, 1952. **Career:** Pvt pract, physician, 1960-; United Am Healthcare Corp, staff; Dearborn United Am Healthcare Corp, resident; Harlem Hosp, internship; Bd Cert Internist, 1962; Highland Park Gen Hosp, chief med, dir med educ, 1973-76; Wayne State Univ, clin asst prof, 1975; United Am Healthcare Corp, vice chmn bd dirs, 1985-01. **Orgs:** Life mem, Nat Asn Advan Colored People. **Military Serv:** AUS, 1953-55. **Business Addr:** Physician, Private Practice, 15521 W 7 Mile Rd, Detroit, MI 48235.*

HARRIS, HELEN B.
Educator, president (organization), executive. **Personal:** Born Mar 6, 1925, High Point, NC; daughter of Willie Boulware and Hattie Whitaker; married Dr Wendell B, Sep 4, 1951; children: Wendell B Jr, Charles B & Hobart W. **Educ:** Bennett Col, BA, 1945; Univ IA, MA, 1952. **Career:** Prismatic Images Inc, exec producer. **Orgs:** Exec dir, YWCA, High Point NC, 1945-48; prog dir, YWCA, Des Moines, 1948-51; pres, League Women Voters, 1965; pres, bd ed, Flint, 1973-74,75-76; bd mem, NBD Genesee Bank, 1980-89; trustee, Comm Found Greater Flint, 1986-89; bd mem emer, Questar Sch Gifted, 1987-89; pres, Flint Area Educ Found, 1988-89; chair, Endowment Campaign; bd mem, Christ Episcopal Ctr; Policy Comt, Community Found Greater Flint; St Neighborhood Educ Auth; bd mem, Flint Pub Schs; secy, Mayors Adv Comn; charter mem, Flint Chap, Delta Sigma Theta; Jack & Jill; Nat Asn Adv Colored People; Delta Sigma Theta, Urban League, ACLU. **Honors/Awds:** First female black mem & first woman pres elected to Flint Bd of Ed; executive producer of film "Chameleon Street," Grand Prize winner, US Sun Dance Festival, 1990. **Business Addr:** Executive Producer, Prismatic Images Inc, 1632 Kensington Ave, Flint, MI 48503.*

HARRIS, HORATIO PRESTON
Dentist. **Personal:** Born Sep 25, 1925, Savannah, GA; son of Horatio and Foustina; married Barbara E Monroe; children: Gary P, Patricia L, Michael M, Dr Conrad W, Nancy E, Dr David M, Cathy C, Roxanne D, Robert H. **Educ:** Howard Univ, BS, 1951, DDS, 1956. **Career:** Dentist (retired). Va, Wash, IBM specialist, 1949; St Elizabeth Hosp, intern, oral surgery, 1956-57; pvt prac dent, Wash, 1957; Bur Dent Health, dent officer, 1960-65; Howard Univ, instr, 1966-67, asst prof, 1967-71; minister, 1973-82, Jehovah's Witness minister, 1982. **Orgs:** courtesy staff oral surgery, Freedman's Hosp; Am Dental Asn; Nat Dental Asn; DC Dental Asn; RT Freeman Soc; Omega Psi Phi. **Honors/Awds:** Honored UAU; The Mother Pearl Achievement. **Military Serv:** USNR, 1943-46. *

HARRIS, INETTA
College teacher. **Career:** Greater Cooper Am Methodist Episcopal Zion Church, Oakland, singer; Mich Tech Univ, asst prof, currently. *

HARRIS, J. ROBERT, II
Consultant, president (organization). **Personal:** Born Apr 1, 1944, Lake Charles, LA; son of James Robert and Ruth E Boutte; married Nathaleen Stephenson, Aug 28, 1965 (deceased); children: Evan Scott & April Ruth. **Educ:** Queens Col, BA, psychol, 1966; City Univ New York, MA, 1969; Berlitz Sch Lang, Conv Spanish & French, 1974. **Career:** Equitable Life Ins Co, res analyst, 1965-66; NBC, mkt res supvr, 1966-69; Gen Foods Corp, group mkt res mgr, 1969-72; Pepsi Co Int, assoc dir res, 1972-74; Intern Mkt Res Pepsico Inc plans, assoc dir; JRH Mkt Serv, pres, currently; QRCA, chmn Prof commt, currently; NYU Sch Continuing Education, Prof Mkt Res . **Orgs:** Am Mkt Assn; dir, rec lectr math & french proj Upward Bound, 1966-67; European Soc Opinion & Mkt Res; pres, brd dir Qualitative Res Consult Assn, 1987-89; consult vol, Urban Consult Group Inc; Explorers Club, 1993-; Natl Assn Advan Colored People; Omega Psi Phi; chmn, Res Ind Coalition; mem, Mkt Res Counc Hon soc. **Honors/Awds:** Grant Franklin & Marsh Col, 1961-65; grant, Howard Univ 1961-65; grant, New York State Reg Sch, 1961-65; David Sarnoff Fel, 1967; Key of Success, Mex City, 1973; 1000 Most Successful Blacks, Ebony Mag; Organizations' Pres Awd for Distinguished Ser; Certificate of Merit for Distinguished Service to the Community Dictionary of International Biography. **Special Achievements:** Frequent speaker and writer on qualitative research topics. **Business Addr:** President, JRH Marketing Services Inc, 2927 41st Ave, Long Island City, NY 71878, **Business Phone:** (718)786-9640.

HARRIS, JACKIE BERNARD
Football player. **Personal:** Born Jan 4, 1968, Pine Bluff, AR; married Letrece; children: Jackie Jr. **Educ:** Northeast La Univ. **Career:** Football player (retired); Green Bay Packer, tight end, 1990-93; Tampa Bay Buccaneers, 1994-97; Tenn Oilers, 1998; Tenn Titans, 1999; Dallas Cowboys, tight end, 2000-01. **Honors/Awds:** All-Pro selection, 1992.

HARRIS, JAMES
Football player, football executive. **Personal:** Born Jul 20, 1947, Monroe, GA; married Vickie. **Educ:** Grambling State Univ, educ. **Career:** Football player (retired), football exec; Buffalo Bills, quarterback, 1969-71; Los Angeles Rams, quarterback, 1973-76; San Diego Chargers, quarterback, 1977-81; Tampa Bay Buccaneers, W Coast scout, 1987-92; NY Jets, asst gen mgr, 1993-96; Baltimore Ravens, dir pro personnel, 1997; Jacksonville Jaguars, gen mgr & vpres player personnel, 2003-. **Orgs:** Subcomt, Nat Football League. **Honors/Awds:** Most Valuable Player, Orange Blossom Classic, 1967; Pittsburgh Courier Player of the Year, 1968; Most Valuable Player, NFL Pro Bowl, 1975; leads the NFC in passing; 36th most influential minority person in sports, Sports Illustrated, 2003; inducted into: SWAC Hall of Fame, Grambling Athletic Hall of Fame & La Sports Hall of Fame, Atlanta Right & Wrong Hall of Fame. **Special Achievements:** One of the first African Ameriacan quarterbacks to start in the National Football League; one of the top 50 most influential minorities in sports. **Business Addr:** Vice President of Player Personnel, Jacksonville Jaguars, 1 Alltel Stadium Pl, Jacksonville, FL 32202, **Business Phone:** (904)633-6000.

HARRIS, JAMES, III. See JAM, JIMMY.

HARRIS, JAMES ALEXANDER
Association executive. **Personal:** Born Aug 25, 1926, Des Moines; married Jacquelyn; children: James, Jr, Jerald. **Educ:** Drake Univ, BA, 1948, MFA, 1955; Drake Div Col, post grad work; OK A&M. **Career:** Kansas City, elem teacher, 1948; Langston Univ, teacher, 1953-54; Des Moines, art, human rel teacher, 1954; Nat Educ Asn, vpres, 1973, pres, 2005-. **Orgs:** Speaker, Nat Assembly Educ Res, Yamagata, Japan, 1974; dir, NEA; NEA Budget Com; Steering Com, NEA Const Conv; first deleg, Am Educr Peoples Rep China; co-chmn, NEA Com Am Revolution - Bicen; IA State Educ Asn; Des Moines Educ Asn; dir, Red Cross Refugee Shelter; Am Friends Serv Com; admin com rels, Forest Ave Baptist Church; Mayors Task Forces Educ & Police-Com Rels; NAEA bd dirs liaison, Nat Asn Art Educ; IA Asn Art Educr; NAACP; Kappa Alpha Psi; dir, Des Moines Chap Boys Clubs Am; US Congress Comt Educ & Labor. **Military Serv:** USAF pilot WwII. **Business Addr:** President, National Education Association, 1201 16th St NW, Washington, DC 20036.

HARRIS, JAMES E.
School administrator, educator. **Personal:** Born Sep 24, 1946, Castalia, NC; married Justine Perry; children: Kasheena & Jamillah. **Educ:** Montclair State Col, BA, 1968, MA, 1970; Pub Serv Inst NJ, 1974; Harvard Univ, summer, 1974; New York Univ, attended 1973-. **Career:** Montclair State Col, asst librn, 1964-67; Camp Weequahic, Lake Como, PA, porter, 1964; Montclair State Col, res counr Upward Bound Project summer,1966-67; Elko Lake Camp, NY, counr, 1965; Bamberger's, Newark, asst dir community rels, 1968; Montclair State Col, counr, 1969-70, asst dean stud, 1970-, cross country coach, 1975-, assoc dean stud & ombuds person, 1986-. **Orgs:** Pres, NJ Asn Black Educr, 1973-; Montclair Civil Rights Comn, 1979-; pres, Nat Asn Advan Colored People Montclair Br, 1983; chmn, NJ Black Issues invention Educ Task Force, 1986-; consult, Educ Testing Serv, Am Col Testing Inc; Ctr Opportunity & Personnel Efficiency, NJ; Nat Orientation Directors Asn; pres, Montclair State Col Asn Black Faculty & Adminr Staff; pres, Educ Opportunity Fund Comt; adv bd, Montclair State Col; NoNJ Counr Asn; Nat Asn Personnel Adminr; Am Personnel & Guid Asn; Am Col Personnel Asn; vchmn, NJ Amateur Athletic Union Women Track & Field Com; bd mgr, NJ Asn Amateur Athletic Union Am; bd trustees, Leaguers Inc; dir,coach, Fed Essex Co Athletic Club Newark; Cross Country Coach Montclair State Col; Legis Aide Com Assemblyman Hawkins; N Ward Block Asn; cert mem, NJ Track & Field Officials Asn; Amateur Athletic Union Officials; chmn, Press Coun Affirmative Action Univ Med & Dent NJ; Urban League Essex County. **Honors/Awds:** Outstanding Black Educator Award; Student Leadership Award, Montclair State Col; Essex Co Volunteer Award; Athlete of the Year Award for Montclair St Coll. **Military Serv:** NJ NatlGuard, cpt. **Home Addr:** 9 Pleasant Ave, Montclair, NJ 07042, **Home Phone:** (973)783-4668. **Business Addr:** Associate Dean Students, Ombudsperson, Montclair State University ersity, Dean of Students Department, Rm 400 Stud Ctr, Montclair, NJ 07043, **Business Phone:** (973)655-4206.

HARRIS, JAMES G., JR.
Executive director. **Personal:** Born Oct 27, 1931, Cuthbert, GA; son of James Sr and Eunice Mitchner; married Roxie Lena Riggs; children: Peter C, Robin M. **Educ:** Hillyer Col, attended 1956; Univ Hartford, BS, 1958. **Career:** State Conn, social worker, 1958-59; EJ Korvette, acct payable supvr, 1959-60; State Conn, social worker, 1960-65; State Off Econ Opportunity, asst dir, 1965-66; Gov John Dempsey, spec asst to gov, 1966-70; Greater Hartford Community Renewal Team, exec dir state civil rights co-ord, 1970-82; Conn Dept Human Resources, comnr, 1983-87; Data Inst Inc, consult, 1987-89; Bethol Ctr Humane Services, consult, 1987-89. **Orgs:** Pres, life mem, Nat Asn Advan Colored People, Greater Hartford Br, 1962-64; secy, Alpha Phi Alpha, 1964-66; chmn, chmn emer, State Conf Nat Asn Advan Colored People, 1967-70; Pres legis chmn, Conn Asn Comt Action, 1975-83; vpres & panelist, New Eng Comn Action Assoc, 1977-80; Gov's Task Force Homeless, 1983-; Adult Educ Study Comn, 1984-; Priorities Comm United Way, 1984-; Gov's Designee Femia Distrib Comt, 1984. **Honors/Awds:** Outstanding Service Award, New Eng Chap, Nat Asn Advan Colored People, 1962; Charter Oak Leadership Award, Hartford Chamber Com, 1964; Distinguished Service Award, Phoenix Soc Hartford 1979; Outstanding Service, New Eng CAP Dir Asn, 1981-83; Hon DHL, New Hampshire Col, 1984; Lifetime Achievement Award, Nat Asn Advan Colored People Conf, CT, 1990. **Military Serv:** USAF, sgt, 4 yrs. *

HARRIS, JASPER WILLIAM
Educator, psychologist. **Personal:** Born Dec 10, 1935, Kansas City, MO; son of Jasper and Mary P; married Joann S Harper; children: Jasper Jr MD. **Educ:** Rockhurst Col, BS, biol, 1958; Univ Mo, MA, 1961; Univ Kans, EdD, 1971, PhD, 1981. **Career:** Univ Kans, res assoc, 1969-77; Kans City Sch Dist, teacher, 1963-69, assoc supt, 1977-86, supt, 1986-, asst supvr, 1988-91; Blue Springs Sch Dist, Spec Educ, exec dir, 1992-. **Orgs:** Phi Delta Kappa Fraternity; Alpha Phi Alpha Fraternity; Jr Chamber Com; Rockhurst Col Alumni Asn; Univ Mo Alumni Asn; vice chmn, United Negro Col Fund; adv bd & chmn educ & youth incentives comn, Urban League; Sci Teachers Asn; Am Educ Res Asn; Am Psychol Asn; Univ Kans Alumni Asn; life mem, Nat Asn Advan Colored People; Asn Supervision & Curriculum Develop, Personnel Res Forum; theta boule, Sigma Pi Phi Fraternity; consult, Kaw Valley Med Soc Health Careers Prog, 1971-; participant, Pres US Comn Employ Handicapped, White House, Wash, DC, 1980; bd trustees, Park Col, 1984-94; Univ Kans, alumni bd mem. **Honors/Awds:** SPOKE Award; US Jaycees for Community Services; Outstanding Young Man of America, 1970; Outstanding Young Educator of Greater Kansas City Jr Chamber of Commerce; Life-time Teaching Certificate in Science for the State of Missouri; Life-time Administrative Secondary Certificate for the State of Missouri; Life-time Superintendent's Certificate; selected reviewer, manuscripts submitted publ Exceptional C, 1984-85; appointed, Mo State, Dept Funding Comn Study Group, Comnr Educ, 1985; appointed assoc ed, Exceptal C J, 1985; Special Education Certification; appointed by the Office of the Secretary of Education, Dept Educ to a review panel for identifying exemplary secondary schools Washington DC, 1985; numerous publications and book chapters. **Business Addr:** Executive Director, Blue Springs School District, Special Education, 1801 NW Vesper, Blue Springs, MO 64015.*

HARRIS, JAY TERRENCE
Media executive. **Personal:** Born Dec 3, 1948, Washington, DC; married Anna Christine; children: Taifa Akida, Jamarah Kai, Shala Marie. **Educ:** Lincoln Univ, BA, 1970. **Career:** Wilmington News-J, gen assignment reporter, 1970, urban affairs reporter, 1970-71, investigative reporter, 1971-73; Wilmington News-J Papers, spec projs ed, 1974-75; Northwestern Univ, instr journ & urban affairs, 1973-75, asst prof journ & urban affairs, 1975-82; Frank E Gannett Urban Journ Ctr, asst dir, 1975-76, assoc dir, 1976-82; Northwestern Univ Medill Sch Journ, asst dean, 1977-82; Gannett News Servs, nat corresp, 1982-84; Gannett Newspapers & USA Today, columnist, 1984-85; Philadelphia Daily News, exec ed, 1985-88; Knight-Ridder, exec ed, Newspaper Div, asst to pres, vpres opers, 1988-94; San Jose Mercury News, chmn & publisher, 1994-. **Orgs:** bd mem, Joint Venture, Silicon Valley Network, Bay Area Council; bd mem, Am Leadership Forum; bd mem, Community Found Santa Clara C; bd mem, Tech Mus Innovation; bd mem, Santa Clara C Mfg Group; trustee, John S & James L Knight Found; bd mem, Am Press Inst; Pacific Coun Int Policy; Coun Foreign Rels. **Honors/Awds:** Public Serv Awards, Assoc Press Managing Ed Asn & Greater PA Chap Sigma Delta Chi; Spec Citation Investigation Minority Employ Daily Newspapers, Nat Urban Coalition, 1979; Par Excellence Award Distinguished Serv Journ, Oper PUSH, 1984; Drum Major Justice Award, Southern Christian Leadership Conf, 1985; Siebert Lect, Mich State Univ, 2000. **Special Achievements:** Co-author of a series of articles on heroin trafficking in Wilmington DE. **Business Addr:** Chairman, Publisher, San Jose Mercury News, 750 Ridder Park Dr, San Jose, CA 95190.*

HARRIS, DR. JAZMINE A
Pediatrician. **Educ:** MD. **Career:** Mem Hosp Salem County, pediatrician, currently; pvt pract, currently. **Honors/Awds:** Pediatric Emergency Medicine Award, 2000; Sidney J. Sussman

Award, 2001-02. **Business Addr:** Physician, 621 Beverly Rancocas Rd Suite 2D, Willingboro, NJ 08046.*

HARRIS, JEANETTE (MOMMA J)
Artist, writer, singer. **Personal:** Born Mar 6, 1952, Bridgeport, CT; daughter of Hugo and Rosetta; married; children: Lonnell Lawson Jr & Lynnette D Lawson. **Educ:** Found Bible Inst, BA, 1998. **Career:** Ethan Allen Furniture, Internal Audit Dept, secy; United Illuminating Co, acct payable clerk; Northeast Utilities, customer serv rep; Southern Conn Gas Co, customer serv rep; performance artist, storyteller, writer, composer, singer, 3D Motivational Entertainment, currently. **Orgs:** Mendelsohn Chorale Conn. **Special Achievements:** Writer, producer & dir, "The Church of Mis-Spent Time", 1996; CCA, first comedy showcase, 2000; 3J Productions; play, "Skyy Piece", produced, 2000; Workshop Presenter, Conn Storytelling Ctr, 2000; Runner-up in "Liars Contest", Nat Asn Black Story Tellers Festival, 2001; auth & publ, "Temporary Insanity", What's A Women to Do?, poetry collection; Radio Hostess for weekly broadcast, "An Encouraging Word". **Business Addr:** Performance Artist, 3D Motivational Entertainment, PO Box 524, Bridgeport, CT 06601, **Business Phone:** (203)366-6778.

HARRIS, JEANETTE G.
Executive. **Personal:** Born Jul 18, 1934, Philadelphia, PA; divorced. **Educ:** Inst Banking, 1970. **Career:** First PA Bank NA, banking officer, bank mgr; dept store bookkeeper, sales clerk. **Orgs:** Urban League; bd dir, YMCA; bd mem, Philadelphia Parent Child Care Ctr; vis prof BEEP; Nat Assn Black Women Inc; Philadelphia Black Bankers Assn; comn orgn dealing sr city; past treas, Ch Federal Credit Union; treas, Merchants Assn Progress Plaza Shopping Ctr. **Special Achievements:** First black female bank mgr in Philadelphia.

HARRIS, JEROME C., JR.
Government official, administrator, president (organization). **Personal:** Born Dec 15, 1947, New York, NY; married Rosemarie Mcqueen; children: Rahsaan, Jamal. **Educ:** Rutgers Univ, BA, 1969, MS, urban planning & pub policy anal, 1971. **Career:** Livingston Col, Rutgers, Dept Community Develop, instr, asst to dean acad affairs, 1969-73; Mayor's Policy & Develop Off, Newark, dir urban inst, 1973-74, urban develop coord, 1974-75; Middlesex County Econ Opportunities Corp, dep exec dir mgt & admin, 1975-77; NJ Educ Opportunities Fund, Dept Higher Educ, asst dir, fiscal affairs, 1977-78, assoc dir budget & fiscal planning, 1978-82; City Plainfield, dir pub works & urban develop, 1982, dep city admin, 1983, city admin, 1983, vpres govt affairs; Essex County, admin; State NJ, asst secy & asst treas; Rowan Univ, Urban & Pub Policy Inst, exec dir, Polit Sci Dept, adj prof; Harris Orgn, pres, currently. **Orgs:** Pres, NJ Jaycees, 1977; vpres, New Brunswick Nat Asn Advan Colored People, 1978-79; pres, NJ Pub Policy Res Inst, 1979-84; chmn, Middlesex City CETA Adv Comt, 1979-83; chmn, NJ Black Issues Conv, 1983-; Int City Mgrs Asn; Am Soc Pub Admin, Conf Minority Pub Admin, Forum Black Pub Admin, NJ Munic Mgrs Asn; bd dir, Plainfield Econ Develop Corp; State NJ, Adv Comt Police Standars; CAMConnect; Capital Corridor CDC; Camden African Am Cult Ctr. **Honors/Awds:** Outstanding Black Educr, NJ Asn Black Educ, 1983; Serv Award, NJ Black United Fund, 1984. **Business Addr:** President, The Harris Organization.*

HARRIS, JOHN, III
Educator. **Personal:** Born in Altoona, PA. **Educ:** Highland Pk Col, Mich; Wayne State Univ, BS; Univ Mich, MS, Behavioral Sci Educ & Educ Admin & Supv, PhD, Educ Admin & Supv. **Career:** Univ Ky, Col Educ, prof & dean; Col Educ Cleveland State Univ, prof & dean; Sch Educ, prof & chmn div educ leadership & Policy Studies; Ind Univ Ctr fro Urban & Multicultrual Educ, dir, assoc dir off sch prog, special asst dean; Detroit Pub Schs, asst prin, 1968-73; Pa State Univ, Univ Pk, asst prof, 1973-76; USDA, state urban curriculum specialist & prog coordr; African Am Studies & Res, prof admin & supv, currently; Comn Diversity Univ Ky, chmn, currently. **Business Phone:** (859)257-3593.*

HARRIS, JOHN B., JR.
Executive. **Career:** Deutsche Bank AG, vpres, eTelecare, chief exec officer & pres, currently. **Business Addr:** Chief Executive Officer, President, Deutsche Bank AG, 60 Wall St, New York, NY 10005, **Business Phone:** (212)250-2500.*

HARRIS, JOHN CLIFTON
Physician. **Personal:** Born Jan 15, 1935, Greensboro, NC. **Educ:** NY Col Podiatric Med; NC Agr & Tech, BS, 1962; Howard Univ, attended 1965. **Career:** Dr Podiatric Med, self employed; Addiction Res & Treat Corp, 1972; Lyndon B Johnson Community Health Ctr, staff podiatrist, 1974-77; Towers Nursing Home, staff podiatrist, 1970-71; 125th St Comm Med Group, 1970-74. **Orgs:** Podiatry Soc State NY; Am Podiatry Asn; Acad Podiatry; NY Co Podiatry Soc; bd dir, Harlem Philharmonic Soc Inc; Nat Bd Podiatry; Nat Asn Advan Colored People; YMCA. **Military Serv:** USAF, med serv spl, 1954-58. **Business Phone:** (212)491-6646.*

HARRIS, JOHN H.
Financial manager. **Personal:** Born Jul 7, 1940, Wynne, AR; married Adele E Lee; children: Cheryl E & Angela M. **Educ:** Southern Ill Univ, BS, 1967; Southwestern Grad Sch Banking, 1974. **Career:** Gateway Nat Bank, vpres, cashier, 1967-74, exec vpres, 1975; Boatmens Nat Bank, opers officer, 1976-77; Sch Dist Univ City, dir finance. **Orgs:** Nat Bankers Asn, 1967-; Am Inst Banking, 1967-77; adv Jr Achievement MS Valley Inc, 1967-77; Bank Admin Inst, 1968-73; dir treas, St Louis Coun Campfire Girls Inc, 1972-73; Phi Beta Lambda; Nat Asn Black Accts, 1974-75; treas, fund dr United Negro Col Fund, 1975; bd dir, Inst Black Studies, 1977; NAACP, US Selective Serv Comm; dir treas, Greely Comm Ctr Waring Sch PTA; dir, King-Fanon Ment Health Ctr, Child Day Care Assoc; supervisory comn, Educ Employees Credit Union; treas, Block Unit 1144; dir, Am Cancer Soc.

HARRIS, DR. JOHN H.
Educator. **Personal:** Born Aug 12, 1940, Memphis, TN. **Educ:** LeMoyne Col, BS, 1962; Atlanta Univ, MA, 1966; Memphis State Univ, PhD, 1990. **Career:** US Peace Corps, pc vol Accra Ghana, 1962-64; LeMoyne-Owen Col, instr, 1967-, div natural sci & math sci, prof, currently; LeMoyne-Owen Col, prof math & Comput sci, currently. **Orgs:** Nat Asn Math, 1986-; Am Math Soc, 1987-; Math Asn Am, 1996-; bd mem, Memphis Urban Math Colaborative, (MUMC). **Honors/Awds:** UNCF Faculty Fellow, 1978; IBM/UNCF Faculty Fellow, 1987-90. **Business Addr:** Professor, LeMoyne-Owen College, Division of Natural Science, Mathematics and Computer Science, 807 Walker Ave, Memphis, TN 38126-6595, **Business Phone:** (901)435-1381.

HARRIS, JOHN J.
Chief executive officer. **Personal:** Born Sep 18, 1951, Plymouth, NC; son of Jerome Harris; married; children: 3. **Educ:** Calif State Univ, BA, 1972; Univ Calif, Los Angeles Grad Sch Mgt, MBA, 1974. **Career:** Carnation Co, mkt mgt trainee, 1974, vpres & gen mgr, 1987-91; Friskies Pet Care Div, vpres & gen mgr, 1991; Nestle SA, sr vpres, 1997; Friskies PetCare Co, pres, 1999; Nestle worldwide, chief exec officer & chief world wide integration officer, 2001; Nestle Purina European oper, ceo, 2002-; Nestle Waters, ceo, exec vpres & chmn, 2008-. **Orgs:** Chmn, Pet Food Insts Brd of Dirs, 1993; Lane Col Brd Dirs. **Special Achievements:** Featured in Forbes, Calif Bus, Men of Courage book. **Business Phone:** (412)1924-2111.

HARRIS, JONATHAN CECIL
Football player. **Personal:** Born Jun 9, 1974, Brooklyn, NY. **Educ:** Univ Va. **Career:** Philadelphia Eagles, defensive end, 1997-98; Cleveland Browns, defensive end, 1999; Green Bay Packers, defensive end, 1999; Oakland Raiders, 2002; free agent, currently.

HARRIS, DR. JOSEPH BENJAMIN
Executive. **Personal:** Born Jun 8, 1920, Richmond, VA; son of Joseph Brown and Alice Burrell; married Pauline Elizabeth McKinney; children: Paula Jo, Joseph C & Joya R. **Educ:** VA Union Univ, BS, 1949; Howard Univ, DDS, 1953. **Career:** CA Howell & Co, pres, 1967-72, chmn bd, 1972-; pvt pract, dentist, currently. **Orgs:** Omega Psi Phi, 1947-; Am Dental Soc, 1953-; MI Dental Soc, 1953-; Det Dental Soc, 1953-; Nat Dental Soc, 1955-; Am Dental Fund, 1980; Sigma Pi Phi, 1970. **Honors/Awds:** Am Soc Dentistry for Children, 1953; Detroit Howardite of the Year, Howard Univ Alumni Detroit, 1991. **Military Serv:** AUS, sfc, sgt, 1943-46; Battle of Normandy; Good Conduct Medal; Victory Medal World War II; Asiatic Pacific Theater with 1 Bronze Star, 1944. **Business Addr:** Dentist, 2431 W Grand Blvd, Detroit, MI 48208, **Business Phone:** (313)895-4300.*

HARRIS, JOSEPH ELLIOT, II
Automotive executive. **Personal:** Born Feb 21, 1945, Boston, MA; son of Joseph E and Muriel K; married Young-Ja Chung, Jun 15, 1983; children: Joy Electra & Joseph E III. **Educ:** Howard Univ, BSEE, 1968; Rochester Inst Technol, MBA, 1976; Northeastern Univ, cert advan studies, 1979. **Career:** Stromberg Carlson, elec engr, 1967-74; Xerox Corp, sr mfg engr, 1974-76; Ford Motor Co, buyer, 1976-78; Polaroid Corp, purchasing mgr, 1978-91; Chrysler Corp, exec special supplier relations, 1991-. **Orgs:** Vice chmn, MNY Enterprise Dev Week, 1988-91; Nat Asn Purchasing Mgt, min bus dev group, 1988-92; Mattapan Co Health, 1989-91; Try-Us, 1992; Nat Minority Supplier Develop, 1992; chmn, Mic Minority bus develop, 1992; Oakland Boy Scout, 1992. **Honors/Awds:** Buyer of the Year, New England Min Purchasing Coun, 1988; Coordinator of the Year, Black Corp Pres New England, 1988; Small Business Advocate of the Year, US Small bus admin, 1989; Min Business Advocate of the Year, Commonwealth Mass, 1990; Top Ten Purchasers, Electronic Buyers News, 1992. **Special Achievements:** Microcomputer Technologies for Minority Sourcing, 1987; A Perfect Match, MNY Business News, 1992; Black Achievers, Boston MA, 1990. **Military Serv:** USAF, ROTC. **Home Phone:** (313)567-0107. **Business Addr:** Executive, Chrysler Corp, 12000 Chrysler Dr, Highland Park, MI 48288-1919, **Business Phone:** (313)252-6094.

HARRIS, JOSEPH JOHN, III
Educator, school administrator. **Personal:** Born Oct 10, 1946, Altoona, PA; son of Joseph John II and Ann M Hart; married Donna Ford, Aug 24, 1988; children: Julie Renee & Khyle Lee. **Educ:** Highland Park Col, AS, 1967; Wayne State Univ, BS, 1969; Univ Mich, AnnArbor, MS, 1971, PhD, 1972. **Career:** Detroit Pub Sch, teacher, asst prin, 1968-73; Highland Pk Pub Sch, consult proj dir, 1973; Pa State Univ, asst prof, 1973-76; Ind Univ, assoc prof,1976-83, prof, chair, ctr dir, 1983-87; Cleveland State Univ, prof, dean,1987-90; African-Am Studies & Res, scholar in residence, currently; Univ Ky, prof & dean, 1990-95, prof admin & supv, 1995-, Pres Comn Diversity, chair, advisor, currently. **Orgs:** Bd dir, Marotta Montessori Sch Cleveland, 1987-90; bd trustees, Greater Cleveland Lit Coalition, 1988-; adv bd, Nat Sorority Phi Delta Kappa,1988-; bd trustees, Nat Pub Radio Affiliate-WCPNW, 1988-; bd dir, Nat Orgn Legal Problems Educ, 1988-91; ed bd, CSU Mag, 1989-; Lexington Arts & Cultural Ctr; Holmes Group Ed Schools, E Lansing. **Special Achievements:** Author: "Education, Society & the Brown Decision," Journal of Black Studies, 1982; "The Outlaw Generation," Educational Horizons, 1982;"Identifying Diamond in the Rough," The Gifted Child Today, 1990; "Public School-Univ Collaboration", Community Education Journal, 1989; "The Resurrection of Play in Gifted.," Journal for the Education of the Gifted,1990; "The Elusive Definition of Creativity", The Journal of Creative Behavior, 1992; "Dissonance in the Education Ecology," Metropolitan Universities, 1991; "The American Achievement Ideology and Achievement Differentials Among Pre adolescent Gifted and Non gifted African Males & Females", Journal of Negro Edu, 1992. **Business Addr:** Professor of Administration and Supervision, Scholar in Residence, University Kentucky, College of Education, 103 Dickey Hall, Lexington, KY 40506-0017, **Business Phone:** (859)257-6169.

HARRIS, JOSEPH PRESTON
Executive. **Personal:** Born Apr 11, 1935, Rome, MS; married Otha L; children: Jacqui & Joe Jr. **Educ:** Chicago Tchrs Col, BE 1956; John Marshall Law Sch, JD, 1964. **Career:** Chicago Bd Educ, teacher, 1956-64; Allstate Ins Co, asst vpres. **Orgs:** Bd dirs, Maywood Proviso State Bank, 1973-76; Ill & Chicago Bar Asn; Nat Asn Advan Colored People. **Home Addr:** 2431 W Grand Ave, Detroit, MI 48208.

HARRIS, JOYCE
Executive. **Educ:** Howard Univ, grad; Johns Hopkins Univ, Baltimore, MBA, mkt. **Career:** USAToday.com, former asst news ed; US Mint, Web Content Office Appln Develop, exec producer, web dir, div chief, currently, spokeswoman, currently. **Business Addr:** Division Chief, US Mint, Web Content Office of Application Development, 801 9th St NW, Washington, DC 20220, **Business Phone:** (202)354-7222.

HARRIS, JUAN
Government official. **Career:** City Paterson, bus Adminr, currently. **Business Addr:** Business Administrator, City of Paterson, 155 Market St City Hall 2nd Fl, Paterson, NJ 07505, **Business Phone:** (973)881-3365.

HARRIS, KAMALA D.
District attorney. **Personal:** Born Jan 1, 1964?, Oakland, CA; daughter of Donald and Shyamala Gopalan. **Educ:** Howard Univ, Wash, DC; Univ Calif Hastings Col Law, JD, 1990. **Career:** Alameda County, dep dist atty, 1990-98; Career Criminal Unit, San Francisco Dist Atty's Off, 1998-; City Atty's off, Chief Community & Neighborhood Div, 2000-. **Orgs:** Founder, Coalition to End the Exploitation of Kids. **Honors/Awds:** Hon Woman of Power, Nat Urban League, 2004; Thurgood Marshall Award, Nat Black Prosecutors Asn, 2005; One of the top 100 lawyers in Calif, The Daily Journal Calif. **Special Achievements:** First woman District Attorney in San Francisco; First African American to serve as top prosecutor in California; First Indian American to serve as district attorney in the United States. **Business Phone:** (415)553-1752.*

HARRIS, KELLY C.
Association executive. **Career:** YMCA Greater Richmond, bd dir, currently. **Business Addr:** Board Director, YMCA Greater Richmond, 2 W Franklin St, Richmond, VA 23220, **Business Phone:** (804)649-9622.*

HARRIS, KENNETH G.
Executive, educator. **Educ:** Tex A&M Univ, Edd, 1993. **Career:** Henderson State Univ, Dept curriculum & Instr, prof & chair, currently. **Orgs:** Pres, Arkadelphia School Board, 2007.

HARRIS, LEE
Journalist. **Personal:** Born Dec 30, 1941, Bryan, TX; married Lois. **Educ:** Calif State Univ, 1968. **Career:** Riverside Press, 1968-72; San Bernardino Sun Telegra, 1972-73; Los Angeles Times, reporter. **Special Achievements:** "L.A. City Hall Turns a Genteel 50", 1978. **Military Serv:** AUS, sp 4, 1964-67. **Business Addr:** Reporter, Los Angeles Times, Times Mirror Sq, Los Angeles, CA 90053.*

HARRIS, LEODIS
Judge. **Personal:** Born Aug 11, 1934, Pensacola, FL; married Patsy Auzenne; children: Courtney, Monique, Darwin. **Educ:** Cleveland Col Western Res Univ, attended 1957; Cleveland Marshall Law Sch, JD, 1963. **Career:** Pvt prac law, 1963-77; Com-

mon Pleas Ct Juvenile Div, juvenile ct judge, 1993. **Orgs:** The Greater Cleveland Citizens League, 1961-; Urban Affairs Com Cleveland Bar Asn, 1975-77; Honorary Trustees, Cleveland-Marshall Law Alumni Asn, 2005. **Honors/Awds:** Service award, Cleveland Jr Women's Civic League, 1978; Freedom Award, Cleveland Nat Asn Advan Colored People, 1979; Man of the Yr, Cleveland Negro Bus & Prof Women, 1979; Silver Award, OH Prince Hall Knights Templar, 1980; publ features, Ebony, Nat Star, Nat Enquirer, Cleveland Plain Dealer Sun Mag; media appearances, Today Show, Good Morning Am Show, British Broadcasting, Canadian Broadcasting Corp, numerous local TV & radio shows; speaks, German & Russian; Award for Advocacy for Juveniles is named in his honor. **Military Serv:** AUS, spec 4th cl, 1957-59. *

HARRIS, LEON L.
Labor activist. **Personal:** Born in Nyack, NY; married Evelyn. **Educ:** Hampton Inst, attended 1950; RI Col Educ, AA, 1956; Harvard Univ, attended 1963. **Career:** John Hope Settlement Providence, athletic instr, 1950-53; Providence, New Eng, phys educ instr, 1954-60; ASFCME AFL-CIO, int rep, 1960-64. **Orgs:** Dir, Civil Rights Res Educ; Retail Wholesale Dept Store Union & AFL-CIOCLC, 1964-; nat life mem, com Nat Asn Advan Colored People; vchmn, Manhood Found Inc; adv bd, recruitment training prog, NY Black Trade Union Leadership Com; pres, Greenwich Village Nat Asn Advan Colored People 8 other chaps; pres, New Eng Golf Asn; nat vpres, United Golf Asn; Am Social Club; chmn, CORE Rochester; lectured several univ; A Philip Randolph Inst; Friends Nat Black Theater. **Honors/Awds:** Honor Award Outstanding Athlete, Am Legion, 1947; 16 Letterman; Kans City Monarchs. **Special Achievements:** First black New England to sign with St Louis Cardinals, 1952.

HARRIS, LEONARD ANTHONY
Baseball player, baseball executive. **Personal:** Born Oct 28, 1964, Miami, FL; son of Arthur and Rebecca Clark; married Carnettia Evan Johnson, Feb 17, 1990. **Educ:** Miami-Dade Col. **Career:** Baseball player (retired), baseball coach; Cincinnati Reds, 1988-89,1994-98; Los Angeles Dodgers, infielder, 1989-93; NY Mets, 1998, 2000-01; Colo Rockies, 1999; Ariz Diamondbacks, 1999-2000; Milwaukee Brewers, 2002; Chicago Cubs, 2003; Fla Marlins, infielder, 2003-05; Wash Nationals, infield coordr, interim hitting coach, 2008; Los Angeles Dodgers, hitting inst, currently. **Orgs:** Optimist Club of Miami, 1990-91. **Business Addr:** Professional Baseball Player, Washington Nationals, Infield Coordinator, RFK Stadium, 2400 E Capitol St SE, Washington, DC 20003, **Business Phone:** (202)675-6287.*

HARRIS, LESLIE E.
Judge. **Personal:** Born May 23, 1948, Chicago. **Educ:** Northwestern Univ, attended 1970; Boston Univ, MA, 1974; Boston Col Law Sch, attenhded 1984. **Career:** Suffolk County, probation officer, 1978-81; Comt Pub Coun Serv, 1987-92; Suffolk County Dist Attys Off, Juv Div, chief, 1992-94; Suffolk County Juv Ct, Judge, 1994-. **Honors/Awds:** Judge of the Yr Award, Mass Judges Conf; Community Serv Award, Mass Bar Asn; 10-Point Coalition Serv Award; Mary Q Hawkes Serv Award, Crime & Justice Found; Distinguished Alumni Award, Boston Col Law Sch. **Business Addr:** Judge, Suffolk County Juvenile Court, Juvenile Court Dept Edward W Brooke Courthouse, 24 New Chardon St 5th Fl PO Box 9663, Boston, MA 02114, **Business Phone:** (617)788-8565.*

HARRIS, LESTER L.
Administrator. **Personal:** Married; children: Michelle, Ernie, Leon & Lester. **Career:** Econ Opportunity Coun of Suffolk Inc, chmn. **Orgs:** Vpres, Deer Pk, NAACP, 1964-70, pres, 1973-74; elected committee man, Babylon Dem Party; Suffolk Co Migrant Bd; Suffolk Co Hansel & Gretal Inc; Deer Pk Civic Asn; Negro Airman Int Inc. **Honors/Awds:** Suffolk Co Humanitarian Award, Suffolk Co Locality Mayor JF Goode & Ossie Davis, 1973. *

HARRIS, LORETTA K
Librarian. **Personal:** Born Nov 20, 1935, Bryant, MS; daughter of Estella Kelley Parker; married James Joe Harris; children: Sheila Lynne Harris Ragin. **Educ:** S Ill Univ, cert, 1954; Kennedy-19King Col, cert, 1971; City Col Chicago-19Loop, dip, 1974; Chicago State Univ, BA, 1983, MSLS, 1990. **Career:** Librarian (retired); Univ Il Libr, photog tech, 1957-59; S Ill Univ Libr, library clerk, 1959-63; Univ Ill Chicago, libr clerk, 1963-68; John Crerar Libr, order librn, 1968-70; Univ Ill Chicago, Library Health Sci, libr tech asst III, 1970-98; Memphis City Sch Syst, substitute teacher, 2005. **Orgs:** Chairperson, Coun Libr & Media Tech Assts, 1977-80, const chairperson, 1980-84, Med Libr Asn Midwest Chap, 1976-98; Health Sci Librn Ill, 1976-98; Ontario Asn Libr Techs, 1977-90; Black women Mid W Proj, 1984, Am Libr Assoc, Standing Comm Libr Ed; Training Libr Supportive Staff Subcomm, 1979-81; Int Fedn Libr & Asn & Insts Printing & Reproduction Comt IFLA annual meeting, 1985; Nat Coun Negro Women, 1986; const chairperson, Coun Libr & Media Tech Assts, 1986-91, chairperson, nominating comt, 1988; Ill Sch Libr Asn, 1990; corresp secy, Nat Assoc Negro Musicians, R Nathaniel Dett Branch, 1993-97; Janice Watkins Award Comm; 1994-95, 1997. **Special Achievements:** Listed in Natl Deans List, 1982-83. **Home Addr:** 4011 Lacewood Dr, Memphis, TN 38115, **Home Phone:** (901)366-9092.

HARRIS, LUCIOUS H
Basketball player. **Personal:** Born Dec 18, 1970, Los Angeles, CA; children: Lucious III. **Educ:** Calif State Univ, Long Beach, attended 1993. **Career:** Basketball player (retired); Dallas Mavericks, guard, 1994-96; Philadelphia 76ers, 1996-97; NJ Nets, 1997-2004; Cleveland Cavaliers, guard, 2004-05. **Honors/Awds:** Long Beach State's Athletic Hall of Fame, 1999.

HARRIS, M. L. (MICHAEL LEE HARRIS)
Football player. **Personal:** Born Jan 16, 1954, Columbus, OH; married Linda; children: Michael Lee II & Joshua. **Educ:** Univ Tampa; Kans State Univ. **Career:** Football player (retired); Hamilton Tiger-Cats, tight end, 1976-77; Toronto Argonauts, tight end, 1978-79; Cincinnati Bengals, 1980-85. **Orgs:** Founder, ML Harris Outreach; Sports World Ministries.

HARRIS, MARCELITE J.
Air force officer. **Personal:** Born Jan 16, 1943, Houston, TX; daughter of Cecil Oneal and Marcelite Elizabeth Terrell Jordan; married Maurice Anthony, Nov 29, 1980; children: Steven Eric & Tenecia Marcelite. **Educ:** Spelman Col, Atlanta, GA, 1964; Squadon Offr Sch, Corresp, Air Univ, Montgomery, AL, 1975; Cent Mich Univ, Wash, DC, 1978; Chapman Col, Colo Springs, CO, 1980; Air War Col, Seminar, Air Univ, Montgomery, AL, 1982; Univ Md, Okinawa, Japan, BS, 1986; Sr Offs in Nat Security, Harvard Univ, Boston, MA, 1989; CAPSTONE, Residence, Nat Defense Univ, Wash DC, 1990; Nat & Int Security Mgt Course, Harvard Univ, Boston, MA, 1994, Sr Mgr Govt, 1995. **Career:** Air force Officer (retired); Head Start, Houston, TX, teacher, 1964-65 Travis Air Force Base, 60th Mil Airlift Wing, asst dir for admin, 1965-67; Bitburg Air Base, West Germany, 71st Tactical Missile Squadron, administrative Offr, 1969-70; Korat Royal Thai Air Force Base, Thailand, 49th Tactical Fighter Squadron, maintenance supvr, 1971-72; Travis Air Force Base, Calif, from job control Offr to field maintenance supvr, 1972-75; Headquarters USAF, Wash, DC, personnel staff Offr & White House social aide, 1975-78; USAF Acad, Colo Springs, Colo, Cadet Squadron 39, air Offr commanding, 1978-80; Mc Connell Air Force Base, Kans, maintenance control Offr, 384th Air Refueling Wing, 1980-81, commander 384th Avionics Maintenance Squadron, 1981-82, commander 384th Field Maintenance Squadron, 1982; Pacific Air Forces Logistic Support Ctr, Kadena Air Base, Japan, dir maintenance, 1982-86; Keesler Air Force Base, Miss, dep commander for maintenance, 1986-88, commander 3300th Tech Training Wing, 1988-90; Tinker Air Force Base, Okla City Air Logistics Ctr, vice commander, 1990-93; Headquarters Air Educ & Training Command, Randolph Air Force Base, dir tech training, 1993-94; Headquarters USAF, Wash, dir maintenance, 1994-97; United Space Alliance, 1997-2002. **Orgs:** Air Force Asn, 1965-; Tuskegee Airmen, 1990-; Miss Gulf Coast Chamber Com, 1987-90; Biloxi Rotary, 1989-90; Delta Sigma Theta, 1980-; Bd Dirs, United Services Automobile asn, 1993; Unite States Rep to the Women in NATO Comm, 1994. **Honors/Awds:** White House Social Aide, Pres Carter, 1977-78; one first two women cadet squadron commanders, USAF Acad, 1978; Woman Year, New Orleans Chap, Nat Sports Orgn, 1989; Outstanding Young Woman of America, 1990; Women of Distinction Award, Thomas W. Anthony Chapter, Air Force Asn, 1995; has received numerous other civilian awards. **Special Achievements:** First Woman Aircraft maintenance officer, USAF, 1969; first woman Avionic sand Field Maintenance Squadron Commander, Strategic Air Command, 1981-82; first woman dir of maintenance in the USAF, 1982; first woman deputy commander of maintenance in the USAF, 1986; Top 100 Afro-American Business & Professional Women, Dollars & Sense Magazine, 1989; first African-American woman brigadier general, USAF, 1990; First African-American woman major general in the United States, 1995. **Military Serv:** US Air Force, 1994-97; Legion of Merit (twice); Bronze Star; Meritorious Service Medal (four times); Air Force Commendation Medal (twice); Distinguished Presidential Unit citation; Air Force Outstanding Unit Award (eight times), with Valor (one time-Vietnam War); Air Force Organizational Excellence Award (twice); Vietnam Service Medal; Republic of Vietnam Gallantry Cross with Device; Republic of Vietnam Campaign Medal; Nat Defense Service Medal; Air Forces Overseas Long Tour Ribbon (twice); Air Force Overseas Short Tour Ribbon, others.

HARRIS, DR. MARION HOPKINS
Educator, vice president (organization). **Personal:** Born Jul 27, 1938, Washington, DC; daughter of Dennis C Hopkins and Georgia Greenleaf; divorced; children: Alan Edward MD. **Educ:** Univ Pittsburgh, MUA, 1971; USC, MPA, 1985; Univ Southern Calif, DPA, 1986. **Career:** Westinghouse Corp, Pittsburgh, housing consult, 1970-71; Univ Pittsburgh, Carnegie-Mellon fel, 1970-71; Dept Urban Renewal & Econ Develop, Rochester, NY, dir prog planning; Fairfax City, Redevel & Housing Auth, exec dir, 1971-72; HUD Detroit Area Off, dep dir housing, 1973-75; US Gen Acct Off, Wash, DC, managing auditor, 1975-79; Dept Housing & Urban Develop Off Asst Sec, sr field officer housing, 1979-90, dir eval div, US Dept Housing & Urban Develop, off mgt & qual assurance, 1991-; Bowie State Univ, Grad Prog Admin Mgt, coordr, prof, 1991-93, Master Pub Admin Prog, prog coordr, vpres finance & admin, 2000-, actg vpres finance & admin, 2005-07, Sch Bus, prof mgt & pub admin, currently. **Orgs:** Fel, Ford Found, 1970-71; pres, USC-WPAC Doctoral Asn, DC, 1979; exec bd mem, SW Neighborhood Assembly, DC, 1979; Black Women's Agenda, 1980; chmn, Housing Comn, DC League Women Voters, 1980-82; Adv Neighborhood Comnr, 1986; sub cabinet, Citizens Adv Bd, Wash Suburban Sanit Comn, 1989-; steering comt mem, Acad Leadership Inst, Univ Md, 1993; co-chair, bd mem, Gov Workforce Investment Bd, 1996-98; Am Soc Pub Admin; presenter, Acad Bus Admin; Gov Workforce Investment Bd Bus Admin; Am Acad Social & Polit Sci, Am Eval Asn; chmn, Educ Comn, Caribbean Am Intercultural Orgn; ex-off mem, Bowie State Univ Found. **Honors/Awds:** Outstanding Performance Award, US Dept Housing & Urban Develop, 1984, 1987; Secretary's Cert Achievement, 1988; Secretary's Group Award, 1990; Merit Award, 1990; Governor Maryland's Transition Team, 1996. **Home Addr:** 10229 Ruthland Round Rd, Columbia, MD 21044. **Business Phone:** (301)860-4000 Ext 23682.

HARRIS, MARION REX
Chairperson, association executive. **Personal:** Born Jun 30, 1934, Wayne County, NC; son of Virginia Harris and Eugene Harris; married Aronul Beauford Edwards; children: Amy, Angelique, Anjanette. **Educ:** LaSalle Ext Corres Law Sch, 1970; A&T State Univ, Hon Doc Humanities, 1983. **Career:** A&H Cleaners Inc, proprietor & chmn bd, 1965-; A&H Coin-Op Laundromat, proprietor & chmn bd, 1970-; Off Min Bus Enterprise Adv Bd, bd mem, 1970-; NC Dept Trans, bd mem, 1972-76; Custom Molders Inc, bd dirs, 1976-83; Int & Domestic Develop Corp, vice chairperson & chief exec officer, 1976-; Rexon Coal Co, chmn bd, 1981-; Vanguard Investment Co, chief exec officer, 1982-84; Cape Fear Reg Bur Community Action Inc, bd dirs. **Orgs:** Fayetteville Area Chamber Com, 1965-; NC Coal Inst, 1976-; dir, Nat Bus League, 1980-; chmn, Rexon Coal Co, 1982-; dir, Middle Atlantic Tech Ctr, 1983-; bd trustees, St Augustine's Col, 1983-; bd trustees, A&T State Univ, 1985-. **Honors/Awds:** Recognition Black Hist Sears Roebuck Co, 1969; Letter Recognition & Excellence Business US Dept Com Off Minority Bus Enterprise, 1972; Businessman of the Yr, Nat Asn Minority Cert Pub Accts, 1982; "Driven" Business, NC Mag, 1983; Horatio Alger Award, St Augustine's Col, 1983; Par Excellence Operation PUSH, 1983. **Military Serv:** 82nd airborne E7 12 yrs; Silver Star; Good Conduct Medal; Army Accom. **Business Addr:** Vice Chairperson, Chief Executive Officer, International Domestic Development Corporation, 4511 Bragg Blvd, Fayetteville, NC 28303.*

HARRIS, DR. MARJORIE ELIZABETH
College administrator. **Personal:** Born Dec 8, 1924, Indianapolis, IN; daughter of T Garfield Lewis and Violet T Harrison-Lewis; married Atty Richard Ray, Nov 20, 1965; children: Frank L Gillespie, Grant G Gillespie, Gordon L Gillespie & Jason Ray. **Educ:** WVa State Col, Inst WVA, BS, 1946; Univ Mich, Ann Arbor, MA, 1975, PhD, 1981. **Career:** Lewis Col Bus, Detroit, MI, fac, 1946-60, admin asst, 1960-65, pres, 1968-2006, property trustee chair, 2006, bd mem, currently. **Orgs:** Bd trustees, Lewis Col Bus, 1950-; bd comnrs, Detroit Pub Libr, 1970-86; regional dir, Gamma Phi Delta Sorority, 1989. **Honors/Awds:** Mayors Award of Merit, Mayor City Detroit, 1979; Spirit Detroit, City Detroit, 1979; Excellence Educator Award, Asn Black Women Higher Educ, 1986; Community Service Award, Detroit Urban League, 1988. **Special Achievements:** Fifty Most Influential Women Detroit, Detroit Monthly Magazine, 1985. **Business Addr:** Property Trustee Chair, Lewis College of Business, 17370 Meyers Rd, Detroit, MI 48235, **Business Phone:** (313)862-6300.

HARRIS, MARY LORRAINE
Government official. **Personal:** Born Jan 18, 1954, Durham, NC; daughter of Greenville E and Mable Freeland. **Educ:** NC Central Univ, BA, 1975; Univ Miami, MS, 1980. **Career:** Metro Dade Transp Admin, prog analyst, 1978-80, prog analyst 3, 1980-81, prin planner, 1981-83, chiConf Minority Transit Officials & chair 1988-;ef urban init unit, 1983-84, asst exec dir, 1984-88, asst dep dir, 1988-90; Metro Dade Co, dept human resources, adminr, 1990. **Orgs:** Bd dirs, League Women Voters, 1988-; Conf Minority Transit Officials & chair 1988-; Metro Dade Off Rehabilitative Servs, Miami, Fla, asst dir, 1989; Greater Miami Opera Guild, 1990-; Metro Dade Women's Asn; Nat Forum Black Pub Adminr; Women's Transp Sem; Nat Asn Female Execs; Am Heart Asn Greater Miami; Nat Asn Advan Colored People; chairperson, COMTO Mid Year Conf; task force Inner City "Say No To Drugs"; Metro Dade County United Way Cabinet. **Honors/Awds:** Gold Award, United Way; Outstanding Black American, State Florida, 1986. *

HARRIS, DR. MARY STYLES
Educator, executive, president (organization). **Personal:** Born Jun 26, 1949, Nashville, TN; daughter of George and Margaret; married Sidney E; children: 1. **Educ:** Lincoln Univ, BA, Biol, 1971; Cornell Univ, PhD, Molecular Genetics, 1975; Rutgers Med Sch, post-doctoral study, 1977. **Career:** Sickle Cell Found GA, exec dir, 1977-79; Morehouse Col Sch Med, asst prof, 1978-; WGTV Channel 8 Univ GA, scientist Residence, 1979-80; Atlanta Univ, asst prof Biol, 1980-81; GA Dept Human Resources, dir genetic servs; Harris & Assoc, pres & genetics consult, currently; BioTech Communs, pres, currently. **Orgs:** Bdvisitors, CDC; bd visitors, Grady Hosp; bd mem, Families First Atlanta; Women's Forum Ga; bd mem, CDC Found; GA Breast Cancer Alliance; Sickle Cell Found. **Honors/Awds:** Outstanding Young women of America,

1977-78; Outstanding Working Woman of 1980, Glamour Mag, 1979-80; Outstanding Georgia Business Woman, Ga Trend Mag, 1999; Woman of Achievement, Young Women Chrisitian Asn, 2002; Distinguished African-American Scientists of the 21 Century; Profiles in Progress Award; Excellence in Radio Broadcasting, Atlanta Med Asn, 2001 & 2002; 10 NIH grants. **Special Achievements:** Leadership Atlanta, 2000; first blacks to enter Jackson high school in Miami. **Business Addr:** President, BioTechnical Communs, 227 Sand Springs Pl Suite 103D-190, Atlanta, GA 30328, **Business Phone:** (404)252-9872.

HARRIS, DR. MARYANN
School administrator, entertainer. **Personal:** Born Jun 10, 1946, Moultrie, GA; married John W; children: Paul & Justin. **Educ:** Knoxville Col, BS, 1969; Wayne State Univ, MA, 1971; Nova Univ, EdD, 1986; Univ Akron, MA, 1992. **Career:** Case Western Res Univ, gerontology supvr, 1972-74; Cuyahoga Community Col, geront consult, 1975-80; City Cleveland, geront consult, 1980-81; Proj Rainbow Asn Inc, exec dir & founder, 1980-; East Cleveland City Sch, bdmem; UAW- Ford Develop & Training Prog, reg coord; story teller, currently. **Orgs:** Sch bd E Cleveland City Sch Dist, 1979-; geront consult, Coun Econ Opportunity Greater Cleveland, 1980-84; grants develop, Cleveland Adult Training, 1980-; pres & sr assoc Grantsmanship, Res Coun, 1980-; exec comt mem, Cuyahoga County Demo Party, 1984; chmn, Youth Comn Nat Asn AdvanColored People, 1985; second vpres, Alpha Kappa Alpha, 1985; Nat Sch Bd Asn Fed Rel Network, 1988-; Ohio Northeast Region Bd; pres, Ohio Community Educ Asn; vpres, Cleveland Asn Black Storytellers. **Honors/Awds:** Gerontology Study Grant USA Admin on Aging, 1969-71; Women's Rights, Practices Policies Community Service Award, 1984; Career Mother of the Year, Cleveland Call & Post Newspaper, 1984; Award of Achievement, Ohio School Boards Asn, 1991-94; Award Winning Author, 1997. **Business Addr:** Storyteller, Cleveland Story Tellers, 1326 E 143 St, East Cleveland, OH 44112.

HARRIS, MELVIN
Government official. **Personal:** Born Feb 9, 1953, Oxford, NC. **Educ:** NC Central Univ, BA, 1975; The Am Univ, MPA, 1977. **Career:** US Off Personnel Mgt, personnel mgt specialist, 1977; Am Fed of State Co & Munic Author, res analyst, 1977-78; Prince Georges Co MD, personnel & labor rels analyst, 1978-79; Dist Columbia Gov, prin labor rels officer, 1979-88; Howard Univ, dir labor & employees rels, 1988-92; City Baltimore, labor comnr; Off Labor & Employee Rels, Fed Aviation Admin, dir, 2004; Off Employ & Labor Mgt, exec dir. **Orgs:** Pres, Alpha Phi Omega, NC Central Univ, 1973-75; Conf of Minority Pub Admin Am Soc for Pub Admin, 1978-; roundtable coordr, Nat Capitol Area Chap Am Soc for Pub Admin, 1980-83; chmn, VA Voter Regis Educ Task Force, 1984; co-founder & treas, Nat Young Prof Forum Am Soc for Pub Admin, 1981-83; bd dir, Nat Coun Asn Policy Sci, 1984-85; bd dir, Nat Capitol Area Chap, Am Soc Pub Admin, 1980-82, 1984-85; Alexandria Forum, 1983-; co-chmn, Young Prof Forum Nat Capitol Area Chap, ASPA; camp dir, Alex Young Dem, 1982; Sponsor, N VA Voter Reg Coalition, 1983; Alex Dem Exec Comn, 1983-84; pres, Alex Young Dem, 1983-84; exec vpres, Va Young Dem, 1984-; Am Univ Title IX Adv Comn, 1984-; chmn, Va Young Dem NVA Fundraiser, 1985. **Honors/Awds:** Nat Asn Schs Pub Affairs & Pub Admin fel, 1975; Chap Serv Award, Nat Capitol Area Chap Am Soc Publ Admin, 1983. **Special Achievements:** Author: New Directions in Personnel, 1976; Starting a County Program for Alcoholic Employees, 1977; co-author: The Supreme Ct and Pub Employment, 1976; Labor Mgt Rels, 1977. *

HARRIS, MICHAEL LEE. See HARRIS, M. L.

HARRIS, REV. MICHAEL NEELY
Clergy, counselor. **Personal:** Born Feb 5, 1947, Athens, GA; son of William T and Mattie Neely Harris Samuels; married Sylvia Ann Jones, Nov 30, 1968; children: Crystal Michele, Michael Clayton. **Educ:** Morehouse Col, BA, 1968; Eastern Baptist Theol Seminary, MDiv, 1975, DMin, 1984. **Career:** Philadelphia Sch Dist, res intern, 1968-69, admin asst; Off Fedr Eval, day-care prog, 1969-71; First Baptist Church of Passtown, pastor, 1971-80; Emmanuel Baptist Church, pastor, 1980-89; Wheat St Baptist Church, pastor, 1989-. **Orgs:** Bd mem, Roosevelt, NY Bd of Educ, 1987-89; chmn, PNBC Home Mission Bd, 1988-90; bd mem, Wheat St Fed Credit Union, 1989-; Wheat St Charitable Found, chmn, 1989-; trustee, Morehouse Sch Religion, 1991-; dir, Sweet Auburn Area Improvement Asn, 1992; mayor's religious adv bd, City of Atlanta, 1992-; convener & adv, Auburn Ave Merchants Asn; Concerned Black Clergy. **Honors/Awds:** Most Outstanding Preacher, Eastern Baptist Seminary, 1975; Man of the Year, Coatesville Club of Nat Negro & Bus Prof, 1978; Man of the Year, Queens County Nat Negro Bus & Prof Women, 1987; Morehouse Col of Ministers Inductee, 1991; Outstanding Achievement in religion, Morehouse Col Atlanta Alumni Chap, 1997. **Special Achievements:** Publication: "The He, Thee, Me Program: A Stewardship Plan to Undergird a Third World Missilogical Ministry in the Context of the Black Church in the USA," 1984. **Business Addr:** Pastor, Wheat St Baptist Church, Corner Auburn Ave, William Holmes Borders Dr NE, Atlanta, GA 30312, **Business Phone:** (404)659-4328.*

HARRIS, MICHAEL WESLEY
Historian, educator. **Personal:** Born Nov 9, 1945, Indianapolis, IN; son of Edwina N Bohannon and Harold I Harris; married Carol Grier Harris (divorced 1982). **Educ:** Ball State Univ, Muncie, Ind, 1966; Andrews Univ, Berrien Springs, Mich, BA, 1967; Bowling Green State Univ, Bowling Green, OH, MM, 1968; Harvard Univ, Cambridge, MA, PhD, 1982. **Career:** Oakwood Col, Huntsville, Ala, instr music/German, 1968-71; Univ Tenn-Knoxville, Knoxville, Tenn, asst prof religious studies, 1982-87; Temple Univ, Philadelphia, Pa, vis asst prof religious studies, 1987-88; Wesleyan Univ, Middletown, Conn, assoc prof hist, 1988-91; Univ Iowa, prof hist world studies, currently; Union Theol Sem City NY, prof church hist, currently. **Orgs:** Co-chair, prog committee, Nat Coun Black Studies, 1988-90; coun mem, Am Soc Ch Hist, 1990-93; Am Historical asn, 1978-; Am Studies asn, 1987-. **Honors/Awds:** Rockefeller Humanities Fel, Rockefeller Found, 1985-86; Research Fel, Smithsonian Inst, 1979-80; Nat Fel Fund Dissertation Fel, 1976-77; History & Theory, 1990-92. **Special Achievements:** Author: The Rise of Gospel Blues: The Music of Thomas A Dorsey in the Urban Church, Oxford Univ Press, 1992. **Business Addr:** Professor, Union Theological Seminary City of New York, Deptartment of Church History, 3041 Broadway 121st St, New York, NY 10027, **Business Phone:** (212)280-1394.

HARRIS, MICHELE ROLES
Executive. **Personal:** Born Jul 10, 1945, Berkeley, CA; daughter of Mahlon Roles and Marguerite Barber Roles; married Joseph Harris. **Educ:** Univ San Francisco, BS, 1978. **Career:** Ted Bates Advert, asst acct exec, 1979-82; Essence Mag, acct exec, 1982-83; Johnson Publ Co, acct exec, 1983-84; Am Heritage Publ, eastern sales mgr, 1984-86; Gannett Co Inc, acct exec, 1986-. **Orgs:** The EDGES Group Inc, co-chair commun comm, 1986-. **Honors/Awds:** Gannett National Newspaper Sales Award, 1995. **Home Addr:** 4 Cedar lane, Croton on Hudson, NY 10520.

HARRIS, NARVIE J.
Educator, elementary school teacher. **Personal:** Born in Wrightsville, GA; daughter of James E and Anna; married Joseph L, Nov 19, 1945 (deceased); children: Daryll Harris Griffin. **Educ:** Clark Col, AB, 1939; Atlanta Univ, MED, 1944; Tuskegee Inst; Univ GA; GA State Univ; Tenn State Univ; Wayne State Univ, Detroit Mich. **Career:** Educator (retired); Decatur County, Ga, home econ & elem teacher, 1939-41; Henry County, Ga, home econ & elem teacher, 1941-42; Calhoun County, GA, home econ, teacher, 1942-43; Albany St Ga St Univ, teacher; DekalbSch Syst, instr coordr, 1944-83. **Orgs:** Royal Oaks Manor Club, 1961-96; pres, Ga Cong Col PTA, 1967-71; vpres, Borders Courtesy Guild, 1979-03; bd dirs, De Kalb Hist Soc, 1981-03; pres, Decatur-Dekalb Retired Teacher Asn, 1987; trustee, Wheat St Baptist Church, 1987-03, reelected, 1995-2000; Church anniversary chair, 1990-92; United Sisterhood Outreach Prog, vol, Christmas prog sponsor, 1992-2000; Nonagenavarian Awards sponsor, 1993; chair, Historian Wheat St Church, 1999-2003; consult, Morris Brown Col & Atlanta Univ; supvr, Ga Asn Inst; secy, tres, ASCD, GA; Ch Sch Bells Award Prog, GA Asn Educrs; chair vololympic, Wheat St Church, 1996; Joseph B Whitehead Boys Club; Fulton County Arts Coun; Dekalb Hist Soc, 2000-03; life mem, NCP; Decater/Dekalb Retired Teachers Asn; Ga Retired Teachers Asn; Dist, Atlanta Alumna chap; trustee, Wheat St Baptist Church; Pi Lambda Theta; Toastmasters Int; Clark Univ Alumnae Asn; Atlanta Univ Alumnae Asn. **Honors/Awds:** BT Wash High Sch, chair, 60th Reunion, 1934; Bronze woman of year, Iota PiLambda Sorty, 1965; co authored, Hist Ga Cong Col PTA Hist, 1970; Ambassador from Ga to West Africa, 1972, Brazil, 1974, England, 1977,Korea, 1980, Kyoto & Tokyo, Japan; co authored Hist Royal Oaks Manor Comm Club, 1979; Cali Colombia, 1981; Clark Col Alumni Dynamic Educr, 1982; Hon Assoc Supt Dekalb Schls, 1985; Distinguished Alumni Achievement Award, Clark Col, 1986; Distinguished Alumni Atlanta Univ, 1987; Moscow, Leningrad-Tibishi, 1989; Plaque for Outstanding Service, Borders CourtesyGuild, 1993; Stylemaker of the Year Award, 1993; MLK Jr Center Volunteer Service Award for Non-Violent Change, 1994; Plaque from Borders Courtesey Guild for Services Rendered, 1994, Honored by Wheat St Bapt Church, 1995; Community Relations Coun, Appointed by Mayor Maynard Jackson, 1993-94; pres, GA Retired Teachers Asn, 1994; Installed Pres GRTA, 1995; pres, Nancy Bridge Club, 1997-00; chair, 12 month Tea at Wheat St Baptist Church; 1998; sch named Narvie J Harris Trad Theme School, Dekalb County, 1999; commencement speaker, Holy Innocent Sch, 2000; plaque of appreciation, NCP, Dekalb County Chap, 2001; Ed Award by Million Man March; chair vol comn, Wheat St Baptist Church; Narvie Harris Excellence in Education Award, Dekalb Nat Asn Advan Colored People, 2002; Atlanta Urban League Prague Community Service Award, Fannie Lou Hamer Prague, 2003; Dynamic Delta, Delta Sigma Theta Sorority Inc; publ book, Ed for Dekalb Afro Am, Arcadia Press. **Home Addr:** 815 Woodmere Dr NW, Atlanta, GA 30318. *

HARRIS, NATHANIEL C., JR.
State government official. **Personal:** Born Jan 1, 1941, Hackensack, NJ; son of Nathaniel C Harris Sr and Susan Satterwhite; married Frazeal Larrymore, Feb 1, 1969; children: Courtney. **Educ:** Hampton Inst Hampton, BS, 1964; Pace Univ NY, MBA, 1979. **Career:** Aetna Life & Casualty, engineering acct mgr, 1966-68; Real Estate & Constr Div, dept head foreign collection & data processing, 1968-71, acct officer, 1971-73; Urban Affairs, staff officer, 1973-75; RE Comn Develop,sr acct officer, 1975-78; Citibank NA, asst vpres, real estate-mkt &planning, 1979-80; Chase Manhattan Bank, vpres real estate, 1980-90; National Westminster Bank, NJ, vpres; Natwest, NJ, Community Development Corp, pres, 1990-96; United Nat Bank, sr vpres, 1996. **Orgs:** Chmn fin comt, bd dir, Energy Task Force, 1979-81; Omega Psi Phi; NAACP; bd dir, 1980-87, Neighborhood Housing Serv New York City; pres, Urban Bankers Coalition, New York City, 1985-87; vpres, Nat Asn Urban Bankers,1986-87; pres, Nat Asn Urban Bankers, 1987-88; pres, Neighborhood Housing Serv, New York City, 1988-; bd trustees, Bloomfield Col, 1991-96, vice chmn, 1994-96; trustee, Montclair, NJ Art Mus; bd pres, Drum twacket Found,2000-. **Honors/Awds:** Banker of the Year, Urban Bankers Coilition, New York, 1989. **Military Serv:** AUS, capt, 1964-70; Vietnam Serv Medal; Vietnam Campaign Medal; Nat Defense Serv Medal. **Business Phone:** (908)429-2365.*

HARRIS, ONA C
Association executive. **Personal:** Born Jun 7, 1943, Detroit, MI; divorced; children: Michael. **Educ:** Wayne Co Community Col, AA; Univ Detroit, BS, health care admin; Univ Detroit Mercy, MS health care & health care admin, currently. **Career:** Carnegie Inst Tech, med asst, 1962-63; Blvd Gen Hosp, Southwest Detroit Hosp, sp chem tech, 1965-77; Qual Clin Lab Inc, suprv sp chem tech, 1977-86; Univ Detroit, tech computer asst, 1986-89; Simon House, vol, 1989-90, asst dir, 1990-92, exec dir, 1992-. **Orgs:** Bd pres, IDS Consortium; adv bd, Crains Nonprofit News; Mich Soc Asn Execs; bd mem, Mich Coalition Against Homelessness; Mich Prof Women's Network; Women's Econ Club; Nat Alliance End Homelessness; coun mem & vice minister, Secular Franciscan Order; bd mem, Wayne Co Neighborhood Leg Serv; bd mem, AIDS Nutrit Servs Alliance. **Honors/Awds:** The Family Award, Sec Franciscan Order, 1994; Crain's Honarary Mention, Crain's Best Managed Nonprofit, 1996; Black Tribute, Messiah Baptist Church, 1997; Drt Excellence, US Dept Housing & Urban Develop, 1997. **Home Addr:** 20527 Hubbell St, Detroit, MI 48235, **Home Phone:** (313)862-3297. **Business Addr:** Executive Director, Simon House, 16260 Dexter Ave, Detroit, MI 48221, **Business Phone:** (313)863-1400.*

HARRIS, OSCAR L.
Government official. **Personal:** Born Jun 27, 1945, Chiefland, FL; son of Rosa Bell and Oscar L Harris Sr; married Alice Mae Wilson; children: Aurthur, Melissa, Lori & Corey. **Educ:** Univ Mass, MRP, 1982. **Career:** Santa Fe Community Col, teacher, 1975; Alachua County Sch, coach, 1972-76; Archer Community Progressive Org Inc, dir, 1978-81; Archer Daycare Ctr, pres, 1986-90; Fla Assoc for Community Action Inc, pres; Cent Fla Comm Action Agency Inc, exec dir, currently. **Orgs:** Fel, Southeastern Leadership Develop Prog Ford Found, 1976-77; coun man,City Archer, 1980; fel, Nat Rural/Urban Fels Prog, 1981-82; Gainesville Chamber Leadership, 1984; Nat Asn Black Pub Admin, 1984; gubernatorial appointee, N Cent Regional Planning Coun, 1992-2000; regional rep, South Eastern Asn Comm Action Agencies, 1998-; secy, Alachua County Affordable Housing Coalition, 1999-; chmn, Comm Action Award Excellence, 2002; Pvt Indust Coun; vpres, Transp Disadvantaged Comn; Vision 2000, Affordable Housing Coalition, Hunger Coalition; bd mem United Way; bd mem, Nat Community Action Partnership; chair, Cent Fla Comm Action Agency. **Honors/Awds:** Grant Ford Found, 1976; Nat Urban Fellows, 1981; Housing Affordability Book Dept Comm Affairs, 1982; Ebony Award, Gainesville Police Dept, 1985; Achievement Award, Alpha Phi Alpha Leadership 1986; Oscar Harris Day in City of Gainesville Feb 4, 1986. **Home Addr:** PO Box 125, Archer, FL 32618. **Business Addr:** Executive Director, Central Florida Community Action Agency, 220 N Main St Suite C, Gainesville, FL 32602.

HARRIS, PAUL CLINTON, SR.
Lawyer. **Personal:** Born Mar 31, 1964, Charlottesville, VA; son of Pauline Jackson; married Monica L, Oct 21, 1989; children: Paul Jr, Alexandra & Alanah Madison. **Educ:** Hampton Univ, BA, 1986; George Washington Univ, JD, 1995. **Career:** VA House Deleg, state legislator, 58th dist rep, 1997-2001; atty, deleg, currently; McGuire, Woods, Battle & Booth, atty; Dept Justice, Civil Div, dep asst atty gen, 2001-02, dep assoc atty gen, 2002-03; Raytheon Co, Enterprise Compliance, sr coun & dir; Shook, Hardy & Bacon LLP, partner, 2003-. **Orgs:** Charlottesville-Albemarle C & Youth Comn; exec comn, Albemarle City Republican; legis action comn, Charlottesville-Albemarle C; Thomas Jefferson Inn Ct; Boys & Girls Club; hon mem, DARE; pres, Stud Body, Hampton Univ; cadet battalion comdr, Army ROTC Cadet Corps. **Honors/Awds:** George C Marshall Leadership Award, VA Mil Inst Found. **Special Achievements:** Won Republican primary with 72 percent of the vote, June 10, 1997; Won general election with 63 percent of the vote, 1997. **Military Serv:** AUS, 1986-90. **Home Addr:** 162 Larkspur Ct, Charlottesville, VA 22902, **Home Phone:** (804)293-7923. **Business Phone:** (202)783-8400.

HARRIS, PEP (HERNANDO PETROCELLI)
Baseball player. **Personal:** Born Sep 23, 1972, Lancaster, SC. **Career:** Calif Angels, 1996; Anaheim Angels, pitcher, 1997-98; Los Angeles Dodgers, 2004. **Honors/Awds:** Texas-Louisiana League All-Star, 2001. *

HARRIS, PERCY G.
Physician. **Personal:** Born Sep 4, 1927, Durant, MS; son of Norman Henry and Glendora; married Evelyn Lileah Furgerson;

children: 12. **Educ:** IA State Teachers Col, attended 1949; Catholic Univ, attended 1951; Am Univ, attended 1953; Howard Univ, BS, 1953, MD, 1957. **Career:** Physician (retired); St Lukes Hosp, asst med dir, 1958-59, out patient clin dir, 1959-61, audit & utilization rev comt chmn, 1962-75, vpres med staff, 1973, secy-treas, 1974, pres-elect, 1975, pres, 1976; Linn County Med Soc, parliamentarian, 1968-77, secy-treas, 1977-78, vpres, 1978-79; Linn County, deputy coroner, 1958-59, coroner, 1959-61, med examr, 1961-00; pvt pract, physician, 1958-99. **Orgs:** Cedar Rapids/Marion Human Rels Coun, 1961-67; founder & pres, Cedar Rapids Negro Civic Orgn, 1961-67; pres, Cedar Rapids Chap, 1964-66; pres, Jane Boyd Community House, 1967-69; Mayor's Comt, Low Cost Housing, 1967; chmn, Mass Immunization Measles, 1968; United Way, Nominating Exec Comt, 1969-72; Non-Profit Housing Corp, 1969; Oakhill-Jackson Econ Develop Corp, 1972-75; founder & pres, Cedar Rapids Community Cable, 1973-83; vpres, Non-Profit Housing Corp, 1973-; bd mem, Oak Hill Eng, 1973-75; Community Mental Health Ctr, Linn County, 1974-82; vpres, Cedar Rapids Cable Commun 1976-83; Kirkwood Community Col, Med Adv Comt, 1976-; Iowa Bd Regents, 1977-89; Iowa Found Med Care, 1977-; Iowa Football Coaches Asn, 1980; Mercy Hosp, Med Liaison Comt; St Luke's Hosp, Pub Rels Comt; Linn County Med Soc; NAACP. **Honors/Awds:** Community Serv Award, NAACP, 1979; Community Bldg Award, B'nai B'rith, 1982; Serv High Sch Athletics Award, 1982; Recipient of Gold-Headed Cane, Mercy Med Laureate, 1998. **Special Achievements:** Auth: "Prime Guidelines to Good Health: Periodic Checkup," Cedar Rapids Gazette, Mar 14, 1979; "Room Rates Vary with Hospital Size, Cedar Rapids Under State Norm," Cedar Rapids Gazette, Jan 16, 1979; "Prescription Drug Price Methods Vary," Cedar Rapids Gazette, Nov 22, 1978; "Hospital Room Rate Breakdown in Cedar Rapids Bares Exceptional Deal," Cedar Rapids Gazette, Sept 27, 1978; numerous other articles. *

HARRIS, PETER J.
Editor, publisher. **Personal:** Born Apr 26, 1955, Washington, DC. **Educ:** Howard Univ, BA, 1977. **Career:** publ, journalist, ed & broadcaster; Baltimore Afro-Am, staff reporter/ed, 1977-78, sports & culture, columnist, 1979-84; Genetic Dancers Mag, ed/publ, 1980; Wherever Dreams Live, author, 1982; The Dispatcher, Int Longshoremen's & Warehousemen's Union, San Francisco, CA, asst ed, 1984-87; Genetic Dancers, founding publ/ed, 1984-91; Forgotten Lang, Statewide Anthology, Calif Poets Schs, Co-ed, 1985; Black Film Rev, Wash, DC, asst ed, 1989-91; Hand Me My Griot Clothes, Black Classic Press, Baltimore, author, 1993; The Drumming Between Us, founding publ/ed, 1994-99; Safe Arms, auth, 2004; The Johnson Chronicles, auth, 2005; Inspiration House, founder & Artistic dir, currently. **Orgs:** Pub rels consult Coun, Independent Black Inst, 1983-. **Honors/Awds:** Award for Lit Excellence, Oakland PEN Josephine Miles. **Business Addr:** Founder, Artistic director, Inspiration House, 7102 Lockraven Rd, Temple Hills, MD 20748-5308.

HARRIS, RAMON
Administrator. **Career:** Xerox Corp, controller, bus mgr, quality mgr; Educ Alternatives Inc, div pres; Exec Leadership Found, Technol Transfer Proj, dir, currently, Inst Leadership Develop & Res, int exec dir. **Business Addr:** Director of Technology Transfer Project, The Executive Leadership Council, Executive Leadership Foundation, 1010 Wisconsin Ave NW Suite 520, Washington, DC 20007, **Business Phone:** (202)298-8235.

HARRIS, RANDALL
Automotive executive. **Career:** Ultimate Pontiac Buick GMC Isuzu, pres, currently. **Business Phone:** (540)898-6200.*

HARRIS, RAYMONT LESHAWN
Football player, consultant, executive director. **Personal:** Born Dec 23, 1970, Lorain, OH; married Leslie; children: Shakia & Elijah. **Educ:** Ohio State Univ, attneded, 1994. **Career:** Football player (retired), Consultant, Executive director; Chicago Bears, running back, 1994-97; Green Bay Packers, running back, 1998; Denver Broncos, running back, 2000; New England Patriots, running back, 2000; Chase Home Finance, mortgage consult, 2004-08; Ohio State Univ, Fisher Col Bus, asst dir, 2008- . **Honors/Awds:** Most valuable player, Ohio State Buckeyes Football Season, 1993; Rookie of the year, 1994. **Business Addr:** Assistant Director, Fisher College of Business, 2100 Neil Ave, Columbus, OH 43210, **Business Phone:** (614)292-0331.

HARRIS, REGGIE (REGINALD ALLEN HARRIS)
Baseball player. **Personal:** Born Aug 12, 1968, Waynesboro, VA. **Career:** Baseball player (retired); Oakland Athletics, pitcher, 1990-91; Boston Red Sox, 1996; Philadelphia Phillies, 1997; Houston Astros, free agent, 1998 &2004; Milwaukee Brewers, 1999; Tampa Bay Devil Rays, 2000 & 2002; Atlanta Braves, 2000; Pittsburgh Pirates, 2001; Newark Bears, pitcher, 2004; Houston Astros, 2005.

HARRIS, REGINALD ALLEN. **See HARRIS, REGGIE.**

HARRIS, DR. ROBERT ALLEN
Conductor (Music), college teacher, composer. **Personal:** Born Jan 9, 1938, Detroit, MI; son of Major L and Rusha Marshall; married Mary L Pickens, Jun 8, 1963; children: Shari Michelle. **Educ:** Wayne State Univ, BS, 1960, MA, 1962; Mich State Univ, PhD, 1971. **Career:** Detroit Pub Schs, teacher, 1960-64; Wayne State Univ, asst prof, 1964-70; Mich State Univ, assoc prof, prof, 1970-77; Wayne State Univ, Detroit, vis prof; Univ Tex, Austin, vis prof; Univ S Africa, Pretoria, vis prof; Northwestern Univ, Sch Music, prof conducting & ensembles, 1977-, dir, currently; Univ S Africa, vis prof. **Orgs:** Dir music, Trinity Church N Shore, 1978-; cochair & choral panel mem, Nat Endowment Arts. **Honors/Awds:** Distinguished Alumni Award, Wayne State Univ, 1983; School of Music Exemplar in Teaching Award; Alumni Asn Excellence in Teaching Award. **Special Achievements:** Compositions for chorus published by Oxford University Press, Boosey and Hawkes, Walton Music, Mark Foster, Alliance Music, and J. S. Paluch. **Business Addr:** Director, Professor of Conducting and Ensembles, Northwestern University, School of Music, 711 Elgin Rd, Evanston, IL 60208.

HARRIS, ROBERT D.
Manager. **Personal:** Born Aug 31, 1941, Burnwell, WV; married Barbara. **Educ:** WV State Col, BA, 1966; Univ Akron Sch Law, JD. **Career:** Firestone Tire & Rubber Co, indust rel trainee, 1966-67; Akron, indust rel rep plant, 1967-69, mgr labor rel, 1971-73, mgr indust rel; Fall River MA, mgr indust rel, 1969-71. **Orgs:** Employers & Assn; exec com Summit Co; comnr Civil Serv Comm Akron, 1977; Am OH & Akron Bar Assns; adv bd, YMCA; Nat Alliance Businessmen's Youth Motivation Task Force; W Side Neighbours; Alpha Phi Alpha frat; Akron Barristers Club; OH Bar, 1976. **Honors/Awds:** Black Exec Exch Prog Nat Urban League; Ebony Success Story. **Military Serv:** AUS, sgt E-5, 1959-62.

HARRIS, ROBERT EUGENE PEYTON
Financial manager. **Personal:** Born Sep 5, 1940, Washington, DC; son of John F and Jane E (deceased); married Yvonne Ramey; children: Lisa & Johanna. **Educ:** Morehouse Col, BA, 1963; Long Island Univ, MBA, 1981. **Career:** Equitable Life Assurance Soc, exp exam; Bronx Community Col Asn Inc, opers mgr. **Orgs:** Vpres, Battle Hill Civic Asn, 1977; 100 Black Men, 1976; Coun Concerned Black Exec New York City, 1980; Illustrious Potentiat Elejmal Temple Shrine, 1987; worshipful master Bright Hope Masonic Lodge, 1981; Asn MBA Execs. **Military Serv:** USAR, ltc, 1964-89. *

HARRIS, ROBERT F.
Government official. **Personal:** Born May 15, 1941, Knight Station, FL; son of James and Gertrude; married; children: Roger & Lisa. **Educ:** Fla A&M Univ, BS, 1964. **Career:** Subcomt Govt Opers, US Senate, chief clerk, dep staff dir; Bd Pub Instr Polk Co, teacher & coach, 1966-72; Comt Govt Affairs, dep dir, 1988; US Postal Serv, vpres diversity develop, 1994. **Orgs:** Chmn & bd dir, Neighborhood Serv Ctr Inc, Lakeland; Cath Soc Serv Central FL; Coun Concerned Citizens Lakeland; Pi Gamma Mu. **Honors/Awds:** All Conf Track & Field; Cleve Abott Award for Track 1963; various track record awards; inductee, Polk Co Schs Hall of Fame, 1997. **Military Serv:** Airborne, first lt, 1964-66.

HARRIS, ROBERT L.
Executive, vice president (organization). **Personal:** Born Mar 4, 1944, Arkadelphia, AR; son of Ben and Lucy; married Glenda Newell; children: Anthony, Regina, Brittany & Phillip. **Educ:** Merritt Col, AA, 1963; San Francisco State Univ, BA, 1965; Univ Calif Sch Law Berkeley, JD, 1972; Harvard Grad Sch Bus, AMP, 1988. **Career:** Vice President (retired); Alameda County Probation Off, dep probation officer, 1965-69; Pac Gas & Elec Co, atty 1972, cent div mgr, 1989-93, vpres community rels, 1994-98, vpres environ affairs. **Orgs:** Pres, Western Region, Kappa Alpha Psi, 1975-79; pres, Nat Bar Asn, 1979-80; admin mem, Blue Shield Calif, 1979-92; Calif State Bar, 1980-81; lawyer fel, adv comn, RH Smith Comn, Howard Univ Sch Law, 1981-83; pres,Wiley Manuel Law Found, 1982-88; secy, Nat Bar Inst, 1982-87; chmn, Legal Comn Oakland Br, Nat Asn Advan Colored People, 1983-87; grand pole march, Kappa Alpha Psi, 1991-95; bd, Port Oakland, 1996-2000; bd mem, co-chair, San Francisco Lawyers Community, 1998-; chmn, Pub Law Sect. **Honors/Awds:** Robert Ming Award, Nat Asn Advan Colored People; UNCF Frederick Patterson Award; C Francis Stratford Award, Nat Bar Asn. **Special Achievements:** Hundred Most Influential Blacks in America on five different occasions, Ebony Mag. **Home Phone:** (510)638-1331.

HARRIS, ROBERT L., JR.
Educator, school administrator. **Personal:** Born Apr 23, 1943, Chicago, IL; son of Robert L and Ruby L Watkins; married Anita B Campbell Harris, Nov 14, 1964; children: Lisa Marie, Leslie Susanne, Lauren Yvonne. **Educ:** Roosevelt Univ, Chicago, IL, BA, 1966, MA, 1968; Northwestern Univ, Evanston, IL, PhD, 1974. **Career:** St Rita Elem Sch, Chicago, IL, 6th grade teacher, 1965-68; Miles Col, Birmingham, AL, instr, 1968-69; Univ Ill, Urbana, IL, asst prof, 1972-75; Cornell Univ, Ithaca, NY, dir, 1986-91, asst to assoc prof, 1975, assoc prof, currently, vice provost, 2000-; ASALH, pres, 1991-93. **Orgs:** Pres, Asn study Afro-Am Life & Hist, 1991-92; chair & memship comt, Am Historical Asn, 1989-94; chair & prog comn, Am Historical Asn, 1995; mem & bd dirs, New York Coun Humanitites, 1983-87; editorial bd, Jour Negro Hist, 1978-96; editorial bd, Western Jour Black Studies, 1990-; Nat Adv Bd, The Soc Hist Educ, 1996-; Nat Historian, Alpha Phi Alpha Fraternity, Inc. **Honors/Awds:** Teaching Afro-Amer History, Am Historical Asn, 1992; Black Studies United States, The Ford Found, 1990; Rockefeller Humanities Fellow, SUNY Buffalo, 1991-92; WEB DuBois Fellow, Harvard Univ, 1983-84; Ford Foundation Fellow, 1983-84; National Endowment for the Humanities Fellow, 1974-75; Carter G. Woodson Scholars Medallion. **Business Addr:** Associate Professor, Vice Provost, Cornell University, 449 Day Hall, Ithaca, NY 14853, **Business Phone:** (607)255-5358.*

HARRIS, ROBERT LEE
Football player. **Personal:** Born Jun 13, 1969, Riviera Beach, FL; married. **Educ:** Southern Univ. **Career:** Football player(retired); Minn Vikings, defensive tackle, 1992-94; New York Giants, defensive tackle, 1995-99. **Honors/Awds:** Rookie of the Year, 1992.

HARRIS, ROOSEVELT
Government official. **Educ:** Valdosta State Univ, MA, pub admin. **Career:** City Brunswick, GA, exec dir community develop, city mgr, currently. **Orgs:** Int City & Co Mgt Asn; Nat Asn Housing Redevelop Off; Community Develops Asn; Nat Asn Pub Adminrs; Lambda Beta Sigma Chap, Phi Beta Sigma Fraternity Inc; Coastal Ga Pan-Hellenic Coun Preserv Technicians GroupInc; Fourteen Black Men Glynn Inc; Brunswick Area Transportation Study; Connecting Link Links Inc. **Special Achievements:** First black city manager Brunswick, GA. **Business Addr:** City Manager, City Brunswick, 601 Gloucester St, Brunswick, GA 31520, **Business Phone:** (912)267-5501.

HARRIS, DR. RUTH COLES
School administrator. **Personal:** Born Sep 26, 1928, Charlottesville, VA; daughter of Bernard A and Ruth Wyatt; married John Benjamin, Sep 2, 1950; children: John Benjamin Jr & Vita Michelle. **Educ:** VA State Univ, BS 1948; NY Univ Grad Sch Bus Admin, MBA 1949; Col William & Mary, EdD 1977; Va Union Univ, LHD, 1998. **Career:** VA Union Univ, instr, 1949-64, head com dept, 1956-59, assoc prof com dept, 1964-69, prof, dir div com, 1969-73, Distinguished prof emer, currently; Sydney Lewis Sch Bus Admin, dir, 1973-81; Sydney Lewis Sch Bus Admin, mem mgt team, 1985-87, acct dept chair, 1988-97. **Orgs:** Equal Oppurtunity Comm AACSB, 1975-76; bd dir, Am Assembly Collegiate Schs bus, 1976-79; adv bd, InterCollegiate Case Clearing House, 1976-79; St Adv Coun Community Serv Continuing Ed Prog, 1977-80; bd dirs, Richmond Urban League, 1979-84; agency eval comm United Way Greater Richmond, 1980-85; appointed, 1983-85 by gov Robb Inter departmental Comm Rate Setting Children's Facilities; bd, Richmond VA Chap Nat Coaltion 100 Black Women; chairperson, Minority Doctoral Fellows Comt, Am Inst Cert Pub Accts, 1990-92; bd dirs, VA Soc CPA's, 1995-98. **Honors/Awds:** Virginia Power, Strong Men a Delver Woman's Club Award for Achievement in Business, 1963; Faculty Fellowship Award United Negro Col Fund, 1976-77; Serwa Award, Virginia Commonwealth Chapter, Nat Coalition of 100 Black-Women, 1989; Teacher of the Year Award, Va Union University, Sears Roebuck Found, 1990; Outstanding Accounting Educator Award, Virginia Society of CPAs & American Institute of CPAs, 1991; Va Heroes, participant, 1991-94,1996-97; Outstanding Faculty Award, Va State Coun Higher Educ, 1992; Nissan, HBCU Fellow, 1992; Bell Ringer Richmond, NAUW, 1992; Ebone Images Award, Northern VA Chapter, Nat Coalition of 100 Black Women, 1993; Distinguished Career in Accounting Award, 1997; Doctor of Humane Letters, 1998; Tenneco Excellence in Teaching nd Women Honoree, 1998. **Special Achievements:** First black woman to pass CPA exam in VA, 1962. **Home Addr:** 2816 Edgewood Ave, Richmond, VA 23222, **Home Phone:** (804)321-3875.

HARRIS, DR. SARAH ELIZABETH
Manager, consultant, executive director. **Personal:** Born Dec 31, 1937, Newnan, GA; daughter of Dan W Gates (deceased) and Sarah L Gates; married Kenneth Eugene; children: Kim Y. **Educ:** Miami Univ, BS 1959, MEd 1967, PhD, 1973; Wilberforce Univ, Wilberforce,Oh, DHL. **Career:** Career Opportunity Prog, univ coor dr, 1970-73; FL Sch Desegregation Expert, consult, 1971-77; Gen Electric Co, mgr sup serv, 1973-75; Urban Rural Joint Task Force, ESAA Proj, proj dir, 1975-76; Sinclair Col, consult, 1976; Inst Educ Leadership George Wash Univ, educ policy fel, 1977-78; Cleveland Sch Desegregation Exp, consult, 1977; Citizens Council OH Schs, staff assoc, 1978-79; Dayton Power & Light Co, dir community rel, 1985; Dayton & Montgomery County Pub Educ Fund, sr consult, 1986; Montgomery County, treas, 1987-91, comnr, 1991-92; Dayton Urban League Inc, pres, 1991-93; cert sem leader & independent consult; Nat Conf Christians & Jews, exec dir. **Orgs:** Bd dir, YSI Inc, currently; pres, Dayton Found; co-chmn, Dayton Dialogue Race Rel (DDRR); Challenge 95 Network; Criminal Justice Comt; Dayton Women's Network; Self-Sufficiency Task Force; bd trustees, Wright State Univ; bd trustees, Sisters Mercy Health Corp; bd trustees, Parity 2000; Delta Sigma Theta Inc; Corinthian Baptist Church. **Honors/Awds:** C Serv Award; Jack & Jill Am Dayton, 1975; Outstanding Woman of the Year, Iota Phi Lamba Dayton, 1978; Salute Career Women, YWCA, 1982; Outstanding Grad Award Dayton Pub Schs, 1983; Top Ten Women, 1983; Induction OH Women's Hall of Fame,

1984; Martin Luther King Nat Holiday Celebration Meritorious Award Community Soc Servs; Bishop Alumni Medal, Miami Univ; Outstanding Community Leader Award, Great Lakes Midwest Reg Blacks Govt, 1986; Dayton Champion Award, Nat Multiple Sclerosis Society, 1987; Mark Excellence Award, Nat Forum Black Pub Add, 1991. Ohio Women's Hall of Fame. **Business Addr:** Board of Director, YSI Inc, 1725 Brannum Lane, Yellow Springs, OH 45387, **Business Phone:** (937)767-7241.

HARRIS, SEAN EUGENE
Football player. **Personal:** Born Feb 25, 1972, Tucson, AZ. **Educ:** Univ Ariz. **Career:** Chicago Bears, linebacker, 1995-2000; Indianapolis Colts, 2001.

HARRIS, SHAWNTAE
Rap musician, singer, actor. **Personal:** Born Apr 14, 1974, Chicago, IL. **Career:** Throwin's Tantrums Rec Label, founder, 2000; Albums: Funkda fied, 1994; Anuthat antrum, 1996; Unrestricted, 2000; Limelite Luv & Niteclubz, 2003; TBC; TV guest appearances: "The Parent Hood", 1997, 1998; "VIP", 2000; TV movie: "Carmen: A Hip Hopera", MTV, 2001; Films: Glitter, 2001; Civil Brand, 2002; Movie compositions: Bad Boys, 1995; Hard Ball, 2001; Like Mike, 2002; Films: Kazaam, 1996; Carmen: A Hip Hopera, 2001; Glitter, 2001; Civil Brand, 2002; 30 Days, 2006; Songs: "Funkda fied", 1994; "Fa AllY'all", 1994; "Give It To Ya", 1995; "Sittin' On Top of the World", 1996; "Ghetto Love", 1997; "That's What I'm Looking For", 2000; "Whatch u Like",2000; "In Love Wit Chu", 2003. **Business Addr:** Rapper, So So Def Recordings, c/o Artistic Control, 685 Lambert Dr NE, Atlanta, GA 30324, **Business Phone:** (404)888-9900.*

HARRIS, SIDNEY E
Educator. **Personal:** Born Jul 21, 1949, Atlanta, GA; son of Nathaniel and Marion Johnson; married Mary Styles, Jun 26, 1971; children: Savaria B. **Educ:** Morehouse Col, BA, 1971; Cornel Univ, Ithaca, NY, MA, 1975, PhD, 1976. **Career:** Bell Telephone Labs, tech staff mem, 1973-78; Ga State Univ, J Mack Robinson Col Bus, Atlanta, GA, assoc prof, 1978-87, dean, 1997-2004, prof comput info systs, currently; Peter F Drucker Grad Mgt Ctr, Claremont Grad Sch, Claremont, CA, prof mgt, 1987-90, chair mgt prog, 1990-91, dean, 1991-96; Property Secured Investment, Los Angeles, corp dir, 1994-95; GM/Hughes Electronics, consult; Coca-Cola Co, consult; Xerox Corp, consult; IBM, consult; Hewlett Packard, consult;, BellSouth Serv, consult; AT&T, consult; Equifax Serv, consult; Lanier Worldwide, consult; AirGate PCS, consult; AMRESCO, consult; AACSB Int, consult; S Bus Admin Asn, consult. **Orgs:** Nat Sci Soc, 1976-; vice chmn, Los Angeles Co Productivity Comn, 1988-91; corp dir, Family Saving Bank, Los Angeles, CA, 1988-; assoc ed, MIS Quarterly, 1989-92; ed adv bd, Bus Forum, 1989-; bd govs, Peter F Drucker Non-Profit Found, NY, 1991-; Beta Gamma Sigma, Nat Honor Soc Bus Sch, 1994-2002; corp dir, Serv Master Co, Chicago, IL, 1995-; bd dir, TransAm Investors, Los Angeles, CA, 1995-; bd trustees, Menlo Col, 1995-; corp dir, Total Serv Syst Inc, 1999-; corp dir, Air Gate PCS, 2000-02; Soc Int Bus Fel, 2002-; Sigma Xi. **Honors/Awds:** Volunteer Service Award, Nat Comput Conf Comt, 1986; Dedicated Science Award, Nat Comput Conf Comt, 1988. **Special Achievements:** Presented & published numerous papers. **Business Addr:** Professor of Computer Information Systems, Georgia State University, J Mack Robinson College of Business, Dept Comput Info Systs, 427 RCB Bldg 35 Broad St NW, Atlanta, GA 30303, **Business Phone:** (404)413-7017.

HARRIS, STANLEY EUGENE
Banker. **Personal:** Born May 19, 1953, Columbus, OH; son of Harvey J Sr (deceased) and Julia Ann V; married Gene C Thomas, Jun 25, 1977; children: Wade T. **Educ:** Univ Notre Dame, BBA, 1975; Stonier Grad Sch Banking, ABA, 1997. **Career:** Ohio Nat Bank, banking mgt trainee, 1980-81, supvr-credit res, 1981-82, credit banking rep, 1982-84, asst vpres/mgr credit res, 1985-87, mgr community develop, 1988-90; Nat City Corp, community reinvestment officer, 1991-92; Nat City Bank, Columbus, mgr pub rels/min bus serv, 1992-94, vpres, regional mgr, 1995-97, vpres & mgr gov accts, 1997-; Franklin Univ, adj prof finance, 1998-01. **Orgs:** Comnr, Ohio Develop Finance Adv Bd, 1986-94; treas, Columbus Area Community Mental Health Ctr, 1988-91; chair, Columbus Found-Community Arts Fund, 1989-97; Treas, 1986-91, First vice chair, 1992-94, chair, 1994-95, Columbus Urban League; trustee, Buckeye Boys Ranch, 1990-94; trustee, I Know I Can Inc, 1990-02; chair, trustee bd, Mt Olivet Baptist Church, 1993-02; vice chair, Ohio Black Legis Caucus Corp Roundtable, 1999-; comnr, Columbus Metro Housing Auth, 2000-; trustee, Project Linden Inc, 2000-02; Project Grad Inc of Colo; Urban Financial Services Coalition, Columbus chapter, 2000-. **Honors/Awds:** Golden Rule Award, J C Penney Co, 1984; Columbus Jaycees, 10 Outstanding Young Citizens, 1986. **Business Addr:** Manager of Government Accounts, National City Bank, 155 E Broad St, Columbus, OH 43251, **Business Phone:** (614)463-8658.*

HARRIS, STEVE
Executive, vice president (organization). **Career:** ABC Radio Network, exec; XM Prog Ctr, vpres; ABC Radio Networks, vpres, multicultural programming, currently. **Honors/Awds:** Black Radio Exclusive Drummer Award; Young Black Programmers Programmer of the Year. **Special Achievements:** Top 25 Most Successful African-Americans in Radio, Radio Ink, 1999. **Business Phone:** (202)895-2327.

HARRIS, STEVE
Actor. **Personal:** Born Dec 3, 1965, Chicago, IL; son of John and Mattie. **Educ:** Northern Ill Univ, BA, drama; Univ Del, MFA, theater. **Career:** Films: Don't Mess with My Sister, 1985; Seven Hours to Judgment, 1988; Sugar Hill, 1994; The Rock, 1996; Lesse Prophets, 1997; Lovers & Liars, 1998; The Mod Squad, 1999; King of the World, 2000; The Skulls, 2000; Minority Report, 2002; Beyond the City Limits, 2001; Bringing Down the House, 2003; Death & Texas, 2004; Diary of a Mad Black Woman, 2005; The Unseen, 2005; Ball Don't Lie, 2008; TV series: Against the Wall, 1994; "Law & Order", 1994-95; "Homicide", 1994; New York Undercover, 1994-95;"Heaven & Hell: North & South, Book III", 1994; "Ally McBeal", 1997; George Wallace, 1997; "The Practice", 1997-2004; Nightmare Street, 1998; "The Mod Squad", 1999; "The Skulls", 2000; "King of the World", 2000; "Minority Report", 2002; "The Batman", 2004-06; "The Unseen", 2005; "Heist", 2006; "Grey's Anatomy", 2006; Protect & Serve, 2007; Eli Stone, 2008. **Honors/Awds:** Q Award, Viewers Qual TV, 1998 & 1999; Image Award, 2004. **Business Addr:** Actor, Williams Morris Agency, 1 William Morris Pl, Beverly Hills, CA 90212, **Business Phone:** (310)859-4000.*

HARRIS, DR. TEREA DONNELLE
Physician. **Personal:** Born Aug 5, 1956, St Louis, MO; daughter of Samuel Elliott and Dixie Kay Gardner. **Educ:** Fisk Univ, BA 1978; Meharry Med Col, MD 1982. **Career:** Henry Ford Hosp, resident, 1983-86; Health Alliance Plan, staff physician, 1986-88; Outer Drive Hosp, Lincoln Park, MI, internist, 1988-91; Mich Health Care Ctr, urgent care physician, 1991-92; Bi-County Hosp, internist, house physician, 1992-93; Henry Ford Hosp, fellow, Div Infectious Dis, 1993-95; Henry Ford Health Syst, Detroit Northwest, staff physician, 1995-. **Orgs:** Nat Med Asn; The Links; life ber, Fisk Alumni Asn; Meharry Alumni Asn; Infectious Dis Soc Am; Am Soc Microbiol. **Honors/Awds:** Outstanding Young Women of America, Alpha Kappa Alpha Sor Inc. **Business Addr:** Physician, Henry Ford Health System, 7800 W Outer Dr, Detroit, MI 48235.

HARRIS, THOMAS C.
Executive. **Personal:** Born Mar 23, 1933, Paterson, NJ; married Betty M Kennedy; children: Thomas Jr, Michael, Elaine Jefferson & Brenda. **Educ:** Fairleigh Dickinson Univ, Teaneck NJ, BS, chem, 1970, surface active chem, 1973; Columbia Univ NY, cosmetic sci, 1972. **Career:** Shulton Inc, chemist, 1968; Revlon Inc, sr chemist, 1974; Ame Cyanand Co, group leader res & develop, 1977; Harris Chem Co Inc, pres, 1977-. **Orgs:** Bd dir, Chamber Com; Rotary Club Int; bd trustee, St Joseph's Med Ctr; assoc minister, Mission Church God; nat corresp secy, Nat Mens Orgn; Cosmetic Chem Soc; Sales & Allied Chem Indust; adv, Youth Christ. **Honors/Awds:** Gold Medal Atlantic Richfield Co Prime Sponsor of Olympic, 1984; Excellence in Business, US Olympics LA. **Military Serv:** AUS, Signal Corp sp 3/c, three years; Nat Defense Serv Medal, 1953-56. **Home Addr:** 602 14th Ave, Paterson, NJ 07504. **Business Addr:** President, Harris Chemical Co Inc, 546 E 30th St, Paterson, NJ 07504.

HARRIS, THOMAS WALTER
Librarian, playwright. **Personal:** Born Apr 30, 1930, New York, NY; son of Melvin and Mary; married Joyce Carter. **Educ:** Howard Univ, BA, 1957; Univ Calif, MA, Los angeles, 1959; Univ Southern Calif, MLS, 1962. **Career:** Appeal Printing Co, staff, 1948-49; Voice Am, writer, 1953-55; Bur Internal Rev, Wash DC, staff, 1956-57; Los Angeles Pub Libr, Los Angeles, Calif, librn lit & fiction dept, 1961; Studio W Channel 22, writer & dir; Inner City Cult Ctr, teacher, 1968; Actors Studio, writer, 1967-74; Pasadena Playhouse, playwright; Los Angeles Citizens Co, producer & dir; Univ Calif, Los Angeles, teacher playwriting, 1966; playwright & writer, currently; Plays: Daddy Hugs & Kisses, 1960; The Relic, 1961; The Selma Maid, 1967; Always with Love, 1970; The Solution, 1970; Mary Queen of Crackers, 1971; Suds, 1973; No Time to Play, 1977; A Streetcar Salad, 1979; Other: Fall of an Iron Horse; All Tigers Are Tame; City Beneath the Skin; Who Killed Sweetie; Beverly Hills Olympics; At Wits End; The Man Handlers; Clothespins & Dreams; Books: The Fall of Archy House, Barnstormer, Flight into the Unknown, 1957; Get Out of My Body, You'll Like It on Mars, Goodbye, Dead Man, 1958; Baby, 1959. **Orgs:** Dramatists Guild; Nat Playwrights Co; Black Theatre Network; Nat Asn Advan Colored People; Am Asn Retired People; Am Fedn State, Co & Munic Employees; Los Angeles Black Playwrights; Alliance Los Angeles Playwright. **Honors/Awds:** Outstanding Contribution to Theatre in Loa Angeles, Citation Los Angeles City Coun, 1967; All CIAA, All Tournament, Howard Univ 1956. **Special Achievements:** Musical: "Suds as Clothespins & Dreams", Pasadena Civic, 1990. **Military Serv:** AUS, Ord Korea, 1951-53. **Business Addr:** Playwright, 630 W 5th St, Los Angeles, CA 90071.

HARRIS, TRICIA R
Executive. **Personal:** Born Feb 16, 1977, Weisbaden, Germany; daughter of Virginia. **Career:** Intellectual Properties Mgt, file cler, secy, exec asst chmn, 1995-96, licensing operations mgr, 1996-97, licensing mgr; Intellectual Properties Mgt, mgr, 1995-96, dir, 1996-99; Tokyo Data Ctr, Rollout, prog consult, 1999-2000; Martin Luther King Jr., Ctr Nonviolent Social Change Inc, managing dir, 2004-04; Political Campaign Mgt, consult, 2004-06; Global Sourcing Off, dir, 2005-07, human resource mgr, currently. **Orgs:** Consult, Corp Social Responsibililty & Diversity Mgt, 2004-05; dir, Martin L. King Mem Found. **Business Addr:** Human Resource Manager, Global PMO, 550 Peachtree St NW, Atlanta, GA 30309.

HARRIS, DR. TRUDIER
Educator, scholar. **Personal:** Born Feb 27, 1948, Mantua, AL; daughter of Unareed Burton Moore and Terrell Sr. **Educ:** Stillman Col, Tuscaloosa, AL, BA, 1969; Ohio State Univ, Columbus, OH, MA,1972, PhD, 1973. **Career:** The Col William & Mary, Williamsburg, VA, asst prof, 1973-79; Univ NC, Chapel Hill, NC, assoc prof, 1979-85, prof, 1985-88, assoc chair, 2005-07; J Carlyle Sitterson prof Eng, 1988-; Univ Ark, Little Rock, AR, William Grant Cooper Vis Distinguished prof, 1987; Ohio State Univ, Columbus OH, vis distinguished prof, 1988. Author: From Mammies To Militants: Domesticsin Black American Literature, 1982; Exorcising Blackness: Historical &Literary Lynching & Burning Rituals, 1984; Black Women In The Fiction ofJames Baldwin, 1985; Fiction & Folklore: The Novels of Toni Morrison, 1991; The Power of the Porch: The Storyteller's Craft in Zora Neale Hurston, Gloria Naylor, & Randall Kenan, 1996; Saints, Sinners, Saviors: Strong Black Women in African American Literature, 2001; South of Tradition: Essays on African American Literature, 2002; Summer Snow: Reflections from a Black Daughter of the South, 2003; editor: Selected Works of Ida B Well Afro-American Fiction Writers After 1955 in the Dictionary of Literary Biography Series, 1984; Afro-American Writers After, 1955: Dramatists & Prose Writers, 1985; Afro-American Poets After, 1955, 1985; Afro-American Writers Before The Harlem Renaissance, 1986;Afro-American Writers From The Harlem Renaissance To 1940, 1987; Afro-American Writers From 1940 To 1955, 1988; The Oxford Companion to Women's Writing in the United States, 1994; New Essays on Baldwin's Go Tell It On the Mountain, 1996 The Oxford Companion to African American Literature, 1997; Call & Response: The Riverside Anthology of the African American Literary Tradition, 1997; The Literature of the American South: A Norton Anthology, 1997. **Orgs:** Mod Lang Asn Am, 1973-; Am Folklore Soc, 1973-; Col Language Asn, 1974-; S Atlantic Mod Lang Asn, 1980-; Langston Hughes Soc, 1982-; Zeta Phi Beta Sorority Inc; fel Nat Res Coun & Ford Found, 1982-83; Rockefeller Fel, Bellagio, Italy, 1994; fel Nat Humanities Ctr, 1996-. **Honors/Awds:** Creative Scholarship Award, Col Lang Asn, 1987; Teaching Award, S AtlanticMod Lang Asn, 1987; First Annual Award of Distinction for the Col of Humanities, 1994; Award for Excellence in Teaching; South of Tradition: Essays on African American Literature, 2002; UNC System Board of Governors' Award, 2005; John Hurt Fisher Award, S Atlantic Asn Dept Eng,2005. **Business Addr:** J Carlyle Sitterson Professor of English, University of North Carolina at Chapel Hil Department of English and Comparative Literature, Greenlaw Hall CB Suite 3520, Chapel Hill, NC 27599-3520, **Business Phone:** (919)962-5481.

HARRIS, VERA D.
Government official. **Personal:** Born Nov 10, 1912, Palestine, TX; daughter of Caesar Albert and Estalla Pryor; married James A, Sep 25, 1963 (deceased). **Educ:** Prairie View A&M Col, BS, 1935; Tex So Univ, MS 1950. **Career:** Government official (retired); S Newspaper Feat, Dallas, home econ lectr, 1935-37; Tex Agr Extens, co extens agent, 1937-73. **Orgs:** Secy, Order E Stars, 1945-46; Prairie View Alumni Asn, 1945-47, secy, 1968-72, chmn, const & bylaws, 1969-70, chmn budget comt, Gamma Sigma Chap; pres, 1945-47, secy, 1972-77; Cambridge Village Civic Club; NRTA & AARP; pres, Gardenia Garden Club; Optim 13 Soc Club, 1970-72; life mem, Young Women's Christian Asn, 1973; chmn, Health Comn, Houston Harris Co, Ret Teachers Asn, 1974; hist, Home Econ Homemaking, 1974; Am Home Econ Asn; Prairie View Alumni Club; Sigma Gamma Rho Sorority; Epsilon Sigma Phi Frat; Tex Home Econ Asn; Home Econ Homemaking; Am Home Econ Asn; Houston Harris Co Ret Teachers Asn; Clint Pk Unit Methodist Church; Nat Asn Extn Home Econs & Nat Asn Ret Fed Employ Sec; Houston Negro C C; pres, Tex Negro Home Dem Agts Asn; Pine Crest Home Demo Club; pres, Houston Harris Co Ret Teachers; life mem, Gulfgate Chap No 941, Young Women's Christian Asn, 1973-; Grand Order Ct Calauthe; vpres, Nat Asn Retd Fed Employees. **Honors/Awds:** Certificate of Recognition, Tex Negro Home Demo Agts Asn, 1947; Certificate of Award, Nat Asn Fash & Access Design, 1957; Distinguished Service Award, Tex Negro Home Demo Agts Asn, 1962; Sigma of Year Merit Award, 1973; "Palm Branch & Laurel Wreaths" Pal Negro Bus & Prof Wom Club,1976; 100 Plus Club, Prairie View Develop Fund, 1976-78; Cooperative Extension Program, Prairie Vew A&M Univ, 1986; Houston Harris County Retired Teachers Asn, 1988; Gardenia Garden Club, Plaque, 40 year member, 1994; Certificate of Merit, Asn Retired Black County Agents, 1991; Framed Memories, Family & Friends, 1992; Sigma Gamma Rho, Dedicated Service,1995; Prairie View A&M Univ, Coop Extension Prog, Certificate of Appreciation, 1997; Houston Harris County Retired Teacher's Awd, 2000;Presented the Hilltopper Award, Prairie View A&M Univ Alumni, 1994. **Special Achieve-**

ments: Woman of the Week, The Informer 1954. **Home Addr:** 5110 Trail Lake Dr, Houston, TX 77045-4035. *

HARRIS, VERNON JOSEPH
Manager. **Personal:** Born May 18, 1926, Washington, DC; son of Vernon J Harris Sr and Beatrice V Robinson; married Georgetta Mae Ross (deceased); children: Elliott F, Cassandra Harris Lockwood, Georgette E H Lee , Wayne J, Verna J H Agen, Dolores A (deceased). **Educ:** Catholic Univ Am, BE, 1952. **Career:** manager (retired); General Elec AESD, mgr, sr engr, cons, project engr, design engr, jr engr, 1952-88; GE aerospace electronics systems. mgr. **Orgs:** pres, past lt governor NY dist Kiwanis & Kiwanis Club N Utica, 1962-95; Col Council SUNY, Col technol Utica, 1968-84; financial officer, Provost Post American Legion; past comdr Provost Post American Legion, 1974-76; treas, Central NY Chap Amer Heart asn, 1975-80; treas, NY State Affiliate American Heart Asn, 1978-80; pres, A Good Old Summer Time, Inc, Utica, NY, 1995-97; bd mem & treas, Cornell Cooperative Extension of Oneida County, 1991-97. **Honors/Awds:** Elfun Territorial Awd, Pub Serv Utica Elfun Soc Gen Elec AESD, 1974-75; Elfun Man of Yr, Utica Chap, Elfun Soc Gen Elec AESD, 1975; nominee Phillippe Awd for Pub Serv, Gen Elec Co, 1977; Phillippe Awd winner for Pub Serv, Gen Elec Co, 1978. **Military Serv:** Hon discharge, AUS Air Corp with rank of Sgt, 1946; NCO incharge of base signal office 387th ASG, Godman Fld KY, Freeman Fld IN, and Lockbourn Fld OH. *

HARRIS, VIRGINIA R.
Artist. **Career:** Sonoma State Univ, quilt artist, currently. *

HARRIS, VITA M.
Executive. **Educ:** Howard Univ, BS, mkt, MBA; Univ MD. **Career:** Draft Direct Worldwide, exec vpres, 2003, chief incite officer, exec vpres & dir insight serv, currently. **Honors/Awds:** 25 Influential Black Women in Bus, Network Jour mag, 2006. **Special Achievements:** Become the first Black female CPA in the state of Virginia. *

HARRIS, DR. WALTER
College administrator. **Personal:** Born Jan 27, 1947, Suttles, AL; son of Walter Sr and Arie L B; married Henrietta Augustus, Apr 17, 1976; children: Ayana Kristi & Askala Almaz. **Educ:** Knoxville Col, Knoxville, TN, BS, 1968; Mich State Univ, East Lansing, MI, MM, 1969, PhD, 1979; Harvard Univ, Cambridge, MA, dipl, 1990. **Career:** Ariz State Univ, Tempe, AZ, coordr, undergrad studies, music, asst dean, Col Fine Arts, actg dean, assoc dean, interim asst vpres acad affairs, vice provost; NC Cent Univ, Durham, NC, provost & vice chancellor acad affairs; Univ NC, Chapel Hill, NC, sr exec fel; Loyola Univ New Orleans, provost, vpres, acad affairs, 2003-. **Orgs:** Pi Kappa Lamda Honorary Fraternity, Mich State Univ, 1968; fel NEH, 1974; Luce Fel, Luce Found, 1977; Int Coun Fine Arts Deans, 1985-; regional chairperson, Am Choral Dir Asn, 1987-; bd dir, Phoenix Symphony Orchestra, 1990-; bd trustees, Phoenix Boys Choir, 1990-; pres, Ariz Alliance Arts Educ, 1991-93. **Business Addr:** Provost, Vice President, Academic Affairs, Loyola University New Orleans, Marquette Hall 221, PO Box 7, New Orleans, LA 70118.

HARRIS, WALTER LEE
Football player. **Personal:** Born Aug 10, 1974, La Grange, GA; married Trina; children: Courtney, London & Summer. **Educ:** Miss State Univ. **Career:** Chicago Bears, defensive back, 1996-2001; Indianapolis Colts, 2001-03; Wash Redskins, corner back, 2004-05; San Francisco 49ers, corner back, 2006- . **Honors/Awds:** NFC Player of the Month; NFC Defensive Player of the Week; Bill Walsh Award. Harris was also selected to rep the NFC in the Pro Bowl, 2007 . **Special Achievements:** NFL Draft, First round pick, No 13, 1996. **Business Addr:** Cornerback, San Francisco 49ers, 4949 Centennial Blvd, Santa Clara, CA 95054, **Business Phone:** (408)562-4949.

HARRIS, WHITNEY G.
Executive director. **Educ:** McNeese State Univ, BS; La State Univ, MS, psychol; Univ Ottawa, theol; Univ Cincinnati, PhD; Union Inst, PhD; Harvard Mgt Develop Prog, cert. **Career:** Spec educ teacher; Union Inst, adj prof; Southern Develop Found, Lafayette, La, youth consult; McNeese State Univ, vpres spec serv & equity, exec dir human rels & social equity, dir, equal opportunity/minority affairs, 1990-01; La Dept Social Serv, impartial hearing officer, 1995-2001; Burton Col Educ, prof, 1996; Eastern Mich Univ, Dept Diversity & Affirmative Action, dir, 2001-05; Minnesota State Cols & Univs, dir diversity, 2005-. **Orgs:** Am Asn Affirmative Action; Phi Kappa Pi Honor Soc; Nat Asn Advan Colored People; Am Civil Liberties Union; Phi Delta Kappa; Nat Human Rights Campaign; Southern Poverty Law Ctr; Am Men's Studies Asn; Mich Equality & The Ruth Ellis Ctr. **Special Achievements:** Author of numerous papers on African-American males published in academic and professional journals including the Journal of African American Studies, the Journal of Men's Studies and Black Issues in Higher Education. **Business Addr:** Director of Diversity, Minnesota State Colleges and Universities, Wells Fargo Place 30 7th St E Suite 350, Saint Paul, MN 55101-7804.*

HARRIS, DR. WILLA BING
Educator. **Personal:** Born Mar 12, 1945, Allendale, SC; daughter of Van Bing and Willa M Lofton Bing; married Dr Jake J Harris, Jun 3, 1972; children: KeVan Bing. **Educ:** Bennett Col, BA, 1966; Bloomsburg State Col, MEd, 1968; Univ Ill, EdD, 1975. **Career:** White Haven State Sch & Hosp, teacher, 1967-69; Albany State Col, instr, 1969; SC State Col Orangeburg, asst prof & suprv grad practicum stud, 1969-70; Univ Ill, Urbana Champaign, Upward Bound, head counr, 1971, asst to major adv, 1971-73; Barber-Scotia Col, asst prof of educ & psychol, 1975-76; Ala State Univ, Montgomery, coord, spec educ, prof & coordr, currently; Cent Ala Regional Educ In-Serv Ctr, coordr, 1985-88, dir, Rural & Minority Spec Educ Personnel Preparation, 1988, assoc prof & coord for special educ, 1976-, dir emotional conflict, teacher preparation program, 1990-98. **Orgs:** Consult Head Start, 1977-80, 1984-85; lay delegate annual conf, Ala W Fla Conf United Methodist Church, 1980-90; bd dir, United Methodist Children's Home, Selma, AL, 1984-94, 1996; Ala State Univ Credit Union, 1984-87; Nellie Burge Comm Ctr 1985-91; Am Asn Mental Deficiency-Mental Retardation; AAUP; Ala Consortium Univ Dirs Spec Ed; Black Child Devel Inst; Coun Excep C; Coun C Behavior Disorders; Div C Commun Disorders, Div Mental Retardation, Teacher Ed Div; Ill Admin Spec Ed; Kappa Delta Pi; Nat Asn Educ Young C; Nat Asn Retarded Citizens; Montgomery City Asn Retarded Citizens; Phi Delta Kappa; Ala State Univ Grad Fac; Ala State Univ Woman's Club; Montgomery Newcomers Club; Tot n Teens; Peter Crump Elem Sch PTA State & Nat Chapt; Metrop United Methodist Church, Adult II Sunday Sch Class; comt chmn, Fund Raising Choir Robes; admin, Organizer United Meth Youth Fel; jurisdictional coordr, Black Methodists Southeastern Jurisdiction Church Renewal, 1989-; bd mem, finance chair, Nat Black Methodists Church Renewal, 1989-; pres, bd dir, United Methodist Children's Home, 1990-94. **Honors/Awds:** USOE Fellow, Univ Ill, 1970-73; Ford Found Fel, Univ Ill, 1972-73; Educator of Year, Ala Asn Retarded Citizens, 1982; Outstanding Educator, Montgomery County Asn Retarded Citizens, 1982; Volunteer Services Award, Montgomery County Asn Retarded Citizens, 1985; Distinguished Alumni Award, C V Bing High Sch, Allendale, SC, 1988. **Home Addr:** 2613 Whispering Pines Dr, Montgomery, AL 36116. **Business Addr:** Professor, Coordinator, Alabama State University, 915 S Jackson St 109 Councill Hall, PO Box 271, Montgomery, AL 36101-0271, **Business Phone:** (334)229-4394.

HARRIS, WILLIAM ALLEN
Sociologist. **Personal:** Born Aug 3, 1937, Providence, RI; son of William A and Ruth Pell; married; children: Rebecca Jackson, Kurt R, Trevor & Jimbo S. **Educ:** Univ Calif, Santa Barbara, BA, 1968; Yale Univ, MA, 1970; Stanford Univ, PhD, 1981. **Career:** Sociologist (retired); 6927th Radio Squadron Mobile, Onna Point, 1958-60; Wesleyan Univ, Ctr Afro-Am Studies asst prof, 1978-82; Univ Vi, res scientist, 1982-87; Clean Sites, res assoc, 1987-90; Univ Iowa, African Am World Studies, visiting fac, 1990-92; Boston Col, Dept Sociol, asst prof, 1992-2000. **Orgs:** Am Sociol Asn, 1977-; Asn Black Sociologists, 1990-; Asn Social & Behav Scientist, 1994-. **Honors/Awds:** NCEA Fel, Black Theatre, 1968; UCSB, Asian Studies, Top Grad, 1968. NDFL Fel, Japanese Lang, 1969; Nat Fel Fund, grad study, 1974-79; Fulbright Res Fel, Beijing, China, 2000-01. **Special Achievements:** Author of: Theatrical Performances, CA & Virgin Islands, 1967-86; Films of Spike Lee, 1995; Theory Construction, Socological Theory, Vol 10, 1992; Upward Mobility Among African Americans, 1996. **Military Serv:** US Air Force, E 3, 1957-60; Completed intensive course in Mandarin Chinese. **Home Addr:** 247 Chestnut Hill Ave Suite 31, Brighton, MA 02135, **Home Phone:** (617)254-6136.

HARRIS, WILLIAM ANTHONY (BILL HARRIS)
Curator, educator. **Personal:** Born Jan 25, 1941, Anniston, AL; son of Edwin and Elizabeth Gay; married Carole McDonald, Oct 7, 1966. **Educ:** Wayne State Univ, BA, 1971, MA, 1977. **Career:** JazzMobile, 1981-83; New Fed Theatre, 1983-85; Wayne State Univ, 1985-90, prof, 1993-; Ctr Creative Studies, 1985-90; Mus African-Am Hist, cur, 1990-. **Orgs:** Bd mem, Detroit Coun Arts, 1987-; bd mem, Inside Out, 1997-. **Honors/Awds:** Paul Robeson Cultural Arts Award, State Mich, 1985; Rosa Parks Vis Scholar Fel, Martin Luther King, Jr, 1987; Writer in Residence Grant, Rockefeller Found, 1988; Art Achievement Award for Alumni, Wayne State Univ, 1989. **Special Achievements:** Publ: Stories About the Old Days (play), 1989; Every Goodbye Ain't Gone, (play) 1989; Robert Johnson: Trick the Devil, 1993; The Ringmaster's Array (poems); Yardbird Suite: Side One (Poems); Riffs & Coda (plays), 1998. Approximately 80 productions of plays written. "He Who Endures" (play) in anthology African American Literature, edited by Al Young; "Every Goodbye Ain't Gone" (play) in anthology New Plays for the Black Theater, edited by Woodie King, Jr. **Military Serv:** AUS, sp4, 1966-68. **Home Addr:** 15 E Kirby Suite 611, Detroit, MI 48202. **Business Addr:** Professor, Wayne State University, College of Liberal Arts and Science, 5057 Woodward Eng Dept, Detroit, MI 48202, **Business Phone:** (313)577-3414.

HARRIS, WILLIAM H
Lawyer. **Personal:** Born Sep 8, 1942, New Orleans, LA; son of William H and Victoria Fontenette; married Cynthia; children: Alisa Carol & William H III. **Educ:** Xavier Univ, BA, 1965; Howard Univ, JD, 1968. **Career:** Dept Housing & Urban Develop, Off Gen Counsel, atty; Greenstein Delorme & Luchs PC, shareholder, 1989-, atty-prin, currently; pvt pract, 1969-. **Orgs:** US Ct Appeals Wash, DC; US Dist Ct; US Ct Claims; Nat Asn Advan Colored People; Am Nat DC & Nat Bar Asn; DC mayor's comn on Rental Housing Prod; Nat Assoc Security Professionals; assoc mem, DC Bldg Indust Asn; Mortgage Bankers Asn Am; Alpha Phi Alpha Fraternity. **Business Addr:** Attorney Principal, Shareholder, Greenstein Delorme & Luchs PC, Real Estate Financing, 1620 L St NW Suite 900, Washington, DC 20036-5605, **Business Phone:** (202)452-1400 Ext 329.

HARRIS, DR. WILLIAM HAMILTON
College administrator, educator, executive. **Personal:** Born Jul 22, 1944, Fitzgerald, GA; son of Robert and Sallie; married Wanda F; children: Cynthia Maria & William James. **Educ:** Paine Col, AB, 1966; Ind Univ, MA, 1967, PhD, 1973. **Career:** Paine Col, instr hist, 1967-69, pres, 1982-88; Ind Univ, lectr, prof hist,1972-82, dir cic minorities fel prog, 1977-82; Univ Hamburg, Ger, ful bright prof, vis prof, 1977-78; Tex Southern Univ, pres, 1988-94; Ala State Univ, pres, 1994-2000; Network Instrnl TV Inc, bd dirs, 2001-, chmn bd & chair exec comt, 2002-; Ft Valley State Univ, interim pres, 2005-06; Tex Col, interim pres, 2008; Ala State Univ, interim pres, pres, 2009-. **Orgs:** Leadership Augusta/Leadership Ga, 1982-84; Augusta Jr Achievement Bd Dir,1984-88, ETS Bd Trustees, 1984-90; UNCF Bd Dir, 1984-88; NAFEO Com Inter col Athletics, 1984-86; Lilly Endowment Inc, Comn Lilly Open Fel, 1984-87,Boy Scouts Am; bd dir, NAFEO, 1985-88; Ga Comn Bicentennial US Const,1986-88; Augusta Chamber Com/Augusta Rotary, 1988; bd dir, Montgomery Area United Way, 1995-; bd dir, Montgomery Metrop YMCA, 1995-; bd dir, Montgomery Chamber Com, 1995-; bd visitors, Air Univ, USAF, 1996-; bd dirs, Leadership Ala, 1996-; bd dir, City erence (SWAC) Coun Pres,1996-97; chair, Ala Coun Col & Univ Presidents, 1997-; Ga Asn Cols. **Honors/Awds:** Susan O'Kell Memorial Award, Ind Univ, Bloomington, 1971; Fulbright Fel,Univ Hamburg, 1978-79; Distinguished Alumni Service Award, Ind Univ, 1991; Doctor of Laws, Honoris Causa, Paine Col, 1991; Distinguished Son of Fitzgerald, Ga Centennial Observance, 1996; Doctor of Humanities, Tuskegee Univ. **Special Achievements:** Author: Keeping the Faith: A Philip Randolph, Milton P Webster; Brotherhood of Sleeping Car Porters, 1977; The Harder We Run, Oxford Univ Press, 1982; One of the Fifty Most Influential Black Georgians. **Home Addr:** 6 Oyster Landing Rd, Hilton Head Island, SC 29928. **Business Addr:** President, Ala State University, President's Office, 915 S Jackson St, 130 Councill Hall, Montgomery, AL 36101, **Business Phone:** (334)229-4202.

HARRIS, WILLIAM J
Educator, writer. **Personal:** Born Mar 12, 1942, Fairborn, OH; son of William Lee and Camilla Hunter; married Susan Kumin, Aug 25, 1968; children: Kate Elizabeth Harris. **Educ:** Cent State Univ, Wilberforce OH, BA, 1968; Stanford Univ, Stanford, CA, MA, 1971, PhD, 1974. **Career:** Educator & Writer: Cornell Univ, Ithaca NY, asst prof, 1972-77; Epoch Mag, poetry ed, 1972-77; Univ Calif, Riverside CA, asst prof, 1977-83; Harvard Univ, Cambridge MA, Andrew W Mellon fac fel, 1982-83; State Univ New York, Stony Brook NY, assoc prof, 1985-92; Minn Review, poetry ed, 1988-92; Norton Anthology Afro-Am Lit, adv ed, 1988; Pa State Univ, assoc prof, 1992-2002; Univ Kans, assoc prof, 2002-; Author: Hey Fella Would You Mind Holding This Piano a Moment, 1974; In My Own Dark Way, 1977; The Poetry & Poetics of Amiri Baraka: The Jazz Aesthetic, 1985; editor: The LeRoi Jones/Amiri Baraka Reader, 1991, second ed, 1999; co-editor, Call & Response: The Riverside Anthology of the African-American Literary Tradition, 1998. **Orgs:** Modern Lang Asn Am, 1971-; Am & Culture Soc. **Honors/Awds:** Outstanding Academic Book for The Poetry and Poetics of Amiri Baraka, Choice Magazine, 1986; Outstanding Teacher Award, Pa State, Col Liberal Arts, 1997; GRF faculty Award, Kansas Univ, 2005. **Home Addr:** 5221 Harvard Rd, Lawrence, KS 66049.

HARRIS, WILLIAM JOSEPH, II
Sculptor. **Personal:** Born Nov 19, 1949, Lansing, MI; son of William and Ella; children: Damon. **Educ:** UCLA. **Career:** Self-employed, sculptor, currently. **Orgs:** Co-chair, Decatur GA Arts festival, 1994-95; vol, African Am Parokaine Experience Mus; bd mem, Decatur-Dekalb Arts Alliance. **Honors/Awds:** Works Catalogued Permanently in the African-American Design Archive at Smithsonian's Cooper-Hewitt Museum Dec Arts, 1994; Earl Pardon Memorial Invitational Award Exhibit, 1994; African Expressions, Spruill Center for the Arts, 1994. **Special Achievements:** Work of Art, which is traveling the US with the Uncommon Beauty in Common Objects, Exhibitions, sponsored by Lila Wallace Readers Digest Fund, National Afro-American Museum; Published 79th Annual Conference of the Association for the Study of Afro-American Life and History, 1994.

HARRIS, WILLIAM M.
School administrator. **Personal:** Born Jan 19, 1932, Middletown, OH; married Mary Buchanan; children: William, Walter & Adrienne. **Educ:** OH State, BS, 1954; Univ ND, MS, 1968. **Career:** Essex Co Col, counr, 1968-69; Rutgers Univ, asst dean students, 1969-71; Rutgers Univ, dir camp ctr & stud act, 1971-77; Univ MS Amherst, dir camp ctr. **Orgs:** Comn Minor Prog; Asn Col Union Intern, 1971-; help alien youth E Orange Bd Educ, 1970-74; Vind Soc, 1971-. **Military Serv:** USAF, Reserves lt col. *

HARRIS, DR. WILLIAM MCKINLEY
Consultant, educator. **Personal:** Born Oct 29, 1941, Richmond, VA; son of William and Rosa Minor; divorced; children: Rolisa, William Jr, Dana & Melissa. **Educ:** Howard Univ, BS, physics, 1964; Univ Wash, MUP, urban planning, 1972, PhD, urban planning, 1974. **Career:** Western Wash State Col, Ctr Urban Studies, dir, 1973-74; Portland State Univ, Black Studies Dept, chmn, 1974-76; Off Afro Am Affairs, dean, 1976-81; Univ Va, prof city planning, 1987-98; planning consult, 1987-; Jackson State Univ, Sch Policy & Planning, Dept Urban & Regional Planning, prof & assoc dean; Mass Inst Technol, Martin Luther King Jr Vis Professor, currently. **Orgs:** Nat Asn Advan Colored People, 1964-; Am Planning Asn, 1976-; Am Inst Cert Planners, 1978-; Charlottesville Planning Comn, 1981-98; bd mem, Develop Training Inst, 1988-; bd dirs, TJ United Way, 1990-98; Charlottesville Bd Zoning Appeals, 1991-98; fel People People's Citizen Ambassador Prog, 1993-96; Fel Am Inst Certified Planners, Urban Affairs Asn, currently. **Honors/Awds:** Portland, Oregon Citizen Year, 1975; Outstanding Service, Community Develop Soc VA, 1984; Teacher of the Year, Monticello Community Action Agency, 1990; Delegation leader to China, Citizen Ambassador Prog, 1992, 1994; Life Time Achievement Award, Planning & Black Community Div Am Planning Asn. **Special Achievements:** Written 30 articles and three books; Black Community Development, 1976; Charlottesville Little League Basketball, coach, championships, 1982, 1988, 1992. "Professional Education of African Americans: A Challenge to Ethical Teaching," Business and Professional Ethics Journal, 1990; "Technology Education for Planners: A Century for African and People of African Descent," African Technology Forum, 1992; "African-American Economic Development in Baltimore," The Urban Design and Planning Magazine, 1993; "Environmental Racism: A Challenge to Community Development," Journal of Black Studies, 1995; "Challenge and Opportunity: Core Cities and Surburbs," 2002; "Urban Segregation in the Deep South: Race, Education, and Planning Ethics in Jackson MS," 2003. **Military Serv:** USAF, rotc cadet.

HARRIS, DR. ZELEMA M.
Chancellor (education). **Personal:** Born Jan 12, 1940, Newton County, TX; children: Narissa, Cynthia Bond & James (Jay). **Educ:** Prairie View A&M Col, BS, 1961; Univ Kans, MS, 1972, EdD, 1976. **Career:** Metro Community Col, coordr curric eval, 1976-77, dir curric eval 1977-78, dir ed opportunity ctr, 1978-80, dir dist serv, 1980; Nat Ctr Voc Ed, consult, 1978-81; Pioneer Community Col, pres, 1980-87; Penn Valley Community Col & Pioneer Campus, pres, 1987-90; Parkland Col, pres, 1990-2006; St Louis Community Col, interim chancellor, chancellor, 2007-. **Orgs:** Eval Spec Off Ed, 1976; consult, McMannis Assoc, 1978-80; bd mem, Black Econ Union, 1981-85; Urban League Greater Kansas City, 1981-90; pres, Nat Asn Advan Colored People, 1982-86; gen chmn, Greater Kansas City, MO United Negro Col Fund Campaign, 1988; Steering Comt, Mayor's Prayer Breakfast; Full Employment Coun; Nat Conf Christians & Jews; Downtown Minority Develop Corp; Pub Bldg Auth; Quality Ed Coalition; co-chair, Kansas City's Jazz Comn; United Way Champaign County; Champaign County Chamber Com; Jr League Champaign-Urbana; Rotary Club Champaign; Urban League Champaign County. **Honors/Awds:** Mary McLeod-Bethune, Alpha Phi Alpha, 1983; Recognition for OutstandingParticipation, UNCF Lou Rawls Parade Stars Fund-Raising TV spec, 1983; Jefferson Award, Channel 4 TV NBC, 1984; Recognition for Service, Adv Comt House Select Comt C Youth & Females, 1984; Protestant of the Year CitationAward, Nat Coun Christians & Jews, 1986; Kansas City Spirit Award, GillisCtr Kansas City, MO, 1987; Leadership Award, Nat CounBlack Am Affairs,1994; Wingspread Award, IL Sect, Am Asn Women Community Col, 1995; Woman of Distinction, Green Meadows Girl Scout Coun, 1996; Marie Y Martin ChiefExecutive Officer Award, Asn Comt Col Trustees, 1997; Athena Award forOutstanding Business Professional Woman, Champaign City Chamber Com, 1997; President of the Year, Am Asn Women Community Col, 1997. **Special Achievements:** One of the 60 Women of Achievement, Mid Continent Coun Girl Scouts, 1983;Developed, "Vocational Evaluation Model," The Mo Adv Coun Voc Educ, 9thAnn Report, 1978; One of the 100 Most Influential Women, Globe Newspaper,1983, 1990; One of the Most Powerful Women in KS City, KS Citian publ by Cof C 1984; One of Nations Most Influential Black Women, Dollars & SenseMag, 1986; One of 30 Women of Conscience, Panel Am Women, 1987; Author,"Meeting the Growing Challenges of Ethnic Diversity," Community, Techn &Jr Col Times, 1990; "Creating a Climate of Institutional Inclusiveness,"Community, Tech & Jr Col Times, 1992; "Leadership for Creating CommunityWithin Institutions"; "Multicultural and International Challenges to theCommunity College: A Model for Collegewide Proactive Response," ERICClearinghouse Community Cols, 1995; "Leadership in Action: LeadingCollectively at Parkland College," Community Col Jour, 1996; "Embracing aNew Vision in the Information Age," Community Col Week, 1996; "From Policyto Action: Implementation of NCA's Statement on Access, Equity, andDiversity," NCA Quarterly, 1997; St. Louis Leader of Distinction, YWCA, 2008. **Business Addr:** Chancellor, St Louis Community College, 300 S Broadway, St Louis, MO 63102, **Business Phone:** (314)539-5000.

HARRIS-DIAW, ROSALIND JUANITA
Publisher. **Personal:** Born Mar 19, 1950, Grand Rapids, MI; daughter of Ruth Boyd Smith and Doyle James; married; children: Lawrence & Donald. **Educ:** Davenport Col Bus, 1970; Patricia Stevens Career Sch, 1973; UNO Omaha, 1981; Metro State Col, African Am Leadership Inst, cert, 1991. **Career:** Omaha National Bank, chartographer, 1975-77; Salt & Pepper Art Studios, owner & operator, 1977-80; Rees Printing Co, grapic artist, 1981; Colorado Homes & Lifestyles, production artist, 1981-82; DK Assoc Excel Serv, Lowry AFB graphic artist, 1982-84; Production Plus/Spectrum Designs, owner & operator, 1984-; Urban Spectrum, publisher, art dir & owner, 1987-. **Orgs:** Pres & publist, Five Points Bus Asn, 1989-; treas, Mothers & Daughters Inc, 1989-; Colo Black Chamber Com, 1990-97; dir, Rocky Mountain Women's Inst, 1994-97; Metro State Col Pres's Community Adv Coun, 1994; Colo Hist Soc African Am Adv Coun, 1994-; Chairs Steering Com, Hiawatha Davis Campaign Better Communities Comt, 1995; Metro State Cols Press' Community Adv Coun; appointed comnr, Mayors Off Art Cult & Film; Co Asn Black Journalists; African-Am Leadership Inst; Nat Coun Negro Women; dir, Girls Scouts Inc; Denver Metro Conv & Visitor's Bur; stapleton Redevelop, Citizen Adv Bd; Mayor's Coun Safe City Summit Task Force; Five Points Bus Asn. **Honors/Awds:** Women of Achievement Nominee, YWCA, 1990; Business Award, CBWPA-Co Black Women Polit Action, 1991; Print Journalist of the Year, CABJ-Co Asn Black Journalist, 1994; MLK Jr Humanitarian Award, Major Wellington E Webb, 1995; Community Newspaper Media Award, Am Legion, 1995; Trailblazer Award, Nat Coun Negro Women, 1997; LOC Million Man March Media Award, 1998; Top 100 Media Award, 1999; Women of Distinction, Girl Scouts, 2000; Corp Award, Bus & Prof Women, 2000; Community Diversity Award, Delta Sigma Theta, Denver Alumae chap, 2000; Dr MLK Business Social Responsibility Award, 2003; Burger King Everyday Hero Award, 2003. **Home Addr:** 5563 Xanadu St, Denver, CO 80239. **Business Addr:** Publisher, President, Urban Spectrum, 2499 Washington St, Denver, CO 80205, **Business Phone:** (303)292-6446.

HARRIS-EBOHON, DR. ALTHERIA THYRA
Educator, executive. **Personal:** Born Jun 26, 1948, Miami, FL; daughter of Andrew Harris Sr and Mary White-Harris; married John Ikpomwenosa Ebohon, Dec 25, 1987; children: Paul, Samson, Terrian Sheyvonne McNeal-Berry, Marquell Hughes-Berry,LaDarius McNeal-Berry, LaDonte' McNeal-Berry & Nigel Berry. **Educ:** Miami-Dade Community Col, AA, 1968; FL Atlantic Univ, BA, 1970; Morgan State Univ, MS, 1972; FL Atlantic Univ, EdS, 1976; Nova Univ, EdD, 1981; Barry Univ, Fla Int Univ; Univ Miami. **Career:** Dade Co Pub Schs, educr; businesswoman, 1988-. **Orgs:** New Mt Zion Missionary Baptist Church Hialeah; Nat Educ Asn, 1970; Baptist training union directress New Mt Zion Missionary Baptist Church Hialeah, 1980-; bd mem, Fla Baptist Convention Inc, 1986; life fel, Int Biographical Asn, Cambridge, England, 1988-; Am Biographical Inst, 1988; Blk Hist Oratorical Comt Sponsor, 1990. **Honors/Awds:** Awards Banquet Honoree by Senator Bob Graham, St Augustine, FL 1986. *

HARRIS-JONES, YVONNE
Consultant. **Personal:** Born in West Palm Beach, FL; daughter of Albert and Mary G Lightfoot Simpson. **Educ:** City Col NY, BA, sociol, 1970; New Sch Univ Soc Res, MA, human resource Mgt, 1977. **Career:** Fed Reserve Bank NY, sr training specialist, 1972-76; Am Stock Exchange, managing dir, Employee Rels, 1976-96; Yvonne Harris Jones Enterprises, pres & chief exec officer, 1997-. **Orgs:** Pres, Zeta Delta Phi Graduate Chap, 1970-76; Soc Hum Res Mgt, 1976-; Coalition 100 Black Women 1977-; adv bd, Murry Bergtraum HS, 1979-96; NY Club, NANBPWC Inc. 1986-; adv bd, Career Opportunity, 1991-2003; adv bd, Medgar Evers Sch Bus & Pub Admin, 1998-; Leadership Am , 1998. **Honors/Awds:** Black Achievers in Indus Award, YMCA Harlem Branch 1979; Corporate Achievement Award, Negro Bus & Prof Women's Clubs Inc, 1985; Mary McCloud Bethune Award, Nat Coun Negro Women, 1991. **Special Achievements:** Contributed article to professional magazines, 1984-2003; Salute to Black Business & Professional Women, Dollars & Sense Mag, 1989. **Business Addr:** President, Chief Executive Officer, Yvonne Harris Jones Enterprises, PO Box 20, Mohegan Lake, NY 10547, **Business Phone:** (914)528-6899.

HARRISON, DR. A. B.
Physician. **Personal:** Born Jan 1, 1909?, Portsmouth, VA. **Educ:** Va State Col, BS; Meharry Med Col, MD, 1930. **Career:** Franklin, VA, pvt pract, 1936-; South Hampton Memorial Hosp, staff mem, 1945; Franklin, VA, City Coun, 1968-74, vice mayor, 1974-76, mayor, 1976-; Provident Hosp, intern.

HARRISON, ALVIN
Track and field athlete. **Personal:** Born Jan 20, 1974, Orlando, FL; son of Albert and Juanita; children: Shraee & Shiyah. **Educ:** Hartnell Col. **Career:** Track & field athlete, currently. **Honors/Awds:** Third Place, USA Juniors Competition, 1993; Winner, Bruce Jenner Classic, 1996; Gold Medal, Olympics, 1996, 2000; First Place, Nat Indoor Track & Field, 1998. **Special Achievements:** Co-author, Go to Your Destiny, 2000.

HARRISON, DR. ANDOLYN
Educator, dean (education). **Educ:** Bowling Green State Univ, PhD. **Career:** Grambling State Univ, Dept Educ Leadership, dean, prof, currently. **Orgs:** Louisiana Educ Consortium (LEC). **Special Achievements:** Has co-authored a chapter in Selected Models of Developmental Education Programs in Higher Education, a chapter in Reading Across The Curriculum, co-author of an article in The Review of Higher Education. **Business Phone:** (318)274-3857.

HARRISON, ANGELA
Manager. **Educ:** Univ San Diego, BA, 1989; Ind State Univ, MBA, 1999. **Career:** Ind State Univ, help desk mgr info technol, 1995-, interim dir multimedia support, 2000-. **Business Addr:** Help Desk Manager, Interim Director, Indiana State University, 200 N 7th St, Terre Haute, IN 47809-9989, **Business Phone:** (812)237-8264.

HARRISON, BEVERLY E
Lawyer. **Personal:** Born Jun 17, 1948, Port Chester, NY. **Educ:** SUNY Oneonta, BA, 1970; Univ Ill, Col Law, JD, 1973. **Career:** Counr Housing & Spec Equal Opport Prog, grad asst, 1970-73; SUNY Oneonta Legal & Affirm Action Affairs, asst pres employ, 1974-81; State Univ NY, Stony Brook, spec asst pres affirm action & equal employ, 1981-83; Nassau Community Col, Human Resources & Labor Rels, assoc vpres, 1983-. **Orgs:** Fac adv, Varsity Cheerleaders, State Univ NY, 1974-81; bd mem, Am Asn Univ Women, 1978-79; bd mem, Planned Parenthood Otsego & Delaware County, 1978-80; Am Asn Affirmative Action Nominating Comn, 1979-80; Univ Fac Senate Fair Employ Practices Comn, 1979-81; State Univ Affirmative Action Coun, 1981-83; bd mem, Am Red Cross Suffolk County, 1981-83; Suffold Comm Develop Corp 1981-83; NY State Pub Employer Labor Rels Asn; Indust Rels Res Asn; Metrop Black Bar Asn; Comt Minority Labor Lawyers; Nat Conf Black Lawyers; Nat Asn Black Women Atty; bd mem, Suffolk County Girl Scout Coun; founder, Asn Black Women Higher Educ. **Honors/Awds:** Public Service Award. **Business Addr:** Associate Vice President of Personal & Labor Relations, Nassau Community College, Office of Human Resources and Labor Relations, Tower 820 8th Fl One Educ Dr, Garden City, NY 11530, **Business Phone:** (516)572-7660.

HARRISON, BOB
Football coach, scout. **Personal:** Born Sep 9, 1941, Cleveland, OH; married Anna Marie Bradley; children: Lorraine Ellen & Barbara Annette; married Faye. **Educ:** Kent State Univ, BS, 1964, MEd, 1969. **Career:** John Adams High Sch, Cleveland, asst head football coach, 1964-66, head football coach, 1967-68; Kent State Univ, assoc admission dir, asst football coach, 1969-70; Univ Ia, asst football coach, 1971-73; NC State Univ, asst coach, 1975-76; Univ Tenn, asst coach, 1977-82; Univ Ga, coach, 1988-91; Atlanta Falcons Prof Football Team, asst coach, receivers coach, 1983-86, col scout, 1994-; Pittsburgh Steelers, asst coach, 1992-93; Boston Col, receivers coach, 1994-96. **Orgs:** Offensive coord, Cornell Univ Ithaca, 1974; Nat Asn Advan Colored People,1982-. **Business Addr:** College Scout, Atlanta Falcons, 4400 Falcon Pkwy, Flowery Branch, GA 30542, **Business Phone:** (770)965-3115.

HARRISON, BOYD G, JR.
Automotive executive. **Personal:** Born Feb 23, 1949, Detroit, MI; son of Boyd G Sr and Jessie Mae Trussel; married Alfreda Rowell, Jul 19, 1969; children: Deonne & Devon. **Educ:** Detroit Col Bus, comput sci, 1972. **Career:** Ford Motor Co, Dearborn, MI, inspector, 1968-72; Chevrolet Cent Off, Warren, MI, comput opers, 1972-85; Ford Motor Co, Minority Dealer Training Prog, Detroit, MI, dealer cand, 1985-86; W Covina Lincoln-Mercury, W Covina, CA, dealer prin, 1986-. **Orgs:** Dir, W Covina Chamber Com, 1988-; Ford Lincoln-Mercury Minority Dealers Asn Polit Action Comt. **Honors/Awds:** Small Bus Person of the Year; American Best & Brightest Young Business Professionals. **Home Addr:** 2260 Omega Circle, La Verne, CA 91750, **Home Phone:** (714)596-9312. **Business Addr:** Dealer Principal, West Covina Lincoln-Mercury, 2539 E Garvey Ave, West Covina, CA 91791, **Business Phone:** (818)966-0681.

HARRISON, DR. C KEITH
Educator. **Educ:** Cerritos Col; W Tex State Univ; Calif State Univ, Dominguez Hill, MS, phys educ; Univ Southern Calif, attended. **Career:** Univ Mich, Ann Arbor, Paul Robeson Res Ctr Acad & Athletic Prowess, founder, 1997-2004; fac, Ariz State Univ, 2004-06; Univ Central Fla, Col Bus Admin, DeVos Sport Bus Mgt Grad Prog, assoc prof, currently; Rush Philanthropic's Hip Hop Summit Action Network, Scholar-in-Residence, currently. **Orgs:** Co-founder, Scholar Baller. **Honors/Awds:** Teacher of the Year, Michigan Univ, 1998; outstanding faculty educator, Wash State Univ.

HARRISON, CALVIN
Track and field athlete. **Personal:** Born Jan 20, 1974, Orlando, FL; son of Albert and Juanita; divorced; children: Jarijah. **Educ:** Hartnell Col, attended 1994. **Career:** USATF, Nike club, track & field athlete, currently. **Honors/Awds:** USA Juniors competition, first place, 1993; Reno Air Games, won 400-meter, 1996; Nike Perfontaine Classic, won 400-meter, 1996; Natl Indoor Track & Field, 400-meter, second place, 1998; Olympics, 4x400-meter, gold medal, 2000. **Special Achievements:** Co-author: Go to Your Destiny, 2000. **Business Addr:** Track, Field Athlete, US Track & Field Inc, 1 RCA Dome Suite 140, Indianapolis, IN 46225, **Business Phone:** (317)261-0500.

HARRISON, CAROL L.
Educator. **Personal:** Born Nov 15, 1946, Buffalo, NY. **Educ:** State Univ NY Buffalo, BA, eng psychol, 1968, PhD 1970. **Career:** Educator (retired); Univ Buffalo, Alumni Assn, 1968-; Am Assn, Univ Prof,1968-; Modern Lang Assn, 1969-; Medailla Col Eng Dept, instr, asst prof,chmn, 1970-73, prof, 1999; State Univ NY, Buffalo, english educ colloquim,1972-; Media-Communications Medaille Col, acting dir, assoc prof, 1974;Int Plaform Asn, 1972-74; Acad Com Buffalo Philharmonic, 1971-73. **Orgs:** Vol work Buffalo Childrens Hosp, 1972; Western NY Consortium Eng & Am LitProf, 1974; Nomination Am Asn Univ Womens Educ Found. **Honors/Awds:** Outstanding Educators Am Award, 1974.

HARRISON, CHARLES
Chief executive officer. **Career:** Crown Energy Inc, chief exec officer, 1987-.

HARRISON, CHRIS
Football player. **Personal:** Born Feb 25, 1972, Washington, DC. **Educ:** Univ Va. **Career:** Detroit Lions, guard, 1996-98; Baltimore Ravens, guard, 1999.

HARRISON, DR. DAPHNE DUVAL (DAPHNE D COMEGYS)
Educator. **Personal:** Born Mar 14, 1932, Orlando, FL; daughter of Alexander Chisholm Duval and Daphne Beatrice Alexander Williams; married Daniel L Comegys Jr; children: Michael Alexander & Stephanie Dolores. **Educ:** Talladega Col, BMus, 1953; Northwestern Univ, MMus, 1961; Univ Miami, Fla,EdD, 1971. **Career:** Marion & Broward Co, FL, music teacher, 1953-66; Broward Co, FL, TV instr,1966-68; Fla Atlantic Univ, asst prof educ, 1969-70; Univ Miami, southern fel, 1969-70; Hallandale Middle Sch, FL, dean of girls, 1970-71; BenedictCol, assoc prof fine arts 1971-72; Moton Ctr Independent Studies,Philadelphia, fel, 1976-77; Univ Calif Los Angeles, NEH African humanities fel, 1979; Univ Md, Baltimore, Africana Studies Dept, assoc prof, chairperson, prof, 1981-96, Ctr Study Humanities, dir, 1996-99, prof emer, 1999-; Fulbright fel, 1986. **Orgs:** Chair music dir, St Andrews Church, Hollywood, Fla, 1960-70; bd mem, Fla State Teachers Asn, 1963-65; bd mem, CTD Fla Educrs Asn, 1965-67; consult, Fla Sch Desegregation Consult Ctr, 1965-70; social planner, New Town Harbison, SC, 1971-72; proj dir, Racism Intervention Develop Proj, Univ Md, 1975-77; proj dir, Summer Inst African & African Am Hist Culture & Lit, 1984-85; Nat Asn Negro Bus & Prof Women; Alpha Kappa Alpha; Asn Study Afro-Am Life & Hist; co-chair, Black Family Comt African Am Empowerment Proj; comnr, Md Comn African-Am Hist & Cult; Sonneck Soc; Int Asn Study Popular Music. **Honors/Awds:** Theodore Presser Award, Talladega Col, 1951; Outstanding Faculty of the Year, Black Stud Union, Univ Md, Baltimore, 1988-89; Most Favorite Fac, Stud Govt Asn, Univ Md, Baltimore, 1989; Classic Blues & Women Singers, Blackwell Press Guide Blues, 1989; NEH Fel Univ Profs, 1992-; Phi Beta Kappa, 1998; Phi Kappa Phi Scholar, 1999; Nat Golden Key Hon Soc. **Special Achievements:** Author: Black Pearls: Blues Queens of the 1920's, Rutgers Univ Press, 1988; Wheelin' on Beale, 1993. **Home Addr:** 5560 Shepherdess Ct, Columbia, MD 21045, **Home Phone:** (410)997-5775. **Business Addr:** Professor Emeritus, University Maryland Baltimore, African American Studies, 1000 Hilltop Circle, Baltimore, MD 21250, **Business Phone:** (410)455-1000.

HARRISON, DELBERT EUGENE
Executive. **Personal:** Born Jan 8, 1951, Flint, MI; son of Eugene Harrison and Audrey; married Mary Hill, Sep 4, 1982; children: Darren, Whitney & Danielle. **Educ:** Wilberforce Univ, Wilberforce, OH, BA, 1978. **Career:** Kemper Ins Co, Long Grove, IL, personnel asst II, 1981-82; Allstate Ins Co, S Barrington, IL, div human resources mgr, 1982-86; Chem Bank NY, Chicago, IL, vpres, dir, human resources, 1987-88; Navistar Financial Corp, Rolling Meadows, IL, vpres, human resources. **Orgs:** Bd trustees, Latino Inst, 1986-90; adv bd mem, Roosevelt Univ, Robin Campus, 1989-; secy, Black Human Resources Network. **Home Addr:** 5727 Ring Ct, Hanover Park, IL 60103. **Business Phone:** (708)734-4500.

HARRISON, DON K., SR.
Educator, psychologist. **Personal:** Born Apr 12, 1933, Nashville, NC; married Algeo O Hale; children: Denise & Don K. **Educ:** NC Cent Univ, BA, 1953; Wayne State Univ, MA, 1958; Univ Mich, PhD, 1972. **Career:** Univ Mich, Guidance & Coun Prog, asst prof, 1972-76; Univ Mich, Guidance & Coun Prog, chmn, 1974-77; Univ Mich Rehab Coun Educ, assoc prof & dir,1975; Wayne State Univ, Voc Rehab, adj asst prof, 1972-97; Univ Mich Rehab Res Inst, assoc prof & dir, 1976-97, prof emer, currently. **Orgs:** Am Psychol Asn; Personnel & Guidance Asn Rehab Couns Traineeship Rehab Serv Admin, 1975; dir, PRIME Inc, MI, 1970-80. **Honors/Awds:** Outstanding Service Award, MI Personel & Guide Asn, 1976. **Military Serv:** AUS, sgt, 1953-55.

HARRISON, FAYE VENETIA
Anthropologist, educator. **Personal:** Born Nov 25, 1951, Norfolk, VA; daughter of James and Odelia B Harper; married William Louis Conwill, May 17, 1980; children: Giles, Mondlane & Justin. **Educ:** Brown Univ, BA, 1974; Stanford Univ, MA, 1977, PhD, 1982. **Career:** Univ Louisville, asst pro anthrop, 1983-89; Univ Tenn-Knoxville, assoc prof anthrop, 1989-97; Univ SC, Columbia, prof anthrop, grad dir women's studies, 1997-; Univ Tenn, Lindsay Young Prof, currently. **Orgs:** CMS Anthrop Women; pres, 1989-91, secy, 1985-87, ed, 1984-85, Asn Black Anthropologists; KEN Rainbow Coalition, 1988-90; Dem Socialists Am, 1990-; bd mem, Am Anthrop Asn, 1990-91; Union Anthrop & Ethnol Sci 1993-98; adv bd, Off Justice, Peace, Integrity Creation, Knoxville Roman Cath Diocese, 1994-97; ed bd, Univ Tenn Press, 1995-97; East Tenn Coalition Abolish State Killing, 1995-97; co-chair, chair, 1998-2003, Int chair, Black Fac & Staff Asn, Univ Tenn-Knoxville, 1995-97; Nat Alliance Against Racist Polit Repression; bd bd, NAACP; Annual Rev Anthrop; ed, bd, Critique Anthrop; assoc ed, Urban Anthrop; ed bd, Identities; ed bd, Womanist Theory & Res. **Honors/Awds:** Samuel T Arnold Fellowship, Brown Univ, 1974-75; Graduate Fellowship, Ford Found, 1976-78; Fulbright-Hays Predoctoral Fellowships, US Dept Educ, 1978-79; Compton Fellowship, Danforth Found, 1981-82; Postdoctoral Fellowship, Ford Found, 1987-88; Certficate of Merit for Scholarly Achievement, Phi Beta Kappa, 1993. **Special Achievements:** Editor & Contributor: "WEB DuBois and Anthropology," special issue, Critique of Anthrop, 1992; editor and contributor: Decolonizing Anthropology, Am Anthrop Asn, 1991, Second ed, 1997; editor and contributor: "Black Folks in Cities Here and There: Changing Patterns of Domination & Response," special issue, Urban Anthropology and Cultural Systems in World Economic Development, 1988; "Women in Jamaica's Urban Informal Economy," New West Indian Guide (reprinted in Third World Women and the Politics of Feminism, Indiana UNV Press), 1988 (1991); "Jamaica and the INT Drug Economy," TransAfrica Forum, 1990; performer: "Three Women, One Struggle," Louisville, KY, INT Women's Day Celebration Dayton, OH, 1989, Black Arts Festival, Summer 1990; author: Writing Against The Grain: Cultural Politics of Difference in Alice Walker's Fiction, Critique of Anthropology, 1993; Foreword, Comparative Perspectives on Slavery, 1993; "The Persistent Power of Race in the Cultural and Political Economy of Racism," Annual Review of Anthropology, 1995; "Give Me That Old Time Religion: The Genealogy and Cultural Politics of an Afro-Christian Celebration in Halifa County, NC," Religion in the South, 1995; co-editor, contributor, African AMR Pioneers in Anthropology, Univ of ILL Press, 1998; contributed entries, "The Blackwell Dictionary of Anthropology," 1998; "The Gendered Politics and Violence of Structural Adjustment: A View from Jamaica;"in Situated Lives: Gender and Culture in Everyday Life, 1997. **Business Addr:** Professor, University of Tennessee, College of Arts & Science, Department Anthropology, 250 S Stadium Hall, Knoxville, TN 37996-0720, **Business Phone:** (865)974-4408.

HARRISON, DR. FRED
Dean (education), educator. **Educ:** Ft Valley State Col, BS, 1971; Univ Ga, M.Ed, 1972; Ohio State Univ, PhD, 1979. **Career:** Univ Ga, exten specialist personnel & staff develop, asst prof exten educ;Ft Valley State Univ, Col Agr, Home Econs & Allied Progs, dean, currently, Coop Exten Prog, adminr, currently. **Orgs:** Exten adminr, Asn Research Dirs Inc, currently. **Honors/Awds:** Award of Excellence, Univ Ga, Col Agr & Environ Sci Alumni Asn, 2003. **Business Addr:** Extension Administrator, Fort Valley State University, College of Agriculture, Home Economics & Allied Programs, 1005 State Univ Dr, PO Box 4061, Ft Valley, GA 31030-4313, **Business Phone:** (478)825-6344.

HARRISON, GEORGE
Clergy. **Career:** First Baptist Church NBC, pastor, currently. *

HARRISON, HARRY PAUL
Educator. **Personal:** Born Jan 10, 1923, Lawrenceville, VA; son of George E and Eliza Green; married Teressa H; children: Vera, Zelma & Agatha. **Educ:** St Pauls Col, BS, 1952. **Career:** Educator (retired); Greenville County Sch Syst, teacher, 1952-55; Bruns County Sch Syst, teacher, 1955-85, bd supvrs, 1976-93, chmn, 1982-93. **Orgs:** Supt, Sunday Sch, 1957-83; pres, Brunswick Teachers Asn, 1968-69; pres, Brunswick Ed Asn, 1970-71; chmn, Poplar Mt Church's Bldg Comn, 1977; chmn, Brunswick County Dem Comn, 1978-90; treas, Brunswick County Nat Asn Advan Colored People, 1978-; dir, Emergency Servs Brunswick County, 1980-; chmn, Brunswick County Social Servs, 1989-90; vice chmn, Planning Dist No 13, 1989-92; S S Community Servs Bd, 1990-. **Honors/Awds:** Back Bone, Nat Asn Advan Colored People, 1976 & 1980; Citizen of the Year, Omega 1981; Outstanding Service, Bethany Baptist Asn, 1984-90. **Military Serv:** AUS, corpl, 1946-47; Army Occupation Medal; WWII Victory Medal. *

HARRISON, HATTIE N.
Government official. **Personal:** Born Feb 11, 1928, Lancaster, SC; married Robert (deceased); children: Robert & Philip. **Educ:** J C Smith; Community Educ Develop; Antioch Col. **Career:** Sr commn aide, 1968-73; del sub-tchr, 1962-73; mayors rep, 1974; NH Sch Pub Reltns Assn, consult, 1970; NH Aerospace Conv; Comm Sensitivity Training Comm Sch Div; MD Gen Assembly Dist 45, delegate mem, currently; Mott Found, consult. **Orgs:** Founder & chmn, Dunbar Comm & Cncl; mem, Steering Com Univ MD; Nat Asn Advan Colored People Comm Sch Workshop; founder, Douglass Teen Club; ward leader, Mothers March, 1950-60; House Del; chair, Rules & Exec Nominations Comt; Md Comn Status Women, 1973-74; Md Comn Women, 1976; Comn Study Domestic Rels Laws, 1976-80; Task Force Permits Simplification, 1979-80; Task Force Youth Employment, 1980-82; Task Force Examine State's Cemetery & Funeral Indust, 1996; Int Community Educ Asn; pres, Md Asn Community Educ; Young Women's Christian Asn; E Baltimore Women's League; Nat Lab Advan Educ; chair, Historic E Baltimore Community Action Coalition. **Honors/Awds:** Outstanding Leadership Award, 1974; Women Year, Alpha Zeta, 1974; Casper R Taylor Jr Founder's Award, House Del, 2005. **Special Achievements:** First African-American woman to chair a legislative committee in Maryland. **Business Addr:** Delegate, Maryland General Assembly, Rm 365 House Off Bldg 6 Bladen St, Annapolis, MD 21401-1991, **Business Phone:** 800-492-7122.

HARRISON, JAMES, JR.
Pharmacist. **Personal:** Born Oct 14, 1930, Pittsburg, PA; married Eunice Kea; children: Wanda, James III & Donna. **Educ:** BS, 1954; Regist Pharmacist, 1956; Univ Freeman's Hosp, Intern 1 Yr. **Career:** Harrison Pharm Inc, pres; Berg Pharm, purchased, 1971. **Orgs:** Sunday Sch Teacher; Boy Scout Leader; adv bd, Bloomfield HS; pres & treas, NJ Pharm; bd dir, Essex Co Pharm Soc. **Business Addr:** President, Harrison Pharm, 634 Martin Luther King Jr Blvd, Newark, NJ 07102.*

HARRISON, JAMES C.
President (Organization). **Career:** Protective Indust Ins Co, pres & chief exec officer. **Business Addr:** President, Chief Executive Officer, Protective Industrial Insurance Company, 2300 11th Ave N, Birmingham, AL 35234, **Business Phone:** (205)323-5256.*

HARRISON, JAY P.
Executive. **Career:** Internet Opers Ctr Inc, pres & cheif tech officer, currently. **Orgs:** Inst Elec & Electronics Engrs. *

HARRISON, LISA DARLENE
Basketball player, basketball coach. **Personal:** Born Jan 2, 1971, Louisville, KY; daughter of Cobble and Larry; married Paul Rogers. **Educ:** Univ Tenn, attended. **Career:** Basketball player (retired), basketball coach; Columbus Quest, guard, 1996-97; Portland Power, 1997-99; Phoenix Mercury, 1999-2003, 2005, asst coach, 2004-05. **Honors/Awds:** Ky High Sch Athletics Hall of Fame, 2001; Named, Outreach coordinator for the athletic department, Univ Louisville; Won "Sexiest WNBA Player". **Special Achievements:** Lisa was once ranked eighth in free throw shooting accuracy at 86.4%, 2001.

HARRISON, MARVIN DANIEL
Football player. **Personal:** Born Aug 25, 1972, Philadelphia, PA; son of Linda. **Educ:** Syracuse Univ, retailing. **Career:** Indianapolis Colts, wide receiver, 1996-2008. **Orgs:** Colts-Star News Gridiron Geography Prog; Indianapolis Housing Agency Develop. **Honors/Awds:** Maxwell Award. **Special Achievements:** Appeared on "Wheel of Fortune"; became the only player ever in the history of the NFL to have six double digit reception games in one single season in the 2002 regular season.

HARRISON, DR. MERNOY EDWARD
School administrator. **Personal:** Born Nov 15, 1947, Denver, CO; son of Doris L Thompson Jackson and Mernoy E; married Frankie Gilliam Harrison, Jun 29, 1974; children: Dara T Harrison & Jelani T Harrison. **Educ:** Stanford Univ, Stanford, Calif, BS, 1969; MBA, 1975; Univ NC, Chapel Hill, NC, PhD, 1988. **Career:** Ravenswood High Sch, East Palo Alto, Calif, teacher; Sequoia Union Sch Dist, Redwood City, Calif, teacher, 1969-70; Kaiser Found, Los Angeles, Calif, teacher, 1970-72; San Mateo County, Redwood City, Calif, analyst, 1973-74; Merrill Intern, 1974; Woodrow Wilson fel, 1974-76; NC Cent Univ, Durham, NC, Controller, 1974-81; Calif State Univ, Sacramento, Calif, vpres, 1981-97; Ariz State Univ, exec vpres admin & finance, chief financial officer, downtown phoenix campus, exec provost & vpres, 1997-. **Orgs:** Treas, Sacramento-Yolo Camp Fire, 1982-86; vpres, Western Asn Col & Univ Bus Officers, 1989-90; pres, 1990-91; mem, bd dir, Nat Asn Col & Univ Bus Officers, 1988; chair, exec comt, Calif State Univ Bus Officers Asn, 1983-85; bd trustees, Stanford Univ, 1992-97. **Business Addr:** Vice President, Provost, Arizona State University, Downtown Phoenix Campus, PO Box 872303, Tempe, AZ 85287-2303, **Business Phone:** (602)496-1000.

HARRISON, MYA MARIE
Dancer, singer, actor. **Personal:** Born Oct 10, 1979, Washington, DC. **Educ:** Univ Md, College Park. **Career:** Albums: Mya, 1998; Fear of Flying, 2000; Singles: "Movin' On", 1998; "It's All About Me", 1998; Film appearances: Chicago, 2002; In Too Deep, 1999; Volcano High, 2001; Chicago, 2002; Dirty Dancing: Havana Nights, 2004; Shall We Dance, 2004; Cursed, 2005; NCIS, 2005; Swap Meet, 2006; Ways of the Flesh, 2006; The Metrosexual, 2007; Cover, 2008; Love For Sale, 2008; Penthouse, 2008; Dancing with the Stars, 2009. **Honors/Awds:** MTV Music Award, 1998 & 2001; Grammy Award, 1999 & 2002; Lady of Soul, 1999; MVPA Award, 1999; Soul Train Music Award, 1999 & 2001; Radio Music Awards, 2001; Teen Choice Awards, 2001; TMF Awards, 2001; VH1 Music Awards, 2001; ALMA Awards, 2002;

ASCAP Pop Music Awards, 2002; Billboard Video Awards, 2003; BMI Award, 2002; Channel Thailand Music Awards, 2002; Channel Thailand Music Awards, 2002; Broadcast Film Critics Association Award, 2003; Phoenix Film Critics Society Award, 2003; Screen Actors Guild Award, 2003; MTV Movie Award, 2005. **Special Achievements:** Best Video, "Lady Marmalade"; Nominee of Best Frightened Performance for cursed, 2005. **Business Addr:** Vocalist, c/o Interscope Records Inc, 10900 Wilshire Blvd, Los Angeles, CA 90024, **Business Phone:** (310)208-6547.

HARRISON, NANCY GANNAWAY
Dentist. **Personal:** Born Oct 20, 1929, Trinity, NC; married Robert; children: Renee & Susan. **Educ:** Shaw Univ, BS, 1950; Howard Univ, DDS, 1954. **Career:** St Elizabeth Hosp Wash DC, intern, 1955; Dent, self-employed. **Orgs:** Acad Gen Dent; treas, Twin City Dent Soc, 1969, 1971; Old N State Dent Soc; NC Dent & Soc; Am Dent Asn Urbn League Guild; Delta Sigma Theta Sorority; secy, Altrusa Ind; vpres & bd dir, Young Women's Christian Asn, 1973-75.

HARRISON, PAUL CARTER
Educator, writer, television producer. **Personal:** Born Mar 3, 1936, New York, NY; son of Paul and Thelma Carter; married Wanda Malone, Aug 6, 1988; children: Fonteyn. **Educ:** Ind Univ, BA, psychol, 1957; New Sch Soc Res, MA, psychol & phenomenol,1962. **Career:** Educator, Television Producer(retired); NSF fel, 1959-60; Howard Univ,asst prof theatre arts, 1968-70; Kent State Univ, assoc prof afro-am lit, 1969; Calif State Univ, prof theatre arts, 1970-72; Univ Massachusetts, Amherst, prof theatre arts & afro-am studies, 1972-76, prof emer, currently; Choice Mag, cult consult, 1973-83; Elan Mag, contrib edtheatre, 1981-83; Rockefeller Found, fel, 1985; Callaloo Mag, contrib &adv ed, 1985-88; Evergreen Col, curric & cult diversity consult, 1986; Columbia Col, Theatre & Music Dept, artistic producer & chmn, 1976-80, writer-in-residence, 1980-2002, prof emer, 2003-; NEA Playwrights fel, 1995; Director plays: "Junebug Graduates Tonight," 1969; "Lady Day: A Musical Tragedy," 1972; "My Sister, My Sister," 1981; "The River Niger,"1987; producer, play: Black Recollections, 1972; conceptualized, directed:"Ain't Supposed to Die a Natural Death," 1970; dir: "In an Upstate Motel, "1981; playwright: "Tabernacle," 1981; "Anchorman," 1988; "The Death of Boogie Woogie," 1980; "Goree Crossing," 1992; developer & producer, television film: playwright, "Leave 'Em Laughin'," CBS-TV, 1981, Stranger On The Square; playwright: "The Experimental Leader," 1965; "The Great Mac Daddy," 1974; author: The Drama of Nommo, Grove Press, NY, 1973; Kuntu Drama: Plays From the African Continuum, 1974; In the Shawdow of the Great White Way, Thunder Mouth Press, 1989; Charles Stewart's Jazz File, 1985; screenwriter: Lord Shango, 1974; Young blood,1978; Gettin' to Know Me, 1980; editor: Kuntu Drama, anthology, Grove Press, NY, 1974; dir, "Food for the GODS," 1994; editor: Totem Voices, Anthology, Grove Press; co-editor: Classic Plays from the Negro Ensemble Co, Univ Pittsburgh Press, 1995; Black Theatre: Ritual Performance in the African Diaspora, Temple Univ Press, 2002; dir: "Trial of One-Short Sighted Black Woman vs Safreeta Mae & Mammy Louise," 1996-2001; CA premiere, "Waiting to Be Invited;" dir, Sty of the Blind Pig, 2002, 2003, 2004; editor: "African American Review Special Issue on Black Theatre, "winter, 1997. **Orgs:** Theatre panel, Ill Arts Coun, 1976-79; panel, NEA Playwrights, 1992; Meet the Composer, Readers Digest Comn, 1992, 1995; exec comm, Nat Black Theatre Summit Golden Pond, 1998; bd govs, African Grove Inst Arts, 1998. **Honors/Awds:** Obie Award, Best Play, "The Great Mac Daddy," 1974; Grant, Ill Art Coun,1984; Audelco Award, Audelco Develop Comm, 1981; Humanitas Prize, 1981;Best director, AUDELCO, 1999.

HARRISON, PEARL LEWIS
Association executive. **Personal:** Born Jun 8, 1932, East Orange, NJ; married John Arnold; children: Lauren Deborah & Adrianne Carol. **Educ:** Juilliard Sch Music NY, cert, 1952. **Career:** Association executive (retired); Pearl Lewis Harrison Piano Studio, dir, 1953-83; Governor's Task Force Suburban Essex Arts Coun, mem, 1978; City E Orange, coord arts/cult, 1979-80, actg dir pub rels, 1986, Dept Arts & Cult Affairs, dir, 1986-90. **Orgs:** NJ Music Educ Coun, 1960-77; Suburban Essex Arts Coun, 1978-82; Friends NJ Opera, 1982-; Resolution Cult Expertise Essex Co Bd, 1983; Essex Co Arts & Cult Planning Bd, 1983-86; bd trustees, United Way Essex & Hudson Co, 1985-86; Black Composers Inc, 1985-; NJ Motion Picture Comn, 1986-; exec dir, E Orange Arts & Cult Inc, 1986-88; E Orange Libr Bd, 1986-90; Hist Soc E Orange, 1999; Pearl Lewis Harrison Fine Arts Scholar Fund, 1994. **Honors/Awds:** White House Citation, Mrs Nancy Reagan music/comn spirit, 1983; Women of the Year Award, Pride & Heritage Int Year Environ Concerns, 1983; State New Jersey Excellence Award, NJ State Sen, 1983; Certificate of Appreciation, Comn Serv, City E Orange, 1983; Annual Black Heritage Pioneer Family Awards, City E Orange, 1986; United Nations Citation, 1989. **Home Phone:** (973)675-2812. *

HARRISON, DR. ROBERT WALKER
Educator, administrator. **Personal:** Born Oct 13, 1941, Natchez, MS; son of Robert and Charlotte; married Gayle Johnson; children: Robert & Seth. **Educ:** Tougaloo SC Col, BS, 1961; Northwestern Univ, MD, 1966. **Career:** Vanderbilt Univ Sch Med, instr, 1972-74, from asst prof to assoc prof, 1974-85; Univ Ark Med Sci, prof, 1985-93; Univ Rochester Med Sch, prof emer, 1993; consult, NIH; Knoll Pharmaceut, consult; Abbott & Roche, consult; Beeslender.com Inc, pres & chief exec officer, currently. **Orgs:** Endocrine Soc; Alpha Phi Alpha. **Military Serv:** USN, lt comm, 1968-70. **Business Addr:** President, Chief Executive Officer, beeSlender.com Inc, 91 Berkeley St Suite 3, Rochester, NY 14607, **Business Phone:** (585)271-6878.

HARRISON, DR. RODERICK
Executive, executive director. **Educ:** Harvard Univ, AB; Princeton Univ, PhD. **Career:** Univ Calif, LA, Afro-Am Studies & Sociol Dept, fac; US Census Bur Racial Statistics Br, chief; Howard Univ, Dept Sociol & Anthrop, fac, currently; Joint Ctr Polit & Econ Studies, Off Res, dir, currently. **Orgs:** Am Statist Soc; founding dir, DataBank. **Honors/Awds:** Roger Herriot Award, Am Statist Soc. **Special Achievements:** Published several books. **Business Phone:** (202)789-3514.

HARRISON, RODNEY SCOTT
Football player. **Personal:** Born Dec 15, 1972, Markham, IL; son of Barbara; married Erika; children: Christian, Rodney Jr & Mikala. **Educ:** Western Ill Univ, gen studies. **Career:** Football Player (Retired); San Diego Chargers, defensive back, 1994-2002; New Eng Patriots, safety, 2003-08. **Honors/Awds:** San Diego Chargers, Defensive Player of the Year, 1996 & 1997; Chargers Co-Defensive Player of the Year, 1996, 1997, 2000 & 2001; Peter King's Defensive Player of the Year, Associated press, 2003; Ed Block Courage Award, 2006; Pro Bowler Twice, 1998, 2001; First-team All-Pro Twice, 1998, 2003. **Business Addr:** Safety, New England Patriots, Gillette Stadium 1 Patriot Pl, Foxboro, MA 02035, **Business Phone:** (508)543-8200.

HARRISON, RONALD E.
Executive, vice president (organization). **Personal:** Born Jan 11, 1936, New York, NY; son of Olive DeVaux Harrison and Edmund Harrison; married; children: Richard, David, Katherine. **Educ:** City Col NY, BBA, 1958; Boston Col, corp community rels prog, 1987. **Career:** Director, Area Manager, Vice President (retired); Pepsi Cola Metro Bottling Co NY, vpres, area mgr; Pepsi-Cola Inc, Cincinnati dir special mkts, 1966, control div Chicago dir training, 1969, mgmt instr Phoenix dir training, 1970, franchise develop NY dir, 1972; Pepsi Bottling Co, area vpres, 1975-79; Pepsi-Cola Co, div vpres, 1979-81; Pepsi-Cola Inc, nat sales dir, 1981-86; PepsiCo, sr vpres, community affairs, 2000-04. **Orgs:** Nat Asn Mktg Develop; Sales Exec Club NY; bd trustee NY Orphan Asylum Soc; mem, Educ Spl Sch Dist Greenburgh; past chair, Bus Policy Review Coun; bd mem, Westchester Coalition; bd mem, NY State Job Training Partnership Coun; mem, Am Mkt Asn; mem, Exec Leadership Coun; mem, Nat Hispanic Corp Coun; mem, Westchester Clubmen; chair, Int Franchise Asn; past chair, Int Franchise Asn Ed Found; mem, Int Franchise Asn Minorities Franchising Comn; chair, Bus Consortium Fund; mem, adv bd, Congressional Black Caucus; founding chmn, Int Franchise Asn, 2005-. **Honors/Awds:** Int Franchise Asn Award, 2005; First Diversity Award, Int Franchise Asn, 2006. *

HARRISON, ROSCOE CONKLIN, JR.
Publicist. **Personal:** Born Sep 20, 1944, Belton, TX; son of Roscoe Conklin Sr and Georgia Dell Moore; married Sandra K Smitha, Aug 27, 1966; children: Corinne Michelle. **Educ:** Temple Junior Col, AA, 1964; Prairie View A & M Univ, BA, 1966; Univ Mary Hardin Baylor, 1967. **Career:** KTEM Radio, announcer, 1960-64; Temple Daily Telegram, reporter, 1966-67; San Antonio Express News, reporter, 1967-68; Jet Mag, assoc editor, 1968-69; KCEN-TV, news bureau chief & reporter, 1970-76; Texas Attorney Gen John Hill, deputy press secy, 1976-79; KCEN-TV, public affairs dir, 1979-93; Scott & White Mem Hosp, assoc dir spec proj; Scott & White Mem Hosp, dir community affairs, currently. **Orgs:** Nat Asn Health Servs Execs, 1994-; Am Soc Health Care Mkt & Pub Rels, 1994-; Tem Bel Heart Asn, bd mem, 1994-; Temple Chamber Com, 1994-; Ebony Cultural Soc, pres; Legislative Adv Comn TX Asn Pub & Nonprofit Hosp; Communities in Sch bd; Baylor Univ Col Arts & Sci, adv coun; Belton Christian Youth Ctr, bd; Temple Bus Growing Ctr, bd; TX A&M Univ, Race & Ethnic Studies Nat Corp Adv Bd; Bell County Judge Comnr Court COM People Disabilities. **Honors/Awds:** Broadcaster of the Year, Texas Farmers Union, 1993; Communicator of the Year, Bell County Communs Prof, 1988; Texas Asn Broadcasters, Distinguished Local Programming, 1977; Jefferson Awards Media Award, Outstanding Public Service, 1990. **Business Addr:** Director of Community Affairs, Scott & White Mem Hosp, 2401 S 31st St, Temple, TX 76508, **Business Phone:** (254)724-1929.*

HARRISON, SHIRLEY DINDY
Executive, vice president (organization), vice president (organization). **Personal:** Born Apr 11, 1951, Syracuse, NY; daughter of Homer Leonard and Eve Uchal; divorced. **Educ:** Syracuse Univ, NY, BFA, 1973. **Career:** Artifacts Syst Ltd, Manchester, NH, graphic artist, 1973-74; PEACE Inc, Syracuse, NY, dir, community devel, 1974-77; Miller Brewing Co, Milwaukee, WI, dir, employee rels & compl, 1977-92; Philip Morris Co Inc, dir diversity mgt & devel, 1992-96, diversity mgt & devel, vpres, 1997. **Honors/Awds:** Community Serv Award, Miller Brewing Co, 1986; Black Achiever, YMCA. **Special Achievements:** 100 Top Bus & Prof Black Women, Dollar & Sense Mag, 1988; 100 Best & Brightest Black Women in Corp Am, Ebony Mag, 1990. *

HARRISON, WENDELL RICHARD
Musician. **Personal:** Born Oct 1, 1942, Detroit, MI; son of Walter R and Ossalee Lockett; divorced 1970; married Pamela Wise, Jan 1, 1970. **Educ:** Highland Pk Jr Col; Detroit Inst Arts Conserv Music. **Career:** Hank Crawford's band, mem; Rebirth Inc, artistic dir, 1978-; musician-clarinetist, saxophonist & composer, currently; Records: Fly By Night, 1990; Forever Duke, 1991; Live In Concert, 1992; Be Boppers Method Book, 1991; Urban Expressions; Something For Pops, 1993; Rush & Hustle,1994; The Eighth House, 2002; Riding With Pluto; Battle of the Tenors; Urban Expressions, 2003; Message from the Tribe: An Anthology of Tribe Records 1972-77, 2004. **Orgs:** Detroit Fedn Musicians Union, 1970; Nat Jazz Serv Orgn, 1991-93; Chamber Music Am, 2002-. **Honors/Awds:** Fellowship Grant, Nat Endowment Arts, 1978, 1992; Distinguished Service Award, Wayne County, 1985; Creative Artist Grant, Arts Found Mich,1992-97; Proclamation, Congressman John Conyers, 1992; Jazz Masters Award, Arts Midwest, 1993; Proclamation, Barbara Rose Collins; Distinguished Artist Award, Detroit City Coun; Creative Artists Grand Award, 2000; Chamber Music America Doris Duke Creative New Works, 2003; Chamber Music Am Residency, 2005. **Business Addr:** Musician, Rebirth Inc, 81 Chandler St, Detroit, MI 48202, **Business Phone:** (313)875-0289.

HARRISON-HALE, DR. ALGEA OTHELLA
Educator. **Personal:** Born Feb 14, 1936, Winona, WV; children: Denise & Don Jr. **Educ:** Bluefield State Col, BS, Ed, 1956; Univ MI, MA, Ed, 1959, PhD, Psychol, Ed, 1970. **Career:** Detroit Pub Sch Syst, teacher; Inkster Sch Syst, Res design, Urban Action Needs Analysis, Wayne County Head start Prog, MI Dept Educ, consult, 1962-66; Highland Park Sch Syst, sch diagnostician, 1968-69; Oakland Univ, prof. **Orgs:** Am Psychol Asn, MI Psychol Asn, Asn Black Psychol, Soc Res Child Develop, Asn Soc & Behavioral Sci; bd trustees, New Detroit Inc, Roeper City & City Schs; Founders Soc, Your Heritage House A Black Mus, Nat Org Women, Child Care Coordr Coun. **Honors/Awds:** Fel, Horace Rackham Predoctoral, 1969-70; US Public Health Grants, 1965-68; graduated second highest member class. *

HARRISON HOPKINS, ESTHER ARVILLA
Lawyer, scientist. **Personal:** Born Sep 18, 1926, Stamford, CT; married T Ewell Hopkins; children: Susan, Thomas Jr. **Educ:** Boston Univ, AB, 1947; Howard Univ, MS, chem, 1949; Yale Univ, MS, biophys chem, 1962, PhD, 1967; Suffolk Univ, JD, 1976. **Career:** Scientist, attorney (retired); Va State Col, fac, 1949-52; New England Inst Med Res, biophysicist, 1955-59; Am Cyanamid Corp, res chemist, 1959-61; Polaroid Corp, scientist, 1967-73, patent atty, 1973-78, sr proj adminr, 1979; Mass Dept Environ Protection, dep gen coun, 1989. **Orgs:** Bd govs, Asn Yale Alumni; chair, Yale Medal Comt; nat bd, YMCA USA; pres-elect, Gen Alumni Asn, Boston Univ; Finance Comt, Town Framingham, MA; corp mem, Cambridge Family, YMCA; hon mem, Boston Univ Women's Grad Club; bd dir & pres, Framingham Region, YMCA; Alpha Kappa Alpha Sorority; Soc Promoting Theol Educ; dean, Stamfort Chap Am Guild Organists; nat scholar, Nat Asn Col Women, 1963; distinguished alumni, Boston Univ Col Liberal Arts, 1975; Phi Beta Kappa; Sigma Xi; Sigma Pi Sigma; Beta Kappa Chi; Sci Res Soc Am. **Honors/Awds:** Training Grant, USPHS, 1962-66; First Parish Award, 1977; Women of Achievement, Mass Fedn Bus & Prof Women's Club, 1979; Woman of the Year, Framingham Bus & Prof Women's Club, 1979; Woman of the Year, Regional Family YMCA, Framingham, 1984. *

HARRISON-JONES, LOIS
School administrator. **Educ:** Va State Univ, BS; Temple Univ, MA; Va Tech Univ, CAGS, EdD. **Career:** Dallas Pub Schs, supt, 1991; Boston Pub Sch, supt, 1991; Howard Univ, Dept Educ Admin Policy, assoc clin prof, 2000-, chair, currently. **Orgs:** Pres, Nat Alliance Black Sch Educrs; dir, Lightspan Inc, 2003-. **Special Achievements:** First African American superintendent of Boston Schools, 1991. **Business Addr:** Associate Professor, Howard University, Department of Education Admistration & Policy, 2441 4th St NW, Acad Support A Rm 223, Washington, DC 20059, **Business Phone:** (202)806-7342.*

HARRISON-SULLIVAN, JEANETTE LAVERNE
Television journalist, executive. **Personal:** Born Dec 4, 1948, Kyoto, Japan; married James Michael Sullivan; children: Katherine, James Brady. **Educ:** Colo State Univ, BA, french, 1968; Univ Calif, Berkeley, masters jour, 1973. **Career:** KPIX-TV, San Francisco, CA, TV news agent, 1973-74; KTVU-TV, Oakland CA, ed, 1973-74; KQED-TV, San Francisco, CA, reporter, 1974-75; KGW-TV, Portland, OR, TV news reporter, 1975-78; WTCN-TV, Minneapolis, MN, TV news reporter, 1978-; KARE-TV, TV news reporter; Bechtel Parsons/Brickerhoff, media rels dir, 1988-92; FleetBoston, Corp Commun, vpres, 1992-98; PFPC Inc, Corp Commun, vpres & managing dir; Eaton Vance

Corp, vpres & mgr pub rels, currently. **Orgs:** Limited Thirty Black Prof Womens Orgn; Nat Hon Phi Sigma Iota, 1970-. **Special Achievements:** Community service at Veteran of foriegn wars, Waite Park, 1984; community service at Gannet Corporation, MN, 1984; wrote & produced 5 TV Series. **Business Addr:** Vice President, Manager of Public Relations, Eaton Vance Corporation, 255 State St, Boston, MA 02109-2617.

HARROLD, AUSTIN LEROY
Government official, clergy, bishop. **Personal:** Born Jan 28, 1942, Omaha; son of Walter W and Madeline Brown; married Gussie; children: Sabrina Butler, Austin Harrold, Jr, Sophia Harrold. **Educ:** Lane Col, TN, BA, sociol, 1964; Interden Theol Ctr & Phillips Sch Theol, Atlanta, MDiv, 1968. **Career:** Mayor Jersey City, exec secy, 1981-85; Interdenominational Christian Community Church, pastor & founder, 1985; US Dept Com, Bur Census, community awareness specialist, 1986-88; Jersey City, Water Dept, dir, 1989-; Barr's Chapel CME Church, ,Paris, TN, first appointment; St Mary CME Church, pastor; W Mitchell CME Church, Atlanta, asst pastor; Lane Chapel CME Church, pastor; Turner Chapel CME Church, Mt Clemens, pastor; Calvary CME Church, Jersey City, pastor; Phillips Memorial CME Church, pastor; Russell CME Church, pastor; Mt Clemens High Sch, teacher; Detroit Dist CME Church Leadership Training Sch, dean; Jersey City's King Solomon Lodge, bishop, currently. **Orgs:** Secy, Mich Nat Black Conv, 1972; bd mem, Oper PUSH, 1975-; exec dir, Concerned Clergy Jersey City, 1980-; Dem Nomination Kansas House Reps 45th Dist; vpres, Jersey City Br Nat Asn Advan Colored People; secy, Interdenominational Ministerial All Jersey City Br Nat Asn Advan Colored People; secy, Interdenominational Ministerial All Jersey City & Vicinity; chaplin, Topeka Jaycees; co-chmn, Employ Task Force Coord Comn Black Comt; secy, Interdenominational Ministerial Alliance Topeka Vicinity; cent mgr, NE Macomb Act Ctr; bd dirs, Macomb County Child Guid Clinic; Mt Clemens Ministerial Asn; pres, Macomb County Chap Nat Asn Advan Colored People; pres, Christ Clemens Elem Sch PTA; WM Excelsior Lodge; vpres, Macomb County Community Human Rels Asn; bd pension, Mich-Ill Annual Conf, Third Epopal Dist CME Church; Mich Dept Educ Voc Rehab Serv; coun mem, Mt Clemens Dist Off; chmn, Mt Clemens Chap, Youth Understanding; Mt Clemens City Comn; Macomb County Off Substance Abuse Adv Coun. **Honors/Awds:** Cert of Merit, Third Episcopals Dist, Christ Methodist Episcopal Church, 1960-62; Effective Christ Leadership, 1960-64; Outstanding Young Men of Am, Bd Educ, 1970, 1976; Dept Sociol Award, Dept Relig & Philos. **Special Achievements:** Selected to spend summer 1963 in Sierra Leone W Africa in Operation Crossroads Africa Project, 1963. **Business Addr:** Bishop, King Solomon Lodge, Jersey City, NJ 07304.*

HARROLD, LAWRENCE A
Manager. **Personal:** Born Apr 4, 1952, Belle Glade, FL; married Phyllis Lea; children: Lawrence Jr, Lamont & James. **Educ:** Hillsborough Community Col, AA, 1975; San Francisco State Univ, BA, 1977, MBA, 1979. **Career:** Pac Tel, mkt off supvr, 1980-81; Westvaco Corp, prod supvr. **Orgs:** Black MBA. **Military Serv:** USAF sgt 4 yrs. **Home Addr:** 1057 Monfredo Dr, Pittsburg, CA 94565, **Home Phone:** (925)432-1710. **Business Addr:** Production Supervisor, Westvaco Corp, 5650 Hollis, Emeryville, CA 94608, **Business Phone:** (510)655-6211.*

HARRY, JACKEE
Actor. **Personal:** Born Aug 14, 1956, Winston-Salem, NC; daughter of Warren Perry and Flossie Perry; married Elgin Charles Williams, Jan 1, 1996 (divorced 2003). **Educ:** Long Island Univ, Brooklyn Ctr, BA, educ. **Career:** Actress, currently; Brooklyn Tech High Sch, hist teacher; TV: "Another World", 1983-85; "227", 1985-89; "The Royal Family", 1991; "Sister, Sister", 1994-99; "To Tell the Truth", 2000; "One on One", 2005;"Everybody Hates Drew", 2006; "The Last Day of Summer", 2007; Broadway productions: A Broadway Musical, 1978; Eubie!; The Wiz; One More Time; For Colored Girls Who Have Considered Suicide When the Rainbow is Enuf, 2000; Lady Day at the Emerson Bar & Grill, 2001; The Boys from Syracuse, 2002; A Christmas Carol, 2004; Too Good To Let Go, 2005; Man Of Her Dreams, 2006; Damn Yankees, 2007, U Got Me Bent And Twisted, 2007, The Sunshine Boys, 2008; JD Lawrence's The Clean Up Woman, 2008; Hairspray, 2009; Films: The Women of Brewster Place, 1989; Ladybugs,1992; The Reluctant Agent, 1996; The Nick at Nite Holiday Special, 2003; You Got Served, 2004; One on One, 2005; All You've Got, 2006; The Man of Her Dreams, 2009; GED, 2009. **Honors/Awds:** Emmy Award, Nat Acad TV Arts & Scs, for outstanding performance by asupporting actress, 1987; Image Award for Outstanding Supporting Actress in a Comedy Series, 1999; Image Award for Outstanding Supporting Actressin a Comedy Series, 2000; Emmy Award, 2004. **Special Achievements:** Golden Globe Nominee for Best Performance by an Actress, Supporting Role Series, Mini Series Motion Picture Made for TV, 1989; First African American actress to win an Emmy award for Outstanding Supporting Actress in a Comedy Series, 2004. **Business Addr:** Actress, PO Box 69248, Los Angeles, CA 90069-0248.

HART, BRENDA G.
Educator. **Personal:** Born Jul 8, 1949, Williamstown, MA; daughter of Thomas A and Adalyne Monroe; divorced; children: Patrick & Katheryn. **Educ:** Boston Univ, BA, 1970; Univ Louisville, MEd, 1972. **Career:** Community Action Comm, manpower coord, 1973; Univ Louisville, Coop Educ Off, asst dir, 1973-77; Univ Louisville, Gen Eng, asst dir, 1977-81, dir, 1981-94, dir, Minority & Women in Engrg Progs, 1994-2001, dir, Student Affairs, 2001-. **Orgs:** Bd dir, Univ Louisville Athletic Bd, 2003-; mem, Univ Louisville Alumni Asn, 2003-. **Honors/Awds:** Received Outstanding Faculty Advisor Award, 1991; Bethune Service Award, Nat Coun Negro Women, 1996; Alumni Scholar for Service, Speed Sch Alumni Asn, 1996; Distinguished Service Award, Univ Louisville, 2001; Founders Award, WEPAN, 2006. **Special Achievements:** Articles published in ASEE journal, 2006. **Business Addr:** Director of Student Affairs, Professor of Engineering Fundamentals, University of Louisville, Rm 208 JB Speed Bldg, Louisville, KY 40292, **Business Phone:** (502)852-0440.

HART, CHRISTOPHER ALVIN
Government official, lawyer. **Personal:** Born Jun 18, 1947, Denver, CO; son of Judson D Hart (deceased) and Margaret Murlee Shaw; married LeeAnn Moore Hart; children: Adam Christopher, Brooke Corinne. **Educ:** Princeton Univ, BSE, 1969, MSE, aerospace eng, 1971; Harvard Law Sch, JD, 1973. **Career:** Peabody Rivlin & Lambert, assoc, 1973-76; Air Transp Assn, atty, 1976-77; US Dept Transp, dep asst gen coun, 1977-79; Dickstein, Shapiro & Morin, assoc, 1979-81; Hart & Chavers, managing partner, 1981-90; Nat Transp Safety Bd, mem, 1990-93; Nat Hwy Traffic Safety Admin, dep adminr, 1993-95; Fed Aviation Admin, asst adminr syst safety, 1995, deputy dir, currently. **Orgs:** Fed Wash Bar Asns, 1973-; Aircraft Owners & Pilots Asn, 1973-; Princeton Eng Adv & Resource Coun, 1975-90; Lawyer Pilots Bar Assn, 1975-; dir/pres, Beckman Place Condo Asn, 1979-83; Fed Communs Bar Asn, 1981-; dir, WPFW-FM, 1983-88. **Special Achievements:** Author: "Antitrust Aspects of Deepwater Ports," Transportation Law Journal 1979; "State Action Antitrust Immunity for Airport Operators," Transportation Law Journal 1981. **Home Addr:** 1612 Crittanden St NW, Washington, DC 20011. **Business Addr:** Deputy Director, Federal Aviation Administration, 800 Independence Ave SW Rm 1040A, Washington, DC 20591.*

HART, CLYDE JAMES, JR.
Association executive, administrator, vice president (organization). **Personal:** Born Nov 29, 1946, Jersey City, NJ; son of Clyde J Hart Sr and Audrey E. **Educ:** St Peters Col, BS, 1972; Catholic Univ, JD, 1975; George Washington Univ, MPP, 1986. **Career:** Hon Aubrey Robinson, law clerk, 1975-77; Akin, Gump, Haver & Feld, atty, 1977-80; Interstate Com Comn, atty, 1980-94; US Senate Com Comt, sr coun, 1994-98; US Maritime Admin, admin, 1998-01; Fed Motor Carrier Safety Admin, adminr, 2000-01; Am Bus Asn, vpres, 2001-. **Orgs:** DC Bar Assn, 1976-; WA Bar Assn, 1976-. **Honors/Awds:** St Peter's Coll, Outstanding Graduate, 1972; MA Maritime Academy, hon doctorate, 1999; ICC Achievement Award, 1990; CVA/BLSA Award, 2000; Annual Award, Cooperstown Conf, 2000. **Military Serv:** Air Force, Sgt, 1965-69; hon discharge. *

HART, EDWARD E.
Physician. **Personal:** Born May 8, 1927; married Joycelyn Reed; children: Edward, Janet, Reed, Cynthia, Jonathan. **Educ:** Univ Toledo, BS, 1946; Meharry Med Sch, MD, 1949; Am Col Surgeons, FACS Fel, 1960. **Career:** ophthalmologist (retired); pvt pract, ophthalmologist. **Orgs:** organizer, Ithaca's civil rights actions, 1960; chmn, Cornell Comn Against Segregation, Ithaca Freedom Walk Comt; partner , Family Reading Partnership. **Military Serv:** USAF, 1954-56. *

HART, DR. JACQUELINE D.
Educator. **Personal:** Born in Gainesville, FL; daughter of Edna M. **Educ:** Lane Col, Jackson, BS 1959; Ind Univ, Bloomington, 1965; Univ Fla,Gainesville, Med, 1970, EdS, 1972, PhD, 1985. **Career:** Alachua Pub Schs, instr, 1967-70; Santa Fe Col, instr, 1972-74; Univ Fla, Equal Opp Prog, dir, 1974-88; Univ Fla, Gainesville, Fla, asst v pres, 1988-99, Equal Opportunity Affirmative Action, vice provost, 1998-; Society as Docta Inc, 1988. **Orgs:** Am Asn Affirmative Action, Nominating Comt; Delta Pi Epsilon; Kappa DeltaPi; bd secy, League Women Voters; legis comt, Comm Status Women, 1983-83; former pres, life mem, Delta Sigma Theta Inc; Am Cancer Soc Bd, 1984-; United Way Alachua Cty, 1985-; Allocation Reviewer Comt; Inst Black Cult Adv Bd, 1988; bd mem, United Nat Asn, Fla Div, 1989. **Honors/Awds:** Leadership Achievement Award, Alpha Phi Alpha, 1981; Leadership Gainesville VIII-City of Gainesville, 1983; Administrative Leadership Award City of Gainesville, 1986; Distinguished Alumni Award, Nat Asn Equal Opportunity Higher Educ, 1989. **Home Addr:** 1911 NW 23rd St, Gainesville, FL 32601, **Home Phone:** (352)377-8210. **Business Addr:** Vice Provost, University of Florida, Equal Opportunity Affirmative Action, 125 Tigert Hall, PO Box 113050, Gainesville, FL 32611, **Business Phone:** (352)392-3008.

HART, MILDRED
Librarian. **Personal:** Born in Wadley, AL; daughter of Ella Mae Underwood Slaughter and Owen Slaughter; married Robert Lewis Hart, Aug 28; children: Monica Lynne. **Educ:** Cuyahoga Community Col; Notre Dame Col, S Euclid, OH; Ursline Col, OH. **Career:** Librarian (retired); E Cleveland Pub Libr, E Cleveland, Ohio, br mgr. **Orgs:** Bd YWCA, N Cent, E Cleveland, Ohio; Bd Coop Exten, Ohio State Univ; Bd Cuyahoga Community Col, Metro Alumni; 4-H Club adv, Coop Exten, Ohio State Univ; moderator Deacon bd, St Marks Presby Church; E Cleveland Kiwanis Club; Bd Berea C Home & Family Serv; Bd NE Ohio Neighborhood Health Serv Inc; Mt Paran Church God. **Honors/Awds:** Outstanding Serv, St Mark's Presby Church; Dedicated & Loyal Serv, E Cleveland Pub Libr.

HART, NOEL A.
Government official. **Personal:** Born Dec 14, 1927, Jamaica, NY; son of Noel A and Louise Mason; married Patricia Spence Cuffee (deceased); children: Noel Jr, Alison, Ira & Jonathan; married Lorraine Booker. **Educ:** NY Univ, BA, 1954; Mt St Mary's, MBA, 1992; Emergency Mgt Inst, Emmitsburg, MD, educ specialist, computs, admin. **Career:** Government official (retired); Exec Develop Prog Nat Fire Acad, Emmitsburg MD, training instr; Peoria Fire Dept, fire marshal, 1977; NY City Fire Dept, 1954-77; John Jay Col, team leader, lectr; Promotional & Career Training Prog, prof; FEMA US Fire Admin, fire prevention specialist; Emergency Mgt Inst, Emmitsburg, MD, educ specialist & group leader, 1987. **Orgs:** Past pres, Comus Sch Club; trustee Port Chester Pub Libr; bd dir, Port Chester Carver Ctr; Intl Asn Black Prof Fire Fighters, 1969-; ward envestryman St Peters Episcopal Church, Prince Peace Episcopal Church; Diocese Coun Episcopal Diocese Central PA; Nat Forum Black Pub Adminrs, 1988-; Chief Officers Resource Comt, 1986-. **Military Serv:** AUS, pfc, 1945-47. *

HART, PHYLLIS D
State government official. **Personal:** Born Aug 8, 1942, Detroit, MI; daughter of James Davidson and Louise Boykin Ransom; married Raymond (died 1987); children: Darlene Annette. **Career:** Ohio Dept Natural Resources, EEO contract compliance adminr, EEO regional prog adminr, currently. **Orgs:** Dem Nat Comm. **Home Addr:** 1091 Ellsworth Ave, Columbus, OH 43206. **Business Addr:** EEO Regional Program Administrator, Ohio Department of Natural Resources, 1050 Freeway Dr N 4th Fl, Columbus, OH 43229, **Business Phone:** (614)995-2293.

HART, RONALD O.
Government official, school administrator. **Personal:** Born Jun 9, 1942, Suffolk, VA; married Ethel D; children: Aprill Jenelle, Ryan O. **Educ:** NC A&T State Univ, BS, Biol 1964; Hampton Inst, MS, Biol 1968; Old Dominion Univ, Cert Admin, 1976. **Career:** John F Kennedy High Sch, 1964-76; Metrop Church Fed C Union, 1966-; Ruffner Jr HS, 1976-; Suffolk City Coun, vmayor, Cypress rep. **Orgs:** Omega Psi Phi Frat; adv, Stratford Terrace Civic League; Nat Educ Asns, Norfolk, Va, 1976-; Odd Fellows Lodge, 1978-; adv, Cypress Comn League, 1976-; Metrop Baptist Church. **Honors/Awds:** Outstanding Educator Elks Lodge Suffolk VA 1975; Man of the Year Omega Psi Phi Frat Suffolk 1979. **Business Addr:** Vice Mayor Cypress Rep, Suffolk City County, 129 Co St, Suffolk, VA 23434.*

HART, TONY
Counselor. **Personal:** Born Jul 27, 1954, Harlem, NY; married Judy Murphy; children: Tonya. **Educ:** State Univ NY, attended 1978, New Paltz, Master Humanistic Educ, 1987. **Career:** Highland Educ Occup Ctr Juvenile Offenders, Orange County Jail, Marist Col HEOP Prog, counr; Green Haven Correctional Facil, correction counr; Marist Col Humanities Dept, part-time col instr; Downstate Correctional Facil, Fishkill, NY, counr, 1989-. **Orgs:** NY State Coalition Criminal Justice; bd mem, Coalition Peoples Rights; Nat Rainbow Coalition; Newburgh Black Hist Comt. **Honors/Awds:** Spec Acad Award, State Univ NY, 1977; Outstanding Serv Award, PreRelease Ctr, Green Haven Correctional Facil, 1986; Martin Luther King Jr Award, Newburgh Mem Comt, 1987; Black Humanitarian Award, Newburgh Free Acad, 1987; Most Deserving Black Award, Newburgh Black Hist Comt, 1989. **Business Phone:** (845)831-6600.

HARTAWAY, THOMAS N
Administrator, clergy. **Personal:** Born Mar 28, 1943, Lonoke County; married Arnice Slocum; children: Katina, Carla, Keith, Thomas III & Britt. **Educ:** Henderson St Teachers Col AR; Inst Pol Gov Batesville Col, attended 1972; Harding Col, attended 1973. **Career:** Ch Christ, st dir christian educ; Carter Mondale Camp, st dep cam coord 1976; Hartaway Assoc Adv & Pub Rel, pres, 1974-76; OKY Radio, gen sales mgr 1972-74; Ch Christ, minister 1968-71; The AR Carrier Newspaper, pub,l 1975-76; The Black Cnsmr Dir, publ, 1976-77; Dixie Ch Christ, pastor, evangelist, currently. **Orgs:** Bd mem, No Little Rock Dwntwn Dev Com; adv bd mem, NLR Comm Dev Agy; bd mem, Cent AR Christian Col; bd mem, consult HOPE Inc No Little Rock AR. **Honors/Awds:** Outstanding Young Men of America Award, 1976; Best Service Award, Pulaski Co Shrf Dept; Outstanding Leadership Award, Conf CME Chs. **Business Addr:** Pastor, Dixie Church Of Christ, 210 Tanglewood St, Fordyce, AR 72114, **Business Phone:** (501)945-9748.

HARTH, RAYMOND EARL
Lawyer. **Personal:** Born Feb 4, 1929, Chicago, IL; son of Daniel W and Helen M; married Fran Byrd; children: Cheryl, Raymond

Jr & Douglass. **Educ:** Univ Chicago Law Sch, JD, 1952. **Career:** Pvt Pract, Atty, currently. **Orgs:** Pres, Ill Conf Br, Nat Asn Advan Colored People, 1962-65; chmn, 1960-62, 1966-69, Handled No Civil Rghts Cases, State & Fed Cts, 1960-72. **Military Serv:** ANG, 1st lt, 1948-64. **Business Addr:** Attorney, 7926 Chapple Ave, Chicago, IL 60616.

HART-HOLIFIELD, EMILY B.
Educator, teacher. **Personal:** Born Oct 29, 1940, St Joseph, LA; divorced; children: Tammylynn & Lynnella. **Educ:** Southern Univ, Baton Rouge, LA, BS, speech & hearing, 1966; Pepperdine Univ, MS, sch mgt & admin, 1974; Univ Calif, Los Angeles. **Career:** Compton Unified Sch Dist, teacher, 1969-80, consult, 1975-78, teacher &speech therapist, 1969-75, sr bd trustee mem, currently; NV Cos, speech therapist, 1968-69; Orleans Parish, New Orleans, teacher, 1978. **Orgs:** Los Angeles County, Trustee Asn, 1977; adv dir, Univ Southern Calif, Acad Educ Mgt, 1978-79; vpres, Compton Community Col, 1978; Calif Dem Party Affirmative Action, 1979-80; pres & bd trustees, Compton Community Col, 1980; dir, Calif State, Long Beach, Math Engineering & Sci Achievement Bd; accrediation, W Hills Col. **Honors/Awds:** Love & Devotion For C Award, Parent Adv Coun Compton, 1972; Woman of Year-Award, Nat Coun Negro Women, 1973; Outstanding Community Serv Award, Nat Asn Adv Colored People, 1975; Educr Dedicated to C, Compton Unified Sch Dist Parent Adv Coun, 1982; Hometown Heroines, 1988; Golden Apple Award, Compton Educ Asn, 1992. **Special Achievements:** First black woman elected tro trustee compton Comm Coll 1975; First black woman elected Los Angeles Co Trustee Assn 1977. **Business Addr:** Senior Board of Trustee Member, Compton Community College, 1111 E Artesia Blvd, Compton, CA 90221.*

HARTLEY, FRANK
Football player. **Personal:** Born Dec 15, 1967, Chicago, IL. **Educ:** Ill Univ. **Career:** Football player(retired); Cleveland Browns, tight end, 1994-95; Baltimore Ravens, 1996; San Diego Chargers, 1997-98.

HARTMAN, HERMENE DEMARIS
Writer, educator, publisher. **Personal:** Born Sep 24, 1948, Chicago, IL; daughter of Herman D and Mildred F Bowden; married David M Wallace (divorced). **Educ:** Roosevelt Univ, BFA, 1970, MPh 1974, MA 1974; Univ Ill, MBA, 1994. **Career:** WBBM-TV-CBS, prod & asst mgr comm affairs, 1973-84; Soul publ, columnist, 1978-; The Hartman Group, pres, 1978-80; City Col Chicago, assoc prof, 1980-83, dir develop & comm, 1983-88; vice chancellor External Affairs, 1988-89; Hartman Publ NDIGO, Chicago, IL, pres & chief exec officer, 1989-, editor-in-chief, currently; Truman Col, assoc prof behav sci; Alliance Bus Leaders & Entrepreneurs, pres. **Orgs:** Am Acad Poets, 1979; adv comm, Arts John F Kennedy Ctr, 1979; adv bd, UnivIll, Sch Art & Design, 1979; exhibit com Chicago Pub Library Cultural Ctr, 1979; exec com Nat adv coun, John F Kennedy Ctr, Wash, DC, 1980; bd dir, Boy Scouts Am; vpres, Chicago Asn Black Journalists; founder, The NDIGO Foundation, 1995. **Honors/Awds:** Hartman has received over 300 awards in her areas of expertise; Outstanding Community Service Award, Hydiah Proj Inc, 2000; Community Spirit Award, Black Women Lawyers Asn, 2000; Media Maker honoree, History Makers, 2001; Winnie Mandela Endurance with Dignity Award, 2001; Black Women's Expo Phenomenal Woman in Communications Award, 2001; Trailblazer in Chicago Journalism Award, Chicago Asn Black Journalists; Ebony Magazine/ Colgate Palmolive Outstanding Mother Award; Crain's Chicago Business Magazine Top 100 Business Leaders list; America's Top Business/Professional Women, Dollars & Sense Mag. **Business Addr:** Publisher, Chief Executive Officer, NDIGO Foundation Hartman Publishing Group, 19 North Sangamon St, Chicago, IL 60607, **Business Phone:** (312)822-0202.

HART-NIBBRIG, HAROLD C
Lawyer. **Personal:** Born Aug 16, 1938, Los Angeles, CA; married Deanna T McKenzie; children: Nand, Jaunice & Lauren. **Educ:** Polit Sci, BA, 1961, JD, 1971. **Career:** Law Off Harold C Hart-Nibbrig, atty, currently. **Orgs:** Vpres, La Black Cong, 1968; Western Ctr Law & Poverty, 1968-71; Martin Luther King fel, Woodrow Wilson Fel Found, 1968; Community Educ Develop & Referral Serv, 1969-; Black Law Ctr Inc, 1971-73; bd dirs, Am Civil Liberties Union, 1973-79; chmn bd, Viewer Spon TV Found KVST-TV, 1973-74; La Co Bar Asn; John M Langston Law Club. **Honors/Awds:** Order of Golden Bruin, Unic Calif, Los Angeles, 1960; Service Award, Calif Jobs Agents Asn, 1974; West Law & Justice Award, Southern Christian Leadership Conf, 1979; Image Award, Nat Asn Advan Colored People, 1980. **Military Serv:** AUS, pfc, 1961-64. **Business Addr:** Attorney, Law Office of Harold C Hart-Nibbrig, 11777 San Vicente Blvd Suite 670, Los Angeles, CA 90049, **Business Phone:** (310)820-7900.

HARTSFIELD, ARNETT L., JR.
Lawyer, educator, firefighter. **Personal:** Born Jun 14, 1918, Bellingham, WA; married Kathleen Bush; children: Maria, Paula Johnson, Charlean Fields, Arnett & Barbara. **Educ:** Univ Southern Calif, BA, econ, 1951; Univ SC, LLB, 1955. **Career:** Lawyer, Educator, Firefighter (retired); City Los Angeles, fireman, 1940-61; pvt pract, 1955-64; Calif Fair Employ, assoc coun, 1964-65; Los Angeles Neighborhood Legal Serv, exec dir, 1965-67; Comt Mediation Ctr, chief mediator, 1967-69; United Way, asst dir, 1970-71; Calif State Univ, Long Beach, asst prof, 1972-74, assoc prof, 1974. **Orgs:** Bd trustees, S Bay Univ Col Law; pres, Los Angeles City Civil Serv Comn, 1973-76, vpres, 1974-75. **Honors/Awds:** Man of Year, Comn Rels Conf S Calif, 1962; Lifetime Achievement Award; Eme Award, 2001; Los Angeles City Fire Station No. 46, named in honor. **Special Achievements:** UCLA's first African American member of the ROTC. **Military Serv:** First Lt, 369th infantry, 1943-46; Bronze Star Medal. **Home Addr:** 8745 S Harvard Blvd, Los Angeles, CA 90047.

HARTSFIELD, JUDY
Judge. **Educ:** Univ Mich, grad; Univ San Diego, law degree. **Career:** Child & Family Serv Bur, judge; Wayne Co Probate Ct, judge, 2004-. **Business Addr:** Judge, Wayne County Probate Court, 2 Woodward Ave, Detroit, MI 48226, **Business Phone:** (313)224-5706.

HARTZOG, ERNEST E.
School administrator, chairperson, business owner. **Personal:** Born Jan 8, 1928, York, PA; married Jeanne Leatrice Shorty; children: Daniel & Sharon. **Educ:** San Diego State Univ, BA, 1955, MA, 1962; New York Univ, MA, 1964; US Int Univ, PhD, 1969. **Career:** San Diego Pub Sch, teacher, 1956-61, counr, 1961-63; San Diego Urban League, 1964-66; San Diego High Sch, vice prin, 1966-67; Lincoln High Sch San Diego, prin, 1967-69; Detroit Pub Sch, 1969-70; Philadelphia Pub Sch, rockefeller int; San Diego Pub Sch, dir neighborhood youth corps; Govt Studies System Philadelphia, prog mgr, 1970-72; Portland Pub Sch, asst supt comm relations staff devel, 1972-92; NME Assoc LLC, partner, currently. **Orgs:** African Meth- odist Episcopal church; Nat Asn Advan Colored People; Martin Luther King Scholar Fund; chmn, Oregon St; Alliance Black Sch Educr;Oregon Sch Activists Asn; United Negro Col Fund; Am Asn Sch Administrators; pres, Nat Alliance Black Sch Educr, 1979-81; vpres, USTA Pac NW Sec, currently; bd dir & chmn, A-MAN Inc, currently. **Honors/Awds:** Bluey Key Nat Honor Society. **Military Serv:** AUYS, sargent, 1946-51. **Business Addr:** Partner, NME Associates LLC, 14130 N W Bordeaux Lane, Portland, OR 97201.

HARVARD, BEVERLY BAILEY
Police chief. **Personal:** Born Dec 22, 1950, Macon, GA; married Jimmy; children: Christa. **Educ:** Morris Brown Col, BA, 1972; GA State Univ, MS, 1980; Federal Bureau of Investigation (FBI) National Academy, graduate, 1983. **Career:** Atlanta Police Dept, police officer, 1972-79, dep chief police, 1982-94; police chief; Atlanta Dept Pub Safety, affirmative action spec, 1979-80, dir pub info, 1980-82; Atlanta Harts field Int Airport, asst security dir, currently. **Orgs:** Bd trustees, Mem Leadership Altanta; secy, Comn Accreditation Law Enforcement Agencies; Police Exec Res Forums; Gov's Task Force Police Stress, Nat Org Black Law Enforcement Exec; mem exec comt, Int Asn Chief Police; Delta Sigma Theta Sor Inc, 1979-; bd dirs, Ga State Univ Alumni Asn. **Honors/Awds:** Outstanding Atlantan, 1983; Alumni of the Year, Morris Brown Col, 1985; Woman of the Year, 1995; YWCA Woman of Year; SCLC Drum Major for Justice Award; Trumpet Award, 1998. **Special Achievements:** One of the 100 Most Influential Georgians. **Business Phone:** 800-897-1910.

HARVELL, VALERIA GOMEZ
Librarian. **Personal:** Born Jun 27, 1958, Richmond, VA. **Educ:** Va State Col, BS, 1978; Pittsburgh Theol Sem, MDiv, 1983; Univ Pittsburgh, MLS, 1983. **Career:** Burr Oaks Regional Libr Syst, chief librn, 1984-85; Newark Public Libr, br mgr, 1985-86; Penn State Univ, head librn, 1986, Africana Res Ctr, fac African Am Studies, currently. **Orgs:** Am Libr Asn; Am Theol Libr Asn; Penn Libr Asn; Black Librn Caucus; Black Librns Caucus. **Business Addr:** Faculty, The Pennsylvania State University, Africana Research Center, 217 Willard Bldg, University Park, PA 16802, **Business Phone:** (814)865-6482.

HARVEY, ANTONIO
Basketball player, basketball coach. **Personal:** Born Jul 6, 1970, Pascagoula, MS; married Kim; children: Aryanna & Kameron. **Educ:** Southern Ill Univ; Connors State Jr Univ; Univ Ga; Pfeiffer Univ. **Career:** Basketball player (retired), basketball coach, radio analyst; CBA: Atlanta Eagles, 1993; NBA: Los Angeles Lakers, 1993-95; NBA: Seattle Supersonics, 2001-02; NBA: Atlanta Hawks, 2002-03; Am Basketball Asn, Portland Reign, gen mgr & head coach; All-Stars Sports Acad, owner; Portland Trail Blazers, radio analyst, currently. **Orgs:** Founder L I Q U I D Sports Found. **Business Phone:** (503)234-9291.

HARVEY, DANA COLETTE
Marketing executive. **Personal:** Born Jan 6, 1971, Detroit, MI; daughter of Vernice Davis Anthony; married Kenneth E Harvey Jr, Aug 16, 1997; children: Kenneth E III. **Educ:** Mich State Univ, BS, 1993; Wayne State Univ, MBA, 1999. **Career:** Hermanoff & Assocs, acct exec, 1996-97; Southland Ctr Rouse Co, 1999-2003; MGM Grand Casino Detroit, mkt mgr; Mills Co, mkt dir, 2003-05; Hotel Assocs, vpres & new bus Mkt mgr, 2006-07; Henry Ford Health Syst, mkt specialist, 2007-. **Orgs:** NBMBAA; AKA Sorority Inc. **Business Addr:** Marketing Specialist, Henry Ford Health System, 2799 W Grand Blvd, Detroit, MI 48202.

HARVEY, ERROL ALLEN
Clergy. **Personal:** Born Aug 5, 1943, Grand Rapids, MI; son of Fred and Elizabeth. **Educ:** Aquinas Col, BA, 1965; Seabury Western Theol Sem, BD, 1969; NY Univ, MPA, 1977; Nat Theol Sem Commonwealth Univ, DDiv, 1991. **Career:** Trinity Cathedral, curate, 1968-70; St Mark's Church, rector, 1970-72; St Andrew's Church, rector, 1972-83; St Augustine's Church, rector, 1983-. **Orgs:** Convener, Episcopal Black Caucus Diocese New York; past pres, Lower East Side Needle Exchange; mem bd dir, Housing Works Inc, currently. **Honors/Awds:** Outstanding Service Award, Council Churches City New York, 1998; DeWitt Reformed Church Community Service Award; Leadership Award, Black Caucus Diocese of New York; James H Robinson Jr Award, Henry St Settlement Cadet Corps; Honorary Doctor of Divinity Degree, Nat Theol Seminary Commonwealth Univ. **Business Addr:** Rector, St Augustine Church, 333 Madison St, New York, NY 10002, **Business Phone:** (212)673-5300.

HARVEY, GERALD
Government official. **Personal:** Born Feb 21, 1950, Macon, GA; married Cotilda Qanterman; children: Marcia & Gerald. **Educ:** Tuskegee Inst, BS, polit sci, 1972; GA Col, MEd, behavior disorder, 1977. **Career:** GA Psycho-Educ Ctr, therapist, 1973-85; City Macon, councilman, 1979-87;City Macon Off Workforce Devel, youth coordr. **Orgs:** Co Chmn, Unionville Neighborhood Improvement Asn. **Home Addr:** 1255 S Clarotina Rd, Apopka, FL 32703-7062.

HARVEY, DR. HAROLD A.
Educator, physician. **Personal:** Born Oct 24, 1944; married Mary; children: 3. **Educ:** Univ W Indies, MB, BS, 1969; Residency, Internal Med, Lemuel Shattuck Hospital, 1972; Residency, Medical Oncology, Lemuel Shattuck Hospital, 1973; Fel, Medical Oncology, New England Medical Center, 1974. **Career:** Queen Elizabeth Hosp, intern; Lemuel Shattuck Hosp, resident; Tufts N Eng Med Ctr, Dept Med, fel med oncol, teaching fel; PA State Univ, assoc prof med; PA State Univ Milton S Hershey Med Ctr, assoc prof med, medoncologist, cancer res, 1974-, prof med, 2004-. **Orgs:** Am Fedn Clin Res; Am Soc Clin Oncol; Am Asn Cancer Res; Am Asn Cancer Educ; Am Cancer Soc; Prev & Res Adv Bd, Pa Cancer Control; Bd Sci Coun, Nat Cancer Inst; Am Bd Intern Med; clin oncol study sect, NIH. **Special Achievements:** Listed in the 'Best Doctor in America', 2007. **Business Addr:** Professor Medicine, Pennsysl vania State University, Milton S Hershey Med Ctr, 500 Univ Dr, Hershey, PA 17033-0850.

HARVEY, JACQUELINE V.
Educator. **Personal:** Born Jan 21, 1933, Gramercy, LA; daughter of Alexander B Pittman and Selena Robinson Pittman; married Herbert J; children: Cassondra Dominique, Gretchen Young, Herbert & Yolonda. **Educ:** Nat Voc Col, Vocational Counseling, 1953; So Univ New Orleans, Soc Mkt Cert, 1969; Xavier Univ, Spec Training, 1970; Loyola Univ, Adv Studies, 1978; Southern Univ New Orleans, New Orleans, LA; LA State Univ, Baton Rouge, LA, 1988; CPM candidate. **Career:** Educator (retired); LA Family Planning Prog, New Orleans, dir community serv, family health counr supvr comn active workers, 1974, scc supvr family health counr, 1970-74; Family Health Inc, team supvr aux health wroker, 1968-69; LA Family Planning Prog New Orleans, aux health worker, 1967-68; Ctr Health Training, state training mgr, 1982-2001; Louisiana Off Pub Health, Family Planning Prog, dir, community serv, 2001. **Orgs:** Consult, Volunteer Mgt, 1967-; consult, Outreach Family Planning, 1967-; pres, Easton Community Schs Adv Coun; Am Pub Health Asn, NAACP; pres, Minority Women Progress; adv bd mem, Orleans Parish, Community Sch Prog, 1970-; past chair, ad-hoc, ed comn, LA Pub Health Asn, 1984-91; Nat Family Planning & Reproductive Health Asn, 1989-; founding mem, past vpres, secy, treas, state dir, LA Initiative Teen Pregnancy Prevention; chair, LITPP Tri Regional Task Force, currently. **Honors/Awds:** Merit Award, Family Health Found, 1971; Community Involvement Plaque, Proj Enable, 1967; Community Service, LA Black Women Progress, 1976; Outstanding Achievement, Women Hist NO LA, 1976; Service Award, Noteworthy Commun Leaders LA, 1981; Merit Award, NO Human Rel, 1982; Out standing Service Award, Nat Asn Neighborhoods, 1987; Service Award, Super Parent Support Network, 1989-90; Community Service Award, North Neighborhood Devt, 1989-90; Outstanding Volunteer Service Award, State LA, 1999; Service Award, Orleans Parish Schs Parental Involvement. *

HARVEY, KENNETH RAY
Executive, football player. **Personal:** Born May 6, 1965, Austin, TX; married Janice; children: Anthony, Marcus & Nathaniel (deceased). **Educ:** Laney Col; Univ Calif, Berkeley. **Career:** Phoenix Cardinals, linebacker, 1988-93; Wash Redskins, 1994-98; Ikoya Productions, Ikoya, TV & film prod co, exec producer, currently; Com cast Sports; Central Union homeless shelter, staff; Leading Authorities Inc, speaker, currently. **Orgs:** Pres, Wash Redskins Alumni Asn; Cent Union homeless shelter. **Honors/ Awds:** Pro Bowler, 1994-97; One of the Washington Redskins 70 Greatest Players. **Special Achievements:** Wrote children books; spokesman for drug awareness programs. **Business Phone:** (202)783-0300.

HARVEY, LINDA JOY
Media executive. **Personal:** Born Jun 11, 1957, Detroit, MI; daughter of Charles Edward and Royetta Lavern Phillips;

divorced; children: Rodgerick Keith Philson & Autumn Joy Philson. **Career:** Booth Broadcasting Inc, promotions asst, 1989-91; Mich Con Gas CPN, boiler operator, 1975-; Fritz Broadcasting Inc, Mix 92.3 WMXD-FM, promotions dir, on-air staff mem, 1991-. **Orgs:** Life mem, NCP. **Business Phone:** (313)569-8000.

HARVEY, LOUIS-CHARLES

Educator, theologian. **Personal:** Born May 5, 1945, Memphis, TN; son of Willie Miles and Mary Jones; children: Marcus Louis, Melanee Charles. **Educ:** LeMoyne-Owen Col, BS, 1967; Colgate Rochester Divinity Sch, MDiv, 1971; Union Theol Sem, MPhil, 1977, PhD, 1978. **Career:** Colgate Rochester-Divinity Sch, prof, 1974-78; Payne Theol Sem, dean, 1978-79, pres, 1989-; United Theological Sem, prof, 1979-; Metrop Am Methodist Episcopal Church, sr minister, 1996-, presiding elder, 2001-. **Special Achievements:** Articles published Journal of Religious Thought 1983, 1987; Rsch grant Assn of Theological Schools 1984-85; pioneered study of Black Religion in Great Britain, 1985-86; biographer of William Crogman in Something More Than Human Cole, 1987. *

HARVEY, MAURICE REGINALD

Executive. **Personal:** Born Sep 26, 1957, Atlanta, GA; son of Cardia B and Charle E; married Kimberly Kay, Mar 15, 1987. **Educ:** Ga State Univ; DeKalb; Atlanta Area Tech. **Career:** Am Presedent Co, MIS dir; Mentis, system programmer; Thacker, data processing mgr; H J Russell & Co, comput programmer; Concept Technologies Corp, pres, currently. **Orgs:** Common Black Data Processor Asn. **Special Achievements:** Developed customs documentation system for international freight. **Business Phone:** (404)847-0999.

HARVEY, MICHAEL P

Chief executive officer. **Personal:** Married; children: Jason. **Career:** Phatco Beverage Co, chief exec officer; Russell Simmons Beverage Co, chief exec officer, currently. **Business Addr:** Chief Executive Officer, Russell Simmons Beverage Co, 2248 N State College Blvd, Foullerton, CA 92831, **Business Phone:** 800-251-1877.

HARVEY, NORMA BAKER

Educator, counselor, administrator. **Personal:** Born Nov 23, 1943, Martinsville, VA; daughter of Nannie Hobson Baker and John T Baker (both deceased); married Dr William R Harvey; children: Kelly R, Christopher, Leslie D. **Educ:** Va State Univ, BS, educ, 1965; Fisk Univ, MA, educ media, 1976. **Career:** Educator (retired); VA & AL, elem sch teacher, 1965-68; State MA Planning Off, admin asst, 1968-70; Tuskegee Inst, res asst, 1974-78; Hampton Univ, bus counr, 1982; Kelech Real Estate Corp, pres, 1981; Pepsi Bottling Co Houghton Inc, secy & treas; Hampton Univ, dir. **Orgs:** Bd mem, Peninsula Coun Arts, 1978-80; Planning & Res Comt United Way 1978-82; bd dirs, United Way, 1978-80; bd dirs, Am Heart Asn, 1981-83; panelist Va Community Arts, 1983-84; bd dirs, Va Symphony, 1983-86; trustee, United Way, 1985-87; bd trustees, Va Symphony, 1987-91; bd trustees, Peninsula Fine Arts Ctr, 1990-; bd trustees, Va Mus Nat Hist, 1990-91; bd trustees, Col William & Mary, 1991-95; bd trustees, Peninsula Chap Nat Conf Christians & Jews; charter mem, Harbor Bank, Newport News. **Honors/Awds:** Int Progs Tuskegee Behavioral Sci Res Tuskegee Inst, 1976; Va Peninsula Community Award, Minority Advocate Bus Award, 1991; Va Peninsula Chamber Com, Minority Bus Advocate Award, 1991; State Va, Minority Advocates Bus Award, 1992; Minority Bus Advocate Award, State Va, 1992; Va Coun Status of Women's Corp Achievement Award, 1993; Community Serv Award, Girls Inc Greater Peninsula; Nat Conf Christians & Jews, Humanitarian Award; Delta Sigma Theta Sorority, Inc; Gamma Iota Chap, Community Serv Award. *

HARVEY, PETER C

Lawyer. **Educ:** Morgan State Univ, BA, 1979; Columbia Univ Sch Law, human rights law rev, JD, 1982. **Career:** NJ State Law & Pub Safety Dept, gen law div, atty, 2003-06; Patterson Belknap Webb & Tyler LLP, partner, currently. **Orgs:** NAAG Corp Responsibility & Securities Working Group; Nat Asn Attys Gen; Nat Bar Asn; Am Bar Asn; Pi Sigma Alpha. **Honors/Awds:** Lawyer of the Year, NJ Law Journals, 2003. **Special Achievements:** First African American to serve as New Jersey Attorney General; Top 10 Black Lawyers Am, Black Enterprise Mag, 2004; 100 Most Influential Black Ams, Ebony Mag, 2005. **Business Phone:** (212)336-2000.

HARVEY, RAYMOND

Music director. **Personal:** Born Dec 9, 1950, New York, NY; son of Lee and Doris Walwin. **Educ:** Oberlin Conserv Music, Oberlin, OH, BMus & MMus, 1973; Yale Sch Music, New Haven, CT, MMA, 1978, DMA, 1984. **Career:** Northfield Mt Hermon Sch, choral dir, 1973-76; Des Moines Metro Opera, assoc conductor, 1976-80; Texas Opera Theater, music dir, 1979-80; Indianapolis Symphony, Exxon, arts endowment conductor, 1980-83; Marion (Indiana) Philharmonic, music dir, 1982-86; Buffalo Philharmonic, assoc conductor, 1983-86; Springfield Symphony Orchestra, music dir, 1986-94; Fresno Philharmonic, music dir, 1993-2000; Kalamazoo Symphony Orchestra, music dir, 1999-; El Paso Opera, music dir, 1995-97, artistic dir, 2007-09; Orchestral perfomances; Detroit Symphony; NY Philharmonic; Buffalo Philharmonic; Indianapolis Symphony; Houston Symphony; Louisville Orchestra; Minnesota Orchestra; Atlanta Symphony; San Diego Symphony; St Louis Symphony; Utah Symphony. **Special Achievements:** Has conducted opera in US, Canada and Italy; has been featured in Ebony & Symphony magazines and is profiled in the book, Black Conductors. **Business Addr:** Music Director, Kalamazoo Symphony Orchestra, 359 S Kalamazoo Mall Suite 100, Kalamazoo, MI 49007, **Business Phone:** (269)349-7759.*

HARVEY, RICHARD CLEMONT, JR.

Football player, business owner. **Personal:** Born Sep 11, 1966, Pascagoula, MS; married Regina; children: Richard Jr & Tiffany. **Educ:** Tulane Univ, BSc, comput info syst. **Career:** Football player (reitred), Business owner; New Eng Patriots, linebacker, 1990-91; Buffalo Bills, 1992-93; Denver Broncos, 1994; New Orleans Saints, 1995-97; Oakland Raiders, 1998-99; San Diego, 2000; businessman, Pleasanton, currently. **Orgs:** Player rep, NFL Players Asn.

HARVEY, RICHARD R

Executive. **Career:** Tuskegee Fed Savings & Loan Assn, Tuskegee, AL, managing officer. **Business Phone:** (205)727-2560.

HARVEY, SANDI

Sales manager. **Career:** Atlantic City Conv & Visitors Authority, dir wash, DC, sales, currently.

HARVEY, STEVE

Actor, entertainer, comedian. **Personal:** Born Jan 17, 1956, Welch, WV; married Mary; children: twin daughters (first wife) & son Wynton. **Educ:** Univ Va, attended. **Career:** Stand up comedian; TV Series: "Me & the Boys", ABC, 1994; "The Steve Harvey Show", WB Network, 1996-2002; "Steve Harvey's Big Time", WB, 2003-; "2005 BET Comedy Awards", host, 2005; "The 2nd Annual BET Comedy Awards", host, 2005; Films: The Fighting Temptations, 2003; Love Don't Cost a Thing, 2003; You Got Served, 2004; Johnson Family Vacation, 2004; Crown Royal Kings of Comedy Tour, host; Racing Stripes, 2005; Steve Harvey Foun, founder, currently; Writer: "HBO Comedy Half-Hour", 1995; "The Original Kings of Comedy", 2006; "Before They Were Kings", 2004; "Don't Trip He Ain't Through with Me Yet", 2006; Producer: "Big Time", 2003; "Pulled Over", 2004; "Mobile Home Disaster", 2005; "Don't Trip He Ain't Through with Me Yet", 2006. **Orgs:** Omega Psi Phi Fraternity Inc. **Honors/Awds:** Naacp Image Award, Outstanding Actor in a Comedy Series, 30th Annual, Outstanding Actor and Outstanding Comedy Series, 31st Annual, Outstanding Actor in a Comedy Series, 32nd Annual, Outstanding Actor in a Comedy Series, 33rd Annual, Entertainer of the Year, 2000; Keeper of the Dream Award, Martin Luher King Jr. **Business Addr:** Comedian, Premiere Radio Networks, 15260 Ventura Blvd, Sherman Oaks, CA 91403, **Business Phone:** (212)445-3900.

HARVEY, WARDELLE G., SR.

Clergy, business owner, activist. **Personal:** Born Jun 12, 1926, Booneville, IN; married Christine P Harvey; children: Marian Jeanette, Wardell, Monica Perirr, Dione. **Educ:** Tri-State Baptist Col, attended 1957; Evansville Col, attended 1958; Inter-Baptist Theol Sem, attended 1962, BTh, DD, 1963, DCL, 1970; Union Theol Sem, DD, 1992. **Career:** Paducah Pub Housing, comnr, 1966-67; City Paducah, city comnr, 1968-75, mayor pro-temn, 1970-72; Greater Harrison State Baptist Church, Paducah, pastor; Cosmopolitan Mortuary, founder & owner; WG Harvey Manor, owner; Greater Love Baptist Church, pastor, currently. **Orgs:** Mayors Adv Bd, 1964-66; vpres, KY Baptists Asn, 1964-66; pres, Baptist Ministers Alliance, Paducah Area, 1965-67; auditor, 1st Dist Asn, 1965; State Voca Ed Bd Chmn Comt Chest, 1965; chmn, RISE Comt, 1995; pres, founder, Non-Partisan League; Inter-Denominational Ministers Alliance, Nat Asn Advan Colored People, Christ Leadership Conf, KY Col, Duke Paducah; Nat Asn Advan Colored People; activist, Civil Rights, Non-Partisan League, Paducah. **Honors/Awds:** Nat Asn Advan Colored People Award, 1990; Outstanding Afro-Am Man, 1995; Civil Rights Hall of Fame, 2000; Civic Beautification Award; Optimist Club Blue Ribbon Award; Voca Indust Ed Award; Pol Know-How, Beta Omega Omega Chap, Alpha Kappa Alpha. **Special Achievements:** First black to hold public office in Western KY; Only black in America to attend a KKK meeting. First African American to be appointed to the Paducah City Commission. *

HARVEY, WILLIAM JAMES, III

Clergy. **Personal:** Born Jun 18, 1912, Oklahoma City, OK; son of Dr William J, Jr and L Mae Johnston; married Betty JenkinsJean Nelson, Dec 25, 1983; children: William J, IV, Janice Faith & Edward Jr. **Educ:** Fisk Univ, Nashville, TN, BA, 1935; Chicago Theol Sem, MDiv, 1938. **Career:** Clergy (retired); Philadelphia, pastor 1939-50; Pinn Mem Baptist Church, Philadelphia, PA, pastor, 1939-50; Va Union Univ, guest preacher, 1946-48; Cheyney St Teachers Col, guest preacher, 1949; Fisk Univ, guest preacher, 1949; Hampton Univ, guest preacher, 1950; Okla City, pastor, 1950-53; Calvary Baptist Church, Oklahoma City, OK, pastor, 1950-54; Church Hist Sch, Langston, OK, prof homiletics religion, 1951-53; PrairieView St Col, guest preacher, 1951-52; Okla St Univ, guest preacher, 1953; Macedonia Baptist Church, Pittsburgh, PA, pastor, 1954-66. **Orgs:** Auditor, Penn Baptist Conv, 1945-50; mem exec bd foreign mission bd, Nat Baptist Conv, 1949-50, exec sec, 1961; vpres, Philadelphia Baptist Ministers Conf, 1950; assoc ed, Mission Herald, 1950-54; Convening Conv Nat Coun Churches, 1951; pres, Oklahoma City Ministers Alliance, 1953; Nat Baptist Conv World Baptist Alliance, London, Eng, 1955; pre-invested, World Baptist Alliance, Rio de Janeiro, Brazil, 1959; vpres, Pittsburgh Baptist Ministers Conf, 1961; treas, Allegheny Union Baptist Asn, 1961-62; Ministers Conf, 1961; Alpha Phi Alpha; Sigma Pi Phi; bd dir, Nat Baptist Conv, USA Inc, 1961; bd dir, Bread World, 1986; bd dir, Africa News, 1987; bd dir, Philadelphia Urban League; life mem, Nat Asn Advan Colored People.

HARVEY, DR. WILLIAM R.

School administrator. **Personal:** Born Jan 29, 1941, Brewton, AL; son of Willie D C and Mamie Claudis; married Norma Baker, Aug 13, 1966; children: Kelly Renee, William Christopher & Leslie Denise. **Educ:** Talladega Col, BA, 1961; VA State Univ, MA, 1966; Harvard Univ, PhD, 1972. **Career:** Sec sch teacher, 1965-66; Southern Ala Economic Opportunity Agency, dep dir, 1966-68; Harvard Intensive Summer Studies Prog, 1969; Harvard Univ, asst to dean govt affairs, 1969-70; Fisk Univ, admin asst to pres, 1970-72; Tuskegee Inst, vpres student affairs,1972-74, vpres, admin servs, 1974-78; Hampton Univ, pres, 1978-; Pepsi Cola Bottling Co, Houghton, MI, owner, chmn, pres, 1986-. **Orgs:** Bd dirs, Newport News S&L, 1980; bd visitors, Univ VA, 1981; bd dirs, Nat Merit Scholarship Corp, 1981; bd dir, Signet Banking Corp, 1989-97; comt mem, Pres, Adv Bd, 1990-; comt mem, US Dept Comt Min Econ Develop Coun,1990-; bd, AM COUN EDUC, 1992; bd, Trigon Blue Cross Blue Shield, 1992; bd, Signet Bank Peninsula; bd dirs, Intl Guaranty Ins Co, 1990-; bd trustees,VIR Mus Fine Arts, 1992; bd trustees, VIR Hist SOC, 1992; AM COUN EDUC CMSGOV Rels; bd, Newport News Shipbuilding, Inc, 1996; bd dir, First Union Nat Bank, 1997; Trigon Blue Cross Blue Shield; Signet Bank. **Honors/Awds:** Harvard Univ, ADE Fellow, 1969; Woodrow Wilson FOUND, Martin L King Fellow, 1968-70, Woodrow Wilson Intern Fellowship, 1970-72; Honorary Degrees: Salisbury State Col, LHD, 1983; Medaille Col, PdD, 1987; Lemoyne-Owens Col, LHD, 1988; VIR Cultural Laureate Award, 1992; Phi Delta Kappa, Harvard Chapter Award, 1992. **Military Serv:** AUS, 1965-65; Army Nat Guard Reserve, 1965-. **Business Addr:** President, Hampton University, Office President, Admin Bldg Room 200, Hampton, VA 23668, **Business Phone:** (757)727-5231.*

HARVEY-SALAAM, DYANE MICHELLE

Teacher, choreographer, athletic coach. **Personal:** Born Nov 16, 1951, Schenectady, NY; daughter of Walter Franklin; married Abdel Rut, Jan 2, 1984; children: Khisekh Nekhekh-Naut. **Career:** Forces Nature Dance Theatre Co, founding mem, prin soloist, 1981-; New York Found for the Arts, artist in residence, 1982-97; Borough Manhattan Community Col, adjunct prof, 1988-97; Lehman Col, adjunct prof, 1989-97; City Ctr Educ Outreach, dance instr, 1993-97; Hofstra Univ, adjunct prof, 1996-97, guest artist, currently; Manhattan E Middle Sch, dance consult, 1997-98. **Orgs:** Actor's Equity, 1973; Screen Actor's Guild, 1977; Forces of Nature Dance Theatre, prinl soloist, founding mem, 1982-; Troupe New York, advisory bd, mem, choreographer, 1997-. **Honors/Awds:** Audience Develop Comn, Audelco, 1983; Nat Coun Arts Achievements, Monarch Merit Award, 1991; second Black Theatre Conference, IRA Aldridge Award,1995. **Special Achievements:** Choreographed "Herizon," 1987, 1996, 1997; "The Women of Plums," 1997; Oiga Mi Voz, 1997; "Ki-Ache Stories From the Belly," collaborated with Peggy Choy and Fred Ito, 1997; "Loves Fire," the Acting Co, evening of plays, 1998; dancer, Fred Benjamin, Eleo Pomare, Alvin Ailey, Ze'eva Cohen, Dianne McIntyre, Your Arms Too Short to Box With God, Timbuktu, TheWiz.; Performed and toured with numerous dance companies. **Home Phone:** (212)289-2057. **Business Addr:** Guest Artist, Hofstra University, 139 Calkins, Hempstead, NY 11549-1000, **Business Phone:** (516)463-5444.

HARVIN, ALVIN

Journalist. **Personal:** Born Feb 20, 1937, NYC; married Norma Ellis; children: A Jamieson, Khary, Demetria. **Educ:** City Col NY, BA, 1967. **Career:** NY Post, sports reporter; NY Times, sports reporter. **Orgs:** Baseball Writers Asn Am; past pres, alumini asn city col new york. *

HARVIN, REV. DURANT KEVIN, III

Clergy. **Personal:** Born Jul 5, 1966, Baltimore, MD; son of Durant Jr and Rev Cynthia S; married Lisa M Clark, Aug 4, 1990; children: Durant K Harvin IV, Dairia Kymber Harvin. **Educ:** Hampton Univ, BA, 1988; Colgate Rochester Divinity Sch, MDiv, 1991. **Career:** Hampton Univ, asst dean, 1987-88; Baber African Methodist Episcopal Church, stud minister, 1988-91; Colgate Rochester Divinity Sch, minority recruiter, 1988-91; Bethel African Methodist Episcopal Church, Baltimore, exec asst pastor, 1991-92; Richard Brown Church, sr pastor; Emmanuel Christian Community Church, pastor. **Orgs:** Vpres, Interdenominational Ministerial Alliance; Youngstown Cms Social Justice; African

Methodist Episcopal Ministerial Alliance, 1991-92; Forest Pk Sr Ctr; nat officer, Nat Asn Black Seminarians, 1989-91; Nat Asn Black Jour, 1987-88; Nat Bd mem, Collective Banking Group; charter mem, CBG's Baltimore Chap; Omega Psi Phi Fraternity; chief exec off, Kingdom Excellence Ministries. **Honors/Awds:** Distinguished Serv, Nat Asn Black Seminarians, 1990, 1991; Distinguished Serv, Colgate Rochester Divinity Sch, 1991. **Special Achievements:** Books: Journey From My Dungeon: Confessions of an African Child of Divorce, 1992; first African-American pastor of the Richard Brown Memorial United Methodist Church in Youngstown. *

HASAN, AQEEL KHATIB
Labor relations manager. **Personal:** Born Sep 10, 1955, Augusta, GA; married Venita Lejuene Merriweather; children: Aqeel. **Educ:** Augusta Area Tech Sch, dipl, 1978. **Career:** Augusta News Rev, columnist, 1978-79; WRDW Radio, broadcaster, 1978-80; Black Focus Mag, columnist, 1982; Employ Planning Consult Inc, pres, 1985. **Orgs:** Counr, Richmond Co Correction Inst, 1876-80; minister, Am Muslim Mission, 1977-80; Richmond Co Bd Educ, 1982-, pres, 1983-84; Richmond Co Bd Health, 1983-84. **Honors/Awds:** Citizen of the Year, Omega Psi Phi Fraternity, 1983; Citizen of the Year, Augusta News Rev, 1983; Outstanding Young Man America, Jaycees Nat, 1984. **Military Serv:** USMC, lance corp, 2 yrs.

HASKINS, CLEM SMITH
Basketball coach, basketball player. **Personal:** Born Jul 11, 1943, Campbellsville, KY; son of Lucy Smith Haskins and Columbus Haskins; married Yevette Penick, May 22, 1965; children: Clemette, Lori & Brent. **Educ:** Western Ky Univ, Bowling Green, KY, BS, 1967, MA, 1971. **Career:** Basketball player, basketball coach (retired); Chicago Bulls, Chicago, IL, prof athlete, 1967-70; Phoenix Suns, Phoenix, Ariz, prof athlete, 1970-73; Wash Bullets, Washington, DC, prof athlete, 1973-77; Western Kentucky Univ, Bowling Green, Ky, dir continuing educ ctr, 1977-78, asst basketball coach, 1978-80, head basketball coach, 1980-86; Univ Minn, Minneapolis, Minn, head basketball coach, 1986-99; Olympic Dream Team II, asst basketball coach, 1996; Goodwill Games, head basketball coach, 1998. **Orgs:** Nat Assoc Basketball Coaches, 1977-; player representative, NBA Players' Assoc, 1971-73; mem, Sherriff Boys & Girls Ranch, 1980-; Sigma Pi Phi, Omicron Boule, 1990. **Honors/Awds:** Kentucky High School Hall of Fame, 1988; First Team Col All-American, NCAA, 1967; NBC Rookie Coach of the Year, 1980-81 (WKY); Ohio Valley Conference Coach of the Year, 1980-81; Kentucky Hall of Fame, 1990; Sunbelt Conference Coach of the Year, 1985-86; Assistant Coach of 1996 US Olympic Gold Medal Team, 1996; Distinguished Alumni, Western Ky Univ, 1996; Hall of Fame, Western Ky Univ; Asniated Press Coach of the Year, 1997.

HASKINS, CLEMETTE
Basketball coach. **Personal:** Daughter of Clem Haskins. **Educ:** BS, broadcasting, 1987. **Career:** NCAA Final Four All-Tournament team, mem, 1986; Univ Dayton, asst women's basketball coach, women's basketball head coach; Hill topper Sports Satellite Network, commentator. **Honors/Awds:** Western's Female Athlete-of-the-Year, 1987; Inducted, Western's Athletics Hall of Fame. *

HASKINS, JAMES W., JR.
Public relations executive. **Personal:** Born Dec 1, 1932, Sandusky, OH; married Janie L Moore; children: Lisa, Scott, Karen, Laura, Ronald, Sondra, Iona. **Educ:** Bowling Green State Univ, BA, 1959; Univ Penn, MSEd, 1975, Doct Cand Educ Admin. **Career:** Ctr Providence Hosp Sch Nursing, bctrlgst-tech, 1960-63, sci instr, 1962; Controls Rdtn Inc, tech, 1961-63; US Atomic Enrgy Comn, chem, 1963-66; Chem & Engr & News, asst ed bur head, 1966-69; DuPont Invitation, res sci writer, 1969-71, ed, 1971-; IUPAC Bk Org Chem, ed; US Acad Sci Host, mcrmlclr chem, 1971. **Orgs:** Am Chem Soc; AAAS; Nat Asn Sci Writers Inc; Soc Tech Comn; Sigma Delta Chi; Int Asn Bus Comn; Black Educ Forum; Urban League; NAACP; Alpha Phi Alpha; Wynfld Residents Asn; Phi Delta Kappa. **Honors/Awds:** Sci Writer Yr, NY Voice, 1972; Legion Hon; Chap 4 Chap, 1973. **Military Serv:** USMC, sgt, 1954-57.

HASKINS, JOSEPH, JR.
Banker. **Personal:** Married; children: one son. **Educ:** Morgan State Univ, BA, econ; NY Univ, MBA; Johns Hopkins Univ, MD, liberal Arts; Wharton Sch, Univ PA, banking cert. **Career:** Chase Manhattan Bank, New York; Chemical Bank, New York, loan officer; Midlantic Nat Bank, New Jersey, loan officer; Coppin State Col, vpres, bus & finance; Prudential-Bache Securities, investment broker; Harbor Bank Md, chmn, pres & chief exec officer, 1987-. **Orgs:** Nat Banker's Asn; Am Banker's Asn; Pres Roundtable; bd mem, Md Banking Sch; Academy Finance; Better Bus Bureau; Greater Baltimore Comt; Villa Julie Col; Associated Black Charities; Md Industrial Devt Financing Authority; dir bd, CareFirst Blue Cross Blue Shield; Morgan State Univ Bus Sch; Security Title, Chairs E Baltimore Bio-Tech Urban Develop Proj & Associated Black Charities. **Honors/Awds:** SBA Financial Advocate of the Year, 1989; Black Outstanding Marylander, 1991. **Business Addr:** Chairman, Chief Executive Officer, Harbor Bank of Maryland, 25 W Fayette St, Baltimore, MD 21201, **Business Phone:** (410)528-1801.*

HASKINS, MICHAEL KEVIN
Public relations executive, consultant. **Personal:** Born Mar 30, 1950, Washington, DC; son of Thomas and Frances Datcher; married. **Educ:** Lincoln Univ, Oxford, Pa, BA, econs, 1972; LaSalle Univ, Philadelphia, Pa, MBA, finance, 1980. **Career:** Fidelity Bank, Philadelphia, Pa, asst mgr, 1972-76; First Pa Bank, Philadelphia, Pa, mkt specialist, 1976-77, asst vpres, 1983-89; Greater Philadelphia CDC, Philadelphia, Pa, sr proj mgr, 1977-80; Emerson Electric, Hatfield, Pa, mkt analyst, 1980-82; Cooper Labs, Lang Horn, Pa, product mgr, 1982-83; Crawley Haskins & Rodgers Pub Rels, Philadelphia, Pa, exec vpres & commun consult, 1989-. **Orgs:** Vpres & secy, Greater Philadelphia Venture Capital, 1983-; dir, Pa Minority Bus Develop Authority, 1988-91; pres, Richard Allen Mus Bd, 1989-91; bd dirs, Philadelphia Coun Community Advan. **Honors/Awds:** Mother Bethel AME Bicentennial Award, 1987; Group Leader, Urban League Philadelphia, 1988. **Business Addr:** Executive Vice President, Communications Consultant, Crawley, Haskins & Rodgers Public Relations, Penn Mutual Towers 510 Walnut St Suite 1300, Philadelphia, PA 19106-3601, **Business Phone:** (215)922-7184.

HASKINS, MORICE LEE, JR.
Financial manager. **Personal:** Born Jun 9, 1947, New Brunswick, NJ; son of Morice L Sr and Mary Toombs; married Jane Segal; children: Rachel. **Educ:** Colgate Univ, BA, 1969; Hofstra Univ Sch Law, JDL, 1978. **Career:** Financial manager (retired); Colony S Settlement House Brooklyn, Soc Studies Curric, coordr, 1969; State Univ NY, Oswego, assoc dean, dir full opportunity prog, 1969-71; NY State Educ Dept, assoc higher educ, 1971-75,Comn Educ Opporunity, exec secy, 1974-75; First Tenn Bank Corp, vpres & mgr estate admin, 1979. **Orgs:** Asn Equality & Excellence Educ, 1978-82; Nat Bar Asn, Memphis, 1979-; AmInst Banking, Memphis, 1979-; Tau Kappa Epsilon; Mediator Memphis City Ctr Dispute Prog, 1979-81; vice chmn, LaRose Sch Title I, 1979-81; Chicasaw Coun; Boy Scouts Am, 1981-84; bd dir, Memphis Black Arts Alliance,1982-86; loan comnr, Tenn Valley Ctr Minority Econ Develop, 1984-87; chmn, bd dir, Dixie Homes Boys Club, 1988-90; bd dir, Agri center Int, Shelby Co Agricenter Comn, 1994-; sec, bd trustees, Grace-St Luke's Episcopal Sch. **Business Addr:** Board of Director, Agricenter International, Shelby County Agricenter Commission, 7777 Walnut Grove Rd, Memphis, TN 38120, **Business Phone:** (901)757-7777.

HASKINS, WILLIAM J.
Consultant. **Personal:** Born Oct 16, 1930, Binghamton, NY; son of William L and Signora; married Bessie White; children: Billy, Terri & Wendell. **Educ:** Syracuse Univ, BA, 1952; Columbia Univ, MA, 1953; NY Univ, cert admin, 1954. **Career:** Boys Club Am, Milwaukee, 1957-60, Richmond, 1960-62; Nat Urban League, exec dir Eliz NJ, 1962-64, mid eastern reg 1964-66, deputy dir, 1966-69; Nat Urban League, assoc dir, 1967; Nat Alliance Bus, nat dir comn rel, 1969-72; Arthur D Little, sr staff consult 1972; Eastern Reg Nat Urban League, dir; Human Resources Social Serv Nat Urban League, nat dir; Urban League Whitney M Young Jr Training Exec Develop & Continuing Educ Ctr, dir, 1986; vpres, Nat Urban League Progs, 1989-94. **Orgs:** Nat Coun Urban League; exec mem, NAACP; Pres, Comn Mental Health; pubmem, Pres Strategy Coun Drug Abuse; bd mem, Nat Coun Black Alcoholism; Alpha Phi Alpha Frat; chmn, Human Environment Ctr Wash DC; 100 Black Men New Jersey. **Honors/Awds:** Many athletic awards, 1948-53; Athlete Year, 1951; Man of Year, 1970; Letterman of Distinction, Syracuse Univ, 1978; Pacesetters Award, Syracuse Univ Black Alumni, 1979; inducted into NY State Athletic Hall of Fame, 1982. *

HASKINS, YVONNE B.
Lawyer. **Personal:** Born Feb 23, 1938, Atlanta, GA; daughter of Joseph H Blakeney and Rozlyn Douthard Blakeney; married Harold J Haskins, Mar 15, 1969; children: Randall, Russell, Kristin. **Educ:** Spelman Col, Atlanta, GA, 1956; Temple Univ, Philadelphia, PA, BS, Summa Cum Laude, 1968; Temple Sch Law, Philadelphia, PA, JD, 1986. **Career:** Univ Pennsylvania, Philadelphia, PA, security specialist, 1972-74; PA Comn Crime & Delinquency, Philadelphia, PA, regional dir, 1974-77; PA Bd Probation & Parole, Philadelphia, PA, regional dir, 1977-86; Schnader, Harrison, Segal & Lewis, Philadelphia, PA, atty, 1986-89; Ballard, Spahr, Andres & Ingersoll, Philadelphia, PA, atty; Yvonne B Haskins Law Off, atty, currently. **Orgs:** Pres, Big Sisters Philadelphia, 1980-88; Pres, Prog Female Offenders, Inc, 1987-; bd mem, West Mt Airy Neighbors Inc, 1989-. **Honors/Awds:** Appreciation Award, Black Pre-Law Soc, Outstanding Service, Univ Penn, 1988-89. **Business Phone:** (215)242-3042.*

HASSELBACH, HARALD
Football player. **Personal:** Born Sep 22, 1967, Amsterdam, Netherlands; married Aundrea; children: Terran. **Educ:** Univ Wash. **Career:** Football player (retired); Calgary Stampeders, defensive end, 1990-94; Denver Broncos, 1994-2001; Green Bay Packers, 2001. **Honors/Awds:** CFL All Star, 1983.

HASSELL, LEROY ROUNTREE, SR.
Judge, lawyer. **Personal:** Born Aug 17, 1955, Norfolk, VA; son of Joseph R Sr and Ruth; married Linda Greene. **Educ:** Univ Va, BA, 1977; Harvard Law Sch, JD, 1980. **Career:** McGuire, Woods, Battle & Boothe, Richmond, VA, lawyer, 1980-89; Supreme Ct Va, Richmond, VA, justice, 1989-2003, chief justice, 2003-. **Orgs:** Dir, Legal Aid Cent VA, 1982-85; dir, Carpenter Ctr Performing Arts, 1984-86; chmn, Richmond Sch Bd, 1985-89; dir, Am Red Cross, 1985-89; adv bd, Massey Cancer Ctr, 1989-; ABA's Comt Continuing Appellate Educ, 1990-; vol, Richmond Pub Sch; bd vis, Regent Univ Sch Law; State Drug Treatment Ct Adv Comt. **Honors/Awds:** Black Achievers Award, YMCA, 1985, 1986; Outstanding Young Citizen Award, Richmond Jaycees, 1987; Outstanding Young Virginian Award, Va Jaycees, 1987; Liberty Bell Award, Am Bar Asn, 1990. **Special Achievements:** First African American chief justice of VA Supreme Court. **Business Addr:** Chief Justice, Supreme Court of Virginia, 100 N 9th St Fl 3, Richmond, VA 23219-1315, **Business Phone:** (804)786-6455.

HASSON, NICOLE DENISE
Association executive. **Personal:** Born Sep 18, 1963, Chicago, IL; daughter of Willie and Beverly Johnson. **Educ:** Western Ill Univ, BA, 1985; Roosevelt Univ, MPA, 1991. **Career:** Western Ill Affirmative Action Off, admin asst, 1985; Nat Opinion Res Co, asst supvr, 1986; Keck, Mahin & Cate, legal asst, 1986; Horwitz, Horwitz & Assoc, legal asst, off mgr, 1986-89; Alpha Kappa Alpha Sorority Inc, off opers asst dir, 1989-. **Orgs:** Pres, Nat Asn Advan Colored People, 1984-; secy, Alpha Kappa Alpha Inc, 1985-; spec events chmn, St Phillip Neri Woman's Bd, publicity chmn, 1988-; Alpha Kappa Alpha Educ Found, 1988-; Kiwanis Int, 1991-; prog chair, Top Ladies Distinct, TTA adv, beautification comt, 1991-; Friends of the Parks, 1991-. **Honors/Awds:** Miss Alpha Phi Alpha, Alpha Phi Alpha, 1983; Alice Motts Scholarship, Alpha Kappa Alpha Educational Foundation, 1990; Woman of Destiny Protege Award, Women of Destiny, 1990; Initiative Award, Friends of the Parks, 1992. **Home Phone:** (312)288-5380. **Business Addr:** Office Operations Assistant Director, Alpha Kappa Alpha Sorority Inc, 5656 S Stony Island Ave, Chicago, IL 60637, **Business Phone:** (312)684-1282.

HASTICK, ROY A
Entrepreneur. **Career:** Caribbean Am Chamber Com & Indust Inc, founder, pres & chief exec officer, currently. **Orgs:** Chase Manhattan Bank Community Develop Bd; Tropical Tv Network; NYC Mayor's Small Bus Adv Bd; Brooklyn Ctr Performing Arts Brooklyn Col; chair, Medgar Evers Col Caribbean Res Ctr Adv Bd; Brooklyn Navy Yard Econ Develop Corp; bd mem, Brooklyn Empowerment Zone. **Honors/Awds:** Nat Award, U.S. Dept Com; Minority Business Advocate of the Year Award; Immigrant of the Year Award, Brooklyn Borough Pres Hon Howard Golden, 1986; West Indian American Achievers Award; Ron Brown Leadership Award. **Business Addr:** President & Cheif Executive Officer, Founder, Caribbean American Chamber of Commerce & Industry Inc, 63 Flushing Ave Mezzanine A, Brooklyn Navy Yard Bldg Suite 5, Brooklyn, NY 11205, **Business Phone:** (718)834-4544.

HASTINGS, ALCEE LAMAR
Congressperson (u.s. federal government). **Personal:** Born Sep 5, 1936, Altamonte Springs, FL; son of Mildred L and Julius C; divorced; children: Alcee II. **Educ:** Fisk Univ, BA, 1958; Howard Univ; Fla A&M Univ, JD, 1963. **Career:** Allen & Hastings, Ft Lauderdale, FL, atty, 1963-66, pvt law pract, 1966-77; Broward County, FL, circuit ct judge, 1977-79; US Dist Ct, judge,1979-89; US House Representatives, Fla 23rd Dist, congressman & rep, 1992-98 & 2002-. **Orgs:** Broward County Bar Asn; Fla Bar Asn; Amn Bar Asn; Nat Bar Asn; Am Trial Lawyers Asn; Broward County Trial Lawyers Asn; Broward County Criminal Defense Atty Asn; Am Arbitration Asn; Broward County Classroom Teachers Asn; Broward County Coun Human Rels; State Fla Educ Comn; Task Force Crime; bd dirs, Urban League Broward County; bd dirs, Broward County Sickle Cell Anemia Found; Fla Voters League; House Rules Comt; House Permanent Select Comt Intelligence; Vchmn, Democratic Select Committee. **Honors/Awds:** Freedom Award, NAACP; Man of the Year, Kappa Alpha Psi, Orlando Chap;NAACP County Award, 1976; Humanitarian Award, Broward County Young Democrats, 1978; Citizen of the Year Award, Zeta Phi Beta, 1978; Sam Delevoe Human Rights Award, Community Rels Bd Broward County, 1978; Man of Year, Comn Italian Am Affairs, 1979-80; Judge Alcee Hastings Day, named in hon, proclaimed City Daytona Beach, Dec 14, 1980; Glades Festival of Afro Arts Award, Zeta Phi Beta, 1981. **Special Achievements:** First African-American to chair the Helsinki Commission. **Business Addr:** Representative, Congressman, US House of Representatives, Florida 23rd District, 2701 W Oakland Pk Blvd Suite 200, Fort Lauderdale, FL 33311, **Business Phone:** (954)733-2800.

HASTINGS, ANDRE ORLANDO
Football player. **Personal:** Born Nov 7, 1971, Macon, GA. **Educ:** Univ Ga. **Career:** Football player (retired),athlete canine trainer; Pittsburgh Steelers, wide receiver, 1993-96; New Orleans Saints, 1997-99; Tampa Bay Buccaneers, 2000; trainer kennel,phoenix. **Honors/Awds:** USA Today Offensive Player Of the Year Award, 1989.

HASTON, DR. RAYMOND CURTISS, JR.
Dentist. **Personal:** Born Jul 24, 1945, Lexington, VA; married Diane Rawls; children: Lisa, Crystal, April & Tasha. **Educ:** Bluefield State, BS, 1967; Howard Univ, DDS, 1977. **Career:** Ap-

pomattox Pub Sch Systs, teacher, 1967-68; Milton Sumners HS, teacher, 1969; DC Pub Sch Syst, teacher, 1969-73; Pvt Practice, dentist, currently. **Orgs:** Nat Dent Asn, 1987; Am Dent Asn, 1987, Gen Acad Dentistry, 1987; Alpha Phi Alpha Frat; NAACP. **Honors/Awds:** Scholars, Nat Sci Found, 1971-72. **Home Addr:** 6425 Battle Rock Dr, Clifton, VA 20124, **Home Phone:** (703)830-5897. **Business Addr:** Dentist, 14393 Hereford Rd, Woodbridge, VA 22193, **Business Phone:** (703)690-2050.

HASTY, JAMES EDWARD
Football player, football coach, talk show host. **Personal:** Born May 23, 1965, Seattle, WA. **Educ:** Wash State Univ, BS, commun. **Career:** Football player (retired), Football coach, Talk show host; New York Jets, defensive back, 1988-94; Kans City Chiefs, 1995-2000; Oakland Raiders, defensive Back, 2001; Bellevue High Sch, asst defensive coach, 2001-04; NFL, ESPN, analyst, 2006-. **Orgs:** Found, Jessica Guzman Scholarship Found; Omega Psi Phi Fraternity Inc. **Business Addr:** NFL Analyst, ESPN, ESPN Plz 935 Midle St, Bristol, CT 06010, **Business Phone:** (860)766-2000.

HASTY, KEITH A
President (Organization), executive. **Career:** Best Foam Fabricators Inc, Chicago, IL, pres & cheif exec officer, 1981-. **Orgs:** Nat Minority Bus Coun. **Business Addr:** President, Chief Executive Officer, Best Foam Fabricators Inc, 9633 S Cottage Grove Ave, Chicago, IL 60628.

HATCHER, BILLY. See HATCHER, WILLIAM AUGUSTUS.

HATCHER, JEFFREY FRENCH
Manager. **Personal:** Born in East Orange, NJ; son of John Cornelius and Cordella Garnes; divorced; children: Troy. **Educ:** Tenn State Univ, attended 1969; New Sch Social Res, attended 1978. **Career:** Spot Time Ltd, Nat TV State Reps, sales mgr, 1979-82; MCA TV, acct exec, 1982-84; Channel Syndication Corp, mkt dir, 1984-85; USA Network, regional mgr affil rels, 1985-. **Orgs:** Nat Acad TV Arts & Scis; Int Radio & TV Soc Inc; Nat Asn Minorities Cable, New York Chap. **Business Addr:** Regional Manager, USA Network, 1230 Ave Of The Americas, New York, NY 10020, **Business Phone:** (212)413-5679.

HATCHER, LIZZIE R
Lawyer. **Personal:** Born Feb 8, 1954, Houston, TX; daughter of Fred Randall and Azzie Wafer Parker; married Sherman Hatcher, Feb 8, 1973; children: Charmonda, Marcus & Madeira. **Educ:** Grambling State Univ, BA, 1975; Southern Univ, JD, 1982; La Tech Univ; Southwestern Univ. **Career:** Thomas M Burns Ltd, Las Vegas, NV, atty, law clerk, 1980-83; Lizzie R Hatcher, Las Vegas, NV, atty, 1983-; Capital Murder Case Defense Panel; Eighth Judicial Dist Ct, paternity referee; Nevada Comn Ethics; pvt pract, atty at law, currently. **Orgs:** Pres, Las Vegas Chap, NBA, 1985-87; Victory Missionary Baptist Church, 1986-; trustee, Victory Missionary Baptist Church, 1987-88; Nat Asn Advan Colored People, Las Vegas Br, 1988-; regional dir, Nat Bar Asn, 1990-; Nev State Bar CLE Comt; Nev State Ethics Comn; Am Immigration Lawyers Asn Nev Chapter. **Special Achievements:** Syst Discriminatory Treat African-Am Capital Cases, Criminal Justice Syst, Howard Univ Criminal Law Symposium, 1990. **Business Addr:** Attorney At Law, Private Practice, 302 E Carson Rd Suite 620, Las Vegas, NV 89101, **Business Phone:** (702)386-2988.

HATCHER, RICHARD GORDON
Politician, college teacher, educator. **Personal:** Born Jul 10, 1933, Michigan City, IN; son of Carlton and Catherine; married Ruthellyn Marie Rowles, Aug 8, 1976; children: Ragen Heather, Rachelle Catherine & Renee Camille. **Educ:** Ill Univ, BS, 1956; Valparaiso Univ, JD, 1959. **Career:** East Chicago, IN, pvt legal pract; Lake County, IN, dep prosecutor, 1960-63; Gary City Coun, councilman-at-large, 1963-66; Mayor Gary, 1967-87; R Gordon Hatcher & Assocs, founder, 1988-; Valparaiso Univ, law prof, 1989, sr res prof & spec asst to dean, currently; Ind Univ Northwest, adj prof african am studies. **Orgs:** Chmn, Human & Resources Develop, 1974; Dem Conf Mayors, 1977; chair, African Am Summit, 1989; Nat League Cities; pres, US Conf Mayors; Nat Conf Black Mayors; Nat Black Polit Conv; vice chair, Nat Dem Comn; Mikulski Comn; Nat Urban Coalition; nat chmn, bd dir, Oper PUSH; exec bd, Nat Asn Adv Colored People; Nat Dem Comn Deleg Selection; founder, Nat Black Caucus Locally Elected Officials; Nat Black Caucus; Ill State Dem Cent Comn; Asn Coun Arts; chair, TransAfrica Inc; Jesse Jackson Pres Campaign; pres, Nat Civil Rights Mus & Hall Fame; bd dirs, Marshall Univ Soc Yeager Scholars; fel Kennedy Sch Govt, Harvard Univ; Ind Bar Asn; Am Bar Asn; Gary Bar Asn. **Honors/Awds:** Urban Leadership Award, Ind Asn Cities & Towns, 1986; Nat League Cities President's Award, 1987; Nat Black Caucus Local Elected Officials Liberty Award, 1987; Outstanding Achievement Civil Rights 10 Annual Ovington Award; Life Member & Leadership Award, Nat Asn Adv Colored People; Man of the Year, Harlem Lawyers Asn; Distinguished Service Award, Capital Press Club; Distinguished Service Award, Jaycees; Employ Benefactors Award, Int Asn Personnel Employ Security; Serv Loyalty & Dedication Award, Black Stud Union, Prairie State Col; Outstanding Citation Year Award, United Viscounts, Ind; Inspired Leadership, Ind State Black Caucus. **Special Achievements:** Among 100 Most Influential Black Americans, Ebony Magazine, 1971; Among 200 most outstanding young leaders of US, Time Magazine, 1974; First Black Elected Mayor of a major American city. **Business Addr:** Senior Research Professor, Assistant to the Dean, Valparaiso University, 651 S Col Ave, Valparaiso, IN 46383.

HATCHER, ROBERT L
Automotive executive. **Career:** Chicago Truck Ctr Inc, pres, currently. **Orgs:** Chmn, Minority Bus Roundtable. **Business Phone:** (773)890-2416.

HATCHER, WILLIAM AUGUSTUS (BILLY HATCHER)
Baseball player, athletic coach. **Personal:** Born Oct 4, 1960, Williams, AZ; married Karen; children: Derek & Chelsea. **Educ:** Yavapai Community Col, Prescott, Az, attended. **Career:** Baseball player (retired), baseball coach; Chicago Cubs, outfielder, 1984-85; Houston Astros, outfielder, 1986-89; Pittsburgh Pirates, 1989; Cincinnati Reds, 1990-92; Boston Red Sox, 1992-94; Philadelphia Phillies,1994; Tex Rangers, 1995; Tampa Bay Devil Rays, first base coach, 1998-99, 2003-05, third base coach, 2000, bench coach, 2001-02; Cincinnati Reds, first base coach, 2006-. **Honors/Awds:** Babe Ruth Award, 1990. **Business Addr:** First Base Coach, Cincinnati Reds, 100 Main St, Cincinnati, OH 45202, **Business Phone:** (513)765-7000.

HATCHETT, ELBERT
Lawyer. **Personal:** Born Jan 24, 1936, Pontiac, MI; married Laurestine; children: 4. **Educ:** Central State Col OH; Univ MI; FL A&M Univ, LLD. **Career:** Hatchett Brown Watermont & Campbell, attny, 1969; Circle H Ranch Otter Lake MI, owner; Hatchett, DeWalt & Hatchett, sr & founding partner, attny, 1968-. **Honors/Awds:** Num awards from local & state orgs for serv to community & outstanding contribs to the pursuit of human rights; Distinguished Alumni Award, FL A&M Univ. **Business Addr:** Trial Attorney Sr Parnter, Hatchett DeWalt Hatchett Hall, 485 Orchard Lake Ave, Pontiac, MI 48341.

HATCHETT, GLENDA A.
Judge. **Personal:** Born Jan 1, 1951?, Atlanta, GA; children: Charles, Christopher. **Educ:** Mount Holyoke Col, BA, polit sci, 1973; Emory Univ Law Sch, 1977. **Career:** Delta Air Lines, legal & pub rels depts; Fulton County, Ga Juvenile Ct, chief presiding judge; Ct Appointed Special Advocates, nat speaker; Sony Pictures Entertainment Inc, Ct Rm TV Show. **Orgs:** Bd mem, Gap; bd mem, Serv Master; bd mem, Columbia & HCA; Nat Ct Appointed Special Advocates Asn, 2003; bd dir, Nat Football League Atlanta Falcons & Hosp Corp Am. **Honors/Awds:** Distinguished Alumna, Mount Holyoke Col; Outstanding Alumni of the Year, Emory Univ Law Sch; Honorary degree, Mount Holyoke Col; Emory Medal, Emory Law Sch; Outstanding Jurist of the Year, Nat Bar Asn; Pound Award, Outstanding Work in Criminal Justice, Nat Coun Crime & Delinquency; Outstanding Community Service Award, Spelman Col Bd Trustees; Thurgood Marshall Award, Nat Asn Advan Colored People; Prism Award, 2003; Woman of the Year, Nat Orgn 100 Black Men Am. **Special Achievements:** Book: Say What You Mean and Mean What You Say; Ga first African-Am chief presiding judge state ct. **Business Addr:** Author, Sony Pictures Entertainment Inc, Judge Hatchett Show, 10202 W Wash Blvd, Culver City, CA 90232, **Business Phone:** (310)244-4000.*

HATCHETT, JOSEPH WOODROW
Lawyer. **Personal:** Born Sep 17, 1932, Clearwater, FL; son of John Arthur and Lula; children: Cheryl Nadine Clark & Brenda Audrey Davis. **Educ:** Fla A&M Univ, BA, polit sci, 1954; Howard Univ Sch Law, LLB, 1959; Naval Justice Sch, cert, 1973; NY Univ, appellate judge course, 1977; Am Acad Jud Educ, appellate judge course, 1978; Harvard Law Sch, prog instr lawyers, 1980, 1990. **Career:** Nat Asn Advan Colored People Legal Defense Fund, coop atty, 1960-66; City Atty, Daytona Beach, spec asst, 1963-66; Mason Fla, gen coun, 1963-66; Daytona Beach Urban Renewal Dept, consult, 1963-66; Mid Dist Fla, asst US atty, 1966-68; Conscientious Objectors, Dept Justice, spec hearing officer, 1967-68; US Atty Middle Dist FL, first asst, 1968-71; Middle Dist Fla, US magistrate, 1971-75; Supreme Ct Fla, justice, 1975-79; US Ct Appeals Fifth Circuit, US circuit judge, 1979-81; US Ct Appeals 11th Circuit, US circuit judge, 1981-99, chief US circuit judge, 1996-99; Akerman Senterfitt & Eidson, Pa, shareholder, 1999-. **Orgs:** Bd dirs, Int Acad Trial Lawyers; Am Judicature Soc; Jacksonville Bar Asn; D W Perkins Bar Asn; adv comt, Appellate Rules; Nat Coun Fed Magistrates; Fla Bar Asn; Am Bar Asn; Nat Bar Asn; bd dir, Am Judicature Soc; Jacksonville Bar Asn; DW Perkins Bar Asn; Fla Chap, Nat Bar Asn; Phi Delta Phi Legal Frat; Phi Alpha Delta Legal Frat; Omega Psi Phi Frat; bd mem, SunTrust Bank; chair, Appellate Practice Group. **Honors/Awds:** Man of the Year Award, Fla Jax Club, 1974; Medallion for Human Relations, Bethune Cookman, 1975; An Accolate for Juristic Distinction Tampa Urban League, 1975; Most Outstanding Citizen, Broward County Nat Bar Asn, 1976; Bicentennial Award, Fla A&M Univ, 1976; Community Service Award, Edward Waters Col, 1976; hon doctor laws, Fla Memorial Col, 1976; Post Graduate Achievement Award, Howard Univ, 1977; High Risk Award, State Action Coun, 1977; President's Citation, Cook County Bar Asn, 1977; Hon LLD, Fla Memorial Col, 1978; Hon LLD, Stetson Law Sch, 1980; Gertrude E Rush Award, Nat Bar Asn, 1995; Hon LLD, Fla A&M Univ, 1996; Hon LLD, Howard Univ, 1998; Anti-Defamation League Jurisprudence Award, 2003; Hall of Fame, Nat Bar Asn, 2005; Spirit of Excellence Award, ABA Comn Racial & Ethnic Diversity Profession, 2007; numerous other awards. **Special Achievements:** First black person appointed to the highest court of a state since reconstruction; First black person elected to public office in a statewide election in the south; First black person to serve on a federal appellate court in the south; Several publications including: Pre-Trial Discovery in Criminal Cases, Fed Judicial Ctr Libr, 1974; Criminal Law Survey-1978, Univ Miami Law Rev; 1978 Devements in FL Law, 1979. **Military Serv:** AUS, first lt, 1954-56; USMCR, lt col, mil judge, 1973-81. **Home Addr:** 106 E College Ave, PO Box 1877, Tallahassee, FL 32301-7750, **Home Phone:** (850)224-9634. **Business Addr:** Share Holder, Akerman Senterfitt & Eidson PA, Highpoint Ctr 12th Fl, 106 E Col Ave, Tallahassee, FL 32301, **Business Phone:** (850)224-9634.

HATCHETT, PAUL ANDREW
Banker. **Personal:** Born May 27, 1925, Clearwater, FL; married Pearlie Young; children: Mrs Paulette Simms, Mrs Pamela Hunnicutt, Paul A II. **Educ:** Hampton Inst Hampton VA, BS, 1951; FL A&M Univ Tlhs, MEd. **Career:** Pinellas Co Sch Syst FL, teacher admin, 1951-71; Clearwater Federal Savings & Loan, personnel dir mkt, 1972-78, asst vpres; clearwater city, comnr, 1981-82. **Orgs:** Pres, Clrwtr Kwns Club E, 1974-; dir, Clrwtr Slvtn Army, 1973-76; chmn, Pinellas Co Housing Auth, 1974-; bd trustees, St Pittersburg Jr Col, 1978-; bd trustees, Med Ctr Hosp, 1978-. **Honors/Awds:** Service award, St Pittersburg Jr Col; Service award, Pinellas Co Housing Auth, 1979. **Military Serv:** AUS, 1st lt korean cnflct. *

HATCHETT, WILLIAM F.
Labor relations manager. **Personal:** Married Ora; children: Craig, Kimberley & Karen. **Educ:** Rutgers Univ, BS, 1950; MA, sch admin. **Career:** Labor relations manager (retired); Verona Pub Sch, staff; Eastern PaLeague, pro basketball; McCoy Job Corps Ctr Sparta WI, set up & oper recreation & phys ed prog; RCA Corp, mgr, 1966-68, employ admin & resources RCA Corp Staff, 1968-87; Performance Training Inc, vpres, 1987. **Orgs:** Consult & presentations Moods & Attitudes Black Man; Lions Club; dir, Little League Prog; bd dir, ARC; comnr, State NJ Pub Broadcasting Auth; adv coun, Econ Career Educ, St Bd Educ, Higher Educ; EDGES Group Inc; Stud Coun, Crown & Scroll, Cap & Skull; chmn, Nat Urban League, Whitney M Young Jr Training Ctr. **Honors/Awds:** Spl Achievement Award, Key Women Am Inc, York Manor, 1982; Whitney M Young Jr Spl Appreciation Award, Nat Urban League Inc, 1990; Hall of Fame, Rutgers Univ Football, 1991; Basketball Hall of Fame, 1994; Nat Football Found & Col Hall of Fame; Distinguished Am Award, Essex county New Jersey Chap, 1996; Hall of Fame, NJ Sports Writer Asn. **Military Serv:** AUS, first lt, 1951-53. **Home Addr:** PO Box 1208, Spotsylvania, VA 22553.

HATCHETTE, MATT
Football player, actor. **Personal:** Born May 1, 1974, Cleveland, OH. **Educ:** Langston Univ; Mercyhurst Col, attended. **Career:** Football player (retired), actor; Minn Vikings, wide receiver, 1997-2000; New York Jets, 2001; Oakland Raiders, 2002; Jacksonville Jaguars, 2003; Amsterdam Admirals, 2003; Film: Playas Ball, 2003; Doing Hard Time, 2004; The Take, 2007; Extra Ordinary Barry, 2008; TV : Doing Hard Time, 2004; How I Met Your Mother, 2008; Boston Legal, 2008; Millionaire Matchmaker, 2009. *

HATHAWAY, CYNTHIA GRAY
Judge. **Personal:** Born Jan 15, 1948, Detroit, MI; married Michael Hathaway. **Educ:** Wayne State Univ, BS; Univ Detroit, MS, criminal justice; Detroit Col Law, JD. **Career:** Wayne County Circuit Ct, Ct Common Pleas Detroit, Mich, ct clerk & gen clerk, 1971-74; Detroit Recorder's Ct, probation officer, judicial asst, 1974-83; Vandeever, Garzia PC, law clerk, 1984-85; Philip R Sever Title Co, title examr, 1985-87; Law Offices Cynthia Gray Hathaway, trial practitioner, 1987-94; Third Judicial Circuit Ct, judge, 1994-. **Orgs:** Michigan Bar Asn; Detroit Bar Asn; Am Bar Asn; Straker Bar Asn; Sports Lawyers Bar Asn; Black Judges MI Bar Asn; life mem, NAACP; Detroit Urban League; former bd mem, Women's Econ Club; bd mem, The Inner City Sub-Ctr; past dir, Reggie McKenzie Found; bd mem, Doorsteps; The Historic Little Rock Baptist Church. **Honors/Awds:** Women of the Year, Nat Black Women Polit Leadership Caucus. **Business Addr:** Judge, Wayne County Circuit Court, 3rd Judicial Circuit, Frank Murphy Hall of Justice, 1441 St Antoine Courtroom 801, Detroit, MI 48226, **Business Phone:** (313)224-2120.

HATTER, HENRY
Engineer. **Personal:** Born May 21, 1935, Livingston, AL; son of Frank and Isabella McIntyre; married Barbara King, Apr 22, 1956; children: Marcus A, Kelly Mays, Henry II & DeAngelo Deloney. **Educ:** Sgnw Valley Col, BS, 1966; E Univ, MS, Physics, 1972. **Career:** Engineer (retired); Chem engr, 1965-69; GM, prod supv, 1970-73, tech, 1971; Buick Mtr Div GMC, sr engr, 1973-96;

MSU, govt educ liasion, 1996; pres, Clio bd educ, 1999-2001; vpres, Hamilton Community Network, 2001. **Orgs:** Secy, Genesee County Republican Party, 1972-76; Clio Bcntnl Comn, 1975; alt deleg, Nat Conv GOP, 1976; Electoral Col, 1976; 7th dist chmn GOP, 1977, 1978; chmn, Old Nwsbys Black Mtr Div, 1976; Gns Co Bicentennial Comn; Flint Riv Beautif Workshop; MI Trvl Commn 1979; pres Old Nwsbys Genesee County, 1981; rep GM Area Wide C C; comnr, Mich Travel Comn, 1978-86; indust ber, Environ Licensing Bd, 1991-; trustee, Clio Bd Educ, 1990-; vpres, Issues & Resolution Comt, Mich Asn Sch Bd, 1995; adv bd Hurley Hosp N Pointe; pres, Genesee County Asn Sch Bds, 1994-96; fin chair, Genesee County Republican Party, 1996-98; Genesee County co-chair, 1998; bd, Clio, currently. **Honors/Awds:** Distinguished Alumnus Award, Sgnw Vly Col, 1978; Salvation Army Humanitarian Award. **Home Addr:** 1238 E Farrand Rd, Clio, MI 48420.

HATTER, TERRY J
Judge. **Personal:** Born Mar 11, 1933, Chicago, IL; married Trudy; children: Susan, Allison, Terry & Scott. **Educ:** Wesleyan Univ, BA, 1954; Univ Chicago Law Sch, JD, 1960. **Career:** Judge (retired); US Veterans Admin, adjudicator, 1960-61; Pvt Pract, 1961-62; Cook Co, asst pub defender, 1961-62; Northern Dist Calif, asst US atty, 1962-66; Eastern Dist Calif, spec asst US atty, 1965-66; Off Econ Opportunity, regional legal serv dir, 1967-70; Western Ctr Law & Poverty, exec dir; Loyola Univ, prof, 1973-75; Off Mayor, exec asst dir criminal justice planning, 1974-75; Calif Super Ct, judge, 1977-80; Fed Dist Ct, Cent Dist Calif, judge, 1980; US Dist Ct, Ctr Dist Calif, chief judge, 1998-2001, judge. **Orgs:** Chief coun, San Francisco Neighborhood Legal Assistance Found, 1966-67; chair & bd Counsilors, Univ S Calif Law Sch; trustee, Mt St Mary's Col; bd mem, Western Justice Ctr Found; bd overseers, Rand Ct Justice Inst. **Military Serv:** USAF, nco-in-charge, 1955-56.

HATTON, DR. BARBARA R.
Educator. **Personal:** Born Jun 4, 1941, LaGrange, GA; divorced; children: Kera. **Educ:** BS, 1962; MA, 1966; MEA 1970; PhD, 1976. **Career:** Nat Defense Educ Act, fel, 1965-66; Europ Parkinson's Dis Asn, fel, 1969-71; SC State Univ, pres, 1992; Tuskegee Inst, dean sch educ; Atlanta Univ, dean educ; Atlanta Pub Sch Syst, teacher; Howard Univ, counr; Federal City Col Wash, asst dir, admis asst, dean stud servs; Stanford Urban Rural Inst; Stanford Univ Sch Educ, prof educ; Ford Found Ed & Cult, dep dir; Knoxville Coll, pres, 1997-2005. **Orgs:** Co-dir, Iniative Improv Educ Governance, 1973; Community Yearbook, 1974-75; chair & bd trust, Ravenswood City Sch Dist; East Palo Alto; Alpha Kappa Alpha Sor; Psi Chi Hon Soc Psychol; Phi Delta Kappa Hon Soc Educ. **Honors/Awds:** Rose Award, Univ Southern Calif; Drum Major for Justice Award, SCLC; Award for Distinguished Post grad Achievement, Howard Univ. **Special Achievements:** First Black Member of Cherokee Country Club, 2002.

HAUGABOOK, TERRENCE RANDALL
Lawyer. **Personal:** Born May 16, 1960, Detroit, MI; son of LaVerne Haugabook; married Maria, Sep 18, 1999; children: Donovan Baker, Terrence Randall II & Tia Rachelle. **Educ:** Univ Mich, BS, 1982; Detroit Col Law, JD, 1991. **Career:** UAW-Ford Legal Svcs Plan, staff atty, 1991-94; Lewis, White & Clay, asn atty, 1994-95; Wayne County Prosecutor's Office, asst Prosecuting atty, 1995-2003; Univ D Mercy, Personal Injury Law, adj prof, 1998-; US Dept Justice, asst United States atty, 2003-. **Orgs:** Alpha Phi Alpha Fraternity Inc, 1979-; Phi Alpha Delta Legal Fraternity, 1990-; Am Bar Asn, 1991-; Mich Bar Asn, 1991-; Wolverine Bar Asn, 1991-; Life Directions Inc, adult mentor, 1993-; Detroit Bar Asn, 1994-. **Honors/Awds:** American Jurisprudence Book Award in Professional Responsibility, Lawyer's Coop Publ, 1991. **Business Addr:** Assistant US Attorney, 211 W Fort St Suite 2001, Detroit, MI 48226, **Business Phone:** (313)226-9157.

HAUGHTON, DR. ETHEL NORRIS
Educator. **Personal:** Born Mar 3, 1956, Petersburg, VA; daughter of Marie Perry Norris and Dr Granville M Norris; married Harold J Sr. **Educ:** East Carolina Univ, BM, 1977; Ohio State Univ, MA, 1978, PhD, 1994;Westminster Choir Col, attended 1986. **Career:** Ohio State Univ, Presidential fel, 1993-94; Ohio State Univ, One-Year Minority fel, 1977-78, grad teaching asst, 1987-88; Va State Univ, assoc prof music, currently. **Orgs:** Ctr Black Music Res; Soc Am Music, 2000; Col Music Soc; Sigma Alpha Iota; PhiKappa Phi. **Honors/Awds:** Finalist, Nat Achievement Scholar Prog Outstanding Negro Stud, 1973. **Business Addr:** Associate Professor of Music, Virginia State University, Department of Music Art & Design, Davis Hall, 1 Hayden Dr, PO Box 9007, Petersburg, VA 23806, **Business Phone:** (804)524-5311.

HAUGSTAD, MAY KATHERYN
Insurance executive, college teacher. **Personal:** Born Oct 18, 1937, Dallas, TX; married Paul; children: Monika Moss, Veronica Moss & Karsten. **Educ:** Southern Univ, BS, 1959; Yale Univ, MS, 1960; Cath Univ, PhD, 1971. **Career:** Howard Univ, res asst, 1961-63, instr, 1963-66; Fed City Col, asst prof, 1968-69; Univ NH, asst prof, 1969-75, dept chmn, 1972-73; Univ Oslo, researcher, 1977-86; Prudential Annuity Serv Ctr, regist rep, agent, 1987-. **Orgs:** Delta Sigma Theta Sor; Sigma Xi; life underwriting, trainer, coun fel, LUTCF. **Special Achievements:** Author, The Effect of Photosynthetic Enhancement on Photorespiration in Sinapis Alba, 1979; Determination of Spectral Responses of Photorespiration in Sinapis Alba by CO2; Burst Effect of O2 & CO2 Compensation Concentrations, Photosynthetica, 1980; author of several publications including: Effect of Abscisic Acid on CO2 Exchange in Lemna Gibba; Yield of Tomato & Maize in Response to Filiar & Root Appl of Triacontanol; Photoinhibition of Photosynthesis: Effect of Light & the Selective Excitation of the Photosystems on Recovery. *

HAVIS, JEFFREY OSCAR
Executive. **Personal:** Born Dec 7, 1966, Chicago, IL; son of James and Thelma; married Teterina, Jul 16, 1993; children: Alexia Jade. **Educ:** Univ Ill Champaign, BS, mkt, 1990. **Career:** Northern Telecom, mkt intern, 1985-89; Otis Elevator, new equipment mgr, 1990-94; Rainbow Elevator Corp, gen mgr, 1994-; Exec Polishing, ceo, 1994-. **Orgs:** Pres, Alpha Phi Alpha Fraternity Inc, 1987-; Minority Com Asn, 1988-90; Inroads Alumni Asn, 1990-; pres, African Am Elevator Prof, 1993-. **Honors/Awds:** Best & Brightest Business Professional, Dollar & Sense Mag, 1994. **Business Addr:** General Mgr, Rainbow Elevator Corp, 12620 Holiday Dr Unit C, Chicago, IL 60803-3235, **Business Phone:** (708)371-7700.

HAWES, BERNADINE TINNER
Computer executive. **Personal:** Born Feb 16, 1950, Washington, DC; daughter of Bernard T and Geneva Childs; married William Hawes, Jul 23, 1971. **Educ:** Lincoln Univ, Lincoln Univ, PA, Phi Beta Kappa, BA, 1972; Univ Pennsylvania, Philadelphia, PA, MA, 1980, ABD, 1980. **Career:** Lincoln Univ, Lincoln Univ, PA, res asst, 1971-72; Univ City Sci Ctr, Philadelphia, PA, dir information systs, 1986-88, dir res mgt, vpres & dir, 2002. **Orgs:** Chairperson, Black Alumni Soc, 1990-91; United Way SE Pennsylvania Fund Allocation, 1987-91; Women Tech, 1986; bd mem, Philadelphia Doll Mus, 1988-91; bd mem, Application Develop Ctr, 1987-91. *

HAWK, CHARLES N., JR.
Educator, school principal. **Personal:** Born Aug 10, 1931, Madison Hts, VA; married Amarylyiss Murphy; children: Charles Nathaniel III, Lloyd Spurgeon & Natalyn Nicole. **Educ:** Northwestern Univ Sch Ed, BS, 1953; Loyola Univ, MA, 1966. **Career:** Chicago Pub Schs, teacher, 1953-56; Hoke Smith High Sch Atlanta, prin, 1957; Perkerson Elem Sch, prin, currently. **Orgs:** Nat Atlanta & GA Elem Prins Asn; Nat Asn Sec Sch Prins, NEA, Atlanta & GA Asn Educ; Alpha Phi Alpha; Phi Delta Kappa, Mason; bd mgrs, YMCA; bd dirs, Ralph C Robinson Boys Club, BSA. **Honors/Awds:** Outstanding Leadership Award, Boy Scouts Atlanta Reg, 1969; Outstanding Leadership Award, YMCA, 1974; Outstanding Leadership Award, Alpha Phi Alpha, 1975. **Business Addr:** Principal, Perkerson Elementary School, 2895 Lakewood Ave SW, Atlanta, GA 30315-5809.*

HAWK, CHARLES NATHANIEL, III
Lawyer, school administrator. **Personal:** Born Oct 25, 1957, Atlanta, GA. **Educ:** Morehouse Col, BA, 1979; Georgetown Univ Law Ctr, JD, 1982. **Career:** Cooper & Weintraub PC, assoc, 1982-83; Morehouse Col, dir off alumni affairs; Hawk Law Firm, atty; Global Com Co, vpres, currently. **Orgs:** Sec Deacon Bd Friendship Baptist Church, 1978-; mem Coun Advan & Support Educ, 1983-; chmn, United Way Campaign Morehouse Col, 1983-; GA Bar Asn, 1983-; off coun, Law Firm Cooper & Assoc, 1983-; legal coun, Nat Black Alumni Hall Fame, 1983-; legal coun, Hank Aaron Found Inc, 1984-; legal coun, Coun Nat Alumni Assoc Inc, 1984-. **Honors/Awds:** Artistic Achievement, Georgetown Univ Church Ensemble, 1982; Service Award, United Negro Col Fund, 1985. **Special Achievements:** Writer & dir: "Black Gold", "Balls, Balloons, and Butterflies". **Business Addr:** Vice President of Legal Affairs, Global Commerce Co, 400 Colony Sq Suite 200, Atlanta, GA 30361, **Business Phone:** (404)870-9033.

HAWKINS, ANDRE
School administrator. **Personal:** Born Aug 1, 1953, Jacksonville, FL; son of Sylvester and Emma J; married Annette Campbell; children: Anika, Alicia & Antoinette. **Educ:** Univ Southern Calif, BA, Hist, 1975; Fla Atlantic Univ, MEd Admin & Super, EdS Admin & Super, 1985. **Career:** Fla Sch Boys, occup counr, 1975-76, classroom teacher, 1976-79; Indian River Community Col, acad counr, 1979, dir educ, 1979-82, dir instrnl serv, 1982-86, asst dean instr, 1986-89, assoc dean Voc Educ, 1989-98, dean voc Educ, 1998-. **Orgs:** Univ S Calif & Fla Atlantic Univ Alumni Asn, 1976-; New Hope Lodge 450, 1981-; Southern Regional Coun Black Am Affairs, 1981-; Fla Adult Educ Asn, 1981-; Fla Adult & Community Educ Asn, 1982-; Am Asn Adult & Continuing Educ FACC, 1982-; Ft Pierce Chamber Com St Luce Leadership, 1983-; pres, 1986, chmn, 1987 Fla Asn Com Cols, Indian River CC Chap; bd dirs, St Lucie Co Learn Read Literary Prog, 1985-87; Nat Coun Instrnl Adminrs, 1986-; bd dirs, Fla Asn Community Cols, 1987, St Lucie Co YMCA, 1987; bd dir, NY Mets Booster Club, 1987-; second vpres, Fla Asn Conn Cols, 1988, vpres, 1989; bd dir, Indian River Community Ment Health Asn Inc, 1989-; treas, Martin Luther King Jr Comorative Community, 1989-; pres elect, Fla Asn Community Cols, 1990, pres, 1991, immediate past pres 1992; SLW Centennial High Sch Adv Coun, 1997-; exe comt bd, Area Agency Aging Palm Beach/Treas Coast; Southern Asn Cols & Schs Accreditation Team; Treasure Coast CNL Collaborative Agencies. **Business Addr:** Dean, Indian River Community College, 3209 Virginia Ave, Fort Pierce, FL 34981.

HAWKINS, ARTRELL, JR.
Football player. **Personal:** Born Nov 24, 1976, Johnstown, PA. **Educ:** Cincinnati col. **Career:** Football player (retired); Cincinnati Bengals, defensive back, 1998-2003; Carolina Panthers, 2004; New England Patriots, corner back, 2005-06; Wash Redskins, 2005; New York Jets, 2008; online radio host, 2 Deep Zone.

HAWKINS, DR. BENNY F
Educator, dentist. **Personal:** Born Feb 27, 1931, Chattanooga, TN; son of Corinne and Bennie; married E Marie Harvey; children: Benny F Jr, Christopher Thomas & Rachel. **Educ:** Morehouse Col, BS, 1952; Meharry Med Col, DDS, 1958; Univ IA, MS, 1972, Cert Periodont, 1972. **Career:** USAF Dent Corps, lt col, 1958-78; Univ IA Col Dent, periodont Grad, dir, assoc prof periodont, 1978-93; Univ Iowa, interim assoc provost, 1993-94, spec adv minority affairs provost & vpres health Sci, 1995-97, Periodont Pre Doctoral Prog, dir, assoc prof periodont, assoc prof emer periodont, currently. **Orgs:** Vestry Trinity Episcopal Church Iowa City, 1980-83; bd dirs, Iowa City Rotary Club, 1982-84, 1991-93, 1998-2000; Human Rights Comn Iowa City, 1983-86; vpres, Univ Dist Dent Soc, 1984-85; pres, Iowa Soc Periodontology, 1985-86; Am Dent Asn; Am Acad Periodontology; Am Asn Dent Schs; Int Asn Dent Res; pres, Omicron Kappa Upsilon Hon Dent Fraternity, Iowa, 1988-89; chmn, Orgn Post-Doctoral Periodont Prog Dirs; pres, Midwest Soc Periodontology, 1992-93; Grant reviewer, Nat Inst Dent & Craniofacial Res. **Honors/Awds:** Omicron Kappa Upsilon Hon Dent Frat Iowa, 1980; Fel, Int Col Dentists, 1984; Distinguished Alumni of the Year Award, Nat Asn Equal Opportunity Higher Educ, 1986; Fel, Am Col Dentists. **Military Serv:** USAF Dental Corps, lt col, 1958-78, Air Force Commendation Medal, 1976. **Business Addr:** Associate Professor Emeritus, University of Iowa, Department of Periodontics, 450 Dent Sci S, Iowa City, IA 52242-1001, **Business Phone:** (319)335-7238.

HAWKINS, CALVIN D
Lawyer, clergy. **Personal:** Born Jun 14, 1945, Brooklyn, NY; son of Wallace and Azalien; married Lennie E James; children: Alia, Alex & Jason. **Educ:** Huntington Col, BA, 1967; Howard Univ, JD, 1970; Wesley Theol Sem, MDiv, 1974. **Career:** US Dept Justice, atty, 1971-74, comm rel specialist, 1971; Am Univ, assoc chaplain, 1971-72; Supreme Ct, IN, 1971; So Dist Ct, IN, 1971; DC Ct Appeals, 1973; Dist Ct DC, 1973; Unitd Ct Appeals DC, 1973; Supreme Ct, USA, 1974; First United Presby Church, Gary, interim pastor; Valparaiso Univ Sch Law, adj prof; Shropshire & Allen, Gary, IN, atty, 1974, currently. **Orgs:** Am Bar Asn; Ind State Bar Asn; Gary Bar Asns; DC Bar Unified; Thurgood Marshall Law Asn; Am Bar Asn; Coun Urban State Local Govt Law Sec; bd trustees, Huntington Col; Ind Republican Platform Comn; Ind Bd Law Examiners; Ind Bar Found; Bd Legal Servs Northwest Ind; Lake County Bar Asn; trustee, US Bankruptcy Ct, Northern Dist Ind. **Honors/Awds:** Social Theological Award, Martin Luther King Jr Hood Theol Sem, 1971; Jonathan M Daniels Fellow Award, 1974; Alumnus of Year Award, Huntington College, 1975; Fellow Award, Chicago Theol Sem, 1976. **Business Addr:** Attorney, Chawkins Law, 4858 Broadway, PO Box 64859, Gary, IN 46408, **Business Phone:** (219)887-2626.*

HAWKINS, COURTNEY TYRONE, JR.
Football player, football coach. **Personal:** Born Dec 12, 1969, Flint, MI. **Educ:** Mich State Univ. **Career:** Football player (retired), Football coach; Tampa Bay Buccaneers, wide receiver, 1992-96; Pittsburgh Steelers, 1997-2000; Beecher High Sch, head football coach & athletic dir, currently. **Business Phone:** (810)591-9260.*

HAWKINS, DR. DORISULA WOOTEN
Educator. **Personal:** Born Nov 15, 1941, Mt Pleasant, TX; daughter of Artesia Ellis Wooten and Wilbur Wooten; married Howard; children: Darrell & Derek. **Educ:** Jarvis Christian Col, BS, 1962; E Tex State Univ, attended 1965; Prairie View A&M Univ, MS, 1967; Tex A&M Univ, attended 1970; Univ Houston, EdD, 1975. **Career:** Jarvis Col, secy & asst pub rels dir, 1962-63; Roxton Sch Dist, instr bus, 1963-66; Prairie View A&M Univ, assoc prof, 1966-96, head gen bus dept, 1976-88; Jarvis christian Col, develop officer, 1996-97, prof bus admin, 1997. **Orgs:** Adv bd, Milady Publ Co; exec bd mem, TX Asn Black Personnel Higher Educ, 1978-83; bd mem, TX Bus Educ (TBEA) Asn, 1978-83; presm Alpha Kappa Alpha,1982-85; chmn, TX Bus Thcr Educ Coun, 1985-87; Nat Bus Educ Assoc; bd trustees, Jarvis Christian Col, 1986-88; pres, Nat Alumni Assoc, 1986-88, 2005. **Honors/Awds:** Dist Business Teacher of the Yr TBEA, 1981; Disting Alumnus Jarvis Coll, 1982; nominee, State Teacher of Yr TBEA, 1982; Disting Alumni Citation(NAFEO), 1986.

HAWKINS, EDWIN
Songwriter, composer, conductor (music). **Personal:** Born Aug 10, 1943, Oakland, CA; son of Dan Lee and Mamie. **Career:** Recording artist; worked with: Buddah Records, 1969-74; Polygram Records, 1975-81; Myrrh Records, 1982; Birthright

Records, 1983-85; Fixit Records, 1992-93; Harmony Records; 1997-98; World Class Records, 1999-2000; Albums: Let Us Go Into the House of the Lord, 1968; Oh Happy Day, 1969; He brew Boys, 1969; Ain't It Like Him, 1970; More Happy Days, 1971; Peace Is Blowin' In The Wind, 1972; Children Get Together, 1972; Wonderful, 1976; The Comforter, 1977; Imagine Heaven, 1982; Love Alive 2, 1993; Music & Arts Seminar Mass Choir, 1983; Angels Will Be Singing with the Music & Arts Seminar Mass Choir, 1984; Have Mercy with the Music & Arts Seminar Mass Choir, 1985; Give Us Peace with the Music & Arts Seminar Mass Choir, 1987; That Name with the Music & Arts Seminar Mass Choir, 1988; Face to Face, 1990; Love Is the Only Way, 1998; Edwin Hawkins Music & Arts Seminar, founder, 1992; Love Fellowship Mass Choir, 2002-. **Orgs:** Founder, pres, Music & Arts Seminar, 1982-. **Honors/Awds:** Grammy Awards, 1970, 1971, 1978 & 1993. **Business Addr:** Singer, Composer, c/o StreamRing Music Network, 80 Remington Blvd, Ronkonkoma, NY 11779, **Business Phone:** (631)588-6218.

HAWKINS, ERNESTINE L
Librarian, executive director. **Personal:** Born Oct 30, 1950, Cleveland, OH; daughter of John Taylor and Odessa; divorced; children: Amanda. **Educ:** Miami Univ, BA, 1974; Case Western Reserve Univ, MLS, 1977. **Career:** Cuyahoga Co Pub Libr, Garfield Libr, ref librn, 1977-87; Cuyahoga Co Pub Libr, Mayfield Regional Libr, ref specialist, 1987-88; E Cleveland Pub Libr, bd liasion, dep dir, 1988-. **Orgs:** Black Caucus ALA, 1978-; Am Librn Asn, 1978-; Pub Libr Asn, 1978-; Ohio Libr Coun, 1988-; bd mem, E Cleveland Neighborhood Ctr, 1988-2003; bd mem, Ohio Libr Coun, 2004-; comt chair, PLA Com-Suc Homeless; bd mem, Black Caucus ALA. **Special Achievements:** Co-author: Stop Talking, Start Doing: Attracting People of Color to the Library Profession. **Business Addr:** Deputy Director, East Cleveland Public Library, 14101 Euclid Ave, East Cleveland, OH 44112, **Business Phone:** (216)541-4128.

HAWKINS, DR. GENE
Educator. **Personal:** Born in Henderson, NC; son of Argenia Sr and Roxie Smith. **Educ:** Glassboro State, BS, 1955; Temple Univ, MA, 1969; Nova Univ, DEd, 1976. **Career:** Dept Ford Twp Pub Schs, math teacher, 1955-64, chmn math dept & coun, 1957-67; Gloucester County Col, dir financial aid, 1968-74; The Col Bd, financial aid serv, dir. **Orgs:** Publicity dir, Nat Asn Advan Colored People, 1963-66; consult, Financial Aid Inst, 1968-78; consult, ETS Upward Bound Col Bd, 1970-74; consult, HEW, 1970-76; NJ Asn Col & Univ Presidents, 1982; exec dir, Glou County Economic Develop, 1970-72; treas, Eastern Asn Financial Aid Admin, 1973-75. **Honors/Awds:** Distinguished Distinguished Alumni Award, Glassboro State, 1971; Black Student Unity Movement Award, Gloucester County Col, 1971; Ten Year Service Award, Col Bd, 1985; Distinguished Educator, NJFOF Dir Asn, 1979; Spec Recognition NY Bd Educ, 1982; Distinguished Service Award, NJ Student Financial Aid Admin, 1989. **Military Serv:** USMC, 1951-53. **Home Addr:** 2130 Bailey Ter, Philadelphia, PA 19145. *

HAWKINS, HERSEY R., JR.
Basketball player, basketball coach. **Personal:** Born Sep 29, 1966, Chicago, IL. **Educ:** Bradley Univ, Peoria, IL, 1988. **Career:** Basketball player (retired), basketball coach; Philadelphia 76ers, 1988-93; Charlotte Hornets, 1993-95, 2001; Seattle Supersonics, 1995-99; Chicago Bulls, 1999-2001; Estrella Foothills High Sch, asst coach, 2006-07. **Honors/Awds:** Bronze medal, Olympic Games, 1988; NBA All-Rookie First Team, 1989; NBA Sportsmanship Award, 1999. **Special Achievements:** NBA Draft, First round pick, No 6, 1988.

HAWKINS, DR. JAMES
School administrator, educational consultant. **Personal:** Born Jul 2, 1939, Sunflower, MS; married Vivian D; children: Lisa & Linda. **Educ:** Western Mich Univ, BS, 1963; Wayne State Univ, MA, 1967; Mich State Univ, PhD, 1972. **Career:** School Aministrator (retired), Educational Consultant: Pontiac Pub Sch, teacher, 1963-67, project dir, 1967-68, prin, 1968-72; Jackson Mich Pub Sch, asst supt, 1973-75, dept supt, 1975-78; Benton Harbor Area Sch, supt, 1978-84; Ypsilanti Pub Schs, supt, 1984-90; Evanston, IL, asst supt, 1990-91; Gary Community Schs, supt, 1991-97; Pontiac Sch System, interim supt, 1997-98; Siebert Brandford Shank & Co, LLC, exec educational liaison, 1999; Oakland Schs, educational consult, 1999; Bd Educ Ypsilanti, interim supt, 2005-06, supt, 2006-09. **Orgs:** Mayors Urban Entrp Com, 1983-84, N Cent Reg Lab, 1984-85; State Partnership Sch Relationship Task Force, 1984-85; Kappa Alpha Psi; Rotary Int; Nat Asn Advan Colored People; pres, Middle Cities Ed Asn, 1984-85; Gamma Rho Boule, 1986; bd dirs, United Way; Govs Comn Community Serv, IN, 1994. **Honors/Awds:** Benton Harbor Citizens Award, 1983; Man of Year, Negro Bus & Prof Womens Club, 1977; Volunteer of the Year, Urban League NW Ind, 1992; Outstanding Community Service Award, Urban League NW Ind, 1993-94; Outstanding K-12, Alumni Administrator of Year, Mich State Univ, 1994; Marcus Foster Outstanding Educator of the Year, Nat Alliance Black Sch Educr, 1994; Dr Martin Luther King Jr Humanitarian Award, Eastern Mich Univ; Marcus Foster Distinguished Educator of the Year Award, Nat Alliance Black Sch Educr; Col of Education Outstanding Alumni Award, Mich State Univ. **Special Achievements:** Authored several articles on educational topics. **Home Addr:** 2144 Collegewood St, Ypsilanti, MI 48197, **Home Phone:** (734)544-5918.

HAWKINS, JAMES C.
Manager. **Personal:** Born Mar 26, 1932, Apalachicola, FL; son of Prudence Hawkins and Harold Hawkins; married Gloria M Edmonds; children: Brian, Cynthia. **Educ:** Univ RI, BSME, 1959; Northeastern Univ, MSEM, 1971; Mass Inst Technol Sloane Sch, 1977. **Career:** Rayethon Co & MIT Labs, sr engr, 1966-68; Nat Radio Co, mgr engrs, 1968-70; consult, 1971-77; Polaroid Corp, mgr, 1973-77, sr mgr, 1978-95, div mgr, 1984, corp dir (retired), 1989-95. **Orgs:** Int & ext consult various organs; past grand knight K of C; mem Actors Guild, ASME; CCD instructor; org & coach basketball team, tennis player, tutor, inst Karate, 1985-; board of directors, Chamber of Commerce, Cambridge, MA, 1989-; East Cambridge Savings Bank; trustee, Mount Auburn Hospital, Cambridge, MA, 1987-; board of directors, YMCA. **Honors/Awds:** Scholarship LaSalle Acad; Cambridge Chamber of Commerce, chairman of the board, 1989-92. **Military Serv:** USAF 1951-55. *

HAWKINS, JOHN RUSSELL, III
Publicist. **Personal:** Born Sep 7, 1949, Washington, DC; son of John; married Michelle Mary Rector; children: John R IV, Mercedes Nicole. **Educ:** Howard Univ, BA, 1971; Am Univ, MPA, 1976; Am Univ Law Sch, JD, 1979; Univ London Law Fac Eng, independent study. **Career:** Fed Trade Comn & US EEOC, personnel mgt spec, 1972-75; Pentagon Counterintelligence Forces AUS, admin ofcr, 1975-77; Theoseus T Clayton Law Firm, law clerk, 1979-80; US EEOC Pub Affairs, asst dir Pub Affairs, 1981-85; AUS Pub Affairs, major, 1986-, dep chief staff mobility & reserve affairs, currently. **Orgs:** Phi Delta Phi Int Law Fraternity, 1978-; pres & chief coun, HRH Commercial Farms Inc NC, 1979-; cub scout leader, Pack 442, 1985-; treas, St John Baptist Home Sch Asn, 1986-; Kappa Alpha Psi. **Honors/Awds:** Sustained Superior Performance, Fed Govt, 1979-85; ed writer, Wash Informer & Wash Afro, 1985-86; Outstanding Young Men of America, 1986. **Military Serv:** AUS, major; Meritorious Service Medal, Army Commendation Medal, Army Achievement Medal. **Home Addr:** 2123 Apple Tree Lane, Silver Spring, MD 20905. **Business Addr:** Deputy Chief Of Staff For Mobility And Reserve Affairs, US Army, Pentagon, Washington, DC 20310.*

HAWKINS, JOHNNY L
Lawyer. **Career:** J L Hawkins & Assoc PC, owner, 1996-; True Substance Records, pres, currently. **Business Addr:** Owner, Attorney, J L Hawkins & Associates PC, 17515 W 9 Mile Rd Suite 740, Southfield, MI 48075-4413, **Business Phone:** (248)557-5551.

HAWKINS, LATROY
Baseball player. **Personal:** Born Dec 21, 1972, Gary, IN. **Career:** Minnesota Twins, pitcher, 1995-2003; Chicago Cubs, pitcher, 2004-05; San Francisco Giants, 2005; Baltimore Orioles, 2006; Colorado Rockies, 2007; New York Yankees, 2008; Houston Astros, 2008-09. **Business Addr:** Professional Baseball Player, Houston Astros, Minute Maid Pk, 501 Crawford St, Houston, TX 77002.*

HAWKINS, LA-VAN
Executive. **Personal:** Born Jan 1, 1960; married Wendy (divorced 2004). **Career:** Kentucky Fried Chicken, staff mktg, 1970-86; Checkers & Bojangles Restaurants, franchise operator, 1986-95; La-Van Hawkins Inner City Foods, chief exec officer, founder & owner, 1995-98; UrbanCity Foods, chmn, ceo, pres, 1998-; Lineage Group Inc, owner, 2002-. **Special Achievements:** Black Enterprise's List of Top 100 Industrial/Service Companies, ranked 93, 1994, 14, 1999, 12, 2000.

HAWKINS, DR. LAWRENCE C. See Obituaries section.

HAWKINS, MARY L
Counselor, educator. **Personal:** Born Jan 1, 331 ?, Columbus, GA; daughter of Bruno and Eva Powell Robinson. **Educ:** Meharry Med Col, Cert Dent Hygene, 1961; Western Mich Univ, BS, 1976, MA, 1979. **Career:** Benton Harbor Area Schs, Benton Harbor, Mich, counselor & educator; Link Crisis Intervention Ctr, St Joseph, Mich; drug prevention educr; Priv Prac, dent hygenist 1961-67; Brrn Co Health Dept, sr dent hygenist, 1967; Brass Found, Chicago, Ill, project co-ord, 1986-87; Mich Rehab, Kalamazoo Mich, substance abuse & voc rehabilitation coun, 1988. **Orgs:** Am Dent Hygenist Asn, 1961; Bus & Prof Women; Am Asn Univ Women; Nat Counr's Asn; Meharry Alumni Asn; Mnority Affairs Co, spec consult, 1973-75; Tri-Co Health Planners Commission, 1970-75; Nat Asn Advan Colored People, 1963; YWCA, 1965; Blossomland United Way, 1983-89; Operation PUSH, 1980; March Dms 1970; EAP; Mich Asn Alcoholism & Drug Abuse Counrs Inc; NAADAC. **Honors/Awds:** Outstanding Dental Hygienist, Meharry's Alumni, 1974; President's Award, Nat Dent Hygienists Asn, 1975. **Home Addr:** PO Box 320, St Joseph, MI 49085-0826. **Business Phone:** (312)874-1223.

HAWKINS, MICHAEL
Basketball player. **Personal:** Born Oct 28, 1972, Canton, OH. **Educ:** Xavier Univ. **Career:** Rockford Lightning, 1995-97, 1998-99; Boston Celtics, 1996-97; Olympiacos, 1997-98; Sacramento Kings, 1998-99; Charlotte Hornets, 1999-2000; Cleveland Cavaliers, 2000-01; FC Barcelona, 2001; Slask Wroclaw, 2001-02; Basketball Club Oostende, 2002-03; Al Jalaa Aleppo, Syrian basketball league, 2005-06. **Honors/Awds:** All-Defensive Team, All-League Second Team, CBA, 1996-97.

HAWKINS, DR. MURIEL A.
Educator. **Personal:** Born Apr 22, 1946, Norfolk, VA; daughter of George and Frieda Robinson Mitchell; children: Jamal Scott. **Educ:** Chicago Med Sch Health Sci, BS, 1975; Citadel, MEd, 1979; Loyola Univ Chicago, PhD, 1988. **Career:** Meharry Med Col, radiographer, 1967-69, Matthew Walker Health Ctr, radiol supvr/clin coordr, 1969-71; Cook County Hosp, Sch Radiol Technol, clin instr, 1971-76; Malcolm X Col, adj instr, 1974-76; Med Univ SC, Col Allied Health Scis, instr/clin instr, 1976-78, Dept Psychiat, res asst & instr, 1978-80; Chicago State Univ, Col Allied Health, coordr stud & community affairs, 1981-87, Col Nursing & Allied Health Prof, asst prof radiol sci, 1984-93, Joint Prog Col Allied Health & Arts & Sci, Health Careers Opportunity Prog, prog dir, 1987-90, dir acad support & develop serv, 1990-92, Col Nursing & Allied Health Prof, dir acad enrichment & outreach prog, 1992-93; Univ Wisc-Oshkosh, Ctr Acad Support & Diversity, Human Serv & Prof Leadership, assoc prof & asst vice chancellor, 1993-. **Orgs:** Kellogg fel, Am Soc Allied Health Prof, 1983-84; ICEOP fel, 1986-87; grants reviewer, Allied Health Spec Proj, Bur Health Prof, 1990, 1991; coordr, Univ Wisc Oshkosh Multicult & Disadvantaged Syst, 1993-; One Oshkosh: Diversity Network, 1993-; Cent Asn Col & Sch, 1994-; peerreviewer, Higher Learning Comn; mentor, Big Bros Big Sisters Fox Valley, 1995-; Diversity Coun, 2000-04; chair, Diversity Innovation Grants Comt, 2001; consult, Multicult Affairs, William Paterson Univ, 2002; bd dir, Tempo Int, 2003-; African Am Studies Comt, 2005-; founding bd mem, Asn Blacks Higher Educ, 2005-; vol mediator, Winnebago Conflict Resolution Ctr, 2006-. **Honors/Awds:** Recognition Award, Women Color UW Syst, 1998; Leadership Award, Div of Acad Support, UW Oshkosh; Appreciation Award, Black Student Union, UW Oshkosh. **Special Achievements:** Role Modeling as a Strategy for the Retention of Minorities in Health Professions, presentation at annual ICBC meeting 1983 & Midwest Allied Health Symposium 1984 subsequently published in Journal of Ethnic Concerns; "Deaning in the Allied Health Professions," presentation at the ASAHP Annual Meeting Pittsburgh, PA 1986; "Successful Coping Strategiesfor Black Graduate Students," Natl Conf AAHE Chicago, IL, 1987; "Profile of An Allied Health Dean," Jour Allied Health, 19:3, 1990; Programs to Promote Minority Student Retention, paper, Annual Black Student Retention Conf, Las Vegas, 1991; "Mentorship and the Retention of First-Year College Students," paper, National Soc of Allied Health Mgt, DC, 1992;"Innovative Programs to Promote Student Persistence," paper, "Convention on College Compostion of Communication," Cincinnati, 1992. **Home Addr:** 602 E Irving Ave, Oshkosh, WI 54901.

HAWKINS, PAULETTE
Executive. **Career:** Warner/Chappell Music Inc, sr dir, vpres licensing, 2007-. **Business Addr:** Vice President of Licensing, Warner/Chappell Music Inc, 10585 Santa Monica Blvd, Los Angeles, CA 90025-4950, **Business Phone:** (310)441-8600.

HAWKINS, ROBERT B.
Manager, salesperson. **Personal:** Born Mar 13, 1964, Marion, IN; son of David and Margaret; married Michele Hawkins, Apr 1, 1992; children: Lauren N, Kayla A. **Educ:** E Mich Univ, BS, indust distrib, 1988. **Career:** Kimberly-Clark, manufacturers rep, 1988-91; Princeton Pharmaceut, sales rep, 1991-93; Bristol-Myers Squibb, assoc territory mgr, 1993-94; Gannett Outdoor, nat acct mgr, 1994-97, transit mgr, currently. **Orgs:** Prof Develop Comt, Pharmaceut Rep's Detroit Excelling, 1991-94; Adcraft Club Detroit, 1994-. **Honors/Awds:** National Acctountant's Award, 1990; Eagle Award, Kimberly-Clark, 1991; Philip Morris, BOB Award, 1995-98; Advertising Salute, Air Force, 1999. **Business Addr:** Transit Manager, Gannett Outdoor, 88 Custer St, Detroit, MI 48202, **Business Phone:** (313)556-7115.*

HAWKINS, STEVEN WAYNE
Lawyer. **Personal:** Born Jul 10, 1962, Peekskill, NY; son of Peter and Ida Marie Boyd. **Educ:** Harvard Univ, BA, Econs, 1984; Univ Zimbabwe, attended 1986; NY Univ, JD, 1988. **Career:** Hon A Leon Higginbotham, Philadelphia, PA, law clerk, 1988-89; Nat Asn Advan Colored People Legal Defense Fund, NY, staff atty, 1989-95; Nat Judicial Col, fac instr, Nat Coalition Abolish Death Penalty, exec dir, 1995-. **Orgs:** Bd trustees, NY Univ, Ctr Int Studies, 1989-; NY State Bar; Bar US Supreme Ct; Bd Dir, Death Penalty Info Ctr; Criminal Justice Comt; Nat Conf Black Lawyers; Am Bar Asn; US Cts Appeal. **Honors/Awds:** Ames Award, Harvard Univ, 1984; Am Jurisprudence Award, NY Univ Law Sch, 1987; Next Generation Leadership Fellow, Rockefeller Found, 1998-99; Civil Rights Advocacy Awards; Public Interest Advocacy Award, Nat Asn Advan Colored People Legal Defense & Educational Fund; Outstanding Graduate Award, NY Univ Pub Int Law Found. **Home Addr:** 823 Glass Ave NE, Olympia, WA 98506, **Home Phone:** (360)570-8744. *

HAWKINS, TRAMAINE (TRAMAINE DAVIS)
Gospel singer. **Personal:** Born Oct 11, 1951, San Francisco, CA; married Walter (divorced); children: Jamie & Trystan; married

Tommy Richardson; children: Demar Richardson. **Career:** Gospel vocalist; Albums: Tramaine Hawkins Live, 1976; Determined, 1983; The Search Is Over, 1986; In The Morning Time, 1986; Child Of The King, 1986; Fall Down (Spirit OfLove), 1986; Freedom, 1987; The Rock, 1987; The Joy That Floods My Soul, 1988; Live, 1990; Tramaine, 1993; Tramaine Treasury, 1993; All My Best to You, 1994; A To a Higher Place, 1994; I Found The Answer, 1995; By His Strength, 2001; All My Best to You Vol 2, 2001; Still Tramaine, 2001; Mega3 Collection, 2002; Light Records Classic Gold: Determined, 2004; Light Records Classic Gold: Tramaine Treasury, 2004; Gospel Goes Gold, 2006; My Everything, 2007; Quint essential EMI Gospel, 2007; I Never Lost My Praise, 2007; Mega 3, 2007; Excellent Lord, 2007; O Happy Day; "I never Lost my Praise", 2007. **Honors/Awds:** Gospel Music Excellence Award, Tramaine Hawkins Live, 1991; Grammy Award; Commun Excellence Black Audiences Awards, Nat Asn Adv Colored People Image Award; Stellar Award; Brit Gospel Music Award; Gospel Music Excellence Award; Dove Award. **Business Phone:** (201)930-1000.*

HAWKINS, WALTER
Clergy, gospel singer. **Personal:** Born May 18, 1949, Oakland, CA. **Educ:** Univ Calif, Berkeley, MDiv. **Career:** Code Records LLC, owner & gospel singer, currently; Love Ctr Ministries Inc, pastor & founder, currently; Albums: Do Your Best, 1972; Going up Yonder, 1975; Love Alive 1, 1975; Jesus Christ Is the Way, 1977; Love Alive 2, 1978; The Hawkins Family Live', 1980; I Feel Like Singing, 1983; Love Alive 3, 1984; Special Gift' Hawkins Family, 1988; Love Alive 4, 1990; New Dawning, 1996; Love Alive, Vol. 5: 25th Anniversary Reunion 1, 1998; Take Courage, 2000; A Song In My Heart, 2005; Compilation: Only the Best, 1990; Light Years, 1995; The Hawkins Family Collection, 1995; New Dawning, 1995; Light Years, 1995; Ooh Wee, 1997; Legends Of Gospel, 2002; The Best of Love Alive, 2002; Mega 3 Collection: Love Alive, 2002; Light Recs Classic Gold: Love Alive, 2004; A Song in My Heart, 2005; The Very Best of Walter Hawkins & the Hawkins Family, 2005. **Honors/Awds:** Numerous honors & awards including one Grammy award win, nine Grammy nominations, three Dove Awards, several Gospel Music Workshop Of America awards, numerous Stellar Award nominations and lifetime achievement recognition. **Business Addr:** Gospel Singer, Owner, Code Records LLC, 360 Grand Ave Suite 158, Oakland, CA 94610, **Business Phone:** (209)543-1917.

HAWKINS, WALTER L
Police officer, military leader, writer. **Personal:** Born Jan 17, 1949, Atlanta, GA; son of Walter and Helen Johnson; married Carol H, Jul 18, 1977; children: Winter L, Michael Donta & Whitney L. **Educ:** Atlanta Police Acad, 1971; Dekalb Col, 1972; Univ Ga, 1977. **Career:** Atlanta Police Dept, police officer, 1971-72, detective, 1972-75; Fulton County Police, sargent, 1975-82; Fulton County Sheriff Dept, sheriff, 1985-87; US Postal Inspection Serv, postal police & chair Atlanta division's diversity com, 1987-. **Orgs:** Nat Asn Advan Colored People; NCOA; Millennial Lodge #537, MF&AM of W; Guiding Light Chapter #923; A-Plus. **Honors/Awds:** Commendation Medal, 1980, 1989; US Army Meritorious Service Medal, 1993; US Postal Service Award, 1995. **Special Achievements:** Fulton County Comissioners Proclamation "Walter Hawkins Day," 1994; Atlanta City, Proclamation, "Walter Hawkins Day," 1994; First Black sargent, Fulton County; Author: "African Biographies," 1992, 1994; author: "African Generals and Flag Officers," 1993. **Military Serv:** AUS, command sgt major, 1968-70; USAR 1970-. **Business Addr:** Diversity Chairman, US Postal Inspection Service, 200 Tradeport Blvd Suite 209, Atlanta, GA 30354-2994, **Business Phone:** (404)765-7382.

HAWKINS, WILLIAM DOUGLAS
Executive. **Personal:** Born May 14, 1946, Los Angeles, CA; son of William D and Marian Parrish; married Floy Marie Barabino; children: William D, Yonnine, Kellie, Todd. **Educ:** Howard Univ, BA, 1968. **Career:** US Congressman Samuel S Stratton, admin assist, 1968-70; Security Pacific Nat Bank, commercial loan officer, 1970-73; Nat Economic Management Asn, sr vpres, 1973-76; Korn Ferry Intl, managing associate, 1976-84; Hawkins Co, pres & ceo, 1984-. **Orgs:** Ed, chair Black Businessmen's Asn of LA, 1975; bd dirs, Boy Scouts of Am, LA Coun, 1979-82; fundraiser, LA Chapter United Negro Col Fund, 1984; Calif Exec Recruiters Asn, 1985; NAACP; chmn, Josephite Lay Advisory Bd, 1988-92; bd of dir, LA Chap Am Red Cross, 1995-97; bd chair, Coll Bound, 1995-98; vpres, LA Archdiocese Catholic Sch Bd, 1994-97. **Honors/Awds:** Award of Merit, Boy Scouts of Am, 1977; Silver Beaver, Boy Scouts of Am, 1989. **Business Addr:** President, Chief Executive Officer, Hawkins Co, 5455 Wilshire Blvd, Ste 1406, Los Angeles, CA 90036.*

HAWKINS-RUSSELL, HAZEL M.
Educator, teacher. **Personal:** Born Jun 11, 1924, Cedar Lake, TX; daughter of Nelse and Evelyn Hawkins; married James (deceased); children: Beverly Ann, Vicki Rochelle. **Educ:** New State Univ, BA, 1944; Univ Redlands, MA, 1965; US Internatl Univ, PhD, 1973. **Career:** Lubbock Independent Sch Dist, teacher, 1944-46; Riverside Unified Sch Dist, teacher, 1947-65; Pupil Servised Riverside Unified Sch Dist, consult, 1965-74, admin, 1970-82; Calif State Univ, assoc prof, 1982-91; Riverside Community Col, adj prof, part time faculty, currently. **Orgs:** Nat Coun Negro Women, 1960; Am Asn Univ Women, 1965; Delta Kappa Gamma, 1965; Alpha Kappa Alpha, 1973; Phi Delta Kappa, 1975; Urban League; Nat Asn Advan Colored People. **Honors/Awds:** Humanitarian Award, Asn Intergroup Rel Educrs; Educator of the Year, Omega Psi Phi, Pi Rho Chapt, 1981; Outstanding Achievement in Education, Riverside YWCA, 1983; Educator Award, Nat Asn Advan Colored People, 1982; Ida L Jackson Graduate Achievement Award, Alpha Kappa Alpha, 1985. **Special Achievements:** First African-Am teacher at Riverside Unified Sch Dist, 1947. **Business Addr:** Part Time Faculty, Riverside City Community College District, 4800 Magnolia Ave, Riverside, CA 92506, **Business Phone:** (909)222-8000.*

HAWTHORNE, ANGEL L.
Television producer, administrator. **Personal:** Born May 31, 1959, Chicago, IL. **Educ:** Columbia Col, BA, 1981. **Career:** WLS-TV, desk asst, 1980; ABC News, desk asst, 1980-81, assignment ed, 1981-85, field producer, 1985-; Univ Tenn, Ctr Telecommunications & Video; Home & Garden TV, exec producer; WVLT-TV/CBS, exec producer; Turner Broadcasting, dir develop; Cornell Univ, Educ TV, asst dir, currently. **Business Addr:** Assistant Director, Cornell University, Educational Television, 410 Thurston Ave, Ithaca, NY 14850-2488.

HAWTHORNE, KENNETH L.
Executive. **Personal:** Born in Mobile, AL; married Eugenia; children: Cecilia Hawthorne Patterson, Bruce, Bart. **Educ:** Pac Western Univ, BBA; Univ Pittsburgh, Teaching Cert. **Career:** exec (retired); NY City Dist Gulf Oil Corp, sales mgr, 1971-73, mkt mgr, 1973-76; Gulf Trading & Transp Co (Gulf Oil Sub), vpres, 1976-81; Gulf Tire & Supply Co (Gulf Oil Sub), pres, 1981-83; Gulf Oil Corp, mgr mgt training dev; KLH & Assoc, pres. **Orgs:** adv bd, Hermann Hosp Soc; bd, Am Cancer Soc; vchmn, Charter Review Comn, bd comnr, chair, Housing Authority, W Palm Beach, FL, 1998-01; chair, W Palm Beach Red Cross, Human Resources Comn. *

HAY, SAMUEL ARTHUR
Educator. **Personal:** Born Mar 26, 1937, Barnwell, SC; son of Thomas Jr and Maebelle Glover H; married Delores Ricks Glover, Jun 1, 1986 (divorced 1988). **Educ:** Bethune Cookman Col, AB, 1959; John Hopkins Univ, AM, 1967; Cornell Univ, PhD, 1971. **Career:** Univ Md Baltimore County, asst prof eng & African Am studies, 1971-74; Purdue Univ, assoc prof & chair person black studies, 1974-78; Wash Univ St Louis, prof & chair person black studies, 1978-79; Morgan St Univ, prof & chairperson theatre, 1979-87; UC Berkeley, vis prof African Am studies, 1987-88; NC Agr & Tech St Univ, prof & head theatre, 1993-2002; Lafayette Col, vis prof govt & law, 2002-. **Orgs:** Founder, Nat Conf African Am Theatre, 1980-87; managing dir, Bullins Mem Theatre, 1987-88; founding archi vist, Ed Bullins Collection, 1988-98; Founder artistic dir, Cottage Theatre, 1988-93; founder, Nat Symp African Am Theatre, 1989-95. **Honors/Awds:** Distinguished Scholar Award, NC Agr & Tech St Univ, 1995; Foundation Medallion, Harvard Univ, 1995; Choice Award, Am Libr Asn, 1995; Am Col Theatre Festival Winner, Kennedy Ctr, 1997. **Special Achievements:** Author of Focus on Literature: Ideas, 1978, Focus on Literature: America, 1978, Afr Amer Theatre, 1994, Ed Bullins: A Literary Biography, 1997, David Richmond, Play Produced at Kennedy Center, 1999. **Military Serv:** AUS, PFC, 1961-63. **Home Addr:** 422 Mccartney St, PO Box 1183, Easton, PA 18044-1183. **Business Addr:** Visiting Professor, Government & Law, Lafayette College, Department of Government & Law, 17 Watson Hall, Easton, PA 18042, **Business Phone:** (610)330-5000.

HAYDEL, JAMES V, SR.
Insurance executive. **Career:** Majestic Life Ins Co Inc, New Orleans, LA, chief exec. **Business Addr:** Chief Executive, Majestic Life Insurance Company Inc, 1833 Dryades St, New Orleans, LA 70113, **Business Phone:** (504)525-0375.

HAYDEN, AARON CHAUTEZZ
Football player. **Personal:** Born Apr 13, 1973, Detroit, MI; married ChaToya Chante, 1998. **Educ:** Univ Tenn. **Career:** Football player (retired); San Diego Chargers, running back, 1995-96; Green Bay Packers, 1997; Philadelphia Eagles, 1998.

HAYDEN, CARLA DIANE
Library administrator, executive director. **Personal:** Born in Tallahassee, FL; daughter of Bruce Kennard Jr and Colleen Dowling; divorced. **Educ:** Roosevelt Univ, BA, 1973; Univ Chicago, MA, 1977, PhD, 1987; Univ Baltimore, hon Doctor Humane Letters, 2000; Morgan State Univ, hon Doctor Humane Letters, 2001. **Career:** Chicago Pub Libr, C's librn & libr assoc, 1973-79, young adult serv coordr, 1979-81; Mus Sci & Indust, libr serv coordr, 1982-87; Univ Pittsburgh, Sch Libr & Info Sci, asst prof, 1987-91; Chicago Pub Libr, chief librn & first dep comnr, 1991-93; Enoch Pratt Free Libr, Baltimore, MD, exec dir, 1993-. **Orgs:** Pub Libr Asn; bd mem, Comn Md Museum African Am Hist & Cult, 1987; Md African Am Museum Corp, 1988-; bd mem, Franklin & Eleanor Roosevelt Inst & Libr; bd mem, Md Hist Soc; Baltimore City Hist Soc; bd mem, Goucher Col; bd mem, Wash Col; Md Pub Broadcasting Comn; Sinai Hosp; Mercy Hosp Adv Bd; Nat Aquarium Baltimore Adv Bd; bd mem, Univ Pittsburgh Sch Info Sci; chair, Am Libr Asn, Comt Accreditation & Spectrum Initiative; pres, Am Libr Asn, 2003-04. **Honors/Awds:** Librarian of the Year, Libr J, 1995; Carver-Wash Award, Baltimore Tuskegee Alumni Asn, 1995; Legacy of Literacy Award, DuBois Circle, 1996; Maryland's Top 100 Women, Warfield's Bus Rec, 1996; Torch Bearer Award, Coalition of 100 Black Women, 1996; Andrew White Medal, Loyola Col, 1997; President's Medal, Johns Hopkins Univ, 1998; Notable Black American Women, 2000; Women of the Year, Ms Mag, 2003; Maryland's Top 100 Women, Daily Rec, 2003. **Special Achievements:** Ed: Venture into Cultures: A Multi-Cultural Bibliography & Resource Book, Am Libr Assn, 1992; author of numerous chapters & articles. **Business Addr:** Executive Director, Enoch Pratt Free Library, 400 Cathedral St, Baltimore, MD 21201-4484, **Business Phone:** (410)396-5430.*

HAYDEN, FRANK F.
Government official, college administrator, chairperson. **Personal:** Born in Quantico, VA. **Educ:** Wayne County Community Col, AA, polit sci, 1973; Univ Mich, BA, gen studies & polit sci, 1976. **Career:** City Detroit, tree artisan, 1966, Dept Parks & Recreation, jr forester, Dept Water & Sewage, govt analyst, pub affairs mgr & exec ed, pub rels dir, currently; Wayne County Community Col, chmn, vice chair, chairperson dist 3, currently. **Orgs:** Wayne County Community Col, District 3; Pub Affairs Coun, Am Water Works Asn; Educ Task Force; Mich Minority Bus Develop Coun; Water People. **Honors/Awds:** Nominated for Coordinator of the Year. **Business Addr:** Chairperson District 3, Wayne County Community College, 801 W Fort St, Detroit, MI 48226, **Business Phone:** (313)496-2887.

HAYDEN, REV. DR. JOHN CARLETON
Educator, clergy. **Personal:** Born Dec 30, 1933, Bowling Green, KY; son of Otis Roosevelt and Gladys Gatewood; married Jacqueline Green; children: Jonathan Christopher Janani Hayden & Johanna Christina Jamila Hayden. **Educ:** Wayne State, BA, 1955; Univ Detroit, MA, 1962; Col Emmanuel & St Chad, LTh honors, 1963; Howard Univ, PhD, 1972; Col Emmanuel & St Chad, MDiv, 1991. **Career:** St Mary's Sch Indian Girls, teacher, 1955; Detroit Pub Schs, teacher, 1956-59; St Chad's Sec Sch, instr, 1962-64; Univ Regina, Anglican chaplain, 1963-67, instr hist, 1965-68; St George's Church, assoc rector, 1968-71, 1973-82, 1986-87 & 1994-, asst, currently; Church Atonement, asst, 1971-72; St Monica's Church, priest-in-charge, 1972-73; Howard Univ, asst prof hist, 1972-78, scholar church hist, 1978-79, Episcopal & Anglican chaplain, lectr church hist, 1994-; Angus Dunn fel, 1973-74, 1978, 1989, 1995 & 1998-2000; Bd Theol Educ, fel, 1978-79; Robert R Moton fel, 1978-79; Morgan State Univ, Dept Hist & Geog, chmn, 1979-86; Holy Comforter Church, St Andrew's Parish, rector, 1982-86; Frostburg State Univ, prof hist, 1986-87; Univ South Sch Theol, assoc dean, 1987-92; Episcopal Off Black Ministries, consult, 1992-94; St Michael & All Angels Church, Adelphi Parish, priest-in-charge, 1992-94; Montgomery Col, adj lectr hist, 1992-94; Coolidge fel, Asn Religion & Intellectual Life, 1998. **Orgs:** Church Hist Soc; bd dir, Asn Study Afro-Am Life & Hist; Am Hist Asn; Southern Hist Asn; parliamentarian, Union Black Episcopalians; Tuxis & Older Boys' Parlaiment Bd, 1963-68; Anglican chaplain, Saskatchewan Correctional Inst, 1963-68; protestant chaplain, Saskatchewan Boys' Sch, 1963-68; chmn youth conf, Saskatchewan Centennial Corp, 1964-67; founding dir, Wascana Student Housing Corp, 1965-68; pres, Saskatchewan Asn Retarded C, 1966-68; lt-gen Saskatchewan, 1967; founding dir, Ranch Ehrlo, 1967-68; chaplain's assoc, Royal Can Mountain Police, Regina; Comn Community Improv; pres, Black Episcopal Clergy, Wash Diocese, 1974-76; bd dirs, Wash Urban League, 1980-87; bd dirs, St Patrick's Episcopal Day Sch, 1981-87; Soc Prom Christian Knowledge USA Bd, 1987-92; secy, bd trustees, St Mary's Episcopal Ctr, 1988-92; bd adv, St Andrew's Sewanee Sch, 1989-; prog comt, KANUGA Conf Ctr, 1989-93, diversity comn, 1996-, bd adv, 1996-2000, bd trustees, 2000-; bd dirs, Evangelical Educ Soc, 1992-98; bd trustees, Wash Episcopal Sch, 1992-. **Honors/Awds:** Faculty Research in the Social Sciences Award, 1973, 1974; Spencer Foundation Award, 1975; Am Philosophical Society Award, 1976; Commn for Black Minsters, Grant, 1976-78; Absalom Jones Award, 1987; Grambling University Award, Grambling State Univ, 1990; Kanuga Conference Center Award, 1991. **Business Addr:** Pastor, St George Church, 160 You St NW, Washington, DC 20001.

HAYDEN, ROBERT C., JR.
Historian, writer, educator. **Personal:** Born Aug 21, 1937, New Bedford, MA; son of Robert C Sr (deceased) and Josephine Hughes (deceased); divorced; children: Dr Deborah Hayden-Hall, Kevin R Esq, Karen E McAdams. **Educ:** Boston Univ, Boston MA, BA, 1959, EdM, 1961; Harvard Univ, Cambridge MA, Cert, 1966; MA Inst Technol, Cert, 1977. **Career:** Newton Pub Sch, sci teacher, 1961-65; Xerox Educ Div, sci ed, 1966-69; Metrop Coun Educ Opportunity, Boston MA, exec dir, 1970-73; Educ Develop Ctr, Newton MA, proj dir, 1973-80; Northeastern Univ, Boston MA, adj fac, 1978; MA Inst Technol, dir, Sec Tech Educ Proj, 1980-82; Boston Pub Schs, Boston MA, exec asst to supt, dir proj develop, 1982-86; MA Pre-Engineering Prog, Boston MA, exec dir, 1987-91; Northeastern Univ, Boston, sr lectr, 1978-01; Lesley Univ, sr lectr, 1992-2005; Univ MA, Boston, lectr, 1993; Art Inst

Boston, lectr, 1994; Schomburg Ctr Res Black Cult, scholar-in-residence, 1994-95; Oak Bluffs Hist Comn, 1998-00; RCH Assoc, founder & pres, currently. **Orgs:** Kappa Alpha Psi Fraternity, 1957; Nat Asn Black Sch Educr, 1976-90; Black Educr Alliance MS, 1980-92; secy, Asn Study Afro-Am Life & Hist, 1995. **Honors/Awds:** Educ Press All-Am Award, Educ Press Asoc Am, 1968; Nat Asn Advan Colored People Serv Award, Nat Asn Advan Colored People, 1973; Human Rels Award, MA Teachers Asn, 1979; Carter G Woodson Humanitarian Award, Omega Psi Phi, 1985; Martin Luther King Jr Award, Boston Pub Schs, 1986; Humanitarian Serv Award, The Spiritual Assembly Baha'is Boston, 1987; Hon Doctors degree, Bridgewater State Col, 1999. **Special Achievements:** Author: Eight AFA Scientists, 1970, Nine AFA Inventors, 1992; Eleven Black Am Doctors, 1992; Boston's Nat Asn Advan Colored People Hist, 1910-1982, 1982; Faith, Cult & Leadership: A History of the Black Church in Boston, 1985; Singing For All People: Roland Hayes—A Biography, 1989; AFAs in Boston: More Than 350 Years, 1991; AFAs & Cape Verdean Am in New Bedford, MA: A History of Achievement and Cot, 1993; A Cult Guide to AFA Heritage in New England, 1992; Multicultural Contributions to Sci, 1996; Sci & Tec: A Rich Heritage, 1997; African Am's on Martha's Vineyard & Nantucket, 1999; co-ed, Changing Lives, Changing Communities: Oral Histories from Action for Boston Cot Develop, 2002. **Business Addr:** President, 22 Menahan St, Vineyard Haven, MA 02568.*

HAYDEN, WILLIAM HUGHES
Investment banker. **Personal:** Born Apr 26, 1940, New Bedford, MA. **Educ:** Southeastern Mass Univ, BS, BA, 1962; New Eng Sch Law, JSD, 1967; New Sch Social Res, cert, 1968. **Career:** Atty Gens Off, MA, 1963-67; US Dept Treas, 1966-67; Pres Comn Civil Disorders, asst dir cong rels, 1967-; NY State Urban Devel Corp, reg dir, 1968-73; Grapetree Bay Hotels Co, gen partner, 1973-75; E End Resources Corp, pres, 1973-75; Metro Appl Res Ctr, sr fel, 1974-75; First Boston Corp, managing dir, 1975-84; Bear Stearns & Co, sr managing dir & partner, 1984-. **Orgs:** Former dir, Wiltwyck Sch Boys, 1976-78; bd dirs, Urban Home Ownership Corp, 1977; bd dirs, United Neighborhood Houses NY City, 1977-; former dir, First Women's Bank NY, 1979; former trustee, vice chmn, Citizen's Budget Comt, City NY, 1981-99; dir, Nat Asn Securities Profs; trustee, NY Law Sch, 1995-; trustee, mem exec comt, New Sch Univ, 1990-; trustee , vice chair, Citizens Budget Comn, City NY, 1983-89; trustee, Nat Asn Advan Colored People Spec Contribution Fund; life mem, Nat Asn Advan Colored People; chair, Get Ahead Found (S Africa Bus Financing Orgn), 1985-98; trustee, African Am Inst, 1985-98; Munic Bond Club NY, 1980-; past chair exec comt, Nat Asn Securities Prof, 1990-93; SIA, Comt Pub & Munic Finance; trustee, Citizen Union, NY, 1998-. *

HAYE, CLIFFORD S
Lawyer. **Personal:** Born Dec 20, 1942, New York; son of Clifford and Sylvia; married Jenelyn; children: Angela & Christopher. **Educ:** Mich State Univ, NC Col, BA, 1966; Columbia Law Sch, JD, 1972. **Career:** Columbia Univ Law Sch, residence adv; US Dept Justice, trial atty, 1972-73; NY Stock Exchange, enforcement atty, 1973-74; Teachers Ins Ann Asn, asst gen coun, 1974, sr coun, currently, TIAA-CREF, minority lawyer, corp coun; Spencer Partners LLC, partner, consult, currently. **Orgs:** Comn elect Charles Evers Gov, 1971; vol atty, Comm Law Off, 1974-78; atty, Indigent Panel Kings Co, 1975-79. **Military Serv:** AUS, First lt, 1966-69. **Business Addr:** Partner, Spencer Partners LLC, PO Box 7333, Bloomfield, CT 06001-7333, **Business Phone:** 800-520-0818 Ext 1495.

HAYES, ALBERTINE BRANNUM
Educator. **Personal:** Born in Lake Providence, LA; married James T. **Educ:** Southern Univ, BS, 1940; Univ Mich, MA, 1952; George Peabody Col Teacher, specialist educ; Univ Okla, EdD. **Career:** Caddo Parish Sch Bd, asst supt comn affairs; Natchitoches Paris Sch La,teacher; Lake Charles City Sch La, teacher; Caddo Parish Sch La, teacher, asst prin charge instr; Booker T Wash High Sch, supr math sci educ; Centenary Col La, lecturer educ; Southern Univ La, prof educ; NE State Univ La, guest prof. **Orgs:** Vpres, Pride Carroll Burial Ins Co Lake Providence La; vpres, Hayes Flower Shop Shreveport, La; v chmn, United Way, 1974; bd dir, Integrated Youth Serv; bd dir, United Way, 1975; bd dir, Shreveport Chap Am Red Cross; dir, Delta Sigma Theta Sorority, currently. **Honors/Awds:** Zeta Woman of the Year, 1965; Educator of the Year. **Business Addr:** Director, Delta Sigma Theta Sorority, PO BOX 3265, Shreveport, LA 71133-3265.*

HAYES, ALVIN, JR. See Obituaries section.

HAYES, ANNAMARIE GILLESPIE
Educator, college teacher. **Personal:** Born Sep 6, 1931, Flint; married Emery M; children: Colon & Marcus. **Educ:** Mich State Univ, BA, MA, MS, PhD. **Career:** Pontiac Pub Schs, Inkster Pub Schs, pub sch teacher; Mich-Ohio Regional Lab, teacher trainer; Mich State Univ, educ specialist; Univ Wis, Madison, res assoc; Wayne State Univ, Col Educ, assoc prof, currently; Williams Col, fel res. **Orgs:** Nat Asn Negro Bus & Prof Women; Nat Asn Black Fin Aid Admin; Nat All Black Educ; Am Educ Res Asn; Asn Study Negro Life & Hist; bd dir, Int Afro-Am Mus; Shrine Black Madonna Detroit; Coun woman Erma Henderson Women's Concerns Conf. **Honors/Awds:** Woman of the Year Award, Mich State Univ, 1971. **Military Serv:** USAF, Europe Award, 1972. *

HAYES, DR. BARBARA E.
Dean (education), educator. **Educ:** Tex Southern Univ, BS; Purdue Univ, MS; Univ Houston, PhD. **Career:** Tex Southern Univ, Sch Pharm, assoc dean acad affairs, Col Pharm & Health Scis, dean & assoc prof pharmacol, currently, RCMI Prog, dir, currently. **Orgs:** Pres, Asn Minority Health Prof Sch, 2005-; mem, Amn Asn Cols Pharmacy; mem, Amn Diabetes Asn; mem, Amn Asn Pharmaceut Scientists. **Business Addr:** Dean, Texas Southern University, College Of Pharmacy and Health Sciences, 3100 Cleburne Ave, Gray Hall Room Suite 240, Houston, TX 77004, **Business Phone:** (713)313-7280.

HAYES, CHARLES
Government official. **Personal:** Born Oct 14, 1943, Catherine, AL; married Muriel. **Educ:** Mobile Bus Col, dipl, 1970; Selma Univ, assoc, 1971; Wallace Community Col, dipl, 1973; Univ S Ala, attended 1983; Dale Carnegie, attended 1984. **Career:** Government official(retired); Wilcox Co, comnr, currently; 4th Judicial Circuit, spec investr dist atty, indigent def comn. **Orgs:** Alberta Comn Health Clin, 1981-84; Asn Co Comnr, 1982-; deacon Salem Baptist Ch, 1982-; dir, Alberta Comn Club, 1983-85; dir, Alberta Community Fire Dept, 1984-; Wilcox Co Democratic Conf; Ala Democratic Conf Black Caucus. **Honors/Awds:** Outstanding Leadership Award, Alberta Comn Club-Alberta AL, 1984. **Military Serv:** AUS, sgt, E-5, 1964-69; Code of Conduct Award. **Home Addr:** 300Patterson rd, Catherine, AL 36728. *

HAYES, CHARLES DEWAYNE
Baseball player, baseball executive. **Personal:** Born May 29, 1965, Hattiesburg, MS. **Career:** Baseball Player (retired), baseball executive; San Francisco Giants,1988-89, 1998-99; Philadelphia Phillies, third baseman, 1989-91, 1995; New York Yankees, 1992, 1996-97; Colorado Rockies, 1993-94; Pitts burgh Pirates, 1996; Milwaukee Brewers, 2000; Houston Astros, 2001; Big League Baseball Acad, owner & operator, currently. **Honors/Awds:** NL Doubles Leader, 1993; Winner, World Series Ring, 1996.

HAYES, DR. CHARLES LEONARD. See Obituaries section.

HAYES, CHRIS
Football player. **Personal:** Born May 7, 1972, San Bernardino, CA; married Aran; children: Christopher Jr, Isaiah & Jeremiah. **Educ:** Wash State Univ. **Career:** Football player (retired); Green Bay Packers, defensive back, 1996; NY Jets, 1997-2001; New Eng Patriots, 2002; New Century Mortgage Corp, staff. **Orgs:** Founder, Chris Hayes Motivational; founder, CEO, 3030 Productions Inc, currently.

HAYES, CURTISS LEO
Educator. **Personal:** Born Jan 10, 1931, Glasgow, VA; married Opal Juanita Owens; children: Janice R Almond, Curtiss L Jr & Collin L. **Educ:** Morningside Col, BA, 1956; Ariz State Univ, MA, 1974; Dallas Theol Sem, ThM, 1980. **Career:** Sec Pub Schs, teacher, 1956-75; Sudan Interior Mission, Christian educ coord, 1980-84; Liberian Baptist Theol Sem, theol instr, 1982-83; Dallas Bible Col, missionary residence 1984-85; Dallas Independent Sch Dist, substitute teacher. **Orgs:** Nat Asn Advan Colored People, 1956; pres, Desert Sands Teachers Asn, 1972; Stull Bill Steering Comm, 1973; Nat Educ Asn, 1973; lic minister, Mt Zion Baptist Church, 1980; instr, Monrovia Bible Inst, 1982. **Honors/Awds:** Diamond Key Award, Nat Forensic League, 1972. **Military Serv:** AUS, corpl 2 yrs; Hon Discharge.

HAYES, DENNIS COURTLAND
Lawyer, government official. **Educ:** Indiana University, BS; Indiana University Law School at Indianapolis, JD, 1977. **Orgs:** NAACP, Attorney, 1985; NAACP, Chief Legal Officer, 1990; NAACP, Interim President and CEO. **Home Addr:** 004850. *

HAYES, DONALD ROSS, JR.
Football player. **Personal:** Born Jul 13, 1975, Century, FL. **Educ:** Univ Wis. **Career:** Carolina Panthers, wide receiver, 1998-2001, 2004; New England Patriots, wide receiver, 2002; Canadian football league: Toronto Argonauts, wide receiver, 2006.

HAYES, EDWARD
Lawyer. **Personal:** Born Jun 19, 1947, Long Branch, NJ; son of Edward and Bessie E Dickerson; married Alice Hall; children: Blair Hall & Kia Hall. **Educ:** Wesleyan Univ, BA, 1969; Stanford Law Sch, JD, 1972. **Career:** Commr Mary Gardner Jones FTC, clerk, 1971; Citizens Commun Ctr, atty, 1972-74; Hayes & White, partner atty, 1974-84; Baker & Hostetler, partner atty, 1984-92; US Dept Health & Human Serv, counr to secy, currently; MVM Inc, sr vpres admin & gen coun, 2002-. **Orgs:** Supreme Ct Bar; DC Bar; bd mem, Nat Capital YMCA; adv comm, African Develop Fund; bd mem, Inst Intl Trade & Develop; bd mem, DC Chamber Comm; Nat Asn Broadcasters; Nat Asn Black Owned Broadcasters. **Special Achievements:** Articles publ Nat Bar Assn. **Business Addr:** Senior Vice President, MVM Inc, 1593 Spring Hill Rd Suite 700, Vienna, VA 22182, **Business Phone:** (703)790-3138.

HAYES, ELEANOR MAXINE
Television news anchorperson. **Personal:** Born Feb 9, 1954, Cleveland, OH; daughter of Jimmy and Ruth. **Educ:** El Instituto Tecnologico de Monterrey, Monterrey, Mex, 1971; Western Col, Oxford, OH, 1972; Oberlin Col, Oberlin, OH, commun & polit sci, 1976. **Career:** WERE Radio, Cleveland, Ohio, anchor & reporter, 1976-79; WTOL-TV, Toledo, Ohio, investigative reporter; WTVF-TV, Nashville, Tenn, anchor; WISN-TV, Milwaukee, Wis, co-anchor, 1983-87; WJW-TV 8, Cleveland, Ohio, co-anchor, 1987, reporter & anchor; WVIZ-TV, "Women?s Health Series", prog host; ACN-TV, anchor; McDonald's Restaurants, owner; Ohio News Network, anchor & reporter, 2005-. **Orgs:** Am Sickle Cell Anemia Asn, 1989-. **Honors/Awds:** Numerous awards including Three Emmy Awards, Nat acad TV Arts & Sci; Volunteer Achievement Award, United Black Fund Greater Cleveland, 1991; National NABJ, UPI & AP reporting honors; inductee, Broadcasters Hall of Fame, 2003. **Business Addr:** Reporter, Ohio News Network, 770 Twin Rivers Dr, Columbus, OH 43215, **Business Phone:** (614)280-3600.

HAYES, ELVIN E.
Executive, baseball player, government official. **Personal:** Born Nov 17, 1945, Rayville, LA; married Erna; children: Elvin Jr, Erna Jr, Erica & Ethan. **Educ:** Univ Houston, attended 1968; Col Md Law Enforcement Acad. **Career:** Basketball player (retired), business owner, government official; SanDiego Rockets, 1968-71, Houston Rockets, 1971-72, 1981-84, 1981-84, Baltimore Bullets, 1972-73, Capital Bullets, 1973-74, Washington Bullets, 1974-81 (retired); Greater Cleveland Ford-Mercury Inc, chief exec officer; Elvin Hayes Ford Inc, owner, currently; Liberty Co Sheriff's Off, res dep, currently. **Orgs:** Iota Phi Theta Fraternity. **Honors/Awds:** All Star every year in the NBA; All Amer every year at Houston; Col Playerof the Yr 1968; only player in NBA history to have more than 1,000 rebounds every year; missed only six of 984 games in pro career; 4th all time minutes played (highest of active players); top active player inrebounds (5th all time); 7th all time scorer (one of 6 NBA players toscore 20,000 pts & pull down 10,000 rebounds); 8th in NBA scoring 1979; 5th in rebounding; 5th in blocked shots; elected to the Basketball Hall of Fame, 1990; named to the NBA's 50th Anniversary All-Time Team, 1996-97; inducted by the San Diego Hall of Champions into the Breitbard Hall of Fame, 2003. **Business Addr:** Owner, Elvin Hayes Ford Inc, PO Box 1547, Crosby, TX 77532.

HAYES, DR. FLOYD WINDOM
Educator. **Personal:** Born Nov 3, 1942, Gary, IN; son of Charles Henry and Thelma Ruth Person; married Charlene Moore; children: Tracy, Keisha, Ndidi & Kia-Lillian. **Educ:** Univ Paris, cert, 1964; NC Central Univ, BA, 1967; Univ Calif, Los Angeles, MA, 1969; Univ MD, PhD, 1985. **Career:** Univ Calif, Los Angeles, instruction specialist, 1969-70; Princeton Univ, lectr dept polit, exec sec Afro-Amer studies, 1970-71; Swarth more Col,Dept Hist, vis lectr, 1971; Univ MD, asst coord Afro-Amer studies, 1971-73, instr, 1971-77; Cornell Univ, instr Africana studies, 1977-78; Close Up Found, prog instruct, 1979-80; Howard Univ, res asst, res felinst ed policy, 1980-81, 1981-85; US Equal Employment Oppor Com, specialasst to chmn, 1985-86; San Diego State Univ, asst prof Africana studies, 1986; NC State Univ, assoc prof; John Hopkins Univ, sr lectr & coord undergrad prog, currently. **Orgs:** Consultant Union Township Sch System, 1971, Comm Educ Exchange Prog Columbia Univ, 1972, MD State Dept Educ, 1973-75; mem, Early Childhood Educ Sub comm FICE US Dept Educ, 1986. **Honors/Awds:** Outstanding Young Men of America, 1977; "The Future, A Guide to Information Sources," World Future Soc, 1977; "The African Presence in America Before Columbus," Black World July 1973; "Structures of Dominance& the Political Economy of Black Higher Education," Inst Study Educ Policy, Howard Univ, 1981; "The Political Economy, Reaganomics, & Blacks,"The Western Journal of Black Studies 1982; "Politics & Education inAmerica's Multicultural Society," Journal of Ethnic Studies 1989;"Governmental Retreat and the Politics of African American Self-Reliant Development," Journal of Black Studies 1990. **Home Addr:** 284 61st St, San Diego, CA 92114, **Home Phone:** (619)263-0444. **Business Addr:** Senior Lecturer, Director, John Hopkins University, Center For African Studies, Greenhouse 118, 3400 N Charles St, Baltimore, MD 21218, **Business Phone:** (410)516-7659.

HAYES, GRAHAM EDMONDSON
Lawyer. **Personal:** Born Nov 2, 1929, Horton, KS; children: Sondra, Karen, Graham II & Alisa. **Educ:** Washburn Univ, AB, 1956; Washburn Univ, JD, 1957. **Career:** Sedgwick Co, dep dist atty, 1958-62; KS Comn Civil Rights, atty, 1970-74; Wichita Comn Civil Rights, examr, 1974, atty, 1975-; Pvt Pract, atty law, currently. **Orgs:** Supreme Ct US; US Ct Claimes; Tax Ct US; US Dist Ct; Circuit Ct US; Supreme Ct Kans; USAF Bd Correction Mil Rec; St Bd Law Examr KS; bd dirs, Kans Trial Lawyers Asn; Am Trial Lawyers Asn; Nat Asn Criminal Def Lawyers; pres, Urban League Wichita; VFW Post 6888; Kappa Alpha Psi. **Honors/Awds:** Appt Exmnr, 1976; Kans State Bd Admis Atty, 1979. **Military Serv:** USAF, 1948-52. **Business Addr:** Attorney, 2459 N Plumthicket Ct, Wichita, KS 67226-1525, **Business Phone:** (316)315-0884.*

HAYES, ISAAC LEE. See Obituaries section.

HAYES, J HAROLD, JR.
Television journalist. **Personal:** Born Apr 21, 1953, McKeesport, PA; son of J Harold Sr and Gladys Burrell; married Iris Dennis, Jan 28, 1984; children: Kristin Heather & Lindsay Victoria. **Educ:** Univ Pittsburgh, Pittsburgh, Pa, BA, speech & commun, 1971-75. **Career:** Urban League Pittsburgh, "Reading is Fundamental" prog, res asst; WSIV-AM, Pekin, Ill, announcer, 1976-77; WRAU-TV, Peoria, Ill, weekend anchor & reporter, 1977-79; KDKA-TV, Pittsburgh, Pa, reporter, 1979-. **Orgs:** Nat Asn Black Journalists, 1987-; trustee, Mt Ararat Baptist Church; spokesman, Negro Educ Emergency Fund. **Honors/Awds:** Recipient of scholarship, Negro Educ Emergency Fund (NEED). **Business Addr:** Reporter, KDKA-TV, News, 1 Gateway Center, Pittsburgh, PA 15222, **Business Phone:** (412)575-2200.

HAYES, JACKI
Executive. **Career:** Ford Employee African Ancestry Network, pres.

HAYES, JAMES C. See HAYES, JIM.

HAYES, JIM (JAMES C HAYES)
Association executive, mayor. **Personal:** Born May 25, 1946, Sacramento, CA; son of Juanita Hayes Metoyer; married Murilda; married Chris Parham, Jan 1, 1974; children: LaNene Hayes-Pruitt & James Jr. **Educ:** Univ Alaska, BA, 1970. **Career:** Joy Elem Sch, Fairbanks, AK, teacher, 1970-71; President's Coun Youth & Job Opportunity, Juneau, AK, bur dir, 1971; Off Gov, Manpower Planning Div, Juneau, dep dir, 1971-72; Off Consumer Protection, Fairbanks, assoc atty-investr, 1972-90, 1991, investr, 1990-91; City Coun Fairbanks, former councilman; State Alaska, Consumer Protection Off, investr; City Fairbanks, mayor, 1992-2001; Love Social Services Ctr, bd dirs, 2001-05; Univ Alaska Bd Regents, regent, 2003-; Lily Valley church, pastor, currently. **Orgs:** Fairbanks City Coun, 1987-92. **Honors/Awds:** Distinguished Alumnus, Univ Alaska, Fairbanks, 2002. **Special Achievements:** First African American to hold the post of Mayor in Alaska. **Business Phone:** (907)474-7211.

HAYES, JONATHAN MICHAEL
Football player, football coach. **Personal:** Born Aug 11, 1962, South Fayette, PA; married; children: 4. **Educ:** Univ Iowa, BS, criminol, 1986. **Career:** Football player (retired); football coach; Kansas City Chiefs, tight end, 1985-93; Pittsburgh Steelers, 1994-96; Univ Okla, asst coach, 1999-2002; Cincinnati Bengals, tight ends coach, 2003-. **Special Achievements:** Considered one of the finest blocking tight ends in the NFL. **Business Addr:** Tight Ends Coach, Cincinnati Bengals, 1 Paul Brown Stadium, Cincinnati, OH 45202, **Business Phone:** (513)621-3550.

HAYES, LAURA
Comedian, actor. **Personal:** Born in Oaktown, CA. **Career:** TV series: "Martin"; "That's Life"; "The Hughley's"; "Bette"; "Kristin";"Politically Incorrect"; "The Parkers", 2003; Finders Keepers, 2005; "All of Us", 2006; "The Sarah Silverman Program", 2007; "Safety Geeks SVI, 2009; Stage shows: Bay Area Black Comedy Competition, host, 1988-96; BET's Comic View, co-host, 1996-98 & 2000; Theater performance: Out on a Twig; Films: I Got the Hook-Up; King of Queens; Miss Laura: Felon to Funny; Def Comedy Jam 1, 1993; The Latham Comedy Collection, 2000-03; Comic View All-Stars, 2002; Beauty Shop, 2005; Low, 2006; Virus, 2006; TV Shows: "Showtime's Queens of Comedy", host; "ABC's Christmas Spec, Sinbad & Friends"; "Health Insurance", 2005; "Neesee's Grave Plot", 2006. **Orgs:** Spokesperson, CalWORKS/Behav Health Care Serv. **Honors/Awds:** Comedian of the month.

HAYES, LEOLA G.
Educator, college teacher, chairperson. **Personal:** Born in Rocky Mount, NC; married Spurgeon S. **Educ:** PhD, 1973; BS; MA; MS, prof dipl. **Career:** NY Inst Blind, teacher, 1953-54; Fair Lawn NJ, teacher handicapped c; Blind Chicago, consult, 1954-57; Fair Lawn NJ, supv spl educ, 1957-64; William Paterson Col, NJ, Spec Educ Dept, chmn, curentlyr. **Orgs:** Drug Abuse Prog, 1973-; CEC; Voc Rehab Soc; AAMD; NJEA; Young People Coun Session, Alpha Kappa Alpha Sorority. **Honors/Awds:** Human Rels Award, Nat Bus & Prof Women; Nat Comn Leaders Award; Hannah G Solomon Award; Ernest Melly Award. *

HAYES, MARION LEROY
Educator. **Personal:** Born Dec 23, 1931, Jefferson Co, MS; son of Lindsey J and Irene Rollins; married Louise. **Educ:** Alcorn State Univ, BS, 1961; South Univ, MEd, 1971. **Career:** Educator (retired); Hazelhurst Pub Sch, teacher, 1961-66; Jefferson Co Sch, asst prin, teacher, 1966-75, supt educ. **Orgs:** Am Asn Sch Admin; Nat Educ Asn; Miss Asn Sch Supts; Miss Asn Educ, Jefferson Co Teachers Asn; bd mem, Copiah-Lincoln Jr Col; planning bd, chmn, town Fayette; bd gov, Educ Secur. **Military Serv:** USAF, E-5, 1950-54; USA, E-5, 1956-60. *

HAYES, MELVIN ANTHONY
Football player. **Personal:** Born Apr 28, 1973, New Orleans, LA. **Educ:** Miss State Univ. **Career:** New York Jets, guard, 1995-96; Tennessee Oilers, 1997.

HAYES, MERCURY
Football player. **Personal:** Born Jan 1, 1973, Houston, TX. **Educ:** Univ Mich, BS, commun, attended. **Career:** Football player (retired), New Orleans Saints, wide receiver, 1996-97; Atlanta Falcons, 1997; Wash Redskins, 1998;Barcelona Dragons, 1999, Montreal Alouettes, 1999-2000; Norfolk Nighthawks, 2002. **Honors/Awds:** Michigan All-time Record consecutive games with reception, 1995-2001.

HAYES, NORMAN A.
Executive. **Career:** Ind State Univ, dir financial aid. **Orgs:** Enrollment Mgt Team Subcomt. *

HAYES, REGINALD
Actor. **Personal:** Born Jul 15, 1969, Chicago, IL. **Educ:** Ill State Univ, BA; N western Military Naval Acad, attended. **Career:** Films: A Family Thing, 1996; Chicago Cab, 1998; Being John Malkovich, 1999; Charlie's Angels, 2000; Stop Thief!, 2004; TV Series: "Getting Personal", 1998; "Roswell", 1999; "Girlfriends", 2000; "Will & Grace", 2000; "Then Came You", 2000; "The Twilight Zone", 2003; "Kim Possible", 2003; Hummingbird Magic, narrator, 2008. **Business Addr:** Actor, c/o United Paramount Network, 11800 Wilshire Blvd, Los Angeles, CA 90025.*

HAYES, RICHARD C.
School administrator. **Personal:** Born Dec 13, 1938, Carbondale, IL; son of William Richard Hayes Sr and Eurma C Jones; married Joyce L Harris, Mar 19, 1961; children: Clinette Steele, Rachaelle Ruff & Richard. **Educ:** BA, 1967; MA, 1975. **Career:** School administrator (retired); Southern Ill Univ, asst dir stud develop, assoc Univ affirm action officer, internal compliance ofcr; Gov's Ofc Human Resources, dir; Ill St Employment Serv, employment coord; Southern Ill Univ, acad adv gen studies; Carbondale, planning operator, 1963-66. **Orgs:** Chmn, Affirmative Action Officers Asn, 1972-; consult, AA/EEO; exec com, Nat AAAO; pres, Carbondale Nat Asn Advan Colored People; Bethel AME Ch; Tuscan Lodge #44 PHA; pres, Serv Sr Jackson County. **Military Serv:** USN, 1956-58. *

HAYES, TEDDY (THEODORE HAYES)
Writer, playwright, musician. **Personal:** Born Oct 20, 1951, Cleveland, OH; son of Evelyn Hayes and Ernest; divorced; children: Kai. **Educ:** Cleveland State Univ, BA, film & tv, 1974. **Career:** Vindicator, ed, 1970; Cleveland Call & Post, part-time reporter, 1970; WSWS-TV, part-time film processor & ed, 1970; community action agency, Dayton, OH, short filmmaker & commun officer, 1970; Melvin Van Peebles Productions, writing asst & office mgr; freelance writer & music video dir; creative writing teacher, London, England, 1990-; SKD Productions, owner, currently. **Orgs:** Crime Writers Asn; Burry Man Writers Ctr. **Honors/Awds:** American Emmy Award. **Special Achievements:** Books: Blood Red Blues, 1998; Dead By Popular Demand, 2000; As Wrong As Two Left Shoes, 2003; Plays: Hondo Gothic, 1987; The Holding Pen, 1987; Break Away Angel, 1997; I Remember Marvin, 2002; The Baskerville Beast, 2003; screenplays: The Day They Came to Arrest the Book, 1987; Panther, 1995; Case No 603, 2003. **Business Addr:** Owner, SKD Productions, Unit 5 14 Birbeck Rd, London W3 6BG, United Kingdom, **Business Phone:** (020)8992-9614.

HAYES, THEODORE. See HAYES, TEDDY.

HAYES-GILES, JOYCE V.
Executive. **Personal:** Born in Jackson, MS; daughter of Isaac and Myrtle Stigger; married Ronald Giles; children: Kristen, Erica. **Educ:** Knoxville Col, BA 1970; Univ Detroit, MBA 1978; Wayne State Law Sch, JD 1985. **Career:** Chrysler Corp, salary admin analyst/supvr, 1971-76; Auto Club MI, compensation adminr, 1976-78; Mich Con Gas Co, dir mat mgt & other managerial positions; MCN Energy Group, vpres corp resources, 2001, DTE Energy, sr vpres customer serv & bd mem, currently. **Orgs:** Nat Black MBA Asn, 1978-; exec comt, Amer Red Cross; Detroit Bar Asn, MI Bar Asn; Nat Purchasing Asn; chairperson personnel comt & vpres bd, YWCA; NAACP; Links Inc; Delta Sigma Theta Sor Inc; pres, Metropol YWCA, 1988-89; Jack & Jill Am; bd chair, Detroit Urban League; Marygrove Coll; Wolverine Bar Asn. **Honors/Awds:** Leadership Detroit Grad Chamber Com, 1982; Minority Achiever in Industry, YWCA, 1984; NAACP 100 Club Award. **Business Addr:** Senior Vice President, Board Member, DTE Energy, Customer Serv, 2000 2nd Ave, Detroit, MI 48226, **Business Phone:** (313)235-4000.*

HAYES-JORDAN, MARGARET
Executive. **Personal:** Born Jan 1, 1943; divorced; children: Fawn & Frederick. **Educ:** Georgetown Univ, Wash, DC, BSN, 1964; Univ Calif-Berkeley, Berkeley, Calif, MPH, 1972. **Career:** San Bernardino Community Hosp, San Bernardino, Calif, staff nurse, 1964-65; Vis Nurse Asn San Francisco, San Francisco, Calif, pub health nurse, 1966-67, pvt duty nurse, 1967-68; Comprehensive Child Care Proj, Mt Zion Hosp, San Francisco, Calif, sr pub health nurse, 1968-71; Lester Gorsline Assocs, Terra Linda, Calif, consult, 1972; US Pub Health Serv, Region IX, Div Resources Develop, San Francisco, Calif, dep dir, 1975-76, Health Planning & Facilities Br, chief, 1976-78; San Francisco Gen Hosp & San Francisco Med Ctr, San Francisco, Calif, assoc adminr outpatient, community emergency serv, 1978-90; Kaiser Found Health Plan, Oakland, Calif, coordr, lic & accreditation, 1983, dir, accreditation & quality assurance, 1983-84; Kaiser Foundation Health Plan Ga Inc, Atlanta, Ga, employ rels mgr, 1984-86, health plan mgr, 1984-86, assoc regional mgr, 1986; Kaiser Found Health Plan Texas Inc, Dallas, Tex, vpres & regional mgr, 1986-; Tex Health Resources, exec vpres corp affairs; Dallas Medical Resource, pres & chief exec officer, 2004-; Mentor Corp, dir, 2007-. **Orgs:** Exec bd mem, Am Pub Health Asn; founder & past dir, Nat Black Nurses Asn Inc; past pres & dir, Bay Area Black Nurses Asn Inc; founder & past dir, Bay Area Black Consortium Quality Health Care Inc; Dallas Assembly; Dallas Citizens Coun; adv bd, Dallas Women's Found; bd dirs, Greater Dallas Community Churches; bd dirs, Tex State Bd Ins High Risk Health Pool; Sch Nursing Adv Coun, Univ Tex, Arlington; adv bd, Women's Ctr Dallas. **Honors/Awds:** Distinguished Alumnus Award, Georgetown Univ, Sch Nursing; Alumni of the Year, Sch Pub Health, Univ Calif, Berkeley; named one of 21 Women of Power and Influence in Corporate America", Black Enterprise Mag; named to the Movers and Shakers list, Bus Week Mag. **Special Achievements:** Numerous articles including "The Interdisciplinary Health Team in Providing Nutrition Assessment", Nutrition Assessment, A Comprehensive Guide for Planning Intervention, 1984; Discovering the Issues: A First Step in Plan Development, December 1974; "Managed Competition Lets Employees Choose". **Business Phone:** (214)523-9034.*

HAYGOOD, WIL
Journalist. **Personal:** Born Sep 19, 1954, Columbus, OH; son of Jack and Elvira. **Educ:** Miami Univ, BA, 1976. **Career:** Columbus Ohio Call & Post, reporter, 1977-78; Community Info & Referal, hotline operator, 1978-79; Macy's Dept Store NY, exec, 1980-81; The Charleston Gazette, copy ed, 1981-83; The Pittsburgh Post Gazette, reporter, 1984-85; The Boston Globe, feature reporter; Wash Post, Style Sect, writer, 2003. **Orgs:** Editors Award, Sunday Mag; New England Associated Press Award; National Headliners Award; National Association of Black Journalists Award; Great Lakes Book Award, 1997; James Thurber Literary Fel; Alicia Patterson Foundation Fel; Yaddo Fel. **Honors/Awds:** Nattional Headliner Award, Outstanding Feature Writing, 1986. **Special Achievements:** Auth: Two on the River, 1986; King of the Cats: The Life and Times of Adam Clayton Powell Jr., 1993; The Haygoods of Columbus: A Family Memoir, 1997; In Black and White: The Life of Sammy Davis Jr., 2003. **Business Addr:** Writer, Washington Post, Sect Style, 1150 15th St NW, Washington, DC 20071.*

HAYLING, WILLIAM H.
Gynecologist, obstetrician. **Personal:** Born Dec 7, 1925, Trenton, NJ; son of Dr & Mrs William Hayling; married Carolyn Anne Mitchem; children: Pamela Hoffman, Patricia Price. **Educ:** Boston Univ, pre-19med, 1945; Howard Univ, MD, 1949. **Career:** NJ Col Med & Dent, assoc prof obstet & gynec, 1960-80; King Drew Med Ctr, asst prof obstet & gynec, 1981-87, chief ambulatory obstet & gynec, 1981. **Orgs:** Pres, 100 Black Men of NJ, 1975-78; bd mem, Jersey City State Col, NJ, 1975-80; pres, Nat 100 Black Men of Am Inc, 1987; founder & pres, 100 Black Men of LA Inc. **Honors/Awds:** Image Award, 100 Black Men of LA, 1982; LA Sentinel Awaed LA Sentinel Newspaper, 1983; Presidential Award Alpha Phi Alpha Fratternity, 1984. **Military Serv:** USY, Med Corps, capt, 1951-53; Bronze Star; Combat Med Badge. *

HAYMAN, WARREN C.
Educator. **Personal:** Born Oct 1, 1932, Baltimore, MD; married Jacqueline; children: Warren Jr, Guy & Julia. **Educ:** Coppin State Col, BS, elementary educ, 1961; Stanford Univ, MA, math, 1967; Harvard Univ, EdD, 1978. **Career:** Coppin State Col, dean educ; Ravenswood City Sch Dist, supt, 1973-77; Ravenswood, asst supt, 1971-73; Belle Haven, elem prin, 1968-71; Baltimore City Schs, elem teacher, 1961-66; Stanford Univ, faculty resident, 1970-73; San Francisco State Univ, instr, 1971-74; US Off Educ, consult, 1968-76; Morgan State Univ, Sch Educ & Urban Studies, asst dean; Baltimore Co Pub Schs, bd mem; Community Col Baltimore Co, Board Trustee, mem, 2007-. **Orgs:** Chmn bd, Nairobi Col, 1970-76; chmn bd, Mid-Peninsula Urban Coalition, 1973-75; reg dir educ, Phi Beta Sigma Frat Inc, 1980; 100 Black Men of Maryland; Coun Urban Bd Educ; Am Asn Sch Adminr. **Honors/Awds:** Good conduct ribbon, AUS, 1955-57; elem math teacher fel, NSF, 1966; exp teacher fel, US Off Educ, 1966; higher educ fel, Rockfeller Found, 1976-78; Distinguished Black Marylander Award; Fullwood Foundation Valued Hours Award; Rotary Club Service Above Self Award. **Military Serv:** AUS, sp/2nd class, 1955-57. **Business Addr:** Board Trustee, The Community College of Baltimore County, 800 South Rolling Rd, Baltimore, MD 21228.*

HAYMON, ALAN
Executive. **Personal:** Born in Cleveland, OH. **Educ:** Harvard Univ, BA, 1977, MBA, 1980, studying econs, currently. **Career:** Haymon Entertainment, founder, chairman, currently. **Special Achievements:** Most successful concert promoter of African-American music; entertainers include: MC Hammer, Eddie Murphy, Bobby Brown, Bell, Biv, DeVoe, New Edition, Patti La Belle, Frankie Beverly, numerous others; Talent Buyer Of The Year. **Business Addr:** Chairman, AH Enterprises, 15 Sevland Rd, Newton Center, MA 02459, **Business Phone:** (617)332-9680.*

HAYMORE, TYRONE
Curator. **Personal:** Born Mar 12, 1947, Chicago, IL; son of Mildred Ernestine Calhoun and T H Haymore. **Educ:** Thornton Jr

Col, AA, 1969; Northeastern Ill Univ, BA, educ, 1986; Ill Inst Munic Clerks, Munic Clerk Cert, 1992. **Career:** Chicago Transit Authority, rail clerk, 1968-; Village Robbins, IL, village clerk, trustee, 1983-87, village clerk, 1989; Village Robbins, 4 yr term, re-elected, clerk, 1993-; Channel 14 Cable TV, First exec producer & dir, 1994-; Robbins Hist Soc Mus, exec dir, curator, currently. **Orgs:** Dir, Comn Youth Bremen Twp, 1983; treas, Black Elected Officials Ill, 1984; Ill Civil Air Patrole; Munic Clerks Ill, 1989-93. **Honors/Awds:** Christian Leadership, Christ Crusader Church Robbins, 1965; Music Scholar Summer Music Camp, Eastern Ill Univ, 1965; Achievement Award, Mayor Robbins Ambulance Fund Dr, 1984; Plaque for Outstanding Service as Treasurer, Black Elected Officials Ill, 1990; Plaque for Outstanding Historian in Robbins, Robbins Recreation & Training Ctr, 1992; Certificate for Professionalism as a CMC, 1993. **Special Achievements:** History Coloring Book entitled, Robbins, Illinois, co-author, 1994. **Business Addr:** Curator, Robbins Historical Society Museum, 13822 S Cent Pk Ave, PO Box 1561, Robbins, IL 60472, **Business Phone:** (708)389-5393.

HAYNES, DR. ALPHONSO WORDEN
School administrator. **Personal:** Born in Brooklyn, NY; married Margaret S Alvarez; children: Thomas, Pia, Mia, Pilar, Alphonso III & Alejandro. **Educ:** Long Island Univ, BA, 1965; Columbia Univ, MS, 1967, MA, 1974, EdD, 1978. **Career:** Educator (retired); NY City Dept Welfare, admin & recreation, 1953-67; Harlem Hosp Ctr, pediatsocial worker, 1967-69; Long Island Univ, dean stud, 1969-79; Norfolk State Univ Sch Social Work, assoc prof & prog dir, 1979-81; Old Dominion Univ, stud affairs, asst dean; Grand Valley State Univ, prof, Sch social work, prof emer. **Orgs:** Nat Asn Soc Workers, 1967; Acad Cert Soc Workers, 1969; staff training consult, Chesapeake Soc Serv, 1979-80; bd mem, Young Adult & Campus Ministry, 1983; Admin, Va Asn Stud Personnel, 1981; Res Focus in Black Ed, 1980; bd mem, Columbia Univ Sch Social Work Alumni Asn. **Honors/Awds:** Pi Gamma Mu Soc Sci Hon Soc, 1962; Karagheusian Memorial Fel, Columbia Univ, 1965-67; Outstanding Educator In America. **Business Addr:** Professor Emeritus, Grand Valley State University, 1 Campus Dr, Allendale, MI 49401-9403.*

HAYNES, BARBARA ASCHE
Educator. **Personal:** Born Jun 26, 1935, Rochester, PA; married Donald F. **Educ:** Chatham Col, BS,NE, 1958; Univ Pittsburgh, MS, NE, 1967, PhD, 1984. **Career:** Educator (retired); Allegheny Gen Hosp Sch Nursing Pittsburgh, instrnursing, 1959-67; Allegheny Community Col, asst prof nursing, 1967-70,assoc prof & dept head, 1970-74, dean life sci & dir nursing prog,1974-79; Col DuPage, instr nursing, 1979-80; Univ Ill Chicago Co Nursing, asst prof gen nursing & dir stud serv. **Orgs:** Secy, Univ Pittsburgh Sch Nursing Alumnae Asn, 1967-69; bd dirs, Pa Nurses Asn 1973-77; chmn, nominating comn Univ Pittsburgh Sch Nursing Alumnae-Asn, 1974; bd dirs, United Ment Health Allegheny Co, 1975-79; prof adv comn, NW Allegheny Home Care Prog, 1976-79; vchmn, conf group teaching Pa Nurse's Asn, 1977-79; community nursing educ, Pa Nurses Asn, 1977-79; adv community, BSN Prog LaRoche Col, 1978-79; reg continuing educ adv comn, Duquesne Univ Group, 1978-79; speaker, Teachers Col Columbia Univ, 1972; speaker, Nat League Nursing-Coun Asn Degree Progs NY, 1974; Sigma Theta Tau Alpha Lambda Chapt. **Honors/Awds:** Chancellors Distinguished Public Service Award. **Special Achievements:** Pub "The Practical Nurse" & "Auto-Education" PA Nurse 1972. *

HAYNES, DR. BRIAN LEE
School administrator. **Personal:** Born Jul 20, 1964, Columbus, OH; son of Lewis Haynes and Sarah; married Jacquelyn Harris, Sep 4, 1999. **Educ:** Ohio State Univ, BA, hist, 1986; Ohio Univ, MS, health, PE, 1987, PhD, Higher Educ, 1991. **Career:** Ohio Univ, stud activities, asst dir, 1988-89, Health Careers Opportunity Prog, asst coordr, 1989-90, coordr minority stud serv, 1990-91; Gettysburg Col, asst dean, inter cultural adv, 1991-92; E Carolina Univ, asst vc stud life, 1992-99; State Univ Syst Fla, dir, student affairs, 1999-2000; FlaInt Univ, asst vpres stud affairs & state dir, 2000-05; Clayton State Univ, Morrow, GA, vpres, div stud affairs, 2006-. **Orgs:** Am Col Personnel Asn; Nat Asn Stud Personnel Adminr; Kappa Alpha Psi Fraternity. **Business Addr:** Vice President for Student Affairs, Clayton State University, Division of Student Affairs, 2000 Clayton State Blvd, Morrow, GA 30260.

HAYNES, CORNELL, JR. See NELLY.

HAYNES, FARNESE N (FARNESE NAOMI HAYNES)
Lawyer. **Personal:** Born Dec 25, 1960, Bluefield, WV; daughter of Jesse Sr and Melda. **Educ:** Am Univ, BA, 1983; Howard Univ Sch Law, JD, 1986. **Career:** Howard Law J, ed-in chief, 1984-86; Leftwich Moore & Douglas, staff atty, 1987; US Dept Agr, staff atty, 1987-93; United Negro Col Fund Inc, gen coun, 1993-. **Orgs:** Delta Sigma Theta Sorority Inc, 1980-; Ineffective Assistance Coun, 28, HOWLJ191, 1985; Supreme Ct PA, 1986; Penn Bar Asn, 1986-93; DC Bar Asn, 1988-; Dist Columbia Ct Appeals, 1988; Md Bar Asn, 1989-; Ct Appeals Md, 1989; US Dist Ct, Dist Md, 1989; J Franklin Bourne Bar Asn, 1990-92; Supreme Ct VA, 1995; US Supreme Ct, 1997; chair, Fundraising Comt; Nat Asn Advan Colored People. **Home Addr:** 11685 Newbridge Ct, Reston, VA 20191-3516, **Home Phone:** (703)620-6629. **Business Addr:** General Counsel, United Negro College Fund Inc, 8260 Willow Oaks Corp Dr, PO Box 10444, Fairfax, VA 22031-8044, **Business Phone:** (703)205-3400.

HAYNES, FARNESE NAOMI. See HAYNES, FARNESE N.

HAYNES, DR. JAMES H.
School administrator. **Personal:** Born Nov 27, 1953, Pensacola, FL; son of Jap and Annie Sims. **Educ:** Pensacola Jr Col, AA, 1973; Morehouse Col, BA, 1975; Ga State Univ, MEd, 1977; Univ Iowa, PhD, Educ Admin, 1979. **Career:** Atlanta Pub Sch Syst, teacher, 1975-77; Philadelphia Training Ctr, asst dir, 1979-80; Fla A&M Univ, dir planning, 1980-83; Morgan State Univ, dir inst res, 1983-84, adj prof educ leadership, 1983-, vpres, Planning & Instnl Res, 1984-88, title III dir, 1988-. **Orgs:** Woodrow Wilson Nat Fellowship Found, 1980; consult, Title III Prog Bowie State Col, 1984-; consult, Asn Minority Health Profession Sch 1982; supvr admin, NTE, GMAT 1984-; secy, Alpha Phi Alpha, Baltimore Morehouse Alumni Club; NAACP; Morehouse Col Nat Alumni Asn; bd dirs, Baltimore Employment Network. **Honors/Awds:** Hon mem, Promethean Kappa Tau; hon mem, Phi Delta Kappa; hon mem, Phi Alpha Theta; Governor's Citation, Baltimore community; Mayor's Citation, Baltimore City. **Home Addr:** 3239 Powhatan Ave, Baltimore, MD 21216. **Business Addr:** Title III Director, Morgan State University, 1700 Cold Spring Lane & Hillen Rd Room 305 D, Baltimore, MD 21251.

HAYNES, JOE A
Executive director. **Career:** Jobs Miss Graduates Inc, exec dir, 2001-. **Business Addr:** Executive Director, Jobs Miss Graduates Inc, 6055 Ridgewood Rd Suite A, Jackson, MS 39211, **Business Phone:** (601)978-1711.

HAYNES, DR. JOHN KERMIT
Educator. **Personal:** Born Oct 30, 1943, Monroe, LA; son of John Kermit Sr and Grace Quanita Ross; married Carolyn Ann Price, Aug 14, 1969. **Educ:** Morehouse Col, BS, biol, 1964; Brown Univ, PhD, develop biol, 1970. **Career:** Brown Univ, Providence, RI, Div Biol, NIH trainee & teaching asst, 1964-70, res fel, 1970-71, vis res prof, 1991-92, adj prof, 1993-2000; Mass Inst Technol, Cambridge, Dept Biol, res assoc & teaching asst, 1971-73; Meharry Med Col, Nashville, TN, asst prof, 1973-78; Morehouse Col, Atlanta, GA, assoc prof & dir off health professions, 1979-81, prof & dir off health professions, 1981-90, David Packard prof Sci & chmn, Dept Biol, 1985-2001, David Packard prof & dean div Sci & Math, 1999-; Clark Atlanta Univ, Atlanta, GA, adj prof, 1980-95; MDIBL, res scientist, 1994. **Orgs:** AAAS; Am Soc Cell Biol; Am Chem Soc; peer reviewer, Nat Sci Found; chmn, bd dir, Afro Arts Ctr, 1970-72; bd dir, Sickle Cell Found, Ga 1980-; bd trustees, Morehouse Col, 1984-87; GRE Biochem, Cell & Molecular Biol Comt Exam, 1989-92; Comn Undergrad Sci Educ; Nat Res Coun, 1994-; chairperson, Minor AFFs Comn; Am Soc Cell Biol, 1994-; Comn Adv Math & Sci Prog Am HighSchs, Nat Res Coun, 1999-; mem, Biol Directorate Adv Comt, NSF, 2006. **Honors/Awds:** David Packard Chair, Morehouse Col, 1985-; Distinguished African American Scientists of Twenteeth Century, 1996; Phi Beta Kappa, 1999. **Special Achievements:** Elected to the New York Academy of Science, 1979; Listed in American Men & Women of Science, 1985-; Listed in Who' Who Among America's Teachers, 1994-; Listed in Who's Who among Black Americans; Listed in Marquis' Who's Who in Science and Engineering; Biography published in Distinguished African American Scientist of the 20th Century, by J.H. Kessler et al., Orxy Press, Phoenix, AZ. **Business Addr:** David Packard Professor, Dean, Morehouse College, Department of Biology, 830 Westview Dr SW, 104 Nabrit-Mapp-McBay Sci Bldg, Atlanta, GA 30314, **Business Phone:** (404)215-2610.

HAYNES, DR. LEONARD L
Government official. **Personal:** Born Jan 26, 1947, Boston, MA; son of Leonard L Jr and Leila Davenport; married Mary Sensley, Aug 10, 1968; children: Leonard IV, Eboni Michelle, Bakari Ali, Jabari & Kenyatta. **Educ:** Southern Univ, Baton Rouge, LA, BA, 1968; Carnegie Mellon Univ, Pittsburgh, PA, MA, 1969; Ohio State Univ, Columbus, OH, PhD, 1975; Ohio State Univ, Hon Doctor Laws, 1990; Tougaloo Col, Hon DHL, 1990; Univ St Thomas, Hon Doctor Laws, 1990; Ala A&M Univ, Hon Doctor Laws, 1990; Stockton State Col, Hon Doctor Laws, 1991; Bridgewater Col, Hon Doctor Pub Admin, 1992. **Career:** Inst Serv Educ, Wash, DC, dir, desegregation unit, 1976-79; Nat Asn State/Land Grant Col, Wash, DC, dir, pub black cols, 1979-82; Southern Univ System, Baton Rouge, LA, exec vpres, 1982-85, prof hist, 1985-88; La Dept Educ, Baton Rouge, LA, asst supt, 1988-89; US Dept Educ, Wash, DC, asst secy, 1989-91; Brookings Inst, adj fac, 1991-92; US Info Agency, dir acad progs, 1992; sr consult & nat educ goals panel, 1993; Univ Md, vis scholar, 1994; Am Univ, sr asst pres, 1994; Fine Host Corp, Greenwich, CT, sr adv, 1995-97; Provost, prof, 1997-99; Grambling State Univ, Grambling, LA, acting pres, 1997-99; DC Pub Schs, sr adv supvr, 1999-2001; US Dept Educ, spec asst secy, 2001-03, Fund Improv Postsecondary Educ, dir, 2003-, White House Initiative on Historically Black Col & Univs, exec dir, 2007-. **Orgs:** Omega Psi Phi Frat, 1968-; Jack & Jill Inc, 1988. **Honors/Awds:** elected, Cosmos Club Wash, DC, Rotary Int Wash; Outstanding Educator Award, Omega Psi Phi Frat; Hist Makers, 2002. **Business Addr:** Executive Director, US Department of Education, Fund for the Improvement of Postsecondary Education, 1990 K St NW 6th Fl, Washington, DC 20006-8544, **Business Phone:** (202)502-7500.

HAYNES, MICHAEL DAVID
Football player. **Personal:** Born Dec 24, 1965, New Orleans, LA; married Cookie Oubre. **Educ:** Northern Ariz Univ. **Career:** Football player (retired); Atlanta Falcons, wide receiver, 1988-93, 1997; New Orleans Saints, 1994-96. **Special Achievements:** Led NFL in yards per reception in 1991 with 22.4.

HAYNES, MICHAEL E.
Government official, clergy. **Personal:** Born May 9, 1927, Boston, MA. **Educ:** Berkshire Christian Col; New Eng Sch Theol, ABM, 1949; Shelton Col. **Career:** Government official, Clergy (retired); Breezy Meadows Camp, prog dir, 1951-62; Robert Gould Shaw House, asst boys worker, 1953-58; Commonwealth MA Yth Serv Div, 1955-57; Norfolk House Ct, soc work staff, 1957-64; Commonwealth MA State Parole Bd, mem; 12th Baptist Church, sr minister, 1964-; House Reps 7th Suffolk Dist, mem, 1965-69. **Orgs:** Chmn, Metro Boston Settlement Asn, 1965-67; bd dir, New Eng Baptist Hosp; Citizen Training Group Boston Juv Ct; Cushing Acad; Gordon-Conwell Theol Sem ; Malone Col; Boys' Club Boston; Roxbury Clubhouse; Mayor's Comt Violence, 1976; New Boston Comt; City Boston Charitable Fund; chmn, gov adv comt State Chaplains; Ministerail Alliance Greater Boston; Gordon-Conwell Bd Trustees, 1976. **Honors/Awds:** "Five Minutes Before Midnight" Evang Missions, 1968; Recipient, LLD Gordon Col, 1969; Dr Pub Serv Barington Col, 1971; pub "Christian-Secular Coop" Urban Mission, 1974; DD Northeastern Univ, 1978; Intervarsity Press Champion, Urban Challenge, 1979; honorary Doctor of Divinity degree, Gordon Col.

HAYNES, PHILIP R
Engineer. **Personal:** Born Feb 25, 1946, Beckley, WV; son of James and Pearl. **Educ:** Devry, AEET, 1973; Ohio State Univ, 1973-75. **Career:** AT&T, programming staff mem, 1969-91; Alpha Protection Syst, electronic protection engr, 1991-; Alpha Funding, dir, 2004. **Orgs:** Nat Tech Asn, 1980-92; Main St Bus Asn, 1992-; MATAH, 1999-. **Business Addr:** President, Alpha Funding, 3000B E Main St Suite 183, Columbus, OH 43209, **Business Phone:** (614)492-9971.*

HAYNES, RICK. See HAYNES, ULRIC ST CLAIR.

HAYNES, SUE BLOOD
Writer, educational consultant, computer scientist. **Personal:** Born Mar 21, 1939, Pine Bluff, AR; married Joe Willis; children: Rodney & Joe B. **Educ:** Seattle Univ, BA, MA, 1974; The Union Inst, PhD, 1978; Bryn Mawr Col, mgt cert, 1979. **Career:** S Seattle Community Col, dir spl prog, 1974-; Seattle Univ, head couns, 1972-74; IBO Data Processing Co Inc, exec officer & owner, 1969-99; The Boeing Co, comput engr, 1965-95, Y2K mgr/consult, 1998-99; Seattle Cult & Ethnic Tours, chief exec officer, currently; Book: A Game of Marbles. **Orgs:** Bd dirs, Educ Talent Search, 1977-; bd dir, New Careers Found, 1978-; editorial bd, The Western Jour Black Studies, 1978-; Alpha Kappa Alpha 1977-; vice pres, bd dir, Coun Black Am Affairs, Western Region, 1978-79; chairperson, founder, The Inner-City Health Careers Proj-jack & Jill Am, 1978-79; vpres, The Union Inst Alumni Bd; WA Intl Bus Network pres, field reader, US Dept Education/Technology; NAACP; ex-sec, NW Black Chamber Commerce Bd, 1997. **Honors/Awds:** Community Service Award, Univ Chicago, 1974; Pub Sch Vol Award, Seattle Pub Sch, 1978; Martin Luther King Jr Memorial Award, Blanks Wooten Prod, 1980; Black Education Award, Western Regional Coun Black Am Affairs, 1980; Computer Design Award, Boeing Defense & Space Div, 1988. **Business Addr:** Chief Execuitve Officer, Seattle Cultural & Ethnic Tours, PO Box 80602, Seattle, WA 98108, **Business Phone:** (206)760-9199.

HAYNES, ULRIC ST CLAIR (RICK HAYNES)
School administrator. **Personal:** Born Jun 8, 1931, Brooklyn, NY; son of Ulric S Haynes Sr and Ellaline Gay; married Yolande Toussaint; children: Alexandra & Gregory. **Educ:** Amherst Col, BA, 1952; Yale Law Sch, JD, 1956; Harvard Bus Sch Advan Mgt Prog, 1966. **Career:** US Dept State, foreign serv officer, 1963-64; Nat Security Coun, staff, 1964-66; Mgt Formation Inc, pres, 1966-70; Spencer Stuart Asn, sr vpres, 1970-72; Cummins Engine Co, vpres mgt develop, 1972-75, vpres Mid-East & Africa, 1975-77; Am Embassy-Algeria, ambassador, 1977-81; Cummins Engine Co, vpres int bus planning, 1981-83; Self-Employed, consult, 1984-85; State Univ NY Col, Old Westbury, actg pres, 1985-86; AFS Int, Intercult Prog, pres, 1986-87; Drake Beam Morin, sr vpres, 1988-91; Hofstra Univ Sch Bus, dean, 1991-96, exec dean univ intl rels, 1996-2000, consult to pres, 2000-03; Rollins Col, adj prof, currently; Drew Univ, int recruiter, currently. **Orgs:** Coun Foreign Rel, 1968-; sel comt, Henry Luce Found Asian Scholars Prog, 1975-; bd dir, Am Broadcasting Co, 1981-84; Rohm & Haas Co, 1981-84; HSBC Bank USA, 1981-; Yale Club NY; chmn, Ind United Negro Col Fund Dr, 1981; bd mem, Environ Prod Corp,

1993-99; US Africa Airways, 1994-96; bd dir, Hemmeter Enterprises Inc, 1994-96; Grand Palais Casino Inc, 1994-96; bd dir, Pall Corp, 1994-; bd mem, Coun Am Ambassador; trustee, Deep Springs Col, 1998-2001; Reliastar Insurance Co NY, 1998-2003; NNCOM Int Inc, 1998-2003; Am Acad Dipl Coun, Am Ambassadors & Atlantic Coun US. **Honors/Awds:** Martin Luther King Humanitarian Award; New York City Martin Luther King Award, Black Christian Caucus Riverside Church; Resolutions of Commendation, Ind State Senate & Assembly, Calif State Senate, City Detroit & LA; Alumni Award, Class 1952; Liberty Bell Award, Ind Young Lawyers Asn; Freedom Award; Ind Black Expo, 1981; Certificate of Appreciation, US Dept State; Honorary LLD, Ind Univ; Honorary LLD, Ala State Univ; Honorary LLD, Fisk Univ; Honorary LLD, John Jay Col; Honorary LLD, Butler Univ & Mercy Col. **Special Achievements:** Member of a team of American diplomats who negotiated the release of the hostages in the American Embassy in Tehran, Iran, 1980-81. **Home Addr:** 2403 Timothy Lane, Kissimmee, FL 34743-3661. **Business Addr:** International Recruiter, Drew University, 36 Madison Ave, Madison, NJ 07940, **Business Phone:** (973)408-3739.

HAYNES, DR. WALTER WESLEY
Dentist. **Personal:** Born Nov 16, 1919, St Matthews, SC; children: Saundra & Donald. **Educ:** Lincoln Univ, AB, 1943; Howard Univ Col Dent, DDS, 1946. **Career:** Dentist (retired); 1st Presbyterian Church Hempstead, deacon, 1962-67; Queens Gen & Tribro Hosp, 1960-65; Hempstead Sch, dentist, 1962-93. **Orgs:** Pres, Queens Clin Soc, 1961-62; Ethical Dent Soc, 1975-77; Am Dent Asn; Nat Dent Asn; 10th Dist Dent Soc; Beta Kappa Chi; Omega Psi Phi. **Honors/Awds:** Man of the Year, Lincoln Univ, 1967; fel, Acad Gen Dent, 1984; Lincoln Univ Founders Day Award Outstanding Achievement, 1999. **Military Serv:** AUS, capt, 1946-48. *

HAYNES, WILLIAM J., JR.
Judge. **Personal:** Born Sep 5, 1949, Memphis, TN; son of William J Haynes and Martyna Q; married Carol Donaldson; children: Paz, Anthony, Maya. **Educ:** Col St Thomas, BA, 1970; Vanderbilt Sch Law, JD, 1973. **Career:** Tenn State Atty, Gen Off, asst atty gen, 1973-77; Tenn State Antitrust & Consumer Protection, dep atty gen, 1978-84, spec dep atty gen special litigation, 1984; Vanderbilt Sch Law, lecturer law, 1987-94; US Dist Ct Middle Dist Tenn, magistrate judge; US Govt, Ct US Dist, Dist Judge, currently. **Orgs:** Am Bar Asn, 1978, 1985, 1988-91; vchair, State Enforcement Comt, Antitrust Section; vpres Nashville Bar Asn, 1980-84; dist atty gen, pro tem Shelby Cty Criminal Ct, 1980; Rotary Int, 1980-90; mem bd dir, Cumberland Museum & Sci Ctr, 1981-87; mem bd prof, esponsibility Tenn Supreme Ct, 1982-84; mem bd dir, Napier Lobby Bar Asn, 1983-84; chmn, antitrust planning comn Nat Asn Atty Gen, 1984; bd adv, Corporate Practice Series, Bureau Nat Affairs, 1989-90. **Honors/Awds:** Bennett Douglas Bell Award, Vanderbilt Sch Law, 1973; Black History Month Award, 1990. **Special Achievements:** Books: State Antitrust Laws, Bureau Nat Affairs, 1988; Fed Exec Asn; The Legal Aspects of Selling & Buying, Shepard's McGraw Hill, 1991. *

HAYNES, WILLIE C., III
School administrator, government official. **Personal:** Born Nov 23, 1951, Opelousas, LA; son of Willie Jr and Watkins Lillie; married Rebecca M Smith; children: Markisha A & Willie C IV. **Educ:** Southern Univ, Baton Rouge, BA, 1973, MA, educ, 1976. **Career:** Clark Lodge No 186, jr deacon, 1975-88; Melville High Sch, asst prin, 1982-88; St Landry Parish Police Jury, Dist 5 juror, 1988-91; Melville Elem Sch, prin, 2009. **Orgs:** Nat Asn Advan Colored People, 1981-88; Gov Coun Phys Fitness & Sports, 1984-87; Acidiana Principal's Asn, 1984-88; mem bd dirs, St Landry Parish Coun Aging, 1985-88. **Business Addr:** Principal, Melville Elementary School, PO Box 485, Melville, LA 71353.*

HAYNES, DR. WORTH EDWARD
School administrator. **Personal:** Born Apr 20, 1942, Webb, MS; son of Shellie (deceased) and Annie Mae; married Linden C Smith; children: Natasha C & Worth Edward. **Educ:** Alcorn State Univ Lorman MS, BS, 1965; Wis State Univ River Falls, MST, 1971; Iowa State Univ Am, PhD, 1977. **Career:** Alcorn St Univ, youth camp dir, 1964; Eva H Harris HS Brookhaven Miss, teacher vocational agr, 1964-69; Hinds Co AHS Utica, teacher vocational agr, 1969-72; Utica Jr Col, dir vocational tech educ, 1972-74; Iowa St Univ Ames, instr agr educ dept, 1974-76, grad student adv, 1976-77; UticaJr Col, dir vocational-tech educ, 1977-; Governors Off Job Develop & Training, exec dir, 1985-86; Div Indust Serv & Fed Prog, ast st dir; Off Vocational Tech & Adult Educ, Bureau Bus & Com & Technol, dir; Miss Dept Educ, Bureau Vocational Community Develop, dir. **Orgs:** Pres, Utica Comm Develop Assoc, 1978-80; pres, Post Sec Voc Dirs Asn, Missi, 1979; chmn, Post Sec St Evaluation Comn Voc Educ Missi, 1980; deacon, vpres, laymen asn; New Hope Bapt Church, Jackson, Miss; Sunday sch teacher New Hope Church; pres, Koahoama County Incubator, Clarksdale, Miss; state leader, State Baptist Asn, 1990. **Honors/Awds:** Outstanding Teacher Award, Miss Econ Devel Council Eva Harris High Sch, Brookhaven, Miss, 1967-69; Man of the Year Award, Alpha Phi Alpha FratNatchez, Miss, 1972; Achievement Award, Gamma Sigma Delta Honor Soc Agr Ames, Iowa, 1976; Outstanding Contributions Agr Educ Iowa, Vocational Educ Asn Ames, 1976; Outstanding Serv, Utica Jr Col, 1984; Outstanding Contribution Econ Develop, Gulf Coast Bus Serv Corp, 1986. **Business Addr:** Director, Mississippi Department of Education, 500 High St, Jackson, MS 39205, **Business Phone:** (601)359-5743.*

HAYSBERT, DENNIS DEXTER
Actor. **Personal:** Born Jun 2, 1954, San Mateo, CA; son of Charles Sr and Gladys Minor; married Lynn Griffith (divorced 2001); children: Charles & Katharine; married Elena Simms, Apr 13, 1980 (divorced 1984). **Educ:** Am Col Dramatic Arts, Pasadena, Calif; Col San Mateo; Am Acad Dramatic Arts. **Career:** Films: Major League, 1989; Navy Seals, 1990; Mr Baseball, 1992; Love-Field, 1992; Suture, 1993; Major League II, 1994; Heat, 1995; Waiting to Exhale, 1995; Amanda, 1996; Insomnia, 1996; Absolute Power, 1997; Major League: Back to the Minors, 1998; How to Make the Cruelest Month, 1998; Standoff, 1998; The Thirteenth Floor, 1999; The Minus Man, 1999; Random Hearts, 1999; Love & Basketball, 2000; What's Cooking?, 2000; Ticker, 2002; Far From Heaven, 2002; Sinbad: Legend of the Seven Seas (voice), 2003; Splinter Cell: Pandora Tomorrow, 2004; Call of Duty: Finest Hour, 2004; Jarhead, 2005; Splinter Cell: Double Agent, 2006; Breach, 2007; Goodbye Bafana, 2007; Cessation, 2008; TV series: "The White Shadow", 1979; "Buck Rogers in the 25th Century", 1980-81; "Code Red", 1981; Grambling's White Tiger, 1981; The Return of Marcus Welby, M.D., 1984; Growing Pains, 1985-88; "Wilder Westen, inclusive", 1988; "Just the Ten of Us", 1988-89; "K-9000", 1991; "Queen", 1993; "Return to Lonesome Dove", 1993; "Halleluja", 1993; "Widow's Kiss", 1996; "The Writing on the Wall", 1996; "Just the Ten of Us", 1988-89; "Now & Again", 1999-2000; "Static Shock", 2001-03; Justice League, 2001-03; 24, 2001-06; "Secrets of Pearl Harbor", 2004; Empire, 2005; "The Unit", 2006-08. **Orgs:** NETDAY. **Honors/Awds:** Golden Globe Award nomination, Actor in a Supporting Role in a Series, 24, 2003; Black Reel Theatrical Award for Best Supporting Actor, 2003; Golden Satellite Award for Best Performance by an Actor in a Supporting Role, 2003; Saturn Award, 2000; Black Reels Award, 2003. **Business Addr:** Actor, c/o Paradigm Talent Agency, 36 N Cresent Dr, Beverly Hills, CA 90210.*

HAYSBERT, RAYMOND VICTOR
Executive. **Personal:** Born Jan 19, 1920, Cincinnati, OH; son of William D and Emma; married Carol Evelyn Roberts, Dec 25, 1945; children: Raymond V Jr, Reginald, Nikita M & Brian R. **Educ:** Univ Cincinnati, BSME, 1945; Wilberforce Univ, BS, math, 1948; Cent State Univ Ohio, BS, bus admin, 1949; Univ Md, DPS, 1984; Sojourner Douglass Col, attended 1996. **Career:** Cincinnati City, boiler oper, 1941-42; Cent State Univ, instr, 1947-52;Parks Sausage Co, gen mgr, exec vpres, 1952-74, pres, 1974-; dir, Equitable Ban corp, 1971-90; dir, S Baltimore Gen Hosp, 1973-84; dir, C & P Telephone Co, 1975-85; dir, Richmond Dist Fed Res Bank, 1984-; dir, Bell Atlantic Corp, 1985-; Forum Caterers, pres & chief exec officer, currently. **Orgs:** Pres, The Hub Orgn, 1979-84; Presidents Round table 1983-; trustee, Univ Md Med Syst, 1984-; chmn, Oper Heartbeat; chmn, Baltimore Urban League;Greater Baltimore Black Chamber Com. **Honors/Awds:** Man of Year, Baltimore Bus League, 1968; Man of Year, Baltimore Mkt Asn,1971; Distinguished Citizen, Square Compass Club, 1973; Irving Blum Award,United Way Cent Md; Honorary Doctor Public Service, Univ Md; Baltimore Business Hall of Fame, Jr Achievement Metrop Baltimore, 1986; Business Executive of the Year, Baltimore Mag, 1988. **Military Serv:** USAF; Tuskegee Airman; Civilian Aide to Sec of Army 6 yrs; various awdars, 1981. **Business Addr:** President, Chief Executive Officer, Forum Caterers Inc, 4210 Primrose Ave, Baltimore, MD 21215.

HAYWARD, ANN STEWART
Television producer, television director, writer. **Personal:** Born Aug 23, 1944, Philadelphia, PA. **Educ:** Simmons Col, AB, 1966; NY Univ, grad, 1970; Am Film Inst, Directing Workshop Women, attended 1978; Stanford Univ, prof jour Knight fel, 1979. **Career:** ABC TV Network, dir res, 1972-73, News Doc Div, assoc producer, producer, dir & writer; KPIX TV, Westinghouse Broadcasting Co, video producer, 1979-80; Group Visionary Prod Inc, writer, reporter & producer, 1980. **Orgs:** Dirs Guild Am; Guild Am.

HAYWARD, GARLAND, SR.
Commissioner, government official. **Career:** Princess Anne Town Commissioners Off, town comnr, vpres, currently. **Business Addr:** Vice president, Princess Anne Town Commissioners Office, 30489 Broad St, Princess Anne, MD 21853-1243, **Business Phone:** (410)651-1818.*

HAYWARD, DR. JACQUELINE C
Journalist, television news anchorperson. **Personal:** Born Oct 23, 1944, East Orange, NJ; married Sidney G. **Educ:** Howard Univ, BA 1966. **Career:** WTOP TV 9, anchorwoman; WAGA TV 5, 1970-72; V Mayor's Ofc, asst to vmayor 1970; City Miami, dir training 1969-70; W*USA 9 NEWS NOW, anchor, currently, vpres, media outreach, 2006-; Documentaries: Sahel: The Border of Hell; Somalia: The Silent Tragedy; We Shall Return. **Orgs:** Delta Sigma Theta Sor; Nat Coun Negro Women; Nat Bus & Prof Women; bd mem, Nat Asn Advan Colored People; Nat Asn Social Workers; past vpres, Boys & Girls Club Greater Wash; Summer Opera Theatre Co; United Black Fund; Montgomery County, Maryland's Hospice Caring. **Honors/Awds:** Women of the 70's Capitol Press Club; Honorary Doctorate, Howard Univ, 1985; Outstanding Woman, Am Asn Univ Women; Woman of Achievement, Nat Multiple Sclerosis Soc; Publishing Citizen of the Year, Kiwanis Club, Toastmasters Club; Emmy Award, 1994; Board of Governors Award, 1995; Washingtonian of the Year, Washingtonian Mag; Dr Edward C Mazique Memorial Award, 1995. **Special Achievements:** The first female in the Wash market to anchor a newscast. **Business Phone:** (202)895-5999.

HAYWARD, OLGA LORETTA HINES
Librarian. **Personal:** Born in Alexandria, LA; daughter of Lillie Florence George Hines and Samuel James Hines; married Samuel E Hayward Jr (deceased); children: Anne Elizabeth & Olga Patricia Hayward Ryer. **Educ:** Dillard Univ, BA, 1941; Atlanta Univ, BS, libr sci, 1944; Univ Mich, MA, libr sci, 1959; La State Univ, MA, Hist, 1977; La State Univ, further study. **Career:** Librarian (retired); Marksville, La, High Sch, teacher, 1941-42; Grambling Col, head librn, 1944-46; New Orleans Pub Libr, librn, 1947-48; Southern Univ Baton Rouge, head ref dept, 1948-74, collection develop librn, 1984-86, head ref dept, 1986-88; Southern Univ, head bus & social sci collections ref dept, 1974-84. **Orgs:** Episcopal Social Serv Community La Episcopal Diocese, 1972-79; banquet community mem, Baton Rouge Conf Christians & Jews, 1982; vice chair, 1985-86, chair, 1986-87, La Libr Assoc Subject Specialists Sect; steering comt, LA Community Develop Libr, 1987-89; secy, treas, vpres, pres, La Chap Special Libraries Asn. **Honors/Awds:** Lucy B Foote Award, Subject Specialists Sect, La Libr Asn, 1990; Roll of Honor Award, La Southern Miss Chap, Spec Libraries Asn, 1995. **Special Achievements:** Introduced and taught the first teacher-librarian courses at Grambling Col, 1945; participated in forming LA Certification standards for teacher-librarians, 1945; First black employed in New Orleans Public Library System as a Branch Libraries, 1947; Publications: "Annotated Bibliography of Works By and About Whitney M Young" Bulletin of Bibliography July/Aug 1974; "Spotlight on Special Libraries in LA" LA Library Asn Bulletin 41 Summer 1979. **Home Addr:** 1632 Harding Blvd, Baton Rouge, LA 70807.

HAYWOOD, DWAYNE A.
Government official. **Career:** City Detroit, Dept Human Serv, exec dir, Bur Community Action & Econ Opportunity, dir; Dept Human Serv, Dir, Currently. **Business Addr:** Director, Bureau of Community Action & Economic Opportunity, Department of Human Services, 235 S Grand Ave Suite 1314, PO Box 30037, Lansing, MI 48909, **Business Phone:** (517)241-7911.

HAYWOOD, GAR ANTHONY
Writer. **Personal:** Born May 22, 1954, Hollywood, CA; son of Jack and Barbara Haywood; married Lynnette, Dec 5, 1981 (divorced); children: Courtney, Erin. **Career:** Comput maintenance technician, 1970-90; Bell Atlantic, field engr, 1976; detective fiction writer, 1987-; television script writer, 1998-; Novelist, writer, currently. **Orgs:** Mystery Writers Am, 1989; Pvt Eye Writers Am, 1988; American Crime Writers League, 1989. **Honors/Awds:** Best First Private Eye Novel, Pvt Eye Writers Am, 1988, "Fear of the Dark"; Shamus Award, Pvt Eye Writers Am, Best First Novel, 1988. **Business Addr:** Author, c/o GP Putnam's Sons, 200 Madison Ave, New York, NY 10016.*

HAYWOOD, GEORGE WEAVER
Executive. **Personal:** Born Sep 30, 1952, Washington, DC; son of John Wilfred Jr and Marie Weaver; married Cheryl Lynn Jenkins, Mar 28, 1987; children: Allison Marie. **Educ:** Harvard col, AB, 1974, Harvard Law Sch, 1979. **Career:** Lehman Brothers inc, assoc, 1982-84, vpres, 1984-86, sr vpres, 1986-88, exec vpres, 1988-91, managing dir, bond trader, 1991-94; Moore Capital Mgt, dir, 1994-98; pvt investor, 1998-; XM radio, bd dir, 2004-. **Orgs:** Bd trustees, Brooklyn Poly Prep Sch, 1992-; bd dirs, Advan Bionutrition; bd dirs, PingTones; bd trustees, New School Univ. **Business Addr:** Board of Directors, XM Satellite Radio Inc, 1500 Eckington Place NE, Washington, DC 20002, **Business Phone:** (202)380-4000.

HAYWOOD, HIRAM H., JR.
Clergy, naval officer. **Personal:** Born Jan 8, 1921, Key West, FL; married Charlean Peters; children: Hiram III, Yolanda, Yvonne. **Career:** Catholic Archdiocese Wash, permanent deacon, assigned Basilica Nat Shrine Immaculate Conception, Nat Catholic Church, currently. **Orgs:** Knights of Columbus 4th deg. **Honors/Awds:** Fed Superior Accomplishment Awards, 1960 1972. **Military Serv:** US Naval Gun Factory Washington & Naval Ordnance Sta Indian Head MD, 32 yrs; USAAF, cadet & sergeant, 1943-46. **Business Addr:** Deacon, Basilica Nat Shrine Immaculate Conception, National Catholic Church, 400 Mich Ave NE, Washington, DC 20001.*

HAYWOOD, DR. L. JULIAN
Educator, physician. **Personal:** Born in Reidsville, NC; son of Thomas W Haywood Sr and Louise V Hayley Haywood; married Virginia Elizabeth Paige; children: Julian Anthony. **Educ:** Hampton Inst, BS, 1948; Howard Univ, MD, 1952. **Career:** Univ Southern Calif, asst prof, 1963-67, LAC/Univ Southern Calif Med

Ctr,dir, CCU, 1966-, assoc prof, 1967-76, sr physician, Comprehensive Sickle Cell Ctr, dir, 1972, Keck Sch Med, prof med, 1976-; Loma Linda Univ, clin,prof med, 1978-; ECG, Dir, 1996-. **Orgs:** AAAS, 1957-; fel, Am Col Cardiol, 1968-; consult, Martin Luther King Jr.Hosp, 1970-; pres, Sickle Cell Dis Res Found, 1978-89; gov comt, Am Col Physics, 1981-; past pres, AHA/Greater Los Angeles Aff, 1983; Am Heart Assoc, 1983-; fel Med Div, 1990-; pres, Asn Physicians LA County Hosp,1991-2006; consult, Calif State Dept Health Hypertension Ctrl Prog-;consult, NHLBI; counr, Asn Acad Minority Physicians, pres elect, 1992-93,pres, 1993-94; Armed Forces Epidemiology Bd, 1996-; HCT Div PHS; pres,Salerni Colegium, USC, 1997-98; pres, Asn Physicians Los Angeles City Hosp, 1997-; prog coordr, Steering Comt, 1997-99; Alpha Omega Alpha; Asn Black Cardiologists. **Honors/Awds:** Certificate of Merit, City Los Angeles, 1982; Certificate of recognition,Nat Med Asn, 1982; News maker of the Year, Nat Asn Med Women, 1982;Distinguished Alumni, Howard Univ 1982; District Service Award, Am Heart Asn /GLAA, 1984; Honoree, Int Med Sect, 1988; Louis Russell Award, Am Heart Asn, 1988; Heart of Gold Award, Am Heart Asn, 1989; Award of Merit,Am Heart Asn, 1991; Outstanding Alumnus-at-Large, Hampton Univ, 1993; Laurente Award, Am Col Physicians, CA Region 1, 1997; Past PresidentsRecognition Award, USC Salerni Collegium, 1999; Best of the Best inMedicine plaque, Black Enterprise, 2001; Certificate of Appreciation,Armed Forces Epidemiology Bd, 2001; Distinguished Service Award, 2001,Certificate of Merit, 2003, Am Col Cardiol; Distinguished Health Educator,Howard Univ Sch Med, 2003. **Special Achievements:** Over 500 sci papers & abstr. **Military Serv:** USN, lt, 1954-56. **Business Addr:** Professor of Medicine, University of Southern California Keck School of Medicine, 1937 Hosp Pl, GNH 8350 9319, Los Angeles, CA 90031, **Business Phone:** (323)226-7116.

HAYWOOD, NORCELL D.
Executive, architect. **Personal:** Born Jan 23, 1935, Bastrop, TX; children: Natalie Dawn, Nan Deliah, David Norcell. **Educ:** Prairie View A&M Col, 1955; Univ Tex, BA, 1960. **Career:** Prarie View A&M Col, instr sch eng, 1960-61; planning dept, 1961; Eugene Wukasch, architect eng TX, 1961-63; O'Neil Ford & Assoc San Antonio, 1963-68; Norcell D Haywood & Assoc San Antonio, 1968-72; Haywood Jordan Mc Cowan SAT Inc, pres, 1972-. **Orgs:** Am Inst Architects; TX Soc Architects; San Antonio Chap Am Inst Architects; Construct Specif Inst; past pres, Minority Architects Inc Tex & LA M Arch, 1971-73; bd dir, San Antonio BRC; life mem, Alpha Phi Alpha; BBB San Antonio Inc; bd prof, FREE; bd dir, Met YMCA; bd dir, Mid Am Region YMCA; sec Nat Org Min Architects; bd dir, Healy Murphy Learning Ctr; Alamo Area Coun Govt Regional Develop & Rev Com; bd dir, Nat Coun YMCA; Univ of TX Schl of Architecture Dean's Coun; bd dir, San Antonio Bus Resource Ctr; coach bd dir, San Antonio Symphony Soc; chmn, Alamo City C of C; life mem, Univ Tex, Univ Develop Bd. **Honors/Awds:** Merit Award, second Bapt Ch San Antonio Am Inst Architects Design Award Prog San Antonio Chap, 1968; Cert commendation Houston Munic Art Commn, 1973-74. **Business Addr:** President, Architect, Haywood Jordan McCowan SAT Inc, 1221 S Ww White Rd, PO Box 20378, San Antonio, TX 78220-3425, **Business Phone:** (210)337-5250.*

HAYWOOD, ROOSEVELT V., III
Chief executive officer, president (organization). **Personal:** Born Feb 6, 1929, Mount Bayou, MS; married Adel; children: 6. **Educ:** Ind Univ, attended 1973. **Career:** Haywood Ins Agency, owner; Haywood & Fleming Assocs Inc, pres & chief execofficer, 1984-. **Orgs:** City Counman, Large Gary; state chmn, Fair Share Orgn; pres, United Coun Midtown Businessmen; founder & pres, Gary's Midtown Voters League;mem adv bd, Gary Urban League; vpres, Gary Nat Asn Advan Colored People;co-founder & pres, Gary Toastmasters; nat mem trustee, Pilgrim Baptist Church. **Honors/Awds:** President's Award, Ind Univ Alumni Asn. **Business Addr:** President, Chief Executive Officer, Haywood & Fleming Assocs Inc, 650 S Lake St, Gary, IN 46403, **Business Phone:** (219)938-5025.

HAYWOOD, SPENCER
Businessperson, basketball player. **Personal:** Born Apr 22, 1949, Silver City, MS; married Iman (divorced 1987); children: Zulekha; married Linda, Nov 30, 1990; children: Nikiah, Shaakira & Isis. **Educ:** Trinidad Jr Col, attended 1967; Univ Detroit. **Career:** Basketball player (retired), business person, motivational speaker; Denver Rockets, 1969-70; Seattle Super Sonics, 1971-75; NY Knicks, 1976-79; Los Angeles Lakers, 1980; European League, Italy, 1981-82; Wash Bullets, 1982-83; Spencer Haywood LLC, owner, currently; PD Entertainment, speaker. **Honors/Awds:** Olympic gold medalist, 1968; NBA All-Star Team, 1972-75; Championship Ring, Lakers, 1979-80; Denver Rookie of the Year, Leading Scorer & Rebounder, MVP; All-Star Game MVP; Sonics, Four-Time First Team, All-Pro. **Special Achievements:** Has developed videotape to aid in the recovery of substance abusers; wrote his autobiography, Spencer Haywood: The Rise, the Fall, the Recovery. **Business Addr:** Motivational Speaker, PD Entertainment, 3225 Johnson Ave Suite 5F, Bronx, NY 10463, **Business Phone:** (718)543-2042.

HAYWOODE, M. DOUGLAS
Lawyer, educator. **Personal:** Born Feb 24, 1938, Brooklyn; divorced; children: Alyssa, Arthur, Helene, Drake, Phillip & Edward. **Educ:** Brooklyn Col, BA, 1959; Brooklyn Law Sch, JD, 1962, LLM, 1967; New Sch Social Res, MA, 1970; PhD. **Career:** NY City Br Nat Asn Advan Colored People, coun, 1962-64; City NY, prof Polit Sci, 1969; Human Resources Admin NYC, assoc gen coun, 1972-74; Pvt Pract Law, currently. **Orgs:** NY City Bar Asn; Nat Conf Black Lawyers; Am Soc Int Law; Int African Ctr; dir, Enterprise 9 Investigation Agency. **Honors/Awds:** Governor personal Appointee, NY Housing Corp. **Business Addr:** Lawyer, Private Practice Law, 71 Maple St, Brooklyn, NY 11225.*

HAZEL, DARRYL B.
President (Organization). **Educ:** Wesleyan Univ, BA, econs; Northwestern Univ, MA, econs. **Career:** N Am Automotive Opers Mkt, mkt prog, strategy mgr, educ & training mgr & mkt res dir; N Am Car Prod Develop, bus planning mgr; Lincoln Mercury Mkt, analyst, mkt mgr, bus mgr, field mgr & pres mkt, 1972-05; Ford Div, gen mkt mgr, 1997; Ford Customer Serv Div, exec dir, 1999; Global Mkt Serv, 2005; Ford Motor Co, sr vpres, 2006-; Ford Customer Serv Div, named pres, 2006-. **Orgs:** Think Detroit Police Athletic League; Alliant Energy; Oakland Family Serv; Congressional Black Caucus Found. **Honors/Awds:** Edward Davis African American Executive of the Year, On Wheels Inc, 2003. **Business Addr:** Senior Vice President, Ford Motor Company, 16800 Exec Pl Dr, PO Box 6248, Dearborn, MI 48126, **Business Phone:** 800-392-3673.*

HAZEL, JANIS D
Executive. **Personal:** Born Jan 19, 1963, Detroit, MI; daughter of Charlie H and Gladys D. **Educ:** Univ Mich, BA, polit sci, 1985; L'Inst de Touraine, Tours France, Intensive French Lang Prog, 1985. **Career:** Cong Black Caucus Found Inc, intern, 1982; US Dept Transp, policy planning intern, 1983; Senator Donald W Riegle Jr, legis aide, 1985-87; Bldg Owners & Mngs Assn Int, legis rep, 1987-89; Cong John Conyers Jr, legis dir, 1989-91; Asn Am Pub TV Stas, mgr advocacy progs, 1991-. **Orgs:** Alpha Kappa Alpha Sorority, 1982-; secy, Pacifica Found, bd dir, 1988-; chmn adv bd, WPFW FM Radio, 1989-94; Nat Black Prog Consortium, 1991-95; Nat Black Media Coalition, 1991-95; Am Women Radio & TV, 1991-; Am Soc Asn Execs, 1992-; Women Govt Rels, 1994-; Telecommunications Policy Roundtable, 1995. **Special Achievements:** Proficient in Fr; Exec producer, Cong Black Caucus Found Inc, legis conf Jazz Issues Forum & Performance, 1989-94. **Business Addr:** Manager, Association of Public Television Stations, 2100 Crystal Dr Suite 700, Arlington, VA 22202, **Business Phone:** (202)887-8413.

HAZELWOOD, HON. HARRY, JR.
Judge, president (organization). **Personal:** Born Oct 8, 1921, Newark; married Ruth Gainous; children: Harry & Stephen. **Educ:** Rutgers Univ, BA, 1943; Cornell Law Sch, LLB, 1945. **Career:** Retired: Atty, 1948; Co Prosecutor, asst, 1956-58; City Newark, municipal judge, 1958-74; City Newark, chief judge, 1970-74; Essex Co Ct, judge,1974-79; Essex Co, super ct judge. **Orgs:** Am Essex Co NJ; Nat Bar Assn; pres, Nat Assn Advan Colored People, 1950. **Special Achievements:** First African-American Judge appointed to the Newark Municipal Court. *

HAZZARD, DR. TERRY LOUIS
School administrator. **Personal:** Born Jul 8, 1957, Mobile, AL; son of Milton and Ora D Sheffield; married Tanya Finkley, Jun 27, 1981; children: Jared Finkley Hazzard. **Educ:** Ala A&M Univ, BS, 1979; Univ Ala, MA, 1980; Fla State Univ, EDS, 1991, Fla State Univ, EdD, 1996. **Career:** Univ Ala, financial aid peer counr, 1979-80, residence hall asst dir, 1980, coord/coop educ, 1980-81; Spring Hill Col, counr/upward bound, 1981-85; Bishop State Community Col, asst dean stud, 1985-91, dean stud, currently. **Orgs:** Alpha Phi Alpha Fraternity; Nat Asn Stud Personal Administrators; Choir Greater Mt Olive #2 Baptist Church; local Performer; vocalist Mobile Opera; Ala Asn Guidance/Counseling; Ala Asn Deans Students. **Special Achievements:** Appeared in movie Under Siege; vocalist, Miss USA Pagent, 1989. publications in the Eric System, "Attitudes of White Students Attending Black Colleges and Universities," 1989, "Affirmative Action and Women in Higher Education," 1989; Vocalist, Governor's Inauguration, Alabama; Publications: Sexual Harrassment: What's Good for the Goose is Good for the Gander; Eric System, 1989. **Home Addr:** 6322 Hillcrest Oaks Dr, Mobile, AL 36693. **Business Addr:** Dean of Students, Bishop State Community College, 351 N Broad St, Mobile, AL 36603-5898, **Business Phone:** (251)405-7089.

HAZZARD, WALTER R., JR. (MAHDI ABDUL RAHMAN)
Basketball coach, basketball player, executive. **Personal:** Born Apr 15, 1942, Wilmington, DE; son of Dr Walter R Hazzard Sr and Alexina Sara Ayers; married Jaleesa Patricia Shepherd; children: Yakub, Jalal, Khalil & Rasheed. **Educ:** Univ Calif, Los Angeles, BS, 1964. **Career:** Basketball player, Basketball coach (retired), Executive; Los Angeles Lakers 1964-67; Seattle Super Sonics 1967-68; Atlanta Hawks 1968-71; Buffalo Braves 1971-73; Golden State Warriors 1972-73; Univ Calif, Los Angeles, head basketball coach, 1984-88, staff associate to the vice-chancellor, 1989; Los Angeles Sports Academy, pres & co-founder,currently. **Orgs:** X-NBA Players Asn; Kappa Alpha Psi Frat; 100 Black Men of Los Angeles. **Honors/Awds:** Coach of 1985 Natl Invitation Tournament championship team; NCAA Player of the Year, 1964; NCAA Tournament Most Outstanding Player, 1964; Pacific Ten Conference Coach of the Year; Father of the Year; Athletes & Entertainers for Kids; Gold Medal, Olympic Basketball Team; Athletic Hall of Fame, UCLA, UCLA Bruins Basketball 1963-64 NCAA Champions, NCAA Men's Division I Basketball Tournament Most Outstanding Player, 1964. **Home Addr:** 1722 S Virginia Rd, Los Angeles, CA 90019, **Home Phone:** (323)735-8356.

HEACOCK, DON ROLAND
Psychiatrist, educator. **Personal:** Born Jun 2, 1928, Springfield, MA; son of Roland T and Lucile LaCour; married Celia Arce; children: Stephan, Roland & Maria. **Educ:** Colby Col, BA, 1949; Howard Univ Col Med, MD, 1954. **Career:** Knickerbocker Hosp, dir, Dept Psychiat, 1970-72; Bronx Psychiat Ctr, diradolescent serv, 1975-79; Mt Sinai Sch Med, Dept Psychiat, clin asst prof psychiat. **Orgs:** Life fel, Am Psychiat Asn; NY Dist Br Am Psychol Asn; NY State Med Asn;life fel, Am Ortho Psychiat Asn; NY Coun Child Psychiat; Am Acad Child Psychiat. **Honors/Awds:** Diplomate Am Bd Psychiat & Neurology 1962; diplomate, Am Bd Child Psychiat, 1965. **Special Achievements:** Ed: A Psyco dynamic Approach to Adolescent Psychiatry, 1980; auth: Black Slum Child Problem of Aggression, 1977; article: Suicidal Behavior in Black and Hispanic Adolescents, Psychiatric Annels, 1990; chapter on Group Therapy with Adolescents by Paul Kymissis. **Military Serv:** AUS, capt, 1956-58. **Business Addr:** Assistant Clinical Professor, Mount Sinai Hospital, 1 Gustave L Levy Pl, PO Box 1230, New York, NY 10029.

HEAD, DENA
Basketball player. **Personal:** Born Aug 16, 1970; daughter of James. **Educ:** Univ Tenn, sports mgt, 1992; Baker Col. **Career:** Basketball player (retired), Ancona, Italy, guard, 1992-94; DKSK, Hungary, 1994-95; Mirande, France,1996-97; Utah Starzz, 1997; Cent Conn State Athletics, asst coach, 2001-; Blue Devils, develop guard & recruiting coordr. **Honors/Awds:** National Championships; The Southeastern Conference Player of the Yr;women's college basketball championship, 1998, 1999; SEC Freshman of the Yr, 1989; AFLAC Assistant Coach of the Yr. **Business Addr:** Assistant Coach, Recruiting coordinator, Cent Conn State Athletics Women's Basketball, 1615 Stanley St, New Britain, CT 06050, **Business Phone:** (860)832-2278.*

HEAD, EDITH
Government official. **Personal:** Born Nov 16, 1927, Autaugaville, AL; married Toysie Lee Head; children: Alberta, Patricia A, Timothy L, Robert W. **Educ:** Wilkins Cosmetology Sch, 1955; Market Training Inst, grad, 1968; Cuyahoga Community Col. **Career:** Clinic Inn Motel, desk clerk, 1969-72; E Cleveland Pub Libr, front off aide, 1972-74; Villa Angela Sch, media aide, 1974-75; City E Cleveland, cmser, 1978-; St James Luthern Church, Hunger Ctr, volunteer, Grand Parents Support Group, pres, currently. **Orgs:** Pres, Orinoco St Club, 1968-82; pres, Community Action Team, 1975; Cuyahoga Democ Party, 1975-; Nat League Cities, 1978-; Ohio Munic League, 1978-; pres, Comn E Cleveland Black Women, 1983-; Omega Baptist Church, correspondance secy, sr usher bd; Helen S Brown Sr Citizens Ctr, choir, sightseers club; Mother's bd, Omega Baptist Church, 2000-. **Honors/Awds:** Honorary Citizen City of Atlanta, 1979; Special Recognition, ECCJC E Cleveland, 1980; Certificate of Appreciation, City E Cleveland, 1984; Outstanding Work, Citizens E Cleveland, 1982; Volunteer of the Year, St James Lutheran Church, Hunger Ctr. **Home Addr:** 12409 Signet Ave, Cleveland, OH 44120. **Business Addr:** President, The Grand Parents Support Group, St James Lutheran Church, 1424 Hayden Ave, East Cleveland, OH 44112.*

HEAD, HELAINE
Television director, stage manager. **Personal:** Born Jan 17, 1947, Los Angeles, CA. **Educ:** Univ San Francisco, BA, 1968. **Career:** Am Conserv Theatre, stage mgr; Univ Southern Calif, Sch Cinema-TV, assoc prof, currently; Broadway prod, Porgy and Bess, The Royal Family, Raisin', Ain't Supposed to Die a Natural Death, prod stage mgr; Theatre prod, Second Thoughts, The Yellow Pin, Orrin, The Effect of Gamma Rays on Man-in-the Moon Marigolds, dir; TV series: "You Must Remember This"; "Wiseguy"; "Tour of Duty"; "My Past Is My Own"; "LA Law"; "Cagney and Lacey"; "St Elsewhere"; "Simple Justice"; "Law and Order"; "Sisters"; "Frank's Place"; "New York Undercover"; "SeaQuest"; "Lena Horne: The Lady and Her Music"; "Dear America: Color Me Dark", 2000; "Soul Food", 2000. **Honors/Awds:** Director's Guild Award, 1993. **Business Addr:** Associate Professor, University of Southern California, School of Cinema-Television, 850 W 34th St, Los Angeles, CA 90089-2211, **Business Phone:** (213)740-3317.*

HEAD, DR. LAURA DEAN
Educator. **Personal:** Born Nov 3, 1948, Los Angeles, CA; daughter of Marvin and Helaine. **Educ:** San Francisco State Col, BA, 1971; Univ Mich, MA, 1974, PhD, develop psychol, 1978. **Career:** Univ Calif-Riverside, 1973-76; Minority fel, Am Psych Asn, 1976-77; Urban Inst Human Develop, proj dir, 1978-80; Far West Lab Educ Res & Develop, proj dir, 1980-81; San Francisco

State Univ, prof black studies, 1978; Col Ethnic Studies, San Francisco State Univ, prof, currently. **Orgs:** Chair, Bd Marin City Multi-Serv Inst, 1978-; chair, Black Child Develop Inst, 1978-81; Comt Sch Crime Calif State Dept Educ, 1981; bd dir, Oakland Men's Proj, 1988-; Comt Organize 20th Anniversary Commemoration 1968 San Francisco State Univ Stud Strike, 1988. **Honors/Awds:** Meritorious Promise Award, San Francisco State Univ, 1984. **Home Addr:** 3614 Randolph Ave, Oakland, CA 94602, **Home Phone:** (510)531-1420. **Business Addr:** Professor, San Francisco State University, College of Ethnic Studies, 1600 Holloway Ave HUM 231, San Francisco, CA 94132, **Business Phone:** (415)338-2309.

HEAD, RAYMOND, JR.
Government official, executive. **Personal:** Born Feb 23, 1921, Griffin, GA; son of Raymond Sr. and Pauline; married Ceola Johnson; children: Cheryl Johnson, Raylanda Anderson, Raymond III. **Educ:** Tuskegee Inst, BS, 1943. **Career:** Cleanwell Cleaners, partner & tailor, 1956-; Griffin Co, city comnr, 1971, mayor, 1977, 1985, mayor pro team, 1975, 1986, 1989; Head Raymond Pressing Club, Owner. **Orgs:** treas, steward Heck Chapel United Meth Ch, 1948; comdr, 1946-51, quartermaster, 1951-, Vaughn-Blake VFW Post, 8480; charter mem, Morgan-Brown Am Legion Post 546; Spalding Improv League; Spalding Jr Achievement; C C GA Assoc Retarded Children; Spalding Pike Upson Co Dept Labor, 1972; bd Family & Children Serv, 1970; del Nat Dem Conv, 1976; vol worker Am Cancer Soc Inc Spalding Co Unit; Cert Lay Sprark United Meth Ch; chmn, Pastor Parish Rel Heck Chapel Red Oak Charge; Griffin Dist Comn Bldg & Loc; United Meth N GA Conf Com Ethnic Minority Local Ch; convener, Griffin Spalding Co Comn Human Rels; pres, NAACP; bd dir, Spalding & Convalescent Ctr; mem trustee, bd N GA Meth Conf; Griffin Spalding Hosp Authority, 1971;vice chmn, bd dir State McIntosh Trail Area Planning & l Comn, 1975; appointed by GA Gov, Carter State Hosp Advisory Coun, 1972; GA Municipal Asn 6th Dist Dir, 1974-75; Dem Nat Convention delegate; GMA Municipal Comn; Spalding Co Health Bd. **Honors/Awds:** Outstanding Community Service, Citizens Spalding Co, 1969; Dedicated Service, Laciso Club, 1971; Outstanding Service Awards, 1st Black Elected Official Caballeros Dlub, 1972; Civic Improv League, 1976; Heck Chapel United Meth Ch, 1977; 8 St Bapt Ch, 1977; Bicentennial Award, Griffin Spalding Bicentennial Comn, 1976; Award, 30 yrs dedicated Serv; Disting Service Award, Mayor, Bus, Religious Ldr, & Civic Ldr, 1977; Ft Valley St Col 38th Annual Award; Man of year Award; Griffin Spalding NNBPW Club, 1977; proclamation, City Griffin; Mayor Raymond Head Jr, lifetime mem, Vauhn-Blake VFW Post 8480; citation, Locust Grove Masonic Lodge 543; Griffin Branch NAACP citation, 1977, Roy Wilkins Freedom Award, 1985; Tuskegee Univ & Spalding County Athletic Halls of Fame, 1985; certificates of appreciation, American Heart Asn; Am Len Post 546; General Griffin Chamber of Commerce award, 1989. **Military Serv:** AUS, s, sgt, 1943-46. *

HEAD, SAMUEL
Government official, consultant. **Personal:** Born Nov 20, 1948, Tampa, FL; son of Grace (deceased); married Karen Grant Head, Oct 24, 1988; children: Samuel Sherman, Shaunda Denise & Jonathan Spencer. **Educ:** Fla A&M Univ, Tallahassee, FL, BS, 1970; Valdosta State Col, Valdosta, Ga, cert govt mgt, 1980; Nat Univ, MS, 1989; Golden Gate Univ, Las Vegas NV, MPA, 1992. **Career:** Atlanta Bd Educ, Atlanta, Ga, educr, 1970-73; Harold A Dawson Real Estate Brokers, Atlanta, Ga, real estate exec, 1973-81; Fed Emergency Mgt Agency, Atlanta, Ga, mgt specialist, 1976-82; Cuban Refuge Operation, Key W Fla, dep fed coord officer, 1980; EG & G Inc, Las Vegas, NV, asst personnel security adminr, 1982-84; Nev Econ Develop Co, Las Vegas, NV, dir com revitalization, 1984-85; Clark County mgr's Off, Las Vegas, NV, sr mgt analyst, 1985-92; City Seaside, asst city mgr, 1992-; Pvt Pract, consult; The Head Group, pres, 1995. **Orgs:** Int City Managers Asn; Am Soc Pub Administrators; Conf Minority Pub Administrators; Nat Forum Black Pub Administrators; Calif League Cities; Nat League Cities; Fla A&M Nat Alumni Asn; Monterey County Film Comn; chmn, State Nev Job Training Coord Coun, 1988-90; chmn, Clark County Minority/Women Bus Coun, 1987-92; Toastmasters Int; pres, Uptown Kiwanis Int Club, 1989-90; pres, Las Vegas Chap, Alpha Phi Alpha Frat, 1983-87; Prince Hall Free & Accepted Masons. **Honors/Awds:** Meritorious Award, Uptown Kiwanis Club, 1988.

HEADLEY, HEATHER
Actor, singer. **Personal:** Born Oct 5, 1974, Trinidad and Tobago; daughter of Eric and Hannah; married Brian Musso, 2004. **Educ:** Northwestern Univ. **Career:** Stage: The Lion King; Aida; albums: This Is Who I Am, 2002; In My Mind, 2006; films: Elmo's Magic Cookbook, 2001; Dirty Dancing: Havana Nights, 2004; TV: "The Rosie O'Donnell Show", 2000; "Walt Disney World Christmas Day Parade", 2002; "Sidewalks Entertainment", 2003; "Breakin' All the Rules", 2004; "An Evening of Stars: Tribute to Stevie Wonder", 2006; "An American Celebration at Ford's Theater", 2006; The Mark Twain Prize: Neil Simon, 2006; An American Celebration at Ford's Theater, 2006; "It's Show time at the Apollo", 2006; Episode dated 12 March 2009, 2009; "The Tonight Show with Jay Leno", 2009; Album: This Is Who I Am, 2002; In My Mind, 2006; Audience of One, 2009. **Honors/Awds:** Tony Award, Aida, 1998; Two Grammy Award, Best Actress in a Musical, Sarah Siddons Award, 2000; R&B/Soul Album of the Year - Solo, 2003; Best R&B/Soul or Rap New Artist - Solo, 2003. *

HEADLEY, SHARI
Actor. **Personal:** Born Jul 15, 1964, Queens, NY; married Christopher Martin, Jan 1, 1993 (divorced 1995); children: Skyler. **Career:** Films: Coming to America, 1988; The Preacher's Wife, 1996; A Woman Like That, 1997; Johnson Family Vacation, 2004; Nothing Is Private, 2007; Belly 2: Millionaire Boyz Club, 2009. TV appearances: "Kojak: Ariana", 1989; "Gideon Oliver", 1989; "Kojak: None So Blind", 1990; "Quantum Leap", 1990; "Walker", "Texas Ranger", 1993; "All My Children", 1991-2005; New York Undercover:, 1995; "Walker, Texas Ranger", 1996; "Cosby", 1996; "413 Hope St", 1997; "413 Hope St.", 1997; "The Love Boat: The Next Wave", 1998; "The Wayans Bros.", 1999; "The Guiding Light", 2001-02; "Half & Half", 2003; "The Bold & the Beautiful", 2004-05; "One on One", 2004; "House M.D.", 2005. **Honors/Awds:** Image Award nomination, 1998. **Business Addr:** Actress, c/o J Michael Bloom & Associates, 233 Pk Ave S 10th Fl, New York, NY 10003, **Business Phone:** (212)529-6500.

HEARD, BLANCHE DENISE
Administrator. **Personal:** Born Aug 9, 1951, Washington, DC; daughter of Albert M Winters Sr and Marlene Coley; married Emanuel F Heard Jr (deceased); children: Latricia Poole, Michael Poole & Mannikka Heard. **Educ:** Montgomery Co Jr Col, attended 1969; Univ Col, attended 1976; Tenn State Univ, attended 1972. **Career:** Am Security Bank, supvr, 1974-75, sr edp auditor, 1976-83; Savings Bank Baltimore, sr edp auditor, 1984-85; US Fidelity & Guaranty, info interity admin, 1985-88, supvr, data security, 1988-93; Comput Based System Inc. **Orgs:** Chair, Elec Data Process Auditors Asn, 1980-81; int secy, EDPP Conf, 1982; Data Processing Mgt Asn, 1986, United Black Fund Greater Baltimore, 1986-87; Black Data Processing Asn; Womens Aux, Baltimore Chap Nat Asn Advanc Colored People; Nat Asn Female Exec. *

HEARD, GAR (GARFIELD HEARD)
Basketball player, basketball coach. **Personal:** Born May 3, 1948, Hogansville, GA; son of Charlie Mae and Preston Martin; married Kathleen Cline (divorced); children: Kim, Jaasmeen, Gyasi & Avery. **Educ:** Univ Okla, BS, 1970. **Career:** Basketball player, coach (retired); Seattle Supersonics, forward, 1970-72; Chicago Bulls, 1972-73; Buffalo Braves, 1973-76; Phoenix Suns, 1976-80; San Diego Clippers, 1980-84; Ariz State Univ, volunteer ast coach, 1982-83; Arzi Phoneix, realtor, 1984-87; Dallas Mavericks, interim head coach, 1993; Indiana Pacers, asst coach, 1993-97; Philadelphia 76ers, ast coach, 1997-98; Detroit Pistons, asst coach, 1998-99, asst head coach & interim coach, 2004; Washington Wizards, head coach, 1999-2000; Detroit Pistons, asst coach, 2004-05. **Honors/Awds:** All Big Eight Conference; MVP in the Big Eight, 1970; MVP in Marshall University Tournament, 1970; NBA Champions, Phoenix Suns, 1976. *

HEARD, GEOFFREY A.
Chief executive officer. **Career:** SERO/Nat Scholar Serv, pres & cheif exec officer, currently. **Orgs:** Bd mem, Henry W Grady Health Syst Found; trustee, The Fulton-DeKalb Hosp Authority, Grady Health Syst. **Business Addr:** President, Cheif Executive Officer, National Scholar Service, 230 Peachtree St Suite 530, Atlanta, GA 30303, **Business Phone:** (404)522-7260.*

HEARD, GEORGINA E
Airline executive, executive. **Personal:** Born Aug 8, 1952, Chicago, IL; daughter of George and Minnie; married Paul Labonne; children: Marc Labonne. **Educ:** Bradley Univ, BS, 1974; DePaul Univ, MS, 1978; Inst Family Therapy, 1979-80. **Career:** Comprehensive Care Families, dir, 1980-82; Inwood Community Ment Health Ctr, Wash Heights, unit chief, 1982-83; United Airlines, human resources staff mgr, 1983-86, personnel adminr, 1986-88, benefits commun mgr, 1988-93, human resources mgr, 1993-; Chicagoland Bus Partners, pres & exec dir, 1998-; United Airlines, dir Govt & Pub Affairs, 2000. **Orgs:** Vpres, Youth Guid, 1993-; chairperson, Nat Asn Advan Colored People Fair Share Corp, Adv Coun, 1993-; vice chmn, Annual Blackbook Music Awards, 1993; OIC Nat Tech Adv Coun, 1994-; dir, Bottomless Closet, 1998-; vpres, Literacy Chicago, 1998-99; Chicago Workforce Bd, 2002-. **Honors/Awds:** Outstanding Young Woman of America, 1984; United Airlines Human Resources Annual Award, 1991; Community Partnership Award, Mutual America, 1999. **Special Achievements:** In-School Consultation: School-based Community Mental Health, Educational Resources, 1981. **Home Addr:** 8832 Gleneagles Lane, Darien, IL 60561.

HEARD, HERMAN WILLIE, JR.
Football player. **Personal:** Born Nov 24, 1961, Denver, CO. **Educ:** Univ Southern Colo, Ft Lewis Col. **Career:** Football player (retired); Kansas City Chiefs, running back, 1984-89.

HEARD, LONEAR WINDHAM
Executive. **Personal:** Married James T. Heard, May 19, 1964 (died 1981); children: four daughters. **Educ:** Rust Col, BA, 1964; Atlanta Univ, GA, MBA. **Career:** Rust Col, sec dir public relations, sec pres, v pres bd trustees; Am Nat Bank Trust, statistical sec; James T. Heard Mgmt Corp, Cerritos, CA, co-mgr, owner, pres; Vermont Slauson, mem bd dir. **Honors/Awds:** McDonald's Golden Arch Award, 1986.

HEARD, MARIAN L
Association executive. **Personal:** Born in Canton, GA; daughter of Ural Noble and Indiana Billinglea; married Winlow, Aug 31, 1993; children: Gregory & Derek. **Educ:** Univ Bridgeport, Jr Col, AA, 1963; Univ Mass, Amherst, BA, 1976; Springfield Col, MEd, 1978. **Career:** Inner-City Children's Ctr, exec dir, 1972-74; Housatonic Community Col, instr, 1976-84; WICC Radio, Bridgeport, CT, radio show moderator, 1977-83; United Way, Eastern Fairfield County, CT, dir, opers, 1981-88, assoc exec dir, 1988-89, pres & chief exec officer, 1989-92, United Way, Mass Bay, pres & chief exec officer, 1992-2004; CVS Corp, dir, 1999-; Oxen Hill Partners, pres & chief exec office, currently; BioSphere Medical Inc, bd dir, 2006-. **Orgs:** Bd mem, Blue Cross & Blue Shield, MA, 1992-; bd mem, Fleet Bank Mass, 1992-; Am Mgt Asn; Exec Women's Group; Nat Bus & Prof Women's Club; Non-Profit Mgt Group; Women Philanthropy; Women in Radio & TV; mem, Dana Faber Cancer Inst. **Honors/Awds:** John H Garber Jr Minority Dev Award, United Way Am, 1988; Golden Tee Award, Cardinal Shehan Ctr, 1990; Community Leadership Award, Girl Scouts, Housatonic Coun, 1990; Women Achievement Award, Big Sisters Asn Greater Boston, 1991; Youth Leadership Community Service Award, Walter Memorial AM Zion Church, 1992. **Special Achievements:** Contributor: CRP Bylaws, 1990; Agency Self-Support Policy, 1981; United Way; Allocation/Distribution Policy, 1982. **Business Addr:** President, Chief Executive Officer, Oxen Hill Partners, 695 Atlantic Ave 8th Fl, Boston, MA 02111, **Business Phone:** (617)526-7979.

HEARN, DR. ROSEMARY
School administrator. **Personal:** Born May 1, 1929, Indianapolis, IN; daughter of Oscar Thomas and Mabel Lee Ward. **Educ:** Howard Univ, BA, 1951; Ind Univ, MA, 1958, PhD, 1973. **Career:** Prof (retired); Lincoln Univ, Jefferson City, Mo, eng prof, 1958-2001, dir hons prog, 1968-72, exec dean acad affairs, 1983-85, spec asst to presacad affairs, 1985-87, dean, Col Arts & Sci, 1989, vpres, acad affairs, 1997-2001, prof emer, currently. **Orgs:** Nat Asn Teachers Eng; Col Lang Asn; reviewer & consult, US Dept HEW, 1977-79; Delta Sigma Theta; secy & bd dirs, Jefferson City United Way, 1983; judge, Miss Community Betterment Awards Competition, 1983; Mo State Planning Comm, Am Coun Educ; Nat Identification Prog, 1983-; Planning Comm, Nat Asn State Land Grant Col & Univ, 1985-; Mid-Miss Asn Col & Univ, vice-chair, exec comm mid-Mo; Miss Asn Social Welfare; reviewer & consult, Am Asn Univ Women; adv panel, Mo Coun Arts, 1987-; reviewer, Am Libr Asn; Comn, Urban Agenda, NASVLGC, 1992-; bd dirs, Mo Humanities Coun, 1995; pres-elect, bd dir, Coun Col Arts & Sci, 1997-. **Honors/Awds:** Outstanding teacher, Lincoln Univ, 1971; Develop Proposals, Dept HEW, dist reader, 1977-79; Phelps-Stokes (West Africa, 1975) NEH, grants received, 1977-80; NEH, Div Res Prog, proposal reviewer, 1980-81; Am Libr Asn, CHOICE, consult-reviewer, 1985-; Comn Service Award, Jefferson City United Way, 1987.

HEARNE, EARL
Government official, administrator. **Personal:** Born Aug 2, 1956, Calvert, TX; son of Earlie and Ellen Foster Rosemond; children: Timothy Earl & Tiffany Charisse. **Educ:** Univ Tex, Austin, TX, BBA, finance, 1979; Tex A&M Corpus Christi, Corpus Christi, TX, MBA, mgt, 1982. **Career:** Univ Tex, Austin, TX, clerk typist I, 1976; Amoco Prod Co, Corpus Christi, TX, admin analyst, 1979-83; Corpus Christi ISD, Corpus Christi, TX, paraprofessional aide II, 1984-85; city Corpus Christi, Corpus Christi, TX, mgt & budget analyst II, 1985-, aso auditor, 1992-; City League City TX, internal audit dir, 1995; City Houston TX, Munic Ct, ade supr, 1996; Galveston County Treasurers Office, asst county treas, 1996-; Galveston County, admin servs mgr, currently. **Orgs:** Nat Asn Advan Colored People, 1987, Gov Finance Officer's Asn, 1989-97, Tex Asn Assessing Officers, 1985-87, United Way Finance Adv Comt, 1987-92, Nueces County Mental Health & Retardation Adv Comt, 1988-90; coordr, Leadership Tomorrow, city Corpus Christi, 1988-92. **Honors/Awds:** Incentive Award, City Corpus Christi, budget reconciliations, 1988-89. **Special Achievements:** Author: Instructional Manual, City Corpus Christi, 1989; 2nd edition, Instructional Procedural Manual - Budget, City Corpus Christi, 1991. **Home Addr:** 3703 Rosedale St, Houston, TX 77004-6409. **Business Addr:** Assistant County Treasurer, Galveston County, Department of Parks and Senior Services, 4102 Main, LaMarque, TX 77568, **Business Phone:** (409)934-8100.

HEARNS, THOMAS
Boxer, boxing promoter. **Personal:** Born Oct 18, 1958, Memphis, TN; son of Lois; married Rena; children: Ronald, Natasha & Thomas Charles K A. **Career:** Boxer (retired), boxing promoter; prof boxer, 1977-2000; Hearns Entertainment Inc, co-owner & boxing promoter, 2000-. **Orgs:** Vol policeman, Detroit Police Dept; World Boxing Coun. **Honors/Awds:** Super Welterweight Champion; Amateur Boxer of the Year Award, 1977; 139 lb Champion, Nat Golden Gloves, 1977; 139 lb Champion, Nat AAU, 1977; WBA World Welterweight Championship, 1980; Fighter of the Year, Boxing Writers Asn, 1980; Fighter of the Year,

Ring Mag, 1980, 1985; WBC Super Welterweight Championship, 1982; WBC Light Middleweight boxing, 1982-86; WBC Light Heavyweight Champion, 1987; WBC Middleweight Championship, 1987; WBO Super Middleweight Champion, 1988-90; IBF Lightweight Championship, 1991; WBA Light Heavyweight Champion, 1992; Cruiserweight Champion, 1995; Cruiserweight title, NABF, 1994; Cruiserweight title, Int Boxing Orgn, 1999. **Special Achievements:** First Black to win boxing titles in five different weight classes.

HEARON, DENNIS JAMES
Computer executive. **Personal:** Born May 18, 1941, New York, NY; son of David Rossignole and Dorothy May Bowles; married Diana Elaine Jackson, Apr 13, 1974; children: Elizabeth & Micheal. **Educ:** City Col NY, New York, NY, BE, mech eng, 1963; Brooklyn Polytech Inst, Brooklyn, NY, MS, indust eng, 1967. **Career:** Grumman Aerospace, Bethpage, NY, Engr, 1963-67; IBM Corp, Somers, NY, asst gen mgr, 1967, Europe, Middle East & Africa team, managing dir, 1999. **Orgs:** Bd mem, United Way Westchester, 1983-84; mentor, Horizon Club, 1989-; chair, Westchester Educ Coalition, 1990-; steering comn, Westchester Acad, 1990-. **Honors/Awds:** Black Achievers Award, Chicago Urban League, 1979; Community Service Award, Horizon Club, Norwalk, Conn Chamber Com, 1990.

HEARST, GERALD GARRISON
Football player. **Personal:** Born Jan 4, 1971, Lincolnton, GA; married Aug 9, 2009; children: 3. **Educ:** Univ Ga, attended 1992. **Career:** Phoenix Cardinals, running back, 1993; Ariz Cardinals, running back,1994-95; Cincinnati Bengals, running back, 1996; San Francisco 49ers, running back, 1997-2003; Denver Broncos, running back, 2004. **Honors/Awds:** Victor Award, 1995; NFL Comeback Player of the Year, Assoc Press, 1995 & 2001; Pro Bowl selection, 1998 & 2000; Doak Walker Award.

HEATH, JAMES E.
Educator, musician. **Personal:** Born Oct 25, 1926, Philadelphia, PA; married Mona Brown; children: Mtume, Roslyn & Jeffrey. **Educ:** Theodore Presser Sch Music, saxophone. **Career:** Educator (retired), musician; The Afro-American State of Evolution, performer, 1976; Woodwinds, Housatonic Comm Col, Bridgeport, instr; Aaron Copland Sch Music, Queens Col, New York City, prof, 1987-98; Louis Armstrong House, adv, 1987-; Jazz Repetory Co; Heath Bros Quartet, Jimmy Heath Quartet; Compositions: "Three Ears", 1988; "In Praise", 1994;"Leadership Suite", 1995; "Sweet Jazz mobile", 1999, "Turn Up the Heath", 2008. **Orgs:** Bd trustees, Thelonious Monk Inst, 1990-; adv bd, Int Asn Jazz Educrs, 2000; adv panel, NY State Coun Arts, 2002. **Honors/Awds:** Jazz Pioneer Award, BMI City Col New York, 1985; Jimmy Heath Day,Wilmington, NC, named in honor, 1985; Honorary Doctor of Humane Letters,Sojourner-Douglass Col, Baltimore, MD, 1986; Jazz Masters Award, Afro-Am Mus, Philadelphia, PA; Walk of Fame Award, Philadelphia Music Alliance,1993; The lonious Monk Institute of Jazz Founders Award, 1994; Presidential Award, Queens Col, 1998; NY State Governor's Arts Award, 2000; Honorary doctorate in music, Julliard, 2002; Leadership Award, Nat Visionary Leadership Project, 2003; Jazz Festival Award, Harstad, Norway; Giants of Black History Award, Greater Harlem Chamber Com, 2004; Don Red man Heritage Award, 2006; Humani tarium Award, honorary Doctorate, Human Letters; Int Asn Jazz Educ, 2006. **Special Achievements:** Composer of over 125 compositions; played saxophone with Howard Mc Ghee, Miles Davis, Dizzy Gillespie, Art Farmer, Clark Terry & Own Bands; recorded 10 albums; performed on 90 albums with other jazz greats; Grammy nominee in 1980, 1993, 1996. **Home Addr:** 11315 34th Ave Suite 3D, Corona, NY 11368.

HEAVY D (DWIGHT MYERS)
Rap musician, actor, executive. **Personal:** Born May 24, 1967, Jamaica, West Indies; son of Clifford and Eulahlee Myers; children: Xea. **Career:** Heavy D & the Boyz, rap singer; singles & albums include: Black Coffee & Nuttin But Love; albums: "Waterbed Hev", 1997; Uptown Recs, pres; Universal Music Group, sr vpres, currently; TV: "Booker", 1990, "Tales from the Crypt", 1992, "Roc", 1993, "Living Single", 1994-96, "Happily Ever After: Fairy Tales for Every Child", 1997, "Martial Law?, 1999, "For Your Love", 2000, "Boston Public", 2000-03, "The Tracy Morgan Show", 2003-04, "Yes, Dear", 2005; "Bones", 2005; "Untitled Music High Project", 2006; Film: New Jersey Drive, 1995, The Deli, 1997, The Cider House Rules, 1999, Life, 1999, Next Afternoon, 2000, Big Trouble, 2002, Black Listed, 2003; Larceny, 2004, Step Up, 2006. **Orgs:** AFTRA, SAG, ASCAP. **Honors/Awds:** Soul Train Award; Two-Time Grammy Nominee (music); Platinum recs for Living Large, 1987, Big Tyme, 1989, Peaceful Journey, 1991; Gold Rec, Blue Funk, 1993. **Business Addr:** Actor, MCA Recordings, 1755 Broadway 8th fl, New York, NY 10019, **Business Phone:** (212)841-8000.

HEBERT, STANLEY PAUL
Executive, lawyer. **Personal:** Born Jun 18, 1922, Baton Rouge, LA; married Mary Lou Usher; children: 6. **Educ:** Univ Wisc, PhB, 1947; Marquette Univ Law Sch, JD, 1950. **Career:** US Govt Off Price Stabilization Milwaukee, investr atty, 1951; Southern Univ Law Sch, asst prof, 1951-52; NC Col Law Sch, assoc prof law, 1952-55; atty pvt pract, Columbus, GA, 1955-56; atty pvt pract Milwaukee, 1956-58; City Milwaukee, City Attorney's Off, asst city atty, 1958-61; State Wisc & Pub Serv Comn Wisc, comnr, 1961-63; US Govt Dept Navy Off Gen Coun Wash DC, dep gen coun, 1963-69; US EEOC, gen coun, 1969-71; Bank Am, vpres asst secy, 1971-76, coun; Gen Coun, Port Oakland, gen coun, 1976-95; Wendell Rosen Black & Dean LLP, 1996-2001; pvt pratice, currently. **Orgs:** Calif Bar Asn; DC Bar Asn; US Supreme Ct; US Ct Appeals; Ga Bar Asn; Fed Bar Asn; Wisc Bar Asn; former chmn, Exec Comt Nat Cath Community Serv; vpres & mem, Exec Comt & Bd Dir United Serv Orgn Inc; chmn, Pastoral Comn Comt on Role Church in Changing Metro, Diocese, Wash DC; Bd Gov John Carroll Soc & Pastoral Comn, Archdiocese, Wash; Exec Comt Wisc Welfare Coun; Exec Comt Int Inst Milwaukee; Exec Comt Madison Comn on Human Rels; Exec Comt Milwaukee & Madison Chaps NAACP; mem bd trustees, Voorhees Col; adv bd, Calif State Univ Hayward; pres, Nat Cath Conf Interracial Justice; Bay Area Urban League; chmn, Calif Atty Gen's Adv Comn on Comt Police Rel; regent, Holy Names Col; mem bd, Wiley Manuel Law Found; Nat dir, bd Marcus Foster Ed Inst; Sigma Pi Phi Frat; Alpha Gamma Boule; Am Asn Port Authorities. **Honors/Awds:** Recip Public Service Award, Delta Chi Lambda Chap Alpha Phi Alpha Frat Inc, 1962. **Military Serv:** Served USAF WW II a/c; Capt USNR, JAG Corp, Retired. **Business Addr:** Attroney Private Pratice, 2733 Mountaingate Way, Oakland, CA 94611, **Business Phone:** (510)531-8874.

HEBERT, ZENEBEWORK TESHOME
Executive. **Personal:** Born Apr 1, 1942, Addis Ababa, Ethiopia; daughter of Teshome Shenqut and Aselefech Aderra; married Maurice Robert, Jan 28, 1968 (deceased); children: Teshome & Rachel. **Educ:** Univ Ill, Col Pharm, BS, 1967. **Career:** Michael Reese Hosp, pharmacist, 1967-70; S Chicago Community Hosp, pharmacist 1971-74; Life Store, owner, mgr 1974-; Arthur Treacher Fish & Chips, owner, mgr 1978; Hebert & Moore Store Men, owner, mgr; Hebert Montissore Sch, owner; Hebert Enterprises, pres, chief exec officer; Frusen Isladje Ice Cream, Chicago, IL, owner, pres, 1987; Nino's Men's Clothing, Chicago, IL, vpres, 1987. **Orgs:** Jack & Jill Am Inc; SNOB Inc; vpres & mem, 87th St & Stony Island Bus Asn. **Honors/Awds:** One of the Top 10 Black Business Women in Chicago; One of the Top 10 Best Dressed Women in Chicago. **Business Addr:** Owner, The Life Store, 1639 E 87th St, Chicago, IL 60617, **Business Phone:** (773)731-2530.

HECKER, BARRY
Scout, radio director. **Personal:** Born in Washington, DC; married Merle. **Educ:** Frostburg State Col, BS, Health, phys educ & recreation; George Washington Univ, WA, DC, MA, educ; Fla State Univ, Tallahassee, FL, PhD, athletic admin. **Career:** Jhon Wooden Basketball Fundamentals Camp, CA, instr, 1971 & 1981; B S Leiden Basketball Club, Dutch Prof League, head coach, 1975-76; George Washington Univ, asst coach; George Mason Univ, dir & asst coach, 1973; Westminster Col, Salt Lake City, UT, dir & head basketball coach, 1976-78; Bertka's Views Nat Scouting Serv, scout; Cleveland Cavaliers, dir player acquisition, 1985-87; Los Angeles Clippers, dir scouting & asst coach, 1994-98, dir player personnel; Las Vegas Bandits, interim head coach & player personnel dir, 1999-2001; The Memphis Grizzlies, asst coach, currently. **Business Phone:** (901)888-4667.

HEDGEPETH, DR. CHESTER MELVIN
Educator. **Personal:** Born Oct 28, 1937, Richmond, VA; son of Chester Sr and Ethel Carter; married Thelma Washington, Aug 16, 1969; children: Chester M III. **Educ:** Blackburn Col, BA, 1960; Wesleyan Univ, MA, 1966; Harvard Univ, EdD, 1977. **Career:** Maggie Walker High Sch, teacher, 1960-65; Macalester Col, instr eng, 1968-71; Col St Thomas, St Paul, MN, instr; Va Union Univ, instr eng, 1966-68, 1971-75; Lesley Col, eng instr; Va Common wealth Univ, coordr Afro-Am studies, 1978-; Univ Md Eastern Shore, dean arts & scis & chmn eng lang, 1983-95, Eng & Modern Lang Dept, actg chair, African Language Proj, prin investr, 1992-98, dir & assoc prof eng, currently. **Orgs:** Phi Delta Kappa Harvard Chap, 1976-; S Atlantic Modern Lang Asn, 1978-; pres, Va Humanities Conf, 1982-83; founding ed, Maryland Rev, 1986-96; Sigma Pi Phi Gamma Theta. **Honors/Awds:** Distinguished Alumnus, Harvard Univ, 1986; Certificate of Merit, Goddard Space Flight Ctr, 1990; Distinguished Alumnus, Blackburn Col, 1992; Freedom's Foundation Award. **Special Achievements:** Author: Afro-American Perspectives in the Humanities, Collegiate Pub Co, 1980, Theories of Social Action in Black Literature, Peter Lang Pub, 1986, 20th Century African American Writers & Artists, ALA, 1991. **Home Addr:** 1008 Schumaker Woods Rd, Salisbury, MD 21801. **Business Addr:** Director, Associate Professor of English, University of Maryland Eastern Shore, African Language Research Project, 1112 Trigg Hall, Princess Anne, MD 21853.

HEDGEPETH, LEONARD
Chief executive officer. **Career:** United National Bank, Fayetteville, NC, chief exec. **Business Addr:** Chief Excutive Officer, United National Bank, 320 Green St, PO Box 1150, Fayetteville, NC 28302, **Business Phone:** (919)483-1131.

HEDGESPETH, GEORGE T., JR.
Financial manager. **Personal:** Born Aug 9, 1949, Richmond, VA; married Portia Meade; children: George III & Sheldon. **Educ:** Lincoln Univ Pa, BA, 1971; Central Mich, MA, 1978. **Career:** Lincoln Univ PA, acct, 1971-72, dir financial aid, 1974-77; Univ Rochester, NY, asst dir stud activ, 1972-74; Moton Consortium Wash, DC, asst dir, 1977-78; Miami Dade Community Col FL, dir financial aid & vet affairs, 1978. **Orgs:** Comn mem, Need Analysis The Col Bd; inst rep, Nat Asn Stut Financial Aid Adminr; S Asn Stud Fin Aid Adminrs; Fla Asn Stud Financial Aid Adminrs; Omega Psi Phi Frat; Tidewater Coun, Boy Scouts Am. **Honors/Awds:** Omega Psi Phi Frat Beta Chap, 1977; Outstanding young men, Am Jaycees Am, 1978. **Home Phone:** (757)420-7120.

HEDGLEY, DAVID RICE, JR.
Mathematician. **Personal:** Born Jan 21, 1937, Chicago, IL; son of Rev David R Sr (deceased) and Christine Kelly (deceased); divorced; children: Angela Kay Garber & Andrea Kim. **Educ:** Va Union Univ, BS boil, 1958; Mich State Univ, BS math, 1964; Calif State Univ, MS math, 1970; Somerset Univ, PhD, comput sci, Il minister, l988. **Career:** So Adhesive Corp, chemist, 1958-59; Ashland Sch System, teacher, 1961-65; Richmond Sch System, teacher, 1965-66; NASA Dryden Flight Res Facility, mathematician, 1966. **Orgs:** Asst prof, AU Col, 1975-78; consult, Mfg Tools Inc, 1982-86; bd mem, Local Black Adv Group, 1984-87; consult, Univ Wash, 1984. **Honors/Awds:** Superior Sustained Award Recognition Award, 1966-87; Best Paper of Year (Scientific) 1976; Nat Exceptional Engr Award, NASA, 1983; Nat Julian Allen Award, NASA, 1984; Nat Space Act Award, NASA 1984; Special Achievement, NASA 1988; Tech Brief Award, 1992; NASA Space Act Award, 1994; Nat Space Act Award, 1998. **Special Achievements:** Numerous scientific publications from 1974-87; Father Of 3D Graphics. **Military Serv:** AUS, E-4, 2 yrs. **Home Addr:** PO Box 1674, Lancaster, CA 93539. **Business Addr:** Chief Research Mathematician, NASA Dryden Flight Research Center, PO Box 273, Edwards, CA 93523, **Business Phone:** (661)276-3311.

HEDGPETH, KIM ROBERTS. See ROBERTS, KIM.

HEDGSPETH, ADRIENNE CASSANDRA
Journalist. **Personal:** Born Aug 29, 1959, Norfolk, VA; daughter of Beulah Hedgspeth Reid. **Educ:** Norfolk State Univ, Norfolk, Va, BA, 1977-81; Conn Sch Broadcast, Farmington, CT, 1985. **Career:** Cincinnati Enquirer, Cincinnati, OH, reporter, summer, 1980; Shoreline Times, Inc, Guilford, CT, reporter, 1981-83; Norwich Bulletin, Norwich, CT, reporter, 1983-84; Register, New Haven, Ct, political columnist, 1989. **Orgs:** NAACP, 1985; Nat Asn Black Journalists, 1989-. **Honors/Awds:** Media Award, Greater New Haven Sec Natl Coun Negro Women, Inc, 1990 Journalism Awards: 1st Place, Sigma Delta Chi, CT Chapter, 1989; National Dean's List, 1981. **Home Phone:** (203)562-4283.

HEFLIN, JOHN F.
Educator. **Personal:** Born 1941, Sweetwater, TX; married Anita Blaz; children: Kyle & Jonathan. **Educ:** NMex Highlands Univ, BA, 1963; Stanford Univ, MA, 1972, PhD, 1977. **Career:** US Dept Interior Denver, Colo, cartographer, 1964-65; Merced Union High Sch, Merced, Calif, teacher & coach, 1965-70; Stanford Univ, asst to dean, 1971-74; Ore Dept D, EEO prog coordr, 1974-76; Portland State Univ, asst prof educ admin. **Orgs:** Portland Urban League; Ore Assembly Black Affairs; Ore Alliance Black Sch Educrs; Calif Teachers Asn; Ore Educrs Asn; Nat Educ Adult; Nat Coun Social Studies; Policy Stud Orgn; Phi Delta Kapp; bd dir, Mid-Peninsula Task Force Integrated Ed; Am Ed Res Asn; ed dir, Nat Advan Asn Colored People; Nat Alliance Black Sch Educr; nat chmn, Res Focus Black Educ, Am Ed Res Asn; comnr, Portland Metro Human Rels Comt; Asn Supervision & Curriculm Develop; Found Leadership Develop Prog, 1970-71. **Business Addr:** Assistant Professor, Portland State University, Educ Admin, PO Box 751, Portland, OR 97207.*

HEFLIN, MARRION
Executive. **Personal:** Born Aug 28, 1963, Akron, OH; son of Lou J and Marion L. **Educ:** Ohio Univ, BBA, 1985, MBA, 1996. **Career:** McDonalds Corp, staff; TMP Worldwide, staff; Huntington Bancshares Inc vpres; KPMG, dir, trans serv group; Prestige Design Group Inc, pres & chief exec officer, 2001-; Nevis Securities LLC, managing dir & chief financial officer, curently; Clark Atlanta Univ, adj prof. **Orgs:** Nat Asn Black Accts; Am Inst Cert Pub Accts; Fla Inst Cert Pub Accts; past pres, Col of Bus Ohio Univ; past bd trustee, On My Own, Inc; past bd trustee, Neighborhood House Inc; Nat Black MBA Asn; past chmn bd, S Fulton Chamber Com; mem bd, Dirs Ohio Univ Alumni Asn; vol investment comt, Metro Atlanta United Way. **Honors/Awds:** Ping Recent Graduate Award, Ohio Univ, 1990; Blackburn-Spence Award, Deppen Award, Templeton Award, Columbus Area Leadership Program. **Military Serv:** United States Army Reserves, cpt, 1982-; 10 Military Ribbons, Served in Operation Desert Storm. **Home Addr:** 7508 Cole Lane, Atlanta, GA 30349, **Home Phone:** (770)969-2577. **Business Addr:** Managing Director, Chief Financial Officer, Nevis Securities LLC, 1180 W Peach St Suite 1150, Atlanta, GA 30309, **Business Phone:** (678)442-7203.

HEFNER, DR. JAMES A
School administrator, educator. **Personal:** Born Jun 20, 1941, Brevard, NC; married Edwina Long; children: Christopher, Jonathan & David. **Educ:** NC A&T State Univ, BS, 1961; Atlanta

Univ, MA, 1962; Univ CO, PhD, 1971; Hon Doctorate Civil Law, Univ S. **Career:** Prairie View A&M Col, teacher, 1962-63; Benedict Col, teacher, 1963-64; Fla A&M Univ, teacher, 1964-65; Univ Colo, teacher, 1965-67; Clark Col, teacher, 1967-71; Atlanta Univ, teacher, 1973-74; Morehouse Col, teacher, 1974-82; Tuskegee Inst, provost, 1982-84; Jackson State Univ, pres, 1984-91; Tenn State Univ, pres, 1991-2005, Thomas & Patricia Frist Chair Excellence Entrepreneurship, 2005-, Regents prof & pres emer, 2005-. **Orgs:** United Negro Col Fund; mem NAACP; Labor & Indstry Com; I-20 Coaltn; Atlanta Univ Ctr Fac Forum; consult, Cong Black Caucus; Nat Inst Pub Mgt, Dept Transp; Am Econ Asn, Indust Rels Res Asn; Nat Inst Pub Mgt; Community Econ Develop Coun; TVA Minority Econ Develop Coun; Mayor's Coun Col & Univ Pres; Coun Families Am; fel, Du Bois Inst; Phi Beta Kappa; MENSA. **Honors/Awds:** NAFEO Achievement Award; Good Guy Award. **Special Achievements:** Author of more than 50 articles on economic research; Books: Black Employment in Atlanta; Public Policy for the Black Community: Strategies and Perspectives. **Business Addr:** President Emeritus, Tennessee State University, 3500 John A Merritt Blvd, Nashville, TN 37209-1561, **Business Phone:** (615)963-5331.

HEGAMIN, GEORGE (GEORGE RUSSELL HEGAMIN)
Football player. **Personal:** Born Feb 14, 1973, Camden, NJ; married Kimbre. **Educ:** NC State Univ. **Career:** Dallas Cowboys, tackle, 1994-97; Philadelphia Eagles, 1998; Tampa Bay Buccaneers, 1999-2000.

HEGAMIN, GEORGE RUSSELL. See HEGAMIN, GEORGE.

HEGGANS, DARRYL
Executive. **Career:** Black Entertainment TV, regional vpres, vpres advert & media, currently. *

HEGGER, WILBER L
Clergy. **Personal:** Born May 6, 1936, Lemoine, LA; son of Luke and Derotha Sam; married Marlene Mouton, Jun 4, 1960; children: Kevin Norbert. **Educ:** Grambling State Univ, Grambling, LA, BS, Math & Sci, 1960; Univ Southwestern LA, Lafayette, LA, post-baccalaureate, 1972-74; Diocese Lafayette, Lafayette, LA, permanent diaconate formation prog, currently. **Career:** Lafayette Parish Sch Bd, Lafayette, LA, math, sci teacher, 1960-72; Univ Southwestern LA, Lafayette, LA, asst football coach, 1972-74; Prudential Ins Co, Lafayette, LA, dist agent, 1974-80; Chubby's Fantastic Cakes, Lafayette, LA, self-employed, 1980-; Diocese Lafayette, Lafayette, LA, dir OBCM, 1989-. **Orgs:** Treas, Grambling Alumni Asn-Lafayette Ch, 1960-; jail minister, Diocese Lafayette, 1986-; chairperson, Ministers Black Catholic Communities, 1988-90; coordr, Lafayette Civil Parish, currently. **Honors/Awds:** Bishop's Service Award, Diocese Lafayette, 1989. **Home Addr:** 201 Becky Lane, Lafayette, LA 70508. **Business Addr:** Co-Ordinator, Lafayette Civil Parish, Lafayette, LA 70501.

HEIGHT, DR. DOROTHY I.
Association executive. **Personal:** Born Mar 24, 1912, Richmond, VA. **Educ:** NY Univ, MA, 1933; NY Sch Social Work. **Career:** New York City Welfare Dept, caseworker, 1934; YWCA, Ctr Racial Justice, dir. **Orgs:** Volunteer, 1937, pres & chmn, Nat Coun Negro Women, 1957-97, pres emer, currenlty; pres, Delta Sigma Theta Sorority, 1947-58; comn bd, US Dept Defense Adv Comn Women, 1952-55; comn bd, New York St Social Welfare Bd, 1958-68; bd govs, ARC, 1964-70; Pres's Community Employment Handicapped; ad hoc comm, Pub Welfare Dept Health Educ & Welfare; consult, African Affairs Sec St; Women's Comm Off Emergency Planning Pres's Comm Status Women; pres community, Equal Employment Oppor; bd dir, CARE; CommRel Serv; bd govs, ARC; nat bd, YWCA; dir, YMCA Ctr Racial Justice; chmn exec comt, Leadership Conf Civil Rights, currently. **Honors/Awds:** Distinguished Service Award, Nat Conf Social Welfare, 1971; Citizens Medal Award Pres Reagan, 1989; Medal Freedom Pres Clinton, 1994; International Freedom Conductor Award, Nat Undeground Railroad Freedom Ctr, 2003; Congressional Gold Medal, 2004. **Special Achievements:** Author of numerous articles. **Business Addr:** Chairman Executive Committee, Leadership Conference on Civil Rights, 10 Fl 1629 K St NW, Washington, DC 20006, **Business Phone:** (202)466-3311.*

HEINEBACK, BARBARA TAYLOR
Hospital administrator. **Personal:** Born Dec 29, 1951, New York, NY; daughter of John and Robella; married; children: 1. **Educ:** Howard Univ, BA, TV commun, 1971; Univ Stockholm, cert lang arts, 1975. **Career:** CBS TV, asst prod, "Face the Nation", 1969-71; Swed Nat Radio Stockholm, freelance journalist, 1972-75; White House, press asst first lady; Commun Satellite Corp, mgr pub rels, 1976-87; Scripps Mem Hosp, San Diego, Calif; America's Cup, chief & dir, currently. **Orgs:** Dir, Wash Urban League; dir, Chamber Com, Chula Vista Calif; PRSA; Nat Asn Health Developers; Pub Rels Soc Am; Nat Soc Fund Raising Exec; Sunrise Bonita Rotary. **Honors/Awds:** Articles in Stockholm's major morning daily "Dagens Nyheter"; Plaques Appreciation, Pres Carter, Pres Tolbert; San Diego Arts Bd; United Negro Col Fund Steering Comm San Diego. **Home Addr:** PO Box 8604, La Jolla, CA 92038-8604. **Business Addr:** Chief of Protocol, Director of Public Relations, America's Cup, 2044 First Ave Suite 300, San Diego, CA 92101-2079.

HEISKELL, MICHAEL PORTER
Lawyer. **Personal:** Born Sep 11, 1951, Ft Worth, TX; married Gayle Regina Beverly; children: Marian Phenice & James Dewitt II. **Educ:** Baylor Univ, BA, 1972; Baylor Law Sch, JD, 1974. **Career:** Dawson Dawson Smith & Snodd, law clerk, 1974-75; Galveston Co, asst dist atty, 1975-80; Johnson Vaughn & Heiskell, atty; United States Atty, asst atty, 1980-84; Johnson Vaughn & Heiskell, partner, atty & coun at law, 1984-. **Orgs:** Del Phi Alpha Delta Law Frat Conv, 1974; mem, Galveston Co Bar asn; vpres sec Galveston Co Young Lawyers asn, 1977-78; Am Bar asn, 1976-77; Tex St Bar asn; Tex Dist & Co Attys Asn; bd dir mem Gulf Coast Legal Found; Disaster Relief Com; Tex Young Lawers Asn; Min Recruit Com Baylor Law Sch; pres, Pi Sigma Alpha Baylor Univ; pres, Agiza Funika Soc Serv Club Baylor Univ; pres, elect Fort Worth Black Bar Asn; vpres, Tarrant County Criminal Defense Lawyers Asn; assoc dir, pres, Tex Criminal Defense Lawyers Asn. **Honors/Awds:** Mr Navarro Jr Col Corsicana Tex, 1971; Lawyer of the Year Award, Tarrant Co Black Bar Assn, 1995, 2000; Tex Criminal Defense Lawyers Asn Presidential Award of Excellence 1994, 1995 & 2003. **Special Achievements:** Frequent Author and Lectr: "Confessions in Texas;" "Guilty Pleas;" "Cross-Examination of Experts in Federal Fraud Investigations;" "Grand Jury Practice in Federal Courts;" "Opening Statements"; "Fundamentals of Federal Representation"; "Effective Federal Pretrial Motions;" "Litigating Multi-Defendant Cases;" "Handling the Narcotics Case;" "Capital Murder Jury Selection;" First African American president of the Texas Criminal Defense Lawyers Assn; Superlawyer, 2003-04; First black to grad from Baylor Law School; First black asst DA Galveston Co. **Business Addr:** Partner, Senior Attorney, Counsellor, Johnson Vaughn & Heiskell, 600 Tex St 2nd Fl, Fort Worth, TX 76102, **Business Phone:** (817)877-5321.

HEMBY, DOROTHY JEAN
School administrator. **Personal:** Born in Greenville, NC. **Educ:** Essex Co Col, AS, lib arts, 1975; Montclair State Col, sociol & social studies, 1975; Kean Col NJ, stud personnel serv, 1977. **Career:** Newark Bd Educ, teacher, 1974-76; Kean Col NJ, Col counr, 1976-77; Passaic Co Community Col, counr & admin, 1978-. **Orgs:** Chmn, HOPE Orgn, 1978-82; NJ EOF Prof Assoc Inc, 1978-; community mem, NJ Assoc Black Educr, 1979-; chmn, Passaic Co Col Stud Life, 1983-84; counr, The Love Jesus Ministry 1983-; NJ Black Issues Assoc, 1984; exec bd & secy, Passaic Co Admin Assoc; advisor & consult, Passaic Co Newman Christian Club, 1983-; exec bd & treas, Passaic County Col Admin Assoc, 1985-88; Am Assoc Coun& Develop; chmn, mission & goals middle state comt, Passaic County Col; bd mem, Human Serv Prog, Passaic City Community Col; co-chair, Alcohol & Drug Awareness Community, 1993-; NJ Higher Educ Consortium; Special Needs C; co-chair, fund raiser community, 1994-. **Honors/Awds:** Counselor of the Year Award, 1993; Excellence Awards, NJ Coun Co Cols, 1995. *

HEMMINGWAY, DR. BEULAH S.
Educator. **Personal:** Born Mar 11, 1943, Clarksdale, MS; daughter of Willie Smith Jr and Pennie Ree; married Theodore; children: Kofi Patrice & Julius Chaka. **Educ:** Coahoma Jr Col, attended 1962; Alcorn State Univ, BS, 1964; NC Cent Univ,MA, 1965; Fla State Univ, PhD, 1981. **Career:** Southern Univ, teacher, 1965-66; Voorhees Col, teacher, 1966-67; Benedict Col, teacher, 1967-72; Fla A&M Univ, Dept Eng, assoc prof language & lit,1972, vpres, prof eng, currently. **Orgs:** Chairperson, Poetry Festival, 1975-82; adv, Lambda Iota Tau, 1975-82; Role& Scope Comt, 1976; Libr Resource Comt, 1977; Jack & Jill Am, 1979-81; bddir, LeMoyne Art Found, 1980-82; Fla Col, Eng Teachers, Undergrad Coun Co-lArts & Sci, 1982-; search comt vpres acad affairs, Fla A&M Univ, 1982;Mothers March Dimes, 1982-; vpres, Nat Coun Negro Women, 1982-; HomecomingComt, 1983; panelist, Fla Div Cult Affairs, 1986; Am Popular Cult Asn,1988; bd mem, Drifters Inc, 1989; pres, Fla A&M Univ Fac Sen, 1995-99; NatCoun Teachers Eng; Col Lang Asn; Curriculum Comt Lang & Lit; Southern Asn-Cols & Schs Editing Comt; Col Level Acad Skills Test Task Force; progchairperson 112th anniv, Bethel Baptist Church; Tallahassee Urban League;Nat Asn Advan Colored People; Am Asn Higher Educ. **Honors/Awds:** Teacher of the Year, Florida A&M Univ, 1987-88; Meritorious Service Award,1988; Winner, Teaching Incentive Award Prog, 1993. **Special Achievements:** Author, publications include: "Critics Assessment of Faulkners Black Characters FL A&M Univ" 1978; "A Comparative Pilot Study by Sex & Race ofthe Use of Slang" Soc for Gen Syst Rsch 1978; "Abyss-Gwendolyn Brooks Women" FL A&M Univ Bulletin; read paper 45th Annual Convention of CollLang Assoc 1985 "Can Computer Managed Grammar Make a Difference That Makesa Difference?"; Author Chapter 4, "Through the Prism of Africanity: APreliminary Investigation of Zora Neale Hurston's Mules and Men,"presented paper at American Popular Culture Assn 1989; "Through the Prismof Africanity," Zora in Florida, 1991; seminar: "Black Women Writers,"1983; workshop: "Teaching English Composition," Bay County EnglishTeachers, Panama City, Florida; read a paper at the Coll Language Assn's58th Annual Convention numerous other publications. **Home Addr:** PO Box 6029, Tallahassee, FL 32314-6029. **Business Addr:** Professor of English, Florida A & M University, Department English, Rm 410 & 414 422 Tucker Hall, Tallahassee, FL 32307, **Business Phone:** (850)599-3465.

HEMPHILL, FRANK
Educator. **Personal:** Born Nov 16, 1943, Cleveland, OH; married Brenda; children: Tracie, Dawn & Frank John Parker Jr. **Educ:** W Ky Univ, BS, 1968; Ky State Univ, MEd, 1975. **Career:** Shaw High Sch, E Cleveland, biol teacher, 1968-71, teaching asst biol, 1971-73, assoc dean students, dir acad asst, 1975; Hiram Col, dir stud acad serv, currently. **Orgs:** Minority Educ Serv Asn; vpres, Black Studie Consortium NE OH. **Honors/Awds:** Martha Jennings Fel, 1971; Outstanding Contribution Award, Alliance Black Consciousness Asn Hiram Ohio. **Home Addr:** 11820 Kenyon, PO Box 181, Hiram, OH 44234-0181, **Home Phone:** (330)569-7623. **Business Addr:** Director, Hiram College, Student Academic Services, Hinsdale 105, PO Box 67, Hiram, OH 44234, **Business Phone:** (330)569-5131.

HEMPHILL, REV. DR. MILEY MAE
Educator, school principal, teacher. **Personal:** Born Jan 8, 1914, Gwinnett County, GA; married John R. **Educ:** Morris Brown Col, AB, 1950; Atlanta Univ, MA, 1957; Col New Truth, DD, 1970. **Career:** Teacher, school principal, educator (retired); Teacher & prin; Gwinnett-Jackson Co & Winder City Sch, curric dir; Ga Dept Educ, reading eng specialist; notary public, 1957-; West Hunter St Baptist Church, assoc minister, 1980-. **Orgs:** Life mem, NEA; GEA; GTEA; ACS; pres, Atlanta Ga Jeanes Curric Dirs; dir, Region IV Fine Arts; pres, Royal Oaks Manor Comm Club; YMCA; pres, Helen A Whiting Soc, 1989-. **Honors/Awds:** Union Baptist Semin, LLD, 1974, LHD, 1976; Bronze woman of the year in Education, 1966; Outstanding Personalities of the South, 1972. **Home Addr:** 896 Woodmere Dr NW, Atlanta, GA 30318-6002.

HEMPSTEAD, HESSLEY JAMES, II
Football player, scout. **Personal:** Born Jan 29, 1972, Upland, CA. **Educ:** Univ Kans. **Career:** Football player (retired); Detroit Lions, guard, 1995-97, scout, 2000.

HEMSLEY, NATE
Football player. **Personal:** Born May 5, 1974, Willingboro, NJ. **Educ:** Syracuse Univ, attended 1996. **Career:** Dallas Cowboys, linebacker, 1997-99; Carolina Panthers, 2001; Miami Dolphins, 2001-02.

HEMSLEY, SHERMAN ALEXANDER
Comedian, actor. **Personal:** Born Feb 1, 1938, Philadelphia, PA. **Educ:** Attended Philadelphia Acad Dramatic Arts; studied with Negro Ensemble Co NY, Lloyd Richards. **Career:** Love Is Inc, owner; Triangle Productions, owner, currently; TV Series: "All in the Family", 1973-75; "The Jeffersons", 1975-85; "Amen", 1986-91; "Dinosaurs", 1991-94; 'Goode Behavior", 1996; "The Hughleys", 1999-2000; "Up, Up, & Away !", 2000; "Mister Ed", 2004; "The Surreal Life", 2005; Stage: The People vs Ranchman, 1968; Purlie, 1970; Don't Bother Me I Can't Cope; I'm Not Rappa port, 1987; The Odd Couple; Norman Is That You?, 1986; Film: Alice in Wonderland, 1985; Screwed, 2000; Mr Ed, 2001; The Father, the Son & the Holy Fonz, 2005; For the Love of a Dog, 2007. **Orgs:** AFTRA, Vinnette Carroll's Urban Arts Corps, Actors Equity Asn, Screen Actors Guild. **Honors/Awds:** NAACP Image Award, 1976, 1987; Hollywood Fgn Press Asn award; Golden Globe award. **Special Achievements:** Emmy Award nominated and NAACP Image Award winning, and Golden Globe nominated American character.

HENCE, MARIE J.
Violinist. **Personal:** Born Jul 2, 1936, Trenton, NJ. **Educ:** New Eng Conserv Music, BM, MM, 1960; Tanglewood, attended 1958; Yale Summer Sch Music & Art, attended 1960. **Career:** Musicians Broadway, music contractor; Shubert Theatres, 1961-74. **Special Achievements:** First female music contractor in Musicians on Broadway. **Home Addr:** 185 W End Ave, New York, NY 10023, **Home Phone:** (212)787-8853. *

HENDERSON, ALAN LYBROOKS
Basketball player, business owner. **Personal:** Born Dec 2, 1972, Morgantown, WV; son of Ray. **Educ:** Ind Univ, BA, biol; Howard Univ Sch Medicine, 1995. **Career:** Basketball player (retired), business owner; Atlanta Hawks, forward, 1995-2004; Dallas Mavericks, 2004-05; Cleveland Cavaliers, forward, 2005-06; Hendu Entertainment, owner, currently; Philadelphia 76ers, 2006-07; Utah Jazz, 2007. **Orgs:** Kappa Alpha Psi Fraternity. **Honors/Awds:** NBA Most Improved Player, 1998. *

HENDERSON, ANGELO B
Journalist. **Personal:** Born Oct 14, 1962, Louisville, KY; son of Roger L and Ruby M Henderson; married Felecia Dixon, Oct 21, 1989; children: Grant. **Educ:** Univ Ky, BA, jour, 1985. **Career:** Walt Disney World, intern/attractions, 1982; WHAS-TV (CBS affiliate), reporting intern, 1983; Wall Street Journal, Cleveland, OH, intern, 1984; Lexington Herald Leader, intern, 1984-85; Detroit Free Press, intern, 1985; St Petersburg Times, staff writer, 1985-86; Courier-Journal, Louisville, KY, bus reporter, 1986-89; Detroit News, bus reporter/columist, 1989-93, city desk reporter, 1993-

95; Wall St J, staff reporter, 1995-97, dep bur chief, currently, sr spec writer/page one, 1998-2000, dep detroit bur chief; Angelo ink LLC, pres & chief exec officer, currently. **Orgs:** Former pres, Detroit Chap Nat Asn Black Journalists; Nat Asn Black Journalists, parliamentarian. **Honors/Awds:** Best of Gannett Award for Business/Consumer Reporting, 1991; Nat Asn Black Journalists Award, Outstanding Coverage of the Black Condition for a series of Business Stories, 1992; 1st Place, Detroit Press Club Found, 1993; Unity Award for Excellence in Minority Reporting for Public Affairs/Social Issues, 1993; Pulitzer Prize for Distinguished Feature Writing, 1999; nations best reporters on race & ethnicity in am, 2000; Asn pastor worship, Vision & Emerging Ministries, Hope United Methodist Church, currently. **Special Achievements:** He also is the first African American to win a Pulitzer for The Wall Street Journal, one of the world's most influential newspapers; He also was named one of "39 African-American Achievers to Watch? in the next millennium by SuccessGuide magazine. **Business Addr:** Deputy Detroit Bureau Chief, Wall Street J News Bur, 500 Woodward Ave Suite 1950, Detroit, MI 48226, **Business Phone:** (313)963-7800.

HENDERSON, AUSTRALIA TARVER
Educator. **Personal:** Born Feb 8, 1942, Ft Worth, TX; married William. **Educ:** Fisk Univ, BA 1964; Ohio Univ, MA 1965; Univ Iowa, PhD, 1975. **Career:** Miami Valley St Col, staff, 1965-66; Pontiac N High Sch, teacher, 1966-69;AWAKE, teacher & dir, 1969; Fla A&M Univ, instr, 1968-71, asst prof,1973-74; Univ Iowa, teaching res fel, 1971-74; Tex Christian Univ, ColHumanities & Social Sci, assoc prof African-Am lit, currently. **Orgs:** Fla A&M Univ Midwest Modern Lang Asn; S Atlantic Modern Lang Asn; Col LangAsn. **Special Achievements:** Book: In loathing & love : Black Southern novelists' views of the South,1954-64, 1978. **Business Addr:** Associate Professor, Texas Christian University, College of Humanities & Social Sciences, 2800 S Univ Dr Reed 225, Fort Worth, TX 76129, **Business Phone:** (817)257-6245.

HENDERSON, BARRINGTON
Singer. **Personal:** Born Jun 10, 1966, Washington County, PA; son of Joyce. **Career:** Albums: Power; Bulls-eye; I Wanna Hold Your Hand; Phoenix Rising, 1998; Ear-Resistible, 2000; "I'm Sorry", writer & singer; The Temptations, 1998; It's All Right to Be Wrong, vocalist; A Little Bit Lonely, vocalist; Awesome, 2001; My Baby; Best Kept Secret, 2003. **Honors/Awds:** Grammy Award. **Business Addr:** Singer, William Morris Agency, 1 William Morris Pl, Beverly Hills, CA 90121, **Business Phone:** (310)859-4000.

HENDERSON, CARL L, JR.
Police officer. **Personal:** Born May 5, 1945, Pelahatchie, MS; son of Carl (deceased) and Mary Sample (deceased); married Eunice; children: Carl Dwaine, Gary Lee & Linette. **Educ:** Prentiss Junior Col, Prentiss, MS, AS, 1966; Univ New Haven, West Haven, CT, BS, 1976. **Career:** Hartford Bd Educ, Hartford, CT, social worker, 1968-71; Hartford Police Dept, Hartford, CT, supervr, lt, 1971-76, sgt, 1979-. **Orgs:** Pres, Hartford Guardians, 1988-92; Hartford Police Union, 1971-. **Honors/Awds:** Community Service Award, Hartford Guardians Inc, 1980, 1987, 1995. **Military Serv:** AUS, sgt, 1976-79; Honorary Service Medal-Good Conduct, 1979. **Home Phone:** (203)242-3415. **Business Addr:** Sergeant, Hartford Police Department, 50 Jenning Rd, Hartford, CT 06120, **Business Phone:** (860)527-7300.

HENDERSON, CEDRIC EARL
Basketball player. **Personal:** Born Mar 11, 1975, Memphis, TN. **Educ:** Univ Memphis, attended 1997. **Career:** Cleveland Cavaliers, forward, 1997-2001; Golden State Warriors, 2001-02; Milwaukee Bucks, free agent. *

HENDERSON, CHERI KAYE
Association executive. **Personal:** Born Feb 3, 1947, Knoxville, TN; daughter of James Noel and Marion Perry. **Educ:** Univ Tenn Knoxville, BS, 1974. **Career:** Knox Co Sch Syst, instr, 1974-76; Metrop Nashville Bd Educ, instr, adult basic educ, 1976-78; Tenn State Dept Econ & Community Develop, asst chief procurement, 1976-78; Minority Bus Opportunity Comt, exec dir, 1978-79; Tenn Minority Supplier Develop Coun Inc, exec dir, 1979-; pres, currently. **Orgs:** Citizens Bank Community Adv Coun; bd dirs, United Way Middle Tenn; bd dirs, Nashville Bus Incubation Ctr; bd mgrs, Northwest Young Men's Christian Asn; Leadership Nashville; bd dirs, Am Heart Asn; Third Nat Bank Econ Develop External Coun; Hugh O'Brien Youth Found; Matthew 25, Nashville Read; chair, United Negro Col Fund, Middle Tenn Campaign, Small/Medium Bus. **Honors/Awds:** Minorities & Women In Business, Women Who Make A Difference, 1992, Nat Award of Excellence, 1990; Minority Business News USA, Women Who Mean Business, 1992; Woman of the Year, Davidson Co Bus & Prof Women, 1991; Executive Director of the Year, Nat Adv Comt, 1983; Alpha Phi Alpha Fraternity Tau Lamba Chapter Public Service Award, 1999; "The Best of Decade," Minority Business News USA, Dallas, TX, 2002. **Special Achievements:** New Minority Business Resource Division for United Way, 1991. **Business Addr:** Executive Director, President, Tennessee Minority Supplier Development Council Inc, 220 Athens Way Suite 105 Metro Ctr Plz I Bldg, Nashville, TN 37228, **Business Phone:** (615)259-4699.

HENDERSON, CHERYL BROWN
Association executive. **Personal:** Born Dec 20, 1950, Topeka, KS; daughter of Rev Oliver L Brown and Leola; married Larry, Aug 5, 1972; children: Christopher. **Educ:** Baker Univ, BS, 1972; Emporia State Univ, MA, 1976. **Career:** Topeka Pub Schs, teacher, 1972-76, counr, 1976-79; KS State, Dept Educ, educ consult, 1979-94; Brown & Brown Asn, owner, 1984-; Brown Found, pres, founder & chief exec officer, 1988-. **Orgs:** St John AME, 1964-; bd mem, Kans State Hist Soc, 1997-; bd mem, Nat Trust for Hist Preservation, 1998-; adv, US Senate Adv Comt-Math & Sci, KS, 1998-; bd mem, Kans Humanities Coun, 1997-; adv, Nat Park Serv-Brown Bd Educ, 1990-; second vpres, Shounee County Republic Women, 1999-; past chair, Mayor's Coun Diversity, 1998-. **Honors/Awds:** Distinguished Alumni Citation, Baker Univ, 1997; Spirit of Topeka, Topeka Convention & Visitors Bur, 1998; Heart-to-Heart Award, Volunteer Ctr, Topeka, 1999; Capitol Citizen Award, Cable TV, 1999; Diversity Council Leadership, City Topeka, Mayor's Office, 1999; Spirit of Amelia Earhart Role Model Award, Amelia Earhart Museum; the Friend of Education Award, Nat Educ Asn, 2005; numerous awards for work and presentations on women's issues; Life Time Achievement Award, Nat Alliance Black Sch Educ; Fight for Justice Award, Southern Univ Law Ctr. **Special Achievements:** Lectured on "Brown v Bd of Ed" numerous campuses, 1988-; developed legislation to establish "Brown v Bd" Natl Park, 1992; Publications: Brown v Bd of Educ: In Pursuit of Freedom & Equality, Teachers Guide; Forty Years After the Brown Decision: Implications, Perspectives and Future Direction, Readings on Equal Educ, vol 13, 1997; "The Brown Foundation Story: Preserving Public History" CRM vol 19, No 2, 1996; one of a group of individuals invited to a reception at the White House in honor of Dr. King and the children of Civil Rights Movement and the 75th Anniv, US Dept of Labor, Women's Bureau, 1994, 1995; "Landmark Decision-Remembering the Struggle for Equal Education", Land and People, The Trust for Public Lands, vol 6, no. 1, 1994; "Schoolhouse Restoration", Preserving Our Recent Past, Historic Preservation Education Foundation, Washington, DC, 1995. **Business Addr:** President, Chief Executive Officer, Brown Foundation, 214 SW 6th Suite 306, Topeka, KS 66603, **Business Phone:** (785)235-3939.

HENDERSON, DR. CORTEZ V.
Educator. **Personal:** Born Jun 8, 1960, Pine Bluff, AR; daughter of Ed and Sue; divorced. **Educ:** Univ Ark, Pine Bluff, BS, 1982; Iowa State Univ, ME, 1987, PhD, 1992. **Career:** St Community Col, dean students; Univ Cent Ark, Conway, vis prof; NewBirth Youth Difference Prog, educ coordr/ grant writer; Univ Ark, Pine Bluff, AR, Ronald E McNair Scholars Prog, prin investr & prog dir, 2003-. **Orgs:** Bd mem, Coun Opportunity Educ, 1997-2000; pres, SW Asn Students Assistance Prog, 1997-2000; Leadership Pine Bluff, 2002; Alliance Candidate Inst, 2002; Pine Bluff Comn C & Youth; Task Force Reinventing Downtown; Nat Asn Advan Colored People; comt mem, Nat TRIO Conf. **Business Addr:** Program Director, Investigator, University of Arkansas, Ronald McNair Scholars Program, 1408 N Univ Dr, MS 4915, Pine Bluff, AR 71601, **Business Phone:** (870)575-8515.

HENDERSON, DAVID
Writer, poet, educator. **Personal:** Born Jan 1, 1942?, New York, NY. **Educ:** Bronx Comm Col, attended 1960; Hunter Col, NY, attended 1961; New Sch Social Res, attended 1962; East West Inst, attended 1964; Univ Without Walls, Berkeley, attended 1972. **Career:** Soc Umbra, co-founder, 1962-; City Col New York, SEEK prog lectr, 1967-69,poet-in-residence, 1969-70; Univ Calif, Berkeley, lectr, 1970-72; fulltime auth, 1973-79; Univ Calif, San Diego, vis prof, 1979-80; Naropa Univ, vis prof, 1981, 1995, 2004; State Univ New York, Stony Brook, vis prof, 1988-89; St. Mark's Poetry Proj, workshop leader, 1995, 2003; New York Found Arts, artist fel, 1999; New Sch, vis prof, 2000; Author: Felix of the Silent Forest, 1967; De Mayor of Harlem, Dutton, 1970; Jimi Hendrix:Voodoo Child of the Aquarian Age, 1978; The Low East, 1980; Neo-California, 1998; Editor: Umbra, co-editor, 1963-68; Umbra Anthology, 1968; Umbra, ed, 1968-74; Umbra/Latin Soul, 1975. **Orgs:** Consult, Nat Endowment Arts, 1967-68, 1980; consult, Berkeley Pub Sch Syst, 1968; NY Pub Sch Systs; Int PEN, 1972-; Arts Comn City Berkeley,1975-77; Afro-Am Triad World Writers Union, 1980-. **Honors/Awds:** Great Lakes College Association of New Writers Award, 1971; New Genre Poetry Grant, Calif Arts Coun, 1992; Artist Grant, Found Contemp Performance Arts, 1999. **Special Achievements:** Henderson wrote the lyrics to composer and pianist Sun Ra's "Love in OuterSpace".

HENDERSON, EDDIE L.
Engineer. **Personal:** Born Feb 25, 1932, Quincy, FL; son of Ennis and Ruby Green; married Velma Dean Hall; children: Tracy, Dionne. **Career:** Engineer (retired); Freedmens Hosp, 1961-67; Am Broadcasting Co News, DC; NABET, engr, 1994. **Orgs:** Local 644 Int Alliance Theatrical Stage Employees; Hillcrest Heights Baptist Church. **Honors/Awds:** Amateur Fighter Golden Gloves, NY, 1949-50; So Conf Air Force Japan, 1953. **Military Serv:** USAF, 1951-55. *

HENDERSON, HON. ERMA L.
Government official. **Personal:** Born Aug 20, 1917, Pensacola, FL; divorced; children: 2. **Educ:** Detroit Inst Technol; Wayne County Community Col; Univ Mich; Wayne State Univ, MA. **Career:** Government official, business owner (retired); Detroit City Coun, city council woman, 1972-90, pres, 1977-90, pres emer, currently; City Detroit, councilman Nicholas Hood, aide; Erma Henderson's Wholistic Health Foods, owner. **Orgs:** Bd mem, Nat Coun Crime & Delinquancy; League Women Voters; Nat Asn Soc Work Inc; Mich Acad Sci Arts & Letters; Asn Black Soc Work WSU; Am Dem Act Bd; Interfaith Act Coun; life mem, NAACP; Nat Coun Negro Women; bd mem, Black-Polish Conf; organizer, Women's Conf Concerns; bd chairwoman, Mich Coalition Against Redlining; co-founder, Black Res Found; Delta Sigma Theta Inc; Alpha Chap, Gamma Phi Delta Sorority; past chairwoman, Women Munic Govt; Nat League Cities; Eta Phi Beta Sorority, Alpha Chap. **Honors/Awds:** Hon Doctor of Humane Letters, Shaw Col, 1974; Michiganian of the Year, Detroit News, 1978; Michigan Women's Hall of Fame, 1990. **Special Achievements:** First black to win against a white opponent in a city-wide non-partisan election; first black woman to serve on Detroit s City Council.

HENDERSON, FRANK S, JR.
Government official. **Personal:** Born Oct 12, 1958, Oakley, KS; son of Frank S and Meade A Jones; married Lorraine M White, Mar 26, 1988; children: Ashley A. **Educ:** Barton County Comm Col, Great Bend, Kans, AA, 1981; Washburn Univ, Topeka, Kans, BA, 1987. **Career:** Kansas Dept Social & Rehabilition Services, Topeka, Kans, mental health activity therapist, 1979-82, social service admin, 1982-85; Kans Dept Corr, topeka, Kans, corrections specialist, 1985-87; Kans Parole Bd, Topeka, KS, vice-chairman, 1988-89, chmn, 1989-90; Kans Crime Victims Compensation Bd, exec dir, 1995-. **Orgs:** Nat Asn Advan Colored People, 1986; vpres, Mental Health Asn, Kans, 1988-90; comnr, Governor's Adv Comn Mental Health & Retardation Servs, 1988-90; Topeka Sunset Optimist Club, 1989-; mem, Nat Asn Blacks Criminal Justice, 1989-; councilman, Kans Criminal Justice Co-ord Coun, 1989-90; Nat Forum Black Public Admin, 1990-; prog chmn, Governor's Martin Luther King Commemoration, 1991. **Honors/Awds:** Special Recognition Award, Third Kans Judicial District, 1987-89; Service Award, Sunset of Optimist Club, 1988. **Business Addr:** Executive Director, Kansas Crime Victims Compensation Board, 700 Jackson Suite 400, Topeka, KS 66612, **Business Phone:** (913)296-2359.

HENDERSON, DR. GEORGE
Educator. **Personal:** Born Jun 18, 1932, Hurtsboro, AL; son of Kidd L Henderson and Lula Mae Crawford Fisher; married Barbara Beard; children: George Jr, Michele, Lea Murr, Joy, Lisa, Dawn Johnson & Faith Mosley. **Educ:** Wayne State Univ, BA, 1957, MA, 1959, PhD, 1965. **Career:** Educator (retired), consult; Church Youth Serv, soc caseworker, 1957-59; Detroit Housing Comn, soc economist, 1960-61; Detroit Urban League, comunity serv dir, 1961-63; Detroit Mayors Youth Comn, prog dir, 1963-64; Detroit Pub Sch, asst supt, 1965-67; USAF Acad, distinguished visiting prof, 1980-81; Univ Okla, David Ross Boyd distinguished prof, 1985, Col Libr Studies, dean, 1996-2000, Sylvan Goldman prof, Regents distinguished prof, prof human rels & dir; Kerr-McGee Presidential prof, 2001; US Dept Def, cosult; US Dept Justice, consult; US Comn Civil Rights, consult; Social Sec Admin, consult; Am Red Cross, consult. **Orgs:** Kappa Alpha Psi Frat; Am Sociol Asn; Asn Black Sociologist; Asn Supr & Curriculum Develop. **Honors/Awds:** Citation for Achievements in Human Relations, Okla State Senate, 1978; Distinguished Community Service Award, Urban League Okla City, 1981; Citation for Affirmative Action Activities in Higher Education, Okla House Rep, 1984; Civilian Commendation, Tinker AFB, 1986; Outstanding Faculty Award, Univ Okla Black People's Union, 1987; Outstanding Contributions, Osan Air Base, Korea, 1987; Trail Blazer Award, Okla Alliance Affirmative Action, 1988; Outstanding Teacher, Univ Okla Black Alumni Asn, 1988; Human Rights Award, Okla Human Rights Comn, 1989; Okla Black Public Administrators Excellence Award, 1990; Martin Luther King Jr Award, Univ Okla, Col Health Black Student Asn, 1990; Distinguished Service Award, Univ Okla, 1992; Black Caucus Award Educational Service, Am Asn Higher Educ, 1992; Outstanding Col Univ Teacher, Okla Found Excellence, 2000; Okla Higher Education Hall of Fame, 2003; Okla Hall of Fame, 2003; Career Achievement Award, Univ Okla Col Educ, 2003; Lifetime Achievement Award, Okla Black Heritage, 2003. **Special Achievements:** Third African-American Appointed to a Full-Time Faculty Position in University of Oklahoma; First African-American to hold an Endowed Professorship in the State of Oklahoma; Publications: Police Human Rel,1981; Transcultural Hlth Care 1981; Physician-Patient Communication 1981; The State of Black OK 1983; The Human Rights of Prof Helpers, 1983; Psychosocial Aspects of Disability, 1984; Mending Broken Children, 1984; College Survival for Student Athletes, 1985; International Business & Cultures, 1987; Our Souls to Keep, 1989; Understanding Indigenous & Foreign Cultures, 1989; Values in Health Care, 1991; Cultural Diversity in the Workplace, 1994; Social Work Interventions, 1994; Migrant's, Immigrants & Slaves,1995; Human Relations Issues in Management, 1996; Our Souls to Keep, 1999; Rethinking Ethnicity & Health Care, 1999;

Ethnicity & Substance Abuse, 2002. **Military Serv:** USAF, a 2c, 1953-55. **Home Addr:** 2616 Osborne Dr, Norman, OK 73069, **Home Phone:** (405)329-8614.

HENDERSON, GERALD (JEROME MCKINLEY HENDERSON)
Television broadcaster, basketball player, business owner. **Personal:** Born Jan 16, 1956, Richmond, VA; married Marie; children: 2. **Educ:** Va Commonwealth Univ. **Career:** Basketball player (retired), television broadcaster, business owner; Boston Celtics, guard, 1979-84; Seattle SuperSonics, 1984-87; NY Knicks, 1987; Philadelphia 76ers, 1987-89; Detroit Pistons, 1989-91 & 1991-92; Houston Rockets, 1991; All state Transp Co Inc, owner & pres; Genesis Adv, rep; Pa Merchant Group, vpres investment mgt; Comcast Sports Net, NBA analyst; RE/MAX Serv, sales assoc, currently. **Business Phone:** (215)654-6166.

HENDERSON, HENRY F., JR.
Executive. **Personal:** Born Jan 1, 1928?. **Educ:** State Univ NY Agr & Tech Inst, attended 1950; William Paterson Univ; Seton Hall Univ; NY Univ; Stevens Inst Technol; Alfred State Col. **Career:** HF Henderson Indust, pres & chief exec officer, 1954-. **Orgs:** Paterson Econ Develop Corp; Comt Common Defense; Regional Plan Asn; Task Force Pub TV; The Century Found; NJ State Employ & Training Comn, comnr, Port Authority Of NY & NJ; chair, Gov Comn Int Trade during admin Gov; Delta Dental Plan NJ; NJ Chamber Of Com; Stevens Inst Technol; NY Theol Sem. **Honors/Awds:** Company of Yr, Black Enterprise Mag; hon doc, Kean Univ; Distinguished Bus Citizen of Yr, NJ Bus & Indust Asn. **Business Addr:** President, Cheif Executive Officer, HF Henderson Industries, 45 Fairfield Pl, West Caldwell, NJ 07006, **Business Phone:** (973)227-9250.*

HENDERSON, HENRY FAIRFAX, JR.
Executive. **Personal:** Born Mar 10, 1928, Paterson, NJ; son of Henry F Henderson Sr. and Elizabeth Hammond; married Ethel Miller Henderson, Dec 19, 1948; children: Kathleen Carter, Kenneth, David, Elizabeth. **Educ:** State Univ NY Alfred, attended 1950; William Paterson Col, Seton Hall Univ; NY Univ. **Career:** Howe Richardson Scale Co, engr, 1950-67; HF Henderson Indust, founder, 1954-67, pres & chief exec officer, 1967-. **Orgs:** Comnr, Port Authority NY & NJ; chmn, Governor's Comn Int Trade; dir, NJ State Chamber Com; World Trade Inst Port Authority NY & NJ; adv bd mem curric, State Univ NY Agr & Tech Inst; bd mem, Partnership NJ; bd trustees, Stevens Inst Technol; bd dirs, Gen Pub Utilities Corp; bd trustees, Community Found NJ; Pres Comn Exec Exchange; Found NJ Alliance Action; adv comt, Essex County Superior Ct. **Honors/Awds:** Outstanding Business Achievement Award, NJ Black Chamber Com; Most Outstanding Minority Business Award, Edmond L Houston Found, 1979; Recognition of Business Achievement, Leaguers Inc, 1982; Black Achievers Entrepreneur of the Year Award, Leaguers Inc, 1982; Contractor of the Year, US Small Bus Admin, 1983; Outstanding Achievement in Business & Public Service Award; Urban League of Essex Co Award; National Association Negro Business & Professional Women Clubs Award; Man of the Year Award; Brotherhood Award, Nat Conf of Christians & Jews Inc, 1984; Man of the Yr 100, Black Men NJ Inc; Distinguished Business Citizen of the Year, NJ Bus & Ind Assoc; received 28th annual Essex Award for Outstanding Service to Business, Industry & Humanity, 1986; National Black MBA Association award; Distinguished Alumni Award, the Passaic Valley High Sch, 1986; Berean Award, United Minority Business Brain Trust Inc, 1988; New Jersey Entrepreneur of the Year Finalist, Arthur Young & Co, 1988; Outstanding Service to Business and Humanity, Hudson County Urban League, 1989; Image Award, St James AME Church, 1990; Honorary Doctor of Laws, Kean College, 1987; Honorary Doctor of Engineering, Stevens Inst Technol. **Home Addr:** 315 Rifle Camp Rd, West Paterson, NJ 07424. **Business Addr:** President, Chief Executive Officer, H F Henderson Indust, 45 Fairfield Pl, West Caldwell, NJ 07006-2630.*

HENDERSON, HERBERT H
Lawyer. **Personal:** Married Maxine D McKissick; children: Cherly Lynne, Sherri Avis Willoughby, Gail Staples, Leslie Jeanine & Michael Renaldo. **Educ:** WVa State Col, BS, bus admin, 1953; George Washington Univ Col Law, JD, 1958. **Career:** Civil Rights & Gen Pract, atty; Marshall Univ, part-time instr black hist, 1967-80; Henderson & Henderson Gen Pract, atty & sr partner, currently. **Orgs:** State pres, WVa Nat Asn Advan Colored People, 1966-86; mgr & supvr, WV Nat Asn Advan Colored People Jobs Prog, 1978-; nat bd dirs, NCP, 1980-; pres, WV Conf; Cabell Co Bar Asn; bd dir, WVa Trial Lawyers Asn; WV State Bar; Nat Bar Asn; Am Trial Lawyers Asn; Mountaineer Bar Asn; dir, Region III Asn Ment Health; chmn & bd trustees, Huntington Dist United Methodist Church; State United Methodist Church Conf; pres, Meth Men's Club; Ebenezer Methodist Church; Kappa Alpha Psi Frat; bd trustees, Morristown Col; fel, WVa Bar Asn. **Honors/Awds:** W Robert Ming Award, Nat Asn Advan Colored People Bd Dirs, 1985; Justitia Officium Award, WVa Univ Col Law, 1989; Hall of Fame, Nat Bar Asn, 1998; TG Nutter Award, NCP, WVa Conf Br; Living Dream Award for Civil Rights, WVa Martin Luther King, Jr Holiday CMS. **Military Serv:** AUS, 1946-49; Korean Conflict, artil officer, 1953-55. **Home Addr:** 440 12 Ave, Huntington, WV 25701. **Business Addr:** Attorney, Senior Partner,

Henderson Henderson & Staples, 711 5th Ave, Huntington, WV 25701-2010, **Business Phone:** (304)523-5732.

HENDERSON, HUGH C.
Government official. **Personal:** Born Dec 3, 1930, Poughkeepsie, NY; married Sandra V Bell; children: Hugh III & Denise. **Educ:** Kent Univ; Univ Ind; Univ Ill; Univ Wis. **Career:** Valley Mold & Iron Co, maintenance electrician, 1949-68; United Steel Workers Am, staff rep 1968-78; State Dept Employ Relat, secy, 1979; State Wis, Labor & Indust Review Comn, comnr, 1986. **Orgs:** Chmn bd, Milwaukee Industrialization Ctr, 1971-; bd dir, Milwaukee UrbanLeague, 1974-79; nat bd, Nat OIC, 1978-; pres, Milwaukee Frontier Club, 1977-79; Int Personnel Mgt Asn, 1979. **Honors/Awds:** Cert of Appreciation, OIC Bd Dir, 1978; Outstanding Community Effort Award, Dane City State Employees Combined Campaign, 1979; Enlightened Leadership, Dedicated Community Service Award, Milwaukee Frontiers Club, 1980. **Military Serv:** AUS, 1950-53; Combat Medal. *

HENDERSON, I. D., JR.
Government official. **Personal:** Born Jul 23, 1929, Lufkin, TX; married Jerlean Eastland; children: Brenda Kay Heads, Lara Wayne Parker, Gwendolyn Joyce McKinley & BruceAnthony. **Career:** Commissioner (retired); F Home Savings & Loans Asn, bldg supr, 1972-79; Lufkin Foundry Inc, mat control, 1971-72; Recinct 2 Angelina County, TX, pres & county comnr, 1979. **Orgs:** Master mason Franfurt Ger, 1962-65; master mason Mistletoe Lodge #31 Lawton OK, 1966-77; master mason Southgate Lodge #42 Lufkin TX, 1978-; deacon, Mt Calvary Bapt Ch Lufkin TX. **Honors/Awds:** Recipient KSM w/1 Bronze, SV Stara; NDSM; GMC w/5 Loops; Purple Heart AUS. **Special Achievements:** First Black Commissioner in Agelina County. **Military Serv:** AUS, sfc-e-7, 1951-70.

HENDERSON, JAMES H.
Government official, educator. **Personal:** Born Apr 20, 1937, Lexington, NC; son of Henry and Callie Spindell; married Joan E Woods; children: Tonya L, James H Jr, James, Jennifer, Janet, Jacqueline & Patricia. **Educ:** Community Col Air Force, AAS Mgt, AAS, Ed Methodology, 1981; Pikes Peak Community Col, AA Gen Studies, 1978; Univ Southern Colo, BS, 1979; Webste rUniv, MA, Mgt, 1982; Univ Northern Colo, MA, Coun, 1983; Harvard Univ,Grad Sch Educ, Insti Mgt Lifelong Educ. **Career:** USAF, educ supt, 1955-81; Ed Ctr Hurlburt Fla, educ coun, 1982-84; Hq Strategic Air Command, command educ counr, 1984, USAF Civil Serv, HQSAC/DPAE, asst dir educ serv, 1989, educ specialist, currently. **Orgs:** Recorder Kadesia Temple 135, 1975-; Am Assn Adult Continuing Educ, 1978; Am Numismatic Assn, 1982; Am Assn Coun Develop, 1982; mid west cord, Mili Educr & Coun Assn, 1983; Natl cert coun, Natl Brd Cert Coun, 1984. **Honors/Awds:** Coun Guide (Mil), 1984; Educ Serv Officers Guide, 1989. **Military Serv:** USAF, Mgt, 26 yrs; Good Conduct Medal; Commendation Medal; Meritorious Service Medal.

HENDERSON, DR. JAMES HENRY MERIWETHER
Educator. **Personal:** Born Aug 10, 1917, Falls Church, VA; son of Edwin Bancroft and Mary; married Betty Francis, Mar 28, 1948; children: Ellen Wimbish, Dena Sewell, James F & Edwin B II. **Educ:** Howard Univ, Wash DC, BS, bot, 1939; Univ WI Madison, MPh, 1940, PhD, plant physiol, 1943. **Career:** Univ Chicago Toxicity Lab, res asst, 1943-45; Carver Res Found Tuskegee Inst, res assoc, 1945-48, 1950-68; CA Inst Tech, res fel, 1948-50; Biol Dept Tuskegee Inst, prof & head, 1957-68; Carver Res Found Tuskegee Inst, dir, 1968-75; Nat Res Coun, consult; NIH's MBRS Prog Tuskegee Inst, prog dir, 1973-87; Comn Undergraduate Bio Sci Wash Carver Found, comnr; Tuskegee Univ, dean, sr res prof bio, emer prof & dean emer; Div Natural Sci Tuskegee Inst, chmn, 1975. **Orgs:** Fel AAAS; Am Soc Plant physiologists; Tissue Culture Asn; Sci Honor Soc; Phi Beta Kappa; Beta Kappa Chi; elder, W minister Presbyterian Church Tuskegee; mem bd trustees, Montreat-Anderson Col, 1973-78; bd mem, Soc Sigma Xi, 1982-85; mem bd trustees, Stillman Col Tuscaloosa AL. 1981-90. **Honors/Awds:** Alumni Award, Howard Univ, 1964 & 1975; eminent faculty award, 1965, faculty Award 1976 & 1980, Tuskegee Inst; UNCF Award for Dist Scholars, 1982; Distinguished Service Award, SS-ASPP, 1984; Lamplighters Award, Beta Kappa Chi, 1984; Golden Key, Nat Honor SOC, 1995; AAAS Mentor Award for Lifetime Achievement, 2001. **Special Achievements:** Published over 50 professional journal articles, review articles, a book, abstracts, and made numerous presentations to professional and lay audiences, also has provided unexcelled leadership in professional organizations including the American Association for the Advancement of Science, the American Society of Plant Physiologists, the Botanical Society of America, the National Institute of Science, the American Institute of Biological Sciences, the Society for the Study of Development and Growth, and the Tissue Culture Association. **Business Addr:** Chairman, Tuskegee University, Div Natural Sci, Carver Research Labs, Tuskegee Institute, AL 36088, **Business Phone:** (334)727-8011.

HENDERSON, JEROME MCKINLEY. See HENDERSON, GERALD.

HENDERSON, JEROME VIRGIL
Football player, athletic director, football coach. **Personal:** Born Aug 8, 1969, Statesville, NC; married Traci; children: Jazmin,

Taylor & Tyler. **Educ:** Clemson Univ. **Career:** Football player (retired), Football coach, Athletic director; New England Patriots, defensive back, 1991-93, 1996; Buffalo Bills, 1993-94; Philadelphia Eagles, 1995; New York Jets, 1997-98, dir player develop & defensive backs coach, 2006-08; Cleveland Browns, def coach, currently. **Business Addr:** Defensive Backs Coach, Cleveland Browns, 76 Lou Groza Blvd, Berea, OH 44017.

HENDERSON, DR. JOHN L.
College administrator, executive. **Personal:** Born Apr 10, 1932, Evergreen, AL; married Theresa Crittenden; children: Dana, Nina & John. **Educ:** Hampton Inst, BS, 1955; Univ Cincinnati, MEd, 1967, EdD, 1976; Inst Afro-Am Studies Earlham Col, 1971; PhD, 1976. **Career:** Univ Cincinnati, 1957-67, asst dean stud, 1968-69, dean stud develop,1972-76; Xavier Univ, res asst, 1967-68, lectr psychol educ, 1970-72; Raymond Walters Col, instr psychol educ, 1969-70; Wilberforce Univ, pres, 1988-2002; Ayers & Assocs Inc, assoc, 2002-; Univ Urban Affairs, dir; Sinclair Community Col, vpres; US Pub Health Serv, Cincinnati, res asst; Sinclair Community Col, Dayton, OH, Am Asn Higher Educ, vpres stud serv. **Orgs:** Cincinnati Br Nat Asn Advan Colored People, 1969; Phi Delta Kappa, 1971; Spec Task Force Study Racial Isolation Cincinnati Pub Schs, 1972-73; Cincinnati Manpower Planning Coun, 1971-72; bd trustees, Cincinnati Sch Found, 1973-75; Develop Educ Adv Comt, OH Bd Regents, 1974; ed bd, NASPA Jour, 1974; bd dir, Dayton Urban League, 1977-; bd dir, Miami Valley Lung Asn, 1978; bd dir, Miami Valley Educ Oppor Ctr, 1978; bd dir, Miami Valley Coun Aging, 1979; ed bd, Jour Develop & Remedial Educ, 1980; Asn Non-White Concerns; Nat Asn Stud Personnel Adminstrs; Am Col Personnel Asn; comnr, Cincinnati Human Rels Comt; chmn, Educ Comt; chmn & bd comnrs, Cincinnati Human Rels Comt; Coun Black Am Affairs. **Honors/Awds:** Honorable Chairman of Cincinnati Black Expo, 1971. **Special Achievements:** First black chairman of college council. **Military Serv:** AUS, first lt, 1955-57. **Business Phone:** (703)418-2815.

HENDERSON, JOYCE ANN
Executive. **Personal:** Born Jan 12, 1947, Oklahoma City, OK; married William Gerald; children: Kevin G & Wm Kelly. **Educ:** Langston Univ, Ok, BS, 1969; Cent State Univ Edmond OK, MS, 1973. **Career:** Harvard Mid Sch OK City Sch Syst, asst prin, 1978-80; Life Guthrie Job Corps Ctr, supvr basic educ & dept head ctr, 1976-78; Orchard Park Girls Sch Ok City Sch Syst, counr, 1974-76; Teacher Corps Univ OK & OK City Sch Syst, teacher corps supvr, 1972-74; Okla City Pub Sch, prin 1980-, dir sch & community serv, currently. **Orgs:** Co-authored, Teachers Guide Black Hist Okla Ok City School Syst, 1970; secy, Okla Chap Alpha Kappa Alpha Sorority, 1973-77; Okla Chap Jack & Jill Am Inc, 1975-; bd mem, Cent State Univ Alumni Asn, 1977-; sec & bd mem, UN Asn Okla City Chap, 1977-; Okla Educ Asn Prins Asn; bd mem & v chairwoman OK Crime Comn, 1978-. **Honors/Awds:** 2nd pl Midwestern Region Outstanding Sorority, Alpha Kappa Alpha Sorority, 1977. **Business Addr:** Director, Oklahoma City Public Schools, 900 N Klein, Oklahoma City, OK 73106.

HENDERSON, DR. LENNEAL JOSEPH
Consultant, educator. **Personal:** Born Oct 27, 1946, New Orleans, LA; son of Marcelle and Lenneal; married Joyce E Colon, May 7, 1989; children: Lenneal C & Lenneal J III. **Educ:** Univ Calif, Berkeley, BA, 1968, MA, 1969, PhD Polit Sci, 1977. **Career:** San Jose State Univ, Afro-Amer Studies, lectr, 1973-75; Shepard & Assoc,1973-74; Morrison & Rowe, sr analyst, 1974; Dukes Dukes & Assocs, San Francisco, assoc consult, 1974-75; Howard Univ, Wash, vis prof polit sci, 1975, prof sch bus & public admin, 1979-87; Rockefeller Found, res fel, 1981-83; Univ Tenn Knoxville, head, prof polit sci, 1988-89; Fed ExecInst, Charlottesville Valif, prof, 1989; Schaefer Ctr Public Policy, Univ Baltimore, sr fel, 1989-, State Md, Henry C Welcome fel, 1989-92; Calvert Inst Policy Res, distinguished prof govt & public admin, currently; NC Ct Univ, Daniel T Blue Endowed Prof Polit Sci, 2001-03; Fielding Grad Inst, part-time fac, 1991-. **Orgs:** Bd dirs, acting pres, Children & Youth Serv Agency; pres, San Francisco, African Am Hist & Cult Soc; Campaign Human Devel; co-ed "Journal on Political Repression"; affiliate Joint Center for Political Studies, Wash,1971-; Conf Minority Public Administrators, 1972-; Am Assn Univ Prof,1972-; educ brd, The Black Scholar Mag; chmn, Citizens Energy Adv Comn, Wash, 1981-; Natl Res Coun, 1983-84; brd trustees, Population Reference Bur; brd dirs, Decision Demographics, Natl Civic League; brd trustees, Chesapeake Bay Found, 1991-98; brd governors, Citizen's Planning and Housing Assn Baltimore, 1990-. **Honors/Awds:** Outstanding Service Award, San Francisco, Afro-Am Hist Soc, 1975; Outstanding Educator of America, 1975; Distinguished Faculty Award, Howard Univ; Kellogg Nat Fel, 1984-87; Distinguished Chair in Teaching, Univ Baltimore, 1992-93; Rockefeller Brothers Fund Mentor, 1999-2002. **Special Achievements:** Author: "Black Political Life in the US", 1972; "Diversity Management in the Baltimore-Washington Metropolitan Area," Maryland Policy Issues, Vol. 2, No. 1, Spring 1999; "Energy Policy and Urban Fiscal Management," Public Administration Review, Vol. 41, Jan. 1981; "Managing Human and Natural Disasters in Developing Nations,", 1994. **Business Addr:** Distinguished Professor of Government & Public Administration, Calvert Institute for Policy research, 1304 St Paul St, Baltimore, MD 21202-2786, **Business Phone:** (410)837-6198.

HENDERSON, LEON C
School administrator. **Personal:** Born Aug 4, 1947, Cincinnati, OH. **Educ:** Xavier Univ, BS, sociol; Wash Univ, MS, sociol, PhD, sociol. **Career:** Carmele Hall, prin & pres; St Alphonsus Ligouri Parish, pres, Parish Coun, vpres; Xavier Univ, Inst Black Catholic Studies, coordr, instr & adminr; Wilberforce Univ, dean stud affairs & develop; Cardinal Ritter Col Prep High Sch, teacher, adminr, pres, currently. **Orgs:** St Louis Archdiocesan Pastoral Coun; trustee, Kenrick-Glennon Sem. **Military Serv:** USN, 1967-71. **Business Addr:** President, Cardinal Ritter College Preparatory High School, 701 N Spring Ave, Saint Louis, MO 63108, **Business Phone:** (314)446-5507.

HENDERSON, LEROY W., JR.
Photographer, educator. **Personal:** Born May 27, 1936, Richmond, VA; married Helen Foy; children: Kerby & Keith. **Educ:** Va State Col, BS, 1959; Pratt, MS, 1965; Nat Acad TV Arts & Sci Film & TV Workshop, cert, 1973. **Career:** Richmond Pub Sch Syst, art teacher, 1959; New York Sch Syst, art teacher, 1962-66; freelance photographer, 1967-; Brooklyn Mus Educ Dept, art teacher, 1968; Bedford-Lincoln Neighborhood Mus, Brooklyn, art teacher, 1968-70. **Orgs:** Emergency Cult Coalition, 1968; bd mem, Aunt Len's Doll & Toy Mus, NY; Kappa Alpha Psi Frat; Full Opportunities Com Acad TV Arts & Sci, 1970-73; African Am Photographers Guild. **Honors/Awds:** Commendation for Heroic Performance, High Sch Mus & Art New York, 1968; Recipient Certificate of Excellence, Mead Libr Ideas Mead Paper Co, 1972; One Show Merit Award, Dir Club Inc & Copy Club, NY, 1974; Photo-Graphic Int Annual Award of Outstanding Art & Photog. **Military Serv:** AUS, specialist 4, 1959-61. *

HENDERSON, LLOYD D.
School administrator. **Personal:** Born Jan 28, 1945, Monroe Co, AL; married Sarah A; children: Cheryl. **Educ:** Ala State Univ, BS, 1964; Univ Wyo, MS, 1971; Auburn Univ, attended 1972. **Career:** School administrator (retired); Monroe Co Training Sch, coach head math dept, 1964-70; Monroe Co Monroeville Ala, instr adult educ, 1965; Univ Wyo, instr physics, 1971; Lurleen B Wallace State Jr Col, instr math & physics, 1971-74, dir stud support & spec prog, 1974. **Orgs:** Am Educ Asn; Nat Educ Asn; SAE-OPP; chmn, trustee bd, First Bethlehem Baptist Church; Covington Co Civic Organ; Free & Accepted Masons, Ala. **Honors/Awds:** Cert Achievement, Fla A & M Univ, 1970. *

HENDERSON, DR. NANNETTE S.
Educator. **Personal:** Born Jun 9, 1946, Washington, DC; daughter of Percival Carlton Smith and Edith Richardson; married Lyman Beecher, Nov 29, 1969; children: Kara Michelle & Kristi Bynn. **Educ:** Howard Univ, BS, 1967, MS, 1969; NC State Univ, PhD, 1973. **Career:** NC St Univ, Raleigh, asst prof plant path; Vance Granville CommunityCol, dir col transfer prog, Sci Dept, chair, 2003. **Orgs:** NC Asn Educr; Am Asn Jr & Community Col; NC Asn Two-Year & Community Col Biologists; Nat Sci Teachers Orgn, 1980-l; Phi Kappa Phi Hon Soc; Beta Kappa Chi Hon Soc. **Honors/Awds:** Excellence in Teaching, NC Dept Community Col, 1987; CASE Teaching Award, 1988; Tar Heel of the Week, News & Observer Newspaper, 1988; O Harris Award, Nat Sci Teachers Asn, 1990. **Home Addr:** 516 W Ridgeway St, Warrenton, NC 27589. **Business Addr:** Chair, Vance Granville Community College, Science Department, PO Box 917, Henderson, NC 27536.*

HENDERSON, RAMONA ESTELLE. See PEARSON, RAMONA HENDERSON.

HENDERSON, REMOND
Government official. **Personal:** Born Sep 21, 1952, Los Angeles, CA; son of Ernestine and Riebert M; married Joann Bukovich Henderson; children: Audra Elizabeth & Riebert Sterling. **Educ:** Cent Wash State Univ, BA, 1974. **Career:** Ernst & Young, Los Angeles, CA, staff & sr acct & auditor, 1974-77; Laventhol & Horwath, Los Angeles, CA, sr acct & auditor, 1977-79; Kaufman & Broad Inc, Los Angeles, CA, internal auditor, 1979-81; Kaufman & Broad Inc, Irvine, CA, controller, 1981; Dept Community & Regional Affairs, internal auditor III, 1982-84; Dept Community & Regional Affairs, Juneau, AK, dep dir, div admin serv, 1984-; Dept Labor & Workforce Develop, admin serv dir, 2003-. **Orgs:** Pres, Juneau Chap Blacks Govt, 1984-89; treas, Blacks Govt, Region X, 1986-88; pres, Region V, 1994-; Alaska Soc Cert Pub Accountants; Am Inst Cert Pub Accountants; co-founder, First Shiloh Missionary Baptist Church, Juneau; Juneau Rotary Club; emergency interim successor, Juneau Assembly Coun; chair, Dr Martin Luther King Jr Commemorative Comt Juneau, 1986-88; Juneau Arctic Winter Games Comt, 1990. **Honors/Awds:** Acad Scholar, Wash Soc CPA's, 1972-74; President's Award, Blacks Govt, Region X, 1985 & 1987; Certificate of Appreciation, City & Borough Juneau, Bus & Prof Women's Club Juneau, 1986; Federal Employee of the Year, Citizens Selection Comt, 1988; Special Achievement Award, 1990. **Business Addr:** Administrative Services Director, Department Of Labor and Workforce Development, Research & Analysis Section, PO Box 25501, Juneau, AK 99802-5501, **Business Phone:** (907)465-2720.

HENDERSON, RICKEY HENLEY (RICKEY NELSON HENLEY)
Baseball player, baseball manager. **Personal:** Born Dec 25, 1958, Chicago, IL; married Pamela; children: Angela, Alexis & Adriann. **Career:** Baseball player (retired), coach; Oakland Athletics, outfielder, 1979-84, 1989-93, 1994-95, 1998; NY Yankees, outfielder, 1985-89; Toronto Blue Jays, 1993; San Diego Padres, 1996-97, 2001; Anaheim Angels, 1997; NY Mets, 1999-2000, spec instr, 2006, first base coach, 2007; Seattle Mariners, 2000; Boston Red Sox, 2002; Los Angeles Dodgers, 2003; Newark Bears, 2004; San Diego Surf Dawgs, Golden Baseball League, 2005-07; New York Mets, spl instr, 2006-07, first base coach, 2007-08. **Honors/Awds:** Gold Glove Award, 1981; Silver Slugger Award, 1981, 1985, 1990; Sporting News Silver Shoe Award, 1982; Sporting News Golden Shoe Award, 1983; American League Championship Series MVP, 1989; American League Most Valuable Player, Baseball Writers' Asn Am, 1990; TSN Comeback Player of the Year Award, 1999; Inducted in to Hall of Fame, 2009. **Special Achievements:** Only American League player to steal at least 100 bases in a single season.

HENDERSON, DR. ROBBYE R. See Obituaries section.

HENDERSON, DR. ROMEO CLANTON
Educator. **Personal:** Born Apr 23, 1915, Salisbury, NC; married Jestina Tutt; children: Gwynette & Patricia. **Educ:** Livingstone Col, AB, 1936; Cornell Univ, MA, 1938; Pa State Univ, EdD, 1950. **Career:** Swift Memorial Jr Col, Rogersville Tenn, instr dean, 1939-43; SC State Col Orangeburg, prof, chmn social sci, dean sch grad studies, 1952-60; DE State Col, prof educ, dean instrn. *

HENDERSON, RONALD
Law enforcement officer. **Career:** St Louis City Police, Bur of Patrol Support, dep chief, chief police; US Marshal for the Eastern Dist of Mo, 2002-. **Orgs:** Int Asn Chiefs Police. **Business Addr:** US Marshal for the Eastern District of Missouri, 111 S 10th St Rm 2319, St Louis, MO 63102-1116, **Business Phone:** (314)539-2212.

HENDERSON, RUTH FAYNELLA
Educator, composer. **Personal:** Born in Kansas City, MO; daughter of Isaiah Hilkiah Henderson Jr and Ophelia Beatrice. **Educ:** Bishop Col, BS, elem edu, 1965; N Tex State Univ, MEd, early childhood, 1975; La Salle Univ, EdD, 1995. **Career:** Dallas Independent Sch Dist, early childhood educr; First Baptist Church Hamilton Pk, minister music, 1969-89; Lighthouse Church God Christ, pianist, 1991-; Willow Grove Baptist Church, minister music, 1992-. **Orgs:** Pres, Christians In Action; founder, Christian Dating & Friendship Ministry; producer, Fruit Fest, 1992. **Special Achievements:** Wrote and composed several songs on Fla Mass Choir album, Jeffrey La ValleyNew Jerusalem Choir album, James Cleveland Gospel Music Workshop albums, DFN Mass Choir album.

HENDERSON, STEPHEN. See HENDERSON, STEPHEN MCKINLEY.

HENDERSON, STEPHEN MCKINLEY (STEPHEN HENDERSON)
Educator, actor. **Personal:** Born Aug 31, 1949, Kansas City, MO; son of Elihue Kelley and Ruby Naomi Johnson; married Pamela Reed, Apr 22, 1978; children: Jamal Stephen. **Educ:** Lincoln Univ, 1968; Juilliard Drama Div, 1970; NC Sch Arts, BFA, 1972; Purdue Univ, MA, 1977. **Career:** State Univ NY, Buffalo, NY, dept chairperson, tenured prof; Actor: 4 Broadway productions, 5 off-Broadway productions, Royal Nat Theatre of Great Britain, Dublin Theatre Festival, 3 Kennedy Center productions; Sundance Theatre Lab Co, 2003; Everyday People HBO film, 2004; The Good Heart, 2009; TV series: New Amsterdam for Fox Television, episodes of LAW AND ORDER, "The Faithful", 2001, "Law & Order: Criminal Intent ",2001, "Access Nation", 2002, "Hitman", 2002, "Heart of Darkness", 2006, "Hostage", 2006, "Conviction", 2006, "Clock", 2006, "Law & Order: Special Victims Unit", 2006; American Theatre Wing's, Working In The Theatre, "August Wilson's Legacy", 2007; Sweetie, 2008. **Orgs:** Soc Stage Dirs & Choreographers; AFA, 1976-; SAG, 1982-; Theatre Auditor, 1988-92; SSDC, 1992-; Special Arts Comm, 1994-98; NY State Coun Arts; Actor's Equity; bd mem, Arts Coun Western NY; steering comm, Actors Ctr, 2001-. **Honors/Awds:** Los Angeles NAACP Theatre Award; Los Angeles Drama Critics Circle Award; New York Drama Desk and Obie Award; Nominee, Black Reel Awards, 2005. **Special Achievements:** Distinquished Alumni Award, Purdue University, College of Liberal Arts; 1996; Olympic Arts Festival Citation in Recognition and Appreciation (as director of the production, ALI!). **Business Addr:** Associate Professor, State University of NY at Buffalo, Department of Theatre & Dance, 189 Alumni Arena, Buffalo, NY 14260-5030, **Business Phone:** (716)645-6898.

HENDERSON, THELTON EUGENE
Judge. **Personal:** Born Nov 28, 1933, Shreveport, LA; son of Eugene M and Wanzie; children: Geoffrey A. **Educ:** Univ Calif, Berkeley, BA, 1956; Univ Calif, Boalt Hall Sch Law, JD, 1962. **Career:** US Army Corporal, 1956-58; US Dept Justice, atty, 1962-63; Fitz Simmons & Petris, assoc, 1964-66; San Mateo County Legal Aid Soc, dir atty, 1966-69; Stanford Univ Law Sch, asst dean, 1968-77; Rosen, Remcho & Henderson, pvt pract, 1977-80; Golden Gate Univ, Sch Law, assoc prof, 1978-80; US DistCt, 9 Circuit, CA, judge, 1980; chief judge, 1997; sr judge; US Dist Court, Northern Dist Calif, chief judge emer, 1997-. **Orgs:** Nat Bar Asn; Charles Houston Law Asn. **Honors/Awds:** American Inns of Court Lewis F Powell Jr Award, 2005. **Military Serv:** AUS, 1956-58. **Business Addr:** Chief Judge Emeritus, US District Court, Northern District of California, 450 Golden Gate Ave 18th Fl, San Francisco, CA 94102, **Business Phone:** (626)577-2255.

HENDERSON, THERESA CRITTENDEN
Educator, school principal. **Personal:** Born Nov 11, 1937, Montgomery, AL; daughter of Willie L and Jacob K; married John L, Jun 28, 1969; children: Dana, Nina & Brent. **Educ:** Univ Cincinnati, BS, educ & fine arts, 1959, MEd, 1969. **Career:** Newark, NJ, pub schs, teacher, jr high, 1959-60; NY City Pub Schs, elem teacher, 1960-64; Cincinnati Pub Schs, art teacher, 1964-83, asst prin, 1983-84, prin, 1984-91, dir, 1992-. **Orgs:** Alpha Kappa Alpha, 1957-; chmn, Urban Arts Comm, Woman's City Club; mem, The Links Inc, 1971-75, chmn fundraising prog, vpres & secy, 1972-; Delta Kappa Gamma, 1988-; pres, Cincinnati Contemp Arts Ctr, 1980-84; Phi Delta Kappa, 1988-; Nat Alliance Black Sch Educrs, 1988-; Cincinnati Opera Bd, 1991-; Playhouse Park Bd. **Honors/Awds:** Honorary Doctorate, Cincinnati Tech Col, 1992; Woman of the Year, Cincinnati Enquirer, 1989; Brotherhood/Sisterhood Award, Nat Conf Christians & Jews, 1992; Excellence in Education Award, 1988, National Blue Ribbon Award, US Dept Educ, 1992. **Special Achievements:** Cincinnati Art Museum Exhibit, local artists, 1960, Discovery 70 Art Exhibit, National Art Exhibit, 1970, Leadership Cincinnati, Class XIV, 1990-91. **Home Phone:** (513)242-3939. **Business Addr:** Director, Cincinnati Public Schools, 3060 Durrell Ave E Hoffman School, Cincinnati, OH 45207, **Business Phone:** (513)961-1724.

HENDERSON, TRACY
Basketball player. **Personal:** Born Dec 31, 1974; daughter of Dorothy Ann Henderson; married; children: Journee. **Educ:** Univ Ga, consumer econ, 1997. **Career:** Atlanta Glory, 1997-98; Nashville Noise, 1998; Cleveland Rockers, ctr, 1999-03. **Honors/Awds:** ABL Rookie of the Yr Award. **Special Achievements:** Top-10 players in the hist, Univ Ga; finalist, Naismith Player of the Yr Award. *

HENDERSON, VIRGINIA RUTH MCKINNEY
Psychologist. **Personal:** Born Feb 19, 1932, Cleveland, OH; daughter of Ruth Berry McKinney and Dr Wade Hampton McKinney; married Perry A; children: Sheryl, Virginia, Perry Jr. **Educ:** Spelman Col, BA, psychol, 1953; Boston Univ, MA, 1955; Univ NMex, PhD, psychol, 1974. **Career:** Psychologist (retired); Mad Metro Sch Dist, sch psychol, 1976-97; Univ NMex, asst prof ped psychiat, 1968-76; Seattle, sch psychol, 1967-68; Cleveland Metro Gen Hosp, psychologist, 1963-65; Cleveland Guidance Ctr, psychologist, 1957-59; Muscatatuck St Sch, dir nursery educ psychologist, 1955-57; Model Cities Day Care Ctr, consult, 1972-74; Madison Sch Dist, spec asst to supt equity & diversity, 1993-97. **Orgs:** Am Psychol Asn, 1968-92; Nat Asn Sch Psychologists, 1976-; Am Asn Ment Def, 1964; bd dir, All Faiths Receiving Home, 1973-76; bd trustees, Mazano Day Sch, 1974-76; bd dir, TWCA, 1977; First Baptist Church of Mad, WI; bd dirs, Wis Nurses Asn; bd dirs, Madison Urban League; Founder mem, Nat Asn Sch Psychologists; pres, Women in Focus; Gen Bd, Am Baptist Churches USA, 1983-92; bd dir, Green Lake Conf Ctr; Wayland Bd, Univ Wisconsin; chair, Minority Student Achievement Comn, Madison Sch Dist; United Way Allocation Comt, 1987-91; pres, bd dirs, African Am Acad; co chair, Mann Educ Opportunity Fund, 1991; Dane County Econ Summit, 1991-93; Jr League of Madison Comn Adv Bd; Madison Civics Club; Dist 4 Carl Perkins, adv comn for MATC, Spec Population; Prog Comt Proj Opportunity; founding mem, pres & bd of dir, African-Am Ethnic Acad; bd dir, Madison C Mus; bd governors, Madison Community found; grand making comt, 1998-01, Asset Builder's Award comn, 1999; bd develop comt, 2000; Evjue Foun; founding mem, Found Madison Pub Schs. **Honors/Awds:** Grand Magna Cum Laude, Spelman Col, 1953; Nat Cert Sch Psychologist, 1992; Distinguished Serv Award, Madison Sch Dist, 1990; Woman Distinction, YWCA, 1990; Citizen of the Yr, Omega Psi Phi Frat, 1991; Madison Mag 50 Most Influential People, 1992, 1997; Tribute to Black Women, 1994; Woman of the Yr Award, Mothers of Simpson St, 1994; African-Am C Festival Award, 1995; Cert Appreciation, Neighborhood Intervention Prog, 1996; Whitney M Young Award, Urban League of Madison, 2000; Community Builder Award, Dane Fund, 2001; Dr.Martin Luther King Jr Award, DAne County, 2003. *

HENDERSON, WADE
Association executive. **Educ:** Howard Univ; Rutgers Univ Sch Law, JD. **Career:** Am Civil Liberties Union, legis coun, lobbyist, Wash Nat Off, assoc dir; Univ DC, David A Clarke Sch Law, Pub Interest Law, Joseph L Rauh Jr prof; Nat Asn Advancement Colored People, WA, bureau dir; Leadership Conf Civil Rights, exec dir, currently, Leadership Conf Civil Rights Educ Fund, coun, currently. **Orgs:** Bar Supreme Ct, DC, NJ. **Honors/Awds:** Bar's William J Brennan Award, DC, 2002; Everett C Parker Award, Off Commun Inc, United Church Christ, 2002; Congressional Black Caucus Chair's Award, 2003. **Special Achievements:** Author of numerous articles on civil rights, human rights & pub policy

issues. **Business Addr:** Executive Director, Leadership Conference on Civil Rights, 1629 K St NW, 10th Fl, Washington, DC 20006-1601, **Business Phone:** (202)466-3311.*

HENDERSON, WILLIAM AVERY
Pilot, military leader. **Personal:** Born Jan 18, 1943, Ann Arbor, MI; son of William and Viola; married Francine, Jul 28, 1990; children: Nicole & Justin. **Educ:** Eastern Mich Univ, BS, social & hist, 1964. **Career:** Pilot (retired); Gen Motors Corp, pilot, 1974-93, chief pilot, 1993; 127th Tactical Fighter Wing, asst chief command post, chief safety, 1977-90; Mich Air Nat Guard Hq, plans officer, dep dir, 1990-93, brig gen, 1993-95, maj gen, 1995; Gen Motors, dir flight opers, 2000. **Orgs:** Kappa Alpha Psi, 1963-; Tuskegee Airmen, 1989-; Nat Guard Asn US, 1977-; Nat Guard Asn Mich, 1977-. **Special Achievements:** First African American brigadier general in the history of the Michigan Air National Guard; First African American to head Gen Motors corp fleet. **Military Serv:** USMC, 1964-74; Distinguished Flying Crosses, 1969, Air Medals eight.

HENDERSON, WILLIAM TERRELLE
Football player. **Personal:** Born Feb 19, 1971, Richmond, VA; married Brigitta; children: William II. **Educ:** NC, BS, phys educ, 1994. **Career:** Green Bay Packers, running back, 1995-2006; Marco Rivera's youth football clinic, instructor. **Orgs:** Am Diabetes Assn; Make-a-Wish Found; Am Red Cross; Big Brothers/Big Sisters; the Leukemia Soc; Crippled Children's Fund. **Honors/Awds:** Pro Bowl, 2005. **Special Achievements:** Stands 12th on the franchise's all-time list; Stands 11th on the Packers' all-time receptions list; "Monday Night Kickoff," WBAY, co-host, 1996; Earned first-team Associated Press All-Pro and NFC Pro Bowl starter accolades, 2004. **Business Addr:** Professional Football Player, Green Bay Packers, 1265 Lombardi Ave, PO Box 10628, Green Bay, WI 54307, **Business Phone:** (920)496-5700.

HENDERSON MOORE, NINA
Executive. **Career:** Black Entertainment TV, pres & chief operating officer. **Honors/Awds:** Nat Asn Advan Colored People Image Awards; Cable Positive Award. *

HENDERSON-NOCHO, AUDREY J
Activist. **Personal:** Born Aug 27, 1959, Sacramento, CA; daughter of Lillian Riccardo; married Kim (divorced 1988); children: Antiquia, Serenia & Asheley. **Educ:** Univ ND, Grand Forks, ND, BA, BS, 1991. **Career:** USAFB NCO Club, Grand Forks, ND, cook, 1984-86; Univ NDak, Grand Forks, ND, student aid, EBT cult ctr, 1986-89, mail sorter, 1989, stud coun, career serv & job placement, 1990-. **Orgs:** Former chairperson, Multi-Ethnic Support Asn, Community Housing Resource Bd, 1987-89; Chairperson, ND Comt Martin Luther King Jr Holiday, 1988; Mayors Human Needs Com, 1990-; Concerned Citizens Against Prejudice, 1990-; NDak Adv Comt US Civil Rights Comn, 1991-93. **Honors/Awds:** Making of the King Holiday Award, 1991. **Business Addr:** Student Cousel, University of North Datkota, 264 Centennial Dr 8382, Grand Forks, ND 58202, **Business Phone:** (701)777-2011.

HENDON, LEA ALPHA
Manager, consultant. **Personal:** Born Mar 27, 1953, Hartford, CT; daughter of Charles Martin and Willie Mae Wilcox Martin. **Educ:** Boston Col, Chesnut Hill MA, BA educ, 1975; Eastern New Mexico Univ, Portales NM, MA Psychol, 1979. **Career:** Boston Pub Schs, Boston, teacher, 1975-77; Allstate Ins Co, Farmington CT, office operations supvr, 1979-80; Aetna Ins Co, Hartford CT, bus syst analyst, 1980-83; Hartford Ins Group, Hartford CT, off automation consult, 1983-85; Aetna Life & Casualty, Hartford CT, recruiter, consult, 1986-. **Orgs:** Adv bd, DP, Post Col, 1987-88; Am Soc Personnel Admin, 1988-; pres, Black Data Processing Asn, Hartford Chapter, 1989-90; sec, ITC-Gavel, 1990-91; Delta Sigma Theta Sorority; NAFE. **Business Addr:** Administrator, Corporate Staffing, Aetna Life and Casualty, 151 Farmington Ave DA09, Hartford, CT 06156, **Business Phone:** (203)273-4008.

HENDRICKS, BARBARA
Opera singer. **Personal:** Born Nov 20, 1948, Stephens, AR; daughter of M L and Della; married Martin T; children: Sebastian Amadeus & Jennie Victoria. **Educ:** Univ Nebr, BS, math & chem, 1969; Juilliard Sch Music, BMus, 1969. **Career:** Ormindo, San Francisco Spring Opera, 1974; Boston Opera; St Paul Opera; Santa Fe Opera; Deutsche Opera; Berlin; Aix-en-Provence Festival; Houston Opera; De Nederlandse Opera stichting; Glyndebourne Festival Opera; Boston Symphony Orchestra; New York Philharmonic; Los Angeles Philharmonic; Cleveland Symphony Orchestra; Philadelphia Orchestra; Chicago Symphony; Berlin Philharmonic; Vienna Philharmonic; London Symphony Orchestra; Orchestre de Paris; Orchestre National de France. **Orgs:** Spec adv inter culturality to the Director General of UNESCO, 1994; founder, Barbara Hendricks Found Peace & Reconciliation, 1998; Swedish Acad Music. **Honors/Awds:** Numerous honors & awards including Dmus, Nebr Wesleyan Univ, 1988; Doctorat Honoris Causa, Univ Louvain, Belg, 1990; Chevalier de la Legiond' Honneur, 1992; Doctorat Honoris Causa, Univ Grenoble, France, 1996; DMus, Juilliard Sch Mus, 2000; Prince of Asturias Award for the Arts, 2000; Lions Club International Award, 2001; Premio Internacional Xifra Heras, 2004. **Special Achievements:** Film: Mimi in La Boheme, 1994. **Business Phone:** (014)281-3821.

HENDRICKS, BARKLEY L.
Artist, educator. **Personal:** Born Apr 16, 1945, Philadelphia. **Educ:** Bpa Acad Fine Arts, cert, 1967; Yale Univ Sch Art, BFA, MFA, 1972. **Career:** Conn Col, artist, asst prof art, 1972-, prof art studio, currently; Univ Saskatchewan, vis artist, 1974; Glassboro State Col, 1974; Pa Acad Fine Arts, instr, 1971, 1972; Offset Lithography Inst, Brandywine Workshop, Philadelphia, PA, artist fel, 1987; People to People, Citizens Ambassador fel, 1991; One Man Exhibitions: Conn Col, New London, CT, 1973, 1984, & 1993; Benjamin Mangel Gallery, Philadelphia, PA, 1981, 1993; Walnut St Theater, Philadelphia, PA, 1983; Brattleboro Mus & Art Ctr, Brattleboro, VT, 1984; Pa Acad Fine Arts, Peale House Gallery, Philadelphia PA, 1985; Housatonic Mus Art, Bridgeport, CT, 1988; Manchester Community Col, Manchester, CT, 1992; Cape May County Art Gallery, Cape May, NJ, 1992; Norwalk Community Col, Norwalk, CT, 1993; Collections: Chrysler Mus, Norfolk, VA; Nat Afro-Am Mus & Cult Ctr, Wilberforce, OH; Conn Comn Arts Collection, Hartford, CT; Forbes Mag Collection, New York, NY; Univ Conn Law Sch, Hartford, CT; Brandywine Offset Inst, Philadelphia, PA; Nat Ctr Afro-Am Artists, Boston, MA; Philadelphia Mus Art, Philadelphia, PA; Pa Acad Fine Arts, Philadelphia, PA; Uris Collection, New York, NY; Exhibitions Group Shows: Philadelphia Art Alliance, Philadelphia, PA, 1968, 1970, 1973, 1992; Conn Col, New London, CT, 1972-93; Benjamin Mangel Gallery, Philadelphia, PA, 1981-93; Erector Sq Gallery, New Haven, CT, 1986; Black Am Art Japan, Tokyo, Japan, 1987; Fine Arts Mus Long Island, Long Island, NY, 1988; Laura Knott Gallery, Bradford Col, Bradford, MA, 1992, 1993; Cent Conn State Univ, New Britain, CT, 1992; Hera Art Gallery, Wakefield, RI, 1993. **Honors/Awds:** Childe Hassam Purchase Award, Am Acad Arts & Letters, 1971, 1977; First Prize, Conn Artist Annual, Slater Mem Mus, 1976; Second Butler Medal, 43rd Annual Midyear Show, Butler Inst Am Art, 1979; Individual Artist Award, 1979, Purchase Award, Conn Comn Arts, 1991; Salute to the Arts Award, Philadelphia, PA, 1984. **Business Addr:** Professor of Art Studio, Connecticut College, New London, CT 06320.*

HENDRICKS, BEATRICE E.
Lawyer. **Personal:** Born in St Thomas, Virgin Islands of the United States. **Educ:** Morgan State Col, BS, 1962; Howard Univ Law Sch, JD, 1972. **Career:** William Morris Agency NY, jr acct, 1962-64; IRS, field agent, 1964-69; Ford Motor Co, staff atty, 1972-74; Acacia Mutual Life Ins, atty, 1974-76; Acacia Mutual, asst coun, 1976-79; Dept Housing & Comm Develop, asst corp coun, 1980-85; A&B Household Serv Inc, pres, half-owner, 1979-85, asst corp coun, con affairs sect, asst Corp Coun, Spec Lit Sect, currently. **Orgs:** Nat Bar Asn; Am Bar Asn; DC Bar Asn; Mich Bar Asn; Alpha Kappa Alpha Sor Inc; Inez W Tinsley Cult Soc; Nat Asn Colored Women Clubs Inc; jr warden, St Mary's Episcopal Church, 1990; bd dir, St Mary's Ct. **Business Addr:** Assistant Corporate Counsel, Special Litigation Section, Enforcement Division, 441 E St NW, Washington, DC 20001, **Business Phone:** (202)727-3885.

HENDRICKS, DR. CONSTANCE SMITH (CONSTANCE KASANDRA SMITH-HENDRICKS)
Educator, administrator. **Personal:** Born Aug 25, 1953, Selma, AL; daughter of Henry Daniel Jr and Geneva Cornelia Glover; divorced; children: Denisha Lunya. **Educ:** Univ Ala, Birmingham, BSN, 1974, MSN, 1981; Univ Ala, Tuscaloosa, grad cert, geront, 1987; Boston Col, PhD, 1992. **Career:** Univ Ala, Birmingham, nursing assoc fac, 1975, instr, 1981-82; Roosevelt Area Family Health Ctr, nurse practr, 1975-76; Univ Hosp, staff RN, 1976-78; Good Samaritan Hosp, dir nursing, 1982-83; Tuskegee Univ, asst prof, 1983-85; John Andrew Hosp, nurse adminr, 1985-87; Auburn Univ, asst prof, 1987-96; Boston Col, grad minority fel, 1989-92; Univ SC, asst prof, 1996-2001; Southern Univ A&M Col, Baton Rouge, assoc prof, 2001-04; Hampton Univ Sch Nursing, dean & prof, currently. **Orgs:** Omicron Delta Kappa, 1981-; SE regional dir, Chi Eta Phi Sorority,1985-89, nat second vpres, 1992-97; Sigma Theta Tau Int, 1985-; choir mem& Bible instr, Greater St Mark Missionary Baptist Church, 1986-; Asn Black Nurse Fac, 1987-; Nat Sorority Phi Delta Kappa, 1988-; state vpres, AlaState Nurses Asn, 1993-96; Nat Z-HOPE Dir, 2002-; bd mem, Kiwanis Int, 2003; Zeta Phi Beta Sorority Inc; pres elect, Theta Delta. **Honors/Awds:** Crawford Andolph Scholar, Chi Eta Phi, Epsilon Chap, 1990; Academic Scholar, Myrtle Baptist Church, 1990, 1992; South Carolina Zeta of the Year, 1998 & 2001; Nat Inst Nursing Res/Nat Institutes Health Mentored Res Scientist Develop Award Minority Investigators, 1999-02; Emerging Nursing Star in Health Disparities Res, Howard Univ div Nursing, 2004; Certificate of Recognition for services rendered with Z-HOPE Inter Nat Women of Colorat the United Nations, Zeta Phi Beta Sorority Inc, 2005; King/Chavez/Parks Scholar-In-Residence Award, Univ Mich, Sch Nursing; South Carolina Womanof Achievement Award, SC Governor's Comn Women; Fac Scholar/Teaching Award, Univ SC Black Fac & Staff Asn. **Special Achievements:** Numeroud publications including Professionalism Showing, 1983; Understanding the Adolescent, 1985; The ABNF Association of Black Nursing Faculty) Journal, 13(4), 87-89; Learning Orientations & Health Behaviors of African-American Early Adolescents in Rural Alabama, 1991; Choosing: An Essential Component of Becoming, 1992; Self-esteem matters: Racial and gender differences among rural Southern adolescents. Journal of National Black Nurses Association, 12(2), 15-23, 2001; A community health promotion partnership model: The South Carolina health connection. Journal ofCultural Diversity, 8(3), 69-78,2001; Fostering self efficacy as anethical mandate in health promotion practice and research; Online Journal of Health Ethics; Yesterday, today and forever: Stepping stones to becoming a Twenty First century leader, 2002; The Adolescent Hope Scale, Copyrighted National Library of Congress, 2004; Psychometric Testing of the Miller Hope Scale With Rural Southern Adolescents, 11(3), 41-50, 2005;The Relationship of Hope and Self-efficacy to Health Promoting Behaviors Among Student-Athletics Attending Historically Black Colleges and Universities, 11(3), 23-40, 2005; The Influence of Father Absence on the Self-esteem and Self-Reported Sexual activity of Rural Southern, 16(6), 118-131, 2005, Here's to your Optimal Whole Health, 2005. **Home Addr:** 612 Kimberly Circle, Selma, AL 36701, **Home Phone:** (757)753-4506. **Business Addr:** Dean, Professor, Hampton University, School of Nursing, Emanicipation Dr & Tyler St, Hampton, VA 23668, **Business Phone:** (757)727-5654.

HENDRICKS, JON
Musician, president (organization). **Personal:** Born Sep 16, 1921, Newark, OH; son of Rev Alexander Brooks and Willie Carrington; married Judith, Mar 26, 1959; children: Jon Jr, Michele, Eric, Colleen & Aria. **Educ:** Univ Toledo, pre-law, 1951. **Career:** Lambert, Hendricks & Ross, singer & songwriter, 1957-62; San Francisco Chronicle, jazz instr; Cal St Univ, jazz instr; Sonoma, jazz instr; Univ Calif, Berkeley, jazz instr; Univ Calif, Los Angeles, jazz instr; Stanford, jazz instr; Evolution of the Blues, writer; TV series: "Somewhere to Lay My Weary Head"; Jon Hendricks & Co, singer & songwriter; Hendricks Music Inc, pres; Univ Toledo, prof jazz studies, 2000-; Films: Jazz Is Our Religion; Hommage a Cole Porter; People I Know; Scheherazade, 2003. **Orgs:** Kennedy Center Honors comt, Wash, DC; dir & host, Annual San Francisco Jazz Festival. **Honors/Awds:** Number One Jazz Singer in the World, London's Melody Maker, 1969; Emmy Award; Iris Award; Peabody Awards; Seven Grammy Awards; hon doctorate, Univ Toledo. **Special Achievements:** Sang with and wrote for King Pleasure, Count Basie, Duke Ellington, Louis Armstrong, Dave Brubeck, Carmen McRae; first American jazz artist to lecture at the Sorbonne in Paris; His fifteen voice group, the Jon Hendricks Vocalstra at the University of Toledo, performed to a standing ovation at the Sorbonne. **Military Serv:** USA 1942-46 Cpl. *

HENDRICKS, LETA
Librarian. **Personal:** Born May 22, 1954, Galesburg, IL; daughter of Mary Martha and Lee B. **Educ:** Western Ill Univ, BA (w/ Honors), 1977; Atlanta Univ, MA, 1979; Univ Ill, MS, 1989. **Career:** Carl Sandburg Col, instructor, 1983; Galesburg Public Libr, special col libr, 1980-89; Knox Col, reference asst, 1986-89, instr, 1989; The Ohio State Univ Libr, minority libr intern, 1989-91, head, Human Ecol Libr, 1991-98, head, EHS Syst/Human Ecol Bibliogr, libr, 1998-, asst prof, currently. **Orgs:** NWSA, 1982-; mem, ALA, 1989-; mem, ACRL, 1989-; mem, Black Caucus ALA, 1990-; mem, Phi Kappa Phi, 1976. **Honors/Awds:** Found Scholar Western Ill Univ, 1976. **Business Addr:** Assistant Professor, Ohio State University, 1813 N High St, Columbus, OH 43210, **Business Phone:** (614)292-6184.

HENDRICKS, MARVIN B.
Molecular biologist. **Personal:** Born Dec 4, 1951, Newnan, GA; son of Margaret Petty and Jimmie Lee; married Helen Porthia Talley, Dec 26, 1971; children: Bridget. **Educ:** Mass Inst Technol, Cambridge, MA, BS, 1973; Johns Hopkins Univ, Baltimore, MD, PhD, 1980. **Career:** African Sci Inst, fel; Fred Hutchinson Cancer Res Ctr, Seattle, WA, fel, 1980-84; Integrated Genetics, Framingham, MA, staff scientist, 1984-87, sr scientist, 1987-89; Repligen Corp, Cambridge, MA, res scientist, 1989-91; Cambridge NeuroScience Inc, Cambridge, group leader, 1991-95; Brigham & Women's Hosp, Boston, MA, res scientist, 1995-97; Millennium Pharmaceut Inc, sr scientist, 1997-. **Orgs:** AAAS, 1976-, NY Acad Sci, 1984-; Am Soc Mech Engrs, 1994-; Am Soc Microbiol. **Honors/Awds:** Scholarship, Mass Inst Technol, 1969; Valedictorian, Cent High Sch, Newnan, GA, 1969; publ 20 Articles in int res Js, 1976-; co-author, articles in two books, 1980-; Post-doctoral Fellowship Awards, Am Cancer Soc, 1980, Ann Fuller Fund, Yale Univ, 1980, Nat Inst Health, 1980. **Special Achievements:** Featured in Ebony Mag, 1988. **Home Addr:** 21 Perry H Henderson Dr, Framingham, MA 01701. *

HENDRICKS, RICHARD D
Executive, executive director. **Personal:** Born May 26, 1937, Glen Cove, NY; son of William Richard Hendricks and Ruth Delamar Hendricks; married Madelyn Williams, Jun 1960; children: Pamela, Jeannette & Natalie. **Educ:** Hofstra Univ, BBA, 1960. **Career:** Executive (retired); Abraham & Straus Dept Stores NY, dept mgr, 1960-65; Johnson Pub Co, adv sales rep, 1965-66; JC Penney Co, buyer; JC Penney Co, merchandise exec, 1966-97; Delamar Mkt Int, consult, 1997; Nichelson Entertainment Group, vpres, 1999, dir corp commun, currently. **Orgs:** Founder, bd mem, QNS Asoc Inc; founder, pres, LISA Prodns; spl lectr, Black Exec

Exchange Prog; lectr, State Univ NY, 1963-64; Black Artist Asn; NAACP; adv bd, Nichelson Entertainment Group, currently. **Honors/Awds:** Outstanding Achievement Award, Int Key Women Am, 1974; Community Service Award, Black Media Inc, 1975. **Home Addr:** 5818 Brushy Creek, Dallas, TX 75252. **Business Addr:** Director- Corporate Communications, Nichelson Entertainment Group, 1402 N Corinth St Suite 115, Corinth, TX 76208, **Business Phone:** (214)808-7583.

HENDRICKS, STEVEN AARON
Public relations executive, executive director. **Personal:** Born Feb 5, 1960, Kansas City, KS. **Educ:** Wichita State Univ, BA, jour, 1982. **Career:** Wichita Eagle-Beacon Newspaper, adv rep, 1981; Pizza Hut Inc, comn asst, 1982, opers mgr, 1982-83; State Kans, asst; Gerdau Ameristeel Corp, Corp Commun & Pub Affairs, dir, currently. **Orgs:** Withita State Univ Football Team, 1978-82; Wichita State Univ Advert & PR Club, 1980-82; Fel Christian Athletes, 1981-82; Advert & PR Club Whichita, 1981-82; Kappa Alpha Psi Fraternity, 1982-; Black Dem Caucus, 1984. **Honors/Awds:** Young Man of America, 1984. **Business Addr:** Director Of Corporate Communications & Public Affairs, Gerdau Ameristeel Corporation, 4221 W Boy Scout Blvd Suite 600, Tampa, FL 33607, **Business Phone:** (813)286-8383.

HENDRIX, DEBORAH LYNNE
Association executive, consultant. **Personal:** Born Nov 30, 1961, Chicago, IL; daughter of Edward Wright Jr and Donna L Radford Wright; married Charles W Hendrix, Apr 6, 1991; children: Catherine Elizabeth & Danielle Marie. **Educ:** Howard Univ, Wash DC, BS, 1983; Roosevelt Univ, Chicago Ill, paralegal cert; Inst Paralegal Training, Chicago Ill, cert, 1984. **Career:** Winston & Strawn Law Firm, corp paralegal, 1984-85; Jr Achievement Chicago Ill, vpres & ed serv, 1985-88; Jr Achievement South Bend, Ind, pres, 1988-91; Jr Achievement Inc, dir, training & sem, 1991-94, vpres diversity, vpres diversity & qual assurance, vpres training, diversity & qual, vpres, training & cult change; Sch Dist Two Harrison, secy, bd educ, pres, currently; CD Global Enterprises, owner, currently; Dale Carnegie adj instr. **Orgs:** NAFE, 1990-; Urban League Col Springs; Am Soc Training & Develop, 1991-; After 5 Christian Bus & Prof Women, 1992-; Workout Ltd, 1997; Goodwill Indust, 1998; Communities Sch, 1998. **Honors/Awds:** Named most outstanding stud, sch human ecol, Howard Univ, 1983; Outstanding Young Women Am, 1988; Chicago's Up & Coming Bus & Prof Women, Dollars & Sense Mag, 1988; Emerging Black Leaders, 1994. **Home Addr:** 635 Sand Creek Dr, Colorado Springs, CO 80916, **Home Phone:** (719)271-2411. **Business Addr:** Owner, CD Global Enterprises, 3554 W Richwoods Blvd, Peoria, IL 61604, **Business Phone:** (309)685-2950.

HENDRIX, IDA
Executive, manager. **Personal:** Born Jun 1, 1952. **Career:** Taubman Centers Inc, Great Lakes Crossing, asst gen mgr; Fairlane Town Ctr, asst gen mgr; Briarwood Mall, gen mgr, currently. **Special Achievements:** Most Influential Black Women Metrop, Detroit, 2001. **Business Phone:** (734)761-9550.*

HENDRIX, MARTHA RAYE
Educator, mayor. **Personal:** Born Aug 17, 1939, Mineral Springs, AR; daughter of Lewis and Flossie Johnson; married Clarence Jr, Aug 5, 1963 (divorced); children: Marcia & Clarisse Renee. **Educ:** Shorter Col, N Little Rock, Ark, AA, 1959; Philander Smith, Little Rock, Ark, BA, 1961; Henderson State Univ, Arkadelphia, Ark, MA. **Career:** Howard County High Sch, Mineral Springs, Ark, teacher, 1961-70; Saratoga Sch, Saratoga, Ark, teacher, 1970-89; Town Tollette, Tollette, Ark, mayor, 1989-; Saratoga Sch Dist, Saratoga, Ark, elem prin, 1990-91, Saratoga Elem Sch, Wyo, prin, currently. **Orgs:** Am Educ Asn, 1961-89; Nat Educ Asn, 1961-89; EHC, 1985-89; Literacy Coun, 1987-89; adv bd, Munic League, 1988-89; Hosp Adv Bd; Ark Munic League, mayor; Rural Develop Comn. **Home Addr:** 301 Peach St, Mineral Springs, AR 71851, **Home Phone:** (870)287-4273. **Business Addr:** Principal, Saratoga Elementary School, 311 W Spring St, PO Box 1710, Saratoga, WY 82331, **Business Phone:** (307)326-8365.*

HENDRY, GLORIA
Actor. **Personal:** Born Mar 3, 1949, Winterhaven, FL; daughter of George C and Lottie Beatrice Sconions. **Educ:** Essex Col Bus; Univ Phoenix, Los Angeles City Col Theatre Acad. **Career:** Los Angeles, legal secy; Films: Live & Let Die, 1973; Black Caesar, 1973; Come Back Charleston Blue; Black Belt Jones, 1974; Hell Up In Harlem; Slaughter's Big Rip-Off; Bare Knuckles; Across 110th Street; For Love of Ivy; Landlord; Pumpkin head II, 1993; South Bureau Homicide, 1996; Lookin' Italian, 1998; Seven Swans, 2005; TV Series: "Women in Law"; "Seeds of Tragedy", 1991; "Law & Order"; "Hunter", 1990; "Doogie Howser"; "Falcon Crest"; "Blue Knight"; "As The World Turns"; "Blooper's & Practical Jokes"; "Another World"; "Love American Style"; "Snoop Sisters"; "Santa Barbara"; "As the World Turns"; "This is The Life"; "Absolute Evil", 2009. **Orgs:** Exec dir, Women Performing Arts Los Angeles, Kwanza Found; Actors' Equity Asn; Am Fedn TV & Radio Artists; Screen Actors Guild; Nat Asn Advan Colored People; Hon Phi Beta Omega Frat Inc Rho Iota Chap. **Honors/Awds:** Black Achiever in US Award; National Association of Tennis Award; After Hours News Award, Newark; I Am Somebody Award; Outstanding Celebrity Award; Key to City Birmingham, Ala Mayor George G Seibels; Key to City, Mayor Kenneth Gibson, Newark, NJ; Kathleen Brown Rice Tennis Award; Buffalo Soldiers Award, 10th Calvary. **Business Addr:** Actor, CASTLE HILL ENTERPRISES, 1101 S Orlando Ave, Los Angeles, CA 90053.*

HENLEY, CARL R
Administrator, u.s. attorney. **Personal:** Born Jul 4, 1955, Los Angeles, CA. **Educ:** Calif State Univ, Los Angeles, BA, psychol, 1977, MS, pub admin, 1980; Whittier Col, Sch Law, JD, 1991. **Career:** Universal Artists, asst spec proj, 1977-, assoc producer; Black Leadership Conf, Calif State Univ, Los Angeles, adv, 1977-; Backyard Prods, vpres, bd dirs, 1978-; Los Angels United Sch Dist, coun asst, 1979; Los Angeles Co, community develop analyst asst, 1979-; HME Subsidiaries, vpres, 1982-; Pvt Pract, lawyer; US Supreme Ct Bar, atty, 2006-. **Orgs:** Pres & co-founder, Youth & Col Div, Nat Asn Advan Colored People, Los Angeles, 1977-80, reg dir, 1980-82; Los Angeles Co Dem Cent Comn, 1978-; exec bd mem, S Cent Planning Coun United Way Am, 1979-80; deleg, Calif Dem State Party, 1982-84. **Honors/Awds:** Honorary Life Member Award, Calif State Univ, Los Angeles, 1977; Honarary President Emeritus, Youth & Col Div, Nat Asn Advan Colored People, Los Angeles, 1980; Community Service Resolution, Los Angeles City Coun, 1980. **Business Addr:** Attorney, United States Supreme Court, 1 First St NE, Washington, DC 20543, **Business Phone:** (202)479-3211.

HENLEY, RICKEY NELSON. See HENDERSON, RICKEY HENLEY.

HENLEY, VERNARD W.
Banker. **Personal:** Born Aug 11, 1929, Richmond, VA; son of Walter A and Mary Crump; married Pheriby Christine Gibson; children: Vernard W Jr, Wade G, Adrienne C. **Educ:** Va State Univ, BS, 1951. **Career:** Banker (retired); Mechanics & Farmers Bank Durham, NC, asst note teller, 1951-52, cashier & head personal loan dept, 1954-58; Consolidated Bank & Trust Co, secy & cashier 1958-69, bd dir, 1961, vpres & secy, 1961, vpres, 1969, exec vpres, 1971, pres 1971, & chmn bd, chief exec officer & trust officer, 1984-01; Unity State Bank Dayton, OH, chief exec officer, 1969. **Orgs:** Bd trustees, Va Museum Fine Arts, exec exhibition & finance comm, 1983, ; bd dir, exec & finance comn, Richmond Renaissance Inc; vchmn, chmn, Audit Comn City Richmond, 1983-88; bd trustees, J Sargeant Reynolds Col Found, 1984; bd trustees, exec & finance comt, Va Union Univ, 1984; lay mem, bd dirs, Old Dominion Bar Asn, 1985; bd trustees, Va Coun Econ Ed, 1985; bd dirs, Va Bankers Asn; bd trustees, Univ Fund Va Commonwealth Univ, 1986; bd trustees, Historic Richmond Found; bd dirs, Retail Merchants Asn Greater Richmond; Kiwanis Club Richmond; Nat Corp Comn United Negro Col Fund; bd dirs, Atlantic Rural Exposition; adv bd, Arts Coun Richmond Inc; adv coun, bd trustees, Salvation Army Boys Club; bd dirs, Va Region, Nat Conf Christians & Jews; Richmond Adv Coun Small Bus Admin, 1989; bd dirs, Cities School Found Va, 1989; bd dirs, vchmn, Va Housing Found, 1989; pres, Va Bankers Asn; bd, Owens & Minor Inc; Audit Com, 1993; Comp & Benefits Com, 1994. **Honors/Awds:** Order of Merit Boy Scouts of America, 1967; Man & Boy Award, Salvation Army Boys Club, 1969; Citizenship Award, Astoria Beneficial Club, 1976; Brotherhood Award, Richmond Chap Nat Conf Christians & Jews, 1979; Order & Citizenship Award, Independent Order St Luke, 1981; The Quest for Success Award, Miller Brewing Co & Philip Morris. **Special Achievements:** First African-American president of the Virginia Bankers Asn, 1993. **Military Serv:** AUS, 1st lt, 2 yrs; Bronze Star, 1954. *

HENRY, ALARIC ANTHONY
Lawyer. **Personal:** Born Jan 14, 1963, Detroit, MI; son of Leonard and Marguerite; married Sharon, Jul 20, 1991; children: Ashley E, Jared C & Conner A. **Educ:** Univ Detroit, BS, 1985; Ga State Univ, JD, 1991. **Career:** K-Mart Corp, asst store mgr, 1985-86; Safeco Ins Co, ins adjuster, 1986-91; Luther, Anderson & Cleary, assoc atty, 1991-96, managing partner, 1996-. **Orgs:** Phi Delta Phi, 1989-; Am Bar Asn, 1991-; Ga Bar Asn, 1991-; Tenn Bar Asn, 1991-; Chattanooga Bar Asn, 1991-; S L Hutchins Bar Asn, 1991-; pres 100 Black Men Chattanooga, Bd member 100 Black Men Am. 1992-2003; 100 Black Men Am, 1996-2003; Tenn Defense Lawyer Org. **Honors/Awds:** Chapter Development Award, 100 Black Men of America, 1999; Member of the year 100 Black Men of Chattanooga, 2002. **Special Achievements:** Listed in Mid-South Super Lawyers as being in top 5% of Attorneys in TN and some surrounding states. **Business Addr:** Managing Partner, Luther-Anderson PLLP, 1110 Market St Suite 500, PO Box 151, Chattanooga, TN 37401-0151, **Business Phone:** (423)756-5034.

HENRY, BRENT LEE
Lawyer, vice president (organization). **Personal:** Born Oct 9, 1947, Philadelphia, PA; son of Wilbur and Minnie Adams; married; children: Adam & Aisha. **Educ:** Princeton Univ, Woodrow Wilson Sch Pub & Int Affairs, BA, 1969; Yale Law Sch, JD, 1973; Yale Sch Art & Archit, urban studies, 1973. **Career:** New Haven Housing Info Ctr, coun, 1973-74; Yale Univ, Dept Afro-Am Studies, lectr, 1973-74; Jones Day Reavis & Pogue, atty, 1974-82; NY Human Resources Admin, dept admin, 1978-79; Greater Southeast Community Hosp Found, dir bus & govt affairs, 1982-84; Howard Univ Sch Bus Admin, adj prof, 1982-94; Med Star Health, sr vpres & gen coun, 1985-2002; Partner's Health Care Syst, vpres & gen coun, currently. **Orgs:** Bd trustees, Princeton Univ, 1969-72, 1999-; adv coun, Princeton Univ, Woodrow Wilson Sch Pub & Int Affairs, 1969-72; staff mem, Concerned Citizens Comn Criminal Justice, Cleveland Found, 1975; bd dirs, Bazelon Ctr Ment Health Law, 1987-98; bd dirs, pres, Nat Health Lawyers Asn, 1988-96, 1994-95; bd dirs, Combined Health Appeal, Nat Capital Area, 1989-93; exec comt mem & chair, Alumni Coun, Princeton Univ, 1994-99; bd mem, Pub Welfare Found, 1996-; bd trustees, Princeton Univ, 1999; Nat Inst Health Adv Bd Clin Res; Am Bar Asn; Nat Bar Asn; Ohio Bar Asn; DC Bar Asn; bd dir, New England Legal Found; bd dir, New England Coun; bd dir, Public Welfare Found; Boston Bar asn; past pres, Am Health Lawyers asn. **Honors/Awds:** Frederick Abramson Award, DC Bar Asn, 1996. **Special Achievements:** Auth: The Provision of Indigent Defense Servs, Greater Cleveland. **Business Addr:** Vice President, General Counsel, Partners Health Care System, 800 Boylston St Suite 1150, Boston, MA 02199-8001, **Business Phone:** (617)278-1000.

HENRY, DR. CHARLES E.
Consultant, educator, entrepreneur. **Personal:** Born Apr 14, 1935, Palestine, TX; son of E W Henry Sr and Ophelia Spencer; married Janice Normandyne OBrien; children: Melvin Wayne & Carolyn Janiece Henry Ross. **Educ:** Tex Col, BS, 1956; Texas Tech Univ, MEd 1971, EdD 1974; Erick sonian psycho ther & psycho neuro immunology, cert, 1980; Continuous Improv Facilitator & Facilitator Inst, cert, 1994; Univ Tex, Total Qual Mgt instr, cert, 1995; Tex Tech Univ, Human Resources mgt, cert, 1996. **Career:** Lubbock Sch Dist Sci Inst, 1956-72; Tex Tech Univ Proj Upward Bound, consult/instr, 1968-72; Tex Tech Univ HSC Sch Med, coordr/instr, 1972-76; Wayland Baptist Univ, adj fac, Educ Admn & Supv, 1997-98, adj prof; Henry Enterprises, educ consult/owner/mgr, currently. **Orgs:** Int Platform Asn; Am Soc Prof Consult; Mental Health Asn; Phi Delta Kappa Educ Fraternity; Alpha Phi Alpha Fraternity Inc; Nat Asn Advan Colored People; Tex Mental Health Counr Asn; Phi Delta Kappa; Am Asn Prof Hypno therapists; Soc Human Resource Mgt; Educ Found rep, Theta Kappa Lambda Chap & Alpha Phi Alpha Fraternity; Lubbock Chamber Com; Am Soc Training & Develop; Lubbock Chamber Com. **Honors/Awds:** Citation Excellence, Tex Col Tyler, 1980; Community Service Award, Alpha Kappa Alpha Sorority, 1978; area 3-G coord, Phi Delta Kappa Educ Fraternity, 1977-78; Presidents Award, Estacado HS PTA, 1975-76; Phi Delta Kappa Int, Service Key Award, 1996, Twenty-Five Year Membership Award, 1997; Thirty year PDK Award, 2002; Inducted, African-American Heroes of Lubbock, Hall of Fame, 2003. **Business Addr:** Educator, Management Consultant, Henry Enterprises, 2345 50th st Suite 104, Lubbock, TX 79412-3943, **Business Phone:** (806)799-7322.

HENRY, DR. CHARLES PATRICK, III
Educator. **Personal:** Born Aug 17, 1947, Newark, OH; son of Charles and Ruth Holbert; married Loretta Crenshaw, Aug 23, 1968; children: Adia, Wesley & Laura. **Educ:** Denison Univ, Granville, OH, BA, polit sci, 1969; Univ Chicago, Chicago, IL, MA,1971, PhD, polit sci, 1974. **Career:** Howard Univ, Wash, DC, asst prof, 1973-76; Denison Univ, Granville, OH, asst prof, dir, asst dean, 1976-80; Atlanta Univ, NEH fel, 1980-81; Univ Calif, Berkeley, CA, assoc prof, 1981, prof African Am Studies, currently; Amenesty Int, chair, 1986-88; Univ Mich, visiting prof, 1993; Nat Coun Humanities, 1994; DRL, US State Dept, off dir, 1994-95; Univ Bologna, Distinguished Chair Am Hist & Politics, 2003. **Orgs:** Congressional fel, Am Polit Sci Asn, 1972-73; nat secy, 1981-83, pres, 1992-94, Nat Coun Black Studies; Int exec comt, 1989-91, chair, bd dir, 1986-88, Amnesty Int USA. **Honors/Awds:** Presidential appointee, Nat Coun Humanities, 1996-2000; Chancellor's Award, Chancellor Birgeneau, 2008. **Special Achievements:** Co-author, The Chitlin' Controversy, University Press of America, 1978; author, Culture & African American Politics, Indiana Press, 1990; author, Ralph Bunche: Model Negro or American Other, New York Univ Press, 1999; author, Jesse Jackson, Black Scholar Press, 1991; editor, In Pursuit of Full Employment, Urban League Review, 1986; editor, Ralph Bunche: Selected, Speeches & Writings, Univ Mich Press, 1995; Foreign Policy & the Black International Interest, Albany SUNY Press, 2000. **Business Addr:** Professor, University of California Berkeley, Department of African American Studies, 674 Barrows Hall, Berkeley, CA 94702, **Business Phone:** (510)642-3426.

HENRY, EGBERT WINSTON
Educator. **Personal:** Born Apr 28, 1930, New York, NY; son of Joseph and Virginia; married Barbara J Henry, Dec 19, 1964. **Educ:** City Univ New York, Queens, BS, 1953, Brooklyn Col, MA, 1959, PhD, 1972. **Career:** Educator (retired); City Univ New York, High Sch Lehman Col, asst prof, 1972-74; Oakland Univ, MI, Dept Bio Sci, prof, dept chair, 1974-95. **Orgs:** ed bd mem, Jour Plant Physiol; bd mem, Kirwood Mental Health Clinic; chair, Mich Electron Microscope Society; bd mem, Greening Detroit; bd mem, Visions Unlimited, Pontiac, MI. **Honors/Awds:** Alumni Award, Oakland Univ, 1991, Dedication and Concern for Student

Award. **Special Achievements:** NIH, Summer Program for Talented Minority High School Students, prog dir, 10 years; Co-published: "Superoxide dismatase activity in ethylene-treated bean absscission zone tissue", Proceedings on the Plant Growth Regular Society of America, pgs 115-128. **Military Serv:** AUS, Sp 3, 1953-56. *

HENRY, FOREST T., JR.
Educator. **Personal:** Born Jan 2, 1937, Houston; son of Forest Sr and Belzora Butler; married Melba J Jennings; children: Felicia Denise & Forest III. **Educ:** Howard Univ, BS, 1958; Tex Southern Univ, MEd, 1971, admins cert, 1972. **Career:** Educator (retired); F T Henry Income Tax & Real Estate Serv, 1958; Carter G Woodson Jr High Sch, Houston, asst football coach, 1959-68, teacher, 1959-68, golf coach, 1960-70, teacher phys educ, head football coach & athletic dir, 1968-70, asst prin, 1971-74, prin, 1974-78; Evan E Worthing Sr High Sch, Houston, prin, 1978-82; Houston Independent Sch Dist, asst supt athletics & extracurricular activ, 1982-84, dir opers, 1989-95; Phillis Wheatley Sr High Sch, Houston, TX, prin, 1984-89. **Orgs:** Pres, Greater Fifth Ward Citizens League, 1972-; exec bd, Bhouston Prin Asn, 1972-; Boys Scout Am; YMCA; TX Asn Sec Sch Prin; Nat Asn Sec Sch Prin; bd dir, N Side Sr Citizens Asn; Houston Asn Supv & Curriculum Develop; Tex State Teachers Asn; Alpha Phi Alpha; Appraisal Rev Bd mem, Harris County Appraisal Dist. **Honors/Awds:** Worthing Scholarship; Nat Sci Summer Fellowship Biology; Community Service Award, Religious Heritage Am. *

HENRY, HERMAN (SKEETER HENRY)
Basketball player. **Personal:** Born Dec 8, 1967, Dallas, TX. **Educ:** Midland Col; Univ Okla. **Career:** CBA, Pensacola Tornados, 1990-91; CBA, Birmingham Bandits, 1991-92; NBA, Phoenix Suns, 1994; Large Rapids Mackers, 1994-95; Real Madrid, Spain, 1994-95; CBA, Sioux Falls Skyforce, 1995-96; Panteras de Miranda, Venezuela, 1995-96; Tuborg Pilsner Spor Kulubu Izmir, Turkey, 1995-96; Montpellie, 1996-97; Cholet Toulouse Illiabum Clube, Portugal, 1997-98.

HENRY, I PATRICIA (PAT HENRY)
Executive. **Personal:** Born Aug 20, 1947, Martinsville, VA; daughter of Ida Walker Pinnix; divorced; children: Hans & Tiffany. **Educ:** Bennett Col, BS, 1969; Harvard Univ; Siebel Inst Brewing Tech. **Career:** Gen Elect Co Inc, systs analyst, 1970; Norfolk & Western Railway, systs analyst, 1971; Ethyl Corp, systs analyst, 1972; EI DuPont de Nemours, staff asst to area head, 1973-77; Miller Brewing Co, brewing mgr, 1977-95, plant mgr, 1995-. **Orgs:** Master Brewers Am, 1983; bd trustees, Carlisle Sch, 1984-86; bd dirs, Main St Financial, 1996; bd trustees, Mem Hosp. **Honors/Awds:** Kizzie Award, Black Women Hall of Fame, 1984; Top Black Achiever, NY YMCA, 1984. **Special Achievements:** First female to hold a Leading Managemant post in any major US Brewery, 1995. **Business Addr:** Plant Manager, Miller Brewing Co, 863 E Meadow Rd, PO Box 3327, Eden, NC 27288-3327, **Business Phone:** (336)627-2204.

HENRY, JO-ANN
Executive. **Career:** US Equal Employment Opportunity Comn, dir human resources; Fed Deposit Ins Corp, dir off diversity & econ opportunity; Georgetown Univ, vpres & chief human resources off, currently. *

HENRY, JOHN WESLEY, JR.
College president, school administrator. **Personal:** Born Jun 3, 1929, Greensboro, NC; son of John Wesley and Carrie Lillian; married Cassandra; children: Dawn Yolanda, John Wesley III, Pamela Michelle, Linda Leverne, BrendaDiane & Robin Karen. **Educ:** NC A&T State Univ, BS, 1955; Chicago State Univ, MEd, 1965; Vet Admin Res Hosp, Chicago, cert personnel mgt, 1964; NY Univ, cert voc testing & eval,1966; Chicago Cosmopolitan Free Sch, cert bus mgt, 1964. **Career:** School administrator, college president (retired); Vet Admin Hosp, Perry Point, Md, manual arts therapist, phys med & rehab serv, 1955-58, actg chief, 1958-60; Vet Admin Res Hosp, Chicago, Voc Testing & Eval, chief, 1960-70; Malcolm X Community Col, City Cols Chicago, Tech & Occup Educ, dean, 1970-71, Acad Affairs, vpres, 1971-73; Denmark SC Tech Educ Ctr, assoc dir, 1973-77; Denmark Tech Col, pres, 1977-85. **Orgs:** Bd mem, Chicago West side Planning Comn, 1970-73; vice chmn, Bamberg Co Indust Develop Comn, 1979; SE Regional Coun Black Am Affairs; bd mem, Am Asn Community & Jr Col, 1979-85; hon life mem, Phi Delta Kappa; Phi Theta Kappa; hon life mem, Phi Beta Lambda; Nat Coun Resource Develop; Nat Asn Tech Educ; Coun Advan & Support Educ; Asn Cols & Univs; Am Asn Rehab Therapy; Nat Asn Equal Opportunity Higher Educ; Am Legion; Disabled Am Veterans Asn; Asn Supv & Curric Develop; Asn Am Cols; Coun Occup Educ; Nat Comn Coop Educ; Pres Round table; Nat Rehab Asn. **Honors/Awds:** Award for Educational Excellence, Southern Leadership Conf; Super Perfomer Award, Va Res Hosp. **Military Serv:** AUS, 1947-51. **Home Addr:** 168 COOPER ST, PO Box 25, Denmark, SC 29042. *

HENRY, JOSEPH KING
Educator. **Personal:** Born Aug 2, 1948, St Louis, MO; son of King and Geraldine; married Diana Edwards. **Educ:** Lincoln Univ, BS, 1973; Boston Univ, MA, 1974. **Career:** Humboldt Elem Sch, St Louis, teacher, 1972-73; Metro Coun Educ Opportunity Inc, coordr, 1974-77; Am Lives, instr, grad teaching asst, 1982; Univ Iowa, instr, grad teaching ast, Introd Afro-Am Soc; grad res ast, 1983-85,Spec Servs, acad coun, 1985-86, grad outreach coun, 1986-87, grad outreach coordr, Grad Col, asst dean, 1992, asst dean recruitment & minority affairs, currently; Cornell Col Mt Vernon, IA, lectr hist, 1985. **Orgs:** Coun, Univ Iowa Upward Bound Prog, 1980; pres, Afro-Am Studies Grad StudAsn, 1982-83; The Nat Asn Col Admis Counrs Asn & Conf, 1985; Nat Coun Black Studies, 1988; The Soc Study Multi-Ethnic Lit US, 1988; Orgn Am Historians, 1988; Joint Ctr Political Studies Assoc Prog; Univ Iowa African Am Coun; patron, St Louis Black Repertory Co; Cote Brilliante Presby Ch; Unitarian Universalist Ch; Nat Asn Grad Admis Prof; bd dir, African-Am Historical Mus & Cultural Ctr. **Honors/Awds:** Martin Luther King Fellowship to Boston Univ, 1973; Phi Alpha Theta Int Honor Soc History, 1974; Black Awards, Honor Cert Recognition, Univ Iowa,1984; Afro-Heart Award, Univ Iowa, African-Am Cultural Ctr, 1997; Certificate of Recognition, Southern Univ, 1998. **Business Addr:** Assistant to the Dean, University of Iowa, Graduate College, 205 Gilmore Hall, Iowa City, IA 52242-1320, **Business Phone:** (319)335-2138.

HENRY, DR. JOSEPH LOUIS
Educator. **Personal:** Born May 2, 1924, New Orleans, LA; son of Varice S Henry Jr and Mabel Valentine Mansion; married Dorothy Lilian Whittle (died 1991); children: Leilani Smith, Joseph L Jr, Ronald, Joan Alison & Peter D; married Gracie Cua, Jan 5, 1995. **Educ:** Howard Univ, DDS, 1946; Xavier Univ, BS, 1948, ScD, 1975; Univ Ill, MS,1949, PhD, 1951; Ill Col Optometry, DHL, 1973; Harvard Univ, MA, 1975. **Career:** Howard Univ, from instr to prof, 1946-51, dir clins, 1951-65, dean,1965-75; chmn bd trustee, Ill Col Optom, 1982-86; Harvard Sch Dent Med,assoc dean/prof & chmn, oral diag & oral radiol, dean, 1990; interim dean,currently; Univ Pacific Sch Dent Med, admin officer & consult, 1999-; Howard Univ Dent Sch, dean emer, currently. **Orgs:** AAAS, 1952 & 1972; pres, Int Asn Dent Res DC Sect, 1968; NIH Nat Adv Coun Health Prof, 1968-72; pres, Greater Wash Periodont Soc, 1970; comnr, USComn Educ Credit, 1973-74; chmn, Asn Black Fac & Admin, Harvard Univ, 1981-83; Inst Med Nat Acad Sci,1981-; chmn, Sect Oral Diag & Oral Med, Am Asn Dent Schs, 1984-85, Acad Oral Diag, radiol & med, chmn, Admin Bd-Coun Sect, 1988; Nat Res Coun, Inst Med Comm Aging Soc, 1984-; Am Optom AsnCoun Clin Optom Care, 1984-; Nat Adv Coun Health Prof, 1990-94; Inst Med Comt, Future Dent Educ. **Honors/Awds:** Awards from Urban League, Nat Asn Advan Colored People, UNCF, 1970;Distinguished Faculty Award, Harvard Univ, 1971; Dentist of the Year, Nat Dent Asn, 1972; Dentist of the Year, DC, 1973; DC Mayors Award, 1975; Presidential Award, Nat Dent Asn, 1976, 1978; Distinguished Faculty Award, Harvard Sch Dent Med, 1981; Founder's Award, Nat Optom Asn, 1985; Alumni Achievement Award, Howard Univ, 1986; Citation from Maryland Legislative House of Delegates for "Outstanding Contribution to Dentistry and Commitment to Excellence in Higher Education", 1986; Distinguished Faculty Award; Organization of Teachers of Oral Diagnosis & Service Award, Am Asn Dent Schs, 1995; Received more than 100 awards and recognitions from various organizations and societies. **Special Achievements:** First African-American to board certified in periodontology; published over 100 articles in journals in Dentistry, Dental Education, Optometry &Health Science. **Military Serv:** USAR 2nd Lt; 2515 Serv Unit pfc, 1942-45; Good Conduct Medal, 1944. **Home Addr:** 60 Marinita Ave Apt A, San Rafael, CA 94901. **Business Addr:** Dean Emeritus, Howard University Dental School, 600 W St NW, Washington, DC 20059, **Business Phone:** (202)806-0440.

HENRY, KARL H.
Lawyer. **Personal:** Born Jan 21, 1936, Chicago, IL; son of Karl H and Almeta Macintyre; married Dolores Davis; children: Marc, Paula. **Educ:** Fisk Univ; LA City Col; Northwestern Univ; Southwestern Univ Law LA, JD, 1969; USC Law Shc Prac Aspects Recording Indus. **Career:** Sys Outlet Shoes, asst mgr, 1962-63; Pabst Brewing Co, merchandising salesman, 1964-68; Green Power Found, mkt sales mgr, 1968; Spartan Missile Proj McDonnel Douglas Corp, sr contracts negotiator, 1969-70, sr employee rels rep, 1968-69; Pvt Pract, atty, 1970-; Juv Ct, referee, 1975-76. **Orgs:** LA Co Bar Asn; Am Bar Asn; Juvenile Cts Bar; Langston Law Club; LA Trial Lawyers Asn; Englewood Youth Asn; Nat Police Asn; John F Kennedy Club; bd dirs, Green Power Found; adv bd, STEP Inc; bd dirs Nat Asn Advan Colored People; pres, Hollypark Homeowner Asn; dir, Spec Prog PUSH. **Business Addr:** Attorney, 2903 W Vernon Ave, Los Angeles, CA 90008.*

HENRY, LISA JENNIFER
Executive. **Career:** Henry's Floral Design, owner & designer. *

HENRY, DR. MARCELETT CAMPBELL
Educator. **Personal:** Born Apr 16, 1928, Langston, OK; married Delbert V Jr; children: Jacqueline M, Sharon R, Delbert V III & Andrea D. **Educ:** Langston Univ, BS, 1949; Univ Okla, Norman, ME, 1963; San Fran State Univ, ME, Admin, 1969; Walden Univ, PhD, Admin, 1973. **Career:** Educator (retired); Anchorage Community Col, AK, Voc Home making Courses,teacher, 1954-55, adult Educ & curriculum develop, teacher & coordr summer teachers workshops, 1958-59; Anchorage Indep Sch, Dist AK Lang Arts & Soc Stud, teacher, 1956-59, teacher & homemaking, 1960-65; Tamalpais Union High Sch, Dist Mill Valley, Calif, dept chmn & teacher & dir occupational training prog, 1966-74; Calif State Dept Educ, mgr summer sch & consplanning & develop, coordr alternative educ & project mgr & cons sec educ, state staff & liaison co supts, dir, 1974-96, chmn, 2002; MC Henry Enterprises, pres, 1997-98. **Orgs:** Real Estate Training, 1959; AK Dept Educ 1964; Marin Co Home Educ, 1966-68; Project FEAST City Col San Fran, 1968; consult, Pace Ctr System Analysis Workshop Tamalpais HS Dist, 1969; adv comn & educ, JC Penny Bay Area, 1969-74; consult, Calif State Dept Voc Educ, 1970; consult, Marin Co Supt Off Corte Madera, Calif, 1970; develop model Tamalpais Union High Sch Dist, 1970; state exec bd, Delta Kappa Gamma Chi, 1971; consult, Project Breakthrough, Tamalpais High Sch Dist, 1972; Calif State Dept, 1973; review & eval, panelist Right Read Prog Higher Educ Wales, 1973; US Senate Select Com Nutrition & Human Needs Wash, DC, 1973; sub-com, Calif Attorneys Gen Consumer Educ, 1975; rep, State Supt Pub Instr Select State Century III Leaders, 1976-78; chmn & conf, adv bd Phi Delta Kappa, 1976-77; pres, Sacramento Phi Delta Kappa, 1977-78; US Presidential Task Force, 1981; pres, Asn Multicultural Coun& Develop. **Honors/Awds:** Mother's Day Recognition Award, 1959; Bouquet of the Day, KBYR Radio Station, 1964; Award of Merit, Calif Dept Justice & Educ, 1975; Award for Leadership, State Bicentennial Active State Dept Educ ARBC Calif, 1976; Women of the Year, Delta Delta Zeta Cha Zeta Phi Beta, San Fran, 1976; Nat Sch Journalism Award, Sch Publ Bicentennial Film Brochure, 1977. **Special Achievements:** Published a Handbook on Multicultural Child Development. *

HENRY, DR. MILDRED M DALTON
Educator. **Personal:** Born in Tamo, AR; children: Delano Hampton, Alvia Hampton Turner, Lawrence Hampton & Pamela HamptonRoss. **Educ:** AM&N Col Pine Bluff, BS, music ed, 1971; Southern IL Univ Edwardsville, MS, counr ed, 1976; Southern IL Univ Carbondale, PhD, counr ed, 1983. **Career:** AM&N Col, sec bus office, 1949-51; St Paul Pub Libr, libr asst, 1956-58; AM&N Col, lib asst & secy, 1968-71; Pine Bluff Sch Dist, music teacher, 1971-75; Southern IL Univ Edwardsville, libr asst, 1975; Watson Chapel Sch Dist, counr, 1976-77; Univ AR Pine Bluff, counr, 1978-80; Southern IL Univ Carbondale, dean's fel, 1980-81, grad asst, 1981; Carbondale Elem SchDist, teacher, 1981-83; CA State Univ, San Bernardino, asst prof, 1983, prof emer, currently; The Provisional Accelerated Learning Ctr, founder, Ceo, currently. **Orgs:** Adv bd, Creative Educrs Inc Riverside, 1983-; city comnr, Fontanta CA, 1984-; exec bd, Rialto/Fontana Nat Asn Advan Colored People, 1984-; pres, Provisional Educ Servs Inc, 1984-; Am Asn Univ Profs; Nat Educ Asn; CA Fac Asn; CA Teachers Asn; CA Asn Coun Develop; Asn Teacher Educrs; CA Black Fac & Staff Asn; CA State Employees Asn; Inland Empire Peace Officers Asn; Nat Asn Advan Colored People; Nat Coun Negro Women; steering comt San Bernardino Area Black Coc; San Bernardino Private Industry Coun. **Honors/Awds:** Leadership Awards, Atlanta Univ & Univ Calif, Los Angeles, 1978 & 1979; Citizen of Day, Radio Station KOTN Pine Bluff, 1980; Outstanding Scholastic Achievement, Black Affairs Coun SIUC, 1981. **Special Achievements:** Publication "Setting Up a Responsive Guidance Program in a Middle School" The Guidance Clinic 1979; First African American to become tenured in the College of Education at California State University. **Business Addr:** Professor Emeritus, California State University, 5500 Univ Pkwy, San Bernardino, CA 92407, **Business Phone:** (909)537-5000.*

HENRY, PAT. See HENRY, I PATRICIA.

HENRY, DR. SAMUEL DUDLEY
Educator. **Personal:** Born Oct 9, 1947, Washington, DC; son of Shendrine Boyce Henry and Dudley Henry; married Ana Maria Meneses, Dec 23, 1988. **Educ:** DC Teachers Col, BS, 1969; Columbia Univ, MA, 1974, EdD 1978. **Career:** Binghamton, eng & social studies teacher, 1971-73; HMLI Columbia Univ Teachers Col, res assoc, 1975-77; Sch Ed Univ MA Amherst, asst prof, 1977-78; Race Desegregation Ctr, NY, NJ, VI & PR, dir, 1978-81; San Jose State Univ, dir Equal Opportunity & Affirmative Action, Sch Social Scis, assoc dean 1987-88, assist vpres Stud Affairs, 1989-92; CSU Northridge, Northridge, CA, Sch Educ, assoc dean (acting) 1988-; Portland State Univ, exec dir, Portland Educ Network, assoc prof educ, 1992-94, dept chair, Curric & Instr, 2000-03, assoc prof, Curric & Instr - educ, coordr doctoral pgm, currently; Urban Fel, 1994-2000; De Pauw Univ, chair ed dept, 1998-99; consult, Media Working Group, currently. **Orgs:** Exec bd, Greenfield Sec Sch Comm, 1977-79; sponsor, Harlem Ebonetts Girls Track Team 1980-81; exec bd, Santa Clara Valley Urban League, 1982-83; exec bd, CAAAO, CA Assoc Affirmative Action Off, 1983-84; Prog Comm No CA Fair Employ Round table, 1983-85; ASCD Assoc Supr Curr Ser, 1984-85; bd dirs, Campus Christian Ministry, 1984-85; chair-drug prevention task force, San Jose Round table; chair, Oregon Comm on Children & Families, 2001-. **Honors/Awds:** Outstanding Service Award Disabled Students, SJSU, 1982-83; Commendation Curr Study Comm East Side Union, HS Dist, 1984; AA in Higher Education, Second Annual Conf on Desegregation in Post secondary, 1984. **Military Serv:** ANG, 1967-71; AUSR, 1972. **Home Addr:** 1186 SW 12th Ct, Troutdale, OR 97060. **Business Addr:** Coordinator of the doctoral program, Associate Professor, Portland State

University, Graduate School of Education, 615 SW Harrison Room 596 SBA, PO Box 751, Portland, OR 97207-0751.

HENRY, SKEETER. See HENRY, HERMAN.

HENRY, THOMAS
Educator. **Personal:** Born Nov 27, 1934, St Louis, MO; married Gemalia Blockton. **Educ:** Lincoln Univ, BS, 1957; harris teachers Col. **Career:** St Louis Co Transportation Community; St Louis System, teacher; FreeLance, commercial artist, 1962; Turner Middle Sch St Louis, head art dept, 1985. **Orgs:** Bd dirs, St Louis Co Grand Jury, 1974-77; bd dirs, Bicentennial St LouisCo; chmn, Dist Aunts & Uncles Give Needy Kids Shoes; resource dir, Inner-City YMCA. **Honors/Awds:** City of Week, KATZ Radio; Honor, Rehab Educ Leavenworth Kans; Outstanding Artist, Sigma Gamma Rho, Mo. **Special Achievements:** Painted Portraits of Many Movie Stars & Celebs. **Military Serv:** AUS pfc 1958-60. **Business Addr:** 2815 Pendleton Ave, St Louis, MO 63113.

HENRY, DR. WALTER LESTER, JR.
Physician, college teacher. **Personal:** Born Nov 19, 1915, Philadelphia, PA; son of Walter Lester and Vera Robinson; married Ada Palmer. **Educ:** Temple Univ, AB, 1936; Howard Univ Med Sch, MD, 1941. **Career:** Physician (retired); Howard Univ, from asst prof to prof, 1953-90, chmn dept med, 1962-73; John B Johnson, prof med, 1973-88. **Orgs:** Am Med Asn; Nat Med Asn; Endocrine Soc; Asn Am Physicians; Nat Asn Advan Colored People; Urban League; Sixth Presby Church; Am Bd Internal Med; fac trustee, Howard Univ, 1971-75; bd gov, Am Bd Int Med, 1971-78; regent Am Col Physicians, 1974-; regent, 1974-80, laureate, 1993, Am Col Physicians. **Honors/Awds:** Master, Am Col Physicians, 1987; Distinguished Teacher Award, Am Col Physicians, 1997. **Special Achievements:** Auth: Black Health Library Guide to Diabetes: Vital Health Information for African Americans; First African American to serve as a Regent in Howard University. **Military Serv:** USMC, maj WW II; AUS, Bronze Star, cluster to Bronze Star, 1942-44. **Home Addr:** 1780 Redwood Terr NW, Washington, DC 20012. *

HENRY, WILLIAM ARTHUR, II
Lawyer. **Personal:** Born Feb 11, 1939, Canalou, MO; married Alice Faye Pierce; children: William III, Shawn. **Educ:** Lincoln Univ, BS, 1962; Georgetown Univ Law Ctr, JD, 1972. **Career:** Xerox Corp, patent atty; IBM, rep, 1964-66; US Patent Off, patent exam, 1966-72; Xerox Corp. **Orgs:** DC Bar; DC Bar Asn; PA Bar; Am Bar Asn; Urban League; Nat Patent Law Asn; Rochester Patent Law Asn; Alpha Phi Alpha Frat. **Military Serv:** AUS, 1 lt, 1962-64.

HENRY-FAIRHURST, ELLENAE L
Executive, business owner, president (organization). **Personal:** Born Jan 6, 1943, Dayton, OH; daughter of Jack J Hart Sr; divorced. **Educ:** Miami Univ, BS, 1965; Univ Detroit, MA, 1978. **Career:** Ford Motor Co, mgr mkt res, 1968-86; Chrysler Corp, dealer candidate, 1986-88; Cumberland Chrysler-Plymouth, pres & gen mgr, 1988-92; Huntsville Dodge Inc, owner, pres & gen mgr, 1992-; Infiniti Huntsville, owner & pres, currently. **Orgs:** Secy bd dirs, Chrysler Minority Dealer Asn, 1989-; bd dirs, Sickle Cell Found, 1989-; bd dirs, Dayton Contempory Dance Co, 1993-. **Honors/Awds:** Dodge Five-Star Award. **Special Achievements:** Chrysler Corp, Five Star Dealer; First minority Infiniti retail owner in the United States. **Business Addr:** President, General Manager, Huntsville Dodge Inc, 6580 Univ Dr NW, Huntsville, AL 35806, **Business Phone:** (256)722-0988.

HENSLEY, WILLIE L.
Military leader, executive director. **Career:** US Dept Veterans Affairs, Ctr Minority Veterans, head, 1995, exec secy, 2006, dir, currently; Dept Veterans Affairs, prin adv, currently; Oper Enduring Freedom, 2001; Oper Iraqi Freedom, 2003. **Military Serv:** AUS, lt colonel, 1995. **Business Addr:** Director, Department of US Veterans Affairs, Center Minority Veterans, 810 Vermont Ave NW Suite 700, Washington, DC 20420, **Business Phone:** (202)273-5400.*

HENSON, DANIEL PHILLIP, III
Executive, executive director, president (organization). **Personal:** Born Apr 4, 1943, Baltimore, MD; son of Daniel P Henson Jr and Florence Newton; married Delaphine S; children: Darren P & Dana S. **Educ:** Morgan State Univ, BA, 1966; Johns Hopkins Univ, 1970. **Career:** Baltimore City Pub Sch, teacher, 1966-67; Metropolitan Life Inst Co, assoc mgr, 1967-74; Dan Henson & Assocs, pres, 1973-77; Guardian Life Ins Co Am, gen agent, 1974-77; US Small Bus Admin, reg adm, 1977-79; Minority Bus Dev Agency, dir, 1979-81; Greater Baltimore Comm, dir, 1981-82; G & M Oil Co Inc, vpres, 1982-84; Struever Bros Eccles & Rouse Inc, vpres; Housing & Comm Develop, comnr, 1993-99; Housing Authority Baltimore City, exec dir, 1993-99; Henson Develop Co, pres, currently. **Orgs:** Bd mem, Home Builders Asn Md, 1981-82; chmn bd, Develop Credit Fund Inc, 1982-; Greater Baltimore Comm, 1982-; bd mem, Baltimore Urban League, 1982-88; bd mem, 1982-, chmn bd, 1990-, Baltimore Sch Arts; chmn bd, Investing Baltimore, Inc; bd mem, Johns Hopkins Univ Inst Policy Studies; bd mem, Ctr Ethics & Corp Policy, 1989-; bd mem, Fed Reserve Bank Richmond, Baltimore Br, 1991-. **Business Phone:** (443)367-8001.

HENSON, DARRIN DEWITT
Actor, choreographer. **Personal:** Born May 5, 1972, Bronx, NY. **Career:** Tv Series: "Dance Grooves", 2001; "BET Open Mic: HIV Testing Day, Violation", 2003; "Sharon Osbourne Show, Retrosexual: 80's", 2004, "Love Me or Leave Me", 2004, "Take It to the Limit", 2004, "In the Garden", 2004, "Fear Eats the Soul", 2004, "Don't Think This Hasn't Been Fabulous",2004, "Bump & Grind", 2006, "The Feeling That We Have", 2007, "The Cost of a T-Shirt", 2007, "No Way Back", 2007, "Eye for an Eye", 2007, "The Vision", 2007; "Glass House", 2008; "Disarmed", 2008; "Lincoln Heights", 2007-08; Movies: Double Platinum, 1999; Longshot, 2000; Salon, 2005; The Fabric of a man, Voice, 2005; Last Stand, 2006; April Fools, 2007; The Hustle, 2008; A Good man is hard to find, Voice, 2008; The Express, 2008; Broad way Dance ctr, teacher Hip Hop, currently; "SoulFood", 2000-; Dance & Entertainment Workshop, founder; Darrin's DanceGrooves, choreographer, actor, currently; Broadway Dance Ctr, fac, currently. **Honors/Awds:** Nominee, Image Awards, 2004, 2005. **Special Achievements:** Has choreographed for Christina Aguilara, Brittany Spears, N'Sync, &Jennifer Lopez. **Business Phone:** (212)582-9304.

HENSON, WILLIAM L.
Educator. **Personal:** Born Aug 7, 1934, Baltimore, MD; son of Lawson and Mattie Ward; married Audrey Mills Henson, Feb 2, 1957; children: Cheryl, Elizabeth, Kathleen. **Educ:** Md State Col, BS, 1955; Penn State Univ, MA, 1957, PhD, 1967. **Career:** Commonwealth Pa, Harrisburg, PA, egg law enforcer, 1957-59; USDA, Fredericksburg, PA, poultry inspector, 1959-63; Pa State Univ, Univ Park, PA, grad res asst, 1963-67, asst assoc dean agr, 1969-84, asst dean agr, 1984-; US Dept Agr, Univ Park, PA, sr agr economist, 1967-84, asst dean; Pa State Univ, Asst Prof Emer Agr Econs, currently. **Orgs:** Minorities Agr, Natural Resources & Related Sci, 1988, pres, 1991-92; Am Agr Econ Asn, 1967-90; Am Econ Asn, 1967; Poultry Sci Asn, 1967-90. **Honors/Awds:** Distinguished Alumni Hall of Fame, Md State Col, 1986; Presidential Citation, Nat Asn Equal Opportunity Higher Educ, 1987; Equal Opportunity Award, Penn State Univ, 1989; Equal Opportunity Award, Econ & Stat Serv, USDA, 1980; Alumni Citizen Award, Black Greeks, Pa State Univ, 1988; Excellence in Advising Award, Pa State Univ, 1996. **Home Addr:** 125 Norle St, State College, PA 16801. **Business Addr:** Assistant to Dean, Penn State University, Col Agr Sci, 201 Agr Admin Bldg, University Park, PA 16802.*

HENTON, GEORGE
Executive. **Educ:** Nat Univ, BS, acct. **Career:** Am Bar Asn, budget dir & analyst; Shoe-Box-Accountant, owner, currently. **Orgs:** African Am Asn Fitness Professionals. **Business Addr:** Owner, Shoe-Box-Accountant, 9425 S Michigan Ave, Chicago, IL 60619, **Business Phone:** (773)821-6418.

HERBERT, ADAM W
School administrator, administrator. **Personal:** Born Dec 1, 1943, Muskogee, OK; son of Addie Herbert; married Karen Herbert, Jan 1, 1980. **Educ:** Univ Southern Calif, BA, polit sci, 1966, MA, pub admin, 1968; Univ Pittsburgh, PhD, urban affairs & pub admin, 1971. **Career:** Univ N Fla, pres, 1989-98; State Univ System, chancellor, 1998-2001, Fla Ctr Pub Policy & Leadership, regents prof & exec dir, 2001-03; Ind Univ, pres, 2003-07, Sch Pub & Environ Affairs & Polit Sci, prof; State Farm Fla Ins Co, dir, 2004-; St Joe Co, dir, 2004-. **Orgs:** Former pres, Nat Asn Schs Pub Affairs & Admin; former chair, NASPAA Comn Peer Rev & Accreditation; br trustees, Nat Acad Pub Admin; bd dirs, Joe Corp, 2004-; chmn bd, Ind Univ Found, currently. **Special Achievements:** First African American chancellor of Florida's ten public universities; First African American president of Indiana University. **Business Addr:** Director, St Joe Company, 245 Riverside Ave Suite 500, Jacksonville, FL 32202, **Business Phone:** (866)417-7133.

HERBERT, MAJ. DOUGLAS A.
Law enforcement officer. **Educ:** Henrico Co Sheriff's Off, Spec Law Enforcement Acad. **Career:** Henrico Co Sheriff Off, jail security div, from corporal to sergeant, 1980-85, shift sergeant, 1985-87, lt, 1987-88, capt, major, jail W adminr, chief dep sheriff, currently. **Special Achievements:** First African Am capt with the Henrico Co Sheriff's Off. **Business Addr:** Chief Deputy, Henrico County Sheriff's Office, 4301 E Parham Rd, PO Box 27032, Richmond, VA 23228, **Business Phone:** (804)501-5860.*

HERBERT, JOHN TRAVIS, JR.
Lawyer. **Personal:** Born Feb 17, 1943, Montclair, NJ; divorced; children: Stephanie, Travis & Suzanne. **Educ:** Seton Hall Law Sch, JD, 1974. **Career:** Allied Chem, corp staff, 1969-72; Rugers Univ, adj prof, 1973-; Johnson & Johnson, atty, corp dir, 1974-76, mgr, 1972-74; Cent Jersey OIC, bd atty; Pitney Bowes, Stamford, CT, Corp Facilities & Admin, vpres, coun, 1983-. **Orgs:** Vol, Parole, 1974-; chmn, BALSA Seton Hall Law Sch, 1973-74; coach, Pop Warner Football, 1975-77; organizer, Franklin Township Youth Athletic Asn, 1976-77; Franklin Township Bd Educ; Am Bar Asn; Nat Bar Asn; NJ Bar Asn; Middlesex Co Bar Asn, 1979-80; bd secy & gen coun, Rutgers Min Bus Co, 1980; bd mem, Westchester Fairfield City Corp Coun Assoc, 1985-; bd mayors, Transp Mgt Round Table, 1985-; corp liason, Nat Urban League Stamford, 1986-. **Business Phone:** (203)504-2779.

HERD, REV. JOHN E
Educator, clergy. **Personal:** Born May 29, 1932, Colbert Co, AL; married Eleanor; children: Arnold & Garland. **Educ:** BS, MS, 1966, AA Cert, 1976. **Career:** Russa Moton High Sch, Tallassee, Ala, instr; Cobb High Sch, Anniston, Ala, instr; Brutonville Jr High Sch, Al, prin; Alexandria High Sch, Ala, prin; New Elam #1 Missionary Baptist Church, pastor; Rocky Zion Baptist Church, Pell City, Ala, pastor, currently. **Orgs:** Alpha Phi Alpha; pres, Calhoun Co Educ Asn, 1972. **Special Achievements:** First Black president of Calhoun County Educational Association. **Military Serv:** USAF, sgt 1/c, 1951-55. **Business Addr:** Pastor, Rocky Zion Baptist Church, 1505 10th Ave S, Pell City, AL 35128, **Business Phone:** (205)338-3231.*

HEREFORD, SONNIE WELLINGTON, III
Physician, civil rights activist. **Personal:** Born Jan 7, 1931, Huntsville, AL; son of Sonnie and Jannie Burwell; married Martha Ann Adams, Nov 1956; children: Sonnie IV, Kimela, Lee, Linda, Brenda, Martha. **Educ:** Ala A&M Univ, BS, 1955; Meharry Med Col, MD, 1955. **Career:** Physician (retired); Oakwood Col, campus physician, 1957-73; Ala A&M Univ, prof histol, 1960-68, prof physiol, 1960-68, team physician, 1962-, campus physician, 1962-73; Huntsville Civil Rights Movement, leader & photogr, 1962-63; Calhoun Col, adj instr, prof anat & physiol, 1996-; consult sickle cell anemia, Delta Sigma Theta, 1971-75; pvt pract, physician. **Orgs:** Chmn, Comt Desegregation Huntsville, AL, 1962-63; vol physician, Boy Scouts & Girl Scouts, 1956-93; vol physician, Golden Gloves Huntsville, 1968-88; Omega Psi Phi. **Honors/Awds:** Distinguished Serv Award, Voter Coord Com Huntsville, AL 1962; Distinguished Serv Award, Oakwood Coll Huntsville, AL, 1973; Meharry Med Col, Twenty-Five Year Serv Award, 1980; Distinguished Serv Award, Community Action Agency, 1980; Oakwood Church, Distinguished Serv Award, 1980; Distinguished Serv Award, Zeta Sorority, 1982; Distinguished Serv Award, Madison County Midwives Asn, 1983; Distinguished Serv Award, Ala A&M Univ Athletic Dept, 1985; Ala Hall of Fame, Inducted Huntsville, 1995. **Special Achievements:** Documentary, "A Civil Rights Journey". guest on Calhoun's 4CTV program "Calhoun Review". **Home Phone:** (256)837-1575. *

HERENTON, DR. WILLIE W
Mayor. **Personal:** Born Apr 23, 1940, Memphis, TN; married Ida Jones; children: Errol, Rodney & Andrea. **Educ:** LeMoyne-Owen Col, BS, 1963; Memphis State Univ, MA, 1966; Southern Ill Univ, PhD, 1971. **Career:** Memphis City Sch Syst, elem sch teacher, 1963-67, elem sch prin, 1967-73; Rockefeller Found, fellow 1973-74; Memphis City Schs, dept supt, 1974-78, supt schs 1979-92; City Memphis, mayor, 1991, 2007-. **Orgs:** Bd dir, Nat Urban League; bd dir, Nat Jr Achievement; Amer Asn Sch Adminstr 1969-80; Nat Alliance Black Educators, 1974-; bd dir, Achievement Memphis 1979-; Nat Urban League Educ Adv Coun 1978; bd dir, United Way Greatr Memphis 1979-. **Honors/Awds:** Raymond Foster Scholar Award, So IL Univ 1970; Alumnus of the Year, LeMoyne Owen Col, 1976; Horatio Alger award, 1988; Municipal Leader of the Year, Am City & County Mag, 2002. **Special Achievements:** The first mayor in the hist of the city of Memphis to be elected to a fourth consecutive term as mayor; Named one of Top 100 Sch Adminr in US & Can Exec Educr Journal 1980, 1984. **Business Addr:** Mayor, City Memphis, City Hall 125 N Main St Rm 700, Memphis, TN 38103.

HERMAN, ALEXIS MARGARET
Government official. **Personal:** Born Jul 16, 1947, Mobile, AL; daughter of Alex Herman and Gloria Caponis; married Dr Charles L Franklin Jr. **Educ:** Xavier Univ, BA, sociol, 1969; Cent State Univ, hon doctorate; Lesley Col, hon doctorate. **Career:** Cath Soc Serv, soc worker, 1969-72; Recruitment Training Prog, outreach worker, 1971-72; Black Women Empl Prog Southern Regional Coun, dir, 1972-74; Dept Labor Recruitment Training Prog, consult supvr, 1973-74; Women's Prog Minority Women Empl Atlanta, nat dir, 1974-77; Orgn Econ Coop & Develop, White House rep; Nat Consumer Coop Bank, founding mem; Women's Bur, Dept Labor, dir, 1977-81; Green Herman & Assocs, vpres, 1981-85; A M Herman & Assocs, founder, pres, 1985-93; Dem Nat Conv Comt, chief exec officer, 1991; Dem Nat Comt, dep chair & chief staff; 1992; Presidential Transition Off, dep dir, 1992-93; White House Off Pub Liaison, dir, asst to the US Pres, 1993-97, secy labor, 1997-2000; Coca-Cola Co, Bias Suit Task Force, chair, 2001-, dir, 2007-; Toyota Motor Corp, N Am Diversity Adv Bd, chair; Cummins Inc, bd mem; Metro Goldwyn Mayer Mirage Inc, bd mem; Prudential, bd mem; Entergy Corp, bd dir, currently; New Ventures Inc, chair & chief exec officer, 2001-; speaker, currently. **Orgs:** Bd mem, Adams Nat Bank; bd mem, DC Econ Develop Finance Corp; Nat Coun Negro Women; Delta Sigma Theta Sorority Inc; bd mem, One Am Found; chair, Sodexho Adv Bd; co-chair, Bush Clinton Katrina Fund. **Honors/Awds:** Dorothy I Height Leadership Award; Sara Lee Frontrunner Award, 1999.

Special Achievements: First African-American to lead the Department of Labor. **Business Phone:** (404)957-9899.

HERMAN, KATHLEEN VIRGIL
Administrator. **Personal:** Born May 17, 1942, Buffalo, NY; children: Jonathan Mark. **Educ:** Goddard Col, BA, 1976; Boston Univ, MS, commun, 1980. **Career:** Pub Info Boston Edison, consult, 1979; Minority Recruitment Big Sister Assoc, coordr, 1980; Coun Battered Women, comt educ dir, 1980; Access Atlanta Inc, dir, 1981; City atlanta, coordr cable commun. **Orgs:** Minorities Cable, Nat Assoc Telecom, Nat Fed Local Programmers, Women Cable; NAACP Media Comt, co-chair; Am Women radio & TV. **Honors/Awds:** Pub, "Minority Participation in the Media", sub comt Telecom Consumer Protection & Finance Comn Energy & Com, US House Reps, 98th Congress.

HERMANUZ, GHISLAINE
Educator, architect. **Personal:** Born in Lausanne, Switzerland; daughter of Max Hermanuz and Manotte Tavernier Hermanuz; widowed 1998; children: Dahoud Walker (died 1998). **Educ:** ETH/Lausanne Switzerland, arch dipl, 1967; Harvard Grad Sch Design, attended 1969; Columbia Univ, MS, urban planning, 1971. **Career:** Candilis, Josic & Woods, architect, 1964-65; Llewelyn-Davies & Weeks, architects, 1967-68; Architects' Renewal Comt Harlem, architect, 1969-71; Urban Design Group City Planning Dept, urban designer, 1972-73; Columbia Univ, Grad Sch Architecture, prof archit; City Col NY, prof archit, prof & dir advising, currently; Hermanuz Ltd, prin, 1988-; Taubman Col Archit, charles moore vis prof, urban design, currently. **Orgs:** Bd trustees, Malcom X Mus; UN Huairou comn. **Honors/Awds:** Fulbright Fel, 1968; German Marshall Fund, 1979; Nat Endowment for Arts, 1982; NY State Council on the Arts, 1984, 1986, 1988, 1994; President's Fund for Excellence in Teaching, 1990; Municipal Art Soc, IDEAS Competition, 1994. **Business Addr:** Professor, Director of Advising, The City College of New York, Convent Ave 138th St, New York, NY 10031, **Business Phone:** (212)650-8731.

HERNANDEZ, AILEEN CLARKE
Consultant, executive. **Personal:** Born May 23, 1926, Brooklyn, NY; daughter of Charles Henry Clarke Sr and Ethel Louise Hall; married Alfonso Rafael (divorced 1961). **Educ:** Howard Univ, BA, magna cum laude, 1947; Univ Oslo, postgrad, Int stud exchange prog, 1947; NY Univ, attended 1950; Univ Calif LA, attended; Univ Southern Calif, attended; Intern Ladies Garment Workers Union, grad labor col, 1951; LA State Univ, MA (highest Hons), 1961. **Career:** Int Ladies Garment Workers Union LA, organizer, asst educ dir, 1951-59, dir pub rel & educ, 1959-61; US State Dept, toured South Am countries specialst labor educ, 1960; Calif Fair Employ Prac Comn, asst chief, 1962-65; US Equal Employ Comn, comnr, 1965-66; San Francisco State Univ, lectr & instr polit sci, 1968-69; Univ Calif Berkeley, instr, urban planning, 1978, 1979; Aileen C Hernandez Asn, owner & pres, 1967-; Howard Univ, res asst, dept govt. **Orgs:** Western vpres, Nat Orgn Women, 1967-70, pres, 1970-71; co-founding mem, Black Women Organized Act, San Fran & Nat Hookup Black Women; life trustee, Urban Inst Wash, DC; bd mem, MS Found Women; bd dirs, Nat Comm Against Discrimination Housing 1969; Am Acad Polit & Soc Sci; Indust Rel Res Asn; Am Civil Liberties Union; Comnr, Foreign Policy Study Found; steering/exec com, co-chair, Nat Urban Coalition; pres, bd trustees, Working Assets Money Fund; bd overseers, Inst Civil Justice Rand Corp; adv, Nat Inst Women Color; treas, Eleanor R Spikes Mem Fund; adv comt, Prog Res Immigration Policy, Rand &Urban Inst; bd mem, ed, comm chair, Death Penalty Focus; bd mem, Meiklejohn Civil Liberties Union; Calif Community Campaign Financing; Nat Asn Advan Colored People; Bd pres, Ctr Common Good; Alpha Kappa Alpha; Bay Area Urban League; co-founder/chair, Coalition Econ Equity; vice chair, San Francisco 2000; comnr, Bay Vision 2020; chair, CA Women's Agenda; chair emer, Citizen's Trust; bd, Pesticide Edu Ctr; bd, Garden Proj; bd, Ctr Women Policy Studies; bd, ex com, Citizen's Comn Civil Rights; bd, ex comm, Ctr Govt Studies; bd, Wellesley Ctrs Res Women; bd, San Francisco Workforce Investment; bd, chair Working Group, San Francisco Redevelop Agency; Prog Resources Comt & WISF Bd, 2001-. **Honors/Awds:** Woman of Year, Community Rels Conf Southern CA, 1961; Postgraduate Achievement Award, Bay Area Alumni Club Disting, Howard Univ, 1967; Public Service Award, Charter Day Alumni Postgrad Achvmnt Labor, 1968; Hon DHL, Southern Vermont Col, 1979; Award from Equal Rights Advocates, 1981;Women Award, Friends of the Community on the Status, 1984; Award Ten Women Who Make a Difference, SF League Women Voters, 1985; Parren J Mitchell Award, SF Black Chamber Community, 1985; Distinguished Service Award, Nat Urban Coalition, 1987; Earl Warren Civil Liberties Award, N Calif ACLU, 1989; Wise Woman Award, Ctr Women Policy Studies, 1989; Silver Spur Award, SF Planning & Urban Res Asn, 1995; Mary Lepper Award, Am Polit Sci Asn, 1996; WAVE award, Alumnae Resources, 1997; Ella Hill Hutch Award, Black Women Organized for Political Action, 1997; Activist of the Year Award, San Francisco Bay Area 100 Black Women, 2001; Ten Women Campaign Award, Flyaway Productions, 2003. **Special Achievements:** Named one of 10 Most Disting Women, Bay Area San Fran Examiner, 1968. **Business Addr:** Owner, President, Aileen C Hernandez Associates, 818 47th Ave, San Francisco, CA 94121-3208, **Business Phone:** (415)752-4506.

HERNANDEZ, MARY N
Librarian. **Personal:** Born Nov 21, 1940, Nashville, TN; daughter of Mary DeWees and Rafael. **Educ:** Fisk Univ, Nashville, Tenn, BA, 1962; Tenn State Univ, Nashville, Tenn, 1967, 1979, MS, 1985; Peabody Vanderbilt, Nashville, Tenn, MLS, 1986. **Career:** Georgetown Neighborhood Library, Branch Mgr., 2006-; Northeast Neighborhood Library, Branch Mgr., 2005-2006; District of Columbia Public Library System, Watha T. Daniel/ Shaw Neighborhood Library, Branch Mgr., 1998-2005; The Univ of Arizona Library, Tuscon, AZ, Fine Arts and African Studies Librarian, 1991-1998; The Univ of Tenn, Chattanooga, TN, Asst Prof, 1988-1991, Head Circ Services, 1989-1991; Tennessee Botanical Gardens and Fine Arts Center, Nashville, TN, Fine Arts Librarian, 1986-1988. **Orgs:** Pres, Art Libraries Soc, TN-KY, 1989-90; ARLIS/ NA Membership Comt, 1990-91, 1993-95; Arts & Education Coun, Southern Writers Conf, 1990-91; Black Caucus, Am Library Asn, 1989-91; president-elect, ARLIS, Ariz, 1993-94; Tucson Jazz Soc, 1991-98; Coun Black Educrs, Tucson. **Honors/Awds:** Dean's Award, Lupton Libr Univ Tenn Chattanooga, 1990; LoPresti Award, ARLIS, SE, 1990-91; NEH Award, 1992-93. **Special Achievements:** Order of Merit, Archdiocese Wash, 2004. **Business Addr:** Branch Manager, Watha T Daniel/Shaw Neighborhood Library, 1701 8th St NW, Washington, DC 20002, **Business Phone:** (202)671-0212.

HERNDON, CRAIG GARRIS
Photographer. **Personal:** Born Jan 23, 1947, Washington, DC; son of Lucy Frances Mills and Garris McClellan; married Valerie Ingrid Naylor, Aug 7, 1988; children: Stacey Arlene, Robert Eric, Marcus Vincent, Monica Amber & Maya Violet. **Educ:** Howard Univ, BA, 1970; Md Inst Col Art, MFA, 2005. **Career:** Potomac Mag, news aide, 1968-72; Wash Post, photogr, 1972; PicSmart Inc, founder & ceo, 2000-. **Orgs:** White House News Photographers Asn; Nat Asn Black Journalists. **Honors/Awds:** Nat Asn Black Journalists, Photographer of the Year, 1996. **Business Addr:** Founder, Chief Executive Officer, PicSmart Inc, 3212 Walnut Dr, Annapolis, MD 21403.

HERNDON, GLORIA E.
Executive. **Personal:** Born Aug 9, 1950, St Louis; married Brent A Herndon. **Educ:** Southern Ill Univ, BA, 1970; Johns Hopkins Univ, MA, 1972, PhD, 1978. **Career:** Am Embassy London, financial economist; Ahmadu Bello Univ Nigeria, res, 1978-79; Brooking Inst, res asst; Johns Hopkins, res asst; African-Am Inst, prog asst; Dept State, escort interpreter; Carnegie Endowment Int Peace Coun Foreign Rels, res asst; Equitable Financial Servs, ins co exec, 1984-; GB Herndon & Assoc, ceo & pres, 1989-. **Orgs:** Accomplished Musician; Mu Phi Epsilon; Nat Econ Asn; Am Soc Int Law; Nat Conf Black Polit Scientist; Nat Coun Negro Women; Nigerian-Am C; US Youth Coun Res initial Black Caucus, 1970-71; planner United Minority Arts Coun; Nat Asn Equal Opportunity Higher Educ; Am Asn Community Col; Asn Community Col Trustees. **Honors/Awds:** Nat Negro Merit Semifinalist, 1967; Distinguished Serv Award S Ill Univ, 1970; Nat Asn Hon Studs; Magna Cum Laude Woodrow Wilson Fel Finalist, 1970; recipient Rockefeller Found. **Special Achievements:** Enterprising Women Hall of Fame, 2006. **Business Addr:** President, Chief Executive Officer, G B Herndon & Asn Inc, 601 Pa Ave NW No 900, Washington, DC 20004.*

HERNDON, HAROLD THOMAS, SR.
Executive. **Personal:** Born Oct 28, 1937, Lincolnton, NC; son of John W Jr and Elizabeth; married Catherine Thompson, Jun 30, 1962; children: Harold Jr, Dwayne, LaShawn, Colin, Cynthia. **Educ:** Bluefield State col, BS, 1959; Univ MAR, MS, 1980. **Career:** St Mary's bd educ, music teacher, 1960-70, adr, 1970-80; Compliance Corp, pres & chief exec officer, currently. **Orgs:** Nat Contract mgt asn; pres, Chesapeake Bay Chapter; Rotary int; St Mary's County Econ Develop cms; soc enterpreneurs & Scientists; mer 100; bd mem, St Mary's Nursing Home; St Mary's Vocational Tech educ coun; bd mem, Tri-County Small Bus Develop ctr. **Honors/Awds:** Pathfinder Award, St Mary's Human Rels com, 1990; Outstanding Business Achievements, MNY Alliance, 1992; other awards from various orgs over the years. **Special Achievements:** Top 100 Black business, Back Enterprise, 1991. **Business Addr:** President, Chief Exeutive Officer, Compliance Corporation, 21617 S Essex Dr Suite 34, Lexington Park, MD 20653, **Business Phone:** (301)863-8070.*

HERNDON, LARRY LEE
Baseball player, athletic coach. **Personal:** Born Nov 3, 1953, Sunflower, MS; married Faye Hill; children: Latasha, Kamilah, Maya & Larry Darnell. **Educ:** Tenn State Univ. **Career:** Baseball player, (retired), Athletic coach; St Louis Cardinals, player, 1976; San Francisco Giants, outfielder, 1976-81; Detroit Tigers, outfielder, 1982-88, hitting coach; Lake land Flying Tigers, batting coach, 2006-. **Honors/Awds:** National League Rookie of the Year, Sporting News, 1976; Willie Mac Award, San Francisco Giants, 1981; World Series champion, 1984. **Business Phone:** (863)686-8075.

HERNDON, PHILLIP GEORGE
Investment banker. **Personal:** Born Jul 3, 1951, Little Rock, AR; son of James Franklyn Herndon and Georgia Mae Byrd Herndon. **Educ:** Villanova Univ, PA, 2 years; Amer Legion Boy's State, 1968. **Career:** Pulaski Co, AR, surveyor; Just for Kicks Inc retail shoe store, owner 1973-74; KATV Little Rock, news reporter 1972; Black Rel Dir Youth Div Gov Winthrop Rockefeller's Re-Election Campaign, 1970; Pulaski Co, elected co-surveyor & 1st black elected official, 1972; Lt Governor Amer Legions Boys State, 1st Black elected 1968; Kip Walton Productions (TV/ Motion Pictures), Hollywood, CA, production asst 1974-78; US Assoc Investment Bankers, Little Rock, AR, investment banker, 1985-87; Blinder, Robinson & Co, Denver, CO, asst manager Bond Department 1987-88; consultant, Colorado African/ Caribbean Trade Office 1988-; consultant, Anisco Enterprises (import/export) 1988-; Manufacturing & Distributing International, sr vp, 1992-. **Orgs:** Dir of Community Relations GYST House, (fund raiser drug rehabilitation program); New Futures for Little Rock Youth, dir, volunteer services. **Honors/Awds:** Natl HS Track Champ Natl & state record holder high hurdles 1968; 1st Black inducted into Little Rock Central HS Hall of Fame 1969; recip over 200 full scholarship offers from coll & Univ nationwide 1969; Million Dollar Club, Blinder, Robinson & Company 1988. *

HERRELL, DR. ASTOR YEARY
Chairperson, educator. **Personal:** Born Feb 13, 1935, Fork Ridge, TN; son of Clarence and Charity; married Doris Vivian Smith; children: Patricia Faye. **Educ:** Berea Col, BA, chem, 1957; Tuskegee Inst, MS Ed, 1961; Wayne State Univ, MI, PhD, inorganic chem, 1973. **Career:** St Augustine's Col, instr, 1961-63; Knoxville Col, prof & chmn, 1963-79; Wayne State Univ, Sci Fac Fel, 1970-72; consult Winston-Salem/Forsyth Co Schs, 1983-85; Winston-Salem State Univ, Chairperson phys sci, adj prof chem, currently. **Orgs:** Am Chem Soc; bd dir, Forsyth Co Environ Affairs Bd; Sigma Xi, 1985-. **Honors/Awds:** Biography display Martin Luther King Libr DC, 1984. **Special Achievements:** Several publ nat & int sci J's-last article publ, 1984. **Military Serv:** AUS, Reserves Pfc, 6 yrs. **Business Addr:** Adjunct Professor of Chemistry, Winston-Salem State University, 601 Martin Luther King Jr Dr W B Atkinson 311, PO Box 19531, Winston-Salem, NC 27110.

HERRING, DR. BERNARD DUANE
Educator, physician. **Personal:** Born in Massillon, OH; son of James and Eva; married Odessa Appling; children: Kevin, Duane, Terez & Sean. **Educ:** Kent State Univ, BS, 1952; Univ Cincinnati Med Sch, MD, 1956; LaSalle Univ, LLB, 1963. **Career:** San Fran Gen Hosp, intern, 1956-57; Brooklyn Vet Hosp, resident, 1957-58; Crile Vet Hosp, resident, 1958-59; Merritt Hosp, teaching, 1966-84; Univ CA Med Sch SF, asst clin prof med; gen pract, currently; Alta Bates Summit Med Ctr, Family Med & Geriatric Med, physician, currently. **Orgs:** Am Bd Family Med; Am Bd Internal Med; Am Col Legal Med; Am Med Writers Asn; Am Diabetes Asn; Am Col Physician; Am Soc Composers & Authors; Am Med Asn; Am Heart Asn; pres, Sunshine Vitamin Co; Am Acad Family Physicians,1983; Am Geriatric Soc, 1989; Watchtower Bible & Tract Soc, 1980-89. **Honors/Awds:** Cited by Phi Beta Kappa, Kent State Univ, 1952. **Special Achievements:** Article: "Kaposi Sarcoma in The Negro" 1963 Jama; "Hospital Priviledges"1965; Cleveland Marshall Law Review; "Pernicious Anemia & The AmericanNegro" Am Practr, 1962; "Hepatoma with Unusual Associations" J. Nat MedAsn, 1973; "Cancer of Prostate in Blacks" J. Nat Med Asn, 1977; ListedBest Doctor Am, 1979; "Unravelling Pathophysiology of Male PatternBaldness" 1985; "Understanding Insulin-Resistance in Type 2 Diaretes," J.National Medical Asn, 2002. **Business Addr:** Physician, 2960 Sacramento St, Berkeley, CA 94702.*

HERRING, CEDRIC
Educator. **Educ:** Univ Houston-Univ Park, BA, Sociol, 1980; Univ Mich-Ann Arbor, MA, Sociol, 1981, PhD, Sociol, 1985. **Career:** Texas A&M Univ, Dept Sociol, from asst pro to assoc prof, 1985-90; Univ Ill Chicago, Dept Sociol, assoc prof, 1990-95, Great Cities Inst, Great Cities scholar, 1995-96, prof, 1995-, Inst Res Race & Pub Policy, founding dir, 1996-98; Inst Govt & Pub Affairs, Univ Ill, assoc prof, 1990-95, prof, 1995-; Ind Univ Minority Fac Recruitment fel. **Orgs:** Am Sociol Asn; Midwest Sociol Soc; Nat Res Coun Selection Panel Ford Found Minority Fel Prog. **Honors/Awds:** Sydney Spivack Dissertation Award, 1985. **Special Achievements:** Numerous Publications including Splitting the Middle: Political Alienation, Acquiescence & Activism, editor of African Ams & the Public Agenda: The Paradoxes of Public Policy & co-editor of Empowerment in Chicago: Grassroots Participation in Economic Development & Poverty Alleviation. **Business Addr:** Professor, Institute of Government and Public Affairs, University of Illinois, 815 W Van Buren St Suite 525, Chicago, IL 60607, **Business Phone:** (312)413-0296.

HERRING, LARRY WINDELL
Dentist. **Personal:** Born Jul 8, 1946, Batesville, MS; married Rubbie P Herring; children: Cedric, La Canas Nicole, Yolanda. **Educ:** TN State Univ, BA, 1967; Meharry Med Col, DDS, 1971. **Career:** Pvt pract, dentist, currently. **Orgs:** Nat Dent Asn; Am Dent Asn; Pan TN Dent Asn; Tri-Lakes Study Club; Shelby Co Dent Soc; NAACP; Omega Psi Phi; Masonic Lodge; W Camp MB Ch. **Military Serv:** USAF, capt, 1971-73. **Business Addr:** Dentist, Private Practitioner, 115 Wood St, Batesville, MS 38606-1826, **Business Phone:** (662)563-5344.*

HERRING, LEONARD
Public relations executive, chief executive officer. **Personal:** Born Oct 1, 1934, Valdosta, GA; son of Leonard Herring Sr and Gussie; children: Leonard III & Lynne Rene. **Educ:** Univ Cincinnati, BA 1960, BS 1964. **Career:** Colgate-Palmolive Co NY Co, San Fran, mktg & sales; Cincinnati Bell Tele, acct mgr, mktg staff asst, 1964-66; Armco Steel Corp, asst personnel dir, 1966-67; Leonard Herring Jr. Enterprises, pub rel officer, 1967-, pres & chief exec officer, currently; Celebrity Tennis Tournament Ltd, chmn, 1976-. **Orgs:** Kappa Alpha Psi, 1960-; Univ Cincinnati Aumni Asn, 1964-; Am Tennis Prof, 1970-; Univ Cincinnati 100 Distinguished Alumni, 1970; Am Tennis Writers Asn, 1970-; Am Tennis Profs, 1970; United Tennis Writers Asn, 1970; Advertising Asn Am, 1972-; vpres, Pub Rel Soc Am, 1972-76; vpres, US Lawn Tennis Asn, 1975-76; Men Achievement World, 1976; bd mem, United Way Los Angeles, 1984-; Screen Actor's Guild, 1992-; Prof Tennis Registry, 2001; US Tennis Asn; US Tennis Prof Registry. **Honors/Awds:** Pub rel consult movies; Amityville Horror; Omen; A Piece Action Part II; Sounder, Cross Creek; Cinci Chap Nat Jr Tennis Leagues Boys & Girls, coach, 1972-74; produced celebrity golf & tennis classics in Carribbean, Mexico; Santa Monica Celebrity Tennis Classic, Malibu CA. **Military Serv:** AUS, lt; news correspondent for the Stars & Stripes in Europe, 1954-56.

HERRING, MARSHA K CHURCH
Marketing executive, entrepreneur. **Personal:** Born Jun 23, 1958, Detroit, MI; daughter of Rogers and Muriel; married Cedric Herring, Jun 25, 1983; children: Christopher Earle & Kiara Nicole. **Educ:** Univ Mich, Ann Arbor, bachelors, gen studies, 1980, masters, pub policy, 1983. **Career:** US Sen Carl Levin, pres asst, 1980-85; Humana Hosp Brazos Valley, dir mktg, 1985-89; Greenleaf Hosp, dir mkt, 1989-90; Christ Hosp, dir ment health mkt, 1991-93; UIC Med Ctr, dir mkt, 1993-2001; M'Powered Commun, prin & chief exec officer, 2001-; MusXcellence, dir mkt, currently; ACCESS Community Health Network, dir prog implementation, currently. **Orgs:** Am Mkt Asn, 1988-; S Suburban Chamber Com, IL, 1992-, chair, health servs comt, 1992-94; adv bd mem, Crisis Ctr S Suburbia, 1992-93; Adv bd, 1998-2001, Alliance Healthcare Strategy & Mkt, 1993-; adv bd, Expo Today's Black Woman, 1997-; HIV adv comt, Ill Dept Pub Health, 2001. **Honors/Awds:** Agape Award, HCA Greenleaf Hosp, 1990; Employee of the Month, Gold Star Award, Christ Hosp, 1993; Recognition Award, Acad Black Women Health Professions, 1994; Phenomenal Woman Award, 1998; Children of the Storm Award, 2003.

HERRING, WILLIAM F.
Executive. **Personal:** Born Jul 28, 1932, Valdosta, GA; son of Coy and Viola; married Janet L; children: William Jr, Paul, Kristi. **Educ:** Wayne State Univ, BA, 1961. **Career:** Houdaille Industries, mgr industrial rels, 1970-73; Detroit Coca-Cola Bottling Co, dir industrial rels, 1973-75; Buick Motor Div GM Corp, asst zone mgr, 1977-79, mgr dealer develop, 1979-; WFH & Assoc, owner. **Orgs:** Detroit Police Community Rel, 1972; life mem, NAACP, 1976; Car & Truck Renting & Leasing Asn,1977; Nat Adv Coun, NAACP, 1983-; bd dirs, Urban League, 1985-88; United Negro Col Fund, 1985-. **Honors/Awds:** Achievement Award, United Fund, 1972. **Military Serv:** AUS, cpt, 1952-54. *

HERRINGTON, PERRY LEE
Consultant, educational consultant. **Personal:** Born Mar 26, 1951, Waynesboro, GA; son of Theodore and Judy Herrington; married Janet Bailey, Sep 27, 1980; children: Jeffrey Bailey, Tiese, Kara & Brittany. **Educ:** Univ Chicago, Chicago, IL, cert, Urban Studies, 1971; Coe Col, Cedar Rapids, IA, BA, 1973; Lindenwood Col, St Louis, MO, MBA, 1986. **Career:** Lynndale Sch, Augusta, Ga, instr educables, 1973-74; Paine Col, Augusta, Ga, dir recruitment & admis, 1974-76; Yoorhees Col, Denmark, SC, dir instnl develop, 1976-78; Am Can Co, St Louis, Mo, labor rels assoc, 1978-87; CSRA Bus League/Augusta Minority Bus Develop Ctr, Augusta, Ga, exec dir, 1987; Fla Agr & Mech Univ, exec dir title III, currently. **Orgs:** Nat Asn Advan Colored People, 1987-; bd dir, exec dir, CSRA Bus League, 1987-; bd dir, treas, Augusta Community Housing Resource Bd, 1987-; Ga Statewide Resource Network Initiative, 1990-; regional vpres, Nat Bus League, 1991-; bd dir, Ga Asn Minority Entrepreneurs, 1991-; bd dir, Augusta Mini Theatre, 1991-; title adminr, Nat Asn Hist Black Col & Univ. **Honors/Awds:** Meritorious Service Award, Vorhees Col, 1978; Sammy Davis Jr "Yes I Can" Award, St Louis Urban League/Am Can Co, 1979-80; Regional MBDA Advocacy Award, Atlanta Regional Off, MBDA/US Dept Com, 1990; Meritorious Service Award, Lucy C Laney High Sch Voc Ed Prog, 1990. **Business Phone:** (850)599-3914.

HERRON, BRUCE WAYNE
Executive, football player. **Personal:** Born Apr 14, 1954, Victoria, TX; married Joyce LaDell Freeman; children: Monica Yvonne, Bruce Wayne Jr, Jordaya, Vance. **Educ:** Univ New Mexico, BA, 1977. **Career:** Football player (retired), executive; Miami Dolphins, 1977-78; Chicago Bears, 1978-82; Accurate Air Express, owner, 1982-83; Metro Media TV Channel 32, acct exec, 1984; Chicago State Univ, dir athletics; Waste Mgt Inc, acct exec, currently. **Orgs:** Dir, Big Brothers & Big Sisters; vol, Better Boys Found; hon chmn, Sicle Cell Anemia, 1982. **Honors/Awds:** Man of the Year, Big Brothers & Big Sisters; Byron Wizzer White, Nat Football League Players Asn. **Business Addr:** Accontant Executive, Waste Management Inc., 1001 Fannin St Suite 4000, Houston, TX 77002-6711.*

HERRON, CAROLIVIA
Writer, educator. **Personal:** Born in Washington, DC; daughter of Oscar S and Georgia C J. **Educ:** Eastern Baptist Col, St Davids, PA, BA, eng lit, 1969; Villanova Univ, MA, eng, 1973; Univ Pa, MA, creative writing, 1985, PhD, comparative lit & lit theory, 1985. **Career:** Harvard Univ, African-Am Studies & Comparative Lit, asst prof, 1986-90; Bunting Inst fel, Radcliffe Col, 1988; Beineke Libr fel, Yale Univ, 1988; Mt Holyoke Col, assoc prof eng, 1990-92; Hebrew Col, vis scholar, 1994-95; Harvard Univ, vis scholar, 1995; Brandeis Univ, vis scholar; Calif St Univ, Chicago, eng prof; Random House Inc, writer; Kar-Ben, writer; Epic Center Stories, multimedia developer, currently; Books: Thereafter Johnnie, novel, 1991; Selected Works of Angelina Weld Grimke, 1991; Nappy Hair, 1997; Always An Olivia, 2007; software, The Function at the Junction; software, The Drum of Anansi. **Orgs:** Classical Asn New Eng, 1986-93; fel Fulbright, Mexico; Beinecke to Yale, Folger Shakespeare Libr Scholar; Nat Endowment Humanities Curric Develop African Am Studies. **Honors/Awds:** Fulbright Post-Doctoral Research Award, US Info Serv, 1985; Visit to Collections Award, Nat Endowment Humanities, 1987; Post-Doctoral Research Award, Folger Shakespeare Libr, 1989.

HERRON, VERNON M.
Consultant, clergy. **Personal:** Born Oct 7, 1928, Charlotte; married; children: 3. **Educ:** Shaw Univ, AB, 1951; Johnson C Smith Univ, MDiv, 1958; Pa State Univ, MPA, 1978; Pittsburgh Theol Sem, Dmin, 1978. **Career:** Clergy, consultant (retired); First Baptist Church, Dallas, pastor, 1952-55; Friendship Baptist Church, Pittsburgh, pastor, 1955-62; Harrisburgh State Hosp, clin psychol, 1958; Allentown State Hosp, clin psychol, 1959; Hopewell Baptist, Jeannette, PA, pastor; Second Baptist Church Joliet, pastor, 1962-68; Mich State Univ, conf planning, 1968; Am Baptist Church HQ, asst sec div soc ministries, 1968-75; Valley Forge, strategic planning, 1969-74; Urban Training Ctr, Chicago, 1970; Valley Forge, planning budget obj, 1974, planning prg obj, 1973; Pub Progs, consult admin mgt, 1975; Shiloh Baptist Church, S Philadelphia, asst minister; St Paul's Baptist Church, W Chester, PA, interim pastor, 1995. **Orgs:** Alpha Phi Alpha Frat; Prince Hall Mason. *

HERRON-BRAGGS, CINDY
Singer, actor. **Personal:** Born Sep 26, 1965, San Francisco, CA; married Glenn Braggs; children: Donovan Andrew, Jordan, Natalia. **Career:** Mem group En Vogue; Albums: "Born to Sing", 1990; "Funky Divas", 1992; "EV3", 1997; "Masterpiece Theatre", 2000; "The Gift of Christmas", 2002; "Soul Flower", 2004; TV series: "Johnnie Mae Gibson: FBI", 1986; "Wally & the Valentines", 1989; "Roc", 1993; "On Our Own", 1994-95; "Saturday Night Live", 1992-97; "Malcolm & Eddie", 1999; "Lexie", 2004; Films: Juice, 1992; Batman Forever, 1995; Deadly Rhapsody, 2001. **Special Achievements:** Miss San Fransisco, 1986; second runner Up in 1986 Miss california; Former Miss Black California. **Business Phone:** (213)556-2727.*

HERVEY, BILLY T.
Aerospace engineer. **Personal:** Born Apr 2, 1937, Naples, TX; married Olivia M Gray; children: Jewel, Marcus, Patrick. **Educ:** BS, 1960. **Career:** Aerospace engineer (retired); AUS Corps Engrs Ballistic Missle Off Atlus, mech engr, 1960-62; Gen Dynamics Corp, Atlas F Missile Prog Altus, mech design engr test conductor; NASA/Johnson Space Ctr Houston; Kennedy Space Ctr Cape Kennedy, NASA & mech engr, 1964-65; Mission Control Ctr Houston Gemini & Apollo Flights, NASA flight controller, 1966-71; Phys Sch Tech Mgr; NASA, Space Shuttle Prog Off. **Orgs:** Gulf Coast Soc; Trinity United Meth Chap; Prince Hall Free & Accepted Masonry; Douglas Burrell Consistory No 56; Ancient Accepted Scottist Rite; Ancient Egyptian Arabic Order Noble of Mystic Shrine N & S Am. **Honors/Awds:** Group Achievement Award, Gemini Missions; Group Achievement Flight Oper Award; Presidential Medal Freedom Award; Apollo Xiii Mission Oper Team; Johnson Spacecraft Ctr EEO Award. **Military Serv:** AUS, 1962-64. *

HESTER, ARTHUR C
Automotive executive. **Personal:** Born Mar 5, 1942, Columbus, MS; married Mae J Howard; children: Zina, Karen, Lisa & Arthur III. **Educ:** US Military Acad, West Point, BS, engineering, 1965; Stanford Univ, MS, indust engineering, 1970; New York Univ, MBA, finance, 1977. **Career:** Gen Motors, begining 1981, plant mgr, Tarrytown, NY, plant mgr, Arlington, begining 1989; Main ChB Inc, ChB Calibration Serv, exec vpres & COO. **Orgs:** Trustee, Asn Grads USMA, 1970-73; Ger-Am Coun Fulda, W Germany, 1973-; bd dirs, Am Youth Activ Fulda, W Ger, 1974-; NAACP; Asn AUS; Armor Asn; Blackhorse Asn; Master Mason; past mem, Asn Black Bus Studs, NYU. **Military Serv:** AUS, 1965-81; Recipient Silver Star, Bronze Star, Purple Heart; Meritorious Serv Medal; Vietnamese Cross of Gallantry with Silver Star; Nominee, Outstanding Junior Officer of the year, 1st Army, 1971.

HEWAN, CLINTON GEORGE
Educator. **Personal:** Born Dec 22, 1936, Montega Bay, Jamaica; son of Daniel and Emily Hewan; married Virginia R, May 20, 1965; children: Monique. **Educ:** Univ Cincinnati, BA, 1969, MA, 1971, PhD, 1991. **Career:** Jamaica Foreign Serv, dep ambassador, Venezuela, Peru, Columbia, 1974-79,dep ambassador, Ethiopia, Nigeria, Ghana, 1971-73, dep high comnr,1980-84; Northern Ky Univ, assoc prof, currently. **Orgs:** Ky Canadian Round Table Assn, 1986-; Am Polit Sci Asn, 1988-; state bd mem, Am Civil Liberties Union, 1989-; Ky Polit Sci Assn, 1989-. **Honors/Awds:** Martin Luther King Jr Service Award, 1996; Alumni Assn Strongest Influence Award, Northern Ky Univ, 1998. **Special Achievements:** Publications: Jamaica and The US Caribbean Basin Initiative, 1994;Situational Ethics and US Foreign Policy, 1998; The Road to the 21stCentury for Jamica Trinidad/Tobago and Barbados, 2001; Politics and International Relations: Jamaica, Trinidad/Tobago, Barbados, 2002. **Military Serv:** Jamaica Defence Force (Reserve).

HEWETT, HOWARD
Singer, composer. **Personal:** Born Oct 1, 1955, Akron, OH; married Mari Molina, Feb 14, 1986 (divorced); married Angela, Jan 1, 1998; children: Anissa; married Nia Peeples (divorced); children: Christopher. **Career:** Mem Vocal Group Shalamar; solo artist, 1986-; albums include: I Commit to Love, 1986; Allegiance, 1992; The Journey, 2001; The Journey Live From the Heart, 2002; Intimate, 2005; Enough, 2006; It's Time, 2006; If Only, 2007; flim: A Fight for Glory, 2003. **Honors/Awds:** Grammy, Compose for Motion Picture & TV for Beverly Hills Cop, 1985. **Business Addr:** Vocalist, c/o Elektra Records, 75 Rockefeller Plz, New York, NY 10019, **Business Phone:** (212)275-4000.*

HEWING, DR. PERNELL HAYES
Educator, college teacher. **Personal:** Born May 13, 1933, St Matthews, SC; married Joe B; children: Rita & Johnny. **Educ:** Allen Univ, BS, 1961; Temple Univ, MEd, 1963; Univ Wis, PhD, 1974. **Career:** Palmetto Leader Newspaper, lino typist gen printer, 1952-57; Allen Univ, Dept Printing, supv, 1958-61, instr, 1961-62; Philadelphia Tribune, lino typist, 1962-63; Allen Univ Columbia, asst prof bus, 1963-71; Palmetto Times Newspaper, woman's ed, 1963-64; Palmetto Post, Columbia, SC, mgr ed, 1970-71; Palmetto Post Weekly Newspaper, co-founder, 1970; Univ Wis, prof bus educ, 1971, prof emer, currently. **Orgs:** Nat Bus Educ, 1950; Sigma Gamma Rho Sorority, 1962; Pi Lambda Theta Nat Hon & Prof Asn Women Educ, 1972; Develop Chap, Univ Wis, Madison, 1973; Wis Coord Coun Women Higher Educ; Delta Pi Epsilon Hon Bus Orgn; Am Bus Commun Asn; founder & dir, Avant-Garde Cult & Develop Orgn; Asn Bus Commun. **Business Addr:** Professor Emeritus, University Wisconsin, 800 W Main St, Whitewater, WI 53190-1790.*

HEWITT, REV. BASIL
Clergy. **Personal:** Born Jan 31, 1926, Colon, Panama; married May Shirley; children: Nidia, Gloria & Chris. **Educ:** Kent Southern Col, BA, 1969; Southern Baptist Theol Sem, MDiv, 1973. **Career:** Clergy (retired); Fifth St Baptist Church, asst pastor, 1967-73; Emmanuel Baptist Church, pastor, 1973-91. **Orgs:** Secy, Laurel Clergy Asn, 1974-75; exec comt, Citizen's Adv Coun Pkwy. **Home Addr:** 11299 Laurel Walk Dr, Laurel, MD 20708.

HEWITT, CHRIS (CHRISTOPHER HORACE HEWITT)
Football player. **Personal:** Born Jul 22, 1974, Kingston, Jamaica; married Tanisha La; children: Azia. **Educ:** Cincinnati Univ. **Career:** Football player (Retired); New Orleans Saints, defensive back, 1997-99.

HEWITT, CHRISTOPHER HORACE. **See HEWITT, CHRIS.**

HEWITT, RONALD JEROME
Executive. **Personal:** Born Oct 31, 1932, Welch, WV; married Deanna Cowan; children: Ronald Jr, Kevin, Robert, Jonathan, Mkonto, Mwanaisha. **Educ:** Fisk Univ, BA, 1955. **Career:** Detroit Housing Comn, supt opers, 1969, asst dir, 1971, dir, 1973; Comm & Econ Develop Detroit, exec dep dir, 1974, dir, 1974-79; Mayor Coleman A Young, exec asst, 1979-; DPT Transp, dir, 1982-85; Detroit Planning Dept, dir, 1985-. **Orgs:** Downtown Dev Authority; Detroit Econ Develop Corp; Ford Councl Urban Econ Develop; CORD; SE MI Coun Govt; Detroit Financial Ctr Task Force; Museum AFA History; Greater Detroit Econ Develop Group; bd dir, Detroit Foreign Trade Zone; Detroit Econ Growth Corp; Detroit-Wayne Port Authority liaison; bd mem, Metropolitan Ctr High Technol, 1985-; bd mem, Local Iniatives Support Corp, 1989-; Detroit Munic Credit Union; Tanahill Soc. **Military Serv:** AUS, 1956-58. **Business Addr:** Director, Detroit Planning Department, 2300 Cadillac Twr, Detroit, MI 48226.*

HEWITT, VIVIAN ANN DAVIDSON
Librarian. **Personal:** Born Feb 17, 1920, New Castle, PA; daughter of Arthur Robert Davidson and Lela Luvada Mauney Davidson; married John Hamilton Jr, Dec 26, 1949 (died 2000); children: John Hamilton III. **Educ:** Geneva Col, BA, 1943; Carnegie Mellon Univ, BS, LS, 1944; Univ Pittsburgh, Grad Stud, 1948. **Career:** Librarian (retired); Carnegie Libr Pittsbgh, sr asst libr, 1944-49; Atlanta Univ Sch Libr Sci, instr & librn, 1949-52; Crowell-Colier Publ Co, researcher asst dir, 1954-56; Rockefeller Found, librn, 1956-63; Mex Agr Prog, Rockefeller Found, librn,

1958; Carnegie Endowment Int Peace, NY, 1963-83; Katharine Gibbs Sch, dir libr info servs, 1984-86; Univ Tex, Austin, fac, Grad Sch Libr & Info, 1985; Coun Foreign Rels, ref asst, 1987-88. **Orgs:** Librn, Carnegie Endowment Int Peace, 1963-83; exec com & sec bd, Graham-Windham Child Care & Adoption Agency, 1969-87; pres, Spec Libr Asn, 1978-79; exec com & secy, Laymens Club Cathedral St John Divine NY; Order St John Jerusalem; Alpha Kappa Alpha; Tower Soc; Geneva Col. **Honors/Awds:** LHD, Geneva Col, 1978; Distinguished Alumni Award, Carnegie-Mellon Univ, 1979; Distinguished Alumni Award, Univ Pittsburgh, 1979; Distinguished Service Award, Black Caucus Am Libr Asn, 1979; Hall of Fame, Spec Libr Asn, 1984; BCALA Leadership in the Profession Award, 1993; Leadership Award, Black Alumni, Carnegie Mellon, 2001; Black Caucus, Am Libr Asn. **Special Achievements:** Pittsburgh's first African-American librarian. **Home Addr:** 862 W End Ave, New York, NY 10025.

HEWLETT, ANTOINETTE PAYNE
Government official. **Personal:** Born in Martinsburg, WV; children: Adora. **Educ:** WV State Col, BA; Columbia Univ, MA, 1961. **Career:** Jefferson Co, teacher, 1960; San Francisco Redevelop, relocation asst, 1962-66; Oakland Redevelop, planner & reloc supvr, 1967-76; City Oakland, dir community devel, 1976-, asst agency dir, 1997; Off Housing & Neighborhood Devel, dir, 1995. **Orgs:** Oakland Mus Asn; Friends Ethnic Art; Nat Forum Black Pub Admin; Am Soc Pub Admin; Nat Asn Housing & Redevel Officials; Community Club of CA; bd dirs, Nat Community Devel Asn, 1984-. **Business Addr:** Assistant Agency Director, City of Oakland, Community & Economic Development Agency, 1 Frank H Ogawa Plz, Oakland, CA 94612.*

HEWLETT, DR. DIAL, JR.
Physician. **Personal:** Born Jul 26, 1948, Cleveland, OH; son of Dial and Lydia; married Janice M Chance; children: Kwasi, Tiffany, Whitney Joy, Brandon. **Educ:** Univ Wis, Madison; Univ Wis, Sch Med, MD, 1976. **Career:** Harlem Hosp Ctr, internship & residency, 1976-79; Harlem Hosp Ctr, chief med residency, 1979-80; Montefiore Hosp & Albert Einstein Col Med, fellowship infectious diseases, 1980-82; NY Med Col, asst prof med, assoc prof clin med, currently; Our Lady Mercy Hosp, chief infectious diseases; Calvary Hosp, consult infectious dis, currently. **Orgs:** chief, infectious diseases Lincoln Med & Mental Health Ctr, 1982-84; Am Soc Microbiology; ed bd, Hosp Physicians Joyrnal; consult, infectious diseases Our Lady Mercy Hosp; Calvary Hosp Terminally Ill; Infectious Diseases Soc Am; consult, infectious diseases Lawrence Hosp; Manhattan Cent Med Soc INMA. **Business Addr:** Associate Professor, New York Medical College, Administration Bldg, 100 Grasslands Rd, Valhalla, NY 10595, **Business Phone:** (914)594-4507.*

HEWLETT, EVERETT AUGUSTUS, JR.
Lawyer, county commissioner. **Personal:** Born Mar 27, 1943, Richmond, VA; married Clothilde. **Educ:** Dickinson Col Carlisle PA, BA, 1965; Golden Gate Univ Law Sch, JD, 1975. **Career:** Univ Calif Berkeley, writer-ed, 1970-75; Bayview-Hunters Point Comn Defender San Francisco, staff atty, 1976-80; Pvt Law Pract, atty, 1980-86; San Francisco Super Ct, ct comnr, 1986, discovery comnr, 2000. **Orgs:** Bd dirs, SF Neighborhood Legal Asst Found, 1979-; bd dir, SF Neighborhood Legal Asst Found, 1979-; hearing officer, SF Residl Rent Stabilization & Arbitration Bd, 1980-82; bd dir, CA Asn Black Lawyers, 1980-; vpres, Counseliers W, 1980; pres, William Hastie Bar Asn, 1984; vchmn, SF Neighborhood Legal Asst Found, 1984; parliamentarian, Wm Hastie Bar Asn, 1980-86; State Bar Comn on Legal Specialization, 1982; Calif State Bar Legal Serv Trust Fund Comn, 1984-85. **Honors/Awds:** Editor of Best Newspaper in its class USAF Hamilton CA & Nakhon Phanom, 1967 & 1968. **Military Serv:** USAF, sergeant, information spec, 1965-69. **Business Addr:** Discovery Commissioner, San Francisco Superior Court, 375 Woodside Dr, Youth Guidance Center, San Francisco, CA 94117.

HEYWARD, ISAAC
Media executive, president (organization). **Personal:** Born Apr 30, 1935, Charleston, SC; son of Rev St Julian (deceased) and Chrestina Capers; children: Regina Vermel Heyward (deceased), Bryant Isaac Heyward. **Educ:** Radio Broadcast Inst, New York, NY, Cert, 1967; Morris Col, Sch Relig, Orangeburg Exten, Cert, 1975. **Career:** WHBI Radio, Newark, NJ, prog announcer & sales mgr, 1965-67; WRNW Radio, Mt Kisco, NY, announcer & dir, 1967-71; WQIZ Radio, St George, SC, announcer & sales mgr, 1971-85; WTGH Radio, Cayce, SC, announcer, sales mgr, general sales & sta mgr & pres, currently. **Orgs:** Assoc ordained minister, St Paul Baptist Church, Orangeburg, SC, 1971; Gospel Music Workshop of Am, 1974; Nat Asn Advan Colored People, SC Br, 1974; Baptist Assn, Orangeburg SC, 1985; mem, Boy Scouts Am Coun, 1986; Nat Fed Blind. **Honors/Awds:** Second Runner-up DJ, Gospel of the Year, Lamb Records, 1978; Best Radio Gospel Prog, Lee's Publ, 1979; Gospel Prom, Gospel Workshop Am, 1982; Community Serv, Am Cancer Soc, 1982, 1983; Living Legacy, Nat Coun Negro Women, 1984; Boy Scouts of Am Service, 1986; Honorary Doctor of Christian Ministry, CE Graham Baptist Bible Sem, 1996. **Military Serv:** AUS, pvt, 1959. *

HEYWARD, JAMES OLIVER
Educator, army officer, college administrator. **Personal:** Born Jul 17, 1930, Sumter, SC; son of Julian H Sr (deceased) and Lue (deceased); married Willie Mae Thompson; children: James O Jr, Julian, Edward. **Educ:** SC State Univ, BS, 1953; Armed Forces Staff Col, 1969; Shippensburg State Univ, MA, 1972. **Career:** Educator (retired); US Army, dep comdr military comdr, 1974-75; Cmdr Training & Doctrine Command Field Element, 1976-79; Ala A & M Univ, prof military sci, 1979-83, dir admis. **Orgs:** Am Asn Collegiate Registrars & Admin Officers; Equal Opportunity Committee, 1986-87; Phi Delta Kappa; chmn, Membership Comt, 1983-84; life mem, Nat Advan Asn Colored People; chap vpres, pres, area dir, Alpha Phi Alpha, 1984-92; Human Rels Coun Huntsville Ala; chmn, Huntsville Citizens Police, quality coun, 1992-94; Steward Bd, secy, St John Am Church. **Honors/Awds:** Man of the Year, Alpha Phi Alpha Chap, 1989; Distinguished Alumini Award, SC State Univ, 1996; Community Service Award, Martin Luther King Jr, 2001; Service Award, Boy Scouts Am Whitney M Young Jr, 2002. **Military Serv:** AUS, Colonel 1953-83; Legion of Merit, Bronze Star, Joint Services Commendation, AUS Commendation Medal, Senior Parachutist Badge; Meritorious Serv Medal. *

HEYWARD-GARNER, ILENE PATRICIA
Executive. **Personal:** Born Apr 9, 1948, Plainfield, NJ; daughter of William W Nesbitt Jr and Bonlyn Pitts Nesbitt; divorced; children: Eric Eugene. **Educ:** Fairleigh Dickinson Univ, BS, chem & math, 1976; NY Univ, MS, chem, 1988; George Wash Univ, master cert, proj mgt, 1995. **Career:** AT&T Bell Labs, tech assoc, 1976-77, sr tech assoc, 1977-79, assoc mem tech staff, 1979-81, tech mgr, 1981-94, div mgr, 1994-97, gen mgr; Parcel Plus, owner; Univ VI, Community & Personal Develop Unit, dir, Community Engagement & Lifelong Learning Ctr, dir, currently. **Orgs:** AAAS, 1982-; Plainfield Teen Proj, 1989-97; Alliance Black Telecommunications Employees Inc, 1990-95; adv coun, Nat Black United Fund, 1991-94; bd mem, Big Brors Big Sisters Essex County, 1992-93; bd, treas, Beacon Sch, 1997; Proj Mgt Inst; Am Mgt Asn. **Honors/Awds:** Honor, Bell Communications Res, 1985; AT&T Architecture Award, 1992; African American Biography Hall of Fame, 1993. **Special Achievements:** Author and co-author, many articles in technical journals such as ACS and Journal of the Soc Plastic Engrs 1976-; author, chap in ACS Symposium Monograph Series 1985; featured in cover story of Black Enterprise 1985; featured in UnFold, 1999. **Business Phone:** (340)693-1101.

HEYWOOD, ANTHONY
Executive. **Career:** Mt Hope Child Care Ctr, exec dir. *

HIATT, DANA SIMS
School administrator. **Personal:** Born in Chickasha, OK; daughter of William Edward Sims and Muriel Crowell Sims; married James H. **Educ:** Langston Univ, BA, hist (summa cum laude), 1968; Univ Kans Sch Law, JD, 1971. **Career:** RH Smith Community, Chicago, IL, Okla City, OK, law fel, 1971-73; City Okla, asst municipal atty, 1974; Darrell, Bruce, Johnson & Sims Asn, pvt pract law, 1975-77; Colo State Univ, teaching asst black hist, Off Vpres Acad Affairs, info specialist, title IX coordr, cncltn officer, 1979-82, Off Equal Opportunity & Diversity, dir, currently; R H Smith Law fel; Denver Chap, Links Inc. **Orgs:** Am Asn Univ Women; Am Asn Affrim Action; dir, Higher Educ Affirm Action; pub affairs chair, Jr League Fort Collins, 1991-92. **Honors/Awds:** Outstandng Young Woman, Zeta Phi Beta Sorority, Okla City, OK, 1975. **Special Achievements:** First African American to become the assistant municipal attorney for the city of Oklahoma City; One of 100 nationally selected Reginald Heber Smith Community Law Fellows. **Business Addr:** Director, Colorado State University, Office of Equal Opportunity & Diversity, 101 Stud Serv Bldg, Fort Collins, CO 80523-1016, **Business Phone:** (970)491-5836.

HIATT, DIETRAH
Journalist, counselor. **Personal:** Born Sep 23, 1944, Washington, DC; married Robert Terry; children: Stephanie Gail & Benjamin Jesse. **Educ:** Howard Univ, BA, 1965. **Career:** US Peace Corps Vol Rep Panama, 1965-67; DC Dept Pub Assistance, social serv rep caseworker, 1968-70; Pierre-Ft Pierre Head Start Prog, vol teachers asst, 1973-74; Huron SD Daily Plainsman, reporter, 1973-74; Nyoda Girl Scout Coun, brownie ldr resource person, 1976-77; Pierre Indian Learning Ctr, sch counr; Sen George Mc govern, comm rep; Pierre Times, ed columnist, currently. **Orgs:** Am Asn Univ Women, 1972-74; treas, Short Grass Arts Coun, 1974-75; vpres, Nat Orgn Women Cent SD Chap, 1975-; Dem Party Precinct Woman, 1976-; chairperson, Hughes Co Dem Comt; co-chaiperson, Cand Task Force SD Womens Caucus; Nat Abortion Rights Action League; State Prof Pract & Stand Comn, Dept Educ & Cult Affairs; Alpha Kappa Alpha. **Honors/Awds:** Nominated Outstanding Young Woman of Am, 1973, 1977; Cand, Pierre Sch Bd, 1976; Cand, SD State Senate, 1978. **Special Achievements:** Choreographed & performed rev of dance & history for AAUW Cultural Study Group 1973; Performed in modern & native Am dance recital for Arts Festival arts workshop 1973.

HIBBERT, DOROTHY LASALLE
Educator. **Personal:** Born Sep 17, 1923, New York, NY; daughter of Arthur Hilbert Sr and Lily Roper. **Educ:** Hunter Col, BA, 1945; Teachers Col, Columbia Univ, MA, 1949; City Col, Grad Div, PD, 1983; Walden Univ, MN, doc, educ, 1991. **Career:** Educator (retired); Bd Educ NY, PS 186 teacher, 1947-59, High Sch 136, math teacher, 1959-68, PS 146 & 36, asst prin, 1969-79, PS 138 actg interim prin, 1979-81, PS 93 asst prin, 1981-85, PS 146, prin, 1985-90; Col New Rochelle, instr, 1990. **Orgs:** vpres, 1976-86, secy, 1987, Int League Human Rights; planning partic, NY State Conf Status of Women; secy, Am Comn Africa 1979-; asst examr, Bd Examrs 1982; conf chair, Bronx Reading Coun, 1985; Nat Asn Advan Colored People; Asn Black Educrs, NY, 1986. **Honors/Awds:** Outstanding Educr, City Tabernacle Church, 1980; Outstanding Prin of the Yr, Morrisana Educ Coun, 1980; publ: "The Role of the Nefers in Egyptian Hist," 1979, "Nubian Egypt and Egyptian Nubia," 1979, "Big Red Newspaper," Brooklyn, NY. **Home Addr:** 90 Meucci Ave, Copiague, NY 11726, **Home Phone:** (631)842-5764. *

HIBBERT, LAWRENCE
Executive. **Personal:** Born in Brooklyn, NY. **Educ:** Rutgers Univ, BS, mech engineering. **Career:** Merrill Lynch Pvt Client Archit Group, asst vpres & network servs mgr; Gen Elec, wired area network engr; AMP Inc/Tyco; Access One Corp, founder & managing partner; MBS Educ Serv & Training, founder & managing partner; BCT Partners Inc, founder, pres & chief technol officer, currently. **Orgs:** Small Bus Develop Sub comt Econ Develop; First Baptist Church Lincoln Gardens. *

HIBBLER, WILLIAM J
Judge. **Personal:** Born Aug 7, 1946, Kennedy, AL; son of Arthur Lee and Mami Lue Foster; married Regina, Sep 7, 1969; children: William II & Aviv. **Educ:** Univ Ill, BS, 1969; DePaul Univ Col Law, JD, 1973. **Career:** Cook County State Attys Off, felony trial atty, 1973-76; Belmonte, Kagan, Hibbler & DePalma, partner, 1976-81; State Attys Off, felony trial supvr, 1981-86; US Dist Ct, Northern Dist Ill, judge, currently. **Orgs:** First vpres, Ill Judges Asn, 1996-99; Cook County Bar Asn; Ill State Bar Asn; Ill Judicial Coun; Nat Black Prof Asn. **Honors/Awds:** Distinguished Service Award, Nat Black Prosecutors Asn, 1991; Albert Elias Award, Nat Coun on Crime & Delinquency, 1997; Jane Addams Award, Ill Dept C & Family Serv, 1999; Appreciation Award, Chicago Crime Comn, 1999; Leadership Award, Juvenile Probation Dept, 1999. **Business Addr:** Judge, United States District Court, Northern District of Illinois, Everett McKinley Dirksen Fed Bldg Rm 1746 20th Fl 219 S Dear, Chicago, IL 60604, **Business Phone:** (312)435-5613.

HICKERSON SMITH, OTRIE B.
Psychiatrist. **Personal:** Born Mar 17, 1936, Coffeyville, KS; married Robert A Sr; children: Claude, Donna, Robert Jr. **Educ:** Howard Univ, BS, 1958; Howard Univ Col Med, MD, 1962; Kings Co Hosp, internship, 1963; Menatl Health Inst, res, 1966. **Career:** Menninger Found, staff mem, 1966-67; Area B Comm Health Ctr, chf 1967-69; Univ Med Ctr, instr, 1969-; Tougaloo Col, 1969-72; VACtr, staff mem, 1969-70; Jackson-hinds Comprehensive Health Ctr, dir mental, 1970-; Tougaloo Col, consult; Jackson State Univ, instr; Am & Psychiat Asn, obsvr consult, 1974-75. **Orgs:** Minority Mental Health Ctr Nat Inst Mental Health; Natl Med Asn; Am Med Asn; Am Psychiat Asn; Community Black Psychiat; MS Med Asn; MS State Dept Mental Health; Delta Sigma Theta Sorority; Friends C MS Head Start Proj; bd mem, Hinds Co Proj Head Start. **Home Addr:** 1134 Winter St, Jackson, MS 39203. **Business Addr:** Psychiatrist, 1021 Arbor Vista Blvd, Jackson, MS 39209, **Business Phone:** (601)948-5572.

HICKLIN, FANNIE
Educator, administrator, curator. **Personal:** Born in Talladega, AL; daughter of Willie Pulliam Frazier and Demus Frazier; divorced; children: Ariel Yvonne Ford. **Educ:** Talladega Col, BA; Univ Mich, MA; Univ Wis, Madison, PhD. **Career:** Educator (retired); Magnolia Ave HS, Avery Inst, Burke HS, Tuskegee Inst, Ala A&M Col, Univ Wis, Madison, previous teaching experience; Univ Wisc, Whitewater, assoc dean faculties, 1974-88. **Orgs:** Pres & mem, State Hist Soc Wis Bd Curs; Cent States Commun Asn; Speech Comm Asn; Alpha Kappa Alpha. **Honors/Awds:** W.P. Roseman Excellence in Teaching Award, Univ Wis-Whitewater, 1970. **Special Achievements:** The first African-American faculty member of University of Wisconsin-Whitewater in 1964. *

HICKMAN, ELNOR B G
Secretary (Office). **Personal:** Born Jan 31, 1930, Jackson, MS; daughter of Lerone Sr and Alma Reed Bennett; married Caloway Hickman, Nov 19, 1983; children: Thelma B McDowell, Marshall L Bennett & Shirley L Bennett. **Educ:** Loop Jr Col, AA, 1975. **Career:** Secretary (retired); Legal Assistance Found Chicago, legal secy, admin supvr & exec secy. **Orgs:** Int dir, Prof Secretaries Int, Great Lakes Dist, 1988-90, int sec, 1990-91, 2nd vpres, 1991-92, first vpres, 1992-93, pres-elect, 1993-94, int pres, 1994-95; pres, Int Asn Admin Prof, Chicago Lake Chap, Ill Div, 1987-88; bd dirs, Int Asn Admin Prof, Chicago Lake Chap, Ill Div. **Special Achievements:** First African Am to hold the position of

pres of the Prof Secretaries Intl; Cert Prof Secy Rating, 1977; One of 100 Women Making a Difference, Today's Chicago Women, 1995.

HICKMAN, FRED. See HICKMAN, FREDERICK DOUGLASS.

HICKMAN, FREDERICK DOUGLASS (FRED HICKMAN)
Broadcaster. **Personal:** Born Oct 17, 1956, Springfield, IL; son of George Henry (deceased) and Louise Winifred (deceased); married Judith Tillman, Feb 20, 1989; children: Mack. **Educ:** Coe Col, Cedar Rapids, Iowa, attended 1974-77. **Career:** KLWW Radio, Cedar Rapids, Iowa, news anchor, 1977; WFMB-FM Radio, Springfield, Ill, news & sports anchor, 1977-78; WICS-TV, sports dir, 1978-80; CNN/Turner Broadcasting, Atlanta, Ga, sportscaster/commentator, 1980-84; WDIV-TV, Detroit, Mich, sportscaster/commentator, 1984-86; CNN/Turner Broadcasting, sportscaster/commentator, 1986; WALR-FM, sports dir, 1992; ESPN, sportcenter anchor, 2005-; NBA Shootaround, host, 2006-07; ESPNews, anchor, 2007-. **Orgs:** Butkus Awards Voting Comt, 1991-; Ga State Univ Athletic Asn Bd. **Honors/Awds:** Cable ACE Award Winner, 1989 &1993; "Sexiest Sportscaster", US TV Fan Asn, 1993. **Special Achievements:** Cable ACE Award nominee, 1988, 1989, 1990, 1991, 1992, 1993; Cable ACE award winner, 1989 and 1993; named "sexiest sportscaster" by U.S. Television Fan Association, 1993. **Business Addr:** Anchor, ESPN, 3800 W Alameda Ave Suite B, Burbank, CA 91505, **Business Phone:** (818)460-7222.

HICKMAN, GARRISON M.
Educator. **Personal:** Born Jan 14, 1945, Washington, DC; married Cynthia Burrowes; children: Michael Barrington. **Educ:** VA Union Univ, BA, 1967; Howard Univ, M Div, 1971. **Career:** Neighborhood Youth Corps Dept Defense, teacher counr, 1967-68; Wash Concentrated Employment Prog, 1968-70; DC City Govt, counr 1971; Stud Affairs & Affirmative Action Capital Univ & Abiding Saviour Lutheran Church, assoc dean. **Orgs:** Nat Collegiate Honor Soc; coord com, Nat Crises Conf Inner City Ministries; nat sec, Conf Inner City Ministries, 1973-74; Ohio reg chmn Coord Com on Nat Crisis 1973-75; Coalition Minority Prof Am Lutheran Ch Col & Univ, 1974-75; Nat Chmn Conf on Inner City Ministries, 1975-76; Am Asn Higher Edn; Nat Pres Am Asn Affirmative Action, 1976-77.

HICKMON, NED
Physician. **Personal:** Born Dec 5, 1934, Bishopville, SC; son of James and Nona; married Consuella Anderson; children: Ned Norman, David Wesley, Cheryl A. **Educ:** SC St Col, BS, 1955; Meharry Med Col, Nashville, TN, MD, 1959. **Career:** Huron Rd Hosp, Cleveland OH, intern, 1959-60; HG Phillips Hosp, St Louis, MO, res obstet & gynec, 1960-62; G W Hubbard Hosp Meharry Med Col, Nashville, chief resob & gynec, 1962-63, US army hosp, Bremerhaven, Ger, chief obstet & gynec, 1963-66; patterson army hosp, Ft Monmouth, NJ, asst chief obstet & gynec, 1966-67; Pvt Prac, Hartford, CT, obstet & gynec, 1968-. **Orgs:** Past dir & pres, Comm Health Serv, Hartford, CT, 1972; Alpha Phi Alpha Frat Inc; Sigma Pi Phi Fraternity Inc. **Military Serv:** AUS, Med Corps, Capt, 4 yrs. **Home Addr:** 21 Bloomfield Ave, Hartford, CT 06105. *

HICKS, DR. ARTHUR JAMES
Educator. **Personal:** Born Feb 26, 1938, Jackson, MS; son of A R and Julia M; married Pearlie Mae Little; children: Arnetta Renee & Roselyn Marie. **Educ:** Tougaloo Col, BS, 1960; Univ Illinois, PhD, 1971; Inst Educ Mgt, Harvard Univ, 1989; Lilly Endowment Liberal Arts Workshop, Col, 1992. **Career:** Grenada City Sch, biol & gen sci teacher, chmn sci div, 1960-64; Univ Ga, Botany Dept, asst prof, 1971-77; Missouri Botanical Gardens, NEA Postdoctoral fellowship, 1976; Nat Sci Found, visiting grants officer, 1987; NCA&T, Biol Dept, curator, prof & chmn, 1977-88, dean, Col Arts & Scis, Prog dir, 1988-. **Orgs:** Am Inst Biological Sci; Am Soc Plant Taxonomists; Asn SE Biologists; Botanical Soc Am; North Carolina Acad Sci; Intern Asn Plant Taxonomists; Mississippi Acad Sci; Sigma Xi; Torrey Botanical Club; past co-pres Gaines Sch PTA Athens, 1973-74; bd dir, NE Girl Scouts Am, 1977; bd trustees, Hill First Bapt Church Athens, 1977; Swim Bd Gov Athens Park & Rec Dist Athens, 1977; Natural Areas Adv Comt North Carolina Dept Natural Resources & Comt Develop, 1978; adv bd, Guilford Co NC Environmental Qual, 1979-87; Nat Inst Health Extramural Asn, 1982; Alpha Phi Alpha; bd trustees, Nat Wildflower Res Ctr, 1991-93; Greensboro Beautiful & Greensboro Bog Garden, 1992-. **Honors/Awds:** Hon mem, Beta Kappa Chi Sci Honor Soc, 1960; senior biology Award, Tougaloo Col, 1960; NSF Summer Fellowship SIU Carbondale, 1961;Univ Illinois Botany Fellowship Urbana, 1968-69; So Fellowship Found Fund fel, Univ Illinois Urbana, 1969-71; NEA fel, Missouri Botanical Garden St Louis, 1975-76; Faculty Award, Excellence Sci & Tech, White House Initiative Historically Black Colleges & Universities, 1988. **Special Achievements:** Author: "Apomixis in Xanthium?" Watsonia 1975 "Plant Mounting Problem Overcome-with the Use of Self-Adhesive Plastic Covering" Torreya, 1976; co-auth, ABibliography Plant Collection & Herbarium Curation. **Business Addr:** Program Director Alliances for Minority Participation, North Carolina Agricultural and Technical State University, College Arts & Sciences, 312 N Dudley St Crosby Hall, Greensboro, NC 27411, **Business Phone:** (919)334-7806.*

HICKS, BRIAN L. See HICKS, SKIP.

HICKS, DR. CLAYTON NATHANIEL
School administrator, association executive, optometrist. **Personal:** Born May 2, 1943, Columbus, OH; son of Amos Nathaniel and Augusta Louvenia. **Educ:** Ohio State Univ, BS, 1964, OD, 1970. **Career:** Ohio Dept Health, microbiologist, 1965-70; Ohio State Univ, Col Optom, clinic instr, 1970-; Driving Pk Vision Ctr, optometrist, 1970-; Ohio Dept Human Servs, optom consult, 1977-; Outcomes Mgt Group Ltd, partner & vpres mkt, 1995-; Nat Optom Asn, pres, meeting & conf planner, 1984-, consult, 1989-, exec dir NOF, currently. **Orgs:** Pres, Columbus Panhellenic Coun, 1975-80; Columbus Inner City Lions Club, 1977-80; bd dir, Neighborhood House Inc, 1979-81; Martin Luther King Holiday Observance Comn, 1981-83; Alpha Phi Alpha Fraternity, 1981-83; Nat Optom Asn, 1983-85; Driving Pk Ment Health Comn, 1984; Nat Coalition Black Meeting Planners, 1984; consult, Annette Cosmetiques, 1989-; exec dir, Alpha Rho Lambda Educ Found, 1989-; Livingston Ave Collaborative Community Develop. **Honors/Awds:** Outstanding Service Award, Alpha Phi Alpha Fraternity, 1981; Optometrist of the Year, Nat Optometric Asn, 1983; Citizen of the Week, WCKX Radio, 1986; Outstanding Alumni Award, Ohio State Univ, 1995; Distinguished Leadership Community Award, Driving Park Area CMS, 1999; Outstanding Service Award, APA, 1999; Human Service Award, AKA, 2002; Community Building Award, Gov Bob Taft, 2003; Political Leadership Award, 29th Dist Citizens Caucus. **Business Addr:** Executive Director NOF, National Optometric Association, 1489 Livingston Ave, Columbus, OH 43205, **Business Phone:** (614)253-5593.

HICKS, D'ATRA
Singer, actor, executive. **Personal:** Born in New York City, NY; daughter of Edna Hicks. **Career:** Several commercials, music videos, theatre appearances; Albums: D'Atra Hicks, 1989; "The Godess is Here", 2003. **Orgs:** AFTRA; SAG; ASCAP. **Honors/Awds:** Toured extensively in Japan; NAACP Image Award Nominee, 1989; New York City Music Award Nominee, 1989. **Special Achievements:** Two Top 10 Records in Japan; Natl Assn Advan Colored People Image Award Nominee, 1989; New York City Music Award Nominee, 1989. *

HICKS, DELPHUS VAN, JR.
Law enforcement officer. **Personal:** Born Feb 6, 1939, Ashland, MS; son of Delphus Van Sr and Gladys Woodson; married Frankie Marie Hamer, Jul 5, 1961; children: Early Hue, James Earl & Diane Lanell. **Educ:** Tenn Law Enforcement Acad, attended 1974; Donhue Barber Col, Memphis, TN, master barber license, 1974. **Career:** Williams Candy Co, stockman, 1961-62; Reichold Chem Inc, inspector, mixer, lead man, 1967-72; Leadman Reichhold Chem Inc, mixer, insp, 1967-72; Hardeman Co, Sheriff Dept, chief, dep sheriff, 1968-72, 1974, 1978, sheriff, 1978-. **Orgs:** Vpres, Tenn Sheriff's Asn, 1978-; West Tenn Criminal Invest Asn, 1980-; 25th Judicial Dist Drug Task Force, 1989-. **Honors/Awds:** Tennessee Outstanding Achievements Award, Gov Lamar Alexander, 1981; Outstanding Sheriff of the Year, Tenn Sheriff Asn, 1988-89. **Special Achievements:** First Black Chief Dep Sheriff Hardeman County, 1974; first Black sheriff in Tennessee, 1978. **Military Serv:** AUS, E-5, 1962-67; Soldier of the Year, 1964; Good Conduct Medal, 1964. **Home Addr:** 503 E Jackson St, Bolivar, TN 38008, **Home Phone:** (901)658-6237. **Business Addr:** Sheriff, Hardeman County, Sheriff Department, 315 W Mkt St, Bolivar, TN 38008, **Business Phone:** (731)658-3971.

HICKS, DORIS ASKEW
School administrator. **Personal:** Born May 24, 1926, Sulphur Springs, TX; married George P (deceased); children: Sherra Daunn Hicks-Chappelle. **Educ:** Butler Col, AA 1946; Bishop Col, BA 1948; Univ TX, MLS, 1959. **Career:** Quit man Independent Sch Dist, teacher, 1950-52; Naples Independent Sch Dist, teacher librn, 1952-54; Bowie Co Common & Independent Sch, multi sch librn, 1654-62; Macedonia Sch Dist Texarkana, sch librn, 1962-69; Rochester City Sch Dist Rochester, sch librn, 1969-73; Rochester City Sch Dist, Rochester, NY, dir learning resources, 1973-81; Largo Community Church, co-chairpersons, currently. **Orgs:** Vpres, Sch Libr Media Section, NY Libr Asn; vpres, Sch Libr Media Section, NY Libr Asn; pres & unit vice chmn, Am Asn Sch Librn, ALA, 1979-80; Mt Olivet Baptist Church Scholarship Com, 1976-; bd mem, Hillside C's Ctr, 1977-81; chair fel, Com Rochester Chap Zonta Int, 1979-80; vpres, Prince George's MD Chapter Links Inc, 1993-97; chmn, libr comt, Largo Comt Church, 1994-; co chairperson, Mature Singles, currently. **Honors/Awds:** Sch Library & Media Program Year, Am Asn Sch Librarians, 1975. **Home Addr:** 3812 Sunflower Cir, Mitchellville, MD 20721. **Business Addr:** Co-Cairpersons, Largo Community Church, 1701 Enterprise Rd, Mitchellville, MD 20721, **Business Phone:** (301)249-2255.

HICKS, DORIS MORRISON
Government official. **Personal:** Born Jun 19, 1933, St Marys, GA; daughter of Eleazar and Renetta Jenkins; married Samuel, Sep 15, 1950; children: Barbara Caughman & Sheryl Stokes. **Educ:** Savannah State Col, Ga, attended 1950, BS, 1954, cert, 1959. **Career:** US Postal Serv, Savannah, Ga, distrib clerk, 1966-72, LSM operator, 1972-74, exam clerk, 1974-77, exam spec, 1977-79; training tech, 1974-79; US Postal Serv, Ridgeland, SC, postmaster, 1979-. **Orgs:** Ed, MSC Newsletter, US Postal Serv, 1975-86; Postal Life Adv Bd, US Postal Serv, 1980-82; chairperson, Women's Prog, US Postal Serv, 1979-83; Rev & Selection Comt, US Postal Serv, 1986-. **Honors/Awds:** Cert & Award, Savannah Asn Retarded C, 1972, 1974; Letter of Commendation, Equal Employ Coun US Postal Serv, 1972; Letter of Commendation, Southern Region, US Postal Serv, 1976; Cert & Award, Postal Life US Postal Serv, 1981; Outstanding Achievement, Savannah Women's Prog, US Postal Serv, 1986. **Business Addr:** Postmaster, US Postal Service, 406 Main St Fed Bldg, Ridgeland, SC 29936, **Business Phone:** (803)726-5528.

HICKS, EDITH A.
Government official, school administrator, school principal. **Personal:** Born Sep 6, 1939, Barnwell, SC; married James Adams; children: Ronald, Curtis, Craig, Paul, Paula & Kevin. **Educ:** Antioch Col, BA, 1974, MA, 1976. **Career:** Bd Educ, NY, para prof, 1967-69, asst prin; Morrisania Comn Corp, training specialist, 1969-70; C Circle Day Care, dir, 1970-75; Community Sch Bd, NY, exec asst, 1975-77; Touro Col, adj prof; Col New Rochelle, instr. **Orgs:** Vpres, Community Sch Bd NY; female dist leader, 78th Assembly Dist NY; chairperson, People's Develop Corp, Comn Planning Bd 3. **Honors/Awds:** Sojourner, Truth Black Women Bus & Prof Group, NY City Chap; Woman of the Yr, Morrisania Community Coun; Outstanding Community Serv, Bronx Unity Dem Club. **Home Addr:** 575 E 168th St, Bronx, NY 10456. *

HICKS, ELEANOR
Government official, educational consultant. **Personal:** Born Feb 21, 1943, Columbus, GA; daughter of Carl and Annie Pearl. **Educ:** Univ Cincinnati, BA, cum laude, 1965; Johns Hopkins Sch Advan Int Studies, MA Int Rels, 1967. **Career:** Thailand Dept State, desk officer, 1970-72; US consult to Monaco & Nice Dept State, 1972-75; Dept State, policy analyst, 1975-76; Dept State Cent Am Affairs, dep, 1976-78; Dept State US Embassy Cairo, dep polit sect, 1979-82; Univ Cin, adv int liaison, 1983; Minds Int, pres, 1996-. **Orgs:** Phi Beta Kappa, Univ Cincinnati (UC) 1964-; Middle E Inst; bd Women's Action Orgn Dept State, 1978; Alpha Kappa Alpha; SW Ohio Transp Authority, 1984-; bd treas, Am Red Cross, 1987-89; Am Assembly, Columbia Univ (US Global Interests in 1990s); dir, Fed Res Br, Cincinnati Br, 1990-; mkt comn, Cin Conv Ctr & Int Visitors Bur. **Honors/Awds:** Honorific award Chevalier De Tastevin, 1973; Civic Award in Int Realm, Cavalieri Del Nouvo Europe (Italy), 1974; scholar award named after her for outstanding arts & sci stud (UC) Ann Eleanor Hicks Award, 1974; Legendary Woman Award, St Vincent's, Birmingham Ala, 1975; Leadership Cincinnati, 1988-; Career Woman of Achievement, YWCA, 1985; Golden Key Nat Hon Soc, 1991-. **Business Phone:** (513)281-7770.

HICKS, ERIC DAVID
Football player. **Personal:** Born Jun 17, 1976, Erie, PA; married Erica; children: Shayla & Rocco. **Educ:** Univ Md, criminol & criminal justice. **Career:** Kansas City Chiefs, defensive end, 1998-06; New York Jets, 2007; Detroit Lions, 2009. free agent, currently. **Orgs:** Hicks Hearts Found, 2001; spokesperson, Am heart Asn. **Honors/Awds:** All-Joe Team, 2000; Football Digest All-Pro, 2000; Ed Block Courage Award, 2001.

HICKS, FOSTER
Teacher, basketball coach, high school teacher. **Career:** People's High Sch, teacher; City Vallejo, coun mem; Hogan High Sch, teacher, basketball head coach, currently. **Orgs:** Solano County Black Chamber Com. **Business Addr:** Basketball Head Coach, Teacher, Hogan High School, 850 Rosewood Ave, Vallejo, CA 94591.

HICKS, H. BEECHER, JR.
Clergy. **Personal:** Born Jun 17, 1944, Baton Rouge, LA; son of H Beecher Sr and Eleanor Frazier; married Elizabeth Harrison; children: H Beecher III, Ivan Douglas, Kristin Elizabeth. **Educ:** Univ Ark, Pine Bluff, BA, 1964; Colgate Rochester, MDiv, 1967, Dr Ministry, 1975; Richmond Va, Sem LLD honorary; George Wash Univ, MBA, 1999. **Career:** Second Baptist Church, intern pastorate, 1965-68; Irondequoit United Church Christ, minister to youth, 1967-68; Mt Ararat Baptist Church, sr minister, 1968-73; Antioch Baptist Church, minister, 1973-77; Metrop Baptist Church, sr minister, 1977-, sr servant, currently; Colgate Rochester Divinity Sch & United Theol Sem, adj prof, 1990. **Orgs:** Chmn Bd, Funeral Dirs, 1985; vpres, Eastern Reg Nat Black Pastors Conf; admin, Nat Black Pastors Conf; bd Coun, Court Excellence; asst secy, Progressive Nat Baptist Convention, Co-chair Am Baptist Ministers Coun D C, pres, Kerygma Assoc, A Religious Consulting Serv; pres, Martin Luther King Fels, Inc; co-chair, Ministers Partnership; bd trustees, United Theol Sem, Dayton, OH. **Honors/Awds:** "Give Me This Mountain" Houston TX, 1976; "Images of the Black Preacher, The Man Nobody Knows" Valley Forge PA, 1977; "The Black Church as a Support System

for Black Men on the Simon Syndrome" Howard Univ; Community Leaders & Noteworthy Am, 1977; Gubernatorial Citation, Serv, 1977; Martin Luther King Fellowship, Black Church Studies, 1972-75; author: Preaching Through A Storm, Zondervan Press, 1987; Correspondence with Cripple Tarsus, Zondervan Press, 1990; My Soul's Been Anchored, Zondervan Press, 1999; Rockefeller Protestant Fellowship; coveted Merrill Fellowship. **Business Addr:** Senior Servant, Senior Minister, Metrop Baptist Church, 1225 R St NW, Washington, DC 20009, **Business Phone:** (202)483-1540.*

HICKS, DR. INGRID DIANN
Educator, writer, psychologist. **Personal:** Born Jun 17, 1958, Flint, MI; daughter of Walter and Barbara Mae; married Thomas E Brooks. **Educ:** BA, psychol, 1980; MS, clinic psychol, 1982; Univ Wisc-Milwaukee, PhD, clinic psychol, 1985. **Career:** Univ Wisc, Med Sch, from asst prof to assoc prof, 1985-91; Med Col, Wisc, pvt pract & consult, 1991-. Author: For Black Women Only: The Complete Guide to a Successful Lifestyle Change-Health, Wealth, Love & Happiness, 1991; For Black Women Only (but don't forget about our men); play & book, 1995; For Black Women Only: Our Lives in the New Millennium, 2001; Black Women Only: Our Relationships; Our Childhood Mother; TV appearance: The Oprah Winfrey Show; Provided numerous seminars & workshops. **Orgs:** Am Psychol Asn, 1985-; Wis Psychol Asn, 1985-; Am Soc Clinic Hypn, 1985-; Nat Asn Black Psychologists, 1985-; Milwaukee Community. **Honors/Awds:** Black Achiever, YMCA, 1990; Kool Achiever, Winston, 1991. **Business Addr:** Clinical, Executive Director, Transformation Services, 1003 E Lyon St, PO Box 511835, Milwaukee, WI 53203, **Business Phone:** (414)933-7083.

HICKS, JESSIE YVETTE
Basketball player. **Personal:** Born Dec 2, 1971; married; children: Jamon Emmanuel. **Educ:** Univ Md, BA, criminal justice, 1993, Bowie State, MA, guid & coun, 1998. **Career:** Juven Saski Baloia, Spain, 1993-94; Eastern Shore, MD, asst coach, 1994-95; Bowie State Univ, asst coach, 1995-97; Utah Starzz, forward-ctr, 1997; Orlando Miracle, forward-ctr, 2000-02; Conn Sun, guard, 2003; San Antonio Silver Stars, forward-ctr, 2003-05. **Honors/Awds:** Kodak All-American Honorable, 1991-92, 1992-93. *

HICKS, JIMMIE, JR.
Executive, business owner, consultant. **Personal:** Married Lynda Phillips; children: 4. **Educ:** Kent State Univ, BA, gen studies. **Career:** Cleveland Heights, police chaplin; City Cleveland Heights, councilman, currently; Hicks Ins Agency, owner, currently. **Orgs:** Ordained Elder, Nat Church God Christ; community relations & recreation comt, 1998-2001; munic servs comt coun, 2002-05; Nat Asn Adv Colored People. **Business Addr:** Chief Executive Officer, Hicks Insurance Agency, 14208 Kinsman Rd, Cleveland, OH 44120-4825, **Business Phone:** (216)752-1958.

HICKS, LEON NATHANIEL
Educator. **Personal:** Born Dec 25, 1933, Deerfield, FL. **Educ:** Kans State Univ, BS; Univ Iowa, MA, MFA. **Career:** Fla A&M Univ, Concord; Lincoln Univ; Lehigh Univ; chmn bd, exec & vpres, Hicks Etch print Inc Philadelphia, 1974; Webster Univ, prof art, 1974-99; Webster Univ, prof emer art, 1999-. **Orgs:** Col Art Asn; Nat Conf Artists; Int Platform Asn; Brandywine Graphic Workshop; Creatadrama Soc; Kappa Alpha Psi. **Honors/Awds:** First prizes for prints & art work, Nat Conf Artists, Mo; Black Artists Art publ, 1969; Am Negro Printmakers, 1966; Directions Afro Am Art, 1974; Engraving Am, 1974; Dict Int Biog, 1974; Mo Arts Award, 2000. **Military Serv:** AUS, 1953-56. **Business Addr:** Professor Emeritus, Webster University, Department of Art, 470 E Lockwood Ave, St Louis, MO 63119, **Business Phone:** (314)968-7006.*

HICKS, MARYELLEN
Judge. **Personal:** Born Mar 10, 1949, Odessa, TX; daughter of Albert G Whitlock and Kathleen Durham; widowed; children: Erin Kathleen. **Educ:** Tex Womans Univ, BA, Grad Work, 1971; Tex Tech Sch Law, DJ, 1974. **Career:** Jusge (retired); Bonner & Hicks, atty law, 1975-77; City Ft Worth, munic ct judge, 1977-82; 231st Judicial Dist Ct, dist judge, 1983-85, sr appellate judge. **Orgs:** Fel, Nat Endowment Humanities, 1980; con secy, Nat Women Achievement, 1985; State Bang TX; Nat Bar Asn; vpres, Nat Coun Negro Women; Delta Sigma Theta Sor Jack & Jill Inc; former pres, Font Work Black Bar Assoc; vpres, Sojourner Truth Community Theatre. **Honors/Awds:** Outstanding Black Women, 1982; Outstanding Black Lawyer, 1982; Female Newsmaker, First Yr Press Club, 1982; Citizen Award, Black Pilots Am, 1986; Citizen of the Year, SS Dillow Elem Sch, 1987; Alumna Award, Tex Woman's Univ, 1989.

HICKS, MICHAEL
Football player. **Personal:** Born Feb 1, 1973, Barnesville, GA. **Educ:** SC State Univ. **Career:** Football player (retired); Chicago Bears, running back, 1996-97.

HICKS, MICHAEL L
Physician. **Personal:** Born Apr 8, 1960, Tuskegee Institute, AL; son of Lee Otis and Lillie R Hicks; married Rhonda M Hicks, Sep 14, 1991; children: Michael Leon II & Maya Michelle. **Educ:** Luther Col, BA, 1981; Univ Ala Birmingham, MD, 1986. **Career:** Roswell Park Cancer Inst, fel gynecologic oncol, 1990-92; St Joseph Mary Hosp, dir gynec oncologist, 1992-; St Joseph Mercy Oakland, Mich Cancer Inst, physician, currently; pvt pract. **Orgs:** Nat Med Asn; AMA; Soc Surg Oncologist; Soc Gynec Oncologist; Am Soc Clin Oncologist; Am Col Obstetricians & Gynecologists. **Special Achievements:** Author of numerous medical articles. **Business Addr:** Gynecologic Oncologist, Michigan Cancer Institute, 44405 Woodward Ave Suite 202, Pontiac, MI 48341, **Business Phone:** (248)858-2270.

HICKS, RAYMOND A
College administrator. **Personal:** Born Jan 1, 1943; married Georgia Hicks; children: Shannan, Michael & Jared. **Educ:** Grambling State Univ, BA, 1968; La Tech, MA, 1971; Southern Ill Univ, phD, 1974. **Career:** Col administartor (retired); Grambling State Univ, interim pres, 1993-94, pres, 1994-97, prof. **Orgs:** Nat Asn Equal Opportunity Higher Educ.

HICKS, ROBERT (ROBERT OTIS HICKS, JR.)
Football player. **Personal:** Born Nov 17, 1974, Atlanta, GA. **Educ:** Miss State Univ. **Career:** Football player(retired); Buffalo Bills, tackle, 1998-2000; Oakland Raiders, line back.

HICKS, ROBERT OTIS, JR. See HICKS, ROBERT.

HICKS, REV. DR. SHERMAN G
Clergy. **Personal:** Born Jun 22, 1946, Brooklyn, NY; son of Charles and Sarah; married Anna Marie Peck, Sep 12, 1970 (divorced 1995); children: Andrea, Geoffrey & Christopher. **Educ:** Wittenberg Univ, BA, polit sci, DD; Hamma Sch Theology, MDiv; Carthage Col, DD; Elmhurst Col, DD. **Career:** Old Lutheran Church, asst bishop, Ill; Metrop Chicago Synod, bishop; First Trinity Lutheran Church, sr pastor, currently; Lutheran Sch Theol, Gettysburg, adj fac; Evangelical Lutheran Church Am, Div Outreach, mission dir, currently. **Orgs:** Bd dirs, Nat AIDS Fund; Bethphage Mission Inc; bd dirs, Community Family Life Servs; bd dirs Lifeline, A Mental Retardation Partnership; bd dirs, AIDS Nat Interfaith Network; bd dir, Lutheran Housing Servs Inc; pres, Interfaith Coun Homeless; bd Comm Renewal Soc. **Honors/Awds:** Wittenberg Univ, Alumni Citation, 1993; Doctor of Divinity, Wittenberg Univ. **Business Addr:** Mission Director, Evangelical Lutheran Church America, Divinity Outreach, Lutheran Ctr, 700 Light St, Baltimore, MD 21230, **Business Phone:** (410)230-2878.

HICKS, SKIP (BRIAN L HICKS)
Football player. **Personal:** Born Oct 13, 1974, Corsicana, TX. **Educ:** Univ Calif, LA. **Career:** Football player (retired); Wash Redskins, running back, 1998-2000; Tenn Titans, running back, 2001-02; Carolina Panthers, 2002-03; Cincinnati Bengals, running back, 2004; Toronto Argonauts, 2005.

HICKS, DR. VERONICA ABENA
Manager. **Personal:** Born Feb 22, 1949, Awate, Ghana; daughter of Stephen Kwani Kokroko and Salone Atawa Dzeble Kokroko; married Anthony M, Jun 6, 1980; children: Esi, Gloria & Tania. **Educ:** Univ Ghana, Legon, BSc, 1971, grad dipl, 1972; Iowa State Univ, Ames, MSc, 1976, PhD, 1980. **Career:** Ministry Agri, Accra Ghana, nutrition consult, 1976-77; ISU Dept Biochem & Biophys, Ames, res fel, 1980-81; Kellogg Co, Battle Creek, nutritionist, 1981-82, mgr nutrition res, 1982-84, dir nutrition, 1984-86, dir, chem & physiol, 1986-. **Orgs:** Infant Health Adv bd, Calhoun County Dept Health, 1983-; adv bd, Iowa State Col Consumer & Family Sci, 1985-88. **Business Addr:** Director, Kellogg Company Science & Techology Center, Chemisty & Physiology, 235 Porter St, Battle Creek, MI 49017.

HICKS, WILLIAM H.
State government official. **Personal:** Born Aug 27, 1925, Littleton, NC; married Margaret; children: Chiquita, Patricia, William & Linda. **Educ:** William Patterson Col, BA. **Career:** New Jersey State, assembly man, 1971-75; State Co Housing, dir. **Orgs:** Bd dir, Paterson Boys Club; Damon House adv equal opportunities ramapocol; alderman patersons fourth ward, 1966-71; Am legion post 268. **Military Serv:** USN, air corps, 1943-46. **Business Addr:** Director, State Ct, 317 Pa, Paterson, NJ 07503.

HICKS, WILLIAM JAMES
Educator, physician. **Personal:** Born Jan 3, 1948, Columbus, OH; married; children: 3. **Educ:** Morehouse Col, BS, 1970; Univ Pittsburgh, Sch Med, MD, 1974; Am Bd Med Examr, dipl, 1974; Am Bd Internal Med, dipl, 1977; Am Bd Med Oncol, dipl, 1981. **Career:** Univ Health Ctr Pittsburgh, Presbyterian-Univ Hosp, internship, 1974-75, residency, 1975-77; Ohio State Univ, Dept Hemat & Oncol, fel, 1977-79; William J Hicks Md, 1979-2002; Grant Medical Ctr, Med Oncology, assoc dir, 1979-, attending staff; Columbus Cancer Clin, staff, 1982-86; OH State Univ, assoc, clinical prof med, 1986-2002; chmn, Internal Med Dept, Grant Med Ctr, 1989-91; Saint Anthony's Med Ctr, attending staff, prof clinical med, 2002; Ohio State Univ, Div Hemat & Oncol, prof clin internal med, 2002-. **Orgs:** Alpha Phi Alpha Fraternity, Inc, 1968-; Southwest Oncology Group, 1979-; ECCO Family Health Ctr, 1979-; Grant Med Ctr, 1979-86; pres, Nat Med Asn, 1982-84; Nat Surgical Adjuvant Breast & Bowel Project, 1982-; pres, Columbus Chapter Nat Med Asn, 1982-84; assoc prin investr, Columbus Community Clin Oncol Prog, 1983-, bd trustees, 1983-, instnl rev bd, 1983-; Franklin County Acad Med, 1983-; Sigma Pi Phi Phi Fraternity Inc, 1985-; Ohio State Med Asn, 1986-; Am Soc Clin Oncologists, 1986-; State OH Comn Minority Health, 1987-; Planned Parenthood Cent OH, 1989-95; vice chmn, State OH Comn Minority Health, 1993-; chmn, Nat Black Leadership Initiative Cancer Columbus Coalition, 1994-; Comn African-Am Males, 2002-. **Honors/Awds:** Human Services Award, Alpha Kappa Alpha Sorority, Alpha Sigma Omega Chapter, 1992; Alpha Excellence Award, Alpha Rho Lambda Chapter Alpha Phi Alpha Fraternity, 1994; Recipient Chairman's Award, Minority Health Comn, 1994; Professional Award, Coun Black Students Admin; 13th Annual Black Business Awards Banquet, 1989. **Special Achievements:** Author, publications include: "Randomized Multicenter Trial of Cytosine Arabinoside with Mitoxantrone or Daunorubicin in Previously Untreated Adult Patients with Acute Nonlymphocytic Leukemia," Leukemia, Vol 4, No 3, p 177-183, 1990; "Photodynamic Therapy for Cutaneous and Subcutaneous Malignant Neoplasms," Archives of Surgery, 124, p 211-216, 1989; Black Enterprise Magazine One of Listed Top Black Physicians, 1988; Columbus Monthly Mag, One of Listed Top Doctors, 1992; numerous others. **Business Addr:** Professor, Ohio State University, Division of Hematology & Oncology, B401 Starling Loving Hall, 320 W 10th Ave, Columbus, OH 43210, **Business Phone:** (614)293-8971.

HICKS, WILLIAM L.
Engineer, construction manager. **Personal:** Born Jan 19, 1928, Yoakum, TX. **Educ:** Col Engr, UC Berkeley, BS, 1954. **Career:** Corps Engrs LA, engr trainee; Daniel Mann Johnson & Mendenhall LA, design engr; Ralph M Parsons Co LA, design engr; Mackintosh & Mackintosh LA, civil engr; Hick Construct Co, owner. **Orgs:** Am Soc & Civil Engrs. *

HICKS, WILLIE LEE
Executive. **Personal:** Born Jan 31, 1931, Bartow, GA; son of Mike and Lula Mae Brinson; married Doris Bowman Culley, Sep 10, 1952; children: Debra, Ajisafe, Kathy & Doris Jumoke. **Educ:** Baruch Sch Bus & Pub Admin, BBA 1960; Heffley & Brown Sec Sch, attended 1956. **Career:** Durojaiye Assn, retailer distributor mfg, 1968-73; African Investment Partnership Ltd, 1974; Durojaiye Trading & Commodity Corp, 1976-; United Mutual Life, 1975-; Mind Power Inc, chmn, 1989-. **Orgs:** Nile-Niger Corp, 1957; pres, Durojaiye Trading & Commodity Corp, 1959-62; HKM Intl, 1967; sec Nat Postal Alliance, 1956; NAACP, 1956; sec Angola Refugee Rescue Com; vpres, Soc African Descendents; African-Am Teachers Asn; numerous other affiliations; vpres, United Peoples Movement. **Military Serv:** USAF A/1C, 1951-55. **Business Addr:** Chairman, Mind Power Inc, 1223 Fulton St Suite 4F, PO Box 254, Brooklyn, NY 11216, **Business Phone:** (718)230-5045.*

HICKS-BARTLETT, SHARON THERESA
Social scientist. **Personal:** Born Nov 22, 1951, Chicago, IL; married David Charles; children: Alani Rosa Hicks. **Educ:** Roosevelt Univ, BA, 1976, MA, 1981; Univ Chicago, MA, 1985; Univ Chicago, PhD, 1994. **Career:** IL Coun Cont Med Educ, prog & activities, sec, 1975-78; Amherst Asn, office mgr, 1978-80; Univ Chicago, convocation coordr, 1980-81; Univ Chicago Urban Family Life Project, res asst, 1985-; Am Jewish Comt, Hands Across the Campus, dir, 1995-98; Terrapin Training Strategies Inc, pres, 1998-. **Orgs:** Instr, Thornton Comm Col, 1982 & 1987; freelance researcher, Better Boys Found, 1985; volunteer Ford Heights Comm Serv Ctr, 1986-; literacy tutor, Literacy Volunteers Am, 1987-. **Honors/Awds:** Art & Science Scholar Award, Roosevelt Univ, 1980-81; Title IX Fellowship for Grad Study, Univ Chicago, 1981-85; Danforth-Compton Dissertation Award, Univ Chicago, 1986-87; American Sociology Society Dissertation Award, Univ Chicago, 1986-87. **Home Addr:** 66 Water St, Park Forest, IL 60466. **Business Addr:** President, Terrapin Training Strategies Inc, PO Box 238, Olympia Fields, IL 60461.

HICKSON, EUGENE, SR.
Executive. **Personal:** Born Jun 10, 1930, Limestone, FL; married Verlene Deloris Stebbins; children: Eugene Jr, Vergena, Edward. **Educ:** Gubton-Jones Col, Mortuary Sci, 1952. **Career:** Arcadian newspaper, printer; Arcadia, FL, mayor, 1971-75; Brown's Funeral Home, embalmer & funeral dir; Hickson Funeral Home, owner, 1960-. **Orgs:** 32 Degree Mason; Shriner; deacon Elizabeth Bapt Ch; chmn C C; second vpres, FA Martician Asn. **Honors/Awds:** Florida Mortician Association Award, Sarasota Womens Club, 1971. **Special Achievements:** First African American elected to the Arcadia City Council. **Business Addr:** Owner, Hickson Funeral Home, 142 S Orange Ave, Arcadia, FL 34266.*

HICKSON, SHERMAN RUBEN
Dentist, army officer. **Personal:** Born Apr 3, 1950, Ridgeland, SC; son of Glover M Hickson Jr (deceased) and Justine Odon; married Eavon Holloway; children: Sherman Jr (deceased), LaTonya, Thurston, Adrienne. **Educ:** SC State Col, BS, 1971; Meharry Med Col Sch Dent, DDS, 1975. **Career:** pvt pract, gen dent, 1977-.

Orgs: SC Dent Asn, 1975; Palmetto Med Dent & Pharm Asn, 1976-87; Nat Dent Asn, 1976-87; Acad Gen Dent, 1978-87; Dickerson Lodge 314 Mason Prince Hall, 1981-87; CC Johnson Consistory 136, 1982-87; Cairo Temple 125 Shriners, 1982-87; Orion Chap 135 Eastern Star, 1986-87; trustee, Friendship Baptist Church; life mem, Nat Asn Advan Colored People; life mem, Omega Psi Phi Fraternity Inc; SC Basketball & Football Off Asn; off, Mideastern Athletic Col Football. **Honors/Awds:** Dentsply Int Merit Award, Meharry Med Col Sch Dent. **Special Achievements:** 2nd degree black, belt World Tae Kwon Do Asn, 1982-87. **Military Serv:** AUS, capt, 2 yrs; Letter of Commendation, 1975-77. *

HICKSON, DR. WILLIAM F, JR.
Dentist. **Personal:** Born Aug 27, 1936, Aiken, SC; son of William F Hickson Sr and Nina; married Charlestine Dawson (divorced); children: Nina R, William F, III & G G Oneal. **Educ:** SC State Col, BS, 1956; Meharry, DDS, 1962. **Career:** Pvt pract, gen dentist; WSSB Radio, SC State Col, radio host, 1985. **Orgs:** Am Nat SC Palmetto Dental Assoc; Cty dental dir, OEO State; pres, Palmetto Dental Assoc; reg consult, HEW Dist IV; mem, Beta & Kappa Chi; Omega Psi Phi; past basileus Alpha Iota Boule; past sire Archon; Nat Bd Missions United Presbyterian; mem, NAACP; Fed Dental Cons; act dir, counr, Orangeburg Sickle Cell Found. **Military Serv:** USY capt 1963-65. **Home Addr:** 121 Weybridge Ct, Orangeburg, SC 29115, **Home Phone:** (803)516-9360.

HIGGINBOTHAM, EVE JULIET
Physician, educator, dean (education). **Personal:** Born Nov 4, 1953, New Orleans, LA; daughter of Luther and Ruby; married Frank C Williams Jr, Jun 7, 1986. **Educ:** Mass Inst Technol, BS, chem engineering, 1975, MS, chem engineering, 1975; Harvard Med Sch, MD, 1979. **Career:** Pac Med Ctr, intern, 1979-80; LSU Eye Ctr, resident, 1980-83; Mass Eye & Ear Infirmary, fel, 1983-85; Head Found fel, 1983; EB Durphy fel, 1984; Univ Ill, asst prof, 1985-90; Univ Mich, assoc prof & asst dean, 1990-94; Univ Md Med Sch, Dept Ophthal Visual Sci, prof & chair; Morehouse Sch Med, dean & sr vpres acad affairs, 2006-. **Orgs:** bd dirs, Women Ophthal, 1980-94; bd dirs, Prevent Blindness Am, Chair Publ Comt, 1990-; bd trustees, Am Acad Ophthal, 1992-95; ed bd, Arch Ophthal, 1994-; Inst Med, 2000; voting mem, FDA Ophthalmic Devices Panel, 2001; Nat Med Asn; Nat Eye Health Educ Prog, Nat Eye Inst; Planning Comt, Nat Eye Health Educ Prog, Nat Eye Inst; dir outreach serv, FCGCF; Maryland Soc Eye Physicians & Surgeons; pres, Baltimore City Med Soc. **Honors/Awds:** Knepp Award, 1984; Beem-Fisher Award, Chicago Ophthal Soc, 1985; Nominee AAMC Humanism Med Award, 2004; Suzanne Veroneaux-Troutman Award; Roman Barnes Achievement Award. **Special Achievements:** Glaucoma textbook including over 30 contributors; first woman to head a university based ophthalmology department in the United States; co-editor, Clinical Guide to Comprehensive Opthalmology; Best Doctors in America for more than a decade, one of the top 10 Baltimoreans in 2000 and among the "Top Docs" in Baltimore and Michigan; published over 100 peer-reviewed articles, and she has co-edited four textbooks in ophthalmology. **Business Addr:** Dean, Senior Vice President, Morehouse School of Medicine, 720 Westview Dr SW, Atlanta, GA 30310, **Business Phone:** (404)752-1500.*

HIGGINBOTHAM, F. MICHAEL
Educator. **Educ:** Brown Univ, AB, 1979; Yale Univ, JD, 1982; Cambridge Univ, LLM, 1985. **Career:** Law clerk; Univ Pa Law Sch, lectr law; Univ Baltimore Sch Law, prof, 1988-. **Orgs:** Chmn, Pub Justice Ctr; Coun Foreign Rels; Asn Am Law Schs Comt Recruitment & Retention Minority Fac; DC Bar. **Special Achievements:** New York University Law Review; Columbia University International Law Journal; Boston University International Law Journal; Howard University Law Journal; University of Illinois Law Review. **Business Addr:** Professor of Law, University of Baltimore School of Law, 1420 N Charles St, Baltimore, MD 21201-5779.*

HIGGINBOTHAM, REV. KENNETH DAY, SR.
Clergy. **Personal:** Born May 1, 1928, Worcester, MA; son of Charles Washington Sr and Olive Mary Elizabeth Bowman; married Ruth Kidd; children: Kenneth Jr, Maretta, Michael, Paul, Stephen, Keith, Andrea & Christopher. **Educ:** Trinity Col, BA, 1950; Berkeley Div Sch, MDiv, 1954; Yale-Berkeley Div Sch, STD, 1983; Yale Divinity Sch, Doctor of Sacred Theology. **Career:** St Philips Church, rector, 1957-68; Tenn State Univ, chaplain, 1968-70; Fed City Col, chaplain, 1970-72; Episcopal Diocese WA, asst bishop, 1971-79; Christ Good Shepherd Church, LA, rector, 1979-93; Diocese Los Angeles, canon ordinary, 1993-; All Saints By The Sea, Santa Barbara, CA, priest in charge, 1993; IBRU Ecumenical International Retreat Conf Ctr, Agbarha Otor, Nigeria, dir gen, 1993-95; Fisk Univ, Meharry Med Col; St Matthews, Pacific Palisades, CA, pastor assoc. **Orgs:** Franklin Co Welfare Bd, 1965-68; GOE reader; dep Gen Conv, 1985; pub adv dir, Blue Cross Calif, 1989-90; bd mem, N Am Regional Comt, St George's Col, Jerusalem, 1990-92; chmn, Comn Ministry, Los Angeles, 1991-; Crenshaw Ctr Hosp, chaplain; pres bd, Good Shepherd Ctr Independent Living; chmn, Diocese An Urban Caucus; Program Group Christian Educ & Leadership Training Diocese Los Angeles; Union of Black Episcopalians; bd mem, Encl Churches, Columbus, OH; Green door; standingcom Diocese Southern Ohio; chmn, Comn Black Ministries; mem, Comn Ministry; US Col Sr Hon Soc; Fellow, Bexley Hall Div Sch; hon canon, St Paul's Cathedral, Los Angeles, CA; hon canon, St Audrew's Cathedral, Warri, Nigeria.

HIGGINBOTHAM-BROOKS, RENEE
Lawyer. **Personal:** Born Jan 3, 1952, Martinsville, VA; daughter of Curtis and Charmion; married Clarence Jackson Brooks, Jun 20, 1975; children: Leigh, Codie. **Educ:** Howard Univ, BA, 1974; Georgetown Univ Law Ctr, JD, 1977. **Career:** Nat Labor Rels Bd, field atty, 1977-79; Dept Health, Educ & Welfare, civil rights atty, 1979-87; Law Off Renee Higginbotham Brooks, pvt pract law, 1987-; Tex Alcoholic Beverage CMS, chair. **Orgs:** NBA, 1979-; Links Inc, 1985-; Tarrant County Trial Lawyers Asn, 1989-; State Bar Tex, 1977-; Jack & Jill AME, 1990-; Col State Bar Tex, 1992; Vice Chairwoman, Howard Univ, 2005-. **Honors/Awds:** Quest for Success Award, Dallas Black COC, 1992; Excellence in Law Award, KAP, 1992. **Special Achievements:** First AFA & first female mem & chair Tex Alcoholic Beverage CMS, 1991. **Business Addr:** Proprietor, Law Office of Renee Higginbotham-Brooks, 1st American Title Bldg, 1612 Summit Ave Suite 230, Fort Worth, TX 76102, **Business Phone:** (817)334-0106.*

HIGGINS, BENNETT EDWARD
Educator, funeral director. **Personal:** Born May 5, 1931, Athens, AL; son of JP Higgins and Bertha; married Shirley Webb, Jul 13, 1957; children: Bennett Dion & Melessa Shawn. **Educ:** Ala Agr & Mech Univ, BS, 1953; Temple Univ; Athens Col. **Career:** Atlanta Life Ins Co, salesman, 1953; Forniss Printing Co, Birmingham, lino type operator, 1953; Clements High Sch, Limestone County Bd Educ, teacher sci, 1957-; Peoples Funeral Home, owner & founder, 1965-, mortician & funeral dir, 1968-. **Orgs:** Pres, Nat Asn Advan Colored People, Limestone, 1978-; secy, Limestone Dem Conf; chmn, Boy Scout Troup No 154; Kappa Alpha Psi Frat. **Honors/Awds:** Recipient good conduct & rifle medals AUS 1954; Keep Am Beautiful City of Athens, 1977; Achievement Award, Kappa Alpha Psi Frat, 1978; Outstanding Service Award, Nat Asn Advan Colored People, 1980; NAACP Lifetime award, NAACP, 2007. **Military Serv:** AUS, corp, 1953-55. *

HIGGINS, CHESTER ARCHER, JR.
Photojournalist. **Personal:** Born in Lexington, KY; son of Johnny Frank and Varidee Loretta Young; divorced; children: Nataki, Chester III. **Educ:** Tuskegee Inst, BS, 1970. **Career:** Photographer, author; Exhibits NY & World-Wide Retrospective; USIA, 1975-76; NY Univ, instr, 1975-78; NY Times, staff photogr, 1975-. **Orgs:** Int Ctr Photog. **Honors/Awds:** Works in Museum of Modern Art; Int Ctr Photog; Libr Cong; Vassar Col; Tuskegee Inst Archive Ford Found Fel, 1972-74; Rockefeller Grant, 1973; Nat Endowment Arts Grant, 1973; African Distinguished Lecturer, 1975; United Nations Award; American Graphic Design Award; Award, Graphics Mag; Int Ctr Photog Grant; Artist Director Club of New York Award; Publishers Award, NY Times. **Special Achievements:** Author: Black Woman, McCalls, 1970; Drums of Life, Doubleday, 1974; Some Time Ago, Doubleday, 1978; Feeling the Spirit: Searching the World for the People of Africa, Bantam Books, 1994; Elder Grace: The Nobility of Aging, Bull Finch, 2000; Echo of the Spirit: A Visual Journey, Random House/Harlem Books, 2004. Published his works in Newsweek, New York Times Sunday Magazine, Fortune, Art News, Essence and Archeology; One of the original photos provided the basis for the three-story photo mosaic at the new Museum of the African Diaspora in San Francisco. **Home Addr:** 57 S Portland Ave, Brooklyn, NY 11217-1301, **Home Phone:** (718)625-2474. **Business Addr:** Staff Photographer, The New York Times, 229 W 43rd St, New York, NY 10036-3959.*

HIGGINS, CLARENCE R., JR.
Pediatrician. **Personal:** Born Sep 13, 1927, E St Louis, IL; son of Clarence and Louise; married Edwina Gray; children: Rhonda, Adrienne, Stephen. **Educ:** Fisk Univ, attended 1948; Meharry Med Col, 1953. **Career:** Homer Phillips Hosp St Louis, internship, 1953-54, pediat res, 1954-56; Baylor Col Med, res fellowship, 1956-57, asst clinical prof pediats; Peds Sec NMA, self employed Pediat, chmn, 1973-; St Joseph Hosp, dir; Higgins Clarence R Jr & Assoc, Pediatrican, currently. **Orgs:** Alpha Phi Alpha Fraternity; Diplomat Am Bd Pediats; Fellow Am Acad Pediats. **Military Serv:** USAF, 1957-59. **Business Addr:** Pediatrician, Higgins Clarence R Jr & Association, 4315 Lockwood Dr Suite 9, Houston, TX 77026, **Business Phone:** (713)672-2586.*

HIGGINS, CLEO SURRY
Educator, dean (education). **Personal:** Born Aug 25, 1923, Memphis, TN; widowed; children: Kyle Everett & Sean Craig. **Educ:** LeMoyne Col, BA, 1944; Univ Wis, MPh, 1945, PhD, 1973. **Career:** Bethune-cookman Col, instr, 1945-46, Div Humanities, actg chmn, 1970-73, chmn, 1973-76, actg acad dean, 1976, prof emer, currently; W Va St Col, vis prof, 1948; Cent Acad High Sch, instr reading, 1958-60; CollierBlocker Jr Col, dean stud perssonel regist instr, 1960-63; Humanities St Johns & River Jr Col, instr, 1964-70; Univ WI, Dept Eng, scholar, 1971. **Orgs:** Fessenden Acad, instr, 1943-44; chmn, Bethune-cookman Col, 1946-48; chmn, Div Humanities, Bethune-Cookman Col, 1948-56; fed mem, Beta Iota Sigma Sigma Gamma Rho Society, 1948; standing mem, Vis Com S Asn Sec Schs & Cols, 1948-56; chap mem, Daytona Br, Chap Links Inc, 1956; speaker, St Louis George Wash Day Observance, 1959; nat pres, Sigma Sigma Gamma Rho Society, 1962-63; asst chmn, SACS Vis Team, 1962; chmn, Bilingualism WI, 1963; exec bd mem, Putnam County Chap, Nat Found Marchof Dimes, 1964; Bi-Racial Comn, Putnam County, 1964-70; vol secy, Putnam City Comn Action Prog, 1966; consult, In-Serv Ed Meeting, Putnam County Sec Schs, 1966; FlaCitizens Comn Humanities, 1972-73; Am Dialect Soc; Nat Coun Teachers Eng; Nat Coun Col Pub Adv; Am Asn Univ Women; Putnam Co Hist Soc; Emanuel United Methodist Church; Womens Serv League. **Honors/Awds:** Outstanding Educrs Am, 1970; Recreation, Charles Dana Fac Scholar, Univ NCF, 1972-73; Woman of the Year, Bethune-Cookman Col, 1975; Panelist, Humanities Prog Disadvantaged, 1976; Higher Educ Assistance Award, 2001. **Special Achievements:** Oratorical contest judge, VFW Voice of Democracy National Program, 1975. **Business Addr:** Professor Emeritus, Bethune Cookman College, 640 Dr Mary McLeod Bethune Blvd, Daytona Beach, FL 32114.*

HIGGINS, ORA A.
Manager. **Personal:** Born Sep 24, 1910, Birmingham, AL; married William Higgins Sr; children: Murrell Duster & William Jr. **Educ:** NWS Univ, BA, personnel admin, 1946, MA, bus law, 1955; NWS Univ, Bus Law, grad work. **Career:** Spiegel Inc, asst personnel mgr 1946-77; fac, Dunbar Voc Evening Sch; Ora Higgins Youth Found, founder & mgr, 1976-. **Orgs:** Chicago Comn Human Rel Employ, State Ill, Dept Personnel Grievance Comn; mem Nat Bus League, Chicago Guid & Personnel Asn; Manpower Comn State Ill; Civil Serv Comn Oral Panel; adv bd Midwest Day Care Ctr; bd dir RehabWorkshop Asn; chmn, Du Sable HS Exemplary Proj; sec bd dir, Joint NegroAppeal; treas Jones Comn HS adv coun; chmn Youth Motivation Prog Chicago Asn Commerce & Indus; gov bd, pres women's auxiliary; mem, Tabernacle Comn Hosp & Health Ctr; mem, Women's Div Nat Conf Christians & Jews; Nat chmn, Women Indust Federated Women's Clubs; chmn Award Comn Dunbar Voc HS advcoun; Provident Hosp Women's Aux; personnel chmn YWCA; Corp Com Fund Chicago; Personnel Mgmt Comn; tech adv comn Dawson Skill Ctr City Col Chicago; personnel mgmt Comn Fund; Loop dept stores, eng Integration Prog, 1950; Alpha Gamma Phi Sor; mem Greenview Comn Coun. **Honors/Awds:** Award Chicago Association Commerce & Industry, 1975; Award Add Info Contrib Bus World Cosmo Sec NCNW, 1978; Merit Employ Award, Chicago Asn Commerce & Indust, 1978; Woman of the Week, WBEE Radio, 1973; Association Organisation Vocational Achievement 100th Year Anniversary Emancipation Proclamation Merit Award, 1963; Chicago Daily Defender Round Table Commerce, 1961; Rosa Gregg Award Bus & Indust, Nat Asn Colored Women's Clubs, 1964; Alpha Gamma Phi Sorrosity Outstanding Progressive Woman, 1967; Distinguished Service Award, Tuskegee Inst, 1967. **Special Achievements:** First African American woman to engineer a major industrial integration program. **Business Addr:** Founder, Manager, Ora Higgins Youth Found, 9424 S Parnell Ave, Chicago, IL 60620-2337.*

HIGGINS, RODERICK DWAYNE
Basketball player, basketball coach, sports manager. **Personal:** Born Jan 31, 1960, Monroe, LA; married Concetta; children: Rick & Cory. **Educ:** Fresno State Univ, attended 1982. **Career:** Basketball player (retired), basketball coach, gen mgr; Chicago Bulls, 1982-85 & 1986; Seattle SuperSonics, 1985-86; San Antonio Spurs, 1985-86; NJ Nets, 1986; Golden State Warriors, 1986-92 & 1994; Sacramento Kings, 1992-93; Cleveland Cavaliers, 1993-94; Golden State Warriors, asst coach,1995-2000, gen mgr, 2004-07; Washington Wizards, asst gen mgr, 2000-04; Charlotte Bobcats, gen mgr, currently. **Honors/Awds:** Athletic Hall of Fame, Fresno State Univ. **Business Addr:** General Manager, Charlotte Bobcats, 333 E Trade St, Charlotte, NC 28202, **Business Phone:** (704)688-8600.*

HIGGINS, SAMMIE L.
Clergy, educator. **Personal:** Born May 11, 1923, Ft Worth, TX; married Elizabeth; children: Pam, Don, Benita, Kim & Garry. **Educ:** Univ Denver, BS, 1954; Western Theol Sem, B.Th, 1963; Merritt Col, AA, 1969; Univ Utah, San Francisco State Col. **Career:** Teacher; methodist clergyman; educr. **Orgs:** Nat Asn Advan Colored People; Omega Psi Phi. **Honors/Awds:** Outstanding Citizen, Ogden, 1964; Outstanding Financial Educ Officer, Polytechnic High Sch, 1970; Outstanding Fac Mem & Teacher, 1972.

HIGGINS, SEAN MARIELLE
Basketball player, basketball coach. **Personal:** Born Dec 30, 1968, Los Angeles, CA; son of Earle. **Educ:** Univ Mich, Ann Arbor, MI, 1990. **Career:** Basketball player, basketball coach; San Antonio Spurs, guard-forward, 1990-91; Orlando Magic, guard-forward, 1991-92; Los Angeles Lakers, guard-forward, 1992-93; Golden State Warriors, guard-forward, 1993-94; New Jersey Nets, guard-forward, 1994-95; Philadelphia 76ers, guard-forward, 1995-97; Portland Trailblazers, guard-forward, 1997-98; Albany Patroons, guard-forward; Las Vegas Stars, asst coach, 2007-. **Orgs:** BTB, asst for Hurricane Katrina victims; Exec Producer: Let's Play H.O.R.S.E. **Honors/Awds:** National Champion, "AP All American",

NCAA Tournament Southeast regional, All-Tournament Team . **Special Achievements:** Set franchise record for Most Consecutive Field Goals in a single game (12) Career high in scoring 29 in 26 minutes. **Business Addr:** Assistant Coach, Las Vegas Stars, 2730 S Rancho St, Las Vegas, NV 89102, **Business Phone:** (702)216-2966.

HIGGINS, STANN
Arts administrator. **Personal:** Born May 16, 1952, Pittsburgh, PA. **Educ:** Columbia Col Commun Arts, BS, graphics & advt, 1979. **Career:** Jordan Tamraz Caruso Advt, art dir, 1985, prod mgr, 1979; Bentley Barnes & Lynn Advt, asst prod mgr, 1978; Starstruk Prod, creative dir, 1985; Raddim Intl Musicpaper, art dir, prod mgr, 1986; Starstruk Prod, pres, Starstruck Properties, chief exec officer, currently. **Orgs:** Bd dirs, chmn graphics Yth Communs, 1985. **Honors/Awds:** Work selected, recipient 2 honors mentions Art Inst Chicago, 1965; District Art Award, Maywood Bd Ed, 1966; Certificate Appreciation, Guest Speaker Advertising Triton Col, 1981. **Business Addr:** Chief Executive Officer, Star-Struck Productions LLC, PO Box 59174, Chicago, IL 60659, **Business Phone:** (773)994-6756.*

HIGGINSEN, VY
Music producer, philanthropist, publisher. **Personal:** Born in Harlem, NY; married Ken Wydro. **Educ:** Fashion Inst Technol, NY, 1970. **Career:** Ebony mag, sales rep, beginnng 1970; WBLS-FM, radio person; NBC TV, reporter; Mama Found Arts, chief exec officer & exec dir, currently; Books: Mama I Want to Sing; This is My Song; The Positive Zone; Harlem Is; Producer: Mama, I Want to Sing; Gospel Is . . . !; This is My Song; Glory, Glory Hallelujah; Mama, I Want to Sing, Part II. **Special Achievements:** First black female radio personality in the prime time New York City market on WBLS; first woman to host a morning show on New York radio at WWRL; first woman in advertising sales at Ebony magazine; first black woman to produce a drama on Broadway with Joe Tuners Come and Gone by August Wilson; first black female writer, producer, director of the longest-running, Off-Broadway musical in the history of American theatre. **Business Addr:** Chief Executive Officer, Executive Director, Mama Foundation for the Arts, The School For Gospel, Jazz and R & B Arts, 149 W 126th St, New York, NY 10027, **Business Phone:** (212)280-1045.*

HIGGINSON, VY
Television producer, administrator. **Personal:** Born in New York, NY; daughter of Reverend and Geraldine; married Kenneth Wydro; children: Knoelle. **Educ:** Fashion Inst Technol, New York, NY. **Career:** WBLS-FM, New York, NY, disc jockey; WRKS-FM, radio host; WWRL-AM, talk show host; NBC-TV, "Positively Black", hostess; Unique NY Mag, publ; Supv Inc, pres & chief exec officer; MAMA Found Arts Inc, chief exec officer & exec dir, 2000-, interfaith minister, 2002. **Special Achievements:** Writer and producer of "Mama I Want to Sing," the longest running off-Broadway African-American musical, first African-American female in advertising at Ebony Magazine, first African-American female radio personality in the prime-time New York radio market, first African-American female to produce another playwrights drama on Broadway, This Is My Song, a collection of gospel songs and spirituals for little children, published and edited Unique NY, a lifestyles magazine. **Business Addr:** Chief Executive Officer, Executive Director, Mama Found Arts Inc, 149 W 126th St, New York, NY 10027.

HIGGS, FREDERICK C.
Executive. **Personal:** Born Jul 3, 1935, Nassau, Bahamas; married Beryl Vanderpool; children: Rory, Linda & Saundra. **Educ:** St John's Col, 1951. **Career:** Lisaro Enterprises Ltd, pres, 1973-; Charlotte St Prop, properties mgr,1971-73; Bahamas Airways, sta mgr, 1965-70; New Providence Div BGA. **Orgs:** Vice chmn, tournament dir, New Providence Div BGA; first vpres, Bahamas Confed Amateur Sports; Mental Health Asn Exec; Scout Asn Bahamas; secy, Amateur Boxing Asn Bahamas. **Honors/Awds:** Intl Golf Tour Champion Nairobi, 1973.

HIGGS, MARY ANN SPICER
Educator. **Personal:** Born May 10, 1951, South Bend, IN; daughter of Bobby Jr and Willa B Thornton; married Jack Spicer IV, Dec 25, 1977; children: Jack V. **Educ:** N Tex State Univ, BA, psychol, 1973; Abilene Christian Univ, MPA, 1975; Drake Univ, MA, 1992. **Career:** Veterans Affairs Recruitment Off, Waco Tex, Dallas Tex, Lincoln NE, Knoxville IA, 1973-89; Herbert Hoover Sr High Sch, eng instr & psychol instr, 1992-2000; Communicator Newspaper, columnist, 1992-2000; Hoover High Drill Team, coach, 1994-; Hoover High Drill Team, English Dept, chmn, 1997-99; Iowa Employment Appeal Bd, vice-chair & mgt rep, 2000-; Des Moines Sch Dist, teacher. **Orgs:** Stud senator, Drake Univ, 1971-72; Zeta Phi Beta Sorority, 1982-86; Veteran's Admin, Nat Civil Rights Adv Coun, 1986-89, eeo counr trainer, Nat Trainer Supervisor's EEO; nat parliamentarian; nat vpres, Zeta Phi Beta Sorority, 1986-90, nat dir leadership develop, 1992-96; stud senate comt, Drake Univ, 1990-92; dir non-traditional grad studs & dir multi-cultural theatre, Drake Univ, 1991-92; co-chair, Hoover High Marketing Comt, 1992; dir, Performing Arts Imani Players, Hoover High, 1992; sponsor, SADD, Hoover High Br, 1992-94; Am Inst Parliamentarians, 1996-97; act so chair, Nat Asn Advan Colored People, 1995-97; Polk County Republican Select Comt, 1996; Nat Black Child Develop, 1998-; Centra City Optimist, 1999-; coordr, Partner In Econ Progress; IA Congressional Comt, 2000-; parliamentarian, Sisters Target, 2000-. **Honors/Awds:** Women's Studies Graduate Student of the Year, Drake Univ, 1992; Teacher of the Year, Hoover High, 1998. **Special Achievements:** Licensed Secondary Education Teacher, certified in English/ Speech and Theatre, 1992; Natl Teaching Board Certification Participant, 2000; Iowa Outstanding Teacher nominee, 2000. **Home Addr:** 6001 Creston Ave Suite 8, PO Box 5055, Des Moines, IA 50321. **Business Addr:** Vice Chair - Management Representative, Iowa Employment Appeal Board, 4th Fl Lucas State Off Bldg 312 E 12th St, Des Moines, IA 50319, **Business Phone:** (515)281-3638.

HIGH, CLAUDE, JR.
Executive. **Personal:** Born Nov 5, 1944, Marshall, TX; son of Claude High and Lolee Coursey; married Nelda Nadine Spencer; children: Kino, Claude, III & Kimberli; married Renee Lea Watkins; children: Danielle & Marissa. **Educ:** Univ Mich, BA, 1974; Oakland Univ, MA, 1977. **Career:** Western Electric, installer, 1964-73; grocery store owner, 1973-74; Flint Bd Educ, caseworker, 1974-75; Pub Serv Employ Agency, employ counr, 1975, employ coordr, 1975-76, exec dir, 1976-81; Action Mgt Corp, pres & ceo, 1981-. **Orgs:** Secy, Burton Neighborhood House Serv Bd, 1980-84; found, Metropolitan Chamber Com, 1986, chmn, 1989-91; bd mem, Flint Chamber Com, 1987-97, chmn, 1995-96; Chairs Personnel Comt, 1989-96; Fair Bankng Coalition, 1990-97; local bd, Fed Emergency Mgt Agency, 1991-; Gen Motors/United Auto Workers Task Force, 1991-92; Sports Found Bd, 1992; treas, Food Bank Eastern MI, 1992-; vice chmn, Axxon Comput Servs, Inc, 1994-2000; vice chair, Insight Bd Dirs, 1995-; Genessee Dist Libraries Bd, 1995-98; Greater Flint Health Coalition, 1996-2000; chmn, Vines Menswear, Inc, 1996-; pres, Flint Inner City Golf Club, 1996; pres, Downtown Kiwanis, 1998-99; comt mem, Buick Open Community Alliance, 2001-; bd mem, Uptown Reinvestment Corp, 2001. **Honors/Awds:** Certificate of Apppreciation, City Burton, 1986; Outstanding Minority Entrepreneur, State Mich, 1991; Senate of Michigan, Resolution No 58, 1991. **Special Achievements:** Author: Dialogue with Marijuana Users, 1980; First Black Chairman of Flint Chamber of Commerce, 1995; First black president of Downtown Kiwanis in Flint; One of first two blacks invited to join, Warwick Hills Country Club, 1991; One of the fastest-growing companies in Michigan, Detroit News Private 100, 1990, 1991-92. **Military Serv:** Nat Defense Cadet Corp, sgt, 1962. **Business Addr:** President, Action Management Corporation, 915 S Grand Traverse, Flint, MI 48502, **Business Phone:** (810)234-2828.

HIGH, FREIDA
Educator, artist. **Personal:** Born Oct 21, 1946, Starkville, MS; married Gebre Hewit Tesfagiorgis; children: 2; married Joab Njekho Meshak Wasikhongo (deceased); children: 2. **Educ:** Graceland Col, AA, 1966; Northern Ill Univ, BS, 1968; Univ Wis, MA, 1970, MFA, 1971; Univ Chicago, PhD. **Career:** Univ Wis, dept studies various exhibitions 1970-, Afro-Amer studies, asst prof art dept; artist-in-residence, 1971, Dept Afro Am Studies, from asst prof to assoc prof, 1971-86, prof, 1986-, chiar, 1990-93; Contemp African & Afro-Am Art, researcher; Trad African Art, major shows cur, 1971, 1972; Prints & Paintings Afro-Am Art, cur, 1972; Wis Acad Arts Letter Sci, one woman show latest reflections, 1974; Ky State Univ, 1974; Studio Museum, NY, 1976. **Orgs:** Nat Conf Artists. **Honors/Awds:** Visual Arts Grant, Wis Arts Bd, 1977; City Arts Grant, Cult Comm Off Mayor, 1977. **Special Achievements:** Numerous exhibitions and publications. **Business Addr:** Professor, University of Wisconsin-Madison, Afro-American Studies & Art Department, Rm 4121 Helen C White Hall 600 N Pk St, Madison, WI 53706, **Business Phone:** (608)263-2338.

HIGHSMITH, ALONZO WALTER
Football coach. **Personal:** Born Feb 26, 1965, Bartow, FL; son of Walter Highsmith; married; children: Brandon Thermilus & 2 children. **Educ:** Univ Miami, FL, BS, bus mgt, 1987. **Career:** Football player (retired), scout, social worker; Fullback: Houston Oilers,1987-90, Dallas Cowboys, 1990-91, Tampa Bay Buccaneers, 1991-92; Kansas City Chiefs, 1993; boxer, 1995-99; Tex Southern Univ, head coach; Green Bay Packers, scout, 1999-; Natl Recruiting Serv, founder, currently. **Business Addr:** Scout, Green Bay Packers Inc, 1265 Lombardi Ave, PO Box 10628, Green Bay, WI 54307-0628, **Business Phone:** (920)569-7500.

HIGHSMITH, CARLTON L.
Executive, president (organization). **Personal:** Born in Greenville, NC; children: Alexis, Jennifer. **Educ:** Univ Wis, BA (econs) & MBA (mkt), 1973; Univ Conn, attended 1980; Duke Univ Fuqua Grad Sch Bus, exec training prog; Dartmouth's Tuck Grad Sch Bus, exec training prog; Harvard Univ Grad Sch Bus, exec training prog. **Career:** Rexham Corp, acct mgr, 1974-76; Amstar Corp, mkt mgr, 1976-83; Specialized Packaging Group Inc, pres, chief exec officer & co-founder, 1983-; Hamden Parks & Recreation Dept, youth basketball coach. **Orgs:** Am Mkt Asn; Am Mgt Asn; Soc plastic Engrs; Inst Packaging Profs; Paperboard Packaging Coun; life mem, Nat Asn Advan Colored People; Urban League Greater New Haven; cult curric comn, New Haven Pub Sch Adv Bd; adv bd, Conn Coalition Achievement Now; bd trustees, Quinnipiac Univ; bd dirs, First City Fund Corp. **Honors/Awds:** Supplier of the Year, Johnson & Johnson, 1987; Tech Merit Award, Can Packaging Asn, 1988; Gold Cylinder Award, Gravure Tech Asn Am, 1989; Business Person of the Year, 2006; Manufacturer of the Year Award, US Dept Com MBDA; Business and Philanthropy Award, New Eng Coun Black Philanthropy; Business Hall of Fame Award, Jr Achievement Southern New Eng; Friend of Education Award, Conn Educ Asn; Freedom Award, Conn Nat Asn Advan Colored People; Shining Star Award, Conn Minority Supplier Develop Coun; Distinguished Alumni Award, Univ Wis, Madison. **Special Achievements:** Designer: Prevent Toothbrush carton, Johnson & Johnson; Bigelow Tea carton; BE List 100, Black Enterprise Mag, 1989-91. **Business Addr:** President, Chief Executive Officer, Specialized Packaging Group Inc, 3190 Whitney Ave Suite 7, Laurel Square Pk, Hamden, CT 06518, **Business Phone:** (203)248-3370.*

HIGHTOWER, ANTHONY
Lawyer, state government official, college teacher. **Personal:** Born in Atlanta, GA; son of John Vincent and Erie Beavers. **Educ:** Clark Col, Atlanta Ga, BA,pol sci, 1983; Univ Iowa, Iowa City Iowa, JD, 1986; Harvard Univ, MPA, 1996. **Career:** Self-employed, Col Park Ga, atty, 1986-; Clark Col, Atlanta Ga, teacher,1988-; City Col Park, Col Park, Ga, city councilman, 1986-90,; Dallas, asst city atty; Clark Atlanta Univ, Atlanta, Ga,adj prof, 1988-; mayor pro team, 1990; State Ga, Atlanta, Ga, state rep, 1991-92; Univ Wis, Off Equity & Diversity Serv, dir; Med Col Georgia, sr legal adv, 2006-. **Orgs:** NAACP, 1979-; Alpha Phi Alpha Frat, 1980, 1982-83; bd mem, Clark Col,1982-83; State Bar Ga, 1986-; Nat Bar Assn, 1986-; Am Bar Assn, 1986-; Natl League Cities, 1986-; Nat Black Caucus Local Elected Offs, 1986-; Georgia Munic Assn, 1986-; bd mem, Fulton County Pub Safety Training Ctr, 1989-. **Honors/Awds:** Appreciation Award, Metro Atlanta Pvt Indus Coun, 1988; Political Service Award, Delta Sigma Theta Sorority Inc, 1988; Leadership Inst Municipal Elected Officials, Univ Ga, 1989. **Business Addr:** Senior Legal Advisor, Medical College of Georgia, AA 211, 1120 15th St, Augusta, GA 30912, **Business Phone:** (706)721-4018.

HIGHTOWER, EDWARD STEWART
Psychotherapist. **Personal:** Born Feb 7, 1940, New York, NY; married Ola Cherry; children: Meredith & Allyson. **Educ:** Bloomfield Col, BA 1964; Yeshiva Univ, MS, 1971; DD, 1994. **Career:** Kings Co Hosp Ctr, exec asst, comm bd 1970-72, assoc dir, 1972-79; Gen Learning Corp, reg mkt dir, 1969-70; Manpower Dev Training Prog, coun supr, 1969; Williamsburg Adult Training Ctr, asst teacher, 1967-69; New Eng Life Ins Co, ins agent, 1979-81; Mutual NY, sales mgr, agency super, 1981-88; pvt pract, hypnotherapist, 1986-; Medgar Evar's Col, NY, instr. **Orgs:** Bd dir, Com Labor Ind Corp Kings, 1973-80; pres, Concerned Citizens Ed Gifted & Talented C, 1978-79; chmn, City NY Community Planning Bd No 9, 1979; pres, Prospect Lefferts Gardens Neighborhd Asn, 1979-80; asst comnr, NY State Div Housing, 1988-95; state committeeman, NY State Democratic Comn, 1981-86; dist leader, 57th Assembly Dist, Kings County; bd dirs, Vannguard Urban Improvement Asn, 1985-86; bd mgrs, Bedford Stuyvesant YMCA; Nat Guild Hypnotists; Alpha Phi Alpha Fraternity. **Honors/Awds:** Outstanding Young Men of America, 1970; Community Leaders of America, 1972; Community Activist Award, Nat Coun Negro Women Flatbush Sec, 1979; Outstanding Community Leader Bedford Stuyvesant Jaycees, 1980; Member of the Year, Nat Guild Of Hypnotist, 1989. **Home Addr:** 134 Maple St, Brooklyn, NY 11225, **Home Phone:** (718)284-1202. **Business Addr:** Hypnotherapist, 134 Maple St, Brooklyn, NY 11225, **Business Phone:** (718)284-1202.

HIGHTOWER, HERMA J
Federal government official. **Personal:** Born in Mesa, AZ; daughter of Mae Kemp Harris and Oliver Harris; married Claude George, Aug 3, 1984; children: Valerie & Kimberly. **Educ:** Ariz State Univ, BA, 1963, MA, 1966, PhD, 1977. **Career:** Roosevelt Sch Dist, classroom teacher, 1963-70; Ariz State Personnel Comn, training officer, 1970-71; Ariz Dept Educ, educ prog consult, 1971-74, dir, ESEA Title I, 1974-76, dep assoc supt schs, 1976-78; Internal Revenue Serv, asst dir 1978-79, asst dir 1980-81, asst dist dir 1985-, district dir 1988; Smithsonian Inst, dir nat progs, currently. **Orgs:** Guest speaker, Challenger Space Ctr, Peoria, 1963; adv bd, Ariz State Univ Model Mobility Women, 1976; adhoc consult, Nat Inst Educ, Nat Coaltion Title I Parents, Lawyers Comn Civil Rights Under Law, 1976; City Phoenix Human Rels Comn, 1977; bd dirs, Phoenix Urban League, 1977-79; adhoc consult, Am Educ Res Asn, 1977; bd dirs, Phoenix Opportunities Indust Ctr, 1978-79; Seattle Opportunities Indust Ctr, 1980-81; bd dirs, Seattle Urban League, 1980-81; Bus Admin Tech Comt, Seattle Jr Col, 1980-81; Sr Exec Asn, 1980-; exec comt, Resurgens Atlanta, 1983-; bd dirs, YWCA, 1985-; nat speaker, motivation/goalsetting; bd dir, United Way Greater Des Moines, 1988-; Rotary Club Greater Des Moines, 1988-; Nexus Breakfast Club; LINKS Inc; Delta Sigma Theta; bd dirs, United Way Cent Md. **Honors/Awds:** Distinguished Service Award, Nat Asn Black Accountants, 1982; Keynote speaker, Governor's Salute Black Women Ariz, 1986; Certificate of Merit, City Atlanta, 1988; Partnership in Administration Award, Gen Serv Admin, 1989; Outstanding Performance Rating, 1990; Regional Commis-

sioner's Leadership Award, 1990; Distinguished Performance Rating, 1991; Meritorious Presidential Rank Award; Coalition of 100 Black Women Award, 1992; Outstanding Performance Rating, 1992. **Special Achievements:** First Black Female in the History of IRS to be Selected for its Executive Program in 1978; First Black Female Director in History of IRS, 1988; First Female Executive in nine-state region, 1988. **Home Addr:** 3105 Edgewood Rd, Ellicott City, MD 21043. **Business Addr:** Director of National Programs, Smithsonian Institute, SI Bldg Rm 153 MRC 010, PO Box 37012, Washington, DC 20013-7012, **Business Phone:** (202)633-1000.

HIGHTOWER, MICHAEL
Government official. **Personal:** Born in College Park, GA; son of Erie. **Educ:** Clark Col Atlanta, BA, Music, 1979. **Career:** GA State Univ Atlanta, admin coordr, asst to dir physical plant oper,1979-; City Hall Col Park, councilman, mayor pro team; Fulton Co Comn, comnr. **Orgs:** Friendship Baptist Church, 1965-, Eta Lambda Chap Alpha Phi Alpha, 1979-,GA Municipal Assoc, 1980-, Nat League Cities, 1980-; South Fulton Chamber Com, 1980-, Airport Intl Jaycees, 1982-, bd dir Jesse Draper Boy's Club, 1983-; Nat Asn Counties, pres, currently; Fulton County Building Authority; Fulton County Water Resources Bd; Grady Memorial Hosp Oversight Comt. **Honors/Awds:** Outstanding Service, HS & Community Atlanta Airport Rotary Club, 1975; Man of the Year Award, Alpha Phi Alpha, 1979; Outstanding Young Men of America Award, Am Jaycees, 1980, 1983; Disting Alumni Award, Men Clark Col, 1980; Outstanding Young People of Atlanta Award, 1980; Disting Community Service Award, Woodward Acad, 1981; Disting Community Service Award, Friendship Baptist Church, 1983; Award of Appreciation, Flipper Temple AME Church, 1984; Professional Man of the Year, 1989. *

HIGHTOWER, STEPHEN LAMAR (STEVE HIGHTOWER)
Executive, petroleum worker. **Personal:** Born Sep 21, 1956, Middletown, OH; son of Elsie Hightower and Yudell Hightower; married Brenda Ware, Oct 3, 1992; children: Quincy, Stephanie, Sabrina & Stephen Jr. **Educ:** Wright State Univ, attended 1978. **Career:** Prudential Environ Technologies Inc, pres; Hi-Mark Corp, pres; Landmark Building Services Inc, pres; NBCSL CRT, primary rep; Hightowers Petroleum Co, pres & chief exec officer, currently. **Orgs:** Black Male Coalition, 1992; pres, SOS Community Inc, 1992; Minority Supplier Develop Coun, 1992; ABC Ohio Contractors, 1992; bd dirs, Junior Achievement, 1992; United Missionary Baptist Church, 1992. **Honors/Awds:** Salesman of the Year, Snyder Realtors, 1979; Top 100 Minority Business, State Ohio, 1981; Toastmaster Int, 1986; Ceco Bldg, Largest Bldg Sold Midwest Region, 1989. **Business Addr:** President, Chief Executive Officer, Hightowers Petroleum Co., 3589 Commerce Dr, Franklin, OH 45004, **Business Phone:** (513)423-4272.

HIGHTOWER, STEVE. **See HIGHTOWER, STEPHEN LAMAR.**

HIGHTOWER, WILLAR H
Executive, county government official, programmer analyst. **Personal:** Born Aug 8, 1943, Greenville, SC; married Pergetta K Smith; children: Willa J, Terri T & Catrice. **Educ:** NC Col, Durham, Maths, 1965; SC State Univ, BS, math, 1964. **Career:** AUS, battery comdr, 1965-67; USAR Defense Personnel Support Ctr, logistician, 1981-89; WSRC, comput programmer, 1967-79, buyer, 1979-89, asst purchasing agt, 1980-89; Lessons Learned, engr, 1989-2000. **Orgs:** Nat Asn Advan Colored People, 1967-; Res Officers Asn, 1968-; city Counman, City Aiken, SC, 1981-; bd dir, Aiken Chap Am Red Cross, 2001-. **Honors/Awds:** Presented Key to the City of Aiken, 1986. **Military Serv:** AUS, LTC, 24 yrs; USAR, 15 yrs, Eighty First ARCOM, Certificate of Achievement, 1979, Medal, 1980. **Home Addr:** 682 Edrie St NE. **Business Addr:** Councilmember District 8, Aiken County, 682 Edrie St NE, Aiken, SC 29801-4208, **Business Phone:** (803)648-3020.

HILDEBRAND, RICHARD ALLEN
Clergy, bishop. **Personal:** Born Feb 1, 1916, Winnsboro, SC; son of Agnes Brogdon; married Anna Beatrix Lewis; children: Camille Ylonne. **Educ:** Allen Univ, BA, 1938; Payne Theol Sch, BD, 1941; Boston Univ, STM, 1948; Wilberforce Univ, DD, 1953; Morris Brown Col, LLD, 1975. **Career:** Bishop (retired); African Methodist Episcopal Church, ordained to ministry, 1936, bishop, 1972; Columbia & Sumter, SC, pastor, 1936-38; Jamestown & Akron, OH, pastor, 1938-45; Providence, pastor, 1945-48; Bayshore, NY, pastor, 1948-49; Wilmington, DE, pastor, 1949-50; Bethel AME Church, NY, pastor, 1950-65; Bridge State AME Church, Brooklyn, pastor, 1965-72; AME Church, Ga 6th Dist, presiding bishop, 1972-76, 1st Dist Philadelphia, bishop, 1976-92. **Orgs:** Pres, Manhattan Dirs Protestant Coun, 1956-60; chmn, Churches New Harlem Hosp, NY, 1957-65; pres, NY Br, Nat Asn Advan Colored People, 1962-64; pres, Atlanta N GA Conf, AME Fed Credit Union, 1972-76; chmn, bd dirs, Morris Brown Col, Turner Sem Interdenominational Theol Ctr, 1972-76, Payne Theol Sem, 1976-; pres, Coun Bishops, AME Church, 1977-; Alpha Phi Alpha, Masons.

HILDRETH, GLADYS JOHNSON
School administrator, educator. **Personal:** Born Oct 15, 1933, Columbia, MS; married Dr Eddie Jr; children: Bertina, Dwayne, Kathleen & Karen. **Educ:** Southern Univ, Baton Rouge, La, BS, 1953; Univ Wis, Madison, MS, 1955; Mich State Univ, E Lansing, PhD, 1973. **Career:** Southern Univ, assoc prof, 1960-68; La State Univ Sch Human Ecol, prof family studies, 1974-90, Sch Human Ecol, prof emer, 1990-; Tex Woman's Univ, Denton, Tex, prof, 1990-; Univ Ky, chair & prof dept family studies, currently. **Orgs:** Delta Sigma Theta, 1970-; consult, Nat Asn Educ Young C, 1974-; Ctr Family Am Home Econ Asn, 1977-79; state chmn aging serv, La Home Econ Asn, 1978-80; Chmn jr div adv coun La State Univ, 1979-80; Phi Upsilon Omicron Southern Univ Home Econ; Omicron Nu Mich State Univ Human Ecol; Nat Coun Family Rels; Sect, TCFR; Tex Consortium Geriatric Educ. **Honors/Awds:** Grad Sch Fel, Mich State Univ Human Ecol, 1970; Thelma Porter Fel, Mich State Univ Human Ecol, 1970; Recipient Los Angeles Home Econ Asn Distinguished District & State Service Award, 1986; Nominated Am Coun Educ Fel; Distinguished Faculty Fellowship Award, La State Univ; Distinguished Service Award, SE Coun Family Rels; Nat Coun Family Rel, Marie Peters Ethnic Minority Award. **Business Addr:** Professor, Chair, University of Kentucky, Department of Family Studies, 316 Funkhouser Bldg, Lexington, KY 40506-0054, **Business Phone:** (859)257-7781.

HILL, ALFRED
Executive. **Personal:** Born Dec 25, 1925, Atlanta, GA; son of Alfred and Fannie M; divorced; children: Alfred III, Gordon, Stanford. **Educ:** Howard Univ, BA, 1952. **Career:** Executive (retired); Newark Lamp Plant, employ speclization; Equal Opportunity & Urban Affairs & Hourly Skill Training, Lighting Bus Group, mgr; Euclid Lamp Plant Gen Ele Co, mgr employee & union rel, 1985; Smythe Cramer Co, realtor, Cleveland, OH. **Orgs:** Nat Urban Affairs Coun, 1972-; Corp Minority Panel; adv, Lamp Bus Div Minority Panel; mem, Hum Rels Coun, Cleveland; Community Leadership Comn; pres & bd mem, Collinwood Community Serv Ctr; bd mem, Karamu House Cleveland Area Coun Hum Rels; mem, Res & Dev Comn Cleveland Urban League. **Honors/Awds:** Frontiersman Community Service Award, 1960. **Military Serv:** USAF, capt, 1952-69. **Home Addr:** 2602 Edgerton Rd, University Heights, OH 44118. *

HILL, ANITA FAYE
Educator, lawyer. **Personal:** Born Jul 30, 1956, Morris, OK; daughter of Albert and Erma. **Educ:** Okla State Univ, BS, psychol, 1977; Yale Univ Law Sch, JD, 1980. **Career:** Wash DC, law firm, 1980-81; US Dept Educ, asst Clarence Thomas, 1981-82; US Equal Employment Opportunity Comn, spec asst Clarence Thomas, 1982-83; Oral Roberts Univ, law prof, 1983-86; Univ Okla, Col Law, prof law, 1986-96; Brandeis Univ, prof, 1998-. **Orgs:** Antioch Baptist Church; Big Brothers Big Sisters, Am Green County, OK; DC Bar, 1980; Nat Women's Law Ctr; Okla Bar Asn; fel, Fletcher Found. **Honors/Awds:** Woman of the Year, Glamour Mag, 1991. **Special Achievements:** Ms mag, wrote article, "The Nature of the Beast," concerning sexual harassment, p 32, 1992; speaker at conf on "Race, Gender & Power in Am," Georgetown Univ Law Sch, Oct 1992; appeared on The Today Show, Oct 1992; speaker at conf at Univ of Pa, 1992; kick off speaker at conf at Hunter Coll; appeared on 60 Minutes, 1992; speaker at Univ of New Mexico; speaker at Rutgers Univ for women lawmakers' conference; Speaking Truth to Power, 1997. **Business Phone:** (781)736-2000.

HILL, ANNETTE TILLMAN
Educator, counselor, elementary school teacher. **Personal:** Born Nov 9, 1937, Copiah County, MS; daughter of Fayette and Martha Coleman; divorced; children: Gerri Lavonne Hill-Chance. **Educ:** Tougaloo Col, BS, 1956; Chicago State Univ, MS, educ, 1971; Jackson State Univ; Univ Miss. **Career:** Educator (retired); Parrish High Sch, sci & math teacher, 1956-60; Chicago Pub Sch, sci teacher, 1960-69; Wendell Phillips High Sch, Chicago, counr, 1969-71; Jackson State Univ, counr, 1971-82; Hazlehurst High Sch, counr, 1982. **Orgs:** bd dirs, Cent Miss Chap, Am Red Cross, 1978-81, 1985-88; adv comn mem, Juv Justice, State Miss, 1981-89; chairperson, Emergency Food & Shelter Adv Comt, Copiah County, 1985-; Copiah County Econ Develop, 1999-; bd dir, Boys & Girls Club S Cent Miss; Develop Plan Early Childhood Educ Serv, Copiah County, MI; Miss Counr Asn; Am Asn Coun & Develop; Multicultural Asn Coun & Develop; Hazlehurst Pub Schs PTA; vpres, Hazlehurst Br, Nat Asn Adv Colored People. **Honors/Awds:** Cert of Achievement, Life Career Develop Syst, 1976; Cert of Appreciation, Nat Found Cancer Res, 1982; Cert of Appreciation, Healthfest Cent Miss Chap, Am Red Cross, 1982, 1983; Nat Appreciation Award, Soc Distinguished High Sch Students, 1983. **Home Addr:** 321 N Massengill St, Hazlehurst, MS 39083. *

HILL, ARTHUR BURIT
Police officer, vice president (organization). **Personal:** Born Apr 2, 1922, New York, NY; son of Victoria Hill and Alton Hill; married Patricia Ruth Smith, Aug 5, 1956; children: Arthur Jr, Ernest, Victoria & Joanne. **Educ:** City Univ, BS, 1966, MPA, 1973. **Career:** Police officer, vice president (retired); NY Police Dept, patrolman, 1946, sgt, 1956; lt 1960; capt 1964; dep inspector, 1967; inspector, 1969; deputy chief, 1969; asst chief, 1971-73; United Parcel Serv, mgt trainee, 1973, vpres pub affairs, 1975; vpres 1975-92. **Orgs:** Life mem, Nat Asn Advan Colored People; dir, Guy R Brewer Dem Club, 1981-; Kappa Alpha Psi; Sigma Pi Phi-Alpha Sigma Boule; Guardsman, 33 degree Mason; dir,NY City Municiple Water Finance Authority; trustee, North General Hospital NY City; vice chmn, Apollo Theater found;dir, Harlem NY. **Honors/Awds:** Commander Honor Legion, NYPD,1950; lay reader NY Diocese Epsicopal Church,1960-; William A Dawson Award, Cong Black Caucus, 1988; Trustee of the Year Award, United Hospital Fund,1993. **Military Serv:** AUS corpl, 1942-46. **Home Addr:** 187-10 Ilion Ave, Jamaica, NY 11412.

HILL, BARBARA A
Consultant, association executive, chief executive officer. **Educ:** Ky State Univ, BS; Wash Univ, St Louis, MO, MS, social work. **Career:** Mich Womens Found, pres & chief exec officer, 2003-; Girl Scouts USA, consult; Nat Off YWCA, USA, consult; Girl Scouts Northern MI, chief exec officer; YWCA, Metropolitan Detroit, chief exec officer; Women Cos Bus Initiative, Milwaukee, WI, chief exec officer; Detroit Empowerment Zone Develop Corp, consult. **Orgs:** Bd trustees, Grant Allocation Comn; Alliance Women Entrepreneurs. **Business Addr:** President, Chief Executive Officer, Michigan Womens Foundation (MWF), 17177 N Laurel Pk Dr Suite 161, Livonia, MI 48152, **Business Phone:** (734)542-3946.*

HILL, BARBARA ANN
Educator. **Personal:** Born Mar 31, 1950, Brooklyn, NY; daughter of Robert Floyd and Delphine Chaplin Floyd; married Larry Hill; children: Vaughn, Kinshasa. **Educ:** Long Island Univ CW Post Ctr, BS, 1974, MS, 1984. **Career:** Howard T Herber Middle Sch, educator; parent involvement Coordr, Tyrrell County Pub Schs, Columbia NC; Columbia HS & MS, Columbia, NC, physical educ teacher. **Orgs:** NY State Pub High Sch Athletic Asn, 1976-92; found, adv, Malverne Girls Varsity Club, 1976-92; track champ Nassau Co HS Girls Track, 1978-84; Nassau Girls Athletic Rep, 1979-92; Black Educator Coalition Malverne HS, 1984-92; found & adv Carter G Woodson Black Studies Club, 1984-92; sec Nassau Co Volleyball Coaches Asn, 1985-87; workshop crd Hempstead Pre-K Reading Workshop, 1984-91; pres, Ludlum PTA, 1985-89; corresponding secy, Nassau County High Sch Athletic Asn, 1990-92; representative, Nassau County High Sch Athletic Coun, 1987-92; treas, PTA, 1990-92; Key Women America Inc, 1986-92, vip, 1990-92; treas, Ludlum PTA, 1989-92; pres, Alberta B Gray-Schultz Middle Sch PTA, 1991-92; Tyrell Elem Sch Parents Planning comn, 1992-93; Community Voices, 1992-95; Church Road Emergency Food Closet, Food Pantry, chair person, 1994; Black Hist Club Prog, Columbia HS & MS, found, adv, 1992-; NC Breast Cancer Screening Program, secy, Tyrrell County Lay Community Adv Bd, 1994-01; NCP, secy, 1998-. **Honors/Awds:** Coach of the Year, 1984, 5 time coach County Championship Track & Field Girls, 1976-79, 1984; eight times Girls Track & Field Divisional & Conference Champions; Nassau County Class C Volleyball Champions, 1992; NY State Volleyball Championship Sportsmanship Award, 1992; NC Governor's Volunteer Award for Children, 1994; Tobacco Belt Volleyball Tournament Champions, 1996, 1998, 2001; Volleyball Coach of the Year, 1996, 1997, 2001. **Business Addr:** Physical Education Teacher, Columbia High School, PO Box 419, Columbia, NC 27925, **Business Phone:** (252)796-8161.*

HILL, BETTY J.
Manager. **Personal:** Born Aug 11, 1948; married. **Educ:** Los Angeles Harbor Jr Col, AA, 1970; Calif State Univ, BA, 1973. **Career:** Compton Urban Corps, counr, 1973-74, chief counselor, 1974-75; City of Compton Urban Corps, asst dir, 1975-76, urban corps dir, 1976-78; City of Compton, manpower program chief, 1978-80, manpower programs dir, 1980-. **Orgs:** Employment Training Adv Comt, Nat Asn Female Execs; Veterans Comn, Compton Nat Asn Adv Colored People; Prime Agent Coun, Los Angeles Reg Coalition Serv Providers; Human Resources Develop Comn; United Way Southeast Agency Exec Comt; Nat Forum for Black Publ Adminrs; Young Men's Christian Asn. **Business Addr:** Manpower Program Director, City of Compton, 205 S Willowbrook Ave, Compton, CA 90220.*

HILL, BOB. **See HILL, ROBERT LEWIS.**

HILL, BOBBY L
Government official. **Personal:** Widowed. **Educ:** Wayne State Univ, BS, bus admin, 1971, educ specialist cert, 1974; Eastern Mich Univ, MA, educ admin, 1973. **Career:** Mt Clemens Community Schs, teacher admin, retired; -; Real Estate Investor, 1980-; United Memorial Funeral Home, partner, 1985; Community Cent Bank, bd dir, dir emer, currently; Macomb County, bd comnr. **Orgs:** Trustee, N Broadway Church Christ; chmn, Midwestern Christian Inst Bd Dir; Mt Clemens Found; Macomb County Comn Growth Aliance; Macomb County Br NAACP Exec Comn. **Honors/Awds:** Ameritech Trail Blazer Award, 1998. **Military Serv:** USAF, retired, 20 yrs. **Home Addr:** 37552 Charter Oaks Blvd, Clinton Township, MI 48036, **Home Phone:** (586)463-5947. **Business Addr:** Director Emeritus, Community Central Bank Corporation, 120 N Main St, Mt Clemens, MI 48043, **Business Phone:** (586)783-4500.

HILL, BRUCE EDWARD
Football player. **Personal:** Born Feb 29, 1964, Fort Dix, NJ. **Educ:** Ariz State Univ, attended. **Career:** Football player (retired); Tampa Bay Buccaneers, wide receiver, 1987-91.

HILL, CALVIN G.
Businessperson, consultant. **Personal:** Born Jan 2, 1947, Baltimore, MD; son of Henry and Elizabeth; married Janet McDonald; children: Grant. **Educ:** Yale Univ, BA, 1969; Southern Methodist Univ, Perkins Sch Theol, 1969-71. **Career:** Dallas Cowboys, running back, 1969-74, team consult, currently; Hawaiians WFL, running back, 1975; Wash Redskins, 1976-77; Cleveland Browns, 1978-81; Baltimore Orioles, vpres/admin personnel, 1987, bd dir; NFL Cleveland Browns, consult; Alexander & Assoc Inc, consult; Peace Corp, spec asst dir; Pepper Co, Pub Rel Rep & Nat Good Will ambassador; Dallas Bank & Trust, Dallas, Tex, com loan officer & asst vpres; Jarvis Christian Col, Hawkins, Tex, develop dir; Bethlehem Steel Co, labor rel Rep; Fleet Financial Serv Providence, RI, consult, currently; Cleveland Browns Football Club, consult, currently; Alexander & Assoc Inc, Washington, DC, consult, currently. **Orgs:** Yale Club Wash, DC; exec bd, Yale Develop Bd; Yale Univ Coun, 1982-86; adv bd, Rand Corp Drug Policy Res Ctr; Delta Kappa Epsilon Fraternity; Battel Chapel Deacons; St Elmo's Soc; Black Stud Yale; Md Athletic Hall Fame. **Honors/Awds:** Pro Bowl NFL All-Star Game, 1969, 1972, 1973-74; NFL Rookie of the Year, 1969; Sporting News NFL Estrn Conf All-Star Team, 1969; All NFL Pro Football Writers America, 1969, 1973; NFL Champ Games, 1970-71; 1000 Yard Club, 1972; Sporting News NFC All-Star, 1973; Jordan Oliver Award; Chester Pla Roche Scholarship. **Business Addr:** Consultant, Alexander & Associates Inc, 4400 Jenifer St NW, Washington, DC 20015, **Business Phone:** (202)237-8686.

HILL, CLARA GRANT
Educator, executive. **Personal:** Born Oct 5, 1928, Hugo, OK. **Educ:** Philander Smith Col, BA, 1952; Memphis State Univ, MA. **Career:** Long view Elem Sch, chairperson, sixth grade teachers, 1963-77, teacher, 1985; Memphis Educ Asn, faculty rep, 1963-; Prof Growth Comt, chairperson,1973-; acting prin, 1972-77. **Orgs:** Comt mem, Curriculum Develop Elem Ed, appointed St Comn Educ, 1977; Memphis Ed Asn; W TN Ed Asn; TN Ed Asn; Nat Ed Asn; exec bd MEA, 1973-76; chairperson, memship comn MEA, 1974-76; chairperson, Status Women Educ MEA, 1977; chairperson, Screening Comt Hiring Staff MEA, 1977-78; chairperson, Black Caucus MEA, 1977; Credentials Comn TEA, 1976; Resultants Comn TEA, 1977; pres, Dept Classroom Teachers TEA, 1976-78; NAACP; exec bd mem, chairperson, Xmas Seals, 1975-76; basileus Sigma Gamma Rho Sor, 1973-75; chairperson, Outstanding Sigma Woman Year, 1973-74; memship Comn Reg & Nat Chapters Sor; YWCA; pres, Optimistic Chartable Soc Club, 1969; Philander Smith Alum Asn; chairperson, Constitution Comt, 1976; pres Les Demonselles Club, 1972; community weeker Heart Fund; Cancer Fund; Birth Defects; teacher Sun Sch, 1964-; pres, Usher Bd, 1972; dir, Chrian Ed, 1966-67; adv, Jr Usher Bd, 1970-; chairperson, Birth month Fellowship, 1973; Ada Cir Missionary Soc; pres, Dept Classroom Teacher TEA, 1977. **Honors/Awds:** Five Outstanding Service Awards, MEA, 1974-77; Leadership Training Award, NEA, 1976; two Community Service Awards, US Congressman Harold Ford TN, 1976-77. *

HILL, COLIN C
Executive. **Educ:** Va Tech Univ, BS, physics; McGill Univ, MS, physics; Cornell Univ, MS, physics. **Career:** Gene Network Sci Inc, chief exec officer, pres, chmn & co-founder, 2000-. **Honors/Awds:** Rising Star Award, Black Enterprise, 2004. **Special Achievements:** Appeared in numerous publications & television segments including The Wall Street Jour, CNBC Morning Call, Nature, Wired, & Economist; named to MIT Technology Review's TR100 list of the top innovators in the world under the age of 35, 2004. **Business Addr:** Chairman & Co-Founder, Chief Executive Officer & President, Gene Network Sciences Inc, 53 Brown Rd, Ithaca, NY 14850, **Business Phone:** (607)257-0332.

HILL, CURTIS T., SR.
Educator, insurance agent, politician. **Personal:** Born Jun 30, 1929, Vernon, OK; son of Curtis L and Virginia; married; children: Sonya L & Curtis. **Educ:** BS, 1950; Dent Tech, 1953; Adviced Life Ins, 1971. **Career:** St Farm Ins Co, agent; Jr High Sch, teacher. **Orgs:** Nat Asn Life Underwriters; vpres, Elkhart Co Life Underwriters; pres, Nat Asn Advan Colored People Chap; pres, Elkhart Urban League; bd dir, Am Cancer Soc; Nat Black Caucus Sch Bd Mem; former life mem chair, Elkhart Nat Asn Advan Colored People; former bd mem, Jaycees; Elkhart Sch Bd; Life Ins Millionaires Club, 1972. **Honors/Awds:** Outstanding Historian Award, Ind Jaycees, 1960; Award for Outstanding Contribution to Education, Ind Sch Bd Asn, 1974. **Special Achievements:** First black candidate for Mayor of Elkhart. **Military Serv:** AUS Res, col (retired). **Business Addr:** Agent, State Farm Insurance Company, 2408 S Nappanee St, Elkhart, IN 46514.

HILL, CYNTHIA D
Lawyer. **Personal:** Born Feb 5, 1952, Bethesda, MD; daughter of Melvin Leroy and Mamie L Landrum. **Educ:** Wellesley Col, BA, 1974; Georgetown Univ Law Ctr, JD, 1977. **Career:** DC Office Consumer Protection, law clerk to admin law judge, 1977-78; League Women Voters Educ Fund, staff atty litigation dept, 1978-84, acting dir litigation dept, 1984-85, dir election serv & litigation, 1985-90; DC Bar, asst exec dir, progs, 1990-. **Orgs:** Admitted to DC Bar; Women's Div Nat Bar Asn, 1977-, Wash Bar Asn, 1978-, Women's Bar Asn, DC, 1979-, Wash Coun Lawyers, 1986-2006; bd dirs, Metro Wash Planning & Housing Asn, 1980-89; Am Soc Asn Execs, 1990-; Nat Asn Bar Execs, 1990-, bd dirs, 1998-2000; Asn Continuing Legal Educ, 1991-; bd dirs, Friends Nat Parks, Gettysburg Inc, 2001-06; mbrshp comte, Gettysburg Fdtn, 2006-. **Honors/Awds:** Phi Beta Kappa. **Business Addr:** Assistant Executive Director for Programs, District of Columbia Bar, 1250 H St NW 6th Fl, Washington, DC 20005-5937, **Business Phone:** (202)737-4700.

HILL, DEBORAH
Labor relations manager. **Personal:** Born Oct 15, 1944, Long Beach, CA; daughter of David and Eva. **Educ:** Calif State Col Long Beach, BA, 1967; Western State Univ Col Law, JD, 1975. **Career:** Shell Oil Co, analyst, 1968-76, sr emp rel analyst, 1976-78, employee rel rep, 1978-82, employee rel asn, 1982-85, serv mgr, 1985-86, sr employee rel rep 1986; human resources mgr. **Orgs:** Chmn, personnel commun, Alpha Kappa Alpha Sor Inc, 1982-86; historian, Intl Asn Personnel Women, 1983; Top Ladies Distinction, 1980-; trustee, bd Wesley Chapel AME Church, 1983-; Links, Inc 1986-; Leadership Long Beach, 1990; bd dir, NCCJ, 1990-; bd dir, CRI, 1990-; bd dirs, trust fund comt mem, State Bar CA, 1991; bd dirs, Bouggess White Scholar Fund, 1990-91.United Way, 1991-. **Business Addr:** Manager, Equilon Enterprises Shell LLC, Human Resources, 20945 S Wilmington Ave, Carson, CA 90810-1039, **Business Phone:** (310)816-2160.

HILL, DEIRDRE HUGHES
Lawyer. **Personal:** Married. **Educ:** Univ Calif, Santa Barbara, BA, polit sci; Loyola Law Sch, JD, 1985. **Career:** Los Angeles Police Dept, inspector gen; Los Angeles Police Comn, pres, 1993-96; Saltzburg, Ray & Bergman LLP, sr assoc, 1990-98; Pvt pract, atty, currently. **Orgs:** State Calif, Calif Sci Ctr Bd Dir, currently. **Business Phone:** (310)481-6700.

HILL, DENNIS ODELL
Educator, basketball coach. **Personal:** Born Nov 25, 1953, Kansas City, KS; son of Buster and Yvonne Marie Bennett James; married Kathryn Kinnear Hill, Sep 4, 1982; children: Erica Nicole & Anthony Jerome. **Educ:** Southwest Mo State Univ, Springfield, MO, BS, 1976. **Career:** Southwest MO State, Springfield, MO, asst basketball coach, 1978-89; Pittsburg State Univ, Pittsburg, KS, head basketball coach, 1989-. **Honors/Awds:** Distinguished Community Service Award, Nat Asn Advan Colored People, Springfield Br, 1988. **Business Addr:** Head Coach, Pittsburg State University, Men, 1701 S Broadway, Pittsburg, KS 66762, **Business Phone:** (316)235-4648.

HILL, DIANNE
Educator. **Personal:** Born Mar 6, 1955, Newark, NJ; children: Tania Regina & Gary Robert. **Educ:** Caldwell Col, BA, 1977; Rutgers Univ, cert, 1982; Jersey City State Col, MA, 1985. **Career:** Newark Bd Educ, teacher, 1976-77; Friendly Fuld Headstart Prog, teacher, policy comm mem, 1977-80; Educ Opportunity Prof Asn, pub rels officer, 1982-86; Caldwell Col, dir educ oppor fund prog, 1980-. **Orgs:** Mem policy coun, Friendly Fuld Headstart, 1983-85; bd mem, Irvington Community Develop, 1985-86, Women's Employ Network; pvt sector rep, Asn Independent Cols & Univs NJ. **Honors/Awds:** Outstanding Black Women of the Year, 1985; Outstanding Alumnae Award, Caldwell Coll BSCU & Faculty, 1985. **Business Addr:** Director, Caldwell College, Ryerson Ave, Caldwell, NJ 07006, **Business Phone:** (201)228-4424.

HILL, DONNA. See NICHOLAS, DENISE.

HILL, DONNA
Writer. **Personal:** Born Aug 6, 1955, Brooklyn, NY; divorced; children: Nichole, Dawne & Matthew. **Educ:** Attended Pace Univ. **Career:** Kianga House, dir, 1988-92; Brooklyn Teen Pregnancy Network, exec dir, 1992-94; Author, romance novels including: Rooms of the Heart, 1990; Indiscretions, 1991; Temptation, 1994; Intimate Betrayal, 1997; Charade, 1998; Chances Are, 1998; Interlude, 1999, Rhythms, 2001; Rockin' Around That Christmas Tree: A Holiday Novel, 2003, Dark Thirst: An Anthology, 2004, Getting Hers, 2005, Guilty Pleasures, 2006, If I Were Your Woman, 2007; co-wrote screenplay, Fire, 2000, Steele-Perkins Lit Agency, currently. **Orgs:** Black Writers Alliance; Novelist Inc; Romance Writers Am. **Honors/Awds:** Community Service Award, Dept Children's Servs, 1993; named Hon State Senator, mayor Lake Charles, LA, 1999; Career Achievement Award, Romantic Times Mag, 1998, 2000. **Special Achievements:** featured in Essence, The Daily News, USA Today, Today's Black Woman, and Black Enterprise magazine. **Business Addr:** Author, Pattie Steele-Perkins, 26 Island Lane, Canandiagua, NY 14424, **Business Phone:** (716)396-9290.

HILL, DULE (KARIM DULE HILL)
Actor, dancer. **Personal:** Born May 3, 1975, East Brunswick, NJ; son of Bert and Jennifer; married Nicole Lyn, Jul 10, 2004. **Educ:** Seton Hall Univ. **Career:** Appeared in numerous commercials; stage roles: Bring in 'da Noise, Bringin 'da Funk; Shenandoah; Films: Sugar Hill, 1993; She's All That, 1999;Men of Honor, 2000; television guest appearances: All My Children; Cosby;Smart Guy; Whisper, 2007; Remarkable Power, 2007; Tv movies: "The Ditchdigger's Daughters", 1997; "Color of Justice", 1997; "Love Songs", 1999; "10.5", 2004; Tv series: "The West Wing", 1999-; "Good Old Boy: A Delta Boyhood", 1988; "The More You Know", 1989; "City Kids", "Ghostwriter: To Catch a Creep: Part 1", 1993; "Sugar Hill?, 1994; "New York News: New York News-","New York Undercover: CAT", 1995; "Cosby: Shall We Dance?", 1997; "Color of Justice, The Ditchdiggers Daughters", 1997; "Smart Guy: Gotta Dance", 1998; "The West Wing: Mr. Willis of Ohio"; "The West Wing: The Crackpots &These Women", "The West Wing: Five Votes Down", "The West Wing: A Proportional Response", "The West Wing", "Chicken Soup for the Soul: Mother's Day", 1999; Love Songs, Shes All That, 1999; "The West Wing: Take This Sabbath Day", 2000; Men of Honor, 2000; "The West Wing: Isaac &Ishmael", "Mad TV:", 2001; "The West Wing: 100,000 Airplanes", "The West Wing: 20 Hours in America: Part 1", 2002; Holes, 2003; "The West Wing: Abuel Banat", "Punk'd:", "The West Wing: Twenty Five", 2003; "The West Wing:No Exit", "The West Wing: The Supremes", "The West Wing: Eppur Si Muove","The West Wing: The Warfare of Genghis Khan", "The West Wing: The Benign Prerogative", 2004; Sexual Life, Edmond, The Numbers, 2005; Edmond, 2005; "Psych", "The West Wing: Welcome to Wherever You Are", 2006; "Hellion, The Guardian",2006; actor, tap dancer, currently. **Honors/Awds:** Dule Hill Day declared Chicago, 1986; screen actors guild awards, 2001, 2002. **Home Addr:** 9100 Wilshire Blvd W Twr 6th FL, Beverly Hills, CA 90212, **Home Phone:** (310)248-6117. **Business Addr:** Actor, Warner Bros Studios, Warner Bros Television, 4000 Warner Blvd, Burbank, CA 91505, **Business Phone:** (818)954-6000.

HILL, ERIC
Football player, president (organization). **Personal:** Born Nov 14, 1966, Blytheville, AR; children: Erica & Arielle. **Educ:** La State Univ. **Career:** Football player (retired), pres; Phoenix Cardinals, linebacker, 1989-93; Ariz Cardinals, 1994-97; St Louis Rams, 1998; San Diego Chargers, linebacker, 1999; Eric Hill Nissan, owner & pres, currently. **Business Phone:** 888-447-5216.

HILL, ESTHER P.
Educator. **Personal:** Born Jun 7, 1922, Rocky Mount, NC; married Samuel W; children: Samesta Elaine. **Educ:** Columbia Univ, BS, 1943, MA, 1954; NY Univ, PhD, 1962. **Career:** Charlotte-Mecklenburg Schs, art teacher, asst supvr, cons, prog asst,1951-72; Univ NC Charlotte, assoc prof art, 1972, prof emer, currently, prof exhibitor prints, jewelry & paintings. **Orgs:** Chmn, Div Higher Ed, NC Art Ed Asn, 1979-81; reg rep, NAEA Com Minority Concerns 1978-81; life mem, NEA; Am Asn Univ Women; Phi Delta Kappa; Alpha Kappa Alpha Sorority; Moles; nat pres, Guys & Dolls Inc; bd trustees, Mint Mus Art. **Honors/Awds:** Service Award, Plaque Guys & Dolls; Doctoral Award, NC Bd Govs, 1979-80; Spirit Square Honoree for Contributions in Arts, Afro-Am Cult Ctr, Gala Celebration, 1981. **Home Addr:** 1624 Madison Ave, Charlotte, NC 28216, **Home Phone:** (704)334-4802. **Business Addr:** Professor Emerita, University of North Carolina, 9201 Univ City Blvd, Charlotte, NC 28223-0001, **Business Phone:** (704)687-2000.*

HILL, FREDERICK W
Educator, vice president (organization). **Educ:** Univ Pittsburgh, BA, 1975, JD, 1978. **Career:** Univ Pittsburgh, adj prof; McDonnell Douglas corp, vpres commun; Chase Manhattan Bank, exec vpres; JP Morgan Chase & Co, exec vpres, 2004; FW Hill LLC, currently. **Orgs:** Mem bd trustees, Univ Pittsburgh; bd dirs, Ad Coun. **Honors/Awds:** Won several awards for teaching excellence. *

HILL, DR. GEORGE C.
Educator. **Personal:** Born Feb 19, 1939, Moorestown, NJ; married Linda; children: Yvette, Kevin, Nicole & Brian. **Educ:** Rutgers Univ, BS, 1961; Howard Univ, MS, 1963; New York Univ, PhD, 1967. **Career:** Squibb Inst Med Res, res invstr 1969-71; Univ Cambridge, Eng, NIH spl res fel, 1971-72; Univ Ky Med Ctr, NIH post-doctoral fellow 1967-69; Colo State Univ, assoc, 1972-85; Meharry Med Col, dir, div biomed sci, vpres,int prog; Vanderbilt Univ, assoc dean diversity med educ, Levi Watkins Jr prof diversity med educ, prof med educ & admin prof, currently. **Orgs:** AAAS; Am Inst Bio Sci; Am Soc Protozoologists; Am Soc Parasitologists;Soc Biological Chem; Sigma Xi; Inst Med Nat Acad Sci; fel, Am Acad Microbiol, 2002. **Honors/Awds:** NIH Research Career Development Award, 1974-79. **Business Addr:** Associate Dean for Diversity, Vanderbilt University, Office for Diversity in Medical Education, 301 Light Hall, Nashville, TN 37235, **Business Phone:** (615)322-7498.

HILL, GEORGE CALVIN
Physician. **Personal:** Born Aug 29, 1925, Johnstown, PA; son of George C and Mosetta Pollard; married Valentine Kay Johnson, Jun 12, 1959; children: Georgia Anne, Janet Marietta & Ellen Valentine. **Educ:** Univ Pittsburgh, PA, BS, 1948; MS, 1954; Meharry Med Col, Nashville, TN, MD, 1954-58. **Career:** Harper Grace Staff, jr attend, 1976; Hutzel Hosp, jr attend, 1974; Brent Gen Hosp, sr attend, 1972; Harper Hosp, 1971; Detroit Gen Hosp, 1971; Wayne St & Med Sch, asst lectr, 1971; Pvt Pract, 1966-69; VA Hosp, staff surg, 1966; Dearborn, 1965-66; Saginaw Mi, 1964-

65; Am Bd Surg, diplo, 1964; Dearborn VA Hosp, instr, 1963-64; gen surg res, 1959-63; Mercy Hosp, internship, 1958-59; self employed Detroit, MI, surgeon, 1966-87; Chrysler Corp, Detroit, MI, plant physician, 1983-91; Detroit Edison, dir of med staff, 1991-95; Ford Motor Co, plant physician; assoc area med dir, Great Lakes area, currently. **Orgs:** Am Col Surgeons; Am Trauma Soc; Int Col Surgeons; Detroit Surg Asn; Detroit Surg Soc; diplomate Am Bd Surg; Am Med Writers Asn; Am Med Asn; Wayne Co Med Soc; Nat Med Asn; Detroit Med Soc; Wolverine Med Soc Speakers Bur; Am Cancer Soc; bd dirs, United Health Org, 1985-; chmn, Comm Occupational Health Safety, Wayne Co Med Soc, 1989-. **Honors/Awds:** Dr. Clarke McDermont Award, 1962, 1963, Chi Delta Mu, 1957. **Military Serv:** USN, 1944-46; AUS, Med Corp, Active Reserve, col, 1983-; Oper Desert Storm, 1990-91; retired 1995. **Home Addr:** 4082 St Andrews Ct, Bloomfield Hills, MI 48302-1774. **Business Addr:** Associate Area Medical Director, 1401 W Fort St, Detroit, MI 48233-8442, **Business Phone:** (313)234-8820.

HILL, GEORGE HIRAM
Executive. **Personal:** Born Apr 13, 1940, Detroit, MI; married Alma Matney; children: Dylan Foster. **Educ:** Wayne State Univ, BA,polit sci, 1962. **Career:** MI Bell Telephone Co, comn consult employ supr & comn supvr, 1963-68; Asst Negro Youth Campaign, exec dir, 1967; Job Oppty Line WJBK-TV, host, 1968-73; Chrysler Corp, labor rel supr & corp personnel staff, 1968-71; Diversified Chem Technol, founder & pres, chmn & cheif exec officer, 1971-. **Orgs:** Treasr, Greater Detroit Chamber Com; bd advs, Univ Detroit Bus Sch; bd mem, MI Minority Bus Develop Corp, 1976-91; secy, Nat Asn Black Automotive Suppliers, 1990; bd adv, Detroit Literacy Volunteers Am; Mich Minority Chem Asn; -adv bd mem, Kraft Foods MBE ; adv bd mem, Procter & Gamble MBE; adv bd mem, Ford Motor Co MBE. **Honors/Awds:** Jr Achievement Award, 1973; Citation Distinguished & Significant Contributions, Wayne Co Community Col; Minority Business man of the Year, State MI, 1978; Outstanding Small Business man of the Year, State MI, 1979. **Special Achievements:** First Black person on a regularly scheduled TV show in the Detroit area, 1968; Honored by Boy Scouts of Am MI Dist, 1973; Sponsor of the First USA competition for Cass Technical High School. **Business Addr:** President and Chief Executive Officer, Founder, Diversified Chemical Technologies Inc, 15477 Woodrow Wilson, Detroit, MI 48238.*

HILL, GILBERT R.
Government official. **Personal:** Born Jan 1, 1931; married Delores Hooks. **Career:** Detroit Police Dept, Detroit, MI, police officer comdr, 1959-89; actor, Beverly Hills Cop, 1985; Detroit City Coun, Detroit, MI, city coun mem, 1990, pres. **Honors/Awds:** Played Sgt Gilbert Todd in Beverly Hills Cop, 1984; Beverly Hills Cop II, 1987; Beverly Hills Cop III, 1994.

HILL, GLENALLEN
Baseball player. **Personal:** Born Mar 22, 1965, Santa Cruz, CA; married Lori; children: Simone, Chanel & Heleyna. **Educ:** Ariz State Univ. **Career:** Baseball player (retired), baseball coach; Toronto Blue Jays, outfielder, 1989-91; Cleveland Indians, 1991-93; Chicago Cubs, 1993-94, 1998-2000; San Francisco Giants, 1995-97; Seattle Mariners, 1998; NY Yankees, 2000; Anaheim Angels, 2001; Modesto Nuts, hitting coach; Calif & Carolina League All-Star Game, coach, 2006; Colorado Rockies, first base coach, 2006-. **Honors/Awds:** World Series Champion, NY Yankees, 2000. **Business Addr:** First Base Coach, Colorado Rockies, Coors Field, 2001 Blake St, Denver, CO 80205-2000, **Business Phone:** (303)292-0200.

HILL, GRANT HENRY
Basketball player. **Personal:** Born Oct 5, 1972, Dallas, TX; son of Calvin and Janet; married Tamia, Jul 24, 1999; children: Myla Grace. **Educ:** Duke Univ. **Career:** Detroit Pistons, forward, 1994-2000; Orlando Magic, 2000-07; Phoenix Suns, 2007-. **Orgs:** Dillard Univ, Malcolm McDonald Scholar Fund, co-founder. **Honors/Awds:** NBA Co-rookie of the Year, 1995; NBA All-Rookie First Team, 1995; NBA All-Star, 1995-98; All-NBA First Team, 1997; IBM Award, 1997; Gold Medal, US Olympic Basketball Team, 1996; Henry Iba Award, Best Collegiate Defensive Player, 1992; Atlantic Coast Conf Player of the Year, 1992; Community Serv Award; NBA Sportsmanship Award, 2005. **Business Addr:** Professional Basketball Player, Phoenix Suns, 201 E Jefferson St, Orlando, AZ 85004, **Business Phone:** (602)379-7900.

HILL, GREGORY LAMONTE
Football player. **Personal:** Born Feb 23, 1972, Dallas, TX; children: jordan. **Educ:** Univ Tex, A&M. **Career:** Kans City Chiefs, running back, 1994-97; St Louis Rams, 1998; Detroit Lions, 1998. **Orgs:** Founder, Greg Hill Time Charitable Found. **Honors/Awds:** NCAA freshman debut record.

HILL, HATTIE
Consultant, executive. **Personal:** Born Jul 6, 1958, Marianna, AR; daughter of Carrie Flowers; married Terry, Nov 22, 1984. **Educ:** Ark State Univ, BA, educ, 1977, MA, coun, 1981. **Career:** TX Rehab Comn, dir training, rehab counr; Hattie Hill Enterprises, founder & chief exec officer, currently. **Orgs:** Am Bus Women's Asn, 1986-90; co-founder, Vision 100; Dallas Women Together, 1989-; Nat Asn Women Bus Owners, 1992-; Dallas Women's Convenant, 1993-; bd mem, Leadership Am, 1993-; exec bd mem, Trinity Med Ctr, 1994-97; African Am Women Entrepreneurs Inc, 1994-; adv bd mem, YWCA Dallas Women's Ctr, 1994-; bd, Presbyterian Hosp; Women's Museum; adv bd,YWCA Metrop Dallas; Soc Int Bus Fel; Fed Res Bank Dallas; Goizueta Bus Sch Emory Univ; Nat African Am Women's Leadership Inst; adv bd, Wyndham Int External Diversity; adv bd, Orleans Customer; vice chmn, mktg & chap rels, MPI Found Bd Trustees, currently. **Honors/Awds:** Today's Dallas Woman of the Year, Today's Dallas Woman, 1995; Best & Brightest African American Business Woman, Dollars & Sense Mag, 1993, Hall of Fame, 1994; Forty Under Forty, Dallas Bus Jour, 1994; Leading Women of the Future, Mirabella Mag; Entrepreneur of the Year, Quest for Success, 2000; Louise Raggio Pathfinder Award, 2001; 25 Most Influential People in the Meeting's Industry, Meeting News Magazine. **Special Achievements:** Articles: "Sensitivity Training: Do it Right!," Texas Banking, May 1994; "South Africa: The Good, The Bad & the Ugly, "Sharing Ideas, Dec 1992; "Tip Off: Diversity," Dallas Business Journal; numerous other article & interviews; author: Women Who Carry Their Men; Smart Women, Smart Choices, Named Hot 25 Speakers by Successful Meetings Magazine; nominee for "Entrepreneurial Excellence". **Business Addr:** Chief Executive Officer, Hattie Hill Enterprises Inc, 5220 Spring Valley St 340, PO Box 802967, Dallas, TX 75380-2967, **Business Phone:** (972)473-3003.

HILL, HENRY, JR.
Banker. **Personal:** Born Mar 19, 1935, Nashville, TN; married Mary E Hill; children: Michael E, Terrill E, Veronica E. **Educ:** Weaver Sch Real Est, cert; Am Inst Banking, dipl, 1981. **Career:** Citizens Savings Bank & Trust Co, br mgr/loan officer, 1963-76, exec vpres, 1976-84, interim pres/interim chief exec officer, 1984, pres/chief exec officer, 1984-. **Orgs:** bd dir, Better Bus Bureau; bd dir, Am Inst Banking; bd dir, Citizens Savings Bank & Trust Co; bd dir, March Dimes Birth Defectd Found; chmn, bd dir, S St Community Ctr; chmn, trustees, bd, Progressive Bapt Ch; Nat Asn Negro Bus & Prof Women's Club Inc, 1986; Jefferson St, Nashville. **Honors/Awds:** Certificate of Appreciation, S St Community Ctr, 1980; Man of the Year, 1986; Graduate of Leadership, Nashville. **Special Achievements:** Profiled in newspaper Nashville Banner, 1984; Profiled in newspaper Nashville Tennessean, 1984. **Business Addr:** President, Chief Executive Officier, Citizens Savings Bank & Trust Company, 1917 Heiman St, Nashville, TN 37208-2409.

HILL, JACQUELINE R
Lawyer. **Personal:** Born May 23, 1940, Topeka, KS; daughter of Boyd Alexander Hill and Noblesse Armenta Demoss Lansdowne; divorced; children: Dana Alesse Jamison. **Educ:** Univ CA Berkeley, BA 1962; Univ Southern CA, Teachers Credential 1966; Southwestern Univ Sch Law, JD, 1972; Calif State Univ, Long Beach, Cert Calligraphy, 1989; W Los Angeles Communiyt Col, Cert Med Billing, 1998. **Career:** Univ Calif Lawrence Radiation Lab, admin exec, 1963-66; LA Unified Sch Dist, math teacher, 1966-73; LA Comm Col Dist, instr, 1972-75; Los Angeles County, dep dist atty, 1973-99; Calif State Univ, Long Beach, instr, 1990-91; Jacque All Trades, pres, 1990, Los Angeles County Dist Atty Off, atty, currently. **Orgs:** Alpha Kappa Alpha Sorority; Calif State Bar; Am Bar Asn; Calif State Adv Group Juvenile Justice & Delinquency Prev, 1983-95. **Honors/Awds:** Legal Book Awards, Southwestern Univ Sch Law, 1969-72. **Business Addr:** Attorney, Los Angeles County District Attorney Office, 18th Fl Suite 301, 210 W Temple St, Los Angeles, CA 90012, **Business Phone:** (213)974-3611.

HILL, JAMES, JR.
Accountant. **Personal:** Born Aug 20, 1941, Baltimore, MD; married Carole Jones, Feb 19, 1972; children: James III & Brian. **Educ:** Central State Col, BS, 1964; Univ Chicago, MBA, (Personnel, Admin & Acct), 1967. **Career:** Union Carbon, cost acct, 1964-65; Alexander Grant & Co, auditor, 1967-69; Chicago Econ Develop Corp, dep dir, 1968-70; Hill Taylor LLC, managing partner, 1972-. **Orgs:** Bd dirs Chicago Commons Assoc, 1970; various comms Am Inst CPAs, 1977; state bd acct StateIL, 1980; bd dirs, IL CPA Soc, 1983-86, Provident Hosp, 1983-86, treas, Better Govt Assoc, 1990-91; lifetime mem, Kappa Alpha Psi Fraternity; Citizen Info Serv; bd dir, Economic Club Chicago; Japan Am Soc; bd trustees, IL Inst Techol; adv comt, Univ Chicago Bus Sch; bd dir, FRAC. **Honors/Awds:** Certificate of Apppreciation, Nat Asn Real Estate Brokers; Cert Merit, Central State Univ Alumni Asn; Outstanding Prof Achievement, Central State Univ; Distinguished Serv Award, Coun Community Serv; Little Gold Oilcan Award, Chicago Econ Develop Corp; Certificate of Apppreciation, Chicago State Univ; Whos Who in the Midwest; Outstanding Young Men Am. **Home Phone:** (312)587-7936. **Business Addr:** Managing Partner, Hill Taylor LLC, 116 S Michigan Ave 11th Fl, Chicago, IL 60603, **Business Phone:** (312)332-4964.

HILL, JAMES A., JR.
Lawyer, government official. **Personal:** Born Apr 23, 1947, Atlanta, GA; married CJ Van Pelt; children: Jennifer Joy. **Educ:** Mich State Univ, BA, 1969; Ill Univ, MBA, 1971, JD, 1974. **Career:** Judge Adv Gen Corp, 1972; Bankers Trust Co, 1970; State Oregon, state treas, 1992; Ore Dept Revenue, hearing officer; Ore Dept Justice, asst atty gen, law clerk; Ill Univ, Consortium Grad Study Bus Blacks fel; Oregon State, state rep & state sen. **Orgs:** Ore State Bar Asn, 1975-; Salem Ore Chap; Nat Asn Advan Colored People;charter mem, Ore Assembly Black Affairs. **Special Achievements:** First African-American State Official, 1992. *

HILL, DR. JAMES A, SR.
Educator, clergy. **Personal:** Born Jun 10, 1934, Chicago, IL; son of Robert E Hill Sr and Fannie M Whitney; divorced; children: Carl J, Jewell Davis, Fannie M, James A Jr & Robert E. **Educ:** Chicago Baptist Col, Sem Dept, 1959; Blackstone Sch Law, LLB, 1962; Am Bible & Divinity Col, ThM, 1966; Clarksville Sch Theol, BD, 1966, THD, 1979; St John's Univ, BA, 1974; Trinity Col, MS, 1976; Gradelupa Col & Sem, San Antonio, TX, DHum, 1988; Faith Evangelical Luthern Sem, Tacoma, WA, DMin, 1989. **Career:** Methodist CME Church, minister, 1950-; Wayne County EOE, dept dir, 1967-69; Wayne County Probation Dept, probation officer, 1969-72; Memphis Urban League, dept dir, 1975-80. **Orgs:** Gov's Comn Human Rights, Fairbanks Human Rels Coun; exec bd, Fairbanks USO, United Fund Comm; chmn, Boy Scouts Am; Fairbanks Ministerial Asn; Anchorage Ministerial Asn; Am Acad Polit & Soc Sci; asst state chaplain, Elks State MI Asn; asst grand chaplainn Elks Nat Asn IBPOE W; prof mem, Adult Educ Asn USA; life mem, AMVETS; Am Counrs Soc; Am Ministerial Asn; Nat Asn Social Workers Inc. **Honors/Awds:** Meritorious Service Certificate, Masonic Order; Meritorious Service Plaques, Inkster Br US Jaycees, 1967-68; Community Service Award, Hon Harold E Ford US Congressman, 1977; Man of the Year, Christian Info & Serv Ctr, 1988; Outstanding Big Brother Award, Angelina Co Juvenile Probation Serv, 1988; Outstanding Family & Community Serv, Hon Charles Wilson US Congressman, 1988; Letters Appreciation, Govs Comn Human Rights State AK; Letters Appreciation, Fairbanks Human Relations Coun; Nat Asn Advan Colored People State Level Serv; Letters of Appreciation, Univ AK; Letters of Appreciation, Mayor City Fairbanks, AK; Plaques, Eastern Star & Masonic Order; Meritorious Service Plaques, Golden Gate Lodge, Sunset Temple, IBPOE W; Certificate Appreciation, S Bend Urban league Oustanding Comn Leadership; Plaque, Laymen Chapel CME Church. **Special Achievements:** First & only black member of the clergy listed in the AK Literary Dir for the State of AK in 1964, Let's Study the Bible 1987, Evangelism for Today, 1985. **Home Addr:** 3733 Juneau St, PO Box 18616, Seattle, WA 98118. **Business Addr:** Minister, Curry Temple CME Church, 172 23rd Ave, Seattle, WA 98122, **Business Phone:** (206)325-9344.

HILL, JAMES H
Public relations executive. **Personal:** Born Aug 11, 1947, Toledo, OH; son of James Hill Sr and Cassie Hill; married Cynthia Carter, Mar 5, 1988; children: Jasmine Dianae. **Educ:** Ohio Univ, Athens OH, BS, jour, 1969; Ohio Univ Grad Sch, Athens OH, attended. **Career:** Owens-Corning Fiberglas, Toledo OH, merchandise supvr, 1970-75; WGTE-TV FM Pub Broadcasting, Toledo OH, dir pub info, 1975-77, producer/writer, 1977-80; S C Johnson, Racine WI, mgr opers, pub rels, 1980-82; Sara Lee Corp, Chicago IL, dir pub rels & communs, 1982-86; Burrell Pub Rels Inc, Chicago IL, pres & ceo, 1986-; Kaiser Found, Health Plan & Hosps, vp commun, 1995-; Hill Commun, pres, currently. **Orgs:** Bd mem, Nat Asn Advan Colored People/Toledo, 1973-75; PCC, 1983-; PRSA, 1983-; co-chmn fundraising, UNCF/Chicago, 1983, mem comt, 1985-; bd mem, C & Adolescent Forum, 1984-86, 1989-; BPRSA, 1985-; Econ Club Chicago, 1986-; bd mem, Travelers & Immigrant Aid, 1989-; pub rels adv comn, Chicago Urban League, 1989-; Oakland Chamber Com; E Bay Community Found; Oakland Mus Calif. **Honors/Awds:** Gold Trumpet, PCC, 1981; Silver Trumpet, PCC, 1981, 1986, 1989; CINE Golden Eagle, 1981; Gold Quil Award of Excellence and Merit, Int Asn Bus Communicator, 1984; Silver Anvil, Pub Rels Soc Am, 1986. **Business Addr:** President, Hill Communication, 111 Broadway Suite 101, Oakland, CA 94607-3730, **Business Phone:** (510)663-6155.

HILL, JAMES L
Association executive, administrator. **Personal:** Born Aug 21, 1928, Austin, TX; married Geraldine Holmes; children: Jacqueline (Howard). **Educ:** Huston-Tillotson Col, BA Ed 1953; Univ Tex, Med, 1962. **Career:** Adminr (retired); Abilene, guid counr, 1959-64; Pt Arthur, dir, pupil personnel, 1968-73, dir testing, 1964-68; CTB/MCGRAW Hill, Manchester MO, eval specialist, 1973-74; Tex state Bd Educ, dir, Off Urban Ed, dep Comnr, 1974-89; Univ Tex, assoc vpres, 1998-2002, exec dir, vpres community & sch rels, 2002-07. **Orgs:** Nat Educ Asn; Tex St Teacher Asn; Tex Personnersnl & Guid Asn; Am Personnel & Guid Asn; Phi Delta Kappa; past mem, bd dir Jefferson Co Ec Opportunity Comn; Tex Urban Adv Coun; Tex Urban Curric & Eval Couns; Huston-Tillotson Col. **Honors/Awds:** Special Alumni Award, 1972; Outstanding Achievement Award,Tex State Dist 50 Rep Dawnna Dukes, D-Austin, 1999; Austin Area Urban League & Whitney M Young, Jr Award, 1999; chosen as one of 30 educators to tour Viet Nam with Bob Hope Troupe to present MEMO; Ex-Students' Asn

Legacy Award. **Special Achievements:** The first African American vice president, Univ Tex, Austin. **Military Serv:** USN, 1948-53.

HILL, JAMES L.
School administrator. **Personal:** Born Oct 22, 1936, Bowling Green, OH; son of Joe L and Flossie Mae Susan; married Carolyn G Hill, Jun 8, 1963; children: Todd Derek, Candace Leah. **Educ:** Ind State Univ, Terre Haute, IN, BS, phys educ, 1965, MS, phys educ, 1966; Cent Mich Univ, Mt Pleasant, MI, specialist educ admin. **Career:** School administrator (retired); Arsenal Tech High Sch, Indianapolis, IN, teacher/coach, 1966-68; Shortridge High Sch, Indianapolis, IN, teacher/coach, 1968-70; Cent Mich Univ, Mt Pleasant, MI, instr, 1970-74; Blue Lake Fine Arts Camp, Muskegon, MI, dir, summer coun prog, 1972-74; Cent Mich Univ, Mt Pleasant, MI, asst prof, 1974-75, acting dean studs, 1975-76, dean studs, 1976-79, vpres, stud affairs, 1979-95. **Orgs:** Phi Kappa Epsilon, 1966-; Mich Stud Affairs Admin, 1976-; Am Coun Educ, 1978-; asst vpres, NASPA Region IV-East, 1980-81; legis comt, Asn Col/Univ Housing Officers, 1980-82; awards comt chair, Nat Asn Stud Personnel Admin, 1989-90. **Honors/Awds:** Indiana Wrestling Hall of Fame Inductee, Ind High Sch Wrestling Coaches' Asn, 1974; Sigma Iota Epsilon Honorary Member, 1979, Mortar Board Honorary Member, 1983, Golden Key National Honorary Member, 1987, Cent Mich Univ; Distinguished Alumni, Ind State Univ, 1989. **Military Serv:** USN, 1956-60; Honorable Discharge. **Home Addr:** 1841 W Pickard St, Mount Pleasant, MI 48858. *

HILL, PROF. JAMES LEE
School administrator, educator. **Personal:** Born Dec 10, 1941, Meigs, GA; son of Willie Lee Hill; married Flo J; children: Deron James & Toussaint LeMarc. **Educ:** T Valley St Col, BS Eng, 1963; Atlanta Univ, MA, Eng, 1968; Univ Iowa,PhD, Am CIV, 1976, 1978; Purdue Univ, post doctoral study, 1981; JohnCarroll Univ, post doctoral study, 1984. **Career:** Winder City Schs, instr Eng, 1964-65; Hancock Cent High, chmn Eng dept,1965-68; Paine Col, instr Eng, 1968-71; Benedict Col, chmn Eng dept,1974-77; Albany State Univ, chmn Eng dept, 1977-96, dean arts & sci,1981-, asst vpres acad affairs & prof eng, currently. **Orgs:** Consult, Nat Res Proj Black Women, 1979-81; secy, Albany Urban League Bd, 1979-81; chair, assoc, asst chair, Conf Col Comp & Commun, 1980-83; chair,vice chair, GA Endowment Humanities, 1981-83; Asn exec, Comm NCTE,1982-83; pres, Beta Nu Sigma Phi Beta Sigma Fraternity, 1983-; chair, Acad Comm Eng-GA, 1983-84; vpres S Atlantic Asn Dept Eng, 1984-85; bd dir, NatFed State Humanities Couns, 1984-87; Asn Col, Section Comm Nat Coun Teachers Eng, 1985-89, chair, 1993-95; Prof Serv: dir, NEA Writer-in-Res Prog Asn, 1982-91; dir, NEH Summer Humanities Inst ASC, 1983, 1984, 1989;Am regional dir Sourn Region Phi Beta Sigma; vis scholar, Nat Humanities Fac; Georgia Desoto Comn; Georgia Christopher Columbus Comn; dir, NCTE Summer Inst Teachers Literature; Beta Nu Sigma, 2009; Advisory comm, Bd of Regents Univ System; Georgia Coun Teachers. **Honors/Awds:** NEH Fellow Atlanta Univ, 1969; NEH Fellow Univ IA, 1971-74; Governor's Award in the Humanities, State Ga, 1987. **Special Achievements:** Publications: "Migration of Blacks to Iowa," "The Apprenticeship of Chester Himes," "The Antiheroic Hero in the Novels of Frank Yerby," A Sourcebook for Teachers of Georgia History; editor, Studies in African and African-American Culture; "Interview with Frank Garvin Yerby;" "Frank Yerby;" "The Foxes of Harrow;" "A Woman of Fancy". **Home Addr:** 2408 Greenmount Dr, Albany, GA 31705. **Business Addr:** Assistant Vice President, Professor, Albany State University, Department of English, Modern Languages and Mass Communication, 504 College Ave Hartnett Hall 329, Albany, GA 31705.

HILL, JAMES O.
Government official, air force officer. **Personal:** Born Sep 5, 1937, Austin; married Eva Marie Mosby; children: Eva Marie, James O II, Dudley Joseph. **Educ:** Howard Univ, BA, 1964; Nova Univ, MPA, 1975. **Career:** Government official (retired); Boys Clubs Newark, asst dir, 1964-68; Boys Clubs Broward Co, FL, dir, 1968-71; City Ft Lauderdale, asst city mgr, manpower analyst, admin asst, 1971-99. **Orgs:** KC, 1968; Elks, 1970-; ARC, 1971-; Govts Crime Prev Task Force, 1971-; Ft Lauderdale Chamber Comn, 1971-; Int City Mgrs Asn, 1972-; Am Soc Pub Admin, 1973-; Seminole Hist Soc, 1975. **Honors/Awds:** Youth Serv Award, 1970; Three Boys Club Serv Awards, 1964-70; Exemplary Former City Employee Award, 1999; Trinity Intl Univ, hon doctorate, 2001. **Military Serv:** USAF, a/1c, 1958-62, Educ achievement award, 1961. **Home Addr:** 450 NW 34th Ave, Fort Lauderdale, FL 33311. *

HILL, JEFFREY RONALD
Marketing executive. **Personal:** Born Nov 14, 1948, Philadelphia, PA. **Educ:** Cheyney State Col, BS, sci, 1972; Pa State Univ, PA, mkt cert, 1974. **Career:** Philip Morris Tobacco Co, NY, sales mgr, 1972-75; 3rd Jazz Record Co & Retail Philadelphia, mgr, 1975-76; Second Story/Catacombs Disco Complex Philadelphia, mgr, 1978-79; Hilltop Promotions Philadelphia, dir, 1979-; Nabisco Inc, mkt sales mgr. **Orgs:** Nat Hist Soc, 1968-77; Black Music Asn; Am Film Inst. **Honors/Awds:** Merit Achievement Award, Am Legion Philadelphia Post, 1963. **Business Addr:** Marketing Sales Manager, Nabisco Inc, 201 Precision Dr, Horsham, PA 19044, **Business Phone:** (215)672-1401.*

HILL, JENNIFER A
Journalist. **Educ:** Case Western Reserve Univ, BA, 1974; Columbia Univ Grad Sch Jour, MS, 1978. **Career:** Atlanta Jour-Const, deputy bus & tech ed; Univ Ga Press, ed, currently. **Business Addr:** Editor, University of Georgia Press, 330 Research Dr, Athens, GA 30602, **Business Phone:** (706)369-6144.

HILL, JESSE, JR.
Executive, president (organization), business owner. **Personal:** Born Jan 1, 1927?, St Louis, MO; son of Jesse Sr and Nancy Dennis Martin; married Juanita Azira Gonzalez, Jan 1, 1995; children: Nancy & Azira. **Educ:** Lincoln Univ, BS, physics & math; Univ Mich, MBA, Actuarial Sci, 1949. **Career:** Executive (retired), president, owner; Atlanta Life Ins Co, actuary, vpres, chief actuary, pres, ceo, 1949-95; Concessions Int, pres, owner, 1979-. **Orgs:** Chmn, campaign Andrew Young, 1972; campaign Maynard Jackson; past chmn, Nat Alliance Businessmen; dir Marta; bd dir, Delta Airlines; past chmn, Atlanta Crime Comn; pres, Enterprise Investments Inc; Am Acad Actuaries; Atlanta Actuarial Club; SE Actuarial Club; bd dir, chmn, Bldg Com Martin Luther King Ctr Social Change; bd dir, Nat Urban Coalition Oppor Funding Inc; Nat Urban League; Voter Educ proj; bd, Boy Scouts Am, Bethune Cookman Col, Provident Hosp; bd dir, Sperry Hutchinson Co; Commun Satellite Corp; Morse Shoe Co; Trust Co Ga; Knight Ridder Newspapers Inc; Nat Serv Indust Inc; chmn retired, Herndon Found. **Honors/Awds:** Received numerous honors & awards from civic & civil rights orgns; EOE Award, Annual Nat Urban League, 1965; Most Distinguished Alumni Award, MO Lincoln Univ, 1970; Abe Goldstein Award, Anti-Defamation League B'nai B'rith, 1973; Hon LLD, Morris Brown Col, Clark Col, 1972 1974; Chung-Ang Univ, 1976; Univ Mich, 1994; Ivan Allen Jr Prize. **Special Achievements:** First Black President of the Atlanta Chamber of Commerce; First Black Member of the Georgia Board of Regents; First Black Member of the Board of Directors for Rich's Department Store. **Military Serv:** Veteran Korean war.

HILL, JIMMY H.
Government official. **Personal:** Born Jun 14, 1948, Macon, GA; son of Harvie and Mertis Hill; married Lucille, Jun 22, 1968; children: Chandra, Jamie & Jennifer. **Educ:** Compton Col, AS, 1977. **Career:** Los Angeles Fire Dept, firefighter, 1973-78, apparatus operator, 1978-79; fire inspector I, 1979-82, fire inspector II, 1982-83, capt I, 1983-85; capt II, 1985-89, battalion chief, 1989-97; fire marshal & dep chief,1997-. **Orgs:** NFPA, 1989-; IFMA, 1999-, bd mem, 2001-; Western Fire Chief Assn; African Am Firefighter Mus. **Special Achievements:** He is the highest ranking African American in the history of the Los Angeles City Fire Department. **Military Serv:** USN, E-5, 1966-70. **Business Addr:** Fire Marshal, Deputy Chief, Los Angeles Fire Department, 200 N Main St Suite 910, City Hall East, Los Angeles, CA 90012, **Business Phone:** (213)485-5969.

HILL, JOSEPH HAVORD
Lawyer. **Personal:** Born Aug 19, 1940, Luverne, AL; son of Huey (deceased) and Arneta Williams; married Jacqueline Bryant Andrews, Jun 30, 1963; children: Jason Joseph Kent Hill. **Educ:** Cent State Univ, Wilberforce, OH, BS, 1962; Akron Univ, Akron, OH, JD, 1972. **Career:** Goodyear Tire and Rubber Co, Akron OH, chemist, 1965-69; Nat Labor Rels Bd, Cleveland Ohio, atty, 1972-76; Montgomery Ward, Chicago IL, sr labor rels atty, 1976-78; McDonald's Corp, Oak Brook IL, sr labor rels atty, 1978-81, staff dir labor rels, 1981-83, dir labor rels, 1983-95; asst vpres, labor rels, 1995; atty, labor rels & human resources, currently. **Orgs:** Alpha Phi Alpha Frat; bd dir, Alpha Phi Alpha Homes Inc, Akron OH, 1972-76; Alpha Phi Alpha Fraternity; Eta Tau Lambda, Akron OH, 1974-76; Nat Asn Advan Colored People; Urban League Chicago; Am Bar Asn; Nat Bar Asn; vpres, Theta Mu Lambda Chapter; Alpha Phi Alpha Fraternity. **Honors/Awds:** Akron Univ Law Review, 1971-72; President's Award, McDonald's Corp, 1981. **Military Serv:** AUS, Artillery (Field), captain, 1963-65. **Business Addr:** Attorney, McDonald's Corp, McDonalds Plz, Oak Brook, IL 60521.*

HILL, JULIA H.
Educator. **Personal:** Born in Kansas City, MO; daughter of Arthur H Hicks and Ethel Williams; married Quincy T (deceased). **Educ:** Lincoln Univ, BS, 1943; Univ Southern Calif, CA, attended 1954; Nova Univ, PhD, 1982. **Career:** Educator (retired); Kans City, Miss Sch Dist, elem sch teacher, 1943-66,consult urban affairs, 1966-67, coordr title I para prof, 1968-75, elem sch prin, 1975-76; Pioneer Community Col, community serv coordr, 1976-79; Northland Work & Training Unit, coordr, 1980-81; Kans City Skill Ctr, eve coordr, 1982-85; coordr, col rel, 1985-92. **Orgs:** Ppres, Kans City, Miss Nat Asn Adv Colored People Br, 1971-80; SW Bell Tele Adv Comn, 1981-94; Kans City, Miss Sch Bd, 1984-96; Kans City Campus Ministers, 1984-94; chair, Kans City, Miss Nat Asn Adv Colored People Br, 1984-99; life mem, Alpha Kappa Alpha Sorority, Beta Omega Chap; heritage life mem, Nat Asn Adv Colored People. **Honors/Awds:** Mo Leon M Jordan Memorial Award, Dist Servs, Kansas City, 1971; Citizen of the Year, Omega Phi Psi Fraternity, Kansas City, MO, 1973; Leadership &Civil Rights, KS City, Mo Baptist Ministers Union, 1974; SCLC Black Woman on the Move, 1975; Othell G Whitlock Memorial Award, 1976; Nat Asn Adv Colored People Civil Rights Award, 1976; Afro-Am Stud Union Distinguished Comn Leadership, 1977; Outstanding Civil Rights, 1978; Outstanding Community Serv, Beacon Light Seventh Day Adventist Church, 1979; Civil Rights Black Archives Award, 1980-81; Harold L Holiday Sr Civil Rights Award, Nat Asn Adv Colored People, 1988; Distinguished Serv Award, Lincoln Univ, Mo Nat Alumni Asn, 1990; Zeta Phi Beta Sorority Outstanding Leadership; Greater Kans City Bus & Prof Women Sojourner Truth Award;Outstanding Women of the Year Award; Girl Scouts of Am Award; Dr Martin Luther King Jr Awards, Oper PUSH. **Special Achievements:** One of the 100 Most Influential Blacks of Kansas City, 1986-88. **Home Addr:** 5100 Lawn Ave, Kansas City, MO 64130. *

HILL, DR. JULIUS W.
Physician. **Personal:** Born Jun 12, 1917, Atlanta, GA; married Luella Blaine; children: Sheila Lorraine. **Educ:** Johnson C Smith Univ, BA, 1933; Univ Ill, BS, MS, 1973; Meharry Med Col, MD, 1951; USC, orthopedic surgery, 1956. **Career:** Self-employed, physician, orthop surgeon, currently. **Orgs:** Pres emer, Golden State Med Asn, 1960-72; bd dir, La Co Hosp Comn, 1963-; Past pres, Nat Med Asn, 1969-70; Nat Med Fellowships Inc, 1970-; Charles RDrew Post grad Med Sch, 1971-; pres, Nat Med Asn Found, 1974-; bd dir, Martin Luther King Hosp, La; Am Med Asn; Riverside Nat Bank, Houston; Calif State Med Asn; Phi Beta Kappa; Sigma Xi; Kappa Alpha Psi; Masons. **Honors/Awds:** Distinguished Serv Award, Nat Med Asn, 1970-71; Outstanding Serv Award, Charles R Drew Med Soc, Los Angeles, Calif. **Military Serv:** AUS, major, 1941-46. **Home Addr:** 1224 S Van Ness Ave, Los Angeles, CA 90019.

HILL, KARIM DULE. See HILL, DULE.

HILL, KENNETH D.
Executive. **Personal:** Born Jan 22, 1938, Bryn Mawr, PA; married C Irene Wigington; children: Kimberly Diane. **Educ:** Temple Univ, Assoc Arch Tech, 1958; Univ PA, Indust Mgt, 1972; Harvard Bus Sch, PMD, 1980. **Career:** Sun Co Inc, central sales trng mgr, 1969-71; Alliance Enterprise, pres, 1971-73; Sun Co Inc, dist mgr, 1973-75, proj mgr corp human res, 1975-76, div mgr mkt, 1976-79, mgr corp citizenship, 1979-84, vice pres pub affairs, 1984-. **Orgs:** Chmn, coun trustees Cheyney State Univ, 1981; bd trustees, Comt Leadership Seminar, 1983; pres, Am Asn Blacks Energy, 1984-86; bd dir, Private Industry Coun, 1984. **Honors/Awds:** Ebony Women's Award, Community Serv Womens Res Network, 1982; James McCoy Founder's Award, NAACP, 1982; Centennial Award, Advan & Image Bldg Cheyney Univ, 1983; Community Service Award, Urban League Philadelphia, 1983. **Military Serv:** AUS, spec 4, 1960-62; Good Conduct Medal, Soldier of the Month, 1960-62. **Business Phone:** (215)339-2000.

HILL, KENNETH WADE
Baseball player. **Personal:** Born Dec 14, 1965, Lynn, MA; married Lorrie Rollin, Nov 30, 1996; children: Ken Jr. **Educ:** North Adams State Col, attended. **Career:** Baseball player (Retired); St Louis Cardinals, pitcher, 1988-91, 1995; Montreal Expos, 1992-94; Cleveland Indians, 1995; Texas Rangers, 1996-97; Anaheim Angels, 1997-2000; Chicago White Sox, 2000; Tampa Bay Devil Rays, 2001. **Honors/Awds:** MLB All-Star Game, 1994. *

HILL, LEO
Administrator. **Personal:** Born Mar 27, 1937, Columbus, TX; married Jacquelyne; children: Leo, Stacy. **Educ:** Los Angeles City Col, attended 1958; Los Angeles State Col, BA, 1961, Grad Work, 1962; Calif Inst Technol, attended 1969; Pepperdine, 1970; Univ Calif, Los Angeles, cert Indust Rel, 1979, cert personnel mgt, 1979; Inst Cert Prof Mgrs, cert Mgt, 1984. **Career:** Administrator, dir (retired); RCA Serv Co, sr job develop admin; Hughes Aircraft Co, head action prog, 1977-81; Lockheed-CA Co, mgr equal opportunity progs, dir, 1981-2004. **Orgs:** Dir, comn prog, Greater LA, Community Action Agency; dir, Prog Monitoring, Neighborhood Youth Corps, Narcotics 1973; asst eeo, 1972, dir personnel, 1972, Econ & Youth Opp Agency, Greater, Los Angeles; personell dir, 1966-71; acting admin officer, 1968-69; dir, Bethune Co Park; mem, comn Florence-Firestone Coun & Case Conf; mem, Los Angeles Area Ed Comm, Men Tomorrow, Hunters Elite Gun Club, Narcotics Task Force; Am Soc Training & Develop; vpres, 1961, treas 1960, Los Angeles State Col Inter-Frat Coun; pres, Kappa Psi Frat. **Honors/Awds:** Sam Berry Tournament Most Valuable Player; Broke-Tied 11 Records Jr Coll Career; CCAA best team 3 yrs; Leading Scorer NCAA Most Valuable; Calif State Univ Los Angeles Hall of Fame (Basketball) 1985. **Home Addr:** 1355 Buckhorn Bend Loop R, Los Angeles, CA 71202.

HILL, MARVIN LEWIS
Executive. **Personal:** Born Aug 19, 1951, Indianapolis, IN; son of Maurice and Luciele Campbell; married Deborah Jill Shaffer, Jun 10, 1989; children: Jessica Ashley & Alison Victoria. **Educ:** Ind State Univ, 1971, criminal justice, 1974. **Career:** Marriott corp, mgr, 1974-78; Steak & Ale Restaurant, corp trainer, 1978-79; MLH dba Sir Speedy, pres, 1979-86; Shaffer-Hill, Express Press Inc, pres, 1986. **Orgs:** Chmn, Kiwanis Int district young children, 1992, governor, I-I District, 1991; coun, Village Hoffman Estates, 1991-94; pres, Wheeling, 1983-85; Citizen Participation org, 1974. **Honors/Awds:** Distinguish Past Lt Governor, Kiwanis Int, 1992; Outstanding dir, Vill Hoffman Estates, 1991.

HILL, MARY ALICE
Association executive. **Personal:** Born Sep 15, 1938, Marlow, GA; married Elton E Hill. **Educ:** NJ Col Com, pub admin, 1956;

Univ Col, urban studies, 1972; Rutgers Univ, certified pub mgr, 1986. **Career:** City Newark, sr budget analyst, 1972-83, mgt info spec, 1985, pres, nat coun negro women. **Orgs:** Am Mgt Assoc; Nat Assoc Black Pub Admin; pres, Newark Sect Nat Coun Negro Women Inc; chmn, US Selective Serv Bd 33; NJ State Univ Med & Dentistry; bd pres, Coun Affirm Action; chair, Metropolitan BC Women's Day, 1983; NJ Bethune Recog Team Steering Comt, 1985; officer, Bethany 43, OES PHA Newark NJ; chair, NJ Rainbow Coalition; chmn UMDNJ-PCAA 1987. **Honors/Awds:** Nomination, Mayor's Committee Service Award, 1980; Rainbow Coalition Service Award, 1984.

HILL, MELBA. See MOORE, MELBA.

HILL, MERVIN E., JR.
Television producer. **Personal:** Born Jul 12, 1947, St Louis, MO. **Educ:** Grand Valley State Col, BA; William James Col, Allendale, MI, attended 1974. **Career:** Black Free Form Theatre Co, Grand Rapids, actor & asst dir, 1971-72; Living Arts Proj, Grand Rapids Bd Educ, drama dir, 1971-72; WOTV, Grand Rapids, mgr, 1973; WGVC-TV, Allendale, MI, asst to producer, 1975-; TV Series: "Arbitration Mr Businessman"; "Portrait of African Journey"; "The Neighborhood". **Business Addr:** Assistant to Producer, WGVC TV 35, Allendale, MI 49401.*

HILL, DR. OBIE CLEVELAND
School administrator, educator. **Personal:** Born Oct 20, 1949, Enterprise, MS; son of John C Hill and Florine E Nichols; married Lois Charles, Nov 11, 1972; children: Demetria & Christina. **Educ:** Nicholls State Univ, BA, Liberal Arts, 1973, Teacher Cert, 1976, MEd,1978; Univ New Orleans, EdD, 1993. **Career:** Sch admin (retired), educator (retired); LaFourche Parish Sch, teacher,1976-79; Nicholls State Univ, asst mens basketball coach, 1979-85, asst prof phys ed, 1985-, dir stud teaching, 1994-98, former dean educ; Southern Univ New Orleans, dean educ, 1998-99. **Orgs:** LaFourche Parish Community & Housing Develop Org, 1995-; La Asn Cols Teacher Educ, 1998-; bd commr, Thibodaux Regional Med Ctr, 2001-. **Honors/Awds:** Nicholls State Univ Athletics Hall of Fame, 1981; Louisiana Asn Basketball Coaches Hall of Fame, 1994; James Lynn Powell Award, Nicholls State Univ Alumni Fel. **Military Serv:** AUS, SFC, Meritorious Service Medal, Army Commendation Medal.

HILL, OLIVER W., SR. See Obituaries section.

HILL, PATRICIA LIGGINS
Educator. **Personal:** Born Sep 18, 1942, Washington, DC; divorced; children: Sanya Patrice & Solomon Philip. **Educ:** Howard Univ, BA, 1965; Univ San Francisco, MA, 1970; Stanford Univ, PhD,1977. **Career:** Univ San Francisco, from instr to assoc prof, 1970-84, dir ethnic studies, 1977-, prof eng, 1984-; Urban Inst for Human Service Inc, research consult, 1976-80; Univ Minn, Upper Midwest Tri-Racial Ctr, resource consult, 1977-78; Nat Endowment Humanities fel, 1978. **Orgs:** Bd dir, W side Ment Health Ctr, 1971-78; SF Community Col Bd, 1972-78; Calif Coun Black Educ, 1973-. **Special Achievements:** Published: "The Dark/Black-Bad Light/White-Good Illusion in Joseph Conrad's 'Heart of Darkness' & 'Nigger of the Narcissus," Western Journal of Black Studies 1979; publications: Roots for a Third World Aesthetic Found in Black & Chicano Poetry, De Colores 1980; "The Violent Space, An Interpretation of the Function of the New Black Aesthetic in Etheridge Knight's Poetry, "Black Amer Lit Forum 1980; General editor, "Call &Response: The Riverside Anthology of the African American Literary Tradition," Houghton Mifflin, 1997. **Business Addr:** Professor, University San Francisco, English Department, 2130 Fulton St, San Francisco, CA 94117-1080.

HILL, RANDAL THRILL
Football player, federal government official. **Personal:** Born Sep 21, 1969, Miami, FL. **Educ:** Univ Miami, BS, sociol. **Career:** Football player (retired); Miami Dolphins, wide receiver, 1991, 1995-96; Phoenix Cardinals, 1991-93; Ariz Cardinals, 1994; New Orleans Saints, wide receiver, 1997; US Dept Homeland Security, agt, currently.

HILL, RAY. See HILL, RAYMOND.

HILL, DR. RAY ALLEN
Educator. **Personal:** Born Sep 16, 1942, Houston, TX; son of Ann Stewart and Cal Hill Jr. **Educ:** Howard Univ, Wash, DC, BS 1964, MS, 1965; Univ Calif, Berkley, PhD, 1977. **Career:** Southern Univ, Baton Rouge, La, instr, 1965-66; Howard Univ, Wash, DC, instr botany, 1966-75; Fisk Univ, Nashville, Tenn, asst prof, 1977-80; EPA, Wash DC, staff scientist, 1978; NASA, Wash, DC, staff scientist, 1979; Univ Calif, San Francisco, Calif, vis research assoc prof, 1985; Lowell Col Preparatory Sch, San Francisco, Calif, instr, 1986-; Purdue Univ, W Lafayette Ind, vis prof botany & plant pathology, 1989, 1990, 1991; Alpha Distributors, owner, 1989-; Genentech Inc, vis scientist, 1992; DOE Fel, staff scientist, 1993. **Orgs:** Mem, Nat Inst Sci, 1968-85, Am Asn Advanced Science, 1972-85, Am Soc Cell Biol, 1972-85, Botanical Soc Am, 1972-85, Information Vis Ctr, 1975-, Alpha Phi Alpha Fraternity 1980-; bd mem, Big Brothers East Bay, 1986-89. **Honors/Awds:** E E Worthing Fel, E E Worthing Trust, 1960-64; Faculty Fel, Howard Univ, 1972; Fel, Ford Found, 1975-77; Faculty Fel, Nat Sci Found, 1975; NASA/ASEE Fel, Stanford Univ, 1983-84; published "Ultrastructure of Synergids of Gossypium hirsutum," 1977 & "Polarity Studies in Roots of Ipomea batatas In vitro," 1965; IISME Fel, genentech Inc, 1992, Calif Mentor Teacher, 1993-97; coach, 1st Place Sci Bowl Team, three times; Lowell Col preparatory, 1995-97; teacher adv, Toshiba/NSTA ExploraVision Awards, 1st & 2nd Place, Lowell Col Preparatory; Einstein fel, finalist, twice. **Business Addr:** Owner, Alpha Distributors, 4700 N Ronald St, Harwood Heights, illunois, CA 60706, **Business Phone:** (708)867-5200.

HILL, RAYMOND (RAY HILL)
Football player. **Personal:** Born Aug 7, 1975, Detroit, MI. **Educ:** Mich State Univ. **Career:** Buffalo Bills, defensive back, 1998, 2000; Miami Dolphins, defensive back, 1998-2000.

HILL, REUBEN BENJAMIN
Lawyer. **Personal:** Born Aug 1, 1938, Indianapolis, IN; son of Joe L and Flossie M; married Sheila; children: Philip, Martin, Nicholas. **Educ:** Ind Univ, attended 1969; Ind Univ Law Sch, attended 1973. **Career:** Ind State Police/Trooper, legal adv, 1964-74; Bingham Summers Welch & Spilman, assoc 1974-75; Marion Co, pros dep 1975-; Flanner House Indianapolis, exec dir, 1975; Social Serv Agency, atty/exec dir; Butler Hahn Little & Hill, atty; Marion Super Ct, Criminal Div 18, judge, currently. **Orgs:** Indianapolis Lawyers Comn; bd dir, Ind Lawyers Comn; bd mem, WYFI- Pub Broadcasting Serv; C's Mus; bd dir, Metro Arts Coun; Am Bar Asn; Indianapolis Bar Asn; Ind Bar Asn; Nat Bar Asn Adv Bd; Indianapolis Repertory Theatre; Kiwanis Club; Indianapolis Mus Art Adv comt; adv bd, Indianapolis Urban League; Inner-City Y's Men Club; Indianapolis 500 Festival Bd Dir IN; Ind Univ Law Sch Min Enrollment Adv Comt; Greater Ind Progress Comt; Ind State Dept Ment Health Bd Dir; Golden Glove Off Ind; bd mem, Selective Serv Syst; dist appeal bd; Alpha Eta Boule; Sigma Pi Phi Fraternity; pres, Flanner House Found; bd mem, Salvation Army; Indianapolis Zoo bd. **Honors/Awds:** Outstanding Ind Citizen Ind Black Bi-Centennial; WTLC Indianapolis Citizen of the Day; WTLC Man of the Year, 1978. **Military Serv:** USAF 1957-61. **Business Phone:** (317)327-3237.*

HILL, DR. RICHARD NATHANIEL. See Obituaries section.

HILL, ROBERT A.
Association executive. **Career:** Nat Asn Minority Auto Dealers, exec dir, 1992; Ford Motor Minority Dealers Asn, exec dir, currently. **Orgs:** Nat Asn Minority Auto Dealers. **Business Addr:** Executive Director, Ford Motor Minority Dealers Association, 16000 W Nine Mile Rd Suite 603, Southfield, MI 48075, **Business Phone:** (248)557-2500.*

HILL, ROBERT BERNARD
School administrator. **Personal:** Born Sep 7, 1938, Brooklyn, NY; married; children: Bernard & Renee. **Educ:** City Col NY, BA, sociol, 1961; Columbia Univ, NYC, PhD, sociol, 1969. **Career:** Bureau Applied Soc Res, Columbia Univ NY, res assoc, 1964-69; Princeton Univ Fordham U, adj faculty, 1969-73; Nat Urban League, Res Dept, dep dir res, 1969-72, dir res, 1972-81; Bureau Census, chmn, mem adv comt black population, 1974; Howard Univ Wash, DC, visiting scholar soc dept sch Human ecology, 1975-77; Bur Soc Sci Res, vpres, sr res assoc, 1981-86; Morgan State Univ, dir, urban res, 1989-98; Westat, sr researcher, 2001-. **Orgs:** Pres, Wash, DC Sociol Soc, 1975; pres, NAACP Chap. **Special Achievements:** Author: The Strengths of Black Families, 1972; Informal Adoption Among Black Families NUL, Res Dept Wash, DC, 1977; Research on the African American Family, Auburn House, 1993; The Strengths of African American Families: Twenty-five Years Later, 1997. **Business Addr:** Senior Researcher, Westat Inc, 1650 Res Blvd, Rockville, MD 20850-3195, **Business Phone:** (301)251-1500.*

HILL, ROBERT J., JR.
Architect. **Personal:** Born Feb 23, 1943, Wilmington, NC; married Sheila G. **Educ:** A&T State Univ, BS, 1971. **Career:** Norfolk Naval Shipyard, archit engr pub works, naval architect. **Orgs:** Soc Prof Naval Engr; Kappa Alpha Psi; YMCA; 35th St Karate Club; A&T Alumni Club. **Honors/Awds:** Letter Commendation, Shipyard Comdr, 1974. **Military Serv:** AUS, 1962-65.

HILL, ROBERT K.
Executive. **Personal:** Born May 12, 1917, San Antonio, TX; married Mildred. **Educ:** Univ Nebr; Inst Banking, 1951. **Career:** Union Pacific RR, 1937-42; Epply Hotel Co, 1942-46; self-employed, 1946-50; Fed Res Bank, 1950-54; Hill Enterprises, founder & mgr, 1954-; Dept Justice, coordr weed & seed program, 1996. **Orgs:** Score counr, Small Bus Admin; secy & treas, NE Placement Asn; Ins Underwriter; Notary Public; Omaha Real Estate Asn; bd dir, Omaha Chamber Com; Bus Develop Corp; United Comm Serv; Nat Conf Christians & Jews; GeneEpply Boys Club; Omaha Safety Coun; Legal Aid Soc; founder & dir Comt, Bank Nebr; int past pres, Frontiers Int; Nat Fed Independent Bus; pres, Central State Golf Asn; past master, Excelsior Lodge 2 Masonic Order; dir, Nat Bus League.

HILL, REV. DR. ROBERT LEE
Clergy, counselor. **Personal:** Born Oct 9, 1931, Birmingham, Uruguay; son of Elcano Hill and Zora; divorced; children: Robert Rowland Renel, Victoria, Shvone & Peter. **Educ:** Universal Life Church Inc, doctorate, Am church law & parliamentary law, 1980; Union Baptist Sem Sch Relig Studies, BS, theol, 1996, MS, theol, 1998. **Career:** Ford Motor Co, roving part inspector; US Postal Serv, clerk; City Det, Zool Dept; Hill Invest & Exterminating Co, pres & ceo; Universal Life Hope, pastor, counr; Community Christian Church, minister. **Orgs:** Detroit Zoo Soc; Detroit Inst Arts; Mayors Clean SweepTeam; United Found Girl Scouts & Boy Scouts; Veterans Foreign Wars, former vice commander; chair, pres, Universal Life Gospel Production; Prince Hall, master mason; Notary Pub Org, 1994; NCP. **Honors/Awds:** Certificate of Appreciation, Detroit Police Second Precinct, 1999; Recognition Award, Detroit City Coun, 1984. **Military Serv:** AUS, capt, 82nd Airborne Div, 1950-53; "Good Conduct" medal; UN Korean Servs F/S.

HILL, ROBERT LEWIS (BOB HILL)
Association executive. **Personal:** Born Feb 23, 1934, Spartanburg, SC; son of Modecai and Texanna Hardy; married Marcia Norcott, Sep 28, 1957; children: Robin Lindsey & Lisa Beth. **Educ:** Southern Conn State Univ, New Haven, BS, educ, 1960; Fairfield Univ, CT, attended 1967; Brandeis Univ, Waltham, MA, cert human resource mgt, 1980. **Career:** New Haven Bd Educ, New Haven, CT, teacher, 1963-65; Community Progress Inc, New Haven, CT, counr & trainer, 1965-67; Opportunities Indus Ctr, New Haven, CT, exec dir, 1968-69; Nat League Cities, Wash, DC, coord nat urban fel, 1969-71, nat dir, vets prog, 1971-78, dir, human resources & public safety, 1978-82; Am Gas Asn, Arlington, VA, vpres consumer & community affairs, 1985-95; Am Asn Blacks Energy, pres, 1992-96 & 1998-2007, immediate past pres & chief operating officer, 2007-. **Orgs:** Diaconate Bd, chancel choir, Peoples Congregational United Church Christ, Wash, DC 1976-; bd, Am Asn Blacks Energy, 1986-92; Peoples Neighborhood Fed Credit Union. **Honors/Awds:** Asn fel, Yale Univ, 1970; Outstanding Achievement Award, Am Veterans Comt, 1974; vis prof, Black Exec Exchange Prog Nat Urban League, 1988; Distinguished Supporter Award Support HBCU's, Dept Interior, 1988; Role Model Achievement Award, Ft Valley State Col, 1989. **Military Serv:** USAF, airman first class, 1952-56; Good Conduct Award; Foreign Service Award. **Business Addr:** Past President, Chief Operating Officer, American Association of Blacks in Energy, 927 15th St NW Suite 200, Washington, DC 20005.

HILL, DR. ROSALIE A.
Educator. **Personal:** Born Dec 30, 1933, Philadelphia, PA; daughter of Joseph Behlin (deceased) and Anna Mae Elliott (deceased); children: Bernadette Hill Amos. **Educ:** Fla A&M Univ, Tallahassee, FL, BS, M.Ed, 1961; FL State Univ, Tallahassee, FL, PhD, 1985. **Career:** Leon Interfaith Child Care Inc, dir; staff dir; Taylor Co Adult Inst, basic educ teacher; Fla A & M, counr; Taylor Co Head Start Prog, dir; Jerkins HS, music teacher; Fla State Univ, res assoc; RA Hill & Assoc, educ consult; Fla A&M Univ, exec asst vpres. **Orgs:** Secy, vpres, pres, Taylor Co Educ Asn, 1966-69; Taylor City Teachers Asn,1961; pres, 1963-65; vpres, Fla State Teachers Asn, 1965; chairperson Dist iII, 1960-66; chairperson, Fla State Teachers Asn, 1965-66; exec bd mem Dist III, 1963-65; Fla Educ Asn Small Co Prob Comt, 1967-69; chairperson Jerkins High Sch, 1964-79; bd mem, Taylor Co Sch Bd; PK Yonge Lab Sch; Leon City Sch Bd, 1974-75; secy, FL A & M Univ Alumni Asn, 1974-76; Nat Asn,1974-; Am Higher Educ Asn; Am Asn Affirmative Action Officers; Zeta Phi Beta Sor; Taylor Co Improvement Club Inc; Tri-Co Econ Coun; Taylor Co Bi-racial Com; Region III Drug Abuse Com; Miss Black Am Pageant; Am Cancer Soc; Hills borough County Community Status of Women; spec proj coord, FLA & M Univ Nat Alumni Asn, 1985-; Nat Asn Advan Colored People; Greater Tampa urban League. **Honors/Awds:** Lewis State Scholarship, 1952-56; Teacher of Year, Jerkins High Sch, 1960; Yearbook Dedication Jerkins High Sch, 1960; Tampa Bay Most Influential Blacks, 1983; Outstanding Alumni Hall of Fame, Fla A&M Univ, 1987; Martin Luther King Education Award, Start Together on Progress Inc, 1988; co-founder, Fla Statewide Alumni Consortium Historically Black Insts, 1985; founder, Conf Educ Blacks, Tampa, 1982. *

HILL, RUFUS S.
Clergy. **Personal:** Born Apr 8, 1923, Raymond, MS; son of Orville A and Mary R Dixon; married Ruth (divorced); children: Rufus, Thomasine, Beverly & Daphane. **Educ:** Miss Indust Col, BA, 1951; State Univ, MA, 1971. **Career:** Shannon, MS, teacher 1951-55; Houston, MS, teacher, 1955-61; New Albany, MS, teacher, 1961-66; Clay City, MS, teacher, 1966-72; Christian Methodist Episcopal Church, clergyman; Universal Life Ins, 1963-65; Union Fed Life Ins, 1965-66; Dixie Car Craft Ctr, owner; four-Way Pest Control Co, owner; Dixie Box Co, owner, 1991-. **Orgs:** Past chmn, Union Co Community Develop Coun, 1963-66; vpres, Clay County Community Fed Credit Union, 1971-74; Miss Loyal Democratic Party; Am Legion Post #252, New Albany; FA Mason Lodge #171; founder, chap NAACP; New Albany Develop Club; Union Co Life; founder, dir, Lee County Drug Dependency Rehab

Ctr Inc, 1989-; founder, dir, Lee County Drug Abuse Prev & Rehab Ctr, 1991; past pres, NAACP, Lee County, 1994. **Military Serv:** AUS, corporal, 1943-46; Campaign Medal, Good Conduct Medal; Bronze Star. **Home Addr:** Verona, MS 38879.

HILL, SANDRA PATRICIA
Social worker, manager. **Personal:** Born Nov 1, 1943, Piedmont, AL; daughter of Edith Palmore Hill and Theotis Hill. **Educ:** Berea Col Berea, KY, BS, 1966; Southern Baptist Theo Sem, MRE, 1968; Univ Mich, MSW, 1977; Cornell Univ, attended. **Career:** Harvard St Baptist Ctr, Alexandria, VA, assoc dir, 1968-73; Harvard St Baptist Ctr, dir, 1974-75; Home Mission Bd, S Baptist Conv, consult, 1977-86, res status, 1987; Southern Baptist Theol Sem, Louisville, KY, vis prof soc work, 1987-88; Empire State Col, Ithaca, NY, mentor, community & human servs, 1989-90; Displaced Homemakers Ctr, peer servs & minority advocacy coord, 1989-98; Dresden House, mgr, currently. **Orgs:** Old, Inc, Alexandria, VA, 1970-75; Asn Black Social Workers, 1974-; Fsecy & treas, Southern Baptist Soc Serv Asn, 1977-82; bd dir, Reach Out Inc Atlanta, 1980; Nat Asn Advan Colored People; Cornell Coop Exten Tompkins Co, 1991-98; bd dirs, vice chair, chair, strategic planning comn, Task Battered Women Tompkins Co, 1992-; chair, 1994-97, vice chair, 1997-98, Soc Work Adv Comn, Cornell Univ; Black Women's Empowerment Group; vpres, Home Econ & Human Ecol Prog Comn. **Home Addr:** 200 S Hanks St, Rome, GA 30165-4160. **Business Addr:** Manager, Dresden House, 18 Albany Villas, Hove BN32SA, United Kingdom, **Business Phone:** (127)373-2173.

HILL, SONNY. See HILL, WILLIAM RANDOLPH.

HILL, DR. SYLVIA IONE-BENNETT
Educator. **Personal:** Born Aug 15, 1940, Jacksonville, FL; daughter of Paul Theodore Sr and Evelyn Harker; children: Gloria Angela Davis. **Educ:** Howard Univ, BS, 1963; Univ Ore, MS, 1967, PhD, 1971. **Career:** Macalester Col, asst prof, 1972-74; Univ DC, Dept Criminal Justice, prof criminal justice, 1974-, Dept Urban Affairs, prof, currently; Union Expermenting Col & Univs, part-time core prof, 1976-. **Orgs:** Sec gen, Sixth Pan African Cong, 1974; founder & co-chairperson, Southern Africa Support Proj, 1978-; founder/mem, Steering Comn Free S Africa Movement, 1984-; treas, bd TransAfrica Forum, 1984-; bd mem, TransAfrica, 1984-90; bd mem, New World Found, 1988-; assoc dir, USA Tour Nelson & Winnie Mandela, 1990. **Honors/Awds:** Nat Certified Councils, 1984-89. **Business Addr:** Professor of Criminal Justice, University of the District of Columbia, Department of Urban Affairs, Social Sciences & Social Work, Rm 407-03 Bldg 41 4200 Conn Ave NW, Washington, DC 20008, **Business Phone:** (202)274-5687.

HILL, TYRONE
Basketball player. **Personal:** Born Mar 19, 1968, Cincinnati, OH. **Educ:** Xavier Univ, BA, 1990. **Career:** Basketball player (retired); Golden State Warriors, ctr forward, 1990-93; Cleveland Cavaliers, 1993-97, 2001-03; Major League Baseball, Naughty Koalas, 1994-95; Hunger Dunkers, 1995-99; Milwaukee Bucks, 1997; Philadelphia 76ers, 1998-2001, 2003; Miami Heat, forward, 2003-04. **Special Achievements:** Hosted the Tyrone Hill All-Star Charity Basketball Game, Cincinnati, 1996.

HILL, VELMA MURPHY
Association executive, psychotherapist. **Personal:** Born Oct 17, 1938, Chicago, IL; married Norman Hill. **Educ:** N Ill Univ, Dekalb; Roosevelt Univ, Chicago, attended 1960; Harvard Univ, MEd, 1969. **Career:** OEO, summer recruit dir, 1964-65; CORE, 1960-64; Am Dem Action Wash, exec dir 1965-66; United Fedn Teachers, asst to pres, Paraprofessional Chap, chairwoman, 1969-79; NY City Training Inst, consult, 1967-68; Serv Employees Int Union, Wash, DC, dir human rights & int affairs; psychotherapist, currently. **Orgs:** Labor Adv Comt, OEO, 1970-71; Trade Union Comt Histadrut Labor Seminar Israel, 1969; Commn Status Women, 1975; bd mem, A Philip Randolph Inst.

HILL, VONCIEL JONES
Judge. **Personal:** Born Sep 23, 1948, Hattiesburg, MS; married Charles Edward Hill. **Educ:** Univ Tex, BA, 1969, JD, 1979; Atlanta Univ, MA, libr sci, 1971; Rice Univ, MA, hist, 1976; Southern Methodist Univ, MDiv, 1991. **Career:** GA Pub Sch, Atlanta, teacher, 1969-70; Prairie View A&M Univ, asst circulations libr, 1971-72; Tex Southern Univ, asst law libr, 1972-76; Pub Utility Comt TX, staff atty, 1979-80; Dallas, Ft Worth Airport, asst city atty; St Luke Community United Methodist Church, asst pastor, 1985-; Dallas Munic Ct, munic ct judge; Pvt Pract, atty, currently. **Orgs:** chair & bd dir, Methodism's Breadbasket, 1983-85; comt chair, Dallas Bar Asn, 1985; secy, JL Turner Legal Asn, 1985; treas, State Bar TX Women & the Law Secy. **Honors/Awds:** Ford Foundation fellow, Atlanta Univ, 1970-71; fellow, Rice Univ, 1974-76. **Business Addr:** Attorney, Law Office of Vonciel Jones Hill, 4347 S Hampton Rd Suite 210, Dallas, TX 75232, **Business Phone:** (214)333-9080.*

HILL, WILLIAM BRADLEY, JR.
Lawyer. **Personal:** Born Mar 3, 1952, Atlanta, GA; married Melba Gayle Wynn; children: Melba Kara. **Educ:** Wash & Lee Univ, Lexington Va, BA, 1974, Sch Law, JD, 1977. **Career:** State Law Dept Atlanta GA, asst atty gen, 1977-90; Atty Gen & Dir, Criminal Div, sr asst, 1982-88; dep atty gen, 1988-90; State Ct Fulton County, judge, 1990-92; Superior Ct Fulton County, judge, 1992; Atlanta, Ga, atty, currently; Ashe, Refuse & Hill, partner, currently. **Orgs:** State Bar Ga, 1977; exec chmn, Wash & Lee Univ Black Alumni Found, 1980-; Ga Comn Dispute Resolution; State Judicial Nominating Comn; Northern Dist Ga Bar Coun. **Special Achievements:** Listed among 2003 The Best Lawyers in America. **Business Addr:** Partner, Ashe, Rafuse & Hill, 1355 Peachtree St NE Suite 500, Atlanta, GA 30309-3232.*

HILL, WILLIAM RANDOLPH (SONNY HILL)
Labor activist. **Personal:** Born Jul 22, 1936, Philadelphia, PA; married Edith Hughes; children: K Brent, Starr & Leah. **Career:** CBS TV, editor, 1977; Teamsters Local 169, secy, treas, bus agent & trust, 1960-93; Lancaster Red Roses Basketball Team, owner, 1975; Eastern Basketball League, basketball player; WPEN Lct Sports & Humanitarian, analyst, 1966-; Sonny Hill, John Chaney Basketball Camp, co-owner, 1975-, exec dir, currently; WIP Sports Radio Talk Show, host, 1986-; WRIT Radio, Temple Univ Basketball, color analyst, 1993-; Pa 76ers, exec advisor to pres, 1996-; First Union Complex, exec advisor to pres & chief exec officer, 1995-. **Orgs:** Pres Charles Baker Mem Summer League, 1960-; adv bd, MacDonald's HS All Am Team, 1978-80; bd dir, Big Bros Assoc Nat Comn, opr PUSH; NAACP; Big Bros; PUSH; pres, founder, Sonny Hill Community Involvement League Inc, 1968-. **Honors/Awds:** Outstanding Community Serv Award, Sports Mag, 1970; human rights award, Comn on Human Rel, 1972; good neighbour award, WDAS Radio, 1973; Oxford Circle JC Award, 1973; Man of Year award, Fishtown, 1973; Man of Year, Nite Owl, 1972-73; Tribune Charities, 1976; Basketball Weekly Player Develop Award, Toyota Motors, 1977; Mutual Radio Broadcaster NBA Championship, 1980; Mellon Bank Good neighbour Award, 1985; John B Kelley Award, 1986; City Hope Spirit Life Award; Whitney Young Leadership Award, Urban League of Pa, 1990; Service Award, Leon H Sullivan Charitable Golf Tournamet, Zion COT center, 1992; EDR's Roundtable Dr Wm H Gray Jr, COT Activist Awd, 1993; honorary doctorate, Temple Univ, 1998; Clarence Farmer Award, Pa Comn on Human Relations, 2001. **Military Serv:** ANG, 1959-65. **Business Addr:** Founder, Executive Director, Sonny Hill League, 429 S 50th St, Philadelphia, PA 19143, **Business Phone:** (215)474-2801.

HILLARD, TERRY
Police officer. **Personal:** Born Jan 1, 1944, South Fulton, TN; married Dorothy; children: 2. **Educ:** Chicago State Univ, BS, MS. **Career:** Police Officer (retired); Chicago Police Dept, Area 2 dep chief patrol, 1995, chief detectives, 1995-98, supt, 1998-2003. **Orgs:** NOBLE; Chicago Westside Police Asn; FBI Nat Acad Asn; S Suburban Chiefs Police Asn; Nat Comn Future DNA Evidence; Domestic Violence Advocacy Coord Coun; adv bd, Ill State Police Forensic Sci Ctr, Chicago. **Honors/Awds:** Police Awards: Police Medal; Superintendent's Award of Valor; Police Blue Star Award; Carter Harrison/Lambert Tree Honorable Mention; Special Service Award, Chicago Community Policing; Special Service Award, Democratic Nat Convention; 3 DPT Commendations; Unit Meritorious Performance Award; Chicago COC Award. **Special Achievements:** First African-American chief of detectives in Chicago. **Military Serv:** US Marine Corps, sgt, 1963-67; Presidential Unit Citation; Vietnam Svc Medal; Good Conduct Medal; Nat Defense Service Medal; Republic of Vietnam Campaign Medal.

HILLIARD, ALICIA VICTORIA
Television journalist. **Personal:** Born Jan 4, 1949, Wadesboro, NC; daughter of George Allen and Annie Louise. **Educ:** Morgan State Univ, BA, 1971; Univ Wis, Madison. **Career:** Baltimore City Hosps, nutrition asst & kitchen asst, 1970; State atty's Off, polit sci intern, 1970-71; Morgan State Univ, pub rels asst, 1971-72; Housing Authority Baltimore City, info asst, 1972-75; WMTV, reporter & producer, 1977-82; Univ Wis, Madison, teaching asst assoc, 1977-78; WISC TV, exec news producer, 1982-88; WHDH TV, news producer, 1988-. **Orgs:** AKA Sorority, Inc, 1971-; Boston Aan Black Journalists, 1988-; Nat Asn Black Journalists, 1988-; mentor & vol, Black Achievers, YWCA, 1992-. **Honors/Awds:** Sword of Hope Award, Am Cancer Soc, 1990; Unity Award/Education, 1990, Unity Award/AIDS, 1990, Univ MSR-Lincoln; Gabriel Awards for coverage Nelson Mandela visit to Boston, 1990; Special Chair Award, AFTRA-SAG, 1991; American Scene Award, New England AFTRA-SAG, 1991; Best Feature, NAT Asn Black Journalists, 1991; Black Achiever, Boston YWCA, 1992; Community Service Award, Veterans Benefits Clearinghouse, 1992. **Business Addr:** Television News Producer, WHDH TV New 7, 7 Bulfinch Pl News Dept 3rd fl, Boston, MA 02114-2913, **Business Phone:** (617)725-0864.

HILLIARD, AMY S
Entrepreneur, marketing executive, chief executive officer. **Personal:** Daughter of Stratford and Gwendolyn; children: Angelica & Nicholas Jones. **Educ:** Howard Univ; Harvard Bus Sch, MBA. **Career:** Bloomingdales, NY, buyer; Gillette Inc, Boston, dir mkt; Lustrasilk, mkt exec; Pillsbury Inc, Baked Goods Div, dir mkt develop, 1992; Burrell Communs Group, sr vpres, Integrated Mkt Servs, dir, 1992-95; Hilliard Mkt Group LLC, pres & chief exec officer, 1995-; Soft Sheen Prods/ L'Oreal, sr vpres mkt, 1998-2000; DePaul Univ, adj prof; Comfort Cake Co, pres & chief exec officer, 2001-. **Orgs:** Bd dirs, Metrop Family Servs. **Honors/Awds:** Chicago Cosmopolitan Chamber of Commerce Leadership Award, 2004; Heritage Award, BCA, 2005; Business Executive of the Year, Delta Sigma Theta; Phenomenal Woman Award for Entrepreneurship; Top Corporate Women to Watch, Bus Monthly; Top Corporate Women, Essence Mag; Boston City Coun Serv Award; Honorary Citizenships of Atlanta & Memphisl; Nat Restaurant Asn; Direct Mkt Asn; Am Advert Found; Black Enterprise Entrepreneurs Conf; Womens Bus Develop Annual Entrepreneurs Conf; United Way Nat Leadership Conf; Int Inst Res. **Special Achievements:** Top 100 Businesswoman, Dollars & Sense; 100 Women Making a Difference, Today's Chicago Woman; 100 People to Watch, N'Digo Mag; Top 100 Black Business & Professional Women, Dollars & Sense. **Business Addr:** President, Chief Executive Officer, Comfort Cake Company LLC, 1243 S Wabash Ave Suite 201, Chicago, IL 60605, **Business Phone:** (312)922-7403.

HILLIARD, DR. ASA GRANT, III. See Obituaries section.

HILLIARD, EARL FREDERICK
Congressperson (u.s. federal government), lawyer. **Personal:** Born Apr 9, 1942, Birmingham, AL; son of William and Iola Frazier; married Mary Franklin, Jun 19, 1966; children: Alesia & Earl Jr. **Educ:** Morehouse Col, BA, 1964; Howard Univ Sch Law, JD, 1967; Atlanta Univ Sch Bus, MBA, 1970. **Career:** Ala State Univ, asst to pres, 1968-70; Pearson & Hilliard Law Firm, partners, 1972-73; Birmingham Legal Aid Soc, regional heber fel, 1970-72; State Ala, state rep, 1970-72, state sen, 1980-92; WJLD-AM FM Radio, owner, 1985-87; US House Rep, cong man, 1993-2003; Pvt Pract, lawyer, currently. **Orgs:** Pres, Am Trust Life Ins Co, 1977-90; Nat Bar Asn, 1979; Alpha Phi Alpha Fraternity Inc, 1980; pres, Am Trust Land Co, 1980-; Morehouse Col Nat Alumni Asn, 1983; NAACP, 1984; bd trustees, Miles Law Sch, 1984-; bdtrustees, Tuskegee Univ, 1986-; chmn, Ala Black Legis Caucus; bd mem, Cong Black Caucus Inst. **Honors/Awds:** Publ, The Legal Aspects of the Franchise Contract, 1970; Father of the year, Nat Orgn Women, 1981; Outstanding Leadership Award, Alpha Phi Alpha Fraternity Inc, 1980; Gen Order of the Gambia. **Special Achievements:** Book: How To Play Bid Whist, 1984; first African American to represent Alabama in the United States Congress. **Business Addr:** Lawyer, 1625 Castleberry Way, Birmingham, AL 35214, **Business Phone:** (205)798-7352.

HILLIARD, IKE (ISAAC JASON HILLIARD)
Football player. **Personal:** Born Apr 5, 1976, Patterson, LA; son of Ivory Sr and Doris; married Lourdes; children: Kye, Kalyn, Leila Marie & Ilysa Jade. **Educ:** Univ Miami, BA, sociol, Fl. **Career:** NY Giants, wide receiver, 1997-2004; Tampa Bay Buccaneers, wide receiver,2005-09. **Special Achievements:** First round pick, NFL Draft, 1997. **Business Addr:** Professional Football Player, Tampa Bay Buccaneers, 1 Buccaneer Pl, Tampa, FL 33607, **Business Phone:** (813)870-2700.

HILLIARD, PATSY JO
Government official. **Personal:** Married Asa G (deceased). **Educ:** San Francisco State Univ, BA, interdisciplinary soc sci. **Career:** Montessori teacher & lectr; E Point City, GA, mayor; WASET Educ Prod Co, co-owner & exec officer, currently. **Orgs:** Atlanta Chap Links; Nat League Cities Human Develop Steering Comt; past chair, GMA Municipal Govt & Admin Policy Comn; Atlanta Chap, Delta Sigma Theta Sorority, Inc; state chair, GMA Unfunded Mundates Day; Ga Municipal Asn. **Honors/Awds:** Meritorious Award, Omega Psi Phi Eta, Omega Chapter, 1993; Government Award, Women Morris Brown Col, 1993; Salute to Women, YWCA Greater Atlanta, Acade Women Achievers, 1993; Public Service Award, Alpha Kappa Alpha; Enhancing Comm Betterment Award, US Conference of Mayors, 1994; Trailblazers Award, Lyceum Div Sec Educ, Atlanta Public; Torch Award, Delta Sigma Theta Sorority, Inc; East Point Mayor & City Council Resolution for Service; Excellence in Government, NAHS; Certificate of Appreciation, Fulton County, Tony Comm, 1995; Race Realtions Award, Resurgence Atlanta, 1994. Realtions Award, Resurgence Atlanta, 1994. **Special Achievements:** Mayor Hilliard is the first female African-America Mayor in the Greater Atlanta Metropolitan Area & first female Mayor of the City of East Point in the 104th year history of the City.

HILLIARD, RANDY
Football player. **Personal:** Born Feb 6, 1967, Metairie, LA; married Lynette. **Educ:** Northwestern State, La. **Career:** Football player (retired) Cleveland Browns, defensive back, 1990-93;Denver Broncos, 1994-97; Chicago Bears, 1998. **Honors/Awds:** N Club Hall of Fame, Northwestern State univ, 2008.

HILLIARD, ROBERT LEE MOORE
Physician. **Personal:** Born Jan 1, 1931, San Antonio, TX; son of Otho Earl and Robbie Moore; married Marilu Moreno; children: Ronald, Bennie Karen Brown, Portia Denise Byas, Robert Jr, Rudyard Lance, Robbie Lesley, Ruby Lucinda, Barbara Felix. **Educ:** Howard Univ, BS, 1951; Univ TX Med Branch, MD, 1956. **Career:** Nat Med Assn, trustee, 1975-81, 1983-84; Nat Med Asn,

pres, 1982-83; TX Bank, dir, 1975-88; Nat Med Fellowships, dir, 1982-; St Mary's Univ, trustee adv bd, 1983-90; TX State Bd Med Examiners, mem, 1984-91, pres, 1989-90; chmn, NMA Judicial Coun, 1988-94; Women's Clinic San Antonio, sr Ob & Gyn, currently; pvt pract, physician, currently. **Orgs:** Chmn, San Antonio Housing Authority, 1969-71; councilman, San Antonio City Coun, 1971-73; commissioned Honorary Admiral TX Navy State TX, 1978; comnr, San Antonio Fire & Police Civil Serv Comn, 1978-80; Hon Div Surgeon 1st Calvary Div US Army, 1983; vice chmn, United Negro Col Fund, 1971-75; vice chmn, City Water Bd San Antonio, 1980-85; chmn City Water Bd, 1986-88. **Honors/Awds:** Dedicated Service, 1973, Distinguished Leadership, 1982 United Negro Col Fund; Benefactor de la Communidad City San Antonio, 1981; Cert of Appreciation, State TX House Reps, 1983; Achievement Award, S Central Region AKA Sorority, 1983; Distinguished Alumnus, Univ Texas Med Branch, 1991; Recipient, Howard Univ, Distinguished Alumnus Award, 1995. **Military Serv:** USAF, capt flight surg, 1957-60. *

HILLIARD, WILLIAM ALEXANDER
Clergy, bishop. **Personal:** Born in Greenville, TX; married Edra Mae. **Educ:** Western Univ, AB; Shaeffer Theol Sem Western Univ, BD; Hood Theol Sem, DD. **Career:** Bishop (retired); African Meth Episcopal Zion Church, bishop; ministerial pastorates, KS, MO, SC, NC; AME Zion Church, elected to Episcopacy; overseas mission work Zion Church Ghana, Nigeria, Liberia, West Africa, 1960; Zion Conf GA, OK, KS, MO, CA, WA, OR, supr. **Orgs:** Chmn, Div Overseas Minis Nat Coun Church Christ; trustee, Livingstone Col; Nom Comn Deg; chmn, Land Use Comn; World Coun Church; Nat Coun Churches; Nat Asn Advan Colored People; Urban League; Christian Com Coun Detroit; Knight Great Band Liberia W Africa, 1975; selected serv leader, Am Relig Del, ind educ develop, China. **Honors/Awds:** John Bryan Sm African Cen Mem Cit, 12th Episcopal Dist AME Zion Church; First AME Zion Rest Home Cit Laurinburg Dist Cen NC Conf; Mayor John H Reading, Off Mayor; Off Com Coun Mel Ravitz; 77th Legis of City Detroit, MI; Ohio House Rep AL Concione; Father of Yr, Mich Conf, 1975; City of Los Angeles Thomas Ley Off.

HILLIARD, WILLIAM ARTHUR
Journalist, editor. **Personal:** Born May 28, 1927, Chicago, IL; son of Felix Henry and Ruth Little; divorced; children: Gregory Stephen, Linda Karen, Sandra Hilliard Gunder. **Educ:** Pac Univ, BA, jour, 1952, Hon Law Degree. **Career:** Journalist (retired); Oregonian Publ Co, 1952-94. **Orgs:** bd dirs, Nat Urban League, 1973-78; chair, Nat Conf Nat Urban League, 1979-80; chair & bd dirs, Fed Res Bank, San Francisco, Portland Branch, 1991-93; pres, Am Soc Newspaper Ed, 1993-; APA Fraternity; Nat Asn Black Journalists; NAACP; adv bd, Alpha Phi Alpha Fraternity, Freedom Forum First Amendment Ctr. **Honors/Awds:** Anti-Defamation League Torch Liberty Award; Publ Serv Award, Univ Ore; Amos E Voorhies Award, 1991; Equal Opportunity Award, Urban League Portland; Presidential Award, Nat Asn Black Journalists; Special Recognition Award, Asian Am Journalists Asn; Sculpture Friendship Award, Native Am Journalist Asn; Distinguished Serv Award, Ore State Univ; Distinguished Serv Award, Western Oregon State Col. **Military Serv:** USN, Seaman 1st Class, 1945-46. *

HILL-LUBIN, DR. MILDRED ANDERSON
Educator. **Personal:** Born Mar 23, 1933, Russell County, AL; daughter of Luther and Mary; married Dr Maurice A Lubin; children: Walter H Hill & Robert T Hill. **Educ:** Paine Col Augusta, BA, 1961; Western Reserve Cleveland, MA, 1962; Indiana Univ, attended 1964; Univ Minn, attended 1966; Howard Univ & African-19Am Inst, 1972; Univ Ill Urbana-19Champaign, PhD, African Studies, 1974. **Career:** Paine Col, instr, asst prof, 1962-65, 1966-70; Hamline Univ, exchange prof, 1965-66; Paine Col, asst prof Eng, dir EPDA prog, 1970-72; Univ Ill, teaching asst, instr, 1972-74; Univ Fla, assoc prof eng, dir eng prog spec admit stud, 1974-77, asst dean grad sch, 1977-80, assoc prof eng & african studies, 1982, assoc prof emer, currently. **Orgs:** Exec comm, Col Comp & Comm (CCCC), 1977-80; pres, FOCUS, 1978-79; panel mem Adv Coun Mellon Humanities Grant UNCF Col Fund, 1980-90; proj Asn coun, Chief State Sch Officers, 1981-82; consult, Am Coun Educ, 1981-; discipline comm African Lit Fulbright Awards, 1983-86; exec comm., African Lit Asn, 1983-89; pres, Gainesville Chap the Links, 1985-87; bd dir, Gainesville/Alachua Co Ctr Excell, 1985-; Alpha Kappa Alpha Sor; pres, African Lit Asn 1987-88; dir, Gainesville-Jacmel Haiti Sister Cities Prog, 1987-92; pres, The Visionaires, 1988-91; Fla Humanities Coun, 1991-95; Santa Fe Community Col District, 1993-. **Honors/Awds:** Alpha Kappa Mu Honor Soc Paine Col 1960; Travel-Study Grant to W Africa African-Amer Int 19; Trainer of Teachers Fellowship Univ Ill, 1973-74; Women of Distinction Award, Gainesville Area, 1992;, Teacher of the Year, Univ Fla, 1994; Susan B Anthony Award, Gainesville Comm on the Status of Women, 1994. **Special Achievements:** Co-editor of "Towards Defining the African Aesthetic" and articles in, "Southern Folklore Quarterly," "Coll Lang Assn Journal"; "Presence Africaine"; "Okike"; Leadership and Achievement Award, Nu Eta Lambda Chapter Alpha Phi Alpha Fraternity 1988; articles, "The Black Grandmother in Literature," in Ngambika, 1986. **Home Addr:** 6211 NW 23rd Lane, Gainesville, FL 32606. **Business Addr:** Associate Professor Emerita, University of Florida, Department of English, 4008 Turlington Hall PO Box 117310, Gainesville, FL 32611-7310, **Business Phone:** (352)392-0860.

HILLMAN, GRACIA
Association executive, executive. **Personal:** Born Sep 12, 1949, New Bedford, MA; daughter of George and Mary Grace; married Robert E Bates Jr; children: Hillman Martin. **Educ:** Univ Mass, Boston, Col Pub & Community Serv, attended 1978. **Career:** Mass Legislative Black Caucus, admin, 1975-77; Mass Dept Correction, exec asst to comnr, 1977-79; Mass Port Authority, pub & govt affairs spec, 1979; Joint Ctr Polit & Econ Studies, coordr, 1979-82; Nat Coalition Black Voter Participation, exec dir, 1982-87; Cong Black Caucus Found, interim exec dir, 1988; Dukakis Pres Campaign, sr advisor cong affairs, 1988; Coun Found, exec consult, 1989-90; League Women Voters US & League Women Voters Educ Fund, exec dir; WorldSpace Found, pres & chief exec officer; US Dept State, sr coordr Int Women's Issues; US Election Assistance Comn, chair, 2005, comnr, currently. **Orgs:** Nat Polit Cong Black Women; secy, United Front Homes Develop Corp, New Bedford, MA, 1972-76; pres, United Front Homes Day Care Ctr, New Bedford, MA, 1973-76; pres, ONBOARD Community Action Prog, New Bedford, MA, 1974-76; chairperson, Mass Govt Serv Career Prog, 1977-78; vice chairperson, Ctr Youth Serv, Wash, DC, 1985-; prog devel consult, Cong Black Caucus Found, 1987. **Special Achievements:** Nominated by President George W Bush and confirmed by unanimous consent of the US Senate on December 9, 2003, to serve an initial two-year term on the US Election Assistance Commission. **Home Addr:** 3524 Tex Ave SE, Washington, DC 20020. *

HILL-MARLEY, LAURYN NOELLE
Actor, rap musician. **Personal:** Born May 25, 1975, South Orange, NJ; married Rohan Marley; children: Zion David, Selah Louise, Joshua & John. **Educ:** Columbia Univ. **Career:** The Fugees, mem; Albums with the Fugees: Blunted on Reality, 1993, The Score, 1996; Solo Albums: The Miseducation of Lauryn Hill, 1998; MTV Unplugged No 2.0, 2002; Film appearances: Sister Act II, 1993; Rhyme & Reason, 1997; Hav Plenty, 1997; Restaurant, 1998; Film: King of the Hill, 1999; Turn It Up, 2000; TV appearances: "As the World Turns", 1991; "Daddy's Girl", 1996; Songs: "If I Ruled the World (Imagine That)", 1996; "The Sweetest Thing", 1997; "All My Time", 1997; "The Miseducation of Lauryn Hill", 1998; "Can't Take My Eyes off of You", 1998; "Doo Wop (That Thing)", 1998; "Lost Ones", 1999;"Ex-Factor", 1999; "Everything Is Everything", 1999; "Mr. Intentional", 2002; "Say", 2006; "Lose Myself", 2007; Africa Unite, 2008. **Orgs:** Founder, The Refugee Proj. **Honors/Awds:** NAACP Image Awards; Outstanding New Artist; Outstanding Female Artist; Outstanding Album; President's Award; American Music Awards; Favorite New Artist; Am Music Award; Favorite R&B/Soul Album; Grammy Award for Album Of The Year, 1998; Grammy Award for Best New Artist, 1998; Grammy Award forR&B Female Vocal, 1998; Grammy Award for R&B Song, 1998; Grammy Award for R&B Album, 1998; Grammy Award for Album Of The Year, 1999; Favorite Female, R&B/Soul Artist, 2000. **Special Achievements:** Nineteen Grammy Nominations; is first of only seven female artists awarded five Grammys in one year. *

HILLS, JAMES BRICKY
Pharmacist. **Personal:** Born Oct 1, 1944, Opelousas, LA; married Beatrice M Hubbard. **Educ:** Tex Southern Univ, Col Pharm, BS, 1971. **Career:** Tex State Univ, Sch Pharm Alumni, bd dir, 1978; Christian Col Am, bd dir, 1985-86, vchmn bd regents, 1985-86; La Porte Neighborhood Ctr, bd dir, 1986; Lava Rock Apothecary, Pasadena, TX, owner, 1991-; La Porte Apothecary Inc, owner, pres, currently. **Orgs:** Bd dir, Harris Co Pharm Asn, 1982; career consult, N Forest ISD Health Prof, 1984; chmn, Universal Serv Admin Co; Church God Christ, 1985; instr, Greater Emmanuel Bible Inst, 1985; consult, Eastwood Health Clinic, 1985; chmn, House Delegates, 1990-91, Tex Pharmaceut Asn; Nat Asn Advan Colored People; LaPorte Chamber Com; vpres, LaPorte Neighborhood Ctr Inc, 1988-; pres, Agape Investment Develop Corp, 1990. **Honors/Awds:** Outstanding Educator, SS Tex SC Church God Christ, 1982; Outstanding Board Member, HCPA, 1984; Outstanding Board Member, CCA, 1986; Pharmacist of the Year, Harris County Pharm Asn, 1990. **Military Serv:** AUS, E-5, 2 yrs. **Home Addr:** 5447 Sue Marie Lane, Houston, TX 77091. **Business Addr:** Owner, Lava Rock Apothecary, 1907 E Southmore St, Pasadena, TX 77502, **Business Phone:** (713)471-3400.

HILLSMAN, GERALD C.
Association executive. **Personal:** Born Jul 7, 1926, Dayton, OH; married Julia. **Educ:** Marjorie Webster Jr Col, AA, 1975; Nat Inst Drug Progs, Cert 1975. **Career:** VA Hosp Brentwood CA, drug consult, 1971-72; VA Hosp, drug consult, 1972-73; USC Hosp, drug consult; Central City Bricks/Kick Proj, founder, prog dir, 1970-. **Orgs:** Pres Partners Progress; hon mem, bd dir W Coast Asn Puerto Rican Substance Abuse Workers Inc; adv bd mem, Cent City Substance Abuse Trng LA. **Honors/Awds:** Outstanding Comm Serv Award Alliance Drug Ed & Prevention Tehachapi 1974; Outstanding Serv Young People San Bernardino 1974; Dynamic Leadership Award, Friends of Bricks, 1974; Resolution CA State Assembly, 1974; Congressional Medal of Merit, Congressman Augustus F Hawkins 1976; num plaques. **Business Addr:** Program Dir, Central City Bricks/Kick Proj, 1925 S Trinity St, Los Angeles, CA 90011.

HILSON, DR. ARTHUR LEE
School administrator, clergy. **Personal:** Born Apr 6, 1936, Cincinnati, OH; son of Shepard and Bertha McAdoo Wilburn; married Florine McClary, Apr 3, 1982; children: Gabrielle, Antionette & David. **Educ:** Wheaton Col, Springfield Christian Bible Sem, Wheaton, IL, bachelor theol; Andover Newton Theol Sem, Newton Ctr, MA, MDiv; Univ Mass, Amherst, MA, MEd, 1974, EdD, 1979. **Career:** Human Resources Develop Ctr, Newport, RI, human rels consult, 1973; Univ Mass, Amherst, MA, admin asst to dean Grad affairs, Sch Educ, 1973-75, dept head, Veterans Assistance & Coun Servs, 1976-78, dept head, Univ Placement Servs, 1978-87, exec dir, Pub Safety, 1987-92; Univ New Hampshire, fac, Am studies stud affairs, 1993-; New Hope Baptist Church, pastor, sr pastor, 1991-; NH Comnr Human Rights. **Orgs:** Phi Delta Kappa; Am Personnel Officers Asn; Eastern Col Personnel Officers Asn; Col Placement Coun; Nat Asn Advan Colored People; bd mem, Am Veterans Comt; chmn, Nat Asn Minority Veterans Prog Adminr; bd mem, Nat Asn Veterans Prog Adminr; bd member, interim dir, Veterans Outreach Ctr, Greenfield, MA; Int Asn Campus Law Enforcement Adminr; Int Asn Chiefs Police; chmn, United Christian Found; charter pres, Amherst Nat Asn Advan Colored People; bd dirs, Western Mass Girl Scouts; bd dirs, United Way Hampshire County. **Honors/Awds:** Kellogg Fellow, Kellogg Found, 1973-74; Martin Luther King Award, 2000. **Military Serv:** USN, CPO/Cmdr, 1954-73; Navy Achievement Medal. **Home Addr:** 2 Joffre Terr, Portsmouth, NH 03801-4915, **Home Phone:** (603)433-7343. **Business Addr:** Senior Pastor, New Hope Baptist Church, 263 Peverly Hill Rd, PO Box 1473, Portsmouth, NH 03801-1473, **Business Phone:** (603)436-3551.

HILTON, STANLEY WILLIAM, JR.
Executive. **Personal:** Born in Philadelphia, PA; son of Stanley W Sr and Jennie Parsons Cooper; divorced; children: Richard H Hilton. **Educ:** Fisk Univ, BA, 1959; Temple Univ, attended 1959. **Career:** Mill Run Playhouse Niles IL, treas, 1969-70; Shubert Theatre, co mgr, Hair, 1969-70; Orpheum Theatre San Francisco, mgr, 1970-74; "My Fair Lady", "Jesus Christ Superstar", "No Place to be Somebody" San Francisco, co mgr; Park & Theatre Opers Art Park Lewiston NY, dir 1974; Evanston Theatre Co IL, bus mgr; Blackstone Theatre Chgo, mgr 1974-86; Emory & Company, owner, 1990-92; real estate and retail entrepreneur; "Pope Joan," Chicago, gen mgr, 1996; "Hair," Chicago, general manager, 1996; Auditorium Theatre, mgr, 1998-99. **Orgs:** coordr ed & vocational couns, Concentrated Employ Prog, Comn, Col Dist San Fran 1971-73; off mgr, Cook Cty Dept Publ Aid Chicago, 1966-70; exec asst, sec Bd Pensions Meth Ch IL, 1965-66; mem Assoc, Theatrical Press Agt & Mgr NY; reg soc worker, IL; cert teacher & vocational couns, CA; comt mem, Art ist Chicago. **Military Serv:** NGR, 1960. *

HILTON, TANYA
Association executive. **Personal:** Married Steven; children: Taylor & Justin. **Educ:** Univ Minn, BA, bus; postgrad study, Eng. **Career:** Am Asn Univ Women, Educ Found, dir, currently. **Business Phone:** (202)728-7602.

HINDS, LENNOX S
Educator, lawyer. **Personal:** Born in Port of Spain, Trinidad and Tobago; son of Arthur and Dolly Stevens; married Bessie; children: Brent, Yvette & Renee. **Educ:** City Col New York, BS, chem; Mass Inst Technol, MS, chem; Univ Minn; Rutgers Sch Law, JD 1972. **Career:** Dir (retired), prof, partner; Nat Conf Black Lawyers, nat dir, 1973-78; Charles Pfizer & Co, staff; Cities Serv Res & Develop Co, staff; Prisoner's Rights Org Defense, dir, 1971-72; Heritage Found, dir, 1969-72; Citgo Corp, res sect chief, 1964-69; City Col New York, Ctr Legal Educ Urban Policy, Charles H Revson Fel, 1979-980; Rutgers Univ, chmn admin justice prog, prof criminal justice, currently; Stevens, Hinds & White PC, partner, currently. **Orgs:** Vpres, Int Asn Dem Lawyers; Intl Bd Orgn Non-Govt; New Jersey Bar Asn; Nat Minority Adv Comn Criminal Justice; Nat Adv Coun Child Abuse; bd mem, Soc Mobilization Legal Proj; past nat secy, Black-Am Law Students Asn; past bd mem, Law Studetns Civil Rights Res Coun; rep, Int Asn Dem Lawyers, 1973-. **Honors/Awds:** J Skelly Wright Civil Rights Award; Asn Black Law Students, Service Award, 1973; Distguished Alumnus Award, Black-American Law Students Asn, 1974. **Special Achievements:** Authored and supervised numerous publications on the issue of human rights and international law. **Home Addr:** 42 Van Doren Ave, Somerset, NJ 08873. **Business Addr:** Professor, Rutgers University, Criminal Justice Department, Lucy Stone Hall B-253 Livingston, New Brunswick, NJ 08903.

HINE, DARLENE CLARK
Educator, president (organization), editor. **Personal:** Born Feb 7, 1947, Morley, MO; daughter of Leveste and Lottie Mr; children: Robbie Davine. **Educ:** Roosevelt Univ, Chicago, BA, 1968; Kent State Univ, Kent, OH, MA, 1970, PhD, 1975. **Career:** SC State Col, asst prof, 1972-74; Purdue Univ, asst prof, 1974-79, interim dir, Africana & Res Ctr, 1978-79, assoc prof 1979-81, vice provost, 1981-85, prof hist, 1985-87; Truth, Newsletter ABWH, ed, 1979-80; Mich State Univ, John A Hannah prof Am hist, 1987-2004, adj prof, 2004-; Univ Del, vis distinguished prof women's studies, 1989-90; Historian, assoc ed, 1995-; Univ SC, Robert E McNair vis prof southern studies, 1996; Roosevelt Univ, Harold Washington vis prof, 1996; Northwestern Univ, Avalon distinguished vis prof, 1997, bd trustee, prof African Am studies & prof hist, 2004-. **Orgs:** Exec coun mem, Asn Study Afro-Am

Life Hist, 1979-81; dir publications, Asn Black Women Historians, 1979; bd dirs, Consortium Social Sci Asn, 1987-91; Yale Univ Coun Comt Grad Sch, 1988-93; nominating comt chair, Am Hist Asn, 1988-89; exec coun, Southern Hist Asn, 1990-93; Asn Study African Life & Hist Carter G Woodson Scholar-in-Residence Comn, 1995; exec comt mem, Nat Acad Critical Studies, 1996-; chair, Comn Women, Southern Hist Asn, 1996-98; prog comt mem, Orgn Am Hist, 1998; Delta Sigma Theta Sorority Inc, 2000; Am Acad Arts & Sci, 2006; Phi Beta Kappa. **Honors/Awds:** Otto Wirth Alumni Award for Outstanding Scholarship, Roosevelt Univ, 1988; Outstanding Book Award, Gustavus Myers Ctr Human Rights, 1990; Letitia Woods Brown Book Award, Asn Black Women Historians, 1990; Special Achievement Award, Kent Univ Alumni Asn, 1991; Outstanding Reference Source Award, Am Libr Asn, 1994; Zora Neal Hurston-Paul Robeson Award, Nat Coun Black Studies Inc, 1995; Letitia Woods Brown Memorial Anthology Prize, Asn Black Women Historians, 1995; Univ Mass, DHL, 1998; Carter G Woodson Medallion, 2001; Purdue Univ, DHL, 2002; Lauinia L Dock Book Award, Am Asn Nursing. **Special Achievements:** One of the Outstanding College Leaders of the 20th Century, 1999; Author of: Black Victory, The Rise and Fall of the White Primary in Texas, 1979, Black Women in White: Social Conflict and Cooperation in the Nursing Profession 1890-50, 1989; Hine Sight: Black Women and the Re-Construction of American History, 1994, Speak Truth to Power: Black Professional Class in United States History, 1996; Coauthor, A Shining Thread of Hope: The History of Black Women in America, 1998. **Business Addr:** Professor of History, Professor of African American Studies, Northwestern University, Department of History, 1881 Sheridan Rd 202 2-320 Kresge Hall, Evanston, IL 60208.

HINES, ALICE WILLIAMS
Housing developer. **Personal:** Born Sep 8, 1921, San Antonio, TX; daughter of Earl and Clara Williams; married Henry Hines (deceased); children: Henry Nelson, William Earl. **Educ:** Prairie View A&M Univ; St Phillip Jr Col, 1940; Samuel Huston Col, BS, 1942. **Career:** Housing developer (retired); San Antonio Sch Syst, substitute teacher; San Antonio, TX Housing Authority, pub housing mgr. **Orgs:** Pres, treas, Nat Asn Housing & Redevelop Officials, local chapter; past pres, treas, vice pres, past sec, Delta Sigma Theta Sorority; Nat Coalition 100 Black Women. **Honors/Awds:** Delta Woman of the Year, Delta Sigma Theta Sorority, 1982. **Special Achievements:** First African American Woman San Antonio Housing Authority manager in TX, 1965. **Home Addr:** 1028 Dawson St, San Antonio, TX 78202. *

HINES, CARL R
Real estate agent. **Personal:** Born Mar 23, 1931, Louisville, KY; married Teresa Churchill; children: 4. **Educ:** Univ Louisville, BS; Louisville Sch Law. **Career:** Housing Opportunity Ctr, exec dir, 1974; KY Gen Assembly Louisville, state rep, 1978-86; Housing Opportunity Cts Inc, city dir, exec dir; Carl R Hines Realty Co, owner, currently. **Orgs:** Louisville Bd Educ, 1968 & 1972; Housing Com Louisville C C, 1985; Housing Task Force Louisville C C; Mayor's Housing Task Force under Mayor Frank Burke; Nat Asn Community Develop; bd dir, State KY Housing Corp; Coun, Nat Ctr Housing Mgt Wash; adv comt, Non-Profit Housing Ctr; vice chmn, Jefferson Co Bd Educ; Dist Lines Subcom Charter Com Merger Louisville & Jefferson Co Schs; former mem bd, Louisville NAACP, W Louisville Optimist Club; past chmn, Shawnee Dist Boy Scouts Am; pres, Just Men's Civic & Social Club; exec secy, Louisville & Jefferson Co Community Action Comn; vice Chmn bd mgrs, YMCA; chmn, Fifth Region KY Sch Bd Asn; Gov's Adv Coun Educ; Fed Rels Network Nat Sch Bd Asn; dir, chair, Nat Caucus Black Sch, Ky City; Asn Realtors. **Honors/Awds:** Various including Air Force Distinguished Flying Cross. **Military Serv:** USAF 3 yrs. **Business Addr:** Owner, Carl R Hines Realty, 1300 W Broadway Suite 206, Louisville, KY 40203.

HINES, DR. CHARLES A.
Military leader, president (organization), college president. **Personal:** Born Sep 4, 1935, Washington, DC; son of Charles A and Grace W; married Veronica Lamb, Aug 24, 1962; children: Tracy, Charles, Kelly, Christina, Michael, Nicholas & Timothy. **Educ:** Howard Univ, BS, phys educ, 1962; Mich State Univ, MS, police admin & pub safety, 1970; AUS Command & Gen Staff Col, master mil arts & sci, 1971; Johns Hopkins Univ, PhD, sociol, 1983. **Career:** President orgnaization, Military Leader (retired); Univ Md, Univ Col, instr & adj prof, 1971; AUS, 1962, dir eval, War Col, 1980-81, comdr fourteenth mil police brigade, 1983-85, dir officer personnel mgt, 1985-87, dir mgt & budget, off dep chief staff personnel, 1987-89, commanding gen chem & mil police training ctrs, commanding gen, Ft McClellan, AL, commandant, mil police sch, 1989; Smithsonian Inst, Protection & Health Serv, dir, 1992; Prairie View A & M Univ, pres, 1994-2002. **Orgs:** Alpha Phi Alpha Fraternity Inc; FBI Nat Acad Assoc; chmn, Tex Mil Strategic Planning Comn. **Honors/Awds:** Nat Boys & Girls Club Hall of Fame, 1992; Outstanding Black Man, Southern Christian Leadership Conf, 1994. **Military Serv:** AUS, enlisted, 1954-57, maj gen, 1962-92.

HINES, COURTNEY
Publisher, executive. **Career:** Shades of Color, publ, chief exec officer, co-owner & exec, 1995-. **Business Addr:** Co-Owner, Executive, Shades of Color, PO Box 5523, Gardena, CA 90019, **Business Phone:** (323)938-9524.*

HINES, DEBORAH HARMON
Educator. **Personal:** Born Sep 6, 1948, Memphis, TN; daughter of Callie Turner Harmon and Jessie Harmon; children: Christopher Jeffrey & Damion Jesse. **Educ:** LeMoyne-Owen Col, BS, 1970; Univ Tenn, PhD, 1977. **Career:** Meharry Med Col, asst prof, 1976-89; Univ Mass Med Sch, assoc dean minority progs, 1989-91, assoc dean, Sch Serv, 1991-94, assoc provost,1994-95, assoc vice chancellor, 1995-, prof cell biol, currently. **Orgs:** NAMME, 1979-; Asn Am Med Col, Minority Affairs Sect, 1989-; trustee, Mechanics Hall, Mkt Comt, 1996-; pres, Community Adv Comt, Worchester State Col, 1994-; bd dirs, Int Ctr Worcester, 1994-97; bd dirs, Centro Las Americas, 1994-97; Visions 2000, 1999-; Ctr AIDS Res, currently; Am Soc Cell Biol. **Honors/Awds:** Tenn Opportunities, Women Sci & Technol, 1996; Distinguished Alumni Citation, NAFEO, 997; Helping Hands Award, LeMoyne-Owen Col, 1998; Educator Award, Nat Asn Negro Bus & Prof Women, 1999; Leadership Award, Worcester NCCJ, 1999. **Special Achievements:** Architect, co-pi, Robert Wood Johnson Worcester Pipeline Collaborative. **Business Addr:** Professor, Associate Vice Chancellor School Services, University of Massachusetts Medical School, 55 Lake Ave N, S1-842, Worcester, MA 01655-0132, **Business Phone:** (508)856-2444.

HINES, GARRETT
Athlete, military leader. **Personal:** Born Jul 3, 1969, Chicago, IL; married Ileana. **Educ:** Southern Ill Univ, BA, biol sci, MA. **Career:** Athlete (retired), military leader; US Olympic Comt, bobsledder, 1998-2003; USAR, lt, 1996-. **Orgs:** Olympic Athletes Prog, Home Depot. **Honors/Awds:** Armed Forces Athlete of the Year, 1998; Silver medal, 4-man bobsled, Winter Olympics, 2002; Brakeman Push Championships, 2000; Silver medal, World Championships, 2003. **Special Achievements:** With Randy Jones, First African American men to win medals at Winter Olympics, 2002; Fourth in 4-man & sixth in 2-man at 2000 World Championships. **Military Serv:** USAR.

HINES, JIMMIE
Automotive executive. **Career:** Edmond Dodge Inc, pres & gen mgr, 1992-96.

HINES, KINGSLEY B
Lawyer. **Personal:** Born Mar 27, 1944, Pasadena, CA; married Camille; children: Tiffany & Garrett. **Educ:** Univ SC, BA, 1966; Loyola Univ, JD, 1969. **Career:** Family Law Ctr, leg servs, 1969-71; Eng Sq Law Ctr LA, 1970-71; Southern Calif Edison Co, atty, 1972-. **Orgs:** Calif Bar Asn; Los Angeles County Bar Asn; Langston Law Club. **Business Addr:** Attorney, PO BOX 6587, Altadena, CA 91003.

HINES, LAURA M. See Obituaries section.

HINES, DR. MORGAN B
Dentist. **Personal:** Born Aug 11, 1946, New York, NY; son of Emmie Hines and Edgar Hines; children: Morgan B Jr. **Educ:** Toledo Univ, attended 968; Meharry Medical Col, DDS, 1973. **Career:** Hubbard Hosp, intern, 1973-74; Maury Co Health Dept, dentist, 1974-75; Meharry Medical Col, dept oral pathology, assoc prof 1975-76; pvt pract, Columbia, Tenn, prof hypn pract, 1976-; pvt pract, Columbia, Tenn, dentist, 1974-. **Orgs:** Prof artist pen & ink, sculpture, oils, pencil; Tenn Arts League, TN Performing Arts Ctr, Columbia State Comm Col, Tenn State Univ; chmn Maury County Fine Arts Exhibit, 1983; piece in collection of art Mid State TN Regional Library, 1985; mem, Tenn Art League, Columbia Creative Arts Guild, Columbia; hospital staff Maury County Hosp; mem, Amer Dental Assoc, Omega Psi Phi Frat Inc, Tenn Sheriff Org, Tenn Black Artist Assoc; bd dirs, Nashville Amateur Boxing Assoc, Maury Co Creative Art Guild, Tenn/Ala/Ga Amateur Boxing Hall of Fame. **Honors/Awds:** Coach of the Year Award Spirit of America, Tournament Decatur Ala, 1981; Tenn Special Deputy Sheriff; numerous art awards; numerous appreciation awards for dedication to youth & boxing; three articles Amateur Boxing Magazine, 1980-82; poem published in "The World Book of Poetry", 1981. **Home Addr:** 418 W 6th St, Columbia, TN 38401, **Home Phone:** (931)388-7555. **Business Addr:** Physician, 418 W 6th St, Columbia, TN 38401, **Business Phone:** (931)388-3336.

HINES, ROSETTA (THE ROSE)
Radio host. **Personal:** Born in Chattnooga, TN; married; children: 1. **Career:** WGPR, mid-day announcer & prog dir, 1998-; WDET, staff; WJZZ, music dir & drive time announcer, mid-day announcer, disc jockey, currently. **Orgs:** Hon mem Nat Asn Media Women. **Special Achievements:** Voted Number One DeeJay in the Metro Area by the Detroit News in 1982, and the Michigan Chronicle included her name in a Top DeeJay Poll in 1985, first black woman in Michigan to earn a degree in broadcast engineering, first Honorary Member of the National Association of Media Women (Detroit Chapter); First Black Woman in Michigan to earn a degree in broadcast engineering. **Business Addr:** Jockey, Radio One Inc, 3250 Franklin Rd, Detroit, MI 48207-4219, **Business Phone:** (313)259-4005.

HINES, WILEY EARL
Dentist. **Personal:** Born Apr 29, 1942, Greenville, NC; married Gloria D Moore; children: Wandria, Wiley, Derrick. **Educ:** Knoxville Col, BS, 1963; Meharry Med Col, DDS, 1971. **Career:** Oak Ridge Nat Labs, biologist, 1963-65; Melpar, biologist, 1965-67; State NC, pub health dentist, 1971-73; Howard Univ, asst clin prof, 1975; Pvt pract, dentist, 1973-. **Orgs:** Am Dental Asn; Old N St Dent Asn; E Med Dent Pharm Soc, Alpha Phi Alpha, IBPOE, Prince Hall Mason; NC Dent Soc; Fifth Dist Dent Soc; Greenville Planning & Zoning Comn, 1981-86; Mental Health Asn; New E Bank Greenville, bd dirs, 1989-99; RBC Centura Bank, bd dirs, 1999-03. **Honors/Awds:** Distinguished Service Award, ANCA, 1984; Presidential Citation, Nattional Association for Equal Opportunity in Higher Educ, 1989; Community Service Award, Eta Nu Chapter of Alpha Phi Alpha, 1991. **Military Serv:** USNR, 1971-73.

HINES, DR. WILLIAM E
Physician. **Personal:** Born Jun 16, 1958, St Louis, MO; son of Bessie M. **Educ:** Northwestern Univ, Evanston, Ill, BA, 1980; Univ Mo Columbia, Columbia, Mo, MD, 1984; Ohio State Univ, Columbus, Ohio, MS, 1988. **Career:** Wayne State Univ, Detroit, Mich, resident physician, 1984-87; Ohio State Univ, Columbus, Ohio, fel, clin instr, 1987-88; Howard Univ, Wash, DC, asst prof, 1989-90; Ind Univ, Gary, Ind, dir-family pract & clin asst prof, 1990-92; Hines Family Care Ctr, pres & chmn, currently. **Orgs:** Nat Med Asn, 1985-, trustee, Region V, 2001; Am Acad Family Physicians, 1984-; prof bd mem, Stud Nat Med Asn Bd Dirs, 1986-94; exec comt mem, Stud Nat Med Asn Bd Dirs, 1987-89, 1990-94; Prof Bd Mem Emer, 1994; Soc Teachers Family Med, 1991-. **Honors/Awds:** Nat Medical Fellowship Award, Nat Med Fel, 1980-81, 1981-82; Percy H Lee Award for Outstanding Alumni Achievement, Middlewestern Province, Kappa Alpha Psi Fraternity Inc, 1984, 1996; Recognition Award, Stud Nat Asn, Region II, 1987; Black Stud Leadership Award, Grad Stud, Ohio State Univ, 1988; Grand Polemarch's Appreciation Cert, Grand Chap, Kappa Alpha Psi Fraternity Inc, 1988; Fac Orientation Award, Soc Teachers Family Med, 1991; Hon Life Mem, Stud Nat Med Asn, 1994. **Business Addr:** President, Chairman, Hines Family Care Center, 13300 New Halls Ferry Rd Suite C, Florissant, MO 63033, **Business Phone:** (314)830-1900.

HINKLE, JACKSON HERBERT
Clergy. **Personal:** Born Dec 17, 1943, Arkansas; children: Herby, Jack & Samantha. **Educ:** Philander-Smith Col, BA; Greenville Indus Col, DD, 1966; Northwestern Univ. **Career:** Cathedral Faith, Inkster, MI, pastor, cathedral hq, 1975-; New Hebron Baptist Church, Little Rock, AR, pastor; St Bethel Baptist Church, Chicago, pastor; Stinson Cathedral Funeral Home; Mobil Video Tape Co, vpres; Cathedral Faith, E Detroit, founder, pastor. **Orgs:** Founder chmn, Back to God Am Comn; founder, pres, Cathedral Christian Acad; founder, dir, Nat Asn Black Soul Winning Christians, 1974. **Honors/Awds:** Certificate of Appreciation, Gov; Outstanding Serv Award, New Bethel Baptist Ch, 1973. **Business Addr:** Founder, Pastor, Cathedral of Faith, 13925 Burt Rd, Detroit, MI 48223, **Business Phone:** (313)533-9673.

HINSON, ANN J.
Librarian, executive, educator. **Personal:** Married Prince Jr, Aug 28, 1954; children: Gerald, Prince L & Terence. **Educ:** Fla A&M Univ, BS; Atlanta Univ, MSLS. **Career:** Fla A&M Univ, fac, 1961-, dept head & librarian, Coleman Mem Libr, asst dir Pub & Info Servs, currently.

HINSON, ROY MANUS
Basketball player. **Personal:** Born May 2, 1961, Trenton, NJ; married Cynthia Chitwood; children: Calvin Chitwood. **Educ:** Rutgers Univ, New Brunswick, NJ, attended 1983. **Career:** Basketball player (retired); Cleveland Cavaliers, 1983-86; Philadelphia 76ers, 1986-89; NJ Nets, 1989-91.

HINTON, ALFRED FONTAINE
Artist, educator, college teacher. **Personal:** Born Nov 27, 1940, Columbus, GA; son of Eddie H and Johnnie Mae Sipp; married Ann Noel Pearlman, Aug 5, 1965; children: Adam, Melina & Elizabeth. **Educ:** Univ Iowa, BA, 1967; Univ Cincinnati, MFA, 1970. **Career:** Toronto Argonaurs, prof football player, 1963-67; Khadejha Primitive Prints Toronto, design consult, 1967-68; Dickinson Col, Carlisle, PA, instr, 1969; Western Mich Univ, asst prof painting & drawing, 1970-77; Univ Mich Sch Art, assoc prof painting, 1977-82, prof, painting, 1982-2007, prof emer art, 2007-. **Orgs:** Artist Gallery 7, Detroit 1970-; coordr, Visual Arts Mich Acad Sci Arts & Letters, 1972-74; Visual Arts Adv Panel Mich Coun Arts, 1973-; bd mem, Mich Coun Arts, 1980-84; exec bd mem, Concerned Citizen's Arts Michi, 1983-86; panelist, Ongoing Mich Artist Prog, Detroit Inst Arts, 1986-88; master panel bd, Detroit Coun Arts, 1987-. **Honors/Awds:** Research grant, Western Mich Univ 1972-73; Flint Inst of Arts All Mich Exhibition Purchase Award, 1972; 16 one-person shows; 40 invitational & group exhibitions; All-Amer, co-capt; Most Valuable Player, Univ of Iowa Football Team, 1961; Creative Artist Grant, Mich Coun for the Arts, 1985; State of Michigan Commission on Art in Public Places, 1986. **Business Addr:** Professor Emeritus, Univ Michigan, School of Art, 2055 Art & Archit Bldg, Ann Arbor, MI 48109, **Business Phone:** (734)936-0684.*

HINTON, CHRISTOPHER JEROME
Photographer, business owner. **Personal:** Born Sep 23, 1952, Raleigh, NC; son of A M and J D. **Educ:** Winston-Salem State

Univ, NC, BA, music, 1975. **Career:** J D Hinton Studio, Raleigh, NC, photographer, 1976-. **Orgs:** Phi Beta Sigma Frat, 1972-; Garner Road Family, YMCA Back A Child Campaign; United Negro Col Fund Campaign, 1989; Natl Assn Advan Colored People Freedom Fund Banquet, annual. **Honors/Awds:** Phi Beta Sigma Frat Award; Business Award, Raleigh Alumnae Chapter Delta Sigma Theta; photography works featured in natl publications such as: Jet Publication, Black Radio Exclusive, Ohio Historical Soc. **Business Addr:** Co-owner, J D Hinton Studio, 515 S Blount St, Raleigh, NC 27601.*

HINTON, GREGORY TYRONE
Lawyer. **Personal:** Born Nov 22, 1949, Barrackville, WV; son of Nathan Hinton and Amelia Hinton; divorced; children: Gregory T II, Hamilton H & Carol Princess Jean. **Educ:** Fairmont State Col, AB, 1978; West Va Univ, Col Law, JD, 1981; Kellogg Leadership Develop Cert, 1995. **Career:** Thorofare Markets Inc, stock clerk/carry-out, 1968-69; Hope Nat Gas Co, casual rouster, 1970-71; Mont Power Co, elec clerk, 1972-73; Gibbs & Hill, elec clerk, 1973-75; N Cent Opportunity Indus Ctr, exec dir, 1975-78; Fairmont City Coun, coun mem, 1977-86, mayor, 1983-85; WV Univ Col Law, consult; atty pvt pract; Fairmont State Col, prof, 1989-. **Orgs:** Mont Valley Asn Health Centers Inc, 1974-; deacon Good Hope Baptists Church, 1974-; hon mem, Magnificent Souls, 1983; hon mem, Am Soc Nondestructive Testing Fairmont State Col Sect, 1984; corp banking & bus law & minority affairs comt, WV State Bar, 1984-86; vis comt, WV Univ Col Law, 1984-87, consult, 1985-; adv bd, WNPB-TV 1984-86; bd mem, Fairmont Gen Hosp, 1985-86; WV adv comt to US Commn Civil Rights, 1985-89; pres, MT State Bar Asn, 1986-88; ethics comn, WV State Bar, 1986-87; NAACP Legal Redress Comt. **Honors/Awds:** Outstanding Young Man of American Jaycees, 1979 & 1984; West Virginia Outstanding Black Attorney, Black Am Law Stud Asn, Morgantown, WV, 1984; West Virginia Outstanding Black Attorney; Special Award as Mayor, WVa State Asn & PER-PDR Tri-State Conf of Councils IBPOEW PA-OH-WV, 1984; Special Award as Mayor, Dunbar HS class, 1947 & 1984; Black Am Law Stud Asn, Morgantown, WV 1985; Outstanding West Virginia Black Attorney; Wiliam A Boram Award, Teaching Excellence, 1996 & 1997; West Virginia Professor of the Year, Carnegie Found Advancement Teaching, 1997; Alumni of Achievement, Fairmont State Univ, 2000. **Special Achievements:** First black elected Mayor to a major city, WV, 1983. **Home Addr:** 700 Locust Ave, Fairmont, WV 26554. **Business Addr:** Professor, Fairmont State University, School of Business, JH 215a 1201 Locust Ave, Fairmont, WV 26554, **Business Phone:** (304)367-4244.

HINTON, HORTENSE BECK
College administrator. **Personal:** Born Apr 27, 1950, Charlottesville, VA; widowed; children: Shani O, Adisa A & Ajamu A. **Educ:** State Univ NY, BA, psychol, 1971; Univ DC, MA, counsel, 1977; Univ Va, EdD, counr educ, 1988. **Career:** Univ DC, sr counr & asst dir spec serv prog, 1971-78; Univ Va, assoc dean& dir summer prep prog off afro-am affairs, 1978-88; Germanna Community Col, dir, stud develop servs; Northern Va Community Col, Manassas Campus, dean studs develop, interim vpres acad student serv, actg vpres, provost, currently, chief admin & acad officer, currently, dean stud develop, currently. **Orgs:** Am Asn Coun & Develop; Nat Asn Women's Deans & Counselors; Am Asn UnivWomen; Am Asn Affirmative Action; clerk, trustee, youth adv, Free UnionBaptist Church; consult, Alcohol & Other Drug Ctr; Va Commonwealth Univ. **Honors/Awds:** Community Service Award, Culpepper Br, Nat Asn Advan Colored People, 1983;Martin L King Jr Faculty Award, Alpha Phi Alpha Inc, Univ Va, 1986-87;Gubernatorial Appointment, Va State Equal Employment Opportunity Coun,1986-94. **Home Addr:** 21325 Mt Pony Rd, Culpeper, VA 22701. **Business Addr:** Provost, Chief Administrative & Academic Officer, Northern Virginia Community College, Manassas Campus, AA 228 6901 Sudley Rd, Manassas, VA 20109-2399, **Business Phone:** (703)257-6664.

HINTZEN, PERCY CLAUDE
Educator. **Personal:** Born Jan 26, 1947, Georgetown, Guyana; son of Vera Malfalda Khan and Percival Coppin; married Joan Alicia McIntosh Hintzen; married Joan Alicia McIntosh, Mar 7, 1985; children: Ian, Shawn, Alicia & Candace. **Educ:** Univ Guyana, Georgetown, Guyana, BS, 1975; Clark Univ, Worcester, Mass, MA, Int Urbanization & Pub Policy, 1976; Yale Univ, New Haven, CT, MA, sociol, 1977; MPhil, comparative sociol, 1977, PhD, comparative polit sociol, 1981. **Career:** Univ Guyana, Guyana, lectr, 1977-78; Yale Univ, New Haven, CT, acting instr, 1978-79; Univ Calif, Berkeley, Calif, assoc prof, 1979-, African Am Studies, assoc prof, chmn, 1994-, Peace & Conflict Studies, dir, 1994-, Ctr Race & Gender, actg dir, 2006-, prof, currently. **Orgs:** Am Sociol Soc, 1979-; Caribbean Studies Asn, 1979, vpres, 2005- 06, pres, 2006-; Am Polit Sci Asn, 1979-81; Adv Comt, Diaspora Summer Seminar, Fla Int Univ, 2004-. **Honors/Awds:** The Costs of Regime Survival, Cambridge Univ Press, 1989. **Business Addr:** Professor & Chair of African American Studies, Acting Director, Center for Race and Gender, University of California, Berkeley, Department of African American Studies, 660 Barrows Hall, PO Box 2572, Berkeley, CA 94720-2572, **Business Phone:** (510)642-0393.

HIPKINS, CONRAD
Executive, chief executive officer. **Career:** Automated Sciences Group Inc, chief exec officer, share holder. **Home Addr:** 1425 Leegate Rd NW, Washington, DC 20012. *

HITCHCOCK, JIMMY DAVIS, JR.
Football player. **Personal:** Born Nov 9, 1970, Concord, NC. **Educ:** Univ NC. **Career:** New England Patriots, defensive back, 1995-97, 2002; Minn Vikings, 1998-99; Carolina Panthers, 2000-01; Detroit Lions, corner back, 2002.

HITE, NANCY URSULA
Television producer, public relations executive. **Personal:** Born Aug 1, 1956, White Plains, NY; daughter of Forest Davis and Jesse. **Educ:** Spelman Col, BA, 1978; Iona Col, MS, 1985. **Career:** WOVX-Radio Station, reporter, 1978-79; Louis-Rowe Enterprises, pub rel exec secy, 1979-; Potpourri WVOX Radio, producer, 1982-; Freelance journalist newspapers & mag, US, 1982-; Int Photo News Serv, mng ed; Conversation Rowe, producer; Nat Photo News Serv, producer & managing ed, 1985-. **Orgs:** Assoc editor, New Rochelle Branch, NAACP, 1985-86; adv, New Rochelle NAACP Youth Coun, 1987; vpres, New Rochelle NAACP; Alpha Kappa Alpha Sor; secy, African Am Guild of Performing Artists; co-founder, African Heritage Educational Forum; co-founder, Ki Africa Taalimu Shule. **Honors/Awds:** Cert, The Publicity Club of New York, 1981-82; Outstanding Young Women of Am, 1986. **Special Achievements:** Researcher "Break Dancing" pub by Shron Publication, 1984; entertainment articles pub in "Right On" & "Class" Magazines Edri Communications. **Business Addr:** Executive Secretary to the Corporation, Louis-Rowe Enterprises, 455 Main St Suite 99, New Rochelle, NY 10801.*

HIXON, MAMIE WEBB
Educator. **Personal:** Born Mar 30, 1946, Indianola, MS; daughter of Sam and Rosa Lee; widowed. **Educ:** Talladega Col, Talladega, BA, Eng, 1967; Univ W Fla, Pensacola, MA, Eng, 1982. **Career:** Escambia Co Sch Dist, Eng teacher, 1967-80; Pensacola Jr Col, instr Eng, 1980-82; Univ W Fla, Writing Skills Lab, dir, 1982-, Dept Eng, asst prof, currently. **Orgs:** Pres, Local chap, Alpha Kappa Alpha Sorority Inc, 1967-; founding pres, Nat Coalition 100 Black Women, Pensacola Chap, 1993-; bd dirs, Alzheimer's Family Servs Inc, 1995-; bd dir, African Am Heritage Soc, 1995-; W Fla Lit Fedn, 1996-; secy, Links Inc, Pensacola Chap, 1997-; bd dir, Panhandle Tiger Bay Club, 1998-. **Honors/Awds:** Soror of the Year, Alpha Kappa Alpha, 1986, 2001; Distinguished Faculty Service Award, Univ W Fla, 1993; Pyramid Builder Award, Nat Asn Advan Colored People, 1994; President's Award for Leadership in Diversity, Univ W Fla, 2000. **Special Achievements:** Associate Editor: When Black Folks Was Colored, 1993-98; Author: Essentials of English Language Research & Education Associates; Real Good Grammar, 1995; Real Good Grammar, Too, Kendall/Hunt Publishers, 1997; editor: Remembering Those Who Can't Remember: A Chapbook, 2002. **Home Addr:** 3075 N 10th Ave, Pensacola, FL 32503, **Home Phone:** (850)433-3326. **Business Addr:** Assistant Professor, Director of Writing Skills Laboratory, University of West Florida, Department of English, Rm 207 Bldg 50 11000 Univ Pkwy, Pensacola, FL 32514, **Business Phone:** (850)474-2987.

HOAGLAND, EVERETT H.
Educator, poet. **Personal:** Born Dec 18, 1942, Philadelphia, PA; married Darrell Steward Forman; children: Kamal, Nia, Ayan & Reza. **Educ:** Lincoln Univ, Pa, BA, 1964; Brown Univ, MA, 1973. **Career:** Philadelphia Sch System, eng teacher, 1964-67; Lincoln Univ, asst dir admis, 1967-69; Claremont Col, Black Studies, instr Afro-Am poetry, 1969-71; Brown Univ, univ fel, 1971-73; NEH fel, 1984; Southeastern Mass Univ, assoc prof eng; Univ Mass, dartmouth, prof emer, 2005-. **Orgs:** Unitarian Universalist Faith, 1973-; clerk corp & bd mem, New Bedford Foster Grandparents Prog, 1976-82; weekly columnist, New Bedford Standard-Times, 1979-82; contributing ed, Am Poetry Rev, 1984-; poet-in-residence, Wm Carney Acad New Bedford, 1985; NAACP; Black Radical Cong, 1999. **Honors/Awds:** Silvera Award for Creative Writing, Lincoln Univ, 1964; Gwendolyn Brooks Award for Fiction, Black World Mag, 1974; Creative Artists Fel, Mass Arts & Humanities Competition, 1975; fel, Artists Found Annual State WidePoetry Competition, 1985; Certificates of Commendation, Community Serv Arts, Mass State Legis, Mass Governor's Off, Mass Senate; US House Representatives; City New Bedford Award, New Bedford NAACP; Poet Laureate, City New Bedford, Mass, 1994-98. **Special Achievements:** Published book, This City and Other Poems; poem "Just Words" set to musicin symphony of Just Words, 1998. **Business Addr:** Professor Emeritus, University of Massachusetts Dartmouth, Department of English, 285 Old Westport Rd, North Dartmouth, MA 02747-2300.

HOARD, LEROY
Football player. **Personal:** Born May 15, 1968, New Orleans, LA. **Educ:** Univ Mich, educ. **Career:** Football player (retired); Cleveland Browns, running back, 1990-95; Baltimore Ravens, 1996; Carolina Panthers, 1996; Minn Vikings, 1996-99. **Honors/Awds:** Rose Bowl MVP Award, 1989; Rookie of the Year, 1990; Pro Bowl, 1994.

HOBBS, DR. ALMA COBB
Administrator. **Personal:** Born Oct 16, 1949, Farmville, NC; daughter of Nathan R Cobb Sr; divorced; children: Steven L. **Educ:** NC Cent Univ, BS, 1970; NC State Univ, MS, 1975, PhD, 1981. **Career:** Windsor NC Exten Serv, home ec & 4-h agent, 1970-73; Davidson Co Exten Serv, 4-h agent, 1974-78; USDA, nat prog leader, 1988-89; Tenn State Univ, adminr, 1981-90; USDA, asst dep admin, 1990-94, dep admin, 1994; Va State Univ, Sch Agr, dean & adminr, currently. **Orgs:** Treas, Arlington Chap Links, 1992-93; vpres, Hendersonville Links, 1982-92; Alpha Kappa Alpha Sorority; Nat Asn Ext Agent 4-h Agents; Epsilon Sigma Phi; Phi Delta Kappa; Nat Asn Family & Consumer Sci; bd mem, Va Pesticide Control Bd. **Honors/Awds:** Numerous awards and honors including Distingusihed Service Award, 1996; Outstanding Professional Achievements Award, 1996; African American Achievers in Agriculture Award, 1996; USDA Honor Award; Nat 4-H Achievement Award. **Special Achievements:** 25 educational publications at Tennessee State University on a variety of issues related to textiles and clothing, 1982-88. **Business Addr:** Dean, Administrator, Virginia State University, School of Agriculture, PO Box 9081, Petersburg, VA 23806-9081, **Business Phone:** (804)524-5961.

HOBBS, DARYL RAY
Football player, football executive. **Personal:** Born May 23, 1968, Victoria, TX; married Tamiyka. **Educ:** Univ Pac. **Career:** Football player(retired); Coach; Oakland Raiders, wide receiver, 1995-97; New Orleans Saints, 1997; Seattle Sea hawks, 1997; Santa Monica Col, offensive cord; Humble, TX, exec,currently. *

HOBBS, DR. JOSEPH
Educator, physician. **Personal:** Born Aug 5, 1948, Augusta, GA; married Janice Polk. **Educ:** Mercer Univ, BS, 1970; Med Col Ga, MD, 1974. **Career:** Am Acad Family Pract, fel, 1979; Med Col Ga, asst prof family med, 1979,instr family med, 1978, chief resident, 1977, family pract res, 1976, medintern, 1975, prof & chmn family med, currently, GAFP Tollison, distinguished chmn, currently, vice dean primary care & community affairs,Coun Grad Med Educ of the Health Resources & Servs Admin, currently, sr. assoc dean, currently. **Orgs:** Richmond Co Med Soc, 1978; vpres, Stoney Med Dental Pharm Soc, 1979; team physician, T W Josey High Sch; Thomas W Johnson Award, Am Acad Family Physicians, 2003. **Honors/Awds:** Recipient Commendation Family Practice Resident, Med Col Ga, 1978; Thomas W. Johnson Award, American Academy of Family Physicians, 2003. **Business Addr:** Professor and Distinguished Chair, Vice Dean for Primary Care and Community Affairs, Medical College Georgia, Department Family Medicine, HB 4012, Augusta, GA 30912, **Business Phone:** (706)721-4074.

HOBSON, CAROL J. See SMITH, CAROL J.

HOBSON, CHARLES BLAGROVE
Executive. **Personal:** Born Jun 23, 1936, Brooklyn, NY; son of Charles Samuel and Cordelia Victoria; married Maren Stange, Jun 24, 1990; children: Hallie & Clara. **Educ:** Brooklyn Col, 1960; Emory Univ, 1976. **Career:** ABC-TV, New York, NY, producer, 1967-71; WETA-TV, Wash, DC, tv producer, 1967-89; Vassar Col, Poughkeepsie, NY, instr, 1969-71; Clark Col, Atlanta, GA, dir mass communs, 1971-76; Visamondo Prod, Montreal, Canada, writer, 1988; Jamaica Broadcasting Corp, consult, 1988; WNET-TV, New York, NY, dir mkt planning, 1989-; Medgar Evers Col, City Univ NY, prof, sr res fel; Vanguard Documentaries Inc, founder, artistic head, currently. **Orgs:** Consult, Nat Endowment Arts, 1976-87, NEH; bd mem, Am Beautiful Fund, 1977-87; exec producer, The Africans, Jumpstreet, Global Links; Writer's Guild Am, African Studies Asn; consult, Greycom Int; consult, Nat Black Arts Festival; bd mem, Am Beautiful Fund; pres & bd dirs, Nat Black Programming Consortium; educ sub-comt, Mus Modern art; consult, Am Jazz Mus, Kans City, MO. **Honors/Awds:** Capital Press Club Award, 1968; Emmy Award NATAS, 1968; Governor's Award, Natl Acad Arts & Sci, 1976; WC Hardy Award, 1981; Natl Black Prog Consortium Award, 1985; Ohio State Award, 1987; One of the Leading TV Producers, Millimeter Magazine; The Japan Prize, 1987; Golden Eagle Award, CINE, 1987; Ohio State Award for Excellence in Educational Programming, 1988; Fulbright Scholar, The University of Munich Amerika Institute, 1996-97; Fulbright Scholar in Munich, Germany, 1996-97. **Special Achievements:** Ranked one of the fifty top producers in the film and television industry by Millimeter magazine. **Military Serv:** AUS, pfc, 1962-63. **Home Addr:** 293 State St, Brooklyn, NY 11201, **Home Phone:** (917)804-8768. **Business Addr:** Founder, Artistic Head, Vanguard Documentaries Inc, 293 State St, Brooklyn, NY 11202-6624.

HOBSON, DONALD LEWIS
Judge, government official. **Personal:** Born Jan 11, 1935, Detroit, MI; son of Oscar Collins and Theresa Lewis; divorced; children: Donna Lynne. **Educ:** Ohio State Univ; Eastern Mich Univ, BSc,

hist; Mich State Univ, MA; Detroit Col Law, JD; Univ Mich; Wayne State Univ Law Sch; Hampton Inst, US Naval Acad; US Naval Justice Sch; Nat Judicial Col; Howard Col; Wayne Community Col. **Career:** Government official, judge (retired); Detroit Pub Sch Syst, social science teacher, 1957-64; Detroit Bd Educ Job Upgrading Prog, coordr; US Dept Justice, Washington; Goodman Eden Millender Goodman & Bedrosian Detroit, assoc partner; Common Pleas Ct, City Detroit, judge; Recorders Ct, Detroit, judge. **Orgs:** Arbit panelist mem, Detroit Regional Adv Coun Am Arbitration Asn; nat execbd & adv bd, Detroit Chap Nat Lawyers Guild; exec bd, Am Trial Lawyers Asn; Nat Bd Coun Legal Educ Opportunities; hearing referee, Mich Civil Rights Comt; secy, Income Tax Review Bd, City Detroit; Mich Supreme Ct's Spec Comm on Landlord-Tenant Problems; Nat Bd Nat Bar Asn; State Bar Mich Rep Assembly; counr, State Bar Grievance Bd; treas, vpres, pres & bd dirs, Wolverine Bar Asn; Nat Asn Equal Opportunity Higher Educ; Omega Psi Phi Fraternity; Phi Kappa Delta Fraternity. **Honors/Awds:** Eastern Mich Univ Alumni Honors Award, 1974; DHL, Shaw Col, Detroit, 1977; Hon Doctor of Laws Degree & DDiv; Black Lawyers, Law Practice & Bar Asn. **Military Serv:** USNR, comdr. **Home Addr:** 2136 Bryanston Crescent S, Detroit, MI 48207. *

HOBSON, MELLODY
Businessperson. **Personal:** Born Apr 3, 1969, Chicago, IL; daughter of Dorothy Ashley. **Educ:** Graduated from St. Ignatius College Preparatory, 1987; Princeton Univ, BA, 1991. **Career:** Ariel Capital Management Senior VP and Dir of Marketing, 1991-2000; Pres. of Ariel Capital Management, 2000-. **Orgs:** Chairman of the Ariel Mutual Funds Board of Trustees; Board of directors: Field Museum, Do Something (nonprofit Organization for young people); Civic Federation of Chicago; Chicago Public Library, Tellabs (Naperville, IL); Princeton Club of Chicago; St. Ignatius Preparatory School Alumni organization; director of three public companies: DreamWorks Animation SKG, Inc., The Estee Lauder Companies Inc. and Starbucks Corp; Board of Governors of the Investment Company Institute, a Term Member of the New York Council on Foreign Relations, and is a former Trustee of Princeton Univ; Member of the Economic club of Chicago, the Commercial Club of Chicago, and the Young Presidents Organization (YPO). **Honors/Awds:** Named a Global Leader of Tomorrow by the World Economic Forum in Davos; One of the 20 Leaders of the Future, Ebony Magazine, 1992; one of 20 Under 30, Working Women Magazine, 1992. **Special Achievements:** Financial contributor to ABC network's Good Morning America and reports on finance for WGN's Minority Business Report. **Business Addr:** Ariel Investments, LLC, 200 East Randolph Dr., Suite 2900, Chicago, IL 60601, **Business Phone:** (312)726-0140.*

HOBSON, MELLODY L.
Marketing executive. **Personal:** Born Apr 3, 1969, Chicago, IL; daughter of Dorothy Ashley. **Educ:** Princeton Univ, Woodrow Wilson Sch Int Rels & Pub Policy, BA, 1991. **Career:** Ariel Capital Mgt, Chicago, vpres mkt, 1991-94; Sr vpres & dir mkt, 1994-00; dir & pres, 2000-; Ariel Mutual Funds Bd Trustees, chmn; bd dir, DreamWorks Animation SKG Inc; bd dir, Estee Lauder Co Inc; Starbucks Corp, dir. **Orgs:** Secy, Princeton Club of Chicago, 1991-; bd dir, Civic Fedn Chicago; bd dirs, Chicago Pub Libr; trustee, Chicago Architecture Found; bd dir, Field Mus; bd dir, Do Something; St Ignatius Prep Sch Alumni org. **Honors/Awds:** Named one of 20 Leaders of the Future, Ebony, 1992; named one of 20 Under 30, Working Women Magazine, 1992. **Business Addr:** President, Ariel Capital Management LLC, 200 East Randolph Dr Suite 2900, Chicago, IL 60601.*

HOBSON, ROBERT R.
Government official. **Personal:** Born Oct 20, 1930, Memphis, TN; children: Mafara, Alicia. **Educ:** Tenn State Univ, BA Govt, 1952; Howard Univ, attended 1957; Johns Hopkins Univ, attended 1959. **Career:** Pres's Comt Equal Employ Off Fed Contract Compliance, sr compliance adv, 1963-71; Nat Urban Coalition, asst to the pres, 1971-73; Off Fed Contract Compliance, assoc dir, 1973-82; White House, sr staff mem. **Honors/Awds:** Merit Awards, OFCCP Labor Dept awards, 1967, 1969, Distinguished Serv Career 1974, Special Achievement, 1975-79, Commendation Excellent Serv, 1976. *

HOBSON-SIMMONS, JOYCE ANN. See SIMMONS, JOYCE HOBSON.

HODGE, ALETA S.
Writer, financial manager. **Personal:** Born May 15, 1954, Indianapolis, IN; daughter of Frank and Doryce Hodge. **Educ:** Stanford Univ, BS, 1976; Indiana Univ, MBA, 1978. **Career:** Ind Univ, instr; Purdue Univ, Indianapolis, instr; Money Counsel Inc, pres, 2003-; auth: Women & Money Common Sense Handbook, 1995; The Value Book, 2001; columnist, The Indianapolis Star, 2000-. **Orgs:** Financial Planner Asn, 1998-; Inst Cert Financial Planners, Stanford Alumni Asn, 2007. **Business Addr:** President, Money Coun Inc, 709 N Pk Ave Suite 202, PO Box 441127, Indianapolis, IN 46202, **Business Phone:** (317)634-8049.

HODGE, DR. CHARLES MASON
School administrator. **Personal:** Born Jun 25, 1938, Seguin, TX; son of Clifford D and Goldie M Campbell; married Elizabeth Howze; children: Gwendolyn & Clinton. **Educ:** Univ Ark, Pine Bluff, BA, 1960; Univ N Tex, MEd, 1969; Univ Tex, EdD, 1976. **Career:** Terrell HS Ft Worth, high sch teacher, 1964-69; Jarvis Christian Col, instr social studies educ, 1969-73; AR Desegregation Ctr Pub Sch, assoc dir, 1973-74; Ark Dept Higher Educ, co ordr human res, 1974-76, asst dir res & planning, 1980; Univ Cent Ark, assoc prof & teacher educ, 1976-80, asst vpres acad affairs, 1980-83, dean, col educ, 1983-89; Lamar Univ,Beaumont TX, dean col educ, 1989; Bowie State Univ, Sch Educ, asst dean, currently, Dept Educ Leadership, interim chmn, currently. **Orgs:** Bd trustees, Robert Morris Col, Philadelphia, 1992-; bd dir, Tex Com Bank-Beaumont, 1991; Sch Deseg Monitoring Team, US Dist Ctr, 1980; Unit Accreditation Bd Nat Coun Accred Teacher Educ, 1986-; Ark State Coun EconEduc, 1987-89; ed bd, Teacher Educ & Pract J; Am Asn Col Teacher Educ; Nat Coun Accreditation Teacher Educ. **Business Addr:** Assistant Dean, Interim Chair, Bowie State University, 14000 Jericho Pk Rd, Bowie, MD 20715-9465, **Business Phone:** (301)860-4000.

HODGE, CYNTHIA ELOIS
Dentist. **Personal:** Born Feb 23, 1947, Troop, TX; daughter of Robert Spencer and Doris Lydia; divorced; children: Delwyn Ray Madkins. **Educ:** Univ Denver, pre-19dent, 1975; Univ Ore Health Scis Ctr Sch Dent, DMD, 1979; Univ NC, Chapel Hill, MPH, 1985; Harvard Univ, MPA. **Career:** Dent C, assoc dent, 1979-82; Post Grad Training Univ NC, 1982-85; Meharry Med Col, Dept Hosp Dent, chairperson, 1985-90; Meharry Med Col, Sch Dent, Nashville, TN, dir, gen pract residency prog, 1985-90; Pvt Pract, gen dent, 1990-; Univ NC, MPH, 1994; Fairrow Dent Ctr, dentist; Univ Conn Health Ctr Sch Dent Med, dir, 2003-, asst dean, Off Community & Outreach Progs, currently. **Orgs:** Nat Dental Asn, 1979-; Am Dent Asn, 1979-; Dent consult, Multnomah County Health Dept Portland, OR, 1979-81; dent consul, Health Adv Bd, Albina Ministerial Alliance, Headstart Prog, 1980-82; dent coordr regional, Nat Dent Asn, 1981-82; Headstart Prog; Infectious Dis Control Comn; Tenn Dent Asn, 1987-; Health & Educ Facil Bd Metrop Davidson County, 1990-; Am Asn Women Dentists, 1990-; Acad Gen Dent, 1994-; Am Asn Pub Health Dent, 1994-; chairperson, Commt Minority Affairs; exec bd, Nashville Cares Inc; Am Cancer Soc Prof Educ Comn; bd advisors, Natchez Col, MS; Inst Health Care Poor & Underserved, Meharry Med Col. **Honors/Awds:** Certificate of Recognition, Wash Monroe High Sch; Award for Participation in Dental Field Experiences, Wash Monroe High Sch, Portland, OR, 1981; valuable contribution to the Scientific Session, Nat Dent Asn, 1988; Award for Scientific Presentation, Nat Dent Asn, 1991, 1992. **Business Addr:** Assistant Dean for Admissions and Outreach, University of Connecticut School of Dental Medicine, 263 Farmington Ave, Farmington, CT 06030.*

HODGE, DEREK M.
Lawyer, government official. **Personal:** Born Oct 5, 1941, St Croix, Virgin Islands of the United States; son of Rexford and Enid; divorced; children: Marisol & Jonathan. **Educ:** Mich State Univ, BA, 1963; Georgetown Univ Law Ctr, JD, 1971. **Career:** Law Firm Hodge Sheen & Finch, partner, 1972; pvt pract, atty, 1978-84; USVI Legis, sen pres, 1984-86; VI Govt Comms Rules, Trade, Tourism & Econ Develop, Conserv Recreation & Cult Affairs, mem, 1984-86; Govt VI, lt gov, 1986-94; US VI, comnr ins; Mackay & Hodge, partner, currently. **Orgs:** Pres, VI Partners for Health, 1980-81; chmn, bd dir, St Dunstan's Episcopal Sch, 1983-84; titular head Dem Party VI, 1983-86; pres, VI Bar Asn, 1984-86 mem, Charlotte Amalie Lawyer Asn. **Honors/Awds:** Appreciation plaque 4-H Club of VI, 1984; Certificate of Merit Small Business Devel Center, 1986; Recognition plaque, Lutheran Social Serv of VI, 1986; Proclamation Fulton Co GA, 1987; Cert of Membership, Joint Ctr Polit Studies Asn Prog, 1987. **Military Serv:** AUS 1967; Army Nat Guard capt, staff judge advocate, 1979-83. **Business Phone:** (340)774-3971.

HODGE, DONALD JEROME
Basketball player. **Personal:** Born Feb 25, 1969, Washington, DC. **Educ:** Temple Univ. **Career:** Basketball player (retired); Dallas Mavericks, ctr, 1991-96; Charlotte Hornets, ctr, 1996.

HODGE, ERNEST M
Automotive executive, chief executive officer, business owner. **Career:** March/Hodge Holding Co, chief exec officer, currently, March/Hodge Automotive Group, co-chief exec officer, currently; Heritage Cadillac Inc, chief exec officer & owner, currently. **Business Phone:** (770)960-0060.

HODGE, MARGUERITE V.
Social worker. **Personal:** Born May 21, 1920, Avondale, PA; married Dee; children: Dee. **Educ:** Howard Univ, BA, 1943; Univ Chicago, 1947. **Career:** Provident Hosp, med social worker, 1944-46; Provident Hosp, psychiatric social worker, 1948-49; Provident Hosp, med social worker, 1947-48; Municipal TB Santorium, med social worker, 1949-51; Field Rep, 1953-60; Agency Coordr, 1960-64; UCLA, field instr, 1966-67; Prof & Vol Serv, supr, 1965-68; UCLA, field instr, 1969-70; Information & Referral Serv, supr, 1968-70; Lung Asn, regional dir, 1970-; Placement Student, field instr, 1974. **Orgs:** Nat Conf Social Welfare; Nat Asn Social Workers; licentiate Royal Acad Health; consult S Ctr Area Welfare Planning Coun; adv com LA Urban League Health & Welfare Comt Head start; SEARCH Bd USC Sch Med; discussion leader Alchololism Conf Welfare Planning Coun, 1962; discussion leader Conf Home Care Welfare Planning Coun & City Hope, 1962; registration chmn, Pacific SW Regional Inst NASW, 1966; serv & rehab comn Am Cancer Soc CA Div Cervical Cancer Screening Sub-comt; bd dir, CA Asn Mental Health, 1973; Prog Planning Com So CA Pub Health Asn; LA Co Inter agy Coun Smoking & Health; Mayor's Adv Coun Handicapped, 1974; adv comt Area IX Regional Med Prog; panel participant TB Asn; Numerous Other Comt; westminster Pres; Alpha Kappa Alpha Sor. **Honors/Awds:** Volunteer Service Award, Patton State Hosp, 1965-66; Community Service Award, El Santo Nino Comn Develop Proj Cath Welfare Bur, 1972; Special Recognition Award, S Ctrl Area Planning Coun, 1973; Recipient, Special Recognition Award, Bd Dir Lung Asn 20 yrs Serv, 1974; Special Award King-Drew Sickle Cell Ctr, 1974; Special Award, Kedren Community Mental Health Ctr.

HODGE, NORRIS
Broker, appraiser. **Personal:** Born Apr 3, 1927, Kingsville, TX; married Ruby Faye; children: Brenda, Theodora, Myrna. **Educ:** BBA, MS, 1964. **Career:** TX Southern Univ, asst prof; Friends Univ Wichita KS, asst prof; Hodge & Co Realtors, currently. **Orgs:** Am Econ Asn. **Honors/Awds:** So Econ Asn Recipient Ford Found Fellowship; Western Econ Asn; Gen Elect Fellowship Univ Chicago. **Business Addr:** Real Estate Agent, Hodge & Company Realtors, 13027 Hiram Clarke, Houston, TX 77045.

HODGE, DR. W. J.
College president. **Career:** Simmons Univ Bible Col, Louisville, Ky, pres & chancellor, 1982-96.

HODGE, WILLIAM ANTHONY
Businessperson. **Personal:** Born Apr 26, 1962, Tuskegee Institute, AL; son of Johnie Albert and Lula Pearl McNair; married Dr Audrey Maria Hodge MD, Dec 16, 1989; children: Alani Maria. **Educ:** Tuskegee Univ, Tuskegee Inst, AL, BS, 1985; Auburn Univ, AL, MS, 1989. **Career:** Purdue Univ Dept Agronomy, W Lafayette, IN, res asst, 1983; Walt Disney World, Epcot Ctr, Orlando, Fl, agri intern, 1983-84; Tuskegee Univ Sch Agri, Tuskegee, AL, teaching asst, 1984-85, soil scientist & water qual tech, 1989-, extension specialist & water qual coop exten prog, 1991-; Oak Ridge National Labs, Oak Ridge, TN, res asst, 1985; Auburn Univ, Auburn, AL, grad res asst, 1986-89; Carter Funeral Home, mgr, funeral dir, 1992-; US Transportation Inc, owner, 1998. **Orgs:** Am Soc Agron, 1983-; Gamma Sigma Delta, 1987; Negro Airmen Int, 1988-; Ala Agri & Forestry Leaders, 1989-; Worshipful master, Prince Hall Masonic Lodge 17, 1990-; Ala Farmers Fedn, 1990-; Ala Funeral Dirs Asn, 1995-; Ala Soil & Water Conserv Soc; bd mem, Bullock Co Hosp, 1997-; Union Springs Housing Authority, 1997-; Southern Region Sustainable Agri Res & Educ. **Honors/Awds:** Outstanding Agronomy Student, Am Soc Agron, 1985; Nat Honarary, Alpha Kappa Mu, 1985. **Home Addr:** PO Box 167, Union Springs, AL 36089. **Business Addr:** Training Coordinator, Tuskegee University, 202 Extension Bldg, Tuskegee, AL 36088.

HODGES, DR. CAROLYN RICHARDSON
Educator. **Personal:** Born Nov 25, 1947, Roebling, NJ; daughter of Luther Kendrick and Mary Catherine; married John Oliver, Apr 8, 1972; children: Daniel Oliver. **Educ:** Arcadia Univ, BA; Beaver Col, BA, 1969; Univ Chicago, MA, Ger lang & lit, 1971, PhD, Ger lang & lit, 1974. **Career:** Univ Chicago, trustee fel, 1969-73; Cent YMCA Community Col, instr ger, 1970-72; Kennedy-King Jr Col, asst prof humanities, 1975-82; Univ Tenn, Knoxville, asst prof Ger, 1982-88, assoc prof Ger, 1988-, Col Arts & Sci, Acad Personnel, assoc dean, chmn, prof Ger lang, currently, Dept Modern Foreign Lang & Lit, head, currently. **Orgs:** Tenn Collab Coun Foreign Lang, 1986-; vpres, Tenn Am Asn Teachers Ger, 1987-89; bd mem, Tenn Foreign Lang Teacher Asn, 1989-92; secy & treas, Southern Comparative Lit Asn, 1990-. **Honors/Awds:** Dissertation Year Award, Ford Found, 1973-74; Faculty Travel Award, 1983; Chancellor's Citation for Extraordinary Service, Univ Tenn, 1987; Merrill Research Award, Col Educ, Univ Tenn, Knoxville, 1990, 1992; Outstanding Advising, Col Lib Arts, 1991. **Home Addr:** 4815 Skyline Dr, Knoxville, TN 37914. **Business Addr:** Professor of German Language, Department Head, University of Tennessee, College of Arts & Science, Department Modern Foreign Lang & Lit, 701 McClung Tower, Knoxville, TN 37996-0470, **Business Phone:** (865)974-3421.

HODGES, CRAIG ANTHONY
Basketball coach, basketball player. **Personal:** Born Jun 27, 1960, Park Forest, IL; married Allison D Jordan, Jan 1, 1996; children: Jibril & Jamaal; married Allison D Jordan, 1996. **Educ:** Calif State Univ, Long Beach, attended 1982. **Career:** Basketball player (retired), basketball coach; San Diego Clippers, guard, 1982-84, Milwaukee Bucks, guard, 1984-88; Phoenix Suns, guard, 1988-89; Chicago Bulls, guard, 1989-92; Chicago State Univ, men's basketball coach; Los Angeles Lakers, shooting coach, currently. **Orgs:** Pres, Operation Unit; Save The Youth; pres, Three Point Inc. **Honors/Awds:** Basketball Digest's Second Team All-Rookie squad, 1982-83. **Business Addr:** Assistant Coach, Los Angeles Lakers, 555 N Nash St, El Segundo, CA 90245, **Business Phone:** (310)426-6000.

HODGES, DR. DAVID JULIAN
Educator, anthropologist. **Personal:** Born Jan 11, 1944, Atlanta, GA. **Educ:** NY Univ, PhD, 1971, MA, 1969; Morris Brown Col, magna cum laude, BA, 1966; Sophia Univ Tokyo, spl grad study, 1967; Columbia Univ, attended 1966; Emory Univ GA, attended 1965; Harvard Univ, post grad study, 1973. **Career:** NY City Youth Bd, sr st club worker, 1965-69; So Educ Found fel, 1965; Woodrow Wilson fel, 1965; So Fel Fund fel, 1969-71; Voorhees Tech Inst NY, part time instr, 1969-70; Nassau Comm Col Garden City, instr, 1970; Am Asn Univ Prof Educ Action Specialist NY Comn Devel Agency, 1969-71; Heritage Musem NY, cur, 1971-73; Cornerstone Change Inc, pres & founder, 1974-; Hunter Col, prof anthrop, 1985, Sch Educ, actg dean, currently. **Orgs:** Adv bd, YMCA, 1970-; PGM Serv Com YMCA Greater NY; AAAS; Phi Delta Kappa; Alpha Kappa Delta; Alpha Kappa Mu; Soc Applied Anthrop; Nat Soc Study Educ; Am Anthrop Asn. **Honors/Awds:** New York University Founder's Day Award, 1973. **Military Serv:** AUS, 1966-68. **Business Addr:** Acting Dean, Professor of Anthropology, Hunter College, Department of Anthropology, Rm N733 695 Pk Ave, New York, NY 10021.

HODGES, HELENE
Association executive, executive director. **Personal:** Born Apr 27, 1949, Schwabach, Germany; daughter of Joseph J and Eugenie Ann Hellwig. **Educ:** Finch Col, attended 1971; St John's Univ, Jamaica, NY, attended 1975, prof dipl, 1979, PhD, 1985. **Career:** Virgin Islands Dept Educ, teacher, 1970-71; NY Bd Educ, teacher & sch dir, 1971-86; Asn Supv & Curric Develop, Alexandria, VA, dir res & info, 1986-93, dir collab ventures, 1993-. **Orgs:** Educ comn mem, Martin Luther King Jr Fed Holiday Comn, 1986-; steering comt mem, NAEP, 1990; selection comt mem, CSSO, Nat Teacher of the Yr Prog, 1991-; Phi Delta Kappa; Nat Alliance Black Sch Educrs; Mid-Atlantic Equity Consortium. **Honors/Awds:** Distinguished Achievement, Educ Press Asn, 1988; Award for Excellence in Educational Journalism. *

HODGES, DR. JACQUELINE
Educator. **Personal:** Married William A Earnest. **Educ:** Huntingdon Col; MEd. **Career:** Stanhope Elmore High Sch, Mill brook, AL, teacher; Wayne County Community Col Downtown Campus, pres. **Orgs:** Bd mem, 1996-99, vpres, 1999-2000, pres, 2001, Huntingdon Col Nat Alumni Asn. *

HODGES, DR. JOHN O.
Educator. **Personal:** Born Jan 26, 1944, Greenwood, MS; son of Tommy James and Samantha Wilson; married Carolyn R Richardson, Apr 8, 1972; children: Daniel. **Educ:** Univ Nantes, France, cert, 1967; Morehouse Col, Atlanta, GA, BA, 1968;Atlanta Univ, Atlanta, GA, MA, 1971; Univ Chicago, IL, MA, 1972, PhD, Religion and Literature, 1980. **Career:** Morehouse Col, Atlanta, GA, dir lang lab, 1969-70; Barat Col, Lake Forest,IL, lectr eng, 1970-72, dir, Afro-Am studies, 1972-75, asst prof eng,1972-75; Univ Chicago, IL, asst dean univ students, 1977-82; Univ Tenn, Knoxville, TN, Dept Relig Studies, asst prof, 1982-88, assoc prof, 1988-, acting head, 1989-90, chair, African & African-Am Studies, 1997-2002. **Orgs:** Modern Lang Asn, 1981-; Am Acad Relig, 1982-; Col Lang Asn, 1982-; S Atlantic Modern Lang Asn, 1983; Langston Hughes Soc; Richard Wright Circle. **Honors/Awds:** Merrill Overseas Fellow, Morehouse, 1966-67; Rockefeller Fellow,Rockefeller Found, 1970-71; Ford Fellow, Ford Found, 1976-78; NEH Fellow, Nat Endowment Humanities, 1984; Outstanding Teacher Award, Univ Tenn Nat Alumni Asn, 1996; Cal Johnson Outstanding Faculty Member, Univ Tenn, 2000-01. **Home Addr:** 4815 Skyline Dr, Knoxville, TN 37914. **Business Addr:** Associate Professor, University of Tennessee, Department of Religious Studies, 509 McClung Tower, Knoxville, TN 37996-0450, **Business Phone:** (865)974-6983.

HODGES, LILLIAN BERNICE
Business owner. **Personal:** Born Apr 2, 1939, Rosebud Island Mar, AR; married Alzetl Joe Nathan; children: Lillian L. **Educ:** Shorter Jr Col, N Little Rock, AR, 1958; TX Women Univ Denton TX, attended1965. **Career:** E Cent Econ Corp, outreach person, 1965-66; Univ AR, nutritionist, 1967; Mr Tax Am, mgr, 1968-74; sunday sch teacher, Beautiful Zion Baptist Church, 1976-80; Local 282, United Furniture Workers Am, rep, 1977-80; countries NAACP, liaison officer, 1985. **Orgs:** Vice chmn, Coalition Better Broadcast, 1968-71; dir, L R Jackson Girls Club Am; vpres, Demo Women Critt Co; ex-sec, Critt Co Improv Asn; pres, NAACP Critt Co, 1972-78; vpres, State NAACP, 1973-75; bd mem, Bd METOG Youth Serv, 1973-75. **Honors/Awds:** Outstanding Participation Univ S Census Bus, 1970; Outstanding Award Minority Bus, Minority Bus Develop, 1975; Outstanding Serv Award, NAACP Local, 1976; Outstanding Religious Work Non-Denominational Coun, 1979.

HODGES, MELVIN SANCHO
Lawyer. **Personal:** Born Jan 1, 1940, Columbia, SC; son of Hilliard Jr and Aubrey; married Ugertha Birdsong; children: Melvin II. **Educ:** Morehouse Col, 1960; UC Santa Barbara, BA, 1965; UC Berkeley, JD, 1969. **Career:** IBM Corp, atty, 1969-72; Hastings Law Col, prof, 1972-73; St Calif, dep atty gen, 1976-78; Chevron USA Inc, atty, 1978-93; pvt practice, atty, 1993-; Dianne Williams Law Off, atty. **Orgs:** Ast treasurer, Am Asn Blacks Energy, 1984-86; Calif Bar Asn; San Francisco Bar Asn; Charles Houston Bar Asn; financial comt, Bay Area Black United Fund, 1982-84; bd trustees, UCSB Found. **Honors/Awds:** Outstanding Legal Service, San Francisco Bar Asn, 1983-84, 1994-97; Outstanding Legal Service, Calif Bar Asn, 1983-84; Distinguished Alumni Award, Univ Calif, Santa Barbara, 1990. *

HODGES, PATRICIA ANN
Executive. **Personal:** Born Mar 24, 1954, Indianapolis, IN; daughter of Jeremiah McKeage and Betty Brooks. **Career:** Ind Sch Deaf, residential asst, 1977-79; Ind Voc Col, interpreter deaf, 1979-83; Ind National Guard, file clerk, 1983-85; Specialized Interpreter Service, pres, 1993-. **Orgs:** Ind Regist Chap Interpreters; Black Deaf Advocate; Indianapolis Resource Ctr Independent. **Honors/Awds:** Distinguished Service Award, State Ind, 1990; Woman of the Rainbow Award, 1991; Nominated Entrepreneur of the Year, Ernest & Young Service, 1991; Breakthrough Woman Award, 100 Coalition of Black Women, 1992. **Military Serv:** USAFR, sargent, 1982-86. **Business Addr:** President, Specialized Interpreter Service, PO Box 88814, Indianapolis, IN 46208, **Business Phone:** (317)328-1584.

HODGES, VIRGIL HALL
Executive, educator, vice president (organization). **Personal:** Born Dec 6, 1936, Atlanta, GA; son of Virgil W and Ruth Hall; married Verna McNeil; children: Virgil Arthur III & Ruth-Ercile. **Educ:** Morris Brown Col, BA, 1958; NY Univ, MA, 1959, cert, 1961. **Career:** Philander Smith Col, asst prof, 1959-61; NY Youth Bd, area adminr, 1961-67; Coney Island Family Ctr, exec dir, 1967-69; NY State Narcotic Control Comt, fac dir, 1969-76; NY State Dept Labor, dir CETA div, 1977-81, dep comt, 1981-91; NY State Martin Luther King Jr Comn & Inst Non violence, exec dir, 1991-95; bd trustees, Morris Brown Col, 2003-04; Instrnl Systs Inc, vpres, currently. **Orgs:** Bd dir, Labor Br, Nat Asn Advan Colored People; bd adv, MLK Jr Ctr Nonviolent Soc Change; pres, Minority Organizers Voter Educ & Registr. **Honors/Awds:** Man of the Year Award, Coney Island Comt, 1968; Alumni Award, Morris BrownCol, 1978; Public Service Award, NY State Nat Asn Advan Colored People,1982; Humanitarian Award, NY Martin Luther King Jr Support Group, 1983; New York Alumni Award, Morris Brown Col, 1987; Distinguished Service Award, New York State Black & Puerto Rican Caucus, 1987; Distinguished Service, Labor Br, Nat Asn Advan Colored People, 1987; Potoker Award, NY State Brotherhood Comt, 1988. **Home Addr:** 4805 Regency Ter SW, Atlanta, GA 30331. **Business Addr:** Vice President, Instructional Systems Inc., Atlanta, GA 30331.*

HODGINS, JAMES WILLIAM
Football player, radio host. **Personal:** Born Apr 30, 1977, San Jose, CA; married Stephanie; children: Isaiah, Isaac & 1 child. **Educ:** San Jose State Univ, BA, sociol. **Career:** St Louis Rams, running back, 1999-02; Ariz Cardinals, fullback, 2003-05; New York Jets, 2006; Voice America Talk Radio, "The O & Hodge Show", show host, currently. **Orgs:** Cardinals Charities.

HODGSON-BROOKS, GLORIA J
Artist, psychotherapist. **Personal:** Born Nov 28, 1942, Hartford, CT; daughter of Marion S Jackson Gill and Charles O Gill; married Peter C. **Educ:** Bennett Col, BA, 1965; Smith Col Sch Social Work, MSW, 1979; Hartford Family Inst, Gestalt-Body Centered Psychotherapy, 1983; Nat Asn Social Workers, cert, 1982; State Conn, cert social work, 1987; Am Bd Examiners Clin Social Work, dipl, 1988. **Career:** Child & Family Serv Inc, social worker, 1974-77; Inter-Agency Serv, social worker, 1974-77; Hartford Family Inst, intern, 1976-78; Pvt Pract, psychotherapist, 1976-78; Child & Family Serv Inc, clin social worker, 1979-80; Dr Isaiah Clark Family & Youth Clin, dir, 1980-81; Hartford Family Inst, assoc, 1978-85; Pvt Pract, psychotherapist, 1978-85; Psychotherapy & Coun Assocs, psychotherapist & partner, 1985-; Brooks & Brooks Ltd, Hartford, Conn, pres, 1985-; Solitude Visual Arts Studio, Hartford, Conn, partner, 1989-. **Orgs:** Nat Asn Black Social Workers, 1972-; Nat Alliance Against Racist & Polit Repression, 1977-85; Nat Asn Social Workers, 1977-; coun minority stud, Trinity Col, 1982-85; staff training, Directions Unlimited, 1984-85; Conn Caucus Black Women Polit Action, 1984-86; assoc mem, PRO Disabled Entrepreneur, 1985-86; workshop leader on goal setting PRO Disabled Entrepreneur Goal Setting Workshops, 1985-86; staff training commun, Sandler Sales Inst, 1986; admin consult, Conn Ctr Human Growth & Develop, 1986; Farmington Valley Arts Ctr, 1986-; adv bd, IAM Cares, 1986-; Int Sculpture Ctr; Am Craft Coun; Am Craft Mus; charter mem, Nat Mus Women Arts; Nat Trust Hist Preserv. **Honors/Awds:** Award, Dr Issiah Clark Family & Youth Clin, 1988. **Special Achievements:** Published "An Exploratory Study of the Diagnostic Process in Gestalt Therapy," Smith College Library 1975, social Worker for Justice Awd Smith College School for Social Work, 1979, art exhibits: International Biographical Centre, 1989, ECKANKAR Creative Art Festival, 1987, 1988, New England Hardweavers, 1987. **Business Addr:** Psychotherapist, Partner, Psychotherapy & Counseling Associates, 483 W Middle Turnpike W Suite 217, Manchester, CT 06040, **Business Phone:** (860)647-0899.

HOFFLER, DR. RICHARD WINFRED, JR.
Physician. **Personal:** Born Jun 22, 1944, Lynchburg, VA; son of Richard Winfred Hoffler Sr and Julia; married Sylvia C; children: Edward & Erika. **Educ:** Hampton Inst, BA, 1966; Meharry Med Col, MD, 1970. **Career:** Youngstown Hosp, intern, 1970, resd, 1971-74; Pvt practice, physician, 1974-90; Staff Physician, Ambulatory Care VAMC, Hampton, VA, 1990-; Tidewater Disability Determination Servs, state agency med consult, 1974-80, chief med consult, 1980-90; pvt pract, currently. **Orgs:** AMA, Norfolk Acad Med, Norfolk Med Soc, Nat Med Asn, state agency med consult, 1974-; Tidewater Disability Determination Servs, chief med consult, 1980-; Sentera Hosps, consulting staff. **Honors/Awds:** Scholar, Hampton Inst, 1963-64. **Home Addr:** 4700 Pickle Barn Ct, Virginia Beach, VA 23455, **Home Phone:** (804)490-4485. **Business Addr:** Physician, 100 Emancipation Dr, Hampton, VA 23667, **Business Phone:** (757)722-9961.

HOFFMAN, JOSEPH IRVINE, JR.
Physician. **Personal:** Born Apr 14, 1939, Charleston, SC; married Pamela Louise Hayling; children: Kathyrn, Kristen, Kara. **Educ:** Harvard Col, AB, 1960; Howard Univ, MD, 1964. **Career:** Lenox Hill Hosp, internship, 1964-66; Hosp Spec Surgery NY, orthopedic res, 1968-71; Joseph Hoffman MD, PC, pres, currently. **Orgs:** Nat Med Assoc, AMA; past pres, Atlanta Med Asn; NAACP, Urban League, Atlanta C C, Omega Psi Phi; cert Am Bd Orthopedic Surg, 1973; fel Am Rheumatism Asn, 1972, Acad Orthopedic Surg, 1977; past pres, 100 Black Men Atlanta. **Military Serv:** USN, 1966-68. **Business Addr:** President, Joseph Hoffman MD PC, 2950 Stone Hogan Connector Rd Bldg 2 Suite A, Atlanta, GA 30331, **Business Phone:** (404)344-9454.*

HOGAN, BEVERLY WADE
College administrator, government official. **Personal:** Born Jul 5, 1951, Crystal Springs, MS; daughter of W D Wade Sr and Mae Ether Easley Wade; married Marvin, Jun 11, 1971; children: Maurice DeShay & Marcellus Wade. **Educ:** Tougaloo Col, Tougaloo, BA, psychol, 1973; Jackson State Univ, Jackson, MS, MPPA, 1990. **Career:** Ment Health Ctr, Jackson, MS, ment health rapist, 1973-74; Hinds County Ment Health Asn, Jackson, MS, exec dir, 1974-80; Miss Ment Health Asn, Jackson, MS, exec dir, 1980-83; Gov Off Fed/State Progs, Jackson, MS, execdir, 1984-87; Coun State Govts, Toll fel, 1987; Miss Workers' Compensation Comn, Jackson, MS, comnr; Tougaloo Col, Health & Wellness Ctr, trustee &Col adminr, dir, vpres, Instnl Advan, pres, 2002-.Dir, Sanderson Farms, Inc, currently. **Orgs:** Southern regional dir, Coun State Planning Agencies, 1985; chairperson, Nat Child Support Implementation Proj, 1986; chairperson, Miss Campaign UNCF Telethon, 1987, 1988; chairperson, Sch Bus Adv Coun, Jackson State Univ, 1988-; pub rels chairperson, Miss Childrens Home Soc, 1990-91; Entergy Mississipii, bd mem, 1999-. **Honors/Awds:** Distinguished Leadership, Citizens Crossroads, 1984; Administrator of the Year, Miss Chap, Am Soc Pub Adminr, 1986; Mississippi Now Distinction,Univ Miss, 1987; United Negro College Fund, Distinguished Leadership Award, 1988; Woman of the Year, Bus & Prof Women, 1989; Mississippi Majesty Awards, honoree, 2003; Eagle Award, 2006. **Business Addr:** President, Tougaloo College, Edward Blackmon Admin Bldg-President's Suite 500 W Co Line R, Tougaloo, MS 39174, **Business Phone:** (601)977-7730.

HOGAN, CAROLYN ANN
Government official, president (organization), consultant. **Personal:** Born Jul 13, 1944, New Orleans, LA; daughter of Elijah Hogan Sr (deceased) and Yolanda Getridge Hogan Mosley. **Educ:** Dillard Univ, BA, 1966; Fisk Univ, MA, 1969; Southern Ill Univ, 1974. **Career:** Dillard Univ, instr, 1969-73; Southern Univ, New Orleans, LA, instr, 1973-75; Orleans Parish Sch Bd, psychologist, 1974-75; City New Orleans, evaluation specialist, 1976-79; Nat Opinion Res Ctr, opinion researcher, 1980-82; Nat Testing Servs, opinion researcher, 1981; Transit Mgt Southeast La, benefits specialist, 1985-86, workers compensation rep, 1986-; Fisk Univ, pres, currently; Int Consult, 1979. **Orgs:** Consult, Albert Wicker Schs Special Educ Class Orleans Parish Sch Bd, 1978; Gestalt Inst Psychodrama, 1978-79; panelist, WDSU-TV Spectrum 50 entitled"A Salute to Women", 1979; Touro Infirmary & La State Univ Med Ctr Psychiatry Sem, 1979; New Orleans Neighborhood Police Anti-Crime Coun, 1983-86; Stress Mgt Workshop Career Track Seminars, 1985; scholar comn Crescent City Chap Conf Minorities Transportation 1986-87; Voters Democratic Nat Comt, president's adv; Nat Asn Female Exec. **Honors/Awds:** APA ABPSI NSF, Visiting Scientist in Psychology, 1971; USPHS Traineeship in Psychology So Ill Univ, 1973-74; researcher for President's Civil Adv Commn; publication "A Black Woman's Struggles in Racial Integration," & "In Defense of Brown," in integrated education in 1980,84 Horace Mann Bond Ctr for Equal Educ; Miss United Negro College Fund; Women's Inner Circle of Achievement Award, 1990, World Decoration of Excellence Award, 1989, Am Biographical Inst; Nobel Peace Prize; Nobel Prize in Medicine.

HOGAN, ED. See HOGAN, EDWIN B.

HOGAN, EDWIN B. (ED HOGAN)
Consultant, president (organization). **Personal:** Born Sep 2, 1940, Cleveland, OH; son of Lonnie N and Helen Marie Brock; married Letitia G Jackson, Jul 26, 1988; children: Edwina R, Bryan C Jackson. **Career:** New Visions Group Inc, pres, 1996; The Suc-

cess Group Inc, sr lobbyist, legis specialist, partner & vpres govt affairs, chief liaison, currently. **Orgs:** Vchmn, Ballet Met, 1990-; vchmn, Maryhaven, 1991-; exec comt, Columbus Nat Asn Advan Colored People, 1989-; COT Connections, 1992-. **Honors/Awds:** Distinguished Service Award; Ballet Met, 1992; Golden Ruler Award, Columbus Sch Bd, 1992; "Edwin B Hogan Day", City of Cleveland, 1990; Certificate of Recognition, Ohio Aty Gen, 1992. **Special Achievements:** DePaul Univ Sch Law Review, 1974; Boston Globe Review, 1976; Toronto Contrast Newspaper, 1973-79. **Military Serv:** USF, A2K, 1957-60. **Business Phone:** (614)221-0971.*

HOGAN, DR. JAMES CARROLL
Biologist. **Personal:** Born Jan 3, 1939, Milledgeville, GA; son of James C, Sr and Leanna Johnson; married Izola Stinson, Nov 29, 1959; children: Pamela Renita Robertson, Gregory Karl & Jeffrey Darryl. **Educ:** Albany State Col, BS 1961; Atlanta Univ, MS 1968; Brown Univ, PhD 1972. Yale Univ, fel, 1973. **Career:** Hancock Co Bd Educ, teacher sci dept & chmn, 1961-66; Atlanta Pub SchS, sci teacher, 1967-68; Atlanta Univ, instr, 1967; Yale Univ, Sch Med, res assoc, 1973-76; Howard Univ, asst prof dept anat, 1976-78; Yale Univ, Vis Faculty Fel; Howard Univ, asst prof grad sch, 1976-78; Univ CT, assoc prof Allied health sci, 1979-82; UCONN Health Ctr, assoc prof & univ dir, 1982-87; Conn Dept Pub Health, Hartford, CT, chief, clin chem & hemat, 1990-, Chief Environ, Chem & Biochem, 2001-03, Sect Chief, Biomonitoring, currently, Health Lab sec mgr, currently. **Orgs:** Founder & chmn, Rhode Isl& Community Sickle Cell Disease, 1970-72; founder, UCONN Health Sci Cluster Progs Parents Auxilary, 1979; vpres, CT's Black Health Prof Network, 1982-86; Pres, Nat Assoc Medical Minority Educators 1985-86; Omega Psi Phi Fraternity Inc; bd adv, Sickle Cell Assoc CT Inc; Urban League, Atlanta Univ Honor Soc, Sigma Xi; AAAS; Am Soc Cell Biology; Nat Assoc Med Minority Educr Inc; NY Acad Sci; Alpha Eta Soc; founder & pres, N Haven (CT) Asn Black Citizens, 1988-;N Haven Community Serv Comn, 1990; adv bd, Greater New Haven State Tech Col, 1989-; founder & pres, CT Chapter Nat Tech Asn, 1988-; bd dirs, A Better Chance Inc; bd dirs, Hartford Alliance Sci & Math; life mem, chair, Educ Comt, New Haven Chap, Nat Asn Advan Colored People; bd dirs, Conn Pub Health Assoc; bd dirs, Nat Tech Asn, 1993-; pres, Immanuel Bapt Ch, Mens Club, 1998-; CT Acad Sci & Engineering, 2002; mem comm (CASE), 2003, mem Chmn 2004-. **Honors/Awds:** Macy Scholar Marine Biological Lab Woods Hole MA, 1978-80; Research Foundation Grant, Univ CT 1979-80; Certified Clinical Laboratory Director, State of CT, 1993; Omega Man of the Year Award, Chi Omicron Chapter, 1992; Frederick G Adam Award, Univ CT's, 2001; Certificate of Recognition, CT Dept Pub Health 2001; NOH Asn of Black Citizen's Outstanding Citizen's Award, 2001; NW Elm City Negro Prof & Business Women's Man of the Year Award, 2002. **Special Achievements:** Twenty-six publications including "An Ultrastructural Analysis of Cytoplasmic Makers in Germ Cells of Oryzias Laptipes," J Ultrastruct Res 62, 237-250; "Regeneration of the Caudal Fin in Killfishes (Oryzias laptipes and Fundulus heteroclitus)" J Cell Biol 91(2), pt 2, p110a; numerous presentations. first African American to hold the position of chief of environmental chemistry at the Connecticut Department of Public Health Laboratory. **Home Addr:** 51 Pool Rd, PO Box 146, North Haven, CT 06473, **Home Phone:** (203)239-3184. **Business Addr:** Section Chief, Health Laboratory Section Manager, Connecticut Department of Public Health, Division of Laboratories, Environ Chem, 10 Clinton St, Hartford, CT 06106, **Business Phone:** (860)509-8540.

HOGAN, WILLIAM E., II
Computer executive, executive. **Personal:** Born Sep 30, 1942, Montgomery, AL; son of William E and D S Hogan; married Shadra Hogan, Sep 4, 1965; children: Shalaun, William E III. **Educ:** Okla State Univ, Stillwater, OK, BS, 1965, PhD, 1973; Southern Methodist Univ, Dallas, TX, MS, 1969. **Career:** Univ Kans, Lawrence, KS, assoc exec vice chancellor, 1978-84; AMIC, Lawrence, KS, pres, 1982-84; Honeywell Inc, Minneapolis, MN, vpres technol & bus develop, 1984-86, vpres staff exec to pres, 1986, vpres corps TQS, 1987-88; vpres, IIO, 1988-; Hogan Co, founder, 1993-, chair & chief exec officer, 1998-. **Orgs:** Chair, Res Adv Bd, Greater Minn Corp, 1989-90; chair, Minn High Technol Coun, 1989-90; chair, Historically Black Res Univ Found Bd, 1990; bd mem, Bethune-Cookman Univ. **Honors/Awds:** Outstanding Young Men in America, Chamber Com, 1977; Plaques for Outstanding Contribution to Minority Programs, Univ Kans Students, 1977, 1979; Outstanding Black Engineer of America, Co & All Historically Black Cols, 1989; International Business Fellow, Indust & Col, 1989. *

HOGGES, RALPH
Executive director, educator. **Personal:** Born Aug 3, 1947, Allentown, GA; son of Laura Burnett Rembert; married Lilia N Pardo; children: Genithia L & Alicia I. **Educ:** Tuskegee Inst, BS, 1971, med, 1972; Nova Univ Ft Lauderdale, EdD, 1977. **Career:** Fla Int Univ, Miami, prin tech, 1972-73, coordr col work-study prog, 1973-74, admin asst dean, 1974-78, assoc dean stud affairs, 1978-; Ctr Minority Res Inc, Miami, exec dir, 1979-; Fla Mem Col, dir, assoc dean,prof, 1984-90; Nova Southeastern Univ, Fischler Grad Sch, dir, prof, 1991-, Inst Pub Policy & Exec Leadership Higher Educ, exec dir, diversity Advi coun, currently. **Orgs:** Kappa Delta Pi, 1971-; Bd trusee, Am InterdenomiNat Univ, 1978-; Fla ColStud Affairs Asn, 1978-; Phi Delta Kappa, 1978-; bd dir, Ctr Minority ResInc, 1979-. **Honors/Awds:** Outstanding Service in Education, Phi Beta Sigma Fraternity, Miami, 1978. **Business Addr:** Executive Director, Diversity advisory Council, Nova Southeastern University, Institute for Public Policy and Executive Leadership, 1750 NE 167th St, North Miami Beach, FL 33162-3017, **Business Phone:** (954)262-8454.

HOGU, BARBARA J JONES
Educator, artist. **Personal:** Born Apr 17, 1938, Chicago, IL; married Jean-Claude Hogu; children: Kuumba. **Educ:** Howard Univ, BA 1959; Gov State Univ, humanities studies, 1992-95; Chicago Art Inst, BFA; Ill Inst technol, MS. **Career:** Chicago Post Off, clerk 1961-64; Robt Paige Designs, designer 1968-69; lecturer 1968; Chicago Public High Schs, Art Inst high schs, 1964-70; Malcolm X Col, asst prof, assoc prof currently. **Orgs:** Southside Comm Ctr, 1971; Third World Press, staff artist, 1973; Nat Conf Artists, vpres, 1973; Art History Sch Art Inst, lect, 1974-79; African Commune Black Relevant Artists; Union Black Artists. **Honors/Awds:** First Print Award Black Aesthetics "69" Serv Award; Malcolm X Umoja Award, 1973. **Home Addr:** PO Box 49425, Chicago, IL 60649. **Business Addr:** Associate Professor, Malcolm X Col, Communs & Fine Arts, 1900 W Van Buren, Chicago, IL 60612, **Business Phone:** (312)850-7334.

HOGUE, LESLIE DENISE
Editor. **Personal:** Born Sep 1, 1966, Detroit, MI; daughter of Dennis O and Katherine F Green; married Earlonzo D, Sep 26, 1997; children: Earlonzo Jr. **Educ:** Wayne State Univ, BA, 1992. **Career:** Surreal Mag, ed, pub, 1992-95; Comput Training & Support Corp, ed, 1995-96; Health Care Weekly Rev, ed, 1996. **Orgs:** Treas, Olive Tree Found, 1997; Inst Health Improv Southeast Mich, 1997, Word Faith Int Christian Ctr, writer, 1998. **Business Addr:** Editor, Health Care Weekly Review, 24901 Northwestern Hwy Suite 316A, Southfield, MI 48075, **Business Phone:** (248)352-3322.

HOLBERT, JOANNE
Educator. **Personal:** Born in Washington, DC; daughter of Lelond. **Educ:** Univ Kans, BS, Home Econ Educ, 1965; Peabody Teachers Col, MA, Educ, 1968; Ind Univ, Bloomington, PhD, Coun, 1975. **Career:** Oakland Univ, asst prof, 1975-77; Wayne St Univ, Col Educ, asst dean, 1977-, assoc prof, currently; City Pontiac, dep mayor, 1986-89; OaklandCounty, county comr, 1995-98. **Orgs:** Alpha Kappa Alpha; Oakland County Chapter, Links Inc; Nat Advan Asn Colored People; Pontiac Urban League; div admin, class schedules, faculty & stud Issues, prog develop, Theoretical and Behavioral Found. **Honors/Awds:** Wonder Woman, Women's Survival Ctr, 1990; Outstanding Women, YMCA Pontiac, 1991. **Business Addr:** Interim Assistant Dean, Associate Professor, Wayne State University, Administrative and Organizational Studies (AOS), Theoretical and Behavioral Foundations (TBF), 341 Col Educ, Detroit, MI 48202, **Business Phone:** (313)577-1721.

HOLBERT, RAY ARTHUR, III
Baseball player. **Personal:** Born Sep 25, 1970, Torrance, CA; married Cecilia. **Career:** San Diego Padres, 1994-95; Montreal Expos, 1998; Atlanta Braves, 1998; Kansas City Royals, infielder, 1999-2000; Tampa Bay Devil Rays, 2000; El Camino Col, asst coach, currently.

HOLBERT, RAYMOND
Educator. **Personal:** Born Feb 24, 1945, Berkeley, CA; son of James Albert Holbert and Carolyn Bernice Gary; married Susan Demersseman, May 26, 1989; children: Onika Valentine, Lauren Dakota & Brian Jaymes. **Educ:** Laney Col, AA, 1964; Univ Calif, AB, 1972, MA, 1974, MFA, 1975. **Career:** City Col San Francisco, art dept, prof art, currently. **Orgs:** Artists Books Advocate, Nat Conf Artists. **Special Achievements:** Exhibits at: San Francisco Art Mus, 1972; Oakland Art Mus, 1973, Berkeley, 1974; Baylor Univ, Waco, TX , 1975; Studio Mus, Harlem, NY, 1977, 1979; Howard Univ, Wash, DC, 1980; Helen Euphrat Gallery, CA, 1982, Brockman Gallery, LA, 1982; Grand Oak Gallery, 1983; LA Mus African Am Art Printmakers, 1984; Calif Mus African Am Art, 1986, San Francisco Art Comn Gallery, 1987; City Art Gallery, San Francisco. **Business Addr:** Professor, City College of San Francisco, Art Department, 50 Phelan Ave, Berkeley, CA 94112, **Business Phone:** (415)239-3000.

HOLCOMBE, ROBERT (ROBERT WAYNE HOLCOMBE)
Football player. **Personal:** Born Dec 11, 1975, Houston, TX. **Educ:** Ill. **Career:** St Louis Rams, running back, 1998-2001; Tenn Titans, running back, 2002-04; Kans City Chiefs, running back, 2005; free agent, currently. **Honors/Awds:** Super Bowl XXXVI; Super Bowl XXXVI; All-Am & All-Far W hons, Prep Football Report. *

HOLCOMBE, ROBERT WAYNE. See HOLCOMBE, ROBERT.

HOLDEN, KIP. See HOLDEN, MELVIN LEE.

HOLDEN, MELVIN LEE (KIP HOLDEN)
State government official, mayor. **Personal:** Born Aug 12, 1952, New Orleans, LA; son of Curtis and Rosa Rogers; married Lois Stevenson Holden; children: Melvin II, Angela, Monique, Myron & Brian Michael. **Educ:** La State Univ, BA, jour; Southern Univ, MA, jour; Southern Univ Sch Law, JD. **Career:** WXOK Radio, Baton Rouge, La, news dir, 1975-77; WWL Radio, New Orleans, La, reporter, 1977-78; WBRZ Channel 2, Baton Rouge, La, reporter, 1978-79; US Census Bur, Baton Rouge, La, pub rels specialist; Baton Rouge City Police, Baton Rouge, La, pub info officer; La Dept Labor Off Workers Compensation, Baton Rouge, La, law clerk; Baton Rouge Metro Coun Dist 2, councilman, 1984-88; La House Representatives, Dist 63, state rep, 1988-2001; Southern Univ Sch Law, Baton Rouge, La, adj prof law, 1991-; La State, Dist 15, senator; Melvin "Kip" Holden & Assocs, rpin, currently; City Baton Rouge, Parish East Baton Rouge, mayor-pres, 2005-. **Orgs:** Xi Nu Lamba Chapter, Alpha Phi Alpha; La Bar Asn; Am Bar Asn; Nat Bar Asn; Greater Baton Rouge Airport Comn. **Honors/Awds:** Best Bets Award, Ctr Policy Alternatives, Wash, DC; Brown Pelican Award; Alumni Hall of Fame, La State Univ; Senator of the Year Award, La Fedn Teachers, 2003; Greater Baton Rouge Pan-Hellenic Council Award, 2003; Distinguished Service Award, Phi Beta Sigma Fraternity Inc, Gulf Coast Region, 2003; Friend of School Psychology Award, La Sch Psychol Asn, 2003; Legislator of the Year Award, Asn Retarded Citizens La, 2003; Blues Foundation Slim Harpo Award, Blues Ambassador, 2005; Academic Distinction Fund Award Winner, 2006; UGS Innovative Leadership Award, 2006; Nat Conference of Black Mayors Valiant Award for Balanced Government, 2006; Military Order of the Purple Heart Distinguished Service Award, 2007; BREC Trailblazer Award, 2007; numerous other awards and honors. **Special Achievements:** First African-American mayor-president of Baton Rouge and East Baton Rouge Parish. **Home Addr:** 234 Rivercrest, Baton Rouge, LA 70807. **Business Addr:** Mayor-President, Office of the Mayor President, 222 St Louis St 3rd Fl, Baton Rouge, LA 70802, **Business Phone:** (225)389-5100.

HOLDEN, MICHELLE Y
Television journalist. **Personal:** Born Mar 31, 1954, Toledo, OH; daughter of Richard and Ammie Edmond; divorced; children: Richard. **Educ:** Univ Toledo, Toledo, OH, 1972-75. **Career:** Television journalist, actor; WDHO-TV, Toledo, Ohio, reporter, 1976; WBNS-TV, Columbus, Ohio, noon anchor, 1978-82, WHAS-TV, Louisville, Ky, noon anchor, 1982-85; WEWS-TV, Cleveland, Ohio, weekend anchor, 1985-88; WBBM-TV, Chicago, Ill, TV news reporter, 1988-90; KTTV-TV, Los Angeles, Calif, TV news reporter, 1990; Encore Cable Host "Trade Secrets," 1992; KCAL-TV, Los Angeles, Calif, freelance reporter, 1993; Spec Corresp Conus Satellite Network OJ Simpson Trial, 1994; Films: Stranger by Night, 1994; Speechless, 1994; TV series: "SeaQuest DSV", 1993; The Positively True Adventures of the Alleged Texas Cheerleader-Murdering Mom, 1993; Without Warning, 1994; "Picket Fences", 1993-94. **Orgs:** Nat Asn Black Journalists, 1982-; Alpha Kappa Alpha Sorority; First Baptist Church, Jeffersontown, KY. **Honors/Awds:** Female Broadcaster of the Year, Nat Asn Career Women, 1987; Ohio Gen Assembly Commendation, 1982; Greater Cleveland Enterprising Women, 1987; Fred Hampton Communications Award, 1989; Emmy Nomination News Reporting, 1991; Emmy Nomination News Writing, 1992.

HOLDEN, HON. NATE
Government official. **Personal:** Born Jan 1, 1929?. **Career:** Government official (retired); Los Angeles County Supvr, asst chief dep; Calif State Senator 1974-78; Los Angeles City Coun, mem, 1987-2003. **Orgs:** LA County Transportation Comn-(LACTC); LA Metropolitan Transit Authority (LAMTA).

HOLDER, ERIC, JR.
Attorney General. **Personal:** Born Jan 21, 1951, The Bronx, NY; son of Miriam Holder and Eric Holder; married Dr. Sharon Malone; children: Maya, Brooke, Eric. **Educ:** Stuyvesant High School, 1969; Columbia Univ, 1973; Columbia Law School, 1976. **Career:** Assoc Judge on the Superior Court of the District of Columbia, 1988; appointed by Bill Clinto as U.S.District Attorney for the District of Columbia, 1993-97; Deputy Attorney General under Janet Reno, 1997-01; private law practice with Covington & Burling, 2001-08; Attorney General of the US, 2009-. **Orgs:** The George Washington Univ Board of Trustees, 1996-97;created Lawyers for One America; on the boards of Columbia Univ, the Save the Children Foundation, and Concerned Black men. **Special Achievements:** First Af Am to serve as Attorney General of the US; named by The Natl Law Journal as one of "The Most 50 Influential Minority Lawyers in America"; named one of the "Greatest Washington Lawyers of the Past 30 Years" by the Legal Times. **Business Addr:** U.S. Department of Justice, 950 Pennsylvania Ave, NW, Washington, DC 20530-0001, **Business Phone:** (202)514-2000.*

HOLDER, ERIC H
Lawyer. **Personal:** Born Jan 21, 1951, New York, NY; son of Eric and Miriam R Yearwood; married Sharon Malone; children: 3. **Educ:** Columbia Col, BA, 1973, JD, 1976. **Career:** US Dept Justice, Pub Integrity Sect, trial atty, 1976-88; Super Ct, Wash, assoc judge, 1988-93; US atty DC, 1993-97; US dep atty gen, 1997-2001; Covington & Burling, partner, 2001-. **Orgs:** Meyer Found; Save C; Concerned Black Men; US Sentencing Comn Ad Hoc Adv Group; chmn, Eastman Kodak External Diversity Adv Panel. **Honors/Awds:** The Best Lawyers in America, 2007; Numerous

Awards. **Special Achievements:** First African American to hold post of US attorney for Washington, DC; First African American to be named deputy attorney general. **Business Phone:** (202)662-5372.

HOLDER, GEOFFREY
Choreographer, actor, artistic director. **Personal:** Born Aug 1, 1930, Port-of-Spain, Trinidad and Tobago; son of Arthur Holder and Louise De Frense; married Carmen deLavallade, Jan 1, 1955; children: Leo Anthony Lamont. **Educ:** Queens Royal Col, native dances, WI, 1948. **Career:** Roscoe Holders Dance O Trinidad, stage debut, co mem, 1942; Metropolitan Opera, solo dancer, 1956-57; Kaufmann Auditorium, dancer, 1956- 60; Show Boat, solo dancer, 1957; Geoffrey Holder Dance Co, concerts, 1956- 60; Musical: Waiting for Godot, performer, 1957; Festival of Two Worlds, Italy, 1958; Festividad, Ballet Hispanico, 1979; Brouhaha, choreographer, 1960; House of Flowers, performer, 1964; Mhil Daiim, 1964; Josephine Bakers Review, dancer, 1964; Three Songs for One, choreographer & costume designer; The Twelve Gates, costume designer, 1964; The Wiz, dir & costume designer, 1975; Timbuktu, dir, costume designer & choreographer, 1978; The Boys Choir of Harlem and Friends, Staged Concert, 1993; KYOT, Phoenix, AZ, voiceover, 1994-; Film appearances: All Night Long, 1961; Doctor Dolittle, 1967; Krakatoa East of Java, 1969; Everything You Always Wanted to Know About Sex But Were Afraid to Ask, 1972; Live and Let Die,1973; Swashbuckler, 1976; Doctor J. Kanye, 1978; Annie, 1982; Boomerang, 1992; Books: Black Gods, Green Islands, 1957; Geoffrey Holders Cookbook, 1974; Boomerang, 1992; Hell A Cyberpunk Thriller, 1995; Hasards ou coincidences, 1998; Goosed, 1999; Geoffrey Holder The Unknown Side, 2002; Carmen & Geoffrey, 2005; Charlie & the Chocolate Factory, 2005; TV appearances: "Stage Your Number", 1953; "Aladdin", 1958; "The Bottle Imp", 1958; "7-Up commercials", 1970 & 1980; "The Tonight Show", 1975; "Good Morning, America", 1976; "Straight Talk", 1976; "The Gold Bug", 1980; "Your New Day", 1981; "Alice in Wonderland", 1983; "Hour Magazine", 1984; "John Grins Christmas", 1986; "Ghost of a Chance", 1987; "The 62nd Annual Academy Awards", 1990; "The Cosby Show", 1988; "Bear in the Big Blue House", 1997; "Cyberchase", 2002 & 2003; KYOT-FM, Phoenix, Arizona, voiceover, 1994-. **Orgs:** Am Fedn TV & Radio Artists; Actors' Equity Asn; Am Guild Musical Artists; Am Guild Variety Artists. **Honors/Awds:** United Caribbean Youth Award, 1962; Clio Awards, 1970, 1971; Drama Desk Award, The Wiz, 1975; Tony Awards, Best Director of a Musical, Best Costumes, The Wiz, 1975; Monarch Award, Nat Coun Cult & Art, 1982; Harold Jackman Memorial Award, 1982. **Special Achievements:** Paintings exhibited at numerous galleries throughout the US and West Indies; recorded albums of West Indian songs and stories. **Home Addr:** 2059 Madison Ave, New York, NY 10037, **Home Phone:** (917)507-4269. *

HOLDER, LAURENCE
Playwright. **Personal:** Born Feb 26, 1939, Brooklyn, NY; son of Barbadian immigrants; married Andrea; children: 3. **Educ:** City Col NY, degree geol, MA, creative writing, 1975. **Career:** Playwright; TV series: "Watch Your Mouth", WNET NBC TV, 1974-75; hist musical Juba, La Mama Co, 1978; "When the Chickens Came Home to Roost", 1982; plays: Zora Neale Hurston, 1990; M: The Mandela Saga, 1995; Monk, 2000; NY Univ; S Mountain Comm Col; Mercy Col; Col New Rochelle & John Jay Col Crim Justice, prof, 1999. **Orgs:** Mem fac, John Jay Col Criminal Justice. **Honors/Awds:** 3 Audelco (Audience Development Comm) Awards; OTTO, Garland Anderson Award, Nat Black Theatre Festival. **Special Achievements:** Is the author of several volumes of poetry and 7 novels. **Home Addr:** 626 Riverside Dr, New York, NY 10031, **Home Phone:** (212)690-7787.

HOLDER, REUBEN D.
Government official, management consultant. **Personal:** Born Mar 21, 1923, New York, NY; son of Orneata and Richard; married Iris A Lumsby, Apr 3, 1948; children: Gregory Stewart. **Educ:** City Col NY; Queens Col City Univ New York Urban Affairs, BA; ExecSem Ctr Kings Point New York; Fed Exec Inst Charlottesville, VA. **Career:** New York Post Off, asst employ officer, 1968; New York Regional US Post Off, regional manpower dev specialist, 1969; US Civil Serv & Comn, fed regional equal employ opportunity rep, 1971; self employed, consult & lectr, 1971-; US Govt Off Personnel Mgt, chief regional staffing div, 1973-; UHURV Joint Develop Corp, chmn bd dirs, 1988-; New York Planning Bd No 12, area rep, 1989-; Holder Mgt Systs Inc, mgt consult & lectr. **Orgs:** Chmn & nat bd dir, 369th Vet Asn, 1978; pres, Black Fed Exec, 1980; bd dir, Queens Br New York Urban League, 1986-87; bd, Urban Renewal Comm S Jamaica; bd, Neighborhood Based Coalition; chmn, Land Use Comm, NY Comm Planning Bd No 12; life mem & pres, Queens Dist; 100 Black Men. **Honors/Awds:** Alpha Sigma Lambda, Upsilon Chap, NY; Deans List Queens Col. **Military Serv:** AUS, sgt, 1942-46; Bronze Star; w/ 6 Battle Stars. **Home Addr:** 177-53 Leslie Rd, Jamaica, NY 11434.

HOLDSCLAW, CHAMIQUE
Basketball player. **Personal:** Born Aug 9, 1977, Astoria, NY. **Educ:** Univ Tenn, attended 1999. **Career:** Wash Mystics, forward & guard, 1999-04; Ros Casares Valencia, 2004-05; Los Angeles Sparks, forward & guard, 2005-07; TS Wisla Can-Pack Krakow, 2006-07; Atlanta Dream, 2009-. **Honors/Awds:** AP, First Team All-American, 1996-99; four-time Kodak All-American; ESPY, Women's college Basketball Player of the Year, 1997-98, 1998-99, Female Athlete of the Year, 1998-99; Preseason All-Am, 1998-99; Consensus Preseason Nat Player of the Year, 1998-99; Preseason SEC Player of the Year, 1998-99; NCAA, Honda-Broderick Cup Award, Most Outstanding Female Athlete, 1998; Female Athlete of the Year Award, Southeastern Conf, 1997-98; Sullivan Award, Nations Best Amateur Athlete, 1998-99; WNBA Rookie of the Year, 1999; Naismith Award, 1998 & 1999. **Business Addr:** Professional Basketball Player, Los Angeles Sparks, 83 Walton St NW Suite 500, Atlanta, GA 30303, **Business Phone:** (404)604-2626.*

HOLLAND, DR. ANTONIO FREDERICK
Educator. **Personal:** Born Dec 5, 1943, Petersburg, VA; son of Garnett G and Carmen T; married Carolyn Turner, Nov 25, 1975; children: Bradley Wilkins & Erik G. **Educ:** Northeastern Univ, BA, 1967, MA, 1969; Univ Mo-Columbia, PhD, 1984. **Career:** Lincoln Univ, div chair, 1970-, Dept Psychol, chmn, Dept Social & Behav Sci, chmn, prof hist, chair, currently. **Orgs:** Alpha Phi Alpha, 1978-; bd mem, Mo Folklore Soc, 1992-; fomer vice chair, fomer chair, Mo Adv Coun Hist Preserv, 1994-2001; vice chair, Mo Ctr Book, 1996-; fomer vpres, pres, 1997-, Mo Mil Hist Soc; bd mem, treas, 1997-; John William "Blind" Boone Found. **Honors/Awds:** Martin Luther King Jr Award, State Mo, 1999; Martin Luther King Drum Major Award, 2007. **Special Achievements:** Co-auth, The Soldier's Dream Continued: History of Lincoln Univ, 1991;co-auth, Missouri's Black Heritage, Univ Mo Press, 1993. **Military Serv:** AUS, Lt Col, 1968-70; Mo Army Nat Guard, 1978-99; Meritorious Serv Medal, 1999. **Business Addr:** Professor of History, Chairman, Lincoln University, 413 Martin Luther King Hall, Jefferson City, MO 65101, **Business Phone:** (573)681-5148.

HOLLAND, BRIAN
Television producer, songwriter. **Personal:** Born Feb 15, 1941, Detroit, MI. **Career:** Holland-Dozier-Holland, song-writer & producing team, currently; Films: Holiday Heart, 2000; Hollywood Rocks the Movies: The Early Years, 1955-70, 2000; An Extremely Goofy Movie, 2000; Frequency, 2000; Riding in Cars with Boys, 2001; The Martins, 2001; Rat Race, 2001; Standing in the Shadows of Motown, 2002; Sorority Boys, 2002; Boat Trip, 2002; Auto Focus, 2002; Monster, 2003; Gothika, 2003; Matchstick Men, 2003; I'll Be There, 2003; Cradle 2 the Grave, 2003; Envy, 2004; Shark Tale, 2004; The 40 Year Old Virgin, 2005; Harsh Times, 2005; Four Brothers, 2005; Glory Road, 2006; Bobby, 2006; Wellkamm to Verona, 2006; Larry the Cable Guy: Health Inspector, 2006; Glory Road, 2006; Larry the Cable Guy: Health Inspector, 2006; Zodiac, 2007; Amazing Journey: The Story of The Who, 2007; License to Wed, 2007; The Nines, 2007; Tv Series: "American Dreams", 2002; "Great Performances", 2005; "Shminiya, Ha-", 2006; "The Sopranos", 2007; "TV Land Confidential", 2007. **Honors/Awds:** Songwriters Hall of Fame, 1988; Rock & Roll Hall of Fame, 1990; BMI Icon Award, 2003. **Business Addr:** Song Writer, Holland Dozier & Holland Productions, 1800 N Highland Ave Suite 124, Los Angeles, CA 90028.

HOLLAND, DARIUS
Football player. **Personal:** Born Nov 10, 1973, Petersburg, VA. **Educ:** Univ Colo. **Career:** Football player (retired), Green Bay Packers, defensive tackle, 1995-97; Kans City Chiefs, 1998;Detroit Lions, 1998; Cleveland Browns, 1999-01; Minn Vikings, 2002; Denver Broncos, defensive tackle, 2003-04. **Honors/Awds:** Gatorade Player of the Yr; named in hon, Darius Holland Day, State NM, 1997; state's Defensive Player, Albuquerque Journal.Super Bowl champion XXXI. **Special Achievements:** Holland earned all-State and all-District honors as a junior and a senior. *

HOLLAND, DORREEN ANTOINETTE
Educator. **Personal:** Born Jul 29, 1968, Charlottesville, VA; daughter of Earl. **Educ:** Va Union Univ, BS, 1990. **Career:** Locust Grove Elem Sch, 5th grade teacher, 1990-93; Northside Christian Sch, 1-4 gr teacher, summer sch; Charlottesville Sch Syst proj yes teacher, 1993-94; Fluvanna County Sch Syst, chap one resource teacher, 1994-. **Orgs:** Secy, Senior Class, 1986-96; freedom funder organizer, Nat Asn Advan Colored People, 1993-; Am Heart Asn, 1993-; art teacher, Bible Study, 1993-; Youth organizer for church, 1993-. **Honors/Awds:** Lettie Pate, 1987; Alpha Kappa Mu, 1986. **Special Achievements:** Senior Queen, NAACP, 1994. **Business Phone:** (434)589-8208.*

HOLLAND, EDWARD, JR.
Songwriter, television producer, singer. **Personal:** Born Oct 30, 1939, Detroit, MI. **Career:** Films: The Martins, 2001; Cradle 2 the Grave, 2003; I'll Be There, 2003; Zodiac, 2007; Albums: The Complete Eddie Holland, Eddie Holland; Songs: "Jamie", "Leaving Here", "Just Ain't Enough Love"; TV: "Funhouse", 2000; "Hard Cases", 2003; "Michael Bubl: Caught in the Act", 2005; Hollad-Dozier-Holland, mem songwriting & producing team, owner, currently. **Honors/Awds:** Inductee, Rock & Roll Hall of Fame, 1990; BMI Icon Award, 2003. **Business Addr:** Owner, Holland-Dozier-Holland, 1800 N Highland Ave Suite 124, Los Angeles, CA 90028.*

HOLLAND, ETHEL M
Nurse. **Personal:** Born Oct 31, 1946, Washington, DC; married Reginald D Johnson. **Educ:** Immaculate Conception Acad, Wash, DC, HSD, 1964; Mt Mrty Col Ynktn SD, BS, 1968; Nursing Catholic Univ Am Wash DC, MS, 1974. **Career:** Walter Reed Army Hosp, Wash, DC, staff nurse, 1968-69; 91st E Vac Hosp Vietnam, asst head nurse, 1969-70; DC Gen Hosp, clin nurse, Dept Pediat, 1970-73; Childrens Hosp Nat Med Ctr, Wash, DC, serv dir, Acute Care, 1974; Dept Health, Bur Comm, coord, currently. **Orgs:** DC Nurses Asn, 1968-88; Sigma Theta Tau Kappa Chapter, Wash, DC, 1974; vol, Ancst Neighborhood Clin, Wash, DC, 1974; Black Nurses Asn Greater Metro Area, 1978-; Ethnic Nurses Adv Health Care Among Minorities, 1978-80; vpres, Registered Nurse Exam Bd, 1979-88. **Honors/Awds:** Inducted into Nat Hon Soc for Nurses; Army Cmndtn Medal Mrtrs Serv Vietnam, 1970; papers presented Nurse Care of Pts who Fail to Thrive 1979; Patterns of Elimination, 1976; Nursing Care of Patients with Sickle Cell Anemia, 1975. **Military Serv:** AUS, First Lt. **Business Addr:** Coordinator, Department of Health, 825 N Capitol St NW, Washington, DC 20002.

HOLLAND, LOUIS A
Executive. **Educ:** Univ Wisc, BS, econ. **Career:** Holland Capital Mgt LP, managing partner & chief investment officer, 1991-; AG Becker Paribas Inc, vpres. **Orgs:** Vice chmn, Univ Wis Found; dir, Assoc Gov Bd Univ. **Honors/Awds:** Distinguished Alumni Award, Wisc Alumni Asn. **Business Addr:** Managing Partner, Chief Investment Officer, Holland Capital Management LP, 1 N Wacker Dr Suite 700, Chicago, IL 60606, **Business Phone:** (312)553-4830.*

HOLLAND, LOYS MARIE
Health services administrator. **Personal:** Born Jun 9, 1950, Carp, MS; daughter of James Lee Flagg and Ora Lee Flagg; married. **Educ:** Loop City Col, Harold Wash Univ, AA, 1971; Nat Col Educ, BA, 1974. **Career:** Chicago Dept Health, clerical supvr, 1975-95, pub health adminr, 1995-, regional adminr, currently; Robert Taylor Initative, dir, 1996-97. **Orgs:** Adv bd, CARDE, 1995-; adv bd, Holman Health Ctr, 1995-; PTA, 1993-, pres, 2000-01, Christ the King Lutheran Sch; Grand Blvd Found, 1995-; bd dirs, Chicago Pub Sch, Homeless Educ Prog. **Honors/Awds:** Outstanding Leadership & Community Service Award, Boys Scouts Am, 1997. **Business Addr:** Regional Administrator, Chicago Department of Health, 4150 W 55th St, Chicago, IL 60609, **Business Phone:** (312)747-1020.

HOLLAND, MAJOR LEONARD
Educator, architect. **Personal:** Born Mar 8, 1941, Tuskegee, AL; son of Soloman M Holland and Emily L Holland; married Sceiva, Dec 28, 1966; children: Mark, Michael & John. **Educ:** Howard Univ, BArch, 1963. **Career:** Fry & Welch Architects, 1966-69; Tuskegee Univ, assoc prof, 1969-; Major Holland Architect & Associates PC, vpres, 1972, pres, currently. **Orgs:** Fry & Welch Architects, 1966-69; Tuskegee Univ, assoc prof, 1969-; Major Holland Architect & Assocs PC, vpres, 1972, pres, currently. **Honors/Awds:** Businessman of the Year, 1978; Faculty of the Year, Dept Archit, Tuskegee Univ, 1978-81; Silver Kappa Alpha Psi Regional Achievement Award, 1983; Archit Design Award for Tuskegee Municipal Complex, 1986; Beaver Award, Boy Scouts Am, 1991; fel, Am Inst Architects, 1992. **Military Serv:** AUS, cengr, 1st lt, 1964-66; Commendation Award, 1965. **Business Phone:** (334)727-4079.

HOLLAND, ROBERT
Chief executive officer, executive, executive director. **Personal:** Born Jan 1, 1940, Albion, MI; son of Robert Sr; married Barbara Jean; children: Robert III, Kheri & Jaclyn. **Educ:** Union Col, BS, mech eng, 1962; Bernard Baruch Col, MBA, 1969. **Career:** Neptune Orient Lines LTD, staff; YUM! Brands Inc, staff; Carver Bancorp Inc, dir; Mobil Corp, engr, 1962-68; McKinsey & Co, assoc & partner, 1968-91; Rokher-J Consult Firm & Holding Co, chmn & chief exec officer, 1981-84, 1991-95; City Mkt Inc, chmn & chief exec officer, 1984-87; Gilreath Mfg, sr vpres/chmn, 1987-91; Ben & Jerry's Homemade Inc, pres & chief exec officer, 1995-96; WorkPlace Integraters, pres & chief exec officer, 1997-2001; Lexmark Int Inc, dir, 1998-; Williams Capital Partners, gen partner & indust specialist, currently. **Business Addr:** Director, Lexmark International Inc, 740 W New Circle Rd, Lexington, KY 40511, **Business Phone:** (859)232-2000.

HOLLAND, ROBIN W
Educator. **Personal:** Born May 23, 1953, Columbus, OH; daughter of Robert R Jackson and Elizabeth W; married Ralph V Holland Jr, Jun 20, 1987. **Educ:** Ohio State Univ, BS, 1974, MA, 1975. **Career:** Columbus Pub Sch, reading teacher, 1975-76, gifted educ teacher, 1977-80, classroom teacher, 1976-86, consult teacher, 1986-89, reading recovery early literacy teacher, 1990-2002, Coach Intervention Specialist, 2002-, Reading Dept & Title I Dept, coord. **Orgs:** Nat Educ Asn, 1975-; Reading Recovery Coun N Am, 1993-; The Order the Daughters the King, 1996-; St Philips

Episcopal Church; Int Reading Asn; Nat Coun Teachers Eng. **Honors/Awds:** Martha Holden Jennings Scholar, Martha Holden Jennings Found, 1990-91. **Business Addr:** Teacher, Salem Elem Sch, Columbus Pub Sch, 1040 Garvey Rd, Columbus, OH 43229-4131, **Business Phone:** (614)365-5351.

HOLLAND, SPENCER H
Educator, president (organization), psychologist. **Personal:** Born Sep 11, 1939, Suffern, NY. **Educ:** Glassboro State Col, AB, 1965; Columbia Univ, AM, 1968, PhD, 1976. **Career:** Burnet Jr HS, teacher, 1965-67; Essex Co Col, asst prof, 1968-73, chmn, psychol dept, 1970-73; Harlem Interfaith Coun Serv, prev ment health teacher, 1974-75; Child Abuse & Neglect Proj Div Pupil Personnel Serv, Wash DC Pub Sch, coordr, 1976-90; Morgan State Univ, Ctr Educ African-Am Males, dir; Proj 2000 Inc, pres, founder & exec dir, currently. **Orgs:** Am Psychol Asn; Asn Black Psychologists, 1972-. **Honors/Awds:** Nat Fel Fund Fel, 1973-76. **Military Serv:** USAF, 1957-60.

HOLLAND-CALBERT, MARY ANN
Registered nurse. **Personal:** Born Jul 12, 1941, New York, NY; daughter of James Kirkland and Doris Wiles Vance; married Clarence E, May 23, 1987; children: Toussaint Michael. **Educ:** Washington Technical Inst, AAS, 1976; Univ of District of Columbia, BSN, 1987-. **Career:** St Elizabeth Hosp, Washington DC, psychiatric nurse coord, 1970-88; Greater Southeast Community Hosp, Washington DC, psychiatric nurse, 1988-. **Orgs:** Nat Council of Negro Women, 1976-; Chi Eta Phi Sorority Inc, 1976-, exec sec 1983-88; Top Ladies of Distinction, 1986-; St Mark Presbyterian Church. **Business Addr:** Psychiatric Nurse, Greater Southwest Community Hospital, 1310 Southern Ave SE 4-East, Washington, DC 20032-4699, **Business Phone:** (202)574-6716.

HOLLAND-CORN, KEDRA (KEDRA NICOL HOLLAND-CORN)
Basketball player. **Personal:** Born Nov 5, 1974. **Educ:** Univ Ga, health & phys educ, 1997. **Career:** San Jose Lasers, guard, 1997-99; Sacramento Monarchs, guard, 1999-2002; Detroit Shock, guard, 2003; Houston Comets, currently. **Orgs:** Fel Christian Athletes. **Business Addr:** Professional Basketball Player, Houston Comets, 1510 Polk St, Houston, TX 77002, **Business Phone:** (713)627-9622.

HOLLAND-CORN, KEDRA NICOL. See HOLLAND-CORN, KEDRA.

HOLLEY, DR. JAMES W
Dentist, government official. **Personal:** Born Nov 24, 1926, Portsmouth, VA; married Mary W; children: James IV & Robin. **Educ:** WVa State Col, BS, 1949; Howard Univ, DDS, 1955. **Career:** Portsmouth City, councilman, 1968-84; City Portsmouth, vice mayor, 1978-80; Maryview Hosp/Portsmouth Gen Hosp, dental staff; City Portsmouth, mayor, 1984-87, 1996-. **Orgs:** Past moderator, Retired Officers Asn, 1996; Mayor Comt Yr, 2005; Norfolk Community Va State Dent Asn; Va Tidewater Dent Soc; Old Dominion Dent Soc; Nat Dent Asn; Am Dent Asn; Pierre Fauchard Acad; Portsmouth Dent Soc; Chicago Dent Soc; Cen Civic Forum; United Civic League; Miller Day Nursery; Gosport Dist Boy Scouts Am; Tidewater Coun Boy Scouts Am; YMCA; United Fund; Portsmouth C C; Citizens Planning Asn; NAACP; founder & chmn, Int Group Clins; past pres & secy, Nat Guardsman; past pres, Portsmouth Sports Club; past pres & founder, NH Negro Golf Asn; Chi Delta Mu; past basileus, Omega Psi Phi; fel, Christian Church; founder, Church coun; past chmn, Church Assembly. **Honors/Awds:** School Bell Award, Portsmouth Teachers, 1960; Achievement Award, Boy Scouts Am, 1962; President Award, Nat Dent Asn, 1963; Omega, Man of Year, 1963; Silver Beaver Award, Boy Scouts Am, 1963; Dentist of Year, Old Dominion Den Soc, 1968; President Award, Old Dominion Soc, 1969; Dental Award, Howard Univ, 1975; Nat Dentist of the Year, 1984; Citizen of the Year, Omega Psi Phi Fraternity, 1984; Delta Sigma Theta Sorority, 1993; Hampton Rds Chap of the Conf of Minority Public Admin, 1996; Honorary Doctor of Laws, W VA State Col, 1996; Honoree member, Minority Police Officers Asn Portsmouth, VA, 1997; DHL, Norfolk State Univ, 2006; Dominion Power Strong Men & Women Award, 2007. **Special Achievements:** First African American mayor in Portsmouth City. **Military Serv:** WW, II. **Business Addr:** Mayor, City of Portsmouth, Department of Economic Development, 200 High St Suite 200, Portsmouth, VA 23704.

HOLLEY, JIM
Clergy, administrator. **Personal:** Born Dec 5, 1943, Philadelphia, PA; son of Charles James Sr and Effie Mae King; married Phyllis Dean Holley (divorced 1982); children: Tiffani Dionne. **Educ:** Wayne State Univ, PhD, higher educ, Detroit, MI; Drew Univ, DMin, econ develop; Chicago Theol Sem, BA, divinity in the old testament, MA, divinity in the new testament; Tenn State Univ, BS, pre-law, MS, int rels. **Career:** Ashland Theol Sem, dean; Little Rock Baptist Church, Detroit, MI, pastor, 1972-; Cognos Advert, pres & chief exec officer, Detroit, 1988-; Country Preacher Foods Inc, pres & chief exec officer, currently; E/W Cargo Airlines, founder & pres, currently; Valet Syst, MI, founder & pres, MI, currently. **Orgs:** Bd mem, Woodward Ave Action Asn; chmn, Budget Personnel & Training Policy & Promotional Appeals; founder & chmn, Detroit Acad Arts & Sci; Bd Police Commissioners. **Honors/Awds:** Michiganian of the Year, Detroit News. **Special Achievements:** Author of several books; is rated by the Detroit Free Press as one of the top five ministers in Michigan; by Crain's Business Magazine as one of the "Foremost Voices in Detroit". **Business Addr:** Pastor, Little Rock Baptist Church, 9000 Woodward Ave, Detroit, MI 48202, **Business Phone:** (313)872-2900.*

HOLLEY, JOHN CLIFTON
Military leader, association executive. **Personal:** Born Jan 8, 1940, Virginia Beach, VA; son of Edward L and Hazel L; married Harriett N, Mar 10, 1962; children: John C & Barbara J Davis. **Educ:** NC A&T State Univ, BS, chem, 1961; Am Univ, polit sci, 1977. **Career:** Military leader (retired), association executive; AUS progressive mgr, key leader, comdr Army units from platoon to brigade, staff officer highest level Dept Army, 1961-91; Maynard Jackson Youth Found, pres, currently. **Orgs:** Am Acad Polit Sci & Social Sci, 1980-; Am Univ Alumni Asn, 1987-; Acad Polit Sci, 1990-; Ben Hill United Methodist Church, treas, Class Benjamin, pres, finance comt, sec, Invest Club, 1991-; pres, NC A&T Alumni Asn, Atlanta chap, 1993-97; lt gov, Kiwanis Int, 1998-99; Asn AUS; Nat Asn Advan Colored People. **Honors/Awds:** NC A&T State Univ, Destinguished Mil Grad, 1961; Man of the Yr, Ben Hill United Methodist Church, 1997, Leadership Award, 1996; Int Civil Rights Ctr & Mus, Sit-in Participants Award, 1998; Mentor of Excellence, Teray Mill Sch, Dekalk County Sch Syst, 1996. **Military Serv:** AUS,col, 1961-91; Combat Infantryman's Badge; Army Paratrooper's Badge; Gen Staff Badge; USAF, War Col, Army Commendation Medal, 1966; Meritorious Serv Medal; US Command & General Staff Col, 1973-83; Bronze Star, 1967; Legion of Merit, 1985, 1988, 1991. **Home Addr:** 100 Creek View Trail, Fayetteville, GA 30214, **Home Phone:** (770)461-3469. **Business Addr:** President, Maynard Jackson Youth Foundation, 100 Peachtree St Suite 2275, Atlanta, GA 30303, **Business Phone:** (404)681-3211.

HOLLEY, DR. SANDRA CAVANAUGH
Educator, pathologist, college administrator. **Personal:** Born Mar 30, 1943, Washington, DC; daughter of Clyde Howard and Rebecca Arthur; children: David Marshall. **Educ:** George Washington Univ, AB 1965, AM 1966, Hon Doctor Pub Serv deg, 1989; Univ Conn, PhD 1979. **Career:** Rehab Ctr Eastern Fairfield Co, speech pathologist, 1966-70; Southern Conn State Univ, speech & lang pathologist, prof, 1970, Sch Grad Studies, dean,currently. **Orgs:** Chmn, Humane Comn City New Haven, 1977-86; bd dir, Am Nat Red Cross S Cent Chap, 1978-84; exec bd, Conn Speech & Hearing Asn, 1971-83; bd dir, NewHaven Vis Nurse Asn, 1977-79; vpres, admin, Am Speech-Language-Hearing Asn, 1983-85; bd dir, Foote Sch Asn, 1985-89; pres, Am Speech-Language-Hearing Asn, 1988. **Honors/Awds:** Danforth fel, Southern Conn State Col, 1973-80; Leadership in Communications Award, Howard Univ, 1987; Fel, Am Speech-Language-Hearing Asn, 1980; Multicultural Founders Award, Southern Conn State Univ, 1994;Milestone Award, Nat Coalition of 100 Black Women, 1994; Distinguished Alumna Award, Dept Speech & Hearing, George Wash Univ, 1997. **Business Addr:** Dean, Southern Connecticut State University, School of Grad Studies, Engleman Hall B018 501 Crescent St, New Haven, CT 06515-1355, **Business Phone:** (203)392-5234.

HOLLEY, SHARON YVONNE
Librarian, administrator. **Personal:** Born Aug 15, 1949, Gainesville, FL; daughter of Rebecca Bryant Jordan and Johnnie Jordan; married Kenneth, Aug 7, 1976; children: Nzinga, Asantewa & Makeda. **Educ:** Santa Fe Community Col, Gainesville, Fla, AA, 1968; Fla Atlantic Univ, Boca Raton, Fla, BA, 1970; Wayne State Univ, Detroit, MI, MSLS, 1972. **Career:** Librarian, Administrator (retired); Buffalo & Erie Co Pub Libr, Buffalo, NY, librn, 1972, coordr urban servs, exten servs adminr. **Orgs:** Afro-Am Hist Asn Niagara Frontier, 1977-; Kwanzaa Comt Buffalo, 1980-; Nat Asn Black Storytellers, 1986-; Black Caucus Am Libr Asn, 1990-; African-Am Librarians Western NY, 1990-. **Honors/Awds:** Certificate of Merit, Buffalo & Erie Co Pub Libr, 1984; Black History & Library Science Award, Empire State Fed Womens' Clubs, 1988; Community Service Award, Nat Asn Bus & Prof Women, 1989; Black Family & Heritage Award, Alpha Kappa Alpha, Xi Epsilon Omega Chap, 1989; Woman of the Year, Zeta Phi Beta Sorority Inc, Kappa Upsilon Zeta Chap, 1997; Uncrowned Queens, Afa Builders Western NY, 2001. **Special Achievements:** Author, African American History Rap, Simon and Schuster, 1989, The African American Book of Values, Doubleday, 1998.

HOLLIDAY, BILLIE. See HOLLIDAY-HAYES, WILHELMINA EVELYN.

HOLLIDAY, DIMETRY GIOVONNI. See HOLLIDAY, VONNIE.

HOLLIDAY, DR. GAYLE
President (organization). **Career:** G&H Consult LLC, pres.

HOLLIDAY, JENNIFER
Singer, actor. **Personal:** Born Oct 19, 1960, Houston, TX; daughter of Omie Lee and Jennie Thomas; married Rev Andre Woods, Mar 21, 1993 (divorced 1995); married Billy Meadows, Jan 1, 1991 (divorced 1991). **Educ:** Berklee Col Music, Boston, PhD, music, 2000. **Career:** Stage performances: Your Arms Too Short to Box with God, 1979-80; Dreamgirls, 1981; Sing, Mahalia, Sing, 1985; TV appearances: "Saturday Night Live", 1982; "The Love Boat", 1986; "In Performance at the White House", 1988; Albums: Dreamgirls, 1981; Feel My Soul, 1983; Say You Love Me, 1985; Get Close to My Love, 1987; Im On Your Side, 1991; On & On, 1995; The Best of Jennifer Holliday, 1996; 20th Century Masters - The Millennium Collection: The Best of Jennifer Holliday, 2000; Duet with Najiyah Through The Storm, 2006; Songs: "And I Am Telling You Im Not Going", 1982; "I Am Changing", 1982; "I Am Love",1983; "Just Let Me Wait", 1983; "Hard Time for Lovers", 1985; "No Frills Love", 1996; "Heart on the Line", 1987; Im on Your Side", 1991; "Love Stories", 1991; "A Womans Got The Power", 2000; "Think It Over", 2000; "And I Am Telling You Im Not Going, 2001 & 2007; "Givin Up", 2007. **Honors/Awds:** Grammy Award, 1981; Tony Award, 1981; Antoinette Perry Award, Best Actress in a Musical, 1982; Drama Desk Award for Outstanding Featured Actress in a Musical, 1981; Theatre Awards Outstanding Broadway Debut, 1982; Drama Desk Award, Best Lead Actress in a Musical, 1982; Grammy Award, Best R&B Performance-Female, 1983; Grammy Award Best New Artist, 1983; Image Award, Nat Asn Advan Colored People, 1983; Grammy Award, Best Inspirational Performance-Female, 1986; Distinguished Alumni Award, Tex Southern Univ; honorary doctoral degree, Berklee Col Music. **Special Achievements:** She is a two-time Grammy Award-winning African-American singer and actress. *

HOLLIDAY, VONNIE (DIMETRY GIOVONNI HOLLIDAY)
Football player. **Personal:** Born Dec 11, 1975, Camden, SC; married Eboni; children: Kali & Joey. **Educ:** NC Univ, BCS. **Career:** Green Bay Packers, defensive end, 1998-2002; Kansas City Chiefs, defensive end, 2003-04; Miami Dolphins, defensive tackle, 2005-08; free agent, currently. **Orgs:** Vonnie Holliday Found, 2001; Kids Company; fund raising efforts of the United Way of Kershaw County in SC, chmn, 2003-04. **Honors/Awds:** South Carolina's Male Professional Athlete of the Year, South Carolina Athletic Hall of Fame, 1999; NFL Defensive Rookie of the Month honor; First Team All-ACC, 1997. **Business Phone:** (404)229-8125.*

HOLLIDAY-HAYES, WILHELMINA EVELYN (BILLIE HOLLIDAY)
Government official. **Personal:** Born in Jacksonville, FL; daughter of Leah Ervin and John; married John (Jackie), Aug 25, 1970; children: Stepson & John W II. **Educ:** NY Univ, BS; Columbia Sch Social Work, grad studies; New Sch Social Res, MA, human resources; Inst Mediation & Conflict Resolution, cert mediator. **Career:** Government Official (retired); New York Dept Social Serv, case worker, 1956-61; New York Off Probation, court reporting officer, 1961-68; New York Police Dept, asst dir & exec dir, 1968-74; Vera Inst Justice & Pretrial Serv Agency, borough dir, 1974-76; Bd Parole, NY, comnr, 1976-84;New York Police Dept, dep comnr community affairs, 1984-94; Mt Vernon Police Dept, dep police comnr, 1994-95, comnr, 1995-96; Pres, NACCP, Manhattan, currently. **Orgs:** Hon pres, Friends N side Ctr Child Develop, 1974-; pres, Mid Manhattan Nat Asn Advan Colored People, 2000-; vpres & bd dir, Wiltwyck Sch Boys; chairperson & bd dir, Wiltwyck Brooklyn Div; bd dir, Exodus House; consult, Equal Opportunity & Womens Career Mag; fel organizer, Harlem Improvement Proj; Delta Sigma Theta; pres, Black Resources & Issues Now(BRAIN); adv, Greater New York Coun Boy Scouts Am & Law Enforcement Explorer Scouts; consult, Key Women Am; Manhattan Urban League; Women Criminal Justice. **Honors/Awds:** Humanitarian Award, New York Chap Continental Soc Inc, 1985; So journer Truth Loyalty Award, Coalition Black Trade Unionists, 1986; Achievement Award, Fedn Negro Civil Assocs New York, 1986; Govt & Community Serv Award, Nat Coun Negro Women, 1989. **Special Achievements:** AME's Top 100 Black Women, 1985. **Business Addr:** President, Mid-Manhattan NAACP, 270 W 96th St, New York, NY 10025, **Business Phone:** (212)749-2323.

HOLLIER, DWIGHT LEON, JR.
Football player, football coach. **Personal:** Born Apr 21, 1969, Hampton, VA; married Chandra, Mar 22, 1997; children: Deandre. **Educ:** Univ NC, BS, speech communications & psychol; Nova S eastern Univ, Davie Florida, MS, Men Health Coun. **Career:** Football player(retired), football coach; Miami Dolphins, linebacker, 1992-99; Indianapolis Colts, linebacker, 2000; coach, Stanly County Schs; coach, Frankfurt Galaxy; Coaching intern, Tony Dungy, Indianapolis in 2004; Nat Bd Cert Counr and Licensed Prof Counr, currently. **Orgs:** Bd residential & support Services; vpres, NFL Alumni Carolinas chapter; vpres, Charlotte Chapter NFL retired players union. **Honors/Awds:** Patterson Metal, univ NC. *

HOLLIMAN, ARGIE N (ARGIE HOLLIMAN-CHIBUZO)
Association executive. **Personal:** Born Jun 8, 1957, Grand Rapids, MI; daughter of John and Mattie M; children: Stephine Bryant, Stephen Bryant & Shawn Bryant. **Educ:** Grand Valley State Univ,

attended 1979; Columbia Sch Broadcasting, BA, commun, 1982. **Career:** WEHB Radio, host & producer, 1980-82; WKWM Radio, news dir, 1982-87; Sarah Allen Family Neighborhood Ctr, tutorial serv dir, 1987-88; S E End Neighborhood Asn, crime prev dir, 1988-92; Creative Commun Ctr, pres; YWCA, vol servs coun ctr coordr, 1990-. **Orgs:** Chmn pub rel, PTA, 1988-89; chmn, Gov's Task Force Youth Initiatives, 1988-89; co-founder, Burton St Church Christ, 1989; co-chmn, pub rel minority affairs, Chamber Com, 1991-92; chmn, Grand Rapids Cable Access Ctr, 1992; co-founder, Oakdale HR Ctr; Coailition Rep Govt; co-chmn, racism rtsk force, YWCA, 1992. **Special Achievements:** host & producer, "It's Time to Talk," 1990; Actress, Community Mental Health Theatre Troupe, 1992. **Business Addr:** Volunteer Coordinator, YWCA, 25 Sheldon Blvd SE, Grand Rapids, MI 49503, **Business Phone:** (616)459-7062 Ext 461.

HOLLIMAN, DAVID L
Executive. **Personal:** Born Sep 13, 1929, Denver, CO; son of Ernest W Holliman Jr (deceased) and Dorothy Taylor Holliman; married Mildred Helms, Dec 23, 1973; children: Rhoda, Lisa & Michael. **Educ:** Regis Col, Denver, CO, BA, econs, 1990. **Career:** Continental Air Lines, Denver, CO, passenger serv opers, 1966-86; United Maintenance Inc, pres, 1972-89; Primalon Int Enterprise Ltd, chief exec officer, 1989-; Queen City Servs, courier serv consult, currently. **Orgs:** Past trustee, Campbell Chapel AME Church Steward Bd, 1942-; Mayor's Bd Appeals; Mayors Black Adv Comn; Colo Black Roundtable; Colo Centennial Ethnic Minority Cou Bi-Centennial Comn; Adv group, Colo Pub Serv Co; past pres, PTA, Barrett Elem Sch. **Honors/Awds:** Grand Inspector General, 330 United Supreme, Coun, NJ, PHA, 1973, 1988; Legion of Honor, Charter Mem, 1974; Hall of Fame, Ira C. Meadows, Knights Templar, 1985; Man of the Year, Knights Templar, 1985; Past Imperial Potentate, Ancient Egyptian Arabic Order Noble Majestic Shrine Jurisdiction, 1988-90; Joseph E Seagram Vanguard Award; Honorary Past Grand Master, Ill, Ark, Tenn & Prov Ont, Texas Jurisdiction; Hon Captain, Syrian Temple No 49, Arabic Foot Patrol; Hon Lieutenant, Denver Police Dept. **Military Serv:** US Coast Guard, Petty Officer 1st Class, 1948-58; graduate of USCG Petty Officer School, Groton, CT; US Navy Firefighting School, Oakland, CA; Honorary capt, Denver Police Dept; Ebony Magazine, One of 100 Most Influential People, 1989. **Home Addr:** 2030 E 11th Ave, Denver, CO 80206-0844.

HOLLIMAN-CHIBUZO, ARGIE. See HOLLIMAN, ARGIE N.

HOLLIN, KENNETH RONALD
School administrator. **Personal:** Born Nov 6, 1948, Yuma, AZ; son of James T and Cleo E Cook; married Michelle Brown; children: Cheyenne, Kenya, James & Antonio. **Educ:** Arizona Western Col, Yuma, Ariz, AA, 1968; Ariz State Univ, Tempe, Ariz, BA, sec educ, 1973. **Career:** Phoenix Job Corps Ctr, Phoenix, Ariz, counr, 1973-75; Phoenix Opportunities Industrialization Ctr, Phoenix, Ariz, counr, 1975-80; Educ Opportunity Ctr, Phoenix, Ariz, counr, 1978-80; Abbey Rents, Phoenix, Ariz, truck driver, 1980-82; Educ Opportunity Ctr, Phoenix, Ariz, counr, 1982-84; Ariz State Univ, Tempe, Ariz, asst dir stud recruitment undergrad admis, 1984-, dir undergrad admis, currently. **Orgs:** Vpres, Ariz Multicultural Student Services Asn, 1987-89; chmn, Chapter I Parent Coun, Phoenix Elementary Sch Dst 1, 1987-89; pres, Garfield Sch PTO, 1987-90;planning comt mem, Statewide Parent Involvement Conf, Ariz Dept Educ, 1988-89; pres, Citizen's Adv Coun, Phoenix Elementary Sch Dst 1, 1989-90. **Honors/Awds:** Affirmative Action Award, Arizona State Univ, 1991. **Business Addr:** Director, K-12 Outreach Undergraduate Admissions, Arizona State University, 600 E Orange St, Tempe, AZ 85281, **Business Phone:** (480)965-3042.

HOLLINGER, REGINALD J
Executive. **Educ:** Williams Col, BA; Harvard Bus Sch, MBA. **Career:** PaineWebber Inc, managing dir & group head; Morgan Stanley & Co, prin; Chase Securities Inc, managing dir; Archway Broadcasting Group LLC, dir, currently; Radiovisa Corp, dir, currently; Quetzal/JP Morgan Partners, managing mem, currently. **Business Addr:** Managing Member, Quetzal / JP Morgan Partners, 1221 Ave of the Americas 40th Fl, New York, NY 10020-1080, **Business Phone:** (212)899-3536.*

HOLLINGSWORTH, ALFRED DELANO
Executive. **Personal:** Born Oct 26, 1942, Jackson, MS; married Hattie. **Educ:** Univ CO, BS; Univ WA, MA. **Career:** Crown Zellarbach, jr exec sales dept, 1965-67; Fiberboard Corp, sales mgr, 1967-68; Sheet Plant Corp, pres, 1968-; Aldelano Packaging Corp, founder, pres & cheif exec officer, 1968-Squat Corp, pres & owner, 1970-. **Orgs:** Bd dir, Black Bus Asn; LAC C Chmn "Hot Seat" prog; Rotary Club; foundr, Christian Bus Ministries; Youth Bus Prog. **Honors/Awds:** Black Businessman of Month, Nat Asn Mkt Develop; Award, US Dept Com. *

HOLLINGSWORTH, JOHN ALEXANDER
Educator, teacher. **Personal:** Born Sep 25, 1925, Owego, NY; son of John Alexander Sr (deceased) and Florence Eve Haley (deceased); married Dr Winifred Stoelting; children: 5. **Educ:** NC A&T State Univ, BS, agr, 1950, MS, adult educ, 1985; NC Cent Univ, MS,biol, 1960; Cornell Univ, attended 1963. **Career:** Educator (retired); Fayetteville City Schs, sci teacher, 1959-68, sci & math coordr, 1968-83; NC A&T State Univ, grad stud, 1983-85, staff develop intern; consult, writer, 1985. **Orgs:** Pres, Fayetteville City Unit NCTA, 1968-71; pres, NC Sci Teachers Asn, 1971-73; Fayetteville Airport Comn, 1973-79; grad stud intern, Maj Int Stress Mgt & Prev Health Care, 1983-85; NEA; NCAE; NEA-R; Black World Found, Nat Mus Am Indian; Ecol Action/Comn Ground; NC Retired Sch Personnel; Nat Retired Teacher Asn; Nat Asn Black Veterans; A&T Alumni Asn; NC Retired Govt Employees Asn; NC Sci Teachers Asn, Inst Noetic Sci. **Special Achievements:** Writer/dir, ESAA Pilot Proj in Math, 1972-80. **Military Serv:** AUS, capt, 1943-46, 1949-57; Served in Germany, Korea, & Hawaii. **Home Addr:** 61 Otalco Dr, Cherokee Village, AR 72529-6407. *

HOLLINGSWORTH, PERLESTA A
Lawyer. **Personal:** Born Apr 12, 1936, Little Rock, AR; son of Eartha Mae Frampton Morris (deceased) and Perlesta G; married Ada Louise Shine; children: Terri, Tracy, Perlesta Jr &a Maxie. **Educ:** Talladega Col, AB 1958; Univ Ariz Law Sch, JD, 1969. **Career:** Ariz City Coun, legal extradition officer, prosecuting atty, 1971; Little Rock City Bd, 1973-76, asst mayor, 1975-76; Arkan Supreme Ct, assoc justice, 1983-85; Hollingsworth Law Firm PA, atty, currently. **Orgs:** Urban League, Nat Asn Advan Colored People; Alpha Phi Alpha; Nat Bar Asn; Am Bar Asn; Sigma Pi Phi Fraternity. **Honors/Awds:** Omega Citizen of the Year, 1975. **Military Serv:** AUS, 1958-60. **Home Phone:** (501)664-7583. **Business Addr:** Attorney, Hollingsworth Law Firm PA, 415 Main St, Little Rock, AR 72201-3801, **Business Phone:** (501)374-3420.

HOLLINS, HUE
Sports manager. **Educ:** Calif State Univ. **Career:** Sports Manager (retired); NBA, referee.

HOLLINS, PROF. JOSEPH EDWARD
School administrator. **Personal:** Born Dec 14, 1927, Baton Rouge, LA; married Louise T; children: Reginald, Larry, Patrice & Stephanie. **Educ:** Leland Col, BS, 1952; NM Styland Univ, attended 1957; Southern Univ, ME, 1969. **Career:** Thomas A Levy, 1950-60; Upper Marengauin, prin, 1960. **Orgs:** Alderman Town Maringouin, 1970. *

HOLLINS, LEROY
Executive. **Personal:** Born Jul 1, 1945, Texarkana, TX; son of Robert (deceased) and Willie Pearl Purifoy (deceased); married Viola Anderson, Sep 21, 1968; children: LeTasha Renea & Shawn Ashley. **Educ:** Bishop Col, Dallas, attended 1970; Tex A&M, Dallas, attended 1975. **Career:** Tex Instruments, Dallas, Emp Serv & Recn Admin, 1970-79; Martin Marietta Astronaut Group, Denver, mgr, employee serv, 1979-. **Orgs:** Pres, Nat Employee Serv & Recreation Asn; pres, co-founder, Denver Area Employee Serv & Recn Asn, 1981-; Educ & Res Found, 1990-91; dep comnr, Amateur Softball Asn; Colo Asn Rec Athletics; Colo Parks & Recreation Asn. **Honors/Awds:** Operational Performance Awards, Martin Marietta Astonaut Group, 1981, 1982, 1990; Jefferson Cup, Martin Marietta Corp, 1982; Publications Award, Nat Employee Serv & Recreation Asn. **Home Addr:** 11701 E Yale Way, Aurora, CO 80014, **Home Phone:** (303)750-0977. **Business Addr:** Manager, Martin Marietta Astronautics Group, PO Box 179, Denver, CO 80201.

HOLLINS, LIONEL EUGENE
Basketball player, basketball coach. **Personal:** Born Oct 19, 1953, Arkansas City, KS; married Angela; children: Christopher, Anthony, Jacqueline & Austin. **Educ:** Ariz State Univ. **Career:** Basketball player (retired), basketball coach; Portland Trailblazers, guard, 1975-80; Philadelphia 76ers, 1980-82; San Diego Clippers, 1982-83; Detroit Pistons, 1983-84; Ariz State Univ, asst coach, 1985-88; Phoenix Suns, asst coach, 1988-95; Utah, 1993; Az, 1995; Vancouver Grizzlies, asst coach, 1995-99, head coach, 1999; Memphis Grizzlies, asst coach, 1999-2000,interim head coach, 2004-. **Honors/Awds:** NCAA Division I Men's Basketball Third Team All-Am AP, 1974; NBA Champions, Portland Trailblazers, 1977; NBA All-Star, 1977; Pacific Division titles, 1993, 1995. **Business Phone:** (901)888-4667.*

HOLLIS, MARY LEE
Business owner, real estate agent. **Personal:** Born May 15, 1942, Miller, GA; married Albert H; children: Naomi M & Pat Ann. **Educ:** Sacramento City & State Col; Real Estate Sch, cert . **Career:** Hollis Small Family Home CCF, owner, dir & broker, currently. **Orgs:** Adv bd, Sacramento Bd Realtors; Sacramento Asn Artists; Sacramento Asn C; Trinity Church Choir. **Business Addr:** Owner, Director, Hollis Small Family Home CCF, 1297 Valley Brook Ave, Sacramento, CA 95831.*

HOLLOMAN, THADDEUS BAILEY
Banker. **Personal:** Born Jun 30, 1955, Newport News, VA; son of Paul and Elsie; married Renee D Brown; children: Thaddeus Jr, Kelsey. **Educ:** Howard Univ, BBA, 1977; Old Dominion Univ, Pub Admin, 1983; Univ VA, VA Bankers Asn, Sch Bank Mgt, 1992. **Career:** Peat Marwick Mitchell & Co, auditor, 1977-79; Stud Loan Mkt Assoc, acct, 1979; Hampton Univ, acct 1979-81; City Newport News Va, auditor 1981-85; Community Fed Savings & Loan, 1985-90; Consol Bank, vpres; Old Pt Nat Bank, vpres, currently. **Orgs:** Bd trustees, C Waldo Scott Ctr HOPE; Newport News Educ Found, currently; 100 Black Men of Am Inc; Newport News Sch Bd; Phi Beta Sigma Fraternity Inc; Va Bankers Asn, 1990; charter mem, citizens review bd, Subsidized Housing, 1991-92; Nat Advan Asn Colored People Newport News Va; Newport News Political Action Comn, currently; treasurer, Peninsula Habitat Humanity; chmn, Bd Zoning Appeals, City Newport News, Va; Beta Gamma Sigma Bus Honor Soc; Newport News Econ & Indust Develop Authority, currently. **Business Addr:** President, Newport News Education Foundation, 12465 Warwick Blvd, Newport News, VA 23606, **Business Phone:** (757)591-4500.*

HOLLOWAY, ARDITH E
Executive. **Personal:** Born Oct 9, 1958, Youngstown, OH; daughter of James E Matthews (deceased) and J Faye; married Kenneth, Aug 28, 1982; children: Steffany & Autumn. **Educ:** Ohio State Univ, BA, speech commun, 1981. **Career:** Gulf Oil, vital source speaker, 1980-82; Metro Page Columbus, sales rep, 1982-84, relief dist mgr, circulation dept, 1984-85; Neighbor News, acct exec, 1985-88; Columbus Dispatch, acct exec, retail advert, 1988-. **Orgs:** United Way Speakers League; Columbus Urban League, resource develop com; Dublin Black Parent Asn, equity com co-chair; Faith Mission, volunteer; Columbus Metrop Club; bd mem, Dahlberg Learning Ctr; bd mem, YMCA Black Achievers. **Special Achievements:** An account exec for The Columbus Dispatch, implemented several new special newspaper supplements: Think Before You Drink, Black History Month, Library Special Section, St Anthony Special Section, Argo & Lehne Gift Guide, America Flora Events Pages, Expo Souvenirs, Buckeye Gymnastics, Discover Downtown, Huntington Center, Mt Vernon Plaza, & Kroger Employment; top salesperson for numerous special sections: Prom Time, Holiday Idea Guide, Dining Guide, Senior Lifestyles, In Time of Need, and Back to School. **Business Addr:** Account Executive, Columbus Dispatch, 34 S 3rd St 5300 Crosswind, Columbus, OH 43215, **Business Phone:** (614)461-8819.

HOLLOWAY, DOUGLAS V
Executive. **Personal:** Born Jul 3, 1954, Pittsburgh, PA; son of Arnold and Hattie Keys; married L Susan Branche, Jun 10, 1990. **Educ:** Emerson Col, BS, 1976; Columbia Univ, Grad Sch Bus, MBA, 1978. **Career:** Gen Foods, asst prod mgr, 1978-79; CBS TV Network, financial anal, 1979-81; CBS Cable, sales rep, 1981-82; TV Cable Week, Time Inc, mgr, nat acct, 1982-83; USA Network, dir, nat acct, 1983-85, vpres, affil rels, 1985-87, sr vpres, affil rels, 1987-2000; Universal TV, pres, network distrib & affil rels, 2000; Cable Investments NBC Universal Cable, pres, 2004-; ValueVision Media Inc, dir, currently. **Orgs:** Pres, Uptown Investment Assoc, 1986-; pres, Nat Asn Minorities Cable, 1990-93, vpres, 1988-90; bd mem, Cable TV Admin & Mkt, 1992-; chmn, Nat Asn Multi-ethnicity Commun. **Honors/Awds:** Forty Under 40 Professional Leadership, Crain NY Bus Mag, 1989; Affiliate Relations Award, Nat Asn Multi-ethnicity Commun, 1990; Vanguard Award, 2000. **Special Achievements:** Journal of Marketing, 1978. **Business Addr:** President, Cable Investments for NBC Universal Cable, 900 Sylvan Ave 1 Cnbc Plz, Englewood Cliffs, NJ 07632, **Business Phone:** (201)735-3568.

HOLLOWAY, DR. ERNEST LEON
School administrator. **Personal:** Born Sep 12, 1930, Boley, OK; married Lula M Reed; children: Ernest L Jr, Reginald & Norman. **Educ:** Langston Univ, BS, voc agr educ, 1952; OK State Univ, MS, 1955; Univ OK, EdD, 1970. **Career:** Tinker Air Field base, 1955; Boley High Sch, sci teacher & prin, 1955-62; Langston Univ, asst prof biol, asst registr, registr, dean stud affairs, prof, vpres admin, actg pres, interim pres, pres, 1979-2005; pres emer, currently. **Orgs:** Comn Leadership Develop; Am Coun Educ; USDA & 1890 Task Force; Coun OK Col & Univ Presidents; Coun 1890 Presidents; Food & Agr Coun State OK; Nat Alliance Black Sch Educrs; Alpha Phi Alpha; Phi Delta Kappa; Nat Asn State Univ & Land-Grant Col; bd dir, Nat Asn Equal Opportunity Higher Ed; bd trustees, Nat 4-H Coun; bd trustees, Presidents Coun Red River Athletic Conf; chair & bd trustees, Presidents Coun OK State Regents Higher Ed; OK Small Bus Develop Consortium, Adv Bd; Prince Hall Masons; Imperial Coun Shriners; United Supreme Coun, AASR, 33E; President's Bd Adv Historically Black Col & Athletics, 2002; Land Grant Pres Asn; Nat Asn Inter collegiate Athletics; adv bd, Historically Black Col & Univl; Alpha Phi Alpha Fraternity Inc. **Honors/Awds:** Distinguished Educator Award; Public Service Award; Martin Luther King Humanitarian Award; Afro-Amer Hall of Fame, 1987; OK Educators Hall of Fame, 1996; OK Higher Education Hall of Fame, 1999; Ok State Univ Alumni Assn Hall of Fame, 2001; Thurgood Marshall Scholar Fund Educ Leadership Award; Educ Leadership Award. **Special Achievements:** Listed in 100 Most Influential Friends by Black Journal, 1977. **Business Addr:** President Emeritus, Langston University, PO Box 1500, Langston, OK 73050.

HOLLOWAY, DR. ERNESTINE
Educator, college teacher. **Personal:** Born May 23, 1930, Clyde, MS. **Educ:** Tougaloo Col, BS; NY Univ, MA; Mich State Univ,

NDEA, stud personnel serv higher educ; Univ Miss, MEd; Univ Southern Miss, Phd, educ admin. **Career:** Professor (Retired); High Sch, teacher, 1952-53; Greenville Pub Schs Systs, sci teacher, 1952-53; Tougaloo Col, sect pres, admin asst to pres, 1953-63, asst dean, 1963-65, dean stud, 1965-85; NASPA J, ed bd, 1972-75; St Dept Educ, Jackson, MS, Div Accreditation, accreditation monitor, 1987, Div St wide Testing, educ technologist, 1987-92; Jackson St Univ, Educ Found & Leadership, Sch Educ, asst prof educ admin, 1992-. **Orgs:** Undergrad prog adv mem, Alpha Kappa Alpha Sorority, 1974-78, bd dir, OperaS, 1975-76; charter mem, Opera S Guild, 1976-; Nat Asn Stud Personnel Admin, 1976-78; Reg III Adv Bd, 1978; res comt, Jackson Mun Separate Sch Dist; Col Comt Nat Asn Women Deans & Counselors; consult, Workshops & Conf Stud Personnel Serv; Phi Delta Kappa Fraternity; Miss Personnel Guid Asn; Southern Col Personnel Asn; Am Miss Asn; United Church Christ Study, NY Univ Nat Def Ed; Miss Asn Minority Sch Admin; Pi Lambda Theta Nat Hon & Prof Asn Educ; Nat Asn Women Deans Admin & Counr; Am Asn Univ Women; Supvr & Curric Develop; Am Asn Univ Women; Yth Task Group, Hinds Co Asn Mental Health. **Honors/Awds:** Award Mich St Univ; Alumnus of the Year, Tougaloo Col, 1971; Miss Black Women, Nat Asn Colored Women's Club, 1976; Hall of Fame Honoree, Tougaloo Col Nat Alumni Asn, 2001.

HOLLOWAY, GERALD
Career: Essex Co Col, Fashion Entertainment Bd, producer & adv, currently. **Business Addr:** Producer, Advisor, Fashion Entertainment Board, Essex County College, 303 University Ave, Newark, NJ 07102-1798, **Business Phone:** (973)877-3418.

HOLLOWAY, HARRIS M.
Businessperson, funeral director, clergy. **Personal:** Born Jan 26, 1949, Aiken, SC. **Educ:** Livingston Col, BS, 1971; Hood Theol Sem, attended 1971; Am Acad-Mc Allister Inst Funeral Serv, PMS, 1974. **Career:** NJ Dept Labor Indust, employ interviewer, 1971-73; Carnie P Bragg Funeral Homes Inc, funeral dir, 1972-78; Perry Funeral Home, funeral dir; Pure Light Baptist Church, Newark, NJ, pastor; Gen Motors Accept Corp, field rep, 1974-84, credit rep, 1984-93, customer rels supvr, 1993-94, acquisitions analyst, 1994-. **Orgs:** Paterson Jaycees, 1975-76; Garden State Funeral Dirs, 1977; Rotary Col Paterson, 1977-78; treas, Teacher Corp Community Coun Peterson, 1979; master mason Mt Zion Lodge No 50. **Honors/Awds:** Named best lighting technician, best stage mgr, best Set Designer, most coop thespian Livingston Col, 1966-71. **Business Addr:** Director, Perry Funeral Home, 34 Mercer St, Newark, NJ 07103.*

HOLLOWAY, JERRY
Educator. **Personal:** Born May 14, 1941, Chicago, IL; married Mary Bowie. **Educ:** Parson Col, BA, 1963; Univ Nev, MEd, 1971. **Career:** Matt Kelly Elem Sch Las Vegas, teacher, 1963-66; Las Vegas, coordr recprog elem studs, 1965-66; coordr summer work experience prog, 1966; Washoe Co Sch Dist Reno, asstd in planing & supvr disadvantaged studs in workexperience prog, 1966; Trainer Jr HS Reno, teacher, 1966-67, teacher, admin asst to prin, vprin, 1968-69, dean studs, 1969-71; Traner Rec Prog City Reno Rec Dept, asst dir, 1970-71; Washoe Co Sch Dist, Reno, intergroup specialist, 1971-72, sch admin, curric coordr, asst supt, Stud Support Serv, Sch Impr Plan, 2007-08. **Orgs:** Reno-Sparks Br Nat Asn Advan Colored People; chap mem past chmn, Black-Coalition Fair Housing Law Com; past chmn, Human Rels Com NV State EducAsn; chmn, comt mem, Cub Scouts Div BSA, Las Vegas; secy treas, Econ OpporBd Washoe Co; vchmn, CETA Manpower Adv Plng Coun; bd dir, YMCA; chmnretired sr ctzns vol prog; commn Equal Rights Citizens; NV Asn Adminr; Nat-Staff Devel Coun; Family Support Am; Nat Asn Elem Sch Prins; LiterateCommunity Comn; NV Cent Off Admin Asn. **Honors/Awds:** President's Medal, Univ NV, 2006. **Business Addr:** Team Member, School Improvement Plan, Washoe County School District, 425 E 9th St, PO Box 30425, Reno, NV 89520-3425.

HOLLOWAY, JOAQUIN MILLER, JR.
School administrator, librarian, vice president (organization). **Personal:** Born Dec 28, 1937, Mobile, AL; son of Joaquin M Holloway Sr and Ariel Williams; married Malvina Murray, Jun 5, 1960; children: Monica, Joaquin III, Josef. **Educ:** Talladega Col, AB, 1957; Ind Univ, MS, 1958, EdS, 1960; Univ Ala, PhD, 1976. **Career:** School administrator (retired); Tex S Univ, instr, 1958-61; Cent High School, instr, 1961-65; Mobile Co Pub Sch Syst, media specialist, 1965-69; Univ S Ala, prof bus, 1969, sr librn & head instrnl media ctr, dir instrnl media ctr. **Orgs:** Consult, Int Paper Co, 1977-80; consult, Necott Devel Co, 1978; consult, Middle States Asn Col & Schs, 1978; bd mem, YMCA Dearborn Br, 1975-86; bd mem, Cine-Tel Comn, 1976-; coun mem, Ala State Coun on the Arts, 1979-; vpres, Culture Black & White, 1969-; host "Holloway House" progressive jazz prog, WKRG AM-WKRG FM Radio, 1969-79; mem Asn Educ Comm & Tech, Minorities Media, Omega Psi Phi Frat, Phi Delta Kappa, Omicron Delta Kappa; licensed lay reader in the Episcopal Ch; co-host of local UNCF Telethon 1983, 1984, 1988. **Honors/Awds:** Fifth Place Award Photog, Allied Arts Coun Competition, 1974; Second Place Award Photog, First Annual Fort Conde Arts Festival, 1979; 3 First Place Awards, Photog Mobile Soc Model Eng 20th SER Conv, 1980; one-man photog shows, including: Percy Whiting Gall, 1985, Tel Fair Peet Gall, Auburn Univ, 1986, Tacon Station Gall, 1986; George Washington Carver Mus, Tuskegee Univ, 1987, Fine Arts Mus S, 1987, Hay Center Art Gall, Stillman Col, 1988, Isabel Comer Mus of Art, 1989; The John L LeFlore Civic Award, 1990; Gladys M Cooper Fine Arts Award, 1991. *

HOLLOWAY, DR. NATHANIEL OVERTON, JR.
Dentist. **Personal:** Born Jan 30, 1926, Holly Grove, AR; son of Nathaniel Holloway Sr; married Dorothy Gladys; children: Jacqueline, Nathaniel III & Rhoda. **Educ:** Tenn State Univ, BS, 1949; Meharry Med Col, DDS, 1953. **Career:** Pvt Pract, dentist. **Orgs:** Past pres, Ypsilanti Bus & Prof League/Washtenaw Dist Dent Soc; Wolverine Dent Soc; Mich State Dent Soc; chmn, ADA Dent Soc; Deacon bd & Trust bd, Plymouth Congregational Church; past gen chmn, NAACP Freedom Fund Dinner; past pres, Detroit Duffers Golf Asn; Alpha Phi Alpha; Beta Kappa Chi. **Military Serv:** USN, 1944.

HOLLOWELL, JOHNNY LAVERAL
Military leader, child care worker. **Personal:** Born Sep 13, 1951, New Orleans, LA; married Angie D; children: Chandler A, Ivory D, Alexandria B. **Educ:** Utica Jr Col, AA, 1971; Alcorn A&M Univ, attended 1972; Columbia Col, BA, 1980; Univ Phoenix, pursuing MBA, grad studies. **Career:** Military leader (retired), Child care worker; US Coast Guard; Willowell Develop Ctr Inc, co-owner, pres & chief exec officer, currently. **Orgs:** Big Brothers Am; life mem, Nat Naval Officers Asn; life mem, Omega Psi Phi Frat; Role Models Unlimited; Rotary Club Int. **Honors/Awds:** Omega Man of the Yr, 1992, Rho Nu Chap; Roy Wilkins Renown Serv Award, Nat Asn Advan Colored People, 1999. **Military Serv:** USCG, CDR; Meritorious Serv Medal, 2 Commendation Medals, 3 Achievement Medals, Letter of Commendation, Meritorious Team Commendation, Good Conduct Award. **Business Addr:** President, Director, Willowell Child Development Center, 909 Med Ctr Blvd, PO Box 57157, Webster, TX 77598-0000.*

HOLLOWELL, KENNETH LAWRENCE
Government official. **Personal:** Born Mar 5, 1945, Detroit, MI; son of Herman JDJ Hollowell Sr and Rachel A Kimble Hollowell; married Patricia J; children: Terrance L & Rhonda L. **Educ:** Wayne County Comm Col, AA, 1979. **Career:** Cook Paint & Varnish Co, rsch tech 1967-71; Teamsters Local Union No 247, bus rep, 1971-80, trustee & bus rep, 1980-82, recording sec & bus rep, 1982-85, vpres & bus rep, 1985-87, pres & bus rep, 1987-88, secy & treasprin Officer, 1988-2002; Detroit Mayor's Off labor, faith based affairs,Liaison, 2003. **Orgs:** Exec commander, Detroit Police Reserves, 1970-94; Dep imperial potentateIntl Shriners, 1975-83; bd mem, Teamsters Nat Black Caucus, 1976-; comnr-,Civic Ctr City Detroit, 1976-94; first vpres, Mich Assoc Masonic Grand Lodges, 1979-; grand master, Ralph Bunche Grand Lodge Int Masons, 1979-81; bd mem, Mich Coalition Black Trade Unionists, 1980-; bd dirs, United Way MI, 1980-86, Metro Agency Retarded Citizens, 1981-94; Indust Rels Res Asn, 1981-2000; Econ Alliance MI, 1982-2002; adv comm., Ctr Volunteerism UCS, 1981-87; dep supreme grand master, Int Masons, 1983-86; supreme grandmaster, Int F&AM Masons, 1986-89; Metro Detroit Convention & Visitors Bur,1986-2002, vice chmn, 1994; bd dir, MI Chap Int Asn Exhibition Mgrs, 1987-93; exec bd mem, Metro Detroit AFL-CIO, 1988-2002; bd mem, Metro Detroit Chap, A Phillip Randolph Inst, 1988-; trustee, Mich Teamsters Joint Coun No 43, 1989-95; NAACP, 1989-; Corp, 1992-2000; bd dir, Robert Holmes Teamsters Retiree Housing Corp, 1990-98; bd dir, Teamsters Credit Union Wayne & Oakland Counties, MI, 1989-; bd dir, Metropolitan Realty Comnr Detroit Police Dept, 1994-98; recording secy, Mich Teamsters Joint Coun No 43, 1995-98; comnr, Youth Sports & Recreation Comn, 2001-; bddirs, Southeast Mich Chap, Am Red Cross, 2002-. **Honors/Awds:** Walter Campbell Community Services Award, Mich United Labor Community Servs Sch, 1977; Goodwill Ambassador Award, Minority Womens Network, 1987; Community Services Award, United Way Southeastern Mich, 1990; Mich Asn Masonic Grand Lodge Community Services Award, 1994; Nelson Jack Edwards Award, (MI CETU), Apr 1994. **Military Serv:** USMC, sgt, 1963-67; Good Conduct Medal, Natl Defense Medal, Vietnam Service Medal, Vietnam Campaign.

HOLLOWELL, MELVIN BUTCH
Lawyer. **Educ:** Albion Col, BA, 1981; Univ Va Sch Law, JD, 1984. **Career:** Mich Dem Party, gen coun, chair; Butzel Long PC, gen coun, atty, partner; Allen Brothers PLLC, lawyer, currently; Nat Asn Advan Colored People, gen coun, legal coun, currently. **Orgs:** Chmn, Freedom Fund Dinner, Nat Asn Advan Colored People, 1995; State Bar Mich; Nat Bar Asn; Wolverine Bar Asn; life mem, US Ct Appeals; co-chair, Citizen Advocacy Comt, US Dist Ct; Detroit Music Hall; Am Red Cross; Detroit Cent Bus Dist Asn; Univ Detroit Jesuit High Sch; Adv Bd, Bank Bloomfield Hills. **Honors/Awds:** First Lifetime Achievement Award, Detroit Chap. **Special Achievements:** Columnist, Mich Chronicle & Jewish News. **Business Addr:** Legal counsel, National Association for the Advancement of Colored People, 4805 Mt Hope Dr, Baltimore, MD 21215, **Business Phone:** (410)358-8900.

HOLLOWELL, MELVIN L.
Surgeon. **Personal:** Born Nov 24, 1930, Detroit, MI; married Sylvia Regina Ports; children: Regina, Dana, Melvin Jr, Danielle, Christopher, Courtney, Sylvia. **Educ:** Wayne State Univ, BS, 1953; Meharry Medical Col, MD, 1959. **Career:** Hutzel Hosp, vice chmn dept urol, 1980-87; Harper Grace Hosp Detroit, med bd, 1983-85, exec comt, 1983-85; Southeast Mich Surg Soc, pres, 1983-84; N Cent Sect Am Urol Asn, exec comt, 1984-86; Samaritan Health Ctr, Sisters Mercy, exec comt, 1985-87, chmn dept surgery, 1985-; Wayne State Univ Col Med, Dept Urol, clinical asst prof; pvt pract, Urologicargry Adults & C, urologist, pres, currently. **Orgs:** Life mem, Nat Asn Advan Colored People; Kappa Alpha Psi Frat; GESU Cath Church; pres, Mich Br Am Urol Asn, 1976-77. **Honors/Awds:** Fellow Am Col Surgeons; Am Col Med Dirs Physician Execs; Royal Col Med; Am Bd Urol. **Military Serv:** AUS Medical Corp capt 1958-62; AUS Commendation Awd/Medal 1961. **Business Addr:** Urological Surgeon, President, 20905 Greenfield Rd, Southfield, MI 48075.*

HOLMAN, ALVIN T.
Manager, consultant. **Personal:** Born Jul 21, 1948, Washington, DC; married Karen. **Educ:** Los Angeles Harbor Col, AA, 1969; Univ Wash, AB, 1970; Mich State Univ, attended 1972. **Career:** Southern Calif Rapid Transit Dist, planning proj mgr; UHURU Inc, proj dir; City of Seattle, comn planning consult; Off Econ & Opportunity Seattle, res consult; State Mich, urban planner, comn planning specialist; Berryman & Assocs, sr planning consult; Gardner & Holman Consult, owner. **Orgs:** Am Inst Planners; Am Soc Planning Officials; Am Soc Planning Consults Nat Asn Housing & Rehab Officials; Nat Asn Planners. **Business Addr:** Research Consult, Gardner & Holman Consult, 3761 Stocker St Suite 103, Los Angeles, CA 90008.

HOLMAN, DORIS ANN
Educator. **Personal:** Born Feb 14, 1924, Wetumpka, AL; daughter of Willie G and Mattie Banks; divorced; children: DeWayne, Douglas, Desiree & Glenn. **Educ:** Ala State Univ, BS, 1944; Univ San Francisco, MA, 1979. **Career:** Educator (retired); Detroit City Sch; Compton Unified Sch Dist, teacher. **Orgs:** NEA; Phi Delta Kappa Beta Phi; Nat Asn Univ Women; rep, CA Teachers Asn StCoun, 1960-62; bd dir, ATEB Corp; chmn, Neg Coun Compton Unified Sch Dist, 1971-73; pres, Compton Educ Asn, 1971-74; bd dir, Compton YMCA, 1970-; regional dir, Nat Tots & Teens, 1972-; chmn, Neighborhood GS A; bd dir, BSA; bd dir, Christian Day Sch Comm Lutheran Church; Int Toastmistress Club; pres, Women Church Comn Lutheran Church, 1977, 1992-94; treas, So Bay Conf Am Lutheran Church Women, 1977; secy, Compton Educ Asn, 1976-77; Compton Sch Dist Compens Educ Adv Coun Sch Adv Coun; bd dir, Mid Cities Sch Credit Union, 1998-; pres, 1993; elect bd, Col & Univ Serv Am Lutheran Church, 1982-88; worthy matron, Gethsemane Chap Order Eastern Star, 1994. **Honors/Awds:** Pro Achievement Award, Enterprise Teachers Asn, 1968; Who Award, Calif Teacher Asn, 1970; Teacher in Political Award Theol Bass Mem, 1972; Nat Sorority Phi Delta Kappa, Soror of the Year, 1994; Ala State Univ Alumni Asn, Los Angeles Chap, Alumnus of the Year, 1989. **Home Addr:** 322 E 135th St, Los Angeles, CA 90061, **Home Phone:** (310)327-0765. *

HOLMAN, FOREST H., JR.
Secretary (office). **Personal:** Born Apr 2, 1942, Birmingham, AL; married; children: Karriem Malik. **Educ:** Tuskegee Inst, BS, 1965; Mich State Univ, MA, 1971, PhD, 1974. **Career:** City Chicago, teacher; Chicago Vice & Lords St Acad Inst, 1968; OIC, instr, 1967-68; State Mi, senate res, 1970-72; Tuskegee Inst, dir Freshman studies & asst prof, 1972-73; City Detroit, exec asst mayor; Mich State Univ, asst prof, Race & Urban Studies, 1974-75; Shaw Col Detroit, adj prof philos & soc inst, 1974-78; Wayne State Univ, adj prof, Polit sci, 1974-80; Mich Consol Gas Co Detroit, mgr environ planning, 1978-. **Orgs:** Dept Black Studies Eastern Mich Univ; counr, Highland Pk Dept Human Resources, MI; counr, Mich Dept Human Resources, 1974-45; Asn Study Negro Life & Hist; Asn Social & Behavioural Sci; Alpha Phi Omega & Kappa Alpha Psi Frat; guest panelist, Summer Bus Inst Wayne State Univ; panelist, Neighborhood Legal Serv. **Honors/Awds:** Cert Recognition Jacob A Citrin Mem Sem & Gov Conf Unemploy. **Home Addr:** 923 Long fellow St, Detroit, MI 48202. *

HOLMAN, KARRIEM MALIK
Association executive. **Personal:** Born Apr 13, 1969, Chicago, CO; son of Forest and Beverly. **Educ:** Howard Univ, BA, 1992. **Career:** Mich Youth Corp, supvr, 1988; Rep John Conyers, D-Mich, legis intern, 1989; Alliance Justice, staff asst, 1992-93; Gov Ann Richards Re-election Campaign, field coordr, 1994; Nat Black Bus Coun, exec asst, legis asst, 1994-. **Orgs:** Legis Consult, Summit 1993 Health Care Coalition, 1994; Participation 2000 PAC, 1994. **Special Achievements:** Participation 2000 PAC: selected from competitive pool of applicants to work on reelection of Gov Ann Richards; One of 5 African-Americans young people to work on a major gubernatorial campaign. **Home Phone:** (202)832-1288. **Business Addr:** Legislative Assistant, National Black Business Council, 1010 Wayne Ave Suite 430, Silver Spring, MD 20901, **Business Phone:** (301)585-6222.

HOLMAN, KWAME KENT ALLAN
Journalist. **Personal:** Born Jul 4, 1953, New Haven, CT; son of M Carl; married Miriam Rudder Holman, Feb 13, 1992; children:

Kevin Alton, Donovan Joseph. **Educ:** Howard Univ, BS, 1977; Northwestern Univ, MS, jour, 1981. **Career:** Dist Columbia Govt, acting press sec to the mayor, 1980; Nat Summit Conf Black Econ Develop, pub rels consult, 1980; C Defense Fund, commun asst, 1980; WTOC-TV, reporter, talk show host, 1982-83; The Newshour with Jim Lehrer, producer & corresp, 1983-93, cong corresp, 1993-. **Orgs:** Nat Asn Black Journalists, occasional speaker; Partners Journ, occasional ed, 1990-; Journalists Round Table, C-Span, occasional panelist, 1993-; Nat Press Club, occasional panelist, 1994-. **Honors/Awds:** George Polk Award for Nat TV Reporting, 1984; Nat News & Docu Emmy, 1985; Local News & Doc Emmy, 1991; Joan Shorenstein Barone Award, 1994. **Special Achievements:** Consulting Writer, "AIDS and Race"-The AIDS Quarterly: Fall 1989 with Peter Jennings, 1989. **Business Addr:** Congressional Correspondent, The Newshour with Jim Lehrer, 3620 S 27th St, Arlington, VA 22206, **Business Phone:** (703)998-2861.*

HOLMES, ALVIN ADOLF
State government official, educator. **Personal:** Born Oct 26, 1939, Montgomery, AL; son of John H and Willie Ann; married Judy (divorced 1970); children: Veronica. **Educ:** Ala State Univ, Montgomery, AL, BS, 1962, MEd, 1972, MA, 1979; Selma Univ, Selma, AL, LLD, 1982; Rochester Bus Inst; Atlanta Univ; Univ Pa; Univ Ala; Jones Sch Law. **Career:** Licensed real estate broker; Ala State Univ, Montgomery, AL, asst prof hist; State Ala, 78th Dist, Montgomery, AL, state rep, 1974-. **Orgs:** State Dem Exec Comt; Dem Party Ala; Nat Asn Advan Colored People; bd dirs, Southern Christian Leadership Conf; Hutchinson Missionary Baptist Church; Kappa Alpha Psi Fraternity, Southern Christian Leadership Conf, Montgomery Improvement Asn. **Military Serv:** AUS, Sp-4, 1962-65; Good Conduct Medal. **Business Addr:** State Representative, State of Alabama, 78th District, 11 S Union St Room 525-A, PO Box 6064, Montgomery, AL 36130, **Business Phone:** (334)242-7706.

HOLMES, ARTHUR
Executive. **Personal:** Born May 12, 1931, Decatur, AL; son of Arthur Jr and Grace L; married Wilma King; children: Deborah H Cook, Rick Fairley-Brown, Sharon H Key & Sharon Fairley-Nickerson. **Educ:** Hampton Univ, BS, chem, 1952; Kent State Univ, MBA, 1967. **Career:** Automated Sciences Group Inc, vpres logistics, 1987-90, exec vpres & coo, 1990, pres & chief exec officer, 1990; Montgomery County Coun, Dept PubWorks & Transp, dir, 2004-. **Orgs:** Omega Psi Phi Fraternity, 1952-; chmn, NAACP, Educ Comm, Montgomery Co, MD, 1993-95; pres, Retired Mil Officers asn, 1994-; comnr, Md Nat Capital Park & Planning Comn, 1994-. **Honors/Awds:** Businessman of the Year, Omega Psi Phi Fraternity, Mu Nu Chap, 1993. **Military Serv:** AUS, material command, dir readiness, 1980-82; AUS, dep of the inspectorgen, 1982-83; AUS for Logistics, asst deputy chief of staff, 1983-84; AUS, AUS Tank-Automotive Command, commanding gen, 1984-87; Distinguished Serv Medal, Legion of Merit, Bronze Star. **Business Addr:** Director, Montgomery County Council, Department of Public Works & Transport, 101 Monroe St 10th Fl, Rockville, MD 20850-2540, **Business Phone:** (240)777-7170.

HOLMES, DR. BARBARA J.
Educator, writer. **Personal:** Born Jun 26, 1934, Chicago, IL; daughter of Wyess Wilhaite and Helyne Wilhaite; married Laurence H; children: Carole, Helyne, Sheryl & Laurence. **Educ:** Talladega Col, attended 1953; Univ Colo, BA, 1973, MA, 1974, PhD, 1978. **Career:** Nat Assessment Educ Progress, writer, 1977-83; State Educ Policy Sem Progco-sponsored Educ Comn States & Inst Educ Leadership, nat coordr; Policy Studies, ECS Former Dir; other educ prof organs, presentations; Consult Recruitment & Retention Minority Teachers, Expertise Teacher Educ, Work Force Literacy; Univ Colorado, Assoc Prof Commun, currently. **Orgs:** Delta Sigma Theta Pub Serv Sor; bd dirs, Whitney M Young Jr Mem Found, 1974-84; fel, Educ Policy Fel Prog, 1982-83. **Honors/Awds:** Phi Beta Kappa Honor Society, 1974; Academic Fellow Whitney M Young, 1973-74. **Special Achievements:** Published over 20 articles & reports. **Business Addr:** Associate Professor Communications, University of Colorado, Campus Box 185, PO Box 173364, Denver, CO 80217-3364, **Business Phone:** (303)315-2230.*

HOLMES, CARL
Executive. **Personal:** Born Jan 6, 1929, Oklahoma City, OK; married Marvella; children: Carla D. **Educ:** Drake Univ, MBA, 1951; LA State Univ, Fire Dept; Southern Methodist Univ, Fire Dept Admin; Univ MD Fire Dept Staff & Command Sch; Motivational Mgt Schs; Okla Univ Equal Opportunity Sem. **Career:** Executive (retired); Okla City Fire Dept, fire chief, 1951-81; Carl Holmes & Assoc, dir, 1980; Carl Holmes Exec Develop Inst, exec dir, 1990-96. **Orgs:** Consult, City Ft Worth, 1979; City Atlanta, 1980; City San Francisco, 1982; nat Fire Acad, WA DC Fire Dept; Int Assoc Fire Instr; assoc mem, Nat Assoc Black Mgrs; fire serv training instr, Okla State Univ; city chmn, Okla Lung Assoc; tech adv Training Mag; instr motivational mgt Phycol Chem Corp; Am Airlines; Tex Light & Power Inc; Okla Natural Gas Inc; Continental Oil Inc; Tex Instrument Inc; consult, City Admin Tech Asst Orlando, FL. **Honors/Awds:** guest lectr, Univ MD. **Home Addr:** 5106 N Lottie Ave, Okalahoma City, OK 73111, **Home Phone:** (405)427-9516. *

HOLMES, CARLTON
Marketing executive. **Personal:** Born Apr 1, 1951, New York, NY; married Dr Thelma Dye; children: Kyle, Arianna. **Educ:** Cornell Univ, BA, 1973; Columbia Univ, Grad Sch Bus, MBA, 1975. **Career:** Lever Bros, asst prod mgr, 1975-77; Johnson & Johnson, prod dir, 1977-82; Drake Bakeries, prod mgr, 1982-83; Block Drug Co, Jersey City, dir new bus develop, 1983-89. **Orgs:** Cornell Black Alumni Asn; Nat Black MBA Asn. **Business Addr:** Director New Business Development, Block Drug Co, 257 Cornelison Ave, Jersey City, NJ 07302, **Business Phone:** (201)434-3000.*

HOLMES, CLAYTON ANTWAN
Football player. **Personal:** Born Aug 23, 1969, Florence, SC; children: Dominique, Colton Jackson & Kenya Briana. **Educ:** North Greenville Univ, Carson-Newman Univ. **Career:** Football player (retired); Dallas Cowboys, defensive back, 1992, 1994-95; Miami Dolphins, 1997; motivational speaker.

HOLMES, CLOYD JAMES
Labor activist, president (organization). **Personal:** Born Nov 23, 1939, Houston, TX; son of Haywood and Charlene Cooper; married Madelyn Holmes Lopaz, Sep 20, 1986; children: Reginald B, Patrice, Cloyd J Jr & Anthony E. **Career:** Ramada Inn, fry cook, 1960-63; Howard Johnson Hotel, fry cook, 1964-66; C W Post Col, Automatique Food Serv, chef, shop stewart, 1966-70; USEU Local 377, Long Island City, NY, bus rep, 1970-71, fin secy, treas, 1971-72, former pres. **Orgs:** Int Found Employee Benefit Plan, 1970-; exec bd mem, vpres, Retail Wholesale & Dept Store Union, 1978; former sec, treas, The Negro Labor Comn; exec vpres, Huntington Boy's Club; former vpres, Nat Asn Advan Colored People, Greenwich Village Br, mem, Huntington Br; A Philip Randolph Inst, 1986, Coalition Black Trade Unionists; Am Cancer Soc, Queen's Br. **Honors/Awds:** Greenwich Village Nat Asn Advan Colored People Br, 1980; The Trade Union Women African Heritage, 1981; NAACP 'Man of the Year', 1983; Negro Labor Comn 'Man of the Year', 1984; Am Cancer Soc Greater Jamaica Unit for Notable Serv in' the Crusade to Conquer Cancer Award', 1984. **Home Addr:** 86-11th Ave, Huntington Station, NY 11746, **Home Phone:** (516)351-9386.

HOLMES, DARICK
Football player. **Personal:** Born Jul 1, 1971, Pasadena, CA; son of Gloria. **Educ:** Portland State Univ. **Career:** Football player (retired); Buffalo Bills, running back, 1995-98; Green Bay Packers, running back, 1998-99; Indianapolis Colts, running back, 1999-00. **Honors/Awds:** Football Digest, "Sweet 16" Rookie Team, 1995. *

HOLMES, DOROTHY E
Psychologist, psychoanalyst. **Personal:** Born Mar 9, 1943, Chicago, IL; daughter of Major Moten Evans and Queen McGee Evans Pryor; married Raymond L M, Jun 29, 1985. **Educ:** Univ Ill, BS, 1963; Southern Ill Univ, MA, psychol, 1966, PhD, clin psychol, 1968. **Career:** Dept Psychol Howard Univ Hosp, assoc prof; pvt prac; Dept Psychol Univ MD, asst prof 1970-73; Univ Rochester, instr & postdoctoral fel, 1968-70; George Wash Univ, Doctor Psychol Prog, dir, currently, Clin Psychol, prof, currently; Baltimore-Wash Psychoanal Inst, training & supvr analyst, currently. **Orgs:** Nat Inst Mental Health; fel Am Psych Asn; Sigma Xi; Am Psychoanalytic Asn; DC Psychol Asn; Baltimore-Wash Inst & Soc Psychoanalysis; bd dir, Nat Regist Health Serv Providers Psychol, 1988-; bd dir, Prof Exam Serv, 1987-. **Special Achievements:** Publ 1 book & 7 sci articles and 3 book reviews. **Business Addr:** Director Doctor of Psychology Program, Professor of Clinical Psychology, George Washington University, 2300 M St NW Suite 910, Washington, DC 20037, **Business Phone:** (202)496-6261.

HOLMES, E SELEAN
Museum curator, consultant. **Personal:** Born Jul 15, 1954, Cincinnati, OH; daughter of Bert L Holmes Sr and Harriet J. **Educ:** Knoxville Col, attended 1972-73; Univ Cincinnati, BA, 1979, MA, 1981-83; Yale Univ, prog African lang, 1983. **Career:** Curator, artist & designer; Yale Univ, fel, prog African lang, 1983; Traveler's Aid Int Inst, foreign lang coordr, 1985; Nat ARO Museum & Cult Ctr, cur, 1985-89; Smith Col, Mwangi Cult Ctr, dir, 1989-90; Arts Consortium African Am Mus, assoc dir, 1991-; Cincinnati Hist Soc, mus ctr dir African Am prog, 1992-96; cult consult, 1996-98; Nat Underground Railroad Freedom Ctr, cur, 1999-2001; DuSable Mus African Am Hist, chief cur & dir exhibs & collections, 2001-05; Northwestern Univ, instr, currently; consult, currently. **Orgs:** Treas, African Am Mus Asn, 1986-89; African Am Studies Asn, 1986-; Mass Asn Women Deans & Adv, 1989-90; dir develop, YWCA, 1990-93; midwest rep, African Am Commentary Mag, 1990; vpres, Univ Cincinnati Friends Women's Studies, 1991-93; Cincinnati Art Museum, 1991-92; bd, Int Visitors Coun, USIA, 1996-99. **Honors/Awds:** Grant for professional development, Alliance Ohio Comt Arts Agencies, 1988; Philo T Farnsworth Video Award, 1993; Certificate of Appreciation, Ohio Crime Prev Asn, 1994; Applause Mag Imagemaker Honoree, 1995; Zora Neale Hurston Outstanding Scholar Award, 1999. **Special Achievements:** Exhibited and sold artwork throughout the 1970s, extensive travel throughout the USA, Africa, Canada, Bermuda, Italy, 1975-96, recognized by the Newspaper Association of America for compiling the Cincinnati Enquirer Black History Month Teacher's Guide, 1996. **Business Addr:** Consultant, Instructor, Northwestern University, School of Continuing Studies, 339 E Chicago Ave, Chicago, OH 60611-3008, **Business Phone:** (312)503-6950.

HOLMES, EARL
Football player, football executive, football executive. **Personal:** Born Apr 28, 1973, Tallahassee, FL; married Tiffany; children: Earl Jr. **Educ:** Fla A&M univ. **Career:** Pittsburgh Steelers, linebacker, 1996-2001; Cleveland Browns, 2002; Detroit Lions, line backer, 2003-05; Detroit Lions, free agent, 2003-. **Orgs:** Kappa Alpha Psi Fraternity, 1994. *

HOLMES, HENRY SIDNEY, III
Lawyer. **Personal:** Born Apr 10, 1944, New York, NY; son of Henry Sidney II and Annie; married Albertha C Middleton (deceased); children: Monique Elizabeth. **Educ:** Columbia Univ, BA, 1976; Hofstra Univ Sch Law, JD, 1979. **Career:** Lever Bros Co, acct mgr, 1969-72; Black Life Discount Stores, owner, 1970-76; Mudge Rose Guthrie Alexander & Ferdon, partner, 1987-95; Winston & Strawn, partner, currently. **Orgs:** Mem NY Bar Asn, 1979-; 100 Black Men Inc, 1983-; bd dirs, Nat Asn Securities Prof, 1985-91. **Military Serv:** AUS, 1966-68. **Home Addr:** 138-42 228 St, Laurelton, NY 11413. **Business Phone:** (212)294-6700.

HOLMES, REV. JAMES ARTHUR
Clergy, historian, chaplain. **Personal:** Born May 27, 1954, Charleston, SC; son of James Arthur Sr and Maranda Phillips. **Educ:** Allen Univ, Columbia, SC, BA, 1976; Interdenominational Theol Ctr, Atlanta, GA, MDiv, 1982; Boston Univ, Boston, MA, STM, 1989, 1989-, ThD. **Career:** Shady Grove AMEC, Blythewood, SC, pastor, 1974-75; Rock Hill AMEC, Columbia, SC, pastor, 1975-76; Lagree AMEC, Sumter, SC, pastor, 1976-77; Am Church SC, Columbia, SC, hist consult, 1987-88; Charleston County Substance Abuse Comn, Charleston, SC, community resource person, 1990-; Boston Univ, asst prof church hist; Shaw Univ, asst prof church hist, currently. **Orgs:** SC Hist Soc, 1985-; Reserve Officers' Asn, 1986-. **Honors/Awds:** Annual Am Fellow, Int African Methodist Episcopal Church, 1989-91; Bishop Fredrick C James Fel, Bishop F C James, 1989. **Special Achievements:** Author, Thirty Bishops South Carolina, 1987; "The Priority Emanuel AME Church: Longest Continuous AME Church in South" AME Review, 1987; contributor, five chaps, African Methodism in South Carolina: A Bicentennial Focus, 1987; various others. **Military Serv:** AUS, capt, chaplain, 1977-86; AUS Reserves, capt, chaplain, 1986-; received Meritorious Service Ribbon, 1986, received Army Achievement Medal, 1985, received Army Serv Ribbon, 1983. **Business Addr:** Assistant Professor, Shaw University Divinity School, 118 E South St, Raleigh, NC 02215, **Business Phone:** (919)716-5517.

HOLMES, JAMES FRANKLIN
Government official. **Personal:** Born Nov 1, 1945, Leesburg, GA; son of Benjamin and Rosa Johnson; married Elaine Durham, Aug 6, 1976; children: Marcel J Holmes. **Educ:** Albany State Col, Albany, GA, BA, 1967. **Career:** US Cen Sub Bur, Detroit, MI, survey statistician, 1968-73; US Census Bur, Detroit, MI, prog coordr, 1973-79; US Census Bur, Kansas City, MD, asst reg dir, 1979-82; US Census Bur, Los Angeles, CA, asst reg director, 1982-83; US Census Bur, Philadelphia, PA, regional dir, 1983-85; US Census Bur, Atlanta, GA, regional dir, 1985-. **Orgs:** Atlanta Econs Club, 1986-; US Census Bur Strategic Planning Comt, 1987-89; Southern Demographic Asn, 1988-; vpres, S Cobb Improvement Asn, 1988-; Atlanta chap, Am Stat Asn, 1990-; vpres, Mableton Tigers Youth Baseball Asn, 1988-. **Honors/Awds:** US Department of Commerce Bronze Medal Award, US Census Bur, 1985; US Department of Commerce Silver Medal Award, US Dept Com, 1989-. **Military Serv:** AUS Reserve, Sergeant first Class, 1970-76. **Business Addr:** Regional Director, US Census Bureau, 101 Marietta St Suite 3200, Atlanta, GA 30303-2700.*

HOLMES, JERRY
Football player, football coach. **Personal:** Born Dec 22, 1957, Hampton, VA. **Educ:** Chowan jun Col,assoc deg, bus admn,1977; W Virginia Univ,Bach degree, 1980; Hampton Univ, MBA; Long Island Univ, MBA. **Career:** NY Jets, 1980-83, 1986-87; Pittsburgh Maulers, 1984; NJ Gen, 1985; Detroit Lions, 1988-89; Green Bay Packers, corner back, 1990-91; Hampton Univ, co-defensive cord & linebacker coach, 1992-94, defensive cord linebacker; W VA, asst football coach, 1994-98; Cleve land Browns, defensive back coach, 1999-00; Wash Redskins, defensive back coach, 2001; San Diego Chargers, defensive back coach, 2002-03, Hampston Univ, head coach,2007-09. **Honors/Awds:** Sporting News USFL All-Star Team, 1984, 1985; Black Coll Natl Champs,Hampton Univ, 1992, 1993; CIAA championships; Ira A Rodgers Award. *

HOLMES, KENNY
Football player. **Personal:** Born Oct 24, 1973, Vero Beach, FL. **Educ:** Univ Miami, attended. **Career:** Football player(retired); Tenn Oilers, defensive end, 1997-98; Tenn Titans, defensive end, 1999-00; NY Giants, 2001-03. *

HOLMES, LARRY
Boxer, businessperson. **Personal:** Born Nov 3, 1949, Cuthbert, GA; married Diane; children: Misty, Lisa, Belinda, Kandy & Larry

Jr. **Career:** Professional kick boxer (retired), businessperson; boxer, 1968-85; Muhammad Ali, sparring partner; Round 1 Bar & Disco, owner; sports wear store, owner; professional boxer; Larry Holmes Enterprises Inc, owner, 2003-. **Honors/Awds:** World Heavyweight Champion, 1978-85; champion, Int Boxing Fed, 1984; undefeated record, 45 professional fights, 31 won by knockouts; One of Ten Outstanding Men in Am, Junior Chamber Com; Inducted into the International Boxing Hall of Fame, 2008. **Business Addr:** Owner, Larry Holmes Enterprises Inc, 91 Larry Holmes Dr Suite 200, Easton, PA 18042, **Business Phone:** (610)253-6905.

HOLMES, LESTER
Football player. **Personal:** Born Sep 27, 1969, Tylertown, MS. **Educ:** Jackson State Univ. **Career:** Philadelphia Eagles, guard, 1993-96; Oakland Raiders, 1997; Ariz Cardinals, 1998-2000. **Honors/Awds:** Rookie of the year, 1993.

HOLMES, DR. LORENE B
Educator. **Personal:** Born Jul 27, 1937, Mineola, TX; daughter of William H Barnes and Jessie M Barnes; married Charles M Sr (deceased) (deceased); children: Charles Jr, James Henry & Jessyca Yvette. **Educ:** Jarvis Christian Col, BS, 1959; Univ N Tex, M Bus Ed, 1966, EdD, 1970. **Career:** Jarvis Christian Col, Div Eight Col Prog, chairperson soc & behav sci, 1971-75, chairperson bus admin dir int progs, 1975-78, Div Social Sci & Bus, chairperson, 1978-81, Div Bus Admin, chairperson, 1981-96, exec asst pres external rels, Career Mgt Serv, dir career planning & placement, currently. **Orgs:** Nat Bus Educ Asn, 1964-; Tex Bus Educ Asn, 1972-; treas, Hawkins Alumnae Chap Delta Sigma Theta Sorority, 1983-, Golden life mem; proposal reader, United States Dept Educ, 1986-2000, bd Hawkins Helping Hands, 1987-94; staff dir, Presidential Search Comt, Jarvis Christian Col, 1987-88; bd dir, Greater Hawkins Chamber Com, 1987-; bd /sec, Hawkins Public Libr Bd, 1988-95; life mem, Jarvis Christian Col/ Southern Christian Inst; Nat Alumni & Ex-Student Asn. **Honors/ Awds:** Publs (approx 15) Prof Jour, 1969-84; Top Lady of the Year, Top Ladies of Distinction Inc, 1982-; Woman of the Year, Hawkins C of C, 1982; Certificates of Honor, E TX Chap of Links Inc; Longview & Tyler TX, 1980 & 1984; Certificate of Appreciation, Am Bus Women's Asn, Lake Country Charter, 1984; T A Abbott Faculty Excellence in Teaching Award, 1988; Business Teacher of the Year, Tex Bus Educ Asn, 1988; Certificate of Appreciation, Shawnee State Univ, 1988; Certificate of Appreciation, Univ North Tex; Exec on Campus Prog, 1989; Heritage Award, 1991; Profiles of East Texas, KLTV, 1991; Jarvis Christian Col First Pioneer Hall of Fame, 1994; Texas State Collegiate Business Teacher of the Year, 1996; 6 chapters in yearbooks, 16 articles published, editorial reviewer for 2 textbooks. **Special Achievements:** Honored by KLTV Channel 7 as one of eight East Texan "Profiles of East Texans—We're Proud of You," filmed for Lou Rawls' Parade of Stars UNCF Telethon, Jarvis Christian College, 1992. **Business Addr:** Director of Career Planning and Placement, Jarvis Christian College, Alumni Reclamanagement Reclamation Program, Hwy 80, PO Box 1470, Hawkins, TX 75765, **Business Phone:** (903)769-5795.

HOLMES, DR. LOUYCO W
Educator, dentist. **Personal:** Born Apr 24, 1924, Washington, DC; son of Naomi and Louyco; married Carleen Watts; children: Richard L. **Educ:** Howard Univ, 1943; Rutgers Col Pharm, BS, 1950; NJ Col Med & Dent, DMD, 1967; Acad Gen Dent, fel, 1982-. **Career:** Dentist, Educator (retired); Holmes Pharm, owner, 1954-63; Gen Dental Pract, dentist, 1967-92; NJ Dental Sch, dental educr & prof clin oper dent, 1967-89. **Orgs:** Pres, 1958-59, NJ Pharm Assoc; vpres, Commonwealth Dent Asn, 1977-79, pres, 1979-80,chmn, Budget Com, 1977; Chi Delta Mu Frat; Nat Dent Asn; House Dels, 1974-77; chmn, Credentials Com, 1975; bd trustees, RL Garner Trust & Fund. **Military Serv:** AUS, sgt, 1943-46. **Home Addr:** 520 Scotland Rd, South Orange, NJ 07079.

HOLMES, MARY BROWN
Labor activist, manager, judge. **Personal:** Born Oct 20, 1950, Charleston, SC; daughter of Vernell P and Rufus; married William; children: Hosea L Banks & Joya N. **Educ:** Johnson C Smith Univ, BA, 1971; Webster Col, MA, 1976. **Career:** Sea Island Comp Health, med social worker, 1974-79; Trident Tech Col, instr, 1980-82; Telamon Corp, dep dir; SC Dept Corrections, admin judge, 1987-. **Orgs:** Elder St Paul Presby Church; Sea Island Comp Health, 1973-74; Ocean Queen OES, 1975; treas, Charleston EOC Comn, 1980; chmn, Nat Black Social Worker Orgn, 1974-; SC Sch Bd Asn 1975-; chmn, St Paul Sch Bd, 1975-. **Honors/Awds:** Notary SC, 1976-86; Outstanding Young Women of America, 1978. **Home Addr:** PO Box 237, Hollywood, SC 29449. **Business Addr:** Chief Judge, 5962 Hwy 165 Suite 200, Ravenel, SC 29470-5514, **Business Phone:** (843)889-8332.

HOLMES, MICHAEL R
Executive. **Personal:** Born in St Louis, MO; married Gail; children: 2. **Educ:** Wash Univ, attended 1979. **Career:** Executive (retired); Monsanto, HR Dept, 1980; Edward Jones, prin partner & chief human resources officer, head hr, 1996-2004. **Orgs:** United Way; Mary Inst & Country Day Sch; Webster Univ; Harris-Stowe State Univ.

HOLMES, ODETTA. See Obituaries section.

HOLMES, PRIEST ANTHONY
Football player, philanthropist. **Personal:** Born Oct 7, 1973, Ft Smith, AR; son of Herman Morris; children: DeAndre, Jekovan, Corion & Jaylenn. **Educ:** Univ Tex, Austin. **Career:** Football player (retired); Baltimore Ravens, running back, 1997-2000; Kansas City Chiefs, running back, 2001-07; philanthropist, currently. **Orgs:** Nat spokesperson, Nat Dairy Coun; fel, Christian Athletes; supporter & benefactor, Children's Miracle Network; spokesperson, Chiefs & Price Chopper MVP Kid prog, 2002-03; founder, Priest Holmes Foundation. **Honors/Awds:** Offensive Player of the Year, San Antonio Light; Civic Leader Award, Nat Consortium Acad & Sports; The Snickers Hungriest Player of the Year, SuperBowl XXXIX; Sportsman of the Year, San Antonio Express-News, 2000; Special Achievement Award, Kansas City Sports Community, 2002; Chiefs Unsung Hero Award, Nat Football League Players Asn, 2002; Father of the Year, Afro-Am Newspapers, 2002; The JB Award, FOX Sports, 2005. **Special Achievements:** Named one of the Top 100 Good Guys in sports by The Sporting News in 2003. **Business Addr:** Founder, Philanthropist, Priest Holmes Foundation, 85 NE Loop 410 Ste 205, San Antonio, TX 78216.

HOLMES, RICHARD BERNARD
Banker. **Personal:** Born Apr 4, 1951, Chicago, IL; son of Robert B and Florence M; married Marion Turner, Jul 2, 1977; children: Reginald B. **Educ:** Chicago City Col, 1968-70; DePaul Univ, 1973-75; Univ Phoenix, BSBA, 1989. **Career:** First Nat Bank Chicago, sr tax acct, 1972-79; Valley Nat Bank, trust tax adminr, 1979-82; Ariz Bank, mgr, trust tax unit, 1982-85; Security Pacific Bank, employee benefit trust admin, 1985-89, Systs conversion proj consult, 1989-90; Bank Am, mgr, employee benefit acct, 1990-92, sr trust officer, 1992-. **Orgs:** Pres, Ariz Asn Urban Bankers, 1988-89; acct dir, United Negro Col Fund, San Diego, Phoenix, 1988-90, 1992-; vpres, Western Region, Nat Asn Urban Bankers, 1989-90, vpres finance, 1991-92, pres, 1996-97; pres, San Diego Urban Bankers, 1993-94. **Honors/Awds:** Man of the Year, Southern Calif Conference of the African Methodist Episcopal Church, 1996. **Military Serv:** USY, sgt, 1971-72; Bronze Star, Vietnam Service Medal, 1972. **Home Phone:** (619)484-3243. **Business Addr:** Vice President, 450 B St Suite 1700, San Diego, CA 92101, **Business Phone:** (619)515-5724.

HOLMES, DR. ROBERT A
Government official. **Personal:** Born Jul 13, 1943, Shepherdstown, WV; son of Priscilla L and Clarence A; divorced; children: Donna Lee Vaughn, Darlene Marie Jackson & Robert A Jr. **Educ:** Shepherd Col, attended 1964; Columbia Univ, MA, 1966, PhD, 1969; Shepherd Col Hon Doctorate Humanities, 2001. **Career:** Harvard-Yale-Columbia Summer Studies Prog, dir, 1968-69; Southern Univ, assoc prof, 1969-70; City Univ New York, Bernard Baruch Col, dir SEEK, 1970-71; Atlanta Univ, prof, 1971-; Ga House Rep, state rep, 1975-; Govt Affairs Comn, chmn; Clark Atlanta Univ, Southern Ctr Studies Pub Policy, dir, 1989-, distinguished prof polit sci, 2002-, dir currently; Ga Gen Assembly, state rep, 2004-. **Orgs:** Pres, Adams Pk Residents Asn, 1972-73; pres, Nat Conf Black Polit Scientists, 1973-74; pres, Asn Social & Behav Scientists, 1976-77; chmn, bd dirs, YMCA SW Atlanta, 1976-78; chmn, bd dirs, Res Atlanta, 1978-79; chair, Ga Legisl Black Caucus, 1990-91; bd dirs, Capitol City Bank, 1995-; chair, bd trustees, Jomandi Theater Co, 1998-; exec coun, Am Polit Sci Asn, 2000-02. **Honors/Awds:** Outstanding Young Man of the Year, Atlanta Jaycees, 1975; Outstanding Legislator's Award, Am Asn Adult Educr, 1978; Alumnus of the Year, Shepherd Col, 1978; Layperson of the Year Award, Metrop Atlanta YMCA, 1989; Chmn, Ga Legis Black Caucus, 1990-91; Amoco Foundation Outstanding Professor Award, Clark-Atlanta Univ, 1992; Fannie Lou Hamer Community Service Award, 1993; Torchbearer Award, Sickle Cell Found Ga, 1996; Legislator of the Year, Nat Black Caucus State Legislators, 1999; Bob A Holmes Freeway, named in honor, 1999. **Special Achievements:** Author/co-author: 25 monographs and books; 75 articles; Editor of two annual publications, The Georgia Legislative Review and the Status of Black Atlanta; First African American in the history of the General Assembly to serve on the Budget Subcommittee. **Business Addr:** Director, Distinguished Professor, Clark-Atlanta University, Southern Center for Studies in Public Policy, 223 James P Brawley Dr, Atlanta, GA 30314, **Business Phone:** (404)880-8089.

HOLMES, ROBERT C
Commissioner, lawyer. **Personal:** Born Mar 20, 1945, Elizabeth, NJ; divorced; children: 1. **Educ:** Cornell Univ, AB, 1967; Harvard Law Sch, JD, 1971. **Career:** Roxbury, cir assoc, 1969-71; State NJ, atty, 1971; Newark Housing Devel & Rehab Corp Newark, exec dir, 1971-74; Newark Watershed Conservation & Development Corp, chief exec, 1979-87; NJ St Dep Comm Affairs, asst commr atty; Rudgers Sch law, clin prof law, currently. **Orgs:** NJ Bar asn; Nat Bar asn; Am Soc Pub Adm; Garden St Bar asn; NAHRO. **Honors/Awds:** Nat hon soc, Cornell Univ; Deans List; 4 yr Teagle Found Scholar; Sr Men's Hon Soc MA NG. **Business Phone:** (973)353-5059.

HOLMES, ROBERT ERNEST
Lawyer, president (organization). **Personal:** Born Jul 24, 1943, New York, NY. **Educ:** NY Univ, BA, 1966; NY Univ Sch Law, JD, 1969; Manhattan Sch Music & Univ Southern Calif, additional study. **Career:** Paul Weiss Rifkind Wharton & Garrison, summer assoc, 1968, part time atty, 1968-69, assoc atty, 1969-71; WA Sq Col of Arts & Sci, guest lectr, 1969-70, adj instr Am Lit, 1970-71; NY Sch Continuing Educ, adj instr Black Am, 1969-70; Motown Record Corp, sr coun, 1971, legal coun, 1971; Columbia Pictures, Music Group, sr vpres, gen mgr, Music Publ Div, pres. **Orgs:** Bd dir, Pacific Psychotherapy Asn, CA; bd dir, Nat Asn Advan Colored People; bd dir, Const Rights Found CA; bd dir, Black Music Asn; pres, Black Entertainment & Sports Lawyers' Asn; assoc couns, Motown Records, 1971-77. **Honors/Awds:** Dean's List, Temple Univ & NY Univ Sch Law; Univ Schlorship NY Univ, NY State Schlorship, NY Univ; Leopold Schepp Fund Schlorship, NY Univ; various debate & pub speking awrads; Am Jurisprudence Prize in Copyright; Military History Award, Temple Univ, 1963; recipient Fulbright-Dougherty Travel Grant, 1967; Samuel Rubin Schlorship Carnegie Fund Schlorship. **Special Achievements:** Author of numerous publs. **Business Addr:** Senior Vice President General Manager, President, Columbia Pictures, Music Publ Div, Columbia Plz E, Rm 231, Burbank, CA 91505.

HOLMES, ROBERT KATHRONE, JR.
Executive, president (organization), chief executive officer. **Personal:** Born Sep 5, 1952, Louisville, KY; son of Robert K Sr and Cecile E Thompson; married Stephanie A Kennedy, Nov 20, 1982; children: Robert K III, Tomika C & Justin C. **Educ:** McKendree Col, Lebanon, IL, bus admin, 1988. **Career:** Kentucky Fried Chicken, Louisville, KY, mgr facilities, 1979-88; Brown-Forman Corp, Louisville, KY, vpres, dir corp servs, 1988; Louisville Real Estate Develop Co, pres & ceo; The Mardrian Group, chmn & asst vpres, currently. **Orgs:** Past pres, Intl Fac Mgt Asn, 1985-; mem, Nat Asn Corp Real Estate Execs, 1988-; mem, Intl Soc Fac Execs, 1989-; prof cert, Certified Com Investment Mem; bd dir, Louisville Real Estate Develop Co. **Honors/Awds:** KFC-Adult Black Achiever, YMCA Black Achiever Program, 1988; Corp Team Work Award, Brown-Forman Corp, 1990; Kentucky Colonel; Leadership Louisville Class, 1989. **Business Phone:** (502)776-2749.

HOLMES, DR. WENDELL P
Funeral director. **Personal:** Born Feb 10, 1922, Brunswick, GA; married Jacquelyne Spence; children: Wendell P Holmes III & Carolyn Holmes Nesmith. **Educ:** Hampton Inst, Pres Class, BS, 1943; Eckels Col Mortuary Sci, pres class mortuary sci, 1947. **Career:** Duval Co Sch Bd, chmn, 1980-84; Holmes & West Funeral Home PA, pres, 1956-86; Wendell Holmes Funeral Dirs Inc, funeral dir, pres, 1986-. **Orgs:** Duval Co Sch Bd, 1969-92; chair & bd dirs, Century Nat Bank, 1976-85; chmn & bd trustees, Bethune Cookman Col; founding sire archon, Gamma Beta Blvd, Sigma Pi Phi Fraternity Inc; bd trustees, chmn, Hampton Univ; Alpha Phi Alpha Fraternity, bd mem, Hampton Univ. **Honors/ Awds:** Hon LLD Degree Bethune-Cookman, 1982; Annual Brotherhood Award, Nat Conf Christians & Jews, 1985; Small Bus man of the Year, Jacksonville Area-Chamber Com; Meritorious Service in Area of Human Relation, Alpha Phi Alpha Fraternity; Silver Bell Award for Significant Contribution to Education, Duval County Classroom Teachers Asn. **Military Serv:** AUS, first lt, QMC, 3 1/2 yrs. **Home Addr:** 12859 Muirfield Blvd S, Jacksonville, FL 32225. **Business Addr:** President, Wendell Holmes Funeral Directors Inc, 2719 W Edgewood Ave, Jacksonville, FL 32209, **Business Phone:** (904)765-1641.

HOLMES, WILLIAM
Executive, minister (clergy). **Personal:** Born Aug 19, 1940, Allendale, SC; married Diane T; children: Renada Irene, Eva Regina. **Educ:** VoorHees Col, BS, math, 1973. **Career:** Mayor, City Allendale, 1976-88; DuPont, sr engr; Allendale Sta Church Christ, radio ministry, currently. **Orgs:** SC Sect Conf Black Mayors; NAACP; Allendale County Indust Develop Bd. **Honors/Awds:** Alpha Chi Hon Soc Beta Chap, Voor Hees Col, 1972. **Special Achievements:** coach, Little League Baseball. **Military Serv:** USAF, legal specialist, staff seargent, 1961-69; Commendation Medal.

HOLMES, WILLIAM B
Law enforcement officer. **Personal:** Born Jan 31, 1937, Trenton, NJ; married Helen Vereen; children: Mark William & Allen C. **Educ:** VA Union Univ, BA, 1959. **Career:** Fed Probation Officers Asn, teacher, 1960-61; Dept Pub Welfare, soc case worker, 1961-62; Mercer Co Welfare Bd, social case worker, 1962-63; State NJ, Div Mental Retardation, social worker, 1963-66; Fed Job Corp, group leader, 1966; State NJ, parole officer, 1966-75; E Dist PA, US probation officer, 1975-. **Orgs:** Bd dir, Lawrence YMCA, 1968-; pres, vpres, Bd Educ, Lawrence Township, 1969-; life mem, past polemarch Kappa Alpha Psi Frat, 1970-71; chmn, Mercer Co, Community Col EOF, 1972-; exec bd, Nat Asn Advan Colored People Trenton. **Honors/Awds:** Pioneer Award for Achievement; Polemarch Award, Kappa Alpha Psi Frat; Certificate of recognition, Lawrence Township Recreation Comn; Certificate of recognition, Lawrence Township Non-Profit Housing; Achievement Award, Distinguish Service Kappa Alpha Frat; Achievement Award, Nat Asn Advan Colored People; Recognition Award for Outstanding service, Lawrence Township. **Military Serv:** AUSR, e-5, 1960-66. **Business Addr:** 601 Market St, Philadelphia, PA 19106.

HOLMES, WILLIE A.
Salesperson, consultant. **Personal:** Born Jul 25, 1928, Warwick, VA; married Addie Smith; children: Audrey, Yolanda & Wendell. **Educ:** Quinn Col, BS, 1961. **Career:** Litton Med Prod, salesman, 1955-68; Equit Life, agent, 1968-69, asst dist sales mgr, 1969, dist sales mgr, 1970; AXA Adv LLC, consult & adv, currently. **Orgs:** Alpha Phi Alpha, 1957; Nat Asn Life Underwriters, 1968-; Career Sales Club, 1974-; Conn Develop Authority, 1976; New Haven Bus & Prof Asn; vpres, Bus Vent; dir, Urbn League Nat Asn Advan Colored People; Quinn Col Alum Asn. **Honors/Awds:** Man of Year, Alpha Phi Alpha, 1965. **Special Achievements:** First & only black member appointed to Connecticut Development Authority. **Military Serv:** AUS, staff sgt, 1952-54. **Home Addr:** 87 Antrim St, West Haven, CT 06516, **Home Phone:** (203)934-7256. **Business Addr:** Consultant, 87 Antrim St, West Haven, CT 06516, **Business Phone:** (203)934-7256.*

HOLMES, WILMA K.
Educator. **Personal:** Born Apr 25, 1933, Washington, DC; daughter of Elton F and Edith T; married Arthur Holmes Jr, Feb 19, 1983; children: Ricki Fairley Brown & Sharon Fairley. **Educ:** DC Teachers Col, Wash, DC, BA, 1956; Stanford Univ, Palo Alto, CA, MA, 1970. **Career:** Vario Sch Syst, teacher, 1964-70; Montgomery Co Pub Sch, teacher, 1964-70, language arts teacher specialist, 1969-70, dir human rels, 1970-84, human rels training coordr, 1970-71, supvr instr, 1987-92, prin, currently; Flower Valley Elem Sch, elem prin, 1992. **Orgs:** Nat Alliance of Black Sch Educ; Am Assn of Sch Adminr; Montgomery Co Alumni Chap; Delta Sigma Theta Soreity; Phi Delta Kappa Sorority; PiLambda Theta Hon Educ Soreity; Nat Coun of Negro Women; conf chair, Elem Sch Admin Assn, 2001; Nat Asn Elem Prin; Nat Asn Advan Colored People, Montgomery County Br; pres, gospel choir class leader, Clinton AME Zion Church; Silver Spring mem, bd dirs, Community Concerts Olrey Links Inc. **Honors/Awds:** Back to Basics & Multiculturalism are not Mutually Exclusive, NEA Human Rights Conf; Creative Solutions to Staff Reduction, Am Asn Sch Adminrs;woman of year, Montgomery County, 1979; Design & Implemented Multiethnic Conv Educ & Consult-Sexism. **Home Addr:** 17104 Blossom View Dr, Olney, MD 20832. **Business Addr:** Principal, Montgomery County Public Schools, 4615 Sunflower Dr, Rockville, MD 20853.

HOLMES, REV. ZAN W., JR.
Educator. **Personal:** Born Feb 1, 1935, San Angelo, TX; widowed 1999; married Carrie Collins, Jan 1, 2001. **Educ:** Huston-Tillotson Col, BA, 1956; Southern Methodist Univ, BD, 1959, STM, 1968. **Career:** Educator (retired); Hamilton Park UMC, pastor, 1958-68; Tex St rep, 1968-72; Dallas Cent Dist, N Tex Conf, 1968-74; Intern Prog, Southern Methodist Univ, assoc dir, 1974-78; St Luke Community United Methodist Church, sr pastor, 1974-02; Perkins Sch Theol, Southern Methodist Univ, assoc prof preaching, 1978-02. **Orgs:** Judicial Coun United Methodist Church; Bd Regents, Univ Tex Syst, regent; Greater Dallas Community Churches, past pres, bd dirs; Comerica Bank, bd dirs; State Fair Tex, bd dirs; Dallas Found, bd dirs; Soc Study Black Religion; Black Methodist Church Renewal; Nat Asn Advan Colored People; Alpha Phi Alpha Fraternity; Legis Comt Tex Const Rev Comn, chair, 1974;Tri-Ethnic Comt, chair, 1971; Dallas Pastor's Asn, pres, 1963; United Methodist Publ House, bd dirs; CDF, Tex adv bd; Chase Bank, ministerial adv bd. **Honors/Awds:** Jr Black Acad Arts & Letters, Living Legend Award, 1991; Huston-Tillotson Col, Humanitarian Award, 1991; Linz Jewelers & Dallas Morning News, LinzAward, 1991; Dallas Peace Ctr, Peace Maker Award, 1990; Peace Maker Award,Dallas Peace Ctr, 1991; Linz Award, Line Jewelers & Dallas Morning News,1991; Humanitarian Award, Houston-Tillotson Col, 1991; Living LegendAward, Jr Black Acad Arts & Letters, 1991; Dillard Univ, hon doctors oflaws, 1993; Huston-Tillotson Col, honorary doctors of divinity, 1970; RustCol, Honorary Doctor of Laws, 2002; Tom Unis Diversity Award, GreaterDallas, Human Rels Comn, 2002. **Special Achievements:** First African American to hold the position of president of Dallas Pastor's Assn, 1963; "Black and United Methodist," in Our Time Under Godis Now, Abingdon Press, 1993; author: Encountering Jesus, Abingdon Press, 1992; When Trouble Comes, CSS Press, 1996; "Enabling the Word to Happen, "in Power in the Pulpit: How America's Most Effective Black Preachers Prepare Their Sermons, 2002; narrator: "Disciple" Bible Study Video, Cokesbury/Graded Press Video, 1987/1992; adv comt publ entitled Songs of Zion, Abingdon Press, 1981; Come Sunday-The Liturgy Zion, Companion to SZO-Abingdon Press, 1990; When Trouble Comes, CSS Publishing Co, Inc, 1996. **Business Addr:** Educator, Los Angeles, CA 90009.*

HOLSENDOLPH, ERNEST
Journalist. **Personal:** Born Oct 31, 1935, Quitman, GA; son of Wallace and Ethel; married Linda Shelby Holensdolph, Jan 8, 1972; children: Nora, Joseph. **Educ:** Columbia Col, BA, 1958. **Career:** Cleveland Press, reporter, 1961-65; E Ohio Gas Co, editor, 1965-67; Wash Star, reporter, 1967-69; Fortune Magazine, assoc editor, 1969-71; NY Times, reporter, 1972-83; Plain Dealer, Cleveland, OH, bus editor, 1983-89; Atlanta J Const, city ed, 1989-91, bus columnist, 1991. **Orgs:** bd dirs, Alumni Asn Columbia Col. **Honors/Awds:** The SABEW Distinguished Achievement Award. **Military Serv:** AUS. *

HOLSEY, BERNARD
Football player. **Personal:** Born Dec 10, 1973, Rome, GA. **Educ:** Duke Univ. **Career:** Football player (retired); New York Giants, defensive end, 1996-99;Indianapolis Colts, 2000; New England Patriots, 2002; Wash Redskins, 2003; St Louis Rams, 2004; Utah Utes, currently. **Business Addr:** Professional Football Player, University of Utah, Utah Utes, 201 S Presidents Circle, Salt Lake City, UT 84112, **Business Phone:** (801)581-7200.

HOLSEY, DR. LILLA G.
Educator. **Personal:** Born Aug 26, 1941, San Mateo, FL; children: Linita. **Educ:** Hampton Univ, BS, 1963; Fla State Univ, MS, 1971, PhD, 1974. **Career:** Lincoln High Sch, 1964-70; Gainesville High Sch, home econ teacher,1970-72; Fla State Univ, grad res asst, 1971 & 1973; E Carolina Univ, adv& assoc prof home econs, 1974-, Dept Bus, Carrer & Tech Educ, assoc prof &grad prog dir, currently. **Orgs:** Nat & Am Home Econ Assn; Am & Voc Assn; NC Consumer Assn; Bethel AME Church; brd trustees, Alpha Kappa Alpha; Kappa Delta Pi & Omicron Nu Hon Soc; Phi Kappa Delta. **Honors/Awds:** Ford Found fel, 1973-74; charter mem, Putnam County Educ Hall of Fame Palatha Fla. **Business Addr:** Associate Professor, Graduate Program Director, East Carolina University, Department of Business & Information Technologies Education, 2309 Bate Bldg, Greenville, NC 27858.

HOLT, DELORIS LENETTE
Educator, writer. **Personal:** Born in East Chicago, IN; daughter of Willis Adams and Pearl Adams; married Chester A. **Educ:** Ball State Univ, BSEd, 1956; Pepperdine Univ, credential, 1969; Univ SanFrancisco, MSEd, 1978. **Career:** Los Angeles City Schs, parent involvement coordr; Cleveland Pub Schs,teacher; Los Angeles City Schs, Follow Through, adv proj; Los Angeles Unified Sch Dist, teacher & author, currently; Book: Heritage, 2007. **Orgs:** Alpha Kappa Alpha; Kinderpress, 1991. **Honors/Awds:** Resolution of Commendation, Los Angles City Coun, 1972; Merit Award, Calif Asn Teachers Eng, 1973; Early Childhood Educ Instrnl Guides Teachers Kinderpress, 1991. **Special Achievements:** Author of books published by Ward Ritchie Press 1971, Childrens Press1973, LA Unified School Dist 1987; published Black Hist Playing Card Deck US Games Systems Inc, 1978. **Business Addr:** Teacher, Author, Los Angeles Unified School District, 419 W 98th St, Los Angeles, CA 90003.*

HOLT, DONALD H.
Executive. **Personal:** Born Jan 22, 1941, Cleveland, OH; married Dianne Williford. **Educ:** J Carroll Univ, BS, BA 1964; Case Wstrn Res Univ, MBA, 1971; Univ Akron, JD, 1976. **Career:** Prmr Indus Corp, asst vpres corp prsnl admin; E OH Gas Co, asst to pres 1969-, spec asst to pres 1968-69, cst anlyst, 1967-68; atty, Donald H. Holt, currently. **Orgs:** Test Urban Leag Greater Cleveland; City Club of Cleveland; United Way Serv; Rotary Club, Cleveland; Blacks in Mgt; NAACP; Alpha Phi Alpha; Nat Urban Affairs Coun; OH State Bar Asn. **Honors/Awds:** Leadership Cleveland Class of 1979-80; Alpha Kappa Psi Men of Achie 1977; 10 Outstanding Young Men Jcs 1973. **Military Serv:** AUS 1st Lt. **Business Addr:** Attorney, Donald H. Holt, 23512 Cedar Rd, Beachwood, OH 44122-1066.*

HOLT, DR. DOROTHY L THOMAS
Educator, administrator. **Personal:** Born Nov 11, 1930, Shreveport, LA; married James S Holt III; children: James IV, Jonathan Lamar & Roderick Lenard. **Educ:** Wiley Col Marshall Tex, BS, 1962; La Tech Univ Ruston, MS, 1973; Northwestern State Univ, 1973-75; E Tex State Univ Com, EdD, 1978. **Career:** Adminr, Educator (retired); Caddo Parish Educ Sec Assoc, pres & founder, 1954-62; Caddo Teachers Assoc, sec, 1973-74; League Women Voters, Shreveport, treas, 1979-82, vpres, 1982-83; La Distrib Educ Assoc, treas, 1979-80, pres, 1980-81; Cent High Alumni Assoc, treas, 1980-93; Nat Assoc Adv Black Am, sec & bd mem, 1983-85; Caddo Asn Educrs, vpres, 1984-85; La Assoc Dist Educ Teachers Awards Comm, chairperson 1984-85; Caddo Parish Sch Syst, coord. **Orgs:** Chmn, Alpha Kappa Alpha Sorority Inc, 1983-85; vpres, Caddo Asn Educr, 1984-85; Phi Delta Kappa, Kappa Delta Pi, Nat Assoc DE Teachers, Am Voc Ed Assoc, La Assoc DE Teachers NEA, YMCA, YWCA; bd trustees, MDEA/AV Dist Ed Prof Develop Award; chmn, Caddo Parish Textbook Comm Dist Educ Teachers; planner & presenter, CPSB Prof Improv In-Service Prog; pres, Ave BC Jr Mission; Allendale Br YWCA Bd Mgt, Caddo Parish Teachers Fed Union, Ed Comm Ave Bapt Church Fed Credit Union; pres, Allendale Br YWCA, 1988-91; Shreveport Reg Arts CNL; vip, Civic Club, 1993; pres, Sigma Rho Omego Chap, Alpha Kappa Alpha Sorority Inc, 1997-98; bd dirs, David Raines Med Ctr. **Honors/Awds:** Outstanding Leadership Awards, Nat DE, 1983: Ave BC Educational Award, 1984; Booker T Washington High School Student Council Award; Appreciation Award, Muscular Dystrophy, HS chmn; Educator of the Year, Finalist; Outstanding coordinator & Fellowship Award, Leadership Develop, USOE; Teacher of the Year Award, La Vocational Asn; DECA Award; Shreveport Times Educator of the Year Award, 1986; Outstanding Leadership Award Huntington HS; Southern Assoc Accreditation Chairperson, 1987; AKA Sorority Civic & COT Award, 1992; Woman of the Year Award, Zeta Phi Beta Sorority, Outstanding Civic & COT, 1991; Afro-American History Month Award, 1993; Distinguished Alumni Award, Wiley Col, 1996; UNCFund Award, 1996; Meritorious Service Award, UNCF, 1998, 1999-01; certificate, David Raines COT Health Ctr; Certificate of Appreciation, Caddo Parish Sch Bd, 2000; Pelican CNL Girl Scouts Award, 2001; Sickle Cell Anemia Service Award, 2002; Founder's Award, Sigma Rho chp, AKA, 2002. **Special Achievements:** Published Articles: Journal of Business Education & Business Education Forum Magazines. Selected one of 100 Women of the Century for Civic & Community Services, 2001. **Home Addr:** 306 Holcomb Dr, Shreveport, LA 71103.

HOLT, DR. EDWIN J.
Educator, counselor, college teacher. **Personal:** Born in Shreveport, LA; son of James S and Sammie Lee Draper; married Dr Essie W; children: Lisa Michele & Rachelle Justine. **Educ:** Cent State Univ, BA, 1958; Ind Univ, MS, 1962; Univ Ariz, EdD, 1971; Univ Tenn, attended 1977. **Career:** Caddo Parish Sch Bd, teacher, 1959-67, guid coun, 1967-68, from asst prin to sch prin, 1968-74, instr dir, 1974-80, asst supt, 1980-90; La State Univ, adj prof, 1972; La Tech Univ, 1973-75; Northeast La Univ, 1973-75; NE La Univ, 1973; Southern Univ, 1976-79; Grambling St Univ, 1980-84; H Enterprises, founder & co-chmn, 1980-81; La State Univ, assoc prof psychol, 1990. **Orgs:** Bd dir, Rutherford House, 1980-84; dir, summer youth work study prog;Trinity Baptist Church, 1980-; co-dir, Afro Am Hist Actvists, Trinity Baptist Church, 1980-; pres, La Alpha Phi Alpha Frat, 1981-83; Shreveport Clean Community, 1981-86; bd mem, Caddo Dist PTA, 1981-90; bd dir, Norwela Coun BSA, 1981-86; appeal bd mem, Selective Serv Syst, 1981-89; bd dir, Coun Aging, 1982-84; bd dir, Am Heart Asn, 1991-; bd mgt, Carver Br, YMCA, 1982-87; Shreveport Proj Sel Sufficiency Task Force, 1984-87; prof mem, Nat Educ Asn; LEA; CAE; Phi Delta Kappa; Caddo Jt Adm Org; board dir Youth Involvement Prog, 1986-89; pres, Delta Kappa Boule; Sigma Pi Phi Fraternity, 1997; Kappa Delta Pi; Hon Soc; auditor, Shreveport Nat Coun Negro Women; licensed La prof counr. **Honors/Awds:** John Hay Fel Williams Col, 1964; Caddo Parish Educ Yr, 1966; NDEA Fel State Col, Ariz, 1968; Southern Fel Fund, Univ Ariz, 1970-71; Man of Yr, Alpha Phi Alpha Fraternity, 1972.

HOLT, DR. ESSIE W.
Educator. **Personal:** Born in Sicily Island, LA; married Dr Edwin J; children: Lisa Michelle & Rachelle Justine. **Educ:** Grambling State Univ, BS; Univ Ark, Fayetteville, MEd, Educ Specialist; Univ Tenn, Knoxville, EdD. **Career:** Educator (retired); LSU-Shreveport, Caddo Parish Sch Bd, classroom teacher, guidance counselor, psychologist, elementary prin, elementary instructional supvr, asst supt curric & instrn, asst supt; La Lic Prof Counr Bd of Examiners, counr; Judson Fundamental Magnet Sch, prin. **Orgs:** Alpha Kappa Alpha Delta Lambda Omega Chapter; Links Inc; NAESP; PTA; bd dir, United Way; bd dir, Rutherford House; bd dir, Juvenile Justice Prog; Vol, Sickle Cell Anemia Dr; bd dir, YWCA; bd dirs; Child Care Services Bd; bd dir, Goodwill Indust; bd dir, LSU Med Ctr Instnl Rev Bd Protection Human Research Subjects, secy trustee bd, Trinity Baptist Church; Women's Auxiliary Orgn. **Honors/Awds:** Zeta Phi Beta Educator Award; Leadership Shreveport Grad CAE Educator Yraward; LA Gov Comm Women life mem PTA recipient; Women Who Have made a Difference Award, LA PTA Service Scroll; Athena Award Recipient, 1998. **Home Addr:** 208 Plano St, Shreveport, LA 71103. **Business Addr:** Professor, La Prof Counr Bd of Examiners, 8631 Summa Ave, Baton Rouge, LA 70809.*

HOLT, FRED D
Clergy. **Personal:** Born Feb 7, 1931, Macon, GA; married Nancy Smith; children: Larry, Kenny, Tim, Tony & Clevetta Rogers. **Educ:** Hartnell Col, AA, Human Serv, 1980; Chapaman Col, BA, sociol, 1982; Goldengate Univ, masters, pub admin, 1984. **Career:** M & H Restaurant, owner, 1973-76; Salinas City Coun, candid, 1979-83; Salinas City Affirm Active Action Bd chap, 1980-82; Sal Rent Mediation Bd, mem, 1981-83; Nadon Enterprise, owner, 1981-85; St James CME Church, Steward Bd, chmn, 1983; Salinas Nat Asn Advan Colored People, chmn, 1983-85; St James AME Church, preacher, 1991-; Holts Record Co, vpres. **Orgs:** Sr deacon Fremont Masonic Lodge No 13, 1958-82; Salinas Chamber Com, 1972-83; pres, Salinas Nat Asn Advan Colored People, 1974-75; life mem, Nat Asn Advan Colored People, 1984; KRS Omega Psi Phi Omicron Nu, 1984-85, basilius, 1994-96; legal redress officer Salinas Br, Nat Asn Advan Colored People, 1995-. **Honors/Awds:** Thalheimer Award Class I, Nat Asn Advan Colored People, 1975-76; Man Of The Year Award, Nat Asn Advan Colored People, 1979; Achievement Award, Nat Asn Advan Colored People, 1984; Omicron-Nu Omega Psi Phi Man of the Year, 1990, 95; Lay Leader Award, 1997. **Military Serv:** Good Conduct Army Commend, 1951; AUS, E-7 Vietnam War, 1967-69; Served in Vietnam, 1968-69; first sargent, 26 yrs; Meritorious Award, 1972; Bronze Star, 1973. **Home Addr:** 1433 Shawnee Wy, Salinas, CA 93906, **Home Phone:** (831)449-2936. **Business Addr:** Preacher, St James AME Church, 588 Martin Luther King Jr Blvd, Newark, NJ 07102, **Business Phone:** (973)621-9122.

HOLT, DR. JAMES STOKES, III
Educator. **Personal:** Born Sep 23, 1927, Shreveport, LA; son of James and Sammie Lee Draper; married Dr Dorothy L Thomas; children: James IV, Jonathan Lamar & Roderick Lenard. **Educ:** Cent State Univ, BS, 1949; LA State Univ, MEd, 1956; Univ AR, EdD, 1973; Lincoln Grad Ctr, San Antoine, Tex, MSA (Master Senior Appraiser), 1989. **Career:** Educator (retired); Caddo Parish Sch Bd, math bio chem instr, 1950-66; State Dept LA, coun

mem state drug abuse, 1972-74; Grad Sch S Univ, fac mem, 1972-79; Southern Univ, div chmn, 1972-79; HHH Real Estate Investments Co, pres, 1981; MRA Nat Asn Master Appraisers, 1982; Southern Univ, prof biol; Holt Real Estate Appraisal Co, Shreveport, owner, 1987; Ruben Real Estate Co, Shreveport, LA, salesman; LA Ins Comn, licensed salesman, 1991; cert real estate property inspector, 1999. **Orgs:** Alpha Phi Alpha Frat, 1947-; Beta Kappa Chi Hon Soc, 1948-; life mem, LEA Teacher orgn, 1955-; life mem, NEA Teacher Orgn, 1960-; Supt Sunday Sch Ave Baptist Church, 1969-92; 3rd Degree Mason AF & AM, 1970-; secy, Shreveport Metro Bd Appeals, 1975-; pres, Lakeside Acres Civic Asn, 1968-; YMCA, Nat Asn Advan Colored People, LA Coun Human Rights; co-chmn, Biol Scholarship Award Comt, 1992; mem 20 yr Celebration Steering Comm for SU-Shreveport; LA Home Mgrs Asn, 1987-; Nat Orgn Black County Officials (NOBCO), 1988-; Shreveport Black Chamber Com, 1988; EAC charter mem; Nat Soc Environ Consult, 1995; Boy Scouts Am, Cherokee Dist, Norweia Coun Dist comnr, 2002-. **Honors/Awds:** Educator of the Year, Caddo Educ Asn; Shreveport Times Award, 1962; Fla State Univ Radiation Biology Award, 1963; Southern Fel Higher Educ Award, Univ AR, 1972-74; Fourth District Distinguished Achievement Award, La Educ Asn, 1974; recipient of Scout Leaders Regional Tr Cert & Scout masters key; Nat Sci Fel Biol Stud, TSU, 1958, Dillard Univ, 1962; Phi Delta Kappa, Univ Ark, 1971; Univ Texas, Academic Year Grant, Nat Sci Found, 1960; Sprit of Scouting Award, Boy Scouts of Am (BSA), 1999; Silver Beaver Award, BSA, 1999; Woodbadge Training Award, BSA, 1999; Whitney Young Award, BSA, 2001; Small Business Man of the Yr, Minority Bus Coun, 2002. **Home Addr:** 306 Holcomb Dr, Shreveport, LA 71103. *

HOLT, JOHN J.
Government official. **Personal:** Born May 7, 1931, Richmond, VA; son of Samuel L and Susie B; married Andrea; children: Gwen, Greg, John, Keth, Derek & Brandon. **Educ:** Va Union Univ, BS, 1961. **Career:** USAF, commun specialist, 1952-56; Univ Md, lab scientist, 1963-69, personnel mgr, 1969-74; Md Port Admin, human resources mgr, 1974-. **Orgs:** Pres, IPMA, 1980-81; Asn Affirmative Action Officers, 1981; Johns Hopkins Univ Metro Planning & Res Comn, 1982-; Venture Grant Comn, 1984-; vpres, MAAAO, 1985-87; bd dir, United Way Cent Md, 1985-87; chmn, United Way Comn Serv, 1985; pres, MAAAO 1987-89; sr arbitrator, Nat Panel Consumer Arbitrators, 1988-. **Honors/Awds:** Furture Business Leaders Am Balt, 1979; Dr Richard H Hunt Scholarship Award, Comn Serv Md; Community Service Award, Gov State Md, 1989. **Special Achievements:** Governor's Citation for Outstanding Service, Baltimore, MD, 1981; Citizen Citation Mayor of Baltimore 1989. **Military Serv:** USAF, sgt, 4 yrs; Nat Defense Servce Medal; Good Conduct Medal. **Home Addr:** 4115 Hanwell Rd, Randallstown, MD 21133, **Home Phone:** (410)655-0216. **Business Addr:** Manager Human Resources, Maryland Port Admin, 2510 Broening Hwy Maritime Center Point Breeze, Baltimore, MD 21224, **Business Phone:** (410)631-1076.*

HOLT, JONATHAN LAMAR
Physical therapist. **Personal:** Son of James S and Dorothy. **Educ:** BS; MS. **Career:** Schumpert Med Ctr, respiratory therapist, currently. **Business Addr:** Respiratory Therapist, Schumpert Medical Center, 5646 S Lakseshore Dr No 3, Shreveport, LA 71118.*

HOLT, KENNETH CHARLES
School administrator. **Personal:** Born Feb 9, 1948, Pine Bluff, AR; son of Curtis Holt Sr and Velma Lovell; married Helen N Reed Holt, Aug 1972; children: Byron Kieth, Derrick Vaughn, Briana Dashon. **Educ:** Univ Ark, Pine Bluff, BS, 1970; Univ Wis, Milwaukee, MS, 1978; supt prog, 1988-. **Career:** Milwaukee Pub Schs, teacher, 1970-80, asst prin, 1980-88, prin, 1988-, stud serv div, dir, currently. **Orgs:** Educ Employment Coun Milwaukee Pub Sch, 1988-; chairperson, WI Dept Pub Instn-Prog Rev Panel AIDS Educ Prog, 1989-; co-chairperson, African Am Male Youth Task Force-Milwaukee Pub Sch, 1989-; exec comm, WI Black Historical Soc, 1989-91; Nat Asn Sec Sch Prin, 1989-; Nat Middle Sch Asn, 1991-. **Honors/Awds:** Distinguished Man of Milwaukee 1989, Top Ladies Distinction Inc, 1989; Warner Cable Co, Black Excellence Award Winner Educ, 1992. **Special Achievements:** Selected to participate in the 1990 WI Admn Leadership Acad, 1989; featured in Ebony, Essence, Black Enterprise and Wall Street Journal, 1990; featured in Newsweek, Sch and Col, Dollars and Cents, Jet, Asn for Supervision & Curriculum Development-UPDATE, New York Times, Educ Week, Exec Educator and New Republic; Milwaukee Times Weekly Newspaper, WITI TV6. Publications: Letter to the editor, The Washington Post, Feb 15, 1991; counterpart to Kenneth B Clark's opposition to the African-American Immersion schools, The Philadelphia Daily News, Mar 22, 1991; "An Island of Hope: Milwaukee's African-American Immersion Schools," The Journal of Negro Education, Fall 1991; "Milwaukee's Radical Answer to Multicultural Education," School Safety, Fall 1991; "A Rationale for Creating African-American Immersion Schools," Educational Leadership, Dec 1991/Jan 1992. **Business Addr:** Director, Milwaukee Public Schools, Div Stud Serv, 5225 W Vliet St, Milwaukee, WI 53208.*

HOLT, LEO E
Judge. **Personal:** Born Jul 2, 1927, Chicago, IL; married Dorothy Considine; children: Pamela & Paula. **Educ:** John Marshall Law Sch, LLB, 1959. **Career:** Judge (retired); Circuit Co Cook Co, judge. **Orgs:** Cook Co Bar Asn; Kappa Alpha Psi Fraternity. **Honors/Awds:** Kappa Alpha Psi Achievement Award, 1971; Richard Westbrook Award, Cook Co Bar Asn, 1975; Robert R Ming Award, Cook Co Bar Asn, 1981; Oper PUSH Community Service Award, 1981; South Suburban Leadership Council Community Service Award, 1985. **Military Serv:** USAF, corpl, 1945-47.

HOLT, LEROY
Football player. **Personal:** Born Feb 7, 1967. **Educ:** Univ Southern Calif, BA, hist, 1990. **Career:** Miami Dolphins, running back, 1990. **Special Achievements:** Honorable mention All-America, junior year; Honorable mention All-Pac 10, sophomore year.

HOLT, MAUDE R
Health services administrator. **Personal:** Born Aug 3, 1949, Thomaston, AL; daughter of Henry J Holt and Naomi Holt Levert; divorced; children: Andre & DeNeal Madry. **Educ:** AL A&M Univ, BS, 1976; Univ Miami, MBA/HA, 1983. **Career:** Rochester Tel, acct clerk, 1972-76; Allstate Ins, supvr, 1976-77; Jackson Mem Hosp, asst adminr, 1978-86; Metro-Dade, adminr; Alcohol & Drug Abuse Servs Admin, adminr, state dir; Dist Columbia, Dept Human Serv, Managed Care Med Assistance Admin, chief, currently. **Orgs:** Delta Sigma Theta Sorority; Eta Phi Beta Sorority; NAACP; Urban League; Coalition Homeless; Black Pub Adminrs; Nat Asn Coalition Bus & Prof Women; Am Bus Women; Fla Voters League; pres, Greater Miami Chap AL A&M Univ Metro-Action Plan. **Business Addr:** Chief, Department of Human Services, Office of Managed Care Medical Assistance Administration, 825 N Capital St N E 5th Fl, Washington, DC 20001, **Business Phone:** (202)442-9074.

HOLT, MELONIE R
Television journalist. **Personal:** Born in Hartford, CT; daughter of Joseph and Jo. **Educ:** Pa State Univ, BA, jour, 1993. **Career:** WCVB-TV, Leo L Beranek fel, 1993-94; WLEX-TV, health reporter & weekend anchor, 1994-96; WSOC-TV, anchor, gen assignment reporter & pub affairs host; WAXN-TV, producer & host; WFTV, gen assignment reporter, 2004-. **Honors/Awds:** Outstanding Achievement in Newscast Daytime, 16th Annual Midsouth Regional Emmy Awards. **Special Achievements:** Was recognized by the Muscular Dystrophy Association three times for raising awareness of neuromuscular diseases. **Business Addr:** General Assignment Reporter, WFTV, 490 E South St, Orlando, FL 32801, **Business Phone:** (407)841-9000.

HOLT, MIKEL
Editor. **Personal:** Born Mar 12, 1952, Milwaukee, WI. **Educ:** Univ WI Milwaukee. **Career:** Sunday Insight, WTMJ-TV, panelist, 1994-; Milwaukee Community Journ, ed & assoc publ, 1976-; Milwaukee Star Times, managing ed, 1975-76, sports ed photo journ, 1974-75; Milwaukee Sentinel, intern, 1968-69; Seabreeze Mag, Milwaukee ed; DJ WCLG, asst prog dir; Naval AP & Group Vietnam, hist writer 1971-72; Comnine Great Lakes IL, media rel officer, 1972-73; Stringer Jet Mag, 1971-72; Malik Commun Inc, prin acct exec, owner, pres & assoc publ, currently; Miller Brewing Co, chief account executive. **Orgs:** Founder, Wisconsin Black Media Asn; bd dir, Messmer High Sch; past mem, NAACP Youth Coun; past co-chmn, Black Awareness Study Group; Milwaukee Black Photo-Journ; WI Black Press; TUJU; vice pres, Asn Stud Afro-Am Life & Hist; founder, Black Res Orgn. **Honors/Awds:** Two-time winner Best Column Award, NNPA; Braggs & Brooks Sports Serv Award, 1974; Letter appreciation for broadcasting, 1972; Community Serv Award, NNPA; Senate Award, State Wis; Black Achievement Award,1976; Community Serv Award, Univ Wis, 977; Community Serv Award, Black Studio Union, 1977; Messner Impact Award, 1993; Men Who Dare Award, 1994; A Phillip Randolph Award, Recipient, 1994; NNPA Award for Best Feature Story, Mayoral Citation, 1996; Peace Achiever Award, 2000; A Philip Randolph Messenger Award, 2000; NNPA Best Columnist Award, 2000; Messmer Award, 2002; Christ The King Achievement Award, 2003. **Special Achievements:** Author, Not Yet Free at Last, 2000. **Military Serv:** USN, Petty officer second class, 1969-73. **Business Addr:** owner & Associate Publisher, Principal Accounts Executive, Malik Communications Inc, 3612 N King Dr, Milwaukee, WI 53212, **Business Phone:** (414)372-8600.

HOLT, RODERICK LENARD
Cardiologist. **Career:** Schunpnet Med Ctr, cardiologist. *

HOLT, TORRY JABAR
Football player. **Personal:** Born Jun 5, 1976, Greensboro, NC; son of Ojetta Holt-Shoffner (deceased); married Carla; children: 3. **Educ:** NC State Univ, sociol. **Career:** St Louis Rams, wide receiver, 1999-08. Jacksonville Jaguars. wide receiver, 2009-. **Orgs:** Founder, Holt Found. **Honors/Awds:** Rookie of the Year, St Louis Rams, 1999; Super Bowl Champion, 1999-2000; ACC Player of the Year; Offensive Back of the Year; Fred Biletnik off Award;0 Wide Receiver of the Year, Nat Football League Alumni, 2003; Most Valuable Palyer, St Louis Rams, 2003 & 2005. **Business Addr:** Wide Receiver, Jacksonville Jaguars, 1 Stadium Place, Jacksonville, FL 32202, **Business Phone:** (904)633-2000.

HOLTE, PATRICIA LOUISE. See LABELLE, PATTI.

HOLTON, MICHAEL DAVID
Basketball player, basketball coach. **Personal:** Born Aug 4, 1961, Seattle, WA. **Educ:** Univ Calif, Los Angeles, attended 1984. **Career:** Basketball player (retired), basketball coach, Television Analyst; Phoenix Suns, 1984-86; Chicago Bulls, 1985-86; Portland Trail Blazers, 1986-88; Charlotte Hornets, 1988-90; Pasadena City Col, asst coach, 1993-94; Portland Pilots, Univ Portland, asst coach, 1994-95, head coach, 2001-06; Comcast SportsNet, currently. *

HOLTON, PRISCILLA BROWNE
Consultant, educator. **Personal:** Born Dec 31, 1921, Hartford, CT; daughter of Edward Ashton and Lucille Ford; married John Lyle, Dec 24, 1944; children: Mary Frances Dickerson, John K & Leslie Lucille Mumenthaler. **Educ:** St Joseph Col Women, BS, 1946; Antioch Univ, MEd, 1971. **Career:** Green Tree Sch, prin, 1969-74; Antioch Univ, dir special educ dept, 1974-77, MEd prog adminr, 1977-80; City Philadelphia, coord head start, 1980-83; Self-employed, consult; Holy Cross Day Care, interim dir, 1989-90. **Orgs:** Chairperson, Foster Grandparents, 1980-85; pres, Children's Village Adv Bd, 1980-85; exec bd mem, Coun Labor & Industs, 1983-87; Delta Sigma Theta Sorority; Pa Acad Fine Arts; Afro-Am Mus, Smithsonian Inst; League Women Voters, Nat Asn Educ Young Children; Wharton Settlement; Del Valley Asn Nursery & Kindergarden Teachers; Penn State, YWCA; Parent Child Ctr, Head Start; Mill Creek Day Care Ctr. **Honors/Awds:** Award, VIP Serv Club, 1980; Recognition of Community Service, Chapel Four Chaplains, 1980; Distinguished Alumni Award, St Joseph Col, 1983; Certificate of Appreciation, Better Boys Found, 1986. **Special Achievements:** TV appearances for toy manufacturer; publications Tips to Parents (weekly) Hartford Chronicle CT; co-authored Teachers Manual for Green Tree School. **Home Addr:** 515 W Chelten Apt 603, Philadelphia, PA 19144-4420. *

HOLYFIELD, EVANDER
Boxer, founder (originator). **Personal:** Born Oct 9, 1962, Atmore, AL; son of Annie Laura; married Paulette (divorced 1991); married Candi Calvana Smith, Jul 3, 2003; children: 2; married Janice Itson, Oct 4, 1996 (divorced 2000); children: Elijah. **Career:** Prof boxer, currently; Evander Holyfield Buick & Subaru, Atlanta, GA, partner, currently; Real Deal Records, founder; Black Family Channel, partner; trainer, currently. **Orgs:** Founder, Holyfield Found. **Honors/Awds:** Bronze Medal, Los Angeles Summer Olympic Games, 1984; WBA Cruiserweight Champion,1986-88; IBF Cruiserweight Champion, 1987-88; WBC WBA IBF Heavyweight Champion, 1990-92; WBA Heavyweight Champion, 1993-94, 2000-01; IBF Heavyweight Champion, 1993-94, 1997-99; WBA Heavyweight Champion, 1996-99. **Special Achievements:** Only boxer ever to become world heavyweight champion four times; TV: "Christmas special of the Fresh Prince of Bel-Air", 1990; appearance on the original BBC Strictly Come Dancing "Champion of Champions" showdown; numerous television appearances. **Business Phone:** (770)460-6807.

HONABLUE, RICHARD RIDDICK
Physician. **Personal:** Born Apr 1, 1948, Staten Island, NY; children: Richard III, Xavier, Michael. **Educ:** Long Island Univ, AA, 1968; Wagner Col, Grymes Hill, BS, 1970; Meharry Med Col, MD, 1974. **Career:** Pildes Opticians NY, optical dispenser, 1968-70; CBS Radio News, editors desk asst, 1969; United Negro Col Fund Pre-Med Prog Fisk Univ, tutor, 1971; Dede Wallace Community Mental Health Serv, consult, 1976; Med Exam Ctr, med dir, 1977; George Wash Univ Sch Allied Health Sci, asst clin prof, 1979; Duke Univ Dept Family Pract, asst clin prof, 1981-87; Suffolk Community Health Ctr; med dir; Tidewater Regional Jail, physician dirr; Family Health Care Ltd, owner, physician, currently. **Orgs:** Buffalo Boyz Motorcycle Club, Williamsburg chap; pres, Resident's Asn, Meharyy, 1976; diplomate, Am Bd Family Pract, 1980; med examiner, Comm Va; Lord Chamberlain Soc; Tidewater TV Adv Comt; Tau Kappa Epsilon; Am Mecd Asn; Am Asn Family Physicians; VAFP; chmn, Reg II Nat Med Asn, 1984-85; pres, Williamsburg Men's Club, 1984; Asn Military Surgeons US; Nat Naval Officers Asn; Frontiers Int; life mem, Nat Asn Advan Colored People; Nat Comn Cert Physician Assistants, 1990-98. **Honors/Awds:** Eagle Scout Award, 1966; Order of the Arrow. **Military Serv:** AUS, Reserves capt med corps, 1975-77; USNR Commander. **Business Addr:** Owner, Family Health Care Ltd, 8025 Belroi Rd, Gloucester, VA 23061.*

HONEYCUTT, ANDREW E.
Educator. **Personal:** Born Jan 28, 1942, Humboldt, KS; son of Ed Lee and Thelma; married Pamela Hatchett, Jun 4, 1977; children: Michael, Andrea, Andrew Jr, Aaron. **Educ:** Ottawa Univ, BA, 1964; Boston Univ, MBA, 1970; Harvard Univ, DBA, 1975. **Career:** Florida A&M univ, Florida Region II Housing ctr, co-dir, 1974-75, mgt Scis div, chair, 1974-77; Texas Southern univ, ctr intl Develop, assoc dir, 1979-81, interim dept head, 1979-80; nat ctr Housing mgt dis, coordr organ develop, 1983-89, vip strategic planning, 1990-91; Savannah State Col, sch bus, dean, 1991, Univ Ark, Pine Bluff, Sch Bus, dean; Anaheim Univ, dean, currently. **Orgs:** chair, Savannah Regional Minority Purchasing coun, 1991-92; bd, First Union Bank, 1991-92; bd, United Way, 1991-92; bd,

Savannah Econ Develop Authority, 1991-92; bd, hospice Savannah, 1991-92; bd, Small bus Asst corp, 1991-92; bd, West Broad YMCA, 1991-92; bd, Pvt Indust coun, 1991-92. **Honors/Awds:** Big Brother Award, Big Brother asn, MA, 1975; Small bus Leardership Award, Small bus , MS, 1979; caya Fellowship, TX, Black Youth Role Model Award, 1983; Fellow Award, nat ctr Housing mgt, DC, 1987. **Special Achievements:** Author, "Foreign Direct Investment Strategies," Detroit Bus Jour, 1988; "The Quality Improvement Process: Learning from Japan," Proceedings, 1989; "Intl Marketing Myopia: A Proposed Cure," Intl mgt, 1989; "mgt Relationship - A mgt Strategy for the 21st Century," 1990; "Competing with Global Quality Control," Journal of bus Strategies, 1990. **Military Serv:** USY Military Intelligence, 1st lt, 1965-68, Airborne, 1966. **Business Addr:** Dean, Anaheim University, School Business, 1240 South State College Blvd 110, Anaheim, CA 92806-5150, **Business Phone:** (813)498-1005.*

HONEYCUTT, JERALD DEWAYNE
Basketball player. **Personal:** Born Oct 20, 1974, Shreveport, LA. **Educ:** Tulane Univ. **Career:** Milwaukee Bucks, forward-guard, 1997-99; Philadelphia 76ers, 1999; OSGPhoenix, Japanese Superleague; Mitsubishi Electric Dolphins, Japanese Superleague, currently. **Honors/Awds:** Louisiana Basketball Hall of Fame, 2006. **Business Addr:** Professional Basketball Player, Mitsubishi Electric Dolphins.

HONORE, STEPHAN LEROY
Lawyer. **Personal:** Born May 14, 1938, Urbana, OH; son of Albert R and Lalu May Dolby; married Flor; children: Francis, Andrew & Stephanie. **Educ:** Capital Univ, BS, 1960; Univ Toledo, JD, 1974. **Career:** Peace Corps Columbia, Dominican Rep, 1961-66; US State Dept AID, 1966-68; Trans Century Corp, 1968-69; Model Cities Prog Toledo, 1970-71; Peace Corps Dominican Rep, 1978-81; Thurgood Marshall Sch Law, law prof, 1974-84; self-employed Houston, TX, atty law, import & export bus, real estate, 1984-; Telecommunications, 1994-. **Orgs:** Stud body pres Capital Univ, 1960-69; presiding justice, stud honor ct, Univ Toledo Col Law, 1973-74; law rev, casenote ed, Univ Toledo Law, 1973-74; bd dir, Immigration Coun Ctr, 1976-78; State Bar Tex; Nat Bar Asn; Houston Bar Asn; Am Immigration Lawyers Asn; pres, Parochial Sch Bd, 1983-88; bd educ, Galueston-Houston Cath Diocese, 1988-94, pres bd, 1992-94; treas, Braeswood Democrats. **Special Achievements:** Articles on criminal & labor law publ in Univ of Toledo Law Review 1973-74. **Business Addr:** Attorney, 4131 Levonshire Dr, Houston, TX 77025-3914, **Business Phone:** (713)664-3208.

HOOD, ARETHA D.
Dentist. **Educ:** DDS. **Career:** Pardise Dental Ctr, dentist, 1997-. **Business Addr:** Dentist, Paradise Dental Center, 19015 W McNichols Rd, Detroit, MI 48219, **Business Phone:** (313)538-0004.

HOOD, CHARLES MCKINLEY, JR.
Government official. **Personal:** Born Aug 9, 1936, Richmond, VA; son of Charles M Sr and Ethel Saunders; married Marion Overton Hood, May 28, 1960; children: Charles III, Brian M, Cheryl E. **Educ:** Hampton Inst, BS, 1959; Univ Richmond; Univ Okla, MA, 1974. **Career:** Government official (retired); AUS, 1960; AUS War Col, fac mem, 1983-84; AUS Europe, Herzogenaurach, Germany, comdr, 1984-86; AUS Army Forces Command, Atlanta, GA, Chief Warplans, 1986-87; US Forces Command, Atlanta, GA, dep J5, 1987-88; US Second Army, Atlanta, GA, chief opers, 1988-90; US Virgin Islands, St Thomas, VI, adj gen, 1990. **Orgs:** APA, 1973-; Asn USY, 1960-; Alumni Asn War Col, 1983-; Adj Gen Asn, 1990-; Nat Guard Asn, 1990-. **Honors/Awds:** Nat Black Heritage Observance Coun, Inc, Humanitarian Serv Award, 1992. **Military Serv:** Usy, major gen, 1990-; Legion of Merit (3), Bronze Star (3), Meritorious Service Medal(3). *

HOOD, DENISE PAGE
Judge. **Personal:** Born Feb 21, 1952, Ohio; married Nicholas III; children: 2. **Educ:** Yale Col, BA, 1974; Columbia Univ Law Sch, JD, 1977. **Career:** City Detroit, lawyer, city atty, 1977-82; Detroit's 36th Dist Ct, judge, 1983-89; Recorder's Ct, judge, 1989-92; Wayne Co Circuit Ct, judge, 1993-94; Eastern Dist Mich, US Dist Ct, judge, 1994-. **Orgs:** Bd dirs, Detroit Bar Asn, 1983-, pres, 1993; pres, Asn Black Judges Mich, 1991-92; chair, Exec Coun, United Church Christ, 1991-93; Detroit Metrop Bar Asn Found Bd; past pres, Detroit Bar Asn; Asn Black Judges Mich; vpres, Olivet Col Bd Trustees; Harper-Hutzel Hosp Bd Trustees; InsideOut Literary Arts Project Bd. **Honors/Awds:** Presidential Award, Asn Black Judges Mich, 1998; Role Model Award, Alternatives for Girls, 1999; Woman of Distinction Award, Ebenezer African Methodist Espicoal Church, 1999; Damon J Keith Community Spirit Award, Wolverine Bar Asn, 2000; Michigan Anti-Defamation League's Women of Achievement Award, 2005. **Special Achievements:** First African American woman elected pres, Detroit Bar Asn, 1993. **Business Addr:** Judge, Eastern District Michigan, 231 W Lafayette Blvd Suite 238, Detroit, MI 48201, **Business Phone:** (313)234-5165.

HOOD, HAROLD
Judge, educator. **Personal:** Born Jan 14, 1931, Hamtramck, MI; son of W Sylvester Hood Sr and Lenore Elizabeth Hand; married Rev Dr Lottie Jones; children: Harold Keith, Kenneth Loren, Kevin Joseph & Karen Teresa. **Educ:** Univ Mich, BA (Phi Eta Sigma Scholastic Honorary), 1952; Wayne State Univ, JD, 1959. **Career:** Judge (retired), educator; Hood, Rice & Charity, atty, 1959-61; City Detroit, asst corp coun, 1961-69; E Dist Mich, chief asst US atty 1969-73; Common Plea Ct, Detroit, judge, 1973-77; Recorders Ct, Detroit, judge, 1977-78; Cent Mich Univ, adj prof; Mich Judicial Inst, fac; Nat Judicial Col, fac; Third Judicial Circuit Mich, judge, 1978-82; Mich Ct Appeals, judge, 1982-2004; Cooley Law Sch, adj prof, currently; Oakland Univ, adj prof, currently. **Orgs:** Am Bar Asn; St Mich Bar Asn; Detroit Bar Asn; dir Am Judicature Soc; Nat Bar Asn; Judicial Coun NBA; Asn Black Judges Mich; trustee/vice chmn, Kirwood Gen Hosp, 1974-79; bd mem, Old Newsboys-Good fels, 1974-, pres, 1987-89; Detroit Renaissance Lions, 1975-; bd mem, NCA/DD Greater Detroit Area, 1976-; bd mem & chmn, Nat Coun Alcoholism, 1979-; Nat Judicial Col, fac, 1980-82; comnr, Mich Judicial Tenure Comn, 1986-94, chmn, 1988-90; chmn, Mich Supreme Ct Comt Stand Civil Jury Instructions, 1987-; chmn, Mich Supreme Ct Task Force Race/Ethnic Issues Courts, 1987-; chmn, 1987; dir, Thomas M Cooley Law Sch, 1988-96; Comner, Off Substance Abuse Serv, St Mich, 1987-92; Golden Heritage Life; Nat Asn Advan Colored People; trustee, First Congregational Chair Detroit; trustee, Mich St Bar Found, 1992-; trustee, Am INNS Ct Found, 1992-; Nat Adv Coun Alcohol Abuse & Alcoholism; trustee, Johnson Inst Found; chair, Ecumenical Theol Sem; chair, Glass Scholarship Found; co-chair, Open Justice Comn St Bar Mich; bd trustee, Mich St Bar Asn, 2006-. **Honors/Awds:** Ted Owens Award, Detroit Alumni Kappa Alpha Psi, 1971; Service Award, Fed Exec Bd, 1972; Northern Province Achievement, Award Kappa Alpha Psi, 1972;City of Inkster Merit Award, City Inkster, Mich, 1976; Distinguished Alumni, Wayne St Univ Law Sch, 1984; "Exec Alcoholism-A Special Problem," Labor-Management Journal, 1988; Judicial Servant Award, Mich Corrections Comn, 1989; Augustus D Straker Distinguished Jurist Award, 1989; Champion of Justice Award, St Bar Mich, 1990; Phillip A Hart Award, Mich Women's Hall Fame, 1991; Martin Luther King Award, Washtenaw County Bar, 1992; Silver Key Award, NCADD, 1996. **Military Serv:** USASC, 1st lt 1952-54; Army Commendation Medal, Korean Serv Medal, Far East Serv Medal, 1954. **Home Addr:** 300 Riverfront Pk Suite 14K, Detroit, MI 48226. **Business Phone:** (517)371-5140.

HOOD, NICHOLAS
Government official, president (organization), founder (originator). **Personal:** Born Jun 21, 1923, Terre Haute, IN; married Elizabeth Flemister; children: Nicholas III, Emory, Stephen & Sarah Cyprian; married Doris Chenault, 1993. **Educ:** Purdue Univ, BS, 1945; N Cent Col, BA, 1946; Yale Univ, BA, divinity, 1949; Olivet Col, hon DD, 1966; Divinity Sch Univ Chicago, hon LittD, LLD, 1966; N Cent Col, hon DD, 1966. **Career:** Government Official (retired); City Detroit, city councilman; Plymouth Church, sr minister; Dixwell Cong Church, asst minister; Cent Cong Church, minister; Cong Churches US, vice mod; Non-Profit Housing Ctr, pres; Fed Nat Mortgage Asn, Cyprian Ctr, founder & adv comm. **Orgs:** Bd mem, Ministers Life & Casualty Union Bd; mem bd trustees, Hutzel Hosp; Indust Housing Study Tour Europe, 1971; US rep World Conf Non-Profit Housing, 1972. **Honors/Awds:** Outstanding member, 1949 class Yale Divinity Sch, 1974; Amistad Award, Outstanding Service to America, 1977. **Special Achievements:** First African-American graduate of North Central College.

HOOKER, DR. BILLIE J.
Educator, administrator. **Educ:** Albany State Col, Ga, eng; Atlanta Univ, libr serv; Ohio State Univ, PhD, educ admin. **Career:** Bennett Col, vpres develop; Del State Univ, vpres univ advan, 1999-; United Negro Col Fund, dir educ servs; TMT Group Inc, sr trainer, currently; Wiley Col, Assoc vpres Develop & Alumni Affairs, 2004-05. **Business Addr:** Senior Trainer, TMT Group Inc, 115 Wholesale Ave, Huntsville, AL 35811, **Business Phone:** (256)536-9717.

HOOKER, DOUGLAS RANDOLF
Executive, government official, vice president (organization). **Personal:** Born Mar 31, 1954, Moultrie, GA; son of Odessa R Walker and H Randolph; married Patrise M Perkins, Feb 17, 1979; children: Douglas Patrick Hooker & Randi Michelle Hooker. **Educ:** Ga Inst Technol, Atlanta, Ga, BS, mech engineering, 1978, MS, technol & sci, 1985; Emory Univ, Atlanta, Ga, MBA, 1987. **Career:** Georgia Power Co, Atlanta, GA, asst section supervisor, 1979-85; Bio-Lab Inc, Decatur, GA, dir of mktg svcs, 1990-; Randolph Group, chief exec officer & pres; City Atlanta, Dept Pub Works, comnr; SL King & Assocs, vpres operations; HDR Engineering Inc, vpres & dept mgr, 2001; State Rd & Tollway Authority, exec dir, 2003-05; PBS&J, southern states dist dir, currently. **Orgs:** Vpres, Ga Tech Minority Alumni Comt, 1982-85; vpres, Nat Soc Black Engineers-Alumni Exten, 1991-; Leadership Georgia[a6]s Class of 1996; Leadership Atlanta[a6]s Class, 2003; Am Coun Engineering Co; Am Pub ransp Asn; Am Pub Works Asn; Nat Soc Black Engineers; bd dirs, Regional Leadership Forum. **Honors/Awds:** Woodruff Scholar, Emory University, 1985-87; Miller-Patillo Honoree, Patilloc Found, 1990; Regional Leadership Forums Service Award, 2004. **Home Addr:** 335 Glenhurst Lane SW, Atlanta, GA 30331, **Home Phone:** (404)696-9163. **Business Addr:** Southern States District Director, PBS&J, 5665 New Northside Dr Suite 400, Atlanta, GA 30328-4617, **Business Phone:** (770)933-0280.

HOOKER, ODESSA WALKER
School administrator. **Personal:** Born Sep 21, 1930, Moultrie, GA; daughter of Anderson Walker and Pauline Walker; divorced; children: Douglas R, Melanie Ann, David A, Margaret P & Darrell W. **Educ:** Paine Coll, BA, 1951; Atlanta Univ, cert, 1951; Univ Cincinnati, MEd, 1967. **Career:** Sch administrator (retired); Barnesville HS, english teacher, 1951-53; Whittemore High Sch, english teacher, 1954-55; Cincinnati Public Sch, elem teacher, 1961-83, elem asst prin, 1983; Fund for Independent Sch Cincinnati Inc, coord; Summerbridge Cincinnati, Inc, founder; Breakthrough Cincinnati, bd trustees emer, currently. **Orgs:** Co-choir dir and organist 1955-, bible class teacher 1977-, Peoples Tabernacle Bapt Church; volunteer organist Chapel Serv Bethesda Oak Hosp 1983-. **Honors/Awds:** First Black Pres Delta Psi Delta Kappa Gamma Intl Cincinnati OH 1986-88; Teachers of Excellence Award at the 23rd General Synod of The United Church of Christ. **Special Achievements:** Published two books: "With Heads Held High: Legacy of My Southern Parents", "Premier African American Role Models of Cincinnati.? one of 10 Cincinnati Enquirer Women of the Year.

HOOKER, OLIVIA J
Psychologist. **Personal:** Born Feb 12, 1915, Muskogee, OK; daughter of Samuel D Hooker and Anita J. **Educ:** OH State Univ, BS, 1937; Columbia Univ TC, MA, 1947; Univ Rochester, PhD, 1962; Am Acad Forensic Psychol, dipl, 2001. **Career:** Psychologist (retired); NY State Dept Ment Health, psychologist, 1947-57; grad fel, Univ Rochester, 1955-57; Kennedy Child Study Ctr, dir psychol & assoc adminr, 1961-83; Fordham Univ, assoc prof clin psychol, 1963-83; Fred S Keller Sch Behavior Analysis, consult, 1988-2000. **Orgs:** Nat Am Advan Colored People, 1945-2001; chair const comt, Am Asn Ment Retardation, 1949-2001; fel Am Psychol Asn, 1958-2001; bd mem, Terenee Cardinal Cooke Servs, 1970-96; bd mem, Kennedy Child Study Ctr, 1986-2001; admin coun, Trinity United Methodist Church; Sigma Xi. **Special Achievements:** Co-author, Comparative Study of Intelligence Variability; read papers at conferences in Bologna, Italy and Cairo, Egypt; first black woman to enlist in the SPARs. **Military Serv:** US Coast Guard, Women's Reserve, Y2c, 1945-46. **Home Addr:** 42 Juniper Hill Rd, White Plains, NY 10607-2104.

HOOKS, BENJAMIN LAWSON
Educator, clergy, lawyer. **Personal:** Born Jan 31, 1925, Memphis, TN; son of Robert B Hooks Sr and Bessie White; married Frances Dancy, Mar 21, 1951; children: Patricia Gray. **Educ:** Le Moyne Col, attended 1943; Howard Univ, attended 1944; De Paul Univ, JD, 1948. **Career:** Clergy (retired), lawyer (retired), educator(retired; atty, 1949-65, 1968-72; Mutual Federal Savings & Loan Asn, co-founder, vpres, dir, chmn, 1955-69; Middle Baptist Church, pastor, 1956-72; asst public defender, 1961-64; Greater New Mt Moriah Baptist Church, pastor, 1964-; Shelby County Criminal Ct, judge, 1965-68; Fed Commun Comn, 1972-78; NAACP, exec dir, 1977-93; Chapman Co, sr vpres, 1993; Fisk Univ, prof soc justice, 1993-2002; Univ Memphis, Dept Polit Sci, adj prof. **Orgs:** Nat Bar Asn, judicial coun; Am Bar Asn; Tenn Bar Asn; bd trustee, LeMoyne-Owen Col; bd dir, Southern Christian Leadership Conf, 1968-72; grand chancellor, Knights Pythias; bd trustee, Hampton Inst; Nat Civil Rights Mus, bd mem; Benjamin L Hooks Instit Social Change, 1996; Tenn Coun Human Relations; Omega Psi Phi. **Honors/Awds:** Howard Univ, LLD (hon), 1975; Wilberforce Univ, LLD (hon), 1976; Cent State Univ, DHL (hon), 1974, LLD (hon), 1976; Masons Man of the Year Award, 1964, Gold Medal Achievement Award, 1972; Optimist Club of America Award, 1966; Lincoln League Award, 1965; Tennessee Regional Baptist Convention Award; Spingarn Award, NAACP, 1986; producer/host,Conversations in Black & White; co-producer, Forty Percent Speaks; panelist, What Is Your Faith?; Presidential Medal of Freedom, 2007. **Special Achievements:** Benjamin L. Hooks Institute for Social Change was established at the University of Memphis. **Military Serv:** AUS, staff sgt, 1943-46.

HOOKS, BRIAN
Actor. **Personal:** Born Jul 27, 1973, Bakersfield, CA. **Career:** Actor, producer, writer; Films: Bulworth, 1998; Thursday, 1998; Beloved, 1998; Q: The Movie, exec producer, 1999; Phat Beach, 1996; High School High, 1996; Austin Powers: The Spy Who Shagged Me, 1999; Obstacles, 2000; 3 Strikes, 2000; The Luau, 2001; The Entrepreneurs, 2003; Soul Plane, 2004; 7eventy 5ive, dir, writer & producer, 2007; Cutlass, 2007; Fool's Gold, 2008; TV series: Runaway Car?, 1997; "Cracker", 1998; "The Parkers", 1999-2000; "The Proud Family", 2003; "Eve", 2003-06; Exec producer: Nothin' 2 Lose, 2000; The Luau, 2001; The Chat room; Malibooty!, 2003; Wifey, 2005; All Starz Live, 2005; 7eventy 5ive, 2007; "Cold Case", 2009. **Honors/Awds:** Nominee, Video Premiere Award, 2001. **Business Addr:** Actor, c/o Michael Greenwald, Don Buchwald & Associates, 6500 Wilshire Blvd Suite 2200, Los Angeles, CA 90048, **Business Phone:** (323)655-7400.*

HOOKS, FRANCES DANCY
Educator, teacher, secretary general. **Personal:** Born Feb 23, 1927, Memphis, TN; daughter of Andrew Dancy and Georgia Graves;

married Benjamin Lawson; children: Patricia Louise & Gray. **Educ:** Fisk Univ, BS, 1949; Tenn State Univ, MS, 1968. **Career:** Shelby County Sch, TN, teacher, 1949-51; Memphis City Sch, teacher, 1951-59, high sch counr admin, 1959-73, counr-pregnant girls, 1976-77; Benjamin L Hooks Inst Social Change, Univ Memphis, secy & mentor, currently. **Orgs:** Organizer People Power Proj, 1968; pres, Memphis Chap, Links Inc, 1968;pres & co-founder, Riverview, KS Community & Day Care Ctr, 1969-73; diryouth activ, Mt Monah Baptist Church, 1973-75; dir, Youth Activ MidBaptist Church, 1973-75; co-chair, Nat Civil Rights Award Affair, 1999;Women Achievement; Women's Found; adv bd, YWCA; bd mem, Memphis CancerFound; bd mem, Memphis Col Art; Nat Asn Adv Colored People. **Honors/Awds:** Outstanding Server, Memphia Vol Placement Prog, TN, 1973; Youth Chap, Scholar Fund, Richmond, VA, Nat Asn Adv Colored People, 1979; Memphis Award, Boston, Nat Asn Adv Colored People, 1980; Honorable Chair Award, KY State Nat Asn Adv Colored People, 1980; Women of Achievement Award, 1997. **Home Addr:** 200 Wagner Pl Suite 408, Memphis, TN 38103. **Business Addr:** Secretary, Mentor, Benjamin L Hooks Institute for Social Change, University of Memphis, 107 Scates Hall, Memphis, TN 38152-3530.*

HOOKS, DR. JAMES BYRON, JR.
Educator, business owner. **Personal:** Born Sep 23, 1933, Birmingham, AL; son of James Byron Hooks Sr and Bessie Ardis Hooks; married Marcell Elizabeth; children: Angelique L, James Byron III, Kimberly M, Jamal B, Joffrey B & Keisha M. **Educ:** Ind Univ, BS, 1955; Roosevelt Univ, MA, 1969; Northwestern Univ, PhD,1975. **Career:** Educator (retired); J M Harlan High, asst prin, 1969-75; exec dir, Talent Inc, 1971; Skiles Middle Sch, prin, 1975; Haven Middle Sch, prin, 1976; Whitney Young, teacher & dean, 1980-92; Hooks & Co Real Estate Investments, owner, 1989-; "Ritual Without Reality," & "Thread The Needle," cable TV producer. **Orgs:** Bd dir, Sullivan House Local Serv Syst, 1984-89. **Military Serv:** USN, first airman, 1955-57.

HOOKS, KEVIN
Movie director, actor. **Personal:** Born Sep 19, 1958, Philadelphia, PA; son of Robert Brooks and Yvonne; married Cheryl; children: 3. **Career:** Films: Sounder, actor, 1972; Aaron Loves Angela, actor, 1975; A Hero Ain't Nothin' But a Sandwich, actor, 1978; Take Down, actor, 1979; Innerspace, actor, 1987; Strictly Business, dir & actor, 1991; Passenger 57, 1992; Fled, 1996; Black Dog, 1998; Lie Detector, 1999; Shallow Hal, actor, 2001; TV series: "J.T.", actor, 1969; "Just an Old Sweet Song", actor, 1976; "The Rookies", actor, 1976; The Greatest Thing That Almost Happened, actor, 1977; "The White Shadow", actor, 1978-81; "Lou Grant", actor, 1978; CanYou Hear the Laughter? The Story of Freddie Prinze, actor, 1979; FriendlyFire, actor, 1979; "Backstairs at the White House", actor, 1979; St. Elsewhere, 1983-84; For Members Only, actor, 1983; "The Powers of Matthew Star", actor, 1983; Fame, 1984; Hotel, 1984; V, 1984-85; "ABC Afterschool Specials", 1986-87; "He's the Mayor", actor, 1986; "Vietnam War Story",1987; "21 Jump Street", 1987; "Once a Hero", 1987; Mariah", 1987;"Midnight Caller", 1988-89; Roots: The Gift, 1988; China Beach", 1988;"CBS Schoolbreak Special", 1988; "Probe", 1988; "Alien Nation", 1989; HeatWave, 1990; "Doogie Howser, M.D.", 1990; Murder Without Motive: The Edmund Perry Story, 1992; "I'll Fly Away", 1992; "Tales from the Crypt", 1993; Irresistible Force, 1993; To My Daughter with Love, 1994; "Homicide: Lifeon the Street", 1996; "Profiler", 1997; Glory & Honor, dir & actor, 1998;"The Hoop Life", 1999; Mutiny, 1999; "Rescue 77", 1999; The Color of Friendship, dir & producer, 2000; "Soul Food", 2000-04; "City of Angels", dir & exec producer, 2000; ER, 2000; "Philly", dir & exec producer, 2001-02; NYPD Blue, 2001-04; "Without a Trace", 2003-04; "Las Vegas", 2003; "Dragnet", dir & co-exec producer, 2003; Sounder, dir & producer, 2003; "Cold Case", 2004; "Line of Fire", 2004; North Shore, 2004; "24", 2004-05; "Lost", 2004-05; "Ghost Whisperer", 2005; Alias, 2005; The Inside, 2005; "Prison Break", dir, 2006-08, co-exec producer, 2006, exec producer, 2006-08; "Lincoln Heights", dir & exec producer, 2007. **Honors/Awds:** Emmy Award, 2001. **Business Addr:** Actor, c/o United Talent Agency, 9560 Wilshire Blvd Fl 5, Beverly Hills, CA 90212, **Business Phone:** (310)273-6700.

HOOKS, MICHAEL ANTHONY
Real estate appraiser, government official. **Personal:** Born Oct 13, 1950, Memphis, TN; married Janet Dean Perry; children: Michael Jr & Kristian Nichole. **Educ:** Lane Col, Jackson, TN, 1969; Memphis State Univ, 1969. **Career:** Shelby County Assessor's Off, dep tax assessor, 1972-77; Gilliam Communs Inc, acct exec; State Tech Inst, lectr & instr; Michael Hooks & Assocs, pres; Memphis, Tenn, city councilman; Shelby County Property Assessor, 1988-92; Shelby County Bd Comnrs, comnr, 1994, reelected, 1998, Memphis Sch, vpres, 2001. **Orgs:** Delegate Tenn Constitutional Conv, 1977; Counman, Memphis, TN, 1979-81; Nat Asn Advan Colored People; PUSH Inc; Knights Pythion; Commitment Memphis; Omega Psi Phi Fraternity; Prince Hall Masonic Lodge; Memphis Downtown Photographic Soc Inc; State Bd Equalization; bd mem, Memphis Sch. **Honors/Awds:** Tenn Asn Assessing Officers; Assessor of the Year, Int Asn Assessing Officers; Soc Real Estate Appraisers; Nat Asn Real Estate Brokers; Memphis Bd Realtors. **Special Achievements:** One of 50 Outstanding Leaders of the Future, Ebony Mag, 1978. **Home Addr:** 2143 S Pkwy E, Memphis, TN 38114. **Business Addr:** Commissioner, District 3, 160 N Main St Suite 450, Memphis, TN 38103.

HOOPER, MICHELE J
Executive. **Personal:** Born Jul 16, 1951, Uniontown, PA; daughter of Percy and Beatrice Eley; married Lemuel Seabrook III, Sep 4, 1976. **Educ:** Univ Penn, Philadelphia, BA, 1973; Univ Chicago, MBA, 1973-75; State Ill, CPA, 1981. **Career:** Baxter Corp, Chicago, parenterals div, 1976-83, dir, coverage & reimbursement, 1983-85, vpres, corp planning, 1985-88, Canada, pres, 1988; Int Bus Group, Caremark Int Inc, corp vpres, pres, currently; Stadtlander Drug Co Inc, pres, chief exec officer; Dir's Coun, co-founder, managing partner, currently. **Orgs:** Chmn bd, Baxter Credit Union Dirs, 1981-88; bd dir, 1985-89, bd chmn, 1988, Joseph Holmes Dance Theatre; Econ Club Chicago, 1986-; bd dir, Lake Forest Grad Sch Mgt, 1987-88, bd, Med Dev Canada, 1988-; Young Pres Org, 1989-; Com 200, 1989-; pres, Nat Asn Corp Dir, currently; adv bd, Am Telecare; adv bd, LEK Consult; adv bd, Equis Corp; Ctr Dis Control Found; Joffrey Ballet & Evanston Northwestern Healthcare; World President's Organization; Exec Leadership Coun; Chicago Network; Nat Asn Corp Dir. **Business Addr:** Managing Partner, The Directors Council, 875 N Mich Ave Suite 2314, Chicago, IL 60611, **Business Phone:** (312)335-0871.

HOOVER, FELIX A
Journalist. **Personal:** Born Jul 17, 1949, Columbus, OH; son of Alfred B and Felicia L O. **Educ:** Ohio State Univ, Columbus, OH, BA, 1970; MA, 1976. **Career:** WLWC-TV, Columbus, OH, reporter, photographer & writer; Franklin Co Pub Defender, Columbus, OH, investr; Columbus Rctrn & Pks Dept, Columbus, OH, arts admn & grant writer; Call & Post, Columbus, OH, sports ed, ad rep, dep gen mgr; Omaha Star, Omaha, NE, advert rep; Columbus Dispatch, Columbus, OH, relig reporter, currently. **Orgs:** Treas, Columbus Asn Black Journalists, 1988-90. **Honors/Awds:** Third Place, Best Series, Asniated Press Soc Ohio, 1989. **Business Addr:** Religion Reporter, The Columbus Dispatch, 34 S Third St, Columbus, OH 43215, **Business Phone:** (614)461-5000.

HOOVER, JESSE
Government official. **Personal:** Born Sep 6, 1918, Tamo, AR; son of William and Magonila Martin; married Dorothy Franks (died 1990). **Educ:** Wayne State Univ, 1952. **Career:** US Postal Serv, personnel action & records supvr, 1946-77; Detroit Postal Employees Union, vpres, 1946-77, bd dir; City of Detroit, Detroit, MI, councilman Hood, admin asst, 1978-90. **Orgs:** NAACP; Freedom Fund; The Moors; 1st Nighters; Sagicornians; bd deacons & trustees Plymouth Cong Ch; Pilot Club Cert Merit, Mens Club, 1968. **Honors/Awds:** US Postal Service Bicentennial Award, 1976; Certificate Appreciation, NAACP, 1976; co-chmn, Annual Easter Teas; Pilot Club Cert Merit; Certificate Appreciation, Easter Tea. **Special Achievements:** First black in the Detroit Postal Employees Union to be appointed as Board of Director. **Military Serv:** AUS staff sgt 1941-45. **Home Addr:** 16825 Normandy St, Detroit, MI 48221. *

HOOVER, THERESSA
Executive. **Personal:** Born Sep 7, 1925, Fayetteville, AR; daughter of James and Rissie. **Educ:** Philander Smith Col, BBA, 1946; NY Univ, MA, 1962. **Career:** exec (retired); Little Rock Meth Coun, assoc dir, 1946-48; Womans Div Christian Serv, field worker, 1948-58; Dept Christian Soc Rels, secy, 1958-65; Sect Prog & Educ Christian Mission, asst gen secy, 1965-68; Womens Div Bd Global Ministries United Meth Ch, assoc gen secy, 1968-90. **Orgs:** bd trustees, Paine Col, 1963-76; del, World Coun Ch Assemblies Sweden, 1968; Nairobi 1975; Vancouver, 1983; bd mem, Ch Women United, 1968; Bossey Ecumenical Inst, 1969-75; Nat Coun Ch, 1969-72; Comn, Ch Participation Develop, 1970; bd trustees, United Theol Sem; Nat Bd YWCA; bd cur, Stephens Col; exec comn, Nat Coun Negro Women; Cent Comn, World Coun Ch, 1983-90; Task Force Racial Justice; dep gen secy, Theressa Hoover United Methodist Ch. **Honors/Awds:** Doctorate of Humane Letters, Bennett Col, 1990; Ark Black Hall of Fame, 2000. **Special Achievements:** Theressa Hoover Community Service and Global Citizen Fund Award was established. *

HOPE, JULIUS CAESAR
Clergy, activist, executive director. **Personal:** Born Sep 6, 1932, Mobile, AL; son of Robert and Zeola King; married Louise Portis, May 21, 1959; children: Rev Julius Escous, Tonya Louise. **Educ:** Ala State Col, BS, 1958; Interdenominational Theol Ctr, MST, 1961. **Career:** Zion Baptist Church, Brunswick, GA, pastor, 1961-70; Polit Action Chair, Brunswick, GA, br Nat Asn Adv Colored People, 1961-78; Ga State Conf Nat Asn Adv Colored People Br, pres, 1967-78; First Baptist Church, Macon, GA, pastor, 1970-78; Nat Asn Advan Colored People, Midwest Region III, nat dir relig affairs, 1978-; New Grace Missionary Baptist Church, Highland Pk, MI, pastor, 1979-; Nat Asn Advan Colored People, Midwest Region III, Relig Affairs Dept, dir, 1988-. **Orgs:** Nat Asn Advan Colored People; Pres Comn Civil Rights, 1977-81; bd dirs, Proj Smile, 1974-76; pres, Ga State Church Sch & Baptist Training Union Cong, 1974-78; dir, Neighborhod Youth Corps, Coastal Area, GA, 1967-78; Alpha Phi Alpha. **Honors/Awds:** Rev Julius C Hope Day, Brunswick, GA, 1970, 1987; Citation, City Glen Cove, NY, 1978; Spec Tribute Community Serv, State Mich, 1982; Outstanding Serv Award, Coun Nat Alumni Asn, 1983; hon degree, Birmingham Baptist Bible Col, 1984; Key to Youngstown, OH, 1988; Proclamation, US Sen Howard Metzenbaum, 1988; Outstanding Serv Award, Ohio Tri-County Nat Asn Advan Colored People, 1989. **Military Serv:** AUS, airman first class. **Business Addr:** Director, National Association for the Advancement of Colored People, Relig Affairs Dept, 17117 W 9 Mile Rd Suite 1021, Southfield, MI 48075.*

HOPE, MARIE H. SAUNDERS
Educator. **Personal:** Born Mar 6, 1927, Detroit, MI; daughter of Leander C Holley and Elvine P Holley; divorced; children: John Jerry Saunders Jr. **Educ:** Bennett Col, BA, elem educ, 1948; Ohio State Univ, MA, elem educ, 1954. **Career:** Educator (retired); Tazewell Co Va Sch bd, elem teacher, 1951-54; Cols Pub Schs, substitute elem schs, 1954-55; elem teacher, Milo elem Prek-K-1, 1955-73; Chap I reading teacher, John XVIII Cath Sch, 1973-75; parent coordr Chap I elem Sch, 1975-87; Life Care Alliance, part time substitute sr dining ctr coordr, 1987-94. **Orgs:** Alpha Kappa Alpha Sorority Inc; Alpha Sigma Omega; Aesthetics Social Club, pres, 1992; Cols S Dist United Methodist Church, assoc lay mem, 1992; United Methodist Church, lay speaker S Dist & W Ohio Conf, 1992. **Honors/Awds:** Women of Character Award, Greater Hilltop Community Develop & Westside Messenger, 1992; Ohio House of Rep, 1992; Women of Character Special Recognition Proclamation, 1992; Sojourner Truth Award, 1994; Voices of Black Women Award, 1996; Black Friend of Freedom soc Inc, 2001; Living Faith Award, 2003; Columbus Pub Schs, Golden Rule Award, 2003. **Special Achievements:** Writer, producer, performer, director, Harriet Tubman: A Moment in History, one-act play, 1992. **Home Addr:** 3988 Karl Rd Suite 37, Columbus, OH 43224, **Home Phone:** (614)267-4674. *

HOPE, DR. RICHARD OLIVER
Educator, sociologist. **Personal:** Born Apr 1, 1939, Atlanta, GA; married Alice Anderson; children: Leah & Richard Jr. **Educ:** Morehouse Col, BA, 1961; Syracuse Univ, MA, 1964, PhD, 1969. **Career:** Metro Appl Res Ctr, res assoc, 1960-72; Brooklyn Col, asst prof sociol, 1968-72; Dept Defense, dir res, 1972-74; Morgan State Univ, chmn & prof, 1974-82; Goddard Space Flight Ctr, res fel, 1976-78; Ind Univ, Indianapolis, Dept Sociol, chmn & prof; Mass Inst Technol, exec dir, 1988-; Woodrow Wilson Nat Fel Found, Thomas R Pickering Foreign Affairs Fel Progs, vpres & dir prog int affairs, currently. **Orgs:** Assoc ed, J Inter-cultural Rels, 1976-; vis lectr, Univ West Indies Mona Jamaica, 1977; mem bd dirs, Moton Found, 1978-; mem bd dir, Urban League, Flanner House Indianapolis, 1982-; Corp Vis Comt, Mass Inst Technol, 1982-. **Special Achievements:** Publications "Racial Strife in the US Military," Praeger Publishing, 1979; "Black Leadership," Black Organizations Univ Press, 1980. **Military Serv:** AUS, civilian GS-15, 1970-74. **Business Addr:** Vice President, Director, Programs in International Affairs, Woodrow Wilson National Fellowship Foundation, Foreign Affairs Fellowship Program, 5 Vaughn Dr Suite 300, PO Box 2437, Princeton, NJ 08540-6313.

HOPKINS, BERNARD
Boxer. **Personal:** Born Jan 15, 1965, Philadelphia, PA; son of Bernard Hopkins Sr and Shirley; married Jeanette; children: Latrice. **Career:** Penn tower hotel, philadelphia, cook; prof boxer, currently. **Honors/Awds:** USBA, world middleweight champion, 1992-94; IBF, middleweight title, 1995; WBC, middleweight title, 2001; WBA, middleweight title, 2001; IBF, world middleweight champion, 1995-05; WBC, world middleweight champion, 2001vJuly 16, 2005; WBA, world middleweight champion, 2001-05; WBO, world middleweight champion, 2004v05; pound for pound first boxer, 2004-05; The ring world light, heavyweight champion, 2006-. **Business Addr:** Professional boxer, c/o Norman Horton, 5780 W Centinela Ave Suite 409, Los Angeles, CA 90071, **Business Phone:** (323)418-0850.

HOPKINS, BRAD. **See HOPKINS, BRADLEY D.**

HOPKINS, BRADLEY D. (BRAD HOPKINS)
Football player, television broadcaster. **Personal:** Born Sep 5, 1970, Columbia, SC; married Kellie, Mar 9, 1995. **Educ:** Univ Ill, BS, speech communs. **Career:** Football player (retired), sports reporter; Houston Oilers, tackle,1993-96; Tenn Titans, offensive tackle, 1997-98; Tennessee Titans,1999-05; wsmv, sportd reporter, 2006-. **Honors/Awds:** Pro Bowl selection, 2000, 2003; All-Pro selection, 2003. **Business Phone:** (615)353-4444.

HOPKINS, DR. DIANNE MCAFEE
Educator. **Personal:** Born Dec 30, 1944, Houston, TX; daughter of Valda Lois Baker and DeWitt Talmadge; married Dale William, Jul 7, 1982; children: Scott McAfee. **Educ:** Fisk Univ, Nashville, TN, BA, 1966; Atlanta Univ, Atlanta, GA, MSLS, 1967;Western Mich Univ, Kalamazoo, MI, EdS, 1973; Univ Wisc-Madison, Madison,WI, PhD, 1981. **Career:** Houston Independent Sch Dist, Houston, TX, librn, 1967-71; Dept Educ Mich,Lansing, MI, sch librn consult, 1972-73; West Bloomfield Sch, West Bloomfield, MI, high sch librn, 1973-74; Univ Mich, Ann Arbor, MI, schlibrn consult, 1974-77; Wis Dept Pub Instr, Madison, dir, sch

librn,1977-87; Univ Wisc-Madison, asst prof, 1987-92, assoc prof, 1992-99, prof& asst dir, 1999, Sch Lib & info Sci, prof emer, currently. **Orgs:** Beta Phi Mu Int Libr Fraternity, 1967; Phi Delta Kappa, 1980; chair, AASL White House Conf Libr & Info Serv Planning & Implementation Comt, 1986-92; ed bd, Sch Libr Media Quarterly, AASL, 1988-91; chair, Educr Sch Lib Media Specialists Sect, AASL, 1989-90; AASL Rep, White House Conf Lib & Info Serv, 1991-; Vision Comn Nat Sch Lib Media Stand, AASL, 1994-98; Intellectual Freedom Comn, Ala, 1991-95; trustee, bd dir, FTRF, 1997-99; bd mem large, Libr Res Round Table, AL, 1997-2000; exec comt, bd dir, Freedom Read Found, 1998-99; ed bd, Sch Libr Media Online J, Am Asn Sch Librns, 1999-2002; External Rev Panel Pool mem, Am Libr Asn, Ala, Off Accrediatation, 1999-; Higher Educ Rep, bd dir, Wis Educ Media Asn, 2000-02; bd dir, Am Civil Liberties Union. **Honors/Awds:** Exceptional Performance Award, Wis Dept Pub Instr, 1982; ALISE Research Award, 1992; Distinguised Service Award, Am Asn Sch Librns; Intellectual Freedom Roll of Honor, Freedom Read Found & Ala Off Intellectual Freedom, 1999; Mandarin Intellectual Freedom Award, Wis, SIRS, 2000. **Business Addr:** Professor Emeritus, University of Wisconsin-Madison, School of Library & Information Science, 600 N Pk St, 4217 White Hall Helen C, Madison, WI 53706, **Business Phone:** (608)263-2955.

HOPKINS, DONALD RAY
Lawyer, government official. **Personal:** Born Nov 14, 1936, Tulsa, OK; son of Carolyn McGlory and Stacey E; divorced; children: Yvonne Ann-Marie. **Educ:** Univ Kans, BA, cum laude, 1958; Yale Univ, MA 1959; Univ Calif Berkeley, JD 1965; Harvard Law Sch, LLM, cum laude, 1969. **Career:** Government offical (retired), lawyer; Univ Calif Berkeley, teaching asst, 1960-63, asst dean students, 1965-67, asst exec vice chancellor, 1967-68; NAACP Legal Defense Fund Inc, staff atty, 1969-70; Pacific Cons, exec vpres, 1970-71; 8th Calif Cong Dist, dist admin, 1971-93; atty, pvt pract, 1981-. **Orgs:** Estate tax examr, US Treas Dept, 1965; Acad Polit Sci; Arbitration Asn Bd Arbitrators; bd dir, Am Civil Liberties Union, No Calif, 1969-71; bd dir, Univ Calif Alumni Asn, 1976-79; bd dir, African Film Soc; bd dir, Travelers Aid Soc; Univ Calif Alumni Asn; Calif State, Nat, Am, Fed,Alameda County Bar Asn; bd dir, Chas Houston Bar Asn; Am Trial Lawyers Asn; Nat Conf Black Lawyers; Nat Lawyers Guild; Calif Asn Black Lawyers; bd dir, Volunteer Parole; advisory bd, Afro Sports hall. **Honors/Awds:** Various achievement awards; Woodrow Wilson Fellow; Phi Beta Kappa; PiSigma Alpha. **Special Achievements:** Contrib auth, "Politics & Change in Berkeley", Nathan & Scott 1979;contrib auth to several periodicals. **Business Addr:** Attorney, 4606 S Garnett Suite 310, Tulsa, OK 74146, **Business Phone:** (918)622-6613.

HOPKINS, DONALD ROSWELL
Physician. **Personal:** Born Sep 25, 1941, Miami, FL; son of J Leonard and Iva Major; married Ernestine, Jun 24, 1967. **Educ:** Morehouse Col, BS, 1962; Univ Chicago Med Sch, MD, 1966; Harvard Sch Pub Health, MPH, 1970. **Career:** San Francisco Gen Hosp, intern, 1966-67; CDC, various positions, 1967-74; Harvard Sch Pub Health, asst prof, 1974-77; Centers Disease Control, asst dir, int health, 1978-84, deputy dir, 1984-87; Carter Ctr & Global 2000, sr consult, 1987-97, assoc exec dir, 1997-. **Orgs:** Am Soc Trop Med & Hygiene, 1965; Inst Med, 1987. **Honors/Awds:** Distinguished Serv Medal, US Pub Health Serv, 1986; Morehouse Col, Hon Doc, 1988; Emory Univ, Hon Doc, 1994; fel MacArthur Found, 1995; Lowell hon doc, Univ Mass, 1997; Nat Order Mali, 1998. **Special Achievements:** Directed: "Smallpox Eradication Program," Sierra Leone, 1967-69; Directed: "Guinea Worm Eradication Initiative at CDC," 1980-87; Author: "Princes & Peasants: Smallpox in History," 1983; "At Carter Center," 1987; led the Guinea worm eradication initiative, which has brought down the number of Guinea worm cases from an estimated 3.5 million in 1986 to approximately 15,500 cases in 2004. **Business Addr:** Associate Executive Director, The Carter Center, 1 Copenhill, 453 Freedom Pkwy, Atlanta, GA 30307, **Business Phone:** (404)420-5100.*

HOPKINS, EDNA J.
Educator. **Personal:** Born Sep 29, 1924, Weatherford, TX; married Fritizer; children: Stephen. **Educ:** Tex Col, BA, 1952; Columbia Univ, MA. **Career:** LA Co Schs, teacher, 1955; Enterprise Sch Dist, teacher, 1958; Educ Workshops, 1965-67, Task Force New Ling Prog, supvr teacher, Task Force Early Childhood Educ, 1970; Compton Unified Sch Dist, Task Force PIRAMID, coordr, 1974. **Orgs:** Chair, PR&R Community Educ Asn, 1965-68; Nat Corp Bd, "Women in Community Service Inc" 1968-; White House Conf Food, Hunger & Nutrit, 1969-; vpres, Nat Coun Negro Women, 1970-; chairperson, Greater LA WIGS Bd, 1970-; Calif Teacher Asn; Nat Educ Asn; Compton Educ Asn; Int Asn Chlidhood Educ; Delta Sigma Theta; Dir Christian Educ LA Dist Christian Meth Epis Church; Dir, Christian Educ Philllip Tem CME Church, 1970; secy & chmn, C Care & Dev Ser Inc; Int Asn Vol Eds; bd dir, Womn Coal Com Comn Acting, 1970-73; bd dir, Teen Age & Mothers, Harriet Tubman Sch, 1970-74; bd dir, LA Coun Chs, 1970-72; Educ Adv Comt PUSH; Bd Advs Am Youth Acting Org Inc, 1974-. **Honors/Awds:** Apple Grammy Teacher of Year, 1968; Award Women in, 1972; Woman of Year, Christian Methodist Episcopal Church Womens Miss Soc, 1972. *

HOPKINS, EDWARD CHARLES
Business owner, air force officer. **Personal:** Born Jan 1, 1973. **Career:** USAF Acad, second lt; Criterion Mgt Consult, pres, founder & owner, currently. **Orgs:** Pres, Davis-Monthan Air Force Base Black Heritage Asn; mem bd dir, Ariz Black Bd Dir Proj. **Special Achievements:** Young Leader of the Future, Ebony Mag, 2003. **Military Serv:** USAF Acad. **Business Addr:** President, Owner, Criterion Management Consulting, 120 S Houghton Rd Suite 138, Tucson, AZ 85748, **Business Phone:** (866)991-8797.

HOPKINS, DR. GAYLE P.
Athletic director. **Personal:** Born Nov 7, 1941, Tulsa, OK; son of Elbert Hopkins and Sophia Jackson Hopkins; married Patricia Cartwright, Sep 22, 1967; children: Alissa & Christopher. **Educ:** Univ Ariz, Tucson, AZ, BA, 1965; San Francisco State, San Francisco, CA, MA, 1972; Claremont Grad Sch, Claremont, CA, PhD, 1978. **Career:** San Francisco State, San Francisco, CA, phys educ coach, 1969-75; Claremont Col, track coach & dir phys educ; Claremont-McKenna, Claremont,CA, assoc prof, 1975-83; Dept Agr, Wash, DC, EEO specialist, 1979-80; Univ Ariz, Tucson, AZ, asst athletic dir, assoc to dir athletics, community & alumni rels, currently. **Orgs:** Pres, Nat Asn Athletic Advs Acads, 1983-; pres, Univ Arizona Black Alumni, 1987-; chmn, Black Studies, Tucson Unified Sch Dist; Ariz C Asn. **Honors/Awds:** Hall of Fame, Drake Univ, Univ Ariz, 1967; Coach of the Year, San Francisco State Univ, 1974; Lyndon Johnson Cong Fel, 1978. **Special Achievements:** Represented the United States in the 1964 Tokyo Olympics as a long jumper; Wildcats' first NCAA champion. **Business Addr:** Associate, University of Arizona, Department of Intercollegiate Athletics, McKale Memorial Ctr, PO Box 210096, Tucson, AZ 85721-0096, **Business Phone:** (520)621-0889.

HOPKINS, DR. JOHN DAVID
Educator. **Personal:** Born Mar 6, 1933, Trenton, NJ; son of John P Sr and Edith Harvey; married Lillian L Henry; children: John III, Kay & Lisa. **Educ:** Lincoln Univ, AB, 1954; Meharry Med Col, MD, 1958; OH State Univ, residency, 1963; Vanderbilt Univ, Fellowship, 1970. **Career:** Educator (retired); Meharry Med Col, assoc prof, 1963-75, dir, 1970-75; Tuskegee VA Hosp, consult, 1965-68; Riverside Hosp, dir, 1972-75; VA Hosp, chief radiology, 1973-75; Norfolk Community Hosp, radiologist, 1975-98, pres staff, 1983-85, chief radiologist; Lake Taylor Hosp, consult radiologist, 1985. **Orgs:** Am Col Radiology; fel, Am Col Nuclear Physicians; Soc Nuclear Med; adv bd, Community Mental Health Ctr; Aeolian Club; Clinical Serv Comn, East VA Sch Med; bd dir, United Givers Fund; bd trustees, Eastern VA Med Sch; Nat Med Asn; Am Med Asn; comnr, Norfolk Pub Health Dept, 1983-. **Honors/Awds:** Guest lecturer; 8 publications; Alpha Omega, Honor Medical Society; Sigma Pi Phi; examiner, Am Bd Radiology, 1983-90; case report, "Adrenal Tumors,"Journal Computed Tomography, 1988. **Military Serv:** AUS, lt col, 1968-70. *

HOPKINS, LEROY TAFT
Educator. **Personal:** Born Aug 19, 1942, Lancaster, PA; son of Leroy T and Mary E. **Educ:** Millersville State Col, BA, 1966; Harvard Univ, PhD, 1974. **Career:** NE Univ, instr ger, 1971-72; Hedwig-Heyle-Schule, W Ger, instr eng, 1974-76; Urban League Lancaster Co Inc, assoc dir, 1976-79, acting exec dir, 1979; Millersville State Col, asst prof ger, 1979, prof ger, currently, Dept Foreign Languages, chmn, currently,Foreign Lang Dept, chair, 1998-. **Orgs:** Bd mem, Lancaster County Libr & Lancaster Neighborhood Health Ctr 1977-; chmn, Pa Delegation White House Conf Libraries, 1978-79; adv comt, Black Hist Pa Hist & Mus Comn, 1979-; Pa Humanities Coun, 1988-94; com person, City Lancasters Overall Econ Develop Prog; first vpres, 1989, pres, 1991-94, Lancaster Historical Soc; bd dirs, DAAD Alumni Asn US, currently. **Honors/Awds:** Travelling Fel, Harvard Univ, 1969-70; Study & Visit Grant Res, German Acad Exchange Serv, 1989 & 1994; Mem Hon Soc, Phi Kappa Phi, 1991 . **Business Addr:** Professor of German, Millersville University, Department of Foreign Languages, McComsey 252 1 S George St, PO Box 1002, Millersville, PA 17551-0302.

HOPKINS, NOVELLETE O
Taxonomist. **Career:** City Atlantic City, dep tax assessor, currently. **Business Addr:** Deputy Tax Assessor, City of Atlantic City, 1301 Bacharach Blvd, Atlantic City, NJ 08401, **Business Phone:** (609)347-5386.

HOPKINS, PEREA M.
Meeting planner. **Personal:** Born Apr 13, 1931, Marshall, TX; daughter of Charles A McCane and Margaret Perea McCane; married Milton M Hopkins Jr EdD; children: Christina Elizabeth. **Educ:** Seton Hill Col, BA, math, 1953. **Career:** Ballistic Res Lab, Aberdeen Proving Ground, MD, mathematician, 1954-60; Spacetrack System Div LG Hanscom Field MA, mathematician, 1960-68; Dynatrend Inc, Woburn, MA, staff acct, 1972-81; IOCS Inc, finance asst, 1981-83; Heritage Meetings & Incentives Inc, acct mgr, 1983-; Krikorian Miller Assoc, Bedford, MA, opers mgr, 1987-93; ECNE, meeting planner. **Orgs:** Am Asn Univ Women, 1953-; Am Math Asn, 1953-68; League Women Voters Bedford, 1969-; chmn human resources, League Women Voters Bedford, 1970-76; bd dir, Boston C's Serv; pres bd dirs, Roxbury C's Serv, 1973-79; charter mem, Middlesex County Chap Links Inc, 1976-; pres, Middlesex County Chap Links, 1976-77; secy, Middlesex County Chap Links, 1978-80; Gov Adv Comt, Am Col Phys, Washington, DC, 1980; chairperson, Middlesex County Chap Links, 1986-88, rec secy, 1988-90; chmn, Bedford-Lexington Br, Am Asn Univ Women, 1986-88; vpres, Bedford-Lexington Br, Am Asn UnivWomen, 1994-96; treasurer, Rho Epsilon Omega, Alpha Kappa Alpha Sorority Inc, 1994-96; secy, Bedford-Lexington Br, Am Asn Univ Women, 2006. **Home Addr:** 8 Hilltop Dr, Bedford, MA 01730. *

HOPKINS, TELMA
Actor, singer. **Personal:** Born Oct 28, 1948, Louisville, KY. **Career:** Tony Orlando and Dawn, singer; Isaac Hayes, backup singer; Films: Future Cop, 1985; The Love Guru, 2008. TV appearances: "Love Boat", 1979; "Bosom Buddies", 1980; "Dance Fever", 1981; "Fantasy Island"; "Gimme A Break", 1983-87; "Circus of the Stars", 1985; "Family Matters", 1989-97; "Half & Half", 2002-06; "Psych", 2008. **Honors/Awds:** Outstanding Supporting Actress in a Comedy Series, BET Comedy Award, 2005. **Special Achievements:** Four times Image Award nominee. **Business Phone:** (310)557-6860.*

HOPKINS, THOMAS FRANKLIN
Educator, research scientist. **Personal:** Born in Culpepper, VA; son of Thomas Hopkins and Dorothy L Atkins Hopkins-Brown; children: Winifred Louise, Thomas M, Charles M, Michael & Arthur G. **Educ:** Calvin Coolidge Col, Boston, BS, 1955; Mich State Univ, MS, 1961; Boston Univ, PhD, 1970. **Career:** Professor (retired); Worcester Found Experimental Biol, res asst, 1949-60, scientist, 1960-70; Univ Conn, assoc prof biol, 1970-75; Univ Md Eastern Shore, Dept Natural Sci, chmn, 1975-86, prof biol, 1986-94. **Orgs:** Am Physiol Soc, 1970-; Nat Sci Teachers Asn. **Honors/Awds:** Publ many jour articles. **Military Serv:** US Marine Corps, Cpl, 1943-46. **Home Addr:** 820 S Schumaker Dr, PO Box 5138, Salisbury, MD 21804, **Home Phone:** (443)260-0748.

HOPKINS, DR. VASHTI EDYTHE JOHNSON
Educator. **Personal:** Born Aug 22, 1924, Virginia; daughter of Louis Tenner and Matilda Ann Robinson; married Haywood Hopkins Sr; children: Haywood Jr, Yvonne Andrews & Sharon. **Educ:** Va Seminary & Col, BS, 1963; St Pauls Col, BS, elem educ, 1967; Univ Va, med, 1969; S western Univ, PhD, educ, 1984. **Career:** Educator (retired); Amherst City Pub Schs, teacher, 1963-67; Lynchburg Pub Schs, teacher, 1967-74; Sandusky Middle Sch, teacher, 1974-82; Va Seminary & Col, prof eng, 1991-97. **Orgs:** Dep organizer, Order Eastern Star Prince Hall Affiliated, 1967-91; Eastern Theol Ctr; Zeta Chap Zeta Phi Beta Sorority; life mem, Univ Va Alumni Asn; life mem, Century Club St Paul's Col; life mem, Nat Educ Asn; life mem, Va Educ Asn; life mem, Lutheran Educ Asn; Daughter Isis, Golden Circle Past LL Ruler; pres, Episcopal Church Women; pres Amity Soc; Bridgette Soc; Nat Sor Phi Delta Kappa Inc; Alpha Tau Chap; Lynchburg Va Chap; Phi Delta Kappa Fraternity; pres, Lynchburg Retired Teachers, 1989-90; pres, Dist F Retired Teachers, 1990-92. **Honors/Awds:** Achievement Award, Order of Eastern Star Chap 40, 1984; Outstanding Achievement Grand Chap, Va Order of the Eastern Star Prince Hall Affiliated, 1984; Golden Poet Award, World of Poetry, 1989-96. **Special Achievements:** Published Poetry in Century Magazine, 1960; Poems published in 1989, 1992.

HOPKINS, WES
Football player. **Personal:** Born Sep 26, 1961, Birmingham, AL. **Educ:** Southern Methodist Univ. **Career:** Football player (retired); Philadelphia Eagles, free safety, 1983-93. **Honors/Awds:** Most Valuable Defensive Player, Cotton Bowl; Defensive Player of the Week, Sports Illustrated; Defensive Player of the Week, NFL; NFC Defensive Player of the Month; Eagles Defensive Most Valuable Player. **Special Achievements:** Has appeared in a documentary film, The Complete History of the Philadelphia Eagles, 2004.

HOPKINS, WILLIAM A
Government official. **Personal:** Born May 27, 1943, Americus, GA; married Desi Page; children: Ellen, Ryan, Christopher & Leslee. **Educ:** Albany State Col, BA, 1968; Ga State Univ, MPA, 1984. **Career:** St Regis Paper Co, asst indust rels, 1967-69; Sentry Ins, dist mgr, 1969-72; Ins Multi Line, territory mgr, 1972-77; Piedmont Ins Agency, pres, 1977-82. **Orgs:** Vpres, Atlanta Alumni KAY, 1976-78; pres, Albany State Alumni, 1980-82; bd mem, Morris Brown Col. **Honors/Awds:** Outstanding Young Men of Am Indust Rels, St Regis, 1969-72; Lt Col, State Ga Gov Staff, 1982. **Military Serv:** AUS, capt, 1962-66. **Home Phone:** (404)346-3965. **Business Addr:** Special Assistant to the Commander, Stof Georgia Director Small Business Affairs, 200 Piedmont Ave Suite 1416, Atlanta, GA 30334.

HOPKINSON, MARK I
Chief executive officer. **Career:** British Gov, US media strategist; British Broadcasting Corp, trained journalist; NewsMark Public Relations, chief exec officer, currently. **Business Phone:** (561)852-5767.*

HOPPER, DR. CORNELIUS LENARD
School administrator, vice president (organization). **Personal:** Born Aug 30, 1934, Hartshorne, OK; son of Claude and Hazel

Pugh; married Barbara M Johnson; children: Adriane, Brian & Michael. **Educ:** Ohio Univ Athens, OH, AB, 1956; Univ Cincinnati Col MEd, MD, 1960. **Career:** Univ WI, instr neurol, 1967-68, asst prof neurol, 1968-71; Tuskegee Inst, med dir, 1971-79; Univ Ala Sch Med, asst clin prof, 1971-79; Univ Calif, special asst health affairs, 1979-83; Univ Calif, vpres health affairs, 1983-2000, emer vpres health affairs, currently. **Orgs:** Consult, Off Spec Progs Bur Health Manpower Educ, NIH, 1972-79; consult, Am Pub Health Asn Div Int Health Prog, 1974-; pres, Ala, St Med Asn, 1974-79; assoc mem, Am Acad Neurol Nat Med Asn; Am Asn Advan Sci; Asn Acad Health Ctrs; Golden St Med Asn; DHEW Nat Adv Coun Prof Standards Review Org (PSRO), 1974-78; Nat Adv Comt Robert Wood Johnson Found Comn Hosp-Med Staff Sponsored Primary Care Group Pract Prog, 1974-82; VA Med Sch Asst Review Comt, 1975-76; Nat Adv Comm Robert Wood Johnson Found Nurse Fac Fellowships Prog, 1976-82; CA Health Manpower Policy Comm, 1981-01; Epilepsy Found Am, Nat Info & Resource Ctr Adv Comt, 1982-; vpres, Calif Asn HMOs Found, 1994-. **Honors/Awds:** Special Research Fellow, Demyelinating Dis Nat Inst Neurol Dis & Blindness, 1967-68; Alumnus of the Year, Ohio Univ, 1985; Medal of Merit, Ohio Univ, 1985; publ including, PSRO, A Current Status Report Proceedings of Sixth Annual Conf on the Southern Region Conf on the Humanities and Public Policy May, 1976; The Health Care Delivery System, A Rural Perspective Contact '72 - Proceedings of the Governor's Health manpower Conference 174, 1972; with CG Matthews & CS Cleeland, Symptom Instability & Thermo regulation in Multiple Sclerosis Neurology 22, 142, 1972; with CS Cleeland and CG Matthews, MMPI Profiles in Exacerbation & Remission of Multiple Sclerosis Psychol Reports 27, 343, 1970; First Recipient Of National Medical Fellowships Founder's Award, 2001. **Military Serv:** USN, Battalion Surgeon 4th Marines, 2 yrs. **Home Addr:** l4201 Skyline Blvd, Oakland, CA 94619. **Business Addr:** Vice President Emeritus for Health Affairs, University of California, 1111 Franklin St 11th Fl, Oakland, CA 94607-5200.*

HOPSON, REAR ADM. DEBORAH PARHAM. See PARHAM HOPSON, REAR ADM. DEBORAH L.

HOPSON, HAROLD THEODORE (SONNY HOPSON)
Executive, entertainer. **Personal:** Born Jan 24, 1937, Abington, PA; children: Ronald, Lynette, Regina, Lisa-Shelia, Harold III, Kelley LynetteWashington, Ashley Lorraine Stanley, Ronald John II & Barry. **Educ:** Philadelphia Wireless Sch, 3 post grad courses, 3rd class Radio Tel Operators License, 1965. **Career:** Harold Randolph & Harvey Schmidt, div Ins Investigator, 1958-65; Philadelphia Tribune, writer/reporter, 1965-66; Pepsi Generation Come Alive Radio Personality, 1965-66; Radio station WHAT-AM Philadelphia, communicator & radio personality, 1965-71, 1980-86; Scene Philadelphia Tribune, entertainment critic & reviewer, 1966-67; Sonny Hopson's Celebrity Lounge, proprietor, 1969-73; WDAS AM-FM Radio Station, asst to pres, 1978; WHTH-FM Radio, owner, 1986-; Steven M Kramer, Attorney at Law, Phila, NY,NJ, LA, special asst, 1977-97; Megastarr Entertainment WHTH Music com, chmn & chief exec officer, 1999-. **Orgs:** Nat Asn Advan Colored People, 1957-; SCLC, 1965-; Nat Asn Radio & TV Announcers, 1965-; Jazz Home Club, 1968-; pres, founder, new chmn,Concerned Communicators, 1971-; organizer, People United Save Humanity, 1971-; co-founder, Nat Black Media Coalition. **Honors/Awds:** Sickle Cell Anemia Research Award, 1966; BSA Cit Award, 1967; Inter Urban Leag Award of Phila, 1967; Disc Jockey of Year Award, 1969; Special Service Award, YMCA, 1968; Mayor of Phila Youth, 1970; Jazz at Home Club of America Achievement Award, 1971; mention in Books The Sound of Philadelphia & The Greatest Muhammad Ali; The Sonny Hopson Stories, Philadelphia Tribune; Life Mag, stories with Richie Allen; Sepia, stories with Major Cox sum & Sonny Wall, 1973; stories with Mojo Magazine, City Paper, New Over Server, Philadelphia Weekly; newspapers, Philadelphia Tribune, 1968, Philadelphia Enquirer, Philadelphia Daily News. **Special Achievements:** Author, Mohammed Ali, 2000. **Military Serv:** USAF, 1954-57. **Business Addr:** Chairman, Cheif Executive Officer, Megastarr Entertainment WHTH Music, 4936 Wynnefield Ave, Philadelphia, PA 19131.

HOPSON, KEVIN M
Scientist, health services administrator. **Personal:** Born May 11, 1959, Roanoke, VA; son of James M; married Deborah Hopson, Feb 14, 1998. **Educ:** Va Tech, BS, biochem & biol, 1983; Hood Col, MBA, 2003. **Career:** Hercules Inc, prod develop mgr, 1983-84, process engr, 1984-87, res chemist, 1987-90; FDA, chemist, 1990-94, consumer safety officer, currently, staff, Bioresearch Monitoring.

HOPSON, MELVIN CLARENCE
Administrator, executive. **Personal:** Born Jun 29, 1937, Sawyersville, AL; son of Lovell Hopson Sr and Irene; divorced; children: Steven, Wayne, Myra. **Educ:** Roosevelt Univ, BA, English, 1966. **Career:** Administrator, Executive (retired); Montgomery Ward, store Mgr, 1968, dir EEO, 1969-80; McDonalds Corp, asst vpres, diversity develop, 1994. **Orgs:** Bd mem & life trustee, Chicago Urban League, 1971-; officer, Rat Pac Inc, 1980-; pres, Chicago Urban Affairs Coun, 1983; bd mem, Chicago NAACP, 1984; Kappa Alpha Psi; bd dirs, YMCA, 1985-. **Honors/Awds:** Man of year Chicago Urban League, 1980. **Military Serv:** USAF, sergeant, 1957-61. *

HOPSON, SONNY. See HOPSON, HAROLD THEODORE.

HORAD, SEWELL D., SR.
Educator, army officer. **Personal:** Born Jan 26, 1922, Washington, DC; married Ella Garnett; children: Sewell D jr & Denise H. **Educ:** Howard Univ, BS, 1942; George Washington Univ, MA, 1973. **Career:** Real estate salesman & bus owner, 1946-; Wash DC Pub Schs, admin officer spec educ, currently, teacher math, sci physically handicapped c, 1958-72. **Orgs:** Lodge Masonic Temple; vice pres "What Good Are We" Club; Oldest Black Clubs in DC; "Pro-duffers" Golf Club of DC. **Special Achievements:** Instrumental in developing new techniques for teaching handicapped children, some have been copyrighted; Author "Fraction Computer", math book designed to solve fractional problems without finding least common denominator; invented an info retrieval system. **Military Serv:** AUS, capt, 1942-46. **Business Addr:** 5511 Illinois Ave NW, Washington, DC 20011.

HORD, DR. FREDERICK LEE (MZEE LASANA OKPARA)
Educator, writer. **Personal:** Born Nov 7, 1941, Kokomo, IN; son of Noel E and Jessie Tyler; divorced; children: Teresa D Hord-Owens, F Mark & Laurel E. **Educ:** Ind State Univ, BS, Speech and Hist, 1963, MS, Speech and Educ, 1965; Union Grad Sch, PhD, Literature and Hist, 1987. **Career:** Educator, Author: Wabash Col, prof black studies, 1972-76; Ind Univ, guest lectr black studies, 1976; Frostburg State Univ, asst dir minority affairs, 1980-84; PANFRE, lectr, 1981-; Howard Univ, prof Afro-Am studies, 1984-87; W Va Univ, dir Ctr Black Cult, 1987-88; Knox Col, prof black studies & chair black studies prog, 1988-; book: Reconstruction Memory, Third World Press, 1991; Life Sentences: Freeing Black Relationships; Third World Press, 1995; co-editor: I Am Because We Are: Readings in Black Philosophy, 1995; book poems After-(h)ours, Third World Press, 1974; lead article, West Virginia Law Review on Black Culture Centers, Summer, 1989; Black Culture Centers: Inside Out. **Orgs:** Consult ed, Nightsun; regional consult, NAMSE; consult, black studies Afro Am Enterprises; founder & pres, Asn Black Cult Ctrs, 1994-; pres, Nat Asn Black Cult Ctr; Nat Coun Black Studies. **Honors/Awds:** Governor's Award, Outstanding Black Male Scholar in Indiana Col & Univ, 1963. **Special Achievements:** Poems & articles in major black journals such as Illinois Issues, Words Work, Black Books Bulletin, The Western Journal of Black Studies, Black American Literature Forum, Obsidian II; featured poet in Fall 1982 issue of The Western Journal of Black Studies. **Business Addr:** Professor, chairman, Knox College, 2 E S St, Galesburg, IL 61401-4999.

HORD, NOEL EDWARD
Executive. **Personal:** Born Jul 10, 1946, Kokomo, IN; son of Noel Ernest and Jessie Mae Tyler; married Cora Eileen, Jul 10, 1966 (deceased); children: Michelle Denise & Noel Daniel. **Educ:** Ind State Univ, Terre Haute, IN, 1967. **Career:** Wohl Shoe Co, Clayton, MO, various responsibilities, 1967-84; Nine West Group, vp operations, 1984-86, svp/gen mgr, 1986-87; Enzol Angiolini Div, pres, 1988-91, group pres, 1991-93; US Shoe Corp, Footwear Group, pres & chief exec officer; BCBG Footwear, pres & chief operating officer, 2001-. **Orgs:** Urban League's Nat Black Exec Exchange Prog; co-founder, Concerned Black Man of Action Youth in Danbury, CT; co-founder, Hord Foundation, Danbury, CT. **Honors/Awds:** James C Taylor Personal Award, Outstanding Work in Human Resources & Career Development, 1980; Footwear News Man of the Year, 1994. **Business Addr:** President, BCBG Footwear, 10250 Santa Monica Blvd, Los Angeles, CA 90067, **Business Phone:** (310)553-2281.

HORN, JOE. See HORN, JOSEPH.

HORN, JOSEPH (JOE HORN)
Football player. **Personal:** Born Jan 16, 1972, Tupelo, MS; married Lacreshia; children: Jhia & Joseph. **Educ:** Itawamba Jr Col. **Career:** Memphis Mad Dogs, 1995; Kans City Chiefs, wide receiver, 1996-99; New Orleans Saints, wide receiver, 2000-06; Atlanta Falcons, 2007-08, free agent, currently. **Honors/Awds:** Saints Offensive Player of the Year, 2000.

HORNBUCKLE, NAPOLEON
Executive. **Personal:** Born Feb 16, 1942, Birmingham, AL; son of Lee E and Louisa Coleman; married Dorothy Jeanne Sadler, Sep 4, 1964; children: Scott & Vance. **Educ:** Tennessee State Univ, Nashville, TN, BA, elec electronics eng, 1964. **Career:** Executive (retired); Motorola Inc, AZ, develop engr mgr, proj engr mgr, proj leader mgr, mkt develop mgr, vpres & dir, vpres & gen mgr, SED, 1990-95; Worldwide Mkt Systs Solutions Group, corp vpres, dir, 1995. **Orgs:** Omega Psi Phi Fraternity, 1964; Armed Forces Commun Asn, 1976-; Electronics Indust Asn, 1976-; Nat Security Indust Asn, 1984-; Nat Asn Advan Colored People, 1987-; Boule, 1988-. **Honors/Awds:** Engineer of the Year, US Black Engr Mag, 1990.

HORNBURGER, JANE M (JANE MELVIN HORNBURGER)
Educator. **Personal:** Born Aug 26, 1928, Fayetteville, NC; daughter of Ella Carter Melvin and Roy D Melvin; married Aug 19, 1950 (divorced). **Educ:** Fayetteville State Univ, BS, 1948; NY Univ, MA, 1950, EdD, 1970. **Career:** Kinston, NCA Pub Schs, teacher, 1948-53; Wilmington, Del Pub Schs, teacher, 1954-66, suv reading/lang arts, 1966-69, dir teacher training, 1969-72, Boston Univ, asst prof, 1972-77; City Univ NY, Brooklyn Col, assoc prof educ serv, 1978-. **Orgs:** Dir, Mass Asn Reading Educrs, 1976-77; NYC Reading Coun; NY State Eng Coun; New Eng Asn Teachers Eng; Int Reading Asn, policy guidelines comt, 1981-83, exec search comn, 1983, bd mem, 1987-90, chap, hq comt, 1989-90; Nat Coun Teachers Eng, comn classroom pract, 1983,1978-81 & 1985-88, comn mem communicating res, 1989-92, ed bd, 1981-84; NY State Reading Asn, chair, 1990-; Bronx Reading Coun, pres, IRA hon coun, 1987-89; Am Asn Univ Profs; Phi Delta Kappa; Pi Lambda Theta; Kappa Delta Pi Episcopalian. **Honors/Awds:** Woman of the Year, Am Asn Univ Women, 1968; Founder's Day Award, NY Univ Bd Trustees, 1971; Named to Talent File, Nat Coun Teachers Eng, 1989; Regional Award in Reading Education, NY State Reading Asn, 1989,Literature Advocate Award, 1990; Leader in Literature, Int Reading Asn, 1991. **Special Achievements:** Author: So You Have an Aide: A Guide for Teachers in the Use of Classroom Aides, 1968; "Deep Are the Roots: Busing in Boston," Journal of Negro Education, 1976; Teaching Multicultural Children, 1976; African Countries and Cultures: A Concise Illustrated Dictionary, 1981; Focus: Teaching English Language Arts, 1981. **Business Addr:** Associate Professor, City University of New York, Brooklyn College, Ave H Bedford 2208 Boylan Hall, Brooklyn, NY 11210, **Business Phone:** (718)951-5738.

HORNBURGER, JANE MELVIN. See HORNBURGER, JANE M.

HORNE, DR. AARON
College administrator, educator. **Personal:** Born Dec 3, 1941, Chipley, FL; son of Albert and Laura; married Myrtle; children: Ericka, Michelle & Aaron Jr. **Educ:** Tenn State Univ, BS, 1968; Roosevelt Univ, MM, 1972; Univ Iowa, MFA, 1973, doctorate musical arts, 1976; Univ New Hampshire Inst Enrollment, mgt dipl, 1990; Harvard Univ, Grad Sch Educ, dipl, 1993. **Career:** College Administrator, Educator (retired); Fla A & M Univ, asst prof, 1968-72; Univ Iowa, lectr, 1973-76; Tex Southern Univ, assoc prof, 1976-77; Northwestern Univ, sr lectr, 1982-89; Northeastern Ill Univ, prof & dir jazz studies, 1977-89, Ctr Inner City Studies, prof music, 1996-97, actng dir, 1998-2001; Bd Govs Univs, asst vice chancellor acad affairs, 1990-2001; Winston-Salem State Univ, Col Arts & Scis, dean & prof music, 2001-07. **Orgs:** Exec bd, Int Asn Jazz Educrs, 1970-; Nat Asn Col Wind & Percussion Instrs, 1972-; Music Educrs Nat Conf, 1977-; bd mem, Duke Ellington Soc, 1988-; Am Asn Higher Educ, 1989-; Black Music Caucus, 1989-; Ill Comm Black Concerns Higher Educ, 1989-; Arts-in-Education; advisor, Alpha Kappa Mu honor Society. **Honors/Awds:** Honored Participant, Lublin Jazz Festival, 1980; Outstanding Service to Jazz, Nat Asn Jazz Educrs, 1981; Presidential Merit Award, Northeastern Ill Univ, 1982; Artist in Residence Grant/Award, Nat Endowment Arts, 1982;Certificate of Excellence, Music Educrs Nat Conf, 1984; Mentor Award, Black Heritage Gospel Choir, Northeastern Ill Univ, 2000; Instructor of the year, Northeastern Ill Univ, 2001; Service Award, Roosevelt Univ, 2001. **Special Achievements:** Music Educators National Conference, Featured Artist, 1978, Woodwind Music of Black Composers, Greenwood Press, 1990, String Music of Black Composers, Greenwood Press, 1991, Keyboard Music of Black Composers, Greenwood Press, 1992, Brass Music of Black Composers, Greenwood Press, 1995. **Military Serv:** AUS, spec-4, 1958-61. **Home Addr:** 122 Scottsdale Dr, Advance, NC 27006, **Home Phone:** (336)998-8095.

HORNE, DEBORAH JEAN
Television journalist. **Personal:** Born Jul 26, 1953, Newport News, VA; daughter of Willie Edward and Daisy Mae Pellman. **Educ:** Hampton Univ, Hampton, VA, BA, 1975; Ohio State Univ, Columbus, OH, MA, 1976. **Career:** Providennce Jour, Providence, RI, gen assignment reporter, 1976-81; WPRI-TV, E Providence, RI, chief reporter, 1981; KIRO 7 Eyewitness News, gen assignment reporter, 1991-, KIRO InColor, creator, KIRO Backstage, creator. **Orgs:** Architectural preservation, bd mem, Elmwood Found, 1989-; bd mem, Big Sister Asn RI, 1986-90; pres, Delta Sigma Theta Inc, 1974-; bd mem, Vol League Rhode Island, 1981-82; vol, Shelter Battered Women, 1983-86; Seattle Domestic Violence Coun; bd mem, Seattle Emergency Housing Serv. **Honors/Awds:** Massachusetts Asniated Press Highest Award, "A Question of Rape," special TV program, 1985; 1st place, features, "Chatham Houses: Washed Away," New England United Press InterNat, 1989; 1st place, continuing coverage, "Ocean Dumping," lead reporter, 1989, 2nd place, spot news, "Coventry Chemical Fire," 1989, Massachusetts Asniated Press Broadcasters Award. **Business Addr:** General Assignment Reporter, KIRO 7 Eyewitness News, 2807 Third Ave, Seattle, WA 98121, **Business Phone:** (206)728-7777.

HORNE, DR. EDWIN CLAY
Dentist. **Personal:** Born Feb 16, 1924, Greensboro, NC; son of Ellis Clay (deceased) and Annie Slade (deceased); married Gene Ann, Aug 23, 1952; children: Carol Anne Horne-Penn & Edwin Christian Horne. **Educ:** NC A&T State Univ, BS, 1947; Univ Pa,

Sch Dent, DDS, 1952. **Career:** Harlem Hosp, assoc attending dentist, 1954-95; Upper Harlem Comprehensive Care Ctr, attending dentist & attending dent supvr, 1985-89; N Cent Bronx-Montefiore Hosp Affiliation, from clin assoc supvr to adj prof clin dent; Columbia Univ Sch Dent & Oral Surg; Univ Pa, Sch Dent Med, adj prof; N Cent Bronx Dent Clin, attending & assoc prof; Pvt Practice, dentist, currently. **Orgs:** Fel, Am Col Dentists; 1st Dist Dent Soc NY; Omega Psi Phi Frat; Sigma Pi Phi Frat; Reveille Club NY; Lions Int Englewood; corp mem; Schomburg Corp, Schomburg Ctr Res Black Cult; sire archon, NE Region Sigma Pi Phi Frat, 1987-88; NC A&T State Univ Alumni; bd dirs, Univ Pa-Metro, NJ Alumni Asn, 1987; exec bd, Univ Pa Dent Sch Alumni Soc, 1989-90; comm mem, visual aids, Annual November Dent Convention, NY City; pres, Univ Pa Dent Sch Alumni Soc Adv to Dean, 1998; mem bd trustees, Schomberg Corp, 1998. **Honors/Awds:** Man of the Year Award, Kappa Omicron Chap Omega Psi Phi Frat, 1970; honored for 40 yrs Meritorious Membership, Omega Psi Phi Frat, 1986; Fifty Year Membership Award, Los Angeles Grand Conclave Omega, 1996. **Military Serv:** AUS. **Home Addr:** 374 Miller Ave, Englewood, NJ 07631, **Home Phone:** (201)567-4767. **Business Addr:** Dentist, 2255 5th Ave, New York, NY 10037-200, **Business Phone:** (212)368-3912.

HORNE, GENE-ANN POLK. **See POLK, DR. GENE-ANN.**

HORNE, GERALD CHARLES
College teacher. **Personal:** Born Jan 3, 1949, St Louis, MO; son of Jerry and Flora; married Savenda, May 25, 1994. **Educ:** Princeton Univ, BA, 1970; Univ Calif-Berkeley, JD, 1973; Columbia Univ, MA, 1978; PhD, 1982. **Career:** Affirmative Action Coordr Ctr, dir coun, 1979-82; Sarah Lawrence Col,prof, 1982-88; Nat Conf Black Lawyers, exec dir, 1985-86; Local 1199 Health & Hosp Workers Union AFL-CIO, spec coun, 1986-88; Univ Calif, Santa Barbara, prof; Univ North Carolina, prof chem, currently, prof commun studies, African & Afro-Am Studies, currently. **Orgs:** Secy & treas, Am Fedn Teachers, Local 2274, 1976-78; chair, Nat Conf Black Lawyers, Intl Comt, 1982-85; chair, Nat Lawyers Guild, Intl Comn, 1988-92; chair, Pears & Freedom Party, 1991-92. **Honors/Awds:** Hope Stevens Award, Nat Conf Black Lawyers, 1983; Getman Service to Students Award, Univ Calif, Santa Barbara, 1990; Carter G Woodson Fellow,Univ Va, 1991-92; City Univ NY, Belle Zeller Visiting Prof, 1993-94; Coun Intl Exchange Scholars, Full bright Scholar & Univ Zimbabwe, 1995. **Special Achievements:** Pub include: Black Liberation & Red Scare: Ben Davis and the Communist Party, London: Assocs Univ Presses, 1994; Reversing Discrimination: The Case Affirmative Action, Intl Publ, 1992; Thinking and Re-thinking US Hist, Coun Intl Books C, 1989; Communist Front? Civil Rights Cong, London:Assoc Univ Presses, 1988; Black and Red: W E B DuBois & Afro-Am Response Cold War, 1944-63, State Univ NY Press, 1986. **Business Addr:** Professor, University North Carolina, Communication Studies, PO Box 3285, Chapel Hill, NC 27599-3195, **Business Phone:** (919)967-6878.*

HORNE, JUNE C
Buyer. **Personal:** Born Sep 3, 1953, New York, NY; daughter of Samuel and Ceceill Sledge; married Frank, Mar 30, 1972. **Educ:** Lab Inst Merchandising, BS, 1971. **Career:** Saks Fifth Ave, exec trainee, 1971-72, asst buyer swimwear, sportswear, 1976-78, buyer swimwear, 1977-79, buyer designer sportswear, 1978-82; Saks Garden City Br, store gen mgr, 1982-84; Saks Fifth Ave, assoc div merch mgr, designer sportswear, 1985-92; dir, designer sportswear, 1986-, sr buyer designer sportswear & ready-to-wear, 1992-. **Orgs:** YMCA Greater NY, Black Achievers, Black Retail Action Group; Fashion Outreach. **Honors/Awds:** Black Achievers in Industry Award, YMCA Greater NY, 1979; Interviewed for NY Times Article "A Buyer's View of the Busy World of Fashion", 1980; "The Shadow Designer,"1999; Buyer Achievement Award, Black Retail Action Group, 1982; Lab Inst Merchandising, Adv Bd Alumnae Award, 1998; 100 Black Men of America Inc, & the Magic Johnson Found, Pioneer Award, 1998; Brag Business Achievement Award, 2003. **Special Achievements:** First black female store gen mgr, Saks Garden City Br, 1982. **Business Addr:** Senior Buyer, Saks Fifth Avenue, 12 E 49th St, New York, NY 10017, **Business Phone:** (212)940-5877.

HORNE, JUNE MERIDETH
Technician. **Personal:** Born Feb 23, 1936, Chicago, IL; daughter of William and Elizabeth Neal; married Brazell, Oct 6, 1954 (deceased); children: Brazell Rodney. **Educ:** Kennedy King Jr Col, attended 1975. **Career:** Technician (retired); Veterans Admin, psychiat tech, 1964-94. **Orgs:** Pres Browder & Watts Inc, 1985; Int Biographical Ctr, Int Order Merit, 1990; Women's Inner Circle Achievement, Am Biographical Inst, 1990; Int Parliament Safety & Peace, 1991, 1992. **Honors/Awds:** Knighthood, 1991, Lofsensic Ursinius Order, Found Ethiopia Netherland; Knighthood, 1992. **Special Achievements:** Emergency Escape Apparatus (invention), US Patent; Order Souberain Et Militaire De La Milice Du Saint Sepuulcre Confederation Chivalry, Australia.

HORNE, LENA MARY CALHOUN
Singer, dancer, actor. **Personal:** Born Jun 30, 1917, Brooklyn, NY; daughter of Edwin F and Lena Calhoun; married Louis J Jones, Jan 1, 1937 (divorced 1944); children: Gail & Edwin; married Lennie Hayton, Jan 1, 1947 (died 1971). **Educ:** Howard Univ, honorary degree; Spelman Col, honorary degree. **Career:** Singer, actor, dancer (retired); Theater appearances include: "Dance with Your Gods," 1934; "Jamaica," 1957; "Tony Bennett & Lena Horne Sing," 1974; "Lena Horne: The Lady & Her Music," 1981, toured major US cities, 1982; "Nine O'Clock Revue," US & Canada, 1961; film appearances include: Duke Isthe Tops, 1938; Cabin in the Sky, 1943; Stormy Weather, 1943; Broadway Rhythm, 1944; Till the Clouds Roll By, 1946; Death of a Gunfighter, 1969;The Wiz, 1978; television appearances include: "Music '55," 1955; "The Perry Como Show," 1959; "Here's to the Ladies," 1960; "Bell Telephone Hour," 1964; "The Cosby Show"; "Sanford & Son"; "The Ed Sullivan Show"; "The Tonight Show"; "The Lena Horne Show," 1959; "The Frank Sinatra Timex Show," 1960; "The Milton Berle Special," 1962; "Lena in Concert," 1969;"Harry & Lena," 197"Keep US Beautiful," 1973; related career: Cotton Club, chorus member, singer, 1933; Noble Sissle's Orchestra, appeared with,1935-36; Charlie Barnet Band, appeared with, 1940-41; writings include: In Person, autobiography, 1950; co-author, Lena, autobiography, 1965; recordings include: Birth of the Blues, 1940; Moanin' Low, 1940; Little Girl Blue, 1942; A Date with Fletcher Henderson, 1944; Till the Clouds Roll By, 1946; Words & Music, 1948; At the Waldorf, 1958; Sands, 1961; Like Latin, 1963; On the Blue Side, 1962; Lena Horne Sings Your Requests, 1963; Lena Goes Latin, 1963; Classics in Blue; Porgy & Bess; The Lady Is a Tramp; First Lady; The One & Only; Standing Room Only; Stormy Weather; We'll Be Together Again, Blue Note Records, 1994; An Evening with Lena Horne, 1994; Seasons of a Life, 2006. **Orgs:** Actors' Equity Asn; Screen Actors Guild; Am Fedn TV & Radio Artists; Am Guild Musical Artists; Am Guild Variety Artists; NAACP; Nat Coun Negro Women; Delta Sigma Theta Sorority Inc. **Honors/Awds:** Page One Award, NY Newspaper Guild; Black Filmmakers Hall of Fame; HandelMedallion, Highest Cultural Award; Drama Desk Award, Best Actress in aMusical; Third Annual Young Audiences Arts Award; Ebony's LifetimeAchievement Award; New York Drama Critics Poll Award, Best Performance byFemale Lead in Musical, "Jamaica," 1958; Female Solo Vocal Performance,1961; Best Female Vocal Performance, 1962; Circle Award, "Lena Horne: TheLady and her Music"; Special Tony Award, 1982; Best Cast Show Album, 1981;Special Citation, Antoinette Perry Special Award, 1981; Spingarn Award,NAACP, 1983; Kennedy Center Honors Award, Lifetime Contribution to Arts,1984; Paul Robeson Award, Actors' Equity Assn, 1985; Pied Piper Award,American Assn of Composers, Authors & Publishers, 1987; Best Jazz VocalPerformance - Duo or Group, 1988; Best Jazz Vocal Performance " Female,1988; Lifetime Achievement Award, 1989; Best Jazz Vocal Performance, 1995;two Grammy Awards. **Special Achievements:** Inducted to Int Civil Rights Walk of Fame, Martin Luther King, Jr NatHistoric Site, 2006.

HORNE, MARVIN L. R., JR.
Manager. **Personal:** Born Mar 5, 1936, Richmond, VA; married Vernell Bell; children: Marvin III, Tracy R, Carl E, Kelly M. **Educ:** VA State Col, BS, Physics, 1957; Howard Univ, Physics, 1960; Univ Rochester, MBA 1975. **Career:** US Naval Weapons Lab, math & physicist, 1960-61; Gen Elec Co, physicist, 1961-63; US Naval Weapons Lab, math & physicist, 1963-65; Eastman Kodak Co, Eng mgr. **Orgs:** Amer Inst of Aero & Astronautics, 1963-67; Tech Mkt Soc Am, 1978-; Sigma Pi Sigma, 1954-57; Kappa Mu Episilon, 1954-57; Alpha Phi Alpha Frat, 1954-; Beta Gamma Sigma, 1975-; chmn, Rochester City Planning comn, 1977-82. **Military Serv:** AUS, first lt, 1957-59; Letter Commendation.

HORNE, SEMMION N
Executive. **Personal:** Children: Raymond N. **Educ:** Dorchester Acad; Spring Garden Inst. **Career:** Horne & Howard Const Co, line mechanic; Somerset Hills & Co Nat Bank, pres. **Orgs:** Pres, NAACP; Rent Leveling Bd; Community Church God; life mem, Wise Owl Club. **Home Addr:** 84 Berry St, Somerset, NJ 08873, **Home Phone:** (732)249-4988. *

HORNE, TONY TREMAINE
Football player, football coach. **Personal:** Born Mar 21, 1976, Queens, NC. **Educ:** Clemson Univ. **Career:** Football player (retired); Football coach; St Louis Rams, wide receiver, 1998-2000; KansCity Chiefs, 2001; speed coach, D1 Sports Training.

HORNE-MCGEE, PATRICIA J
School administrator, executive director. **Personal:** Born Dec 23, 1946, Ypsilanti, MI; daughter of Louise Hardwick Horne and Lacy Horne Sr; married Columbus McGee, Aug 4, 1979. **Educ:** Mich State Univ, BA, 1968; Univ Mich, MSW, 1971; Eastern Mich Univ, MA, 1973; Univ Mich, infant mental health cert. **Career:** Mich State Dept Social Serv, caseworker, 1968-69; Ann Arbor Model Cities, social coordr, 1970-72; Washtenaw Co Community Coordinated Child Care, exec dir, 1971-74; Ferris State Univ, asst prof, 1974-79; Mercy Col Detroit, assoc prof & prog dir social work dept, 1979-88; Wayne Co Intermediate Sch Dist, assoc dir, 1987-94; Wayne State Univ, adjunct prof, 1988-; Washtenaw Community Col, Ann Arbor, MI, adjunct prof, 1989-; Univ Calif, Los Angeles, mgt fel, 1993; Wayne County Regional Educ Serv Agency, dir, 1994-99; Washtenaw Co Head Start, dir, 1999-. **Orgs:** Sec Huron Valley Asn Black Social Workers, 1971-; head start consult, Wayne Co, Washtenaw Co, Region V, Emprise Design, CSR, 1980; planning comnr, City Ypsilanti, 1982-96; bd mem, Huron Valley Girl Scouts, 1983-, second vpres, 1988-94; pres, Ann Arbor Delta Sigma Theta, 1985-87; Nat Asn Social Workers; Zoning Bd Appeals City Ypsilanti; vpres, Mich Coun, Delta Sigma Theta Sorority. **Honors/Awds:** Program of Achievement Award, Nat Head Start Asn, 1999. **Home Addr:** 925 Frederick St, Ypsilanti, MI 48197. **Business Addr:** Director, Washtenaw Co Head Start, 1661 Leforge Rd, Ypsilanti, MI 48197, **Business Phone:** (734)484-7119.

HORNSBY, DR. ALTON, JR.
Educator, editor, college teacher. **Personal:** Born Sep 3, 1940, Atlanta, GA; married Anne R; children: Alton III & Angela. **Educ:** Morehouse Col, BA, hist, 1961; Univ Tex, MA, hist, 1962, PhD, hist, 1969. **Career:** Southern Educ Found fel, 1966-68; Woodrow Wilson fel, 1961-62; Tuskegee Inst, instr hist, 1962-65; independent ed, 1975; Morehouse Col, Dept Hist, asst prof, actg chmn, 1968-71, assoc prof, 1971-74, chmn, 1971-98, prof,1974, Fuller E Callaway prof hist, 1989-; Rockefeller Humanities fel, 1977-78; Ed bd, Atlanta Hist J; ed bd, Western J Black Studies; ed, JNegro Hist. **Orgs:** Chmn, St Comt Life & Hist Black Georgians, 1968-; Exec comt mem, Asn Study Afro-Am Life & Hist, 1977-; Danforth Found Assoc, 1978-81; pres & adv comt mem, Southern Conf Afro-Am Studies, 1979-; pres & prog comt chair, Asn Soc & Behavioral Scientists, 1984-85; int comt mem & exec comt mem, Southern Hist Asn, 1988-; Conf Ed Hist J; Plantation Socs Am; Nat CounBlack Studies; Orgn Am Historians; Ga Asn Historians; Phi Alpha Theta; PhiBeta Kappa. **Honors/Awds:** Teacher of the Year, Alpha Phi Alpha, Morehouse Col, 1971-72; Distinguished Scholar Award, United Negro Col Fund, 1982-83; WEB DuBoisAward, 1989; Atlanta Regional Fed Employers Award, 1989; Distinguished Serv Award, Ga Asn Historians, 1990; Distinguished Historian Award, APEXMus, 1993. **Special Achievements:** Ed: The Dictionary of 20th Century Black Leaders, 1985; The John and Lugenia Burns Hope Papers, 1975-84; The Journal of Negro History, 1976-; author, works include: In the Cage: Eyewitness Accounts of the Freed Negroin Southern Society 1987-29, 1971; The Black Almanac, 4th rev edition, 1977; The Negro in Revolutionary Georgia, 1972; Chronology of African-American History, 1991; Milestones in 20th-Century African-American History, 1993; articles and reviews in: Journal of Negro History; Journal of American History; Alabama Historical Review; and numerous others; lecturer: Ohio State Univ; Martin Luther King Jr Historic District; Paine College; Jackson State Univ; numerous others; consultant: So Assn of Colleges and Secondary Schools; National Endowment for the Humanities; Georgia Endowment for the Humanities; National Research Council; "Black Public Education in Atlanta, Georgia: From Segregation to Segregation," Journal of Negro History, 1991. **Business Addr:** Fuller E Callaway Professor, Morehouse College, Department History, 830 Westview Dr SW, Atlanta, GA 30314-3773.*

HORRY, ROBERT KEITH
Basketball player. **Personal:** Born Aug 25, 1970, Hartford, MD; son of Robert Sr and Lelia; married Keva I Develle, Jul 5, 1997; children: Robert Cameron & Ashlyn. **Educ:** Univ Ala. **Career:** Houston Rockets, forward, 1992-96; Phoenix Suns, 1997; Los Angeles Lakers, forward, 1996-2003; San Antonio Spurs, forward-ctr, 2004-. **Honors/Awds:** All-Rookie Second Team, Nat Basketball Asn, 1993; Championship, Nat Basketball Asn, 1994, 1995. **Special Achievements:** First round pick, No 11, Nat Basketball Asn Draft, 1992; TV show appearances: David Letterman Show, Episode 398, 1995; Jack and Jill, Episode 4, 1999; Passion Soap Opera, Episodes 62, 66-67, 1999. **Business Addr:** Professional Basketball Player, San Antonio Spurs, 1 AT&T Ctr, San Antonio, TX 78219, **Business Phone:** (210)444-5000.

HORSFORD, ANNA MARIA
Television producer, actor. **Personal:** Born Mar 6, 1948, New York, NY; daughter of Victor A and Lillian Agatha Richardson. **Educ:** Inter-Am Univ Puerto Rico, attended 1967; Manhattan's Sch Performing Arts. **Career:** Stage appearances: Coriolanus, 1965; In the Well of the House, 1972; Perfection in Black, 1973; Les Femmes Noires, 1974; Sweet Talk, 1975; For Colored Girls Who Have Considered Suicide/When the Rainbow Is Enuf, 1978;Peep, 1981; Movies: An Almost Perfect Affair, 1979; Times Square, 1980; The Fan, 1981; Love Child, 1982; Class, 1983; Crackers, 1984; Presumed Innocent, 1990; Mr. Jones, 1993; Once Upon a Time When We Were Colored, 1995; One Fine Day, 1996; Set It Off, 1996; Dear God, 1996; Kiss the Girls, 1997; At Face Value, 1999; Dancing in September, 2000; Nutty Professor II: The Klumps, 2000; Jacked, 2001; Along Came a Spider, 2001; How High, 2001; Minority Report, 2002; Friday After Next, 2002; Justice, 2004; Guarding Eddy, 2004; My Big Phat Hip Hop Family, 2005; Ganked, 2005; Angel from Montgomery, 2006; Broken Bridges, 2006; Gridiron Gang, 2006; Trade, 2007; I Tried, 2007; Pretty Ugly People, 2008; TV appearances: "The Good News", 1978; "Watch Your Mouth", producer, 1978; "An Almost Perfect Affair". 1978; "The Guiding Light,"1979; "Times Square," 1979; "Love Child," 1981; "Bill," 1981; "Crackers,"1982; "Benny's Place," 1982; "A Doctor's Story". 1984; "Nobody's Child"; "Amen," 1986-91; "Rhythm & Blues," 1992-; "The Wayans Bros"; "The Chronicle", 2002; "The Bernie Mac Show", 2004;

"Entourage", 2005-06; "The Shield, 2005-08; "Entourage", 2005; "Heist", 2006; "Grey's Anatomy", 2005-07; "Everybody Hates Chris", 2008; "Las Vegas", 2008. **Orgs:** Variety Club Am; pres, Black Women Theatre, 1983-84; Screen Actors Guild,Am Fedn TV & Radio Artists; Actor's Equity; Sigma Gamma Rho Sorority Inc. **Honors/Awds:** Best Comedy Actress, Brooklyn Links, 1963; Outstanding Leadership Award, NAACP, 1973.

HORTON, ANDRE (ANDREANA SUK HORTON)
Skier. **Personal:** Born Oct 4, 1979, Anchorage, AK. **Career:** Skier (retired), exec; Stewart Sports, skier; Nat Brotherhood Skiers, nat youth dir & competition dir, currently. **Orgs:** US Ski & Snow Bd Asn, athlete bd rep, currently; AK state champion, 1998; First place, Mt Bachelor's NW Cup Finals, 2001. **Special Achievements:** First African American selected to US Ski Team Develp Prog, 2000; First African American to win an FIS race in Europe, 2001. **Business Addr:** National Youth Director, Competition Director, National Brotherhood of Skiers, 525 E 53rd St Suite 418, Chicago, IL 60615.

HORTON, ANDREANA SUK. See HORTON, ANDRE.

HORTON, ANDREANA SUKI (SUKI HORTON)
Skier. **Personal:** Born May 3, 1982, Anchorage, AK; daughter of Garry and Elsena. **Educ:** Univ Alaska Anchorage, BS, jour & pub rels, currently. **Career:** National Brotherhood of Skiers, Western Region Elite Ski Team, mem & competition dir, currently. **Orgs:** Nat Brotherhood Skiers Ski Club. **Honors/Awds:** US Ski Teams Junior Development Croup, 1997; AK State Champion, 1998; second pl, Western Region Downhill FIS series, 2001; Athlete of the Year, NBS, 2001; ranked No 1 in Age Group. **Special Achievements:** Fifth American at Snow Basin Nor Ams.

HORTON, CARL E.
Marketing executive, chief executive officer, president (organization). **Personal:** Born Apr 11, 1944, Philadelphia, PA; son of W S Horton and Dorothy L; married Phyllis Sims, Apr 1, 1969; children: Meredith & Carl Jr. **Educ:** Morgan State Col, BA, 1967; Univ Pa, Wharton Grad Div, MBA, 1972. **Career:** Executive (retired); Gen Foods Corp, asst prod mgr, 1972-73; Xerox Corp, sr mkt consult, 1973-76; Heublein Inc, prod mgr, 1976-80; Jos E Seagram,sr prod mgr, 1980-86, group mkt dir, 1986-87, vpres group mkt dir,1987-92, dir bus dev, 1992-94; Absolut Vodka, vpres mkt, 1994; AbsolutSpirits Co, pres & chief exec officer, 2001. **Orgs:** Kappa Alpha Psi Fraternity, Stamford Alumni, Morgan State Col, 1965-; advbd, CEBA Awards, 1989-; bd dir, Cigna, NY, 1990-. **Honors/Awds:** Black Achievers Award, NY City YMCA, 1985; Blackbook Awards, Dollars &Sense Mag, 1990. **Military Serv:** AUS, 1967-69.

HORTON, DR. CARRELL PETERSON
Educator, college teacher. **Personal:** Born Nov 28, 1928, Daytona Beach, FL; daughter of Preston S Peterson and Mildred Adams; divorced; children: Richard. **Educ:** Fisk Univ, BA, 1949; Cornell Univ, MA, 1950; Univ Chicago, PhD, 1972. **Career:** Cornell Univ, grad asst, 1949-50; Fisk Univ, instr & res assoc, 1950-55; Meharry Med Col, stat anal, 1955-66; Fisk Univ, prof psychol & admin, 1966, Div Social Sci, dir, dean acad affairs, 1996-99, Dept Psychol, chair, emer prof, currently; Ford Found, IBM, fac fel, 1969-71; Health Serv Res, consult, 1977-80; NSF, consult, 1979; Nat Res Coun, consult, 1979; Fisk Univ, Acad Affairs, Dean, 1996-97. **Orgs:** Bd dir, Rochelle Training Ctr, 1968-84; bd dir, Wesley Found, 1977; bd dir, Samaritan Pastoral Coun Ctr, 1983; Bd Higher Educ & Campus Ministry, UM Church, 1983-86; bd mem, 18th Ave Family Enrichment Ctr, 2000-. **Honors/Awds:** Urban League Award, Jacksonville, FL, 1949; article in professional journals. **Home Addr:** 2410 Buchanan St, Nashville, TN 37208-1937. **Business Addr:** Emeritus Professor, Fisk University, 1000 17th Ave N, Nashville, TN 37208-3051.*

HORTON, CLARENCE MICHAEL
Executive. **Personal:** Born in Chicago, IL. **Career:** Capital Rec; Interscope Rec; Universal Rec, sr vpres prom, currently. **Business Addr:** Senior Vice President of Promotions, Universal Records, 1755 Broadway 7th Fl, New York, NY 10019, **Business Phone:** (212)373-0600.

HORTON, DOLLIE BEA DIXON
Executive. **Personal:** Born Apr 19, 1942, Fort Valley, GA; daughter of Lillian Byrd Dixon and Hezzie Dixon; married Cornelious Horton Jr, Nov 3, 1963; children: Alre Giovanni & Roderick Cornelious. **Educ:** Fort Valley State Col, Fort Valley, GA, BS, 1964, MS, 1974; Atlanta Univ, cert, French, 1966; USAF, cert, 1974; Univ Mich, Ann Arbor, MI, cert, 1975; Thomason Real Estate Sch cert, 1978; Phelps-Stokes, Wash, DC, cert, 1978; Am Asn Community & Jr Cols, Kiawah Island, SC, cert, 1982; Georgia Ins Pre-license Sch, cert, 1988. **Career:** Pearl Stephens High Sch, Warner Robins, GA, teacher, 1964-67; Fort Valley State Col, admin asst, 1967-74, asst dir develop & placement, 1974-76, acting dir col & community rels, 1976-77, dir col & community rels, 1977-80; HA Hunt High Sch, Fort Valley, GA, teacher, Spanish, 1968-69; Peach County Bd Educ, Fort Valley, GA, adult educ teacher, 1969-71; Warner Robins Air Logistics Ctr, Robins Air Force Base, GA, personnel staffing specialist, 1980-82; Valmedia

Inc, owner, 1982; City Fort Valley, Utility Bd Comnrs, 1995-; Fort Valley State Univ, Pub Serv Ctr, dir, 1999-. **Orgs:** Bd dirs, Peach County Fort Valley Chamber Com; Int Toastmistress Clubs Am; vpres, Gia Coalition Black Women; Ga Asn Broadcasters; Nat Asn Broadcasters; Fort Valley State Col Comt Chamber Com; Mid Ga Minority Media Asn; Vogue Socialite Club. **Honors/Awds:** Black Georgian of the Year, 1983; Radio Station Owner of the Year, 1983; Broadcaster of the Year, Black Col Radio. **Business Addr:** Director, Fort Valley State University, 1005 State Univ Dr, Fort Valley, GA 31030, **Business Phone:** (478)825-6060.

HORTON, EARLE C
Lawyer. **Personal:** Born Mar 9, 1943, Tampa, FL; son of Earle Horton and Helen Belton Horton; children: Brett & Earle III. **Educ:** Fisk Univ, BA, 1964; Cleveland State Univ, JD, 1968. **Career:** Thunder Bay Community, pres; Graves & Horton LLC, atty, currently. **Orgs:** First Black Law Firm OH; spec coun Atty Gen OH; Am Bar Asn; OH State Bar Asn; Cleveland Bar Asn; John Harlan Law Club; Cleveland Fisk Univ Club; NAACP, Urban League, Norman Minor Bar Assoc. **Honors/Awds:** Recipient Meritorious Service Award, Cleveland Bar Asn, 1971; District Service Award, John Harlan Law Club, 1973. **Business Phone:** (216)696-2022.

HORTON, JOANN
College administrator, executive, consultant. **Personal:** Born in Lenoir, NC. **Educ:** Appalachian State Univ, BA, MA, fr; Ohio State Univ, PhD, higher educ admin. **Career:** Olive-Harvey Col, curric coordr, acad vpres, provost; Tenn Dept Gen Serv, asst comnr; Iowa Community Col System, state adminr; Tex Southern Univ, pres, 1993-95; Am Coun Educ, sr fel, 1995-; Kennedy-King Col, Chicago, pres, 1998; Baltimore City Community Coll, acting vpres, 2005, interim vpres acad affairs, chief acad officer; Team Masters Inc, founder & pres, currently; Pac Crest, chief oper officer, inst facilitator, currently. **Honors/Awds:** Distinguished Alumnus, Appalachian State Univ; Commendation from House Chamber, Tex Legis, 1995. **Special Achievements:** First female president of Texas Southern University. **Business Addr:** Institute Facilitator, Chief Operating Officer, Pacific Crest, 906 Lacey Ave Suite 211, Lisle, IL 60532, **Business Phone:** (630)737-1067.

HORTON, LARKIN, JR.
Executive, consultant. **Personal:** Born Feb 18, 1939, Lenoir, NC; married Patricia Richardson; children: Larkin III & Gregory Derwin. **Educ:** Catawba Valley Tech Inst, assoc elect, 1960; Gen Electric Control Sch, Master Controls, 1961; Clever-Brooks Pressure Vessels, Cert Pressure Vessels, 1961; Caldwell Community Col, Cert Powder Activated Tools, 1972; Cert massage therapy, 1998. **Career:** Executive (retired); E Finley Auto Laundry, owner; City Lenoir, councilman; Horton's Electric Co, owner & contractor; prof photographer; Elec Consult & Safety Specialist, ANSI, NIOSHA, & UL, instr. **Orgs:** Trustee, St Paul AME Ch; bd dir, Nat Cancer Soc; Caldwell Friends Inc, 1984-85; Gov Crime Prevention Comn; inspector, Int Asn Elect Inspectors; bd mem, Nat Cancer Soc, 1983. **Honors/Awds:** Value Analysis Award, Burlington Ind, 1980-82; Man of the Year, Am Legion, 1984; Lenoir Police Explorer Post 246, Appreciation Plaque, 1990; first Volunteer Service Award, 1986; Resolution Appreciation, City Lenoir, Lenoir City coun, Key City, 1991; Dr Martin Luther King Jr Award, 1991; Richard Allen Humanitarian Award, St Paul Am Chap, 2003. **Home Addr:** 445 Arlington Cir NW, PO Box 242, Lenoir, NC 28645-1256, **Home Phone:** (828)754-4267. *

HORTON, LARNIE G., SR.
Government official, clergy. **Personal:** Married Katrena B; children: Larnie Glenn, Jr, Langston Garvey. **Educ:** Morris Brown Col, AB; Univ NC, Chapel Hill; Duke Univ, MDiv; Nat Theo Sem & Col. **Career:** Saxapaw, NC, pastor, 1960-64; Kittrell Col, NC, acad dean, 1961-62, pres, 1966-73; Emanuel AME Church, Durham, pastor, 1964-66; Gov Minority Affairs, spec asst, 1973-. **Orgs:** Bd trustees, Vance County Tech Inst, 1968; bd dir, Soul City Found, 1968; bd dir, Nat Lab Higher Educ, 1970; consult, Am Asn Jr Col, 1970-72; Nat Asn Advan Colored People; Merchants Asn Chapel Hill; Alpha Phi Alpha Fraternity; C of C, Henderson, NC; fel Woodrow Wilson & Rockefeller; bd giv, Univ NC Sixteen Constituent Insts. **Honors/Awds:** Nat Alumni Asn Award, Stillman Col, 1970; Civic Achievement Award, Morris Brown Col, Nat Alumni Asn.

HORTON, LEMUEL LEONARD
Manager. **Personal:** Born Jun 29, 1936, Fort Valley, GA; married Yvonne Felton; children: Lorna Y Hill. **Educ:** Fort Valley State Col, BS, 1964. **Career:** Civil Serv Robins AFB, Ga, warehouseman, 1958-65; State Ga, community serv consult, 1965-68; Ft Valley State Col, dir stud union, 1968-71; Res Group, assoc, 1971-73; New York Life, field underwriter, 1973-; Gold Kist Inc, mgr employee rels, 1973-. **Orgs:** Pres, Resurgens Int Asn Quality Circles, IRRA, 1980-81; pres, vpres & bd mem, Ga Chap Epilepsy Found; pres, TAPS Epilepsy Found; Int Mentoring Asn. **Honors/Awds:** Presidential Citation, Nat Asn Equal Opportunities Higher Educ, 1983. **Military Serv:** AUS, sp2, 3 yrs; AUS, Res command sgt, maj, 40 yrs; Army Achievement Medal, 1982, Army Commendation Medal, 1983, Meritorious Service Medal, 1986. **Business Addr:** Manager, Gold Kist Inc, 244 Perimeter Ctr Pkwy NE, PO Box 2210, Atlanta, GA 30346-2397, **Business Phone:** (770)393-5000.

HORTON, OSCAR J
Executive. **Personal:** Born Jul 22, 1952, Camden, AR; married Miriam; children: Kelli & Alisan. **Educ:** Univ Ark, psychol. **Career:** International Truck & Engine: Credit Co, Oper Mgr Mfg, VP Labor Relations, vpres & gen mgr; Sun State Int Trucks, pres & owner, currently. **Orgs:** Tampa Chamber Com, 1999; Tampa Urban League, 2000; USF Stavros Ctr, 2002; In-Roads, 2002; bd mem, Tampa Museum Art, 2002; bd mem, Goodwill Ind, Sun Coast, 2002; bd trustees, USF Found, 2003; bd mem, Bank Tampa, 2004; Boys & Girls Club Tampa. **Business Addr:** President, Owner, Sun State International Trucks LLC, 6020 Adamo Dr, Tampa, FL 33619, **Business Phone:** (813)621-1331.

HORTON, RAYMOND ANTHONY
Football player, football coach. **Personal:** Born Apr 12, 1960, Tacoma, WA; married Leslie; children: Taylor. **Educ:** Univ Wash, BA, soc, 1983. **Career:** Football player (retired), football coach; Cincinnati Bengals, corner back,nickel back & safety, 1983-88, coach, 1997-2001; Dallas Cowboys, safety, 1989-92; Long Shots, driving range, Seattle, WA, owner; Wash Redskins, asst defensive backs coach, 1994-96; Detroit Lions, sec coach, 2002-03; Pittsburgh Steelers, asst defensive backs coach, 2004-07, defensive backs coach, 2007-. **Orgs:** Organizer, Ray Hope Food Dr, Dallas, TX. **Business Addr:** Defensive Backs Coach, Pittsburgh Steelers, 3400 S Water St, Pittsburgh, PA 15203, **Business Phone:** (412)432-7800.

HORTON, STELLA JEAN
Management consultant, teacher, executive director. **Personal:** Born Aug 16, 1944, Durham, NC; children: Braheim Knight. **Educ:** St Augustine's Col, attended 1964; A&T State Univ, BS, 1966; State Univ Rutgers, MEd, 1972, EdD, 1986. **Career:** Orange County Bd Educ, teacher, 1966-69; Rutgers State Univ, assoc prof, 1970-76; Alternative Sch, Camden Bd Educ, teacher & prin, 1976-80; Camden Ctr Youth Develop, exec dir, 1980-; Educ Training & Enterprise Ctr, sr mgt consult & sr training specialist, currently. **Orgs:** Consult, NJ Dept Educ, 1980-84; Urban League Camden Co, 1981-83; vpres, Camden City Bd Educ, 1983-84, 1980-; 5th Legislative Dist, NJ Sch Bds, 1983-. **Honors/Awds:** Serv Young People, Juvenile Resource Ctr Inc, 1979; Community Serv, NJ Asn Black Social Workers, 1982. **Home Addr:** 1412 Van Hook St, Camden, NJ 08104. **Business Addr:** Senior Management Consultant, Senior Training Specialist, Education Training Enterprise Center, 313 Market St, Camden, NJ 08102.*

HORTON, SUKI. See HORTON, ANDREANA SUKI.

HORTON, WILLIE WATTISON
Baseball player, baseball executive. **Personal:** Born Oct 18, 1942, Arno, VA; married Lillian. **Career:** Baseball player (retired), baseball executive; Detroit Tigers, out fielder, 1963-77, comt mem, 2000, spec asst to pres, 2003-; Tex Rangers, outfielder, 1977; Cleveland Indians, outfielder, 1978; Oakland Athletics, outfielder, 1978; Toronto Blue Jays, outfielder, 1978; Seattle Mariners, outfielder, 1979-80. **Honors/Awds:** American League All-Star Team, 1965, 1968, 1970, 1973; Most Valuable Player, Seattle Mariners, 1979; American League Comeback Player of the Year, Sporting News, 1979; Afro-American Sports Hall of Fame, 1992; Namedin honor, The Willie Horton Baseball and Softball Diamonds, 2004. **Special Achievements:** First black ballplayer so honored by the Tigers, stands next to the statue of Ty Cobb, a noted racist; Biography, "The People's Champion: Willie Horton", Immortal Investments Publ, 2005. **Business Addr:** Special Assistant to the President, Detroit Tigers, 2100 Woodward Ave, Detroit, MI 48201, **Business Phone:** (313)471-2255.

HOSKINS, MICHELE
Executive. **Personal:** Divorced. **Career:** Michele Foods Inc, owner, founder & chief exec officer, 1984-. **Honors/Awds:** The Entrepreneurial Women Award, 1998; Madam Walker Entrepreneurial Award, 1999; Phenomenal Women Award, 2000; Entrepreneur of the Year, Womens Foodservices Forum, 2002. **Special Achievements:** Author: Sweet Expectations: Michele Hoskins' Recipe for Success, 2004; First African American vendor with Costco!. **Business Phone:** (708)331-7316.

HOSKINS CLARK, TEMPY M.
Educator. **Personal:** Born Oct 25, 1938, Hazen, AK; married Wilber L Hoskins; children: Jamele, Monroe & Brian McKissic. **Educ:** Philander Smith Col, BA, 1963; Western MI Univ, MA, 1971. **Career:** Grand Rapids Bd Educ, elem prin; McKinley Upper Grade Ctr Chicago IL, vocal music teacher; S Middle Sch Grand Rapids MI, vocal music teacher, chmn. **Orgs:** Minister, mus True Light Bapt Ch Grand Rapids; bd dir, Blue Lake Fine Arts Camp; pres, Negro Bus & Prof Club Inc; Delta Sigma Theta Sor; pres, local chap Delta Sigma Theta; travel abroad summer, 1972 with hs students Belgium Holland England & France.

HOSTEN, DR. ADRIAN OLIVER
Physician, educator. **Personal:** Born in Grenada, WI; married Claire C; children: Karen & Lester. **Educ:** Atlantic Union Col, BA, 1958; Howard Univ, MD, 1962. **Career:** Bates Memorial High Sch, prin, 1954-55, instr, 1966-68, asst prof,1968-72; Med Intensive Care Unit Howard Univ Hosp, dir, 1968-75; Howard

Univ, chief nephrology div, 1967-87; assoc prof, 1972-82; prof 1982-; chmn Dept med, 1988-. **Orgs:** Nat Med Asn, 1968-; Am Soc Nephrology, 1971-; Int Soc Nephrology, 1973-; Fel Am Col Physicians . **Business Addr:** Chairman, Howard University Hosp, 2041 Georgia Ave Nw, Washington, DC 20060.*

HOUSE, JAMES E.
Executive, consultant. **Personal:** Born in Goldsboro, NC; son of Edward AE and Cleo Peoples. **Educ:** Howard Univ, BS, mech eng, 1963. **Career:** McDonnell Douglas Corp, St Louis, test & struct engr, 1963-67; Fairchild Hiller Corp, stress analyst, 1967-68; Boeing Co Seattle, res engr, 1968-72; Eckenberge Group, Wash, DC, pres, 1970-; WIPCO Inc St Croix,vpres treas, 1972-77; Nat Asn Minority CPA Firms, Govt DC, Jones & Artis Co Wash, DC, consult, 1981-86; JBH Assocs, consult, 1986-87; USDA, Off Small & Disadvantaged Bus Utilization, sr exec serv, dir, 1991-93, Off Small & Disadvantaged Bus Utilization, Dep Agr, dir, currently; DMBE, VA, dir, 1994-96. **Orgs:** Pres, Stud Govt Sch Eng & Arch, Howard Univ, 1962; secy, Republican Cent Comn Prince Georges County, MD, 1982-84; chmn, Md Frederick Douglass Scholar Fund, 1984-; Va Black Republican Coun, 1984-96; VI C C Econ Develop Comn, VI Businessmens Asn, Minority Bus Develop Org, St Croix Howard Univ Alumni Asn, Alpha Phi Omega; chmn, Black Republican Coun Prince Georges County, MD, 1984-85; co-chmn, Reagan-Bush, 1984; Comn Prince Georges County, MD, 1984; chmn, Md Black Republican Coun, 1985-87; vicechmn, Md State Republican Party, 1986-90; bd mem, Nat Coun 100, 1986-; Nat Asn African Am Bus Owners, pres, 1989-; Comt Purchase From People Who Are Blind or Severley Disabled, Ability One. **Honors/Awds:** Civil Rights Student Leader, 1959-62; Touring Debater Intl AFSC Peace Caravan, 1960; Service Award, Alpha Phi Omega, 1961; Distinguished Military Student Award, 1962; The News American Baltimore, 1974; Memorial Year Award, Nat Asn Black Mfgrs Inc, 1975; Achievement Award, Estate Profit Civic Asn VI, 1978; Achievement Award, Nat Asn Minority CPA Firms Wash DC, 1978; Achievement Award, Md Minority Contractors Asn, 1986-87; Republican of the Year, 1987; elected delegate, White House Conf Small Bus, 1986; Bush delegate, Md Republican Nat Convention, 1988; md chmn, Nat Black Republican Coun, Bush-Cheney, 2000. **Home Addr:** 14011 Old Stage Rd Suite A, Bowie, MD 20720, **Home Phone:** (301)262-7714. **Business Addr:** Director, Office of Small and Disadvantaged Business Utilization, Department of Agriculture, 14th & Independence Ave SW 1566 S Bldg, Washington, DC 20250-9501, **Business Phone:** (202)720-7117.

HOUSE, KYLA N
Administrator. **Career:** Am Elec Power, col rels adminr, currently. **Orgs:** Leadership Tulsa Class 29; bd mem, YMCA. **Business Addr:** College Relations Administrator, American Electric Power, 212 E 6th St, Tulsa, OK 74119, **Business Phone:** (918)599-2677.*

HOUSE, MICHAEL A
Journalist. **Personal:** Born Jul 13, 1941, Louisville, KY; son of William T Hodges and Jamesetta; married Doris J House; children: Robert, Margoit & William; married Doris J House. **Educ:** Howard Univ, attended 1965; Baruch Col, City Univ New York, MBA, 1974. **Career:** Ford Motor Co, staff; Mobil Oil Corp, staff; Rockwell Int; Amalgamated Pub Inc, pres; Call & Post Newspapers Inc, pres & chief operating officer; Mayor Frank G Jackson, Cleveland, OH, press secy & spokesman; Cleveland's Cable TV Public Access Channel, gen mgr, 2006-08; Chicago Defender, pres, 2008-. **Orgs:** Pres, Nat Asn Market Developers; 100 Black Men New Jersey; Urban League Greater Cleveland; The Hunger Network; Minority Organ Transplant Educ Prog. **Honors/Awds:** Publisher of the Year, Natl Newspaper Publ Asn, 2003. Publisher of the Year, Philadelphia Tribune. **Military Serv:** AUS, first lt, 1965-67. **Business Addr:** President, Founder, Executive Director, Chicago Defender, 200 S Mich Ave, Chicago, IL 44120-1396, **Business Phone:** (312)225-2400.

HOUSE, MILLARD L.
Educator, founder (originator), school administrator. **Personal:** Born Jan 28, 1944, Langston, OK; married Anna Shumate; children: Milton, Signee & Millard II. **Educ:** Langston Univ, BA, 1966; Northeastern St Col, MA, 1971. **Career:** Gilcrease Jr HS, soc sci instr, 1966-70; Dept Human Rel Tulsa Pub Sch, dir, 1970-; Marian Anderson Elem Sch, sch adminr; KIPP Tulsa Col Preparatory, founder & prin, currently. **Orgs:** NEA OK Educ Asn; Supvrs & Dir, Tulsa Asn Curric; Tulsa Pub Sch Affirmative Action Com; Urban League; Nat Asn Advan Colored People; Langston Univ Alumni Asn; YMCA; Kappa Alpha Psi; Phi Delta Kappa; Royal Housa Club; StJohn's Bapt Ch; Mayor's Comn Comt Relations. **Honors/Awds:** Outstanding Young Men Am Award, US Jaycees, 1973; Kappa Yr Award, Kappa Alpha Psi 1974-75; Principal of the Year; Outstanding Administrator of the Year.

HOUSE, N GERRY
School administrator. **Personal:** Married Lee; children: 2. **Educ:** NC A&T Univ, BS; Southern Ill Univ, MS; Univ NC, Chapel Hill, PhD. **Career:** Teacher; jr & sr high sch guidance coun; prin & asst suptd; Memphis City Schs, supt; Inst Stud Achievement, pres, chief exec officer, 2000-. **Orgs:** Am Asn Sch Admin; Phi Delta

Kappa; Nat Asn Black Sch Educrs; bd dir Woodrow Wilson Found; Nat Adv bd Nat Ctr Study Privatization Educ; bd trustees, Adelphi Univ; bd trustees Educal Testing Serv, 2002-05. **Honors/Awds:** Phi Delta Kappa Leadership Award; Martin Luther King Achievement Award; Communicator Year, Memphis Chap Pub Rels Soc; Richard R Green Award for Urban Educ, 1998; Nat Supt Year, Am Asn Sch Admin, 1999; Harold W McGraw Award for Excellence in Educ, 1999; Alumni Leadership Award, Univ NC, 2000; Doctorate Educ Admin, Univ NC; Hon Doctor of Humanities Degrees, Rhodes Col & Lemoyne Owen Col, Memphis, TN. **Special Achievements:** Named twice to the Executive Educator Magazine's listing of Top 100 Executive Educators in Education; Honored by Long Island Business News Magazine for Commitment to Fostering Excellence in Education, 2005. **Business Addr:** President, Chief Ececutive Officer, Institute for Student Achievement, 1 Hollow Lane Suite 100, Lake Success, NY 11042-1215, **Business Phone:** (516)812-6700.

HOUSTON, ALICE K.
Executive. **Educ:** Univ Louisville, MS, stud personnel serv, 1975. **Career:** Univ Louisville, asst & assoc dir financial aide; Johnson-Houston Corp, dir admin & finance; Houston-Johnson Inc, vpres admin; Active Transp Co, pres; Automotive Carrier Serv, chief exec officer, currently. **Orgs:** Nat Urban League; African Am Venture Capital Fund; Muhammad Ali Ctr; Reg Leadership Coalition; Community Partnership Bd; Jewish Hosp HealthCare Serv Bd; W Louisville Econ Alliance Adv Comt. **Special Achievements:** Black Enterprise's Top 100 Industrial/Service companies, ranked #38, 1999, #24, 2000. **Business Addr:** Chief Executive Officer, Automotive Carrier Services Inc, 620 W Shipp Ave Suite A, Louisville, KY 40208, **Business Phone:** (502)635-7440.*

HOUSTON, DR. ALICE V.
Educator. **Personal:** Born in Baton Rouge, LA. **Educ:** S Univ, BA, 1953; La State Univ, MEd, 1956; Univ Tex, PhD, 1974. **Career:** Educator (retired); teacher, 1953-68; S Greenville Elem Sch, Baton Rouge, prin, 1968-69; Beechwood Elem Sch, E Baton Rouge Parish Sch Bd, prin, 1969-75; E Baton Rouge Parish Sch, supr res & prog eval, 1976-77, supr eval state & fed progs, 1976; Okla City Pub Schs, dir curriculum, 1977-82; Seattle Pub Schs, asst supt, 1982-91; Human Resources Recruitment & Develop, dir, 1991-96, Early Childhood Educ, dir, 1996-98. **Orgs:** Exec coun, Asn Supvr & Curric Develop, 1979-81; exec bd, Nat Alliance Black Sch Educr, 1975-79; Phi Delta Kappa; Kappa Delta Pi; Nat Advan Asn Colored People; Zeta Phi Beta; bd dirs, United Way King Co. **Honors/Awds:** Award, Plaque Girl Scouts 1964; Award, Plaque Zeta Phi Zeta, 1970; Award, Doctoral Fed Univ Tex, 1972-73; Outstanding Serv, Nat Alliance Black Sch Educrs Recognition, 1974-77, 1977-79; Outstanding Prin of Year, 1975; Outstanding Contrib Area Educ, 1977; Citizen of the Year, Omega Psi Phi Recognition, 1981; Award, All Stud Okla City Okla Black Liberated Arts Ctr, 1982; Award providing Excellence in Educ, Benefit Guild Asn Martin Luther King Jr, 1985; Award of Merit for Community, Serv Alpha Phi Alpha, 1986. **Home Addr:** 1802 17th Ave, Seattle, WA 98122. *

HOUSTON, ALLAN WADE
Executive, basketball player. **Personal:** Born Apr 20, 1971, Louisville, KY; son of Wade; married Tamara, Aug 24, 1996; children: Remie, Allan, Rowan & Jade. **Educ:** Univ Tenn, BA, african Am studies. **Career:** Basketball player (retired), exec; Detroit Pistons, guard, 1994-96; NY Knicks, guard, 1996-2005; ESPN Radio, broadcaster; Top Gun Leather, founder, currently; Allan Houston Enterprises Inc, pres & chief exec officer, currently; H2O Prods, founder & pres, currently; NY Knicks, asst to the pres for basketball operations, currently; UNK NBA. co found, currently. **Orgs:** Founder & pres, Allan Houston Found, currently; Kappa Alpha Psi Inc. **Special Achievements:** First round, 11th pick, NBA Draft, 1993. **Business Addr:** Founder, President, Allan Houston Foundation, 350 5th Ave Suite 5936, New York, NY 10031, **Business Phone:** 800-806-8647.

HOUSTON, BOBBY
Football player. **Personal:** Born Oct 26, 1967, Washington, DC; children: Taylor. **Educ:** NC State Univ. **Career:** Green Bay Packers, linebacker, 1990; NY Jets, 1991-96; Kans City Chiefs, 1997; San Diego Chargers, 1997-98; Minn Vikings, linebacker, 1998.

HOUSTON, CISSY (EMILY CISSY DRINKARD HOUSTON)
Gospel singer. **Personal:** Born Sep 30, 1933, Newark, NJ; daughter of Nicholas (deceased) and Delia (deceased); married John (divorced 1993); children: Whitney; married Freddie Garland (divorced 1956); children: Gary. **Career:** Drinkard Singers, mem; Sweet Inspirations, gospel group singer, 1963-69;Albums: Sweet Inspiration, 1968; What the World Needs Now is Love, 1968; Cissy Houston, 1971; Cissy Houston, Private Stock, 1977; Warning Danger, 1979; Step Aside for a Lady, 1980; (with Chuck Jackson) I'll Take Care of You, 1992; Face to Face, 1996; Presenting Cissy Houston; The Long & Winding Road; Cissy Houston; Think It Over, Warning Danger; Step Aside For A Lady; I'll Take Care Of You, 1992; Face To Face; Atlantic Rec; Muscle Shoals; New York; night club singer, currently; New Hope Baptist Church, Radio Choir, dir, currently; TV: "Taking My Turn", 1984; " Vernon John's Story', 1994; Film: The Wiz, 1978; The Preachers

Wife, 1996. **Orgs:** Ceo & pres, Whitney Houston Found, 1988-. **Honors/Awds:** Medal for Distinguished Humanitarian Leadership, Univ Med & Dent, NJ, 1992; Pioneer Award, Rhythm & Blues Found, 1995; Grammy Award for Best Traditional Soul Gospel Album, 1996 & 1998. **Special Achievements:** Film: T Author: How Sweet the Sound: My Life with God & Gospel, 1998. she recorded the song "Family First" for the soundtrack to the movie Daddy's Little Girls in 2006. **Business Addr:** Singer, c/o House of Blues Music, 8439 Sunset Blvd Suite 404, West Hollywood, CA 90069, **Business Phone:** (323)848-5100.*

HOUSTON, IVAN J
Insurance executive. **Personal:** Born Jun 15, 1925, Los Angeles, CA; son of Norman O Houston and Doris Talbot Young; married Philippa Jones; children: Pamela, Kathi & Ivan A. **Educ:** Univ Calif Berkeley, BS, 1948; Univ Manitoba, actuarial sci; Life Off Mgt Inst, fellow; Am Col Life Underwriters, charter life underwriter. **Career:** Insurance executive (retired); Actuary, 1948; Actuarial & Policy owners Serv Div, supr, 1950, admin asst charge, 1952, asst sec actuarial, 1954, actuary, 1956, bd dir exec com mem, 1959, vpres actuary, 1966; Golden State Mutual Life Ins Co, pres, chief exec officer, 1970, chmn bd, chief exec officer, 1980-90, chmn bd, 1991-99. **Orgs:** Asn Conf Consulting Actuaries; Am Acad Actuaries; Am Soc Pension Actuaries; Int Actuarial Asn; past pres Los Angeles Actuarial Club; Kappa Alpha Psi Frat; Sigma Pi Phi Frat; past bd Regents Loyola Marymount Univ; corp bd, United Way Los Angeles Inc; past bd dir, Calif C C; past chmn bd dir, Los Angeles Urban League; past bd dir, Pacific Indemnity Co; former chmn bd dir, M&M Asn; former bd dir, Los Angeles C C; former chmn bd Life Off Mgt Asn, 1979-80; bd dir, First Interstate Bank CA, Pacific Thesis Group; former bd, Kaiser Alum & Chem Corp, Metromedia, Family Savings & Loan; comnr, Los Angeles Human Rels Comm. **Special Achievements:** First African-Am elected bd dir Am Life Ins Asn; appointed Knight, Order of St Gregory the Great, by Pope John Paul II, 1993. **Military Serv:** AUS, sgt major, 1943-45; Purple Heart; Bronze Star; Combat Infantryman's Badge.

HOUSTON, DR. JOHNNY L
Administrator, mathematician, computer scientist. **Personal:** Born Nov 19, 1941, Sandersville, GA; son of Bobby Lee and Catherine Vinson; married Virginia Lawrence; children: Mave Lawrence & Kaiulani Michelle. **Educ:** Morehouse Col, BA, 1964; Atlanta Univ, MS, 1966; Universite Strasbourg, France, attended 1967; Univ Ga, attended 1969; Purdue Univ, PhD, 1974. **Career:** Atlanta Univ, chmn math & comput sci, 1975-81; Lawrence Livermore Nat Lab, vis scientist, 1979, 1983; Fort Valley State Col, coord comput sci, 1981-83, Callaway prof comput sci, 1983-84; Elizabeth City State Univ, vice chancellor acad affairs, 1984-88, Dept Math & Comput Sci, prof, 1984-88, sr res prof, 1988-2008, coordr comput Sci, 1988-96, CSSV Ctr, dir, 1996-2008, African Studies Prog, dir, 2002-08, Textbooks & Learning Mat Prog, 2002-08, exec secy emer, currently; NASA Langley Res Ctr, vis scientist, 1989. **Orgs:** Dir, Black Cult Ctr, Purdue Univ, 1972-73; exec secy, Nat Asn Math, 1975-89; vis scientist, Nat Ctr Atom Res, 1976; co-dir, Nat Conf Math & Phys Sci, Boulder, 1979; pres, chmn the bd, Int Trade & Develop Corp, 1979-86; consult, Math, Comput Sci Spec NIH-MARC Rev Comn, 1982-86; Am Math Soc; Asn Comput Mach; Math Asn Am; Nat Asn Math. **Honors/Awds:** Merril Scholar, Univ de Strasbourg France, 1966-67; Distinguished Service Award. **Home Addr:** 602 W Main St, Elizabeth City, NC 27909. **Business Addr:** Executive Secretary Emeritus, Elizabeth City State University, Department Math & Comput Sci, Rm 124 Lester Hall Parkview Dr, Elizabeth City, NC 27909, **Business Phone:** (252)335-3361.

HOUSTON, KAREN GRAY. See GRAY, KAREN G.

HOUSTON, KENNETH RAY
Football player, football coach, counselor. **Personal:** Born Nov 12, 1944, Lufkin, TX; son of Herod; married Gustie Marie Rice; children: Kenneth Christian & Kene. **Educ:** Prairie View A&M, BSM, guid coun, 1967. **Career:** Football player (retired), coach; Am Football League, Houston Oilers, defensive back, 1967-72; Nat Football League, Wash Redskins, 1973-80; Wheatley High Sch, coach; Westbury High Sch, coach, coach; Houston Oilers, coach, 1982-85; Univ Houston, coach, 1986-90; Tex Independent Sch Dist, counselor, currently. **Honors/Awds:** NFL Record for Touchdowns On Interceptions (9), Houston, 1967-71; Byron Whizzer White Award for Humanitarian Service, NFL Players Asn, 1980; Pro Bowl, 1970-76; Pro Football Hall of Fame, 1986. **Special Achievements:** Listed in 100 Greatest Football Players by Sporting News, 1999; Named one of the 70 Greatest Redskins. **Business Addr:** Counselor, Texas Independent School District, 4400 W 18th St, Houston, TX 77092-8501, **Business Phone:** (713)556-7025.

HOUSTON, LILLIAN S.
Educator. **Personal:** Born Oct 24, 1946, Tyler, TX; married David. **Educ:** Tex Col, BA, 1966; E TX State Univ, MS, sociol, 1975. **Career:** Nursing Home Admin Wiley Col, instr, prog dir. **Orgs:** Tex Nursing Home Asn; Nat Caucus Black Aged; Am Asn Retired Persons; Cole Hill CME Church, Tyler, TX; Local CYF Christian Youth Fellowship; dir, Cole Hill CME Church; bd dir, Tyler City Libr, Tyler, TX; Am Col Nursing.

HOUSTON, SEAWADON L (HOUSTON SEA)
Banker, vice president (organization). **Personal:** Born Aug 29, 1942, Liberty, MO; son of Samuel Houston and Thelma Merical; married Carole L Floyd, Jun 1976; children: Brenda, Toni, George & Michael. **Educ:** Golden Gate Univ, BA bus; Univ Wash, banking Sch; Stanford Sloan Prog, grad. **Career:** Wells Fargo Bank, trainee, 1965-66, several mgt positions, 1966-84, sr vpres, 1984-90, exec vpres, 1990-. **Orgs:** Bay Area Urban Bankers Asn; bd mem, Consumer Bankers Asn; bd mem, Golden Gate Univ; adv bd, Nat Asn Urban Bankers; adv bd, Stanford Sloan. **Military Serv:** USAF, sgt, 1960-65; Far East Airman of the Year, 1963. **Business Addr:** Executive Vice President, Wells Fargo Bank, 455 Market St 4th Fl, San Francisco, CA 94105, **Business Phone:** (415)477-6020.

HOUSTON, WADE
Business owner, basketball coach. **Personal:** Born Oct 9, 1944, Alcoa, TN. **Educ:** Univ Louisville, BS, MS, educ psychol 1966. **Career:** Basketball coach (retired), businessman; Univ Louisville, asst coach, 1976; Univ Tenn, Knoxville, Tenn, head coach, 1989-94, JHT Holdings, pres& chief exec officer, 2001; Johnson-Houston Travel Agency, owner, currently. **Orgs:** Univ Louisvilles Athletic Hall Fame; KY Athletic Hall Fame. **Honors/Awds:** Spalding Univ, hon doctorate, 2002. **Special Achievements:** First African Am player at the Univ of Louisville; First Black Head Coach in the Southeastern Conference.

HOUSTON, DR. WHITNEY ELIZABETH
Music producer, actor, singer. **Personal:** Born Aug 9, 1963, Newark, NJ; daughter of John and Cissy; married Bobby Brown, Jul 18, 1992 (divorced 2007); children: Bobbi Kristina Houston Brown. **Career:** Albums: Whitney Houston, 1985; Whitney, 1987; I'm Your Baby Tonight, 1990; Bodyguard Soundtrack, 1992; The Preacher's Wife Soundtrack, 1996; My Love is Your Love, 1999; Whitney: The Greatest Hits, 2000; Love, Whitney, 2001; Just Whitney, 2002; Films: Bodyguard, 1992; Waiting to Exhale, actress, 1995; The Preacher's Wife, actress & exec producer, 1996; Cinderella, actress & exec producer, 1997; Whitney Houston: Fine, exec producer, 2000; The Princess Diaries, producer, 2001; The Princess Diaries 2: Royal Engagement, producer, 2004; 13 Going on 30, 2004; CMT Greatest Moments: Dolly Parton, 2006; CMT: The Greatest - 40 Days That Shaped Country Music, 2006; Sing Star Pop, 2007; Daddy's Little Girls, 2007; TV program: "The Cheetah Girls", exec producer, 2003-06; Singles: "Saving All My Love for You", 1985; "How Will I Know", 1986; "Greatest Love of All", 1986; "I Wanna Dance with Somebody (Who Loves Me)", 1987; "Didn't We Almost Have It All", 1987; "So Emotional", 1988; "Where Do Broken Hearts Go", 1988; "I'm Your Baby Tonight", 1990; "All the Man That I Need", 1991; "I Will Always Love You" 1992; "Exhale (Shoop Shoop)", 1995; "Being Bobby Brown", 2005; "Biography", 2006; "20 to 1", 2006; "Frank - Der Wedding planer", 2007; "So You Wanna Be a Pop star", 2007; "30 Rock", 2007; Nippy Inc, owner, currently. **Orgs:** Founder, Whitney Houston Found C. **Honors/Awds:** Key to the City of Newark; Grammy Award, 1986, 1988, 1994 & 2000; Top Female Pop Vocalist; Best Female Video Award, MTV, 1986; UNCF honoree, 1990; Image Award, NAACP, 1994, 1997, 1999, 2000; Entertainer of the Year, 1994; Honorary Doctorate, Grambling State Univ; Soul Train Music Awards, 1994; World Music Awards, 1994; Juno Award, 1994; Soul Train Music Awards, 1995, 1996; American Music Award, 1997; ASCAP Pop Award, 1997; Nickelodeon Kids Choice Awards, 1998; People's Choice Awards, 1998; Trumpet Pinnacle Award, 1998; Dove Award, 1998; International Artist of the Year, Bambi Germany, 1999; Brazil Dance Music Award, 1999; NJR Music Awards, 2000; Japan Gold Disc Awards, 2001; Meteor Ireland Music Award, 2001; Lifetime Achievement Award, Women's World, 2004; NJ Walk of Fame Inductee, 2006. **Business Addr:** Artist, Nippy Inc, 60 Pk Pl, Newark, NJ 07102, **Business Phone:** (973)824-8886.

HOUSTON, WILLIAM DEBOISE
School administrator. **Personal:** Born Mar 10, 1940, Quincy, FL; son of Albert and Ada; married Elizabeth Shorter; children: William Carril, Kendra, Karli & Kylean. **Educ:** SC State Col, BSEd, 1963; NC A&T Univ, MEd, 1972; Lehigh Univ, admin cert, 1975. **Career:** School administrator(retired); Easton Area Sch dist, teacher, 1964-74; Shawnee Intermediate Sch, asst prin, 1975. **Orgs:** Vpres Easton City Coun; chairperson, Easton Econ Develop, Police Fire & Health Bd City Easton; co-host, Channel 39 Black Exposure TV Show; Pa State Ed Asn; Am Asn Health Phys Ed & Recreation, Women's League Voters, Nat Asn Advan Colored People Exec Bd; bd mem, Easton Boys Club, Pvt Indust Coun; pres, Pride & Joy Ed Nursery Inc, South Side Civic Asn; bd trustees, Union AME Church; pres, Easton City Coun. **Honors/Awds:** Certificate of Appreciation, Nat Asn Advan Colored People, 1967 & 1982; Rainbow Festival Award, Bahai, 1981; First Black Councilman City of Easton Pa Certificate, Nat Asn Advan Colored People; Easton City Counc, 1985-87 & 1988-90. **Home Addr:** 201 Reese St, Easton, PA 18042. *

HOUSTON, WILLIE LEWIS
Museum director. **Personal:** Born Aug 21, 1948, Pensacola, FL; married Oct 1990. **Educ:** Adelphi Univ, BA, 1978. **Career:** African Am Mus, mus dir, 1981-, musician cur, currently. **Orgs:** pres, United Fed Tribal Chiefs, 1995; Civil Serv Employees Asn Nassau County, NY; co-chair, Unity Comn. **Honors/Awds:** Community Service Award, Concerned Citizens for Roslyn's Youth, 1991; Community Serv Award, NY State Assembly 18th Dist, 1994; Community Service Award, Nassau County exec, 1996, 1998; Community Serv Award, Nassau County Legislator, 1997, 1999; Community Serv Award, Nat Asn Univ Women, 1998; Man of the Yr Award, Hempstead Community, 2002. *

HOUZE, JENEICE CARMEL WONG
Educator. **Personal:** Born in New Orleans, LA; married Harold Emmanuel Houze; children: Harold Emanuel Jr, Miles Peter. **Educ:** Xavier Univ, LA, BA, 1959; Univ San Francisco, MA, 1980; California State Univ, LDS. **Career:** Chicago Sch Dist, teacher, 1959-65; Torrance Unified Sch Dist, teacher, 1965-, mentor teacher, 1991-; staff, develop clin teaching Rowland Heights, CA, 1983-84; Hawthrone School Dist, consult, 1998. **Orgs:** secy, 1983-93, Xavier Univ of LA Alumni; CA Teachers Asn, 1966-; Nat Educ Asn, 1966-; Torrance Teachers Asn, 1966-; Parent Teachers Asn, 1966-; Sci Leadership, team mem, 1993-; Dist Sci Workshop on Sci Framework, 1982-83; coord, Career Awareness Prog, Lincoln Sch, 1982-84; proj writing team mem, Lincoln Elem Sch, 1983-84; Olympic Field Day chairperson, budgeting asst, coord ECT Musical Holiday Presentation, 1983-84; facilitator Workshops, Lincoln Elem Sch, 1983-87; curriculum writer Gifted & Talented Prog, Lincoln Elem Sch, 1983-86; Univ St Francis Alumni, 1986-87; Lang Arts Steering Comt, 1995-; Rdg Task Force, site mentor & lead teacher, 1995-97; mentor, Beginning Teacher Support Assessment, 1992-00; lead teacher, 1990-00, trainer Peer Quality Rev, 1996-98. **Honors/Awds:** Honorary Service Chairperson, PTA Asn, 1983-84; Honorary Serv Award, Torrance PTA, 1986-87; Recipient US Educators to Japan, 1992. **Business Addr:** Mentor Teacher, Elementary Mentor Teacher, Torrance Unified Sch Dist, Elem, 2335 Plaza del Amo, Torrance, CA 90504.*

HOVELL, YVONNE
Automotive executive, president (organization), chief executive officer. **Educ:** Howard Univ, BS, pharmaceut sci; Univ Ill Med Ctr, MD, pub health. **Career:** Univ Chicago, Hosp Pharm; Univ Ill, Int Health & Pub Health, fac; E Tulsa Dodge, pres & chief exec officer, 2001-. **Orgs:** Bd dir, Tulsa Metro Chamber; Founders Asn, Univ Wisconsin; Nat Automobile Dealers Asn; Ment Health Asn; Jr League Tulsa; Ok Work Force; Found Schs. **Honors/Awds:** Five-Star Dealership Award, DaimlerChrysler Motors. **Business Addr:** President, Chief Executive Officer, E Tulsa Dodge, 4627 S Mem Dr, Tulsa, OK 74145, **Business Phone:** (918)663-6343.*

HOWARD, ANICA
Chief executive officer, association executive. **Educ:** Spelman Col, BS, eng; GA Inst Technol, BS, indust eng; Duke Univ Fuqua Sch Bus, MBA. **Career:** Xantus Corp, exec dir & dir oper, 1994-99; Christianseeds.com, pres & ceo, 1999-2000; Miragent Commun, ceo, currently. **Orgs:** Southern regional dir, Nat Black MBA Asn, 1998-99; Nat Black MBA Asn Bd Dirs, 1998-01; coo, Nat Black MBA Asn; chair, Bethlehem Ctr Nashville; bd dir, Nashville Ballet. **Business Addr:** Chief Executive Officer, Miragent Communications, 216 Centerview Dr Suite 330, Brentwood, TN 37027, **Business Phone:** (615)377-1334.

HOWARD, AUBREY J
Executive. **Personal:** Born Mar 23, 1945, Memphis, TN; married Patricia Claxton; children: Adrian K. **Educ:** Southwestern Univ, Memphis, BA, 1972. **Career:** Prev Med Ctr, acting dir, 1972; Proj Aging, asst dir, 1973; Intergovernmental Coord Dept Shelby County Govt, assoc dir res, 1974; Beale St Nat Historic Found, exec dir, 1975; Doyen Asn Inc, pres, 1977-83; TESCO Develop, dir develop, 1983-85; Belz/Curits Outdoor Operations, mgr real estate operations, 1985-; Belz Enterprises, proj dir new hotels & com develop, 1986-; Ment Health Serv, dep dir, 1992; Midtown Ment Health Ctr, chief exec officer, currently. **Orgs:** Fel, Nat Endowment Humanities, 1977; chmn, Midtown Memphis Ment Health Ctr, 1980-82; pres, Ballet S Inc, 1980-82; Mason, NAACP; bd mem, Memphis Oral Sch Deaf, 1985; Memphis Crisis Stabilization Ctr, 1985; State Tenn Dept Ment Health & Ment Retardation, 1986-94; Tenn Asn Mental Health Orgs. **Honors/Awds:** Aubrey J Howard Founders Award, named in honor. **Business Addr:** Chief Executive Officer, Midtown Mental Health Center, 427 Linden Ave, Memphis, TN 38128, **Business Phone:** (901)577-9470.

HOWARD, BRIAN
Basketball player. **Personal:** Born Oct 19, 1967, Winston-Salem, NC. **Educ:** NC State Univ. **Career:** Basketball player (retired), owner; Omaha Racers, 1990-92; Dallas Mavericks, 1992-93; Francorosso Torino, 1993-94; Sioux Falls Sky force,1994-95; ASVEL Villeurbanne, 1995-97; Efes Pilsen, 1997-98; Olympique Antibes, 1998-99; Paris Basket Racing, 1999-2000; 2002-03; Strasbourg IG, 2000-01; ES Chalon-sur-Saone, 2001-02; CB Bilbao Berri, 2003-04; Mlekarna Kunin, 2004-05; Brian Howard's Basketball Acad, owner, currently.

HOWARD, CALVIN JOHNSON
Law enforcement officer. **Personal:** Born Oct 17, 1947, Miami, FL; son of Norman and Mary Magdalene Johnson Ferguson; divorced; children: Tara Evette, Christian Calvin Deon, Arlethia Michelle, LaTonya Linnell, Cortenay DeMaun, LaToya Linnett, Troy Everett, Jabari Deon, Christian Jerrod Jameel. **Educ:** Tarrant County Jr Col, Hurst TX, AA Law Enforcement; Univ Tex, Arlington TX; Abilene Christian Univ, Garland TX, BS, Criminal Justice. **Career:** Law enforcement officer (retired); Dade County Seriff's Off, Miami FL, dep Sheriff, 1969-70; Tarrant County Sheriff's Off, Ft Worth TX, dep Sheriff, 1970-72; Dallas Police Dept, Dallas TX, police officer, 1972, retired sr corporal, 1993; sr spec adv Minister Interior. **Orgs:** Founder, Tex Peace Officers Asn, Dallas Chapter, 1975-77, First state vpres, 1977-82; vice chmn, Southern Region, Nat Black Police Asn, 1980-84, chmn, 1984-92, nat chmn, 1988-90; Nat Asn Advan Colored People, Cong Task Force, Dallas Chapter, 1987; Inspiring Body Christ, Dallas, TX, 1992; Dallas & Grand Prairie Tex Nat Asn Advan Colored People, 1989. **Honors/Awds:** Appreciation Award, Tex Peace Officers Asn, Dallas Chapter, 1986; Leadership Award, Southern Region NBPA, 1987; Dallas Community Rels Comn, 1988; Outstanding Law Enforcement Officer Award, Greater Dallas; Cot Rels Comn, Renault Robinson Nat Award, Nat Black Police Asn, 1988. **Military Serv:** USY, SFC, SA AUS Intelligence; , USF, SSG, 1965-71; Tex Army Nat Guard, Airborne Medic; Ret AUS, 1994. *

HOWARD, CAROL. See HAMMOND, CAROL H.

HOWARD, DALTON J., JR.
Lawyer, u.s. attorney. **Personal:** Born in Vicksburg, MS; married Marian Hill. **Educ:** Parsons Clge, BS, 1964; Howard Univ Sch Law, JD, 1974. **Career:** Gary Sch City, teachr, 1968-69; Mutual NY, field underwriter, 1968-69; law stud, 1971-74; Wash Tech Inst, instr, 1974-75; Neighborhood Legal Serv Prog, managing atty, 1975-. **Orgs:** Vpres dir, Movin' on Inc, 1974-; Nat Bar Asn; Am Bar Asn; Asn Trial Lawyers Am; DC Bar Asn; Sigma Delta Tau Legal Frat; Recreation Assistance Bd, OBC, 2005. **Honors/Awds:** AUS, bandsman, 1969-71. **Business Addr:** Attorney, 1429 Good Hope Rd SE, Washington, DC 20002.*

HOWARD, DESMOND KEVIN
Football player, television talk show host. **Personal:** Born May 15, 1970, Cleveland, OH; son of James D and Hattie V Dawkins Shockley. **Educ:** Univ Mich, BA, commun, 1992. **Career:** Football player (retired), TV analyst; Wash Redskins, wide receiver, 1992-94; Jacksonville Jaguars, 1995; Green Bay Packers, 1996; Oakland Raiders, 1997-98; Green Bay Packers, 1999; Detroit Lions, wide receiver, 2000-01; ESPN, coll football analyst, currently. **Orgs:** Peer facilitator & prog adv, Beale Harden Beale Inc, 1990; employee, Habari Gani, 1992; chmn, Nat Consortium Acad & Sports, 1992; chmn, NCAA Found, 1992; spokesperson, Spec Olympics, 1992. **Honors/Awds:** Heisman Trophy, Downtown Atheletic Club, 1991; Player of the Year, Walter Camp Found, 1991; Offensive Player of the Year, Maxwell Award, 1991; NCAA Offensive Player of the Year, ABC Sports, 1991; Most Valuable Player, Super Bowl XXXI, 1997. **Special Achievements:** 100 Black Men, 1992. **Home Addr:** 6622 Villa Sonrisa Suite 820, Boca Raton, FL 33433, **Home Phone:** (407)561-0707.

HOWARD, DONALD R.
Engineer, chemical engineer. **Personal:** Born Oct 13, 1928, Wightman, VA; married Virdie M Hubbard; children: Jada Marni & Donald Jr. **Educ:** BS, 1959. **Career:** IITRI, 1956-64; Mobil Oil Corp, 1964-68; Commonwealth Edison Co, prin chem engr, 1968. **Orgs:** AICHE; Am Chem Soc; Prof Black Chemists & Chem Engrs; Carter Temple CME Church. **Military Serv:** USMC, 1951-53.

HOWARD, DR. ELIZABETH FITZGERALD
College teacher, librarian, writer. **Personal:** Born Dec 28, 1927, Baltimore, MD; daughter of John Mac Farland Fitzgerald and Bertha McKinley James; married Lawrence C; children: Jane Howard-Martin, Susan C & Laura L. **Educ:** Harvard Univ, Radcliffe Col, AB, 1948; Univ Pittsburgh, MLS, 1971, PhD, 1977. **Career:** Boston Pub Libr, c librn, 1952-56; Episcopal Diocese Pittsburgh, resource librn, 1972-74; Pittsburgh Theol Sem, librn, 1974-77; Univ Pittsburgh, vis lectr, 1976-78; WVA Univ, asst prof, 1978-85, on leave sr librn, prof emer, 1993-; Univ Maiduguri, Nigeria, fac, 1981-82, assoc prof, 1985-89, prof, 1989-93. **Orgs:** Dir, Radcliffe Alumnae Asn, 1969-72; bd trustees, Ellis Sch, Pittsburgh, 1970-75; trustee, Magee Womens Hosp, 1980-94; Episcopal Diocese Pittsburgh Cathedral Chap, 1984-86; bd mem, QED Commun, 1987-94; bd mem, Beginning With Books, 1987-93; bd mem, US Bd Books Youth, 2000-02; Pittsburgh Chap, LINKS Inc; Am Libr Asn, C Lit Asn, Soc C Book Writers. **Honors/Awds:** Cand Bd Dirs, Harvard Alumni Asn, 1987; Libr Sci Hon, Soc Beta Pi Mu. **Special Achievements:** Author Articles in Professional Journals; author professional nonfiction, Am as Story, 1988; author children's books, Train to Lulu's House, Chita's Christmas Tree, 1989, Aunt Flossie's Hats, 1991; Mac and Marie and the Train Toss Surprise, 1993; Papa Tells Chita a Story, 1995; What's in Aunt Mary's Room, 1996; America as Story (2nd edition, with Rosemary Coffey), 1997; When Will Sarah Come, 1999; Virgie Goes to School with Us Boys, 2000; LULU's Birthday, 2001; Flower Girl Butterflies, 2004. **Home Addr:** 825 Morewood Ave, Pittsburgh, PA 15213. **Business Addr:** Professor Emeriti, West Virginia University, PO Box 6201, Morgantown, WV 26506.*

HOWARD, ELLEN D
Association executive, executive director. **Personal:** Born Apr 8, 1929, Baltimore, MD; daughter of Lucious Norman Dolvey and Louise Tignor; divorced; children: Harold H Jr & Larry K. **Educ:** Morgan State Col, BS, 1951; Johns Hopkins Univ, MA, 1968. **Career:** Educ Talent Search US Off Educ, exec dir; MD Educ Opportunity Ctr, exec dir, currently. **Orgs:** Bd trustees, Col Entrance Exam Bd; DE DC Md Asn Financial Aid Admin; 4th Dist Dem Orgn, Baltimore City; Nat Asn Stud Financial Aid Admin; Nat Coun Negro Women; Md Personnel & Guid Asn; Nat Educ Asn; YWCA; Nat Asn Advan Colored People; Baltimore Pub Sch Teachers Asn; Delta Sigma Theta Inc; Baltimore Continental Soc Underprivileged C Inc; Town & Country Set; Baltimore Chap Moles Inc; Girl Scouts Cent, Md Nominating Coun; Nat Vol Planning Prog Mgt & Audits Girl Scouts, USA; Phi Delta Gamma, Gamma Chap Nat Hon Fraternity Grad Women; Phi Lambda Theta Chi Chap Nat Hon & Prof Asn Women Educ; Enon Baptist Church; Girl Scouts Cent Md; Md Personnel & Guid Asn; Baltimore Urban League & League Women Voters; Pub Sch Adminr & Supvr Asn. **Honors/Awds:** Certificate of Appreciation, Am Biog Inst, 1975; Community Servive Certificate, 1974; Certificate of Achievement, Morgan Col, ROTC, 1974; Am Legion Award; InterNat Women's Year Award; Outstanding Woman in Youth Development, Baltimore Alumni Chap Delta Sigma Theta Inc; Hall of Fame, MECEO; Maryland State Award for Outstanding Services. **Special Achievements:** Author, Financial Aid for Higher Educ. **Home Addr:** 3220 Yosemite Ave, Baltimore, MD 21215. **Business Addr:** Executive Director, Maryland Educational Opportunity Center, 10451 Twin Rivers Rd Suite 247, Columbia, MD 21044, **Business Phone:** (410)997-9036.

HOWARD, GLEN
Executive. **Personal:** Born Sep 12, 1942, Detroit, MI; son of Green (deceased) and Rebecca Hall (deceased); married Sheila Perkins Howard, Feb 8, 1964 (divorced 1981); children: Sheryce, Glen Jr. **Educ:** Wayne County Community Col, attended 1973. **Career:** A & P Tea Co, asst mgr, 1960-67; Detroit Edison, meter reader, 1967-68; The Drackett Co, sales rep, 1968-70; United Beverage Co, area mgr, 1970-76; Great Lakes Beverage Co, area mgr, 1976-85; Coors Brewing Co, community rels field mgr, 1986-. **Orgs:** Nat Asn Advan Colored People, 1973-; bd dirs, Food Indust Coun; bd dirs, Detroit Chamber Com, 1989-; adv coun mem, Detroit Chap, Southern Christian Leadership Conf, 1990-. **Honors/Awds:** Community Service Award, Detroit Fire Dept; Meritorious Service Award, City of Detroit, Recreation Dept; Appreciation Award, Tuskegee Airmen Inc, Detroit Chap.

HOWARD, GLEN
Clergy. **Personal:** Born May 20, 1956, Oakland, CA; married Marian Byrd. **Educ:** La Tech Univ, BS Psychol, 1980; Gammon Theol Sem, MDiv, 1984. **Career:** Marc Paul Inc, mgt, 1976-79; Xerox Corp, sales & mkt, 1980-81; United Methodist Church Iowa Conf, pastor, 1984-. **Orgs:** Sec Ankeny Ministerial Asn, 1985. **Business Addr:** Pastor, United Methodist Church, 206 SW Walnut, Ankeny, IA 50021.

HOWARD, GREGORY ALLEN
Screenwriter, playwright. **Personal:** Born Jan 1, 1962?, Norfolk, VA. **Educ:** Princeton Univ, am hist. **Career:** Playwright, screenwriter & author; CBS, story ed; guest lectr, Howard Univ; Screenwriter: Fox, "True Colors", 1988; CBS, "The Royal Family"; CBS, "Teach"; ABC, "Where I live", story ed; "21 Jump Street"; Remember The Titans, 2000; Drummer Boy; We Are A Chain; Baptism In Fire. **Orgs:** Kennedy Ctr Circles; founder & creator, Howard Lonsdale Scholar; Alvin Ailey Partner; bd mem, Ctr Creative Community. **Honors/Awds:** Paul Robeson Award, 2004; Christopher Award; Heartland Film Festival Award; Best Picture Award, Nat Asn Advan Colored People; Excellence Award, Orgn Black Screenwriters; Black Cinema Cafe Award. **Special Achievements:** Only screenwriter selected to write essays for German Publisher Bernard Taschen's Greatest of All Time. **Business Addr:** Screenwriter310-859-4462, William Morris Agency, 151 El Camino Dr, Beverly Hills, CA 90212, **Business Phone:** (310)274-7451.

HOWARD, GWENDOLYN JULIUS
Educator, president (organization). **Personal:** Born Nov 15, 1932, Brooklyn, NY; divorced; children: Calvin & Lisa C. **Educ:** Bethune Cookman Col, BS, 1956; Univ Northern Colo, MS, 1974, EdD, 1976. **Career:** Sunlight Beauty Acad-Kingston Jam Cri Deliq Task Force Mod Cities, assoc, 1968-70; SE Reg NANB & PW Clubs, gov, 1970-73; Gala Travel Inc, Miami, co-owner; Dade Co Public Sch, Sch liaison juvenile justice support prog. **Orgs:** Sigma Gamma Rho, 1967-; pres, Epsilon Chap Gamma Phi Delta, 1978-81; pres, Sigma Gamma Rho, Gamma Delta Sigma Chap, 1980-82; pres, Miami Chap Top Ladies Distinction Inc, 1983-87; exec bd, YWCA NW, 2 yrs; adv coun, Miami Dade Community Col, 1984. **Honors/Awds:** Appreciation Award Excellence, Civic & Social Club, 1971; Nat Asn Bus & Prof Women's Club, 1971; Achievement Awards, Sigma Gamma Rho, 1976, MAB &P's Women Clubs, 1976, Gamma Phi Delta Sor, 1976; nominee, Fla Women Hall Fame, 1984; Greater Miami Outstanding Influential Blacks, 1984; Top Lady of the Year, 1985-86. **Business Addr:** School Liaison Education Specialist, Dade Co Public School, Juvenile Justice Support Prog, 3300 NW 27th Ave, Miami, FL 33142.

HOWARD, JOHN MILTON
Lawyer. **Career:** DC Mental Health Advocacy Trust, Mental Health Lawyer, Pvt pract, currently. **Business Addr:** Lawyer, Private Practice, 1532 Upshur St NW, Washington, DC 20011-7008, **Business Phone:** (202)723-5919.

HOWARD, DR. JOHN ROBERT
Educator, lawyer. **Personal:** Born Jan 24, 1933, Boston, MA; married Mary Doris Adams; children: Leigh Humphrey. **Educ:** Brandeis Univ, BA, 1955; New York Univ, MA, 1961; Stanford Univ, PhD, 1965; J Du Pace Univ, 1985. **Career:** Univ Ore, asst prof, 1965-68; Rutgers Univ, assoc prof, 1969-71; State Univ NY, dean & prof, 1971-80, prof sociol, 1971-, Div Social Sci, distinguished serv prof, currently; Pvt Pract, atty, 1986-. **Orgs:** United Way Westchester, 1976-78; Inst Urban Design, bd adv, 1978-; Soc Study Social Prob, vpres, 1978-79; St Theater Inc, 1978-80; Friends Nueberger Mus, 1982-85. **Honors/Awds:** Publ Lifestyles the Black, WW Norton, 1969; The Cutting Edge, J B Lippincott Publ, 1974; Urban Black Politics, Annals Am Acad, 1978. **Special Achievements:** Published various articles. **Business Addr:** Attorney, 271 N Ave, New Rochelle, NY 10801-5104, **Business Phone:** (914)235-2235.*

HOWARD, JULES JOSEPH, JR.
Executive. **Personal:** Born Aug 24, 1943, New Orleans, LA; son of Jules J Sr and Ophelia; divorced; children: Gwendolyn. **Educ:** Calif State Univ, BA, bus admin, 1975, MBA, 1977. **Career:** City of Carson, exec asst, 1973-79; Comput Careers Corp, mgr, 1979-81; Great 400 Group Int, exec dir, 1981, sr recruiter, currenlty. **Orgs:** Vpres, Carson Lions Club; Kappa Alpha Psi Fraternity; Carson Br Nat Asn Advan Colored People; Calif Inst Employment Coun; Calif Asn Personnel Consults. **Business Addr:** Executive Director, Senior Recruiter, Great 400 Group International, 500 E Carson St Suite 105, Carson, CA 90745, **Business Phone:** (310)549-2170.

HOWARD, JUWAN ANTONIO
Basketball player. **Personal:** Born Feb 7, 1973, Chicago, IL; son of Leroy Watson Jr and Helena Howard. **Educ:** Univ Mich, BA, commun, 1995. **Career:** Wash Wizards, forward, 1994-2001; Dallas Mavericks, forward, 2001-02, 2007-; Denver Nuggets, forward, 2002-03; Orlando Magic, forward, 2003-04; Houston Rockets, forward, 2004-07. **Orgs:** Fab Five, Univ Mich, 1991-94; nat spokesman, Nat Basketball Asn; founder, Juwan Howard Found. **Honors/Awds:** NBA All-Star, 1996; Good Guys in Sports, The Sporting News; Chopper Travaglini Award. **Business Phone:** (214)747-6287.

HOWARD, KEITH L.
Optometrist. **Personal:** Born Feb 27, 1940, Buffalo, NY; son of Robert B Sr and Annie C; married Patricia; children: Jennifer, Kristopher. **Educ:** AA, BS, OD, 1966. **Career:** Optical Corp, partner, 1968; pvt pract, 1969; Melnick, Howard, Grzankowski Opt, prof corp formed, 1974; Southern Tier Optometric Ctr, vpres, partner, 1979-; Coun Optom Ctr, Optometrist, currently. **Orgs:** dir, Nat & Am Optom Asn; Nat Eye Res Found Optom Exten Prog, Olean YMCA; Olean Community Chest; EGO Health Studios Inc; bd mem, State Bd Optom, 1985-89, 1989-93; bd mem & Region I dir, Nat Optom Asn, 1988-89; past pres, Nat Optom Asn, 2000. **Honors/Awds:** Olean YMCA Man Year, 1970; one of two black optometrists, NY State; Founders Award, Nat Optom Asn, 2000; President Medal Honor, Illinois Col Optom, 2000. **Business Addr:** Assistant Secretary, Editor, National Optometric Association, 168 N Union St, Olean, NY 14760, **Business Phone:** (716)372-9464.*

HOWARD, DR. LAWRENCE CABOT
Consultant, educator. **Personal:** Born Apr 16, 1925, Des Moines, IA; son of Charles Preston Howard and Louisa Maude Lewis; married Elizabeth Fitzgerald, Feb 14, 1953; children: Jane, Susan & Laura. **Educ:** Drake Univ, BA, 1949; Wayne State Univ, MA, 1950; Harvard Univ, PhD, 1956. **Career:** Hofstra Univ, instr & asst prof, 1956-58; Brandeis Univ, asst prof 1958-63; Peace Corps, Phillippines, assoc dir, 1961-63; Ctr Innovation NY St Dept Educ, assoc dir, 1964; Univ WI, dir human rel inst, 1964-67; Danforth Found, vpres, 1967-69; Univ Pittsburgh, dean, Grad Sch Pub & Int Affairs, 1969-73, prof, 1973-94, prof emer, 1994-; Chatham Col, distinguished vis prof, 1995-98; Govt Bahamas, mgt consult, 1986-94; Pub Policy Assoc, pres, currently. **Orgs:** Consult US Off Edn State Dept Bur Extnl Res; mem res & adv brd Comn Econ Develop; Natl Adv Comn Tchr Corps, 1967-69; Pgh World Affrs Coun, 1969-; Pgh Hist & Landmarks Found; mem exec Coun, Nat Assn Sch Pub Affrs Admin, 1971-73; Am Soc Pub Admin, 1972-; trustee, Ch Soc Col Work, Drake Univ, St Augustine Col, Seabury Western Theol Sem, Epis Diocese of Pgh; Harvard Grad Soc Advan Study & Res; Dep Epis Diocesan Conv; bd mem, Episcopal Relief & Develop Fund, 2001-. **Honors/Awds:** Man of the Yr, Alpha Phi Alpha, 1949; Disting Alumnus Awd, Drake Univ,1971; natl pres, COMPA, 1979-80; Full bright Prof, Univ Maiduguri, Nigeria,1981-82; Phi Beta Kappa. **Special Achievements:** Authored "American Involvement in Africa South of the Sahara 1800-1860 (Harvard Dissertations in American History and Political Science)"; Lawrence Cabot Howard Doctoral Research Award; co-author, "Publ Admin, Balancing Power & Accountability"; contrib articles to professional jours. **Military Serv:** AUS, 1943-45. **Home Addr:** 825 Morewood Ave, Pittsburgh, PA 15213. **Business Addr:** Professor Emeritus, University of Pittsburgh, Graduate School of Public & International Affairs, 3601 Posvar Hall, Pittsburgh, PA 15260, **Business Phone:** (412)648-7618.

HOWARD, DR. LEON
Educator. **Personal:** Born Jan 1, 1958?. **Career:** Ala State Univ, pres, 1983-91. *

HOWARD, LEON W., JR.
Executive. **Personal:** Born May 3, 1935, Pittsburgh, PA. **Educ:** Univ Pgh, attended 1974-; PA State Univ, attended 1968; licensed as broker 1971. **Career:** Robt C Golden, real estate, 1956-57; Surety Underwriters Inc, vpres, 1970-73; Nationwide Ins Co, agency agreement, 1972-; Howard Leon W Jr Ins, broker, cur. **Orgs:** Past chmn Labor & Indus Com Pgh NAACP 1974; past pres Pgh Branch NAACP 1975; pres, COPP; past vpres, PABU; bd dir, Black Catholic Ministries & Laymen's Coun; exec bd mem Pgh Chap NAACP; exec bd mem Homewood-Brushton YMCA; commr City Pgh, Dept of City Planning; nat Assn, Sec Dealers; Pgh Life Underwriters Asn Inc; Nat Asn, Life Underwriters; Ins Club of Pgh Inc. **Honors/Awds:** Outstanding Contribution to the Struggle for Human Rights Award, Western PA Black Polit Assembly. **Military Serv:** AUS paratrooper. *

HOWARD, LESLIE CARL
Administrator, lawyer. **Personal:** Born Jun 18, 1950, Aberdeen, MD; son of Willis C and Ethel B; married Corrine Felder; children: Kevin, Keith & Kenneth. **Educ:** Howard Univ, BA, 1980; Community Col, Baltimore, AA, 1971, cert electronics, 1982; Baruch Col, MPA, 1984; Johns Hopkins Univ, cert, 1989-90; Univ Baltimore, Sch Law, JD, 1997. **Career:** MD Dept Human Resources, caseworker II, 1975-77; Mayor Baltimore, spec asst, 1979-82; Neighborhood Housing Serv Baltimore, prog dir, 1982-83; Mayor Detroit, spec asst, 1983-84; Neighborhood Housing Serv, Baltimore, from neighborhood coord asst dir to neighborhood dir, 1985-87; Hartford County, MD, housing coordr, 1987-89; City Baltimore Develop Corp, develop dir, 1989-96; Eubie Blake Nat Jazz Inst & Cult Ctr, exec dir, 1996-2000; Priv Pract, atty, 2000-. **Orgs:** Pres, Coppin Heights Community Corp; Nat Urban fel Class, 1983-84; organizer & pres, Alliance Rosemont Community Orgn Inc, 1987-91; founding pres, MD Low Income Housing Coalition, 1989-91; steering comt mem, Baltimore Neighborhood Resource Ctr, 1990-92; vpres, Bd Govs, MD ACLU, 1999-; atty law, Coppin Heights Community Develop Corp, bd dir. **Honors/Awds:** Summer Scholarship, Peabody Preparatory Sch, 1967; Governor's Certificate of Appreciation; Wilson Park Community Service Award; Community Service Award, 1989-90; Mayor's Certificate, 2000. **Home Addr:** 2322 Harlem Ave, Baltimore, MD 21216, **Home Phone:** (410)566-0146. **Business Addr:** Attorney, 441 E 22nd St, Baltimore, MD 21202, **Business Phone:** (410)566-5223.

HOWARD, LILLIE PEARL
Educator, school administrator. **Personal:** Born Oct 4, 1949, Gadsden, AL; daughter of Walter Moody and Zola Mae; married Willie D Kendricks (divorced 1986); children: Kimberly Denise & Benjamin Richard. **Educ:** Univ S Ala, Mobile, BA, 1971; Univ NMex, Albuquerque, MA, 1972, PhD, 1975; Harvard Univ, Cambridge, grad inst educ mgt, 1988. **Career:** Ford Found, fel, 1971-75; Wright State Univ, Dayton, OH, assoc prof eng, 1980-85, Col Lib Arts, from asst dean to assoc dean, 1982-87, prof eng, 1985-, asst vpres acad affairs, 1987-88, assoc vpres acad affairs, 1988-94, undergrad educ & acad affairs, assoc provost, 1994-99, assoc provost acad affairs, dean univ, vpres res, prof Eng & sr vpres curric & instr, currently. **Orgs:** Am Asn Higher Educ; Ohio Bd Regents Comn Enhancement Undergrad Educ; Ohio Bd Regents Comn Articulation & Transfer; Nat Asn Women Deans, Adminr & Counrs; Nat Asn Acad Affairs Admin; consult & evaluator, NCA, Review Coun. **Honors/Awds:** Woodrow Wilson Finalist, 1971; President's Award for Excellence, Wright State Univ. **Special Achievements:** Author of Zora Neale Hurston, 1980, editor of Alice Walker and Zora Neal Hurston, 1993, numerous articles and book chapters on African American literature. **Business Addr:** Senior Vice President for Curriculum & Instruction, Professor of English, Wright State University, 240 Univ Hall, Dayton, OH 45435, **Business Phone:** (937)775-2097.

HOWARD, LINWOOD E.
Banker, manager. **Personal:** Born Mar 12, 1954, Roanake Rapids, NC; son of Alexander M and Norma; married Denise Laws; children: Marcellus, Jeniene. **Educ:** Livingstone Col, BS, 1976; Univ NC Chapel Hill, advan, attended 1984. **Career:** First Union Nat Bank, br mgr, 1976-86, consumer banking br mgr & vpres, 1986-93; Crestar Bank, mkt mgr, sr vpres, 1993; Downtown Norfolk, bd dir, currently; SunTrust Bank, area mgr, currently. **Orgs:** bd mem, Greenville Chamber Comt, 1992; bd mem, Greenville Area Coun, 1992; dir, United Neighborhood Econ Devel Corp, 1991; bd dirs, Downtown Norfolk Coun; Norfolk State Univ Sch Bus. *

HOWARD, DR. LYTIA RAMANI
Educator, clergy. **Personal:** Born May 6, 1950, Atlanta, GA; daughter of G LaMarr and Gwendolyn. **Educ:** Spelman Col, BA,

1971; Univ Tenn, MACT, 1973; Atlanta Univ, MA, 1978, EdD 1979; Interdenominational Theol Ctr, MRE, 1984. **Career:** Spelman Col, instr, asst prof, 1973-83, asst dean acad, 1983-85; Ga Inst Technol, dir special prog, minority & special prog, asst dean; New Hope COGIC, co-pastor, currently; intl pres, The Sunshine Band, Church of God in Christ, Inc 1986-. **Orgs:** Mem Alpha Kappa Delta Sociological Honor Soc, Mid-South Sociological asn, Nat Asn for Women Deans Administrators and Counselors, Southern Christian Leadership Coun, Phi Delta Kappa, Amer Soc for Engrg Educ; bd mem Nat Consortium for Grad Degrees for Minorities in Engrg Inc 1985-86; mem Nat Action Coun for Minorities in Engrg, Nat Asn Minority Engrg Program Administrators, United Asn Christian Counselors; chairperson bd dirs Hinsley Day Care Ctr 1986; bd trustees New Hope Church God in Christ 1986. **Special Achievements:** Outstanding Young Women of America; Who's Who Among Black American. **Home Addr:** 371 Lynnhaven Dr SW, Atlanta, GA 30310. **Business Addr:** Co-Pastor, Church of God in Christ, 440 Gardner St SW, Atlanta, GA 30310.

HOWARD, M W
Clergy, school administrator. **Personal:** Born Mar 3, 1946, Americus, GA; son of Moses William Sr and Laura Turner; married Barbara Jean Wright; children: Matthew Weldon, Adam Turner & Maisha Wright. **Educ:** Morehouse Col, BA, 1968; Princeton Theol Sem, MDiv, 1972. **Career:** Reformed Church AM, exec dir Black Coun, 1972-92; New York Theol Sem, pres, 1992-99; Bethany Baptist Church, pastor, 1999-. **Orgs:** Ordained minister Am Baptist Churches, 1974; moderator, Prog Combat Racism World Coun Churches, 1976-78; pres, Nat Coun Churches, 1979-81; provided X-mas services US Hostages Iran, 1979; bd trustees, Nat Urban League, 1981-88; bd trustees, Independent Sector, 1981-86; trustee, Children's Defense Fund, 1981-86; pres, Am Comn Africa; Sigma Pi Phi Fraternity; Chaired Ecumenical delegation which accompanied the Rev Jesse Jackson to obtain release Lt Robt Goodman in Damascus, Syria; human rights advisory group, World Coun Churches, 1989; chair religious comn, Welcome Nelson Mandela to New York, 1990; Coun Foreign Rels, 1997-; exec comt, Asn Theol Schs, 1994-2000. **Honors/Awds:** Hon Dr of Divinity Degree, Miles Col & Central Col, 1979-80; citations Mayors of Philadelphia, PA & Americus, GA, 1981-84; Distinguished Alumnus Award, Princeton Sem, 1982; Hon Dr of Humane Letters Morehouse Coll, 1984; Citations from the NJ ST Assembly; The City of Waterloo, Iowa; The Township of Lawrence, NJ; The Touissant Loverture Freedom Award, NY Haitian Community; Chaired the Seminar against bank loans to South Africa in Zurich, Switzerland in 1982; The Measure of A Man Award. **Business Addr:** Pastor, Bethany Baptist Church, 275 W Market St, Newark, NJ 07103, **Business Phone:** (973)623-8161.

HOWARD, DR. MAMIE R (MAMIE HOWARD GOLLADAY)
School administrator. **Personal:** Born Nov 24, 1946, Pascagoula, MS; daughter of E Howard. **Educ:** Pensacola Jr Col, AS, 1971, BS, 1976; Univ Ala, MS, 1979, PhD, 1988. **Career:** DW McMillan Hosp, gen duty rn, 1967-71, supvr, 1971-76; Jefferson Davis Jr Col, instr, 1976-78; Pensacola Jr Col, dept chair allied health ed, 1978-90; CS Mott Community Col, Flint, Mich, dean, sch health & human scis, 1990; Sullivan County Community Col pres, currently. **Orgs:** Am Nurses Asn, 1971-, USA Alumni Asn; consult, Escambia Sickle Cell Disease Found, 1979-82; UAB Alumni Asn, 1979-, Committee for Allied Health Educ, 1981-, AAWCGC 1982-; bd of dir, Fla Lung Asn, 1983-90; chief exec officer, State Mgmt Ltd, 1985-86; dir, large Lung Asn, 1986-90; Alpha Kappa Alpha; chair, PRIDE Committee Am Lung Asn, 1989-90; Am Lung Asn Bd, Genesse County, Mich, 1991-. **Honors/Awds:** Honor Award, Kappa Delta Pi Grad Honor Soc, 1981-; Selected as a Leader of the 80's, FIPSE, 1982; honored by the gov as an Outstanding Black American, 1988; Leadership Award, Pensacola Chamber Com, 1990; Outstanding Educt, Alpha Kappa Alpha Sor, 1990. **Home Phone:** (313)239-1513. **Business Addr:** President, Sullivan County Community College, 112 College Road, PO Box 4002, Loch Sheldrake, NY 12759-4002, **Business Phone:** (845)434-5750 Ext 4261.

HOWARD, MICHELLE
Naval officer. **Personal:** Born Jan 1, 1964?; daughter of Phillipa and Nick; married Wayne K Cowles. **Educ:** US Naval Acad, BS, 1982; USY Command & Gen Staff Col, MA, Military Arts & Sci, 1998. **Career:** Expeditionary Warfare Div, dep dir; OPNAV, 2006; US Navy, secy navy sr military asst. **Honors/Awds:** Captain Winifred Collins Award, Secy Navy & Navy League 1987; Meretorious Serv Medal; Navy Commendation Medal; Navy Achievement Medal; Nat Defense Medal; Armed Forces Expeditionary Medal; Armed Forces Serv Medal; Southwest Asia Serv Medal; NATO Medal; Kuwaiti Liberation Medal; Kuwaiti Liberation Medal; Meretorious Serv Medal; Navy Commendation Medal; Navy Achievement Medal; Nat Defense Serv Medal; Armed Forces Expeditionary Medal; SW Asia Serv Medal; Armed Forces Serv Medal; NATO Medal; Kuwait Liberation Medal; Kuwait Liberation Medal. **Special Achievements:** first African American woman to command a ship in the U.S. Navy. **Business Addr:** Senior Military Assistant, United States Navy, 701 Pennsylvania Ave NW Suite 123, Washington, DC 20004, **Business Phone:** (202)737-2300.*

HOWARD, MILTON L.
Architect, executive. **Personal:** Born Sep 3, 1927, Hurtsboro, AL; married Dolores Allen; children: Mark, James. **Educ:** Ky State Col; Univ Ill. **Career:** Milton Lewis Howard Assocs Inc, architect & owner, currently. **Orgs:** Am Inst Archits; Nal Coun Archit Regis Bds; Guild Religious Archit 1; Bldg Bd Appeals City Hartford; asst treasr, Bloomfield Housing Authority; Am Inst Architects, S Arsenal Everywhere Sch, Hartford, CT; Am Asn Sch Admin, S Arsenal Everywhere Sch, Hartford, Conn. **Honors/Awds:** Bus Leadership Award, Greater Hartford Chamber Com. **Military Serv:** AUS, 1950-52. **Business Addr:** Owner, Milton Lewis Howard Associates Inc., 1 Regency Dr, Bloomfield, CT 06002.*

HOWARD, NORMAN
Manager. **Personal:** Born Jan 30, 1947, Johnson City, TN; married Nancy Goines; children: Erick, Nicole, Nichelle. **Educ:** Georgetown Univ Inst Comparative Polit & Econ Syst, dipl, 1972; Benedict Col, BS, 1974; Univ Detroit, MBA, 1979. **Career:** Ford Motor Co, Casting Div & Transmission & Chassis Div, salary admin, 1974-81, sales opers staff, affirmative action prog coordr, 1981-82, supvr sales pers & training, 1982-83, Ford World HQ, personnel & orgn staff, ind rels analyst, 1983-85, Dearborn Glass Plant, mgr ind rels dept, 1985-99; Greektown Casino, vpres human resources, 1999-. **Orgs:** Pres, Phi Bet Lambda, 1973-74; Delta Mu Delta, 1973-74; chmn, Gesu Boy Scout Troop 191 Comt, 1982-85; pres, Detroit Chap Bendict Col Alumni Club, 1984-; Greater Detroit Area Health Coun. **Honors/Awds:** Outstanding Service Recognition Award, Gesu Boy Scout Troop 191 Detroit 1983, 84, 85; Distinguished Alumni Citation, Nat Asn Equal Opportunity Higher Educ, 1986. **Military Serv:** USAF, sgt, 4 yrs. **Business Addr:** Manager, Greektown Casino, 459 Lafayette Blvd, Detroit, MI 48226.

HOWARD, NORMAN LEROY
Administrator. **Personal:** Born May 22, 1930, New York, NY; married Barbara; children: Karen, Dale, Steven. **Career:** Consolidated Edison Co NY Inc, equal employ oppurtunity coordr; New York City Dept Parks, playground dir, 1948-51; NYCPD, detective, 1952-72; Inst Mediation & Conflict Resol, consult, 1972-73. **Orgs:** 100 Black Men Inc; Boys Yesteryr; 369th Vet Asn; K C St Patricks Coun; Retired Guardians NYCPD; Int Black Police Asn; Welterweight boxing champion amatuer NY City Dept Parks 1943-44; Middleweight Champion Amatuer Met AAU, 1945; Air Force Mem Found; Air Force Asn. **Honors/Awds:** Combat Cross for Bravery, NYCPD, 1955. **Special Achievements:** 15 awards for Bravery & Excellent Police Work NYCPD; First black detective assigned to 40th squad Bronx 1954. **Military Serv:** AUS, pvt e1, 1950-52; Good Conduct Medal. **Business Addr:** 4 Irving Pl, New York, NY 10003.

HOWARD, OSBIE L
Executive. **Personal:** Born Feb 9, 1943, Memphis, TN; son of Osbie L Sr and Bertha S; married Rose O Ollie; children: John, Kendra & Nathan. **Educ:** Memphis State Univ, BBA, 1967; Wash Univ, MBA, 1971. **Career:** Executive, pres (retired); Exxon Co, finan analyst, 1971-72; Memphis Bus Resource Ctr, finan specialist, 1972-74; Tenn State Bd Accountacy, CPA, 1973; Banks Findley White & Co CPA's, tax mgr, 1974-78; Shelby Cty Govt, asst chief admins officer, 1978-79; Tenn Valley Ctr for Minority Economic Devel, exec vpres, 1979-88; Secured Capital Developers, partner, 1988-91; City Memphis, Treas Div, treas & dir; United Am Healthcare Corp Health Plan Tenn Inc, pres & chief exec officer. **Orgs:** Treas & co-founder, New Memphis Develop Corp, 1976; bd dir, West Tenn Venture Capital Corp, 1981; Grad Bus Sch fel, Consortium Grad Study Mgt, 1969; treas, Ind Develop Corp Memphis & Shelby Co, 1980-91. **Honors/Awds:** Alumni Entrepreneur Award, Bus Minority Coun, Sch Bus, Wash Univ, 1991. **Home Addr:** 190 Dubois Dr, Memphis, TN 38109-7444.

HOWARD, PAUL LAWRENCE
Lawyer. **Personal:** Born Sep 22, 1951, Waynesboro, GA; son of Paul L Howard Sr and Gussie P; married Petrina M Moody, Jun 2, 1990; children: Jamila, Paul L III & Simone. **Educ:** Morehouse Col, AB, 1972; Emory Univ Sch Law, JD, 1976. **Career:** City Atlanta, munic ct, dep solicitor; Fulton Co, dist atty's off, asst dist atty; Thomas, Kennedy, Sampson & Patterson, assoc; Fulton Co, State Ct, solicitor, dist atty, currently; Off Local Child Fatality Rev, Ga Dept Human Resources, chairperson, currently. **Orgs:** Bench & bar comt, Gate City Bar; Nat Bar Asn; Atlanta Bar Asn; Ga Bar Asn; Ga Solicitors Asn; Ga Supreme Ct Bar; Nat Asn Advan Colored People; Urban League. **Honors/Awds:** Good Guy Award, GA Women's Political Caucus; Atlanta Community Prevention Coalition's Outstanding Effort to Stop the Violence Award; Gammon Theological Seminary's Outstanding Committee Service Award; Achievements in Law, Morehouse Col, 1992; Providence Baptist Church Law, 1992; Georgia Asn of Black Women Attorneys, 1992; Criminal Justice Coordinating Council Eagle Award for Prosecution, 2003. **Special Achievements:** First African American district attorney in Georgia. **Military Serv:** Georgia National Guard, e-2, 1972-78. **Business Addr:** District Attorney, Fulton County, District Attorney's Office, 136 Pryor St SW Rm 301, Atlanta, GA 30303, **Business Phone:** (404)730-4980.

HOWARD, RAY F.
Government official, executive director. **Personal:** Born Oct 5, 1945, Troy, AL; son of Arthur (deceased) and Maudie L Bennett (deceased); married Sharon G Harvey Howard; children: Leslie R, Joy R. **Educ:** Cleveland State Univ, BBA, 1970; Case Western Res Univ Sch Mgt, Cleveland, OH, MBA, 1972. **Career:** Bausch & Lomb & UCO, Rochester, NY, mgr, planning & prod, customer serv, 1973-81; CIBA Vision Care, Atlanta, GA, nat customer serv mgr, 1981-85; GMD, Dunwoody, GA, prod mkt dir, 1985-87; Proj Mkt Group, Atlanta, GA, pres, 1987-89; US Treas Dept, Internal Rev Serv Div, San Jose, CA, asst dist dir, 1989-, dir, currently. **Orgs:** Am Mgt Asn, 1975-81; Sales & Mkt Execs Club, 1983-89; Am Soc Training & Develop, 1987-89; Sr Execs Asn, 1989-; Rotary Club Int, 1994-; Prod Develop & Mgt Asn. **Honors/Awds:** Sales & Mkt Awards, Bausch & Lomb & CIBA Vision, 1976-85; Achievement Award, United Way, 1989; Excellence Award, Atlanta Dist, IRS, 1990; Commissioners Award, 2000. **Military Serv:** USAF, 1964. **Business Addr:** Director, US Treasury Department Internal Revenue Service, 68 Sewall St, Augusta, ME 30308, **Business Phone:** (207)622-1508.*

HOWARD, RAYMOND
Lawyer, government official. **Personal:** Born Mar 13, 1935, St Louis, MO; married Dorothy J; children: Raymond, Monica, Heather & Angelique. **Educ:** Univ Wis, BA; St Louis Univ, JD. **Career:** MO State Senate, senator; St Louis Municipal judge; Howard Law Firm, atty, personal injury, family law, malpractice, real estate & bus law, currently. **Orgs:** St Louis Christian Ctr; bd dirs, Urban League; bd dirs, atty, Nat Asn Advan Colored People; bd dirs, Metrop Young Men Christian Asn; bd dirs, Gateway Nat Bank; Nat Bar Asn; Am Bar Asn; St Louis Bar Asn; Am Trial Lawyers Asn; pres, St Louis Congress Racial Equality. **Honors/Awds:** Outstanding Man of America, Jr Chamber Com; St Louis Argus Newspaper Award; Outstanding Man of Kappa Alpha Psi, Kappa Alpha Psi; Distinguished Service Award, St Louis Bar Asn; Distinguished Service Award, Lawyers Asn; Vashon High School Hall of Fame; Distinguish Service Award, St Louis Univ. **Special Achievements:** Second African American elected to the MO Senate; author of MO's Fair Employment Law, Fair Housing Law, Public Accommodation's Law, Tuition Scholarship Law; won over 200 cases; tried cases before US Supreme Court. **Military Serv:** Paratrooper, 82 Airborne, lt. **Business Addr:** Attorney, Private Practice, 7912 Bonhomme Suite 104, Saint Louis, MO 63105, **Business Phone:** (314)721-6622.

HOWARD, SAMUEL HOUSTON
Executive. **Personal:** Born May 8, 1939, Marietta, OK; son of Nellie Gaines and Houston; married Karan A Wilson; children: Anica & Samuel II. **Educ:** Okla State Univ, BS, 1961; Stanford Univ, MA, 1963. **Career:** White House, spec asst fel, 1966-67; Howard Univ, dir, 1967-68; HEW, consult secy, 1967-69; TAW Int Leasing Corp, vpres finance, secy, treas, 1968-72; Phoenix Community Group Inc, founder, pres, 1972-; Meharry Med Col, vpres finance, 1973-77; Hosp Affiliates Int Inc, vpres, 1977-81; Hosp Corp Am, vpres, treas, 1981-85, sr vpres pub affairs, 1985-1988; Phoenix Holdings, chmn, pres, chief exec oficer, 1989-. **Orgs:** Numerous memberships including Phi Kappa Phi; Blue Key; Beta Gamma Sigma; Delta Sigma Pi; Alpha Phi Alpha; Human Rels Coun; Cordell Hall Coun; Lariats; Sigma Epsilon Sigma; Fed Am Hosp; Finance Exec Inst, Bd Nashville Br NAACP; Utah Sch Bus Adv Bd; TSU Presidents Adv Bd; St Thomas Hosp Bd Counselors; chmn, Nashville Conv Ctr Comn; Am Hosp Asn; chmn, Nashville Chamber Com; dir, Corp Child Care; former dir, Genesis Health Ventures; former trustee, Fisk Univ; nat chmn, Easter Seals Inc, 2000-03; Nat Bipartison Comn Future Medicare; dir, O'Charley's Inc; trustee, Fisk Univ; founder & dir, 100 Black Men Middle Tenn; chmn Urban League Middle Tenn. **Honors/Awds:** Numerous awards and honors including Business Hall of Fame, Okla State Univ, 1983; Small Business Executive of the Year Award, Nashville Bus Jour, 1995; Outstanding CEO Award, 1997; Human Relations Award, Nat Conference Christians and Jews; Philanthropist of the Year; Nashvillian of the Year; Distinguished Businessman of the Year. **Business Addr:** Chairman, President, Chief Executive Officer, Phoenix Holdings Inc, 216 Centerview Dr Suite 300, Brentwood, TN 37027-3226, **Business Phone:** (615)377-9480.

HOWARD, SHERRI
Fashion model, athlete, actor. **Personal:** Born Jun 1, 1962, Sherman, TX; daughter of Eugene and Barbara. **Educ:** Calif State Univ, Los Angeles, BS, elec engineering. **Career:** Athlete, actress, fashion model, coach; Olympic athlete, 1984-88; The Scorpion King, actor, 2002; TV appearances: "Profiler", 1997; "Beverly Hills 90210", 1999; "Diagnosis Murder", 1999; "X-files", 2000; "Martial Law", 2000; "No Fare", 2000; "Criminal Minds", 2007; Head Girls/Sprints Coach. **Orgs:** Screen Actor's Guild; AFTRA. **Honors/Awds:** Gold Medal, 4x400 meter relay, Olympics, 1984; Silver Medal, 4x400 meter relay, Olympics, 1988; Athlete of the Year. **Special Achievements:** Appeared in numerous commercials. **Business Addr:** Actor, c/o Ross Stephens Artist Management, 3760 Cahuenga Blvd Suite 209, Studio City, CA 91604, **Business Phone:** (818)760-0801.

HOWARD, SHIRLEY M.
Educator, college teacher. **Personal:** Born Dec 15, 1935, Chicago, IL; married Johnnie; children: Patrice, Paula & Christopher. **Educ:** Cook Col Sch Nursing, dipl, 1960; DePaul Univ, BSN, 1969, MS, 1972. **Career:** Gov's State Univ, res grant, 1972-75;

Village Nursing Serv, co-owner; nursing admin, instr, publ health nurse; HEW Proj, nursing educ & res, author & proj dir; Gov State Univ, prof health sci, Health Sci Instructional Prog, coord. **Orgs:** Nat League Nursing; Asn Rehab Nurses; Deans & Dirs Coun Baccalaureate & Higher Degree Progs; consult, Robbins Human Resource Ctr; Independent Peoples Party; PTA; bd mem, Family Health Ctr; adv bd, Kennedy-King Col Nursing Alumni; bd mem, Comprehensive Comn Health Planning & Develop Coun. **Honors/Awds:** Cert Merit, Youth Motivation Comn & Chicago Merit Employ Comn, 1971-72. **Business Addr:** Professor, Governors State University, Park Forest, IL 60466.

HOWARD, STEPHEN
Basketball player. **Personal:** Born Jul 15, 1970, Dallas, TX. **Educ:** DePaul Univ. **Career:** Utah Jazz, forward, 1992-94, 1997; San Antonio Spurs, 1996-97; Seattle Supersonics, forward, 1997-98; Al Hilal, 2006-.

HOWARD, SUSAN E
Writer, lecturer. **Personal:** Born Apr 9, 1961, Fort Wayne, IN; daughter of John Howard Sr and Ferdie A Webster Howard. **Educ:** Syracuse Univ, Syracuse, NY, BS, 1983. **Career:** Frost Illustrated, Fort Wayne, IN, intern, 1978; Jour-Gazette, Fort Wayne, IN, intern, 1978-79; Daily Orange (campus paper), Syracuse, NY, ed ed, 1982; Courier-Jour, Louisville, KY, intern, 1982; Atlanta Jour-Const, Atlanta, GA, sports writer, mag writer, 1983-88; Newsday, Melville, NY, news reporter, feature writer, 1988; Ind Univ-Purdue Univ Fort Wayne, lectr, currently. **Orgs:** NABJ, 1983-; Nat Black Women's Health Proj, 1988-. **Honors/Awds:** NABJ, first place in sports reporting, 1986; first place sports reporting, Atlanta Asn Black Journalists, 1986; Front Page Award, Irene Virag & Edna Negron, feature reporting, 1989; Newsday Publisher's Award, for news project on segregation on Long Island, 1990. **Home Addr:** 4 Lawrence Hill Rd, Huntington, NY 11743-3114. **Business Addr:** Lecturer, Indiana University-Purdue University Fort Wayne, Classroom-Med Bld Rm 143, Melville, NY 11747-4250, **Business Phone:** (260)481-5441 Ext. 19134.

HOWARD, TANYA MILLICENT
Computer engineer. **Personal:** Born May 4, 1968, Chapel Hill, NC; daughter of Charlie Edward and Sadie Ann Graves. **Educ:** Howard Univ, Wash, DC, BS, engineering, 1991. **Career:** Close-Up Found, Alexandria, VA, transportation clerk, 1989-; Dept Defense, Wash, DC, tech clerk, 1989-; Martin Marietta, Air Traffic Systs, systs engr, 1991-. **Orgs:** Region II secy, Nat Soc Black Engrs, 1990-91; chairperson, Inst Electrical & Electronics Engrs, 1990-91; comt chair, Springfield Baptist Church, 1990-91; news ed, Howard Engr Mag, 1989-91; secy, Howard Univ Sch Engineering, 1989-90; Toastmasters Inc, 1991-92; Nat Asn Female Execs, 1991-92. **Honors/Awds:** Academic Award, Nat Soc Black Engrs, 1990. **Home Addr:** 4613 Sargent Rd, Washington, DC 20017. **Business Addr:** Systems Engineer, Martin Marietta - Air Traffic Systems, 400 Virginia Ave SW, Washington, DC 20024.

HOWARD, TY
Football player. **Personal:** Born Nov 30, 1973, Columbus, OH. **Educ:** Ohio State Univ. **Career:** Football player (retired); Ariz Cardinals, defensive back, 1997-98; Cincinnati Bengals, defensive back, 1999; Tenn Titans, defensive back, 2000.

HOWARD, VERA GOUKE
Educator. **Personal:** Born in Brooklyn, NY; married. **Educ:** Baruch Col, BBA, 1958; NY Univ, MA, 1969. **Career:** NY City Bd Educ, 1963-71; Brooklyn Col, adj instr; Manpower Develop Training, teacher; Brooklyn Col, prog lectr; NY Dept Welfare, social worker investr; NY Inst Technol, counr, 1971-. **Orgs:** NY City Personnel Guid Asn; Black Alliance Educrs; vol counr, Long Island Asn Black Counr.

HOWARD, DR. VIVIAN GORDON
Educator. **Personal:** Born Apr 22, 1923, Warsaw, VA; married Roscoe C (deceased); children: Linda G, Roscoe C Jr & Roderick W. **Educ:** Va State Univ, BS, 1946, MS, elem educ, 1960, MS, 1966, EdD, math, 1969; Hermenet San Francisco, certified coach mgt, 1984; Action Technol, certified guide, 1985. **Career:** Educator (retired); Va State Univ, prof math, 1969; Nat Inst Health, extramural assoc, 1981; Longwood Col, vis prof math, 1983-84; Va Tech, vis prof math, 1984-85; Howard Enterprises, founder. **Orgs:** Consult, Nat Inst Educ, 1974-76; math consult, DC Schs; assist orgn mathlabs Anacostia schs 1975-77; dir, Secondary Prog Gifted Math Sci & Eng, DC Schs, Mediax Corp, Ct, 1976; workshop leader Nat Level-Metric System & Math Labs; Va crd & nat bd Nat Coalition of 100 Black Women, establishing 6 chapters 1983-; Va crd Adolescent Pregnancy Child Watch of Children's Defense Fund, 1984-. **Honors/Awds:** Bronze Award, Int Film Fest "Roads to Mathematics through Phys Educ Art Music & Educ" Industrial Arts VSU Prog, US Office Educ Dept Health Educ & Welfare, 1972; Distinguished Teacher, Sch Natural Sci VSU, 1979; Human Relations Award Education, Minority Caucus, Va Educ Asn NEA, 1984; Outstanding Political Service Award, Womens Vote Proj Atlanta, 1984. *

HOWARD, WARDELL MACK
Opera singer. **Personal:** Born Apr 11, 1934, Shreveport, LA; son of Arthur Mitchell and Lubertha Williams; married Shirley, Jan 20,

1991; children: Merlin W. **Educ:** NY Univ, 1976; Univ Calif, Los Angeles, music; Prof Theater Inst Los Angeles Civic Light Opera. **Career:** The Roger Wagner Choral, soloist, 1980-85; The Los Angeles Master Choral, 1980-85; The Los Angeles Cult Affairs, choral-conductor, 1985-; Opera Roles Performed: La Boheme, Colline, Puccini; "Don Giovanni, Leporello, Mozart; Tremonisha, Parson Alltalk, Scott Joplin; Univ Calif Opera Theatre, mem; Album: Mostly Broadway, 2005; singer, currently. **Orgs:** Los Angeles Master Choral; The Roger Wagner Choral; The City of Los Angeles Cultural Affairs. **Honors/Awds:** Southern Calif Motion Picture Coun Contribution to The Entertainment Industry, 1986; Saints & Sinners, Great Artist Award, 1986, 1988; Women's American ORT, Golden Names For Israel, 1980. **Military Serv:** AUS, PFC, 1957-79. **Home Addr:** 8746 Tobias Ave Suite 7, Panorama City, CA 91402, **Home Phone:** (818)891-4226. **Business Addr:** Singer, 8746 Tobias Ave Suite 7, Panorama City, CA 91402, **Business Phone:** (818)891-4226.

HOWARD-COLEMAN, BILLIE JEAN
Educator, nurse. **Personal:** Born Jul 31, 1950, Chicago, IL. **Educ:** Univ Ill, Chicago, BSN, 1973; Loyola Univ, MSN, 1976. **Career:** Univ Ill Hosp, staff nurse, 1973-76; Univ Ill Col Nursing, instr, 1976-77; Michael Reese Hosp, clin specialist, 1977-78; Univ Ill Col Nursing, asst prof, 1978-81; Univ Chicago Hosp, supvr, 1981-83; Nursing Provident Med Ctr, assoc dir, 1983-84; Chicago St Univ, asst prof nursing, 1984-; Chicago St Univ, asst prof nursing, 1987; Chicago Bd Educ, sch nurse, teacher, 1987; Chicago pub high sch, teacher, currently. **Orgs:** Ill Sch Health Asn; past mem, Sigma Theta Tau, March Dimes Perinatal Nursing Adv Coun; Chicago Teachers Union, Local one. **Honors/Awds:** School Nurse of the Year, Chicago, 2001. **Home Addr:** 338 S Harper Ave, Glenwood, IL 60425. **Business Addr:** Teacher, Chicago Public Schools, 125 S Clark, Chicago, IL 60628, **Business Phone:** (773)553-2688.

HOWE, PROF. RUTH-ARLENE W.
Educator. **Personal:** Born Nov 21, 1933, Scotch Plains, NJ; daughter of Grace-Louise Randolph Wood and Curtis Alexander; married Theodore Holmes, Jun 29, 1957; children: Marian, Curtis, Helen & Edgar. **Educ:** Wellesley Col, AB, 1955; Simmons Col, MSW, 1957; Boston Col, JD, 1974. **Career:** Nat Inst Ment Health, fel, 1956-57; Cleveland Ohio Cath Youth Serv Bur, case worker, 1957-61; Tufts Delta Health Ctr, Mound Bayou, Miss, housing develop consult, 1969-70; Simmons Col Sch Social Work, instr soc pol, 1970-78; Law & Child Develop Proj, DHEW/ACYF Funded B C Law Sch, asst dir, 1977-79; Boston Col Law Sch, from asst prof law to prof law, 1977-2008, prof emer, 2009-; Mary Ingraham Bunting Inst, Radcliffe Col, Hermon Dunlap Smith fel law & social/pub policy, 1994-95. **Orgs:** Bd mem, Boston League Women Voters, 1963-68; clerk, Grimes-King Found Elderly Inc, 1972-; guardian adv litem, Mass Family & Probate Ct, 1979-; ABA Tech NCCUSL Uniform Adoption & Marital Property Acts, 1980-83; Mass Gov St Comn Child Support Enforcement, 1985; Mass Adv Comn Child Support Guidelines, 1986-89; Mass Gov/ MBA Comn Legal Needs C, 1986-87; NCCUSL Uniform Putative & Unknown Fathers Act Reporter, 1986-88; ed bd, Family Advocate, ABA sect Family Law, 1989-95, 2001-; Mass Supreme Judicial Ct Comn, Study Racial & Ethnic Bias Courts, 1990-94; US State Dept, Study Group Inter country Adoption, 1991-97; adv, Black Law Stud Asn; treas, Black Alumni Network. **Honors/Awds:** Wellesley scholar, Wellesley Col, 1955; Cited Contribution Legal Educ, Mass Black Lawyers Asn, 1983; Honorary Award, Mass Black Legis Caucus, 1988; Honorary Award, Boston Col Law Sch Alumni Asn, 1996; Honorary Award, Mus Afro-Am Hist; The BC Law Class, 2008. **Special Achievements:** Numerous publications in the areas of family law, foster care, adoption and social services including "Parenthood in the United States", Oxford Univ Press, 2000; "Race Matters in Adoption" ABA Family Law Quarterly, 2008 Fiftieth Anniversary Issue. **Business Addr:** Professor Emeritus, Boston College, Law School, 885 Centre St EW322, Newton Center, MA 02459-1163.

HOWELL, AMAZIAH, III
Executive. **Personal:** Born Oct 12, 1948, Goldsboro, NC; son of Amaziah and Theresa Reid; married Jessica McCoy, Jul 8, 1978; children: Joy Elizabeth, Aimee Denise. **Educ:** Johnson C Smith Univ, Charlotte, NC, attended 1968; NY Inst Credit, attended 1970; Amos Tuck Sch Bus, Dartmouth Univ, minority bus exec prog. **Career:** Manufacturers Hanover Trust Co, credit investr, 1968-72; Off US Senator James L Buckley, special asst, 1973-76; Wallace & Wallace Fuel Oil Co, mkt mgr, 1978-79; Asn Minority Enterprises NY Inc, exec dir, 1976-77, 1979-81; Las Energy Corp, Roosevelt NY, vpres, 1981-85; Howell Petrol Prod Inc, Brooklyn, NY, pres & chief exec officer, 1985-. **Orgs:** Am Asn Blacks Energy; Brooklyn Chamber Com; exec bd, Brooklyn Sports Found; Comn Students African Descent NY City Bd Educ; Comt Econ Develop; bus adv coun, Dist Community Sch; adv bd & oversight comt, chmn, Downtown Brooklyn Community; Environ Action Coalition; vpres, Halsey St Black Asn; Helen Keller Servs Blind; Latimer Woods Econ Develop Corp; exec adv coun, Long Island Univ; adv coun, Metrop Transit Authority; NY & NJ Minority Purchasing Coun; planning comt, vpres, chmn, Pub Sch 282; adv comt, US Courthouse Foley Square; Cornerstone Baptist Church; NY Water Bd. **Honors/Awds:** United States Jaycees, JCI Senator, 1981; Outstanding Minority Business, Nat Minority Bus

Coun, 1987; Robert F Kennedy Memorial Award to Minority Business, Brooklyn Chamber Com, 1989; Minority Supplier of the Year Award, NY & NJ Minority Purchasing Coun, 1989 & 1990; Supplier of the Year Regional Award Winner, Nat Minority Supplier Develop Coun, 1990; regional winner of the Entrepreneur of the Year, Merrill Lynch, Ernst & Young Mag, 1990; Small Businessman of the Year, NY Chamber Com & Indust, 1990; Green Star Award, Environ Action Coalition, 1992; New York City Business Advocate Award, Mayor Rudolph W Giuliani, 1994; Building Brick Award, NY Urban League, 1994. **Business Phone:** (718)855-4400.*

HOWELL, CHESTER THOMAS
Executive. **Personal:** Born Mar 23, 1937, Tarentum, PA; son of Hunter Lee and Jessie Leona Sharp; married Loretta J Lewis, Jan 18, 1964; children: Tracey Lynn, Jennifer Lynne & Hunter Lee II. **Educ:** Allegheny Tech Inst, 1968; Third Dist African Methodist Episcopal Theol Inst, 1994. **Career:** Executive (retired); Veterans Admin Hosp, nursing asst, 1961-68; Atlantic Design Corp, elec engr, 1968-72; Xerox Corp, Pittsburgh, dist bus mgr, chief financial officer, 1972-96. **Orgs:** Free & Accepted Masons, Prince Hall, 1970-79; pres, Metropolitan Area Minority Employees, Xerox, 1979; deacon, E End Baptist Tabernacle, Bridgeport, 1981-88; Cent Baptist, Syracuse, 1988-90; Human Rights Comn, Harrison Township Sch Dist; Habitat Humanities, Family Nurture Comt; Ed Rev Bd, Valley Daily News Dispatch. **Honors/Awds:** Black Achievers Award, Young Mens Christian Asn, 1980; ordained African Methodist Episcopal minister, local deacon, Bethel AMEC, 1992; ordained local elder, Bethel AMEC, Tarentum, Pa 15084, 1996. **Military Serv:** USAF, airman 1st class, 1955-59.

HOWELL, GERALD T
Insurance executive. **Educ:** Tenn State Univ, BS, cum laude, 1936. **Career:** Universal Life Ins Co, agent & other offices, 1941-61, agency dir, 1961-66, dir agencies, 1967, vpres & dir agencies, 1968-79, sr vpres & dir field opers, 1980-85, first vpres & secy & ceo, 1986-89, pres & ceo, 1990-95, chmn bd, 1995, Memphis, TN. **Orgs:** Nat Ins Asn; Nat Asn Advan Colored People; Emmanuel Epis Ch Alpha Phi & Alpha; Mason; Shriner. **Honors/Awds:** Sportsmen's Club Special Serv Award, Nat Ins Asn 1974; Blount Award, Nat Ins Asn, 1974. **Military Serv:** AUS, ETO first sargent, 1942-45.

HOWELL, MALQUEEN
Educator. **Personal:** Born Apr 3, 1949, Calhoun County, SC. **Educ:** BA, 1971, MA, 1972. **Career:** Benedict Col, eng instr. **Orgs:** Founding pres, Calhoun County Jr Improv League, 1966; Nat Asn Advan Colored People; adv panel, St Human Affairs Comn; Study & Preservation Black Hist; Art & Folklore Simons-Mann Col, 1973; voter educ proj & Heart Fund Campaign; United Way; Alpha Kappa Alpha. **Business Addr:** Instructor, Benedict College, 1600 Harden St, Columbia, SC 29204.

HOWELL, RACHEL
Human services worker. **Personal:** Born May 28, 1961, Detroit, MI; daughter of Carmen Perry and L C Howell; children: Bruce Howell & Ariana Howell. **Educ:** Franklin, basic EMT, 1986-87; Detroit EMS Training Acad, EMT-S, 1990; Detroit Receiving Hosp, advance cardiac life support, 1996; Superior Med Educ, paramedic, 1996-97. **Career:** E Jefferson Mkt, Detroit, Mich, cashier/lottery, 1980-84; Barnes & Noble (WCCC), Detroit, Mich, cashier/clerk, 1984-87; Detroit Fire Dept, Detroit, Mich, EMT, 1987-90, specialist, 1990-97, paramedic, 1997-; Int Union Operating Engineers, Local 547, from Union steward to chief steward, 1998-2003, EMMTTA rep, 2005-. **Honors/Awds:** Life Saver of the Year, Detroit E Medl Control, 1990-91; Life Saver of the Year, 100 Club, 1990-91. **Business Addr:** EMMTTA Representative, International Union of Operating Engineers Local 547, 24270 W Seven Mile Rd, Detroit, MI 48219, **Business Phone:** (313)532-2022.

HOWELL, ROBERT J., JR.
Executive. **Personal:** Born Feb 24, 1935, New York, NY; married Elestine. **Educ:** New Sch, MA; NY Univ, PhD. **Career:** Prof Recruitment & Replacement, spl asst dir personnel, 1967-68, chief, 1968-72; Cornell Grad Sch & Indust Labor Rel, consult, 1970-71; Div Employ, dep dir, 1972-74; NY State Civil Serv Commision Prof Cand Internal Pub Personnel Asn, oral examr; Human Resources Admin; Personnel Admin. **Orgs:** 100 Black Men. **Military Serv:** Sp 4, 1958-60. **Business Addr:** 271 Church St, New York, NY.*

HOWELL, ROBERT L
Educator. **Personal:** Born Oct 29, 1950, Paterson, NJ; son of David Sr and Sarah Alice Howell; married Yolanda Feliciano, Apr 10, 1976; children: Roberto M Jr, Danielle Elsie Sarah & Reynaldo Pressly. **Educ:** William Patterson Col, BA, 1971, ME, 1974. **Career:** Paterson Pub Sch, teacher, 1971-88, vice prin, 1988-89, prin, 1990, Eastside High Sch, prin, Sch 29, prin, currently. **Orgs:** Nat Educ Asn, 1971-; NAACP, 1973-; Nat Asn Elem Sch Principals, 1990-; bd dir, Positive Impact, 1992-; Nat Asn Sec Sch Principals, 2000-. **Honors/Awds:** Teacher of the Year, PS #12, Paterson, NJ, 1977; Governor's Teacher Recognition Award, NJ Governor's Office, 1988; Educator's Award, Phi Delta Kappa,

1992; Educator's Award, OPP, 1993; Educator's Award, Chauncey Brown Comt, 2000. **Business Addr:** Principal, Paterson High Schools, School 29, 88 Danforth Ave, Paterson, NJ 07501, **Business Phone:** (973)321-0290.

HOWELL, SHARON MARIE

Executive, dean (education). **Personal:** Born Dec 6, 1950, Minneapolis, MN; daughter of Tyler Jackson Jr and Juanita Olivia Marino. **Educ:** Xavier Univ La, BS, 1972; Univ St Thomas, St Paul, MA, 1985; Midwest Canon Law Soc Inst, Mundelein, IL, attended 1985; St Paul Sem, St Paul, MN, attended 1986. **Career:** Acad Natural Sci Philadelphia, Avondale, PA, res asst, 1972-74; 3M Co, St Paul, MN, anal chemist, 1974-76; Control Data Corp, Bloomington, MN, chemist, 1976-78; Minneapolis Inst Art, asst coordr exhibs, 1978-79; Minn State Dept Agr, St Paul, MN, anal chemist, 1979-80; Home Good Shepherd, St Paul, MN youth worker, 1980-83; Church St Leonard Port Maurice, pastoral minister, 1983-84; Univ St Thomas, St Paul, MN, dir multicultural & stud serv, dir diversity initiatives; Archdiocese St Paul & Minneapolis, St Paul, MN, intern, 1984-86; Black Cath Concerns, liaison, 1986; Archdiocesan Cms Black Cath, exec secy, 1986; Univ St Thomas, dir, asst dean & stud reconciliation & ombudsperson, currently. **Orgs:** Bd mem, Comn Evangelization, 1983-86; Asn Pastoral Ministers, 1984; assoc mem, Canon Law Soc Am, 1984; bd mem, Comn Ministry, 1985-89, chair, 1987-89; Minn Interfaith Coun Affordable Housing, 1988-90; bd dirs, Greater Minneapolis Coun Churches, 1989-91; Leadership St Paul, 1989-90; Sisters St Joseph, Carondelet, St Paul Prov; bd dirs, Cath Charities, 1990-95; bd trustees, Col St Catherine, St Paul, 1994; Coalition Ministerial Asn. **Business Addr:** Assistant Dean, Student Reconciliation & Ombudsperson, University St Thomas, 1000 LaSalle Ave Suite 110, Minneapolis, MN 55403, **Business Phone:** (651)962-6461.

HOWELL, WILLIAM B

Clergy. **Personal:** Born Feb 19, 1932, High Point, NC. **Educ:** Winston Salem State Col, BS, 1965; La Salle Univ Corr Sch, Chicago, LLB; ITC Gammon Theol Sem, MDiv, 1970; Brantridge Forest Col Eng, hon DD, 1972; Daniel Payne Col, DD, 1975. **Career:** Clergy (retired); High Point NC, law enforcement officer, 1953-62; Southern Pines Pub Sch, NC, teacher, 1965-67; NC TN GA Conf, pastorates; Turner Theol Sem Ext Prog, teacher theol, 1973; ML Harris United Methodist Church, minister. **Orgs:** Pres, Columbus Ga chap Oper PUSH; ordained decon & elder, United Methodist Church; vice-chmn, bd missions, S Ga Conf, 1972; vice chmn, Ministry S Ga Conf, 1972; Ga State Senate, 1972; mem bd dir, YMCA, 1973-74; pres, Columbus Phoenix City, Ministerial Alliance; Nat Asn Advan Colored People; Gammon Sem Alumni Asn; Comn Religion & Race S Ga Conf Chaplain WK. **Honors/Awds:** Scholarship Award, Bd United Methodist Church, 1967; Ada Stovall Award Academic Achievement, 1970; Dr Martin & Luther King Award Distinguished Service, 1974; Humanitarian Award, Am Red Cross, 1974.

HOWLETT, WALTER, JR.

Chairperson, president (organization). **Educ:** Univ Ala, BS, acct, 1981, CPA, 1983. **Career:** Booker T Washington Insurance Co Inc, chmn, pres & chief executive officer, currently; A G Gaston Construction Co Inc, pres & chief exec officer, currently. **Orgs:** AmSouth Bank Birmingham; Bus Coun Ala; Birmingham Chamber Com; Univ Ala Birmingham Sch Bus Adv Bd; United Way Cent Ala; Jr Achievement Ala; Boy Scouts Am. **Business Addr:** CEO, A G Gaston Construction Co Inc, 310 18th St N Suite 500, PO Box 697, Birmingham, AL 35203-0697, **Business Phone:** (205)328-0376.*

HOWROYD, JANICE BRYANT

Entrepreneur. **Personal:** Born Jan 1, 1953?, Tarboro, NC; married Bernard Howroyd, 1983; children: Katharyn, Brett. **Educ:** NC A&T Univ. **Career:** ACT*1 Personnel Servs, founder & pres, 1978-, chmn, currently. **Orgs:** Nat Asn Women Bus Owners; bd dirs, Urban League Los Angeles; bd dirs, Greater LA Dept African Am Chamber Comn. **Honors/Awds:** Minority Enterprise Develop Week Achievement Award, US Dept of Com, 1992; Entrepreneur of the Yr, AT&T Univ, 1994; Spirit of American Enterprise Presidential Award, 2005. **Special Achievements:** Numerous television shows: "The Oprah Winfrey Show" and "The Tavis Smiley Show"; Been twice named by the Star Group as one of the 50 Leading Women Entrepreneurs of the World, the first African-American woman honored. **Business Addr:** Founder & Chairman, Chief Executive Officer, ACT*1 Personnel Services, 5334 Torrance Blvd, Torrance, CA 90503, **Business Phone:** (310)370-5939.*

HOWZE, JOSEPH LAWSON

Clergy. **Personal:** Born Aug 30, 1923, Daphne, AL; son of Albert Otis and Helen Artamesa. **Educ:** Ala State Jr Col; AL State Univ, BS, 1948; St Bonaventure Univ, attended 1959; Phillips Col, bus mgt, 1980. **Career:** Mobile Cent High Sch, teacher, 1952; Cath Sch, St Monic, Okla, teacher, 1952; Roman Catholic Church, ordained priest, 1959; pastor in various churches including: Charlotte, Southern Pines, Durham, Sanford, Asheville, 1959-72; Natchez-Jackson, MS, aux bishop, 1973-77; Biloxi, MS, bishop, 1977, bishop emer, currently. **Orgs:** Trustee, Xavier Univ, New Orleans; MS Health Care Comn; NCCB & USCC; educ comt, USCC; Social Develop & World Peace Comt; liaison comt, Off Black Catholics, NCCB; bd dirs, Biloxi Reg Med Ctr; Dem; KC Knights St Peter Claver. **Honors/Awds:** Received many honorary degrees from various universities including: Univ Portland, 1974; Sacred Heart Col, 1977; St Bonaventure Univ, 1977; Manhattan Col, 1979; Bible Crusade Col, 1987; Belmont Abbey Col, 1999. **Special Achievements:** Became one of few Black bishops in history of Catholic Church in US; first Bishop of the New Diocese of Biloxi MS 1977; first Black Catholic bishop to head a Catholic Diocese in the USA since 1900. **Business Addr:** Bishop Emeritus, Diocese Biloxi, 1790 Popps Ferry Rd, Biloxi, MS 39532-1189, **Business Phone:** (228)702-2111.

HOWZE, KAREN AILEEN

Lawyer, consultant, editor. **Personal:** Born Dec 8, 1950, Detroit, MI; daughter of Manuel and Dorothy June Smith; children: Charlene, Karie & Lucinda. **Educ:** Univ Southern Calif, BA, 1972; Hastings Col Law, JD, 1977. **Career:** Detroit Free Press, reporter, 1971; San Francisco Chronicle, reporter, 1972-78; News day, Long Island, asst ed, 1978-79; Gannett Newspapers, Rochester, NY, asst managing ed/Sunday features ed, 1979-80; USA Today, founding ed, 1981, managing ed/systs, 1982-86, managing ed/int ed, 1986-88; Gannett Co Inc, Corp News Systs, ed, 1988-90; mgt consult, 1990-; Howze & Assocs, atty 1990-; Howard Univ, Sch Communs, lectr, 1990-92; Adoption Support Inst, pres/founder, 1990-; Am Univ Sch Commun, prof, 1991-94; DC Superior Court, Family Div, Remedial Project, spec master, 2000-01; Am Bar Asn, Ctr C & Law, dir, Adolescent Health Progs, 2001-02; Magistrate Judge, DC Superior Ct Family Ct, 2002-. **Orgs:** Nat Assn of Black Journal; past mem Sigma Delta Chi; past mem Women in Commun; mem, Alameda Co Comm Hlth Adv Bd; guest lect local comm col; mem, Amer Society of Newspaper Editors; vice-chair, Minority Opportunities Comm, Amer Newspaper Publisher's Assn; bd of directors, North AMR CN Lon Adoptable Children; bd mem, IST; bd mem Chelsea School; chap mayor'saCOM on Placement of Children in Family Homes; State of Am Bar ASN, licensed to practice law; Am Bar Asn, 1993-; mem, Probate Educ Comt; chmn, Super Ct DC Adoption Rules Advisory. **Honors/Awds:** Business Woman of the Year, Spellman Alumni, Wash, DC, 1986; Sr Ed, And Still We Rise, interviews with 50 Black Americans by Barbara Reynolds,1987. **Special Achievements:** Publications: And Still We Rise, Interviews with 50 Black Americans by Barbara Reynolds, 1987; Making Differences Work: Cultural Context in Abuse and Neglect Practice for Judges and Attorneys, 1996; Health for Teens in Care, 2002. **Business Addr:** Family Court Magistrate Judge, DC Superior Court, Moultrie Courthouse, 500 Indiana Ave NW, Washington, DC 20001, **Business Phone:** (202)879-1061.*

HOYE, CHERRON. See JOYCE, ELLA.

HOYE, WALTER B.

Journalist. **Personal:** Born May 19, 1930, Lena, MS; son of William H Sr and Lou Bertha Stewart; married Vida M Pickens Hoye, Aug 28, 1954; children: Walter B II, JoAnn M. **Educ:** Wayne St Univ, BA, 1954; Univ Calif San Diego, attended 1973. **Career:** Journalist (retired); Mich Chronicle Newspaper, sports ed & columinst, 1964-68; San Diego Chargers Football Club, asst dir pub rels, 1968-76; NFL media Rel, Super Bowl, 1972-75; SD Urban League Neighbourhood House Asn, pub info off, 1976; Educ Cult Complex, dir support syst, supvr, 1988-91. **Orgs:** vpres, San Diego Urban League, 1972-75; prog rev panelist, United Way CHAD, San Diego County, 1972-74; bd dirs, Red Cross San Diego, County, 1975-77; bd dirs, Pub Access TV, 1977-79; treas, San Diego Career Guidance Asn, 1981-82; adv bd, KPBS TV 15, 1983-84; Int Asn Auditorium Managers, 1978, 1990-91; Rocky Mountain Asn Stud Financial Aid Adminr, 1988. **Honors/Awds:** Nominator, Outstanding Young Men/Women of America, 1976-85; Citizen of Month, San Diego, 1979; Certificate of Recognition, California Legislative Assembly, 1989. **Home Addr:** 6959 Ridge Manor Ave, San Diego, CA 92115. *

HOYLE, DR. CLASSIE G.

Educator, college teacher, dean (education). **Personal:** Born Mar 26, 1936, Annapolis, MD; daughter of Nathaniel Daniel Gillis and Truma Lawson Elliott; married Daniel C, Aug 21, 1955; children: Dennis James & Lynne Valarie Jones. **Educ:** Morgan State Univ, BS, 1958, MS, 1968; Univ Iowa, PhD, 1977. **Career:** Lab scientist, 1958-59; sci teacher, 1960-68; Morgan St Univ, sci teacher, 1968-73; grad teaching asst, 1974-76; Coop Educ, coordr, 1976-77; Career Serv Placement Ctr, asst dir, 1977-78; Univ Iowa, dir affirmative action, 1978-82; Clarke Col, vpres acad affairs, 1982-85; Univ Iowa, Iowa City, IA, asst dean, 1985-90; NIH/NIGMS, Bethesda, MD, health scientist admin, 1990-. **Orgs:** Senatorial Scholar, 1954-58; Beta Kappa Chi, 1957; Alpha Kappa Mu, 1957; Kappa Delta Pi, 1958; Nat Sci Teachers Asn; Asn Educ Teachers Sci; Nat Asn Biol Teachers; Nat Sci Fel, 1965-68; den mother Cub Scouts, 1968-74; chairperson, courtesy comm Morgan St Univ, 1969-72; admin asst, Mt.Lebanon Bapist Church, 1970-73; secy treas, Fed Credit Union, 1970-73; secy, Morgan St Univ, 1972-73; Higher Educ Title III Grant, 1973-75; SoFel Fund, 1975-76; Iowa pres Am Coun Educ Nat Identification Prog, 1979-81; pres, Phi Delta Kappa, 1980. **Home Addr:** 2089 Forest Dr, Annapolis, MD 21401. **Business Addr:** Health Scientist Administra-

tor, National Institutes of Health, National Institute of General Medical Science, 5333 Wbard Ave WW-NIGMS-Rm 950, Bethesda, MD 20892, **Business Phone:** (301)496-7941.

HOYT, HON. KENNETH M

Judge. **Personal:** Born Jan 1, 1948?, San Augustine, TX. **Educ:** Tex Southern Univ, AB, 1969, Thurgood Marshall Sch Law, JD, 1972. **Career:** Pvt pract, 1972-85; city atty, 1975-81; 125th Civil Dist Ct, State Tex, presiding judge, 1981-82; State Tex Col Trial Advocacy Prog, fac, 1981-82; 125th Civil Dist Ct, State Tex, presiding judge, 1981-82; Tex Southern Univ, Thurgood Marshall Sch Law, adj prof, 1983-84; First Dist Ct Appeals Tex, justice, 1985-88; US Dist Ct, CJA Comt, chair, judge, currently. **Business Addr:** Federation Judge, US District Judge, US Courthouse, Rm 11144 515 Rusk Ave, Houston, TX 77002, **Business Phone:** (713)250-5611.

HOYT, BISHOP THOMAS L

Clergy, educator. **Personal:** Born Mar 14, 1941, Fayette, AL; married Ocie Harriet Oden; children: Doria & Thomas III. **Educ:** Evansville Col & Lane Col, BA, 1962; Interdenominational Theol Ctr, MDiv, 1965; Union Theol Sem, STM, 1967; Duke Univ, PhD, 1975. **Career:** Jefferson Pk Methodist, assoc pastor, 1965-67; St Joseph CME, pastor, 1967-70; Fawcett Memorial, pastor, 1970-72; Interdenominational Theol Ctr, prof, 1972-78; Howard Univ, prof, 1978-80; Hartford Sem, prof new testament, 1980-94; Nat Coun Churches, NY, pres, 2004-05; Christian Methodist Episcopal Church, Dept Lay Ministry, chmn, currently. **Orgs:** Soc Biblical Lit; Am Acad Religion; Soc study Black Religion; Theol Comn Consult Church Union; bd dirs, CT Bible Soc; Christian Methodist Church; Alpha Phi Alpha; Nat Asn Advan Colored People; Faith & Order Comn Nat Coun & World Coun Churches; bd dirs, Inst Ecumenical & Cult Res. **Honors/Awds:** Rockefeller Doctoral Fel; Nat Asn Equal Opportunity Higher Educ award; participant, Bilateral Dialogue between Methodist/Roman Catholic Churches; African Methodist Episcopal Zion/Christian Methodist Episcopal Unity Comm. **Home Addr:** 80 Girard Ave, Hartford, CT 06105. **Business Addr:** Chairman, Christian Methodist Episcopal Church, Department of Lay Ministry, 9560 Drake Ave, Evanston, IL 60203, **Business Phone:** (312)683-6831.

HOYTE, DR. ARTHUR HAMILTON

Educator, physician. **Personal:** Born Mar 22, 1938, Boston, MA; married Stephanie Hebron; children: Jacques. **Educ:** Harvard Col, BA, 1960; Columbia Univ Col Physicians & Surgeons, MD, 1964; San Francisco Gen Hosp, intern ship, 1965; Pres Hosp, resident, 1968. **Career:** Kaiser Found Hosp, 1968-70; E Palo Alto Neighbourhood Health Ctr, 1969-70; Off Econ Opportunity, med officer, 1970-71; consult Health Care Serv,1971-; Georgetown Univ Sch Med, asst prof,1971-; dir, Off Minority Stud Develop, Georgetown Univ. **Orgs:** Medico-Chirurgical Soc DC, 1974-; DC United Way; Coalition Health Adv, 1975-; Boys Club Washington, 1975-; pres, DC Sci Fair Asn, 1976-77; Presidential Task Force, 1976. **Honors/Awds:** Civil Service Award, Wash Region Med Prog, 1975. **Military Serv:** USAR, 1969-74. **Business Phone:** (202)687-1602.

HOYTE, JAMES STERLING

Lawyer, college administrator. **Personal:** Born Apr 21, 1944, Boston, MA; son of Patti Ridley and Oscar H; married Norma Dinnall, Dec 12, 1964; children: Keith Sterling & Kirsten Dinnall. **Educ:** Harvard Univ, BA, 1965, Law Sch, JD, 1968, Grad Sch Bus, Mass, PMD cert,1971, Kennedy Sch Govt, 1986. **Career:** Arthur D Little Inc, sr staff, 1969-74, 1979-82; Mass Sec State, Boston, Mass, dep secy, 1975-76; Mass Port Authority, secy-treas, dir admin, 1976-79; Commonwealth Mass, cabinet secy, secy Environ Affairs, 1983-88; Coate, Hall & Stewart, partner, 1989-91; Mass Horticultural Soc, interimexec dir, consultant, 1991-92; Attorney; Harvard Univ, assoc vpres & asst to pres, 1992-, adj lect pub policy & title IX coordr, currently. **Orgs:** Am Bar Asn; secy, Mass Black Lawyers Asn; bd dir, OpportunitiesIndusrialization Ctr Greater Boston, 1976-83; Nat Bar Asn, 1978-, LongRange Planning Comm, United Way Mass Bay, 1978; bd dir, Roxbury Multi ServCtr, 1979-87; chmn, bd trustees, Environ Comm, Boston Harbor Asn, 1989-;exec comm, bd dir, 1,000 Friends Mass, 1989-; bd trustees, Univ Hosp, 1989. **Honors/Awds:** Ten Outstanding Young Leaders, Greater Boston Jaycees, 1967; Black Achiever Award, Greater Boston YMCA, 1978; Alpha Man of the Year, Epsilon Gamma Lambda Chap Alpha Phi Alpha Frat, 1984; Governor Francis Sargent Award, Boston Harbor Asn, 1986; Frederick Douglass Award, Greater Boston YMCA, 1987. **Business Phone:** (617)495-1548.

HRABOWSKI, DR. FREEMAN ALPHONSA, III

Writer, educator. **Personal:** Born Aug 13, 1950, Birmingham, AL; son of Freeman and Maggie; married Jacqueline Coleman; children: Eric. **Educ:** Hampton Inst, BA, 1970; Univ Ill, Urbana-Champaign, MA, math, 1971, PhD, higher educ admin & statist, 1975. **Career:** Univ Ill Urbana-Champaign, math instr, 1972-73, admin intern, 1973-74,asst dean, 1974-76; Alab A&M Univ Normal, assoc dean, 1976-77; Coppin State Col, Baltimore, dean arts & scis div, 1977-81, vpres, academic affairs, 1981-87; Univ Md, Baltimore County, vice provost, 1987-90, exec vpres, 1990-92, interim pres, 1992-93; Univ Md, Catonville, pres, 1992-

;Books: Beating the Odds & Overcoming the Odds; Focusing on parenting &high-achieving African American males & females in science. **Orgs:** Alpha Phi Alpha; sr class pres, Hampton Inst, 1969-70; Baltimore City Life Museums; adv coun, Florence Crittenton Servs Inc; Peabody Inst, Johns Hopkins Univ; evaluator, Middle States Asn Col & Sch; Baltimore Equitable Soc; Unity Md Med Sys; Am Coun Educ, Constellation Energy, Baltimore Comm Found; Ctr Stage, Greater Baltimore Comm; Joint Ctr Polit & Econ Develop,McCormick & Co; Mercantile Safe Deposit & Trust Co; Merrick & France Found; Suburban Maryland High-Technol Coun; Asn Am Col & Univ; CarnegieInst; Marguerite Casey Found; Corvis Corp; consult, Nat Sci Found; NIH; Univs & Sch Systs. **Honors/Awds:** Outstanding Alumni Award, Phi Delta Kappa, Hampton Univ; Outstanding Community Service Award, Tuskegee Univ; Marylander of the Yr; USM Frederick doughlas award; Mc Graw Prize; BETA Award; NSF EDR Achievement Award; Edward Bouchet Leadership Award, MNY Grad Educ, Yale Univ; honorary degree, Princeton Univ; honorary degrees, Duke Univ; honorary degrees, Univ Ill; honorary degree, Univ Ala-Birmingham; honorary degree, Gallaudet Univ; honorary degree, Goucher Col; honorary degree, Med Univ SC & Binghamton Univ; Americas Best Leaders, U.S. News & World Report, 2008. **Special Achievements:** Co-author, Oxford Univ Press, beating odds, raising academically successful african Am Males, 1998, overcoming odds, 2002. **Business Addr:** President, University of Maryland-Baltimore County, 1000 Hilltop Circle, Baltimore, MD 21250, **Business Phone:** (410)455-3880.

HUBBARD, AMOS B.
Educator. **Personal:** Born May 11, 1930, Dora, AL; son of A B Hubbard; married Irene Windham; children: Melicent Concetta. **Educ:** Ala State Univ, BS, 1955; Ind Univ, MS, 1960; Univ Tenn; Univ Ala, Tuscaloosa; Mich State Univ; Univ Tulsa, OK. **Career:** Educator (retired); Carver HS Union Springs, AL, teacher & coach, 1955-58; Riverside HS Northport, AL, teacher, 1958-68; Col Educ Ach Prog, Stillman Col, dir, 1968-72, dir educ develop prog, 1972-74, athl dir, 1972-79, dir spec serv prog, 1976, coord instr, teaching-learning, 1975, dir spec progs, 1977-87, dean studs, 1988-95. **Orgs:** Kappa Alpha Psi; Brown Presbyterian Church; Kappa Delta Pi, 1973; Phi Delta Kappa, 1973; comn mgt, Barnes Br Young Men's Christian Asn, 1965-68; Tuscaloosa Civic Ctr Comn, 1971, Family Coun Serv, 1974; Kiwanis Tuscaloosa; Ment Health Bd; Narashino City Sister City Comn; Tuscaloosa Co Community Housing Resources Bd. **Honors/Awds:** Certificate of Achievement Award, Educ Improvement Project Soc Asn Col & Sch, 1973; Distinguished Service Award, United Fund Tuscaloosa City, 1973. **Military Serv:** AUS, corpl, 1951-53. *

HUBBARD, HON. ARNETTE RHINEHART
Lawyer. **Personal:** Born Jan 11, Stephens, AR; married; children: Gregory. **Educ:** John Marshall Law Sch, JD, 1969; Southern Ill Univ, BS. **Career:** Lawyers Comn Civil Rights Under Law, staff atty, 1970-72; pvt pract, 1972-; Chicago Cable Comn, Chicago, IL, comnr, 1985-89; Chicago Bd Election Comnrs, Chicago, IL, comnr, 1989-97; State Ill Circuit Ct, Cook Co Judicial Circuit, judge, 1997-. **Orgs:** Nat Bar Asn, 1975-; Nat Asn Advan Colored People; pres, Cook Co Bar Asn; pres, Asn Election Comn Off Ill; adv comm, Election Authority, State Bd Elections State Ill; exec bd, Ill Asn Co Off; exec comm, Int Asn Clerks, Recorders, Election Officials & Treas; bd dirs, Alpha Kappa Alpha Sorority; pres, Southern Ill Univ Alumni Asn, 1994-; Chicago Network; Women's Bar Asn Ill. **Honors/Awds:** Clarence Darrow Award; Obelisk Award for Education & Community Service, 2000; Scroll of Disting Women Lawyers, Nat Bar Asn, 2001. **Special Achievements:** First female president of the National Bar Association, 1981-82. **Business Addr:** Judge, State of Illinois Circuit Court, Cook County Judicial Circuit, 2005 Richard J Daley Ctr 50 Wash St, Chicago, IL 60602, **Business Phone:** (312)603-5907.*

HUBBARD, CALVIN L
Artist, educator. **Personal:** Born Jul 23, 1940, Dallas, TX; son of Ressie and CrinerMildred; married Evelyn McAfee Hubbard, Dec 21, 1968; children: Katrina, Tyletha & Yuressa. **Educ:** Aspen Sch Contemp Art, CO, attended 1963; Tex Southern Univ, Houston, BAE, 1966; Rochester Inst Technol, MST, 1971. **Career:** Educator (retired). Houston Independent Sch Dist, teacher, 1969-70; City Sch Dist, Rochester, NY, teacher, 1970-96; Nazareth Col, coordr art show, 1986-87; Turtle Pottery Studio & Gallery, owner & dir, 1987-; Eureka Lodge #36, jr warden, 1990-91; Eureka Lodge #36, worshipful master, 1995-96. **Orgs:** Bd mem, Woodward Health Ctr, 1988. **Honors/Awds:** Outstanding Leader Sec Educ, 1976; Martin Luther King Cultural Art Award, Colgate Divinity Sch, 1984; Recognition Outstanding Teacher, Univ Rochester, NY, 1986; Dewitt Clinton Award, 1998. **Special Achievements:** Published in Black Art in Houston, Texas Southern Univ, 1977. **Military Serv:** AUS, Sgt, 1966-69; Vietnam Service Award, Army Craft Contest, 1969. **Business Addr:** Owner, Turtle Pottery Studio & Gallery, 594 Brown St, Rochester, NY 14611, **Business Phone:** (585)328-7060.

HUBBARD, JAMES MADISON, JR.
Dentist. **Personal:** Born in Durham, NC; married Gloria Carter; children: Linda Rose, James III & Phillip. **Educ:** NC Cent Univ, BS, 1945; Howard Univ, DDS, 1949; Univ Calif Los Angeles, MPH, 1974. **Career:** Jersey City Med Ctr, intern, 1949-50; Durham, pvt pract, 1950-62; Lincoln Hosp Durham, chief attend oral surg; dentist pvt pract, currently. **Orgs:** Pres, W Manchester Med Dent Ctr; Hollywood Presb Hosp, Hollywood, Calif; bd dir & dent dir, CompreCare Health Plan; bd mem & chmn, Second Baptist Church Credit Union; life mem, Nat Asn Advan Colored People; 32nd degree Mason & Shriner; Kappa Alpha Psi Fraternity. **Honors/Awds:** Alexander Hunter Dental Society Award, 1963; Award for Achievement, Calif Dental Col, 1973. **Military Serv:** AUS, Dent Corps, capt, 1955-57. **Home Addr:** 5018 Valley Ridge Ave, Los Angeles, CA 90043. **Business Addr:** Dentist, 600 W Manchester Ave, Los Angeles, CA 90044.

HUBBARD, JEAN P.
Educator. **Personal:** Born Mar 5, 1917, Bedford, VA; married Portia. **Educ:** Wilberforce Univ, BS, 1941; Ohio State Univ, MA, 1945; Dayton Art Inst Univ CA, further study; Tulane Univ. **Career:** Educator (retired); Tenn State Univ, assoc prof, 1947-50; Art Dept Cent State Col, chmn, 1950-55; Southern Univ, instr, 1955-64; Dept Fine Arts Southern Univ, chmn, 1964. **Orgs:** Am Asn Univ Prof; Col Art Asn Am Paintings permanent collection, CarverMus Tuskegee AL; commn Mural Southern Univ New Orleans; Blacks LA & their contiribution to Culture of State of LA.

HUBBARD, JOSEPHINE BRODIE
Executive. **Personal:** Born May 11, 1938, Tampa, FL; married Ronald C; children: Ronald Charles & Valerie Alicia. **Educ:** Fl A&M Univ, BS hon, 1958; Univ South Fla, MA hon, 1968. **Career:** Howard W Blake H S, teacher, 1958-63; Chicopee H S, teacher, 1965-66; NB Young Jr H S, guid counr, 1968-69; Univ South Fla, proj upward bound counr coord, 1969-71, spec serv dir & acad adv; Wright State Univ, acad adv, 1973; Edwards Air Force Base, sub teacher, 1974-75, guidance counr, 1978-80; Dept Army West Ger, guid counr, 1978-80, collateral duty assignment, ed serv officer, 1980-81; Nellis Air Force Base, guid counr, 1981-83; Family Support Ctr, chief prog, 1983-87, asst educ serv officer, 1987-, dir, currently; Hubbard Family Ministries Inc, pres, dir, currently. **Orgs:** Rep, Family Support Ctr; dir, Vol Agencies Orgn, 1983-; Southern NV Chap Federally Employed Women Inc, 1983-; Fed Women's Prog Interagency Coun, 1983-; scholar chmn, Nellis Noncommissioned Officers Wives' Club, 1985. **Honors/Awds:** Sustained Superior Performance Award, Family Support Ctr, Chief Prog, 1985-86; Tactical Air Command Certificate Recognition Special Achievement, 1985; Notable Achievement Award, Dept Air Force, 1985; Sustained Superior Performance Award, Family Support Ctr, 1990-92. **Business Addr:** President, Director, Hubbard Family Ministries Inc, 4633 W El Prado Blvd, Tampa, FL 33629, **Business Phone:** (813)831-5114.

HUBBARD, LAWRENCE RAY
Interior designer. **Personal:** Born Oct 23, 1965, Pittsburgh, PA; son of Sylvia; children: John Perez, Hassan Perez. **Educ:** NY Univ, BA & BS, 1986. **Career:** Detroit Police Off, 1987-94; Viggiano Interiors, pres & owner, 1988-. **Orgs:** Optimist Club; Am Soc Interior Designers. **Special Achievements:** Appearances & articles: Detroit News; Detroit Free Press; WDIV-TV; Michigan Chronicle. **Business Phone:** (313)869-2523.*

HUBBARD, PAUL LEONARD
Government official, businessperson, president (organization). **Personal:** Born Oct 31, 1942, Cincinnati, OH; son of Paul and Sylvia; married Georgia; children: Paul Anthony & Melissa (stepdaughter). **Educ:** Ohio Univ, BS, bus ed, 1961-65; Wayne State Univ, Detroit, MI, SSW,1969-71; IBM Exec Mgmt Training, Cert, 1980; AMA, Exec Training Pres, Cert 1982. **Career:** Stowe Adult Ed, instructor 1965; Detroit Public Sch, teacher 1965-71; Wayne County CC, consultant 1971-74; Downriver Family Neighborhood Serv, assoc dir, 1971-74; New Detroit Inc, sr vpres; DHT transportation,1979-89, pres, 1989-93; City Toledo, dir neighborhoods & housing, 1993-; franchisee, Captain D's LLC, 2005-. **Orgs:** Chmn, MI Bell Consumer Adv Group, 1984-89; chmn, Metro Youth Prog Inc,1983-87; Nat vpres, Nat Assoc Black Social Workers, 1982-86; US Selective Serv Bd, 1985-87; Inter Nat Exchange Bd Dirs, 1985-; chmn, MI Supreme CtSubcomt, 1986-; pres, Detroit Chap Nat Asn Black Social Workers; Coun Polit Educ; bd dir, Goodwill Industries Greater Detroit; bd dirs, Grand Valley Univ; bd dirs, Mary grove Col; bd dirs, Southwest Hosp; bd dirs,Channel 56; Fed Home Loan bank. **Honors/Awds:** Outstanding Serv Award, Det chap, Nat Asn Black Social Workers, 1975;Lafayette Allen Sr Distinguished Serv Award, 1979; Detroit City Coun Testimonial Resolution for Community Servs, 1980; NABSW alumni year award,1981; Gentlemen Wall St Serv Award, 1984; Am Cancer Soc serv award, 1985; Black Enterprise Magazine serv award, 1987; Nat Welfare Rights serv award, 1988. **Business Addr:** Franchisee, Captain D, 2060 W Laskey Rd, Toledo, OH 43613, **Business Phone:** (419)473-0227.

HUBBARD, PHILIP GREGORY
Basketball player, basketball coach. **Personal:** Born Dec 13, 1956, Canton, OH; married Dr Jackie Williams; children: Whitney & Maurice. **Educ:** Univ Mich, attended 1980. **Career:** Basketball player (retired), Basketball coach: Detroit Pistons, 1979-82, Cleveland Cavaliers, 1982-89; NY Knicks, scouting coordr; 1993-94; Atlanta Hawks, asst coach, 1997-98; Golden State, asst coach, 2002; Wash Wizards, asst coach, 2003-. **Orgs:** US 1976 Olympic Basketball Team; Cavalier's rep & hon coach, OH Spec Olympics. **Honors/Awds:** Team leader & one of the best sixth men, Nat Basketball Asn. **Special Achievements:** Nominee, Walter Kennedy Award, 1984; only Cavalier to play in all 82regular season games, 1982-83; Staff that ranks as the longest tenured unit in the Eastern Conference. **Business Phone:** (202)661-5100.*

HUBBARD, REGINALD T.
Automotive executive. **Career:** Metrolina Dodge Inc, pres & chief exec officer, currently. **Business Phone:** (704)553-1988.*

HUBBARD, STANLEY
Executive. **Personal:** Born Oct 29, 1940, San Marcos, TX; son of Raymond William and Virginia Algeray Byars; married Dorothy Irene Brice Hubbard, Aug 28, 1965 (died 2001); children: Kimberly M, Stanley Jr, Thaddaeus B, Horace B (deceased), Raymond W II & Duane C. **Educ:** San Antonio Community Col, TX, AA, mid mgt, 1979; Antioch Univ Ohio, BA, labor studies, 1995. **Career:** Executive (retired); Various elec contractors, San Antonio, TX, from apprentice to journeyman, 1963-73; San Antonio Building Trades, San Antonio, TX, prog recruiter, 1973-79; AFL-CIO, Wash, DC, building trades prog coordr, 1979-81; IBEW, Wash, DC, int rep, 1981-2002. **Orgs:** Exec bd mem, IBEW Local No 60, 1969-73; bd mem, Tex State PTA, 1976-79; Greater Wash, DC br, APRI, 1983-; bd mem, Clinton Boys & Girls Club, 1985-89; pres, Surratts/Clinton Dem Club, 1989, 1992; bd dirs & gen mem, Safety Equipment Inst, 1997-2000. **Honors/Awds:** Wall Street Journal Award, San Antonio Community Col, WSJ, 1976; Texas Life Membership, Tex State PTA, 1977. **Special Achievements:** IBEW's first African-American apprentice in the state of Texas. **Military Serv:** AUS, specialist 4, 1959-62. **Home Addr:** 6916 Northgate Pkwy, Clinton, MD 20735-4057, **Home Phone:** (301)868-4762.

HUBBARD, TRENIDAD AVIEL. **See HUBBARD, TRENT.**

HUBBARD, TRENT (TRENIDAD AVIEL HUBBARD)
Baseball player. **Personal:** Born May 11, 1966, Chicago, IL; married Angela; children: Jaylen. **Educ:** Southern Univ. **Career:** Colo Rockies, outfielder, 1994-96; San Francisco Giants, 1996; ClevelandIndians, 1997; Los Angeles Dodgers, 1998-99; Atlanta Braves, 2000; Baltimore Orioles, 2000; Kans City Royals, 2001; San Diego Padres, 2002-03; Chicago Cubs, 2003; Class AAA teams, Durham Bulls, Round Rock Express and Iowa Cubs, 2005. *

HUBERT, JANET LOUISE
Actor. **Personal:** Born Jan 13, 1956, New York, NY; married James Whitten, Sep 3, 1990 (divorced); children: Elijah Issac; married Larry Kraft, 2005. **Educ:** Juilliard Sch; Loyola Unic, acct. **Career:** Alvin Ailey dance co; TV series: "The Fresh Prince of Bel Air", 1990-93; "New Eden", 1994; "What About Your Friends", 1995; "All My Children", 1999; "The Job", 2001-02; "The Bernie Mac Show", 2000-04; "Christmas at Water's Edge", 2004; "One Life to Live", 2005; Films: Agent on Ice, 1986; White Man's Burden, 1995;California Myth, 1999; 30 Years to Life, 2001; Neurotica, 2004; Proud, 2004; Stage credits include: Sophisticated Ladies; Cats, Broadway. **Business Addr:** Actress, Michael Slessinger & Associates, 8730 Sunset Blvd Suite 270-W, West Hollywood, CA 90069, **Business Phone:** (310)657-7113.

HUCKABY, HENRY LAFAYETTE
Physician. **Personal:** Born Jul 26, 1934, Crockett, TX; married Audria Mae Rain (divorced 1989); children: Seneca Kay, Arthur Craig, Sophia Katherine. **Educ:** Prairie View Agr & Mech Univ, BS, 1956; Meharry Med Col, MD, 1965. **Career:** Houston Indepenent Sch, sch teacher, 1959-61; Harlem Hosp NY, internship-surgeon, 1965-66, residency-gen surg,1966-70; Columbia Presby Hosp, residency plastic surg, 1970-72; Baylor Col Med, clinical instr plastic surg, 1973-77, attend plastic surgeon, 1974-87; Pvt Pract, plastic & reconstructive surg, 1974-87, hand surgeon, cosmetic surgeon, critical wound surgeon, burn surg, 1974-87, micro-vascular surgeon, 1982-. **Orgs:** Houston Med Forum; Nat Med Asn. **Military Serv:** AUS, first lt, 1956-58. **Business Addr:** Private Practitioner, 2619 Holman St, PO Box 13687, Houston, TX 77004.*

HUCKABY, MALCOLM
Basketball player. **Personal:** Born Apr 7, 1972. **Educ:** Boston Col, attended 1994. **Career:** Miami Heat, guard, 1997; Fileni JE, Italy, 1997; US Trust Bank, Boston, vpres; Bank Of America, fin adv. **Orgs:** Bd mem, Big Brothers Big Sisters of Mass Bay; Athlete Advisory Brd, Sports Legacy Inst, 2008. **Honors/Awds:** Boston College Varsity Club Athletic Hall of Fame, 2004.

HUDDLESTON, WILLIAM EMANUEL. **See LATEEF, DR. YUSEF.**

HUDGEONS, LOUISE TAYLOR
School administrator, dean (education). **Personal:** Born May 31, 1931, Canton, OH; married Denton Russell. **Educ:** Roosevelt Univ, Chicago, BS, 1952; Univ Chicago, AM, 1958; Ill Univ, EdD,

1974; Govs State Univ, MBA, 1977. **Career:** School administrator, Dean(retired); Mich Blvd Garden Apts, acct, 1952-55; Chicago Pub Schs, teacher, 1955-67; State Ill, Bus Off Educ, supvr, 1967-69; Chicago State Univ, asst prof,assoc prof, chmn, asst dean, acting dean, 1969-78; Eastern NM Univ, Col Bus, dean, 1978-; Cent State Univ, Sch Bus Admin, dean. **Orgs:** Consult, VA Polytech Inst, 1966; N Cent Asn Evaluating Teams, 1968-74; chmn, Col & Univ Div, Ill Bus Educ Asn, 1970; consult, Ill State Univ, 1971; chmn, Evaluation Supt Pub Schs, IL, 1972; consult, Cent Syst Res,1973; consult, US Off Educ, 1975; consult, Minn Bus Opportunities Comn, 1976-78; consult, Jwl Osco Co, 1977-78; consult, Govs State Univ, 1978; fel Am & Assembly Col Schs Bus, 1978. **Special Achievements:** Co-author, Your Career in Mrktng Mcgraw Hill, 1976; numerous speaking; several articles published.

HUDLIN, REGINALD ALAN
Movie producer, movie director, administrator. **Personal:** Born Dec 15, 1961, Centerville, MO; son of Warrington W and Helen Cason. **Educ:** Harvard Univ, BA, 1983. **Career:** Films: Reggie's World of Soul, 1984; The Kold Waves, 1985; House Party, 1990; BeBe's Kids, 1992; Boomerang, 1992; The Great White Hype, 1996; The Ladies Man, 2000; Servicing Sara, 2002; TV work includes, "Cosmic Slop", HBO, 1994; "The Last Days of Russell", ABC, 1995; "The Ride", 1998; "Richard Pryor: The Funniest Man Dead or Alive", 2005; "Bring That Year Back 2006: Laugh Now, Cry Later", 2006; Ill State Arts Coun, artist-in-residence, 1984-85; Ogilvy & Mather Advert Agency, NY, copywriter, 1986; Univ Wisc, Milwaukee, vis lectr film, 1985-86; Black Panther, writer, 2004; Hudlin Bros Inc, producer, screenwriter & film maker, currently; Black Entertainment TV network, pres entertainment & chief prog exec, 2005-. **Orgs:** Co-founder, Black Filmmakers Found, 1978. **Honors/Awds:** Grantee, Production of the Year, Black Filmmaker Found, 1983, 1985 & 1986; Best Film Award, Black Cinema Soc, 1984; fel, Nat Endowment Arts, 1985; Lillian Award, Delta Sigma Theta Sorority, 1990; Filmmakers Trophy, US Film Festival, 1990; Key to the City of Newark, 1990; Black Filmmakers Hall of Fame, 1990; Nancy Susan Reynolds Award, Ctr Pop Options; Clarence Muse Award, 1991; Starlight Award, Black Am Cinema Soc, 1993. **Special Achievements:** First African-American animated film producer. **Business Addr:** Producer, Filmmaker, Hudlin Bros Inc, Tribeca Film Ctr, 375 Greenwich St 6th Floor, New York, NY 10013.*

HUDSON, CHARLES LYNN
Baseball player. **Personal:** Born Mar 16, 1959, Ennis, TX; married Nikki. **Educ:** Prairie View A&M Univ, BA, 1981. **Career:** Baseball player (retired); Philadelphia Phillies, pitcher, 1983-86; New York Yankees, pitcher, 1987-88; Detroit Tigers, pitcher, 1989. **Honors/Awds:** Pitcher of the Year, 1982; named to Baseball Digest Rookie team, 1983.

HUDSON, CHERYL WILLIS
Publisher, arts administrator. **Personal:** Born Apr 7, 1948, Portsmouth, VA; daughter of Hayes Elijah III and Lillian Watson; married Wade Hudson, Jun 24, 1972; children: Katura J & Stephan J. **Educ:** Oberlin Col, BA (cum laude), 1970; Ratcliffe Col Publ Procedures Course, 1970; Northeastern Univ, graphic arts mgt courses, 1972; Art Studs League, NY; Parsons Sch Design, 1976. **Career:** Houghton Mifflin Co, art ed & sr art ed, 1970-73; Macmillan Publ Co, designer, design mgr, 1973-78; Arete Publ Co, asst art dir, 1978-82; freelance designer spec projs, 1979, 1985-88; Paperwing Press & Angel Entertainment, art dir, freelance design consult, 1982-87; Just Us Books, co-founder & ed dir, 1988-; Book: Bright Eyes, Brown Skin; Many Colors of Mother Goose; Come By Here, Lord: Everyday Prayers for Children; Hold Christmas In Your Heart; What Do You Know, Snow!; What a Baby!; Hands Can & Construction Zone. **Orgs:** Soc C's Book Writers & Illurs, 1989-; Nat Asn Black Book Publ, 1990-92; bd dirs, Multicult Publ Exchange, 1990-98; Black Women Publ, 1990-92; adv bd, Small Press Ctr, 1999-. **Honors/Awds:** Stephen Crane Library Award, Newark Pub Libr, 2000; inductee, InterNat Literary Hall of Fame, 2003. **Special Achievements:** Author of Afro-Bets ABC Book, 1987, Afro-Bets 123 Book, 1988, Selection In The Multicolored Mirror: Cultural Substance in Literature for Children and Young Adults, 1991, Multiculturalism in Children's Books, 1990, Good Morning, Baby, 1992, Good Night, Baby, 1992, co-author of Bright Eyes, Brown Skin, 1990, Kwanzaa Sticker Activity Book, Scholastic Inc/Just Us Books, 1994, Glo Goes Shopping, 1998, Come by Here Lord, 2001, Langston's Legacy, 2002, articles have appeared in Edited by Violet Harris, Teaching Multicultural Literature in Grades K-8; "Creating Good Books for Children," A Black Publishers Perspective; Speaks Frequently on Topics Related to Creative Publishing of Books for Children, Focusing on African American Themes. **Business Addr:** Co-founder, Editorial Director, Just Us Books Inc, 356 Glenwood Ave Suite 3, East Orange, NJ 07017, **Business Phone:** (973)676-4345.

HUDSON, CHRIS. See HUDSON, CHRISTOPHER RESHERD.

HUDSON, CHRISTOPHER RESHERD (CHRIS HUDSON)
Football player. **Personal:** Born Oct 6, 1971, Houston, TX. **Educ:** Univ Colo, bus, 1995. **Career:** Football player (retired); Jacksonville Jaguars, defensive back, 1995-98; Chicago Bears, 1999; Atlanta Falcons, 2001. **Orgs:** Colorado Buffaloes. **Honors/Awds:** Jim Thorpe Award, 1994.

HUDSON, DIANNE ATKINSON
Television producer, journalist. **Educ:** Ohio Univ, BA, broadcast journ. **Career:** Assoc Press, broadcast news writer, 1976; TV Series: "The Oprah Winfrey Show", exec producer & producer, 1986, 1994-03; "I Hate the Way I Look", sr producer, 1994; "ABC Afterschool Specials", sr producer, 1994; Oprah Winfrey, spec adv; Harpo Productions, vpres; Oprah Winfrey Found & Oprah's Angel Network, pres. **Orgs:** Bd trustee, Howard Univ, 2005-. **Honors/Awds:** Outstanding Talk Show, 1986; Nominee, Daytime Emmy Awards; received nine Emmy Awards. **Special Achievements:** Establishing Oprah's Book Club. **Business Addr:** Executive Producer, Harpo Productions The Oprah Winfrey Show, Harpo Studios, 110 N Carpenter St, Chicago, IL 60607, **Business Phone:** (312)633-0808.*

HUDSON, DON R
Editor. **Personal:** Born Sep 9, 1962, Shreveport, LA; son of David Hudson Sr and Gladies; married Miriam Caston Hudson, Dec 29, 1984. **Educ:** Northwestern State Univ, 1980; Northeast La Univ, BA, broadcast jour, 1983. **Career:** Monroe News-Star world, sports writer, ed, 1981; Atlanta J-Const, asst sports ed, Ark Gazette, sports ed; Orlando Sentinel, Sunday sports ed; Lansing State J, managing ed, 1999; Jackson Clarion-Ledger, sports writer, managing ed, currently. **Orgs:** Nat Asn Black Journalists; Associated Press Sports Eds; Orlando Black Achievers Prog. **Honors/Awds:** Orlando YMCA, The Orlando Sentinel's Black Achiever, 1991-92. **Business Addr:** Managing Editor, The Clarion-Ledger, PO Box 40, Jackson, MS 39205-0040, **Business Phone:** (601)961-7230.

HUDSON, ELBERT T.
Executive. **Career:** Broadway Fed Bank , Los Angeles, CA, pres & chief exec officer, 1972-92, chmn exec comt, currently. **Orgs:** Calif Bar asn; mem exec comt & chmn, audit comt, Golden State Mutual Life Ins Co;chair bd Trustees, Angeles Funeral Home pre-need Fund; mem bd La Trade Tech Col Found. **Business Addr:** Chairman of the Executive Committee, Broadway Federal Bank, 4800 Wilshire Blvd, Los Angeles, CA 90010, **Business Phone:** (323)634-1700.*

HUDSON, ERNIE
Actor. **Personal:** Born Dec 17, 1945, Benton Harbor, MI; son of Maggie Donald; married Linda Kingsberg, May 25, 1985; children: Andrew & Ross; married Jeannie Moore, Jan 1, 1963 (divorced 1982); children: Ernest Jr & Rocky. **Educ:** Wayne State Univ, BA; Yale Univ Sch Drama, MFA; Univ Minn, PhD. **Career:** Janitor; Chrysler Corp, machine operator; MI Bell, customer rep, Actor, currently; TV: "The Next Generations", 1979; "High cliffe Manor", 1979; "White Mama", 1980; "Love on the Run", 1985; "The Last Precinct", 1986; "Broken Badges", 1990; "Angel Street", 1992; "Wild Palms", 1993; "The Cherokee Kid", 1996; "Oz", 1997-2003; "Clover", 1997; "Michael Jordan: An American Hero", 1999; "Nowhere to Land", 2000; "A Town Without Christmas", 2001; "HRT", 2001; "10-8: Officers on Duty", 2003; "Fighting the Odds: The Marilyn Gambrell Story", 2005; "Desperate Housewives", 2006; "Certifiably Jonathan", 2007; "Final Approach", 2007; "Las Vegas", 2007; "Gus's Dad May Have Killed an Old Guy", 2007; "Psych", 2007; "guest appearances on various tv shows; film: Lead belly, 1976; The Main Event, 1979; The Octagon, 1980; The Jazz Singer, 1980; Penitentiary II, 1982; Going Berserk, 1983; Two of a Kind, 1983; Joy of Sex, 1984; Ghostbusters, 1984; Weeds, 1986; Leviathan, 1989; Trapper County War, 1989; Ghostbusters II, 1989; The Hand That Rocks the Cradle, 1992; Sugar Hill, 1993; No Escape,1993; The Cowboy Way, 1994; Airheads, 1994; The Crow, 1994; Congo, 1995; The Substitute, 1996; For Which He Stands, 1996; Mr Magoo, 1997; Operation Delta Force, 1997; Leviathan, 1997; Fakin' Da Funk, 1997; October 22, 1998; Stranger in the Kingdom, 1998; Butter, 1998; Shark Attack, 1999; Stealth Fighter, 1999; Paper Bullets, 1999; Lillie, 1999; Interceptors, 1999; Hijack, 1999; Everything's Jake, 2000; Red Letters, 2000; The Watcher, 2000; Miss Congeniality, 2000; Anne B Real, 2002; The Ron Clark Story, 2005; Sledge: The Untold Story, 2005; Marilyn Hotchkiss' Ballroom Dancing & Charm Sch, 2005; Miss Congeniality 2: Armed & Fabulous, 2005;Halfway Decent, 2005; Hood of Horror, 2006; Nobel Son, 2006; Hood of Horror, 2006; 21 Guns, 2006. **Honors/Awds:** Universe Readers Choice Award, Best Supporting Actor Genre Motion Picture, 1995; Golden Satellite Award, Best Performance Actor in a Television Series, Drama, 1999. **Military Serv:** USMC. **Business Phone:** (310)656-0400.

HUDSON, FREDERICK BERNARD
Writer, television producer, management consultant. **Personal:** Born Oct 29, 1947, Chicago, IL; son of Joseph T and Nellie Parham; married Yvonne. **Educ:** Wayne State Univ, BA, 1969; Yale Law Sch, attended 1970; New Sch Social Res, MA, 1975; Am Inst Planners, registered city planner cert, 1979. **Career:** Odyssey House, NJ, adminr, 1971-73; Afarm Assocs, res assoc, 1975; City Univ NY, fac mem, 1975-76; City Univ Res, prog consult, 1975-76; Elon Mickels & Assocs, proj dir, 1976-78; Detroit City Coun, staff analyst, 1978-79; Southern Ill Univ, vis asst prof & coordr, 1979-80; Frederick Douglass Creative Arts Ctr, dir pub rels, 1981-82; Centaur Consult, pres, 1983-; Col New Rochelle, 1986-87; Am Bus Inst, educ officer, 1986-89; producer television movies: Things We Take & Undercover Man; Take it to Hill, 1995-99. **Orgs:** Spec prog asst, Nat Urban League, 1973-75; Asn Independent Video & Filmmakers; Am Planning Asn; Am Mgmt Asn; community consult, AT&T, 1974; community consult, Coro Found, 1980; community consult, Reality House, 1982; instr, Dist Coun 37, 1989-; organizer, Nat Action Network, 1995-; October 22 Movement, 2000-; Int Action Ctr, 2000-; Mensa, Film Video Arts, Am Mgt Asn, currently. **Honors/Awds:** Citation of Merit, 1969, 1973-74; Mayors Commendation for the City of Newark, New Jersey Certificate of Merit, 1974; New Writers Citation, PEN, 1984; Service Award, DC 37, 2000. **Special Achievements:** Author of What's In a Number? An Eval of a Title I Prog, 1975, poems: Black Scholar, Obsedian,1980, Anthology of Magazine Verse, short story, "The Peach Tree," 1982, play, The Indenture of Simon Hastings, 1988, has published in many literary magazines, including the Massachusetts Review and The Black Scholar. **Business Addr:** President, Centaur Consult, 1510 E 172 St Apt 4, Bronx, NY 10472.

HUDSON, HEATHER MCTEER
Mayor. **Personal:** Daughter of Charles V; married Abe Jr. **Educ:** Spelman Col, BA, sociol, 1998; Tulane Univ, JD. **Career:** McTeer & Assocs Law Firm, atty; Lennys Sub Shop, co-owner; City Greenville, mayor, 2003-, Agape Storage Christian Ctr, mem. **Orgs:** Teen ministry leader, Agape Storge Christian Ctr; co-founder, Proj Give Back; exec dir, McTeer Found; Mission Miss; Alpha Kappa Alpha Sorority Inc; Miss Bar Asn; Am Trial Lawyers Asn; Wash County Bar Asn; Magnolia BarAsn; Spelman Col Alumnae Asn; Rotary Club; Miss Municipal League. **Honors/Awds:** The 50 Most Beautiful Women in the World, Essence Magazine, 2005. **Special Achievements:** First African-American and female mayor of Greenville, Mississippi. **Business Addr:** Mayor, City of Greenville, 340 Main St, Greenville, MS 38701, **Business Phone:** (662)378-1538.*

HUDSON, DR. JAMES BLAINE
Educator, dean (education). **Personal:** Born Sep 8, 1949, Louisville, KY; son of James Blaine Hudson II and Lillian Williamson Hudson; married Bonetta M Hines; children: Maya F, Travis M & Kenwyn K. **Educ:** Univ Louisville, BS, 1974, MEd, 1975; Univ Ky, EdD, 1981. **Career:** Sch Educ Univ Louisville, admin coord, 1974-75; W Louisville Educ Prog, Univ Louisville, admin coord, 1975-77, from asst dir to dir 1977-82; Haggin fel, Univ Ky, 1977-78; Univ Louisville, assoc dir; Univ Louisville Preparatory Div, assoc dir, 1982-92; Pan-African Studies, asst prof, 1992-98, assoc prof, chmn, 1998-2003, assoc dean, 1999-2003, acting dean, 2003-05, dean, 2005-. **Orgs:** APGA, KPGA, ACPA 1976-; MENSA 1984-; chair, Kentucky African Am Heritage Comn, 2000-. **Honors/Awds:** Nat Merit Scholar, 1967; Black Faculty Staff Member of the yr, Univ Louisville, 1982; Martin Luther King Jr Dream Award, Mayor's off, 2002. **Home Addr:** 4255 North Western Pkwy, Louisville, KY 40212-2930. **Business Addr:** Dean, Professor, College of Arts and Sciences, Univ of Louisville, Louisville, KY 40292.

HUDSON, JENNIFER KATE
Singer, actor. **Personal:** Born Sep 12, 1981, Chicago, IL; daughter of Samuel Simpson (deceased) and Darnell Hudson; married David Daniel Otunga; children: David Daniel Otunga Jr. **Educ:** Dunbar Voc Career Acad, attended 1999. **Career:** Album: Dream girls, 2006; Singles: "And I Am Telling You I'm Not Going", 2006; All Dressed in Love, 2007; Spotlight", 2008; TV: "On-Air with Ryan Sea crest", 2004; "HBO First Look", 2006; "Film '72", 2007; Movies Rock, 2007; Elmo's Christmas Countdown, 2007; Making of 'Sex & the City, 2008; "Entertainment Tonight", 2008; "Live with Regis & Kathie Lee", 2008; Michael Jackson Memorial, 2009. An Evening of Stars: Tribute to Patti LaBelle, 2009. **Honors/Awds:** WAFCA Award, 2006; SEFCA Award, 2006; Screen Actors Guild Awards, 2006; Satellite Award, 2006; PFCS Award, 2006; NYFCC Award, 2006; NBR Award,2006; Sierra Award, 2006; Pauline Kael Breakout Award, 2006; Oscar Award,2007; BAFTA Film Award, 2007; BET Award, 2007; Black Reel Award, 2007;Critics Choice Award, 2007; COFCA Award, 2007; Golden Globe, 2007; Image Award, 2007; Breakthrough Performance Award, 2007; Teen Choice Award, 2007. **Special Achievements:** Third African American celebrity, and the first African American singer,to grace the cover of Vogue magazine; One of 115 people invited to join AMPAS in 2007. **Business Addr:** Actor, William Morris Agency, 151 El Camino Dr, Beverly Hills, CA 90212.

HUDSON, DR. JEROME WILLIAM
Educator. **Personal:** Born May 9, 1953, Washington, DC. **Educ:** Univ MD, BA, 1975; George Wash Univ, Grad Cert, 1980; Am Inst Hypnotherapy, PhD 1986. **Career:** YMCA, asst phys dir, 1977-78; Wesley Early Childhood Ctr, dir, 1978-79; Shore Up Inc, dir training & employment, 1979-; Romejoy Inc, Salisbury, MD, chief exec officer, 1986-. **Orgs:** Adj fac mem, Salisbury State Col, 1978-80; gov state adv coun, Office C & Youth, 1978-; dir training & employment, Shore Up Inc, 1979-87; state adv comt mem, Office C & Youth, 1980-; selection comt mem, Foster Care Review

Bd, 1980-87; selection comt mem, Foster Care Review Bd, 1980-; lectr univ & cols, 1980-; bd dir, Heart Asn, 1980-81; vpres, Wicomico County Coun Social Serv, 1980-81; lecr, Afro-Am Hist Week Phi Delta Kappa, 1982; bd dir, Md Pub Broadcasting-Chem People Adv Bd; bd dirs, March Dimes, 1983, YMCA 1984-90; Salisbury Chap Jaycees, 1986-; founder, Rural Opportunity for Minority Enterprise Scholar, 1990-. **Honors/Awds:** Key to the City of Salisbury, 1978; Employee of the Year Shore Up Inc, 1981; Producer C & Youth Conf Gov MD, 1981; Enthusiastic Award, MD State Dept Educ, 1985-86. **Special Achievements:** Outstanding Young Men of America, US Jaycees 1981. **Home Addr:** PO Box 3305, Salisbury, MD 21802. **Business Addr:** Chief Executive Officer, Romejoy Inc, 1115 Tuscola Ave Suite 1A, Salisbury, MD 21801, **Business Phone:** (410)543-0713.

HUDSON, KATE. See BRYANT, JOY.

HUDSON, KEITH
Executive. **Personal:** Born Mar 4, 1954, St Louis, MO; married Janeice Fay Gipson. **Educ:** OFallon Tech Sch, Electronics, 1974. **Career:** Hudson Embassy, store mgr, 1972-75; Metro Advert, acct exec, 1977; Teds One Stop, salesman, 1975-78; Teds One Stop Inc, vpres Sales & mdse, 1978-; Platinum Plus Records & Tapes, pres 1979. **Orgs:** Dem Orgn, 1973; Black Music Asn, 1977. **Honors/Awds:** Gold record, RCA Records & Tapes, 1977. **Home Addr:** 4667 Tesson St, St Louis, MO 63116. *

HUDSON, LESTER DARNELL
Lawyer. **Personal:** Born Mar 4, 1949, Detroit, MI; married Vivian Ann Johnson. **Educ:** Fisk Univ, BA, 1971; Boston Col, Law Degree; Law Sch Brighton, MA, 1974. **Career:** Bell & Hudson, atty & sr partner; City Boston Law Dept, intern, 1972-73; Boston Legal & Asst Proj, legal intern, 1972; Boston Col, legal internlegal asst, 1973-74. **Orgs:** Detroit Bar Asn; NBA; ABA Young Lawyers sect; Urban League; PUSH Detroit; NAACP Crime Task Force comt. **Honors/Awds:** Award for Leadership & Scholarship, Scott Paper Co Found, 1971; Martin Luther King Award, Leadership & Comn Involvement, 1974.

HUDSON, MERRY C.
Government official. **Personal:** Born Dec 25, 1943, Baltimore, MD; married Robert L Hudson; children: Alicia; Stephen. **Educ:** Howard Univ, BA, 1965, JD, 1968; George Wash Univ, LLM, 1972. **Career:** Howard Univ, acad scholar, 1961-68; Equal Employ Opportunity Comn, supvry atty, 1971-72; Univ Md, affirmative action officer, 1975-76; Pvt Pract Law, 1976-78; Univ Md, consult, 1976; State Md, Comn Human Rels, chief hearing examr, 1978-. **Orgs:** Treas, DC Links Inc, 1985-; Nat Asn Admin Law Judges; Nat Bar Asn; Alpha Kappa Alpha. **Honors/Awds:** Cert of Appreciation, State Md, Personnel Dept, 1980; Citation Distinquished Serv, Nat Judicial Col, 1982, Distinguished Alumni Award, Nat Asn Equal Opportunities, 1986. **Home Addr:** 1216 Edgevale Rd, Silver Spring, MD 20910.

HUDSON, PAUL C.
Banker, entrepreneur. **Educ:** Univ Calif, Berkeley, BA, polit sci; Boalt Hall Sch Law, juris doctorate, 1973. **Career:** Broadway Fed Savings & Loan, pres & chief exec officer, currently. **Orgs:** Los Angeles NAACP; Boy Scouts Am; Chmn, Community Redevelop Agency; State Calif & Dist Columbia bars; Community Build, Inc. **Honors/Awds:** Local Community Heroes, 2007. **Special Achievements:** Company ranked 13 Black Enterprise Top Financial Companies List, 1992. **Business Phone:** (323)634-1700.*

HUDSON, DR. ROBERT LEE
Educator, physician. **Personal:** Born Oct 30, 1939, Mobile, AL; son of Robert L and Claudia M Jackson Hudson Graham; married Merry Brock; children: Alicia & Stephen. **Educ:** Lincoln Univ, BA, 1962; Howard Univ, MD, 1966. **Career:** Howard Univ Ctr Sickle Cell Disease, physician coord, 1971-72, dep dir, 1972-75; Howard Univ, asst prof, 1971-75; pvt pract, physician, currently; Children's Nat Med Ctr, physician, currently. **Orgs:** Columbia Hosp Women; DC Gen Hosp; mem bd dir, Capital Head Start, 1971-75; med cons Capital Head start, 1971-76; Med Soc DC; Am Acad Pediatrics; Medico Chirurgical Soc DC; Am Heart Asn. **Business Addr:** Physician, 2600 Naylor Rd SE, Washington, DC 20020.

HUDSON, DR. ROY DAVAGE
Educator, administrator. **Personal:** Born Jun 30, 1930, Chattanooga, TN; son of James Roy and Everence Wilkerson; married Constance Joan Taylor, Aug 31, 1956; children: Hollye Hudson Goler & David K Hudson. **Educ:** Livingstone Col, BS, 1955; Univ Mich, MS, 1957, PhD, 1962; Lehigh Univ, LLD, 1974; Princeton Univ, LLD, 1975. **Career:** Univ Mich Med Sch, asst prof, 1961-66; Brown Univ Med Sch, assoc prof, 1966-70; Brown Univ Grad Sch, assoc dean, 1966-69; Hampton Univ, pres, 1970-76; Warner Lambert, Parke-Davis, vpres, pharmaceut res planning, 1977-79; Upjohn Co, pharmaceut res, dir cent nervous system res, 1981-87, Pharmaceut Res & Develop, Europe, vpres, 1987-90, corp vpres pub rels, 1990-92; Univ Mich, ML King/C Chavez/R Parks vis prof, 1989; Guid Clin, exec dir & chief exec officer, 1994; Livingstone Col, interim pres, 1995-96. **Orgs:** Danforth Fel, Danforth Found, 1955-62; bd dir, Peninsula Chamber Com, 1970-76; bd dir, United Va Bankshares, 1971-76; bd dir, Chesapeake & Potomac Telephone Co, 1972-76; chmn, Va State Comn Selection Rhodes Scholars, 1973; bd dir, Am Coun Educ, 1973-76; bd dir, Parke-Davis Co, 1974-76; bd trustees, Nat Med Fel, 1990-92; bd dirs, Comerica Bank, 1990-95; adv bd, Kalamazoo Math & Sci Ctr, 1990-92. **Honors/Awds:** Scholarship Award, Omega Psi Phi Fraternity, 1954-55; Distinguished Alumni Medallion, Livingstone Col, 1969; Outstanding Civilian Service Award, AUS, 1972; Award of Merit for Continuous Service to Humanity, Omega Psi Phi Fraternity, 1974; Award for Exemplary Leadership, Omega Psi Phi Fraternity, 1978. **Military Serv:** USAF, staff sgt, 1948-52. **Home Addr:** 7057 Oak Highlands Dr, Kalamazoo, MI 49009-6508, **Home Phone:** (269)372-7556.

HUDSON, STERLING HENRY
Educator, college administrator. **Personal:** Born Jul 6, 1950, Hot Springs, VA; son of Sterling H Hudson Jr; married Cheryl White; children: Tara L. **Educ:** Hampton Univ, BA, 1973, MA, 1979; Ga State Univ, Capella Univ. **Career:** Hampton Univ, admissions counr, 1973-77, asst dean admis, 1977-82; Elizabeth City State Univ, dir admis & recruitment, 1982-83; Morehouse Col, dir admis, 1983-93, asst vpres acad affairs & dir admis, dean freshmen, 1991-96, Admis & Enrollment Mgt, vice provost, 1996-98, Admis & Rec, dean, 1998-, dir PSP, currently. **Orgs:** Nat Asn Col Admis Counr, 1973-; Am Asn Col Deans Registr Admis Officers, 1973-; Kappa Delta Pi, 1979-; Atlanta Urban League, 1984-; rep, Univ Ctr Ga, 1984-86; coun col level serv, Col Bd, 1985-88; Golden Key Hon Soc, 1999-; Iota Phi Theta Fraternity Inc. **Honors/Awds:** Most Outstanding Graduate Brother, Iota Phi Theta 1980; Fleischman Foundation UNCF Study Grant, 1986; Student Government Campus Leader Award, 2000. **Business Addr:** Dean, Director, Morehouse College, Office of Admissions and Records, 830 Westview Dr SW, Atlanta, GA 30314-3773, **Business Phone:** (404)215-2748.

HUDSON, DR. THEODORE R.
Educator, writer, college teacher. **Personal:** Born in Washington, DC; married Geneva Bess; children: Eric & Vicki. **Educ:** Miner Teachers Col, BS; NY Univ, MA; Howard Univ, MA, PhD. **Career:** Educator (retired); Univ DC, prof eng, 1964-77; Am Univ, adj prof lit, 1968-69, 1991; Howard Univ, grad prof eng, 1977-91, consult, 1991. **Orgs:** Vpres, Duke Ellington Soc; ed, Ellingtonia; behind-the scenes vol, Smithsonian Inst; pres, Highland Beach City Asn. **Honors/Awds:** Most Distinguished Literature Scholar Award, Col Lang Asn, 1974. **Special Achievements:** From LeRoi Jones to Amiri Baraka, Lit Works, Duke Univ Press, 1973; Numart in periodicals and books; Officer Brother, The Venerable Order of St John. **Home Addr:** 1900 Lyttonsville Rd Suite 315, Silver Spring, MD 20910. *

HUDSON, TROY
Basketball player, singer. **Personal:** Born Mar 13, 1976, Carbondale, IL. **Educ:** Univ Mo; Southern Ill univ, attended 1998. **Career:** Yakima, Sioux Falls, Continental Basketball Asn, 1997-98; Utah Jazz, 1997-98; Los Angeles Clippers, guard, 1997, 1998-2000; Orlando Magic, 2000-02; Minn Timberwolves, guard, 2002-07; Golden State Warriors, 2007-08. **Special Achievements:** Minnesota's second-leading scorer during the 2003 Playoffs; released a rap album entitled: The Stress of Both Worlds under the name T-Hud, 2006; album: Undrafted. *

HUDSON, WILLIAM THOMAS
Government official. **Personal:** Born Dec 14, 1929, Chicago, IL; son of Cornelius and Mary. **Educ:** NWS Univ, BS, 1953; Univ Chicago, MA, 1954; Harvard Univ, MPA, 1982. **Career:** Bur Retirement & Survivors Ins Balt, claims authorizer, 1963-64; Hders Retirement & Survivors Ins, employee devel officer; Comn EEO WA, detail edto pres; Ret & Survivors Ins, spec asst for EEO to dir, 1964-65; Off SecDept HEW WA, dep EEO Officer, 1966-67; Off Secy Dept Transp WA, cons, prog mgr internal EEO prog, Nat Urban league Conv, resource, 1967-70; Off Civil Rights USCG WA, chief, 1970-83; US Dept Transp, dept dir civil rights, 1983-. **Orgs:** Sr Exec Asn; Phi Delta Kappa; Hon Soc Men Ed. **Honors/Awds:** Silver Medal for Meritorious Achievement, 1974. **Military Serv:** AUS, 1954-56. *

HUDSON-WEEMS, DR. CLENORA
Educator. **Personal:** Born Jul 23, 1945, Oxford, MS; daughter of Matthew Pearson and Mary Cohran Pearson; married Dr Robert E Weems Jr; children: Sharifa Zakiya. **Educ:** LeMoyne Col, BA, 1967; L Universite de Dijon, France, Cert, 1969; Atlanta Univ, MA, 1971; Univ Iowa, PhD, 1988. **Career:** Delaware State Col, asst prof, 1972-73; Southern Univ New Orleans, asst prof eng, 1976-77; Del State Col, dir black studies, asst prof eng, 1980-85; Ford Doctoral Fel, 1986-87; Grad Col Fel, Univ Iowa, 1986-87; Ford Dissertation Fel, 1987-88; Banneker Honors Col, assoc prof, 1988-90; Univ Mo, Columbia, assoc prof, 1990, prof, currently. **Orgs:** Ed bd mem, Western Jour Black Studies, Wash State Univ; Col Lang Asn, 1970-; African Heritage Studies Asn, 1985-; Asn Study African-Am Life & Hist, 1992-; Women's Intl League Peace & Freedom. **Honors/Awds:** Nat Endowment for the Humanities, 1981; Committee on Institution Cooperation, 1983; Ford Fellowships, 1986-88; Honorary Outstanding Black Delawarean, 1986; Key to the City, Memphis, 1994; Black Woman of the Year, Alpha Kappa Alpha, 1994; Proclamation, State Tenn House Rep, 1994; Proclamation, Mo Legislative Black Caucus, 1994; Resolution, Memphis City Coun, 1994; Scholarly Achievement & Leadership Award, Western Jour Black Studies, 1995; Carter G Woodson Award, Shelby State, 1996; Toni Morrison Soc Book Award, 1998; Alumni Award, LeMoyne-Owen Col, 1998; Distinguished Lect Award, LeMoyne-Owen Col, 1999. **Special Achievements:** Author: Emmett Till: The Sacrificial Lamb of the Civil Rights Movement, 1994; Africana Womanism: Reclaiming Ourselves, 1993, "Africana Womanism: An Historical, Global Perspective for Women of African Descent" in Calland Response: African-American Literacy Tradition, 1997; "Self-Naming and Self-Defining: A Reclamation;" Sisterhood, Feminism and Power, 1997; Soul Mates, a novel, 1998; "Toni Morrison's World of Topsy-Turveydom: A Methodological Explication of New Black Literary Criticism," Western Journal for Black Studies, 1986; "The Tripartite Plight of African-American Women in Their Eyes Were Watching God and The Color Purple," Journal of Black Studies, 1989; "Cultural and Agenda Conflicts in Academia: Critical Issues for Africana Women's Studies," Western Journal of Black Studies, 1989; "Claude McKay: Black Protest in Western Traditional Form," Western Journal of Black Studies, 1992; "From Malcolm Little to El Hajj Malik El Shabazz: Malcolm's Evolving Attitude toward Africana Women", Western Journal of Black Studies, 1993; Co-author: Twayne US Authors Series, Toni Morrison, 1990; Interview with American Audio Prose Library, Inc, 1995; "Africana Womanism: An African Centered Paradigmin an African Centered Discipline", Western Journal of Black Studies, 1997; "Resurrecting Emmett Till", Journal of Black Studies, 1998; "20th Century African American Literature," An Historiographical & Bibliographical Guide to the African American Experience, Greenwood Publishers; Edited: Guest editor for a special issue on Africana Womanism for the Western Journal of Black Studies (Fall 2001); A Guide to Africana Studies (Africa World Press), 2005. **Business Addr:** Professor, University of Missouri, Department Eng, 107 Tate Hall, Columbia, MO 65211.

HUDSPETH, GREGORY CHARLES
College teacher, dean (education), educator. **Personal:** Born Oct 1, 1947, San Antonio, TX; son of Charles and Louise Menefee; married Dollie Rivers, Dec 26, 1970; children: Gregory Jr & Brandon. **Educ:** Huston-Tillotson Col, BA, 1970; St Marys Univ, MA, 1975. **Career:** Northside Independent Sch Dist, San Antonio, TX, teacher & coach, 1971-78;St Philips Col, San Antonio, TX, assoc prof, 1978, Arts & Sci, prof &dean. **Orgs:** Alpha Phi Alpha Fraternity Inc, 1968; chmn, Dem Party, 1980; pres, Fac Senate, 1983-86, 1988; trustee, Target 90/ Goals, San Antonio, 1985-89;Deacon, Mt Zion First Baptist Church, 1987; vpres, Huston-Tillotson Col Alumni Asn, San Antonio, 1990. **Honors/Awds:** San Antonian of the Day, WDAI Radio, 1970; Black Am Polit Sci, Am PolitSci Asn, 1988; Trail Blazer, Texas Pub Asn, 1991. **Home Addr:** 1707 Palmer Vw, San Antonio, TX 78258-7279.

HUESTON, OLIVER DAVID
Psychiatrist. **Personal:** Born Oct 23, 1941, New York, NY; divorced; children: Michael & David. **Educ:** Hunter Col, BA, 1963; Meharry Med Col, MD, 1968. **Career:** Harlem Hosp, chief resident pediat, 1970-71; Columbia Univ Col Physicians & Surgeons, attending pediatrician, 1971-72; Harlem Hosp, gen psychiat resident, 1972-74, fel child psychiat, 1974-75; Josiah Macy fel, 1972; Self Employed, 1985. **Orgs:** Pediatrician Flower 5 Ave Hosp Martin L King Evening Clin, 1971; Josiah Macy Fellow 1971-72; clin physician, NY State Drug Abuse Control Com; Ambulatory Drug Unit 13 Harlem Hops; St Albans Martyr Episcopal Church. **Military Serv:** USAFR, 1968-71. **Business Addr:** Physician, Oliver D Hueston MD, 843 Barbara Dr, Teaneck, NJ 07666.

HUFF, JANICE WAGES
Meteorologist. **Personal:** Born Sep 1, 1960, New York, NY; daughter of Dorothy L Wages; married Kenneth E Huff, Dec 3, 1983. **Educ:** Fla State Univ, Tallahassee Fla, BS, Meteorol, 1982. **Career:** Nat Serv, Columbia, SC, weather trainee, 1978-80; WCTV-TV, Tallahassee, Fla, weather intern, 1982; WTVC-TV, Chattanooga, Tenn, meteorol, 1982-83; WRBL-TV, Columbus, Ga, meteorol, 1983-87; KSDK-TV, St Louis, Mo, meteorol, 1987-90; KRON-TV, San Francisco, Calif, meteorol, 1990-95; NBC 4, meteorol, 1995-. **Orgs:** Nat Hon Soc, Secy Stud Coun, Varsity Cheerleader, & Miss Shamrock, 1978; Am Meteorol Soc, 1981-; Nat Asn Black Journalists, 1986-; Alpha Kappa Alpha Sorority, 1986-; Nat Acad TV Arts & Scis. **Honors/Awds:** Weathercasting, Seal Approval, Am Meteorol Soc, 1985; TV Emmy Best Weathercaster, Nat Asn TV Arts & Scis, 1988; Golden Heart Award; Miracle Makers Media Award, 2004. **Business Addr:** Meteorologist, WNBC-TV, 30 Rockefeller Plz, New York, NY 10112, **Business Phone:** (212)664-2903.

HUFF, LEON ALEXANDER
Composer, musician, television producer. **Personal:** Born Apr 8, 1942, Camden, NJ; children: Leon II, Inga, Bilail, Erika, Debra & Dietra. **Career:** Atlantic Rec, songwriter; Excel Rec, founder, 1966; Philadelphia Intl Rec, co-founder & vice chmn, 1971-; Mighty Three Publishing Co, founder; songwriter & producer; Soundtrack: "Great Performances", 2005; Silence Is Golden, 2006; Songwriter: "Only The Strong Survive", Little Manhattan,

2005; "I Wanna Know Your Name", Roll Bounce, 2005; "You'll Never Find Another Love Like Mine", Guess Who, 2005; "Love Train" & "Now That We Found Love", Hitch, 2005; Composer: Mean Johnny Barrows, 1976; The Out-of-Towners, 1999; The Honeymooners, 2005. **Honors/Awds:** Key to City of Camden; Record World Producer-Writer of Decade Award; Best Rhythm & Blues Producers Award, Nat Asn TV & Recording Artists, 1968-69; numerous Grammy nominations and awards; The Number 1 Song Publishing Award; The Number 1 Record Company Award; The Soul of America Music Award, 1992; Philadelphia Music Alliance Walk of Fame Award, 1993; inducted into Songwriters Hall of Fame, 1995; Impact Award of Excellence, 1996; Grammy Lifetime Achievement Award, 1999; Inaugural Lifetime Achievement Award, Philadelphia Music Conf, 2000; Dance Music Hall of Fame, 2005; Ahmet Ertegnn Award by the Rock and Roll Hall of Fame, 2008; Mulford Street renamed as Leon Huff Way in Camden, NJ, 2009. **Special Achievements:** Over 300 gold and platinum singles & albums. **Business Addr:** Co-Founder, Vice Chairman, Philadelphia International Records, 309 S Broad St, Philadelphia, PA 19107, **Business Phone:** (215)985-0900.

HUFF, LORETTA LOVE (LORETTA L BOOKER)
Executive, president (organization). **Personal:** Born May 16, 1951, Chicago, IL; daughter of Andrew E and Lois Orr; married. **Educ:** Howard Univ, BS, psychol, 1972; Univ Chicago, MBA, finance, 1983. **Career:** Sears Roebuck & Co, programmer, 1972-74, office mgr, 1974-78, consumer res serv mgr, 1978-80, survey consult, 1980-81; Continental Bank, commercial lending, 1981-83, col rels, 1983-84; Apple Comput Inc, Cupertino, CA, staffing consult, 1988-89, col rels consult, 1989-90, compensation specialist, 1990-93, prog mgr, 1993-94; Sega Am, hr mgr, 1994-95; Softbank Forums, hr dir, 1995-97; Merlin Consult, pres, 1997-; Sagent Technol Inc, vpres human resources, 1999-2000; PDI/Dreamworks, head human resources, 2001; Univ Phoenix, fac; Kraft Inc, corporate recruiter; Merlin Venture Partners LLC, pres; Emerald Harvest Consult LLC, pres & prin consult, currently. **Orgs:** Nat Black MBA Asn, 1980-94; seminar dir, Werner Erhard & Asn, 1985-87; bd dir, Northern Cook Co Pvt Ind Coun, 1986-89, mem, 1989-, pres, 1990-91; secy, treas & vpres, Career Mgmt Comm, Univ Chicago Women's Bus Group, 1987; personnel bd mem, City Sunnyvale, 1999-2003; Int Mgt Consults, 1999-2000; Nat Speakers Asn; Black Profs Coaches Alliance; Int Coach Fed; Delta Sigma Theta Sorority Inc; Palo Alto/Bay Area Alumnae. **Honors/Awds:** Minority Business Enterprise of the Year, 2004. **Home Addr:** 2606 W Estes Way, Phoenix, AZ 85041. **Business Addr:** President, Principal Consultant, Emerald Harvest Consulting LLC, 2606 W Estes Way, Phoenix, AZ 85041, **Business Phone:** (602)454-7787.

HUFF, LOUIS ANDREW
Educator, consultant. **Personal:** Born Jan 1, 1949, New Haven, CT; married Suzanne Elaine Cooke; children: Elaine Kai. **Educ:** Howard Univ, BA, econ bus fin, 1971, MA, econ, 1974, PhD, econ, 1981. **Career:** Fed Res Bd, economist, 1971-74; Lincoln Univ, asst prof, 1977-80; CBC ResInst, pres, 1980-82; Univ New Haven, asst prof, 1980-82; 1st Buffalo Corp,economist/stockbroker, 1983-; PA State Univ, asst prof econ; Wilmingtoncol, adj fac; Alliance Consulting, LLC, financial adv, currently. **Orgs:** Bd mem, CBC Inc, 1982-; Western Econ Soc, 1983-; econ consult, RIE Ltd,1983-; host & producer, Economist Corner, 1984-; chairperson housing,NAACP Reading Chap, 1984-; Atlantic Econ Soc, 1984-. **Honors/Awds:** Research Study Award, Nat Chap Eastern States, 1979; Outstanding Young Manin America, 1981. **Special Achievements:** Article published Atlantic Economic Journal 1985; Presented papers at numnat econ confs including Montreal Canada, 1983, Rome Italy, 1985. **Business Addr:** Financial Advisor, Alliance Consulting LLC, 4 Daniels Farm Rd, Trumbull, CT 06611, **Business Phone:** (203)257-6342.*

HUFF, LULA LUNSFORD
Executive. **Personal:** Born in Columbus, GA; daughter of Walter T and Sally; married Charles E Jr, Jun 11, 1972; children: Tamara Nicole. **Educ:** Howard Univ, Wash, BA, 1971; Atlanta Univ, Atlanta, MBA, 1973; State Ga, CPA, 1978. **Career:** Ernst & Young, CPA Firm, Columbus, GA, acct, auditor, 1973-76; Consolidated Govt Columbus, Columbus, GA, chief internal auditor, 1976-84; Troy State Univ, Phoenix City, AL, Acct Dept, instr, 1979-89, chmn, 1980-87, dir personnel mgt grad prog, 1984-85; Pratt & Whitney, UTC, Columbus, GA, sr financial officer, cost analyst, 1984-85, financial supvr, 1985-89, controller, 1989-96; Columbus Consolidated Govt Tag & Tax Off, Muscogee County tax comnr, 1997-. **Orgs:** YMCA, Ga Soc CPA; Urban League; PUSH; Nat Asn Advan Colored People; Howard Univ Alumni Asn; Nat Coun Negro Women; Jack & Jill Am Inc; Links Inc; Delta Sigma Theta Sorority Inc; bd mem, Girl Scouts; Am Inst CPA's; Leadership Columbus, GA; Uptown Columbus; Dale Carnegie; St Anne Cath Church; Delta Mu Delta Nat Bus Honor Soc; Iota Phi Lambda Sorority Inc. **Honors/Awds:** Outstanding Service Award, St Benedict Cath Church, 1971-76; Outstanding Achievement & Service Award, First African Baptist Church, 1975; Certificate of Merit for Excellent Community Leadership & Contribution to Good Government, Congressman Jack T Brinkley, 1976; Outstanding Woman of the Year, Delta Mu Delta Nat Bus Honor Soc, Ledger Enquirer Newspaper, 1976; Achievement Award, Links Inc, 1976; Black Excellence Award, Nat Asn Negro Bus & Prof Women's Clubs Inc, 1977; Professional Woman of the Year Award, Iota Phi Lambda Sorority Inc, 1977; Distinguished Black Citizen Award, WOKS Radio, 1978; Business Woman of the Year Award, Iota Phi Lambda Sorority Inc, 1979. **Business Addr:** Muscogee County Tax Commissioner, Columbus Consolidated Government Tag & Tax Office, 100 10th St E Wing, PO Box 1441, Columbus, GA 31901, **Business Phone:** (706)653-4208.

HUFF, WILLIAM. See Obituaries section.

HUFFMAN, RUFUS C.
Association executive, executive. **Personal:** Born Feb 5, 1927, Bullock County, AL; married Callie Iola Harris; children: Rufus, Jr, Henry. **Educ:** Ala State Univ, BS, 1952, MEd, 1966; NY Univ. **Career:** Techer Prin Coach; Russell Co Bd Educ, prin, 1947-49; Augusta Co Bd Educ Prattville AL, 1951-53. **Orgs:** Bullock Co Bd Educ Union, Springs, AL, 1953-56; Randolph Co Bd Educ Cuthbert GA, 1956-63; pres, Union Springs, NAACP, 1966-70; chmn Bullock Co Coordntg Com 1966-70; coordr treas mgr, Seasha Fed Credit Union Tuskeegee Inst, AL, 1968-70; chmn, Bullock Co Recreational Bd 1973; S educ field dir, NAACP Spec Contrib Fund Inc, 1985; co-founder, SE Self-Help Asn; organizer treas mgr, SEASHA Fed Credit Union; consult, OEO Comprehensive Health Prog & Ford Found Leadership Develop Prog; pres, Bullock Co Teachers Asn; pres, Bullock Co Athletic Asn; life mem, NAACP; v pres, Bullock Co Improvement Orgn; mem bd dir, S Poverty Law Ctr; Leadership Develop Prog Selection Comt; Union Springs Adv Comn City Coun; Great Books Western World Salesman; Distrib Success Motivation Inst. **Honors/Awds:** Teacher of Yr, Bullock Co, 1963-64; Joshua A Smith Award, Outstanding Leadership Educ Human Develop South; Cert Honor NAACP Club 100. *

HUGER, JAMES E., SR.
Executive. **Personal:** Born in Tampa, FL; married Phannye Brinson; children: James Ermine, Jr, Thomas Albert, II, John Leland. **Educ:** Bethune Cookman Col; WVa State Col; Univ Mich. **Career:** Executive (retired); Bethune-Cookman Col, bus mgr, from admin asst to pres, assoc treas; Alpha Phi Alpha Frat Inc, gen secy; City of Daytona Beach, Fl, dir community develop, 1994. **Orgs:** Life mem, Alpha Phi Alpha Frat, Nat Asn Advan Colored People; Elks; Masons; Am Legion; Asn Study Negro Life & Hist; Sigma Pi Phi Frat; Civic League, Civitan, Shrine; bd dirs: Fla Health Care, Fla League Cities Intergovernmental Rel Comn, pres, bd dirs, Stewart Treat Ctr, SERC/NAHRO's Comn & Redevelop Comn, The United Methodist Church, Volusia Gov Employees Credit Union; pres bd dirs, Rape Crisis Ctr Volusia Co Inc; chmn, United Nations Comn, 1985; Dr Martin L King Birthday Commemoration Comn; pres, Volusia County Asn Retarded Citizens; bd dirs, State Ment Health Asn; Rev Panel, Developing Inst HEW Wash DC; State Comn Aging; Fla Bar Grievance Comn; Southern Growth Policy Bd; Rotary Int; CMS Future S; minority enterprise develop comn, Dept Com; Gov Martin Luther King Comn, 1992; King Ctr Community Develop, adv comt mem, 1992-94, secy, 1992; Metro Bd Greater Daytona Beach YMCA, 1992-93; Bethune-Cookman Col Southern Col Alumni Asn, pres, 1992-93; pres, Nat Community Developt Asn, 1992-93. **Honors/Awds:** Charles W Green Award, Outstanding Serv Humanity; Man of the Yr, Alpha Phi Alpha Frat; ADR Year, Bethune Cookman Col Award, Medallion Outstanding Contrib Local Govt; Award Achievement, Nat Asn Advan Colored People; Humanitarian Award Nat Asn Advan Colored People; Equality Day Award, Nat Org Women; Fla Asn Retarded Citizens & Volusia Asn Retarded Citizens; Distinguished Serv Award, United Nations, 1985; Cert Appreciation, Halifax Hosp Med Ctr, 1985; Links Inc, 1985, Stewart Memorial United Methodist Chap, 1986; Distinguished Serv Award, Award Thank You, 1986; Ray Sims Award, Outstanding Contrib Fight Against Heart Dis, 1986; Dedication Jimmy Huger Circle Asn Retarded Citizens Volusia County, 1986; Plaque Appreciation Mary McLeod Bethune Ctr, 1986; Award Appreciation, Rape Crisis Ctr Volusia County, 1986; Living Legacy Cert Recog, Nat Caucus & Ctr Black Aged, 1992; US Dept Housing & Urban Develop, Region IV, Award Spl Recognition, 1993; Cert Appreciation, Asn Retarded Citizens, Volusia County Inc, 1993; Bronze Service Award, Am Heart Asn, 1993; Cert Appreciation, Volunteer R & R Chmn, 1993; Volunteer of the Year, Fla Alcohol & Drug Abuse Asn, 1993; Citizen of the Day, City Miami Beach, 1993; Award Excellence, King Ctr, Atlanta GA, 1993; Award Appreciation, James E Huger Day Adv Comt Ctr Community Develop, 1993; Volusia County Coun, 1993; Volunteer of the Year, Fla Alcohol & Drub Abuse Asn, 1993; J Saxton Lloyd Distinguished Serv Award, Civic League Halifax Area Inc, 1994; Larry J Kelley Community Serv Award, 2000; Herbert Davidson Man of theYr, United Way, 2001; Distinguished Alumni Award, Bethune-Cookman Col, 2002; Beautiful Award, Keep Daytona Beach, 2003. **Special Achievements:** Dedicated James E Huger Living Learning Center, Bethune-Cookman College, 1990; Dedicated James E Huger Adolesence Complex, Stewart Marchman Center, 1994; author: Huger's Hist of the Halifax Hosp Associated, 1998; Disaster Preparedness Guidebook for Community Develop Prof, 1998; Disaster Preparedness Guidebook for the DeLand Dist, 1999. **Military Serv:** USM, sgt major, 4 yrs. **Home Addr:** 935 Sycamore St, Daytona Beach, FL 32114, **Home Phone:** (386)253-2135. *

HUGER, RAYMOND A
Executive. **Educ:** Bernard Baruch Col, BA; Fordham Univ, MBA. **Career:** Paradigm Solutions, founder, chmn & ceo, 1991-; IBM, field engr, sales & mkt & exec mgt positions, regional mgr. **Special Achievements:** Listed in "Top Entrepreneurs" by US Black Engr & Info Technol, 2004. **Business Addr:** Founder & Chairman, Chief Executive Officer, Paradigm Solutions, 9715 Key W Ave Fl 3, Rockville, MD 20850, **Business Phone:** (301)468-1200.*

HUGGINS, CLARENCE L.
Physician. **Personal:** Born Apr 25, 1926, Birmingham, AL; son of Clarence and Lucille; married Carolyn King; children: Patricia, Clarence III, Daphne. **Educ:** Morgan St Col, BS, 1950; Meharry Med Col, MD, 1958; Huron Rd Hosp, Cleveland, Surg Res, 1963; Am Bd Surg, dipl, 1964. **Career:** Cleveland Transit Syst, med dir, 1969-72; Cleveland Acad Med, bd dir, 1974-76; Medic-Screen Health Ctr, pres, 1974-84; Shaker Med Ctr Hosp, chief surg, 1982-84; Metrohealth Hosp Women, chief surg, 1989-; City E Cleveland, OH, dir health, 1990; pvt pract, gen surgeon, currently. **Orgs:** Fel, Am Col Surgeons, 1966; pres med staff, Forest City Hosp, Cleveland, 1970-73; pres bd trustees, Hough-Norwood Family Health Ctr, 1974-78; dir, First Bank Nat Asn, 1974-85; mem adv bd, Robert Wood Johnson Found Nat Health Serv Prog, 1977-83; dir, Ohio Motorist Asn, AAA 1979-85; Seventy Second Am Assembly, Columbia Univ, 1986. **Military Serv:** AUS, 1st Lt Airborne Inf, 1944-46, 1951-52. **Business Addr:** General Surgeon, 13944 Euclid Ave, Cleveland, OH 44112.*

HUGGINS, HOSIAH, JR.
Management consultant. **Personal:** Born Aug 17, 1950, Chicago, IL. **Educ:** Univ Akron, BA 1974; Newport Univ, MPA 1988. **Career:** Amalgamated Stationers, vpres sales, 1974-80; Xerox Corp, mkt exec, 1980-83; Insight & Attitudes Inc, pres; Zebraa Commun, chmn & chief exec officer, currently. **Orgs:** Bd dirs, Urban League Cleveland, 1978-80, YMCA, 1979-85; nat pres, Nat Asn Mgt Consult, 1985-; Inst Mgt Consult. **Honors/Awds:** Outstanding Scholastic, Phi Beta Sigma, 1974; Outstanding Young Man of Am, 1982; Man of the Year, Bel-Aire Civic Club, 1983; "1983 Most Interesting People" Cleveland Mag.

HUGGINS, LINDA JOHNSON
Real estate agent. **Personal:** Born Nov 15, 1950, Oklahoma City, OK; daughter of Wallace C Johnson (deceased) and Wanda Fleming Johnson; married Howard Huggins III, Jun 10, 1972; children: Andrea Yvette & Valerie Diane. **Educ:** Langston Univ, Langston, Okla, BS, math educ, 1972; Webster Univ, St Louis, Mo, MA, bus admin/mgt, 1977. **Career:** Real estate agent (retired); Southwestern Bell Telephone Co, Kans City, Mo, engr, 1972-75, area mgr, 1976-2000; Century 21-Suburban, real estate agent, 1981-. **Orgs:** Pres, St Louis Chap, 1980-; St Louis Real Estate Bd, 1981-; Mo Real Estate Asn, 1981-; Nat Asn Advan Colored People, 1988-; publicity chair, 1990-91, parliamentarian, 1996-98, vpres, 1999-00, pres, 2001-02, Alpha Kappa Alpha Sorority; YWCA, 1988-; Greater Mt Carmel Baptist Church, St Louis, Mo; Community Network SBC; Langston Univ Nat Alumni Asn. **Honors/Awds:** Distinguished Alumni, Nat Asn Equal Opportunity, 1988; Mother of Merit, Nat Benevolent Asn; Unsung Heroine Community Service Award, Top Ladies Distinction. **Business Addr:** Real Estate Agent, Century 21-Suburban, 12765 New Halls Ferry Rd, Florissant, MO 63033, **Business Phone:** (314)921-6500.

HUGGINS-WILLIAMS, DR. NEDRA
Educator, businessperson. **Educ:** Fisk Univ; Univ Utah, PhD. **Career:** Educator (retired), BusinessPerson; Nat Defense Univ, prof, Global Training Solutions, 2003-. **Orgs:** African Studies Asn.; bd visitor, Bennett Col Women; bd mem, Middle Tennessee Big Brothers & Big Sister, bd mem, Nat Bar Asn; mem,Alpha Kappa Alpha Sorority. **Honors/Awds:** US Medal, Pub Serv, Dept Defense. **Special Achievements:** First African American female faculty member of the National Defense University.

HUGHES, ALBERT
Movie director. **Personal:** Born Apr 1, 1972, Detroit, MI. **Career:** dir, producer, writer & cinematographer; Films: Menace II Society, co-producer, writer & dir, 1993; Dead Presidents, producer, writer & dir, 1995; American Pimp, cinematographer, producer & dir, 1999; Scratch, exec producer, 2001; From Hell, exec producer & dir, 2001; TV: "Touching Evil", exec producer, 2004. **Business Phone:** (310)550-4000.

HUGHES, ALLEN
Movie director, movie producer. **Personal:** Born Apr 1, 1972, Detroit, MI; son of Aida. **Career:** Film/TV director & producer; Films: Menace II Society, story writer & co-producer, 1993; Dead Presidents, producer & story writer, 1995; American Pimp, producer, 1999; From Hell, exec producer, 2001; TV series: Touching Evil, exec producer, 2004; Knights of the South Bronx, 2005. **Honors/Awds:** Independent Spirit Award nomination, best

first feature, 1994; Grand Jury Prize nomination for documentary, Sundance Film Festival, 1999. **Business Phone:** (310)550-4000.

HUGHES, BERNICE ANN
Educator. **Personal:** Born Apr 10, 1959, Medina, TN; daughter of Rena L Hughes. **Educ:** Middle Tenn State Univ, BSW, 1982, MA, 1991. **Career:** Middle Tenn State Univ, phys plant supvr, 1982-88, housing area coordr, 1988-92, housing assoc dir, personnel & develop, 1992; Abraham Baldwin Agr Col, dean & proj dir, currently. **Orgs:** Exec bd, Tenn Asn Col & Univ Housing Officers, 1988-92; Alpha Kappa Alpha, 1992-. **Honors/Awds:** Superior Pacesetter Award, Abraham Baldwin Agr Col. **Business Phone:** (229)391-5140.

HUGHES, DR. CARL D.
Clergy, educator. **Personal:** Born in Indianapolis, IN; married Louise. **Educ:** WVa State Col Inst, BS, 1942; Wharton Sch Finance Univ PA, MA, 1943; Christian Theol Sem, BD, 1957; Christian Theol Sem, MA, 1958; Christian Theol Sem, M.Div, 1972; Cent Baptist Theol Sem IN, DD, 1975; IN Univ Sch Law Wayne State Univ & Univ Detroit, Post Grad Studies. **Career:** Mt Zion Baptist Church Indianapolis, ministers asst, 1952; Second Baptist Church Lafayette, 1952-56; St John Missionary Baptist Church, 1956-60; Christian Educ Methodist Baptist Church, Detroit, dir, 1960-61; Bethel Baptist Church E Detroit, pastor, 1961; Hughes Enterprise Inc, vpres treas; Detroit Christian Training Ctr, dean; Bus Educ Detroit Pub Sch, teacher; Church Builder & Bus Educ Detroit Pub Sch, dept head; Calvary Dist Asn Detroit, instr; Wolverine State Conv SS & BTU Cong MI, former instr; Nat Baptist SS & BTU Cong, instr; Central Bible Sem, instr. **Orgs:** Comt YMCA; Comt NAACP; Grand Bd Dir Kappa Alpha Psi Nat Col Frat; Mason; budget comt Nat Negro Bus League; treas, St Emma Mil Acad Parent Asn Detroit; chmn, bd trustees, Todd-Phillips C Home Wolverine State Missionary Baptist Conv Inc; chmn, Finance Pastors' Div Nat Baptist Cong Christian Educ. **Honors/Awds:** Received First John L Webb Award, Nat Baptist Conv, 1948; Auth "The Church Organized For Meaning Ministry" & "Financing Local Church Property".

HUGHES, CATHERINE LIGGINS
Media executive. **Personal:** Born Apr 22, 1947, Omaha, NE; daughter of William A Woods and Helen E Jones Woods; children: Alfred Charles Liggins, III. **Educ:** Creighton Univ, Omaha, NE, attended 1969; Univ Nebr, Omaha, NE, attended 1971; Harvard Univ, Cambridge, MA, attended 1975. **Career:** Howard Univ, sch commun, admin asst, 1971-73; WHUR-FM col radio station, asst, 1973-75, vpres & gen mgr; WYCB-AM, pres & gen mgr, late 1970s; Radio One Inc, founder; WOL-AM, owner; WOL-AM, owner; WMMJ-FM, owner; WWIN-AM/FM, owner;WERQ-FM/WOLB-AM, owner; WKYS-FM, owner; WJZZ-FM, owner; WCHB-AM/WCHB-FM, owner. **Orgs:** Bd mem, United Black Fund, 1978-88; bd mem, DC Boys Girls Club, 1983-86; chmn, Community Comm Corp, 1985-87; Wash Post Recall Comn, 1987. **Honors/Awds:** Woman of the Year, Wash Woman, 1987; People's Champion Award, Nat Black Media Coalition, 1988; Kool Achiever Communications, 1988; Woman of the Year, Women at Work of the Nat Capital Area, 1989; The Cathy Hughes TV Show, 1989; Honorary deg, Sojourner Douglass Col, Baltimore, 1995; Lifetime Achievement Award, Wash Area Broadcasters; Distinguished Service Award, Nat Asn Broadcasters, 2001; Madam CJ Walker Award, Ebony Mag, 2002; Golden Mike Award, Broadcasters Found; Lifetime Achievement Award, Nat Asn Black Owned Broadcasters; Essence Magazine Award, 2002. **Special Achievements:** First African-American woman to head a publicly traded company; First African-American to attend Duchesne Academy of the Sacred Heart, a prestigious Catholic girls' school in Omaha; Selected as 100 Who Have Changed the World by Ebony Mag. *

HUGHES, GEORGE MELVIN
Educator. **Personal:** Born Aug 26, 1938, Charlotte, TN; married Evelyn Benson; children: Vickie L, George M Jr. **Educ:** TN State Univ, BS, 1961, MEd, 1963; Univ WI-19Milwaukee, Post Grad studies, 1968; Cardinal Stritch Col, Post Grad studies, 1983; Indiana Univ, Post Grad studies, 1986. **Career:** Lafollette Elem Sch, teacher, 1963-68; Parkman Middle Sch, asst prin, 1968-71; Garfield Elem Sch, asst prin, 1971-74; Lee Elem Sch, prin. **Orgs:** Bd dir, Carter Child Develop Ctr, 1981, Girl Scouts Am, 1987, Phi Delta Kappa Milwaukee Chap, 1987; panelist US Dept Educ Ctr Systs & Prog Develop Inc, 1987; consult Indianapolis Sch Syst, 1987, Muscogee County Sch Dist Columbus GA, 1987; life mem, NAACP; consult Southwest Educ Develop Lab TX. **Honors/Awds:** Special Recognition, Lee Sch Parent-Teacher Orgn, 1983; Spec Visit US Educ Sec William J Bennett, 1986; apptitude Property Tax Review Bd Mequon, 1986-; invited White House Rose Garden Pres reception release book entitled "What Works, Educating Disadvantaged Children"; received Nat Recogniton by US Dept Educ part RISE effective sch prog Milwaukee Pub Schs. **Military Serv:** USAF, ROTC, 2 yrs, TN State Univ.

HUGHES, GEORGE VINCENT
Automotive executive, president (organization). **Personal:** Born Apr 8, 1930, New York, NY; son of Marion Hughes and Lewis Hughes; children: Deirdre & Vincent. **Educ:** Col City New York, MBA, 1954. **Career:** George Hughes Chevrolet, pres, currently. **Honors/Awds:** Alpha Phi Alpha, 1950-. **Military Serv:** USY, 82nd Airborne Infantry, capt, 3 yrs. **Home Addr:** PO Box 6697, Freehold, NJ 07728. **Business Addr:** President, George Hughes Chevrolet, 3712 ROUTE 9, PO Box 6697, Freehold, NJ 07728, **Business Phone:** (732)462-1324.

HUGHES, HARVEY L.
Lawyer. **Personal:** Born May 7, 1909, Port DePosit, MD; married Ethel C. **Educ:** Univ Pittsburgh Terrell Law Sch, LLB, 1944. **Career:** Off VA, Accredited Present Claims, 1955; Harris & Hughes Law Firm, partner; N Capitol Corp, gen coun. **Orgs:** Wash Bar Asn, 1946; Legal Fraternity Sigm Delta Tau, 1946; Nat Bar Asn, 1954; DC Bar Asn, 1972; counr, St Martin's Boys Club, 1972; Alpha Phi Alpha Fraternity; Fairmount Heights Civic Club.

HUGHES, HOLLIS EUGENE, JR.
Executive. **Personal:** Born Mar 14, 1943, Tulsa, OK; son of Hollis Eugene Sr. and Suzan Marie Brummell; married Lavera Ruth Knight, Aug 26. **Educ:** Ball State Univ, BS, Soc Sci, 1965, MA, Sociol, 1968. **Career:** S Bend Community Sch Corp, teacher & coach, 1965-69; Model Cities Prog & City S Bend, exec dir, 1969-74; Housing Asst Off Inc, pres & dir, 1974-; United Way St Joseph Co, pres, currently. **Orgs:** Am Planning Asn, 1975; Nat Asn Housing & Redevelop Officials, 1978-; Am Mgt Asn 1979-89; Alpha Phi Alpha Frat Inc, 1966-; Alpha Phi Omega Serv Frat, 1967-; pres elect Ball State Univ Alumni Coun, 1974-; pres & bd mem, Family & Children Ctr, 1978-79; trustee, S Bend Community Sch Corp & Pub Library; vpres, S Bend Community Sch Corp & Pub Library, 1978-; vpres, S Bend Community Sch Corp, 1980-81; life mem, NAACP; pres, S Bend Community Sch Corp, 1981-82; pres, South Bend Pub Library Bd Trustees, 1984-85; Adv Comt US Comn Civil Rights; bd trustees Art Ctr Inc S Bend; trustee, Mem Hosp; bd trustees, Mem Hosp Found, 1987-90; bd mem, Youth Servs Bureau; bd mem, Community Educ Round Tabledir, S Bend-Mishka Chamber Com, 1987-; dir, Project Future St Joseph County, 1987-; trustee, Ball State Univ, 1989-; Ball State Univ Black Alumni Asn, 1989-; vpres, Visions Progress, 1986-; bd dirs, St Joseph County Minority Bus Develop Coun, 1991. **Honors/Awds:** Outstanding Citizen of IN Award, IN Civil Rights Comn, 1976; George Award, Outstanding Community Serv Mishawaka Enterprise Record, 1977; Distinguished Black Alumni, Ball State Univ Alumni Asn, 1989; Benny Award, Ball State Univ Alumni Asn, 1988. **Business Addr:** President, United Way St Joseph Co, 3517 E Jefferson Blvd, PO Box 6396, South Bend, IN 46660-6396, **Business Phone:** (574)232-8201.*

HUGHES, ISAAC SUNNY
Mathematician. **Personal:** Born Jun 29, 1944, Zachary, LA; married Anna Ceaser; children: Timothy, Troy, Jessica. **Educ:** Grambling Univ, BA, 1966; Univ NC, Pub Admin, 1974. **Career:** King George co, VA, supvr, 1984-87; Naval Surface Weapons Ctr, mathematician, 1967-; Co Sch Bd, 1989-90, 1993-95. **Orgs:** Worshipful Master KG Masonic Lodge No 314, 1978; cub master Boy Scouts Am, 1978-81; bd mem, Zoning Appeals KG, 1981; Wetland Bd KG, 1982; tie breaker Bd of Supervisors KG, 1983; bd trustee-chair, Antioch Baptist Church KG; Worthy Patron Guiding Star Chapter No 216; Fredericksburg Consistory No 346; Magnus Temple No 3; United Supreme Coun, 33rd Degree Masons, Asst Dist Dep Grand Master. **Honors/Awds:** Outstanding Performance, 1974, High Quality Performance, 1978, Spec Achievement, 1983, Super Performance, 1984, Dept navy; Secy of the Yr, Prince Hall Masons of VA, 1984; Distinguished Community Serv, 1989; Super Performance, 1990; Super Performance, 1991; Super Performance 1992; Super Performance, 1993; Super Performance, 1994. **Special Achievements:** The first African-American elected to the King George Co. Board of Supervisors. **Home Addr:** 10325 Oak Tree Dr, King George, VA 22485. *

HUGHES, CAPT. JIMMY FRANKLIN, SR.
Law enforcement officer. **Personal:** Born Apr 10, 1952, Tuscaloosa, AL; son of Lee Marvin and Maryann Stanley; married Juanita Price, May 29; children: Trina Woodberry, Jimmy Jr & Jared. **Educ:** Youngstown State Univ, AS, 1989, BS, 1992, MS, 1997; Northwestern Univ, Acad Police Staff & Comdr, SPSC-22, 1986; FBI Nat Acad, Sect 193, grad; Ohio Peace Officers Training Acad, police instrs cert, 1985; additional educ, training law enforcement. **Career:** Youngstown Police Dept, patrol officer, 1977-81, detective sgt, 1981-87, lt, 1987-95, capt, 1995-, chief police, currently. **Orgs:** Mid-Am Teakwon Do Asn; Nat Black Police Asn; pres, Black Knights Police Asn; Mahoning County Drug & Alcohol Addiction Bd; Mahoning County United Way Distribution Comt; Youngstown Urgan League; Nat Asn Advan Colored People Youngstown; assoc mem, Buckeye Elks Lodge No73 IBPOE. **Honors/Awds:** Gold Medals, Ohio Police Olympics; Meritorious Service Award, Youngstown Police Dept; Buckeye Elk Youth Athletic Awards; Community Service Award, Black Knights Police Asn; Commendation of Professionalism, Youngstown Police Dept; Departmental Commendations & Community Recognition Awards. **Special Achievements:** First African American promoted in the city's history to the rank of Captain, the Police Departments' highest rank. **Home Addr:** 3239 Oak St, Youngstown, OH 44505, **Home Phone:** (330)743-6335. **Business Addr:** Captain, Chief of Police, Youngstown Police Department, 116 W Boardman St, Youngstown, OH 44503, **Business Phone:** (330)742-8900.

HUGHES, JOHNNIE LEE
Miner. **Personal:** Born Nov 18, 1924, Coalwood, WV; son of George Hughes and Florine Westbrooke; married Sarah Etta Gibson; children: Leonard C Jones, Jacqueline Lee Jones & Moseley. **Career:** Miner (retired); Osage W Va, mayor, 1959-61, 1968-70; Off Am Asian Free Labor Inst Wash DC Turkey, instr mine safety, 1979; Consolidated Coal Co, mine worker, 1995. **Orgs:** Pres, UMWA 2122, 1978-80; Mine Com/Safety Com; Coal Miners Polit Action Community. **Honors/Awds:** Miner to Mayor publ Ebony Edition, 1972; consult to Turkey Publ Miner's Jour, 1980. **Special Achievements:** First Black chief of police Monongalia Co WV; First Black mayor State of WV. **Military Serv:** USMC, Cpl, 1942-46.

HUGHES, DR. JOYCE A.
Lawyer, college teacher, educator. **Personal:** Born Feb 7, 1940, Gadsden, AL; daughter of Bessie Cunningham Hughes and Solomon Hughes Sr. **Educ:** Carleton Col, Northfield, MN, magna cum laude, BA, 1961; Univ Madrid,Spain, cert, 1962; Univ Minn Law Sch, cum laude, JD, 1965. **Career:** John Hay Whitney fel, 1962-63; Univ Minn, assoc prof law, 1971-75; Northwestern Univ, vis assoc prof law, 1975-76, assoc prof law, 1976-79,prof law, 1979-; Univ Calif, Hastings Col Law, vis prof law, 1991. **Orgs:** Trustee, Carleton Col, 1969-94; dir, First Plymouth Bank, 1971-82;trustee, Nat Urban League, 1972-78; Am Bar asn; Nat Bar Asn; Ill Bar Asn;Cook County Bar Asn; dir, Chicago Bd Educ, 1980-82; dir, Fed Home Loan Bank Chicago, 1980-84; Phi Beta Kappa, 1961; Black Women Lawyers Greater Chicago. **Honors/Awds:** Fulbright Scholar, 1961-62; Alumni Achievement Award, Carleton Col Northfield, Minn, 1969; Achievement, Minn Afro-American Lawyers, 1972;Service Award, Black Law Stud Asn, Univ Minn Law Sch, 1974; Kizzy Award, Black Women Hall Fame Found, 1979; Woman of the Year, Zeta Phi Beta Sorority Inc, Chicago, 1982; Service Award, Nat Alliance Black Sch Educr, 1982; Woman of the Year, Coalition United Community Action, Chicago, 1983; Achievement, Minn Minority Lawyers Asn, 1983; 100 Top Bus & Prof Women,Dollars & Sense Magazine, 1986; Superior Public Service, Cook County Bar Asn, 1987; Distinguished Service, Black Women Lawyers Asn Greater Chicago,1993; Woman of Achievement and Role Model Day, Bennett Col Founder's,1993; Honorary Doctor of Laws, Carleton Col Northfield, Minn, 2001; Leno O Smith Award, Black Women Minn Aty, 2002; Clyde Ferguson Award, Asn Am Law Sch, Minority Groups Sect, 2002. **Special Achievements:** First Black female tenure-track law professor at a majority school, 20years after such a person was a professor at a predominantly Black law school. **Business Addr:** Professor of Law, Northwestern University School of Law, 347 E Chicago Ave, Chicago, IL 60611.

HUGHES, KORI
Public relations executive. **Educ:** Hampton Univ. **Career:** Law Off Willie E Gary, pub rels dir, currently. **Business Addr:** Director of Public Relations, Law Off of Willie E Gary, 221 E Osceola St, Stuart, FL 34994, **Business Phone:** (772)288-0771.

HUGHES, LARRY
Basketball player. **Personal:** Born Jan 23, 1980. **Educ:** St Louis Univ, attended 1991. **Career:** Philadelphia 76ers, 1998-2000; Golden State Warriors, 2000-02; Wash Wizards, guard, 2002-05; Cleveland Cavaliers, guard, 2005-08; Chicago Bulls, 2008-. **Business Addr:** Professional Basketball Player, Chicago Bulls, 1901 W Madison St, Chicago, IL 60612, **Business Phone:** (312)455-4000.

HUGHES, MAMIE F.
Civil rights activist, community activist. **Personal:** Born May 3, 1929, Jacksonville, FL; married Judge Leonard; children: Leonard, III, Kevin, Stefan, Patrick, Amy. **Educ:** Fisk Univ, BA, 1949; Univ Mo, attended 1951. **Career:** Community activist (retired); Mo Pub Sch System, teacher, 1951-52, 1957-62; Greenville, teacher, 1954-56; Fed Agency Reg Dir Action, 1985; Head Start, vol, 1968-69; St Joseph Cath Sch, vol teacher, 1962-63; The Jackson Co Legislature, charter mem, 1972-78; Carver Neighborhood Ctr, mem adv comn, 1985; New Metzl Ad Touts Support, civil rights leader; Samuel U. Rodgers Community Health Ctr; Samuel U Rodgers Community Health Ctr, bd chmn. **Orgs:** Cath Interracial Coun, 1959-63; former bd mem, HPEED, 1965-66; founding comn, Vol Serv Bur; bd mem, United Campaign Vol, 1964-68; vol, Martin Luther King Jr HS; Greater KS Coordinating Comn Int Women's Yr; Jackson Co Child Welfare Adv Com; Panel Am Women; chmn, Comn Aging; chmn, Fed Exec Bd; past chmn, Health & Welfare Comn; KC Mo Fair Housing Comn; vol, parent, 1965-66; foster, Parent 1966-67; St Joseph Sch PTA; pres, Greater KC Minority Women's Coalition Human Rights; recording secy, Greater KC Hearing & Speech Ctr; bd mem, Truman Med Ctr; vchmn, Mid-Am Regional Coun, 1972-78; Parker Sq Housing Corp; Lincoln Black Archives; KC Crime Comn; YMCA Urban Servs; Manpower Adv Mem, Nat Coun Negro Women; Nat Advan Asn Colored People; Jack & Jill Am Inc; Greater KC Links Inc Serv Urban Youth De LaSalle Eduenter; Beautiful Activists Vol Serv Woolf Bros & Germaine Monteil; exec dir, Black Econ Union, 1981-86; ombudsman, advocate, the Bruce R. Watkins Drive project, 1987-01. **Honors/Awds:** Community Service Award; Service Award, Nat Advan Asn Colored People; Freedom Fund Dinner Com. *

HUGHES, MARK
Basketball player, basketball coach. **Personal:** Born Oct 5, 1966, Muskegon, MI; married Ronna; children: Mark Jr, Madelyn & Jackson. **Educ:** Mich State Univ. **Career:** Basketball player (retired), basketball coach; Detroit Pistons, 1991; Scaini Venezia, 1991-93; Grand Rapids Hoops, 1995-98, head coach, 1997-2002; Toronto Raptors, 1996; Orlando Magic, asst coach, 2002-04; Sacramento Kings, asst coach, 2006-. **Business Phone:** (916)928-0000.

HUGHES, ROBERT DANAN
Football player, banker. **Personal:** Born Dec 11, 1970, Bayonne, NJ; married Tifanni; children: Jessicah Briana, Joseph Alan, Taurin Isaiah & Savana Rienne. **Educ:** Univ Iowa, commun. **Career:** Milwaukee Brewers, wide receiver, 1991-92; Kans City Chiefs, wide receiver, 1993-98; Bank Am, 1999; US Bancorp; US Bank Home Mortgage, originator, currently. **Orgs:** Danan Hughes Annual Give Back Benefit Inc. **Business Addr:** Home Mortgage Originator, US Bank Home Mortgage, 10401 Holmes Rd, Kansas City, MO 64131, **Business Phone:** (816)508-6544.

HUGHES, TYRONE CHRISTOPHER
Football player. **Personal:** Born Jan 14, 1970, New Orleans, LA. **Educ:** Univ Nebr, BS, consumer sci. **Career:** Football player (retired); New Orleans Saints, cornerback, 1993-96; Chicago Bears, kick returner, 1997; Dallas Cowboys, kick returner, 1998.

HUGHES, VINCENT J
State government official. **Personal:** Born Oct 26, 1956, Philadelphia, PA; son of James and Ann; married Reneee. **Educ:** Temple Univ. **Career:** Penn Legis Black Caucus, chmn, 1991-94; Pa St Senate, House Representatives, St rep, 1987-94, Dist 7, senator, 1994-; elected Minority Caucus Chair, 2009. **Orgs:** Chmn, Pa Legis Black Caucus; chmn, Health & Welfare Comt; St Gov & Labor Rels Comt; bd dir, Penn Higher Educ Assistance Agency; coun, St Government's Eastern Regional Conf Comt Health & Human Serv; founding mem, Democratic Study Group; bd mem, Philadelphia Commercial Develop Corp; Philadelphia Welfare Pride & Blacks Educating Blacks About Sexual Health Issues; co-founder; democratic chair, Children First; Senate Pub Health & Welfare Comn; Appropriations, Educ & Policy; Am Fed St Co & Munic Employees Union; Prince Hall Grand Lodge Free & Accepted Masons; Phildelphia Int Airport Adv Bd; Father's Day Rally Comn; trustee, Mt Carmel Baptist Church. **Business Phone:** (717)787-7112.

HUGHLEY, D L (DARRYL LYNN HUGHLEY)
Comedian, actor. **Personal:** Born Mar 6, 1963, Los Angeles, CA; son of Charles and Audrey; married LaDonna, 1986; children: Tyler, Ryan & Kyle. **Career:** Stand-up comedian, actor; Appeared on Def Comedy Jam, HBO; host, Comic View, BET, 1992; TV series: "Double Rush," 1995; "The Hughleys," actor, writer, co-producer, 1998; "Studio 60 on the Sunset Strip", 2006-07; Films: Inspector Gadget, 1999; DL Hughley Goin' Home, 1999; The Orgininal Kings of Comedy, 2000; The Brothers, 2001; VH1 Big in 03, 2003; Scary Movie 3, 2003; Soul Plane, 2004; Shackles, 2005; Cloud 9, 2006; The Adventures of Brer Rabbit, 2006; K&R: Part 1, 2 & 3, 2007; What Kind of Day Has It Been, 2007; Studio 60 on the Sunset Strip, 2007; Doubting Thomas, 2008. **Orgs:** Omega Psi Phi Fraternity. **Business Addr:** Actor, Barash & Altman Inc, 9100 Wilshire Blvd Suite 1000 W, Beverly Hills, CA 90212-3413.

HUGHLEY, DARRYL LYNN. See HUGHLEY, D L.

HUGHLEY, STEPHANIE
Dancer, chief executive officer. **Educ:** Kent State Univ, BS; Antioch Col, MEd. **Career:** Negro Ensemble Co, gen mgr; Atlanta Comt, Olympic Games Cult Olympiad, theatre & dance producer; Atlanta Cult Community, 1987-92; Nat Black Arts Festival, artistic dir, 1987-92, founding artistic dir, chief exec officer bd dirs, currently, exec producer, currently; NJ Performing Arts Ctr, vpres programming, 1995-99; Dance Theater Boston, dancer; Elma Lewis Sch Fine Arts, dancer; African/Caribbean & Ballet Co, dancer; Alvin Ailey Am Dance Theater, consult; Pittsburgh Symphony Orchestra, consult; Nat Music Ctr Wash, consult. **Orgs:** Bd Metro Atlanta Arts & Cult Coalition; Atlanta Conv Ctr & Visitors Bur; Asn Theatrical Press Agts & Mgrs. **Business Phone:** (404)730-7315.*

HUGINE, DR. ANDREW, JR.
Educator, president (organization). **Personal:** Born in Green Pond, SC; married Abbiegail Hamilton; children: Andrew III & Akilah. **Educ:** SC State Univ, BS, math; Mich State Univ, MS, math, PhD, higher educ, instnl res. **Career:** Univ Year Action Prog, dir; Southern Asn Col & Schs Self- Study, asst dir & dir; Acad Affairs, asst vpres; SC State Univ, interim exec vpres, interim vpres, pres, Stud Govt Asn, pres, prin investr, currently; Mich State Univ, teaching asst; Ivenia Brown Elem Sch, Stud Coun, pres; Colleton High Sch, Stud Coun, pres. **Orgs:** Williams Chapel AME Church, Orangeburg, SC; Omega Psi Phi Fraternity; Edisto Masonic Lodge; Edisto United Way Bd Dirs; chmn bd trustees, Orangeburg Consol Sch Dist Five. **Honors/Awds:** Received numerous awards and recognition for his participation in these activities and organizations. **Business Addr:** Principal Investigator, South Carolina State University, 300 Col St NE, PO Box 7574, Orangeburg, SC 29117-0001, **Business Phone:** (803)536-7013.*

HULETT, ROSEMARY D
School administrator. **Personal:** Born Sep 17, 1954, Chicago, IL; married Melvin D. **Educ:** Chicago State Univ, BSEd, 1975; MSEd, 1980. **Career:** Archdiocese Chicago Cath Sch Bd, head teacher, 1975-77, headstart dir, 1977-78; Chicago Bd Educ, Special Educ, teacher, 1978-80; Chicago State Univ, dir alumni affairs, 1980-; Gov State Univ, interim assoc vpres, develop & alumni res, currently, dir alumni relations, currently. **Orgs:** River Oaks Coop Towne House Memorial Comn; River Oaks Coop Towne House Fin Comn; Nat Asn Educ Young C, 1975-77; Coun Excep Educ, 1978-79; exec secy/treas, Chicago State Univ Alumni Asn, 1980-; chmn, CASE V Career Advan Women & Minorities Comn, 1985-88; bd mem, Case V Bd Dir, 1987-89; ceo, Alumini Asn, Gov State Univ, currently. **Honors/Awds:** Teacher of the Year Award, Nat Asn Educ Young C, 1976; Special Education Teaching Certificate, Chicago Bd Educ, 1979; Certificate of Recognition for Alumni, Admin Coun Advan Sec Educ, 1980; Outstanding Young Professional Award, Chicago Coalition Urban Prof, 1986. **Business Addr:** Associate Vice President, Director of Alumini Relations, Governors State University, Institutional Advancement & Alumni Relations, 1 Univ Pkwy, University Park, IL 60466, **Business Phone:** (708)534-4128.

HULL, AKASHA GLORIA
Educator. **Personal:** Born Dec 6, 1944, Shreveport, LA; daughter of Robert T and Jimmie; married Prentice R, Jun 12, 1966 (divorced 1983); children: Adrian L Prentice. **Educ:** Southern Univ, BA, 1966; Purdue Univ, MA, 1968, PhD, 1972. **Career:** Univ Del, Newark, instr, 1971; Univ Del, asst prof, 1972-77; Univ Del, assoc prof, 1977-86; Black Am Lit Forum, adv ed, 1978-86; Univ Del, prof Eng, 1986-88; Stanford Univ, visiting scholar, 1987-88; Univ Calif-SantaCruz, prof womens studies & lit, 1988-2000, chair women's studies dept, 1989-91, prof emerita, womens studies & lit, 2000-. **Orgs:** Co-project dir, Black Women's Studies project, 1982-84; Mellon Scholar, Wellesley Ctr Res Women, 1983; comn co-chair, Modern Language Asn; Nat Women's Studies Asn; adv & consult, Black Am Lit Forum, Feminist Studies; Col Lang Asn; Modern Lang Asn Am; Nat Asn Advan Colored People; Alpha Kappa Alpha; Am Humanities Division Faculty Fellowship, Asn of Univ Women, 1990-91; Nat Humanities Ctr, 1994-95. **Honors/Awds:** Nat Institute of Women of Color Award, 1982. **Business Addr:** Professor Emeritus, University of California, Santa Cruz, Humanities 1 Suite 503, 1156 High St, Santa Cruz, CA 95064-1016, **Business Phone:** (831)459-2696.

HULL, BERNARD S., SR.
Engineer. **Personal:** Born Aug 1, 1929, Wetipquin, MD; married Marion Hayes; children: Karla L, Bernard S II. **Educ:** Howard Univ, BS, 1951; Univ Md. **Career:** Engineer (retired); Tamarach Triangle Civic Asn, exec bd; White Oak Fed Credit Union, vpres, 1972-77; Naval Mat Command, Wash DC, corp planning div hq, 1985; Naval Surf Weapons Ctr, White Oaks, MD, Col rela rep; Naval Surf Weapons Ctr, Silver Spring, MD, res mech engr adv planning staff, 1987. **Orgs:** Life mem, Nat Asn Advan Colored People. **Honors/Awds:** Distinguished Able Toastmaster Award, 1974. **Military Serv:** AUS. *

HULL, EVERSON WARREN
Government official. **Personal:** Born Oct 14, 1943, Nevis; married Melverlynn Surilina Spears; children: Randolph E, Cecilia A. **Educ:** Howard Univ, BA, 1970, PhD, 1977; Univ MD, MA, 1974. **Career:** Fed Nat Mort Assoc, economist, 1973-76; Am Petrol Inst, sr economist, 1976-78; TRW Inc, sr economist, 1978-79; Cong Res Servs, head money & banking quantitative econs, 1979-83; US Dept Labor, dep asst secy policy, 1983-. **Business Addr:** Deputy Assistant Secretary, US Department Labor, 200 Const Ave NW, Washington, DC 20210.*

HULL, DR. GEORGE, JR.
Educator. **Personal:** Born Sep 30, 1922, Indianola, MS; married Jewell, Jan 1, 1947; children: George Ronald & Sharon Elaine. **Educ:** Alcorn State Col, BS, 1945; Tenn State Univ, MS, 1949; OH State Univ, PhD, entom, 1957. **Career:** Tenn State Univ, asst instr boil, 1948-49, from instr to prof, 1949-64, chmn lower div biol; Grambling col, Dept Biol Sci, of & head, 1964-66; Fisk Univ, Dept Biol, prof & chmn, Div Nat Sci & Math, dir, 1977-, prof emer, currently. **Orgs:** Pres, Fisk-Meharry-Tenn State Sigma Xi Club, 1960-61; regional dir, Nat Inst Sci, 1973-74; pres, Nashville Club, 1973-75; regional vpres, Beta Kappa Chi, 1975; Sigma Xi; Frontiers Int; pres, Nashville Alumini Chap; AAAS; Entom Soc Am. **Military Serv:** USN 1944-46. **Home Addr:** 4212 Enchanted Ct, Nashville, TN 37218. **Business Addr:** Professor Emeritus, Fisk University, Department of Biology, 1000 17th Ave N, Nashville, TN 37208-3051, **Business Phone:** (615)329-8500.*

HULL, STEPHANIE J
School principal. **Educ:** Harvard Univ, PhD, 1992. **Career:** Wellesley Col, asst to pres & sec & adj asst prof; The Brearley Sch, head, currently. **Honors/Awds:** First African Am to lead New York's Brearley Sch. **Business Addr:** Head, Brearley School, 610 E 83rd St, New York, NY 10028, **Business Phone:** (212)744-8582.*

HUMES, EMANUEL I., SR.
Executive. **Personal:** Born Jan 12, 1928, Miami, FL; married Lillie. **Career:** Menelek Construction Co Inc, chmn bd dir; Bethlehem Steel Corp, sub-foreman, 1950-70; Niagra Frontier Housing Develop, field supt; BAW Construct Co; supt & coordr; Urban Syst Housing Co, mgr; Church God Prophecy, minister, 1950-70; E I Humes Cleaning & Janitorial Serv, 1971-; Manlil Mgt Corp, 1973-; Humall Enterprieses; E I Humes Construct, 1971-; Church God Prophecy, SS sput, 1974. **Orgs:** Greater Jefferson Businessmen's Asn; life mem, NAACP. **Honors/Awds:** achievement award, Black Enterpise Mag; Top 100, 1974; Service Medal, Nat Defense . **Military Serv:** AUS, med corp corpl, 1953-55. *

HUMMINGS, ARMENTA ADAMS. See ADAMS, ARMENTA ESTELLA.

HUMPHREY, HOWARD JOHN
Engineer. **Personal:** Born Nov 5, 1940; son of Easton; married Bernadette Barker; children: Hayden, Lynette. **Educ:** NY Univ, BE, 1969; Univ Mich, Am Electric Power Spons Mgt Training Prog, 1976. **Career:** Am Elec Power Serv Corp, group mgr civil eng div, 1988, mgr mat handling div, 1983-88, sect head mat handling div, asst sect head, sr engr, assoc engr, engr technol, 1967-; Cl Ford Power Plant Solid Waste Disposal, specialist. **Orgs:** Reg Prof Engr NJ, OH & WV; Am Soc Civ Engr; chmn, Am Coal Ash Asn. **Special Achievements:** First Black Department Head in the American Electrical Power Service Corporation. **Business Addr:** Group Manager, American Electric Power Service Corporation, 30 S Nevada Ave Suite 602, Columbus, OH 43216.*

HUMPHREY, KATHRYN BRITT
Educator. **Personal:** Born Jan 24, 1923, Champaign, IL; daughter of Jesse and Vennie; widowed. **Educ:** Parkland Jr Col, social studies; Univ Ill Urbana, social & med studies. **Career:** Educator (retired). Champaign Park Dist, Phys Educ Pub Sch Recess, youth dir, 1941-44; domestic serv worker, 1941-53; Univ Ill, Col Vet Med, natural sci lab asst, Microscopic Anat, histol technician, 1955-87. **Orgs:** Black Caucus Sch Bd Mems, cent region, 1970-76; co-founder, Gamma Upsilon Psi, Scholar Promotion, 1973-; Univ Ill, Young Women's Christian Asn; Nat Coun Negro Women; Carver Park Improvement Asn; Univ Ill Employee Credit Union, vice chmn, 1976-; City Champaign Township Bd, 1986-90; Champaign-Urbana Mass Transit Bd, 1990-; bd mem, Champaign Community Schs, Dist 4, 1970-76; Urban League or Champaign County; Occupational Indust Coun; Vet Med Col, Univ Ill, affirmative action comt; Mt Olive Baptist Church, Missionary Dept, pres, bd Christian Educ, Baptist Gen State Convention, Women's Auxiliary, past vpres, Cent Dist Asn Ill, past pres. **Honors/Awds:** Recipient of Service Award, Urban League; Service Award, Young People's Dept Cent Dist Asn; Service Award, Bapt Gen St Conv Ill Young People's Dept. *

HUMPHREY, MARGO
Educator, writer, artist. **Personal:** Born 1942, Oakland, CA; daughter of James Dudley and Dorothy Reed; married Thais Valentine Nysus (divorced). **Educ:** Merritt City Col, 1963; Calif State-Hayward, Hayward, CA, attended 1968; Calif Col Arts & Crafts, attended 1973; Stanford Univ, Palo Alto, CA, MA, 1974. **Career:** Golden State Mutual Life Ins Co, purchase, 1968; Stanford Univ, teaching asst, 1972-74; Ford Found fel, 1980-81; Univ S Pacific, Suva, vis fac; Univ Calif, Santa Cruz, asst prof art, 1985; Univ Tex, San Antonio, visiting assoc, 1987; Margaret Trowell Sch Fine Art, Kampala, Uganda, 1987; Univ Benin, Benin, Nigeria, artistic specialist, 1987; Yaba Tec Inst, Nigeria, artistic specialist; Art Inst Chicago, visiting assoc, 1988-89; Tiffany fel, 1988; Univ Md, grad dir, 1991-93, assoc prof, 1989-; NEA grant; Nat Gallery, Harare, Zimbabwe, vis fac. **Orgs:** NAACP; "Eight" Inst Contemp Art Va Museum Richmond, 1980; design costume & stage sets comn, Oakland Ballet Co, 1990; US Info Agency Arts Am Prog. **Honors/Awds:** State Honor Proclamation, Mayor Henry Cisneros; Marcus Foster Award for Teaching Excellence, Oakland Pub Sch, 1986; Louis Comfort Tiffany Award; James D Phelan Award in Printmaking. **Special Achievements:** The 1970's prints & drawings of Afro-Americans, Mus of the Center of Afro-Am Artists Inc, Boston 1980; Honored as first American to open the American Section, National Gallery of Art, Lagos, Nigeria; author and illustrator of the children's book, "The River That Gave Gifts"; work was selected by the Stanford Committee for the Arts, to be presented to Duke Ellington in an Honorary Degree Ceremony. **Home Addr:** 4310 Notre Dame St, Hyattsville, MD 20783-1909. **Business Addr:** Associate Professor, University of Maryland, Department of Art College, 1211 E Art/Sociol bldg, College Park, MD 20742, **Business Phone:** (301)405-1445.

HUMPHREY, MARIAN J
Banker. **Career:** Med Ctr State Bank, Okla City, OK, chief exec. **Business Addr:** Chief Executive, Medical Center State Bank, 1300 N Lottie, Oklahoma City, OK 73117, **Business Phone:** (405)424-5271.

HUMPHREY, MARION ANDREW
Judge, clergy. **Personal:** Born Nov 2, 1949, Pine Bluff, AR; son of Doris L Pendleton; married Vernita Gloria Thomas, Dec 27, 1986;

children: Marion Andrew Jr. **Educ:** Princeton Univ, BA, 1972; Harvard Divinity Sch, MDiv, 1978; Univ Aak Law Sch, JD, 1979. **Career:** State Ark, asst atty gen, 1981, circuit ct judge, 1993-; self-employed, law pract, 1982-86, 1987-89; Allison Mem Presbyterian Church, pastor, 1984-; City Little Rock, asst city atty, 1986, munic judge, 1989-92; Pulaski Co Courthouse, circuit judge, currently. **Orgs:** Ark C Hosp, 1992-; Lyon Col; Little Rock Rotary Club, 1991-; NCP; NBA, judicial coun, 1989-; Princeton Alumni Asn Ark. **Home Addr:** 2115 S Arch St, Little Rock, AR 72206, **Home Phone:** (501)375-3345. **Business Addr:** Circuit Judge, Pulaski County Courthouse, First Division, Rm 420 401 W Markham St, Little Rock, AR 72201, **Business Phone:** (501)340-8590.

HUMPHREY, ROBERT CHARLES
Football player. **Personal:** Born Aug 23, 1961, Lubbock, TX. **Educ:** NMex State Univ. **Career:** NY Jets, 1983-90; Los Angeles Rams, corner back, kick returner, 1990-91; San Diego Chargers, defensive back, 1991.

HUMPHREY, SONNIE
Manager. **Educ:** Hunter Col, New York, NY, BA, 1976. **Career:** Hunter Col News, reporter, 1974-76; Arts Bulletin, ed, 1981; Souvenir, jr ed, 1985-88; Jackie Robinson Found, 1991-96; Ed-Newsletter, Zeta Delta Phi Sorority, currently. **Orgs:** Bd mem, YGB Leadership Training, 1971-; coordr, Luncheon & Fashion Event, 1980-89; award coordr, Nat Coalition 100 Black Women Candace Awards, 1982-89; talent coordr, Motown Returns Apollo; United Negro Col Fund Auxiliary Comn, 1984-; vpres, New York Coalition 100 Black Women, 1986-; pres, Zeta Delta Phi Sorority, 1987-; spec events coordr, UNCF Michael Jackson Benefit, 1988; vol, New York Host Comn Grammys, 1991; presenter, Black History Makers Award, 1991; New York Women's Agenda, 1993-. **Honors/Awds:** Outstanding Service, Zeta Delta Phi Sorority, 1974, 1977 & 1986; Service To Youth Award, Kennedy Community Ctr, 1975, 1978; Outstanding Young Women, 1982; Achievement Award, New York Coalition 100 Black Women, 1984; Community Service, Joseph P Kennedy Community Ctr, 1985; CBS-TV Adv Comn Black Hist Month Moments, 1995-. **Special Achievements:** Poems, "Black Women," 1977, "Young, Gifted and Black," 1980. **Home Addr:** 3531 Bronxwood Ave, Bronx, NY 10469. *

HUMPHRIES, CHARLES, JR.
Obstetrician, gynecologist. **Personal:** Born Apr 14, 1943, Dawson, GA; married Monica Tulio; children: Charlie Christopher. **Educ:** Fisk Univ, BA, 1966; Meharry Med Col, MD, 1972. **Career:** Pvt pract, physician, currently. **Orgs:** Omega Psi Phi Fraternity; Dougherty Co Med Soc; Ga State Med Asn; Med Asn Ga; asst treas, Ga State Affil Univ Ill, 1972-73; Southwest GA Black Health Care Providers. **Military Serv:** USN, lcdr, 1976-78. **Home Addr:** 3520 Wexford Dr, Albany, GA 31707. **Business Addr:** Physician, 802 N Jefferson St, Albany, GA 31701.

HUMPHRIES, DR. FREDERICK S
College administrator. **Personal:** Born Dec 26, 1935, Apalachicola, FL; son of Thornton Humphries Sr and Minnie Henry; married Antoinette McTurner, Aug 20, 1960; children: Frederick S jr, Robin Tanya & Laurence Anthony. **Educ:** Florida A&M Univ, Tallahassee, Fla, BS (magna cum laude), 1957; Univ Pittsburgh, Pittsburgh, Pa, PhD, 1964. **Career:** Pvt tutor sci & math, 1959-64; Fla A&M Univ, Tallahassee Fla, assoc prof, 1964-66, prof chem, 1968-74, Col Curric Prog, prog dir, 1967-68, pres, 1985-2001, regent prof, currently; Univ Minn, asst prof chem, 1966-67; Inst Servs Educ, Wash, DC, prog dir summer conf & thirteen-col curric prog, 1968-74, three-univs grad prog humanities, 1970-74, innovative instnl res consortium, 1972-73, study sci capability black col, 1972-74, interdisciplinary prog, 1973-74, two-univ grad prog sci, 1973-74; Tenn State Univ, Nashville, Tenn, pres, 1974-85, pres emer, 1985-. **Orgs:** Am Asn Higher Educ; AAAS; Am Asn Univ Profs; Am Chem Soc; Am Asn Minority Res Univs; Nat Asn Advan Colored People; bd dirs, Am Cancer Soc; bd, Barnett Bank; bd, Pride; bd dirs, YMCA, 1987; Vis comt, Mass Inst Technol, 1982; Joint Comt Agr Develop, 1982; chmn, Adv Comt Off Advan Pub Negro Col, 1982; secy, Am Coun Educ, 1978; Int Platform Asn; Nat Merit Scholar Corp; chmn, Nat Asn State Univs & Land Grant Cols; bd dirs, Walmart Corp; bd dirs, Brinker Int; Pres Bill Clinton, White House Adv Comt Historically Black Cols & Univs; pres & chief exec officer, Nat Asn Equal Opportunity Higher Educ, 2001-03. **Honors/Awds:** Frederick S Humphries Day, City Indianapolis, 1975; Outstanding Citizen of the Year Award, Nashville Chap, Omega Psi Phi, 1976; Certificate of Appreciation, Gcv Tenn, 1982; Certificate of Appreciation, Dept Health & Human Servs, 1983; leadership grant, Prudential Life Ins Co Found, 1988; Centennial Medallion, Fla A & M Univ; Bicentennial Medal Distinction & Distinguished Alumnus Award, Univ Pittsburgh; Thurgood Marshall Award for Higher Education, Johnson Publ Co, 1991; Drum Major for Justice Award for Higher Education, Southern Christian Leadership Conf, 1993; Floridian of the Year, Orlando Sentinel, 1997; Trumpet Award for Education, Time Warner, Turner Broadcasting Syst, 2001; Lifetime Achievement Award, Nat Asn Black Engrs, 2001; numerous honorary doctrorate degrees. **Military Serv:** AUS, Security Agency, officer, 1957-59. **Business Addr:** President Emeritus, Tennessee State University, 3500 John A Merritt Blvd, Nashville, TN 37209, **Business Phone:** (615)963-5000.

HUMPHRIES, JAMES NATHAN
Lawyer. **Personal:** Born Feb 15, 1958, Detroit, MI; son of Andrew John and Mary Jane; married Diane D Rogers, Dec 14, 1985 (deceased); children: Charneise N Newton, Keyontay S, Karlea T & Kalon J. **Educ:** Univ Mich, BGS, 1980, JD, 1984. **Career:** Mich State Univ, Cooper Extension Prog, 4H youth agent, 1984-87; Detroit City Coun Research Div, anal, 1987-89; City Dearborn, Legal Dept, asst corp coun, 1989-95; Detroit Bd Educ, asst gen coun, 1995; Dept Fed State & Local Grant Develop & Prog Compliance, interim exec dir; Pvt Pract, atty, currently. **Orgs:** Mich Bar Asn, 1986-; Wolverine Bar Asn, 1986-; Detroit Bar Asn, 1986-; Detroit Officials Asn. **Business Addr:** Interim Executive Director, Department of Federal, State & Local Grant Development & Program Compliance, 3011 W Grand Blvd Suite 450 Fisher Bldg, Detroit, MI 48202, **Business Phone:** (313)873-7661.

HUMPHRIES, JAY (JOHN JAY HUMPHRIES)
Basketball player, basketball coach. **Personal:** Born Oct 17, 1962, Los Angeles, CA; married Angelica; children: Britni, Courtni, Jden & Xavier. **Educ:** Univ Colo, attended 1984. **Career:** Basketball player (retired), basketball coach; Phoenix Suns, guard,1984-88; Milwaukee Bucks, guard, 1987-92; UtahJazz, shooting guard, 1992-95, Boston Celtics, guard, 1994-95; Chinese CBA, assoc head coach, 2001; Inchon ET Land Black Slamer, asst coach, Phoenix Suns; head coach, 2002-07; Reno Bighorns, head coach, currently. **Honors/Awds:** Big Eight All-Conf Team; All-Am & Big Eight All-Defensive Team; BigEight's All-Freshman team. *

HUMPHRIES, PAULA G
Judge. **Educ:** Univ Mich; Wayne State Univ Law Sch. **Career:** State Mich, asst state atty, 1979-84; Mich Senate, minority coun, 1984-87; 36th Dist Ct, ct magistrate; Mich 36th Dist Ct, judge, 1988-. **Military Serv:** Operation Desert Storm, veteran, 1991; Judge Advocate Gen Br, ltcol. **Business Addr:** Judge, Michigan 36th District Court, 421 Madison Ave, Detroit, MI 48226, **Business Phone:** (313)965-8622.

HUNDON, JAMES HENRY
Football player. **Personal:** Born Apr 9, 1971, San Francisco, CA. **Educ:** Portland State Univ. **Career:** Football player (retired); Cincinnati Bengals, wide receiver, 1996-99; SanJose Sabercats, prof football player, 2001-04.

HUNIGAN, COL. EARL
Army officer. **Personal:** Born Jul 29, 1929, Omaha, NE; married Lazell Phillips; children: Kirk & Kris. **Educ:** Univ Mich, BBA, 1952. **Career:** Civil Serv Comn, investr, 1956-60, personnel specialist, 1962-63; USAF, mgt analyst, 1960-62; FAA, personnel specialist, 1963-68; US Coast Guard, dep dir civil personnel, 1968-69; Dept Transp, spec asst, asst secy admin, 1969-71; S Region FAA, exec officer, 1971-73; Food & Nutrit Serv US Dept Agri, dep admin mgt, 1973-78; Smithsonian Inst, dir personel training, 1985; E&L Assocs, mgt consult; Ebenezer African Methodist Episcopal Church, Ft Wash, Md, adminr, 1990. **Orgs:** Alpha Phi Alpha; Nat Asn Advan Colored People; Urban League; Phalanx; Am Soc Pub Admin. **Honors/Awds:** Sustained Super Performer, 1957-58, 1961 & 1971; Spec Act, 1963-73; Quality Step Increase, 1968; Distinguished Mil Instr Award, 1969-71. **Military Serv:** AUS, col, retired. **Home Addr:** 46875 Grissom St, Sterling, VA 20165-3575.

HUNN, DOROTHY FEGAN
Health services administrator. **Personal:** Born Sep 1, 1928, Chandler, OK; daughter of John Fegan and Willie Fegan; married Myron Vernon; children: Myron Vernon, Jonathan Scott & William Bruce. **Educ:** Memorial Hosp Sch Nursing, RN, 1952; Compton Community Col, AA, 1969; CSU Dominguez Hills, BA, 1976; Pepperdine Univ, MPA 1977; CSU Long Beach, PhN, 1984. **Career:** Health Serv Admin; Prof Nursing & RCFE Admin. **Orgs:** Alpha Kappa Alpha Sorority; Phi Delta Kappa Sorority; Nat Asn Univ Women; Auxillary to Angel City Dental Soc, JUGS; Links Inc; First United Methodist Church. **Home Addr:** 820 Clemmer Dr, Compton, CA 90221.

HUNN, MYRON VERNON
Dentist. **Personal:** Born Aug 9, 1926, Sequndo, CO; married Dorothy Louise; children: Myron Jr, Jonathan & William. **Educ:** La State Col, BA, 1954; Howard Univ, DDS, 1958. **Career:** Pvt practice, dentist. **Orgs:** Compton Optimist Club; Comn, Redev Agency; personnel bd, City Compton, 1967-70; bd dirs, YMCA, 1970-73; pres, trustee bd United Methodist Church, 1970-73; Nat Dent Asn; Am Dent Asn. **Military Serv:** AUS, 1951-54. **Business Addr:** 1315 N Bullis Rd 4, Compton, CA 90221.

HUNT, BETTY SYBLE
Government official. **Personal:** Born Mar 13, 1919, Forest, MS; married IP Hunt; children: Irvin D, Vera H Jennings, Garland H & Vernon. **Educ:** Scott Co Training Sch, dipl, 1935; Jackson State Univ, BS, 1964; Univ Miss, Reading, attended 1969; Miss Col, attended 1979. **Career:** Jackson State Bookstore, asst mgr, 1950-65; Canton Pub Sch, teacher, 1968-73; Packard Elec, assembler, 1973-85; Hinds Co, MS, election comnr. **Orgs:** Founder, JSU Campus Ministry Methodist Students, 1957; chairperson, United Givers Fund, 1968-69; Election Comn Asn Miss, 1980; 100 Black Women Coalition, 1982; delegate, Co Dem Convention, 1984; pres, Women Progress Miss Inc, 1983-85; pres, Miss Chap Nat Coalition 100 Black Women. **Honors/Awds:** Certificate, March of Dimes, 1968; Community Excellence Award, Gen Motors, 1974; Award, Pin United Methodist Women, 1984; Certificate, Three Quarter Way House, 1984. **Home Addr:** 11517 Evelake Ct, North Potomac, MD 20878-2592. **Business Addr:** Election Commissioner, Hinds Co Dist 5, Hines Co Court House, Jackson, MS 39215, **Business Phone:** (601)968-6555.

HUNT, CHARLES AMOES
Librarian. **Personal:** Born Jan 21, 1950, Montclair, NJ; son of William Henry and Juliet Adele Carter Bey. **Educ:** MTI Bus Col, Newark, NJ, comput programmer, 1968; Doane Col, Crete, Nebr, BA, 1973; Doane Col, Omaha, Nebr, teaching cert, 1973; Syracuse Univ, Syracuse, NY, MSLS, 1975; Univ Pac, Stockton, Calif, pub mgt, 1996; Calif State Univ-Stanislaus, Turlock, Calif, law, 1999; Humphreys Col, Stockton, Calif, law, 2000. **Career:** Chicago Pub Libr, Chicago, Ill, br librn, 1975-78; Atlantic Richfield Co, Los Angeles, Calif, technical librn, 1978-79; Calif State Univ-Fullerton, Fullerton, Calif, ref librn, 1979; Kiddy Col Eng Sch, Mishima City, Japan, eng instr, 1979-81; Stockton-San Joaquin County Pub Libr, Stockton, Calif, adult serv librn, 1981-91, supervising librn, 1991-98; Univ Pac, Stockton, Calif, ref librn, 2001; San Joaquin Delta Col, Stockton, Calif, adj facility, 2001-. **Orgs:** Guest reviewer, Ref Books Bulletin Edl Bd, Am Libr Asn, 1975-79; Black Caucus Am Libr Asn, 1975-78, 1981-; reviewer, Booklist mag, Am Library Asn, 1976-79; Yelland Memorial Scholar Minority Students Comt, Calif Libr Asn, 1987-88; vpres/pres-elect, 1990-91, pres, 1991-92, Community Info Sect, Pub Libr Asn Ala; chair, CIS Nominating Comt, 1993 & 1994; Off Literacy & Outreach Serv Adv Comn, Ala, 1998-00. **Honors/Awds:** Undergrad Scholar, Turrell Fund, E Orange, NJ, 1969-73; Jr Semester Abroad Prog, Doane Col, 1972; Grad fel, Syracuse Univ, 1974-75; Gold Award for Best Newsletter, Manteca, Calif, Kiwanis, 1988; United Way San Joaquin County, Recertification Team, Stockton, Calif, 1994 & 1995; City-paid tuition, Univ Pac, Stockton, Calif, 1996. **Special Achievements:** "Role of the Public Manager in a Changing Environment", 1996. **Home Addr:** 1209 W Downs St, Stockton, CA 95207, **Home Phone:** (209)951-5385.

HUNT, CLETIDUS
Football player. **Personal:** Born Jan 2, 1976, Memphis, TN. **Educ:** Ky State Univ. **Career:** Football player (retired); Green Bay Packers, defensive tackle, 1999-2004; New York Dragons, 2007.

HUNT, DARROLD VICTOR
Conductor (music). **Personal:** Born Jun 29, 1941, New Bedford, MA; son of Edward and Vera Watkins. **Educ:** New Bedford, Inst Technol, New Bedford, MA, 1963; Juilliard Sch, New York,NY, BS, 1969, MS, 1970. **Career:** SUNY Purchase, Mt Vernon, NY, instr, 1968-70; Brooklyn Col, New York, NY, asst prof, 1970-73, assoc prof & conductor, 1977-79; Urban Philharmonic Soc, Wash, DC, music coord, 1970-; Baltimore Sym, Baltimore, MD, apprentice & asst conductor, 1973-77. **Orgs:** Bd, funding comm, DC Humanities Coun, 1985-89; bd, minority outreach comm, Epilepsy Found Am, 1988-2001; music comm, DC Comn Arts & Humanities, 1988-89. **Honors/Awds:** The Frederick Douglass Memorial Award, 1992. **Special Achievements:** Listed in Who's Who in Entertainment. **Business Addr:** Music Coordinator, The Urban Philharmonic Society, 1711 T St NW Suite 9, Washington, DC 20009-7109, **Business Phone:** (202)387-4448.

HUNT, EDWARD
Executive. **Career:** Stop Shop & Save, CEO, co-owner, 1976-; E & S Mkt, pres, currently. **Business Addr:** President, E & S Markets Inc, 1401 Bloomfield Ave, Baltimore, MD 21227, **Business Phone:** (410)233-7152.*

HUNT, EUGENE
Banker, vice president (organization). **Personal:** Born Jul 19, 1948, Augusta, GA; son of Alfred Hunt Sr and Mabel Williams; divorced; children: Brian Eugene. **Educ:** Augusta Col, BBA, 1971; Augusta Col, post-baccalaureate study, 1978-79. **Career:** Citizen & Soc Nat Bank, Nations Bank, mgr 1975, dir, 1976, asst banking officer, 1977, banking officer & br mgr, 1980-; asst vpres in charge, Govt Banking Div, 1984. **Orgs:** Treas, Good Shepherd Baptist Church Inc, 1971-; sec, Cent Savannah River Area Bus League, 1976; pres, Cent Savannah River Area Bus League, 1979; tech adv bd, Opportunity Indus Center, 1977-80; bd dirs, Augusta Sickle Cell Ctr, 1977; loan exec, Nat Alliance Businessmen, 1979-80; Governor's Educ Review Comn, 1983-84; past chmn, Ga Dept Tech & Adult Educ, 1985-. **Honors/Awds:** Service Award, Nat Alliance Businessmen, 1977; Service Award Good Shepherd Baptist Church Inc, 1978; Appreciation Award Cent Savannah River Area Youth Employment Opportunity Inc, 1979; Businessman of the Year, Augusta Black Historical Soc, 1983; Businessman of the Year, Augusta Chap Delta Sigma Theata, 1984. **Business Addr:** Staff, Bank Am, 2870 Central Ave, Augusta, GA 30909-3905, **Business Phone:** (404)828-8249.

HUNT, ISAAC COSBY, JR.
School administrator, lawyer, commissioner. **Personal:** Born Aug 1, 1937, Danville, VA; married Elizabeth Raucnell; children: Isaac

III. **Educ:** Fisk Univ, BA, 1957; Univ Va, Law Sch, LLB, 1962. **Career:** Lawyer, school administrator, commissioner, (retired); Securities & Exchange Comn, staff atty, 1962-67; Nat Adv Comn Civil Disorders, team leader, 1967-68; RAND Corp, res staff, 1968-71; Cath Univ Am, asst prof Law, 1971-77; Jones Day Renvis Pogue, assoc, 1977-79; Dept Army, prin dep gen coun, 1979-81; Antioch Sch Law, dean; US Securities & Exchange Comn, comnr, 1996. **Orgs:** Co-chair, DC Consumer Goods Bd, 1974-76; bd gov, Soc Am Law Teachers, 1976-79; troop comt mem, Boy Scouts Am Troop 52, 1982; chair, Sasha Bruce Youthwork Inc, 1987. **Honors/Awds:** Outstanding Civilian Service Award, Dept Army, 1981. *

HUNT, JAMES, JR. See Obituaries section.

HUNT, JEFFREY C.
Government official. **Personal:** Born Oct 30, 1968, Detroit, MI; son of Clyde Cleveland and Anne Ruth Ellis. **Educ:** Howard Univ, BA, 1991. **Career:** US House Reps, legis asst, 1991; New World Technol Inc, chmn & chief exec officer, 1995; City Detroit Cable Commun Comn, Dept Elections, sr training specialist, chmn, currently, comnr, currently. **Orgs:** Detroit Democratic Club, 1996-; chmn, founder, Tomorrow's Leadership Today, PAC, 1996-; bd mem, Am Heart Asn, 1995-; heath allocation comn mem, United Way Community Servs, 1995; Million Man March Asn, 1995-; founder,Ambitious Students Involved in Community Serv, 1987-; master mason, Mt Pavan Price Hall Affiliated, 1992-. **Honors/Awds:** Presidential Fellowship, Lyndon Baines Johnson Found, 1991. **Special Achievements:** Conducted Excel Leadership Prog, 1994; MI Political Leadership Prog, 1995; Greater Detroit Chamber of Commerce, Leadership Detroit, 1996. **Business Phone:** (313)224-2100.

HUNT, MAURICE
Educator. **Personal:** Born Dec 16, 1943, Birmingham, AL; son of Percy Benjamin Hunt Sr and Ora Lee Lawson; married Mary Elizabeth Sain, Aug 6, 1966; children: Michael Phillip. **Educ:** Ky St Col, BS, 1966; Iowa Univ, attended 1971; Drake Univ, MSE, 1975. **Career:** Good Shepherd High Sch, coach, 1965-66; Glen Park Ambridge Elem Schs,instr, 1967-69; Tolleston High Sch, instr & coach, 1967-69; Grinnell Col, instr & coach, 1969-77; Cent St Univ, asst prof & coach, 1977-79; Morehouse Col, instr & coach 1979-. **Orgs:** Grinnell, IA Youth Comn, 1969-71; Am Football Coaches Asn 1970-; Wrestling Fedn, 1970-73; Iowa Lions Club, 1972-77; Drake Relays Comn, 1973-77; Iowa Human Rights Comn 1976-77; Rater, NAIA, 1978; Sheridan Black Col Pollster. **Honors/Awds:** Athletics Hall of Fame, Kentucky State University, 1991; Phyllis Wheatley Award, Women's Federated Clubs, 1991. **Special Achievements:** Coach of Year Atlanta Daily World Newspaper, Atlanta Constitution Journal, SIAC, 100 Percent Wreatling Club 1979, Atlanta Extra Point Club 1980-83, 1987-88. **Business Addr:** Physical Education Instructor, Morehouse College, 830 Wview Dr, Atlanta, GA 30314, **Business Phone:** (404)681-2800.

HUNT, DR. PORTIA L
Educator, psychologist, consultant. **Personal:** Born Feb 12, 1947, East St Louis, IL; daughter of Ethel and Luches. **Educ:** Southern Ill Univ, Edwardsville, BS, educ & psychol, 1971, MS, counr educ, 1972; Ind State Univ, Terre Haute, Ind, PhD, coun & psychol serv, 1975. **Career:** State Comm Col, counr, 1971-73; Portia Hunt & Assocs, psychologist, 1979-; Eclipse Mgt Consult Group, pres, 1986-; Temple Univ, prof coun psychol, 1975-, Coun Psychol Prog, prog coordr. **Orgs:** Delaware Valley Assoc Black Psychologists, 1976-; Nat prog chair, Assoc Black Psychologists, 1979; adv bd pres, Eastern Col Cushing Counseling Act 101, 1980-86; bd mem, Ch World Inst, Temple Univ, 1980-86; Philadelphia Desegration Sch Dist; bd mem, ABRAXAS Found, 1985-; Survivors Move Bombing Philadelphia & W Philadelphia Consortium Mental Health Ctr, consult, 1985-86. **Honors/Awds:** Professional Affairs Serv Award, Delaware Valley Asn Black Psychol, 1983; Psychology Award, Serv Black Comn, Alliance Black Social Worker, 1985; Psychology Award, Delaware Valley Asn Black Psychologists, 1986; Kathryn Sisson Phillips Fellowship Scholar, 1974; Women to Watch Award, Bus Jour Philadelphia, 1995. **Business Addr:** Professor Counseling Psychology, Program Coordinator, Temple University, Weiss Hall 267 1701 N 13th St, Philadelphia, PA 19122-6085, **Business Phone:** (215)204-1586.

HUNT, RICHARD HOWARD
Sculptor. **Personal:** Born Sep 12, 1935, Chicago, IL; son of Howard and Inez Henderson; divorced. **Educ:** Art Inst Chicago, BA, 1957; Belli Bare; Univ Chicago, attended 1955. **Career:** Advant-Grade Sculptures, sculptor, creator; Sch Art Inst Chicago, teacher, 1961; Univ Ill, Chicago, dept arch & art, 1962; Yale Univ, vis prof; Purdue Univ, vis prof, 1965; Northwestern Univ, vis prof, 1968; Mich State Univ, E Lansing, MI, vis prof, 1997. **Orgs:** Perm col art, Mus Chicago, Cleveland, Houston, NY, Buffalo, Milwaukee, Israel; work was exhibited in Artists of Chicago & Vicinity Exhbtn 1955-56; 62nd, 63rd, 64th Am Exhib of Art Inst of Chicago; Carnegie Intrnat Exhib in Pitts 1958; Mus of Mod New York City 1959; one-man Exhib in NYC, Chicago; participated in exhib Ten Negro Artists from US; First World Festival of Negro Arts, Dakar, Senegal 1966. **Honors/Awds:** Recip 6 Major Awards & Flwshps. **Military Serv:** First African-American sculptor to be honored with a retrospective exhibition at the Museum of Modern Art in New York in 1969. **Home Addr:** 1017 W Lill Ave, Chicago, IL 60614, **Home Phone:** (773)929-6161.

HUNT, RONALD JOSEPH
School administrator, athletic coach. **Personal:** Born Dec 19, 1951, Uniontown, PA; married Karen Elaine Hill; children: Lynnette & Angela. **Educ:** Slippery Rock St Col, BS Health, Phys Ed 1973, MEd Admin & Curriculum, 1975. **Career:** Slippery Rock State Col, asst dir admis, 1979-, temp instr phys ed, 1979, actg coord spec serv, 1974, grad asst, 1973, asst football coach, 1973-77, asst basketball coach, 1978-79; National City Bank, vpres, Regional Commercial Lending, 2008-. **Orgs:** Bd dir, Connie Hawkins Basketball Inc, 1978-80; bd dir, W Side Comn Act Ctr, 1979-80; bd dir, Lawrence County Coun Comn Ctrs, 1979-80. **Honors/Awds:** Outstanding Athletic Am, 1973; Outstanding Man Comn, Jaycees, 1979.

HUNT, SAMUEL D. See Obituaries section.

HUNTER, BRIAN LEE
Baseball player. **Personal:** Born Mar 5, 1971, Portland, OR. **Career:** Houston Astros, outfielder, 1994-96; Detroit Tigers, 1997-99; Seattle Mariners, 1999; Colo Rockies, 2000; Cincinnati Reds, 2000; Philadelphia Phillies, 2001; Houston Astros, outfielder, 2002-03; St Louis Cardinals, outfielder, 2004; Kans City Royals, 2005. *

HUNTER, BRIAN RONALD
Baseball player, scout. **Personal:** Born Mar 4, 1968, Torrance, CA; married Stephanie; children: Zachary. **Career:** Baseball Player (retired), scout; Atlanta Braves, 1991-93, 1999, scout, curently; Pittsburgh Pirates, 1994; Cincinnati Reds, 1994-95; Seattle Mariners, 1996; St Louis Cardinals, 1998; Philadelphia Phillies, 2000; NY Mets, scouts; Washington Nationals, scout.

HUNTER, BRYAN C.
Financial manager, president (organization). **Personal:** Born Oct 24, 1961, Kingston, Jamaica; son of Calvin and Monica Chong; married Kimberly A; children: Christopher & Nicole. **Educ:** Harvard Univ, AB, 1983; Univ Chicago, Grad Sch Bus, MBA, 1988. **Career:** Arthur Andersen & Co, sr consult, 1984-85; First Nat Bank Chicago, profit planner, 1985-87, sr trader, vpres, 1987-94; ABN AMRO Bank, trading mgr, vpres, 1994-99; Chicago Mercantile Exchange, dir currency prod, 2000, FXMarketSpace, chief operating officer, 2006-07; prin & owner, Asteri Capital Management LLC, 2007-. **Orgs:** Alumni interviewer, Harvard Club Chicago. **Business Addr:** Owner, Principal, Asteri Capital Management LLC, Chicago Mercantile Exchange, Chicago, IL 60614.

HUNTER, C. J. (COTTRELL J HUNTER)
Athlete, athletic coach. **Personal:** Born Dec 14, 1968, Washington, DC; married Marion Jones; children: Ahny & Coryatt. **Educ:** Pa State Univ, BA, political sc. **Career:** Athlete (retired), Athlete Coach; world shot-put champion; Cardinal Gibbons High Sch, coach, currently. **Honors/Awds:** World Indoor silver medalist, 1995; World Champion, 1999; World Track and Field Champ Seville, Spain, gold medal; 3-time USA national champion; USA Olympic team member, 2000. **Business Addr:** Coach, Cardinal Gibbons High School, 1401 Edwards Mill Rd, Raleigh, NC 27607, **Business Phone:** (919)834-1625.

HUNTER, CECELIA CORBIN
Government official, association executive, executive director. **Personal:** Born Jul 8, 1945, Jersey City, NJ; daughter of Leander M Corbin and Margaret Nelson Corbin; divorced; children: Alicia Stacey. **Educ:** Harvard Univ, John F Kennedy Sch Govt, MPA, 1982. **Career:** Atlanta Off Mayor Maynard Jackson, dir fed rels, 1974-81, chief staff, 1990-91, dir olympic coord, 1991-94; ICMA Retirement Corp, mgr, eastern region, 1982-90; 1996 Atlanta Paralympic Games, vpres operations & serv, 1994; Teachers's Retirement System, exec dir, 2001-05; City Atlanta, Audit Comt & Atlanta Pub Safety Authority, exec, currently. **Orgs:** Bd mem, Atlanta Area Coun Campfire Girls, 1976-80; W End Neighborhood Develop Corp, 1980-; asst secy, bd dirs, ICMA Retirement Corp, 1983-88; charter mem, 100 Black Women Metro Atlanta, 1987; trustee, Catalyst Mag, 1989-; bd dirs, Atlanta Bus League, 1991-; bd dirs, Zoo Atlanta, 1991-; bd dirs, chair eeo comt, Atlanta Comt Olympic Games, 1991-94. **Honors/Awds:** Word Processing, Spring Cover Story, 1975; Atlanta Constitution-Intown Extra, "Atlanta's Complete Count Committee", 1980; Tribute to African-American Business and Professional Women, Dollars & Sense Mag, 1990; OIC Champion, 1994; Atlanta's Top 100 Black Women of Influence. **Business Addr:** Association Executive, City of Atlanta, Ethics Office, 68 Mitchell St SW Suite 3180, Atlanta, GA 30303, **Business Phone:** (404)330-6286.

HUNTER, CECIL THOMAS
Educator. **Personal:** Born Feb 5, 1925, Greenup, KY; married Gloria James; children: Mildred C, Charlene James, Rosalind H Levy, Roderick & Gloria. **Educ:** Wash Jr Col; FL A&M Univ. **Career:** Brownsville Mid Sch, teacher math. **Orgs:** Chmn, Cath Soc Serv; chmn, Govt Ctr Auth; chmn, Escambia Co Health Facil Auth; comt mem bd dir, Sacred Heart Found; Saenger Mgt bd dir; Finance Comt & Gen Govt Comt City Coun; past mem, Hospice - NW Fla Area Agency Aging; St Anthony's Cath Church; Knights Columbus; Jack & Jill Am; Kappa Alpha Psi Fraternity; Nat Asn Advan Colored People. **Honors/Awds:** Diocesan Medal of Honor; Secular Franciscan Peace Award. **Military Serv:** WWII, veteran. **Home Addr:** 1330 E Scott St, Pensacola, FL 32503. **Business Addr:** Teacher Mathematics, Brownsville Middle School, 3100 West Strong St, Pensacola, FL 32501.*

HUNTER, CHARLES A
Educator, clergy. **Personal:** Born May 7, 1926, Longview, TX; son of Ivernia Charlott and Wallace Alvin; married Annie Alexander; children: Alpha A, Rhonda A, Rhasell D, Byron C & Rosalyn A. **Educ:** Bishop Col, BA, 1947; Howard Univ, BD, 1950; Philadelphia Divinity Sch, MTh, 1954, ThD 1958; Univ N Tex, MS, 1971. **Career:** Bishop Col, prof sociol, 1961-72, 1975-88; Hope Presbyterian Church, Dallas, pastor, 1962-68; Dallas Independent Sch, sociol res, 1969-72, 1974-75; St Luke Presbyterian Church, Dallas, co-pastor 1969-80; Univ Tex, Arlington, assoc prof 1972-73; Dallas County Community Churches, dir church & community, 1989-; Synod Sun, moderator, 1991-93. **Orgs:** Dir, United Cmps Christian Fel, 1959-61; coordr, Amigos, 1968-; bd mem, Greater Dallas Housing Opportunity Ctr, 1969-; Dallas Theater Ctr 1974-83; Red Cross Dallas, 1975-81; Dallas Citizens/Police Relations Bd, 1981-88; bd mem, Trinity River Authority, 1983-89; moderator, Grace Presbytery, 1985; moderator, Synod of the Sun, 1991-93. **Honors/Awds:** Trail Blazer Award, Bus & Professional Women, 1966; Outstanding Alumni, Bishop Col Alumni Asn, 1966; Fair Housing Award, Greater Dallas Housing Opportunity Ctr, 1972; Volunteer Award, First Lady's Vol, TX, 1980. **Home Addr:** 2329 Southwood Dr, Dallas, TX 75224. **Business Addr:** Director of Department of Church and Community, Greater Dallas Community of Churches, 624 N Good Latimer Expy, Dallas, TX 75204, **Business Phone:** (214)824-8680.

HUNTER, CLARENCE HENRY
Public relations executive. **Personal:** Born Nov 1, 1925, Raleigh, NC; son of Wade H and Katie L; married Mary Ransom; children: Karen, Beverly, Katherine & Andrew. **Educ:** New York Univ, BS, 1950. **Career:** Journ & Guide Norfolk Va, reporter, bureau mgr, 1950-53; Ebony Mag Chicago Ill, assoc editor, 1953-55; Post-Tribune Gary Ind, reporter, 1955-62; WA Evening Star WADC, reporter, 1962-65; US Comn Civil Rights WA DC, dir info, 1965-69; WA Journ Ctr WA DC, assoc dir, 1969-71; Howard Univ, dir univ rel & publ, 1971-73; General Motors Public Relations, staff asst, 1973-78, Rochester Products Div, dir communs & public relations, 1978-88, AC Rochester Div, mgr pub affairs commun, 1988-. **Orgs:** Public Relations Society Am; Austin Steward Prof Society; United Way Greater Rochester; Martin Luther King Jr Festival Comn; GM Civic Involvement Prog. **Honors/Awds:** Howard Coles Community Award, Asn Black Communicators, Rochester Chap, 1984; Distinguished Achievement Award, Black Bus Asn Greater Rochester, 1991; Kathryn B Terrell Award for Distinguished Volunteer Serv, Urban League Rochester, 1991. **Military Serv:** US Marine Corps, Sgt, 1944-46. **Business Addr:** Manager Public Affairs, Communications, Gen Motors Corp., AC Rochester Div, PO Box 92700, Rochester, NY 14692.

HUNTER, COTTRELL J. See HUNTER, C. J.

HUNTER, DAVID
Educator, clergy. **Personal:** Born Aug 3, 1941, Enterprise, MS; son of Sandy (deceased) and Laura; married Mary Williams; children: David Cornell, Christopher Dante. **Educ:** Alcorn State Univ, BS, 1964; Cleveland State Univ, MEd, 1974; Cent Bible Col, BA, 1976; Trinity Theol Sem, Newburgh, IN, doctoral candidate, currently. **Career:** E Cleveland Schs, teacher, 1969-82; Bright Star Missionary Baptist Church, pastor, 1972-. **Orgs:** Life mem, Alpha Phi Alpha, 1965-; Oper PUSH; Nat Asn Advan Colored People; E Cleveland Bd Educ, pres, 1988-89, 1991; pres, E Ministerial Alliance, 1994-95. **Honors/Awds:** Acad Scholarship, Alcorn State, 1962. **Business Addr:** Bright Star Missionary Baptist Church, 13028 Shaw Ave, Cleveland, OH 44108.*

HUNTER, DR. DAVID LEE
School administrator. **Personal:** Born Sep 10, 1933, Charlotte, NC; son of Annie L Boulware; married Margaret Plair; children: Karen Leslie & Jocelyn Jeanine. **Educ:** Johnson C Smith Univ, BS, 1951; Atlanta Univ, MS, 1964; Nova Univ, Ed.D,1979. **Career:** Carver Col & Mecklenburg Col, instr math, 1957-63; Cent Piedmont Community Col, instr math, 1963-71, coordr col transfer prog, 1971-73, dir,personnel, 1973-75, vpres, dean, gen studies, 1975, dean arts & sci. **Orgs:** Fin sec bd trustees, Little Rock AME Zion Church, 1973; Am Soc Pub Admin, 1974-; admin, NC Asn Community Col Instnl, 1975-; bd dir, Charlotte Rehab Homes Inc, 1978; rep, CPCC League Innovation Community Col, 1979-; bd dir,ARC 1979; bd dirs, Southern Reg Coun Black Am Affairs; NC SRCBAA. **Military Serv:** AUS, corpl, 1953-55.

HUNTER, DOROTHY
College teacher. **Personal:** Divorced. **Educ:** Huston-Tillotson Univ, BS, MS, math. **Career:** Huston Tillotson Univ, instr, currently. *

HUNTER, EDWINA EARLE
Educator, business owner. **Personal:** Born Dec 29, 1943, Caswell County, NC; daughter of Edgar Earl Palmer and Bessie Catherine Brown; married James Weldon Sr, Jul 2, 1966; children: James W Jr, Anika Z & Isaac Earl. **Educ:** Spelman Col, BA, 1964; Smith Col, MAT, 1966. **Career:** Vint Hill Farms Sta, post chapel choir dir, 1967-68; El Paso Community Col, instr music, 1975-76; Prince George's Co Sch, music teacher, 1969-72, dir vocal music, 1979; Kinder musik with Miss Winnie, owner, currently; Edwina Hunter Studio, owner, currently; Chair, Piano Festival, The Greater Laurel Music Teachers' Asn. **Orgs:** Secy, Columbia Chap NAASC, 1984-, pres, 1986-90; pres, Columbia Chap Nat Alumnae Asn Spelman Col, 1987-; secy & treas, NE Region, Nat Alumnae Asn Spelman Col, 1992-; MSTA Greater Laurel Music Teachers Asn NEA, MENC, MMENC; Suzuki Asn; Nat Asn Advan Colored People. **Honors/Awds:** Distinguished Alumni Award, NAFEO, 1989; Alumna of the Year, NAASC, Columbia, MD Chap, 2001. **Special Achievements:** Recording "Children's Songs for Games from Africa", Folkways FCS 77855, 1979. **Business Addr:** Owner, Edwina Hunter Studio, 10721 Graeloch Rd, Laurel, MD 20723, **Business Phone:** (301)953-2891.

HUNTER, FREDERICK DOUGLAS
Lawyer. **Personal:** Born Jan 30, 1940, Pittsburgh, PA; son of Charlie and Elizabeth; married Rosie M Kirkland; children: Frederick D & Deborah R. **Educ:** Univ Pittsburgh, BS, 1961, PhD, 1967; Univ Md, JD, 1974. **Career:** Lubrizol Corp, assoc gen coun, chief patent coun, currently; EI Dupont De Nemours & Co, corp coun, 1972-89; W R Grace & Co, sr res chem, 1967-72. **Orgs:** Am Bar Asn; Delaware Bar Asn; Dist Columbia Bar Asn; AOA Fraternity; Am Intellectual Property Law Asn; Chem Mfrs Asn. **Honors/Awds:** Published 5 papers on various sci jour. **Home Addr:** 17310 Bittersweet Trail, Chagrin Falls, OH 44023. **Business Addr:** Chief Patent Counsel, The Lubrizol Corporation, 29400 Lakeland Blvd, Wickliffe, OH 44092-2298, **Business Phone:** (216)943-4200.

HUNTER, GIGI
Actor, dancer, fashion designer. **Personal:** Born Jun 26, 1960, Washington, DC. **Educ:** Duke Ellington Sch Arts, Wash, DC. **Career:** Danced for TV shows: "Solid Gold"; "Fame"; "Broadway musical: The Wiz";"Cold Case", 2006; "I Know My Kid's a Star", actress, 2008; Danced for the Films: Coming to America, 1988; Mac & Me, 1988; Lambada, 1990; Rent, 2005;Dark Streets, 2008; Gigi Hunter Collection, owner & designer, currently. **Honors/Awds:** Magic Johnson Salute to African-American Designers, 1999. **Business Addr:** Owner, Fashion Designer, GiGi Hunter Collection, 719 S Los Angeles St Suite 332, Los Angeles, CA 90014, **Business Phone:** (213)624-6898.

HUNTER, IRBY B.
Dentist. **Personal:** Born Jul 12, 1940, Longview, TX; married Staphalene Johnson; children: Constance A, Irby B. **Educ:** Tex Col Tyler, BS, chem, 1961; Tuskegee Inst Ala, MS, chem, 1963; Univ Tex, Houston, DDS, 1968. **Career:** Atlantic & Richfield Houston, chem, 1964-68; Houston ISD, teacher ad ed, 1965-68; Dr WA Hembry Dallas, dentist gen, 1968-70; dentist gen, 1971-. **Orgs:** Am Dent Asn, 1965-; pres, MC Cooper Dent Soc Dallas, 1974-78; pres, Golf St Dent Assn Tex, 1978-; Steering Comt, Small Sch Task Force Dallas ISD, 1979-; mem bd, Community Health Ctrs Dallas Inc, 1979-; Sir Orchun, Sigma Pi Phi Frat Dallas, 1979. **Honors/Awds:** Special Alumni Award, Tex Col Tyler, TX, 1980. **Business Addr:** Dentist, 2826 E Illinois Ave, Dallas, TX 75216-3422.*

HUNTER, JAMES MACKIELL
Lawyer. **Personal:** Born Feb 7, 1946, Macon County, GA; son of Elton and Odessa; married Lorraine Dunlap; children: Adrienne, Michelle & Hillary. **Educ:** Ft Valley State Univ, BS, 1968; Howard Univ, JD, 1973; Harvard Univ, Pract Inst Lawyers, 1991. **Career:** US Equal Employ Opportunity Comn, trial atty, 1973-76, suprv trl atty 1976-78; M James Hunter & Assoc, prin partner 1978-81; M&M Products Co, vpres, gen coun, 1981-90; Hunt, Richardson, Garner, Todd & Cadenhead, partner, 1990-93; Schnader, Harrison, Segal & Lewis, partner, 1993-2000; Holland & Knight LLP, partner, 2000-. **Orgs:** Bd mem Atlanta Judicial Comn, 1978-; bd visitors, Grady Hosp, 1983-; Clayton Jr Col 1984-; Atlanta Jr Col Bd 1986; gen coun, 100 Black Men Atlanta, Inc, 1986-2000; 100 Black Men Am, nat gen coun, 1987-2001; bd mem, Nat Alliance Bus SE Region, 1987-2001; gen coun, Leadership Atlanta, 1988-93; nat coun, Nat Black Col Hall Fame Found Inc, 1988-2001; Goodwill IDS N GA, 1999-2001. **Honors/Awds:** Knox Award, Ft Valley State 1968; Omega Psi Phi Award, 1968; Outstanding Atlantans, 1978; Outstanding Gans, 1984. **Military Serv:** USAR, 1968-74. **Business Addr:** Partner, Holland & Knight LLP, 1 Atlantic Ctr 1201 W Peachtree St NE Suite 2000, Atlanta, GA 30309-3400, **Business Phone:** (404)817-8493.

HUNTER, REV. JAMES NATHANIEL, II
Clergy. **Personal:** Born Aug 16, 1943, Glasgow, VA; son of James N Sr and Helen Louise Strawbridge; married Sharron Joy Condon, Jul 22, 1972. **Educ:** St Paul'sCol, BA, 1966; Bexley Hall, BD, 1969; State Univ New York, Geneseo, MA, 1970. **Career:** Sch Dist Rochester, teacher, 1970-72; DEP Interior, prin, counr, teacher, 1972-83; Kila, Inc, employ counr, 1983-85; Fairbanks Resource Agency, suv, homeliving specialist, 1985-88; St Jude's Episcopal Church, vicar, 1988-, Jubilee Ctr, exd, 1992-; Univ Alaska, Fairbanks, adj prof. **Orgs:** Secy, Breadline, Inc, 1985; Tanana Conf Churches, 1985; Union Black Episcopalians, 1988; chair, Alaska Interfaith Impact, 1988; secy, Comn Ministry-Episcopal, 1990-94; dean, Tanana Interior Deanery, 1990-92; secy, past pres, 1989, Kiwanis Club N Pole; consult, Food Bank Fairbanks; elected to city coun, Mayor Pro Temp, 1998; Diocese Alaska Standing Comt. **Honors/Awds:** COT Leader Award, Martin Luther King, Jr, 1988; Outstanding Board Member, Breadline, Inc, 1989; Memorial Award for Outstanding Leadership, Fairbanks Resource Agency, 1988; Bexley Hall, Rossister Fellowships, 1988, 1991; Award to study in Israel, Episcopal Church USA Domestic & Foreign Ministry, 1990; Citizen of the Year, North Pole Chamber of Commerce, 1996; Vice Mayor, 1996. **Special Achievements:** First African American to serve on city council of North Pole; first African American priest to serve in Diocese of Alaska and only one so far; first African American to work as principal of elementary school system in Yukon-Kuskovian area. **Business Addr:** Vicar, Executive Director, St Jude, Jubilee Center, PO Box 55458, North Pole, AK 99705, **Business Phone:** (907)488-9329.

HUNTER, JERRY L.
Lawyer. **Personal:** Born Sep 1, 1942, Mt Holly, NC; son of Samuel and Annie B. **Educ:** NC A&T State Univ, BS, 1964; Howard Univ Sch Law, JD, 1967. **Career:** Roundtree, Knox, Hunter & Parker, atty, partner law firm. **Orgs:** DC Occupational Safety Bd, 1994-97; US Supreme Ct Bar; US Dist Ct (MD &DC); US Ct Appeals; DC Ct Appeals; US Ct Claims; Nat Bar Asn; Am Bar Asn; DC Bar Asn; Asn Plaintiffs Trial Atty; Sigma Delta Tau Legal Frat; Alpha Kappa Mu Honor Soc; Kappa Pi Int Hon Art Soc; Asn Trial Lawyers Am. **Honors/Awds:** American Jurisprudence Award for Academic Achievement in Legal Methods & History. **Special Achievements:** Co-auth article, "Current Racial Legal Developments", 12 How-L J 299, Spring 1966. **Business Addr:** Partner, Roundtree, Knox, Hunter & Parker, 1822 11th St NW, Washington, DC 20001-5015, **Business Phone:** (202)234-1722.

HUNTER, REV. JOHN DAVIDSON
Consultant. **Personal:** Married Lucile Chandler; children: Louise, John D Jr, Joshua, Phillip & Jackie Owens. **Educ:** Selma Univ, HS, grad opelika. **Career:** Protective Indust Ins Co, rep, 1962-81; Pilgrim Health Life Ins Co, rep, 1981-. **Orgs:** Tabernacle Baptist Church, 1941-; NAACP, 1950-; Dallas City Voters League, 1975-; Selma City Coun, 1976-84; President's Democratic Club Ala, 1977-85; Selma Black Leadership Coun, 1979-85; exec comt, Southwest Ala Sickle Cell Anemia Asn, 1984-85; minister, Rocky Br Baptist Church. **Honors/Awds:** Received twenty prof achievement awards & four community service awards. **Home Addr:** 1818 Martin Luther King St, Selma, AL 36701.

HUNTER, JOHN W.
Government official. **Personal:** Born Apr 18, 1934, Union, MS; son of Frank and Estella; married RoseMary White, Jul 3, 1956; children: Eric & Shawn. **Educ:** CS Mott Comm Jr Col, bus arts, 1969. **Career:** Government official (retired); 7th Dist Cong Black Caucus Polit Action Comt No 659, chmn; Genesee County Bd Health, bd dir; Genesee County Bd Comn, county comn, 1974-86; Genesee County Rd Comn, comnr. **Orgs:** Bd dir, Nat Asn County Welfare & Soc Serv Comn, Genesee Memorial Hosp, 1975-84, Model Cities Econ Develop Corp; chairperson, Genesee County Human Serv Comn; precinct delegate, former delegate, State Democratic Convention; Urban League, Nat Asn Advan Colored People, Elks Vehicle City Lodge 1036. **Honors/Awds:** Leadership Award, Black Bus & Professor Womens Organization, 1978; Frederick Douglass Award, National Association Black Bus & Professor Women Organization, 1987; A Philip Randolph Civic Right Award, 1989; National Media Womens Award, 1991. **Special Achievements:** First black to be named to road commission, 5th black to serve in the State of Michigan as road commissioner; Ambulatory Wing at Genesee memorial Hospital in Flint MI was named The John W Hunter Wing, 1984. *

HUNTER, KIM L
Executive, chief executive officer. **Personal:** Born Jun 30, 1961, Philadelphia, PA; son of Talmadge Edward Milton and Alberta May. **Educ:** Univ Wash, BA, bus admin, 1982; Univ St Thomas, MA, int mgt, 1988; Darthmonth Col, cert minority bus exec prog, 1992, cert advan minority bus exec prog, 1993; Northwestern Univ, cert advan mgt educ prog, 2000. **Career:** Pharmaseal, Div Baxter Corp, sales rep, 1982-86, mkt mgr, 1986-89; Int Commun & Advertising Network, exec vpres & gen mgr, 1989-90; Langrant Found, founder & pres, 1998-; Lagrant Commun, founder, pres & chief executive officer, currently. **Orgs:** Pres, Black PR Soc Calif Inc, 1991-94; vpres pub rels, Mus Art Contemporaries, 1993-94; KCET Business Partners Comt, 1994-95; bd mem, Next Wave Learning, 1995; comnr, City Los Angeles Animal Regulation Dept, 1996-99; pres, Am Cancer Soc, Cent Los Angeles Unit, 1998-2000; bd secy, Planned Parenthood Los Angeles, 1999-2000; bd mem, Calif Coun Humanities, 2000-; chmn, Lagrant Found; Am Cancer Soc. **Honors/Awds:** Marketing Incentinve Trip Award, 1988; Innovative Achievement in Business Communication Award, 1994; Outstanding Graphic Design Business Award, City Los Angeles, Dept Airports, 1994; Certificate of Merit, Am Cancer Soc, 1994. **Business Addr:** President, Chief Executive Officer, Lagrant Communications, 626 Wilshire Blvd Suite 700, Los Angeles, CA 90071-2300, **Business Phone:** (323)469-8680.

HUNTER, KIMBERLY ALICE
Executive. **Personal:** Born Jan 31, 1962, Chicago, IL; daughter of Eric Earl Graham and Eleanor Lucille Graham; married Bryan Charles, Jun 18, 1983; children: Christopher Elliot & Nicole Evelyn. **Educ:** Harvard & Radcliffe Col, AB, 1983; Univ Chicago, Grad Sch Bus, MBA, 1988. **Career:** First Nat Bank Chicago, vpres, 1983-89; Banc One Capital Markets, managing dir, 1989-2000; Corn Products Int Inc, dir, 2001-04, treasr, 2004-. **Orgs:** Bd dirs, Nat Asn Corporate Treas; Harvard Club Chicago Alumni Interviewer, YWCA Circle Friends. **Honors/Awds:** Black MBA Magazine Inaugural Top 50 Under 50. **Business Addr:** Corporate Treasurer, Corn Products International Inc, 5 Westbrook Corporate Ctr, Westchester, IL 60154, **Business Phone:** (708)551-2637.

HUNTER, LINDSEY BENSON
Basketball player. **Personal:** Born Dec 3, 1970, Utica, MS; married Ivy; children: 2. **Career:** Detroit Pistons, guard, 1993-2000, 2003-; Milwaukee Bucks, guard, 2000-01; Los Angeles Lakers, guard, 2001-02; Toronto Raptors, guard, 2002-03; Pistons, point & shooting guard, 2003-04. **Orgs:** Nat Basketball Asn; bd dir, Daybreak Homeless shelter, currently. **Honors/Awds:** NBA All-Rookie Second Team, 1994. **Special Achievements:** First round, tenth pick, NBA Draft, 1993. **Business Addr:** Professional Basketball Player, Detroit Pistons, 2 Championship Dr, Auburn Hills, MI 48326, **Business Phone:** (248)377-0100.

HUNTER, LLOYD THOMAS
Physician. **Personal:** Born Feb 6, 1936, Des Moines, IA; married Janice; children: Cynthia, Laura, Elizabeth. **Educ:** Univ Nebr, AB, 1957, MD, 1962. **Career:** Univ Southern Calif, staff; Univ Calif Los Angeles, Assoc Prof; pvt pract, physician, currently. **Orgs:** Diplomate Am Bd Pediat; fel Am Acad Pediat; La Pediat Soc; Charles R Drew Med Soc; Am Med Asn; Nat Med & Asn; Golden State Med Asn; Calif Med Asn; La Pediat Soc; Kappa Alpha Psi Frat; Nat Asn Advan Colored People; Los Angeles Urban League; Alpha Omega Alpha Med Hon Soc. **Honors/Awds:** Merit award Army commendation medal; 1962; Univ NE Regents Schlrshp 1961-62. **Military Serv:** AUS, med corps, capt, 1963-65, Merit award Army commendation medal. **Business Addr:** Physician, 4050 Kenway Ave, Los Angeles, CA 90008.*

HUNTER, DR. MAE M
President (Organization). **Career:** President (retired); Teacher Asn Chicago, pres aids found, currently. **Business Addr:** President Aids Foundation, Retired Teacher Association of Chicago, 220 S State St Suite 2100, Chicago, IL 60604, **Business Phone:** (312)939-3327.

HUNTER, OLIVER CLIFFORD, JR.
Physician. **Personal:** Born Feb 20, 1935, Kilgore, TX; married Shirley; children: Oliver, III, Stephen, Stephanie, Sherri. **Educ:** Tex Southern Univ, BS, 1956; Univ Tex Med Sch, MD, 1963. **Career:** Harris Co, TX, pvt pract, 1967; Baylor Col, instr, 1967-73; Univ Tex M D Anderson Cancer Ctr; Memorial Hermann Hosp, Houston, TX; Intracare Med Ctr, Houston, TX; Methodist Hosp Syst, Houston, TX. **Orgs:** Harris County Med Soc; Tex & Nat Med Asn; Tex & Am Soc Int Med; Houston Med Forum; life mem, Kappa Alpha Psi; Nat Bd Med Examiners, 1964; Am Bd Internal Med, 1970; Univ Tex Med Br Alumni Asn, 1974; Tex Southern Univ Alumni, 1975; Trinity Methodist Church; MacGregory Pk Civic Club; Big Bro; Cal Farley's Boy's Ranch; Nat Jewish Hosp. **Honors/Awds:** Outstanding Alumnus, Tex Col, 1974. **Military Serv:** AUS, pfc, 1963. **Business Addr:** Physician, The Methodist Hospital System, 6565 Fannin St, Houston, TX 77030.*

HUNTER, PATRICK J., SR.
Educator. **Personal:** Born Oct 29, 1929, Elberton, GA; married Mildred R Powell; children: Patrick J Jr, Kim M Brown, Michael A & Jeffrey M. **Educ:** Univ Bridgeport Conn, BA, 1958, MS, 1959; NY Univ, PhD. **Career:** Conn Dept Social Serv, caseworker, 1960-62; Birdgeport Inter-Group Coun Conn, exec dir, 1963-66; Community Training & Employ, Stamford, Conn, execdir, 1966-68; Housatonic Community Col, dept chmn, 1975-81; Housatonic Community Col, prof emer, currently. **Orgs:** Rotary Int Bridgeport Conn, 1963-66; pres, SW Regional Ment Health Bd, 1986-87; Conn State Mental Health Bd, 1987; planning coun, United Way Greater Bridgeport; bd mem, SW Conn Ment Health; Greater Bridgeport Catchment Area; adv bd, Greater Bridgeport Regional Ment Health; vpres, Ment Health Social Club Greater Bridgeport Area. **Honors/Awds:** Citizen of Year, College Charles Young Post, 1963; Achievement Award, Radio Station WICC, 1963; Outstanding Educator 1972. **Military Serv:** AUS, corpl, 1952-54; Korean Medal. **Business Addr:** Professor Emeritus, Housatonic Community College, Psychology Department, 900 Lafayette Blvd, Bridgeport, CT 06604, **Business Phone:** (203)332-5200.

HUNTER, RHONDA F
Lawyer. **Career:** Law Off Rhonda Hunter, atty, currently. **Orgs:** Pres, Dallas Bar Asn, 2004-05, bd dirs, Nat Conf Bar. **Business Phone:** (214)698-5900.*

HUNTER, RICHARD C
School administrator. **Personal:** Born May 4, 1939, Omaha, NE. **Educ:** Univ Omaha, BA, elem educ, 1961; San Francisco State Col, MA, elem educ, 1967; Univ Calif, Berkeley, EdD, sch admin, 1971. **Career:** Berkeley, CA, sch teacher, asst prin, prin; Richmond, Va, Pub Sch, supt; Dayton, Ohio, supt; Tokyo, Japan, teacher; Richmond, VA, prin; Seattle, asst dep supvr; Richmond, VA, Bd Educ, assoc supvr; Valentine Mus Dominion Nat Bank, staff; Richmond Chamber Comn, staff; St Paul Col, fac; Baltimore City Pub Schs, Baltimore, Md, supt; Dept Defense Educ Activity, US Govt, Arlington, VA, assoc dir educ, 1998; Univ NC, Chapel Hill, prof educ leadership, 1999-2000; Univ Ill, Urbana-Champaign, Dept Educ Orgn & Leadership, dept head, 2000-03, prof, 2000-. **Orgs:** Inst rep, Am Asn Col Teacher Educ, 2002-05; Ill Coun Profs Educ Admin, 2005; Ill Asn Sch Adminr, 2005; Educ Admin Alumni Asn, Champaign, Ill, 2005; Nat Alliance Black Sch Educr, Wash, DC, 2005; Chapel Hill, NC, Urban Rev, 2005; Kappa Alpha Psi; Phi Delta Kappa. **Honors/Awds:** Good Government Award, Richmond First Club; Univ Richmond, Hon Doctorate. **Special Achievements:** Numerous publications including All things to all people, special circumstances influencing the performance of African-American superintendents. Education and Urban Society, 2005; Tettegah, Sharon and Hunter, Richard C Education and Technology: Issues in Applications of Policy and Administration in K-12 Schools, Advances in Educational Administration, Volume 8, Oxford, England: JAI-Elsevier Science. **Business Addr:** Professor, University of Illinois at Urbana-Champaign, Educational Organization & Leadership, 337 Educ Bldg 1310 S 6th St MC 708, Champaign, IL 61820.

HUNTER, REV. SYLVESTER
Clergy. **Personal:** Born Mar 28, 1949, Pensacola, FL; married Janice Hunter, 1973; children: Sylvester & Chole. **Educ:** Wiley Col, BS, 1975; Houston Bible Inst, 1984; Concordia Theol Sem, 1987; Garrett Theol Sem, Master Theol Studies, 1991. **Career:** Ford Aerospace & Comn Corp, financial cost analyst, 1980-84, sr property coord, 1984-86; Magnavox Electronics Sys, sr contract property analyst, 1986-89; One Church One Offender Inc, exec dir, 1991-92; Union Baptist Church, asst to pastor, 1992-98, sr minister, 1998-, sr pastor, currently. **Orgs:** Alpha Phi Alpha; Kappa Tau Delta; vpres, Nat Asn Advan Colored People; chmn, bd dir, Fort Wayne Urban League; bd dir, Ind Minority Consortium; bd dir, Aids Task Force; chmn, InterdenomiNat Ministrial Alliance; fac mem, Congress Christian Educ, Gen Ind State, congress pres, 2000-. **Honors/Awds:** Young Black Achiever, 1986; Honorary Doctorate of Divinity Degree, St Thomas Christian Col. **Military Serv:** US Marine Corp, first lt, 1973-79. **Home Addr:** 2525 Palisade Dr, Fort Wayne, IN 46806. **Business Addr:** Senior Pastor, Union Baptist Church, 2200 Smith St, Fort Wayne, IN 46803.

HUNTER, TEOLA P.
Government official, association executive, consultant. **Personal:** Born Feb 5, 1933, Detroit, MI; daughter of T P and Olivia Cranon; children: Denise Hughes Ciccel, Jeffrey & Anthony. **Educ:** Univ Detroit, BS, 1958; Wayne State Univ, MEd, 1971. **Career:** Detroit Pub Sch Syst, teacher, 1958-72; Buttons & Bows Nurseries & Preparatory Schs, founder, owner & operator, 1971-85; Mich House Reps, mem, 1980-82; Pro Tempore, elected speaker, 1989; Wayne County, Health Community Serv, dep dir, 1992-93, co clerk, 1993; Sloan/Hunter Group, founding partner, consult, currently. **Orgs:** Vpres, Womens Equity Action League; Pi Lamda Theta; Links, Greater Wayne County Chap; bd dirs, Downriver Community; chair, bd dirs, Diversified Youth Servs; Delta Sigma Theta Sorority; Citizens Adv Comt,Wayne County Youth; adv bd mem, Childrens Aid Soc; bd mem, Omni Care, Qual Assurance Comt; bd dirs, Detroit Urban League; Nat Asn Advan Colored People;founder, Resource Endowment Aiding Children Together Love; Nat Asn County Recorders, Election Officials & Clerks; Univ Detroit Mercy, Presidents Cabinet; Womens Econ Club; bd dirs, Blue Cross Blue Shield Mich; intern exec dir, Coleman A Young Found, 2001. **Honors/Awds:** Path Finders Award, Black Students Oakland Univ, 1982; Citizen of the Year Award, Detroit Medical Soc, 1985; Outstanding Citizen Award, Gentleman Wall St, 1985; Black Legis Hon Black Hist Month, Blue Cross & Blue Shield,1986; Award of Merit for Outstanding Achievement & Leadership Develop &Community Rels, Core City Neighborhoods Inc, City of Detroit, 1986;Outstanding Public Service, Wayne Co Comm Col, 1991; Image Maker Award,1992; Annual Millie Award, Women Pol Caucus, 1995; Outstanding Public Leadership Award, Mich State Univ, 1996; US Point of Lich Rec Award, 1997; YWCA Women of Achievement, 1998; Heritage Award, Ford Motor Co, 1999. **Special Achievements:** First female speaker pro tempore in Michigan; First female to be elected Wayne County Clerk. **Business Addr:** Member of Board of Directors, Blue Shield of Michigan, 600 Lafayette E, Detroit, MI 48226, **Business Phone:** (313)225-9000.

HUNTER, TONY WAYNE
Football player. **Personal:** Born May 22, 1960, Cincinnati, OH. **Educ:** Univ Notre Dame, BS, econ, 1984. **Career:** Football player (retired); Buffalo Bills, tight end, 1983-84; Los Angeles Rams, tight end, 1985-86. **Honors/Awds:** All-Rookie teams, UPI & Pro Football Weekly; won 4 letters for Notre Dame; Playboy All-Am, NEA All-Am Sr; All-Am; OH Player of the Year.

HUNTER, TORII KEDAR
Baseball player. **Personal:** Born Jul 18, 1975, Pine Bluff, AR; son of Theotis and Shirley; married Katrina Hall; children: Cameron & Torii Jr. **Career:** Gulf Coast League Twins, centerfielder, 1992-96; New Britain Rock Cats, centerfielder, 1996-98; Minn Twins, outfielder, 1997-07; Los Angeles Angels, 2008-. **Honors/Awds:** Gold Glove Awards, 2001, 2002, 2003; All-Star selection, 2002, 2007, 2009. **Business Addr:** Professional Baseball Player, Los Angeles Angels of Anaheim, 2000 E Gene Autry Way, Anaheim, CA 92806-6143, **Business Phone:** (714)940-2000.*

HUNTER, DR. WILLIAM ANDREW
Educator. **Personal:** Born Sep 6, 1913, N Little Rock, AR; son of Jessie D Hunter and W J C Hunter; married Alma Rose Burgess. **Educ:** Dunbar Jr Col, Little Rock, AR, AA, 1933; Wilberforce Univ, Wilberforce, OH, BS, 1936; Iowa State Univ, Ames, IA, MS, 1948, PhD, 1952. **Career:** Dunbar High Sch, Little Rock, AR, instr Math & Sci, 1936-42; Tuskegee Inst, AL, prof of educ, 1950-57, dean sch educ 1957-73; AACTE, Wash, DC, dir of multi cult res proj, 1973-74; Iowa State Univ, dir res inst studies educ, 1974-79; Col Educ Iowa State Univ, prof of educ 1979-83, prof emer, curric & instr, 1983-. **Orgs:** Kappa Alpha Psi Frat, 1936-; pres, Am Asn Col Teacher Educ, 1973-74; Nat Teacher Exam Adv Bd Educ Testing Serv, 1973-78; consult, Iowa Dept Pub Instr Human Relations, 1975; life mem, Tuskegee AL Civic Asn; Nat Educ Asn; Phi Delta Kappa; Kappa Delta Pi; Phi Kappa Phi; chmn, Comn Christian Unity & Inter religious Concerns, Nat GEO Conference of the United Metho dist Church, 1995-2000. **Honors/Awds:** Outstanding Serv Teaching Profession, Tuskegee Univ, 1972; Alumni Distinguished Achievement Award, Iowa State Univ, 1973; Lagomarchino Lauerate Award, Col Educ, Iowa State Univ. **Special Achievements:** Author & editor: "Multicultural Education Through Competency-Based Teacher Education", 1974; coauthor with Liem Nguyen: "Educational Systems in Southeast Asia in Comparison with those in the United States", 1979. **Military Serv:** AUS, seregent, 1942-46; Good Conduct Am, N African, European Theater. **Home Addr:** 2202 Country Club Ct, Augusta, GA 30904. **Business Addr:** Professor Emeritus, College of Education Iowa State University, 1550 Beardshear Hall, Ames, IA 50011-2021, **Business Phone:** (515)294-9591.

HUNTER-GAULT, CHARLAYNE
Journalist. **Personal:** Born Feb 27, 1942, Due West, SC; daughter of Charles and Althea; married Ronald, 1971; children: Chuma; married Walter Stovall (divorced); children: Susan Stovall. **Educ:** Wayne State Univ, 1961; Univ Ga, BA, 1963; Wash Univ, Russell Sage fel, 1968. **Career:** The New Yorker, reporter; The New York Times, reporter; The MacNeil/Lehrer Newshour, reporter & nat affairs corresp, 1978-97; Nat Pub Radio, chief corresp Africa, 1997-99, foreign corresp, currently; CNN, Johannesburg Bur Chief, 1999-2005. **Honors/Awds:** Emmy Awards; Journalism Awards;, 1986 George Foster Peabody Award for Excellence in Broadcast Journalism;, 1990 Sidney Hillman Award; Good Housekeeping Broadcast Personality of the Year Award; American Women in Radio and Television Award. **Special Achievements:** First African American woman to graduate from the University of Georgia in 1962, reported on Apartheid in 1985, is author of In My Place 1992, is the recipient of more than two dozen honorary degrees. **Business Phone:** (202)513-2300.

HUNTER HAYES, TRACEY JOEL
Librarian. **Personal:** Born Jan 20, 1966, Philadelphia, PA; son of William and Osalee Barbara Jenkins Hunter; married Kathleen Jean Butler, Jul 26, 1992; children: Tracey Joel, Jalaal Aqil & Makkah Imani. **Educ:** Lincoln Univ, BS, philos, 1987; Univ Pittsburgh, Sch Libr & Info Sci, MLS, 1989; Va Union Univ, Sch Theol, Divinity, 2004. **Career:** Univ Pittsburgh, SLIS, libr asst, 1988, resident asst, 1988; Free Libr Philadelphia, C librn, 1989-92; Lincoln Univ, spec collections librn, 1992; Am Libr Asn, Ala minority fel, 1992-; Ky State Univ, asst dir, 1993-95; Southern IL Univ Carbondale, asst undergraduate librn, 1995-96; Temple Univ, ref & CD librn, 1996-98; Hampton Univ Libr, asst dir, 1998; Lincoln Univ, dir alumni rel, Langston Hughes Mem Libr, dir, currenly, assoc prof, currently, Alumini Asn, pres, currently. **Orgs:** Groove Phi Groove, 1985; Concerned Black Men Inc; Nat Delegate, 1987; Black Caucus Am Libr Asn, 1989; Am Libr Asn, 1990-; chmn, Mayors Adv Comt Homeless, 1990; Free & Accepted Masons, PHA, Hiram 5 Philadelphia, 1991; vpres, Lincoln Univ Alumni Asn, 1992-93, pres, 1997-; Ky Asn Blacks Higher Educ, 1994-95; Rotary Int, 1994-96; trustee, Lincoln Univ, 2000-02. **Honors/Awds:** W Fales Prize in Philosophy, Lincoln Univ, 1987; Univ Pittsburgh, State Libr Scholar, 1988-89; Outstanding Young Man of the Year, 1989-90; Community Service Award, Philadelphia Mayors Office, 1990; Hon Delegate, White House Conf Librs, 1991; US Voting Delegate, Int Fed Libr Asn, 1991; participant, Snowbird Leadership Inst, 1993; Achievement Award, Black Caucus Am Library Asn, 1994-95; Alumni Achievement Award, Lincoln Univ, 1998; Men Making a Difference Award, Congressman Chaka Fattah, Model Cities Am, 1998. **Special Achievements:** workshop & lecture, Sixth Annual Virginia Hamilton Conference, 1990; Storytelling, Free Library of Philadelphia, 1991; lecture & publication, PA Black Conference on Higher Education, 1992; ALA Fellowship Report, "Not New Just Different"; Lecture, Shepherd College, 1992; Lecture, Villanova University, 1992; Associationn of Research Libraries Leadership and Career Development Program Inaugural Group, 1997-98. **Home Addr:** 1635 W Diamond St, Philadelphia, PA 19121, **Home Phone:** (215)232-4262. **Business Addr:** President, Lincoln University, 1570 Baltimore Pke, PO Box 179, Lincoln University, PA 19352, **Business Phone:** (610)932-8300.

HUNTLEY, LYNN JONES
Lawyer, president (organization). **Personal:** Born in Fort Lee, VA; daughter of Lawrence N and Mary Ellen. **Educ:** Fisk Univ, attended 1965; Barnard Col, AB, sociol, 1967; Columbia Univ Sch Law, JD, 1970. **Career:** Bernard Baruch Col, teaching asst, 1969-70; Judge Motley US Dist Ct NY, law clerk, 1970-71; Nat Asn Advan Colored People Legal Defense & Educ Fund Inc, asst coun, 1971-73; NY City Comn Human Rights, gen coun, 1973-75; Nat Asn Advan Colored People Legal Defense Fund Inc, asst coun, 1975-78; US Dept Justice Civil Rights Div, sect chief spec litigation sec, 1978-81, dep asst atty gen, 1981-82; The Ford Found, prog officer, 1982-87, dep dir charge human rights & social justice prog, 1987-91, Rights & Social Justice Prog, dir, 1991-; Southern Educ Found, pres, 2002-. **Orgs:** Nat Bar Asn; NY State Bar; chair, Fed Women's Prog Adv Comn US Dept Justice; Black Affairs Prog Adv Comn; bd dirs, Sheltering Arms Children's Serv; Nat Asn Advan Colored People; columnist, Essence Mag; NY State Sentencing Guidelines Comn; secy, Black Am Law Studs Asn; Columbia Law Review; bd mem, The Legal Aid Soc; NYS Govs Adv Comt Black Affairs; bd trustees, Barnard Col. **Honors/Awds:** First Black Woman on Columbia Law Rev; Spl Commendation Award, US Dept Justice; Sr Exec Serv Outstanding Performance Award & bonus, US Dept Justice; Outstanding Performance, Ford Found; Thurgood Marshall Award, Asn Bd NY; Lucy Terry Prince Award, Lawyer's Comt Civil Rights. **Special Achievements:** Co-editor, Beyond Racism: Embracing an Interdependent Future in 2000 & Beyond Racism: Race and Equality in Brazil, South Africa and the United States in 2001. **Business Addr:** President, Southern Education Foundation, 135 Auburn Ave NE 2nd Fl, Atlanta, GA 30303.*

HUNTLEY, RICHARD FRANK. See Obituaries section.

HURD, BRIDGET G.
Government official. **Career:** St John Health, Warren, corp community rels coordr; Greater Detroit Area Health Coun, Communs & Corp Affairs, dir, vpres, currently.

HURD, DAVID JAMES
Musician, educator. **Personal:** Born Jan 27, 1950, Brooklyn, NY. **Educ:** Juilliard Sch, attended 1967; Oberlin Col, BMus, 1971; Univ NC Chapel Hill, attended 1972; Berkeley Divinity Sch Yale, BMus; Church Divinity Sch Pac, DMus; Seabury Western Theol Sem, LHD. **Career:** Trinity Parish, asst organist, 1971-72; Duke Univ, asst dir choral activ, asst chapel organist, 1972-73; Church Intercession NYC, organist & music dir, 1973-79; composer; Gen Theol Sem, prof church music, organist, 1979-; Yale Inst Sacred Music, visiting lectr, 1982-83; Manhattan Sch Music, organ fac, 1984-; All Saints Church music, dir, 1985; Church Holy Apostles, music dir, currently. **Orgs:** New York Chap Am Guild Organists, 1966-; Theta Chap Pi Kappa Lambda 1971-; vchmn, Standing Comn Church Music, 1976-85; concert organist, Phillip Trucken Brod Artist Rep, 1977-; aristic adv comt, Boys Choir Harlem, 1978-; Asn Anglican Musicians, 1979-; organ recitalist, AGO Biennial Nat Conv Minneapolis, 1980; Liturgical Comm Episcopal Diocese NY, 1982; organ recitalist, AGO Biennial Nat Conv, 1986. **Honors/Awds:** First Prize Organ Playing, Int Cong Organists, 1977; First Prize Organ Improvisation, Int Cong Organists, Philadelphia, 1977, premiered in Ljubljana, Slovenia at the International Saxophone Congress, 2006. **Special Achievements:** Diploma in improvision Stichting Intl Orgelconcours Goud The Netherlands1981. **Business Addr:** Music Director, Church of the Holy Apostles, 296 9th Ave, New York, NY 10001.

HURD, DR. JAMES L P
Musician, educator, organist. **Personal:** Born Aug 2, 1945, Bonham, TX. **Educ:** Washburn Univ, BA, music, 1967; Am Conservatory Music, MMus, 1968; Univ Southern Calif, MusD, 1973. **Career:** Calvary Baptist Church, Topeka, KS, organist dir, 1962-69; Protestant Chapel, KS Boys Sch, Topeka, organist choir dir, 1964-67, 1968-69; Cult Arts Div Topeka Recreation Comn, head music, 1965-67; Lawndale Presby Church Chicago, choir dir, 1967-68; Blessed Sacrament Cath Church,Chicago, IL, organist, 1967-68; Ward African Methodist Episcopal Church Los Angeles, CA, organist dir, 1969-73; Orgn & Mgt Analyst State Hwy, ComnKS, 1969-70; El Camino Col, prof music, 1973-; First Pres Church Inglewood, organist & dir Music 1973-96; Long Beach City Col, organ instr, 1973; Calif St Univ, organ prof; Dominguez Hills, organ prof; Calif St Univ, Long Beach, organ prof; St Andrew's Presby Church, Redondo Beach, CA, organist & dir music, currently; First Baptist Church of Palos Verdes, CA, organist & dir, currently. **Orgs:** Am Guild Organists; Kappa Alpha Psi; Phi Mu Alpha; Adjudicator Music Teachers Assn Calif; brd dirs, pres, Airport Marina Coun Serv, 1995-2005; brd dir, Westchester YMCA, currently. **Honors/Awds:** Outstanding Young Men of America, US Jaycees, 1980; City of Los Angeles Mayor's Certificate of Appreciation, Music Contributions to the Community. **Special Achievements:** Featured organ recitalist for

several chapters of ther American Guild of Organists, and presented in organ concerts across the united States andEurope. **Business Addr:** Professor, El Camino College, 16007 Crenshaw Blvd, Torrance, CA 90506, **Business Phone:** (310)660-3701.

HURD, DR. JOSEPH KINDALL
Surgeon. **Personal:** Born Feb 12, 1938, Hoisington, KS; son of Joseph Kindall Sr and Mildred Mae Ramsey; married Jean Elizabeth Challenger, Jun 20, 1964; children: Joseph Kindall III & Jason Hansen. **Educ:** Harvard Col, AB (magna cum), 1960, MD, 1964. **Career:** Harvard Med Sch, clin instr surg, 1972-; Lahey Clinic Found, gynecologist, 1972-, chmn, dept gynecol, 1988-2000; Coun Dept, chmn, 1991-99; Tufts Med Sch, asst clin prof, Obstet, gynec, 1996. **Orgs:** Soc Boston; bd dir, Freedom House Inc; bd dirs, Crispus Attucks Day Care Ctr; bd dirs, Roxbury Med Dent Group; Am Fertility Soc; Charles River Med Soc; AMA; Nat Med Asn; coun, Massachusetts Med Soc; Am Uro-Gynecol Soc; Am Asn Gynecol Laporoscopy; Alpha Chap, Phi Beta Kappa; bd govs & bd trustees, Lahey Clin, 1977-91, finance & exec comt, 1987-90; pres, New Eng Med Soc, 1980; counr, Harvard Med Alumni Asn, 1990-93, dir, 1990-93, pres, 2004; Iota Chi Chap, Omega Psi Phi; Sigma Pi Phi Fratrernity, 1991-; Massachusetts Sect Am Col Obstet, gynec, 1993-96; Sire Archon, Beta Beta Boule, Sigma Pi Phi Fraternity, 2006-08. **Honors/Awds:** Spencer B Lewis Award, Coleus Soc, Harvard Med Sch, 1990. **Military Serv:** AUS, maj, 1970-72; Army commendation medal, 1972. **Home Addr:** 18 Emerson Rd, Wellesley, MA 02481-3419. **Business Addr:** Gynecologist, Lahey Clinic Medical Center, Department of Gynecology, 41 Mall Rd, Burlington, MA 01805.

HURD, WILLIAM CHARLES
Physician, ophthalmologist. **Personal:** Born May 17, 1947, Memphis, TN; son of Leon (deceased) and Doris; married Rhynette Northcross; children: Bill Jr, Ryan. **Educ:** Univ Notre Dame, BS, 1969; Mass Inst Technol, MS, 1972; Meharry Med Col, MD, 1980. **Career:** Gen Elect Corp, systs engr, 1969-70; Tenn State Univ, asst prof, 1972-76; Univ Tenn, intern, 1980-81, resident physician, 1982-85; Memphis Health Ctr, med consult, 1981; Memphis Emergency Specialists, consult physician, 1982-84; Methodist Hosp, staff physician, 1985-; pvt pract, physician, currently. **Orgs:** Bd dirs, Vis Nurse Asn, 1985-. **Honors/Awds:** All Am Track Athlete at Nortre Dame, 1697-69; Athlete of the yr, Notre Dame Univ, 1968; World Record Holder at 300 yd Dash Indoors, 1968-72; Rhodes Scholar Semi Finalist, 1969; Prof Musician & Winner at serveral Nat Jazz Fest Competition; Harvey G Foster Award, Univ Notre Dame, 1992; Hold US Patent on a Medical Instrument; NCAA, Silver Anniversary Award, 1994. **Special Achievements:** Semi Annual Medical Mission trips to Mexico, Brazil, Senegal, and Africa. **Business Addr:** Physician, Ophthalmologist, Private Practice, 220 S Claybrook St Suite 504, Memphis, TN 38104, **Business Phone:** (901)276-4844.*

HURDLE, HORTENSE O MCNEIL
School administrator. **Personal:** Born May 20, 1925, Marlin, TX; daughter of Leroy McNeil and Annie Mae Williams McNeil-Wade; married Clarence, Jan 15, 1949; children: Clarence II & Gaile Evonne. **Educ:** Prairie View Univ, BS, 1947; Sacramento State Univ, MA, 1973, MS, 1974. **Career:** School administrator (Retired); Fed Govt, employee, 1947-57, elem teacher vpres, 1957-64; Compensatory Educ, dir, 1964-68; Del Paso & Heights Sch Dist, elem sch prin, 1968-86. **Orgs:** Co-founder, Concerned Citizens Greater Sacramento, 1976; Les Belles Artes Club, 1985-90; FWR Iota Phi Lambda Sorority, asst regional dir, 1989-93; western regional dir, 1997-; Sacramento Iota Phi Lambda Sorority; Calif Admin Asn CTA; ed, Young Child; Nat Alliance Black Educr; Sacramento Black Educr; Women Div Dem Women; Nat Asn Advan Colored People; Phi Beta Delta Frat; XI Field Chap; Negro Coun Women; trustee, Shiloh Baptist Church. **Honors/Awds:** B'nai B'rith Outstanding Award, 1966; Distinguished Community Serv Award,Sacramento Chamber Com, 1967; Outstanding Sorority, Far Western Region,Iota Phi Lambda Sorority, 1980; Outstanding Service Award, Beta Tau Chap,Iota Phi Lambda, 1989; Outstanding Service Award, Western Region, Nat Alliance Black School Educr, 1991. **Special Achievements:** Resolution 53 Assembly Dist & Progessive 12, 1970. **Home Addr:** 1370 40th Ave, Sacramento, CA 95814.

HURSEY, JAMES SAMUEL
Educator. **Personal:** Born May 9, 1931, Bridgeton, NJ; married Joyce Langston Washington; children: Joni Hursey-Young & Jennifer Elizabeth. **Educ:** Glassboro St Col, BS; Va St Col, attended 1955. **Career:** Bridgeton Housing Authority, comnr, 1958-84; Bridgeton City Coun, councilman, 1982-85; Cumberland County Utilities Authority, 1985-90; Bridgeton Sch Syst, teacher, 1994, City of Bridgeton, vice chmn, comnr, currently. **Orgs:** Nat Asn Advan Colored People; bd dir, Child Develop Ctr, 1984-94; Nat Black Caucus, NJ; Asn Black Elected Officials; secy, Hur-Ed Inc; chmn, Cedar Hill Mem Park, 1980; bd dir, YMCA. **Military Serv:** USN, 1955-58. **Business Addr:** Commissioner, Cumberland County Utilities Authority, 333 Water St, Bridgeton, NJ 08302, **Business Phone:** (856)455-7120.

HURST, BEVERLY J.
Association executive. **Personal:** Born Jan 16, 1933, Oberlin, OH; married Charles G Hurst Jr; children: Chaverly Kikanza. **Educ:** Howard Univ, BA, 1963, MA, 1968. **Career:** Gen Acct Off Wash, secy, 1951-56; Crile VA Hosp, med secy, 1956-61; Howard Univ, admin asst, 1963-64, res asst, 1964-67; DC Dept Pub Health, res &training specialist, 1967-68; New Careers Proj TRD, remedial educ supvr, 1968-69; Model Cities Teacher Aide Proj Kennedy-King Col, coordr, 1969-70; Ill Inst Social Policy, eval analyst, 1970-71; Chicago Urban League, res dir, 1972-76; Community Serv Admin, prog analyst, 1980-82; US Railroad Retirement Bd, equal employ specialist, 1982-84; US Corps Engrs, equal employ opportunities mgr, 1984-. **Orgs:** Author: various articles papers & reports for professional journals; consult, Youth Group Homes Proj DC Dept Pub Welfare; community specialist, Wash Concentrated Employ Proj United Planning Org; res consult Georgetown Univ Inst for Urban Serv Aides; AL Nellum & Assoc; consult, various other firms & asn; Am Sociol Asn; Am Acad Polit & Social Sci.

HURST, ROBERT (BOB HURST)
Musician. **Personal:** Born Oct 4, 1964. **Career:** Bebob Music Inc, The Tonight Show, musician, currently; Do the Right Thing, musician, 1989; Branford Marsalis: The Music Tells You, musician, 1992; Mommy's Day, lightning designer, 1997; The Wood, composer, 1999; Brown Sugar, composer & conductor, 2002; Diana Krall: Live at the Montreal Jazz Festival, actor, 2004; Ocean's Twelve, musician, 2004; Burned, writer & dir, 2006; TV series: "Great Performances", musician, 2007; Univ Mich Sch Music, Theatre, & Dance, assc prof, currently. **Orgs:** Bd dir, John Coltrane Found. **Honors/Awds:** Four Emmy Awards; five Grammy Awards. **Business Phone:** (734)615-1265.

HURST, RODNEY LAWRENCE
Government official, executive director. **Personal:** Born Mar 2, 1944, Jacksonville, FL; married Ann; children: Rodney II, Todd. **Educ:** Fla Jr Col; Edward Waters Col. **Career:** Corp Pub Broadcasting, fel grant, 1969-70; Greater Jacksonville Econ Opportunity, proj dir, 1971-73; City Jacksonville, proj dir, 1973-75; Self Employed, ins salesman, 1975-; CILB, exec dir, 1996; Edward Waters Col, Community Develop Corp, dir, currently. **Orgs:** ins & underwriter, Prudential, 1965-69; Welfare & Soc Serv Policy Steering Comt; Nat Asn County; Jacksonville Coun Citizen Involvement; City Coun Financial & Rules Comn; Cable TV Comn; chmn, Agr & Recreation Comn; Nat Asn Advan Colored People; Urban League; bd mem, Boy's Club; adv coun mem, Ribault Sr High Sch; Consortium Aid Neglected & Abused C. **Honors/Awds:** Man of Yr, Jacksonville Club, 1960. **Special Achievements:** Co-host "Feedback" WJCT-TV, 1969-71. **Military Serv:** USAF, a/2c, 1961-65. **Business Addr:** Director, Edward Waters College, Community Develop Corp, 1658 Kings Rd, Jacksonville, FL 32209-6199.*

HURT, PATRICIA
Lawyer. **Career:** Essex County, dep admin, prosecutor. **Special Achievements:** First African American and First Woman to serve as prosecutor in Essex County.

HURTE, LEROY E.
Conductor (music), artistic director, writer. **Personal:** Born May 2, 1915, Muskogee, OK; son of Charles and Dora Grayson; married Hazel. **Educ:** Los Angeles City Col; Juilliard Sch Music; Tanglewood Music Workshop; Fresno State Col; Victor Valley Col. **Career:** Symphony Orchestra, Inglewood Philharmonic Asn, conductor; Angel City Symphony Orch, founder & conductor; Los Angeles Comt Symphony, guest conductor; Calif Jr Symphony, guest conductor; Kings Co & Symphony, guest conductor; Fresno Philharmonic; Hanford Choral Soc, choral conductor; Tamarind Ave SDA Church; Inglewood Philharmonic, conductor, 1988; Los Angeles Philharmonic Orchestra, guest conductor; Lyric Mag, ed & publ; Books: The Magic of Music; So You're the Choir Director: A Handbook for the Choir and Its Director. **Orgs:** Pres, Rotary Club, 1985-86; Nat Asn Negro Musicians. **Honors/Awds:** Achievement Award, Nat Asn Media Women, 1973-74; Commendation, City Los Angeles; Proclamation honoring Inglewood Symphony Orchestra, Inglewood,CA, 1985; Paul Harris fel, Rotary Club; Phi Theta Kappa. **Special Achievements:** Author of 3 books. **Business Addr:** Symphony Conductor, PO Box 1945, Apple Valley, CA 92307.*

HUSKEY, BUTCH (ROBERT LEON)
Baseball player, athletic coach. **Personal:** Born Nov 10, 1971, Anadarko, OK. **Career:** Baseball player (retired), Athletic coach; New York Mets, infielder, 1993, 1995-98; Seattle Mariners, 1999; Boston Red Sox, 1999; Minn Twins, 2000; Colo Rockies, 2000; Cleveland Indians, 2001; Cameron Univ, asst coach. **Orgs:** Sterling Silver Award; Doubleday Award, 1991-95.

HUTCHERSON, BERNICE B R
Educator. **Personal:** Born Apr 14, 1925, Newton, KS; daughter of Albert Ray Sr and Henrietta; married Hubert W; children: Pamela Dineen & Karla Michelle. **Educ:** Langston Univ, BA, 1950; Chicago Teachers Col, attended 1952; Univ Kans, MSW, 1969; Univ Chicago, Social Worker Teachers Cert, 1973. **Career:** Chicago Pub Schs, reading teacher; Social worker, 1954-72; Wichita State Univ, prof, social work, 1970, geront fac chair, 1996, prof emer, currently. **Orgs:** Pres, Kans Co Social Workers Asn; Wichita Area Comm Action Program; Nat Asn Social Workers; Kans Conf Social Welfare; pres, Kans Multicultural Asn Substance Abuse; Sedgwick Co; Kans Ment Health Asn Bd; Sr Citizens Bd; Am Pub Welfare Asn; Am Asn Univ prof; charter mem, Wichita OIC Bd; Acad Cert Social Workers; Suicide Prev Serv Counr; past pres, Youth Dept Calvary Baptist Church; Wichita Alumnae Delta Sigma Theta; Matron KF Valley 97 OES; Nat Coun Negro Women; Nat Asn Advan Colored People; Family Planning Wichita Health Dept; Kans Off Minority Bus Enterprises; Bd Educ 259 Prof Speakers Bur. **Honors/Awds:** Elder Housing Facility, Wichita City Coun, 1980; Phi Kappa Phi; Service Award, Wichita State Univ Alumni Asn, 1994. **Special Achievements:** Recipient of numerous community, professional and academic accolades. **Business Addr:** Professor Emeritus, Wichita State University, School of Social Work, 1845 Fairmount Campus, PO Box 154, Wichita, KS 67260-0154, **Business Phone:** (316)978-7250.

HUTCHERSON, DR. HILDA
Educator, writer, gynecologist. **Personal:** Born Jan 21, 1955, Tuskegee, AL; daughter of John Hutcherson and Bernice; married Frederic Fabiano, 1986; children: Lauren, Steven, Andrew & Freddie. **Educ:** Stanford Univ, human biol; Harvard Med Sch; Univ Calif, San Francisco, medintern. **Career:** Vanderbilt Clinic Ambulatory Services, New York, NY, med dir, 1986-89; Columbia Presbyterian Med Ctr, New York, NY, dir, 1986-89; Columbia Col Physicians & Surgeons, New York, NY, asst prof, 1986-, dir, 1988, admissions comt mem, 1998, & assoc dean, 2002-; Columbia Presbyterian Med Ctr, New York, NY, asst attending, 1987- & co-dir, 1997, 2001-; AOL, love & sex coach, currently; Books: Having Your Baby: A guide for African American Women; What Your Mother Never Told You About Sex & Pleasure: A Woman's Guide to Getting the Sex You Want; Need & Deserve. **Orgs:** Fel, Am Col Obstet & Gynecol; assoc mem, Am Fertility Soc; Am Med Asn; Nat Med Asn; pres, The Women's Sexual Health Found. **Honors/Awds:** Award of Excellence in biological research, 1972; America's Leading Physicians, 2001; Gender Equity Teaching Award, 2002-03. **Special Achievements:** One of America's Leading Physicians, Black Enterprise Mag; one of the Top Doctors in New York in the Castle Connoly Guide; included in the Best Doctors in America 2005-06 database. **Business Addr:** Assistant Professor of Clinical Obstetrics, Columbia University, 16 E 60th St Suite 480, New York, NY 10022, **Business Phone:** (212)326-8554.

HUTCHINS, FRANCIS L., JR. (MICKEY HUTCHINS)
Educator, physician. **Personal:** Born Jul 8, 1943, Ridley Park, PA; son of Francis L and Mercedes; married Sandra (died 1999); children: Keisha & Francis L. **Educ:** Duquesne Univ, BS, biol, 1965; Howard Univ, MD, 1969. **Career:** Lankenau Hosp, intern, 1970; Ob-Gyn, resident, 1973; Temple Univ Hosp, Dept Obstet & Gynec, asst prof & dir family planning, 1975-77; Thomas Jefferson Univ, Dept Obstet & Gynec, asst prof, 1977-81, clin assoc prof, 1991-98; Lankenau Hosp, Dept Obstet & Gynec, dir res & educ & dir family planning, 1977-81; Commonwealth Pa, Dept Health, consul to obstet, gynec, & family planning adolescents, 1980; Hahnemann Univ, Dept Obstet & Gynec, asst prof, 1981-84, dir family planning, dir ambulatory affairs & community med, 1981-84, dir Maternal/Infant Care Proj, dir, Div Obstet, 1983-84, Dept Obstet, actg chmn, 1984, assoc prof clin obstet & gynec, 1984-98, clin assoc pres, 1985, chmn, 2000-01, prof, 2000-02; Booth Maternity Ctr, med dir, 1985-86; Plan Parenthood Pa, med dir, 1985; City Philadelphia, Dept Maternal & Child Health, med dir, 1985-86; Grad Hosp, dir gynec & women's servs, 1992; Graduate Hosp, vice chmn, 1993-95, chmn, 1995-98, clin prof, 1998-2000; Roxborough Memorial Hosp, fac, 1998-2000; Fibroid Ctr, dir, currently; consult obstet & gynec, 2001-02; Drexel Univ, prof obstet & gynec, 2004-; consult, 2004-; pvt pract, currently; Howard Univ Col Medicine, Dept Obstet /Gynec, prof & chmn, 2000-01. **Orgs:** Nat Med Asn, 1973-; Obstet Soc Philadelphia, 1973-; fel Am Col Obstetricians/Gynecologists, 1976; Am Soc Colposcopy & Colpamicroscopy, 1977-; Philadelphia Col Surgeons, 1978-; Am Asn Gynec Laparoscopists, 1987-; Am Fertility Soc, 1989-; bd dirs, Marriage Coun Philadelphia, 1991; bd dirs, Family Planning Coun SE Pa, 1992; Int Soc Gynecologic Endoscopy; Philadelphia Col Physicians; Am Fertil Soc; mem, Hope fibroids inc, 2005. **Special Achievements:** Author: "Developments in Contraceptive Prescribing Family Planning", Philadelphia Medicine, April 1979; "Outcome of Teenage Pregnancies, "Medical Aspects of Human Sexuality, January 1980; "Adolescent Pregnancy Among Black Philadelphia, "Urban League of Philadelphia, February, 1981; "Uterine Fibroids Current Concepts and Management", The Female Patient, Oct 1990; "Myomectomy after Selective Preoperative Treatment with a Gonadotropin-Releasing Hormone Analog," The Journal of Reproductive Medicine, vol 37, number 8, Aug 1992; producer of video tape, Diabetes and Pregnancy, Clinical Issues in Female Patient, series 127, tape 12703, 1983; contributing editor: Federation Licensing Examination, McGraw-Hill, 1986; Pre-Test Foreign Medical Graduate Examination In Medical Science, McGraw-Hill, 1987. **Military Serv:** USN, lt cmdr, 1973-75. **Business Addr:** Physician Consultant, **Business Phone:** (610)940-5666.

HUTCHINS, JAN DARWIN
Businessperson, president (organization). **Personal:** Born Feb 11, 1949, Danville, IL; married Teri A Hope. **Educ:** Yale Col, BA,

1971. **Career:** KRON-TV, sports dir; KPIX-TV Westinghouse, sports, anchor & reposter, 1974-80; WIIC-TV Cox Broadcasting, sports reporter, 1972-74; AT&T Long Lines, sales supvr, 1971-72; SF Giants Baseball, prog dir, 1993-94; Golf Pro Intl, dir communications, 1994-95; AC Media, pres, 1997-. **Orgs:** Mem Health & Wisdom. **Honors/Awds:** Los Gatos Town Council.

HUTCHINS, LAWRENCE G, SR.
Association executive, vice president (organization). **Personal:** Born Sep 13, 1931, Danville, VA; son of James E Sr (deceased) and Alfrezia Mimms (deceased); married Rebbie Jacobs, Jun 14, 1952; children: Karen H Watts, Lawrence Jr, Gary & Gerald. **Educ:** VA State Col, Petersburg, VA, 1954-56; VCU, Richmond, VA, 1972-74. **Career:** Nat Asn Lett Carriers, exec vpres 496, 1962-69, pres, Richmond Branch 496, 1969-78; VA State Asn, pres, 1970-78; asst, Nat bus agt, 1978-82; Nat bus agt, 1982-87; vpres, 1987-. **Orgs:** Pres, Richmond Branch A Philip Randolph Inst; chmn, const comn, Crusade Voters, Richmond; co-founder, Black Metro Little League, Richmond; trustee, Second Baptist Church, S Richmond; adv bd, United Way; co-chair, Richmond Chap MDA. **Military Serv:** Army, cpl, 1952-54. **Business Addr:** Vice President, National Association of Letter Carriers, 100 Indiana Ave NW, Washington, DC 20001-2144, **Business Phone:** (202)393-4695.

HUTCHINS, REV. MARKEL
Civil rights activist, consultant, clergy. **Personal:** Born Jan 1, 1977, Stone Mountain, GA; son of Leon and Dorothy. **Educ:** DDiv. **Career:** AME Church, minister; methodist pastor; Nat Youth Connection, founder, 1995, nat pres & ceo; MRH LLC, managing prin & ceo, currently. **Orgs:** DeKalb County Bd Educ; Rainbow/PUSH Coalition. **Special Achievements:** First black person elected student body president at Stone Mountain High School; featured as one of the most eligible bachelors by Ebony Magazine. **Business Addr:** Managing Principal, Chief Executive Officer, MRH LLC, 3330 Cumberland Blvd Suite 500, Atlanta, GA 30339, **Business Phone:** (610)864-1008.

HUTCHINS, MICKEY. See HUTCHINS, FRANCIS L., JR.

HUTCHINSON, EARL OFARI
Writer, columnist. **Personal:** Born Oct 8, 1945, Chicago, IL; son of Earl and Nina; married Barbara, Mar 5, 1988; children: Sikivu & Fanon. **Educ:** Calif State Univ, Los Angeles, BA, 1969; Pac Western Univ, PhD, 1992. **Career:** Books: The Myth of Black Capitalism, 1970; The Mugging of Black America, 1990; Black Fatherhood I, 1992, vol II, 1993; The Assassination of the Black Male Image, 1994; Blacks & Reds: Race & Class in Conflict, 1919-90, 1995; Betrayed: A History of Presidential Failure to Protect Black Lives, 1996; Beyond OJ: Race, Sex, & Class Lessons for Americans, 1996; The Crisis in Black & Black, 1998; The Disappearance of Black Leadership, 2000; The Emerging Black Primates, 2006; columnist, currently. **Orgs:** The Writers Guild; pres, Nat Alliance Positive Action. **Honors/Awds:** The Gustavus Myers Award; Outstanding Book Award, 1995; Nat Black Journalist Award. **Business Addr:** Author, Journalist, Hutchinson Communications, 5517 Secrest Dr, Los Angeles, CA 90043.

HUTCHINSON, DR. GEORGE
School administrator, educator. **Personal:** Born Dec 19, 1938, Albuquerque, NM; son of John and Leona; married Gwen Pierce. **Educ:** Calif State Univ Los Angeles, BS, 1969, MS, 1971; United States Int Univ, PhD, 1977; Nat Univ, San Diego, Calif, Post Doctoral Law, 1988. **Career:** Calif State Univ, assoc dean educ support serv, 1986-; San Diego State Univ, asst prof dept of recreation, 1973-79, asst dean, 1974-77, assoc dean, 1978-81, col prof studies & fine arts, assoc prof dept recreation, 1979-94, dir stud outreach serv dir 1981, assoc prof emer, 1994-. **Orgs:** Adv Counc Minority Officer Recruiting US Navy, 1977-; mem at large Industry Educ Council Greater San Diego 1980-; Phi Kappa Phi; mem bd dirs, Am Cancer Soci, 1984-; Athletic Adv Comm, 1985-; Senate Comm Minority; Calif Acad Partnership Prog, 1985-; Naval Reserve Officers Asn, Navy League of the US; San Diego Chap, Urban League; State Bar Calif, 1988-; pres, Boy Scouts Am Explorers Division, 1988-. **Honors/Awds:** Hon Mem, US Navy ROTC Selection Bd Chief of Naval Opers Washington DC, 1979-82; Distinguished Alumna San Diego Comm Leadership Develop, 1980; Hon Mem, Phi Kappa Phi San Diego State Univ, 1980-86; Role Higher Educ in Educ Reform Adolescents 1988; Meeting the Challenge of Technol, 1988; Letter of Commendation, Mayor, City San Diego, 1989; Proclamation, Bd Supvrs, 1990; Resolution, Assemblyman Chacon 75th District, 1990; San Diego Urban League, Letter of Commendation, 1991; Nat Black Child Dev Inc, Certificate of Apppreciation, 1992; San Diego Housing Comn, Proclamation, 1992. **Special Achievements:** 11 publications including "Trends Affecting Black Recreators in the Professional Society," California Parks and Recreation Society Magazine 1981. **Military Serv:** USN capt 21 yrs; Letter of Commendation for Outstanding Serv to the Navy & Marine Selection Bd, 1979-91; Meritorious Serv Medal, 1980; Letter of Commendation,1981; Gold Star for Excellence in Recruiting 1981; Gold Wreath Awd for Excellence in Recruiting, 1982-92; Navy Achievement, 1989; 2nd Meritorious Serv Medal, 1990; 37th Gold Wreath for Excellence in Recruiting, 1990. **Home Addr:** 318 Gravilla St, La Jolla, CA 92037. **Business Phone:** (619)594-4964.

HUTCHINSON, JAMES J., JR.
Executive. **Personal:** Born Sep 22, 1947, Chicago, IL; divorced; children: Kelley, Jimmy. **Educ:** Dartmouth Col, BA, 1969; Amos Tuck Sch Bus Admin, MBA, 1971. **Career:** First Nat Bank Chicago, coop loan officer, 1971-74; S Side Bank, exec vpres, 1974-80; Inter-Urban Broadcasting Co, vpres, 1977-81; Inter-Urban Broadcasting Co, pres, 1984-; Inter-Urban Rental Systs, pres, 1985-; Inter-Urban Broadcasting New Orleans Partnership, exec vpres, gen partner, 1980-86; Savannah Cardinals Baseball Club, secy, 1986-; Inter-Urban Broadcasting Group, pres, 1986-; Family Advocacy & Neighborhood Serv, exec dir, currently. **Orgs:** Adv bd mem, New Orleans Reg Vo-Tech Inst, 1982-; exec comt mem, Chambers Small Bus Coun, 1984; radio vpres, Greater New Orleans Broadcasters Asn, 1984-85; comn New Orleans Exhibs Hall Auth, 1986-; chmn, Urban League Greater New Orleans, 1986-; YMCA Greater New Orleans; United Way; Metrop Area Comt; LA Calif Mus Pvt Indust Coun; Greater NO Tourist & Conv Comn; Mayor Morials Superbowl Task Force; AP Tureaud Comn; Mayor Morials Bus Devel Coun; Bus Task Force Educ. **Honors/Awds:** Outstanding Achievement Award, Citizens Cultural Found, 1978; Distinguished Serv Award, Blackbook Urban League Greater New Orleans, 1981; Metropolitan Area Comt Leadership Forum, 1983. **Special Achievements:** one of the Ten Outstanding Black Businessmen in Chicago Award, 1979; one of the Ten Best Dressed Men in New Orleans Men of Fashion. **Business Addr:** Executive Director, Family Advocacy & Neighborhood Serv, 5700 Read Blvd, PO Box 50157, New Orleans, LA 70150-0157.*

HUTCHINSON, JEROME
Executive. **Personal:** Born Jul 23, 1926, Louisville, KY; married Eleanor; children: Jerome, Jr, Seretha R. **Educ:** Univ Louisville, AB, 1951; Sch Bus Admin & Seminars Small Bus Admin, grad. **Career:** Admiral Finance Co, credit investgr, 1954-55; Falls City Brewing Co, sales & pub rel rep 1956-66; Small Bus Admin, mgt specialist, 1966-69; Econ Develop & Now Inc, Louisville , exec dir, 1969-70; Jonah Enterprises Inc, Louisville, vpres, 1970-71; Jerome Hutchinson & Assoc Inc, pres; Hutchinson & Assoc Inc, chief exec officer, currently. **Orgs:** Bd mem, IMBE Wash, 1969-70; bd mem, Louisville OIC, 1970-72; chmn bd dir, Continental Nat Bank KY, 1973-75; bd mem & chmn Finance, Com River Reg Mental Health Corp, 1974-75; chmn bd dir, Plymouth Urban Ctr, 1974; Alpha Gardens Block Watch Club. **Honors/Awds:** SBA Regional Mgt Award, 1968; Citizen of Day Award, WLOU Radio, 1973; Ambassador of Goodwill Citation City, Louisville, 1974. **Military Serv:** USN, 3rd class petty officer World War II. **Business Addr:** Chief Executive Officer, Hutchinson Associates Inc, 1147 W Ohio St Suite 305, Chicago, IL 60622, **Business Phone:** (312)455-9191.*

HUTCHINSON, LOUISE DANIEL
Historian. **Personal:** Born Jun 3, 1928, Ridge, MD; married Ellsworth W Hutchinson Jr; children: Ronald, David, Donna, Dana, Victoria. **Educ:** Miner Teacher Col, Prairie View A&M, Howard Univ, 1952; Am Hist & Afro-Am Studies, Grad Hons, Sociol. **Career:** Historian (retired); Nat Portrait Gallery SI, res harmon collection, 1971, educ res spec, 1972-73; Nat Capitol Parks E Wash, educ res spec, 1973-74; Anacostia Mus Smithsonian Inst, hist, dir res, 1974-86. **Orgs:** Bd mem, SE Neighbor House, 1968-70; bd dir, Wash Urban League, 1968-70; mem bd, SE Unit Am Cancer Soc, 1969-; chmn supt, Coun Arts Educ, DC Pub Sch, 1972-74; Nat Asn Negro Bus & Prof Women's Club Inc, 1973-; exec comt bd, DC Citizens Better Pub Educ, 1974-76; Frederick Douglass Mem & Hist Asn, 1974-, Douglass ad hoc community, Nat Capitol Parks E; planning comn bicent Smithsonian Inst; Anacostia Hist Soc. **Honors/Awds:** Author: "The Anacostia Story, 1608-30", 1977, "Out of Africa, From Kingdoms to Colonization", Smithsonian Press, 1979, "Anna J Cooper, A Voice from the South", Smithsonian Press, 1981; Exhibit Black Women, Achievements Against the Odds Smithsonian Traveling Exhib Service. *

HUTCHISON, DR. HARRY GREENE
College teacher, educator. **Personal:** Born Apr 12, 1948, Detroit, MI; son of Mary Robinson and Harry. **Educ:** Wayne State Univ, Detroit, Mich, BA, econ, 1969, MA, econ, 1975; Univ Mich, Ann Arbor, MBA, 1977; Wayne State Univ Law Sch, JD, 1986; Univ Oxford, dipl, 2000. **Career:** Detroit Edison, Detroit, Mich, bus analyst, 1971-74; Ford Motor Co, Troy,Mich, financial analyst, 1977-80; Lawrence Technol Univ, Southfield, Mich, asst prof econ & law, 1981-89; Lathrup Village, Mich, atty & counr, 1987-89; Univ San Diego, vis prof, 1992. Univ Detroit, Detroit, Mich, from asst prof law, to prof law, 1989-2001, fac dir London law prog & prof law, 1998-2000; First Am Bank, bd dir, 1991-94; Univ San Diego Law Sch, vis prof law, 1992; Univ Bristol, fac law, 1998-99; Wayne State Univ, fractional time prof, 2000, vis prof, 2001-02, prof & dir grad studies, 2003-04, law prof, 2002-06; George Mason Univ Sch Law, vis prof, 2005-06, prof law, 2006-. **Orgs:** Senior policy analyst, Mackinac Ctr, 1987-; chair, Nat Asn Securities Dealers arbit panels, 1990-98; AAA Securities Arbit Panels; bd adv,Heartland Inst, 1990-; Mich Civil Rights Comn, 1991-93. **Honors/Awds:** Barnes Award for Faculty Scholarship, Univ Detroit Mercy, Sch Law, 1993 & 2001. **Special Achievements:** Published numerous articles; Article listed in Top Ten List of Labor Law Articles. **Business Addr:** Professor, George Mason University School of Law, 3301 Fairfax Dr Room 321 Arlington Campus, Arlington, VA 48202, **Business Phone:** (703)993-8980.

HUTCHISON, DR. PEYTON S.
School administrator, consultant. **Personal:** Born Mar 24, 1925, Detroit, MI; son of Gladys Palace Smith and Harry Greene; married Betty L Sweeney; children: Peyton Jr, Allison Leigh & Jonathan Alan. **Educ:** Wayne State Univ, BS, Educ, 1950, MEd, 1955; Northern Ill Univ 1969; Mich State Univ, PhD 1975. **Career:** Detroit Pub Schs, admin asst 1966-73, asst prin, 1964-65; City Col Chicago, supervising dir, 1973-75; Chicago Urban Skills Inst, vpres1974-75, pres, 1975-84, exec dean; Roosevelt Univ, adj prof, 1984-94; Hutchison Assoc (consulting business) currently; Richard J. Daly Col, exec dean /dir; Knoxville Col, interim pres. **Orgs:** Teacher, Detroit Public Sch, 1950-54; dir, Green Pastures Camp Detroit Urban League 1959-65; asst prin, Detroit Public Sch, 1964-65; matl develop suprv Detroit Pub Sch, 1965-67; sr level res assoc, Mich State Univ, 1968-69; chmn, bd dir, Classic Chorales Inc, 1983-; chmn, Col Univ Unit Am Assoc Adult Cont Educ, 1983-; trustee, Knoxville Col, 1984-; mem Alpha Phi Alpha; division dir, pres, 1992-93, Am Asn Adult/Continuing Educ; exec comt, Am Cancer Soc. **Honors/Awds:** Pres, Phi Delta Kappa, Wayne State Univ, 1963; Mott Doctoral fel, Charles Stewart Mott Found, 1968; Carl Sandburg Award, Friends Chicago Pub Libr,1984; Community Service Award, Univ Chicago Int Kiwanis 1985; Phi Kappa Phi Nat Hon Soc; Phi Beta Sigma Hon Soc; Listed in Who's Who in American Education & Who's Who in Black America; Hall of Fame, Am Asn Adult/Continuing Educ. **Military Serv:** AUS sgt 1944-46. **Home Addr:** 688 Old Elm Rd, Lake Forest, IL 60045.

HUTSON, TONY
Football player. **Personal:** Born Mar 13, 1974, Houston, TX. **Educ:** Northeastern State Univ. **Career:** Football player (retired), Dallas Cowboys, tackle, 1997-99; Wash Redskins, guard, 2000.

HUTTON, DAVID LAVON
Educator, teacher. **Personal:** Born in Kansas City, MO. **Educ:** Cent Miss State Univ, BS, 1963; Hall Recognition, 1963; Univ Miss, Kans, MA, 1974. **Career:** Educator (retired); Paseo High Sch, teacher, 1965-79; Lincoln Acad N, teacher, 1981-91; JA Rogers Acad, curric coordr, 1991-95; Ladd Sch, voltutor, 1998. **Orgs:** AFT, 1965-; bd dirs, Ray Co Sesquicentennial Comn, 1970-71; trustee, Bethel AME Church, 1979-92; Nat Asn Adv Colored People, 1983-; Bldg & Expansion Bethel AME Church, 1983-; pres, Voices Bethel AME Church, 1994-95; Million Man March, 1995; ambassador, Alvin Ailey Dance Troupe, 1996; vol docent, Bruce Watkins Cult Ctr, 1997; Mid-town Kiwanis, 1998-; Nat Coun African-Am Men; sr adult coun pres, Bethel AME Church; tax-aide counr, AARP. **Honors/Awds:** Hall of Recognition, Cent Miss State Univ, 1963; Outstanding Sec Educr,1975. **Military Serv:** AUS, sp/4, 3 yrs; medal of good conduct, 1956-59. *

HUTTON, GERALD L.
Educator, consultant. **Personal:** Born in Pittsburg, KS; married Marjorie. **Career:** Lincoln & HP Study Schs, Springfield, Mo, teacher; Springfield Pub Schs, pub info rep; St Louis NW HS, athletic dir & bus educ instr; St Louis Educ TV, Zoning Pk Bd, community comnr, pub television-utilization consult; Ancient Egyptian Arabic Order Nobles Mystic Shrine N & S Am, officer. **Orgs:** Am Guild Variety Artists; Anerucah Fed TV & Radio Artists; Am Equity Asn; Royal Vagabonds St Louis Mens Civic Club; St Louis Area Bus Teachers Asn; Kiwanis Club; Nat Advan Asn Colored People; St Louis Br; hon past, potentate PHA Shriners; United Supreme Coun, PHA So Jurisdiction 33rd deg, Soloist World Series Games, St Louis, 1967, 1968; life mem, Kappa Alpha Psi. **Honors/Awds:** Festival Appreciation Award, Sigma Gamma Rho Sorority Inc & Zeta Sigma chap Afro-am Arts. **Special Achievements:** Book: High School & College Typewriting.

HUTTON, MARILYN ADELE
Lawyer. **Personal:** Born Jul 21, 1950, Cincinnati, OH. **Educ:** Fisk Univ, BA, 1972; Harvard Law Sch, JD, 1975; Hague Acad Int Law, cert, 1983. **Career:** US Senator Lloyd M Bentsen, legislative aide, 1975-76; The Procter & Gamble Co, corp coun, 1976-81; Cincinnati Queen City Bowling Senate, corp secy, 1980-82; NAACP, legislative coun, 1986-87; Arlington Co, Va, Human Rights Commn, 1992-; Va State Coal & Energy Commn, 1994-; Nat Educ Assoc, atty human & civil rights spec, currently. **Orgs:** Legal adv comm, Nat Bowling Assoc, 1978-80; mem, Int Bar Assoc, Am Soc Int Law, Am & Fed Bar Assocs, Dist Columbia Bar Assoc, Am Assoc Art Museums, Corcoran Gallery Art; mem, US Ct Military Appeals, US Ct Appeals Fed Circuit, US Ct Appeals Dist Columbia Circuit, Dist Columbia Courts Appeals. **Special Achievements:** Author American Soc of Intl Law 1986, annual meeting report 1987. **Business Addr:** Attorney, National Education Association, 1201 16th St NW, Washington, DC 20001, **Business Phone:** (202)833-4000.

HUTTON, DR. RONALD I
Dentist. **Personal:** Born Jul 23, 1949, High Point, NC; son of Joseph E Hutton (deceased). **Educ:** Hampton Inst, BA, 1971;

Howard Univ Col Dentistry, DDS, 1975; Kimbrough Army Hosp, Gen Pract Residency, 1975-76. **Career:** Winston-Salem Dental Care, dentist; Army Dental Corp, dentist, 1975-78; pvt pract, currently. **Orgs:** Am Col Dent; Asn Mil Surgeons US; Old N State Dental & Soc; NC 2nd Dist Dental Soc; Am & Nat Dental Asns; Acad Gen Dent; Zoning Bd Adjustments, Town Lewisville; bd trustees, Big Brothers-Big Sisters; bd trustees, Summit Sch Winston-Salem, NC; exec bd, Old Hickory Boy Scout Coun. **Honors/Awds:** Organized society fel Campus of Hampton Inst, 1969; Mastership, Acad Gen Dent. **Military Serv:** AUS, dentist, 1975-78; AUS Reserves, col. **Home Addr:** 1220 Brook Acres Trail, Clemmons, NC 27012. **Business Addr:** Physician, 201 Charlois Blvd, Winston-Salem, NC 27103, **Business Phone:** (336)718-1800.

HUYGHUE, MICHAEL L.
Football executive. **Personal:** Born Sep 21, 1961. **Educ:** Cornell Univ; Univ Mich, Law. **Career:** World League of Am Football; Detroit Lions, gen coun, vpres admin, 1993-94; Jacksonville Jaguars, sr vpres football opers; Axcess Sports & Entertainment LLC, ceo, currently. **Orgs:** Sports Lawyers Assoc; bd of trustees, alma mater; MPS Group. **Business Addr:** Chief Executive Officer, Axcess Sports & Entertainment LLC, 1 Independent Dr Suite 2602, Jacksonville, FL 32202, **Business Phone:** (904)301-3000.*

HYATT, HERMAN WILBERT, SR.
Physician, clergy. **Personal:** Born Feb 19, 1926, South Pittsburg, TN; son of Robert Charles and Wilma Vance; married Elizabeth; children: Monique, Monica, Hamilton, Richard, Robert, Herman Jr. **Educ:** Tenn A&I State Univ, BS, 1949; Meharry Med Col, MD, 1956; Lincoln Univ Law Sch, JD, 1972; San Jose Bible Col, San Jose, CA, BA, 1986; Christian Bible Col & Seminary, MS, 2001, admin, 2002. **Career:** Kern Gen Hosp, res pediatrrician, 1957-59, Pediat Dept, chief, 1963; AME Church, dist dir youth cong, 1964-75; St James African Methodist, pastor, 1967-77; San Jose Hosp, Dept Pediat, chmn, 1971-72, Alexian Brothers Hosp, 1973-74; Mt Hermon African Methodist Episcopal Church, founder & pastor; pvt pract pediatrician, currently. **Orgs:** Alpha Kappa Mu Nat Honor Soc, 1948; ordained itinerant elder, Bishop H Thomas Prim, 1966; life mem, Nat Asn Advan Colored people; Parents Helping Parents; vpres, Interdenominational Ministers Alliance, 1987-; Calif Conf, African Methodist Episcopal Church, bd examiners, currently; assoc dir, Calif Conf, African Methodist Episcopal Church. **Honors/Awds:** Special Recognition Award, Santa Clara Human Rights Comn, 1988; Commendation, City San Jose, 1989-90; Special Award, Urban League, 1988; Monrovia Col, Honorary Doctor of Humanities, 1987; San Jose City Col, Honorary Asn Art, 1988; Man of the Year, San Jose, Calif Citizen's Group, 1989; Valley of Hearts Award, Parents Helping Parents, 1992. **Special Achievements:** Published book, A Cry for Help, 1991; Wrote, directed and produced 3-act play for the Young People's Department of the California Conference of the African Methodist Episcopal Church, 1992; Book, "Reflections and Meditations From a Mountain," 2003. **Military Serv:** AUS, sgt, 1946. **Business Addr:** Pediatrician, 12 S 14th St, San Jose, CA 95112, **Business Phone:** (408)295-2693.*

HYDE, DR. MAXINE DEBORRAH
Neurosurgeon, physician. **Personal:** Born Jan 18, 1949, Laurel, MS; daughter of Sellus and Ann McDonald. **Educ:** Tougaloo Col, BS, biol, 1970; Cleveland State Univ, MS, biol, 1973; Case Western Res Univ, MD, 1977; Am Bd Neurol Surg, dipl. **Career:** Univ Hosp, internship gen surg, 1977-78, residency neurosurg, 1978-82; Guthrie Clinic, neurosurg staff, 1982-87; Canoga Park, CA, pvt pract, neurosurg, 1987-; Beacon Hope Scholar Found Inc, founder. **Orgs:** Cong Neurol Surgeons; Alpha Omega Alpha Hon Med Soc, 1977; Calif Neurosurg Soc; Am Asn Neurol Surgeons. **Honors/Awds:** Black Women Who Make It Happen, Nat Coun Negro Women, 1989; Strong Men & Women Excellence Leadership Award, 1996; DHL, Tongaloo Col, Tongaloo, Miss. **Special Achievements:** Second African-American Female Neurosurgeon; Publications: "5-Hydroxytryptophan decarboxylase & monoamine oxidase in the maturing mouse eye", 1973; "The Maturation of 5-hydroxytryptophan decarboxylase in regions of the mouse brain", 1973; "The maturation of indoleamine metabolism in the lateral eye of the mouse", 1974; "The maturation of monoamine oxidase and 5-hydroxyindole acetic acid in regions of the mouse brain", 1974; "Re-expansion of previously collapsed ventricles", 1982; Featured Story, Ebony, 1983; Featured in first edition of Medica, 1983; Featured story Am Med News, 1984; First Register as one of "the best of the new generation-those who exemplify in their professional lives the qualities of courage, originality, ingenuity, vision and selfless service", Esquire mag, 1984. **Business Addr:** Founder, Beacon of Hope Scholarship Foundation, 7230 Med Ctr Dr Suite 300, West Hills, CA 91307.

HYDE, DR. WILLIAM R. See Obituaries section.

HYLER, LORA LEE
Radio journalist, president (organization). **Personal:** Born Oct 4, 1959, Racine, WI; daughter of Leona McGee and Haward. **Educ:** Univ Wis-Milwaukee, Milwaukee, Wis, BA, Mass Commun, 1981. **Career:** WISN Radio, an ABC Affiliate, Milwaukee, WI, news reporter, 1980-84; Wisconsin Natural Gas Co, Racine, Wis, commun writer, 1984-88; Journal Commun, Milwaukee, Wis, commun mgr, 1988-91; Wis Elec Power Co., Milwaukee, pub info rep, 1991-2001; Hyler Commun, pres & chief exec officer, 2004-. **Orgs:** Public Relations Soc Am, 1990-; Wis Black Media Asn. **Business Addr:** President, Cheif Executive Officer, Hyler Communications, 11512 N Port Washington Rd Suite 201A, Milwaukee, WI 53092, **Business Phone:** (262)241-5380.

HYLTON, ANDREA LAMARR
Librarian. **Personal:** Born Dec 12, 1965, Martinsville, VA; daughter of Gloria Mae Hodge and Vallie Walker. **Educ:** James Madison Univ, Harrisonburg, BS, 1988; NC Cent Univ, Durham, MLS, 1990. **Career:** Blue Ridge Regional Libr, Martinsville, VA, libr asst, 1987; Spotsylvania County Sch Bd, Spotsylvania, VA, librn, 1988-89; NC Cent Univ, Durham, NC, grad asst, 1989-90; Family Health Int, Research Triangle Park, NC, intern, 1990; First Union Securities; Duke Energy Co; Johnson C. Smith Univ, info sci librn, currently. **Orgs:** Va Educ Media Asn, 1986-90; pres, NC Cent Univ Stud Chap Am Libr Asn, 1989-90; treas, NC Cent Univ Stud Chap Spec Libr Asn, 1989-90; NC Cent Univ Sch Libr & Info Sci Curric Comt, 1990; stud staff mem, Am Libr Asn, Nat Conf, 1990. **Honors/Awds:** Special Talent Award, NC Cent Univ, 1989; Jenkins-Moore Scholar, Sch Libr & Info Sci, NC Cent Univ, 1990. **Business Addr:** Information Sciences Librarian, Johnson C. Smith University, Libr 216 100 Beatties Ford Rd, Charlotte, NC 28216, **Business Phone:** (704)371-6747.

HYLTON, KENNETH N., SR.
Lawyer. **Personal:** Born Jul 7, 1929, Roanoke, VA; son of S W Hylton; married Ethel Washington; children: Kenneth N Jr, Keith Norman, Kevin Nathaniel. **Educ:** Talladega Col, BA; Wayne State Univ, MA; Boston Univ Sch Law, JD. **Career:** Bailer, Lee, Long, Brown & Cain, partner, 1957-62; Wayne Co, MI, pub adminr; Swainson, Dingell, Hylton & Zemmol, partner, 1962-67; Civil Rights Comn, State Mich, referee, 1962-67; Nat Advan Asn Colroed People, Housing Corp, counsel; Dingell, Hylton & Zemmol, partner, 1967-77; Kenneth N Hylton & Assocs, 1977-80; Hylton & Hylton PC, sr partner & atty, 1980-. **Orgs:** Eastern & Western Fed Dist Ct Bar Mich; 6th Circuit US Ct Appeals Bar; Supreme Ct US Bar; Va State Bar; Mich State Bar; Detroit Bar Asn; Wolvernine Bar Asn; Am Bar Asn; Nat Lawyers Guild; Am Judicature Soc; Workmen's Compensation Section & Condemnation Comt; Am Trial Lawyers Asn; former chmn, State Bar Grievance Bd State Mich; Alpha Phi Alpha Fraternity; Nat Advan Asn Colored People; pres & chmn bd dirs, Westlawn Cemetery Asn Detroit; bd dir, Nat Housing Conf, Wash, DC; secy bd & gen coun, Omnibank, Detroit, MI. **Military Serv:** AUS, first lt, 1953-56. **Business Addr:** Attorney, Hylton & Hylton PC, 613 Griswold St Suite 315, Detroit, MI 48226-3978, **Business Phone:** (313)843-8850.*

HYLTON, TAFT H.
Manager. **Personal:** Born Jun 22, 1936, Washington, DC; divorced. **Educ:** BS, 1959; Washington Conservatory Music; Wash Inst Music. **Career:** Dept of Human Serv DC Govt, chief & Payments Br; Ofc Budget & Mgmt Sys DC Govt, budget & accounting analyst; choral conductor; tcht private piano; Voices of Expression Choral Ensemble, fndr dir. **Orgs:** Am Choral Dir Asn; dir of sr choir New Bethel Bapt Ch; dir Anthem Choir Allen AME Ch; Cosmopolitan Choral Ensemble; Am Light OperaCo; Negro Oratorio Soc; 12th St Christian Ch; Univ Soc Piano Tchrs. **Honors/Awds:** Work Performance Award; Pub Health Serv NIH, 1963; Eligible Bachelor featured, Ebony Mag, 1974.

HYMAN, EARLE
Actor. **Personal:** Born Oct 11, 1926, Rocky Mount, NC; son of Zachariah and Maria Lilly. **Educ:** Amer Theatre Wing; Actors Studio. **Career:** NY State Am Negro Theatre, performer, 1943; Films: The Lost Weekend, 1945; The Bamboo Prison, 1954; The Possession of Joel Delaney, 1972; House Party Playhouse, various roles 1974; The Green Pastures, Coriolanus, 1979; Fighting Back, 1982; Gandahar, 1988, Light Years, 1988; TV movies & Series: "Love of Life",1951; The Green Pastures, 1957; "Play of the Week", 1959-60; "The Cosby Show", 1984-92; "Thunder cats", 1985; "A Man Called Hawk", 1989; "Cosby", 1997; "The Moving of Sophia Myles", 2000; "Moonshine Over Harlem", 2001;"A Look Back", 2002; "Recovering the Life of Canada Lee", 2006. **Orgs:** Reader, Am Found Blind. **Honors/Awds:** Show Business Award, 1953; Seagram Vanguard Award, 1955; Theatre World Award, 1956; GRY Award, Norwegian, Oslo, Norway, 1965; ACE Award, 1983; Norwegian State Award, 1984. **Special Achievements:** Nominated for an Emmy Award in 1986. **Home Addr:** 484 W 43rd St, New York, NY 10036, **Home Phone:** (212)594-8663.

HYMAN, MARK J
Executive. **Personal:** Born Apr 25, 1916, Rocky Mount, NC; son of Joshua and Eliza Vick; married Mable V, Sep 19, 1947 (deceased); children: Beverley & Linda. **Educ:** NY Univ, BA, MA; Temple Univ, PhD. **Career:** The Way Publishing Co, chmn; Mark Hyman Assocs Inc, pres. **Orgs:** Chmn, Philadelphia Urban League; chmn, Howard Univ Alumni Club Philadelphia; chmn, Philadelphia Press Club; chair, Edythe Ingraham Hist Club; Omega Psi Phi Fraternity; dir, Nat Pub Rels; vpres, Philadelphia Am Cancer Soc; founder & bd mem, Aro Hist & Cult Mus, Philadelphia. **Honors/Awds:** Mary McLeod Bethune Medallion, Bethune Cookman Univ; Philadelphia Tribune Front Page Award; ASOd Press Broadcast Award; Afro American Historical Museum Award; Pennsylvania State Legislature Award. **Special Achievements:** Books: Blacks Before America, Vol I, II, III, 1979; Blacks Who Died for Jesus, A History Book, 1983; Black Shogun of Japan, 1986; The America that killed King: Fact & Fiction, 1991. **Military Serv:** AUS, 2nd lt, 1940-43. **Home Addr:** 5070 Parkside Ave Suite 1122, Philadelphia, PA 19131.

HYMES, JESSE
Executive, real estate executive. **Personal:** Born Feb 13, 1939, St Joseph, LA; married Addie B; children: Kenneth, Tracey & Trina. **Educ:** Univ Chicago, MBA, 1972; Purdue Univ, AAS, 1970. **Career:** Meade Elec Co, draftsman estimator, 1969; financial analyst, 1972; plant acct, 1974; control syst adminr, 1975; Joseph Schlitz Brewing Co, plant controller, asst controller, 1975; Hymes Appraisals & Realty Group, residential real estate appraiser & owner, currently. **Orgs:** Nat Asn Advan Colored People; jr advr Achievement, 1975-76; art coun, 1975-76; bd dir, Urban Arts, 1976; pres, Nat Parent Teacher Asn, 1977; adv dom, Boy Scouts Am, 1977. **Honors/Awds:** Cogme fellowship grant, 1972; Urban League Black Achiever Award, NY YMCA, 1977. **Military Serv:** AUS, sp 4, 1962-65. **Business Addr:** Owner, Residential real estate appraiser, Hymes Appraisals & Realty Group, 1001 S Marshall St, PO Box 130, Winston-Salem, NC 27101.

HYNSON, CARROLL HENRY, JR.
State government official. **Personal:** Born Dec 28, 1936, Washington, DC; son of Adel and Carroll; children: Michelle Hynson Green, Lejuene Tarra, Marcus Carroll, Brandee Carol. **Educ:** Pa State Univ, sociol & polit sci, 1959; Am Univ, summer course, sociol; Morgan State Univ, BA, 1960. **Career:** Sonderling Broadcasting Co, chief announcer/actg prog dir, 1965-75; Hynsons Real Estate, off mgr, 1975-76; Ceda Corp, pub affairs specialist, 1976-77; Provident Hosp Inc, asst vpres develop & pub rels, 1978-80; Balt/Wash Int Airport, dir off trade develop, 1980-84; MD State Lottery Agency, dep dir sales, 1984-88, dep dir pub affairs, 1984-. **Orgs:** life mem, Phi Beta Pi Com Frat, 1973; vpres, Scholar Scholars Comn, 1984; bd dir, Epilepsy Found MD, 1982; adv bd, Baltimore Convention Bur, 1982; Kappa Alpha Psi Fraternity; vice chmn, Anne Arundel Co/Annap Bicentennial Comm. **Special Achievements:** Host/producer, It Ain't Necessarily So-CBS, 1976; Host/producer, The C Thing WRC-TV & Back to School Spec, Washington WHG-TV. **Home Addr:** Severna Park, MD 21146. **Business Addr:** Deputy Director Public Affairs, MD State Lottery Agency, Plz Off Ctr Suite 204, 6776 Reisterstown Rd, Baltimore, MD 21215.*

HYPOLITE, DR. CHRISTINE COLLINS
Educator. **Personal:** Born Nov 20, 1956, New Orleans, LA; daughter of Harold and Shirley; married Shelby J, Jul 10, 1993. **Educ:** Nicholls State Univ, BA, 1978, MEd, 1980; La State Univ, PhD, 2003. **Career:** Lafourche Parish Schs, teacher, 1979-94; Nicholls State Univ, asst prof, 1994, Dept Teacher Educ, assoc prof, currently. **Orgs:** Nat Sci Teacher Asn, 1995-; Nat Coun Teachers Math, 1995-; Asn Curric Develop, 1995-; bd chair, Bayonland Families Helping Families, 1997-. **Honors/Awds:** Teacher of the Year, Jaycess, 1991; Faculty Member of the Month, Nicholls State Univ, 2003. **Special Achievements:** Listed in Who's Who Among Am Teachers, 2005, 2006. **Business Addr:** Associate Professor, Nicholls State University, Department of Teacher Education, 243 Polk Hall, PO Box 2035, Thibodaux, LA 70310, **Business Phone:** (985)448-4314.

HYSAW, GUILLERMO LARK
Automotive executive. **Personal:** Born Dec 19, 1948, Bakersfield, CA; son of Guillermo and Georgia; married Kimberly, Nov 7, 1987; children: S Jamal, Immari A & Megan Ashley. **Educ:** Oakland Univ, BA, 1972; Claremont Grad Sch, MA, 1991, MBA, 1993, AMBA, 1996. **Career:** Gen Motors Corp, staff, 1971-87; Toyota, Lexus Div, sr mkt rep admin, 1987-88, venture capital planning mgr, 1988-89, nat advert mgr, 1989-91, nat bus develop mgr, 1991-92, nat mkt develop mgr, 1992-93, nat fleet mkt opers mgr, 1993-97, corp mgr used vehicle dept, 1997-2000, corp mgr, mkt rep, 2000-02, vpres diversity, 2002-06; Mach-1 Autogroup, partner, currently. **Orgs:** Chair, 100 Black Men Los Angeles, Inc; vpres, Nat Asn Black MBA, Los Angeles; life mem, Nat Comm, NAACP; Nat External Fundraiser, Alpha Phi Alpha Frat; bd dirs & pres, Compton Comm Col Found; bd dirs, Drew Med Hosp; nat co-chairperson mkt, 100 Black Men Am, Inc; strategic planning mem, Nat Econ Develop; exec mgt, Gen Motors Inst Bd Regents, 1990; Nat Asn Advan People Color; Beta Psi Lambda. **Honors/Awds:** Peter F Drucker Graduate Management Award, 1990; Corporate Profile Award, Black Enterprise Mag, 1991; Corporate Role Model Award, African Male Achievers Network, 1992, 1993, 1994. **Special Achievements:** Sports Illustrated Magazine, cover,

1969, Black Enterprise, corp profile article, 1991, Jet Magazine, corp profile article, 1997, over 200 Black Newspapers, corp profile article, 1997, Sphinx Magazine, corp profile article, cover, 1998. **Business Addr:** Partner, Mach 1 Autogroup, 1001 Avenido Pico Suite C 258, San Clemente, CA 92673, **Business Phone:** (714)889-9140.

HYTCHE, DR. WILLIAM P. See Obituaries section.

I

IBEKWE, LAWRENCE ANENE
Educator, school administrator. **Personal:** Born Apr 17, 1952, Onitsha, Nigeria; son of Eusebius and Marcelina Ibekwe Ozumba; married Theresa Ibekwe Nwabunie, Mar 23, 1989; children: Lynn, Lawren & Lawrence Jr. **Educ:** Marshall Univ, Huntington, WV, 1979; Philander Smith Col, Little Rock, AR, BA, bus admin, 1981; Univ Ark, Fayetteville, MS, mgt, 1983. **Career:** State Sch Bd, Holy Rosary Teacher's Col, Nigeria, libr asst, 1975-78; Ark Commemorative Comt, Old State House, security officer, 1983-84; Philander Smith Col, instr, 1984-91; Shorter Col, assoc prof, 1984-, Dept Bus & Appl Sci, head, 1987-88, 1991, acad dean, currently; Ark Dept Heritage, Mgt Proj Anal, 1992-93. **Orgs:** Adv, Phi Beta Lambda, Philander Smith Col, 1986-; chmn, Ark Asn Nigerians, Supv Coun, 1986; chmn, Constitution Review, 1986, 1989, 1992; adv, Ark Asn Nigerian Studs, 1986-88; adv, Constitution Review, 1987; treas, Elite Social Club, 1987-; Knight Columbus, 1987-; Bd Adv, Little Rock Job Corp Prog, 1989-91; campus coordr, Fed Funded Int Studies Prog, 1990-93; treas, Nigerian Professionals Ark, 1991-92. **Honors/Awds:** Award of Recognition for Advising, PBL Bus Club, 1986-89; Outstanding Young Men of America, Jaycees, 1981; several Outstanding Leadership and Performance Awards; Man of the Year Award, 1991. **Home Addr:** PO Box 164431, Little Rock, AR 72216. **Business Addr:** Academic Dean Academic Affairs, Shorter College, 604 N Locust St, North Little Rock, AR 72114, **Business Phone:** (501)374-6305.

IBELEMA, DR. MINABERE
Educator. **Personal:** Born Dec 9, 1954, Bonny, Nigeria; son of Violet Eredappa and Ebenezer Tamunoibelema; married Jan 8, 1994 (divorced 2004); children: Danielle Boma & Ibim. **Educ:** Wilberforce Univ, Wilberforce, OH, BA, 1979; Oh State Univ, Columbus, OH, MA, 1980, PhD, 1984. **Career:** Cent State Univ, Wilberforce, OH, assoc prof, 1984-91; Eastern Ill Univ, Charleston, IL, assoc prof, 1991-95; Univ Ala, Birmingham, assoc prof commun studies, 1995-. **Orgs:** Asn Educ Jour & Mass Commun, 1987-; African Studies Asn, 1992-. **Honors/Awds:** Honorable Mention, Munger Africana Libr, African Thesis Competition, Calif Inst Technol, 1982. **Special Achievements:** Co-author, Afro-Optimism: Perspectives on Africa's Advances, New York: Praeger, 2003. **Business Addr:** Associate Professor, University of Alabama, Department of Communication Studies, 15 St Office Bldg, Birmingham, AL 35295-2060, **Business Phone:** (205)934-6297.

IBN MCDANIELS-NOEL, MUHIYYALDIN MALAK ABD AL MUTA'ALI
Naval officer. **Personal:** Born in Salem, NJ; married; children: three. **Educ:** BBA, bus admin; MBA, indust rels & arbit, personnel mgt; MDiv, Islamic studies law; DMin, Islamic studies & Muslim-Christian rels. **Career:** US Navy, chaplain, Lt, 1996-. **Orgs:** NCP; APA; Black Ministers Conf; consult, The Ctr Study Religious Freedom; VIR Wesleyan Col; Nat Conf Cot Justice; Am Muslim Coun; Muslim Military Mbr Asn; Alpha Eta Pho Aviation; Nat Naval Officers Asn; Military Chaplains Asn; Alumni Asn; Salem Comn Col; Wilmington Col; Am Islamic Col; Lutheran Sch Theol Chi; Muslim Stud Asn; Univ Chi; Old Dominion Univ; dir, Islamic Charities Hampton Rds. **Special Achievements:** First Muslim chaplain in the history of the US Navy. **Military Serv:** US Navy; Joint Silver Commenation Medal, Joint Silver Achievement Medal, Navy & Marine Corps Achievement Medal, Combat Action Ribbon; Joint Meritorious Unit Award; Navy Unit Commendation; Meritorious Unit Commendation; Battle "E" Ribbon; Good Conduct Medal; Naval Reserve Meritorious Silver Medal; Navy Expeditionary Medal; Nat Defense Silver Medal; SW Asia Silver Medal; Humanitarian Silver Medal; Sea Silver Deployment Ribbon; Navy & Marine Corps Overseas Silver Ribbon; Kuwait Liberation Medal Kingdom of Saudi Arabia; Kuwait Liberation Medal, Kuwait; Rifle Sharpshooter Medal; Pistol Expert Medal; Volunteer Medal; Armed Forces Service Medal. **Business Addr:** Chaplain, Commander, Carrier Air Wing EIGHT, Unit 60109, FPO, AE 09504-4406, **Business Phone:** (757)433-2089.*

IBRAHIM, ABDULLAH (ADOLPH JOHANNES DOLLAR BRAND)
Pianist, composer. **Personal:** Born Oct 9, 1934, Cape Town; married Sathima Bea Benjamin; children: Tsakwe & Tsidi. **Educ:** Univ Cape Town. **Career:** Jazz Epistles, pianist & composer, 1949-61; Tuxedo Slickers, pianist &composer, 1949-61; Willie Max Big Band, pianist & composer, 1949-61; Dollar Brand Trio, band leader, 1962-65; Liberation Opera, Kalahari,composer, 1978; Marimba Mus Ctr & Ekapa Rec, dir; AS-Shams Rec Co; Cape Town, S Africa, karate instr; Ekaya, band leader, 1983-; M7 Acad S African Musicians, Cape Town, founder; Discography: Ekaya, 1983; Zimbabwe, 1983; Water From an Ancient Well, 1985; Mindif, 1988; Blues for a Hip King,1989; African River, 1989; No Fear, No Die, 1990; Mantra Mode, 1991; Knysna Blue, 1993; Yarona, 1995; Cape Town Flowers, 1997; African Suite, 1999; Ekapa Lodumo, 2001; African Magic, 2002; Senzo, 2008. **Orgs:** Nat Endowment Arts. **Honors/Awds:** Rockefeller Grant, 1968; Silver Award, 1973; Grand Prix Award, 1973; Talent Deserving Wider Recognition, Downbeat Mag, 1975; Gresham Col, London, UK, guest lectr, 2000. **Business Addr:** Composer, Hotel Chelsea, 222 W 23rd St, Hotel Chelsea Suite 314, New York, NY 10011.*

ICE, DR. ANNE-MARE
Pediatrician. **Personal:** Born Mar 16, 1945, Detroit, MI; daughter of Lois Tabor and Garnet Terry. **Educ:** Fisk Univ, BA, Chem, 1966; Howard Univ Col Med, MD, 1970; Milwaukee C Hosp, Internship residency pediat, 1973; Madonna Univ, MSBA, 1996. **Career:** Wayne State Univ Col Med, clinical asst prof; Interval Med Ctr, pediat physician; pvt practice, pediat, 1973-. **Orgs:** Am Bd of Pediat; Natl Med Assoc; Links Inc; Delta Sigma Theta Inc. **Honors/Awds:** Community Pediatrician Award, Coalition Reduce Infant Mortality, 1997; Sojourner Truth Humanitarian Award, Nat Asn Negro Bus & Prof Women Detroit Chap, 1998. **Business Addr:** Pediatrics Physician, 22341 W 8 Mile Rd, Detroit, MI 48219, **Business Phone:** (313)836-0062.*

ICE CUBE (OSHEA JACKSON)
Actor, rap musician. **Personal:** Born Jun 15, 1969, Los Angeles, CA; son of Doris and Hosea; married Kimberly, Jan 1, 1993; children: Darryl, O'Shea & Kareema. **Educ:** Phoenix Inst Technol, attended 1988. **Career:** Rap musician; actor; NWA, mem, 1988-90; albums: AmeriKKKa's Most Wanted, 1990; Death Cert, 1991; The Predator, 1993; War & Peace Vol 1, 1999; War & Peace Vol 2, 2000; Next Friday, 2000; Gone in Sixty Seconds, 2000; Save the Last Dance, 2001; Jay & Silent Bob Strike Back, 2001; How High, 2001; Ali G Indahouse, 2002; Friday After Next, 2002; The Hot Chick, 2002; Blade II, 2002; All About the Benjamins, 2002; Hollywood Homicide, 2003; Lethal Injection, 2003; Grand Theft Auto: San Andreas, 2004; Harsh Times, 2005; Beerfest, 2006; Waist Deep, 2006; films: Next Friday, 2000; Ghosts of Mars, 2001; All About the Benjamins, 2002; Barbershop, 2002; Friday After Next, 2002; WC: Bandana Swangin - All That Glitters Ain't Gold, 2003; Torque, 2004; Barbershop 2: Back in Business, 2004; Are We Done Yet?, 2005, 2007; xXx: State of the Union, 2005; First Sunday, 2008. **Honors/Awds:** Blockbuster Entertainment Award for Favorite Action Team, 2000; MECCA Movie Award-Acting Award, 2002. **Special Achievements:** Premiere mag, guest movie reviewer, Straight Out of Brooklyn, 1991; The Predator entered Billboards pop & black charts at Number 1, 1993. **Business Addr:** Actor, Creative Artists Agency, 9830 Wishire Blvd, Beverly Hills, CA 90212-1825.

ICE-T (TRACY MORROW)
Actor, rap musician. **Personal:** Born Feb 16, 1958, Newark, NJ; married Darlene. **Career:** Rapper, Actor, currently; Rapper, recs include: "The Coldest Rap," 1982; Rhyme Pays, 1987; Power, 1988; Colors, motion picture soundtrack, 1988; The Iceberg & Freedom of Speech Jack Hustler," 1991; O G-Original Gangster, 1991; Body Count, 1992; Home Invasion, 1993; films: Breakin', 1984; New Jack City, 1991, Ricochet, 1992; Trespass, 1993; Surviving The Game, 1994; Johnny Mnemonic, 1995; Players, 1997; Judgement Day, 1999; The Heist, 1999; Leprechaun in the Hood, 2000; 3000 Miles to Gracel&, 2001; Lexie, 2004; TV: New York Undercover, 1994-98; Players, 1997-98; Law & Order: Special Victims Unit, 2000-; Beyond Tough, co-exec producer & host, 2004; Smoke Out Festival 2003, 2005; "Law & Order", 2005; The Magic 7, 2006; "Law & Order: Spec Victims Unit", 2006; "Outside", 2007; "Burned", 2007; "Law & Order: Special Victims Unit", 2008; The Magic 7, 2008. **Special Achievements:** Lollapalooza, performer, 1991.

IDEWU, OLAWALE OLUSOJI
Physician, educator. **Personal:** Born in Abeokuta Ogun, Nigeria; son of George B Idewu and Rali Idewu; married Linda, Sep 24, 1994; children: Ayodele & Olanrewaju. **Educ:** Blackburn Col, BA, 1959; Heidelberg Univ; Freiburg Univ, W Ger, MD, 1966;Am Bd Otolaryngol, Head & Neck Surg. **Career:** Ear, Nose & Throat Health Ctr, physician/owner, currently; NW Univ, Dept Otolaryngol & Maxillofacial Surg, Chicago, IL, instr. **Orgs:** AMA; Iowa Medical Soc; fel, Am Acad Otolaryngol; fel, Am Col Surgeons; fel, Int Col Surgeons; Am Acad Otolaryngol, Allergy; fel, Rotary Club Int, Harris. **Honors/Awds:** Distinguished Person, Nigerian-Am Forum, 1990. **Special Achievements:** Scholar to study Med, Heidelberg Univ, 1960; Nigerian Folk Tales. **Military Serv:** Air Force res, maj, 1985-91. **Business Phone:** (941)235-2131.

IFALASE, DR. OLUSEGEN (ERLIN BAIN)
Clinical psychologist. **Personal:** Born Sep 25, 1949, Nassau, Bahamas; son of Clifford Bain and Jennie Bain; children: Akilah-Halima, Kwasi Rashidi & Jamila Rashida. **Educ:** Univ Miami, BA, 1980, PhD, 1986. **Career:** Ctr Child Devel, psychologist, 1979-82; Miami Ment Health Ctr, dir substance abuse, 1982-84; Dept Youth & Family Devel, clin psychologist, 1985-92; Ujima Assocs Inc, exec dir, 1986-. **Orgs:** Ment Health Asn Dade Co, 1982-, Chiumba Imani African Dance Co, 1983-, Nat Black Alcoholism Coun, 1984-; pres, S Fla Asn Black Psychologists, 1986-; consult, Informed Families, 1986, Switchboard Miami, 1986; Kuumba Artists Asn, 1986; consult, Family Health Ctr Miami, 1987. **Honors/Awds:** Nat Minority fel grant, 1978-83; Community Service Award, Welfare Mothers Dade, 1982; Appreciation Award Dade Co Sch Bd, 1986; Inner City Task Force, 1986. *

IFILL, GWEN
Journalist. **Personal:** Born Sep 29, 1955, Queens, NY; daughter of O Urcille and Eleanor. **Educ:** Simmons Col, BA, commun, 1977. **Career:** Boston Herald-Am, reporter, 1977-80; Baltimore Evening Sun, reporter, 1981-84; Wash Post, polit reporter, 1984-91; New York Times, Cong & White House corresp, 1991-94; NBC News, Wash DC bur, chief Cong & polit corresp, 1994-99; Wash Week (fmrly Wash Week in Review), panelist & guest moderator, 1992-99, moderator & managing ed, 1999-; Newshour With Jim Lehrer, sr polit corresp, currently; Public Broadcasting Serv, moderator & managing ed, currently. **Orgs:** Nat Assoc Black Journalists; chair, Robert F Kennedy Memorial Jour Awards; bd mem, Univ Md's Philip Merrill Col Jour; bd mem, Harvard Inst Polit; Am Acad Arts & Scis. **Honors/Awds:** Fifteen honorary degrees. **Business Addr:** Senior Correspondent, The NewsHour with Jim Lehrer, PO Box 473, Warsaw, MO 65355, **Business Phone:** (866)678-6397.

IGE, DR. DOROTHY
Educator. **Personal:** Born in Parma, MO; daughter of Rufus and Florida Belle. **Educ:** Southeast Mo State Col, BS, 1971; Cent Mo State Univ, MA, speech commun; 1973; OH State Univ, PhD, speech commun, 1980. **Career:** Bowling Green State Univ; Ind Univ Northwest, Gary, IN, prof commun,1985-, Col Arts & Sci, dean, 2002-08, interim vice chancellor acad affairs, 2004-05. **Orgs:** Fel Am Coun Educ, 2002. **Honors/Awds:** Best Teacher Letter of Recognition, Bowling Green State Univ; IUN Teaching Award, 1991; FACET Award, Ind Univ Northwest, 1994. **Business Addr:** Dean College of Arts & Sciences, Professor of Communication, Indiana University Northwest, Tamarack Hall Room 58, Gary, IN 46408, **Business Phone:** (219)980-6731.

IGE, DR. DOROTHY W K
Educator. **Personal:** Born Apr 18, 1950, Parma, MO; daughter of Rufus A and Florida B Madden; married Adewole A; children: Olufolajimi Wm. **Educ:** Southeast Mo State Univ, BS, speech, 1971; Cent Mo State Univ, MA, speech commn, 1973; Ohio State Univ, PhD, speech educ, 1980. **Career:** Webster Grove Schs, speech & drama teacher, 1971-77; DOD Dependents Schs, drama teacher, 1977-78; Bowling Green State Univ, fac & field exp cord,1980-84; Ind Univ, Dept Commun, fac, dean arts & sci, 2002-, dept chair,currently, interim vice chancellor acad affairs & tenured prof commun, currently. **Orgs:** Pub adv brd, Bowling Green State Univ, 1980-83; assoc, Ohio State Univ Black Alumni, 1980-; Phi Delta Kappa, 1980-; speech commun mem & assoc black caucus pres, legislative coun, Black Opportunities Task Force, 1981-87; State Ohio Brd Redesign Educ Progs, 1982; pres & prog chairperson, Women Investing Together, Human Rels Comn, Bowling Green State Univ, 1984; fel Am Coun Educ, 2002. **Honors/Awds:** Academic Scholarship Certificate, Southeast Mo State Univ, 1970; Third World Peoples Award, Bowling Green State Univ, 1984; IUN Teaching Award,1991; FACET Award, Minority Studies, IUN, 1994. **Special Achievements:** Published over 20 articles & book chapters on communication education for minorities, the Community of Disabilities & women, 1981-87. **Business Addr:** Chair & Dean of Arts & Sciences, Tenured Professor of Communication, Indiana University Northwest, Department of Communication, 3400 Broadway Tamarack 54, Gary, IN 46408, **Business Phone:** (219)980-6731.

IGHNER, BENARD T.
Musician, singer. **Personal:** Born Jan 18, 1945, Houston, TX. **Career:** Almo Publ Co, staff writer; Alamo Music Corp, singer; singer, music arranger, rec engineer; Single: Con Alma, 1967; Never Again, 1967; Album: Rock Requiem, 1971; Nobody Does It Like Me, 1974; Body Heat, 1975; Magic Lady, 1975; Who Is This Bitch Anyway, 1975; Little Dreamer, 1979; The Planet Is Alive,Let It Live, 1984; Sum Serious Blues, 1993. **Special Achievements:** Received $ Gold & Platinum Awards for his classic "Everythinh must Change" in 1974; Appeared in Jack Nicholson film "The Two Jakes" & also in "227" for TV. **Military Serv:** AUS, pfc, 1962-65. **Business Addr:** Singer, Alamo Music Corporation, 1416 N La Brea, Los Angeles, CA 90028.*

IGINLA, JAROME
Hockey player. **Personal:** Born Jul 1, 1977, Alberta;son of Elvis Iginla and Susan Schucard. **Career:** St. Albert Raiders, 1991-93; Kamloops Blazers, Western Hockey League,1993-96; Dallas Stars, Natl Hockey League, prof hockey player, 1995; Calgary Flames, Natl Hockey League, right wing, 1995-02, capt, 2003-. **Honors/Awds:** George Parsons Trophy, 1995; Four Broncos Mem Trophy, 1996; All-Star First Team, Canadian Hockey League,

1996; All-Star First Team, Western Hockey League, 1996; gold medal, World Junior Championships, 1996; All Rookie Team, Natl Hockey League, 1996-97; gold medal, World Championships, 1997; Team Canada Gold Medal, Olympics, 2002; Maurice Richard Award, 2002, 2004; Art Ross Trophy, 2002; Lester B. Pearson Award, 2002; Scurfield Humanitarian Award, 2002; gold medal, Winter Olympics, 2002; World Cup of Hockey Championship, 2004; Memorial Cups; King Clancy Memorial Trophy, 2004. **Business Addr:** Professional Hockey Player, Calgary Flames, Canadian Airlines Saddledome, PO Box 1540 Sta M, Calgary, AB, Canada T2P 3B9, **Business Phone:** (403)777-4646.*

IGLEHART, LLOYD D.
Lawyer. **Personal:** Born Apr 20, 1938, Dallas, TX; son of Lloyd and Helen Waggoner; married Vivian, Jun 20, 1964; children: Lloyd III, Stanley, Llauryn, Robyn. **Educ:** Lincoln Univ MO, BS, 1961; Howard Univ, JD, 1969; Columbia Univ, MPH, 1976. **Career:** Met Life Ins Co, atty, 1969-73; RCA Consumer Electronics, atty, 1973-74; Univ Md Hosp, Baltimore, MD, adminr, 1976-80; Pvt Pract, atty, 1983-. **Orgs:** Nat Health Lawyers Asn; Am Bar Asn; Nat Bar Asn; WA Bar Asn; PA Supreme Ct; Supreme Ct TX; DC Ct Appeals; US Supreme Ct; Phi Alpha Delta Law Fraternity; Alpha Phi Alpha Fraternity; Sigma Delta Tau Legal Fraternity. **Military Serv:** AUS, 1961-63. **Business Addr:** Attorney, 1717 K St NW, Washington, DC 20036, **Business Phone:** (202)508-3671.*

IKE, ALICE DENISE
Lawyer. **Personal:** Born Mar 25, 1955, Washington, DC; daughter of William Howard Jr and Allyre Owens. **Educ:** Univ Md, Baltimore County, BA, 1977, Sch Law, JD, 1981. **Career:** Morgan State Univ, part-time inr, 1984, 1985; Legal Servs Inst, legal intern, 1980-81; Legal Aid Md Inc, staff atty, 1981-82; City Baltimore, Off State's Atty, asst states atty, 1983-85; Univ Md, Baltimore County, part-time inr, 1990-; Dept Health & Ment Hyg, Off Atty Gen, asst atty gen, 1985-. **Orgs:** DC Bar Asn, 1982-; State Md Bar Asn, 1981-; Alliance Black Women Attys, 1982-; Foster Care Review Bd Baltimore City, chap bd, 1986-. **Business Addr:** Assistant Attorney General, Department of Health and Mental Hygiene, Office of the Attorney General, 300 W Preston St Suite 302, Baltimore, MD 21201, **Business Phone:** (410)767-6646.*

ILOANI, GWENDOLYN SMITH
Businessperson. **Personal:** Children: Brandon, Bryan, Corey. **Educ:** Colgate Univ, BA, 1976; Univ of Hartford, MBA. **Career:** Chairman, Pres and CEO of Smith Whiley & Co.; previously Managing Director at Aetna Inc. **Orgs:** Member of the Board of Trustees of Colgate Univ and the Univ of Connecticut Foundation; Treasurer of the Greater Hartford Chapter of Jack and Jill of America; Charter Member of the Marathon Club, Natl Assoc of Securities Professionals, and the Natl Assoc of Investment Companies; member of the Epsilon Omicron Omega Chapter of Alpha Kappa Alpha Sorority; The Farmington Valley Chapter of The Links Incorporated; First Congregational Church of Bloomfield; life member of NAACP. **Honors/Awds:** Chase Medallion from Eastern Connecticut State Univ. **Special Achievements:** Named one of the Eight Remarkable Women of 2008 by the Hartford Business Journal; named one of the "75 Most Powerful Blacks on Wall Street" and one of the "50Most Powerful Black Women in Business" by Black Enterprise Magazine. **Business Addr:** 242 Trumbull St., Hartford, CT 06103-1213, **Business Phone:** (860)548-2513.*

IMA, KAFI. See JETER-JOHNSON, SHEILA ANN.

IMES, MO'NIQUE
Actor. **Personal:** Born Dec 11, 1967, Baltimore, MD; daughter of Steven Jr and Alice; married Mark Jackson, Dec 25, 1997 (divorced); children: Mark Jr & Shalon; married Sidney Hicks, May 20, 2006; children: Jonathan & David. **Career:** Films: 3 Strikes, 2000; Baby Boy, 2001; Two Can Play That Game, 2001; Half Past Dead, 2002; Good Fences, 2003; Soul Plane, 2004; Hair Show, 2004; Shadowboxer, 2005; Domino, 2005; Phat Girlz, 2006; Beerfest, 2006; Farce of the Penguins, voice, 2006; Welcome Home, Roscoe Jenkins, 2008; Precious: Based on the novel push by Sapphire, 2009; Steppin: The Movie, 2009; TVseries: "The Parkers", 1999; Moesha, 1999-2000; "The Parkers", 1999-2004; "The Queens of Comedy", 2001; Platinum Comedy Series: Roasting Shaquille O'Neal, 2002; "Good Fences", 2003; "Heroes of Comedy: Women on Top", 2003; 3rd Annual BET Awards, 2003; Shaq's All Star Comedy Roast 2, 2003; TV in Black: The First Fifty Years, 2004; Pryor Offenses, 2004; "The Bernie MacShow", 2004; "Mo'Nique's Fat Chance", 2005; "Mo's House", 2006; Entertainment Tonight, 2006-08; Mo'Nique's F.A.T. Chance: The Road to Paris, 2007; "Celebrity Family Feud", 2008. **Honors/Awds:** Image Award for Outstanding Actress, Comedy Series, 2001, 2002, 2004,2005; Black Reel Award, 2004. Nominee, BET Comedy Award, 2005. **Special Achievements:** Author of Skinny Women Are Evil, 2003. **Business Addr:** Actor, Big City Artist Management, 6047 Tampa Ave Suite 302, Tarzana, CA 91356, **Business Phone:** (818)705-0411.*

IMHOTEP, AKBAR
Artist. **Personal:** Born Dec 22, 1951, Perry, GA; son of Carrie L Ridley and Robert Hart; children: Akilah, Garvey, Sara-Maat. **Educ:** Georgia Tech, 1977; Paine Col, BA. **Career:** Proposition Theatre, actor, 1977-79; Ctr for Puppetry Arts, puppeteer, 1979-86; Wren's Nest, storyteller residence, 1986-; self-employed storyteller & puppeteer, 1986-; The Arts Mach, puppetry & storytelling, currently. **Orgs:** Kawanda/Kwanzaa Network, founder/exec dir, 1993-94; Metro-Atlanta Kwanzaa Assn, chairman, 1986-92; Assn of Black Storytellers, 1991-; Puppeteers of Am, 1986-; Omega Psi Phi, 1971-; NAACP, 1989-; Nation of Islam, 1975-78. **Honors/Awds:** Metro-Atlanta Kwanzaa Assn, Mzee Olutunji Award, 1992; WACP, Kwumba Award, 1990. **Special Achievements:** Performances throughout the southeastern US, 1989-; performances in three consecutive NBAF, 1988, 1990, 1992; performances in Jazz and Heritage Festival, 1994; published three volumes of poetry, 1982, 1988, 1994. **Business Addr:** Storyteller, Actor, Poet, The Arts Mach, PO Box 11386, Atlanta, GA 30303, **Business Phone:** (404)688-3376.*

INCE, HAROLD S.
Dentist. **Personal:** Born Jan 7, 1930, Brooklyn; married Mary Ann Jackson; children: Nancy, Harold Jr. **Educ:** BS, 1951; DDS, 1956. **Career:** Pvt pract, dentist, currently. **Orgs:** Am Dent Asn; Conn Dent Asn; New Haven Dent Asn; First New Haven Nat Bank; Urban League; Bias Stanley Fund; Alpha Phi Alpha. **Military Serv:** USAF, capt, 1956-58. **Business Addr:** Dentist, General Dentistry, 226 Dixwell Ave Suite 206, PO Box 3021, New Haven, CT 06511-3456, **Business Phone:** (203)776-9391.*

INGRAM, EDITH J.
Judge, teacher. **Personal:** Born Jan 16, 1942, Sparta, GA; divorced. **Educ:** Ft Valley State Col, BS, elem educ, 1963. **Career:** Moore Elem Sch, Griffin, GA, teacher, 1963-67; Hancock Cent Elem, Sparta, GA, teacher, 1967-68; Hancock County Probate Ct, judge, 1968-. **Orgs:** Macedonia Baptist Church Choir, 1951-; Hancock County Womens Club, 1964-; State Nat & Int Asn Probate Judges, 1969; comt chairwoman, Ga Coalition Black Women, 1980-; Ga Gen Assembly. **Honors/Awds:** Achievement Award, Nat Asn Advan Colored People, 1969; Cert of Merit, Booker T, Wash, 1973; Outstanding Citizen's, Fulton County, 1978; Outstanding Courage Southern Polit Arena, Atlanta Br Nat Asn Advan Colored People, 1979. **Business Addr:** Judge, Hancock County Probate Court, Courthouse Sq, Sparta, GA 31087.*

INGRAM, GAREY
Baseball player, athletic coach. **Personal:** Born Jul 25, 1970, Columbus, GA. **Career:** Baseball player (retired), baseball coach: Los Angeles Dodgers, outfielder, 1994-97; Columbus Catfish, hitting coach; Great lakes loons, hitting coach, 2007-08; Connecticut Defenders, hitting coach, currently. *

INGRAM, GREGORY LAMONT
Artist. **Personal:** Born Apr 10, 1961, Greensboro, NC; son of Bradley and Mary L. **Educ:** New York Dept Cult Affairs, cert, 1985. **Career:** New York Housing Asn, artist consult, 1994-95; Harmony Visions Gallery, dir, 1994; GLI Graphics & Consults, pres, 1995-. **Orgs:** Consult, Rush Philanthropic Arts Found, 1994-98; New York Greenthumb Proj, Brooklyn, NY; vol, Comm Bd 5 Brooklyn NY, 1996-99; St Paul Comm Chap, 1997; Americorps, Black Chap Educ, 1997-99; vol, Brooklyn Parks, 1997-98; United Comm Ctrs' Residency; Americorps: Blacks Chap Educ. **Honors/Awds:** Citizens Week Awards. **Home Addr:** 485 Fountain Ave, Brooklyn, NY 11208. **Business Addr:** Artist, President, GLI Graphics & Consultants, 485 Fountain Ave Apt 1E, Brooklyn, NY 11208, **Business Phone:** (347)405-6177.

INGRAM, JAMES
Songwriter, musician. **Personal:** Born Feb 16, 1956, Akron, OH; married Debbie; children: 6. **Career:** Musician, songwriter, currently; Albums: "Yah Mo Be There", 1983; "It's Your Night", 1983; Never Felt So Good, 1988; It's Real, 1989; The Power of Great Music, 1991; Always You, 1993; Forever More: The Best of James Ingram, 1999; Singles: Just Once, 1981; One Hundred Ways, 1981; Baby, Come to Me, 1982; How Do You Keep the Music Playing, 1983; "She Loves Me (The Best That I Can Be)", 1984; There's No Easy Way,1984; What About Me, 1984; "Always", 1986; "Never Felt So Good", 1986; "Somewhere Out There", 1987; "Better Way", 1987; "A Natural Man (You Make Me Feel Like)", 1989; "It's Real", 1989; "I Wanna Come Back", 1989; "I Don't Have The Heart", 1990; "Secret Garden", 1990; "Get Ready", 1991; "When Was The Last Time The Music Made You Cry?", 1991; "Where Did My Heart Go", 1991; "The Day I Fall In Love", 1994. **Special Achievements:** First artist in the history of pop music to win a Grammy Award without having released his own album; guest vocalist, Michael McDonald's In the Spirit holiday album, 2001; His 1994 composition "The Day I Fell in Love", from the movie Beethoven's Second (on which he dueted with Dolly Parton)was nominated for an Oscar. **Business Addr:** Musician.

INGRAM, KEVIN
Executive. **Personal:** Born in Philadelphia, PA. **Educ:** Mass Inst Technol, BChE, 1980; Stanford Univ, Western Electric Res Scholar Eng; Stanford Univ Grad Sch Bus. **Career:** Goldman Sachs & Co, vpres, 1988; Lehman Brothers, assoc; Deutsche Morgan Grenfell, managing dir. **Special Achievements:** Listed as one of 25 "Hottest Blacks on Wall Street," Black Enterprise, 1992. *

INGRAM, DR. LAVERNE
Physician. **Personal:** Born Mar 1, 1955, Lawrenceville, VA; daughter of Lydia House and James; married Robert Dean. **Educ:** Va Union Univ, Richmond, Va, BS, biol, 1977; Harvard Univ, Cambridge, MA, attended 1975; Va Commonwealth Univ, Richmond, VA, attended 1978; Eastern Va Med Sch, Norfolk, VA, MD, 1981. **Career:** Med Col Va, Richmond, VA, lab asst, 1972-73, lab specialist, 1973-78; Howard Univ Hosp, Wash, DC, med intern, 1981-82; radiol res, 1982-85; US Navy, Norfolk, VA, head, radio dept, 1985-87; US Navy, Portsmouth, VA, staff radiologist, 1987-90; Univ Tex Health Sci Ctr, Houston, TX, staff radiol, 1990-, chief mammography, currently; LBJ Hosp, interim chief diag imaging serv, currently. **Orgs:** Life mem, Nat Naval Officers Asn; Soc Aid Sickle Cell Anemia; Big Brother Big Sister, 1986-; Nat Med Asn; vice chair, Am Red Cross, NE Houston, 1998; Alpha Kappa Alpha, Am Roentgen Ray Soc. **Honors/Awds:** Distinguished Service Award, Nat Naval Officers Asn, 1988; Deans Excellence Award, UTHSC, 1997-98, 2000-01. **Military Serv:** USN, lt, comdr, 1985-90, USNR, comdr, 1992-; Navy Commendation, 1987; Certificate of Appreciation, 1988, 1989; Navy Achievement Award, 1990. **Business Addr:** Interim Chief of Diagnostic Imaging Services & Assistant Professor, University of Texas, Department of Radiology, 5656 Kelley St, Houston, TX 77026, **Business Phone:** (713)566-5440.

INGRAM, PHILLIP M
Computer executive. **Personal:** Born Nov 14, 1945, Detroit, MI; son of Henry and Marion Martin Lewis; divorced; children: Marc J Ingram. **Educ:** Wayne State Univ, Detroit, MI, BFA, indust design, 1971, MBA, 1978. **Career:** Gen Motors Eng, Warren, MI, proj engr, 1964-78; Am Motors Corp, Detroit, MI, prin engr, 1978-79; Systemation Corp, Detroit, MI, pres, 1979-80; Detroit Inst Technol, Detroit, MI, assoc prof, 1980-81; Gen Automation, Detroit, MI, dist sales mgr, 1980-82; The Comput Group Inc, Novi, MI, pres & founder, 1982-. **Orgs:** Engineering Soc Detroit, 1975. **Honors/Awds:** Reviewer, Nat Sci Found Cause Grant Progs, 1980. **Business Addr:** President, Founder, The Computer Group Inc, 41252 Vincenti Ct, Novi, MI 48375, **Business Phone:** (248)888-6900.*

INGRAM, STEPHEN ANTHONY
Football player. **Personal:** Born May 8, 1971, Cheverly, MD; married Robyn. **Educ:** Univ Md, BS, criminal justice. **Career:** Tampa Bay Buccaneers, tackle & guard, 1995; Jacksonville Jaguars, 1999.

INGRAM, VALERIE J.
Television journalist, television producer. **Personal:** Born Dec 5, 1959, Chicago, IL; daughter of Bettie J Rushing Ingram and Archie R Ingram. **Educ:** Loyola Univ, Chicago, IL, 1990; Columbia Col, Chicago, Il, BA, radio, writing, 1979. **Career:** WUSN Radio US99, Chicago, IL, senior sales assistant, 1984-85; CBS Radio Network, Chicago, IL, office manager, 1985-87; WBBM-AM Radio, Chicago, IL, associate producer, 1987-; WFLA, reporter, currently. **Orgs:** Member, radio ad hoc committee, International Lutheran Layman's League, 1990-; mem, National Association of Black Journalists, 1990-; mem, Lutheran Women's Missionary League, 1989-; secretary, Minority Employees Association, CBS Inc, 1985-90; Leader, Gospel Choir, 1989-, youth group officer, St Paul Lutheran Church Austin, 1986-88; Sunday school teacher, HS, 1988-90. **Honors/Awds:** Outstanding Volunteer, Aid Association for Lutherans Branch #385, 1989. **Business Addr:** Reporter, WFLA, 4585 140th Ave N, Clearwater, FL 33760.*

INGRAM, WILLIAM B.
Consultant, educator, president (organization). **Personal:** Born May 5, 1935, Lillesville, NC; married Dora Rebecca Plowden (deceased); children: Katrina, Eric & Elaine. **Educ:** Lincoln Univ, BA, 1961; Univ Southern Calif, MA, pub admin, 1977. **Career:** D'Lora's Boys Home, co-owner, 1968-73; La County Mus, chief mus operations, 1970-73; Riverside City Col, training consult, 1977-; B&D Financial Serv, owner, 1980-; Orange County Probation, training consult, 1981-; Supervising Dep Probations Officer, 1961-87; teacher, Moreno Valley Sch, 1984. **Orgs:** Vpres, Calif Sch Bd Asn, 1979-; pres, Calif Coalition Black Bd Mems, 1982; pres, Nat Caucus Black Bd Mems, 1982-84; dir, Perris Valley Martin Luther King Found, 1983-85; Calif Correction, Probation & Parole Comt, 1984-85; pres-elect, Riverside Co School Bd Asn, 1985-86; bd dirs, Coalition Calif Black Bd Mems; comnr, Riverside County Juvenile Justice; pres, Calif Sch Bd Asn, 1989; vpres, Nat Sch Bd Asn; bd dir, Nat Sch Bd Asn, 1991-94; pres, Nat Sch Bd Asn, 1997-98. **Honors/Awds:** Community Service Award, Los Angeles Bd Supervisors, 1980; Outstanding Bd Mem, Nat School Bd Asn, 1983; Proclamation Riverside Bd Supervisors, Blacksupporter/Achievement, 1984. **Military Serv:** AUS, corpl 1953-56.

INGRAM-SAMPSON, BARBARA JO
Manager. **Personal:** Born Apr 25, 1962, Omaha, NE; daughter of Robert Lewis and Lillian Reech Ingram; married Aaron L, Sep 14, 1996; children: Alyse Nicole. **Educ:** Iowa State Univ, BA, archit, 1985; Metrop Tech Inst; Univ Calif Los Angeles, archit, 1991. **Career:** Archit freelance consult, 1991-92; Harold Williams Assoc, Design Team, 1992-93; Am Stores Properties Inc, CADD planner, 1993-95; Valentine Crane Brunjes Onyon Architects, proj coordr, 1995-. **Orgs:** Chair mem, youth comt counsr, Calvary Baptist Church, 1993-, Sr High, youth mentor, 1996; archit design

studio juror, Univ Utah, 1995-. **Honors/Awds:** Dean Award, Alpha Chi Omega, Grad Sch Archit & Planning, Univ Calif Los Angeles, 1991; SNW Thesis Award, 1991. **Special Achievements:** Created water color, "Dod", 1984; UCLA, Grad School of Architecture and Planning, The Next Generation Thesis Exhibit, 1991, The Architectural Forum, developer, organizer, 1990, Women in Environmental Design Conference, San Francisco, representative, 1991. **Business Addr:** Project Coordinator, Valentiner Crane Brunjes Onyon Architects, 524 S 600 E, Salt Lake City, UT 84102, **Business Phone:** (801)575-8800.

INGRUM, ADRIENNE G
Publishing executive. **Personal:** Born Mar 21, 1954, St Louis, MO; daughter of Clister Jack and Leontine Yvonne Pulliam; married Arn Reginald Ashwood, May 24, 1977 (divorced 1996). **Educ:** Georgetown Univ, Wash, DC, BS, intl economics. **Career:** Harvard Univ, Boston, MA, staff asst, 1977-79; Grosset & Dunlap, New York, NY, assoc editor, 1980-82; Putnam Berkley Group, New York, NY, vpres & exec editor, 1982-90; Waldenbooks, Stamford, CT, publ & vpres, Longmeadow Press, 1990-94; Crown Publishers, vpres & dir of trade paperback publishing, 1994-96; publ, HarperCollins Publishers, currently. **Orgs:** Women's Media Group; Go On Girl! Book Club. **Home Addr:** 43 St Nicholas Place, New York, NY 10031, **Home Phone:** (212)283-6466. **Business Addr:** Publisher, HarperCollins Publishers, 10 E 53rd St, New York, NY 10022, **Business Phone:** (212)207-7000.

INNIS, ROY EMILE ALFREDO
Association executive. **Personal:** Born Jun 6, 1934, St Croix, VI; son of Alexander Innis and Georgianna Thomas Innis; married Doris Funnye; children: Roy (deceased), Alexander (deceased), Cedric, Patricia, Corinne, Kwame, Niger, Kimathi & Mugabe. **Educ:** City Col NY, 1952-56. **Career:** Vick Chem Co, res chemist, 1958-63; Montefiore Hosp, res chemist, 1963-67; Harlem Commonwealth Coun, dir, 1967-68; Metrop Applied Res Ctr New York, res fel, 1967; Cong Racial Equality, assoc dir, 1968, nat dir, 1968-81, nat chmn, 1981-, chief exec officer, currently. **Orgs:** Mem bd, New York Urban Coalition, Haryou Act, Harlem Commonwealth Coun, exec dir; Coalition Fairness Africa; Hudson Inst; Daemen Col; Am Alliance Better Sch; Landmark Legal Found; Nat Ethnic Coalition Orgn; Nat Rifle Asn; African Am Fund Higher Educ; assoc mem Fraternal Order Police. **Military Serv:** AUS, sgt, 2 Yrs. **Home Addr:** 800 Riverside Dr, New York, NY 10032. **Business Addr:** National Chairman, Chief Executive Officer, Congress of Racial Equality, 817 Broadway Fl 3, New York, NY 10003, **Business Phone:** (212)598-4000.

IONE, CAROLE
Clergy, psychotherapist. **Personal:** Born May 28, 1937, Washington, DC; daughter of Hylan Garnet Lewis and Leighla Whipper; married Salvatore J Bovoso, Jan 1, 1971 (divorced 1982); children: Alessandro, Santiago & Antonio. **Educ:** Bennington Col, 1959; Helix Training Prog, psychother & the Healing Arts, 1987; Chinese Healing Arts Ctr, Qi Gong Therapist, 1991; Nat Guild Hypnotists, Advan Clin Hypnotherapist, 1994. **Career:** Renaissance Poets Series, co-founder, 1960; Renaissance House, Inc, artistic dir, 1960; Dream, J & Notebook Workshops, instr, 1980-; Essence Mag, contrib editor, 1980-82; Manhatten Theatre Club, dir, writers performance, 1980-82; Women's Mysteries, dir, 1987-; Live Letters, artistic dir, 1974-; The Pauline Oliveros Found, founder, 1985-, vpres, co-artistic dir; Deep Listening Inst, artistic dir, currently. **Orgs:** Poets & Writers, Inc, 1979-; Nat Writers Union, 1988-; The Inl Womens Writing Guild, 1988-; The Author's Guild, Inc, 1991-. **Honors/Awds:** New York State Council on the Arts and Poets and Writers, Inc, for Live Letters Presentation 1979-; Rockefeller Foundation & Nat Endowment for the Arts, for Njinga, The Queen-King, a play w/music and pageantry, 1987-91; South Carolina Comm for the Humanities, for A Diary of Reconstruction, 1985; Fellowships to the Macdowell Colony, Yaddo, Edward; Albee Foundation, The Writers Room. **Special Achievements:** Scripts: Njinga the Queen-King; A Diary of Reconstruction; Mirage, A Friend; New York City, Evidence; Script devel for Rizzoli Productions, NYC; Publications: This is a Dream, Mom Press, 2000; Pride of Family, 4 generations of Amer Women of Color, Summit Books, 1991, Avon Books, 1992; The Coffee Table Lover, The Country Press, 1973; Unsealed Lips, Capra Press, 1990; Piramada Negra, The Country Press, 1973, Live Letters, Press, 1991; Contemporary Literary Criticism, 1989; Fiction, Reviews and Articles in: The Village Voice, New Dawn, Oui, Ms American Film Ambassador, Working Women; Oggi; Vogue; Christian Science; Monitor; Essence; Arcadie; Revue Literature; Readings and Presentations: Skidmore College, New School for Social Research, Teachers and Writers Collaborative, City College of New York, Columbia Green Comm Coll, Seattle Douglass-The Truth Library, The College of Charleston, Avery Institute, The New York Public Library, The Actors Institute, Manhattan Theatre Club, Natl Public Radio, CBS Nightwatch, The Open Center, SUNY, New Paltz, Omega Institute, Esalen Institute, New York Geneological Society, Shomburg Center, NY Public Library and Others. **Home Addr:** 156 Hunter St, Kingston, NY 12401, **Home Phone:** (914)339-5776. **Business Addr:** Artistic Director, Deep Listening Institute, 77 Cornell St, Kingston, NY 12401, **Business Phone:** (845)338-5984.

IRBY, GALVEN
Government official. **Personal:** Born Sep 29, 1921, Laurens, SC; son of Henry D and Grace L; married Delores Virginia Odden, Dec 17, 1957; children: Barbara J, Grace M, Kelley R Garrett, Vickie L Strickland, Sandra M Garrett, Galven C, Craig R. **Educ:** Youngstown Univ, attended 1948; Howard Univ, LLB, 1952. **Career:** Government official (retired); Republic Iron & Steel Mills & Fabrication, 1940-49; US Postal Serv, part time postal clerk, 1950-63; State Ore, dept Employ Security, claims supvr, 1954-63; Veterans Admin, legal disability rating supt, 1972-86. **Orgs:** bd controls, Pacific Lutheran Univ; bd controls, adv, Concordia Col, 1973-75; dept admis, exec & nat bd, Am Lutheran, 1978-79; sre, N Pacific Dist, Portland Conf, 1965-67; Alpha Phi Alpha Fraternity; bd controls, Pacific Lutheran Univ, 1988-94; Alpha Phi Alpha & Nat Asn Advan Colored People Sch Mentoring Project, 1989-; numerous others. **Honors/Awds:** Public Service Award, US Veterans Admin, 1969; Superior Performance Award, 1975; Public Appreciation Award, 1975; NAT Commanders Award, Disabled Am Veterans, 1982. **Military Serv:** USY, sgt, 1942-45; 31 months of Overseas duty; Bronze Star; Good Conduct Award. *

IRBY, MARY
Automotive executive. **Personal:** Born Oct 19, 1944, Columbus, MS; daughter of Robert and Lettie B Swopes; divorced; children: Cassandra Delk, Robert Smallwood & Joseph Smallwood. **Educ:** Bowling Green State Univ, BLS, 1989; Cent Mich Univ. **Career:** Gen Motors Corp, spokeswoman, dir commun, 1968-. **Orgs:** Second vpres, Girl Scouts USA, 1987-89; bd mem, Leadership Saginaw Alumni, 1994-; bd mem, Reuben Daniels Found, 1994-; bd mem, Big Brothers Big Sisters, 1994-; Pub Rel SocAm White Pines Chap, 1994-; Saginaw Community Found, Distribution Comn, 1995; Alpha Kappa Alpha Sorority. **Business Addr:** Director Communications, General Motors Corporation, Metal Fabricating Division, 1450 Stephenson Hwy, Troy, MI 48007-7025, **Business Phone:** (248)696-2054.

IRELAND, RODERICK LOUIS
Supreme court justice. **Personal:** Born Dec 3, 1944, Springfield, MA; married; children: Helen Elizabeth & Michael Alexander. **Educ:** Lincoln Univ, BA, 1966; Columbia Univ Law Sch, JD, 1969; Harvard Law Sch, LLM, 1975, N eastern Univ, PhD, Law, Policy & Soc Prog, 1998. **Career:** Harvard Ctr Law & Educ, staff atty, 1970-71; Roxbury Defenders Comt, chief atty, dep & exec dir, 1971-73; Harvard Law Sch, teaching fel, 1972-78, adj fac, 1978-; Mass Civil Serv Comn, hearing officer, 1973-75; Roxbury Dist Ct Clin, legal coun, 1974-77; Burnham, Stern & Shapiro, assoc, 1975; Mass Exec Off Admin & Fin, asst secy & chief legal coun, 1975-77; Boston Juvenile Ct, judge, 1977-90; Bd Appeal Motor Vehicle Liability Policies & Bonds, chmn, 1977; Col Criminal Justice, N eastern Univ, adj fac, 1978-; Mass Appeals Court, judge, 1990-97; Judicial Youth Corps, adv & teacher, 1990-; Mass Supreme Judicial Ct, justice, 1997-; New York Univ Law Sch, fac mem Appellate Judges Sem, 2001-. **Orgs:** Bd dirs, Columbia Law Sch Alumni Asn; Mass Bar Asn; Boston Bar Asn; ABA; Mass Black Lawyers Asn; NY Bar Asn Bd Dirs Proj Aim; bd dirs, First Inc; bd dirs, Roxbury YMCA; bd dirs, Mass Minority Coun Alcoholism; Omega Psi Phi; Lincoln Alumni. **Honors/Awds:** St. Thomas More Award, Boston Col Law Sch; Recipient, 10 Outstanding young leaders of Boston Award, Boston Jaycees, 1979; 10 Outstanding Men of America Award, US Jaycees, 1980; Boston Covenant Peace Prize, 1982; Haskell Cohn Distinguished Judicial Service Award, Boston Bar Asn; 1990; Judicial Excellence Award, Mass Judges Conference, 1996; The Judicial Excellence Award, Mass Bar Asn, Lawyers Weekly Newspaper, 2001; several honorary Doctor of Law degrees; Friend of Justice Award; Massachusetts Bar Found; 2008. **Special Achievements:** First African American justice On Massachusetts Supreme Court in its over three hundred year history; author of Massachusetts Juvenile Law, 2d edition, published by West Publishing, 2006. **Business Addr:** Justice, Supreme Judicial Court, Massachusetts Judicial Branch, 1 Pemberton Square Suite 2500, John Adams Courthouse, Boston, MA 02108-3107, **Business Phone:** (617)557-1000.

IRMAGEAN, U.
Artist. **Personal:** Born Apr 9, 1947, Detroit, MI; daughter of Theodore Curry and Mamie Lee Sago Curry; divorced; children: Sundjata T Kone. **Educ:** Wayne State Univ Monteith Col, attended 1966; Grove Str Col, AA, 1974; CA Col Arts & Crafts, BFA, 1976. **Career:** Isabelle Percy W Gallery CA Col Arts & Crafts Oakland, exhibit, 1979; NY Carlsberg Glyptotek Mus Copenhagen Denmark, rep, 1980; Los Medanos Col Pittsburg, CA, exhibit artist, 1980; Berkeley Art Ctr CA, exhibit, 1981; Galerie Franz Mehring Berlin, Germany, exhibit, 1981; SF Mus Modern Art, exhibit, 1981; Ctr Visual Arts Oakland CA, exhibit, 1985; Spanish Speaking Citizens Found, Oakland, CA, guest art instr, 1989; E Oakland YouthDevelop Ctr, Oakland, CA, mural instr, 1989; City Sites, CA Col Arts &Crafts, artist mentor, 1989; Berkeley Art Ctr, exhibitor, 1988; San Francisco State Univ, exhibitor, 1989; Koncepts Cult Gallery, Oakland, CA, art instr, 1989; Ebony Mus, Oakland, CA, exhibitor coord, 1989-90; Hatley Martin Gallery, CA, exhibit, 1990; Capp St Gallery, San Francisco, CA, pubart installation, 1991; Ebony Mus, cur, 1994-95. **Orgs:** Juror Vida Gallery SF, CA 1981; coordr, US participation 11 Bienal del Grabado De Am Maracaibo, Venezuela 1982; juror, Festival at the lake, Craft/Art Market, Oakland, CA, 1989; Berkeley Juneteenth Asn Inc, 1992; Art & Creative Writing Youth Competition Prog, Golden State Life Ins. **Honors/Awds:** Amer Artist Today in Black & White Vol 11 1980 author Dr H L Williams; exhibit Dept De Bellas Artes Guadaljara, Mexico 1982; exhibit Brockman Gallery Prod LA, CA 1982; Hon mem Sigma Gamma Rho Sor, 1986; Daniel Mendelowitz "A Guide to Drawing" 3rd ed Holt Rinehart and Winston 1982, 4th ed revised by Duane Wakeham 1988; Outstanding Women of the Twentieth Century, Sigma Gamma Rho Sorority, 1986; Certificate of Appreciation, St Augustine's Church, 1988; feature, The Aurora, 1987, Sigma Gamma Rho Sorority, 1987; The CA Art Review, 2nd edition Amer Reference, Inc, 1988; Amer artist, 2nd edition, References, 1989; 1st Place, Best of Show, Ebony Museum, Expo 89-90, 1990; Black Scholar, vol 20, no 3 & 4, Black World Foundation (cover), 1990; Feature, Eugene White's Kujionia Magazine, 1990. **Special Achievements:** Selected publications: Anthology of Contemporary African-American Women Artists, 1992, A Guide to Drawing, 1993, Poetry: An American Heritage, 1993; Smell This 2, UC Berkeley, 1991; exhibitions: Prague, Czechoslovakia, Art of Ecology: Recycling the Collective Spirit, 1991, Richmond Art Center, Looking Out Looking In, 1992, Bomani Gallery, 1992; Voices of the Dream; African American Women Speak, Venice Johnson, Chronicle Books. **Business Addr:** Artist, 832 37th Ave, Berkeley, CA 94601.

IROGBE, KEMA
Educator, college administrator. **Personal:** Born Mar 30, 1956, EBU, Nigeria; son of Onwuanukwu and Eunice Iyanwa; married Helen Irogbe, Feb 15, 1993; children: Kumama. **Educ:** Instituto Allende, Mexico, BA, 1978; Jackson State Univ, BA, 1980, MPPA, 1982; Atlanta Univ, PhD, 1987. **Career:** Ga Southern Univ, asst prof, 1990-91; Bridgewater State Univ, instr, 1987-90; Curry Col, adj prof, 1988-90; SC State Univ, adj prof, 1993-; Claflin Univ, int prog, prof & dir, 1991-. **Orgs:** Campus coordr, Pi Sigma Alpha; campus coordr, Pi Gmama Mu; Am Soc Public Admin; Nat Conf Black Political Scientists; Am Politicial Sci Asn; dir, Afrofest. **Honors/Awds:** Faculty of the Year, Claflin Col, 1996; NEH Summer Fellowship, Harvard Univ, 1995; MIT Summer Fellowship, MIT, 1990. **Special Achievements:** Author: The Roots of US Foreign Policy Toward Apartheid South Africa, 1969-85, published by The Edwin Mellen Press, NY, 1997; contributor, The Alexis de Tocqueville Tour: Exploring Democracy in America, published by C-Span, 1997. **Home Addr:** 1600 Columbia Rd Apt E-3, Orangeburg, SC 29115. **Business Addr:** Professor, Director, Claflin University, International Program, Rm 6 Trustee Hall 400 Magnolia St, Orangeburg, SC 29115-9970, **Business Phone:** (803)535-5277.

IRONS, EDWARD D.
Educator, college administrator. **Personal:** Born Aug 29, 1923, Hulbert, OK. **Educ:** Wilburforce Univ, BS bus admin; Univ Minn, MA, hosp admin, 1951; HarvardUniv, PhD. **Career:** Riverside Nat Bank, Houston, Tex, partner, 1964, prin organizer, pres; Fla A&M Univ, fac; Howard Univs bus sch, founding dean; Atlanta Univ ctr, Altanta, GA, prof; City Wash, DC, Off Banking & Financial Inst DC, supt; Irons & Assocs, pres; Clark-Atlanta Univ Sch Bus Admin, econ prof, dean, finance prof, currently; consolidated State Inst, adminr; Investment Survey Div, Agency Int Develop, chief; Florida A&M Univ, asst bus mgr. **Orgs:** Atlanta Life Ins Corp; Lincoln Nat Life Corp; mem, BE Bd Economists. **Business Addr:** Dean, Clark Atlanta University, School of Business Administration, 200A Wright Hall, Atlanta, GA 30314, **Business Phone:** (404)880-8420.

IRONS, HON. PAULETTE R
Judge. **Personal:** Born Jun 19, 1953; married Alvin L Irons; children: Marseah & Paul. **Educ:** Loyola Univ, BBA; Tulane Univ, JD. **Career:** Systs engr, 1976-83; construction estimator, 1984-92; atty, small bus consult, 1992-93; Paulette Irons Law Firm, 1992-; La State, Dist 95, rep, 1992-94; La State Dist 4, sen, 1994-2004; Civil Dist Ct Parish Orleans, Judge, currently. **Orgs:** La Women's Caucus; La Legis Black Caucus; Women's Network Nat Conf State Legislatures; League Women's Voters; Am Asn Univ Women; Nat Order Black Elected Legislators; sen vice chair, La Legis Women's Caucus; Pub Interest Law Found; Tulane Law Women; Parent-Teacher Orgn; La League Women Voters; New Orleans Oncol Nurses Breast Cancer Prevention, La Initiative Teen Pregnancy Prev; New Orleans Area Literacy Coalition. **Honors/Awds:** Alliance for Good Government, Legislator of the Year, 1995; Women For a Better Louisiana. **Business Addr:** Judge, Civil District Court for the Parish of Orleans, 421 Loyola Ave Rm 200 C, New Orleans, LA 70112.

IRONS, SANDRA JEAN
Educator. **Personal:** Born Jul 17, 1940, Middlesboro, KY; daughter of Rosa Green Carr (deceased) and Roy Carr (deceased); married Lethenius Irons (divorced 1978). **Educ:** Ky State Univ, Frankford, KY, BS, 1960; Purdue Univ, W Lafayette, MAT, 1965; Indiana Univ, Gary, IN, MS30. **Career:** State Ohio Dept Pub Welfare, Dayton, OH, caseworker, 1960-61; Gary Community Sch Corp, Gary, IN, teacher, 1961-71; Gary Teachers Union, Gary, IN, pres, 1971-. **Orgs:** Vpres, Am Fedn Teachers, 1974; sec, Indiana Fed Teachers, 1996; pres, NW Ind Fedn Labor, 1995-97; treas, NW Ind Coun Teachers Unions, 1984; New Revelation Baptist Church; pres, Ment Health Asn, Lake County, 1984-88, 1996. **Honors/Awds:** Fel, Nat Sci Found, 1961-65; Gary Comn on the Status of Women, 1973-75; Beirne Award, 2002. **Business Addr:** President, Gary Teachers Union, 1401 Virginia St, Local No 4 AFT, Gary, IN 46407.*

IRVIN, CHARLES LESLIE
Lawyer. **Personal:** Born Mar 2, 1935, Corpus Christi, TX; son of Joseph and Louise; married Shirley Jean Smith; children: Kimberley Antoinette, Jonathan Charles. **Educ:** Tex Southern Univ, BA & LLB, 1964; Cornell Univ, exec develop course, attended 1984; Wharton Sch Bus, financial course, attended 1985. **Career:** US Dept Labor Kans City, MO, atty, 1964-67; US Dept Labor Chicago, atty, 1967-73; Texaco Inc, sr atty; div atty Midland, TX, 1988-89; atty, Denver, CO, 1989-90, regional coun, 1990; managing atty, admin, White Plains, NY; atty, pvt prac, currently. **Orgs:** TX & CO Bars Asn, 1964-; US Supreme Ct; 9th & 5th Cir Ct Appeals, TX Bar Found. **Military Serv:** AUS, sergeant, E-5 1955-58. **Business Addr:** Attorney, 6156 Andershire Dr, Conroe, TX 77304, **Business Phone:** (936)441-6158.*

IRVIN, DENNIS J.
President (organization), chief executive officer. **Career:** Highland Community Bank, pres & chief exec officer, currently. **Orgs:** Nat Bankers Asn. **Business Addr:** President, Chief Executive Officer, Highland Community Bank, 1701 W 87th St, Chicago, IL 60620, **Business Phone:** (773)881-6800.*

IRVIN, KEN
Football player. **Personal:** Born Jul 11, 1972, Rome, GA. **Educ:** Univ Memphis. **Career:** Football player (retired); Buffalo Bills, defensive back, 1995-2001; New Orleans Saints, defensive back, 2002; Minn Vikings, defensive back, 2003-05.

IRVIN, MICHAEL JEROME
Football player, entertainer. **Personal:** Born Mar 5, 1966, Fort Lauderdale, FL; son of Walter and Pearl; children (previous marriage): Myesha Beyonca; married Sandi Harrell, Jan 1, 1990; children: Chelsea, Michael & Elijah. **Educ:** Univ Miami, BA, bus mgt, 1988. **Career:** Football player (retired), analyst; Dallas Cowboys, wide receiver, 1988-2000; ESPN, Nat Football League, analyst. **Honors/Awds:** NFL Alumni, Wide Receiver of the Year, 1991; Pro Bowl, 1991, 1992, 1993, 1994, 1995; Inducted Pro Football Hall of Fame, 2005; Professional Football Hall of Fame, 2007; Super Bowl champion XXVII, XXVIII, XXX. **Special Achievements:** Film Appearances: The Year of the Yao, 2004; The Longest Yard, 2005; The Comebacks, 2007.

IRVIN, MILTON M
Executive. **Personal:** Born in East Orange, NJ. **Educ:** US Merchant Marine Acad; Univ Penn, Wharton Sch Bus & Finance, MBA. **Career:** Salomon Brothers Inc, trader, 1977, vpres, 1979, dir, sr mgr, 1992-99; Paine Webber, managing dir, 1988-90; Chase Manhattan Bank, lending officer; UBS, Dept Grad training Fixed Income, Rates & Currency, managing dir & global head. **Orgs:** Bd dir, Wharton Univ Penn; founder & past bd mem, Exec Leadership Coun; bd dir, Harlem Sch Arts; NJ Bd Recreation; adv comt, Pension Benefit Guaranty Corp. **Special Achievements:** Listed as one of 25 "Hottest Blacks on Wall Street," Black Enterprise, 1992. **Business Addr:** Advisory Board Member, The Wharton School of University of Pennsylvania, 3451 Walnut St, Philadelphia, PA 19104, **Business Phone:** (215)898-5000.*

IRVIN, MONFORD MERRILL
Baseball player, executive. **Personal:** Born Feb 25, 1919, Haleburg, AL; son of Cupid Alexander and Mary Eliza Henderson; married Dee; children: Pamela Irvin Fields & Patti Irvin Gordon. **Educ:** Lincoln Univ, attended 1942. **Career:** Baseball player (retired), coach; Negro League, Newark Eagles, 1937-48; Cuban Winter League, baseball player; NY Giants, baseball player, 1949-55; Chicago Cubs, baseball player, 1956; NY Mets, scout, 1967-68; Off Baseball Comnr, spec asst to the comnr, 1968-84; Diversified Capital Corp, vpres. **Orgs:** Comt Baseball Veterans, Nat Baseball Hall Fame. **Honors/Awds:** Negro League East All-Star team, 1941, 1946-48; Mexican League MVP, 1942; Puerto Rican League MVP, 1945-46; Baseball Hall of Fame, 1973; Lincoln University Alumni Hall of Fame, 1988. **Special Achievements:** One of the first black players to be signed after baseball's color line was broken by Jackie Robinson in 1947; first Negro League Player to lead Major League Baseball in RBI with 121, 1951; featured in television shows & films including: "Baseball", 1994; "The Top 5 Reasons You Can't Blame", 2005; "War Stories with Oliver North", 2006. **Military Serv:** Buck sgt 1313 GS Engineers - ETO, 1943-45. **Home Addr:** 11 Douglas Ct S, Homosassa, FL 34446. **Business Addr:** Member, National Baseball Hall of Fame, Committee on Baseball Veterans, 25 Main St, PO Box 590, Cooperstown, NY 13326.

IRVIN, REGINA LYNETTE
State government official. **Personal:** Born Sep 13, 1963, Columbia, MS; daughter of Eugene and Carolyn J Barnes. **Educ:** Alcorn State Univ, BA, 1985; Thurgood Marshall Sch Law, JD, 1988. **Career:** Magistrate Karen K Brown, law clerk, 1988; Dept Navy, Naval Sea Syst Command, atty, 1988-89; Atty S Ralph Martin Jr & Benjamin W Spaulding Jr, law clerk, 1989; Atty Raymond Register, law clerk, 1989-90; Secret & ASC, law clerk, 1989-90; Dept Veterans Affairs, claims examr, 1991; Miss Dept Human Servs, child support enforcement officer, 1992-93; Miss Dept Human Servs, admin hearings Officer, 1993-2000; Miss State Dept Health, br dir, 2000-. **Orgs:** Basileus, anti basileus, grammateus, 1983-84, Alpha Kappa Alpha Sorority; secy, Polit Sci Soc, 1983-84; pres, Social Sci Soc, 1984-85; gen mem, Am Bar Asn, 1985-88; vpres, Phi Alpha Delta Law Fraternity Int, 1985-88; vpres, NBA, Black Law Studs Asn, 1985-88; gen mem, State Bar Tex, Studs Div, 1985-88; staff mem, Thurgood Marshall Law Review, 1985-88. **Honors/Awds:** Scholastic Scholarship, Barrister's Wives, 1986-87; BCI, Outstanding Leadership Award, 1989; TMSLR, Book Review Editor, 1987-88; Nat Dean's List, 1988-89. **Special Achievements:** Author: case comment, Thurgood Marshall Law Review, vol 12, num 1, p 271, Fall 1986. **Home Addr:** 1212 Maxwell St, Columbia, MS 39429.

IRVIN, SEDRICK
Football player, football coach. **Personal:** Born Mar 30, 1978, Miami, FL. **Educ:** Mich State Univ. **Career:** Football player (retired); football coach; Detroit Lions, running back, 1999-2000; asst coach, Gulliver Preparatory Sch; asst coach, Univ Ala, currently.

IRVINE, DR. CAROLYN LENETTE
Educator. **Personal:** Born Mar 7, 1947, Quincy, FL; daughter of Robert L Green and Jessie M Jones McCloud; married Freeman R Irvine Jr, Nov 28, 1977; children: Fredreka R & Freeman R III. **Educ:** Fla A&M Univ, Tallahassee, Fla, BS, 1970; Univ Fla, Gainesville, Fla, MS, 1975; Fla State Univ, Tallahassee, Fla, PhD, 1989. **Career:** Shanks High Sch, Quincy, Fla, speech & english teacher, 1976-77; Fla A&M Univ, Tallahassee, Fla, speech teacher, 1975-76, 1983-, english teacher, 1978-83, dept Eng, assoc prof, currently. **Orgs:** Jack & Jill Am Inc, 1988-90; Asn Teachers Am, 1989-90; Fla Speech Commun Asn, 1984-91; Phi Delta Kappa, 1984-91. **Honors/Awds:** Cert of Appreciation, Miracle Temple Daycare Ctr. **Business Addr:** Associate Professor of Speech Communication, Florida A&M University, Department of English, 304 Tucker Hall Room 410, Tallahassee, FL 32307, **Business Phone:** (850)599-3799.

IRVING, CLARENCE LARRY, JR.
Lawyer. **Personal:** Born Jul 7, 1955, Brooklyn, NY. **Educ:** Northwestern Univ, BA, 1976; Stanford Univ Law Sch, JD, 1979. **Career:** Kirkland E Ellis, summer assoc, 1977; Breed Abbott & Morgan, summer assoc, 1978; Hogan & Hartson, assoc, 1979-83; US Rep Mickey Leland, legislative dir & coun, 1983-87; US House Rep Subcomn Telecomm & Finance, sr coun, 1987-92; Nat Telecommunications & Info Admin, asst secy com & dir, 1993-99; Irving Info Group, pres & chief executive officer, currently. **Orgs:** Nat Bar Asn, 1980-; Precinct capt Wash DC Democratic Party, 1983-84; Nat Conf Black Lawyers Comn Task Force, 1983-; Variety Club Greater Wash, 1985-; chair, House Rep Fair Employment Practices Comt, 1985-87; bd vis, Stanford Law Sch; bd mem, House Rep Child Care Ctr; co-chair, Am Bar Asn, Electronic Media Div, Comt Communications Law. **Honors/Awds:** Pres, Stanford Law Sch Class of 1979; Outstanding Young Man Am, Jaycees, 1979. **Business Addr:** President, Chief Executive Officer, Irving Information Group, Washington, DC.*

IRVING, OPHELIA MCALPIN
Librarian. **Personal:** Born Apr 4, 1929, Gadsden, AL; daughter of Jerry McAlpin and Lamae Prater McAlpin; married Charles G Jr; children: Cyretha C. **Educ:** Clarks Col, AB, 1951; Atlanta Univ, attended 1952; Syracuse Univ, MLS, 1958, 1973; Drexel Inst Tech, attended 1966; NC Cent Univ, attended 1982. **Career:** Ctr High Sch Waycross, librn, 1951-54; Spencer Jr High Sch Columbus, librn, 1954-55; St Augustine's Col Raleigh, librn, 1955-68; NC State Libr Raleigh, asst chief info ser sect, 1968-91; Shaw Univ, Raleigh, resource librn p/t, 1992-. **Orgs:** Alpha Kappa Alpha Sor, 1954-; NC Libr Asn, 1955-; Jack & Jill Am Inc, 1961-73; Am Libr Asn, 1963-; YWCA, 1965-; NC Line Users Group, 1982-; Microcomput Users Group NC, 1983-; Top Ladies Distinction; Continental Societies Inc, 1990; Links Inc, 1991. **Honors/Awds:** Faculty Fellowship, St Augustine Col Raleigh, NC, 1964; NC Road Builders' Award, 1991; Order of the Long Leaf Pine Award, 1991; appointed to the NC State Library Commission, 1992; BCALA Distinguished Award, 1992; NCLA Life Membership Award, 1997; docent Emeritus Award, NC Mus Hist, 2002. **Home Addr:** 533 E Lenoir St, Raleigh, NC 27601, **Home Phone:** (919)833-3658. **Business Addr:** Librarian, Shaw University, 118 E S St, Raleigh, NC 27601, **Business Phone:** (919)546-8200.

IRVING, TERRY DUANE
Football player. **Personal:** Born Jul 3, 1971, Galveston, TX; married Frankie; children: Breana. **Educ:** Mc Neese State Univ, BS, elec eng. **Career:** Football player(retired); Ariz Cardinals, linebacker, 1994-98.

ISAAC, BRIAN WAYNE
Administrator. **Educ:** NY Univ, BA, 1976, MA, pub admin, 1984. **Career:** Long Island Lighting Co, training & educ coordr, 1977-79, EEO admin, 1979-84, employ serv admin, 1984-. **Orgs:** Pres, Manhattan Spokesman Club, 1977-78; The Edges Group Inc. *

ISAAC, EARLEAN
Judge. **Personal:** Born Feb 11, 1950, Forkland, AL; daughter of Robert Percy and Mary Virginia Smith; married Johnny L, Apr 24, 1971; children: Johnny L Jr, Jamaine L & Janetha L. **Career:** Greene County Judge Probate, Eutaw, AL, license clerk, 1971-75, chief clerk, 75-89, judge, 1989-. **Orgs:** St Paul United Methodist Church, 1988. **Honors/Awds:** Citizen of the Year Award, Kappa Alpha Psi Fraternity, 1989. **Special Achievements:** First Black Woman Probate Judge in Alabama. **Home Addr:** 288 Lloyd Chapel Rd, Forkland, AL 36740, **Home Phone:** (205)289-3866. **Business Addr:** Judge, Greene County Judge of Probate, 400 Morrow Ave, PO Box 790, Eutaw, AL 35462, **Business Phone:** (205)372-3340.

ISAAC, DR. EPHRAIM
Historian, scholar, educator. **Personal:** Born May 29, 1936, Nedjio, Ethiopia; son of Ruth and Yishaq; married Sherry Rosen; children: Devorah Esther, Raphael Samuel & Yael Ruth. **Educ:** Concordia Col, BA, philosophy, chemistry, 1958; Harvard Divinity Sch, M Div, 1963; Harvard Univ, PhD, 1969; Calif Univ, New York, DHL; LittD. **Career:** Harvard Univ, from instr to lectr, 1968-71, from assoc prof to prof, 1971-77, Divinity Sch, vis prof; Hebrew Univ, lect, 1977-79; Bard Col, vis prof, 1981-83; Princeton Univ, vis prof, Relig & African Am Studies,1995-2001; Princeton Univ, vis, prof; Inst Semitic Studies, dir,currently; Yemenite Jewish Fedn Am, pres, currently; Inst Relig & Pub Policy, dir, currently. **Orgs:** Pres, Ethiopian Stud Asn N Am, 1959-62; chorale dir, Harvard Grad Chorale, 1962-64; treas, Harvard Grad Stud Asn, 1962-65; chmn, Comn Ethiopian Literacy, 1963-68; dir gen, Nat Literacy Campaign Ethiopia, 1966-72; bd mem, African Studies Heritage Asn, 1969-73; bd mem, Am Asn Ethiopian Jews, 1973-; vice chmn, Ethiopian Famine Relief Comn, 1984-; fel, Butler Col; fel, Dead Sea Scrolls Found. **Honors/Awds:** Ethiopian National Prize for literacy, 1967; NEH Research Grant, 1976; Fellow Endowment for the Humanities, 1979; Faculty Fund Research Grants, Harvard Univ; United Nations Associations of Ethiopia Peace Award; Society of Ethiopian Established in Diaspora Education Award; Peacemaker Award; Best teacher of the Year; Ephraim Isaac Prize in African Studies in honor, named in honor, 1999; honorary degrees, John J. Col CUNY, Addis Ababa Univ, Ethiopia; NEH Fellowship. **Special Achievements:** Outstanding Educators of Am, 1972; Author of numerous articles on Ethiopian and Jewish studies; Author of Ethiopic book of Enoch, Doubleday, 1983, a history of religions in Africa; first professor hired in Afro-American Studies at Harvard Univ. **Business Addr:** Director, Institute on Religion and Public Policy, 1620 I St NW Suite LL10, Washington, DC 20006, **Business Phone:** (202)835-8760.

ISAAC, JOSEPH WILLIAM ALEXANDER
Physician. **Personal:** Born Jan 1, 1935?; son of Agatha Henry and Timothy; married Gertrude Harris; children: Charles, Zoe, Joseph A. **Educ:** City Col, NY, BS, 1967; Howard Univ, MD, 1971; Am Bd Obstet & Gynec, Dipl. **Career:** Freedmens Hosp, Wash DC, med intern, 1971-72; Howard Univ, Wash, DC, resident obstet & gynec, 1972-76; Norfolk Health Dept, family planning phys, 1976-77; Norfolk & Portsmouth, VA, pvt pract, obstet & gynec, 1977-; Portsmouth Gen Hosp, chmn dept obstet & gynec, 1985-88; Norflk Comm Hosp, chmn dept obstet & gynec, 1991-98; Portsmouth Gen Hosp, pres med staff, 1993. **Orgs:** Am Med Asn, 1975-; Nat Med Asn; Norfolk Med Soc, 1976; Norfolk Acad Med, 1977-99; Portsmouth Chamber Com, 1978; Med Adv Comt Tidewater March Dimes, 1979; Am Col obstet & gynec, 1979, vpres, 1986-90, pres, 1990-92; Old Dom Med Soc; pres, Norfolk Med Soc, 1985-87; Cent Tex Med Found. **Military Serv:** AUS, sgt, 1959-62. **Home Addr:** 712 Elderberry Ct, Chesapeake, VA 23320. **Business Addr:** Physician, 549 E Brambleton Ave Suite 4, Norfolk, VA 23510.*

ISAAC, TAMEIKA
Business owner, city council member. **Personal:** Married Jamie L; children: Tamia. **Educ:** Hampton Univ, BS, 1994; Spring Valley High Sch; Univ SC Sch Law, PhD, 1997. **Career:** Jabber, Gray & Isaac, PA, partner, currently; councilwoman, Columbia City Coun, currently. **Orgs:** Am Bar Asn Young Lawyers Div; SC Bar & Richland County Bar Asn; pres, Columbia Lawyers Asn; SC Black Lawyers Asn; bd mem, Am Red Cross SC Blood Serv. **Honors/Awds:** Woman of Distinction Award, Area Girl Scouts, 2004; Lincoln C Jenkins Award, Columbia Urban League, 2005. **Special Achievements:** First African-American to win an at-large seat on on Columbia City Council; the first African-American female to be elected to Columbia City Council; youngest ever to be elected to Columbia City Council in either gender or race; Named as one of the Top 20 under 40 by the State newspaper. **Business Phone:** (803)254-8868.*

ISAAC, TELESFORO ALEXANDER
Clergy. **Personal:** Born Jan 5, 1929, San Pedro Macoris, Dominican Republic; son of Simon and Violet Francis; married Juana Maria Rosa-Zorrilla, Aug 30, 1961; children: Juan Alexander, Marcos Alexander & Miriam Elizabeth. **Educ:** Instituto Vazquez, 1950; Sem Haiti, 1958; Universidad de Santo Domingo, 1969; Seminario Episcopal del Caribe, MDiv, 1971. **Career:** Clergy (Retired); Morey Hardware Store, Porvenir Sugar Mill, clerk, 1950-54; San Gabriel Episcopal Church, vicar, 1958-61; Jesus Nazarene Episcopal Church, vicar, 1961-65; San Andres Episcopal Church, vicar, 1965-69; San Esteban Episcopal Church, vicar, 1971-72; Dominican Republic Diocese, diocesan bishop, 1972-91; Diocese Southwest Fla, asst bishop, 1991. **Orgs:** Founder, prin, San Gabriel & Jesus Nazarene Schs, 1959-62; co-

founder, Dominican-Am Lang Inst, 1964-; bd trustees, Church World Serv, 1966-91; founder, San Marcos & San Andres High Schs, 1966-70, prin; chair, Caribbean Episcopal Seminary, 1975-76, bd; founder, pres, bd dir, Ctr Theol Sch, 1975-91; pres, Ctr Rehab, Handicapped, 1985-91, bd dir; chair, bd dir, Asn Human Rights, 1991. **Honors/Awds:** Doctor of Divinity, City Univ Los Angeles, 1977; Distinguished Citizen, San Pedro de Macoris, 1983. **Special Achievements:** La Labor Educativa de la Iglesia Episcopal Dominicana, 1971.

ISAACS, PATRICIA
Executive, executive director. **Personal:** Born May 6, 1949, Georgetown, Guyana; daughter of Violet Isaacs; married Morty Greene; children: Krystal Louise. **Educ:** DC Teachers Col; S Eastern Univ. **Career:** McDonalds Corp, Mich Region, dir opers, 1975-91, regional vpres, 1991-96, Jamaica's first McDonald's Restaurant, managing dir, 1996-. **Orgs:** Detroit Chamber Com; bd mem, Homes Black C; Black Owners Asn. **Business Addr:** Managing Director, McDonalds Corp, 2111 McDonald, Oak Brook, IL 60523, **Business Phone:** (630)623-3000.*

ISAACS, STEPHEN D
Safety engineer. **Personal:** Born Feb 22, 1944, Boston, MA; children: Athelia & Stephanie. **Educ:** Howard Univ, BMech Engineering, 1969, MBA, 1973. **Career:** Office Mgmt & Budget, Opers Res Analyst, 1973-76; US Nuclear Reg Comn, prog analyst, 1976-77; US Nuclear Reg Comn, FOIA officer, 1977-86; Fed Aviation Admin, aviation safety inspector, 1986-. **Orgs:** Am Soc Mech Engrs, 1973-; Am Soc Access Profs, 1980-86; acct exec, Int Monetary Founding Group Inc, 1984-86; bd dirs, Special Air Serv Inc, 1983-85; Wash Soc Engrs, 1985-. **Military Serv:** USCG, E-4 intelligence specialist, 1969-71. **Home Addr:** 1907-2nd St NW, Washington, DC 20001. **Business Addr:** Aviation Safety Inspector, Federal Aviation Administration, Flight Standards Service, 800 Independence Ave SW, Washington, DC 20590.

ISAACS-LOWE, ARLENE ELIZABETH
Financial manager. **Personal:** Born Oct 17, 1959, Kingston, Jamaica; daughter of Lawrence G and Barbara C Davis; married Walter J IV, Jul 26, 1986; children: Walter J V. **Educ:** Howard Univ, Wash, DC, BBA, 1981; Fordham Univ, New York, NY, MBA, 1990. **Career:** VSE Corp, Alexandria, VA, staff acct, 1981-84; West World Holding Inc, New York, NY, sr acct, 1984-87, acct mgr, 1987-; Metropolitan Life, New York,NY, financial analyst, 1987-88, mgr, 1988-89, controller, 1989-92, portfolio mgr, 1992-; Moody's Investors Servs, sr vpres, currently. **Orgs:** Natl Urban League, 1988-; Natl Assn Black Accts, 1989-; Natl Black MBA, 1990-; Beta Gamma Sigma Honor Soc, Fordham Univ, 1990; bd mem, Rheedlen Found,1991-; BEEP. **Special Achievements:** America's Best & Brightest, Dollars & Sense Mag, 1991; 100 Most Promising Black Women in Corporate America, Ebony Mag, 1991. **Home Phone:** (718)712-5565. **Business Phone:** (212)553-7841.

ISADORE, HAROLD W.
Lawyer, librarian. **Personal:** Born in Alexandria, LA. **Educ:** Southern Univ, BS, 1967; Southern Univ Sch Law, JD, 1970; SUNY Buffalo Law Sch, Cert, 1978. **Career:** US Dept Labor Off Solicitor, atty, 1970-73; Baton Rouge Legal Aid Soc, atty, 1973-74; Pub Defender Baton Rouge, atty, 1974-75; Southern Univ Sch Law, assoc law librn; Pvt Pract, currently. **Orgs:** Am Bar Asn, Nat Bar Asn, Delta Theta Phi Law Frat, Am Asn Law Librs, Kappa Alpha Psi Frat, Inc. **Honors/Awds:** Service award, Student Bar Asn, Southern Univ Law Sch, 1970; Hypotext Security Devices, Southern Univ Publisher, 1979; Hypotext Civil Procedure, Vols 1 & 11 S Univ Publisher, 1980-81; Humanitarian Award, Louis A Martinet Legal Soc; Staff Award, Southern Univ Law Ctr, 1980-81, 1985-87, 1990-94. **Business Addr:** Lawyer, Private Practitioner, PO Box 10565, Baton Rouge, LA 70813, **Business Phone:** (225)343-9326.*

ISHMAN, DR. SYBIL RAY
Educator. **Personal:** Born Jul 25, 1946, Durham, NC; married Reginald E. **Educ:** Univ NC, Greensboro, BA, 1968; Univ NC, Chapel Hill, MA, 1971, PhD, 1983. **Career:** NC Cent Univ, grad asst, 1969-71, instr, 1970-72; NC State Univ, eng instr, 1972-76, asst prof, 1979-85; Howard Univ, eng instr, 1976-77; Nazareth Col, adj prof, 1985-86, eng instr, 1986, 1988, 1990, 1992; Rochester Inst Technol, NTID Eng Dept, chair, 1986-91, Dept Lib Arts Support, asst prof, assoc prof, currently. **Orgs:** Am Asn Univ Women; Modern Lang Asn; Nat Coun Teachers Eng; TESOL; Nat Smart Set Durham Chap. **Honors/Awds:** Who's Who Among Outstanding Black Collegians, 1972; Teaching Effectiveness Recognition Student Award, NC State Univ, 1984. **Business Phone:** (585)475-2444.

ISIBOR, EDWARD IROGUEHI
Educator, engineer. **Personal:** Born Jun 9, 1940, Benin City, Nigeria; married Edwina Williams; children: Ekinadose & Emwanta. **Educ:** Howard Univ, BSc, Civil Engineering, 1965; Mass Inst Technol, MSc, Transp Engineering, 1967; Purdue Univ, PhD, Transp Engineering, 1970. **Career:** Mass Inst Technol, res asst, 1965-67; Purdue Univ, res asst, 1967-69; Cleveland State Univ, Afro-Am Cult Ctr, dir, 1970-71; NE Ohio Areawide Coord Agency, Cleveland, transp engr, 1972; Fla Int Univ, Dept Civil Eng, assoc prof & head urban syst prog, 1973-75; Tenn State Univ, Sch Eng & Tech, dean, 1975, prof civil & environ eng, currently. **Orgs:** Tau Beta Pi Hon Soc, 1964; Sigma Xi Hon Soc, 1970; Am Soc Eng Educ; Transp Res Bd, WA, DC; Ohio Soc Prof Engrs; C C Reg Engr, OH; Am Soc Civil Engrs. **Honors/Awds:** Nashville's Living Legends, Governor's Traffic Safety Comt; Honored in the White House, Washington by President Reagan; A day named in honor, City & Staff Nashville, Tennessee; Honored life mem, ASCE. **Special Achievements:** A Day Named in Honor by the City and Staff of Nashville, Tennessee; published numerous articles & books. **Business Addr:** Professor, Tennessee State University, Department Civil Engineering, 3500 John A Merritt Blvd, Nashville, TN 37203, **Business Phone:** (615)963-5432.

ISLER, MARSHALL A., III
Executive, real estate developer, vice president (organization). **Personal:** Born Jan 9, 1939, Kinston, NC; son of Marshall A Jr and Louise Douglas; married Verna Harmon Bradford, Jun 14, 1996; children: Valerie L, Bryan C. **Educ:** Howard Univ, BSEE, 1962; George Wash Univ, MEA, 1971; Harvard Univ, PMD, 1977. **Career:** Johns Hopkins Univ Applied Physics Lab, space sys officer, 1967; Naval Air Sys Command, satellite proj engr, 1971; Nat Bureau Standards Law Enforcement Standards, security syst prog mgr, 1973; Sen John Tunney, sci adv, 1974; Nat Bureau Standards Dept Com Ctr Consult Prod Tech, dep dir, 1978; Parametric Inc, pres; Isler Assoc, pres; Downtown Develop Corp, exec vpres, currently. **Orgs:** Howard Univ Alumni Assoc, Omega Psi Phi Frat, SBF Credit Union; assoc Urban Land Ins; Durham Bus & Prof Chain; Durham Chamber Com; Nat Home Builders Assoc; Mayor's Downtown Redevelop Comt Durham; pres, Abiding Savior Lutheran Church Durham, NC, 1989-91; vpres, Bus & Prof Chain Durham, NC, 1989-90; Bd Dir, Dispute Settlement Ctr Durham, NC, 1989-90; Human Rels Comt, Durham NC Chamber Com, 1990-91; Churches Action, Durham, NC, 1990-. **Honors/Awds:** Congressional Fellowship, 1973-74. **Military Serv:** USN Lt 1962-67; USNR, Comdr, 1967-. **Business Addr:** Executive Vice President, Downtown Develop Corporation, 201 Hay St, Fayetteville, NC 28301, **Business Phone:** (910)484-4242.*

ISLEY, ERNIE (ERNEST BERNARD ISLEY)
Musician, singer. **Personal:** Born Mar 7, 1952, Cincinnati, OH. **Career:** The Isley Brothers, music band mem, 1973-; guitarist, drummer, singer & songwriter, currently; Albums: Shout!, 1959; Twist & Shout, 1962; Twisting& Shouting, 1963; This Old Heart of Mine, 1966; Soul on the Rocks, 1967; It's Our Thing, 1969; The Brothers Isley, 1969; Live at Yankee Stadium, 1969; Get Into Something, 1970; In the Beginning, 1971; Givin' It Back,1971; Brother, Brother, Brother, 1972; 33, 1973; Live It Up, 1974; The Heat Is On, 1975; Harvest for the World, 1976; Go for Your Guns, 1977; Showdown, 1978; Timeless, 1978; Winner Takes All, 1979; Go All the Way, 1980; Grand Slam, 1981; Inside You, 1981; The Real Deal, 1982; Between the Sheets, 1983; Greatest Hits, Vol 1, 1984; Masterpiece, 1985; Smooth Sailin', 1987; Spend the Night, 1989; High Wire, solo album, 1990; Tracks of Life, 1992; Live, 1993; Beautiful Ballads, 1994; For The Love of You, 1995; The Isley Brothers Live, 1996; Mission to Please, 1996; Shake it Up Baby: Shout, Twist & Shout, 2000; Eternal, 2000; Love Songs, 2001; 20thCentury Masters - The Millenium Collection: The Best of the Isley Brothers, 2001; Body Kiss, 2003; Here I Am: Isley Meets Bacharach, 2003; Live It Up, 2004; Rebound, 2005; # Karaoke Revolution Party, 2005; The Sentinel, 2006; Code Name: The Cleaner, 2007; Superbad, 2007; Pineapple Express, 2008. **Honors/Awds:** Rock & Roll Hall of Fame, 1992. **Business Addr:** Musician, c/o Varese Sarabande Records Inc, 11846 Ventura Blvd Suite 130, Studio City, CA 91604, **Business Phone:** (818)753-4143.

ISLEY, MARVIN
Musician. **Personal:** Born Aug 18, 1953, Cincinnati, OH. **Career:** The Isley Brothers, musician, 1973-84 & 1991-97; Isley-Jasper-Isley, group mem, 1984-87; Albums: Shout, 1959; Twist & Shout, 1962; This Old Heart of Mine, 1966; Soul on the Rocks, 1967; Its Our Thing, 1969; The Brothers, 1969; Doin' Their Thing, 1969; Brother, Brother, Brother, 1972; 33, 1973; Between the Sheets, 1983; Broadway's Closer To Sunset Boulevard, 1984; Caravan Of Love, 1985; Different Drummer, 1987; Beautiful Ballads, 1994; Mission to Please, 1996; The Early Years, 2000; Singles: Caravan Of Love, 1985; "Insatiable Woman", 1986; "8th Wonder of the World, 1987; "Givin' You Back the Love", 1988; Tracks of Life, 1991; Live!, 1993; Mission to Please, 1996; Eternel, 2001; Body Kiss, 2003; Baby Makin' Music 2006. **Orgs:** Spokesperson, Am Diabetes Asn. **Honors/Awds:** Rock & Roll Hall Of Fame, 1992.

ISMAIL, QADRY RAHMADAN
Football player, football coach. **Personal:** Born Nov 8, 1970, Newark, NJ; married Holly, Apr 8, 1995; children: 3. **Educ:** Syracuse Univ, speech commun, 1992. **Career:** Football player (retired), Football coach; Minn Vikings, wide receiver,1993-96; Miami Dolphins, 1997; Green Bay Packers, 1997; New Orleans Saints, 1998; Baltimore Ravens, 1999-2001; Indianapolis Colts, 2002; West Boca Raton Community High Sch, coach, currently. **Orgs:** Spokesperson, Drug Abuse Resistance Educ. **Honors/Awds:** Track Athlete-of-the-Year; All-Am hons, Track & Field News; Martin Luther King Citizenship Award; Offensive Player of the Week, AFC, 1999. **Business Addr:** Coach, West Boca Raton Community High School, 1501 NW 15th Ct, Boca Raton, FL 33486, **Business Phone:** (561)338-1400.

ISMAIL, RAGHIB RAMADIAN (ROCKET ISMAIL)
Football player. **Personal:** Born Nov 18, 1969, Elizabeth, NJ; son of Ibrahim and Fatma; married Melani; children: Noe & Imani. **Educ:** Univ Notre Dame. **Career:** Football player (retired); Toronto Argonauts (CFL), running back, 1991-93; Oakland Raiders, 1993-95; Carolina Panthers, wide receiver, 1996-98; Dallas Cowboys, 1999-2002. **Honors/Awds:** All-American, 1989, 1990; Walter Camp Award, 1990; Grey Cup MVP, 1991; Sprint Runner, NCAA Indoor Championships.

ISMAIL, ROCKET. **See ISMAIL, RAGHIB RAMADIAN.**

ISMIAL, SALAAM IBN
Association executive, founder (originator). **Personal:** Born in Jersey City, NJ. **Educ:** Robert Walsh Sch Bus, 1979; Kean Col, NJ, 1982; Union County Col, 1983. . **Career:** Elizabeth Youth Coun, pres 1982-84; Union County Col, vpres, 1983; NAACP, youth pres 1984; EYC After Sch Prog Rec Dept, coordr, 1984-85; United Youth Coun Inc, chmn & founder, currently; Salaam Ismial Communs, owner. **Orgs:** Youth leader Local Chap, CORE, 1973; chmn, Kean Col Black Stud Union, 1982; pres, Elizabeth Youth Coun, 1982-85; Black Issue Convention, Southern Christian Leadership, 1984, Progressive Rainbow Alliance NJ, 1985; pres, United Youth Coun Inc; coordr, Union African Stud Orgs, Col Org Statewide; bd, Urban League Essex Co Pediats Aid Foster Care, 1989. **Honors/Awds:** Medal of Honor Elizabeth Boys Scouts, 1972; Outstanding Service Award, Kean Black Stud Union, 1982; CommServ Elizabeth Youth Coun, 1983; Life Time Membership, NAACP, 1984. **Business Addr:** Chairman, Founder, United Youth Council Inc, PO Box 142, Hillside, NJ 07205, **Business Phone:** (973)297-8865.

ISOM, EDDIE (EDDIE L ISOM)
Hotel executive. **Educ:** Livingstone Col. **Career:** Marriott Corp, food & beverage dir; Howard Univ Hotel, dir food, gen mgr.

ISOM, EDDIE L. **See ISOM, EDDIE.**

ISRAEL, MAE H
Journalist. **Personal:** Born Apr 8, 1953, Robeson County, NC; daughter of Samuel L Israel and Mae C Israel. **Educ:** Univ NC, Chapel Hill, BA, jour, 1975. **Career:** Greensboro Daily News, reporter, 1975-80; Charlotte Observer, reporter, assignment editor, 1980-89; Wash Post, ed, 1989-. **Orgs:** Women Communs, 1977-79; Southeastern Black Press Inst, 1977-79; pres, Charlotte Area Asn Black Journalists, 1985-89; Nat Asn Black Journalists, 1978-; Wash Area Asn Black Journalists, 1989-; Delta Sigma Theta. **Honors/Awds:** Press Award, Feature Writing, NC Press Asn, 1977; Excellence in Writing, Landmark Commun, 1978; News Writing, Feature Writing, Black Media Asn, 1985, 1986. **Business Addr:** Editor, The Washington Post Montgomery Edition, 51 Monroe St Suite 500, Rockville, MD 20850, **Business Phone:** (202)334-7582.

ISRAEL, STEVEN DOUGLAS
Football player. **Personal:** Born Mar 16, 1969, Lawnside, NJ; married Lorae; children: Averi Lorae & Ashley Shardae. **Educ:** Univ Pittsburgh, econ. **Career:** Football player (retired); Los Angeles Rams, defensive back, 1992-94; San Francisco 49ers, 1995-96; New England Patriots, 1997-99; New Orleans Saints, 2001.

ITA, LAWRENCE EYO
Educator. **Personal:** Born Dec 1, 1939, Calabar, Nigeria; married Autumn Dean; children: Eyo & Ekanem. **Educ:** London Univ, BSC, 1962; Univ Mich, PhD, 1970. **Career:** Commonwealth Assoc, engineering consult, 1970-72; Bur Assoc Serv, dir, 1974-77; Univ Nev, assoc prof, 1978; Col Southern Nev, prof, currently. **Orgs:** Am Soc Engineering Educ, 1974-; Int Soc Solar Energy, 1975-; Am Soc Heat Refrig & Air-Cond Engrs, 1976-. **Special Achievements:** Publs Jour of Chem & Engineering Data, 1974-76. **Business Addr:** Professor, College of Southern Nevada, 6375 W Charleston Blvd, Las Vegas, NV 89146.

IVERSON, ALLEN
Basketball player. **Personal:** Born Jun 7, 1975, Hampton, VA; married Tawanna Turner, 2001; children: Tiaura, Messiah, Allen II (Duece) & Isaiah Rahsaan. **Educ:** Georgetown Univ. **Career:** Philadelphia 76ers, guard, 1996-2006; Denver Nuggets, guard, 2006-. **Honors/Awds:** NBA Draft, First round pick, 1996; NBA Player of the Week, 1997; NBA All Rookie Team, 1997; Schick Rookie of the Year Award, 1997; All-NBA First Team, 1999; NBA Most Valuable Player, 2001; NBA All-Star Game Most Valuable Player, 2005. **Special Achievements:** First rookie in history to score 40 points or more in four consecutive games. **Business Addr:** Professional Basketball Player, Denver Nuggets, 1000 Chopper Circle, Denver, CO 80204, **Business Phone:** (303)405-1100.

IVERSON, JOHNATHAN LEE
Circus performer. **Personal:** Son of Sylvia Iverson. **Educ:** Univ Hartford's Hartt Sch, voice performance, 1998. **Career:** Ringling

Bros & Barnum & Bailey, circus ringmaster, currently. **Orgs:** Charismatic Goodwill Ambassador; virtuoso tenor. **Honors/Awds:** Seeing Placido Domingo perform in Japan, 1989; Barbara Walter's, 10 Most Fascinating People, 1999; singing at the intermission for Luciano Pavarotti's Concert in Central Park; performing in a live show on Broadway for two weeks, 1993. **Special Achievements:** The first African-American ringmaster of a major U.S. circus in 1999 at the age of 22. **Business Addr:** Ringmaster Red Unit, c/o Ringling Bros & Barnum & Bailey Circus, 8607 Westwood Center Dr, Vienna, VA 22182, **Business Phone:** (703)448-4000.*

IVERY, DR. CURTIS L.
College administrator. **Educ:** Tex A&M Univ, BS, pol sci & journalism; West Texas St, MA, phsycol; Univ Arkansas, doc, edn admin. **Career:** State Ark, commissioner Hum Serv, 1985;El Centro Col, vpres; Mt View Col Of Dallas County Community Col Dist, vpres & act pres; Wayne County Community Col Dist, chief exec officer; Wayne County Community Col, chancellor, currently. **Orgs:** Detroit Comm Bank; New Detroit Inc; Detroit Urban League. **Honors/Awds:** Natl Excellence in Leadership Award, 2004; Walter E Douglas Humanitarian Award, 2004; Michiganian Of The Year Award, 2005; Outstanding Global Leadership, 2006; Best College President Award, 2006; Outstanding Child/Family Advocate Award, 2006; **** Excellence in Education Award; News Maker Of The Year Award, 2008; Man Of Excellence, 2008. **Special Achievements:** First African-American appointed to the governor's Cabinet in Arkansas; Author : "Journeys Of Conscience", 2005; "Fatherhood : Reclaiming Our Legacy"; "Urban Crisis In America". **Business Addr:** Chancellor, Wayne County Community College, 801 W Fort St, Detroit, MI 48226, **Business Phone:** (313)496-2510.

IVERY, EDDIE LEE
Football player, football coach. **Personal:** Born Jul 30, 1957, McDuffie, GA; married Anna; children: Tauvia Edana & Eddie Lee Jr. **Educ:** Ga Tech, BS, Indus Mgmt, 1992. **Career:** Football player (retired), player develop asst; Green Bay Packers, running back, 1979-88; Thomson High Sch, coach, 1988-90; Ga Tech athletics staff, asst strength & conditioning coach; Ga Tech Athletic Asn, player develop asst, currently; Outreach Inc, resource coordr. **Honors/Awds:** Senoir Year, All-Time NCAA Single Game Rushing Record; Nat Stud-Athlete Day Giant Steps Award, 1992. **Special Achievements:** Finished eighth in the Heisman Trophy ballotting; All-America honors by the Associated Press & United Press International, 1978. **Business Phone:** (404)894-3961.

IVERY, JAMES A
Federal government official. **Personal:** Born Jan 5, 1950, Zebulon, NC; son of Eugene Copeland and Dorothy; divorced; children: Jacinda D I & Toshiba I. **Educ:** Fayetteville State Univ, Fayetteville, NC, BS, 1972; Bucknell Univ, Lewisburg, PA, MPA, 1982. **Career:** Wake County Pub Schs, Raleigh, NC, instr & coach, 1972-74; Internal Revenue Serv, Raleigh, NC, revenue officer, 1974-76; US Dept Health & Human Serv, Wash, DC, spec asst dir, Off Intergovernmental affairs, asst dep undersecretary, currently. **Orgs:** Life mem, Alpha Phi Alpha Frat, 1977; Nat Forum Black Pub Admin, 1986; Mt Zion Baptist Church, Arlington, VA, 1986; bd dirs, Potomac Massage Training Inst, 1995. **Honors/Awds:** Outstanding Young Men of America, 1985; Distinguished Black Col Grad, Nat Asn Equal Opportunity Higher Educ, 1988. **Special Achievements:** Published, "Say Brother Column,", Essense Mag, 1986. **Business Addr:** Assistant to Deputy Undersecretary, US Dept of Health & Human Services, Office of InterGovernmental Affairs, 200 Independence Ave SW Rm 618E, Washington, DC 20201, **Business Phone:** (202)720-2511.

IVEY, ARTIS LEON, JR.
Actor, rap musician. **Personal:** Born Aug 1, 1963, Compton, CA; son of Jackie Jones and Artis; married Josefa Salinas, May 18, 1996. **Career:** Albums: It Takes a Thief, 1994; Gangsta's Paradise, 1995; My Soul, 1997; Fantastic Voyage: The Greatest Hits, 2001; El Cool Magnifico, 2002; The Return of the Gangsta, 2006; Three Days to Vegas, 2007; Chinaman's Chance, 2008; Steal Hear, 2008; The Lost Archives of Quincy Taylor, 2009; Songs: "County Line", 1993; "Gangsta Paradise", 1995; "1,2,3,4", 1996; "Fantastic Voyage", 1994; "Mama, I'm in Love'"; TV series: "Sabrina, the Teenage Witch", 1996; "Hitz", 1997; "Muppets Tonight", 1997; "The Nanny", 1998; "Malcolm & Eddie", 1999; "18 Wheels of Justice", 2000; "Futurama", 2001; "Robbery Homicide Division", 2002; Red Water, 2003; Dracula 3000, 2004. **Honors/Awds:** Billboard Music Award, 1994, 1996; American Music Award, 1996; Nominated for Grammy Award, 1994-96; MTV Video Music Award, 1996, 1997; won ASCAP Award, 1997. **Special Achievements:** Co-hosted the MOBO Awards in the UK in 2005; nominated several times for MTV Music Awards and Grammy Awards. *

IVEY, HORACE SPENCER
Educator. **Personal:** Born Nov 13, 1931, DeLand, FL; married Barbara Edwards; children: Lawrence, Derek, Chandra, Allegra & Elliot. **Educ:** Smith Col Sch Soc Work; Univ Conn, MSW, 1956; Syracuse Univ, 1962. **Career:** State Univ Hosp, social worker, 1956-61, case worker, 1958-60, supvr, 1961-62; State Univ NY Upstate Med Ctr, assoc prof, dir, social worker serv. **Orgs:** Nat Asn Social Workers; Acad Certified Soc Workers; Med Social Work Sec; Healther Serv Comn Coun Aging; Am Hosp Asn Coun Vols; Syracuse Univ Rehab Coun. **Special Achievements:** Publications: "Factors in Selection of Patients for Home Chemo-Therapy",1956; "Hospital Abortion Program Implication for Social Work Planning & Serv Delivery", 1971; numerous others. **Business Addr:** Associate Professor, State University of New York Upstate Medical Center, 750 E Adams St, Syracuse, NY 13210.

IVY, JAMES E
Police officer. **Personal:** Born Sep 13, 1937, Memphis, TN; son of John and Mary Wells Coleman; married Sally Gibbs Ivy, Jan 23, 1980; children: Jacqueline, Pamela & Gwendolyn & Bridgette. **Educ:** Memphis State Univ; Univ N Fla; Nat Exec Inst, Nat FBI Acad. **Career:** Police officer (Retired); Memphis Police Dept, Memphis, TN, police officer, 1963-73, lt, 1973-79, capt, 1979-81, inspector, 1981-83, chief inspector, 1983-84, dep chief, 1984-88, dir, 1988-95. **Orgs:** Int Asns Chiefs Police; Memphis Metrop Asn Chiefs Police; Nat Exec Inst Alumni Asn. **Honors/Awds:** Outstanding Achievement, Governor Ned McWherter, 1988; Dedicated Community Serv, Breath Life SD A Church, 1990; Outstanding Religious Serv, Gospel Temple Baptist Church, 1991; Dedicated Community Serv, Moolah Temple #54. **Special Achievements:** First Black Director to Memphis Police Dept.

IZELL, BOOKER T
Newspaper executive. **Personal:** Born Feb 14, 1940, Auburn, AL; son of Davis WalKer; married Birdie M Carpenter, May 1, 1962; children: Gwendolyn R. **Educ:** Wright State Univ, acct, 1968-70. **Career:** Dayton Newspaper, circulation mgr, 1965-78; Springfield Newspaper, circulation dir, 1978-84; Cox Enterprises Inc, mgr human resources develop, 1987-93; Atlanta Jour & Const, single copy mgr, 1984-87, vpres community affairs / workplace diversity, 1993; Booker T Izell Assoc, pres, currently. **Orgs:** Nat Asn Advan Colored People, 1975; Nat Asn Black Journalists, 1986; bd mem, Atlanta Bus Forum, 1991; bd mem, Atlanta Art & Bus, 1992; Atlanta Chamber Com, 1992; Southern Circulation Mgr Asn, 1992-95; bd mem, Alliance Theatre Arts, 1993; Regional Leadership Found, 1993; Newspaper Asn Am, 1994; trustee, Clayton State Univ, 1996. **Honors/Awds:** Glenn L Cox Award, Dayton Newspaper, 1975; Ohio President Award, 1983. **Military Serv:** US Marines, 1958-61. **Business Addr:** President, Booker T Izell Associates, 3019 Duke of Gloucester, East Point, GA 30344, **Business Phone:** (404)768-5423.

IZRAEL, JIMI
Journalist. **Personal:** Divorced. **Educ:** B.A. in Communications from Cleveland State Univ; Master of Fine Arts Degree from Spalding Univ. **Honors/Awds:** Presidential Fellow at Case Western Reserve Univ. **Special Achievements:** Moderates The Barbershop for Natl Public Radio's Tell Me More with Michel Martin; blogs The Hardline for Washington Post-backed, The Root.com; Primary Colors for TV One Online; his opinion appears in Los Angeles Times, Salon.com, Philadelphia Inquirer, Chicago Tribune, Atlanta Journal-Constitution, American Spectator, The Plain Dealer; author of The Denzel Principle. *

J

J., RAY (WILLIE RAYMOND NORWOOD JR.)
Singer, executive. **Personal:** Born Jan 17, 1981, McComb, MS; son of Willie Norwood and Sonja Bates-Norwood. **Career:** Albums: Everything You Want, 1997; This Ain't a Game, 2001; Raydiation, 2005; Tv: "The Sinbad Show", 1993; "The Enemy Within", 1994 "Moesha", 1996; "Aftershock: Earthquake in New York", 1999; "Source Sound Lab", 2000; "The Proud Family", 2001; "Black Sash", 2003; "Christmas at Water's Edge", 2004; "One on One", 2005; "Love Triangle", 2006; films: Mars Attacks!, 1996; Steel, 1997; Superstar, 2007; KnockOut Entertainment, Los Angeles, CA, prin, chief exec officer, currently. **Business Addr:** Chief Executive Officer, KnockOut Entertainment, 10960 Wilshire Blvd Suite 2150, Los Angeles, CA 90024-3807.*

JACKET, BARBARA JEAN
Athletic director, educator. **Personal:** Born Dec 26, 1936, Port Arthur, TX; daughter of Raymond Jacket and Eva Mae Getwood-Pickney. **Educ:** Tuskegee Inst, BS, 1958; Prairie View A&M Univ, MS, 1968; Univ Houston,advan studies, 1976. **Career:** US World Championships, head coach, 1986; Van Buren High Sch, phys educ teacher; Lincoln High Sch, phys educ teacher; Prairie View A&M Univ, womens track & field, head coach, dir athletics, prof phys educ, currently. **Orgs:** Nat Col Athletic Asn; Nat Asn Intercollegiate Athletics; Southwestern Athletic Conf. **Honors/Awds:** Tuskegee Athletic Hall of Fame, 1987; Coach of the Year, Cross Country Southwestern Athletic Comt, 1987; Coach of the Year, Indoor Southwestern Athletic Conf, 1987; Coach of the Year, NAIA Indoor & Outdoor Nat Championship, 1987; Joe Robercher Award, Athletic Congress, 1992, The Presidents TAC Award, 1992; Yellow Rose of Texas Award (2), Gov Ann Richards, 1992; Texas Womens Hall of Fame, Texas Womens Conf, 1992; Southwestern Athletic Conference Hall of Fame; NAIA Hall of Fame; Prairie View A&M University Hall of Fame. **Special Achievements:** Second Black female to coach an Olympic team. **Business Addr:** Professor of Physical Education, Prairie View A&M University, PO Box 1500, Prairie View, TX 77446, **Business Phone:** (936)261-9100.

JACKS, ULYSSES
Lawyer. **Personal:** Born Jan 15, 1937, Coatesville, PA; son of Fred Douglas and Mable; married Esterlene A Gibson; children: Marcus U & Eric D. **Educ:** Va Union Univ, BS, 1959; La Salle Col, acct, 1967; Howard Univ Law Sch, JD (Cum Laude), 1970. **Career:** Philadelphia Pub Schs, teacher, 1964-67; Equal Employ Opportunity Comn, decision writer, 1969-70; Howard Law Sch, admin asst univ coun; Csaplar & Bok, assoc, 1970-77; Massachusetts Highway Dept, dep chief coun, 1977-. **Orgs:** Teaching fel, Howard Univ Law Sch, 1969-70; Massachusetts Black Lawyers; Massachusetts Bar Asn; Am Bar Asn; dir, Opportunities Indust Ctrs Greater Boston, 1982-88; dir, Codman Square Housing Corp, 1988-90; dir, Commonwealth Coop Bank, 1991-. **Special Achievements:** Development Editor for Howard University Law Journal, 1968-69. **Military Serv:** AUS, sgt, 1960-62. **Business Addr:** Deputy Chief Counsel, Massachusetts Highway Department, 10 Pk Plz, Boston, MA 02116, **Business Phone:** (617)973-7810.

JACKSON, DR. ADA JEAN WORK
President (organization), educator. **Personal:** Born in Nashville, TN; daughter of Lucuis Work Jr and Josephine Wilson; children: Andrea Eva Fitzpatrick Collins. **Educ:** Tenn State Univ, BS, 1959, ME, 1965; George Peabody Col Teachers, EdS, guid & couns, 1975; Vanderbilt Univ, PhD, educ admin, 1981. **Career:** Educator (retired), President; Metro Pub Sch, reading specialist, 1964-76, careers spec, 1976-77, guid counsr, 1977-79, asst prin, 1979-83, coordr stud referrals, 1983-85, admin, Comprehensive High Sch, 1985-95, US Dept Educ, reviewer, 1989-2000; United Methodist Church, Black Col Fund, asst gen secy, 1995-97; prin; J'S Serv Concept, owner. **Orgs:** Alpha Delta Omega; Alpha Kappa Alpha; 1957-; Miss Nat Educ Asn; TEA; Nat Educ Asn, 1959-; Phi Delta Kappa 1972-; Nat Asn Sec Sch Prin, 1978-; nat pres, Nat Pan-Hellenic Coun, 1985-89; interim asst gen secy, United Methodist Church Black Col Fund, 1995, dir, 1996; Coalition 100 Black Prof Women; Urban League; Urban League Guild; life mem, Nat Asn Advan Colored People; Nashville Dem Women Soc; Top Ladies Distinction; pres, Nashville Chap, 1996-2000; Leadership Brentwood, 1999-2000; scholarship bd, Am Baptist Col; nat pres, Tenn State Univ Alumni Asn, currently. **Honors/Awds:** Woman of the Year, Gordon United Methodist Women's Honoree, 1964; National Leader of America Award, Nat Asn Equal Opportunity Higher Educ, 1980; Black Outstanding Leader Award, 1986; Soror of the Year, Alpha Kappa Alpha, 1987; Woman of the Year, Nat Bus & Prof Womens Orgn, 1987; Professional Woman of the Year, Nat Asn Negro Bus & Prof Women, 1987; Distinguished Service Award, Tenn Black Caucus State Legis, 1988; Woman of the Year, Gordon United Methodist Church; Nat Outstanding Community Leadership Award, NCP, 1992; Distinguished Bell Ringers Image Award, Bennett Col, 1996; Distinguished Service Award, Coalition of 100 Black Women, 1999; Outstanding Living Legend Service Award, Tenn State Univ, 1999.

JACKSON, AGNES MORELAND
Educator. **Personal:** Born Dec 2, 1930, Pine Bluff, AR; married Harold A Jr; children: Barbara R Arnwine & Lucretia D Peebles. **Educ:** Univ Redlands, BA, eng, 1952; Univ Wash, MA, eng lit, 1953; Columbia Univ,PhD, philos, 1960. **Career:** Spelman Col, instr, 1953-55; Boston Univ, Col Basic Studies, Liberal Arts,instr, asst prof, 1959-63; Calif State Univ, Los Angeles, from asst prof to assoc prof, 1963-69; Pitzer Col, Intercollegiate Dept Black Studies,eng prof, 1969, Peter S & Gloria Gold prof, 1992-97, prof emer, 1997-;Sojourner Truth Lectr, Claremont McKenna Col, 2000-01; consult. **Orgs:** Soc Values Higher Educ Cent Comt, 1971-74; Danforth Asn Prog, 1971-; bdtrustees, pres, Pomona Unified Sch Dist, 1981-89; nominating comt, bd dir,Span Trails Girl Scout Coun, 1981-90; Phi Beta Kappa, Univ Redlands,1982-; Pomona School Board. bd dirs, Modern Lang Asn, 1985-88; AAUP; Am Asn Univ Women. **Honors/Awds:** Grad Fel Award, United Church Christ Danforth, 1952-59; Southern Fel Fund Award, 1955; Distinguished Serv Award, Univ Redlands Alumni Asn, 1973; Cross-Disciplinary Post-Doctoral Fel Award, Soc Values Higher Educ. **Business Addr:** Professor Emerita, Pitzer College, 1050 N Mills Ave, Claremont, CA 91711.

JACKSON, ALFRED THOMAS
Athletic coach, executive. **Personal:** Born May 30, 1937, Issue, MD; married Clarice Cecelia Brooks; children: Michael, Karen & Damien. **Educ:** Fisk Univ, BS, 1964. **Career:** Grand Union Co, Elmwood Park NJ, 1965-69, mgr training & develop, 1974-75, admin Training & develop, 1975; NBC NY, admin training & devel 1976,mgr & org Develop, 1976, dir & org Develop 1978, dir training, 1979-80,employee devel & coun, 1980, emp coun & develop & AA, dir, 1986-91;diversity & employee coun, dir, 1991-92; Diversity & Strategic Planning Scholastic Inc, dir, 1992-96; ATJ Enterprises, LLC, founder & pres, 1996-. **Orgs:** Pres, Better Hu-

man Rels Coun, Bloomfield, NJ, 1973-78; chmn comt, Adv Brd Bloomfield Col, 1973-77; brd trustees, Bloomfield Col NJ, 1977-78; brd, Am Red Cross Metro NJ. **Honors/Awds:** Black Achievers Award Harlem Ymca NY, 1971. **Military Serv:** AUS, E-2, 1960; Out standing Trainee of the Cycle, AUS, 1960. **Home Addr:** 214 Elmwynd Dr, Orange, NJ 07050. **Business Addr:** President, Founder, ATJ Enterprises LLC, PO Box 826, South Orange, NJ 07079-9998, **Business Phone:** (301)259-2055.

JACKSON, ALPHONSE
Social worker, state government official. **Personal:** Born Nov 27, 1927, Shreveport, LA; married Ruby H McClure; children: Lydia & Angela. **Educ:** Southern Univ, BA, 1944; NY Univ, MA. **Career:** LEA, pres, 1965-70, past vpres; teacher; NEA, state dir; State La, St rep Dist 2, 1972-92; Early Head Start Ctr, lobbyist; Caddo Community Action Agency, social worker, currently; Alphonse Jackson Jr Early HeadStart Ctr, social worker, currently. **Orgs:** Nat Dept Elem Prin; Shreveport Bicent Comt; LA House Reps, Health & Welfare Comt; La Legis Black Caucus. **Military Serv:** World War II. **Business Phone:** (318)629-1900.

JACKSON, ALPHONSO
Government official. **Personal:** Born Sep 9, 1945, Marshall, TX; married Marcia A Clark-Jackson, Jun 18, 1988; children: Annette, Lesley. **Educ:** Turman State Univ, BS, polit sci, 1968, MA, educ admin, 1969; Wash Univ Sch Law, JD, 1973. **Career:** City St Louis, dir pub safety, 1977; St Louis Housing Authority, exec dir; Laventhol & Horwath, St Louis, MO, dir consult serv; Univ Mo, spec asst chancellor & asst prof; Dept Pub & Assisted Housing, WA, DC, dir; Dallas Housing Authority, pres & chief exec officer, 1989-96; Am Elec Power-Tex, Austin, TX, pres, 1996-01; US Housing & Urban Develop Dept, dep secy & chief operating officer, 2001-04, secy, 2004-. **Orgs:** fel Apsen Inst; Chairperson, DC Redevelop Land Agency Bd; chmn, Gen Serv Comn, State Tex; Nat Comn Am's Urban Families; Nat Comn Severely Distressed Pub Housing; Kappa Alpha Psi Fraternity. **Business Addr:** Secretary, US Dept of Housing & Urban Develop, 451 7th St SW, Washington, DC 20410.*

JACKSON, ALTERMAN
Educator. **Personal:** Born Feb 28, 1948, Bronx, NY. **Educ:** Lincoln Univ, BA, 1970; Millersville State Col, ME, 1973. **Career:** City Lancaster, personnel asst, 1970-71; Sch Dist Lancaster, dir 1971-72; Millersville Univ, asst dir, counr, 1972-76; Lancaster Rec Comn; supvr, 1974-76; Hahnemann Univ Sch Med, dir, admis, 1976; Harrisburg Area Community Col, vpres stud affairs/enrollment mgt, dir Admis & Mkt, 2004. **Orgs:** Pres, 307-Acad Fel, 1968-69; Lancaster City Co Human Rel Comn, 1971; comnmem, King-Clemente Memorial Scholar Fund Trinity Luth Church, 1972-77;regist rep, Pa State Ed Asn, 1972-77; Pa Black Conf Higher Educ, 1973-76,NE Med Schs, 1976-77; bd dirs, Nat Asn Med Minority Educ, 1976-77; registrep, Asn Am Med Col, 1977; Omega Psi Phi. **Honors/Awds:** Outstanding Young Men of America, 1976.

JACKSON, ALVIN B., JR.
Government official. **Personal:** Born Mar 21, 1961, Miami, FL; son of Gussye M Bartley; married Dorothea U. Jackson, Mar 12, 1983; children: Alvin Bernard III, Carla, Desarae, Doreen, Kavell, Nicola, Sharonette, Tiffini. **Educ:** Univ Md, Col Park, MD, BA, govt & polit, 1982. **Career:** Urban Resources Consul, Washington DC, admin aide, 1979-81; Birch & Davis Asn, Silver Spring MD, govt conf coordr, 1982-83; Ft Lauderdale Col, Miami FL, dir admin, 1984; Real Estate Data Inc, Miami FL, county coordr, 1985-88; Opa-Locka Com Develop Corp, Pastor, The Church of the Kingdom of God, 1984-97; Opa-Locka FL, com revitalization specialist, 1988; Town Eatonville FL, town adminr, 1988-90; City Eustis, dir human servs, 1990-93; Econ Develop Comn Mid-Florida, Lake Co, coordr, 1993-96; Dep County Mgr, Lake Co Bd, co comnr, 1996-01; S Fla Water Mgt Dist, dep exec dir, govt & pub affairs, currently. **Orgs:** Am Soc Pub Admin, 1985; secy, King Clubs Greater Miami, 1987-88; chmn, Day Care Comt, 1987-88, area pres, Dade County PTA/PTSA; Fla State Comt African American Hist, 1988, chair, 1998; Fla League Cities Black Elected, 1988; Preserve Eatonville Community Inc, 1988-; Zora Neale Hurston Ad Hoc, 1988-90; state chmn, Progress Inc; coun mem, Fla State Hist Preserv Coun, 1988-94; bd dir, Ctr Drug Free Living, 1989-91; bd dirs, Lake Sumter Mental Health & Hosp, 1990-93; Golden Triangle Kiwanis, vpres; Lake County Urban Network; HRS Health & Human Serv Local Bd; Fla Dept Educ Tech Comn Mkg Educ; bd dirs, Fla Waterman Hosp Found, 1994-96; bd regents, Leadership Lake, 1994-. **Honors/Awds:** City Manager, Mayor's Award, 1991; Wall of Fame, Eustis High Sch, 1992; Apple From the Teachers Award, 1989; Washington Day Parade Marshall, 1995; Community Service Award, Orlando Sentinel/Lake County League Cities, 1995; Community Service Award Bus Develop, 1995; Outstanding Community Service Award, 1995; Black Achiever of Central Florida Award, 1997. **Home Addr:** PO Box 124, Eustis, FL 32727-0124. **Business Addr:** South Florida Water Management District, County Manager's Office, 3301 Gun Club Rd, West Palm Beach, FL 33406, **Business Phone:** (561)686-8800.*

JACKSON, DR. ANDREW
Educator, sociologist. **Personal:** Born Feb 2, 1945, Montgomery, AL; married Hazel Ogilvie; children: Yasmine Nefertiti. **Educ:** Yale Univ, study prog, 1966; Alabama State Univ, BA, 1967; Univ Nairobi Kenya, Ed, 1970; Univ Calif, Santa Barbara, MA Ed, Psych, 1970, MA, 1972, PhD, soc, 1974. **Career:** Desegregation Inst Emergency Sch Aid Act, consult, 1977; Fisk Univ, adj prof, 1978-; US Dept Labor, HBC faculty fel, 1980; Nat assoc equal oppty higher ed, consult, 1981; Tenn St Univ, prof soc, 1973-, head, Dept Africana Studies. **Orgs:** Pres, Assoc Social & Behavioral Scientists Inc, 1983-84; mem, Ed Bd Jour Soc & Behavioral Sci, 1984-; chairperson, bd dir, Sank of a Dance Theatre, 1984-; mem, Am Soc Assoc, Am Acad Political & Soc Sci, Southern Soc Assoc, Am Assoc Univ Prof, Kappa Alpha Psi, Islamic Ctr Inc; life mem, Asn Social & Behavioral Scientists Inc. **Honors/Awds:** Delegate Crisis Black Family Summit, NAACP, 1984; Article "Illuminating the Path to Community Self-Reliance" Journal of Soc & Behavioral Sci 1984; Textbook Sci of Soc, 1985; article "Apart he id, the Great Debate and Martin Luther King Jr" The AME Church Review, 1985. **Business Addr:** Professor, Tennessee State University, Department of Africana Studies, 3500 John A Merritt Blvd, Nashville, TN 37203.

JACKSON, ANDREW PRESTON (SEKOU MOLEFI BAAKO)
Library administrator. **Personal:** Born Jan 28, 1947, Brooklyn, NY; son of Walter L Sr and Bessie Lindsay. **Educ:** York Col, Jamaica, NY, BS, 1990; City Univ NY, MLS, libr sci; Queens Col, City Univ NY, Flushing, NY, MLS, 1996. **Career:** NY Agency Child Develop, coordr personnel serv, 1971-76; Robinson Chevrolet, Novato, CA, customer rels mgr, 1976-78; Langston Hughes Community Libr & Cult Ctr, Corona, NY, exec dir, 1980-; York Col, City Univ NY, adj prof, 2001-; Roosevelt Pub Libr, Training, Develop & Opers, consult, 2005-; author; essayist; lecturer. **Orgs:** Bd mem, Elmhurst Hosp Ctr, 1983-97; life mem, Nat Asn Adavn Colored People; NY Black Librarians Caucus; York Col Alumni, Inc; adv coun, York Col; exec bd, Am Lib Asn; community adv bd, Louis Armstrong House & Archives, 1998-; bd dir, Dollars Scholars, Corona-East Elmhurst chapter, 1998-; bd educ, People African Ancestry, 1999-; Poet Laureate Queens Selection Comt, 1999-; NY State Freedom Trial Community, 1999-2002; NY Libr Asn; bd trustees, Renaissance Charter Sch, 2000-; bd mem, Queens Col; Queens Borough Pres's Community Coun, 2002; pres, Black Caucus Am Libr Asn, 2004-06; past pres, Black Caucus Am Libr Asn 2006-08. **Honors/Awds:** Ombudsman Award, 1982; East Elmhurst Track Club, Community Service Award, 1986; Outstanding Leadership in Queens Award, Queens Fedn Churches, 1988; York Col, City Univ NY, Dean's List, 1990; Man of the Year, Nat Asn Negro Bus & Prof Women's Clubs Inc, 1991; African Americans of Distinction Award, NY State Gov, 1994; Distinguished Graduate Award, Nat Asn Equal Opportunity Higher Educ, 1994; Fulfilling the Dream Award, WCBS-TV, 1996; Distinguished Alumni Award, York Col Alumni Inc, 1996; Scroll of Honor, 4W Circle Arts & Enterprise Inc, 1996; Community Service Award, Nat Coun Negro Women Inc, North Shore Chap, 1997; Community Service Award, E Elmhurst Alumni Asn, 1998; Outstanding Contribution Award, Combined Treas Agencies, 1999; Lamplighter of the Year, Queens Borough Pl, 1999; BCALA Library Advocacy Award, 1999; Community Service Award, FDNY African Heritage Soc, 2000; Appreciation Award, Grace Episcopal Church, 2001; Cultural Award & Exemplary Community Service Award, Key Women Am Inc, 2002; Community Activist Award, United Progress Dem Club, 2002; Community Service Award, Corona Cong Church, 2002; Excellence in Leadership, Empress Life Members Guild, 2002; Citation of Honor, Queens Borough Pres, 2002; Community Person of the Year, Delta Beta Zeta chapter. **Special Achievements:** Contributing Author-Foreword, African American Almanac, 9th and 10th Editions, 2003, 2008; "If You Want to Know the Secrets of the World, Read a Book!", Turn The Page and You Don't Stop Sharing Successful Chapters in Our Lives With Youth, 2006; "In the Tradition: The Legacy of Culture Messengers From Langston Hughes to Tupac Shakur", 2006. **Military Serv:** USAF, E-5, 1964-68; Bronze Star, 1967. **Home Addr:** 94-24 30th Ave, East Elmhurst, NY 11369. **Business Addr:** Executive Director, Queens Library, Langston Hughes Community Library & Cultural Center, 100 01 Northern Blvd, Corona, NY 11368.

JACKSON, ANGELA
Poet, playwright, writer. **Personal:** Born Jul 25, 1951, Greenville, MS; daughter of George and Angeline Robinson. **Educ:** Northwestern Univ, BA, Eng & Am lit, 1977; Univ Chicago, MA, humanities, 1995. **Career:** Ill Arts Coun, poets-in-the-Sch prog, 1974-76, 1979-83; Stephens Col, writer in residence, 1983-86; Columbia Col, 1986-88, writer in residence, 1988-92; Framingham State Col, writer in residence, 1994; Howard Univ, lectr, 1995-97; Sch Art Inst, fac, creative writing prog, 1998; freelance writer & editor, 1998-. **Orgs:** OBAC Writers Workshop, 1970-90; Ebony Talent Found Aux, 1977; First World, 1977-78; Ill Arts Coun Lit Panel, 1979-81, 1992; fel Coordinating Coun Lit Mag, 1981-85, sec 1983, pres 1984, treas, 1985; ETA Playwright Discovery Iniative, 1991-98. **Honors/Awds:** NEA Creative Writing Fellowship, 1980; America Book Award, 1985; Book of the Year Award, 1994; Carl Sandburg Award, Chicago Pub Libr, 1994; Daniel Curley Award, IAC Arts Coun, 1997; Creative Writing Fellowship, Ill Arts Coun, 2000. **Special Achievements:** Author, Dark Legs & Silk Kisses: The Beatitudes of the Spinners, 1992; "Shango Diaspora," 1980; "Comfort Stew," 1997; And All These Roads Be Luminous: Poems Selected & New, 1998. **Home Addr:** 5527 S Wentworth Ave, Chicago, IL 60621. **Business Addr:** Poet, Author, 2693 Lakeshore Blvd West Suite 11, Toronto, ON, Canada M8V 1G6, **Business Phone:** (416)259-3365.

JACKSON, DR. ANNA MAE
Educator. **Personal:** Born Apr 10, 1934, Wetumpka, AL; daughter of Moses E and Alice M; children: Stevan & Sean. **Educ:** Bowling Green State Univ, BA, 1959; Univ Denver, MA, 1960; Colo State Univ, PhD, 1967. **Career:** State Home & Training Sch Lapeer Mich, staff psych, 1960-61; State Home & Training Sch Wheat ridge Colo, chief psych, 1962-68; Univ Colo Health Sci Ctr, assoc prof psych, assoc prof, assoc dean. **Orgs:** Consult, US Homes Inc, 1975-78; visiting lecturer, Afro-Am Studies Dept, 1971-73; adv bd, Sch Comn & Human Srer; Assoc Black Psych, pres Denver Rocky Mountain Chap, 1993-94; Nat Advan Asn Colored People Park Hill Br, 1982-83; Denver Urban League. **Honors/Awds:** Woman of the Year, Regina's Soc and Civic Club, 1977; Woman of Achivement,Denver Alumnae Chap Delta Sigma Theta Sor, 1976; Founders Award, Asn Black Psychologists, 1987; Distinguished Chapter Service Award, Denver-Rocky Mountain Chapter Asn Black Psychologists, 1987; Distinguished Psychologist, Assoc Black Psychologists. *

JACKSON, ART EUGENE, SR.
Executive. **Personal:** Born Jan 14, 1941, Saint Louis, MO; married Nodie Elnora Scales; children: Andrea Annette, Art Eugene Jr. **Educ:** Lincoln Univ. **Career:** McDonnell Douglas, stock keeper, 1966-69; Freeman Shoe Co, mgr sales, 1969-85; Mc Donnell Douglas, tool & parts ctrl spec. **Orgs:** NAACP, 1953; club scout leader Boys Scout Am, 1972; pres, City Northwoods, 1974; treas & pk bd, City Northwoods, 1982; alderman, City Northwoods, 1983-; treas, Normandy Baseball League. **Honors/Awds:** DECA, Trainer St Louis Pub Sch, 1980-81. **Military Serv:** USAF, aic, 4 yrs; Good Conduct, Sharp Shooting, 1959-64. **Business Addr:** Tool & Parts Control Specialist, Mc Donnell Douglas, Mc Donnell Blvd, Saint Louis, MO 63134.

JACKSON, ARTHUR D., JR.
Judge, legal consultant. **Personal:** Born Oct 31, 1942; married Suellen Kay Shea; children: Christopher Daniel, Kyle Joseph, Courtney Kathleen. **Educ:** Ohio Northern Univ, BS, BMusEd, 1964, JD, 1968. **Career:** City Dayton Dept Law, negotiator & asst city atty, 1968-70; Jackson & Austin, atty law, 1969-71; City Dayton, asst city prosecutor, 1970-71; Dept Justice S Dist Oh, asst US atty, 1971-74; Dayton/Mont Co Crim Justice Ctr, legal spec/instr, 1974-75; Skilken & Jackson, atty, 1975-77; Dayton Municipal Ct, judge. **Orgs:** Choir dir, Epworth Meth Church, 1964-67; deputy dir, Pub Defender Asn, 1975-76; instr, Sinclair Comn Col, 1975-; hearing officer, Ohio Civil Rights Comn, 1975-76; exec comn, Mont Co Emergency Serv Coun; Dayton Performing Arts Fund Bd; pres, Dayton Ballet Co Bd; adj prof law, Univ Dayton Col Law, 1977-. **Honors/Awds:** Outstanding Actor-Musical Dayton Co, 1980; State Certified EMT Paramedic, 1981 & 1984. **Business Addr:** Attorney, 3rd Pine St, Seattle, WA 98101.

JACKSON, ARTHUR HOWARD
Executive. **Personal:** Born Mar 27, 1956, Bronx, NY; son of Arthur H and Minnie Belle McChaney-Jackson. **Educ:** Am Col, BA, MA, bus & technol, PhD bus & ethics; Joint Ctr Polit Studies, cert Govt mgt; George Wash Univ, paralegal studies; John Hopkins Univ, community Planning, attended. **Career:** DC Govt, contracting engr, 1990-99; AHJ Group, pres & chief exec officer, 1999-. **Orgs:** Mayor's Task Force Govt Finance, 1994-98; adv Mayor Wash DC, MB Focus Group, 1994-98; nat vpres, Fighting 54th Inc, 1994-; precinct coordr, Unify Beautify Campaign, 1995; bd consumer adv, Giant Foods Stores, 1998-2000; adv bus develop, Southwest Hill Asn, 1999-; bus consult, Fundraising Network Inc, 1999-; planning comt, Mayor's Neighborhood Action Proj, 1999-2000; aids benefit planning Comt, Race Cure, 2000. **Honors/Awds:** Named Outstanding Young Leader U.S. Jaycees, 1988; Ted Hagans Award, Govt DC, 1998; Community Serv Award, Prince Georges Chamber Com, 1998; Serv Award, Cong Heights Post Office, 1999; Outstanding Serv Award, City Seat Pleasant, MD, 1999; Freedom Fund Award, Nat Asn Advan Colored People. **Special Achievements:** Elected in 1975 as the youngest elected city councilman in US history at age 18; author of "Hope City" script; at age 14, youngest reporter in the history of The Afro American Newspaper; actor: Deep Impact, Pelican Brief, Fat City; author, Marion Barry Warrior for the People, 2000. **Business Phone:** (202)271-5522.

JACKSON, DR. ARTHUR JAMES
Educator. **Personal:** Born Jan 11, 1943, Union Springs, AL; married Beverly Fennoy; children: Monica D. **Educ:** Wayne State Univ, BS, 1972, Sch Med, MS, 1976, PhD, 1979. **Career:** Wayne St Univ, grad asst, 1974-76, grad asst, 1976-79; Tenn State Univ, Dept Phys Sci, adj fac, currently; Meharry Med Col, Dept Biomed Sci, Div Prof Educ, assoc prof anat & vice chair, currently. **Orgs:** Treas, Alpha Omega Alpha; Black Med Asn. **Honors/Awds:** Pre-Alumni Council Award for Excellence in Teaching, Meharry Med Col, 1980; Kaiser-Permanente Award for Excellence in Teaching, Meharry Medical Col, 1980; Award for Excellence in Teaching, Black Med Asn, Wayne St Univ. **Special Achievements:**

Published numerous books. **Business Addr:** Associate Professor of Anatomy, Vice Chair, Meharry Medical College, Department of Anatomy, WBS B116 1005 DB Todd Blvd, Nashville, TN 37208, **Business Phone:** (615)327-6712.

JACKSON, DR. ARTHUR ROSZELL
School administrator. **Personal:** Born Aug 16, 1949, Fort Dix, NJ; son of Arthur and Elouise Fussell; married Celeste Budd, Jun 25, 1983; children: Kyle Arthur & Tamara Sheree. **Educ:** State Univ NY, BA, 1971, MA, 1977; Univ MA, Amherst, MA, EdD, 1988. **Career:** Educ Opportunity Prog, State Univ NY, acad counr, 1971-72; State Univ NY Binghamton, asst dir stud financial aide, 1972-77; Financial Aid Serv Univ Mass, assoc dir, 1977-82; Financial Aid Serv Univ Mass Amherst, dir, 1982-90; Eastern Conn State Univ, assoc dean stud affairs; Norfolk State Univ, vpres stud affairs, 1997-2000; West fied State Col, vpres stud affairs, currently. **Orgs:** Vice chmn New England Col Bd 1984-86; liaison/consult, Nat Consortium Educ Access 1985-87; vpres, Eastern Asn Stud Financial Aid Admins 1986; pole march, pres Hartford Alumni Chap Kappa Alpha Psi, 1986-87; Nat Conf Black Retention 1986, Col Bd Nat Forum, 1986; bd dir, MA Higher Educ Assistance Corp, I988-; pres, Eastern Asn Stud Financial Aid Admin, I989;Conn state dir, Nat Asn Stud Personnel Admin, 1993-95; chmn, Educ Resource Inst, 1994-96; Sigma Pi Phi Fraternity, 1994; Minority Undergraduate Fellows Prog, NASPA, 1997-2000; adv Bd, Norfolk Acad, 1998-2000; adv bd, White Oak Sch, 2000. **Honors/Awds:** Network on Equity & Excellence Award, Nat Asn Stud Personnel Admin, 1992; Speaker Nat Asn Student Personnel Adminrs 1995; Golden Key Honor Soc, 1997; Found Excellence, Asn Col & Univ Housing Org, 1999. **Special Achievements:** President Clinton Post Secondary Education Transition Task Force, 1992-93. **Business Addr:** Vice Chancellor of Student Affairs, University of North Carolina, 9201 University City Blvd, charlotte, NC 28223.

JACKSON, AUBREY N.
Dentist. **Personal:** Born Feb 11, 1926, Lynchburg, VA; married Laura Thompson; children: Aubrey, Kelly, Carl. **Educ:** Bluefield State Col, BS, 1949; Howard Univ, attended 1950; Meharry Med Col, DDS, 1954. **Career:** Dent Clin Salem, pvt practice, currently. **Orgs:** NDA; Am Dent Asn; past pres, WVa Med Soc; WVa State Dent Soc; pres, Mercer-Mcdowell Dent Soc; Mcdowell Co Health Coun; Chas Payne Dent Study Club; Bluefield Study Club; chmn exec comn, Nat Advan Asn Colored People; pol coun, Coun Southern Mountains; treas, Alpha Zeta Lambda Chap Alpha Phi Alpha; treas, Upsilon Boule Sigma Pi Phi. **Military Serv:** USN, PhM 3rd cl, 1944-46. **Business Addr:** Dentist, 107 Main St, Hc 52 Box 165, Keystone, WV 24852, **Business Phone:** (304)862-3338.*

JACKSON, AUDREY NABORS
Executive. **Personal:** Born Jul 10, 1926, New Orleans, LA; daughter of Raymond Nabors Sr and Beluah Carney Nabors; married Freddie Sr, Jul 26, 1946 (deceased); children: Claudia J Fisher, Beverly J Franklin, Freddie Jr (deceased), Sharyll Muri Curley-Etuk, Antria Curley Wilson & Zefron Curley. **Educ:** Southern Univ, Lab Sch, Baton Rouge, LA, attended; Southern Univ & A&M Col, Baton Rouge, LA, BA, 1951, med, 1966; Chicago Teachers Col, attended 1959. **Career:** Librarian (retired); JS Dawson High Sch, librn, 1951-54; Southdown HS, librn 1954-55; Chaneyville High Sch Zachary LA, librn, 1955-81; La Legis Bureau, secy, 1979, 1980; Clerk Court's Off, abstractor, 1982; La Senate Docket, legis session, 1982, 1983, 1984; census taker, 1990; Nabors Bid Tabulation Serv, pres/owner. **Orgs:** Usher, Greater PhiLa delphia Baptist Church; golden life mem, treas, DST Sorority Inc, 1971-75, 1979; YWCA Author Comm; life mem, Southern Univ Alumni Fed; charter mem, Women in Mainstream; fin chair, La Womens Pol Caucus, 1984-85, treas, 1985; 1st vice chair, Baton Rouge Womens Pol Caucus, 1984-85, treas, 1985-; treas, Friends Int, 1982-; La Retired Teachers Asn; La Democratic Fin Coun; Nat Retired Teachers Asn; Mayor Press Comn Needs Women, 1982-85; exec bd LLA, sch librn, 1977-79; secy, Human Resource & Develop CRP, 1978-80; lib dept, pres, La Asn Educators, 1967-69, 1977-78; treas, 1973, vpres, 1973-74, Rural Prog Adv Bd; Nat Educ Asn; treas, La Women in Polit, 1986-; treas, Baton Rouge Women's Politics, 1986-; life mem, Southern Univ Alumni Fed; Am Asn Retired Persons; life mem, Am Lib Asn,; adv comt, Am Asn Sch Librarians; Centroplex, 1991-; vol, Baton Rouge City Ct; bd dir, Doug Williams Found, 1988; La Democratic State Cent Comt, Dist 64, elect unopposed, 1992-96, 1997-2002; secy, treas, Sixth Congressional Dist La, 1993-; Woman Greater Baton Rouge Coun, 1998-2004; City-Parish Planning & Zoning Comn, 200104; vpres, 1999-2000, pres-elect, 2000-01, pres, 2001-02, treas, 2003-, Kiwanis; vol, FAAA; chair, City Planning & Zoning Comn, 2003-04; comnr & chmn, Recreation & Pk Comn For the Parish E Baton Rouge, 2005-.

JACKSON, HON. AVA NICOLA
Lawyer. **Personal:** Born Nov 10, 1957, Preston, MS; daughter of Enos and Alma; married Charles G Woodall, Nov 13, 1981; children: Raphael Kenzell Jackson Woodall & Amanda Nicola Jackson Woodall. **Educ:** Univ Miss, BS, social work & pub admin, 1979, Sch Law, JD, 1981. **Career:** Morris & Jackson, assoc atty, 1981-82; N Miss Rural Legal Serv, managing atty, 1983-90, exec dir, 1990-, exec asst, currently. **Orgs:** Magnolia Bar Asn, 1981-; Miss Bar Asn, 1981-; pres, Zeta Phi Beta Sorority, 1985-. **Honors/Awds:** Service Award, NCP, Kemper County Br, 1986; Leadership Award, NMRLS, 1991; Legal Services Laywer of the Year, Miss Bar Asn, 1992; Zeta of the Year, Zeta Phi Beta, 1993. **Special Achievements:** First female executive director of the North Mississippi Rural Legal Services. **Home Phone:** (662)236-4167. **Business Addr:** Executive Director, Executive Assistant, North Mississippi Rural Legal Service, 5 Co Rd 1014, PO Box 767, Oxford, MS 38655, **Business Phone:** (662)234-8731.

JACKSON, DR. BENITA MARIE (BENITA MARIE JACKSON-SMOOT)
Physician. **Personal:** Born Aug 14, 1956, Englewood, NJ; daughter of Benjamin and Gloria. **Educ:** Mount Holyoke Col, BA, 1978; Howard Univ, Col Medicine, MD, 1982; Emory Univ, MPH, 1989. **Career:** Prev med residency prog, Ctrs Disease Control, dir; Howard Univ Hosp, epidemic intelligence officer & prev, 1984-86; Morehouse Sch Med, Internal Med, 1987-89; Group Health Prev Public Health, Emergency Med, staff physician; Ohio State Univ, Col Pub Health, asoc dean, dir & asst prof, currently. **Orgs:** Nat Med Asn; Am Pub Health Asn; Natural Med Asn; Am CLG Prev Med; Am Pub Health Asn; Asn Teachers Prev Med. **Honors/Awds:** Nat Achievement Scholarship Finalist for Outstanding Negro Students, 1974. **Business Addr:** Assistant Professor, Ohio State University, Div Epidemiol & Biostatistics, 320 W 10th Ave B-115 Starling-Loving Hall, Columbus, OH 43210.

JACKSON, BERNARD H
Lawyer. **Educ:** City Col New York, BA; Brooklyn Law Sch, JD; NY Law Sch, grad work. **Career:** Lawyer (retired); Bronx Criminal Ct, judge; Police Dept, legal staff; US Atty, asst; Dyett Alexander Dinkins, atty; OEO NE Region, area coodr; Civilian Complaint Rev Bd NY, exec dir; Pete Rozells Nat Football League, asst comnr; Gov NY, spec asst; Urban Crisis Am WEVD Radio, host; NY Supreme Ct, justice, 1987-90; Endispute, vpres, sr judicial officer; White & Case, coun, 1990. **Orgs:** Bd dir, Settlement Housing Fund; S Bronx Overall Econ Develop Corp; 100 Black Men; Police Athletic League NY; Nat Multiple Sclerosis Soc NY; Urban Leag; Mayor John Lindsay's Com City Marshals; Citizens Union NYC; founding mem, Neighbourhood Legal Serv Prog; Nat Asn Advan Colored People; Asn Bronx Comn Orgns; Taft Youth & Adult Ctr; guest lectr, John Jay Col New Sch Soc Res Bernard M Baruch Col; host, NY Urban League Presents WBLS-FM; mediator, Ctr Mediation & Conflict Resolution; arbitrator, first Judicial Dept NY Bar; US Supreme Ct; US Customs Ct; Fed Circuit Dist Cts; Am Bar Asn; Fed Bar Coun; Bronx Co Bar Asn; Harlem Lawyers Asn. **Honors/Awds:** Community Service Award, South Bronx Overall Develop Corp, 1992-; Outstanding Achievement Award, ASPIRA, 1991.

JACKSON, BEVERLY ANNE
Executive, television director. **Personal:** Born Nov 29, 1947, Philadelphia, PA; daughter of Frank E Jackson Sr. and Alice M McConico; children: Michelle Marie. **Educ:** Penn State Univ, BA, speech, broadcasting, 1969; Chas Morris Price Sch Advertising & Journalism, advertising certificate, 1972. **Career:** Sch Dist of Philadephia, substitute teacher, 1969-70; US Cencus Bureau, ade clerk, 1970-71; RCA Service CPN, special projects inr, 1971-72; KATZ-TV Television, advertising sales, sales asst, 1972; KYW-TV, Westinghouse Broadcasting CPN, production asst, 1972-74, assoc producer, 1974-76, dir, 1976-91; "The Joan Rivers Show," dir, 1991-; "Gossip, Gossip, Gossip with Joan Rivers," dir, 1992-; & VVerVe Graphix video, pres, owner, currently. **Orgs:** DRRs Guild of Am; AMR Women in Radio & TV; DST; volunteer Big Sister, Big Sisters of Philadelphia 1980; Intl TV Asn; Nat Academy of TV Arts and Sciences; SOC of Motion Picture and TV ENRs; Intl Brotherhood of Electrical Workers; Nat Black Media Coalition; Nat Asn of Female EXEs; Cherry Hill MNY Civic Asn. **Honors/Awds:** Nat Academy of Television Arts & SCIs, Philadelphia Chapter, Most Outstanding Television Talk Program, Series Emmy, for "Time Out," Beverly A Jackson, dir, 1987-88. **Special Achievements:** First AFA female dir hired by KYW-TV; believed to be the first AFA woman to direct a television program in the history of Philadelphia broadcast television. **Business Addr:** Director, Joan Rivers Show, CBS Broadcast Ctr, 555 W 57th St, New York, NY 10019.

JACKSON, BEVERLY JOYCE
Television producer, educator. **Personal:** Born May 17, 1955, Detroit, MI; daughter of Laura Grogan and Samuel. **Educ:** Univ Mich, Ann Arbor, Mich, BA, 1977. **Career:** WTOL-TV, Toledo, Ohio, news reporter, 1977-79; WGBH-TV, Boston, Mass, news reporter, 1982-83; WCVB-TV, Boston, Mass, producer, 1983-85; CBS News, New York, NY, producer, 1985-88; ABC News, New York, NY, producer, World News Tonight, 1988-93; NBC News, sr producer; Columbia Univ, adj prof. **Orgs:** NAB; Delta Sigma Theta Sorority Inc; vpres, Nat Asn Black Journalists, 1984-85. **Honors/Awds:** United Press International Award, 1984; Black Achievers Award, United Press Int, 1985; Gabriel Award, Nat Catholic Asn Broadcasters & Commun, 1990; Judge's Award, World Hunger Media Awards, 1990, CINE Golden Eagle Award, 1992; George Washington Medal of Honor, 1992; Gabriel Award, 1992; Gold Hugo-Chicago International Film Festival, 1993.

JACKSON, BO (VINCENT EDWARD JACKSON)
Football player, baseball player, actor. **Personal:** Born Nov 30, 1962, Bessemer, AP; son of A D Adams and Florence Bond; married Linda Garrett, Sep 5, 1987; children: Morgan, Garrett & Nicholas. **Educ:** Auburn Univ Sch, BS, Human Sci, 1995. **Career:** Football player, baseball player (retired), actor; Kansas City Royals, baseball player, 1986-90; Los Angeles Raiders, football player, 1987-90; Chicago White Sox, baseball player, 1991, 1993; Calif Angels, baseball player, 1994; Bo Jackson Elite Sports Complex, co-owner & chief exec off, currently. Films: Fakin' Da Funk, 1997; The Pandora Project, 1998. **Orgs:** Pres, Health South Sports Med Coun. **Honors/Awds:** Heisman Trophy Winner, Auburn Univ, 1985; American League All-Star Team,1989; Jim Thorpe Legacy Award, 1992; AL Comeback Player of the Year Award,1993; Col Football Hall of Fame, Natl Football Found, 1999; Tony Conigliaro Award, 1993. **Special Achievements:** First man to be named to both the Baseball All-Star game and the NFL's Pro Bowl.

JACKSON, BOBBY
Basketball player. **Personal:** Born Mar 13, 1973, East spencer, NC; son of Sarah Jackson. **Educ:** Univ Minn, sports mgt. **Career:** Denver Nuggets, guard, 1997-98; Minn Timber wolves, 1999-00; Sacramento Kings, guard, 2000-05; Memphis Grizzlies, point guard, 2005-06; NO Oklahoma City New Orleans Hornets, guard, 2006-08; Houston Rockets, 2008; Sacramento Kings, 2008-. **Honors/Awds:** Big Ten Player of the Yr; Defensive Player of the Yr; All-Final Four Team,NCAA; Most Valuable Player, Midwest Region; Sixth Man of the Year, 2002, 2003. **Special Achievements:** Schick All-Rookie Second Team, 1997, 1998. **Business Addr:** Professional Basketball Player, Sacramento Kings, ARCO Arena, One Sports Pkwy, Sacramento, CA 95834, **Business Phone:** (916)928-0000.*

JACKSON, BOBBY L. See Obituaries section.

JACKSON, BRENDA (BRENDA L JACKSON)
Executive. **Personal:** Born Oct 27, 1950, Aberdeen, MD. **Educ:** Prairie View A&M Univ, BS, home econs, 1972. **Career:** Dallas Power & Light Co, home serv adv, 1973-78, supvr consumer serv, 1978-81, community prog mgr, 1981; TXU Bus Serv, exec vpres, 2002; Oncor Elec Delivery Co, sr vpres elec asset ownership, 2003; TXU Elec Delivery, sr vpres customer/community serv, 2004-. **Orgs:** Vol, Tom Paukins Campaign Cong, 1978; bd dirs, Dallas Co Chap, Am Heart Asn; bd visitors, Bishop Col, Mus Afro-Am Life & Cult, 1979-; Dallas Black C C; Am Home Econs Asn; Tex Home Econs Asn; N Tex Home Economist Bus Am Asn; Blacks Energy; trustee, Teacher Retirement Syst Tex; Baylor Col Dent; Dallas Mus Art; Metrop YWCA; N Tex Comn; Dallas Opera; Presbyterian Hosp; Dallas Symphony. **Honors/Awds:** Award of Merit, Am Heart Asn, 1978; ATHENA Award, Greater Dallas Chamber. **Special Achievements:** Author (with Charlene Clark): The Children's Help Your Heart Cookbook, 1978. **Home Addr:** 5539 McCommas Blvd, Dallas, TX 75206. **Business Addr:** Senior Vice President, TXU Electric Delivery, 1601 Bryan St, Dallas, TX 75201-3411, **Business Phone:** (214)812-4600.*

JACKSON, BRENDA L. See JACKSON, BRENDA.

JACKSON, BURNETT LAMAR, JR.
Dentist. **Personal:** Born Jan 31, 1928, Athens, GA; married Dorian Sara Gant; children: Burnett Lamar, Stephen Mouzon. **Educ:** Ky State Col, BS, 1950; Meharry Med Col, DDS, 1960. **Career:** Dent Tuskegee, AL, pvt pract, 1961-68, Philadelphia 1969-; John A Andrew Hosp, Tuskegee Inst, chief dent serv, 1961-68; Temple Univ Philadelphia, pub health dentist 1968-70; W Nice Town-Fioga Neighbourhood Health Ctr, chief dent serv, 1970-. **Orgs:** Secy, John A Andrew Clinic Soc, 1965-68; Acad Gen Dent; Com Greater Tuskegee, AL, 1966-68; Macon Co Action Com, 1965-68; secy, Philadelphia County Dent Asn, Jackson, 1969-70, New Era, 1972; Ala Dent Soc. **Military Serv:** AUS, 1951-52. **Business Addr:** Physician, 3450 N 17 St, Philadelphia, PA 19140.*

JACKSON, CARLOS
Law enforcement officer. **Career:** Denver Sheriffs Dept, Dep, capt, maj, currently. **Special Achievements:** Highest ranking African American in the Denver Sheriffs Department; first African American major in the Denver Sheriffs Dept. **Business Phone:** (720)865-9557.

JACKSON, CAROL E
Judge. **Personal:** Born Aug 9, 1952, St Louis, MO. **Educ:** Wellesley Col, BA, 1973; Univ Mich Law Sch, JD, 1976. **Career:** Thompson & Mitchell, atty, 1976-83; Mallinckrodt Inc, coun, 1983-85; US Dist Ct, Eastern Dist Mo, magistrate, 1986-92, dist judge, 1992, chief judge, 1992-; Wash Univ, adj prof law, 1989-92. **Orgs:** Trustee, St Louis Art Mus, 1987-91; Nat Asn Womens Judges; Fed Magistrate Judges Asn; Miss Bar Asn; St Louis Co Bar Asn; Metro St Louis; Mound City Bar Asn; St Louis Lawyers Asn; Mo Bar; Bar Asn Metro St Louis; Lawyers Asn St Louis. **Special Achievements:** First woman appointed to the federal bench in the Eastern District of Missouri; first United States Magistrate Judge to be appointed to the United States District Court in that district. **Business Phone:** (314)244-7540.

JACKSON, CHARLES ELLIS. See Obituaries section.

JACKSON, CHARLES N., II
Association executive. **Personal:** Born Mar 16, 1931, Richmond, VA; son of Miles M. and Thelma Manning; married Marlene

Mills; children: Renata, Andrea, Charles III. **Educ:** Va Union Univ, BS, 1958; Temple Univ, Post Grad, 1976; Miss Southeastern Univ, Post Grad, 1976. **Career:** The Nat Urban Coalition, vpres admin & finance; Agency Int Devl, sr auditor chief accnt; IRS Intell Div, spec agt; Phila, auditor & treas vol tech; Soc Am Foresters, Bethesda, MD, dir, finance & admin, 1991, sr dir & chief forest officer, currently. **Orgs:** Asst bd mem, Wash Hosp Nat Asn Accts; nat Soc Pub Accts Am Acctg Asn; Am Mgmt Asn Accredited; Accreditation Coun Acctg. **Military Serv:** USAF, 1951-55. **Business Addr:** Senior Director, Chief Financial Officer, Soc Am Foresters, 5400 Grosvenor Lane, Bethesda, MD 20814-2198.*

JACKSON, CHARLES RICHARD, JR.
Executive. **Personal:** Born Jun 18, 1929, Yonkers, NY; married Mary Alice Crockett; children: Steven, Marc. **Educ:** Lincoln Univ, attended 1950; Adelphi Univ, BA, 1953; Baruch Sch, MPA, 1959; City Col NY, attended 1960. **Career:** Yonkers Police Dept, det, 1952-67; Westchester Co Sheriff Dept, chief criminal investr, 1968-72; 3 State Narcotic Strike Force, comdr, 1970-72; Con Edison Urban Affairs, asst to vpres, 1973; consult, Polaroid Corp, 1973-74; consult, Boston Police Dept, 1973; lectr, Univ Okla, 1973; City Mgr, asst, 1974-75; Nat Football League, asst dir security, 1975-. **Orgs:** Urban Affairs Task Force, 1966; US Gov Presidential Task Force Drug Abuse, 1973; Col Mainland, 1973-75; pres, Int Narcotic Enforcement Officers Asn, 1977; Int Asn Chiefs Police; FBINA; NYPD Hon Legion; Nat Sheriff Asn; NY State Asn Chiefs Police; Am Soc Indust Security; Non Comn Officers Asn. **Honors/Awds:** Distinguished Police Serv Dept Awards, 1952-73; NY City Detective Educ Asn, 1968; Humanitarian Award, Portchester Citizens Anti-Poverty Asn Inc, 1975; Gold Medal Award, 1992; Distinguished AMR, Nat Football FND & Hall Fame, 1992. **Special Achievements:** One of 10 Outstanding Police Officers in US W Grand Jurors Award, 1971; auth: "Coop with Police," 1968; "The Impact of Drugs on the Sport of Football," 1976. **Military Serv:** USY, sp/4, 1954-55. *

JACKSON, CHERYLE
Association executive, president (organization), chief executive officer. **Personal:** Born in Chicago, IL; married Charles. **Educ:** Northwestern Univ, attended, 1988. **Career:** Regional vpres gov & pub affairs; Nat dir state & local gov affairs; Senior-level gov affairs positions with Amtrak; Nat Pub Radio, vpres communs & brand mgt, dir corp communs & dir corp identity & info; Ill Gov, dir communs; Chicago Urban League, pres & chief exec officer, currently. **Honors/Awds:** First Woman To Lead The Social & Civil Justice Organisation; First Female President & CEO of Chicago Urban League. **Business Addr:** President, Chief Executive Officer, Chicago Urban League, 4510 S Mich Ave, Chicago, IL 60653, **Business Phone:** (773)451-3607.*

JACKSON, CHRIS WAYNE. See ABDUL-RAUF, MAHMOUD.

JACKSON, CLARENCE A
Automotive executive. **Career:** Royal Dodge Inc, chief exec officer, currently. **Special Achievements:** Co is listed No 88 on Black Enterprise's list of top 100 auto dealers, 1994.

JACKSON, CORNELIA PINKNEY
Educator. **Personal:** Born in Marietta, GA; daughter of Louise Williams Pinkney-Hemphill and Cleveland Pinkney; married Ernest Jr, Aug 7, 1950; children: Andrea & Glenn. **Educ:** Clark Col, attended 1948; Wayne State Univ, MA; Mich State Univ; Conn St Col. **Career:** Educator (retired); elem sch, 1955-63; Pontiac Sch Dist, resource teacher, 1963-87. **Orgs:** Pres, Pontiac Educ Asn, 1965-66; Nat Educ Asn Conv, 1967-; World Confederation Orgn Teaching Prof, 1973-77; bd dir, Mich Educ Asn; bd dir, Nat Educ Asn; Nat Educ Asn Comt & Prgm & Budget; charter mem, Theta Lambda Omega AKA. **Honors/Awds:** Scholarship Clark Col, 1944; Nat Defense Educ Act grant Ssholar, Conn St Col, 1966; Hilda Maehling Fel, 1968; Honoree Connie Jackson Award, MEA.

JACKSON, CURTIS JAMES, III. See FIFTY CENT.

JACKSON, DAMIAN JACQUES
Baseball player. **Personal:** Born Aug 16, 1973, Los Angeles, CA. **Career:** Cleveland Indians, infielder, 1996-97; Cincinnati Reds, 1997-98; San DiegoPadres, infielder, 1998-2001, 2005; Detroit Tigers, 2002; Boston Red Sox, 2003; Chicago Cubs, 2004; Kansas City Royals, 2004; Wash redskins, 2006; Orange County Flyers, Currently. *

JACKSON, DARCY DEMILLE (WILMA LITTLEJOHN JACKSON)
Journalist. **Personal:** Born in Chicago, IL; daughter of Rev R L Littlejohn and Sophia O; married Gordon C; children: Carole Harris, Linda Luten, Shelley Bethay & Jill Jackson Lewis. **Educ:** Univ Mich, BGS 1977; Mich State Univ, cert, 1977; Oakland Univ, advan study 1978; Leadership Flint Training, cert, 1988. **Career:** ANP, NPI, ed, feature writer, 1960-65; Sepia Mag, columnist, 1963-82; Howard Univ, guest lectr, 1981; Manulife Ins Co, consult, 1981-82; Jordan Col, instr, 1982-83; Mott Community Col, instr, 1982-85; Time Shares Inc, consult, 1982-83; The Flint Jour, columnist & feature writer, 1982-; Dear Wilma, columnist, 1982-; Univ Mich, guest lectr, 1983-85; Creative consult Gail Mazaraki, consult 1984-85; Travel consult/Monarch Travel, 1987-; Medi-Rary Lit Serv, ed Adv, 1987-89; About Books, rev serv, currently. **Orgs:** NAMW Inc Media Women, 1975-85; founder, Flint Chap NAMW Inc, 1975-85; charter mem The Links Inc, Flint Area Chap, 1980-85; bd, YWCA Public Affairs, 1981-83; Phi Delta Kappa Educ Frat, 1983-85; bd dir, MI League Human Serv; Public Affairs Comn; Top Ladies Distinction, Grand Blanc Arts Guild Paint & Palette Art Group, Univ MI Alumni Asn; Nat Asn Black Journalists; Leadership Flint, 1987-89; delegate, Int Caribbean Conf, Women Aglow, 1988; bd, Univ Mich Alumni Bd Soc; treas, bd gov, Univ Mich Alumni Soc, 1995-97; Eta Phi Beta Sorority Inc; founding chap/charter mem, Delta Tau Chapter; treas, Alumni Bd Gov's, 1997-99; bd certified, Christian Counr Asn. **Honors/Awds:** Woman of Yr, Media Women, 1976-85; Darcy DeMille Mag Award; Human Rel Award, Mayor City Flint, 1982; "Special Tributes" State MI, 1978; Links Service Award, 1984; NAMW Commun Award, 1989; Honors Award/Community Serv, Genesee Area Intermediate Sch Dist, 1989; conducted: Writer's Workshops, Univ Mich-Flint, 1984-89; creative writing seminars, Mott Community Col, 1987-89; YWCA, Nina Mills Women of Achievement Award, nominee, 1994-95; Choice Award, Nat Negro Bus & Prof Women Inc, 1997. **Special Achievements:** Author, Minute Musings, 2006. **Home Addr:** 7517 Oceanline Dr, Indianapolis, IN 46214. **Business Addr:** Last Word, Inc, PO Box 53657, Indianapolis, IN 46214.

JACKSON, DARNELL
State government official, judge. **Personal:** Born Feb 2, 1955, Saginaw, MI; son of Roosevelt and Annie L; married Yvonne K Givens, Jul 29, 1978; children: Brandon D, Elliott S. **Educ:** Wayne State Univ, BA, 1977; Sch Law, JD, 1981; Kalamazoo Valley Community Col, AS, law enforcement, 1993. **Career:** Wayne State Univ, Free Legal Aid Clin, stud atty, 1979-81; Allan & Jackson PC, atty at law, 1983-85; Motivational speaker, 1983-; City Saginaw, Attys Off, atty, 1985-86; County Saginaw, Prosecutors Off, asst prosecutor, 1986-89, dep chief asst, 1990-93; Braun Kendrick, atty law, 1989-90; Delta Col Univ Ctr Mich, criminal justice instr, 1990-96; City Saginaw Police Dept, dep chief police, 1993-96; State Mich, Off Drug Control Policy, dir, 1996-01; Saginaw County, 70th Judicial Dist Ct, judge, 2001-06, 10th Judicial Circuit Ct, judge, 2006-. **Orgs:** bd dirs, Mr Rogers Say No to Drugs Prog, 1991-95; Multicultural Adv Comn, Saginaw Valley State Univ, 1991-96; bd dirs, Saginaw Cty Child Abuse & Neglect Coun, 1994-96; bd dirs, Westchester Village Essex Manor, 1994-96; chair, State MI, Drug Educ Adv Comn, 1996-01; Dare Adv Bd, State MI, 1996-01; bd dirs, United Way Saginaw County,1996-; Mich Youth Gang & Violence Task Force, 1997-01; co-chair, State MI, African Am Male Health Initiative Steering Comt, 1997-01; exec comn, Southeast Mich High Intensity Drug Trafficking Area, HIDTA, 1997-01; co-chair, Partnership For A Drug-Free Mich Steering Comn, 1997-. **Honors/Awds:** Award Prof Excellence, FBI, Saginaw County Gang Crime Task Force, 1995; Frederick Douglass Award for Community Serv, MI State Legis, 1991; Award for Effort in War on Drugs, Saginaw Police Dept, Special Operations Unit, 1989; Spec Tribute for Community Serv, MI State Legis, 1985; Community Serv Award, Free Legal Aid Clinic, Wayne State Univ, 1980, 1981. **Business Addr:** Judge, 10th Judicial Circuit Ct, Saginaw County Governmental Center, 111 S Mich Ave, Saginaw, MI 48602, **Business Phone:** (989)790-5488.*

JACKSON, DARRELL DUANE
Lawyer, colonial administrator. **Personal:** Born Aug 7, 1965, Cleveland, OH; son of William L Jackson Sr and Mary D; divorced. **Educ:** The Col William & Mary, BA, 1987; George Mason Univ Sch Law, JD, 1990. **Career:** Fairfax County Pub Sch, substitute teacher, 1985-92; Jay B Myerson Esquire, law clerk, 1988-89; Krooth & Altman, summer assoc, 1989; Honorable Leonie M Brinkema, judicial law clerk, 1990-91; Hon Marcus D Williams, judicial law clerk, 1991-92; County Fairfax, asst county atty, 1992-2000; Office US Atty, asst US attny, 2000-04; George Mason Univ Sch Law, asst dean & dir minority affairs, 2004-. **Orgs:** Va State Bar, 1991-; Fairfax County Bar, 1993-; Northern Va Black Attorneys Asn, treas, 1992-; Chantilly High Pyramid Minority Student Achievement Comt; Marymount Univ Paralegal Adv Comt, 1993-. **Special Achievements:** Author, The Sunset of Affirmative Action?: The City of Richmond vs JA Cronson Co, 1990; speeches: "Survival in Law School," 1990; "Judicial Clerkship," 1992. **Business Addr:** Assistant Dean, Director of Minority Affairs, George Mason University School of Law, 3301 Fairfax Dr Rm 237, Arlington, VA 22201, **Business Phone:** (703)993-8197.

JACKSON, DEBORAH BYARD CAMPBELL
Association executive, manager. **Personal:** Born Oct 23, 1947, Bluefield, WV; married. **Educ:** Bluefield State Col, BA, 1968; Union Grad Sch, PhD; Human Resource Develop, 1978. **Career:** Ctr Human Rel, prof asst; Univ Md Eastern Shore, workshop mgr, conf mgr, currently. **Orgs:** Minority Involvement Prog, Nat Educ Asn, coordr; Asn Fed Credit Union, first African Am pres; CT Educ Asn, first African Am exec dir; WV Educ Asn; Delta Sigma Theta; Nat Coun Negro Women; Nat Educ Asn; Nat Asn Advan Colored People; Zonta Int. **Home Addr:** 7901 Prentice Ct, Fort Washington, MD 20744. **Business Addr:** Conference Manager, University of Maryland Eastern Shore, Office of International Programs, Trigg Hall Rm 1104, Princess Anne, MD 21853-1299, **Business Phone:** (410)651-6543.

JACKSON, DR. DENNIS LEE
Educator. **Personal:** Born Feb 18, 1937, Pachuta, MS; married Annie Earl Anderson (deceased); children: Donna, Danna, DeAnna & Dennis II; married Althea Yvonne Tucker; children: China. **Educ:** Alcorn A&M Col, BS, 1959; Univ Miami, M.Ed, 1969, Ed.D, 1977. **Career:** Oakley Training Sch, teacher, 1959-64; Utica High Sch, teacher, 1964-65, prin, 1965-68; Orange County Pub Schs, sr admin, 1971-91, dir, 1991-. **Orgs:** Nat Asn Advan Colored People, 1960-; Am Educ Res Asn, 1968-; Fla Assoc Sch Admin, 1971-; Leadership Orlando, 1980-; supporter, Urban League, 1980-. **Honors/Awds:** Scholar 4-H Club, 1955; NDEA fel, Univ Miami, 1968. **Military Serv:** AUS, Spc-4 Army Res, 10 yrs. **Home Addr:** 6000 Park Hamilton Blvd, Orlando, FL 32808. **Business Addr:** Director, Orange County Public Schools, 445 W Amelia St, Orlando, FL 32801-1127, **Business Phone:** (407)317-3237.

JACKSON, DERRICK ZANE
Journalist. **Personal:** Born Jul 31, 1955, Milwaukee, WI; son of Samuel T and Doris; married Michelle D Holmes, Aug 16, 1980; children: Marjani Lisa Jackson, Omar Holmes & Tano Holmes. **Educ:** Univ Wisc, Milwaukee, BA, Mass Commun, 1976; Harvard Univ. **Career:** Milwaukee Courier, WI, reporter, 1970-72; Milwaukee J, WI, sportswriter, 1972-76; Kans City Star, MO, sportswriter, 1976-78; Newsday, Melville, sportswriter, NY city reporter, 1978-85, New Eng bur chief, 1985-88; Boston Globe, MA, columnist, assoc ed, 1988-; Simmons Col, part time fac journalism, currently; Grace United Methodist Church, scoutmaster & adv. **Orgs:** Nat Asn Black Journ, 1977-; Boston Asn Black Journ, 1985-. **Honors/Awds:** First Place, Newsday Annual Award, Sportswriting, 1984; First Place, Newsday Annual Award, Deadline News, 1985; Meyer Berger Award, Columbia Univ, 1985; First Place, Meyer Berger Award for NY City Reporting, Columbia Univ, 1986; Best New Columnist, Boston Mag, 1989; 2nd Place, Commentary, Nat Asn Black Journ, 1990; Unity Awards, Lincoln Univ; five-time winner, Nat Asn Black Journalists; Sword of Hope Commentary Award, New England Div Am Cancer Soc; Human Rights Award, Curry Col; Honorary Degree, Episcopal Divinity Sch, Salem State Col, Cambridge, Mass. **Business Addr:** Columnist, Associate Editor, Boston Globe, 135 Morrissey Blvd, Boston, MA 02107, **Business Phone:** (617)929-3088.

JACKSON, DEXTER LAMAR
Football player. **Personal:** Born Jul 28, 1977, Quincy, FL; married Tina; children: Jazmine & Daisia. **Educ:** Fla State Univ, BS, human & family sci, 2001. **Career:** Tampa Bay Buccaneers, defensive back & safety, 1999-2002, 2004-05; Ariz Cardinals, 2003; Cincinnati Bengals, free agt, 2006-09. **Orgs:** Buccaneer Stud Adv Bd, 2002. **Honors/Awds:** Tallahassee Democrats Big Bend Offensive Player of the Year; Super Bowl MVP (XXXVII); Super Bowl champion (XXXVII). **Business Addr:** Professional Football Player, Cincinnati Bengals, One Paul Brown Stadium, Cincinnati, OH 45202, **Business Phone:** (513)621-3550.

JACKSON, DONALD J
Executive. **Personal:** Born Sep 18, 1943, Chicago, IL; son of John Wesley and Lillian Peachy; married Rosemary; children: Rhonda & Dana. **Educ:** Northwestern Univ, BS, radio, TV & film, 1965. **Career:** WVON-RADIO, sales mgr, 1967-70; WBEE-RAD, acct exec, 1966-67; RH Donnelly, salesman, 1965-66; Cent City Prods, founder, 1971, pres, 1984, chief exec officer, currently. **Orgs:** Bd Mem, NW Univ "N" Men's Club, 1974; Oper PUSH; Chicago Urban Leag; AMA; Chic Symphony Soc; Art Inst Chic; Chicago Econ Club; Nat Asn TV Programming Execs; NAACP; bd chmn, DuSable Museum African Am Hist; bd mem, Gateway Found; bd mem, Chicago Jr; bd mem, Columbia Col; Chicago Minority Bus Develop Coun Inc; founder, Alliance Bus Leaders & Entrepreneurs; Jr Achievement Chicago. **Honors/Awds:** Blackbook's Ten Outstand Black Bus People, 1976; 'community service award', Ill Nurs Asn & Nat Med Asn, 1975; Chic Jaycees award, 1974; Sickle Cell Anemia Award, 1972. **Special Achievements:** TV programs include: programs include: The Bud Billiken Back-to-School Parade, the first and only televised black parade; MBR: Minority Business Report, the first nationally syndicated business show highlighting minorities; The Stellar Gospel Music Awards, which Jackson began in 1985; and Know Your Heritage, the first televised quiz show featuring African American students. **Military Serv:** USN, lt JG, 1972. **Business Addr:** Founder, Chairman, Chief Executive Officer, Central City Productions Inc, 212 E Ohio St Suite 300, Chicago, IL 60611, **Business Phone:** (312)654-1100.

JACKSON, DOROTHY R.
Lawyer. **Personal:** Born in Brooklyn, NY; daughter of Ollie (deceased) and Willamina Belton; married William W Ellis, PhD; children: Samantha Dorian Smith. **Educ:** Lincoln Univ, BA, 1971; Seton Hall Univ Law Sch, JD, 1978; Harvard Uni, John F Kennedy Sch Govt, SMG, 1989; Jackson State Univ, cert, 1990. **Career:** New York City Bd Educ, teacher Eng, 1971-84, educ ad-

minr, 1984-85; Vincent L Johnson ESQ, law asst, 1985-86; Congressman Edolphus Towns, chief staff, 1986-89; Samdor Enterprises LTD, pres, chief exec officer, 1989-91; Congresswoman Barbara-Rose Collins, chief staff, 1991-92; US House Reps, Speaker Thomas S Foley, spec coun, 1992; Congresswoman Eddie Bernice Johnson, chief staff; legis coun congressman Donald M Payne; Dem Cong Campaign Comt, dir voter participation; Am Gaming Asn, vpres govt affairs, currently. **Orgs:** Pres, NY Urban League, Brooklyn Br, 1986-88; Pres, Bridge Street AME Church Legal Soc, 1987-88; fel, Harvard Univ John F Kennedy Sch Govt, 1989; by-laws comt, legis rep, Alpha Kappa Alpha Sorority Inc; Stuyvesant Heights Lions Club; adv bd, Kings County Hosp Develop Project; bd dirs, Young Techocrats Inc; Women's Campaign Network; Nat Asn Negro Bus & Prof Women's Clubs; League Women Voters; Joint Ctr Polit & Econ Studies. **Honors/Awds:** Concerned Women of Brooklyn, Woman on the Move Award, 1988; Public Affairs Award, Mid-Brooklyn Civic Asn, 1989; Civil Rights Award, Nat Black Police Asn, 1990. **Special Achievements:** Elected delegate: Judicial, 1985-87; NY State United Teachers; United Fedn Teachers. **Business Addr:** Vice President of Government Affairs, The American Gaming Association, 555 13th St NW Suite 1010 E, Washington, DC 20004, **Business Phone:** (202)637-6500.*

JACKSON, DUANE MYRON
Educator, zoo keeper. **Personal:** Born Jan 6, 1948, Chicago, IL; son of Rev A P and Harriet Jackson; married Fleda M, May 18, 1974; children: Kimya & Kari. **Educ:** Morehouse Col, BA, psychology, 1974; Univ Ill, MA, biological psychology, 1976, PhD, 1984. **Career:** Clark Col, asst prof, 1981-87; Morehouse Math & Sci Upward Bound Prog, curr coord, 1991-; Zool Atlanta, cur insects & res scientist; Morehouse Col, assoc prof, Dept Psychol, currently. **Orgs:** Animal Behav Soc, 1977-; Am Asn Zoo & Aquariums, 1992-; bd gov, Nat Conf Undergrad Res, 1993-; counr, Coun Undergrad Res, 1994-; Int Soc Behav Ecol, 1994-. **Honors/Awds:** Paul Mussen Award Psychol, Morehouse Col, 1974; Nat Fellow Award, Ford Found, 1979-80; Short Term Visitor Fellow, Smithsonian Inst, 1993; Res Experience Undergrads, Nat Sci Found, 1994. **Special Achievements:** Animal Activ & Presence of Docent Inteaction: Visitor Behav Zoo Atlanta,Visitor Behav, 1994; Motivations Drive Prejudice & Discrimination: Is the Scientific Community Really Objective, J R & Adams, A Multicultural Prism: Voices from the Field, 1994; numerous other publication; Article: Who was Charles Turner, 2009. **Military Serv:** AUS, Army Security Agency, sgt, 1967-71; Armay Commendation Medal, Vietnam, 1969. **Business Addr:** Associate Professor, Morehouse College, Department Psychology, Nabrit-Mapp-McBay Hall 2nd Fl 830 Westview Dr, Atlanta, GA 30314, **Business Phone:** (404)681-2800.

JACKSON, DWAYNE ADRIAN
Insurance executive. **Personal:** Born Aug 3, 1955, New York, NY; son of George and Ina Stockton; married Cheryl, Sep 20, 1984; children: David & Courtney. **Educ:** Westfield State Col, BA, 1977. **Career:** Crawford & Co Ins Adjusters, adjuster, 1977-79; Mass Mutual, second vpres, 1979-98; Hamilton Sunstrand Div United Technologies, 1998-2000; United Technologies, Leadership Progs, mgr, 2000-. **Orgs:** Chartered life underwriter, Am Soc CLU/CHFC, 1990-; bd dirs, Jr Achievement, 1993-96; bd dirs, Dunbar Community Ctr, 1993-; bd dirs, NAACP, Springfield Chap, 1993-96; bd dirs, Goodwill Industs, 1994-96; bd dirs, Vis Nurses Asn, 1995-96; pres bd dirs, Dunbar Community Ctr, 1996.

JACKSON, EARL
Artist. **Personal:** Born Nov 12, 1948, Ann Arbor, MI; divorced; children: Daniel. **Educ:** Washtenaw Community Col; Eastern Mich Univ. **Career:** Artist; Exhibitions: African Am Museum Hist, Detroit Washtenaw Community Col; Univ Michigan Museum Art; Chicago's Museum Sci & Industry; Nat Gallery Art, Dakar, Senegal. **Orgs:** Nat Conf Artists, 1983-; Ann Arbor Art Asn; founding mem, African Am Cult & Hist Museum.Ann Arbor, MI; Apex Museum, Atlanta, GA; Marietta/Cobb Museum Art; Georgia Registry Artist. **Honors/Awds:** Best Miniature Paintings, African World Festival, Detroit, MI, 1983; The Willow Run High School Hall of Fame, Ypsilanti, MI 1998. **Business Addr:** Artist, Professional Picture Framer, Jackson Studio, 1063 7 Springs Cir, Marietta, GA 30068-2660, **Business Phone:** (770)321-6842.

JACKSON, EARL, JR.
Microbiologist. **Personal:** Born Sep 4, 1938, Paris, KY; son of Earl Sr and Margaret Elizabeth Cummins. **Educ:** Ky State Univ, BS, 1960; Univ Conn, Northeastern Univ, Univ Paris; Northeastern Univ Boston, MA, MS, 1986. **Career:** Microbiologist (retired); Hydra Power Corp, chem analyst, 1964-68; Massachusetts Gen Hosp, sr res analyst dept anesthesia, 1968-81, microbiologist dept med, 1981-95. **Orgs:** Am Soc Microbiol; Am Assoc Advan Sci; Ky State Univ Alumni Assoc; NE Asn Clinical Microbiol & Infectious Disease; Am Asn Clinical Chem; NY Acad Sci. **Honors/Awds:** Outstanding and Distinguished Community Leaders and Noteworthy, Am Citation 1977; Distinguished Alumni of the Year, Nat Asn Equal Opportunity Citation 1986; inductee, Ky State Univ Hall of Fame, 1986. **Special Achievements:** spec articles publ "Hemoglobin-O2 Affinity Regulation, 43(4), 632-642", 1977 J Applied Physiology; "Measurement of Levels of Aminoglycosides and Vancomycin in Serum", May 1984 pp 707-709 J Clinical Microbiol. *

JACKSON, EARL J.
Clergy. **Personal:** Born Mar 11, 1943, Chattanooga, TN; son of James C (deceased) and Kathryn C; married Ms Barbara Faye Anderson; children: Earl Darelwin, Roderick Lamar. **Educ:** Tenn A&I State Univ, attended 1965; Am Baptist Theol Sem, 1966; The Detroit Baptist Sem, ThG, BTh, DD, 1969; The Emmanuel Bible Col, BA, MDiv, MRE, 1978. **Career:** New Bethel Baptist Church, Warren County, KY, pastor, 1968-, radio ministry, 1969; KY Dept Human Resources, sr employ interviewer, 1970-. **Orgs:** Bowling Green Warren Co Chap Nat Asn Advan Colored People; IAPES Employ Serv Organ; Bowling Green Alumni Kappa Alpha Psi Fraternity Bowling Green Noon Kiwanis Club; Bowling Green Warren Co Jaycees, 1971-73; bd dir, Bowling Green War Memorial Boy's Club, 1979-; asst chmn bd, Bowling Green Human Rights Comn, 1976-79; bd dirs, Bowling Green Noon Kiwanis Club; worshipful master House Solomon Ancient & Accepted Scottish Rite Masons of the World, 1981-90; grand dep inspector gen, The House of Solomon 767 Ancient & Accepted Scottish Rite Masons of the World; pres, Ky State Missionary, Baptist Missionary & Educ conv, Bowling Green, KY, currently. **Business Addr:** Radio Minister, Pastor, New Bethel Baptist Church, 801 Church St, Bowling Green, KY 42101.*

JACKSON, EARLINE
School administrator. **Personal:** Born Mar 26, 1943, Columbia, SC; children: Tanyl Lea & Tamara P Newsome. **Educ:** Molloy Col, BA, psych/sociol, 1982. **Career:** Cornell Univ, FDC Pilot Prog, exec bd mem educ planning, assessment, 1974-77; LI Minority Alliance Inc, educ, remedial serv prog coordr, 1978-82; ABWA Pandora Chap, chairperson educ comn, 1983; Molloy Col, assoc dir st thomas aquinas prog, currently. **Orgs:** Founder & exec dir, FDC Asn Nassau Co Inc, 1972-79; exec bd mem, Nassau Co Rep Licensed FDC Asn NYS Inc, 1973-78; bd mem, Daycare Coun Nassau Co Inc, 1974-78; bd mem Comm, Adv Bd Roosevelt NY, 1976-78; Nassau Co Rep, Cornell Univ, FDC Prog Planning Comm, 1978; chairperson emer, FDC Asn Nassau Co Inc, 1979. **Honors/Awds:** Meritorious Service & Achievement FDC, Asn Nassau Co Inc, 1978. **Business Addr:** Associate Director Of Saint Thomas Aquinas Program, Molloy College, Rockville Centre, 1000 Hempstead Ave, PO Box 5002, Rockville Centre, NY 11570-5002.

JACKSON, EDGAR NEWTON
Educator. **Personal:** Born Apr 20, 1959, Washington, DC; son of Joan F J Clement and Edgar Newton Jackson Sr. **Educ:** Univ DC, WA, DC, BS, 1987; Grambling State Univ, Grambling, La, MS, 1989; Howard Univ, WA, DC, postgrad studies, 1990; Univ Nmex, Albuquerque, NM, PhD, 1995. **Career:** Warner Theatre, WA, DC, box office mgr, 1979-81; Howard Univ, WA, DC, aquatic mgr, 1981-, instr, 1989-; Univ DC, WA, DC, adj instr, 1987-88; Grambling State Univ, Grambling, La, instr, 1988-89; Univ NMex, Albuquerque, NMex, teaching asst, 1990-91, athletic dept intern, 1991; Howard Univ, asst prof, head swim coach, 1991-98; Fla State Univ, asst prof, 1998-2003, assoc prof & dept chmn, 2003, Sport Mgt Rctrn Mgt & Phys Educ dept, instr, currently. **Orgs:** Am Alliance Health, Phys Educ, Rctrn & Dance, 1983-; mem, Coun for Nat Coop Aquatics, 1984-; chair, Aquatic Safety Comm, Am Red Cross, 1985-; mem, Nat Rctrn and Pk asn, 1985-; mem, Nat Org for Athletic Develop, 1987-; mem, N Am Soc for the Sociol Sport, 1987-; life mem, Omega Psi Phi; life mem, NAACP, Grambling State Univ Alumni asn, Univ the DC Alumni asn; mem, Kappa Delta Pi; life mem, Wash Urban League; mem, Phi Delta Kappa; pres, FL Ahperd, 2001-02. **Honors/Awds:** Certif of appreciation, Am Red Cross, 1984; Intl & Multicultural Award, Univ of the DC, 1987; Omega Man of Yr, Alpha Omega Chap, 1993, CHI Omega Chap, 2001. **Business Addr:** Instructor, Florida State University, Sport Mgt Rctrn Mgt & Phys Educ, Tallahassee, FL, **Business Phone:** (850)644-4813.

JACKSON, DR. EDISON O.
College administrator. **Personal:** Born in Heathsville, VA; married Florence; children: Terrance & Eulaynea. **Educ:** Howard Univ, BS, zool, 1965, MA, coun, 1968; New York Theol Sem, MDiv; NRutgers, State Univ NJ, Doctorate Educ, 1983. **Career:** Legal Aid Agency Dist Columbia, offender rehab proj, 1967-68; Fed City Col, sr coun instr, 1968-69; Essex Co Col, dean stud affairs, 1969-74, vpres stud affairs, 1974-80, exec vpres & chief acad officer, 1983-85; Upsala Col East Orange, adj fac; Compton Community Col, pres, 1985-89; City Univ NY, Medgar Eves Col, pres, 1989-09. **Orgs:** Am Asn Higher Educ; Am Personnel & Guid Asn; Am Col Personnel Asn; Eastern Asn Col Deans & Adv Stud; Nat Asn Student Personnel; Nat Coun Crime & Delinquency; Calif Asn Community Col; Nat Asn Equal Opportunity Higher Educ. **Honors/Awds:** New York State Governor's Award for African-Americans of Distinction, 1993; Rutgers University Distinguished Service Award, 1993; New York Chapter American Jewish Committee Community Relations Award, 1993; Dr Martin Luther King Jr Humanitarian Award, Shirley Chisholm Cult Inst C, 1995; Community Service Award, Delta Sigma Theta, 1996; Educational Leadership Award, Nat Comt Furtherance Jewish Educ, 1999; Community Award, Cong Rec, Congressman Ed Towns, 2000; Education Award, Church Women United Brooklyn Inc, 2000. **Special Achievements:** Author: "Can College Make Better Correctional Officers," in Federal Probation, Sept 1973; "On The Need for Teachers: A Position Statement,"Black Issues in Higher

Education, Oct 1988; "The Community & Minority Students, A Crucial Agenda," Western Interstate Commission for Higher Edu, July 1989. **Business Addr:** President, City University of New York, Medgar Evers College, Bedford Bldg B3009 1650 Bedford St, Brooklyn, NY 11225, **Business Phone:** (718)270-5000.

JACKSON, DR. EDWARD R.
Educator, administrator. **Personal:** Born May 24, 1942, New Iberia, LA; son of Leona Strauss and Oliver; married Nedra Clem, Dec 19, 1975; children: Chris, Corey, Robert, Edward II & Camy. **Educ:** Univ Southwestern La, Lafayette, LA, BA, 1963; Marquette Univ, Milwaukee,WI, MA, polit sci, 1965; Univ Iowa, Iowa City, IA, PhD, polit sci, 1968. **Career:** Southern Univ, Baton Rouge, LA, from asst prof polit sci to dept chmn,1968-70, chancellor, 1988; Fisk Univ, Nashville, TN, assoc prof polit sci, 1970-76; Howard Univ, Wash, DC, assoc prof polit sci, 1976-79; Natl Aeronautics & Space Admin, Admin & Support dirate, admin officer; SC State Col, Orangeburg, SC, Dept political science, chmn, 1979-86, vice provost acad affairs, 1986. **Honors/Awds:** Honorable Mention, Woodrow Wilson Fellowship, 1963; Faculty Intern, Natl Sci Found, 1967-68. **Special Achievements:** Has published articles in several professional journals.

JACKSON, ELIJAH
Executive, u.s. attorney, president (organization). **Personal:** Born Feb 9, 1947; married Mary. **Career:** Prestige Airways, pres; Navcom Aviation, pres; Navcom Systs Inc, pres, currently. **Orgs:** Inst Navig; LORAN Working Group; Wildgoose Asn. **Honors/Awds:** NCP Award; Business Achievement Award; Christian Churches Award. **Special Achievements:** CPN ranked 61 on the Black Enterprise list of top 100 industrial companies, 1992. **Business Phone:** (703)361-0884.

JACKSON, EMORY NAPOLEON
Association executive, consultant, president (organization). **Personal:** Born Oct 29, 1937, Magnolia, MS; son of Aaron Napoleon and Juanita Gordon; married Adrea Perry; children: Lisa A & Charles L. **Educ:** Newark State Col, MA counselling; Morehouse Col, BA, 1961; Adler Inst Psychotherapy, 1974. **Career:** UN Int Sch, teacher, 1962; NY Urban League, comm org, 1967; Nat Med Asn, consult; Int Asn Official Human Rights Agencies, consult; Econ Develop Nat Urban League, dep dir; Off Manpower Dev & Training Nat Urban League, nat dir; US Dept Housing Urban Develop, spec & from asst to secy, 1976-77; Urban League Eastern MS, pres, 1977-80; DOE NY City Human Resources Admin, dep comnr, 1980; City NY, Dept Sanit, dep comnr, 1983-86; We Care About NY Inc, pres, 1986; State NY, Dormitory Authority, dir off Opportunity progs, currently. **Orgs:** Vpres, US Team Handball Fed & Olympic Com Chmn Community Housing Resources Bd Boston; bd dir, Boston Pvt Inc; bd dir, Boston Metro Nab Nat Urban League fel; Nat Urban League, 1969. **Honors/Awds:** Highest scorer team handball N Am, 1965-70; Outstanding achievement, Boston City Coun Resolution, 1980; Community Serv Boy Scouts-Brooklyn Dist, 1987, 88 & 89; Community Service Girl Scout, Coun Greater NY, 1988. **Home Addr:** 1333 President St, Brooklyn, NY 11213. **Business Addr:** Director, Dormitory Authority of the State of New York., Office of Opportunity Programs, New York, NY.

JACKSON, ERIC SCOTT
School administrator, educator, athletic coach. **Personal:** Born Jan 26, 1964, Ann Arbor, MI; son of Geraldine and Lionel; children: Davis & Brooks. **Educ:** Eastern Mich Univ, BS, hist, 1987, Masters Prog, hist; Univ Cincinnati,Masters Prog, coun. **Career:** Ypsilanti High Sch, Ann Arbor, MI, freshman coach football, 1985-86; Univ Cincinnati, grad asst football, 1987-89; Univ Cincinnati, head grad asst football, 1988; Cornell Univ, freshman coach football, 1989-91; Alma Col,head track coach, asst football coach, 1991; Las Vegas Aces, prof spring football league, asst football coach, 1992; Idaho, sec coach, 1993; Alma Col, defensive coordr & PE supvr; Princeton Univ, defensive backs coach, currently. **Orgs:** Track, Athletic Cong, 1991-; Am Football Coaches Asn, 1991-; network comn, Black Coaches Asn, 1992; Off Publ Princeton Football Asn. **Home Phone:** (517)463-1359. **Business Addr:** Defensive backs coach, Princeton University, Princeton Football Association, 21 Jadwin Gym, PO Box 71, Princeton, NJ 08544, **Business Phone:** (609)258-3514.

JACKSON, ESTHER COOPER
Editor. **Personal:** Born Aug 21, 1917, Arlington, VA; daughter of George Posea and Esther Irving; married James Edward, May 7, 1941; children: Harriet Jackson Scarupa & Kathryn Jackson Seeman. **Educ:** Oberlin Col, AB, 1938; Fisk Univ, MA, 1940. **Career:** Southern Negro Youth Congress, exec secy, 1940-50; Nat Urban League, educ dir, 1952-54; Nat Bd Girls Scouts Am, social worker, 1954-; Freedomways Magazine, ed; WEB Du Bois, co-ed; Black Titan & Paul Robeson, co-ed; The Great Forerunner, co-ed. **Orgs:** Parents Teachers Asn. **Honors/Awds:** Rosenwald Fel, 1940-41; Rabinowitz Fund Grant, 1962-63; William L Patterson Foundation Award, 1978; Nat Alliance of Third World Journalists, 1981; Harlem School of the Arts Award, 1987; Lifetime Achievement Award, New York Asn Black Journalists, 1989. **Home Addr:** 21 St James Pl, Brooklyn, NY 11205. *

JACKSON, EUGENE D.
Executive. **Personal:** Born Sep 5, 1943, Waukomis, OK; son of Joseph Gordon and Queen Esther Royal; married Phyllis; children:

Stephanie, Bradley, Kimberly, Aisha, Bakari, Shasha. **Educ:** Univ MSR, Rolla, BS, 1967; Columbia Univ, MS, 1971. **Career:** Colgate Palmolive NYC, indust engr 1967-68; Black Econ Union NYC, prod, proj engr, 1968-69; Interracial Coun Bus Opportunity NYC, dir maj indust prog, 1969-71; Unity Broadcasting Network, pres & chmn, 1993; World Af Network, chair, chief exec officer, currently; Queens Inner-Unity Cable Syst, vice chair. **Orgs:** Howard Univ Intl Sponsors Coun; Alpha Phi Alpha Fraternity, Lincoln UNIV, PA, bd; NACME. **Business Phone:** (404)521-6120.*

JACKSON, FELIX W.
Physician. **Personal:** Born Sep 6, 1928, Woodville, MS. **Educ:** Ill Col, optometry. **Career:** Am Sch, self instr optomoligist; Strip Founders Inc, purchasing agent; USPOe, carrier; FW Jackson Enterprises, owner. **Orgs:** Pres, Nat Asn Advan Colored People, 1965-67; bd exec vpres, Forsyth Century Art, 1964-68; vice chmn, Model Cities Bd, 1968-70; Winston SalemRedevel Comn, 1974. **Honors/Awds:** Rep All Am City Event, 1965. **Special Achievements:** First black opth of NC state. **Military Serv:** AUS. **Home Addr:** 533 N Liberty St, Winston-Salem, NC 27101.

JACKSON, FRANK
Educator. **Personal:** Born 1929, Mound City, IL; married Hope Turk, May 29, 1993; children: Wallace Turk, Michael Turk, Diane Brooks & Bonnie Alexis. **Career:** Educator (retired); USN, instr. **Orgs:** Community Develop Comm, 1989-93; pres, NAACP, Vallejo br, 1991-2002, sect dir, 1999-; Fighting Back Partnership, 1992-93; Human Relations Comm,1993-99; chair, Am Red Cross, Solano Co chap, 1994-98; Civil Service Comm, 2000-. **Honors/Awds:** Humanitarian of the Year, Am Red Cross, 1995; Citizen of the Year, Omega Psi Phi, 1999. **Military Serv:** USAAF, corporal, 1946-48; Sustained Superior Award, Dept Navy, 1987.

JACKSON, FRANK DONALD
Government official, mayor, administrator. **Personal:** Born Jul 25, 1951, Luling, TX; son of Willie Louise Smith and Robbie Sr; married Marian Elaine Jones; children: Tracy, Ayanna, Chelkh & Okofo. **Educ:** Prairie View A&M Univ, BA, geog, 1973. **Career:** USS Long Beach CGN9, div off, 1973-76; USS Coral Sea CU43, div off, 1976-77; Naval Beach Group Det Mar 1-79, officer charge, 1979, first lt beachmaster unit II, 1977-79; NROTC Prairie View, navigation/operation officer, 1979-82; USNR, lt comdr; Mobile Mine Assembly Group Det 1310, commanding officer; Prairie View Messenger, ed/pub; Prairie View Vol Fire Fighter Asn, pres; Prairie View A&M Univ, Memorial Stud Ctr, dir 1982-87, dir auxiliary serv, 1987-, govt affairs officer, currently; Craft Opportunity 2215 Galveston Tex, Commanding Officer, 1988-; mayor, Prairie View, TX, 2002-. **Orgs:** Prince Hall Mason, 1970; Alpha Phi Alpha, 1971; Gamma Theta Upsilon, 1972; city Counman, City Prairie View, 1982-92; Phi Alpha Theta, 1983; Nat Naval Officers Asn, 1985; Waller County Hist Comn & Soc, 1989-; County Comner-Waller County, 1991-96, reelected, 1996-2000; Chamber Com. **Honors/Awds:** Man of the Year, Memorial Stud Ctr Adv Bd, 1985; publ, Prairie View Messenger, 1984-88; Staff Member of The Year, Prairie View A&M Univ, 1988-89. **Military Serv:** USNR, comdr, 1973-; 2 Navy Achievement Medal, Navy Commendation Medal, 1989. **Business Addr:** Mayor, City of Prairie View, 300 US Hwy 290 E, PO Box 817, Prairie View, TX 77446, **Business Phone:** (936)857-3711.

JACKSON, FRANKLIN D. B.
Executive. **Personal:** Born Mar 21, 1934, Cypress, AL; son of J H Jackson and Mary; divorced; children: Franklin K, Debra R, Sabrina F, Delilah E, Jacquelyn R. **Educ:** Univ N Colo Greeley, BS, Bus Admin, 1976, MS, Pub Admin, 1977; Webster Col St Louis, MS, Health & Hosp Admin, 1979. **Career:** Executive (retired); EEOC, employment opportunity specialist, 1976-78; HUD, fair housing & EO spec, 1978-; Jackson's Enter Ltd, pres & owner, 1980. **Orgs:** Publicity chmn, Univ Colo,t Manuel, 1972; historian, Kappa Alpha Psi Fratenity, 1975-; band leader, Happy Jacks Combo & Dance Band; Am Soc Pub Admin, 1976-; bd dir, Occup Industrialization Ctr, 1977-; res chmn, Police Comn Denver, 1977-78. **Honors/Awds:** Award Acad Achievement, Fitzsimons Army Med Ctr, 1976; Cert Appreciation, Optimist Int NE Denver, 1978; Outstanding Serv Award, Denver Alumni Chap, Kappa Alpha Psi, 1978; Univ S leadership award, Am Conf leadership, 1978. **Military Serv:** AUS, 1st sgt paratroopers; Bronze Stars Meritorious Serv; Medal of Gallantry with palm. **Home Addr:** 9931 E Ohio Ave, Denver, CO 80247. *

JACKSON, FRED CAPERS. **See JACKSON, FRED H.**

JACKSON, FRED H (FRED CAPERS JACKSON)
Pilot. **Personal:** Born Mar 12, 1933, Bridgeton, NJ; son of Fred H Jackson, Sr and Hortence P Steward Jackson; married Linda Lee Brokaski, Oct 5, 1991; children: Pamela, Antionette, Cheri, Fred, II, Courtney Page, Heather Schulte, Holly Schulte & Lisa Pullan. **Career:** Pilot (Retired); Eastern Air Lines, pilot, 1967-91. **Orgs:** Negro Airman Int; asst scout master, Troop 254, 1969-74; Black Airline Pilot's Asn; NJ Bd Real Estate Salesman; Nanticoks - Lenni - Lenape Native Am Tribe. **Military Serv:** USAF, major, 1953-67; Combat Crew Medal; NJ Air Nat Guard, 1967-73; National Defense Service Medal; Good Conduct Medal, Flight Instr. **Home Addr:** 5 Deland Pk B, Fairport, NY 14450.

JACKSON, FRED JAMES, SR.
Administrator. **Personal:** Born Jun 11, 1950, High Point, NC; son of Mary Jane Walker; divorced; children: Marrian Ann, Fred James Jr, Patrice M. **Educ:** Monterey Peninsula Col; Sacramento State Univ, BA, 1977; Univ Md; Armed Forces Inst, cert; Univ San Diego. **Career:** Boulder Col, veterans affairs officer, 1978-79; Hiram Johnaosn High Sch, head golf coach; McClellan AFB Logistic Ctr, procurement mgr, 1975-87; Black Rose Enterprise Publ, pres, chief exec officer, 1986-; The Drug Intervention Network Inc, exec dir, 1987-92; USDA, procurement officer, 1992-94; Grant Joint Union Sch Dist, eng teacher, dept chair, 1994-96; Sacramento Unified Sch Dist, Hiram Johnson High, lead teacher, comput educ, 1995-; Hole One Jr Golf Club Inc, dir, currently. **Orgs:** City Sacramento, Mayors Drug Gang Task Force, 1987-93; AAAS, Black Church Proj, 1992-95; Nat Educ Asn, 1994-; Calif Teachers Asn, 1994-; Nat Asn Black Sch Educr, 1995-; peer counseling, leadership coordr, tobacco drug and alcohol program coord, 1996-, State Calif. **Honors/Awds:** Youth Authority Certificate of Appreciation, 1979; Certificate of Appreciation, Asn African American Women, 1988; Certificate of Recognition, State of Calif Assembly, 1996; Senate Certificate of Recognition, 1996. **Special Achievements:** The Balcony, poem, 1994; They Call Me Names, book of poetry, pulitzer nomination, 1994; Lightning, Master of the Blues, fiction, pulitzer nomination, 1994; Passion In Black, poetry, pulitzer nomination, 1992; One Race, Many Cultures, book of historical poetry, 1998. **Military Serv:** AUS, 1967-75 USAR, 1975-87; Four honorable discharges, the Viet Nam Cross of Gallantry, 1969; two presidential citations; and many more. **Business Addr:** Director, The Hole In One Jr Golf Club Inc, PO Box 5283, Sacramento, CA 95817, **Business Phone:** (916)705-4653.*

JACKSON, FREDDIE
Singer, composer. **Personal:** Born Oct 2, 1956, Harlem, NY. **Career:** Night club performer; back-up vocalist/cameo soloist with Melba Moore, 1984; Mystic Merlin, singer; Albums: Rock Me Tonight, 1985; Just Like The First Time, 1986; Don't Let Love Slip Away, 1988; Do Me Again, 1990; Time For Love, 1992; Here It Is, 1994; At Christmas, 1994; Private Party, 1995; For Old Times Sake: The Freddie Jackson Story, 1996; Anthology, 1998; Life After 30, 1999; Live In Concert, 2000; On Tour, 2001; It's Your Move, 2004; Personal Reflections, 2005; Transitions, 2006; Greatest Hits, 2007; composer with Paul Laurence, currently. **Honors/Awds:** Am Black Gold Award, Outstanding Male Artist, 1986. **Special Achievements:** Grammy nomination for Best New Artist, 1985; Film: King of New York. **Business Addr:** Singer, Wenig-Lamonica Associates LLC, 580 White Plains Rd, Tarrytown, NY 90028, **Business Phone:** (914)631-6500.

JACKSON, FREDERICK LEON
Educator. **Personal:** Born Aug 15, 1934, Albany, NY; married Mildred Helen Hagood; children: Leon K, Anthony W. **Educ:** Oregon State Univ, BS, 1976; Portland State Univ, MS, 1977. **Career:** Portland Pub Schs, handicapped teacher, 1976-81, sixth grade teacher, 1981-84, integration coordr, 1984-86, stud transfer coord, 1986-. **Orgs:** Dir, Portland Asn Teachers, 1978-86; KRS, 1983-85; basileaus, 1985-86; Omega Psi Phi; chmn minority project, Ore Educ As, 1984-85; Ore Alliance Black Sch Ed, 1985-87. **Honors/Awds:** Leadership Award, 1982; Leadership Award, Minority Ore Educ Asn, 1984; Man of the Year, Omega Psi Phi Zeta Nu, 1986, 1987. **Military Serv:** USAF, E-6 tech sgt, 1952-72; Outstanding Unit Award. **Business Addr:** Coordinator, Portland Pub Schs, Stud Transfer, 8020 NE Tillamook, Portland, OR 97213.*

JACKSON, GARNET NELSON
Writer, columnist, educator. **Personal:** Born May 27, 1944, New Orleans, LA; daughter of Carrie Brent Sherman; married Anthony Jackson, Jan 2, 1970 (divorced); children: Damon. **Educ:** Dillard Univ, BA, 1968; Eastern Mich Univ, 1972. **Career:** Flint Bd Educ, teacher; Self Employed, publ, author, 1989-; Flint Ed, columnist, 1989-90; Flint J, columnist, 1990-94; Modern Curric Press, Simon & Schuster, author, pioneer Biographies Concept, 1990-94. **Orgs:** NAACP, 1987-; Sylvester Broome Book Club, 1990-; The Greater Flint Optimist Club, 1993-; Int Reading Asn, 1996; Am Libr Asn, 1996. **Honors/Awds:** Rejoti Publ, Honorable Mention for Outstanding Poetry, 1987; Educator of the Year Award, Nat Asn Advan Colored People, 1991; Harambee Medal, Nat Asn Advan Colored People, 1991; Dorothy Duke Evans Educator of the Year, 1991; Award for Children's Lit, Mt Zion Church, 1991; City Flint, Off Mayor, Proclamation of Outstanding Citizenship, 1992; State Mich, Gov Engler, Letter of Commendation, 1992; Christa McAuliffe Special Tribute Award, State Mich, 1992; Congressional Record, Proclamation of Outstanding Citizenship, US Cong, 1992; Certificate of Special Recognition, US Senator, Don Reigle, 1992; Special Tribute Award, Civil Park Sch, 1992; Zeta Phi Beta Finer Womanhood Hall of Fame, Zeta Phi Beta Sorority, 1993. **Business Addr:** Writer, 3519 Applewood Ln, Grand Blanc, MI 48439, **Business Phone:** (810)695-9157.

JACKSON, GARY MONROE
Lawyer. **Personal:** Born Nov 10, 1945, Denver, CO; son of Floyd M Jr and Nancelia Elizabeth; married Regina Lee, Sep 30, 1986; children: Michael Mascotti & Tara Mascotti. **Educ:** Univ Redlands, 1963-64; Univ Colo, BA, 1967, Sch Law, JD, 1970. **Career:** Denver Dist Atty Off, chief trial dep, 1970-74; US Atty Off, asst US atty, 1974-76; DiManna, Eklund, Ciancio & Jackson, partner, 1976-82; DiManna & Jackson LLP, partner, lawyer, 1982-; US Dist Ct, chair & mem; Colo Supreme Ct, chair & mem. **Orgs:** Founder, pres, Sam Cary Bar Asn; bd dirs, Col Trial Lawyers Asn; bd trustees, Denver Bar Asn, 1980-81; chair, Comt Conduct, 1982-86; Am Col Trial Lawyers; Am Bd Trial Advocates; vpres, Colo Bar Asn; Best Lawyers Am. **Honors/Awds:** Special Commendation, US Dept Justice, 1976; Wiley A Branton Award, Nat Bar Asn, 2001; Lifetime Achievement Award, Sam Cary Bar Asn; Order of the Coif, Univ Colo. **Home Addr:** 330 Garfield St, Denver, CO 80206, **Home Phone:** (303)322-2528. **Business Addr:** Lawyer, Partner, DiManna & Jackson LLP, 1741 High St, Denver, CO 80218, **Business Phone:** (303)320-4848.

JACKSON, GEORGE
Chief executive officer, president (organization). **Educ:** Oakland Univ, BS, human resource develop; Cent Mich Univ, MA, bus mgt Detroit Cooley High Sch, MA, bus mgt. **Career:** DTE Energy, dir customer mkt; United States Navy, personnel & human rel; Mich Consol Gas Co, Econ Develop Exec, Detroit City, City Planning & Develop Dept, interim dir; Detroit Econ Growth Corp, pres & chief exec officer, currently. **Orgs:** City Detroit Econ Develop Orgn; Detroit Regional Chamber; Greater Detroit Foreign Trade Zone; Am Arab Chamber Com Mich. **Honors/Awds:** Distinguished Alumni Achievement Award, 2003. **Business Addr:** President, Chief Executive Officer, Detroit Economic Growth Corporation, 500 Griswold St Suite 2200, Detroit, MI 48226, **Business Phone:** (313)963-2940.

JACKSON, GERALD E.
Executive, chief executive officer, president (organization). **Personal:** Born Apr 13, 1949, Chicago, IL; son of Bruce and Hazel; married Denorsia, Oct 31, 1974; children: Gerald Jr, Gavin & Syreeta. **Educ:** Olive Harvey Col, 1972; Roosevelt Univ, BBA, 1975. **Career:** Licensed pvt investr; certified real estate broker; Chicago Police Dept, Chicago, IL, police officer; GEJ Security, chief exec officer & pres, 1982-. **Orgs:** Chatham Bus Asn, 1989; bd mem, Rosenblum Boys & Girls Club, 1989; Chicago Asn of Com & Indust, 1986; Nat Org Black Law Enforcement Execs; Kappa Alpha Psi; Nat Burglar Alarm Asn; Am Soc Indus Security Assoc. **Honors/Awds:** Recipient Meritorious Service Award, United Negro College Fund, 1987; Pioneering Spirit Award, Rosenblum Boys & Girls Club, 1989; Entrepreneur of the Year Award (Finalist), Stein & Co, 1988, 1990. **Business Phone:** (312)994-0516.

JACKSON, GERALD MILTON
Lawyer. **Personal:** Born Jan 8, 1943, Cleveland, OH; son of Albert and Mary L; married; children: Alisa, Carmen & Jason A. **Educ:** Ky State Univ, BA, 1967; Univ Colo Sch Law, post grad legal training, 1968; Case Western Res Univ Sch Law, JD, 1971. **Career:** Jackson Law Cuyahoga Co Juv Detention Home, supvr, 1965; Cuyahoga Co, Dept Welfare, case worker, 1967-68; Univ Colo, Minority Students Enrichment & Scholar Prog, dir, 1968; Cleveland Trust Co, acct, 1969; EEO Comn US Govt, case anal, 1970; E Cleveland, asst law dir, 1971; Ohio Gen Assembly, legis advocate, 1971-72; Reginald Heber Smith Community Lawyer fel, 1971-73; Lawyers Housing ABA & Cleveland Bar, asst dir, 1972-75; John M Harlan Law Club Inc, vpres, 1975-76; Alexander Jackson & Buchman, atty partner law firm; Jackson Law Co, owner, atty & legal serv consult, currently, sr partner, currently. **Orgs:** Organizer chmn, Black Am Law Stud Asn, Case Western Univ Sch Law, 1970-71, Induction Soc Benchers, 2001; vice chmn, Cleveland Chap, Nat Conf Black Lawyers, 1974-75; NBA; dist rep, Ohio Asn Black Atty, 1974-75; Am Bar Asn; NH Bar Asn; Ohio Bar Asn; Bar Asn Great Cleveland; Cleveland Lawyers Asn; Nat Asn Advan Colored People; Citizens League Cleveland; Legal Aid Soc; vpres, Case Western Res Law Sch Alumni Asn, 2002-03. **Honors/Awds:** Recipient MLK & Award, Baccus Law Sch, 1970-71; co-designer, BALSA Emblem 1971; certificate of appreciation, Bar Asn Greater Cleveland, 1973-75. **Business Addr:** Owner & Attorney, Senior Partner, Jackson Law Co, 3673 Lee Rd, Shaker Heights, OH 44120-5108, **Business Phone:** (216)752-8000.

JACKSON, GILES B
Judge. **Personal:** Born Mar 1, 1924, Richmond, VA; son of Bessie A and Roscoe C; married Mary Ever, 1964; children: Mignon Carter, Yvette Townsend & Yvonne Jackson. **Educ:** VA State Univ, BA, 1948; Southwestern Univ, JD, 1953; Univ Southern Calif, attended 1968; Univ Calif Berkeley, Judicial Col, attended 1977. **Career:** Judge (retired); Pvt pract, atty, 1954-66; Los Angeles Co Super Ct, comn, judge pro tem, 1966-77; Los Angeles Judicial Dist, judge, 1977-86. **Orgs:** Los Angeles Co Bar Asn; life mem, Nat Asn Advan Colored People; life mem, DAV. **Military Serv:** USMC, NCO, 1943-46. **Home Phone:** (310)641-0281.

JACKSON, GORDON MARTIN, JR.
Journalist, writer, manager. **Personal:** Born Jul 3, 1954, Portsmouth, VA; son of Melveen Sr and Gordon; divorced; children: Gordon III, Gregory. **Career:** Minority Opportunity News, sr ed, 1993-94; Dallas Weekly, actg mgr ed, 1995-97; Healthy Living, dir mkt/commun, 1997-98; Urban Press Syndicate, owner/gen mgr, 1997-; Denver Weekly News, ed-in-chief, 1998-99. **Orgs:** parlimentarian, Dallas/Ft Worth Asn Black Communicators, 1994-97; Nat Asn Black Journalists, 1996-; Colo

Asn Black Journalists, 1997-; Colo Press Asn, 1997-; Am Psychiat Asn, 1997; Colo Black Chamber Com, 2000-; 100 Black Men, Colo Chap, 2000-. **Honors/Awds:** A Phillip Randolph Messenger Award Educ, Nat Newspaper Publ Asn, 1998; A Phillip Randolph Messenger Award Civil Rights, 1997; Colo Black Roundtable President's Award, 1990. **Special Achievements:** Featured in Colorado Black Leadership Profiles, 2000. *

JACKSON, GOVERNOR EUGENE
Financial manager. **Personal:** Born May 5, 1951, Linden, TX; married Linda Kay Sueing; children: Governor Eugene III. **Educ:** E Tex State Univ, BS, 1973; N Tex State Univ, MEd, 1978. **Career:** E Tex State Univ, Sam Rayburn Memorial Stud Ctr, bldg serv supr, 1969-73; DeVry Inst Tech, assoc dean studs, 1973-76; Tex Woman's Univ, dir financial aid, 1976-. **Orgs:** Nat Asn Stud Fin Aid Adminstr, 1973-80; SW Asn Stud Financial Aid Admin, 1973-80; admin coun, Tex Woman's Univ, 1977-80; Voter Regist Com Dallas,1978-80; admin bd, St Luke Methodist Church, 1978-80; nominating co, Tex Stud Financial Aid Adminr, 1979. **Honors/Awds:** Leadership Award, E Tex State Univ, 1969-70, 1970-71; Outstanding Young Man of America, Jaycees, 1979. **Business Addr:** Director, Texas Woman University, 304 Administrative Dr, PO Box 425408, Denton, TX 76204.

JACKSON, GRADY O'NEAL
Football player. **Personal:** Born Jan 21, 1973, Greensboro, AL. **Educ:** Knoxville Col, Business and Physical Educ. **Career:** Oakland Raiders, defensive end, 1997-2001; New Orleans Saints, 2002-03; Green Bay Packers, defensive tackle, 2003-05; Atlanta Falcons, 2006-; Jacksonville Jaguars, 2007; Atlanta Falcons, 2008; Detroit Lions, 2009-.

JACKSON, GRANT DWIGHT
Baseball player, athletic coach. **Personal:** Born Sep 28, 1942, Fostoria, OH; married Millie; children: Gayron, Debbie, Yolanda & Grant II. **Educ:** Bowling Green State Univ, Bowling Green, OH. **Career:** Baseball player (retired), baseball coach; Philadelphia Phillies, pitcher, 1965-70; Baltimore Orioles, pitcher, 1971-76; NY Yankees, pitcher, 1976; Pittsburgh Pirates, pitcher, 1977-81 & 1982; Montreal Expos pitcher, 1981; Kans City Royals, pitcher, 1982; Pittsburgh Pirates, pitching coach, 1983; Cincinnati Reds, pitching coach, 1994-95; AAA Indianapolis Indians, Cincinnati Reds, coach; The Durham Bulls Baseball Club, coach, 2000; Rochester Red Wings, pitching coach, 2003-05. **Orgs:** Baltimore Orioles. **Honors/Awds:** Nat League All-Star Team, 1969; Winning pitcher of the last game of theWorld Series; World Series Champs, Pittsburgh Pirates, 1979; PA SportsHall of Fame Western Chp, 2000. **Special Achievements:** First African-American pitching coach for the Pittsburgh Pirates; Havecapacity for Pub Rels; advanced scouting & minor league Coord; SpeakSpanish fluently. **Home Phone:** (724)941-1396.

JACKSON, GREG ALLEN
Football player, football coach. **Personal:** Born Sep 26, 1966, Hialeah, FL; married Dina; children: Greg Jr & Jayden. **Educ:** Fairleigh Dickinson Univ, commun, 2004. **Career:** Football player (retired), Football coach; New York Giants, defensive back, 1989-93; Philadelphia Eagles, 1994-95; New Orleans Saints, 1996; San Diego Chargers, 1997-2001; Tulane Univ, coach, currently. **Business Addr:** Assistant Coach-Linebackers, Tulane University, James W Wilson Jr Center, New Orleans, LA 70118, **Business Phone:** (504)862-8000.

JACKSON, GREGORY
Automotive executive. **Personal:** Born Jul 12, 1957, Detroit, MI; son of Roy and Doris; married Jackie B, Aug 7, 1982; children: Anika S & Gregory J. **Educ:** Morris Brown Coll, BS, acct; Atlanta Univ, Grad Sch Bus, MBA, finance & mkt. **Career:** Arthur Andersen & Co, sr acct, 1980-82; Stroh Brewery Co, controller, 1982-84; Kastleton Co, pres, 1984-91; Prestige Auto Group, founder & pres, currently. **Orgs:** Nat Automobile Dealers Asn; Mich Auto Dealers Asn; Nat Asn Minority Auto Dealers; Gen Motors Minority Dealers Asn; Nat Am Advan Colored People; Kappa Alpha Psi Fraternity. **Honors/Awds:** Black Enterprise 100; Named Auto Dealer of the Yr, Black Enterprise, 2005. **Special Achievements:** Black Enterprise's list of Top 100 Auto Dealers, ranked No 20, 1999, No 3, 2000, ranked No 1, 2001. **Business Addr:** Founder, President, Prestige Auto Group, 7401 N Clio Rd, PO Box 189, Mount Morris, MI 48458, **Business Phone:** (810)686-2310.

JACKSON, HAL (HAROLD BARON JACKSON)
Executive, chief executive officer. **Personal:** Born Nov 3, 1915, Charleston, SC; son of Eugene Baron and Laura Rivers; married; children: Harold Baron Jackson Jr, Jewell McCabe & Jane Harley. **Educ:** Troy Conf Acad Vt; Howard Univ. **Career:** WBLS, Group, Inner City Broad casting Corp, chmn; Hal Jackson Prod, pres & chief exec officer; Hal Jackson's Talented Teens Int Talent Prog, chief exec officer, founder, exec producer, currently. **Orgs:** New York Local; Nat Bd, Am Fedn TV & Radio Artists. **Honors/Awds:** Numerous honors and awards including: Man of Year Award, Beverly Hills Chap Nat Asn Advan Colored People; "Image Awards"; First President Award Broadcasting; Award for Work among youth Pres JF Kennedy; Disc Jockey of the Year, Fair Play Comn & charitable endeavors; Hall of Fame, Nat Asn Broadcasters, 1990; William Bethany Award, 1991; Candace Award, Coalition of 100 Black Women, 1991; Honored for 50 years of broadcasting by the House of Representatives; "Radio Living Legend Award," 1992; Radio Hall of Fame, 1995; "Pioneering Achievements in Black Radio", hon, Smithsonian Inst Wash, DC, 1997; Inductee, Broadcasting & Cable Hall of Fame, 2001. **Special Achievements:** First radio personality to broadcast three daily shows on three different New York stations; Leading pioneer in radio & TV industries established many firsts as black man in this field; partic host national cerebral Palsy Telethon; color comment for home games of NY Nets ABA Basketball Team; Narrator Intern for national syndicate of radio sports for HEW to recruit young people for medical & social service careers; numerous other programs on radio & TV for various fund raising & civic causes. **Business Addr:** Chief Executive Officer, ICBC Broadcast Holdings, Inc., 3 Pk Ave, New York, NY 10016, **Business Phone:** (212)592-0413.

JACKSON, HAROLD BARON. See JACKSON, HAL.

JACKSON, HAROLD BARON, JR.
Lawyer. **Personal:** Born Dec 28, 1939, Washington, DC; son of Harold and Julia; divorced; children: Julie, Tiffany, Jaime. **Educ:** Marquette Univ, BA, 1964; Marquette Univ Law Sch, JD, 1967. **Career:** Milwaukee County, asst dist atty, 1968; Milwaukee Bd Sch Dir, pres, 1970-72; Jackson & Clark Atty, partner, 1970-73; Marquette Univ Law Sch, prof law, 1972-73; circuit ct judge; Milwaukee Metrop Sewerage Dist, sr coun, 1986, sr staff atty, currently. **Orgs:** Exec bd, Milwaukee Jr Bar Asn, 1970; chmn, Criminal Law Sect Milwaukee Bar Asn, 1972; pres bd dir, Sojourner Truth House; chmn bd dir, Benedict Ctr Criminal Justice; bd dir, Athletes Youth. **Honors/Awds:** Outstanding Jurist Award, Friends in Law, 1982; Man of the Yr, Milwaukee Theol Inst, 1978; Winner of American Jurisprudence Awards Constitutional Law, Criminal Law & Jurisprudence. **Home Addr:** 1756 N Hi Mount Blvd, Milwaukee, WI 53208. *

JACKSON, HAROLD JEROME
Journalist. **Personal:** Born Aug 14, 1953, Birmingham, AL; married Denise Estell Pledger, Apr 30, 1977; children: Annette Michelle & Dennis Jerome. **Educ:** Baker Univ, Baldwin, KS, BA, 1975. **Career:** Birmingham Post-Herald, Birmingham, AL, reporter, 1975-80; United Press Int, Birmingham, AL, reporter, 1980-83, state news ed, 1983-85; Philadelphia Inquirer, Philadelphia, PA, asst nat ed, 1985-87; The Birmingham News, Birmingham, AL, ed bd, 1987-94; The Baltimore Sun, ed bd, Baltimore, MD, 1994; The Philadelphia Inquirer, Ed Page, coordr, 1999-2004, dep ed, 2004-07, ed, 2007-. **Orgs:** Nat Asn Black Journalists, 1980-; Westminster Presby Church, 1964-. **Honors/Awds:** Achievement Award, Writing, Asniated Press, 1978; Merit Award, Writing, UPI, 1987; Green Eyeshade, Writing, Soc Prof Journalists, 1989; Hector Award, Writing, Troy State Univ, 1990; APA Award, Writing, Ala Press Asn, 1990; Journalist of the Year, Nat Asn Black Journalists, 1991; Pulitzer Prize, Ed Writing, Columbia Univ, 1991; Citizenship Award, Birmingham Emancipation Asn, 1993; Alumnus of the Year, Baker Univ, 1992. **Home Addr:** 57 Fox Hollow Lane, Sewell, NJ 08080. **Business Addr:** Editorial Page Editor, The Philadelphia Inquirer, PO Box 8263, Philadelphia, PA 19101, **Business Phone:** (215)854-2555.

JACKSON, HAROLD LEONARD, JR.
Financial manager. **Personal:** Born Sep 26, 1955, Columbia, SC; son of Harold L Sr and Orion Virginia Meaders; married Deborah Ann Knox, Feb 12, 1983; children: Matthew G & Jennifer E. **Educ:** Tex A&M Univ, Col Sta, BBA, finance, 1977. **Career:** Dresser Atlas, Houston, TX, off supvr, 1977-83; Macy's, Houston, TX,assoc, 1984; Continental Airlines, Houston, TX, rev acct supvr, 1984-85; City Houston, Houston Tex, fin analyst, div mgr grants, 1985-. **Orgs:** Nat Forum Black Public Admin, 1987-88; Govt Finance Officers Assn, 1988-. **Business Addr:** Divisional Mgr, City of Houston, 901 Bagby Houston TX 77002, PO Box 1562, Houston, TX 77002.*

JACKSON, HENRY RALPH
Clergy, founder (originator). **Personal:** Born Aug 22, 1915, Birmingham, AL; married Cheri J Harrell; children: Zita J. **Educ:** Daniel Payne Col, BA; Jackson Theol Sem, BD; Wilberforce Univ, LlD; Campbell Col, DD; Allen Univ, HHD; Monrovia Col. **Career:** N Memphis Dist AME Church, presiding elder; Bethal AME Church, MinimumSalary Dept, founder & dir, pastor, currently. **Orgs:** Gen conf, AME Church, 1944-80; founder & pres, Brotherhood AME Church; gen bd, AME Church; pres, Christian Brotherhood Homes Inc; co-chmn, Comn Move Equality; Thirty Second Degree Mason; State Dem Exec Comt; hon mem, State County Munic Employees AFL-CIO; founding father, Memphis Goodwill Boys Club; Goodwill Boys Club; Mallory Knights Charitable Orgn; Memphis Welfare Rights Orgn; JUGS Inc; Co-Ettes Inc Congressman Harold Ford. **Honors/Awds:** National Association Advance Colored People Meritorious Service Awards, Brotherhood AME Church; Man of the Year, IBPOE; Citizens Award, Local 1733, AFSCME; Outstanding Tennesse Award, Gov Ray Blanton. **Business Addr:** Pastor, Bethel AME Chuch, 405 3rd Ave, Pompano Beach, FL 33060.

JACKSON, DR. HERMOINE PRESTINE
Psychologist. **Personal:** Born Mar 11, 1945, Wilmington, DE; daughter of Herman P Sr and Ella B Roane. **Educ:** Elizabethtown Col, BA, 1967; OH State Univ, MA, 1979, PhD, 1991. **Career:** Wilmington Pub Sch, teacher 1967-68; Philadelphia Pub Sch System, teacher 1968-74; Cent Mich Univ, instr, 1979-81; State NY W Seneca Develop Ctr, psych, 1981-90; NY State Div Youth, Buffalo Residential Ctr,psychologist, 1990-94; Va State Dept Juvenile Justice; bermuda corrections ctr. **Orgs:** Am Psych Assoc; Am Assoc Ment Retardation; Coalition of 100 Black Women. **Honors/Awds:** Outstanding Instr, Cent Mich Univ, 1981. *

JACKSON, HIRAM
Executive. **Career:** DMC Technologies, pres & chief exec officer; GlobalView Technologies, pres & chief exec officer; Genesis Energy Solutions LLC, pres & chief operating officer, currently. **Orgs:** Founder, ACCESS Am; exec bd mem, NAACP, Detroit Br; chair, Freedom Fund Dinner; Charles H Wright Museum African Am History; Freedom Inst. **Business Phone:** (313)962-9060.

JACKSON, DR. HORACE
Association executive. **Personal:** Born Feb 19, 1935, Opelika, AL; son of Howard Taft and Emma Lee; divorced; children: David, Michael & Karen M Stewart. **Educ:** Tenn A&I State Univ, BS, 1957; Wash Univ, MA, educ, 1969; Wash Univ, PhD, 1976. **Career:** Chattanooga Pub Schs, curric resource teacher, 1957-68; Rutgers Col, lectr, 1973-74; Va Polytech Inst, asst prof, 1974-75; E St Louis Ctr, coordr acad progs, 1976-77; Magnet Sch Enrich Prog, St Louis Univ, lead instr, 1978-80; St Louis Pub Schs, div asst, 1980-83; Mika Info Serv, pres, 1983-89; Chattanooga Area Urban League, dir progs, 1989-90; Partners Econ Progress, mgr minority bus develop; Southeast Indust Develop Asn, spec proj coordr. **Orgs:** Kappa Alpha Psi, 1954-; Kappa Delta Pi, 1970-; Phi Delta Kappa, 1970-; Chattanooga African Am Chamber Com, currently; coordr proj, Southeast Indust Develop Asn. **Home Addr:** 5240 Polk St, Chattanooga, TN 37410, **Home Phone:** (423)821-2091. **Business Addr:** Coordinator of Projects, Southeast Industrial Development Association, 535 Chestnut St, Chattanooga, TN 37402, **Business Phone:** (423)424-4245.

JACKSON, INEZ AUSTIN
Executive. **Educ:** Int Sch Design, attended 1964. **Career:** Design Innerphase Inc, Silver Spring, MD, pres, currently. **Orgs:** Camellia Soc Potomac Valley. *

JACKSON, ISAIAH ALLEN
Conductor (music). **Personal:** Born Jan 22, 1945, Richmond, VA; son of Isaiah and Alma Alverta Norris; married Helen Caroline Tuntland; children: Benjamin, Katharine & Caroline. **Educ:** Harvard Univ, BA, (cum laude), 1966; Stanford Univ, MA, 1967; Juilliard Sch, MS, 1969, DMA, 1973. **Career:** Bach Soc Orchestra, music dir, 1965-66; Juilliard String Ensemble NYC, founder & conductor, 1970-71; Am Sym Orchestra, asst conductor, 1970-71; Baltimore Sym Orchestra, asst conductor, 1971-73; Rochester Philharmonic Orchestra, assoc conductor, 1973-87; Flint Sym Orchestra, MI, music dir & conductor 1982-87; Royal Ballet London England, prin conductor, 1986; Dayton Philharmonic Orchestra, music dir, 1987-95; music dir, l987-90; Queensland Sym Orchestra, Australia, prin guest conductor, 1993-95; Youngstown (OH) Sym, music dir, 1996-; Canberra (Australia) Sym Orchestra, prin guest conductor, 1996-97; Pro Arte Chamber Orchestra Boston, mus dir, 2000-05, conductor emer, currently. **Orgs:** Mem bd dir, Ralph Bunche Scholar Fund, 1974-87; music panel, NY Coun Arts,1978; guest conductor, NY Philharmonic, 1978; guest conductor, Boston Pops, 1983, 1990-94; Detroit Sym Orchestra, 1983, 1985; Cleveland Orchestra, 1983-84, 1986-87, 1989-92; Guest conductor, San Francisco Sym, 1984; Toronto Sym, 1984, 1990, 2002; Orchestre de la Suisse Romande, 1985,1988; BBC Concert Orchestra, 1987; guest conductor, Berlin Sym, 1989-95; Signet Soc Medal For The Arts, Harvard Univ, 1991; Dallas Sym, 1993; Houston Sym, 1995; Royal Liverpool Phil, 1995; trustee, Boston Athenaeum, 2001-; Hochstein Sch Music & Dance. **Honors/Awds:** First Govs Awards for the Arts Commonwealth of VA Richmond, 1979; Signet medal, Signet Soc, Harvard Univ, 1991. **Special Achievements:** First African-American to be appointed to a music directorship in the Boston area. **Business Addr:** Conductor Emeritus, Pro Arte Chamber Orchestra of Boston, 107 Brighton Ave Suite 1, Boston, MA 02134.

JACKSON, JACQUELYNE JOHNSON
Educator. **Personal:** Born Feb 24, 1932, Winston-Salem, NC; divorced; children: Viola Elizabeth. **Educ:** Univ Wis, BS, 1953, MS, 1955; Ohio State Univ, PhD, 1960. **Career:** John Hay Whitney fel, 1957-59; NSF Fel, 1957-; Southern Univ Baton Rouge, assoc prof, 1959-62; Univ Colo, Boulder, fel, 1961; Jackson State Col, prof, 1962-64; Howard Univ, asst prof, 1964-66; NIH Fel, 1966-68 & 1977-78; St Augustine's Col, vis prof, 1969-; Univ NC, Chapel Hill, fac, 1977-78; Howard Univ, prof, 1978-85; Duke Univ, instr & assoc prof med sociol, 1966-98, assoc prof emer med sociol, 1998-. **Orgs:** Life mem, Tuskegee, Ala Civic Asn, 1959-; Am Soc Aging; former mem bd dir, Carver Res Found, Tuskegee Univ, 1970-87; dir, Nat Coun Black Aging, 1975-; Am Sociol Asn; Southern Sociol Soc; Geront Soc Am; bd dirs, Nat Coun Aging; former pres, Asn Social & Behav Scientists; former chairperson, Caucus Black Sociologists; Ctr Immigration Studies, 1997-. **Honors/Awds:** Received numerous awards from Am Psychiat

Asn, OSU, AAHA & ABS. **Special Achievements:** Author: "These Rights They Seek", 1962; "Minorities & Aging", 1980; approximately 100 chapters in books and articles since 1962. **Business Addr:** Associate Professor Emeritus, Duke University, School of Medicine, PO Box 3878, Durham, NC 27710.

JACKSON, REV. JAMES CONROY. See Obituaries section.

JACKSON, JAMES E., SR.
Insurance executive, president (organization). **Personal:** Born Feb 4, 1943, Roberta, GA; son of J B WornumC and Dollie; divorced; children: James Jr, Nsombi, Jawara, Brandon, Barenda. **Career:** Allstate Ins Co, agency owner, 1971-; Dunhill Staffing Systs, chief exec officer akland & Macomb franchise's, 1996-; Poole & Jackson Ins Agency, owner & chief exec officer, 2001-. **Orgs:** Nat Asn Advan Colored People, 1978; Optimist Club Detroit, 1991, pres, 1998. **Honors/Awds:** Michigan Sales Leader, Allstate Ins, Auto Ins, Territory 3, 1998; FLPI Production, Territory 3, 1998, Life Ins, Territory, 3, 1998, Personal Property, Territory 3, 1998; Motor Club, 1998. **Special Achievements:** First minority chief exec officer & owner of a Dunhill Staffing Systs Franchise. **Military Serv:** AUS, sergeant, 1962-65. **Home Addr:** 454 Wishbone, Bloomfield Hills, MI 48304, **Home Phone:** (248)723-6682. **Business Addr:** Senior Account Agent, Allstate Insurance Co, 17051 W 10 Mile Rd, Southfield, MI 48075, **Business Phone:** (248)443-0000.*

JACKSON, JAMES GARFIELD
Law enforcement officer. **Personal:** Born Oct 24, 1933, Columbus, OH; son of George and Sarah; married Mary; children: James II & Jason. **Educ:** FBI Nat Exec Inst, attended; Harvard Univ, John F Kennedy Sch Gov, attended. **Career:** Columbus Div Police, officer, 1958-67, sgt, 1967-71, lt, 1971-74, capt, 1974-77, dep chief, 1977-90, chief, 1990-. **Orgs:** Major City Chiefs Asn; Int Asn Chiefs Police; Ohio Asn Chiefs Police; Nat Black Law Enforcement Execs. **Honors/Awds:** Lloyd Sealey Award, Nat Orgn Black Law Enforcement Exec, 2005. **Special Achievements:** First black police chief in the Columbus Div Police; Only person in the Columbus Div Police to place first on three written promotional examinations for sergeant, capt & dep chief; Testimony for minorities & females helped bring about a federal court finding from which 75% of current black & female officers have benefited through employ, assignment, promotion, back pay or a combination thereof. **Military Serv:** USMC, sgt, 1951-54. **Home Addr:** 1349 Bryden Rd, Columbus, OH 43205, **Home Phone:** (614)645-6003. **Business Addr:** Chief of Police, Columbus Division of Police, 120 Marconi Blvd, PO Box 15009, Columbus, OH 43215, **Business Phone:** (614)645-4600.

JACKSON, JAMES HOLMEN
Executive. **Personal:** Born Oct 5, 1949, Newark, NJ; married Lynda P Valrie; children: Lamarr. **Educ:** Compu-Train, comput operator, 1970; ICBO Rutgers Univ, bus mgt, 1974; Bloomfield Col, BA, 1979. **Career:** Moldcast Lighting Div, asst mgr qc, 1972-79; Condor Int Corp, treas, 1979-80; Internal Revenue Serv, revenue officer, 1980-83; Jacmin Inc, pres; JS Minor Corp, consult. **Orgs:** Treas, Citizens Improvement League, 1979-82; pres, Montgomery Ave Block Assoc, Irv, NJ, 1979-83; chmn bd, Sugar Bear Prods; bd dirs, People's Comn Corp; Budget Construction Co; chmn, Tenant Assoc 111 So Harrison E, Orange, NJ. **Military Serv:** AUS; Honorable Discharge, 1972. **Business Addr:** Owner, President, Jacmin Inc, 210 Pinehurst Ave, Scotch Plains, NJ 07076, **Business Phone:** (201)642-7019.

JACKSON, DR. JAMES SIDNEY
Educator, behavioral scientist. **Personal:** Born Jul 30, 1944, Detroit, MI; son of Pete James and Johnnie Mae Wilson Taylor; married Toni C Antonucci; children: Ariana Marie & Kendra Rose. **Educ:** Mich State Univ, BS, psychol, 1966; Univ Toledo, MA, psychol, 1970; Wayne State Univ, PhD, social psychol, 1972. **Career:** Lucas Co Family Ct, Toledo, OH, probation counr, 1967-68; Wayne State Univ, urban studies fel, 1969-70; Univ Mich, Ann Arbor, from asst prof to assoc prof 1971-85, dir, Nat Survey Black Am, 1980, prof psychol 1986-94, assoc dean, Rackham Grad Sch, 1988-92, Inst Gerontology, fac assoc, 1988-, Sch Pub Health, prof health behav & health educ, 1990-, Fogarty Sr Postdoctoral Int Fel, 1993-94, Daniel Katz Distinguished Univ Prof Psychol, 1995-, Prog Res Black Am, Inst Social Res, dir, res group dynamics, 1996-, Ctr Afro-American & African Studies, dir, 1998, Ctr Res Ethnicity, Cult & Health, fac assoc, 2001-04, Inst Social Res, dir, 2005-; Ford Foundation, sr postdoctoral fel, 1986-87; Univ Minn, Hill distinguished visiting prof, 1995; Univ Tokyo, vis prof, 2001. **Orgs:** Fac assoc, Inst Soc Res, 1971-85; chmn, Nat Asn Black Psychologists, 1972-73; chmn, Asn Adv Psychol, 1978-80; bd dir, Pub Comt Mental Health, 1978-83; chair, Social Psychol Training Prog, Univ Mich, 1980-86; fac assoc, Ctr Afro-Am & African Studies 1982-; mem comt status black, Am Nat Res Coun, 1985-; res scientist, Inst Social Res, 1986-; mem bd trustees, Asn Adv Psychol 1986-; chair, Task Force, Gerontological Soc Am, 1989; Nat Adv Mental Health Coun, NIMH, 1989-; Data Analysis Res Network, Nat Collegiate Athletic Asn, 1989-, chair, 1994-; Grad Record Exam Comn, 1990-93; prog comn, Am Psychol Soc, 1990-91; adv bd, Brookdale Nat Fel Prog, Humanities, Behav & Social Sci, 1990-; bd dirs, Ronald McDonald House, 1993-99; Fed Behav, Psychol & Cognitive Sci, 1994-; co-chair, Wayne State Univ, Inst Gerontology, 1994-; US Census Bureau, Adv Comm African Am, 1994-2004; bd trustees, Greenhills Sch, 1997-; nat adv comn mem, Boston Museum Sci Traveling Exhibition Aging, 1998-2000; Nat Inst Aging, Bd Scientific Counrs, 2000-04; Nat Res Coun, Comm Pop, Panel Race, Ethnicity & Health Later Life, 2001-02; Nat Occup Res Agenda, 2001; Am Psychol Asn, Delegation UN World Conf Race, 2001; chair-elect, AAAS, 2002-03, chair 2003-04; Nat Acad Sci, Inst Med, 2002. **Honors/Awds:** Distinguished Faculty Achievement Award, Univ Mich, 1975-76; Robert W Kleemier Award, Outstanding Res Aging, 1994; Harold R Johnson Diversity Award, Univ Mich, 2000; Peace & Social Justice Award, Soc Peace, Conflict & Violence, Am Psychol Asn, 2000; Distinguished Career Contribution to Research Award, Soc Psychol Study Ethnic Minority Issues, Am Psychol Asn, 2001; Lifetime Award, Comn Mental Health Coun, 2002. **Special Achievements:** Published numerous books, chapters and scientific articles on international, comparative studies of immigration, race and ethnic relations, physical and mental health, etc. **Business Addr:** Professor, Director, University of Michigan, Institute for Social Research, 426 Thompson St, Ann Arbor, MI 48106-1248.

JACKSON, JANET DAMITA JO
Actor, entertainer, singer. **Personal:** Born May 16, 1966, Gary, IN; daughter of Joseph Jackson and Katherine Jackson; married James Debarge, Sep 7, 1984 (divorced 1985); married Rene Elizondo, Mar 31, 1991 (divorced 2000). **Career:** Studio Albums: Janet Jackson, 1982; Dream Street, 1984; Control, 1986; Janet Jackson's Rhythm Nation, 1989; janet., 1993; Design of a Decade, 1995; The Velvet ope, 1997; All For You, 2001; Damita Jo, 2004; 20 Y.O., 2006; DVD: The Rhythm nation Compilation, 1997; Design of a Decade, 1997; The Velvet Rope Tour - Live In Concert, 1999; All For You special edition, 2001; Live in Hawaii, 2002; From Janet. to Damita Jo, 2004; TV Series: Good Times, 1977-79; A New Kind of Family, 1979-80; Different Strokes, 1980-84; Fame, 1984-85; Films: Poetic Justice, 1993; Nutty Professor II: The Klumps, 2000; "Why Did I Get Married", 2007; Music Videos: Dream Street, 1984; What ave You Done For Me Lately, 1986; Nasty, 1986; When I Think Of You, 1986; Control, 1986; Let's Wait A while, 1987; The Pleasure Principle, 1987; Diamonds, 1988; 2300 Jackson Street, 1989; Miss You Much, 1989; The Knowledge, 1989; Rhythm Nation, 1989; Escapade, 1989; Alright, 1990; Come Back To Me, 1990; Black Cat, 1990; Love Will Never Do (Without You), 1990; The Best things in life re free (Janet& Luther aren't in the video), 1992; That's The Way Love Goes, 1993; If 1993; Again, 1993; Because of Love, 1993; Any Time, Any Place, 1994; Throb (Saturday Night live performance), 1994; You Want This, 1994; Whoops Now, 1995; What 'll I Do, 1995; Scream, 1995; Runaway, 1995; Twenty Foreplay, 1996; Got 'Til It's Gone, 1997; Together Again, 1997; Together Again (Deeper Remix), 1997; I Get Lonely, 1998; Go Deep, 1998; You, 1998; Luv Me(Janet Doesn't appear in the video), 1998; Every Time, 1998; Boyfiend/Girlfriend, 1999; Whats it gonna be, 1999; Doesn't Really Matter, 2000; All for You, 2001; Someone To Call My Lover, 2001; Son Of A Gun, 2001; Feel It Boy, 2002; Just A Little While, 2004; I Want You, 2004; All Nite (Don't Stop), 2004; R&B Junkie (not released), 2004; Gotta Getcha, 2005; Call On Me feat, 2006; So Excited Feat, 2006; With U, 2007. **Honors/Awds:** American Music Awards, Favorite R&B Female Artist; World Music Awards, Outstanding Contribution to Rhythm and Blues; American Society of Composers, Authors and Publishers Award, 1995; American Music Awards, Award of Merit, 2000; Entertainer of the Yr, Nat Asn of Black Owned Broadcasters, 2002; Essence Award, 2002; Governor's Award, Recording Academy, 2002; Touching a Life Award, Behind the Bench, 2004; received more than 150 awards including Grammy Awards; American Music Awards; MTV Video Music Awards; MTV Movie Awards; MTV Japan Video Music Awards; Billboard Music Awards; Soul Train Music Awards; MTV Europe Awards; Nickelodeon Kids' Choice Awards; Radio Music Awards; BMI Pop Awards; NBA / Touching a Life Awards; World Music Awards; VH- Fashion Awards; Blockbuster Entertainment Awards; Golden Globes; Essence Awards; Japan Gold Disc Awards; Rolling Stone Readers Choice Awards; Oscar Awards (Academy Awards); AIDS Project LosAngeles (APLA); Hollywood Walk of Fame; Ebony Magazine Awards; IFPI Platinum Europe Awards; Source Awards; Dutch Grammys TMF Awards; BPI UK Sales Awards; GLAAD Media Awards; Playboy Magazine Entertainment Awards; Inter Nat Dance Music Awards; ACE (American Cinema Awards); ARIA Awards (Australian Sales Awards); Emmy Awards (Academy of Television Arts &Sciences); Dutch Edison Awards; Narm Awards (Nat Asn of Recording Merchandisers); Nat Alumnae Asn Of Spelman Awards; Nat Asn Advan Colored People Image Awards; CORE (Congress of Racial Equality); Starlight Foundation Awards; Ctr for Population Options; Channel V Awards; Dansk Grammy Awards (Danish Music Awards); Brazilian TVZ Video Awards; Bravo Awards; Swiss Sales Awards (Switzerland Sales); Radioscope Awards; BMG Music Club Sales Award; DMC DJ Awards; Performance Magazine Awards; LEAP Awards. **Special Achievements:** The only performer male or female to be nominated for Grammy Awards in Pop, Rock, Dance, Rap and R&B, and the first female recording artist of color to be nominated for a Producer Of The Year Grammy; only woman singer in the history of Rock & Roll to score 5 back to back #1 studio albums on the Billboard Album's chart; nominated for Oscar Award Best Music, Original Song for:Poetic Justice (1993) in 1994. **Business Addr:** Entertainer, Grabow & Associates Inc., 4219 Creekmeadow Dr, Dallas, TX 75287-6806.

JACKSON, JANET E.
Judge, president (organization), chief executive officer. **Personal:** Married; children: Harrison. **Educ:** Wittenberg Univ, BA, hist, 1975; Natl Law Ctr, George Wash Univ, JD, 1978. **Career:** Ohio Atty Gen Off, asst atty gen, 1978-80, asst chief civil rights sect,1980-82, chief crime victims compensation sect, 1982, chief work comp sect, 1983-87; Sindell, Sindell & Rubenstein, atty, 1982-83; Franklin County Munic Ct, judge, 1987-97, admin, 1992; Columbus City, atty, 1997-03; United Way Cent, Ohio, pres & chief exec officer, 2003-. **Orgs:** Columbus Bar Assn; Natl Conf Black Lawyers; Women Lawyers Franklin County; Ohio State Bar Assn; brd dirs, Action C; brd trustees, Wittenberg Univ; Columbus Mortar Brd Alumni Club; pres, Col Metropolitan Club; bd mem, Leadership Colombus; bd mem, Franklin Univ; bd mem, Marty's Kids Foundn. **Honors/Awds:** Distinguished Barrister Award, Natl Conf Black Lawyers, 1988; Outstanding Accomplishments Award, Franklin County Dem Women, 1988; Community Serv Award, Metrop Dem Women's Club, 1989; Warren Jennings Award, Franklin County Ment Health Brd, 1989; Dr Martin Luther King Jr Humanitarian Award, Columbus Educ Assn, 1991; Women of Achievement Award, YWCA, 1992; Citizen's Award, Columbus Assn Educ Young C, 1993; Citations Award, Pi Lambda Theta, 1993; John Mercer Langston Award, Natl Conf Black Lawyers & Robert B Elliot Law Club, 1994. **Special Achievements:** Blue Chip Profile, 1992; Inducted into Ohio Women's Hall of Fame in 2001. **Business Addr:** Chief Executive Officer, President, United Way Central Ohio, 360 S 3rd St, Columbus, OH 43215.*

JACKSON, JANINE MICHELE
Journalist. **Personal:** Born Jan 30, 1965, Wilmington, DE; daughter of Wagner and Arva Marshall; married Jim Naureckas, Jan 1, 1997. **Educ:** Sarah Lawrence Col, BA, 1985; New Sch Social Res, MA, sociol, 1992. **Career:** FAIR, res dir, prof dir, currently; FAIR Mag, An Extra, contrib; Labor at the Crossroads, host, 1994-. **Orgs:** Labor at the Crossroads, 1994-. **Honors/Awds:** Communicator of the Year, Metro NY Labor Press Coun, 1996. **Business Phone:** (212)633-6700.

JACKSON, JAREN
Basketball player, basketball coach. **Personal:** Born Oct 27, 1967, New Orleans, LA; married Terri. **Educ:** Georgetown Univ. **Career:** Basketball player (retired), basketball coach; NJ Nets, guard, 1989-90; Wichita Falls Texans, CBA, 1990-91; Dayton Wings, WBL, 1991; La Crosse Catbirds, CBA, 1991-92; Golden State Warriors, 1992; Los Angeles Clippers, 1992-93; La Crosse Catbirds, CBA, 1993-94; Portland Trailblazers, 1993-94; Philadelphia 76ers, 1994-95; Pittsburgh Piranhas, CBA, 1995; Ft Wayne Fury, CBA, 1995-96; Houston Rockets, 1996; Wash Wizards, 1996-97; San Antonio Spurs, 1997-2001; Orlando Magic, guard, 2001-02; CBA, Gary Steelheads, coach; Pittsburgh Xplosion, head coach, 2007-. **Orgs:** Founder, New Orleans Youth Org; founder, Back on the Block Found. **Honors/Awds:** NBA World Champion San Antonio Spurs, 1999; Spalding 3-Point Champion (McDonald's Championship-Milan, Italy), 1999. **Business Addr:** Head Coach, Pittsburgh Xplosion, 200 James St Suite 302, Monreville, PA 15146, **Business Phone:** 877-410-9900.

JACKSON, JESSE L., JR.
Congressperson (U.S. federal government). **Personal:** Born Mar 11, 1965; son of Jesse Louis Jackson Sr; married Sandi; children: Jessica Donatella, Jesse III. **Educ:** NC A&T State Univ, BS, 1987; Chicago Theol Seminary, MA, 1990; Univ Ill Law Sch, JD, 1993. **Career:** Nat Rainbow Coalition, nat outreach field dir; US House Rep, Sec Dist, IL, congressman, 1995-. **Orgs:** Pres, "Keep Hope Alive" Polit Action Comt; Democratic Nat Comt; Oper PUSH, vpres-at-large. **Honors/Awds:** Hon deg Chicago Theol Seminary, NC A&T State Univ, Govrs State Univ, Prairie State Col, Morehouse Sch Med. **Special Achievements:** Co-author: Legal Lynching, 1996; It's About the Money, 1999; Legal Lynching II, 2001; A More Perfect Union: Advancing New American Rights, 2001, with Frank E Watkins. Ebony Magazine, 50 Leaders of the Future. **Business Addr:** Congressman, US House of Representatives, 2419 Rayburn House Off Bldg, Washington, DC 20515-1302, **Business Phone:** (202)225-0773.*

JACKSON, REV. JESSE LOUIS
Clergy, civil rights activist, government official. **Personal:** Born Oct 8, 1941, Greenville, SC; son of Noah Robinson and Helen Burns; married Jacqueline Lavinia Brown, Jan 1, 1963; children: Sanitita,Jesse Louis Jackson Jr, Jonathan, Yusef DuBois J & Jacqueline Lavinia. **Educ:** Univ Ill, attended 1960; NC A&T Univ, BA, 1964; Chicago Theol Sem, DD,MDiv, 2000. **Career:** Greenville, SC Civil Rights Movement, leader, 1960; Serv Statewide TV Prog, dir, 1962; Operation PUSH, nat pres, 1972-83; Greensboro, NC Civil Rights Movement, mem, 1963; NC Intercoll Coun Human Rights, pres; Gov Stanford's Off, liaison officer; Cong Racial Equality, field rep South Eastern region, 1965; Bapt Church, ordained minister, 1968; The Nat Rainbow Coalition, founder & pres, 1984-96; CNN Network, "Both Sides With Jesse Jackson", host, 1992-2000; Rainbow PUSH Coalition, founder & pres,

1996-. **Orgs:** Assoc minister, Fel Missionary Baptist Church; nat dir, SCLC Oper Breadbasket, 1967; Nat dir, Coord Coun Community Orgn, 1966-71; Active Black Coalition United Comt Action. **Honors/Awds:** Greensboro Citizen of the Year 1964; Chicago Club Frontier's Intl Man of the Year, 1968; Presidential Award, Nat Med Asn, 1969; Humanitarian Father of the Year, Nat Father's Day Community, 1971; Presidential Medal of Freedom, 2000. **Special Achievements:** Second African American to mount a nationwide campaign for President of the US; author, Straight From The Heart, Fortress Press, 1987; Appointed by President Clinton as the Special Envoy to Africa, 1997; co-author, Legal Lynching: Racism, Injustice, and the Death Penalty, 1996; co-author, It's About Money, 2000. **Business Phone:** (773)373-3366.

JACKSON, JIM
Basketball player. **Personal:** Born Oct 14, 1970, Toledo, OH; married. **Educ:** OH State Univ, attended 1993. **Career:** Dallas Mavericks, guard, 1992-96; NJ Nets, 1996-97; Philadelphia 76ers, 1997-98; Golden State Warriors, 1998; Portland Blazers, 1998-99; Atlanta Hawks, 1999-2001; Cleveland Cavaliers, 2000-01; Miami Heat, 2001; Sacramento Kings, 2002; Houston Rockets, 2003-04; Phoenix Suns, forward-guard, 2005-06; Los Angeles Lakers, 2006. **Orgs:** Founder, James Arthur Jackson Found. **Special Achievements:** NBA Draft, First round pick, No 4, 1992.

JACKSON, JOHN
Mayor. **Personal:** Born Jan 17, 1948, Hayneville, AL; married Katie Welch; children: Nina S & Kevin John. **Educ:** Tuskegee Inst, Cert, Qual Control, 1966; Univ Mich, Ins Exec, 1969. **Career:** Ford Motor Co, final inspector, 1969-72; Life Ins GA, ins exec, 1973-79; City White Hall, mayor. **Orgs:** Chmn bd, Sellers Mem Christian Church; Stud Non violent Co ordr Comn. *

JACKSON, JOHN
Landscape architect, chief executive officer. **Personal:** Born Aug 14, 1961, New York, NY; son of John Jr and Lucille; married Jul 3, 1983 (divorced); children: John Jackson IV. **Educ:** Mississippi State Univ, bachelor landscape architecture, 1983. **Career:** Pickering Firm, landscape architect, 1983-87; Toles Associates, dir landscape archit, land planning & chief operating officer, 1987-90; Jackson Person & Assocs Inc, pres & chief exec officer, 1991-. **Orgs:** Am Planning Asn, 1984-; comt chmn, 1991-, Am Soc Landscape Architects, 1986-; vice chmn, Coun Fed Procurement Architects & Engrs, 1995-. **Honors/Awds:** Planning Award of Excellence, Tenn Am, 1992; West Tennessee Small Business Award, US Small Bus Admin, 1993; Small Business Award, Memphis Bus Jour, 1994; Tennessee Small Business of the Year, US Small Bus Admin, 1995; Supplier of the Year Award, Nat Minority Supplier Develop Coun, 1996. **Business Phone:** (901)523-9150.

JACKSON, JOHN
Football player. **Personal:** Born Jan 4, 1965, Camp Kwe, Japan; married Joan; children: Josh & Jordan. **Educ:** Eastern Ky Univ, BA, police admin, 1988. **Career:** Football player (retired); Pittsburgh Steelers, tackle, 1988-97; San Diego Chargers, 1998-99; Cincinnati Bengals, 2000-01. **Orgs:** John & Joan Jackson Found.

JACKSON, JOHN H.
Civil engineer. **Personal:** Born Jun 8, 1943, Boonville, MO; son of Louis R and Elnora Smith Campbell; married Mae Jones Jackson. **Educ:** Univ MO, BS, civil eng, 1968; Univ Houston, MBA, finance, 1975. **Career:** Dow Chemical, design engr, 1968-72, proj engr, 1974-83; J F Pritchard & Co, design engr, 1972-74; City Miami, asst dir pub works. **Orgs:** Am Soc Pub Admin, 1983-; Nat Forum Black Pub Admin, 1984-; Nat Asn Advan Colored People. **Home Addr:** 8506 SW 103rd Ave, Miami, FL 33173, **Home Phone:** (305)271-9039. *

JACKSON, JOHNNY, JR.
Legislator, association executive. **Personal:** Born Sep 19, 1943, New Orleans; married Ara Jean; children: Kenyatta Shabazz. **Educ:** Southern Univ, BA, 1965; Univ New Orleans, attended 1966. **Career:** Logan Cab Co, dispatcher, 1958-61; Sears Gentilly, porter, 1961-65; Desire Community Ctr, exec dir, 1963-73; Social Welfare Planning Coun, comt orgn, 1965-68; Dist 101, state rep, 1973-77; State La, coun mem, 1986-94; La Legis Black Caucus, founding mem. **Orgs:** Munic & Prochial Gov't Comn, 1972-77; Health & Welfare Comn House, 1972-77; Joint Comn Health & Welfare, 1972-77; subcomt mem, Career & Sec Educ, 1972-77; House Comn Educ, 1972-77; subcomt mem, Health & Ment Disorders, 1972-77; joint comt mem, Spec Educ, 1972-76; Gov Blue Ribbon Comn, Southern Univ Crisis, 1972; New Orleans Community Schs, 1973-77; spec comt mem, Stud Concerns, 1974-76; Gov Comn St Rev Sharing, 1974; Gov Comn Adv Valorem Taxes, 1975; Desire Credit Union, 1975-77; pres, OSEI Day Care, 1975-77; LA Legis Gov Food Stamps Adv Comt, 1977; House Comn Ways & Means, 1977; Joint Comn Legis Coun, 1977; New Orleans Jazz & Heritage Found; St Roch Comn Improvement Asn; Nat Black Found; Desire Comt Housing Corp Affiliated; Desire Area Comt Coun Affiliated; Desire/FL Sr Citizens Prog; Boy Scouts Am; Urban League; Nat Asn Advan Colored People; Free Southern Theatre; Desire Community Ctr; bd mem, Northern Sickle Cell Anemia Found; bd mem, Greater Northern Asn Retarded Citizens.

JACKSON, JONATHAN
Association executive, president (organization). **Personal:** Daughter of Jesse and Jacqueline. **Career:** PUSH-Excel, pres bd, currently; Jesse L Jackson Sr Productions, secy, currently; Jacqueline Inc, pres, currently. **Orgs:** Pres, Citizenship Educ Fund, currently. **Business Addr:** President of the Board, PUSH-Excel, 930 E 50th St, Chicago, IL 60615, **Business Phone:** (773)373-3366.

JACKSON, DR. JULIUS HAMILTON
Scientist, educator. **Personal:** Born Jan 6, 1944, Kansas City, MO; son of Virgil Lawrence Sr and Julia Esther Jones; married Patricia Ann Herring, Dec 22, 1979; children: Rahsaan Hamil, Sajida Lazelle & Ajani Josef. **Educ:** Univ Kans, Lawrence, KS, AB, 1966, PhD, 1969. **Career:** Purdue Univ, W Lafayette, NIH res fel, 1969-71, res assoc, 1971-72; Meharry Med Col, Nashville, TN, asst prof microbiol, 1972-76, assoc prof, chmn microbiol, 1981-85, dir, hybridoma res support facility, 1985-87; Mich State Univ, E Lansing, assoc prof microbiol, 1987-. **Orgs:** Am Soc Microbiol; Am Soc Biol Chemists, 1982-; chmn, Comt Equal Opportunities for Minority Groups, Am Soc Biochem & Molecular Biol, 1992. **Honors/Awds:** William A Hinton Research Training Award, Am Soc Microbiol, 2000. **Business Addr:** Professor, Michigan State University, Department Microbiology & Molecular Genetics, 2215 Biomedical Physical Sciences East Lansing, East Lansing, MI 48824-4320, **Business Phone:** (517)884-5398.

JACKSON, KAREN DENISE
Engineer. **Personal:** Born Jan 14, 1947, Chicago, IL; daughter of William Jesse and Kathryn; married Raymond, Apr 24, 1971; children: Cheo Oronde Diallobe & Ahkil Asaad Diallobe. **Educ:** Elmira Col, BS, math & chem, 1976; Mich State Univ, BSEE, 1984. **Career:** Gen Motors, foreman, 1977-82; Motorola, software engr, 1984-. **Orgs:** Ariz Coun Black Engrs & Scientists, vpres, computer camp chmn, 1986-; WordWizards Toast Masters, charter secy-treas, 1987-; Chmn, ACBES Summer Computer Camp, 1989-92; co-founder of business group for black women, Strictly Business. **Honors/Awds:** Black Engineer of the Year for Community Service, US Black Engr Magazine, 1992; The Career Communications Group; ACBES, High Five Award, 1991. **Special Achievements:** First Black history radio program in Corning NY, 1974; created KomputerEd Tools, 1996. **Home Addr:** 7748 S Rita Lane, Tempe, AZ 85284-1502. **Business Addr:** Software Engineer, Motorola Government Electronics Group, 8201 E McDowell Rd Hayden Bldg, Scottsdale, AZ 85257-3893, **Business Phone:** (602)441-1197.

JACKSON, KAREN EUBANKS
Association executive. **Educ:** Morgan State Univ, BA, sociol. **Career:** YWCA, Houston Health Initiative, prog mgr; Newark Dept Welfare, social worker; Sisters Network Inc, partner, founder & ceo, currently. **Orgs:** Int Breast Cancer Res Found; Ctr Res Minority Health; Am Soc Breast Dis; Consumers Liaison Group; Nat Breast Cancer Coalition; Susan G Komen Breast Cancer Found, African Am Nat Adv Comt; Baylor Methodist Breast Care Ctr Adv Coun. **Honors/Awds:** Certificate, Nat Breast Cancer Coalition Proj Lead; Certificate, Encore plus Breast Health Educr; Certificate, Am Cancer Soc Spec Touch Breast Health & Look Good-Feel Better; Breast Cancer Hero, Lifetime TV. **Special Achievements:** co-author, Breast Cancer in African American Women: The Evolution of the Sisters Network Inc, Breast Diseases: A Year Book Quarterly, 2003; Her story has also been included in an HBO special: Cancer: Evolution to Revolution and in several breast cancer related books: Breast Cancer Black Women, My Mother?s Breast & Celebrating Life. **Business Addr:** Founder, Chief Executive Officer, Sisters Network Inc, 8787 Woodway Dr Suite 4206, Houston, TX 77063, **Business Phone:** (713)781-0255.*

JACKSON, DR. KEITH HUNTER
Educator. **Personal:** Born Sep 24, 1953, Columbus, OH; married Violet Smallhorne; children: Kamilah & Akil. **Educ:** Morehouse Col, BS, 1976; Ga Tech Univ, BSEE, 1976; Stanford Univ, MS, physics, 1979, PhD, 1982. **Career:** Hewlett Packard Labs, tech staff, 1981-83; Howard Univ, asst prof, 1983-88; Rockwell Int, Rocketdyne Div, tech staff, 1988-91; Lawrence Berkeley Nat Lab, staff scientist, 1991, Ctr X-Ray Optics, dir; Fla A&M Univ, vpres res, currently. **Orgs:** Pres, Nat Soc Black Physicists, 2002-; founding dir, Nat Asn Equal Opportunity Higher Educ, 2002-03; Am Phys Soc; Optical Soc Am; Army Res Lab Tech Assessment Bd; exec comt mem, Advan Light Source. **Special Achievements:** Published numerous articles and books. **Business Addr:** Vice President for Research, Florida A&M University, Office of the Vice President for Research, 410 Foote-Hilyer Admin Ctr, Tallahassee, FL 32307, **Business Phone:** (850)412-5102.

JACKSON, KEITH JEROME
Football player, radio broadcaster. **Personal:** Born Apr 19, 1965, Little Rock, AR; children: Keith Jr. **Educ:** Okla Univ, BS, communs, 1988. **Career:** Football player (retired), Radio broadcaster; Philadelphia Eagles, tightend, 1988-91; Miami Dolphins, tight end, 1992-94; Green Bay Packers, tightend, 1995-96; Ark Razorbacks football radio broadcasts, color commentator, currently. **Orgs:** Omega Psi Phi. **Honors/Awds:** Rookie of the Year, Sporting News, 1988. **Special Achievements:** College Football Hall of Fame, 2001; Six Pro Bowl selection, 1988, 1989, 1990, 1992, 1993 & 1996; Five All-Pro selection, 1988, 1989, 1990, 1992 & 1996. **Business Phone:** (501)324-7562.*

JACKSON, KEITH M.
Executive. **Personal:** Born Nov 22, 1948, Springfield, IL. **Educ:** Dartmouth Col, BA, 1971; Columbia Univ, MS, 1975. **Career:** Sahara Energy Corp, pres; Trans Urban East Orgn Inc NYC, consult econ dev & mkt analysis, 1971-73; Rep Charles B Rangel US House Reps Wash, legis asst, 1973-74; Cong Black Caucus Inc, exec dir.

JACKSON, KENYA LOVE
Executive. **Personal:** Born Nov 25, 1963, Flushing, NY; daughter of James G Newman II and Gladys Maria Knight. **Educ:** Univ San Diego, BA, 1986. **Career:** Cedar Sinai Hosp, Los Angeles CA, lab res technician, 1982-84; Jeremiah's Steak House, Dallas TX, asst mgr, head cashier, 1984-85; Marquee Entertainment, Los Angeles CA, asst exec vpres, 1986-87; Shakeji Inc, Las Vegas NV, exec adminr, 1987-; Kenya's Cakes Stars, Las Vegas NV, owner, 1994-. **Orgs:** Secy & treas, Newman Mgt Inc, 1987-; corp dir, KNS Prod Inc, 1987-; corp dir, Knight Hair Care Inc, 1988-; secy & treas, Ms G Inc 1988-; pres, Kenya's Kitchen Inc, 1993. **Business Addr:** Owner, Kenya's Cakes of the Stars, 1301 E Sunset Rd, Las Vegas, NV 89120, **Business Phone:** (702)450-7661.

JACKSON, KEVIN
Athlete, athletic coach. **Personal:** Married Robin; children: Cole, Trinity, Bailee & Brynn. **Career:** US Olympic Athlete, freestyle wrestler, 1992, freestyle wrestling coach, currently. **Honors/Awds:** USOC Wrestler of the Year, 1991; Gold Medalist, World Champion, 1991; Champion, Pan Am Games, 1991, 1995; Gold Medalist, Olympic Games, Barcelona, Spain, 1992; Amateur Wrestling News Man of the Year, 1992; John Smith Award, USA Wrestling Freestyle Wrestler of the Year, 1995; US Nat Wrestling Hall of Fame. **Special Achievements:** One of only five U.S. wrestlers to claim three career World-level titles. **Business Addr:** Wrestling Coach, US Olympic Training Center, 1 Olympic Plz, Colorado Springs, CO 80909, **Business Phone:** (719)578-4500.

JACKSON, KEVIN ALLEN
Executive, government official. **Personal:** Born Aug 27, 1962, Chicago, IL; son of Allen Jackson and Elizabeth; married Paula Jackson, Jul 17, 1992; children: Ryann Elizabeth. **Educ:** Northeastern Illinois Univ, BA, pre-law, 1986; Roosevelt Univ, Graduate Div, 1988; Columbia Coll, Graduate Div, 1990. **Career:** Various Firms, Law clerk/paralegal, various firms, 1982-86; US OPM, personnel management specialist, 1986-90; JEG, Inc, pres/chief financial officer, 1989-; US DOL/OSHA, management analyst, 1990-97, regional training officer, 1997-. **Orgs:** United Negro College Fund, Fund Raising Bd member; Operation Push, past member, volunteer; InterNat Film & Video Festival, panel member; Midwest Radio & Music asn; Rat Pack InterNat, asst to chair, exec Bd mem; Am Society Public Administrators; Chicago Metro Staffing Coun; InterNat Personnel Management asn. **Honors/Awds:** USDOL, Special Act Award, 1999, 2000; Special Act/Group Award, 1999, Performance Award, 1999; USOPM, Impact Award, 1990. **Special Achievements:** Stageplay optioned, "Pearl's Place", 2000; screenplay optioned, "chiba", 1998-99; stageplay produced, "About Men.", 1991, 1992, 2000; exec prod, R&B album, "Soul Child", 1999; CBS teleplay, "Great American Family", 1994. **Business Addr:** Regional Training Officer, US Dept Labor & OSHA, 230 So Dearborn Suite 3244, Chicago, IL 60604, **Business Phone:** (312)353-6628.

JACKSON, KEVIN L
Executive. **Personal:** Born Mar 23, 1956, Washington, DC; son of Thomas and Dorothy; married Michelle, Jun 19, 1993; children: Bruce & Kevin Nolan. **Educ:** Lehigh Univ, BS, 1978; Univ Minnesota, mgt principles; Defense Syst Mgt Col, defense contractor finance. **Career:** NCR Corp, acct mgr, 1978-82; Honeywell Fed Syst, acct mgr, 1982-87; Honeywell Inc, mkt develop mgr, 1987-90; Alliant Techsystems, mgr, AF Prog, 1990-98, dir bus develop, 1998-; Sports Enhancements Inc, bd mem, 1997-; Alliant Techsystems, Inc, dir bus develop. **Orgs:** Vpres, AFA-DW Steele Chap, 1995-. **Honors/Awds:** NCR Century Point Club, 1979, 1980, 1981; Pacesetter Award for Sales Excellence, 1983, 1985, 1986; Honeywell Top Performer Award, 1989; Alliant Great Performer Award, 1994. **Business Addr:** Director of Business Development, Alliant Techsystems, 5050 Lincoln Dr, Edina, MN 55436-1097, **Business Phone:** (703)412-5997.

JACKSON, LA TOYA YVONNE
Entertainer, actor. **Personal:** Born May 29, 1956, Gary, IN; daughter of Joseph and Katherine; married Jack Gordon, 1989. **Career:** Singer, dancer, television star, exec currently; Albums: You're Gonna Get Rocked, 1988; Imagination, 1986; TV series: "We Are the World", 1985; "Late Night with David Letterman", 1989; "Hola Raffaella!", 1993; "Howard Stern", 1994-95; "So Graham Norton", 1999; "Larry King Live", 2003; "V Graham Norton", 2003; "Show de Cristina, El", 2004; "Michael Jackson's Boys", 2005; "Airport", 2005; "Armed & Famous", 2007; Ja-Tail Enterprises LLC & Ja-Tail Records, owner, currently; Studio Albums: La Toya Jackson, 1980; My Special Love, 1981; Heart

Don't Lie, 1984; Imagination, 1986; La Toya, 1988; Bad Girl, 1989; No Relations, 1991; Formidable, 1992; From Nashville to You, 1994; Stop in the Name of Love, 1995; Lady Blues, 2008, Startin' Over, 2009. **Honors/Awds:** Outstanding Song Awards, 1985. **Special Achievements:** Worked with Nancy Reagan's Just-Say-No Anti Drug campaign, 1987; Geraldo, guest appearance; posed for Playboy mag, 1989; Bob Hope's Easter Vacation in the Bahamas, tv special, participant, 1989; La Toya: Growing Up in the Jackson Family, autobiography, co-author with Patricia Romanowski, Dutton, 1991; She received a Grammy nomination for Best Reggae Recording; One of five Outstanding Song Awards at the 1985 World Popular Song Festival in Japan, for her single "Baby Sister"; She was one of the recipients of a Grammy Award for Record of the Year as a vocalist for "We Are the World"; She is the spokeswoman for "Star Ice". **Business Addr:** Singer, Owner, Ja Tail Records, Ja Tail Enterprises LLC, 8306 Wilshire Blvd Suite 528, PO BOX 7158, Beverly Hills, CA 90211, **Business Phone:** (323)934-9268.

JACKSON, LARRON DEONNE
Accountant, football player. **Personal:** Born Aug 26, 1949, St Louis, MO; divorced; children: Laresa, Temple & Larron Jr. **Educ:** Missouri Univ, BS, 1971. **Career:** Football player (retired), executive; Denver Broncos, 1971-74; Atlanta Falcons, 1975-76; Monsanto Chemicals, mgt trainee, 1970; Touch-Ross, jr & sr staff acct, 1972-74; Jackson & Montgomery Tax & Acct Serv, 1975; Jackson & Assocs Fin Serv, acct, 1975. **Honors/Awds:** Outstanding Col Athlete Am, 1971; NFL All-Pro Rookie team, 1971; hon bd mem, Mathew-Dickeys Boys Club, 1971.

JACKSON, LARRY EUGENE
Engineer. **Personal:** Born Feb 18, 1943, Chicago, IL; married Roberta O Staples; children: Crystal, Robyn & Larry Jr. **Educ:** Purdue Univ, BSME, 1967. **Career:** Inland Steel Co, sr engr, 1967-75; Kaiser Eng Inc, proj eng, 1977. **Orgs:** Am Inst Stl Engr Mem, Lake Area United Way Budget Comn; Racing Chmn, INSki Coun; pres bd dir, Gary & Bldg; Alpha Phi Alpha; Front Int Gary Chap Art Pub AISE, 1970. **Business Addr:** 35 E Wacker Dr, Chicago, IL 60601.

JACKSON, LEE ARTHUR
Government official. **Personal:** Born Apr 14, 1950, Lynch, KY; son of Sylmon James and Marie Stokes; married Carolyn Bates, Jun 3, 1978; children: Michelle Tarese. **Educ:** Univ Ky, BA, 1973; Ky State Univ, CPM, 1990. **Career:** Dept Employment Serv, field off mgr. **Orgs:** Dist dir, Alpha Phi Alpha, 1972; St Luke Lodge #123, 1972; pres, Ky Asn State Employees, 1990-; vchmn, Am Fed Teachers; Fed Pub Employees, 1992; chmn, Community Action Coun Brothers Policy Bd; Ky Am Water Co Consumer Adv Coun; pres, AFT-Ky; vpres, Ky State AFL-CIO; bd mem, Lexington Pub Libr, KY. **Special Achievements:** First African American to head the Kentucky Association of State Employees. **Home Addr:** 2804 Mt McKinley Way, Lexington, KY 40517-3814. **Business Addr:** President, Kentucky Association of State Employees, PO Box 4110, Frankfort, KY 40604-4110, **Business Phone:** (502)875-2273.

JACKSON, LENWOOD A
Judge. **Personal:** Born Jan 11, 1944, Concord, GA. **Educ:** Miami Univ, Oxford, OH, stud, 1965; Harvard Univ law sch, Cambridge, MA, Hons, Summer Sch, 1965; Morris Brown Col, Atlanta, Ga, BA, cum laude, 1966; Emory Univ, Sch Law, JD, 1969. **Career:** CIEO fel, 1965; City Atlanta, Planning Dept, intern, 1967; OEO Reg Coun, law clerk, 1968; Johnson & Jordan, law clerk, 1968-69; Emory Neighborhood Law Office, legal asst, 1969; Nat Labor Rels Bd LA, atty; Ga Gen Assembly, intern, 1969; Patterson, Parks & Franklin, atty; Latimer Haddon & Stanfield, assoc atty, 1971-72; City Ct Atlanta, Munic Ct Atlanta, judge, 1992-. **Orgs:** Am Bar Asn; Nat Bar Asn; Ga Bar Asn; Atlanta Bar Asn; Gate City Bar Asn; Nat Org Legal Probs Educ; Phi Delta Phi Legal Fraternity; Alpha Phi Alpha Fraternity; exec comt, Nat Coun Sch Attys; Butler St, YMCA. **Military Serv:** USY, sgt, 1969-. **Home Addr:** 104 Trinity Ave SW, Atlanta, GA 30312, **Home Phone:** (404)658-6919. **Business Addr:** Judge, City of Atlanta, Municipal Court of Atlanta, 150 Garnett St SW, Atlanta, GA 30303, **Business Phone:** (404)658-6940.

JACKSON, LEO EDWIN. See Obituaries section.

JACKSON, LESLIE ELAINE. See SOUTH, LESLIE ELAINE.

JACKSON, LILLIAN
Association executive. **Personal:** Born in Montgomery, AL. **Educ:** Troy State Univ, AA; Ala State Univ, BA, MA. **Career:** Nat Asn Advan Colored People, Metro Montgomery Br, dir; Ala State Nat Asn Advan Colored People, pres.

JACKSON, LISA P.
Government Official. **Personal:** Born Feb 8, 1962, Philadelphia, PA; married Kenny Jackson; children: Marcus, Brian. **Educ:** Bachelor degree, summa cum laude, Tulane Univ School of Engineering, 1983; master's in engineering from Princeton Univ, 1986. **Career:** Assistant Commissioner for Land Use Management; Assistant Commissioner for Compliance and Enforcement, worked 16 years as an employee of the US EPA; Dept of Environmental Protection (DEP), 2002; Commissioner of the state's DEP, appointed by Governor Jon S. Corzine, 2006; Chief of Staff to Governor Jon S. Corzine, 2008-09; Administrator of the EPA, 2009-. **Special Achievements:** First Af Am to serve as the Administrator of the EPA, 2009-. **Business Addr:** U.S. Environmental Protection Agency, Ariel Rios Bldg, 1200 Pennsylvania Ave., N.W., Washington, DC 20460, **Business Phone:** (202)272-0167.*

JACKSON, DR. LUKE
Dentist. **Personal:** Born Sep 17, 1919, Recovery, GA; married Shirley Ann Lead; children: Charles L, Wayne D, Shirlee Barnetta, Shirlene Elizabeth & Luke Jr. **Educ:** Ga St Col, BS 1942; Atlanta Univ, attended 1946; Meharry Med Col, DDS, 1951. **Career:** Meharry Med Col, instr prosthetic dent, 1951-53; Pvt Pract, dentist, 1953-. **Orgs:** Bd organiser Peoples Bank Chattanooga, 1974-; Nat Bd Dent Examr; Pan-Tenn Dent Asn; George W Hubbard Dent Soc; Bus Div Chattanooga Coun Comt Action, 1963-68; bi-racial Mayor's Comt, 1963; bldg coun; bd mgt, Henry Br YMCA, 1965-70. **Military Serv:** USNR WW II. **Business Addr:** Dentist, 5124 Lantana Lane, Chattanooga, TN 37416.*

JACKSON, LURLINE BRADLEY
Executive. **Personal:** Born in Dallas, TX; daughter of Henry Bradley (deceased) and Alice Young (deceased). **Educ:** N Tex State Univ, 1956; El Centro Jr Col, 1974; Richland Col, 1978; Respiratory Ther Sch, 1980; Tarrant Co Jr Col, nursing home admin, 1983. **Career:** Presbyterian Hosp, Dallas, respiratory ther; Caring Med Supply Co, founder, owner, pres, ceo, currently. **Orgs:** Nat vpres, Lincoln Alumni Asn, Dallas, 1990-92; Dallas Chap, Nat Asn Advan Colored People; vpres, NCW; Nat Caucus & Ctr Black Aged; speaker, Altzheimer, Dallas Chap. **Honors/Awds:** Iota Phi Lambda, Psi Chap, 1968; Welcome House Inc, Nat Coun Negro Women Inc, Oak Cliff Sect, 1983; Dallas Metro Club, Nat Asn Negro Bus & Prof Women, 1989; Wash-Lincoln Alumni Asn Dallas, 1989; FDR Award, She-Roes & He-Roes, 1990. **Special Achievements:** Lurline Bradley Jackson is the first black students to attend North Texas State College, 1956.

JACKSON, PROF. LUTHER PORTER, JR. See Obituaries section.

JACKSON, MANNIE L
Executive. **Personal:** Born May 4, 1939, Illmo, MO; married Cathy; children: Cassie & Candace. **Educ:** Univ Ill attended 1960; Univ Detroit, mkt & econ. **Career:** Gen Motors, 1968; Honeywell Inc, various positions, 1968, Commun Serv Div, vpres & gen mgr, 1981-87, Corp Mkt, vpres; Harlem Globetrotters Int Inc, owner, chmn & chief exec officer, bd dirs, currently; Boxcar Financial Holdings, chmn, currently. **Orgs:** Founding mem, Exec Leadership Coun, pres; Am Red Cross Bd Gov, 2000-. **Honors/Awds:** Naismith Memorial Basketball Hall of Fame, 2006; Basketballs Human Spirit Award. **Special Achievements:** One of Americas "40 Most Powerful Black Executives", Black Enterprise Mag, 1988, 1993; first African American owner of a major international sports organistration. **Business Addr:** Board of Directors, Harlem Globetrotters International Inc, 400 E Van Buren St Suite 300, Phoenix, AZ 85004, **Business Phone:** (602)258-0000.

JACKSON, MARCUS
Executive, president (organization), chief executive officer. **Career:** Provo Arabia Ltd, Saudi Arabia, proj engr, 1980-83; Kan City Power & Light Co, engr, 1974-80, asst dir power supply, sr dir power supply, vpres power prod, sr vpres power supply, exec vpres, coo, 1996-99, exec vpres, cfo, 1999-2000; SEMCO Energy Corp, chmn, pres & ceo, 2001-03.

JACKSON, MARIE O
Judge. **Personal:** Born Aug 14, 1947, Pittsburgh, PA; daughter of Warren Joseph Oliver and Nettie Marie Wall; children: Toney, Vincent, Alphonso & Ana. **Educ:** Mt Holyoke Col, BA, 1969; Harvard Law Sch, JD, 1972. **Career:** Cambridge & Somerville Legal Servs, gen trial work, 1972-74; Tufts Univ, vis lectr, 1973-74; MA Comn Against Discrimination, staff dir, 1974-76; Div Hearing Officers, admin justice, 1976-77, Exec Off Admin & Finance, gen coun, 1977-80; Dist Ct, Dept Trial Ct Cambridge Div, justice, 1980-97; Dist Woburn, presiding justice, 1997-98; Cambridge Dist Ct, judge, 1998-. **Orgs:** Bd & Regional Dir, Nat Asn Women Judges, 1981-84; Nat Coun Juvenile & Family Ct Judges, 1981-89; Greater Boston Youth Symphony Orchestra 1985-87; Nat Conf Christians & Jews, 1985-87; Alpha Kappa Alpha Sor Psi Omega Chap; Middlesex Co Dist Atty's Child Sexual Abuse Task Force, 1985-86; Gov's Task Force Correction Alternatives, 1985-86, Foster Care, 1986-87; bd Judge, Baker Guid Ctr, 1987-94; Dist Ct Standards Comn for Care & Protection & CHINS cases, 1990; bd dirs, Adolescent Consult Servs, 1996; PRS, MAS Black Judges Conf, 1998-; Racial & Ethnic Access & Fairness Adv Bd, 2000-; Comn Pub Trust & Confidence, 2001-03; Boston Inn Court, 2002-. **Honors/Awds:** Outstanding Young Leader Boston Jaycees, 1981; Leadership Massachusetts Black Lawyers, 1981; Sojourner Truth Award, Nat Asn Negro Bus & Prof Women, 1986; Community Justice Award, MA Justice Resource Inst, 1985; Achievement Award, Cambridge YWCA, 1985; Leadership Achievement & Service Awards; Sesquicentennial Alumnae Award, Mt Holyoke Alumnae Asn, 1988. **Special Achievements:** First Justice of the Woburn District Court. **Business Addr:** Justice, Cambridge District Court, 40 Thorndike St, Cambridge, MA 02141, **Business Phone:** (617)494-4350.

JACKSON, MARK A.
Basketball player, executive. **Personal:** Born Apr 1, 1965, Brooklyn, NY; married Desiree Coleman, Jul 29, 1990; children: Mark II, Christian, Micah & Heavyn. **Educ:** St John's Univ, St Vincents Col, Jamaica, NY, commun arts, 1987. **Career:** Basket Player (retired), Analyst; NY Knicks, guard, 1987-92, Los Angeles Clippers, 1992-94; Ind Pacers, 1994-96, 1997-2000; Denver Nuggets, 1996-97; Toronto Raptors, 2000-01; Utah Jazz, 2002-03; Ordained Minister, 1996; Players Wear Int, co-owner, currently; Houston Rockets, 2003-04; Yankees Entertainment & Sports network, NJ Nets, analyst, currently; ABC, analyst, currently; mem, ABC studio show. **Orgs:** United Negro Col Fund; mem, Wheelchair Charities. **Honors/Awds:** Rookie of the Year, NBA, 1988; NBA All-Star, 1989. **Business Phone:** (646)487-3600.

JACKSON, MARY
Financial manager. **Personal:** Born Jan 7, 1932, Lumpkin, GA; daughter of Adie Beauford Jr and Ida B Robinson; married Arthur L, Jul 2, 1965; children: Richard L George III & Cynthia A George. **Educ:** Albany St Col, Albany GA, BEd, 1953; Anchorage Ak Community Col, ABus, 1980, BS, 1997; Columbia State Univ, BS, 1997. **Career:** Sheraton Hotel, Wash DC, payroll supvr, 1963-66; Westover AFB MA, procurement clerk, 1966-68; Edwards AFB CA, procurement clerk, 1968-71; Elmendorf ABF AK, purchasing agent, 1971-75; Automotive Parts, Anchorage AK, purchasing agent, 1975-78; Alaska Village Electric, Anchorage AK, purchasing mgr, 1978-95; EMJ Travel, 1995. **Orgs:** Delta Sigma Theta Sorority, 1952; educ adv, Anchorage Community Col, 1977-79; comt mem, Kimo News Adv Coun Prog, 1978-80; Alpha Delta Zeta, Phi Theta Kappa Honor Soc, 1978; St Grand Loyal Lady Ruler, Order Golden Circle, 1982-89; past st pres, Alaska St Fedn BPW/USA, 1983-84; past illustrious commandress, Daughter Isis, 1980-81; past dir, Int Affairs Purchasing Mgt, 1983-84; past sec, Soroptimist Int, 1984; past chmn, Job Serv Exec Comt, 1985; past chmn, Anchorage Community Block Grant Develop(HUD), 1986-95; grand worthy matron, Prince Hall GC Order Eastern Star, 1987-90; strategic long range comt, Links, Ak Chapter, 1992; Imperial Court Daughters Isis, chmn Imperial Directress the Year, 2003-04; Nat Coun Negro Women; local 100 Black Women. **Honors/Awds:** Outstanding Service Award, purchasing mgt, 1983-84; Woman of the Year, Nat Bus Women, 1984; Outstanding Achievement Leadership, Prince Hall Masons F&AM, 1988; Community Service Award, Alaska Black Caucus, 1988; Imperial Deputy of the Desert, Isiserettes, 1988-; Community Service Award, Zeta Phi Beta Sorority, 1989; Outstanding Service Award Public Relations, Imperial Ct, Daughters Isis, 1990; Employee of the Quarter, Alaska Village Electric, 1992; Outstanding Accomplishment, North Future Bus & Prof Women's Club, 1992; Outstanding Letters Recognition, Gov Alaska, Outstanding Commission Service, 1995. **Home Addr:** 8539 Crosspointe Ct, Antelope, CA 95843.

JACKSON, MATTIE J
Labor activist, vice president (organization). **Personal:** Born Oct 3, 1921, Livingston, TX; widowed; children: Gail Lavarra. **Educ:** Johnson Bus Col, Healds Bus Col; San Francisco State Univ, Cert Completion Awd. **Career:** Labor activist, Vice president (retired); Koret Calif, garment worker, shop steward, 1947-67; ILGWU, bus agent, 1967-70, int vpres, head. **Orgs:** Commnr SF Bd Appeals, 1967-; Nat Asn Advan Colored People Adv Bd, SF Comm Col, Social Concerns Commn Jones UM Church; exec bd, SF Labor Coun; exec bd, Nat Negro Coun Women. **Honors/Awds:** 'Salute to Women of Labor Award', Senate Indust, 1983; Certificate of Appreciation, USO, 1984; Apri Salute to Labor, A Philip Randolph Inst, 1987. **Home Addr:** 524 Belvedere St, San Francisco, CA 94117.

JACKSON, MEL (MELTON JACKSON)
Actor. **Personal:** Born Oct 13, 1970, Chicago, IL. **Career:** Films: Scenes for the Soul, 1995; Soul Food, 1997; Carmin's Choice, 1997;Dancing in September, 2000; An Invited Guest, 2000; Dirty Hearts, 2000;Automatic, 2001; Deliver Us From Eva, 2003; Detective Morgan, Motives,2004; Movie: To Sir, with Love II, 1996; Little Richard, 2000; Playingwith Fire, 2000; Dancing in September, 2000; Tv series: "Midnight Ma",1995; "In the House", 1997-98;"Living Single", 1997-98; "DAG", 2000; "TheDivision", 2004; Tv movies: "To Sir With Love 2", 1996; "George Wallace",1997; "Temptations", 1998; "Little Richard", 2000; "Playing With Fire",2000; "Automatic", 2001; "Deliver Us from Eva", 2003; "The Making of Motives", 2004; "Flip the Script", 2005; "The Black Man's Guide to Understanding Black Women", 2006; "Abduction of Jesse Bookman", producer, 2009; Am Majic Entertainment, owner,currently; Stone Manners Agency, owner,

currently. **Honors/Awds:** Best Performance by an Actor, 2008. **Business Phone:** (323)655-1313.

JACKSON, MELTON. See JACKSON, MEL.

JACKSON, MICHAEL JOSEPH. See Obituaries section.

JACKSON, MICHAEL RAY (MIKE JACKSON)
Baseball player. **Personal:** Born Dec 22, 1964, Houston, TX. **Career:** Baseball Player (Retired); Philadelphia Phillies, pitcher, 1986-87; Seattle Mariners, 1988-91, 1996;San Francisco Giants, 1992-94; Cincinnati Reds, 1995; Cleveland Indians, 1997-99; Houston Astros, 2001; Minnesota Twins, 2002; Chicago White Sox, pitcher, 2004. **Honors/Awds:** Led NL in games pitched, 1993. *

JACKSON, MICHAEL W
Judge, district attorney. **Personal:** Born Nov 18, 1963, Fayetteville, TN. **Educ:** Centre Col; Fla State Col Law, law deg. **Career:** Ala 4th Judicial Circuit, asst dist atty, dist atty, currently; Selma Muni Ct, munic judge; pvt pract, atty, currently. **Orgs:** State Dem Exec Comt. **Special Achievements:** The only African-American currently serving as District Attorney in Alabama. **Business Addr:** District Attorney, 4th Judicial Circuit, 105 Lauderdale St, PO Box 987, Selma, AL 36702-0000, **Business Phone:** (334)874-2540.

JACKSON, MIKE. See JACKSON, MICHAEL RAY.

JACKSON, MILES M.
School administrator, educator. **Personal:** Born Apr 28, 1929, Richmond, VA; son of Miles M Sr and Thelma; married Bernice R, Jan 10, 1955; children: Milles III, Marsha Bethards, Muriel & Melia Phifer. **Educ:** Va Union Univ, BA, 1955; Drexel Univ, Col Info Sci, MS, 1956; Syracuse Univ, Newhouse Sch Commun, PhD, 1973. **Career:** Free Libr, Philadelphia, ref res librn, 1956-58; Hampton Univ, head librn, 1958-62; Am Samoa, territorial librn, 1962-64; Atlanta Univ, Trevor Arnett Libr, dir, 1964-67; proff, Tehran univ, 1968-69; State Univ NY, assoc prof, 1969-75; Univ Hawaii, dean & prof, 1975-95, prof & dean emer, 1995-. **Orgs:** Am Libr Asn, 1958-; Asn Libr & Info Sci Edu, 1969, pres, 1969-70; bd mem, Hawaii Libr, 1984-92, pres, 1984-86; bd mem, Cent YMCA, 1986; Winward Y's Men, 1996-; Hawaii State Libr Adv Coun, 1996-98; Hawaii Coun Humanities, 2000. **Honors/Awds:** Sr Fulbright Award, Lectr Tehran, Iran, 1968-69; Harold Han cour Travel Award, S Pac, 1978. **Special Achievements:** Editor: Pacific Island Studies, 1986; Int Handbook of Contemp Develop in Librarianship, 1981, Auth: Comparative & Int Librarianship, 1970; Linkages Over Space & Time, 1991; And They Came, 2001. **Business Addr:** Professor, Dean Emeritus, University of Hawaii, Library & Information Science Program, 303A POST Bldg 1680 E West Rd, Honolulu, HI 96822, **Business Phone:** (808)956-7321.

JACKSON, MILLIE (MILDRED JACKSON)
Singer, actor. **Personal:** Born Jul 15, 1944, Thompson, GA; married; children: Keisha & Jerroll. **Career:** Albums: Millie Jackson, 1972; Hurts So Good, 1973; I Got To Try It Once,1974; Caught Up, 1974; Still Caught Up, 1975; Free & In Love, 1976; Feelin' Bitchy, 1977; Lovingly Yours, 1977; Get It Out'cha System, 1978; A Moment's Pleasure, 1979; Royal Rappin's, 1979; Live & Uncensored, 1979; For Men Only, 1980; I Had To Say It, 1980; Live, 1980; Just a Li'l BitCountry, 1981; Hard Times, 1982; Millie Jackson "Live & Outrageous", 1982;E.S.P. (Extra Sexual Persuasion), 1983; Imitation of Love, 1986; The Tidels Turning, 1988; Back To The Shit, 1989; Young Man, Older Woman, 1991;Young Man, Older Woman: Cast Album, 1993; Rock N' Soul, 1994; It's Over,1995; The Sequel, It Ain't Over, 1997; Not for Church Folk!, 2001; Singles: "Will You Love Me Tom", 1989, "Young Man Older Woman", 1991,"Check in the Mail, 1994"; "An Imitation of Love"; "Something You Can Feel"; "Living With A Stranger"; "Taking My Life Back"; "Love Quake";"Chocolate Brown Eyes"; "Breaking Up Somebody's Home"; "The Lies That We Live"; "Did You Think I Wouldn't Cry"; "Butt-A-Cize"; "Leave Me Alone";Compilations: Pimps, Players & Private Eyes, 1992, Wild Women Do Get the Blues, 1996; Films: Cleopatra Jones; Wigstock; Spring Records, recording artist; Jive/Zomba Records, recording artist; soul singer, currently; KKDA, radio show host, Dallas, TX; Weird Wreckuds, owner, currently;a ctress, currently. **Orgs:** Whodini; Facts Life. **Honors/Awds:** Best Female R&B Vocalist, Cash Box Magazine. **Business Addr:** Owner, Weird Wreckuds, PO Box 491000, College Park, GA 30349.

JACKSON, NORMAN A.
Association executive, basketball coach. **Personal:** Born Nov 16, 1932, New York, NY; married Nellie; children: Deborah, Norma, Leona. **Educ:** Tuskegee Univ, attended 1955. **Career:** Association executive (retired); Minority Affairs Fla State Univ, dir, 1970-72; Col Entrance Exam Bd So Regional Office Atlanta, asst dir, 1972-74; Fla Comn Human Relations Comn, exec dir; Student Comt Serv St Petersburg Jr Col, dir, 1965-70; Gibbs Jr Col, FL, athletic dir & dept chmn; St Petersburg, FL, chmn dept physical educ & athletic dir, 1959-65; Univ AR, instr; Res Devel FL Jr Col, asst dir. **Orgs:** Pres So Asn Black Admin, 1973-74; cons, lecturer & writer, Fla Equal Access; Nat Coun Measurement Edn; Phi Delta Kappa; Nat Asn Fin Asst Minority Students; Nat Alliance Black Sch Educator; AACJC; Am Pers & Guidance Asn; Fla Asn Comt Col; Fla Asn Fin Aid Admins; So Asn Financial Aid Admins; Fa Educ Res Asn; Nat Vocational Guidance Asn. **Honors/Awds:** Basketball Coach Yr, 1964; fel, Kellogg, NDEA, Seeing Eye Corp; grants, UOES, So Educ Found. **Military Serv:** AUS 1 lt.

JACKSON, OLIVER L
Educator, artist. **Personal:** Born Jun 23, 1935, St Louis, MO; son of Oliver Lee and Mae Nell. **Educ:** Ill Wesleyan Univ Bloomington, IL, BFA, 1954-58; Univ Iowa, Iowa City, IA, MFA, 1961-63. **Career:** Educator (retired), Artist; St Louis Comm Coll, St Louis, MO, art instr, 1964-67; Washington Univ, St Louis, MO, art instr, 1967-69; Southern IL Univ, E St Louis IL, instr, 1967-69; Oberlin Coll, Oberlin OH, Afro American Studies, assoc prof, 1969-70; California State Univ, Sacramento, prof of art, 1971-2003; Univ of Hawaii, Hilo, Vis Artist, 2001; Univ of Hawaii, Hilo, Vis Artist, 2005. **Honors/Awds:** Natl Endowment for the Arts, Awd in Painting, 1980; Nettie Marie Jones Fellowship in the Visual Arts, 1984; Art Matters, Inc, New York, NY, Artist Grant, 1988; Fleishhacker Foundation, Eureka Fellowship in Painting, 1993; Flintridge Found Awards in the Visual Arts, Award in Painting & Sculpture, 2004.

JACKSON, OSCAR JEROME
Physician. **Personal:** Born Dec 17, 1929, Fairfield, AL; son of William and Lillian; divorced. **Educ:** Howard Univ, BS; Howard Univ, MD. **Career:** Gen Surgical, internship & residency; pvt pract, physician, 1963-; John Hale Med Soc, pres, currently. **Orgs:** Am Bd Surg, 1963; fel, Am Col Surg, 1967; clin instr surg, Univ Calif; attending surgeon, Mt Zion Hosp; dir, John Hale Med Plan; chmn, United Health Alliance; pres, Bus & Prof Asn; pres, John Hale med soc; Omega Phi Psi Fraternity. **Honors/Awds:** Professor Of Chemistry Prize, Howard Univ. **Military Serv:** Busaf, capt, 1956-59. **Business Addr:** President, John Hale Medical Society, 1342 Haight St, San Francisco, CA 94117, **Business Phone:** (415)552-0916.*

JACKSON, OSHEA. See ICE CUBE.

JACKSON, PAMELA J.
Government official. **Personal:** Born Jun 9, 1967, Louisville, KY; daughter of Philip M and Donna W. **Educ:** Univ Pa, BA, econ, 1988; Wayne State Univ, MA, econ, 1993. **Career:** Univ Pa Tutoring Ctr, counr, adv, 1985-88; Pryor, Govan, & Counts, investment banking assoc, 1986-87; In Black, Bus Bus Pubation, sales mgr, 1987-88; City Detroit, asst Mayor, 1988-. **Orgs:** 1990 Census Complete Count Comt, pub rels sub-com crd, fundraising subcom crd, 1990-91; Amandla Mandela Detroit Comt, logistics-opers crd, 1990; Wayne State Univ-City Detroit Consortium, steering comn, co-chair, 1991-; Colman A Young Found, Scholar com crd, recipient liaison, 1992-. **Honors/Awds:** elected Precinct Delegate, Detroit, 1992. **Special Achievements:** Two Showings: abstract artistic paintings, 1990-91; photographic work urban Am Honored as emotionally moving & techly well done. **Business Addr:** Assistant to the Mayor, City of Detroit, Mayor's Office, 1126 City County Bldg, Detroit, MI 48226, **Business Phone:** (313)224-3164.

JACKSON, PAZEL, JR.
Banker, executive. **Personal:** Born Feb 21, 1932, Brooklyn, NY; son of Pazel and Adalite; children: Karen, Pazel, Peter, Allyson. **Educ:** City Col NY, BCE, 1954, MCE, 1959; Columbia Univ, MBA, 1972. **Career:** NYC, civil engr, 1956-62; Worlds Fair Corp NYC, chief design, 1962-66; NY City Dept Pub Works, dep gen mgr, 1966-67; New York Dept Bldgs, asst comn, 1967-69; Bowery Savings Bank, NY, sr vpres, 1969-86; Chem Bank NY, Residential Mortgage Div, sr credit officer, 1986-95; JPMorgan Chase, sr vpres, 1995-00; Carver Bancorp Inc, dir, 1997-. **Orgs:** Dir, Nat Housing Partnership Corp; NY State Urban Develop Corp; New York Housing Develop Corp, Battery Park City Authority, Bedford Stuyvesant Restoration Corp; bd dir Community Serv Soc, Citizens Housing & Planning Coun; NY Prof Engrs Soc, Am Soc Civil Engrs; NY Bldg Cong, City Col Alumni Asn; Lambda Alpha; Columbia Univ Alumni. **Honors/Awds:** Man of the Year, Brooklyn Civic Asn, 1967; Special Award, Paragon Fed Credit Union, 1968. **Military Serv:** AUS, lt, 1954-56. **Home Addr:** 135 Rutland Rd, Brooklyn, NY 11225. **Business Addr:** Director, Carver Bancorp Inc, 75 W 125th St, New York, NY 10027.*

JACKSON, PRINCE ALBERT
Educator. **Personal:** Born Mar 17, 1925, Savannah, GA; married Marilyn Stuggles; children: Prince Albert, III, Rodney Mark, Julia Lucia, Anthony Brian & Philip Andrews. **Educ:** Savannah State Col, BS, 1949; New York Univ, MS, 1950; Univ Kans, PostGrad, 1962; Boston Col, PhD, philos, 1966. **Career:** William James High Sch Statesboro, teacher, sci & math, 1950-55; Savannah St Col, fac, 1955; Savannah St Col, assoc prof, math & physics, 1966-71; Savannah St Col, Savannah, GA, pres, 1971-78. **Orgs:** Athl dir, St Pius X HS Savannah, 1955-64; mgr, YMCA, Savannah, 1962; teaching fel vis instr, Boston Col, 1964-66; vice chmn, St PiX Educ Coun, 1967; life mem, NAACP, 1968; adv, Comn Devel Corp, 1969; vpres, Bd Pub Educ Savannah & Chatham Co, 1971; Educ Comn US Cath Conf, 1971; Southern Regional Educ Bd, 1971-74; Chatham-Savannah Charter Study Comn; Bd dir, United Way; TACTICS Nat Policy Bd; St Jude Guild; adv bd, March Dimes; adv comn, Nat Assessment Educ Progress; Am Asn St Cols & Univ; Nat Asn Equal Educ Oppurtunity; Nat Sci Found Panel; Exec Comn; Am Asn Univ Prof; NEA; Ga Teachers Educ Asn; Nat Sci Teachers Asn; Nat Coun Teachers Math; Am Educ Res Asn; Nat Coun Measurement Educ; Nat Inst Sci Bd; bd dirs, Ga Heart Asn; Goodwill Inds; ARC; BSA, trustee, Ga Econ Coun. **Honors/Awds:** Outstanding leadership service award, Savannah State Col, Nat Alumni Asn, 1967. **Special Achievements:** Man of Year, Alpha Phi Alpha, 1960 & 67; Southern Region Man of Year, the Frogs Inc, 1967. **Military Serv:** USNR, 1942-46.

JACKSON, RANDELL
Basketball player. **Personal:** Born Jan 16, 1976. **Educ:** Fla State Univ, attended 1998. **Career:** Ft Wayne Fury, 1998; Dallas Mavericks, 1999; Washington Wizards, forward,1999; Gallitos de Isabela, 2002; Bnei Hasharonm, 2002-03; Villa Duarte deCalero, 2003; Maccabi Givat Shmuel Israel Premier League, 2004-05; Xinjiang Gyang Hui Flying Tigers, China, 2005-06; Union Atletica, Uruguay Primera League, 2006-07; Central Entrerriano Guale guaychu, Argentina, 2007; Panteras de Aguascalientes, Mexico, 2007; Tokyo Apache, Japan, 2007-.

JACKSON, RANDOLPH
Judge. **Personal:** Born Oct 10, 1943, Brooklyn, NY; son of James Titler and Rathenia McCollum; children: 2. **Educ:** NY Univ, BA, 1965; Brooklyn Law Sch, JD, 1969. **Career:** New York State Guard, lt col; Mudge Rose Guthrie & Alexander, assoc atty, 1969-70; Pvt Pract Law, 1971-81; New York City Family Ct, hearing examr, 1981; Civil Ct, Housing Part, judge, 1981-87; Civil Ct, judge, 1987-88; Supreme Ct Brooklyn NY, justice, 1988-. **Orgs:** Life mem, Nat Bar Asn, 1971-; Brooklyn Bar Asn, 1971-; Crown Hgts Lions Club, 1980-; Sigma Pi Phi, 1986-; life mem, NAACP, 1990-. **Special Achievements:** Book, "How to Get a Fair Trial By Jury", 1978; "Black People in the Bible," 2002. **Business Addr:** Justice, Supreme Court, Kings County, 360 Adams St, PO Box 21525, Brooklyn, NY 11201, **Business Phone:** (718)643-2116.

JACKSON, RANDY (RANDALL DARIUS RANDY JACKSON)
Music producer, actor, broadcaster. **Personal:** Born Jun 23, 1956, Baton Rouge, LA; son of Herman and Julia; married Elizabeth (divorced 1990); children: Taylor; married Erika Riker, Dec 29, 1995; children: Zoe & Jordan. **Educ:** Southern Univ, BA, music, 1979. **Career:** Music producer & speaker, currently; played bass & keyboards on over 1000 records; Columbia Rec, vpres; MCA Rec, sr vpres; Univ Calif, Los Angeles, teacher, rec ind classes; TV series: Bubblegum Babylon, 2002; "American Idol: The Search for a Superstar", judge, 2002-08; "E! True Hollywood Story", 2003-04; "Late Night with Conan O'Brien", 2004-08; "General Hospital", 2004; "Jimmy Kimmel Live!", 2004-08; "Dr. Vegas", 2004; "The Tonight Show with Jay Leno", 2004-07; "Tavis Smiley", 2004; Kevin Hill, 2005; Randy Jackson, 2005; What Did ITV Do for Me?, 2005; "The View", 2005-07; "The Late Late Show with Craig Ferguson", 2005-07; "Late Show with David Letterman", 2006-08; "Ellen: The Ellen De Generes Show", 2006-08; "Entertainment Tonight", 2007-08; Stax Records 50th Anniversary Concert, 2008; "Randy Jackson Presents America's Best Dance Crew", exec producer, 2008; Album: Randy Jackson's Music Club, Vol. 1, 2008; Singles:"Dance Like There's No Tomorrow", 2008; "Real Love", 2008. **Business Addr:** Actor, PMK & HBH, 8500 Wilshire Blvd Suite 700, Los Angeles, CA 90211, **Business Phone:** (310)289-6200.*

JACKSON, RAYMOND DEWAYNE
Football player. **Personal:** Born Feb 17, 1973, East Chicago, IN; married Natalie; children: Ami & P Shai. **Educ:** Colorado State Univ. **Career:** Football player (retired); Buffalo Bills, defensive back, 1996-98; Cleveland Browns, defensive back, 1999-2001. **Honors/Awds:** Rookie of the Year, 1996.

JACKSON, DR. RAYMOND T
Educator. **Personal:** Born Dec 11, 1933, Providence, RI; son of Beulah B and Raymond T; married Inez Austin; children: Andrea C & Yewande K. **Educ:** New Eng Conserv Music, BMus, 1955; Juilliard Sch Music, BS, 1957, MS, 1959, DMA 1973; Am Conserv Music Fontainebleau, France, dipl, 1960. **Career:** Univ RI, asst prof music, 1968-75; Mannes Col Music, NY, instr, 1970-77; Concordia Col, Bronxville, NY, asst prof music, 1970-77; Howard Univ, prof piano, 1977-, chmn piano div & appl music studies, 1986-88, chmn Dept Music, 1989-92, coordr stud & fac concerts, 1990-. **Orgs:** Organist & choir dir, Congdon St Baptist Church, 1948-57; concert pianist US, Europe, S Am, 1951; organist & choir dir, Trinity Lutheran Church, Tenafly, NJ, 1957-60; organist & choir dir, Trinity Lutheran Ch Bogota, NJ, 1961-72; lect & recitalist Classical Piano Music composer, African decent Adjudicator Col & Univ Piano Master Classes, 1963; organist second, Church Christ Scientist, NY, 1972-77; organist First Church Christ Scientist Chevy Chase, Md, 1978-; piano rec artist, Performance Rec Black Artist Series, 1982; substitute organist, First Church Christ Scientist, 1993; pres, Raymond Jackson Music Forum; Baldwin Piano Roster Distinguished Performing Artists;

honarary mem, Chopin Club Providence, RI, 1966; founder & dir, Jackson Classical Piano Found Inc, 1999. **Honors/Awds:** George W Chadwick Medal, New Eng Conserv Music, Boston, 1955; prizewinner, Nat Asn Negro Musicians, 1957; New York Town Hall Debut Award, 1959; fel, Eliza & George Howard Found, 1960 & 1963; fel, John Hay Whitney Found, 1965; prizewinner, Int Piano Competition Rio De Janeiro, 1965; prizewinner, Marguerite Long Int Piano Competition, Paris, 1965; prizewinner, Jugg Inc; fel, Ford Found 1971-73; fel, Roothbert Fund, 1971-73; Outstanding Faculty Award, Howard Univ, 1998. **Home Addr:** 1732 Overlook Dr, Silver Spring, MD 20903. **Business Addr:** Professor, Pianist, Howard University, College of Arts and Sciences, 2455 6th St NW, Washington, DC 20059, **Business Phone:** (202)806-7082.

JACKSON, REBBIE (MAUREEN REILETTE BROWN)
Musician, dancer, singer. **Personal:** Born May 29, 1950, Gary, IN; daughter of Joseph and Katherine; married. **Career:** Albums: Centipede, 1984; Reaction, 1986; R U Tuff Enuff, 1988; Rebbie Jackson Collection, 1996; Yours Faithfully, 1998; Fly Away. **Business Phone:** (212)833-8500.*

JACKSON, REGGIE MARTINEZ
Executive, sports manager, baseball player. **Personal:** Born May 18, 1946, Wyncote, PA; son of Martinez and Clara; married Jennie Campos, Jan 1, 1968 (divorced 1972). **Educ:** Ariz State Univ. **Career:** Baseball player (retired), executive; Kansas City Athletics, outfielder, 1967; Oakland Athletics, outfielder, 1968-75; Baltimore Orioles, outfielder, 1976; NY Yankees, outfielder, 1977-81; Calif Angels, outfielder 1982-86; Oakland Athletics, outfielder, 1987, hitting coach, part-time, 1991; ABC Sports, field reporter & color commentator; NY Yankees, spec adv to gen partner, 1993; Viking Components, dir new bus develop. **Orgs:** Former nat chmn, Amyotrophic Lateral Sclerosis; pres, Mr October Found Kids. **Honors/Awds:** Americal League Most Valuable Player, 1973; Hon Big Brother of the Year, Big Bros & Sisters Prog, 1984; Baseball Hall of Fame, 1992. **Special Achievements:** Listed in "The 100 Greatest Baseball Players" by Sporting News, 1999; Cameo appearances in the films including: The Naked Gun: From the Files of Police Squad!; Baseketball; & The Benchwarmers.

JACKSON, DR. REGINALD LEO
Educator. **Personal:** Born Jan 10, 1945, Springfield, MA; son of Katharine Edwards and Leo Jackson. **Educ:** Yale Univ Sch Art & Archit, BFA, MFA, 1970; State Univ New York, Stony Brook, NY, MSW, 1977; Union Inst Cincinnati, OH, PhD, commun, visual anthrop, 1979; Massachusetts Inst Technol, Community Fels Prog, 1981. **Career:** Yale Univ Sch Art & Archit, instr, 1970; Quinnipiac Col, asst prof, filmmaking, 1972; Biomed Comn, asst media prod, dir, 1972-74; Simmons Col, tenured prof photo commun, prof commun, 1974-95, prof emer, 1999-; Olaleye Commun Inc, founder & pres, 1986-; Photog Collective Community Change, coordr, 1995-97; African Univ Col Commun, Accra Ghana, W Africa, assoc dean; Fulbright fel, 2000-01. **Orgs:** Founding mem, Heightened Black Awareness, 1973; consult, New York State HEOP Higher Educ Opportunity Prog, 1975; Poetry Lives Series, McDougal Littel & Co, 1976; African Heritage Inst Simmons Rev Photo & Essay-Ghana Simmons Col, 1976; co-chmn, legis Comn, METCO-MA Coun Educ Opportunity, 1977-; consult, Eng High Sch, 1977-; consult, Charles E Mackey Mid Sch Photo, 1979-; fel, Ford Found, 1980-81; Ford Found Post Doctorate fel, Mass Inst Technol, 1980; Comn Fel, Mass Inst Technol, 1980; Smithsonian Res Fel, Mus Nat Hist, 1981; FATE, 1989; Nat Conf Artists; pres, Community Change Inc, 1992-93; Mass Asn; pres, United Neighbors Lower Roxbury; proj review comt co-chair Parcel 3; Roxbury Strategic Master Plan Oversight Comt; Black Community Info Ctr; Massachusetts Asn Ment Health; WGBH Community Adv Bd. **Honors/Awds:** Res grants, Simmons Col, 1975, 1977 & 1980; Artist Residence, African Am Master Artists-in-Residency Prog, Northeastern Univ Boston, 1978-; Mass Arts & Humanities Grant, 1979; James D Parks Spec Award, Nat Conf Artists, 1979; Crystal Stair Award-twice, African Am Alumni Asn, Simmons Col; Man of the Year, Simmons Col, 2007. **Business Addr:** President, Olaleye Communications Inc, Aba Gallery, 85 Windsor St, Boston, MA 02120, **Business Phone:** (617)445-3303.

JACKSON, RICARDO C
Judge. **Personal:** Born Aug 27, 1935, Philadelphia, PA. **Educ:** Va Union Univ, Richmond, VA, BA, 1962; Howard Univ Sch Law, WA, DC, JD, 1965; Howard Univ Sch Law, WA, DC, Juris Dr, 1969. **Career:** Co Ct Philadelphia Co, Clerk, 1955-56; Pa Dept Pub Asst, caseworker, 1962; Nix & Nix, Philadelphia, PA, 1966-69; Danford Builders Inc, Philadelphia, PA, gen coun, 1966-70; pvt pract, 1969; Nat Dir OEO, spec consult, 1970; Redevelop Authority City Philadelphia, Legal Staff Gen Coun, contract atty, 1970-77; Munic Ct Philadelphia, judge, 1977-81; US Dept Labor, secy rep, 2000-02; Philadelphia Ct, judge, currently. **Orgs:** Co-chmn, mem, vice chmn, Philadelphia Bar Asn; 1969; pres, Barristers' Asn Philadelphia, 1970-74; chmn, Philadelphia Urban Coalition, 1970-71; Nat Bar Asn; Am Bar Asn; Pa Bar Asn; Pa Trial Lawyers Asn; Am Arbitration Asn; Am Judicature Soc; Pa Conf State Trial Judges; Comt 1000, Pa Comn Sentencing, 1992. **Honors/Awds:** Certificate of Appreciation, Disciplinary Bd Supreme Ct Pa, 1976; Community Service Award, Veterans Foreign Wars, 1979; Legion of Honor Membership, Chapel Four Chaplains, 1980; Award for Dedication, Dept Legal & Real Estate Studies, Temple Univ, 1989. **Special Achievements:** Co-Author of Report of the Philadelphia Bar Association's Special Committee on Pennsylvania Bar Admission Procedures - Racial Discrimination In Administration of the Pennsylvania Bar Examination, Temple Law Quarterly, Vol. 44, No. 2, Winter, 1971; Handling Death Penalty Cases, Benchbook (Chapter), March, 1993. **Military Serv:** AUS, ord supply specialist, 1958-61. **Business Addr:** Judge, Philadelphia Courts, First Judical District of Pennsylvania, Rm 143 City Hall 800 Spring Garden St, Philadelphia, PA 19107, **Business Phone:** (215)686-7948.

JACKSON, RICHARD E., JR.
Government official, educator. **Personal:** Born Jul 18, 1945, Peekskill, NY; married Ruth Sokolinsky; children: Tara, Alice, Abigail & William. **Educ:** Univ Bridgeport, BA, math, 1968. **Career:** Peekskill City Sch, math teacher, 1968; dir, Neighborhood Youth Corps Community Action Prog, 1968; United Way Westchester, bd dirs, 1969; Peekskill Field Libr, bd dirs, 1974; Westchester Co Republican Comt, co committeeman, 1975; Peekskill City Republican Comt, vice chmn, 1976; City Peekskill, councilman, 1979-84, mayor, 1984-91, dep mayor, 1993; Peekskill Housing Authority, bd mem, 1982; City Peekskill, dep mayor, 1982-84, mayor, 1985-91; NY Dept Motor Vehicles, comnr, 1995-2000. **Orgs:** Educ Comt, Nat Asn Advan Colored People, 1981-83; Westchester Co Bd Ethics, 1984; chmn, Peekskill Indust Develop Corp, 1985-91; pres, Region I, Am Asn Motor Vehicles Admin, 1997; chmn & adv bd mem, Govt Technol Conf, 1997; NY State Auto-Theft & Ins Fraud Bd, 1997. **Honors/Awds:** National Science Foundation Award. **Special Achievements:** First African American Mayor in New York State. *

JACKSON, RICHARD H.
Executive. **Personal:** Born Oct 17, 1933, Detroit; married Arlena; children: Deirdre, Gordon, Rhonda. **Educ:** Univ MO; Univ Wichita, Walton Sch, Com, 1971. **Career:** Nat Energy Corp, IL, vpres Opers, 1975-; Gits Bros Mfg Co, Chicago, vpres eng; Boeing Corp, mem; Beech Aircraft, engr; NASA, Dept Defense, mem. *

JACKSON, RICKEY ANDERSON
Football player. **Personal:** Born Mar 20, 1958, Pahokee, FL; married Norma; children: Rickeyah. **Educ:** Univ Pittsburgh. **Career:** Football player (retired); New Orleans Saints, linebacker, 1981-93; SanFrancisco 49ers, linebacker, 1994-95. **Honors/Awds:** Defensive Most Valuable Player, E-W Shrine Game; ABC Player of the Game vs Penn St, 1980; New Orleans Saints Hall Fame; All-Century Team, Fla High Sch Asn, 2007.

JACKSON, ROBERT, JR.
Journalist, columnist. **Personal:** Born Jan 15, 1936, Chicago, IL; son of Robert and Lucille; married; children: Dawn, Robert III & Randall. **Educ:** Colo State Col, BA, 1957; Northwestern Univ, Columbia Col, addn study. **Career:** Int News Serv, reporter 1958; Chicago Am Chicago Today, reporter, 1958-69; WBEE Radio Chicago, reporter, 1964; Chicago Bulletin, ed-writer, 1965; Chicago Urban League, writer-producer, 1966; CCUO, dir pub info, 1969-70; Argonne Nat Lab, dir pub info, 1970-73; Provident Hosp & Training Sch, dir publ rel; Reg Alcoholism Info Prog Nat Coun Alcoholism, field dir, 1975-; Rocky Mountain News, news staff writer, currently. **Orgs:** Chicago Newspaper Reporters Asn, 1965; Sigma Delta Chi,1965; United Black Journalist 1968; Coun Advan Sci Writing, 1971; Atomic Industrial Form, 1971; publ rel Soc Am, 1971; bd dir, S Shore YMCA, 1972; Hosp Publ Rel Soc, 1974. **Honors/Awds:** Nomination for Asn Press Award, 1965; Nomination for Pulitzer Prize, 1963, 1988; Community Service Award, Urban League of Metropolitan Denver; The NAACP's Community Service Award; The Malcolm X Award, Black Student Alliance at Metro State Col; Coors, Distinguished Citizen Award; Public Service Award, United Negro Col Fund; Five Points Business Asn, Award; Distinguished Service Award, The Hispanics of Colorado; Outstanding Journalist in Print Award, The Colorado Asn of Blacks in Journ, 1993; Lifetime Achievement Award, 1999; Awards from the American Legion, The Denver District Attorney's Office & several Denver area Schools. **Business Addr:** News Staff Writer, Denver Rocky Mountain News, 400 W Colfax Ave, Denver, CO 80204, **Business Phone:** (303)892-5399.*

JACKSON, ROBERT ANDREW
Advertising executive, vice president (organization), executive director. **Personal:** Born May 16, 1959, Reedville, VA; son of Robert Albert and Lucy; married Felicia Lynn Willis Jackson, Sep 1, 1985; children: Robert Andrew II. **Educ:** Fla A&M Univ, Tallahassee, BS, 1981, MBA, 1983. **Career:** Leo Burnett Advert, Chicago, IL, 1983-85; Bozell Advert, Chicago, IL, 1985; Burrell Commun Group, Chicago, IL, vpres & client serv dir, 1986-. **Orgs:** Alpha Phi Alpha; FAMU Alumni Asn; Targeted Advert Prof; Chicago Advert Fedn, Ctrs New Horizon. **Business Addr:** Vice President, Client Service Director, Burrell Communications Group, 233 N Michigan Ave Suite 2900, Chicago, IL 60601-5704.*

JACKSON, ROBERT E.
Association executive. **Personal:** Born Feb 10, 1937, Reading, PA; married Carol A Norman; children: Robert E jr, Jeannine, Monique & Gregory. **Career:** Food Serv Albright Col, dir, 1971; Schuylkill Valley Restaurant Asn, pres, 1974-76. **Orgs:** Second vpres, PA Asn Blind; pres, Berks Co Asn Blind; bd dirs, Camp Conrad Weiser; NACUFS. **Military Serv:** AUSR, E-5, 1955-62. *

JACKSON, RONALD G
Manager, executive. **Personal:** Born Sep 7, 1952, New Orleans, LA; married Brenda J Bellamy; children: Ronald Jr, Tiffany & Joseph. **Educ:** Jackson State Univ, BA, 1974; Howard Univ, MSW, 1975; Antioch Sch Law, JD, 1985. **Career:** Sen Thad Cochran, staff asst 1974-77; Southern Miss Legal Serv, paralegal 1977; Miss Gulf Coast Jr Col, instr 1978; Harrison Co Head Start Prog, proj dir 1978-79; Univ Southern Miss, asst prof 1979-83; Nat Urban League, policy analyst; US Catholic Conf, policy adv; Nat Asn Social Workers, NASW, gov rels assoc, lobbyist; DC Catholic Conf, exec dir, currently. **Orgs:** Nat Asn Advan Colored People, 1979-84; Omega Psi Phi Inc, 1981-; Midtown Montessori Sch, 1985-; St Ann's Infant & Maternity Home, 1989-; Covenant House, Wash DC; Policy Comm Catholic; bd mem, Charities. **Special Achievements:** First African-American staff assistant for Senator Thad Cochran, 1974-77. **Home Addr:** 5611 Leon St, Camp Springs, MD 20746. **Business Addr:** Executive Director, DC Catholic Conference, 145 Taylor St NE, PO Box 29260, Washington, DC 20017, **Business Phone:** (301)853-5342.

JACKSON, RONALD LEE
Educator, government official. **Personal:** Born Jul 13, 1943, Kansas City, MO; married Hattie Robinson; children: Taj & Yasmira. **Educ:** Harris Jr Col, AA, 1963; Wash Univ, AB, 1965; Southern Ill Univ, attended 1976. **Career:** Ill State Univ, admis coun, 1969-70; Wash Univ, asst dir admis, 1970-73, asst dean 1973-; Higher Educ Coord Coun, Admis Comn, 1970-73; St Louis Comn Africa, 1975-76; US Sen John Danforth, asst. **Orgs:** Coun Black Affairs, Ill State Univ, 1969-70; fel CORD, 1973; Leadership St Louis, 1982-83; bd mem, New City Sch, 1984-86; Urban League, Educ Comt, 1984-; chmn, United Way Comn Wide Youth Panel, 1986-87; Minority Bus Advocate Eastern MO, 1986; bd mem, Cardinal Ritter Col Prep HS, 1987-; vpres, Westlake Scholar Comn. **Military Serv:** AUS, 1st lt, 1966-69. **Business Addr:** Assistant to Senator, US Senator John C Danforth, 815 Olive Room 228, Saint Louis, MO 63101.

JACKSON, DR. ROY JOSEPH, JR.
Chemist, educator. **Personal:** Born Feb 8, 1944, Cotton Port, LA. **Educ:** Southern Univ, Baton Rouge, LA, BS, 1965, MS, 1969; Univ Calif, San Diego, PhD, chem, 1975. **Career:** Dow Chem Co, res chemist, 1968; Southern Univ, instr, 1969-70, grad asst, 1967-69; Univ Calif, teaching asst, 1970-75; Shell Developing Co, res chemist, 1975-. **Orgs:** Am Chem Soc; Kappa Delta Pi; Alpha Phi Alpha; Black Action Comt. **Special Achievements:** Numerous contributions to the study of photochemistry. **Military Serv:** AUS, capt, 1965-67, Bronze Star Medal. **Home Addr:** 12707 Havant Cir, Houston, TX 77077-2226. **Business Addr:** Senior Research Chemist, Shell Development Company, Westhollow Research Centre, Hwy 6 S, Houston, TX 77077.*

JACKSON, ROY LEE
Baseball player. **Personal:** Born May 1, 1954, Opelika, AL; married Mary. **Educ:** Tuskegee Inst, Tuskegee, AL. **Career:** Baseball player (retired), instructor; NY Mets, pitcher, 1977-80, Toronto Blue Jays, pitcher, 1981-84, San Diego Padres, pitcher, 1985; Minnesota Twins, pitcher, 1986; Ala base ball instr, currently. **Honors/Awds:** Voted Most Valuable Player Award, baseball Tuskegee Inst, 1974 & 1975; Appalachian All-Star Team. **Home Phone:** (334)741-9953.

JACKSON, DR. RUDOLPH ELLSWORTH
Educator, physician. **Personal:** Born May 31, 1935, Richmond, VA; son of Samuel and Jennie; married Janice Diane Ayer; children: Kimberley R, Kelley J, Rudolph E Jr & Alison D Ligon. **Educ:** Morehouse Col, BS, 1957; Meharry Med Col, MD, 1961. **Career:** Educator (retired), physician; St Jude Childrens Res Hosp, asst mem hemat, 1969-72; Nat Heart Lung & Blood Inst, chief sickle cell disease br, 1972-77; Howard Univ Sch Med, assoc prof, dept pediat, 1977-79; MeharryMed Col, chmn dept pediat, 1979-83; Morehouse Sch Med, act chr dept pediat, 1984-90, prof pediat, AIDS Res Consortium, dir; Asn Minority Health Professions Schs AIDS Res Consortium, dir; Off Int Health Progs, assoc dir. **Orgs:** AMA; Nat Med Asn; Am Soc Hemat; adv comt, DHEW sickle cell disease, 1971-72; Sigma Xi Scientific Soc, Howard Univ, 1978-; Nat Adv Coun Nat Inst Arthritis Diabetes Digestive Kidney Diseases NIH DHEW, 1979-83; AsnMed Sch Pediatric, 1980-89;; Alpha Omega Alpha Med Soc, Meharry Med Col,1980-; adv comt mem, DHEW lead poisoning, 1984; Pediat Task Force, Ageny Health Care Policy Res, 1991-96; adv comt, Ctr Disease Control, DHHS,1991-2003; Am Acad Pediat, 1991-95; Pediat Task Force, Am Acad Pediat,1992-96. **Honors/Awds:** DHEW Superior Serv Award; Federal Exec Institutes Award; LW Diggs Meritarious Serv Award; Consult, Committee Select Nominees for Nobel Prize in Medicine; NMA Certificate of Recognition for Scientific council. **Military Serv:** USN, lt cmdr, 5 yrs. **Business Addr:** Founding Members, MoreHouse School Medical, 720 Westview Dr SW, Atlanta, GA 30310-1495, **Business Phone:** (404)752-1703.

JACKSON, RUSSELL A
School principal. **Personal:** Born Feb 26, 1934, Philadelphia, PA; married Elois; children: Cheryll Renne & Charles Russell. **Educ:**

Cheyney State Col, BA, 1956; Temple Univ, MA, 1962, EdD, 1970. **Career:** Philadelphia Pub Sch, teacher, asst prin & elem prin; Chester, Pa, asst supt; E Orange Pub Sch, supt, 1968-72; Roosevelt Sch Dist No 66, supt; Howard Univ, Dept Educ Admin & Policy, asst prof, currently. **Orgs:** Am Asn Sch Adminr; Ariz Sch Admin Inc; Phi Delta Kappa Fraternity; pres, Nat Alliance Black Sch Educ, 1970-72; pres, Greater Phoenix Supr Asn, 1974-75; exec comn, Ariz Found Blind. **Military Serv:** USN, 1958.

JACKSON, RUSTY
Executive. **Personal:** Born in Greenville, SC; daughter of James Russell and Georgia. **Career:** Trans World Airlines, New York, NY, flight attend; IBM Corp, Columbia, SC, mkt support representative; Lanier Bus Products, Atlanta, Ga, mkt support mgr; Lexitron Corp, Wash, DC, territory mgr; Wash Convention Ctr, Wash, DC, special asst gen mgr, 1981-84; Coors Brewing Co, Wash, DC, CR reg mgr & Nat group mgr, 1984; Resolutions Inc, pres; Henderson Event Mgt, vpres, managing dir, 2005-. **Orgs:** Bd mem, Nat Kidney Found, 1988-91; bd mem, Leukemia Soc, 990-91; bd mem, DC Chamber Comm, 1990-95; bd mem, Metro Wash YMCA, 1990-92; bd mem, Wash Women League; bd chmn, United Negro Col Fund; Comns adv bd, Ladies Prof Golf asn. **Honors/Awds:** Dollars & Sense African Am Bus & Prof Women, 1989; DC NAACP Presidents Award, 1985; Public Service Award, Nat Assn Black Co Officials, 1988; Distinguished Golf Award, Nat Negro Golf Assn, 1987. **Business Addr:** Vice President, Henderson Event Management, 84 Villa Rd, Greenville, SC 29615, **Business Phone:** (864)298-1342.

JACKSON, DR. RUTH MOORE
Library administrator. **Personal:** Born Sep 27, 1938, Potecasi, NC; daughter of Jesse Thomas Sr and Ruth Estelle Futrell; married Roderick Earle, Aug 14, 1965; children: Eric Roderick. **Educ:** Hampton Inst, Hampton, VA, BS, bus, 1960; Atlanta Univ, Atlanta, GA, MSLS, 1965; Indiana Univ, Bloomington, IN, PhD, 1976. **Career:** Va State Univ, Petersburg, VA, librn, 1965-69; Ind Univ, Bloomington, IN, teaching fel/vis lectr; Va State Univ, Petersburg, VA, assoc prof, 1976-84; Univ N Fla, Jacksonville, FL, asst dir libraries, 1984-88; WVa Univ, Morgantown, WV, dean, univ libraries, 1988-98, spec asst to provost, 1999; Wichita State Univ Libraries, dean, 1999; Univ Calif, Riverside, univ librn, currently. **Orgs:** Am Libr Asn, 1976-; Asn Col & Res Libraries, 1984-; WVa Libr Asn, 1991-99; Am Mgt Asn, 1976-84; chair, WVa Higher Educ Libr Resources Adv Coun, 1988-98; chair, WVa Acad Libr Dir's Group, 1989-97; chair, WVa Acad Libr Consortium, 1991-98; Coalition for Networked Info, 1990-99; WVa Legis Comt, 1994-99; Addison-Wesley Higher Educ, tech bd, 1996-97; HW Wilson Adv Bd, 1999-; CODDL, Kans Regent's Univs, 1999-. **Honors/Awds:** US Off Educ Fel, US Off Educ, 1969-71; Competitive Research Award, Ind Univ, 1973; Southern Fel Found Fel, SFF, 1973-74; Nat Fac Minorities Res Fel, 1979-80; Outstanding Alumni Award, Hampton Inst, 1980; Distinguished West Virginian Award, 1992; Non-Italian Woman of the Year, 1992. **Business Addr:** University Librarian, University Of California, Riverside, 900 Univ Ave Rivera Libr 1st Fl, Riverside, CA 92521, **Business Phone:** (951)827-3221.

JACKSON, SAMUEL L
Actor. **Personal:** Born Dec 21, 1949, Washington, DC; married LaTanya Richardson; children: Zoe. **Educ:** Morehouse Col, dramatic arts. **Career:** Actor, currently; Stage productions: A Soldiers Play, 1981; The Piano Lesson, 1987; Sally & Prince, 1989; The District Line, 1990; Two Trains Running, 1990; Home; Fences, Seattle Repertory Theater; Distant Fires, Coast Playhouse, 1993. Films: Together for Days; Ragtime, 1981; Raw, 1987; Sch Daze, 1988; Sea of Love, 1989; Do the Right Thing, 1989; Mo' Better Blues, 1990; Def by Temptation, 1990; Goodfellas, 1991; Jungle Fever, 1991; Jumpin' at the Boneyard, 1992; White Sands, 1992; Patriot Games, 1992; True Romance, 1993; Menace II Society, 1993; National Lampoon's Loaded Weapon I, 1993; Amos & Andrew, 1993; Jurassic Park, 1993; Against the Wall, 1994; Assault at West Point, 1994; The Court Martial of Johnson Whittaker, 1994; Fresh, 1994; Pulp Fiction, 1994; Kiss of Death, 1995; Die Hard With A Vengeance, 1995; A Time to Kill, 1996; The Long Kiss Goodnight, 1997; Eve's Bayou, 1997; 187, 1997; Jackie Brown, 1998; The Negotiator, 1998; Sphere, 1998; Deep Blue Sea, 1999; Star Wars Episode I, 1999; Any Given Wednesday, 2000; Rules of Engagement, 2000; Shaft, 2000; Unbreakable, 2000; The Caveman's Valentine, 2001; The 51st State, 2001; Changing Lanes, 2002; Star Wars Episode II, 2002; XXX, 2002; The House on Turk Street, 2002; Basic, 2003; SWAT, 2003; Blackout, 2003; HBO movie, Unchained Memories: Readings from the Slave Narratives, reader, 2003; XXX 2, 2004; Twisted, 2004; Kill Bill Vol 2, 2004; Home of the Brave, 2006; Black Snake Moan, 2006; Snakes on a Plane, 2006; Resurrecting the Champ, 2007; Jumper, 2008; TV: "The Displaced Person", 1976; "The Trial of the Moke', 1978; "Uncle Tom's Cabin", 1987; "Dead Man Out", 1989; "Dead & Alive: The Race for Gus Farace", 1991; "Simple Justice", 1993; "Against the Wall", 1994; "ESPY Awards", 2002; 2004: "A Light Knight's Odyssey", 2004 (voice); "The Boondocks", 2006; "Freedomland", 2006; "Afro Samurai", 2007. **Orgs:** Just Us Theater Co, cofounder; Negro Ensemble Co. **Honors/Awds:** Best Supporting Actor, Jungle Fever, Cannes Film Fest,1991; New York Film Critics Award, Jungle Fever, 1991; nominated, Academy Award, Best Supporting Actor, Pulp Fiction, 1995; Outstanding Supporting Actor in a Motion Picture, 1997; Artists of Vision Award, 1999; Career Achievement Award, Acapulco Black Film Fest, 1999; received a star on the Hollywood Walk of Fame, 2000; Essence Awards, honoree, 2001; Outstanding Actor in a Motion Picture, 2006. **Business Addr:** Actor, International Creative Management, 8942 Wilshire Blvd, Beverly Hills, CA 90211.

JACKSON, SAMUEL S., JR.
Educator. **Personal:** Born Nov 8, 1934, Natchez, MS; married Margaret Atkins; children: Sharon, Orlando, Sheila & Samuel III. **Educ:** Alcorn State Univ, BS, agr educ & gen sci; Antioch Col, MS, educ admin. **Career:** Lincoln Attendance Ctr, high sch teacher, sch prin, 1957-66, 1967-68; Wilberforce Univ, assoc dir coop educ, 1968-70, dean stud, 1970-78; Cent St Univ, assoc dean stud, 1978-83, vpres stud affairs, 1983-96, spec asst pres, 1995-96. **Orgs:** Phi Delta Kappa; Am Personal Guid Asn; Nat Asn Stud Personnel Adminr; Am Col Union Asn; Nat Col Housing Asn; Admis & Fin St & Nat Orgn; Ohio Stud Personnel Asn; Omega Psi Phi Fraternity; Nat Asn Advan Colored People. **Honors/Awds:** Scholar, NSF, 1966-67; S GA Awards, Wilberforce Univ, 1980-85; Man of the Year, Omega Psi Phi Fraternity; Hall of Honors, Alcorn St Univ, 1995. **Military Serv:** AUS, spec serv, 1955-57. **Home Addr:** 1615 Spillan Rd, Yellow Springs, OH 45387.

JACKSON, SANDRA STEVENS
Government official, banker. **Personal:** Married Jesse Jackson Jr. **Career:** US Info Agency, Pub Dipl Prog, former sr coordr; Export-Import Bank, Off Cong & External Affairs, vpres, currently. **Business Phone:** (202)565-1594.

JACKSON, DR. SHIRLEY ANN
Government official. **Personal:** Born Aug 5, 1946, Washington, DC; married Morris; children: Alan. **Educ:** Mass Inst Technol, SB, physics, 1968, PhD, physics, 1973. **Career:** Fermi Nat Accelerator Lab, resident assoc theoretical physicist, 1973-76;Europ Orgn Nuclear Res, vis sci assoc, 1974-75; Bell Telephone Labs, technol staff, 1976-92; Rutgers Univ, prof physics, 1991-95; Nuclear Regulatory Comn, chair, 1995-99; Rensselaer Polytech Inst, pres, 1999-. **Orgs:** Amn Physicists Soc; New York Acad Sci; Sigma Xi; Nat Inst Sci; Comt for Educating & Employing Women Scientists & Engineers; MIT Corp, bd trustees, 1975-85; Lincoln Univ, 1980-; Nat Acad Sci, 1981-82; Nat Acad Eng; pres, AAAS, 2004; chmn, AAAS Bd Dirs, 2005; Am Philos Soc, 2007. **Honors/ Awds:** Ford Foundation, Advanced Study Fellowship, 1971-73, Grant, 1974-75; Martin Marietta Corp, Fellowship, 1972-73; First African American female to receive PhD from MIT and the first in the nation to get a doctoral degree in physics; Thomas Alva Edison Award, 1993; Golden Torch Award, National Society Black Engs, 2000; 100 Women of Excellence Award, Albany-Colonie, 2000; Immortal Award, Associated Black Charities, 2001; Richtmyer Memorial Lecture Award, American Association Physics Teachers, 2001; Community Citizenship Award, Troy Rehabilitation & Improvement Program, 2006. **Special Achievements:** The first woman to win the Black Engineer of the Year Award by US BlackEngineer & Information Technology magazine; First African-American tobecome a Commissioner of the U.S. Nuclear Regulatory Commission. **Business Addr:** President, Rensselaer Polytechnic Institute, 110 8th St, Troy, NY 12180.*

JACKSON, STANLEY LEON
Basketball player. **Personal:** Born Oct 10, 1970, Tuskegee, AL. **Educ:** Univ Ala, Birmingham. **Career:** Basketball player(retired); Minn Timber wolves, guard, 1993-94; Fla Beach dogs, guard, 1995-96; Caceres, guard, 1996-97; Sevilla, guard, 1997-98; Quad City Thunder, guard, 1998-99; Dijon, guard, 1999-00; ES Chalon-Sur-Saone, guard, 2000-05; Strasbourg, guard, 2006. *

JACKSON, STEVEN WAYNE
Football player, football coach. **Personal:** Born Apr 8, 1969, Houston, TX; married; children: Dominique & Stephen. **Educ:** Purdue Univ. **Career:** Football player (retired), football coach; Houston Oilers, defensive back, 1991-96; Tenn Oilers, defensive back, 1997-99; Wash Redskins, safeties coach, currently. **Honors/ Awds:** Ed Block Courage Award, 1998. **Business Phone:** (703)478-8900.

JACKSON, STUART WAYNE
Sports manager, athletic coach. **Personal:** Born Dec 11, 1955, Reading, PA; son of Harold Russell and Pauline Virginia Artist; married Susan Taylor; children: Lauren, Taylor, Erin & Yanna. **Educ:** Seattle Univ, WA, BA, bus mgt, 1978. **Career:** IBM, Los Angeles, CA, Mict Rep DPD, 1978-81; Univ Ore, Eugene, OR, asst coach, 1981-83; Wash State Univ, Pullman, WA, asst coach, 1983-85; Providence Col, Providence, RI, asst coach & head recruiting coordr, 1985-87; NY Knicks, asst coach, 1987-89, head coach, 1989-90; Nat Basketball Asn (NBA), NY, dir basketball oper, 1991, exec vpres basketball opers, currently; Univ Wis Badgers, head basketball coach, 1992-93, 1993-94; Vancouver Grizzlies, pres & gen mgr, 1994, head coach, 1997-2000. **Orgs:** Nat Asn Basketball Coaches. **Honors/Awds:** Father of Year, Nat Father Year Comt, 1990.

JACKSON, SUZANNE FITZALLEN
Artist, educator. **Personal:** Born Jan 30, 1944, St Louis, MO; daughter of Roy Dedrick and Ann Marie (Butler); divorced; children: Rafiki C D Smith-Mhunzi. **Educ:** SF State Univ, BFA, 1966; Otis Art Inst, studied with Charles White & Noel Quinn, 1968; Yale Univ, Sch Drama, MFAD, 1990. **Career:** Painter, poet, 1960-; Desert Sun Sch, faculty, 1982-85, currently; Freelance scenic & costume designer, 1987-94; St Mary's Col Maryland, scenographer, asst prof, 1994-96; Savannah Col Art & Design, prof painting, 1996. **Orgs:** United Scenic Artists, Local 829, 1990-; Costume Soc Am, 1990-. **Honors/Awds:** Int Latham Found Humane Soc & Kindness to animals, Scholarships, 1961; Grand Prize, Eyes & Ears Found, Int Year of the Child Billboard Competition; Nomination for the First Nat Award in the Visual Arts, 1981; Idyllwild Sch Music & the Arts, Asniates Fel for Etching/Book Making & Dance, 1982-84; Nat Museum of Women in the Arts, charter artists, registry, 1987; Cave Canem African-American Poets, fel, 1996-; several others. **Special Achievements:** Numerous solo and group museum exhibitions, 1960-; numerous others. **Business Addr:** Faculty, Desert Sun School, 15 W 41st St, Savannah, GA 31401-8984, **Business Phone:** (912)233-8177.

JACKSON, TAMMY
Basketball player. **Personal:** Born Dec 3, 1962. **Educ:** Univ Fla, rcrn, 1985. **Career:** Italy, Sweden, Japan & France; Houston Comets, forward-center, 1997-98, 1999-2002; Wash Mystics, 1998; Santa Fe Community Col, asst coach, 2004. **Honors/Awds:** WNBA Championships, 1997; Japanese League Championships; all-SEC first-team. Won Bronze Medal, 1992. **Special Achievements:** Florida honored her as an SEC Great with the school's pick, 2003. *

JACKSON, TERRY (TERRANCE BERNARD JACKSON)
Football player. **Personal:** Born Jan 10, 1976, Gainesville, FL; son of Willie. **Educ:** Fla Univ, BA, bus & mkt. **Career:** San Francisco 49ers, running back, 1999-2005. **Honors/Awds:** Leadership Award; All-SEC Award; Spec Teams Player of the Week, NFC, 2003. *

JACKSON, TIA
Basketball player, basketball coach. **Personal:** Born Apr 21, 1972, Salisbury, MD. **Educ:** Univ Iowa, BA, media studies film, 1995. **Career:** Iowa Hawkeyes, guard, forward; Va Commonwealth Univ, asst coach, 1996-99; Phoenix Mercury, guard, forward, 1997; Stanford Univ, asst coach, 1999; Univ Calif, Los Angeles, CA, Bruin, recruiting coordr, asst coach, 2000-05; Duke Women's Basketball, coaching staff, 2005-07; Univ WA women's basketball, head coach, 2007-. **Orgs:** Women's Basketball Hall of Fame. **Special Achievements:** Earned NCAA Mideast Regional All-Tournament honors. **Business Addr:** coach, University of Washington women's basketball, 3910 Montlake Blvd Graves Bldg Room 101, PO Box 354070, Seattle, WA 98195-4070, **Business Phone:** (206)543-2200.*

JACKSON, TOM
Football player. **Personal:** Born Apr 4, 1951, Cleveland, OH. **Educ:** Louisville Univ, Bus. **Career:** Football player (retired); Denver Broncos, line backer, 1973-86; ESPN Inc, NFL studio analyst, 1987-. **Honors/Awds:** MO Valley Conf Player of the Yr, 1970, 1972; most valuable player, Denvers Broncos, 1974, 1976-77; Am Bowl; Blue-Gray Game; Broncos Ring of Fame, 1992. **Special Achievements:** Pro Bowl 1977, 1978-79; All-Pro Bowl, 1977-78. **Business Addr:** NFL Studio Analyst, ESPN Inc, 935 Mid St, Bristol, CT 06010-1001, **Business Phone:** (203)585-2000.

JACKSON, TOMI L.
Association executive. **Personal:** Born Nov 28, 1923, Dallas, TX; daughter of Thomas Stephens and Ida Stephens; children: Joanne Ragan & Linda Marlane Craft. **Educ:** Wayne State Univ, BA, 1940. **Career:** Channel 2 TV, 1950; Channel 7 TV, 1965; Det Water & Sewerage Dept, 1979; Tomi Jackson & Assoc, pub rel. **Orgs:** Area vpres, Am Women in Radio & TV; bd mem, Women's Advert Club Detroit; bd mem, United Found; Travelers Aid Soc. **Honors/Awds:** Demmy Award, United Found, 1981. **Home Addr:** 11424 E Rembrandt Ave, Mesa, AZ 85212-4169. *

JACKSON, TONYA CHARISSE
Executive, administrator. **Personal:** Born Feb 28, 1959, Indianapolis, IN; daughter of Fred and Loretta; married Jerry Smallwood; children: Eddie Jackosn & Justin Smallwood. **Educ:** Purdue Univ, BS, comput tech, 1981; George Mason Univ, MS, mgt info systems, 1987; Univ Va, exec training prog, 1998. **Career:** Thomas & Skinner, mgr systems develop, 1977-84; Planning Res Corp, mgr, financial systems, 1984-87; Freddie Mac, mgr, prod develop, 1987-89, dir, strategic systems planning, 1989-90, dir, corp bus re-engineering, 1990-91, dir, mgt & control systems, 1991-92, dir, nat & distressed acct, 1992-93, dir, customer & mkt interface, 1993-94, dir, nat revenue acct, 1994-95, dept head, transaction processing, 1996-97, vp, transaction processing, 1997-2001, vpres customer care, currently. **Orgs:** Chair, Sisters SON Found, 1997-; vice chair, Phillips Progs C & Families, 1998-; chair, Women's Mortgage Indust Network, 2002-. **Honors/Awds:** Best Manager Award, Freddie Mac; Gold Award for Excellence in Customer Service, Freddie Mac; Rookie

Officer of the Year, Freddie Mac, 1997; Y2K Leadership, Freddie Mac. **Business Addr:** Vice President of Customer Care, Freddie Mac, 8250 Jones Branch Dr, McLean, VA 22102-3110, **Business Phone:** (703)903-2000.

JACKSON, TYOKA
Football player. **Personal:** Born Nov 22, 1971, Washington, DC; married Tenique; children: 2. **Educ:** Pa State univ. **Career:** Miami Dolphins, defensive end, 1994-95; Tampa Bay Buccaneers, 1996-2000; St Louis Rams, defensive end, 2001-05; Detroit lions, 2006-07. **Orgs:** Get Into the Game; the Rams Reader Team; Bowl-a-RAM-a; Make a Wish Found; founder, Tyoka's Troops with Am Red Cross; leader, Jackson Investment Company, 2008. **Special Achievements:** Nominee for the Walter Payton Man of the Yr award. **Business Addr:** Owner, Jackson Investment Company, 125 Yuma St SE Suite 101, WashingtonDC, WA 20032.*

JACKSON, VINCENT EDWARD. See JACKSON, BO.

JACKSON, W. SHERMAN
Educator, college teacher. **Personal:** Born May 21, 1939, Crowley, LA; married Frances P McIntyre; children: Sherlyn, Sherrese & W Sherman II. **Educ:** Southern Univ, AB, 1962; NC Cent Univ, MA, 1963; Ohio State Univ, PhD, 1969. **Career:** Alcorn Col, Lorman, MS, instr, 1963-64; Cent State Univ, instr, 1966-68; Univ Lagos, Nigeria, sr fulbright lectr, 1972-73; Miami Univ, assoc profam const hist & law, 1969-. **Orgs:** Pres/founder, Asn Acad Advan, 1969; pres, Oxford Nat Asn Adv Colored People, 1979; consult, NEH; ed consult, Pentagon Ed Testing Serv. **Special Achievements:** Author : The Anglo-Norman Nobility in the Reign of Henry I: The Second Generation. **Business Addr:** Associate Professor, Miami University, 272 Upham Hall, Miami, OH 45056, **Business Phone:** (513)529-5137.

JACKSON, WALTER KINSLEY
Clergy. **Personal:** Born Mar 28, 1914, Boley, OK; son of Adelaide and Eddie; married Eula Lee Wilhite; children: Waltine. **Educ:** Bishop Col, AB, 1937; OK Sch Rel, BTh, 1947; Morris Booker Mem Col, DDiv, 1955; Okla Sch Rel, DDiv, 1964; Union Theol Sem, 1966. **Career:** Corinth Baptist Church, Ardmore OK, pastor; t John Mission Bapt Church,minister, 44 yrs, sr pastor, pastor emer, currently. **Orgs:** Bd trustees, Bishop Col Dallas, Tex; bd dir, Med Cent State Bank; Gov Comon Rehab of State of OK; Coalition of Civic Leadership of OK City; bd dir,Progressive Bapt Nat Conv; bd dir, Okal Mission Bapt State Conv; pres, Okla Baptist State Conv, 1966. **Honors/Awds:** Viola P Cutler Award, Urban League Okla City, 1970; DHL, Virginia Sem, Lynchburg, VA. **Business Addr:** Pastor Emeritus, St John Missionary Baptist Church, 5700 N Kelley Ave, Oklahoma City, OK 73111.*

JACKSON, WARREN GARRISON
Executive. **Personal:** Born in Yonkers, NY; son of Charles R. and Ethel R. Garrison; married Christena V, Sep 7, 1952; children: Tenley Ann, W Garrison, Terrance V. **Educ:** Manhattan Col, Riverdale, NY, BS, 1952. **Career:** NY Times, New York, NY, asst circulation mgr; Amsterdam News, New York, NY, circulation dir; Circulation Experti, Hartsdale, NY, founder, pres & chief exec officer, 1968-. **Orgs:** Vice chair, Jackie Robinson Found, 1989-; trustee, Jackie Joyner Kersee Found, 1989-; trustee, White Plains Hosp, 1990-. **Honors/Awds:** OIC Achievement, OIC Am, New Eng Region, 1986; Outstanding Achievement, Omega Phi Si, 1988; Business Award, New York Chapter, LINKS, 1991. **Special Achievements:** First black circulation inspector for the New York Times in the early 1950s; first black circulation director of a major New York newspaper, the now-defunct New York nickerbocker. **Business Addr:** President, Chief Executive Officer, Circulation Experti, 707 Westchester Ave Suite 309, White Plains, NY 10604.*

JACKSON, WAVERLY ARTHUR, JR.
Football player. **Personal:** Born Dec 19, 1972, South Hill, VA. **Educ:** Va Tech. **Career:** Carolina Panthers, defensive tackle, 1997-98; Indianapolis Colts, 1998-2002, free agent, currently.

JACKSON, WILEY, JR.
Clergy. **Personal:** Born Jan 16, 1953, Atlanta, GA; son of Wiley Jackson Sr; married Mary Ann, Mar 20, 1993; children: Wiley Jackson III. **Educ:** S Ga Col; Dekalb Cent Col, AD; Beulah Heights Bible Col, BA. **Career:** Frito-Lay Inc, 1971-81; Gospel Tabernacle, pastor & founder, chief exec officer, 1982-. **Orgs:** Nat Religious Broadcasters; Churches Uniting Global Mission; Fellowship, Inner City Word Faith Churches; Pentecostal Fellowship, N Am; bd preachers, Morehouse Col; Word Action; Fellowship Pastors; bd dir, Fellowship Inner City Word Faith Ministires. **Honors/Awds:** Honarary Doctorate Divinity. **Special Achievements:** Book: Born to Overcome, 2002. **Business Addr:** Chief Executive Officer, Founder, Gospel Tabernacle, 277 Clifton St, Atlanta, GA 30317-2122, **Business Phone:** (404)370-3800.*

JACKSON, WILLIAM ALVIN
Automotive executive. **Personal:** Born Sep 20, 1950, Chicago, IL; son of Elnora and James; married Rita F, Jul 13, 1991; children: Richard A, Alyssa B & Danielle L. **Educ:** Loyola Univ, BSBA, 1975. **Career:** L-M Division Ford Motor Co, zone mgr, 1975-79; Volkswagen Am Inc, district sales mgr, 1979-82, advertising productions superior, 1982-84; shows & exhibits mgr, 1984-87; Jones Transfer Co, vpres sales & mkt, 1987-89; Chrysler Int Corp, merchandising mgr, 1989-93, France & Spain, regional sales & mkt mgr, 1993-96, int fleet sales mgr, 1996. **Orgs:** Mentor, Detroit Big Brother Prog, 1990-93; founder, bd dirs, Tia Nedd Organ Donor Found. **Honors/Awds:** Ambassador's Award, Alpha Phi Alpha, 1966; Certificate of Recognition, US Dept Com, Export Assistance Ctr. **Special Achievements:** Proficient in French. **Home Addr:** 3283 Springbrook Ct, West Bloomfield, MI 48324-3252.

JACKSON, WILLIAM E
Educator. **Personal:** Born Dec 1, 1936, Creedmoor, NC; married Janet. **Educ:** NC Cent Univ, BA, 1958; New York Univ, MA, 1961; Univ Pa, PhD, 1972. **Career:** City Co, NY, 1961-64; Univ PA, instr, 1967-70; Yale Univ, asst prof ger; Univ Va, fac, 1981-2005, chmn, 1991-, assoc prof emer, Dept Ger, 2005-. **Orgs:** Am Asn Teachers Ger; NC Cent Alumni. **Honors/Awds:** Outstanding Faculty Award, African-Am Affairs, 1999; Univ Teaching Award, Univ Va, 2005. **Special Achievements:** Author: Reinmar's Women , Amsterdambenjamins 1980; publs in "Neophilologus" "Colloquia Germanica" & "Germanica Studies in Honor of Otto Springer".

JACKSON, WILLIAM ED
Executive. **Personal:** Born Aug 6, 1932, Mason, TN; son of Willie B and Mabel E Harris; married Toria Catherine Hubbard, Oct 30, 1951; children: William E Jr, Michael A & Michelle D. **Educ:** Wilson Jr Col, Chicago, IL, 1950-51, 1958-59; Univ Ill, Chicago, Chicago, IL, CBA, cert 1989-90. **Career:** Ill State Police, Crestwood, IL, trooper, 1957-63; IBEW Local 1031, Chicago, IL, bus agent, 1963-66; Schieffelin & Somerset Co, Chicago, IL 1968-94, vpres, sr vpres, cent region mgr, 1981-94; WEJAC Inc Trucking, pres, currently. **Orgs:** Chmn, Sky Ranch Found, Chicago Branch, 1981; Int Bus Adv Coun, 1989-91; bd vis, NC Cent Univ, 1986-; Link Unlimited, Chicago, 1987-; IL Racing Bd Comm, 1995-; St Xavier Col, Chicago; Nat Asn Sickle Cell Disease; QBG Found. **Honors/Awds:** Black Achievers of Industry Award, YMCA, NY, 1973; Sky Ranch Foundation Man of Year, New York, 1981; Industry Award, Inner City Liquor Asn, 1982; Blackbook National Business & Professional Award, New York, 1982; Outstanding Citizen Award, Clark College Alumni Asn, 1990. **Military Serv:** Army, Sgt, 1952-54; Soldier of Year, 1953. **Business Addr:** President, WEJAC, 7149 S Exchange, Chicago, IL 60649, **Business Phone:** (773)768-4310.

JACKSON, WILLIAM R
Psychotherapist, businessperson. **Personal:** Born Aug 28, 1945, Souix Falls, SD; son of Juanita R Clardy; married Jacqualine, Nov 30, 1996; children: Felicia Overton & Kimberly Overton. **Educ:** Washburn Univ, BEd, 1968; Ball State Univ, MA, 1975. **Career:** Great Clips Inc, franchisee, 1989-; Dr Bayless & Assoc, psychotherapist, 1989-. **Honors/Awds:** Million Dollar Club, Great Clips Inc, 1998. **Military Serv:** USAF, maj, 1968-88; Meritorious Service Medal, 1986 & 1988; Commendation Service Medal, 1982 & 1988; Luke Air Force Base, AZ, Outstanding ADR of the Year, 1985 & 1986. **Home Addr:** 6121 W Corrine Dr, Glendale, AZ 85304, **Home Phone:** (602)486-2192. **Business Addr:** President/Owner, SCOE Inc, dba Great Clips.

JACKSON, WILLIE BERNARD, JR.
Football player. **Personal:** Born Aug 16, 1971, Gainesville, FL. **Educ:** Univ Fla, BS, telecommun, 1993. **Career:** Dallas Cowboys, 1994; Jacksonville Jaguars, wide receiver, 1995-97; Cincinnati Bengals, 1998-99; New Orleans Saints, 2000-01; Atlanta Falcons, 2002; Washington Redskins, 2002; AAFL, 2008-. *

JACKSON, WILLIS RANDELL, II
Athletic director, educator, athletic coach. **Personal:** Born Sep 11, 1945, Memphis, TN; son of Willis Randell and Louise Hallbert; married Patricia F Crisp, Jan 21, 1991; children: Ericka, Hasani & Jamila. **Educ:** Rochester Jr Col, cert, 1965; ND State Univ, BS, 1967; SIU Edwardsville, MS & Admin Cert, 1980. **Career:** Rochester Lourdes High Sch, head wrestling coach, 1967-68; Soldan High Sch, head wrestling coach, 1969-71; Lincoln Sr High Sch, head wrestling coach, 1971-74, athletic dir, 1973-74; E St Louis Sr High Sch, head wrestling coach, 1974-84, athletic dir, 1974-81; Hughes Quinn Jr High Sch, head girls track coach, 1985-91, teacher, currently; Dr Jack's Sports Ltd, chief exec officer, currently. **Orgs:** Ill Wrestling Coaches & Off Assoc, 1974-; NWCOA Wrestling Coaches & Off Assoc, 1974-; Nat Basketball Coaches Assoc, 1985-; Nat Athletic Dirs Assoc, 1974-; pres, Grandmaster Athletic Asn; Southern Cross #112 Prince Hall Mason, 1975-. **Honors/Awds:** Illinois State Athletic Director of the Year, Dist 15, 1977 & 1978; Coach of Year, Wrestling E St Louis Jour, 1975. **Business Addr:** Teacher, Hughes Quinn Rock Jr High School, 1000 Ohio Ave, East St Louis, IL 62201-1355, **Business Phone:** (618)583-8421.

JACKSON, WILMA LITTLEJOHN. See JACKSON, DARCY DEMILLE.

JACKSON, YVONNE RUTH
Executive. **Personal:** Born Jun 30, 1949, Los Angeles, CA; daughter of Giles B and Gwendolyn Lackey Battle; married Frederick Jackson Jr, Mar 24, 1989; children: Cortney, Douglass. **Educ:** Spelman Col, BA, histoty, 1970; Harvard Univ Sch Bus, PMD, 1985; Baruch Col, CUNY, MBA. **Career:** Sears Roebuck & Co, from asst dept mgr to dept mgr, 1970-71, asst buyer & asst retail sales mgr, 1972-77, personnel mgr, 1977-79; Avon Products, Inc, exec recruiter emp relations mgr & dir human resource, 1979-85, dir mfg, redeployment & dir human resource int, 1985-87, vpres int & human resources, 1987-93; Burger King Corp, sr vpres worldwide human resources, 1983; Pfizer Inc, sr vpres, 2003-. **Orgs:** Spelman Col, bd trustees, 1996-; Spelman Corp Women's Roundtable, chair, 1994-; bd mem, Women's Foodserv Forum, 1995; adv bd mem, Catalyst, 1993-; bd mem, Inroads S Fla, 1996-; bd mem, Girls Inc; bd mem, Adv Coun acct firm Price-Waterhouse; bd mem, Inst Womens Policy. **Honors/Awds:** YMCA, Black Achiever, 1986; YMCA of Greater NY, Y's Woman Achiever, 1992; Spelman Col Alumini Asn, Bus Achievement Award, 1993; 2004 Alumni of the Year, Spelman Col. **Business Addr:** Senior Vice President, Pfizer Inc, Human Resources Orgnisation & Environment, 235 E 42nd St, New York, NY 10017-5755, **Business Phone:** (212)361-8374.*

JACKSON, YVONNE RUTH
Vice president (Organization). **Personal:** Born Jun 30, 1949, Los Angeles, CA; daughter of Giles and Gwendolyn; married Frederick Jackson Jr, Mar 24, 1989; children: Cortney & Douglass. **Educ:** Spelman Col, BA; Harvard Bus Sch, mgt develop cert. **Career:** Avon Products; Sears; Roebuck & Co; Compaq Comp Corp, human resource head; Burger King, human resource head; Pfizer Inc, human resource head, beginning 2002; Corp Human Resources, leadership team & sr vpres, 2004-. **Orgs:** Vice chmn, Bd Trustees Spelman Col; Bd Inst Women's Policy Res; Adv Bd Catalyst. **Honors/Awds:** Black Achiever, YMCA, 1986; Y's Woman Achiever, YMCA of Greater NY, 1992; Bus Achievement Award, Spelman Col Alumini Asn, 1993; Alumni of the Year, Spelman Col, 2004. **Business Addr:** Senior Vice President of Corporate Human Resource, Pfizer Inc., 235 E 42nd St, New York, NY 10017, **Business Phone:** (212)733-2323.*

JACKSON-BENNETT, ROSALIND
Executive director. **Career:** US Office Diversity & Inclusion Avon Products, dir, currently. **Business Addr:** Director, US Office of Diversity and Inclusion for Avon Products Inc., 1345 Ave of the Americas, New York, NY 10105-0196.

JACKSON-FOY, LUCY MAYE
Educator. **Personal:** Born Sep 28, 1919, Texas; daughter of Louise Jackson and L J Jackson; married Joseph Daniel Foy, Dec 11, 1954. **Educ:** A&T Col, Ohio State, Prairie View Col, Tex Woman's Univ; N Tex State Col; Kans State Teachers Col; Kans Univ; Kans Cent Mo State Univ; Univ Mo. **Career:** Educator (retired); Veteran Admin, 1946-50; A&T Col, 1950-54; Hamilton Park High Sch, 1954-62; Kans City Mo Sch Dist, voc coordr, 1963-84. **Orgs:** Eta Phi Beta, 1968-74; Nat Rehab Asn; Counc Except C; Mo State Teachers Asn; Disabled Am Veterans; Nat Coun Teachers Math; Nat Asn Advan Colored People; Nat Coun Negro Women; Eta Phi Beta Sor; exec bd dirs, Kans City Asn Ment Retarded C; Comt Davis Brickle Report; Spec Educ Adv Com; Community Serv Greater Kans City; co-founder Shelly Sch Ment Retarded; vol, Adult Basic Educ Prog; Health Care AARP Bd Kans City; pres, Washington-Lincoln High Sch Club, 1987-88; bd, Women's Chamber Com Kans City. **Honors/Awds:** Outstanding Sec Educ Am, 1974-75; Certificate, Nat Wis Law Alumni Asn, 1987-88. **Military Serv:** Women's Army Corps, 1942-45; Good Conduct Medal. **Home Addr:** 1414 E 28 St, Kansas City, MO 64109-1214.

JACKSON-GILLISON, ESQ. HELEN L
Lawyer. **Personal:** Born Jul 9, 1944, Colliers, WV; daughter of George W Sr and Helen L; married Edward L Gillison Sr; children: Edward L II. **Educ:** W Liberty State Col, BS, 1977; WVa Univ Col Law, JD, 1981. **Career:** Helen L Jackson-Gillison Law Off, atty, 1981-, sr partner, currently. **Orgs:** WVa State Bar; WVa Trial Lawyers Asn; Mountain State Bar Asn; Hancock Co Bar Asn; Am Bar Ass; Nat Bar Asn; Am Trial Lawyers Asn; Weirton Bus; Prof Womens Club. **Honors/Awds:** Black Attorney of the Year Award, WVa Col Law, 1986. **Special Achievements:** First African American female to began her own private law practice in Weirton, WVa; First African American female to serve on the Audit & Budget Committee and the Unlawful Practice of Law Committee, WVa State Bar; First African American appointed to the WVa North Community College Board of Trustees. **Business Addr:** Attorney, Senior Partner, Helen L Jackson-Gillison Law Offices, 3139 W St, Weirton, WV 26062, **Business Phone:** (304)748-7116.

JACKSON-LEE, SHEILA
Congressperson (U.S. federal government). **Personal:** Born Jan 12, 1950. **Educ:** Yale Univ, BA, 1972; Univ Va, Law Sch, JD, 1975. **Career:** Houston City Coun, atty, 1990-94; US House Reps, congresswoman, 1995-. **Orgs:** Founder, member & co-chair, Cong C's Caucus; founder, member & co-chair, Afghan Caucus; founder, member & co-chair, Pakistan Caucus; founder, member & co-chair, Algerian Caucus. **Honors/Awds:** Drum Major Award for Public Service, Revelation Urban Develop Inst, 2005; Phillip

Burton Immigration & Civil Rights Award, 2006; Top Women in the Sciences Award, Nat Tech Asn Scientists & Engrs; Legislator of the Year, Nat Ment Health Asn. **Special Achievements:** Hailed by "Congressional Quarterly" as one of the 50 most effective members of Congress and by "U.S. News and World Report" as one of the 10 most influential legislators in the House of Representatives; first African American women At-Large members of the Houston City Council; authored several immigration bills, such as H.R. 750, the "Save America Comprehensive Immigration Act of 2007"; hailed by Ebony magazine as one of the "100 Most Fascinating Black Women of the 20th Century"; one of the most influential and prolific legislators on Capitol Hill, Houston Chronicle. **Business Addr:** Congresswoman, United States House of Representatives, 2435 Rayburn Bldg, Washington, DC 20515.*

JACKSON-RANSOM, BUNNIE
Business owner, executive. **Personal:** Born in Louisburg, NC; daughter of Burnal James Hayes and Elizabeth Day Hayes; divorced; children: Elizabeth Jackson, Brooke Jackson, Maynard Jackson III & Rae Yvonne Ransom. **Educ:** NC Col, BS, 1961; NC Cent Univ, MS, bus, 1969. **Career:** Pvt Consult Serv, 1972-76; First Class Inc, pres & founder, 1975-; BJT, Inc, Owner & Operator, 1979-83; SOS Band, Inc, staff, 1980-84, 1989-92; GA State Univ, instr, 1981-90, 1995; Atlanta Artists Mgt Inc, mgt servs CAMEO, 1983-89. **Orgs:** Nat Am Advan Colored People; Delta Sigma Theta Sorority; Link Inc; 100 Black Women; Atlanta Asn Black Journalists. **Honors/Awds:** Certificate Appreciation, Atlanta Pub Schs, 1974; Nat Media Women, Atlanta Chap, Community Leader Int Scope, 1975; Bronze Jubilee Award, 1984; President Award, Atlanta Asn Black Journalists, 1984, 1991, 1993. **Special Achievements:** Top 100 Black Bus & Prof Women, Dollar & Sense Magazine, 1985. **Business Phone:** (404)505-8188.

JACKSON ROBINSON, TRACY CAMILLE
Marketing executive. **Personal:** Born Jun 4, 1966, Detroit, MI. **Educ:** Univ Mich, Dearborn, BSE, 1987, Ann Arbor, MBA, 1990. **Career:** Three M Corp, mfg engr, 1987-88; Kraft Foods, brand asst, 1990-91, assoc brand mgr, 1991-92, proj mgr, 1993-94, brand mgr, 1994-97; Amtrak, central region mktg dir, 1997-. **Orgs:** Alpha Kappa Alpha Sorority, comt mem, 1984-; Girl Scouts Am, troup leader, 1991-95; Uhlich Children's Home, bd mem, 1994-; Nat Black MBA Asn, 1993-; Transportation Mkt & Community Asn, treas, currently. **Business Addr:** Central Region Marketing Director, Amtrak, National Railroad Passenger Corporation, 60 Mass Ave, Washington, DC 20002, **Business Phone:** 800-872-7245.

JACKSON-SMOOT, BENITA MARIE. See JACKSON, DR. BENITA MARIE.

JACKSON-TEAL, RITA F.
Educator. **Personal:** Born Apr 26, 1949, Memphis, TN; children: Rashel, Janette & Teal. **Educ:** Tenn State Univ, BS, 1971; Univ Mich, MA, 1973; Ed D; Memphis State Univ1989. **Career:** Argonne Lab Argonne IL, stud trainee, 1971; Rust Col Holly Springs, MS, math instr, tutor, 1973-75; Lincoln Lab Lexington MA, vis scientist, 1974; LeMoyne-Owen Col Memphis, math instr, 1975-78; dir Spec Serv, Upward Bound & Learning Resource Ctr. **Orgs:** Coord Dual-Degree Eng Prog, 1977-80; chairperson, Greek Letter Comn, 1978-80; mem, Cult & Ath Comm Rust Col; Freshman Comt, Orientation Comt, Acad Standing Comt, Acad Task Force Cluster Coop Ed Delta Sigma Theta; Delta Sigma Theta; Alpha Kappa Mu, Beta Kappa Chi; Kappa Delta Pi; vpres, TN Assoc Spec Prog, 1983-85; chairperson, Delta Sigma Theta Scholar Comt, 1984-85; reg chairperson, Southeastern Assoc Ed Opportunity Prog Personnel SAEOPP Annual Conf, 1985; pres, Tenn Asn Spec Prog, 1985-87; chmn, SAEOPP Scholarship Comt, 1986-87; chmn, SAEOPP Constitution Comt, 1985-87; secy, SAEOPP, 1987. **Business Addr:** Director of Special Services, LeMoyne-Owen College, 807 Walker Ave, Memphis, TN 38126.

JACOB, JOHN EDWARD
Executive. **Personal:** Born Dec 16, 1934, Trout, LA; son of Emory and Claudia Sadler; married Barbara May Singleton, Mar 28, 1959; children: Sheryl Rene. **Educ:** Howard Univ, BA, 1957, MSW, 1963. **Career:** US Post off, parcel post sorting mach oper, 1958-60; Baltimore City Dept Pub Welfare, caseworker, 1960-63, child welfare case work suprv, 1963-65; Wash Urban League, dir ed & youth incentives, 1965-66, branch off dir, 1966-67, assoc exec dir admin, 1967-68, actg exec dir, 1968-70, spec lectr, 1968-69; Howard Univ Sch Social Work, spec lectr, 1968-69; Wash Urban League, dir soc work field work stud unit, 1968-70; Eastern Reg Nat Urban League, dir com org training, 1970; San Diego Urban League, exec dir, 1970-75; Wash Urban League, pres, 1975-79; Nat Urban League, exec vpres, 1979-81, pres & chief exec officer, 1982-94; Anheuser-Busch Cos Inc, bd dirs, 1990-2006, exec vpres global commun & chief communs officer, 1994-2006; Morgan Stanley, bd dir; Coca-Cola Enterprises Inc, bd dir; LTV Corp, bd dir; NY NEX New York, bd dir; Continental Corp, bd dir; Nat Westminster Bancorp, bd dir; Howard Univ, chmn emer; Edward Jones, mem investment policy adv comt, currently. **Orgs:** Kappa Alpha Psi, 1954; Nat Assoc Social Workers, 1961-; consult, Nat Coun Negro Women, 1967-69, Nat Urban League, 1968-69; chmn bd trustees, Howard Univ, 1971-78, chmn, 1988; consult, Timely Investment Club, 1972-75; Judicial Nominating Comt DC, 1976-79; dir, Local Initiatives Support Corp, 1980-; Advertisement Review Bd, 1980-83; adv comt mem, NY Hosp, 1980-83; dir A Better Chance, 1980-83; dir, NY Found 1982-85; corp dir, NY Telephone Co, 1983-; dir, Nat Conf Christians & Jews, 1983-88; Rockefeller Univ Coun, 1983-88; chmn, Emer Bd trustees Howard Univ; Legal Aid Soc; Drucker Found; Nat Conf Bd; Econ Policy Inst; Nat Parks Found & Local Initiatives Support Corp. **Honors/Awds:** Whitney M Young Award, Wash Urban League Inc 1979; Special Citation Atlanta Club Howard Univ Alumni Asn, 1980; Atty Hudson L Lavell Soc Action Award, Phi Beta Sigma, 1982; Exemplary Service Award, Alumni Club Long Island Howard Univ, 1983; Achievement Award, Zeta Phi Beta, 1984, Cleveland Alumni Chap Kappa Alpha Psi, 1984; Alumni Achievement Award, Alpha Psi Atlanta Club Howard Univ, 1984; Nat Kappaman Achievement Durham Alumni Chapter Kappa, 1984; Black book's Bus & Professional Award, Dollars & Sense Mag, 1985; Achievement Award, Peoria Alumni Chap Kappa Alpha Psi,1985; Forrester B Washington Award, Atlanta Univ Sch Social Work, 1986; United Way of America's Nat Professional Leadership Award, 1989. **Military Serv:** AUS, reserve capt, 1957-65; Airborne Parachutist Badge, 1958. **Home Addr:** 2409 Wexford Woods Ct, St Louis, MO 63131. **Business Addr:** Member Investment Policy Advisory Committee, Edward Jones, 12555 Manchester Rd, St Louis, MO 63131, **Business Phone:** (314)515-2000.

JACOBS, DR. DANIEL WESLEY, SR.
Clergy, administrator. **Personal:** Born Aug 26, 1933, Aragon, GA; son of Daniel Lott (deceased) and Fannie Lou Cosby Jacobs Pannell (deceased); married Mary Louise Jenkins, Jun 4, 1955; children: Daniel Jr, Reginald Eugene & Dana Michelle. **Educ:** Morris Brown Col, BA, 1951-55; Turner Theol Seminary, MDiv, 1959-62; Emory Univ, PhD, 1965-67; Columbia Theol Seminary, 1987-. **Career:** Clergy, Administrator (Retired); E Atlanta Dist, AME Church, presiding elder, 1971-72; Allen Temple, AME Church, pastor, 1972-77; St James AME Church, pastor, 1977-80; Steward Chapel AME Church, pastor, 1980-82; St Mark AME Church, pastor, 1982-85; Turner Theol Seminary, dean, pres, 1985. **Orgs:** Pres, Atlanta AME Ministers Union, 1970; pres, Deans coun, Interdenominational Theol Ctr; prs, Columbus Phenix City Ministers Alliance, 1978-80; housing comn chmn, Atlanta NAACP, 1973-77; sec elect, Christian Counsel Metropolitan Atlanta, 1977. **Honors/Awds:** Doctor of Divinity Degree, Faith Col, 1984; Doctor of Divinity Degree, Payne Theol Seminary, 1986; Excellence in Leadership, Columbus Phenix City Ministers Alliance, 1979; Distinguished Alumnus, Turner Theol Seminary, 1986; Excellence in Theol Educ, Turner Stud Fellowship, 1987. **Home Addr:** 440 Dartmouth Dr SW, Atlanta, GA 30331.

JACOBS, DANNY ODELL
Educator, chairperson, physician. **Personal:** Born Sep 7, 1954, Camden, AR; son of Felix and Helen; divorced; children: Nia & Daniel. **Educ:** Harvard Univ, AB, 1975; Wash Univ, MD, 1979; Harvard Sch Pub Health, MPH, 1989. **Career:** Harvard Med Sch, asst prof surg, 1989-92, assoc prof surg, 1993-; Brigham & Women's Hosp, physician mem, nutrition support, 1992-95, sr surgeon, 1993-, assoc prog dir, clin res, 1995-98, dir, metabolic support svcs, dir, lab surg metab; Creighton Univ Sch Med, Omaha, NE, chmn & Arnold W Lempka Distinguished Prof Surg; Duke Univ Health System, Dept Surgery, chair, 2003-, David C Sabiston Jr prof, currently. **Orgs:** Am Soc Parenteral & Enteral Nutrition, 1987-; Soc Univ Surgeons, 1990-; Asn Acad Surg, 1991-; Am Col Sugeons, fel, 1992-; Soc Black Acad Surgeons, 1992-; Soc Surg Alimentary Tract, 1994-; New England Surg Soc, 1994-; Soc Critical Care Med, 1994-. **Honors/Awds:** Association for Academic Surgery, Residents Research Award, 1983; Univ of Pen, Jonathan Rhoads Surgery Resident Award, 1985; Greater Boston YMCA, Black Achievement Award, 1990; American Society Parenteral Nutrition, Stanley Audrick Research Scholar Award, 1990; Brigham & Womens Hospital, Matson Award for Training, 1993; Robert Wood Johnson Minority Medical Faculty Development Award, 1989; Stanley Dudrick Research Scholar Award, 1990. **Special Achievements:** Over 100 publications. **Business Addr:** Chair, David C Sabiston Jr Professor, Duke University Health System, Department of Surgery, DUMC 3704, Durham, NC 27710, **Business Phone:** (919)681-3445.

JACOBS, ENNIS LEON
Lawyer. **Personal:** Born Jan 19, 1954, Tampa, FL; son of Ennis Sr and Vetta; married Ruth, Aug 15, 1976; children: Bron & Jasmine. **Educ:** Fla A&M Univ, BS, Magna Cum Laude, tech, 1976; Fla State Univ Col Law, JD, 1986. **Career:** Eastman Kodak Co, syst analyst, 1976-80; RCA Corp, syst rep, 1980-82; Fla Pub Serv Comn, staff atty, 1986-89; Fla Atty Gen, staff atty, 1989-91; Fla Sen, staff atty, 1991-93; Fla Legis House, staff atty, 1993-; Fla Pub Serv Comn, 1998-; Williams Jacobs & Assoc LLC, atty, currently. **Orgs:** Pres bd, Tallahassee Habitat Humanity; Nat Bar Asn; Am Bar Asn; Leon County Guardian Ad Litem. **Special Achievements:** Author, "State Regulation of Information Services," Barrister, ABA Young Lawyers Division, Spring 1991. **Business Phone:** (850)222-1246.

JACOBS, REV. GREGORY ALEXANDER
Clergy, lawyer. **Personal:** Born Mar 10, 1952, Bilwaskarma, Nicaragua; son of Solomon N and Lynette G; married Beverly C Jacobs, Sep 30, 1978; children: Charlotte Elizabeth & Stephanie Nicole. **Educ:** Princeton Univ, AB, 1974; Columbia Univ Sch Law, JD, 1977; Bexley Hall Divinity Sch, MDiv, 1995. **Career:** Thompson Hine & Flory, partner; St Philip's Episcopal Church, vicar; Diocese Ohio, bishop's asst, 1999-2001; Trinity Episcopal Cathedral, Canon Mission & Ministry, currently. **Orgs:** Bd dirs, Minority Contractors Assistance Prog, 1985-97; bd dirs, trustee, Diocese Ohio, Episcopal, 1989-94; African-Am Archives Auxiliary, 1990-95; area bd dirs, Society Bank, 1990-95; convenor, Black Episcopal Seminarians, 1991-95; chair, United Negro Col Fund Foundations, 1991-95; Diocesan Coun, 1996-99; bd dir, Inter Act Cleveland, 1999-; adv bd, West Side Ecumenical Ministry, 2001-. **Home Addr:** 3330 Elsmere Rd, Shaker Heights, OH 44120, **Home Phone:** (216)991-5176. **Business Phone:** (216)774-0409.

JACOBS, HAZEL A.
Manager, government official. **Personal:** Born Sep 25, 1948, Blakely, GA; daughter of Leamon and Pearlia Jewell; married Claude, Jul 24, 1970. **Educ:** Ga State Univ, BS, 1982, MPA, 1986. **Career:** City Atlanta, GA, admin asst, 1970-71, 1973-74, office mgr, 1974-78, legis policy analyst, 1978-; Atlanta Charter Comn, admin asst, 1971-73, dir res policy anal; Adv bd, Fulton county, currently. **Orgs:** Am Asn Pub Admin, 1984-; Nat Asn Prof Women, 1985-; Nat Forum Black Pub Admin, 1985-.

JACOBS, LARRY BEN
Chemical engineer, clergy. **Personal:** Born Dec 15, 1959, Arlington, GA; son of Mattie C Jackson and Tommy L; married Carolyn Laverne Malone, Nov 24, 1984; children: Matthew, Leah, Christopher. **Educ:** Tuskegee Inst, Cert 1980, BS, chem, 1984. **Career:** Int Paper Co, co-op engr, 1980; Procter & Gamble, co-op engr, 1982; Weyerhaeuser Co, prof intern, 1984-86; Hercules Inc, process engr, 1986-88; Gen Elect Co, Burkville, AL prod engr 1988-91; Hoechst Celanese Corp, Salisbury, NC, develop engr, 1991-; Charlotte, NC, bus reengr, 1992-96, activity base cost coordr, 1996-97; BP, sr chem engr, 1997-; First Decatur AME Zion Church, pastor, 1998-. **Orgs:** AIChE, 1980-86; assoc mem, Tech Asn Pulp & Paper Indus, 1980-86; steward & choir president Turner Chapel AME Church, 1984-86; educ chmn, Columbus MS Coalition Black Orgn, 1985-86; corresp, The Jackson Advocate, 1986; toastmaster, Toastmaster's Int, 1986-; math tutor, Asbury UM Church, 1987; secy, Tuskegee Univ Eng Alumni Asn, 1988-; Soldiers Memorial AMEZ Church Steward, 1991-; Salisbury, NC sch adv chair, 1992-93; bd dirs, Rowan Co, NC Red Cross, 1994-; adv bd, City Salisbury, 1994-; vpres, Leadership Roman, 1997; First Decatur Mission AMEZ Church, pastor, 1997-; secy, Decatur Many Develop Asn, 1999-; pres, Decatur Ministerial Network, 2001. **Honors/Awds:** "Down Route 82" Manuscript "The Jackson Advocate" 1986; Best Speaker & Best Evaluator RAAP Toastmasters Club 1986-87; NCA Gov Volunteer Award, 1992. **Military Serv:** USAF, Reserves, airman First class, 3 yrs; Armed Forces Comm & Electronics Assoc Citation, Cert Merit. **Business Addr:** Pastor, First Decatur A M E Zion Church, 106 11th Ave NW 303D Beltline Pl, PO Box 301, Decatur, AL 35603, **Business Phone:** (256)340-9100.*

JACOBS, PATRICIA DIANNE
Executive, lawyer. **Personal:** Born Jan 27, 1950, Camden, AR; daughter of Felix H and Helen M Tate; divorced; children: Branden Kemiah, Brittne Katelyn-Helen, Bradley Kareem-Felix. **Educ:** Lincoln Univ, BA, 1970; Harvard Law Sch, JD, 1973. **Career:** Lincoln Univ, asst dir financial aid, 1970; Exxon Corp, legal assoc, 1973-75; John Jay Col Criminal Justice, asst prof, 1974-75; Lincoln Univ, dir & trustee, 1983-; K-Com Micrographics Inc, pres. **Orgs:** asst min coun, US Senate Small Bus Comt, 1975-77; pres, Am Asn MESBICS Inc, 1977-83; dir, Wider Opportunities Women, 1983-; dir, Coop Assistance Fund, 1983-. **Honors/Awds:** Regional Atty Advocate Small Bus, DC Small Bus Admin, 1982; Lincoln Alumni Award, Lincoln Univ, 1981; Woman Owned Bus Enterprise Award, US Dept Transp, 1987; Alumni Achievement Award, Lincoln Univ, 1990. **Special Achievements:** Under 30 Achievement Award, Black Enterprise, 1978. *

JACOBS, REGINA
Track and field athlete. **Personal:** Born Sep 28, 1963, Los Angeles, CA; daughter of Cecilia Jacobs; married Tom Craig. **Educ:** Stanford Univ, BA, 1990; Univ CA-Berkeley, MBA, 1992. **Career:** Track & Field Athlete (retired); Middle & long-distance track athlete. **Orgs:** Researcher, Inst Study Sport & Soc. **Honors/Awds:** Sixth World Championships Athletics, Athens, silvermedal, 1997; WorldChampionships, Sevilla, silvermedal, 1999. **Special Achievements:** First woman to break the 4-minute barrier, 2003; set a world record in the indoor 1500 m with a time of 3:59.58, becoming the first woman to break 4minutes in the event. *

JACOBS, SYLVIA MARIE
Educator. **Personal:** Born Oct 27, 1946, Mansfield, OH; daughter of Murval Aletha Cansler Jacobs Porch and Love Jacobs; married Levell Exum, Jun 20, 1980; children: Levell Rickie Exum & Sylvia Agnes Jacobs Exum. **Educ:** Wayne State Univ, Detroit, MI, BS, 1969, MBA, 1972; Howard Univ, Wash, DC, PhD, 1975.

Career: McKerrow Elem Sch, Detroit, MI, teacher, 1969-72; Fed City Col, Wash, DC, vis lectr, 1973; Univ Ariz, Pine Bluff, AR, asst prof, 1975-76; NC Cent Univ, Durham, NC, assoc prof, 1976-82, prof, 1982-, dept chair, 1992-99; Univ NC, Chapel Hill, vis prof, 1982; Univ Fla, Gainesville, NEH, seminar leader, 1988. **Orgs:** Delta Sigma Theta, 1968-; African Studies Asn, 1976-; co-convener, Southeastern Regional Sem African Studies, 1983-87; nat dir, 1984-88, co-publications dir, 1995-97, Asn Black Women Historians; Nat Coun Negro Women Inc, 1985-; Southern Poverty Law Ctr, 1985-; Comt Status Minority Historians & Minority Hist, Orgn Am Historians, 1987-90; NAACP, 1987-; exec coun, mem, Asn Study African Am Life & Hist ASALH, 1995-; Orgn Am Historians; Am Historical Asn. **Honors/Awds:** Letitia Brown Memorial Publication Prize, Asn Black Women Historians, 1984, 1992; Distinguished Achievement Award, Howard Univ Alumni Club, 1985; Lorraine A Williams Leadership Award, ABWH, 1997; Mary McLeod Bethune Service Award, ASALH, 1997; John Blassingame Award, 2006. **Special Achievements:** Editor, works include: Black Americans & Missionary Movement in Africa, 1982; 36 articles, 1975-01; 9 book reviews, 1975-01; author: The African Nexus: Black American Perspectives on the European Partitioning of Africa, 1981; Carter G. Woodson Medallion, 2006. **Home Addr:** 4109 Cobscook Dr, Durham, NC 27707, **Home Phone:** (919)493-1024. **Business Addr:** Professor, Director of Undergraduate Studies, North Carolina Central University, Department of History, 204 Edmonds Class Rm Bldg, Durham, NC 27707, **Business Phone:** (919)530-7932.

JACOBS, TIM
Football player. **Personal:** Born Apr 5, 1970, Washington, DC; married Valerie, Jun 29, 1997; children: Taylor Arden. **Educ:** Delaware Univ. **Career:** Football player(retired), Cleveland Browns, corner back, 1993-95; Miami Dolphins, defensive back, 1996-97.

JACOX, KENDYL (KENDYL LAMARC JACOX)
Football player. **Personal:** Born Jun 10, 1975, Dallas, TX. **Educ:** Kans State Univ, soc sci. **Career:** San Diego Chargers, guard, 1998-01; New Orleans Saints, guard, 2002-05; Miami Dolphins, guard, 2006; free agent, currently. **Honors/Awds:** All-Big 12 hons, 1997. **Special Achievements:** Selected to play in E W Shrine All-Star game, 1998. *

JACOX, KENDYL LAMARC. See JACOX, KENDYL.

JACQUES, CORNELL
Executive. **Personal:** Born Jul 12, 1949, Detroit, MI; son of Hernando and Hazel J; married Elaine Tribble, Aug 31, 1974; children: Monique S. **Educ:** Journeyman Air Traffic Controller, 1979; Mercer Univ, BBA, 1980. **Career:** Federal Aviation Admin, Journeyman Air Traffic Controller, 1974-81; Central Vending Co., route supvr, 1983-85; Lockheed IMS, resident parking consult, 1985-86; City Detroit, parking comn coordr, 1986-88; Lockheed Martin IMS, consult, asst vpres, 1989-91, munic serv vpres, 1991-94, regional vpres, 1995; ACS State & Local Solutions Inc, regional vp, currently. **Orgs:** Int Parking Inst, 1985-; Nat Forum Black Pub Admin, 1992-; Kappa Alpha Psi Fraternity, 1968-. **Honors/Awds:** Special Achievement Award, Federal Aviation Admin, 1980; IMS President's Awd, 1999. **Military Serv:** US Air Force, sgt, 1969-73. **Business Addr:** Regional Vice President, ACS State & Local Solutions Inc, 2828 N Haskell, Dallas, TX 75204, **Business Phone:** (214)841-6111.

JACQUET, NATE
Football player. **Personal:** Born Sep 2, 1975, Duarte, CA. **Educ:** Mt San Antonio Col; San Diego State Univ. **Career:** Indianapolis Colts, wide receiver, 1997; Miami Dolphins, wide receiver, 1998-99; San Diego Chargers, wide receiver, 2000; Minn Vikings, wide receiver, 2001; Carolina Panthers, wide receiver, 2002; Chicago Bears, wide receiver, currently. **Honors/Awds:** Rookie of the year, 1997.

JAGGERS, GARLAND
Social worker, writer. **Personal:** Born Mar 24, 1933, Detroit, MI; son of Bennie and Garland; divorced; children: Howard Robinson, Leslie Moorer, Dr Kim Jaggers & Melanie Jaggers. **Educ:** Wayne State Univ, BA, 1957, MSW, 1962. **Career:** Univ Detroit, adj prof; Creative Strategies Inc, chief exec officer, 1968-; Nat Black United Fund, exec dir, 1982-84; Community Case Mgt, interim dir; Proctor Publ LLC, author, currently. Author: Black Arts Magazine, 1967; To The Poet in You, 1981; Activate Your Leadership, 1981; Fog: An Analysis of Catholic Dogma, 1999. **Orgs:** Chmn bd, Mich Black United Fund, 1972-83. **Military Serv:** AUS, PFC, 1957-59. **Home Addr:** 1739 Canton St, Detroit, MI 48207, **Home Phone:** (313)923-5085. **Business Addr:** Author, c/o Proctor Publications LLC, 1832 Midvale St, PO Box 2498, Ypsilanti, MI 48197, **Business Phone:** (734)480-9900.

JAKES, T D. See JAKES, BISHOP THOMAS DEXTER.

JAKES, BISHOP THOMAS DEXTER (T D JAKES)
Clergy, playwright, writer. **Personal:** Born Jun 9, 1957, South Charleston, WV; son of Ernest Sr and Odith Jakes; married Serita Ann Jamison, Jan 1, 1981; children: Jamar, Jermaine, Cora, Sarah & Thomas Dexter Jr. **Educ:** Ctr Bus Col, attended 1972; W Va State Col, attended 1976; Friends Univ, BA, MA, 1990, doctorate ministry, 1995. **Career:** Greater Emmanuel Temple of Faith, pastor, 1979-96; radio ministry, "The Master's Plan," 1982-85; television show, "Get Ready," 1993-98; TD Jakes Ministries, 1994-; The Potter's House, pastor, 1998-; The Potter's House of Dallas Inc, founding pastor, chief exec officer, 2002-; author, T D Jakes Ministries, owner, currently. **Honors/Awds:** Gospel Heritage Award for Ministry, 1996; Stellar Found, Excellence Award, 1996; Gospel Music Asn, Dove Seal, for Woman, Thou Art Loosed: Songs Healing & Deliverance, 1997; Grammy & Dove Award nominations, Outstanding Contemporary Gospel Album, for Live at Potter's House, 1999; named one Top Five Religions Innovators, CNN & Time Magazine, 2001; named one of the 56 Most Intriguing Blacks, Ebony, 2001; Grammy & Dove Award nominations, Outstanding Contemporary Gospel Album, for Storm Is Over, 2002; Stellar & NAACP Image Awards for Outstanding Gospel Album, 2002; Chmn's Award, Nat Religious Broadcasters, 2002. **Special Achievements:** Author: Woman, Thou Art Loosed, 1993; Naked and Not Ashamed, 1995; The Harvest, 1995; Can You Stand to Be Blessed?, 1995; Daddy Loves His Girls, 1996; Help! I'm Raising My Children Alone, 1996; Lay Aside the Weight, 1997; The Lady, Her Lover, and Her Lord, 1998; Maximize the Moment: God's Action Plan for Your Life, 2000 (reached No 3 on NY Times Business Best Sellers List); Experiencing Jesus: God's Spiritual Workmanship in the Beleiver, 2000; The Great Investment: Faith, Family, and Finance, 2001; God's Leading Lady, 2002 (reached No 4 on NY Times Hardcover Best Sellers List); Co-author: Behind Closed Doors, Gospel play, 2000; produced Sacred Love Songs CD (named one of yr's top Gospel Albums, Billboard, 1999); Woman Thou Art Loosed stage production reached No 1, Gospel Play Honors, 1999; recognized by Time magazine as "America's Best Preacher," 2001; created Dexterity Sounds music label in collarboration with EMI Gospel, 2001.

JAM, JIMMY (JAMES HARRIS, III)
Music producer, songwriter, executive. **Personal:** Born Jun 6, 1959, Minneapolis, MN; married Lisa Padilla; children: Tyler James, Maximillian Lee & Isabella B. **Career:** Flyte Tyme Prods Inc, co-producer & songwriter, currently. **Honors/Awds:** American Music Award, Best R&B Single, 1986; Grammy Award, Producer of the Year, 1986; Best Dance Recording, 2001; Academy Award, 1993; Essence Award, 2002. **Business Addr:** Co-Producer, Flyte Tyme Productions Inc, 4100 W 76th St, PO Box 398045, Edina, MN 55435, **Business Phone:** (952)897-3901.

JAMAL, AHMAD
Artist, composer. **Personal:** Born Jul 2, 1930, Pittsburgh, PA; divorced; children: Sumayah. **Career:** George Hudson Orchestra touring 1940s, jazz pianist; Four Strings, player, 1950; Caldwells, accompanist, 1951; formed own trio, 1951; Okeh Recs, Cadet Recs, rec contract; performer: Jazz Alley Downtown Seattle; Georges Chicago; Joe Segals Jazz Showcase; Voyager West St Louis; Ethyl's Place; Fairmont Hotels; Cricket Theater Hennepin Ctr; Apollo Theatre Town Hall; Rainbow Grill (Waldorf Astoria); The Embers; Village Gate; Iridium; The Village Vanguard; "Digital Works", "Rossiter Rd", "Live at the Montreal Jazz Festival", Atlantic Recs; Ellora Mgt, musician, currently; albums: All of You; Jamal Plays Jamal; At The Penthouse; Extension; The Awakening; Freelight; Naked City Theme; One; Digital Works; Crystal; Pittsburgh; Chicago Revisited; Live in Paris '92; Ahmad's Blues; Poinciana; Telarc Recording Artist; I Remember Duke, Hoagy & Strayhorn, 1995; Chicago Revisited, 1994; Birdology Distributed by Polygram, "Live In Paris"; 1994; The Essence, Part 1, 1996; The Essence, Part 2, 1997; Nature, The Essence Part III; 1998 Atlantic; Birdology, "Olympia 2000," 2000; Recordings: "Waltz for Debby", 1980; Birdology: "Live in Paris", 1992, 1996; "Big Byrd", 1996; " In Search Of", 2003; "After Fajar", 2005. **Honors/Awds:** Am Jazz Masters Award, NEA, 1994; Djangod 'Or Award, 1996; Arts & Culture Recognition Award, 2001; Am Jazz Hall of Fame, NJ Jazz Soc, 2003; Gold Medallion, 2004. **Special Achievements:** Only artist to have an LP in the album top ten of nat charts for 108 consecutive weeks But Not For Me, performed 2 years with Philip Morris Tour around the world: Berne Jazz Festival 1989, Pittsburgh, 1990, 1996, performing at the Umbria Jazz Fesitval in Italy, also in Finland, Blues Alley in Georgetown, The Blackhawk, Yoshi's in San Francisco/Oakland, "Crystal", Hal Leonard Publications has published The Ahmad Jamal Collection of a collection of piano transcriptions. **Business Addr:** Musician, Ellora Management, 11 Brook St, PO Box 755, Lakeville, CT 06039, **Business Phone:** (860)435-1305.

JAMERSON, JOHN W
Dentist. **Personal:** Born Apr 26, 1951, Savannag, GA; son of JW, Jr and Dorothy Breaux; married Sheanon Brown, Dec 28, 1978; children: Desiree Maria, Elizabeth Rene, Amanda Louise, JW IV, Charles Martin Breaux & Amelia Morgan. **Educ:** Morris Brown Col; Savannah State Univ, BS, 1974; Howard Univ, DDS, 1980. **Career:** Westside Comprehensive Health Ctr, dentist, 1980-82; pvt pract, dentist, 1982-. **Orgs:** Vpres, bd dir, King-Tisdell Found, 1987-89, 1991-93; Dept Family & C Serv, 1994-, vpres, bd dir, 1997-2000, pres, 1999-; Ga Dent Asn, 1996-; Southeast Dist Dent Soc, 1999-; fel Acad Dent Int, 1999; St Matthews Episcopal Church, 1999-; fel Int Col Dent, 2000; hon fel, Ga Dent Asn, 2000. **Honors/Awds:** Man of The Year, Alpha Phi Alpha Fraternity Inc, 1974, 1986, 1993. **Business Addr:** Dentist, John W Jamerson III, 315 E Henry St, Savannah, GA 31401, **Business Phone:** (912)232-6171.

JAMES, ADVERGUS DELL
School administrator. **Personal:** Born Sep 24, 1944, Garden City, KS; son of Advergus D Sr and Helen Lee; married Anna Flave Glenn; children: Anthony David & Adam Glen. **Educ:** Langston Univ, BS, 1966; Okla State Univ, MS, 1969. **Career:** Langston Univ, asst registr, 1966-69; Langston Univ, dir admis & record,1969-70; Prairie View A&M Univ, dir, 1970-85, dir admis & financial aid,1986-88, dir financial aid, 1988-98, Stud Financial Serv, exec dir financial serv, 1998; Tuskegee Univ, Stud Financial Serv, dir, currently. **Orgs:** Consult, State Stud Financial Asst Training, 1979-80; pres, Tex Asn Stud Financial Aid Admin, 1981-82; Tex Guaranteed Stud Loan Adv Bd, 1984-86;Nat Coun Stud Financial Aid Admin, 1985-86; bd dirs, Depelcin Ctr, 1986;adv bd, Outstanding Rural Scholars, 1990-; bd dir, Adv Comt, Greater E Tex Higher Educ Authority, 1995-; bd dirs, Tex Asn Stud Financial Aid Admin;bd dir, Greater Tex Found; Tex Higher Educ Coord; Alpha Phi Alpha Fraternity; charter mem, Prairie View Optimist Club. **Honors/Awds:** Distinguished Alumni Award, Nat Asn Equal Opportunity, 1991; Top Administrator, Prairie View A&M Univ, 1992-93. **Home Addr:** 7611 Hertfordshire Dr, Spring, TX 77379. **Business Addr:** Director of Financial Aid Department, Tuskegee University, PO Box 830659, Tuskegee, AL 36083-0659, **Business Phone:** (334)727-8746.

JAMES, ALEXANDER, JR.
Executive. **Personal:** Born Nov 2, 1933, Branchville, SC; married Dorothy Jones; children: Audrey D, Gregory A & Kevin ES. **Educ:** City Col NY, BE, 1961; NY Univ, Grad Eng, MSEE, 1963, Grad Bus Admin, MBA, 1986. **Career:** Bell Tele Lab, engr, 1961-68; Mkt Monitor Data Inc, oper mgr, 1968-69; EF Shelley & Co Mgt Cons, sr vpres, 1969-75; Citibank NA, vpres, 1975-82; Group 88 Inc, sr vpres. **Orgs:** Inst Elec & Electronics Engr; Am Mgt Asn; bd dir, Group 88 Inc Consult; bd dir, Urban Home Ownership Corp; chmn trustees, Pilgrim Baptist Church; commnr, Middletown Twp Human Rights Comm, 1976-80; Nat Black MBA Assoc, 1984. **Honors/Awds:** Community Achievement Award, Nat Asn Negro Bus & Prof Women's Clubs, 1978. **Military Serv:** AUS, splist 2nd cl, 1953-55. **Home Addr:** 11 Sir Paul Ct, Middletown, NJ 07748-3542. **Business Addr:** Senior Vice President, Group 88 Inc, 1 Penn Plz Fl 29, New York, NY 10119, **Business Phone:** (212)239-8899.*

JAMES, DR. ALLIX BLEDSOE
College administrator, clergy. **Personal:** Born Dec 17, 1922, Marshall, TX; son of Samuel Horace James Sr and Tannie E; married Susie B Nickens; children: Alvan Bosworth & Portia V. **Educ:** VA Union Univ, AB, 1944, MDiv, 1946; Union Theol Sem, ThM, 1949, ThD, 1957; Univ Richmond, LLD, 1971; St Paul's Col, DD, 1981. **Career:** Third Union Baptist Church, minister; Mt Zion Baptist Church, minister; Union Zion Baptist Church, minister; Va Union Univ, instr biblical studies, 1947-50, dean students, 1950-56, dean sch theol, 1956-70, vpres, 1960-70, pres, 1970-79, pres emer, 1979-85, 1990-, chancellor, 1985-93. **Orgs:** Bd dir, Nat Exec Bd, Nat Conf Christians & Jews Inc; co-founder, pres & bd dir, Richmond Gold Bowl Sponsors; bd dir, Nat Coun Am First Freedom; pres & bd trustees, Black Hist Mus & Cult Ctr Va Inc; educ task force chmn, Richmond Tommorrow; founder, chmn & bd dir, Leadership Round table; bd dir,Va Elec & Power Co; bd dir, Consolidated Bank & Trust Co; Univ Adv Coun, Am Coun Life Ins; bd dir, Beekne Investment Co Inc; Alpha Phi Alpha Fraternity; Sigma Pi Phi Fraternity Inc; Alpha Beta Boule; bd trustee, Moore St Baptist Church; bd dir, Va Ctr Inclusive Communities; hon bd mem, Bells for Peace. **Honors/Awds:** Outstanding Achievement Award, Beta Gamma Lambda Chap, Alpha Phi Alpha, 1981; Good Government Award, Richmond First Club, 1985; MF Manuel Community Service Award, Metrop Bus League, 1991; Exemplary Vision Award, Full wood Foods Inc, 1992; The Shirley A Hart Award, Int Ministers Wives Asn, 1992; Community Appreciation Dinner honoree, 1994; UNCF Flame Bearer of Education Award, 1997; Excellence in Leadership Award, VA Power Strong Men & Women, 2000; Citation, Liberian Asn & Gye Nyame Ministries, 2001. **Special Achievements:** First African-American to serve as president of Virginia State Board of Education; Association of Theological Schools in the US; National Conference of Christians and Jews, Virginia Region; first African-American chairman, Richmond Planning Commission; Board of trustees, Virginia Union University named the restored University Chapel in Coburn Hall, The AllixB James Chapel, 1992; guest of the Government of Republic of Taiwan to explore possibilities for educational cooperation, 1976; conferences with European theological educators from Germany, Switzerland, Italy, France and England, 1969; study of higher education in USSR, 1973; contributing editor, The Continuing Quest; author: Calling a Pastor in a Baptist Church; Three Score and Ten Plus: The Pilgrimage of an African-American Educator, 1922-27; numerous articles, local & national publications & professional journals. **Home Addr:** 2956 Hathaway Rd Suite 302, Richmond, VA 23225, **Home Phone:** (804)320-3655. **Business Addr:** President Emeritus, Va Union University, 1500 N Lombardy St, Richmond, VA 23220, **Business Phone:** (804)257-5600.

JAMES, ANTHONY R
Executive. **Personal:** Born in Lake Alfred, FL. **Educ:** Polk Community Col, AA, eng, 1970; Univ S Fla, BS, elec eng, 1973. **Career:** Executive (retired); Procter & Gamble Co, elec & instrumentation mgr, prod dept mgr, resident engr; NASA Kennedy Space Ctr, eng asst; Southern Co, Ga Power Co, maintenance supt, cent cluster mgr, safety & health supvr, 1978, Southern Co Servs, safety & health supvr, bd mem, African Am ceo, exec vpres, Savannah Elec & Power, vpres power generation & sr prod officer, 2000-01, chmn, pres & ceo, 2001-04, Southern Co Servs, exec vpres, 2005-08, Shared Servs Group, pres, 2005-08. **Orgs:** Bd mem, Southeastern Elec Exchange; Rotary Club Savannah; Am Asn Blacks; Ash Tree Orgn; Ga Chamber Com; Prof Asn Ga Educrs; Savannah Econ Develop Authority; Boy Scouts Am, Coastal Empire Coun Inc; Asn Edison Illuminating Co Chambers Com; Edison Elec Inst Chambers Com; 100 Black Men Savannah. **Honors/Awds:** Black Engineer of the Year, Career Commun, 2004. **Special Achievements:** co-author, The Shoulders of Giants; only black CEO in the Southern network; one of the "50 Most Important Blacks in Technology," Career Commun, 2005.

JAMES, ARMINTA SUSAN. See Obituaries section.

JAMES, DR. BETTY HARRIS
Educator. **Personal:** Born Jun 21, 1932, Gadsden, AL; daughter of William and Mary Etta Wacasey; married Joseph E (deceased); children: Cecilia Denise James Joyce, Tyrone Michael & Tyshaun Michele. **Educ:** Univ Pitts, BS Educ, MEd, 1971, PhD, 1974; Marshall Univ, MA, 1976. **Career:** WV St Col, prof educ, 1974-84, spec asst pres, 1981-84; Livingstone Col, assoc vpres, acad affairs, 1984-86; Appalachia Educ Lab, dir, regional liaison ctr, 1986-. **Orgs:** Pres, Charleston Br Nat Asn Advan Colored People, 1979-81; Comm Coun Job Corps, 1979-; consult, WV Human Rights Commn, 1980-; Phi Lambda Theta Hon Soc, Kappa Delta Phi. **Honors/Awds:** Danforth Asn, 1976; Fac Meritorious Service Award, WVa St Col, 1977; Meritorious Service Livingstone Col Stud Govt, 1985. **Business Addr:** Director, Appalachia Educational Laboratory, 1031 Quarrier St Atlas Bldg, PO Box 1348, Charleston, WV 25301, **Business Phone:** (304)347-0400.

JAMES, DR. BETTY NOWLIN
Executive director, administrator. **Personal:** Born Feb 16, 1936, Athens, GA; married Lewis Francis; children: Beth Marie Morris & Dewey Douglas Morris III. **Educ:** Fisk Univ, BA, 1956; Univ Houston, MEd, 1969, EdD, 1975. **Career:** Houston Ind Sch Dist, teacher & music specialist, 1958-71, fed prog asst, 1972-74, assoc dir res & eval, 1975-76; Univ Houston, Downtown, coord instr planning & eval, 1976-80, dir inst res, 1980-83, dir inst serv, 1983-; Tex Higher Educ Coord Bd, Access & Equity Div, asst comnr, 2000; Alpha Kappa Alpha Sorority Inc, exec dir, 1999-. **Orgs:** Phi Delta Kappa Res Fraternity, 1976-; allocations rev panel, United Way, 1983-; worksite coordr, Tenneci Inc Cities Sch Pro, 1984; top black achiever award comt mem, Human Enrichment Life Prog, 1985-; Black Achiever Selection Comt Chair, Riverside Gen Hosp, 1986; exec bd, Houston YWCA, UNCF, Patterson Awards Comt UNCF. **Honors/Awds:** Top Worksite Award, Tenneco Inc, 1984; Outstanding Woman Award, Univ Houston-Downtown Houston, YWCA Bd, 1985; HELP Outstanding Black Achiever Award, Human Enrichment Life, 1985. **Business Addr:** Executive Director, Alpha Kappa Alpha Sorority Inc, 5656 S Stony Island Ave, Chicago, IL 60637, **Business Phone:** (773)684-1282.

JAMES, CARRIE HOUSER
Educator. **Personal:** Born Nov 6, 1949, Orangeburg, SC; daughter of Alfred Houser Sr and Lula Bell Riley; divorced; children: Gabrielle DeAnna, Claudia Michelle & Louis Maxx. **Educ:** Univ SC, Columbia, SC, BSN, 1971; Catholic Univ Am, Wash, DC, MSN, 1974; SC State Col, Orangeburg, SC, 1990; Univ SC, Columbia, SC. **Career:** C Hosp Nat Med Ctr, Wash, DC, clin specialist, 1974-76; Univ SC-Col Nursing, Columbia, SC, instr, 1976-78; Richland Mem Hosp, Columbia, SC, dir nursing, C Hosp, 1977-84; SC State Univ, Orangeburg, SC, asst prof, 1984-; Edisto Health District, Orangeburg, SC, consult, child birth educator, 1986-89; Reg Med Ctr, Orangeburg, SC, relief staff nurse-pt, 1988-96, child birth educ & LCHS health educ, 2000-; Low Country Healthy Start/TRMC, perinatal health educator, 2003-04; Low Country Healthy Start, perinatal health educator, 2004-. **Orgs:** Sec, Orangeburg County, Ambulance Comt, 1987-; recorder, SACS steering comt, SC State Col, 1988-90; treas, SC Nurses Found, 1988-93; pres, SC Nurses Asn, 1990-94; Congress Econ, Am Nurses Asn, 1990-94; Maternal, Infant, Child Health Coun SC, 1990-98; Alliance 2020 Leadership Team, 1992-; chair, Constituent Assembly, ANA, 1994-96; ANA; ANA'S Ctr Ethics & Human Rights, 1994-97; pioneer nurse, Tri County Black Nurses Asn, 1995; Delta Sigma Theta, Inc 1999-; bd dir, Orangeburg County First Steps, 2000-; Tri-County Comn Alcohol & Drug Abuse, 2000-04; LLR Bd Nursing, 2004-07; pres-elect, Ctr Am Nurses; moderator, Community Adv Panel Albemarle Coop-Orangeburg Plant, 2004; Am Cancer Soc, Community Action Team & Relay Life Planning Comt Orangeburg County. **Honors/Awds:** Five Year Service Pin, Richland Mem Hosp, 1982; Excellence in Education, Edisto, District Nurses Asn, 1989; appreciation certificate, Howard Sch Pub Health & Brigham & Women's Hosp, 1989-99; Outstanding Nursing Alumni, USC Col Nursing, 1995; Twenty Year Service, SC State Univ, 2003; President's Award, SCNA, 2002. **Special Achievements:** Founder & facilitator for Celebrations, a support group for African Graduate of Leadership South Carolina, 1992; American Women who are breast cancer survivors, 2000; Graduate of Leadership Orangeburg County, 2004. **Business Addr:** Assistant Professor of Nursing, South Carolina State University, 1890 Res & Exten, PO Box 7336, Orangeburg, SC 29117, **Business Phone:** (803)536-8465.

JAMES, CHARLES HOWELL, II
Executive. **Personal:** Born Nov 22, 1930, Charleston, WV; married Lucia Jeanette Bacote; children: Sheila, Stephanie, Charles III, Sarah. **Educ:** Univ Pa, Wharton Sch Finance & Com, BS, 1953; WVa State Col. **Career:** Retired; James Produce Co, salesman, 1956-60; James Produce Co, secy treas, 1961-63; James Produce Co, sec treas & gen mgr, 1963-67; James Produce Co, pres & gen mgr, 1967-72; C H James & Co, pres chmn, 1972-91; The James CRP, chmn & chief exec officer, 1981; W Va State Col, special adv pres, 1992-96, vip admin, 1994. **Orgs:** bd trustees, United Fund Kanawha Valley, 1967-75; commr & sec bd Kanawha Int Airport Auth, 1969-79; bd trustees, First Bapt Ch, 1969-98; Rotary Club Charleston 1970-; bd dir, Buckskin Coun BSA, 1970-73; bd dir, Charleston C C; dist adv coun, Small Bus Admin, 1971-89; bd dir, Indust adv coun OIC's Am, 1972-; Sire Archon, 1974; chmn Mayor's Com on Interstate Understructure Charleston, 1973; vpres Mountain State Businessmen's Asn WV, 1974-75; pres Alpha Iota Lambda Chap, 1974-76; chmn, Charleston C C FFA Ham Bacon & Egg Show; US C C; Assoc WVa Asn Retail Grocers; bd dir, Charston Progress Asn Econ Devel; life mem Alpha Phi Alpha Frat; Upsilon Boule Sigma Pi Phi Frat; life mem, Nat Asn Advan Colored People. **Honors/Awds:** Hon soc Beta Gamma Sigma; Cent WV Airport Authority award, Air transp syst WV, 1969-79; US SBA MNY Small BUS Person of the Year, WV Dist & Philadelphia Region, 1984; Future Farmers Am Hon Farmer, 1975; Charleston BUS & Professional Men's Club Businessman of the year, 1983; OIC Corporate Support award, 1984; Kanawha County WV Famous Person award, 1988; Bus Leadership award, Alpha Phi Alpha Midwestern Region, 1989; PRSial award, WV State Col, 1990. **Special Achievements:** Top 100 businessmen, Black Enterprise Mag, 1974-90. **Military Serv:** USAF capt 1953-56. **Business Addr:** Chairman, Cheif Executive Officer, The James Corporation, Charleston, WV 25314.*

JAMES, CHARLES L.
Educator. **Personal:** Born Apr 12, 1934, Poughkeepsie, NY; married Rose Jane Fisher; children: Sheilah Ellen & Terri Lynn. **Educ:** State Univ NY New Paltz, BS, 1961; State Univ NY Albany, MA, 1969. **Career:** Spackenkill Sch Poughkeepsie NY, elem teacher eng, 1961-67; Dutchess CommCol Poughkeepsie NY, instr eng, 1967-69; State Univ NY Oneonta NY, asst prof & assoc prof, 1969-73; post grad fel Yale Univ Danforth Found, 1971-72; Swarthmore col, assoc prof, 1973; Swarthmore col, prof & chmn, prof emer currently; Clare Hall Col, Eng, vis assoc prof, 1981; Eugene M Lang Fac, fel, 1984-85; George Becker Fac, fel, 1992-93; Sara Lawrence Lightfoot, prof emer, 1997. **Orgs:** Am Asn Univ Prof; Modern Lang Asn; Col Lang Asn. **Honors/Awds:** Summer seminar National Endowment for the Humanities, 1978; National Endowment for Humanities, 1990. **Special Achievements:** Author: "The Black Writer in Am" Albany State University New york 1969; From the Roots: Short Stories by Black Americans; Harper and Row, 1975. **Military Serv:** AUS sgt 1955-57. **Business Addr:** Professor Emeritus, Swarthmore College, Department English Literature, 500 College Ave, Swarthmore, PA 19081, **Business Phone:** (610)328-8000.

JAMES, CHARLES LESLIE
Insurance executive. **Personal:** Born Sep 23, 1939, Montecello, AR; son of Mamie James; married Elaine James, Mar 16, 1966. **Educ:** Am Col Life Underwriters, CLU, 1969; Sacramento City Col, AA, 1970; San Francisco State Univ, BS, 1981. **Career:** Golden State Mutual Life Ins Co, vpres, 1961-; Mirador Diversified Servs Inc, bd dirs. **Orgs:** Life Underwriters Asn Los Angeles, 1981-; Soc Fellow Lime Mgt, 1981-; Soc Chartered Life Underwriters, 1989; Black Agenda, vpres, 1989; YMCA Los Angeles, 1989; Hugh O'Brian Youth Found, adv bd, 1990; Los Angeles County Sheriff Found, 1989 & 1993. **Honors/Awds:** Certificate of Appreciation, County Los Angeles, 1990; Appreciation & Recognition, Los Angeles County Sheriff's Dept, 1992. **Special Achievements:** Hall of Fame, John C Fremont High School, 1993. **Home Addr:** 3652 Kensley Dr, Inglewood, CA 90305, **Home Phone:** (310)677-4017. **Business Addr:** Vice President, Golden State Mutual Life Ins Co, 1999 W Adams Blvd, Los Angeles, CA 90018, **Business Phone:** (213)731-1131.*

JAMES, CHERYL
Rap musician. **Personal:** Born Mar 8, 1964, Brooklyn, NY; married Gavin Wray, Dec 24, 2000; children: 2. **Educ:** Queensborough Community Col. **Career:** Films: Stay Tuned, 1992; Who's the Man?, 1993; Raw Nerve, 1999; TV series: "Sisters in the Name of Rap", 1992; "Saturday Night Live", 1994; "The John Larroquette Show", 1994; "3rd Annual VH1 Hip-Hop Honors", 2006; Sears Roebuck & Co, telephone customer-serv rep, 1985; Salt-N-Pepa, mem group, 1985-; Albums: Hot, Cool & Vicious, 1986; A Salt with a Deadly Pepa, 1989; Blacks' Magic, 1990; A Blitz of Salt-N-Pepa, 1991; Juice, 1992; Brand New, 1998; For Our Children; Concert, contributor, 1993; GavFam Music Inc, owner. **Honors/Awds:** Ablum "Push It," gold single, 1988; A Salt with a Deadly Pepa, gold, 1988; Hot, Cool & Vicious, platinum, 1988; Nat Acad Rec Arts & Sci, Grammy Award nomination, rap category, 1989. **Special Achievements:** Ranked No 83 on VH1's 100 Greatest Women of Rock N Roll. *

JAMES, CLARENCE L., JR.
Executive. **Personal:** Born Oct 13, 1933, Los Angeles, CA; son of Clarence and Marguerite; married Patricia Douglas; children: Clarence III, Craig. **Educ:** John Muir Col, AA, 1952; OH State Univ, BS, 1956; Cleveland State Univ, JD, 1962; Case Western Reserve Univ, pub mgt science certificate, 1968. **Career:** Cleveland Legal Aid Soc, civil dir 1964-68; City of Cleveland, Dir of Law & Dep Mayor 1968-71; James Moore & Douglas, attorney-at-law, 1971-77, chmn; State of OH, atty general 1972-77; US Copyright Royality Tribunal, chmn, comm, 1977-81; The Keefe Co, vpres Domestic Affairs & General Coun, 1981-83; govt relations & pub affairs firm, 1983-95; Manatt Phelps & Phillips, partner, 1995-. **Orgs:** Pres Law School Alumni Assoc, 1970-71; overseers Cleveland Marshall Col of Law, 1970-77; v pres, Legal Aid Soc of Cleveland, 1972-73; Trustee Cleveland Bar Assoc, 1972-75; dep state coord, CA Carter & Mondale Pres Campaign, 1976; state coord, NJ DeRose for Governor campaign, 1977. **Honors/Awds:** Chamber of Commerce Awd, 1969. **Business Addr:** Partner, Manatt Phelps & Phillips, 1 Metro Ctr, 700 12th St NW Suite 1100, Washington, DC 20005-4075.*

JAMES, DANIEL, III
Air Force officer. **Personal:** Son of Daniel "Chappie" Jr (deceased) and Dorothy Watkins (deceased); married Dana. **Educ:** Univ Ariz, Tucson, BA, psychol, 1968; Air Command & Staff Col, 1981; Nat Security Mgt Course, 1992. **Career:** Airforce officer (retired); Cam Ranh Bay Air Base, South Vietnam, forward air controller, 1969-70; Williams AFB, Ariz, squadron instr pilot, 1970-72, squadron flight training class comdr, 1972-73; Headquarters USAF, Washington, DC, air opers staff officer, 1973; Udorn Royal Thai Air Force Base, Thailand, squadron asst flight comdr, 1974-75; Nellis Air Force Base, Nev, squadron pilot, 1975-76, squadron flight comdr, 1976-78; Kelly Air Force Base, 149th Tactical Fighter Group, TX, weapons tactics officer, 1978-79, 182nd Tactical Fighter Squadron, group pilot, unit pilot, 1979-82, unit comdr, 1982-83, comdr, 1983-88, C flight, pilot, 1988-89, 149th Tactical Fighter Group, command post asst officer-in-charge, command post officer-in-charge, 1989-92, 149th Tactical Fighter Wing, vice comdr, 1992-94, 149th Opers Group, comdr, 1994-95; Headquarters Tex Nat Guard, Austin, adj gen, 1995-02; Air Nat Guard, Arlington, Va, dir, 2002-06. **Orgs:** Chmn, Greater Austin Qual Coun, 1998-99; bd dirs, Greater Austin Chamber Com. **Honors/Awds:** Garvey-Woodson Award, Black United Fund Tex, 1995; Outstanding Service Award, Texas STARBASE Exec Adv Bd, 1995-1996; Benjamin D. Foulois First Flight Award, Air Force Asn, Tex, 1997; Central Texas Combined Federal Campaign Community Service Award, 1997-98; Honored Patriot Award, Selective Serv Syst, 1998 & 1999; Commendation for Military Service, Joint Session Tex Legislature, 1999; The Palmetto Patriot Award, SC, 1999. Distinguished Achievement Award, Tuskegee Airmen Nat Hist Mus, 2003. **Special Achievements:** "Military-State Partnerships: A Winning Relationship for All," National Guard Review, 1997. **Military Serv:** USAF, 1968-06; Distinguished Service Medal, Legion of Merit, Distinguished Flying Cross, Meritorious Service Medal, Air Medal with silver and bronze oak leaf clusters, Air Force Commendation Medal, Air Force Achievement Medal, Presidential Unit Citation, Air Force Outstanding Unit Award, Combat Readiness Medal, National Defense Service Medal with two bronze stars, Vietnam Service Medal with four bronze stars, Global War on Terrorism Service Medal, Air Force Longevity Service Award Ribbon with silver and three bronze oak leaf clusters, Armed Forces Reserve Medal with gold hourglass, Small Arms Expert Marksmanship Ribbon, Air Force Training Ribbon, Vietnam Gallantry Cross with silver star, Republic of Vietnam Campaign Medal. *

JAMES, DARRYL FARRAR
Clergy. **Personal:** Born Jul 3, 1954, Bridgeport, CT; son of Laurayne and Anthony Francis Sr. **Educ:** Howard Univ, BA, 1976; Interdominational Theol Ctr, MA, 1977; Yale Divinity Sch, MDiv, 1979. **Career:** Trinity Cathedral, lay assistant to dean, 1979-81; St Matthew's & St Joseph's, assistant priest, 1981-85; Messiah-St Bartholomew Episcopal Church, rector, 1985-. **Orgs:** Nat bd mem, Project Equality Inc; African Male Cms; Aids Task Force; Cms Ministry, 1988-91; past pres, Howard Univ Alumni, Chicago Chap, 1990; Cathedral Shelter, 1986-90; Urban Strategy Cms, 1989; Interfaith Coun Homeless, 1979; Kappa Alpha Psi, Chicago Alumni Chap. **Honors/Awds:** Scholarship, Yale Divinity Sch, 1977; Alpha Kappa Alpha Monarch Award, 1994; Chicago Alumni Achievement Award, Kappa Alpha Psi. **Business Addr:** The Reverend, Messiah St Bartholomew Episcopal Church, 8255 S Dante Ave, Chicago, IL 60619, **Business Phone:** (312)721-3232.*

JAMES, DAVA PAULETTE
School administrator, counselor. **Personal:** Born in Sharon, PA. **Educ:** Westminster Col, BA, 1974; Hampton Inst, MA, 1978; Iowa State Univ, PhD, 1985. **Career:** Hampton Inst, grad asst women's div, 1976-78; Slippery Rock State Col, asst dir admis-

sions, 1978-79; Youngstown State Univ, acad adv, 1980-85; Marshalltown Community Col, Iowa Valley Community Col Dist, prof, counr & adv, currently. **Orgs:** Nat Acad Advising Asn; vpres, Nat Asn Negro Bus & Prof Women's Clubs Ohio Valley Club; bd mem, Nat Asn Advan Colored People; Urban League. **Honors/Awds:** Outstanding Young Women of America, listed in 1982; cert & trophy Meritorious Vol United Negro Col Fund Youngstown Area Campaign, 1982-85. **Business Addr:** Professor, Counselor, Advisor, Marshalltown Community College, Iowa Valley Community Col Dist, 3700 S Ctr St, Marshalltown, IA 50158.

JAMES, DR. DAVID PHILLIP
Educator, consultant. **Personal:** Born Sep 2, 1940, Greenville, NC; son of John Oscar and Lula Forbes; married Janie Russell; children: Lauren Nicole & Joi Melissa. **Educ:** Elizabeth City State Univ, NC, BS, 1962; Georgetown Univ, Wash, DC,MA, 1971; Nova Univ, Fort Lauderdale, FL, EdD, retention & supporting-fields, 1978. **Career:** Pittsburgh County, NC, teacher & coach, 1962-63; Clarke Col, VA, socialsci teacher & coach, 1963-67; Pub Schs, Wash, DC, social sci teacher &coach, 1967-71; Prince George's Community Col, educ admin, 1971-, deaneduc develop degree & exten centers & spec progs, currently; part-timeconsult, self-employed, 1978-. **Orgs:** Nat Coun Community Serv & Continued Educ, 1973-; Adult Educ Asn, 1978-; Am Asn Higher Educ, 1982; pres, Int Mentoring Asn, 1989-; Student Retention. **Honors/Awds:** Numerous awards and honors including Hon Grad, Elizabeth City State Col,NC, 1962; Outstanding Teacher of the Year, Washington, DC Pub Sch, 1971;Phi Alpha Theta Int Award, Georgetown Univ, 1971; OutstandingAdministrator Award, Prince George Community Col, 1988; Honorary MentionRecipient, Md Asn Higher Educ Outstanding Educator, 1989. **Special Achievements:** First Black Associate Dean, Prince George's Community Col, 1979; Authored,"Black Issues in Higher Education", 1988, "Increasing the Retention Rates of Black & Minority Students Through Mentoring & Tutorial Services at Prince George's Community College", 1989. **Home Addr:** 5007 Satan Wood Dr, Columbia, MD 21044.

JAMES, DION
Baseball player. **Personal:** Born Nov 9, 1962, Philadelphia, PA. **Career:** Baseball player (retired); Milwaukee Brewers, outfielder, 1983-85; Atlanta Braves, outfielder, 1987-89; Cleveland Indians, 1989-90; NY Yankees, 1992-93, 1995-96; Chunichi dragons, 1994. **Honors/Awds:** Rookie of the Yr, 1984. *

JAMES, DONNA ANITA
Executive, president (organization). **Personal:** Born Jun 30, 1957; married Larry; children: Christopher Michael, Justin Michael. **Educ:** NC A&T, accounting, 1979. **Career:** Executive (retired); Coopers & Lybrand, Columbus, OH, auditor, 1979-81; Nationwide, Columbus, OH, various accounting positions, 1981-90, Opers & Treas Servs, dir, 1990-93, exec asst to Nationwide chief exec officer & chmn, 1993-96, Human Resources Div, vpres, 1996-98, sr vpres, chief human resources officer, 1998-2000, exec vpres, chief admin officer, 2000-2003; Nationwide Strategic Investments, Columbus, OH, president, 2004; Lardon Assocs, pres, 2006-. **Orgs:** NC A&T, exec adv coun; bd mem, Am Foreign Servs; bd mem, Intimate Brands Inc; bd mem, Ohio Col Access Network; Columbus Chapt Links; AICPA. **Honors/Awds:** Women of Achievement, YWCA, 1999; Spirit of Advocacy, DeVry, 2001; Diversity Award, Working Mother Mag, 2001. **Special Achievements:** First African-American woman president of Nationwide Strategic Investments. *

JAMES, ELDRIDGE M.
Educator. **Personal:** Born Mar 23, 1942, Eunice, LA; married Betty Lea Stewart; children: Rona La Ne & Heath Elridge Floront. **Educ:** Grambling State Univ, BS, 1966; Wayne State Univ, MEd, 1969; Mich State Univ, PhD, 1973. **Career:** Ford Motor Co, supvr, 1966-68; CJ Miller Elem Sch; Great Lakes Steel Corp, dir educ, 1968-70; Ecorse HS, teacher, 1968-70; Great Lakes Steel Corp, indus instr, 1969-70; Mich State Univ, grad asst, 1972; Grambling State Univ, assoc prof, 1973-74; Quachia Parish Bd Educ, asst prof & clin prof, 1974-; NE LA Univ, mem grad fac, asst prof sec & coun educ, 1975-76. **Orgs:** La Indust Arts Asn; Am Vocat Asn; La Asn Pub Sch Adult Edn; So Asn Counr Educ & Supervision; La State Reading Coun; Asn Supr & Curriculum Develop; Phi Delta Kappa; Scottish Rite Mason King Solomon's Lodge; Omega Psi Phi. **Special Achievements:** Wrote several articles & books for Grambling College; Dean's list of outstanding graduates Michigan State University. **Military Serv:** USN, 1960-62. **Business Addr:** Assistant Professor, Northeast Louisiana University, Sec Coun Educ, Monroe, LA 71202.

JAMES, EUGENIA H
Government official. **Personal:** Born Feb 23, 1954, Chicago, IL; daughter of John and Gladys Ward; divorced; children: Jeneena Eugenia. **Educ:** Worsham Col Mortuary Sci, cert, 1974. **Career:** AA Rayner & Sons Funeral Home, mortician, 1974-77; City Dallas, ct opers, 1983-88, jail opers mgr, 1988-90, purchasing agent, 1990-96, asst dir human servs, 1996-. **Orgs:** Chair, Nat Inst Govt Purchasing, 1993-95; bd mem, Ex-Offico, Dallas Youth Servs Corp, 1996; Nat Forum Black Pub Adminrs; Nat Asn Purchasing Mgrs; Am Pub Works Asn. **Business Addr:** Assistant Director, Department of Environmental and Health Services, City of Dallas, 1500 Marilla St, Dallas, TX 75201, **Business Phone:** (214)670-5113.

JAMES, DR. FELIX
Clergy, educator. **Personal:** Born Nov 17, 1937, Hurtsboro, AL; son of Leroy Sr and Blanche Clark; married Florence Bernard, Aug 7, 1985. **Educ:** Fort Valley State Col, GA, BS, 1962; Howard Univ, DC, MA, 1967; Ohio State Univ, Columbus, PhD, 1972; New Orleans Baptist Theol Seminary, New Orleans, MA, christian educ, 1991. **Career:** Columbia Pub Sch, SC, instr social studies, 1962-64; Howard Univ, DC, reserve book librarian, 1965-67; Tuskegee Inst, instr hist, 1967-70; Southern Ill Univ, Carbondale, asst prof hist, 1972-74; Southern Univ New Orleans, chmn hist dept, 1974-75, prof hist, 1979-; Salvation Baptist Church, pastor, moderator; Mt Zion Miss Baptist, assoc, currently. **Orgs:** State dir, Asn Study Afro-Am Life & Hist, 1973-, co-chair prog comm, 1979-80, exec bd; New Orleans Martin Luther King Steering Comm, 1977-; fac coun, Southern Univ New Orleans, 1980-85; vice-chair arrangement comm, ASBS Annual Meeting New Orleans, 1983; exec bd, La Hist Asn, 1984-86; adv bd, Annual City-Wide Black Heritage Celebration, 1985-; comnr, New Orleans Bicentennial Comm, 1987-91; consult, Ethnic Minorities Cult Ctr, Univ N Iowa, 1988; sr warden, DeGruy Lodge, Prince Hall Free & Accepted Masons, 1989; bd dir, S Christian Leadership Conf, 1983-; worshipful master, DeGruy Lodge No 7, Prince Hall Free & Accepted Masons, 1991-; Illustrious Comman Kadosh, Eureka Consistory, No 7-Masons. **Special Achievements:** Author of books like: The American Addition: History of a Black Community, Univ Press of America, 1978; contributor to Dict of Amer Negro Biography, 1982, Dict of Louisiana Biography, 1986, Black Leadership in the 20th Century, 1989, Edn of the Black Adult in the US, 1989, and Twentieth Century Black Leaders, 1989. **Business Addr:** Professor, Southern University at New Orleans, Department of Arts and Humanities, Bldg 29B 6801 Press Dr, New Orleans, LA 70126, **Business Phone:** (504)286-5154.

JAMES, FRANK SAMUEL, III
Lawyer. **Personal:** Born Aug 10, 1945, Mobile, AL; son of Frank S Jr; married Jothany Dianne Williams; children: David RF, Jothany Michelle, Julia Dianne. **Educ:** Campbell Col, BS, 1973; Univ AL, JD, 1978; US Army War Col, grad, 1990. **Career:** Fed Judge Virgil Pittman, law clerk, 1978-80; US Dept Justice, asst us atty, 1980-86; Univ AL Sch Law, prof, asst dean, 1986-90; Berkowitz, Lefkovits, Isom & Kushner, Partner, atty, 1990-. **Orgs:** Am Bar Asn, 1978-, AL State Bar, 1978-, Birmingham Bar Asn, 1980-; Bd YMCA Metro Birmingham, 1996-; coun Synod Mid South, 1985-86; moderator, mem coun Birmingham Presbytery, 1986; pres bd, 1988-90, chmn bd, 1991-, Alabama Capital Representation Resource Ctr, 1991-; dir, Columbia Theol Sem, 1991-99; trustee, Farrah Law Soc, 1990-; trustee, The Presbytery Sheppards & Lapsley, 1990-98. **Honors/Awds:** Author Contingent Fees Domestic Relations Actions, 3 Jour Legal Prof 209, 1978; elected to bench & bar, Legal Hon Soc, 1978; author with Charles W. Gamble, Perspectives on the Evidence Law of Alabama: A Decade Evolution 1977-87, 40 Alabama Law Review 95, 1988; author, "Protecting Final Judgments: A Critical Overview Provisional Injunctive Relief Alabama," 20 Cumberland Law Review 227, 1990; Distinguished Alumnus, Campbell Univ, 1987. **Military Serv:** AUS, Reserve, Colonel, 1965-95; Bronze Star, Air Medal, Purple Heart, Army Commendation Medal, Meritorious Service Medal, Army Achievement Medal, Combat Infantryman's Badge, AUS Infantry Officer Candidate Hall Fame, 1991. **Business Addr:** Attorney, Partner, Berkowitz, Lefkovits, Isom & Kushner, SouthTrust Tower 420 N 20th St Suite 1600, Birmingham, AL 35203, **Business Phone:** (205)250-8317.*

JAMES, FREDERICK C.
Bishop. **Personal:** Born Apr 7, 1922, Prosperity, SC; married Theressa Gregg. **Educ:** Allen Univ, BA, 1943; Howard Univ, MDiv, 1947. **Career:** AME Episcopal Church, ordained ministry; Friendship AME Church Irmo SC, pastor, 1945; Mem AME Church Columbia SC, bishop, 1946; Wayman AME Church Winnsboro SC, bishop, 1947-50; Chappelle Mem AME Church Columbia SC, bishop, 1950-53; Mt Pisgah AME Church Sumter SC, bishop, 1953-72; AME Church Dallas, bishop, 1972-. **Orgs:** Bd dir, Greater Little Rock Urban League; chmn bd, Shorter Col; founder, Mt Pisgah Apts, Sumter, James Ctr, maseru, Lesotho, Mem Nat Interfaith Comt Fund Open Soc Dem Clubs; Odd Fels, Masons, Shriners; dean Dickerson Theol Sem, 1949-53; pres, Sumter br NAACP, 1959-72; World Conf Church & Soc Geneva, 1966; chmn, Wateree Community Actions Agency, 1969-72; bishop Botswana, Lesotho, Swaziland, Mozambique, South Africa, Namibia, 1972-76; presiding bishop, AR OK, 1976-; chmn, Comn Missions AME Church, 1976-; Nat Coun Church Christ USA, 1979-; hon consult, gen representing Lesotho AR & OK, 1979-; deleg, World Meth Coun Honolulu, 1981; secy, AME Coun Bishops, 1981; Bd Trustees, Allen Univ. **Business Addr:** Bishop, African Methodist Episcopal Church, 604 Locust St, North Little Rock, AR 72114.

JAMES, FREDERICK JOHN
Lawyer. **Personal:** Born Sep 1, 1938, Chicago, IL; son of John Henry and Frances Harris; married Barbara L Penny; children: Frederick J & Edward A. **Educ:** Univ Chicago, attended 1958; San Francisco State Col, BA, 1968; UC Berkeley Grad Sch Bus, MBA, 1972; UC Berkeley Boalt Hall Sch Law, JD, 1973. **Career:** Wells Fargo Bank, field auditor, 1964-66; Del Monte Corp, mgt trainee, 1966-68; Ctr Real Estate & Urban Econs, res asst, 1970; Law Off Hiawatha Roberts, law clerk, atty, 1972-74; Law Off Frederick J James, atty, 1974-; Calif State Univ, lectr, 1976; sole practitioner, currently. **Orgs:** Treas, Black MBA Asn, Berkeley, CA, 1973; bd mem, Men Tomorrow, 1977; bd, mem/legal coun, Northern Calif Black C C & Oakland Alameda Co Black Chamber Com, 1978-; bd mem, Comnrs Oakland Housing Authority, 1983-89; pres, Alameda Co Dem Lawyers, 1986; Charles Houston Bar Asn; Nat Bar Asn; Am Bar Asn. **Honors/Awds:** Academic Scholarship, Univ Chicago, 1955-58; Certificate of Recognition for Legal Services to Poor, Charles Houston Bar Asn, 1979; Certificate of Appreciation for Writing Judicare, Grant Proposal, 1979. **Military Serv:** AUS, e-4, 1962-64. **Business Addr:** Attorney, Law Office of Frederick James, 7717 Edgewater Dr Suite 130, Oakland, CA 94621, **Business Phone:** (510)839-5708.

JAMES, GERRY M
Executive. **Personal:** Born Mar 15, 1959, Little Rock, AR; son of Cleo Charles; married Darlene James, Aug 24, 1985; children: LaTasha, Gerry III & Danielle. **Educ:** Univ Ark, Pine Bluff; Chicago State Univ, Chicago IL, BS, bus mgt, 1979. **Career:** Johnson Prods Co, asst office mgr, 1978-83, distribr spec markets, sales mgr, 1983-86; Gillette Co, Lustrasilk, territory acct mgr, 1989-93; New York Life Ins Co, field underwriter, financial planner, 1986-89; JM Prod Inc, regional sales mgr, retail & prof, 1993-95; Ecoco Inc, nat sales mgr, vpres, sales & mkt, chief operating officer, 1995-. **Orgs:** Bd mem, Campaign for a Drug Free Westside. **Business Addr:** President, Chief Operating Officer, Ecoco Inc, 1830 N Lamon Ave, Chicago, IL 60639-4512, **Business Phone:** (773)745-7700.

JAMES, GILLETTE ORIEL
Clergy. **Personal:** Born May 5, 1935; son of Samuel and Ethlyn; married Rosa Vernita Ferguson; children: Jennifer. **Educ:** God's Bible Sch & Col, Cincinnati, AB, 1959; Univ San Francisco, BA, 1968; Am Baptist Sem W, MDiv, 1970, DMin, 1976; Oxford Univ, Eng. **Career:** Christian Union Church, WI, pastor, 1959-60; Western Union, tel rec, 1962-65; Grace Baptist Church, San Francisco, organizer & pastor, 1963-69; Beth Eden Baptist Church, Oakland, CA, asst pastor & minister christian educ, 1970-71, sr pastor, 1971-. **Orgs:** Dean, Baptist Ministers Union Oakland, 1971-85; pres, bd dirs, Social Serv Bur Oakland, 1976-79; vpres, Northern CA Credit Union, 1976-79; pres, Black Am Baptists Northern Calif, 1977-84; vpres, Black Am Baptists, 1985-90; exec secy, Calif State Baptist Conv, 1985-86; vpres, Baptist Ministers Union Oakland, 1986-; chmn, Community Earthquake Disaster Comt, 1989-91; Mayor's Earthquake Relief Fund, 1989-91; pres, Black Am Baptist, 1991-; exec comt mem, Western Comn Ministry, 1992-; trustee, Am Baptist Sem W, 1992-. **Honors/Awds:** Caliborne Hill Award, Am Baptist Sem W, 1970; Outstanding Immigrant Award, Int Inst E Bay, 1977; Distinguished Serv Award, Baptist Ministers Union Oakland, 1985; 4th Annual Black Clergy Award, Bayview Multipurpose Sr Serv. **Military Serv:** AUS, chaplain's asst, 1961-62; Good Conduct Medal, 1961, Rifle Marksman Medal, 1962. **Home Addr:** 2400 Havenscourt Blvd, Oakland, CA 94605. *

JAMES, HAWTHORNE
Entertainer. **Personal:** Born in Chicago, IL; son of John Copage and A M Alene. **Educ:** Univ Notre Dame, BA, 1974; Univ Mich, MA, 1975. **Career:** Films: Disco Godfather, 1979; Penitentiary II, 1982; The Color Purple,1985; I'm Gonna Git You Sucka, 1988; Patty Hearst, 1988; Ricky 1, 1988;Othello, 1989; The Color Purple; The Doors, 1991; The Five Heartbeats,1991; The Fresh Prince of Bel-Air, 1992; The Water Engine, 1992; TheHabitation of Dragons, 1992; Caroline at Midnight, 1994; I'm Gonna Get YouSucka; Speed, 1994; Se7en, 1995; Heaven's Prisoners, 1996; Sparks, 1997;Campfire Tales, 1997; Amistad, 1997; The Art of a Bullet, 1999; AuggieRose, 2000; Code Blue, 2000; Past Present, 2002; The Dist, 2003; Plant Oneon Me, 2004; Boss'n Up, 2005; Today You Die, 2005; The System Within,2006; Hood of Horror, 2006; Dir, The Stick Up Kids, 2008 TV Series: "Hill Street Blues", 1984-86;"What's Happening Now!", 1985-86; "Amazing Stories", 1986; "Cheers", 1987;Police Story: The Freeway Killings, 1987; The Water Engine, 1992; "TheFresh Prince of Bel-Air", 1992; The Habitation of Dragons, 1992; The Heartof Justice, 1992; "Frasier", 1993; "The Adventures of Brisco County Jr. ",1994; Martin, 1994; "The Good News", 1997; "Sparks", 1997; NYPD Blue,1998; "City of Angels", 2000; Roswell, 2001; "The District", 2003;"Charmed", 2002-04; "ER", 2004; "Carnivale", 2005; "Stargate SG-1", 2006. **Honors/Awds:** Los Angeles Drama-Logue Award, 1982 & 1989; Los Angeles Weekly Award,1987; Jury Prize, 2005; Winner, Ted Lange Ira Aldridge Actg Competition. **Business Phone:** (818)972-1747.

JAMES, HENRY CHARLES
Basketball player. **Personal:** Born Jul 29, 1965, Centreville, AL; married Carmen; children: 6. **Educ:** St Marys Univ, BS, comput sci. **Career:** Basketball player (retired); Spanish League, forward, 1988-89; CBA, Wichita Falls Texans, 1988-94; Cleveland Cavaliers, 1990-92, 1997-98; Scavolini Pesaro, Italy, 1992-93;

Utah Jazz, 1992-93; Sacramento Kings, 1993; Los Angeles Clippers, 1993-94; CBA, Sioux Falls Skyforce, 1994-96; Houston Rockets, 1995-96; Atlanta Hawks, 1996-97. **Honors/Awds:** All-League second team, CBA, 1993, 1996; All-League first team, CBA, 1994; Most Valuable Player, CBA Playoffs, 1996; CBA Championship, 1996.

JAMES, DR. HERBERT I
Scientist, manager. **Personal:** Born Mar 30, 1933, St Thomas, Virgin Islands of the United States; married Christine M Stolz; children: Herbert Jr & Robyn. **Educ:** Hampton Inst, BS; Clark Univ, MA, PhD; DB Hill Train Cs, ins broker; DB Hill Train Cs, investment broker; LaSalle Ext Univ, bus mgt. **Career:** DB Hill & Co, br mgr; DB Hill & Assoc, br mgr; Clark Univ, teacher asst; St Thomas HS, teacher; Exp Col VI, teacher; Hampton Inst, teacher; ESB Inc, res sci, 1965-76; Xerox Corp, scientist, 1976-80; personnel mgr, 1980-. **Orgs:** Electrochem Soc; AAAS; Instrument Soc Am; Beta Kappa Chi; Alpha Kappa Mu; NY Acad Sci; exec bd, Bucks Co Boy Scouts; bd dir, Freedom Valley Coun Girl Scouts; Nat Asn Advan Colored People; scholar, Hampton Inst. **Honors/Awds:** VI Public Affairs Award, 1965; JFK Library Minority Award; Presidential US Commendation Award. **Home Addr:** 49 Cumberland Dr, Mississauga, ON, Canada L5G 3N1, **Home Phone:** (416)278-6722. **Business Addr:** Manager, Xerox Corporation, Joseph C Wilson Center for Technology, Bldg 128 800 Phillips Rd, Webster, NY 14580, **Business Phone:** (585)423-5090.

JAMES, DR. HERMAN DELANO
School administrator, educator. **Personal:** Born Feb 25, 1943, St Thomas, VI; son of Henry James and Frances Smith James; married Marie Gray; children: Renee, Sybil & Sidney. **Educ:** Tuskegee Inst, BS, 1965; St Johns Univ, MA, 1967; Univ Pittsburgh, PhD, 1972. **Career:** Univ Pittsburgh, asst prof, 1971-72; Univ Mass, asst prof, 1972-78, assoc provost, 1975-76, asst chancellor, 1976-78; Calif St Univ, vice provost, 1978-82; Rowan Univ, vpres, 1982-84, pres, 1984-98, dir, 1990, distinguished prof, 1998-. **Orgs:** Cherry Hill Minority Civic Asn, 1982-84; bd mem, NJ Educ Computer Network, 1983-; chair-colleges, Gloucester County United Way, 1985; bd dirs, Am Asn State Cols & Univs; bd trustees, Middle States Asn; vice chair, Pres Coun, 1996; bd dirs, S Jersey Industs; bd dirs, NJ St Chamber Com; hon trustee, NJ Symphony Orchestra; Am Coun Educ Comn Leadership Dev; Labor/Higher Educ Forum; Am Coun Educ; adv comt, Am Asn St Cols & Univs; Camden Educ Alliance; bd trustees, NJ Futures; Martin Luther King Comn. **Honors/Awds:** Fellowship, NIH, 1968-71; Young Black Achiever, Boston YMCA, 1977; Outstanding Educator, Williamstown Civic Asn, 1984; Eileen Tosney Award, Am Asn Univ Adminr, 1994; Honorary Doctor of Laws, Tuskegee Univ, 1996. **Business Addr:** Distinguished Professor, Rowan University, 201 Mullica Hill Rd, Glassboro, NJ 08028.*

JAMES, JEROME KEITH
Basketball player. **Personal:** Born Nov 17, 1975, Tampa, FL; children: Jamarcus. **Educ:** Fla A&M Univ, pre law, 1998. **Career:** Sacramento Kings, ctr, 1998-2000; KK Buducnost Podgorica, Yugoslavia, 2001;Super Sonics, ctr, 2001-05; New York Knickerbockers, 2005-09; Chicago Bulls, 2009-. **Honors/Awds:** All-MEAC honoree, 1997-98. *

JAMES, DR. JIMMIE, JR.
College administrator. **Personal:** Born Jul 5, 1938, Hattiesburg, MS; son of Jimmie James, Sr and Annie M Rogers James; married Carrie Green, Jun 2, 1962; children: Michael Renwick. **Educ:** Jackson State Univ, BME, 1960; Roosevelt Univ, Chicago Musical Col, attended 1960; Univ Wisc, MS, 1966; Univ Southern Miss, PhD, 1973. **Career:** Earl Travillion High Sch, dir bands, 1959-66; Jackson State Univ, assoc dir bands, 1966-80, dir musical activities, 1980-83, chmn & prof, dept music, 1983-. **Orgs:** Phi Delta Kappa, 1980-2002; minister music, Pearl St AME Church, 1980-2002; nat talent hunt dir, Omega Psi Phi, 1990-94; connectional dir music, AME Church, 1992-2000; Gamma Boule, 1998-2000; sire archon elect, sire archon, 2001-02, Sigma Pi Phi; bd dirs, Jour Black Sacred Music. **Honors/Awds:** Named Evaluator, Nat Asn Schs Music, 1988; Distinguished President Award, Optimist Int, 1988-89; Lib Arts Spotlight on Scholars, Jackson State Univ, 1989; Distinguished Lt Governor Award, 1989-90; Scroll of Honor, Omega Psi, 1994. **Special Achievements:** Guilmant's Sonata in D Minor, Original Band Transcription, 1966; Methods and Perspectives of Urban Music Education, contributor, 1983; Organizing the Church Music Ministry for the 21st Century, 1989; Songs of Praise, contributor, 1998; Auth: Organizing the Church Music Ministry for the 21st Century; Co-Auth: The Mississippi Black Bankers & Their Institutions; Named Hon La State Rep; first African-American to receive Ph.D. degree from the Univ of Southern Mississippi. **Business Addr:** Chairman, Professor of Music, Jackson State University, Department of Music, 1400 J R Lynch St, PO Box 17055, Jackson, MS 39217, **Business Phone:** (601)979-2141.

JAMES, JOHN A
Executive, administrator. **Personal:** Born in Starkville, MS. **Educ:** MS Valley State Univ, BS, sociol; Univ Toledo, guid, 1965; Wayne State Univ, bus admin, 1969-72. **Career:** Chrysler Corp, Personnel & Labor Rels, 1969-78; James Group Int, chmn & chief exec oficer, currently. **Orgs:** Alpha Phi Alpha; Booker T Wash Bus Asn; 100 Black Men of Greater Detroit; bd dirs, Charles H Wright Mus African Am Hist; Dept Transp Adv Comn, Detroit, MI; bd dirs, Detroit Econ Growth Corp; bd dirs, Detroit-Wayne Co Port Authority; Econ Club Detroit; life mem, Nat Asn Advan Colored People; trustee, Hartford Baptist Church; Renaissance Club Detroit; bd mem, Wayne Co Econ Develop Corp; Minority Bus Develop Coun; Boys & Girls Clubs SE Mich; Detroit Regional Chamber; Nat Asn Black Automotive Suppliers. **Honors/Awds:** Citizen of the Year, Hartford Memorial Baptist Church, 1984; Minority Supplier of the Year, MI Minority Bus Develop Coun, 1985; Distinguished Minority Business Man of the Year, MI Dept Com, 1987; Corporate Man of the Year, Minority Women's Network, 1988; Minority Women's Network Man of the Year Award, 1988; Gold Pentastar Award, Chrysler Corp, 1993; Distinguished Alumni, MS Valley State Univ, 1993; Optimist of the Year, 1995; Business Hall of Fame Laureate for Junior Achievement of SE Michigan, 1996; Hank Aguirre Humanitarian Award, MMBDC, 1998; Ford Entrepreneurial Role Model, 1998; Michigan Entrepreneur of the Year for Service, Ernst Q Young, 1998; Ernst & Young Entrepreneur of the Year Finalist, Kauffman Ctr, 1998; Ford Q1 Award, Renaissance Global Logistics, 2001; GM Supplier of the Year, Elec Syst, JASCO, 2003-04; Visteon Facility PPM VQA Award, Motor City Logistics, 2003; GM Supplier of the Year. Motor City Express, 2006-07; Ford Manufacturing Excellence Award, Renaissance Global Logistics, 2006; Urban Wheels Award Supplier of the Year, 2007. **Special Achievements:** Top 100 Black Businesses, Black Enterprise Mag, 1995-98; inductee, Junior Achievement, SE MI Bus Hall of Fame, 1996. **Military Serv:** AUS, CEngr, Commissioned Officer, 1966-69, Bronze Star. **Business Addr:** Chairman, Chief Executive Officer, James Group International, 4335 W Fort St, Detroit, MI 48209, **Business Phone:** (313)841-0070.*

JAMES, JOSEPH J
Executive. **Personal:** Born in Glen Ridge, NJ. **Educ:** Union Col, Schenectady, NY, BS; NY Univ, attended. **Career:** Prince George's County Econ Develop Corp, pres & ceo; Corp Econ Opportunity, pres & ceo, curerntly; Mainstream Bus Enterprises LLC, managing mem, currently; SC Scientific Inc, pres & ceo, currently. **Orgs:** Am Asn Enterprise Zones; Int Econ Develop Coun; Southern Asn Utilization Biomass Resources; Int Coun Shopping Ctr; Am Tennis Asn. **Special Achievements:** First African American in his current position. **Business Addr:** President, Chief Executive Officer, Corporation for Economic Opportunity, 116 Wildewood Club Ct, Columbia, SC 29223, **Business Phone:** (803)462-0153.

JAMES, JUANITA T.
Publishing executive. **Personal:** Born Oct 1, 1952, Brooklyn, NY; daughter of Compton Carew and Nora Corlette; married Dudley Norman Williams Jr, Apr 9, 1988; children: Dudley Norman III. **Educ:** Princeton Univ, BA, 1974; Columbia Univ Grad Sch Bus, MBA, 1982. **Career:** Thomson-CSF Inc, purchasing agent, 1974-76; Time Life Books Inc, ed research, 1976-78, ed admin, 1978-81; Time Inc, financial analyst, 1981-83; Time Life Books Inc, vpres human resources, 1983-86; Time Life Libraries Inc, pres & chief exec officer, 1987-90; Book Month Club Inc, vpres & dir specialty clubs, 1990-92, sr vpres, ed, 1992-; Rouse Co, dir; Pitney Bowes Inc, vpres, Direct Mkt Strategy & Bus Develop, currently. **Orgs:** Nat Black MBA Asn, 1982-; Nat Urban League, 1982-; bd mem, The Green Door, 1984-88; trustee, Princeton Univ, 1984-; mem, Nat Coalition of 100 Black Women, 1986-; Black Women In Publishing; The Women's Media Group; Nat Asn Advan Colored People. **Honors/Awds:** Black Achievers Industry Award, Harlem YMCA, 1979; Andrew Heiskell Award Community Serv, Time Inc, 1982; Alumni Serv Award, Asn Black Princeton Alumni, 1988; Achievement Award, Greater New York chapter, Links Inc, 1988; Hall of Fame Award, Nat Asn Negro Bus & Prof Womens Clubs, 1990; Achievement Award, Corp Women's Network, 1994; Distinguished Service Award, Columbia Univ Grad Sch Bus. **Business Addr:** Vice President, Pitney Bowes Inc, 1 Elmcroft Rd, Stamford, CT 06926-0700.*

JAMES, KAY COLES
State government official, executive director. **Personal:** Born Jun 1, 1949, Portsmouth, VA; married Charles. **Educ:** Hampton Inst, Hampton, VA, BS, 1971. **Career:** NRLC, Wash, DC, dir pub affairs, White House Task Force Black Family, 1986-88; Nat Comn C, comnr, 1987; US Dept HHS, Wash, DC, asst secy pub affairs, 1989; One to One, Wash, DC, exec vpres, 1990, sr vpres & chief exec officer, 1991; White House Off Nat Drug Control Policy, assoc dir, 1991; Commonwealth Va, secy health & human resource, 1993; Family Res Coun, sr vpres, 1993; US Off Personnel Mgt, dir, 2001-; Joint Financial Mgt Improv Prog, chmn, 2004-. **Orgs:** Dir publ, Nat Right Life Comt, 1985; bd mem, Nat Comn C, 1988; bd dirs, Amerigroup Corp. **Special Achievements:** Publishes, Never Forget. **Business Addr:** Director, US Office of Personnel Management, 1900 E St NW, Washington, DC 20415-1000.*

JAMES, KEVIN PORTER
Administrator. **Personal:** Born Aug 2, 1964, Wichita, KS; son of James Jr and Alice Jean. **Educ:** Dodge City Community Col, AA, gen studies, commun technol, 1984; Univ Ariz, BA, radio TV, pub rels, 1988. **Career:** Univ Ariz, Luke Olson, men's basketball mgr, 1984-88; vpres event mgt serv, asst mgr, southwest region, 1988-90; Orlando Magic, Brian C Wiliams, mgr, 1991-; Fred L Slaughter, NBA scout, recruiter, 1992-. **Business Phone:** (303)256-0020.

JAMES, LAWRENCE W
Executive. **Personal:** Born May 15, 1956, Columbus, OH; son of Lois Belton James and Elijah Larry; married Adrienne C, Jun 17, 1978; children: Aaron Vincent & Brandon Michael. **Educ:** Wittenberg Univ, BA, 1978; Northwestern Univ, MBA, 1980. **Career:** Proctor & Gamble, asst brand mgr, 1980-83; Borden, product mgr, 1983-85; Ross Labs, mkt mgr, 1985-88; Lens Crafters, dir mkt, 1988-92; Primetime Mgt Inc, pres, 1992-94; Choice Care, dir spec health plan, 1994-96; Middletown Reg Health Syst, vpres, 1996; Ctr Multicultural Competence Healthcare Orgns pres, ceo, currently. **Orgs:** Middletown Action, 1996-2000; bd, Arts Middletown, 1997-99; Middletown Int, 1997-99; bd, Middletown Adolescent Leaders Achieve, 1998-; bd, Middletown YMCA, 1998-; bd, Middletown Social Health Ctr, 1999-; steering comn, Middletown Ownership Coun, 2000-. **Business Addr:** President, Chief Executive Officer, The Center for Multicultural Competence in Healthcare Organizations, 4555 Lake Forest Dr 650 Wlake Ctr, Cincinnati, OH 45242, **Business Phone:** (513)563-3004.

JAMES, LEBRON
Basketball player. **Personal:** Born Dec 30, 1984, Akron, OH; son of Gloria; married Savannah Brinson; children: LeBron Jr & Bryce Maximus. **Career:** Cleveland Cavaliers, star guard, 2003-. **Honors/Awds:** Mr Basketball, OH, 2001; Rookie of the Yr, 2004; Nat Rookie of the Year in 2004; Basketball Assn, 2004; NBA All-Star, 2005, 2006, 2007; NBA All-Star Game MVP, 2006; All-NBA, 2005, 2006, 2007; NBA Eastern Conference Champions, 2007; NBA Most Valuable Player in 2009. **Special Achievements:** Member of the USA Gold Medal-winning Olympics Team in 2008. **Business Addr:** Professional Basketball Player, Cleveland Cavaliers, 1 Ctr Ct, Cleveland, OH 44115-4001, **Business Phone:** (216)420-2000.*

JAMES, LETITIA
City council member. **Personal:** Born in Brooklyn, NY. **Educ:** CUNY's Lehman Col, attended; Howard Univ, Wash, DC, law sch educ; Columbia Univ, Grad Sch Intl& Pub Affairs. **Career:** Legal Aid Soc, pub defender; Brooklyn Regional Off, atty; New York City Coun, city councilwoman, 2003-, committee chair, currently. **Orgs:** Founder, Urban Network. **Special Achievements:** First asst atty gen in Charge of the Brooklyn Regional Off. **Business Addr:** City Councilman, New York City Coun, 250 Broadway Suite 1815, New York, NY 10007, **Business Phone:** (212)788-7081.*

JAMES, MARQUITA L
Educator. **Personal:** Born Nov 9, 1932, Philadelphia, PA. **Educ:** Wilberforce Univ, BA, 1955; Seton Ahll Univ, S Orange, NJ, MA, 1966; Candidacy NY Univ, PhD, 1974. **Career:** Wyandanch Schs, Wydandanch NY, chmn, 1964-68; Freeport NY, Afro-Am Hist curr coor, 1968-69; Nassau Comm Col, Garden City, Long Island NY, assoc prof hist, prof hist polit sci & geog, currently. **Orgs:** Asn Univ Profs; Asn Afro-Am Educ; Am Hist Asn; Afro-Am Black Heritage Asn; Cong Racial Equal; Coun Interracial Books Child; Alpha Kappa Alpha Sor; Nat Black Feminist Org; pres, Nassau-Suffolk Br Asn Study Afro-Am Life & Hist. **Honors/Awds:** Listed among black Elders in Black History Museum Hempstead LI NY; Nat Defense Educational Award, Teachers Col, Columbia Univ, NY; Martin Luther King jr Graduage Fellow Award, NY Univ, 1968-71; InterNat Education Award, Univ Ghana, Legon, W Africa, 1969; Chancellors Award, State Univ NY, 1981. **Business Addr:** Professor, Nassau Community College, Department of History, Political Science & Geography, 1 Education Dr Bldg G-G224, Garden City, NY 11530.

JAMES, MITCHELL. See RICHMOND, MITCH.

JAMES, OLIVE C. R.
Library administrator. **Personal:** Born Dec 4, 1929, New York, NY; daughter of Audley C Roach and Edith E Brown Roach; married Edmond Austin James (divorced 1965); children: Alan E, Karen Straughn, Jeffrey A, Christopher E. **Educ:** City Col New York, New York, NY, BS, 1950, grad work, 1952; Rutgers UNIV, MLS, 1965, New York UNIV, grad work, 1976. **Career:** Queens Col, CUNY, New York, NY, reference librn & DEPT head, 1966-76; Stanford UNIV, Stanford, CA, libr DEPT chief, 1976-80; Libr Congress, Washington DC, DIV chief, 1980-87; Yale UNIV, New Haven, CT, consult, 1985-86; San Francisco State UNIV, San Francisco, CA, libr DIR, 1987-92; librn emer. **Orgs:** ASO Col & Resource Librs, EXEC bd, UNIV librs section, prog & language planning COMN, EXEC COMT bibliographic instr section-;Friends San Francisco Pub Libr, bd, 1988-; PRES, Ocean Beach Homeowners ASN, 1991-; PRES, Stanford UNIV Librns Assembly, 1979-80. **Honors/Awds:** UCLA Senior Fellow, Coun Res Libr, 1987; Fellowship Consultants Program, ASN Res Librs, 1982; USS DEPT EDUC, UNIV Maryland, Fellowship libr ADMIN Develop Prog, 1973; DEPT EDUC, France, Assistante de Langue Anglais, 1952-53; Member four National Honor Societies: French, Spanish, Education, Librarianship. *

JAMES, PEGGI C
Association executive. **Personal:** Born Dec 4, 1940, Dothan, AL; divorced; children: Rose, Roddy & Rolaunda. **Educ:** Ala State

Univ, BS, 1967. **Career:** Grimsley HS Ashford Ala, teacher, 1967-69; Human Resource Develop Corp, exec dir, 2001-. **Orgs:** Ala Asn Community Action Agencys; NEA; Les Vingts Socialietes Club; Dothan Asn Women's Clubs; NAACP; bd dirs, Civic Ctr Opera House; Southeatern Asn Community Action Agencies. **Honors/Awds:** 4-yr scholar, Ala Asn Women's Clubs, 1957; HC Trenholm acad award, 1958; Dothan woman of year, 1974; Ala woman achievement, 1974. **Business Addr:** Executive Director, Human Resource Develop Corp, 100 George Wallace Dr, PO Box 311407, Enterprise, AL 36331, **Business Phone:** (334)347-0881.

JAMES, RICHARD L.
Educator, school administrator. **Personal:** Born Jul 31, 1926, Asheville, NC; married Velma A Kinsey. **Educ:** Hampton Inst Va, BS, 1949; Univ Mich, MMus, 1951; Univ Md, EdD, 1968. **Career:** Prince George's County, teacher, 1958-67; Am Asn Cols Teacher Educ, assoc dir, 1968-73; Morgan State Univ, Baltimore, teacher educ, assoc dean, 1973-75; Sch Educ Morgan State Univ, acting dean. **Orgs:** Commun comn Asn Teacher Educrs; Asn Higher Educ; Multicultural Educ Com Am Assoc Col Teacher Educ; Omega Psi Phi. **Special Achievements:** Author educ publs. **Military Serv:** AUS, 1945-46.

JAMES, DR. ROBERT D.
School administrator. **Personal:** Born Aug 24, 1950, New Rochelle, NY; son of Shirley Clark and Everett Lanier; married Cheryl D Holley, Feb 28, 1971; children: Ayanna Laura, Anika Laren & Jamaal Malik. **Educ:** State Univ NY, Brockport, BS, 1972, MS, 1975; State Univ NY, Albany, Ed.D. **Career:** Baden St Settlement Coun Ctr, asst dir, 1973-74; State Univ NY, Brockport, counr, 1974-77, Educ Opportunity Prog, dir, 1977-79, EOC, exec dir,1979-87, Off Spec Prog, actg sr assoc, 1987-91, State Univ NY Cent Off,assoc vice chancellor off spec progs, 1991-99, assoc provost, 1995-, assoc vice provost opportunity progs, currently; Pub Employ Rels Bd, mediator &fact finder, 1985-; NY State Martin Luther King Jr Inst Non Violence,interim dir, 1991; Hunter Col, consult, 2001; Millersville Univ, consult,2003; US Dept Educ, consult. **Orgs:** Consult, Univ Rochester Ct Ment Health Team, 1974-79; consult, Ctr Urban Ethnic Affairs, 1975-77; bd mem, Catholic Youth Orgn, 1979-87; bd mem,YMCA, Rochester, 1979-85; bd mem, Urban League, Rochester 1984-88; bd mem-,Legal Aid Soc, 1984-86; bd mem, Am Diabetes Asn, 1984-86; mediator & factfinder, NY State Pub Employ Rel Bd, 1985-; former dir & pres, Tri-State Consortium Opportunity Progs, 1988-; bd dir, Nat Guard Challenge Prog,1997-; consult, Montclair St, 2000; bd governors, Finger Lakes Occup Educ Ctr. **Honors/Awds:** Outstanding Service Award, State Univ NY, 1988; Arthur A Schomburg Distinguished Service Award, Asn Equality & Excellence Educ Inc, 1989;Distinguished Service Award, State Univ NY, 1990; Distinguished Service Award, Tri State Consortium, 1991; Man of the Year Award, Tri-State Consortium, 2001; Governor's Award Outstanding Service in Education;Outstanding Alumni Award, State Univ NY. **Home Addr:** 206 Exec Dr, Guilderland, NY 12084. **Business Addr:** Associate Vice Provost for Opportunity Programs, State University of New York College at Brockport, 350 New Campus Dr, Brockport, NY 14420-2914, **Business Phone:** (585)395-2796.

JAMES, ROBERT EARL
Banker. **Personal:** Born Nov 21, 1946, Hattiesburg, MS; son of James Sr and Jimmie; married Shirley B; children: Robert II, Anne, Rachelle. **Educ:** Morris Brown Col, BA, 1968; Harvard Univ, MBA, 1970. **Career:** Armco Steel Corp Middletown, OH, accounting trainee 1967; C & S Natl Bank Atlanta, GA, mgt trainee, 1969; Savannah Tribune Savannah, GA, publ; Carver State Bank, Savannah, GA, pres, 1971-. **Orgs:** Gen partner, Atlantic Investors; trustee mem, Morris Brown Col; White House Conf Small Bus; dir, Ga Telecommunications Comn; Int Bus Fel, 1983; chmn bd, Nat Bankers Asn, 1990-92. **Business Addr:** President, Carver State Bank, 701 Martin Luther King Jr Blvd, PO Box 2769, Savannah, GA 31402.*

JAMES, RONALD
Executive, president (organization), chief executive officer. **Personal:** Born Dec 3, 1950, Port Arthur, TX; married Renee; children: Joshua & Jordan. **Educ:** Doane Col, Crete, Nebr, BBA, 1971; Creighton Univ, Omaha, Nebr, 1977. **Career:** US W Commun, Minneapolis, Minn, executive officer, 1971-96; Ceridian Corp, Human Resources Group, pres & chief exec officer, 1996-98; Ctr Ethical Bus Cultures, Minneapolis, Minn, pres & chief exec officer, 2000-. **Orgs:** Dir, St Paul Co; dir, Automotive Indust Holding Inc; co-chair, Action C Comunity, 1991-; United Way Minneapolis; dir, Ceridan Corp; dir, Great Hall Investment Funds Inc; bd dirs, Tamarack Funds; bd dirs, Bremer Fin Corp; bd dirs, Allina Hosps & Clins; bd dirs, Best Buy Co Inc. **Honors/Awds:** Oustanding Young Alumni, Doane Col, 1982; Honor D Award, Hall of Fame, 1988; Top 25 Black Managers, Black Enterprise, 1988; KARE-11 Board of Governor's Award, 1992. **Business Addr:** President, Chief Executive Officer, Center for Ethical Business Cultures, 1000 LaSalle Ave, Minneapolis, MN 55403-2005, **Business Phone:** (651)962-4120.

JAMES, RONALD J.
Lawyer, executive director. **Personal:** Born Apr 8, 1937, Centerville, IA; son of Raymond B and Jennie M Smith; married Patricia O'Donnell; children: Catlin, Kelly, Shannon, Ronald Jr, Kevin. **Educ:** Univ Mo, AB, 1959; Am Univ Wash Col Law, JD, 1966; Southern Ill Univ, MA, 1972. **Career:** EEO Comn, regional atty, 1972-75; Waterloo IA Comn Human Rights, exec dir, 1967; Waterloo IA, asst Co atty, 1967-69; OEO, spec asst to dir, 1970-71; spec atty to con to pres, 1971-72; Congressman James Bromwell, staff asst, 1963-64; US Dept Labor, admin wage & hour div, 1975-77; Squire Sanders & Dempsey, partner, 1977-03; US Dept Homeland Security, Chief Human Capital Officer, 2003-. **Orgs:** Am Bar Asn; Nat Bar Asn; IA Bar Assn; Supreme Ct Bar; Urban League; Ohio Bar Asn. **Honors/Awds:** Nat speech honorary Delta Sigma Rho. **Military Serv:** AUS, First lt, 1960-63; USAR capt. **Business Addr:** Chief Human Capital Officer, US Dept Homeland Security, Washington, DC 20528.*

JAMES, SHARPE
Politician, mayor, government official. **Personal:** Born Feb 20, 1936, Jacksonville, FL; married Mary Mattison; children: John, Elliott & Kevin. **Educ:** Montclair State Col, BA, hon doctor laws, 1988; Springfield Col, MA, phys educ; Wash State Univ; Columbia Univ; Rutgers Univ. **Career:** Pub off, S ward councilman; Newark Pub Schs, teacher; Essex Co Col, prof, 1968-86; City Newark, NJ, coun mem, 1970-86, council man-at-large, 1982-86, mayor, 1986, 90, 2002; NJ State Senate, sen, 1999, 2002; Am Dem Party, politician. **Orgs:** Founder, Little City Hall Inc; charter mem & pres, Org Negro Educrs; exec, Scholar Assistance Guid Asn; bd mem, Nat League Cities; US Conf Mayors; exec comt, Newark Collaboration Group. **Honors/Awds:** Distinguished Alumni Award, Montclair State Col; NJ State Tennis Asn Champion; Newark Sr Tennis Champion; City Livability Award, 1991; Top 100 influential black Americans, Ebony, 1991; Honorary Doctorate, Drew Univ, 1991, 1992; Most Valuable Public Official Award, City &State, 1992; inducted, NJ Elected Officials Hall of Fame, 1999; Arts Leader sr, Little City Hall Inc; charter mem & pres, Org Negro Educrs;hip Award, US Conf Mayors & Am Arts, 2002; Mayor of the Year, NJ Conf Mayors, 2003. **Special Achievements:** Second African American Mayor of Newark, NJ; First Newark mayor to run unopposed when he sought re-election, 1990. **Military Serv:** AUS, Europ.

JAMES, SHERRI GWENDOLYN
Lawyer. **Personal:** Born in Columbus, GA; daughter of Johnny and Zelma. **Educ:** Georgetown Univ, BA, 1984; Univ Ga Law Sch, JD, 1988. **Career:** District Atty Off, asst regional coun, 1991-. **Orgs:** Am Bar Asn; Nat Bar Asn; GA Asn Black Women Atty. **Business Phone:** (912)562-1083.

JAMES, SIDNEY J.
School administrator, army officer, president (organization). **Personal:** Born Jun 25, 1935, Columbia, MS; married Margie Pope; children: Kenja. **Educ:** Alcorn State Univ, BS, health & phys educ, 1958; Univ Southern MS, MS, col coun, 1972, Specialist's Ed Admin, 1981; Marquette Univ, Cert Mgt Training Inst, 1980. **Career:** Prentiss Normal & Indus Inst, coach & teacher, 1960-67, dean students, 1967-73, dir spec progs, 1973-81, pres, 1981-. **Orgs:** Adv bd, First Fed Savings & Loan, 1984; Phi Delta Kappa, 1980-; vpres, City Planning Comn, Columbia, MS, 1981-; Miss State Job Training Coord Coun, 1983-; Shriner 33 Mason. **Honors/Awds:** Coach of the Year, Southern Intercollegiate Cong Co, 1965; Outstanding Service Award, SAEOPP, 1981; Distinguish Service Award, Phi Delta Kappa, 1983. **Military Serv:** AUS, specialist E4, 2 yrs. **Home Addr:** 1200 Maxwell Ave, Columbia, MS 39429. *

JAMES, STEPHEN ELISHA
Government official. **Personal:** Born May 19, 1942, Montgomery, AL; son of Hazel Todd and Elisha; married Janie, Apr 5, 1964 (divorced 1989); children: Lydia Yvonne Boseman & Stephen Christopher James. **Educ:** Case Western Reserve Univ, Cleveland, BA, 1970, MSLS, 1971; Univ Wis, Madison, PhD, 1983. **Career:** Cleveland Pub Libr, Cleveland, librn, 1969-73; Atlanta Univ, Atlanta, prof, 1976-87; Pub Libraries Saginaw, Saginaw, asst dir, 1987-90; Libr Mich, Lansing, div dir, 1990-. **Orgs:** Intellectual freedom comt, Mich Libr Asn, 1988-92; accreditation comt, Am Libr Asn, 1990-92; Kappa Delta Lambda chap, Alpha Phi Alpha, 1991-. **Honors/Awds:** Beta-Phi-Mu, Am Libr Asn, 1984. **Military Serv:** USN, E-4, 1962-66. **Business Phone:** (517)373-1580.

JAMES, TONI-LESLIE
Costume designer. **Personal:** Born Jun 11, 1957, McKeesport, PA; daughter of Leslie Burrell and Alice B; married David Higham, Feb 28, 1981; children: Cosima B. **Educ:** Ohio State Univ, BFA, 1979. **Career:** Theatre Arts, costume designer, currently. **Orgs:** United Scenic Artists Local 829; Sokka Gakki Int. **Honors/Awds:** Audelio Awards, Audelio Award Nominations, 1990, 1991; Drama-Logue Award, Drama-Logue, 1991; Drama Desk Nominations, Drama Desk, 1991, 1992; Am Theatre Wine Award, 1992; Tony Nomination, 1992. *

JAMES, TORY STEVEN
Football player. **Personal:** Born May 18, 1973, New Orleans, LA; married Angela. **Educ:** La State Univ. **Career:** Denver Broncos, defensive back, 1996-99; Oakland Raiders, 2000-02;Cincinnati Bengals, corner back, 2003-06; New England Patriots, defensive-back, currently. **Honors/Awds:** First-team All-Southeastern Conf hons, 1994. **Business Phone:** (508)543-8200.*

JAMES, TROY LEE. See Obituaries section.

JAMES, VENITA HAWTHORNE
Journalist, editor. **Personal:** Born Jul 8, 1955, Des Moines, IA; daughter of Peter and Frances; married Daryl James, Aug 3, 1984; children: Jahara & Akil. **Educ:** Lincoln Univ, BA, 1977. **Career:** Ariz Repub, asst city ed, 1991-94, dep metro ed, 1994-97, sr ed, 1997-, W Valley, gen mgr & sr ed, 2004-. **Orgs:** Pres, Ariz Asn Black Journalists, 1998-; Nat Asn Black Journalists, 1985. **Business Phone:** (602)444-8222.

JAMES, WILLIAM
Educator. **Personal:** Born May 10, 1945, Augusta, GA; son of Harriet Martin and Hinton; married Avis Cooper; children: Kevyn & William. **Educ:** Morehouse Col, BA, 1967; Howard Univ, JD, 1972; Atlanta Univ, MSLS, 1973. **Career:** Fed City Col, lectr, 1972; Fed Trade Comn, law clerk, 1972; Atlanta Univ, grad asst, 1972-73; Univ Tenn, asst prof & asst librn, 1973-77; Univ Ky, from asst prof law & law librn to assoc prof law & law librn to prof law & dir law libr, 1977-88; Villanova Univ, prof law & dir law libr, 1988-, assoc dean info serv, 1995-. **Orgs:** AALS; LSAC; Asn Am Law Sch Comn Libr; bd adv, Legal Ref Serv Quart; Am Asn Law Libr; Comn Placement, Educ, Minorities, Scholar & Grants; chair, Minorities Comn, 1985-87; chair, Scholar & Nomination Comn, Southeastern Asn Law Librn. **Special Achievements:** Numerous publications including Law Libraries Which Offer Service to Prisoners, 1975; Recommended Collections for Prison Law Libraries , 1975; Legal Reference Materials and Law Library Services, 1976; written annotated bibliographies for Law and Psychiatry, 1979. **Military Serv:** AUS, e-5, 1969-71. **Home Addr:** 15 Cypress Lane, Berwyn, PA 19312. **Business Addr:** Professor of Law & Director of the Law Library, Associate Dean for Information Services, Villanova University, School of Law, 299 N Spring Mill Rd Libr Garey Hall, Villanova, PA 19085-1597, **Business Phone:** (610)519-7023.

JAMES, REV. WILLIAM M.
Executive. **Personal:** Born Jun 4, 1916, Meadville, MS; son of Warren and Rosa Ann; married Juanita; children: Edward. **Educ:** Mt Beulah Col, AA; Butler Univ, BS, B Sacred Lit; Drew Univ, BD MA; Univ Chicago, Drew Univ, grad courses. **Career:** Multi Ethnic Ctr Ministry Northeastern Jurisdiction United Methodist Church, dir; Metro Comt United Methodist Ch NY, sr minister; Trinity United Meth Ch Bronx, pastor; ordained deacon, 1938; elder, 1940; Drew Univ, dir. **Orgs:** Officer Nat Bd Educ Methodist Church; organizer, founder, Ministerial Interfaith Asn admin Halem Col Asst Prog; Harlem Interfaith Harlem Coun Asn; Found Harlem; pres, New York City Br NAACP; chmn bd, Harlem Urban Develop Corp; founder, Young People's Found. *

JAMES, WYNONA YVONNE
Consultant. **Personal:** Born Dec 7, 1953, Sacramento, CA; daughter of Robert and Estelle James; divorced. **Educ:** Allan Hancock Col, 1974-75; Middle Tenn State Univ, BS, 1978; Univ Colo, 1995; Fuller Theol Sem, 1996-97. **Career:** USAF, chief, Air Force suggestion prog, 1992-95, human resources dir, 1995-96, qual consult, 1996-97, mgt analyst & consult, 1997-; Franklin Covey, consult, 1994-2000; Air Nat Guard Training & Educ Ctr & Military Acad, vis consult. **Orgs:** Nat Asn Suggestion Syst, 1987-95; pres, Rocky Mountain Employee Involvement Asn Chap, 1993-94; Employee Involvement Nat Task Force, DOD Rep Awards Comt, 1993-94; vpres, Rocky Mountain Employee Involvement Asn, 1994-95; secy & mem chair, Toastmasters Int, 1995-96; bd mem, Girl Scout Wagon Wheel Coun, 1995-96; Am Cancer Soc, 1995-96; mem comt, Employee Involvement Asn, 1996-97; Knoxville Lace Soc, 2000-01; team leader, Pikes Peak Habitat Humanity, 2000; Nat Quilt Asn, 2001-02; Knoxville Quilters Guild, 2002-03; Beck Cult Mus, 2002-03; East Tenn Hist Soc, 2002-. **Honors/Awds:** Civilian of the Year Award, Twenty first Space Wing-Space Command, 1991; Competant Toastmaster Award, 1995; Outstanding Civilian of the Quarter, Twenty first Space Wing-Space Command, 1996; Air Force Commendation Medal Civilian Award, 2000. **Special Achievements:** Movie extra in film Switchback, 1997. **Home Addr:** PO Box 5573, Colorado Springs, CO 80931, **Home Phone:** (719)556-0261. **Business Addr:** Visiting Consultant, National Air Guard Training & Education Center & Military Academy, 400 IG Brown Dr McGhee Tyson Air Nat Guard Base, Louisville, TN 37777, **Business Phone:** (865)985-3677.

JAMES-FOSTER, JOY LYNNE
Educator. **Personal:** Born Jul 31, 1967, Knoxville, TN; daughter of Joseph and Joyce; married Jerry Foster, Jul 21, 2002; children: Kennedy. **Educ:** Univ Tenn, Knoxville, BS, educ, 1990, elem educ, 1994, EdS, holistic teaching, 1999, admin, 1999, doctorate, educ, 2004. **Career:** Knox Co Sch, Powell Elem Sch, teacher, 1994-2003, West View, teacher asst, 1987-94, curric facilitator, 2003-04; Univ Tenn & Dept Health, vis scholar asst ship, 1997; Beaumont Magnet Sch, asst prin, 2004-05; Blue Grass Elem Sch, asst prin, 2005-; Univ Tenn Knoxville, grad res asst, 2000-04;

Univ Tenn, black grad opportunity fel, 2000-03; Teacher of The Year Program Tennessee Dept Education, judge, 2005-Present. **Orgs:** Phi Delta Kappa, 2000; Kappa Delta Pi, 2000; Knoxville Area Chamber Partnership, 2000; panel mem, Educ Testing Serv, 2000. **Home Addr:** 1124 Ferncliff Way, Knoxville, TN 37923, **Home Phone:** (865)470-3165. **Business Addr:** Assistant Principal, Blue Grass Elementary School, 8901 Blue Grass Rd, Knoxville, TN 37922, **Business Phone:** (865)539-7864.

JAMISON, ANTAWN CORTEZ
Basketball player. **Personal:** Born Jun 12, 1976, Shreveport, LA; married Ione Rucker, Jul 1, 2003. **Educ:** Univ NC, attended 1997. **Career:** Golden State Warriors, forward, 1998-2003; Dallas Mavericks, 2003-04; Wash Wizards, forward, 2004-; USA Nat Team, currently. **Honors/Awds:** John Wooden Award, Col Player of the Year, 1997-98; Naismith Award, Col Player of the Year, 1997-98; Bronze Medal, FIBA World Championship, US Nat Team, 2006. **Business Addr:** Professional Basketball Player, Washington Wizards, Verizon Ctr 601 F St NW, Washington, DC 20004, **Business Phone:** (202)661-5100.

JAMISON, BIRDIE HAIRSTON
Judge. **Personal:** Born Jul 1, 1957, Martinsville, VA; daughter of Irvin Spencer Sr and Ida Dalton; married Calvin D Jamison Sr, Aug 14, 1982; children: Calvin D Jamison Jr. **Educ:** Col William & Mary, Williamsburg, VA, BBA, 1979; Marshall Wythe Sch Law, Col William & Mary, Williamsburg, VA, JD, 1982. **Career:** George W Harris, Jr & Assoc, Roanoke, VA, assoc atty, 1982-84; Roanoke Commonwealth Atty, Roanoke, VA, asst commonwealth atty, 1984-88; VA Polytechnic Inst, Blacksburg, VA, adjunct instr, 1983-88; VA Atty Gen, Richmond, VA, asst atty gen, 1988-90; Richmond Commonwealth Atty, Richmond, VA, deputy commonwealth atty, 1990-91; Gen Dist Ct, Richmond, VA, judge, Currently. **Orgs:** Delta Sigma Theta, Inc, 1978-; Old Dominion Bar Asn, 1982-; Corresponding secy, Girlfriends, Inc, 1984-; pres, Roanoke Chapter Old Dominion Bar Asn, 1985-87; bd mem, Big Brother & Big Sister, 1990-; bd mem, Garfield Memorial Fund, 1990-; Jack & Jill, Inc, 1990-. **Honors/Awds:** SERWA Award, Coalition 200 Black Women, 1992; Virginia Heroes Award, 1992; Alumini Achievement Award, Richmond Alumini chapter. **Business Addr:** Judge, General District Court, 800 East Marshall, Richmond, VA 23219-1998, **Business Phone:** (804)780-6437.*

JAMISON, GEORGE R., JR.
Football player. **Personal:** Born Sep 30, 1962, Bridgeton, NJ; married Arnella. **Educ:** Univ Detroit, BA, hum res develop, 1990. **Career:** Football (retired): Philadelphia Stars, linebacker, 1984; Baltimore Stars, 1985; Detroit Lions, 1987-93, 1997-98; Kansas City Chiefs, 1994-96; Detroit Lions, hon capt, currently. **Honors/Awds:** Lions' Block award recipient,1998.

JAMISON, ISAAC TERRELL
Executive. **Personal:** Born Jun 30, 1969, Baltimore, MD; son of Joan Jenkins and Issac Jamison; married Aticha M, Jul 28, 2001. **Educ:** Tuskegee Univ, attended 1992. **Career:** Morton Int Salt Co, sales rep, Jackson, MS, 1993-94, Pittsburgh, 1994-96, nat sales mgr, 1996-99, region sales admin mgr, 1999-2002, marketing business segment mgr, 2002-. **Orgs:** Life mem, Kappa Alpha Psi Fraternity, 1993-; bd mem, African Am Comt, Nat Kidney Found, 1995; bd trustee, Tuskegee Univ, 1994. **Special Achievements:** Morton Salt Company, Salarium Society, Top Salesman, 1997, 1998. **Home Addr:** PO Box 2085, Roswell, GA 30077. **Business Addr:** Regional Sales Administration Manager, Morton International Salt Co, 11111 Houze Rd Suite 105, Roswell, GA 30076.

JAMISON, JUDITH ANN
Executive, dancer, artistic director. **Personal:** Born May 10, 1943, Philadelphia, PA; daughter of John Jamison Sr and Tessie B; married Miguel Godreau, Jan 1, 1972 (divorced 1974). **Educ:** Fisk Univ, attended 1962; Univ Arts, Philadelphia, PA, attended 1964; Judimar Sch The Dance. **Career:** Alvin Ailey Am Dance Theater, prin, 1964-80, dancer & choreographer, 1980-89, artistic dir, 1989-; guest appearances in various organizations including: Am Ballet Theatre; Harkness Ballet; San Francisco Ballet; Dallas Ballet; Vienna State Opera; Munich State Opera; Hamburg State Opera; choreographer: Divining, 1984; Mefistofele, Judith Jamison: The Dance maker; Double Exposure, 2000; Here Now, 2002; The Jamison Project, dir, 1988-89; TV Series: "The Cosby Show", actor, 1985; "A Tribute to Alvin Ailey", actor, 1990. **Orgs:** Bd mem, Coun Arts; Harper Festival Chicago, 1965; Festival Negro Arts Dakar Senegal, 1966; Edinburgh Festival, 1968; Women's Choreography Initiative; founder, BFA Prog, The Ailey Sch & Fordham Univ. **Honors/Awds:** Dance Magazine Award, 1972; Key to City of New York, 1976; Distinguished Service Award, Harvard Univ, 1982; Distinguished Service Award, Mayor of New York City, 1982; Philadelphia Arts Alliance Award; The Franklin Mint Award; Candace Award, Nat Coalition 100 Black Women; received honorary doctorates from various universities including: Univ Arts; Mary mount Col; Middlebury Col; Manhattanville Col; Outstanding Choreography for "Dance in America: A Hymn For Alvin Ailey,", Prime time Emmy Awards, 1999; Kennedy Center Honoree, 1999; Emmy Award; American Choreography Award for Outstanding Choreography; Algur H Meadows Award, Southern Methodist Univ, 2001; Nat Medal of Arts, Pres George Bush, 2001; "Making a Difference" Award, NAACP ACT-SO, 2003; Paul Robeson Award, Actors Equity Asn. **Special Achievements:** Co-author, Dancing Spirit, 1993. **Business Addr:** Artistic Director, Alvin Ailey American Dance Theater, The Joan Weill Center for Dance, 405 W 55th St, New York, NY 10019, **Business Phone:** (212)405-9000.

JARMON, JAMES HENRY, JR. See Obituaries section.

JARREAU, ALWYN LOPEZ
Actor, singer, songwriter. **Personal:** Born Mar 12, 1940, Milwaukee, WI; son of Emile and Pearl; married Phyllis Hall, Jan 1, 1964 (divorced 1968); children: Ryan; married Susan Player, Jan 1, 1977; children: Ryan. **Educ:** Ripon Col, BS, psychol, 1962; Univ IA, MS, voc rehab, 1964. **Career:** Singer & songwriter; Albums: We Got By, 1975; Glow, 1976; Look to theRainbow, 1977; All Fly Home, 1978; This Time, 1980; Breaking Away, 1981; Lis for Lover, 1986; Heart's Horizon, 1989; Al Jarreau, 1992; Tenderness, 1994; Best of Al Jarreau, 1996; Tomorrow Today, All I Got, 2000; Accentuate the Positive, 2004; Al & Lou, 2004; Lean on Me, 2004; R&B Soul, 2005; Givin' It Up, 2006; Look To The Rainbow: Live in Europe, 2008; Love Songs (Rhino), 2008; Christmas (Rhino), 2008. **Honors/Awds:** Grammy Award, 1981; Italian Music Critics Award, 1977; winner, Readers'Poll Down Beat Mag, 1977-79; Grammy Award, 1978-79; five Grammy Awards; honored with a star on the Hollywood Walk of Fame, 2001; Literacy Champion Award, 2002; French Music Academy Awards. **Special Achievements:** Film: Touched by an Angel, 1997; A Taste of Us: The Movie, 2007; Soundtrack: Warner Bros, Girls Know How, 1982; Universal pictures, Moonlighting, 1984; Motown, Never Explain Love, 1989; The Fighting Temptations, 2003; Against the Ropes, 2004. **Business Phone:** (310)288-4545.

JARRETT, GERALD I, SR.
Educator, lawyer. **Personal:** Born Jul 18, 1947, Newark, NJ; son of Nelson and Zelma; married Karen Jordan, Aug 3, 1985; children: Laini, Gerald Jr, Brandon & Michael. **Educ:** Western New Mex Univ; Youngstown State Univ, BA, 1971; Seton Hall Sch Law, JD, 1974. **Career:** State NJ Labor Dept, hearings officer, 1977-79; State NJ ade law judge, 1979-81; Pvt Pract, atty, 1981-85; NJ Assembly Majority Leader Off, legal asst, 1985-86; NJ Pub Defender Off, pub defender, 1986-97; Essex County Col, adj prof, 1996; St Augustine Col, asst prof, 1997. **Orgs:** Treas, 1983-84, pres, 1984-85, Garden State Bar Asn; chair ade law section, Nat Bar Asn, 1979-81; Kappa Alpha Psi, 1968-; bd & exec secy, Essex Newark Legal Serv, 1981-85. **Home Addr:** 10913 Bexhill Dr, Raleigh, NC 27606-9512.

JARRETT, VALERIE B.
Government official. **Personal:** Born Nov 14, 1956, Shiraz, Iran; daughter of James Bowman and Barbara Bowman; divorced; children: Laura. **Educ:** Stanford Univ, AB, psychol, 1978; Univ Mich Law Sch, JD, 1981. **Career:** Pope Ballard Shepard & Fowle Ltd, assoc, cre banking; Sonnenschein, Carlin, Nath & Rosenthal, Real Estate Dept, assoc; City Chicago, Dept Law, dep corp coun finance & develop, Off Mayor, dep chief staff, Dept Planning, actg comnr, Dept Planning & Develop, comnr; Chicago Stock Exchange, chmn, 2004-; The Habitat Co, exec vpres & managing dir, currently. **Orgs:** Lambda Alpha Int; Ctr Int Bus Educ & Res; pres, SE Chicago Comn; Ncp Legal Defense & Educ-Chicago Fund, dir; Local Initiatives Support Corp; The Econ Club Chicago; Nat Coun Urban Econ Develop; dir, Leadership Greater Chicago, 1988-89; chmn bd dirs, Chicago Transit Authority; bd dirs, Navigating Consult; chmn Univ Chicago Hosp; exec coun, Metropolis 2020; dir, USG Corp; dir, Harris Insight Funds; dir, Joyce Found. **Honors/Awds:** Women's Bus Develop Ctr, Gov Support Award, 1992. **Special Achievements:** Consolidated Dept Planning, Econ Develop and Urban Renewal, 1992; implemented a model prog for the revitalization of three Chicago neighborhoods, 1992; created a bus express unit to cut red tape to serv Chicago bus, 1992. **Business Addr:** Executive Vice President, Managing Director, The Habitat Co, 350 W Hubbard St 5th Fl, Chicago, IL 60610, **Business Phone:** (312)527-5400.*

JARRETT-JACKSON, MARY FRANCIS
Executive. **Personal:** Born Feb 15, 1931, Nickolasville, KY; daughter of Bronaugh and Gladys Bridges; married Clarence, Mar 29, 1986; children: Ernest L Jarrett & Ruth E Jarrett-Cooper. **Educ:** Howard Univ, BS, 1952; Atlanta Univ, MA, 1988. **Career:** Executive (Retired); Detroit Police Dept, deputy chief western operation, 1958-94; Wayne County Juvenile Detention Facility, chief asst dir, 1995-2000; Wayne County Sheriff's Dept, deputy admin, 2000. **Honors/Awds:** MI Senate Resolution 902, 1986; Induction Int Women Police Hall of Fame, 1986; Detroit City Coun, Testimonial Resolution, 1987; Women's Economic Club, Detroit's Dynamic Women, 1992. **Special Achievements:** Apprenticeship, Serology & Trace Evidence, Scotland Yard Laboratories, London, England, 1972. **Home Addr:** 20006 Robson St, Detroit, MI 48235, **Home Phone:** (313)342-2139.

JA RULE (JEFFREY ATKINS)
Rap musician. **Personal:** Born Feb 29, 1976, Queens, NY; married Aisha, 2001; children: Britney, Jeffrey & Jordan. **Career:** Albums: Venni Vetti Vecci, 1999; Rule 3:36, 2000; Pain Is Love, 2001; The Last Temptation, 2002; Blood in my Eye, 2003; R.U. L.E, 2004; Caught Up, 2005; Exodus, 2005; The Mirror, 2009; Welcome to Rule York, 2009 Films: Turn It Up, 2000; The Fast & the Furious, 2001; Half Past Dead, 2003; "Inked", 2005; "South Beach", 2006; Films: Turn It Up, 2000; The Fast & the Furious, 2001; Half Past Dead; 2002; Scary Movie3, 2003; The Cookout, 2004; Shall We Dance, 2004; Back in the Day, 2005; Assault on Precinct 13, 2005; Furnace, 2006; Half Past Dead 2, 2007; Don't Fade Away, 2009; The INC Records, co-owner, 1999. **Orgs:** Founder, LIFE Camp. **Honors/Awds:** Artist of the Year, Vibe, 2001; World's Best-Selling Rap Artist, World Music Awards, 2001; Best Solo Artist, GQ, 2002; Male Artist of the Year,Teen Choice Award, 2002; Source Award Won for R&B/Rap Collboration of the Year, 2003; Source Award Won for Phat Tape Song of the Year, 2004. **Business Addr:** Rap Musician, A & M Records, 825 Eigth Ave Fl 23, New York, NY 10019, **Business Phone:** (212)333-8000.

JARVIS, CHARLENE DREW
School administrator, president (organization). **Personal:** Born 1941, Washington, DC; daughter of Charles R Drew. **Educ:** Roosevelt High Sch, attended 1958; Oberlin Col, BA, 1962; Howard Univ, MS, 1964; Univ Md, PhD, neuropsychol, 1971; Amherst Col, DHL; George Wash Univ, Doctor of Pub Serv. **Career:** Howard Univ, instr psychol, 1965, prof; Nat Inst Ment Health, pre-doctoral fel, res scientist, 1978; DC City Coun, coun woman, 1979-00; Southeastern Univ, pres, 1996-; Montgomery Col, prof. **Orgs:** former chair, Coun Govts; chairperson, pres-elect, DC Chamber Com; Greater Wash Bd Trade; chair, Community Bus Partnership Comn; bd dir, BB & T Bank; bd dir, Nat Asn Independent Col & Univ; chair, DC City Coun, Comt Econ Develop; exec comt mem, Fed City Coun; Wash Chap, Am Red Cross; Breast Cancer Task Force Dept Health & Human Serv; Women's Health Initiative, NIH; Nat Mus Health; Nat Bone Marrow Prog. **Honors/Awds:** 1999 Washingtonians of the Year, Washingtonian Mag, 1999; Brotherhood-Sisterhood Award, Nat Conf Community & Justice, 2002; Outstanding Support, Women's Bus Ctr; received numerous honors & received more than 100 awards. **Business Addr:** President, Southeastern University, 501 1st St SW, Washington, DC 20024-2788.*

JASON, JEANNE. See WRIGHT, JEANNE JASON.

JASPER, ED. See JASPER, EDWARD VIDEL.

JASPER, EDWARD VIDEL (ED JASPER)
Football player. **Personal:** Born Jan 18, 1973, Tyler, TX. **Educ:** Tex A&M Univ, agr. **Career:** Football player (retired); Philadelphia Eagles, defensive tackle, 1997-98; Atlanta Falcons, defensive tackle, 1999-04; Oakland Raiders, defensive tackle, 2005. *

JASPER, KENJI NATHANIEL
Writer. **Personal:** Born Jan 1, 1976; son of Melvin and Angela. **Educ:** Morehouse Col, 1997. **Career:** Inst Preserv & Study African Am Writing, instr; WTTG, Fox 5's Newsbag, on-air personality, 1986-87; Black Entertainment TV Teen Summit, founding cast mem, 1989-93; Books: Dark, 2001; Dakota Grand, 2002; Seeking Salamanca Mitchell, 2004; The House on Childress Street, 2006; Beats, Rhymes & Life, 2007; Snow, 2007; What We Love & Hate About Hip Hop; The Armory Press, chief exec officer & ed. **Business Addr:** Author, c/o Random House Inc, 1745 Broadway, New York, NY 10019.

JASPER, LAWRENCE E
Insurance executive. **Personal:** Born Oct 25, 1946, Philadelphia, PA; son of Lawrence Jasper (deceased) and Geraldine (deceased); married Diana Lundy; children: Laurette & Dawn. **Educ:** ICA; LUTC. **Career:** Debit Agt, 1968-69; Supr, 1969-71; Serv Asst Spectrum Arena, supr, 1971-74; Pilgrim Life Ins Co, from asst to vice pres, 1974, vpres, currently. **Orgs:** Nat Asn Advan Colored People; Young Great Soc;, 19 St Bapt Ch Youth Dept; Interest Bus Training Black & Youth. **Honors/Awds:** Man of Year, Pilgrim Life Ins, 1970, 1972. **Special Achievements:** First Black in mgmt Pilgrim Life; first man to receive Man of Year Award twice; youngest man & only black on bd dir at Pilgrim Life. **Military Serv:** Sgt, E-5 drill instr, 1968. **Business Addr:** Vice President, Pilgrim Life Insurance Company (Pilgrim Mutual Insurance Co), 8049 Wchester Pike, Upper Darby, PA 19082.

JAVERY, MICHAEL
Manager. **Personal:** Born Aug 16, 1953, Slidell, LA; son of George Jr and Inez Gaddie; married Peggy Veronica, Jul 2, 1994; children: Ryan Michael. **Educ:** West Hills Col, BSEE, 1974. **Career:** USN, avionics officer, 1971-77, sr test engr, 1984-88, chief test opers eng, 1987-88, chief final assembly & test, 1988-89, chief TPS appln, 1988-89, sr staff engr advan mfg technol, 1989-91; Lockheed Martin Corp, test engr, mgr, TPS large struct, 1991-97, dir, mfg & test, 1997-, vpres prod opers, currently. **Orgs:** YMCA, 1991-. **Honors/Awds:** Astronaut Silver Snoopy, MCC-NASA, 1978; Operational Performance Award, MMC, 1982; Space Shuttle Launch Honoree, MMC, 1982, 1992; Mission Success Award, MMC, 1990; Black Engineer, Outstanding Tech Con-

trib, 1992. **Military Serv:** USN, avionics officer, 1971-77; Good Conduct Medal, Vietnam Veteran. **Home Addr:** 102 Maumus Ave, New Orleans, LA 70131, **Home Phone:** (504)394-2886. **Business Addr:** Vice president of production operations, Lockheed Martin Corporation, 6801 Rockledge Dr, Bethesda, MD 20817, **Business Phone:** (301)897-6000.

JAY, DR. JAMES M.
Educator. **Personal:** Born Sep 12, 1927, Fitzgerald, GA; son of John B and Lizzie W; married Patsie Phelps; children: Mark E, Alicia D & Byron R. **Educ:** Paine Col, AB, 1950; Ohio State Univ, MSc, 1953, PhD, 1956. **Career:** Ohio State Univ, postdoctoral fel, 1956-57; Southern Univ, from asst prof to prof, 1957-61; Wayne State Univ, from asst prof to prof, 1961-94, prof emer, 1994-; ed bd mem, J Food Protection, 1981-97; Univ Nev, Las Vegas, adj prof, 1994. **Orgs:** Fel Am Soc Microbiol, 1956-; fel IFT, 1958-; comt mem, Nat Acad Sci, 1984-87; Nat Adv Comt Microbiol Criteria Foods, USDA, 1987-94; panel mem, Inst Food Technol, 1991-95; Wayne State Univ Acad Scholars, 1994; Sigma Xi; Int Asn Food Protect. **Honors/Awds:** Probus Award, Wayne State Univ, 1969; Distinguished Alumni Award, Paine Col, 1969; Founders Award, Detroit Inter-Alumni Coun, United Negro Col Fund, 1986; Michigan Science Trailblazer Award, Detroit Sci Ctr, 1987; Waksman Outstanding Teacher Award, Soc Indust Microbiol & Biotechnol,1988; Faculty Research Award, Sigma Xi Chap, Wayne State Univ, 1988; fel Inst Food Technologists, 1996-; Outstanding Teacher Award, Soc Indust Microbiol, 1996; fel Am Soc Microbiol, 1997; fel Int Asn Food Protection, 1999. **Special Achievements:** Author of Modern Food Microbiology, 1975. **Military Serv:** AUS, sgt, 1946-47. **Business Addr:** Professor Emeritus, Wayne State UNiversity, Department of Biological Sciences, 1360 Biol Sci Bldg, Detroit, MI 48202, **Business Phone:** (313)577-2873.

JAYCOX, MARY IRINE
Public relations executive. **Personal:** Born Aug 19, 1939, Camphill, AL; daughter of Eddie B Knight and Betty Busby; married James Curtis; children: James Jr, Sharon, Mary & Thomas. **Educ:** Univ Northern Iowa, BA, 1984, MA, 1986. **Career:** Har-lin Pre-Sch Erie Pa, parent coordr, 1966-67; Sears Roebuck & Co, div mgr, 1973-80; KBBG-FM Waterloo Iowa, talk show host, 1981-84; Dubuque City Festivals, prom dir, pub info coordr. **Orgs:** Freelance feature writer Waterloo Courier, Tel Herald Dubuque; housing analyst, Comn Housing Resource Bd; YMCA mem & publicity comn, Waterloo, 1985-86; comnr, Cable Comn Teleprogramming. **Honors/Awds:** Best Com Script, 1984, Best Short Script, Univ Northern Iowa, 1984. **Home Addr:** 1600 Shelby Dr, Dyersburg, TN 38024-3439. **Business Addr:** Public Information Coordinator, City Dubuque, 13th & Central, Dubuque, IA 52001, **Business Phone:** (319)589-4116.

JAYNES, DR. GERALD DAVID
Educator. **Personal:** Born Jan 30, 1947, Streator, IL; son of Homer and Lorraine Greenwood; married Patricia Hall; children: Vechel & Hillary. **Educ:** Univ Ill-Urbana, BA, 1971, MA, 1974, PhD, 1976; Yale Univ, MA, 1984. **Career:** Univ Penn, asst prof econ, 1975-77; Yale Univ, asst prof econ, 1977-81, assoc prof econ, 1981-84, prof econ & African American Studies, 1984-; Nat Res Coun, study dir Comm Status Black Am, 1985-89, chair, African & Afro-American Studies, 1990-96. **Honors/Awds:** Adj fel, Joint Ctr for Polit Studies 1982; Bd economists BlackEnterprise Mag, 1984-95; Council of Economic Advisors to President of Nat Urban League, 2007-. **Special Achievements:** Book "Branches Without Roots, Genesis of the Black Working Class," Oxford Univ Press 1986; "A Common Destiny: Blacks and American Society"; ed with R.Williams Jr. ed. Encyclopedia of African American Society, 2004. **Military Serv:** AUS, spl 5th class, 3 yrs; Viet Nam Service, 1966-67. **Business Addr:** Professor of Economics & African American Studies, Director of Graduate Studies, African American Studies, Yale University, Department of Economics, Rm 202 28 Hillhouse Ave, PO Box 208268, New Haven, CT 06520-8268, **Business Phone:** (203)432-3586.

JEAN, KYMBERLY
Business owner, founder (originator), president (organization). **Personal:** Born Dec 31, 1963, Chicago, IL; daughter of P Jean and H Jean. **Educ:** Los Angeles City col, AA, 1985. **Career:** Opposites Attract, pres & founder, 1989-. **Orgs:** Toastmaster; Womens Referral Ser; Nat Asn Women bus owners; BLK Women's Network. **Special Achievements:** The Oprah Winfrey Show, 1991; Jet Magazine, 1992; The Phil Donahue Show, 1992; Essence Magazine, 1993.

JEAN, NELUST WYCLEF (WYCLEF JEAN)
Rap musician, guitarist. **Personal:** Born Oct 17, 1972, Croix-des-Bouquets, Haiti; son of Gesner; married Marie Claudinette. **Career:** Rapper, guitarist, recording artist & producer, 1993-; Albums: The Carnival, 1997; The Ecleftic: 2 Sides II a Book, 2000; Masquerade, 2002; The Preacher's Son, 2003; Greatest Hits, 2003; Welcome to Haiti: Creole 101, 2004; The Carnival II: Memoirs of an Immigrant, 2007; TV series: "Postcards from Buster", 2004; "Rock the Paint", 2005; Film: Life, 1999. **Special Achievements:** Nominated for two Grammy Awards, including Best Rap Album for the Carnival, 1998; was nominated for Best Hip-Hop Act at the 2000 MTV Europe Music Awards; in 2005, he earned a Golden Globe nomination for his track entitled "Million Voices" featured on the soundtrack to the film Hotel Rwanda. **Business Phone:** (212)833-8000.*

JEFF, DJ JAZZY (JEFFREY ALLAN TOWNES)
Singer, chief executive officer. **Personal:** Born Jan 22, 1965, Philadelphia, PA. **Career:** Albums: Rock the House, 1987; He's the DJ, I'm the Rapper, 1988; Greatest Hits, 1988; Andin This Corner.., 1989; Homebase, 1991; Code Red, 1993; Before the Willennium, 2000; Boom Shake the Room, 1993; The Magnificent, 2002; The Magnificent EP, 2002; Platinum & Gold Collection, 2003; In the House, 2004; The Very Best of DJ Jazzy Jeff & the Fresh Prince, 2006; The Return of the Magnificent, 2007; Singles: I'm Looking for the One (To Be with Me), 2005; We Live in Philly, 2005; How I Do, 2005; Cobbs Creek, 2005; Girls Ain't Nuthin' But Trouble, 2006; For Da Love of Da Game, 2006; Break It Down, 2006; My Peoples, 2006; wrote theme song & appeared on television sit-com: "Fresh Prince of Bel Air"; exec producer: Who is Jill Scott?, Words & Sound, Vol One, 2000; A Touch Of Jazz Inc, founder & chief exec officer, currently. **Honors/Awds:** Grammy award for "Parents Just Don't Understand", 1988 & "Summertime", 1991. **Business Addr:** Founder, Chief Executive Officer, A Touch of Jazz Inc, 444 N 3rd St Suite C9, Philadelphia, PA 19123, **Business Phone:** (215)928-9192.

JEFF, GLORIA JEAN
State government official. **Personal:** Born Apr 8, 1952, Detroit, MI; daughter of Doris Lee and Harriette Virginia Davis. **Educ:** Univ Mich, Ann Arbor, MI, BSE, civil engineering, MSE, civil engineering, Masters Urban Planning; Carnegie-Mellon Univ, Prof Prog Urban Transp, cert; Indiana Univ & Purdue Univ Am Asn State Hwy Transp Off Mgt Inst, cert. **Career:** S Eastern Mich Transp Authority, prin planner, prog analyst, equip engr, 1976-81; Mich Dept Transp, Multi-Regional Planning Div, Lansing, MI, div adminr, 1981-84, Urban Transp Planning Div, div adminr, 1984-85, Bur Transp Planning, asst dep dir, 1985-90, dep dir, 1990; Univ Mich, Col Archit & Urban Planning, Ann Arbor, MI, adj prof, 1988; Fed Hwy Admin, dep adminr, 1998-; Mich Dept Transp, dir, 2003-. **Orgs:** Am Planning Asn, Transp Planning Div; bd dirs, 1988, vpres, 1989-90, pres, 1990, Am Planning Asn, Mich Chap; Mich Soc Planning Off; Am Inst Cert Planners; bd dirs, Univ Mich Alumni Asn; Women's Transp Sem; bd dirs, Univ Mich Col Archit & Urban Planning Alumni Soc; chair, Univ Mich Col Engineering; Transp Res Bd, Statewide Multi-modal Transp Planning Comt; Delta Sigma Theta Sorority; vice chair, Intermodal Issues Comt, Am Asn State Hwy & Transp Off; vice chair Miss Valley Conf, Strategic Issues Comt, 1990-. **Honors/Awds:** Achievement Award, Mich Chapter, Conf Minority Transp Off, 1990; Distinguished Alumni Award, Univ Mich, 1991; Young Engr of the Year, Detroit Chapter, Nat Soc Prof Engrs, 1979; Young Engr of the Year, Detroit Chapter, Soc Women Engrs, 1979; SEMTA Bd Dirs Resolution of Commendation Achievement Award, 1979; active with high sch studs pursuing sci & engineering educ. **Special Achievements:** First African American female deputy administrator for the FHA. **Business Addr:** State Transporation Bldg, 425 W Ottawa St, PO Box 30050, Lansing, MI 48909.*

JEFFCOAT, JAMES WILSON
Football player. **Personal:** Born Apr 1, 1961, Long Branch, NJ; married Tammy; children: Jaren, Jackson, Jacqoline & Jasmine. **Educ:** Ariz State Univ, BA, commun, 1983, MBA. **Career:** Football player (retired), football coach; Dallas Cowboys, defensive end, 1983-94, asst coach, 1998-2000, defensive ends coach, 2000-05; Buffalo Bills, 1995-97; Univ Houston, defensive line coach; Plano West High Sch, defensive end coach, 2008-; Bally Total Fitness, partner; All state insurance agency, owner, currently. **Orgs:** Boys Clubs; Leukemia Soc; Make-A-Wish Found; Sickle Cell Anemia Found; Special Olympics. **Honors/ Awds:** Unsung Hero Award, NJ Sportswriter's Asn, 1991; Super Bowl Champion. **Special Achievements:** Dallas Cowboys' Man of the Year nominee, 1990.

JEFFERIES, CHARLOTTE S.
Educator, u.s. attorney. **Personal:** Born Mar 8, 1944, McKeesport, PA. **Educ:** Howard Univ, BS, 1966; Rollins Col, attended 1967; Duquesne Univ Sch Law, JD, 1980. **Career:** Seminole Co FL, teacher, 1966-67; OIC Erie, dir coun, 1967-70; Urban Coalition RI, health planner, 1970-71; Stud Serv Oic RI, dir, 1971-72; Career Devel Brown Univ, assoc dir, 1973-77; Neighborhood Legal Serv Mckeesport, legal intern, 1978-79; Off US aty Dept Justice, law clerk, 1979-80; Hon Donald E Ziegler Judge US Dist Ct & Western Dist Pa Off US Atty, law clerk, 1980-81; Horty Springer & Mattern PC, partner, 1981; Horty Springer Publications, res ed, currently. **Orgs:** Appellate moot court bd, Duquesne Univ, 1979-80; chmn, Merit Selection Panel US Magistrates Western Dist Pa, 1987-88; Delta Sigma Theta Inc; Allegheny County Bar Asn; Pa Bar Asn; Am bar Asn; Nat Bar Asn; Homer S Brown Law Asn; Soc Hosp Atty Western Pa; city counperson, City Duquesne; YWCA Mc Keesport; NAACP; Howard Univ Alumni Club; Allegheny County Air Pollution Adv Comt; munic Adv comt; Nat Health Lawyers Asn; Am Health Lawyers Asn. **Honors/ Awds:** Richard Allen Award, Outstanding Civic contrib, 1980. **Special Achievements:** Outstanding Student of the Year, Black Amer Law Student Asn, Duquesne Univ Chap, 1980. **Business Addr:** Attorney, Horty Springer & Mattern PC, 4614 Fifth Ave, Pittsburgh, PA 15213, **Business Phone:** (412)687-7677.*

JEFFERIES, GREG LEMONT
Football player. **Personal:** Born Oct 16, 1971, High Point, NC. **Educ:** Univ Va. **Career:** Football player (retired); Detroit Lions, defensive back, 1993-98; Miami Dolphins, defensive back, 1999-2000.

JEFFERIES, MARY
Manager. **Career:** Community Action Organization Inc, dir, currently.

JEFFERS, BEN L.
Government official, business owner. **Personal:** Born Jun 18, 1944, Lake City, FL; married Salomia Lawson. **Educ:** Mt State Univ; A&T U; McNeese State Univ. **Career:** LA Health & Human Res Admin, dir div mgt; LA Health & Human Resources Admin, dir; LA Comn Human Rels Rights & Responsibilities, dir; Gov Edwin Edwards, cong aide; LA Democratic Party, chair; Dem Natl Conv, LA, deleg, 2000, 2004; Louisiana Democratic Party Exec Comt, 6th Congressional Dist, DNC at-large, 2004-; Ben Jeffers Inc, chief exec officer, currently; Vanderbilt Consulting LLC, sr advisor, currently. **Orgs:** Chmn LA Coalition for Social Serv Prog; state adv bd Comprehensive Hlth Planning; mem Dvlpmntl Disabilities Coun; Nat Rehabltatn asn; LA Rehab Asn; Am Soc Training & Devel; Am Pub Welfare Asn; LA Health Asn; Kiwanis Club Lake Charles; Am Legion; Prince Hall Masons; past mem bd dir, Advertising & Press Clubg SW LA; past bd mem, Foreman-reynaud Br YMCA; gen mgr, Lake Charles Newsleader; former Exec asst to Pub Newsleader Newspapers in LA & MS; ed, Pub Lake Charles Times; State Manpower Planning Cncl; mem NAACP; Was a super delegate in 2008 presidental election nomination, 2008; Bd mem, Regents Advisory Coun, Post Secondary Education; bd mem, Grambling State Univ Found. **Special Achievements:** First African American elected to chair Louisiana Democratic Party. **Military Serv:** USMC, sgt, 1963-67. **Home Phone:** (225)383-9724. **Business Addr:** DNC At-Large, Louisiana Democratic Party, 6th Congressional District, PO Box 4016, Baton Rouge, LA 70821, **Business Phone:** (225)346-5400.

JEFFERS, CLIFTON R.
Lawyer, president (organization). **Personal:** Born Feb 8, 1934, Roxboro, NC; son of Theron and Clara; married Mary R Lloyd; children: Kwame. **Educ:** Tenn State Univ, AB, 1956; Hastings Col Law Univ, CA, JD, 1964. **Career:** State Calif, state dep atty, 1964-69; US Dept Housing & Urban Develop, reg admin, 1969-76; State Calif, chief asst state pub defender, 1976-84; James & Jeffers, pres, 2002, sr partner, currently; Univ Calif, Berkeley, guest lectr criminal; Stanford Univ Law Sch, guest lectr; Univ Southern Calif Sch Law, guest lectr. **Orgs:** Pres, San Francisco Nat Asn Advan Colored People, 1966-69; San Francisco Coun Churches, 1967-72; San Francisco Econ Opportunities Coun, 1967-68; bd dir, Am Civil Liberties Union Northern Calif, 1969-73; bd dirs, Lawyers Club, San Francisco, 1981-82; bd dir, Bar Asn San Francisco, 1984-; founding pres, William Hastie Lawyers Asn; bd dir, Frederick Douglas Haynes Gardens; gen coun, 3rd Baptist Church; bd dir, Calif Rural Legal Assistance Found; founding mem, San Francisco Black Leadership Forum; trustee, 3rd Baptist Church; bd dir, Nat Asn Advan Colored People; bd dir, First Dist Appellate Proj; co-founder, State Bar Standing Comn Legal Serv Criminal Defendants; Calif Asn Black Lawyers; co-founder & dir, Third Baptist Gardens Inc; Afro-Am Agenda Coun; Nat Calif & San Francisco Bar Asn; Charles Houston Bar Asn; Am Judicature Soc. **Honors/Awds:** Outstanding Pres Award, Nat Asn Advan Colored People, 1967, 1969; Am Jurisprudence Award; Equal Employ Opportunities Award, US Dept Housing & Urban Develop; Cert of Fair Housing Achievement, US Dept Housing & Urban Develop; Meritorious Serv Award, Nat Asn Advan Colored People; Outstanding Performance Award, US Dept Housing & Urban Develop; Cert of Honor, San Francisco Bd Supervisors. **Military Serv:** USAF, lt, 1956-59. **Home Addr:** San Francisco, CA 94122. **Business Phone:** (415)433-6542.*

JEFFERS, EVE (EVE JIHAN JEFFERS)
Rap musician, actor. **Personal:** Born Nov 10, 1978, Philadelphia, PA; daughter of Jerry Jeffers and Julie Wilcher. **Career:** Albums: Let There Be Eve: Ruff Ryders' First Lady, 1999; Scorpion, 2001; Eve-Olution, 2002; Films: Barbershop, 2002; XXX, 2002; Barbershop 2, 2004; TV Series: "Eve," 2003-06; "Spider-Man", 2003; "Third Watch", 2003; "The Woodsman," 2004; "The Cookout," 2004; "One on One", 2004; "Saturday Night Live", 2005; Flashbacks of a Fool, 2008. **Honors/Awds:** Video Music Award, 2004; Grammy Award, 2002. **Business Addr:** Rapper, Actress, Interscope Records, 2220 Colorado Ave, Santa Monica, CA 90404, **Business Phone:** (310)865-1000.

JEFFERS, EVE JIHAN. See JEFFERS, EVE.

JEFFERS, GRADY ROMMEL
Executive. **Personal:** Born Jul 11, 1943, New York, NY; son of Robert and Alberta; married Maryann P; children: Anna, Debbie, Michael & Alberta. **Educ:** Bernard Baruch Col; Manhattan Com-

munity Col, AA, 1973. **Career:** Bankers Trust Co, asst vpres commercial loan group; Franklin Nat Bank, mgr, 1969-74; Republic Nat Bank, vpres, 1980-. **Orgs:** Nat Bankers Asn mem Masons; 100 Black Men; Minority Bus & Develop; Nat Asn Acct; Urban Bankers Coalition; secy, exec bd, Private Industry Coun, 1989-. **Honors/Awds:** Nom White house Fellowship. **Military Serv:** USAF, 1961-65. *

JEFFERS, JACK
Musician. **Personal:** Born Dec 10, 1928; son of Rose Elizabeth Bosfield and George William Jeffers; married Cynthia Rogers; children: Laura & Lee. **Educ:** Northeastern Univ, BS, 1951; New York Univ Sch Law, JD, 1982. **Career:** State Univ NY, prof emer music. **Orgs:** Chmn, 7 Arts Chap CORE, 1964-66. **Military Serv:** AUS, sp3, 1956-58. **Home Addr:** 119 Manhattan Ave, New York, NY 10025. *

JEFFERS, SHEILA B
Educator. **Personal:** Born Dec 4, 1954, New York, NY; daughter of Carl H Sr; divorced; children: Clifton Lamar & Terri Anika Prudhomme. **Educ:** State Univ New York, Oneonta, BS, 1975; Webster Univ, MA, 1985; Syracuse Univ, MSW, 1992; Univ Fla, PhD, 2003. **Career:** USAF, squadron cmdr, 1980-89; Salvation Army New York, dir infant mortality, 1990-91; Syracuse Community Health Ctr, dir CMCM, 1991-92; FL A&M Univ, exten specalist, 1992-, asst prof agr sci & coop exten serv, currently. **Orgs:** Life mem, Int Black Women's Cong; Am Asn Anthropologists; secy-treas, Asn Black Anthropologists; NAACP, 1992-; Nat Asn Behav Sci, 1999-; Soc Med Anthropologists, 1999-; Inst African Am Health, 2000-; dir, Proj HEALTH, Fla A&M Univ, Inst African Am Health. **Honors/Awds:** Outstanding Achievement Award,Syracuse Univ, Corp Access Partnership, 1992; Service Award, Bd County Commissioners, 1995; FAc Develop FEI, Univ Fla, 1995-03; Outstanding Accomplishments in the Field of Breast Cancer, Spellman Col, 2000; Hon Supporter Breast Cancer, Susan G Komen Breast Cancer Found, 2001. **Special Achievements:** Numerous publications and presentations including Lifting While We Climb: Removing Breast Cancer Treatment for African American Women. Reaching For The Cure. Making A Difference Conference, Susan G Komen Foundation, Washington DC 2000; Spirituality and Black Women's Health. Oral Presentation, The Association of Social and Behavioral Scientists Sixty Fifth Annual Conference. Community Action: Reviewed, Renewed and Revitalized. March 22-25, 2000. **Military Serv:** USAF, capt, 1980-89; Air Force Commendation Award with one oak leaf cluster. **Business Addr:** Assistant Professor, Florida A&M University, Perry Paige Bldg Rm 306C S, Tallahassee, FL 32308-5596, **Business Phone:** (850)561-2924.

JEFFERSON, ALPHINE WADE
Educator. **Personal:** Born Dec 31, 1950, Caroline County, VA; son of Horace Douglas and Ellie Mae Lewis; divorced. **Educ:** Univ Chicago, AB, 1973; Duke Univ, MA, 1975, PhD, 1979. **Career:** Duke Univ, Oral History Inst, instr, 1974, Inst Policy Sci Res, assoc & coordr oral interviews, 1974, instr social sci, 1976; Northern Ill Univ, Dept Hist, instr, 1978-79, Ctr Black Studies, fac assoc, 1978-85, asst prof dept hist, 1979-85; Harvard Univ, Andrew W Mellon post doctoral fel, 1982-83; Southern Methodist Univ, vis asst prof hist & interim dir African-Am studies, 1984-85, asst prof hist, 1984-89; Col Wooster, OH, assoc prof hist, 1989-96, prof & chair, 1996-99, Dept Hist, prof, First VPres, 2006-. **Orgs:** Reader, Nat Endowment Humanities, 1980-; consult, Dwight Correctional Ctr Humanities Proj, 1980-81; reader, Newberry Libr Inst, Chicago, 1984-; reader, Scott Foresman & Co, 1984-; adv bd Int Jour Oral Hist, 1986-; bd dir, African Heritage Cult Arts League, 1986-; bd dir, Int Theatrical Arts Soc, 1988-; bd dir, Huang Int Inc, 1988-; Dallas Independent Sch Dist, African-Am Adv Bd 1988-; Am Hist Asn; Asn Study Afro-Am Life & Hist; first vpres, Oral Hist Asn, vpres & pres, 2006-07; Org Am Historians; Nat Coun Black Studies; Ill Coun Black Studies; Du Sable Mus African Am Hist. **Honors/Awds:** Alexander White Scholar, Univ Chicago, 1972-73; The Promise of World Peace Award, Am Bahai, Dallas, TX, 1986; Most Popular Professor Award, Southern Methodist Univ Stud Body, 1986; The Margareta Deschner Teaching Award, Southern Methodist Univ Women's Studies Coun, 1986. **Special Achievements:** Numerous publications, chapters in books, articles, reviews and numerous papers presented at professional conferences. **Home Addr:** 530 Forest Creek Dr, Wooster, OH 44691, **Home Phone:** (330)264-8680. **Business Addr:** First Vice President, The College of Wooster, Department of History, 1189 Beall Ave, Wooster, OH 44691, **Business Phone:** (330)263-2455.

JEFFERSON, ANDREA GREEN
Marketing executive. **Personal:** Born Oct 9, 1946, New Orleans, LA; daughter of Herman and Bernice Johnson; married William, Jun 13, 1970; children: Jamila, Jalila, Jelani, Nailah & Akilah. **Educ:** Southern Univ, BA, 1969; Rutgers Univ, MEd, 1970; Univ New Orleans, EdD, 1979; Harvard Grad Sch Educ Mgt, 1989. **Career:** Southern Univ New Orleans, dir financial aid, 1980-81, vice chancellor student affairs, 1988-92; New Orleans Pub Schs, admin intern, 1982-83, supvr math, 1983-84, instructional specialist, 1985-86, dir instr/staff develop, 1986-87, dir area I schs, 1987-88; Grambling State Univ, coordr/doctoral prog, 1992-94. **Orgs:** Bd mem, Nat Cou Negro Women, 1984-88; past secy, fundraising chair, Links New Orleans Chap, 1986-; President's Coun Tulane Univ, 1991-; Women's Nat Democratic Club, 1991-; bd mem, Cong Black Caucus Found, 1992-; past chair/issue forum chair, Cong Black Caucus Spouses, 1992-95; Stanley S Scott Cancer Res Ctr, 1993; pres, Amistad Res Ctr, 1994-; bd supervisors, Southern Univ, 1995-; La State Univ Med Ctr. **Honors/Awds:** Role Model, YWCA, 1993. **Special Achievements:** Publication Board, Initiatives, scholarly journal of the National Assn of Women in Education, 1990-93; The College Student Affairs Journal, 1991-93; Ethnic Women Newsletters, editor, 1992-93; The Changing Faces of Aids, 1993; Congressional Black Caucus Spouses Publication. **Business Phone:** (504)862-3222.

JEFFERSON, ANDREW L. See Obituaries section.

JEFFERSON, DR. ARTHUR
School administrator. **Personal:** Born Dec 1, 1938, Alabama; children: Mark & Michael. **Educ:** Wayne State Univ, BS, 1960, MA, polit sci, 1963, EdD, 1973. **Career:** Detroit Pub Schs, asst regional supt, 1970-71, regional supt, 1971-75,interim gen supt, 1975, gen supt, 1975-90, supt emer, currently; Univ Mich, distinguished vis prof, 1990-95. **Orgs:** Nat Polit Sci Hon Soc; Pi Sigma Alpha; Nat & Mich Couns Soc Studies; Am Mich Asn Sch Adminr; Coun Basic Educ; Metrop Detroit Soc Black Educ Adminr; Nat Alliance Black Sch Educr; Nat Rev Panel Study Sch Desegregation; bd trustees, Wayne State Univ Alumni Asn, 1968-71; Am Civil Lib Union; Nat Asn Advan Colored People; bd dir, Coun Great City Sch; bd trustees, Detroit Econ Growth Corp; bd dir, Detroit Educ TV Found; bd adv, Detroit Pre-Employment Training Ctr; bd dir, Detroit Teachers CreditUnion; Econ Club Detroit; bd dir United Found; PTA Urban Adv Task Force; chair, bd trustees, Mus African Hist; bd dir, Col Bound Kids Learning Ctr. **Special Achievements:** First Black Superintendent, 1974. **Business Addr:** Superintendent Emeritus, Detroit Public Schools, 250 E Harbortown Dr Apt 701, Detroit, MI 48207-5016.

JEFFERSON, AUSTIN, JR.
Clergy. **Personal:** Born in Aiken, SC; married Evelyn Griffin; children: Leonard A, Harry P, Evelyn L, Gene A. **Educ:** Temple Sch Theol, 1953; Moody Bible Inst; New Era Sem; Eastern Sem; Universal Bible Inst, Masters, Bible Study, 1974. **Career:** Cleric, currently. **Orgs:** Bd Foreign Missions; chmn, Bd St Home; Nat Baptist Conv; Methodist Christian Coun; adv bd, Eastern Sem; vpres, New England MS Conv, 1971; Even Conf.

JEFFERSON, CLIFTON
Funeral director, mayor. **Personal:** Born Sep 10, 1928, Lynchburg, SC; son of John and Cassie McDonald; married Gwendolyn W; children: Carolyn, Chrishinda, Lamont & Latisha Lenora. **Educ:** SC St Col, BS, 1946; Univ MD, 1954; SC St Col, MA, 1968. **Career:** Fleming Sch, sci teacher 1955-57; Mt Pleasant HS, asst prin 1957-77; Bishopville Middle Sch, prin, 1977-87; Lynchburg SC, mayor 1975-77; Jefferson Funeral Home, owner. **Orgs:** Chmn admin bd, Warren Chapel United Meth Sch; deleg, SC Dem Conv; SC Morticians Asn; Nat Asn Advan Colored People; Kappa Alpha Psi; United Meth Ch; Black Mayors SC; NEA; SCEA; LCEA; SC Mun Asn. **Honors/Awds:** Man of Year, SC Mortician Asn, 1976; Achievement Award, Kappa Alpha Psi, 1977; Dedicated Serv Award, Mt Pleasant HS, 1977. **Special Achievements:** First black mayor in Lynchburg, SC. **Business Addr:** Owner, Jefferson Funeral Home, 130 Mc Intosh St, Lynchburg, SC 29080, **Business Phone:** (803)437-2332.

JEFFERSON, FREDERICK CARL, JR.
School administrator. **Personal:** Born Dec 30, 1934, New Orleans, LA; married June Greene; children: Crystal, Frederick, Christian. **Educ:** Hunter Col, BS Music, 1957, MA Music, 1959, MA Guid, 1967; Univ Mass, Amhurst, EdD 1981. **Career:** SUNY Albany, prog assoc, 1971-73; Univ Rochester, dir educ oppor prog, 1973-76, dir minority stud affairs & assoc dean stud, 1976-85, asst prof, dir urban sch & educ, 1996-99, prof emer, currently. **Orgs:** Action for a Better Community, 1976-; United Way, 1978-; vice chmn bd Dirs, PRIS2M 1978-84; Nat Training Labs; consult New Perspectives Inc; William Warfield Scholarship Fund; Primary Ment Health Proj; Austin Steward Prof Soc, 1985-; Roundtable on Educ Change, 1987-; Urban League Rochester; asst prof Grad Sch Educ & Human Develop, Univ Rochester. **Honors/Awds:** Volunteer Serv Awards, United Way, 1978-86; ABC Serv Award, Action for a Better Community, 1979-86; PRIS2M 1983; Hispanic Leadership Award 1985; Haggai Chapter Community Award, 2007. **Special Achievements:** Publ "Creating a Multicultural Perspective" Asn Col Unions Int Bulletin, 1986. **Business Addr:** Professor Emeritus, University Rochester, Warner Sch Educ and Human Develop, PO Box 270425, Rochester, NY 14627-0425.*

JEFFERSON, GARY SCOTT
Airline executive. **Personal:** Born Nov 4, 1945, Pittsburgh, PA; son of Willard M; married Beverly J Allen, Dec 30, 1967; children: Gary S & Kelly J. **Educ:** Ind Univ PA, Ind, BA, 1967. **Career:** United Airlines Corp, vpres pub affairs. **Orgs:** Chicago Urban League; Nat Asn Advan Colored People; Chicago Econ Club; pres, Clinton's Welfare Work Reform Prog; Chicago Coun Race Rels; bd dirs, Chicago Coun Urban Affairs, 1999-2000. **Honors/Awds:** Distinguished Alumni Award. **Special Achievements:** Listed as 50 top black executives in corporate America.

JEFFERSON, GREG BENTON
Football player, teacher. **Personal:** Born Aug 31, 1971, Orlando, FL; married Twana; children: Victoria & Samantha. **Educ:** Univ Cent Fla, BS, criminal justice. **Career:** Philadelphia Eagles, defensive end, 1995-2000; Evans High Sch, teacher,2006; Orlando Predators, 2006-07.

JEFFERSON, HILDA HUTCHINSON
Educator. **Personal:** Born Jun 19, 1920, Charleston, SC; married James L Jefferson Jr; children: Marjorie, Leon, Charles, Herman, Edward & Jerome. **Educ:** Avery Norm Inst, Cert, 1940; Tuskegee Inst, BS, Home Econ, 1944; Allen Univ, Advan Studies, 1954; SC State Col, Advan Studies, 1955. **Career:** Educator (retired); Stark Gen Hosp, asst dietician, 1944-45; 6 Mile Jr HS, sci teacher, 1945-46; Macedonia HS, home econ teacher, 1946-47; Avery HS, dietician, 1948-50; Baptist Hill HS, home econ teacher, 1950-53; Lincoln HS, sci teacher, 1955-58; Wallace HS, home econ teacher, 1958-69; St Andrews Parish HS, home econ teacher, 1969-82; Charleston SC, coun mem, 1975; City Charleston, Mayor Pro Tem, 1976, 1984, 1992. **Orgs:** New Israel RE Church, 1920-, NAACP, 1950-, Charleston Cty Democratic Women, 1976, Charlestons Art & Hist Comn, 1976-, Nat League Cities, 1976-; chmn, Traffic & Transp Comn, 1980-; Charleston Area Comt, Rel Comn, 1980, SC Gov Comn Hwy Safety, 1980; mem bd, Carolina Art Asn, 1980, Charleston Mus, 1980-, Trident United Way, 1982-; Coun Govt, 1983-; chmn, Black Portrait Study Comn, 1984-85; pres, Gamma Zeta Chap Zeta Phi Beta, 1984-86; secy, Charleston Cty Munic Asn, 1985-; porgy & bess adv comn Catfish Row Co Inc, 1985-; adv coun, Charleston Area Sr Citizens Serv, 1985-. **Honors/Awds:** Outstanding Contrib & Meritorious Serv, Vol Community, Charleston Fed Womens & Girls Clubs, 1972; Outstanding Service & Dedication in the Fields of Education, 1976, Politics, 1976, Service, 1979,84; Royal Light Award Woman of the Year, 1976; 1st Black Woman Home Econ of the Year for Charleston Cty & SC, 1976; Recognized by Gamma Xi Omega Chap Alpha Kappa Alpha, 1977, Phi Beta Sigma, Omega Psi Phi; Contrib to Women Award, YWCA 1980; Safety Recognition of Dedicated & Outstanding Serv to the Citizens of SC-SC Governors Comm on Hwy, 1982; Outstanding Serv to Community, 1983. **Special Achievements:** First Black Woman City of Charleston selected Mayor Pro Term, 1976, 1984, 1992.

JEFFERSON, HORACE LEE
Dentist. **Personal:** Born Oct 10, 1924, Detroit, MI; married Betty Lou Brown; children: Linda, Eric, Judith, Michael. **Educ:** Highland Park Jr Col, 1948; Univ Mich Dental Sch, DDS, 1952. **Career:** Retired; Ford Motor Co, staff, 1946; Lincoln Motor Car Co, 1952; Dentist, 1948-53; Herman Keifer City Hosp Detroit, staff sr dentist, 1954-71; pvt pract, dent, 1954-99. **Orgs:** Detroit Dist Dental Soc; Mich Dent Asn; Am Dent Asn, 1953; Wolverine Dental Soc; Afro-Am Mus detroit; Alpha Phi Alpha Fraternity; Nat Asn Advan Colored People; Delta Dental Plans Mich; Acad Gen Dent. **Honors/Awds:** Clinical Presentation 15th Review, Detroit Dist Dental Soc, 1957; Wolverine Dental Soc, 1971; forum Presentation Gamma Lambda Chap AOA 1973. **Military Serv:** AUS, 1944-46; Meritorious Unit Award. **Business Addr:** 10040 Puritan, Detroit, MI 48238.*

JEFFERSON, JAMES E. See Obituaries section.

JEFFERSON, DR. JOSEPH L
Counselor, educator. **Personal:** Born Nov 8, 1940, Pensacola, FL; married Ida C Wedgeworth; children: Eric, Clynita & Steven. **Educ:** Tex Southern Univ, BS, econs, 1968, MA, coun, 1971; Ohio State Univ, PhD, counr educ, 1974. **Career:** Tex Southern Univ, grad fel, 1970-71; Voc Guid Houston, counsr, 1971; Tex Southern Univ, admin asst dean col arts & sci, assoc dir, Off Inst Res, prof coun & asst prof educ, currently. **Orgs:** Am Educ & Res Asn; Phi Delta Kappa; Asn Inst Res; Am Coun Asn; Tex Couns Asn; Kappa Alpha Psi Fraternity; Houston Jr club; Houston Lion's Club. **Military Serv:** AUS, sp E5, 1962-65. **Business Addr:** Professor of Counseling, Texas Southern University, 3100 Cleburne St, Houston, TX 77004.

JEFFERSON, KAREN L.
Librarian. **Personal:** Born Oct 30, 1952, Eglin AFB, FL; daughter of Henry S and Agnes McLean. **Educ:** Howard Univ, Wash, DC, BA, 1974; Atlanta Univ, Atlanta, GA, MSLS, 1975. **Career:** Moorland-Spingarn Res Ctr, Howard Univ, Wash, DC, manuscript librn, 1976-80, sr manuscript librn, 1980-87, curator, 1987-93; Nat Endowment Humanities, Wash, DC, humanities adminr; Robert W Woodruff Libr, Atlanta Univ Ctr, Head Archives & Spec Collections, currently. **Orgs:** Co-ed, African Am & Third World Archivist Roundtable Newsletter, 1987-93; bd mem, African-Am Educ Archives Proj, 1989-93; Black Caucus ALA 1972-; Soc Am Archivists, 1983-; Mid Atlantic Region Archives Conf, 1982-; Acad Cert Archivists, 1989-. **Business Addr:** Head of Archives & Special Collections, Robert W Woodruff Library, Atlanta University Center, 111 James P Brawley Dr SW, Atlanta, GA 30314, **Business Phone:** (404)978-2000.*

JEFFERSON, LINDA
President (Organization). **Career:** Burrell Communs Group LLC, sr vpres & dir media, 2004-. **Orgs:** Arbitron Inc. **Business Phone:** (312)297-9753.*

JEFFERSON, MARCIA D.
Librarian, educator. **Personal:** Born Jan 2, 1935, Jamaica; daughter of Jacob A Dyer (deceased) and Marjorie Lewis

(deceased); married Eugene Jefferson, Apr 2, 1966; children: Denise, Darryl. **Educ:** Brooklyn Col, Brooklyn, NY, BA, 1957; Rutgers Univ Sch Libr Sci, NB, NJ, MLS, 1959; State Univ NY, Stony Brook, NY, MALS, 1987. **Career:** Brooklyn Pub Libr, NY, page & librn trainee, 1954-63; Bayshore & Brightwaters Pub Libr, NY, ref librn, 1963-66; Staff-Libr & UST, NY Worlds Fair, 1965; Patchogue-Medford Schs, NY, sch librn, 1966-67; Bayshore & Brightwaters Pub Libr, ref librn, 1969; Suffolk County Community Col, Selden, periodicals librn, 1978, prof, 2001. **Orgs:** SC Libr Asn, 1978; bd trustee & elected mem, Patchogue-Medford Libr, 1989; Black Caucus & ALA, 1989; vpres, acad div SC Libr Asn; vpres, Data & Story Libr, 1990. *

JEFFERSON, MARGO
Journalist. **Personal:** Born in Chicago, IL; daughter of Ron and Irma. **Educ:** Univ Chicago Lab Sch; Brandeis Univ, BA; Columbia Univ, MS, jour. **Career:** Columbia Univ, instr; NY Univ, instr; Vogue Mag, ed; Newsweek Mag, ed; NY Times, critic, 1993, 2003. **Honors/Awds:** Pulitzer Prize, criticism, New York Times, 1995.

JEFFERSON, OVERTON C.
Educator, lawyer. **Personal:** Born in Port Arthur, TX; married Marjorie; children: Robert & Olida. **Educ:** Xavier Univ, New Orleans, AB, 1949; NC Cent Univ, JD; NY Univ Sch Law, LLM. **Career:** Tex Southern Univ Sch Law, asst prof, 1953-58; Houston Legal Found, centoff dir, 1985. **Military Serv:** AUS, 1942-45. **Business Addr:** Lawyer, 609 Fannin Ave Suite 1909, Houston, TX 77002.

JEFFERSON, PATRICIA ANN
Appraiser. **Personal:** Born Nov 26, 1951, Richmond County, NC. **Educ:** Augusta Col, BBA, 1973. **Career:** GA Power Co, customer serv rep, 1969-73; Black Stud Union Augusta Col, secy, organizer, 1971-73; Augusta/Richmond Co Human Rels Comn, from admin asst to dir, 1974-81; Augusta Focus Newspaper, gen mgr, 1982-87; Pat Jefferson Realty, Appraisals, cert residential appraiser, 1987-; Jefferson Appraisal Co, cert residential appraiser, currently. **Orgs:** Eta Theta Zeta Sorority, founder, dir, Spiritualettes, 1974-; Spirit Creek Bapt Ch; bd, Am Red Cross; bd, CSRA BUS League; Nat Asn Real Estate Appraiser; Appraisal Inst, affiliate; bd mem, Ga Real Estate Appraisers Bd; bd mem, Operation Self Help. **Business Addr:** Certified Residential Appraiser, Jefferson Appraisal Co, 1126 11th St, Augusta, GA 30901.

JEFFERSON, REGGIE
Baseball player, athletic coach. **Personal:** Born Sep 25, 1968, Tallahassee, FL; married Kay; children: Shayna, R J, Jannay & Jalen. **Educ:** Univ S Fla, BA, bus admin, 2003. **Career:** Baseball player (retired), athletic coach; Cincinnati Reds, infielder, 1991; Cleveland Indians, 1991-94; Seattle Mariners, 1994; Boston Red Sox, 1995-99; Japanese league, 2000; Tampa Bay Devil Rays, spring training camp, guest instr, 2004; Albuquerque Isotopes, Fla Marlins, hitting coach; Univ S Fla, asst coach, 2005, hitting coach, 2006-. **Special Achievements:** Eighth in American League in batting average (.319), 1997.

JEFFERSON, ROBERT R.
Government official. **Personal:** Born Sep 21, 1932, Lexington, KY; married Katie E Scott (died 1998); children: Robert Jr & Stanley. **Educ:** Ky State Col, BA, Hist, Polit Sci, Biol, 1967, MA, Pub Affairs, 1974. **Career:** Government official (retired); IBM, assembler, 1959; US Pub Health Hosp, various positions, 1957-74; US Bur Prisons, sr case mgr, 1974-83; Lexington Fayette Urban County, coun mem, 1988-. **Orgs:** Comt organizer, Whitney Young Sickle Cell Ctr, 1973-74; acting exec dir, Urban Co Human Rights Comn, Lexington, 1974; past dist rep & mem, Supreme Coun; chmn, Human Rights Comn, 1969-83; Black & Williams Community Ctr; Nat Conf Christians & Jews; LFUC Urban League, CORE, Bluegrass Black Bus Asn, Agency Exec Forum; bd mem, Nat League Cities, 1993-95; bd mem, KY League Cities, 1990-2000. **Honors/Awds:** Outstanding Service Award, LFUCG Human Rights Comn, 1985; Distinguished Service Award, Micro City Govt, 1985; Outstanding Service Award, Lima Dirve Seventh Day Adventist Church, 1981; Distinguished Service Award, KY State Univ, 1981; Brotherhood Award, NCCJ, 1979; Honorary Doctorate Degree, Micro City Univ, 1975; Minority Affairs Community Distinguished Services, 1973; Several Omega Psi Phi Fraternal Awards; Outstanding Achievement in Fair Housing Award for individual, 2007. **Military Serv:** USAF, 1947-54; USAFR, 1954-68. *

JEFFERSON, ROLAND SPRATLIN
Physician. **Personal:** Born May 16, 1939, Washington, DC; son of Bernard S and Devonia H Spratlin; married Melanie L Moore; children: Roland Jr, Rodney Earl, Shannon Devonia, Royce Bernard. **Educ:** Univ S CA, BA Anthropology 1961; Howard Univ, MD 1965. **Career:** Martin L King, Jr Hosp, assoc prof, 1972-75; Dept Rehab, consult, 1972-78; Watts Health Found, staff psychiatrist, 1973-80; Asn Black Motion Picture & TV Producers, pres/founding mem, 1980-81; pvt pract, physician. **Orgs:** Writers Guild Am W; Nat Med Asn; bd dir, Am Sickle Cell Found, 1973-76; bd adv Brockman Gallery, 1976-78. **Honors/Awds:** Grassroots Award, Sons Watts, 1977; Golden Quill Award, Abffriham Found, 1977; Nat Asn Advan Colored People Image Award, 13th Annual, Nat Asn Advan Colored People Image Awards, 1980; Award Merit Black Am Cinema Soc, 1989; Special DRRs Award, 24th Annual Nat Asn Advan Colored People Image Awards, 1992; Producer, Writer, Dir, Feature Film "Perfume", 1989. **Special Achievements:** First Place, Film Drama Black Filmmakers Hall of Fame 1980; author of 4 novels, The School on 103rd Street (1976), A Card for the Players (1978), 559 to Damascus (1985), Damaged Goods, (2003). **Military Serv:** USAF capt 1969-71. **Business Addr:** Physician, 3870 Crenshaw Blvd, Los Angeles, CA 90008-1828, **Business Phone:** (323)299-4508.*

JEFFERSON, SHAWN (VANCHI LASHAWN JEFFERSON)
Football player. **Personal:** Born Feb 22, 1969, Jacksonville, FL. **Educ:** Univ Cent Fla, bus admin. **Career:** Football player (retired); San Diego Chargers, wide receiver, 1991-95; New Eng Patriots, 1996-99; Mellon Bank, internship, 1998; Atlanta Falcons, 2000-02; Detroit Lions, wide receiver, 2003; Any Occasion Catering Co, co-owner, currently. **Orgs:** Ducks Unlimited. **Business Addr:** Co-Owner, Any Occasion Catering, 2137 N Courtenay Pkwy, Merritt Island, FL 32953, **Business Phone:** (321)459-1673.*

JEFFERSON, VANCHI LASHAWN. See JEFFERSON, SHAWN.

JEFFERSON, WALLACE B
Lawyer. **Personal:** Son of William and Joyce; married Rhonda; children: 3. **Educ:** Univ Mich, BA, polit philos, 1985; Univ Tex Sch Law, JD, 1988. **Career:** Groce Locke & Hebdon Inc, Appelate Sect, atty; Tom Crofts & Sharon Callaway, owner, 1991; Supreme Ct, Austin TX, US atty gen, 2001-03, chief justice, 2004-. **Orgs:** Pres, San Antonio Bar Asn, 1998-99; William S Sessions Am Inn Ct, 1999; Am Bar Asn. **Honors/Awds:** 40 Under 40 Rising Star, San Antonio Bus Jour, 1996; Outstanding Young Lawyer, San Antonio Young Lawyers Asn, 1997; Outstanding Alumnus Award, Univ Tex Sch Law, 2005; Distinguished Alumnus Award, James Madison Col. **Special Achievements:** First African American Chief Justice of the Supreme Court of Texas. **Business Addr:** Chief Justice, The Supreme Court of Texas, 201 W 14th St, PO Box 12248 Capitol Sta, Austin, TX 78701, **Business Phone:** (512)463-7899.

JEFFERSON, HON. WILLIAM JENNINGS
Congressperson (u.s. federal government). **Personal:** Born Mar 14, 1947, Lake Providence, LA; son of Mose and Angeline Harris; married Andrea Green; children: Jamila Efuru, Jalila Eshe, Jelani, Nailah & Akilah. **Educ:** Southern Univ A& M Col, Baton Rouge, LA, BA, eng & polit sci, 1969; Harvard Univ, Cambridge, MA, JD, 1972; Georgetown Law Ctr, LLM, 1996. **Career:** US Ct Appeals, 5th Circuit, Judge Alvin B Rubin, judicial clerk, 1972-73; US Senator J Bennett Johnston, Wash, DC, legis asst, 1973-75; Jefferson, Bryan & Gray, New Orleans, La, founding partner, 1976; Louisiana State Senate,mem, 1979; Baton Rouge, La, mem, 1980-90; US House Reps, Wash, DC, Second Dist La, mem, 1991-2009. **Orgs:** La Bar Assn; Am Bar Assn; Nat Bar Assn; DC Bar Assn; chair, Cong Black Caucus Found, 2001-; sr mem, Ways & Means Comt; House Comt Budget; co chair,Africa Trade & Investment Caucus; Cong Caucus Brazil & Nigeria; trustee, Greater St Stephen Full Gospel Church. **Honors/Awds:** Legislator of the Year, Alliance Good Govt; AP Tureaud Community Legal Services Award; Louisiana Political Museum & Hall Of Field, 2000; Distinguished Service Award, Wash Int Trade Assn, 2002; Iberville Award, New Orleans Mag, 2002; Maritime Service Award, Wash, DC Propeller Club, 2004. **Special Achievements:** First African-American to be elected to Congress in Louisiana since Reconstruction. **Military Serv:** AUS, judge advocate gen, capt, 1969.

JEFFERSON-BULLOCK, JALILA
Lawyer. **Personal:** Married Torey. **Educ:** Harvard Col, AB, eng; Univ Chicago, MA, humanities; Harvard Law, JD. **Career:** La Dist 91, atty & state rep, currently. **Orgs:** La State Bar Asn; Am Bar Asn; Nat Bar Asn; Bd dirs, REAL; vpres, CHESS; bd dirs, Lindy's Pl; bd dirs, CASA; bd dirs, Books You; bd dirs, New Orleans Jazz Orchestra; Adv Comt, Dress Success; Adv Comt, WOW Home Ownership Prog; Stud Nat Community. **Honors/Awds:** Servant of the Year, Nat Coun Negro Women. **Business Addr:** Attorney, State Representative, Louisiana District 91, 3313 S Saratoga St Suite 7, New Orleans, LA 70115, **Business Phone:** (504)896-1478.*

JEFFERSON-FORD, CHARMAIN
Law enforcement officer. **Personal:** Born Oct 2, 1963, Detroit, MI; daughter of Walter L Patton and Hercules; children: Krysten N. **Educ:** Wayne State Univ, Detroit, Mich, 1981-87. **Career:** Detroit Pub Schs, Detroit, Mich, clerk, 1978-81; Hudson's Dept Store, Detroit, Mich, model, 1979-81; Grand Value Pharmacy, Detroit, Mich, pharmacy teacher, 1981-88; City Southfield, Southfield, Mich, police officer, 1988-; Drug Abuse Resistance Educ, officer, 1991-. **Orgs:** Pres, Future Homemakers Am, 1980-81. **Honors/Awds:** First black female police officer in Southfield, MI. **Home Addr:** 27070 Pebblebrook St, Southfield, MI 48034, **Home Phone:** (248)350-2354. **Business Addr:** Police Officer, City of Southfield Police Department, Crime Prevention Bureau, 26000 Evergreen Rd, Southfield, MI 48034, **Business Phone:** (248)796-5300.

JEFFERSON-JENKINS, CAROLYN
High school principal, president (government). **Personal:** Born Sep 19, 1952, Cleveland, OH; daughter of James and Ruby; married Kenneth B Jenkins, Sr., Apr 19, 1997. **Educ:** Western Col, BA, Social Sci & Educ, 1974; John Carroll Univ, MEd, Admin & Supv, 1981; Kent State Univ, EdS, 1985; Cleveland State Univ, PhD, 1991. **Career:** Cleveland Heights, Univ Heights Schs, prin, 1993-95; Jr Achievement Inc, vpres, 1996-98; League Women Voters US, pres, 2002. **Orgs:** Pres, Bus & Prof Women Pikes Peak Region, 1997-98; Phi Delta Kappa; Asn Supv & Curriculum Develop; Nat Asn Sec Sch Prin; Nat Coun Social Studies; Adv Comn, Citizens Project Colo Springs; Aspen Inst, Democracy & Citizenship Project. **Honors/Awds:** Ivy Young Willis Award, Cabrini Col, 1999; BPW Woman of the Year, Pikes Peak, 1998; Good Gonernment Volunteer Award, Carrie Chapman Catt, 1995; Who's Who Among Successful African-Americans; Who's Who in American Education; Outstanding Young Woman in America Award; Civic Leadership Award, Nat Coalition Black Civic Participation; Distinguished Alumni Award, Civic Leadership Cleveland State Univ; Good Housekeeping Award for Women in Government; National Women's Hall of Fame. **Special Achievements:** Book: One Man-One Vote: The History of African-American Vote in the United States; Current Issues in Global Education; first African American woman to head the League of Women Voters of the United States. *

JEFFERSON-MOSS, CAROLYN
Government official. **Personal:** Born Sep 20, 1945, Washington, DC; married Alfred Jeffrey Moss. **Educ:** Howard Univ, BA, polit sci, 1970, MA, pub admin, 1974. **Career:** Reps C Diggs & A Hawkins, cong Black caucus legislative dir, 1970-71; Exotech Systems Inc, sr asso, proj dir, 1971-74; Black Group Inc, sr assoc, dir survey res, 1974-75; Mark Battle Assoc Inc, sr assoc dir mkt, survey res div, 1975-78; Dept Com, dep to asst secy cong affairs, 1978; VaSecy Admin; Fairfax County, dir State & Local Affairs; Common Wealth Va,Dom Resources, dir corp pub policy, 2005-; Capitol Square Preservation Council, Legislative, currently. **Orgs:** Alpha Kappa Alpha Inc, 1968; Met Dem Women's Club, 1974. **Honors/Awds:** Fel, Advan Studies Polit Sci Ford Found Joint Ctr Polit Studies, 1970-71. **Business Addr:** Director of Corporate Public Policy, Common Wealth of Virgnia, 1111 E Main St Suite 901 Richmond, Richmond, VA 23219.

JEFFREY, RONNALD JAMES
Writer, lecturer. **Personal:** Born Mar 11, 1949, Cheyenne, WY; son of John Thomas and Lillian Leola Carter; married Marilyn Mansell, Dec 10, 1978; children: Keeya & Kaylee. **Educ:** Chadron State Col, BS, sociol & anthropology, 1972; Univ Northern CO, MS, communs, 1976. **Career:** Laramie County Community Col, instr, 1980; Univ Wyoming, instr; Off Youth Alternatives, dir, 1971-. **Orgs:** Bd mem, Cheyenne Child Care Ctrs, NAACP, 1984; consult, 1975-; lect, 1975-; Bd mem, Juvenile Justice Adv Bd, 1984-; dir Rocky Mountain Federal Bank, 1988-89; pres, Wy Asn Marriage & Family Therapist, 1986-88; clinical mem, Am Asn Marriage & family Therapy. **Honors/Awds:** George Washington Honor Medal, Freedom Found, 1977; Distinguished Service Award, Cheyenne Jaycees, 1978; Jefferson Award, Am Ins Pub Serv, 1980; Phi Delta Kappa Award, Serv Educ, 1986. **Special Achievements:** Co-author: "A Guide for the Family Therapist"; "COT Hero". torch bearer for Olympic Games, 1996. **Business Addr:** Director, Office of Youth Alternatives, City Cheyenne, 1328 Talbot Ct, Cheyenne, WY 82001, **Business Phone:** (307)637-6480.*

JEFFREYS, JOHN H
Management consultant. **Personal:** Born Mar 27, 1940, Youngsville, NC; married Constance Little; children: Gregory & Alvin. **Educ:** Shaw Univ, AB, sociol, 1962; Univ Ga, MA, pub admin, 1975, ABD/DPA, 1985. **Career:** Rowan County Salisbury, NC, Anti Poverty Prog, Neighborhood Serv Ctr, dir, 1964-67; City Hickory, dir human resources, 1967-70; US Adv Comn Intergovernmental Rels, intern, 1969-70; Univ Ga, Fanning Inst Leadership, leadership develop specialist, sr pub serv assoc & sr fanning fel emer, currently. **Orgs:** Consult, Int Asn City Mgrs, 1983; Pub Safety Personnel, St Croix, 1984; Am Soc Training & Develop, 1984; parliamentarian, Ga Asn Black Elected Off, 1984; pub safety & criminal justice comn, Nat Asn Counties; charter mem, Nat Asn Blacks Criminal Justice. **Honors/Awds:** Man of the Year, Phi Beta Sigma Delta Mu Sigma Chap, 1977, 1981 & 1983; Outstanding Management Instructor, Ga Clerks Asn, 1983. **Special Achievements:** First Black elected in the Clarke County, Ga, 1982; First Black intern in US Advisory Commisson Intergovernmental Relations. **Home Addr:** 140 Jones Dr, Athens, GA 30606. **Business Addr:** Senior Public Service Associate, Senior Fanning Fellow Emeritus, University of Georgia, Fanning Institute for Leadership, 286 Oconee St Suite 200N, Athens, GA 30602-1999, **Business Phone:** (706)255-2564.

JEFFRIES, FRAN M
Journalist. **Personal:** Born Jul 21, 1959, Yanceyville, NC; daughter of William and Elizabeth; married Lawrence Mu-

hammed, Jul 1, 1989. **Educ:** Am Univ, BA, 1982; Ind Univ, MA, 1984. **Career:** Post-Tribune, Gary Ind, reporter, 1984-87; The Courier-Jour, copy ed, reporter, asst city ed, neighborhoods ed, suburbun ed, 1996-; Sun-Sentinel, S Fl, educ ed, 1998-2005; Atlanta J Constitution, features ed, 2005-. **Orgs:** Nat Asn Black Journalist; Soc Prof Journalists; Zenger-Miller mgt trainer; Louisville Asn Black Journalist. **Business Addr:** Features Editor, Atlanta Journal-Constitution, 72 Marietta St NW, Atlanta, GA 30303, **Business Phone:** (404)526-5384.

JEFFRIES, FREDDIE L.
Engineer, executive director. **Personal:** Born Apr 12, 1939, Gates, TN; son of Freddie R and Lora (deceased); married Helen A Ginn, Jan 29, 1971; children: Elizabeth, Terri, Joyce, Lee. **Educ:** Tenn State Univ, BSCE, 1961; Univ Mich, MSE, 1970; Indust Col Armed Forces, dipl, 1984; George Wash Univ, MPA, 1984. **Career:** Nat Oceanic & Atmospheric Admin, Rear Admin; United S Dept Com, Coast & Geodetic Survey, engr, environ sci serv admin engr; Soc Am Mil Engrs, dir, 1970; Nat Oceanic & Atmospheric Admin, Atlantic Marine Ctr, dir, 1999. **Orgs:** Am Cong Surveying & Mapping; Am Soc Photogrammetry, 1961-73. **Honors/Awds:** Distinguished Grad Award, Tenn State Univ, 1991; Special Achievement Awards, 1986, 1987; Unit Citations, 1974, 1988; Karo Award, 1979. *

JEFFRIES, GREG (GREG LEMONT JEFFRIES)
Football player. **Personal:** Born Oct 16, 1971, High Point, NC. **Educ:** Univ Va. **Career:** Football player (retired), Detroit Lions, defensive back, 1993-98; Miami Dolphins, corner back, 1999-00. *

JEFFRIES, GREG LEMONT. See JEFFRIES, GREG.

JEFFRIES, LEONARD
Educator. **Personal:** Born Jan 19, 1937, Newark, NJ. **Educ:** Lafayette Col; Columbia Univ, PhD. **Career:** NY State Comn Educ, Task Force on Deficiency Correction Curric Regarding People Color, former consult, former mem; City Col NY, Dept African Am Studies, chmn, 1992, prof of polit sci, currently. **Orgs:** African Heritage Studies Asn; Nat Black United Front. **Business Addr:** Professor Political Science, City College New York, Department of African American Studies, 535 E 80th St, New York, NY 10021, **Business Phone:** (212)650-8651.

JEFFRIES, DR. ROSALIND R (NANA ESSIE ABIBIO)
Artist, educator. **Personal:** Born Jun 24, 1936, New York, NY; daughter of Edmond Felix Robinson and Mary Gibson; married Leonard Jeffries Jr, Nov 29, 1965. **Educ:** Hunter Col, BA 1963; Columbia Univ, MA, 1968; Yale Univ, PhD, 1990. **Career:** US Govt USIS, Abidjan, & Ivory Coast, W Africa, dir exhib 1965-66. Group Seminars, Africa, co-leader, 1966-72; Brooklyn Mus, lectr 1969; San Jose St Univ, asst prof 1969-72; City Univ New York, art hist, artist & prof, 1972-; African Am Hist & Cult Mus, cur; Bishop's Bible Col Church God Christ, New York, NY, asst prof, 1991; Jersey City Univ, Jersey City, asst prof, currently; Sch Visual Arts, New York, NY, teaching fac, currently; Metrop Mus Art, New York, cur. **Orgs:** Col Arts Asn; CA St Art Historians; Nat Conf Artists; bd dirs, Kem-Were Sci Consortium, 1986-; dir art & cul, Asn Study African Classical Civilizations, 1986-; Blacklight Fel, Black Presence Bible, 1991-; Nat Coun Black Studies. **Honors/Awds:** Negro Music & Art, 1969; Arts Achievement Award, Pres Senegal, 1986; Enstooled Queen Mother, Ashantehene Traditional Govt Ghana, 1988; Q Kingdom Award, United Nations, 1998; Int Black Women Congress Award, 1999; Arthur Schomburg Fac, Ramapo Col. **Special Achievements:** Essays appear in books Black Women in Antiquity and African American History, 2001; Instrumental in Production of Class Room Textbook "African History: A Journey of Liberation", Peoples Publishing Group, Saddle Brook, NJ, 2001. **Business Addr:** Teaching Faculty, School of Visual Arts, 209 E 23rd St, New York, NY 10010-3994, **Business Phone:** (212)592-2000.

JELLERETTE DEJONGH, MONIQUE EVADNE
Writer, graphic artist. **Personal:** Born Feb 26, 1959, Los Angeles, CA; daughter of Carole and Alphonso; married Robert Charles deJongh, Jr, Apr 20, 1990; children: Dylan, Jordan. **Educ:** Boston Univ, Sch Arts, assoc degree fine arts, 1981. **Career:** NY Times Sunday Mag, asst art dir, 1986-87; Genigraphics Inc, comput graphic artist, 1987; Thing of Beauty Prod, 1987-88; Times Sq Studios, art dir, 1987-91; Brownstone Underground, founder & art dir, 1990-; MTV Graphics, electronic designer, 1993-94; Doubleday Publ Group; Book: How To Marry A Black Man. **Orgs:** Jack & Jill Am, Queens Chap, NY. **Special Achievements:** Whitney Houston & Disney, Touchstone, are making movie version of book, "How To Marry A Black Man". *

JELLS, DIETRICH
Football player. **Personal:** Born Apr 11, 1972, Erie, PA. **Educ:** Univ Pittsburgh. **Career:** Football player (retired); New England Patriots, wide receiver, 1996-97; Philadelphia Eagles, 1998-99.

JEMISON, AJ D
Executive. **Career:** Fairlane Town Ctr, gen mgr; Tampa, Fla mall, mgr; Taubman Co, gen mgr; Beverly Ctr, gen mgr, 2005-. **Orgs:** Vol, Hillborough Comn Status Women; bd mem, Children's Home; bd mem, Girl Scouts Suncoast Coun; bd mem, Lowry Park Zoo; W Cent Fla PBS Sta; HARC; bd mem, Fla State Fair Authority; Tampa Org Black Affairs; Tampa Bay Conv & Visitors Bur. **Honors/Awds:** Volunteer of the Year, Dress for Success, 2004; Minority Businessperson of the Year, Tampa Bay Metro Mag, 2004; Bay News 9 Everyday Hero, 2005; Executive Woman of the Year, Network Exec Women, 2005. **Business Addr:** General Manager, Beverly Center, 8500 Beverly Blvd, Los Angeles, CA 90048, **Business Phone:** (310)854-0071.

JEMISON, DR. MAE CAROL
Educator, astronaut, physician. **Personal:** Born Oct 17, 1956, Decatur, AL; daughter of Charlie and Dorothy Green; divorced. **Educ:** Stanford Univ CA, BChE, African & African Am studies, 1977; Cornell Univ, MD, 1981. **Career:** Univ SC Med Ctr, Los Angeles, intern, 1982; Peace Corps West Africa, staff doctor, 1983-85; CIGNA Health Plans CA, gen practr, 1985-87; NASA, astronaut, 1987-93; Dartmouth Col, Montgomery fel, 1993, adj prof, currently; The Jemison Group, founder & pres, 1993-; Discovery Channel, World of Wonder series, host & tech consult, 1994-95; Jemison Inst Advan Technol, dir, 1995-2002; BioSentient Corp, founder & pres, 1999-. **Orgs:** Bd dir, Scholastic Inc; bd dir, The Keystone Ctr; bd dir, Nat Urban League; bd dir, Gen-Probe Inc; AAAS; Houston's UNICEF; Aspen Inst; dir, Valspar Corp; Am Chem Soc; Asn Space Explorers; Alpha Kappa Alpha Sorority; World Sickle Cell Found; founder & chair, Dorothy Jemison Found for Excellence; Nat Inst Sci Inst Med. **Honors/Awds:** Essence Award, Essence Mag, 1988; ScD, Lincoln Univ, 1991; DHL, Winston Salem Col, NC, 1991; Du Sable Museum Award, 1992; Mae C Jemison Academy, named in honor, 1992; Nat Women's Hall of Fame, 1993; Kilby Science Award, 1993; Turner Trumpet Award, 1993; selected as one of the top seven women leaders in a Presidential Ballot Nat straw poll conducted by The White House Project, 1999; Tribute to a Black American Award, Nat Conf Black Mayors, 2003; Ford Freedom Award Scholar, 2003; Rotary Club Chicago's ROTARY/One Award; Doctor Humanities, Princeton Univ. **Special Achievements:** First African American female to enter into space, September 12, 1992; listed in "50 Most Beautiful People in the World" by People magazine, 1993; appeared in the PBS documentary, "African American Lives", 2006. **Business Addr:** President, Founder, The Jemison Group, PO Box 591455, Houston, TX 77259-1455, **Business Phone:** (281)486-7918.

JEMISON, REV. DR. THEODORE JUDSON
Clergy. **Personal:** Born Aug 1, 1918, Selma, AL; son of Rev David V and Henrietta; married; children: Bettye Jane, Dianne Frances & Theodore Judson. **Educ:** Ala St Col, BS, 1940; VA Union Univ, DM, 1945, DD, 1971; Natchez Col, DD, 1953. **Career:** Baptist Church, ordained minister; Mt Zion Baptist Church, Staunton, pastor, 1945-49; Mt Zion First Baptist Church, Baton Rouge, pastor, 1949; Nat Baptist Conv USA, pres, 1982-94. **Orgs:** Gen secy, Nat Baptist Conv USA Inc; 1953; Nat Coun Churches US; LA Rights Comn; Baton Rouge Community Rels Comt; NAACP; pres, Frontiers Intl, Baton Rouge Chap; Alpha Phi Alpha; Shriner; Mason. **Honors/Awds:** Citizen of the Year For Outstanding Contributions in civics, recreation,education, religion, City Baton Rouge; Minister of the Year, Nat Beta Club, 1973; Distinguished Service Award, E Rouge Education Asn, 1973.

JEMMOTT, HENSLEY B
Executive. **Personal:** Born Mar 14, 1947, New York, NY; son of Hensley Barton and Alice Lucille Lee; married Lynn Hooper; children: Hensley & Dara. **Educ:** Syracuse Univ, BA, 1968; Columbia Univ, MBA, 1973. **Career:** Squibb Corp, financial analyst, 1973-78; Am Stand, sr financial anal, 1978-79; Am Cyanamid Co, Am Far E Div, mgr planning, 1979-81; Lederle Int, mgr mkt res, 1981-91; Wm Douglas McAdams Inc, vpres, 1991-93; Torre, Renta, Lazor, vpres, 1993; UniWorld Group Inc, mgt supv, 1993-; Am Cyanamid Co, prod mgr. **Orgs:** Bd dir, Urban League Manhattan, 1977-79; bd dir, Am Lung Asn, NJ, 1983-85, dir, 1984-87; Omega Psi Phi. **Business Addr:** Management Supervisor, UniWorld Group Inc, 100 Ave of the Americas, New York, NY 10013-1699, **Business Phone:** (212)219-7108.

JENIFER, DR. FRANKLYN GREEN
College president. **Personal:** Born Mar 26, 1939, Washington, DC; son of Joseph and Mary Green; married Alfleda, Jan 1, 1964; children: Brenda, Tracey & Ivan. **Educ:** Howard Univ, Wash, DC, BS, 1962, MS, 1965; Univ Md, Coll Pk, MD, PhD,1970. **Career:** U.S. Dept Agr, MD, plant pathologist, 1963-70; Col pres (retired); Livingston Col, Rutgers Univ, NB, NJ, prof biol, 1970-79, Biol Dept, chairperson, 1974-77; Rutgers Univ, Newark, NJ, assoc provost, 1977-79; NJ Dept Higher Ed, Trenton, NJ, vice chancellor, 1979-86; Mass Bd Regents Higher Ed, Boston, MA, chancellor, 1986-90; Howard Univ, Wash, DC, pres, 1990-94; Univ Texas, Dallas, pres, 1994-2005. **Orgs:** Bd dir, Chevron Texaco Inc; bd dir, United Way Metrop Dallas; monitoring comt mem, La Desegregation Settlement; bd trustee, Univ Res Asn Inc; Dallas Citizens Coun; bd dir, N Tex Comn; bd trustee, Tex Health Res Inst; Dallas Citizens Coun, Greater Dallas Chamber Com; Adv Coun Jacob's Ladder; Dallas Ctr Performing Arts Pres Adv Coun; Monitoring Comn La Desegregation Agreement. **Honors/Awds:** Honary LLD, Babson Col, 1990; Honary LLD, Mount Holyoke Col, 1990; Honary DHL, Univ Med & Dentistry NJ, 1989; Honary Doctor of Education, Wheelock Col, 1990; Honorary Doctor of Science, Bowdoin Col, 1992; LLD, Univ Mass, Amherst, 1992; DHL, Kean Col, NJ, 1992; Honorary Doctor Science, Essex County Community Col, 1992.

JENKINS, ADAM, JR.
Manager. **Personal:** Born Sep 9, 1942, N Carrollton, MS; married Margaree Gordon; children: Veronica, Randolph, Darryl. **Educ:** Alcorn A&M Col, BS, 1967; Univ Omaha, attended 1968; Miss State Univ, attended 1969; Miss Col, MBA, 1975. **Career:** Utica Jr Col, cashier, 1967-68, bus mgr, 1969-; Hinds Jr Col, Raymond Campus, vpres bus servs. **Orgs:** Consult Natchez Jr Col; Miss Jr Col Bus Mgrs Assoc; Nat Asn Cols & Univs Bus Officers; Nat Educ Asn; Miss Teachers Asn; Nat Asn Advan Colored People; secy treas, Phi Beta Sigma, 1971-72; Hinds Jr Col, Raymond Campus, develop found bd mem, currently. **Business Addr:** Development Foundation Board Member, Raymond Campus, PO Box 1100, Raymond, MS 39154-1100.*

JENKINS, DR. ADELBERT HOWARD
Educator. **Personal:** Born Dec 10, 1934, St Louis, MO; son of Helen Howard and Herbert; married Betty Lanier; children: Christopher. **Educ:** Antioch Col, BA, 1957; Univ Mich, MA, 1958, PhD, 1963; Dipl Clin Psychol, ABPP. **Career:** A Einstein Med Col, post doctoral fel, 1962-64, asst instr, instr 1964-67; New York Univ Med Ctr, asst prof, 1967-71; New York Univ, New York, NY, assoc prof, 1971, dir undergrad studies psychol, 1982-86 & 1989-93, assoc prof emer, currently. **Orgs:** Training consult, Veterans Admin Med Centers, Bronx, Brooklyn; Am Psychol Asn, 1964-; New York State Psychol Asn, 1966-; Nat Asn Black Psychol, 1968-; fel, Soc Personality Assessment, 1974-; pres, div theoret & philospsychol, 2003-04. **Honors/Awds:** Scholar of the Year, Nat Asn Black Psychologists, 1983; Martin L King Jr Award, New York Soc Clin Psychologists, 1984; M L King, Jr-Rosa Parks Vis Prof, Psychol, Univ Mich, 1987; Golden Dozen Award, Excellence in Teaching, New York Univ, Fac Arts & Sci, 1988. **Special Achievements:** Numerous publications including "Psychology and African Americans, A Humanistic Approach", 1995; Humanistic psychology and multiculturalism, 2001; Individuality in cultural context: The case for psychological agency, 2001; A humanistic approach to Black psychology, 2004; Creativity and resilience in the African American experience. The Humanistic Psychologist, 2005. **Business Addr:** Associate Professor Emeritus, New York University, Department of Psychology, Rm 203 715 Broadway, New York, NY 10003, **Business Phone:** (212)998-7937.

JENKINS, DR. ALTHEA H.
Librarian, educator. **Personal:** Born in Tallahassee, FL; daughter of Samuel and Florence Brown; children: James C II. **Educ:** Fla A&M Univ, BSLS, 1963; FL Atlantic Univ, LD Cert, 1970; Fla State Univ, MSLS, 1972; Nova Univ, EdD, 1977. **Career:** Librarian (retired); Indian River Sch Bd, sch media specialist, 1963-71; Fla State Univ, grad asst, 1971-72; Miami-Dade Community Col, libr dir, 1972-80; Univ S Fla Sarasota, libr dir, 1980-91; Am Libr Asn, Chicago, IL, exec dir, 1991-2001; Fla State Univ, dir univ libr. **Orgs:** Pres, Fla Asn Col & Res Libr, 1983-85; Eckerd Col Bd Trustees, 1984-; First vpres, Delta Kappa Gamma, 1986-; Phi Delta Kappa, 1987-; Sarasota County United Way Bd, 1987-; pres, Fla Libr Asn, 1988-89; Sarasota County Hist Comn, 1988-; Sarasota County Community Found, 1988-; Sarasota Chamber Com, 1989; Delta Sigma Theta, 1990-; Am Asn Higher Educ, 1997-2001; Am Libr Asn; Asn Col & Res Libr; Nat Sci Digital Libr; Asn Col Res Libr; Southeastern Libr Network; bd mem, TLT Group. **Honors/Awds:** Certificate of Appreciation, Newtown Libr Planning Bd, 1981; Certificate of Appreciation, Sarasota-Manatee Phi Delta Kappa, 1984; "She Knows WhereShe is Going", Girls Clubs of America Award, 1989. **Special Achievements:** First African American executive director of the Association of College & Research Libraries.

JENKINS, ANDREW
Administrator, activist. **Personal:** Born Jul 20, 1936, Philadelphia, PA; son of William and Madeline Green; married Patricia A Green Jenkins, Oct 25, 1958; children: Eric, Denise, Andrea, Andrew. **Educ:** Antioch Univ, BA, Human Servs, 1982; Jamerson's Sch Ministry, ordained minister; True Holiness Temple, Inc, Sch Ministerial Concepts, attending. **Career:** Mantva Comt Planners, pres, 1967-85; City Philadelphia, Liaison Officer Anti-Poverty Agency, 1971-79; City Philadelphia, Chmn Mayor's Citizen Adv Comt, 1977-79; Mt Vernon Manor Apts, pres, 1978-85; Mantva Primary Health Ctr, pres, 1984-85; First United Baptist Church Male Chorus, vice pres, 1984-85; Mantva Comt Develop Corp, vice pres, 1984-85; Philadelphia Redevelop Authority, dir relocation & prop mgt, exec dir; City Philadelphia, dep mayor. **Orgs:** Pres Mantua Community Planners, 1967-79; Dir, Univ PA Commun Develop, 1969-71; Community Organizer Univ PA, 1969-71; liaison officer Philadelphia Ant Pov Action Comt, 1971-79; pres, Mt Vernon Apartments, 1978-; exec bd, West Philadelphia Partnership Inc, 1983-89; Am Legion George J Cornish Post, 1983-85, Nat Forum Black Admin, 1984-85; Mayor Wilson Goode's Labor Std Bd, 1985, Philadelphia Redevelop Authority Labor Mgt Comt; real estate comt bd mem, Martin Luther King Village Comt Asn

Inc; bd mem, Stinger Square Corp. **Honors/Awds:** Man of the Year, Philadelphia Jaycees, 1971; Outstanding Young American, Nat Jaycees, 1972; Good Leadership Citations, Mayor Bill Green City Coun & Gov Thornburgh, 1982; Outstanding Leadership, West Philadelphia C C, 1984; City Council Citations, 1983-84; Congressman Bill Gray Award, 1982; Young Great Social Award, 1985; Mantua Committe Leadership Award, 1985; COT Support Award, James Schuller Mem Boxing Gym, 1997; God Work Award, Maria Scott Ensemble Serv, 1996; COT Service Award, African Am COT, Whitney Young CNF, 1994; Role Model Award, Dr. Inez Thompson & Gospel Singer Thomasina James, 1995; City Philadelphia Retirement Award, 1992. **Military Serv:** USAF, airman sec class, 4 yrs; Citation for Community Relation Basketball, 1957. *

JENKINS, ANDREW JAMES
Senator (u.s. federal government). **Personal:** Born Jun 27, 1941, Brooklyn, NY; married Michelle Rios; children: Andrew Jr & Alexandra. **Educ:** Fordham Univ, Soc Sci, 1969; Fordham Univ Law Sch, JD, 1972. **Career:** City Univ New York Col, adj prof; Jenkins Aings & Johnson Law Firm, atty; NY State Senate, senator, 1983-90. **Orgs:** Parliamentarian Guy R Brewer Dem Club; Knights Pythias. **Honors/Awds:** Nat Hon Soc.

JENKINS, AUGUSTUS G, JR.
Funeral director. **Personal:** Born Aug 24, 1943, New York, NY; son of Augustus G Sr and W Louise Johnson; married Nellie Kirkland, Jul 12, 1970; children: Natalie & Ashley. **Educ:** Cent State Univ, Wilberforce, Ohio, BS, 1965; Ohio State Univ, Columbus, Ohio, MS, 1966. **Career:** Jenkins Funeral Chapel, New York, NY, owner, funeral dir & operator, 1970-; Black Tennis & Sports Found, New York, NY, founder & vice chair, 1977-; prof pilot & flight instr, 1985-; Nat Cash Regist, systems engr; Int Bus Mach, systems engr. **Orgs:** Founder, Nat Asn Advan Colored People Bergen County, NJ; bd mem, Lions Club; bd mem, Harlem YMCA; Nat Negro Golf Asn; Omega Psi Phi Frat; Englewood Social Club. **Military Serv:** AUS Signal Corps, 1966-68. **Home Addr:** 144 Lake St, Englewood, NJ 07631. **Business Addr:** Owner, Operator, Jenkins Funeral Chapel, 1893 Amsterdam Ave, New York, NY 10032, **Business Phone:** (212)926-5979.

JENKINS, BARBARA WILLIAMS
Librarian. **Personal:** Born Aug 17, 1934, Union, SC; daughter of Johncie Sartor Williams and Ernest N Williams; married Robert A; children: Ronald & Pamela. **Educ:** Bennett Col, BA; Univ Ill, MSLS; Rutgers Univ, PhD. **Career:** Circulation libr; ref & documents libr; SC State Col, Whittaker Libr, libr, 1957-62, head librarian, 1963-71, libr dir, 1962-87, dean libr & info serv, 1974-97, dean emeritus libr & info serv, 2000-. **Orgs:** SC Lib Asn; SE Lib Asn; Am Lib Asn; Am Soc Info Sci; Alpha Kappa Mu Hon Soc; Am Asn Univ & Profs; lib consult instr; co-adj fac, Rutgers Univ; assoc dir, Inst Libr Correction Inst; NAACP; Delta Sigma Theta Inc; S Atlantic Reg dir, 1968-70; Nat Comn Constitution by-laws, 1971-75; Links Inc; pres, Orangeburg Chap, 1975-77; treas, Black Caucus Am Libr Asn, 1976-78; adv com, SC Mus Comn; vice area dir, Southern Area Links Inc, 1979-83; Land Grant Libr Dirs Asn, 1979-85; chmn, Ala Black Caucus, 1984-86; pres, SC Libr Asn, 1986-87; bd dirs, SOLINET Southeastern Libr Network, 1989-; bd dirs, SC African Am Heritage Coun; bd dirs, chmn, currently, Harvin Clarendon County Libr; bd dirs, SC Archives & History Found; bd dirs, Ellorec Heritage Mus. **Honors/Awds:** John Cotton Dana Award; Design & Planning Award, MF Whittaker Libr; Boss of the Year Award, Orangeburg Chap Prof Secretaries Asn, 1980; Service Award, 1980; Land Grant, Libr Dir Asn, 1984; President's Award, SC Libr Asn, 1987; Distinguished Service Award, SC State Col, 1991; Culture Keeper Award, Black Caucus Ala, 1999; Clarendon County Nat Coun Negro Women Hall of Fame, 2001; inducted SC State Univ Hall Fame, 2004. **Home Addr:** 102 S Boundary St, Manning, SC 29102. **Business Addr:** Dean Emeritus, South Carolina State University, Miller F Whittaker Library, 300 Col St NE, Orangeburg, SC 29117, **Business Phone:** (803)536-7000.

JENKINS, BILLY LEON, JR.
Football player. **Personal:** Born Jul 8, 1974, Los Angeles, CA; children: Khalil. **Educ:** Howard Univ. **Career:** St Louis Rams, defensive back, 1997-99; Denver Broncos, 2000-01; Green Bay Packers, 2001; Buffalo Bills, 2002.

JENKINS, BOBBY G
Executive. **Personal:** Born Sep 30, 1939, Detroit, MI; married Clara Gibson. **Educ:** Wayne State Univ, BS, 1966. **Career:** Executive (retired); Ford Motor Co, Mich Truck Plant, 1964, Lincoln-Mercury Div, Chicago, admin mgr, 1968-69, Chicago, zone mgr, 1969-71, gen field mgr, mkt sales. **Orgs:** Beta Gamma Hon Soc, 1967; adv bd, African Am New Car Dealers. **Honors/Awds:** Top marketing student of year, Sales Mkt Execs Detroit, 1967. **Military Serv:** USN, 1957-60.

JENKINS, CARLTON J.
Banker, president (organization). **Educ:** Dartmouth Col, BA; Univ Calif Los Angeles, exec mgt prog. **Career:** Los Angeles Local Develop Corp, bd dirs, mayoral appointee; Los Angeles Develop Reform Comn, mem; Kroger Co; Founders Nat Bank Los Angeles, chief executive officer, pres & chmn, 1991-99; OneNetNow.com LLC, prin & chief exec officer, 1999-01; The Fred Meyer Co, dir; Kroger Co, dir; Dryades Savings Bank, founder, dir & prin; Yucaipa Corp Initiatives Fund, partner. **Orgs:** Calif State Bd Educ; Univ Calif Los Angeles Med Ctr; trustee, Univ W Los Angeles Sch Law. **Special Achievements:** Company is ranked No 14 on Black Enterprise's list of Top 100 financial companies, 1994. *

JENKINS, CAROL ANN
Journalist. **Personal:** Born Nov 30, 1944, Montgomery, AL; married Carlos Hines. **Educ:** Boston Univ, BS, 1966; NY Univ, MA, 1968. **Career:** WOR-TV, co-anchor reporter, 1970-71; Straight Talk WOR- TV, moderator, 1971-72, new reporter; ABC-TVREASONOR/SMITH Report Eyewitness News, corr, 1972-73; WNBC-TV, news corr, 1973-96; Greenstone Media, bd chair; Women's Media Ctr, pres & founding mem bd of dir, currently; media & polit analyst. **Orgs:** Am Fedn TV & Radio Artists; Writers Guild Am E; Nat Acad Arts & Scis; Int Radio & TV Soc; Am Women Radio & TV; Nat Asn Media Women; US bd, African Med & Res Found; bd, Ms Found Women & Feminist Press. **Honors/Awds:** Service Award, Harlem Prep Sch, 1971; Outstanding Achievement Award, Ophelia DeVore Sch, 1972; Outstanding Achievement Award, Ala State Univ, 1972; Outstanding Achievement Award, Jour Alpha Wives, 1974; hon doctorate, Col New Rochelle; hon doctorate, Marymount Manhattan Col; Lifetime & InterNat Reporting Achievement Award, Asn Black Journalist, NY Chapt; Front Page Award, Daily News; Mother of the Year, Nat Mothers Day Comt; Woman of the Year, Police Athletic League; Humanitarian of the Year, Abbot House; Distinguished Alumna, NY Univ. **Special Achievements:** Co-Author: Black Titan: A.G. Gaston and the Making of a Black American Millionaire; A frequently sought speaker and moderator, she also conducts media training seminars and private sessions for women across the country; executive producer of the PBS documentary, What I Want My Words To Do To You, which won the Freedom of Expression Award at the Sundance Film Festival in 2003. **Business Addr:** President, Women Media Center, 350 Fifth Ave Suite 901, New York, NY 10118.

JENKINS, CHIP
Athlete, lawyer. **Educ:** Villanova Sch Law, JD. **Career:** US Olympic Team, Men's Track & Field, 1992; athlete; U.S. Patent Off, atty, currently; real estate investor, currently. **Honors/Awds:** Gold Medalist, Olymic Games, US Men's Track & Field, 4x400 relay, 1992.

JENKINS, CYNTHIA. See Obituaries section.

JENKINS, DERON CHARLES
Football player. **Personal:** Born Nov 14, 1973, Saint Louis, MO; children: Syrus. **Educ:** Univ Tenn, degree, psychol. **Career:** Football player (retired), Baltimore Ravens, defensive back, 1996-99; San Diego Chargers, defensive back, 2000; Tenn Titans, defensive back, 2001; Carolina Panthers, defensive panthers, 2002; Austin Wranglers, 2004; Nashville Kats, 2005-06. **Honors/Awds:** All-Rookie Team, 2004.

JENKINS, EDMOND THOMAS
Educator. **Personal:** Born Apr 4, 1930, Cleveland, OH; son of James and Amy. **Educ:** Howard Univ, BA, 1953; Western Reserve Univ, MA, 1956, MSSA, 1966; Moreno Acad Sociodrama Psychodrama & Group Psychother, Cert, 1968. **Career:** Educator (retired); Tenn A&I State Univ, instr 1956-60; Garden Valley Neighborhood House, teen group worker acting dir, 1960-64; Ionia State Hosp Criminally Insane, clinical sw supvr, 1966-69; Case Western Reserve Univ, asst prof, assoc prof, 1969-92, assoc prof emer, 1992; E Cleveland Theatre, artistic dir. **Orgs:** Cert Nat Asn Social Workers; life mem, Nat Advan Asn Colored People; Asn Advan Social Work Groups; bd dir, Cleveland Sight Ctr; bd trustees, Cleveland Sight Ctr. **Honors/Awds:** Appreciation Award, St Andrews Episcopal Church, 1980; Outstanding Professor Award, Asn Black Stud Social Workers, 1980; Teacher of the Year, Alumni Asn 1982. **Military Serv:** AUS, corpl, 2 yrs; Good Conduct Medal, Korean Serv Medal. **Business Addr:** Professor Emeritus, Mandel School of Applied Social Sciences, Case Western Reserve University, 10900 Euclid Ave, Cleveland, OH 44106, **Business Phone:** (216)368-2290.*

JENKINS, ELIZABETH AMETA
Counselor, educator. **Personal:** Born Mar 11, 1929, Brooklyn, NY; daughter of Ameta A Hackett-Hunte and Lionel A Hunte; divorced; children: Roland, Roderick, Howard, Rebecca & Leah. **Educ:** Molloy Col, BA, social psychol, 1977; Hofstra Univ, MA, 1985. **Career:** Nassau Co Dept Social Serv, social work aid, 1965-68; Econ Opportunity Coun Roosevelt, NY, summer youth dir & community organizer, 1970-72; Alliance MNY Group Leaders Inc, activities planner & parent coord, 1972-77; Molloy Col, St Thomas Aquinas Prog, prog counr. **Orgs:** Asn Equality & Excellence Educ, 1979; Long Island Coun Stud Perspective Admin, 1981-; Asn Black Women Higher Educ, 1977-; Higher Educ Opportunity Prog, Prof Orgn Long Island Region, 1978; Am Asn Univ Women, 1977; Am Bus Womens Asn, 1984; pres, Roosevelt Scholar Asn, 1958-75; founding secy, Nassau & Suffolk Health Syst Agency, 1976-78; Nassau Co Task Force Status Women, 1977-79. **Honors/Awds:** Ten Year Plaque for Dedicated Service, Molloy Col, 1987; Ten Year Pin for Dedicated Service to Higher Education Opportunity Program Professional Organization, State Educ Dept Higher Educ Opportunity Prog, 1990; Distinguished Service Medal, Molloy Col, 2001; 25-Year Service Medal, Molloy Col, 2002. **Home Addr:** 50 Holloway St, Freeport, NY 11520. **Business Addr:** Program Counselor, Molloy College, Kellenberg 001 1000 Hempstead Ave, Rockville Centre, NY 11570, **Business Phone:** (516)678-5000 Ext 6732.

JENKINS, ELLA LOUISE
Musician, singer. **Personal:** Born Aug 6, 1924, St Louis, MO. **Educ:** Wilson Jr Col, assoc degree, 1947; Roosevelt Col, 1948; San Francisco St Col, BA, sociol, 1951. **Career:** Freelance musician, singer & rec artist; Smithsonian Folkways Rec, rec artist. **Orgs:** Prog dir, YWCA, 1952; Music Educ Nat Conf; Int Platform Asn; Am Soc Composers. **Honors/Awds:** Pioneer in Early Television Citation; Parent's Choice Award; Lifetime Achievement Award, KOHL Educ Found; Meritorious Service Award, Cook County C's Hosp; Grammy Lifetime Acheivement Award, 2004; Nominee, Grammy Best Musical Album for Children for Sharing Cultures with Ella Jenkins, 2005; GRAMMY Award for Best Musical Album for Children for celebration: A Tribute to Ella Jenkins, 2005; Nominee, Grammy for Best Best Musical Album for Children for Ella Jenkins and a Union of Friends Pulling Together, 2000; Nominee, Grammy for Best Musical Album for Children for Ella Jenkins and a Union of Friends, 1999; Chicagoan of the year, Chicago Magazine, 2005. **Special Achievements:** Is called the the first lady of children's folk song; received a salute from the Ravinia Festival; has served as a U.S. delegate to Hong Kong, China and the former Soviet Union with the John F. Kennedy Center for the Performing Arts. **Business Addr:** Musician, 1844 N Mohawk St, Chicago, IL 60614.*

JENKINS, EMMANUEL LEE
School administrator. **Personal:** Born Aug 7, 1934, Greenville, NC; widowed; children: Darel, Gregory, Jerome & Tamara. **Educ:** Howard Univ, BA, pharm, 1956; Long Island Univ, MS, educ, 1974. **Career:** School administrator (retired); Rhodes Med, pharm, 1956; Moore-Schley Cameron & Co, customers broker, 1960-70; US Merchant Marine Acad, dir admis, 1970-95. **Orgs:** Officer, Lakeview Educ Comn, 1968-73; rep, Col Bd, 1973-; rep, Nat Asn Col Admis Officers, 1974-; mem, Col Bd Coun, 1982-83. **Honors/Awds:** Special Achievement Award, USMM Acad, 1975; Special Achievement Award, 1983. **Military Serv:** USN, cmdr; Bronze Medal, Superior Fed Serv Maritime Admin, 1978. *

JENKINS, FERGUSON ARTHUR
Baseball player. **Personal:** Born Dec 13, 1942, Ontario;married Maryanne (died 1991); children: 2; married Lydia. **Career:** Baseball player(retired), association executive; Pitcher: Philadelphia Phillies, 1965-66, Chicago Cubs, 1966-73, 1982-83; Texas Rangers, 1974-75, 1978-81; Boston Red Sox, 1976-77; Cincinnati Reds, pitching coach, 1992-93, roving pitching instructor; Chicago Cubs, pitching coach; Canadian Baseball League, commissioner, 2003. **Orgs:** Chmn, Fergie Jenkins Found Inc, currently. **Honors/Awds:** Cy Young Memorial Award, Nat League, 1971; 20-game winner, six straight years; Nat League All-Star Team, 1967, 1971, 1972; inducted to Canadian Baseball Hall of Fame, 1987; inducted to Baseball Hall of Fame, 1991; Canadian Athlete of the Year, 1967, 1968, 1971, 1974; Lou Marsh Trophy,1971; Order of Canada, 1987; commissioner of the now-defunct Canadian Baseball League, 2003; inducted to Texas Rangers Hall of Fame, 2004. **Special Achievements:** The only Canadian honored in the National Baseball Hall of Fame in Coopers town, New York; most strike outs than any other pitcher in Cubs history with 2038. **Business Addr:** Chairman, Fergie Jenkins Foundation Inc, 67 Commerce Pl Suite 3, St Catharines, ON, Canada 60613, **Business Phone:** (905)688-9418.

JENKINS, FRANK SHOCKLEY
Publisher, poet, writer. **Personal:** Born Apr 11, 1925, Seattle, WA; married Lynn Hamilton; children: Frank Alexander & Denise. **Career:** US Merchant marine, 1942-52; US Post Off, 1952-68; Time-DC Los Angeles, freight handler, 1969-73; Hollywood, actor, 1973-; Shockley Press, poet & publ; Publ: I Didn't Start Out To Be A Poet, 1977, 1981; Black Mac Say, 1981; works included in Emmy Award Prog, 1982; Voices of Our People, In Celebration of Black Poetry, 1982; play: Nobody, 1997; From Behind My Eyes, poetry, 1998; Driving While Black in Beverly Hills, 2001. **Orgs:** Screen Actors Guild; Teamsters 357; Screen Extras Guild, AFTRA.

JENKINS, HARRY LANCASTER
Dentist. **Personal:** Born Apr 22, 1932, Columbus, GA; married Janie R; children: Harry, Timothy, Anthony, Gary. **Educ:** Morehouse Col, AB, 1955; Meharry Med Col, DDS, 1962. **Career:** Tuskegee Veterans Admin Hosp, internship, 1963; Maryview Hosp Portsmouth, VA, staff; Portsmouth Gen Hosp; Norfolk Community Hosp, staff mem; Self-employed, dent surgeon, currently. **Orgs:** Am Cancer Soc; Am Youth Orgn; Eureka Bus & Prof Club; adv bd, Va State Civil Rights Comn. **Military Serv:** AUS, 1952. **Business Addr:** Dentist, 3349 Portsmouth Blvd, Portsmouth, VA 23701.*

JENKINS, DR. HERMAN LEE
School administrator. **Personal:** Born May 7, 1940, Montgomery, AL; married Margaret Stephenson; children: Gloria & Herman Jr.

Educ: Clark Univ, BA, 1974, PhD, 1983. **Career:** Southern Christian Leadership Conf, comt organizer civil rights activist, 1965-69; fel/pres Metrop Appl Res Ctr, 1967-68; Clark Univ, dir community rels, 1972; Am Int Col lectr, 1976; Queens Col, exec asst to pres, 1978-80, vpres; HL Jenkins Geog Analysis Inc, pres & chief exec officer, 1978-; Self-employed, artist mapmaker, 1961-. **Orgs:** Nat Asn Advan Colored People; 100 Black Men Inc; Asn Am Geogr. **Honors/Awds:** Jonas Clark Scholar, Clark Univ, 1977. **Military Serv:** AUS, pfc, 3 yrs. **Home Addr:** 24120 Northern Blvd, Douglaston, NY 11362.

JENKINS, JAMES
Football player. **Personal:** Born Aug 17, 1967, Staten Island, NY; divorced; children: 3. **Educ:** Rutgers Univ. **Career:** Football player (retired); Wash Redskins, tight end, 1991-2000; Lifetime Fitness Alpharetta, personal trainer; Cologne Falcons, head coach,currently. **Honors/Awds:** Ed Block Courage Award, 1997.

JENKINS, JIM
Chief executive officer, president (organization). **Personal:** Born in Detroit, MI. **Educ:** Tenn State Univ, Bachelor's Degree, elec eng. **Career:** Turner Construct Co, purchasing mgr; Jenkins Construct Inc, pres & chief exec officer, 1989-. **Orgs:** Bd dir, Detroit Regional Chamber. **Business Phone:** (313)625-7200.*

JENKINS, DR. JIMMY RAYMOND
School administrator. **Personal:** Born Mar 18, 1943, Selma, NC; married Faleese Moore; children: Lisa, Ginger Cartwright & Jimmy Jr. **Educ:** Elizabeth City State Univ, BS, biol, 1965; Purdue Univ, MS, Biol Educ, PhD, 1972. **Career:** Elizabeth City State Univ, asst prof biol, 1972, asst acad dean, 1972, assoc prof biol, 1973, vice chancellor acad affairs, 1977, chancellor, 1983-95, chancellor emer, 1995-; Edward Waters Col, pres, 1997-2005; Livingstone Col, Salisbury, NC, pres, 2006-. **Orgs:** NC Humanities Comt, 1980; Gov Oversight Comt, Nat Caucus Black Aged; Elizabeth City Chap Kiwanis Intl; NC Bd Sci & Tech; Am Asn Higher Ed. **Honors/Awds:** Distinguished Alumni, NAFEO; Outstanding Young Men in America; Boss of the Year, Elizabeth City State Univ, 1978; Jimmy R Jenkins Science Building, named in honor, Elizabeth City State Univ. **Home Addr:** 1304 Parkview Dr, Elizabeth City, NC 27909. **Business Addr:** President, Livingstone College, 701 W Monroe St, Salisbury, NC 28144, **Business Phone:** (704)216-6153.

JENKINS, JOHN
Mayor, president (organization). **Educ:** Bates Col, Lewiston, Maine, BA, psychol. **Career:** John Jenkins Acad Personal Develop, owner, 1970-97; Bates Col, dir housing, 1986-88; Dirigo Corp, pres, 1988-97; City Lewiston, ME, mayor, 1993-97; State Senator, ME, 1996-98; Multi-Cultural Develop, UNUM, dir, currently; Peptalk, pres & owner, currently; Dirigo Corp, pres, currently. **Orgs:** Maine Healthcare Proj; Muskie Sch Pub Serv; Partners Ending Hunger; Maine Conserv Sch; Maine Sports Legends; Boy Scouts - Pine Tree Coun; Bates Dance Festival. **Honors/Awds:** Community Service Award, Chamber Com; Community Leadership Award, Maine Develop Found; City Livability Award, US Conf Mayors; World Martial Arts Champion; Maine State Sports Hall of Fame; Lewiston-Auburn Sports Hall of Fame; Mr Maine Physique, 1977; -"Outstanding Trio National Achiever Award", Nat Coun Educ Opport, 1996; Community Service Award, Chamber Com, 1997. **Special Achievements:** World Martial Arts Champion, five times; World Martial Arts Hall of Fame, inductee; Lewiston-Auburn and Maine Sports Hall of Fame, inductee. **Business Addr:** Presidnet, Owner, Peptalk, PO Box 7205, Lewiston, ME 04243-7205, **Business Phone:** (207)783-3413.*

JENKINS, JOSEPH WALTER
Management consultant. **Personal:** Born Jan 28, 1941, East Orange, NJ; son of Joseph and Annabelle Clarke; married F Louise Diaz; children: Khalil & Medinah (deceased). **Educ:** Tenn State Univ, BBA, 1963; Farleigh Dickinson Univ, MBA, mgmt, 1979. **Career:** Gen Motors, prod control coordr, 1963; Ford Motor Co, engineering analyst, 1966; Travelers Ins Co, asst mgr, personnel admin, 1968; Chubb Corp, eeo mgr 1974, asst vpres, human resources; City of E Orange, bus adminir, 1986-90; J W Jenkins & Co, pres 1990; Neward Bd Educ, Pensions & Benefits Mgr, 1991-96; Chase Manhattan Bank, benefit consult, 1996-98; City E Orange, city admin, 1998-. **Orgs:** Ams Sailing Asn; pres, Community Day Nursery, 1992; Omega Psi Phi Fraternity. **Honors/Awds:** Black Achievers Award, Harlem Br, YMCA, 1976; Outstanding Serv Optimist Club Orange, E Orange, 1979; Outstanding Citizen Award, Eagle Flight New Jersey, 1988. **Home Addr:** 7 Mountain Dr, West Orange, NJ 07052. **Business Addr:** City Administrator, City of East Orange, 44 City Hall Plz, East Orange, NJ 07017-4104, **Business Phone:** (973)266-5310.

JENKINS, JULIUS
Educator, chancellor (education), college president. **Career:** College president (retired); Concordia Col, Selma, AL, pres, chancellor. **Honors/Awds:** lifetime achiever, Black Clergy Caucus (African American Pastors of the LCMS).

JENKINS, KENNETH JOE
Clergy, educator. **Personal:** Born Sep 8, 1954, Detroit, MI; son of Roger and Lucy; married Karen L, May 24, 1980; children: Joel D, Jessica D, Jaimi D & Jonathan K. **Educ:** Eastern Mich Univ, BS, 1977, MA, 1983; Cent Bible Col Assemblies God. **Career:** Ypsilanti Pub Sch, sub-teacher, com educ person, 1975-78; Detroit Pub Schs, teacher, 1978-; sch staff adminr, 2001; sch asst prin, 2002; charter pastor, SW MI AGAPE, 2002; Redemption Love Christian Ctr, pastor, currently. **Orgs:** Minister, Church God Christ, 1974-91; Phys Educ Adv Comt, Detroit Pub Sch, 1985-98, High Sch Coaches, 1985-93, Physical Fitness Comt, 1984-98. **Honors/Awds:** Educator's Achievement Award, Booker T Washington Bus Asn, 1998. **Special Achievements:** Detroit Public Schools, physical education, fitness accountability test, 1993-95. **Business Addr:** Pastor, Redemptive Love Christian Center, 12190 Conant St, Detroit, MI 48212, **Business Phone:** (313)893-6275.

JENKINS, DR. KENNETH VINCENT
School administrator. **Personal:** Born in Elizabeth, NJ; son of Thomas Augustus and Rebecca Meredith Williams; divorced; children: 4. **Educ:** Columbia Col, NY, BA; Teachers Col, Columbia Univ, NY, MA & PhD. **Career:** South Side High Sch, Rockville Ctr, NY, chmn eng dept, 1965-72; consultantin English, NYS Dept Educ, Albany 1965 - 1972; Regents Question Committee Eng, Albany 1966-71; Nassau Community Col, supvr adj fac, prof eng & afro-am lit, Dept Afro-Am studies, chmn, 1974-; mem, exe bd. **Orgs:** Afro-Am Inst, NY; Mensa, dv bd mem, Radio Sta WBAI-FM NY, 1972-85; Consult Eng, convener, chmn bd dir, Target Youth Ctrs Inc, NY, 1973-75; chmn,pres, Nat Bd Pac Found, 1973-80; chmn, Nassau County Youth Bd, 1979-98;Phi Delta Kappa; Asn Study Afro-Am Life & Hist; Coun Black Am Affairs;Exec bd, NY African Studies Asn; African Heritage Studies Asn; Gov 's NY State Coun Youth 1986-93; Schomburg Corp, 1989-93; bd mem, Long Island Community Found, 1989-98; bd mem, NY State Youth Support Inc, 1990-93. **Honors/Awds:** Baker Award, Columbia Univ; Martin Luther King Jr Award, Nassau County,1989; 100 Black Men Special Service Award, 1994; David K Kadane Family Serv Award; LI Award, Nat Coun Negro Women, 2002; MLK Award, Celebration Com Nassau County, 1990; Nat Coun Negro Women Award 2003; Community Awards. **Special Achievements:** Author of essays, short stories, reviews, "Last Day in Church."; owner" Black Books and Artifacts". **Military Serv:** US Nat Guard. **Business Addr:** Professor of English, Chairperson, Nassau Community College, Department of African-American Studies, 1 Education Dr Bldg H 124, Garden City, NY 11530, **Business Phone:** (516)572-7157.

JENKINS, LOUIS E
Clinical psychologist, educator. **Personal:** Born Dec 20, 1931, Staten Island, NY; married Althea L; children: Le Toia M. **Educ:** Union Col, BS, 1954; Univ Nebr, MA, 1959; Pepperdine Univ, MA, Psychol, 1970; Pa State Univ, PhD, Clinical Psychol, 1973. **Career:** Pepperdine Univ, assoc prof psychol, 1970-75; LA Union SDA Sch, teacher, 1959-64; LA City Sch, teacher, 1964-65, counr, 1965-66, sch psychologist, 1966-69; Martin Luther King Jr Gen Hosp LA, Dept Psychol & Human Behavior, staff psychologist; CA Fam Study Cent Downey, CA, pvt pract; Loma Linda Univ, Dept Psychol, dept chair, currently. **Orgs:** Nat Asn Advan Colored People; Soc Clin Psychol; Psychol Relig; Am Psychol Law; Family Psychol; Soc Psychol Study Ethnic Minority Issues; Am Psychol Soc; Am Asn Christian Counr; Acad Clin Psychol; Am Bd Prof Psychol; Coun Grad Dept Psychol. **Military Serv:** AUS Med Corp sp3 1954-56.

JENKINS, LUTHER NEAL
Aerospace engineer. **Personal:** Born Mar 21, 1968, Newport News, VA. **Career:** NASA Langley Res Ctr, aerospace engr, 1990-. **Orgs:** Omega Psi Phi Fraternity, Inc. **Honors/Awds:** Ebony, 50 Leaders of Tomorrow, 1992. **Business Addr:** Aerospace Engineer, NASA Langley Research Center, Mail Stop 432, Hampton, VA 23681, **Business Phone:** (757)864-8026.

JENKINS, MELVIN
Football player. **Personal:** Born Mar 16, 1962, Jackson, MS. **Educ:** Univ Cincinnati. **Career:** Canadian Football League, Calgary, 1984-86; Nat Football League, Seattle Seahawks, 1987-90, Detroit Lions, cornerback, 1991-94; Atlanta Falcons, 1993. *

JENKINS, MELVIN E
Physician, educator. **Personal:** Born Jun 24, 1923, Kansas City, MO; son of Melvin and Marguerite; married Maria Parker; children: Janis, Carol, Lore & Ingrid. **Educ:** Univ Kans Col Med, AB, 1944, MD, 1946. **Career:** Freedman's Hosp, internship, 1946-47, pediat residency, 1947-50, from asst pediatrician to assoc pediatrician, 1950-69; Howard Univ Col Med, clin instr, 1951-54, clin asst prof, 1954-55, from asst prof to assoc prof, 1957-69, Dept Pediat & Child Health, prof chmn, 1973-86, prof emer, currently; Johns Hopkins Univ, pediatric endocrinol, 1963-65, lectr, dept of pediatrics, 1974; Univ Nebr Med Ctr, pediatrician, 1969-73, dir pediat endocrine clin, 1969-73, prof & vice chmn, dept pediat, 1971-73; George Wash Univ, profial lectr child health & develop, 1973-; Hosp Sick C, attending staff, 1973-91; Childrens Hosp Nat Med Ctr, DC, sr attending pediatrician, 1973-; Freedmen's Hosp, chief pediatrician, 1973-86; NIH, consult, 1973-. **Orgs:** Chmn pediat sect, Nat Med Asn, 1966-69; chmn med records comt, Freedmen's Hosp, 1966; med sch rep, Howard Univ Coun Admin, 1967, 1974; ed chief, Pediatric Newsletter, Nat Med Asn, 1970-83; adv bd, Human Growth Inc, 1971; Policy Adv Comn Ctr Urban Affairs, 1971-73; bd dirs, Urban League Nebr, 1971-73; med dir, Parent Ctr, 1971-73; pres bd dirs, Comprehensive Health Asn Omaha Inc, 1972-73; bd mem, Howard Univ Hosp, 1974-88; campus rep, Endocrine Soc, 1974-80; med adv comt, Nat Found March Dimes, 1974-78; Nat Adv Res Resources Coun, NIH, 1974-78; med adv comt, Nat Pituitary Agency, 1975-78; examiner, Am Bd Pediat, 1975-88, bd mem, 1983-89; Pediat Surg Comn, Am Bd Surg, 1984; chmn, Health Task Force; Sigma Xi; Med Chirurgicalc DC; AAAS; Black Child Develop Inst Inc; Alpha Omega Alpha. **Honors/Awds:** Golden Apple Award, South African Med Asn, 1963; Recognition for Outstanding Contributor to Growth of Pediatric Section, Nat Med Asn, 1966-69; Outstanding Achievement Award, Southern Christian Leadership Conf, 1972; Outstanding Scholar-Teacher Award, Howard Univ, 1984; Outstanding Contributor, Citation City Coun, DC, 1984; Leadership in Medicine Award, Univ Kans, 1989. **Business Addr:** Professor Emeritus, Howard University College of Medicine, Department of Pediatrics, 520 W St NW, Washington, DC 20059, **Business Phone:** (202)806-6270.

JENKINS, MELVIN LEMUEL
Lawyer. **Personal:** Born Oct 15, 1947, Halifax, NC; son of Solomon Green and Minerva; married Wanda Holly, May 20, 1972; children: Shelley, Melvin Jr, Dawn & Holly Rae-Ann. **Educ:** NC A&T State Univ, BS 1969; Univ Kans Sch Law, JD, 1972. **Career:** Legal Aid Soc Kans City, MO, staff atty, 1972; US Dept Housing & Urban Develop, staff atty, 1972-73; US Commun Civil Rights, reg atty, 1973-79; US Comn Civil Rights, Cent Reg Off, dir, currently; Univ KS Sch Law, Benton fel. **Orgs:** Bd dir, Joan Davis Spec Sch, 1984-; Nat Bar Asn; NE Bar Asn; Mayors Human Rel Comn Kansas City, MO; Alpha Phi Omega Serv Fraternity; Omega Psi Phi Fraternity; Smith fel, Legal Aid Soc. **Honors/Awds:** Civil Rights Award, Blue Valley Lodge Masons. **Home Addr:** 8015 Sunset Circle, Grandview, MO 64030-1461, **Home Phone:** (816)761-2416. **Business Addr:** Director, US Commission on Civil Rights, Central Regional Office, 400 State Ave Suite 908, Kansas City, KS 66101, **Business Phone:** (913)551-1400.

JENKINS, MONICA
Manager. **Personal:** Born Apr 7, 1961, San Francisco, CA; daughter of James and Marie Taylor. **Educ:** Univ Santa Clara, CA, BS, 1983. **Career:** First Nationwide Bank, San Francisco, CA, customer serv rep, 1983-85, state sales trainer, 1985-90; Nordstrom, San Francisco, CA, sales assoc, 1989-90; Pacfic Gas & Electric Co, San Francisco, CA, human resources assoc, 1989-90, human resources rep, EEO & diversity unit, 1990-. **Orgs:** CHOCS, 1990-; ACHRC, 1990-; BEA, 1990-. **Business Phone:** (415)973-5853.

JENKINS, NEDRA
Lawyer. **Personal:** Born 1969; daughter of John. **Educ:** Univ Chicago, BA & MA, Social Sci, 1991; Univ Calif, Los Angeles, Sch Law, JD, 1994. **Career:** City Compton, Office City atty, 1994; Wilson & Becks, assocs, 1995-96; Office of the County Counsel, 1996-. **Orgs:** State Bar CA, 9th Circuit Ct Appeal & US District Ct - Central Dist, 1994-; U.S. Supreme Ct, 2005-; Black Women Lawyers Asn Los Angeles; bd mem, Calif Asn Black Lawyers, 2003-04; adv bd, Hollywood Black Film Festival,1999-; Am Bar Asn; Nat Bar Asn; Calif Asn Black Lawyers; Calif Women Lawyers; Los Angeles County Bar Asn; Univ Calif Los Angeles Black Alumni Asn; Pasadena Tournament Roses; State Bench Bar Coalition, 2004; Local Bench Bar Coalition, 2005; Lanterns Comt; Mt Wash Homeowners Alliance; Bar Leaders Conf Comt, 2005. **Honors/Awds:** Distinguished Woman Award, Top Ladies Distinction, Pasadena Chap, 2005.**Special Achievements:** Southern California Super Lawyers Rising Star- Employment Law by Law & Politics Magazine and the publishers of Los Angeles Magazine, 2005, 2006, 2007. **Business Addr:** Principal Deputy County Counsel, Office of Counsel, Los Angeles County, 1 Gateway Pl 24th Fl, Los Angeles, CA 90012, **Business Phone:** (213)922-2526.

JENKINS, OZELLA
Manager. **Personal:** Born Aug 13, 1945, Roanoke Rapids, NC. **Educ:** NC Cent Univ, attended 1964; Howard Univ, attended 1965; Cornell Univ, attended 1974. **Career:** C&P Tel Co, customer serv rep, 1964-71; Pitts Motor Hotel, restaurant mgr, 1964-72; Sheraton Wash Hotel, conv mgr; asn dir, Nat Asn Health Serv Exec. **Orgs:** Nat Coun Negro Women 1962-; Nat Asn Catering Execs; Nat Coalition Black Mtg Planners 1984-; bus mgr Wash Chap JUGS Inc, 1984; vpres, Bonaire Homes Asn, 1985. **Honors/Awds:** Cert Daughters Am Revolution, 1979; Recognition Excellence Successful Meeting Mag 1982,84,86; cert/plaque Meeting Planners Int, 1984; plaque Nat Urban League 1985, US Marshal Service, 1985, Metro Police Dept Wash DC, 1985. **Business Addr:** Association Director, National Association of Health Services Executives, 8630 Fenton St Suite 126, Silver Spring, MD 20910.

JENKINS, WANDA JOYCE
Health services administrator. **Personal:** Born Jun 20, 1946, Kansas City, MO; daughter of S J Holly, Sr; married Melvin L Jen-

kins Sr, May 20, 1972; children: Dawn, shelley, Melvin Jr & Holly. **Educ:** Kans State Col, Pittsburg, BSW, 1969; Univ KS, MSW, 1974. **Career:** YMCA, asst dir, 1974-75; Rainbow Ment Health Ctr, social worker, 1975-80; Community Support, Res Health, coordr, 1980-86; Andrews Way Group Home, dir, 1986-89; Swope Pkwy Health Ctr, 1989-; Univ KS, Sch Social Work, field instr, 1990-94; Washburn Univ, Sch Social Work, field instr, 1992-97. **Orgs:** Leadership prog, Greater Kans City COC, 1985; Nat Asn Black Social Workers; Mo Asn Social Workers; AKA; chair, Ward Chapel Am Church, Steward Bd. **Honors/Awds:** Social Worker of the Year, MO Asn Social Workers, 1997; Social Worker of the Year, Kansas City Asn Social Worker, 1997; Woman of the Year, Ward Chapel Am Church, 2000. **Business Addr:** Coordinator of Community Support Services, Swope Parkway Health Center Family Group, 3801 Blue Pkwy, Kansas City, MO 64130, **Business Phone:** (816)923-5800.

JENKINS, WOODIE R
Consultant, government official. **Personal:** Born Jun 18, 1940, Washington, DC; son of Rev Woodie R Jenkins Sr and Laura B Berry Washington; married Ramona M Hernandez, Jun 21, 1968; children: Tammy Monique. **Educ:** Howard Univ, BS, Physics, 1964; NM St Univ, MS, Mech & Indust Engineering, 1972. **Career:** Government official (retired), Consult; Nat Range Opers, WSMR, NM, physicist, 1964-70; Quality Assurance Off, WSMR, gen engr, 1970-77; Quality Evaluation Div, WSMR, chief, 1977-82; AUS Training & Doctrine Command's Syst Analysis Activity, WSMR, spec staff asst tech dir, 1980; Las Cruces, NM, city counr, 1980-85, mayor protem, 1982-85; High Energy Laser Prog Off, WSMR, assoc prog mgr plans & opers, 1982-84; High Energy Laser Systs Test Facility, White Sands Missile Range, chief test opers, 1984-93; S Cent Coun Govts Inc, transp planner, 1993-96; Jenkins Consult Serv, chief exec officer, 1996-. **Orgs:** AUS Tech Liaison Rep Am Defense Preparedness Asn, 1975-; Registered Prof Engr, 1979-96; WSMR Speaker's Bur, 1979-82; Polit Action Comn Dona Ana County Nat Asn Advan Colored People Br, 1979-85; bd dirs, White Sands Fed Credit Union, 1979-85; WSMR Comdrs Comt Hisp & Black Employ, 1980-85; Transp Communs & Pub Safety Policy Comn Nat League Cities, 1980-83; Dep Activity Career Prog Mgr Engrs & Scientists WSMR, 1981-93; lect circuit, NMex Jr Col; vchmn bd dirs, Southern NMex Human Develop Inc, 1985-97; NMex Statewide Health Coord Coun, 1985-86; chmn, Las Cruces Extra Territorial Zoning Comn, 1987-92; vpres bd dirs, Las Cruces YMCA, 1988-89. **Honors/Awds:** Certificate of Nobility, NMex Secy State, 1982; WSMR Commander's Award, 1983; Certificate of Appreciation for Public Service, State NMex, 1989;NMex Distinguished Public Service Award, State NMex, 1990. **Business Addr:** Cheif Executive Officer, Jenkins Consult Service, 700 Turner Ave, Las Cruces, NM 88005-1327, **Business Phone:** (505)524-1726.

JENKINS-SCOTT, JACKIE
Health services administrator, college president. **Personal:** Born Aug 18, 1949, Damascus, AR; married James M Scott; children: Amal James, Amber Dawn. **Educ:** Eastern MI Univ, BS, 1971; Boston Univ Sch Social Work, MSW, 1973; Radcliffe Col, Post Grad Res Prog, 1975. **Career:** Commonwealth MA Dept Pub Health, dir treatment serv reg mgr, 1973-77; Roxbury Court Clinic, exec dir, 1977-83; City Boston Pub Health Comn, Comnr, 1998; Dimock Community Health Ctr, pres & chief exec officer, 1983-04; Wheelock Col, pres, currently. **Orgs:** Trustee, Cousens Fund, 1985-92; pres, Newton Chap Jack & Jill Am, 1985, Delta Sigma Theta; vpres, MA League Health Ctrs, 1987; secy, Mass Pub Health Asn, 1987-88, Consortium Black Health Ctr Direct, 1987; bd mem, NAT Cooperative Bank. **Honors/Awds:** Outstanding Contribution Social Worker with Five Years or Less Experience Mass Chap of the Nat Asn Social Workers 1975; "Alcohol Abuse Among Black Women" Douglass Pub 1976; Lady of the Year Award, Proj Understanding, 1978; Kathleen Crampton Award, Massachusetts League Neighborhood Health Ctrs. **Business Addr:** President, Wheelock College, 200 The Riverway, Boston, MA 02215-417, **Business Phone:** (617)879-2213.*

JENNINGS, BENNIE ALFRED
Executive director. **Personal:** Born Nov 21, 1933, Port Gibson, MS; married Mildred B Blackburn; children: Sharon, Marion & Brenda. **Educ:** Alcorn Univ, attended 1957; Grambling State Univ, BS, sec educ, 1960. **Career:** Chesebrough-Ponds Inc, mach adjustor, 1960-63; Gen Dynamics, Elec Boat Div, draftsman & apprentice trang admin, 1963-70; Opportunities Industrialization Ctr, New London County Inc, CT, exec dir, currently. **Orgs:** Nat Asn Advan Colored People; Nat Coun Negro Women; Blacks In Govt. **Honors/Awds:** Distingushed Service Award, USAF; Management Development Institute Award, GE Corp, NY, 1976; Gold Key Award, Opportunities Industrialization Ctr Am, Philadelphia, 1979; 10 Year Service Award, Opportunities Industrialization Ctr Am Philadelphia, 1980; Dr M L King Jr Comm Service Award, Club Cosmos New London, CT 1980. **Military Serv:** USAF, A/3c, 1951-55. **Business Addr:** Executive Director, Opportunities Industrialization Center of New London County Inc, 106 Truman St, New London, CT 06320, **Business Phone:** (860)447-1731.

JENNINGS, BERNARD WAYLON-HANDEL
Activist, scholar, chairperson. **Personal:** Born Jun 21, 1968, Bronx, NY; son of Allan Winston and Louise Aiken. **Educ:** Fla Memorial Col, Miami, Fla, BA, 1991; Fla Int Univ, cert course, 1991; Fla A&M Univ, MS, applied social sci pub admin, 1993. **Career:** City N Miami Mayor's Econ Task Force, intern, 1987; State Rep Elaine Gordon, campaign coordr, 1988, 1990; Fla Memorial Col, intern vpres stud develop, 1990, stud govt asn pres, 1990-91; Metro-Dade County Comn, comn aide comnr Charles Dusseau, 1991-92; Fla A&M Univ, Sch Grad Studies Res & Continuing Educ, grad asst dean grad studies, 1992-92, Campus Alcohol & Drug Res Cent, dir, 1992-93; Gulf Atlantic Indust Supply Inc, 1993; Animation Concepts Inc, chief exec officer & shareholder, 1993-; Fla Memorial Cole, Social Sci Div, prof, 1994-; Metro-Dade County Comn, comn aide chmn bd Arthur E Teele, Jr, 1994; Metro-Dade Transit Agency, transp customer rep, 1994-. **Orgs:** Founder, pres, United Stud Against Drugs, 1987; Stud Govt Asn, 1987-; pres, Fla Memorial Col Stud Govt Asn, 1990-; Comput Sci Asn; Big Brother, Big Sister, Proj Initiative; Kappa Alpha Psi Fraternity Inc; Kiwanis Club; Fla Memorial Col Bd Trustees, 1990, 1991; Nat Asn Advan Colored People; Citizens Crime Watch Community Comt; chmn adv bd, URGENT Inc; Modern Free & Accepted Masons, Loyal Patterson No 373; Biscayne Gardens Civic Asn; co-founder, nat coordr, & parliamentarian, Nat Stud's Support Coun Africa. **Honors/Awds:** Police Explorer, N Miami Police Dept, N Miami, Fla, 1986; Awarded Key to the City, 1986; Acad Deans List, 1987; Award of Appreciation, United Stud Against Drugs, 1987; Acad Award Cert, 1988; Plaque, Appreciation for Efforts, Prospect 89; Acad Hon Roll, 1989, 1990, Fla Memorial Col; Cert Acad Excellence, Alpha Phi Alpha Fraternity, Inc, Delta Psi Chapter, 1988; Cert Appreciation, TF-101 City Miami, 1988; Volunteer of the Yr Dade County, Cert Appreciation, Flagler Fed Dir Vol Agency's, 1988. **Special Achievements:** Culture Fest 92 in Cote d Ivorie, West Africa, seminar host & keynote speaker, 1992; First African/African-American Summit in Abidjan, Cote d' Ivorie, West Africa, national delegate, 1991; Campaign coordinator for numerous public officials. Second African, African-American Summit in Liberville, Gabon, Central Africa, national coordinator, 1993. **Home Addr:** 14910 S River Dr, Miami, FL 33167, **Home Phone:** (305)953-4153.

JENNINGS, DEVOYD
Executive. **Personal:** Born Sep 10, 1947, Los Angeles, CA; son of William and Margaret; married Gwendolyn Barbee, Jan 1, 1980; children: Shawn, Mark & Demeka. **Educ:** Texas Wesleyan Univ, BS, mkt, 1972. **Career:** Tex Univ, staff asst, 1973-77, customer rep, 1977-85, sr rep, 1985-95, ct affairs specialists, staff asst; Fort Worth Metropolitan Black Chamber Com, pres & chief exec officer, currently. **Orgs:** Pres, Ft Worth Minority Leaders, 1981-88; chmn, Ft Worth Metro Bl Ch, 1986-93; Ft Worth United Way, 1987-93; trustee, Tex Wesleyan Univ, 1987-; North Texas Commn, 1992-; chmn, Tex Asn A A Chambers, 1993-97; US African Am Chambers, 1993-, vice chmn, 1993-95. **Honors/Awds:** Tandy Corp, Mkt & Sales, 1968; United Negro Col Fund Service, 1976; Texas Leg Black Caucus, Merit, 1981; Human Relation Comm, Comm Serv, 1983; Malcolm X Award, Arlington Tex Nat As'n Advan Colored People, 1994; Small BUS ADM, Small BUS Advocate of the Year, 1997; honored by North Tex Cms for chairing Mentor-Entrepreneur prog, 1997-2000. **Special Achievements:** Executive Insights For Small Bus, Input, 1993. **Business Addr:** President, Cheif Executive Officer, Fort Worth Metropolitan Black Chamber of Commerce, 1150 South Freeway Suite 211, Fort Worth, TX 76104, **Business Phone:** (817)871-6538.

JENNINGS, DOMINIQUE
Actor. **Personal:** Born Oct 30, 1958, Stockholm, Sweden. **Career:** Films: Sesame Street, 1969; Bad Influence, 1990; Die Hard 2, 1990; A Low Down Dirty Shame, 1994; Sketch Artist II: Hands That See, 1995; Se7en, 1995; 50 Cent: Bulletproof, 2005; TV Series: "Knots Landing", 1991; "Living Single", 1993; "Martin, "1995; "The Fresh Prince of Bel-Air", 1995; "Hang Time", 1995; "Bay watch Nights", 1996; "The Wayans Bros", 1996; "Life with Roger", 1997; "Spawn",1997-99; "Sunset Beach," 1997-99; "The Jamie Foxx Show", 1999; "Angel, "1999; "Dead Last", 2001; "The Zeta Project", 2001-03; "That's Life", 2002;"44 Minutes: The North Hollywood Shoot-Out", 2003. **Business Addr:** Actor, Arlene Thornton & Associates, 12711 Ventura Blvd Suite 490, Studio City, CA 91604, **Business Phone:** (818)760-6688.*

JENNINGS, EVERETT JOSEPH
Engineer, executive, president (organization). **Personal:** Born Oct 9, 1938, Shelby, NC; son of Everett and Ardietha M C; children: Sharon B & Carl E. **Educ:** Cath Univ, attended 1952; St Mary's Univ, BBA, 1959, BSIE, 1961; Univ Iowa, attended 1963; Univ Oklahoma, 1967. **Career:** San Antonio Fair, Inc, dir, planning & scheduling, 1964; Meridian Engineering, proj dir, 1968; Branson Ultra Sonics, sr engr, 1976; Evanbow Construct, dir construct mgt, 1986; State NJ, Dept Transp, asst comnr, 1990; Tish Inc, vpres, oper, 1991; Jennings Assoc Inc, pres, currently. **Orgs:** Vpres, Am Inst Engr, 1965-68; pres, Am Asn Cost Engr, 1985-88; lt gov, Kiwanis Int, 1988-91; vpres, Habitat NJ, 1990; secy, Goodwill Indust Am, 1992; vpres, Newark Boys Chorus Sch; treas, SHARE Inc; treas, Newark Improv Prog; pres, Montclair Soc Engr; pres, United Hosp Med Ctr Found; bd mem, Metrop YMCA; East Orange Bd Educ; founder, chmn, African Am stud Engr Fund. **Honors/Awds:** Scholastic Honor Award, State Rhode Island, 1949; Outstanding Leadership Award, Leaguers, Inc, 1986; Medal of Honor for Education, Distinguished Men's Club, 1990. **Military Serv:** USAF, 1st lt, 1952-54. **Home Addr:** 1610 Corcoran St NW, Washington, DC 20009, **Home Phone:** (202)232-1736. **Business Addr:** President, Jennings & Associates Inc, 44 S Munn Ave, East Orange, NJ 07017, **Business Phone:** (973)672-1562.

JENNINGS, LILLIAN PEGUES
Psychologist. **Personal:** Born in Youngstown, OH; daughter of Paul and Jessie; children: Dan & Kim. **Educ:** Youngstown State Univ, BSEd, 1954; Univ Pittsburgh, MEd, 1967, PhD, 1971; Univ MD, Post-Doctoral Study. **Career:** Warren Schs, teacher, 1954-57; Youngstown Schs, teacher, prog dir, 1957-66; ed consult, 1966-67; Edinboro State Col, coordr black studies, prof ed & reading clinic, 1968-71, affirm action officer, 1972; Youngstown Pub Sch, head start prog dir, res staff assoc, multiple ed res teams; James Madison Univ, Col Ed, assoc dean emerita, currently; HCA, clinical psychologist, prog supvr, currently. **Orgs:** Alpha Kappa Alpha, Va Asn Sch Psychol, Int Reading Asn; served on mayors comn Human Resources Pittsburgh, 1966-67; bd dir, Dr Barber's Ctr for Exceptional Children Erie; Phi Delta Kappa, Delta Kappa Gamma; chmn, NCATE, Dept Ed Accred Teams; Harrisonburg School Bd, Va Arts Comn, Nat Alliance Black Sch Ed; licensed Prof Counr; vchair, Harrisonburg Sch Bd Va; chaired multiple Accreditation teams; mem, WIB. **Honors/Awds:** Res grants Ford Found, Erie Found, NSF. **Special Achievements:** Multiple Pubs, 1986-87; author of multiple pubs & monographs. **Business Addr:** Associate Dean Emerita, James Madison University, College of Education and Human Services, 800S Main St, Harrisonburg, VA 22807, **Business Phone:** (540)568-6108.

JENNINGS, MARGARET ELAINE
Consultant. **Personal:** Born May 22, 1943, Gadsden, AL; daughter of Izora Torbert Jones and Spencer Small Jr; married Jarvis C (divorced 1987); children: Terrence A Hall, Regina Lynn Hall Clay & Jason D. **Educ:** Cuyahoga Community Col, Cleveland, OH; Bowie State Col, Bowie, MD, 1977; Univ Southern Calif, WA, DC, MPA, 1980. **Career:** Value Engineering Alexandria, VA, programer & analyst, 1975-77; Fed Res Bd, WA, DC, data base admin, 1977-79; Booz Allen & Hamilton, Bethesda, MD, data base designer, 1979-86; Advanced Technol, Reston, VA, sr systs analyst, 1986-89; Perot Systs, Herndon, VA, sr systs analyst, 1989-90; Booz Allen & Hamilton, Bethesda, Md, sr systs analyst & asst prog mgr, 1990-. **Orgs:** Local Conf Coord, 1984, fund raising, 1985, pub rels, 1986, vpres, 1986-87, pres, 1987-91, nat exec dir, 1991-, Black Data Processing Asn. **Honors/Awds:** Conducted Work Related Sem, 1987-90, Outstanding Leadership Award, 1988, 1990, Managed Nat Conf, 1991, Solicited & Acquired Corp Sponsorship, Increased Chap Mem, Black Data Processing Asn. **Home Addr:** 7102 Good Luck Rd, Lanham, MD 20706-3711. **Business Addr:** Associate Government Systems Division, Booz Allen & Hamilton Inc, 4330 EW Highway, Bethesda, MD 20814, **Business Phone:** (301)951-2200.*

JENNINGS, DR. ROBERT RAY
Educator, school administrator. **Personal:** Born Nov 15, 1950, Atlanta, GA; son of Forrest Sr and Mary Beeman. **Educ:** Morehouse Col, BA, Sociol, 1972; Cert Gifted Educ 1975; Univ Ga, Cert Adult Basic Educ, 1978; Clark Atlanta Univ, MA, Educ Psychol, 1974, EdS, Educ Specialist in Interrelated Learning, 1979, EdD, Educ Admin & policy studies, 1982.; Ga State Univ Sch Educ, attended. **Career:** Atlanta Univ, asst to dir pub rels, 1973; Atlanta Pub Sch, Hoffman reading coordr, 1973-76; Literacy Action Inc Atlanta, reading consult, 1974-75; Reading Learning Ctr Inc E Point, dir, 1975-79; Atlanta Pub Schs, teacher gifted, 1976-79; Atlanta Univ, consult dean's grant proj, 1979-80; Atlanta Area Tech Sch, part-time prof, 1979-84; Equal Employ Comm US Govt, equal opportunity specialist, 1979-82; Morris Brown Col Atlanta, assoc prof, 1982-84; US Equal Employ Oppor Comn, Atlanta Dist, off comnn rep off dir, 1982-84, Wash, employee develop specialist, 1984-85; asst vpres, develop & placement, Atlanta Univ, 1985-88; Norfolk State Univ, vpres, develop,1988-91; Albany State Univ, vp instnl advan, 1991-97; NC Agr & Tech State Univ Found, vice chancellor Develop & Univ Rels & chief exec officer, 1997-98; Wake Forest Univ, Babcock Grad Sch Mgt, Futur Focus 2020, execvpres & chief opers officer; Ala A&M Univ, 2006-. **Orgs:** Pres, Atlanta Univ Nat Alumni Asn, 1979-81; bd dirs, Exodus Right-to-Read Prog Adult Literacy Prog, 1980; bd adv, Volunteer Atlanta, 1980-84; parlimentarian Coun Except C Atlanta Area Chapter, 1980-81; bd dirs, Parents Anonymous Ga, 1981-84; bd trustees, Atlanta Univ, 1981-85; founder& ed-in-chief Alumni Update Leadership Atlanta, 1982-; Self-Study Eval Comt, Morris Brown Col, 1983-84; bd dirs, Planned Parenthood, 1983-87;exec bd, Leadership Atlanta, 1986-87; vpres, Coun Advan Pub Black Cols & Univ, 1989-; Ncp Educ Legal Adv bd, chair, 1987-; Leadership Albany,1992-93; SW Ga Comprehensive Health Ist bd, 1992-; Cot Rels Coun & TurnerJob Corp, Inc, Albany Ga, bd, 1996-98; Am Lung Asn, Albany Chap, bd, 1994-; West End Church Christ; Am Asn Higher Educ, 1988-; Am Biog Inst, hon mem, bd adv, 1987-; Coun Advan & Support Educ, 1984-; Phi Delta Kappa, 1982-. **Honors/Awds:** Outstanding Achievement Award, Economic Opportunity Atlanta 1972; Outstanding Serv Award Atlanta Inquirer Newspaper, 1972; Director's Award Fred-

erick Douglass Tutorial Inst Morehouse Col, 1972; Outstanding Service Award, Student Nat Educ Asn, 1972; Award of Excellence Stud Miss Teacher'sAsn, 1972; WSB TV & Radio Fel, 1975; Teacher of the Year Home Park Sch Atlanta, 1976; Award of Excellence Wm Finch Sch PTA, 1976; Appreciation Award for Outstanding Leadership SM Inman Sch PTA, 1976; Outstanding Chapter Mem of the Year, Atlanta Univ 1979; Best of Service Award, Frank Lebby Stanton Sch Atlanta, 1979; Alumnus of the Year, Atlanta Univ, 1980; Special Serv Award, Coun Exceptional C, Atlanta, 1981; Special Serv Award, Nat Bd Dirs, Atlanta Univ Alumni, 1981; Phi Delta Kappa Prssional Fraternity Educ, 1982; cited by Atlanta J & Const Newspaper as one of Atlanta's Most Outstanding Volunteers, 1982; Outstanding Serv Award, United Way Metro Atlanta, 1984; Outstanding Atlantan, 1986. **Special Achievements:** First Recipient Leadership Award in Educ, Delta Sigma Theta Sor, 1986. **Home Addr:** 2005 King George Lane SW, Atlanta, GA 30331-4917. **Business Addr:** Executive Vice President & Cheif Operating Officer, Executive Vice Pres/COO, Future Focus 2020 c/o Wake Forest University, Babcock Graduate School of Management, Reynolda Station, PO Box 7208, Winston-Salem, NC 27109, **Business Phone:** (336)758-5217.*

JENNINGS, SYLVESTA LEE
Banker. **Personal:** Born Jan 30, 1933, Halifax; son of Anthony and Luella Freeman; married Lillie Flippen, Jun 10, 1960; children: Mitchell. **Educ:** NC A&T State Univ, Greensboro NC, BS, 1958; Univ Va, Sch Consumer Banking, dipl, 1968; Rutgers Univ, Stonier Grad Sch Banking, dipl, 1972. **Career:** First State Bank, Danville, VA, chmn & pres, 1988-. **Orgs:** Danville Chamber Com, 1989; Nat Bankers Asn, 1989; Prince Hall Masons Va; Danville, Va Sch Bd; Southside Va Bus & Educ Comt; Kappa Alpha Psi Fraternity. **Honors/Awds:** National Association for Equal Opportunity in Higher Education Award, 1989. **Special Achievements:** Research selected for library at Rutgers Univ, Harvard Univ, and ABA, 1972. **Military Serv:** AUS, 1953-55. **Home Addr:** 113 Cambridge Cir, Danville, VA 24541-5237. **Business Phone:** (804)793-4611.*

JENSEN, MARCUS CHRISTIAN
Baseball player. **Personal:** Born Dec 14, 1972, Oakland, CA. **Career:** Baseball player (retired); San Francisco Giants, catcher, 1996-97; Detroit Tigers, catcher, 1997; Milwaukee Brewers, catcher, 1998 & 2002; St Louis Cardinal, catcher, 1999; Minn Twins, catcher, 2000; Boston Red Sox, catcher, 2001; Tex Rangers, catcher, 2001; NY Yankees, catcher, 2003; Reno Silver Sox, catcher; Golden Baseball League, 2005-06; Oakland Athletics, hitting coach, currently. **Honors/Awds:** Gold medal, United States Olympic baseball team, 2000. **Business Addr:** Coach, Oakland Athletics, McAfee Coliseum, 7000 Coliseum Way, Oakland, CA 94621, **Business Phone:** (510)638-4900.*

JENSEN, DR. RAY M
Executive. **Educ:** Howard Univ. **Career:** Ford Motor Co, Minority Supplier Develop, mgr, Supplier Diversity Develop, dir, currently. **Orgs:** Billion Dollar Roundtable. **Business Addr:** Director Minority Supplier Development, Ford Motor Co, 1 American Rd, Dearborn, MI 48121, **Business Phone:** (313)322-3000.

JENSEN, RENALDO MARIO
Automotive executive, air force officer. **Personal:** Born Jun 29, 1934, New York, NY; son of Doris Davis and Octive; married Alicia Clark, Jan 26, 1959; children: Renaldo M, Malinda L. **Educ:** Howard Univ, Washington, DC, BS, mech eng, 1958; Air Force Inst Technol, Dayton, OH, MS, aerospace eng, 1966; Purdue Univ, West Lafayette, IN, PhD, aerospace eng, 1970. **Career:** Air force officer, automotive executive (retired); USAF, officer, 1958-78; Malstrom Air Force Base, MT; Wright Patterson Air Force Base, Air Force Sch Technol, fac, 1967-74; Ford Motor Co, Dearborn, MI, aerospace engr advan concepts aerodynamics, 1978-86, dir minority supplier develop, 1987-2005. **Orgs:** New Detroit Inc, 1987-; Greater Detroit Chamber Com, 1987-; bd dir, Minority Bus Dir, Try Us, 1987-; bd dir, Nat Minority Bus Develop Coun, 1988-; bd dirs, Plum Hollow Country Club, 1995-; Am Soc Mech Engrs; Am Inst Aeronaut & Astronaut; Combustion Inst; Mil Opers Res Soc; Alpha Phi Alpha Fraternity; Tau Beta Pi Eng Hon Soc. **Honors/Awds:** Distinguished Service Award, Wis Minority Purchasing Coun, 1988. **Special Achievements:** Minority Suppliers Hall of Fame. **Military Serv:** USAF, lt col, 1958-78; Missile Combat Crew Award, 1970, Air Force Commendation Medal. *

JERKINS, JERRY GAINES
Clergy. **Personal:** Born in Loxley, AL; married Naomi Donald; children: Cntr, Gerald, Jennifer, Jacqueline. **Educ:** Austin Peay Univ, BS, 1972; N TN Bible Inst, D Evang. **Career:** St John Baptist Church Clarksville, TN, pastor, 1967-; Haynes Chapel Baptist Church, pastor. **Orgs:** Clarksville Ministerial Asn; ministerial rep, C C; corres secy, Pastor's Conf Nat & Baptist Conv Am; PTA; bd, Children Ctr Hilldale Methodist Church; pres, Missionary Baptist St Conv; bd, United Givers Fund; adv bd, Montgomery Co Welfare Dept; adv bd, Youth Challenge Ctr; pres, Dist Pastor's Conf; bd, Salvation Army; NAACP; gospel Programmer, Radio Sta WJZM. **Military Serv:** Mil serv, sgt, 14 yrs. **Business Addr:** Pastor, St John Missionary Baptist Church, 662 South 52Nd St, Richmond, CA 94804, **Business Phone:** (510)233-1779.

JERKINS, RODNEY
Music producer, songwriter, musician. **Personal:** Born Sep 16, 1977, Pleasantville, NJ; son of Frederick and Sylvia; married Joy Enriquez; children: 1. **Career:** Many albums including "Gina Thompson - Nobody Does It Better", 1996; "No Authority - Keep On", 1997; "Brandy - Never Say Never", 1998; "Coko - Hot Coko", 1999; "Spice Girls - Forever", 2000; "Rhona - Rhona", 2001; "Brandy - Full Moon", 2002; "Blaque - Torch", 2004; "Joy Enriquez - Atmosphere Of Heaven", 2005; "Janet Jackson - Discipline", 2008; "Natasha Uncontrollable", 2009; Guest raps: Anesha Birchett - "Get Ready" with Mase, 2005; The Darkchild Allstars - "We Are Family", 2006; The Pussycat Dolls With Diddy, Lil Wayne, & Fatman Scoop - When I Grow Up (Darkchild Remix)", 2008. **Honors/Awds:** Dove Award; Grammy Award. **Business Phone:** (212)833-7442.*

JEROME, JOSEPH D
Clergy. **Personal:** Born Oct 17, 1951, Port-au-Prince, Haiti; son of Thelamon and Marie K. **Educ:** Suffolk Co Community Col, 1983; Long Island Univ, CW Post, 1985; Seabury-Western Theol Sem, MDiv, 1991. **Career:** Family Consult Serv, 1984-86; Suffolk Child Develop, 1985-87; US Legalization & Naturalization Serv, 1987-89; St John's Episcopal Hosp; Interfaith Med Ctr; Diocese Long Island, Church St Luke & St Matthew, priest; St Philips Episcopal Church; Provincial Coun, clergy rep; St Gabriel's Episcopal Church, Hollis, NY, interim rector; All Saints' Episcopal Church, rector, currently. **Orgs:** Union Black Episcopalian, 1983-; La Union Hispanica, 1983-87; African People Org, 1985-87; clergy, Asn Episcopal Black, 1989-; Am Bible Lit, 1991-; Alban Inst, 1991-; Diocesan AIDS Comn, 1991-; Nat Asn Advan Colored People, Long Island, 1991-. **Business Addr:** Rector, All Saints' Episcopal Church, 43-12 46th St, Sunnyside, NY 11104, **Business Phone:** (718)784-8031.

JEROME, DR. NORGE WINIFRED
Educator. **Personal:** Born Nov 3, 1930; daughter of McManus Israel and Evelyn Mary Grant. **Educ:** Howard Univ, BS, magna cum laude, 1960; Univ Wis, Madison, MS, exp food & human nutrit, 1962, PhD, human nutrit, 1967. **Career:** Univ Wis, Madison, Dept Foods & Nutrit, res asst, 1960-62, Sch Home Econ & Nat Inst Res on Poverty, res assoc, 1966-67; Howard Univ, Wash, DC, instr food & nutrit, 1962-63; Kans Univ Med Ctr, Dept Diet & Nutrit, asst prof, 1967-69, Dept Human Ecol, assoc prof, 1969-72, Dept Prev Med & Community Health, asst prof nutrit, 1969-70; from asst prof to assoc prof, Dept Human Ecol, 1970-74; Dept Community Health, assoc prof, 1974-78, Dept Prev Med, prof, 1978-95, Community Nutrit Div, dir, 1981-95, Sch Med, nutritionist, anthrop, assoc dean minority affairs, 1996-98, Prev Med & Pub Health, prof emer, 1996-; Nutrit Anthrop Communicator, ed, 1974-77; Ed Resources Ctr, dir, 1974-77; Campbell Soup Co, res adv, 1979-81; Bristol Myers Co, media rep, 1981-82; AID, Bur Sci & Technol, Off Nutrit, dir, 1988-92; Solar Cookers Int, bd dir, 1992-2000, pres, 1998-2000; Community Health Scholars Prog, W K Kellogg Found, prog evaluator, 1998-. **Orgs:** Panelist, White House Conf Food Nutrit & Health, 1969; acad adv, Children's Advert Review Unit, 1974-78; founder & chairperson, Coun Nutrit Anthrop, 1974-77; World Food & Nutrit Study Nat Acad Sci, 1976; fel Am Anthrop Asn; fel Soc Appl Anthrop; Soc Med Anthrop; Am Pub Health Asn; Am Dietetic Asn; Soc Behav Med; adv bd, J Nutrit Planning, 1977-84; founder & chmn, Comn Nutrit Anthrop, 1978-79; fel Am Soc Nutrit Scis, 1978-; Am Soc Clin Nutrit, 1978-; US Assoc Club Rome, 1980-97; Mayor's Task Force Food & Hunger, 1983-88; bd mem, Urban League, Greater Kans City; fel Am Col Nutrit, 1986-; pres, Asn Women Develop, 1991-93; Black Health Care Coalition, 1992-2002; bd dir, Coop Develop Found; bd trustees, Univ Bridgeport; bd trustees, Child Health Found; Soc Epidemiol Res; AAAS; NY Acad Sci; Inst Food Technologists; Sigma Delta Epsilon; Beta Kappa Chi. **Honors/Awds:** Tuition Scholarships & Dean's Honor Roll, Howard Univ, 1956-60, Pepperidge Farm Inc Award, Outstanding Jr, 1958-59, Beta Kappa Chi, Sci Honor Soc, 1959; Omicron Nu, 1961; Matrix Award, Women Commun Inc, 1976; Dairy Council Merit Award, Greater Kans City, 1977, 1988; First Higuchi/Irvin Youngberg Research Achievement Award, Univ Kans, 1982; Spotlight Award, Women's Bur, US Dept Labor, 1990; Life time Achievement Award, Inst Caribbean Studies, 2002. **Home Addr:** 14402 W 68th St, Shawnee, KS 66216-2149. **Business Addr:** Professor Emerita Preventive Medicine & Public Health, KU Medical Center, Department of Preventive Medicine and Public Health, 3901 Rainbow Blvd, PO Box 1008, Kansas City, KS 66160-7313.

JERRARD, PAUL
Hockey coach. **Personal:** Born Apr 20, 1965. **Educ:** Lake Super State Col, BA, sports mgt. **Career:** Kalamazoo Wings, player coach, 1992-94; Hershey Bears, 1994-97; Lake Superior State Univ, asst coach, 1997-98, 1999-2002; Colo Avalanche, 2002-03; Hershey Bears, 2003-05; Iowa Stars Hockey, asst coach, 2005-. **Business Addr:** Assistant Coach, Iowa Stars Hockey, 833 5th Ave, Des Moines, IA 50309, **Business Phone:** (515)237-8277.

JERVAY, MARION WHITE
Lawyer. **Personal:** Born Mar 26, 1948, Mt Olive, NC; married. **Educ:** Univ NC Wilmington, BA, 1971; Nat Law Center, Geo Wash Univ Wash, DC, 1974; Sch Law Duke Univ Durham, NC, JD, 1976. **Career:** New Hanover County Bd Educ Wilmington, eng teacher, 1972; Norfolk City Schs, teacher, 1972-73; Wade & Roger Smith Attys, Law Raleigh, res asst, 1975; Hon Earl W Vaughn, NC Ct Appeals Raleigh, res asst, 1976-77; Liggett Group Inc Durham, NC, corp atty, 1977; Duke Clin Res Inst, Contracts Mgt & Strategic Develop, dir, 2000-. **Orgs:** NC State Bar; NC Bar Asn; Wake Co Bar Asn; NC Asn Black Lawyers; ABA; Am Bus Women's Asn.

JERVAY, PAUL REGINALD, JR.
Newspaper executive. **Personal:** Born Oct 25, 1949, Atlanta, GA; son of Paul Reginald Sr (deceased) and Brenda Yancey (deceased); married Evelyn Harrison, Jul 24, 1988; children: Jeneea, Adria, Shenay Dunston & Kelvin Dunston. **Educ:** NC Cent Univ, Raleigh, NC, BS, 1971. **Career:** The Carolinian Newspaper, Raleigh, NC, publisher, 1971-; Advantage Advertising, consult. **Orgs:** Owner & treas, Nay-Kel Educ Ctr; bd chairperson, Triangle Opportunities Industrialization Ctr Raleigh Inc. **Honors/Awds:** Service Award, St. Augustine's Col, 1983. **Business Addr:** Publisher, The Carolinian Newspaper, PO Box 25308, Warrenton, NC 27611, **Business Phone:** (919)834-5558.

JERVAY-PENDERGRASS, DR. DEBRA
Educator. **Educ:** Emerson Col, BS, commun disorder, 1973; Univ Pittsburgh, MA, speech-lang path, Georgetown Univ, PhD, linguistics. **Career:** Speech-language pathologist; Lt Joseph P Kennedy Inst, Dept Educ, Off Spec Educ Progs, co-dir, 1997-2001; Childrens Inst; Howard Univ, Dept Commun Disorders researcher, adj asst prof; poet; Montgomery County Pub Schs, Div Early Childhood Progs & Servs, speech-lang pathologist & Linguist, storytellers123, currently. **Special Achievements:** Research and project are featured in "Roots of Reading," the first of a five part Reading Rockets literacy television series that began airing on PBS stations nationally in 2002; Featured in Black Enterprise Mag. **Business Addr:** Speech-Language Pathologist & Linguist, Founder, Storytellers123, PO Box 15114, Chevy Chase, MD 20825.*

JESSUP, GAYLE LOUISE (GAYLE JESSUP FRANKLIN)
Executive, journalist. **Personal:** Born Jul 26, 1957, Washington, DC; daughter of Cedric B Jessup and Theresa W Jessup; married Charles L Franklin Jr, Aug 1, 1987; children: Charles Jessup Franklin. **Educ:** Howard Univ, BA, commun, 1978; Northwestern Univ, MSJ, broadcasting, 1982. **Career:** WTOC-TV, Savannah, GA, reporter, hostess, 1982-84; WGXA-TV, Macon, GA, anchor, reporter, 1984-86; WSB-TV, Atlanta, GA, assoc producer, 1986-87; WHMM-TV 32, Washington, DC, producer, hostess, 1987-; In-Focus Productions, president, 1991-. **Orgs:** Natl Assn of Black Journalists, 1990-; Montgomery County NAACP, 1989-; scholarship committee head, Doug Wiliams Foundation, 1989-91; mentor, Mentors Inc, 1989-; American Federation of Television & Radio Artists, 1988-. **Honors/Awds:** PBS Promotion and Advertising Award Nominee, PBS, 1988; Act-So Merit Award, Montgomery County NAACP, 1990; Georgia School Bell Award, Georgia State Board of Education, 1983; New York Times Scholarship, The New York Times Co, 1981; Gannett Journalism Scholarship, The Gannett Co, 1977. **Home Phone:** (301)299-8696. **Business Addr:** Producer, Hostess, WHMM-TV 32, 2222 4th St. NW, Washington, DC 20059, **Business Phone:** (202)806-3215.

JESSUP, MARSHA EDWINA
College teacher, educator, executive director. **Personal:** Born Nov 8, 1944, Washington, DC. **Educ:** Howard Univ, BS, 1967; Univ Mich, MS, 1971; Cath Univ, attended 1973;Temple Univ, attended 1978. **Career:** Smithsonian Inst, free-lance sci illus, 1967-68; Howard Univ Col Med, asst med illus, 1968-69; US Dept Agr Grad Sch, fac mem, 1971-74; Armed Forces Inst Path, med illus, 1972; NIH, med illus, 1972-74; Dept Media Resources, chief med illus, dir; Univ Med & Dent NJ, Robert Wood Johnson Med Sch, Surg Dept, adj assoc prof, dir media resources, currently, consult, customized training & indust out reach, dir, currently. **Orgs:** NE region bd gov rep, Asn Biomed Commun Dirs, 1982-84; chmn, Asn Med Illustrators, 1986-87. **Honors/Awds:** Cited, Civic & Career Serv, Silver Spring MD Bus & Prof Womens Club, 1973;US Civil Serv Task Force, 1974. **Business Addr:** Director, University of Medicine & Dentistry of New Jersey, Robert Wood Johnson Medical School, Department Media Resources, 675 Hoes Lane, Piscataway, NJ 08854-5635.

JETER, CLIFTON B
Executive. **Personal:** Born Feb 22, 1944, Martinsville, VA; son of Clifton B Jeter Sr and Naomi Winston Jeter; married Diane R Bates; children: Sheree, Amani & Aja. **Educ:** Howard Univ, BA, 1967; Am Univ, MBA, 1970, MD, CPA, 1972; Harvard Univ, advan mgt prog, 1991. **Career:** Executive (retired); Peoples Involvement Corp, controller, 1967-69; Peoples Develop Corp, finance vpres, 1969-74; Howard Univ, internal auditor, 1974-75; Wolf & CO, CPA's, mgr, 1975-77; John F Kennedy Ctr Performing Arts, controller, 1977-84, dir finance, 1985-91, chief financial officer, vpres facilities. **Orgs:** Treas Quality Construct Co, 1974-77; Nat Inst Tennis Develop, 1975-77; Alpha Phi Alpha; Am Inst CPA'S; MD Asn CPA'S DC Inst CPA'S; Nat Black MBA Asn; Nat Asn

Black Accts; Am Mgt Asn; Asn Practicing CPA'S; Harvard Club Wash; chmn bd, Ag Fed Credit Union, currently.

JETER, DELORES DEANN
Pharmacist. **Personal:** Born Mar 11, 1949, Union, SC. **Educ:** Univ SC, Col Pharm, 1973, PhD, pharm admin. **Career:** Funderburks Drug, intern, 1972; Moncrief Army Hosp, intern, 1973; Richland Mem Hosp, clin pharm, 1973; Millers Pharm, reg pharmacist & mgr, 1974. **Orgs:** Am Pharmaceut Asn; Palmetto & Med Dent Pharmaceut Asn; Alcoholic & Drug Abuse Coun; organist, Calvary Baptist Church; Islam Grand Ct Daughters Isis. **Honors/Awds:** Cit day, Columbia, SC. **Business Addr:** 827 N Main St, Lancaster, SC.

JETER, DEREK (DEREK SANDERSON JETER)
Baseball player. **Personal:** Born Jun 26, 1974, Pequannock, NJ; son of Charles. **Educ:** Univ Mich. **Career:** NY Yankees, infielder, 1995-, capt, 2003-. **Orgs:** Turn 2 Found. **Honors/Awds:** Am League Rookie of the Yr, 1996; Joan Payson Award, 1997 All-Star Team selection, 1998-99; World Series Most Valuable Player, 2000; Most Valuable Player, All-Star Game, 2000; Babe Ruth Award, New York Chapter BBWAA,2000; Play of the Yr, ESPY, 2002; Gold Glove Award winner, 2003-05; AL Hank Aaron Award, 2006; Silver Slugger Award winner, 2006-08; he was named 8 on the Sporting News' list of the 50 greatest current players, 2009. **Business Addr:** Professional Baseball Player, NewYork Yankees, 880 River Ave, Bronx, NY 10452, **Business Phone:** (718)293-4300.*

JETER, DEREK SANDERSON. See JETER, DEREK.

JETER, JOSEPH C., JR.
Engineer. **Personal:** Born Aug 16, 1961, Philadelphia, PA. **Educ:** Taylor Univ, BA, Commun, 1983, BS, System Analysis & Political Sci, 1983. **Career:** Taylor Univ, minority recruitment coord, 1980-83, minority fund raising & planner, 1982-83; Applied Energy Servs, intern, 1982; Bell Pa, asst mgr network engrg; seminar writer & career planning, self-employed 1983-; minority recruitment writer & consultant, self-employed, 1983-; career planning writer & consultant, self-employed 1983-. **Orgs:** Vpres, Black Cultural Soc, 1980-82; ed writer, Taylor Univ, 1982-83; pres Adv Comn, Minority Recruitment Taylor Univ, 1982-83; Stud & Econ Leadership Forum, 1982-83. *

JETER-JOHNSON, SHEILA ANN (KAFI IMA)
Writer, publisher. **Personal:** Born Mar 4, 1952, Indianapolis, IN; daughter of Helen L and Linzie E Jeter; married Lawrence E Johnson, Apr 20, 1980; children: Shelette Veal. **Educ:** Ind Univ-19Purdue Univ Indianapolis, 1973; Draughons Bus Col, 1982; Martin Univ, BA, communs, 1991. **Career:** LS Ayres & Co, PBX operator, 1970-73; Gen Motors Corp, 1973-96; Twelve Gates Publ, former publ, 1986-88; Indianapolis Star, reporter, 1988. **Orgs:** vpres, Midtown Writers Assn, 1989-; founding pres, Intl Black Writers, Indianapolis Chap, 1988. **Honors/Awds:** Outstanding Black Women of Indianapolis, NCNW, 1990. **Special Achievements:** Auth, Before It's Too Late, Twelve Gates Publ, 1986. **Business Addr:** Publisher, Twelve Gates Publ, PO Box 19869, Indianapolis, IN 46219.*

JETT, ARTHUR VICTOR, SR.
Executive, building inspector. **Personal:** Born Dec 16, 1906, Union Springs, AL; married Katie; children: Kay Baker A. **Educ:** Morehouse Acad, attended 1928; Chicago Tech Sch. **Career:** Bankhead W Contractors & Develop Inc, pres; Atlanta Bd Educ Estimating & Plan Reading, instr masonry trades, 1948-51; Masonry Trades & Utica Inst,instr, 1932-34; Bricklayers Union Local 9 AFL, bus agt, 1940-44; Masonary Trades, apprent com, 1946-50; bldg contractor, 1952-; Dept Labor, adv Com,1967-69. **Orgs:** Atlanta Urban League, 1944-74; YMCA; bd dir, bd mem & treas, Atlanta Br, Nat Asn Advan Colored People; bd, Nat Child Welfare League Am; United Way; pres bd, Gate City Day Nursery Asn; bd mem treas, Consolidated Mortgage & Investment Co; Atlantic Chamber Com; Nat Conf Social Welfare; first Congregations Chap; UCC; vice chmn, Deacon Bd Morehouse Col Alumni Asn. **Honors/Awds:** Good Neighbor Award, Nat Conf Christians & Jews, 1972; life mem, Nat Asn Advan Colored People; plaque, Nat Asn Advan Colored People, 1974. *

JETT, JAMES
Football player. **Personal:** Born Dec 28, 1970, Charlestown, WV. **Educ:** WVA. **Career:** Football player (retired); Los Angeles Raiders, 1993-94; Oakland Raiders, wide receiver, 1995-2002. **Honors/Awds:** Seven time All-Am; Gold Medal, US Olympics, 1992; West Virginia University Sports Hall of Fame, 2002. *

JEWELL, CURTIS T
Executive, president (organization). **Personal:** Born Sep 8, 1943, Richmond, VA; son of Thelma and Fletcher; married Beverly Ann Cheeks, Aug 15, 1995; children: Neonu Allen, Nia, Curtis II, Sisi, Clay Johnson & Leah Johnson. **Educ:** Park Col, attended 1975. **Career:** Rubicon, admin dir, 1967-72; U Hurer Drug Prog, exec dir, 1972-75; Int Inc, pres, 1975-79; State Ohio, chief off human serv, 1978-79; Nationwide Ins Co, automated sales agent, 1979-85; Praxis Consult Group Inc, pres & chief exec officer, 1987-89; Excel Mgt Systems Inc, founder, pres & chief exec officer, 1989-. **Orgs:** Bd trustees, Special Ties, 1994-; bd trustees, Community Shelter Bd, 1996-97; bd trustees, Greater Columbus Arts Coun, 1996-97; bd trustees, Young Men Destiny, 1997; bd trustees, NBPC, 1998-; bd trustees, COSI, 1998-; bd trustees, Short N Bus Asn, 2000; bd, Franklin County Workforce Policy, 2000. **Honors/Awds:** Small Business Person of the Year, US Small Bus Admin, 1994; African American Male Business Owner of the Year, OAAABO, 1994; Businessman of the Year, Black President's Roundtable Asn, 1994; Business First, Fast Fifty List, 1997 & 1998. **Military Serv:** USN, E-4, 1963-68. **Business Addr:** President, Chief Executive Officer, Excel Management Systems Inc, 691 N High St 2nd Fl, Columbus, OH 43215, **Business Phone:** (614)224-4007 Ext 221.

JEWELL, TOMMY EDWARD, III
Judge. **Personal:** Born Jun 30, 1954, Tucson, AZ; son of Bobbie L and Tommie E Jr; married Angela Juzang, Apr 4, 1981; children: Taja Marie & Thomas IV. **Educ:** NMex State niv, BA, 1976; Univ NMex, JD, 1979. **Career:** Soc Albuquerque Inc, staff atty legal aid, 1979-; Rocky Mountain, regional dir; Jewell, Jewell Kelly & Kitson, Albuquerque, NM, partner, 1981-84; State NMex, Albuquerque, NM, metrop ct judge, 1984-91, Second Judicial Dist Ct, judge, 1991-. **Orgs:** Omega Psi Phi Fraternity Inc, 1974-; Black Am Law Stud Asn, 1977-79; Adv comt, Juv Justice, 1978-; comt mem, Gov Juv Code Task Force, 1979-; fel Reginald Heber Smith, Howard Univ Sch Law, 1980-81; Nat Bar Asn, 1980-; bd dirs, State Justice Inst. **Honors/Awds:** Dean's Award, Univ NMex Sch Law, 1978-79; Outstanding Young New Mexican, NMex Jaycees, 1986. **Business Phone:** (505)841-7392.

JEWETT, KATRINA ANN
Lawyer. **Educ:** Clark Atlanta Univ; Emory Univ, Sch Law. **Career:** YKK Corp Am, corp atty; Miller Martin PLLC, atty, currently. **Business Addr:** Attorney, Miller Martin PLLC, 1000 Vol Bldg, Chattanooga, TN 37402, **Business Phone:** (423)756-6600.*

JIGGETTS, DANNY MARCELLUS
Businessperson, broadcaster. **Personal:** Born Mar 10, 1954, Brooklyn, NY; son of Floyd and Hattie Campbell; married Karen; children: Lauren, Kristan. **Educ:** Harvard, BS; MBA; Northwestern Univ. **Career:** Football player (retired), broadcaster: Chicago Bears, 1976-82; Nat 1st Bank Chicago; Proctor & Gamble, sales rep; Bd Urban Affairs NY, field rep; USFL, NBC-WMAQ TV; CBS Sports; ABN & LaSalle Bank, asst vpres; CBS sports & WBBM-TV Chicago, sports broadcaster; WSCR Radio, Fox-TV, WFLD, broadcaster, currently, Comcast SportsNet Chicago, broadcaster, currently. **Orgs:** Better Boys Found, Nat Hemophilia Found, Spec Olympics, Nat Sudden Infant Death Syndrome Found, Midwest Assoc SickleCell Anemia, March Dimes, Harvard Alumni Assoc. **Honors/Awds:** Leadership Award, BPO Elks Youth; Football 3 times All Ivy New England; Track 2 times All Ivy; Football All Am, 1976; inducted, Harvard Varsity Hall Fame. **Business Addr:** Broadcastor, Comcast SportsNet Chicago, 350 N Orleans St Suite S1 100, Chicago, IL 60654, **Business Phone:** (312)222-6000.*

JOBE, BEN
Educator, basketball coach. **Personal:** Born Mar 2, 1933, Nashville, TN; son of Arthur and Mary B; married Regina W, May 30, 1969; children: Bryan A & Gina B. **Educ:** Fisk Univ, BS, 1956; Tenn State Univ, MS, 1963; Univ Tenn, 1963; Southern Univ, attended 1966. **Career:** Educator, basketball coach (retired); Talladega Col, head basketball coach, 1964-67; AL State Univ, head coach, 1967-68; SC State Univ, head coach, 1968-73; Univ SC, asst coach, 1973-78; Univ Denver, head coach,1978-80; Denver Nuggetts NBA, asst coach, 1980-81; GA Tech Univ, asst coach, 1981-82; AL A&M Univ, head coach, 1982-86; Southern Univ, head coach, 1986-96; Tuskegee Univ, head coach, 1996-00; Southern Univ, head coach, 2001-03. **Orgs:** Kappa Alpha Psi, 1954-00; Tenn Ed Cong, 1956-60; Nat Ed Asn, 1956-60;Health, Phys Ed & Recreation Asn, 1958-60; NAIA Coaches Asn, 1964-73; NatAsn Basketball Coaches, 1973-00; Los Angles Asn Basketball Coaches,1986-96. **Honors/Awds:** Coach of the Year, NAIA (District 6), 1969; Coach of the Year, SIAC, 1969,1984, 1985, 1986; Coach of the Year, Rocky Mount in, 1979; Coach of theYear, NABC, 1988; Coach of the Year, SWAC, 1988, 1989; Black CollegesCoach of the Year, 1993. **Special Achievements:** Conducted basketball clinics in AL, SC, CO, West Africa, LA, FL, TN, NY,Guam, 1964-99; "How to Build a Basketball Program" presented in Holland,1993. **Home Addr:** 1311 Old Montgomery Rd, Tuskegee, AL 36088. *

JOBE, SHIRLEY A.
Librarian. **Personal:** Born Oct 10, 1946, San Bernadino, CA; daughter of Fines and Luejeannia; children: Robyn. **Educ:** Texarkana Col, AA, 1966; East Tex State Univ, AB, 1968; Simmons Col, MSLS, 1971. **Career:** John F Kennedy presial Libr, head librn, 1971-84; Boston Globe Newspaper Co, head librn, currently. **Orgs:** Vpres, MA Black Librns Network, 1984-86; volunteer, Soup Kitchens feed homeless; volunteer visit incarcerated persons Ma prisons. **Honors/Awds:** Educ Prof Developop, Act Grant, 1970; Black Achiever's Award, Boston, 1987. **Business Addr:** Library Director, The Boston Globe, 135 Morrissey Blvd, PO Box 55819, Boston, MA 02205-5819, **Business Phone:** (617)929-8803.*

JOE, DR. LONNIE
Physician, association executive. **Personal:** Married Anne Joe. **Educ:** Univ Mich Sch Med, MD, 1978. **Career:** Providence Hosp, intern, residence, 1983; pvt pract, physician internal med & pulmonary pract, 1984-; Detroit Med Soc, pres, currently; Mich State Med Soc, dir, currently. **Orgs:** Nat Med Asn; Comt Fed Legis, Mich State Med Soc; bd mem, Awards & Nominating Comt, Off Med Develop & Alumni Rels; bd trustee mem, Wayne County Med Soc. **Home Addr:** 22255 Greenfield Rd Suite 300, Southfield, MI 48075, **Home Phone:** (248)557-5227. **Business Addr:** President, Detroit Medical Society, 580 Frederick Douglas, Detroit, MI 48202, **Business Phone:** (313)832-7800.

JOE, WILLIAM (BILLY)
Football player, football coach. **Personal:** Born Oct 14, 1940, Aynor, SC. **Educ:** Villanova Univ, BA, econ; Cheyney State Univ, BA, hist; Antioch Col, MA, sec educ. **Career:** Football player (retired), football coach; Denver Broncos, football player, beginning 1963; Buffalo, 1965; Miami Dolphins, 1966-67; NY Jets,1968-69; Stoke broker; Univ MD, asst, 1970-71; Cheyney State Col, head coach, 1972-78; Philadelphia Eagles, running backs coach, 1979-80; Cent State Univ, OH, head coach; Fla A&M Univ, head coach, 1994-05; head football coach, Division II, Miles College, 2007-. **Orgs:** Kappa Alpha Psi Fraternity; pres, Am Football Coaches' Assn, 1995. **Honors/Awds:** All-Am hons; Most Valuable Player award, 1962; Silver Medal, Shot put, Pan Am Games, 1963; PA State Conf Coach of the Yr, 1978; NAIA Nat Championship, 1990, 1992; Nat Coach of the Yr, Pigskin Club; Nat Coach of the Yr, 100 Percent Wrong Club of Atlanta; Mid-Eastern Athletic Conf Coach of the Yr, 1995, 1996; FAMU Hall of Fame; National Football Foundation's College Football Hall of Fame.

JOHN, ANTHONY
Executive. **Personal:** Born Feb 19, 1950, New York, NY; son of Maggie Seriven and Alfred S; married Elmira Cooper; children: Genean Corrinda Jessica. **Educ:** Ohio State Univ, Columbus, OH, BS, comput sci, 1977; Fairleigh Dickinson Univ, Paterson, NJ, MBA, 1981. **Career:** AT&T, Piscataway, NJ, comput programmer, 1978-80; self-employed comput programmer, 1981-90; Dow Jones, S Brunswick, NJ, systs proj mgr. **Orgs:** Nat treas, BDPA, 1982-84; pres, NJ Chap, Black Data Processing Asn, 1983-84; pres, S Jersey Black Data Processing Asn, 1987; Burlington Co Concerned Black Men, 1989-; treas & bd trustees, Rossville AMEZ Church, 1989-. **Military Serv:** USAF, staff sgt, 1971-78. **Home Addr:** 16 Crosswick Pl, Willingboro, NJ 08046.

JOHN, DAYMOND
President (Organization). **Personal:** Born 1969, Brooklyn, NY. **Career:** Red Lobster, waiter; FUBU Found, founder, 1997; FUBU Entertainment, founder, 2000; Fubu The Collection, founder & chief exec officer, currently. **Honors/Awds:** Entrepreneurs of the Year, Nat Asn Advan Colored People; Congressional Achievement Award for Entrepreneurship; Essence Award. **Business Addr:** Chief Executive Officer, Founder, Fubu The Collection, 350 5th Ave Suite 6617, New York, NY 10118, **Business Phone:** (212)273-3300.

JOHN, DR. MABLE
Association executive, clergy. **Personal:** Born Nov 3, 1930, Bastrop, LA; daughter of Mertis and Lillie John; widowed; children: Jesse P, Joel D, Otis D & Limuel C. **Educ:** Wayne State Univ, RN; Crenshaw Christian Ctr Sch Ministry, divinity degree, 1986; DDiv, 1993. **Career:** Motown Records, recording artist & mgr, 1956-60; Stax Records, recording artist, 1966; Ray Charles Raelettes, lead singer & mgr, 1969-; Otis Music Group, owner/publisher, 1971-; Joy In Jesus Ministries, founder, 1986-. **Orgs:** Nat Asn Sickle Cell Dis, 1979; founder, Joy Community Outreach, 1986-; Urban League, Los Angeles Chap, Welfare Work, 1997. **Honors/Awds:** Letter of Commendation, President Clinton, 1993-2000; Rhythm & Blues Hall of Fame, Inductee, 1994; Heroes & Legends, Inductee, 1994; Letter Commendation, Senators Boxer & Feinstein, 2000. **Special Achievements:** First female solo artist signed to Berry Gordy's Tamla label, 1960; #6 hit "Your Good Thing Is About to End," 1966. **Business Addr:** Founder, Joy Community Outreach to end Homelessness, Joy in Jesus Outreach, 1621 Virginia Rd, Los Angeles, CA 90019, **Business Phone:** (323)731-9315.

JOHNICAN, MINERVA JANE
Executive. **Personal:** Born Nov 16, 1939, Memphis, TN; daughter of John Bruce Johnican Sr. and Annie M Rounsoville Johnican. **Educ:** Central State Col, 1957; TN State Univ, BS, 1960; Memphis State Univ, Graduate Study, 1965. **Career:** Memphis City Schools, elementary sch teacher, 1960-65, elem school librarian, 1965-79; Shelby County Govt, county commissioner, 1975-82; Memphis City Govt, city councilwoman at large, 1983-87. **Orgs:** Chmn pro-tem Shelby Co Bd of Comm 1976-77; pres Gazell Public Relations & Adv Co 1976-78; mem Natl Assoc of Counties Natl Bd 1978-81; past pres, TN County Commission As-

soc, 1980-81; Alpha Kappa Alpha Sor, 1958-; budget chmn, Memphis City Council, 1984; pres, Alpha Termite & Pest Control Inc, 1982-88, pres, Gazelle Broadcasting, Coy Inc; pres & owner of Commonwealth Consultants, Ltd. **Honors/Awds:** Distinguished History Makers Award Mallory Knights Org 1976; "A Salute to Minerva Johnican" Memphis Community Leaders 1977; Outstanding Women in Politics Alpha Kappa Alpha Sor 1978; Outstanding Leadership Award Coca Cola Co of Memphis 1979; Women of Achievement "COURAGE" Award Network Womens Org 1984; First Black to be elected to an At-Large Council the City of Memphis (received 40% of white votes cast); Person of Equality Award Memphis NOW Chapter; Citizen of the Yr Award Excelsior Grand Chapter of Order of the Eastern Star; 1986 NCCJ Govt Serv Award & TN Educ Assoc Humanitarian Award, 1986. **Home Addr:** 1265 Dunnavant St, Memphis, TN 38106. **Business Addr:** President, Chief Executive Officer, 631 Madison Ave, Memphis, TN 38103, **Business Phone:** (901)526-0458.*

JOHNON, BILL E. See JOHNSON, WILLIAM EDWARD.

JOHNS, DR. JACKIE C
Dentist. **Personal:** Born Jul 14, 1953, Belle Glade, FL; son of Mattie M Johns and Gonte Johns. **Educ:** Tex Col, BS (Cum Laude) 1976; Prairie View A&M Univ, MS 1976-77; Col Med & Dent NJ, DMD, 1981. **Career:** Dr AS Ford, dent, 1981-82; Dr CJ Beck, dentist, 1981; Dr RL Levine, dent, 1982-83; US Vets Admin Outpatient, dent, 1983-84; Dr Thomas Scholpler, dent, 1983-84; Jackie C Johns & Assoc, dent, currently. **Orgs:** Am FL Dental Asn; NE Regional Bd Palm Beach Co Dental Asn; The Acad Gen Dent; Alpha Omega Frat; Westboro Bus & Prof Women Orgn; Family & Comprehensive Dent, Boynton Bch, FL; Family & Comprehensive Dent, Belle Glade, FL; Int Cong Oral Implantologist; Family & Comprehensive Dent WPB Fort Pierce FL. **Honors/Awds:** Nationally recognized in Journal of the Nat Dental Asn for active participation in the 1978 Health Fair at NJ Dental School; Comm Serv Citations for work on voters registration drives; Pinacle Award by Being Single Magazine Chicago Ill, 1989; Professional Achievement Award, Black Achievement, Glades Alumnae Chapter, Delta Sigma Theta Sorority Inc, 1991. **Military Serv:** AUS, Reserve capt. **Home Addr:** 685 S Main St, Belle Glade, FL 33430, **Home Phone:** (561)996-1010. **Business Addr:** Dentist, Jackie C Johns & Assoc, 2100 45th St Suite A8, West Palm Beach, FL 33407, **Business Phone:** (561)842-5619.

JOHNS, JAMIE
Association executive. **Career:** Notary Signing Agent & Instr, 1997-; Notary Access Asn, pres & owner, 1999-. **Orgs:** Nat Notary Asn; Ambassador, Carson Chamber Com; Federal Employees W Credit Union; Nat Adv Coun, GoGetNotary.com & GoGetLoan.com, 2005; J and E GuestCare. **Honors/Awds:** Nat Notary of the Year, Nat Notary Asn, 2004; Martin Luther King Jr Drum Major Award, CAL-State Dominquez, 2004. **Special Achievements:** Ebony Magazine, Speaking of People, March, 2004. **Business Addr:** Owner, President, Notary Access Association LLC, 2286 E Carson St Suite 312, Long Beach, CA 90749, **Business Phone:** 877-954-8093.*

JOHNS, MARIE C.
President (Organization), vice president (organization), executive. **Personal:** Married Wendell L; children: Richard. **Educ:** Ind Univ, John F Kennedy Sch Govt, BS; Univ Va, Darden Grad Sch Bus Admin, Masters Pub Admin. **Career:** retired: Bell Atlantic Wash, vpres external affairs; Landmark Systs Corp, dir; Verizon DC, pres. **Orgs:** Wash Performing Arts Soc; Greater Wash Bd Trace; Helen Hayes Awards; Fed City Coun; founding chair, Wash DC Technol Coun; Sr Bd Stewards Metrop Af Methodist Episcopal Church; past chair, YMCA Metrop Wash Bd Dirs; past pres, DC Chamber Com; past chair, Leadership Wash; Trustee, Howard Univ; alumna Indiana Univ. **Honors/Awds:** honor doctorate, Trinity Col, 1999; recipient, numerous awards bus & civic leadership; Twenty-Five Most Influential Black Women in Business, Network Journal, 2003.

JOHNS, MICHAEL EARL
Consultant. **Personal:** Born Jan 14, 1945, Alexandria, VA; children: Michael E Jr. **Educ:** Howard Univ, BA, econ, 1968; Wharton Sch Finance, MBA, mgt info & control syst, 1972. **Career:** IBM Corp, syst engr, 1968-71; Xerox Corp, financial mgr, 1972-78; The Prism Corp, pres; Unity CMS, Mkt Res Div, dir, currently. **Orgs:** Market Res Asn, 1980-, DC Chamber Com, 1984-. **Business Phone:** (202)526-0503.

JOHNS, POLLYANNA (POLLYANNA JOHNS KIMBROUGH)
Basketball player. **Personal:** Born Nov 6, 1975, Bahamas. **Educ:** Univ Mich, attended 1998. **Career:** Player (retired); Coach; Charlotte Sting, 1998; Cleveland Rockers, 2000-01; Miami Sol, ctr,2001-02; Cleveland Rockers, ctr, 2003; Houston Comets, ctr, 2004; Southern Tech Wild Cats, asst coach, currently. **Business Addr:** Assistant Coach, Southern Tech Wild Cats, 5605 77 Center Dr Suite 270, Charlotte, NC 28217.*

JOHNS, DR. SONJA MARIA
Surgeon. **Personal:** Born May 13, 1953, Washington, DC; daughter of Ralph L E and Jannie Austin; children: George Wheeler Jr, Ashante, Chiquita, Maria Wheeler. **Educ:** Howard Univ Col Liberal Arts, BS, 1976; Howard Univ Col Med, MD, 1978; Howard Univ Hosp Family Practice Residency, cert completion, 1981; Aerospace Med Brooks AFB, San Antonio, TX, cert, 1989; Harvard Univ, Nat Security Prog, 1900. **Career:** Nat Health Plan Inc, physician attendance, 1981-82; Women's Med Ctr, family practitioner, 1983; DC Air Nat Guard, chief hosp serv; Warsaw Med Ctr, family physician, 1983-91; Med Squadron, Andrews Air Force Base, MD, commander, 1991-96; Westmoreland Health Serv, family practitioner, founder, owner, 1991-; state air surgeon & inspector gen, dean, 1996; Beaumont Juvenile Ctr, med dir, 1991-97; Northern Neck Regional Jail, med dir, 1996-99; Hanover Juvenile Correctional Ctr Barrett Juvenile Correctional, med dir, 1997-99. **Orgs:** Am Acad Family Physicians; Nat Med Assoc; Am Med Assoc; Nat Advan Asn Colored People; Assoc Military Surgeons; Northern Neck Med Soc; vpres, Tapp Hosp; co-founder, Black Bus & Prof Coalition; bd mem, Richmond Co Comn Serv Assoc Inc; soloist soprano, Comn Chorus; Northern Neck Convention Choir; Northern Neck Choral Soc; adv, 4-H Club Richmond Co; pres, Tappahannock Kiwanis Club. **Honors/Awds:** Physician's Recognition Award, Am Med Assoc, 1981-88. **Military Serv:** Air Nal Guard, Col; Meritorious Service Medal, Air Force Commendation, Perfect Attendance, Air Force Longevity, Nat Defense, Outstanding Unit. **Business Addr:** Owner, Founder, Westmoreland Health, PO Box 1120, Warsaw, VA 22572-0640.*

JOHNS, STEPHEN ARNOLD
Insurance executive. **Personal:** Born Aug 21, 1920, Chicago, IL; son of Stephen and Bennie F Shannon; married Tanis Fortier, May 24, 1966; children: Brenda Johns Penney. **Educ:** Roosevelt Col, BA, 1947; FLMI Life Off Mgt Asn, 1959; Calif Lutheran Univ Am Col Life Underwriters, 1964. **Career:** Jackson Mutual Life Chicago, 1942-47; methods analyst, 1957; Agency Educ & tn, dir, 1960; Asst Agency off 1962; Asso Agency, dir, 1964; asn agency, dir, 1970; Golden St Mutual Life Ins Co, vpres agency, dir, 1974-80; sr vpres & chief mkt officer, 1980-83, retired 1985. **Orgs:** Mem bd dir, Golden St Mutual Life Ins Co; Life Underwriters' Asn of LA LANCCP; Urban League; Kappa Alpha Psi. **Military Serv:** AUS, s & sgt, 1943-46. **Home Addr:** 5221 Angeles Vista Blvd, Los Angeles, CA 90043.

JOHNS KIMBROUGH, POLLYANNA. See JOHNS, POLLYANNA.

JOHNSON, ADDIE COLLINS
Educator. **Personal:** Born Jan 1, 1928?, Evansville, IN; daughter of Stewart Collins and Willa Shamell Collins; married John Q, Sep 6, 1958 (deceased); children: Parker Collins. **Educ:** Howard Univ, BS, 1956; PBB Hosp, dietetic internship, RD, 1957; Framingham State Col, MEd, 1968. **Career:** Boston Lying In Hosp, therapeut dietitian, 1957-61; Harvard Sch Pub Health Res, dietitian, 1963-64; Hour Glass Newspaper Kwajakin MI, ed, 1965-66; Foxborough Pub Sch, teacher, 1968-2000; Univ Mass, Harbor Campus Dept Nursing, nutritionist, 1980-88; Bridgewater State Col, asst prof, 1982-94; Foxborough High, teacher consumer & family sci, 1994-2000; real estate sales assoc, Century 21 Florence Kates, Sharon, Mass, 2001-. **Orgs:** Bd dir, Finance chmn, Mass Home Econ Asn; Am Dietetics Asn; Soc Nutrit Educ; Am Home Econ Asn; Circle Lets Inc; Delta Sigma Theta Sorority Inc; Mass Teachers Asn; Links Inc; pres, Boston Chap Links Inc; nominating comt, Nat Links Inc, 1978-79; Am Asn Univ Women; chairperson, pres, Iota Chap, Delta Kappa Gamma, 1989-; Nat Sci Found, Proj Seed, 1992; Nat Asn Advan Colored People. **Honors/Awds:** Presenter, Northeast Regional Social Studies Conf, 1984-85; Area Achievement Award, Delta Kappa Gamma, 2001. **Business Addr:** Real Estate Sales Associate, Century 21 Florence Kates, 21 S Main St, Sharon, MA 02067, **Business Phone:** (781)784-6771.

JOHNSON, ADRIENNE
Basketball player. **Personal:** Born Feb 5, 1974; daughter of Albert Johnson and Yvonne. **Educ:** Ohio State, attended 1996. **Career:** Cleveland Rockers, guard, 1997-98; Orlando Miracle, 1999-02; Connecticut Sun, guard, 2003-04; Seattle Storm, 2005; Louisiana Tech Lady Techsters, 2007-08. **Honors/Awds:** All-Big Ten, Third Team; Most Improved Player Award, Leadership Award, OH State; Sixth Man Award; Hometown Hero award, 2001. *

JOHNSON, ALBERT JAMES
Golfer. **Personal:** Born Aug 20, 1943, Phoenix, AZ; son of Eddie and Albert; married Beverly (divorced); children: Kevin A Johnson. **Educ:** Univ Ariz, BS, mgt, 1965. **Career:** Golf player (retired); Harlem Globletrotters, player 1965-67; Univ AZ, asst coach 1968-72; Matthew Chevrolet & Orielly Chevrolet, Tucson, AZ, salesman, 1972-84; City of Tucson, Parks & Recreation, Starter II supervisor. **Orgs:** Active 20-30 Serv Club 1970-72; Randolph Mens Golf Club 1976-; Desert Trails Mens Club 1969-74; Univ AZ & Alumni Club 1970-73; deacon & elder Trinity Presb Ch 1969-73; Saguaro Mens Club, 1984-91. **Honors/Awds:** All Western Athletic Conference, Basketball, 1963, 1964-65; City Tucson, Tom Price Memorial Golf Tournament Winner, 1990. **Special Achievements:** The first black assistant basketball coach in the Western Athletic Conference, 1972.

JOHNSON, ALBERT WILLIAM, SR.
Automotive executive. **Personal:** Born Feb 23, 1926, St Louis, MO; son of Oscar William and Anna; married Marion, Feb 2, 1952; children: Albert W Johnson Jr, Donald King Johnson & Anthony Johnson. **Educ:** Univ Ill, Champaign, Ill, BS, 1942; Univ Chicago, Chicago, IL, degree hosp admin, 1955; Lincoln Univ, attended. **Career:** Al Johnson Cadillac-Saab-Avanti & Leasing Inc, Tinley Park, IL, pres, 1971-; United Pub Workers Union, former regional dir; Homer Phillips Hosp, St Louis, MO, former admitting supvr, asst admin & bus mgr. **Orgs:** Chmn bd, Variety Club Childrens Charities, 1987-; Ill Sports Facilities Authority, 1988-; bd mem, Thresholds Psychiatric Rehab Ctr, 1990; citizens com, Univ IL; bd dirs, Better Bus Bur Metro Chicago; vpres, Variety Club IL, Chicago Chapter; bd mem, Seaway Nat Bank; Execs Club Chicago; Platformers Club; Metro club; Unicorn Club; life mem, Nat Asn Advan Colored People; Chicago United; sponsor, Chicago Berry-Johnson Bus & Prof Person Recognition Annual Award; founder, Messanger Found; founder, People United Save Humanity Found; Orland Park Lions Club; hon mem, Oaks Club; bd dirs, Ingalls Memorial Hosp; pres, Pyramid Trotting Asn. **Honors/Awds:** Time Magazine Quality Dealer Award, 1975; Certificate of Excellence, Cosmopolitan Chamber Com; Partner in Progress Award, Chicago Asn Com & Indust; Businessman's Award, Woodlawn Orgn; Black Excellence Award, Cultural Community, PUSH; Top 100 Black Businessmen Award, Black Enterprise magazine; Humanitarian Award, Mayor Richard Hatcher, Gary, IN; Certificate of Apppreciation, St Bernard's Hosp; Cert Recognition, Univ Detroit; Appreciation Award, CUS Nat Honor Soc; Cert Merit, Adv Mgt Dealers, Oldsmobile; Appreciation Award, Cosmopolitan Chamber Com; Certificate of Apppreciation, Chatham Business Asn; Certificate of Apppreciation, Gen Motors Corp; Coun Deliberation Award; Humanitarian of the Year Award, Coalition United Community Action. **Special Achievements:** Black Businessman of the Year, Black Book NPSA; Man of the Year, Coalition for United Community Action. **Business Phone:** (312)429-6600.

JOHNSON, ALEX. See JOHNSON, ALEXANDER HAMILTON.

JOHNSON, ALEXANDER HAMILTON (ALEX JOHNSON)
Banker. **Personal:** Born Oct 3, 1924, Greensboro, AL; son of Rev Alexander Johnson and Erma; married Delores Mitzie Russel; children: Alexander III. **Educ:** Calif Pacific Univ, BA, Pub Admin, 1978, MA, Mgmt, 1980. **Career:** Banker (Retired); Federal Aviation Admin, personnel staffing spec, 1968-70, chief civil rights staff, 1970-74; US Equal Employ Opportunity Comn, compliance suprv, 1974-81; Ariz Bank, mgr, vp, 1992. **Orgs:** Pres Am Fed Govt Empl, 1968; clerk session, Southminster Presbyterian Church, 1980-84; chmn bd, Southminster Social Serv Agency, 1981; pres, Southwest Area Conf, Nat Asn Advan Colored People, 1982-84; chmn, Reg I Nat Asn Advan Colored People, 1984-85; keeper records, Phoenix Alumni Kappa Alpha Psi, 1984-86; Sigma Pi Phi, Gamma Mu Boule, 1988; Maricopa County Comn Trial Court Appointments, 1989. **Honors/Awds:** Outstanding Citizen Maricopa City, Nat Asn Advan Colored People, 1978; Award for Caring Phoenix City Human Serv Community, 1980. **Military Serv:** AUS, corpl, 1943-47.

JOHNSON, ALMETA ANN
Lawyer. **Personal:** Born Mar 11, 1947, Rockingham, NC; daughter of V Louise Johnson Noel; divorced; children: Cesseli A Cooke, Harry E Cooke IV. **Educ:** Johnson C Smith Univ, BA, 1968; Ohio State Univ, JD, 1971. **Career:** Metzenbaum Gaines Finley & Stern, law clerk, 1969-70; Ohio State Univ, res asst, 1970-71; Benesch Friedlander Mendelson & Coplan, assoc atty, 1971-75; City Cleveland, chief police prosecutor, 1975-80; pvt pract, atty, currently; Village Woodmere, law dir, 1983-86; E Cleveland City Coun, mem, 1987; Almeta Johnson & Assocs, atty, currently. **Orgs:** Chmn, E Cleveland Citizens Adv Comn, 1973-75, 1988-; chmn, E Cleveland Charter Rev Comn, 1976; bd mem secy treas, OH Law Opportunity Fund; Am Bar Asn; Bar Asn Greater Cleveland; OH State Bar Asn; Black Women Lawyers Asn; Alpha Kappa Alpha. **Honors/Awds:** Lett Civil Liberties Award, Ohio State Univ Col Laws, 1971; One of Ten Most Influential Women in greater Cleveland, The Plain Dealer, 1975; Nat Asn Advan Colored People Outstanding Young Citizen Cleveland Jaycees, 1976. **Business Addr:** Attorney, Almeta Johnson & Associates, 489 E 260th St, Euclid, OH 44132, **Business Phone:** (216)261-4700.*

JOHNSON, ALVIN ROSCOE
Executive. **Personal:** Born Oct 15, 1942, Alton, IL; son of Cyrus L Johnson and Jennie C Keen; married Thelma Marie Hart; children: Brent Alvin, Dirk Cyrus. **Educ:** Univ Edwardsville, Southern IL, BS, Bus Admin 1972, MBA, 1982. **Career:** Olin Corp, mgr train & develop, 1962-77, mgr personnel, 1977-80; Babcock Industries Inc, svp human res & admin, 1980-93; Yale New Haven Hosp, vpres employee rels. **Orgs:** Dir, Am Red Cross, Girl Scouts, Urban League, Acct Babcock Inc, 1982-; treas & golden life mem, NAACP;bd dir, Alumni Assoc Ex; chair, deacons, Immanuel Baptist Church; Sigma Pi Phi; hr coun, Manufactures Alliance Prod Innovation, 1982-; life mem, SIUE Alumni Assoc Ex bd dir, 1975-77. **Military Serv:** AUS, sgt, E-5, 1966-68. *

JOHNSON, ANDREW L, JR.
Lawyer. **Personal:** Born Oct 4, 1931, Youngstown, OH; married Joan Carol Phillips; children: Andrew III & Paul. **Educ:**

Northwestern Univ, BS, 1953; Cleveland State Univ, Sch Law, JD, 1959. **Career:** Shaker Heights Munic Ct, acting judge, 1970-; Pvt Pract, atty, 1960-; Real Estate, ownership, 1962-. **Orgs:** Trustee, Bar Asn Greater Cleveland, 1970-73; chmn bd, trustees, Forest City Hosp Cleveland, 1970-76; Trust Shaker Lakes Regional Native Ctr, 1977-; pres, Bar Asn Greater Cleveland, 1978-79; labor arbitrator, Major Steel Companies NE, OH; hearing examr, Ohio Civil Rights Comn; founding mem & first pres, Cleveland Lawyers Asn Inc; Cleveland Coun Human Rels; pres, Home Owners Title Corp Cleveland; vpres, Northwestern Univ Alumni Club Cleveland; life mem, Alpha Phi Alpha Fraternity; charter mem, Judicial Coun, Nat Bar Asn; charter mem, Eighth Judicial Conference; pres, bd trustees, Forest City Hosp; managing partner, Tower Mgt Co, chmn, Adv Comt; Forest City Hosp Found; life mem, Nat Asn Advan Colored People; Nat Urban League; Sigma Pi Phi Fraternity. **Honors/Awds:** Merit Award, Northwestern Univ Col Arts & Sci, 1979; Law Day Award, Cleveland Lawyers Asn, 1969; Meritorious Service Award, Cleveland Bar Asn, 1970; Alumnus of the Year Award, Northeastern Univ, Col Arts & Sci, 1979. **Military Serv:** AUS, specialist 4th class, 1953-55. **Business Addr:** Attorney, 1205 W 110th St Suite 131, Cleveland, OH 44119, **Business Phone:** (216)651-6000.

JOHNSON, ANNE-MARIE
Actor, vice president (organization). **Personal:** Born Jul 18, 1960, Los Angeles, CA; married Martin Grey, Jan 1, 1996. **Educ:** Univ Calif, Los Angeles, theatre. **Career:** Actress, currently; TV Series: "In the Heat of the Night", 1988-93; "In Living Color", 1993-94; "Spiderman", 1994; "Melrose Place", 1995-96; "Smart Guy", 1997; "JAG", 1995; "The X Files", 2000; "Strong Medicine", 2001; "Rock My Baby", 2004; "That's So Raven", 2006; "Adventures in Boss Sitting", 2006; "Navy NCIS: Naval Criminal Investigative Service", 2007; "Bones", 2007; "House of Payne", 2007; "CSI: Crime Scene Investigation", 2007; TV movies: "His Mistress", 1984; "Dream Date", 1989; "Lucky &Chances", 1990; "steroid", 1997; "Through the Fire", 2002; Films: I'm Gonna Git You Sucka, 1988; The Five Heartbeats, 1991; Strictly Business,1991; Down in the Delta, 1998; Pursuit of Happiness, 2001; Life & Drawing, 2001; That's So Raven: Raven's Makeover Madness, 2006. **Orgs:** Natl vpres, Screen Actors Guild, 2005-. **Business Addr:** Natl Vice President, Screen actors Guild, 5757 Wilshire Blvd 7 Flr, Los Angeles, CA 90036, **Business Phone:** (323)954-1600.

JOHNSON, ANTHONY MARK
Basketball player. **Personal:** Born Oct 2, 1974, Charleston, SC. **Educ:** Col Charleston, BBA, 1997. **Career:** Sacramento Kings, guard, 1997-98; Atlanta Hawks, guard, 1998-2000; Orlando Magic, 1999-2000; Cleveland Cavaliers, 2000-01; NJ Nets, guard, 2001-03; Ind Pacers, guard, 2003-06; Dallas Mavericks, 2006-07; Atlanta Hawks, 2006-07; Sacramento Kings, 2007-08; Orlando Magic, currently. **Orgs:** Owner, AJ Custom Doors and Windows. **Honors/Awds:** Player of the Yr, Trans Am Athletic Conf, 1997; First Team All-TAAC, 1997. **Business Addr:** Professional Basketball Player, Orlando Magic, 8701 Maitland Summit Blvd, Orlando, FL 32810, **Business Phone:** (407)916-2400.*

JOHNSON, DR. ANTHONY MICHAEL
Physicist, educator. **Personal:** Born May 23, 1954, Brooklyn, NY; son of James W and Helen Weaver; married Adrienne Steplight, Jun 2, 1975; children: Kimberly, Justin & Brandon. **Educ:** Polytechnic Inst NY, BS, Physics Magna Cum Laude, 1975; City Col City Univ NY, PhD, Physics, 1981. **Career:** AT &T Bell Labs, sr tech assoc, 1974-77; doctoral can, 1978-81; result rafast optics & electronics; AT & T Bell Labs, mem tech staff, disting mem; Quantum Phys & Electron Res Dept; Disting Mem Tech Staff, 1988-95; Photonic Circuits Res Dept, 1990-95; NJ Inst Tech, chairperson & distingprof, Appl Phys & prof, Elect & Comput Eng, 1995-2003; found prof,optics &photonics & disting prof physics, 2003; Univ MD, Ctr Advan Studies Photonics Res, dir, 2003-, prof phys & prof comp sci & elect eng, 2004-,Wilson H. Elkins profship, Univ System Md, 2004-. **Orgs:** Am Phys Soc, 1977-; Nat Soc Black Physicists, 1980-, tech prog co-chair,1989; Optical Soc Am, 1982-; Inst Elec & Electron Engrs, 1982-; symp organizer Ultrashort Pulses in Optical Fibers, 1985, vchmn, Tech Prog Com,Ultrafast Optical Phenomena, 1985, symp organizer Ultrashort Non linear Pulse Propagation in Optical Fibers, 1988, Ann Mtg Optical Soc Am, 1985; AAAS, 1986-; tech coun, Optical Soc Am, chmn, Tech Group on UltrafastOptical Phenomena, 1986-87; tech prog comm Ann Meeting the Optical Soc Am,1986, 1987, 1988; tech prog comm, Ultrafast Optics & Electronics for the Conf Lasers &Electro-Optics, 1986, 1987; chmn, Tech Prog Subcom Conf on Lasers and Electro-Optics, 1988, 1989, tech prog co-chair, 1990; R W Wood Prize Comm, Optical Soc Am, 1989, chair, 1990; topical ed, Optics Letters,1989-91; Optics News adv comm, 1989-91; sci & tech adv bd, J the Nat Tech Assn, 1989-; vpres, Optical Soc Am, 2000-; Basic Energy Scis Adv Comt, Dept Energy. **Honors/Awds:** Undergrad res award, Sigma Xi, 1975; Coop Res Fel, AT&T Bell Labs, 1975; chap in books on laser usage, 1984, 1989; var patents in optics &electronics; guest ed, Inst Elec & Electron Engrs, J Quantum Electron spec issue, February, 1988; Distinguished Tech Staff Award, AT&T Bell Labs, 1988; Minds in Motion Award, Sci Skills Ctr, Brooklyn, NY, 1989; Distinguished Alumnus Award, Polytechnic Univ, 1993; Black Engineer of the Year Special Recognition Award, 1994; Edward

A. Bouchet Award of the APS, 1996; Science Spectrum Magazine Trailblazer Top Minority in Science Award, 2005. **Special Achievements:** Publisher:"New Approach to the Measurement of the Nonlinear Refractive Index of Short (**Business Phone:** (410)455-1977.

JOHNSON, ANTHONY SCOTT
Football player, chaplain. **Personal:** Born Oct 25, 1967, Indianapolis, IN; married Shelly; children: Taylor, Kylie, Gabriel, Sierra & Elijah. **Educ:** Univ Notre Dame. **Career:** Football player (retired), Chaplin; Indianapolis Colts, running back, 1990-93; New York Jets, 1994; Chicago Bears, 1995; Carolina Panthers, 1995-99; Jacksonville Jaguars, 2000, team chaplain, currently. **Honors/Awds:** Indianapolis Colts, Fan Club Player of the Year, 1992; Max Noble Award, 1992. **Business Addr:** Team Chaplin, Jacksonville Jaguars, One Stadium Pl, Jacksonville, FL 32202, **Business Phone:** (904)633-6000.

JOHNSON, ARGIE K
School administrator. **Personal:** Born Jan 1, 1939. **Educ:** John C. Smith Col, Charlotte, NC; BS, biol; Long Island Univ, Brooklyn, NY, MS; City Univ New York, Baruch Col, MS. **Career:** Veterans Admin Hosp, Brooklyn, NY, res biochemist; New York City Sch Syst, teacher, prin, dep community supt, dep chancellor instr; Chicago Pub Schs, supt, 1993-95. **Orgs:** Nat Coun Negro Women; Nat Alliance Black Sch Educr; Phi Delta Kappa Honor Soc; Delta Sigma Theta Sorority. **Honors/Awds:** Outstanding Achievement Award, Nat Am Advan Colored People; Educator of the Year, Asn Black Sch Educr, New York; Leadership in Education Award; Super Principal Award.

JOHNSON, ARTHUR E
Executive, vice president (organization), president (organization). **Educ:** Morehouse Col, BA, 1968. **Career:** IBM Fed Systs Div, software engr, 1969, gen mgr div, exec asst, pres & chief operating officer, 1992; Loral Corp Fed Systs Group, pres, 1994-96; Lockheed Martin Corp, Systs Integration Group, pres, 1997, Info & Serv, pres & chief operating officer, 1997-99, vpres, Corp Strategic Develop, 1999-2001, sr vpres, Corp Strategic Develop, 2001-; IKON Off Solutions Corporation, bd dir, currently. **Business Phone:** (301)897-6000.

JOHNSON, DR. ARTHUR J.
Vice president (organization), association executive, educator. **Personal:** Born in Americus, GA. **Educ:** Morehouse Col, BS, sociol & polit sci, 1948; Atlanta Univ, MS, sociol. **Career:** Fisk Univ, res fel, 1949-50; Wayne State Univ, sociol fac, 1965, dir community rels dept, 1979, vpres univ rels, 1992-95, prof emer, currently; Nat Asn Advan Colored People, Detroit Chap, pres, 1992; Mich Civil Rights Comn, dep dir; Detroit Pub Sch Syst, dep supt. **Orgs:** Bd mem, Pub Broadcasting Serv; bd mem, Am Symphony Orchestra League; bd mem, Detroit Sci Ctr; bd mem, Detroit Symphony Orchestra; bd mem, Detroit Inst Arts. **Honors/Awds:** DHL, Wayne State Univ, 1998; Honored with Arthur L Johnson Endowed Scholar, Sch Social Work, Detroit, 2002; Hall of Fame, Inter Nat Heritage. **Special Achievements:** Articles: "Stock Pickers Up Yonder; The Canadian Market: So Familiar, So Different", New York Times Magazine, June 12, 1988, "Is Your City Ready for the Big Leagues", Nation's Cities Weekly, January 25, 1988, p. 6, "The Pennsylvania Challenge", Maclean's, April 23, 1984, p. 26, "Israel's Broken Coalition", Maclean's, April 2, 1984, "A Barometer of Violence", Maclean's, March 5, 1984, "The Collapse of a Nation", Maclean's, February 20, 1984; author, Breaking the Banks. **Business Addr:** Professor Emeritus, Wayne State University, 3222 Fac Admin Bldg, Detroit, MI 48202, **Business Phone:** (313)577-2150.

JOHNSON, ARTHUR T
Government official. **Personal:** Born Oct 29, 1947, Earlington, KY; married Dorothy Radford; children: Belinda & Joy. **Educ:** Earlington HS, 1967; Austin Peay State Col, 1968. **Career:** City Earlington, councilman, 1972-83, mayor. **Orgs:** Membership, Earlington Volunteer Fire & Rescue Squad, 1967-; Membership, Earlington Civic Club, 1972-, pres, Earlington Jaycees, 1982; Junior Adv, rep Goodyear Tire & Rubber Co, 1983-84; bd dir, Pennyrile Area Develop Dist Pennyrile Housing Corp. **Honors/Awds:** Citzen of the Year, Hopkins Countains Progress, 1976; Man of the Year, Hopkins Countians Progress, 1985; Black Man of the Year, Black Award Coun, 1985.

JOHNSON, AVERY
Basketball player, basketball coach. **Personal:** Born Mar 25, 1965, New Orleans, LA; married Cassandra, Jul 1, 1991; children: Christianne & Avery Jr. **Educ:** NMex Jr Col, Hobbs, NM, 1984; Cameron Univ, Lawton, OK, 1985; Southern Univ, Baton Rouge, LA, 1988. **Career:** Basketball player (retired), basketball coach; Seattle SuperSonics, guard,1988-90; Denver Nuggets, 1990-91, 2001-02; Houston Rockets, 1992; Golden State Warriors, 1993-94, 2003-04; San Antonio Spurs, 1994; Dallas Mavericks, 2002-03, asst coach, 2004-05, head coach, 2005-; Katrina Rescue Ride, co-host, 2005. **Orgs:** Bd dirs, Project Turn Around, currently; Bd dirs, Hunger Busters, currently. **Honors/Awds:** Home Team Community Service Award, Fannie Mae Found; Western Conference Coach of the Month, 2005; NBA Coach of the Year, 2005-06;

NBA All-Star Team Coach, 2006; NBA Coach of the Year Award, 2006. **Business Phone:** (214)747-6287.

JOHNSON, AYUBU. See JOHNSON, BENJAMIN EARL.

JOHNSON, BARRY
Executive. **Educ:** Yale Univ, BA; Harvard Univ, MBA. **Career:** Disney, Bertelsmann Music Group, Sony Music, mem mgt team; iClique Corp, founder & chief exec officer; MSBET, chief exec officer; Staubach Co, vpres, 2002; Acresh LLC. pres & chief exec officer, currently. **Orgs:** Instr, Nat Found Teaching Entrepreneurship; entrepreneurial instr, Georgetown Law Ctr Harrison Inst. **Business Addr:** President, Chief Executive Oficer, Acresh LLC, 4700 Wisconsin Ave Suite 200, Washington, DC 20001, **Business Phone:** (202)449-4677.

JOHNSON, BEN D.
Insurance executive. **Career:** Winnfield Life Ins Co; Winnfield Funeral Homes; Winnfield Casket Co, Natchitoches, LA, chief exec & owner, currently. **Orgs:** Founder, Ben D. Johnson Educ Found. **Honors/Awds:** Man of the Year, Natchitoches Chamber Com, 1969; Hon state senate, 1972; Humanitarian service award, Nat Asn Advan Colored People; Hon Doctorate in Humanities, Northwestern State Univ, 1998. **Business Addr:** Chief Executive, Owner, Winnfield Life Insurance Co, 315 N St, Natchitoches, LA 71457.

JOHNSON, BEN E.
Manager. **Personal:** Born Jan 31, 1937, Ashley County, AR; married Marlene; children: Jan, Paula, Jay. **Educ:** Univ WI Milwaukee, BS, 1975, Cert Pub Admin, 1987. **Career:** Alderman Dist, alderman; Milwaukee Common Coun, pres; City Milwaukee, city clerk; Milwaukee Enterprise Ctr N, small bus coordr, currently. **Orgs:** Black Caucus, Nat League Cities; Dist vpres, WI League Munic Exec Comn; joint cong state senate co supv & alderman; legis serv ctr Nat League Cities Human Resources Comn; Milwaukee Area Manpower Coun; Mil Urban Oserv; bd chmn, Milwaukee Soc Develop Comn; Milwaukee Econ Develop Comm; corp mem, Milwaukee Urban League; bd dir, CHPASW; adv com, SE WI Reg Plan Comn; NAACP; bd, Greater Milwaukee Coun Arts Child; Milwaukee Rec Task Force; Sch Breakfast Coalition; bd Milwaukee Pabst Theater Bd; Milwaukee Hear Soc Bd; Milwaukee Youth Serv Bur Plan Com; Milwaukee House Task Force; adv bd, Sickle Cell Anemia Found; adv bd, Harambee Re-vit Proj; Milwaukee Repretory Theatre Bd; Milwaukee Perf Arts Ctr Bd; Milwaukee Caucus Aging; Milwaukee Forum; N Side Bus Asn Fed; N Side Pol Action Ctr Found. **Honors/Awds:** Commission Service Award, First Baptist Church; Community Award, CC Rider; Commission Service Award, Milwaukee Little League; Commission Service Award, Upper Third St Merchants; Legis Award, Comm Pride Expo; Commission Service Award, Youth Develop Ctr; Commission Service Award, Milwaukee Theol Inst; Bicen Award, Cent City; Recog & Appreciation Milwaukee Sch of Engr Scholar Univ of WI Milwaukee, 1955; Cent City Business Federal Civic Award, 1975; Walnut Improvement Council Civic Award, 1975. **Business Addr:** Small Business Coordinator, Milwaukee Enterprise Ctr - N, 2821 N 4th St, Milwaukee, WI 53212, **Business Phone:** (414)372-3609.*

JOHNSON, BENJAMIN EARL (AYUBU JOHNSON)
Arts administrator. **Personal:** Born Apr 23, 1943, Brooklyn, NY; children: Brian, Marilyn, Jerri, Nicole. **Educ:** Housatonic Community Col, AA, 1974; Univ Bridgeport, BS, 1979. **Career:** ABDC Inc, proj dir; vis lectr/artist, Sacred Heart Univ, 1974; CABHUA New Haven CT, pres, 1976-77; Hosuatonic Community Col, vis lectr, 1976-79. **Orgs:** Bd dirs, Art Resources New Haven CT, 1976; bd dirs, Channel 8 Affirmative & Action New Haven CT, 1974; lectr/art Bapt Correctional Ctr, 1974-78; coordr/art Harambee Festival, 1975; commr CT Commn on the Arts 1976-80; Thirdstream. **Honors/Awds:** Best in show painting Barnum Festival, 1976; First prize painting oils Barnum Festival 1977; First prize painting watercolor Barnum Festival 1979. **Military Serv:** USF, E-4, 8 yrs. *

JOHNSON, BENNETT J
Salesperson, executive, government official. **Personal:** Born in Chicago, IL; son of Bennett J Sr and Kathryn Burnice Hill Samples. **Educ:** Paine Col, GA, 1948; Roosevelt Univ, chem, math, 1950; Univ Calif, Los Angeles, eng sci, 1955, grad degree, 1956; Real Estate Inst Chicago, mortgage banking, 1973. **Career:** Path Assoc, salesman; Fuller Products Co, salesman; Chicago Courier Newspaper, salesman; PF Collier, salesman; Chicago Pub Schs, high sch teacher, 1957-60; Los Angeles County Probation Dept, probation counr; Ill State Employment Serv, methods & procedures advr, 1961-66; US Dept Defense, Chicago, personnel mgt specialist, 1966-68; Talent Assistance Fund, dir, 1969-71; UCI Group Inc, chair, 1970-; US Dept Com, regional dir, 1971-72; Merit Trust, dept dir, 1972-73; Ill Govs Office Human Resources, asst dir, 1973-74; Path Press Inc, pres, begin 1982; Third World Press, vpres, currently. **Orgs:** Vpres, Nat Asn Advan Colored People, Evanston Br, 1965-66, pres, 1979-83, 1989-91, 1995-2002; regional coordr, Nat Youth Work Comt, 1956-58, Ill State Conf Brs, exec comm, currently; Greater State St Coun, bd, 1972-97; founder, N Cook County Off Econ Opportunity. **Business**

Addr: Vice President, Third World Press Inc, 7522 S Dobson Ave, Chicago, IL 60619, **Business Phone:** (773)651-0700.

JOHNSON, BERNETTE JOSHUA
Judge. **Personal:** Born Jun 17, 1943, Donaldsonville, LA; daughter of Frank Joshua Jr and Olivia Wire; divorced; children: David Kirk & Rachael Denise. **Educ:** Spelman Col, Atlanta, BA, 1964; La State Univ, Law Sch, JD, 1969; Spelman Col, Hon Doctorate Laws. **Career:** Nat Asn Advan Colored People, Legal Defense Fund, cot organizer, 1964-66; US Dept Justice, summer intern, 1967; New Orleans Legal Assistance Corp, atty, 1969-73; self-employed, lawyer, 1973-77; AFNA Nat Educ Found, dir, 1977-81; City New Orleans, dep city atty, 1981-84; State La, judge, justice, 1984-; La Supreme Ct, assoc justice, 1994-. **Orgs:** Secy, Nat Bar Asn, judicial coun, 1992-96; pres, Spelman Col Alumnae Asn, 1992-94; fin secy, Omicron Nu Zeta Chap, Zeta Phi Beta Sorority, 1992-94; pres, Southern Christian Leadership Conf, 1989-94; dist dir, Nat Asn Women Judges, 1992-94; bd mem, YWCA, 1992-94; bd pres, New Orleans Legal Assistance Corp, 1994-96; Martinet Legal Soc, 1995; chair-elect, Nat Bar Asn, judicial coun, 1996-97; trustee bd, Greater St Stephen Full Gospel Baptist Church; New Orleans Chap, Links Inc; Am Bar Asn. **Honors/Awds:** Ernest N Morial Award, New Orleans Legal Assistance Corp, 1992; Role Model Award, YWCA, 1992; Citizenship Award, Nat Asn Advan Colored People, 1996; AP Tureaud Citizenship Award, La State Conf, Nat Asn Advan Colored People. **Special Achievements:** One of the first African-American women to attend the Law School at Louisiana State University; First woman elected to the Civil District Court in New Orleans. **Business Addr:** Associate Justice, Louisiana Supreme Court, 301 Loyola Ave, New Orleans, LA 70112, **Business Phone:** (504)568-8062.

JOHNSON, BETTY JO
Educator. **Personal:** Born Aug 14, 1940, Rankin Cty, MS; daughter of Louise Hayes and Louis; divorced. **Educ:** Piney Woods Sch, Miss, AA, 1960; Tougaloo Col, Miss, BA, 1964; Jackson State Univ, Miss, MEd, 1971; Memphis State Univ, Memphis, EdD, 1975. **Career:** Jackson Pub Sch System, Miss, teacher, 1964-67; Lawyers Comn Civil Rights Under Law Jackson, Miss, legal secy, 1967-69; City Health Improv Proj, Univ Miss Med Ctr, fiscal spec, 1970; Miss Dept Pub Welfare Title IV, planning & eval specialist, 1972-73; Comn Ed Exten Jackson, Miss, curricspec Headstart, 1972; Alcorn State Univ, vis instr, 1973; Memphis State Univ, grad asst, 1973-76; Ariz State Univ, assoc prof, 1976-78; Shelby State Community Col, head dept, gen & early childhood educ, prof, 1978-89; LeMoyne-Owen Col, co-ordr, prof, early childhood educ, 1989-96; SW Tenn Community Col, dept chair educ, 1996-, prof educ, currently. **Orgs:** Kappa Delta Pi, 1976-; Nat Asn Educ Young C, 1976; Phi Delta Kappa, 1978-; Asn Childhood Educ; Tenn Asn Young C; Memphis Urban League; Delta Sigma Theta; Memphis May Ed Com; Memphis Asn Young C; Tenn Asn Supv & Curric Develop, 1988-; bd examiners, Tenn Dept Educ. **Honors/Awds:** Women Color Struggle, A Consortium Doctors, Atlanta, Ga, 1991; Tennessee Outstanding Achievement Award, 1992. **Home Addr:** 6107 Selkirk, Memphis, TN 38103, **Home Phone:** (901)794-1857. **Business Addr:** Professor of Education, Southwest Tennessee Community College, Department Developmental Studies, Rm 220 A Bldg Union Ave Campus, PO Box 780, Memphis, TN 38101-0780, **Business Phone:** (901)333-5345.

JOHNSON, BEVERLEY ERNESTINE
Government official, business owner, president (organization). **Personal:** Born May 16, 1953, Chevenly, MD; daughter of Joanne Juanita Scott and Ernest Charles Lane; married Allen (divorced 1983); children: Allen II. **Educ:** Univ Md, College Park, Md, BS, 1985. **Career:** Dept Housing & Urban Develop, Wash, DC, housing mgt officer, 1980-87; Boston Redevelopment Authority, Boston, Mass, dep dir community/economic devlop, 1987; BEVCO Assoc Inc, pres, currently. **Business Addr:** President, BEVCO Associates Inc, 25 Goodrich Rd Suite 2, Boston, MA 02130, **Business Phone:** (617)522-7003.

JOHNSON, BEVERLY
Singer, actor, fashion model. **Personal:** Born Oct 13, 1952, Buffalo, NY; married Danny Sims; children: Anansa; married Billy Potter, Jan 1, 1971 (divorced 1973). **Educ:** Northeastern Univ, pre-law; Brooklyn Col. **Career:** Glamour Mag, prof fashion model, 1971; Halston, runway model; NatAirlines, television ad singer; Vogue Mag, cover model, 1974; Elle Mag,cover model; Revlon Cosmetics, prof model; Phil Anastasia, singer; Don'tLose the Feeling, solo singer; films: Land of Negritude, 1975; Ashanti,1979; National Lampoon's Loaded Weapon 1, 1992; Meteor Man, 1992; How toBe a Player, 1997; 54, 1998; Down 'n Dirty, 2000; Crossroads, 2002; RedShoe Diaries 15: Forbidden Zone, 2002; TV series: "She's Got the Look",2008; shows: Oprah Winfrey Show, guest appearance; Arsenio Hall Show,guest appearances; JC Penney Portrait Studio/Wilhelmina Modeling Agency,promotional tour nat young model search promoter, 1992. **Orgs:** Africare; Atlanta Black Educ Fund; AIDS Awareness Campaign. **Special Achievements:** Author, Guide to a Life of Beauty, Times Books, 1981; Amoekar Industries is selling wigs and cosmetics under the brand name Beverly Johnson. **Business Phone:** (213)882-6900.

JOHNSON, BILL WADE
Executive. **Personal:** Born May 9, 1943, Idabel, OK; married Barbara. **Educ:** Central Okla State Univ, BA, 1965. **Career:** Night Training Okla City OIC, supvr, 1965-68; Okla City, OIC, dir 1968-70; OIC Int, field specialist 1970-71; OIC Pittsburgh, PA, exec dir, 1970-71; OIC Chicago IL, exec dir, 1976. **Orgs:** Chmn, Frederick Douglass HA, 1965-68; City Chicago Manpower Planning Coun; Convenor Region III OIC's Am; chmn bd dir, Career Develop Inc; chmn bd, Hill Dist Fed Credit Union 1975-76; mem bd dir, Ozanam Strings; Kappa Alpha Psi Frat; Chicago Assembly; numerous other comt, boards & couns. *

JOHNSON, BRENT E.
School administrator, consultant. **Personal:** Born Jan 17, 1947, Springfield, MA; son of Alvin and Matilda Edmonds; divorced; children: Jacye Arnee. **Educ:** Hampton Inst, BS, 1968; West Ga Col, MA, 1975; Atlanta Univ. **Career:** Presbyterian Church, USA, personnel dir, 1974-78; AMTAR Inc, v pres, 1977-80; Atlanta Univ, dir admis, 1980-86; Consortium for Grad Study Mgt, St Louis, MO, dir mkt & recruiting, 1986-89; The Success Factor, Atlanta, GA, managing prin, 1989-; Clark Atlanta Univ, Sch Bus Admin, Atlanta, GA, asst dean & dir MBA prog. **Orgs:** Nat Hampton Alumni Assn, 1972-; pres & bd mem, NW YMCA, 1975-78; pres, Atlanta Univ Staff Assembly, 1981-84; chmn & founder Minority Admis Recruitment Network, 1981-86; consult, Grad Mgt Admis Coun, 1984; chmn, Minority Affairs Adv Comm, Grad Mgt Admis Coun, 1986-89. **Honors/Awds:** Contributor Black Collegian Mag, 1980-; Developed Destination MBA Prog, Natl Black MBA Asn, 1987; recognized for work with minorities in MBA progs, African-Am MBA Asn, Univ of Chicago, 1990. **Military Serv:** USNG, staff sgt, 3 yrs. *

JOHNSON, C. CHRISTINE
Educator. **Personal:** Born Jun 19, 1928, Jackson, MS; daughter of Cornelius and Simon; children: Edward Christian. **Educ:** Univ Md Munich, MS, 1960. **Career:** NY St Div Human Rights, field rep, 1971; Hamilton Col Clinton, NY, dir Higher Educ Opportunity Prog & trustee, 1972-. **Orgs:** Air Force Asn; Retired Officers Asn; pres, NY St Higher Educ Oppor Prof Orgn; NY St pres, Am Asn Non-White Concerns (now Am Asn Multi-Cultural Coun & Develop); NY St Health Sys Agency; bd visitors, Cent NY Psychiat Ctr; NY State's only Forensic Psychiat Ctr; Prof Bus Women's Asn; NAACP; Nat & NY State Asn Human Rights Workers; Opera Guild; rep, Urban Renewal Prog Dayton, OH, 1958; Joint Protestant/Catholic Choir; City Planning; Tri-State Mental Health Bd; pres, Rome Day Care Ctr; Black Women Higher Educ; NY State Higher Educ Opportunity Prog/Prof Orgn; bd visitors, CentNY Psychiat Ctr, pres; Frontiers Inst; Tri-State Consortium Opportunity Progs Higher Edu. **Honors/Awds:** NOW Unsung Heroine Special Award Honor for Achievement Working, Young Col Women, 1978; nom Female Heroine of Year, Pac Air Force, 1969; Hamilton Col Alumni Council Bell Ringer Award for Outstanding Achievement Meritorious Service, 1991; African Americans Distinction Award, NY governor Mario Como, 1994. **Military Serv:** USAF, maj, 1950-70; Vietnam Hon Medal first Class; Outstanding Munitions Officer 1962; Recomm Viet People-To-People Prog Partic; Bronze Star; USAF Comt Medal. **Business Addr:** Director of the Higher Education Opportunity Program, Hamilton College, 198 College Hill Rd, Clinton, NY 13323, **Business Phone:** (315)859-4398.

JOHNSON, DR. CAGE SAUL
Educator, scientist. **Personal:** Born Mar 31, 1941, New Orleans, LA; son of Cage Spooner and Esther Georgiana Saul; married Shirley (died 1999); children: Stephanie & Michelle. **Educ:** Creighton Univ Col Med, MD, 1965. **Career:** Univ Southern Calif, instr med, 1971-74, from asst prof med to assoc prof med, 1974-88, prof med, 1988-, Comprehensive Sickle Cell Ctr Southern Calif, dir, currently. **Orgs:** Chmn, Adv Comt, Genetically Handicaped Persons Prog, Calif Dept Health Serv, 1978-; vice-chmn & bd dir, Sickle Cell Self-Help Asn Inc, 1983-88; secy, EE Just Soc, 1985-93, pres, 1993-95; secy & bd dir, Sickle Cell Dis Res Found, 1986-94; rev comm chmn, Nat Heart Lung & Blood Inst, 1989-91; Alpha Omega Alpha. **Special Achievements:** Co-author: "Liver involvement in sickle cell disease", 1985; "Blood rheology and hyperviscosity syndromes", 1987; Pulmonary complications of sickle cell disease. Seminars in Respitory Medicine, 1988; "Vaso occulusion in Sickle cell Disease Current concepts and unanswered questions", 1991; "Chronic renal failure in sickle cell disease: Risk factors, clinical Course and morality. Annals of Internal Medicine", 1991. **Military Serv:** AUS, maj, 1967-69; Air Medal with "V". **Business Addr:** Professor of Medicine, Director, University of Southern California, 2025 Zonal Ave RoomR 306, Los Angeles, CA 90033.

JOHNSON, CALIPH
Lawyer, educator, executive director. **Personal:** Born Oct 3, 1938, St Joseph, LA; married Cheryl Helena Chapman. **Educ:** Univ Md, BA, 1964; San Jose State Univ, MA, 1968; Univ San Francisco Sch Law, JD, 1972; Georgetown Univ Law Ctr, LLM, 1973. **Career:** City Oakland, CA, admin analyst, 1970-72; Oakland Citizens Comn, Urban Renewal, exec dir, 1970-72; Georgetown Univ Law Ctr, Inst Pub Int Rep, grad fel, 1972-73, atty, 1972-73; Off Gen Coun Equal Employ Opportunity Comn, appellate atty, 1973-75; Thurgood Marshall Sch Law, SW Inst Equal Employ, Tex Southern Univ, asst prof, dir, 1975-78; Univ Miaduguri, Nigeria, consult, 1978-80; Off Lawyer Training Legal Serv Corp, advocacy trainer, 1978-80; Equal Employ Opportunity Comn, hearing examr, 1979-80, Off Gen Coun, appellate atty; Title VII Proj, Nat Bar Asn, Bd Dir Gulf Coast Legal Found, fac; A A White Dispute Resolution Inst, fac; US Naval War Col, Oceans Law Dept, researcher, 1993; SW Inst Dispute Resolution, founder & dir, currently. **Orgs:** Chair, State Bar Tex, ADR Sect & Coun, 1999-00; Comn Law Off Exon, Am Bar Asn; labor law sect, Nat Bar Asn; civil litigation comt mem, Fed Bar Asn; Civil Procedure & Clin Sect Asn Am Law Schs; bd dirs, Houston Neighborhood Justice Prog; Task force Law Prof Teaching ADR; adv bd & bd dirs, A A White Dispute Resolution Inst; chair, City Houston Ethics Comt; Am Arbit Asn; Houston Better Bus Bur. **Special Achievements:** A response to crises of enforcing fair employment, Houston Lawyer, 1975;course material on fair employment literature, Tex Southern Univ, 1976; integrated clinical current module, Texas Southern Univ & HEW, 1978-80; teamsters US Impact on Seniority Relief TX So NBA Law Rev, 1979; Book review, Let Them Be Judges, Howard Univ Law Journal, 1980. **Military Serv:** USN, lt, 3yrs; Naval Res Legal Serv Off, Corpus Christi, TX, comndg officer, 1990-92; US Naval Surface Pac Fleet, actg force judge advocate, 1992. **Business Addr:** Director, Founder, SouthWest Institute for Dispute Resolution, 5330 Griggs Rd, PO Box 66, Houston, TX 77004.

JOHNSON, CARL EARLD
Executive. **Personal:** Born Dec 3, 1936, New York, NY; son of Francis and Gwendolyn; married Mozelle Baker, Jun 6, 1961; children: Brian A & Carla D. **Educ:** City univ NY, BS, 1958, MBA, 1963. **Career:** Western Elec, human resources assoc, 1963-68; Mobil Oil Corp, human resources mgr, 1968-86; Campbell Soup Co, acting dir, gov compliance, 1986-90; Philip Morris Co, credit mgr, affirmative action, 1990-91; Summit Bank, vpres, employee rels & compliance prog, 1991-. **Orgs:** Vpres, Task Force Youth Motivation, 1969-75; vis prof, Black Exchange Prog, 1970-; Medgar Evers Col Curric Develop Comn, 1974-76; Soc Human Resources Mgt, 1976-; Inst Mgt Consult, 1986-; The EDGES Group, 1990-; chair employ coun, Nat Urban Affairs Coun, NJ, 1991-; The Lions Club, 1992-; fed, Hisp Bankers Asn NJ; NJ Urban Bankers Asn. **Special Achievements:** Shattering the Glass Ceiling, 1993; Employment Discrimination in the State of NJ, 1985; Employment Discrimination in NY, 1985; Employers Should Outline Job Terms and Conditions, 1985. **Military Serv:** AUS, Reserve, capt, 1958-70. **Business Phone:** (609)987-3406.

JOHNSON, CARL ELLIOTT
Mechanical engineer. **Personal:** Born Oct 4, 1956, Houston, TX; married Mary Ann Jean; children: Patric, Cristina, Carren. **Educ:** Prairie View A&M Univ, BSME, 1979. **Career:** Union Carbide, maintenance engr, 1979-83; Monsanto Chemical Co, sr process engr, 1984-85, process supvr, 1985-, utilities supvr. **Orgs:** Corp solicitor United Way, 1985-; youth basketball, YMCA, 1987; Speakers Bur.

JOHNSON, CAROL DIAHANN. **See CARROLL, DIAHANN.**

JOHNSON, DR. CARRIE CLEMENTS
Educator. **Personal:** Born Jan 2, 1931, Atlanta, GA; daughter of Lucile Clements and Emanuel Clements; married Alfred James; children: Alfia Katherine. **Educ:** Morris Brown Col, Atlants, Ga, BS, 1951; Columbia Univ, New York, MA,1954; State Univ New York, Buffalo, EdD, 1978. **Career:** Educator (retired); Fulton County Bd Educ, Atlanta, Ga, high sch teacher, 1951-61; Morris Brown Col, Atlanta, Ga, dir career planning & placement, asst prof, 1961-67; State Univ Col, Buffalo, counr, 1967-71, dir counserv, 1971-83, assoc dir, 1977-78, asst prof bus studies, 1983-85; dir classified staff develop Fulton County Schs, 1986-88; Fulton County Bd Educ, Atlanta, Ga, exec dir, 1988-95; Johnson & Johnson, pres. **Orgs:** Nat Urban League Sorority, 1966-67; assoc dir, VISTA Training; Am Personnel & Guid Asn, 1967-; vpres Jack & Jill Am Inc, 1974; HEW fel, US Govt Dept HEW, 1979-81; bd dir, Buffalo Area Engineering Awareness Minorities, 1982; bd dir, Child Develop Inst Buffalo, 1983; scholar comn, Buffalo Urban League, 1984; Zeta Phi Beta; Links Inc; adv coun, Atlanta Tech Inst, 1995-98; bd dir, NAACP, 1996; personnel bd, Fulton County Bd Ethics, currently. **Honors/Awds:** Regioanl Teacher of the Year, 1959; Guide Grad Opportunities Minorities, 1971; HEW Fel, US Govt Dept HEW, 1979; Life Long Learning Award, Alpha Kappa Alpha Sorority, Buffalo, NY, 1984; Exemplary Award, Ga Staff Develop Coun, 1990. **Home Addr:** 3965 Old Fairburn Rd SW, Atlanta, GA 30331.

JOHNSON, CARROLL JONES
Mayor, school administrator. **Personal:** Born Mar 1, 1948, Blackville, SC; daughter of Louise Felder Jones and Rufus Jones; divorced; children: F Kelvin Johnson, Herman N Johnson & Wayne Johnson. **Educ:** Voorhees Col, Denmark SC, BS, 1978; Univ SC. **Career:** Barnwell Sch Dist, Macedonia Elem Sch, Blackville SC, literacy coordr, 1980-; mayor Blackville SC. **Orgs:** Barnwell County Help Line; Barnwell County Community Improvement Bd; Nat Asn Advan Colored People. **Honors/Awds:** Community Service Award, Delta Sigma Theta, 1987; Public Service Award, Alpha Kappa Alpha, 1988; Citizen of the Year,

Omega Psi Phi, 1989; Woman of the Year, Barnwell County Chamber Com, 1989. **Home Addr:** PO Box 305, Blackville, SC 29817.

JOHNSON, CARROLL RANDOLPH, JR.
Executive, clergy. **Personal:** Born Jun 13, 1951, Baltimore, MD; son of Carroll R Sr and Delores Patricia; married Muriel Minor Johnson, Aug 29, 1970; children: Duane, Sherry, Keith. **Educ:** Johns Hopkins, Univ, BA, 1972. **Career:** C & P Telephone, bus off asst mgr, 1972-77; Praise Recording Co, prs, 1977-79; Bell Atlantic, comput consult, 1979-87; Evergreen CPN, 1987-; Maximum Life Christian Church, pastor; Zamar Music Group; Maximum Life Christian Church, Bishop, currently. **Orgs:** Baltimore Coun Self-Esteem; Baltimore Cable Access Corp; Mid-Atlantic Diocese-Bibleway Churches. **Special Achievements:** Mayor's Citation, Outstanding Community Service, 1992; Maximum Life Songs, released gospel album, 1991. **Home Phone:** (410)298-1238. **Business Addr:** President, Zamar Music Group, 1928 Woodlawn Dr, Baltimore, MD 21207, **Business Phone:** (410)597-9925.

JOHNSON, CARYN ELAINE. See GOLDBERG, WHOOPI.

JOHNSON, CATO, II
Executive. **Personal:** Born Aug 26, 1947, Memphis, TN; son of Cato and Frankie Scales; married Georgette Alexander, May 12, 1976; children: Cato III. **Educ:** Memphis State Univ, BS, educ, 1970, MS, educ, 1971; Tenn Sch Banking, Vanderbilt Univ. **Career:** Memphis State Univ, manpower specialist, 1971-73, asst dir, 1981-83; Gen Motors Acceptance Corp, field rep, 1971-74; First Tenn Bank, personnel asst, 1974-75; First Tenn Nat Corp, affirmative action coordr, 1975-78, personnel adminr & affirmative action coordr, 1978-80, mgr personnel, 1980-81; Regional Med Ctr, vpres corp affairs, 1983-85; Methodist Health Systs, sr vpres corp affairs, 1985-. **Orgs:** Memphis Conv & Visitors Bur; Kiwanis; Gov's Coun Health & Physical Fitness; Tenn Human Servs Adv Coun; Jr League Memphis Bd; pres's coun, LeMoyne-Owen Col; bd dirs, Tenn Comprehensive Health Ins Pool; adv comn, Sr Citizen's Servs; pres coun, LeMoyne-Owen Col; Arts Park, Memphis Arts Festival; co chair, Mayor WW Herenton Transition Team, Parks & Facitities Comn; exec comt, Memphis & Shelby Co Sports Authority Bd; Goals Memphis Race Rels Comn; Mayor's Mud Island Task Force; Memphis & Shelby Co Med Soc; pres, Univ Memphis Nat Alumni Asn; Jim Rout, Shelby Co Mayor-elect, transition team, Don Sundquist; Gov Tenn, transition team; chair, Southwest Tenn Community Col Bd Advisors; chmn, TennCare Med Care Adv Comt; vice chair, Needs Assessment Comt. **Honors/Awds:** Appeared on numerous radio and TV talk shows. **Home Phone:** (901)377-2164. **Business Addr:** Senior Vice President of Corporate Affairs, Methodist Health Systems, 1211 Union Ave, Memphis, TN 38104, **Business Phone:** (901)516-7000.

JOHNSON, CHARLES
Educator, physician. **Personal:** Born Jul 28, 1927, Acmar, AL; married Carol Ann; children: Carla & Charles. **Educ:** Howard Univ, BS, 1953, MD, 1963; DC Gen Hosp, Internship Med, 1964. **Career:** Lincoln Hosp, pvt pract, 1967-70; Duke Univ Med Ctr, Durham, NC, from asst prof med to assoc prof med to prof med, 1970-96, prof emer med, 1996, spec adv chancellor, health affairs, 1997; physician, currently. **Orgs:** Durham Acad Med; Kappa Alpha Psi, 1950-; Am Soc Int Med; Am Col Physicians; Am Diabetes Asn; adv comn, Minority Students NC; pres, Old N State Med Soc, 1973-75; chmn, Reg III Nat Med Asn, 1975-78; secy, House Delegates Nat Med Asn, 1975-77; dir, Nat Med Asn, Africa Health Proj, 1975-80; bd admis, Duke Univ Col Med 1976-81; vis speaker, House Delegates Nat Med Asn, 1977-79; speaker, House Delegates Nat Med Asn, 1980-81; bd trustees, Nat Med Asn, 1982-88, secy bd trustees, 1984-86, chmn, bd trustees, 1986-88, pres-elect, 1989-90, pres, 1990-91; Doric Lodge 28,Durham Consistory 218, Shriner, Zafa Temple 176, 33rd Deg Mason, St Titus Epis Church. **Honors/Awds:** Disting Kappaman Achievement Award, Durham Alumni Chap, 1978; Elected Outstanding Physician of the Year, 1980; Medal for Distinguished & Meritorius Service, Duke Univ, 1997. **Special Achievements:** First black faculty member, Duke Univ. **Military Serv:** USAF, sgt, 1946-49, capt 1953-57, Jet Fighter Pilot. **Home Addr:** 1209 E Pointe Dr, Durham, NC 27712, **Home Phone:** (919)620-9107. **Business Addr:** Professor Emeritus, Duke University Medical Center, 1209 E Pointe Dr, Durham, NC 27712, **Business Phone:** (919)575-2532.

JOHNSON, CHARLES BERNARD
Journalist. **Personal:** Born Mar 9, 1954, Detroit, MI; son of Bessie Mae Gayden and Ira B; married Tara Halsey Johnson, Jul 1, 1989; children: Janay & Julius. **Educ:** Mich State Univ, E Lansing, MI, BA, journ, 1975. **Career:** The Flint J, Flint, MI, sports columnist, 1975-88; Black Entertainment TV Sports Report, Wash, DC, panelist, 1988-; USA Today, Wash DC, sports writer, 1988-. **Orgs:** Pres, Nat Asn Black Jour Mid Mich Chap, 1986-87; Sports task force steering comt, Nat Asn Black Journalists, 1989-. **Honors/Awds:** Man of the Year, Flint Golden Gloves, 1982; In Appreciation for Effort, Greater Flint Wrestling Coaches Asn, 1984; Central Flint Optimists Club, 1985; Honored for Community Serv, Nat Asn Media Women Inc, 1987; Hon Inductee, Greater Flint Afro-Am Hall of Fame, 1988; 'Sports Journalist for the Year', Nat Asn Black Journalists, 2000. **Special Achievements:** Made his movie debut in 2006, portraying himself as a boxing writer in "Rocky Balboa. **Business Addr:** Sports Writer, USA Today, 7950 Jones Br Dr 7th Fl, McLean, VA 22108-0605, **Business Phone:** (703)854-5944.

JOHNSON, CHARLES E.
Administrator, educator. **Personal:** Born Jul 1, 1946, Woodville, MS; married Bessie M Hudson; children: Vanessa Lashea, Adrianne Monique, Andrea Melita & Krystal Charlese. **Educ:** Alcorn State Univ, BS, 1968; Southern Univ, MEd, 1971. **Career:** Bay St Louis Sch Dist, teacher 1967-69; Wilkinson County Sch Dist, teacher, 1969-71, supt educ, 1976-97; Brookhaven Sch Dist, teacher, 1972-73; Amite County Sch Dist, teacher, 1974-75. **Orgs:** Nat Asn Advan Colored People; Miss Teachers Asn; Miss Asn Sch Superintendents; Miss Cattlesmen Asn; Nat Cattlesmen Asn. **Honors/Awds:** Charles E Johnson Classroom Bldg, Centreville, Miss, 1980; Charles EJohnson Admin Bldg, Woodville, Miss, 1997. **Home Addr:** 852 W St, Woodville, MS 39669.

JOHNSON, CHARLES EDWARD, JR.
Baseball player. **Personal:** Born Jul 20, 1971, Fort Pierce, FL; married Rhonda Thompson, Dec 3, 1994; children: Brandon & Beau. **Educ:** Univ Miami. **Career:** Baseball player (retired); Florida Marlins, catcher, 1994-98 & 2001-02; Los Angeles Dodgers, catcher, 1998; Baltimore Orioles, catcher, 1999-2000; Chicago White Sox, catcher, 2000; Colorado Rockies, catcher, 2003-04; Tampa Bay Devil Rays, catcher, 2005. **Orgs:** Portland Sea Dogs Hall of Fame. **Honors/Awds:** Rawlings Gold Glove Award, 1995-98; Topps Rookie Team, 1995; Baseball America, Top Defensive Catcher in the Nat League, 1996; USA Baseball Alumni Player of the Year, 1997; World Series champion, 1997; Most Improved Marlin Award, South Florida BBWAA, 1997; Twice All-Star, 1997 & 2001; Hall of Fame, Portland Sea Dogs, 2006.

JOHNSON, DR. CHARLES EDWARD
Scientist. **Personal:** Born Feb 24, 1938, Dallas, NC; son of Lydia D and Ira G; married Gladys E Hawkins; children: Nikolas, Andre, Sean, Markus & Karari. **Educ:** Morgan State Univ, BS, 1960; Univ Cincinnati, PhD, 1966. **Career:** Morgan State Univ, prof biol, 1973-74; Community Col Baltimore, lectr, 1974; The Union Cincinnati, adjunct prof, 1980-81; Procter & Gamble Co, sect head, 1981-88; Clairol Inc, Stamford, CT, mgr & dir, 1988-. **Orgs:** AAAS, 1980-83; Am Soc Microbiol; bd trustees, W End Health Clinic, 1980-82. **Honors/Awds:** NDEA Fel. **Special Achievements:** 'Lethal Toxin of Bacillus cereus I. Relationships and Nature of Toxin, Hemolysin, and Phospholipase', 1967; Patent detergent composition containing protedytic enzymes elaborated by Thermactinomyces Vulgaris 15734, 1972. **Business Addr:** Director, Technical Support, Clairol Inc, 1 Blachley Rd, Stamford, CT 06902, **Business Phone:** (203)357-5134.

JOHNSON, CHARLES EVERETT
Football player. **Personal:** Born Jan 3, 1972, San Bernardino, CA; married Tanisha; children: Charles III. **Educ:** Univ Colo, BA, mkt. **Career:** Pittsburgh Steelers, wide receiver, 1994-98; Philadelphia Eagles, 1999-2000; New Eng Patriots, 2001; Buffalo Bills, 2002. **Honors/Awds:** Ed Black Courage Award, 1994; All-Big Eight Offensive Player of the Year. **Special Achievements:** The first Colorado player to ever surpass the 2000-yard career.

JOHNSON, CHARLES FLOYD (JAZZ VOYD JOHNSON)
Lawyer, television producer. **Personal:** Born Feb 12, 1942, Camden, NJ; son of Orange Maull and Bertha Ellen Seagers; married Anne Burford, Jun 18, 1983; children: Kristin Suzanne. **Educ:** Univ Del, 1961; Howard Univ, BA, 1962; Howard Univ Sch Law, JD, 1965. **Career:** Howard Berg Law Off, atty, 1965; US Copyright Off, atty, 1967-70; Swedish Ministry Justice, Stockholm, Sweden, atty, 1970; Universal TV, prod coordr, 1971-74, assoc prod, 1974-76, producer, 1976-82, supv producer, 1982-, exec producer, 1985-; TV series: "The Six Million Dollar Man", actor, 1974; "Kojak", actor, 1975; "The Rockford Files", producer, 1975-80, supv producer, 1977-79, assoc producer, 1975-76; Hellinger's Law, 1981; "Simon & Simon", 1981; "Bret Maverick", 1981; "Magnum, P.I.", producer, 1983, supv producer, 1984-86, co-exec producer, 1980-88; Revealing Evidence: Stalking the Honolulu Strangler, exec producer, 1990; "Quantum Leap", co-exec producer, 1993; The Rockford Files: A Blessing in Disguise, exec producer, 1995; The Rockford Files: If It Bleeds.. It Leads, producer, 1999; "First Monday", co-exec producer, 2002; "JAG", co-exec producer, 1997-2004, actor, 1999-2005; "Navy NCIS: Naval Criminal Investigative Service", co-exec producer, 2004-07 & 2007-08; Films: Silverfox, writer & exec producer, 1991. **Orgs:** Vice chmn, Media Forum, 1978-82; Asn Black Motion Picture & TV Producers, 1980-82; bd, Kwanza Found, 1985; bd, Am Independent Video Filmmakers, 1985-90; Caucus Producers, Dirs & Writers, 1990-; Crossroads Theatre Arts Acad, 1990; Screen Actors Guild Am; bd, Producers Guild Am; Writers Guild Am; Nat Acad TV Arts & Sci; Am Film Inst; OPP. **Honors/Awds:** Numerous awards including Emmy Award, Rockford Files, Best TV Drama, 1978; 3 Emmy Nominations for: Rockford Files, 1978-79, 1979-80, Los Angeles Area Emmy Award Winner for producing and performing in a KCET/PBS Special "Voices of Our People, A Celebration of Black Poetry", 1981; Commendations, City Los Angeles, 1982, 1993; Commendation, Calif State Legis, 1982; Commendation, Calif State Senate, 1982; Magnum PI, 1982-83 & 1983-84; Alumni Achievement Award, Stony Brook Col Prep, 1979; Outstanding Alumnus, Howard Univ Alumni Club So CA, 1982; Outstanding Alumnus Award, Howard Univ, 1985; Commendation, Hawaii State Senate, 1988; Commendation, Hawaii House Rep, 1988; Commendation, City Honolulu, 1988. **Special Achievements:** Books: "The Origins of the Stockholm Protocol", 1970; co-author, Black Women in Television, 1990. **Military Serv:** AUS, sgt, 1965-67; Army Commendation Medal, 1967.

JOHNSON, CHARLES H.
Educator. **Personal:** Born Mar 5, 1932, Conway, SC; married Vermelle J; children: Temple & Charles H Jr. **Educ:** SC State Col, BS, 1954; SC State Col, med, 1969. **Career:** Educator (retired); Claflin Col, Orangeburg, SC, dean stud, educr & prin pub sch, 1962-67, 1967-96. **Orgs:** SC Stud Personnel Asn; Southern Col Personnel Asn; Nat Stud Personnel Adminrs; Nat Educ Asn; Prof Club; bd dir, Orangeburg Co Coun Aging; Veterans Foreign Wars; bd dir, Orangeburg United Fund; bd trustees, Trinity United Methodist Church; Omega Psi Phi; IBPO Elks World; SC State Univ Alumni; life mem, NCP; vis, Chaflin Col; life mem, PTA; bd dirs, United Way; bd dirs, Palmetto Lou City Health Systs; comn mem, Orangeburg Area Develop Ctr; charter mem, Hon Alumni Asn, Africa Univ, 2000. **Honors/Awds:** Various Naval Awards & Citations; Honorary Doctorate Aspen, Univ, 1997; Hall of Fame, Chaplin Col, 1998; Presidential Citation, Chaplin Col, 1999. **Military Serv:** USN, petty officer. **Home Addr:** 691 Bramble Lane, Orangeburg, SC 29115, **Home Phone:** (803)534-8783. *

JOHNSON, CHARLES H
Lawyer. **Personal:** Born May 24, 1946, New Haven, CT; son of Charles H and Helen Taylor. **Educ:** Hotchkiss Sch, Lakeville, CT, 1964; Yale Univ, BA, 1968; Yale Univ Law Sch, JD, 1972. **Career:** Montgomery McCracken Walker & Rhoads, atty pvt practice, 1972-75; US Food & Drug Admin, asst chief counsel 1975-79; US Equal Employ Opportunity Comn, supervisory trial atty, 1978-79; Conn Gen Life Ins Co, atty, 1979-82; New England Mutual Life Ins Co, counsel & asst secy, 1982-93; atty, pvt practice, 1993-99; Whittier Law Sch, Los Angeles, CA, adjunct prof, 1995; La Superior Ct, contracts analyst, 1999-. **Orgs:** Nat Bar Asn. **Military Serv:** AUS, Hon Discharge, 1976. **Business Phone:** (213)974-5422.*

JOHNSON, CHARLES LEE
Dentist. **Personal:** Born Dec 18, 1941, Atlanta, GA; son of Willie James and Ollie Moore; divorced; children: Nichole Denise, Charlena Natasha. **Educ:** Morris Brown Col, BS, 1964; Meharry Med Col, 1965; Howard Univ, DDS, 1969; Univ MD Provident Hosp, cert oral surgery internship, 1970; Walter Reed Hosp; Emory Univ; Med Col GA; Int Congress Oral Implantology (Paris), post doctoral studies, 1972. **Career:** Metro-Atlanta Doctor's Clinic; Ben Massell Char Dent Clinic, staff, 1972-; Atlanta Col Med & Dent Asst, consult, 1972-; Fulton City Dept Corrections, asst dir, dept dent, 1990-95; Pvt practice, dent, currently. **Orgs:** Dean Pledgees & Probates, Phi Beta Sigma, 1962; Pres, Med Tech Class, Meharry Col, 1964-65;Am Endodontic Soc; Am Soc Clinical Hypnosis; Jamaica Dent Soc; Am Dent Asn; GA Dent Asn; vpres, N Ga Dent Soc; Acad Gen Dent; Morris Brown Col Alumni Asn; Am Cancer Soc; Atlanta C C; Phi Beta Sigma, 1962; Howard Univ; vpres, Chi Delta Mu, 1966; dean, Probates & Pledgees Chi Delta Mu, 1966; vpres, Local Chaptre; Butler St YMCA, 1972; exec bd dir, Atlanta Urban League; St Anthony Catholic Ch; Academy Gen Dent; vpres, N Ga Dent Soc; reviewer, Med Review Inst Am, 2000. **Honors/Awds:** Football scholarship, Morris Town Col, 1960; Acad Scholarship, GA Higher Educ Asn, 1964-69; Honorary mem, Beta Beat Beta Scientific Honor Soc; Wall of Tolerance Awd, 2001. **Business Addr:** Dentist, 549 Joseph E Lowery Blvd NW, Atlanta, GA 30310.*

JOHNSON, CHARLES RICHARD
Cartoonist or animator, educator, writer. **Personal:** Born Apr 23, 1948, Evanston, IL; son of Benjamin Lee and Ruby Elizabeth Jackson; married Joan New, Jun 1970; children: Malik & Elizabeth. **Educ:** Southern Ill Univ, BA, 1971, MA 1973; State Univ NY, Stony Brook, PhD, 1976. **Career:** Chicago Tribune, cartoonist, reporter, 1969-70; St Louis Proud, art staff, 1971-72; Univ Wash, asst prof, 1976-79, assoc prof, 1979-82, prof eng, 1982-, writer & cartoonist, currently; Seattle Review, fiction ed, 1978-; Author: Charlie's Pad, 1970; Black Humor, 1970; Half-Past Nation Time, 1972; Faith & Good Thing, 1974; Chrlie Smith & Fritter Tree, 1978; Oxherding Tale, 1982; Booker, 1983; Sorcerer's Apprentice, 1986; Being & Race: Black Writing since 1970, 1988; Pieces of Eight, 1989; MiddlePassage, 1990; Rites of Passage: Stories about Growing up by Black Writersfrom around the World, 1993; On Writers & Writing, 1994; Black Men Speaking, 1997; Still I Rise; A Cartoon Hist African Ams, 1997; Dreamer, 1998; Africans in America: America's Journey through Slavery, 1998; I Call Myself an Artist: Writings by & about Charles Johnson, 1999; A Treasury of North American Folktales, 1999; Was Born a Slave: An Anthology of Classic Slave Narratives, 1999; Sacred Fire: The QBR 100 Essential Black Books, 2000; Soulcatcher & Other Stories, 2001; Turning the Wheel: Es-

says on Buddhism & Writing, 2003; Dr. King's Refrigerator: Other Bedtime Stories, 2005. contributor to numerous anthologies & TV series. **Orgs:** Bd mem, former dir, Assoc Writing Prog Awards Series in Short Fiction. **Honors/Awds:** Named jour alumnus of the year, Southern Ill Univ, 1981; Gov Award for Lit, State Wash, 1983; Callaloo Creative Writing Award, 1983; Citation in Pushcart Prize's Outstanding Writers sect, 1984; Writer's Guild Award for Best Children's Show (Booker), 1984; Writers Guild Award for bestchildren's show, 1986; Nat Book Award, 1990; Hon Doctor of Humane Letters, Southern Ill Univ, 1995; Hon Degree of Doctor of Letters, State Univ NY, Stony Brook, 1999; Pac Northwest Writers Asn Achievement Award, 2001; Metrop King Co County Author Recognition Award, 2001; American Academy of Arts & Letters Award for Literature, 2002. **Special Achievements:** Nomination for PEN/Faulkner Award, PEN Am Ctr, 1987; Winner of National Book Award in Fiction for his novel Middle Passage. **Business Addr:** Professor, University of Washington, Department of English, PO Box 354330, Seattle, WA 98195-4330, **Business Phone:** (206)543-9865.

JOHNSON, CHARLES RONALD, SR.
Legislator, lawyer. **Personal:** Born Feb 17, 1951, New York, NY; married Nancy Bradford; children: Jessica Ashley, Charles Ronald Jr. **Educ:** Dartmouth Col, AB, 1971; Univ Calif, Berkeley, JD, 1974. **Career:** Bronx County NY, asst dist atty, 1974-75; Sen Minority Leader NY, criminal justice analyist, 1975-76; atty, pvt prac, 1976-78; 76th Assembly Dist NY, assemblyman, 1978-80. **Orgs:** Pres, DeWitt Clinton Alumni Asn, 1979-80. **Honors/Awds:** Man of the Yr Award, NY City Housing Police Guardians Asn, 1979; Man of the Yr, Bronx Lebanon Hosp Ctr; Comn Leadership Award, 1980; Legislator of the Yr, Nat Urban Coalition, 1980. **Business Addr:** 1188 Grand Concourse, Bronx, NY 10451.*

JOHNSON, CHARLES V.
Judge. **Personal:** Born Jun 11, 1928, Malvern, AR; son of Charlie and Laura Miller; married Lazelle S; children: James W Brown, Tracy L, Terri Lynn. **Educ:** Ark Agri Mech & Normal Col, Pine Bluff, BA, 1954; Univ WA, School Law, Seattle, 1957. **Career:** Judge (retired); atty pvt pract, 1958-69; Municipal Court Seattle, judge, 1969-80, presiding judge 1971-72; State WA King County Superior Court, judge, 1981-98; Presiding Judge King County Superior Court, 1989-93. **Orgs:** Bd dir, WA State Mag Asn; charter mem, Judicial Coun, Nat Bar Asn; Seattle-King County Branch-Bar Liaison Comt; Am Judicial Soc; Phi Alpha Delta; treas, Cent Area Comn Civil Rights, 1963-70; First AME Church, 1960-; chmn bd mgmt, E Madison Branch, 1964-69, bd dir; pres, Metro Branch, 1972-73; YMCA; pres, Seattle Br, NAACP 1959-63; pres, NW Area Conf, 1965-71; Nat Legal Comn; chmn, Seattle Model Cities Adv Coun, 1968-72; Seattle Lawyers Comt Civil Rights, 1968-69; adv comt, US Comn Civil Rights; pres, Am Judges Asn, 1981-82; nat pres, Sigma Rho Hon Soc, 1954-55; Bd mem, Nat Ctr State Courts, 1985-90. **Honors/Awds:** Distinguished Citizens Award, Model Cities Seattle, 1973; First Citizens Award, Seattle, 1973; Man of the Year Award, Alpha Phi Alpha, 1973; Distinguished Community Award for United Way; YMCA Serv Youth Award; Benefit Guilds Martin Luther King Community Serv Award; Links Human Rights Award; Award for Distinguished Serv, Seattle-King County Bar Asn, 1991; Distinguished Serv Award, Nat Ctr State Courts; Distinguished Alumnus, Univ Wash, Sch Law, 1992; Municipal League King County, Distinguished Service Award, 1994; King County, Public Official of the Year Award, 1994; Wash State Bar Asn, Outstanding Judge Award, 1994. **Military Serv:** Univ S Army, Staff/Sgt, 1948-52. **Home Addr:** 3513 SW Hanford St, Seattle, WA 98126. *

JOHNSON, CHERYL P.
Chief executive officer. **Career:** Coalition Temporary Shelter (COTS), shelter dir, 1990; Coalition on Temporary Shelter, chief exec officer, currently. **Business Phone:** (313)831-3777.*

JOHNSON, CLARISSA. See Obituaries section.

JOHNSON, CLARK W
Association executive. **Educ:** Grambling State Univ, BS, chem; Univ Denver, MS, chem; Pepperdine Univ, MA, bus admin; Univ Calif Anderson Sch Bus, exec mgt course. **Career:** Lockheed Martin Corp, staff; Soc Advan Mat & Process Engineering, int vpres, int sr vpres, int pres, 2003-04, int treas; Nat Sec Prog Orgn Satellite Syst Div, El Segundo, CA, syst engineering proj mgr, currently. **Orgs:** NASA Space Sta Materials & Processes Control Bd. **Honors/Awds:** Pioneer of the Year Award, Nat Soc Black Engrs, 2004. **Special Achievements:** First African American president of the Advancement of Material & Process Engineering. *

JOHNSON, CLEVELAND, JR.
Executive. **Personal:** Born Aug 17, 1934, Eufaula, AL; son of Cleveland Johnson Sr and Arline Petty Johnson; married Joan B Maloney; children: Keith Michael, Genevieve Carolyn, Kelly Marie & Cleveland III. **Educ:** Tri State Univ Ind, BS, 1955; Adelphi Univ; NY Police Acad Police Sci Prog, 1959; NY Univ, M Pub Admin, 1975. **Career:** NYPD, Detective Div, 1959-65; Investors Planning Corp Am, 1960-65; Islip Dept COT Affairs, dir, 1965-70; Town Islip Housing Authority, exec dir, 1966-71, dir personnel, 1969-70, dep town supvr, 1969-71; Johnson Diversified Inc, pres, 1969-; County Suffolk Riverhead NY, dep county exec, 1972-79; SUNY Farmingdale, exec asst pres, 1979-81, vpres, prof bus, 1981-89; FCD Const Corp, pres, 1981-88; Allstate Life Ins Co, dir, 1983-; Dent World, Inc, bd dir, 1985-87; Moran Equity Fund, dir, 1990-95; US Dept HTH & Human Serv, regional dir, 1990-93; Johnson Consult Assoc, pres, 1993, chmn adv bd, currently; MARIGA Commun Corp, vpres, 1993-97; ValueCare Inc, vpres, 1997-; HTH Care Receivable Funding Corp, exec vpres, 1995-98; Family & Housing Develop Serv, Inc, exec vpres. 1998-; GRC, Resonance Inc, pres, 1998-99; Magnetic Resonance Ctr Inc, pres, 1998-2002; Int Am Life Ins Co, dir, 1999-; OXY Med Ctr Am, chmn & ceo, 2000-; IPO Russia Inc, chmn, bd adv, 2002-. **Orgs:** Chmn, Selective Serv Syst, Local Bd #2, 1966-79; bd dir, WLIW-TV Channel 21, 1986-92; nat co-chmn, Nat Black Republican Coun, 1988-90; pres, Cent Islip Bd Ed, 1972-80; founding pres, New York State Black Republican Coun, 1974-78; chmn, Selective Serv Syst, Local Bd 118, 1980-2001; pres, Cornell Coop Extension, Suffolk County, 1994-2001; illustrious dep-at-large, United Supreme Coun, AASR, Prince Hall Affiliation, 1994-; bd, Suffolk Cty Girl Scout Coun, 1996-2000; hon bd, Long Island Aquarium; chmn, Suffolk County Jail Comn, 1999-2001; chmn, Credentials Comn, Nat Black Rep Comn; chmn, Econ Develop Comn Nat Black Rep Comn; NY State Grand Lodge Educ Comn; adv coun, Southside Hosp; pres, adv comn Equal Opportunity, State Univ Farmingdale; pres, adv coun & assoc trustee, Dowling Col; pres emer, Urban League Long Island; Bay Shore Cent Islip Br Nat Asn Advan Colored People; Acad Polit Sci, Columbia Univ; former vpres, Long Island Hlth & Hosp Planning Coun Inc, bd trustees. **Honors/Awds:** Public Serv Award, Islip Spanish Am Coun, 1966; Comm Serv Award, Carleton Park Civic Asn, 1966; Award for Comm Relations, Nat Coun Negro Women, 1968; Civic Achievement Award, NY State Grand Lodge Prince Hall Masons, 1969; Distinguished Alumni Award, Tri State Univ, 1969; Sovereign Grand Inspector General 33rd Degree AASR Prince Hall Affiliation, 1974; Presidential Award, 1984; Distinguished Serv Award, Am Asn Affirmantive Action, Region II, 1993; Distinguished Citizen Award, WAS Times FND, 1996; Frederick Douglass Award, LI Coun, Afro Am Republicans, 1996; Renoun Serv Award, King David Consistory No 3 AASR, 2000; Outstanding Voluntary Leadership Award, Cornell Coop Extension, 2000; Cert Congratulations, Commander's The Rite, A.A.S. R., Orient NY, 2000; Presidents Award, Cornell Coop Extension, 2001; Excellence in Parenting Award, Am Family Coalition, Nat Parents Day Coun, 2002. **Military Serv:** USY, spc-4, 1957-59, Reserves, 1st sgt, 1959-66. **Home Addr:** 47 Doral Lane, Bayshore, NY 11706. **Business Addr:** Chairman-Advisory Board, Johnson Consulting Associates, PO Box 5190, Bayshore, NY 11706, **Business Phone:** (516)969-0386.

JOHNSON, CLINISSON ANTHONY
Judge. **Personal:** Born Nov 16, 1947, Memphis, TN; married Andrea Yvonne Morrow; children: Collin Anthony; Terrence GalonTiffany Gayle. **Educ:** Fisk Univ Nashville, BA, hist, 1969; Univ Tenn Law Sch Knoxville, JD, 1972. **Career:** City Atty's Ofc Memphis, part-time pub defender 1972-74; Ratner Sugarmon Lucas & Salky Law Ofc Memphi, asso assy, 1972-76; Shelby Co Pub Defenders Ofc Memphis, asst pub defender 1974-75; Memphis Municipal Ct System, city ct judge div IV 1976-. **Orgs:** Tenn Bar Asn; Memphis & Shelby Co Bar Asn; Nat Bar Asn; Nat Advan Asn Colored People, 1985. **Business Addr:** Judge, City Memphis Munic Court, 128 Adams Ave, Memphis, TN 38103.

JOHNSON, CLINTON LEE
Clergy, manager, government official. **Personal:** Born Mar 16, 1947, Mobile, AL; son of Alfred F and Clara Chapman; married Barbara Gibson, May 20, 1972; children: Ginnessa L, Ashley T & Clinton Jr. **Educ:** Ala A&M Univ, Mobile, AL, BA, gov & soc, 1969; Univ Southern Ala, Mobile, AL, MA, honors rehab cons, 1973; Mobile Col, Mobile, AL, BA, honors, 1982. **Career:** Maneger (retired), pastor, coun; State Ala Vocational Rehab Serv, supvr; Bethlehem Baptist Church, Citronelle, pastro; Mobile City Coun, Mobile, AL, vpres, 1985-; Shiloh Baptist Church, Mobile, AL, pastor, 1988-; Mobile City Coun, Dist 3, coun pres, councilman, currently. **Orgs:** Ala State Employees Asn; Nat Rehab Asn; Ala Rehab Asn; Nat Rehab Coun Asn; Nat Rehab Asn Supvr; past bd mem, Goodwill Indust; past bd mem, Mobile Asn Blind; bd mem, Independent Living Ctr; Mobile Regional Planning Comn; SCLC; Nat Asn Advan Colored People; Alpha Phi Alpha Fraternity; Boys Club Am; past mem, Leadership Ala; chmn, Ala A&M Univ Bd Trustees; Nat Baptist Convention USA Inc; Ala State Baptist Convention; Mobile Baptist Sunlight Dist Asn; Baptist Ministers Conf InterdenomiNat Ministerial Alliance; asst dir, Congress Christian Educ. **Honors/Awds:** Service Award, InterdenomiNat Ministers Alliance, 1986; Service Award, Boys Club Am, 1987; Citizen of the Year, Palestine Temple 16, 1985; Citizen of the Year, Alpha Phi Alpha Fraternity, 1985; Two Honorary Doctorate degree in Religion; Outstanding Young Man in America; Certified Rehabilitation Counselor. **Special Achievements:** Outstanding Young Man in America. **Business Addr:** Councilman, Mobile City, PO Box 1827, Mobile, AL 36633-1827, **Business Phone:** (251)208-7441.

JOHNSON, COLLIS, JR.
Dentist. **Personal:** Born Nov 17, 1946, Oklahoma; son of Ruby and Collis; married Marsha Michele Jones; children: Jonathan Ashley, Rachael Christine & Laura Michelle May. **Educ:** Langston Univ Okla, BS, 1969; Meharry Med Col, Tenn, DDS, 1973; Martin Luther King Gen Hosp, gen res, 1974. **Career:** Denver, pvt pract, gen dent, 1977-; Pilot City Health Ctr, Minneapolis, gen dent dept, 1974-77. **Orgs:** Am Dental Asn; Nat Dental Asn, 1977-; asst treas, Alpha Phi Alpha Inc; Denver Urban League; pres, Clarence T Holmes Dental Soc, 1986; bd dental examiners, State Colo, 1997-2001; Colo Dental Bd. **Honors/Awds:** Board of DRRs, Concorde Career CLG. **Home Addr:** 1756 Vine St, Denver, CO 80206, **Home Phone:** (303)322-1177. **Business Addr:** Physician, 1756 Vine St, Denver, CO 80206, **Business Phone:** (303)322-1177.

JOHNSON, COSTELLO O
Executive, president (organization), chief executive officer. **Personal:** Born Feb 14, 1938, Chicago, IL; son of Adrian and Dorothy; married Eunita Flemings Johnson, Aug 26, 1967; children: Gina Perry, Pamela Eatman & Darin. **Educ:** Chicago Acad Fine Arts, BA, 1962; Ill Inst Technol; Univ Ill. **Career:** Montgomery Wards, designer, space planner, 1968-68; Contract Interiors, designer, space planner, 1968-70; Desks Inc, sales assoc, 1970-73; Haworth Chicago, pres, 1973-79; Costello Johnson & Assocs, pres, 1979-89; Costello Johnson Corp Off Syst Inc, chief exec officer & pres, 1989-. **Orgs:** Dir, Urban Gateways; dir, Metrop Family Serv; Friends Comt, Jesse Owens Found; exec bd mem, Chicago Minority Bus Develop Coun; co-chmn & fundraiser, Marcy Newberry Asn; Alpha Phi Fraternity. **Business Addr:** President, Chief Executive Officer, Costello Johnson Corporate Office Systems Inc, 833 W Jackson Blvd Fl 6, Chicago, IL 60607, **Business Phone:** (312)421-7200.

JOHNSON, CYNTHIA
Association executive, community activist. **Personal:** Born Aug 19, 1958, Detroit, MI; daughter of Willie L and Beverly Johnson; married Hoskins (divorced); children: Wallace, Tyhecia & Henry. **Educ:** Wayne County Community Col, AA, 1989; Walsh Col, BBA, 1992. **Career:** Wayne County Neighborhood Legal Ctr, prog consult, 1992-94; Inkster Schs, crisis intervention consult, 1994-95; Wayne County Govt, intern, 1994-95, victim's witness asst, 1995; GOGIRLS, dir, 1995-. **Business Addr:** Executive Director, Giving Our Girls Incentive (for) Real Life Situations (GOGIRLS), 29999 Pine St, Inkster, MI 48141.

JOHNSON, CYNTHIA L. M.
Lawyer. **Personal:** Born Mar 1, 1952, Detroit, MI; daughter of Robert Alexander (deceased) and Frances E (deceased); children: Alexandra, Lauren, Joshua. **Educ:** Univ Michigan, BA, 1973; Master Pub Health, 1975; Detroit Col Law, JD, 1984. **Career:** Detroit Med Found & Mich HMO Plans Inc, dep dir, 1975; New York City Health Hosp Corp, sr health analyst, 1976-77; United Autoworkers healthcare, consult, 1977-83; Mich Ct Appeals, judicial law clerk, 1983-89; Mich Supreme Ct, judicial law clerk, 1985-87; Clark Hill PLC(Clark, Klein & Beaumont, PLC), partner, 1987-. **Orgs:** Mich Bar Asn; Wolverine Bar Asn; Nat Asn Advan Colored People; Delta Sigma Theta Sorority; bd dirs, Lula Belle Stewart, 1994-98; finance committee, Mercy Health Care Corp, 1993-98; bd dirs, Ronald McDonald House Detroit, 1996. **Business Addr:** Partner, Clark Hill PLC, 500 Woodward Ave Suite 3500, Detroit, MI 48226-3435, **Business Phone:** (313)965-8263.*

JOHNSON, CYRUS EDWIN
Executive. **Personal:** Born Feb 18, 1929, Alton, IL; son of Cyrus L and Jennie Cornelia Keen (deceased); married Charlotte E Keniebrew; children: Judie & Rene. **Educ:** Univ Ill, BS, 1956, MA, 1959; Harvard Bus Sch, 1974. **Career:** Farmer, 1946-50; Urbana Lincoln Hotel, asst mgr, 1953-59; Ill Bell Telephone Co, dist mgr, 1959-72; Gen Mills Inc, vpres; MGO Facilities & Serv, dir. **Orgs:** Dir, AULT Inc, Lifespan Inc; former trustee, Gen Mills Found, Nat Minority Bus Campaign; former dir, Abbot-Northwestern Hosp; former deans adv council Purdue Univ, Bus Sch, Harvard Bus Sch Asn; bd dir WVa State Col Found, 1988-; Bus Adv Bethune-Cookman Col Div Bus, 1989-; nat bd dir, Girl Scouts USA, 1990-. **Honors/Awds:** Am Legion Scholarship Award, 1943; fel Chicago Defender Roundtable Com, 1967; Portraits of Success Award, Purdue Univ, Old Masters, 1975. **Military Serv:** AUS, 1950-52. **Business Addr:** Vice President, Director, MGO Facilities & Service, PO Box 1113, Minneapolis, MN 55440.

JOHNSON, DARRIUS DASHOME
Football player. **Personal:** Born May 18, 1973, Terrell, TX. **Educ:** Univ Okla. **Career:** Football player (retired); Denver Broncos, cornerback & safety, 1996-99; Kans City Chiefs, cornerback, 2003.

JOHNSON, DAVE
Basketball player. **Personal:** Born Nov 16, 1970, Morgan City, LA. **Educ:** Syracuse Univ, attended. **Career:** Portland Trail Blazers, guard & forward, 1992-93; Chicago Bulls, 1994; Pasta Baronia Napoli, 1997-98.

JOHNSON, DAVID E.
Banker. **Personal:** Born Aug 4, 1960, Jackson, MS; son of Earnest; married Doris Martin, Mar 11, 1989; children: D. **Educ:**

Jackson State Univ, BS, magna cum laude, 1982; Am Inst Banking, 1983-87;Hinds Community Col, AA, summa cum laude, 1987; LOU State Univ SchBanking, 1992; Cannon Financial Inst Trust Sch, Pepperdine Univ & Univ NCCharlotte, 2002. **Career:** AM South Bank, supply clerk, 1979-80, records clerk, 1980-82, mgt trainee,1982-83, asst mgr & acct profitability analyst, 1983-84, credit analyst,1985, asst vpres & asst br mgr, 1985-89, vpres & br mgr, 1989-93, vpres &regional community develop officer, 1993-2000, vpres & trust adminr,currently. **Orgs:** Choir pres & musician, 1972-, Nat Asn Urban Bankers; Sunday sch supt,1987-; bd trustees, Zion Chapel Church God Christ, 1989-; charter mem,treas, Jackson Chap, 1992; pres, Youth Act Coun, 1994-; chmn, Bldg FundComt, 1994-; adv bd, Jackson State Univ Continuing Educ Learning Ctr,1998; bd dir, Minority Capital Fund, 1999; United Way, donor investmentcomt, 1999. **Honors/Awds:** Professional Black Achiever of the Year, YMCA, 1984; Bus ManagementAcademic Award, 1982, Pre's List Scholar, 1982, National Dean's ListScholar, 1981, Jackson State Univ; Leadership Jackson, 1998; OutstandingYoung Men of America, 1984, 1989, 1996, 1998; Leadership Mississippi, 2001. **Business Addr:** Vice President, Client Services Officer, Am South Bank, 109 Webster Cir, Jackson, MS 39201, **Business Phone:** (601)968-4794.

JOHNSON, DAVIS
Executive. **Personal:** Born Feb 23, 1934, Detroit, MI; son of Hubert; married Alphia Bymun, Jun 21, 1958; children: Cheryl Rene Johnson. **Educ:** Wayne State Univ; Harvard Univ; Mich State Univ; Investment Sem; Notre Dame. **Career:** Investors Diversified Serv Inc, sales rep, 1966-69, dist sales mgr, 1969-72, div sales mgr, 1972; Johnsons Financial Serv Inc, chief exec officer. **Orgs:** Nat Asn Securities Dealers; Nat Asn Advan Colored People; Booker T Washington Bus Asn; Cotillion Club; Big Ten Alumni Asn; Metro Contractors; Jugs African Med Asn. **Military Serv:** AUS, corpl, 1952-54. **Home Addr:** 19160 Parkside St, Detroit, MI 48221. *

JOHNSON, DENNIS
Executive, president (organization). **Career:** NBC TV Networks, from page, mgr, dir; ABC TV Networks, vpres & exec producer; Osmond TV; Showtime Entertainment Group, Showtime Networks, sr vpres; Omni Broadcasting Network Inc, pres & gen mgr, currently; Dennis Johnson Prods, film & television prod co. **Special Achievements:** First African Am to hold the position of sr vpres at Showtime Entertainment Group; organized musical & comedy specials starring: Elton John, Michael Jackson, Gladys Knight, Jim Carrey, Tommy Davidson, Tim Allen, Elaine Boosler, Paul Reiser, Dionne Warwick & Drew Carey. **Business Phone:** (702)938-0467.

JOHNSON, DINAH
Writer, educator. **Personal:** Born in Charleston, SC; daughter of Douglas Johnson Sr and Beatrice Taylor. **Educ:** Princeton Univ; Yale Univ, PhD, 1988. **Career:** Books: Quinnie Blue; Sitting Pretty; Sunday Week; All around Town; African Am Review; The Best of the Brownies' Book; Splash; Telling Tales; In Daddy's Arms I am Tall; Presenting Laurence Yep; Nobody's Brat: Life Through the Eyes of Military Kids; Beautiful by Design: The Story of African American Children's Literature, co-producer; edited various publications including: The Collected Works of Langston Hughes, Volume 11:The Works for Children; African American Review, Vol. 32, no.1; The Best of The Brownies' Book; Presenting Laurence Yep; Telling Tales: The Pedagogy & Promise of African Am Literature for Youth; Univ SC, prof eng, currently. **Honors/Awds:** The Best of The Brownies' Book Award, Children's Book Council/NCSS, 1997. **Business Addr:** Professor, University of South Carolina, 513 Humanities Office Bldg, Columbia, SC 29208, **Business Phone:** (803)777-2345.

JOHNSON, DONN S
Journalist. **Personal:** Born May 9, 1947, St Louis, MO; son of Ivory M Dodd (deceased) and Clyde E Sr; married Earlene Beverly Breedlove, Jun 1, 1969; children: Lauren Beverly Johnson. **Educ:** St Louis Comm Col Florissant Valley, AA, 1976; Webster Col, BA, 1977. **Career:** KWK Radio St Louis, newsman & disc jockey, 1970-72; WIL Radio St Louis, newsman & dir comm rel, 1972-78; KTVI Channel 2 St Louis, anchor & reporter, 1978-; St Louis Am Newspaper, columnist. **Orgs:** Mem adv bd, Mass Commun Forest Park Comm Col, 1972-; Greater St Louis Black Journalists Asn, 1979-; St Louis Press Club, 1980; vpres, St Louis Chap, Am Fedn Radio & TV Artists (AFTRA); bd, St Louis Gateway Classic Fund. **Honors/Awds:** Howard B Woods Mem Award, Jour Black Stud Asn, Webster Col, 1977; Best News Story of the Year Award, Greater St Louis Black Journalists Assoc, 1978; Black Excellence in Journalism Award, Greater St Louis Black Journalism Asn, 1978, 1984, 1986, 1988-89; Unity Awards in Media, Lincoln Univ, 1985; Media Award, Gifted Asn, MO, 1987; Media Award of Excellence, Mo Asn Community & Jr Col, 1990; Emmy (local), Acad TV Arts & Sci, 1989. **Military Serv:** AUS, corpl, 1966-67. **Business Addr:** Anchor, Reporter, KTVI Channel 2, 5915 Berthold Ave, Saint Louis, MO 63110, **Business Phone:** (314)644-7560.

JOHNSON, DONNA ALLIGOOD
Executive. **Personal:** Born Oct 25, 1956, Detroit, MI; daughter of Douglas Lacy and Cynthia Elvira Vincent; married Curtis Charles, Jun 27, 1987. **Educ:** Tufts Univ, BS, 1978. **Career:** BBDO, acct coordr, 1978-79, asst acct exec, 1980-82, acct exec, 1983-85, sr acct exec, 1985-88; Citicorp POS Info Servs, mktg mgr, 1988-90, prod mgr, 1991; TSS, vpres, 1992-95; MasterCard Int, vpres acceptance develop, vpres new mkts, currently. **Orgs:** Bd mem, Am Red Cross, 1997; Nat Asn Advan Colored People. **Honors/Awds:** YMCA Black Achievers, 2002. **Home Addr:** 668 Glenbrook Rd, Stamford, CT 06906-1433, **Home Phone:** (203)353-8730. **Business Addr:** Vice President of New Markets, MasterCard International, 2000 Purchase St, Purchase, NY 10577, **Business Phone:** (914)249-2000.

JOHNSON, DORIS ELAYNE
Educator, librarian. **Personal:** Born Jul 13, 1954, Orangeburg, SC; daughter of Angie Pearl Glover Johnson and Roscoe Johnson Sr; children: LaTroy Damon. **Educ:** SC State Col, Orangeburg, SC, 1976; Clark Atlanta Univ, Atlanta, Ga, MSLS, 1990. **Career:** SC State Univ, Orangeburg, SC, libr tech asst, 1982-89, librn, ref & info specialist, instr, 1991-, Interim Coordr Collection Develop, currently. **Orgs:** Atlanta Law Libr Asn, 1989-; Am Libr Asn, 1989-; SC Libr Asn, 1991-; Delta Sigma Theta Sorority. **Honors/Awds:** Minority Stipend, Atlanta Law Libr Asn, 1990; Delta of the Year, 1997. **Home Addr:** 820 Corona Dr, Orangeburg, SC 29115-6307. **Business Addr:** Interim Coordinator of Collection Development, South Carolina State University, Miller F. Whittaker Library, 300 College Ave, Orangeburg, SC 29117, **Business Phone:** (803)536-7045.*

JOHNSON, DOROTHY M
Nurse. **Personal:** Born Aug 18, 1922, Indianapolis, IN; daughter of Gilbert Hooks and Leola; widowed; children: Arlene J Beesing. **Educ:** Mohawk Valley Community Col, AASN, 1972; State Univ NY, Utica, BSN, 1982. **Career:** Nurse (retired); Registered nurse. **Orgs:** Nat Black Leadership Initiative on Cancer; chair, Las Vegas Coalition, 1994; chair, Health Comm, Theta Theta Omega Sorority, 1994; Women's Health Coalition, Las Vegas, 1997; Am Cancer Soc, Regional Coun; Witness Proj Sponsoring Org, 2000; Prince Hall Masonic Family, NY Chap; founder, Las Vegas Coalition; United Assembly 72. **Home Addr:** 5324 W Rancher Ave, Las Vegas, NV 89108, **Home Phone:** (702)655-3752.

JOHNSON, DOROTHY TURNER
Librarian, educator. **Personal:** Born Jan 18, 1915, Dublin, GA; daughter of Thomas and Eva Montgomery; married Harold Martin (died 1977). **Educ:** Spelman Col, Atlanta, Ga, AB, 1938; Univ Wis, Madison, Wis, BS, libr sci, 1949; Western Reserve Univ, Cleveland, Ohio, MS, libr sci. **Career:** Librarian, Educator (retired); Dade County Public Schs, Homestead, Fla, teacher, 1934-36; Fla Normal & Indust Inst, St Augustine, Fla, librn, 1939-41; Spelman Col, Atlanta, Ga, asst librn, 1941-42; Detroit Public Libr, Detroit, MI, children's librarian, 1949-50; Cleveland Pub Library, Cleveland, Ohio, head, classrooms div, 1950-65; Cuyahoga Com Col, Cleveland, Ohio, head, libr technol, 1965-80. **Orgs:** Am Libr Asn, 1956-80; Asn Univ Profs, 1975-80; Urban League Guild, 1975-; ACLU, 1965; Alpha Kappa Alpha Sorority, 1947. **Honors/Awds:** Fulbright Scholar, US Office Educ, 1976; Dorothy T Johnson Guild, 2000-. **Special Achievements:** Author: One Day, Mother (Un Dia, Madre), 1996. **Military Serv:** AUS (WAAC), PFC, 1942-45. **Home Addr:** 315 Grand Magnolia Ave Suite 20108, Celebration, FL 34747, **Home Phone:** (407)566-8668.

JOHNSON, DOUGLAS H.
Educator. **Personal:** Born May 1, 1943, Bolivia, NC; married Shirley L. **Educ:** Cheyney St Col, Cheyne, PA, BA, 1969; Univ RI, Kingston, degree community planning, 1971; Mass Inst Technol, PhD. **Career:** Univ Rhode Island, asst prof community planning; Wilmington Metro Area Planning Coun, Wilmington, DE, summer intern, 1970; Inst, community planning, 1974-; Community Planning CPAD, asst prof, 1974-; State Rhode Island, Providence, consult Off Continuing Educ, 1974. **Orgs:** Prin, vpres, Community Found, 1973-; ed, Nat Asn Planners, Newsletter, 1973-75; Am Soc Planning Off; Nat Asn Planning; Am Asn Univ Profs; United Work-Study Fel, US Dept Housing & Urban Develop, 1969-71. **Honors/Awds:** Award, Am Inst Planning, 1971; National Fellowship Fund Award; Academician of the Year, Mass Inst Technol, 1976-77. **Business Addr:** Graduate Curriculum Community Planning, Kingston, RI 02881.

JOHNSON, DWAYNE DOUGLAS (THE ROCK)
Actor, wrestler. **Personal:** Born May 2, 1972, Hayward, CA; son of Ata Maivia and Rocky; married Dany Garcia, 1997. **Educ:** Univ Miami, Coral Gables, Fla, BS, criminol & physiol, 1995. **Career:** Canadian Football League, Calgary Stampeders, pract team, 1995; World Wrestling Entertainment, prof wrestler, 1996-2001; actor, currently; Films: The Mummy Returns, 2001; The Scorpion King, 2002; The Rundown, 2003; Walking Tall, 2004; Be Cool, 2005; Doom, 2005; Johnny Bravo, 2006; Southland Tales, 2006; Spy Hunter, 2006; Reno 911!: Miami, 2007; The Game Plan, 2007; Get Smart, 2008; TV guest appearances: "Star Trek Voyager", 1995; "That '70s Show", 1998; "DAG", 2000; "Saturday Night Live", 2002. **Special Achievements:** Autobiography: The Rock Says The Most Electrifying Man in Sports Entertainment, 2000.

JOHNSON, EARL
Engineer. **Personal:** Born Jun 25, 1943, Gilmer, TX; son of Lunnie and Ella; married Pamela G Huddleston, Nov 18, 1990; children: Marla A. **Educ:** Electronic Technical Inst, 1967-68; Mesa Jr Col, 1975-76. **Career:** Conic Corp, electronic assembly, 1967-68; Ryan Aeronical, electronic assembly, 1968-69; Ketema Aerospace & Electronics, jr engr, 1969-90; John Sound Lab, pres, owner, 1990-. **Military Serv:** USY, sgt, 1964-67. **Business Phone:** (619)258-8342.

JOHNSON, EARVIN (MAGIC JOHNSON)
Executive, basketball player, basketball coach. **Personal:** Born Aug 14, 1959, Lansing, MI; son of Earvin Sr and Christine; married Earleatha (Cookie); children: Andre, Earvin III & Elisa. **Educ:** Mich State Univ. **Career:** Basketball Player, coach (retired), executive; La Lakers, guard, 1979-92, 1996, head coach, 1994, minority owner, 1996-; Magic Johnson Enterprises, owner & chief exec officer, 1992, chmn & chief exec officer, currently; Johnson Develop Corp, chmn & chief exec officer, currently; The Magic Hour, Fox, host, 1998. **Orgs:** Magic Johnson Found; AOL; Am Express; Farmers Ins; Fortune Mag; Wash Mutual; Rochester Inst Technol; Samsung; Best Buy; Sun Microsystems; Univ Calif, Irvine; Choice Hotels; Arden Realty, Glaxo SmithKline Pharma; TheCoca-Cola Co; Muscular Dystrophy Asn; co-chair, UN Day; bd trustees, Am Cancer Soc Found; co-chair, VP Al Gore's White House Community Empowerment Bd. **Honors/Awds:** World Class Athlete, MI St; NBA Player of the Week; Schick Pivotal Player Award; won 2 playoff MVP Awards; NBA MVP, 1987, 1992; Gold Medal, US Olympic Basketball Team, 1992; Excellence in Community Leadership Award, Boston Col, 1998; PRAME Presidents Award, 1998; Ronald H Brown Award for Leadership, 2000; Lifetime Achievement Award, Friars Club CA, 2002; Naismith Memorial Basketball Hall of Fame, 2002; Person of the Year, Savoy mag, 2003; Entrepreneur of the Year, Crenshaw Chamber Com. **Special Achievements:** Autobiography, Magic, 1983; one of the country's most influential businessmen by Fortune magazine; one of the 100 Most Powerful People in Los Angeles. **Business Addr:** Chairman, Chief Executive Officer, Johnson Develop Corporation, 5005 Riverway Suite 500, Houston, TX 77056, **Business Phone:** (713)960-9977.

JOHNSON, EDDIE BERNICE
Congressperson (U.S. federal government). **Personal:** Born Dec 3, 1935, Waco, TX; divorced; children: Dawrence Kirk Jr. **Educ:** Univ Notre Dame, St Marys Col, nursing cert, 1955; Tex Christian Univ, Fort Worth, TX, BS, 1967; Southern Methodist Univ, Dallas, TX, MPA, 1976. **Career:** Veterans Admin Hosp, Dallas, TX, nurse; Tex State House Rep, mem, 1972-77; Dept Health, Educ & Welfare, regional dir, 1977; US Dept Health, Educ & Welfare, adminr, 1977-81; Sammons Enterprises Inc, asst to pres, 1981-87; Vis Nurse Asn, vpres, govt affairs, 1981-87; Eddie Bernice Johnson & Assocs, founder; Tex State Senate, 1987-93; US House Rep, 30th Congressional Dist Tex, congresswoman, 1993-; Tex Democratic Delegation, sr democratic dep whip & chmn, currently. **Orgs:** Am Nurses Asn; Links Inc, Dallas chap; Dallas Black Chamber Com; Nat Asn Advan Colored People; Girlfriends Inc; Alpha Kappa Alpha Sorority; past pres, Nat Coun Negro Women; past vpres & secy, Nat Order Women Legislators; bd dir, Sunbelt Nat Bank; chair, Congressional Black Caucus, 2001-. **Honors/Awds:** LLD, Bishop Col, 1979; LLD, Jarvis Christian Col, 1979; LLD, Tex Col, 1989; LLD, Paul Quinn Col; LLD, Houston-Tillotson Col; Scholar Award, United Negro Col Fund, Dallas, 1992; Juanita Craft Award in Politics, Nat Asn Advan Colored People, 1989; Heroes Award, Nat Asn Advan Colored People, 2000; President's Award, Nat Conf Black Mayors, 2001; Visionary Award, Nat Orgn Black Elected Legis Women, 2001; Woman of the Year, 100 Black Men Am, 2001; 25th Anniversary Outstanding Achievement Award, Nat Black Caucus State Legislators. **Special Achievements:** Bernice Johnson became the first woman and the first African-American to ever represent the Dallas, Texas area in Congress when she was elected to the United States House of Representatives in 1992. **Business Addr:** Congresswoman, US House of Representative, 1511 Longworth House Office Bldg, Washington, DC 20515, **Business Phone:** (202)225-8885.

JOHNSON, EDDIE C.
Judge. **Personal:** Born Jun 1, 1920, Chicago, IL; married Olivia; children: Edward & Ella. **Educ:** Roosevelt Univ, AB; John Marshall Law Sch, JD; Loyola Univ, attended. **Career:** Atty, Judge (retired); pvt pract, atty, 1952-65; Brooks, Rhett & Johnson,1953-55; Gayles, Johnson & Handy, 1957-61; Ellis, Westbrook & Holman,Gillen & Owens, 1961-65; Jones, Ware & Greaud, official coun; Circuit Ct,Cook County, IL, judge, 1965-91. **Orgs:** Cook Co & Nat Bar Asn, Judical Coun NBA. **Honors/Awds:** Distinguished Service & Alumnus Award, John Mouskell Law Sch; The Push-Foundation Award; Meritorious Service Award & Judicial Career ServiceAward, Ill Judicial Coun.

JOHNSON, EDMOND R.
Lawyer. **Personal:** Born Jun 26, 1937, Plymouth, NC; married Thelma Crosby; children: Edrenna Renee, Erica Ronelle. **Educ:** NC Cent Univ, BA, 1959; Howard Univ, JD, 1968. **Career:** DE Tech Comm Col, teacher law clerk, 1968-69; pvt pract law, 1970-; Edmond R Johnson & Assoc, atty, currently. **Orgs:** NC Acad Trial Lawyers; NC State Bar; Nat & Am Bar Asns; NC Black Lawyers Asn; Nat Asn Advan Colored People; Alpha Phi Alpha. **Business Addr:** Attorney, Edmond R Johnson & Assoc, 916 W 5th St Suite 202, Charlotte, NC 28202.*

JOHNSON, EDNA DECOURSEY
Educator. **Personal:** Born Jun 1, 1922, Baltimore, MD; married Laurence Harry, Sep 30, 1956. **Educ:** Coppin St Col, BS, 1944; Johns Hopkins Univ, Post Grad, Work Consumer & Law, 1954; Rutgers Univ, Cert Group Dynamic Human Relations, 1956; Univ Winconsin, Cert Finance Money Mgt, 1966. **Career:** Educator (retired); Baltimore City Pub Schs, elementary teacher, 1944-63; Baltimore Urban League, dir consult serv, 1963-78; Comm Coll of Baltimore & other Comm Clgs, part-time instr, 1975-92; Northwest Baltimore Corp, exec dir, 1979-82; MD Food Bank, prog dir, 1979-82; Nat Assoc Negro Bus & Prof Womens Clubs Inc, prog dir, 1979-82. **Orgs:** Secy, Devel Urban League's consumer educ prog, 1963; past gov dist, Nat Asn Negro Bus & Prof Womens Clubs, 1967-71, 1973-75; past Nat Corresp, 1971-73; Heritage United Church Christ, 1971-73; past pres, Baltimore Club Mid Atlantic ABWA, 1970-73; bd mem, Consumers Union First Black Woman, 1972-84; Consumer adv, Am Egg Bd, 1979-84; bd mem, Nat Coalition Consumer Educ, 1982-86; Zeta Phi Beta Sorority Alumni. **Honors/Awds:** National Sojourner Truth Meritorious Service Award, Truth Baltimore Club &Nat Asn Negro Bus & Prof Womens Club Inc, 1974; Lambda Kappa Major, 1972;The Pilomathians, 1982. **Special Achievements:** Hundred Outstndng Women Delta Sigma Theta Sorority. **Home Addr:** 3655 Wabash Ave, Baltimore, MD 21215.

JOHNSON, EDWARD ARNET
Basketball player, radio host, president (organization). **Personal:** Born May 1, 1959, Chicago, IL; married Joy; children: Jade Alexis & Justin Edward. **Educ:** Univ Ill, BA, hist. **Career:** Basketball player (retired), color commentator, pres (organization); Kans City Kings, forward & guard, 1981-85; Sacramento Kings, 1985-87; Phoenix Suns, 1987-91, color analyst, currently; Seattle SuperSonics, 1991-93; Charlotte Hornets, 1993-94; Olympiacos BC, 1994-95; Ind Pacers, 1995-96; Houston Rockets, forward, 1996-99; HoopsHype, staff; Teamfone Inc, pres & co-founder, currently. **Honors/Awds:** NBA Sixth Man Award, 1989. **Special Achievements:** Released an instructional DVD called Eddie Johnson's Jumpshot and Offensive Skills.

JOHNSON, DR. EDWARD ELEMUEL
Educator. **Personal:** Born in Crooked River, Jamaica; son of Rev Edward E and Mary Elizabeth Blake; married Beverley Jean Morris; children: Edward E, Lawrence P, Robin Jeannine, Nathan J & Cyril U. **Educ:** Howard Univ, BS, 1947, MS, 1948; Univ Colo, PhD, 1952. **Career:** Southern Univ, Baton Rouge, LA, prof & assoc dean univ, 1955-72; Los Angeles State Univ Med Sch, clin prof psychiat, 1969-72; United Bd Col Develop, dir, 1972-74; NJ Robert Wood Johnson Med Sch, prof psychiat, 1974-. **Orgs:** Panelist, Sci Fac Develop Nat Sci Found, 1978-82; site visitor, NIH, 1978-; consult, Bell Lab, Holmdel, NJ, 1982-85; bd trustees, Crossroads Theatre Co, 1983-; bd dirs, PSI Assoc Inc, 1984-. **Honors/Awds:** Fel, AAAS; life mem, The Soc Sigma Xi; Pi Gamma Mu Nat Soc Sci Hon Soc; Psi Chi Nat Psychol Hon Soc; Beta Beta Beta Biol Honor Soc, Thirty-third Degree Mason, Prince Hall Affiliation; Sigma Pi Phi Fraternity; Alpha Phi Alpha Fraternity. **Special Achievements:** Over 50 scientific publications including book chapt. **Military Serv:** AUS, irst Lt, 1951-53. **Home Addr:** PO Box 597, East Brunswick, NJ 08816. **Business Addr:** Professor of Psychiatry, Department of Psychiatry, Robert Wood Johnson Medical School 675 Hoes Lane, Piscataway, NJ 08854, **Business Phone:** (732)235-4700.

JOHNSON, EDWARD M
Executive. **Personal:** Born Jan 15, 1943, Washington, DC. **Educ:** BArch, 1967; Master, City Planning, 1970. **Career:** Architects & Urban Planners, 1969-; JJ Lord Construction Co, pres; Edward M Johnson & Assoc PC, owner, currently. **Orgs:** Am Inst Architects; Design Review Panel DC; Dept Housing & Community Develop. **Honors/Awds:** Recip, US Housing & Urban Dev Fel; Doxiodus Fel; Urban Transp Fel. **Business Addr:** Owner, Edward M Johnson & Assoc PC, 3612 12th St NE, Washington, DC 20017, **Business Phone:** (202)526-3610.

JOHNSON, ELAINE MCDOWELL
Government official. **Personal:** Born Jun 28, 1942, Baltimore, MD; daughter of McKinley and Lena Blue; married Walter A Johnson, 1978 (divorced); children: Nathan Murphy Jr, Michael Murphy; married Walter Johnson, Jan 20, 1978. **Educ:** Morgan State Univ, BA, 1965; Univ MD, MSW, 1971, PhD, 1988. **Career:** Government official (retired); State MD, acting regional dir, 1971-72; Nat Inst Drug Abuse, pub health adv, 1972-76, Div Community Asst, deputy dir & dir, 1976-82, Div Prevention & Communs, dir, 1982-85; ADAMHA, exec asst to admin, 1985; Nat Inst Drug Abuse, deputy dir, 1985-88, dir, Off Substance Abuse Prevention, 1988-90; ADAMHA & SAMHSA, acting admin, 1990-92; Ctr Substance Abuse Prev, dir, 1992; Friends Res Inst, Prin Investigator. **Orgs:** Ordained officer, Presbyterian Church 1981-84; nat dir, drug abuse prevention prog Zeta Phi Beta Sor, 1986-92; consult, US Information Agency, US State Dept; Links Inc. **Honors/Awds:** National Services Youth Award, Links Inc, 1986; National Award, Outstanding Leadership Improving Health Care Black Community, Nat Med Asn, 1988; Prevention Award, Defining & Advancing Sci Prevention, Nat Drug Info Ctr Families Action, 1988; F Elwood Davis Award, Govt Official Responsive Needs Youth, Boys & Girls Clubs, 1989; Nat Coun Alcoholism & Drug Dependence Inc; President's Meritorious Award, Outstanding FDL Leadership, 1991; National Leadership Award, Nat Fed Parents, 1991; President's Distinguished Service Award, Outstanding Fed Leadership, 1993. **Special Achievements:** Author: "Cocaine: The Am Experience," The Cocaine Crisis, D Allen, ed, NY Plenum Press, 1987; "The Impact of Drug Abuse on Women's Health," Pub health Reports, 1987; "The Gov's Response Drug Abuse Problems Among Minority Populations," Journal of the Black Nurses Asn; "Preventing Alcohol Abuse: A Move Towards a National Agenda," Principles and Practices of Student Health, Found, Vol 1, H Wallace, et al, eds, Third Party Publ CPN, 1991. *

JOHNSON, ELLIS BERNARD
Football player. **Personal:** Born Oct 30, 1973, Wildwood, FL; married Simone; children: Nichole & Ellis Bernard Jr. **Educ:** Univ Fla. **Career:** Football player (retired); Indianapolis Colts, defensive tackle, 1995-2001; Atlanta Falcons, 2002-03; Denver Broncos, 2004.

JOHNSON, ERIC G
Executive. **Personal:** Born Mar 29, 1951, Chicago, IL; son of George Eillis and Joan Betty; married Pamela Johnson, Apr 8, 1979; children: Lecretia, Erin, Cara & John. **Educ:** Babson Col, BAS, 1972; Univ Chicago, MBA, 1977. **Career:** Proctor & Gamble, staff, 1972-75; Johnson Prod, pres & chief exec officer, 1988-92; Baldwin Ice Cream Co, pres & chief exec officer, 1992-; Baldwin Richardson Foods Co, pres & chief exec officer, 1997-. **Orgs:** Young Presidents Orgn; bd dirs, Dr Martin Luther King Ctr; bd dirs, Chicago State Univ; bd trustees, Babson Col; Olympia Fields Country Club; bd trustees, Glenwood Sch Boys; Comn Econ Develop; bd dirs, Nat Am Advan Colored People; bd trustees, Rochester Inst Technol, 2000-; chmn, Develop Comt; Securities Comt. **Honors/Awds:** Leadership Award, Boy Scouts Am; Annual Recognition Award, 100 Black Men Am; Humanitarian Award, Willi Wilson Found; Chicago State Col; Hon Doctor Lett; Freedom Award, Lincoln Mem, Jobs, Peace. **Special Achievements:** Lifelink Celebrity Challenge; The Ideal Black Gold Trade Show; Ranked 44 in the Black Enterprise's Top 100 Industrial/Service Companies list, 1999. **Business Addr:** President, Chief Executive Officer, Baldwin Richardson Foods Co, 20201 S LaGrange Rd Suite 200, Frankfort, IL 60423, **Business Phone:** (866)644-2732.

JOHNSON, ERMA CHANSLER (ERMA JOHNSON HADLEY)
School administrator, president (organization). **Personal:** Born Jun 6, 1942, Leggett, TX; married Lawrence Eugene; children: Thelma Ardenia. **Educ:** Prairie View A&M Univ, BS, 1963; Bowling Green State Univ, MEd, 1968. **Career:** Turner High Sch, teacher, 1963-67; Bowling Green State Univ, grad asst,1967-68; Tarrant County Jr Col, Dist Fort Worth, TX, assoc prof, 1968-72, asst dir personnel, 1973-74, dir personnel, 1974-81, humr consult, vice chancellor human resources, vice chancellor admin, currently. **Orgs:** Consult, Col & Univ US Civil Comn Serv, 1972-; Pres, Fannie M Heath Cultural Club, 1974-75, 1978-80; Ft Worth Am Revolution Bicentennial Comt,1974-76; bd dir, 1974-78, treas, 1977-78, Ft Worth-Tarrant County Supportive Outreach Serv; Task Force 100, 1976; vpres, Ft Worth Minority Leaders & Citizens Coun, 1976-78; Ft Worth Pub Transp Adv comt, 1976-80; bd dir, Community Devel Fund, 1976-80; Ft Worth Girls Club, 1976-81, pres, 1979-81; Ft Worth Keep Am Beautiful Task Force, 1977-78; comm vice chairperson, bd dir, United Way of Metropolitan Tarrant County, 1979; Ft Worth Cent Bus Dist Planning Coun, 1979-81; seminar leader Col & Univ Personnel Asn, 1980-; pres, Tex asn Black personnel Higher Educ, 1981-83; Ft Worth Citizens on the Move, 1983; Forum Ft Worth; secy, Mt Rose Baptist Church; bd dir, Ft Worth Black Chamber Com; charter mem, Tarrant County Black Hist & Genealogical Society; Rotary Club Ft Worth; pres, Links Inc; secy bd dir, Mt Rose Child Care Ctr; chmn oper comt, Dallas/Ft Worth Airport Bd; chmn, Dallas/Ft Worth Intl Airport Bd, 1987. **Honors/Awds:** Grad Asstship, Bowling Green State Univ, 1967-68; One Week Ed & Prof Devel Act Grant in Voc Ed, 1969, four week, 1970; Listed in Outstanding Ed Am, 1972; Outstanding Young Women Am, 1975; Fort Worth Black Female Achiever of the Year, 1977; Distinguished Leadership Award, 2009. **Special Achievements:** Nominated for Outstanding Teacher, Tarrant County Jr Coll, 1971. **Home Addr:** 2362 Faett Court, Fort Worth, TX 76119. **Business Addr:** Vice Chancellor for Administration, Tarrant County Junior College, 1500 Houston, Fort Worth, TX 76102.

JOHNSON, ERNEST KAYE, III
Surgeon. **Personal:** Born Feb 7, 1950, Ocala, FL; son of E K and Delores; married Clara Perry; children: Ernest IV, Clara Delores. **Educ:** Univ Fla, Pre-Med, 1971; Meharry Med Col, MD, 1975. **Career:** Student Nat Med Asn, vpres, 1973-74; Meharry House Staff Assoc, vpres, 1975-76; Hubbard Hosp Meharry Med Col, Gen Surgery, 1980; Infinity III Inc, vpres, 1983-85. **Orgs:** Matthew Walker Surg Soc, 1975-87, RF Boyd Med Soc, 1975-87; Nashville Acad Med, 1980-83; Tenn Med Asn, 1980-83; Alpha Phi Alpha; Apollo Club, 1990-91. **Honors/Awds:** Hon mem US House of Reps, 1983; Hon Dep Sheriff Nashville Davidson Co, 1984. **Business Addr:** Physician, 3803 Hydes Ferry Pike, Nashville, TN 37218.

JOHNSON, ERNEST L.
Banker, lawyer. **Personal:** Born Aug 24, 1950, Ferriday, LA; son of Evans Sr and Florence; married Pamela Taylor, Oct 30, 1992; children: Emanuel, Louisa, Ernest II. **Educ:** Grambling State UNIV, BS, 1973; Southern UNIV Sch Law, JD, 1976. **Career:** Johnson, Taylor & Thomas, sr partner, 1980-89; Southern UNIV Law CTR, pro; Life Savings Bank, chair bd, pres, currently; pvt pract, atty, currently. **Orgs:** LOU NCP, evp, 1991-; LOU State Bar ASN, 1976-; Louis A Martinet Legal SOC, 1986-; Project Invest BLK, bd; Church Point Ministries Feed Family, bd; louisiana community develop capital fund. **Honors/Awds:** NCP, NAT PRS Leadership Award, 1992; Louis A Martinet Legal SOC, Leadership Award, 1991; JK Haynes EDU FND, The Prestigious Seervice Award, 1990; Southern UNIV Law CTR, Earl Warren Fellowship, 1973-76; Scotlandville Man of the Year Award, Scotlandville Jaycees, 1990; the Kelly Alexander Award, 1997; Human Rights Leadership Award, Freedom Magazine's, 2000. **Special Achievements:** Lead counsel, Clark v Roemer, restructuring LOU judical system; general counsel, LOU state conference of NCP, first vip, 1991; co-host, Legally Speaking Program. *

JOHNSON, ERVIN, JR.
Basketball player. **Personal:** Born Dec 21, 1967, New Orleans, LA. **Educ:** Univ New Orleans, general studies, 1997. **Career:** Basket ball player (retired); Seattle Super Sonics, center, 1993-96; Denver Nuggets, 1996-97; Milwaukee Bucks, 1997-03, 2005-06; Minnesota Timber wolves, ctr, 2003-05. **Honors/Awds:** ROBIE Award for Humanitarianism, 2002; Community Assist Award, 2003; Honorable Mention All-American, Assoc Press; MVP of the NABC All-America Game, 1993. *

JOHNSON, EUNICE WALKER
Publishing executive, secretary (organization). **Personal:** Born in Selma, AL; daughter of Nathaniel D Walker and Ethel McAlpine Walker; married John H; children: John Harold & Linda. **Educ:** Talladega Col, BA; Loyola Univ, MA; Univ Chicago; Northwestern Univ, J; Ray-Vogue Sch Design, interior decoration. **Career:** Johnson Pub Co Inc, secy treas, currently. **Orgs:** Women's Bd Art Inst Chicago, 1967-; Women's Bd Univ Chicago; United Negro Col Fund; Women's Bd Lyric Opera; Fashion Group; Nat Found Fashion Inst; bd dir, Talladega Col; trustee, Harvard St George Sch, Chicago; bd mem, Pk-Kenwood Women's Aux, IL. **Honors/Awds:** Received several awards including: The Chicagoan of the Year Award, The Boys & Girls Club of Chicago, 1987; Outstanding Black College University Alumnus Award, Ala a & M Univ Asn, 1990; The Trumpet Award, 1999; Frederick D. Patterson Founders Award, 2001, Harold H. Hines Benefactors Award, 2002, United Negro Col Fund. **Business Addr:** Secretary, Treasurer, Johnson Publishing Company Inc., 820 S Mich Ave, Chicago, IL 60605, **Business Phone:** (312)322-9200.

JOHNSON, EUNITA E
Executive, trader. **Personal:** Born Jul 21, 1939, Chicago, IL; daughter of Ella Peters Flemings and Amos Flemings; married Costello, Aug 26, 1967; children: Gina Perry, Pamela Eatman & Darin. **Educ:** Wilson City Col, attended 1957-59; Nat Col Educ, attended 1974-77. **Career:** Eucos Manufacturing, owner, 1970-74; Costello Johnson & Assocs, vpres, 1979-89; Corp Off Systems Inc, vpres, 1989-, secy, co-chief exec officer, currently. **Orgs:** Chair, Chicago Community, Jessee Owens Found; Chicago Regional Purchasing Coun; pres, Dempster & Chicago Ave Merchants Asn, 1971-74; chap pres, N Shore Chap Jack & Jill Am, 1978-92; Chicago Urban League, 1989-. **Honors/Awds:** Outstanding Business Women of the Year, Southside County Ctr, 1988. **Business Addr:** Co-Chief Executive Officer, Corporate Office Sytems Inc, 833 W Jackson Blvd 6th Fl, Chicago, IL 60607, **Business Phone:** (312)421-7200.

JOHNSON, EZRA RAY
Football player. **Personal:** Born Oct 2, 1955, Shreveport, LA; married Carmen. **Educ:** Morris Brown Col. **Career:** Football player (retired); Green Bay Packers, defensive end, 1977-87; Indianapolis Colts, defensive end, 1988-89; Houston Oilers, defensive end, 1990-91. **Honors/Awds:** Hall of Fame, Green Bay Packers, 1997. **Special Achievements:** Ranked among NFC leaders with 14 1/2 quarterback sacks, 1983. *

JOHNSON, F. RAYMOND
Executive. **Personal:** Born May 10, 1920, Richmond, TX; married; children: Bernarde, Sheryl & Floyd. **Educ:** Southern Calif Col Bus, attended 1953. **Career:** Self-Employed, pub acct, 1955-65; Opportunity Industrialization Ctrs Am, job develop specialist, 1965-68; S Cent Improv Action Coun, dep dir,1968-70; Usina Community Develop Corp, exec dir, 1970-74; Barker Mgt Inc, gen mgr, 1974-78; Calif Housing Finance Agency, state housing consult, 1978; Hjima Housing Corp, dir, 1978-83. **Orgs:** Chmn, Hjima Community Develop Corp, 1978-83; Nat Asn Advan Colored People; YMCA; Brotherhood Crusade. **Honors/Awds:** Cong Citation Asst Minority Entrepreneurs Bus Develop La Co. **Military Serv:** AUS, sgt, 1941-45.

JOHNSON, FRAN (RAGLIN JOHNSON)
Executive. **Personal:** Born Jan 5, 1939, Chicago, IL; daughter of Ernestine Conway and Leon Covington; married; children: Hu-

mont Berry II, Derek C Berry, T David, Mark E & Maria L. **Educ:** Chicago State Univ, BS, 1973, MSed, 1975; Univ Cincinnati, EdD, 1981. **Career:** Chicago State Univ, dir, spec train unit, 1973-77; Kennedy King Col, prof, 1977-80; Greater Cincinnati Chamber Com, dir, YES Prog, 1980-83; Univ Cincinnati, 1981-; Elite Travel Serv, founder & owner, 1983-; Chicago Bd Educ, Michael Reese Hosp; Job Opportunity Better Skills, asst dir; Ctrl YMCA Col, dir, secretarial training. **Orgs:** African Travel Asn, 1977-; Pvt Industry Coun, 1983-89; Int Am Travel Agency Soc, 1983-; trustee, United Way, 1989-; Withrow Local Sch Coun Bd, 1989-; trustee, Cincinnati Local Develop Coun, 1990-; Xonta Int, 1992-; Greater Cincinnati Bus Owners Bd, 1992-; Nat Asn Advan Colored People. **Honors/Awds:** Summer Jobs Merit Award, Pres US Am, 1984; Woman Enterprise, US Small Bus, 1991; Woman of the Year, YWCA, 1992; Black Achiever, YMCA, 1992. **Special Achievements:** African Appointment Book, 1990-95. **Business Phone:** (513)861-8555.

JOHNSON, FRANK
Basketball player, basketball coach. **Personal:** Born Nov 23, 1958, Weirsdale, FL; married Amy; children: Lindsay & Natalie. **Educ:** Wake Forest Univ, BS, 1981. **Career:** Basketball player (retired), basketball coach; Wash Bullets, 1981-88; Houston Rockets, 1988-89; Varise, Rimini, Italy, 1989-92; Phoenix Suns, 1992-94; Phoenix Suns, asst coach, 1997-2000, head coach, 2001-03; Spokesman, Suns community relations dept. **Orgs:** Nat Basketball Asn. **Honors/Awds:** All-Rookie, 1982; All-Am, AP & UPI; All-ACC; Outstanding player in Aloha Classic.; Three time All-Star, 1980-82. **Special Achievements:** First black head coach of Phoenix Suns.

JOHNSON, FRANK J., SR.
Publisher, chief executive officer. **Personal:** Born Sep 1, 1939, Hope, AR; son of Odell Johnson Sr and Jettie Irene Wingfield Johnson; married Betty J Logan; children: Troy & Frank Jr. **Educ:** Calif State Univ Fresno, BA, Educ, 1963. **Career:** Fresno Colony Sch Dist, teacher, 1963-69; Grapevine Mag, publ & edn, 1969-84; W Fresno Sch Dist, prin & counr, 1970-74, dist supt, 1975-79; Who's Who of Black Millionaires Inc, chief exec officer & publ, currently. **Orgs:** Phi Beta Sigma Fraternity, 1959-; W Coast Black Publs Assn, 1979-; exec dir, Non-Profit Housing Assn Inc (NOAH), 1995-. **Honors/Awds:** Outstanding Teacher, West Fresno Sch Dist, 1969, Admin 1977; First Black Sch Dist Supt in Central CA, 1975-79; Civil Service Brd Fresno CA1977-81; Outstanding Achievement Education & Publisher, Alpha Phi Alpha Fraternity, 1978; Outstanding Educator, Calif Black Sch Brd Assn, 1989. **Special Achievements:** Author, Who's Who of Black Millionaires, 1984. **Military Serv:** AUS; Community Service Award, 1974. **Business Addr:** Chief Executive Officier, Publisher, Who's Who Black Millionaires Inc, PO Box 12092, Fresno, CA 93776, **Business Phone:** (209)233-3944.

JOHNSON, FRANK J., JR.
Association executive. **Personal:** Born Jan 30, 1930, Marshall, TX; son of Leedonia Johnson and Fury J Johnson; married May Joyce Wood; children: Teri & Valerie. **Educ:** Univ Wash, BA; Univ Ore, addn study. **Career:** Association executive (retired); Nat Educ Asn; Nat Educ Asn, Teacher Rights Div, mgr; Nat Educ Asn, Minority Involvement Prog, former coordr; Shoreline Sch Syst, Seattle, WA, former teacher, eng dept head; SEA ScopeAsn Newspaper, ed. **Orgs:** Pres, Shoreline Educ Asn, 1964-65; exec bd, Greater Seattle; Coun Teacher Eng; partic, NCTE Conv; SEA Scope Adv Bd; chmn, Right Read Comt; chmn, Comt Prof PSCTE; consult & speaker, Sec Sch & Leadership Conf Stud Govt & Parliamentary Procedure; chmn bd, Finance Mt Zion Baptist Church; pres bd dir, Mt Zion Baptist Church Fed Credit Union; pres, Beta Omicron Chap; Phi Beta Sigma. **Honors/Awds:** John Hay Fel, Univ Ore, 1964. **Special Achievements:** Author of several publ. **Home Addr:** 8068 Inverness Ridge Rd, Potomac, MD 20854. *

JOHNSON, DR. FRED D.
Educator, consultant. **Personal:** Born Mar 7, 1933, Fayetteville, TN; married Dorothy G; children: Fredna & Sheraldine. **Educ:** Tenn State Univ, BS; Univ Memphis, MEd; Univ Tenn, PhD, admin &leadership, 1974. **Career:** Educator (retired), consultant; Shelby County Schs, sci teacher 1954-67,sci supvr, 1967-68, asst supt instr, 1968-77; Shelby County Bd Educ,interim supt, 1977-99, exec dir; La Bd Regents, consult, 1994-97; Christian Bros Univ, adj prof; NSF, prog officer; McKenzie Group, sr consult, currently; Univ Memphis, Col Educs Ctr, adj prof, educr, asst supt. **Orgs:** BSCS; Nat Conv Prog, 1972; Area Conv, chmn, 1974; NSTA 1985; NEA 1985; ASCD 1985; AAAS 1985; NASS1985; KDP 1985; AASA 1985; Optimist 1985; NAACP1985; NAACP; Nat Sci Found, NSF, prog officer, 1986-87; Memphis Symphony,1998-01; Memphis Zoo, 2001; Facing History & Our Selves, 2001; Nominations Comt, chair, 2002-. **Honors/Awds:** Outstanding Teacher Award, Tenn Acad Sci, 1971; District Service Award,NAACP, 1983; District Role Model, NABSE, 1994; Educator of the year, UnivMemphis, 1999; Science Teacher of the Year; Distinguished Science Educator Award; National Science Teachers Association Distinguished Service Award; National Conference of Community & Justices Humanitarian Award, NSTA's most prestigious award "the Robert H. Carleton" Award, 2009. **Military Serv:** AUS, e-5, 1955-57. **Business Addr:** Consultant, 8890 Bridlewood Lane, Cordova, TN 38016, **Business Phone:** (901)751-4005.

JOHNSON, FREDERICK DOUGLASS
Educator. **Personal:** Born Mar 28, 1946, Chattanooga, TN; married Jacqueline Faith Jones; children: Kyle. **Educ:** Oakwood Col, Huntsville, attended 1966; Union Col Lincoln, NE, attended 1968; NE Weslyan Univ, BA, 1972; Univ NE, MA, 1980. **Career:** Randolph Sch, Lincoln NE, teacher, 1972-75, team leader, 1976-83; Belmont Sch, Lincoln NE, asst prin curriculum coord, 1983-86; asst prin, Park Elem Sch, Lincoln, NE. **Orgs:** Phi Delta Kappa, Nat Ed Asn; Nebr State Educ; Lincoln Educ Asn; Lincoln Pub Sch Minority Connection; Guidance Study Comt; Personnel Recruitment Comt; Allan Chapel Seventh-Day-Adventist Church; Am Legion, Kiwanis, Malone Community Ctr; bd mem, Allan Chapel Church, Child Guide Ctr Lincoln; Nebr Weslyan Career Ctr. **Military Serv:** AUS E-5 1 1/2 yrs; Good Conduct Medal, Asian Serv Medal. **Business Addr:** Assistant Principal, Park Elementary School, 714 F St, Lincoln, NE 68521.

JOHNSON, FREDERICK E.
Engineer. **Personal:** Born Jun 24, 1941, Detroit, MI; son of Tommie L and Naomi H; married Sandra A; children: Frederick II & Seth. **Educ:** Wayne State Univ, BEE, 1964; Syracuse Univ, MEE, 1969. **Career:** Engineer (retired); IBM Endicott Lab, line printer test mgr, instrumentation & mech analysis, mgr prod develop, engr mgr proj off, mgr RAS design, instructor, develop; WUCI Radio Station, former pres; FESAJ Enterprises, TQM Specialist, pres; Binghamton Univ, adj instr. **Orgs:** Exec comm New York, Pa Health Systems Agency; adv engr, tech asst, engr, IBM; pres, bd dirs, Broome Ct Urban League; pres, Iota Theta Lambda Chap Alpha Phi Alpha, 1977-79; treas, bd dir, New York, Pa Health Systems Agency; trustee, Trinity AME Zion Church; pub chmn, Broome Cty NAACP, Alpha Phi Alpha, Iota Theta Lambda, Buddy Camp Assoc, 1970; chmn, Minority Bus Adv Comn, Broome City, NY; IEEE. **Home Addr:** 313 Patio Dr, Endicott, NY 13760, **Home Phone:** (607)748-0519.

JOHNSON, GENEVA B.
Association executive, executive director. **Personal:** Born in Aiken County, SC; daughter of Pierce Bolton and Lillie Mae. **Educ:** Albright Col, BS 1951; Case Western Res Univ, MSSA, 1957. **Career:** YWCA Houston, prog dir; Wernersville State Hosp PA, psychiat socialworker; Childrens Aid Soc, supvr; United Way Berks Co, asst exec dir; United Way DE, dir; United Way Greater Rochester, assoc exec dir; United Way Am, sr vpres; Family Serv Am, pres, chief exec officer, 1983-2004; VistaCare Inc, dir, 2004-. **Orgs:** Consult, Coun Jewish Feds; consult, YWCA; Nat Fel Prog, WK Kellogg Found; Nat Urban League; Big Brothers & Big Sisters Am; Nat Asn Advan Colored People; bd dir, Nat Ctr Learning Disabilities; Found Ctr; Ind Univ Ctr Philanthropy; Case Western Reserve Univ, Mandel Ctr Nonprofit Orgs; Salzburg Sem; Nat Ctr Nonprofit Bd; Wis Energy Corp & Wis Elect & Power Co; fel, Nat Acad Pub Admin. **Honors/Awds:** Hon Doctor Humanities, Albright Col, 1983; Distinguished Service Award,Case Western Reserve Univ, 1983; F Ritter& Hettie L Shumway DistinguishedService Award 1986; Award for Outstanding Service, Nat Urban LeagueMovement. **Special Achievements:** Top 100 Black Business & Professional Women of America, Dollars & Sense Mag, 1986; One of twenty women selected to attend the Jerusalem Women Seminar held in Israel and Egypt. **Business Addr:** Director, VistaCare Inc, 4800 N Scottsdale Rd Suite 5000, Scottsdale, AZ 85251, **Business Phone:** (480)648-4545.

JOHNSON, GEORGE, JR.
Firefighter. **Personal:** Born Apr 15, 1934, Warrenton, GA; children: Inc. **Educ:** Inst Tech; GA Tech; Schell Sch Marking & Mgt. **Career:** Richmond Ca Fire Dept, various positions, 1968-70; chief, 1970-. **Orgs:** E Augusta Action Comm; Augusta-Richmond Co Hum Rel Task Force; GA Asn for Black Elected Officials; Dem Party of GA; Eureka Grand Lodge; NAACP; CSRA. **Honors/Awds:** Involvement Council Award, 1971-72; Big Brother Certification appreciation, GA Asn Retarded Children Inc. **Military Serv:** AUS, sgt, 1951-64. **Home Addr:** 3712 Columbia Dr, Martinez, GA 30907. **Business Addr:** Chief, E Richmond Co, Fire Department, 2618 Richmond Hill Rd, Augusta, GA 30906, **Business Phone:** (706)771-2800.

JOHNSON, GEORGE ELLIS, SR.
Consultant. **Personal:** Born Jun 16, 1927, Richton, MS; son of Charles and Priscilla; married Joan B; children: Eric, John, George Jr & Joan Marie. **Career:** SB Fuller, 1944; Johnson Prod Co Inc, pres & chief exec officer, 1954-89, consult, 1989-. **Orgs:** Independence Bank Chicago; bd dir, Commonwealth Edison Co; Indecorp Inc;Am Health & Beauty Aids Inst; George E Johnson Educ Fund; George E Johnson Found; Babson Col; Boy Scouts Am; Chicago Orchestral Asn; Chicago Sunday Evening Club; Chicago Urban League; Dearborn Park Corp; nat adv comt,Interracial Coun Bus Opportunity; vpres, Jr Achievement Chicago; LyricOpera Chicago; Chicago United; Econ Club of Chicago; The Com Club; Nat Asn Advan Colored People; Nat Asthma Ctr, Northwestern Mem Hosp; Protestant Found Greater Chicago; Northwestern Univ; The Hundred Club Cook; Greater Chicago; chmn, Indecorp. **Honors/Awds:** Abraham Lincoln Ctr Humanitarian Serv Award, 1972; D of Bus Admin, Xavier Univ, 1973; D of Humanities, Clark Col, 1974; D of Com Sci, The Col of the Holy Cross, 1975; DL Babson Col, 1976; DHL Chicago State Univ, 1977; DLFisk Univ, 1977; DL Tuskegee Inst, 1978; Am Black Achievement Award, EbonyMag, 1978; DHL Lemoyne-Owen Col, 1979; Harvard Club Chicago Pub Serv Award, 1979; DL Lake Forest Col, 1979; Horatio Alger Award, 1980; Babson Medal, 1983; Hall of Fame, JA Chicago Bus, 1985. **Special Achievements:** Started his own business Johnson Products Co Inc, a hair care co which achieved listing on Am Stock Exchange in 1971 as First black-owned co to be listed on a maj stock exchange; First African-American to be elected a director on the board of Commonwealth Edison. **Home Addr:** 180 E Pearson St, Chicago, IL 60611. *

JOHNSON, GEORGIA ANNA LEWIS
Physician, publisher. **Personal:** Born Feb 1, 1930, Chicago, IL; daughter of Robert L. Lewis and Sarah Lewis Scoggins; children: Barbara, Ruth, Mary. **Educ:** West Mich Univ, attended 1951; Univ Mich Med Sch, MD, 1955. **Career:** Evanston IL, intern, 1955-56; Ypsilanti St Hosp, physician, 1960-65; Ingham Co Health Dept, physician, 1967-69; Int Med Col, asst prof, 1969-75; Mich State Univ, dir adolescent serv; Olin Health Ctr, staff physician, 1969-87; Georgia A. Johnson Publ Co, publ, currently. **Orgs:** Nat Asn Advan Colored People; Am Med Asn; MSMS; Ingham Co Med Soc; Alpha Kappa Alpha Sorority; AEI Women's Med Fraternity; Kappa Rho Sigma Hon Sci Fraternity; Sickle Cell Anemia Found; bd trust, Capital Area Comp Health Plan Asn; chmn Adv Comt, Health Serv Agency; bd dir, Comp Family Health Proj; hospitality comn, Mich Publishers Asn, 1989-; Great Lakes Booksellers Asn, 1990-. **Honors/Awds:** Scholarship, Jessie Smith Noyes Sch, 1951-55; District Alumna Award, West Mich Univ, 1972. **Special Achievements:** Publications: Towpath to Freedom, 1989; Webster's Gold, 1990; published by Georgia A Johnson Publishing Company, The Baby Who Knew Too Much, 1993; Black Med Graduates of the Univ of Michigan & Selected Black Michigan Physicians, 1995; Facts, Artifacts and Lies, or the Shackling of Women (comments on the socialization of women); Michigan Senior Olympian, track, 1996-; USA Track & Field, 1997-; Natl Sports Classic, 1997-; XIII World Veterans Athletic Championship, 1999; MI State Champion, USA Power Lifting. **Home Addr:** 2608 Darien Dr, Lansing, MI 48912-4538. **Business Addr:** Publisher, Georgia A. Johnson Publishing Company, 2608 Darien Dr, Lansing, MI 48912-4538.*

JOHNSON, GEORGIANNA
Administrator. **Personal:** Born Dec 13, 1930, Asheville, NC; daughter of Amelia Starks and William Fisher; married Eugene W Smith, Jul 30, 1950; children: Eugenia Smith Sykes. **Educ:** Empire State Univ, NY, 1976; Long Island Univ, NY, BA, sociol, 1976; Hunter Col, NY, MA, Sociol. **Career:** NY State Employ Off, NY, claims examr, 1950-63; Sherman Thursby, NY, ins adjuster, 1963-68; Hosp Joint Diseases, NY, case aide, 1968-79; Orthop Inst, NY, social work asst, 1979-86; Drug, Hosp & Health Care Employees Union, Local 1199, NY, pres, 1986; Quest Serv Inc, facil dir, currently. **Orgs:** Alpha Kappa Alpha Sorority, 1986; Black Trade Unionists, 1986; Coalition Union Women, 1986; bd mem, Nat Alliance Party, 1989; Nat Asn Advan Colored People. **Honors/Awds:** Equality for Social Justice Award, Health PAC, 1987; Supportive Spirit Award, 37 Women Comn, 1987; Outstanding Achievement Award, NY Urban League, 1987; Service/Action Beyond Call of Duty Award, Cent Brooklyn, 1988; Labor Recognition Award, Nat Asn Advan Colored People, 1988. **Home Phone:** (215)765-0144. **Business Addr:** Facility Director, Quest Services Inc, 1169 Philipsburg-Bigler Hwy, Philipsburg, PA 16866, **Business Phone:** (814)342-1515.

JOHNSON, GERALDINE ROSS
Lawyer. **Personal:** Born May 13, 1946, Moline, IL; married John T; children: Christine E, Glenda R & John T Jr. **Educ:** Augustana Col, BA, 1968; Univ PA Sch Social Work, MSW, 1974; Univ IA Col Law, JD, 1982. **Career:** Linn Co IA Dept Social Servs, caseworker, 1968-69; Children's Serv City St Louis, intake case worker, 1969-70; Get Set Day Care, presch teacher, 1970-72; Franciscan Mental Health Ctr, social worker, 1974-78; Davenport Civil Rights Comn, atty, 1984-86; City Davenport Legal Dept, atty, 1986-. **Orgs:** Iowa State Bar Asn, Scott Co Bar Asn; Sounds Peace Choral Group, 1981-86; Davenport Civil Rights Comn, 1982-84; bd dirs, Family Resources Inc, 1982-; Delta Sigma Theta Pub Serv Sor Inc, 1984-; volunteer United Way, 1986; guest speaker, Upward Bound, Marycrest Sociol Dept, Merit Employ Coun, Blackhawk Col Alpha Ctr; Tabernacle Baptist Church Moline IL; Pulpit Community, 1986. **Special Achievements:** Survey of sex educ literature on file in the British Library by request, 1984.

JOHNSON, GLENN T.
Judge. **Personal:** Born Jul 19, 1917, Washington, AR; son of Floyd and Reola Thompson; married Elaine Bailey; married Evelyn Freeman (deceased); children: Evelyn A & Glenn Jr. **Educ:** Wilberforce Univ Xenia, OH, BS, 1941; John Marshall Law Sch Chicago, JD, 1949, SJD, 1950. **Career:** Judge (retired); State Ill, asst atty gen, 1957-63; Metro Sanitary Dist Greater Chicago, sr atty, 1963-66; Circuit Ct Cook Co, IL, judge, 1966-73; Appellate Ct Ill 1st Dist, justice, 1973-94. **Orgs:** Trustee, Woodlawn AME Ch, 1960-; Judicial Coun Nat Bar Asn, 1970-; Bench & Bar Section Coun, Ill Bar Asn, 1983; fel Am Acad Matrimonial Lawyers, 1972-; World Asn Judges, 1973-; trustee John Marshall Law Sch Chicago; Judicial Coun African Methodist Episcopal Ch, 1976-;

fel Ill Bar Found, 1984-; Nat Asn Advan Colored People; Urban League; YMCA; Chicago Boys & Girls Club; Cook County Bar Asn, Chicago Bar Asn; The Original Forty Club Chicago; Am Bar Asn. **Honors/Awds:** Citation of Merit John Marshall Sch Law, 1970; Judge of Year Cook, County Bar Asn, 1973; Certificate of Appreciation, Ill State Bar Asn, 1975-76; Outstanding Serv, Nat Bar Asn, 1970. **Special Achievements:** Work paper (Madrid, Spain) Sentencing Procedures in the US of America, 1979; Work paper San Paulo, Brazil) Recent Trends in Family Law in the US, 1981; Work paper (Cairo, Egypt) The Legal Response To Child Snatching In US, 1983. **Military Serv:** AUS, chief warrant officer-3, 1942-46; NG, 1950-59; Reserve, 1959-63. **Home Addr:** 5050 S Lake Shore Dr, PO Box 2203, Chicago, IL 60615-3217, **Home Phone:** (312)493-1628.

JOHNSON, GOLDEN ELIZABETH
Lawyer, educator. **Personal:** Born Mar 21, 1944, Newark, NJ. **Educ:** Douglass Col, AB, 1965; Rutgers Newark Sch Law, JD, 1971. **Career:** Spec Res Lab, microbiologist, 1965-68; Newark Legal Serv, intern, 1969; W Kinney Jr HS, teacher, 1969; US Atty Off, intern, 1970; State NJ, dep atty & gen, 1971-72; Comn Leagl Action Workshop, proj dir, 1972-74; Newark Munic Ctr, judge, 1974-77; Hoffmann-La Roche Inc, atty, 1974; Rutgers Law Sch, prof, 1976-; Hoffman La Roche Inc, gen atty, 1977-. **Orgs:** NJ Col Med & Denist Bd Concerned Citizens, 1972-75; NJ Adv Bd US Comn Civil Rights, 1973-77; liaison, City Newark Essex Co Fed Dem Women, 1977; Nat Coun Negro Women; chap mem, Asn Black Women Lawyers; 100 Women Integration Govt; Rutgers Newark Sch Law Alumni Asn; NJ State Bar Asn; Essex Co Bar Asn; Garden State Bar Asn; Bd Govt & Exec Comn, Nat Bar Asn; pres, Women's Div Nat Bar Asn; bd trustees, NJ State Opera; bd trustees & chmn, Newark-Essex Co Legal Serv & Joint Law Reform; bd dir, Cent Ward Girls Club; bd dir, Leaguers Inc; NAACP; Guild Legal Serv; hon mem, Zeta Alpha Iota, 1977; Douglass Soc. **Honors/Awds:** Community Serv Award, Rutgers Law Sch, 1972; Community Serv Award, Donald Tucker Civic Asn, 1974; Achievement Award, Essex Co Civic Asn, 1975; BlackWoman Achievement Award, COM-BIN-NATION, 1975; Award, Nat Coun Negro Women, 1975; Achievement Award, NJ Reg Fedn Colored Women's Club, 1975; outstanding Achievement, NJ Fedn Colored Women's Club, 1975; Achievement Award, Delta Sigma Theta, 1975; Community Serv Award, Newark Title 1 Cent Parents Coun, 1975; Achievement Award, Neward Sect Nat Coun Negro Women, 1975; Award Excellence, Oper PUSH, 1975; Community Serv Award, Roosevelt Homes Housing Proj, 1975; Achievement Award, Nat Asn Negro Bus & Prof Women's Clubs, 1975; Community Serv Award, Essex Co Legal Serv, 1975; Serv Award, Newark Housing Coun Comn, 1976; Distinguished Serv Award, Seton Hall Univ, 1976; Cert Appreciation, Cent Ward Girls Club, 1976; Oper PUSH Tidewa Women Achievement Award, 1976; Achievement Award, Dr Martin Luther King Jr Comn Ctr, 1976; Achievement Award, Guyton-Callahan Post 152, 1976; Outstanding Woman of Year, NJ Jaycee-ETTES, 1977; Alumni Roster Super Merit, E Side HS, 1977; Outstanding Young Woman Am, 1975, 1977.

JOHNSON, HANK
Congressperson (U.S. federal government). **Personal:** Married Mereda Davis Johnson, Esq. **Educ:** Clark College, Bachelors Degree; Texas Southern University, JD. **Career:** Johnson & Johnson Law Group LLC, Lawyer; DeKalb County Commissioner. **Orgs:** House Armed Services Committee; House Committee on the Judiciary; House Committee on Small Business. **Business Addr:** 1133 Longworth House Office Building, Washington, DC 20515, **Business Phone:** (202)225-1605.*

JOHNSON, HAROLD R.
Educator. **Personal:** Born Jan 9, 1926, Ontario;son of Catherine Johnson and Lee Johnson; married Marion; children: Robert Harold, Karen Elizabeth & Alan Douglas. **Educ:** Patterson Collegiate Inst, Windsor; Univ Western Ontario, BA, 1950; Wayne State Univ, MSW, 1957. **Career:** Windsor Labor Comn Human Rights, exec dir, 1951-57; Int Union United Brewery Soft Drink & Distillery Workers Am; United Comm Serv Met Detroit, planning consult, 1957-61; Neighborhood Serv Orgn Detroit, assoc dir, 1961-69; Univ MI, Sch Social Work, prof social work, 1969-95, Health Behavior & Health Educ, prof, 1976-95, dean, 1981-93, spec coun pres, 1993-94, secy,1994-95, prof emer social work, 1996-, dean emer, 1995-; Office Youth Serv State MI, dir, 1970; Univ Regina, 1978; Univ Toronto, vis fac, 1978-84; Temple Univ, fac, 1978; Univ MI Senate, chmn. **Orgs:** Nat Asn Social Workers; chmn, Met Detroit Chap, 1963-64; Mayor's Develop Team Detroit, 1967; Wayne Co Planning Comn, 1968-69; Ctr Urban Studies Wayne State Univ, 1969; City Detroit-Charter Revision Comn, 1971; consult, Mich Comn Corrections, 1972; US Dept Justice, 1972; Famiy Neighborhood Serv So Wayne Co, 1972; Met Fund, 1971; pres, Asn Gerontology Higher Educ, 1979; consult, Province Alberta, 1979; fel, Gerontological Soc; Acad Certified Social Workers; Asn Black Soc Workers; chmn, Blue Ribbon City Comt Wayne Co; vpres & chmn, Prog Com Northeastern Wayne Co Child Guidance Clinic; Detroit Public Sch Res Panel; vchmn, Mich Comm Criminal Justice; comnr, Am Bar Asn, 1985-91, 1993-98; consult, Yeungnam Univ, Republic Korea, 1984-; consult, Univ IA, 1987; consult, Chicago COT Trust, 1992-97. **Honors/Awds:** Alumni of the Year Award, Wayne State Univ, 1985. **Special Achievements:** Author of numerous reports & papers. **Military Serv:** Royal Canadian Armoured Corps sgt. **Home Addr:** 3000 Glazier Way, Ann Arbor, MI 48105. **Business Addr:** Professor Emeritus, Dean Emeritus, University of Michigan, School of Social Work, Rm 3768 SSWB 1080 S Univ, Ann Arbor, MI 48109, **Business Phone:** (734)763-5971.

JOHNSON, ESQ. HARRY E, SR.
Lawyer, educator, association executive. **Personal:** Born Sep 29, 1954, St Louis, MO; married Karen; children: Jennifer, Harry Jr, & Nicholas. **Educ:** Xavier Univ, BS, polit sci; Wash Univ, pub admin; Thurgood Marshall Sch Law, JD. **Career:** Tex Southern Univ, Thurgood Marshall Sch Law, adj prof, currently; Alpha Phi Alpha Fraternity Inc, pres; Wash DC Martin Luther King Jr Nat Memorial Proj Found Inc, pres & ceo, currently. **Orgs:** Nat Bd Dirs Big Bros Big Sisters Am, 2001; coun pres, Nat Pan Hellenic Coun; Nat Bar Asn; Am Bar Asn; Nat Asn Advan Colored People; Boy Scouts Am; 100 Black Men. **Business Addr:** President, Chief Executive Officer, Washington DC Martin Luther King Jr National Memorial Project Foundation Inc, 401 F St NW Suite 334, Washington, DC 20001, **Business Phone:** 888-484-3373.

JOHNSON, HARVEY
Government official, mayor. **Personal:** Born in Vicksburg, MS; married Kathy Ezell; children: Harvey III & Sharla. **Educ:** Tennessee State Univ, BS, Polit Sci; Univ Cincinnati, MS. **Career:** Miss Gaming Bd, comnr; City Jackson MS, mayor, 1997-2005; Jackson State Univ, prof. **Orgs:** Miss Munic League; Metro Jackson Chamber Com; Nat Urban Fel Inc; Comn Cols Southern Asn Cols & Schs. **Special Achievements:** First African American mayor of Jackson, MS.

JOHNSON, DR. HENDERSON A, III
Executive, school administrator, dentist. **Personal:** Born Dec 19, 1929, Nashville, TN; son of Minerva Hatcher Johnson and Henderson A Johnson; married Gwendolyn Gregory, Jun 14, 1952; children: Gregory Paul, Andrea Lynn & H Andrew IV. **Educ:** Fisk Univ, BS(Hons), 1950; Springfield Col, MA, MS, 1951; Med Col VA, RPT, 1952; Western Reserve Univ Sch Dent, DDS, 1959. **Career:** School administrator (retired), dentist; H Andrew Johnson DDS, Inc, pres, 1959-89; Western Reserve Sch Dent, clin instr, 1966-69; Highland View Hosp, staff, 1985; Pvt Pract Dent, 1988-; Mgt Office Design Inc, pres, 1982-86; Enhancement Project Cuyahoga Community Col, dir Dent Prog, 1985-89; Cuyahoga Community Col, dist dir, 1986-94. **Orgs:** Chmn, Cuyahoga Community Col Found, 1971-84, chmn emer, 1991; pres, Shaker Heights Pub Libr 1978-83; dir, Cleveland Pub Radio WCPN, 1983-89; vpres, Ctr Human Rels, 1984-88; vpres, Cleveland Pub Radio WCPN, 1986-89; Ohio Educ Broadcast Network Comn, 1988-91, bd, 1992, vice chair, 1995-; consult, Metro Heights Hosp Found; Comn Accreditation Am Phys Ther Asn. **Honors/Awds:** Citizen of the year, Omega Psi Phi Fraternity, Cleveland, 1974; Distinguished Alumni Award, Fisk Univ, 1976; Elected to the International Col of Dentists, 1986; Alumni Achievement Award, Fisk Univ, 1998; Independence Award, MetroHealth Ctr Rehabilitation, 1998. **Military Serv:** USAF, First Lt, 1953-54. **Home Addr:** 20876 Fairmount Blvd, Cleveland, OH 44118-4840. **Business Addr:** Dentist, 2475 E 22nd St Suite 204, Cleveland, OH 44115, **Business Phone:** (216)566-7770.

JOHNSON, HENRY
Educator. **Personal:** Born Mar 15, 1937, Atlanta, GA; son of Dr K M Johnson; children: Eric, Ian, Stephanie & Rhonda. **Educ:** Morehouse Col, BA; Atlanta Univ, MSW; Univ Mich, post-grad fel, Menninger Found. **Career:** Ft Wayne State Sch, psychiat social worker, 1960-62; Menninger Clin Kans,trainee post-grad psyciat social work, 1962-63; WJ Maxey Boys Training Sch, Mich, dir group care & coun div, 1964-70; Northville State Hosp Soc Serv Dept, conx group serv 1966-69; Opportunity Sch Educ, Univ Mich, assoc dir prog educ 1970-72; Univ Mich, vpres stud serv, 1972-90, vpres community affairs, 1990, Alumni Assn, sr consult, 1992, vpres student affairs emer, currently. **Orgs:** Trustee Ann Arbor Sch Dist, 1968-74; atty gen adv brd, State Mich, 1972; United Fund chmn, Univ Mich, 1973; regional vpres, NASPA IV-E, 1976-78; NCent Assn, consult evaluator, 1984; sire archon, Sigma Pi Phi Frat, 1986-88; trust adv brd Charitable Trust; state brd Mich Assn emotionally Disturbed C; chmn, Washtenaw United Way; Univ Mich, Alumni assn, srconsult, 1992-; Henry Johnson Assoc Urban Ministry, Presbytery Detroit. **Honors/Awds:** Huron Valley Social Worker of the Year, 1973; Inst Higher Educ, Harvard Univ, Cert, 1984; Paul Harris Fel, Rotary Int, vpres, emeritus, Univ of, MI,1996-. **Special Achievements:** First African American administrator at University of Michigan, 1972. **Business Addr:** Vice President for Student Affairs Emeritus, University of Michigan, 911 N Univ Ave, Ann Arbor, MI 48109, **Business Phone:** (734)763-4003.

JOHNSON, HENRY WADE
Media executive. **Personal:** Born Jun 13, 1947, Boston, MA; son of Henry and Helen Wade; married Naja Griffin; children: Shavi Kharim Uhuru & Damani Kharim Ode. **Educ:** Harvard Col, BA, 1970. **Career:** PBS-Boston, WGBH-TV, filmmaker, 1970-79; Blackside Inc, producer, developer, 1979; Rainbow TV Workshop, vpres prod, 1979-84; TV series prod, 1985-89; Warner Bros TV, vpres prod, currently. **Orgs:** African-Am Entertainment Coalition; bd dir, Westside Prep; Black Filmmakers Found; Dirs Guild Am; Asn Producers & Assoc Producers. **Honors/Awds:** Man of the Year, Am Soc Lighting Designers, 1991; Sandra Eves Manly Team Player Award, Nat Asn Advan Colored People, 1993. **Special Achievements:** Producer: "Two of Hearts," 1979; "The Children Shall Lead," 1979; "Righteous Apples," "The Young Landlords," "The Grand Baby"; television series: "Growing Pains," 1985-90; "Just the Ten of US," 1987-90; developer/producer: "Eyes on the Prize," 1979. **Home Addr:** 920 S Genesee Ave, Los Angeles, CA 90036, **Home Phone:** (213)936-6306. **Business Addr:** Vice President, Warner Bros TV, 3400 Riverside Dr, Burbank, CA 91522, **Business Phone:** (818)846-1403.

JOHNSON, HERMON M., SR.
Executive, government official, insurance agent. **Personal:** Born May 5, 1929, Gilbert, LA; son of Samuel Vanora and Comay Anderson; married Alfreta Thompson; children: Hermon, Jr, Cheryl Lynn, Darryl, Josef. **Educ:** Southern Univ, Baton Rouge, BS, 1955; Miss Valley State Col, elem teacher cert, 1959. **Career:** Magnolia Mutual Life Ins Co, off mgr, 1955-59; Myrtle Hall Sch, teacher, 1964-66; community & action specialist, 1966-68; Tufts Delta Health Ctr, econ develop specialist, 1967-73; Community Health Educ, dir, 1973; Dept Patient Health Serv & Resource Coord, dir, 1973-; Paul Revere Life Ins Co, sales rep; Poultry Farms Inc, stock agt; Hermon Johnson Ins, ins agent, currently. **Orgs:** Dir, Mound Bayou Credit Union, 1960-71; vice-mayor, Alderman Mound Bayou, 1961; pres, Mound Bayou Develop Corp, 1961-63; asst ctr dir, Delta Health Ctr, 1975-77; pres, Delta Housing Develop Corp; Am Legion Post 220; Mound Bayour Civic Club; Mound Bayou Conversation & Recreation League; trustee, Bethel AME Church. **Honors/Awds:** Rookie of the Yr Award, 1995; Achiever Award, 1986-87; Challenger Award, 1990; Life ANA Award, 1991. **Military Serv:** AUS, corp, 1951-53. **Home Addr:** PO Box 262, Mound Bayou, MS 38762. **Business Addr:** Insurance Agent, Hermon Johnson Insurance, 201 NW Main Ave, Mound Bayou, MS 38762-7800.*

JOHNSON, HESTER
Automotive executive. **Career:** Metro Lincoln-Mercury Inc, vpres, gen mgr.

JOHNSON, I S LEEVY
Executive, president (organization), funeral director. **Personal:** Born May 16, 1942, Richland County, SC; married Doris. **Educ:** Benedict Col SC, BS, 1965; Univ SC Sch Law, JD, 1968; Univ Minn, Mortuary Sci. **Career:** SC Gen Assembly; Benedict Col, instr; Funeral Dir, licensed embalmer; Johnson Toal & Battiste PA, pres, atty, 1976-; Leevy Johnson Funeral Home Inc, owner, currently; Columbia Develop Corp, dir; First Union Bank Carolinas, dir; First Union Nat Bank SC & Southern Bank & Trust Co, dir; Victory Savings Bank, dir. **Orgs:** fel, Am Bar Asn; Am Col Trial Lawyers; chmn bd trustees, SC State Col; mem exec comt & bd dirs, First Union Nat Bank SC. **Honors/Awds:** Order of the Palmetto Award, 1999; Durant Award, SC Bar; Complete Lawyer Award, Univ SC Sch Law; John W Williams Award, Richland County Bar; Matthew J Perry Medallion, Columbia Lawyers Asn. **Special Achievements:** One of the first three African-Americans elected to the South Carolina General Assembly since reconstruction, and was the first African-American elected President of the South Carolina Bar. **Business Addr:** Attorney, Johnson Toal & Battiste PA, 1615 Barnwell St, Columbia, SC 29201-2925, **Business Phone:** (803)252-9700.*

JOHNSON, IOLA VIVIAN
Journalist. **Personal:** Born Oct 10, 1950, Texarkana, AR. **Educ:** Univ Ariz, polit sci & jour, 1971. **Career:** Wash Post DC, summer intern, 1969; AR Daily Wildcat Univ Ala, staff writer, 1971; KVOA TV Tucson, reporter, anchor/photogr, 1971-73; The Periscope Tucson, managing ed, 1972-73; WFAA TV Dallas, anchor, reporter & talk show host, 1973-85; KTVT-TV CBS 11, reporter, currently. **Orgs:** Wigma Delta Chi, 1968; Am Women Radio & TV; Nat Asn Black Journ; chmn pub comt, Dallas Chap Links Inc; Am Quarter Horse Asn; Tex Palimino Horse Breeders Asn. **Honors/Awds:** Best Anchor Person in Dallas, Ft Worth Dallas Morning News Readers Poll, 1980; Most Popular Woman in Dallas, Dallas Mag; Life Time Achievement Award, Dallas Forth-Worth Asn Black Communicators. **Special Achievements:** First woman and the first African American to write for the ten o'clock news for the NBC affiliate KBOA in Tucson, Arizona; first woman and the first black news anchor in Dallas. **Business Addr:** Reporter, KTVT-TV CBS 11, 5233 Bridge St, Fort Worth, TX 76103.*

JOHNSON, DR. IVORY
College teacher, school principal, executive director. **Personal:** Born Jun 11, 1938, Oakland, MS; married. **Educ:** Harris Teachers Col, St Louis, AA, 1960; BA, 1962; St Louis Univ, M.Ed, 1969; PhD, 1974. **Career:** St Louis Bd Educ, teacher, 1962-69; NDEA fel, 1968; Urban Rural Teacher Renewal Inst, St Louis Pub Sch Syst, consult, 1974; Berkeley Sch Dist, St.Louis, elem sch prin; St Louis Univ, instr; Ferguson-Florissant Reorganized Sch Dist, Title I, prog dir, Fed Progs, exec dir, currently. **Orgs:** Mo State Teachers Asn; St Louis Suburban Prin Asn; Mo Asn Elem Sch Prin;

White House Conf Educ; Nat Asn Elem Sch Prin; Urban League; YMCA; Mo PTA; bd dirs, Metroplex; Kappa Alpha Psi; northeast coordr, Learn & Serv. **Honors/Awds:** J Jerome Peters Professionalism Award, Kappa Alpha Psi, 1975. **Business Addr:** Executive Director, Ferguson-Florissant School District, 1005 Waterford Dr, Florissant, MO 63033, **Business Phone:** (314)506-9089.

JOHNSON, J. BERNARD
Entrepreneur. **Personal:** Born Oct 4, 1942, New Bern, NC; son of Jethro Johnson (deceased) and Clarestine Royal; married Zandra Sue Troxler, Nov 1967; children: Zaundra Yolanda, Rhonda Pillar. **Educ:** NCA Col Durham, BS, bus admin, 1964; Univ Pa, Wharton Sch, MBA, 1973. **Career:** Stern's Dept Store, buyer trainee, 1964-65; IBM corp, regional adr, 1965, 1967-71; Peat Marwick Mitchell, bus consult, 1971-73; Region F HTH Planning Corp, asst dir, 1973-75; EF Hutton, stockbroker, 1975-77; Barclays Am, financial analyst, 1977-79; YoRhon Packaging, chief exec officer, 1979; SB & J Enterprises Inc, pres, currently. **Orgs:** Chmn, bod, bd finance, First Baptist Church-W; budget adv chmn, City Charlotte; small bus adv chmn, Charlotte Chamber Com; bd dirs, The Employers Asn; bd dirs, United Way; bus adv, bd visitors, Johnson C Smith Univ; bd treas, United Family Serv, 2 yrs; bd mem, Pvt Indust Coun; chmn, Charlotte/Mecklenburg Schs; Vocational Devel adv Coun. **Honors/Awds:** Certificate of Appreciation, Cent Piedmont Community Col, 1985; Participation Cert, United Way Leadership Devel, 1987; Certificate of Appreciation, Charlotte Bus League, 1986; Certificate of Appreciation, City of Charlotte, 1985, 1987; Certificate of Appreciation, United Family Services, 1988; Certificate of Appreciation, NC Dept Public Instruc, 1987. **Military Serv:** USY, spc 4, 1965-67. **Business Addr:** President, SB & J Enterprises Inc, PO Box 32051, Charlotte, NC 28202, **Business Phone:** (704)376-0018.*

JOHNSON, J. LEON
Lawyer. **Personal:** Born Aug 22, 1961, Searcy, AR; married Tamara, Jun 19, 2003; children: James, Bowman. **Educ:** Harding Univ, BS, 1983; Univ Arkansas, Sch Law, JD, 1988. **Career:** Wilson & Assoc, assoc partner, 1991-01; Pulaski Co Circuit Judge, 2000; atty, 2001-; Arkansas Atty Gen, 2003. **Orgs:** Pres, W Harold Flowers Law Soc; bd of dirs, Ronald McDonald House; American Studies Bd, Harding Univ. **Honors/Awds:** Alumni of Year, Harding Univ, 2003. **Business Addr:** Attorney, 323 Cent Suite 1050, Little Rock, AR 72201, **Business Phone:** (501)223-3071.*

JOHNSON, DR. JAMES EDWARD
School administrator. **Personal:** Born Sep 1, 1931, Cuthbert, GA; married Mable Lumpkin; children: James Jr, Meryl & Joni. **Educ:** Morehouse Col, BS, 1956; Atlanta Univ, MA, Ed Adm, 1971, EdD, Ed Adm, 1980. **Career:** School administrator (retired); DeKalb County Schs, teacher, 1956-57; Atlanta Pub Schs, teacher, 1957-60; Herff Jones Co, mfr rep, 1961-69; Atlanta Pub Sch, coordr personnel, 1969-71, prin, 1971-73, dir personnel, 1973-74, dir employee rels & personnel, 1976, assoc supt, 1994. **Orgs:** Secy chmn, Scholarship Comn Alpha Phi Alpha Frat, 1955-; del, Nat Educ Asn Atlanta Teacher Asn & GA Asn Educs, 1956-; committeeman Radcliffe PresbyCh, 1956-; committeeman scoutmaster BSA, 1957-; Worker YMCA 1961-; Official Quarterback Club, 1957-; Jr C of C, 1962-64; Atlanta C of C, 1963-64; bd dir, Grady Homes Boys Club, 1965-; del, Am Asn Sch Personal Admins, 1970-71; consult GA Sch Bd Asn, 1975; consult GA C of C, 1976; Asn Educ Neg, 1976-; consult, MS Educ Serv Ctr, 1976; consult, GA Asn EducLeaders, 1976; consult, GA Asn Educs, 1976; consult, Prof Asn GA Educrs, 1977. **Honors/Awds:** Deans List Morehouse Col; Beta Kappa Chi Sci Hon Soc; Top Salesman Award, Herff Jones Co; Dist Serv Award, Morehouse Col; EPDA; fel Doctoral Cand, Atlanta Univ. **Military Serv:** USMC, sgt, 1951-54. **Home Addr:** 425 Fielding Lane SW, Atlanta, GA 30311. *

JOHNSON, JAMES H.
Labor activist. **Personal:** Born Aug 5, 1932, Mohobe, MS; son of Eugene G and Leesie Sowell; married Carrie B Miller; children: Carrie Arlena, Michele Francine, Yolanda Clarice, Vivian Jamie. **Educ:** Wells HS Chicago, IL. **Career:** Labor activist (retired). Kentile Flrs Inc, Chicago, IL, prod worker, 1956-69; URW Akron, OH, field rep, 1969-77, dist dir, 1977-96; Cent Church God, assoc pastor, 1973-84, pastor, 1984-87; pastor, Johnson Memorial Church God, 1987. **Orgs:** Organizer & first pres, Bellwood Community, 1976-79; bd dir & adv, A Philip Randolph, 1980-83; Nat Asn Advan Colored People, 1980; bd dirs, IPAC, 1983-. **Military Serv:** USMC, pfc, 1952-55; Nat Defense Serv; Korean Serv Medal, w/2 stars; UN Serv Medal; Korean PUC. *

JOHNSON, DR. JAMES KENNETH
Surgeon, physician. **Personal:** Born Oct 9, 1942, Detroit, MI; son of William R and Frances C Brantley; married Jean E Hayes, Jul 11, 1965; children: Kalyn J Johnson & Kendell J Johnson. **Educ:** Wayne State Univ, Detroit, MI, BS, 1964; Meharry Med Col, Nashville, TN, MD, 1969; Yale Univ, New Haven CT, 1973-76. **Career:** Strong & Johnson MD, PC, Detroit, MI, physician, surgeon, 1976-; Southwest Detroit Hosp, Detroit, MI, med dir, vpres med affairs, 1986-. **Orgs:** Pres, Detroit Med Soc, 1988-. **Honors/Awds:** Distinguished teacher, Dept Family Practice, Wayne State Univ Med Sch, 1983. **Military Serv:** AUS, major, 1971-73. **Home Addr:** 6506 Spruce Dr, Birmingham, MI 48009. **Business Addr:** Vice President of Medical Affairs, Southwest Detroit Hospital, 2401 20th St, Detroit, MI 48216, **Business Phone:** (313)496-7700.

JOHNSON, JAMES WALTER
Lawyer. **Personal:** Born May 12, 1941, Washington, DC; married Eva M Murdock; children: Kimberely, Stephanie & Christopher. **Educ:** Howard Univ, BS, 1963; George Wash Univ, MS, 1969, JD, 1971. **Career:** Lockheed Missile & Space Co, assoc engr, 1963-64; US Patent Off, examiner, 1965-66; Mitre Corp, staff, 1968-71; Commun Satellite Corp, patent atty, 1971-74; GE Co, div patent consult, 1974-78; Intelsat, patent consult; Air Line Pilots Asn, managing atty, currently. **Orgs:** DC Bar Asn; Pa Bar Asn; Nat Bar Asn; Am Patent Lawyers Asn; reg, US Patent Atty; Kappa Alpha Psi; VA Bar Asn. **Military Serv:** AUS, capt, 1966-68. **Business Addr:** Managing Attorney, Air Line Pilots Association, 535 Herndon Pkwy, Herndon, VA 20170, **Business Phone:** (703)689-4323.

JOHNSON, JARED MODELL
Executive, school administrator. **Personal:** Born Oct 31, 1960, Milwaukee, WI; son of Wilbert David and Florence Ladon. **Educ:** Milwaukee Area Tech Col, 1980; UNIV WIS, Milwaukee, 1984. **Career:** Aspii Contracting & Develop Corp, pres. **Orgs:** Milwaukee Pub Sch. *

JOHNSON, JAY
Radio broadcaster. **Personal:** Born Apr 2, 1947, Louisville, KY; married Arneda Moncure; children: Jason Troy, Tiffany Faye. **Educ:** Triton Col. **Career:** WGRT Radio, announcer, 1968-71; WVON Radio, announcer, 1971-75; WBBM-TV, announcer, 1974-75; WISH-TV, reporter & host, 1978-85; WTLC-FM, prog dir, 1975-; "Solid Gold Soul", ABC Radio, host, currently; Jay Johnson Ent, pres. **Orgs:** bd mem, Am Lung Asn; consult, Ind Black Expo, Ctr for Leadership Develop; comt mem, PAXI 10th Pan Am Games, 1986-87. **Honors/Awds:** Air Personality, Prog Dir of the Yr, Billboard mag, 1974,80,82; Air Personality, Prog Dir of the Yr, Black Radio Exclusive mag, 1977-79, 1985-86; Super Jay Johnson Day City of Indianapolis, 1977; Outstanding Serv as Host, UNCF, 1978-85; Excellence Award Oper PUSH, 1981; Success Award, Black Woman Hall of Fame Found, 1984. **Military Serv:** AUS, 3 yrs. *

JOHNSON, JAZZ VOYD. See JOHNSON, CHARLES FLOYD.

JOHNSON, JEAN
President (organization), chief executive officer. **Educ:** BS, bus admin; MS, energy, environ & nat resource law; Juris doctorate degree; assoc degree, criminal justice. **Career:** Fortune 5 Co, practicing lawer; Legal Watch Inc, pres & chief exec officer, 1997-. **Orgs:** Bd govs, Nat Bar Asn; bd dirs, Houston Minority Bus Coun; bd dirs, Houston Womens Bus Coun; Women's Bus Enterprise Nat Coun's Nat Leadership Forum; pres, Houston Lawyers Asn; Houston Bar Asn; State Bar Tex; bd dir, Women Impacting Public Policy, bd dir, NatInstitute for the Severely Disabled & AVANCE. **Special Achievements:** First Vice Chair of the National Bar Association's Women Lawyers Division. **Business Phone:** (713)864-9997.*

JOHNSON, JEH CHARLES
Lawyer. **Personal:** Born Sep 11, 1957, New York, NY; son of Jeh Vincent and Norma Edelin; married Susan DiMarco Johnson, Mar 18, 1994; children: Jeh Charles Jr & Natalie M. **Educ:** Morehouse Col, BA, 1979; Columbia Law Sch, JD, 1982. **Career:** Paul Weiss Rifkind Wharton & Garrison, assoc, 1984-88, partner, 1992-98, atty, 2001-, partner, currently; Asst United States Atty, SDNY, 1989-91; Gen Counsel US Air Force, 1998-2001. **Orgs:** Dir, The Legal Aid Soc, 1994-98; dir, New York Hall Sci, 1998; dir, Film Soc Lincoln Ctr, 1995-98; trustee, Adelphi Univ, 2001-; Am Law Inst; vice chair, Asn Bar city. **Honors/Awds:** Benjamin E Mays Service Award, Morehouse Col, 2003; Milton S Gould Award, NY Univ Law Sch. **Business Addr:** Partner, Attorney, Paul Weiss, Rifkind Wharton & Garrison, 1285 Ave of the Americas, New York, NY 10019-6064, **Business Phone:** (212)373-3093.

JOHNSON, JEH VINCENT
Architect, lecturer. **Personal:** Born Jul 8, 1931, Nashville, TN; son of Charles Spurgeon and Marie Burgette; married Norma Edelin; children: Jeh Charles & Marguerite Marie. **Educ:** Columbia Col, AB, 1953; Columbia Univ, MArch, 1958. **Career:** Paul R Williams, architect, designer, draftsman, 1956; Adams & Woodbridge Architects, designer, 1958-62; Gindele & Johnson PC, architect pres, 1962-80; Vassar Col, lectr art & design, 1964-2001; LeGendre Johnson McNeil Architects, partner 1980-90; Jeh V Johnson, FAIA, architect 1990-. **Orgs:** Am Inst Arch, 1963-; founder, Nat Org Minority Arch, 1972-; New York St Arch Registration Bd, 1973-84; dir, Bank Hudson, 1977-01; consult, Dutchess County Planning Bd, 1984-; Sigma Pi Phi; dir Scenic Hudson, Inc, 1996-. **Honors/Awds:** Students Medal AIA, NY, 1958; William Kinne Fel Traveling Fel, Europe, 1959; elected Fel, Am Inst Arch, 1977; designed over 300 major projects & 4300 housing units 1963-02. **Military Serv:** AUS, sargent, 1953-55. **Business Addr:** Professor, Vassar College, 202B New Eng Bldg, Poughkeepsie, NY 12604, **Business Phone:** (914)437-5472.

JOHNSON, JERRY CALVIN
Athletic coach, educator, athletic director. **Personal:** Born Jun 20, 1920, Tulsa, OK; married Vaster M; children: Jerry C Jr, Wandra Haywood & Oliver. **Educ:** Fayetteville State Univ, BS, 1950; Columbia Univ, MA, 1951. **Career:** Educator, Basketball Coach (retired); Ridgeview High Sch, teacher, coach, 1951-58; LeMoyne Owen Col, athletic dir & coach, prof health phys educ & recreation, 1959, head coach & adj prof educ. **Orgs:** Vol, Am Red Cross, 1959-; consult, Nat Youth Sports Prog, 1972-82; bd dir, Memphis Shelby City Old Age, 1975-80; adv coun, Tenn State Bd Educ, 1984-; vpres, Southern Intercollegiate Conf, 1984; Memphis Sports Authority; Tenn Gov Adv Coun C Disabilities; Boys Club Memphis; Amateur Athletic Union; Black Coaches Asn; Memphis Black Bus Asn. **Honors/Awds:** Coach of the Year, NCAA 100% Wrong Club, 1975; Faculty Member of the Year, LeMoyne Owen Col, 1980; Recreation Award, Memphis Park Comn, 1985; State Basketball Coach of the Year, 1999; Honorary Doctorate, LeMoyne Owen Col, 1999; SIAC Hall of Fame; Vanguard Club Achievement Award; Kodak Coach of the Year; Vanguard Club Coach of the Year; Fayetteville Hall of Fame Inductee; Black Col Legend Award; John Thompson-Martin Luther King Jr Classic Coaches Award; SIAC Basketball Coach of the Year. **Special Achievements:** Ranked First among active NCAA Division II Coaches.

JOHNSON, JERRY L.
Executive. **Personal:** Born Dec 4, 1947, Freeport, IL; son of Charles W and Katherine Moseley; married Raye Sandford, May 17, 1968; children: Jeri Lynne & Jonathan Wellesley. **Educ:** Northeast Mo State Univ, Kirksville, Mo, BS, educ & psychol, 1969; Northern Ill Univ, DeKalb, Ill, MS, 1970; Western Ill Univ, Macomb, Ill, educ specialist cert; Mass Inst Technol, Cambridge, Mass, MS, mgt, 1983. **Career:** Galesburg Pub Sch Dist, 205, Galesburg, Ill, prin, 1972-76; NWB Tel Co, Minneapolis, Minn, mgt asst, 1976-81, dist plant mgr, 1981-82; NWB Inf Technol, Omaha, NE, chief exec officer, 1984-85, pres & chief exec officer, 1985; US West Inc, Denver, Colo, vpres-residence planning, 1986-87; US W Home & Personal Serv, Phoenix, Ariz, vpres & gen mgr, 1987-90; US W Commun, Inc, Western Region, Network & Technol Serv, Seattle, Wash, vpres, 1990-92, Network & Technol Serv, vpres, 1993; Safeguard Sci, exec vpres; eMoney Adv Inc, pres, 2002-. **Orgs:** Int Soc Sloan; Vis Comt, Sloan Sch Mgt, Mass Inst Technol; Sigma Pi Phi Boule; Kappa Alpha Psi. **Honors/Awds:** The Title "One of Top 25 Most Powerful Black Executives in Corporate America", 1988, "40 Most Powerful Black Executives", Black Enterprise Mag, 1993. **Home Addr:** 5435 154 Ave SE, Bellevue, WA 98006. **Business Phone:** (610)684-4662.

JOHNSON, JESSE J.
Writer, military leader. **Personal:** Born May 15, 1914, Hattiesburg, MS; married Elizabeth C. **Educ:** Tougaloo Col, AB, 1939; Am Exten Sch Law, LLB, 1950; Hampton Inst, MA, 1964. **Career:** Military leader (retired), writer; USY, lt col, 1942-62; Books: Ebony Brass Signed, 1967; Ebony Brass, 1970; Black Soldiers; Black Armed Forces Officers, 1736-71, 1975; The life and times of U.G. Johnson: Civic and spiritual leader in the Missouri Ozarks: A vignette, 1985. **Honors/Awds:** Doctors of Humane Letters, Tougaloo Col, 2001; Appreciation Award, class of 1952, Va State Univ, 2002. **Military Serv:** USY, lt col, 1942-62. *

JOHNSON, JIMMIE (JIMMIE O JOHNSON, JR.)
Football player, football coach. **Personal:** Born Oct 6, 1966, Augusta, GA. **Educ:** Howard Univ, consumer studies, 1989. **Career:** Football player (retired), Football coach; Wash Redskins, tight end, 1989-91; Detroit Lions, 1992-93; Kansas City Chiefs, 1994; Philadelphia Eagles, 1995-98; Coach: South Carolina, running backs coach, 2001; Shaw Univ, off cord, 2002-03; Texas Southern, off coach, 2004-05; Minnesota Vikings, tight end coach, currently. **Business Phone:** (952)828-6500.

JOHNSON, JIMMIE O, JR. See JOHNSON, JIMMIE.

JOHNSON, JOAN B.
Executive, chairperson, chief executive officer. **Personal:** Born Jan 1, 1929; married George E (divorced 1989); children: Eric. **Career:** Johnson Products Co, Chicago, IL, 1954, vpres, 1965-75, treas & dir, 1975-89, chairwomen & chief exec officer, 1989-98.

JOHNSON, JOE T.
Football player. **Personal:** Born Jul 11, 1972, Cleveland, OH. **Educ:** Univ Louisville. **Career:** Football player (retired); New Orleans Saints, defensive end, 1994-2001; Green Bay Packers, defensive end, 2002-03. **Honors/Awds:** Rookie of the Year, 1994; Pro Bowl, 1998, 2000; Comerback Player of the Year, 2000; Nat football league, 2000; All-Pro Selection, 2000.

JOHNSON, JOHN
Association executive. **Career:** Wayne County Neighborhood Legal Servs, staff atty, supervising atty, dep dir; National Consumer Law Ctr, staff atty; UAW Legal Serv Plans, managing

atty; Legal Aid & Defender Asn, chief counl; NAACP, Detroit Br, exec dir, exec comt currently. **Business Addr:** Executive Committee, NAACP-Detroit Chapter, 2990 E Grand Blvd, Detroit, MI 48202, **Business Phone:** (313)871-2087.

JOHNSON, JOHN
Writer, insurance executive. **Personal:** Born Jun 20, 1938, New York, NY; son of John and Irene; divorced. **Educ:** Ciyt Col NY, BA, 1961, masters, 1963; St. Thomas Aquinas Col, D Lit, 1991. **Career:** NYC Bd Educ, teacher & asst prin, 1960-67; Lincoln Univ, assoc prof, fine arts, 1967-68; ABC News, NY, producer, dir, writer & doc unit, 1968-71; ABC Evening News, NY, corresp, 1971-72; WABC-TV, NY, reporter, 1972-85, anchor, 1985-95; WCBS-TV, NY, anchor, 1995-96; WNBC-TV News, NY, anchor, sr corresp, 1996-97; Author: The Black Power Revolt, 1968; Only Son: A Memoir, 2002; One Man Art Show: John Johnson: Bridges (Recent Paintings), 2003; Walter Wickiser Gallery, Soho, NY, 2003; John Johnson: American Portraits: Recent Paintings, 2004; Group Art Show: Walter Wickiser Gallery, Chelsea, NY, 2005; insurance exec, currently. **Orgs:** AFTRA; DGA. **Honors/Awds:** Best Enterprise Reporting Award, AP, 1977; Emmy, Best Sports Progamming, 1978; Best Documentary Award, AP, 1979; Emmy, Best Spot News, 1982; Emmy, Best Service News, 1982; Nat Broadcast Award for Outstanding Spot News, VPI, 1982; Emmy, Best Investigating Reporting, 1983; Lifetime Achievement Award, NY Asn Black Journalists, 1997; Communications Hall of Fame, City Col NY, 2000. **Military Serv:** Reserve Officers' Training Corps. **Business Addr:** Broadcast Journalist, Author, PO Box 547, Palisades, NY 10964, **Business Phone:** (845)638-2898.

JOHNSON, JOHN J
Association executive. **Personal:** Divorced; children: Gloria, Don, Kavin & Felita. **Educ:** Sojourner-Douglass Col, BS. **Career:** Ky Inst Community Dept, trainer, 1968-69; Southern Ky Econ Opportunity Coun, dir field operations & training, equal opportunity officer, 1969-70; Louisville-Jefferson County, Community Action Comm, supv, 1971-75; Louisville-Jefferson County, Human Rels Comm, assoc dir, 1975-77; Ky Comm Human Rights, dir community serv, 1977-84; Community Action Agency, exec dir, 1984-86; Nat Asn Advan Colored People, Voter Educ Dept, nat dir, 1986-89, Labor Dept, nat dir, 1988-, dir prog, currently, chief progs off, currently; Armed Services & Veteran Affairs Dept, from exec asst to the exec dir, 1989, nat dir, 1990-. **Orgs:** Nat Asn Advan Colored People, Life & Golden Heritage, 1963-; Lampton Baptist Church; Nat Urban League, local chap; nat bd dirs, A Philip Randolph Inst; nat bd dirs, Nat Coalition Black Voter Participation; alternate comnr, Martin Luther King Jr Fed Holiday Comn; bd dirs, Nat Comt Pay Equity; numerous other memberships, 1972-. **Honors/Awds:** Human Service Award, Mae St Kidd Auxiliary, 1984; Distinguished Service in Social Action Nat Award, Phi Beta Sigma Fraternity, 1985; Award of Merit, Ky Conf, Nat Asn Advan Colored People, 1986, Award of Appreciation, 1986; Golden Apple Leadership Award, Ky Dept Educ, 1987; Ambassador of Goodwill Award, City Franklin, KY, 1989; Nat Services Program Award, US Bur Census, 1990; US Dept of Defense Award, 1991; Whitney M Young Jr Award; John J Johnson Avenue, named in honor, 1993. **Business Addr:** Chief Programs Officer, Director of Programs, National Association for the Advancement of Colored People, 4805 Mt Hope Dr, Baltimore, MD 21215-3297, **Business Phone:** (410)358-8900.

JOHNSON, JOHN THOMAS
Physician. **Personal:** Born Feb 8, 1942, St Louis, MO; married Geraldine Ross; children: Christine E, Glenda R, John T Jr. **Educ:** Parsons Col, BS, 1967; Philadelphia Col Osteop Med, DO, 1974. **Career:** Davenport Med Ctr, intern, 1974-75, resident, 1975-76; Pvt Pract, physician, 1976-. **Orgs:** Am Osteop Asn, 1976-; Iowa Osteop Med Asn, 1976-; Scott County Med Soc, 1976-; bd dirs, Davenport Med Ctr; vol physician Silver Gloves, Boy Scouts, 1985. **Honors/Awds:** Roast Sepia Guild, 1977; Certificate of Appreciation, The Honor Community, 1982; Recognition Award, Christian Community Serv, 1982; Calvary SDA Church, 1983; Certificate of Appreciation, Sr Citizens, 1985; Recognition Award, Davenport Medical Ctr, 1986. **Military Serv:** AUS, e4, 1963-65.

JOHNSON, JOHN WILL
Lawyer, college teacher. **Personal:** Born Nov 6, 1934, Claiborne Parish, LA; children: John jr, Julian & Juan. **Educ:** Southern Univ Baton Rouge, BA, 1957; Howard Univ Sch Law, JD, 1962; Georgetown Univ Law Ctr, LLM, 1964. **Career:** US Dept Justice Wash, trial lawyer, 1964-68; Ohio Bell Tel & Co Cleveland Corp ABA, gen atty, 1968-72; AT & T, atty, 1972; NY Law Sch, adj law prof, 1978-. **Orgs:** Nat Bar Asn; NY Bar Asn; Ohio Bar Asn; DC Bar Asn; LA Bar Asn. **Honors/Awds:** Distinguished Service Award, Excellence Law Sch & Prof, New York Law Sch. **Military Serv:** Active military duty, 1957-59. **Business Addr:** Attorney, 2 5th Ave Suite 53, New York, NY 10022, **Business Phone:** (212)777-2068.

JOHNSON, JOHNNIE LOUIS
Lawyer. **Personal:** Born Nov 1, 1946, Nesbit, MS; son of Johnnie Louis Johnson II and Beulah M Merriweather; married Bethiness Theodocia Walker, Jun 7, 1970; children: Johnnie L IV, Gregory Lloyd, Justice Millsaps & Ahmad Nakeill. **Educ:** Morris Brown Col, BA, 1967; Ohio Northern Univ, JD, 1970. **Career:** Dept Justice, asst us atty, 1970-73; Equal Employ Opportunity Comn, asst reg atty, 1973-75, spec asst to comnr, 1975-78, dir trial team II, 1978-81, sr trial coun, 2003-, asst gen coun, 1981-83, dir, Legal & Spec Polit Div, 1983-84, dir spec proj, 1984-85. **Orgs:** Pres, BF Jones Bar Asn, 1970-73; pres, Bd Dirs, Memphis & Shelby City, Legal Serv Asn, 1972-74; first vpres, Memphis Chap, Fed Bar Asn, 1972-74; pres, Morris Brown Col Alumni Assoc, 1985-92; pres, Mediterranean Villa Cluster Asn, 1986-; bd dirs, Ohio Northern Univ Law Alumni Assoc, 1988-; mediator, DC Mediation Serv, 1989-; mediator, Multi-Door Disput Resolutim Ctr, 1990-; pres, Nat Coun EEOC Locals 216, 1998-; pres, AFGE Local 2667, 1998-. **Honors/Awds:** Donnie Delaney Commission Defense Award, 1974; Outstanding Young Man of America, 1979; lectr, Ohio Northern Univ, Col Law, 16th annual Law Rev Symp. **Special Achievements:** Participant in Old Dominion 100 Mile Endurance Run, 1979; Empire State Run Up 1979, 1980; New York City Marathon, 1979, 1980; Marine Corp Marathon 1979, 1980, 1981; JFK 50 Miler 1980. **Home Addr:** 11644 Mediter Ct, Reston, VA 20190-3401, **Home Phone:** (703)471-0848. **Business Addr:** Senior Trial Counsel, Equal Employment Opportunity Commission, 1801 L St NW Suite 7214, Washington, DC 20507, **Business Phone:** (901)544-0136.

JOHNSON, DR. JOHNNY B
Educator. **Personal:** Born Feb 17, 1920, Rison, AR; married Mildred Mazique; children: Johnny Jr, Mrs Patricia Berry & Revawn. **Educ:** Agri Mech & Normal Col, BS, 1948; Mich State Univ, MS, 1948, MA, 1955; Univ Ark, EdD, 1963. **Career:** Educator (retired); Agri, Mech & Normal Col, dean, 1949-61; Univ Ark-Pine Bluff, prof, 1963-73, actg chancellor, 1973-74 & 1976-86, vice chancellor acad affairs, 1974-86, prof, provost & coo, 1985-86; Kiwanis Ga Dist, governer. **Orgs:** Ark Educ Asn; Nat Educ Asn; Am Asn Higher Educ, 1949-86; fel, Southern Educ Found, 1962; trustee, Kiwanis Int Found, 1975-86. **Special Achievements:** Author: A Trail from Poverty to Univ Administator, Vantage Press, 1998; Listed Outstanding Educators of America, 1975. **Military Serv:** AUS, tech sgt, 1942-45; Bronze Star; Outstanding Civilian Service Award, Army Reserve Officers' Training Corps, 1974. **Home Addr:** 67 Watson Blvd, Pine Bluff, AR 71601.

JOHNSON, JON D.
Chairperson, state government official. **Personal:** Born Aug 17, 1948. **Educ:** Southern Univ, BS; Loyola Univ, MBA. **Career:** Teacher, 1969-71; City New Orleans, Mayor's Human Rights Comn, mem, 1974-80; La State House Reps, state rep, 1980-85; La State Senate, state senator, 1985-2002; commodity broker; New Orleans Health Corp, chmn, currently. **Orgs:** Nat Asn MBA Execs; Urban League Greater New Orleans. **Business Addr:** Chairman, New Orleans Health Corp, 1008 Jourdan Ave 2nd Fl, New Orleans, LA 70117, **Business Phone:** (504)947-7775.

JOHNSON, JONATHAN F
Executive. **Career:** Community Pride Food Stores Inc, ceo, 1992; Market Place Holdings Inc, pres & ceo, currently. **Orgs:** Bd trustee, Va Union Univ; Richmond Community Hosp. **Business Addr:** President, Chief Executive Officer, Market Place Holdings Inc, 1301 W Broad St, Richmond, VA 23220, **Business Phone:** (804)353-7760.*

JOHNSON, JOSEPH
Journalist, educator. **Personal:** Born Jan 18, 1940, New York, NY; son of Alonzo D Johnson Sr and Lillian Mae Young; married Harriet Nicole Luria, Aug 1, 1967; children: Jeremiah Joseph. **Educ:** Columbia Univ, BA, 1970; Columbia Univ Teachers Col, MA, 1973; New Sch Social Res, additional studies; Columbia Univ, grad fel art hist & archaeol. **Career:** City Univ City Col, teacher, 1970-71; Ramapo Col NJ, assoc prof lit, 1971-, co-chairperson African Am Inst; Reed Cannon & Johnson Publ, ed & publ, 1973-77; Crisis Mag, book ed. **Orgs:** Chmn, Black Lit Panel NE Modern Language Asn, 1974. **Honors/Awds:** Published poetry book, At the Westend, 1976; published "Hot" Telephone Book, 1977; published Tight, Lee Lucas Press, 1978. **Home Addr:** 365 S End Ave, New York, NY 10280. **Business Addr:** Associate Professor of Literature, Ramapo College of New Jersey, B 206 505 Ramapo Valley Rd, Mahwah, NJ 07430, **Business Phone:** (201)684-7411.

JOHNSON, JOSEPH A.
Educator. **Personal:** Born Jun 9, 1925, Columbus, OH; married Olivia Scott. **Educ:** Allen Univ, BS; Columbia Univ, MBA; NY Univ, MA. **Career:** Bus mgr, 1950-56; Allen Univ, Columbia, SC, asst prof bus, 1968-70, spec servs dir, 1970-73, dir gen studies, 1973-, fed projects dir, 1973-. **Orgs:** Phi Delta Kappa; Province Pole march; Kappa Alpha Psi; chmn, Jacks Columbia Jack & Jill; Bethel AME Church. **Military Serv:** AUS, 1943-45. **Business Addr:** Director, Allen University, Federal Projects, Columbia, SC 29204.

JOHNSON, DR. JOSEPH B.
School administrator. **Personal:** Born Sep 16, 1934, New Orleans, LA; son of Sidney T and Lillie Mickens; married Lula Young; children: Yolanda Dixson, Joseph III, Juliete & Julie. **Educ:** Grambling State Univ, BS, 1957; Univ Colo, Boulder, MS, 1967, EdD, 1973; Harvard Univ, cert, 1976. **Career:** Booker T Washington High Sch, Shreveport, teacher, 1962-63; Greenville Park High Sch, teacher, 1963-69; Univ Colo, Boulder, exec asst to pres, 1975-77; Grambling State Univ, pres, 1977-91; Talladega Col, pres, 1991-98. **Orgs:** NAFEO, Amer Coun Educ, Amer Asn Univ Admins; Officer, YMCA, 1977; Kappa Alpha Psi Fraternity, AME Church; bd trustees, State Colls & Univ State La, chmn, Pres' Coun, 1982-83; chmn Pres's Coun, S western Athletic Conf, 1982-84; Gov's Economic Devel Comm, 1984, comm on cols SACS, 1985; chmn, LA delegation SACS, 1985; Steering Comm for Historically Black Cols; adv Office Educ Res Improvement, US Dept Educ, 1987; mem bd advisors, Who's Who in South & Southwest; bd of dir, Univ of CO Alumni Asn, Boulder, 1989-92; Nat Collegiate Athletic Asn, Pres Comn, 1989-93; Am Asn State Cols & Univs Comm on Humanities. **Honors/Awds:** National Alliance of Business Leadership Award, 1984; Honorary Doctors Law, Western Mich Univ, 'Jewish National Fund Tree of Life Award', 1985; 'Distinguished Service to Education Award', Harris-Stowe State Col, 1987; Distinguished Alumni Achievement Award, Univ of Colo; Thur good Marshall Educ Achievement Award, 1988; Asn of Social & Behavioral Scientists Inc, WEB Dubois Award, 1988; 'Honorary Doctor of Philosophy', Gandhigram Rural Univ, India, 1988; named to La Black History Hall of Fame, 1991. **Military Serv:** AUS, Sgt, 1958-62.

JOHNSON, JOSEPH DAVID
Executive, president (organization), chief executive officer. **Personal:** Born Oct 26, 1945, Poplar Bluff, MO; son of Archie and Curley; married Julie Hamilton; children: Joy Laurice & Joelle Devon. **Educ:** Lincoln Univ, BS, educ, 1968, MS, educ admin, 1969. **Career:** Gen Mills Inc, comp per mgt, 1969-72; Dayton Hudson Corp, sr comp specialist, 1972-73; Int Multifoods Corp, div per mgr, 1973-75; Xerox Corp, various per mgt pos, 1975-83; vpres human resources, 1983-88; The Telein Group Inc, pres & ceo, 1988-. **Orgs:** Life mem, Alpha Phi Alpha Fraternity, 1965-; co-founder, Exchange Inc, Prof Asn, 1973-74; bd dir, Eltrex Indust, 1982-83; pres adv bd, Eltrex Ind, 1984-; bd dirs United States Acad Decathalon, 1986-; Am Comput Asn; Nat Asn Corp Black Profs; Nat Asn Advan Colored People; SCLC; Urban League; PUSH; Lincoln Univ Alumni Asn; bd adv, Univ S Calif Ctr Orgn Effectiveness; exec exchange prog, Nat Urban League; Exec Leadership Coun. **Honors/Awds:** Community Service Award, Orange County Links, 1985; Outstanding Alumni Achievement Award, Lincoln Univ, 1986-87; subject of case study on human resources at the Harvard Business School, 1985; Honorary Doctorate of Laws, Lincoln Univ. **Military Serv:** AUS, (military intelligence) 1st lt, 1970-72; Distinguished Military Graduate Lincoln Univ ROTC Program 1968. **Business Addr:** President, Chief Executive Officer, Telen Group Inc, 4281 Katella Ave Suite 109, Los Alamitos, CA 90720-3587, **Business Phone:** (714)952-4444.

JOHNSON, DR. JOSEPH EDWARD, JR.
Educator. **Personal:** Born Jan 1, 1934?, Wilmington, DE; son of Joseph E Sr (deceased) and Dorothy Dean (deceased); married Karen E Denton; children: Kevin. **Educ:** Cent State Univ, BS, 1957; Seton Hall Univ, MA, 1965; Univ Mass, EdD, 1976. **Career:** Educator (retired); Burnett J High Sch, teacher, 1959-66; Wilm Pub Sch, vprin, 1966-68, prin, 1968-71, dir presonnel & employe rel, 1971-75, asst supt, 1975-77, supt, 1977-78; New Castle Co Sch, dep supt instr, 1978-81; Red Clay Coun Sch Dist, supt, 1981-90. **Orgs:** Am Asn Sch Admin; Phi Delta Kappa Educ Frat; Nat Alliance Black Sch Educs; Kappa Alpha Psi Frat; Sigma Pi Phi Boule; past chmn, bd dir, Del Div Am Cancer Soc, 1987-98; bd dir, Boys Club Del 1985-98; bd dirs, Del Futures; Historical Soc Del; bd dirs, YMCA Delaware, currently. **Honors/Awds:** Superintendent of the Year, Delaware, Delaware Chief Sch Officers, 1989. **Military Serv:** AUS, 1st Lt, 1957-59, Reserve Capt, 1959-66. **Business Addr:** Board of Directors, YMCA, 101 N Wacker Dr, Chicago, IL 60606, **Business Phone:** 800-872-9622.*

JOHNSON, DR. JOSEPH F
College teacher, administrator. **Personal:** Married Rowena Peterson-Johnson; children: Katrina. **Educ:** Fayetteville State Univ, BS, biol educ, 1968; Va State Univ, MEd, sci educ, 1973; Va Polytech Inst & State Univ, CAGS, educ admin, 1981, EdD, educ admin, 1981. **Career:** Richmond Pub Schs, supvr opers & serv; Durham County Schs, asst supt; New Hanover County Schs, assoc supt; Univ NC Wilmington, assoc prof educ; Winston-Salem/Forsyth County Schs, assoc supt admin & support serv; Fayetteville State Univ, Sch Educ, dean & prof educ leadership, 1997-2002, 2004-06, prof educ leadership & coordr master sch admin prog, 2002-04, vice chair, Grad Coun, 2003-04, dir & prof educ leadership prog, 2006-07, prof educ leadership prog, 2006-, HRRC/IRB Comt chair, 2007-. **Orgs:** Cumberland County Libr & Info Ctr Bd Trustees, 1997-2003, chair, 2001-03; Cumberland County Schs Qual Coun, 1999-; chair, NC Comn Raising Achievement & Closing Gaps, 2006-; NC State Libr Comn, 2006-. **Business Addr:** Professor of Educational Leadership Program, Fayetteville State University, Department of Educational Leadership & Foundations, 1200 Murchison Rd, 257 Butler Bldg, Fayetteville, NC 28301-4298, **Business Phone:** (910)672-1700.

JOHNSON, JOSHUA
Photographer. **Personal:** Born Dec 30, 1949, Sumpter, SC; son of William and Marjorie; married Phyllis Graham; children: Terrence

& Derrick. **Educ:** Eastman Kodak Co Rochester NY, Photogr Courses, 1976; Rochester Inst Tech, 1975 & 1977; Rutgers Univ Col, BS, Mgt; NY Microscopical Soc, attended 1981. **Career:** NJ Med Sch & CMDNJ, asst med photogr, 1968-70; NJ Dent Sch, prin bio meddent photogr, 1970-; Univ Med & Dent NJ, biomed photogr & mgr photogr serv, 1984-. **Orgs:** Biology Photographer Asn; NY Microscopical Soc; Lecturer Dentists & Cental Stud Intra Oral Photog; illusr, Many Articles Highly Recognized Nat & Int Dent J; co-founder & First Black Dent Photogr, Educ Commun Ctr NJ Dent Sch; Am Bus Mgt Assoc. **Honors/Awds:** Male Role Model Award, Nat Assn Negro Bus & Prof Women's Club, 1998. **Special Achievements:** Illusr dent textbooks dentists & asst, Four Handed Dentistry Dentists & Asst, 1974; 2nd Book Clinical Mgt Head Neck & TMJ Pain & Dysfunctions,1977; Artical "Clinical Cameraman" Bio med Commun J, 1980. *

JOHNSON, JOYCE COLLEEN
Government official. **Personal:** Born Oct 24, 1939, Terre Haute, IN; married Ronald E. **Educ:** Ind State Univ, BS, 1961. **Career:** Government official (Retired); US Dept Housing & Urban Develop, equal opportunity specialist, 1973-78, multifamily housing rep, 1978-83, dir fair housing & equal opportunity, 1983-91, housing consult, real estate owned br, 1991. **Orgs:** Tutor Boy's Club, 1968-71; educ coordr, Int Toastmistress, 1980-83; botanical mgr, Deco-Plants, 1980-82; consult, Am Cancer Soc, 1982-; regional secy, Alpha Pi Chi Sorority 1983-; housing adv, Nat Asn Advan Colored People, 1984-85. **Honors/Awds:** Scholarship Alpha Pi Chi Sor, 1965; co-author of book Certificate Achievement US Dept Army, 1966; Recognition of Community Involvement NAACP, 1984; Certificate of Excellence Alpha Pi Chi Sor, 1985. **Home Addr:** 9662 Cypress Pine St, Orlando, FL 32827-6852. *

JOHNSON, JULIA L.
Government official. **Personal:** Born Jan 18, 1963, Clermont, FL; daughter of Abraham and Gloria. **Educ:** Univ Fla, BS, bus admin, 1985, Sch Law, JD, 1988. **Career:** Maguire, Voorhis & Wells, assoc, 1988-90; Dept Community Affairs, asst gen coun, 1990-92, legis affairs dir, 1991-92; Fla Pub Serv Comn, comnr, 1992-99, chmn, 1997-99, chmn Internet Task Force, 1999-2001; Fla Power & Light, pres, 1995-2003; Milcom Technologies, sr vpres communs & mkt, 2000-01; Mas Tec Inc, dir; North Western Corp, dir; Netcommunications LLC, pres, 2000-; Allegheny Energy Inc, dir, 2003-. **Orgs:** Nat Asn Regulatory Utility Comnrs, commun's comn; Govs State Energy Adv Coun; State Fla Women's Polit Caucus; Leon County Govt Mgt Efficiency Coun; bd dir, chmn, Boys & Girls Club Big Bend; bd mem, Women Execs State Govt; bd mem, Univ Fla Nat Black Alumni Asn; Women's Polit Caucus; Tallahassee Women Lawyers; Tallahassee Barristers Asn; Nat Bar Asn; Tallahassee Urban League; Dept Energy, Nat Asn Regulatory Utility Comnrs Energy Market Access Bd; mem, Fl bd educ; mem, Department of Energy/Nat Asn Regulatory Utility Comnr Energy Mkt Access Bd. **Honors/Awds:** Twelve Great Women Of Florida, 1994; America's Best & Brightest Business & Professional Men and Women, 1994; Ebony Magazine's Young Leaders of the Future, 1993; Hall of Fame, Univ Fla; Fla Blue Key; Human Relations Award, City Gainesville; Most Outstanding Minority Graduate Award, Univ Fla. **Special Achievements:** Consumer Bulletin, Column featured in 12 Florida African-American Newspapers. **Business Addr:** Director, Allegheny Energy Inc, 800 Cabin Hill Dr, Greensburg, PA 15601-1689.

JOHNSON, JULIANA CORNISH
Manager, founder (originator), president (organization). **Personal:** Born Jun 26, 1957, Salisbury, MD; daughter of Jerome and Julia; married Douglas K, Feb 14, 1989. **Educ:** Cornell Univ, BA (w/Honors) 1978; Harvard Grad Sch Bus, MBA, finan, 1982. **Career:** Chase Manhattan Bank, intern 1978; Huntington Nat Bank, sr analyst 1979-80; The World Bank, intern, 1980; Am Tel & Tel Co, mgr 1982-89; AMACAR Group, founder & pres, currently. **Orgs:** Harvard Alumni Asn, 1982-89, Harvard Grad Sch Bus Black Alumni Asn, 1982-89; Nat Black MBA Asn, 1983-89; sponsor, Oakland Ensemble Theatre, 1984-89; bd dirs, Bay Area Black United Fund 1985-89. **Honors/Awds:** Woodford Memorial Public Speaking Award. **Special Achievements:** Top 50 Fast Track Young Executives Business Week Magazine 1987. **Business Phone:** (704)365-0569.

JOHNSON, HON. JUSTIN MORRIS
Judge. **Personal:** Born Aug 19, 1933, Wilkinsburg, PA; son of Oliver Livingstone Johnson and Irene Olive Morris Johnson; married Florence Elizabeth Lester Johnson, Jun 25, 1960; children: William Oliver, Justin Llewellyn & Elizabeth Irene. **Educ:** Univ Chicago, BA, 1954, Law Sch, JD, 1962; Univ VA, Graduate Program for Judges, 1983. **Career:** Partner/sole proprietor, Johnson, Johnson, & Johnson, 1962-77; Bd Educ, Sch Dist Pittsburgh & Pittsburgh-Mt Oliver Intermediate Unit, asst solicitor, 1964-70, solicitor & asst secretary, 1970-78; Berkman Ruslander Pohl Lieber & Engel, partner, 1978-80; Superior Court PA, judge, 1980-; Duquesne Univ Sch Law, adj prof, 1985-90. **Orgs:** Active elder East Liberty Presbyterian Ch; Nat Conf Bar Examiners, 1969-83; PA Bd Law Examiners, 1969-89, vice chmn, 1975-83, chmn, 1983-89; bd trustees, Mercy Hosp, 1976-93, Southside Hosp, 1978-88, United Way Allegheny Co, 1979-90; Pittsburgh Theol Sem, 1985-93; Carnegie Mellon Univ, 1988-93, 1995-; Princeton Theol Sem, 1992-; Urban League Pittsburgh; hearing comn, PA Supreme Court Disciplinary Bd; past pres & dir, Neighborhood Legal Serv Asn; Am Bar Asn, Nat Bar Asn, PA Bar Asn, Homer S Brown Law Asn; fel, Am Bar Found; adv comt, Nat Consortium on Violence Res, currently. **Honors/Awds:** Bond Medal, Univ Chicago, 1954; Dr Martin Luther King Jr Citizen's Medal, 1973; Top Hat Award, 1981; Homer S Brown Service Award, 1982; Man of the Year, Bethesda Presbyterian Church, 1983; President's Award, PA Trial Lawyers Asn, 1983; Award of Merit, Pittsburgh Young Adult Club, 1983; St Thomas More Award, 1985; Public Service Award, Pittsburgh chapter, ASPA, 1986. **Special Achievements:** Second African-American to serve in Pennsylvania Superior Court. **Military Serv:** USAF, aircraft comdr, 1956-59; USAFR, maj, 1963-73. **Home Addr:** 4911 Ellsworth Ave, Pittsburgh, PA 15213-2806, **Home Phone:** (412)683-7424. **Business Addr:** Judge, Superior Court of Pennsylvania, 330 Grant St Suite 2702 Grant Bldg, Pittsburgh, PA 15219, **Business Phone:** (412)565-3604.

JOHNSON, KALANOS VONTELL
Manager. **Personal:** Born Sep 23, 1971, Toccoa, GA; son of Reginald and Rosilyn. **Educ:** Fort Valley State Univ, BS, social work, 1995; Univ Akron, MA, urban planning, 1997. **Career:** Ga Ctr Youth, prog specialist, 1995; Univ Akron, res asst, 1995-96; summit County Bd MR/DD, intern, 1996-97; Macon-Bibb County Planning & Zoning Comn, city planner, 1997-98; Fulton County Dept Pub Works, transp planner, 1998-2000; Atlanta Regional Comn, prin planner, 2000-; B&E Jackson & Assoc, proj mgr, 2002-04; Wilbur Smith Assocs, 2004-06; Delon Hampton & Associs, Chartered, currently. **Orgs:** Am Planning Asn, 1996-; Inst Transp Engineers, 1999-; Omega Psi Phi Fraternity, Inc, 1994-; Fort Valley State Univ Alumni Asn, 1995-. **Honors/Awds:** Outstanding Young Man of America, 1998; sr scholar, Omega Psi Phi Fraternity, Inc, 1994; SIAC All Conf Acad Football Team, 1992. **Home Addr:** 8606 Collins Dr, Jonesboro, GA 30236, **Home Phone:** (678)613-3670. **Business Addr:** Business Development Manager, Southern Region, Delon Hampton & Associates, Chartered, 229 Peachtree St NE Suite 1510 International Towers, Atlanta, GA 30303, **Business Phone:** (404)524-8030.

JOHNSON, KELLEY ANTONIO
Football player. **Personal:** Born Jun 3, 1962, Carlsbad, NM. **Educ:** Los Angeles Valley Col; Univ Colo. **Career:** Football player (retired); Denver Gold, wide receiver, 1985; Canadian Football League, Ottawa Rough Riders, 1986; Indianapolis Colts, 1987; Detroit Lions, 1989.

JOHNSON, KENNETH L.
Association executive. **Personal:** Born Feb 19, 1965, Jacksonville, FL; son of Theodore J and Minnie R. **Educ:** Bethune Cookman Col, BS, 1988. **Career:** Daniel Webster Elem Sch, teacher, 1990-92; Drug Enforcement Admin, Chicago Field Div, intelligence analyst, minority affairs coordr, 1992-95; Family Rescue Inc, dir devel & commun, 1995-97; Fundraising Prog, devel consult, 1997-00; Chicago Youth Ctr, dir devel; Nat Alumni Coun, United Negro College Fund, pres; Nat Chicago Inter Alumini Coun, pres. **Orgs:** UNCF Bd Insts & Mem; UNCF Advisory Bd, Chicago; bd dir, Kaboomes Track Club, Lawndale Community Church; bd dir, Nat Black Col Hall Fame; adv coun, Am Med Asn, Stop America's Violence Everywhere; Interfaith Coun Homeless; bd dir, Boy Scouts Am DuSable Dist, Chicago Area Coun; judge, Cook C Election; Chicago Pub Sch Sci Fair Symposium, Officers Asn; vpres & trustee, Lay Coun, J Claude Allen Christian Methodist Episcopal Church. **Honors/Awds:** Chicago Inter-Alumni Council/UNCF, Outstanding Serv Award, 1994, Outstanding Alumni of the Year Award, 1994; Special Recognition Award, Exec Off Pres, Off Nat Drug Control Policy; Commemorative Plagues Outstanding Contributions Field Drug Law Enforcement, DEA, 1993-95; Exemplary Performance Award, Dept Army, Ill Nat Guard Counter-Drug Support Prog, 1992. **Special Achievements:** Chicago Marathon, 1998. **Military Serv:** USAFR, human relations officer, 1990-; USAFR, first lieutenant.

JOHNSON, KENNETH LAVON
Judge. **Personal:** Born Jul 26, 1937, Columbia, MS; son of Geylon and Minnie O; married Carolyn Elizabeth Dischert, Sep 5, 1970; children: Sara Elizabeth, Jennifer Lorraine. **Educ:** Southern Univ & A&M Col, BA, 1959; Howard Univ Law Sch, LLB, 1962. **Career:** Judge (retired); US Dept Justice, trial atty, 1967-69; Baltimore Lawyers Comn Civil Rights Under Law, exec dir, 1969-70; pvt law pract, 1970-82; Univ Baltimore Sch Law, prof, 1988; Villa Julia Col, prof, 1988; judge. **Orgs:** Nat Asn Advan Colored People. **Honors/Awds:** Distinguished Community Service, Baltimore Frontier Club, 1974; Md 7th Congressional Dist Award, Congressman Parren J Mitchell, 1981; Outstanding Community Service Vanguard Justice Soc, 1982. **Military Serv:** AUS, Judge Advocate Gen Corps, capt, 1962-66; Military Justice Sect, chief, 1964-66; Nat Defense Military Medal, 1966. *

JOHNSON, KENYA
District attorney. **Career:** Fulton County Ct, GA, asst dist atty. **Business Phone:** (404)730-4983.*

JOHNSON, KERRY GERARD (KERRY KRAFT)
Graphic artist, cartoonist or animator. **Personal:** Born Sep 30, 1966, Nashville, TN; son of Dorothy Johnson; married Tawanda Williams Johnson; children: Deandria & Autumn. **Educ:** Ohio State Univ, attended 1989; Columbus Col Art & Design, BFA, 1989. **Career:** Ohio State Univ, cartoonist, 1988-89; Purpose Mag cartoonist, 1991; This Week, graphic artist, 1990-92; North Hills News Record, graphic artist, 1992-; Kerry Kraft Studios, owner & operator, currently; Pittsburgh Post-Gazette, graphic journalist, 1994-; Knight-Ridder Tribune Graphics Network, ed, illustr; Pittsburgh Tribune Rev, dep graphics ed; Baltimore Sun, graphics dir, currently. **Orgs:** Quill & Scroll Honor Soc, 1984; Publicity dir, Alpha Phi Alpha Fraternity, Inc, 1988-89; NAB; Pittsburgh Black Media Fed; NCP; Soc Newspaper Design; Pa Publishers Asn, 1995; Nat Asn Black Journalists, 1996; Soc Prof Journalists; Asn Am Ed Cartoonists. **Honors/Awds:** The Black Greek Coun Award, 1989; Citizen of the Week, Communicator News, 1991; Top 25 Under-Thirty Finalist, Urban Profile, 1992; Pittsburgh Black Media Found Award, 1993-96; Feature Illustration, Pa Publishers Asn, 1995-96; Nat Asn Black Journalists, Feature Illustration, 1996; Golden Quill Award, 1996. **Special Achievements:** Youth Page, Youth Purpose, 1992; Driving Park Libr, Art Exhibition, 1991; North Hills News Record, Communicator News, various illustrations; Kerry Kards & Kerry Klothes. **Business Phone:** (724)934-6630.

JOHNSON, KEVIN MAURICE
Basketball player, executive. **Personal:** Born Mar 4, 1966, Sacramento, CA; son of Lawrence Johnson and Georgia West. **Educ:** Univ Calif, Berkeley, CA, BA, polit sci, 1987; Harvard Divinity Sch,Summer Leadership Inst, attended 2000. **Career:** Basketball player (retired), executive; Cleveland Cavaliers, guard, 1987-88; Phoenix Suns, 1988-98, 2000; NBC, "The NBA," studio commentator, 2000-01; The Kevin Johnson Corp, owner, pres & chief exec officer,currently. **Orgs:** Founder, St HOPE Corp. **Honors/Awds:** All-NBA Second Team, 1989, 1990, 1991, 1994; NBA Most Improved Player, 1989; J Walter Kennedy Citizenship Award, 1991; NBA All-Star, 1990, 1991,1994; Ring of Honor, 2001. **Special Achievements:** Appeared in the Video Games NBA Jam, NBA Jam Tournament Edition, NBA Hangtime, NBA Jam Extreme & NBA Jam, 2003. **Business Addr:** President, Chief Executive Officer, The Kevin Johnson Corporation, PO Box 10743, Phoenix, AZ 85064, **Business Phone:** (602)957-7100.

JOHNSON, KEVIN N.
Basketball coach. **Personal:** Born in Indianapolis, IN; married Sheila Marie; children: Mitchell Edward. **Educ:** Ind State Univ, BS, phys educ, 1989. **Career:** Nat Football League, Indianapolis Colts, asst trainer; Ind Pacers, asst athletic trainer, 1990-94; Wash Wizards, head athletic trainer, 1994-95, 2000-01; NBA All-Star Game, Wash, DC, eastern Conf athletic trainer, 2001; Philadelphia 76ers, head athletic trainer, currently. **Orgs:** Nat Athletic Trainers Asn. **Honors/Awds:** Distinguished Alumni Award, Ind State Univ, 1996. **Business Phone:** (215)339-7625.*

JOHNSON, KEYSHAWN
Football player. **Personal:** Born Jul 22, 1972, Los Angeles, CA; son of Vivien Jessie Johnson; married Shikiri Hightower; children: Maia & Keyshawn Jr. **Educ:** Univ SC. **Career:** Football player (retired), tv broadcaster; NY Jets, wide receiver, 1996-99; Tampa Bay Buccaneers, 2000-03; Dallas Cowboys, wide receiver, 2004-05; Carolina Panthers, 2006; ESPN, tv broadcaster, currently. **Honors/Awds:** First team All-American, The Sporting News, 1995; First player selected in the NFL Draft, 1996; Pro Bowl, 1998. **Special Achievements:** Author, Just Give me the Damn Ball!: The Fast Times and Hard Knocks of an NFL Rookie, 1997; First player in NFL history to score a touchdown on MNF with four different teams; Hosts a weekly show on SIRIUS Satellite Radio's NFL Radio titled "Taking it to the House". **Business Addr:** Television Broadcaster, ESPN, ESPN Plaza 935 Middle St, Bristol, CT 06010, **Business Phone:** (860)766-2000.

JOHNSON, KIMBERLY LYNN (KIMBERLY L THOMAS)
Association executive. **Educ:** Wayne State Univ. **Career:** Talented Youth Develop Inc, founder, exec dir & pres, currently. **Orgs:** Epic Group plc. **Business Addr:** Founder & Executive Director, President, Talented Youth Development Inc, 26753 Evergreen Meadows Ct, Southfield, MI 48076, **Business Phone:** (313)492-0946.*

JOHNSON, LANCE
Baseball player. **Personal:** Born Jul 6, 1963, Cincinnati, OH. **Educ:** Univ S Ala. **Career:** Baseball player (retired); St Louis Cardinals, outfielder, 1987; Chicago White Sox, 1988-95; New York Mets, 1996-97; Chicago Cubs, 1997-99; New York Yankees, 2000. **Honors/Awds:** World Series Champion, 2000; one of four players to lead a Major League in triples as many as five times.

JOHNSON, LARRY DEMETRIC
Basketball player. **Personal:** Born Mar 14, 1969, Tyler, TX; married Celeste Wingfield, Jan 1, 1994; children: Larry Jr, Lance & Lasani. **Educ:** Odessa Jr Col; Univ Nevada, Las Vegas, attended 1991. **Career:** Boxer (retired), basketball player (retired), business owner; Police Athletic Boxing League, boxer, 1978-82; Charlotte Hornets, forward, 1991-96; NY Knicks, 1996-2001; 6001 Hair Studios, owner, currently. **Honors/Awds:** NBA Rookie

of the Year, 1992; NBA All-Rookie first team, 1992; All-NBA second team, 1993; Olympic Dream Team II, 1996; Metlife Community Assist of the Month Award. **Special Achievements:** NBA Draft, first round pick, No 1, 1991. **Business Addr:** Owner, 6001 Hair Studios, 6001 The Plaza, Charlotte, NC 28215, **Business Phone:** (704)535-2722.

JOHNSON, LATONYA
Basketball player. **Personal:** Born Aug 17, 1975, Winchester, TN; daughter of Jesse and Helen. **Educ:** Memphis, attended 1998. **Career:** Utah Starzz, forward, 1998-02; San Antonio Silver Stars, forward, 2003; Houston Comets, forward, 2004; Chicago Blaze, forward, 2005; Asst Dir Basketball, Memphis tigers, 2007-. **Orgs:** Olympic Festival S, 1994; Breast Health Awareness spokesperson. **Honors/Awds:** USA Today Freshman of Influence, 1994; Great Mid w Conf Newcomer Year, 1995; Basketball Times All-American, 1996, 1998. *

JOHNSON, LAVERA
Personal: Born in St Louis, MO. **Educ:** NW Mo State Univ, Maryville, educ; NY Univ, french; New Sch Social Res, NY City, Human Resources. **Career:** Teacher; Univ Wis, Danforth fel; The Brooklyn Hosp; Amalgamated Life Ins Co; c TV Workshop; Nichols Sch, bd mem; Sheehan Mem Hosp, bd mem; human resources consult; Advan Refractory Technologies Inc, vpres human resource; NanoDynamics, S Buffalo, human resources dir, currently. **Orgs:** Soc Human Resources Profs. **Business Phone:** (716)853-4900.

JOHNSON, LAWRENCE E
Lawyer, city council member. **Personal:** Born Sep 22, 1948, Waco, TX; children: Daphne, Lawrence Jr, Demitria & LaShunia. **Educ:** Prairie View A&M Univ, BS, elect engineering, 1971; George Wash Univ, JD, 1975. **Career:** Ins salesman, 1969; IBM, design engr, 1970; Gen Electric Corp, sales engr, 1971-72, patent engr, 1972-76; City Waco, city coun mem, 1990-98; Lawrence Johnson Assoc, atty, currently. **Orgs:** Pres bd, Legal Serv Corp, 1983; pres bd, Mitchell Funeral Home, 1982-85; dir, HOT Legal Serv, 1981-85; secy, pres bd, 1990, McLennan Community Col Bd Trustees. **Honors/Awds:** City of Waco May Pro-Tem, 1991-92, 1996-97. **Business Addr:** Attorney, Lawrence Johnson Associate, 801 Wash Ave Suite 400, Waco, TX 76701-1260, **Business Phone:** (254)756-7041.

JOHNSON, LECTOY TARLINGTON
Physician. **Personal:** Born Nov 28, 1931, Tyler, TX; married Helen Collier; children: Lectoy Tarlington, III, Lynelle Teresa. **Educ:** Tex Col, Tyler, TX, BS, chem, 1952; Howard Univ Col Med, MD, 1956; Wash Univ, St Louis, anesthesiol, 1960; Am Bd Anesthesiol, dipl, 1963. **Career:** Riverside Gen Hosp, Houston, chmn dept anesthesiol, 1960-68; St Joseph Hosp, Houston, chmn dept anesthesiol, 1970-80, acad chief anesthesiol, 1970-80; Univ Tex Med Sch, Houston, act chmn dept anesthsiol, 1973; pvt pract, physician, currently. **Orgs:** Harris County Med Soc; Tex Med Soc; Nat Med Soc; Int Anesthesia Res Soc; Undersea Med Soc; Fel Am Col Anesthesiol, 1963-; Houston Surgical Soc; med dir, Ocean Corp Houston, 1970-78; chmn bd dir, Asn Anesthetists Houston, 1970-80; comm chmn, Boy Scouts Am WL Davis Dist, 1974-75; pres, Gulf coast Anesthesia Soc, Houston, 1979-80; bd dir, Stand Saving & Loan, Houston, 1984-; life mem, Kappa Alpha Psi Frat. **Honors/Awds:** Certificate of Excellence, Gulf Coast Chap Inhalation Therapists; Outstanding Instructor Award, St Joseph Hosp Surgical Dept. **Business Addr:** Physician, 3612 Parkwood Dr, PO Box 784, Houston, TX 77021.*

JOHNSON, LEON
College administrator, chairperson. **Personal:** Born Jul 14, 1930, Aiken, SC; married Janie L; children: Leon Jr, Lisa J. **Educ:** SC State Col, BS, 1955, MS, 1959; Mich State Univ, MD; State Col Univ MD. **Career:** Chairperson, college administrator (retired); Clemson Univ, asst count agent, 1955-62; Univ Md, extension agent com & resource Develop, ; Gov comn on migratory & seasonal farm labour, chair, 1997-03. **Orgs:** Md Asn County Agr Agents; Teamwork Planning Comn; charter founding mem, Community Develop Soc; Community Resource Develop Task Force; SEMIS Work Group Com; Task Force Community Develop Prog; pres, Somerset County Comn Action Agency; Tri-county Migrant Co; vpres, Somerset County Civic Asn; Delmarva Adv Coun Migrat Com; Princess Anne Area Chamber Com; bd dirs, Coston Recreation Coun; Somerset County Civil Defense bd; community orgn, Progress Inc; bd dirs, Somerset County Head Start; Propress Inc; Zion Hill Baptist Church; Omega Psi Phi Frat; Epsilon Sigma Phi Frat; Delmarva Ecmenical Agency Rural Coalition; bd dir, Md Churches United Bd Recognitions Countys Head & Start Prog; Migrant Prog; Community Action Agency. *

JOHNSON, LEON F.
Police officer, mayor. **Personal:** Born May 19, 1926, Salem, NJ; son of Elsie and Elwood; married Margaret Ford, Feb 17, 1946 (deceased); children: Nancy Brown, Kathryn Watford. **Career:** police officer (retired), mayor; Salem County Jail, corrections officer; Spec Police, Salem City, 1955-60, police officer, 1962-88, sgt; Salem City, councilman, 1988-92; Salem City, mayor, 1991-. **Orgs:** lifetime mem, Fraternal Order Police; Am Legion, Post 444; lifetime mem, Mt Hope Methodist Church, Salem. **Honors/Awds:** Nat Policeman of the Year, 1968-69; Policeman of the Year, 1971-72; NCP Award, 1992; Seven Day Adventist, 1992; Mt Picah Church Award, 1992. **Military Serv:** USY, sgt, 1945-46. **Business Addr:** Mayor, City of Salem, 1 New Mkt St, Salem, NJ 08079, **Business Phone:** (609)935-4550.*

JOHNSON, DR. LEROY
College president, clergy. **Personal:** Married Simmie Mae; children: Leana & Leroy Johnson Jr(deceased). **Educ:** Chapman Univ; Kans State Univ, PhD. **Career:** Miles Col, Birmingham, AL, pres & chancellor, 1986-89; Missionary Temple CME Church, pastor, 1989-. **Special Achievements:** First African American to receive a line officer's commission under the Navy Reserve Officer Candidate Program. **Military Serv:** AUS, Chaplain Corps, col, 1963-86;received 25 mil awards.

JOHNSON, LESLIE
Basketball player. **Personal:** Born Jan 12, 1975, Ft Wayne, IN. **Educ:** Western Ky Univ, attended 1998. **Career:** Wash Mystics, forward, 1998. **Honors/Awds:** AP All-American, Honorable Mention, 1998; Kodak All-Am, Honorable Mention, 1994; US Basketball Writers, Third Team, 1994; earned All-Sun Belt Conference honors; National Freshman of the Year. *

JOHNSON, LESTER B., III
Lawyer. **Personal:** Born Dec 4, 1953, Savannah, GA; son of Lester B Jr and Constance M; married Salyon H, May 24, 1975; children: Ayesha K, Khalil A, Faisal B. **Educ:** Col Holy Cross, AB, 1975; Univ Miami, JD, 1978. **Career:** Community Lawyers Inc, law clerk, 1976-77; Ga Legal Serv Progs Inc, staff atty, 1978-80; Martin, Thomas & Bass, PC, assoc, 1980-82; Martin & Johnson, PC, partner, 1983-86; Lester B Johnson III PC, owner, 1986-; Savannah-Chatham Bd Ed, sch bd atty, 1991-; City Savannah, asst city atty. **Orgs:** Nat Bar Asn, 1979; pres, Savannah Bar Asn, 1980; State Bar Ga, 1980-; bd mem, Masjid Jihad, 1980-; bd mem, Historic Savannah, 1988-; pres & secy, Montgolfier Soc, 1992-; Hospice Savannah Found, 1995-; grammateus, Alpha Lambda Mu Boule, 1996-. **Honors/Awds:** Annual Award, Masjid Jihad, 1986; Citizen of the Yr, Omega Psi Phi, 1999. **Business Addr:** Attorney, Lester B Johnson III PC, 216 W Broughton St Suite 201, PO Box 8285, Savannah, GA 31401-8285, **Business Phone:** (912)238-5100.*

JOHNSON, LILLIAN MANN
Educator, administrator. **Personal:** Born Dec 18, 1948, Springfield, MA; daughter of Donald and Ruth Freeman; married Thornton B Johnson, Jr, Jun 26, 1971; children: Joshua, Zachary. **Educ:** Cent State Univ, BS, 1970; Cent Mich Univ, MSA, 1985. **Career:** JC Penney Co, merchandise presentation supvr, 1980-83; Cent Mich Univ, prog coordr, ctr rep, 1983-87; Wright State Univ, acad adv univ div, 1987-89, asst dir, career servs, 1989, asst dir, Bolinga Ctr, 1989-92, dir Bolinga Ctr, 1992-00, adj instr, 2001, asst dean, 2001 & coordr mentoring progs, 2001. **Orgs:** vpres, Am Asn Univ Women, WSU Branch, 1996-; pres, Alpha Kappa Alpha Sorority, 1996-; corres scy, Alpha Kappa Alpha Sorority, 1994-96; pres, Orgn Black Fac & Staff, 1996-97; vpres, Wright State Univ, 1995-96; bd mem, Dayton Art Inst Outreach, 1993-; Phi Delta Kappa Fraternity, 1985-88; Nat Asn Advan Colored People; Dayton Urban League; bd mem, Buckeye Trails Girl Scouts; bd mem, Montgomery County Arts Coun. **Honors/Awds:** Alpha Woman of the Year, Alpha Phi Alpha Fraternity, 1995. **Special Achievements:** One Woman Art Exhibit, Wright State Univ, 1996; Art Exhibit, Greene City Libr, 1977. **Business Addr:** Assistant Dean, Coordinator, Wright State University, 3640 Colonel Glenn Hwy, Fairborn, OH 45324, **Business Phone:** (937)775-3333.*

JOHNSON, LINDA DIANNE
Optometrist. **Personal:** Born Feb 5, 1954, Richland, MS; daughter of Adam and Gertrude; married James Walter Carson Jr, Apr 28, 1984 (divorced 1988); children: James Walter III. **Educ:** Jackson State Univ, BS, 1974; Ind Univ Sch Optometry, OD, 1978. **Career:** Jackson Hinds Comprehensive Health Ctr, dir optom clin, 1978-. **Orgs:** Nat Optom Asn, pres, 1997-99; sec, treas, Miss Optom Asn; Southern Coun Optometrists; Am Red Cross; chair, Cent Miss Chapter, 1995-97; Jackson State Univ; bd mem, Nat Alumni Asn; pres, Miss Optom Asn. **Honors/Awds:** Outstanding Professional Achievement Award, Jackson State Univ Nat Alumni Asn, 1980; Distinguished Service Award, Jackson State Univ, Hinds Alumni Chapter, 1982; Optometrist of the Year, Nat Optom Asn, 1993; Am Red Cross Cent Miss Chap, 1994; Employer of the Year, Jackson Hinds Comprehensive Health Ctr, 1997. **Special Achievements:** First African American female optometrist in the state of Mississippi. **Home Addr:** 5420 I 55 N Suite D, Jackson, MS 39211. **Business Addr:** Director, Jackson-Hinds Comprehensive Health Center, 2775 Medgar Evers Blvd, Jackson, MS 39207, **Business Phone:** (601)364-5106.

JOHNSON, LIVINGSTONE M.
Judge. **Personal:** Born Dec 27, 1927, Wilkinsburg, PA; married Leeburn; children: Lee Carol, Oliver Morris, II, Judith Lee, Livingstone James, Patricia Lee. **Educ:** Howard Univ WA DC, AB, 1949; Univ MI Law Sch, JD, 1957; Col St Judiciary, Grad Nat, 1973. **Career:** Johnson & Johnson Law Firm, patner, 1957-73; County Solicitor, asst, 1962-73; Fifth Jud Dist PA, judge, 1973; Allegheny Co Ct Common Pleas, sr judge, currently. **Orgs:** Panel Judges; past bd mem, NAACP, 1962-68; Urban League, 1963-68; Am Bar Asn; Am Bar Found; Am Judicature Soc; PA Bar Asn; Allegheny County Bar Asn; bd gov, 1967-74, Pub Serv Comn, 1965-; asn trial lawyres crime; Crt Allegheny County Bar Asn; PA Conf St Trail Judges; bd Dir St Peters Child Develop Ctrs Inc; ARC; Boys Club Western PA; Ile Elegba Inc; Bus & Job Develop Corp Comt Rel Agency; Azanan Strongs Inc; Greater Pittsburg Civic League; BS Am; Omega Psi Phi; NAACP. **Honors/Awds:** Louis Caplan Human Relations Award, 1975; honors, Dist Flying Cross; commendation Medal; oak leaf; nominated, Judges Awards, Allegheny County Bar Asn, 2006. **Military Serv:** USAF, 1st lt, 1949-54. **Business Addr:** Senior Judge, Allegheny County court common pleas, 701A City County Bldg, Pittsburgh, PA 15233, **Business Phone:** (412)350-5266.*

JOHNSON, LLOYD A.
Government official. **Personal:** Born Aug 5, 1932, Boston, MA; son of Clarence Lionel and Louise Amelia Dixon; married Constance Riley; children: Scott A & Alison E. **Educ:** Howard Univ, BA, 1954; Aldephi Univ, MSS, 1957; Georgetown Univ Law Ctr, JD 1984. **Career:** Worked troubled indust & families under pub & private auspices, 1954-66; Local Community Corps, exec dir, 1966-69; Community Develop Agency, dir evalutation & res, 1966-69; Urban Ctr Columbia Univ, dir, 1969-74; US House Representatives, sub comt postal operations & serv, labor coun subcomt labor, chmn; Lloyd & Connie Johnson, owner, currently. **Orgs:** Acad Cert Social Workers; Nat Bar Asn; Nat Asn Social Workers; bd dir, Am Orthopsychiatric Asn; Nat Asn Social Workers; Acad Cert Social Workers. **Honors/Awds:** Outstanding Alumni Award Nominee, Howard Univ. **Business Addr:** Owner, Lloyd & Connie Johnson, 1121 Holton Lane, Takoma Park, MD 20912-7536, **Business Phone:** (301)431-4568.

JOHNSON, LONNIE DEMETRIUS
Football player. **Personal:** Born Feb 14, 1971, Miami, FL; married Ushanda; children: Tyrone. **Educ:** Fla State Univ. **Career:** Football player (retired); Buffalo Bills, tight end, 1994-98; Kansas City Chiefs, tight end, 1999.

JOHNSON, LONNIE G.
Inventor. **Personal:** Born Oct 6, 1949, Mobile, AL. **Educ:** Tuskegee UNIV, BS, Mech Engineering, 1973, MS, Nuclear Engineering, 1976, PhD. **Career:** USF Weapons Lab, acting chief Space Nuclear Power Safety section, 1978-79; Jet Propulsion Lab, senior systs engr, Galileo Proj, 1979-82; engr, Mariner Mark II Spacecraft series Comet Rendezvous & Saturn Orbiter Probe missions, 1987-91; USF, Advan Space Systs Requirements mgr nonnuclear strategic weapons tech, 1982-85; Strategic Air Command, chief data mgt br, 1985-87; Johnson Res Develop Co Inc, founder and pres, 1991-. **Orgs:** Georgia Alliance Children; Hank Aaron "Chasing the Dream" Found; Bd Dir Commonwealth Nat Bank. **Honors/Awds:** Pi Tau Sigma National Engineering Honor Society, 1973; USF Commendation Medal, 1984; inducted, Inventor's Hall of Fame, 2000; Golden Torch Award, Nat Soc of Black Engineers, 2001; honorary science doctorate, 2001. **Special Achievements:** Inventor of Super Soaker water gun. **Military Serv:** USF. **Business Addr:** President, Founder, Johnson Research & Development, Inc, 263 Decatur St, Atlanta, GA 30312, **Business Phone:** (404)584-2475.*

JOHNSON, LORRETTA
Executive. **Personal:** Born Oct 29, 1938, Baltimore, MD; married Leonard; children: Leonard Jr, Jeffrey, Kevin. **Educ:** Coppin State Univ Baltimore MD, BS 1976. **Career:** Baltimore City Pub Schs, paraprofessional 1965-70; Baltimore Tchrs Union, paraprofessional chirperson 1970-76; Am Fedn Teachers, intl vpres, 1978; Baltimore Teachers Union, pres paraprofessional chap, 1978-; Md Am Fedn of Teachers, AFL-CIO, pres; Personal Choice Benefits Inc, adv bd, currently. **Orgs:** Exec bd Met AFL-CIO 1978; conS research of Better Schs 1980. **Honors/Awds:** Community Serv Award United Way campaigh 1976; Vol Serv Award MD State AFL-CIO COPE 1977; Meritous Achievemnt Award United Tchrs of New Orleans 1977; Meritous Achievement Award A Phillip Randolph Inst 1978. **Business Addr:** President, Baltimore Teachers Union, 5800 Metro Dr Suite 2, Baltimore, MD 21215.*

JOHNSON, LUCIEN LOVE
Physician. **Personal:** Born Dec 26, 1941, New Orleans, LA; children: Lucien III, Kimberly, Yewande. **Educ:** Purdue Univ, BS, 1962; Howard Univ, MD, 1966. **Career:** Pvt Pract, physician, cardiol, currently. **Orgs:** Am Med Asn; Nat Med Asn; Calif Med Asn; exec secy, Orgn Harmonisation Bus Law Africa. **Special Achievements:** Has written and published two articles in medical journals. **Military Serv:** AUS, capt, 1966-67. **Business Addr:** Cardiologist, 3756 Santa Rosalia Dr, Los Angeles, CA 90008.*

JOHNSON, LUTHER E
Executive, graphic artist. **Personal:** Born Feb 23, 1966, Warrensville Heights, OH; son of Luther and Ann; married Althea, May 29, 1999; children: Brandon & Stephen. **Educ:** Columbus Col Arts & Design, BFA, illus & fine art, 1989. **Career:** Alexander Enterprises, art dir, 1989-91; Modeworks Inc, mural artist, 1992-

94; Columbus Pub Schs, art instr, 1994-96; 1 X-Design, mural artist, 1995-96; Univ TV, graphic designer, 1996-; Chocolate Barbie Prods, 1998-; Chocolate Barbie Prods, Detroit, MI, co-owner multi-media specialist; Art shows & accomplishments: Ohio State Univ, Columbus, OH, 1993, 1994, 1995; Columbus Christian Academy, Columbus, OH, 1995; Martin Luther King Center, Columbus, OH, 1995; Malcolm Brown Gallery, Cleveland, OH, 1996; Electric Lizard, owner, currently; WhiteBlox, Inc, IT Project Mgr, currently. **Orgs:** Alpha Phi Alpha Fraternity, 1986; Great Lakes Info Archit Asn. **Honors/Awds:** First Prize, Banner Competition, Detroit Festival Arts, 1996, 1997; Technology Achievement Award, Comput & Info, Wayne State Univ, 1998; Telly Award. **Business Addr:** Graphic Designer II, University Television, 77 West Canfield, Detroit, MI 48201, **Business Phone:** (313)577-2032.

JOHNSON, MAGIC. See JOHNSON, EARVIN.

JOHNSON, MAMIE PEANUT
Baseball player, nurse, manager. **Personal:** Born Sep 27, 1935, Ridgeway, SC; daughter of Gentry Harrison and Della Belton Havelow; married Charles; children: Charlie. **Educ:** NC A&T Univ, nursing. **Career:** Baseball player (retired), Manager, coach; Wash Recreational Baseball League, St Cyrians team, 1940-50; Negro Leagues, Indianapolis Clowns, pitcher, 1953-55; nurse, 1950-90; Negro Baseball League's Memorabilia Shop, mgr, 1990-; All-star baseball teams, coach, currently. **Orgs:** Founder, They Played Baseball Found, 1999-. **Honors/Awds:** Mary McLeod Bethune Continuing Legacy Award. **Special Achievements:** The President and Mrs. Clinton have honored Ms. Johnson at the White House as a female baseball legend & First female pitcher to play in the Negro Leagues. **Business Addr:** Founder, They Played Baseball Foundation, PO Box 1622, Mitchellville, MD 20717.*

JOHNSON, MARCO
College president, college administrator. **Career:** Los Angeles, firefighter, paramedic; Antelope Valley Med Col, founder, pres & dir, currently. **Orgs:** Bd dirs, Antelope Valley Col Found. **Business Phone:** (661)726-1911.

JOHNSON, MARGIE N.
Educator, dean (education). **Personal:** Born Aug 21, 1938, Jacksonville, TX; daughter of E J (deceased) and Vivian; divorced. **Educ:** Prairie View A&M Univ, RN/BS, 1960; Ind Univ, MS, 1963; Tex Woman's Univ, PhD, 1977. **Career:** Educator (retired); Jarvis Christian Col, Col nurse, 1960-61; Univ Calif, Los Angeles, Neuropsychiatric Div, staff nurse, 1961-62; Fort Dodge Col, intern, 1962-64; Wayne State Univ, asst prof, 1965-72; Dept Nursing, Univ Ibadan, Nigeria, dep dir, 1974-77; Nat Inst Ment Health, Doctoral Fel, 1975-77; Tex Woman's Univ, assoc prof, 1987-88; Tuskegee Univ, Sch Nursing & Allied Health, dean & prof, 1988-98. **Orgs:** Am Asn Cols Nursing; past alt delegate Tex, Am Nurses Asn, 1962-; Nat League Nursing, 1968-; Sigma Theta Tau, 1976-; Phi Lambda Theta, 1978-88; Nat Black Nurses Asn, 1982-; Am Nurses Found, 1982-; Asn Black Nursing Fac Higher Educ, 1988-. **Honors/Awds:** Chi Eta Phi, Nat Honors Soc Black Nurses, 1990; Distinguished Scholar in Residence Nursing, Clemson Univ, 1985-86. **Special Achievements:** Author, with Morakinyo, "Role Perception and Role Enactment," Int J Nurs Studies, 1983; with others, Goad, Canada, "Attitudes Toward Nursing-Males," Jour Nrs Edu, 1984; with Beard, Psychosocial Stress and Blood Press, J Blk Ns Asn, 1987; with Arnold Nieswiadomy, "Chart Reading and Anxiety," Jour Nur Educ, 1989. **Home Addr:** Rte 3 PO Box 617, Jacksonville, TX 75766, **Home Phone:** (903)589-8190. *

JOHNSON, MARGUERITE ANNIE. See ANGELOU, DR. MAYA.

JOHNSON, DR. MARGUERITE M.
School administrator. **Personal:** Born Sep 23, 1948, Wilmington, DE; daughter of Norris R Milburn (deceased) and Elizabeth Milburn; married George Stephen, Aug 1971; children: Stephanie M & Stephen M. **Educ:** Morgan State Univ, Baltimore, MD, BA, 1966-70; Indiana Univ PA, Indiana, PA, MA, 1976; Temple Univ, Philadelphia, PA EdD, 1987. **Career:** Delaware Tech & Community Col, Northern Branch, gen educ develop, instr, co-ordr, 1970-73, Stanton Wilmington Campuses, acting dir continuing educ, dir continuing educ, 1979, Stanton Campus, acting asst dir, continuing educ, 1973-75, asst dir continuing educ, 1975-79, off pres, exec dean instruct & student servs, 1992, Terry Campus, vpres, campus dir, 1994. **Orgs:** Am Asn Women Community Col; Am Asn Univ Women, Dover Chap; Nat NE Region, AACC Rotary Downtown Club, Dover; DE Cent Delaware Econ Develop Coun. **Honors/Awds:** Distinguished Kellog Fel, 1989-90; Outstanding Service Award, Nat Coun Black Am Affairs, Northeast Region, 1991; Special Service Award, Brandywine Prof Asn, 1991; Leadership Award, Asn Black Women Higher Educ, 1993; People To Watch, Delaware Today Mag, 1995.

JOHNSON, DR. MARIE LOVE
Consultant, president (organization), executive director. **Personal:** Born Dec 18, 1925, South Bend, IN; married Arthur (deceased). **Educ:** Ind Univ, BS, 1951; Univ Hartford, Med, 1953; Univ Conn, PhD, 1978. **Career:** East Hartford Bd Educ, spch path, 1949-60, supvr 1960-77; Shadybrook Lang & Learning Ctr, clin dir, 1971-76, exec dir, 1977-78; self-employed, consult, currently. **Orgs:** Pres, Hartford Alumnae Chap Delta Sigma Theta, 1954-56; bd fin Town Vernon, 1963-65; clin & Cert bd, Am Speech & Hearing Asn, 1969-75; pres,Conn Speech & Hearing Asn, 1971-75; pres, JGM Corp, 1971-78; fel, Am Speech & Hearing Asn, 1972; chmn bd mgrs, YMCA 1976-78; vpres, Am Speech & Hearing Asn, 1977-78. **Honors/Awds:** Community Service, Delta Sigma Theta, 1966; Honors, Conn Speech & Hearing Asn, 1970; Tribute Luncheon, Conn Speech & Hearing Asn, 1975; CRT named Arthur & Marie Johnson Early Childhood Training Ctr in their honor, 1996; Lifetime Achievement Award, 2007. **Special Achievements:** Editor: The Collected Poetry of Arthur Lyman Johnson. **Home Addr:** 78 Warren Ave, PO Box 2026, Vernon-Rockville, CT 06066.

JOHNSON, MARJORIE LYNN
Association executive, lecturer, writer. **Personal:** Born Oct 26, 1961, Beloit, WI; married Dale B Johnson; children: Dale Austin. **Educ:** Spelman Col; Long Island Univ, JD. **Career:** Prudential-Bache Securities; Life Underwriters Training Coun; Stay-At-Home Mother Motherhood Network, founder & pres, 1994-. **Orgs:** Am Bar Asn. **Honors/Awds:** Bus honor, Fortune 500 Bus Leadership Prog, The Young Lions Club. **Special Achievements:** Published the MotherSpeak newsletter; author, "So, You're a Stay-At-Home Mother," 1996. **Business Phone:** (212)501-6479.*

JOHNSON, MARK A
Executive, president (organization). **Personal:** Born Aug 10, 1950, Washington, DC; son of Walter R and Charlotte M; married Vera-Marie, Jul 12, 1975; children: Maya & Marci. **Educ:** Bowie State Univ, BS, 1972; Univ Md, MBA, 1979. **Career:** Suburban Trust Bank, employment mgr, 1972-75; Central Intelligence Agency, personnel officer, 1975-77; AT&T Long Lines, acct supvr, 1977-80; Sallie Mae, vpres bus develop, 1980-97; Mark Johnson & Assocs, bus adv serv, pres, 1997-. **Orgs:** Kappa Alpha Psi Fraternity, Inc, 1970-; bd dirs, Black Ski, DC, 1984-; Nat Brotherhood Skiers, 1984-; Nat Black MBA Asn, 1990-; bd dir, Kappa Alpha Psi Found Md, 1991-; US Ski Coaches Asn, 1992-; US Ski Asn, 1992-; Nat Asn Advan Colored People, 1994-. **Honors/Awds:** Humanitarian Award, Kappa Alpha Psi, 1984; Athletic Hall of Fame, Bowie State Univ, 1986; Distinguished Service, Prince Georgians on Camera, Public Access CATV Inc, 1987. **Special Achievements:** Alpine Pre-Course, Level 1, Certified Ski Race Coach, 1994.

JOHNSON, DR. MARK S.
Chairperson, medical researcher. **Personal:** Born Jun 3, 1951, Newark, NJ; son of Jay Robert and Ann Stevenson; married Marlyn; children: Asha Harare, Kwende Aaron, Zuri Anne & Maia. **Educ:** Coe Col, BA, 1974; Univ Md, NJ, Med Sch, MD, 1979; Univ NC, Chapel Hill, MPH, 1989. **Career:** Univ NC, Dept Family Med, Chapel Hill, clin instr, 1982-84; Meharry Med Sch, residency dir, 1984-86; Univ S Ala, asst dean, 1986-91; NJ Med Sch, Dept Family Med, fac, 1991-, prof & chair, currently. **Orgs:** Nat Med Asn; Southwest Ala Sickle Cell, 1981-82, 1987-91; Am Acad Family Physicians, Am Pub Health Asn; NJ Acad Family Physicians; Am Soc Hypertension; pres, Asn Depts Family Med, 2003-05; Asn Black Cardiologists; Int Soc Hypertension Blacks; Soc Teachers Family Med; CAS rep, AAMC; New Jersey Task Force for Prevention of Obesity, 2002-06. **Honors/Awds:** America's Best Family Physicians; Top Docs in America. **Special Achievements:** Author of numerous health articles, book chapters, and reviews; United States Preventive Services Task Force, member. **Business Addr:** Chairman, Professor, New Jersey Medical School, Department of Family Medicine, 183 S Orange Ave, BHSB E-1557, Newark, NJ 07103, **Business Phone:** (973)972-7979.

JOHNSON, MARLENE E.
Government official. **Personal:** Born Jul 1, 1936, Milwaukee, WI; daughter of Edward Jay and Elizabeth Leher; married John Odom; children: Jan, Paula & Jay. **Educ:** Univ Wis, Milwaukee, BS, 1979. **Career:** Boston Store, saleswoman, 1954-64; WXIX-TV Channel 18 Milwaukee, TV hostess, 1962; Milwaukee Pub Sch Syst, social improvement instr, 1966-70; First WI Natl Bank, teller, 1973-75; City Milwaukee, alderman, 1980-; City Milwaukee, WI, alderwoman, 1980. **Orgs:** Century mem, Boy Scouts Am Milwaukee Banner E Div, 1974-75; pres, Women's Aux Milwaukee Courier, 1975-76; Bd dirs, Book fellows-Friends Milwaukee Pub Lib, 1976-80; div leader, YWCA Leader Luncheon, 1977; bd dir, Milwaukee Symphony Orches, 1977-80; lifetime mem, Nat Asn Advan Colored People, 1980; bd dir vchmn, MECCA, 1988-92; vpres bd dir, Milwaukee United Way,1988; Milwaukee Redevelop Auth, 1980-92; bd dir, Milwaukee Conv & Vis Bur;OIC-GM; Pabst Theater Bd Dirs; Nat League Cities Comn & Econ Develop Steering Comn; vpres, WI League Municipalities Sixth Senate Dist; chairwoman, 1980-92; Milwaukee Area Tecnical Col Bd, 1990-92; bd dir, Pvt Indust Coun, 1990-91; comn, Milwaukee Metrop Sewerage Dist, 1994-95. **Honors/Awds:** Quota Buster Award, YMCA, Milwaukee, 1975; Women in Our Lives, 1978; Milwaukee Women Today, 1979; Mayoral Proclamation, 1985; Milwaukee Realist Presidential Award, 1986; Award of Excellence in Community Serv, CYD,1990; Citation by the Senate State of WI, 1987; Outstanding Public Service Award, Gamma Phi Delta, 1992; Inducted into African-American Biographies Hall of Fame in Atlanta, GA, April 1994. *

JOHNSON, DR. MARTIN LEROY
Educator. **Personal:** Born Dec 31, 1941, Westminster, SC; son of James Courtney and Beatrice Williams; married Jo Ann Clinkscales; children: Yolandra & Martin II. **Educ:** Morris Col Sumter, SC, BS, 1962; Univ GA Athens, GA, MEd, 1968, EdD, 1971. **Career:** Anderson, SC, math teacher & chmn, 1962-67; Univ GA, grad asst, 1967-71; Rutgers Univ New Brunswick, asst prof math educa, 1971-72; Univ MD, Col Park, from asst prof to assoc prof, 1972-86, dir, Minorities Sci & Engineering Prog, 1979-80, dir, Dept Curric & Instr, 1980-85, prof educ, 1986-, chair, Dept Curric & Instr, 1994-2001, prof math, currently, Urban & Minority Educ, assoc dean, 2001-, MD Inst Minority Achievement & Urban Educ, dir, currently. **Orgs:** Col Educ fac, 1972-; Vpres, Res Coun Diag & Prescriptive Math, 1978-80; consult, Nat Sci Found, 1984-85, prog dir 1985-86, 1987; pres, MD Coun Teachers Math, 1985-86; chair, Res Adv Comm, Nat Coun Teachers Math, 1988-89; ed bd mem, J Res Math Educ, 1991-94, chair, 1993-94; prs, Res CNL Diag & Prescriptive Math, 1993-95; Am Educ res Asn; Benjamin Banneker Asn, Inc, 1997-99; Nat Asn Math; Asn Math Teacher educators; MD Asn Teacher Educators; Nat Bd Dir, Sch Sci & Math Asn, 1998-2000; Campus Model Excellence, univ MD, 2005. **Honors/Awds:** Fulbright Scholar Nigeria, 1983-84; Distinguished Minority Faculty Member, Univ MD, Col Park, 1985; Mathematics Educator of the Year, MD Coun Teachers Math, 1989; Excellence Award, Black Fac & staff Asn, Univ MD, Col Park. **Special Achievements:** Has authored Guiding Each Child's Learning of Math - Char Merill 1983, and co-authored A Diagnostic Approach to Instruction, K-8 elementary school mathematics textbooks, Mathematics In Action; "How Primary Children Think and Learn", Changing the Faces of Mathematics: Perspectives on African Americans , has been recognized as a campus model of excellence by the Office of Multi-Ethnic Student Education (OMSE)?a unit of the Academic Affairs Division of the University of Maryland in 2005, has edited numerous articles-Journal for Research in Mathematics Education, The Arithmetic Teacher, and NCTM publications. **Business Addr:** Professor of Mathematics, Associate Dean, University of Maryland College of Education, Department of Curriculum and Education, 3119 Benjamin Bldg, College Park, MD 20742, **Business Phone:** (301)405-2337.

JOHNSON, MARVIN R
Chief executive officer, marine corps officer. **Educ:** Univ Fl, BS, mat eng; GA State Univ, MBA, decision sci. **Career:** Nuclear submarine officer (retired), Chairman & Chief executive officer; USN, nuclear submarine officer, 1991-97; The Tennessee Valley Authority; British Energy & Southern Calif; Edison; CipherLink, co-founder & chief exec officer, 1999-2002; ikobo Inc, chief exec officer, 2002-05; Nutrition Systs Inc, founder, chmn & chief exec officer, 2005-. **Military Serv:** USN, nuclear submarine officer, 1991-97. **Business Addr:** Chief Executive Officer, Chairman, Nutrition Systems Inc, 2255 Cumberland Pkwy Bldg 100 Suite 100, Atlanta, GA 30060, **Business Phone:** (678)360-8701.*

JOHNSON, MARVIN R, JR.
Chief executive officer, president (organization). **Educ:** Univ Fla, BS; GA State Univ, MBA. **Career:** Indus Int Inc, product develop mgr; CipherLink Inc, pres & ceo; Ikobo, ceo, pres, currently. **Business Addr:** President, Chief Executive Officer, Ikobo, 1355 Terrel Mill Rd Bldg 1466, Marietta, GA 30067, **Business Phone:** (678)483-4562.

JOHNSON, MARYANN
Executive. **Personal:** Born Oct 11, 1948, Memphis, TN; daughter of William and Maryann. **Educ:** Griggs Bus Col, attended 1967. **Career:** Jerry Butler Prods Inc, from exec asst to pres, 1968-74; A&M Rec, Inc, off mgr, Nat tour coordr, 1975-79; Lorimar TV Prods, from exec asst to pres, music, 1984-85; Twentieth Century Fox Film Corp, exec asst, off mgr, 1987-95, mgr, TV music admin, assoc dir, TV music admin, 1997, dir, TV music admin, 1998-. **Orgs:** Jr Achievement, sponsor, 1972-73; secy, Wilshire United Methodist Church, Coun Ministries, 1975-77; United Methodist Women, rep, 1978-; Nat Asn Advan Colored People, 1979-80; Nat Asn Female Exec, 1980; Nat Acad Rec Arts & Scis, 1985-; hon mem, Sigma Gamma Rho Sorority, 2008. **Honors/Awds:** Bethune Recognition Award, Nat Coun Negro Women Corp Honoree, 2002; Artistic Excellence Award, Sigma Gamma Rho Sorority, 2003; NewsCorp's Exellence Award, Nominees Trophy, 2004. **Special Achievements:** First African-American woman exec in Fox's music dept, 1999. **Business Addr:** Director of TV Music Administration, Twentieth Century Fox Film Corp, 10201 W Pico Blvd Bldg 19/131, Los Angeles, CA 90035.

JOHNSON, MATHEW
Educator, writer. **Personal:** Born Aug 19, 1970, Philadelphia, PA; married. **Educ:** Earlham Col, BA; Columbia Univ, MFA. **Career:** Writer, educator; MTV, copywriter; Temple Univ; Rutgers Univ; Roosevelt Univ; Columbia Univ; Bard Col, asst prof lit prog; writer, currently; Univ Houston, Creative Writing Prog, asst prof,

currently; Time Out mag, columnist, "Utter Matness"; Books: Drop, 2000; Hunting in Harlem, 2003; John Constantine Hellblazer: Papa Midnite, 2006; The Great Negro Plot: A Tale of Conspiracy & Murder in Eighteenth-century New York, 2007; Incognegro, 2008. **Honors/Awds:** Thomas J Watson Fel; Hurston/Wright Legacy Award. **Special Achievements:** publ novel, Drop, 2000, Hunting Harlem, 2003; graphic novel: Incognegro. **Business Addr:** Assistant Professor, University of Houston, Creative Writing Program, 4800 Calhoun Rd, Roy Cullen Bldg Rm 229, Houston, TX 77004, **Business Phone:** (713)743-3015.

JOHNSON, MELVIN CARLTON, III (TRAVIS DAVIS)
Football player. **Personal:** Born Apr 15, 1972, Cincinnati, OH; children: Adonis. **Educ:** Univ Ky. **Career:** Tampa Bay Buccaneers, defensive back, 1995-97; Kansas City Chiefs, defensive back, 1998.

JOHNSON, MELVIN RUSSELL
Physician, military leader. **Personal:** Born Aug 26, 1946, Courtland, VA; married Joyce. **Educ:** Hampton Inst, BA, 1968; Meharry Med Col, MD, 1972. **Career:** Brooke Army Med Ctr, res internal med, 1972-73; Cape Fear Valley Hosp, assoc staff internist, 1975-77; Womack Army Hosp, staff intern, 1976, chief pulmonary dis, 1976-77, chief dept med, 1977-80; Wm Beaumont Army Med Ctr, staff pulmonologist, asst ch pulmonary dis, 1980; pvt pract physician, currently. **Orgs:** Omega Psi Phi Frat, 1971; Nat Asn Resd & Interns, 1972; Am Col Physicians, 1973; C A Whittier Med Soc, 1973; Nat Med Asn, 1974; Am Med Asn, 1975. **Honors/Awds:** National Defense Ribbon, 1972; Fel, Pulmonary Dis Brooke AMC, 1978-80. **Military Serv:** AUS, mc lt col, 1975. **Business Addr:** Physician, 3451 Victoria Blvd, PO Box 1406, Hampton, VA 23661, **Business Phone:** (757)723-9380.*

JOHNSON, MERTHA RUTH
Educator. **Personal:** Born in Jackson, MS; children: Victoria M. **Educ:** Jackson State Univ, BS, 1956; Univ San Francisco, MEd, 1977, MPA, 1983. **Career:** Chicago Sch Syst, educr, 1960-66; E Chicago Sch Syst, educr, 1967-70; Manpower Training Prog, adminr & teacher, 1966; OICW, adminr & teacher; San Mateo Sch Dist, educ, 1970-81; Neighborhood Housing Servs, exec dir, 1982-83; Atlanta Sch Syst, instr, currently. **Orgs:** Parlimentarian, Nat Coun Negro Women; Bus & Prof Women's Club; Atlanta Fedn Teachers; Nat Asn Advan Colored People; SCIC; consult, Lit Proj Black Cacus, GA State Legis; Atlanta's Ministry Int Stud. **Honors/Awds:** Lectr & consult, Multicultural Educ & Black History; Oak Tree Award, Outstanding Teacher of the Year; Nat Endowment for the Humanities Fel, 1994; Eli Wallace Research Fellow, 1993. **Special Achievements:** Workshop Crd Zora Neale Hurston Exhibit; consult, SETCLAE, African Images Publications; participated in development of model curriculum for teaching Dr King's non-violent principles in schools; African Infusion Methodol; Great Books discussion leader; contributing writer: Color Mag; Atlanta Voice; author "Black History Study Manual"; publ "A Study of the Leadership Factors Involved in the Operation of a Successful Neighborhood Housing Program"; selected poetry. **Business Addr:** Instructor, Atlanta School System, 45 Whitehouse Dr SW, Atlanta, GA 30314, **Business Phone:** (404)758-8871.

JOHNSON, MERVIL V.
Executive. **Personal:** Born Dec 20, 1953, Fort Worth, TX. **Educ:** Tx Chritian Univ, BA, Spanish & French, 1976; , bus sch, 1977; TX Christian Univ, M Pub Admin, 1982. **Career:** City Ft Worth, admin asst, 1978-79; City Ft Worth Library, spanish & french instr, 1980-83; North Central TX Coun Govts, reg clearing house coordr, 1980-84; ICMA Retirement Corp, serv rep, 1984; Tarrant County Fatherhood Coalition, vice chair, currently. **Orgs:** Chmn, univ liaison Urban Mgt Assts N TX, 1982-84; chmn, newsletter Conf Minority Pub Admin, 1983-84; Phi Sigma Iota Soc Lang, 1975-; Intl City Mgt Asn, 1981-; Am Soc for Public Admin, 1981. **Honors/Awds:** ITT Fellow, Intl Teleph & Teleg, 1976-77; Clarence E Ridley Scholar, TX City Mgt Asn, 1980-81; ICMA scholarship, Intl City Mgt Asn, 1981; NCTCOG Urban Fellow, N Central TX Coun Govts, 1980-82. **Business Addr:** Vice Chair, Tarrant County Fatherhood Coalition, 1320 S University Dr Suite 600, Fort Worth, TX 76107, **Business Phone:** (817)413-4400.

JOHNSON, MICHAEL
Automotive executive, president (organization), chief executive officer. **Personal:** Born Sep 8, 1959, Detroit, MI; son of Ernestine and Eural; married Cheryl R Batchelor, Sep 29, 1990; children: Michael Byron. **Educ:** Wayne State Univ, BA, 1983; Univ Detroit Sch Law, JD, 1986. **Career:** Dreisbach Cadillac, serv rep, 1977-87; UAW, staff attorney, 1987-89; Gen Motors, dealer cand, trainee, 1989-90; Durand Chevrolet-Geo-Pontiac-Olds Inc, pres & ceo, 1991-.

JOHNSON, MICHAEL
Athlete, journalist, executive. **Personal:** Born Sep 13, 1967, Dallas, TX; son of Paul Sr and Ruby; married Kerry; children: Sebastian. **Educ:** Baylor Univ, BA, mkt, 1990. **Career:** Athlete (retired), journalist, executive; US Olympic Team, track & field, 1992 & 1996, athlete, 2000; Baylor Track & Field, consult; BBC, UK, tv athletics pundit; Daily Telegraph, column writer; Ultimate Performance, founder, currently; Michael Johnson Performance, pres, currently. **Honors/Awds:** Male Athlete of the Year, Track & Field News, 1990; First Place 400 meters, Mobile 1 Invitational, 1991; Gold Medalist, World Track & Field Championships, Tokyo, 1991; First Place 200 meters, Mobile IAAF Grand Prix, 1991; Olympic Games, Gold Medalist, 1992; Historic Double-Gold Medalist, 1996; Gold Medal 400m, Goodwill Games, 1998; World Record Holder, 1996; Gold Medal, World Record 43.18, World Championship, Seville, Spain, 1999; AAU Sullivan Award, 1997; Tex Sports Hall of Fame, 1998; Ten Outstanding Young Americans Award, 1999; Gold Medal, Summer Olympics; U.S. Track & Field Hall of Fame, 2004; Jesse Owens Award, 3-time winner. **Special Achievements:** Broke own record for 200 meter, World Track and Field Championships, 1991; first to win 400-meter race at two consecutive Olympics. **Business Addr:** President, Michael Johnson Performance, 6051 Alma Dr, McKinney, TX 75070.

JOHNSON, MICHAEL ANTHONY
Educator. **Personal:** Born Jan 15, 1951, New York, NY; children: Dieynaba. **Educ:** NY City Tech Col, AA, 1971; City Col NY, Pre-Med, 1973; Empire State Col, BS, Sci Educ 1985. **Career:** Sci Skills Ctr Inc, exec dir, 1980, prin, 1996-; DMC Energy, consult, 1981-84; Energy Task Force, sci writer, 1982-83; NY City Tech Col, res proj, 1983-84. **Orgs:** Pres, Stud Alumni Asn, Empire State Col, 1982-86; NY Acad Scis; AAAS. **Honors/Awds:** Positive Father of the Year Award, 1984; Outstanding Young Americans, 1985; Clark Fellow in Sci & Math Educ Columbia Univ, 1986; Outstanding Achievements in Comm PHNC, 1986; Professional Award, Nat Assoc Negro Bus & Prof Women, 1987; Recognition Award, Women's League Sci & Med, 1987. **Business Phone:** (718)789-7513.*

JOHNSON, MICHAEL L
Lawyer. **Personal:** Born Aug 1, 1958, Bonn, Germany; son of Martinus and Barbara; married Andrea, Aug 22, 1980; children: Christopher, Carl & Alyse. **Educ:** Berklee Col, BS, music educ, 1979; Wayne State Univ, MEd, 1981; Univ Mich, Law Sch, JD, 1986. **Career:** Dickinson Wright, Law Firm, atty assoc, 1986-89; Ameritech, Advert Serv, atty, 1989-92; Ameritech-Mich, regulatory atty, 1993-94, Tel Indust Serv, vpres gen coun, 1994; Pay Phone Serv, vpres gen coun, 1994; Satellite Imaging Corp, vpres sales & bus develop, 2006-. **Orgs:** Mich State Bar, 1986-; Am Bar Asn, 1987-; Detroit Bar Asn, 1987-94; Wolverine Bar Asn, 1987-93; Ill State Bar, 1994-; Chicago Bar Asn, 1995-. **Home Addr:** 1757 Tanager Way, Long Grove, IL 60047, **Home Phone:** (847)540-1115. **Business Phone:** (832)237-2900.

JOHNSON, MICHELE
Salesperson. **Personal:** Born Aug 12, 1959, Brooklyn, NY. **Educ:** Boston Univ, BS, 1981; Fordham Univ. **Career:** CBS Inc, clippings coord, 1981-82, admin asst, 1982-83, sr sales asst, 1983-86; JP Martin Assoc Inc, exec asst, 1986-87; Taylor Made Press, sales rep. **Orgs:** CBS Black Employ Assoc, 1981-86; Nat Assoc Black MBA's 1986-; Assoc MBA Execs 1986-; Advantage Club NY 1986-; dir, Union Bapt Church Youth Comn, 1986-; volunteer Roosevelt Ctr Comn Growth, 1987-. **Business Addr:** Sales Representative, Taylor Made Press, 100 Water St, Brooklyn, NY 11201, **Business Phone:** (718)858-1668.*

JOHNSON, MILDRED H
Educator. **Personal:** Born Jan 1, Cleveland, OH; daughter of Owena Bradshaw; married John B, Jan 29, 1949 (died 2002). **Educ:** W Va State Col, BA; Wayne State Univ, MA; Univ Detroit, MA. **Career:** Detroit Metropolitan Mutual Ins Co, office mgr, 1948-63; Detroit Pub Schs, teacher, 1963-76, learning disability teacher, 1976-80, teacher consult, 1980-89; Educ Guidance Tutoring Ctr, dir & owner, 1986-. **Orgs:** Phi Delta Kappa Honors Fraternity; Nat Asn Negro Bus & Prof Women; Gamma Phi Delta Sorority; Womens Div, United Negro Col Fund. **Honors/Awds:** Greater Rising Star, Grand Chap, Urban Bible Col; Order of Eastern Star, Detroit. **Home Addr:** 19167 Sorrento, Detroit, MI 48235. **Business Addr:** Owner, Director, Education Guidance Tutoring Ctr Inc, 17500 W McNichols, Detroit, MI 48235.

JOHNSON, MILTON D.
Executive. **Personal:** Born May 27, 1928, Sour Lake, TX; married Robbie Russell; children: Paula & Pamela. **Educ:** Paul Quinn Col, BBA, 1951. **Career:** Victoria, TX, teacher, 1956-64; Union Carbide Corp, employee rels assoc, 1964-. **Orgs:** Bd educ, La Marque Ind Schs, 1972-; chmn adv bd, First State Bank Hitchcock, TX; pres, C C, 1974. **Military Serv:** AUS, 1951-53. **Business Addr:** PO Box 471, Texas City, TX 77590.

JOHNSON, MIRIAM B.
Businessperson. **Personal:** Born in Washington, DC; married Norman B. **Educ:** Miner Teachers Col, Wash, DC; Brooklyn Col, attended 1972. **Career:** Black Music makers Inc, exec dir; Husband's Law Off, off mgr. **Orgs:** Vol secy, NAACP, Brooklyn Br; bd dir, Brooklyn Asn Mental Health; mem exec bd, Brooklyn Bur Comn Serv; chairperson, Mental Health Comt Health Syst Agency Dist Bd; Urban Comn Episcopal Diocese, Long Island; parliamentarian historian of Brooklyn Lawyers Wives; prog chairperson, Greater NY Links Inc; former mem, Relations Comt Cent YWCA; exec bd, Stuyvesant Comm Ctr; gen chmn, City Wide Com Looking Glass Ball a fund raising play ball for the construct & devel Mac Donough St Comm Ctr, Bedford-Stuyvesant. **Honors/Awds:** Community Service Award, Berean Baptist Church, 1950 & 1974; NY Amsterdam News; Mac Donough St Comm Ctr, 1963; awarded baccalaureate degree in Sociology cum laude.

JOHNSON, MITCHELL A
College teacher, football player, executive director. **Personal:** Born Mar 1, 1942, Chicago, IL; son of Mitchell and Marcella; divorced; children: Mitchell Matthew & Margo K. **Educ:** Univ Calif Los Angeles, BA, 1965. **Career:** Football Player, School administrator (retired), executive director; Wash Redskins, prof football player, 1972; Student Loan Mkt Asn, sr vpres, 1973-94; MAJ Capital Mgt Inc, pres, 1994-; Eldorado Bankshares Inc, dir; Citizen Investment Trust, trustee, Fed Agr Mortgage Corp, dir, currently. **Orgs:** Funding pres, Wash Asn Money Managers, 1982-; bd dir, Arena Stage, 1987-; bd dir, Mentors Inc, 1990-; bd dir, Nat Rehab Hosp. **Business Phone:** 800-879-3276.

JOHNSON, NATHANIEL J, SR.
Educator. **Personal:** Born Oct 1, 1940, Philadelphia, PA; son of Lucius James and Violet Beatrice Branch; married Fannie Mary Long. **Educ:** LaSalle Univ, Philadelphia, PA, BA, comp & info sci, 1990; Univ Tex, Austin, MBA, 1993. **Career:** Kirk Eng Corp, math technician, 1965-67; Sch Dist Philadelphia, programmer, 1967-68; RCA Corp, New York, NY, sr systs, 1968-70; Electronic Data Systs, New York, NY, systs engr, 1970-72; Hertz Corp, New York, NY, New York Data Ctr, mgr, 1973-80; Amerada Hess Corp, Woodbridge, NJ, mgr comput servs, 1980-83; SCT Resource Mgt Corp, Malvern, PA, exec dir, comput serv, 1983-87; Milwaukee County, Milwaukee, WI, Info Mgt Serv Div, mgr, 1987-88; Prairie View Agr & Mech Univ, exec dir info systs, 1990-94; Comput & Commun Serv, exec dir; NJJ Assoc, owner, 2006-. **Orgs:** Fin Aide Adv Comt, Wayne County Community Col, 1984-85; Asn Comput Machinery, 1987-88; Soc Info Mgt, 1987-88; Govt Mgt Info Systs, 1987-88; In Plant Mgt Asn, 1987-88; Minorities Comput Related Occup, 1987-88; MIS Curric Adv Bd, Marquette Univ, 1987-88; bd dir, Tex Asn State Supported Comput & Commun, 1992-; Asn Comput Machinery, 1994-95; Marquette Univ, Comput Sci Curric Comt, 1994-95; Soc Info Mgt, 1995; Info Technol Client Coun, 1995; Diversity Team, Nat Exchange Carrier Asn, 1996-99; Int Facil Mgt Asn, 1998-99; Asn Col & Univ Adminrs, 2000-05; Info Technol Fin Mgt Asn, 2000-05; Steering Comt, Common Solutions Group, 2002-03. **Home Phone:** (713)890-4286. **Business Addr:** Owner, NJJ Associates, 4540 Lakes Edge Suite 3, West Chester, OH 45069-8675, **Business Phone:** (617)201-4322.

JOHNSON, NIESA
Basketball player, basketball coach. **Personal:** Born Feb 7, 1973, Clinton, MS. **Educ:** Univ Ala, BA, human health serv, 1995. **Career:** Basketball player (retired), basketball coach: Long Beach Stingrays, guard, 1996-98; Seattle Reign, 1998; Charlotte Sting, guard, 1999-01; Detroit Shock, guard, 2001; North ridge Matadors, Calif State Univ, asst coach. **Honors/Awds:** Nat Player of the Yr, 1995. **Special Achievements:** Finalist, Naismith Award; two-time All-American; one of the best in SEC history, ESPN.com; one of the five-best players in the history of the conference, Nancy Lieberman. *

JOHNSON, NORMA HOLLOWAY
Judge. **Personal:** Born Jan 1, 1932?, Lake Charles, LA; daughter of Henry L and Beatrice Williams; married Julius A, Jun 18, 1964. **Educ:** DC Teachers Col, BS, 1955; Georgetown Univ Law Ctr, JD, 1962. **Career:** Sch teacher; Dept Justice, trial atty, 1963-67; DC, asst corp coun, 1967-70; Superior Ct DC, judge, 1970-80; US dist ct, fed judge, (1980-97); chief fed judge, sr judge, currently. **Orgs:** Fel, Am Bar Found; dir, Nat Asn Black Women Attys; Am Judicature Soc; Nat Bar Asn; Am Bar Asn; Wash Bar Asn; Nat Asn Women Judges; dir, DC St Law; dir, Judiciary Leadership Develop Comt. **Special Achievements:** First black woman to lead federal court in nation's capital. **Business Addr:** Senior Judge, US District Court, District of Columbia, Rm 2315 333 Const Ave NW, Washington, DC 20001, **Business Phone:** (202)354-3500.

JOHNSON, NORMAN B.
Lawyer. **Personal:** Born in Lake Charles, LA; married Julius A. **Educ:** DC Teachers Col, BS, 1955; Georgetown Univ Law Ctr, JD, 1962. **Career:** Dept Justice, trial atty, 1963-67; DC, asst corp coun, 1967-70; Superior Ct DC, judge, 1970-. **Orgs:** Dir, Am Judicature Soc; dir, Nat Asn Women Judges; Nat Asn Black Women Attys; Nat Bar Asn; Wash Bar Asn; Am Bar Asn. *

JOHNSON, DR. NORRIS BROCK
College teacher, educator. **Personal:** Born Apr 29, 1942, Chicago, IL; divorced. **Educ:** Mich State Univ, BA, eng & art, 1965, MA, am lit, 1967, MA, anthrop, 1972, PhD, anthrop, 1976. **Career:** Univ NC, Chapel Hill, Dept Anthrop, fac mem, 1977, from asst prof to assoc prof, 1979-91; prof, 1992-; Univ Tokyo & Waseda Univ, Tokyo, Japan, Fulbright Hays lectr, 1985-86; 13th Century Zen Buddhist Temples & Temple Gardens, res, 1985-86; NC State Univ, Sch Archit, Dept Landscape Design, vis assoc prof, 1988;

Spencer Found grant, 1990; Zen Buddhist Temple Gardens, Kyoto, Japan, res, 1992, 1998; Inst Res Social Sci, Univ NC, res grant & curric technol enhancement grant, 2000; Penland Sch Crafts, resident scholar, 2003. **Orgs:** Fac assoc, Nat Humanities Fac, 1980-; fel Am Anthrop Asn, 1980-; fel Inst Arts & Humanities, Univ NC, 1989, 1997; fel Landscape Archit Dumbarton Oaks, Wash, DC, 1990-91; Chapman fel, Inst Arts & Humanities, Univ NC, 1994; Asn Black Anthropologists; bd mem, Soc Humanistic Anthrop. **Honors/Awds:** Honigmann Lect, Church Reconciliation, 1983; Fulbright Award, Japan-Waseda Univ & Univ Tokyo, Komaba, 1985-86. **Business Addr:** Professor, University North Carolina, Department Anthropology, 301 Alumni Building, Chapel Hill, NC 27599-3115, **Business Phone:** (919)962-2389.

JOHNSON, OLRICK
Singer, football player, executive. **Personal:** Born Aug 20, 1977, Miami, FL; son of Lena; married Amirah Brown, 2004. **Educ:** Fla A&M Univ, theater educ. **Career:** Football player (retired), singer, executive; Minn Vikings, linebacker, 1999; NY Jets, linebacker, 1999; New Eng Patriots, linebacker, 2000; Video appearances: "Brighter Day"; "Shook"; "Happy & You Know It"; "NFL Super Bowl XXXVI & XXXVII Gospel Fest", Word Network, BET; "NFL Kick Off Bash"; "Deco Drive"; Albums: Bless My Soul, 2004; How Did We Get Here. **Honors/Awds:** Silver Knight Award, Miami Herald. **Business Addr:** Owner, Singer, Olyric Entertainment, RJC Management, 5925 NE 80 Ave, Portland, OR 97218-2891, **Business Phone:** (503)595-3000.

JOHNSON, DR. OTIS SAMUEL
School administrator, mayor. **Personal:** Born Mar 26, 1942, Savannah, GA; son of Lillian Brown Spencer and Otis Johnson; divorced. **Educ:** Armstrong State Col, AA, 1964; Univ Ga, AB, 1967; Atlanta Univ, MSW, 1969; Brandeis Univ, PhD, 1980. **Career:** City Savannah Model Cities Prog, dep dir, 1969-71; Simmons Col Social Work, spec instr, 1975-76; Savannah State Col, asst prof, 1976-80, assoc prof, 1981-87, prof, 1987-91, Dept Soc Sci, head, 1980-84, Dept Social Work, 1985-88, prof social work & sociol, 1987-91, Sch Social Sci & Lib Arts, 1998; City Savannah, alderman, 1982-88; Housing Authority Savannah, comnr, 1989; Chatham Savannah Youth Futures Authority, exec dir, 1988-98; Savannah City, mayor, currently. **Orgs:** Acad Cert Social Workers, 1971-; secy, Ga Chap, Nat Asn Social Workers, 1984-86; Asn Study Afro-Am Life & Hist; Cent Baptist Church Trustees; Alpha Kappa Delta Socio Hon Soc; Pi Gamma Mu Social Sci Hon Fraternity; bd dirs, Nat Coun Community Ment Health Ctr, 1988-91; Am Legion; Black Community Crusade C; C's Defense Fund; Nat Community Bldg Network; bd mem, Mary Reynolds Babcock Found, 1996-. **Honors/Awds:** Social Worker of the Year, SE GA, Nat Asn Social Workers, 1984; Social Worker of the Year, GA Chap, Nat Asn Social Workers, 1995; Named Healthy Hero by Amerigroup Community Care, 2008. **Military Serv:** USN, 1959-62, received hon discharge; Naval Reserve, 1962-65. **Business Addr:** Mayor, Savannah City, Civic Ctr, Savannah, GA 31401, **Business Phone:** (912)651-6550.*

JOHNSON, PAMELA. **See ROSHELL, PAMELA P.**

JOHNSON, PARKER COLLINS
School administrator. **Personal:** Born Oct 17, 1961, Boston, MA; son of John Quincy III and Addie Collins. **Educ:** Williams Col, BA, 1984; Harvard Univ, Cambridge, Mass, EdM, 1990. **Career:** Fitchburg State Col, asst dir admis, 1984-85; Bentley Col, asst dir admis, 1985-87; Tufts Univ, Medford, MA, asst dir admis, 1987-89; Harvard Univ, Cambridge, MA, grad stud, 1989-90; Am Coun Educ, Washington, DC, researcher, 1990; Calif State Univ, Northridge, CA, counr, 1990-92; Gettysburg Col, Cult Advan, dean, 1992-96; Asn Am Cols & Univs, assoc dir curric, 1996-; Univ Southern Calif, Ctr Higher Educ Policy Anal, res asst, 1998; Univ British Columbia, first yr coordr, 2002-04; Soc Intercultural Educ Training & Res, secy, currently. **Orgs:** Nat Asn Col Admis Counselors, 1984-89; Greater Boston InterUniv Coun, 1985-89; vpres, bd dirs, Fitchburg Comt Action Ctr, 1985; mem-at-large, New Eng Consortium Black Admis Counselors, 1985-89; vol, Boston Youth Risk, 1986-89; external co-chair, New Eng Consortium Black Admis Counselors Inc, 1987-89; Am Asn Higher Educ, 1987-; bd mem, Mass Pre-Engineering Prog, 1988-90; Trans Africa Inc Boston Chap, 1987-90; YMCA; comt mem, Int Progs Comt, 1989-94. **Honors/Awds:** Outstanding Community Service Award, African Am Ctr, Tufts Univ, 1989. **Business Addr:** Secretary, Society for Intercultural Education Training & Research, Centre for Intercultural Commun Continuing Studies, W 4th Ave Suite 261-1917, Vancouver, BC, Canada BCV6J1M7.

JOHNSON, PATRICE DOREEN
Journalist. **Personal:** Born Jul 17, 1952, New York, NY; daughter of Irma Levy and Wilbourne. **Educ:** Barnard Col, BA, 1974; Columbia Univ Grad Sch Jour, MSJ, 1976. **Career:** Dauntless Books, asst ed, 1974-75; Encore Am & Worldwide News, assoc ed, 1976-80; Newsweek Magazine, researcher/reporter, 1981-96; Money Magazine, reporter 1997-2001; Independent writer, currently. **Orgs:** Panelist Am's Black Forum TV show, 1978-79; mem, Nat Alliance Third World Journalists, 1980-85. **Home Addr:** 355 West 85 St, New York, NY 10024, **Home Phone:** (212)595-0683.

JOHNSON, PATRICIA ANITA
School administrator, administrator, curator. **Personal:** Born Mar 17, 1944, Chicago, IL; children: David, Todd. **Educ:** Oberlin Col, BA, 1961; Grad Sch Community Devel, Fellowship, 1983; US Int Univ, MFA, 1985. **Career:** Brockman Gallery Prods, curator, 1976-78; New Visions Gallery, owner, 1978-82; Multicultural Arts Inst, curator, 1982-83; San Diego Community Col Dist, cultural affairs coordr, 1982-85; S Dallas Cultural Ctr City Arts Prog, dir, 1985-. **Orgs:** Exhib consult, Multicultural Arts Inst, 1981-83; grant recipient, CA Arts Coun, 1983-85; Catfish Club San Diego, 1983-85; adv comt, San Diego Arts Festival Bd, 1985; bd mem, City of San Diego Pub Arts Adv Bd, 1985; founder, INROADS an organ of Black Prof Singles, 1985. **Honors/Awds:** Achievement in Fine Arts Award, City of Los Angeles, 1978; Achievement in Fine Arts San Diego Black Achievement Awdars, 1985; Community Service Award, San Diego Chap Nat Asn Advan Colored People, 1985.

JOHNSON, PATRICIA DUREN
Executive, government official. **Personal:** Born Oct 22, 1943, Columbus, OH; daughter of James and Rosetta J; married Harold H Johnson Jr, Dec 25, 1965; children: Jill Johnson. **Educ:** Ohio State Univ, Columbus, BS, educ, 1965; Univ Mich, Grad Sch Mgt, Ann Arbor, 1984. **Career:** Teacher, 1966-72; ITT Hartford, Portland, OR, sales rep, 1972-73; UHP Healthcare, Managed Healthcare Servs, vpres; Wellpoint Health Networks; Blue Cross Calif, Woodland Hills, CA, sr vpres govt servs, 1975, nat mkt officer, gen mgr; P Johnson & Assocs, pres, currently; Qual & Productivity Comn, Los Angeles, CA, comnr, currently. **Orgs:** pres, Delta Sigma Theta Sorority, 1964-65; Am Hosp Asn, 1976-; Women Health Admin, 1979-; bd dir, Am Cancer Soc, 1988-94. **Honors/Awds:** Women of Achievement, YWCA, 1979; Black Woman of Achievement, Nat Asn Advan Colored People, 1987. **Special Achievements:** Author of ABC's of Medicare, 1976; author of How Kids Earn Money, 1978; One of 10 Corp Black Women, Essence Mag, 1989; One of 100 Best and Brightest Black Women in 1990, Ebony Magazine. **Business Addr:** Commissioner, Quality and Productivity Commission, 565 Kenneth Hahn Hall Admin, 500 W Temple St, Los Angeles, CA 90012, **Business Phone:** (213)974-1431.

JOHNSON, PATRICIA L
Educator, lawyer. **Personal:** Born Jan 29, 1956, New York, NY; daughter of Mamie Johnson. **Educ:** John Jay Col, BA, 1977, MA, 1979; Cornel Univ Sch Law, pre-law prog, 1978; Rutgers Sch Law Newark, JD, 1985; Off Ct Admin NY Frontline Leadership, cert, 1988. **Career:** Bur Alcohol Tobacco & Firearms, stud aide, 1977; US Res Serv, br mgr, 1979-82; Bronx Family Ct, notifications supvr, 1982-83; Bronx Dist Attys Off, legal asst, 1983-85; Judicial Friends, law intern, 1985, asst dist atty, 1985-86; Bronx Pub Admin Off, assoc coun, 1986-88; John Jay Col Criminal Justice, New York, NY, adj prof, 1986, prof, currently; Bronx Surrogate's Ct, Bronx, NY, dep chief clerk, 1988-. **Orgs:** Black Women Attys, 1981-; Nat Bar Asn,1983-; Phi Alpha Delta Law Frat Int, 1983-; Prof Bus Women, 1985-; Nat Asn Advan Colored People, 1985-; Nat Women's Polit Caucus, 1985-; Asn Black Law Students Serv Black Comn, 1985; Black Entertainment & Sports Lawyers Asn, 1986-; recording sec, Black Bar Asn Bronx Co, 1986-; corresp sec chair prog bd, Black Bar Bronx, 1987-89; exec dir, founder, Black Entertainment &, Sports Tribune, 1989-; Big Sister, Big Sisters Inc, 1989; chairperson, Entertainment & Sports Law Comm Metrop Black Bar Asn, 1989-. **Honors/Awds:** Outstanding Achievement Award Distinction Rutgers Women's Rights Reporter, 1985. **Special Achievements:** Battling the motion picture assoc of American movie rating of "The White Girl" published in NY Law Journal, 1988. **Business Addr:** Professor, John Jay College of Criminal Justice, Rm 422T 899 Tenth Ave, New York, NY 10019, **Business Phone:** (212)237-8000.

JOHNSON, PAUL EDWIN
Psychologist. **Personal:** Born Dec 27, 1933, Buffalo, NY; son of Maggie J; married Shirley Ann Williams; children: Paula Rene, Darryl Edwin. **Educ:** Talladega Col AL, AB, Psychol, 1955; Harvard Univ, MA, MS, Psychol, 1957; Hartford Semnry Fed, CT, Master-Devnity, 1958; Auburn Univ, MEd, Couns Psychol, 1974, EdD, Counc Psychol, 1980. **Career:** Psychologist (retired); N congregational Ch NY, NY, assoc minister, 1958-62; US Army, chaplain (ltc, ret) 1962-82; AL Dept MH & MR, consul III-MR div, 1972-79, dir quality assurance-MR Div, 1979-94; Pvt Practice, psychologist & minister; congregational-Christian Ch Montgomery, AL, 1980-94. **Orgs:** Bd dir, Montgomery Coun Aging, 1982-84; chmn, Legislative Strike Force Am Mental Health Coun Asn, 1983-84; pres, Ala Mental Health Coun Asn, 1983-84; consult, Ala Dept Pub Safety-Acad, 1983-85; consult, Ala Coun Higher Educ (HBC's), 1984-85; exec comn, Montgomery Area United Way, 1984-86; Ala Bd Examiners Coun, 1986-90; Delta Phi Kappa; Alpha Phi Alpha. **Military Serv:** AUS chaplain (ltc, ret) 21 yrs; Silver Star; Bronze Star (3); Meritorious Svc; Army Comm Med (3) 1962-72; Air Medal (3), Vietnamese Cross of Gallantry; Master Parachutist Badge. **Home Addr:** 118 Elm Dr, Montgomery, AL 36117. *

JOHNSON, PAUL L.
Photojournalist. **Personal:** Born Oct 27, 1943, Savannah, GA; married Angelyne Russell; children: Monifa Ife & Ayeola Binta. **Educ:** Matriculated Savannah State Col; Univ Ghana; Univ S Ill; Univ Fla. **Career:** Acad Black Culture, dir Savannah Model Cities Culture Ctr, 1969-72; profthree free TV pub serv progs, 1971-72; Acad Black Culture Inc, co-founder; KTUL-TV, news photographer. **Orgs:** Bd dir, Inner City Community Ctr, 1970-72; art instr, local cap agency, EOA, 1970; slide lectures, Savannah State Col, pub schs & libraries; PUSH; Asn Study African Am Life & Hist; Nat Asn Advan Colored People. **Honors/Awds:** Year scholarship, Omega Psi Phi, 1961; Outstanding Young Man of American Award, 1972. **Military Serv:** AUS, spl 5, 1967-68. **Business Addr:** News Photographer, KTUL-TV, PO Box 8, Tulsa, OK 74101.

JOHNSON, PAUL LAWRENCE
Judge. **Personal:** Born Sep 23, 1931, Coatesville, PA; married Dorothy Elizabeth Flowers; children: Bruce Michael, Darryl Lawrence. **Educ:** St Paul's Col, attended 1953. **Career:** Judge (retired); Lukens Steel Co, shearman, 1957-63; estimator, 1963-70; Timestudy Tech, 1970-84; Coatesville City Coun, pres, 1980-85; Supreme Ct Pa, dist justice, 1985-93. **Orgs:** Bd mem, Citadel Fed Credit Union, 1972-; pres, Trustees Hutchinson Church 1972; pres, Lancaster County Chap Credit Unions, 1984-87; bd, Coatesville Sr Citizens Ctr, 1983-88, 1996-, pres, 1998-00; United Way, 1987-90; City of Coatesville Authority, 1998-; exec bd, Brandyville YMCA, 1999-; pres, Coatesville Area Sch Dist. **Honors/Awds:** Outstanding Community Service Award J Frederic Wiese, 1984. **Military Serv:** AUS, corpl, 1954-56. **Home Addr:** 514 Elm St, Coatesville, PA 19320. *

JOHNSON, PEPPER (THOMAS PEPPER JOHNSON)
Football player, football coach. **Personal:** Born Jul 29, 1964, Detroit, MI; children: Dionte. **Educ:** Ohio State Univ, coun & phys educ. **Career:** Football player (retired), Football coach; New York Giants, linebacker, 1986-92; Cleveland Browns, 1993-95; Detroit Lions, 1996; New York Jets, 1997-98; New Eng Patriots, asst coach, 2001-, inside linebackers coach, 2001-03, defensive line coach, 2004-; Pepper Johnson Enterprises, founder. **Orgs:** March Dimes; Make a Wish Found; Children's Leukemia Found; Pepper Johnsons Youth Found; Michael Landon Found; Carol M Baldwin Breast Cancer Res Found; Dylan MalaMala Cystic Fibrosis Found; Trey Whitfield Found. **Honors/Awds:** Ohio State Hall of Fame, 2001. **Business Addr:** Assistant Coach, Defensive Line Coach, New England Patriots, One Patriot Plz, Foxborough, MA 02035, **Business Phone:** 800-543-1776.

JOHNSON, PHYLLIS CAMPBELL
Government official, administrator. **Personal:** Born Jul 21, 1954, Fort Worth, TX; daughter of Mira G and Ann Miller. **Educ:** Univ Tex, BA, commun, 1979, MA, urban affairs, 1984. **Career:** Tex Instruments, mfg supvr, 1979-82; N Cent Tex Coun Govts, urban fel, 1984; City Fort Worth, TX, human serv coordr, 1984-87, admin asst, 1987-88, fiscal serv admin, 1988-. **Orgs:** Kappa Delta Pi Hon Soc, Univ Tex, Arlington, 1979-; Neighborhood Adv Coun, 1983-; Urban Mgt Asst N Tex, 1984-; Tex Munic League, 1985-; Network Exec Women, 1985-; secy, N Tex Conf Minority Pub Admins, 1986-87; vpres, Nat Forum Black Pub Admins, 1987-88; Tarrant County League Women Voters, 1987-88; Nat Asn Advan Colored People; Fort Worth Metrop Black Chamber Com; Minority Leaders & Citizens Coun. **Honors/Awds:** Notable Woman of Tex, Awards & Hon Soc Am, 1984-85; Outstanding Young Women of Am, 1986; Leadership Fort Worth Award, Fort Worth Chamber Com, 1988. *

JOHNSON, PHYLLIS MERCEDES
Executive. **Personal:** Born Apr 17, 1919, Hutchinson, KS; married James P; children: Beverly. **Educ:** Lincoln Univ, BS, 1941; Wash Univ, MA, 1965; S Ill Univ, attended 1968. **Career:** Executive (retired); Teacher home econ, 1942-46; Mo Div Empl Sec, dist mgr, 1951-79. **Orgs:** Alpha Kappa Alpha; pres, St Louis Personnel & Guid Asn; Mo Personnel & Guid Asn; Nat Asn Advan Colored People; Urban League; Int Asn Personnel Employ Sec; Am Asn Univ Women. **Honors/Awds:** Merit Award, St Louis Personnel & Guid Asn, 1973. **Home Phone:** (636)946-1559.

JOHNSON, DR. POMPIE LOUIS, JR.
Banker. **Personal:** Born Dec 19, 1926, Pocatello, ID; son of Pompie L Sr and Nellie B; married Marylynn T Hughes; children: Tamara & Karen. **Educ:** Ind State Univ, BA, 1950; Boston Univ Sch Law, JD, 1952; Am Savings & Loan Inst, dipl, 1967; Am Inst Banking, dipl, 1971. **Career:** Boston MA, atty, 1952-55; Mutual Omaha Ins Co, sales & claims, 1956-60; Golden State Mutual Life Ins Co, planning specialist, 1960-62; Safety Savings & Loan Asn, vpres-mgr, 1963-66; Security Pacific Nat Bank, vpres-mgr, 1967-72; Calif Fed Savings & Loan Asn, vpres corp savings, 1973. **Orgs:** Bd dir, Watts Ca Econ Dev Comn, 1973-76; asst treas, Calif State Rep Control Comn, 1974-78; bd dir, Inglewood Calif Chamber Comn, 1975-78; bd dir, Inglewood Calif Merchants Asn, 1975-78; pres, SW Los Angeles Rotary Club, 1979-80; bd dir, Gardena Calif Econ Dev Comm, 1983-; Rotary Int, Dist 5280, Gov Rep, 1994-95; Rotary Int, Dist 5280, chmn Club Serv, 1995-96. **Honors/Awds:** Deleg, Perm Org Comn Rep Nat Conv, 1972; Unsung Hero Award LA Newspaper, 1972; del, Rotary Int Conv Rome, Italy, 1979; Rotarian of the Yr, Los Angeles Rotary, 1982. **Military Serv:** USAF, cprl, 1945-46.

JOHNSON, R. BENJAMIN
Government official. **Personal:** Born Jul 14, 1944, Marion, AR; son of Robert Lee and Willie B Clay; married Jacqueline Vassar,

Dec 6, 1975; children: Nancy, Rahman, Endesha, Jua & Sekou. **Educ:** Indiana Univ; Antioch Col; Tufts Univ; Prince George's Community Col MgtInst. **Career:** WSBT TV, news reporter & host afternoon talk show; Action Inc, dir employ;Manpower Assistance Prog, manpower specialist; Youth Advocacy Prog, dir,1971-73; St Joseph County Credit Union, mgr/treas, 1975-77; Credit UnionInst Nat Ctr Urban Ethnic Affairs, dir, 1977-79; White House Off ConsumerAffairs, dir consumer progs/spec asst consumer adv pres, 1979-81; NatCredit Union Admin, spec asst chmn bd, 1981-82; Black Resource Guide Inc,pres, 1981-; Dept Consumer & Regulatory Affairs, Wash, adminr busregulation admin, 1983-87, adminr housing & environ regulation admin,1987-88; special asst mayor, 1988-89; Dept Pub & Assisted Housing, dir,1989-91; White House Off Pub Liaison, dep asst pres, 1993-2001; BICO Inc,exec vpres & dir, 2001-; Rapid HIV Detection Corp, officer & dir. **Orgs:** Chmn, S Bend Black Voters Asn; vpres, Valley Chap Credit Unions; chmn, StJoseph County CETA Adv Bd; publ, The Black Resource Guide; mem, AFLAC's board. **Honors/Awds:** Distinguished Government Service Award, 1987 & 1990; Outstanding Professionals Award, Bus Exchange Network, 1987; hon doctorate, Morgan State Univ, 1998; hon doctorate, Ark Baptist Church, 1999. **Special Achievements:** Numerous publications including in New Credit Union Management Systems,1969, The Community Development Credit Union, 1977 & 1979, The BlackResource Guide, 1981-91. **Military Serv:** AUS; Hon Discharge. **Business Addr:** Executive Vice President, Director, BICO Inc, 3116 Valhalla Dr, Burbank, CA 91505, **Business Phone:** (818)842-7179.

JOHNSON, RAFER
Athlete, television sportscaster, sports promoter. **Personal:** Born Aug 18, 1935, Hillsboro, TX; married Betsy Thorsen, 1971; children: Jennifer & Josh. **Educ:** Univ Calif, Los Angeles. **Career:** Decathalon athlete; People to People Intl; sports broadcaster; Peace Corps recruiter; Special Olympics Southern Ca, chmn bd governor, currently. **Orgs:** CA Special Olympics, co-founder, gov's bd chair, 1992-; CA State Recreation Commission; Fair Housing Congress; Fellowship of Christian Athletes; Campus Crusade; Dept of Health, Edu & Welfare, Committee on Mental Retardation. **Honors/Awds:** Sportsman of the Year, Sports Illustrated, 1958; Gold medal, decathelon, Olympics, 1960; Athlete of the Yr, Assoc Press, 1960; Inducted, United States Olympic Hall of Fame, 1983; inducted California Hall of Fame, The California Museum, 2009. **Special Achievements:** Film appearances: Sergeant Rutledge, 1960; The Sins of Rachel Cade, 1961; Tarzan & the Great River, 1967; Free to Be. You & Me, 1974; License to Kill, 1989; autobiography, The Best That I Can Be, 1998; 1968 with Tom Brokaw, 2007. **Business Addr:** Chairman, Special Olympics Southern California, 5875 Green Valley, Cir Suite 200, Culver City, CA 90230.*

JOHNSON, RAGLIN. See JOHNSON, FRAN.

JOHNSON, RALPH C
Chief executive officer, president (organization). **Personal:** Born Dec 4, 1941, Pittsburg, TX; married Nadine; children: Stacie. **Educ:** Oakwood Col, BS, 1964; Wichita State Univ, MS, 1967. **Career:** Fox & Co, Kans City, staff acct, 1964-71; Ala A&M Col, assoc prof, bus adminr, 1967-68; Ralph C Johnson & Co PC, founder, 1971-, pres & chief exec officer, currently. **Orgs:** Lic CPA, KS, 1966, MO, 1971; Am Inst CPA's. **Business Addr:** President, Chief Executive Officer, Ralph C Johnson & Company PC, 106 W 11th St Suite 1630, Kansas City, MO 64105-1817, **Business Phone:** (816)472-8900 Ext 302.

JOHNSON, RAY
Executive. **Personal:** Born Dec 13, 1935, Port Gibson, MS; son of Norah Johnson; divorced; children: Raymond Bradle & Fredrick Norman. **Career:** Executive (retired); McDonald's Corp, Nat oper adv bd; McDonald's Restaurants, owner-operator 10 stores; Ray Johnson Enterprises Inc, pres & chief exec officer. **Orgs:** Ariz State Athletic Comm, chmn-comnr, 1981-83; pres, Round-One Prod, 1983-86; chmn, Ariz State Liquor Community, 1983-; comnr, City Phoenix Civil Serv Community, 1986-; dept review bd, Phoenix Police Dept, 1990. **Honors/Awds:** Phoenix AZ Human Resource Businessman of the Year, 1980; AZ & US Small Businessman of the Year, 1984; hon doctorate, Alcorn State Univ, 1997. **Military Serv:** USAF, active, 4 yrs, resv, 4 yrs. **Home Addr:** chicago, IL 60611-5910.

JOHNSON, RAYLEE TERRELL
Football player. **Personal:** Born Jun 1, 1970, Chicago, IL; married Diann (divorced); children: Brooke, Brecena, Brandy & Bryce. **Educ:** Univ Ark, bus educ. **Career:** San Diego Chargers, defensive end, 1993-03; Denver Broncos, defensive end, 2004. *

JOHNSON, RAYMOND L
Police chief. **Personal:** Born Apr 20, 1936, Arkansas; son of Grady and Lucy; children: Ava. **Educ:** Calif State Univ, Sacramento, BA, attended; State CA, lifetime teaching credential. **Career:** Bakersfield, CA, police dept; CA Hwy Patrol, chief southern div; City Inglewood, Police Dept, chief police; Off Criminal Justice Planning, exec dir, currently. **Orgs:** Pres, Peace Officers Asn, Los Angeles Co; CA Peace officers Asn; CA Police Chiefs; Inter-Agency Chief officers; Int Asn Police Chiefs; Los Angeles Co Police Chiefs Asn; S Bay Police Chiefs; Am Mgmt Asn; Nat Org Black Law Enforcement Exec; Los Angeles-Lusaka Zambia Sister City Comn; Sen Task Force Child Abuse; Nat Criminal Justice Asn; Asn Black Law Enforcement Exec; CA Dist Atty Asn; bd dir, Oscar Joel Bryant Asn; dir, Homer Garrott Scholarship Found; bd adv, Los Angeles Child Passenger Safety Asn; hon bd, Am Cancer Soc; Asn Black Law Enforcement Exec; Am Mgt Asn; Automobile Club S Calif; Traffic Safety Advisors Prog; Boy Scouts Am Task Force; State Task Force Ga & Drugs; CA Coun Criminal Justice; CA Dist Atty Asn; rep/accreditation task force, CA Peace officers Asn; CA Police Chiefs Asn Inc; dir, Scholarship Found; Independent Cities Asn, LA Co; Inglewood Coalition Alcohol & Drugs; Inter-Agency Chief Officers; Int Asn Police Chiefs Narcotics & Dangerous Drugs Comt; bd mem, Loved Ones Homicide Victims; bd mem, LA Child Passenger Safety Asn; LA Co Police Chiefs Asn; Nat Asn Blacks Criminal Justice; Nat Criminal Justice Asn; chmn, Awards Comt, Nat Org Black Law Enforcement Exec, 1989; bd dirs, Oscar Joel Bryant Asn; pres, current bd, LA Co; chmn, Uniform Reporting Comt Gangs; Police Found; Police Mgt Asn; Sen Task Force Child Abuse; S Bay Police Chiefs/Criminal Justice Admin Asn; hon mem, Special People Involved Community Endeavors. **Military Serv:** USMC. **Business Addr:** Executive Director, Office of Criminal Justice Planning, 1130 K St Suite 300, Sacramento, CA 95814, **Business Phone:** (916)324-9140.

JOHNSON, RAYMOND L., SR.
Lawyer. **Personal:** Born Jul 31, 1922, Providence, RI; son of Jacob and Lelia; married Evelyn Allen Johnson, Sep 30, 1950; children: Raymond L Jr, Marjorie, Robert A. **Educ:** Howard Univ, Wash, DC, BS, 1950; Rochester Gen Hosp, Rochester, NY, med tech, 1951; Howard Univ Sch Law, Wash, DC, JD, 1956. **Career:** Mathew C Long, gen prac law; All Cts CA, admitted practice, 1964; Grp Health Asn, asst lab supvr, 1953-56; Cedars Lebanon Hosp, med tech; Mt Sinai Hosp, med tech; Univ Hosp, chief med tech, 1957-61; Advanced Bio-Chem Lab, asst med lab supvr; US Congressman Edward R Roybal, special asst, 1962-68; Charles R Drew Med Sch, asst prof law; UCLA Med Sch, asst prof law; County Los Angeles, Los Angeles, CA, special coun; pvt pract, atty, Los Angeles, CA, currently. **Orgs:** Chmn, Hosp Health & Welfare Comn Westside br Nat Advan Asn Colored People; Health Coun & Med-Legal Consult Watts-U So Calif; gen coun, W Adams Comn Hosp; State Bar Calif; licensed lab tech; Nat Adv Health Coun; med-legal Coins Calif Bar; arbitrator, Am Arbitration Asn; Judge Pro Tem panel La Mun Ctr; adminr, Small Bus Develop Ctrs; AMA; La Trial Layers Asn; State Bar Calif Jucicial Comn; Am Arbitration Asn; Fed Off Econ Opportunity; Law Off Mgt Com La Co Bar Asn; La Town Club; Am Soc Hosp Attys; Calif State Bar; judge pro tem, Los Angeles Superior Court; pres, Howard Univ Law Alumni Asn. **Honors/Awds:** Alumni award, Howard Univ, 1961; Outstanding Achievement Award, Howard Univ; Watts Outstanding Achievement Award, 1966; Outstanding Attorney Award, Los Angeles Sentinel, 1976. **Military Serv:** USAF, Air Force Cadet Pilot, 1943-45. **Business Addr:** Attorney, 3756 Santa Rosalia Dr Suite 220, Los Angeles, CA 90008-3606, **Business Phone:** (323)299-3900.*

JOHNSON, DR. RAYMOND LEWIS
Educator. **Personal:** Born Jun 25, 1943, Alice, TX; son of Johnny Virginia; married Claudette Willa Smith; children: Malcolm Patrice. **Educ:** Univ Tex, BA, 1963; Rice Univ, PhD, 1969. **Career:** Univ Md, from asst prof to assoc prof, 1968-80, prof math, 1980-, chair, 1991-96, prof appl math & scientific comput, currently; Inst Mittag-Leffler, vis mem, 1974-75; Howard Univ, prof, 1976-78; McMaster Univ, vis prof, 1983-84. **Orgs:** Bd gov, Inst Math & Its Appln, 1993-96; scientific adv comt, Math Sci Res Inst, 1994-98, trustee, 1998-; bd dirs, Nat Asn Mathematicians, 1994-96; MIE advisory bd, Spelman Col, 1994-; bd gov, MAA, 1998-. **Honors/Awds:** Distinguished Minority Faculty, 1986. **Business Addr:** Professor of Mathematics, University of Maryland, Department of Mathematics, Math Bldg 2107, College Park, MD 20742-4105, **Business Phone:** (301)405-7061.

JOHNSON, REBECCA M.
Educator, teacher. **Personal:** Born Jul 10, 1905, Springfield, MA; daughter of William D and Harriet B. **Educ:** Fisk Univ, BA, 1927; Northwestern Univ, attended 1934, Springfield Col, 1943; Columbia Univ, MA, 1948. **Career:** Educator (retired); Columbia SC Pub Sch Dept, elem teacher, 1927-35, jr high math teacher, 1935-43; Charleston SC Educ 24 Hr Camp Unemployed, dir, 1935; Springfield MA Pub Sch Dept, jr high math teacher, 1943-46, prin, 1947-75; Mount Holyoke Col, vis lectr; Springfield Col, vis lectr; Am Int Col, vis lectr; Rebecca M Johnson Elem Magnet Sch. **Orgs:** Springfield Nat Asn Adv Colored People Bd, 1960-89; bd mem, Springfield Child Guid Clin Inc, 1985-89; co-chair, Scholar & Educ Resource Network Urban League, 1985-89; Alpha Kappa Alpha Sorority; Delta Kappa Gamma Hon Soc Women Educ; chmn scholar comt mem, St John's Congregational Church; Black-Jewish Dialogue Community; John Brown Archives Community, St John's Church; bd dirs, Springfield Tech Community Col. **Honors/Awds:** Woman of the Year, Harambee Holiday, 1975; Black History Award, Trailblazers US Post Off, 1987; Woman of the Year, B'Nai Brith Springfield Chap; Educ Award, First Black Pub Sch Prin, Springfield; Human & Community Serv Award, Springfield Muslim Mission; Dedicated Serv Award, Springfield Tech Communtiy Col, MA Bd Regional Community Cols; Spirit & Dedication Freedom 350 Years Black Presence MA Award, Mus Afro-Am Hist. *

JOHNSON, REGGIE VEL. See VELJOHNSON, REGINALD.

JOHNSON, RENARD U
President (Organization), chief executive officer. **Educ:** Univ Tex, El Paso, BA, bus admin. **Career:** Mgt Assistance Co Am, sr vpres oper, 1984-94; Mgt & Eng Technologies Int Inc, founder, pres & chief exec officer, 1994-. **Orgs:** Paso del Norte Group; bd mem, El Paso Hispanic Chamber Com; bd mem, Boys & Girls Club El Paso; El Paso Asn Performing Arts. **Honors/Awds:** Small Business Person of the Year. **Business Addr:** President, Chief Executive Officer, Management & Engineering Technologies International Inc, 8600 Boeing Dr, El Paso, TX 79925-1226, **Business Phone:** (915)772-4975.*

JOHNSON, DR. RHODA E
Educator. **Personal:** Born Nov 14, 1946, Bessemer, AL; daughter of Foy Barge Sr and Peacolia Dancy Barge; married Ruffer, Jun 7, 1968; children: Ryan & Robert. **Educ:** Tuskegee Inst, Tuskegee, BS, 1968; Univ Mich, Ann Arbor, MI, AM, 1970; Univ Ala, Tuscaloosa, AL, PhD (sociol), 1980. **Career:** Univ Mich, Ann Arbor, MI, Horace H Rackham fel, 1968-69, stud res asst, 1969-70; Tuskegee Inst, Tuskegee, AL, instr, 1970-74, asst prof, 1977-81, assoc prof & dir MARC, 1981-86; Ford Found fel, Southern Educ Found, 1975-77; Univ Ala, Tuscaloosa, AL, instr, 1975, vis prof & acting dir, 1985-86, chair, 1986-91, assoc prof women's studies, 1986-. **Orgs:** Poverty & Ment Health Rural S, CSRS/USDA, Carver Found, 1978-83; steering comm, 21st Century Leadership Proj, 1989-; bd mem, Nat Voting Rights Museum, 1994-; bd mem, Nat Review Bd, Ala Hist Comn. **Special Achievements:** Editor of Women's Studies in the South, Kendall/Hunt, 1991. **Business Addr:** Associate Professor, University of Alabama, Department of Women, PO Box 870272, Tuscaloosa, AL 35487-0272, **Business Phone:** (205)348-9556.

JOHNSON, DR. RHODA E
Educator. **Personal:** Born Nov 14, 1946, Bessemer, AL; daughter of Foy Barge Sr and Peacolia Dancy Barge; married Ruffer Johnson, Jun 7, 1968; children: Ryan & Robert. **Educ:** Tuskegee Inst, Tuskegee, BS, 1968; Univ Mich, Ann Arbor, MI, AM, 1970; Univ Ala, Tuscaloosa, AL, PhD (sociol), 1980. **Career:** Univ Mich, Ann Arbor, MI, Horace H Rackham fel, 1968-69, stud res asst, 1969-70; Tuskegee Inst, Tuskegee, AL, instr, 1970-74, asst prof, 1977-81, assoc prof & dir MARC, 1981-86; Ford Found fel, Southern Educ Found, 1975-77; Univ Ala, Tuscaloosa, AL, instr, 1975, vis prof & acting dir, 1985-86, chair, 1986-91, assoc prof women's studies, 1986-. **Orgs:** Poverty & Ment Health Rural S, CSRS/USDA, Carver Found, 1978-83; steering comm, 21st Century Leadership Proj, 1989-; bd mem, Nat Voting Rights Museum, 1994-; bd mem, Nat Review Bd, Ala Hist Comn. **Special Achievements:** Editor of Women's Studies in the South, Kendall/Hunt, 1991. **Business Addr:** Associate Professor, University of Alabama, Department of Women, PO Box 870272, Tuscaloosa, AL 35487-0272, **Business Phone:** (205)348-9556.

JOHNSON, RICHARD HOWARD
Government official. **Personal:** Born Jan 7, 1931, Jersey City, NJ; son of Richard S and Della H; married D Winona (deceased); children: Sandra J Harris & Richard Nicholas. **Educ:** VA Union Univ, BA, sociol (Cum Laude) 1953; Boston Univ Sch Social Work, MA 1955. **Career:** Government official (retired); Camp Downingtown, dir 1953-55; AUS Hosp, chief psychiat sw 1955-57; Hawthornden State Hosp, psychiat social worker 1957-59; Cuyahoga Co Court Common Pleas, marriage counr 1959-65; Maternal & Child Health, coord neighborhood serv 1965-68; Hough Parent-Child Ctr, dir 1968-72; Parent & Child Ctrs Head Start Bur OCD-DHEW, chief 1972-96; Parent Involvement Br HSB, ACYF, DHHS, chief social serv, 1975-91. **Orgs:** Kappa Alpha Psi Frat; Boule-Sigma Pi Phi Frat; Nat 30-Yr Oldtimers; COSPICS; NAEYC; NASW; NCBCD. **Honors/Awds:** Developed Parent Educ Curricula; Exploring Parenting, 1976; Exploring Self-Sufficiency, 1982; Dept Award, 1986; Looking at Life, 1986; Dept Leadership Award, 1987. **Military Serv:** AUS, specialist 3rd class 2 yrs, 1955-57. **Home Addr:** 13721 Lockdale Rd, Silver Spring, MD 20906.

JOHNSON, RITA FALKENER
Interior designer. **Personal:** Born in Arlington, VA; married Waldo C Falkener. **Educ:** Academie Julien Paris, 1965; Grande Chaumi re Paris, 1967; Pratt Inst, BFA, 1964. **Career:** Esq residential & com interior design; Essence Mag, home ed, 1975-77. **Orgs:** Allied Bd Trade; Nat Home Fashions League Inc Prof showcase; YWCA Designers' Show house, 1976; Designers' Show house, 1977; YWCA Show house, 1977. **Business Addr:** 50 Pierrepont St, Brooklyn, NY 11201.

JOHNSON, R.M.
Writer. **Personal:** Born Apr 1, 1968. **Educ:** Columbia Col; Howard Univ, radiation therapist cert, 1994; NE La Univ, BS,

1995; Chicago State Univ, MFA. **Career:** Little Co Mary Hosp, radiation therapist, 1995; The Harris Men, 1999; Father Found, 2000; The Harris Family, 2001; Dating Games, 2002. **Military Serv:** AUS, 1986-91. **Home Addr:** 7600 N Bosworth Ave, Chicago, IL 60626. **Business Addr:** Writer, c/o Simon & Schuster, 1230 Avenue of the Americas, New York, NY 10020-1586.*

JOHNSON, ROBERT
Health services administrator, chief executive officer. **Educ:** Tennessee State Univ, BS, biol, 1963; Univ Mich, MS, 1971. **Career:** King County Hosp Ctr, Brooklyn, from asst dir to assoc exec dir, 1971-74, actg exec dir, 1974-76; Gen Hosp, Washington, DC, exec dir, 1976-86; St Louis Regional Health Care Corp, pres & chief exec officer, 1986-89; St Louis Regional Med Ctr, chief exec officer, 1986-89; Grady Health Syst, pres & chief exec officer, 1989-93; Grady Mem Hosp, chief exec officer, 1989-93; Detroit Med Ctr, exec vpres, vpres & chief operating officer, 1993-2000; Robert B Johnson & Assocs, pres, 2000-; RBJ Enterprises LLC, chmn & chief exec officer, 2006-. **Military Serv:** USAF Med Serv, corp officer, 1963-69. **Business Phone:** (248)888-0949.

JOHNSON, ROBERT
Government official. **Career:** Nat Credit Union Admin, spec asst, chmn bd consumer progs, dir; Advocate Ester Peterson, spec asst; Bus Regulation Admin, adminr, 1983-87; Housing & Enviorn Admin, adminr; DC, Dept Pub Assisted Housing, dir; Off Pub Liaison, assoc dir, 1993-96, spec asst, pres, 1996-99, asst to pres, White House Off pres's Initiative One Am, dir, 1999-00; Charlotte Sting, WNBA, owner; Black Entertainment TV, founder & chief exec officer; RLJ Cos, founder & chmn, currently. **Special Achievements:** First African-American majority owner of a major sports franchise, 2002; Under Mr. Johnson's leadership, BET became the first African American-owned company publicly traded on the New York Stock Exchange. **Business Addr:** Founder and Chairman, The RLJ Companies, 3 Bethesda Metro Ctr Suite 1000, Bethesda, MD 20814-6347, **Business Phone:** (301)280-7700.*

JOHNSON, ROBERT (BOB JOHNSON)
Automotive executive, executive. **Personal:** Born Jul 15, 1937, Chicago, IL; son of Ben Charles and Thelma Fisher Payne; married Carolyn P Williams, Feb 4, 1984; children: Craig M & Laura L Barnett. **Educ:** Chicago Teachers Col, Chicago, IL, 1965; State Univ NY, attended 1996. **Career:** Allstate Ins Co, Chicago, IL, agent, 1968-78; Bob Johnson Chevrolet Inc, Buffalo, NY, pres, 1981-85; Bob Johnson Chevrolet, Rochester, NY, pres, 1985-; Bob Johnson Automotive Group, NY, chief exec officer, currently; State Univ NY Col, Buffalo, community fel, 1985. **Orgs:** Gen Motors Minority Dealer Asn, 1983-84; bd mem, United Way Rochester, 1990-91; bd mem, Rochester Auto Dealers Asn, 1992-98; chair, Rochester Urban League, 1993-95; bd mem, NY Auto Dealers Asn, 1993-98; bd mem, St Josephs Villa, 1994-98; bd mem, Rochester Chamber Com, 1995-98; bd mem, Frontier Telephone Co Rochester, 1996; bd mem, Nat Urban League, 1996; pres, Brockport Ford, Brockport, NY, 1996-. **Honors/Awds:** Time Magazine Quality Dealer Award, NY, 1998. **Special Achievements:** Top 100 Dealers by Black Enterprise Magazine in the year 1986-98. **Military Serv:** USAF, airman 1st Class, 1954-58. **Business Addr:** Chief Executive Officer, Bob Johnson Automotive Group, 1271 Ridge Rd W, West Rochester, NY 14615, **Business Phone:** (716)663-4040.

JOHNSON, ROBERT B.
Educator. **Personal:** Born Aug 19, 1928, Fair Bluff, NC; married Virginia J; children: Ronald Hal & Jacquelyn Foster. **Educ:** A&T State Univ, BS, 1950, MS, 1959. **Career:** HS Loris, SC, sci teacher, 1955-63; Coastal Jr Col, chem instr, 1959-61; Pleasant Grove Elem Sch Rains, SC, prin, 1963-67; Mullins Sch Dist, SC, elem sch prin, 1968-; Lower Marion County, supt. **Orgs:** Mullins City Coun, 1970-82; Pee Dee Reg Develop Coun; Human Resource Develop Coun. **Business Addr:** Superintendent, Lower Marion County, Sch District No 3, Rains, SC 29589.

JOHNSON, ROBERT E
Administrator. **Personal:** Married Michelle; children: Jasmine & Alexander. **Educ:** Morehouse Col, BS; Univ Cincinnati, MS, Ohio Sate Univ, PhD. **Career:** Central State Univ, exec dir mkt & enrollment mgt; Univ Dayton, Ohio, vpres enrollment mgt, 2004. **Special Achievements:** First Black to hold the position in the Univ Dayton 153-year history. **Business Addr:** vice president, University of Dayton, 300 Col Park, Dayton, OH 45469, **Business Phone:** (937)229-1000.*

JOHNSON, ROBERT H.
Educator. **Personal:** Born Nov 24, 1938, New York, NY; divorced; children: Vietta. **Educ:** Smith Univ, BS, 1960; Long Island Univ, MS, 1964; St John's Univ, PhD, 1970. **Career:** Pharma-Verona Chem Co, chemist, 1961-62; Human Affairs Res Ctr, consult, 1970-72; R H Clark & Assoc, partner, 1974-; Long Island Univ, teacher, 1964-75; Medgar Evers Col CUNY, teacher, 1975-76, dean students, 1977-84, prof chem, 1984-99, prof emer, currently. **Orgs:** Am Chem Soc; AAAS; NY Acad Sci; Asn Black Chemists & Engr; bd trustee, Nat Black Sci Stds Org, 1972-74; chair, Crown Hts Youth Collective, 1979; Fed Drug Addict Prog. **Honors/Awds:** Outstanding Young Men of America, 1971; Outstanding Educators of America, 1973. **Business Addr:** Professor Emeritus, Medgar Evers College, City University of New York, Department of Physical, Environmental & Computer Sciences, 1150 Carroll St, Brooklyn, NY 11225, **Business Phone:** (718)270-6022.

JOHNSON, ROBERT JUNIUS
Executive. **Personal:** Born Mar 19, 1929, Richton, MS; son of Charles Davis Johnson and Priscilla Dean Johnson; married Patricia Sutton, 1992; children: Robert II & Kemberly Nicole. **Career:** Johnson Prod Co Inc, dir distrib, currently. **Business Addr:** Director of Distribution, Johnson Products Company, 8522 S Lafayette Ave, Chicago, IL 60620-1398, **Business Phone:** (312)483-4100.

JOHNSON, ROBERT L.
Executive. **Personal:** Born Apr 8, 1946, Hickory, MS; married Sheila (divorced); children: Paige, Brett; married Maxine. **Educ:** Univ IL, BA, 1968; Woodrow Wilson Sch Pub int Affairs, Princeton Univ, MA, 1972. **Career:** Corp Pub Broadcasting; Wash Urban League; Hon W E Fauntroy, Congr Delegate DC, pres secy; Nat Cable TV Asn, vpres govt rel, 1976-79; Black Entertainment TV, founder, pres & ceo, 1980-00; RLJ Develop LLC, 2001-; NBA Charolotte expansion team, owner, 2003-; NBA Charlotte Sting, mgt, 2003-; Charlotte Sting WNBA, owner, currently. **Orgs:** black entertainment TV; vpres govt affairs NCTA, 1978-79, bd dirs, 1982-84; bd mem, hilton hotels corp; american film inst; advertising coun; bd mem, bd governors nat cable academy; bd mem, walter kaitz found; bd mem, gen Mills; bd mem, wash metro cable club; bd mem, dist cablevision; bd mem, US Airways; bd mem, United Negro Col Fund; bd governors, Rock & Roll Hall Fame . **Honors/Awds:** President Award, NCTA, 1982; Image Award, NAACP, 1982; Pioneer Award, Capital Press Club, 1984; Business of the Year Award, DC Chamber Com, 1985; Cablevision Magazine's 20/20 Vision Award, 1995; Communicator's Award, Black Radio Exclusive; CEBA Award, World Ins Black Commun Inc; Distinguished Alumni Award, Princeton Univ; Turner Broadcasting Trumpet Award, 1993; Executive Leadership Council Award, 1992; Hall of Fame Award, Broadcasting and Cable Magazine, 1997; Grand Tam Award, CTAM; Good Guys Award, Nat Women's Political Caucus, 1997; Humanitarian of the Year, TJ Maxwell Found, 2002. **Special Achievements:** Named to Social Security Panel by Pres George W Bush, 2001. **Business Addr:** Owner, Charlotte NBA Franchise, WNBA Charlotte Sting, 333 E Trade St, Charlotte, NC 28202, **Business Phone:** (704)688-8600.*

JOHNSON, ROBERT L.
Educator, physician. **Personal:** Born Aug 7, 1946, Spartanburg, SC; son of Robert and Clalice Brewton; married Maxine Gilchrist, Jun 24, 1972. **Educ:** Alfred Univ, BA, 1968; Col Med & Dent NJ, MD, 1972. **Career:** Martland Hosp, pediat intern, 1972-73, pediat resident, 1973-74, dir adolescent Med, 1976-78; St Michael's Med Ctr, dir adolescent Med-clin; C Hosp NJ, dir adolescent Med, 1976-; New York Med Sch, asst attending physician, 1976-84; Univ Med & Dent NJ, asst prof clin pediat, 1976-83, assoc prof clin pediat, 1983-89, assoc prof clin psychiat, 1989-, prof clin pediat, 1989-, NJ Med Sch, prof pediat, 1995-, chmn pediat, 2001-05 & currently, Sharon & Joseph L Muscarelle Endowed Dean, 2005-, Adolescent & Young Adult Med, dir, currently; Univ Hosp, dir adolescent Med, 1978-. **Orgs:** Fel, Am Acad Pediat, 1974-, Sect Adolescent Health Care, 1974-, fel, Am Acad Pediat, New Jersey Chap, 1974-; Comn Adolescence; Soc Adolescent Med; Comn Sports Med & Accident Prev, 1976-78; bd mem, Adolescent Health Ctr Door, 1977; bd trustees, Frost Valley YMCA; bd deacons, Union Baptist Church, 1978-; bd trustees, Day Care Coord Coun, 1980-81; vpres Health Affairs, Int Ctr Integrative Studies, 1980-; bd dirs, Inst Develop Youth Progs, 1983-; bd trustees, Newark Boy's Clubs, 1984-; bd dirs, Sex Info & Educ Coun US, 1988-; Carnegie Corp, Substance Abuse Adv Comn, 1989-; credentials comt chair, 1990-, treas, 1990-91, secy, 1991-, New Jersey State Bd Med Examrs; AAP, Comt Careers & Opportunities, chair, Nat Task Force Access Minority C Health Care, chmn, 1991-; Oregon Health Plan Bd Med Examrs, adv comt, 1992; ed bd, Pediat Rev. **Honors/Awds:** Exceptional Merit Award, Univ Med & Dent New Jersey, Newark, NJ, 1982-83; Citizen Year Award, NJ Asn Black Social Workers, Essex Chap, 1988; New Jersey Pride Award in Health, 1989; Roe v Wade Anniversary Award, NJ Coalition Abortion Rights, 1989; Community Service Award, Alpha Kappa Alpha Sorority, 1989; January 19, 1989 proclaimed Dr. Robert L Johnson Day, City Newark, NJ; Outstanding Achievement Award, Centennial Comm Orange, 1989; Recognition Award, Sunshine Club Newark & Friends, 1990; Outstanding Service in Health Awareness Award, NJ Perspectives Mag, 1992. **Special Achievements:** Author: "The Sexual Abuse Boys," New York State Journal Med, p 132, 1989; "Contraception for Adolescents," Female Patient, p 52-55, 1978; co-author: "Roundtable: Adolescent Patient," Female Patient, p 57-63, 1977; "Problem Behaviors Adolescence: A Clinical Perspective," Am Journal Family Therapy, p 72-75, 1985; "Sexual Victimization Boys," Journal Adolescent Health Care, p 372-376, 1985; "Replacing Work Pediatric Residents: Strategies &Issues", Pediatrics, p 1109-1110, 1990; "Depression in Inner City Adolescents Attending an Adolescent Med Clin", Journal Adolescent Health, p 316-318, 1991; "Acquired Immunodeficiency Syndrome: New Jersey High Sch Studs Knowledge, Attitudes & Behaviors", AIDS Educ & Prev, p 21-30, 1991; "Sexual Behaviors African-Am Male Col Studs & Risk HIV Infection", Journal Nat Med Asn, 1992; Books: Race Tree, 2000; Strength for Their Journey, 2002. **Business Addr:** Sharon & Joseph L Muscarelle Endowed Dean (Interim), Pediatrics Chair & Professor, University of Medicine and Dentistry of New Jersey, New Jersey Medical School, 185 S Orange Ave MSB C671, Newark, NJ 07101-1709, **Business Phone:** (973)972-4538.

JOHNSON, ROBERT T.
District attorney. **Personal:** Born Feb 18, 1948, Bronx, NY; son of Robert and Olga; married Dianne Renwick; children: 4. **Educ:** City Col NY, BA, philos, 1972; New York Univ Sch Law, JD, 1975. **Career:** Legal Aid Soc, criminal defense atty, 1975-78; New York City Criminal Ct, judge, 1986; New York State Supreme Ct, actg justice, 1986-88; Bronx Co, NY, dist atty, 1989-. **Orgs:** Past pres, bd dirs, New York State Dist Atty Asn; adv bd, Bronx Sch Law; Bronx County Bar Asn; Black Bar Asn Bronx County; Puerto Rican Bar Asn; bd mem, Bronx Urban League. **Honors/Awds:** David S Michaels Memorial Award for Courageous Efforts in Promoting Integrity in the Criminal Justice System, New York State Bar Asn, 1997. **Special Achievements:** First black to hold position of district attorney in New York state; Longest serving District Attorney in Bronx history, 2005. **Military Serv:** USN, 1968-70. **Business Addr:** District Attorney, Bronx County, 198 E 161st St, Bronx, NY 10451, **Business Phone:** (718)590-2000.

JOHNSON, RON
Football player. **Personal:** Born Sep 21, 1958, Monterey, CA. **Educ:** Calif State Univ, Long Beach. **Career:** Hamilton Tiger-Cats (Canadian Football League), 1982-84; Portland Breakers(USFL), 1985; Philadelphia Eagles, wide receiver, 1985-89.

JOHNSON, RONALD CORNELIUS
Administrator. **Personal:** Born Oct 2, 1946, Amelia County, VA; married Bessie; children: Aisha. **Educ:** VA St Col, BA, 1969; Univ Cincin, MA, 1973; Xavier Univ, MEd, 1977. **Career:** Ronson Mgmt Corp, pres; US Dept of HUD, specialist asst; Univ DC, dir inst in comm & public serv; US Dept of Housing & Urban Dev, mgt analyst; Model Cities Program, admin; The Jewish Hospital, 1st coordr employee relations. **Orgs:** Pres, Ronald C Johnson Asso Inc; bd dir, Bushido Inc; services on nat panel Am Acad for Ed Dev; nat chmn, Conf of Minor Pub Admin, 1975-76; Nat Cncl Am Soc for Pub Adminstrn, 1975-76; chmn, Fairfax Cty Urban Leag; Rural Am Inc; Nat Asn Hous & Rehab Off; NAACP; Nat Com on Responsive Philantropy. **Honors/Awds:** ASPA Apprec Award; Jewish War Vet Award; Urban Leag Serv Award; Conf of Min Pub Admin Award; Danforth Fellow. **Military Serv:** AUSR, 1st lt. **Business Addr:** 1331 H St NW, Washington, DC 20005.

JOHNSON, ROY EDWARD. See Obituaries section.

JOHNSON, ROY LEE
Executive. **Personal:** Born Jun 30, 1955, Charleston, MS; son of James and Viola Sayles; married Vicki Jo Williams, May 10, 1980. **Educ:** Fisk Univ, Nashville, Tenn, BS, 1977; Michigan State Univ, E Lansing, MBA, 1990. **Career:** Ford Motor Co, Detroit, Mich, financial analyst, 1977-83; The Stroh Brewery, Detroit, Mich, mgr financial planning, 1983-91, dir financial planning, 1991-97, vpres financial planning, 1998-99; Handleman Co, vpres budgeting & forecasting, vpres bus support & analysis, 2005-. **Orgs:** Nat Black MBA Asn. **Business Addr:** Vice President Business Support, Ananysis, The Handleman Co, 500 Kirts Blvd, Troy, MI 48084, **Business Phone:** (248)362-4400.

JOHNSON, ROY STEVEN
Journalist, columnist, television sportscaster. **Personal:** Born Mar 19, 1956, Tulsa, OK; son of Roy and Ida Mae Brooks Jenkins; married Barbara Y; children: Edwyn Lawrence & Anna Brooks. **Educ:** Stanford Univ, CA, BA, 1978. **Career:** Sports Illustrated, writer, reporter, 1978-81, sr ed, 1989-94, asst managing ed spec projs, 2002-05; NY Times, sportswriter, 1981-87; Atlanta Journal-Constitution, columnist, 1987-89; Money Mag, sr ed, 1994-; Savoymag, founding ed-in-chief, 2000-02; Vanguarde Media, ed dir; sportswriter,currently; AOL Black Voices, columnist, currently. **Orgs:** Nat Asn Black Journalists, 1985-; Int Amateur Athletic Asn; bd dir, Arthur Ashe Athletic Asn; founder & pres, Roy S Johnson Found; bd dirs, Homeboy Golf Tournament. **Honors/Awds:** Service Award, NY Asn Black Journalists, 1996; Communicator of The Year, Nat Black MBA Asn, 1997. **Special Achievements:** Author: Magic's Touch, Addison-Wesley, 1990; Outrageous, Simon-Schuster, 1992. **Business Addr:** Columnist, AOL Black Voices, New York, NY 10020.

JOHNSON, RUTH W
College administrator, educator. **Personal:** Born in New York, NY; daughter of Herbert and Ruth Moore; divorced; children: Kgositsile. **Educ:** Bronx Community Col, AAS, 1967; Hunter Col, BS, 1972; Columbia Univ, MS, 1975; Fairleigh Dickenson Univ, PhD, 1987. **Career:** Roosevelt Hosp, psychiat clinical specialist, 1977-79; Col New Rochelle, asst prof nursing, 1979-84, acting asst dean & prof, 1984-85, assoc dean, sch nursing, 1989-98; Nat League Nursing, dir, Coun Affairs, Baccalaureate & Higher

Degree Prog, Coun Nurse Exec, 1989-95; Col New Rochelle, dir, Sch New Resources, 1995-98; SC State Univ, Dept Nursing, chmn & prof; Fayetteville State Univ, Dept Nursing, assoc prof, currently. **Orgs:** Vpres, Asn Black Nursing Fac Higher Educ, 1992-94, pres, 1994-96; bd mem, Phillipino Nurses Network, 1999-2001; bd mem, Jour Minority Nurse, 1999-2001; ed bd mem, Jour Holistic Nursing, 1999-2001; bd mem, Orangeburg Calhoun Technical Col LPN Prog, 1999-2001; SC African-Am Nurse Scholars, 2000-01; bd mem, Low Country Area Health Educ Ctr, 2001. **Honors/Awds:** Outstanding Contribution Award, Col New Rochelle, 1989; Excellence in Nursing/Cultural Diversity Award, Phillipino Nurses Asn, 1992; Outstanding Achievement Award, Black Nurses Asn, 1994. **Special Achievements:** Author, "African American Voices, Health Educator Speak Out," American Jnl of Nursing, 1995. **Business Phone:** (910)672-1021.

JOHNSON, SAM
Automotive executive. **Career:** Metro Lincoln Mercury Inc, Charlotte, NC, chief exec; Universal Ford, Inc, Richmond, VA, chief exec; Metro Ford Sales Inc, Tupelo, MS, chief exec; Cross Creek Lincoln Mercury Subaru, Inc, Fayetteville, NC, chief exec; Metro Lincoln Mercury Inc, exec; Sam Johnson Lincoln Mercury Inc, cheif exec, currently. **Orgs:** Am Int Automobile Dealers Asn; Nat Congress. **Honors/Awds:** The prestigious dealer of the year, 1990; Black Enterprise Auto Dealer of the Year, 1994. **Special Achievements:** First two-time recip of the Award- auto dealer of the year; BE's top 100 list since 1975; first earned the prestigious dealer of the year designation in 1990 . **Business Addr:** Cheif Executive Officer, Sam Johnson Lincoln Mercury Inc, 5201 E Independence Blvd, Charlotte, NC 28212.*

JOHNSON, SARAH H.
Government official, social worker. **Personal:** Born Mar 10, 1938, Charleston, SC; divorced. **Educ:** Clark Col, attended 1957; Elkins Inst, Grad, attended 1974. **Career:** Greenville MS, councilwoman, 1985; Mississippi Action for Comm Edn, area dir, 1971-74. **Orgs:** Secy, Weddington Wlm Sch, 1964-65; Exec secy, Star Inc, 1967; secy, Delta Min Nat Coun Ch, 1968-71; brd dir, Black Meth Ch & Renewal, 1971-73; fel, MS Inst Politics, 1972; gen brd ch soc, UMC, 1972-76; Govs Compre Health Planning Adv Coun, 1974-75; radio lic course, rec FCC 1st Class RadioteleOprtrs Lic; Child Develop Group MS; v ch person, Mississippi Adv Comm US Civil rights; mem, Cont Commt Intl Womens Year. **Honors/Awds:** Elks Serene Lodge No 567, Civil Liberties Plaque; First black elected off of Greenville, 1974; Tallahatchie Co Dev League, Silver Cup Out standing Civic Achiev, 1974; Sunflower Co Nat Assn Advan Colored People Plaque Outstanding Civic Achievment, 1974; Elks Serene Lodge No 567, Civil Liberties Citation for Courageous Struggle Against Injustice 1973; Elite Civic & Soc Club Citation Outstanding Achiev Polit, 1974; Queen City Lodge FM & AM, Woman Yr Award, Utility Club Inc, 1973 & 1975. *

JOHNSON, SARAH YVONNE
School administrator. **Personal:** Born Aug 17, 1950, Los Angeles, CA; married Frank Johnson Sr; children: Frank Jr & Ingrid Yvette. **Educ:** Tuskegee Inst, BS, 1972; Harvard Univ, EdM, 1973. **Career:** Penn Cult Ctr, assoc dir, 1973-75; Beaufort City Bd Educ, spec educ teacher, 1975-76; Renaissance Wives Headstart Prog, educ dir, 1976; Vacca Campus State Sch Delinquent Youth, prin, 1976-. **Orgs:** Ala Juv Justice Asn, 1979-, Harvard Club Birmingham, Positive Maturity Adv Bd, 1981-85. **Honors/Awds:** Outstanding Young Women of Am Nomination, 1975,83; Outstanding Serv Award, Miles Col Community Sports Prog, 1981; Outstanding Serv Award, Positive Maturity Foster Grandparent Prog, 1981. **Special Achievements:** First Black Prin, Vacca Campus. **Business Addr:** Principal, Alabama Youth Service, Vacca Campus 8950 Roebuck Blvd, Birmingham, AL 35206.

JOHNSON, SHANNON (SHANNON REGINA JOHNSON)
Basketball player. **Personal:** Born Aug 18, 1974, Hartsville, SC; daughter of Robert Brockington and Jo-Ann Bennett. **Educ:** Univ SC, retailing, 1996. **Career:** Columbus Quest, guard, 1996-98; Orlando Miracle, 1999-02; Fenerbache,Turkey, 1999-2000; Ros Casares, Valencia, Spain, 2001-02; All-FIBA World Championship Team, mem, 2002; Conn Sun, guard, 2003; San Antonio Silver Stars, guard, 2004-06; Detroit shocks, 2007; Houston Comets, 2008; Seattle Storm, 2009-. **Orgs:** USA Basketball team. **Honors/Awds:** First Team All-SEC in 1994, 1995 and 1996; USA World University Games, gold medal, 1997; ABL Championship, 1997, 1998; ABL Eastern Conference, All-Star Team, 1997-98; inducted into Univ SC Hall of Fame; Summer Olympics, gold medal, 2004. **Business Addr:** Professional Basketball Player, Seattle Storm, 3421 Thorndyke Ave W, Seattle, WA 48326.*

JOHNSON, SHANNON REGINA. See JOHNSON, SHANNON.

JOHNSON, SHARON REED
School administrator. **Personal:** Born Aug 25, 1944, Wichita, KS; divorced; children: Michael. **Educ:** Northern Ill Univ, BA, sociol, 1972; Roosevelt Univ, MA, urban studies, 1973; Univ Manchester, England, Cert Environ Design & Social Planning, 1973. **Career:** Northeastern Ill Planning Comn, intern 1972-73; W NY Bd Educ, teacher, 1974, coordr gifted ed & asst prin; PS No 3, prin; Gifted & Bilingual Educ, grants, affirmative action & special events, prin assigned superindent's off; W New York Sch Dist, Memorial High Sch, prin alternative, currently. **Orgs:** Fin secy, St Nicholas Tennis Club, 1983-84; pres, Mayor's Coun Youth/Sr; commun rep, N Hudson Headstart; asst affirm action officer, W NY Bd Educ; bd mem, Hudson City Coordr Gifted Ed; State Coordr Gifted Ed, W NY Adminr Asn; St James Episcopal Church Vestry; Nat Asn Elem Sch Prin; Montclair Drifters. **Honors/Awds:** Northeastern Ill Planning Comn, Tuition Grant, 1972-73. **Special Achievements:** Principal of the first elementary school to be completely wired for the Internet in W New York. **Business Addr:** Principal of Alternative, Memorial High School, 5501 Pk Ave, West New York, NJ 07093.

JOHNSON, SHEILA (SHEILA CRUMP JOHNSON)
Entrepreneur, president (organization), chief executive officer. **Personal:** Born in Pennsylvania; married William T Newman Jr, Sep 24, 2005 (divorced); children: Paige & Brett; married Hon. William T. Newman, Jr, Sep 24, 2005. **Career:** BET, co-founder, 1980-97, vpres corp affairs; WNBA, Wash Mystics, team pres, managing partner & gov, 2005-; Salamander Hospity, pres & chief exec officer, 2005-; Lincoln Holdings LLC, partner, currently. **Orgs:** Bd dir, Univ Va, Sorensen Inst Polit Leadership; Parsons New Sch Design; Sheila C Johnson Performing Arts Ctr. **Special Achievements:** First African-American Woman to be an owner or partner in three professional sports franchises; First African-American Female Billionaire. **Business Addr:** President, Chief Executive Officer, Salamander Hospitality, 100 W Washington St, Middleburg, VA 20118, **Business Phone:** (540)687-3710.

JOHNSON, SHEILA ANN
Librarian. **Personal:** Born Apr 11, 1955; daughter of Edna; married Fadhilika Atiba-Weza, Feb 10, 1990; children: Onaje Weza & Thandiwe Weza. **Educ:** Spelman Col, cum laude, BA, pre-law history, 1976; Atlanta Univ, MSLS, 1978; Touro Law Ctr, attending 2000-. **Career:** Lawrence Livermore Lab, tech info specialist, 1977-78; US Environ Protection Agency Region V, 1978-79; Amherst Col, Sci Libr, head, 1979-80; Brooklyn Pub Libr, Sci & Indust Div, div chief, 1980-93, 1997-; Off Congressman Major R Owens, dep dir, 1995-96. **Orgs:** New York Black Librarians Caucus, 1999-; Am Libr Asn, 1999-; Am Libr Asn; NY Bar Asn; Black Law Stud Asn; Am Civil Liberties Union. **Honors/Awds:** Merit Award, Spelman Col Nat Alumnae Asn; Volunteers Service Award, Kings City Juvenile Offenders Prog; Distinguished Service Awd, Nat Asn Equal Opp Higher Educ; Women of Achievement Award, New York City Coun. **Business Addr:** Division Chief, Brooklyn Public Library, Grand Army Plaza, Brooklyn, NY 11238, **Business Phone:** (718)230-2100.

JOHNSON, SHEILA CRUMP. See JOHNSON, SHEILA.

JOHNSON, SHEILA MONROE
Librarian. **Personal:** Born Nov 27, 1957, Southern Pines, NC; daughter of Esther M Monroe; married Michael Leon, Feb 14, 1982; children: Jade Taylor Johnson. **Educ:** Winston-Salem State Univ, Winston-Salem, BA, 1980; Univ NC, Greensboro, MLS, 1987. **Career:** Carpenter Libr Bowman Gray Sch Med, Winston-Salem, circulation supvr, 1982-85; Forsyth Co Pub Libr, Winston-Salem, head, periodicals & docs, 1985-. **Orgs:** Am Libr Asn, 1988-; NC Libr Asn, 1986-; newsletter co-ed, Remco NCLA, 1986-; pres, Alumni Asn UNC, Greensboro Dept Libr & Info Studies, 1989-90; New Roundtable NCLA, 1986-. **Honors/Awds:** Minority Scholarship, Medical Libr Asn, 1985; Young Careerist Award, New Members Roundtable, NCLA, 1989. **Home Phone:** (919)945-3488. **Business Addr:** Head Periodicals, Documents, Forsyth County Public Library Business Science, 660 W 5th St, Winston-Salem, NC 27101, **Business Phone:** (919)727-2220.

JOHNSON, SHIRLEY
Librarian. **Personal:** Born in Baltimore, MD; daughter of George Marshall and Virginia Williams; married Edward. **Career:** Enoch Pratt Free Libr, Baltimore, Md, 1969-; librn, 1989-, br mgr, currently. **Orgs:** Md Libr Asn, 1985-; Univ Baltimore Alumni Asn, 1987-; Am Libr Asn, 1988-; Black Caucus Am Libr Asn, 1988-; Univ Pittsburgh Alumni Asn, 1989-; Am Lib Asn Off Literacy & Outreach Serv, OLOS, 1996-98; SSRT Coretta Scott King Task Force, 1998-99; Black Caucus Am Libr Asn, 2000-; Pub Libr Asn, 2003-. **Honors/Awds:** Esther J Piercy Award, Enoch Pratt Free Libr, 1994; Metropolitan United Methodist Ch Book Lovers Award, 2003. **Business Phone:** (410)396-0946.

JOHNSON, DR. SHIRLEY B
Association executive. **Career:** United Teachers Dade Co, secy-treas, acting pres, currently. **Orgs:** Am Fed Teachers, Vienna Chap, pres. **Business Addr:** Acting President, Secretary-Treasure, United Teachers of Dade, 2200 Biscayne Blvd, Miami, FL 33137, **Business Phone:** (305)854-0220.

JOHNSON, PROF. STEPHANIE ANNE
Educator. **Personal:** Born Aug 19, 1952, Harrisburg, PA; daughter of Dr Lawrence J and Virginia E. **Educ:** Emerson Col, Boston, 1974; San Francisco State Univ, MA, 1994; Univ Calif-Berkeley, MFA, 1999. **Career:** Black Filmmakers Hall Fame, lighting designer, 1980-90; The Five Heartbeats, film electrician; Visions of the Spirit: Alice Walker, film gaffer & many other films, videos & industrials; guest lectr: Univ CA, Berkeley, Atlanta, San Fran State Univ, De Melkweg, Amsterdam; Lighting Designer: NY, CA, Paris, Bombay; One person show-Sargent Johnson Gallery, S.F, 2006; Visual & Public Art Dept, Calif State Univ, Monterey Bay, co-chair, 2006-, prof, currently. **Orgs:** Int Asn Stagehands & Theatical Employees, IATSE, 1993-; Int Asn Lighting Designers, IALD. **Honors/Awds:** Nat Endowment Fel, Design Arts, 1983; Headlands Ctr Arts, artist-in-residence, 1995; Margaret Calden Hayes Prize, 1999; Wallace Gerbode Design Fel, 1999. Calif State Univ Res grants, 2004, 2006. **Special Achievements:** Many solo & group exhibs: Spelman Coll Mus of Art, NY Pub Libr, The Richmond Art Ctr, CA; Hist Oakland Cemetery, GA; Falkirk Art Ctr, CA, Southern Pac RR Sta; Photos of work & writings publ in Skin Deep: Women Writing on Color, Cult & Identity & Aleph Beth; exhibit, DeYoung Mus, San Francisco, 1999: Civic Arts Commisioner - City of Berkeley, 2007. **Home Addr:** 2740 Mabel St, Berkeley, CA 94702. **Business Addr:** Professor, California State University Monterey Bay, Visual & Public Art Department, 100 Campus Ctr, Seaside, CA 93955-8001, **Business Phone:** (831)582-3693.

JOHNSON, STEPHEN A
Lawyer. **Personal:** Married. **Educ:** Baruch Col, BBA, acct, 1983; Wayne State Univ, JD, 1987. **Career:** Gen Motors Corp, finance analyst, 1983-87; Pricewaterhouse Cooper LLP, partner, 1987-. **Orgs:** One Hundred Black Men, 1997-. **Business Addr:** Partner, Price Waterhouse Coopers LLP, 300 Madison Ave, New York, NY 10017, **Business Phone:** (203)539-3581.

JOHNSON, STEPHEN L
Executive. **Personal:** Born Dec 14, 1944, Denver, CO; son of Mary Helen Bess; married; married; children: Chemaine D, Scott S & Matthew R. **Educ:** Univ Denver, BS, 1966; Univ San Francisco, 1980. **Career:** The Denver Post, reporter/ed, 1970-74; Bank Am, sr pub info officer, 1975-79; First Interstate Bank, vpres pub rels, 1979-83; First Nationwide Financial Corp, a subsid Ford Motor Co vpres & dir corp communs & appt First vpres subsid, 1987; appointed sr vpres, 1988; Union Bank Calif, sr vpres, dir, pub rel & govt affairs, currently. **Orgs:** Trustee, Calif Neighborhood Housing Found, 1980-85; dir, Communs Bridge (Los Angeles), 1984-87 finance chair mayor's Comt Housing Homeless; conf bd, Pub Affair Exec Comt, 1987-92; adv bd, San Jose State Univ, 1987-90; trustee, Fine Arts Mus San Francisco, 1996-. **Honors/Awds:** Directors Award for Public Service, Calif Neighborhood Housing Found, 1980; Honoree, JFK Sch Govt, Harvard Univ Housing Scholar, 1988. **Military Serv:** AUS, Capt, 1966-70; Bronze Star; Vietnam Serv Medals; Company comdr in Vietnam 1968.

JOHNSON, STERLING
Judge. **Personal:** Born May 14, 1934, Brooklyn, NY; married Barbara; children: Sterling III, Alicia Daniels, Jennifer. **Educ:** Brooklyn Col, BA, 1963; Brooklyn Law Sch, LLB, 1966. **Career:** New York City Police Dept, officer, 1956; Southern Dist, asst US atty, 1967-70; Civil Complaint Review Bd, exec dir, 1970-74; DEA, exec liaison officer, 1974-75; Spec Narcotics Prosecutor's Off, spec narcotics prosecutor, 1975; US Dist Ct, fed judge , 1991-. **Orgs:** Bd dir, Police Athletic League, 1975-; chmn, Drug Adv Task Force Nat Adv Comt CDR USNR Annapolis, 1975-; US Sentencing Comn, comnr, 1999-. **Honors/Awds:** Distinguished Service Award, Asn Voluntary Agencies Narcotic Treatment, 1977; Distinguished Black American, Drug Enforcement Admin, 1979. **Military Serv:** USNR, capt. **Business Addr:** Federal Judge, U.S. District Court for the Eastern District of New York, 225 Cadman Plz E, Brooklyn, NY 11201, **Business Phone:** (718)260-2460.*

JOHNSON, T J
Automotive executive. **Career:** Team Ford-Mercury Inc, Tarboro, NC, dealership, owner, currently; Crossroads Ford-Mercury Inc, Jesup, Ga, dealership, owner, currently; Summerville Ford-Mercury Inc, Summerville, SC, dealership, owner, currently. **Special Achievements:** Listed as #82 of 100 top auto dealers, Black Enterprise, 1992. **Business Addr:** Owner, Summerville Ford Mercury, 103 Old Trolley Rd, Summerville, SC 29485, **Business Phone:** (843)873-3550.*

JOHNSON, TALIB. See SOULCHILD, MUSIQ.

JOHNSON, THEODORE, SR.
Military leader. **Personal:** Born Aug 23, 1920, Ft Mitchell, AL; married Mattie E Butler; children: Theodore Jr, Winfred O, Frederick L, Larry E, Welton C, James C & Jeffrey M. **Educ:** Stockton State Col, Pomona, NJ, BS, 1978, MA, 1982; Kean Col, NJ, Union, NJ, MA, coun, 1982; Univ Md; Brookdale Community Col, community ment health. **Career:** Military leader (retired); AUS, Field Artil Brigade Battery, 829 Tank Destroyer Batallion Shipped, Southampton, Eng, basic training, 1941; Le-Harve France Siefried Line Ger, 1944; SW Pac, 1945, stateside 1946-50, Korea, 1950; Ger Occup, duty, 1952-55; AUS, Signal Corp & Res & Develop Lab, 1955-64; Va Blind Ctr Hines Hosp, rehab, 1965; AUS, 1964. **Orgs:** Exec dir & nat pres, Nat Asn Advan Colored People, 1973; Red Bank Community Ctr Inc, Title I Adv Comt &

Adv Comt Proj Seed; exec comt mem & vpres, chmn, Vet Affairs; pres, Red Bank Br Nat Asn Advan Colored People; VFW 438, Disabled Vet Orgn, Prince Hall Masonic Lodge, Oswitchee Lodge 785. **Honors/Awds:** Pres Award, Greater Red Bank Br, Nat Asn Advan Colored People, 1980; Am Theater Oper Medal; European African Mediter & Europe Theater, Asiatic Pacific Theater Oper Medal. **Special Achievements:** Motion Picture Photog. **Home Addr:** 248 Leighton Ave, Red Bank, NJ 07701. *

JOHNSON, THOMAS H
Evangelist. **Personal:** Born Aug 5, 1932, Longview, TX; son of Allen Groggs Sr and Gladys Johnson Morrison; married Maggie L Stewart, Sep 27, 1958; children: Crystal Louise Johnson-Turner & Cathi Lynn Wilson. **Educ:** Southwestern Christian Col, Terrill, Tex, BA, 1955. **Career:** Madison Ave Ch Christ, evangelist 1955-. **Orgs:** Nat Asn Advan Colored People, 1975-; minister, Madison Ave Ch of Christ Wichita 1980; chmn, Jamie Harris Livertransplant Fund, 1987; Christian Question & Answer Panelist. **Business Addr:** Evangelist, Madison Avenue Church of Christ, 1740 N Madison Ave, Wichita, KS 67214, **Business Phone:** (316)265-0583.

JOHNSON, THOMAS PEPPER. See JOHNSON, PEPPER.

JOHNSON, TIFFANI TAMARA
Basketball player. **Personal:** Born Dec 27, 1975, Charlotte, NC. **Educ:** Univ Tenn, attended 1998. **Career:** Sacramento Monarchs, 1998; Phoenix Suns, 1998; Houston Comets, center,200004; seattle storm, 2006. **Honors/Awds:** Sixth Player Award. *

JOHNSON, TIMOTHY JULIUS, JR.
Artist. **Personal:** Born Dec 30, 1935, Chester, SC; son of Lois Peay and Timothy J Johnson Sr; married Patricia B Hoye; children: Darryl Julius & Dianne Patrice. **Educ:** Mich State Univ, 1956. **Career:** Visual Display Arts Chanute AFB IL, supvr, 1979-82; US Govt Air Force, illusr. **Orgs:** Leader & comm B mem, Boy & Girl Scouts Am, 1964-70; Alpha Phi Alpha, 1955-; libr bd mem, Village Rantoul, IL, 1979-82; The River Art Group, 1983-84. **Honors/Awds:** 1st place, Chanute Fine Arts Festival; 2nd place, paintings, 3rd place, sculptures in Urbana, St Fair; 1st place & Best of Show in the Danville Fine Arts Festival; 1st & Best of Show, Tech Exhibit Peoria; Best of Show, Black Heritage week Chanute AFB, 1982.

JOHNSON, TOBE
Educator. **Personal:** Born Sep 16, 1929, Birmingham, AL; son of Evelyn and Tobe; married Goldie Culpepper; children: Tobe III & Cheryl. **Educ:** Morehouse Col, BA, 1954; Columbia Univ, PhD, 1963. **Career:** Ealeton Inst Polit & Nat Ctr Educ polit fac fel, Dem Pres Nom Conv, 1954; Columbia Univ, fel, 1954-55; Prairie View A&M, instr, 1956-57; Prairie View, asst prof, 1961-62; Univ Pittsburgh, vis assoc prof, 1956-66; John Hay Whitney fel, 1959-60; Carleton Col, prof, 1968; Morehouse Col, Dept Polit Sci, distinguished chair, from asst prof to assoc prof, 1958-66, prof, 1967-, Avalon prof polit sci, currently, Div Humanities & Social Scis, interim dean, currently; Ford Found, res fel, 1968-69; United Negro Col Fund, distinguished fel, 1981-82. **Orgs:** Dir, Urban Studies Prog Former Coun; Am Polit Sci Asn; Bd Examrs Educ Testing Serv, Grad Rec Exam Polit Sci, 1972-76; Am Soc Pub Admin; Conf Ministry Pub Admin Bd, United Way Atlanta; S Ed Found; Nat Asn Reg Coun; Atlanta Reg Comm Hons, Phi Beta Kappa; Nat Acad Pub Admin, 1981-. **Special Achievements:** NUmerous publications including "The Nature and Status of Black Studies", 1965; "The Black College as System", 1974; "Black Metropolitanization," Joint Center for Political Studies," , 1974; The Atlanta Regional Metropolitan Transit System. **Military Serv:** USA, s-sgt, 1949-52. **Business Addr:** Avalon Professor of Political Science, Interim Dean of Humanities and Social Science, Morehouse College, Department of Political Science, 830 Westview Dr SW, Atlanta, GA 30314.

JOHNSON, DR. TOMMIE ULMER
Educator. **Personal:** Born Jun 23, 1925, Gary, IN; daughter of Abraham Ulmer and Mosell Sadler Ulmer; married Walter H, Mar 24, 1951 (deceased). **Educ:** Wayne State Univ, BS, 1961, MEd, 1964, EdD, 1971. **Career:** City Detroit, senior stenographer, 1948-59; Detroit Pub Schs, teacher, 1961-68; Ford Foundation fel, 1971; Wayne State Univ, asst prof, 1971-76; Wayne State Univ, assoc prof, 1976-; vis prof, Norfolk State Univ, 1978; Wayne State Univ, asst provost, 1985-. **Orgs:** Sponsor, Delta Pi Epsilon Wayne State Univ Grad Chap, 1980-; Mich Occup Teacher Educ Asn, 1982-; Alpha Kappa Alpha Sororoty; life mem, Nat Asn Advan Colored People; asst treas & trustee, Second Baptist Church Detroit; Am Educ Res Asn; Am Voc Asn; Mich Bus Educ, Nat Bus Educ Asn; Women's Econ Club; vpres, Iota Phi Lambda, 1974-91. **Honors/Awds:** President's Bonus Award, Wayne State Univ, 1991-93; Detroit Western International High School Hall of Fame, 1993. **Special Achievements:** Published "The Retail Community as a Classroom" Journal of Education for Business, 1985. **Business Addr:** Assisstant Provost for Affirmative Action, Wayne State University, 4129 Fac Admin Bldg, Detroit, MI 48202.

JOHNSON, TRE
Football player. **Personal:** Born Aug 30, 1971, New York, NY. **Educ:** Temple Univ, social admin, 1993, MSW. **Career:** Wash Redskins, guard, 1994-00, 2002; Cleveland Browns, 2001.history teacher, Landon Sch, currently. **Honors/Awds:** Pro Bowl alternate, 1996; Pro Bowl, 1999. *

JOHNSON, TROY DWAN
Football player. **Personal:** Born Oct 20, 1962, New Orleans, LA. **Educ:** Southeastern LA Univ; Southern Univ. **Career:** Denver Gold, wide receiver, 1985; St Louis Cardinals, 1986-87; Pittsburgh Steelers, 1988; Detroit Lions, 1989.

JOHNSON, ULYSSES JOHANN, JR.
Educator, teacher, counselor. **Personal:** Born Aug 11, 1929, Winter Haven, FL; married Thelma Mae Simmons, Aug 9, 1967 (deceased); children: Marcus A & Melanie Aida. **Educ:** Fisk Univ, BS, 1951; Univ Denver, MS, 1955; Tenn Tech Univ, EdS, 1973. **Career:** Educator, teacher, counselor (retired); Rochelle Jr Sr High Sch, teacher, counr, coach, 1951-69; Polk Community Col, counr, 1969-71, DSS Spec, dir 1971-73, couns dir, 1973-86. **Orgs:** Pres, Cent Fla Guidance Asn, 1972-73; master, Samson Lodge 142 F & A M Masons, 1980-84; charter mem, FSC Chap, Phi Delta Kappa, 1983-86; Century Soc, Mid-Fla Med Serv Found, Winter Haven Hosp; pres, Fla Asn Community Col; Am Asn Coun Devel; Nat Asn Advan Colored People; Kappa Delta Pi; Kappa Alpha Psi. **Honors/Awds:** Man of the Year Award, Kappa Alpha Psi, 1975; Outstanding Boys, St Chr Post 201 Am Legion Dept, FL, 1984; Man of the Year, Lakeland Alumni Chap, 1985; Cameo Award, Winter Haven Little Theater, 1986; Administrator of the Year, AACJ Colg SCABBA, 1986. **Military Serv:** AUS corporal 1952-54; Good Conduct Medal, French Cord War, 1953. **Home Phone:** (813)293-1966.

JOHNSON, VANEESE
Entrepreneur, consultant, public speaker. **Educ:** Vista Jr Col, AA; Univ Calif, Los Angeles, mgt develop entrepreneurs, 2003; Kellogg Sch Mgt, advan mgt educ prog, 2003; Univ Ill & Kellogg Sch Mgt, adult migrant eng prog, 2003; Univ Calif, Los Angeles, MDE cert, 2003; Harvard Bus Sch, entrepreneurial training, 2004. **Career:** Serv coordr; serv supvr; acct mgr; regional sales mgr; speaker; bus teacher & trainer; On The Move Staffing Services LLC, founder & pres, 1998-. **Orgs:** African Am Bus Summit; San Francisco Black Chamber Com; Jobs 4 Youth; Jewish Voc Serv; bd mem, Northern Calif Supplier Develop Coun; bd mem, Calif Staffing Professionals; mem, Nat Coalition 100 Black Women Inc; Renaissance Entrepreneurship Ctr. **Honors/Awds:** 100 Black Women for Entrepreneur of the Year; Entrepreneur of the Year, Renaissance Entrepreneurship Ctr, 2000; Vol of the Year, Northern Calif Supplier Develop Coun, 2002; Supplier of the Year, Northern Calif Supplier Develop Coun, 2003; Small Bus Employer of the Year, SF Mayor's Comm on Persons with Disabilities, 2004; Madame CJ Walker Entrepreneur of the Year Award, 2004. **Special Achievements:** Recognized in Black Enterprise mag, Professional Black Women's Inc mag. **Business Addr:** Founder, President, On the Move Staffing Services LLC, 275 Fifth St, San Francisco, CA 94103, **Business Phone:** (415)957-1137.

JOHNSON, DR. VANNETTE WILLIAM
School administrator, educator. **Personal:** Born May 27, 1930, Little Rock, AR; son of Charlie and Laura Delorius Miller; married Delois V Davis, Aug 8, 1959; children: Juliette Laureen Lewis, Alberta Lynnette Shelton, Melanie Annette Dumas &Leontyne Delois Howard. **Educ:** Ark AM&N Col, BS, 1952; Univ Ark, MEd, 1961, DEd, 1970. **Career:** Merrill HS, teacher, asst coach, 1952-57; Ark AM&N Col, asst coach & instr, 1957-62, head football coach, 1962-74; Southern Educ Found, fel, 1967-70; Univ Ark, Pine Bluff, head football coach, athletic dir, 1974-75, actg dept chair & athletic dir, 1980-83, dept chair & athletic dir, 1983-84, dept chair, prof 1984-; compilance coordr, currently. **Orgs:** Comnr, Ark Comn Human Relations, 1977-81; justice peace Jefferson County, 1977-; pres, Jefferson Cty Black Caucus 1978-; vpres, Ark Black Caucus, 1981-; corp bd, Jefferson Comprehensive Care Ctr, 1981-; educ community, Pine Bluff Chamber Com, 1982-; Comn Pine Bluff Transportation Comn, 1982-; long range planning, Pine Bluff Chamber Com, 1985; NAACP; Pine Bluff/Jefferson County Clean & Beautiful Community, 1982-85, 1992-; Pine Bluff Convention Ctr Community, fin community, 1977-; Literacy Coun Jefferson County, adv bd, 1987; secy, Jefferson County Democratic Cent Comt, 1990-; pres, Jefferson County Black Elected officials Asn, 1990-; fin comt chmn, Jefferson County Quorum Ct, 1989-; Democratic State Comt, 1990-; Nat Asn Collegiate Dir Athletics; secy-treas, Ark Dem Party. **Honors/Awds:** Inductee Legends Hall of Fame, Southwestern Athletic Conf, 2007; Golden Lion All American Quarterback. **Home Addr:** 1905 Collegiate Dr, Pine Bluff, AR 71601. **Business Addr:** Compliance Coordinator, Professor, University of Arkansas, Pine Bluff, AR 71601, **Business Phone:** (870)534-3835.

JOHNSON, VERDIA EARLINE
Executive. **Personal:** Born Jul 14, 1950, Fort Worth, TX; married Everett N Johnson Jr. **Educ:** Howard Univ, BA, mkt, 1972; NY Univ, MBA, mkt, 1974. **Career:** Colgate Palmolive, NY, asst prod mgr, 1974-77; Standard Brands, NY, sr prod mgr, 1977-81; Nabisco Brands, NJ, sr prod mgr, 1981-84; BCI Mkt Inc, NY, dir mkt, 1984-85; Black Enterprise Mag, NY, advert dir, 1985-86; JEM Group Inc, pres; Gannett Outdoor Co, vpres sales; Graham Gregory Bozell Inc, managing dir; Stedman Graham & Partners, vpres & gen mgr; Footsteps, pres & co-founder, currently. **Orgs:** Nat Asn Mkt Developers; Faith Love Christian Ctr's Jack & Jill Am; Am Asn Adv Agencies. **Honors/Awds:** NJ Black Achievers Award. **Special Achievements:** TV & Radio appearance: CNBC "Power Lunch"; host of other radio stations; featured in MORE Mag & On Wheels Mag; named one of 25 Most Influential Women in Business, Network Mag, 2001; Outstanding Women in Marketing & Communication, Ebony Mag, 2001. **Home Addr:** 7002 Blvd E Suite 8I, Guttenberg, NJ 07093.

JOHNSON, DR. VERMELLE JAMISON
School administrator. **Personal:** Born Aug 2, 1933, Islandton, SC; married Charles Harry; children: Charles H Jr, & Temple Odessa. **Educ:** SC State Col, BS, 1955, MEd, 1969; Univ SC, PhD, 1976. **Career:** Ala State Col, 1956-57; Fed Employee, 1957-62; Pub Sch SC, teacher1962-68; Claflin Col, prof & chairperson, dept bus admin, 1985; SC State Col, asst prof bus educ, 1969, provost, dir, chair, Comt Acad Affairs & Licensing, currently; Univ NDak, instr; Univ RI, instr. **Orgs:** State secy, SC Bus Ed Asn; Alpha Kappa Mu Hon Soc; Delta Mu Delta Nat Bus Frat; Phi Delta kappa Hon Soc; Iota Phi Lambda Bus Sor; Nat Bus Ed Asn; SC State Bus Ed Asn; Alpha Kappa Alpha Sorority; Daughter Elk; IBPOE W; Sunday sch teacher Trinity United Methodist Church; pres, Conf Chief Acad Officers Southern States, 1991-. **Special Achievements:** Author, "So You Think You're Ready to Teach", 1964; "Bus Educs Have Atremendous Bill to Fill", 1970; "A Look at Today's Increased Opptys for Adequately Prepared Bus Grad in SC", 1972; " Bus Ed A Momentous Challenge in the 70s"; First minority female president of Conference of Chief Academic Officers of the Southern States. **Business Addr:** Chair, South Carolina State College, Committee on Academic Affairs and Licensing, 300 Col St NE, Orangeburg, SC 29117, **Business Phone:** (803)536-7190.*

JOHNSON, VICKIE ANNETTE
Basketball player. **Personal:** Born Apr 15, 1972, Shreveport, LA; daughter of Susie. **Educ:** La Tech, sociol & psychol, 1996. **Career:** NY Liberty, forward & guard, 1997-06; San Antonio Silver Stars, forward &guard, 2006-. **Honors/Awds:** Most Valuable Player, LA Tech, 1995-96; LA Player of the Yr, 1996; Vote das a starter for the Women's Nat Basketball Asn All-Star Game, 2001. **Business Addr:** Professional Basketball Player, San Antonio Silver Stars, 1 AT T Ctr, San Antonio, TX 78219, **Business Phone:** (210)444-5000.*

JOHNSON, VINCENT L
Lawyer. **Personal:** Born Aug 12, 1931, Brooklyn, NY; married Gertrude; children: Vincent Jr & Melissa. **Educ:** Brooklyn Col, BA, 1958; St John's Univ, LLB, 1960, JD, 1963. **Career:** Fields & Rosen, asst atty, 1960-61; Kings Co, asst dist atty, 1968; Laufer & Johnson, partner; Pvt Pract, atty, currently. **Orgs:** Brooklyn Bar Asn; Phi Alpha Delta Law Fraternity; bd dir, 100 Black Men NY, 1970-90; bd dir, Nat Asn Advan Colored People, 1956-75. **Honors/Awds:** Subject Police Atheltic League Post Police Atheltic League, 1964. **Military Serv:** USAF, airman 1st class, 1951-55. **Business Addr:** Attorney, 26 Ct St Suite 309, Brooklyn, NY 11242, **Business Phone:** (718)858-1313.

JOHNSON, VINNIE
Basketball player, radio host, executive. **Personal:** Born Sep 1, 1956, Brooklyn, NY. **Educ:** McLennan Community Col, Waco, TX, 1977; Baylor Univ, Waco, TX, phy seduc, 1979. **Career:** Basketball player (retired), business exec; Seattle SuperSonics, 1979-81; Detroit Pistons, player, 1981-94, radio analyst, currently; San Antonio Spurs, 1991-92; Piston Modules LLC, chmn bd, currently; Piston Automotive, chmn & chief exec officer, 1995-; Piston Group, chmn, 1996-. **Orgs:** Detroit Chamber Com; Mich Minority Bus Develop Coun. **Honors/Awds:** Mem, NBA championship teams, 1989, 1990; Michigan Sports Hall of Fame; New York Sports Hall of Fame. **Business Addr:** Chairman, Chief Executive Officer, Piston Automotive LLC, Piston Group, 4015 Michigan Ave, Detroit, MI 48210, **Business Phone:** (313)897-1540.

JOHNSON, VIRGINIA ALMA FAIRFAX
Dancer. **Personal:** Born Jan 25, 1950, Washington, DC; daughter of James L and Madeline Murray. **Educ:** NY Univ, dance, 1969; Fordham Univ. **Career:** Dancer (retired); Guest appearances: Capitol Ballet, Chicago Opera Ballet, Wash Ballet, Baltimore Civic Youth Ballet, Stars of World Ballet, Australia, Detroit Symphony, Nat Symphony, Eugene Ballet; Film: A Piece of the Action, 1977; TV appearances: "Dance in America"; "Ancient Songs of Children"; "Night of 100 Stars"; Maymount Col White House appearances for Pres Carter & Reagan, solo concert; Blanche duBois in a Streetcar Named Desire for PBS Great Performances; A Creole Giselle, NBC; Dance Theatre Harlem, prin dancer, 1969-97. **Orgs:** Hon mem, Alpha Kappa Alpha Sorority. **Honors/Awds:** Young Achiever Award, Nat Coun Women United States, 1985; Outstanding Young Woman of America, Nat Coun Women, 1985; Dance Magazine Award, 1991.

JOHNSON, WALDO EMERSON
Research scientist, educator. **Personal:** Born Mar 13, 1955, Americus, GA; son of Waldo Emerson Sr and Addie Ben. **Educ:**

Mercer Univ, Macon, GA, BA, 1977; Univ Mich, Ann Arbor, MI, MSW, 1979; Sch Social Serv Admin, Univ Chicago, PhD, 1993. **Career:** Ga Sw Col, Upward Bound, proj coordr, 1979-82; Alpha Phi Alpha Frat Inc, asst exec dir, progs, 1982-85, develop consult, 1985-; Firman Community Servs, Chicago, IL, dir, youth & family servs, 1987-90; Loyola Univ Chicago, Chicago, IL, vis asst prof, sch social work, 1991-96; Northwestern Univ, Univ Chicago Joint Ctr Poverty Res, fac affiliate; Princeton Univ, Fragile Families & Child Well-Being Study, Network scholar, investr, 1995-; Univ Chicago, Sch Social Serv Admin (SSA), asst prof, assoc prof, currently, Ctr Race, Polit & Cult, dir, currently. **Orgs:** Chicago Chap, Black Social Workers; Task Force Effective Progs & Res, Nat Campaign Prevent Teen Pregnancy; Working Group Male Family Formation & Fertility, Fed Interagency Forum Child & Family Statist; secy, bd dirs, Proj IMAGE, 1985-91; Southside Br, Nat Asn Advan Colored People; founding mem, Arts Forum Urban Gateways, Chicago; Ill Chap, Nat Asn Social Workers; Coun Social Work Educ; Nat Coun Family Rels; Asn Pub Policy Anal & Mgmt; Metropol bd, Chicago Urban League; Paternal Involvement Project, adv bd; AIDS Walk Chicago; bd dir, Tulane Univ, Sch Social Work, Porter-Cason Inst Advan Family Practice. **Honors/Awds:** Grad Fellowship, Univ Mich, Ann Arbor, MI, 1978-79; Dist Serv Award, Alpha Phi Alpha Frat Inc 1984; Doctoral Fel, Coun Social Work Educ Wash, DC, 1985-88; Dedicated Service Award, Child Life Network Am Red Cross, 1988; President's Service Award, IOTA Delta Lambda Chap, Alpha Phi Alpha, 1998. **Special Achievements:** Consulting editor: Social Work, A Journal of the National Association of Social Workers. **Business Addr:** Director, Associate Professor, University of Chicago, School of Social Service Administration, Ctr Study Race Polit & Cult, 969 E 60th St, Chicago, IL 60637, **Business Phone:** (773)702-1250.

JOHNSON, WALLACE DARNELL
Consultant, athletic coach. **Personal:** Born Dec 25, 1956, Gary, IN; son of Roy and Myrtle Moody. **Educ:** Ind State Univ, Terre Haute, IN, acct, 1979. **Career:** Peat Marwick, Chicago, IL, staff acct, 1983-84; Interstate Develop & Supply Corp, Indianapolis, IN, treasurer, 1985-88; Montreal Expos, Montreal, Quebec, baseball player: 1981-83. 1984, 1986-90; San Fransisco Giants, 1983; Atlanta Braves, coach, 1995-97; Chicago White Sox, coach, 1998-02; W D Johnson & Assoc, pres, currently. **Orgs:** Gamma Gent Alumni Assn, 1977-; treasurer, Main Street Gary, 1991-. **Honors/Awds:** Academic All-American, COSIDA, 1979; McMillan Award for Leadership, Ind St Univ, 1979; Post-Graduate Scholarship Recipient, Natl Col Athletic Assn, 1979; Most Valuable Player, Fla State League, 1980; Athletic Hall of Fame, Ind St Univ, 1985; American Assoc All Star Team, 1985. **Business Addr:** President, W D Johnson & Associates, 4629 Washington St, Gary, IN 46408.*

JOHNSON, WALTER LEON. See JOHNSON, WILLIAM LEON.

JOHNSON, WALTER LOUIS, SR.
Government official. **Personal:** Born Jan 2, 1949, Bastrop, LA; son of Samuel and Dorothy Williams Bolden; married Esther Robinson, Mar 30, 1973; children: Walter II & Erik. **Educ:** San Francisco City Col, San Francisco, AA, 1969; St Mary's Col, Moraga, CA, BA, 1984. **Career:** City Oakland, Oakland, CA, dir retirement systs, 1972-. **Orgs:** Nat Forum Black Pub Adminr; Am Soc Pub Adminr; Nat Conf Pub Employees' Retirement Systs; Calif Asn Pub Retirement Systs. **Military Serv:** AUS, sgt first Class, 1977, Soldier of Year. **Home Addr:** 4108 Fairway Ave, Oakland, CA 94605. **Business Addr:** Director of Retirement Systems, City of Oakland, Retirement Systems, 150 Frank H Ogawa Pl 3rd Fl, Oakland, CA 94612, **Business Phone:** (510)238-3994.

JOHNSON, WALTER THANIEL, JR.
Lawyer. **Personal:** Born May 18, 1940, Greensboro, NC; son of Walter T Sr and Gertrude Alexander; married Yvonne Jeffries, Apr 20, 1985; children: Walter III, Vernon K, Lisa Yvonne & Shannon Tamara. **Educ:** A&T State Univ, BS, 1961; Duke Univ Sch Law, JD, 1964; Univ NC Chapel Hill Govt Execs Inst, l98l, Justice Exec Prog, l984. **Career:** Frye & Johnson, atty; Guilford Co Super Ct, asst dist atty, 1968-69; USAF, judge adv, 1965-68; Law Off Elreta Alexander, assoc, 1964-65; Redevel Com Greensboro, relocation adv, 1962-63; Pub Storage & Warehousing Inc, secy, exec comnr, 1971-76; Barjo Inc, secy, exec comnr, 1973-; Duke Univ Law Sch, adj prof law, 1975-; NC Cent Sch Law, adj prof, 1985-87; Barbee & Johnson, partner, 1987-88; Barbee Johnson & Glenn, partner, 1988-. **Orgs:** Vpres planning, United Way Greensboro 1969-71; chmn, Greensboro County Bd Educ, 1970-; bd mem, Eastern Music Festival, 1972-76; chmn bd trustee, Univ NC, 1974-; Bd Govs NC Bar Asn, 1975-; chmn, NC Inmate Grievance County Com, 1975-; Greensboro Bd Dirs NC Nat Bank, 1976-; chmn, NC Parole Comt, 1981-85; Citizens Comt Alternatives Inceration, 1981-83; vpres, Asn Paroling Authorities, 1982-85; vice chmn, Greensboro Vision, 1985-; bd mem, Greensboro Economic Develop Coun, 1988-. **Honors/Awds:** Outstanding Young Men of NC, 1970, Freedom Guard Award, NC Jaycees, 1970-71; Distinguish Service Award, Greensboro Jaycees, 1970; Peacemaker Award, Carolina Peacemaker Newspaper. **Military Serv:** USAF, capt, 1961-68. **Home Addr:** 1306 W Wendover Ave, Greensboro, NC 27408, **Home Phone:** (336)279-8312. **Business Addr:** Partner, Barbee Johnson & Glenn, 102 N Elm St, PO Box 21401, Greensboro, NC 27401, **Business Phone:** (336)379-1630.*

JOHNSON, WARREN S.
Executive. **Personal:** Born Apr 7, 1947, Philadelphia, PA; married Peggie A Parham; children: Warren S. **Educ:** Hampton Inst, BA, Ec, 1969; Temple Univ, 1975. **Career:** PA Bell & Tele, mgt dev trainee, 1969-70; PA Hosp, training specialist personnel, generalist, 1970-73; Fischer & Porter Co, mgr compensation & benefits, 1973-. **Orgs:** Am Compensation Asn, 1976; exec at large Philadelphia Survey Grp, 1976-; Am Soc Personal Admin, 1977-; consult, YMFT Workshop, Alliance of Bus. **Business Addr:** ABB Instrumentation, 125 E Co Line Rd, Warminster, PA 18974, **Business Phone:** (215)674-6000.*

JOHNSON, WAYNE ALAN
Consultant. **Personal:** Born May 22, 1961, Springfield, MA; son of Karl Anthony Sr and Beverly May Riley; married Terri Clara Colbert Johnson, Jun 1, 1991; children: Brent W, Alana S. **Educ:** George Washington Univ, BBA, 1983; Univ Wis-Madison, MBA, 1984; Georgetown Univ WA, DC, JD, credits. **Career:** Freedom Fed Savings, record dept mgr, 1976-79; US House of Reps Hon Edw P Boland, staff asst, 1980-83; IBM, mktg rep, 1985-88, mktg progs mgr, 1989-90, mkt mgr, 1990-; consult, 1992-. **Orgs:** Consult/participant IBM Adopt-A-School, 1985-86; Nat Black MBA Asn, 1986-88; Nat Asn Advan Colored People, 1989; Montgomery County Church Christ, 1999-. **Honors/Awds:** Col Scholarship Award, Emhart Corp, 1979; MBA Fel Award, Consortium Grad Study, 1983; IBM 100% Club, 1986, 1987, 1991. **Home Addr:** 2 Marigold Ct, Silver Spring, MD 20906. **Business Addr:** Consultant, IBM, 800 N Frederick Ave bldg 183, Gaithersburg, MD 20879, **Business Phone:** (202)595-9566.*

JOHNSON, WAYNE J
Lawyer. **Personal:** Born Mar 21, 1958, Oakland, CA; son of Benjamin Francis and Juanita; married Miriamne, Nov 18, 1980; children: Kisha M, Afiya Tanzania, Zuberi Ogbonna & Jelani Bakari. **Educ:** Univ Calif, Berkeley, AB, 1979; Univ Calif, San Francisco, Hastings Col Law, JD, 1983. **Career:** Off US Congressman Ronald V Dellums, adm aide, 1979-85; Off Coun Nat Asn Advan Colored People, San Francisco Region, assoc, 1985-86; Castlemont High Sch, asst wrestling coach, 1986-89; Law Off Moore & Moore, coun, 1987; Oakland High Sch, head wrestling coach, 1989-92; Law Off Wayne Johnson, chief coun, 1992-. **Orgs:** Exec bd, Congressman Ronald V Dellums, 1984-98; adv bd, Alameda Co Econ Develop, Urban Revitalization Comn, 1993-97; Econ Develop Alliance Bus, 1998; exec bd, Congresswoman Barbara Lee, 1998. **Special Achievements:** Largest settlement in Oakland, CA history for excessive police force, 2001. **Business Addr:** Chief Counsel, Law Offices of Wayne Johnson, 445 Bellevue Ave, Oakland, CA 94610, **Business Phone:** (510)451-1166.

JOHNSON, WAYNE LEE
Consultant. **Personal:** Born Oct 28, 1953, Hartford, CT; son of Hubert L Johnson and Betty Hawthorne Johnson; married Bertha J; children: Jamaal Trumaine, Marquis Jawaan & Brittnee Nicole. **Educ:** Grambling State Univ, BA, 1975; Univ Hartford Grad Sch Bus. **Career:** Hartford Ins Group, work measurement analyst 1975-77, sr work measurement analyst 1977-79, mgt consult 1979-86; Citytrust, vp, 1986-89; Hartford Neighborhood Housing Servs, exec dir, 1990-91; Fox Middle Sch, teacher, 1991-93; State Conn, social worker, 1993-97, childrens servs consult, 1997-. **Orgs:** Asn Internal Mgt Consults, 1981-89; Toastmasters Int, 1982-84; bd dirs, IMPACT, 1985-89; Blue Hills Child Care Ctr Hartford 1986-91; bd dirs, Hartford Proud and Beautiful, 1990-91; pres, Windsor Giants, 1994-96; CT Childrens Alliance 2000-02; Child Fatality Review Panel 2001-01; instr, Police Officer Stands &Training Coun, 2001-03. **Honors/Awds:** Honor, Grambling State Univ, 1973; Dean's List, Grambling State Univ, 1974-75. **Special Achievements:** Wrote article, Starting Up a New Internal Management Consulting DepartmentAIMC Forum, 1988. **Business Addr:** Childrens Services Consultant, Department of Childrens & Families, 250 Hamilton St, Hartford, CT 06106, **Business Phone:** (860)418-8231.

JOHNSON, WENDELL L., JR.
Executive. **Personal:** Born Dec 10, 1922, Lexington, KY; married Rose E Vaughn; children: Wendell III, Edith, Jeffrey & Brian. **Educ:** Hampton Inst, BA, 1947; Atlanta Univ, MSW, 1949. **Career:** Chicago Welfare Dept, caseworker, 1949-51; Cook Co Hosp, med soc worker, 1951-52; Psychopathic Hosp, psychol soc worker, 1952-56; Chicago Housing Authority, asst dept dir mgt & dept exec dir, 1956-. **Orgs:** S Side Cent Comt Work, 1965-66; Grand Blvd Oakwood Community Coun, 1965-66; 2nd Dist Police Workshop, 1965-66; bd mem, Cit Adv Comt Joint Youth Dev Comt, 1967-69; pres, Neigh Inst Adv Comt; comt adv bd, Cabrini-Green Unit Cook Co Dept Pub Assistance, 1967-70; 8th Dist Police Workshop, 1967-76; bd mem, N Area Bd, Chicago Youth Ctrs, 1968-71; Chicago Chap Nat Asn Housing & Redev Officials, 1968-76; Boy Scouts Am; Nat Asn Advan Colored People; mem trustee, Lilydale First Baptist Church; Roseland Heights Comm Asn; Hampton Inst Alumni; Atlanta Univ Alumni; 1st Tee Golf Club. **Honors/Awds:** Award, appreciation of serv resid coun Cabrini-Green Homes, 1966-76; Cert of Appreciation, Kiwanis Club N Cent Chicago, 1967; Superior Public Service Award, Chicago Asn Com & Ind, 1973; Great Guy Achievement Award, WGRT-RADIO, 1973; commend for ded to pub serv, 1973; Cert of Appreciation, Chicago Youth Ctr, 1976; Bronze Star; Purple Heart. **Military Serv:** AUS, tech sgt, 1943-45. **Business Phone:** (312)567-7758.

JOHNSON, WENDELL NORMAN. See Obituaries section.

JOHNSON, WENDY ROBIN
Buyer. **Personal:** Born Dec 26, 1956, New York, NY; daughter of Clarence Woodson Jr (deceased) and Dolores Elizabeth Dominguez; married Keith Andrew Hill, Sep 12, 1992. **Educ:** Elizabeth Seton Col, AAS, liberal arts, 1980; Marymount Manhattan Col, BBA, finance, 1983; Manhattan Col, Bronx, MBA, 1987. **Career:** RCA Records, buyer specialist, 1976-83; PolyGram Records Inc, mgr purchasing, 1983-85; Kraft Foods Corp, assoc buyer, 1985-86; buyer, 1987-95, sr buyer, 1995-. **Orgs:** Delta Sigma Theta Sorority Inc, 1979-; troop leader, Girl Scout Coun Greater NY, 1983-; Nat Asn Female Execs, 1984-; founder, We Buy, 1988-; asst dean, Learning Ctr Canaan Baptist Church, 1988-; instr, Jr Achievement Project Bus, 1989-; Co-founder Nuff Said!, 1992. **Honors/Awds:** Outstanding Young Women of America, 1984. **Special Achievements:** Crossroads, 1993. **Business Phone:** (914)335-2927.

JOHNSON, WILBUR EUGENE
Lawyer. **Personal:** Born Mar 1, 1954, Columbia, SC. **Educ:** Univ SC Aiken; Augusta Col GA, BA, hist, 1976; Univ SC Law Ctr, JD, 1979. **Career:** Fel Earl Warren Legal Training Prog, 1976-79; Richland Co Pub Def Agy, law clerk, 1977-79; Palmetto Legal Serv, staff atty, 1979-; Off Atty Gen SC, asst atty gen, 1979-94; Young Clement Rivers LLP, partner, currently. **Orgs:** SC Bar Asn; Urban League Guild; Kwanza Comn, 1979-; SC Bar Comt; SC Bar Law Related Educ Comt; Am Bar Asn; bd mem, Charleston Metro Chamber Com; bd mem, Community Found; bd mem, Roper & St Francis Health Found; bd mem, SC State Chamber Com; bd mem, Charleston County Disabilities Bd; Trust Pub Land SC Adv Coun, 2005-; Fedn Defense & Corp Coun, 2006-. **Honors/Awds:** Outstanding Col Athelete Am, 1973-74. **Business Addr:** Partner, Young Clement Rivers LLP, 28 Broad St, Charleston, SC 29401, **Business Phone:** (843)724-6659.

JOHNSON, WILHELMINA LASHAUN
Financial manager. **Personal:** Born Aug 13, 1950, Ft Worth, TX. **Educ:** TX Christian Univ, BS, 1983; Univ TX Arlington, 1987. **Career:** City of Ft Worth, admin intern, 1979, admin asst, 1979-83, admin analyst, 1983. **Orgs:** Conf Minorities Assoc, 1979-, Urban Mgt Asn North TX, 1979-, Am Soc Pub Admin, 1980; Intl City Mgt Assoc, 1980-, Nat Forum Black Pub Admin, 1984-.

JOHNSON, WILLARD RAYMOND
Educator. **Personal:** Born Nov 22, 1935, St Louis, MO; son of Willard Johnson and Dorothy Neoma Stovall; married Vivian Robinson; children: Caryn L & Kimberly E. **Educ:** Pasadena City Col, AA, 1955; Univ Calif, Los Angeles, BA, 1957; Johns Hopkins Sch Advanced Int Studies, MA, 1961; Harvard Univ, PhD, 1965. **Career:** Ford Found Foreign Area Training fels, 1959, 1960, 1963, 1964; John Hay Whitney Found Oppurtunity fel, 1961; Mass Inst Technol, from asst prof to assoc prof, 1964-73; Circle Inc, Boston, exec dir & chief exec officer, 1968-70; Mass Inst Technol, prof polit sci, 1973-96; resident fel, Rockefeller Ctr Belagio, Italy, 1987; Fulbright fel, 1987; Mass Inst Technol, prof emer polit sci, 1996-. **Orgs:** Vpres, African Heritage Studies Asn, 1978; Am Polit Sci Asn, 1965-; Nat Econ Asn, 1971-82; Nat Conf Black Polit Scientists, 1971; US Nat Comt, UNESCO, 1960-66; bd mem, Boston New Urban League, 1967-72; bd mem, Nat Scholar Fund Negro Stud, 1958-59; New England Polit Sci Asn, 1966-69; Coun Foreign Rels, 1973-97; Black Forum Foreign Affairs, 1976-78; Asn Study Afro-Am Life & History 1968-72; bd mem, Asn Concerned African Scholars, 1977; nat co-chmn, Asn Concerned African Scholars, 1983-89; bd mem, World Univ Serv, 1958-60; bd mem, Interfaith Housing corp, 1970; chmn bd, Circle Complex, Roxbury, 1970-72; dir, Africa Policy Task Force McGovern Pres Campaign, 1972; Dem Party Adv Coun Foreign Affairs Study, 1976; pres, TransAfrica Inc, Boston Chap, 1981-90; bd mem, Trans Africa Inc Nat, 1977-95; dir, Bus Mgt Econ Develop Res Proj, 1973-95; dir, Communs Component African Am Issues Ctr & Mass Inst Technol Ctr Int Studies, 1982-91; founder & sr adv, Boston Pan-African Forum, 1996-; founder, Kansas Inst African Am & Native Am Family Hist, 1991-; pres, Kansas Inst African Am & Native Am Family Hist, 1997-. **Honors/Awds:** Research Grant, Ctr Int Studies, Mass Inst Technol, 1971; Research Grant, Technol Adaptation Proj, Mass Inst Technol, 1973-74; Black Achievers Award, Boston Young Men Christian Asn,1899; Black Men of Vision Award, Boston Mus African Am Hist, 1992; Fulbright Seminar, Indonesia, 1991. **Special Achievements:** Publications such as articles and book chapters on issues of African development and foreign relations, and economic and political development of American inner-city areas. **Business Addr:** Professor Emeritus of Political Science,

Massachusetts Institute of Technology, Department of Political Science, E53-367 77 Mass Ave, Cambridge, MA 02139, **Business Phone:** (617)253-2952.

JOHNSON, WILLIAM A
Government official, college administrator. **Personal:** Born Aug 22, 1942, Lynchburg, VA; son of William A Johnson, Sr and Roberta Davis Johnson; married Sylvia M Johnson; children: Kelley M, Kristin R, Wynde A & Sylvia McCoy. **Educ:** Howard Univ, BA, 1965, MA, 1967. **Career:** US Supreme Ct, stud aide, 1966; Nat Hwy Users Conf Wash, legis analyst, 1966-67; Genesee Community Col Flint, instr polit sci, 1967-71; Urban League Flint Mich, dep exec dir, 1971-72; Urban League Rochester, pres & chief exex officer, 1972-93; City Rochester, NY, mayor, 1994-2005; Rochester Inst Technol, minett prof, 1996-97, distinguished prof public policy, currently. **Orgs:** Co-founder, Com More Rep Govt; organist, New Bethel CME Church, 1975-91; co-founder Black Leadership Study Group; trustee, Monroe Community Col Rochester NY, 1976-82; NY St Employ & Training Coun, 1977-83; vice chmn, 1978-79, chmn 1979-83, pres, Urban League Rochester Econ Develop Corp, 1985-93; civil serv comnr, City Rochester, 1980-90; bd dirs, Eltrex Indust Inc, 1982-93; co-founder, Austin Steward Prof Soc, 1985-90; mediator, Factfinder, NYS Pub Employ Rels Bd, 1985-93; Sigma Pi Phi Fraternity, Gamma Iota Boule, 1987-, sire archon, 1994-96; chairperson, 1992-93, bd dirs, vice chairperson, New Futures Initiative Inc, 1988-91; NY State Bd Social Work, 1988-93; Univ Rochester Grad Sch Educ, trustees vis comt, 1991-; Grapter, 1996-98; Nat Conf Black Mayors, 1994-2005; Rochester Philharmonic Orchestra, trustee, 1996-; Partners for a Livable Community, trustee, 1997-, chmn, 2002-; US Conf Mayors, Adv bd, 1998-, trustee, 2001-; Eureka Lodge No 36, Free & Accepted Masons, Prince Hall, 1998-; exec comm, New York State Conf Mayors, 1999-2005; Nat League Cities, chair, comm & regional develop task force, 2002-03. **Honors/Awds:** Honor soc, Pi Sigma Alpha, 1967; Jefferson Award for Outstanding Public Service, Am Inst Pub Serv, 1986; Doctor of Humane Letters, KeuKa Col, 1990; Doctor of Laws, St John Fisher Col, 1998; doctor of humane letters, Rochester Institute of Technology, 1999; One of 10 US Public Officials of the Year, Governing Magazine, 1999; Disting Alumni Award for Post-grad Achievement, Howard Univ, 2003. **Special Achievements:** First African-American elected mayor of the City of Rochester, New York. **Home Addr:** 165 Castlebar Rd, Rochester, NY 14610, **Home Phone:** (716)244-7511. **Business Addr:** Distinguished Professor Public Policy, Rochester Institute Technology, 92 Lomb Memorial Dr, Rochester, NY 14263-5608, **Business Phone:** (585)475-4407.

JOHNSON, WILLIAM ARTHUR
Football player, football coach. **Personal:** Born Jan 27, 1952, Bouthwyn, PA; married Barbara; children: Marcia, Kendra, Jared & Jazmyn. **Educ:** Widener Univ. **Career:** Football player (retired), football coach; Houston Oilers, wide receiver, 1974-80; Montreal Alouettes, wide receiver, 1981; Atlanta Falcons, wide receiver, 1982-87; Wash Redskins, wide receiver, 1988; Morehouse Col, coach; Atlanta Falcons, dir player prog, 1994-2005, asst strength & conditioning coach, 2005-. **Orgs:** Alpha Sigma Phi Fraternity. **Honors/Awds:** Comeback Player of the Year, Nat Football League, 1983; Falcon's Top Punt Returner of All-Time; Pro Bowl, 1975, 1977, 1983; Col Football Hall of Fame, 2000; Pennsylvania Sports Hall of Fame, 2000. **Business Phone:** (770)965-3115.

JOHNSON, WILLIAM C.
Executive. **Personal:** Born Jul 1, 1930, New York, NY; children: William C Jr, Anthony C (deceased), Anita C & Robert W. **Career:** Executive (retired); First California Funding Inc, sr vpres. **Orgs:** Am Legion Jackie Robinson Post 252. **Military Serv:** USN, sr chief petty officer, 30 yrs; Vietnam Service Medals, Good Conduct Medal, European Occupation Nat Defense. **Business Addr:** Senior Vice President, First California Funding Inc, 6820 La Tijera Blvd Suite E15, Los Angeles, CA 90045.

JOHNSON, WILLIAM EDWARD (BILL E JOHNON)
Football player, football coach. **Personal:** Born Dec 9, 1968, Chicago, IL. **Educ:** Mich State Univ. **Career:** Football player (retired), Football coach; Cleveland Browns, 1992-94; Pittsburgh Steelers, 1995-96; St Louis Rams, defensive tackle, 1997; Philadelphia Eagles, 1998-99; McKinley high sch, coach, currently. **Honors/Awds:** Football Coach of the Week, Buffalo Bills High Sch, 2007. **Business Addr:** Football Coach, McKinley High School, 2323 17th st NW, Canton, OH 44708, **Business Phone:** (330)438-2750.

JOHNSON, WILLIAM L.
Psychologist, psychoanalyst. **Personal:** Born May 23, 1932, NYC; son of Richard and Artimeza Ward; married Vera Peterkin; children: Toni Ann, Hillary Sloan. **Educ:** Queens Col, BA, 1953; New Sch Soc Res, MA 1955; City Col, MS, 1957; Yeshiva Univ, PhD Clinical Psychol, 1964; Adelphi Univ; Inst Advanced Psychological Studies, Post doctoral Dipl Psychoanalysis, 1968. **Career:** USAF, Mitchel AFB, personal psychologist personal lab, 1957; Kings Pk St Hosp, clinical Psychologist, 1959; NYS Rehab Hosp, psychologist, 1959-62; Falkirk Hosp Central Valley NY; US Peace Corps Ankara Turkey; NY St Training Sch Boys, consult psychologist; Orange Co Ment Health Clinics, chief psychologist, 1962-64; Pvt Practice, psychoanalyst, 1964-. **Orgs:** Am Psychol Asn, 1957-74; St Psychol Asn, 1959-74; pres, Orange Co Psychol Asn, 1963-64; Asn Black Psychologist, 1972-74; Adelphia Univ Postdoctoral Soc, 1969-74. **Honors/Awds:** Alvin Johnson Prize Scholarship, New Sch Soc Res, 1953. **Business Addr:** Psychologist, Psychoanalyst, 300 Mercer St Apt 3k, New York, NY 10003, **Business Phone:** (212)982-4094.*

JOHNSON, WILLIAM LEON (WALTER LEON JOHNSON)
Football player. **Personal:** Born Jul 13, 1974, Morganton, NC. **Educ:** Univ NC. **Career:** New York Jets, running back, 1997-2000; Chicago Bears, 2001-02; San Diego Chargers, 2003-04; free agent, currently.

JOHNSON, WILLIAM PAUL
Consultant. **Personal:** Born Jul 17, 1963, Washington, DC; son of William Paul and Elizabeth Ann. **Educ:** Univ Wash, Wash DC, BBA, 1988; Syracuse Univ, attended 1983; Howard Univ, Wash, MEd, 1993. **Career:** Harry Diamond Labs, Adelphi MD, comput specialist, 1981-87; US Treasury, Bur Engraving & Printing, Wash DC, comput specialist, 1987-89; Comput Info & Support Servs, consult, co-owner, 1987-91; coach, Nat High Sch Comput Competition Team, 1988-95; Comp-U-Staff, Silver Springs MD, comput analyst, progr, 1989-90; McDonald-Bradley Inc, McLean, sr progr, analyst, 1989-94; Tonya Inc, sr consult, 1994-99; US Dept HUD, mgt info specialist, dep adminr, currently. **Orgs:** Pres, Univ Wash DC Data Processing Mgt Asn, 1986-87; educ chairperson, Black Data Processing Asn, 1987-91; founder, pres, Univ Wash Black Data Processing Asn, 1987-88; chairperson, Univ Wash DC Col Bus Stud Adv Coun, 1988; pres, Black Date Processing Asn, Washington DC Chapter, 1991-95. **Honors/Awds:** Syracuse Univ Academic Scholarship Award, 1981-83; Marion S Barry Scholarship Award, Univ Wash DC, 1987; Member of the Year, Washington DC Chapter Black Data Processing Asn, 1988-91; Nat member of the Year, Black Data Processing Asn, 1991; Numerous Leadership Awards, 1991-95. **Home Addr:** 849 Venable Pl NW, Washington, DC 20012. **Business Addr:** Deputy Administrator, US Dept Housing & Urban Develop (HUD), 451 C St SW Rm 4258, Washington, DC 20005, **Business Phone:** (202)708-3368.

JOHNSON, WILLIAM RANDOLPH
Chemist. **Personal:** Born Jul 25, 1930, Oxford, NC; son of William R Sr and Marina Townes; married Wendolyn; children: Wendolyn, Pamela, William III. **Educ:** NC Cent Univ, BS, 1950; Univ Notre Dame, MS, 1952; Univ Pa, PhD, 1958. **Career:** Chemist (retired); Prairie View Agr & Mech Col, fac, 1952-53; Fla Agr & Mech Univ, prof chem, 1958-61; W R Grace & Co, res chem, 1961-63; Philip Morris Res Ctr, sr scientist, 1963-66; Va Union Univ, adj prof, chem, 1963-81. **Orgs:** Nat Asn Guardsmen. **Special Achievements:** Publ: Jour Polymer Sci, 1960; 9 US pat, publ Jour of Org Chem 1971; 3 publ Tobac Sci 1973; 2 publ Nature 1973; 3 publ Chem & Ind 1973, 1975, 1979. **Military Serv:** Army Chem Corps corpl, 1953-55. **Home Addr:** 1001 Spottswood Rd, Richmond, VA 23220. *

JOHNSON, REV. WILLIAM SMITH
Clergy, executive. **Personal:** Born Apr 24, 1941, Salisbury, MD; son of Delcie Mae Markland and Alonzo Lester Johnson; married Jacqueline Andrea Dennis; children: William Jr & Andrea. **Educ:** Univ MD, Eastern Shore, BS, 1963; Eastern Bible Inst, dipl pastoral min, 1985; Salisbury State Univ, grad study; Howard Univ Divinity Sch, grad study; Capitol Bible Sem, grad study. **Career:** Wicomico Co Bd Educ, teacher, 1963-64; US Govt, comput programmer, 1964-65; Detroit Lions, prof football player, 1965; Sussex Co Bd Educ, teacher, 1965-66; EI duPont De Nemours Co Inc, syst specialist, 1966-. Wallace Temple African Methodist Episcopal Zion Church, pastor, 1991-96; Mount Hope AME Zion Church, pastor, 1996-99. **Orgs:** Adv bd mem, Wicomico Co Housing Authority, 1983-84; adv bd mem, Wicomico Co Sch Rezoning Community; NAACP; Prince Hall Mason; asst pastor, St James AME Zion Church; life mem, Salisbury High Asn. **Honors/Awds:** Distinguished Alumni of Year, NAFEO, 1983; Ordained Elder AME Zion Church, 1986; Outstanding Service Award for Church Serv Assistance; Univ MD Eastern Shore, Athletic Hall of Fame. **Home Addr:** PO Box 1225, Salisbury, MD 21802.

JOHNSON, WILLIAM T
Banker, chief executive officer. **Career:** OmniBanc Corp, chmn, ceo. *

JOHNSON, WILLIAM THEOLIOUS
Lawyer. **Personal:** Born Dec 24, 1943, Columbus, OH; son of Andrew and Thelma; married Gloria Kindle, Jun 12, 1966; children: Michael & Michelle. **Educ:** Capital Univ, AB, 1968; Capital Univ, Ohio State Univ, JD, 1972. **Career:** Dunbar Kienzle & Murphey Law Firm, atty, 1972-75; Johnson & Ransier Co LPA, managing partner, 1975-79; Pvt Pract, atty, 1979-; KBLE OH Inc, pres. **Orgs:** Chmn, Black Am Law Stud Asn; chmn, Law Day; Phi Alpha Delta Law Fraternity; vpres, Stud Bar Asn; nat chmn, Elections Comn Am Bar Asn Law Stud Div; pres, Franklin Co Legal Aid & Defender Soc; vice chmn, Franklin Co Ment Health & Retardation Bd; bd mem, spec coun Columbus Urban League; trustee, Columbus Zoo; trustee, Ohio Found Independent Col; nat chmn, Minority Affairs Comn Nat Cable TV Asn; legis comn, NCTA; trustee, Franklin Co Pub Defender Comn; ruling elder, Bethany Presbyterian Church; Columbus, Am Nat Bar Asns; hearing officer, Ohio Civil Rights Comn; hearing officer, Ohio Dept Educ; arbitrator, United Steelworkers; Nat Cable TV Asn; Ohio Cable TV Asn; pract, Supreme Ct US, US Ct Appeals, US Dist Ct & US Tax Ct. **Honors/Awds:** Outstanding Young Man in Columbus, Columbus Jr C C, 1972; Outstanding Community Service Award, Columbus Bar Asn, 1978; Gold Key Award; Lutheran Brotherhood Scholar; Hugh H Huntington Award; American Jurisprudence Book Award; Law Book Award, W Publ Co Const; Community Service Award, Columbus Bar Asn. **Special Achievements:** Selected as one of the Ten Outstanding Young Men in Columbus. **Business Addr:** Attorney, 124 S Wash Ave, Columbus, OH 43215.

JOHNSON, WILLIE
Government official, musician. **Personal:** Born May 26, 1925, Florence, SC; son of Luther and Evelener Richardson; married Fredericka Helen Gadsden, 1946; children: Franklin Lewis. **Educ:** Wayne State Univ, 1970; Cass Tech HS, cert accomplish, 1971; Mich Career Inst, cert grad, 1974. **Career:** Government official (retired); Wayne County Gen Hosp, Wayne County guard, 1951-78; Wayne County, dep sheriff, 1961-68; Kaufman & Broad Homes, supvr, 1961-69; State Mich, asst chief fire & safety officer, 1978; Personal Accomplishment, songwriter, 1955; City Inkster, city councilman, 1990; minister music, vocalist, 1992. **Orgs:** Inkster, Nat Asn Advan Colored People, 1974-; Cent Wayne County Sanitation Authority, 1975-77; Inkster Civil Defense Policy Bd, 1975-; comn mem, Nankin Transit Comn, 1977-; Broadcast Music Inc, 1984-; publ, Wiljoe MusicBMI, 1984-; producer, Inkster's New Sounds "Inkster's New Sound" label,1984-; Nashville Songwriters Asn Int, 1990; Broadcast Music Inc, 1984-; Nat Black Caucus; bd mem, Mich Asn Govt Employees, 1991. **Honors/Awds:** Certificate of appreciation, Wayne County Bd Comn, 1978; special tribute, State Mich, Sen Plawecki & Rep Wm Keith, 1978; Distinguished Employee of the Year, Walter P Reuther Psychol Hosp, 1981; First Place Trophy at Sumpter Township Rodeo for compositions & vocalist, 1988. **Special Achievements:** Won lawsuit as private citizen in state supreme ct to return money to citizens Home Owners' Org, 1971-78. **Military Serv:** USN, seaman 1st class, 1943-46; Asia/Pacific Campaign Medal; Good Conduct Medal; personal letter from secy of Navy; WWII Victory Medal. **Home Addr:** 4066 Durand Ct, Inkster, MI 48141. *

JOHNSON, WILLIE F
Commissioner, chief executive officer. **Educ:** Allen Univ, SC, BA, sociol; Univ Pa, MSW. **Career:** State Pa, Off Social Servs, comnr; City Philadelphia, Off Mayor, Off Employment & Training, exec dir; Fidelity Systs Inc, pres & chief exec officer; PRWT Servs Inc, founder, chmn & chief exec officer, currently; Transitional Work Corp Inc, chmn bd dirs, currently; PRWT Holding Co, chmn & chief exec officer, currently. **Orgs:** Urban League Philadelphia; Philadelphia Tribune; African-Am Chamber Com; Am Heart Asn; Philadelphia-based Berean Inst; Cheyney Univ Found; United Way Southeastern Pa; Am Red Cross; Philadelphia Zoo; Girard Col; West Ins; Del River Port Authority Blue Ribbon Panel; Philadelphia Workforce Investment Bd; Community Serv Develop Corp. **Business Phone:** (215)569-8810.*

JOHNSON, WILLIE F
Executive, commissioner, founder (originator). **Personal:** Born Sep 27, 1939, Jacksonville, FL; children: Thandeka. **Educ:** Allen Univ, BA, sociol, 1961; Univ Penn, MSW, 1970. **Career:** SC Pub Sch, teacher, 1961-64; Nat Biscuit Co, foreman, 1965-66; Youth Develop Ctr S Philadelphia, counr, 1966-68; Youth Develop Ctr Philadelphia, counr, 1961-64, exec dir, 1972-74; Commonwealth Pa Dept Pub Welfare, Southern Reg, comnr, off youth serv; Fidelity Systems Inc, pres & chief exec officer; PRWT Servs Inc, chmn & prin, currently; PRWT Holding Co, chmn & chief exec officer, currently. **Orgs:** Urban League Philadelphia; The Philadelphia Tribune; African-Am Chamber Com; Am Heart Asn; The Cheyney Univ Found; United Way Southeastern Pa; Am Red Cross; Philadelphia Zoo; Girard Col; West Ins; Del River Port Authority Blue Ribbon Panel; Philadelphia Workforce Invest Bd; Community Serv Develop Corp; chmn bd dirs, Transitional Work Corp Inc. **Business Addr:** Chairman, Chief Executive Officer, PRWT Servs Inc, 1835 Mkt St Suite 800, Philadelphia, PA 19103, **Business Phone:** (215)569-8810.

JOHNSON, WYNEVA
Lawyer. **Personal:** Born Oct 28, 1948, Greenwood, MS. **Educ:** Wheaton Col, BA, 1971; Univ Pa, JD, 1974; Georgetown Univ Law Ctr, LLM, 1977. **Career:** Howard Jenkins Fr Nat Labor Rel Bd, coun to bd mem; US Atty's Off, Asst US Atty, currently. **Orgs:** Admitted PA Bar, 1974; admitted MS Bar, 1976; exec bd Wheaton Col Alumnae Asn; chmn, Comn Black Alumnae. **Honors/Awds:** Nominee, Outstanding Young Women America, 1976. **Business Addr:** Assistant United States Attorney, US Attorney's Office, 555 4th St NW, Washington, DC 20530, **Business Phone:** (202)514-6600.

JOHNSON-BLOUNT, THERESA
Librarian. **Personal:** Born Jan 11, 1952, Lafayette, LA; daughter of Willie Johnson and Rosella Veazie Johnson; married William III, Mar 20, 1976; children: Tyaisha Alyce, Wilicia Ellen & Remus Allen. **Educ:** Southern Univ, Baton Rouge, LA, BS, mkt, 1973; Grad Sch, La State Univ, Baton Rouge, LA, 1989; Tex Woman's Univ, Denton, TX, MLS, 1990. **Career:** Mid-County Dirt Pit, Port Arthur, TX, asst Mgr, 1973-75; Wilson's Jewelers, Baton Rouge, LA, invoice clerk, 1976-77; US Coast Guard, Baton Rouge, LA, storekeeper, 1975-78; Woman's Hosp Neonatology Unit, acquisitions librn, consult, 1985-; Tulane Med Ctr Neonatology Unit, acquisitions librn, consult, 1985-; La State Univ, Troy H Middleton Libr, libr assoc II, 1979-90, librn, 1990-91, soc sci United Nations specist librn, 1991-95; Rehab Hosp Baton Rouge, Vol Servs Dept, librn; res librn, 1996-99; Southern Univ A&M Col, Off Grants & Sponsored Progs, res info assoc, 1999-. **Orgs:** Libr Staff Asn, 1980-; Am Libr Asn, 1988-; Ala Black Caucus, Govt Round Table, 1990-; Spec Libr Asn, 1988-, bulletin ed, 1992-94; LSU, Int Hospity Found, host family, 1988-, Black Fac & Black Staff Caucus, 1985-, Black Studs Support Group, 1985-89; RHA rep, TWU, Mary Hufford Hall, 1989-90; libr consult, AMR Therapeutic Recreation Asn; elected vice chair, LLA GODORT, 1995-96, chair, 1996-97. **Honors/Awds:** Scholarship, Beta Phi Mu; acad scholar, Tex Woman's Univ; Donna Jean Billington Scholar; Graduate Assistant Award Library/LRC, Tex Woman's Univ; Certificate of Appreciation, Tex Woman's Univ & Nat Alumnae Asn; Service Award, La State Univ; author, "Pull a String for Results: Strings Used as Therapeutic Activities," Sch Libr Media Activities Monthly, June 1991; author, "Making Sausages: Old Fashioned Boudin," Southern Living, November 1983; author, Cooking from Bayou Courtableau, 1984; author, Lagniappe Cookbook, 1984; Outstanding Family Award, Family Serv Greater Baton Rouge; ASPECT Host Family, 1996-97. **Special Achievements:** Author of articles including "International Year of the Family: Libraries Can Be a Family Educational Affair," Documents to the People, 1994; "United Nations Depository Collection at Troy H Middleton Library," Louisiana Library Assn, LLA Bulletin, 1992; "Characteristics of Automoted Acquisitions Systems in Organizations Belonging to the Assn For Higher Education of North Texas," Texas Woman's Univ, ERIC, 1992; "A Selected List of Basic Health Science Reference Sources," American Therapeutic Recreation Assn, Newsletter, 1992; "Nutty Popcorn Balls," Southern Living, 1988; "Making Sausages: Old Fashioned Boudin," Southern Living, 1983; "Pull a String for Results: Strings Used as Therapeutic Activities," School Library Media Activities Monthly, 8(2), p 31-33, Oct 1991; "A Selected List of Basic Health Science Reference Sources," American Therapeutic Recreation Assn Newsletter, 8(1), p 8, Jan/Feb 1992; "Characteristics of Automated Acquisitions Systems in Organizations Belong to the Assn of Higher Education," ERIC Clearinghouse, Syracuse Univ, 1992; Special Libraries Assn, LA/Southern Mississippi Chapter, bulletin editor; TWU, Booking Binding Workshop, organizer, 1990; Southern University Recreation Dept, banquet organizer, 1992. **Military Serv:** USCG, SK3, 1975-78. **Home Addr:** 8926 High Point Rd, Baton Rouge, LA 70810.

JOHNSON-BROWN, DR. HAZEL WINFRED
Educator, nurse. **Personal:** Born Oct 10, 1927, West Chester, PA; daughter of Garnet Henley and Clarence L; married David B. **Educ:** Harlem Hosp Nursing, Dipl, 1950; Villanova Univ, BS, 1959; Columbia Univ Teacher's Col, MS, 1963; Cath Univ, PhD, 1978. **Career:** Letterman Gen Med Ctr, instr, 1963-66; Valley Forge Gen, supvr, 1966-67; US Army, med res & develop command proj, dir, 1967-73; Univ MD Sch Nursing, dir & asst dean, 1976-78; US Army Hosp, Seoul, Korea, asst nursing, 1978-79; Georgetown Univ, Sch Nursing, asst prof, 1983-84, adj prof, 1985; George Mason Univ, prof sch nursing, 1986, prof emer, currently. **Orgs:** Am Nurses Asn, 1957-; Sigma Theta Tau, 1977-; Asn AUS, 1978-; lifetime mem, Nursing Educ Alumnae Asn Teachers Col Columbia Univ; honorary mem, Chi Eta Phi Alpha Chap, Nat Black Nursing Sor, Delta Sigma Theta. **Honors/Awds:** Recognition Award, Tuskegee Inst Sch Nursing, 1981; Henry O Flipper Award, Mili Law Section Nat Bar Asn, 1981; Distinguished Prof of Nursing & Mili Sci, Prairie View A & M Univ, 1981; Bethune Tubman Truth Award, Black Women Hall of Fame Found, 1981; Roy Wilkins Meritorious Serv Award, NAACP; American Black Achievement Award, Bus & Prof Ebony Mag, 1983; Golden Heart Award, 1983; Black Nurse of Yr, Greater Wash Area Black Nurses Asn, 1984; Nat Inst Women Color Award, 1984; Candace Award, Nat Coalition of 100 Black Women, 1984; Army Commendation Medal with oak leaf cluster. **Special Achievements:** Guest lectr: Georgetown Univ; Univ of Md, George Mason Univ Sch of Nursing, natl/local TV & radio interview participation, 1979-82, Women's Issues & Prof Nursing, Night Watch, 1983, The Different Drummer Series, African-Am hist month programming, PBS-TV, 1983-84, first African-Am woman Gen in hist of Mili Serv, one of 100 Black Bus & Prof Women, Dollars & Sense Mag, 1985. **Military Serv:** AUS Nurse Corps, brigadier gen; Evangeline C Bovard Army Nurse of the Yr Award 1964; Army Commendation Medal, 1966; First Oak Leaf Cluster Nurse of Yr, Dr Anita Newcomb McGee Award, Daughters of the Am Revolution, 1971; Legion of Merit, 1973; Meritorious Serv Medal, 1979; Order of Mili Med Merit, 1983; AUS ROTC Serv Award, 1983; Distinguished Serv Medal, 1983. **Business Addr:** Professor Emerita, George Mason University, School of Nursing, 4400 University Dr, Fairfax, VA 22030-4444, **Business Phone:** (703)993-1300.

JOHNSON-CARSON, DR. LINDA D
Health services administrator, optometrist. **Personal:** Born Feb 5, 1954, Richland, MS; daughter of Adam and Gertrude; divorced; children: James III. **Educ:** Jackson State Univ, BS, 1974; Indiana State Univ, Sch Optometry, Dr Optometry, 1978. **Career:** Jackson Hinds Comprehensive Health Ctr, dept head, Optometry, 1978-. **Orgs:** Mississippi Optometric Asn, mem, 1978-, asst to grad & undergrad comn, 1979-81, legis comn, 1989-, pub rels co-chair, 1989-90, chmn, 1991-93, develop & retention chair, 1993-, pres; Southern County Optometrists, 1974-; Nat Optometric Asn, bd dir, 1974-, trustee at large, 1981-83, region III trustee, 1983-85, secy, 1989-93, vp, 1993-95, pres-elect, 1995-97, pres, 1997-99; bd dir, central Miss chap Am Red Cross, 1988-; exec bd, Am Red Cross Central Miss Chap, 1989-; Am Optometric Asn, 1978-80, 1989-; exec comn, AOA Community Ctr, 1992-96; Am Red Cross Central MS, chap chair volunteer servs, 1988-91, second vchair, bd dirs, 1991-93, vchair, bd dirs, 1993-95, chair, bd dirs, 1995-97. **Honors/Awds:** 'Professional Achievement', Jackson State Univ, Nat Alumni Asn, 1980; Distinguished Service, Jackson Hinds Alumni Chap, Jackson State Nat Alumni Asn, 1982; hon mem, Beta Beta Beta Biological Honor Soc, Jackson State Univ, 1984; Certificate of Appreciation, Ms Optometric Asn, 1990; Volunteer of the Month, Am Red Cross Central Ms Chap, 1990; Certificate of Appreciation, Jackson State Univ, Dean Libr, 1991; Optometrist of the Year, Nat Optometric Asn, 1993; Am Red Cross, Central MS Chap, J Tate Thigpen Award, 1994; JC Penney Golden-Rule Award, Top 10 Finalist Award, 1997; You've Made a Difference Award, Comt Working to Unite Youth Org, Rawkin County, 1997; MS Comnr, Volunteer Serv Commendation, 1996-97; Optometrist of the Year, AM Optometric Asn, 2008. **Special Achievements:** First black female optometrist in Mississippi, 1978. **Home Addr:** 2400 Ladd St, Jackson, MS 39209. **Business Addr:** Department Head of Optometry/Director, Jackson Hinds Comprehensive Health Center, 3502 W Northside Dr, PO Box 3437, Jackson, MS 39213, **Business Phone:** (601)362-5321.

JOHNSON COOK, SUZAN DENISE
Clergy, educator. **Personal:** Born Jan 28, 1957, New York, NY; daughter of Wilbert T and Dorothy C; married Ronald Cook, Oct 11, 1991; children: Samuel David. **Educ:** Emerson Col, BS, 1976; Columbia Univ Teachers Col, MA, 1978; Union Theological Seminary, MDV, 1983; United Theological Seminary, Doctor Ministry, 1990. **Career:** NBC, tv producer; Austrilian Broadcasitng Corp, tv producer; CBS, tv producer; Mariners' Temple Baptist Church, sr pastor; Bronx Christian Fellowship, sr pastor; Multi Ethnic Ctr, exec dir & founder; NY Police Dept, chaplain; Harvard Univ, Divinity Sch, visiting prof; White House, Domestic Policy Coun, 1993; Faith Initiatives, HUD secy, 1994-97; JONCO Productions Inc, co founder, chief exec officer, currently. **Orgs:** vpres, NY Coalition 100 Black Women; Am Baptist Churches; founder, Multi Ethnic Ctr. **Honors/Awds:** Essence Woman, Essence Magazine, 1983; YWCA Award, 1986; Young Achievers, Nat Coun Negro Women, 1988. **Special Achievements:** Book: Preaching In Two Voices, Judson: Valley Forge, 1992; Wise Women Bearing Gifts, Judson: Valley Forge, ed, 1988; Too Blessed to be Stressed Words of Wisdom for Women on the Move, 1998; first African American woman to be elected to an American Baptist Church. **Business Addr:** Pastor, Jonco Productions, Peck Slip Station, PO Box 226, New York, NY 10272-0226, **Business Phone:** (212)289-4374.*

JOHNSON-CROCKETT, DR. MARY ALICE
Physician. **Personal:** Born May 6, 1937, Anderson, SC; daughter of William P and Bernice McAlister; married Edward D Crockett Jr (deceased); children: Edward D III, Alison V & Sharon P. **Educ:** Howard Univ, Col Liberal Arts, BS, 1958; Howard Univ, Col Medicine, MD, 1962. **Career:** Freedman Hosp, intern, 1963; DC Gen Hosp, Vet Admin, Howard Univ, resident internal med, 1963-66; Walter Reed Army Med Ctr, med officer, 1966-67; Vet Admin Hosp Downey, IL, staff physician, 1967-69; Community Group Health Found Inc, staff physician & acting med dir, 1969-72; JB Johnson Nursing Ctr, med dir; Home Care Serv Bur, med officer, med dir, 1972-; Hospice Care DC, med dir, 1979-82; pvt prac, internal med & geriatrics. **Orgs:** Consult, Income Maintenance Admin, 1971-86; health physician, Law Enforcement Agency Admin & Consumer Prod Safety Comn, 1975, 1976-77; mem exec comn, Potomac PTA, 1976-81; track physician, Bowie Race Track, 1977-81; prof adv comt, Hospice Care DC, 1983-; UpJohn, 1985-; steering comt, Sidwell Friends Sch, 1984-85; parent, Support Group Youth Choir Plymouth Congregation UCC; consult, Nat Health Serv, 1972-82; pres, W Henry Greene Friends Music Soc, 1988-; bd mem, Metrop DC Geriatrics Soc; bd mem, Am Geriatrics Soc. **Honors/Awds:** Lucy Moten Fellowship Award, Howard Univ, 1957; Intern of the Year, Howard Univ, 1963; Hospice Award, Hospice Care DC, 1983; Ronald C Newman Award, Jackson-Newman Found Inc, 1987. **Business Phone:** (202)895-0327.

JOHNSON-CROSBY, DEBORAH A.
Executive. **Personal:** Born Jan 15, 1951, Chicago, IL; divorced; children: Malik Fanon. **Educ:** Univ Wis, BA, 1974. **Career:** Mt Sinai Hosp, staff worker bus office, 1969; North side Comn Credit Union, loan clerk, community rels, 1970-71; Concentrated Employ Prog, staff worker; Oper Breadbasket, pub rels dir, 1972-73; Milwaukee Times, reporter, 1973-74; Milwaukee Star Times, managing editor, 1974-75; Milwaukee Bus Federation, dir; freelance journalist; communs consult. **Orgs:** Black Media Alliance WI; Pub Rels Comt; information officer Black Comt Student Alliance, 1972-73; Milwaukee Asn; bd dirs Peck ham Jr HS, 1974.

JOHNSON-HELTON, KAREN
College administrator. **Personal:** Born May 20, 1947, Cincinnati, OH; daughter of James C Payne and Ruth Lee; married Malcolm, Jun 29, 1995. **Educ:** Ohio Univ, Athens, OH, BA, 1969; Atlanta Univ, Atlanta, GA, MSW, 1976; Univ Mich, Ann Arbor, MI, 1978; Tex A&M Univ, attended 1992. **Career:** LeMoyne-Owen Col, Memphis, TN, dir planning, 1976-82; Mary Holmes Col, West Point, MS, fed progs coordr, 1982-86; Rust Col, Holly Springs, MS, proposal writer, 1986-87; Wiley Col, Marshall, TX, assoc vpres, 1987-88, asst pres, 1988-99, dir sponsored progs, 1999-, vpres instnl advan, currently. **Orgs:** Dist comn, Cub Scouts America, 1986-87; steering comt mem, Top Ladies Distinction, 1989-; pub rels comt mem, Zonta Int, 1989-; Third Anti-Basileus, 1990-93; State Tex Dem Party, 1992-; Zeta Phi Beta Sorority, 1992-96; bd mem, Harrison Co United Way, 1997-2004; bd mem, Links Inc, 2003-; Marshall Rotary Club, 2003-; Nat Rep UNCF. **Honors/Awds:** Congressional Proclamation, Outstanding Services to Youth, Congressman Harold Ford, 1981; Certificate of Professional Merit, US Dept Educ, 1986, 1987; Certificate of Outstanding Achievement, US Dept Educ, 1996, 1997; Nat Asn Advan Colored People Award, 2004. **Business Addr:** Vice President for Institutional Advancement, Wiley College, Office Community Relations & Sponsored Programs, Rm 116 Willis King Admin Bldg, 711 Wiley Ave, Marshall, TX 75670-5199, **Business Phone:** (903)927-3300.

JOHNSON-ODIM, DR. CHERYL
Educator. **Personal:** Born Apr 30, 1948, Youngstown, OH; daughter of Elayne Jeffries; married Carlton Odim; children: Chaka Malik, Rashid Jamil & Maya Ruth. **Educ:** Youngstown State Univ, BA, 1972; Northwestern Univ, MA, 1975, PhD, hist,1978. **Career:** Fulbright Hays Dissertation Year fel, 1976; Univ Ibadan, Nigeria, resaffil, 1976; Loyola Univ, Chicago, Afro-Am Studies, dir, 1978-, asst prof, 1978-80; Northwestern Univ, African Studies, asst dir, 1980; Monti cellofel, 1990; Loyola Univ, Chicago, assoc prof, Hist Dept, chairperson; Columbia Col, Liberal Arts & Sci, prof hist, dean; Dominican Univ, Acad Affairs, dean provost, vpres, currently. **Orgs:** Co-chairperson, Ill Coun Black Studies, 1979-; co-chairperson, memship Asn Black Women Historians, 1979-; bd mem, Chiaravalle Montessori Sch, 1980; co-chair elected bd, Women's Caucus, African Studies Asn, 1988-; edbd, Nat Women's Studies Asn Jour, 1992; chair, Joan Kelly Prize Comt, Am Hist Asn; bd dir, Am Coun Learned Soc; bd dir, African Studies Asn; advbd, Ctr Womens & Gender Studies, Rutgers Univ; ed bd, Jour Womens Hist; Vivian G Harsh Soc. **Special Achievements:** Published many books like: Women and the Nation (University of Illinois Press, 1997); "Mirror Images and Shared Standpoints: Black Women in Africa and in the African Diaspora" in Issue: A Journal of Opinion, 1996. She is also a well published poet. **Business Addr:** Dean Provost, Vice President of Academic Affairs, Dominican University, 7900 W Division St Parmer Hall Suite 110, River Forest, IL 60305, **Business Phone:** (708)524-6813.

JOHNSTON, ANNA KATHERINE. **See TAYLOR, ANNA DIGGS.**

JOHNSTON, CHARLENE B.
Educator. **Personal:** Born Mar 6, 1933, New York, NY; daughter of Louis and Rosenda Batson; married Wallace O, May 23, 1992; children: Leana Cunningham Wilkerson & Glen Batson Cunningham. **Educ:** NY Community Col, AAS, dental hyg, 1953; NYU, BS, dent health ed, 1974,MA, community health ed, 1977; Virginia Poly Tech, EDD, higher ed admin, 1990. **Career:** Clin dent hyg pvt pract; Hostos Community Col, prof dent hyg, 1974-75; NYC Community Col, prof dent hyg, 1975-80; Northern Va Community Col, dir denthyg prog, 1980-95. **Orgs:** Delta Sigma Theta Sorority, 1978-; Am Dent Hyg Assn, 1980-; Afro-Am Mus Art, Tampa, FL, 1996-; dir pub rels, Afro-Am Club Hernando City, FL,1997-; past pres, Hernando Performing Arts Ctr Guild. **Honors/Awds:** Scroll of Honor, Jamaica Club Nat Assn Negro Bus & Prof Women's Clubs, 1975; Distinguished Service Award, Northern Va Community Col, 1979; Award or Appreciation for Educating, Proctor & Gamble, 1980.

JOHNSTON, ERNEST
Journalist. **Personal:** Born Nov 25, 1938, Roanoke Rapids, NC; son of Bessie W (deceased) and Ernest Johnston Sr (deceased); divorced; children: Tanya White & Rhonda Cox. **Educ:** NC A&T State Univ, BS, 1960; Columbia Univ, interracial reporting fel, 1972. **Career:** Star-Ledger, reporter, 1964-68; New York Post, reporter, 1968-73; Long Island Press, reporter, 1973-75; Herald News, copy ed, 1975-77; New York Amsterdam News, managing ed, 1977-81, prog coordr, pub info, tech writer, seniors Comm Serv prog, currently; freelance writer, 1981-87; Nat Urban League, commun specialist, pub rels & commun dept, 1987-95;

Crossroads Theatre, dir pub rels, 1996-97; LeJay Assoc, pres, currently. **Orgs:** Vpres, New York Press Club, 1968-69; Nat vpres, chairperson, pub rels comm & ed, NC A&T State Univ Nat Alumni Asn, A & T Today, Aggie Pride; pres, Northern New Jersey chap, 1978-83, pres, New Jersey shore chap, cent, 1990-93, NC A&T State Alumni Asn; Men's Club, Elmwood Presbyterian Church, 1985-90; co-chairperson, Pastor Nominating Comm, Bethel Presbyterian Church, pres, Men's Club; regional dir, NE region, A&T Alumni Asn, 1993-95; mem adv bd, Breast Cancer Ctr Harlem. **Honors/Awds:** Service Award, Black Spectrum Theatre Co, 1979; Contribution to Mankind Award, Caribbean Am Designers & Models, 1980; World Service Award, Harlem YMCA, 1981; Special Recognition Award, northern New Jersey chap, 1982, NAFEO Award, 1995, NC A&T State Alumni Asn; First Place Black & White Photo Award, New Jersey Chamber Com, East Orange, 1985; Alumni Achiever, 1991. **Special Achievements:** Managing editor of The Negro Almanac, a reference work African Americans, 1981, 1990, first black reporter at the Star Ledger. **Military Serv:** AUS, Sp4, 1962-64.

JOHNSTON, DR. GLADYS STYLES
School administrator, college administrator. **Personal:** Born Dec 23, 1942, St Petersburg, FL; daughter of John Edward and Rosa Moses; married Hubert Seward Johnston, Jul 30, 1966. **Educ:** Cheyney Univ, BS, Social Sci, 1963; Temple Univ, MEd, Educ Admin, 1969; Cornell Univ, PhD, 1974. **Career:** College administrator (retire); Chester Sch Dist, Chester, PA, teacher, 1963-66; W Chester Sch Dist, PA, teacher, 1966-67, asst prin, 1968-69, dir summer sch, 1969-71, prin, 1969-71; Chester County Bd Educ, Chester, PA, dir head start, 1967-69; Cornell Univ, teaching asst, 1971-72, res asst, 1972-74; Rutgers Univ, educ admin & supv, asst prof, 1974-79, chairperson, 1979-83, assoc prof, 1979-83, chairperson dept mgt, 1983-85; Col William & Mary, Williamsburg, VA, visiting prof, 1982-83; Ariz State Univ, Col Educ, Temple, AZ, dean & prof, 1985-91; DePaul Univ, Chicago, IL, provost & acad vpres; Univ Nebr Kearney, chancellor, 1993-02 . **Orgs:** Bd dirs, Found Sr Living, 1990-91; bd dirs, KAET TV; bd dirs, Educ Law Ctr, 1979-86; adv coun bd trustees, Cornell Univ, 1981-86; bd trustees, Middlesex Gen Univ Hosp, 1983-86; Am Educ Res Asn; Asn Supv & Curriculum Develop; Am Asn Col Teacher Educ; Nat Conf Prof Educ Admin; exec comt mem, Nat Collegiate Athletic Asn; chair div II, chair bd dir, Am Asn State Col & Univ; mem bd dir, Am Coun Educ; chair, Omaha Br Fed Reserve Bank Kansas City. **Honors/Awds:** Outstanding Alumni, Temple Univ; Andrew D. White Fellowship, Cornell Univ; Phi Kappa Phi Honor Soc; Alpha Phi Sigma National Honorary Scholastic Fraternity, Cheyney State Col. **Special Achievements:** Book: The Emerging Redefinition of Federal Educational Policy: Implications for Educational Excellence, Journal of Educational Evaluation and Policy Analysis; The Carnegie Report: A Retrospective, Journal of Arizona School Board Association, Fall 1986; Rule Administration and Hierarchical Influence of the Principal: A Study of Teacher Loyalty to the Principal, Educational Administrative Quarterly, Fall 1986; Research and Thought in Administration Theory: Developments in the Field of Educational Administration, 1986. *

JOHNSTON, HENRY BRUCE
Administrator. **Personal:** Born Jul 4, 1927; married Cora Virginia Jackson; children: Geraldine, Mark, Lisa & Steven. **Educ:** State Univ Farmingdale, NY, AAS; State Univ Stoney Brook, NY, MA, BS. **Career:** Suffolk Co Hum Rights Comn, exec dir, 1985; State Univ Farmingdale, instr criminal justice; Suffolk Community Col, instr criminal justice; Police Acad Suffolk Co Police Dept, instr; Globe-Trotters Prof Basketball Org, mem. **Orgs:** Bd dir, LI Sickle Cell Proj Nassau & Suffolk; bd dir, Suffolk Rehab Ctr; bd dir & adv bd, Suffolk Co Youth Servs; bd dir, Diocesan Task Force Poverty & Racism Nassau & Suffolk; bd dir, Crime Control Coun, Suffolk Co; bd dir educ, NCCJ; bd dir Awards Comt SCPD; bd dir, Boy Scouts Am Suffolk Co; bd dir, Phi Beta Sigma Frat; bd dir, Econ Opportunity Coun Suffolk Co; bd dir, Urban League Suffolk Co; bd dir, Alcoholism Adv Comn Suffolk Co; NYCPD Youth Squad PAL Div; Nat Asn Advan Colored People; Lions Club, Hauppauge, NY; bd ed Grievance Comt Hauppauge High Sch. **Honors/Awds:** Hunting PAL Award, 1958; Top Basketball Official, 1960-61, 1969; Police Youth Award, SCPD, 1961-62; Medal for Bravery, SCPD, 1964; Outstanding Basketball Official, 1966; Meritorious Service, SCPD 1967; Masons Recognition Award, King Tyre Lodge, 1967; Professionalization Award, SCPD, 1969; Man of Year, NANBPW, 1974; Black Standard Union, SU Farmingdale, 1975. **Military Serv:** AUS, 1st sgt, 1942-45; European-African Middle E Service Medal, Serv Medal, Purple Heart, Asiatic Pacific Service Medal.

JOHNSTON, JULIA MAYO. **See MAYO, DR. JULIA A.**

JOHNSTON, WALLACE O.
Consultant. **Personal:** Born Nov 8, 1929, New York, NY; son of Wallace Johnston and Mary Smith Johnston; married Charlene; children: Asao, Toshio, Paige, Leana & Glen. **Educ:** City Col NY, BME, 1963, grad mech eng study, 1967; US Dept Defense, environ eng, 1968. **Career:** Engineer (retired); New York City Bd of Educ, eng, 1959-68; Hannaham & Johnston, partner, 1968-76; Wallace Johnston Engs, proprietor, chief engr, 1976-97. **Orgs:** Bd dir, NY Assn Consult Engrs, 1974-76; Natl Soc Prof Engr, 1967-; tutorial dir, life mem, Kappa Alpha Psi, 1979; Nat Tech Assn, 1982-; Math Assn Am; past pres, brd dir, Fla Engrs Soc; fel African Sci Inst. **Honors/Awds:** Tech Paper Building Systems Designs NY City 1976; Honorable Mntn Lincoln Wldng Inst Ohio, 1961; Design Award, BSA Progressive Arch, 1971; Licensed Engineer, Fla Brd Prof Licensing, 1967; Design Award, Rochester NY,Convention Ctr, 1993. **Special Achievements:** Library of Congress, Copyright, blinking lighted Kappa Alpha Psi Diamond; designed air cond system for 450,000 sq ft, NYCTA office building; published technical paper "Unique Air Curtain Installation Solves Difficult Airport Problem" in 1969. **Military Serv:** USAF, airmn, First class, 4 yrs; Good Cndct, Korean Theatre, Am Defense,1950-54; Korean War Service Medal, Republic of South Korea. **Home Addr:** 11250 Riddle Dr, Spring Hill, FL 34609.

JOHNSTONE, LANCE
Football player. **Personal:** Born Jun 11, 1973, Philadelphia, PA. **Educ:** Temple Univ. **Career:** Oakland Raiders, defensive end, 1996-2000, 2006; Minnesota Vikings, defensive end, 2001-05. **Orgs:** Founder, The Urban Renaissance Youth Found. *

JOINER, DR. BURNETT
School administrator. **Personal:** Born Nov 10, 1941, Raymond, MS; son of Burnett Joiner Sr and Arcine; married Inez Dixon; children: Michael & Christopher. **Educ:** Utica Jr Col, AA, 1962; Alcorn State Univ, BS, 1964; Bradley Univ, MA,1968; Univ SC, PhD, 1975. **Career:** Oliver Sch Clarksdale, MS, prin, 1968-71; York Sch Dist 1, asst supt sch, 1971-73; SC Col, Orange burg, SC, asst prof, 1974-75; Atlanta Univ,Atlanta, GA, exec dir & assoc prof, 1975-80; Grambling State Univ, exec acad dean & prof, 1984-91; LeMoyne-Owens Col, pres, 1991; Livingstone Col, pres, 1977-2000; Benedict Col, Acad Affairs, sr vpres, currently. **Orgs:** Ouachita Valley Boy Scouts, 1982-; charter mem, Grambling Lions Club,1983-; consult, US Dept Educ, 1983-85; comnr, LA Learning Adv Comn,1984-85; comnr, LA Internship Comn, 1984-85; Nat Inst Educ Study Group Teacher Educ; chair, Col Educ Univ SC Stud Adv; Curric Comt Sch Educ, SC State Col; Ruston-Lincoln C C; vice chairperson, Comt Social Concerns Lewis Temple Church; bd dir, Teacher Educ Coun, State Col & Univ; Am Asn Col Teacher Educ; Gov Internship Comn & Learning Adv Comn. **Special Achievements:** Publications, "The Teacher Corps Policy Board; Three Perspectives on Roleand Function" 1979; "A Documentation Primer; Some Perspectives from the Field" 1979; "New Perspectives on Black Education History" Book Review for the Journal of Negro History in progress; "Identifying Needs and Prioritizing Goals Through Collaboration" 1978; "Education That Is Multicultural; A Process of Curriculum Development" 1979; "The Design, Implementation and Evaluation of a Pre-Service Prototype Competency-Based Teacher Education Model" 1975; "Maximizing Opportunities for Professional Improvement" 1983; Improving Teacher Education: A Conscious Choice, co-author. **Business Addr:** Senior Vice President for Academic Affairs, Benedict College, Department of Academic Affairs, 1600 Harden St, Columbia, SC 29204, **Business Phone:** (253)705-4749.

JOINER, CHARLES
Football coach, football player. **Personal:** Born Oct 14, 1947, Many, LA; married Dianne; children: Jynayna & Kori. **Educ:** Grambling State Univ, BS, bus admin, 1969. **Career:** Football Player (retired), football coach; Houston Oilers, 1969-72; Cincinnati Bengals, 1972-75; San Diego Chargers, 1976-86, wide receivers coach, 2008-; Gulf Oil Co, management trainee, 1971; Kans City Chiefs, asst coach, 2001-08. **Honors/Awds:** Four varsity letters Grambling; named All Pro & All AFC second team, AP and UPI, 1980; MVP and Most Inspirational Player, San Diego Chargers, 1983; established NFL record for most pass receptions (716); played in Pro Bowl, 1976, 1979, 1980; testimonial in Lake Charles on "Charlie Joiner Day," May 15, 1982 & Nov 20, 1986; Pro Football Hall of Fame, 1996. **Home Addr:** 9223 Petersham Dr, Houston, TX 77031. **Business Addr:** Wide Receivers Coach, San Diego Chargers, PO Box 609609, San Diego, CA 92160-9609.

JOLIVET, LINDA CATHERINE
Librarian. **Personal:** Born Mar 5, 1950, New Orleans, LA; daughter of Fred Douglas Jolivet and Nancy Evans Jolivet; children: Shakira N Scott. **Educ:** Univ Southwestern La, Lafayette, LA, BA, 1974; Univ Calif, Berkeley, Berkeley, CA, MLIS, 1988; San Francisco State Univ, San Francisco, CA. **Career:** Lafayette Parish Sch Bd, Layfayette, LA, teacher, 1975-80; Oakland Post Newspaper Group, Oakland, CA, advert asst, 1980-81; Berkeley Pub Libr, Berkeley, CA, libr asst, 1982; Univ Calif, Berkeley, Berkeley, CA, clerical asst, 1982-83, libr asst, 1983-84; Oakland Pub Libr, Oakland, CA, libr asst, 1984-86, ref libr, currently; East Bay Negro Hist Soc Mus-Libr, Oakland, CA, curator-librn, 1986-87; Stanford Univ, Palo Alto, CA, asst librn, 1989-90; Col Alameda, Alameda, CA, librn, 1990; African Am Mus & Libr, reef libr. **Orgs:** Founder, dir, bd Adesua Bea Learning Ctr & Educ Servs, 1982; Am Libr Asn, 1985-91; secy 1990, coord, scholar comt, 1991, Calif Librn Black Caucus, Northern Chap; program asst, Nat Black Child Develop Inst, East Bay Area Affiliate, 1990-91; Northern Calif Ctr Study of Afro-Am Life & Cult, 1991. **Honors/Awds:** Graduate Minority Fellowship, Univ Calif-Berkeley, 1984-85; Graduate Equity Fellowship Award, San Francisco State Univ, 1990-91. **Special Achievements:** Author: Preparations of Librarians to Serve a Multicultural World, Women Library Workers Journal, 1988; African and African American Audiovisual Materials: A Selected Bibliography, Stanford University Libraries, 1990. **Business Addr:** Librarian, College of Alameda, 555 Atlantic Ave, Alameda, CA 94501, **Business Phone:** (510)522-7221.

JOLLEY, SAMUEL DELANOR
College administrator, school administrator, college president. **Personal:** Born Feb 1, 1941, Fort Valley, GA; son of Samuel and Mary; married Jimmye Hambry, Dec 24, 1963; children: Terena J Washington & Samuel D III; married. **Educ:** Fort Valley State Col, BS, 1962; Atlanta Univ, MS, 1965; Ind Univ, EdD, 1974. **Career:** High sch math teacher; Fort Valley State Col, instr math, 1967-70, from asst prof math to assoc prof math, 1970-82, Div Educ, chmn, 1983-85, Sch Arts & Sci, dean, 1985-93; Morris Brown Col, pres, 1993-. **Orgs:** Omega Psi Phi Fraternity, 1960-; Sigma Pi Phi Fraternity, 1991-; Atlanta Univ Ctr, 1993-; bd mem, Univ Ctr Ga, 1993-; bd mem, Univ Community Develop Corp, 1993-; Am Coun Educ, 1993-; bd dir, Atlanta Paralympics Org Comt, 1994-; adv bd, Salvation Army, 1995-; 100 Black Men Atlanta, 1995-; Alpha Kappa Mu Honor Soc; Phi Delta Kappa Educ Fraternity; Beta Kappa Chi Sci Honor Soc; Math Asn Am; Golden Key Nat Honor Soc; NCP; Atlanta Chamber Com; Fort Valley State Col Nat Alumni Asn; Atlanta Univ Ctrs Coun Presidents; Atlanta Systemic Initiative Adv Coun; stewards bd, Allen Temple AME Church, Comm Finance; Fort Valley State Col, Nat Alumn Asn. **Honors/Awds:** Omega Man of the Year, Omega Psi Phi Fraternity, 1985, 1993; Honor, Nat Asn Advan Colored People. **Special Achievements:** One of the Fifty Most Influential African American Males in Georgia, Leadership Atlanta Ga Informer, 1994-95. **Home Addr:** 4410 Pk Ctr Dr SW, Atlanta, GA 30331. **Business Addr:** President, Morris Brown Collage, 643 Martin Luther King Jr Dr NW, Atlanta, GA 30314, **Business Phone:** (404)739-1000.

JOLLEY, WILLIE
Singer. **Personal:** Born Sep 3, 1956, Washington, DC; married Dee Taylor; children: William & LaToya. **Educ:** American Univ, BA, 1978; Wesley Theological Seminary, MA, 1983. **Career:** Jingle singer & jazz vocalist, 1974-90; drug & violence prevention coordinator, Wash, DC, pub Schs, 1990-91; Willie Jolley Worldwide & Inspir Tainment Plus, full-time motivational speaker, pres & chief exec officer, 1991-; Tv, pgm host, American Public TV, 2009-. **Orgs:** Nat Speakers Assoc, 1991-; pres, Nat Capital Speakers Assoc, 1995-96. **Honors/Awds:** Best Male Jazz Vocalist Washington Area Music Asn Award, 1986, 1989, 1990; Best Male Inspirational Vocalist Washington Area Music Asn Award, 1991,1992; Outstanding Motivational & Inspirational Speaker of the Year,Toastmasters Int, 1999; Hall of Fame. **Special Achievements:** Author of two international best selling books. **Business Addr:** President, Owner, Willie Jolley Worldwide Inspir-Tainment Plus, PO Box 55459, Washington, DC 20040, **Business Phone:** (202)723-8863.

JOLLY, ELTON
Educator, association executive. **Personal:** Born Oct 15, 1931, Claymont, DE; son of Ozella Jones and Elton; married Rowena Mozelle Anderson, Sep 22, 1956; children: Elton Brett & William David. **Educ:** Cheyney Univ, Cheyney, PA, BS, elem educ, 1954; Temple Univ, Philadelphia, PA, MS, educ admin, 1964. **Career:** Educator, Associate Executive (Retired); Philadelphia Bd Educ, Philadelphia, PA, teacher & adminr, 1954-65; Opportunities Industrialization Ctrs Am, Philadelphia, PA, exec vice chairman, 1965, pres. **Orgs:** Nat Alliance Bus, 1984-; Black Leadership Forum, 1978-; NAACP, 1960-; founding chmn, Nat Youth Advocacy, 1980-; Nat Assessment Governing Bd, 1987-90; Nat Youth Employ Coalition, founding chmn, currently. **Honors/Awds:** James Duckrey Outstanding Alumni Award, Cheyney Univ, 1978; Job Training Professional of the Year, NAB, 1988; Achievement Award, NAACP, 1988; Secretary of Education Citation for Service, Off Educ, 1989; Secretary of Labor Special Service Award, Dept Labor, 1989. **Military Serv:** AUS, Sp 3, 1954-56; received Good Conduct Medal, Outstanding Leadership Award. **Home Addr:** 6001 Drexel Rd, Philadelphia, PA 19131, **Home Phone:** (215)879-0742.

JOLLY, MARVA LEE
Educator. **Personal:** Born Sep 11, 1937, Crenshaw, MS; daughter of Mattie Louise Williams Pitchford and Floyd Pitchford, Sr; divorced. **Educ:** Roosevelt Univ, BS, 1961; Gov State Univ, MA, 1974. **Career:** Univ Chicago Lab Schs, teacher, 1961-65; Chicago Youth Ctr Head Start, teacher, 1965, dir, 1965-69; Chicago Youth Ctr, Chicago, IL, dir Headstart, 1967-77; Chicago Commons Child Devel, prog dir, 1969-74; Suburban Health Syst Agency, Chicago, IL, educr coord, 1977-82; Chicago State Univ, prof ceramics & practicing artist, asst prof Art, currently. **Orgs:** Pres, Artisan Twenty First Gallery, 1981-85; self-taught ceramic & sculptor artist, 1981-;; bd dir, Urban Traditions, 1984-; bd mem, African Am Artist Roundtable, 1985-; bd dir, Chicago Cult Ctr, 1986-; sponsor, C Int, 1986-; cur, Saphire & Crystals Black Women's Art Exhib, 1987; Exhibs Comn Chicago Cult Ctr; vol, Southside Comm Art Ctr; cur, Earthstones & Rainbow Colors Clay & Textile by Black Chicago Artists; founder, Mud Peoples Black Women's Resources Sharing Workshop. **Honors/Awds:** Best of Category, Black Creativity Mus Sci & Indust, 1984; Invitational Exhib Changing Perceptions, Columbia Col Gallery; Am Visions

Afro-Am Art, 1986; Artist in Residence Lakeside Group, 1988. **Special Achievements:** Top Ten Emerging Black Chicago Artists, 1986-87. **Home Addr:** 5326 Hyde Pk Blvd, Chicago, IL 60615. **Business Addr:** Assistant Professor, Chicago State University, Department of Arts, 9501 S King Dr, Chicago, IL 60628-1598, **Business Phone:** (773)995-2000.

JOLLY, MARY B
School administrator, personal trainer. **Personal:** Born Oct 23, 1940, New Orleans, LA; daughter of Oliver and Audrey Leufroy; married Herbert Nicholas; children: Helaina, Nyla & Chanelle. **Educ:** Loyola Univ, BS, 1975; Univ New Orleans, MS, 1982. **Career:** Jefferson Parish Sheriff's Off, personnel dir, 1976-80; Loyola Univ, personnel dir, 1980-88; New Orleans Pub Sch Syst, personnel admin, 1988-. **Orgs:** Consult Human Resources, EEO, Policies & Procedure; Col & Univ Personnel Admin; La Equal Opportunity Asn; exec bd mem, Int Info Asn Personnel & Payroll Syst Users Group; regional conf prog chair, Am Asn Affirmative Action, 1986; pres bd, Personnel Mgt Asn; New Orleans Metro Chap, Am Soc Personnel Admin, 1986-87; Cross Keys Hon Serv Soc Loyola Univ; Rels Community United Way Greater New Orleans. **Honors/Awds:** Outstanding Service Community, Urban League New Orleans, 1984; Outstanding Contribution, City New Orleans, 1984. **Home Addr:** 7121 Reed Blvd, New Orleans, LA 70127, **Home Phone:** (504)241-8373. **Business Phone:** (504)286-2861.*

JONAS, DR. ERNESTO A
Physician. **Personal:** Born Nov 13, 1939, Panama, PA; son of Harold L and Laura Maria Anderson de; married Mary E Cullen, Jan 15, 1965; children: Jorge A Jonas & Clarissa M Jonas. **Educ:** Univ Nueva Leon, Monterrey, Mexico, MD, 1966; Nassau Univ Med Ctr, E Meadow, NY, residency training, internal med; St ElizabethOs Med Ctr, Boston, MA, cardiovasc training. **Career:** Nassau Univ Med Ctr, div emergency med, chief, 1973-76, coronary care unit, dir, 1976-79, div cardiol, chief (retired), cardiovasc training prog, dir, ending 1997; State Univ NY, Stony Brook, asst prof med, 1973-88, assoc prof med, currently; pvt pract, currently. **Orgs:** Fel, Am Col Physicians, 1977-; fel, Am Col Cardiol, 1981-; mem & exec comt, Dept Med, State Univ NY, Stony Brook; mem & bd dirs, Nassau Chap, Am Heart Asn; Physician Educ Comn, Am Heart Asn. **Honors/Awds:** Excellence in Teaching Award, State Univ NY, Stony Brook, 1980; D'istinguished Service Award', Asn Black Cardiologists, 1987; Distinguished Leadership Award, Am Heart Asn, 1992. **Special Achievements:** Author of articles in medical journals. **Home Addr:** 8 Villas Cir, Melville, NY 11747. **Business Addr:** Physician, 510 Hicksville Rd, Massapequa, NY 11758, **Business Phone:** (516)795-2626.

JONES, A. LORRAINE
Executive, business owner. **Career:** Kleenize-Benje Carpet Specialists, Asbury Park, NJ, pres & owner, 1977-. **Orgs:** Past pres, Nat Asn Women Bus Owners, NJ Chap; chair, Asbury Park Zoning Bd; Nat Asn Bd. **Honors/Awds:** Business Women of the Year, NJ Asn Women Bus Owners, 1988; Small Business Advocate of the Year Award, US Small Bus Admin, 1997. **Special Achievements:** First Minority Woman ever to hold the office of President of the New Jersey Association of Women Business Owners. **Business Addr:** Owner, President, Kleenize-Benje Carpet Specialists, 613 Prospect Ave, Asbury Park, NJ 07712-6327, **Business Phone:** (732)774-1314.

JONES, AARON DELMAS
Football player, president (organization). **Personal:** Born Dec 18, 1966, Orlando, FL. **Educ:** Eastern Ky Univ, attended 1984. **Career:** Football player (retired), pres; Pittsburgh Steelers, defensive end, 1988-92; New England Patriots, 1993-95; Miami Dolphins, 1996; Gold Mech Servs Inc, pres, currently; Excel Speed & Fitness Training LLC, pres, currently. **Orgs:** Pres & comnr, S Cent Athletic Asn. **Honors/Awds:** Defensive player of the Year, Eastern Ky; Defensive Player of the Year, Ohio Valley Conference Co. **Business Addr:** President, Excel Speed & Fitness Training LLC, 8199 Bright Meadow Dr, Orlando, FL 32818, **Business Phone:** (407)466-5637.

JONES, ALBERT ALLEN
Clergy. **Personal:** Born Apr 2, 1913, New Orleans, LA; married Beaulah Mae Houston. **Educ:** Xavier Univ, PhB, AB, 1952. **Career:** Pub Sch, teacher; Bapt Training Union Asn Ministers Alliance, teacher; Union Bapt Theol Sem LA, instr. **Orgs:** Ast dir, Dept Christian Ed 1st Dist Missionary Bapt Asn; dir, Bapt Training Union LA Bapt St Conv S & Region; mem bd trustees, 1st Dist Missionary Bapt Asn; former pres, Mem Ponchartrain Pk Improvement Asn DD, conferred Inter-bapt Theol Ctr. **Military Serv:** World War II vet, sgt.

JONES, ALBERT C.
Educator, executive. **Personal:** Born May 20, 1946, Fort Lauderdale, FL; son of Milton L and Rhodie; married Carolyn; children: Alison; married Carolyn W, Sep 3, 1977; children: Alison C. **Educ:** Edward Waters Col, BS, 1968; Univ Northern Colo, MA, 1974. **Career:** Sch Bd Broward County, educr, 1968-; City Hollywood, recreation supvr, 1968-; Realty 2000 Realtors, realtor, 1979-88; Broward Community Col,prof, 1981-93; City Dania Beach, comnr, 1993-97; Quest Ctr, Hollywood, FL, teacher, 2001; Everglades High Sch, dean; S Broward Hosp Dist, chmn bd, currently. **Orgs:** Fla Alliance & Health, Phys Educ, Recreation Dance, 1979-96; Broward County Asn Phys Educ, 1979-96; Omega Psi Phi; Zeta Chi Chap, 1988-; fel Nat League Cities, 1993-97;, founding mem, vp, 1995-; Col Gardens Neighborhood Asn, Inc; Black Elected Officials Broward County, 1997-;pres, New Republican Club Broward County, 1999-; chmn, Diversity & Cult Outreach Comt, 1999-; S Broward Hosp Dist Bd, 1999, secy treas, 2000-; pres, Jerome E Gray Republican Club; outreach chmn, Broward Republican Exec Comt. **Honors/Awds:** Teacher of the Year, Broward County Asn Phys Educ, 1991; Community Service Educator of the Year, FL Alliance, Health, Phys Ed, Recreation Dance, 1995; Outstanding Politician Award, Men United for Positive Action, 1996; Dedicated Service Award, City of Dania Beach, 1997; Citizen of the Year, Col Gardens Neighborhood Asn, 1998. **Special Achievements:** City Dania Beach, comnr, 1993-97; Appointed by Governor of Fla to the S Broward Hosp Dist, 1999-. **Business Addr:** Chairman of the Board, South Broward Hospital District, 3501 Johnson St, Hollywood, FL 33021-5421, **Business Phone:** (954)987-2000.

JONES, ALBERT J.
Educator. **Personal:** Born Nov 25, 1928, Pittsburgh, PA; married Hattie E; children: Jeffrey L & Bertina M. **Educ:** Md State Col, BS; Univ Pittsburgh, MEd. **Career:** Educator (retired); Somerset High Sch, sci teacher, 1954-56; William C Jason High Sch, physics teacher, 1956-66; Seaford High Sch, physics teacher, 1966-71; Del Tech Comm Col, coun, 1971-94, adult ed coord, 1974-87, test coordr, 1988-94. **Orgs:** Omega Psi Phi; Am Asn Physics Teacher, 1966-71; DE Col Counrs Asn, 1971-74; Sussex Co Counr Asn, 1971-74; Laurel Del Town Coun, 1971-75; DE Col Coun Asn, 1971-94; Suffex Co Coun Asn, 1971-94; Del Coun Personnel Asn, 1971-94; Del Foster Child Rev Bd, 1979-80; bd dir, Sussex Co Sr Serv Inc, 1991-95; Del Retired Sch Personnel Asn, 1995-96; bd dir, Laurel Sr Ctr, 1996; charter mem, adv bd, Laurel Star, 1996-2000; adv bd, Morning Star Publ. **Honors/Awds:** Athletic Hall of Fame, Univ Md Eastern Shore, 1975. *

JONES, ALEXANDER R.
Public relations executive. **Personal:** Born Jan 21, 1952, Washington, DC. **Educ:** Mass Inst Tech, BS, 1974. **Career:** Nat Comn Law Enforcement & Soc Justice, Ch Scientology, assoc dir, 1985. **Orgs:** Ed, Unequal Justice-Under The Law, 1979-80; exec dir, Citizens Comn Community Involvement, 1985. **Honors/Awds:** Author, newspaper column, Law & Social Justice, 1980. *

JONES, ALFREDEAN
School administrator, baseball player. **Personal:** Born Sep 30, 1940, Jonesville, SC; married Betty Jean Smith; children: Pamela, Shelia & Dean. **Educ:** SC State Col, BS, 1963; NC A&T State Univ, MS, 1972; Lehigh Univ, cert, 1975. **Career:** Baseball player, school administrator (retired); Chicago Cubs Minor-s,player, 1963-67; NJ Correctional Syst, supvr recreation, 1964-67; Easton Area Sch Dist, teacher, 1967-75, adminr, 1975-87, asst prin, 1978, interim prin, 1981, prin, 2000-02; Boys & Girls Club, Easton; Easton Housing Authority, bd chmn. **Orgs:** Bd dirs, Educ Day Care Ctr; C Home Easton; vpres, Easton Br Nat Asn Advan Colored People; deacon, Grace Baptist Church, Phillipsburg; Lehigh Valley Christian High Sch Adv Bd. **Honors/Awds:** Certificates of Appreciation Graduating Class, 1984, Children Home of Easton, 1985, Easton Branch Nat Asn Advan Colored People, 1986; The fourth annual Thomas W. Bright Young Ambassador Community Serv Award, 2005. **Home Addr:** 155 Reese St, Easton, PA 18042. *

JONES, ALICE ELEY
Historian, writer. **Personal:** Born Jan 7, 1949, Murfreesboro, NC; daughter of Fred and Iris D; widowed. **Educ:** NC Cent Univ, BA, 1973, MA, 1986. **Career:** NC Cent Univ, prof, 1987-92, asst prof, human scis, 2003; Historically Speaking, owner, 1992-; Minnie Troy Publ, owner, 2002-. **Orgs:** Bd mem, Preserv-NC, 1992-94. **Honors/Awds:** Stagville Fellowship, NC Dept Cultural Resources, 1985-86; Educator of the Year, NC Cent Univ, 1992; Gertrude S Carraway Award, Preserv-NC, 1997; Minnie Fuller Memorial Scholarship, VISTA volunteer. **Special Achievements:** Publication, "Sacred Places and Holy Ground: West African Spiritualism at Historic Stagville Plantation", 1998; curator "African American Builders and Architects in NC 1526-1998", 1998; "Africans in NC", UNC-Center for TV, 1998; African American Heritage Trail, Duke Univ, 1999. **Home Addr:** 309 Union St, Murfreesboro, NC 27855. **Business Addr:** Owner, Historically Speaking, 23 Poinciana Dr, Durham, NC 27707, **Business Phone:** (919)688-8736.*

JONES, ALMA WYATT
Educator. **Personal:** Born Nov 19, 1939, Montgomery, AL; married Melvin O, May 30, 1965. **Educ:** Ala State Univ, MEd, 1966; Eastern Ky Univ, attended; Purdue Univ, attended; Univ Ala, post grad study, attended. **Career:** Teacher (retired); Tuscaloosa City Schs, teacher, 1959-93; Tuscaloosa Chap, Links Inc. **Orgs:** AARP, State Legislative Comn, 1997-; bd dir, Ala Educrs Asn, 1998-99; pres, Ala Retired Teachers Asn, 1999-2000; bd dir, McDonald Hughes Community Ctr; Zeta Phi Beta Sorority Inc; Beta Eta Zeta Chap; second vpres, AARP, Tuscaloosa County Chap Unit 146; Ala Educ Retirees Asn. **Honors/Awds:** Teacher of the Year, Cent High-West Campus, 1990; St Paul African Methodist Episcopal Church First Women Steward; McDonald Hughes Community Center Outstanding Service. **Special Achievements:** Developed the ninth grade social studies curriculum guide for Tuscaloosa city schools; developed "Law, The Language of Liberty," series supplemental materials for Alabama social studies teacher; piloted program: "Teaching Economics Education," for ninth grade. **Home Addr:** 1605 Montrose Dr S, Tuscaloosa, AL 35405-3627, **Home Phone:** (205)345-5514.

JONES, AMMIA W.
Clergy. **Personal:** Born Jan 31, 1910, Mesic, NC; married; children: 4. **Career:** Town of Mesic, former comnr, Clergyman, currently. **Orgs:** Past pres, Mesic Branch, Nat Asn Advan Colored People. **Home Phone:** (252)745-3208.

JONES, ANDRUW RUDOLF
Baseball player. **Personal:** Born Apr 23, 1977, Willemstad, Netherlands Antilles; son of Henry and Carmen; married Nicole Derick; children: Druw & Madison. **Career:** Atlanta Braves, outfielder, 1996-2007; Los Angeles Dodgers, 2007; Texas Rangers, currently. **Honors/Awds:** Minor League Player of the Year, 1995; NL Gold Glove-CF, 1998-99; All-Star, 2000, 2002-03, 2005-06; Silver Slugger Award, 2005; Hank Aaron Award, 2005; Player of the Month, 2005; Major League Player of the Year, 2005. **Special Achievements:** Youngest player to hit a home run in World Series history . **Business Phone:** (972)432-3604.*

JONES, DR. ANN R
Educator. **Personal:** Born Jul 5, 1921, New Castle, PA; married Paul L (deceased); children: Connie E Rose. **Educ:** Livingstone Col, BA, 1944; Univ Pittsburgh, MSW, 1964, PhD, 1978. **Career:** Educator (retired); Irene Kaufmann Ctr, prog dir, 1952-60; Anna Heldman Ctr, prog dir 1960-64; Action Housing, dir training 1964-66; Community Action, dir training, 1966-70; Univ Pittsburgh, prof emeritus, interim dir affirmative action, 1989-91. **Orgs:** Provost adv comn, Womens Concerns; dir, Soc Work Field Educ; nom comn, Nat Coun Soc Work; site visitor, Nat Coun Social Educ Work; adv, comn Allegheny C Youth Serv; pres, Hazelwood Neighborhood Coun; bd dir, Three Rivers Adoption Coun. **Honors/Awds:** Post-Gazette Distinguisg0 Woman, 1969; Distinguish Alumni, Univ Pittsburgh, 1985; Foster Parents Support Award, 1996; Person of the Year, Three Rivers Adoption Council, 1997. *

JONES, ANNETTE MERRITT. See MERRITT CUMMINGS, ANNETTE.

JONES, ANNIE LEE
Clinical psychologist, educator. **Personal:** Born Apr 10, 1949, Augusta, GA; daughter of Thelma Holliday Jones and Lester Jones; married William James Drislane. **Educ:** Augusta Col, BA, 1971; Boston Veteran's Admin Med Ctr, intern, 1975; Univ Tenn, PhD, clin Psychol, 1976; NY Univ, Grad Sch Arts & Sci, postdoctoral. **Career:** Knoxville Bd Educ Handicapped Children's Serv & Headstart Psychologist, citywide coordr, 1975-76; Dillard Univ, asst prof psychology, 1976-77; Harbor Dept Veterans Affairs, clin psychologist, 1977-; HIP Ment Health Serv, clin psychologist, 1990-93; pvt pract, currently; Harlem Family Inst, fac. **Orgs:** Am Psychol Asn; Asn Black Psychologists; Nat Alliance Black Educr; Am Col Forensic Examiners. **Honors/Awds:** Troutt Fel. **Business Addr:** Clinical Psychologist, NY Harbor Department of Veterans Affairs, Department of Veterans Affairs Extended Care Center, 8701 Midland Pkwy, Jamaica, NY 11432, **Business Phone:** (718)658-4648.

JONES, ANTHONY, JR.
Government official. **Personal:** Born Sep 21, 1933, New York, NY; son of Anthony and Pearl; married Arnoline Whitten; children: Leslie Ann & Anthony Arnold. **Educ:** NY Univ, BS, 1958, MS, 1964. **Career:** Government official (retired); Bd Educ NYC, sci teacher, 1959-69; Bedford Stuyvesant Restoration Corp, dir employ, 1969-79; OIC NY, div mgr,1979-81; So Bronx Develop Orgn Inc, proj dir, 1981-87, dir Employ & Training; NY City Police Dept, dir victim & volunteer serv, 1987-95. **Orgs:** Kappa Alpa Psi New York Chapter, 1956-65; comt mem, Mayors Comt Adoption, 1973-75; comt mem, Alexander's Dept Store Affirmative Action Comt, 1973-75; Rotary Club Brooklyn, NY, 1975-79; Exec comn, Manpower Planning Coun NY City, 1975-79. **Honors/Awds:** Nat Sci Alfred Univ, NY, 1964; Foundation, Univ Puerto Rico, 1966. *

JONES, ANTHONY WARD
Executive, manager. **Personal:** Born Aug 15, 1947, Wilmington, NC; son of William Jones Sr and Mary Elizabeth Frasier; married Linda, Dec 27, 1988; children: Marilouise Elizabeth. **Educ:** Hampton Univ, BS, mkt, 1969; UCLA, MBA. **Career:** Munch-A-Million, vpres mkt, 1987-89; Surface Protection Ids, mgr, sales, 1989-91; Universal Paints & Coatings, pres; Front Row Mgt Corp, mgr, currently. **Special Achievements:** Gold and platinum records: Car Wash, MCA Records, 1977; In Full Bloom, Warner

Bros Records, Strikes Again, Warner Bros Records. **Business Addr:** Manager, Front Row Management Corporation, 2345 New Bern Ave, Raleigh, NC 27610, **Business Phone:** (919)231-1712.

JONES, ARNOLD PEARSON
School administrator, chancellor (education), army officer. **Personal:** Born in Chicago, IL; son of Arnold and Tommie; married Joan L; children: Victoria, Arnold, Douglas. **Educ:** Western Mich Univ, BS, 1950; DePaul Univ, MEd, 1955; Univ Ill Urbana, PhD, 1972. **Career:** Retired; Chicago Pub Schs, teacher, sch psychologist, prin, 1965, asst supt schs, 1967-69; Malcolm X Col, vpres acad, 1969-70; Northeastern Ill Univ, prof psychol, spec asst to pres, 1971-78; City Cols Chicago, exec vice chancellor human resources & labor relations, prof emer. **Orgs:** Comm Human Rights Comn, 1981-83; bd dirs, ACLU; educ task force, Chicago Urban League; life mem, Nat Asn Advan Colored People; mem educ core comm Chicago United; Alpha Phi Alpha; nat pres, Am Bridge Assoc, Natl Assoc of Affirm Action; sch bd nominating comm City of Chicago. **Honors/Awds:** Phi Beta Kappa. **Military Serv:** AUS, capt, 2 yrs. *

JONES, ARTHUR L
Law enforcement officer, radio host. **Personal:** Born Jun 12, 1946, Milwaukee, WI; son of Robert and Addie; married Orelia, Aug 7, 1965; children: Derrick & Terrence. **Educ:** Marquette Univ, assocs; Univ Wis-Milwaukee, Bachelors. **Career:** Law Enforcement officer (retired); Milwaukee Police Dept, police officer, police patrolman, 1976-78, detective, 1978-87, lt detectives, 1987-89, capt police, 1989-92; dep inspector police, 1992-96, chief police, 1996-2003; 1290 WMCS, talk radio staff guest host, 2003-. **Orgs:** Am Police Asn; Major Cities Chiefs Asn; Milwaukee Co Law Enforcement Exec; Nat Org Black Law Enforcement Execs; Police Exec Res Forum; Wis Chiefs Police Asn. **Honors/Awds:** Love in Action Image Award, Career Youth Develop, 1997; Thanks for Pulling for the Kids Memorial Award, Boys & Girls Club, 1998; Men of Distinction Award, Mt Zion Assembly, 1999; Dedication Award, Milwakee Pub Schs, 1999; Distinguished Service Award, Nat Asn Advan Colored People, 2001; Policeman of the Year Image Award, 2001. **Special Achievements:** First African American Chief for the City of Milwaukee, 1996. **Home Addr:** 6820 N 112th Ct, Milwaukee, WI 53224, **Home Phone:** (414)935-7200. **Business Addr:** Staff Guest Host, 1290 WMCS, 4222 W Capitol Dr, Milwaukee, WI 53216, **Business Phone:** (414)444-1290.

JONES, DR. BARBARA ANN POSEY
School administrator, educator. **Personal:** Born Jun 23, 1943, Oklahoma City, OK; daughter of Alma Vertena Inglemon and Weldon Burnett; married Mack H, Apr 1, 1964; children: Patrice Lumumba, Tayari A & Bomani B. **Educ:** Univ Okla, AB, 1963; Univ Ill, AM, 1966; Ga State Univ, PhD, 1973. **Career:** Univ Ill, Champaign-Urbana, IL, teaching & res asst, 1963-66; Tex Southern Univ, instr, 1966-67; Atlanta Univ, instr, 1968-69; Clark Col, Dept Bus Admin & Econ, from asst prof econ to prof econs, 1971-87, chairperson, 1971-80, Southern Ctr Studies Pub Policy, sr res assoc, 1981-87; Ahmadu Bello Univ, Dept Econ, Zaria, Nigeria, sr lectr, 1983-84; Prairie View A&M Univ, Dept Econs & Finance, head, 1987-89, Sch Bus, dean, 1989-97; Ala A&M Univ, Sch Bus, prof & dean, 1997-, prof, currently. **Orgs:** Bd dirs, Nat Econ Asn, 1971-2000, secy & treas, 1975-80, pres, 1987; bd trustees, Clark Col, 1973-74 & 1975-79; bd ed adv, Rev Black Polit Econ,1975-; hon mem, Alpha Kappa Mu Honor Soc, 1978; hon mem, Delta Mu Delta Honor Soc, 1991; bd dirs, Southern Bus Admin Asn, 1993-2004, secy & treas, 1996-2000, pres, 2003; bd dir, Int Asn Mgt Educ, 1994-97, exec comt mem, 1995-97, candidacy comt mem, 1992-95, accreditation task force implementation comt mem, 1992-94; bd dirs, Am Assembly Col Schs Bus, 1994-97, exec comt mem, 1995-97; bd dirs, HBCU, Bus Deans Round table, 2002-, pres, 2005-06; mem, AACSB. **Honors/Awds:** Russell Bull Award, Serv Civil Rights, 1963; Outstanding Independent Woman, Univ Okla, 1963; Eleanor Roosevelt Foundation Research Award, 1965;Most Devoted Educator Award, Clark Col, 1974; Outstanding Teacher Award, Stud Govt Asn, Clark Col, 1977-78; Outstanding Teacher, Clark Col, 1980; Distinguished Professor, Delta Sigma Theta, 1981-83; Teacher of the Year, Clark Col, Dept Bus Admin & Econ, 1985-86; US Small Business Administration Award of Excellence, 1995; Teacher of the Year, Kappa Alpha Psi Fraternity, Prairie View A&M Univ, 1996-97; Academic Partner Support Award, AAMU Bus & Indust Cluster, 2000. **Home Addr:** 4926 7 Pine Circle, Huntsville, AL 35816. **Business Addr:** Professor, Dean, Alabama A&M University, School of Business, PO Box 429, Normal, AL 35762.

JONES, BEN F
Educator, artist. **Personal:** Born May 26, 1942, Paterson, NJ. **Educ:** William Paterson Col, BA, 1963; NY Univ, MA, 1967; Pratt Inst, MFA, 1983. **Career:** Nat Endowment Arts, fel grant, 1974-75; NJ State Coun Arts, fel grant, 1977-78, 1983-84; Nat Conf Art, pres, 1978-80, vpres, 1981-84; Sulaimaan Dance Co, chmn bd, 1981-83; New Jersey City Univ, prof art, currently. **Orgs:** NJ Printmaking Coun, 1979-; World Printmaking Coun, 1980-; Nat Conf Artists; bd mem, Friends Music & Art Hudson Co, 1985; mem bd adv, Woodson Found NJ; Montclair Art Mus; African-Am Community. **Honors/Awds:** First Pl & Second Pl, art competition, Atlanta Life Ins, 1982-83; Grant Jersey City State Col, 1982-83; Career Development Award, Passaic Co Community Col, Patterson, NJ, 1984; Excellence in the Arts, Delta Sigma Theta Sorority, 1985. **Special Achievements:** Arts exhibited at many galleries and museums throughout the country. **Business Addr:** Professor Art, Artist, New Jersey City University, 2039 Kennedy Blvd, Jersey City, NJ 07305, **Business Phone:** (201)200-3030.

JONES, BENJAMIN A
Association executive, clergy. **Personal:** Born in Mobile, AL; son of Margaret. **Educ:** Col Lifelong Learning, attended 1994; Univ Mich, MSW, 1995. **Career:** Pentecostal Churches Apostolic Faith, assoc minister, asst to pastor, ordained elder, currently; Drug Strategies, bd mem; Nat Coun Alcoholism & Drug Dependence, Greater Detroit Area, exec dir, pres & chief exec officer, currently. **Military Serv:** Nat Guard, nuclear biol chem specialist, 6yrs. **Business Addr:** President, Chief Executive Officer, The National Council on Alcoholism & Drug Dependence, Greater Detroit Area, 4777 E Outer Dr, Detroit, MI 48234, **Business Phone:** (313)369-5400.

JONES, BENJAMIN E
Executive. **Personal:** Born Sep 8, 1935, New York, NY; married Delcenia R; children: Leslie & Delcenia. **Educ:** Brooklyn Col, BA, 1971; Pace Univ, MBA, 1974. **Career:** Radio Recepter Co, admin, 1959-60; ESX Div Paal Corp, acct, 1962-66; Gen Precision Inc, sr contract admin, negotiator & signer, 1966-71; Capital Formation Inc, Econ Develop Found, New York, pres, 1971-; Interracial Coun Bus Opportunity NY, prog dir, 1971; MBA Mgt Consult Inst, Columbia Univ, dir, 1973; Lightning Supply Inc, pres & owner, currently. **Orgs:** Fed Exec Bd, Minority Bus Opportunity Community, 1972-; bd dir, Upper Park Ave Community Asn, Day Care Ctr, 1974-; Am Mgt Asn; Nat Bus League; Coun Concerned Black Execs; Nat Asn Black Mfrs; Asn MBA Execs; Nat Asn Advan Colored People; One Hundred Black Men Inc; Uptown Chamber Community; NY Urban League; Am Asn MESBICS; vice chmn & treas, Nat Minority Bus Coun. **Military Serv:** USAF, 1955-58. **Business Addr:** President, Owner, Lighting Supply Inc, 85 Franklin Rd, Dover, NJ 07801, **Business Phone:** (973)361-9292.

JONES, BERNIE
Journalist. **Personal:** Born Jun 21, 1952, Baltimore, MD; son of Sumoria Clacks and Newbern L; married Beverly Harvey (divorced 1985); children: Linsay Morgan. **Educ:** Univ NC, Chapel Hill, NC, BA, 1974. **Career:** Baltimore News Am, asst news ed, 1980-81, night news ed, 1981-82; San Diego Union, CA, assist news ed, 1982-85, politics ed, 1985-86, asst news ed, 1986-88, news ed, 1988-95; Opinion Pages, San Diego Union-Tribune, ed, 1995-. **Business Addr:** Editor, San Diego Union-Tribune, Opinion Pages, 350 Camino de la Reina, PO Box 120191, San Diego, CA 92112-0191, **Business Phone:** (619)293-1208.

JONES, BERTHA DIGGS
Social worker, administrator. **Personal:** Born in Richland, GA; divorced; children: Betty Jean. **Educ:** Cent Sch Bus, Buffalo, attended 1968. **Career:** Diggs Assoc Urban Affairs, pres; FEPC, consult, 1945; EEA-WDP, supvr. **Orgs:** Consult to chmn, Buffalo Housing Auth, 1942; organizer, Jr Club Nat Asn; Negro Bus & Prof Women, NY, 1945; statewide organizer & exec dir, State Baptist Cong, 1956-69; adv comt, NY Div Housing, 1961-69; Pres Adv Coun Pace Univ NY, 1966-77; adv coun, Corsi Labor/Mgt Inst Pace Univ, 1966-77; bus consult, NY Dept Com, 1970-71; secy, State Labor Dept, 1973-75; Urban League; Nat Asn Advan Colored People; bd dir, Brooklyn Chap Am Red Cross;Am Acad Polit & Soc Sci Ctr; nat hon mem, Lambda Kappa Mu Sor. **Honors/Awds:** Silver Cup, Nat Rep Coun, 1948; Sojourner Truth Award, 1964; Meritorious Service Award, State Am Legion Unit; Service Award, Vis Nurse Asn Brooklyn, 1967-69; Certificate of Service, NY Labor Dept, 1975; Community Service Award, Woman of the Year, Philadelphia Church Universal Brotherhood, 1977. **Special Achievements:** Author of Home & Family Seminars, 1956; continuous publ newsletters, 1935-77.

JONES, BERTHA H.
Educator. **Personal:** Born Oct 30, 1918, Earle, AR; married Joseph R; children: Malcolm. **Educ:** Ill State Univ, BE; Ball State Univ, MA; Northwestern Univ; Mich Univ; Loyola Univ; Indiana Univ; NW & Purdue Univ. **Career:** Speech teacher, 1951-56; English teacher, 1956-59; counr, 1959-69; Gary Pub Sch Educ Talent Search, dir, 1969-. **Orgs:** IN Proj Dir & Assoc chmn vice chmn; IN Pers & Guidance Assoc; Am Personneland Guid Asn Dele Ind; adv bd, Ind Univ NW Campus; spec serv, Mid W Assoc Stu Fin Aid Admin; Upward Bound adv bd Metro Corps OEO Deleg Agency bd dir; Delta Sigma Theta; YWCA Teen Comm, bd dir; Van Buren Bapt Church; Urban League, Consumer Ed Task Force Ind Univ. **Honors/Awds:** Award of serv to stud, 1974; Ind Personnel & Guid Asn Merit Award, 1973; Pi Lambda Theta; Hon Soc for Women in Ed, 1961. **Special Achievements:** Elected Supreme first Anti-basileus of Nat Sorority of Phi Delta Kappa1969, 1971. **Business Addr:** 2131 Jackson St, Gary, IN 46407.

JONES, DR. BETTY B.
Educator. **Personal:** Born May 4, 1935, Columbia, SC; daughter of William A and Minnie M Brown; married S Preston, Feb 21, 1959; children: Allen Preston & Anthony Paul. **Educ:** Hampton Univ, BS, 1956; Cath Univ Am, MSW, 1965; Univ Mich, PhD, 1981. **Career:** Educator (retired); Campfire Girls, Wash, DC, staff, 1960-68; Bay City Pub Schs, social worker & admin, 1970-77; Delta Col, vpres instr & learning serv, 1977-2001. **Orgs:** Am Assn Univ Profs, 1977-; Am Sociol Soc, 1980-; Midland Hist Soc, 1995-; Natl Orgn Biblical Storytellers, 2002-. **Honors/Awds:** Taggart Award, Mich State Univ, 1994; Outstanding Leadership, Delta Col,2001; MLK Award for Outstanding Service, Dow Chem Co, 2001. **Special Achievements:** Author: Stories of My People: Story of Afr Amer community in Midland, Michigan, 1996; established Intl scholarship endowment in recognition of their joint support to global education in student learning; and to honor Dr. Jones rsquo; legacy in global international education at Delta College.

JONES, DR. BETTY JEAN TOLBERT
Educator. **Personal:** Born Jul 14, 1943, Charleston, SC; daughter of Helen Grant Tolbert and Fred W Tolbert; married Donald W, Nov 27, 1965; children: Tracey. **Educ:** Hampton Inst Va, BS, 1965; Fairfield Univ, CT, MA 1970; Univ Va, EdD, 1990; Princeton Univ, post-doctoral study. **Career:** Dolan Jr High Sch, Conn, sci teacher, 1965-68; Fairfield Univ, grad study, 1968-69; Lane High Sch, teacher, 1973-74; Charlottesville High Sch, Va, biol teacher, 1974-, Sci Dept, chairperson, 1994-; Univ Va, Charlottesville, Va, clin instr, 1986; Univ Va Ctr Biol Timing, biol researcher, 1993-2001; bd dirs, Links Inc; Martin Luther King fel; NASA, Goddard Space Flight Ctr, fel, Woods Hole, Mass Marine Biol Lab, fel; Hope Col Nat Biol Linking Prog, fel; Woodrow Wilson fel; Howard Hughes fel; Univ Calif, Berkeley, Nat Bio tech Forum, fel; Univ Kans, Med Ctr Human Genome Proj, fel; Tufts Univ, Wright Sci Ctr, fel; Fulbright Memorial Fund Scholar to Japan, 2001. **Orgs:** Nat Asn Biol Teachers, 1965-; Am Asn Univ Women, 1970-; Va Asn Sci Teachers, 1973-; treas, Barret Day Care Ctr Bd, 1973-; Am Asn Higher Educ, 1973-; Am Asn Higher Educ Black Caucus, 1973-; bd dirs, Charlottesville Educ Asn, 1974-; Nat Educ Asn; participant Parent-Edn Conf Univ Va; Alpha Kappa Mu; Beta Kappa Chi Nat Honor Soc; Delta Sigma Theta Sorority; Kappa Delta Pi; Friends Within; Jr League Charlottesville; Family Serv Bd Charlottesville; Va Sci Leadership Asn; bd Emergency Food Bank Charlottesville; bd dirs, Va Fund Humanities & Pub Policy; Am Mus Sci & Energy; vpres, Charlottesville chap; vpres & bd dirs, Gordonsville Friends Libr; fel Nat Sci Found. **Honors/Awds:** Charlottesville Public Schools Outstanding Educator Award; Radio Shack Award for Teaching Excellence in Mathematics, Science & Technology. **Home Addr:** PO Box 6429, Charlottesville, VA 22906. **Business Addr:** Biology Teacher, Charlottesville High School, 1562 Dairy Road, Charlottesville, VA 22903.

JONES, DR. BILLY EMANUEL
Government official, physician. **Personal:** Born Jun 11, 1938, Dayton, OH; son of Callie Jones and Paul Jones; children: Alexander. **Educ:** Howard Univ, BS, 1960; Meharry Med Col, MD, 1965; NY Med Col, residency psychiat, 1969; NY Univ, Robert Wagner Grad Sch Pub Serv, MS, 1990. **Career:** Metropolitan Hosp CMHC, asst dir, 1971-73; Coney Island Hosp Dept Psy chiat, assoc dir, 1973-74; Fordham Hosp, Dept Psy chiat, dir, 1974-77; New York Medical Col, Dept Psychiatry & Behavioral Sci, dir, 1977-90, clin prof, currently, Med & Ment Health Ctr, Dept Psy chiat, 1977-88, med dir,1988-90; NY City, Dept Ment Health, Ment Retardation & Alcoholism Servs, comnr, 1990-, Health & Hosps Corp, pres & chief exec officer, 1992-94; Magellan Behavioral Health Serv, sr vpres & chief med officer pub solutions Div, 1997-2001; City Col New York, adj med prof; B Jones ConsultServ, personal therapist & chief consult, currently; sr health & mentalhealth care adminr. **Orgs:** Dip, Am Bd Psychiat & Neurol, 1977-; pres, Black Psychiatrists Am, 1978-80; community serv bd, New York, 1980-90; fel Am Psy chiat Asn, 1983-; NYS Alcohol Drug Abuse & Ment Health Block Grant Community, 1983-90; 100Black Men; Am Col Psychiatrists; New York Acad Med; Nat Med Asn; Am Public Health Asn; Am Col Physician Exec. **Special Achievements:** Manic Depressive Illness Among Poor Urban Blacks, Am Jour Psy chiat Vol 138#9 May, 1981; "Survey of Psychotherapy with Black Men" Am Jour Psy chiat Vol 139 #9 Sept, 1982; author of numerous articles on African Americans. **Military Serv:** AUS, Major, 1969-71. **Business Addr:** Personal Therapist, Chief Executive Officer, B Jones Consulting Services, 56 Hamilton Terr Suite 1, New York, NY 10031, **Business Phone:** (212)234-5649.

JONES, BOB
Media executive, vice president (organization), manager. **Personal:** Born Jul 4, 1936, Ft Worth, TX; son of Ocie (deceased) and Ruby Faye. **Educ:** USC, 1953-58. **Career:** La Herald Dispatch, entertainment ed, 1957-68; Rogers & Cowan, acct exec, 1968-70; Motown Records, publ mgr, 1970-75, exec dir, press & art rel, 1975-87; MJJ Prods, vpres, communs & media rels, 1987-2004, pub rel mgr. **Orgs:** Bd dir, USO, 1977-83, vpres, 1983-84; bd dir, Hollywood C of C; chmn, bd dir, Beverly Hills, Nat Asn Advan Colored People, 1971-83; pres, Black Public Rel Soc Southern Calif, 1985-87; pres, Black Pub Rels Soc Am, 1988-89. **Honors/Awds:** Image Awards, 1973-74; Nat Black Showcases, 1986; Par Excellence Award, Oakland, CA; Pioneer of Excellence, NY, 1989; Black Radio Exclusive, Soul Train, Jack the Rapper, Black Public Relations Society Special Awards of Achievement,

1989; Nat Asn Advan Colored People, 25th Anniversary Image Awards, Sterling Award, 1993; Prame Award, Nat Asn Market Developers; Los Angeles Sentinel, Sentinel Men of the Year; Black Entertainment Television, primetime television documentary, "Bob Jones Godfather Black Hollywood," produced by Belma Johnson; Fred Snowden Humanitarian Award, Greater Los Angeles African-Am Chamber Com, 1995; Special Friend, Hollywood Arts Coun, 1996; Champion Honoree, Black Radio Excl Mag.

JONES, BOBBY M.
Baseball player. **Personal:** Born Apr 11, 1972, Orange, NJ. **Career:** Colo Rockies, pitcher, 1997-99; NY Mets, 2000; Norfolk Tides, 2002; San Diego, pitcher, 2002; NY Mets, pitcher, 2002; Richmond Spiders, 2003; Omaha Royals, 2003; Boston Red Sox, pitcher, 2004; Charlotte Knights, pitcher, 2005; Detroit Tigers, Double-A Erie, 2006. *

JONES, HON. BONNIE LOUISE
Lawyer, judge. **Personal:** Born Feb 3, 1952, Philadelphia, PA; daughter of William Smith and Thelma Mills. **Educ:** Lincoln Univ, BA, 1970; NC Cent Univ Sch Law, JD, 1982. **Career:** VA Legal Aid Soc, law clerk, 1982-83; Newport News Police Dept, permits examnr, 1983-85; Hampton Roads Regional Acad Criminal Justice, training/eval specialist 1985-86; Blayton Allen & Assocs, assoc atty, 1986-88; self-employed atty, Hampton VA, 1988-; McDermott, Roe & Sons, atty, 1992-96; Col William & Mary, Sch Law, adj prof, 1994-97; City Hampton Gen Dist Court, judge, 1996-2002, chief judge, currently. **Orgs:** Phi Alpha Delta Law Fraternity, 1982-; Big Brother/Big Sisters Peninsula, 1985; Am Bar Asn, 1986; VA Bar Asn, 1986; Asn Trial Atty Am; Penn Bar Asn, 1987-; Hampton Bar Asn, 1988-92; coun vpres, Int Training Commun Coun II, 1988-89; Comn Chancery Hampton Circuit Ct; pres, bd dirs, Girls Inc Greater Peninsula. **Home Addr:** 24 Fields Dr, Hampton, VA 23664. **Business Addr:** Chief Judge, City of Hampton General District Court, 236 N King St, PO Box 70, Hampton, VA 23669, **Business Phone:** (757)727-6260.

JONES, BOOKER TEE, SR.
Association executive. **Personal:** Born Jun 30, 1939, Mesic, NC; son of Hezekiah and Mary; married Loretta Johnson; children: Hilda Davis, Booker T Jr, Marietta & Coretta. **Educ:** LaSalle Ext Univ, AA, acct, 1959; Cent Appraiser Soc, real estate appr designation, 1971; Nat Ctr Housing Mgt, housing mgt cert, 1981. **Career:** Executive (retired); Kingsborough Realty Inc, real estate salesman, 1963-67; One Stop Home Sales Co, owner, broker, appraiser, 1967-74; Booker T Jones Real Estate Brokers, pres, real estate broker, 1972-; DPT HUD, real estate appraiser, 1972-73; Costal Progress Inc, coordr, adminr, 1977-80; Twin Rivers Opportunity Inc, housing dir, 1980-85, exec dir, 1985. **Orgs:** Pres, United Communities Asn Net Inc, 1975-85; bd dir, Craven County Fed Credit Union, 1979-82; vice chmn bd, Pamlico County Bd Ed, 1980-85; chmn bd dir, NC Section 8 Housing Asn Inc, 1984-85, bd mem, 1985-; appointee, Pamlico County Planning Bd, 1991; appointee, Low Income Housing Task Force, New Bern, NC, 1991; bd dir, chmn, Costal COT Develop Corp, 1991; bd dir, NC Housing Finance Agency, 1994-; bd dir, Appointed NC Gov mem NC Housing Finance Agency, 1994-; bd trustees, Pamlico Community Col, 2000-04. **Honors/Awds:** Outstanding Service, United Way, 1977; Leadership Training, Nat Citizen Participation Coun Inc, 1979; NC Gov's Appointment Pamlico Cty Transp Efficiency, 1982; Exemplarary Serv, NC Sect 8 Housing Asn Inc, 1984; appointed local adv comt, 1988-; adv bd, NC Dept HUD, 1988-; Outstanding Service Award, 1989-90, 15 Year Employment Longevity Honor, 1992, Twin Rivers Opportunities Inc; Distinguished Guest Honors, Cong woman Eve Clayton, Cong man Mel Watts, & NC Gov Jim Hunt, 1991. **Home Addr:** PO Box 68, Grantsboro, NC 28529.

JONES, BRENT M.
Photographer, educator, journalist. **Personal:** Born Feb 11, 1946, Chicago, IL; married Ingrid. **Educ:** Columbia Col, BA, 1969. **Career:** Opportunity Industrialization Training Ctr, eng instr & asst dir pub rels, 1969-70; Columbia Col, instr creative writing, 1969-70; Black Asn Enterprises, chief photog, 1970-73; Chicago Art Inst, teacher; one-man exhibitions; US Rep; second World Black & African Festival Arts & Culture; freelance photographer & writer, currently. **Orgs:** Founding mem, Chicago Alliance African Am Photogr. **Business Addr:** Photographer, 1137 E 101 St, Chicago, IL 60628.

JONES, BRIAN KEITH
Football player. **Personal:** Born Jan 22, 1968, Iowa City, IA. **Educ:** Univ Tex; Univ Calif. **Career:** Indianapolis Colts, linebacker, 1991; New Orleans Saints, linebacker,1995-98.

JONES, C D. See JONES, CHARLES D.

JONES, CALDWELL
Basketball player. **Personal:** Born Aug 4, 1950, Mc Gehee, AR. **Educ:** Albany State Univ, attended. **Career:** Basketball player (retired); San Diego Conquistadors, 1973-75; Kentucky Colonels, 1975; St Louis Spirits, 1976; Philadephia 76ers, 1976-82; Houston Rockets, 1982-84; Chicago Bulls, 1984-85; Portland Trail Blazers,1986-89; San Antonio Spurs, 1989-90.

JONES, CARL
Executive. **Personal:** Born Jan 1, 1955?, Tennessee. **Educ:** El Camino Col, attended. **Career:** Business Owner (retired), Licensing; Designers Screen Printing, founder, 1982-85; Surf Fetish, founder, 1985-90; Cross Colours Clothing, pres, 1990-94; pvt lic apparels. **Home Addr:** 1370 1/2 Laveta Ter, Los Angeles, CA 90026. *

JONES, CAROLYN G.
Consultant, president (organization). **Personal:** Born Aug 5, 1943, Chattanooga, TN; daughter of Clyde Goolsby and Paralee Johnson Goolsby; married Edward G Jones, Nov 26, 1980; children: Larketta, Harry Charles, Arthur, Edward Lee. **Educ:** Emory Univ Atlanta, BS 1976. **Career:** Metro Hosp West, dir med rec, 1972-74; Erlanger Alton Park Health Ctr, admin asst, 1974-76; Chattanooga State Community Col, prog dir, 1976-81; CJ Enterprises Inc, pres & chief exec officer, currently. **Orgs:** Chairperson, Ed Comt Chatta Area Med Rec Coun, 1984-85; chairperson, Pub Rel CAMRC 1983-84; mem By-Laws Comt TMRA, 1983-84; co-dir Nursing Guild Hawkinsville Bapt Church, 1984-85; Chatt Minority Bus Develop, 1984; Chamber Com; Polit Actia Comt, Nat Coalition 100 Black Women Chatt Chapter; Chatt Area Urban League; Chatt Leadership Grad; Nat Asn Community Health Ctr; Hawkinsville Missionary Baptist Church. **Honors/Awds:** Woman of the Year, Glenwood Bus & Prof Women's Club, 1982; Outstanding Achievement Off, Minority Bus Develop, 1983; Serv Bus Award Chatt Minority Bus, 1984; Entrepreuner of the Year, 1985; House Resolution No 1, TN House Rep, 1986; Business of the Year, Urban League, 1987; Hamilton County Minority Small Business Person Award, Small Bus Admin, 1990; Small Business Person of the Year, Chamber Com, 1990; Chatt "Women of Distinction", 1997; ATHENA Award; Jane Cozby Henderson "Woman of Achievement"; Admin Award for Excellence; Heroes of Public Housing; "Fifteen Women That Make A Difference;" Women in Business Advocate of the Year Award. **Home Addr:** 324 Willow Glen Rd, Chattanooga, TN 37421. **Business Addr:** President, Chief Executive Officer, CJ Enterprises Inc, 7010 Lee Hwy Suite 214, Chattanooga, TN 37421.*

JONES, CEDRIC
Football player. **Personal:** Born Apr 30, 1974, Houston, TX; son of Annette. **Educ:** Univ Okla. **Career:** NY Giants, defensive end, 1996-2000. **Honors/Awds:** All-Am first team, The Sporting News, 1995. *

JONES, CHARISSE MONSIO
Journalist. **Personal:** Born Sep 2, 1965, San Francisco, CA; daughter of Charles Milton and Jean Stephanie Laing. **Educ:** Univ Southern Calif, Los Angeles, CA, BA, 1987. **Career:** Wave Newspaper, Los Angeles, CA, intern, 1985; Los Angeles Herald Examr, Los Angeles, CA, reporter, 1986-88; Los Angeles Times, Los Angeles, CA, reporter, 1989-93; NY Times, reporter, 1993-97; USA Today, reporter, 1997-; Nat Pub Radio, commentator; Essence mag, contributing writer. **Orgs:** Bd mem, Black Journalists Asn Southern Calif, 1989-93; Nat Asn Black Journalists, 1986-; Golden Key Honor Soc, 1984-; USC Mentor Prog, 1990-93. **Honors/Awds:** Los Angeles Press Club Award For Riot Coverage, 1992; Co-writer one of 10 stories to win 1993 Pulitzer Prize for riot coverage; finalist for Livingston Award, 1993. **Special Achievements:** "Shifting: the story of Black women", HarperCollins Publ. **Business Addr:** Reporter & New York Correspondent, USA Today, 7950 Jones Branch Dr, McLean, VA 22108-0605.*

JONES, CHARLES
Educator. **Personal:** Born May 12, 1946, Bronx, NY; son of Charles and Mae; married Linda Marie Coggshall. **Educ:** BS, 1969; MS, 1972; Columbia Univ, PhD. **Career:** Cent Conn State Univ, grad asst, 1970-72, dir educ opportunity prog & asst basketball coach, 1970-, dir, educ support serv, dir athletics & dir intercollegiate athletics, 1994-2007. **Orgs:** Hartford Bd Approved Umpires, 1969; Kappa Delta Pi, 1970; coordr, Annual Thanksgiving Food Drive Deprived Families New Britain Area, 1970-; Nat Asn Basketball Coaches, 1970-; CT State Employees Asn, 1970-; bd mem, CT Commn Higher Educ Accrediting Team, 1972; fac adv, Ebony Choral Ensemble, 1974-;pres, Black Admin Staff Inst Cent; field reader, govt grants; Phi DeltaKappa Sect Conn Assoc Educ Opportunities Prog; coordr, Minority Youth BusConf; bd dirs, Cent Conn State Univ Alumni; pres, CT Asn Educ Opportunity Prog, 1991-92; treas, New England Asn Educ Opportunity Prog Personnel,1992; trustee, Friendship Ctr; trustee, New Britian Found; Nat Collegiate Athletic Asn, Men's Basketball Rules COM; originator, Endowed Scholar Fund Disadvantaged Stud. **Honors/Awds:** Minority Alumni Award; Afro-American Organization Student Award; Puerto Rican Union Recognition Award; Harrison J Kaiser Alumni Service Award,Cent Conn State Univ, 1989; Advisor of the Year, Ctr Conn State Univ,1990-91; Distinguished Service Award, 1991-92; Impact Award, Vin Baker Found, 2001. **Special Achievements:** Co-host of cable TV series "Pioneers". **Business Addr:** Director of Athletics, Director of Intercollegiate Athletics, Central Connecticut State University, 1615 Stanley St, PO Box 4010, New Britain, CT 06050-4010, **Business Phone:** (860)832-3038.

JONES, CHARLES, III. See DARA, OLU.

JONES, CHARLES D (C D JONES)
State government official, lawyer. **Personal:** Born Mar 25, 1950; married Carol Charles. **Educ:** Southern Univ, BA, JD; Univ Ill, MA; Northwestern Univ Dist Atty Sch, attended. **Career:** Asst dist atty, 1976-79; La State Senate, atty, Dist 17, state rep, 1980-92, atty, Dist 34, state senator, 1992-. **Orgs:** La Bar Asn; Northern La Legal Assistance Corp; bd dirs, La Sickle Cell Anemia Asn, currently. **Military Serv:** USAR, capt, 1976-79. **Home Phone:** (318)325-2644. **Business Addr:** Senator, Louisiana State Senate, District 34, 141 Desiard St Suite 315, Monroe, LA 71201, **Business Phone:** (318)362-5469.

JONES, CHARLES GADGET
Basketball player. **Personal:** Born Apr 3, 1957, McGehee, AR. **Educ:** Albany State Univ, attended 1979. **Career:** Played in CBA, 1979-80, 1982-85; played in Italy, 1981-82; Philadelphia 76ers, 1983-84; San Antonio Spurs, 1984; Chicago Bulls, 1984-85; Wash Bullets, 1986-93; Detroit Pistons, 1993-94; Houston Rockets, 1995-98. **Honors/Awds:** All-Metro Conf second team; conf player of week twice; NBA Championship, Houston Rockets, 1995.

JONES, CHARLES RAHMEL
Basketball player. **Personal:** Born Jul 17, 1975, Brooklyn, NY. **Educ:** Rutgers Univ; Long Island Univ. **Career:** Chicago Bulls, guard, 1998-99; Los Angeles Clippers, 1999-2000; SCMontecatini, 2000-01; Ionikos NF Thessaloniki, 2001-02; Brooklyn Kings, 2003; Maccabi Rishon Le-Zion, 2003-04; Libertad Sunchales, 2003-04; PBCLukoil Akademik Sophia, 2004-05; Strong Island Sound, 2005; Albany Patrons, 2005; Gimnasia Esgrima Comodoro Rivadavia, guard, 2005. **Honors/Awds:** All-Star Game, 2004; Bolivian League Champion, 2005.

JONES, CHARLIE (CHARLIE EDWARD JONES)
Football player, football coach. **Personal:** Born Dec 1, 1972, Hanford, CA. **Educ:** Fresno State Univ, speech communs major. **Career:** Football player (retired), football coach: San Diego Chargers, widereceiver, 1996-99; New Orleans Saints, wide receiver; Fresno City Col, coaching staff, currently. **Business Addr:** Coaching Staff, Fresno City College, 1101 E Univ Ave, Fresno, CA 93741, **Business Phone:** (559)442-4600.*

JONES, CHARLIE EDWARD. See JONES, CHARLIE.

JONES, CHERYL ARLEEN
Television producer, manager. **Personal:** Born Sep 2, 1963, Portsmouth, VA; daughter of Donna R and Maxwell Jones. **Educ:** Va Polytech Inst & State Univ, BA, 1986. **Career:** Discovery Networks, mgr, daytime programming, 1986-91, sr account mgr, 1991-93; Discovery Pictures, sr account mgr, 1993-96; Discovery Channel Pictures, dir program mgt, 1996-; Pub Broadcasting Serv, Prog Ddevelop & Independent Film, sr dir, currently. **Orgs:** Nat Acad Cable Programming, 1986-; Nat Acad TV Arts & Sci, 1988-; Int Documentary Asn, 1990-; Museum Broadcasting, 1992-; Am Women Radio & Television, 1991-92; Women Cable, 1987-92; big sister, Big Sister Wash, Metrop Area, 1992-. **Business Addr:** Senior Director Program Development, Independent Film, Public Broadcasting Service, 1320 Braddock Pl, Alexandria, VA 22314, **Business Phone:** (703)739-5150.

JONES, CHESTER RAY
Government official, lawyer. **Personal:** Born Nov 9, 1946, Jackson, MS; son of William Jones Sr and River Lee Clark; married Queen Jackson; children: Jaala & Heddie Rabekah. **Educ:** Tougaloo Col, BA, sociol, 1968; Miss Col Sch Law, JD, 1978; Harvard Univ Grad Sch Educ, Inst Employment & Training Admin summer, 1981. **Career:** Abbott House Irvington-on-Hudson NY, child care worker, 1968; Repub Philippines, peace corps volunteer, 1968-70; Govrs Off Job Develop & Training, equal employment opportunity, 1978-85; Miss State Dept Pub Welfare, staff atty, 1988-89; Miss State Dept Human Serv, sr atty, 1989-; Sanders Law Firm, atty, currently. **Orgs:** Alpha Phi Alpha Frat Inc, 1965; Miss State Bar Asn, 1979; Hinds County Bar Asn, 1979; Am Trial Lawyers Asn, 1979; Nat Inst Employ Equity, 1982; Am Legion (Post 214), 1984; Nat Urban League, 1984; Magnolia Bar Asn 1985-. **Special Achievements:** Harvard Univ's Inst Employment & Training Admin summer, 1981. **Military Serv:** US Coast Guard, third class petty officer, four yrs; Good Conduct Award, 1974. **Home Addr:** 312 Robinhood Rd, Jackson, MS 39206. **Business Addr:** Attorney, Sanders Law Firm, 133 S Com St, PO Box 565, Natchez, MS 39121-0565, **Business Phone:** (601)445-5570.

JONES, CHRIS (CHRISTOPHER CARLOS JONES)
Baseball player. **Personal:** Born Dec 16, 1965, Utica, NY. **Career:** Cincinnati Reds, outfielder, 1991; Houston Astros, 1992; Colo Rockies, 1993-94; New York Mets, 1995-96; San Diego Padres, 1997; Ariz Diamond backs, 1998; San Francisco Giants, 1998; Milwaukee Brewers, 2000; Newark Bears, mgr, 2004-06; Kannapolis Intimidators, mgr, currently. **Business Phone:** (704)932-3267.*

JONES, CHRISTINE MILLER
Educator, government official. **Personal:** Born Dec 25, 1929, Navasota, TX; daughter of Christine M Jones; married Robert E

Jones Sr; children: Robert E Jones Jr. **Educ:** Huston Tillotson Col, Austin, TX, BA, 1949; George Washington Univ, Wash, DC, attended. **Career:** Prince George's Co Bd Educ, pub sch teacher; Md State Govt, state delegate, 1982-94, asst floor leader, 1994. **Orgs:** Nat Educ Asn; Md State Teacher's Asn; Prince George's Educr Asn; Nat Conf Christians & Jews; Prince George Mental Health Asn, 1980; Md Legis Caucuses; Oxon Hill Dem Club; John Hanson Women's Club; Southern PG Bus Prof Women's Club; Nat Asn Advan Colored People; Delta Sigma Theta; The Links. **Honors/Awds:** Service Award, Delta Sigma Theta Sor, 1982; Service Award, Prince George Coalition Black Affairs, 1983; Service Award, Links Inc, 1983; Service Award, Md State Teachers Asn, 1984. **Business Addr:** Teacher, Prince George's County Board of Education, 4518 Beech Rd, Temple Hills, MD 20748.*

JONES, CHRISTOPHER CARLOS. **See JONES, CHRIS.**

JONES, CHRISTOPHER TODD
Football player. **Personal:** Born Aug 7, 1971, West Palm Beach, FL. **Educ:** Univ Miami, Fla, BA, criminal justice. **Career:** Philadelphia Eagles, wide receiver, 1995-97; Oakland Raiders, 1999.

JONES, CLARA STANTON
Librarian, educator, civil rights activist. **Personal:** Born May 14, 1913, St Louis, MO; daughter of Ralph Herbert and Etta James; married Albert Dewitt Jones, Jun 25, 1938; children: Stanton, Vinetta, Kenneth. **Educ:** Milwaukee State Teachers Col, 1930; Spelman Col, Atlanta, GA, AB, 1934; Univ Mich, Ann Arbor, MI, ABLS, 1938. **Career:** Librarian (retired). Dillard Univ, New Orleans, LA, ref librn, 1938, 1942-44; Southern Univ, Baton Rouge, LA, cataloger, 1940-41; Detroit Pub Libr, Detroit, MI, ref, br librn, 1944-70, dir, 1970-78; Univ Calif, Berkeley, regents lectr, 1979-80. **Orgs:** Nat Asn Advan Colored People, 1940-; Women's League Peace & Freedom, 1950-; Am Civil Liberties Union, 1960-; acting pres & pres, Am Libr Asn, 1976-77; UN Asn, 1980-; Nat Coun Negro Women, 1980-. **Honors/Awds:** Distinguished Service to Librarianship Award, Am Libr Asn Black Caucus, 1970; Distinguished Alumnus Award for Outstanding Service to the Library Profession, Univ Mich, Sch Libr Sci, 1971; Athena Award for Humanitarian Service as an Alumna, Univ Mich, 1975; Distinguished Service to the Community Award, Wayne County Community Col, 1978; Lifetime Member Award, Am Libr Asn, 1983; Honorary Doctor of Humane Letters: Shaw Univ, Detroit, MI; NC Cent Univ, Durham, NC; St Johns Univ, Jamaica, NY; Pratt Inst, Brooklyn, NY; Ball State Univ, Muncie, IN; Grand Valley State Univ, Allendale, MI; Wayne State Univ, Detroit, MI; Northern Mich Univ, Marquette, MI; Spelman Col, Atlanta, GA. **Special Achievements:** First African-American president of the American Library Association; first African American and the first woman director in the Detroit Public Library System, 1970. **Home Addr:** 5121 Camden St, Oakland, CA 94619. *

JONES, CLARENCE J., JR.
Government official, president (organization). **Personal:** Born Apr 17, 1933, Boston, MA; son of Clarence J and Elizabeth Middleton; married Wanda Hale, Sep 3, 1983; children: Meta, Nadine, Mark, Michael, Melissa, Kenneth & Mark Duane. **Educ:** Winston-Salem State NC, BS, 1955; Goddard Col, MS. **Career:** City Boston, youth worker, 1960-65, dir youth activ comn, 1968-72, dirhuman rights, 1972-76, dep mayor, 1976-81; Boston Juvenile Ct, probation officer, 1965-68; Boston Redevelop Authority, chmn & bd dirs, 1989-. **Orgs:** Pres, Winston-Salem State Alumni; vpres, Winston-Salem State Univ, 1984-; chmn trustees, 12th Baptist Church; bd mem, Girls & Boys Clubs; bd dirs,Citizenship Training Groups, Boston Juvenile Court. **Honors/Awds:** Outstanding Citizen, Afro-Am Police, 1980; Outstanding Alumnus,Winston-Salem State Univ, 1983; Martin Luther King Jr Drum Major for Peace, 1986. **Military Serv:** AUS, Pfc, 1955-57; Good Conduct Medal. **Business Addr:** Chairman, Board of Directors, Boston Redevelopment Authority, 1 City Hall Sq, Boston, MA 02201, **Business Phone:** (617)722-4300.

JONES, CLARENCE THOMAS
Football player. **Personal:** Born May 6, 1968, Brooklyn, NY; married Shari; children: Clarence III. **Educ:** Univ Md. **Career:** Football player (retired); New York Giants, tackle, 1991-93; St Louis Rams, 1995; New Orleans Saints, 1996-99; Carolina Panthers, 1999-2000.

JONES, HON. CLYDE EUGENE
Lawyer. **Personal:** Born Dec 5, 1954, Birmingham, AL; son of Bennie and Clyde M; married Julia Norment; children: Jakarra Jenise & Jasmine Jekesha. **Educ:** Knoxville Col, BA, 1976; Univ Miss, Pre Law Cleo Fel, 1976; Samford Univ, Cumberland Sch Law, JD, 1979. **Career:** Jefferson County Family Ct, law clerk, baliff, 1979-80; 10th Judicial Circuit, Ala, dep dist atty, 1980; 5th Judicial Circuit Ala, asst dist atty, 1980-84; Penick, Williams & Jones, atty partner, 1985-87; pvt pract, 1987-; 10th Judicial Circuit, State Ala, circuit judge, 2002. **Orgs:** Vpres, Nat Pan Hellenic Coun, 1975-76; undergrad dist rep, Omega Psi Phi Fraternity Inc, 1975-76; Senator Jr Law Class Cumberland Sch Law, 1977-78; law clerk, Shores & Larkin, 1978; stud prosecutor, law clerk, Jefferson County Off, 1978-79; pres, Young Dem Macon County, 1981-84; Ancient Egyptian Arabic Order Nobles Mystic Shrine, 1984-; Shriner, Mizraim Temple 119, 1984-; bd dirs, Magic City Bar Asn, 1985-86; vpres, Magic City Bar Asn, 1987, pres, 1990, bd dirs, 1991; Vestavia-Hoover Kiwanis Club; Magic City Jaycees; Alpha Phi Chap; deacon, 6th Ave Baptist Church; Birmingham Alumni Asn; Birmingham Bar Asn. **Honors/Awds:** Basileus, Omega Psi Phi, 1974-76; hon mem, Atty Gen Staff State Ala, 1979; Proclamation, Clyde E Jones Day, Mayor Tuskegee, Ala, 1984; Leadership Birmingham, 1989 Class; Leadership, Birmingham Alumni Asn, 1990-; 101 Black Men of Birmingham, 1990. **Home Addr:** 1009 Willowbrook Rd, Birmingham, AL 35215. **Business Addr:** Attorney, 710 Criminal Justice Ctr Rm L-06 801 N Richard Arrington Jr, PO Box 10005, Birmingham, AL 35203, **Business Phone:** (205)325-5395.

JONES, COBI N'GAI (COBI N'GAI JONES)
Soccer player, athletic coach. **Personal:** Born Jun 16, 1970, Westlake Village, GA. **Educ:** UCLA, attended. **Career:** Soccer player (retired), Athletic Coach; Coventry City, midfielder, 1992; US Nat Soccer Team, midfielder, 1992-2004; Vasco da Gama, brazel, midfielder, 1996; Los Angeles Galaxy, midfielder, 1996; Major League Soccer, asst coach, currently. **Orgs:** Univ Calif Los Angeles, attended. **Honors/Awds:** Summer Olympics, Barcelona, 1992; World Cup Soccer Team, 1994; Player of the Year Award, Galaxy supporters group, 2006; Inducted into UCLA Hall of Fame, 2002. **Special Achievements:** One of only two USA players to have played every minute in both the 1994and 1998 FIFA World Cups. **Business Addr:** Interim Coach, Los Angeles Galaxy, The Home Depot Ctr 18400 Avalon Blvd Suite 200, Carson, CA 90746, **Business Phone:** 877-342-5299.

JONES, CURLEY C
Librarian. **Personal:** Born Feb 23, 1941, Rossville, TN; son of Cleve and Susie Palmer. **Educ:** Univ Rochester, BA, 1994; Univ Buffalo, MLS, 1997, advan studies cert, Info & Libr Studies, 2006; NYU, dipl paralegal studies, 2001. **Career:** Rochester City Sch Dist, Roch, NY, teacher intern, 1969-70, sub teacher, 1970-72; Univ Ill, grad stud, 1976-77; Univ Utah, Marriott Libr, educ psychol sub specialist, librn, currently. **Orgs:** Life mem, Am Libr Asn, 1972; Chicano Bib Univ Utah, 1973; Mountain Plains Libr Asn, 1973; Black Bib Univ Utah, 1974, compiler, 1977, ed suppl, 1981; Utah Hist Soc; life mem, Nat Asn Advan Colored People, 1984; Asn Study Negro Life & Hist. **Honors/Awds:** Civil Rights Worker of the Year, 2001. **Home Addr:** 377 E 700 S, Salt Lake City, UT 84111. **Business Addr:** Librarian, University Utah, Marriot Library, 295 S 1500 E Rm 327, Salt Lake City, UT 84112.

JONES, CYNTHIA R.
Chief executive officer. **Personal:** Married Kenneth Parks. **Career:** Jones Worley Graphic Design Consults, chief exec officer & pres, currently. **Orgs:** Vice chair, bd dir, Atlanta Business League, 2009. **Business Phone:** (404)876-9272.

JONES, DAMON
Football player. **Personal:** Born Sep 18, 1974, Evanston, IL. **Educ:** Univ Mich, Univ Southern Ill. **Career:** Jacksonville Jaguars, tight end, 1997-2001.

JONES, DAMON DARRON
Basketball player. **Personal:** Born Aug 25, 1976, Galveston, TX; son of Renee Lee and Willie. **Educ:** Univ Houston, sociol, 1997. **Career:** NJ nets, 1998-99; Golden State Warriors, 1999-00; Continental Basketball Assn, Idaho; Boston Celtics, guard, 1999; Vancouver Grizzlies, 2000-01; Detroit Pistons, guard, 2001-02; Sacramento Kings, guard, 2002-03; Milwaukee Bucks, guard, 2003-04; Miami Heat, guard, 2004-05; Cleveland Cavaliers, point guard & shooting guard, 2006-08; Milwaukee Bucks, 2008-09; Free agent, Currently. **Orgs:** Contribr, Pistons' Fannie Mae Found partnership. **Honors/Awds:** Sixth Man of the Yr Award, Intl Basketball Assn, 1997-98; Newcomer of the Yr, 1999; All-League First Team hons, Continental Basketball Assn, 1999; IBA Sixth Man of the Year Award, 1997-98. *

JONES, DARYL L.
State government official, air force officer, president (organization). **Personal:** Born Aug 31, 1955. **Educ:** Baylor Univ, BS, MS; Air Force Acad, Colorado Springs, Colo, BS, 1977; Univ Miami Sch Law, Miami, FL, JD, 1987. **Career:** USAF, phantom pilot, 1977-84; 11th Circuit US Ct, Judge Peter T Fav, fed judicial clerk, 1987-88; PR Nat Guard, pilot, 1988-89; Dade County Atty's Off, aviation div, 1988-90; Fla House Rep, 1990-92; Fla Sen, sen, 1992-02; Dallas Baptist Univ, Bus Sch, adj prof, 1997-02; St Edwards Univ, Grad Sch Mgt, adj prof, 2004-; Dept Air Force, secy designate; Air War Col, Air Univ, mobilization asst; pvt pract atty; Maxwell AFB, col, currently; Tex Instruments, prog mgr, bus develop mgr; D L Jones & Assocs Inc, pres, currently. **Orgs:** Orange Bowl Comt; bd govs, Fla Chamber Com; exec comt, Leadership Fla Bd Regents; adv bd, Dade Community, AvMed Miami; presidential appointee, bd visitors, USAF Acad, 1995-02; Gov Select Task Force Election Procedures Stand & Technol, 2000-01; bd dirs, Am Bankers Ins Group, 1995-99; Gov Comn Sustainable S Fla, 1995-97; Proj Mgt Inst; adv bd, Martin Luther King Jr Inst Nonviolence, 1994-00; pres, Nat Stud Bar Asn, Univ Miami. **Honors/Awds:** Iron Arrow Award, Univ Miami. **Special Achievements:** First African American civilian secretary of US Air Force. **Military Serv:** USAF, F-4, phantom pilot, 1977-84; PR Air Nat Guard, A-7D corsair II pilot, 1988-89; USAF Reserves, 1989-91; Maxwell AFB, col, currently. **Business Phone:** (512)914-5063.*

JONES, DAVID L
Executive, vice president (organization). **Personal:** Born Dec 30, 1950, Charles City, VA; son of Joseph H Sr and Vernell Jones; married Pauline R, Aug 20, 1983; children: Eric Anthony & Christopher David. **Educ:** Williams Col, BA, 1974; Univ NC Sch Bus, 1985; Kellogg Sch Bus, Northwestern Univ, 1987, 1996; Duke Univ, Fugua Sch Bus, 1998. **Career:** GMAC, credit mgr, 1983-85, sales mgr, 1985, asst control branch mgr, 1985-87, bus develop mgr, 1987-88, control br mgr, 1988-90, asst mgr-plans, 1991-93, vp-plans, 1993-; vpres consumer credit, currently. **Orgs:** Adv bd, Credit Res Ctr, Purdue Univ, 1993-; adv bd, Highland Park Comn, High Sch, 1994-; diversity comt, Farmington Pub Schs, 1996; bd mem, Junior Achievement of SE Mich, 1996. **Honors/Awds:** Outstanding Role Model, Concerned Black Men Asn, 1994. **Home Addr:** 29764 Harrow Dr, Farmington Hills, MI 48331. **Business Addr:** Vice President of Consumer Credit, General Motors Acceptance Corp, 3044 W Grand Blvd, Detroit, MI 48202, **Business Phone:** (313)556-0709.

JONES, DAVID R.
Executive, lawyer. **Personal:** Born Apr 30, 1948, Brooklyn, NY; son of Thomas R; married Dr Valerie King; children: Russell, Vanessa. **Educ:** Wesleyan Univ, BA, 1970, MA, 1982; Yale Law Sch, JD, 1974. **Career:** US Senator Robert Kennedy, senate intern, 1967; Fed Dist Judge Constance Baker Motley, law clerk, 1974-75; Cravath Swaine & Moore, litigation assoc, 1975-79; NY City Mayor Koch, spec adv, 1979-83; NY City Youth Bur, exec dir, 1983-86; Wesleyan Univ, trustee, 1984-96, trustee emeritus, 1996-; Community Serv Soc NY, pres & chief exec officer, 1986-; NY Hist Soc, trustee, 1994; Wildlife Conserv Soc, bd trustees. **Orgs:** Thomas J Watson fel, Thomas J Watson Found, 1970; pres, Black Agency Execs New York, 1988-94; bd mem, Carver Fed Savings & Loan Asn, 1989-95; vice chair, Primary Health Care Develop Corp, 1993-95; bd mem, NY City Health & Hosp Corp, 1993-98; bd mem, Capital & Phys Develop Comt, Upper Manhattan Empowerment Zone, 1996-00; vice chmn adv bd, New York City Independent Budget Off; vice chair, Nat Comn Responsive Philanthropy, 1998; bd mem, Prospect Pk Alliance; adv bed meme, New York State Senate Medicaid Reform Task Force; adv bd mem, Sch Pub Affairs, Baruch Col; bd mem, New York Found, 1998-03. **Honors/Awds:** City Univ New York, DHL, 1999. **Business Addr:** President, Chief Executive Officer, Community Service Society of New York, 105 E 22nd St, New York, NY 10010, **Business Phone:** (212)254-8900.*

JONES, DEACON. **See JONES, GROVER WILLIAM, JR.**

JONES, DELISHA MILTON
Basketball player. **Personal:** Born Sep 11, 1974, Riceboro, GA; daughter of Beverly Milton. **Educ:** Univ Fla, attended 1997. **Career:** Portland Power, 1998; LA Sparks, ctr, beginning 1999; Lavezzini Basket Parma, coach, 2001-02; UMMC Ekaterinburg, coach, 2002-04; Gambrinus Brno, coach, 2005-06; Ros Casares Valencia, coach, 2006-; Wash mystics, forward, 2005-07; Los Angeles Sparks, 2008-. **Honors/Awds:** U.S. Olympic Festival, 1994; SEC Player of the Week, 1995, 1996, 1997; All-SEC first team, 1996, 1997; University of Florida, President's Recognition Award, 1997; Wade Trophy recipient as top senior in the country, 1997; NCAA Mideast Regional, Most Outstanding Player, 1997; Wade Trophy, 1997; Southeastern Conference Player of the Year, 1997; Second player of the Year, 1997; World University games, 1997; Most Outstanding Player, NCAA Mideast Regional, 1998; FIBA World Championship, 1998; Olympic Cup gold medal, 1998, 1999, 2000; named to WNBA All-Star team, 2000; Opals World Challenge, 2002; FIBA World Championship, 2002; Euro league Championship, 2003; Euro league, 2005, 2006; Olympic Games, gold medal, 2008. **Special Achievements:** American Basketball League Draft, #2 pick, 1997; WNBA Draft, #4 pick, 1999; second woman to coach a men's professional basketball team. **Business Addr:** Professional Basketball Player, Los Angeles Sparks, 888 S Figueroa St Suite 2010, Los Angeles, CA 90017, **Business Phone:** (213)929-1300.*

JONES, DELORES
Administrator. **Personal:** Born Apr 4, 1954, Chicago, IL; daughter of Josephine Walls and Rufus Charles. **Educ:** Kent State Univ, Kent, OH, BA, jour & pub rels, 1976; Ohio State Univ, MA, jour & pub rels, 1980; Boston Col, Cert, corporate community rel, 2001. **Career:** Burns Pub Rels, Cleveland, OH, communications specialist, 1976; Tribue Chronicle, Warren, OH, asst ed & reporter, 1976-79; Ohio Edison Co, Akron, OH, sr info rep, 1980-97; Kent State Univ Sch Jour, part-time instr, 1989; First Energy Corp, Community Initiatives, dir, 1997-. **Orgs:** Pub Rels Soc Am, Akron Area Chap, 1981-; bd dirs, Pub Rels Soc Am, 1983-89; Nat Sci Teachers Asn, 1983-; secy, Pub Rels Soc Am, 1987; pres, Pub Rels Soc Am, 1988; Corporate Vol Coun, Vol Ctr Summit County, 1987-; Ohio Crime Prevention Asn, 1989-; Summit County Victim Assistance Prog, bd trustees, 1990-2004; secy, Summit County

Victim Assistance Prog 1991; chairperson pub rels comt, Summit County Victim Assistance Prog, 1993-2004; Kent State Univ Sch Jour & Mass Communications, pub rels sequence adv & sem judge 2003-; ed, Around the House Newsletter, The House the Lord, 2002-; Akron Civic Theatre, Muticultural Prog Coun, 2002-; co-chair, Summit County Social Servs Adv Bd, Finance Forum, 2005-. **Honors/Awds:** Leadership Ohio Class V, 1998; Governor's Award for Excellence in Energy, 2005. **Special Achievements:** Coord, Academic Challenge, a high school quiz program on WEWS-TV5; first African American reporter and assistant editor with The Tribune Chronicle, Warren, Ohio; first African American pres of the Public Relations Society of Amer, Akron Chapter; Expanded FirstEnergy's Harvest for Hunger Food Drive across three states, which was recognized by Second Harvest Foodbank for raising more than 4 million pounds of food since 2000; chair, AkronReads Business Partnership with Akron Public Schools, which helped raise student reading scores and is recognized by Gov. Taft as a model for Ohio, 1999-; established FirstEnergy's partnership with Habitat for Humanity, providing nearly $10 million since 2002 to build more than 150 energy efficient homes. **Business Addr:** Community Initiatives Director, FirstEnergy Corporation, 76 S Main St, Akron, OH 44308, **Business Phone:** (330)384-5022.

JONES, DR. DENEESE LAKAY
School administrator, educator. **Personal:** Born Aug 9, 1952, Dallas, VA; daughter of Ben and Theresa Robinson; married Stephen Clyde, Mar 2, 1974; children: Stephanie Roberts & Monica Martin. **Educ:** Tex Woman's Univ, BS, 1974; Tex A&M Univ, MEd, 1988; PhD, 1991. **Career:** Univ KY, asst prof, 1991-97; Study Acad Achievement Learning Environs Ctr, co-founder & dir, 1994-; Univ Ky, assoc prof, 1997-, assoc dean,1998-2002, Am Coun Educ fel, 2002-03, President's Comn Diversity, chair, 2002-05; Longwood Univ, Col Educ & Human Services, prof & dean, 2005-. **Orgs:** Am Educ Res Asn, program chair, The Renaissance Group, Col Reading Asn, 1989-; Int Reading Asn, 1989-; spec study group chair multicultural edu, Am Asn Cols Teacher Educrs, 1992-, chair comt multicultural educ, 2001-03; Am Educ Res Asn, 1992-; Nat Reading Conf, 1992-; Nat Asn Multicultural Educ, 1993-. **Honors/Awds:** LU Chi Award 2008, LU Citizen Leader Award 2008, LU Athletic Training Appreciation Award 2008, President's Award, Asn Teacher Educrs, 1998, 2000; Most Notable Alumna,Tex A&M Univ, 1999; Mildred M Bailey Award Outstanding Faculty, Phi Beta Sigma, 2000; Exceptional Achievement Award Teaching & Advising, Univ Ky, Col Educ, 2000; Literacy Research Award, 2002; Torch of Excellence Award, 2003; Teacher Who Made A Difference, 2003, Notable Alumni for TAMU, 1998; Outstanding Alumni, College of Education, TAMU 2006. **Special Achievements:** Publications: "An Exploration of Prospective Teachers' Literacy Instructional Practices: Expectations vs Actual Usage," in Balanced Reading Instruction; Reading Diagnosis and Remediation: Instructors Manual; "Meeting the Faith Challenge of Rearing Sons and Daughters," in Women to Women: Perspectives of Fifteen Afro-Amer Christian Women, 1996; Preparing Student Teachers for Pluralistic Classrooms, 1998; publications in Black Issues in Higher Education, 2003; invited speaker at Int Learning Conf, London, England, 2003. **Business Addr:** Professor & Dean, Longwood University, College of Education & Human Services, Hull Bldg, Hull Education Center, 201 High Street Suite 137, Farmville, VA 23901, **Business Phone:** (434)395-2051.

JONES, DONALD W.
Educator. **Personal:** Born Dec 7, 1939, Trenton, NC; married Betty Jean Tolbert; children: Tracey La Verne. **Educ:** Hampton Inst Va, BS, bus mgt, 1962; Fair field Univ Conn, MA, Corp &Political Commun, 1969; Ohio Univ, PhD, 1973. **Career:** Educator (retired); NY City Dept Labor, labor mgt prac adj, 1965-66; Urban League Westchester Co Inc, assoc dir in charge econ develop & employ, training adv, field rep, 1966; Norwalk Job Orientation Prog, instr, 1967-68; New Haven Redevel Agency, housing develop officer, 1968-70; UnivVa, Charlottesville, asst prof, Minority Affairs, asst pres, prof, Off Minority Procurement Prog, dir, Darden Minority Bus Exec Prog, founder,1998. **Orgs:** Chmn, Time & Pl Comn; Middle Atlantic Reg; Nat Hampton Alumni Asn; Panel Disc Nat Hampton Alumni Asn; part Invit, Sem Deseg Pub Higher Educ; vpres, pres, Nat Black Caucus; Speech Commun Asn; Int Commun Asn; S Asn Black Admin Personal; Am Asn High Educ; Nat Educ Asn US; Int Platform Asn; LibComn Ohio Univ, 1971-72; exec sec, Inst Self-Study Proj Univ Va; Community Col Admin Comn Univ Va; Afro-Am Std Com Univ Va; exec secy, Presidential Admin Comn Comm Col Univ Va, 1972-74, chmn, 1974; Presidential Admin Comn Educ & Employ Opportunity; Oblig & Rights Univ Va, 1975; past pres, NC 4-H Clubs; NY Hampton Alumni Club; pres, Interfrat Coun Unit Negro Col Fund,1973; chmn, Plan Comn Univ Va Comn Col Artic Conf; Va Community Col Conf Univ Va, 1974; Nat Hampton Alumni Asn, Mid Atlantic Prog. **Honors/Awds:** Outstanding Service in University Area for Human Relations, Black Stud Univ Va, 1976; Queen Elizabeth of England Medal, Charlottesville Albermarle Bicent Community, 1976; United Negro Col Fund Vol Leadership Award, United Negro Col Fund, 1977; Thomas Jefferson Area United Way Award, 1977. **Special Achievements:** First Director of the OMPP.

JONES, DONELL
Songwriter, television producer, singer. **Personal:** Born May 23, 1973, Chicago, IL; son of Bobby Jones; children: Four Daughters. **Career:** Singer, currently; Vocal arrangements for Madonnas Bedtime Stories, 1994; Albums : My Heart, 1996; Where I Want to Be, 1999; Scary Movie 2, 2001; Life Goes On, 2002; Journey Of A Gemini, 2006; Best of Donell Jones, 2007. **Orgs:** Kappa Alpha Psi Fraternity Inc. **Honors/Awds:** Am Music Awarrd, Best Soul & R&B New Entertainer, 2001. **Business Addr:** Artist, LaFace Rec, 6 W 57th St, New York, NY 10026.

JONES, DONNA L. (DONNA ROSS-JONES)
Music publisher. **Personal:** Born Apr 18, 1959, Detroit, MI; daughter of Fred Ross and Carol; married David, Sep 16, 1990; children: Evyn & Nicholas. **Educ:** USC, Entrepreneur Prog, 1994. **Career:** Int Serv, owner, 1980-82; Creative Entertainment, vpres, 1982-88; Transition Music, owner, founder & pres, currently. **Orgs:** Nat Acad Recording Arts & Sci, 1982-; NMPA, 1982; Asn Independent Music Publ, 1996; Bd Mem, North Los Angeles County Regional Cr. **Honors/Awds:** Entrepreneur of the Year, EMBOL-LA, 1996; Certificate of Achievement; TEmerging Entrepreneur Award; Emmy Award. **Special Achievements:** One of the Top 50 Most Powerful Women, Hollywood Reporter, 1996, recognized by Black Enterprise as One of 17 Top Rising Stars in Entertainment, 1996, USC Business Enterprise Network. **Business Addr:** President, Founder, Transition Music Corp, 11288 Ventura Blvd 709, Studio City, CA 91604, **Business Phone:** (323)860-7074.

JONES, DONTAE' ANTIJUAINE
Basketball player. **Personal:** Born Jun 2, 1975, Nashville, TN. **Educ:** NE Miss Community Col; Miss State Univ. **Career:** NY Knicks, forward, 1996-97; Boston Celtics, forward, 1997-98; ABA, forward; Greece League, forward; Turkey League, forward; Italian League, forward; Korean Basketball League, forward; free agent, currently.

JONES, DORINDA A. See Obituaries section.

JONES, DUANE L.
Executive. **Personal:** Born Mar 11, 1937, Duquesne, PA. **Educ:** Univ Pittsburgh, BS, 1959; Univ Oslo, Sorbonne Univ, Paris, adv study, 1963; NY Univ, MA, 1970. **Career:** Prince Edward Co Farmville VA, Eng dept, 1965; Harlem Prep, Eng dept, 1965-67; NY Univ, Opportunities Prog, Eng prog coordr, 1967-71; Black Theatre Alliance, exec dir, 1976-; Antioch Col, TV Film Negro Ensemble Co Nat Black Theatre, actor; Opera Ebony Richard Allen Ctr, stage dir, 1985; Caribe Magazine, guest editor. **Orgs:** New York City Mayor's Comn Culture, Art, 1979-81; Alpha Phi Alpha Actors Equity Negro Actors Guild; bd dirs, PRIDE on TV, 1980. **Honors/Awds:** Phyllis Wheatley Scholarship, Univ Pittsburgh, 1955; PA St Scholarship, Univ Pittsburgh, 1955-59; Phelps-Stokes Fellowship, Lectr Univ of Niamey Niger, 1975.

JONES, EDDIE CHARLES
Basketball player. **Personal:** Born Oct 20, 1971, Pompano Beach, FL; married Trina; children: Alexis, Chelsie & Noah. **Educ:** Temple Univ. **Career:** Los Angeles Lakers, forward-guard, 1994-99; Charlotte Hornets, 1999-2000; Miami Heat, 2001-04; Memphis Grizzlies, forward-guard, 2005-07; Miami Heat, 2007; Dallas Mavericks, guard, 2007-. **Orgs:** Founder, Eddie Jones Found. **Honors/Awds:** NBA All-Rookie First Team, 1995; Schick Rookie Game, NBA All-Star Weekend, MVP, 1995; NBA All-Star, 1997, 1998; Ranked 1st in the NBA in Steals Per Game, 1999-00. **Business Phone:** (214)747-6287.

JONES, DR. EDITH IRBY
Physician. **Personal:** Born Dec 23, 1927, Conway, AR; daughter of Robert and Mattie; married James Beauregard; children: Gary Ivan, Myra Jones Romain, Keith Irby. **Educ:** Knoxville Col, BS, mchem & biol & physics; Northwestern Univ, clinical psychol, 1948; Univ Ark Sch Med; W Va Col Med, postgrad, 1965; Cook Co Graduate School, postgrad, 1966; Methodist Hospital, postgrad, self assessment course, internal med, 1974; Baylor Col Med, cont ed, pract therapeutics, 1977; Univ Tex Med Review, fundamentals therapeutrics, 1977; Hermann Hosp, cardiopulmonary course, 1978; Am Heart Asn, adv cardiopul life support course, 1978. **Career:** Univ Hosp, intern, 1952-53; gen practice, Ark, 1953-59; Baylor Affiliated Hosps, res, 1959-62; pvt practice, TX, physician; Baylor Col, asst prof, clinical med; Univ Tex, asst prof, clinical med; Riverside Hosp Med Staff, exec comn, secy staff; Prospect Med Lab, dir; Houston Coun Alcoholism, adv bd; Comn Revising Justice Code Harris Co; Mercy Hosp Comp Health Care Group, secy, bd dir; Jones Coleman & Whitfield, partner; Universal Healthplan Inc, med dir; Jones Properties, co-owner, CEO. **Orgs:** Admin comn, Univ TeX Sch Med; pres, Nat Med Asn; Houston Am Revolution Bi centennial Comn; pres, Ark Med, Dental & Pharmaceutical Asn; chmn, Internal Med Comn, St Eliz Hosp; med adv, Selective Bd 60; bd dir & chmn, Comn Homemakers Serv Family Serv Ctr; chmn, first pres, Delta Res & Educ Found; bd dir, Houston Coun Human Rels; Comn Hypertension, chmn, Scientific Coun, bd dir, Nat Med Asn; bd, Third Bank Control Grp; Tex Health Asn; comn Drug Abuse, Houston ISD; adv med bd, Visiting Nurses Asn; bd dir, Sudan Corp; bd dir, Afro Am BookDistributors; med adv bd, Planned Parenthood Houston; chmn, SW Volunteers Delta one Am; Questions & Answers Health Care, KCOH Monthly Radio; Knoxville Col, bd trustees, past chmn; The Links Inc; Delta Sigma Theta; pres, Gamma Mu chp; Drug Use Bd, Mutual Asn Prof Serv; Minority Health Resource Ctr; Resource Person Network Off; chmn, HELP Inc; Am Task Force Health Haiti. **Honors/Awds:** Golden Anniversary Award, Zeta Phi Beta, 1970; Distinguished Service Award, Houston Sect Nat Coun Negro Women, 1972; service to promote the efficient administration of justice, Am Judicature Soc, 1973; Woman of Year, Kato Models, 1974; Lois Allen Humanitarian Award, 1975; cert recognition, contribution field med, Antioch Baptist Ch, 1975;life mem, Nat Coun Negro Women; Houston League of Business & Professional Women Achievement Award, 1977; citation for volunteer service, Eta Phi Beta, 1978; Edith Irby Jones Day, State Arkansas, 1979; President's Distinguished Service Award, Knoxville Col Nat Alumni Asn, 1979; Exemplary Serv & Support Prof Educ, 1979; Nat Black Col Alumni Hall of Fame, 1985; Internist of the Year, Am Soc Internal Med, 1988; Recognition for Leadership Support, 1992; Special Award, Asn Black Cardiologists, 1994; Cert Appreciation, City Houston, 1995; Outstanding Accomplishment & Performance, Stud Nat Med Asn, 1995; Award for Promotion Improved Econ, Houston Urban League, 1995; Award for Great Contribution Field Med Area Gerontology, Am Gerontology Soc, 1996; Special Recognition for Promotion of Positive Lifestyles, Houston Parks, 1996; Award for Outstanding Accomplishments, Delta Sigma Theta, 1998; Eagle Award, 1999; Awd for Contribution to Health of Haiti, UNCF, 2000; mem of the year, Asn Black Cardiologists, 2000. **Special Achievements:** First African American admitted to Univ of AR School of Med; numerous publ; first woman to be elected president of the National Medical Association. **Business Addr:** Physician, Internal Medicine, 2601 Prospect St, Houston, TX 77004, **Business Phone:** (713)529-3145.*

JONES, DR. EDWARD (LARRY JONES)
Optometrist. **Personal:** Born Aug 12, 1957, Seattle, WA; son of Edward Louis and Dorothy M Bond; married Maxine S, Jul 4, 1988. **Educ:** Univ WA, BA, 1981; Pac Univ, doctorate, BS, 1985. **Career:** Eyes Rite Optical, 1986-2008, 1989-96; JC Penney Optical, 1992-96; Vista Optical, 1985-2000; Dr Edward Lawrence Jones & Asn Inc, optometrist, currently. **Orgs:** Hon co-chair, PI Omicron Sigma, 1978; bd mem, Nat Optom Asn, 1981-2000, 1995-98. **Special Achievements:** Dyslexia is Complexia, 1986-87.

JONES, EDWARD LEE
Football player, boxer, actor. **Personal:** Born Feb 23, 1951, Jackson, TN. **Educ:** Tenn State Univ, BS, health & phys educ. **Career:** Football player, Boxer (retired), Actor; Dallas Cowboys, defensive lineman, 1974-78, 1980-89; Professional Boxer, 1979; Imperial Investors, partner; Films: Semi-Tough, actor, 1977; The Double McGuffin, actor, 1979; Necessary Roughness, actor, 1991; TV series: "Different Strokes", guest appearance. **Orgs:** Omega Psi Phi fraternity. **Honors/Awds:** Pro Bowl, 1981-83; MVP 1982; All Pro 1981 NEA, 1982.

JONES, DR. EDWARD LOUIS
Writer, historian, educator. **Personal:** Born Jan 15, 1922, Georgetown, TX; son of Henry H and Elizabeth Steen; married Lynne Ann McGreevy, Oct 7, 1964; children: Christopher & Teresa; married Dorothy M Showers, Mar 1, 1952 (divorced 1963); children: Cynthia, Frances & Edward Lawrence. **Educ:** Univ Wash, BA, philos, 1952, BA, speech, 1955, BA, far eastern; Univ Gonzaga, JD, 1967. **Career:** Educator (retired). Hollywood Players Theatre, prod, dir, 1956-58; Roycroft Leg Theatre, prod, dir, 1958-59; Wash St Dept Pub Asst, socworker, 1958; Seattle Water Dept, cost acct clerk, 1960-61; St Wash, atty gen off, 1963-66; Seattle Opport Indust Ctr, supvr, 1966-68; Univ Wash, asst dean, adv, lectr, 1968-87. **Orgs:** Consult, St Atty Gen Adv Comn Crime, St Supvr Coun; vpres, Wash Comn Consumer Interests, Nat Coun Crime & Delinq; bd mem, Nat Acad Adv & Asn; ed, Nat Acad Adv Asn J; Nat Asn Stud Personnel Admin, Am Acad Polit & Soc Sci; Smithsonian Asn; hist adv, Anheuser Busch. **Honors/Awds:** Moot Ct Contest, First Place, 1953. **Special Achievements:** Author: Profiles in African Heritage, Black Zeus, 1972; Tutankhamon, King of Upper & Lower Egypt, 1978; Orator's Workbook, 1982; The Black Diaspora: Colonization of Colored People, 1989; co-auth, Money Exchange Flashcards, Currency Converters, 1976; From Rulers of the World to Slavery, 1990; Pres Zachary Taylor & Senator Hamlin: Union or Death, 1991; Why Colored Am Needan Abraham Lincoln, 1992; Forty Acres & a Mule: The Rape of Colored Am, 1995; Mister Moonman, 2001. **Military Serv:** AUS, second Lt, 1940-46. *

JONES, ELAINE R
Association executive, lawyer. **Personal:** Born Mar 2, 1944, Norfolk, VA. **Educ:** Howard Univ, AB, 1965; Univ Va, LLB, 1970. **Career:** NAACP Legal Defense & Educ Fund, pres, dir-coun, 2004, pres & dir-coun emer, 2004-. **Orgs:** Nat Bar Asn; Old Dominion Bar Asn; Va Trial Lawyers Asn; Int Fedn Women

Lawyers. **Honors/Awds:** Panel arbitration Am Stock Exchange; Delta Sigma Theta Sor; Recognition Award, Black Am Law Students' Asn Outstanding Legal Serv Comm 1974; Specical Achievement Award, Nat Asn Black Women Attys, 1975; Sara Lee Frontrunner Award, 1998; Joseph E. Lowery Lamplighter Awardee, 2003; Holds nine honorary degrees & the highest honor awarded Univ Va. **Special Achievements:** First AFA female law student at the Univ of Virginia's law school. Received the recognition of many organizations, including the Sara Lee Foundation, National Newspaper Publishers Association, Southern Christian Leadership Conference, Olender Foundation, National Association of Black Women Attorneys, and others. **Business Phone:** (212)965-2200.*

JONES, DR. ELNETTA GRIFFIN
Educator. **Personal:** Born Jul 7, 1934, Mullins, SC; married Aaron Mullins; children: Aaron Daryl. **Educ:** SC State Col, BS, 1957; Shippensburg State Col, ME, 1972; Am Univ, DEd, 1979. **Career:** Educator (Retired); Rosenwald High Sch, teacher, 1957-59; AUS & Air Force,Educ Develop Ctr, Wiesbaden, Germany, staff, 1960-63; AUS Infantry Ctr, Ft Benning, GA, teacher, 1964-66; AUS Infantry Ctr, Ft Benning, GA, teacher,1969-70; Shippensburg Univ, Act 101 Prog, from asst dir to dir, 1972-786, acad affairs, asst vpres, 1979-80, spec acad progs, assoc dean, 1980-82,dean spec acad progs, 1982-99. **Orgs:** Penn Asn Develop Educrs; Penn Black Conf Higher Educ; Phi Delta Kappa; Nat Acad Adv Asn; Nat Polit Cong Black Women; The Shippensburg Civic Club; Delta Sigma Theta Inc; Nat Asn Develop Educrs; coun trustee, Shippensburg Univ Pa, 2008. **Honors/Awds:** Outstanding Humanist Award, Shippensburg Univ Black Alumni, 1985. **Special Achievements:** Five publications including contributor to "Research in Higher Education", 1983, The Amer University Press Washington, DC.

JONES, ELVIN R.
Educator. **Personal:** Born Oct 7, 1945, Mobile, AL; son of Johnny M Jones; married Sondra, Nov 19, 1966; children: Beverly. **Educ:** BA, 1966; MEd, admin, 1972. **Career:** Cleveland Pub Sch, teacher, 1966-72; E Cleveland City Schs, teacher, 1972-74, home sch liaison, 1975-77, prin, 1977-96; dir, pupil serv,1996-99, supt, 1999. **Orgs:** Nat Asn Elem Sch Principals; Nat Asn Black Sch Educators; Kappa Alpha Psi;Phi Delta Kappa Prof Educ Asn; life mem, NAACP; Inter City Yacht Club; St Andrews Episcopal Church. **Honors/Awds:** Outstanding Contributor to United Negro Col Fund, UNCF, 1978, 1983;Alumnus of the Yr, St Augustine Col, 1984; Educator of the Yr, Alpha Kappa Alpha, 2000. **Military Serv:** AUS, capt, 1969-71. **Home Addr:** 19436 Scottsdale Blvd, Shaker Heights, OH 44122. **Business Addr:** Superintendent, East Cleveland City Schools, 15305 Euclid Ave, East Cleveland, OH 44112, **Business Phone:** (216)268-6580.

JONES, SEN. EMANUEL DAVIE
Automotive executive, senator (u.s. federal government). **Personal:** Born Apr 1, 1959, Atlanta, GA; son of Leroy and Ethlyn; married Gloria, Apr 6, 1990; children: Emanuel II, Elam D & Emani. **Educ:** Univ Pa, BSEE, 1981; Columbia Univ, MBA, 1986. **Career:** Int Bus Mach Corp, prod engr, 1981-84; Arthur Anderson, consult, 1986-88;Ford Motor Co, dealer cand, 1988-92; Legacy Ford Mcdonough, founder, 1992; Legacy Toyota Union City, founder, 1998; Legendary Ford-Mercury Marion, 1998; Ansa Automotive, founder, 2002; Interstate Cooperation Comt, sec, currently; Ga State Senate, Dist 10, senator, 2004-. **Orgs:** Leadership Henry, 1993-; dir, Henry County Chamber Com, 1994-96; dir, Henry County Rotary Club, 1994; dir, Henry County High Sch Scholar Found,1994-; United Way Henry County, Adv Bd, 1995-; Ga Dept Labor, Adv Bd, 1994-; chmn & stewardship ministry, Shiloh Baptist Church, 1994-95. **Honors/Awds:** Businessman of the Year, Henry County High Sch, 1993; Businessman of the Year, Henry County Police Dept, 1993; Distinguished Service Award, Shiloh Baptist Church, 1994; Top Profit Dealer, Ford Motor Co, 1994; Atlanta Regional Entrepreneur of the Year, US Dept Com, 1996; Atlanta Minority Service Firm of the Year; Businessman of the Year, Alonzo Crim High Sch,1996. **Military Serv:** AUS, Corps Engrs, capt, 1980-; Distinguished Service Award, Army Serv Ribbon. **Business Addr:** Senator, The Georgia State Senate, District 10, 302B Coverdell Off Bldg, Atlanta, GA 30334, **Business Phone:** (404)656-0502.

JONES, EMIL
State government official, senator (u.s. federal government). **Personal:** Born Oct 18, 1935, Chicago, IL; son of Emil Jones Sr and Marilla Mims; married Lorrie Stone, Nov 19, 2005; children: Debra Ann, Renee L, John M & Emil III. **Educ:** Loop Jr Col, AA; Roosevelt Univ, bus admin, 1955; Chicago State Univ, DHL. **Career:** Lic sanit engr; Dem Orgn 21st Ward Regular, precinct capt, 1962-70; Southern Dist Water Filtration Plant, mem exec bd orgn & chlorine engr, 1964-67; Chicago City Coun, sec to alderman, 1967-73; Dem Orgn 34th Ward Regular, precinct capt, 1971, exec secy, 1971, pub rels, 1972; Ill House Reps, state rep, 1973-83; Ill State Senate, 14th Dist, state sen & pres, 1983-. **Orgs:** Morgan Pk Civic League; Nat Conf State Legis; Nat Black Caucus State Legis; bd dir, Forum Sen Pres; bd dir, State Legis Leaders Found. **Honors/Awds:** Friend of Education Award, Ill State Bd Educ; Illinois Delta Kappa Appreciation; Leadership Award, Coalition to Save Chicago Schs; Civil Rights Award, Ill Dept Human Rights; Award for Assisting Disadvantaged Youth, Chicago Urban League; Hall of Fame, Tilden Tech Inst, 2004; Paul Simon Public Service Award, Ill Hunger Coalition, 2004; Man of the Year Award, Best Buddies, 2005; Let Talent Shine Award, Col Summit, 2005; John R. Hammell Award, Chicago Chap ACLU, 2005; Dave Peteron Award, Chicago Teacher Union, 2006; Lifeline Award, Community Mental Health Coun, 2006; One of 100 Most Influential Black Americans, Ebony Mag, 2006; numerous other awards and honors. **Business Addr:** State Senator, President, Illinois General Assembly, Senator 14th District, 327 Capitol Bldg, Springfield, IL 62706, **Business Phone:** (217)782-2728.

JONES, EMMA PETTWAY
Educator, legal consultant. **Personal:** Born Jul 29, 1945, Boykin, AL; daughter of Allie and John B; married J (divorced); children: James, John, Tracy & Malik. **Educ:** Albertus Magnus Col, 1978-80; NH Col, Manchester, BS, 1981, MBA, 1985; City Univ New York, Law Sch Queens, JD, 1988. **Career:** New Haven Fed Credit Union, organizer & mgr, 1979-81; EMA Assoc, pres, 1980-86; Jones Turner & Wright, legal asst, 1986-87; Williams & Wise, legal intern, 1987; Yale Univ, Provost Dept, researcher; Malik Orgn, New Haven, founder, currently; independent consult. **Orgs:** Exec dir, People Actg Change New Haven, CT; consult & trainer, Legal Assistance New Haven, CT; Pub Housing Prog Tenant Rep Coun; NH Col, Orgn Develop Inst; Cheyney State Col, Fair Haven Mediation Prog; exec dir, Conn Afro-Am Hist Soc; chairperson, Nat Econ Develop & Law Ctr; vice pres, YWCA, New Haven. **Honors/Awds:** Received numerous Certificates of Excellence & Outstanding Service Awards. **Home Addr:** 286 James St, New Haven, CT 06513, **Home Phone:** (203)624-5760. **Business Addr:** Founder, Malik Organization, 286 James St Suite 284, New Haven, CT 06513, **Business Phone:** (203)752-1214.

JONES, ENOCH
Clergy. **Personal:** Born Aug 19, 1922, Biloxi, MS; children: Stephen, Enoch Lee, Janet. **Educ:** Am Bapt Sem, BTh, 1954; Fisk Univ, BA, 1956, MA, 1957; Scarrit Col, additional study; Houston Tillotson Col, hon doctorate degree. **Career:** Friendship Bapt Church, pastor, 1952-61; ABT Sem, teacher & dean chapel, 3 yrs; 15th Ave Baptist Church, pastor, 30 yrs, pastor emer, currently. **Orgs:** Nat Bapt Convention USA Inc, 1956; TN BM&E Conv; trustee, ABT Sem; minister prisoners at state prison; conducts joint worship serv with Woodmont Bapt Church & White Church; viewed yearly by 50,000 on TV; Beta Epsilon Hon Soc. **Honors/Awds:** Winner of Outstanding Sermon of Year Award, Nat Bapt Convention Inc; named for Leadership Nashville, 1977-78; hon dep sheriff, Davidson County, 1977; invited to Washington to partcipate in Inauguration of Pres Carter; judge, Best Sermon of the Year, Nat Bapt Pulpit of Natl Bapt Conv Inc; guest preacher, John B Falconer Lect & Monrovia Liberia, 1978; col aide de camp, Gov Staff, 1978; hon sgt-at-arms, TN St House of Reps; hon del, US House of Rep 1980; recipient of three battle stars for serv in Italy 92nd Inf Div 3yrs. **Business Addr:** Pastor Emeritus, Fifteenth Avenue Baptist Church, 1215 9th Ave N, Nashville, TN 37208.

JONES, ERNEST, SR. See Obituaries section.

JONES, ESQ. ERNEST EDWARD
Lawyer, association executive, chief executive officer. **Personal:** Born Nov 21, 1944, Savannah, GA; son of Orlando and Luella Williams; married Denise Rae Scott, Feb 14, 1981; children: Jamal Jones & Kahlil Jones. **Educ:** Dickinson Col, Carlisle, PA, AB, econs, 1966; Temple Univ Sch Law, Philadelphia, PA, JD, 1972. **Career:** Dist Atty's Off, Philadelphia, PA, asst dist atty, 1972-74; Temple Univ Sch Law, Philadelphia, PA, gen coun, 1974-77; Community Legal Serv, Philadelphia, PA, dep dir, 1977-79, exec dir, 1979-83; Greater Philadelphia Urban Affairs Coalition, exec dir, 1983-98; Philadelphia Workforce Develop Corp, pres & chief exec officer, 1998-. **Orgs:** Corp dir, First Union Corp, 1987-; Nat Bar Asn, 1988; chair, Philadelphia Housing Authority, 1991-92; Devereux Found, 1993-; Philadelphia Bar Asn; chair, Black Alliance Educ Options. **Military Serv:** AUS, Korea, co comdr, 1967-69. **Business Addr:** President, Cheif Executive Officer, Philadelphia Workforce Development Corporation, 1617 John F Kennedy Blvd 13th Fl, Philadelphia, PA 19103-1813, **Business Phone:** (215)963-2117.

JONES, ERNEST LEE
Football player. **Personal:** Born Apr 1, 1971, Utica, NY; married Maria; children: Andrea & Deja. **Educ:** Ore Univ. **Career:** Football Player (Retired); New Orleans Saints, defensive end, 1995; Denver Broncos, 1996-98; Carolina Panthers, 1998-99.

JONES, ERVIN EDWARD
Physician. **Personal:** Born Oct 4, 1938, Lake City, SC; married Pauline; children: Vincent, Yvette, Michael. **Educ:** Franklin Sch Sci & Arts, attended 1959; Montgomery County Community Col; Morris Col, attended 1957. **Career:** Philadelphia Col Osteop Med, med tech, 1973; Norristown, PA, coun bd, 1974. **Orgs:** Chmn, Opportunity Coun, 1968-69; past mem, Norristown Adv Comn, 1968-70; past mem, Norristown Jaycees, 1970-72; chmn, Pub Safety Pa Police & Dept, 1974-; chmn negot comm Boro, 1976-77; chmn, Norristown House Comn, 1977; Mt Zion American Methodist Church. **Honors/Awds:** Won state supreme ct dec subpoena power of Boro Coun 1976; hon mem young Dem of Montg Cnty 1976. **Special Achievements:** First black Chairman Public Safety Boro 1974; Second black elected council Boro, 1974. *

JONES, EVERETT LEROI. See BARAKA, IMAMU AMIRI.

JONES, DR. FERDINAND TAYLOR
Psychologist, educator. **Personal:** Born May 15, 1932, New York, NY; son of Ferdinand Taylor and Esther Lillian Harris Haggie; married Myra Jean Rogers, Nov 26, 1967; children: Joanne Esther Jones-Rizzi & Terrie Lynn. **Educ:** Drew Univ, AB, 1953; Univ Vienna, PhD, 1959. **Career:** Riverside Hosp, NY, staff psychologist, 1959-62; Westchester County Community Ment Health Bd, chief psychologist, 1962-67; Lincoln Hosp Ment Health Serv, NY, training consult, 1967-69; Sarah Lawrence Col, Bronxville, NY, psychol fac, 1968-72; Brown Univ, dir psychol serv, 1972-92, prof psychol & lectr psychiat human behav, 1972-97, prof emer psychol, 1997-, dir emer psychol serv, currently; Univ Dar es Salaam, visprof, 1993-94; Oberlin Col, vis prof, 1997-98; Univ Cape Town, vis prof, 1999; Sarah Lawrence Col, guest faculty member. **Orgs:** Pres, Westchester Cnty Psychol Assoc, 1967-69; bd dirs, Women & Infants Hosp, 1983-89; bd dir, Am Orthopsychiatric Assoc, 1984-87; scholar-in-residence, Schomburg Ctr Res Black Culture, 1987; pres, Am Orthopsychiatric Asn, 1989-90; ed, Intl Asn Jazz, 1997-; Am Psychological Asn; Assoc Black Psychologist; Am Assoc Univ Profs Soc Psych Study Social Issues. **Honors/Awds:** Distinguished Service Award West century Psychology Asns, 1972; Charles HNichols Award Brown University, Afro-American studies Dept, 1980; Alumni Achievement Award in Science, Drew University, 1988; Elizabeth H. LeDucAward for Teaching Excellence, Brown Univ, 1997. **Special Achievements:** Co-author of Triumph of the Soul: Cultural & Psychological Aspects of African American Music, 2001. **Military Serv:** USY sp3, 1953-56. **Home Phone:** (401)331-1039. **Business Addr:** Professor Emeritus of Psychology, Director Emeritus of Psychological, Brown Univerity, 89 Waterman St, PO Box 1853, Providence, RI 02912, **Business Phone:** (401)863-7586.

JONES, FLORESTA DELORIS
Educator, journalist. **Personal:** Born Dec 14, 1950, Hopewell, VA. **Educ:** Berry Col, BA, 1972; Mich State Univ, MA, 1975. **Career:** State J Lansing, MI, Detroit Free Press, staff writer intern, 1974; Richmond Afro-Am, staff writer, reporter, 1975-76; State Off Min Bus Enterprise, prog info office, ed spec, 1976-78; Va State Univ, adj fac, 1977-78; Georgian Court Col, dir & adj fac educ opport fund prog, 1978-82; Brookdale Community Col, writing team fac, 1982-. **Orgs:** NJ Educ Opport Fund Prof Asn; Am Asn Univ Women; Women Commun; Int Commun Asn; Nat Asn Advan Colored People; Soc Prof J; Asn Equality & Excellence Educ; Young Women's Christian Asn, Annual Womens Conf Comn; Goodwill Chorus Petersburg, VA. **Honors/Awds:** Scholarship Award; Nat Scholar Serv & Fund Negro Studies, 1969; Sigma Tau Delta English Honorary Fraternity, Berry Col, 1970-72; Alpha Chi Beta Georgia College Honour, Berry Col, 1971-72; Graduate Fellowships & Grad Assistantships, Mich State Univ, 1972-74. **Special Achievements:** Articles Publ in Detroit Free Press, Lansing State Jrnl, Richmond AFRO, US Info Agency & other newspapers. **Business Addr:** Writing Team Faculty, Brookdale Community College, Applied Humanities Inst, Lincroft, NJ 07738.

JONES, FRANCIS R
Association executive, restaurateur. **Career:** United Airlines, supvr stewardess servs, personnel adv; McDonald's, owner & operator, currently. **Orgs:** Pres, Nat Black McDonald's Operators Asn; bd mem, Ronald McDonald's C's Charities; bd mem, Austin Metrop Bus Resource Ctr; People Assisting Homeless. **Honors/Awds:** Economic Justice Award. **Special Achievements:** First African American woman to serve as president of the National Black McDonald's Operators Association.

JONES, FRANK
Mayor, police chief, security guard. **Personal:** Born Oct 25, 1950, Sellers, SC; son of John and Pearl Melton; married Sylvia G, Apr 1974; children: Dennis, Tyrone & Deon Jones. **Educ:** Marion-Mullins Voc, Agr Mechanics, 1967-70; State SC Law Enforcement, Basic Law Enforcement, 1974; Francis Marion Col, Sci & Law, 1976; Florence Darlington Tech, Jail Removal Initiative 1983. **Career:** Hargrove Groceries, Sellers, SC, clerk; Latta Police Dept, Latta, SC, policeman, 1971-73; Marion Police Dept, Marion, SC, lt policeman, 1973-87; SC Criminal Justice Acad, Columbia, SC, First Line Supvr, 1983-85, Traffic Radar Operator, 1987-88; Jones Groceries, Marion, SC, owner; Mcleod Hosp, Florence SC, security guard; Town Sellers SC, mayor & chief policeman. **Orgs:** Adv, Sellers Jr Policeman Dept. **Honors/Awds:** Outstanding Policeman of the Year, Marion Jaycees, 1977-88; Hazardous Material Training, Familiy Line System, 1981; Guest, Rel Prog, Mcleod Hosp, 1988; Law Enforcement Torch Run, SC Law Enforcement, 1989; Outstanding Community Worker, Baptist Educ & Missonary, 1989. **Military Serv:** Coordr Mil Police, pvt.

JONES, FRANK BENSON
Clergy, pilot. **Personal:** Born Aug 21, 1938, Kansas City, MO; son of Benson and Frankie Helen Boyd; married Mary S McClendon;

children: Eleanor, Angela, Gregory & Mia. **Educ:** California State Univ, Dominguez Hills, BA, 1995. **Career:** Jones Comput Syst, pres, 1983-; United Air Lines, pilot, 1966-86; Pentecostal Temple, pastor, 1992-. **Orgs:** Ed, Black Panther Newspaper, 1969; dir, Contra Costa County Emergency Food & Med Serv, 1972-73; pres, PPCP Fed Credit Union, 1971-72; ed, Richmond Crusader Newspaper, 1973-75; secy & treas Comm Developers Inc, 1973-76; ecumenical dir, Church of Acts, 1977-78; pastor Church of Acts, 1977-83. **Military Serv:** USAF, Capt 1957-66; Air Medal with 8 Clusters; Air Force Commendation Medal.

JONES, FREDDIE
Football player. **Personal:** Born Sep 16, 1974, Cheverly, MD. **Educ:** NC State Univ. **Career:** Football player (retired); San Diego Chargers, tight end, 1997-2001; Ariz Cardinals, tight end, 2002-04; Carolina Panthers, tight end, 2004-05. **Honors/Awds:** Rookie of the Year, Col & Pro Football Weekly, 1997.

JONES, FREDRICK E
Automotive executive. **Career:** Fred Jones Pontiac-GMC Truck Inc, Brookfield, ceo, 1984; IHOP Corp, owner, currently. **Orgs:** Chmn trustee bd, Canaan Baptist Church; lifetime mem, Nat Asn Advan Colored People officer, Wis Auto & Truck Dealers Asn. **Special Achievements:** First black men in Milwaukee to open a new car dealership. **Business Addr:** Owner, IHOP Corporation, 13000 Capital Dr, Brookfield, WI 53005-2438, **Business Phone:** (262)781-1300.

JONES, DR. G DANIEL
Clergy. **Personal:** Born in Norfolk, VA; son of George Raymond (deceased) and Estelle Campbell (deceased); married Geraldine S Saunders; children: Bryant Daniel. **Educ:** Va Union Univ, BS, 1962; Andover Newton Theol Sch, MDiv, 1966; Howard Univ's Divinity Sch, DMin, 1978. **Career:** Ministry St John Baptist Church Woburn, MA, pastor, 1965-67; Messiah Baptist Church Brockton, MA, pastor, 1967-73; Zion Baptist Church Portsmouth, VA, pastor, 1973-82; Norfolk State Univ, Norfolk, VA, undergrad instr, philos religion, 1973-82; Sch Theol, Va Union Univ, grad adj, 1979-82; Grace Baptist Church Germantown, Philadelphia, PA, sr pastor, 1982-. **Orgs:** Hampton Inst Minister's Conf, 1973; ministers coun, Am Bapt Churches S, 1974-76, vpres, 1981-82, pres, 1998-2002; bd mem, Lutheran Home Germantown, 1986-94; pres, Ministers Coun, Philadelphia Baptist Ass, 1987-90; Philadelphia Baptist Asn, 1996-98; adv bd chair, Urban Theol Inst, currently; gen bd, Am Baptist Churches, USA; exec comt bd, Lott Carey Baptist Foreign Mission Com; chair, The Centennial Comn. **Honors/Awds:** Human Relations Award, Omega Psi Phi Frat Inc Portsmouth, VA, 1979 & 1982; Citations from City of Portsmouth, Va & Sch Bd, 1980 & 1982; Key to City of Brockton, MA, 1983; First Place Sermon Contest, Am Baptist Churches, PA & DE, 1984; The Jubilee Service Award, Philadelphia Fisk Alumni Club, 1988; Man of the Year, Grace Baptist Church, Germantown, 1989; Citations from City of Philadelphia & House of Representatives, Commonwealth Penn, 1996. **Special Achievements:** Doctoral Thesis, "Educational Ministries in the Black Baptist Churches of Norfolk and Portsmouth Virginia". **Business Addr:** Senior Pastor, Grace Baptist Church of Germantown, 25 W Johnson St, Philadelphia, PA 19144, **Business Phone:** (215)438-3215.

JONES, GAIL HORNE. **See BUCKLEY, GAIL LUMET.**

JONES, GARY
Theatrical director. **Personal:** Born Jun 29, 1942, Chicago, IL; son of Leonard and Jessie Tolbert. **Educ:** Ill Inst Tech Inst Design, 1964. **Career:** Kungsholm Min Grand Opera Chicago, scenic designer & prin puppeteer, 1969-71; Blackstreet USA Puppet Theatre, dir, founder, 1975-; Int Heart Expo, Takamatsu, Japan, 2004; Apejay Schs, New Delhi, India, artist in residence, 2004. **Orgs:** UNIMA-USA Union InterNate de la Marionnette, Puppeteers Am; Los Angeles Arts Recovery Grant, 1992. **Honors/Awds:** Los Angeles Arts Recovery Grant, 1992; Disney KJLH Crystal Castle Award, Outstanding Achievement, 1997. **Special Achievements:** Designed exec prods Porgy & Bess, Carmen, The King & I, My Fair Lady, Gypsy, 1969-71; 5 week sold out engagement at the Smithsonian Inst Div of Performing Arts, 1980, 1982, 3 month tour of Iceland, W Ger, Holland, Portugal, 1984, his work has been written about in countless reviews and newspaper articles. **Business Addr:** Director, Blackstreet USA Puppet Theatre, 4619 W Washington Blvd, Los Angeles, CA 90016, **Business Phone:** (323)936-6091.

JONES, GARY DEWAYNE
Football player. **Personal:** Born Nov 30, 1967, San Augustine, TX; married Tina Haskins, 1992. **Educ:** Tex A&M Univ. **Career:** Pittsburgh Steelers, safety, 1990-91, 1993-94; New York Jets, safety, 1995-96.

JONES, GAYL
Writer, educator. **Personal:** Born Nov 23, 1949, Lexington, KY; daughter of Franklin and Lucille Wilson; married Bob (died 1998). **Educ:** Connecticut Col, BA, 1971; Brown Univ, MA, 1973, DA, 1975. **Career:** Univ Mich, Ann Arbor, MI, prof eng, 1975-83; writer, currently. Author: Chile Woman, 1974; BOP, Blacks on paper, 1975; Corregidora, 1975; Eva's Man, 1976; White Rat: Short Stories, 1977; Song for Anninho, 1981; The Hermit-Woman, 1983; Xarque & Other Poems, 1985; A Life Distilled: Gwendolyn Brooks, Her Poetry & Fiction, 1987; Presence Africaine: Revue Culturelle du Monde Noir/Cultural Review of the Negro World, 1987; The Graywolf Annual Seven: Stories From the American Mosaic, 1990; Black-Eyed Susans/Midnight Birds: Stories By & About Black Women, 1990; Callaloo: A Journal of African-American & African Arts & Letters, 1994; Liberating Voices: Oral Tradition in African American Literature, 1994; The Healing, 1998; Mosquito, 1999. **Orgs:** Fel Nat Endowment Arts; fel Mich Soc Fellows. **Honors/Awds:** Award, Howard Found, 1975; Fiction Award, Mademoiselle, 1975; National Endowment for the Arts grant, 1976; Henry Russell Award, Univ Mich, 1981. **Business Addr:** Writer, Beacon Press, 25 Beacon St, Boston, MA 02108, **Business Phone:** (617)742-2110.

JONES, GAYNELLE GRIFFIN
Government official, lawyer. **Personal:** Born Nov 20, 1948, Dallas, TX; daughter of Marvin C Griffin; married Robert Allen, Dec 26, 1986; children: 3. **Educ:** Emerson Col, BA, 1969; Boston Col Law Sch, JD, 1972. **Career:** Boston Legal Assistance Proj, atty, 1972-73; State Mutual Life Assurance Co, coun, 1973-75; Boston Edison Co, coun, 1975-79; Ouachita Parish Dist Atty's Off, asst dist atty, 1981-82; Jones, Jones, & Jones, partner,1979-82; Harris Co Dist Atty's Off, asst dist atty, 1982-89; Southern Dist Tex, asst US atty, 1989-92; First Ct Appeals, justice, 1992; Vinson & Elkins LLP, atty, 1993; Southern Dist Tex, US atty, 1993-98; Hewlett-Packard Co, Houston Off, assoc coun, litigation coun, dir stand bus conduct, currently; Univ Houston, Litigation Skills Prog, fac, Dir, Phoenix House Foundation, currently. **Orgs:** State Bar Tex, grievance comn, continuing legal educ, lectr; Nat Col Dist Attys, fac; Atty Gen's Adv Inst; Houston Trial Lawyers Asn; trustee, Cate Sch; Wheeler Ave Baptist Church; Nat Asn Advan Colored People; Houston Bar Asn, community affairs sub comn. **Honors/Awds:** Outstanding Arson Prosecution, Tex Adv Coun, 1989; Prosecutor of the Year, Int Asn Credit Card Investigators, 1991; Star Achievement Award, Nat Forum Black Pub Adminrs, 1993; Pioneer Award, Nat Asn Black Prosecutors, 1994;Bessie Colman Trail Blazer Award, Women Who Did; Judge Edward R Finch Speech Award, Am Bar Asn, 1995; Super Achiever Award, Young African Am Achievers, 1995. **Business Addr:** Director of Statndards of Business Conduct, Hewlett-Packard Co, Houston Off, 20555 State Hwy 249, PO Box 61129, Houston, TX 77055.

JONES, GEORGE H.
Educator. **Personal:** Born Feb 21, 1942, Muskogee, OK; son of George H and Bernice Weaver. **Educ:** Harvard Col, BS, 1963; Univ Calif, Berkeley, PhD, 1968. **Career:** Inst Health, Univ Geneva, Switzerland, 1968-71; Univ Mich, asst prof zool, 1971-75, from assoc prof biol to prof biol, 1975-89; Emory Univ, prof biol, 1989, grad dean, vpres res, 1989-95, Goodrich C White prof biol, 1996-, chmn dept biol, currently, actg dean; Helen Hay Whitney Found, fel; Ford Found, fel, 1982. **Orgs:** NY Acad Sci; Am Soc Micro biol; Am Soc Bio chem & Molecular Biol. **Honors/Awds:** Univ Teaching Award, Univ Mich, 1989; Goodrich C White Professorship, 1996; Scholar/Teacher Award, Emory Univ, 1998. **Business Addr:** Professor, Chairman of Biology, Emory University, Department of Biology, O Wayne Rollins Res Ctr, 1510 Clifton Road NE Room 2001, Atlanta, GA 30322.

JONES, GERALD WINFIELD
Government official. **Personal:** Born Jun 27, 1931, Jetersville, VA; son of Emmett Jr and Daisy Peachy L (deceased); married Ann H; children: Crenshaw, Cassandra Coleman, Lessie & Eric. **Educ:** Va State Col, BA, 1952; Howard Univ, LLB, 1960. **Career:** Dept Justice, Civil Rights Div, atty, 1960-65, supervising atty chief voting sect, 1965-, acting deputy asst atty gen, 1994. **Orgs:** Mem bd dirs, Melwood Hort Training Ctr, 1975-83; Nat Bar Asn; Govt Lawyers Sect Nat Bar Asn. **Honors/Awds:** Superior Performance Award, 1964, Special Commendation Award, Dept Justice, 1972; Attorney General Distinguished Service Award, 1973, 1983; Attorney General Award for Upward Mobility, 1978; Senior Executive Service Meritorious Award, 1982, 1985-89; Presidential Rank Meritorious Executive Award, 1990. **Military Serv:** AUS, 1st lt, 1952-55. **Business Addr:** Acting Deputy Assistant Attorney General, PO Box 66128, Washington, DC 20035-6128, **Business Phone:** (202)307-2767.

JONES, GERALDINE J.
Educator, teacher. **Personal:** Born Jul 30, 1939, Seaford, DE; daughter of Thomas and Marion; divorced; children: Monica. **Educ:** DE State Col, BS, 1961; Central MI, MA, bus admin, 1977; Temple Univ,1986; Capella Univ, PhD; Eastern Baptist Theological Seminary, MDiv, 1999. **Career:** Division Social Servs, social worker, 1962-64; Head Start Camden Summer,social worker, 1965, dir, 1971; Migrant Prog Summer, home coord, 1974; public speaker; soloist; free-lance writer; parent educr, 1990-; Parent Early Educ Ctr; Capital Sch Dist, vis teacher, 1975-. **Orgs:** Nat Educ Asn; Del State Educ Asn; DE Asn Vis Teachers; Capital Asn; Tri-Co Investment & Savings Asn; Int Asn Pupil Personnel Workers; adv coun, DE Adolescent Prog, 1985-89; Delta Sigma Theta; Nat Coun Negro Women;Whatc oat United Methodist Church; DE State Col Alumni Asn; Kent Co Alumni Asn; vol teacher Black Studies DE Youth Servs, 1980-; Kent County Chap DE State Col Alumni; treas, Wm C Jason Alumni; Del Asn Certified Vis Teachers; Miss Alumni 1986-87; past pres, Del State Col, Nat Alumni Asn; JH Wms Ensemble, Yesterday's Youth, Gospel ensemble; United Methodist Church, General Conference, delegate, 1992, Penisula Delaware Conference,delegate, NE Jurisdictional Conference, delegate, 1992, Annual Conf,delegate, 1990-; UMW, Peninsula Del Conf, past pres, 1990-; NE Jurisdiction, UM Church; Delta Sigma Theta; treas, Sussex Co Alumni Asn. **Honors/Awds:** African-Am scholarship fund, John Wesley United Methodist Church;Presidential Citation, NAFEO, 1993; Barnabas Award, UMC, Pen-Del Conference, 1990; scholarships, James R Webb; poem pub IAPPW Jornal, 1974;Sigma Iota Epsilon Central MI, 1979; Youth Service Award, What coat United Methodist Church, 1984; Alumnus of the Year, Delaware State Col, 1985;Certificate of Appreciation, Nat Asn Advan Colored People Cent Del Br,1985; Service Award, Peninsula Conf United Methodist Women; Sigma Iota Epsilon Honor Society, Central Michigan, 1978; African-American leaders in Delaware, 1994; Recipient of the Alberta Brown Award, UMC, Martin Luther King Celebration, Pen-Del Conf, 1993; Governors Award for Volunteerism,1998; African-American History Award, Mt Enon Baptist Church, 1998; Delta Women of the Century. **Special Achievements:** Capital Attendance Program, organizer, originator, program to encourage positive school attendance & drop out prevention; CPP, Community Partnership Program, Organizer & Originator, 1993. **Home Addr:** 368 Post Blvd, Dover, DE 19904, **Home Phone:** (302)674-1977. **Business Addr:** Visiting Teacher, Capital School District, 945 Forest St, Dover, DE 19904, **Business Phone:** (302)672-1931.

JONES, GERI DUNCAN
Association executive. **Personal:** Born Nov 28, 1958, Chicago, IL; daughter of Grandee and Carrie Gates; married Michael A Jones, Jan 13, 1979; children: Michael A II, Marlon G & Marcus E. **Educ:** Eastern Ill Univ, Charleston, IL, BA, 1979; Keller Grad Sch Bus Mgt, Chicago, IL, attended 1982. **Career:** Charles A Davis & Assoc, Chicago, IL, acct exec, 1979-83; Debbies Sch Beauty Cult, Chicago, IL, pub rels dir, 1983-84; Am Health Beauty Aids Inst, Chicago, IL, acct exec, 1984-88, exec dir, 1988-. **Orgs:** Zeta Phi Beta Sorority, 1976-; Chicago Soc Asn Exec, 1985-; bd dirs, Heritage Afro Am Beauty Indust, 1988-; Am Soc Asn Exec; nat adv comm, Madame C J Walker Spirit Awards; adv bd, Urban Call; Trade Mag Unbran Retailers; bus admin, St Titus Missionary Baptist Church, 1999-. **Honors/Awds:** Excellence Award, Universal Col Beauty, 1988; Outstanding Business & Professional African American Women, Blackbook, 1990. **Special Achievements:** Listed as one of the top 25 Black Women in Black Enterprise Magazine in 1994. **Business Addr:** Executive Director, American Health & Beauty Aids Institute, PO Box 19510, Chicago, IL 60619-0510, **Business Phone:** (708)333-8740.

JONES, GRACE (GRACE MENDOZA)
Singer, actor. **Personal:** Born May 19, 1948, Spanish Town, Jamaica; married Atila Altaunbay (divorced); children: Paulo. **Educ:** Syracuse Univ, theater. **Career:** Former model; actress, singer & peformance artist, currently; Films: Conant he Destroyer; Deadly Vengeance; Grace Jones-One Man Show; Grace Jones-State of Grace; Siesta; Straight to Hell; Vamp; A View to a Kill; Boomerang, 1992; Palmer's Pick Up, 1999; albums include: Portfolio, 1977; Warm Leatherette; Fame; Portfolio; Living My Life; Nightclubbing; Inside Story; No Place Like Home, 2006; TV: "A Reggae Session", 1988; "Bellezasal agua", 1993; "Beast Master", 1999; "Wolf Girl", 2001; "Shaka Zulu: The Citadel", 2001; No Place Like Home, 2006. Falco Damn, We Still Live,Chelsea On The Rocks, 2008. **Special Achievements:** Ranked No 82 on VH1's 100 Greatest Women of Rock N Roll; ranked No 19 in Channel 5's World's greatest supermodel; Top model for fashion magazines Vogue and Elle, numerous appearances in Stern.

JONES, GREG
Football player. **Personal:** Born May 22, 1974, Denver, CO. **Educ:** Colo Univ. **Career:** Football player (retired), Wash Redskins, linebacker, 1997-2000; Chicago Bears, 2001; Ariz Cardinals,2002; Houston Texans, 2002.

JONES, GREGORY ALLAN
Insurance executive, vice president (organization). **Personal:** Born Aug 15, 1955, New York, NY; son of Alline and Willie; married Sharon, Aug 30, 1980; children: Kimberly & Gregory Jr. **Educ:** Lehman Col, BA, 1977; Insu Inst Am, ARM, 1989. **Career:** Am Int Group, underwriter, 1977-79; INA special risk, jr underwriter, 1979-82; Chubb & Son, sr underwriter, 1982-86; Albert G Ruben & Corp, vpres, 1986-90; Near North Brokerage, sr vpres, 1990-95; USI Entertainment Ins Servs / Max Behm, sr vpres, 1995-2005; C M Meiers Co Inc, vpres prod ins, 2005-. **Orgs:** Black Filmmakers Found, 1990-; Am Filmmakers Inst, 1992-. **Honors/Awds:** Athelete of the year, Lehman Col, 1977. **Business Addr:** Vice President, C. M. Meiers Company, Inc, 21045 Califa St Suite 100, Woodland Hills, CA 91367, **Business Phone:** (818)224-6145.

JONES, GREGORY WAYNE
Insurance executive. **Personal:** Born Dec 29, 1948, Newark, OH; son of Gordon and Mildred; married Helen, Feb 6, 1968; children: Brian & Derek. **Educ:** Franklin Univ, BA, bus, 1974; Hood Col,

MA, 1981; Univ Pa Wharton Sch, MBA, 1984. **Career:** State Farm Ins Co, underwriter, 1969-75, personnel rep, 1975-81, div mgr, 1981-85, exec asst, 1985-88; dep regional vpres 1988-93, regional vpres, 1993-, vpres, 1998-2001, pres, sr vpres & chief exec officer, 2001-. **Orgs:** Founder,100 Black Men Sonoma Co, 1989-93; bd trustee, Calif State Univ Northridge, 1993-; bd, Los Angeles Jr Achievement, 1993-; bd trustee, Wellness Community, 1994; bd, mem, Los Angeles Chamber Com, 1995-; 100 Black Men LA, 1996-; Bd adv, Los Angeles Minority Develop Group, 1996-; chmn, Nat Asn Advan Colored People; chmn, Los Angeles Urban League; bd trustee, Nat Urban League; bd trustee, Franklin Univ. **Honors/Awds:** Empowerment Achievement Award, 1995; Credit Innovator Award, 1995; Bronze Leadership Award, Jr Achievement Am, 1996; Corporate Trailblazer Award, Dollars & Sense Mag, 1998. **Military Serv:** AUS, nat guard, sp4, 1968-73. **Business Addr:** President & Chief Executive Officer, Senior Vice President, State Farm Insurance Company, 1 State Farm Plz, Bloomington, IL 61710, **Business Phone:** (309)663-5111.

JONES, GROVER WILLIAM, JR. (DEACON JONES)
Football player, football executive, football coach. **Personal:** Born Apr 18, 1934, White Plains, NY; married Tiki; children: Monica. **Educ:** Ithaca Col, BS. **Career:** Football player (retired), Football coach, Football Executve; Chicago White Sox, player, scout, instr, minor league mgr, 1955-75; Houston Astros, hitting coach, 1976-82; NY Yankees, scout, 1983; San Diego Padres, hitting coach, 1984-87; Baltimore Orioles Minor League, hitting coach, advance scout, 1987. **Honors/Awds:** Westchester Co & Ithaca Col Hall of fame; Appleton WI Baseball Hall offame; Nations Top Am League Player, 1951; Silver Bat Award Winner, 1956. **Special Achievements:** First Black Man Recog Hall of Fame Cooperstown. **Military Serv:** Mil, 1957-58.

JONES, GUS
Association executive. **Career:** Mich Black Horsemen's Asn, pres. **Business Addr:** President, Michigan Black Horsemen, 29716 Briarbank Ct, Southfield, MI 48034, **Business Phone:** (810)438-0812.*

JONES, GWENDOLYN J
Librarian. **Personal:** Born Oct 31, 1953, Holly Springs, MS; daughter of Willie Payton and Mary E Johnson; married Willie Frank, Oct 30, 1971; children: Anthony Tyrone & Clarissa Danyell. **Educ:** Northwest Jr Col, Senotobia, MS, AS, 1978; Rust Col, Holly Springs, BS, 1984. **Career:** Rust Col, Holly Springs, MS, tech serv asst, 1979-. **Orgs:** Jones Grove Missionary Baptist Church, 1983-; pres, Pastor's Aid, 1985-. **Honors/Awds:** Agency Parent Year Award, ICS Headstart Inc, 1979-80; Certificate of Appreciation, Rust Col Int Alumni Asn, 1986; Certificate of Appreciation, Jones Grove MB Church, 1987; Certificate of Appreciation, Holly Springs/Marshall Co, Rust Club, 1992; Certificate of Post Matron's Jurisdiction MS, 1994. **Home Addr:** 123 Old Hwy 7 S, Holly Springs, MS 38635. **Business Addr:** Technical Service Assistant, Rust College, Leontyne Price Library, 150 Rust Ave Libr 201, Holly Springs, MS 38635, **Business Phone:** (601)252-8000.

JONES, H THOMAS
President (Organization), executive. **Personal:** Born Sep 28, 1944, Maxton, NC; son of Henry Thomas Sr and Nannie Ruth Webb; married Joyce McDougald, Dec 30, 1965; children: Thomasia Elva. **Educ:** Amarillo Jr Col, Amarillo, TX, 1964; Pembroke State Univ, Pembroke, NC, BS, acct, 1972; Central Mich Univ, Mount Pleasant, MI, MA, bus, 1979. **Career:** Carolina Power & Light Co, Raleigh, NC, 1972; Southeastern Utilities Develop Inc, pres & chief exec officer, currently. **Orgs:** Rotary Club, 1988-91; bd mem, Am Cancer Soc, 1989-91; vice chmn, Columbus County Minority Bus Coun, 1989-90; chmn, Columbus County Youth Enrichment Coun, 1990-91; bd mem, United Carolina Bank, 1990-91; bd mem, Columbus County Hosp, 1990-91. **Honors/Awds:** Alpha Man of the Year, Alpha Phi Alpha Fraternity, 1982. **Military Serv:** USAF, Sgt, 1963-67. **Home Addr:** 314 Edgewood Circle, Whiteville, NC 28472. **Business Phone:** (910)843-4131.

JONES, HANK (HENRY W JONES)
Pianist, composer, bandleader. **Personal:** Born Jul 31, 1918, Vicksburg, MS. **Career:** Hot Lips Page Band, 1944; Onyx Club, pianist, 1944; freelance player; CBS, staff, 1959-76; Village Vanguard, mem; Great Jazz Trio, pianist, 1976; Cafe Ziegfeld, solo pianist, 1980; Albums: Albums: Urbanity, 1947; Bop Redux, 1977; I Remember You, 1977; Ain't Misbehavin, 1978; In Japan, 1979; The Jazz Trio of Hank Jones, 1994; Sarala, 1995; Darji's Groove, 1998; The Touch: Rockin' in Rhythm/Lazy Afternoon, 2002; The Talented Touch/Porgy & Bess, 2004; Saturday of Thunder, 2005; For My Father, 2005; Complete Recordings, 2005; Hank & Frank, 2006; West of 5th, 2006; Verve Music Group, pianist, currently. **Honors/Awds:** Jazz Masters Award, Nat Endowment Arts, 1989; Big Band and Jazz Hall of Fame, 2000; Jazz Living Legend Award, Am Soc Composers, Authors & Publs. **Business Addr:** Pianist, Verve Music Group, 1755 Broadway Fl 3, New York, NY 10019, **Business Phone:** (212)331-2000.

JONES, HARDI LIDDELL
Federal government official. **Personal:** Born Nov 2, 1942, St Louis, MO; son of Jamesetta B Liddell and Thomas H E; married Yvonne A Thompson Jones, Nov 16, 1963; children: Miriam Yvette, Sandra Lynnette. **Educ:** St Paul's Col, BS, 1962;Univ MD-Col Park, attended 1963; George Wash Univ, attended 1965. **Career:** US Naval Oceanog Off, phys oceanogr, 1962-63; US Fish & Wildlife Serv, phys oceanogr, 1963-65; US Naval Oceanog Off, phys oceanogr, 1965-67; Underwater Syst Inc, oceanogr, 1967-71; US Naval Oceanogr Off, equal opportunity officer, 1971-74; Bur Reclamation US Dept Interior, dir off equal opportunity, 1974-81; US Dept Treasury IRS, asst to the comnr, 1981-89; IRS, Off Chief Coun, special asst to assoc, 1989, dir, Equal Employment, currently. **Orgs:** Pres, Prince George's County Club Frontiers Int, 1980-82; chmn bd dirs, Combined Comns Action Prince George's County MD, 1981-; Sigma Pi Phi Frat Beta Mu Boule, 1981-; chmn, labor & industry comn, Prince George's Co MD Nat Asn Advan Colored People, 1983-; chmn bd trustees St Paul's Col Lawrenceville VA, 1985-88; life mem, Kappa Alpha Psi Frat Inc; vpres, Prince George's Nat Asn Advan Colored People, 1990-; pres, Prince George's Country Club Frontiers Int, 1991-; pres, Prince George's County Br NCP, 1991-; Beta Mu Boule, Sigma Pi Phi Fraternity, Sire Archon, 1993-. **Honors/Awds:** Cit Oceanogr of the Navy, 1974; Community Serv Award, Combined Communities in Action, 1981; Distinguished Alumnus St Paul's Col, 1985; Presidential Award, Prince George's Nat Asn Advan Colored People, 1987; Meritorious Honor AIM-IRS, 1988. **Home Addr:** 10215 Buena Vista Ave, Lanham, MD 20706. *

JONES, HAROLD M.
Musician. **Personal:** Born Mar 25, 1934, Chicago, IL; son of William Henry and Rosetta; married Wanda J Hudson, Jul 10, 1953; children: Ernest Milton, Louis Eugene & Antar Patrice. **Educ:** Sherwood Music Sch, cert; Juilliard Sch Music, dipl, 1959. **Career:** Flutist & educator: Metrop Music Sch; Tremont YMHA; Bronx House Music Sch; Merrywood Music Camp; Juilliard Sch Music; Prep Div, Westchester Sch Music; Westchester Conserv Music; Manhattanville Col; Manhattan Sch Music; Prep Div, City Univ New York; The Antara Ensemble, founder, dir, conductor; Solo performances: Symphony New World; Munic Concerts Orchestra & Am Symphony Orchestra; The Conserv Orchestra Brooklyn Col; Chamber Orchestra Black Am Music Symposium; S Ark Symphony; The Philharmonic Greensboro, NC; Jackson Symphony Orchestra; Recordings include: Vivaldi Concerti, Max Goberman; Island in the Sun, Harry Belafonte; Trio for Flute, Oboe, Piano, Howard Swanson; Poem for Flute & Harp, N Mondello; Robeson; POV, John Lewis; Harold Jones; From Bach to Bazzini; Afternoon Fantasies; Just As I Am, Antara Rec; Let Us Break Bread Together, Leonarda Rec; numerous recital, orchestra, ensemble & theatrical appearances. **Orgs:** Bd mem, NY Flute Club, 1965-, pres, 1976-79; Nat Flute Asn, 1979; Am Fedn Musicians, Local 802; Chicago Civic Orchestra; fac mem, Brooklyn Col. **Honors/Awds:** Outstanding Woodwind Player Award, Juilliard Sch Music; Key to the City of Jackson, Tennessee, 1991. **Home Addr:** 100 W 94 St, New York, NY 10025. **Business Addr:** Flutist, Antara Records, 2065 Fifth Ave 127th St, PO Box 20384, New York, NY 10025, **Business Phone:** (212)866-2545.

JONES, HELEN HAMPTON
Librarian. **Personal:** Born Jun 9, 1941, Portsmouth, VA; daughter of George Livingston Sr (deceased) and Helen Bowen; married James W Jones Jr (divorced 1974); children: Ginger R, Jewell W. **Educ:** Livingstone Col, Salisbury, NC, BS, 1962; Syracuse Univ, Syracuse, NY, MS, 1975. **Career:** Norfolk State Univ, Norfolk, VA, clerk, stenographer & typist, 1963-75, actg libr dir, 1976, asst acquisitions librn, 1976-79, acquisitions librn, 1979-88, actg asst dir personnel, 1989-90, collection mgt librn, 1988-91; Elizabeth City State Univ, acquisitions librn, 1997-. **Orgs:** Chmn, Portsmouth Pub Sch Bd, 1982-86; charter appointee, Portsmouth Munic Finance Comt, 1972-74, 1978-80; vice chair, Portsmouth Parking Authority, 1979-80; chmn, Portsmouth Pan Hellenic Coun, 1966-67; Va Libr Asn; SE Libr Asn, Am Libr Asn. **Honors/Awds:** Most Valuable Employee, Va Govt Employees Asn, 1986; Citizen of the Year, Eureka Club, Inc, 1984; Medallion Award, Brighton Rock AME Zion Church, 1984. **Home Addr:** 1006 Robinson Rd, Portsmouth, VA 23701. *

JONES, HENRY LOUIS
Football player. **Personal:** Born Dec 29, 1967, St Louis, MO. **Educ:** Univ Ill, psychol, 1990. **Career:** Football player (retired); Buffalo Bills, defensive back, 1991-2000; Minn Vikings, 2001; Atlanta Falcons, 2002. **Honors/Awds:** Pro Bowl selection, 1992; All-Pro selection, 1992.

JONES, HENRY W. See JONES, HANK.

JONES, HERBERT C.
Physician. **Personal:** Born Aug 1, 1936, Demopolis, AL; son of Tom Allen Jr and Bettie Mae Young; married Bessie Chapman Jones, Jun 13, 1958; children: Sandra Jo Jones, Nancy Gayle Jones, Herbert Chapman Jones, Lisa Carol Jones. **Educ:** Talladega Col, AL, attended 1956; Ind Univ, Bloomington, IN, AB, 1957, MD, 1961. **Career:** Univ Ill Med Ctr, Chicago, IL, residency, 1965-68; self-employed surg, Atlanta, GA, physician, 1968-; Cascade Med Ctr, physician, currently. **Orgs:** former chmn, Otolaryngol Sec, Nat Medl Asn, 1969-; fel, Am Acad Otolaryngol, 1969-; Am Col Surgeons, 1972-; Ga State Med Asn; Nat Asn Advan Colored People; dir, Am Acad Otolaryngol, 1993-; dir, Am Bd Otolaryngol, 1994-. **Honors/Awds:** Alpha Omega Alpha Honor Society, 1961; Father of the Year, Concerned Black Clergy of Atlanta, 1987; Outstanding Physician in Otolaryngology, Black Enterprise Magazine, 1988; Physician of the Year, Atlanta Med Asn, 1990. **Military Serv:** USAF, capt, 1961-65. **Business Addr:** Physician, Cascade Medical Center, 2600 Martin Luther King Jr Dr Suite 302, Atlanta, GA 30312.*

JONES, HORACE F
Executive, army officer. **Educ:** Southern Univ, BS, MA, counr; Univ Denver, EdD, guid & coun. **Career:** Army officer (retired), executive; AUS, artillery staff officer, comdr troops, Training Ctr, training unit comdr, staff officer, N Am Aerospace Defense Command, sr intelligence dir, Defense Intelligence Col, vice dean, lt col, 1983; Advan Resource Technologies Inc, founder, 1986-, pres & chief exec officer, currently. **Honors/Awds:** Northern Viriginia Urban League Corporation Award, 1994-96; Fast 50 Award, Wash Technol Newspaper; Fantastic 50, Va Chamber Com, 1997; Fast 50 Award, Va Technol, 1997; FastTrack Enterprise Award for Best Business Practices, 1997. **Special Achievements:** Top 100 African American-owned companies in the US, Black Enterprise Mag, 1998; Top Black Technol Entrepreneurs, US Black Engr & Info Technol mag, 2004. **Military Serv:** AUS, 1958-83. **Business Addr:** President, Chief Executive Officer, Advanced Resource Technologies Inc, 1555 King St Suite 400, Alexandria, VA 22314, **Business Phone:** (703)682-4740.

JONES, DR. HOWARD JAMES
Educator, writer. **Personal:** Born Jun 19, 1944, Benton, LA; son of Elnora Morris and Woodrow; married Joyce Kemp, Dec 12, 1971; children: Jonora Kinshasa & Howard James III. **Educ:** Southern Univ, Baton Rouge, LA, BA, 1966; Howard Univ, Wash, DC, MA, 1968; Wash State Univ, Pullman, WA, PhD, 1975. **Career:** Educator (Retired); Grambling State Univ, Grambling, LA, instr, 1967-70; Univ S Miss, Hattiesburg, MS, asst prof, 1974-76; Prairie View A&M Univ, Prairie View, TX, instr, 1976-78; Tex Southern Univ, Houston, TX, asst prof, 1978-82; Prairie View A&M Univ, Prairie View, TX, assoc prof, 1985; Humanities Texas. **Orgs:** Secry & treas, Southern Conf Afro-Am Studies Inc, 1979-; vpres, Asn Caribbean Studies, 1989-. **Honors/Awds:** Graduate Studies Fellow, Southern Fel Fund, 1970-75; Acad Scholar Holder, La Acad Sch, 1962-66. **Special Achievements:** Written many books including, Their History, 1997; The Red Diary: A Chronological History of Black Americans in Houston, 1991. **Home Addr:** 6747 Ridgeway, Houston, TX 77087, **Home Phone:** (713)641-9738.

JONES, DR. I. GENE
School administrator, vice president (organization). **Educ:** Jarvis Christian Col, BA, 1942; Ball State Univ, MA, 1963; Univ Mich, PhD,1974. **Career:** Denver Pub Schs, teacher & admin asst, 1954-62; Ball State Univ, asst prof, 1962-64; Cent Community Col, instr, Inglewood, CA, 1964-66; Unified Sch Dist, reading resource & curric devel spec, 1966-68; Eastern Mich Univ, asst prof educ, 1969-73; GA State Univ, adj fac, 1975-78; Albany State Col, asst dean acad affairs, 1973-78; St Paul's Col, vpres acad affairs, 1978-, provost, 1988. **Orgs:** Bd dirs, YWCA, Denver, 1960-62; bd dirs, United Way Dougherty City, 1975-78; team capt, GA Heart Fund Asn, 1977-78; N Mex First; adv comt, N Mex Off African Am Affairs. **Honors/Awds:** Am Book Co textbooks publ, 1967; Exxon Fel Am Coun Educ Educ Leadership Devel, 1975; Distinguished Alumni Award, Jarvis Christian Col, 1985; Presidential Citation, Nat Asn Equal Opportunity Higher Educ, 1986. **Home Addr:** 1601 Penn St NE Winrock Villas H 10, Albuquerque, NM 87110, **Home Phone:** (505)884-4049. *

JONES, IDA KILPATRICK. See WHITE, IDA MARGARET.

JONES, IDA M.
Teacher, business owner, lawyer. **Personal:** Born Aug 18, 1953, Omaha, NE; daughter of Jonathan and Mary; married Curtis Darrell Bryant, 2002; children: Kenneth, Eugene, Kamali & Jamilla. **Educ:** Creighton Univ, Omaha, NE, BA, 1974; New York Univ, New York, NY, JD, 1977; UCLA, Cert Online Educ, 2004. **Career:** Legal Aid-Criminal Appeals, New York, NY, assoc appellate coun, 1977-79; Legal Aid Soc, Omaha, NE, staff atty, 1979-81; Univ Nebr, Omaha, NE, assoc prof, 1981-87; Calif State Univ, Fresno, CA, prof, 1987-. **Orgs:** Alpha Sigma Nu, 1974-; NY Bar Asn, 1978-; Nebr Bar Asn, 1982-95; Am Bus Law Asn, 1985-; Beta Gamma Sigma, 1985-; vpres, Western Bus Law Asn, 1988, pres, 1990; Calif Bar Asn, 1990-; vpres, Bd, Fresno Cert Develop Corp. **Honors/Awds:** Research Awards, Calif State Univ, Fresno, 1987-91; Research Awards, UNO, 1987; Meritorious Performance, Calif State Univ, Fresno, 1988, 1990; Craig School Business Award, Educ Innovation, 1990; First recipient, Verna Mae & Wayne A Brooks Professor of Business Law, 1996-99; Excellence in Teaching Award, 1999; Technology in Education, Provost Awards, 2006. **Home Addr:** 5382 N Angus, Fresno, CA 93710, **Home Phone:** (559)228-1040. **Business Addr:** Professor, California State University, Craig School of Business, Finance & Bus Law Department, 5245 N Backer Ave, Fresno, CA 93740-8001, **Business Phone:** (559)278-2151.

JONES, INGRID SAUNDERS
Executive. **Personal:** Born Dec 27, 1945, Detroit, MI; daughter of Homer L and Georgia Lyles; divorced. **Educ:** Mich State Univ,

BA, educ, 1968, Eastern Mich Univ, MA, educ, 1972. **Career:** Detroit Wayne County Child Care, Coord Coun, Detroit, Mich, exec dir, 1974-77; Atlanta City Coun, Atlanta Urban fel, Atlanta, GA, spec asst, 1977-78; City of Atlanta, Atlanta, GA, legis analyst Atlanta City Coun pres, 1978-79, exec asst mayor, 1979-81; Coca-Cola Co, Atlanta, GA, dir urban affairs, 1987-88, asst vpres urban & govt affairs, 1988-92, vpres, corp external affairs, 1992, sr vpres, Global Community Connections, currently; Coca-Cola Found, chairperson, 1992-. **Orgs:** Bd dirs, UNICE; bd dir, Atlanta Neighborhood Develop Corp; bd dir, Cent Atlanta Progress, Cong Black Caucus Found; bd dir, Nat Minority Supplier Develop Coun; bd dir, Exec Leadership Coun Found; The Woodruff Arts Ctr; GA Dept Indust, Trade Tourism; bd dir, Just Us Theater Co; bd dir, United Way Metro Atlanta; Metrop Community Found; Atlanta Empowerment Zone Corp; The Atlanta Bus League; The Links; bd dir, Delta Sigma Theta Sor; Soc Int Bus Fel; Atlanta Women's Network; Int Women's Forum; bd dir, Nat Forum Black Pub Admin. **Honors/Awds:** 100 Black Business & Prof Women Award, Dollar & Sense Mag, 1978; 100 Black Female Corp Execs, Ebony Mag, 1990; Nat Equal Justice Award, Nat Asn Advan Colored People, 1997; Distinguished Community Serv Award, Atlanta Urban League, 1996; Woman Looking Ahead Woman of the Year, 2002; DECA Award, Atlanta Bus Chronicle; Herbert H Wright Community Serv Award, Nat Urban Legaue; Corp Pioneer Award, Bethune-Dubois Fund; Women Who Make A Difference Award, Nat Coun Res Women; Hon Doctor of Humanities, Mich State Univ; Women of Achievement Award, YWCA. **Home Addr:** 1639 Stokes Ave SW, Atlanta, GA 30301. **Business Addr:** Senior Vice President of Global Community Connections, Chairperson, The Coca-Cola Co, PO Box 1734, Atlanta, GA 30301, **Business Phone:** (404)676-3525.

JONES, IRMA RENAE
Police officer. **Personal:** Born Feb 20, 1942, Uriah, AL; daughter of Willie Virginia Harris and Lamb Virginia; married Robert Lloyd, Jan 7, 1980; children: Lisa White, Tiffany Dotson & Robin. **Educ:** Wayne County Community Col, AA, 1973; Wayne State Univ, BS, 1982; Eastern Mich Univ, MLS, 1989. **Career:** NY Univ, clerk typist, 1960-64; Columbia Univ, clerk typist, 1965-68; Pac Bell Telephone, operator, 1968; Bethlehem Steel, typist, 1968-71; WXYZ-TV, typist clerk, 1971-72; Detroit Partition Co, secy, 1972-77; Detroit Police Dept, police officer, 1977-. **Orgs:** Adv, DPD Law Enforcement Explorers, 1988-; bd mem, BUOY 13, 1988-; NAACP, 1991-; adv comt, C Ctr Outpatient, 1991-93; adv comt, Burton Detention Ctr, 1991-94. **Honors/Awds:** Officer of the Year, Detroit Police, 1994; Plymouth United Church Christ Community Serv, 1994; Dedication to Exploring, Detroit Police Law Enforcement Explorers, 1994; Devoted & Untiring Work to Detroit Police Law Enforcement Explorer Post 1313, Boy Scouts Am, 1994. **Business Addr:** Community Relations Officer, Detroit Police Department 13th Precinct, 4747 Woodward, Detroit, MI 48201, **Business Phone:** (313)596-1364.

JONES, JACQUE DEWAYNE
Baseball player. **Personal:** Born Apr 25, 1975, San Diego, CA; children: Jacque Jr. **Educ:** Southern Calif. **Career:** Minnesota Twins, outfielder, 1999-2005; Chicago cubs, Outfielders, 2006-07; Detroit Tigers; Florida Marlins, 2008; Newark Bears, 2009-. **Honors/Awds:** Olympic Bronze, Atlanta, 1996. *

JONES, JACQUELINE VALARIE
Journalist. **Personal:** Born Aug 7, 1954, Washington, DC; daughter of Melvin C and Alice; children: Tony. **Educ:** George Wash Univ, BA, jour, 1976; Cleveland State Univ, Eng, 1980. **Career:** Mutual Broadcasting & Mutual Black Network, tape ed, 1975-77; UPI, Atlanta, reporter, 1977-78; Cleveland Plain Dealer, reporter, 1978-80; Balt Eve Sun, reporter, 1980-81; Wash Star, reporter, 1981; Detroit Free Press, reporter, copy ed, 1981-84; Mpls Star Tribune, copy ed, 1984-87; NY Newsday, adm ed, night city ed, asst city ed & copy ed, 1987-92; Phila Daily News, city ed, 1992-95; Milwaukee Jour Sentinel, sr ed, local news, 1995-97; Wash Post, asst city ed, 1997; Pa State Univ, Col Commun, sr lectr, currently. **Orgs:** Vpres print, Nat Asn Black Journalists Parliamentarian, 1989-95; Accrediting Coun Educ Jour & Mass Commun. **Business Addr:** Senior Lecturer, Pennsylvania State University, Col Commun, 217 Carnegie Bldg Suite 217, University Park, PA 16802, **Business Phone:** (814)865-9582.

JONES, JAKE
Automotive executive. **Personal:** Born Aug 9, 1967, Hollandale, MS; married Veronica Nyhan Jones, May 29, 1999. **Educ:** Carleton Col, BA, 1989; Miss Delta State Univ, 1990; Carnegie-Mellon Univ, MS, 1992. **Career:** US Dept Hamilton Health Sci, health policy analyst, 1992-95; Health Care Financing Admin, sr health policy analyst, 1995-96; US Senator Carol Moseley-Braun, legis asst, 1996-99; AFL-CIO, legis rep, 1999-2000; DaimlerChrysler Corp, sr mgr legis affairs, currently. **Orgs:** Black MBA Asn, 1990-92; pres, Black Grad Stud Orgn, Carnegie Mellon Univ, 1991-92; be mem, Bright Beginning Inc, 2002-05. **Honors/Awds:** Otto Davis Award, Carnegie Mellon Univ, 1992. **Military Serv:** USAR, specialist E-4, 1985-93; Expert Infantry, 1986. **Business Addr:** Senior Manager Legislative Affairs, DaimlerChrysler Corp, 1401 H St NW, Washington, DC 20005.

JONES, JAMES ALFIE
Football player. **Personal:** Born Feb 6, 1969, Davenport, IA. **Educ:** Northern Iowa univ, BS, 1992. **Career:** Football player (retired); Cleveland Browns, defensive tackle, 1991-94; Denver Broncos, 1995; Baltimore Ravens, 1996-98; Detroit Lions, 1999-00; Jones' Tire Service, co-owner. **Orgs:** Spokespeople, First Family Pledge. **Honors/Awds:** Cleveland Browns, Edge NFL Man of the Year, 1993; Humanitarian Award,Cleveland Touchdown Club, 1993; Ed Block Courage Award, detroit lions,2000; "Unsung Heroes" Award, detroit lions, 2000.

JONES, JAMES B
Automotive executive. **Career:** Macon Chrysler-Plymouth Inc, chief exec officer. **Special Achievements:** Co is ranked No 20 on the Black Enterprise list of Top 100 auto dealers, 1994.

JONES, JAMES EARL
Actor. **Personal:** Born Jan 17, 1931, Arkabutla, MS; son of Robert (deceased) and Ruth Williams; married Cecilia Hart; children: Flynn & Shaquonique; married Julienne Marie Hendricks, Mar 15, 1982 (divorced). **Educ:** Univ Mich, BA, 1953; Am Theatre Wing, dipl, 1957. **Career:** Plays: Romeo & Juliet; Wedding in Japan; Sunrise in Campobello; Much Ado About Nothing; The Sleep of Prisoners; The Birds; The Caine Mutiny; Velvet Gloves; The Tender Trap; Arsenic & Old Lace; The Desperate Hours; The Pretender; The Cool World; King Henry V; Measure for Measure; The Blacks; A summer Nights Dream; The Apple; Moon on a Rainbow Shawl; Infidel Caesar; The Merchant of Venice; The Tempest; Toys in the Attic; PS 193; Macbeth; The Love Nest; The Last Minstrel; Othello; The Winter's Tale; Mr Johnson; Next Time I'll Sing to You; Blood knot; King Lear; Of Mice & Men; Paul Robeson; Master Harold & The Boys; Fences, 1987-88; Films: Dr Strangelove; The Comedians; The Man; The River Niger; Swashbuckler; BingoLong Traveling All-Stars & Motor Kings; Exorcist II, The Heretic; The Greatest; The Last Remake of Beau Geste; A Piece of the Action; Allan Quartermain & the Lost City of Gold; The Bushido Blade; Conan the Barbarian; Blood Tide; Gardens of Stone; Matewan; Conan the Barbarian; Coming to America; Field of Dreams; Three Fugitives; Into Thin Air; The Grand Tour; Scorchers; I Can't Lose; The Hunt for Red October; Sommersby; Excessive Force; Meteor Man; Patriot Games; Sneakers; Clear & Present Danger; Clean Slate; Sandlot; Confessions: Two Faces of Evil; Cry the Beloved Country; Looking for Richard; Gang Related; The Annihilation of Fish; Undercover Angel; Finder's Fee; The Papp Project; voice of King Mufasa in The Lion King; voice of Darth Vader in the Star Wars Trilogy; Clear & Present Danger, 1994; Jefferson in Paris, 1995; The Beloved Country Cry, 1995; A Family Thing, 1996; Gang Related, 1997; Casper: ASpirited, voice, 1997; The Lion King II: Simba's Pride, 1998; The Annihilation of Fish, 1999; Martin: Our Friend, 1999; Fantasia 2000, 1999;On the QT, 1999; Undercover Angel, 2000; Finder's Fee, 2001; Star Wars Episode III Revenge of the Sith, voice, 2005; The Sandlot 2, voice, 2005; Robots, voice, 2005; Scary Movie 4, narrator, 2006; Click, vioce, 2006; The Benchwarmers, 2006; TV appearances: "The Defenders; East Side/ WestSide"; "Camera 3"; "Look Up & Give"; "The Cay; King Lear"; "Big Joe & Kansas"; "UFO Incident"; "Jesus of Nazarath"; "The Greatest Thing That Almost Happened"; "Guyana Tragedy, The Story of Jim Jones"; "Me & Mom";"Paris"; "The Golden Movement, An Olympic Love Story"; "Sojourner"; "A DayWithout Sunshine"; "Gabriel's Fire"; "Pros & Cons"; "Under One Roof"; "Homicide", 1997; "What The Deaf Man Heard", 1997; "Alone", 1997; "Merlin", voice, 1998; "Anatomy of a "Homicide: Life on the Street", 1998; "Summer's End", 1999; "Santa & Pete", 1999; "The Washington Monument: It Stands for All", 2000; "Feast of All Saints", 2001; "A Light Knight's Odyssey", voice, 2004, 2006; TV: "Three Miners from Everwood", 2003; "The L Word", 2004; "The Tipping Point", 2004; "The Reading Room", 2005; "The Magic 7", 2006; "The Trail of Tears: Cherokee Legacy", 2006; "Welcome Home Roscoe Jenkins", 2008. **Orgs:** Screen Actors Guild, Actors Equity Asn; Am Fedn TV & Radio Artists; Nat Coun Arts; bd dir, Theatre Commun Group; Nat Rifle Asn Am. **Honors/Awds:** The Village Voice Off-Broadway Awards, 1962; Theatre World Award, 1962; Drama Desk Award, 1964, 1967, 1969, 1970; Obie Award, 1965; Tony Award for Best Actor, Great White Hope, 1969, Best Actor, Fences; Golden Gate Award, 1975; Golden Hugo Award, 1975; Gabriel Award, 1975; Grammy Award, 1976;Medal for Spoken Language, Am Acad Arts & Letters, 1981; inducted into Theatre Hall of Fame, 1985; Antoinette Perry Award, 1987; Outer Critics Circle Award, 1987; Emmy Award, Soldier Boys, 1987; ACE Award, 1989; Emmy Award, Heatwave, 1990; Jean Renoir Award, Los Angeles Film Teachers, 1990; Commonwealth Award, Bank DE, 1991; Emmy Award, Gabriel's Fire, 1991; Hall of Fame Image Award, NAACP, 1992; Nat Medal of the Arts, 1992; Image Award for Outstanding Lead Actor in a Drama Series, Mini-Series or Television Movie, 1993; Joseph Plateau Life Achievement Award, 1995; US Nat Board of Review Career Achievement Award, 1995; Method Fest Lifetime Achievement Award, 2001; John F Kennedy Centre Honour, 2002. **Special Achievements:** Golden Globe Nominee for Best Performance by an Actor in a TV-Series-Drama, 1992. **Military Serv:** AUS, officer. **Business Addr:** Actor, Horatio Productions, PO Box 610, Pawling, NY 12564-0610.

JONES, PROF. JAMES EDWARD
College administrator, educator, government official. **Personal:** Born Jun 4, 1924, Little Rock, AR; son of Alice J Truman; married Joan Cottrell Turner; children: Evan & Peter. **Educ:** Lincoln Univ, BA, 1950; Univ Ill, Inst Labor & Indust Rels, MA, 1951; Univ Wis, Sch Law, JD, 1956. **Career:** US Wage Stabilization Brd, ind rels analyst, 1951-53; US Dept Labor, legisatty, 1956-63, counsel labor rels, 1963-66, Div Labor Rels & Civil Rights,assoc solicitor; Office Labor Mgt Policy Develop, dir, 1966-67; Div Labor Rels & Civil Rights, assoc solicitor, 1967-69; Univ Wis, Madison, vis proflaw & indust rels, 1969-70; Inst Res Poverty, assoc, 1970-71; Inst Rels Res Inst, dir, 1971-73; Ctr Equal Employ & Affirmative Action, Indust Rels Res Inst, dir, 1974-93; Univ Wis, prof, 1970-82; John Bascom, prof law, 1983-91; Nathan P Feinsinger, prof labor law, 1991-93; prof emer, 1993-; United States to the Federal Service Impasses Panel 1978-82; State of Wisconsin to the Manpower Planning Council, 1971-76; Wisconsin Task Force on Comparable Worth 1984-86; City of Madison to the Police and Fire Commission, 1973-77, 1994-95. **Orgs:** Nat Bar Assn; State Bar Wis; Am Bar Assn; UAW, 1970-; Nat Res Coun; adv comt, Nat Acad Scis, 1971-73; Nat Acad Arbitrators, 1982-; Wis Gov's Task Force Comparable Worth, 1984-86; Phi Kappa Phi, 1987; Madison Sch Dist Affirmative Action Adv Comt, 1988-91; US Supreme Ct; Indust Rels Res Assn; United Auto Workers Bd Public Review. **Honors/Awds:** Dept Labor, Sec Labor Career Service Award, 1963; John Hay Whitney Fellow; Smongeski Award, 1988; Lincoln Univ, Alumni Achievement Award, 1967; Prof of the Year, UW Leo Studs, 1986; Hilldale Award, Social Sci Div, 1991; Martin Luther King Humanitarian Award, City Madison, Wis, 1991; C Clyde Ferguson Award; Jr Memorial Award, Am Assn Law Schools Minority Group Sect,1993; Distinguished Service Award, Wis Law Alumni Assn, 1995; Distinguished Alumni Award, Univ Ill, 1996; Teachers Achievement Award, Soc Am Law,1998; Legacy Award, Dunbar High Sch Alumni, Assn, 1999; NBA Hall of Fame, 1999. **Special Achievements:** Race in America, 1992; contribr articles, chaps & prof publs. **Military Serv:** USN, 1943-46. **Business Addr:** Professor Emeritus, Univeristy of Wisconsin, Law School, Rm 9108 975 Bascom Mall, Madison, WI 53706, **Business Phone:** (608)262-2440.

JONES, JAMES F.
Basketball coach. **Personal:** Born Feb 20, 1964, Orange, TX; son of Herman and Edna Davis; married Rebecka, Sep 10, 1994; children: Rachel. **Educ:** Univ Albany, BA, 1986, MA, 1995. **Career:** Univ Albany, asst coach, 1990-95; Yale Univ, asst coach, 1995-97; Ohio Univ, asst coach, 1997-99; Yale Univ, Head Coach, 1999-; Villanova Univ, asst coach, 2007. **Orgs:** Nat Asn Basketball Coaches; New York State Basketball Coaches Asn; Black Coaches Asn. **Home Phone:** (203)432-1485. **Business Addr:** The Joel E Smilow Head Coach, Yale University, Department of Yale Athletics, 20 Tower Pkwy, PO Box 208216, New Haven, CT 06520-8216, **Business Phone:** (203)432-1485.

JONES, JAMES MCCOY
Educator. **Personal:** Born Apr 5, 1941, Detroit, MI; son of Arthur McCoy Jones and Marcella Hayes-Jones; married Olaive Burrowes; children: Shelly & Itenash. **Educ:** Oberlin Col, BA, psychology, 1963; Temple Univ, MA, 1967; Yale Univ, PhD, 1970. **Career:** Franklin Inst, Philadelphia, psychol res, 1964-66; Harvard Univ, asst prof soc psychol, 1970-74, assoc prof soc psychol, 1974-76, vs prof, 1978; Educ Develop Ctr, Exploring Childhood Proj, sr scholar, 1973-74; Guggenheim Fel, 1973; Boston Office Lawrence Johnson & Assocs, dir, 1974-76; Nat Inst Adv Studies, staff dir, 1976-77; APA MNY Fel Prog, dir, 1977; Am Psychol Asn, dir, 1977-, affirmative action officer, 1986-, exec dir, 1987-91; APA Pub Interest Directorate, Inaugural dir; Univ Delaware, prof psychol, 1982-, vis distinguished prof, 1981-82, prof & dir, Black Am Studies, 2005-. **Orgs:** Exec dir, Pub Int Am Psychol Asn, 1987-91; Asn Black Psychologists; pres, Soc Psychol Study Soc Issues; educ consult, J Personality & Soc Psychol; J Clin Psychol; Psychol Bulletin; NIMH Small Grant Review Comt; assembly Behavioral Sci, 1973-77; adv bd, WEB Dubois Res Inst; Comt Res Review Comn, Roxbury, MA, 1970-74; Am Psychol Asn; Am Psychol Soc; Soc Personality & Social Psychol; Soc Psychol Study Ethnic Minority Issues; Soc Exp Social Psychol; Am Educ Res Asn; Asn Behavioral Scientists Med Educ; DC Psychol Asn; Am Sociol Asn; AAAS. **Honors/Awds:** Glen Grey Mem Scholar, Oberlin Col, 1959-63; NIMH Predoctoral Fel, 1967-70; Hon Sterling Fel, Yale Univ, 1968-69; John Simon Guggenheim Fel, 1973-74. **Special Achievements:** Author: "Prejudice and Racism", 1997; "The Black Experience"; "A Compelling Interest: Weighing the evidence on racial dynamics in higher education", 2003; "Essays in honor of a Social Activist and scholar", 2004; "Reflecting on the Nature of Prejudice", 2004; James M.Jones Lifetime Achievement Award, APA Minority Fel Prog. **Business Addr:** Professor, Director, University of Delaware, Department of Psychology, 224 Wolf Hall, Newark, DE 19716, **Business Phone:** (302)831-2489.

JONES, JAMES R
Executive, business owner, consultant. **Personal:** Born Apr 1, 1944, Morristown, NJ; son of James E and Elizabeth B; married Janet Watkins-Jones, Feb 12, 1967; children: Jill, Jackie & Jimmy. **Educ:** Univ Nebr, BS, sec educ & libr sci, 1966; Cent Mich Univ, MA, mgt personnel, 1979. **Career:** Prof football player & teacher, 1966-70; NY Jets Prof Football Club, asst dir personnel, 1970-72; Jersey Cent Power & Light Co, mgr employ & asst to vpres, 1972-80; Gannett Co Inc, dir affirmative action & employee rels, 1980-

84, vpres employee rels, 1984-91; John Hopkins Univ, vpres human resources, 1991-95; Franciscan Health Syst, sr vpres human resources, 1995-96; Inova Health Syst, vpres human resources, 1996-97; Reebok Int Inc, Reebok Div, sr vpres human resources & chief human resources officer, 1997; Jimmy Jones & Assocs, owner, currently. **Orgs:** Kappa Alpha Phi; bd trustees, Exec Leadership Coun; Black Human Resources Network; Edges; Soc Human Resources Mgt; sr vpres, Human Resources Roundtable; trustee, Reebok Found; Conf Bd's Chief Adminr Officer's Coun. **Business Addr:** Owner, Jimmy Jones & Associates, 45 Pk Pl S 102, Morristown, NJ 07960, **Business Phone:** (973)605-8301.

JONES, JAMES V
Automotive executive. **Personal:** Born May 16, 1942, Jackson, NC; son of James and Viola M Brown; divorced; children: James III. **Educ:** NC Central Univ, Durham NC, law degree, 1976. **Career:** Ozone Ford Ltd, Ozone Park, NY, pres, 1987-. **Business Phone:** (718)296-2222.

JONES, JENNIE Y.
Educator, teacher, executive director. **Personal:** Born May 26, 1921, Woodlawn, IL; widowed; children: Johnetta, Harry, Jerry & Danny. **Educ:** Southern Ill Univ, Carbondale, BEd, 1942; Univ Ill, MA, 1949. **Career:** Head Start SIU, regional training officer, 1970-74, prog dir, 1973; Carbonate Sch Dist 95, teacher, 1948-70; Southern Ill Univ, Carbondale, Child Develop Lab, asst prof & dir minority affairs, currently. **Orgs:** Bd dirs, Ill Asn Educ Young C; Delta Kappa Gamma; adv comt mem, Training &Tech Asst Model Cities; bd dirs, State Comn Coordinated Child Care; adv comt mem, Lincoln land Community Col. **Honors/Awds:** Hon Advisory Consult Award, Jackson County, Mental Health Bd, IL Asn Head Start Dirs, 1975. **Business Addr:** Director, Southern Illinois University, 1168 SIU, Carbondale, IL 62901.

JONES, JENNIFER
Opera singer. **Personal:** Born in Wilmington, DE; children: 3. **Educ:** Curtis Inst Music, BM, 1975. **Career:** Grant Martha Baird Rockefeller & Found Philadelphia Orchestra Competition, soloist, 1973; Philadelphia Orchestra, soloist, 1973; Los Angeles Philharmonic, soloist, 1976, 1978 & 1980; Israeli Philharmonic, soloist, 1976 & 1980; NY Philharmonic, soloist, 1979; Houston Grand Opera, alto soloist, 1980; Montreal Symphony, soloist, 1980; opera singer, currently.

JONES, DR. JESSE W.
College administrator. **Personal:** Born Jan 16, 1931, Troup, TX; married LaBelle; children: Penola Washington, Tacora Ballums, Phelisha, Jesse Jr, David, Stephen &Lilla. **Educ:** Tex Col, BS, 1954; Univ Utah, advan work, attended 1956; Highlands Univ, MS, 1956; Ariz State Univ, PhD, 1963, DSc, 1993. **Career:** TX Col, instructor of chem, 1956-58; AZ St, rsch assoc, 1958-63; TX Col, chmn/prof 1963-68; Bishop Col, chmn & prof, 1968-; Baylor Univ, prof, currently. **Orgs:** Pres, Bishop Col Fed Credit Union, 1969-85; vchmn, City Dallas Bd Adjustment, 1977-82; pres, Dallas City Democratic Progressive Voters League, 1977-85; vchmn, Dallas Environ Health Comn, 1983-; Am Chem Soc; fel, Am Sci Soc; sec, Searcy's Youth Found; fel, Am Inst Chemists. **Honors/Awds:** Salutatorium EJ Scott High School, 1950; Outstanding Citizenship Mu Gamma Chapter, Omega Psi Phi, 1976; Silver Beaver Award, Boys Scouts Am, 1983; Craft Award in Politics Dallas Chapter, NAACP, 1984; UNCF Distinguished Scholar, 1986; Tex Black Legislator's Citizenship Award, 1987. **Business Addr:** Professor, Baylor University, Department Chemistry & Biochemistry, Baylor Univ Sci Bldg, 1 Bear Pl Suite 97348, Waco, TX 76706, **Business Phone:** (254)710-6842.

JONES, JILL MARIE
Actor. **Personal:** Born Jan 4, 1975, Dallas, TX. **Educ:** Tex Women's Univ. **Career:** Dallas Cowboys, cheer leader; Dallas Mavericks, dancer; TV series: "Girlfriends", 2000; "City Guys", 2000; "American Dream"; "The Sharon Osbourne Show", 2004; "35th NAACP Image Awards", co-host, 2004; "BET Comedy Awards", 2004; "106 & Park Top 10 Live", 2005; "All Shades of Fine: 25 Hottest Women of the Past 25 Years", 2005; Films: City Guys, 2000; Girlfriends, 2000-06; Redrum, 2007; Universal Remote, 2007; The Perfect Holiday, 2007; Major Movie Star, 2008; The Longshots, 2008. **Orgs:** Alpha Kappa Alpha Sorority. **Special Achievements:** Featured in King magazine, 2002; first woman to host "2004 NAACP Image Awards" program. **Business Addr:** Actress, United Paramount Network, 11800 Wilshire Blvd, Los Angeles, CA 90025, **Business Phone:** (310)575-7000.*

JONES, JIMMIE DENE
Consultant. **Personal:** Born Feb 26, 1939, Childress, TX; married Thelma Wilkerson; children: Vickie Harris, Jimmie D Jr, Amanda Lene Scott & Darryl Bryan. **Educ:** St Marys Col, BSBA, 1973; George Wash Univ, MBA, 1978; Col Financial Planning, Cert, 1984. **Career:** Law Engineering, personnel dir, 1979-86; bus consult, 1982-; J&L Financial Serv, owner 1986-. **Orgs:** Northern Va Minority & Prof Bus Assocs, 1984; chmn, exec, LB Bailey Found Youthful Entrepreneurs. **Honors/Awds:** Proclamation for Volunteer as Financial Counselor, County Exten Off, 1986. **Military Serv:** AUS, cmd sgt, maj E9; Army Commendation Medal, Bronze Star. **Home Addr:** 10019 Lake Jackson Dr, Manassas, VA 20110. **Business Addr:** Consultant, 14760 Independent Lane, Manassas, VA 20112, **Business Phone:** (703)794-8759.

JONES, JIMMIE SIMS
Football player. **Personal:** Born Jan 9, 1966, Lakeland, FL; children: Jimmeria & Jimmie Jr. **Educ:** Univ Miami, Fla. **Career:** Football player (Retired); Dallas Cowboys, defensive tackle, 1990-93; Los Angeles Rams, 1994; St Louis Rams, 1995-96; Philadelphia Eagles, 1997. **Honors/Awds:** Extra Effort Award, NFL, 1995; True Value Hardware Man of the Year Award, St Louis Rams, 1995.

JONES, JOHNNIE ANDERSON
Lawyer. **Personal:** Born Nov 30, 1919, Laurel Hill, LA; son of Henry E and Sarah Ann Coats; married Sebell Elizabeth Chase (divorced); children: Johnnie Jr, Adair Darnell, Adal Dalcho & Ann Sarah Bythelda. **Educ:** Southern Univ, BS, psychol, 1949; Southern Univ Law Sch, JD Law, 1953. **Career:** Universal Life Ins Co, ins agent, 1947-48; US Post Off, ltr carrier, 1948-50; Southern Univ Law Sch, law sch stud, 1950-53; LA State Bar Asn, lawyer, 1953-; Jones & Jones, sr lawyer, currently. **Orgs:** Nat Asn Advan Colored People, 1936-; Asst parish atty City Parish Govt, 1969-72; Frontiers Club Int, 1962-; Alpha Phi Alpha Frat, 1972-; state rep, LA House Rep, 1972-76; sr lawyer, Jones & Jones Atty Law, 1975-. **Honors/Awds:** Frontier man of the year, Frontiers Col Int, 1962; Cert of appreciation, LB Johnson & HH Humphrey, 1964; plaque Alpha Kappa Alpha Sorority, 1972; Most Outstanding Mount, Zion First Bapt Church, 1970. **Military Serv:** AUS, warrant officer, 1942-46; Good Conduct Medal, 1942-46. **Business Addr:** Attorney, Jones & Jones Attorneys-at-Law, 263 3rd St Suite 702, Baton Rouge, LA 70801-1703.*

JONES, DR. JOSEPH
Educator. **Personal:** Born Jun 3, 1928, Albany, GA; son of Joseph and Hattie Turner; married Etta M; children: Josetta I & Robyn M Thomas. **Educ:** Morris Brown Col, BS, 1950; Northwestern Univ, MSc, 1952; Ohio State Univ, PhD, 1960. **Career:** St Augustine's Col, Dept Biol, head, 1952-57, acad dean, 1966-69, Acad Affairs, vpres, 1969-72, Title III Proj, coordr; Univ Sci & Technol, Ghana, W Africa, Fulbright-Hays prof, 1972-73; Tex Southern Univ, dean grad sch, prof biol, assoc vpres res & grad studies, currently; consult strategy planning & educ. **Orgs:** Dir, teacher sci, Nat Sci Found & Atomic Energy Comn Inst; fel Ohio Acad Sci; Sigma Xi Sci Hon Soc; Alpha Mu Hon Soc; Ohio Acad Sci; Am Soc Parasitologists; Nat Sci Teacher Asn; Am Mus Nat Hist; Alpha Phi Alpha Frat. **Honors/Awds:** Spec Danforth Grad Fel, 1958; United Negro Col Fund Fel, 1959; Sr Fulbright-Hays Professorship, Ghana W Africa, 1972; Delaney Educator of the Year Award, 1981; Int Educator Award, 1993. **Business Addr:** Associate Vice President for Research & Graduate Studies, Dean of the Graduate School, Texas Southern University, Department of Biology, 3100 Cleburne St, Houston, TX 77004, **Business Phone:** (713)313-7941.

JONES, K. C.
Basketball coach, basketball player, executive. **Personal:** Born May 25, 1932, Taylor, TX; son of K C Jones Sr and Eula Daniels; children: 6. **Educ:** Univ San Francisco, attended 1956. **Career:** Basketball player, basketball coach (retired), executive; Boston Celtics, 1958-67, asst coach, 1978-79, 1982-83, 1996-97, head coach, 1983-88, vpres basketball opers, 1988-89; Brandeis Univ, head coach, 1967-70; Harvard Univ, asst coach, 1970-71; Los Angeles Lakers, asst coach, 1971-72; ABA San Diego Conquistadors, head coach, 1972-73; Capital Bullets/Wash Bullets, head coach, 1973-76; Milwaukee Bucks, asst coach, 1976-77; Seattle Supersonics, asst coach, 1989-90, head coach, 1990-92; Detroit Pistons, asst coach, 1994-95; ABL New England Blizzard, 1997-99; Univ Hartford, spl asst to dir athletics & commentator, currently. **Orgs:** Kappa Alpha Fraternity. **Honors/Awds:** Olympic Gold Medal, USA Basketball Team, 1956; Eight Championship Rings; Bay Area Hall of Fame, 1986; Naismith Memorial Basketball Hall of Fame, 1989. **Special Achievements:** Only African American coach to win multiple NBA championships as solely ahead coach. **Military Serv:** AUS, 1956-58.

JONES, K MAURICES
Writer. **Career:** Author: Say It Loud; Spike Lee & The African American Filmmakers.

JONES, KATHERINE COLEMAN
Educator. **Personal:** Born Jun 23, 1931, Louisville, KY; daughter of Theodore Roosevelt and Lillian Russell McDowell; married Chester, Jun 30, 1955; children: Kim Joan Wallace. **Educ:** Univ Louisville, BA, elem educ, 1953, MA, admin, 1972, EdS, 1974; Kent Sch Social Work, cert, 1973; Spalding Univ, cert African Am Ministries, 1998. **Career:** Educator (retired); Jefferson County Schs, elem teacher, 1953-67, social worker, 1967-68, urban rural dir, 1968-77, stud affairs liaison, 1977-85. **Orgs:** Nat Asn Advan Colored People; League Women Voters; Black Womens Polit Caucus; Govs Club; State Adv Educ Improvement, 1984; Commonwealth Inst Teachers; bd mem, Nat Conf Christians & Jews; dir social concerns, Watson Mem Baptist Church; Black Family Conf; bd dirs, YMCA; Progressive Nat Baptist Conv. **Honors/Awds:** Teacher of the Year, Louisville Pub Schs, 1967; Teacher of the Year, Durrett HS, 1981; Special Award, NAACP, 1984; Special Award, Nat Conf Christian & Jews, 1986; Mary McLeod Bethune Award, 1990; Adult Black Achiever, 1996; Adult Black Achiever, YWCA, 1996. **Home Addr:** 500 Brook Stone Way, Louisville, KY 40223-2652, **Home Phone:** (502)245-7014.

JONES, DR. KATHERINE ELIZABETH BUTLER
Educational consultant, writer. **Personal:** Born Mar 19, 1936, New York, NY; daughter of Meme Elgitha Clark Butler (deceased) and Theodore Harold Butler (deceased); married Hubert; children: Karen, Lauren, Harlan, Renee, Lisa, Hamilton, Cheryl & Tanya. **Educ:** Mt Holyoke Col, BA, econ & sociol, 1957; Simmons Col, MA, urban educ, 1967; Harvard Univ, EdD, admin & social policy, 1980. **Career:** Boston Pub Schs, teacher, 1958-59; Newton Pub Schs, coord ed prog, 1966-76; Simmons Col, instr, 1967-69; Newton Pub Schs Metrop Coun Educ Opportunities Prog, dir & founder, 1967-76; Sch Systs Pub & Independent MA, consult, 1968-; Wheelock Col, instr, 1976; Cambridge Pub Schs, supvr staff & prog, 1977-81; self-employed educ consult; Deeper Roots Publs, author, currently; Books: Garnets, Diamonds & Other Black Jewels, Am Visions, 1998; They Called It Timbukto, Orion Mag, 1998; Civil Rights Movement in Newton, 1960-80, 2002; Baseball & Madame St Clair, Harvard Rev, 2003; An American Odyssey, Deeper Roots. **Orgs:** Bd dir, METCO, 1966-73; bd trustees, Mt Holyoke Col, 1973-78; Newton Sch Comt, 1978-85; minority affairs comt, Nat Assoc IN Schs, 1984-89; bd, Boston C's Serv, 1985-; bd, Family Serv Asn, 1986-, vice chairperson, 1989-91; Mass Coalition Homeless, 1989-99; Newton Fair Housing; Equal Rights Comt. **Honors/Awds:** Ed Excellence Scholarship to Student Black Citizens of Newton, 1976; Serv METCO City of Newton, 1976; Contrib to Integrated Ed METCO Boston Staff, 1976; Serv Above Self Newton Chamber Com, 1974; Doctoral Dissertation Sch Consolidation in Newton, 1980; Citizens Who Make a Difference ContribMental Health MA Assoc Mental Health, 1982; Tribute to 350 years BlackPresence in Massachusetts Honoree, Museum Afro-Am History, 1988;Nominating Com for Alumnae Trustees Mt Holyoke Col, 1990-92; SchombergScholar in Black Culture NYK Pub Libr, 1991-92; Award Black AlumnaeConference, Mt Holyoke Col, 1994; Fac Boston Univ, Afro-Am Studies Prog,1993-95; Newton Citizen Recognition of Distinction, 1994; Family HistoryExhibitor Museum our Nat Heritage, Lexington, MA, 1995; Discovery AuthorNon-Fiction, New England Pen Writers, 1996. **Special Achievements:** Served as first black member in Newton School Committee from 1978 to 1985. **Home Phone:** (617)332-8183. **Business Addr:** Author, Deeper Roots Publications, 2100 Red Gate Rd, Orlando, FL 32818, **Business Phone:** (407)293-8666.

JONES, DR. KELSEY A.
Educator. **Personal:** Born Jul 15, 1933, Holly Springs, MD; married Virginia Bethel Ford; children: Kelsey Jr, Cheryl Darlene Campbell-Smith, Eric Andre & Claude Anthony. **Educ:** Miss Indust Col, AB (Magna Cum Laude), 1955; Garrett Theol Seminary NWUniv, MDiv, 1959; Univ Mich Med Ctr, clin pastoral care & coun, 1960;Wesley Med Ctr, post grad cert, 1967; Miss Indust Col, DD, 1969; NatParole Inst, Nat Coun Crime & Deliquency-State Univ New York, Albany, Sch Criminal Justice-Inst Man & Science, cert, 1970; Geroge Mason Univ, cert, 1984. **Career:** Fed City Col (UDC Mt Vernon Campus), vis lectr, Black hist, 1973-75; INTER/MET, dir Bacc & Liason consult, 1973-77; Univ DC, Van Ness Campus, prof social sci 1972-77, chmn dept soc/behav sci, 1977-78, prof, Dept Criminal Justice, 1978-94, chmn 1979-91, pres, spec asst environ health, Occup Safety & Inst Security 1984-86; justice prof emer, cur; The ThinkTank Emer Manor, resident faclitator. **Orgs:** Sec NY/WA Annual Conf Vis Chpl Meth Pop Cook County Jail 1956-58; aptd staff Recep-Diag Cntr MI Correct Comn, 1961; sec KS/MO Annual Conf, 1962-70; delegate Gen Conf of Christ Meth Epis Ch, 1966; chmn, St Bd Probation & Parole, 1967; delegate Centennial Session Gen Conf 1970; Dean Leadership Educ ea of 3 confs of 3rd Episcopal Dist; Acad Criminal Justice Scientists; N Atlan Conf Criminal Justice Educators; Inst Criminal Justice Ethics; Nat Criminal Justice Asn, Northeastern Asn Criminal Justice Educators; Am Soc Indust Security; Nat Asn Chiefs Police, Am Soc Pub Admin; Am Asn Higher Educ; Phi Alpha Frat Mu Lamda Chap DC; first vpres Wichita Urban League; bd dirs Bros Inc; LEAP com deseg pub schools, Wichita; Cur Soc. **Honors/Awds:** Presidential Citation, Nat Asn Equal Opportunities Higher Educ; Alumnus of the Year; Distinguished Service Award, Howard Univ; Distinguished Service Award, Univ DC; Lorton Stud Govt Asn contribution to the Lorton Prison Proj; Awarded certificate for workshop on Crime Prevention for Collegesand Universities, Campus Crime Prevention Programs, 1985. **Special Achievements:** Public speaker; written and published many papers and articles. **Home Addr:** 5427 Kansas Ave NW, Washington, DC 20011, **Home Phone:** (202)723-1378. **Business Addr:** Resident Facilitator, Takoma Pk, PO Box 60379-0379, Washington, DC 20039-0379.

JONES, DR. KENNETH LEROY
Surgeon. **Personal:** Born in Kinston, NC; children: Kathryn, Amber, Jonathan. **Educ:** Amherst Col, BS, 1973; Howard Univ Col Med, MD, 1978. **Career:** US Pub Health Serv Johns Hopkins Hosp, gen surgery resident, 1978-83; Advanced Indust Med Inc, vice pres & med dir; E Coast Health Org Inc, pres med dir. **Business Addr:** 300 W Clarendon 240, Phoenix, AZ.

JONES, KIMBERLY DENISE (QUEEN BEE)
Rap musician. **Personal:** Born Jul 11, 1975, Brooklyn, NY; daughter of Linwood and Ruby Mae. **Career:** Albums: Hard Core, 1996; Notorious KIM, 2000; La Belle Mafia, 2003; The Naked Truth, 2005; The Dance Remixes, 2006; The G.O.A.T Mixtape, 2007; Vintage, 2009; Films: She's All That, 1999; Long shot, 2000; Juwanna Mann, 2002; Gang of Roses, 2003; You Got Served, 2004; Nora's Hair Salon, 2004; Superhero Movie, 2008; TV Series: Fuse's Summer Jam X, 2003; American Dreams, 2003; Lil Kim: Countdown to Lock down, exec producer, 2006; The Game, 2007;Singles: Chillin" Tonight; Queen Bee Records, ceo,1999-. **Orgs:** Lil' Kim Cares. **Honors/Awds:** Soul Train Lady of Soul Award, Best R&B/Soul or Rap Music Video, 1998; Best Video, "Lady Marmalade," MTV Video Music Award, 2001; Best Rap Performance by a Duo or Group, Grammy Awards, 2003; Best Video from a Film for "Lady Marmalade", MTV Video Music Award, 2003; Best Female Hip-Hop Artist, American Music Award, 2003; Grammy Awards, 1997, 2002, 2003, 2008; Female Artist of the Year Source Award, 2003; Most Stylish Artist of the Year MOBO Award, 2003. **Special Achievements:** Ranked 34 on VH1's 50 Greatest Hip Hop Artists; Ranked 71 on VH1's 100 Sexiest Artists. **Business Addr:** Singer, c/o Atlantic Records, 1290 Avenue of the Americas 28 Fl, New York, NY 10104-0101, **Business Phone:** (212)707-2000.*

JONES, KIRK. See FINGAZ, STICKY.

JONES, LAFAYETTE GLENN
Marketing executive. **Personal:** Born Feb 17, 1944, Cincinnati, OH; married Wanda S Harriel; children: Kevin, Keith, Melanie, Glenn, Tara. **Educ:** Fisk Univ, BA, 1965; Howard Univ, attended 1966; Stanford Univ, cert mktg mgt, 1976. **Career:** Job Corps, ABT Assoc, Westinghouse Learning Corp YMCA, dir prg acct, 1965-67; State WOL, Sonderling Broadcast Co, dir pub rels, 1967-69; Imperial Margs Food Div, Lever Bros Co, Golden Glow, prod mdse asst, 1969-70; Pillsbury Co, Refrig Foods Div, prod mgr; Birds Eye Div, Gen Foods Corp, Orange Plus, assoc prod mgr, 1970-72; Procter & Gamble; Pillsbury Co; Kraft Foods, mkt exec; Hunt Wesson Foods Div, Norton Simon Inc, Hunts Manwich & Tomato Pastem, mkt mgr, 1974-79; Am Health & Beauty Aids Inst, exec dir; Johnson Prod Co, Chicago, vpres mkt & sales, 1979-; Supreme Beauty Prod, Chicago, IL, vpres & gen mgr, 1988-; Segmented Mkt Serv Inc, pres & chief exec officer, currently. **Orgs:** Bd dir, hon Am Youth Fedn, 1972-74; vpres, bd trustee, Mardan Educ Ctr; Nat Asn Mkt Develop; Urban League. **Honors/Awds:** Frederick Douglas Patterson Award, National Business League, 1987. **Business Addr:** President, Chief Executive Officer, Segmented Marketing Service Inc, 4265 Brownsboro Rd Suite 225, Winston Salem, NC 27106-3425.*

JONES, LARRY. See JONES, DR. EDWARD.

JONES, LARRY WAYNE
Aerospace engineer. **Personal:** Born Jul 8, 1950, Mt Pleasant, TX; son of Don G and Dorothy T; married Beverly Pope Jones, Mar 12, 1976; children: Martin, Thomas & Andrew. **Educ:** US Naval Acad, Annapolis, MD, BS, 1973; US Dept Defense, Fort Belvoir, VA, defense systs mgt col, 1985; Purdue Univ, MS Mgt, 1997. **Career:** Pratt & Whitney, Div United Technologies Corp, dir customer support prog, 1979-, vpres, Mil Customer Support, currently. **Orgs:** United States Naval Acad Alumni Asn. **Military Serv:** USMC, ltcol, res, 1973; Pilot Wings USN, 1975. **Business Addr:** Director, Vice President, Pratt & Whitney, 400 Main St M/S 181-42, PO Box 109600, East Hartford, CT 06108, **Business Phone:** (860)565-4321.

JONES, DR. LAWRENCE N.
School administrator, dean (education). **Personal:** Born Apr 24, 1921, Moundsville, WV; son of Eugene W and Rosa L; married Mary Ellen Cooley; children: Lynn Walker Huntley & Rodney Bruce. **Educ:** WVa State Col, BS, educ, 1942; Univ Chicago, MA, hist, 1948; Oberlin GradSch Theol, BD, 1956; Yale Univ Grad Sch, PhD, religion, 1957, 1961. **Career:** Dean (retired); Oberlin Grad Sch, Lucy Monroe Fel, 1956; Rockefeller Brothers, Rockefeller Doctoral Fel, 1959-61; Fisk Univ, dean chapel, 1960-64; Union Theol Seminary NY, dean prof, 1965-75; Howard Univ Divinity Sch, dean prof, 1975-91, dean emer, 1991-. **Orgs:** United Church Pod World Ministries, 1975-81; consult, Lilly Endowment Inc, Cong Natl Black Churches, Grad Theol Union 1983; chmn, Civil Rights Coord Comm Nashville, 1962-64; pres, Soc Study Black Religion, 1974-77; secy assoc, Theol Sch, 1981-82; bd mem, WHMM TV Pub Adv Bd, 1984-. **Honors/Awds:** Rosenwald Scholarship Rosenwald Fund, 1942; LLD, WVA State Col, 1965; DHL, Jewish Theol Seminary, 1971; DD, Chicago Theol Seminary, 1975; DD, Shaw Univ, 1986; DD, Episcopal Theol Seminary in Va, 1992. **Military Serv:** Quartermaster capt, 1943, 1946, 1947, 1953. **Home Addr:** 1206 Devere Dr, Silver Spring, MD 20903. *

JONES, LAWRENCE W.
Educator. **Personal:** Born Feb 6, 1942, Newport News, VA; married Lolita Diane Grey; children: Lawrence W Jr & Leonard W. **Educ:** Hampton Inst, VA, attended 1964; State Teachers Col Bowie, BS, educ 1967; Univ Mass Amherst, EdD, 1973. **Career:** Bd Educ NYC, teacher, 1967-73; Univ Mass, teaching asst, 1970-73; Univ Mass Brooklyn, COP Prog supvr stud teaching, 1971-73; Youth Action Neighborhood Youth Corp, remedial coord, 1973; Univ NY, Medgar Evers Col, asst prof, educ, 1974-77; Bd Educ NY, teacher reading specialist, 1977-; Community Sch, Newark, consult educ, 1978; Mayor Newark, spec asst educ prog, 1979. **Orgs:** Omega Psi Phi Fraternity, 1972-; consult wedn, Pro Day Care Ctrs Pvt Sch NY, 1975-; One Hundered Black Men, 1978-. **Honors/Awds:** Innovation in Teaching Dissertation, Univ Mass, 1973; Pub Classroom Mgt Ind Instn, 1973-74; Community Serv Awards, Brooklyn COP & Community Life Ctr, 1974-78; Measuring Children's Growth Reading Expanding Reading Exp, 1978.

JONES, LEANDER CORBIN
Educator. **Personal:** Born Jul 16, 1934, Vincent, AR; son of Lander Corbin and Una Bell; married Lethonee Angela Hendricks (died 2006); children: Angela Lynne & Leander Corbin. **Educ:** Univ Ariz, Pine Bluff, BA, 1956; Univ Ill, MS, 1968; Union Grad Inst, PhD, 1973. **Career:** Educator (retired); Chicago Pub Sch, eng teacher, 1956-68; Peace Corps Vol, Eng teacher, 1964-66; TV producer City Col Chicago, 1968-73; Meharry Med Col, communications media specialist, 1973-75; Western Mich Univ, Black Americana studies, from assoc prof to prof, 1975-2003, African studies prog, chmn, 1980-81, Black caucus, co-chmn, 1983-84; Corbin 22 Ltd, pres, 1986; 7 art workshop Am Negro Emancipation Centennial Authority, dir; bd dirs, Kalamazoo Civic Players, 1981-83; pres, Black Theater Kalamazoo, 1978-85; Mich Black Repertory Theatre, dir dramaturg, 1987-90; Ransom Street Playhouse, Kalamazoo, exec prod, 1993. **Orgs:** Kappa Alpha Psi, 1953-; mem exec comt, DuSable Mus African Am Hist, 1970-; pres TABS Ctr 1972-; AAUP 1973-; Nat Coun Black Studies, 1977-; mem, Prisoners Progress Asn, 1977-82; chmn, Comn Against Apartheid, 1977-90; Mich Coun Black Studies, 1977-96; chmn, Kalamazoo Community Rels Bd, 1977-79; Popular Cult Asn, 1978-; SAfrica Solidarity Orgn, 1978-90; Mich Orgn African Studies, 1980-97; comdr Vets Peace Kalamazoo, 1980-91; pres, Black Theatre Group Kalamazoo Civic Players, 1980-83; bd dirs, Kalamazoo Civic Players, 1981-83, Mich Community Crime and Delinq, 1981-83; pres, Corbin 22 Ltd, 1986-; secy bd, Lester Lake Corp, 1992-; designer progs theatre & TV hard educate. **Special Achievements:** TV Series; Roof Over My Head, WDCN, Nashville, 1975, acted in & dir several plays Kalamazoo, 1979-02, Fade to Black, 1986-95; author: Africa Is for Reel, Kalamazoo, 1983. **Military Serv:** AUS, pfc, 1956-58. **Home Addr:** 2226 S Westnedge Ave Suite 222, Kalamazoo, MI 49008.

JONES, DR. LEE
Educator, school administrator. **Personal:** Born Jul 4, 1965, Newark, NJ; son of Levi and Carrie (deceased). **Educ:** Del State Univ, BA, 1987; Ohio State Univ, MA, 1989, MBA, 1992, PhD, 1995. **Career:** Ohio State Univ, resident life dir, 1988-90, dir retention, 1990-93, asst to the vpres, 1993-95; Wash State Univ, dir & asst prof, 1995-97; Fla State Univ, assoc dean & assoc prof, 1997-2004; Univ Wis, Whitewater, dean sch grad studies & prof educ found, currently. **Orgs:** Acad Human Resource Develop; Am Asn Higher Educ; Nat Asn Equal Opportunity; Am Soc Training & Develop; Am Soc Quality; founder, Future Univ Orgn, 1993-; founder, brothers Acad. **Honors/Awds:** Presidential Social Responsibility Award, Kent State Univ, 1997; Distinguished Image Award, Wash State Univ, 1997; Dedication Award, Keystone Col, 1999; Visiting Scholar Award, Univ Ala Birmingham, 1999; Alumni Award, Nat Asn Equal Opportunity, 2000. **Special Achievements:** National public speaker, 1990-, producer and show host of TV talk show host, 1995-, has completed four edited books and one single authored book. **Business Addr:** Dean of Graduate Studies, Professor of Educational Leadership, University of Wisconsin, School of Graduate Studies, Roseman Hall 2013 800 W Main, Whitewater, WI 53190, **Business Phone:** (608)472-1100.*

JONES, LEELAND NEWTON, JR.
School administrator, city council member. **Personal:** Born Jun 15, 1921, Buffalo, NY; son of Leeland N Sr and Julia M Anthony; married Carlita Murphy, May 5, 1945; children: Dr Leeland Anthony Murphy Jones, Dr Johnaaron Murphy Jones, Carlita C M J Perkins. **Educ:** Univ Buffalo, BA, anthrop, 1947; Univ Buffalo Law Sch, attended 1951. **Career:** School administrator (retired); Met Serv Acct, owner; Erie County, supvr, 1948; Buffalo City, coun, 1950-54, pres, proterm city coun, 1953-54; NY State Com vs Discrimination, field rep, 1957-60; Buffalo Urban League, assoc dir, 1964-67; NYS Educ Dept Adult Educ, task force dir; Erie Community Col, asst vpres; OJT Prog, JET Chamber Com, dir. **Orgs:** Organizer & treas, US Stud Asn, 1946; Am Leg; 32nd Prince Hall Mason, Shrine; past pres, Black Hist Found; past pres trustee, Uni Buffalo; bd UB Alumni Asn; pres, Int Veterans Asn; pres, Chef de Gare Veterans Asn; exec comt, AAA Western & Central NY; bd mem, Jesse Ketchum Scholars Awards Comt; chair, State & Local Americanism; assoc minister, Bethel Am Methodist Episcopal Church; bd, Buffalo & Erie County Hist Soc; City Buffalo Charter Revision Comn, chmn, Ethics Task Force, 1998. **Honors/Awds:** Man of the Year, Jr Chamber Com; UB Football Scholarship, 1940; Bison Head Honor Society, 1942; Outstanding Young Man Award, Buffalo City, 1951; Civil Liberties Award, IBPOE; National Elks Oratorical Scholarship Winner; Man of the Year, City of Buffalo, 1988; UB Athletic Hall of Fame, 1990; Family Life Award, Urban League, 1994; Twentieth Century 100 Outstanding Western New Yorkers, Channel 2; MLK Man of the Year, UAW; 20 Outstanding Citizens of the 20th Century, WGRZ-TV. **Special Achievements:** First African American on an integrated University of Buffalo football team; First African-American elected to public office in Buffalo. **Military Serv:** AUS, lt. **Home Addr:** 89 E Depew Ave, Buffalo, NY 14214. *

JONES, LEMUEL B.
Secretary (office). **Personal:** Born Mar 3, 1929, Norway, SC; married Mary Jamison; children: Mark, Karla, Jarret & Eric Jamison. **Educ:** BS, 1952. **Career:** EI DuPont Co, operator chem, 1952-65; Prod & Qual Assurance, foreman, 1965-72; equal employ off, personnel asst, 1972. **Orgs:** Nat Asn Advan Colored People; vpres, PTA; vpres, Sunday Sch Conv; Kappa Alpha Psi Frat. **Honors/Awds:** AUS Achievement Award. **Military Serv:** USN, 1946-48; AUSR, maj, 1952-. *

JONES, LENOY
Football player. **Personal:** Born Sep 25, 1974, Marlin, TX. **Educ:** Tex Christian Univ. **Career:** Football player (retired); Houston Oilers, linebacker, 1996; Tenn Oilers, 1997-98; Cleveland Browns, 1999-02.

JONES, REV. LEON C. See Obituaries section.

JONES, LEONARD WARREN
Lawyer. **Personal:** Born Sep 20, 1965, Washington, DC; son of Lawrence and Lolita. **Educ:** Norfolk State Univ, BS, 1988; Col Ins, MBA, 1992; Thomas M Cooley Law Sch, JD, 1992. **Career:** Pvt Pract, currently. **Orgs:** Omega Psi Phi Fraternity, Inc; 100 Black Men Inc. **Military Serv:** AUS Reserves, capt. *

JONES, LEORA SAM
Athlete. **Personal:** Born Aug 11, 1960, Mt Olive, NC; daughter of Ernest Jones Ruthie and Mae Jones. **Educ:** Louisburg Jr col, asso,1980; East Carolina Univ, 1982. **Career:** Bayer Pharmaceuticals, mkt asst, 1985-86; First Citizens Bank, phillipsburg machine operator, 1989-90, 1992-; Natl Olympic Handball Team, 1992. **Orgs:** Colorado Team Handball, ASN, vip, 1992-. **Honors/Awds:** USA Team Handball Player of the Yr, 1984, 1986, 1988, 1991; Sam Jones Day, 1984, 1988, 1992; USTHF, 3-time Olympian, 1984, 1988, 1992; James E Sullivan Award, Team Handball Athlete of the Yr, 1991; Athlete of the Yr,U.S. Olympic Comt, 1998. **Home Addr:** 110 Elmore St, Mt Olive, NC 28365, **Home Phone:** (919)658-4081. *

JONES, DR. LESLIE FAYE
Educator. **Personal:** Born Oct 5, 1970, Napoleonville, LA; married Johnny Hamilton, Nov 23, 2003. **Educ:** Nicholls State Univ, BS, 1991, MEd, 1992; La State Univ, PhD, 1996. **Career:** St James Parish Sch Dist, teacher, 1992-97; Lafourche Sch Dist, asst prin, 1997-98; Assumption Sch Dist, prin, 1998-2000; Nicholls State Univ, asst prof, 2000-06, assoc prof & minor cheramie endowed prof, currently. **Orgs:** Am Educ Res Asn, 1996-2000; La Educ Res Asn, 1996-2000; La Asn Prinicpals, 1998-2000; Nicholls State Univ Alumni, 1999-; La Prof Educ Admin, 2002-. **Honors/Awds:** Teacher of the Year, St James High Sch, 1993; Huel Perkins Fel, La State Univ, 1995; Another Success Story Award, Nicholls State Univ, 2003. **Special Achievements:** Author: "Ties That Bind"; Jour of Higher Educ, 1998; "Measuring Effective Training," Jour of Effective Teaching, 2001; A Principal's Perspective, In Eugene Kennedy, Raising Standardized Test Scores: An Administrator's Guide, California, Corwin Press, 2003; Presentations: Reform: What Have We Learn?, Four Perspectives of Effective Teaching, Improving Literacy in Mathematics and Reading through Parental Involvement, Hawaii Intl Educ Conf, Waikki, Hawaii, 2005; The Challenges of Principal of this Era, Am Assn of Colls of Teacher Educ Conf, San Diego, CA, 2006. **Business Addr:** Associate Professor, Minor Cheramie Endowed Professor, Nicholls State University, College of Teacher Education, 906 E 1st St Polk Hall, PO Box 2035, Thibodaux, LA 70310, **Business Phone:** (985)448-4344.

JONES, LESTER C
Automotive executive, consultant. **Career:** Pasadena Lincoln-Mercury Sales Inc, chief exec officer & owner; Econ Opportunity Ctr, adv bd mem, financial servs consult, currently. **Business Phone:** (603)594-8513.

JONES, DR. LEWIS ARNOLD
Consultant, physician. **Personal:** Born Sep 16, 1950, Detroit, MI; son of Lewis Arnold Jones Sr and Berlene J; married Pamela D Jennings, Nov 14, 1992; children: Jennifer Tiffany, Alicia Dawn & Lewis Alexander. **Educ:** Wayne State Univ, 1972; Univ Mich Med Sch, MD, 1978; Diagnostic Radiol Residency, Providence Hosp, 1982. **Career:** Tri-County Radiol PC, radiologist, 1983-84; Harper Hosp, radiologist, 1984, dir gastrointestinal radiol div, 1984; Wayne State Univ Sch Med,clin instr, 1985-92, asst prof radiol, 1992-97; Karmanos Cancer Inst, 1992; Mich Dept Community Health, physician consult, 1997-2000; Henry Ford Health Syst, Dept Diagnostic Radiol, staff radiologist, 2000-02; Genesys Physicians Integrated Diagnostics, diagnostic radiologist, 2002-; pvt pract, physician, currently; Ingham Regional Med Ctr, radiolo-

gist & dir breast imaging, currently. **Orgs:** Radiological Soc N Am, 1979-; bd dirs, Am Cancer Soc, Oakland City Mich Div, 1988-; Am Col Radiol, 1989-; Asn Univ Radiologists, 1993-; AMA,1994-; community adv & mem, Karmanos Cancer Inst, 1994; co-investr, NIH Women's Health Initiative, Detroit Clin Ctr, 1996-97. **Honors/Awds:** Outstanding Radiol Resident Award, Providence Hosp, 1982; Vol Leadership Award, Am Cancer Soc, 1988; Life Serv Award, Am Cancer Soc, 1990;Frederick Douglass Award, New Metropolitan Detroit Club Nat Asn Negro Bus & Prof Women's Clubs Inc, 1996. **Special Achievements:** First winner of the Essence Magazine/Preferred Stock Cologne "What a Man Contest," 1995; Named co-chair of the "Year of the Women's Health" steering comt state of Mich(Michigan Department of Community Health), 1996; "Partners for Life" a woman's health seminar, created and presented by Lewis A Jones, MD & Florine Mark, chief exec officer, Weight WatchersInt, 1996. **Business Addr:** Radiologist, Director of Breast Imaging, Ingham Regional Medical Center, 401 W Greenlawn, Lansing, MI 48910.

JONES, LISA PAYNE
School administrator. **Personal:** Born Dec 30, 1958, Camp Zama, Japan; daughter of Charles Benjamin Payne Jr and Eleanor Towns Hamilton; married Peter Lawson, Oct 12, 1985; children: Ryan Charles, Leah Danielle & Evan Cooke. **Educ:** Eastern Mich Univ, BBA, 1980; grad, Case Western Reserve Univ, bus courses, 1982-85. **Career:** AmeriTrust Co NA, general analyst I, 1980-82, II, 1982-85, III, 1985-86; Cuyahoga Metro Housing Authority, mkt mgr, 1986-88, leasing & mkt mgr, 1989, leasing & transfer mgr, 1990-91, mkt coordr, 1992-94. **Orgs:** Delta Sigma Theta Sor Inc, 1978-; project bus consult, Jr Achievement, 1982-83; Cleveland Br, Nat Asn Advan Colored People, 1982-; chairperson, 1983, treas, 1984-85, Operation Greater Cleveland: Big Vote, 1983-85; Urban League Greater Cleveland, 1985-; Nat Black MBA Asn Inc, 1986; League of Women Voters, 1987; Am Mkt Asn, 1987-89; trustee, Shaker Hts Alumni Asn, 1988-95; bd mem, Shaker Schs Found, 1990-94; second vpres, Shaker Hts PTO, 1995-96; Co-chairperson, PTO Strategic Planning Comt, 1997-99; Shaker Heights Alumni Assoc, exec dir, 1995-98; Democratic Precinct, rep, 1998-; Jr League Greater Cleveland, 1998-99. **Honors/Awds:** Achievement Award, EMU Col Bus Acad, 1978; Honors Award, Delta Sigma Theta Inc EMU, 1979. **Home Phone:** (216)561-8988. **Business Addr:** Registar, Shaker Heights Board of Education, 15600 Parkland Dr, Shaker Heights, OH 44120, **Business Phone:** (216)295-4324.

JONES, LOREAN ELECTA
Government official. **Personal:** Born Jun 29, 1938, Arlington, TN; daughter of Earnest and Alcorna Harris; married Jimmie, Oct 1, 1954 (deceased); children: Gale Carson, Dale J, Elna Brunetti, Ervin C, Denise Jimenez, Dennis R,Teresa Y & Terry O (deceased). **Educ:** Owen Col, AA, 1968; Le Moyne-Owen Col, BA, 1970; Memphis State Univ, MS, 1977. **Career:** Government official (retired); State TN Dept Ment Health, social worker, 1970-75; State TN Dept Corrections, parole officer, 1975-78; US Dist Cts Western Dist TN, probation officer, 1978-84, fed drug treatment specialist, 1984-90, supv probation officer, 1990-92, dep chief probation officer, 1992-98. **Orgs:** Bd trustees, Gov TN Arlington Develop Ctr, 1972-73; Comt mem, Black on Black Crime Task Force, 1979-; Fed Probation Officers Asn; PUSH, 1980; life mem, Nat Asn Advan Colored People, 1980; historian, Nat Coun Negro Women, 1983; TN Selective Service Local Bd 38; secy, Le Moyne Owen Alumni Asn; Am Probation & Parole Asn; Am Asn Coun & Develop; Nat Alliance Bus Youth Motivating Task Force, 1982-83; secy, treas, Seast Region Fed Probation Officers Asn, 1983-85. **Honors/Awds:** Citizen of the Week Award, WLOK Radio Station, 1978; Distinguished Leadership Award; Outstanding Serv to the Human Serv Profession, 1987; Nat Cert Counrs Cert. **Special Achievements:** First female probation & parole officer, WD TN, 1978. **Home Addr:** 1520 Netherwood Ave, Memphis, TN 38106. *

JONES, LUCIUS. See Obituaries section.

JONES, MABLE VENEIDA
Insurance executive. **Personal:** Born Sep 20, 1950, Detroit, MI; daughter of James U Jones and Fannie Jones. **Educ:** Eastern Mich Univ, BS, spec educ, 1972; Iowa State Univ, MS, guid & coun, 1973; Wayne State Univ, 1978; Lasalle Univ, doctoral cand, currently. **Career:** Wayne State Univ, Upward Bound, dir, 1973-76; Ford Motor Corp, indust rels prog dir, 1976-80; AAA Mich, employee rels area mgr, employee servs area mgr, training & develop area mgr, exec loan, Detroit strategic planning proj, crime task force, sales admin area mgr, group servs area mgr, br mgr, dir sales adminr, currently. **Orgs:** Women's Economic Club; bd mem, Neighborhood Servs Orgn; bd mem, Booker T Washington Bus Asn; ARO Mus; UNF; youth develop bd, Urban League; bd mem, Ennis; Nat Asn Advan Colored People. **Honors/Awds:** Miss Teamwalk, March Dimes, 1984; Minority Achiever Award, YWCA, 1985; Volunteer of the Year, AAA Mich, 1986; Outstanding Service Award, AAA Mich, 1990-93; Silver Anniversary Achievement, Upward Bound, 1992; Ossawa Sweet Award, Wolverine Bar, 1994; Leadership Award, UNCF, 1997; Community Service Award, BTWBA, 1998. **Home Addr:** 35479 Heritage Lane, Farmington, MI 48335, **Home Phone:** (248)471-5293. **Business Addr:** Director Sales Administration, AAA of Michigan, 1 Auto Club Dr, Dearborn, MI 48126, **Business Phone:** (313)336-1500.

JONES, DR. MARCUS EARL
Educator. **Personal:** Born Jan 7, 1943, Decatur, IL; son of George and Bernetta Mayweather; married Diann, Jan 1, 1971 (divorced 1982); married Valerie Daniel, Jan 1, 1983; children: Anthony, Malik, Omar, Taisha, Samira, Malaika, Na'el, Amina, Jamia & Punch. **Educ:** Southern Ill Univ Carbondale, BA, geog, 1965; Chicago State Univ, MA, geog, 1969; Univ Ghana, Cert, 1968; Southern Ill Univ, PhD, geog, 1978. **Career:** Southern Ill Univ Carbondale, ombudsman, 1972-73; FL A&M Univ, asst prof geog, 1973-76; Univ So FL Tampa, vis prof geog, 1976-77; Morris Brown Col, chair & prof geog, 1978-85; Valdosta State Col, prof geog, 1986-87; Chicago Pub Schs, teacher, 1988-89; SC State Univ, adjunct prof, 1991-2002; Univ NM, vis prof, 2002; Claflin Univ, Orangeburg, SC, assoc prof, 1990-2003, prof, currently. **Orgs:** Asn Am Geogrs; Southeastern Asn Geogrs; Asn Social & Behavioral Scientists Inc; African Studies Asn; West African Res Asn, 1991-92; Nat Asn African-Am Studies, area coordr, 1998; Asn Study Class African Civilizations; SC Coun Social Studies, Claflin Univ, 1999-2002. **Honors/Awds:** Grant to study in Egypt, Fulbright-Hays Commission, 1994; Fulbright Research Scholar, Am Univ Cairo, 1995-96. **Special Achievements:** Author: Black Migration in the United States with Emphasis on Selected Central Cities, Century Twenty One Publishing, 1980; Lower Socio-Economic and Minority Households in Camden County GA, Atlanta Univ, 1987; article "Black Counterstream Migration: New and Return Migrants to the South," 1965-78, Nat Coun Black Studies, 1982; "Black Fatherhood in North America: Historical, Sociological, and Spiritual Perspectives", & "The Changing Roles of Egyptian Women: Pre-Socialists to Post-Socialists Eras," Proceedings Nat Asn African-Am Studies. **Business Addr:** Associate Professor, Claflin University, Department of History & Sociology, 400 Magnolia St, Orangeburg, SC 29115-9970, **Business Phone:** (803)535-5466.

JONES, MARCUS EDMUND
Television journalist. **Personal:** Born Feb 12, 1960, Washington, DC; son of Clarance and Lillie Brown; married Janice Lyons, May 28, 1983; children: Nathan Aaron Alexander. **Educ:** Boston Univ, Boston, BS, 1982; Temple Univ. **Career:** Daily Evening Item Lynn, Mass, columnist, 1976-78; Boston Globe, Boston, Mass, corresp, 1977-78; WILD-AM, Boston, Mass, news anchor & reporter, 1977-82; WQTV, "Boston Live!," Boston, Mass, producer & host, 1980-81; Satellite News Channel, Stamford, Conn, news assoc, 1982-83; WEZN-FM, Bridgeport, Conn, news reporter, 1984; WUSA-TV, "Eyewitness News," Wash, DC, reporter trainee, 1984-85; WGBH-TV, "Ten O'Clock News," Boston, Mass, news reporter, 1986-91, "The Group", videotape ed, 1991-92; WBZ-TV, "News 4," Boston, Mass, freelance reporter, 1993; Lowell Cable TV, "News Ctr 6," Lowell, Mass, news dir, 1992-94; Northeastern Univ, Boston, Mass, jour dept, lectr, 1991-94; New England Cable News, Newton, Mass, freelance reporter, 1994-95; WFXT "Fox 25 News Ten," Dedham, Mass, freelance reporter, 1995; Newschannel 8, Springfield, Va, Wash, DC reporter, 1995-96; Prince George's County "CTV News," Channel 15, Largo, Md, freelance reporter & video tape ed, 1996; Fairfax Network, "School Scene," Channel 21, Annandale, Va, freelance reporter & videographer video tape ed, 1996-98; Arlington Co Info Channel 31, Arlington, Va, freelance, videographer & video tape ed, 1997; Fairfax Co Govt Channel 16, Fairfax, Va, freelance videographer & video tape ed, 1998; FBI Acad, FBI Training Network, Quantico, Va, assoc producer, 1999. **Orgs:** Nat Asn Black Journalists, 1989-; Nat Asn Advan Colored People, 1970-82; Boston Asn Black Journalists, 1989-95; Wash Asn Black Journalists, 1995-. **Honors/Awds:** Emmy Award nominee, two categories, feature & spec reporting, Boston, New England Chapter Nat Acad TV Arts & Scis, 1990; Emmy Award nominee, one category, news event, Boston, NE Chapter, NATAS, 1991; Outstanding Anti-Smoking Report, Am Lung Asn, 1990. **Home Addr:** 5549 Hobsons Choice Loop, Manassas, VA 20112-5465.

JONES, MARCUS EDWARD
Football player. **Personal:** Born Aug 15, 1973, Jacksonville, NC; married Bethany. **Educ:** Univ NC. **Career:** Tampa Bay Buccaneers, defensive tackle, 1996-2002.

JONES, MARGARET B
Library administrator. **Personal:** Born Mar 11, 1932, Haines City, FL; daughter of John and Elizabeth Byrd; married Glover E; children: Edmond D, Glover E Jr, Lisa Jones-Landers, Cedric A & Leslie Jones-Wil son. **Educ:** Fla A&M Univ, BS, 1953; Atlanta Univ, MSLS, 1969; Fla A&M Univ, MEd, 1985. **Career:** Wash Junior Col & High Sch, librn, 1955-60; Fla A&M Univ, librn & asst prof, 1960-78; NC Central Univ, adj prof, 1978-80; Fla A&M Univ, librn, 1981-95, assoc dir libraries, 1996-99, develop officer, 2001-. **Orgs:** Consult, FAMU-Library; Am Libr Asn; Phi Delta Kappa; North Fla Libr Asn; Kappa Delta, Pi Nominee, 1985; Fla Assoc Media Educ, 1975. **Honors/Awds:** Superior Accomplishment Award, Fla A&M Univ, 1990-91; Service Award, 1993-94, 1997-98; Cert Achievement, Panhandle Library Access Network, 1996; Black Achievement Award, Jefferson County Fla, 1997. **Special Achievements:** "Six Decades of Research" Fla A&M Univ, 1995; co-author "School Media Specialization Undergraduate Library Science Program" Fla A&M Univ, Journal of Media & Library Service, Vol 24, p 2, 1987; Spanish Language proficiency. **Home Addr:** 273 Martin Rd, Monticello, FL 32344, **Home Phone:** (850)997-3827. **Business Addr:** Development Officer, Florida A&M University, Coleman Libr Rm 315, Tallahassee, FL 32307, **Business Phone:** (850)599-8576.

JONES, MARILYN ELAINE
Government official. **Personal:** Born in Waco, TX; children: Spencer. **Educ:** Tex Woman's Univ, MA, 1970, BS, 1972, PhD, 1978. **Career:** Early Childhood Educ Tex Woman's Univ, consult, 1970-74; Tex Woman's Univ, prof/lab instr, 1972-74; Paul Quinn Col, counr/placement dir, 1974-83; Prairie View A&M Univ, instr, 1980-84; Gen Land Off State Tex, field rep. **Orgs:** Delta Sigma Theta Sor; NAACP; Nat Asn Young C; APGA; Tex Coalition Black Democrats; Eastern Star; city councilmem first female elected, 1980-84; vpres, Heart Tex Coun Govs 1982-84; mayor, Pro-Tem Waco City Coun, 1983. **Honors/Awds:** Serv Awards, Phi Delta Kappa Inc Gamma Upsilon Chapt, Citizens of Waco, Waco City Council, Heart Tex Coun Govrs; Quality of Life Award, NTSU/TWU Alumni, 1981; Women of the Yr, Progressive Women Wichita, KS, 1982. **Home Addr:** 1604 Harrison Ave, Waco, TX 76704.

JONES, MARION
Athlete. **Personal:** Born Oct 12, 1975, Los Angeles, CA; daughter of George and Marion; married CJ Hunter, Oct 3, 1998 (divorced); married Obadele Thompson, Feb 24, 2007; children: 1. **Educ:** Univ NC, attended 1997. **Career:** Athlete (retired); USA track & field inc, track & field athlete. **Honors/Awds:** The 2-time World 100m champion, 1997, 1999; 2-time World 4x100m champion,1997, 2001; World LJ bronze medalist, 1999; Olympic 100m, 200m & 4x400mchamp, bronze medal in LJ and 4x100m, 2000; World 200m gold medalist,2001; World Cup 100m gold medalist, 2002; USA Champion, 100m & 200m, 2002;13-time USA Outdoor Champion, 4 in LJ, 4 in 100, 5 in 2002; USA Outdoor100m Champion, 2006. **Special Achievements:** First woman to win five track & field medals in one Olympiad, 2000;Belize's Sports Ambassador at Sydney Olympics; first female track and field athlete to win five medals at a single Olympics in Sydney - gold in the 100m, 200m and 4x400m relay, and bronze in the long jump and 4x100relay. *

JONES, MARKEYSIA DONTA
Football player. **Personal:** Born Aug 27, 1972, Washington, DC; son of Thomas Jones; children: Tavia Lachelle. **Educ:** Univ Nebr, BA, acct & bus admin, 1994. **Career:** Pittsburgh Steelers, linebacker, 1995-98; Carolina Panthers, 1999; Chicago Bears, 2005; New Orleans Saints. **Honors/Awds:** First-Team All-Big Eight, AP, Coaches, 1994; Nebr co-weight lifter of the Yr, 1993; Nebraska Football Hall of Fame Inductee, 2007.

JONES, MARSHA REGINA
Journalist. **Personal:** Born Jan 26, 1962, Brooklyn, NY; daughter of Iona Louisa Williams and Eudolphin; married Donald Collins, May 24, 1996; children: Hollis Danielle. **Educ:** Nazareth Col, Advanced Placement Courses Spanish, 1978-80; Purdue Univ, BA, Jour, 1980-84. **Career:** Purdue Exponent Newspaper, reporter, 1981-83; Purdue Reports Magazine, reporter, 1983-84; Black Cultural Ctr Newspaper, reporter, 1983-84; About Time Magazine, editorial asst/reporter 1984-88, asst ed, 1988-89; Project KID, commun consult, 1988-90; SUNY Brockport, NY, mktg commun mgr, 1989-93; Rochester Bus Magazine, Rochester, NY, contributing ed, 1989-93; Roc Live/After Dark, host/producer, 1991; Rochester Metro Challenger, contributing ed, columnist, 1991-; Rochester Museum & Science News, contributing ed, 1992; The Communicator, Rochester Assn of Black Communicators, ed, 1993; Hillside Children's Center, public relations coordinator, 1993-95; Scene Entertainment Weekly, contributing ed, 1995-97; Camp Good Days & Special Times, public relations dir, 1995-96; Planned Parenthood, mktg communications coord, 1997-. **Orgs:** Soc Prof Journalists, 1980-, Nat Asn Black Journalists, 1988-, East HS Ebony Culture Club; Black Scholars Mentor Program Urban League Rochester NY Inc, 1985-89; Black Scholars Alumni Comm Urban League Rochester Inc, 1985-89; Amer Red Cross Minority Screening Campaign Comm, 1985-88; Village Gate Theater, 1985-88; 1986, sec, 1991, Rochester Assoc Black Communicators; Rochester Purdue Alumni Assoc; bd mem, R Nelson Mandela Scholarship Fund, 1989-93; SUNY Brockport Faculty Senate, 1990-91; City Newspaper Editorial Advisory Bd, 1990-93; vice pres, Montgomery Neighborhood Center Youth Adv Bd, 1990-93; Rochester Asn Black Communicators Film Festival, 1991; Rochester asn Black Communicators, pres, 1992-94; Guyanese Am Asn, 1992; United Negro Col Fund Commn, 1992; Boys & Girls Club of Rochester, bd dir, 1994-, Bowl-a-thon Commt, 1993-95;Hillside's Working Together Team, 1993-95; Bill Klein's 13th Annual Academy Awards Committee, publicity chair, 1995-; Hillside Art Diversity Project, co-chair, 1995; Asn Women Commun. **Honors/Awds:** Black Scholar Award Urban League of Rochester NY Inc, 1980; Purdue Reamer Honorary Soc Purdue Univ, 1983 (first black student to be inducted in honor society, to hold office in honor society, to be elected to exec council); Howard G McCall Award Purdue Univ Black Cultural Ctr, 1984; Grand Prix Award Purdue Univ 1984; Matrix Award nominee, Women in Communications, 1988; published A People's Pledge, 1989; UNV Photographer's ASN of AMR's President's Award, 1991; SUNY Brockport's Black Male Support Group Award, 1992; Natl Leadership Council's Capitol Award, 1991. **Special Achievements:** "My

Father's Child, My Mother's Daughter," Visions & Viewpoints: Voices of the Genesee Valley, 1993; "Friendship 1337," Visions & Viewpoints: Voices of the Genesee Valley, 1994, The Healing Power of Friends, "She Was Right" 1997. **Home Phone:** (716)288-6661.

JONES, MARVIN MAURICE (SHADE TREE)
Football player. **Personal:** Born Jun 28, 1972, Miami, FL; married Alexsandra; children: Maya, Daryl & Marvin M Jones Jr. **Educ:** Fla State Univ. **Career:** Football player (retired); New York Jets, linebacker, 1993-2003. **Orgs:** Founder,Marvin Jones Charitable Foundation. **Honors/Awds:** Rotary-Lombardi Award, 1992; Dick Butkus Award, 1992; Florida State Hall of Fame, 2000.

JONES, MAXINE
Singer, songwriter, actor. **Personal:** Born Jan 16, 1965, Paterson, NJ; children: Maya. **Career:** En Vogue, mem group, 1988-2001, 2004-; Albums include: Born to Sing, 1990; Remix to Sing, 1991; Funky Divas, 1992; Run away love, 1993; Greatest Hits, 1998; EV3, 1997; Gift Of Xmas, 2002; Soul Flower, 2004; Essentials, 2005; Hold On & Other Hits, 2005, TBA, 2009; Singles include: "Hold On," "Lies," "Free Your Mind," "This Is Your Life", "My Lovin' (You're Never Gonna Get It)", "Desire", "Yesterday"; Films: Batman Forever, 1995; TV: "A Different World", 1993; "Roc", 1993; "Saturday Night Live", 1997. **Orgs:** R&b Group En Vague. **Honors/Awds:** Born to Sing, platinum, 1990. *

JONES, MEREDITH J.
Government official. **Personal:** Born Mar 24, 1948, Hartford, CT; daughter of Cyril J and Rose Randolph. **Educ:** Swarthmore Col, BA, 1968; Yale Law Sch, JD, 1974. **Career:** Chickering & Gregory, partner, 1983-86; Bechtel Financing Serv, Inc, sr coun, 1986-93; Nat Oceanic & Atmospheric Admin, gen coun, 1993-94; Fed Community Comn, Cable Serv Bur, chief, 1994; Nat Oceanic & Atmospheric Admin, Gen Coun, currently. **Orgs:** Asn Bar City NY; Fed Commun Bar Asn; Nat Asn Minorities Cable. **Business Phone:** (202)377-1400.*

JONES, MERLAKIA KENYATTA
Basketball player. **Personal:** Born Jun 21, 1973, Montgomery, AL. **Educ:** Univ Fla, pub rctrn, 1995; Old Dom Univ, 1996. **Career:** Santaram, Portugal, 1996-97; Cleveland Rockers, guard, 1997-03; Detroit Shock, guard, 2004. **Orgs:** Professional women's sports organization. **Honors/Awds:** Voted Eastern Conf Res, WNBA All-Star Game, 2000; named E Team inaugural WNBA All-Star Game; named Kodak All-Am; All-Am, Assoc Press; three-time All-SEC First Team selection. *

JONES, DR. MICHAEL ANDREA
Psychologist, clergy. **Personal:** Born Aug 6, 1937, Atlanta, GA; married Linda; children: Gattie. **Educ:** Ga State Univ, BA, attended; Atlanta Univ, MA, attended; Am Univ, ED, attended. **Career:** Morris Brown Col, dir; Mitchell Chapel Church, pastor. **Orgs:** Soc Christian Leadership, 1959-; Am Christian Atlanta Asn Educrs; GA Asn Educrs; GA Coun Christians, 1977-; Soc Christian Leadership Conf; United Youth Adult Conf; NAACP; Atlanta Christian Coun, 1975-. **Business Addr:** Pastor, Fayetteville Parish AME, PO Box 430, Fayetteville, GA 30214.

JONES, MICHAEL ANTHONY
Football player. **Personal:** Born Apr 15, 1969, Kansas City, MO; married Leslie; children: Taelor, Moriah & Ashley. **Educ:** Univ Mo. **Career:** Football player (retired); Los Angeles Raiders, linebacker, 1991-94;Oakland Raiders, 1995-96, 2002; St Louis Rams, 1997-2000; Pittsburgh Steelers, 2001-02. **Orgs:** Founder, Michael Jones Foundation.

JONES, MICHAEL B
Physician. **Personal:** Born Aug 17, 1969, Reynolds, GA; son of Leroy and Minnie; divorced. **Educ:** Morris Brown Col, BS, 1992; Medical Col Georgia, MD, 1996. **Career:** Emory Univ, resident psychiatry, 1996-97; Mercer Univ, resident internal med, 1997-2000. **Orgs:** Am Med Asn, 1999-; Nat Med Asn, 1999-; APA, 1991-. **Honors/Awds:** US Achievement Academy Natural Sciences Honor Award, 1991. **Business Addr:** Associate, Doctor, 3840 St Bernard Ave, New Orleans, LA 70122, **Business Phone:** (504)283-4182.*

JONES, MICHAEL DAVID
Football player. **Personal:** Born Aug 25, 1969, Columbia, SC; married. **Educ:** NC State Univ. **Career:** Phoenix Cardinals, defensive end, 1991-93; New England Patriots, 1994-97;St Louis Rams, 1998; Tenn Titans, 1999.

JONES, MICHELE S
Army officer. **Personal:** Born in Baltimore, MD. **Educ:** Fayetteville State Univ, BS, bus admin, MA, mgt & intl rels. **Career:** USAR, staff, 1982, chief adv, squad leader, sect leader, platoon sgt, first sgt, command sgt maj, 2002-. **Honors/Awds:** Meritorious Service Award, Nat Asn Advan Colored People, 2003; Legion of Merit; Meritorious Service Medal; Army Commendation Medal; Army Achievement Medal; Good Conduct Medal; Nat Defense Serv Medal; Armed Forces Reserve Medal. **Special Achievements:** First female selected as class president at the US Sergeants Major Academy; first female to serve as a division CSM; first woman to serve as the CSM of any of the Army's Components, Active or Reserve. **Business Addr:** Command Sergeant Major, US Army Reserve, Office of the Chief, 2400 Army Pentagon Suite 2B548, Washington, DC 20310-2400, **Business Phone:** (703)697-1784.

JONES, MICHELE WOODS
School administrator, consultant. **Personal:** Born Oct 3, 1945, Los Angeles, CA; daughter of David A Francis and Mary Ellen Harris; married Reginald L, Jan 3, 1988; children: Sjaun & Leasa. **Educ:** Phoenix Col, AA, 1965; Univ Calif, Berkeley, BA, hist, 1969, grad study, hist, 1970; Calif State Univ, Hayward, MS, educ psychol, 1979. **Career:** School adminstrator (retired), consultant. Univ Calif, Berkeley, co-dir spec summer proj, 1968, Educ Opportunity Prog, counr, 1968-70, tutorial staff coordr, 1970-72, counr coordr, 1972-73, Stud Info Ctr, asst dir, 1973-77, Stud Learning Ctr, asst dir, 1977-81, prin stud affairs officer, 1981-83, dir stud activ & servs, 1983-89, asst to vice chancellor & staff ombudsperson, 1989-91; Newport News Sch Dist, consult; City Hampton Social Servs Multicultural Comun & Problem Solving, consult; Cobb & Henry Publishers, pres; Va Dept Transp, Hampton Rd region, sr consult, currently. **Orgs:** Pres, sec, Alpha Kappa Alpha sorority, 1967-; campus liaison, Black Alumni Club, Univ Calif, Berkeley, 1969-; bd dirs, Calif Alumni Asn, Univ Calif; Asn Black Psychologists; Educ Res Coun, 1979-; adv bd, Ctr Study, Educ & Advan Women, Univ California, Berkeley; hon mem, Golden Key Nat Honor Soc, 1985; hon mem, Delta Delta Delta sorority, 1986; Nat Asn Stud Personnel Admin; Nat Orientation Dir Asn; Soroptimist Int; Univ & Col Ombudsman Asn, 1989-; bd dirs, Nat Asn Black Pub Sch Admin, 1990-; prog dir, Hampton Chap, Jack & Jill of Am; Int Personnel Mgt Asn; Nat Conf Dialogue & Deliberation. **Honors/Awds:** Order of the Golden Bear, 1975-; Outstanding Black Women of California, 1981-82; Recognition Award, African Students' Asn, Univ Calif, Berkeley, 1982; Rosalie M Stern Award, Calif Alumni Asn, 1984; Citizen of the Year award, Basileus-Epsilon Mu/Omega Psi Phi Fraternity, 1986; Black Alumnae of the Year, Black Alumni Club, Univ Calif, Berkeley, 1987; Outstanding Service Award, Univ Calif, Berkeley, 1988; Management & Professional Achievement Award, Univ Calif, Berkeley, 1991; The Berkeley Citation, Univ Calif, Berkeley, 1991; Michelle Woods Scholarship established in her honor by Alpha Kappa Alpha Sorority. **Business Addr:** Senior Consultant, Virginia Department of Transportation, 401 E Broad St, Richmond, VA 23219, **Business Phone:** (804)786-5128.

JONES, MICHELLE
Financial manager, secretary (government). **Personal:** Born May 10, 1954, Columbus, OH; daughter of Ralph and Ora. **Educ:** Ohio State Univ, attended 1975; Columbus State County Col, attended 1983. **Career:** Columbus Pub Sch, secy, 1974-83; United Way Franklin County, secy, 1983-85, commun coord, 1985-. **Orgs:** Women in Commun Inc, 1985-87; Youth Advocate Serv, 1988-91. **Business Phone:** (614)227-2784.

JONES, MILTON H., JR.
Executive, chief financial officer. **Personal:** Born Jul 25, 1952, Atlanta, GA; son of Milton H Sr and Helen E; married Shelia Pitts; children: Milton C & Tiffany M. **Educ:** Univ Notre Dame, BBA, acct, 1974. **Career:** Peat, Marwick, Mitchell & Co, 1974-77; Citizens & Southern Nat Bank, 1977-91; Nat Bank, exec vpres, 1991-, Dealer Financial Services Group, pres,1997; Bank of America, chief financial officer, coo, global quality &productivity exec, 2003, pres, 2007-. **Orgs:** Exec com, Leadership Atalanta; Leadership GEO, Class, 1992; chair,Tech wood Park Inc; Metropolitan Atlanta YMCA; exec com, Southwest Atlanta YMCA; Atlanta Urban Bankers Asn; Salvation Army Boys & Girls Club, advcoun; GEO Coun Child Abuse, adv bd; chmn, bd, Atlanta Econ Dev Corp; bd, Atlanta Local Dev Corp. **Honors/Awds:** Atlanta Urban Bankers Asn, Pioneer Award, 1992; Nations Bank, Hero Award,1992. **Business Addr:** Global Quality and Productivity Executive, Bank of America, 121 W Trade St Suite 15, Charlotte, NC 28202, **Business Phone:** (704)386-5478.

JONES, MONIQUE
Executive. **Career:** Icon Entertainment, sr vpres, finance & admin, currently. **Business Addr:** Senior Vice President of Finance, Administration, Icon Entertainment, The Quadrangle 4th Fl 180 Wardour St, London W1F 8FX, United Kingdom, **Business Phone:** (442)07494-8100.*

JONES, NANCY REED
President (Organization), executive, chief executive officer. **Personal:** Born Jun 15, 1928, Bamberg County, SC; daughter of Aaron and Josie Bell; married Oct 1, 1950 (widowed); children: Pat Jernan Jones Hagood, Wendy. **Educ:** Temple Univ, attended 1956; Claflin Col, BS, 1958; SC State Col, MS, 1961; Univ SC, 1964. **Career:** Bamberg Co Bd Educ, 1948-80; Nat Testing Serv, 1977-78; Augusta, GA, Bd Educ, 1979-89; Victoria Slipper Retail & Mfg Co, pres & chief exec officer, 1985-. **Orgs:** Union Baptist Chruch; Am Educ Asn; Am Guid Asn; dir guid, Bamberg Ehrhardt High Sch; pres, Pastors Aid Club. **Honors/Awds:** Guid Award, 1978; Teacher of the Yr, 1983; Alpha Kappa Sorority Award, 1990; Delta Sigma Thada Award, 1991. **Business Addr:** Chief Executive Officer, President, Victoria Slipper Retail & Manufacturing Company, 119 Palmelto Ave, PO Box 499, Denmark, SC 29042, **Business Phone:** (803)793-5719.*

JONES, NAPOLEON A, JR.
Judge. **Personal:** Born Aug 25, 1940, Hodge, LA; children: Lena L. **Educ:** San Diego State Univ, BA, 1962, MSW, 1967; Univ San Diego Sch Law, JD, 1971. **Career:** Dept Adult Parole & Community Serv, stud prof asst, 1965-66; Santa Clara Co Welfare Dept Foster Home Placement, 1966-67; CA Rural Legal Asst Modesto, atty, 1972-73; Defenders Inc, San Diego, atty, 1973-75; Jones & Adler, San Diego, atty, 1975-77; San Diego Munic Ct, judge, 1977-82; San Diego Supreme Ct, judge, 1982-94; US Dist Ct, judge, 1994-. **Orgs:** Calif Black Atty Asn; Sigma Pi Phi Fraternity; Kappa Alpha Psi Fraternity; Nat Asn Women Judges; Nat Bar Asn; pres, Earl B Billiam Bar WASN; mentor, Nia UMOIA Valencia Pk Elem Sch; bd visitors, Sch Soc Work, San Diego State Univ; Reginald Heber Smith fel, 1971-73; bd mem, Proj Restore-Women's Drug Treat Prog; adv bd, Friend Friend; dir, USD Law Alumni Asn Bd, 1994-95; adv bd mem, Family Literacy Found; bd mem, Community Partnership Comn; found & pres, SDSU's Black Stud Coun; Bus Adv Bd, Office Educ, San Diego Co, 1997-; Fed Judicial Coun Calif State, 1997-. **Honors/Awds:** Distinguished Alumni, Sch Soc Work Merit; Judge of the Year, Calif Asn Black Lawyers, 1993; Hon Doctor Laws, Calif Western Sch Law, 1994; Judge of the Year Award, La Asn, 1995; Judicial Excellence Award, Dep Dist Atty Asn, 1995; Expression of Appreciation, San Diego Co Bar Asn, 1995; Judicial excellence Award, Dep Dist Atty Asn, 1996; Certificate of Appreciation, State Bar Calif & Univ Calif, 1996; FBI Appreciation Award, Dept Justice, FBI/DEA African Am Hist Celebration, 1997. **Business Addr:** Judge, US District Court, Southern District of California, 940 Front St Fl 2 Suite 2125, San Diego, CA 92101-8912, **Business Phone:** (619)557-2993.

JONES, NASIR
Rap musician. **Personal:** Born Sep 14, 1973, Queensbridge, NY; son of Olu Dara and Fannie Ann. **Career:** Albums: Illmatic, 1994; It Was Written, 1996; I Am, 1999; Nastradamus,1999; Stillmatic, 2001; Street's Disciple, 2004; Hip Hop Is Dead, 2006; Untitled, 2008; Distant Relatives, 2009; Films: Belly, 1998; Ticker, 2001; Sacred Is the Flesh, 2001; God's Son, 2002; Uptown Girls, 2003; Vapors, 2009; Songs: "Halftime", 1992; "It Ain't Hard to Tell", 1994; "The WorldIs Yours", 1994; "If I Ruled the World", 1996; "Nas Is Like", 1999; "Hate Me Now", 1999; "One Mic", 2002; "Made You Look", 2002; "I Can", 2003;"Thief's Theme", 2004; "Just a Moment", 2005; "Hip Hop Is Dead", 2006; "Can't Forget About You", 2007; Ill Will Rec, founder. **Honors/Awds:** Youth Summit Award, Hip Hop Youth Summit, 2002. **Special Achievements:** Launched clothing line Esco. **Business Phone:** (212)833-8000.*

JONES, NATHANIEL, SR.
Government official. **Personal:** Born Oct 3, 1948, New Orleans, LA; married Brenda; children: Natalie, Nathaniel & Natash. **Educ:** Southern Univ, attended 1973. **Career:** King Triumph BC, mem, 1969; Southern Univ Recreation Club, vpres, 1970-72; Prince Hall Masons, mem, 1973; Lutcher & Gramercy Jaycees, mem, 1984. **Orgs:** Rive Parishes Improv League, 1972; chmn, Building & Planning Comn, 1975 & 1981; bd dirs, La Black Music Asn Caucus, 1982, 1983; United Steel Workers Am; La Munic Asn; Nat League Cities, 1983; Lutcher-Gramercy Jaycees, 1984; dist coordr, Nat Black Caucus LEO, 1984; Nat Asn Advan Colored People. **Honors/Awds:** Worked Summer Youth in Drug Prog, 1985. **Business Addr:** Alderman, Town Lutcher, PO Box 456, Lutcher, LA 70071.*

JONES, NATHANIEL JAMAL
Executive. **Personal:** Born Jan 14, 1967, Memphis, TN; son of Fred and Naomi; married Jeanette, Feb 18, 1996. **Educ:** Tenn State Univ, BS, bus admin. **Career:** Int Paper, acct, 1992-94; Mid-S Coliseum, acct, 1994-96; Summitt Mgt, prod mgr, currently; Star Entertainment, pres, currently. **Honors/Awds:** Tenn State Univ, Alumni Award, 1998. **Business Phone:** (901)603-8963.

JONES, NATHANIEL R
Administrator, judge, lawyer. **Personal:** Born May 13, 1926, Youngstown, OH. **Educ:** Youngstown Univ, BA, 1951, LLB (JD), 1956. **Career:** Judge (retired), sr counsel; Fair Employ Prac Comn, City of Youngstown, Ohio, exec dir, 1956-59; pvt pract, attny, 1959-60; US Atty Northern Dist, Ohio, asst, 1960-67; Nat Asn Advan Colored People, gen coun, 1969-79; US Attny No Dist OH, former asst attny; US Ct Appeals Sixth Circuit, judge, 1979-2002; Blank Rome LLP, sr coun, currently. **Orgs:** Asst gen coun, Comt on Civil Disorders, 1967-68; co-chmn, Civilian-Mil Task Force on Mil Justice, 1972; co-chair, Cincinnati Bar Asn/Black Lawyers Asn Cincinnati Round Table; adv Comt mem, Urban Morgan Int Human Rights Inst; Potter Stewart Inn Court; Am Bar Asn; chair, Am Bar Asn Africa Law Initiative; Comn on Opportunities for Minorities in the Profession; Am Arbitration Asn; Nat Bar Asn; Fed Bar Asn; Ohio State Bar Asn; Cincinnati Bar Asn; Mahoning County Bar Asn; Alpha Delta Boule, Sigma Pi Phi Fraternity; Buckeye Lodge IBPOE; 33rd Degree United Supreme

Coun; Kappa Alpha Psi Fraternity; Metropolitan Club, Covington, KY. **Honors/Awds:** Headed three-man team which investigated grievances of black servicemen in W Ger; Metropolitan Club Award, 2005. **Special Achievements:** First African Am appointed as assistant US Attorney for the Northern District of Ohio, Cleveland. **Business Addr:** Senior Counsel, Blank Rome LLP, 1700 PNC Ctr 201 E 5th St, Cincinnati, OH 45202.

JONES, NETTIE PEARL
Writer, school administrator, educator. **Personal:** Born Jan 1, 1941, Arlington, GA; daughter of Delonia Mears Whorton and Benjamin; divorced; children: Lynne Cheryl Harris. **Educ:** Wayne State Univ, Detroit, MI, BS, sec educ, 1963; Marygrove Col, Detroit, MI, MEd, reading, 1972; Fashion Inst Technol, New York, NY, advert, communs, 1973-76. **Career:** Detroit Bd Educ, Detroit, MI, teacher sec social studies, eng, reading, 1963-72; Royal George Sch, Greenfield Park, Que, teacher sec eng, 1966-68; Martin Luther King Sch, New York, NY, teacher reading, 1971-72; Wayne State Univ, Detroit, MI, lectr, vis writer, 1986-87; Chmn Wayne Co Comnr, Detroit, MI, writer, 1988; Wayne Co Community Col, Detroit, MI, teacher devel reading, 1988; Mich Technol Univ, Houghton, MI, asst prof, writer residence, 1988-89, minority affairs asst vpres, 1989; NY Univ, Gallatin Sch Individualized Study, fac, currently; Boricua Col, fac; Montclair State Univ, fac; Essex Co Col, fac; City Univ New Yorks Medgar Evers Col, fac; Book: Fish Tales, 1984; Mischief Makers, 1989; Detroit: Beauty in This Beast; Anita at the Battle of the Bush; Thomas on the Hill: Dark Town Strutters Ball; Television program: "Abrilaharris Quest"; Story: "When Crack Comes Home" 1989. **Orgs:** Detroit Women Writers, 1985; Am Asn Univ Prof, 1986. **Honors/Awds:** Yaddo Fellow Writer, 1985; Contemporary Literary Criticism Yearbook, Notable New Artist, 1985; Michigan Council of the Arts Award, 1986; Two Michigan Council for Arts and Cultural Affairs Awards, 1987 & 1989; National Endowment for the Arts Individual Artist Award, 1989; Carnegie Award, 1995; Centrum Award, 1995; Michigan Technological University's Visionary Award, 1999; Gallatin School's Student Choice Award, 2003. **Special Achievements:** Named one of "Ten Best New Fiction Writers of 1984 by The New York Times. **Business Addr:** Faculty, Gallatin School of Individualized Study, 22 Wash Sq N, New York, NY 10003, **Business Phone:** (212)998-7370.

JONES, DR. NINA F.
School administrator. **Personal:** Born Jul 30, 1918, Madison, GA; daughter of Hallie Flemister and Sumner Flemister; married William M; children: William M Jr & Steven L. **Educ:** Cent YMCA Col, AB, 1938; Chicago Teachers Col, MEd, 1942; Loyola Univ, Chicago, EdD, 1975. **Career:** School administrator (retired); Chicago Public Schs, teacher, 1942, prin, 1965, dist supt, 1969, asst supt personnel, 1975, sec bd examrs, 1983-88. **Orgs:** Alpha Kappa Alpha Sorority, 1940; Alpha Gamma Pi Sorority, 1967; Pi Lambda Theta. **Home Addr:** 9156 S Constance, Chicago, IL 60617.

JONES, NOLAN E
Government official. **Personal:** Born Dec 11, 1944, Houston, TX; son of Ernest and Hester Neal Ross. **Educ:** Tex Southern Univ, Houston, BA, 1968; Swarthmore Col, PA, post baccalaureate, 1969; Wash Univ, St Louis, MO, MA, 1973, PhD, 1975. **Career:** Univ Mich, Ann Arbor, MI, asst prof, 1973-78; NCLS, Human Resources Comt, Wash, DC, comt dir, 1978-, group dir, 1995-2003, dep dir; Nat Govs Asn, dep dir, office fed rels, currently. **Orgs:** Secy, Nat Conf Black Polit Scientist, 1976-78; secy, Allen Adams Fed Credit Union, 1989-92; coun mem, Am Polit Sci Asn, 1990-92; Nat Guard Youth Found, 1999-. **Honors/Awds:** Grad Fel, Pub Law, Edna F Gellhorn, 1970-72; Woodrow Wilson Doctoral Dissertation Fel, 1972-73; The Order of the Palmetto, State SC, 1985; Honorary Tar Heel, State NC, 1989; Excellence in Emergency Management Award, Fed Emergency Mgmt Agency, 1993; The Patrick Henry Award, Nat Guard Asn United States, 1996; Distinguished Service Award, Nat Ctr for State Cts, 2002; 25th Year Award, Nat Govs Asn, 2003. **Military Serv:** USAF, airman second class, 1962-65. **Business Addr:** Deputy Director, Office of Federal Relations, National Governors Association, 444 N Capitol St Suite 267, Washington, DC 20001-1512, **Business Phone:** (202)624-5360.

JONES, ORLANDO
Actor, writer, television producer. **Personal:** Born Apr 10, 1968, Mobile, AL. **Educ:** Col Charleston, attended 1990. **Career:** Actor, writer, currently; A Different World, writer & actor, 1987-88; Roc Live, exec story editor, 1993; The Sinbad Show, producer, 1993; Sound fX, host, 1994; Mad TV, actor & segment writer, 1995-97; appeared as actor: Herman's Head, 1991; King of the Hill, 1997; In Harm's Way, 1997; Sour Grapes, 1998; Woo, 1998; Office Space, 1999; Liberty Heights, 1999; Magnolia, 1999; Waterproof, 1999; New Jersey Turnpikes, 1999; From Dusk Till Dawn 3: The Hangman's Daughter, 2000; The Replacements, 2000; Bedazzled, 2000; Double Take, 2001; Say It Isn't So, 2001; Evolution, 2001; Tortoise Vs Hare, 2002; The Time Machine, 2002; Drumline, 2002; Biker Boyz, 2003; The Runaway Jury, 2003; 7Up, spokesperson, 1999-2002; House of D, 2004; LA Rush, 2005; Looking for Sunday, 2006; Looking for Sunday, 2006; Primeval, 2007; Tv: Girlfriends, 2003; Father of the Pride, 2004-05; The

Evidence, 2006; The Adventures of Chico & Guapo, 2006; Everybody Hates Chris, 2007; Men in Trees, 2007; Ghost Whisperer, 2007; Untitled Victoria Pile Project, 2008; New Amsterdam, 2008; Black Poker Stars Invitational, 2008; Writer: A Different World, 1991; Roc, 1992; The Sinbad Show, 1994; Mad TV, 1995; The Orlando Jones Show, 2003; The Adventures of Chico & Guapo, 2006; Bufu, 2007; Producer: The Sinbad Show, 1994;The Orlando Jones Show, 2003; The Adventures of Chico & Guapo, 2006; Bufu, 2007. **Business Phone:** (212)586-5100.

JONES, OZRO T., JR.
Clergy, bishop. **Personal:** Son of Bishop & Mrs Ozro T Jones; married Regina Shaw Jones; children: Stephen, Soren. **Educ:** Temple Univ, BS, 1945; Temple Univ, MA, 1946; Temple Univ Sch Theol, STB; Temple Univ, STM, 1953; Temple Univ Sch Relig & Philos, STD 1962. **Career:** Young People's Ch of Holy Temple, leader, 1941; Ch of God in Christ to Liberia W Coast Africa, missionary, 1949; Mem Ch of God in Christ, pastor, 1953; Holy Temple Ch of God in Christ, assoc pastor, 1963; Commonwealth PA Ch God Christ, juris bishop, 1973-; Holy Temple Ch of God in Christ, pastor, bishop, currently. **Orgs:** Organized Tuesday Night Young People's Ch Serv; Sons of Gideon; Dau of Ruth; Young People's Choral of Holy Temple; Upper Room Fel; Pentecostal Stud Youth Conf; Big Bros & Big Sisters Fel; bd mem, Oppty Indsln Ctr Inc; Coun Christian Missionaries in Liberia; assoc ed, YPWW Quarterly Topics; co ed, The Christian View of Life; pres, Int Youth Cong Of Church of God in Christ; began Christ Seeks You youth rallies; writer of 3 hymns. **Honors/Awds:** Church of God in Christ, Elevated to 2nd Assistant Presiding Bishop, 1997. **Business Addr:** Bishop, Holy Temple Church God In Christ, Commonwealth Pa, 334 N 60th St, Philadelphia, PA 19139.*

JONES, PATRICIA. See SPEARS JONES, PATRICIA KAY.

JONES, PATRICIA YVONNE
Government official. **Personal:** Born Oct 22, 1956, Muskegon, MI; daughter of Theo and Juanita Henry; children: Dwayne. **Educ:** Muskegon Community Col, practical nursing dipl, 1978, AS, 1978; Grand Valley State Col. **Career:** Hackley Hosp & Med Ctr, lic prac nurse II, 1978-; City Muskegon Heights, council woman; Muskegon County Brd Commissioners. **Orgs:** Mich Lic Practical Nurse Asn, 1978; Nat Asn Advan Colored People, 1981; bdmem, Muskegon Community Col Adv Bd, 1982; Harriet J Cole Order EasternStars, 1983; gen mem, Nat Black Caucus Local Elected Official, 1983; gen mem, Muskegon Heights Bd Com, 1984; vpres, Muskegon Black Women Polit Caucus, treas, 1990-, vpres, 1992; pres, Mich Women Munic Govt, 1990,pres-elect, 1993; pres, 2400 Reynolds Block Club 1990-; Muskegon Heights Econ Develop, 1990-; Muskegon County Black Womens Caucus. **Honors/Awds:** Outstanding Cit Achiev, Muskegon Heights High Sch, 1974, 1984 &1989; Outstanding Comm Serv, Muskegon County Black Womens Polit Caucus, 1989; Outstanding Achievement, Census Bur, 1989; Cert Policy Drugs in Community Program, Michigan State Univ, 1990.

JONES, PAUL E.
College administrator. **Educ:** MBA. **Career:** Durham Tech Community Col, coordr continuing educ, Currently. *

JONES, PERCY ELWOOD
Physician. **Personal:** Born Jun 25, 1940, Richmond, VA; married Nora; children: Sabrina, Christopher. **Educ:** Va Union Univ, attended 1961; Meharry Med Col, MD, 1968; Am Bd Path, dipl. **Career:** Med Col, VA, path resident, path intern, 1968-73; L Richardson Memorial Hosp, chief staff, pathologist; Path Lab Kindred Hosp, med dir; pvt pract, physician, currently. **Orgs:** Am Soc Clin Pathologists; Old N State Med Soc; Nat Med Asn; Kappa Alpha Psi Fraternity; Greensboro Med Soc; Guilford Co Med Soc; Hayes-Taylor YMCA; fel, Col Am Pathologists; fel, Am Soc Clin Pathologists; life mem, Nat Asn Advan Colored People. **Military Serv:** USAF, maj, 1973-75. **Home Addr:** 1807 W Market St, Greensboro, NC 27403. **Business Addr:** Physician, 1807 W Market St, Greensboro, NC 27403.*

JONES, PETER LAWSON
Lawyer, state government official. **Personal:** Born Dec 23, 1952, Cleveland, OH; son of Charles Whitman and Margaret Diane Hoiston; married Lisa Payne, Oct 12, 1985; children: Ryan Charles Jones, Leah Danielle Jones & Evan Cooke Jones. **Educ:** Harvard Col, BA, 1975; Harvard Law Sch, JD, 1980. **Career:** Hon Yvonne B Burke US House Rep, pres & leg aide, 1975-76; Carter-Mondale Pres Campaign, writer & spokesman, 1976; Carter-Mondale Transition Planning Group, transition Officer, 1976-77; Off Intergovt Rels & Congional Affairs HUD, liaison Officer, 1977; Dyke Col Cleveland Ohio, instr, 1980, 1983; Supreme Ct Ohio, law clerk, 1982-83; Ohio Works Co, pres, 1984-85; Shaker Heights, Ohio, councilman, 1984-91; grad, Leadership Cleveland Prog, 1985; Roetzel & Andress, partner & atty, currently; Cuyahoga County, comnr, 2002-. **Orgs:** Pres, bd trustees, Metrop Strategy Group; treas, Harvard Law Sch Asn Cleveland, 1986-, co-gen coun, 1995-; exec comn, Cuyahoga County Dem Party, 1986-; bd trustees, Ct Community Serv Agency; State Cent & Exec

Comts, Ohio Dem Party; life mem, Cleveland Br Nat Asn Advan Colored People; bd trustees, Shaker Youth Baseball League; Mt Zion Congregational Church, UCC; adv bd, Shoes & Clothes Kids; adv bd, Sr Corps Retired Execs; Ohio State Bar Asn; Cleveland Bar Asn. **Honors/Awds:** Harvard Rhodes Scholar Nom; Harvard Nat Scholar; Paul Revere Frothingham Scholar; Currier House Sr Creativity Award; Meritorious Achievement Award, US Dept HUD, 1977, PUSH-Excel Prog, 1981; Eastside Coalition Comm Service Award, 1986; Inductee, Shaker Heights Alumni Asn Hall Fame, 1987; Outstanding Young Clevelander Pub Serv Jaycees, 1989; Black Hist Month Community Service Award, East Ohio Gas Co WZAK-FM, 1992; Good Neighbor Cert Appreciation, United Area Citizens Agency, 1992; Dem Year Award, Shaker Heights Dem Club, 1996; Emerging Polit Leaders Prog, 1997; Proj Interchange Israel Sem, 1998; Legislator of the Year Award, Ohio Sch Counrs Asn, 2000; Ohio Hunger Hero Award, Asn Second Harvest Foodbank, 2000; Comn Award, Ctr Families & C Fathers & Families Together, 2000; Families First Award, Ctr Families & C, 2000; Cert Recognition, Northeast Ohio Breast Cancer Coalition, 2001. **Special Achievements:** First African-American nominated to run for lieutenant governor of the State of Ohio; "The Family Line" a full length play produced at Harvard Coll 1975, Ohio Univ, 1976; staged reading at the E Cleveland Community Theatre 1985; Selected "Ohio Super Lawyer" by the Law & Politics Mag, 2004-06. **Home Addr:** 3532 Norwood Rd, Shaker Heights, OH 44122-4968, **Home Phone:** (216)561-8988. **Business Addr:** Commissioner, Cuyahoga County, Board Of County Commissioners, 1219 Ontario St 4th Fl, Cleveland, OH 44113, **Business Phone:** (216)443-7182.

JONES, DR. PHILLIP ERSKINE
Educator. **Personal:** Born Oct 26, 1940, Chicago, IL; son of Dorothy R; married Jo Lavera Kennedy; children: Phyllis & Joel. **Educ:** Univ Iowa, BS, phys educ, 1963, MA, phys educ, 1967; PhD, 1975. **Career:** Flint Community Sch, Phys Educ & Psychol, teacher, 1967-79; Univ Iowa, coord educ opportunities prog, 1968-70, dir spec support serv, 1970-75, asst vpres & dir affirmative action, 1975-78; adj asst prof educ, 1975-78; assoc dean student serv & adj asst prof educ, 1978-83; dean student serv & adj asst prof educ, 1983-89, assoc vpres acad affairs & dean students, 1989-97, vpres student serv & dean students, currently; US Ethnic Prof Exchange Prog W Germany, representative; Sister Cities Int; Carl Duisberg-Gesellschaft; Inst Auslandsbeziehungen. **Orgs:** Iowa City Human Relations Comn, 1972-74, chair, 1974-75; consult redevelop training prog educr, HOSE; field reader, Grad & Prof Opportunity Prog US Off Educ 1978; consult, US Dept Housing & Urban; field reader, Spec Prog US Off Educ, 1980-87. **Honors/Awds:** Access Award, Introspect Youth Serv, Chicago, 2004. **Special Achievements:** Numerous publications including "Special Education & Socioeconomic Retardation", J Spec Educators Vol 19 No 4 1983; Commentary: "Student Decision Making, When and How", "College/Career Choice, Right Student Right Time Right Place"; proceedings 1972. **Business Addr:** Vice President Student Services & Dean of Students, University of Iowa, 114 Jessup Hall, Iowa City, IA 52242.

JONES, PHILLIP MADISON
Executive. **Personal:** Born 1958. **Career:** Intellectual Properties Mgt Inc, chairman, chief exec officer. **Business Phone:** (404)814-0080.

JONES, POPEYE (RONALD JEROME JONES)
Basketball player. **Personal:** Born Jun 17, 1970, Dresden, TN; married Amy; children: Justin, Seth & Caleb. **Educ:** Murray State Univ, attended 1992. **Career:** Basketball player (Retired); Dallas Mavericks, forward, 1993-96, 2002-03; Toronto Raptors, 1996-98; Boston Celtics, 1998-99; Denver Nuggets, 1999-2000; Wash Wizards, forward, 2000-02; Golden State Warriors, forward, 2003-04. **Honors/Awds:** OVC's Athlete of the Year, 1991, 1992. *

JONES, QUINCY DELIGHT
Composer, music arranger or orchestrator, television producer. **Personal:** Born Mar 14, 1933, Chicago, IL; son of Quincy Delight Sr and Sarah J; married Jeri Caldwell, Jan 1, 1957 (divorced 1966); children: Jolie Jones Levine; married Ulla Andersson, Jan 1, 1967 (divorced 1974); children: Martina Jones & Quincy Jones III; married Peggy Lipton, Jan 1, 1974 (divorced 1990); children: Kidada & Rashida. **Educ:** Berklee Sch Music; Seattle Univ; Boston Conserv; honorary doctorate, Univ Pa. **Career:** Rock Band, founder; Lionel Hampton band, mem; music arranger & composer; music dir, 1961; Mercury Rec, vpres, 1964; Films: The Wiz; In Cold Blood; In the Heat of the Night; Blues for Trumpet & Koto; The Color Purple, exec producer; The Making of The Italian Job, 2003; Get Rich or Die Tryin,2005; music producer: Off the Wall; Thriller; Qwest Recs, owner & founder,1981-; Dept State tour of Near East, Middle East, & South Am, Dizzy Gillespie Orchestra, co-organizer, 1956; Barchlay Disques, Paris, musicdir, 1956-60; independent composer, conductor, 1965-; works include: Brand New Bag, Sounds Stuff Like That, Walking in Space, This is How I Feel about Jazz, Back on the Block, producer, 1990; Vibe magazine, founder,1993; Qwest Rec, owner; Q west Broadcasting, chmn & chief exec officer. **Honors/Awds:** Big Band and Jazz Hall of Fame, 1988; received 27 Grammy Awards and over 50 Grammy nominations; 1979 production of Off the Wall sold over 8 million copies and at that time a record breaking four top-10

singles; album, The Dude received an unprecedented 12 Grammy nominations in 1981 and won 5Grammy Awards; 8 Grammy nominations in 1983 (most by one person in a year); Polar Music Prize, 1994; ABAA Music Award for efforts to aid African famine victims, and for conceiving and giving leadership to USA for Africa, producing the album, We Are the World; numerous others including honorary degrees from Loyola Univ and Seattle Univ; Frederick D Patterson Award, 1999; John F Kennedy Center Honors, 2001; French LTgiond' Honneur medal, 2001. **Special Achievements:** Auth Q: The Autobiography of Quincy Jones, 2002; nominated for Oscar Awards for four film scores.

JONES, QUINCY DELIGHT, III
Music producer, songwriter, actor. **Personal:** Born Dec 23, 1968, London, England; son of Ulla Anderson and Quincy D Jones Jr; married Koa (divorced); children: 2; married Ulla Andersson (divorced 1974); children: Martina & Quincy III; married Jeri Caldwell (divorced 1966); children: Jolie Jones Levine. **Educ:** Berklee Col Music. **Career:** Actor, music producer & writer; LL Cool J's album, co-producer &co-writer, 1993; YoYo's album, co-producer & co-writer, 1993; music: Fresh Prince of Bel-Aire; Out All Night; NBC-TV, Menace II SOC, Hughes Bros Prod, 1993; Q D III Sound Lab, owner, currently; Films: Wiz on Down the Road, 1978; We Are the World, 1985; Michael Jackson: History on Film -Volume II, 1997; Fantasia 2000, 1999; Austin Powers in Goldmember, 2002. **Honors/Awds:** Twenty Seven Grammy Awards & Grammy Legend Award. **Special Achievements:** Numerous honors including 79 Grammy Award Nominations.

JONES, RANDY
Athlete. **Personal:** Born Jun 24, 1969, Winston-Salem, NC; married Cheri; children: Roman & Marissa. **Educ:** Duke Univ, BA, 1991. **Career:** SunTrust Bank, Atlanta, GA, comput technician; US Olympic Comt, bobsledder, currently. **Honors/Awds:** Nat Brakeman & Side Push Championships, 1992 & 1995; Silver Medal 4-man Bobsled, Winter Olympics, 2002. **Special Achievements:** With Garrett Hines, first African Am men to win medal in Winter Olympics, 2002. **Business Addr:** Bobsledder, US Olympic Committee, 1 Olympic Plz, Colorado Springs, CO 80909, **Business Phone:** (719)632-5551.

JONES, RANDY KANE
Lawyer. **Personal:** Born Oct 25, 1957, Jacksonville, NC; son of Henry and Julia Mae Saunders; children: Randy. **Educ:** Univ NC, BA, 1979, Sch Law JD, 1982. **Career:** Judge Advocate Gen's Corps, atty, 1983-86; US Atty, Dept Justice, asst, 1987-. **Orgs:** Fed Bar Asn, 1984-, Am Bar Asn, 1985-, Christian Fellowship Cong Church, 1985, BE SLA, 1986-; Parlimentarian Earl B Gilliam Bar Asn, 1988-; mem bd, California Asn Black Lawyers, 1989-92; Chmn, Veterans Affairs NAACP San Diego Br, 1989-; Nat Bar Asn, 1989-, regional dir, 1991-93; pres, Earl B Gilliam Bar Asn, 1990-91, mem bd, 1987-; bd mem, San Diego County Crime Victims, 1991-94; Leadership, Educ, Awareness, Develop, grad, 1991; NC State & Ca State Bar Asn; San Diego County Bar Asn; vpres, Urban League San Diego Chapter; Nat Bar Asn, 1993-95; bd mem, Voices for Children, 1993-; pres, Nat Bar Asn. **Honors/Awds:** Honorary Doctor Laws, Claflin Col; 100 Most Influential Leaders, Ebony Mag, 1998. **Military Serv:** USN, lt, 3 yrs; Defense Coun Quarter, 1983-86; USNR, CDR, 1987-. **Business Addr:** Assistant, United States Attorney's Office, Department Justice, PO Box 66078, Washington, DC 20035-6078, **Business Phone:** (202)305-0025.*

JONES, RAYMOND DEAN
Judge. **Personal:** Born Nov 30, 1945, Pueblo, CO; married Carolyn S; children: Latoya Bryant, Ruth Marie, Raymond Dean II. **Educ:** Colo Col, BA, polit sci, 1967; Harvard Univ Sch Law, JD, 1971. **Career:** Judge (retired); Colo Supreme Ct, clerk to chief justice, 1971-72; Holme Roberts & Owen, atty, 1972-74; Met Denver Dist Atty Consumer Off Prosec Consumer Defrauders, chief coun, 1974-77; Denver Co Ct, judge, 1977-79; Denver Dist Ct, judge, 1979-87; Colo Ct Appeals, judge, 1988-03. **Orgs:** bd dir, New Dance Theatre Inc, 1972-, CO State Bd Law Exam, 1973-; vpres, bd dir Denver Oppurtunity Inc, 1974-; St Bd CO Humanities Prog, 1977, Gov Task Force Labor Legis, 1976, Gov Task Force Employ Agencies, 1976; pres, Sam Cary Bar Assoc; bd trustees, Denver Bar Asn; CO Bar Asn; Am Bar Asn; bd gov, Nat Bar Asn; sec CO Dem Party; chmn CO Black Caucus, 1973-74; deleg, Dem nat Conv, 1976; Am Judges Asn, CO Assoc Dist Judges, Bar State CO, Fed Dist CO, 10th Fed Circuit, US Supreme Ct; fac Nat Judicial Col Reno NV; bd trustees Colo Col Colorado Springs; Colo Coun Arts; numerous community bds; bd dirs & founder, Cleo Parker Robinson Dance; bd dirs, Denver Consumer Credit Counseling Serv, currently. **Honors/Awds:** Marshal of the Class, Harvard Univ Law Sch, 1971; Barney Ford Community Award, Law & Justice, 1977; listed, The Am Bench, 1977; author "A Search for Better Police Serv & An End Police-Community Tensions Black Urban Neighborhoods & An Examination of Community Control Police" 1971; numerous community awards, Denver & Colorado. **Business Addr:** Lawyer, The Holt Group LLC, 1675 Broadway Suite 1130, Denver, CO 80202, **Business Phone:** (303)225-8500.

JONES, REGGIE (REGINALD LEE JONES)
Football player. **Personal:** Born May 8, 1971, Kansas City, KS. **Educ:** La State Univ. **Career:** Carolina Panthers, wide receiver, 1995-96; Kansas City Chiefs, 1997; San Diego Chargers, 2000-01. **Honors/Awds:** All-America honors, seven times, La State Univ.

JONES, REGINALD LEE. See JONES, REGGIE.

JONES, DR. RENA TALLEY
Educator, college teacher. **Personal:** Born Aug 3, 1937, Pine Mountain, GA. **Educ:** Morris Brown Col, BA, 1960; Atlanta Univ, MS, 1967; Wayne State Univ, PhD, 1974. **Career:** Educator, Col Teacher (retired); Lee Co Bd Educ, instr, 1960-61; Fulton Community Bd Educ, instr, 1961-66; NSF grant, 1966-67; Wayne State Univ, grad asst, 1967-73; Spelman Col, from asst prof biol to prof biol, 1973-2006, chair biol, dir; Macy Summer Inst Premed Educ, 1977; Chautauqua-type Prog Rnat Sci Found, reviewer, Health Careers Off, dir; Wash, DC, partic, pre-med health careers advs & conf. **Orgs:** Health Careers Comn; adv, Atlanta Univ Ctr, Vio Hon Soc; AAAS; Am Soc Microbiol; Ga Acad Sci; assoc mem, Sigma Xi; Beta Kappa Chi; Nat Sci Hon Soc; dir, Spec Health Careers Opportunity Grant; judge, Sci Fair Sec Schs. **Honors/Awds:** Teaching Assitantship, Wayne State Univ, 1967-73; Tenneco Excellence in Teaching Award, United Nego Col Fund, 1989-90. **Special Achievements:** Books: General Biology Laboratory Manual, 1977; Life in the Laboratory, 1980; Experiments in General Biology, 1987.

JONES, RICHARD JULIUS
Association executive. **Educ:** Central State Univ, 1964-66; Toledo Univ, 1972-74; Upsala Col, mgt, 1980; Bradley Univ, mgt, 1982. **Career:** Boys & Girls Club, Toledo, unit dir, NY, guidance dir, Newark, unit dir, Peoria, exec dir, Am, nat staff, Stockton, asst exec dir, pres, ceo, currently. **Orgs:** Chmn bd, Peoria Housing Authority, 1980-90; Human Rel Comn, 1982-87; Bradley Univ Chief Club, 1984; vpres, Kiwanis Club, 1985; Ill Coun Aging, 1985; pres, United Way Exec Dir Asn, 1987; pres, Optimist Club, 1987; bd mem, Rotary Club, 1989. **Honors/Awds:** Man of the Year, Boys & Girls Club Toledo, 1974; Staff Award Man/Boy, Boys & Girls Club of Newark, 1977; Nat Keystone Adv, Boys & Girls Club Am, 1984; Community Servics of the Year, Peoria Housing Authority, 1985, 1987, 1988; Citizen of the Year Award, 1987, 1988; Outstanding Community Leader, 1987; Outstanding Leader, Peoria Action Agency, Peoria InterCity Youth Coun, 1987; Community Leader Award, Peoria Sch Dist, 1987; Citizen of the Year, Peoria Christian Leadership Coun, 1988; Outstanding Staff Award, Boys & Girls Club Peoria, 1990. **Home Phone:** (209)478-3854. **Business Phone:** (209)466-1264.

JONES, RICHARD TIMOTHY
Actor. **Personal:** Born Jan 16, 1972, Japan; son of Clarence; married Nancy, Oct 1, 2009; children: Aubrey, Sydney & Elijah. **Career:** Films: Helicopter, 1993; What's Love Got to Do with It, 1993; Renaissance Man, 1994; Jury Duty, 1995; Johns, 1996; Black Rose of Harlem, 1996; The Trigger Effect, 1996; Kiss the Girls, 1997; Event Horizon, 1997; Goodbye Lover, 1998; The Wood, 1999; Dirty Down Under.. Up Here, 1999; AuggieRose, 2000; Lockdown, 2000; Book of Love, 2002; G, 2002; Moonlight Mile, 2002; Phone Booth, 2002; Twisted, 2004; Collateral, 2004; Finding Neo, co-producer, 2004; Breach, co-producer, 2004; Soul Plane, 2004; Time Bomb,2005; Traci Townsend, 2005; Guess Who, 2005; Cutting Room, 2006; The Package, 2006; Why Did I Get Married?, 2007; Vantage Point, 2008; TV series:?In the Heat of the Night: Who Was Geli Bendl?, 1994; Brooklyn South, 1997-98; Incognito, 1999; "Judging Amy", 1999-2005; The Extinction of the Dinosaurs, 2002; The Cook of the Money Pot, 2002; Second String, 2002; Full-Court Miracle, 2003; Paradise, 2004; Sex, Love & Secrets, 2005;Riding the Bus with My Sister, 2005; Talk Show Diaries, 2005; Dream a Little Dream, 2005; "Sex, Love & Secrets", 2005; Time Bomb, 2006;Girlfriends, 2007; "Terminator: The Sarah Connor Chronicles", 2008. **Honors/Awds:** Nomination, Image Award, 2000. **Business Addr:** Actor, c/o Innovative Artists, 1505 10th St, Santa Monica, CA 90401, **Business Phone:** (310)656-0400.*

JONES, RICHMOND ADDISON
Graphic artist, watercolorist. **Personal:** Born Jul 9, 1937, Chicago, IL; son of Silas Philip and Mabel Betty Crouse; married Christine Ann Osada; children: Philip Frederick. **Educ:** Univ Ill, 1956-57; Am Acad Art, AA, 1957-59; Sch Visual Arts, 1959-61; Lill St Ceramic Studio; Univ Ill; Palette & Chisel Acad Fine Arts, Chicago. **Career:** Batten Barton Durstine & Osborn, asst & assoc art dir, 1961-66; J Walter Thompson Co, art dir, 1966-68; Jones James & Jameson Inc, pres, 1968-69; Fuller Smith & Ross, art dir, 1969-70; Richmond A Jones Graphics, owner & designer 1970-2000; watercolor painter, currently. **Orgs:** Int House Asn, 1959-62; dir & mem, Sponsors Educ Opportunities, 1965-70; founder, vp, mem Group for Advert Progress (Devel Minority Opportunities) 1966-70; dir, mem Ill Epilepsy League, 1972-74; dir, mem, Soc Typographic Arts, 1972-; mem, Am Inst Graphic Arts, 1975-; Chicago Press Club, 1980, Chicago Assoc Com & Industry, 1986; Miss Watercolor Soc; NE Watercolor Soc; Ill Watercolor Soc; Nat Watercolor Soc; Mo Watercolor Soc; Palette & Chisel Acad Fine Arts; Univ Ill Pres Coun. **Honors/Awds:** Highest Readership (2 awards) Design News, 1966; Published Art Direction Mag, 1968; Selected Top Creative Visual Talent Amer Showcas,e 1978-; winner, Max Award for brochure produced for Underwriters Labs Inc, TCR Graphics, 1985; judge for Typographers Int Awd Prog, 1985; judge for awards prog Acad for Health Serv Mkt, Am Mkt Assoc, 1986. **Military Serv:** AUS, sgt, 1962-68; Marksmanship, Good Conduct Medal, Cert of Achievement, 1963-64. **Home Phone:** (773)588-4900. **Business Addr:** Painter, 2530 W Eastwood Ave, Chicago, IL 60625, **Business Phone:** (773)588-4900.

JONES, ROBERT ALTON
Lawyer. **Personal:** Born Jan 30, 1944, Houston, TX; son of Robert J and Gloria C; married Velma Chester Jones; children: Jessica Elizabeth. **Educ:** Tex Southern Univ, BA, 1969; Thurgood Marshall Sch Law, Houston, TX, JD, 1972. **Career:** Univ Houston, part-time prof; Teamster's Local 968, official, 1969-73; Anderson Hodge Jones & Hoyt Inc, Houston, TX, stockholder & vpres, 1974-; Pvt Pract, atty, 1983-; Robert A. Jones & Assoc, criminal defense atty, currently. **Orgs:** Houston Lawyer's Asn; State Bar TX; ABA; TX Crim Defense Lawyer's Asn; Bus & Prof Mens Orgn; Phi Alpha Delta; US Dist Ct, So & Eastern Dist TX; participant, Am Bar Asn Sem Criminal Defense Litigation; bd mem, The Ensemble Theatre; Trial Advocacy Inst, TDCLA, Sam Houston Univ, Huntsville, TX, 1997; and others. **Honors/Awds:** Recipient acheivement awards from Stud Govt & Stud Bar Asn; Am Jurisprudence awards, Debtors & Creditors Rights & Oil & Gas; Alumnus of the Year, Tex Southern Univ. **Business Addr:** Criminal Defense Attorney, Robert A Jones & Associates, 2211 Norfolk Suite 600, Frost Nat Bank Bldg, Houston, TX 77098.*

JONES, ROBERT BERNARD
Educator, musician. **Personal:** Born Oct 2, 1956, Detroit, MI; son of Evelyn Jones and Jimmie Fletcher; married Bernice, Oct 11, 1986; children: Robert Bernard Jones II & Arnesia Nicole. **Educ:** Wayne State Univ, BA, 1979. **Career:** Wayne State Univ, student asst, 1974-79, affil fac; Detroit Pub Sch, broadcast technician, 1979-86; WDET-FM, dir, Detroit Radio Info Serv, 1986-94, broadcast sales mgr, 1994; Self-employed, blues musician, educator, 1994-. **Orgs:** Founding mem, Detroit Blues Soc, 1986-; adv bd, Friends Sch Music Festival, 1993-; adv bd, Detroit Radio Info Serv, 1994-. **Honors/Awds:** Hall of Fame, Detroit Monthly Mag, 1990; Best Blues Instrumentalist, Metro Times Mag, 1990, 1991. **Special Achievements:** Ann Arbor Folk Festival, Performer, 1992; Henry Ford Museum, "Roots of Rhythm," Program MC & Participant, 1994; Old Songs Festival, Albany, NY, Performer, 1994; "The Blues Experience," 4-part Lecture/Performance, Monroe, Mich, Library System, 1994; Chicago Blues Festival, Performer, 1995.

JONES, REV. ROBERT EARL
Clergy. **Personal:** Born Feb 11, 1942, Franklinton, NC; married Karen; children: Darrell Amani. **Educ:** Houston-Tillotson Col, BA, 1965; Yale Univ, MDiv, 1969, STM, 1970; United Theol Sem, DMin, 1994. **Career:** Quinnipiac Col, sem instr, 1968-69; Fair Haven Parents Ministry, exec dir, 1967-74; Yale Divine Sch, asst prof, 1970-74; Southern Conn State Col, adj prof 1974-75; New Haven Anti-Poverty Agency, dep dir, 1974-75; Grand Ave United Church Christ, asst pastor 1974-77; Col Hill Community Church, UP, asst pastor, sr pastor, currently. **Orgs:** Adv bd, Conn Mental Health Ctr, 1974-77; bd pres, Black Coalition New Haven, 1970-75; vpres, pres, Nat Coalition Econ Justice; consult, Nat Acad Churches in transition 1970-75; Nat Alliance Bus New Haven, 1970-72. **Honors/Awds:** Richard Allen Achievement Award, 1970; Albert B Beebe Award, 1970; Foundation Nation Service Award, Wash Times, 1996. **Business Addr:** Senior Pastor, College Hill Community Church, Presbyterian USA, 1547 Philadelphia Dr, Dayton, OH 45406, **Business Phone:** (937)278-4203.

JONES, ROBERT LEE
Football player. **Personal:** Born Sep 27, 1969, Blackstone, VA; married Maneesha; children: Cayleb, Levi & Isaiah. **Educ:** East Carolina Univ. **Career:** Football player (retired); Dallas Cowboys, linebacker, 1992-95; St Louis Rams, linebacker, 1996-97; Miami Dolphins, linebacker, 1998-2000; Wash Redskins, linebacker, 2001. **Orgs:** Champions Christ Ministry. **Honors/Awds:** Defensive Rookie of the Year, United Press Int, Nat Football League, 1992; All-Pro, USA Today, 1994; Defensive Player of the Week, Am Football League; East Carolina University Hall o Fame, 2004. **Special Achievements:** First Pirate to be selected in the first round of the NFL Draft.

JONES, ROBERT WESLEY
Executive. **Personal:** Born Jul 24, 1929, Boston, MA; son of John and Lillian Evans; married Elaine S Savory; children: Todd, Stacy & Austin. **Educ:** Howard Univ, 1950; New York Univ, BS, 1956; New York Law Sch, Cert New York Bar, 1960. **Career:** City New York, dep comr, 1964-66; Pianta Dosi & Assoc, vpres, 1966-68; Burnett Constr Co, ex vpres, 1968-70; New York Univ, adj prof, 1972; Robert W Jones & Assoc Inc, pres, currently. **Orgs:** Citizens Housing & Planning Coun, 1974-; mem bd adv, New York Univ Real Estate Inst, 1974-; exec comt, Asn Better New York, 1975-; chmn, Tougaloo Col Bd Trustees, 1980-, chmn emeritus, 1996; pres, Independent Fee Appraisers, 1984-; mem bd adv, Fed Nat Meeting Asn, 1985-; bd gov, New Sch Soc Res, Milano Grad Sch, 1993; Exec Comt 14th St Local Develop Comt, 1993; sr advr,

Columbia Partners Invest Mgt LLC, 1996; dir, Landon Butler Co, 1996; Brown-Tougaloo Rels community, 1999. **Honors/Awds:** DHL, 1996. **Military Serv:** USMC, sargent, 1950-53; Purple Heart, 1952. **Home Addr:** 2 5th Ave, New York, NY 10011. **Business Addr:** President, Robert W Jones & Associates Inc, 2 Fifth Ave, New York, NY 10011-8842, **Business Phone:** (212)929-5318.

JONES, RODREK EDWARD
Football player. **Personal:** Born Jan 11, 1974, Detroit, MI. **Educ:** Univ Kans, human develop & family living. **Career:** Cincinnati Bengals, tackle, 1996-2001; St Louis Rams, tackle, 2002; Wash Redskins, 2003.

JONES, ROGER CARVER
Football player. **Personal:** Born Apr 22, 1969, Cleveland, OH; married Angela. **Educ:** Tenn State univ. **Career:** Football player (retired); Tampa Bay Buccaneers, defensive back, 1991-93; Cincinnati Bengals, 1994-96; Tenn Oilers, 1997.

JONES, RON. See JONES, RONALD LYMAN.

JONES, RONALD JEROME. See JONES, POPEYE.

JONES, RONALD LYMAN (RON JONES)
Administrator. **Personal:** Born Mar 29, 1945, Dayton, OH; son of Major E and Cecile E; children: Dana L Bullock, David & Aubre. **Educ:** Cent State Univ; Fisk Univ. **Career:** Battelle Memorial Inst, trainer, 1974-88, personnel mgr, BPMD, 1980-88; Online Comput Libr Ctr Inc, mgr, employee rel & develop, 1988-91, mgr human resources, 1991-93, dir admin serv, 1993-, ed asst, dir human resources, currently. **Orgs:** ASTD, pres Cent Ohio Chap; PACO; ASTD, Black Caucus. **Military Serv:** AUS, First Lt, 1968-70; Bronze Star, Army Commendation Medal.

JONES, RONDELL TONY
Football player. **Personal:** Born May 7, 1971, Sunderland, MD. **Educ:** Univ NC. **Career:** Denver Broncos, defensive back, 1993-96; Baltimore Ravens, 1997.

JONES, ROSALYN EVELYN
Lawyer. **Personal:** Born Apr 26, 1961, Frankfurt, Germany; daughter of Harry T. **Educ:** Harvard Raddiffe Col, AB, 1983; Oxford Univ, St John's Col, 1984; Harvard Law Sch, JD, 1987. **Career:** Gibson, Dunn & Crutcher, atty, 1987-89; Rosenfed, Meyer & Susman, atty, 1989-91; Manatt, Phelps & Phillips, partner, atty, 1991-97; Rosalyn E Jones, atty, 1997-. **Orgs:** Bd dir, Black Entertainment & Sports Lawyers Asn; Am Bar Asn, 1993-; Calif Bar, 1987-; Dist Columbia Bar, 1988; Phi Beta Kappa, Harvard Radcliffe Col; Harvard Knox fel, St John's Col, Oxford Univ. **Business Phone:** (310)286-9826.*

JONES, ROSCOE T., JR.
Dentist. **Personal:** Born Jan 25, 1935, Washington, DC; married Marva A J; children: Nancy Ellen. **Educ:** Howard Univ, BS, 1958; Howard Univ, DDS, 1965. **Career:** Self-employed, dentist, 1968-; Dental Clin Ft Belvoir, AUS Dental Corp, actg chief, 1966. **Orgs:** Robert T Freeman Dental Soc, 1970; Acad Gen Dentistry, 1973-; treas, Metro Dental Asn Chartered, 1978-; Sunday sch teacher All Souls Unitarian Church, 1970-77; DC Dental Soc. **Honors/Awds:** Outstanding Cadet, Howard Univ. **Military Serv:** AUS, ROTC, 1959; AUS, cpt , served 2 1/2 yrs. **Business Addr:** Dentist, 1238 Monroe St NE, Washington, DC 20017.

JONES, ROSEMARY M
Executive. **Educ:** NY State Univ, BA Bus Admin, 1972. **Career:** IBM, Supplier Div Prog, SE region, 1995-2002; Turner Broadcasting System Inc, Supplier Div Prog, dir, 2002-. **Orgs:** Chair, Ga Women Bus Coun Bd Dirs, 2004-05; Asian-Am Chamber Com Ga; Am Hotel & Lodging Multicultural Adv Bd; CP Plasma Adv Bd; Ga Minority Supplier Develop Coun. **Business Addr:** Director of Supplier Diversity, Turner Broadcasting System Inc, Supplier Div Prog, 1 CNN Ctr 14th Fl S Tower, Atlanta, GA 30303, **Business Phone:** (404)827-1315.*

JONES, ROY (ROY LEVESTA JONES)
Rap musician, boxer, basketball player. **Personal:** Born Jan 16, 1969, Pensacola, FL. **Career:** Boxer (retired), rap musician; prof boxer, 1989-2004, basketball player, currently, rap musician, currently; Brevard Blue Ducks, currently; Singles: "Y'all Must've Forgot," 2001; "I Smoke, I Drank," 2004; "Can't Be Touched," 2004; Album: Round One, 2002; Release the Beast, 2006. **Honors/Awds:** Golden Gloves Champion, 1986, 1987; Silver Medal, Seoul Olympic Games, 1988; Fighter of the Year, Ring Mag, 1994; World Boxing Council championship belt; World Boxing Asn championship belt; IBF Middleweight champion, 1993-94; IBF Super Middleweight champion, 1994-97; WBC Light Heavyweight champion, 1997-02; WBA Heavyweight Champ belt, 2003. **Special Achievements:** First undisputed light-heavyweight champ of the world since Michael Spinks relinquished the title in 1985; Film appearances: Matrix Reloaded, Enter the Matrix & The Devil's Advocate. **Business Addr:** Rap Musician, 3165 Spreading Oak Dr SW, Atlanta, GA 30311, **Business Phone:** (404)696-0099.

JONES, ROY LEVESTA. See JONES, ROY.

JONES, SAMUEL
Basketball player, basketball coach. **Personal:** Born Jun 24, 1933, Laurinburg, NC; son of Samuel and Louise K; married Gladys Chavis; children: Aubre, Phyllis, Michael, Terri & Ashley. **Educ:** NC Col, BS. **Career:** Professional basketball player (retired), basketball coach; Boston Celtics, 1957-69; NC Central Univ, head basketball coach; New Orleans Jazz Basketball Team, LA, asst coach; Fed City Col, Washington, dir athletics, 1969-77; Blue Ribbon Sports, NIKE Shoe Div, head of promotions; DC Public Sch, Wash, DC, athletic dir, 1989; Montgomery Blair High Sch, substitute teacher, currently. **Orgs:** Kappa Alpha Psi. **Honors/Awds:** North Carolina Hall of Fame, 1980; Naismith Hall of Fame, 1984; Black Athletes Hall of Fame, 1985; Nelms Hall of Fame; CIAA Hall of Fame, NCCU Athletic Hall of Fame. **Special Achievements:** One of 50 Greatest Players in NBA History, 1996. **Military Serv:** AUS. **Business Addr:** Substitute Teacher, Montgomery Blair High School, 51 Univ Blvd E, Silver Spring, MD 20901-2451, **Business Phone:** (301)649-2800.

JONES, SAMUEL L., III
Actor. **Personal:** Born Apr 29, 1983, Boston, MA; son of Sam Jones II. **Career:** Films: Snipes, 2001; Zigzag, 2002; Glory Road, 2006; Home of the Brave, 2006; Krews, 2009; TV series: "A Thousand Words", 2000; "Smallville", 2001-; "Capitol Crimes", 2003; "Smallville: Chloe Chronicles", 2004; "Forsaken", 2004, "ER", 2005; "7th Heaven", 2006; "For One Night", 2006. **Business Addr:** Actor, c/o Warner Bros TV, 15301 Ventura Blvd Suite E, Sherman Oaks, CA 91403.*

JONES, SARAH
Poet, playwright, actor. **Personal:** Born Nov 29, 1973, Baltimore, MD. **Educ:** Bryn Mawr Univ. **Career:** Bryn Mawr Col, Mellon Minority fel; Van Lier Literary fel, 1998; Plays: Surface Transit, 2000; Bamboozled, 2000; Famous, 2000; Women Can't Wait, 2000; Waking the American Dream, 2002; I Am Ali, 2002; Bridge and Tunnel, 2005; Hip-Hop: Beyond Beats & Rhymes, 2006; Good Hair, 2009. **Honors/Awds:** Grand Slam Championship, 1997; Best One Person Show, HBO Apen Comedy Arts Festival; Tony Award; Obie Award; Helen Hayes Award; Calloway Award, New York Civil Liberties Union. **Special Achievements:** Two Drama Desk nominations; first artist in history to sue the Federal Communications Commission for censorship; made numerous TV appearances on HBO, NBC, ABC, CBS, PBS, CNN. **Business Addr:** Actor, 302A W 12 St Suite 121, New York, NY 10014.*

JONES, SELWYN ALDRIDGE
Football player. **Personal:** Born May 13, 1970, Houston, TX. **Educ:** Colo State Univ, attended. **Career:** Football player (retired); Cleveland Browns, 1993; New Orleans Saints, defensive back, 1994; Seattle Seahawks, 1995-96; Denver Broncos, defensive back, 1997-98.

JONES, SHALLEY A
Banker, vice president (organization). **Personal:** Born Sep 17, 1954, Moorehead, MS; daughter of Robert Lee and Rosie Lee; divorced; children: Shantea K & Ernest J II. **Educ:** Univ Miami, BA, 1975; Fla Int Univ, MSM, 1983. **Career:** First Union NAT Bank, asst vpres, loan processing mgr, 1976-84, asst vpres, regional mgr, 1984-85; Chase Fed Bank, first vpres, 1985; SunBank Miami, NA, CRA & Consumer Compliance, vpres, 1994-95; Fannie Mae, dir community investment; S Fla Partnership Office, dir, 1994-2003; Fannie Mae, housing & community develop Midwest region, vpres, 2003-. **Orgs:** AKA Sorority, Inc, 1974-; pres, Miami-Dade Urban Bankers Asn, 1987-89; Nat Black MBA Asn, S Fla chap, 1990-; exec pres, Nat Asn Urban Bankers, 1991-92; Metro-Miami Action Plan, chp, 1991-94; adv bdm, UNF, 1991-93; Eastern Fin Credit Union, dir, 1993-94; bd, NCP, Miami-Dade chap, 1992-94; life mem, bd mem,Dade County Housing Finance Authority, 1996-. **Honors/Awds:** S Fla Bus Jour, Up & Comers Award/Banking, 1989; Dollars & Sense Magazine, Am Best & Brightest, 1991; Am Banker Newspaper, Top 40 Banker Under 40, 1992; Banker of the Year, Miami Dade Urban Bankers ASN, 1992; Unsung Hero Award, City Miami, 1992. **Business Addr:** Vice President, Fannie Mae, 3900 Wisconsin Ave NW, Washington, DC 20016-2892, **Business Phone:** (202)752-7000.*

JONES, SHARON DIANA. See CHARIS.

JONES, SHERMAN J
School administrator, consultant. **Personal:** Born Jan 12, 1946, Newport News, VA; son of Sherman E and Leola Mae Jones; married J Janice, Dec 22, 1967; children: Kimberely & Sherman E. **Educ:** Williams Col Am Studies, BA, 1968; Harvard Univ Gen Mgt, Finance & Organizational Behavior, MBA, 1970, Admin, Planning & Policy Analysis, EdD, 1978. **Career:** Raymond James Financial Services, independant advisor, 1966-; Cresap, McCormic & Padget Inc, mgt consult, 1972-75; Acad Educ Develo Inc, mgt consult, 1975-77; Harvard Grad Sch, teaching fel, 1976-77; Fisk Univ, vpres admin, 1977-80, vpres & acting dean univ, 1980-82; Tuskegee Univ, exec vpres & prof mgt, 1982-91; Clark Atlanta Univ, provost vpres acad affairs prof bus admin, 1991-93; Southern Normal Sch, pres, headmaster, chief exec officer, 1993. **Orgs:** Asst to pres, Woodrow Wilson Admin Intern, Central State Univ, Ohio, 1970-71; bd dir, Better Bus Bur Nashville Middle Tenn Inc, 1978-82; mgt comt, John A Andrew Community Hosp, 1982; adv coun, Am Inst Managing Diversity, Inc, 1984-; bd adv, 1986-92, bd trustees, St Andrews Sewanee Sch; bd dir, YMCA, Brewton; bd dir, Harvard Alumni Asn, 1991-93; chmn, Havard Grad Sch Educ, 1990-91; Nashville Comn Foreign Affairs. **Special Achievements:** Difficult Times for Private Black Colleges," Change mag March 1984; "Adapting Governance, Leadership Style & Mgt to a Changing Environment," Black Colleges & Universities: Challenges for the Future, Antoine Garibaldi, ed, Praeger, 1984; Fac Involvement Col & Univ Decision-Making, unpublished doctoral dissertation, 1978; Faculty Involvement in Coll & Univ Decision Making, in Managing Turbulence & Change, John D Millett, editor, Jossey-Bass, Autumn 1977. **Home Addr:** 1151 Briarcliff Pl NE, Atlanta, GA 30306. **Business Addr:** Independent Financial Advisor, Raymond James Financial Services, 6555 Chapman Hwy, Knoxville, TN 37920, **Business Phone:** (865)579-2776.

JONES, PROF. SHIRLEY JOAN
School administrator. **Personal:** Born Nov 26, 1931, New York, NY; children: Susan & Sande Jr. **Educ:** New York Univ, MA, 1954, MSW, 1964; Columbia Univ, DSW, 1977. **Career:** New York Univ Sch Social Work, asst prof, 1967-70; State Univ New York Stony Brook, assoc prof, 1972-78; New York Univ Metro Studies, adj prof, 1973-77; Univ Southern MS, dean prof, 1978-89; State Univ NY, Albany, Sch Social Welfare, prof, distinguished serv prof & prof emer, 2002-. **Orgs:** Bd dir, Nat Alliance Bus, 1982-85; Comn Child Support Enforcement, 1985; bd dir, Gov Off Vol Citizen Participant, 1985; Nat Asn Black Soc Workers; Nat Asn Social Workers; Coun Social Work Educ; Int Asn Social Work; State Constitutional Change Comt, 1986-87; Int Comn Nat Asn Social Workers; comnr, Accrediation Coun Social Work Educ; US Census Bur, Minority Adv Comt, 2000; expert panelist, Nat Head Start Dept Health & Human Serv. **Honors/Awds:** Woman of the Year, Hattiesbg City Businessmen's Club, 1981; Waldoff's Achievement, 1983; Social Worker of the Year, MS Chap, Nat Asn Black Social Workers, 1983, Dedicated Service Award, 1986; Distinguished Service Award, Gov Off Vol Citizen Part, 1983; Certificate of Appreciation DHHS,OHDS, AFCYF, 1986; Martin Luther King Award, State Univ NY, Albany, 1993; Elected Secretary State Univ New York, Albany Univ Senate, 1993, 1994; City of Albany Award, Human Rights, 1994; Distinguished Professor, 1994; Elected Senator, State Univ NY, Albany, 1995. **Business Addr:** Distinguished Service Professor, Professor Emeritus, University at Albany, State University of New York, School of Social Welfare, Rm RI 111 1400 Washington Ave, Albany, NY 12222.

JONES, SONDRA MICHELLE
Educator, vice president (organization). **Personal:** Born Sep 7, 1948, Norfolk, VA. **Educ:** Morgan State, BA, 1970; Univ Pa, Sch Edn, grad work; Harvard Univ Grad Sch Educ; Temple Univ, attended 1977. **Career:** Health & Welfare Coun, social work trainee, 1966; STOP Prog Norfolk, VA, rec counr, 1967; Health & Welfare Coun, Baltimore, social work trainee, 1968; St Martin's Day Care Ctr, Baltimore, teacher, 1971-72; Develop Disabilities Day Care Ctr, PA, educ dir comn coord teacher, 1972-73; Buck Lane Mem Community Day Care Ctr, Haverford, PA, dir, 1976-; Ctr Families & C, head start dir, vpres C Youth & Family Serv, currently. **Orgs:** Alliance Black Soc Workers; Ivy Club Alpha Kappa Sor; Nat Asn Educ Young C; Phil Asn Retarded C; Child Welfare League Am; Phil Coord Child Care Coun 4 C; Nat Coun Black Child Develop; Black Child Develop Inst. **Business Addr:** Vice President of Children Youth & Family Services, Head Start Director, Center for Families and Children, 4500 Euclid Ave, Cleveland, OH 44103, **Business Phone:** (216)432-7200.

JONES, SPENCER
Clergy, vice president (organization). **Personal:** Born Mar 24, 1946, Poplar Bluff, MO; son of Frank and Evelina; married Kathy AE Drake; children: Daliz E, Trayon D, Shemen A, Melinet MB. **Educ:** Cent Bible Col, BA, religion, 1972. **Career:** Southside Tabernacle, pastor, currently; elected Bishop, 1999. **Orgs:** Alternate presbytery Assemblies of God; vpres Stud Govt; Nat Inner-City Workers Conf; bd mem, Chicago Teen Challenge; Decade Harvest Comt; speaker at the 1989 Gen Coun; pres, Local Sch Coun, 1988-; community rep, 1990-; block club pres, 1986-; Black Rep Assemblies of God; Beat Rep Chicago Police Dept; Nat Black Fel, vpres; Evangel Col, bd of dir, currently. **Honors/Awds:** The Pentecostal Minister; Alumnus for CBC, 1990; Honor Society Sigma Beta Theta, 1972; Outstanding Citizen, Proclamation from the United States House of Representatives. **Special Achievements:** Article in The Pentecostal Evangel, 1984. **Military Serv:** AUS, sp4, 1966-67. **Business Addr:** Pastor, Southside Tabernacle, 7724 S Racine Ave, Chicago, IL 60620-2926.*

JONES, STANLEY BERNARD
College administrator, administrator. **Personal:** Born Mar 18, 1961, Greenwood, SC; son of Herbert C Jr and Maggie P. **Educ:** Radford Univ, BS, 1984, MS, Educ, 1987. **Career:** Radford Univ, asst dir admis, dir, spec stud serv; Hanover Co, educ adminr, hon chmn, 2002; Lee-Davis High Sch, prin. **Orgs:** VA Admin Coun Black Concerns; treas, EEO; Nat Asn Advan Colored People; Nat Asn Student Personnel Adminr; Assoc Handicapped Student Serv Prog Post-sec Educ; Omega Psi Phi Fraternity. **Honors/Awds:** Outstanding Young Man of America, 1985; Outstanding Service Award, Radford Univ Chapter Nat Asn Advan Colored People, 1988. *

JONES, STAR
Television talk show host, journalist, lawyer. **Personal:** Born Mar 24, 1962; daughter of James Byard and Shirley. **Career:** Kings Co (NY) Dist Att's Off, prosecution staff mem, 1986-91, sr asst dist atty, 1991-92; Ct TV, corresp, 1991; NBC -TV, legal corresp, 1992-93; Jones & Jury, host/co-owner, 1994-; ABC-TV, The View, host, 1997-2006; HGTV, House Hunters, host; Author: "You Have to Stand for Something, or You'll Fall for Anything," 1998. **Orgs:** Alpha Kappa Alpha; bd dir & trustee, E Harlem Sch; G&P Found Cancer Res; God's Love We Deliver; int adv bd, Girls Inc; founder, Starlet Fund. **Special Achievements:** Author of two best-selling books.

JONES, TAMALA
Actor. **Personal:** Born Nov 12, 1974, Pasadena, CA. **Career:** Film appearances: How to Make an American Quilt, 1995; Booty Call, 1997; Can't Hardly Wait, 1998; The Wood, 1999; Blue Streak, 1999; Next Friday, 2000; Turn It Up, 2000; How to Kill Your Neighbor's Dog, 2000; The Ladies Man, 2000; Kingdom Come, 2001; The Brothers, 2001; Two Can Play That Game, 2001; On the Line, 2001; Head of State, 2003; Nora's Hair Salon, 2004; Long Distance, 2005; American Dreams, 2007; Daddy Day Camp, 2007; TV guest appearances: "ER," 1995; "JAG," 1996; TV series: "Dangerous Minds," 1996; "Veronica's Closet," 1997-99; "For Your Love," 1998; "One on One," 2001; "Couples," 2002; "The Tracy Morgan Show," 2003; "Accidental Love," 2005; "Ghost Whisperer," 2006; "CSI: Miami," 2006; "Short Circuitz", 2007; "Studio 60 on the Sunset Strip", 2007. **Special Achievements:** One of "The 10 Sexiest Women of the Year", Black Mag, 2000, 2001. **Business Phone:** (310)656-0400.

JONES, TEBUCKY
Football player. **Personal:** Born Oct 6, 1974, New Britain, CT; children: Tenbucky Jones Jr & 2 children. **Educ:** Syracuse Univ, child & family studies, 1998. **Career:** Player (retired); Coach: New Eng Patriots, defensive back, 1998-2002, 2006-07; New Orleans Saints, 2003-04; Miami Dolphins, safety, 2005; New Britain Golden Hurricanes, def backs coach, currently. **Orgs:** Founder, Tebucky Jones Found. **Honors/Awds:** USA Today Connecticut Player Of the Year, 1993. **Business Addr:** 76 Adams St, New Britain, CT 06052-1222.

JONES, THEODORE CORNELIUS
Educator, dentist. **Personal:** Born Sep 29, 1941, Jackson, MS; married Clintoria Inge; children: Dana, Vann, Margo, Kristen, Karrin. **Educ:** Tougaloo Col, BS, 1962; Howard Univ, DDS, 1966; Walter Reed, cert, 1969; cert, 1970; Tufts Univ, attended 1973. **Career:** Miss pvt pract, 1970-71; Jackson Hindscompr Health Ctr, staff dentist, 1972-73; Univ Miss Sch Dent, asst prof 1974-; Pvt Pract, 1974-; Howard Univ, extramural pract, 1975. **Orgs:** Am Dent Asn; Nat Den Asn; Am Asn Orthodontists; Miss Dent Asn; Miss Dent Soc; Jackson-Tougaloo Alumni Club; pres, Tufts Asn Orthodon; AlphaPhi Alpha; Musica Sacra Singers; New Stage Theatre. **Military Serv:** USAF, capt, 1966-68.

JONES, THERESA C
Automotive executive, business owner, chief executive officer. **Personal:** Widowed; children: Michelle, Jason & Joseph. **Educ:** St Mary?s Col, BA; Wayne State Univ, MS. **Career:** Northwestern Dodge Inc, owner, pres & chief exec officer, currently. **Orgs:** Pres, Daimler Chrysler Minority Dealer Asn, 1994. **Business Addr:** Owner, President, Chief Executive Officer, Northwestern Dodge Inc, 10500 W 8 Mile Rd, Ferndale, MI 48220, **Business Phone:** (248)399-6700.*

JONES, THERESA DIANE
Government official. **Personal:** Born Jun 7, 1953, Erie, PA; daughter of Parker P and Mable R. **Educ:** Edinboro State Col, BA 1976. **Career:** Pinellas Oppor Coun Inc, sr outreach worker 1976-77; Info & Referral, suicide intervention spec 1977; City St Petersburg, relocation Officer, 1977-80, admin serv Officer 1980-86, MBE coord 1986-93; Tampa Gen Healthcare, MBE coord 1993-96; City St. Petersburg, MBE coord 1996-98; bus assistance Mgr, 1998-2002; community affairs dir, 2002-. **Orgs:** Bd dirs Pinellas Oppor Coun Inc 1984-89; bd govs St Petersburg Area Chamber Com 1985; co-chair Community Alliance 1985; real estate assoc LouBrown Realty & Mortgage Inc 1985-88; secy Nat Forum Black Pub Adminrs, Tampa Bay Chap 1986-88; pres, Fla Asn MBD Offs, 1996; pres, West Coast Chap, Nat Minority Supplier Develop Coun FL, 1990, 1994; chair, Midtown Wealth Building Task Force; bd dirs, R Club Child Care, Inc, 2003-. **Honors/Awds:** Grad Presial Classroom for Young Ams 1971; Grad Leadership St Petersburg 1984; Up & Comers Award, Price Waterhouse 1988. Presidential Award, Greater Fla Minority Develop Coun, 1989; Tampa/St. Petersburg Minority Bus Develop Ctr, in appreciation enthusiastic support minority-owned bus, 1991; EEO/MBE Award; Outstanding Public Service, Nat Forum Black Pub Adminrs, Tampa Bay Chap, 2000; Tip Hat Award, St. Petersburg Area Chamber Com, 2003; Community Service Leadership Appreciation Award, St. Petersburg Wealth Buiding Coalition, 2003. **Home Addr:** PO Box 3986, St Petersburg, FL 33731. **Business Addr:** Community Affairs Director, City of St Petersburg, PO Box 2842, St Petersburg, FL 33731, **Business Phone:** (727)893-7357.

JONES, THERESA MITCHELL
Executive. **Personal:** Born May 12, 1917, Denison, TX; married Artis; children: Leroy, Pat, Michael & Anthony. **Educ:** Compton Col Calif, AA, 1951; Univ Pacific, BS, 1973. **Career:** LA County Bur Pub Assistance, clerk-typist, 1951-55; Beauty Salons, propr3, 1956-66; Real Estate, part-time salesman, 1961-74; Elem Sch, teacher, 1971-74; City Stockton Comn Develop Renewal Redevelop Agency, relocation Real estate asst. **Orgs:** Nat Beauty Culturist League, 1959-66; dir, SE Ctr, 1968-70; dir, WICS San-Joaquin Co, 1970; assoc mem, Stockton Real Estate Bd, 1972-75; organizer, dir Progressive Youth Compton; supr Jr Ch. **Honors/Awds:** Woman of the Yr Award, LA Alpha Lambda Chap of Theta Nu Sigma Sor, 1966; Award UOP Comt Involvement Prog, 1973.

JONES, THOMAS L.
Lawyer. **Personal:** Born Jan 12, 1941, Greenwood, MS; married Nettie Byrd; children: Martilla R, Nicole L, LaTanya Dionne, Thomas II. **Educ:** Tougaloo Col, BS, chem, 1963; Howard Univ Law Sch, JD, 1971. **Career:** US Peace Corps, Philippines, 1963-65; Cook Co Circuit Ct, probation officer, 1965-66; Neighborhood Consumer Info Ctr, Wash, Hward Univ, prog dir 1970-71; Fed Hwy Admin, Wash, spl asst chief coun, 1971-73; Continental Tel Co, asst vpres & legal atty, 1973-85. **Orgs:** Am Bar Asn; Nat Bar Asn; DC Bar Asn, 1972; Practicing Law Instr; Phi Alpha Delta; adv couns Fed City Col Psychol Dept; Urban League. **Military Serv:** AUS, sp/5, 1966-68. **Business Addr:** Partner, McFadden, Evans & Sill, 2000 M St NW Suite 260, Washington, DC 20036.

JONES, THOMAS WADE
Chief executive officer, executive. **Personal:** Born 1949, Philadelphia, PA; children (previous marriage): Nigel; married Adelaide Knox, 1975; children: Evonne, Michael & Victoria. **Educ:** Cornell Univ, BA, MA; Boston Univ, MBA. **Career:** Athur Young & Co, prin, 1978-82; John Hancock Mutual Life Ins Co, sr vpres & treas, 1982-89; TIAA Cref, chief financial officer & exec vpres finance & planning, 1989-93, pres & chief operating officer, 1993-97, vice chmn & dir, 1995-97; Travelers Group, vice chmn & dir, 1997-98; Salomon Smith Barney Asset Mgt, chmn & chief exec officer, 1998; Citigroup Global Investment Mgt, chmn & chief exec officer; Citigroup Asset Mgt, chmn & chief exec officer; TWJ Capital LLC, prin, bd dir & sr partner, currently; Fox Entertainment Group Inc, dir, currently. **Orgs:** Bd dirs, Fed Home Loan Mortgage Corp; bd dirs, Philip Morris; trustee, Cornell Univ; bd overseers, Cornell Med Col; bd dirs, Altria Group, Cornell Univ, trustee emer. **Honors/Awds:** Named one of Top 50 Blacks in Corporate America, Black Enterprise; ranked No 5 Most Powerful Black Executive, Fortune, 2002; Hon Doctorate, Howard Univ; Hon Doctorate, Pepperdine Univ; Hon Doctorate, Col New Rochelle. **Business Addr:** Board of Director, Senior Partner, TWJ Capital LLC, Six Landmark Sq Suite 404, Stamford, CT 06901, **Business Phone:** (203)359-5610.*

JONES, DR. TONI STOKES
Educator. **Personal:** Born Jul 25, 1954, Detroit, MI; daughter of LeRoy and Hermalene; married Louis E, Jul 20, 1996; children: Emmanuel Stokes. **Educ:** Wayne State Univ, BS, 1978, MEd, 1988, PhD, 1998. **Career:** Rancho High Sch, Las Vegas, NV, teacher, Detroit Pub Sch, teacher; Burbank Middle Sch, teacher, Osborne High Sch, teacher; Cass Tech High Sch, teacher; Volkswagen Am Inc, sr training develop specialist, 1986-88, 1989-94; The Emdicium Group, Inc, instrnl designer, 1994-99; Detroit Col Bus, lectr, 1995; Univ Phoenix, lectr, 1997-99; Univ Mich, Dearborn, lectr, 1998-99; Eastern Mich Univ, asst prof, 1999, assoc prof, dept teacher educ, educ media & technology prog, currently. **Orgs:** Asn Educ Community & Technol, 1994-2001; Mich Asn Comput 1999-; Int Soc Tech Educ, 1999-; secy, E Mich Univ Col Educ Coun, 2000-; Int Soc Technol Educ, 2000-; past bd dir, MACUL, 2000-; Nat Coun Accreditation Teacher Educ, 2004-. **Honors/Awds:** Int Award of Excellence for Tech Publication, Society for Tech Commun, 1987-88; Natl Award of Excellence for Tech Publications, 1987-88; Will Jackson Award, The Emdicium Group Inc, 1998; Faculty Fel Award, East Mich Univ Acad Serv Learning, 1999. **Special Achievements:** Numerous presentations and publications. **Business Addr:** Associate Professor, Eastern Michigan University, College of Education, 315 John W Porter Bldg, Ypsilanti, MI 48197, **Business Phone:** (734)487-3260.

JONES, TONY EDWARD
Football player. **Personal:** Born May 24, 1966, Royston, GA; married Kamilla Orr, Feb 14, 1992; children: 3. **Educ:** Western Carolina Univ, BS, mgt, 1989. **Career:** Football player (retired); Cleveland Browns, tackle, 1988-95; Baltimore Ravens, 1996; Denver Broncos, 1997-2000. **Orgs:** Charter mem, Ty Cobb Museum. **Honors/Awds:** Pro Bowl, 1998.

JONES, VELMA LOIS
Educator. **Educ:** Lemoyne-Owen Col, BA; Columbia Univ, MA; Memphis State Univ, Mich State Univ, grad study. **Career:** Hyde Park Elem Sch Memphis, instr; LeMoyne Owen Col, Mich Col & Memphis Univ, master teacher stud teachers; Cypress Jr HS Memphis, instr math. **Orgs:** Memphis Educ Asn; exec bd, Memphis Educ Asn; parliamentarian co-founder mem chairperson Memphis chap Nat Educ Asn Black Caucus; del, TN Educ Asn Rep Assembly, 1970-79; del Nat Educ Asn Rep Assembly 1971-79; pres, W TN Educ Asn; bd dirs, TN Educ Asn; Nat Coun Teachers Math; TN Coun Teachers Math; Memphis area Teachers Math; NEA concerns Com; TN Educ Asn; vpres, Memphis Dist Laymen's Coun CME Ch; secy, Soc Rel Missionary Soc W TN Ann Conf CME Ch; asst secy, W TN Ann Conf & chairperson com soc concerns; parliamentarian TN Conf NAACP Br; Women's Missionary Coun CME Ch; Compilation com revise Chap Discipline; staff Leadership Fel Prog & Pre-Boule Workshop Alpha Kappa Alpha Sor; S Eastern Reg Dir; Memphis Chap Am Inst parliamentarians; N Memphis Area Adv Coun; Nat Coun Negro Women; TN State Educ Asn; vice chair person Shelby Co Housing Auth; Am Inst Parliamentarians; dir, Christian Educ Trinity Christian Meth Epis Ch. **Honors/Awds:** First woman pres Memphis Br, Nat Asn Advan Colored People; Comn Serv Award, 1958, 1978; Excellent Leadership & Outstanding Serv Awards, Alpha Kappa Alpha, 1966-70; Women of the Yr, 1970; Cert Merit Award, Nat Asn Advan Colored People, 1972; Women of the Yr, 1974; Missionary of the Yr, 1975; Twenty Most Prominent Memphians, 1975; Women Making Hist, 1976; Brotherhood Award, 1977; Outstanding Woman S Eastern Reg; Outstanding Woman of the Yr Award, Nat Asn Advan Colored People, Women's Nat Conf, 1980; Numerous other civic awards. **Business Addr:** Mathematics Instructor, Cypress Junior High School, 2109 Howell Ave, Memphis, TN 38108.

JONES, HON. VERA MASSEY
Judge. **Personal:** Born Jan 1, 1943. **Educ:** Fisk Univ, BA, hist, 1965; Univ Detroit Law Sch, 1969. **Career:** Univ Detroit Urban Law Prog, clin div, 1967, res div, 1968-69; Pvt Pract, atty, 1969-70; Legal Aid & Defender Asn Detroit, dep defender, 1970-73; Detroit Recorders Ct, Traffic & Ordinance Div, referee, 1973-79, judge, chief judge; State Mich, Circuit Ct, Judge, currently. **Orgs:** Founding mem, Nat Asn Women Judges, secy, 1982-83; Mich Black Judges Asn; Nat Asn Advan Colored People, Womens Comn; Delta Sigma Theta; State Bar Mich, Judicial Conf. **Honors/Awds:** Rated Outstanding, Detroit Bar Asn, 1990. **Special Achievements:** Rated preferred & well-qualified, Civic Searchlight, 1990. **Business Addr:** Judge, State of Michigan, 3rd Circuit Court, 2 Woodward Ave, Detroit, MI 48226, **Business Phone:** (313)224-5261.

JONES, VERNON A., JR.
Clergy. **Personal:** Born Sep 19, 1924, Brunswick Co, VA; son of Vernon A and Harriet Rhodes Simmons; married Lillian Clark; children: Cecilia, Harriett, Vernelle. **Educ:** Va Union Univ, AB, 1945; Bishop Payne Div Sch, BD, 1948; Va Theol Sem, MDiv. **Career:** Clergy (retired); St Stephen's Church, Petersburg, VA, rector, 1953-57; St Andrew's Episcopal Church, Tuskegee Inst, rector, 1960-90; vicar, 1957-60. **Orgs:** Secy, Coun Episcopal Diocese, AL, 1975-78; Soc Increase Ministry. *

JONES, VICTORIA C.
Television producer, television journalist. **Personal:** Born Dec 30, 1947, Denver, CO; daughter of Marvin K Dillard and Pearl E Reagor; children: Lisa A Camille Jones. **Educ:** Western Univ, BA, BS, 1972; Harvard Univ, EDM, 1979. **Career:** WB2-TV, "People Are Talking", co-creator, 1979-80, "Coming Together", creator, 1980-81, producer, 1980; WHDH-TV, producer, 1982-95, exec producer & sr producer; Strand Theatre, exec dir, 2002-; Special Projects: "Journey of Courage," 1988; "Mandela's visit to Boston," 1990; "Save Our Children.Save Our Neighborhood," 1992; "Million Man March," 1995; "Voices of Violence," 1996. **Orgs:** Bd visitors, Bunker Hill Community Col; bd mem, Nat Mus Am Indian; bd mem, Nat Asn Black Journalists; co-founder, Coalition 100 Black Women, Boston Chap; pres, Boston Asn Black Journalists. **Honors/Awds:** Emmy, New Eng Emmys, 1977-96; Nat NAACP Special Image Award, 1983; Iris Award, 1984, 1989, 1990; Outstanding Award for Excellence, Ohio State, 1986; Tribute to Excellence, YWCA, 1990. **Business Addr:** Executive Director, Strand Theatre, 543 Columbia Rd, Dorchester, MA 02125, **Business Phone:** (617)282-8000.*

JONES, VICTORIA GENE
Public relations executive. **Personal:** Born Jan 30, 1948, Oakland, CA; daughter of Eugene Leocadio Balugo and Lottie Emelda Charbonnet; divorced; children: Brandon Wells. **Educ:** Pepperdine Univ, Malibu, CA, BS, bus mgt, 1983; Golden Gate Univ, MBA, 1999. **Career:** Southern Calif Gas Co, pub affairs ref ctr supvr, 1973-74, community rels rep, 1974-79, prof employ adminr, 1979-80, pub affairs rep, 1980-82, acct exec, 1982-84, community involvement energy progs adminr, 1984-85, market servs mgr, 1985-88; Pac Enterprises Corp, state govt affairs mgr & lobbyist, 1988-95; The Clorox Co, mgr gov't rels, 1995, dir, Clorox Co Found, currently. **Orgs:** Pres, Capitol Network, 1992; Inst Govt Advocates, 1988-95; Women Advocacy, 1988-95; Calif Elected Women's Asn Educ & Res, 1988-95; Am Asn Blacks Energy, 1988-95; Sacramento Urban League, 1989-95; Los Angeles Urban League, 1980-88. **Honors/Awds:** Black Woman of Achievement, Nat Asn Advan Colored People Legal Defense & Educ Fund, 1990; Mayor's Cert Appreciation Community Involvement, City Los Angeles, 1990; Cert Recognition, Calif State Assembly, 1990. **Business Addr:** Manager of Government Relations, Community Relations, The Clorox Co, 1221 Broadway, Oakland, CA 94619, **Business Phone:** (510)271-2971.

JONES, DR. VIDA YVONNE
School administrator. **Personal:** Born Aug 30, 1946, Collinston, LA; daughter of Willie L and Helen Taylor; married Abdul LaBrie

(divorced 1974); children: Ghania. **Educ:** San Francisco State Univ, San Francisco, CA, BA, 1969; Univ Calif, Berkeley, CA, MA, city planning, 1972; Univ Calif, San Francisco, CA, PhD, 1986. **Career:** Univ Calif, San Francisco, CA, from asst planner to assoc planner, 1972-75, sr planner, 1975-77, prin analyst, 1977-87, Inst Health & Aging, asst dir, training & admin, 1987, Acad Geriat Resource Prog, adminr, currently. **Orgs:** Chair, bd dirs, Bay Area Lupus Found, 1987-88; chair, Minority Outreach Comn, 1985-87; Nat Forum Black Pub Adminr; Am Sociologist Asn; Am Planners Asn. **Home Addr:** 32726 Bass Lake St, Fremont, CA 94536. **Business Addr:** Administrator of Academic Geriatric Resource Program, University of California, Office of the Vice President for Health Affairs, 1111 Franklin St 11th Fl, Oakland, CA 94607-5200, **Business Phone:** (510)987-9706.

JONES, VIOLA
Government official, mayor. **Personal:** Born Apr 27, 1933, Goodnight, OK; daughter of John W and Jeanette Hardimon; married Charles H Jones II, Feb 2, 1952; children: Charlesetta, Carolyn, Cynethia & Charles III. **Educ:** Langston Univ, Langston, OK, BS, 1973. **Career:** Langston Univ, Langston, OK, youth specialist community dev, 1972-82; City Langston, mayor. **Orgs:** Langston Beautiful Federated Club, 1972-; chairperson, Okla Baptist State Missionary Pres's Inc, 1981-; missionary pres, St Mark Dist, 1987-; Bus Prof Women, 1988-. **Honors/Awds:** Dedicated Servs, Langston Univ, 1982; Water Systs Achievement Mgt, Okla Rural Water Asn, 1988; Completing Hours for Municip Officers, Okla Municip League, 1988; Most Outstanding Woman, Gov's Off, 1990; Most Outstanding Citizen, Okla Baptist State Conv, 1990. **Home Addr:** 316 S Melvin B Tolson, Coyle, OK 73027, **Home Phone:** (405)466-2596.

JONES, VIVIAN R
Executive, president (organization), chief executive officer. **Personal:** Born Sep 4, 1948, Chicago, IL; daughter of German and Annie; divorced; children: Victoria LeVance. **Educ:** Kennedy-King Col, AA, 1980; Chicago State Univ, BA, 1986, MSEd, 1988. **Career:** Ada S McKinley, caseworker, 1986-88; Dept C & Family Serv, child protective investr, 1989-91; PSI, adminr, 1990-92; Lifelink, foster care supvr, 1992-94; ABJ Community Servs Inc, founder, pres & chief exec officer, 1992-. **Orgs:** Nat Asn Black Social Workers, Chicago Chap, 1992-; Child Welfare League Am, 1995-; Child Care Asn Ill, 1995-; Nat Asn Advan Colored People, Chicago Chap, 1998-; Nat Polit Cong Black Women, 1998-; Nat League Negro Women, 1998-; Rainbow Coalition, Oper Push, 1999-. **Honors/Awds:** Kizzy Awards, Kizzy Found, 1996-97. **Special Achievements:** The Wiz, exec producer, 1999; The Great Nitty Gritty, exec prod, 1999. **Business Addr:** Chief Executive Officer, President, ABJ Community Services Inc, 1507 E 53rd St, Chicago, IL 60649, **Business Phone:** (773)667-2100.

JONES, WALTER
Lawyer. **Personal:** Born Oct 7, 1946, Chicago, IL; son of Walter and Ruby; divorced. **Educ:** Univ Ill-Champaign, BA, 1969, Col Law, JD, 1972. **Career:** Household Finance Corp, in-house corp coun, 1972-73; Northern Dist Ill, asst US atty, 1973-77; US Attys Off, Criminal Div, dep chief, 1977-80, chief, 1980-83, spec litigation coun, 1983-86; Curiel & Jones, partner, 1986-91; Pugh, Jones, Johnson & Quandt, PC, vpres & partner, 1991-. **Orgs:** Chair, Am Bar Asn, Prosecution Function Comn, 1981-84; Ill State Bar Asn; Cook County Bar Asn; chair, Seventh Circuit Litigation Rev Comn; Ill chair, Seventh Circuit Bar Asn, Comn Criminal Law & Procedure; Chicago Bar Asn; fel Am Bd Criminal Lawyers; fel & former chair, Am Coll Trial Lawyers; fel Int Acad Trial Lawyers. **Special Achievements:** Am Bar Asn, Criminal Justice Mag, ed, 1986-96. **Business Addr:** Vice President, Partner, Pugh, Jones, Johnson & Quandt, P.C.?s Litigation Practice Group, 180 N LaSalle St Suite 3400, Chicago, IL 60601-2807, **Business Phone:** (312)768-7800.

JONES, WALTER
Football player. **Personal:** Born Jan 19, 1974, Aliceville, AL; married Valeria; children: Rafael, Waleria & Walterius. **Educ:** Fla State Univ, BS, criminol. **Career:** Seattle Seahawks, tackle, 1997-. **Honors/Awds:** Mississippi Jr Col Player of the Year, Jackson Clarion-Ledger, 1994; Rookie of the Month, 1997. **Special Achievements:** First round pick No 6, NFL Draft, 1997; first off Lineman in Seahawks history to go to Pro Bowl; Bldg Blocks for Kids prog to Evergreen Hosp, Kirkland for a new pediat playroom. **Business Addr:** Tackle, Seattle Seahawks, 11220 NE 53rd St, Kirkland, WA 98033, **Business Phone:** (425)827-9777.

JONES, WILBERT
Chief executive officer, food consultant. **Personal:** Born Mar 14, 1964, Clarksdale, MS. **Educ:** Loyola Univ, Chicago, BS, chem, 1986. **Career:** Kraft Foods, product dev mgr, 1985-93; Healthy Concepts, pres, 1993-. **Orgs:** Les Amis d'Escoffier Soc Chicago, 2002-; adv bd mem, Common Threads Found, 2001-. **Honors/Awds:** Technol Res Award, Kraft Foods, 1989, 1990; Purple Reflection Award, Nat Coun Negro Women, 1997; Urban Leadership Center Award, Univ Ill, 2004; Chicago Official Unity Day Award, US Dept Enegry Chicago Officia,l 2005; Chicago Chefs of Cuisine Asn Award, Am Culinary Fed, 2008. **Special Achievements:** Contributor:The Heart or the Matter: The African American's Guide to Heart Disease, Heart Treatment and Heart Wellness by Hilton Hudson M.D. and Herbert Stern PH.D; Back To The Table by Art Smith (Oprah Winfrey's Presonal Chef); Contributing Ed, Prepared Foods Magazine, 1998-; Freelance Special Features Writer Black Entertainment Television's website (www.BET.com) 2001-. **Business Addr:** President, Healthy Concepts Inc, 1400 N Lake Shore Dr Suite 4F, Chicago, IL 60610, **Business Phone:** (312)335-0031.

JONES, WILLIAM ALLEN
Lawyer. **Personal:** Born Dec 13, 1941, Philadelphia, PA; son of Roland E and Gloria T; married Dorothea S Whitson; children: Zoey, Rebecca, Gloria & David; married Margaret Smith, Sep 24, 1965 (divorced 1972). **Educ:** Temple Univ, BA, magna cum laude, 1967; Harvard Bus Sch, MBA, 1972; Harvard Law Sch, JD, 1972. **Career:** Walt Disney Prod, atty, 1973-77, asst treas, 1977-79, treas, 1979-81; Wyman Bautzer Rothman Kuchel Silbert, atty, 1981-83; MGM UA Entertainment Co, vpres, gen coun corp & sec; United Artists Corp, sr vpres, corp gen coun, 1986-91; Metro Goldwyn-Mayer Inc, exec vpres, gen coun & secy, 1991-94, exec vpres, Corp Affairs, 1995-97, sr exec vpres & secy, 1997-. **Orgs:** History Honor Soc, 1967; German Honor Soc, 1967; Polit Sci Hon Soc, 1967; bus mgr, Los Angeles Bar Jour, 1974-76; Am Bar Asn, 1974-; State Bar, CA, 1974-; Los Angeles City Bar Asn, 1974-; bd dir, Harvard Bus Sch Asn, S CA, 1985-88; bd trustees, Marlborough Sch; bd gov, Inst Corp Coun, 1991-94; bd dirs, The Nostalgia Network Inc, 1990-94; Pathe Commun Corp, bd dirs, 1991-92; bd dirs, Metro-Goldwyn-Mayer Inc., 1991-92; bd trustees, Flintridge Preparatory Sch, 1993-96; Motion Picture Asn Am, 1995-; bd dirs, Santa Monica Chamber Com, 1996-98; bd dirs, Calif Chamber Com, 2001-04; vice chmn, bd visitors, Temple Univ, 2003-; bd dirs, Motion Picture & TV Fund Corp, 2003-. **Honors/Awds:** President Scholar, Temple Univ, 1967; Diamond Achievement Award, 2001. **Military Serv:** USAF, airman, first class, 4 yrs. **Home Phone:** (818)240-1337. **Business Addr:** Senior Executive Vice President, Secretary, Metro-Goldwyn-Mayer Inc., 2500 Broadway St, Santa Monica, CA 90404.

JONES, WILLIAM BARNARD
Executive. **Personal:** Born Nov 20, 1957, St Louis, MO; son of Alice Narvelle Dunn; married Phyllis, Sep 7, 1985; children: Tanya Nichole, William Barnard II, Ryan Laroy Willard & Ciara Alice Hope. **Educ:** Wash Univ, St Louis, BA, 1980. **Career:** Anheuser-Busch, sr consult, develop, 1989-90, Nat budget adr, 1990-92, exe asst to vpres, 1992-93, nat mgr, field sales, 1993-95, sales dir of Mich, 1994-95, vpres region sales, 1995-99; Bus Development Group, vpres, corp off, 1999-. **Orgs:** Inroads Inc, 1980-. **Honors/Awds:** Corporate Trailblazer Award, Dollar & Sense Magazine, 1997; Dollars & Sense, Sentinal Newspaper Special Achiever, 2001. **Business Addr:** Vice President, Anheuser-Busch Inc, Business Development Group, 1 Busch Pl, Saint Louis, MO 63118-1852, **Business Phone:** (314)552-1100.

JONES, DR. WILLIAM BOWDOIN
Lawyer, ambassador, consultant. **Personal:** Born May 2, 1928, Los Angeles, CA; son of William T and LaVelle Bowdoin; married Joanne F Garland, Jun 27, 1953; children: Lisa Jamison, Stephanie A Marioneaux & Walter C. **Educ:** Univ Calif, Los Angeles, AB, 1949; Univ Southern Calif, JD, 1952. **Career:** Educator, ambassador, lawyer (retired); Pvt Prac, atty-at-law, 1952-62; US Foreign Serv Officer, dipl, 1962-84; US Dept State Washington, dep asst secy state, 1969-73; US Dept State, Paris France, chief, US mission to UNESCO, 1973-77; US Dept State chmn US-Japan cult conf, Hawaii, 1973; US Dept State, ambassador to Haiti, 1977-80; Hampton Univ, diplomat-in-residence, 1980-81; Univ Va, ambassador in residence, 1984-85; Woodrow Wilson Found, Princeton, NJ, fel 1986-87; US House Rep SubComt Western Affairs, staff dir, 1987; Int Bus Law Firm, partner, 1988-91; Hampden Sydney Col, Sydney, VA, bd trustees, 1992-, adj prof, 1991; Pepperdine Univ, distinguished vis prof, 1993; Hampdon & Sydney Col, Johns prof polit sci, Malcolm R Myers Distinguished chair, 1999-2000, ambassador in residence & William A Johns prof polit sci, 2001-07. **Orgs:** Sigma Pi Phi-Boule; Kappa Alpha Psi; Washington Intl Club; CA Bar; Dist Columbia, US Sup Ct; Bar the US Ct Intl Trade, 1988; bd dirs, Am Asn UN-,Nat Capital Region, 1996-; US Coun, UN Univ, 1997-; James Madison Soc, Hampden-Sydney Col, 1996-; bd dir, Ctr Leadership in Pub Affairs, Hampdon-Sydney Col, 1998-; bd dir, Nat Capitol Asn UN; US Coun UN Univ,Tokyo; bd trustees, Hampdon-Sydney Col, 2000-. **Honors/Awds:** Outstanding Public Service, CA, Legislature, 1972; Merit Award, Alumni Univ So CA, 1981. **Special Achievements:** First African American to be named chief of the US Mission to UNESCO, Paris. **Home Addr:** 4807 17th St NW, Washington, DC 20011, **Home Phone:** (202)722-1808.

JONES, WILLIAM C.
Obstetrician, gynecologist. **Personal:** Born Oct 22, 1933, Richmond, VA; married Evora Williams; children: Lisa, Mark, Lori, Michael, David, Lydia. **Educ:** Va State Col, BS 1953; Howard Univ, 1959; Meharry Med Col, MD 1963; Duke Univ Med Ctr, 1968. **Career:** Hubbard Hosp, Meharry Med Col, residency & internship, 1963-67; Duke Univ & affil hosp, Durham, NC, fel, Endocrinology, 1967-68; Physician Obstet/Gynec, pvt pract, Richmond, VA, 1968-. **Orgs:** Am Col Obstet/Gynec; Richmond Acad Med; Richmond Med Soc; Old Dominion Med Soc; Am Bd Obstet & Gyn; Kappa Alpha Psi Frat. **Military Serv:** AUS, 1st Lt, 1954-56. **Business Addr:** Physician Obstetrics & Gynecology, William C Jones, 2809 N Ave Suite 200, Richmond, VA 23222.

JONES, WILLIAM EDWARD
Educator. **Personal:** Born Jul 4, 1930, Indianapolis, IN; married Janet; children: Leslye. **Educ:** Butler Univ, BS, 1956; Ind Univ, MS, 1960. **Career:** Crispus Attucks High Sch, teacher, 1957-61; Ind State Univ, counr, instr, vice prin, dean, 1964-68; Broad Ripple High Sch, prin, 1970. **Orgs:** Consult, HEW; Urban Sch Affairs, Ohio State Univ; Midwest Equal Opportunity Ctr; Desegregation Nat Asn; Sec Sch Prin; Phi Delta Kappa; Ind Sec Sch Adminr; adv coun, Danforth Found; elder, Witherspoon United Presb Church; Greater Indianapolis Progress Com; Kappa Alp Psi; Nat Asn Advan Colored People; Urban League; Danforth Sch Adminr, 1975-76; Broad Ripple Merchants Asn. **Special Achievements:** First African-American principal of Broad Ripple High School. **Military Serv:** USAF, 1952-55. **Business Addr:** Principal, Broad Ripple High School, 1115 E Broad Ripple Ave, Indianapolis, IN 46220.

JONES, WILLIAM JAMES
Business owner, educator. **Personal:** Born Aug 6, 1969, Brooklyn, NY; son of William and Arlene. **Educ:** Kansas City Art Inst, Kansas City, MO, BFA, 1992; Pratt Inst, MPS, fine arts, 1998. **Career:** New York, Dept Personnel, art dir & opers specialist, 1993-94, graphic arts, 1995-96; Times Custom Publ, Essence, Black Enterprise, graphic designer & freelance, 1993-96; IV Design, art dir, 1996-2000; New York Bd Educ, Rikers Island Educ, 1997-99; Bd Educ City New York, 1998-2000; Univ Col Educ Winneba, lectr, 2000-01; Latina Connections/Urban Frontier Indust, Wash, design mgr, 2001-; Col New Rochelle, Sch New Resources, instr, 2002-. **Orgs:** Nat Asn Graphic Artists; Soc Pubation Designers; Am Inst Graphic Artists; Design Mgt Inst; Graphic Artists Guild. **Special Achievements:** Publications: Black Enteprise; Vibe; Essence; The Source. **Home Addr:** 1720 Bedford Ave Suite 11A, Brooklyn, NY 11225, **Home Phone:** (718)771-3007.

JONES, DR. WILLIAM JENIPHER. See Obituaries section.

JONES, DR. WILLIAM O.
Clergy. **Personal:** Born in Covington, TN; married Helen Crombie; children: 4. **Educ:** Moody Bible Inst; Ky State, BS; Gammon Theol Sem, B.D; Murrys Theol Sem, D.D. **Career:** Chattanooga Bible Ctr, dean & dir; Home Mission Bd Soc Baptist Conv,1975-; pastorates TN, KY. **Orgs:** Chaplain, CCC Camp, 1935-37; asst secy, Nat BYPU Bd, 1947-54; ed, Intermed Nat BYPU Quartly; precinct chmn, 12 5 Dist . **Military Serv:** AUS, 1941-45.

JONES, WILLIE
State government official, executive director. **Personal:** Born Oct 16, 1932, Seaboard, NC; married Jacqueline J Gibbs; children: Sharon von Hulsebus & Kurtis. **Educ:** Long Island Univ, BA, 1964; Pace Univ, MBA, 1974. **Career:** NJ Hwy Authority, dir human resources, 1988-. **Orgs:** Soc Human Resources Mgt; Nat C of C; Nat Asn Mfrs; Nat Bus League; Corp Urban Affairs Adv Comt; Pub Affairs Coun; Nat Minority Purchasing Coun; Econ Develop Coun; comt mem, NE region; Nat Urban Affairs Coun; Nat Urban League; Golden Heritage Nat Asn Advan Colored People; Nat Urban Coalition; EDGES Group, Food Markets Inst; adv bd, Felician Col; Artist Family Theater Proj; Nat Asn Mkt Develop; Mil Acad Selection Comt; Toastmaster Int; USAF Speakers Bur; Gen Hap Arnold Air Soc; Ancient Free & Accepted Masons; NY Educ Adv Eastern Dist; Nat Hon Soc, Pi Gamma Mu. **Honors/Awds:** Red Hot Scouting Award; Merit Award, Black Media; Spec Humanitarian Award, Supermarkets Gen Corp; Outstanding Achievements Award, Perth Amboy Br, Nat Asn Advan Colored People; First Affirmative Action Award, Cong Racial Equality; Roy Wilkins Meritorious Serv Award, NJ Nat Asn Advan Colored People Urban Progs; Civil Rights Award, Hoboken Branch, Nat Asn Advan Colored People. **Military Serv:** USAF, 20 yrs. *

JONES, YVONNE DE MARR
School administrator, civil rights activist. **Personal:** Born in Dayton, OH; divorced; children: Diane R-Singh, Bercenia & Shelley Smith. **Educ:** Hunter Col, BA, 1947, MA, 1955. **Career:** School administrator (retired), civil rights activist; Elmsford Pub Schs, 1955-84; Westchester Conn Col. **Orgs:** Bd, Greenburgh Neighborhood Ctr; chair Westchester, Martin Luther King Jr Inst; pres, St Francis Episcopal Church, ECW; pres, Westchester Asn Study Am Life & History; past branch pres, White Plains Greensburgh, Nat Asn Advan Colored People. **Honors/Awds:** Comm Merit Award, Operation PUSH Westchester 1976; Achievement Award, Westchester Co Club BPW, 1978; Key Women of Westchester Award 1987; Conn Service Award, NCW, Westchester Section, 1989; Appreciation Award, Woodburn Correctional, 1989; Appreciation Award, Sing-Sing Prison, 1990; Connecticut Enhancement Award, Nat Asn Black Social Workers, 1991; Community Colleg Awards, Mercy Col Westchester, 1995. **Home Addr:** 118 N Evarts Ave, Elmsford, NY 10523, **Home Phone:** (914)592-6425.

JONES, DR. YVONNE VIVIAN
Educator. **Personal:** Born Jul 29, 1946, New York, NY; daughter of Ernest and Irene Washington; married Sylvester Singleton;

children: Michael Kenneth. **Educ:** Am Univ, BA, 1971, PhD, 1976. **Career:** Eugene & Agnes E Meyer Found, assoc dir, 1971-74; Univ Louisville, asst prof, 1975-81, assoc prof, anthrop, 1981-, Dept Pan Africian Studies, chair, prof, currently. **Orgs:** Pres bd, Planned Parenthood, Louisville Inc, 1977-81; chair, Minority Group Ment Health Prog Review Comn, Nat Inst Ment Health, 1979-82. **Honors/Awds:** Outstanding Scholar Graduate Level, Am Univ, 1976; Outstanding Young Woman of America, 1978. **Business Addr:** Professor, Department of Pan African Studies, 430 Strickler Hall 4th Fl E Wing, Louisville, KY 40292, **Business Phone:** (502)852-2428.

JONES, ZOIA L.
Educator, president (organization). **Personal:** Born Oct 2, 1926, Iota, LA; daughter of Elena Laws (deceased) and Joseph (deceased); married Everette, Sep 27, 1947; children: Zoia Sylvia Jones-Blake. **Educ:** TX Southern Univ, BS, home econ (cum laude), 1960, MEd, guid, 1976; certelem educ, 1963; Prairie View A&M Univ, cert special educ, 1981. **Career:** Educator (retired), president; Evangeline Parish, Rougeau, LA, teacher, 1944-47; Tex Southern Univ, 1960-61; HISD, Houston, TX, teacher, 1961-90; Houston-Harris County Project, volunteer coord, 1967; Magnet Sch, ade task team, 1975; Globe Advocate, past columnist; Houston Informer, past columnist; KCOH Radio Sta, past moderator; Nat Coun Negro Women Inc, Dorothy I Height Sect, pres, nat exec comm-at-large mem, currently; New Pleasant Grove BC, minister, 2003-. **Orgs:** VISTA; Houston COC; Women COT Serv, 1968-70; NAACP; Black Art Ctr; Black Art Museum; RGM Rose Mary Grand Chapter OES TX; UNF; golden life mem, DST, Houston Metropolitan Alumnae Chap, charter officer; May Week Comm; charter bd mem, Adopt Black Children Comm; Eta Phi Beta Sor Inc; life mem, Asn study Negro Life & Hist; past activities, Houston Teachers Asn; TX Classroom Teachers Asn; TX State Teachers Asn; NEA; All Nations Rescue Mission; charter officer, McGregor Park Women, pres; past columist, Forward Times; TX Southern Univ, Nat Alumni Asn; comnr, Civil Ct 3 Harris County; New Pleasant Grove Baptist Church, Sr Mission II; pres, Sunday Sch, teacher,youth supvr, Young Women's Auxiliary; exec nat Comm & local pres, Nat Coun Negro Women, 2000-; chair, Delta Dear Task Force, Delta Sigma Theta Sorority Inc. **Honors/Awds:** Distinguished Service Award, Houston Classroom Teachers Asn; Letter of Commendation, President George Bush, 1990; Letter of Commendation, Sen Lloyd Bentsen, 1990; Letter of Commendation, Sen Phil Graham, 1990; Resolutions of Commendation, TEX Senate & House Rep,1990; Distinguished Service Award, Humanitarian Civil Rights, 1994, Houston-Harris County Retired Teachers Asn; Human Relations Award, Tex State Teachers Asn, Houston Ed Asn, 1994; Distinguished Award, YWA, 1997; Women of Wonder, Nat Gala, Wash, DC; Mary McLeod Bethune Award, Comm Leaders Pacesetter, 2003. **Special Achievements:** Attended the White House Briefing for Afr Amer Leaders; attended 45thCelebration of Civil Rights Movement, Eta Phi Beta Soroity Inc, Xi Chapter, Founders Day Speaker, 1994, Mt Lebanon Baptist Church, Women's Day Speaker, 1994, first "Hall of Fame" inductee, National Council of Negro Women, Dorothy I Height Sect, 1994-95. **Home Addr:** 3417 Charleston, Houston, TX 77021. **Business Addr:** President, National Council of Negro Women Inc, Dorothy I Height Section, 3417 Charleston St, Houston, TX 77021, **Business Phone:** (713)747-3727.

JONES-GRIMES, DR. MABLE CHRISTINE
Educator, home economist. **Personal:** Born Dec 6, 1943, Malden, MO; daughter of Albert Jones and Anna Mae Turner Jones; married James Robert Grimes, Dec 21, 1969; children: Ori Brandon Jones Grimes. **Educ:** Univ Mo-Columbia, BS, 1965, MS, 1968, PhD, 1976. **Career:** Educator (retired); Univ Mo, Coop exten Serv, home economist, 1965-68, 4-H Program, youth specialist & asst prof, Human Develop & Family Studies, AA/EEO Off & dir diversity, Univ Outreach & Ext; Delta Head start Prog, home economist, 1968-69. **Orgs:** Am Home Econ Asn, 1965-; Nat Coun Family Rels, 1980-; fac adv, Delta Tau Chap, Alpha Kappa Alpha Sorority, 1983-; bd mem, Planned Parenthood Inc, 1985-; pres, Kappa Chi Omega Chap, Alpha Kappa Alpha Sorority Inc,1986-87; Chamber Com, Women's Network, 1986; pres, bd dirs, Planned Parenthood Cent Mo, 1988-90. **Honors/Awds:** Meritorious Service Award, State 4-H Off, 1983; Inst Mgt Life Long Learning, Harvard Univ, 1984; fel, Nat Inst Adult & Continuing Educ, Univ Ga, 1989-90. **Special Achievements:** University of Missouri South African Faculty Exchange Program with University of Western Cape, 1989; Presentation & Article, "Race and Leadership Styles of Women" 1988; Consultant, trainer in cultural diversity & inter cultural communications, 1990-93.

JONES-HENDERSON, NAPOLEON
Educator, artist. **Personal:** Born Nov 23, 1943, Chicago, IL; son of Maxine Unger and Woodrow; children: Mamemaeli Di & Lylana Von. **Educ:** Thw Sorbonne Stud Continum, Paris, France, 1963; The Sch Art Inst Chicago, BFA, 1971; Northern Ill Univ, MFA, DeKalb, IL, 1974. **Career:** Museum Nat Ctr Afro-Am Artists, Roxbury, MA, dir educ, 1975-76; Res Inst African & African Diaspora Arts Inc, Roxbury, MA, exec dir, 1979-; Vermont Col Norwich Univ, Montpelier, VT, adj prof, 1989-; Benedict Col, Columbia, SC, 1999-2000; artist, currently; The Harriet Wilson Project, art dir, currently. **Orgs:** Bd mem, Mass Health Comn, 1983-87; African Am Assoc Museums World Craft Coun; Am Craft Coun; Soc Am Goldsmiths; Enamelist Soc; Col Art Assoc; AFRICOBRA; bd dir, Artists Found, 1986-92; bd dir, Unitarian Unversalist, 1986-; bd dir, Celebration Black Cinema, 1987-92; pres, Nat Conference Artists Inc, 1997-99. **Honors/Awds:** Traveling fellowship, Art Inst Chicago, 1971; "FESTAC" US zone rep, Lagos, Nigeria, 1977; Museum Afro-American History, African Meeting House, 350 Years Black presence Commonwealth Mass, 1988; NEFA, New Forms Award, Artist's Projects, 1994; Mayor Boston's, Award Recognition for Outdoor Sculpture Exhibit, 1999; Award for Cultural Contributions, Tri-Ad Veterans League Inc, 1999; Official Citation for Cultural Excellence, Mass State Senate, 1999.

JONES-SMITH, JACQUELINE
Executive. **Personal:** Born Nov 5, 1952, Bronx, NY; married Joshua; children: Joshua Smith Jr. **Educ:** Swarthmore Col, BA, 1974; Syracuse Univ, MLS, 1978; Am Univ Sch Law, JD, 1984. **Career:** MAXIMA Corp, syst librn, 1979-85, dir clearing house oper, 1980-81, sr libr syst consult, 1981-84, div mgr, 1984-85, exec vpres & bd mem, 1995-96, pres & chief oper officer; Montgomery County, asst county atty, 1985-87; Fed Election Comn, staff atty, off gen coun, 1987-89; Consumer Prod Safety Comn, chmn, 1989-96; Good Hope Union United methodist Church, pastor, currently. **Orgs:** Am Bar Asn; NatT Bar Asn; MAR State Bar Asn. **Business Phone:** (301)459-2000.

JONES-TRENT, BERNICE R
Librarian. **Personal:** Born Apr 22, 1946, Michie, TN; daughter of E C Ray and Ellen Hodge; married Julius, Jun 16, 1984. **Educ:** Jackson State Univ, Jackson, MS, BA (cum laude), 1968; Rutgers Univ, New Brunswick, NJ, MLS, 1969; Rutgers Univ, SCILS, New Brunswick, NJ, PhD candidate, 1984-. **Career:** Newark Bus Libr, Newark, NJ, jr librn, 1969-70; Rutgers-Dana Libr, Newark, NJ, bus librn, 1970-82; Rutgers Univ, Libr Sch, New Brunswick, NJ, acting dir, prof, develop studies, 1982-83; Rutgers Univ Libr, New Brunswick, NJ, staff develop librn, 1983-84; Rutgers-Kilmer Libr, New Brunswick, NY, pub servs librn, 1984-85; Old Dominion Univ Libr, Norfolk, VA, head, reference dept, 1985-87; Norfolk State Univ, Norfolk, VA, dir libr, 1987-89; Montclair State Col, Upper Montclair, NJ, dir lib, 1989-. **Orgs:** Am Libr Asn (ALA), 1975-; Asn Col & Res Librs, 1975-; Black Caucus ALA, 1974-; Libr Admin & Mgmt Asn, 1978; chair, Leadership Discussion Group and Women Admin Discussion Group, 1988-90; Alpha Kappa Alpha Sorority Inc, 1965-; charter mem, New Jersey Black Librarians Network, 1975-. **Honors/Awds:** Acad Scholar, Jackson State Univ, 1964-68; Title II B Scholar, Rutgers Univ, 1968-69; County Comt Woman, East Orange, NJ, 1984-85; Scholar, Spec Librs Asn, 1968. **Special Achievements:** Article, 'Keeping Pace with Changes in the Curriculum and in the Student Body', The American Mosaic Public & Access Services, Quarterly Volume 1, Number 3. **Home Addr:** 2217 Crossing Way, Wayne, NJ 07470. **Business Addr:** Director of Library Services, Montclair State University, Sprague Library, Upper Montclair, NJ 07043, **Business Phone:** (201)893-4301.

JONES-WILSON, FAUSTINE CLARISSE
Educator. **Personal:** Born Dec 3, 1927, Little Rock, AR; daughter of James Edward Thomas and Perrine Marie Childress Thomas; married James T Jones, Jun 20, 1948 (divorced 1977); children: Yvonne Dianne Jones & Brian Vincent Jones; married Edwin L Wilson Sr, Jul 10, 1981. **Educ:** Dunbar Jr Col, dipl, 1946; Univ Ark, AB, 1948; Univ Ill, AM, 1951, EdD, 1967. **Career:** Gary, IN Pub Schs, teacher, 1955-62, librn, 1964-67; Univ Ill, Urbana, teaching asst, grad stud, 1962-64, Univ Ill, Chicago, Col Educ, asst prof, 1967-69; Federal City Col, assoc prof, adult educ, 1970-71; Howard Univ,Dept Educ, asst prof, 1969-70, prof educ, actg dean, 1991-92, prof emer, 1993-. **Orgs:** Nominating Comt, Am Educ Studies Asn, 1974-75, Prog Comt, 1975-76, ExeCoun, 1976-79, 1985-86, Butts lect com, 1978-79, nominating comt chair, 1981-82, pres, 1984-85; exec bd, John Dewey Soc NBA79, 1988-90, nominating comt chair, 1992; exec bd, Soc Profs Educ, 1981-87, nominating comt chair,1979; pres, Howard Univ Chap, Phi Delta Kappa, 1986-87, Exec Comt,1986-87; chair, E Coast Steering Comt, Nat Coun Educating Black C,1986-88, 1990-92, bd dir, 1986-98, third vpres, 1992-94; Adv Coun,Charlotte Hawkins Brown Historical Found Inc; numerous honors. **Honors/Awds:** Outstanding Alumni Award, Detroit Chap, Nat Dunbar Alumni Asn, 1973; Frederick Douglass Award, Nat Black Press Asn, 1979; Distinguished Alumna,NAFEO/UAPB, 1984; Distinguished Scholar/TCR, Howard Univ, 1985; Gertrude ERush Award, NBA, 1990. **Special Achievements:** Author: The Changing Mood in Am: Eroding Committment?, 1977; A TraditionalModel of Educational Excellence: Dunbar High School of Little Rock, AR,1981; "External Crosscurrents and Internal Diversity: An Assessment ofBlack Progress 1960-80," Daedalus, 1981; "The Black Family," AFA Almanac(formerly the Negro), 1983, 1989, 1993; "Why Not Public Schools," Journalof Negro EDU, 1992; Editor in Chief Emerita, Journal of Negro Education;"Alleviating the force of Poverty on urban poor Children," in Early ChildDevelopment & Care, 1992; co-editor Encyclopedia of AFA EDU, GreenwoodPress, 1996; co-author: Paul Laurence Dunbar High School of Little Rock,AR: Take From Our Lips a Song, Dunbar to Thee, 2003; former Senior fellow,Phelps Stokes Fund, former associate editor, Journal of EDU for StudentsPlaced at Risk, Johns Hopkins Univ/Howard Univ. **Home Phone:** (301)596-5328. **Business Addr:** Professor Emeritus of Education, Howard University, School of Education, 2441 4th St NW, Washington, DC 20059, **Business Phone:** (202)806-7340.

JORDAN, DR. ABBIE H.
Educator. **Personal:** Born in Wilcox County, GA; daughter of Samuel Williams and Leah Jones Williams; married J Wesley; children: W Kenneth. **Educ:** Albany St Col, BS, 1949; Atlanta Univ, MA, 1953; Univ Ga, PhD, 1979. **Career:** Savannah St Col, from dir to asst prof, 1965-79; founder & dir, The Consortium Doctors Ltd, 1989-; Tuskegee Inst, instr; Atlanta Univ Complex, instr reading; Jr HS Ben Hill County, prin; Veterans Sch, prin & instr; GA-SC Read Conf, org & dir; Savannah Morning News, ed-op columnist; Savannah St Col Reading Inst, founder. **Orgs:** Adv Comn IRA Resol Comn, 1974-; exec sec & treas, Savannah Hosp Authority, 1975-; Adv Comn Ga Hist Found, 1974-80; Telfair Art Acad, 1975-80; Basic Ed & Reading, 1977-78; exec bd, Nat Asn Advan Colored People, 1977-83; coord & founder, Soc Doctors Inc, 1986-; founder & dir, The Consortium Doctors Ltd, 1989, chair, YMCA. **Honors/Awds:** Outstanding Teacher of the Year, 1973. **Special Achievements:** Featured in Essence Mag, 1976; Novelet "Ms Lily", 1977; authored numerous articles; featured in Atlanta Constitution Journal, June 1988; Jet, Sept28, 1992, Oct 5, 1992. **Home Phone:** (912)354-4634. **Business Addr:** Founder, Director, The Consortium of Doctors Ltd, PO Box 2040, Savannah, GA 31404, **Business Phone:** (912)238-1234.

JORDAN, ANDREW
Football player. **Personal:** Born Jun 21, 1972, Charlotte, NC. **Educ:** W Carolina. **Career:** Minn Vikings, tight end, 1994-97, 1999-2001; Tampa Bay Buccaneers, 1997; Philadelphia Eagles, 1998.

JORDAN, ANNE KNIGHT
Government official. **Personal:** Born in Tampa, FL; married Carl R; children: Carmen A Jordan Cox, Karen T & Harold K. **Educ:** Howard Univ, AB, 1949, post grad, 1955; Savannah State Col, 1957; Catholic Univ, 1958; Univ Ga, continuing educ, 1968; Armstrong State Col, 1972. **Career:** Soc Sec Agency Baltimore, clerical, 1941-42; Dept Pub Welfare Wash, staffoster care serv, 1943; Dept Anatomy & Pharmacol Howard Univ Wash, secy,1948-49; US Civil Serv Comn Invest Wash, clerical, 1953; Savannah, teacher spec educ, 1956-57; Tots & Teens Savannah Chap, 1965; Grasshoppers Socio-Civic Club, 1973; Adopt-A-Family MS Delta Poverty Area, 1970; Jr Nat Med Asn, 1970; Happy Homemaker, ed, 1970. **Orgs:** Exec bd, Speech & Hearing, 1958-60; Nat Asn Advan Colored People Nat Conv NY, 1959, MN, 1960; life mem & exec bd mem, Nat Asn Advan Colored People,1959-61; exec bd mem, March Dimes; Nat Found Savannah Chap, 1960; League Women Voters; Ga Coun Human Rels, 1960; pres, Woman's Aux Ga State Med Asn, 1961-62; basileus Sigma Gamma Rho, 1961-62; delegate Nat Coun Cath Women, 1964; White House Conf Health Nutrition & Food, 1969; pres, Woman's Aux Nat Med Asn, 1969-70; chmn adv bd, 1970-71; dir, SE region Nat Asn Black Military Women, 1996-04; Nat Black Catholics Cong IX. **Honors/Awds:** Sigma of the Year Award, Sigma Gamma Rho, 1962; Int Platform Asn, 1976;Hist Preserv Am, 1976; cert, State Ga, Univ Ga, Ga Defense Dept teach Civil Defense Courses; cert season color analyst & fitness consult, 1984. **Military Serv:** AUS, WAC, 1943-46. **Home Addr:** 1627 Mills B Lane Blvd, Savannah, GA 31405.

JORDAN, B DELANO
Lawyer. **Personal:** Born Jan 23, 1970, Nashville, TN; son of Dr George L Jr; married Toupazer, Mar 3, 1995; children: Alexis, Alayna & Selene. **Educ:** Va Tech Col, BS, elec engineering, 1994; William & Mary Sch Law, JD, 1999. **Career:** Litton Poly-Sci, quality assurance engr, 1994; Canon Va Inc, elec engr, 1994-96; NASA Langley Res Ctr, law clerk & patent contractor, 1997-98; Harness, Dickey & Pierce Assocs, 1999-2001; Kenyon & Kenyon LLP, assoc atty, 2001-. **Orgs:** Inst Elec & Electronic Engineers, 1994 & 1999-; bd dirs, Coop Hampton Roads Orgn Minority Engineers, 1995-96; Omega Psi Phi Inc, 1995-; State Bar Mich, 1999-. **Honors/Awds:** CALI Excellence Award in Patent Law, Williams & Mary Sch Law, 1998; Legal Skills Hon, 1997 & 1998; Moot Court Bar, 1998. **Business Addr:** Associate Attorney, Kenyon & Kenyon LLP, 1500 K St NW, Washington, DC 20005-1257, **Business Phone:** (202)220-4226.

JORDAN, BETTYE DAVIS
Entrepreneur. **Personal:** Born Sep 14, 1946, Tampa, FL; daughter of Lee and Ethel; children: Lisa Darlene Walker & Christopher Charles White II. **Educ:** Univ Tampa, BS, med technol, 1968. **Career:** B Davis Enterprises, owner; Harambee Enterprises, pres. **Orgs:** Bd mem, Fla Med Technol Asn, 1979-; exec bd mem, Nat Asn Advan Colored People, 1980-86; bd mem, Women's Survival Ctr, 1981-83; vpres, Pride Joy Enterprises, 1982-85; Movie Guild, 1984-86; vpres, Nat Asn Adbvan Colored People, 1986-; Civic Rev Bd, Tampa Urban League, 1987; bd mem, Col Hill Develop & Comm Cv Org, 1987; vipers, Nat Asn Advan Colored People, 1989-91. **Honors/Awds:** Medical Technologist Award, Univ Community Hosp, 1982. **Home Addr:** 1804 E 21st Ave, Tampa, FL 33605, **Home Phone:** (813)248-6744. **Business Addr:** President, Harambee Enterprises, 3525 N 22nd St, Tampa, FL 33605.

JORDAN, BRIAN O'NEIL
Baseball player. **Personal:** Born Mar 29, 1967, Baltimore, MD; married Pam; children: Briana & Bryson. **Educ:** Richmond Univ.

Career: Atlanta Falcons, safety, 1989-91; St Louis Cardinals, outfielder, 1992-98;Atlanta Braves, 1998-01, 2005-06; Los Angeles Dodgers, outfielder,2002-03; Texas Rangers, outfielder, 2004. Atlanta braves, 2005-06; Tv pre game analyst, currently. **Honors/Awds:** NL All-Star Team, 1998. *

JORDAN, CAROLYN D
Investment banker, lawyer. **Personal:** Born Mar 7, 1941, Fort Worth, TX. **Educ:** Fisk Univ, BA, 1963; Howard Univ, JD, 1966; Texas A & M Com; Eastfield Col. **Career:** Libr Cong, copyright examr, 1966-68; Va Regional Los Angeles, veterans claims adjudicator, 1968-69; Econ & Youth Opportunities Agency, Los Angeles, prog mgt specialist, 1969-70; Compton Calif, dep city atty, 1970-71; Herman A Eng, atty, 1971-72; US Senate, Banking, Housing & Urban Affairs Comn, coun, 1974-92; Nat Credit Union Admin, exec dir, 1998-2001, Neighborhood Credit Union, coun exec comt mem & sr vpres retail opers, 2005-, vice chair, currently; Pryor, McClendon, Counts & Co Inc, Investment Bankers, sr vpres. **Orgs:** Delta Sigma Theta Sorority, 1975-78; bd mem, Links Inc; State Bar Calif; Nat Bar Asn; Bar Dist Columbia; Nominating Comt, Tex Opers Coun. **Honors/Awds:** Award for Contributions to Small Business, Nat Asn Black Manufacturers; Award for Community Service, Delta Sigma Theta Sorority; Award for Contributions to the Field of Law, Nat Bar Asn. **Special Achievements:** First African American to serve as executive director of the National Credit Union Administration; First African-American Counsel to US Senate Banking Housing & Urban affairs Committee of US Senate. **Business Addr:** Vice Chair, Senior Vice President of Retail Operations, National Credit Union Administration, 1775 Duke St, Alexandria, VA 22314-3428, **Business Phone:** (703)518-6321.

JORDAN, DR. CAROLYNE LAMAR
School administrator. **Personal:** Born in Augusta, GA; daughter of Peter and Serena James; married Lawrence M; children: Lara Gayle & Samuel Lamar (deceased). **Educ:** Fisk Univ, BA, 1960; New England Univ, MMus, 1970; Harvard Univ, EEd,1977. **Career:** Hamilton Cent Sch, dir music, 1962-67; Lexington Pub Sch, supvr music,1967-70; Salem St Col, prof psychol, music, 1971-83; Suffolk Univ, asst pres, 1983-88; Fell Smith Col, pres, 1986-87; Le Moyne Owen Col, vpres acad affairs, 1988-90; Harvard Univ, vis scholar, 1990-91; Maryville Univ, assoc dean grad studies, 1992-93; Fed Express Corp, corp trainer, 1993-95; Cape Cod Comm Col, dean acad affairs, 1995-99; Lamar-Jordan Assoc Inc, pres, currently. **Orgs:** Friends Nat Ctr Afro Am, 1971-73; Am Psychol Assn, 1977-; trustee, Cambridge Friends Sch, 1980-84; exec brd, Natl Am Friends Serv Comt, 1983-; chairperson, Long Range Planning Comm Suffolk Univ; renway consortium Retention Comt; pres, Human Resources Cons; past pres, Alpha Kappa Alpha Sorority, Boston chap; exec brd, ACE & NIP, 1985; exec brd, Freedom House, 1985; former brd, phis Urban League; Family Serv phis; phis Symphony Orchestra; Porter Leath Children's Ctr, phis; Young Women Christian Assn; natl pres, Soc Inc, 1997-2001; sr fel, Am Coun Educ, 1999; phis Symphony League, 2002-. **Honors/Awds:** Ford Found Grant Harvard Univ, 1975-77; Radcliffe Grant to Grad Women,1975; Distinguished Service Award, Salem St Col, 1980; Outstanding Young Women of Jaycees, 1982; Humanities Post Doct Grant Harvard Univ; Am Coun Educ. **Business Addr:** President, Lamar-Jordan Associates Inc, HERS Inc, 2826 Cent Ave, Memphis, TN 38111.

JORDAN, CHARLES WESLEY
Clergy. **Personal:** Born May 28, 1933, Dayton, OH; son of David Morris and Naomi Azelia Harper; married Margaret Crawford, Aug 2, 1959; children: Diana & Susan. **Educ:** Roosevelt Univ, BA, 1956; Garrett-Evangelical Theol Sem, MDiv, 1960. **Career:** Clergy (retired); United Methodist Church, minister, 1960; Woodlawn United Methodist Church, pastor, 1960-66; Rockford Ill Urban Ministries, dir 1966-71; Northern Ill Conf Cou, prog staff, 1971-82; Chicago Southern Dist, supt, 1982-87; St Mark United Methodist Church, Chicago, IL, sr pastor, 1987-92; elected bishop, 1992; Iowa Area United Methodist Church, bishop, 1992-2000; Claremont Sch Theo, bishop residence. **Orgs:** Comnr, Rockford Housing Authority, 1967-71; bd dir, United Methodist Bd Global Ministries, 1972-80; United Methodist Coun Ministries, 1980-88; bd trustees, 1982-97, elected life trustee, 2000, Garrett-Evangelical Theol Sem; bd mem, United Methodist Church & Soc, 1992-2000, pres, 1996-2000; Project Image, 1987-92; bd dir, Chicago Community Mental Health Coun, 1989-92; bd dir, Cent Iowa Health Syst, 1992-2000; bd dir, Mid-Iowa Coun Boy Scouts Am, 1995-2000; pres, Iowa Ecumencial Ministries, 1999-2000; Sigma Pi Phi fraternity; life mem, Kappa Alpha Psi Frat; Sigma Pi Phi; life mem, Nat Asn Advan Colored People; life mem, Black Methodists Church Renewal. **Honors/Awds:** Hon doctorate, Morningside Col, 1994; Hon doctorate, Rust Col, 1995; Hon doctorate, Simpson Col, 2000; delegate, United Methodist General Conf, 1976, 1980, 1984, 1988, 1992; Achievement Award in Religion, Chicago Alumni Kappa Alpha Psi Frat, 1986; Hall of Fame, Wendell Phillips High School 1989. **Military Serv:** AUS, pfc, 1953-55. **Home Addr:** 1014 Deborah St, Upland, CA 91784, **Home Phone:** (909)946-6785.

JORDAN, HON. CLAUDIA J.
Judge. **Educ:** Univ NC, BA, 1975; Univ Colo Sch Law, Boulder, 1980. **Career:** Colo Pub Defender's Off, Denver Off, trial atty, 1982-87; sole practitioner, 1987-94; Denver County Ct, judge, 1994-, Currenly. **Orgs:** Colo Bar Asn; Sam Cary Bar Asn; Denver Bar Asn; Colo Women's Bar Asn. **Honors/Awds:** Black Hall of Fame, Colo; Woman of the Year, 2001; Colo BPW Key to the City, El Paso, Texas; Judicial Excellence Award, CU Law Sch. **Special Achievements:** First African-American female judge in the state of Colorado. **Business Addr:** Judge, Denver County Court, 1437 Bannock St Room 230, Denver, CO 80202, **Business Phone:** (720)865-7930.

JORDAN, DARIN GODFREY
Football player. **Personal:** Born Dec 4, 1964, Boston, MA; married Andrea Hayes; children: Jonah & Jenelle. **Educ:** Northeastern Univ, BA, speech commun, 1988. **Career:** Pittsburgh Steelers, 1988; Los Angeles Raiders, 1990; San Francisco49ers, line backer, 1991-94. **Special Achievements:** Elected to the Northeastern Univ Hall of Fame, 2002. *

JORDAN, DAVID LEE
Educator, city council member. **Personal:** Born Apr 3, 1933, Greenwood, MS; son of Cleveland Jordan and Elizabeth Jordan; married Christine Bell; children: David Jr, Joyce Jordan Dugar, Donald & Darryl. **Educ:** Miss Valley State Univ, BS, 1959; Univ Wyo, MS, 1969. **Career:** Teacher (retired), city councilman; Greenwood Voters League, pres, 1965-; The Greenwood Pub Sch Syst, sci teacher, 1970-; Greenwood City Council, pres, 1985; Mississippi State Senate, Greenwood City, councilman, 1993-. **Orgs:** Leflore Co Br & Nat Asn Advan Colored People, 1960-; Leflore Co & Dem Exec Comt 1976-; Nat Dem Platform Civil Rights Adv Comt, 1978; chmn, Miss Valley State Univ Nat Alumni Asn, 1980; Miss Municlpal Asn; Miss Wayport Authority Adv Coun; chmn, Investigate State Off Comt; vchmn, Elections Comt; vchmn, Legislative Reapportionment; chmn, Agriculture Comt; chmn, Educ Comt; chmn, Finance Comt; chmn, Forestry Comt; chmn, Labor Comt; chmn, Municipalities Comt; chmn, Tourism Comt. **Honors/Awds:** Govt Merit Award, Govt Off, 1974; JH White Memorial Award, Miss Valley State Univ Nat Alumni Asn, 1977; Committee Service Award, Omega Psi Phi Frat, 1977-79; attendee, White House Meet Pres Carter, White House Staff 1978-79. **Military Serv:** AUSR pfc 1960-62. **Business Addr:** Greenwood City Councilman, Mississippi State Senate, Greenwood City, Rm 405D NC, PO Box 1018, Jackson, MS 39215, **Business Phone:** (601)359-6234.

JORDAN, DR. DEDRA R
Manager, entrepreneur. **Personal:** Born Aug 10, 1953, Portsmouth, VA; daughter of Paul Wilson and Delores Wilson; married Melvin C Jordan; children: Milton Ray Dixon II. **Educ:** Cert Strategic Mgt Human Resources; Va State Univ, BS; James Madison Univ, MA, Educ; Kennedy-Western Univ, PhD. **Career:** VA Beach Pub Schs, band teacher, 1976-77; Norfolk Pub Schs, teacher, 1978-81; Super Eng & Electronics Co, personnel mgr, indust security supvr, 1981-90; Casde Mfg, personnel mgr/ indust security supvr, 1990-93; Norfolk Airport Auth, dir employee & community rels, 1994-98; SE Pub Serv Auth, human resources analyst, res trainer, 1999-2001; PEMCO, HR coord, 2001-02; FSS Alutiiq JV, human resources mgr, 2002-03; New Horizons Regional Educ Ctr, - human resources dir, currently; BET Consult Serv, founder, currently; Lorman Educ Serv, prin consult, owner, currently. **Orgs:** Int Personnel Mgt Asn; Soc Human Resource Mgt; Employ Mgt Asn; Children's Ctr, 2003; Am Soc Training & Develop; Nat Asn Female Execs; Am Bus Women's Asn; Alpha Kappa Alpha; Virginia & Tidewater Asn Sch Personnel Adminr. **Honors/Awds:** Creative Application Award, Yoder-Heneman HR Mgt (small co), Soc HR Mgt, 1995; InterNat Who's Who of Professional, 1995; Sterling Who's Who Directory, Executive Edition; A Phillip Randolph Award, Outstanding EEO & Affirmative Action, Airport Authority, 1998. Numerous other leadership awards. **Home Phone:** (757)405-3783. **Business Phone:** (757)405-3783.

JORDAN, EDDIE
U.S. attorney, district attorney. **Personal:** Born Jan 1, 1953?, New Orleans, LA. **Educ:** Wesleyan Univ; Rutgers Univ Sch Law, attended 1977. **Career:** US atty (retired), district atty; Southern Univ, 1981-84; New Orleans, asst US atty, 1984-94; Eastern Dist La, US atty, 1994-2001; Orleans Parish, dist atty, 2003-. **Business Addr:** District Attorney, Orleans Parish, 619 S White St, New Orleans, LA 70019, **Business Phone:** (504)822-2414.

JORDAN, EDDIE (EDWARD MONTGOMERY JORDAN)
Basketball coach, basketball player. **Personal:** Born Jan 29, 1955, Washington, DC; married; children (previous marriage): Justin, Eddie Jr & Paul; married Charisse; children: Jackson & Skylar. **Educ:** Rutgers Univ, BA, health & phys educ, 1977. **Career:** Basketball player (retired), basketball coach; Cleveland Cavaliers, basketball player, 1977; NJ Net, 1978-80; Los Angeles Lakers, 1980-81; Nat Basketball Asn World Championship Squad, 1982; Portland Trail Blazers, 1983-84; Boston Col, asst coach, 1986-87; Rutgers Univ, asst coach, 1988; Sacramento Kings, asst coach, head coach, 1996-97; NJ Nets, coaching staff, 1999-03; Wash Wizards, head coach, 2003-. **Orgs:** Vol asst, Rutgers Univ. **Honors/Awds:** E Regional Most Valuable Player, 1976; hon mention All-Am, 1977. **Business Addr:** Head Coach, Wash Wizards, 601 F St NW, Washington, DC 20004, **Business Phone:** (202)661-5050.*

JORDAN, EDDIE J, JR. (EDDIE JACK JORDAN)
Government official. **Personal:** Born Oct 6, 1952, Fort Campbell, KY; son of Eddie J Jordan Sr and Gladys McDaniel (deceased); married Charmaine E, Jul 1974; children: Aisha Zakiya, Chad-Hassan Akil & Julian Khalid. **Educ:** Wesleyan Univ, Middletown, CT, BA, 1974; Rutgers Law Sch, Newark, NJ, JD, 1977. **Career:** Southern Univ Law Sch, prof, 1981; US Atty's Off, assist US atty, 1984-87; Sessions & Fishman, assoc, 1987-90, partner, 1990-92; Bryan, Jupiter & Lewis, coun, 1992-94; US Dept Justice, US atty, 1994-2001; Orleans Parish, La, dist atty, 2003-; Pepper, Hamilton & Scheetz, assoc. **Orgs:** Bd govs, LA State Bar Asn, 1984; bd dirs, 1989-94, vpres, bd dirs, 1991-93, Planned Parenthood LA; bd dirs, Metropolitan Area Community, 1990-94; bd dirs, St Thomas/Irish Channel Consortium, 1990-94; adv comm human rels, Human Rels Comn, City N Orleans, 1993; NAACP, 1993-95; adv comt, Atty Gen's, 1998-2000; adv bd, Reducing Alcohol Accessibility Youth; bd dirs, New Orleans chap Fed Bar Asn; adv bd, Pediat AIDS Prog; adv bd, New Orleans Community, Teach Am; vice chair, Atty Gen's Adv Comm, Subcomt Controlled Substances/ Drug Abuse Prev; bd dirs, Reducing Alcohol Accessibility Youth; Chap Fed Bar Asn; adv bd, Pediat AIDS Prog; adv bd, New Orleans community Teach Am; vice chair, Atty Gen's adv comms, subcomm Controlled Substances/Drug Abuse Prev; subcomts Justice Progs & Organized Crime/Violent Crime. **Honors/Awds:** A P Tureaud Award, Louis A Martinet Legal Soc, 1992; Outstanding Prosecutor Award, Victims & Citizens Against Crime, 1995; David Ellis Byrd Award, Nat Asn Advan Colored People, New Orleans Chap, 1997; Distinguished Public Service Award, Crimefighters Asn New Orleans, 1998. **Special Achievements:** In Search of the Meaning of RICO, LA State Bar Assn; Changing Carnival's old ways is a progressive step, The Times Picayune; Recent Dev in the Law Manual, LA State Bar Assn, 1985-96; Louisiana Appellate Practice Handbook, Lawyers Cooperative Publishing, contributing author. **Business Phone:** (504)571-2820.

JORDAN, EDDIE JACK. See JORDAN, EDDIE J, JR.

JORDAN, EDWARD MONTGOMERY. See JORDAN, EDDIE.

JORDAN, EMMA COLEMAN
Educator, lawyer, civil rights activist. **Personal:** Born Nov 29, 1946, Berkeley, CA; daughter of Myrtle Coleman and Earl; children: Kristen Elena & Allison Elizabeth. **Educ:** Calif State Univ, BA, 1969; Howard Univ, JD, 1973. **Career:** Stanford Law Sch, teaching fel, 1973-74; Univ Santa Clara, asst prof, 1974-75; White House, fel, 1980-81; Atty Gen US, spec asst, 1981; Univ Calif, Davis, fac; Georgetown Univ Law Ctr, prof law, 1987-. **Orgs:** Pres, Soc Am Law Teachers, 1986-88; exec comt, Asn Am Law Schs, 1988-91, pres-elect, 1991-92, pres, 1992-93; Nat Conf Black Lawyers; Nat Bar Asn; Am Soc Int Law; pub mem, Calif State Bd Dent & Exmnrs; Am Asn Law Schs Sects Com Law & Contracts, Minority Groups; Charles Houston Bar Asn; bd dir, Calif Asn Black Lawyers; chmn, Calif St Bar Financial Inst Comn; chmn, AALS Financial Inst & Consumer Financial Serv Sect; bd mem, Consumer Action; adv comm, Nat Consumer Union Northern Ca; Am Law Inst. **Honors/Awds:** Outstanding Academic Achievement Award, Phi Alpha Delta, 1973; Clyde Ferguson Award, Asn Am Law Schs, 2005. **Special Achievements:** First African-American tenured professors at Harvard Law School; Publishing works include: Co-editor with Anita F Hill, Race, Gender and Power in America, Oxford University Press, 1995; Lynching: The Dark Metaphor of American Law, Basic Books, spring 1999; Litigation without representation; The Need for Intervention to Affirm Affirmative Action, Harvard Civil Liberties Civil Rights Law Rev 1979, "After the Merger of Contribution & Indemnity, What are the Limits of Comparative Loss Allocation" AR St Law Rev 1980; "Problems & Prospects of Participation in Affirmative Action Litigation" UC Davis Law Rev 1980; Limitations of the Int Lega Mech Namibia 1972; Articles include: "Ending the Floating Check Game," Hastings Law Review, 1986; "Taking Voting Rights Seriously," Nebraska Law Review, 1986. **Business Addr:** Professor of Law, Georgetown University, 578 McDonough 600 New Jersey Ave NW, Washington, DC 20001-2075, **Business Phone:** (202)662-9402.

JORDAN, ERIC BENET. See BENET, ERIC.

JORDAN, FREDERICK E.
Civil engineer, executive. **Personal:** Born Apr 27, 1937, Loveville, MD; son of Lewis E. **Educ:** Howard Univ, BSCE; Stanford Univ, MSCE. **Career:** Sandrestrom Air Force Base Greenland, asst chief engr pvt pract, 1968; W Asn Minority Consult Engr, pres, 1974; Am Soc Civ Engr SF Sect, dir, 1974; Nat Coun Minority Consult Engr, pres, 1976-77; Bonelli, Young , Wong & Biggs, San & Fran, div civ-struct engr; Bechtel Corp San Fran & Charles T Main Consult Engrs, Boston, struct engr; Riverside Dept Pub Works Riverside CA, civ engr; LA Air Def Command, dir civ engr; US Environ Protect Agency, tech adv; FE Jordan Assocs Inc, prin, pres & chief exec officer currently. **Orgs:** Nat Soc Prof Engr;

consult Engrs Asn US; Struct Engrs Asn CA; Soc Am Mil Engrs; fed mem, pres, chmn bd, dir Engr Soc Com Manpower Training Inc; founding mem, first chmn, North Calif Coun Black Prof Engrs; vpres, San Fran Forum Am Soc Civ Engrs; mem engr adv & bd, Calif State Univ San Fran; San Fran Engr Coun; pres, bd dir Bay Area Urban League Inc, 1972-73; pres, San Francisco Black Chamber Com, 1989-94; pres, Calif Asn Better Govt, 1990-91; councilman, San Francisco Pvt Indust Coun; councilman Calif, Dept Transport Bus Coun; Comnr, San Francisco Parking & Traffic Comn; comnr, Calif State Comn on the Status of the African Male. **Honors/Awds:** Bay Area & State Calif outstanding civil engr comn activity, Am Soc Civ Engr, 1967-68; distinguished alumni award, Bay Area Howard Univ Alumni Club, 1972; Distinguished Black Sci & Eng, US Oakland Mus Asn, 1973; Governor's Award, Best Small Bus Contractor, State CA, 1993; Minority Serv Firm, Five Western States, 1993; One of Ten Outstanding Bus in the US, 1993; several Publs, 20 other awards. **Military Serv:** USAF, 1st Lt. **Business Addr:** President, Chief Executive Officer, FE Jordan Associates Inc, 90 New Montgomery St Suite 1320, San Francisco, CA 94105, **Business Phone:** (415)243-9080.*

JORDAN, GEORGE LEE, JR.
Dentist. **Personal:** Born Nov 2, 1935, Norfolk Co, VA; married Marguerite W; children: George III & Bernard. **Educ:** Cent State Univ, BS, 1957; Fisk Univ, MA, 1963; Meharry Med Col, DDS, 1971. **Career:** Protsmouth VA, teacher, 1958-62; WA DC, teacher, 1963-64; Phoenix, sci teacher, 1964-67; Meharry Med Col, instr, 1971-72; Mich State Univ, asst prof, 1972-76; Lakeside Health Ctr, dir, 1972-75; Pontiac Sch Dist, consult, 1974-77; Olin Health Ctr, dir, 1975-76; Va Clin, PC, dent dir, 1977-86; pvt pract, dentist, 1986-. **Orgs:** NAACP; Pontiac Area Urban League. **Honors/Awds:** Outstanding Teacher Jaycees, WA, DC, 1962; Outstanding Citizen, Omega Psi Phi, 1967; Citation, Pontiac Schs, 1977. **Military Serv:** AUS, res, 2nd lt, 1957-58. **Business Addr:** Dentist, 960 Greenbrier Circle, Chesapeake, VA 23320, **Business Phone:** (757)420-8002.

JORDAN, GEORGE WASHINGTON, JR.
Executive. **Personal:** Born Mar 11, 1938, Chattanooga, TN; son of George W Jordan Sr and Omega Davis; married Fredine Sims; children: George Washington III. **Educ:** Tuskegee Univ, BSEE, 1961; GA Inst Tech, MSIM, 1978; Emory Univ, mgt inst, 1976. **Career:** Boeing Co, engr, 1961-65; Gen Elec Co, engr, 1965-66; Lockheed-Georgia Co, engr & mgr, 1966-. **Orgs:** Life mem, Alpha Phi Alpha Fraternity, 1957-; Nat Mgt Asn, 1966-; sr mem, Am Inst Aero Astro, 1973-; Merit Employees Asn, 1975-; Asn MBA Execs, 1978-; Inst Mgt Sci, 1978-; chmn, Atlanta Zoning Bd, 1978-84; Nat Mem, Flt Sim Tech Comm AIAA, 1984-; Nat Asn Advan Colored People, 1985-; Am Mgt Assoc, 1991; Smithsonian Nat Assoc, 1991; United Way (VIP); bd deacons, Christian Fel Baptist Church, coun Christian ed, youth leadership coun, Sunday sch teacher, royal ambassador counr, fin comm, asst treas, chmn march bd, bus mgr; Bd trustees, Shorter Col. **Honors/Awds:** Dollars & Sense, Outstanding Business & Professional Award, 1991. **Home Addr:** 120 Moss Creek Walk, Fairburn, GA 30213. **Business Addr:** Manager, Lockheed, 86 S Cobb Dr, Marietta, GA 30063-0001.

JORDAN, DR. HAROLD WILLOUGHBY
Physician, educator. **Personal:** Born May 24, 1937, Newnan, GA; son of Edward P (deceased) and Dorothy W; married Geraldine Crawford; children: Harold II, Vincent, Karen & Kristie. **Educ:** Morehouse Col, BS, 1958; Meharry Med Col, MD, 1962; G W Hubbard Hosp, rotating internship, 1963, med residency, 1964; Vanderbilt Univ Hosp, psychiat residency, 1967. **Career:** Meharry Med Col, Dept Psychiat clin instr, 1965-67, instr, acting dir outpatient dept, 1967-68, asst prof, dir psychiat outpatient clinic, 1968-71, prof, chmn dept psychiat, 1979-97; Vanderbilt Univ Hosp, courtesy staff mem, 1967-, clin instr, 1968-72, clin asst prof, 1972-; Florence Crittendon Home, psychiat consult, 1967; State Div Voc Rehab Intensive Treatment Ctr, psychiat consult, 1967-71; Fisk Univ Stud Couns Ctr, psychiat consult, 1969-71; Tenn Dept Mental Health, Mental Retardation, asst comnr, 1971-75, comnr, 1975-79; Tenn State Univ, psychiat consult, 1984-; Cumberland Hall Hosp, attending physician, 1985-; pvt pract, currently. **Orgs:** NAACP, 1957, Am Psychiat Asn, 1967, Am Asn Univ Profs, 1967, R F Boyd Med Soc, 1968, Nat Med Asn, 1970, Black Psychiatrists Am, 1973, Tenn Med Asn, 1975, Nashville Acad Med, 1975, Am Asn Chmn Psychiat, 1979, Alpha Omega Alpha Honorary Med Soc, 1980, Sigma Pi Phi. **Honors/Awds:** Certificate of Recognition, Nashville Chap, Asn Black Psychologists, 1976; certificate of appreciation, Joseph P Kennedy Jr Found, 1976; certificate of recognition, Metro Atlanta Chap Nat Asn Human Rights Workers, 1976; awarded plaque, Nat Asn Black & Social Workers, 1977; plaque, Harriet Cohn Mental Health Ctr, 1979; plaque, Meharry Med Col Class, 1980; President's Award, Meharry Med Col, 1987. **Special Achievements:** Harold W Jordan Habilitation Center, dedicated in Nashville, TN, 1987. **Military Serv:** AUS, Reserve, capt, 1963-69; Tennessee Army Nat Guard, Lt col, 1974-81. **Home Addr:** 4204 Kings Ct, Nashville, TN 37218. **Business Addr:** Psychiat, 2401 Parmer Place, Nashville, TN 37203, **Business Phone:** (615)327-6606.

JORDAN, J PAUL
Executive, chief executive officer, president (organization). **Personal:** Born in Duquesne, PA; son of William and Rebecca; divorced. **Educ:** Univ Mich; Univ Detroit, BS. **Career:** Jordan & Assoc, ceo; Meadow Village Partnership, ceo; Ujama Develop Co, ceo. **Orgs:** Adv bd, Fed Res Bank; adv bd, Fed Home Loan Bank; multicultural comt, Greater Milwaukee Conv & Visitors Bur; Nat Black Comt; dist dir, Am Defense Preparedness Asn; adv bd, US Small Bus Asn; pres, Milwaukee Minority Chamber Com. **Home Phone:** (414)933-6000. **Business Phone:** (414)226-4105.

JORDAN, J. ST. GIRARD
Lawyer. **Personal:** Born Feb 29, 1944, Philadelphia, PA; son of Henderson and Emma Jane; married L Elaine Bullock; children: Daniel, Mark, Chonda, Kijsa. **Educ:** Temple Univ, ABS, 1969, BS, 1970; Univ Pa, Law Sch, JD, 1973. **Career:** SmithKline Corp, financial analyst, 1967-69, sr mkt res analyst, 1960-70; Black Book TV Prod, vpres & treas, 1969-72; Norden Labs Lincoln & VPO Inc, Omaha, corp officer; Goodis Greenfield Henry Shaiman & Levin, assoc, 1973-74; SmithKline Corp, group gen coun, 1974-, asst gen coun, asst secy, 1986-87, gen coun, dir & secy, Consumer Products Inc, 1987; WKW Inc, coun, 1990; consult activities before Expert Comt Drug Dependence, Geneva, Switzerland; UN Coun Narcotic Drugs, Vienna, Austria, 1989-92; Menley James Inc, coun; Municip Tax Bur Inc, coun, 1980-97; Saint Assocs, currently. **Orgs:** Pres, Barristers Asn Philadelphia Inc, 1976-77; Nat Bar Asn; Am Bar Asn; Pa Bar Asn; Philadelphia Bar Asn; NJ Bar Asn; Camden County Bar Asn; legal comt, United Negro Col Fund Dr, 1977; vice chmn, AHI Law Comt, Wash, DC; pres, Philadelphia Fed Black Bus & Prof Orgs; Nat Asn Advan Colored People; Mt Zion Baptist Church; United Fund Way; Neighborhood Servs Comn, adv bd, Christian St Young Women's Christian Asn; bd dirs, United Comn United Way Agency, 1982-84; chmn, AHI Law Comn, 1982; exec comt, Barristes Asn Philadelphia, 1986-87; Delta Epsilon, Southern NJ; Govt Affairs Comn Proprietry Asn; bd, Camden County Girl Scouts, NJ, 1991-92; Fed Judiciary Mediation Bd, 1992-; Municip Tax Bur, official coun, 1995-; Philadanco, secy bd, currently. **Honors/Awds:** Outstanding Student Award, Temple Univ, 1968; Tribune Outstanding Citizen Centennel Award, 1984. **Military Serv:** USAF, A/1C, 1962. **Home Addr:** 6 Rockledge Ct, Marlton, NJ 08053, **Home Phone:** (856)767-3984. **Business Phone:** (215)438-5840.*

JORDAN, JACQUELYN D.
Educator, nurse. **Personal:** Born Mar 3, 1948, Waterbury, CT; divorced; children: Ayanna & Derek. **Educ:** Mattatuck Community Col AA, nursing; Western Conn State Univ BS, nursing; Yale Univ MS, neuroscience nursing; Adelphi Univ, PhD, nursing, 1995. **Career:** Mount Sinai Hosp, clinic nurse supt, 1982-86; Univ Conn, asst prof nursing, 1985-86; Bristol Hosp, patient care mgr, 1986-88; Bridgeport Hosp, head nurse, neuro intensive care unit, 1988-89; Western Conn St Univ, assoc prof, nursing, 1989-98; Howard Univ, asst dean, undergrad nursing, 1998; Towson Univ, Dept Nursing, chair, currently. **Orgs:** Asn Black Nursing Fac Higher Educ, 1990-; Sigma Theta Tau, 1982-; Nat Black Nurses Asn, 1991; Nat Polit Cong Black Women, 1989; bd dir, Nat Polit Cong Black Women, 1997. **Honors/Awds:** Nurse Educator Award, USF, 1991, 1992; Prof Trailblazer's Award, Negro Bus& Prof Women's Clubs, 1984; Dissertation Award, Yale Univ Chap, Sigma Theta Tau, 1994; Dissertation Award, Asn Black Nursing Fac, 1994; Professional Award, Southern CT Black Nurses Asn, 1998. **Special Achievements:** Certified clinic nurse specialist, med & surgical, 1991. **Military Serv:** USY, Sp5, 1966-69. **Home Addr:** 7806 Regal Ct, Clinton, MD 20735, **Home Phone:** (301)877-3274. **Business Addr:** Chairperson, Towson university, Burdick Hall Room 134 8000 York Rd, Towson, MD 21252-0001, **Business Phone:** (410)704-4212.

JOR'DAN, JAMILAH R.
Executive. **Career:** Partnership for Quality Child Care, founder & president, currently. **Orgs:** Vpres, Nat Asn Educ Young C. **Business Addr:** Founder, President, Partnership for Quality Child Care, 228 S Wabash Ave Suite 1000, Chicago, IL 60604.

JORDAN, JOHN EDWARD
Dentist, executive. **Personal:** Born Nov 17, 1930, Nashville, TN; son of John E and Mary Richardson; divorced; children: John E III. **Educ:** Lincoln Univ, PA, BA, 1952; Meharry Med Col, Dent Sch, DDS, 1957; Fisk Univ; Wayne State Univ; Lincoln Univ, post grad courses; Univ Tenn Dent Sch; Univ Ark; Meharry Med Col Sch Dent. **Career:** dent pvt pract, 1958-; Jordan Copy Svc, owner, 1960-87; Shirts Unlimited Clothing Store, partner, 1972-79. **Orgs:** vpres, bd of dirs, Northeast Mental Health Ctr, 1978-85; Middle Baptist Ch, laymen, pres, 1985-95, trustee, 1983-89, superintendent, 1990-95, sanctuary choir, pres, 1992-95 trustee bd, vp, 1992-95, men's choir, 1980-95; Memphis City Baptist Laymen, corresponding secy, 1990-93, fin secy, 1986-87; chmn, dental health Shelby Co Dental Soc Pen TN Dental Asn 1965-89; participant, dentist Memphis Health Fair 1984-89; chmn, Memphis Shelby Co Headstart Policy Coun, 1985-87; chmn, contact rep Memphis Br Afro-Am Historical Asn 1980-89; pres, Hyde Park Hollywood Comn Develop Block Club, 1992; bd of dir PMA; chmn, Headstart Policy Coun, 1986-87; chmn, Dental Health Month Shelby Cty Dental Soc NDA; bd of dirs, Pres Hooks Dimick Day Care, 1989; Memphis Neighborhood Watch, 1990; Evergreen Optimist Club, vp, 1991-93; Hyde Park Neighborhood Coalition, pres, 1993-95; Lewis Ctr Senior Citizens, 1993-95; Austin St Neighborhood Watch, 1992-95; Kappa Alpha Psi, Germantown Alumni Chapter, 1992-95. **Honors/Awds:** US House Representatives Proclamation, Congressman Harold Ford, 1982; Certificate of Achievement, Middle Baptist Church, 1984; Dental Health Week Achievement Award, ADA Shelby Co Dental Soc Pan TN Dental Asn, 1984; Certificate, Northeast Mental Health Ctr Bd Dirs, 1984; Plaques, Shelby Cty Dental Soc for dedication to Dentistry 28 yrs, North Memphis Tennis Club-Thanks, 1986; appreciation for Outstanding Contributions, NE CMTY Mental Health Cntr, 1985; Meharry Medical College Presidents Award, 1982; certificates from Douglass Optimist Club charter member, Natl Childrens Dental Health Month, 1985-87; Middle Baptist Church in appreciation, 1984, Government Lamar Alexander appreciation for helping senior citizens; Dr Martin Luther King Award, Positive Mental Attitude Asn, 1985; honorary mem, Hyde Park Alumni Assoc, 1983; Proclamation Stof TN Rep Larry Turner Pride-damp, 1985; Plaque, Northeast Community Health Ctr, 1985; Outstanding Service Plaque, PMAA Bd Dirs, 1991; Plaque & Certificates, Evergreen Optimist Club. **Business Addr:** Dentist, 2154 Chelsea Ave, Memphis, TN 38108, **Business Phone:** (901)274-2400.*

JORDAN, JOHN WESLEY
Clergy. **Personal:** Born Sep 10, 1941, Edenton, NC; son of Earl Holley and Annie Louise; divorced; children: Johann, Christian & Stanley. **Educ:** Elizabeth City State Univ, BS, eng, 1963; Teachers Col, Columbia Univ, MA, eng, 1964; A Phillip Randolph Inst, attended 1973; Columbia Univ, adv study, 1974; NC State Univ, attended 1976. **Career:** Savannah State Col, instr humanities, 1964-66; Elizabeth City State Col, instr humanities, 1965; Claflin Col SC, instr humanities, 1966; Hampton Univ, instr humanities, 1966-67; New York City Bd Educ, eng teacher, 1967-74; HQ USAG Ft Bragg, NC, personnel actions spec, 1975-77; Camp Casey, Korea, awards & decorations spec, 1977-78; Ft Bragg, NC, ID card sargent, NCOIC, 1978-81; Ft Shafter, HI, Non-Commissioned Officer Charge, personnel actions, 1982-84; Fort Drum NY, personnel actions sergeant, SFC & E7, 1984-86; personnel admin ctr supvr, HHC First Bn 7th FA 1986-88, supvr Transition Ctr, 1989-91; Watertown Correctional Facility, Watertown, NY, eng teacher, GED prog summer, 1988; Watertown Urban Mission, Watertown, NY, dir Oper Breakthrough, 1988-89; Faith Fel Christian Sch, vol eng teacher, 1990-91; City Refuge Christian Church, Great Bend, NY, pastor, 1988-; Carthage Cent Schs, sub teacher, 1999-. **Orgs:** Ed, Refuge Flame City Refuge Christian Church, HI, 1982-84; Metro-Jefferson Pub Safety Building, 1984-; vol minister, Watertown Correctional Facility Watertown, NY, 1984-; vol lay relig leader, Ft Drum Prayer, Bible Study, Fel, 1984-88; Watertown, Jefferson County, Nat Asn Advan Colored People, 1988-; Cape Vincent Correctional Facility, 1988-; relig adv bd, Watertown & Cape Vincent Correctional Facilities 1988-; registered & cert foster father, 1989-2005; Gov Correctional Facilities, 1991-92; vpres, Full Gospel Bus Men's Fel Int, Ft Drum, Charthage Chap, 1985, pres, 1986; chmn worship comn, Ft Drum Gospel Servs; speaker Full Gospel Bus Men's Fel Int; bd mem, New Gate Prison Ministry; bd sch, Faith Fel Christian Sch, 1990-95, 1990-; bd mem, Barnabas Ministries, 1997-; steering comt, Communities That Care, Jefferson County, NY, 1998; bd mem, Alcohol & Substance Abuse Coun, 1998; Rotary Int Watertown, NY Noon Club, 2005-. **Honors/Awds:** Omega Psi Phi Fraternity Undergrad Scholarship, 1962; Grad Scholarship, 1963; American Spirit Honor Award, Ft Jackson, SC, 1975; Administration Ft Ben Harrison IN; first Annual Freedom Fund Award, Watertown & Jefferson County Nat Asn Advan Colored People, 1989; USA Pastor of the Year, DaySpring Cards, 1998; Dewitt Clinton Masonic Award, 1999. **Special Achievements:** 8 trips to Haiti as part of Barnabas Ministries pastor training in Haiti, 1997-. **Military Serv:** AUS, sgt First class, 1975-88; Army Commendation Medal, first Oak Leaf Cluster; Army Achievement Medals; Certificates Appreciation; Meritorious Service Medal, 1988. **Home Addr:** PO Box 321, Great Bend, NY 13643, **Home Phone:** (315)775-9785. **Business Addr:** Pastor, City of Refuge Christian Church, 32500-32504 New York State Hwy suite 3, PO Box 321, Great Bend, NY 13643, **Business Phone:** (315)493-6463.

JORDAN, JOSEPHINE E C
Transportation consultant. **Personal:** Born Dec 13, 1935, Philadelphia, PA; daughter of Clarence Connor and Josephine Connor; married Rev Harry A Sr (deceased). **Educ:** Allied Corp, bus cert, 1971. **Career:** Amtrak, res & info agt. **Orgs:** Daughter Isis, 1983-; Heroines Jericho, 1983-; Past Worthy Matron, Hadassah Chap No 91 OES, 1985-87; Ct Cyrenes, 1987-; Order Golden Circle; Past Royal Perfect Matron Faith & Fidelity, Ladies Circle of Perfection; Past Dist Dep, Past Dist Lectr, 4th OES Dist. **Home Addr:** 2202 Airacobra St, Levittown, PA 19057.

JORDAN, JOY A
Dentist. **Personal:** Daughter of Eugene. **Educ:** Howard Univ Sch Dentist, DDS. **Career:** Pvt pract, Cleveland, OH. **Orgs:** Pres, Nat

Dent Asn; Adv Bd, Church & Dwight's Arm & Hammer Oral Care Div; rep, Greater Cleveland Dent Soc; pres, East Cleveland City Schs Bd Educ; Am Asn Women Dentists; Am Dent Asn; secy, Black Women's Polit Action Comt; coun woman, East Cleveland City Coun. **Honors/Awds:** Martin Luther King Jr Award, NAACP; Women of Achievement, YWCA, 2004. *

JORDAN, KENNETH ULYS
Educator. **Personal:** Born Apr 10, 1944, South Pittsburg, TN; divorced; children: Kenneth II & Michael. **Educ:** Univ Tenn, BS, 1966; Vanderbilt Law Sch, JD, 1974. **Career:** Gen Foods Corp, employ specialist, 1970-71; Nat Alliance Bus Men, loan ed exec, 1970-71; Fair Employment Practices Clinic, assoc dir, 1974; Vanderbilt Univ Law Sch, asst dean, 1975-76, opportunity develop officer & dir, 1977-81; Meharry Medical Col, exec asst pres & interim vpres, 1981-82, vpres admin & gen coun, 1981-83; Air Univ, Air Command & Staff Col, resident stud, 1983-84; US Dept Justice; Justice Mgt Div, staff, 1986-87; Governors Task Force Housing, exec asst, 1987-88; Air, Mil Dept Ten, staff, 1988-95; Nat Comt Employer Support Guard & Reserve, dir, 1997-2000; City Atlanta, chief operating officer, 2001-. **Orgs:** Family & C Servs; Nashville Urban League; Univ Club Nashville; Nashville Bar Found; United Way Middle Tenn; Tenn State Museum Fund; Vanderbilt Univ Credit Union; Asn Vanderbilt Alumni; Napier-Looby Bar Asn; East Coast Chap; AMVETS; Am Legion; Air Force Assoc; VFW; bd, Nat transportation Safety, 1995-97; Vanderbilt Bar Asn; pres, Law Stud Civil Rights Res Coun; Black Am Law Stud Asn; dir, Tenn Housing Develop Agency, 1987-90; Tenn Task Force Supply Minority Teachers, 1988-95; Napier-Looby Bar Asn; Vet Foreign Wars. **Honors/Awds:** US Law Week Award, Vanderbilt Univ Law Sch, 1974; Performance Award, Nat Transportation Safety Bd, 1995-97; Walter P Murray Distinguished Alumnus Award, Asn Vanderbilt Black Alumni, 1995. **Military Serv:** Minot AFB, second lt, 1966-68; Udorn Royal Thai AFB, first lt, 1968-69; Mac Dill AFB, coordr, 1969-70. **Home Addr:** 224 M St SW, Washington, DC 20024-3602. **Business Addr:** Chief Operating Officer, City of Atlanta, 55 Trinity Ave SW, Atlanta, GA 30335-0300, **Business Phone:** (404)330-6100.

JORDAN, KEVIN
Baseball player. **Personal:** Born Oct 9, 1969, San Francisco, CA. **Educ:** Univ Nebr. **Career:** Baseball player (retired);Brisbane Bundits, 1993-97; Philadelphia Phillies, 1995-2001; Cincinnati Reds, 2002; Detroit Tigers, 2003. *

JORDAN, LEROY A
Administrator. **Personal:** Born Dec 27, 1941, Murphysboro, IL; married Johnetta Williams; children: Laura, Loralean & Jennifer. **Educ:** So IL Univ, BS, Elem Educ, 1964; Sangamon State Univ, MA, Educ Admin, 1972; Ill State Univ, ABD, 1997. **Career:** Hopkins Park Pembroke Township Sch, teacher, 1964-65; Sch Dist 186 Springfield IL, teacher adult educ & prin, 1965-69; State Bd Educ Div Vocational Tech Educ, consult res & develop, 1969-72; Sangamon State Univ, asst dir applied studies, 1972-75, dir applied studies & experimental learning, 1975-81, dean innovative & experimental studies, 1982-85, asst supvr, 1990-91, dir, res & develop, 1992-98; Inst Recovery Racisms, facilitator, currently. **Orgs:** IL Asn Sch; educ adv com,Springfield Jr League; corp bd dir, Meml Hosp Springfield Jr League; corp bd dir, Meml Hosp; pres bd educ, Springfield; Nat Sch Bd Asn, 1976-82; pres bd dir, Statesmen Drum & Bugle Corps, 1978-81; Nat Com Campaign Human develop Nat Cath Conf, 1979-82. **Honors/Awds:** Outstanding Leadership Award, Black Caucus Sangamon State Univ, 1979-80; Cert Appreciation, Bd Control Springfield Area Voc Ctr, 1979-80; Outstanding Citizen, Springfield, IL Urban League, 1980. **Business Addr:** Facilitator, Institute for Recovery from Racisms, PO Box 13559, Detroit, MI 48213, **Business Phone:** (313)521-7777.

JORDAN, MARJORIE W.
Manager. **Personal:** Born Jan 12, 1924, New Orleans, LA; widowed; children: Cornelius, Emmett. **Educ:** Dillard Univ, BA, 1944; Univ Chicago; Univ Cincinnati; Col Comn Serv Comn Health Adminr. **Career:** Cincinnati Health Dept, coordr health progs; Housing Opportunities Made Equal, dir. **Orgs:** Nat Asn Black Soc Workers; OH Pub Health Asn; Prof Soc Pub Health Workers OH; Nat Conf Soc Welfare; mem Bd, Nat Non-Profit Housing Corp; bd mem, sec, exec com mem 7 Hills Neighborhood Houses Inc; exec com, Easy Riders Inc; bd, Urban League; ARC; Am Cancer Soc; co-chmn, Consumer Affairs Comn Fed; exec bd, chmn, Consumer Forum; exec com, Hosusing Opportunities Made Equal Inc; Unitarian Universalist Serv Com Bd; Womans City Club; Social Serv Assn. **Honors/Awds:** Recipient Service Award, Am Cancer Society, 1972.

JORDAN, MICHAEL
Basketball player, entrepreneur. **Personal:** Born Feb 17, 1963, Brooklyn, NY; son of James R Jordan Sr and Deloris Peoples; married Juanita Vanoy, Sep 2, 1989 (divorced 2006); children: Jeffrey Michael, Marcus James & Jasmine Mickael. **Educ:** Univ NC, BA, geog. **Career:** Basketball player (retired), entrepreneur; Chicago Bulls, guard, 1984-93, 1995-99; Chicago White Sox, minor league player, 1994-95; Launched own line of athletic clothing, JORDAN Brand, a subdivision of NIKE, 1997; Wash Wizards, part owner, 1999-2001, shooting guard, 2001-03; Charlotte Bobcats, part owner, currently. **Honors/Awds:** NBA Most Valuable Player, 1988, 1991, 1992, 1996; All-NBA First Team, 1987-93, 1996, 1997; NBA Defensive Player of the Year, 1988; NBA All-Defensive First Team, 1988-93, 1996, 1997; NBA Finals Most Valuable Player, 1991, 1992, 1993, 1996, 1997; NBA All-Star, 1985, 1987-93, 1996-98; NBA All-Star Most Valuable Player, 1988, 1996; NBA Rookie of the Year, 1985; Gold Medal, US Olympic Basketball Team, 1984, 1992; founder, Michael Jordan Celebrity Golf Classic, to raise money for United Negro Col Fund, 1989; Jim Thorpe Award, 1992; Award for the Century's Greatest Basketball Player, Sports Illustrated, 1999; Greatest Athlete of the Century, ESPN, 1999; Jackie Robinson Foundation Award. **Special Achievements:** Selected as one of the 50 Greatest Players in NBA History, 1996; selected as 100 Most Powerful People In Sports, Number One, 1997; named to Greatest Chicagoans of the Century; Michael Jordan's statue, United Ctr, Chicago. **Business Addr:** Part Owner, Charlotte Bobcats, 333 E Trade St, Charlotte, NC 28202, **Business Phone:** (704)688-8600.

JORDAN, MICHELLE DENISE
Lawyer. **Personal:** Born Oct 29, 1954, Chicago, IL; daughter of John A and Margaret O; divorced. **Educ:** Loyola Univ, BA (magna cum laude), 1974; Univ Mich Law Sch, JD, 1977. **Career:** States Atty Off Cook Co, asst state atty, 1977-82; pvt law pract, 1982-84, 2003-; Ill Atty Gen Off, trial atty trial div, dep chief environ control div, 1984-90; Hopkins & Sutter Law Firm, partner, 1991-93; US Environ Protection Agency Region five, dep regional adminr, 1994-2001; US Dept Justice, spec asst US atty, 1998-2001; Rainbow/Push Coalition, nat dir fund develop, 2001-03; Ill Dept Pub Aid, asst dir, 2003; sole Practitioner, 2003-. **Orgs:** Chicago Bar Asn, 1977-, Cook County Bar Asn, 1977-, Ill State Bar Asn, 1978-; Nat Bar Asn, 1980-, Prof Women's Auxiliary Provident Hosp, 1981-82; bd mem, Loyola Univ Alumni Asn, 1984-87; subcomt co-chmn, Chicago Bar Asn, Young Bar Asn, 1986-87; investr, investigations, 1986-87, Hearing Div, 1987-88, Chicago Bar Asn, Judicial Evaluation Comt; Child Witness Proj, Task Force, 1987-88; environmental law comt mem, Chicago Bar Asn, 1989; Art Inst Chicago, 1990. **Honors/Awds:** Operation PUSH Womens Day Award, 1978; instr, Chicago Bar Asn, Young Lawyers Intensive Trial Pract Prog, 1986; America's Top 100 Business & Professional Woman, editorial bd Dollars & Sense Mag, 1988; instr, Ill Atty General's Training Prog, 1988; Susan E Olive Nat EEO Award, US EPA, 1996. **Business Phone:** (312)886-9262.

JORDAN, MONTELL DUSEAN
Singer. **Personal:** Born Dec 3, 1968, Los Angeles, CA; children: Sydney & Skyler. **Educ:** Pepperdine Univ, BS, commun. **Career:** Def Jam, vocalist; Songs: "This Is How We Do It"; "Falling"; "I Like, What's On Tonight"; "Supa Star", 2003; Albums: This is How We Do It, 1995; Let's Ride, 1998; Get It On. Tonite, 1999; Montell Jordan, 2002; Life after def, 2003; Freedom Writers, 2007; How She Move, 2007; Step Brothers, 2008. **Orgs:** Kappa Alpha Psi Fraternity. **Special Achievements:** First Def Jam R&B artist to hit Number 1 on pop chart, This Is How We DoIt, 1995; 1995 MTV Video Music Award nominations and 1995 Grammy Awardnomination. **Business Phone:** (212)229-5200.*

JORDAN, PATRICIA
Educator. **Personal:** Born Sep 26, 1951, New York, NY; daughter of Clifford James and Juanita James; married Jack M, Apr 1, 1992; children: Alexa Juanita. **Educ:** Vassar Col, BA, 1972; City Col, MS, 1976; Hofstra Univ, PhD, 1991. **Career:** Cross High Sch, math instr, 1972; Lee High Sch, math instr, 1972-73; Park East High Sch, math instr & advisor, 1973-74; Martin Luther King Jr High Sch, math instr & dean, 1974-76; Malverne High Sch, math instr, 1976-80; Roslyn High Sch, math instr, 1980-2001. **Orgs:** Asn Black Psychologist; NAACP; adv bd mem, NYC Dept Juvenile Justice. **Honors/Awds:** American Teacher Award for Mathematics, Walt Disney Co, 1993; New York State Teacher of the Year, NY State Dept Educ, 1993; Humanitarian Award, Lakeview, NY-NAACP, 1993.

JORDAN, PATRICIA CARTER
Government official. **Personal:** Born Jan 23, 1946, Washington, DC; daughter of Nelver Sherman and Olivette Glaude; married Richard O Jordan Jr, Aug 21, 1965; children: Orisha Katrina Jordan. **Educ:** Howard Univ, Wa, DC, BA, sociol; Top 40 Mgt Training Prog, City NY, grad; Columbia Univ Grad Sch Arts & Scis, grad. **Career:** City NY Bd Educ, asst to deputy chancellor; City NY High Div, mgt consult; Communs Inst, NY, commun supvr; Foundation Change Inter-Racial Books Children, consult & instr; Pub Educ Asn, consult; US Dept Justice, Community Rels Serv, community rels specialist & trainer; Hunter Col Dept Urban Affairs, res asst & adjunct lectr; HARYOU-ACT Assoc, res assoc; Columbia Univ Grad Sch Arts & Sci, res & teaching asst; City NY Housing Preserv & Develop & Off Housing Mgt & Sales, admin mgr. **Orgs:** Dir res & develop, Black Citizens Fair Media, 1971-; Chairperson Bd dir, Upper Manhattan Mental Health Inc; bd mem, Found Minority Interest Media. **Honors/Awds:** Author, "Youth in the Ghetto-A Study of the Consequences of Powerlessness and a Blueprint for Change", HARYOU-ACT, 1964. *

JORDAN, PAUL SCOTT. **See JORDAN, RICKY.**

JORDAN, RANDY LOMENT
Football player, football coach. **Personal:** Born Jun 6, 1970, Manson, NC; married Romonda; children: Raven, Jalen & Justin. **Educ:** Univ NC, BS, speech & commun, 1993. **Career:** Football player (retired), Football coach; NC Univ, 1989-92; Los Angeles Raiders, 1993; Jacksonville Jaguars, running back, 1995-97; Oakland Raiders, 1998-2002; Oakland Raiders, special teams asst coach, 2003; Nebr Cornhuskers, asst coach & running backs, 2004-07; Texas A&M Univ, running backs coach, 2008-. **Orgs:** Fel, Christian Athletes. **Honors/Awds:** NFL Unsung Hero Award, 2001; Ed Block Courage Award,2001. *

JORDAN, REGGIE
Basketball player. **Personal:** Born Jan 26, 1969, Chicago, IL. **Educ:** Southwestern Univ; NMex State Univ, jour. **Career:** Basketball player (retired); Grand Rapids Hoops, Conn Basketball Asn, guard, 1991-93; Yakima Sun Kings, Conn Basketball Asn, 1993-94, 1994-95; Los Angeles Lakers, 1994; Sioux Falls Skyforce, CBA, 1995-96; Atlanta Hawks, 1996; Portland Trail Blazers, 1996; Minn Timberwolves, 1996-99; Wash Wizards, guard, 2000. **Honors/Awds:** All-League first team, Conn Basketball Asn, 1996; All-Defensive team, Conn Basketball Asn, 1993, 1996.

JORDAN, RICHARD
Football player. **Personal:** Born Dec 1, 1974, Holdenville, OK; son of Ray and Jannie; children: 5. **Educ:** Mo Southern State Univ. **Career:** Football player (retired), coach; Detroit Lions, linebacker, 1997-02; radio sports personality; local high sch, coach, currently. **Honors/Awds:** MIAA Defensive Most Valuable Player, 1996; MSSU Athletic Hall of Fame, 2006.

JORDAN, RICKY (PAUL SCOTT JORDAN)
Baseball player. **Personal:** Born May 26, 1965, Richmond, CA. **Career:** Baseball player (retired), baseball coach; Philadelphia Phillies, infielder, 1988-94; Calif Angels, 1995; Seattle Mariners, 1996; Ronald Reagan High Sch, coach, 2002. **Orgs:** Diabetes Help; Kids Basketball Camp; Baseball Camp; Homeless People. **Honors/Awds:** Player of the Year, Phillies Orgn, 1987. **Special Achievements:** Film appearance: High Hopes: The Anatomy of a Winner, 2003; Thirsty first National League Player to hit Home run in First Major League At Bat.

JORDAN, ROBERT
Educator, pianist. **Personal:** Born May 2, 1940, Chattanooga, TN; son of Ira Jordan and Mamie McCamey Jordan. **Educ:** Eastman Sch Music, BM, 1962; Juilliard Sch, MS, 1965; Goethe Inst German Lang, 1965; Hochschulc fur Musik, Germany, 1967; Sorbonne, Paris, 1969. **Career:** Triad Presentations Inc, bd dir, adv coun; Morgan State Univ, artist-in-residence, 1976-78; Univ Del, artist-in-residence, 1979; State Univ NY, Fredonia, Sch Music, prof piano, 1980-2004, asst to dir, 1988-89, Kasling lectr, 1996, prof emer, 2004-; Northern Mich Univ, vis Martin Luther King Prof, 1987; Univ Mich, Ann Arbor, vis prof, 1991. **Orgs:** Inaugurated Minority Scholar Fund, Univ Del, 1979. **Honors/Awds:** Fulbright Scholar, Ger, 1965-67; recipient, four different awards, 1975; Chancellors Award for Excellence in Teaching, State Univ NY. **Special Achievements:** One of 13 pianists chosen nationally to commission a composition from an American composer & give world premiere at Kennedy Center, 1976; established the Mamie and Ira Jordan Minority Music Scholarship and Scholastic Achievement award at SUNY-Fredoria, 1997; concert tour of Japan, Oct 1999; Appearances in recital and with orchestra on four continents; appeared as soloist with Prague Symphony, Bavarian Radio Orchestra, Buffalo Philharmonic, Baltimore Orchestra, Chattanooga Orchestra, Erie Chamber Orchestra; recitals in capital cities, including appearances at Avery Fisher Hall, Alice Tully Hall, Kennedy Center; Silver Jubilee concert celebrations in Suriname, South America, Paris, France-,and USA; Orion Master Recordings; recent appearances at the Festival in LeTouquet. **Business Addr:** Professor Emeritus, State University of New York, School of Music, 280 Cent Ave, Fredonia, NY 14063, **Business Phone:** (716)673-3111.

JORDAN, ROBERT A.
Social worker. **Personal:** Born Dec 4, 1932, Atlanta, GA; married Edna Fraley. **Educ:** Clark Col, AB, 1958; Atlanta Univ, MA, 1969; Univ GA, attended 1973. **Career:** Fulton County Sch Syst, teacher, 1961-66; Atlanta Pub Sch Syst, teacher, 1966-72, reading teacher, 1972-, social worker, 1972; Jazz Radio Prog, Stat WYZE, co-host. **Orgs:** Bd dir, Atlanta Asn Educ(past vpres); Ga Educ Asn; Nat Educ Asn; Prof Rights Comn Asn Am Educators; educ chmn, Forward Ga Assembly; pres, Jazz Disciples Club; State Dem Party; Phi Beta Sigma; bd trustees, Ebenezer Baptist Church. **Special Achievements:** Articles written "Parent Input In Publ Schs" & "Why SAT Scores Are Low"; appeared on Radio (WRNG) & TV (ch 5, 2, 11, 30); collector of Jazz Records five thousand albums; interviewed for article "State of Jazz in Atlanta", Constitution Nwspaper; aauthor article "Profile of a VIP"; article

"What's Wrong with Education". **Military Serv:** AUS pfc 1953-55. **Business Addr:** 1890 Bankhead Hwy, Atlanta, GA 30318.*

JORDAN, DR. ROBERT HOWARD, JR.
Television journalist. **Personal:** Born Aug 31, 1943, Atlanta, GA; son of Robert H and Millicent Dobbs; married Sharon E Lundy, Dec 20, 1970; children: Karen Millicent. **Educ:** Roosevelt Univ, Chicago, Ill, BA, 1975; Northeastern Ill Univ, MA, speech, 1994; Loyola Univ, PhD, philos educ, 2000. **Career:** WSM TV, Nashville, Tenn, reporter & announcer, 1970-73; WGN TV, Chicago IL, reporter & anchor, 1973-78, 1980-, "News at Nine", weekend anchor, currently; CBS News Midwest Bur, Chicago, Ill, reporter, 1978-80; Jordan & Jordan Commun Inc, founder & owner, 1997-. **Orgs:** Am Fedn Radio & TV Artists, 1972-; Chicago Asn Black Journalists, 1983-; bd dir, John G Shedd Aquarium, 1987-; bd dir, Evanston Hosp Corp, 1987-; Chicago Lung Asn; Chicago Sinfonietta Aquarium; Safer Found; Night Ministry. **Honors/Awds:** Black Achievers of Industry Award, YMCA Metrop Chicago, 1975; Appreciation Award, Chicago Dent Soc, 1976; Master of Ceremony, Black & Hispanic Achievers Indust, 1985-89. **Special Achievements:** Many writing credits including two screenplays, Anthony's Key & Multi-Man, written articles for the Chicago Tribune. **Military Serv:** AUS, surgical asst, spc 4th class, outstanding trainee, company D, 9th BN US-ATCI, 1965-68. **Business Addr:** Anchor, Reporter, WGN-TV, 2501 Bradley Pl, Chicago, IL 60618-4718, **Business Phone:** (773)528-2311.

JORDAN, SANDRA D
Educator. **Personal:** Born Dec 3, 1951, Philadelphia, PA; married Byron N, Jul 21, 1973; children: Nedra Catherine & Byron Neal II. **Educ:** Wilberforce Univ, BSEd, 1973; Univ Pittsburgh Law Sch, JD, 1979. **Career:** US Dept Justice, asst US atty, 1979-88; US Dept Independent Coun, Iran Contra, assoc coun, 1988-91; Univ Pitt Law Sch, assoc prof law, prof law, currently. **Orgs:** Homer S Brown Law Asn, 1979-; Nat Bar Asn, 1979-; disciplinary bd, Supreme Ct Pa, 1990-94; vice chair, Pa Judicial Conduct Bd, 1994-. **Honors/Awds:** US Attorney General Special Commendation, 1984; Exceptionally Qualified for Judiciary, Allegheny County Bar Asn, 1992. **Special Achievements:** Published "Classified Information & Conflicts," Columbia Law Review vol 91, No 7, 1991. **Home Addr:** 100 Dewey St, Pittsburgh, PA 15218, **Home Phone:** (412)241-4211. **Business Addr:** Professor of Law, University of Pittsburgh School of Law, Rm 529 3900 Forbes Ave, Pittsburgh, PA 15260, **Business Phone:** (412)648-1988.

JORDAN, STANLEY
Composer, jazz musician. **Personal:** Born Jul 31, 1959, Chicago, IL; married Sandra kilpatrick; children: Julia. **Educ:** Princeton Univ, BA, music theory & compos, 1981; Ariz State Univ, music ther. **Career:** Jazz guitarist & composer; Sedona Books & Music, owner, currently; Albums : "Touch Sensitive", 1983; " Magic Touch", 1985; " One Night With Blue Note Preserved"; "Hideaway", 1986; " Standards, Volume 1", 1987; "Blind Date", 1987; "Flying Home", 1988; "Morning Desire"; "Artists Against ApartheiSunCity"; "RU Tuff Enough"; "Cornucopia'', 1990; "Stolen Moments", 1991; "Stanley Jordan Live in New York", 1998; "Relaxing Music for Difficult Situations I", 2003; "Ragas", 2004; "Dreams Of Peace", 2004. **Orgs:** Am Music Ther Asn. **Honors/Awds:** Award, Reno Jazz Festival; two Grammy nominations. **Special Achievements:** Has played with Dizzy Gillespie, Benny Carter, Quicy Jones, MichalUrbaniak, and Richie Cole. **Business Addr:** Jazz Musician, c/o The Management Ark, 116 Village Blvd, Princeton, NJ 08540.

JORDAN, STEVE RUSSELL
Football player, manager. **Personal:** Born Jan 10, 1961, Phoenix, AZ; married Anita. **Educ:** Brown Univ, BS, civil eng, 1982. **Career:** Football player (retired), Manager; Minn Vikings, tight end, 1982-94; Ryan Co Inc, sr project mgr, dir construction, currently. **Orgs:** Bd fel, Brown Univ; adv bd mem, Nat Football Found; Col Hall Fame; Phx Thunder birds; bd dir, Brown Sports Found, 1996-; chmn, Leukemia Golf Classic; bd mem, Cystic Fibrosis Found; Nat Missing Children's Found; Multiple Sclerosis Soc; Steve R Jordan Endowed Scholar Minority Athletes, Brown Univ, 2000. **Honors/Awds:** NCAA Silver Anniversary Award, 2006. **Special Achievements:** Pro Bowl, 1986, 1987, 1988, 1989, 1990 & 1991. **Business Addr:** Director of Construction, Ryan Companies US Inc, One N Central Ave Suite 1300, Phoenix, AZ 85004-4418, **Business Phone:** (602)322-6100.

JORDAN, REV. TERNAE T
Clergy. **Personal:** Born Dec 3, 1955, Chattanooga, TN; son of Melvin and Maggie Jordan; married Angela Faye Jordan, Dec 24, 1977; children: Ternae Jordan Jr, Dejuan Jordan & JaMichael Jordan. **Educ:** Univ Tennessee, BS, Business Education, 1977. **Career:** Johnson & Johnson, Territorial Sales mgr, 1978-79; Chattanooga Sch System, trainer/teacher/coordinator; Natl Life & Mutual of Omaha Ins Co, sales agent, 1981-83; KBL Enterprises, exec vice pres, 1983-88; Greater Progressive Baptist Church, sr pastor, 1989-; Stop the Madness Inc, founder & pres, 1993-2001, Value-Based Initiative, prog dir, 2001-; Unlimited Dimensions Management Corp, chief exec officer, 2002-. **Orgs:** Paul Clarke Foundation, 1993-; Stop the Madness Inc, founder, 1993-; Park and Recreation Comners; Community Outreach Advisory Coun, Ivy Tech College; Harvard School Divinity, participant, 2000. **Honors/Awds:** Am Institute of Public Service, Jefferson Awd, 1993; Journal Gazette Newspaper, Citizen of the Year, 1997; NAACP-Fort Wayne, Elizabeth Dobynes Awd, 1998. **Business Addr:** Senior Pastor, Greater Progressive Baptist Church, 2215 John St, Fort Wayne, IN 46803, **Business Phone:** (260)744-6235.

JORDAN, THURMAN
Accountant. **Personal:** Born Dec 2, 1938, Harrisburg, IL; son of Joseph and Lutishia; married Teiko Ann; children: Eric, Neal & Philip. **Educ:** Roosevelt Univ, BSBA, 1966; Univ Chicago, MBA, 1982; Univ Ill, CPA, 1972. **Career:** Unisource Network Serv, pres & chief exec officer; Arthur Andersen & Co, audit mgr, 1966-76. Signode Corp, vpres, controller, 1976-88; Chicago Osteop Health Systs, vpres & chief financial officer, 1989-94; Financial consult, 1994-95; Meris Labs Inc, sr vpres & chief financial officer, 1995-97; Spectra llc & Detroit Chassis, vpres & chief financial officer; Magnys Innovative Solutions, chief financial officer. **Orgs:** Ill Soc CPA's Am Inst CPA; Alumni Chicago Forum; former mem, Chicago United; vice chmn, Oper & Effectiveness Comn; Agency Serv Com Comn Fund; bd mem, United Way Chicago, Evanston Art Ctr; bd mem, Bd Trustees, Gould Acad; bd dirs, Northlight Theater; Econ Club Chicago & MAPI. pres, Evanston Art Ctr. **Honors/Awds:** Black Achiever Award, YMCA, 1974. **Military Serv:** AUS, PFC, 1961; Outstanding Trainee Award. **Home Addr:** 2743 Ridge Ave, Evanston, IL 60201, **Home Phone:** (708)491-0393. **Business Phone:** (313)571-2100.

JORDAN, VERNON EULION
Executive, lawyer. **Personal:** Born Aug 15, 1935, Atlanta, GA; son of Vernon and Mary; children: 9; married Shirley; children: Vickee J Adams. **Educ:** DePauw Univ, BA, 1957; Howard Univ Law Sch, JD, 1960; Harvard Univ, Inst Polit, John F Kennedy Sch Govt, fel, 1969. **Career:** Nat Urban League Inc, pres & chief exec officer, 1972-81; United Negro Col Fund, exec dir; Voter Educ Proj, Southern Regional Coun, dir; US Off Econ Opportunity, atty, consult; Nat Asn Advan Colored People, GA field dir; GA & AK, pvt legal pract; Akin, Gump, Strauss, Hauer & Feld, LLP, sr exec partner, 1982-99, of-coun, 2000-; dir, Am Express Co; dir, Dow Jones & CoInc; dir, J C Penney Co Inc; dir, Sara Lee Corp; dir, Xerox Corp; Lazard Freres & Co LLC, sr managing dir & bd dir, 2000-. **Orgs:** Am Revolution Di-Centennial Comn, 1972; Presidential Clemency Bd, 1974; Adv Coun Social Security, 1974; Secretary State's Adv Comt South Africa,1985; Points Light Initiative Found, President's Adv Comt, 1989; trustee, DePauw Univ; trustee, Howard Univ; trustee, LBJ Found; trustee, Nat Acad Found; Intl Adv Comt Daimler-Chrysler; Alfalfa Club; AAAS; Metropolitan Club; Univ Club; bd gov, The Joint Ctr Polit & Econ Studies, 1998-; sradv, Shinsei Bank Ltd; Iraq Study Group; Omega Psi Phi; Sigma Pi Phi; Coun on Foreign Relations. **Honors/Awds:** Barnard Medal of Distinction; Spingarn Medal, 2001; Civil Rights Trumpet Award, 2003; Received honorary degrees from over 55 Cols & universities throughout the US. **Special Achievements:** Author, Vernon Can Read!, 2002. **Business Addr:** Senior Managing Director, Lazard Freres & Co LLC, 30 Rockefeller Plz, New York, NY 10020, **Business Phone:** (212)632-6000.

JORDAN, DR. WILBERT CORNELIOUS
Physician. **Personal:** Born Sep 11, 1944, Wheatley, AR; son of William and Annie Mae. **Educ:** Harvard Col, AB, 1966; Case Western Res Univ, MD, 1971; UCLA, MPH, 1978. **Career:** Ctr Dis Control, epidemiologist, 1973-76; US Pub Health Svcs, lt comdr, 1973-78; Los Angeles County, area pub health chief, 1979-83; Drew Med Sch, assoc prof, 1979-87; King-Drew Med Ctr, dir grad educ; UCLA, asst prof, pub health; King-Drew Med Ctr, Oasis Clin, dir & founder, currently. **Orgs:** Life mem, NAACP 1978-; sec bd PSRO Area XXIII, 1980-84; chmn bd, Minority AIDS Project LA City, 1984-87; bd mem, NAMME 1984-87; Coalition Against Black Exploitation 1985-87; chmn bd, Sallie Martin Found, 1986-87; dir, Nat Conv Gospel Choirs & Choruses Inc; Undersea Med Soc; Am Venereal Dis Asn, Assoc Am Med Col, Nat Med Asn; pres Inglewood Physicians Assoc; liaison Nat Assoc Minority med Educrs; chmn, Black Los Angeles AIDS Comn; ed, S Cent AIDS Newsletter; bd dir, AIDS Res Alliance. **Honors/Awds:** Outstanding Physician of Year, SNMA, 1973; Recognition Award, NAMME, 1984; Recognition Award, NAMME, 1988; Recognition for Service, Warwick Found, 1990; Recognition for Service, Brotherland Crusade, 1991; Physician of the Year, Charles R Drew Med Soc, 1992; Man of the Year, Los Angeles Sentinel Newspaper, 1992; Special Humanitarian Award, Tau Eta Psi Nursing Sorority, 1992. **Business Addr:** Medical Director, King Drew Medical Center, 12021 S Wilmington Oasis Clinic, Los Angeles, CA 90059, **Business Phone:** (310)668-4213.

JORDAN, WILLIAM CHESTER
Educator. **Personal:** Born Apr 7, 1948, Chicago, IL; son of Johnnie Parker and Marguerite Jane; married Christine Kenyon Hershey, May 30, 1970; children: Victoria Marie, John Mark, Clare Kenyon & Lorna Janice. **Educ:** Ripon Col, AB, 1969, DHL, 2001; Princeton Univ, PhD, 1973. **Career:** Princeton Univ, instr, 1973-74, lectr, 1974-75, from asst to assoc prof, 1975-86, prof hist, 1986-; Univ Pa, vis lectr, 1981-82; Swarthmore Col, vis assoc prof, 1985; Dickinson Col, morgan lectr, 1985; Behrman, sr fel humanities, 1989-94; Shelby Cullom Davis Ctr Historical Studies, dir, 1994-99. **Orgs:** Counr, Medieval Acad Am, 1998-2001; assesseur, Int Comt Hist Sci, 2000-; fel Medieval Acad Am; Am Historical Asn; Am Coun Learned Soc; Am Philosophical Soc; Soc Study French Hist; Soc Study Crusades & Latin E; Haskins Soc. **Honors/Awds:** Haskins Medal, Medieval Acad Am, 2000; Teaching Award, Princeton Univ; Behrman Award, Princeton Univ. **Special Achievements:** Author: Louis IX and the Challenge of the Crusade, 1979; From Servitude to Freedom, 1986; The French Monarchy and the Jews, 1989; Women and Credit, 1993; The Great Famine, 1996; Europe in the High Middle Ages, 2001; contributed few publications. **Business Addr:** Professor, Princeton University, Department of History, 232 Dickinson Hall, Princeton, NJ 08544, **Business Phone:** (609)258-4165.

JOSEPH, ABRAHAM
Accountant. **Personal:** Born Mar 12, 1954, Kingsland, GA; son of Abraham Sr and Maude R; married Denese Joseph, May 26, 1990; children: Arika, Bianca & Andre. **Educ:** Morris Brown Col, BS, 1977; Troy State Univ, MS, personnel mgmt, 1983. **Career:** Ga Dept Revenue, tax auditor, 1977-85; Army Audit Agency, auditor, 1985-87; AJ's Acct & Tax Serv, owner & acct, 1987-; Dept Navy, supvr auditor, 1988-; Black Data Processing Assocs, nat vpres finance, currently. **Orgs:** Alpha Phi Alpha, 1973-; Morris Brown Col Alumni, 1977-; treas, Camden Co Black Bus Asn, 1987-; acct/trustee, St Paul AME Church, 1988-; nat asst treas, Blacks Govt, 1988-2001; bd mem, Camden Kings Bay Chamber, 1990-92; Nat Asn Black Accts, 2004-; Am Soc Military Comptrollers, 1987-; Asn Govt Accts, 2000-; bd mem, Black Data Processing Assocs, Austin Chap, TX; life mem, Blacks In Govt; secy, Sons Allen Grant AME. Worship Ctr, Austin, TX; treas, Kinlaw Community Ctr. **Honors/Awds:** Community Service Award, Morris Brown Col Alumni, 1990; Business Award, Camden County Black Bus Asn, 1992. **Home Phone:** (912)729-5127. **Business Addr:** National Vice President of Finance, Black Data Processing Associates, 9500 Arena Dr Suite 350, Largo, MD 20774, **Business Phone:** 800-727-2372.

JOSEPH, DAVID E
Executive, chief executive officer, president (organization). **Career:** Specialized Servs Inc, chmn & ceo, currently. **Business Addr:** Chairman, Chief Executive Officer, Specialized Services Inc, 23077 Greenfield Rd Suite 470, Southfield, MI 48075, **Business Phone:** (248)557-1030.*

JOSEPH, JAMES ALFRED
Chief executive officer, educator. **Personal:** Born Mar 12, 1935, Opelousas, LA; married Mary Braxton; children: Jeffrey & Denise. **Educ:** Southern Univ, BA, 1956; Yale Univ, BD, MA, 1963; SE Univ, LLD, 1982; Univ MD, DPS, 1984. **Career:** Claremont Col, chaplain & prof, 1969-70; Irwin-Sweeney-Miller Found, exec dir, 1970-72; Cummins Engine Co, vpres, 1972-77; US Dept Interior, undersec, 1977-81; Yale Divinity Sch, vis prof, 1981-82; Coun Found, pres, 1982-95; Duke Univ, Southern Africa Ctr Leadership & pub values, exec dir, Pract Pub Policy Studies, prof, currently. **Orgs:** Pitzer Col, 1972-77; chmn, US Comn Northern Marianas, 1980-86; bd dir, Cummins Engine Found, 1981-87; Colonial Williamsburg, 1981-87; Coun Foreign Rel, 1981-85; bd Visitors, Duke Univ 1981-83; adv Comt, US Dept State, 1982-84; bd dirs, Africare 1982-; Hague Club, 1983-87; bd dir, Brooking Inst, 1985-; Salzbert sem, 1985-; Atlantic Coun, 1985-; UN Assoc,1986-; adv comt, Nat Acad Sci, 1982-83; bd dir, C Defense Fund, 1983-; Leader-in-Residence, Hart Leadership Prog; the chmnEmeritus, Childrens Defense Fund; dir, Management and Training Corporation; Bd mem, Advisors of the Kenan Inst Ethics, Duke Univ. **Honors/Awds:** Public Service Award, Yale Afro Am Alumni, 1976; Business Person of the Year, Nat Asn Concerned Bus Studies, 1974. **Special Achievements:** Co-editor, Three Perspectives on Ethnicity, 1972; Author: The Charitable Impulse, 1989; Remaking America, 1995; Ambassador to South Africa from January 1996 to November 1999; First and only US ambassador to present his credentials to President Nelson Mandela. **Military Serv:** Med Serv Corps, First lt, 1956-58. **Business Phone:** (919)660-3659.

JOSEPH, JENNIFER INEZ
School administrator, educator. **Personal:** Born Mar 25, 1948, New Amsterdam, Guyana; daughter of Vincent Percival Chung and Inez Gwendolyn Chung; married Richard A Joseph, Jul 27, 1968; children: Mark Vincent, R Anthony, Robert Lionel. **Educ:** British Open Univ, BA, 1975; Harvard Grad Sch Educ, MEd, 1984. **Career:** Univ Ibadan, Nigeria, publ, admin officer, 1976-79; Oxford Univ, Eng, clin trial coordr, 1979; Dartmouth Col, asst affirmative action officer, 1980-81, asst dir, career & employ servs, 1981, dir, intensive acad support prog, asst dean freshmen, 1981-85, asst dir, admis & financial aid, 1985-86, sr assoc dir, admis & financial aid, 1986-89; Ctr Dis Control, Epidemiol Prog Off, assoc dir, 1989-90; Morehouse Col, exec asst pres, 1991-92, vpres, policy & planning, 1992-. **Orgs:** Co-chair, Asn Black Admin & Financial Aid Officers Ivy League & Sister Schs, 1985-89, 1987-88; consult, adv bd mem, Emory Univ & Pew Charitable Trusts Sci & Math Prog, 1989-90; co-founder, coord comt chair, Saturday Youth Enrichment Prog, Atlanta, GA, 1990-; adv bd mem, Atlanta Youth Enrichment Prog, 1991-. **Honors/Awds:** Performance Award, Ctrs Dis Control, 1990. **Special Achievements:** CDC's

Med Detectives: At the Forefront Pub Health, J Nat Stud Med Asn, 1991; Coun Freely Elected Heads Govt, Int Observer Team, Guyana Elections, 1992; At Home Election Day, Atlanta J & Const, 1992.

JOSEPH, KERRY
Football player. **Personal:** Born Oct 4, 1973, New Iberia, LA. **Educ:** McNeese State Univ. **Career:** Cincinnati Bengals, 1996; London Monarchs, quarterback, 1997; Wash Redskins, slot back, 1997; Rhein Fires, safety, 1998; Seattle Seahawks, defensive back, 1998-01, Ottawa Renegades, quarter back, 2003-05; Saskatchewan Rough riders, 2006-07; Toronto Argonauts, 2008-. **Honors/Awds:** Most valuable player & conf player of the year, McNeese State, 1995; James J Corbett Mem Award, 1995; state's offensive football player of the year, La Sports Writers Assn, 1995; Rogers AT&T CFL Offensive Player of the Week, 2004; CFL's Most Outstanding Player Award, 2007. **Business Phone:** (416)322-9650.*

JOSEPH, LLOYD LEROI
Manager. **Personal:** Born Sep 18, 1934, Los Angeles, CA; son of Al Lee and Blondine; married Jeannette S Jones, Dec 18, 1981; children: Darnetta. **Career:** KIIX Channel 22, Los Angeles, chief broadcast audio eng, 1963; RPM Recording Studio, Los Angeles, chief recording eng, 1965-66; Genisco Technol Corp, Compton, test eng, 1967-69; CB Sound, Los Angeles, recording eng, 1969; KNXT/CBS News, Los Angeles, newsreel soundman, 1969-77; Universal Studios, Universal City, transfer prod recordist, 1977-; Films: Melvin & Howard, Psycho III, Best Little Whore House in Texas; Promise Kept: The Oksana Baiul Story; Televison Series: "Columbo", "Magnum PI", "Murder She Wrote", "Simon & Simon"; Documentaries: Blacks in the Media, Plight of the Jews in Russia. **Honors/Awds:** Emmy Award, TV, 1976. **Military Serv:** USN, AUS, E-5, 1950-57. **Home Phone:** (818)564-1545. **Business Addr:** Sound Recordist, Universal City, 100 Universal Plz, Universal City, CA 91608, **Business Phone:** (818)777-1295.

JOSEPH, RAYMOND ALCIDE
Journalist. **Personal:** Born Aug 31, 1931, San Pedro de Maco, Dominican Republic. **Educ:** Univ Chicago, MA, 1964; Wheaton Col, BA, 1960; Moody Bible Inst, dipl, 1957. **Career:** Wall St J, Div Dow Jones, financial reporter; Haiti-Observateur, co-ed; Embassy Haiti, ambassador, currently. **Orgs:** Found printshop Wis Mission Haiti, 1950; ed, Creole Mmthly "Reyon & Lumie"; translated, ed, publ, New Testament Creole Am Bible Soc, 1960; organizer, daily pol bd cast Haiti French; ed, "Le Combattant Haitien" French & Eng. **Business Addr:** Ambassador, Embassy of Haiti, 2311 Massachusetts Ave NW, Washington, DC 20008, **Business Phone:** (202)332-4090.

JOSEPH-MCINTYRE, MARY
Administrator. **Personal:** Born Jan 12, 1942, Shreveport, LA; children: Jarrett. **Educ:** Contra Costa Jr Col, attended 1962; Willis Col Bus, attended 1963; Univ Calif, attended 1966; Univ San Francisco, continuing educ, bus admin, 1983. **Career:** Univ Calif, Berkeley, secy, 1963-78, coordr sec pool, 1968-71, psychol dept, 1972-74;N Peralta Jr Col, secy pres, 1971-72; Oakland Met Enterprises, adv asst, 1975-76, exec dir 1976-79; Dukes, Dukes & Assoc, project adminr, 1979-83; "Sweet Touch", owner, 1984-; City Oakland Youth Adv Comn, staff liaision, 1989-91; City Oakland, Off Parks & Recreation, adv serv mgr, 1989-; Alameda County Youth Serv Forum Mem, 1989-; Third Ace, Inc, bd secy, 1989-. **Orgs:** Nat Frat Stud & Teachers, 1958-60; Nat Asn Advan Colored People, 1961-65; League Women Voters, 1964-70; vol, Kilimanjaro House, 1968; Black Caucus, 1968-69; Nat Contract & Mgt Asn, 1977-; Negro Women Bus & Prof Inc, 1977-84. **Honors/Awds:** PRS, TAPS Prog; Albany Youth Coun, 1959-60; March of Dimes Award, Alameda County, 1960; Northen Calif Adoption Agency; Outstanding Merit Increase, Univ Calif, 1968. **Home Addr:** 3922 Turnley Ave, Oakland, CA 94605.

JOSEY, DR. E. J. See Obituaries section.

JOSEY, LERONIA ARNETTA
Government official. **Personal:** Born in Norfolk, VA; children: Quenton C. **Educ:** Spelman Col, BA, 1965; Univ Md Sch Soik & Comm Plang, MSW, 1973; Syracuse Univ, Col Law, JD & Maxwell Sch Citizenship Pub Affairs, MPA, 1977. **Career:** US Dept Housing & Urban Develop, Wash, DC, atty, 1977-81; Md Parole Comn, comnr, 1981-; Leronia josey & Assc Llc,Maryland, pres & ceo,2005-. **Orgs:** Pres, Nat Asn Black Women Atty, 1983-; dir, Echo House Found, 1978-82; MedEye Black Bd, 1981-82; Luic Carroll Jackson Mus, 1982-; bd mem,Leadership Maryland. **Honors/Awds:** Third honorable graduate, Spelman Col; law school senate award, 1977;White House fel finalist, 1977; Maryland's Top 100 Women, 1966. **Home Addr:** 3700 Locheam Dr, Baltimore, MD 21207. **Business Addr:** Commissioner, Maryland Parole Commission, Ste 601 1 Investment Pl, Towson, MD 21204.

JOSEY-HERRING, ANITA MARIE
Judge. **Personal:** Born Sep 19, 1960, Portsmouth, VA; daughter of Edward and Katie; married Albert Herring Esq, Jun 22, 1997; children: 1. **Educ:** Va Commonwealth Univ, BA, 1983; Georgetown Univ Law Ctr, JD, 1987. **Career:** Occup Safety & Health Admin. Dept Labor, paralegal specialist, 1984-85; KOH Systs Inc, law clerk, 1985-87; Judge Herbert B Dixon, Jr, judicial clerk, 1987-88; Pub Defender Serv, staff atty, 1988-94, dep dir, 1994-97; Superior Ct, DC, assoc judge, dep presiding judge family div, 2000-. **Orgs:** Nat Bar Asn; Women Lawyer's Div, Greater Wash Area Chap, Community Outreach Comn; Wash Bar Asn; Fed Bar Asn; DC Superior Ct Domestic Violence Coun, 1994-; co-chair, DC Superior Ct Task Force Families & Violence, Domestic Violence Task Force Treatment Subcommittee, 1994-95; Greater Wash Urban League; Delta Sigma Theta Sorority; fac mem, Nat Legal Aid & Defender Training Conf. **Special Achievements:** Georgetown Legal Ethics Law Journal, Georgetown Univ, 1980. **Business Addr:** Deputy Presiding Judge, Superior Court of District Of Columbia, 500 Indiana Ave NW, Washington, DC 20001, **Business Phone:** (202)879-1574.

JOSHUA, DR. ALEXA A
Physician. **Career:** Pvt practioner, internal med, currently. **Business Addr:** Physician, 3741 McDougall, Detroit, MI 48207-2345, **Business Phone:** (313)921-4327.

JOURNEY, LULA MAE
Government official. **Personal:** Born May 8, 1934, Doddsville, MS; divorced; children: Larry, Callie Sanders, Linda, Ronnie, Marilyn Kirk & Blondina. **Educ:** Delta Indust Inst Bus Sch, Doddsville, MS, 1954; Mkt Training Inst, Indianapolis IN, attended 1958; Purdue Univ, attended 1979. **Career:** Ctr Twp Trustees Off, investr, Marion County Home, asst supvr, supvr investr, asst chief supvr oper, 1965-. **Orgs:** Pres, Indianapolis Pre Sch, 1972; bd dir, Citizens Neighborhood Coaltion, 1976-; city-county counr, 10th Dist City-County Coun, 1976-; bd dir, Mapleton/Fall Creek Asn, 1977-; chmn, Mem Comt, Am Bus Women Asn, 1981; state coordr munic women govt, Nat League Cities, 1982-; minority leader dem caucus, City-County Coun, 1985; Health & Corp Mgt, mem. **Honors/Awds:** Key to the City, City-County Coun, 1976; Cert Coop, Beyond Call Duty Ctr Twp Trustees Off, 1978; Cert of Appreciation, Indianapolis Pre-sch, 1978; Suprv of the Month, Ctr Twp Trustees Off, 1979; Cert, IN Asn Motorcycle Clubs, 1983. **Home Addr:** 2020 N New Jersey St, Indianapolis, IN 46202. *

JOWERS, JOHNNIE EDWARD, SR.
Association executive. **Personal:** Born Jul 1, 1931, Lynchburg, SC; son of Loro (deceased) and Bernice (deceased); married Paltine Horton, Sep 30, 1956; children: Johnnie E Jr & Deborah J. **Educ:** Shaw Univ, AB, 1957; NCA Cent Univ, MS, 1958; Johns Hopkins Univ, cert, advan studies educ, 1964; NYK Univ, cert org & admin, 1965. **Career:** Edgecombe Co Bd Educ, sec sch teacher, 1958-59; Salvation Army, phys dir, 1959-60, prog dir, 1960-63, unit dir, 1963-68; Baltimore City Schs, sec sch teacher, 1968-74; Salvation Army, exec dir, 1974-96; CARE Inc, spec educ teacher, 1997-. **Orgs:** Trustee, Progressive First Baptist Church, 1975-; corresp secy, Shaw Univ Alumni Asn, 1975-; Baltimore club pres, Frontiers INT Inc, 1979-80; United Way Cent MAR Speaker's Bur, 1978-94; chmn, Shaw Univ Nat Homecoming Banquet, 1990; area co-chmn, Shaw Univ Capital Campaign, 1991-; chaplin, Baltimore Frontiers Club, 1992-; Greensboro Shaw Univ Alumni Asn; Soc African Am Am Profs; Northeast Region Manpower Develop Comt; Nat Comn; Nat Adv Group. **Honors/Awds:** Student of the Year, Shaw Univ, 1953; Outstanding TCR Award, Baltimore City Schs, 1970; Man & Boy Award, Salvation Army Boys Club, 1973; Distinguished Serv Award, Salvation Army, 1984; Distinguished Alumni Award, NC Cent Univ, 1998; Distinguished Award, Shaw Univ, 1998. **Special Achievements:** History of Intercollegiate Athletics at Shaw Univ, 1958; "Boosting Your Speeches," 1989; "Publicity: Everybody's Job," 1989. **Military Serv:** USY, pfc, 1954-56; Expert Rifleman, Good Conduct Medal. **Home Addr:** 2800 E Coldspring Lane, Baltimore, MD 21214, **Home Phone:** (410)254-1557. **Business Addr:** Trustee, Progressive First Baptist Church, 3220 Garrison Blvd, Baltimore, MD 21216, **Business Phone:** (410)664-6454.

JOY, DANIEL WEBSTER
Judge. **Personal:** Born Apr 15, 1931, Middleton, NC; son of Andrew and Mattie Griffith; married Ruby M Collins; children: Darryl & Kathry. **Educ:** State Univ NY, Albany, BA, 1952; Brooklyn Law Sch, JD, 1957. **Career:** Judge (retired); Rent & Rehab Admin, chief coun, 1967-70, comnr, 1970-73; Housing Preserv & Develop Dept, comnr, 1973-83; Queens Co Civil Ct, judge, 1984-85; Supreme Ct, justice, 1985-2000. **Orgs:** New Hope Lutheran Church, Jamaica, NY, 1973-; Asn Bar City NY, 1976-83; Edwin Gould Found, 1980-; Queens Co Bar Asn, 1981-; bd chmn, Macon B Allen, Black Bar Asn, 1982-; Nat Bar Asn, 1983-; Nat Treas, Lutheran Men in Mission, 2002; pres, AALA Chap. **Honors/Awds:** Community Service Award, Lambda Kappa Mu Sorority, 1996; Seeds of Hope Award, Wheat Ridge Ministries. **Military Serv:** AUS, pfc, 1952-54. **Home Addr:** 14438 168th St, Jamaica, NY 11434-4815.

JOYCE, ELLA (CHERRON HOYE)
Actor. **Personal:** Born Jun 12, 1954, Chicago, IL; daughter of Bunnie Hoye; married Dan Martin. **Educ:** Eastern Mich Univ; bus Col; Yale Repertory Theater, trained with Lloyd Richards. **Career:** Ford Motor Co, secretary; actress, theater experience includes: Don't Get God Started, Two Trains Running, Milestones in Drama, The First Breeze of Summer, Chapter, Ma Rainey's Black Bottom; film experience includes: Stop or My Mom Will Shoot, 1992; Set It Off, 1996; Her Married Lover, 1999; Clockin' Green, 1999; Frozen Hot, 2000; Bubba Ho-tep, 2002; Salvation,2002; Salvation, 2003; Who Made the Potatoe Salad, 2005; Forbidden Fruits, 2005; My Nappy Roots, 2005; Lost Signal, 2006; A Simple Promise, 2008; Busted, 2009; Preacher's Kid, 2009. television appearances: Newlywed Game; Search for Tomorrow; One Life to Live; Roc, 1991-94; Choices, 1992; Selma, Lord, Selma, 1999; Stranger Inside, 2001; The Old Settler, 2001; What About Your Friends: Weekend Getaway, 2002; My Wife and Kids, 2003; Eve, 2004; Frozen Hot, producer, 1999; Clockin Green, assoc producer, 2000; What About Your Friends: Weekend Getaway, 2002; "Eve", 2004. **Honors/Awds:** Audelco Best Dramatic Actress, for Black Theater Excellence; TOR Award for Best Dramatic Actress, in Off-Broadway category; Cass Tech Hall of Famer. **Special Achievements:** Author, Kink Phobia: Journey Through A Black Woman's Hair, 2002. *

JOYNER, CLAUDE C.
Government official, chief financial officer. **Personal:** Born Nov 8, 1950, New Haven, CT; son of Minnie (deceased) and Claude (deceased); married Dolores Brandow, Nov 21, 1987. **Educ:** Maple Springs Baptist Bible Col & Sem, MRE, 1997; Cent State Univ, BS,1974; Pepperdine Univ, MBA, 1983. **Career:** Lincoln Nat Life Ins Co, system designer, 1974-76; First Interstate Bank, operations officer, 1977-79; Aerospace Corp, programmer, 1979-80; Transaction Tech Inc, systs analyst, 1980-84; Electronic Data Systs, sr systs analyst, 1984-85; Booz Allen & Hamilton, assoc, 1985-86; Contel ASC, sr syst analyst, 1986-87; Computer Based Systs Inc, staff analyst, database adminr, 1987-91; Joyner Design Ltd, chief financial officer, 1990-; Crystal City, Va, sr database specialist, 1991-96; US Patent Trademark Off, comput Specialist, 1996-. **Orgs:** Deaf Pride Inc, 1980-86; stud outreach comn, Nat Black MBA Asn, 1984-87;educ chairperson, Black Data Processing Asn, DC Chap, 1985-87; sunday sch teacher, 1986-94, lic minister, 1991-, asst supt, 1992-94, Mt Sinai Baptist Church; staff vol, treas, Mt Sinai Outreach Ctr, 1987-94; treas, Right Way Ministries Inc, 1992-96, chmn trustee bd, 1997-; disciple training dir, 1994-, sunday sch teacher, asst training union dir, 1995-, dir nenevolence Comn, 1997-, Kendall Baptist Church. **Home Addr:** 4102 Buck Creek Rd, Temple Hills, MD 20748-4931. **Business Addr:** Computer Specialist, US Patent & Trademark Office, 2131 Crystal Dr Suite 1100A, Alexandria, VA 22202, **Business Phone:** (703)305-9352.

JOYNER, GORDON L
Lawyer, county commissioner. **Personal:** Born Feb 11, 1950, Fort Valley, GA; son of Henry W and Helen L; children: Ashley & Shannon. **Educ:** Morehouse Col, Atlanta, GA, BA (summa cum laude), 1972; Harvard Law Sch, Cambridge, MA, JD, 1975. **Career:** Kilpatrick & Cody Law Offices, Atlanta, GA, atty, 1975-78; Am Bar Asn, Wash, DC, asst dir, 1978-79; US Dept Housing & Urban Develop, Wash, DC, legal coun, dir fair housing enforcement, 1979-82; Atlanta Munic Ct, Atlanta, GA, judge, 1985-87; Fulton County Bd Commissioners, comnr, 1987-; self-employed atty, currently. **Orgs:** Secy, Atlanta Harvard Club, 1983; chmn, Fulton County Bd Elections, 1985-87; life mem, Nat Asn Advan Colored People; Nat Urban League; exec bd mem, Atlanta Nat Asn Advan Colored People; Alpha Phi Alpha Frat; Mayor's Task Force Pub Educ; Southern Christian Leadership Conf. **Honors/Awds:** Phi Beta Kappa; Government Executive-In-Residence & Vis Prof, Morehouse Col, 1981-82; Official Guest of Israel & Germany Governments, 1989-90. **Business Addr:** Attorney, 945 Ashby Cir NW, PO Box 92816, Atlanta, GA 30314-0816, **Business Phone:** (404)524-2400.

JOYNER, IRVING L
Lawyer, educator. **Personal:** Born Dec 11, 1944, Brooklyn, NY; son of McLean Spaulding and Dorothy; divorced; children: Lauren, Kwame & Tuere. **Educ:** Long Island Univ, Brooklyn NY, BS, 1970; Rutgers Univ Sch Law, Newark NJ, JD. **Career:** United Church Christ Comt Racial Justice, New York NY, dir criminal justice, 1968-78; Currie & Joyner, Raleigh NC, atty law, 1978-80; Nat Prison Proj ACLU, Wash, DC, staff atty, 1980-81; Currie, Pugh & Joyner, Raleigh NC, atty law, 1981-85; NC Cent Univ Sch Law, Durham, NC, atty, 1985-. **Orgs:** Pres, NC Asn Black Lawyers, 1977-; NC State Bar, 1977-; Nat Bar Asn, 1977-; NC Acad Trial Lawyers, 1977-; Federal Bar Adv Coun, 1985-. **Honors/Awds:** Outstanding Contribution to Racial Justice, Asn Black Law Studs, 1977; Paul Robeson Award, Black Am Law Stud Asn, 1977; Professor of the Year, NCCU Stud Bar Asn, 1985; Living Legacy Award, OA Dupree Scholar Found, 1987; Outstanding Contribution to Civil Rights, Wake Forest Black Law Stud Asn, 1987; President's Award, La-Grange, Frink Alumni & Friends Asn, 1991; Lawyers of the Year Award, NC Asn Black Lawyers, 1995; Outstanding Teacher's Award, NC Cent Univ Law Sch Stud Bar Asn. **Special Achievements:** Author of The Black Lawyer in NC, article, 1988; Conflicts of Interest, article, 1988; Police Misconduct Litigation CLE manuscript and Law Review article, 1991; Preparation and Use of Requests for Jury Instructions, CLE manuscript, 1988; Criminal Procedure in NC, book, 1989; Supplements to Criminal Procedure in NCA, 1991-94; The Status of

Africa-Am Lawyers in NC, article, 1992. **Business Addr:** Attorney, North Carolina Central University Law School, 1512 S Alston Ave, Durham, NC 27707, **Business Phone:** (919)560-5255.

JOYNER, LAUREN CELESTE
Lawyer. **Personal:** Born in Brooklyn, NY. **Educ:** Univ NC, BA, psychol, 1989; Georgetown Univ Law Ctr, JD, 1992. **Career:** Kings County, asst dist atty, 1992-93; MasterCard, mgr, 1996-98; Am Express, mgr, 1998, dir, 2000-. **Orgs:** Team leader, New York Cares, 1995-; Children's Aid Soc, Yes Prog mentor, 1997-; Am Bankruptcy Inst, 1998-. **Honors/Awds:** President's Award, MasterCard, 1998; Chairman's Award, Am Express, 2000. **Business Addr:** Director, American Express, 40 Wall St, New York, NY 10005, **Business Phone:** (212)640-3172.

JOYNER, LEMUEL MARTIN
Administrator. **Personal:** Born Jun 20, 1928, Nashville, TN; married Barbara; children: Lemuel Jr, John M, Christopher A, Dennis L, Victor P, Lonnie. **Educ:** Univ Notre Dame, BFA, 1957, MFA, 1969. **Career:** st marys col, asst prof; St. Christophers Workshop, designer ch interiors; Liturgical Artist, 1958-65; St Mary's Col Notre Dame, asst prof art, 1965-71; Office Inter-Cultural develop, spl asst pres, 1970; Day Treatment Ctr, co-develop; Menatl Health Ctr St Joseph City Inc, art therapist, 1985. **Orgs:** Am Art Therapists Asn; S Bend Art Asn; S Bend St Acad; Nat Coun Artist; Alpha Phi Alpha; Ctr Integrative Healing S Bend's Memorial Hosp. **Honors/Awds:** Excellence in Teaching Award, St Mary's Col, 1969; Outstanding Contribution to Standard Life Award; Model Upward Bound Prog, 1966; Black Dimensions In Am Art, 1969; Rev Anthony J Lauck CSC Award.

JOYNER, OSCAR ALBERT
Executive. **Personal:** Born Jan 27, 1975, Dallas, TX; son of Tom Sr and Dora. **Educ:** Darden Univ; Fla A&M Univ, mkt & finance, 1998. **Career:** ABC Radio Networks, producer, 1997-99; Joyner & Assoc, chief exec officer, 1999-2003; Reach Media Inc, pres & chief operating officer, 2003-. **Orgs:** Bd mem, Tom Joyner Found, 1998-; Omega Psi Phi Inc, 1995-; bd dir, Nat Black MBA Asn; 100 Black Men Am. **Honors/Awds:** Benjamin L Hooks Award; Freedom Fighter Award, Nat Am Advan Colored People; Civic Community Award, NV Mag, 2003. **Business Addr:** President, Chief Operating Officer, Reach Media Inc, 13760 Noel Rd Suite 750, Dallas, TX 75240-7336, **Business Phone:** (972)789-1058.

JOYNER, RUBIN E
School administrator. **Personal:** Born Dec 5, 1949, Trenton, NJ; married Phyllis A; children: Zanada & Ciarra. **Educ:** Rider Univ, BA, 1973; Trenton State Col, MEd, 1977; Temple Univ, EdD in progress. **Career:** East Windsor sch syst, guidance counr; Monmouth Univ, dir educ opport prog; Ocean County Col, dir educ opport, 1982-86; Rider Univ, dir educ opport prog, 1987-. **Orgs:** NJ Ed Opp Asn, 1978; Am Asn Coun Dept, 1979; Soc Spec & Ethnic Studies, 1979; Monmouth Col, dir black stud Union, 1979-85; co-founder, Acceleration Comput Sci Prog, 1983-85; Orgn Black Unity, dir, 1985; founder, Access Prog, 1986; co-chairperson, Stud Leadership Educ Opport, 1986. **Honors/Awds:** Appreciation award for black student union, Monmouth Col, 1984; Outstanding Young Men of the Year, 1985; Inductee Hall of Honor, Lawrence High Sch, NJ, 1997. **Business Addr:** Director Education Opportunity Program, Rider University, 2083 Lawrenceville Rd, Vona Annex six, Lawrenceville, NJ 08648-3099.

JOYNER, SETH
Sports promoter, football player. **Personal:** Born Nov 18, 1964, Spring Valley, NY; married Wanda; children: Jasmine. **Educ:** Univ Tex, El Paso. **Career:** Football player (retired), sports promoter; Philadelphia Eagles, linebacker, 1986-93; Ariz Cardinals, 1994-96; Green Bay Packers, 1997-98; Denver Broncos, 1998; All Am Speakers, sports speaker, currently. **Honors/Awds:** Pro Bowl, 1991, 1993, 1994; Defensive Player of the Year, Asniated Press, 1991; NFL Player of the Year, Sports Illustrated, 1991; Super Bowl XXXIII, 1999. **Special Achievements:** TV appearance: "Rome Is Burning, " 2005-06. **Business Addr:** Sports Speaker, All American Speakers, 200 Alexander Dr Suite 208, Durham, NC 27707, **Business Phone:** (919)403-7004.

JOYNER, THOMAS. See JOYNER, TOM.

JOYNER, TOM (THOMAS JOYNER)
Radio host, business owner. **Personal:** Born Jan 1, 1949, Tuskegee, AL; married Dora (divorced); children: Thomas & Albert; married Donna Richardson. **Career:** Chicago Radio Sta, disc jockey; KDKA, Dallas, Tex, morning air personality, 1983-93; WGCI Chicago, afternoon host, 1985-93; Tom Joyner Morning Show, host & producer, 1993-; REACH Media Inc, founder, chair, majority owner, 2003-. **Honors/Awds:** Trumpet Award, 2002; Cong Black Caucus, Mickey Leland Humanitarian/Relig Award. **Business Addr:** Owner, REACH Media Inc, PO Box 801565, Dallas, TX 75380-1565, **Business Phone:** (972)789-1058.

JOYNER-KERSEE, JACKIE
Athlete. **Personal:** Born Mar 3, 1962, East St Louis, IL; daughter of Alfred and Mary; married Bob Kersee, Jan 11, 1986. **Educ:** Univ Calif, LA, BA, 1985. **Career:** Track & field athlete (retired), association executive; track & field athlete, 1987-98; Richmond Rage, prof basketball player, 1996-98; Jackie Joyner-Kersee Found, founder, chairperson & dir, currently. **Orgs:** Jackie Joyner-Kersee Found; Univ Calif Alumni Asn, LA; Athletic Cong Athletics Adv Bd; St Louis Sports Comn. **Honors/Awds:** Silver Medalist, Los Angeles Olympics, American Record Holder in Heptathlon, 1984; American Outdoor Record Holder in Long Jump, 1985; Univ Calif Scholar Athlete, LA, 1985; James E Sullivan Award for Most Outstanding Amateur Athlete, 1986; Broderick Cup for Collegiate Woman Athlete of the Year, 1986; Most Valuable Player, Univ Calif, LA, 1986; American Indoor Nats Champion Long Jump, 1986; World Record in Heptathlon, Goodwill Games, Moscow, US Olympic Festival, 1986; Outstanding Athlete of the Goodwill Games, Soviet Life mag, 1986; Olympia Award for Outstanding Athlete in Sports, Scholarship and Leadership, 1986; City of Hope Victor Award, 1986, 1987; Woman Athlete of the Year, Track & Field News, 1986, 1987; St Louis Athlete of the Year, 1986; Amateur Sportswoman of the Year,1 986, 1987; Jesse Owens Memorial Award, 1986, 1987; Gold Medalist, Heptathlon, Long Jump, World Championship, Rome, 1987; US Record in 100m Hurdle, 1988; Gold Medalist in Long Jump, Seoul Olympics, 1988; Essence Award, 1988; AAF's World Trophy, 1989; Honorary Degree, Univ Mo, 1989; Gold Medal, US Olympic Team, 1992; Robie Award, Jackie Robinson Found, 1994; USA Track & Field (USATF) Hall of Fame, 2004. **Special Achievements:** First Woman to score 7,000 points in a Heptathlon event. **Business Addr:** Chairperson, Director, Jackie Joyner-Kersee Foundation, 101 Jackie Joyner-Kersee Circle, East St Louis, IL 62204, **Business Phone:** (618)274-5437.

JUDGE, DR. PAUL QANTAS
Executive. **Personal:** Born Mar 5, 1977, Baton Rouge, LA; son of Paul and Mary Judge. **Educ:** Morehouse Col, BS, 1998; Georgia Tech, MS, 2000, PhD, 2002. **Career:** NASA, res asst, 1995-98; Ga Tech, researcher, 1998-2003; IBM, developer, 1998; Cipher Trust, chief tech officer, 2000-. **Orgs:** IRTF; Anti Spam Research Group, founder; IEEE; ACM. **Special Achievements:** About 20 publications in academic journals & conferences; regularly speaks at leading industry events including Federal Trade Commission, RSA Conference & congressional panels; featured in hundreds of media outlets including CNN, Business Week, and The Wash Post; MIT's Technol Review Magazine, TR100-100 Top Young Innovators in the World, 2003; The Network Journal "40 Under 40"; Black Enterprise "50 Most Powerful Players Under 40". **Business Addr:** Chief Technology Officer, Cipher Trust Inc, 4800 Northpoint Pkwy Suite 400, Alpharetta, GA 30022, **Business Phone:** (678)969-9399.

JUDSON, DR. HORACE AUGUSTUS
College administrator, college president, educator. **Personal:** Born Aug 7, 1941, Miami, FL; married Beatrice Gail; children: Tamara Renee, Sonya Anita, Sojourner Maria & Jessica Gail. **Educ:** Lincoln Univ, BA, 1963; Cornell Univ, PhD, 1970; Lincoln Univ, DSc, 1994. **Career:** Cornel Univ, res fel, 1965-69; Bethune-Cookman Col, asst prof, 1969; Morgan State Col, assoc dean, 1973-74, from asst prof to assoc prof, 1969-72; Morgan State Univ, vpres acad affairs, 1974-79, prof, 1974-86, Col Sci, assoc dean & dean, Col Sci Improvement Prog, assoc dir & dir, chair chem dept; Calif State Univ, provost & vpres acad affairs & dean col letters & sci, 1994; State Univ NY Col, Plattsburgh, pres & chancellor, 1994-2004; Grambling State Univ, pres, 2004-. **Orgs:** Am Chem Soc; Am Asn Higher Educ; Omega Psi Phi; Miner Inst Bd; Am Asn Univ Admin; Intl Asn Univ, Pres; Am Asn State Col & Univ; bd dir, Res Found State Univ NY; bd trustees, Trudeau Inst; bd dir, Clinton Cty Area Develop Corp; Boy Scouts Am, Adirondack Coun Adv Bd; Am Chem Soc; Sigma XI; Kappa Delta Pi; Phi Kappa Phi; Sigma Beta Delta. **Honors/Awds:** Award for Professional Excellence, Nat Tech Asn, 1984. **Special Achievements:** Several articles in the Journal of American Chemical Society, 1970. **Military Serv:** AUS, md civ aide to secy, 1975. **Business Addr:** President, Grambling State University, 403 Main St, Grambling, LA 71245, **Business Phone:** (318)247-3811.

JULIAN, PERCY L., JR. See Obituaries section.

JUNIOR, E J
Executive, football player, football coach. **Personal:** Born Dec 8, 1959, Salisbury, NC; married Yolanda, Jan 1, 1993; children: Adam, Aja, E J IV, Kyle, Ashley, Shandon, Torren & Cameron. **Educ:** Univ Alabama, degree pub rel. **Career:** Football player (retired), coach; St Louis Cardinals, linebacker, 1981-88; Miami Dolphins, linebacker, 1989-91; Tampa Bay Buccaneers, linebacker, 1992; Seattle Seahawks, linebacker, 1992-93, coach, 1994; Miami Dolphins, dir player develop progs, 1996-98; Dade County Pub Sch, Admin 5000 Role Models Excellent, 1999-2003; Overtown Youth Ctr, exec dir, 2003-; Minnesota Vikings, minority intern coach; Jacksonville Jaguars, minority intern coach, 2005; Southwest Baptist Univ, linebackers coach, 2006-, defensive coordr, currently. **Orgs:** Asst youth pastor, Bethel Full-Gospel Baptist Church,; Kappa Alpha Psi Fraternity Inc; NFL Player Progs, Steering Comt; motivational speaker. **Honors/Awds:** Alabama's Team of the Decade, 1970; Strength Coaches All-American team; All-SEC Defensive Player of the Year, 1980; Sr Bowl, Outstanding Defensive Performer, 1981; named to several All-Rookie teams 1981; Pro Bowl, 1984, 1985; ordained, 1997; Nashville, TN, Public Schools Hall of Fame, 2006; Senior Bowl Hall of Fame, 2007; Lombardi Award finalist. **Business Addr:** Linebackers Coach, Defensive Coordinator, Southwest Baptist University, 1600 Univ Ave, Bolivar, MO 65613, **Business Phone:** (417)328-5281.

JUNIOR, MARVIN
Singer. **Personal:** Born Jan 31, 1936, Harrell, AR. **Career:** The Dells, lead baritone & mem, 1952-; Albums (With the Dells): Oh What a Night, 1957; It's Not Unusual, 1965; There Is, 1968; Love Is Blue, 1969; The Dells' Musical Menu/Always Together, 1969; The Dells' Greatest Hits, 1970; Like It Is, Like It Was, 1971; Freedom Means, 1971; Sweet As Funk Can Be, 1972; The Dells Sing Dionne, 1972; Give Your Baby a Standing Ovation, 1976; The Dells, 1973; The Mighty Mighty Dells, 1974; The Dells vs. The Dramatics, 1975; The Dells' Greatest Hits Volume 2, 1975; We Got To Get Our Thing Together, 1975; No Way Back, 1976; They Said It Couldn't Be Done But We Did It, 1977; Love Connection, 1977; New Beginnings, 1978;Face to Face, 1979; I Touched a Dream, 1980; Whatever Turns You On, 1981; One Step Closer, 1984; The Second Time, 1988; On Their Corner, 1992; I Salute You, 1992; Dreams of Contentment, 1993; Bring Back the Love: Classic Dells, 1996; I Touch a Dream/Whatever Turns, 1998; Reminiscing, 2000; Open Up My Heart: The 9/11 Album, 2002; Hott, 2003; (With Michael Ross): We Finally Meet, 1995; Last Love Letter, 1996; The Wailers Band, guitarist, currently; Solo album: Wailin' For Love, 2007; Jah Roots, 2008. **Business Addr:** Lead Baritone, The Original Dells Inc, PO Box 1133, Harvey, IL 60426-7133, **Business Phone:** (708)474-1422.*

JUNIOR-SPENCE, SAMELLA E.
Educator, musician. **Personal:** Born Dec 15, 1931, Chattanooga, TN; married Ester James; children: Avis & E J. **Educ:** Spelman Col, AB, 1953; La State Univ, Music Educ, 1957; George Peabody Col, PhD, 1977. **Career:** Educator (retired), musician; Leland Col, instr & dir, 1956-57; Jarvis Christian Col, 1957-59; Livingstone Col, prof, 1959-60; E Baker High Sch & Elem Sch, teacher, 1961-63; Carver Jr High Sch, teacher, dir & chmn, 1963-68; Highland Heights Jr High Sch, teacher, 1969-71; Isaac Litton Jr High Sch, 1971-74; Joelton High Sch, asst prin, 1974-75; Cumberland Jr High Sch, prin, 1975-78; Pearl High Sch, prin, 1975-78; Whites Creek Comprehensive High Sch, assoc prin; East High Sch, prin, 1978-86. **Orgs:** Choir dir & minister, Mt Zion Bapt Ch; First Bapt Ch; Disciples Christ Ch; asst organist, First Bapt Ch; choir dir, minister of music & pres, Spelman Club; pres, vpres, secy & comm chmn, Delta Sigma Theta Inc; treas, Nat Coun Negro Women; treas, Black Expo; secy, Albany State Col Wives; com chmn, Nat Educ Asn; comm chmn, Mo Nat Educ Asn; com chmn, Tex Educ Asn;com chmn, Nat Asn Sec Sch Principals; com chmn, Tex Asn Sec Sch Principals; com chmn, Asn Supv & Curric Develop; com Chmn, Asn Teacher Educrs; com chmn, Phi Delta Kappa; com chmn, Am Asn Univ Women; com chmn, Nashville Pin; pres-elect, Middle Region Tex Educ Asn; chmn, Metro Coun Teachers Educ; Nat Fel Ch Musicians; Nat Asn Advan Colored People; vice-chmn bd, Oper PUSH; bd dir, Leadership Nashville Found, 2006-07. **Honors/Awds:** Molly Todd Cup, Nashville CABLE, 1998. **Business Addr:** Director of Board, Leadership Nashville Foundation, PO Box 190498, Nashville, TN 37219.

JUPITER, CLYDE PETER
Executive. **Personal:** Born Oct 31, 1928, New Orleans, LA; married Pat (Schofield) Jupiter, Nov 27, 1987; children: Carol A Gariboldi, Lisa A Jupiter-Byles, Joan C, Jeannie Ritchie, Deanna, Matthews, Mike Schank, Steve Schank, Chris Schank & Erika Schank. **Educ:** Xavier Univ New Orleans, BS, Physics, 1949; Univ Notre Dame S Bend, MS, Physics, 1951. **Career:** Teaching Fel, Univ Notre Dame S Bend IN, 1949-50; Lawrence Radiation Lab, Livermore CA, 1956-64; Gen Atomic Co San Diego, staff sci, 1964-69; EG&G Inc Santa Barbara, mgr radiation physics dept, 1969-70; EG&G Inc Albuquerque, dir appl sci, 1970-71; EG&G Inc Las Vegas, mgr radiation & environ sci dept, 1971-75; US Nuclear Reg Comn, tech asst dir res, 1975-78, prog mgr waste mgt 1978-82; Howard Univ Sch Engineering, adj prof nuclear Engineering prog, 1981-86; US Nuclear Regulatory Comm, sr policy analyst Off policy eval, 1982-86; Jupiter Corp, pres, 1986-2001, chmn & founder, chief operating officer, 2001-. **Orgs:** Am Nuclear Soc, 1965-; bd dir, Am Nuclear Soc, 1976-79, 1994-97; Alpha Phi Alpha Fraternity, 1947-; NAACP; Health Physics Soc; AAAS. **Honors/Awds:** Fel Am Nuclear Soc, 1980. **Military Serv:** AUS sp-3 1954-56.

JUSTICE, DAVID CHRISTOPHER
Broadcaster, baseball player, television journalist. **Personal:** Born Apr 14, 1966, Cincinnati, OH; son of Robert and Nettie; married Halle Berry, Dec 31, 1992 (divorced 1997); married Rebecca Villalobos, Feb 8, 2001; children: Dionisio, Raquel & David Jr. **Educ:** Thomas More Col, Criminal Justice, 1983-85. **Career:** Baseball player (retired), broadcaster, television journalist; Atlanta Braves, outfielder & infielder, 1989-96; Cleveland Indians, 1997-2000; NY Yankees, 2000-01; Oakland Athletics, 2002; ESPN, baseball telecasts, commentator; YES Network, NY Yankees, game & studio analyst, contributor, currently. **Honors/Awds:** Nat League Rookie of the Year, Baseball Writers Asn Am, 1990; Nat League Player of the Month, 1990, 1991; AL Comeback Player of the Year Award, 1997; World Series Champion, 1995, 2000; ALCS Most Valuable Player, 2000. **Business Phone:** (646)487-3600.

K

KAALUND, SEKOU H
Financial manager. **Personal:** Born Jun 29, 1975, Raleigh, NC; son of Jackie Mburu and Barry; married Jennifer, Sep 2, 2000. **Educ:** Univ Granada, Spain, 1995; Hampden-Sydney Col, BA, 1997; Duke Univ, MPP, 1999. **Career:** White House Off Gen Coun; SK Solutions, pres, 1998-99; Fed Res Bank NY, sr bank examiner & sr relationship specialist, 1999; JPMorgan Worldwide Securities Serv, managing dir, head bus develop pvt equity fund serv, currently. **Orgs:** Chair corp develop fundraising, Next Gen Network, 2000-03, vpres, 2003-; asst treas, Kappa Alpha psi, 2003-; Banking on our Future, 2002-; Urban Financial Services Coalition, 2003-. **Honors/Awds:** Nat Youth of the Year Finalist, Boys & Girls Club Am, 1992; Merit Scholar, Hampden-Sydney Col, 1993; Ford Foundation/AED, Woodrow Wilson Fel, Public Policy, 1996; President's Award for Excellence, Fed Reserve Bank, 2001; Nat Orator of the Year, Urban Financial Service Coalition, 2002; President's Award. **Special Achievements:** Featured Ebony magazine 22 "Young Leaders of the Future". **Business Addr:** Managing Director, Head of Business Development for Private Equity Fund Services, JPMorgan Chase Bank, JPMorgan Worldwide Securities Services, 231 Grand St, New York, NY 10013, **Business Phone:** (212)334-0555.

KADREE, MARGARET ANTONIA
Physician, educator, college teacher. **Personal:** Born Jun 25, 1952, Tunapuna, West Indies; daughter of Fitzroy Vidale and Ella; married Adegboyega J Kadree, Apr 24, 1976; children: Temilade, Shijuade, Yewande, Hafsa. **Educ:** NY Univ, BA, 1979; State NY Buffalo Sch Med, MD, 1983. **Career:** Morehouse Sch Med, asst prof med, 1993-, chief infectious dis, 1993-, dir clin residence prog, 1984-, dir HIV prev youth, Subproject MSM Zambian HIV Prev Proj, 1993-; Ctr Dis Control, guest researcher, 1994-, dir, clin res prog, 1994-, Ctr Devices, 1997; pvt pract, physician, currently. **Orgs:** Food & Drug Admin, Microbiologic Devices Comt, 1994-; Ga State Task Force AIDS, 1994-; Am Lung Asn, Educ Comt, 1994-; Atlanta Metrop TB Task Force, 1993-; vice chair, Our Lady Mercy High Sch, Annual Giving Comt. **Honors/Awds:** Dean's Award, State Univ NY Buffalo Sch Med, 1983; Outstanding Resident, Upjohn Pharmaceut Co, 1986. **Special Achievements:** Auth: "AIDS," Washington Post, health section, June 1991; "Adolescents and HIV," New York City Cable, December 1992; "HIV and AIDS," Washington View Magazine, February 1992; "How Safe is Safe Sex?", Ebony Mag, July 1994. *

KAFELE, BARUTI KWAME
School principal, writer, public speaker. **Personal:** Born Oct 22, 1960, Orange, NJ; son of Norman G Hopkins and Delores C James; married Kimberley Broughton, Jun 3, 1989; children: Baruti H. **Educ:** Middlesex County Col, AS, 1985; Kean Univ, BS, mgt sci & mkt, 1986; New Jersey City Univ, MA, educ admin. **Career:** NY City Bd Educ, teacher, 1988-89; Baruti Publ, owner, pres, publ, 1990-; E Orange Bd Educ, teacher, 1992-; Sojourner Truth Mid Sch, prin, 1997-00; Newark Technol High Sch, prin, currently; nat educ consult, currently. **Honors/Awds:** Phi Kappa Phi Nat Hon Soc, 1986; Lambda Alpha Sigma Lib Arts & Sci Hon Soc, 1986; Black Stud Union Acad Achievement Award, 1986; UB & US Lit Achievement Awards, Best New Writer Male, 1991; East Orange Sch Dist & Essex County Pub Schs Teacher of the Yr, 1996-97; Dist & Co Teacher of the Yr. **Special Achievements:** Auth: A Black Parent's Handbook to Educating Your Children, 1991; Goal Setting: For Serious Minded Black Folks, 1991; A Black Student's Guide to Goal Setting, 1992; Goal Setting: A Black View, 1992; A Handbook For Teachers of African American Children, 2004. **Business Addr:** Principal, Newark Technol High School, 187 Broadway, Newark, NJ 07104, **Business Phone:** (973)481-5962.*

KAIGLER, MARIE. See KAIGLER-REESE, MARIE MADELEINE.

KAIGLER-REESE, MARIE MADELEINE (MARIE KAIGLER)
Broadcaster, counselor. **Personal:** Born Jan 25, 1945. **Educ:** Fisk Univ, BA, 1965; Wayne State Univ, attended 1969, 1983. **Career:** Wayne County Juvenile Ct, caseworker aide, 1965-66; Mich Employment Security Comn, employ counr, 1966-67; Northern Systs Co, behav counr, 1967-70; Detroit Bd Educ, sch community agent, 1970-78; Wayne County Community Col, part-time instr, 1969-82; WJLB, People Want to Know, co-host & producer, 1972-79; MORE, group individual instr & sem instr, 1975-85; Wayne State Univ, Col Educ, res asst dean's off, 1985-86; WXYT, radio journalist; Republican Nat Conv Mich, alt del, 1988. **Orgs:** Exec bd chair polit awareness, Mich Asn Coun & Develop, 1989-90; chair educ bd dir, Am Asn Univ Women, 1990; chair & exec bd, Republican Women's Forum, 1986-; chair polit awareness, Mich Employ Coun Asn, 1987-. **Honors/Awds:** Michigan Citizen Newspaper articles: "The Single Homemaker," Oct 8-14, 1989, p. 6, "Aging Black Leadership," Sept 24-30, 1989, p. 6, "Being Black Is Not Enough," Sept 17-23, 1989, p. 6, "Why Republican?," Jul 30- Aug 5, 1989, p. 6, "The Black Agenda 1900-00: Get Real!," Apr 9-15, 1989, p. 6; Certificate of Appreciation, Guest Lecturer, College of Nursing, Wayne State University, 1988; Most Inspiring Counselor, Oakland Community College, 1982; "Appreciation Service" commendation, President of the U S, Washington, DC, 1981; candidate, state representative, 1990; candidate, Wayne County Commissioner, 1990; various others. **Special Achievements:** Was a candidate for Michigan State House of Representatives, 5th Dist, 2000. *

KAISER, ERNEST DANIEL
Editor, writer. **Personal:** Born Dec 5, 1915, Petersburg, VA; son of Ernest B and Elnora B Ellis; married Mary G Orford, 1949 (deceased); children: Eric & Joan. **Educ:** City Col NY, attended 1935-38. **Career:** Erie Railroad, Jersey City, NJ, redcap, 1938-42; Negro Quarterly, NewYork, ed staff, 1943; Cong Indust Orgn, Polit Action Comt, New York, shipping clerk, 1944-45; NY Public Libr, Schomburg Ctr Res Black Cult, NY City, mem staff, 1945; Arno Press, ed, reviewer & consult; Crowell-Collier, ed, reviewer & consult; Beacon Press, ed, reviewer & consult; McGraw-Hill Book Co, ed, reviewer & consult; RR Bowker Co, ed, reviewer & consult; Books: Black Titan: W. E. B. DuBois, Beacon Press, co-ed, 1970; In Defense of the People's Black & White History & Culture, 1971; No Crystal Stair: A Bibliography of Black Literature, co-ed, 1971; The Correspondence of W. E. B. DuBois, Vol I: Selections, 1877-34, co-ed, 1973; The Correspondence of W. E. B. DuBois, Vol II: Selections, 1934-44,co-ed, 1976; The Correspondence of W. E. B. DuBois, Vol III: Selections,1944-63, co-ed, 1978; Harlem: A History of Broken Dreams, co-author, 1974; A Freedomways Reader: Afro-America in the Seventies, ed & contibr, 1977; Paul Robeson: The Great Forerunner, ed & contibr, 1978. **Honors/Awds:** Plaque, Kappa Sigma Chap Sigma Gamma Rho, 1982; Humanitarian Award, Harlem Sch Arts 1985; Ernest D Kaiser Index to Black Resources, named in honor, Schomburg Ctr, 1985; African Heritage Award, 2006. **Home Addr:** 3137 95th St, East Elmhurst, NY 11369, **Home Phone:** (718)899-7719. *

KAISER, JAMES GORDON
Executive. **Personal:** Born Feb 28, 1943, St Louis, MO; son of Samuel Arthur and Jane Aileen; married Kathryn Juanita Mounday; children: Lauren Elizabeth. **Educ:** Univ Calif Los Angeles, BA, 1966; Mass Inst Technol, MS, 1973. **Career:** Corning Glass Work Corning NY, sales rep, 1968-70, sales promotion specialist, 1970-72, product line mgr, 1973-75, bus planning mgr, 1975-76, gen mgr sales & mkt, 1976-79, mgr new bus develop, 1979-81, bus mgr, 1981-84, vpres & gen mgr, 1984-86, sr vpres, 1986-92; Enseco Inc, pres & chief exec officer, 1992-94; bd dir, Sunoco Inc, 1993-; Quanterra Inc, 1994-96; Avenir Partners, Inc, chmn & chief exec officer, 1998-; Ridgeway Avenir LLC, 2001-; Pelican Banners & signs Inc, chmn & chief exec officer, 2001-03; bd mem, Dartnell Enterprises Inc; Kaiser Rigeway LLC, mgr; Lexus Memphis, chmn & chief exec officer, currently. **Orgs:** Bd mem, Stanley Works, 1992-99; bd dirs, Int Asn Environ Testing Labs, 1994; bd trustees, Keystone Ctr, 1993; bd dirs, Wharton Spencer Stuart Dirs Inst; founding mem, past pres, past bd mem, Exec Leadership Coun; bd mem, Toyota Lexus Minority Dealers Asn; bd mem, Kaiser Serv LLC; bd mem, MeadWestvaco. **Honors/Awds:** Houghton Award, Total Quality Corning Inc, 1992; The Partner Development Award, Soc of Black Profs, 1991; Honorary Doctorate, Humane Letters, Fla A&M Univ, 1988; Blue Ribbon Giver's Award, Corning Hosp & Founders Pavilion, 1991. **Special Achievements:** First African American vice president at Enesco Inc. **Military Serv:** USNR jg 2 yrs; Navy Achievement Medal, Nat Defense Medal, 2 Bronze Stars Vietnam Svcs, Republic of Vietnam Campaign Medal. **Home Addr:** 111 Falcon Hills Dr, Highlands Ranch, CO 80126. **Business Phone:** (901)362-8833.

KAISER-DARK, PHYLLIS E
Government official. **Career:** The White House, Off Mgmt & Budjet, confidential asst, 1996, confidential asst adminr, 2000; Off Mayor, Wash, DC, exec asst city adminr, 2001-. **Business Addr:** Executive Assistant, Government of the District of Columbia, Office of the Mayor, 1350 Pennsylvania Ave NW, Washington, DC 20502, **Business Phone:** (202)727-9418.

KALU, ND. See KALU, NDUKWE DIKE.

KALU, NDUKWE DIKE (ND KALU)
Football player. **Personal:** Born Aug 3, 1975, Baltimore, MD; son of Dike and Carolyn; married; children: Karolyn. **Educ:** Rice Univ, attended 1997; BA, 2002. **Career:** Philadelphia Eagles, defensive end, 1997, 2001-05; Wash Redskins, 1998-2000;Houston Texans, 2006-08; NFL, free agent, 2009-. **Honors/Awds:** NFC Defensive Player of the Week, 2002; Jack Edelstein Memorial Award, 2003; Mickey Herskowitz Award, 2006. *

KAMAU, KWADWO AGYMAH
Writer. **Personal:** Born in Barbados. **Educ:** Bernard M Baruch Col, City Univ NY, BBA, 1981, MS, 1985; Va Commonwealth Univ, MFA, 1992. **Career:** NY Off Econ Develop, res asst, 1983-85; UN Secretariat, res asst int econ & social affairs, 1984; NY Dept Invest, statistician, 1985-86; NY State Dept Taxation & Finance, Off Tax Policy Analysis, sr economist, 1986-89; Va Commonwealth Univ, adj prof, 1989; New Va Review, ed asst, 1991-92; Richmond Free Press, copy ed, 1992-93; freelance copy ed & proofreader, 1993-94; writer, 1994-; Centrum & Ucross Found, writer-in-residence, 1998; Book: Flickering Shadows: A Novel; Pictures of a Dying Man. **Honors/Awds:** Wall Street J Award, 1981. **Special Achievements:** Novels include Flickering Shadows, 1996; Pictures of a Dying Man, 1999. **Business Addr:** Writer, Faith Childs Literary Agency, 915 Broadway Suite 1009, New York, NY 10010, **Business Phone:** (212)995-9600.

KAMAU, MOSI (ANTHONY CHARLES GUNN WHITE)
Educator. **Personal:** Born May 5, 1955, Chicago, IL. **Educ:** Univ Minn, BFA, 1979; Florida State Univ, MFA, 1983; Temple Univ, PhD, African-Am Studies, 1989. **Career:** Tutle Contemporary Elem Sch, pottery instr, 1977-78; Talbot Supply Co Inc, welder;, 1979-80; Florida State Univ, asst prep, 1980-81; Williams Foundry, foundryman, 1981-82; St Pauls Col, asst prof art, 1984-89. **Orgs:** Nat Coun Black Studies; African Am Asn Ghana; African Heritage Asn. **Honors/Awds:** Int Exchange Scholarship, Univ Minn to Univ Ife Ile, Ife, Nigeria, 1976-77; Sculpture/$5000 Nat Endowment of the Arts, Visual Arts, Washington DC, 1984-85. **Military Serv:** USN Reserve E-3, 1984-90; grad with honors, 1984. **Home Addr:** 1639 W Grange Ave, Philadelphia, PA 19141, **Home Phone:** (215)924-7145.

KAMOCHE, JIDLAPH GITAU
Educator. **Personal:** Born Dec 1, 1942, Kabete, Kenya; married Charity Njambi; children: Nyakio & Kamoche Gitau. **Educ:** Amherst Col, BA, 1967; Univ Mass, MA, 1969; State Univ NY, Buffalo, PhD, 1977. **Career:** Inst Int Educ, NY, fel, 1968-69; State Univ Col, Buffalo, asst prof hist,1972-77, African & Afro-Am, dir; Univ Okla, asst prof hist, African & Afro-Am Studies, dir, assoc prof, 1977-; Univ Okla, Col Arts Res, fel,1979-80. **Orgs:** Vpres, Asn Black Personnel, Univ Okla, 1978-79. **Special Achievements:** Author of several articles and book reviews in several scholarly jouranals from 1977; Author, Afro-American Life & History, 1977; "Umoja", 1980. **Business Addr:** Associate Professor, University of Oklahoma, Department of History, Rm 403A W Lindsey, Norman, OK 73019, **Business Phone:** (405)325-6001.

KANE, EUGENE A
Columnist. **Personal:** Born May 15, 1956, Philadelphia, PA; son of Eugene and Hattie. **Educ:** Temple Univ, BA, 1980. **Career:** The Philadelphia Bulletin, reporter, 1980; The Milwaukee J, reporter, 1981-85, features writer, columnist, 1985, J Sentinel, columnist, currently. **Orgs:** Wisconsin Black Media Asn, 1984-; Nat Asn Black Journalist, 1994. **Honors/Awds:** First Place Commentary, Am Socy Sunday & Features Edits, 1989; John S Knight Fel, Stanford Univ, 1992-93. **Business Addr:** Metro Columnist, The Milwaukee Journal-Sentinel, 333 W State St, Milwaukee, WI 53201, **Business Phone:** (414)223-5521.

KANE, DR. JACQUELINE ANNE
Educator. **Personal:** Born Aug 27, 1946, New York, NY; daughter of Jacqueline Jones and Philip Gough. **Educ:** Morgan State Univ, AB, 1968; State Univ New York Col, Oneonta, MS, 1974; State Univ New York, Albany, PhD, 1997. **Career:** New York City Dept Soc Serv, caseworker, 1968-70; State Univ New York Col, Oneonta, coordr consult & acad adv, 1970-75; New York State Educ Dept, dir resource ctr higher educ, 1976-81, assoc higher educ opportunity, Bur Higher Edu Opp Prog, 1976-99, Off Col & Univ Eval, 1999-; State Univ New York, Albany, adj instr, 1984-88, 1996-98; JAK Prod, pres, currently. **Orgs:** Bd mem, Asn Black Women Higher Educ, 1978-92, 1997-; NY State Planning Comn, Am Coun Educ Nat Ident Proj, 1980-92, 1999-; Albany NY Alumnae Chap Delta Sigma Theta Sor, 1983-98; Albany Area Chap Am Red Cross, 1984-97; pres, Capital Chap Asn Black Women Higher Educ, 1989-92; chair, adv comn, MNY Women's issues, Ctr Women Govt, 1997-. **Honors/Awds:** Outstanding Young Woman of America, 1978, 1981; Scholarship Award, Delta Sigma Theta Sor Inc, 1981; Hilda H Davis Award for Distinguished Leadership & Service; SAGE, scholarly j black women, 1988; Wave Award, NOW, 1994; African American Women of Distinction, Albany Branch Nat Asn Advan Colored People, 1996. **Home Addr:** 30 Limerick Dr, Albany, NY 12204-1742. **Business Addr:** Associate Higher Education, New York State Education Department, 5N Mezzanine Educ Bldg, Albany, NY 12234, **Business Phone:** (518)474-2593.

KANI, KARL (CARL WILLIAMS)
Fashion designer, president (organization). **Personal:** Born in Brooklyn, NY. **Career:** Threads for Life, designer, 1990-93; Cross Colours, 1991-94; Karl Kani Infinity Inc, founder, pres & chief exec officer, 1995-; Kani Inc, dir. **Orgs:** Bd mem, Nat Asn Advan Colored People; bd mem, Urban League. **Special Achievements:** Developed entrepreneurial program for 24 elementary schools in Los Angeles, through which students learn to run their own businesses by marketing and selling close-out designs by Kani. **Business Phone:** (213)626-6076.

KAPLER, GABE (GABRIEL STEFAN KAPLER)
Baseball player. **Personal:** Born Aug 31, 1975, Hollywood, CA; married Lisa; children: Chase Ty Rio & Dane Gabriel Ri. **Educ:** Moorpark Jr Col. **Career:** Baseball player (retired); Detroit Tigers, 1998-99; Tex Rangers, 2000-02; Colo Rockies, 2002-03; Yomiuri Giants, Japan League, 2004; Boston Red Sox, 2003-06;

Milwaukee Brewers, 2008; Tampa Bay Rays, 2009-. **Orgs:** United States Congress, 2006; Founder, Gabe Kapler Found. **Honors/ Awds:** Southern League MVP award, 1998; Southern California Jewish Sports Hall of Fame, 2006; BoSox Club Man of the Year, 2006; National League Comeback Player of the Year Award. **Special Achievements:** South Atlantic League All-Star OF, 1996; Florida State League All-Star OF, 1997; Double-A All-Star OF, 1998; Baseball America First team Minor League All-Star OF, 1998; Southern League Most Valuable Player, 1998; Baseball Weekly Minor League Player of the Year, 1998; The Sporting News Minor League Player of the Year, 1998; USA Today Minor League Player of the Year, 1998; Detroit Tigers Minor League Player of the Year, 1998; Southern League All-Star OF, 1998. *

KAPPNER, DR. AUGUSTA SOUZA
School administrator, educator. **Personal:** Born Jun 25, 1944, New York, NY; daughter of Augusto Souza and Monica Fraser; married Thomas; children: Tania & Diana. **Educ:** Barnard Col, NY, AB, 1966; Hunter Col, NY, MSW, 1968; Columbia Univ, NY, DSW, 1984. **Career:** St Univ, NY Sch Social Welfare, Stony Brook, asst prof, 1973-74; La Guardia Community Col Queens, NY, assoc prof, 1974-78, dean continuing educ, 1978-84; City Univ NY, New York, NY, univ dean, acad affairs,1984-86; Borough Manhattan Community Col NY, pres, 1986-92; US dept Edn,asst sec voc & adult edn , Wash, 1993-95; Bank Str Col Ed, NY, pres, 1995-. **Orgs:** Bd dirs, Natl Coun Black Am Affairs; NY State Child Care Comn; New York City Temporary Comn on Early Childhood & Child Caring Progs; vice chair, brd trustees, Mary mount Manhattan Col; chmn, Mary mount Manhattan Col Pres Search Comt; pres, chair & bd dirs, Women's Ctr Educ & Career Advancement; New York City Panel Edn Policy. **Honors/Awds:** Hall of Fame, Hunter Col, 1987; Columbia University Medal of Excellence,1988; Barnard Col Medal of Distinction, 1988; Certificate of Achievement, Comptroller of the City of New York, 1990; Community Service Award, Hawks Intl Inc, 1990; Humanitarian Award, Harlem Sch Arts, 1990. **Business Addr:** President, Bank Street College of Education, 610 W 112 St, New York, NY 10025.

KARANGU, DAVID
Automotive executive. **Personal:** Born Jan 1, 1967, Atlanta, GA. **Educ:** Morgan State Univ, BS, mkt. **Career:** Benz Augusta, pres, chief operating officer; Fairway Ford Augusta, pres, chief operating officer. **Orgs:** Bd Dir, Augusta Prep Sch; bd dir, Boys & Girls Club, Augusta; bd dir, MCG Health Syst, 2005-. **Business Addr:** President, Chief Operating Officer, Fairway Ford of Augusta Inc, 4333 Washington Rd, Evans, GA 30809-9512, **Business Phone:** (706)854-9200.

KARPEH, ENID JUAH HILDEGARD
Lawyer. **Personal:** Born Apr 4, 1957, Mainz, Germany; daughter of Martin Sieh Jr and Marion Catherine White Cooper. **Educ:** Univ Penn, BA, int rels, 1979; NY Univ Sch Law, New York, JD, 1983. **Career:** O'Donnell & Schwartz, assoc atty, 1983-85; WNET, 13, NY, assoc gen coun, 1986-88; MTV Networks Inc, NY, coun law & bus affairs, 1988-90; CBS Broadcasting Inc, NY, independent legal coun, 1990; Arts & Entertainment Network, dir, legal & bus affairs; Kidsites 3000 Inc, co-founder & pres, currently. **Orgs:** Bar Asn City NY; Black Entertainment & Sports Lawyers Asn. **Business Addr:** Co-Founder, President, Kidsites 3000 Inc, New York, NY 10011.

KASHIF, GHAYTH NUR (LONNIE KASHIF)
Consultant, writer, television journalist. **Personal:** Born Sep 9, 1933, Raeford, NC; son of Lonnie Smith (deceased) and Annie Mae Bethea Dale; married Hafeeza N A; children: Alif-Ahmed, Rul-Aref, Shazada Latifa & Sadara Barrow. **Educ:** Keesler Commun Chenute USAF, dipl (tech mass commun), 1953; Univ Md Grant Tech, CA, 1953; NY Sch Writing, dipl, 1955. **Career:** Muhammad Speaks Bilalian News, Wash bur chief, 1968-78; Bilalian News AMJ, ed, 1978-81; Int Graphics Kashif News Serv, consult writer, 1981-85; Int Graphics/IQraa Mag, consult, 1981-87; Int Inst Islamic Thought, ed, 1987; Am J Muslim Social Scientists, consult, 1986-87; J Iqraa & Open Mag & Metrop Mag, exec ed, 1982-84, 1985; Warner Cable TV, VA, Islam in Focus,TV dir & producer; Masjidush-Shora, Wash, DC, imam, 1990; Am Muslim Coun, Wash, DC, dir; Black Cong Watch, ed, 1990; Int Inst Islamic Studies, VA, in-house ed; Books: Sacred Journey, 1986; Questions, The Quranic Response. **Orgs:** Pres & chmn, Bilalian News, 1978-81; dir, secy & treas, Metro Mag, 1982-83; rep, Black Media, 1982-83; dir commun, Majdush Shura; Bilalian Econ Develop Corp, 1985-87; dir, Shaw Bus, 1985; Nat Red Cross, 1985; Capital Press Club, 1985; Org 3rd World J NNPA, 1987; dir, The Roundtable Strategic Studies, 1989. **Honors/Awds:** Fred R Doug Award, HU (Muhammad Speaks), 1977; 1st Annual Freedom Journal Award, Univ DC, 1979; Excel in Journalism, CM Found, 1979. **Military Serv:** USAF, sgt; Distinguished National Defense Service Medal; Good Conduct Medal, 1955. *

KASHIF, LONNIE. See KASHIF, GHAYTH NUR.

KASLOFSKY, THOR
Government official. **Personal:** Born Feb 25, 1970, San Francisco, CA; son of Leslie Kaslof and Norma Krieger. **Educ:** John Jay Col Criminal Justice, BA, pub admin, 1997; MBA Baruch Col, City Univ NY, attended. **Career:** City NY, Mayor's Off, events captain, Off Opers, policy analyst, project planner, Off Mgmt & Budget, budget analyst, 1993-98, Dept Homeless Serv, Div Facil Maintenance & Develop, dep dir budget & policy, 1998-2001; dir regulatory & oversight compliance; San Francisco Redevelopment Agency, asst proj mgr, currently. **Orgs:** Community Bd #8 Brooklyn NY; John Jay Alumni Asn; Police Res Asn. **Honors/ Awds:** Nat Dean's List, 1994-97; Kyug Hyup Academic Scholarship, 1996. **Special Achievements:** Published "Race Relations in America: Not So Black and White", John Jay's Finest, 1994. **Business Addr:** Assistant Project Manager, San Francisco Redevelopment Agency, 1 S Van Ness Ave 5th Fl, San Francisco, CA 94103, **Business Phone:** (415)749-2464.

KAUFMAN, MEL. See Obituaries section.

KAZADI, MUADIANVITA MATT
Football player, football coach. **Personal:** Born Dec 20, 1973, Kinshasa, Democratic Republic of the Congo; married Monique; children: Ra-sun, Isis & Rohon. **Educ:** Tulsa Univ, BA, 1997; Univ Mo, ME, 2006. **Career:** Football player (retired), Football coach; St Louis Rams, linebacker, 1997-2001; Barcelona Dragons, 2001-02; Buffalo Bills, 2002; Kans City Chiefs, strength & conditioning asst, 2006-. **Business Phone:** (816)920-9300.

KAZI, ABDUL-KHALIQ KUUMBA
Editor, writer, consultant. **Personal:** Born Dec 15, 1951, New Orleans, LA; son of Wilbur F and Yvonne Gavion; married Sandra Pierre; children: Zijazo, Ambata, Mandela, Ahmad, Jathiya. **Educ:** Tulane Univ, attended 1971; Univ New Orleans, attended 1986; Stanford Univ, attended 1993. **Career:** Moret Press, printer, 1971-80; Figaro Newspaper, prod assoc, 1980-81; Black Collegiate Serv Inc, copy ed, 1981-83, assoc ed, 1983-86, managing ed, 1986-, prod mgr, 1989-; Worldwide Concepts Inc, ed, writer, 1992-; Times-Picayune Publ Corp, ed, 1994-. **Orgs:** Founding mem, Black Runners Orgn, 1980-; Nat Asn Black Journalists, 1988-89; Am Muslim Coun, 1992; Coun Am-Islamic Relations, 1994; founder, Holy Land, 1994. **Honors/Awds:** Unity Award Media, Lincoln Univ MO, 1985, 1989-90; Keynote Speaker/Black Hist, US Dept Agr, 1986; keynote speaker, Black Students on White Campuses Conf, GA State Univ, 1989; guest panelist, Print Jour Seminar, Southern Univ New Orleans, 1989; keynote speaker, Alpha Phi Alpha-Cornell Univ, 1991-; Keynote Speaker, Univ NC-Wilmington, 1993; Speaker, African Holocaust Conf, Bowling Green State Univ, 1993. **Home Addr:** 22 Chatham Dr, New Orleans, LA 70122. *

KEA, ARLEAS UPTON
Lawyer, government official. **Personal:** Born Mar 31, 1957, Weimar, TX; daughter of Henry and Lillie Mae Upton; married Howard E Kea, Apr 19, 1986; children: Chase, Arlyce Mallory. **Educ:** Univ Tex, BA, 1979; Univ Tex Sch Law, JD, 1982. **Career:** US Dept Labor, benefits rev bd atty, 1982-85; Fed Deposit Ins Corp, sr atty, Fidelity Bd Claims, 1985-89, sr coun, Criminal Restitution, 1989-91, asst gen coun, 1994-96, acting dep gen coun, 1995, ombudsman, dir div admin, currently. **Orgs:** US Supreme Ct Bar; State Bar Tex; Nat Bar Asn; Fed Bar Asn, 1985-87; secy, Nat Conf Black Lawyers, 1982-88; Alpha Kappa Alpha Sorority; chmn bd stewards, Lomas African Methodist Episcopal Zion Church, 1988-90; vchair, Tutor & Mentoring Prog. **Honors/ Awds:** FDIC Spec Achievement Award, 1987-89; Outstanding Woman, Lomax African Methodist Episcopal Zion Church, 1990. **Business Addr:** Director, Federal Deposit Insurance Corporation, Division of Administration, 550 17th St NW, Washington, DC 20429, **Business Phone:** (202)898-1000.*

KEARNEY, ESQ. ERIC HENDERSON
Lawyer, publisher. **Personal:** Born Oct 27, 1965, Cincinnati, OH; son of Jasper William and Rose Powell; married Jan Michele, Dec 23, 1995; children: Emerson Celeste Flora. **Educ:** Darmouth Col, AB, 1985; Univ Cincinnati, Col Law, JD, 1989. **Career:** Strauss & Troy, atty, 1989-94; Sesh Commun, pres, 1995-, chief exec officer, currently; Cohen, Todd, Kite & Stanford, LLC, partner atty, 1995-; Gile, Hanover, French Presse Inc, pres, 1998; Cincinnati Herald, publ; Ohio, Dist 9, state sen, currently. **Orgs:** Trustee, Amateur Athletic Comn 2012, 1997; pac founder & treas, African Family Asn Small Bus Commun; steering comt mem, Nat Underground Railroad Freedom Ctr; trustee, Greater Cincinnati African Family Asn C; trustee, Downtown Cincinnati; exec commun, Greater Cincinnati Conv & Visitors Bur; trustee, Independent Living Options; trustee, Cincinnati Zoo. **Honors/ Awds:** Black Achiever, YMCA, 1991; Volunteer Recognition Award, Cincinnati Union Bethel, 1995. **Business Addr:** President, Chief Executive Officer, Sesh Communications, 354 Hearne Ave, Cincinnati, OH 45229-2818, **Business Phone:** (513)961-3331.

KEARNEY, JESSE L
Lawyer. **Personal:** Born Jan 14, 1950, Gould, AR; son of Thomas James and Ethel Virginia Curry; married Sheryl Rene Rogers Kearney, Dec 21, 1977; children: Phillip James & Jessica Leigh. **Educ:** Univ Ark, Fayetteville, AR, BA, polit sci, 1973; Univ Ark, Sch Law, JD, 1976; Nat Judicial Col, Reno, NV, Cert, 1989. **Career:** Kearney Law Office, atty, Magnolia, AR, 1976-77, Pine Bluff, AR, 1981-82; State Ark, Office Atty Gen, Little Rock, AR, asst atty gen, 1977-79; State Ark, Off Gov, Little Rock, AR, spec asst Gov, 1979-81; Ark State Claims Comn, Little Rock, AR, comnr, 1981; Cross, Kearney & McKissic, Pine Bluff, AR, atty partner, 1982-89, 1990-; State Ark Judicial Dept, Pine Bluff, AR, ciruit chancery ct judge, 1989-90; atty pvt pract, currently. **Orgs:** W Harold Flowers Law Soc, 1977-, Jefferson County Bar Asn, 1981-, Ark Bar Asn, 1977-, Ark Trial Lawyers Asn, 1987-, Am Bar Asn, 1977-, Am Trial Lawyers Asn, 1984-. **Business Addr:** Attorney, 1022 W 6th Ave, PO Box 6606, Pine Bluff, AR 71601-4034, **Business Phone:** (870)536-4056.

KEARSE, AMALYA LYLE
Judge. **Personal:** Born Jun 11, 1937, Vauxhall, NJ; son of Robert Freeman and Myra Lyle Smith. **Educ:** Wellesley Col, BA, 1959; Univ Mich Law Sch, Ann Arbor, JD, 1962. **Career:** Hughes Hubbard & Reed, assoc, 1962-69; NY Univ Law Sch Wash Sq, adj lectr, 1968-69; US Ct Appeals, 2nd Circuit, judge, 1979-. **Orgs:** Exec comt, Lawyers Comt Civil Rights Under Law, 1970-79; Am Law Inst; fel Am Col Trial Lawyers; Pres's Comt Selection Judges, 1977-78; Nat Asn Advan Colored People LD&E Fund 1977-79; bd dir, Nat Urban League 1978-79. **Honors/Awds:** Cum Laude; Order of the Coif; Jason L Honigman Award for Outstanding Contrib Law Rev Edit Bd. **Special Achievements:** Second African American and first woman to serve in the Second Circuit of the US Ct of Appeals; Nominated for Attorney General by President Clinton; five-times national champion Bridge Player and has written, translated and edited many books on bridge. **Business Addr:** Circuit Judge, US Ct Appeals, 40 Foley Sq, New York, NY 10007.*

KEARSE, GREGORY SASHI
Publisher, association executive, editor. **Personal:** Born Feb 13, 1949, Brooklyn, NY; divorced; children: Nina Monique. **Educ:** Howard Univ, BA, eng, 1974, Commun Res, PhD candidate. **Career:** NY Times, internship, 1969; WABC-TV NY, news asst, writer, 1970-71; Etcetera Mag, assoc ed, 1971-72; Mutual Black Radio Network, news ed, writer, 1974-78; Howard Univ Press, ed, 1978-85, ed consult, 1985-88; Applns Syst, tech writer, 1989; Kearse & Legall Inc, pres & chief exec officer; Bluelight Publ Co, pub, pres & chief exec officer, currently; Publ: Ebony Mag; Encore; Modern Black Men Mag; Essence Mag; Wash African-Am Newspaper Column ist; Chess Life; Karate Illustrated; The Continenet Newspaper, writer, book rev ed; African Faces Mag, ed-in-chief; Campus Lifestyle Mag; New Directions; Chronicle Higher Educ; Scottish Rite Jour, Phylaxsis Notes, Masonic Digest, managing ed. **Orgs:** St John's 12, Prince Hall Grand Lodge, Mt Vernon Chap 1 (Royal Arch Masons); Nat Rifle Asn; Sigma Delta Chi Soc Prof Journalists; Auth League & Auth Guild Am; Am Asn Univ Presses; Wash Area Publ Asn; Big Bros Greater Washington; Am Fedn TV & Radio Artists; Johnathon Davis Consistory 1 (Supreme Coun 33rd Degree); Scottish Rite Res Soc; Phylaxis Soc. **Honors/Awds:** Writer's Digest Creative Writing Award, 1970; Radio Commentary Award, 1976; Public Serv Award, Sec Labor, 1977. **Business Addr:** President & Chief Executive Officer, Publisher, Bluelight Publishing Company, 15147 Deer Valley Terr, Silver Spring, MD 20906-6224, **Business Phone:** (301)899-3146.

KEATON, WILLIAM T.
College president. **Educ:** AM & N Univ; Howard Univ. **Career:** Ark Baptist Col, Little Rock, AK, pres & chancellor, currently. **Business Addr:** President, Chancellor, Arkansas Baptist College, 1600 Bishop St, Little Rock, AR 72202, **Business Phone:** (501)372-6883.*

KEE, JOHN P. (JOHN PRINCE KEE)
Gospel singer, clergy. **Personal:** Born in Durham, NC; married Felice Sampson; children: 7. **Educ:** Yuba Conserv. **Career:** Discography: "There is Hope", 1990; "Churchin Christmas", 1992; "Churchin", 1992; "Lilies of the Valley", 1993; "Color Blind", 1994; "Just Me This Time", 1994; "Never Shall Forget", 1994; "Wash Me", 1994; "We Walk By Faith", 1994; "Yes Lord", 1994; "Wait on Him", 1994; "Show Up", 1995; "Stand", 1995; "Livin on the Ultimate High", 1995; "Christmas Album", 1996; "Thursday Love", 1997; "Strength", 1997; "Any Day", 1998; New Life Community Choir, founder; Gospel vocalist; New Life Fel Ctr, founder & pastor, 1995-. **Honors/Awds:** GMWA Excellence Award Best New Urban Contemporary Female Group, 1991; GMWA Excellence Award Best Video Concert, 1992; Stellar Award best Music Video, 1992; GMWA Excellence Award for Contemporary Male Vocalist of the Yr, 1992; GMWA Excellence Award for Contemporary Choir of the Yr, 1992; GMWA Excellence Award Best Contemporary Album of the Yr & Producer of the Yr, 1992, 1994; Billboard Music Award No1 Gospel Artist, 1992; Billboard Music Award for 1 Gospel Album, 1992; Stellar Award Best Traditional Album, 1993; Inside Gospel Award Best Male Artist, 1994; Grammy Nomination, 1996, 1999, 2001, 2004; Stellar Award, 2002. **Business Addr:** Pastor, New Life Fellowship Ceter, 1337 Samuel St, Charlotte, NC 28206, **Business Phone:** (704)377-4004.*

KEE, LINDA COOPER (LINDA G COOPER WALTON)
Management consultant. **Personal:** Born Jun 1, 1954, Jacksonville, FL; daughter of Freddie and Benjamin Groomes;

married Steven Kee, Apr 25, 1998. **Educ:** Fla State Univ, BS, 1974; Ind Univ, MBA, 1977; Nat Multicultural Inst, cert. **Career:** Hallmark Cards, budget analyst, 1977-80, mgr sales admin, 1980-85, dir minority affairs, 1985-92; LGC & Assocs, pres, 1992-. **Orgs:** Black MBA Asn; Alpha Kappa alpha Sorotity, 1972-; Soc Human Resource Mgt; treas, GKC Chap Links; Women's Employ Network; Urban League Greater Kansas City; Full Employ Coun; Mo State Bd Mediation; Defense Adv Comn. **Honors/Awds:** 100 Most Influential African Americans, KC Globe Newspaper, 1992, 1993-97; Up & Comers Award, Jr Achievement, 1995; Dollars & Sense. **Special Achievements:** Often cited in various national publications. **Business Addr:** President, LGC & Associates, 1601 E 18th St Suite 120, Kansas City, MO 64105, **Business Phone:** (816)842-0542.

KEE, MARSHA GOODWIN
Government official. **Personal:** Born Oct 3, 1942, Durham, NC; daughter of Lewis Marshall Goodwin and Margaret Catherine Kennedy Goodwin; divorced. **Educ:** Spelman Col, Atlanta, GA, BA, 1964; Atlanta Univ, Atlanta, GA, MA, 1969. **Career:** NC Cent Univ, Durham, NC, instr sociol, 1966-72; NC State Univ, Raleigh, NC, instr sociol, 1973-74; Durham Col, Durham, NC, counr/dir, 1974-80; NC Off State Personnel, Raleigh, NC, personnel analyst, 1980-89; County Durham, NC, dir, equal opportunity/affirmative action, 1989-. **Orgs:** Delta Sigma Theta Sorority Inc, 1967-; Int Personnel Mgt Asn, 1985-; NAACP, 1987-; Nat Forum Black Pub Admin, 1989-; NC Minority Women's Bus Enterprise, 1989-; Fin Secy, NCCU Educ Advan Found, 1989-; chap mem, Durham Alummae Chap, currently. **Honors/Awds:** Alpha Kappa Delta, Nat Sociol Honor Soc, 1965; Outstanding Young Women in America, 1975; Outstanding Soloist, White Rock Baptist Church, 1985; Outstanding Soloist, St Joseph's AME Church Lay Orgn, 1988; Pastor's Soloist, 1989. **Business Phone:** (919)560-0024.

KEELER, VERNES
Executive, business owner, president (organization). **Career:** V Keeler & Assoc Inc, New Orleans LA, owner, pres & chief exec, 1971.

KEELS, JAMES DEWEY
Mayor. **Personal:** Born Jan 12, 1930, Blackfork, OH; son of G Dewey and Hulda Howell; married Dorothy M Wilmore; children: James Dewey Jr & Tawana Lynn Simons. **Educ:** Univ Cincinnati Eve Col, 1971. **Career:** Mayor (retired); US Post Off, postal clerk, 1953-78, supvr del & collection, 1979-80; Village Woodlawn, coun, 1969-71, mayor, 1972-79; Address Info Systs, mgr, 1981-85. **Orgs:** Exec officer & treas, Ohio Mayors Asn; Cincinnati Postal Employ Credit Union, 1969-; Hamilton County Munic League, 1972-79; Woodlawn Action Club; Valley Young Men's Christian Asn, Cincinnati; cmdr, John R Fox No 631 Ame League, 1960-64; New Hope Baptist Church; past exec vpres, Nat All Fed Employ, 1969-72, vpres, 1989-93, 1995-96, pres, 1994-, Gallia Econ Develop Asn; pres, Emancipation Celebration Comt, 1989-94; finance chmn, Gross Br, Young Men's Christian Asn, 1980-88. **Honors/Awds:** Ky Colonel Hon, Or KY Col Commonwealth, 1971; Award of Merit, Pride Mag, 1979; Outstanding Community Service, Gen Assembly Ohio Senate, 1979; Elected member, Govs Ohio Exec Comn, Ohio Rural Develop Partnership, 1993. **Special Achievements:** First black mayor for the Village of Woodlawn, 1972; first black chairman to the Post Office Credit Union, 1974-75; first black elected officer treasure of Ohio Mayor Association, 1978. **Military Serv:** AUS, corpl, 1951-53. **Home Addr:** 1041 Vaughn Rd, Bidwell, OH 45614. *

KEEMER, EDGAR B.
Physician. **Personal:** Born May 18, 1913, Washington, DC; children: 6. **Educ:** Ind Univ, BS; Meharry Med Col, MD, 1936. **Career:** Detroit Inner City, gynecology, 1939-. **Orgs:** Active militant civil rights struggle & Women's right abortion; forced USN accept black Drs, 1943; Nat Asn Repeal Abortion Laws; Kappa & Alpha Psi; pres, Surf Club; Mich Pub Health Asn; Big Game Hunting Safaris Africa; medadv, Clergy CounProb Pregnancy. **Honors/Awds:** Cit Yr, 1974; Feminist Yr nomination, Nat Assn Soc Workers, 1974. **Special Achievements:** Published many articles, Therapeutic Abortion Pub.

KEENE, PAUL F., JR.
Artist, educator. **Personal:** Born Aug 24, 1920, Philadelphia, PA; son of Paul F and Josephine B; married Laura Mitchell, Dec 24, 1944; children: Paul-Jacques, Lydia B. **Educ:** Philadelphia Sch Indust Arts, 1941; Temple Univ, Tyler Art Sch, Philadelphia, PA, BFA, BS, educ, 1947, MFA, 1948; Academie Julien, Paris, France, cert, 1952. **Career:** Educator (retired), artist; Tyler Sch Art, instr, 1947-48; Centre D'Art Haiti, dir courses, 1952-54; John Hag Whitney, fel, 1952, 1954; Philadelphia Col Art, prof, 1964-68; Bucks County Community Col, prof, 1968-85. **Honors/Awds:** Temple Alumni Award, 1967; Alumni Award, Philadelphia Col Art, 1972; Vandersee Award, Brandywine Workshop, 1990. **Special Achievements:** Art in America, new talent, 1954. **Military Serv:** Army Air Corp, signal corp, 2nd lt navigator, 1940-45. *

KEENE, SHARON C.
Executive. **Personal:** Born Feb 27, 1948, Philadelphia, PA. **Educ:** Morgan State Univ, BS, 1970; Univ PA, MLA, 1976. **Career:** Nat Park Serv, chief planning & federal prog, 1980-.

KEENON, UNA H R
Judge. **Personal:** Born Dec 30, 1933, Nashville, TN; daughter of Charles L and Mary L Gowins; children: Gregory M Rhodes & Patrick Washington. **Educ:** Tenn State Univ, BA, 1954; Cleveland State Univ, Col Law, JD cum laude, 1975; Ashland Theol Sem, currently. **Career:** Judge (retired); Cuyahoga County Welfare Dept, social worker, 1957-60; Cleveland Pub Schs, teacher, 1960-74; Legal Aid Soc, atty, 1975-78; Cuyahoga County Pub Defender, Juvenile Div, atty-in-charge, 1978-80; Johnson, Keenon & Blackmon Law Firm, partner, 1980-83; UAW Legal Servs Plan, managing atty, 1983-86; E Cleveland Munic Ct, judge, 1986-2005. **Orgs:** AKA Sorority, 1952-; Black Women Polit Action Comt, founding pres, 1982-86, bd mem, 1986-; NCW, 1986-; bd mem, YWCA, Northern Br, 1989-; bd mem, Nat Asn Advan Colored People, 1992-; bd mem, Hitchcock House, 1992-; bd mem, COT Guidance, 1992-; Cleveland Metrop Bar Asn. **Honors/Awds:** Meritorious Service Award, E Cleveland Black Police Officers Asn, 1988-89; Servant Award, St James Lutheran Church, 1990; Role Model for Women Award, Women Community Serv, 1992; E Ohio Gas Honor Award, 1992; Woman in Service Award, 1993; MLK Jr Altruism Award, E Cleveland Citizens Sound Gov, 1993; Hitchcock Center Award, 1993. **Special Achievements:** Chronical (Past Editor), Official Newsletter of the Association of Municipal County Judges Association. **Home Addr:** 16148 Cleviden Rd, East Cleveland, OH 44112, **Home Phone:** (216)932-5090. *

KEFFERS, JAMIE L
City commissioner. **Career:** US Parole Comn, comnr. **Business Addr:** Commissioner, US Parole Commission, 10th St Constitution Ave NW, Washington, DC 20530, **Business Phone:** (301)492-5990.

KEGLAR, SHELVY HAYWOOD
Psychologist, executive. **Personal:** Born Dec 13, 1947, Charleston, MS; son of Minnie M Keglar Miller and John H Ratliff; married Robbia Steward, Mar 7, 1970; children: Shelvy Jr, Robalon, Skyler, Ronelle & Stanford. **Educ:** Kaskaskia Jr Col, Centralia, Ill, assoc degree, 1966-68; Ark State Univ, Jonesboro, Ark, BA, sociol, 1968-70, MA, rehab coun, 1974; Ind Univ, Bloomington, Ind, PhD, educ psychol, coun psychol, 1979. **Career:** Hamilton Ctr, Terre Haute, Ind, assoc dir, 1974-84; Atterbury Job Corps, Edinburgh, Ind, psychologist, 1979-; Midwest Psychol Ctr Inc, Indianapolis, Ind, pres, 1984-; Ind Consortium Mental Health Serv Res, fac, currently. **Orgs:** Vpres, mem chmn, 1988-89, pres, 1986-87, Nat Black Child Develop Inst, Indianapolis affiliate; pres, Terre Haute Minority Bus Assoc, 1983-84; pres, Ind Asn Black Psychologists, 1982-84; Am Psychol Asn; Asn Black Psychologists; Soc Clin & Exp Hypn. **Honors/Awds:** Service Award, Strong-Turner Alumni Club, Ark State Univ, 1988; Outstanding Service Award, Ind Asn Black Psychologists, 1984; Outstanding Alumnus, Ark State Univ, 1991; Centralia Sports Hall of Fame, 1991; America's Best and Brightest Business and Professional Men, Dollars & Sense Mag. **Special Achievements:** Author: "Workfare and the Black Family," Black Family, vol 6:2, 1986; "Alcohol & Drug Abusers in a Family Practice Resident's Ward," w/M Clarke, Alcohol & Research World, 4, 1980. **Military Serv:** AUS, SP 4, 1971-73; Post Commendation Award. **Home Addr:** 9208 Fordham, Indianapolis, IN 46268, **Home Phone:** (317)872-9727. **Business Addr:** President, Midwest Psychological Center Inc, 3676 Washington Blvd, Indianapolis, IN 46205, **Business Phone:** (317)923-3930.

KEITH, HON. DAMON JEROME
Judge. **Personal:** Born Jul 4, 1922, Detroit, MI; son of Perry A and Annie L Williams; married Rachel Boone, Oct 18, 1953 (died 2007); children: Cecile, Debbie & Gilda. **Educ:** WVa State Col, AB, 1943; Howard Univ Law Sch, LLB, 1949; Wayne State Univ Law Sch, LLM, 1956. **Career:** Off Friend Ct, City Detroit, atty, 1951-55; Wayne County, bd supervisors, 1958-63; Keith, Conyers, Anderson, Brown & Wahls, Detroit, Mich, sr partner, 1964-67; Eastern Dist Mich, chief US judge, 1967-77; US CtAppeals, 6th Circuit Ct, Detroit, Mich, judge, 1977-95, sr judge, 1995-. **Orgs:** Chmn, Mich Civil Rights Comn, 1964-67; trustee, Med Corp Detroit; trustee, Interlochen Arts Acad; trustee, Cranbrook Sch; Citizen's Adv Comn Equal Educ Opportunity Detroit Bd Educ; vpres, United Negro Col Fund Detroit; first vpres emer, Detroit Chap Nat Asn Advan Colored People; comn mgt, Detroit YMCA; Detroit Coun Boy Scouts Am; Detroit Arts Comn; Am Bar Asn; Nat Bar Asn; Mich Bar Asn; Detroit Bar Asn; Nat Lawyers Guild; Am Judicature Soc; Alpha Phi Alpha; Detroit Cotillion; Univ Notre Dame Law Sch, Adv Coun; bd trustees, Univ Detroit Mercy; vice chmn, Detroit Symphony Orchestra; Leukemia Soc Am Inc. **Honors/Awds:** Spingarn Medalist, 1974; received numerous honorary degrees from various universities including: Univ Mich; Howard Univ; Wayne State Univ; Mich St Univ; NY Law Sch; Detroit Col Law; W Va St Col; Univ Detroit; Atlanta Univ; Ohio St Univ; Cent Mich Univ; Eastern Mich Univ; Morehouse Col; NY Law Sch; Hofstra Univ; DePaul Univ; Yale Univ; Western Mich Univ; Tuskegee Univ; Lincoln Univ; Menorah Award, Afro-Asian Inst Histadrut Israel, 1988; Governor's Minuteman Award, The Rotary Club Lansing, 1991; Champion of Justice Award, State Bar Mich, 1991; C Francis Stratford Award, Nat Bar Asn, 1992; Martin Luther King Jr Freedom Award, Progressive Nat Baptist Conv, 1992; Thurgood Marshall Award, Wolverine Bar Asn, 1993; Alumni Award for Distinguished Postgraduate Achievement, Howard Univ, 1994; Earl Burru Dickerson Award; Trumpet Award, Turner Broadcasting Syst, 1991, 2000; Spirit of Excellence Award, Am Bar Asn, 2001; dr, Howard Univ, 2008. **Special Achievements:** Named one of 100 Most Influential Black Americans, Ebony Magazine, 1971, 1977; Publications: "We the People Have Lots to Celebrate," Detroit Free Press, 1987; "Ashmore: Hearts and Minds: The Anatomy of Racism from Roosevelt to Reagan," University of Michigan Law Review, 1983; "A Responsibility to Serve Black Community," Detroit Free Press, 1988. **Military Serv:** AUS, 1943-46. **Business Addr:** Senior Judge, US Court of Appeals, Sixth Circuit, 540 Potter Stewart US Courthouse, 100 E 5th St, Cincinnati, OH 45202, **Business Phone:** (513)564-7000.

KEITH, FLOYD A
Football coach, executive director. **Personal:** Born Aug 22, 1948, St Marys, OH. **Educ:** OH Northern Univ, BS, educ. **Career:** Miami Univ, offensive backfield coach, 1970-73; Univ Colo, offensive backfield coach, quarterback & receiver coach & passing game coordr, 1974-78; Howard Univ, head football coach, 1979-82; Univ Ariz, running back coach, 1983; Ind Univ, quarterback coach & passing game co-coordr, 1984-92; Univ RI, head football coach, 1993-99; Black Coaches Asn, Black Coaches & Adminrs Off, exec dir, 2001-. **Orgs:** Guest & panelist, ESPN. **Special Achievements:** Appeared in HBO Sports documentaries over the past three years; appeared in NBC & ABC specials; frequent participant on numerous national sports talk shows; one of The 101 Most Influential Minorities in Sports, Sports Illustrated, 2004. **Business Addr:** Executive Director, Black Coaches Association, Black Coaches & Administrators Office, 201 S Capitol Ave Suite 495, Indianapolis, IN 46225, **Business Phone:** (317)829-5600.*

KEITH, KAREN C
Athletic coach. **Personal:** Born Apr 16, 1957, Boston, MA; daughter of Albert Keith and Margaret Stokes Keith. **Educ:** Fla State Univ, BS, 1978; Boston Col, MA, M Ed admin & supv, 1989. **Career:** Beth Israel Hosp, Brookline MA, phlebotimist, 1978-83; US Youth Games Team, coach, 1980-81; Newton South High Sch, coach, 1981-83; Brown Jr High Sch, Newton MA sci & phy educ teacher, sports coach team leader, adminr, 1981-87; Boston Col, head coach track & field, 1989. **Honors/Awds:** mem, New England Select Side Rugby Team, 1985-86; first Coach of the Year, Div first Region 1987; Hall of Fame Sagamore Award, Brookline High Sch, 1988.

KEITH, DR. LEROY, JR.
Executive, school administrator, businessperson. **Personal:** Born Feb 14, 1939, Chattanooga, TN; son of Roy and Lula; married Anita Halsey; children: Lori, Susan, Kelli & Kimberly. **Educ:** Morehouse Col, BA, 1961; Ind Univ, MA, 1968, PhD, 1970; Bowdoin Col, LLD, 1990. **Career:** Chattanooga Pub Sch, sci teacher, 1961-66; Neighborhood Serv Prog, Chattanooga TN, dir, 1966-68; Ind Univ, Human Rels Comt, exec secy,1968-69, Bur Educ Placement, admin asst, 1969-70; Dartmouth Col, asst prof educ, William Jewett Tucker Found Internship Prog, dir, 1970-71, asst deancol, asst prof educ, 1971-72, assoc dean & asst prof educ & urban studies,1972-73; Univ Mass Syst, assoc vpres, 1973-75; Mass Bd Higher Ed,chancellor, 1975-78; Univ DC, exec vpres, 1978-82; Aspen Inst Humanistic Studies, Alvin & Peggy Brown fel, 1980; Univ Md, vpres policy & planning,1983-87; Morehouse Col, Atlanta, GA, pres, 1987-94; Carson Prod Co, chmn, 1998-2000; Keystone Group, bd dir; Phoenix Series Fund, bd dir; Stonington Partners Inc, partner; Diversapack Co, dir, currently; Almanac Capital Mgt, managing dir, currently. **Orgs:** Ttrustee, Phoenix Funds Family, 1980-; One to One Mentoring Partnership; bd, Savannah Bus Group; Found Mem Med Ctr; Telfair Mus Art; First CityClub; Savannah Area Chamber Com; CEO Coun Savannah Area Chamber Com; dir, Value Am; Phi Beta Kappa; trustee, Evergreen Invest; trustee, St Andrews Episcopal Sch, bethesda, Md; treas, Capital Formation & Enterprise Develop; bd dir, Siskin Childrens Inst. **Honors/Awds:** Resolution for Outstanding Achievement Award, Tenn House Reps, 1976; Distinguished Alumni Service Award, Ind Univ, Bloomington, 1977. **Special Achievements:** Hundred Top Young Leaders in American Academy, Change Magazine & American Council on Education, 1978; First African American to hold chancellor of the Massachusetts Board of Higher Education.

KEITH, LUTHER
Editor, executive director. **Personal:** Married Jacqueline Hall-Keith; children: Erin. **Educ:** Univ Detroit, jour, 1972. **Career:** Wayne State Univ, Journ Inst Minorities, founding dir, 1985-87; Detroit News, gen assignment reporter, bus ed, asst managing ed, sr ed; ARISE Detroit, exec dir, currently. **Orgs:** Vpres, Nat Asn Black Journalists; bd mem, Rosa Parks Scholar Found; bd mem, Plowshares Theater Co. **Honors/Awds:** Mich Journ Hall of Fame, 1995. **Special Achievements:** First African-Am sportswriter for a major Detroit daily newspaper, 1973; first African-Am reporter assigned to the state capital bureau in Lansing, 1979; first African-Am newsroom ed at The Detroit News, 1982. **Business Addr:** Executive Director, ARISE Detroit!, 5830 Field St Suite 103, Detroit, MI 48213, **Business Phone:** (866)942-7474.

KEITT, LIZ ZIMMERMAN
Consultant, purchasing agent. **Personal:** Born Nov 28, 1938, Cameron, SC; married Joseph L; children: Vincent Lewis &

Marvin. **Educ:** Claflin Univ, BS, phys educ, 1970; SC State Col, MEd, 1974. **Career:** Orangeburg County, former mayor pro team; Claflin Univ, purchasing agt, pres; Claflin Univ Gospel & Choir, adv, 1974-78; Mt Carmel Bapt Church, Cameron, SC, supt, 1971; Project Life: Positeen Prog, founder & dir, 1992-. **Orgs:** Chairperson, Lower Savannah Grassroots Adv Comt, 1976-; Claflin Col Nat Alumni Asn; Dem Women's Club, 1977-79; coordr, Ward III Voters, 1978; Miss Black Universe Pageant, Orangeburg Co, reg dir, 1979; Nat Asn Advan Colored People State; Student Govt Asn; Alpha Kappa Sor; Beta Zeta Omega Chapter Alpha Kappa Alpha Sorority, Inc; Int Alumni Asn Claflin Univ. **Honors/Awds:** Outstanding Community Leader, 1975; Outstanding Adv, Nat Asn Advan Colored People, 1976-77; Outstanding Service, 1978. **Special Achievements:** First African American who served in the Orangeburg City Council; first woman ever to serve as Mayor Pro Tem, and served the City of as Mayor for three months; first woman president of the Eastern Intercollegiate Athletic Conference. **Business Addr:** Founder, Director, Project Life: Positeen, 349 Summers Ave, Orangeburg, SC 29115, **Business Phone:** (803)534-4263.*

KELLER, C RANDOLPH
Public prosecutor. **Career:** City Shaker heights, chief prosecutor, currently. **Business Phone:** (216)491-1443.

KELLER, DR. EDMOND JOSEPH
School administrator, educator. **Personal:** Born Aug 22, 1942, New Orleans, LA; married Genevieve Favorite; children: Vern A & Erika V. **Educ:** La State Univ, New Orleans, BA, 1969; Univ WI, Madison, MA, polit sci, 1970, PhD, polit sci, 1974. **Career:** Univ Wis, Nat Defense Educ Act, title IV fel, 1969-71; Univ Nairobi, Inst Develop Studies, vis res fel, res assoc, 1972-73; Ind Univ Bloomington, from asst prof to assoc prof, 1974-83; Ford Found, fel, 1971-72, Middle E & Africa Field Res fel, 1972-73, fel, 1981-82; Nat Fellowship Fund, fel, 1981-82; Comm Inst Coop, dir cic minority fel prog, 1982-83; Univ Calif Santa Barbara, chmn black studies, 1983-84, from assoc prof to prof, 1983-90, Dept Black Studies, chair, 1983-84, assoc dean grad div, 1984-87, actg dean; Univ Calif, Los Angeles, Am Coun Educ fel, 1987-88, Academic Affairs, Off Pres, fac asst, 1988-90, African studies, prof & vpres, polit sci, 1990-; James S Coleman African Studies Ctr, dir, 1992-2001; President's Task Force Black Stud Eligibility, exec dir, 1988-90; Globalization Res Ctr, dir, 2001-; consult. **Honors/Awds:** Dissertation Research Fellowship, Ford Found, 1972-73; African-Am Scholars Council Post-Doctorate, 1976-77; Post Doctorate, Nat Fel Fund, 1980-82; Rodney Higgins Award of the National Conference of Black Political Scientists, 1981; Ford Found Post Doctorate Ford Found, 1981-82; Eminent Scholar, Norfolk State Univ, 1983; Distinguished Lecturer in Pan Africanist Studies, Ind State Univ, 1987; African Studies Association Distinguished Africanist, 2008. **Special Achievements:** Contributed numerous publications; monographs: Education, Manpower and Development: The Impact of Educational Policy in Kenya, 1980 & Revolutionary Ethiopia: From Empire to People's Republic, 1988. **Military Serv:** AUS, E-5 3 yrs. **Business Addr:** Director, Globalization Research Center-Africa, 405 Hilgard Ave, 10359 Bunche Hall, Los Angeles, CA 90095, **Business Phone:** (310)825-2566.

KELLER, MARY JEAN
Controller. **Personal:** Born Nov 6, 1938, Mt Vernon, NY; daughter of Raymond Mizell and Grace McNair Mizell; children: Ericka Keller. **Educ:** NY Univ, Sch Com, BS, 1960; Columbia Univ, MS, 1978. **Career:** Controller (retired). Hoffberg & Oberfest, Cert Pub Acct's; Bedford Stuyvesant Restoration Corp, asst treas/dir fin; Foreign Policy Study Found Inc, treas; Lisc Inc, controller. **Orgs:** St. Paul Church Orchestra; Sisters Assisting SAfrica; Black Child Develop Inst, NY Affil. **Home Addr:** 198 E 91st St, Brooklyn, NY 11212, **Home Phone:** (718)774-7135. *

KELLEY, DR. DELORES G.
Educator, state government official. **Personal:** Born May 1, 1936, Norfolk, VA; daughter of Stephen and Helen Jefferson; married Russell Victor Jr; children: Norma, Russell III & Brian. **Educ:** VA State Col, BA, philos, 1956; NY Univ, MA, educ, 1958; Purdue Univ, MA, speech commun, 1972; Univ MD, PhD, am studies, 1977. **Career:** NY City Protestant Coun, dir christian educ 1958-60; Plainview JHS, teacher eng, 1965-66; Morgan State Univ, instr eng, 1966-70; Purdue Univ, grad teaching fel speech, 1971-72; Coppin State Col, Lang Lit & Philos, dept chmn, 1976-79, dean lower div, 1979-89, prof communs, 1990-; Md State Deleg (elected from 42nd dist), 1991-94; Md State Sen, 10th Dist, 1995-. **Orgs:** Alpha Kappa Alpha, 1955-; Vol Host Family Baltimore Coun Int Visitors1976-; Roots Forum Proj Grant Md Com Humanities & Pub Policy 1977;evaluation team, Hood Col Md State Dept Educ 1978; reviewer & panelist,Nat Endowment Humanities, 1979-80; chairperson, Adv Coun Gifted & TalentedEduc Baltimore City Sch, 1979-; bd, Harbor Bank Md, 1982-; fel Am CounEduc, 1982-83; exec bd, Baltimore Urban League; sec, Md Dem Party 1986-90;bd, Inst Christian Jewish Studies, 1989-; pres, Black/Jewish ForumBaltimore, 1990-92; chair, Baltimore Chap, Nat Polit Cong Black Women,1993-95; pres-elect, Gov's Comn Adoption, 1995-; deleg, White House ConfAging, 1995; Md Comner Criminal Sentencing Policy, 1996-98; WomenLegislators Md, 1997-98; pres, Women Legislators MD, 1998-99; Gov's CounAdolescent Pregnancy, 1998-; Md Medicaid Adv Comm, 1998-; Atty Gen's & LtGov's Family Violence Coun, 1998-; Md Comn Infant Mortality, 1999-;Baltimore County Schs Strategic Planning Task Force, 1999-; State CommCriminal Sentencing Policy, 1999-;Task Force Common Ownership Communities, 2005-06; State Traumatic Brain Injury Adv Bd, 2005-; Comt Unemployment InsOversight, 2005-06; co-chair, Task Force Study Identity Theft, 2007; Work Group Cult Competency & Workforce Develop Mental Health Prof, 2007-; Task Force Study Develop Disabilities Admin Rate-Payment Syst, 2007-; chair, Executive Nominations Committee, 2007; co chair, Joint Committee on Access to Mental Health Services, 2007. **Honors/Awds:** PhD Thesis "Rhetorical Analysis of 1884-1888 Controversy, Response ofPresbyterian Church in US to Evolution", 1977; Gov's appt State Com onValues Educ, 1980; Baltimore Jewish Coun Fact-Finding Mission to Israel,1987; Coppin Critical Reading Grant, Nat Endowment for the Humanities,1988-89; Women Legislative Leader Award, Md Comn Women, 1995; Champion forChildren Award, Maryland Foster Care Rev Bd, 1996; First Annual RacialJustice Award, YWCA Greater Baltimore, 1996; Maryland's Top 100 Women,Daily Rec, 1996, 1999, 2004; Dorothy Beatty Memorial Award, Women's LawCtr, 1997; Legislator of the Year Award, Domestic Violence Network Md, 1998. **Business Addr:** State Senate, Maryland State Senator, Rm 302 James Sen Off Bldg 11 Bladen St, Annapolis, MD 21401.

KELLEY, JACK ALBERT
Museum curator, educator, police officer. **Personal:** Born Aug 23, 1920, Alberta;son of Frank A and Fannie Cobbs; married Rose Lee Conley (died 1999); children: Jacqueline K Waters, Pamela K Lamar, Keith A & Elizabeth R. **Educ:** Calif State Univ, Fresno, BA, phys educ, 1946. **Career:** Museum curator, Educator, Police officer (retired); Fresno City Police Dept, sergeant detective, 1949-71; Calif St Univ Fresno, coordr law enforcement training proj, 1972-80; Fresno City Col, curator; Fresno County African Am Cult Mus; African Am Hist & Cult Mus San Joaquin Valley, pres, 2003. **Orgs:** Lifetime mem, Varsity Footbball; YMCA; Gamma Xi Chap Phi Beta Sigma Frat; past pres, Past Potentate Saphar Temple 117; past vice chmn, Model City Bd; Shriners; Black Educr Fresno. **Honors/Awds:** Community service Awards, City of Fresno, 1971; Phi Beta Sigma Fraternity, 1980, United Black Men, 1988; African Methodist Episcopal Church, Northern Conf, 1994; Martin L King Jr Community Service Award, 1995. **Special Achievements:** First African American policemen for the Fresno Police Department; One ofFresno's Fabulous "100" Citizens, 1985; One of only five African-American sto be honored- KSEE 24 TV, Fresno, 1995; Honaray mention in Little American Football, 1942. **Military Serv:** USY tank corps, sgt, 1942-44. **Home Addr:** 5295 E Tulare, Fresno, CA 93727.

KELLEY, ROBERT W.
State government official. **Personal:** Born Nov 25, 1940, Nashville, TN; children: Robert Jr, Lanedria & Christopher Shea. **Educ:** Tenn State Univ, BS, 1963; Syracuse Univ, attended 1963; Foreign Serv Inst, attended 1966; US Int Univ Steamboat Springs CO, attended 1970. **Career:** Nashville Urban League, assoc dir, 1969-70; Met Nashville Educ Asn, dir field serv, 1970-72; Meharry Med Col, prog officer, mat mgr hosp & health serv; S St Community Ctr, dir; OIC Inc, 1978-80; Tenn State Univ, proj dir, instr Div Cont Educ, 1982-83. **Orgs:** Alpha Phi Alpha Frat; Nat Asn Advan Colored People; Urban League; Psi Delta Kappa Educ Fraternity; Nat Educ Asn vpres Civitan Int NW Nashville, 1974-75; Nashville Chap Nat Asn Human Rights Workers, Nat Bd, 1974; Transformed Liberty Inc, 1987. **Honors/Awds:** Honorary Sgt At Arms Tenn State Senate, 1971; pub, writer, volunteer, summer issue Peace Corps Vol Mag, 1971; pub Tenth Anniversary Issue US Peace Corps Mag "A Plan for Future Peace;" The Peace Corps, World Beyond War Award, 1987. **Special Achievements:** One of 20 to file a federal lawsuit challenging sch segregation Nashville,leading to the 1956 US Dist Court order to desegregate Nashville schs. *

KELLEY, WILLIAM E.
Association executive. **Personal:** Born Feb 15, 1939, Los Angeles, CA; son of Laura Mae and LeRoy Sr (deceased); married Joann Oliver, Sep 23, 1968; children: Darren LeRoy, Jason Wardell. **Educ:** Whittier Col, BA, 1960; US Naval War Col, attended 1972; George Wash Univ, MS, 1972. **Career:** Association executive (retired); Int Comn YMCA, fel, 1960-61; YMCA Los Angeles, prog dir, 1961-62; Smith, Bucklin & Assoc, acct exec, 1990; Nat Asn Corp Treas, exec dir; Cong Award Found, chief exec officer & nat dir, 2001-04. **Orgs:** Nat Naval Officers Asn, 1972-; Am Soc Asn Exec, 1989-; Naval Order US, 1990; Retired Officers Asn, 1990-; Disabled Am Veterans, 1990-. **Honors/Awds:** Alumni Achievement, Lancer Soc Whittier Col, 1989. **Military Serv:** USN, capt, 1962-90; Joint Serv Medal, Legion of Merit, Vietnam Serv.

KELLEY, WILLIAM MELVIN
Educator, writer. **Personal:** Born Nov 1, 1937, New York, NY; son of William and Narcissa Agatha; married Karen Isabelle Gibson; children: Jessica & Tikaiji. **Educ:** Harvard Univ, attended 1961. **Career:** Free-lance writer & photographer; State Univ NY, Geneseo, writer in residence, 1965; New Sch Social Res, instr, 1965-67; Univ Paris, Nanterre, guest lectr am lit, 1968; Univ W Indies, Mona, guest instr, 1969-70, Sarah Lawrence Col, prof creative writing, 1989-; auth: A Different Drummer, 1962, Dancers on the Shore, 1964, A Drop of Patience, 1965, Dem, 1967, Dunford Travels Everywhere, 1970; articles, "If You're Woke You Dig It", New York Times Mag, 1962; "The Ivy League Negro", Esquire, 1963; "An Am in Rome", Mademoiselle, 1965; "On Racism, Exploitation, & the White Liberal", Negro Digest, 1967; "On Africa in the United States", Negro Digest, 1968; Dancers on the Shore, Howard Univ Press, 1983; Taos Inst Art, guest lectr. **Honors/Awds:** Dana Reed Literary Prize, Harvard Univ, 1960; Bread Loaf Scholar, 1962; John Jay Whitney Found Award, 1963; Rosenthal Foundation Award, Nat Inst Arts & Letters, 1963; Transatlantic Review Award, 1964; Black Academy of Arts & Letters Prize for Fiction, 1970. **Business Addr:** Professor of Creative Writing, Sarah Lawrence College, One Mead Way, Bronxville, NY 10708.

KELLMAN, DENIS ELLIOTT
Lawyer, executive. **Personal:** Born Jul 6, 1948, New York, NY. **Educ:** Yale Col, BA, 1970; Harvard Law Sch, JD, 1975; Harvard Bus Sch, MBA, 1975. **Career:** Le Boeuf Lamb Leiby & Macrae, assoc atty; Columbia Pictures Industs Inc, counr; Bertelsmann Music Group, dir legal & bus affairs; atty, currently. **Orgs:** Int Fedn Phonogram & Videogram Producers; British Phonograpic Industry; Black Music Asn; Harvard Bus Sch Black Alumni Asn; Harvard Law Sch Black Alumni Asn; chmn, Black Entertainment & Sports Lawyers Asn. **Business Addr:** Chairman, Black Entertainment & Sports Lawyers Association, PO Box 441485, Fort Washington, MD 20749-1485, **Business Phone:** (301)248-1818.

KELLOGG, CLARK CLIFTON, JR.
Basketball player, broadcaster. **Personal:** Born Jul 2, 1961, Cleveland, OH; married Rosy; children: Talisa, Alex & Nicholas. **Educ:** Ohio State Univ, attended 1996. **Career:** Basketball player (retired); Ohio State Univ, 1979-82; Ind Pacers, draft pick, 1982, tv analyst, color commentator, currently; ESPN, basketball analyst, 1990; Big East Network; Prime Sports; CBS Sports, game analyst, 1993-94; NCAA Tournament, studio co-host, 1994-97; CBS Sports, studio & game analyst, 1997-. **Orgs:** Bd dirs, Com Nat Bank. **Honors/Awds:** NBA All-Rookie Team; All-Big Ten & Most Valuable Player Honors, 1982. **Business Addr:** Game Analyst, CBS Sports, 51 W 52nd St, New York, NY 10019.

KELLOGG, GEORGE EARL
Executive. **Personal:** Born Oct 20, 1944, Brooklyn, NY; son of William and Mable. **Educ:** Univ NDak, BBA, 1967; Baruch Col, MBA, 1973. **Career:** Chase Manhattan Bank, position eval analyst, 1967-75; Airco Inc, compensation & employ rep, 1975-76; Hoffmann-LaRoche Inc, assoc personnel mgr, 1976-78; Revlon, Inc, mgr human resources, 1978-86; GK Consult Inc, pres, 1986-96; Drake Beam Morin, adj outplacement consult, 1996-98; Cent Park Conservancy, dir human resources, 1996-98; Bugle Boy Indust, dir human resources, 1999. **Orgs:** Delta Sigma Pi Prof Bus Fraternity, 1970-; Am Compensation Asn, 1976-78; Roche Black Coalition, 1977-78; Nat Black MBA Asn, 1980-83; Soc Human Resources Mgt, 1980-; Human Resources Asn New York, 1997-; Mercy Col Adv Bd, 1997-98; Community Health Care Asn NY. **Honors/Awds:** High Achievement Award, Roche Black Coalition, 1977; Certificate of Recognition, Nat Black MBA Asn, 1983; Certificate of Merit, Am Mgt Asn, 1997; Certificate of Appreciation, Baruch Col Pre-Prof Mentor Prog, 1998. **Special Achievements:** Thesis, "The Unionization White Colar & Prof Workers in Today's BUS", 1973; East Ramapo Sch District Home Bound, tutor, 1990-96; Classical Productions Chorale, performer, 1990-93; Baruch Col Society Mentor's, mentor, 1997-; Mercy Col Convocation, speaker, 1998. **Home Addr:** 414 County Club Lane, Pomona, NY 10970-2558, **Home Phone:** (845)354-6829.

KELLOGG, REGINALD J.
Clergy. **Personal:** Born Jul 2, 1933, Ann Arbor, MI. **Educ:** Assumption Sem & Col, BA, 1961; Univ Laval, MA, 1965; Univ Bordeaux, France, lic lit 1967. **Career:** Cent Cathedral High Sch, Toledo, OH, teacher, 1961-65; Holy Trinity Sch, Milwaukee, teacher, 1966; St Francis Col Kitwe, Zambia, teacher, head lang dept, 1967-70; Cent Cathedral High & Ft Wayne, IN, teacher, asst prin, 1970-72; Bishop Luers High Sch, Ft Wayne, IN, teacher; Cathedral Church Diocese, El Paso, priest, assoc pastor; St Francis Basilica, Italy, tour dir, Eng-speaking confessor, currently. **Orgs:** Secy, Am Asn Teachers France & Spain. N Ind Chap, 1970-72; Nat Black Cathedral Clergy Caucus, 1970-93.

KELLUM, ANTHONY O
Executive, real estate executive. **Personal:** Born May 5, 1965, Virginia; married Doreen A, Jun 25, 1994; children: Bryann, Anthony, Nicole & Nathan. **Career:** Kellum Financial Group LLC, pres, chief exec officer, 1994-. **Orgs:** Vpres, Mich Mortgage Brokers Asn, 1999-2000; comt mem, Detroit Sym Orchestra, 2000-01; bd mem, Boysville, 2000-01; comt chait, Mich Mortgage Brokers Asn, 2000-01; adv comt, Lewis Col Bus, 2000-01. **Honors/Awds:** Humanitarian Award, WJLB Clothes for Kids, 1998; Service Award, Mich Mortgage Brokers Assn, 2000; Honorary Award, WQBH, 2000; DHL, Lewis Col Bus, 2001. **Special Achievements:** Property is Power & Family is Job One, speaker,

1977-00; WCHB AM, Finacially Speaking Host, 2000; Front Page News, Kellum Report, writer, 2000. Anthony was the first African-American President of the Michigan Mortgage Brokers Association. **Business Addr:** Chief Executive Officer, President, Kellum Financial Group LLC, 39555 Orchid Hill Pl Suite 600, Novi, MI 48075, **Business Phone:** (248)557-6060.

KELLY, ADRIENNE LORRAINE. See LUMPKIN, ADRIENNE KELLY.

KELLY, BRIAN (BRIAN PATRICK KELLY)
Football player. **Personal:** Born Jan 14, 1976, Las Vegas, NV; married; children: Brian, Kiaran & Kyu Blu. **Educ:** Univ SC, attended 1998. **Career:** Tampa Bay Buccaneers, defensive back, 1998-2007; Detroit Lions, 2008; Free agent, currently. **Honors/Awds:** ESPY Awards, 2003; MTV Video Music Awards, 2004; Super Bowl Champion XXXVIII. **Business Addr:** Corner Back, Detroit Lions, 222 Republic Dr, Allen Park, MI 48101, **Business Phone:** (313)216-4000.

KELLY, BRIAN PATRICK. See KELLY, BRIAN.

KELLY, CHRIS
Rap group, singer. **Personal:** Born Aug 11, 1978, Atlanta, GA; son of Donna. **Career:** Kris Kross, rap duo mem, 1992-96, 2007-; Albums: Totally Krossed Out, 1992; Best of Kris Kross Remixed 1992, 1994, 1996; Da Bomb, 1993; Young, Rich & Dangerous, 1996; Gonna Make U Jump, 1998; Singles: "Jump", 1992; "Warm It Up", 1992; "I Missed the Bus", 1992; "It's a Shame", 1993; "Alright", 1993; "I'm Real", 1993; "I'm Real", 1994; "Tonite's tha Night", 1995; "Live & Die for Hip Hop", 1996. **Business Phone:** (212)833-4494.*

KELLY, ERNECE BEVERLY
Educator. **Personal:** Born Jan 6, 1937, Chicago, IL; daughter of William and Lovette Nathalia. **Educ:** Univ Chicago, AB, 1958, MA, 1959; Northwestern Univ, PhD, 1972. **Career:** Univ of Wis, asst prof, 1978-81; Kingsborough Community Col, assoc prof eng, currently. **Orgs:** Col Lang Asn, 1972-; dir, Nat Coun Teachers Eng, task force racism & bias teaching Eng, 1970-80; exec comm, Conf Col Compos & Commun, 1971-74; Humanities Coun NY; Speakers Humanities, 1992-99. **Honors/Awds:** Res grant, City Univ NY, 1989; scholar residence, Schomburg Ctr Res Black Culture, 1988; Awarded summer seminar, Nat Endowment Humanities, 1978. **Special Achievements:** Has done film reviews in Crisis Magazine and NYK area newspapers, 1991-, has written 138 Commonly Used Idioms, student booklet, 1989, Searching for American National Council of Teachers of English, 1972, Points of Departure, John Wiley & Sons, 1972, film and drama review, New York Beacon. **Home Addr:** 286 10th St, Brooklyn, NY 11215, **Home Phone:** (718)832-3772. **Business Addr:** Associate professor of English, Kingsborough Community College, 2001 Oriental Blvd, Brooklyn, NY 11235, **Business Phone:** (718)368-5000.

KELLY, FLORIDA L. See Obituaries section.

KELLY, REV. DR. HERMAN OSBY
Clergy. **Personal:** Born Feb 28, 1954, Jacksonville, FL; son of Herman; married Linda M Kelly, Sep 1, 1984; children: H Osby III & Tiffany Marie. **Educ:** Morehouse Col, BA, 1975; Springfield Col, MEd, 1976; Boston Univ, MDiv, 1983; Memphis Theol Sem, DMin, 2000. **Career:** Mt Zion AMEC, pastor, 1986-89; RI Col, chaplain, 1987-89; St James AMEC, pastor, 1989-93; Meridian Community Col, instr, 1990-93; Friendship African Methodist Episcopal Church, pastor, 1993-98; La State Univ, instr, 2000-; Bethel African Methodist Episcopal Church, pastor, 2000-. **Orgs:** Nat Asn Advan Colored People, 1989-93; life mem, Kappa Alpha Psi; Black Fac & Staff Asn, La State Univ, 2000-; La Interfaith Conf, 2000-; mentor, fac friend, Football Team mem, La State Univ. **Honors/Awds:** Man of the Year, Nat Asn Advan Colored Peop, 1992; Special Citation, City of Meridian, MS, 1993. **Special Achievements:** Published, "Spiritual Formation of Young Leity in Bethel AME Church," 2000. **Business Addr:** Pastor, Bethel African Methodist Episcopal Church, 1358 S St, Baton Rouge, LA 70802, **Business Phone:** (225)344-6931.

KELLY, IDA B.
Business owner. **Personal:** Born Jun 2, 1925, Yazoo, MS; children: 7. **Career:** Pizza Queen Inc, Detroit, Mich, owner, currently. **Orgs:** Nat Asn Advan Colored People. **Honors/Awds:** Businesswoman of the Year, Nat Asn Bus & Prof Women, 1988. **Business Addr:** Owner, Pizza Queen Inc, Cobo Hall Conf Ctr, PO Box 1002, Detroit, MI 48231, **Business Phone:** (313)259-1100.

KELLY, JAMES CLEMENT
Clergy. **Personal:** Born Sep 29, 1928, Bethlehem, PA; married Loretta; children: Lynne, James Jr, Susan. **Educ:** VA Union Univ, BA, 1964; VA Union Sch Rel, MDiv, 1967. **Career:** Calvary Baptist Church, Clergyman, Pastor Emer, founder. **Orgs:** At Large BSA; Queens Fed Churchs; Rotary Club Jamaica; Prog Nat Bapt NY; life mem, NAACP; NY Mission Soc; vpres, Home Mission bd; PNBC; Admin bd Am Baptist Churchs Metro NY pres Calvary Baptist Fed Credit Union. **Honors/Awds:** Recipient, CIB Badge. **Special Achievements:** fellowship hall will be named in honor of Rev. James C. Kelly, pastor emeritus.

KELLY, JAMES JOHNSON
Military leader. **Personal:** Born Mar 29, 1928, High Point, NC; son of Nathan (deceased) and Elsie Johnson (deceased); married Sallie Mae Williams; children: Eva Mae Kelly-Jones, Thomas Edward Kelly, Cheryl Yvonne Kelly-Oliver. **Educ:** Univ Md, 1957; Our Lady the Lake Univ, BA, 1971, MEd, 1973. **Career:** Military leader (retired). USAF, opers officer, sqdrn comdr, remote air base comdr, sr pilot & expert weapons controller, int pilot, maj, 1971; city San Antonio, TX, Planning Comnr, 1988, vice chmn, 1990-93. **Orgs:** NCP, S Poverty Law Ctr, Retired Officers Asn; Disabled Am Vets, County Workers Coun San Antonio; San Antonio Club OLLU, San Antonio; Lackland AF Base Officers Club, Chap No 5 DAV; lifetime mem, Tex Cong PTA; Star W Masonic Lodge 24, New St Mark Missionary Bapt Church, San Antonio; former mem bd trustees, Our Lady Lake Univ; former pres, OLLU Alumni Asn; adv Brentwood Jr H PTA; chmn, Brentwood Athletic Booster Club; St John Bosco PTC; treas, John F Kennedy H Athletic Booster Asn; pres, Bethel Neighborhood Coun, 1986-91; pres, County Workers Coun, San Antonio, TX, 1987-91; Tex Democratic Party, 1992-; Nat Asn Advan Colored People, 1958-; SCLC, 1962-; Am Asn Retired Persons, 1986-. **Honors/Awds:** UN Service Medal; National Defense Medal; Outstanding Unit Award, USAF; Good Conduct Medal w/3 OLC, USAF; ROKPUCE; WW II Occupation Medal Japan; Nominated for Third Annual Martin Luther King Jr Distinguished Achievement Award, Bexar County, SA, TX, 1989; Community Distinguished Service Award, 1994. **Special Achievements:** First black candidate for city council Dist 6, San Antonio, TX, 1977; first black budget officer, Edgewood Urban-Rural Coun, 1977. **Military Serv:** Army and USAF maj, 1946-71; Legion of Merit; Meritorious Serv Medal; WW II Victory Medal; Korean Serv Medal; AUS Commendation Medal; USAF Commendation Medal w/2 OLC. **Home Addr:** 5010 Enid St, San Antonio, TX 78237. *

KELLY, JOHN PAUL
Banker, consultant. **Personal:** Born Mar 8, 1941, New Orleans, LA; son of John P Sr and Dorothy M Jones; married Lethia A Robinson, Sep 19, 1981; children: John P III, Byron M Smith, Phillip L Smith, Kelli C Smith & Lauren E. **Educ:** Manhattan Col, Bronx, NY, BS, 1963; City Univ NY, MS, 1965. **Career:** Citicorp, NY, asst vpres, 1970-74; Midwest Nat Bank, Indianapolis, IN, pres, 1974-83; Unibind Wash, DC, managing partner, 1987; MMB & Assocs, Wash, DC, partner, 1988; Dryades Savings Bank, staff; Founder's Nat Bank, Los Angeles, pres & chief exec officer; Enterprise Fed Savings Bank, pres& chief exec officer; Brookstone Financial Group Inc, chmn, pres & chief exec officer; Independence Federal Savings Bank, chief lending officer, currently. **Orgs:** Kappa Alpha Psi, 1965-; bd mem, Indianapolis Chamber Com, 1979-85; statetreas, Air Force Asn, 1979-81; bd mem, Citizens Gas & Coke Utility, 1980-85; bd mem & secy, Indianapolis Airport Authority, 1981-85; Gov Ind Fiscal Policy Adv Coun, 1981-85; chmn, Capital Fund Dr, 1982; bd mem, Nat Bus League, 1987-; bd mem, Am Soc Asn Exec, 1988-; Nat Ctr Missing & Exploited C; pres, Nat Bankers Asn, Wash, DC. **Honors/Awds:** Four-Year Academic Scholarship, Manhattan Col, 1959; Academic Scholarship, City Univ NY, 1964. **Military Serv:** USAF, capt, 1963-70; Air Commendation Award. **Business Addr:** Chief Lending Officer, Independence Federal Savings Bank, 1229 Conn Ave NW, Washington, DC 20036, **Business Phone:** (202)626-0417.

KELLY, DR. JOHN RUSSELL
Government official, president (organization). **Personal:** Born Nov 18, 1947, Utica, MS; son of John H; married Bernell Topp; children: Jon Felice & Kristi Bernell. **Educ:** Alcorn State Univ, BS, 1970; Wayne State Univ, MEd, 1972; Univ Southern MS, PhD, 1979. **Career:** AUS, educ specialist, 1971-72; MS Coop Ext Serv, youth develop specialist, 1973-79; Sea Grant Adv Serv, marine specialist, 1979-83; USN Family Serv Ctr, dir; Univ Southern MS, adj prof, currently. **Orgs:** Pres, Res Mgt Inc, 1981; dep dir, Navy Family Serv Ctr, 1983-90; pres, gov bd, Phillips Col, 1985-93; pres, MS div Am Cancer Soc, 1986-88; gen vpres, Alpha Phi Alpha Frat, 1987-91; pres, Harrison Co United Way, 1987-89; pres, J & B Printing Inc; DBA Print Shack, 1987-93; vice chair, 1997, chair, 1999, Am Cancer Soc Nat Bd Dirs; chair, Gulf Coast Med Ctr Bd Trustees, 2001. **Honors/Awds:** Outstanding Young Man in America, Nat Jaycees, 1979, 1982. **Military Serv:** AUS, sargent.

KELLY, JOSEPH WINSTON, JR.
Football player. **Personal:** Born Dec 11, 1964, Sun Valley, CA; son of Joe Sr. **Educ:** Univ Wash, attended 1986. **Career:** Cincinnati Bengals, linebacker, 1986-89; New York Jets, 1990-92; Los Angeles Raiders, 1993; Los Angeles Rams, 1994; Green Bay Packers, 1995; Philadelphia Eagles, 1996. **Honors/Awds:** AFC Championship Game; NFL Championship Game.

KELLY, LEONTINE T C
Bishop. **Personal:** Born Mar 5, 1920, Washington, DC; daughter of David D Turpeau and Ila M Turpeau; married Gloster Current (deceased); children: Angela & Gloster Jr; married James David; children: John David & Pamela. **Educ:** W Va State Col, attended 1941; Va Union Univ, attended 1960; Union Theol Sem, Richmond, VA, MDiv, 1969. **Career:** Bishop (Retired); Asbury United Methodist Church, Richmond, VA, pastor, 1976-83; United Methodist Church, Nashville, TN, mem nat staff, 1983-84; Calif-Nev Conf, San Francisco, CA, bishop, 1984-89; Galilee United Methodist Church, Edwardsville, VA, pastor; Va Conf Coun Ministries, staff mem; Sch teacher. **Honors/Awds:** Drum Major for Justice Award, Martin Luther King, Jr; Grass Roots Leadership; Christian Leadership Conference Award. **Special Achievements:** The first African-American woman bishop was Leontine T.C. Kelly, elected in 1984.

KELLY, MARION GREENUP
Association executive. **Personal:** Born Nov 28, 1947, Baton Rouge, LA; married Harlan H; children: Ingrid, Ian. **Educ:** H Sophie Newcomb Col Tulane Univ, BA, 1969; Tulane Univ, MEd, 1970. **Career:** Headstart, tchr, 1970-71; Neighborhood Coordr, asst exec dir, 1971-73; Mayors Office New Orleans, city partic coordr, 1975; city's Human Rels Comt, Deputy Dir; Audubon Park Comn, Asst Dir & Bus Mgr. **Orgs:** Nat Asn Planners, 1971-73; Am Soc & Planning Officials, 1971-74; Honors Educ Soc, 1970-73; Gr New Orleans Presch Asn, 1970-74; Childrens Bur New Orleans, 1973-74. **Honors/Awds:** Civic Organization awards, pub schs Baton Rouge, 1963-64. **Business Addr:** City Hall BE10, New Orleans, LA 70112.

KELLY, MICHAEL RAYMOND (MIKE RAYMOND KELLY)
Baseball player. **Personal:** Born Jun 2, 1970, Los Angeles, CA. **Educ:** Ariz State Univ. **Career:** Baseball Player (retired); Atlanta Braves, outfielder, 1994-95; Cincinnati Reds, outfielder, 1996-97; Tampa Bay Devil Rays, outfielder, 1998-99; Colorado Rockies, outfielder, 1999. **Honors/Awds:** Golden Spikes Award, 1991.

KELLY, MIKE RAYMOND. See KELLY, MICHAEL RAYMOND.

KELLY, R (ROBERT KELLY)
Singer. **Personal:** Born Jan 8, 1967, Chicago, IL; son of Joann. **Career:** Singer, songwriter, producer, dancer; USBL, Atlantic City Seagulls, basketball player, 1997; Albums: Born into the '90s, 1992; 12 Play, 1993; R Kelly, 1995; TP-2.com, 2000; The Best of Both Worlds, 2002; Chocolate Factory, 2003; The R. in R&B Collection, Vol. 1, 2003; Happy People & U Saved Me, 2004; Unfinished Business, 2004; TP-3: Reloaded, 2005; Remix City Vol. 1, 2005; Double Up, 2007; Hot singles include: Sex Me (Parts 1 2); Bump N' Grind; Your Body's Callin; self-titled album, 1998; Shaft, 2000; Osmosis Jones, 2001; Drumline, 2002; Old Sch, 2003; Fun with Dick & Jane. 2004; Trapped in the Closet: Chapters 1-12, 2005, 2007. **Honors/Awds:** NAACP Image Award, Outstanding Song, 1997; Grammy, Award, Best Song Written for a Motion Picture, 1998; Am Music Award, Favorite Male R&B & Soul Artist, 2000; Billboard Award, 2003; Winner of Grammy Award. **Business Addr:** Vocalist, c/o Jive Records, 137-139 W 25th St, New York, NY 10001, **Business Phone:** (212)727-0016.

KELLY, ROBERT. See KELLY, R.

KELLY, THOMAS, JR.
Financial manager. **Personal:** Born Apr 2, 1951, Augusta, GA; married Geraldine; children: Thomas III & Tiffany Nicole. **Educ:** Augusta Col Sch Bus, BBA, Augusta Col, MBA, 1978. **Career:** Med Col GA Talmadge Memorial Hosp; gen assountant, 1973-74, cost Accountant, 1974-75, fiscal & affairs analyst, 1975-76, asst hosp adminstr, 1976-78, assoc hosp adminr; Med Col Ga Health System, sr vpres, cfo, currently. **Orgs:** Hosp Financial Mgt Asn; chmn, Internal Audit Com Health Ctr Credit, 1977-79; loan exec, United Way Agency, 1978-79. **Business Addr:** Senoir Vice President, Chief Financial Officer, Medical College of Georgia Health System, 1120 15th St, Augusta, GA 30912, **Business Phone:** (706)721-0211.

KELSEY, JOSEPHINE
School administrator, president (organization), executive director. **Career:** Ctr Creative Studies, pres, 1991-93; Mich Guild Artists & Artisans, exec dir; Humane Soc Huron Valley, exec dir, currently. **Orgs:** Mayor's Comn State Art Fairs. **Special Achievements:** First chief executive officer of the corp formed by the merger of the Coll of Art & Design & the Inst of Music & Dance. *

KELSO-WATSON, ANGELA R.
College administrator. **Personal:** Born Mar 21, 1961, Guthrie, OK; daughter of JM and Ruth Harris; married Cleovis Watson II, Jun 5, 1993; children: Crystal Kelso & Jade Watson. **Educ:** BS, 1991; MBA, 1995. **Career:** Langston Univ, secy receptionist, pres off, 1980-82, secy pres off, 1982-84, exec asst to pres, 1984-95, exec asst pres assoc vpres for admis, 1995-97, chief staff, pres off, 1997-2000, acting vpres admin & fiscal affairs, 2000-01, vpres admin & fiscal affairs, 2001-. **Orgs:** Nat Asn Col & Univ Bus Officers, NACUBO; Okla Asn Col & Univ Bus Officers;chmn, Langston Econ Develop Authority; Langston Univ Nat Alumni

Asn;charter mem, Epsilon Epsilon Chap, Phi Beta Delta Honor Soc; Alpha KappaAlpha; Women Higher Educ; Mt Zion Missionary Baptist Church. **Honors/Awds:** Distinguished Service Award, Langston Univ, 1981; Award for 20 years ofservice to Langston Univ; APPLAUSE Award. **Special Achievements:** First woman to serve as Vice President for Administrative and Fiscal Affairs at Langston University & first African American woman to this position in any institution of higher education in Oklahoma. **Business Addr:** Vice President, Administrative & Fiscal Affairs, Langston University, Page Hall Room 218, PO Box 1500, Langston, OK 73050, **Business Phone:** (405)466-3259.

KEMP, EMMERLYNE JANE
Musician, songwriter. **Personal:** Born May 6, 1935, Chicago, IL; daughter of Robert Louis (deceased) and Janie Lee Harris (deceased); divorced. **Educ:** Northwestern Univ, piano, 1954; Monterey CA, MPC, 1960; Berklee Sch Music, Boston, MA, jazz subjects, 1965; New York Univ, music educ, 1971. **Career:** Beth Eden Bapt Church 1st Concert, 1942; Berkeley Little Theater, class piano, 1950; theater show piano, 1958; Santa Clara Col, concert with jazz group, 1961; Radio & TV com voice overs, 1966; CBS-TV, staff, 1968; Ballad of Box Brown, creator, 1974; Musicals: Bubbling Brown Sugar, 1975-76; Tomorrow's Woman; Someone To Sing To, 1992; First Awakening. **Orgs:** Harlem Arts Alliance. **Honors/Awds:** First place, National Talent Competition, Bapt Ushers, Washington, DC, 1953; Second place, Golden State Chap, Nat Asn Negro Musicians, 1954; National Endowment for the Arts Grant, San Francisco Choral Artists, 1977; ASCAP Awards; Audelco Pioneer Award. **Military Serv:** AUS, specialist grade 4, 1956-59. **Home Addr:** 626 Riverside Dr, New York, NY 10031. *

KEMP, LEROY PERCY (DARNELL FREEMAN)
Automotive executive. **Personal:** Born Dec 24, 1956, Cleveland, OH; son of Leroy Percy Sr and Jessie Bell; married Linda Diane Isabell, Nov 16, 1991; children: Brandon Elliott, Jordan Lee & Mercedes Christina. **Educ:** Univ Wis-Madison, BBA, mkt, 1979, MBA, mkt, 1983. **Career:** Burrell Advertising, acct exec, 1985-87; Clairol Inc, Consumer Prod Div, assoc product mgr, 1987-89; Ford Motor Co. Minority Dealer Training Prog, 1989-91; Forest Lake Ford Inc, pres & owner, 1991-; wrestler, currently. **Orgs:** Ford Lincoln Mercury Minority Dealer Asn; Nat Asn Minority Automobile Dealers; USA Wrestling Nat Governing Body; Raise His Praise Worship Ctr. **Honors/Awds:** Nat Wrestling Hall of Fame, inductee, 1989; George Martin Wisconsin Wrestling Hall of Fame, 1983; Pan Am Games, Two-time Gold Medalist, 1979-84; Seven-time Nat Freestyle Wrestling Champion; two-time Ohio State High School Wrestling Champion, 1973-74. **Special Achievements:** First American to become Three-time World Freestyle Wrestling Champion, 1978, 1979, 1982; at age 21, the youngest American to win world championships, 1978. **Business Addr:** President, Owner, Forest Lake Ford Inc, 231 19th St SW, Forest Lake, MN 55025, **Business Phone:** (651)464-4600.

KEMP, SHAWN T.
Basketball player, basketball executive. **Personal:** Born Nov 26, 1969, Elkhart, IN. **Educ:** Univ Ky, attended 1989; Trinity Valley Community Col, attended 1989. **Career:** Basketball player (retired), basketball executive; Seattle SuperSonics, forward, 1989-97; Cleveland Cavaliers, 1997-2000; Portland Trail Blazers,2000-02; Orlando Magic, 2002-03; Shawn Kemp Basketball Clinic, owner, currently. **Honors/Awds:** NBA All-Star, 1998. **Special Achievements:** Ranked 12th in the NBA in scoring, averaging 20.5 ppg in 1999; ranked14th in the NBA in rebounds per game, averaging 8.8 in 2000.

KENAN, RANDALL G.
Writer, educator. **Personal:** Born Mar 12, 1963, Brooklyn, NY. **Educ:** Univ North Carolina, Chapel Hill, NC, BA, 1985. **Career:** Alfred A Knopf, New York, NY, editor, 1985-89; Sarah Lawrence Col, Bronxville, NY, lecturer, beginning 1989; Vassar Col, Poughkepsie, NY, lecturer, 1989-; Columbia Univ, New York, NY, lecturer, beginning 1990. **Honors/Awds:** New York Foundation of the Arts Grant, 1989; MacDowell Colony Fellowship, 1990; author: A Visitation of Spirits, Grove Press, 1989; Let the Dead Bury Their Dead, Harcourt, Brace, 1992. **Special Achievements:** Author: A Visitation of Spirits, Grove Press, 1989; Let the Dead Bury Their Dead, Harcourt, Brace, 1992. **Business Addr:** Lecturer, Vassar College, Durham, NC 27708.*

KENDALL, JOHN S.
Lawyer. **Personal:** Born in Chicago, IL. **Educ:** University of Dayton, Bachelors Degree, 1985; The Ohio State University, JD, 1990. **Career:** Northrop Defense Systems Division, Communications Systems Engineer; Sughrue, Mion, Zinn, McPeak & Seas, Law Clerk. **Orgs:** Chairman, Metropolitan Reclamation District of Greater Chicago Civil Service Board; Vice Chair of Development, 100 Black Men of Chicago. **Honors/Awds:** Allstate Insurance Company's "From Whence We Came" award; Connection Enterprise's "Men of Excellence Award" and Cook County Bar Association's "J. Earnest Wilkins Award.". **Special Achievements:** Wrote two articles: "Federal Protection Against Unfair Competition" and "Intellectual Property: Don't Lose Your Most Valuable Asset.". *

KENDALL, LETTIE M.
Educator, government official. **Personal:** Born May 2, 1930, Magnolia, AR; married Robert B; children: Yvonne, Sharon, Donald & Ronald. **Educ:** Ariz Bapt Col, BS, 1951; Bishop Col, 1951; Tenn State Univ; Austin Peay State Univ, MA, 1974; Austin Peay State Univ, EdS, 1979. **Career:** Woodruff County Sch Syst, teacher, 1951-52; Clarksville & Mont City Sch,1961; Byrns L Darden Sch, 1966; Moore Elem & Cohen Schs, prin, 1977-; Clarksville Sch; Ringgold Elem Teacher. **Orgs:** Clarksville Mont City Educ Asn; past mem, TEA, MTEA, NEA; Kappa Delta Pi; Dept Byrns L Darden Sch; Middle Tenn Coun IRA; attended numerous workshops; County Comnrs Asn Tenn; Adv Comt EEO bd, Ft Campbell, KY; Sch Com County Ct; Nat Asn Advan Colored People; Clarksville Community Develop Comn; vice chmn, Recreational & Hist bd County Comn; past dirn St John Baptist Church Sunday Sch; Montgomery County, Dist 13 County Comnr, 2006-. **Honors/Awds:** Honored with a park named in her name, 2006.

KENDALL, MICHELLE KATRINA
Pharmacist, executive. **Personal:** Born Aug 5, 1952, Detroit, MI; daughter of Louis A Cayce and Evelyn Cayce; married Jeffrey M, May 20, 1989; children: Christopher M. **Educ:** Wayne State Univ, BA, biol, 1983, BS, pharm, 1987. **Career:** Wayne State Univ, stud res asst, 1972-84; C Hosp, pharm intern, 1984-87; Perry Drug Store Inc, pharm supvr, 1987-. **Orgs:** Detroit Pharmacy Guild; Lambda Kappa Sigma, 1986-; Adv Bd, Crockett Voc Ctr, 1992-. **Home Phone:** (313)342-8084. **Business Addr:** Pharmacy Supervisor, Perry Drug Stores Inc, 5400 Perry Dr, Pontiac, MI 48340, **Business Phone:** (313)538-2780.

KENDALL, ROBERT, JR.
Lawyer. **Personal:** Born Feb 11, 1947, Thomaston, GA; married Lolita Marie Toles; children: Yolanda Yvette & Robert III. **Educ:** Ft Valley State Col, BS, Educ, 1969; Tex State Univ Sch Law, JD, 1973. **Career:** US Dept Justice, atty, asst dir civil div, currently. **Orgs:** Phi Beta Sigma Fraternity, 1968; Phi Alpha Delta Law Fraternity, 1969. **Honors/Awds:** Special Achievement Awards for Sustained Superior Performance of Duty, US Dept Justice, Wash, DC, 1977, 1985, 1989, 1990 & 1992. **Military Serv:** AUS, E-5 2 yrs; Bronze Star. **Business Addr:** Assistant Director, Attorney, US Dept of Justice, Office of Immigration Litigation, 950 Pennsylvania Ave NW, PO Box 878, Washington, DC 20530-0001, **Business Phone:** (202)353-1555.

KENDRICK, CAROL YVONNE
Counselor. **Personal:** Born Jan 29, 1952, New York, NY; daughter of E Curtis and Marguerite Holloway; married John A DeMicco, May 6, 1989. **Educ:** New York Univ, BA, 1974; New York Univ Sch Law, JD, 1977. **Career:** Off Bronx Dist Atty, asst dist atty, 1977-81; New York Life Insurance Co, assoc coun, 1981-97; AnnTaylor, asst gen coun, 1997-2002; Hahn Hessen LLP, contract litigation atty, 2003-04; MetLife, sr coun; Song of Noway, prodn mgr; Desert Song, stage mgr. **Orgs:** Speaker, Minority Interchange, 1983-84; treas, Riverside Opera Ensemble, 1984-. **Honors/Awds:** Best & Brightest Black Women in Corporate America, Ebony Mag, 1990. **Home Addr:** 92 Pinebrook Rd, New Rochelle, NY 10801, **Home Phone:** (914)235-1976. **Business Addr:** Treasurer, Riverside Opera Ensemble, 488 Madison Ave 14th Fl, New York, NY 10022.

KENDRICK, CURTIS L
Librarian. **Personal:** Born Jun 13, 1958, Queens, NY; son of Ercell Curtis and Marguerite Sanford Holloway; married Mary Beth Souza. **Educ:** Brown Univ, Providence, RI, BA, 1980; Simmons Col, Boston, MA, MLS, 1984; Emory Univ, Atlanta, GA, MBA, 1992. **Career:** Brown Univ, Providence, RI, libr asn specialist, 1981-83; Oberlin Col, Oberlin, OH, asst to dir librs, 1984-86; State Univ New York, Stony Brook, NY, head, circulation dept, 1986-90; Info Consult, Decatur, GA, ceo, 1990-92; Harvard Univ, asst dir librs, 1992-98; Columbia Univ, dir; City Univ NY, univ libr, 2004-. **Orgs:** Am Libr Asn, 1983-; Asn Col & Res Librs, 1985-; Libr Admin & Mgmt Asn, 1990-; Libr Info Technol Asn, 1990-. **Honors/Awds:** Beta Phi Mu, Nat Honor Soc, 1983; Fac Travel Res Grant, SUNY, Stony Brook, 1989; Title II-B Fel, US Dept Educ, 1983; Emory Scholar Fel, 1990-92; 'George Mew Organisation & Management Award', 1992. **Special Achievements:** Author, A User-Centered View of Document Delivery & Interlibrary Loan, Library Admin and Mgmt, 1994; The Competitive Advantage of Librarians, Managing Resource Sharing in the Electronic Age, 1996; The Design & Operation Off-site Storage in Support of Preservation Programs, Erice 96 Conservation and Restoration of Archive & Library Materials Conference, 1996; Performance Measures of Shelving Accuracy, Journal of Academic Librarianship, 1991; Minority Internship/Scholarship in Library and Information Sciences, College & Research Libraries News, 1990; Cavalry to the Rescue, Col & Research Libraries News, 1989. **Home Addr:** 30 Glenburn Rd, Arlington, MA 02474, **Home Phone:** (617)643-7639. **Business Addr:** University Librarian, City University of New York, 535 E 80th St 5th fl, New York, NY 10075, **Business Phone:** (212)794-5481.

KENDRICK, JOY A.
Lawyer. **Personal:** Born in Burlington, NC; daughter of Charles and Sarah L. **Educ:** Univ NC, Chapel Hill, BA, 1977; State Univ NY, Buffalo, JD, 1981; Ind Univ, MBA, 1985. **Career:** Alamance Tech Col, orientation librn, 1977-78; Cora P Maloney Col, acad coordr, 1980-81; Neighborhood Legal Serv Inc, staff atty, 1981-83; law clerk, 1979-81; NCR Corp, bus intern, 1984; JA Kendrick Bus Enterprises Inc, pres, 1985-; Law Off Joy Kendrick, managing coun, 1985-. **Orgs:** bd mem, Chamber Com, 1987-90; Erie County Bar Asn; NY State Bar Asn; Am Bar Asn; Leadership Buffalo, 1988; bd, Buffalo Pvt Industry Coun, 1990-; Buffalo Bus, contrib writer; bd dir, Minority Bus Coun; bd dir, Housing Asst Ctr. **Business Addr:** President, Lawyer, JA Kendrick Business Inc, Statler Twr, 107 Delaware Ave Suite 1534, Buffalo, NY 14202-3015, **Business Phone:** (716)855-2251.*

KENDRICK, L JOHN, SR.
Executive. **Personal:** Born May 13, 1932, Monticello, KY; son of Wesley and Marie; divorced; children: L John Jr, Rozalind Denese Hopgood & Debra Jo Hopgood. **Career:** Kendrick Paper Stock Co, ceo, 1954-. **Orgs:** Jefferson County Chamber Com, 1968-81; Jefferson County NCP, 1968-92; chmn, Jefferson County Housing Authority, 1972-74; Just Mens Club, 1969-72; Govs Club, 1990-; finance comt, Corinthian Baptist Church. **Honors/Awds:** Cert Recognition Efforts Recycling, 1988; Governors Corp Recycling Award, State Ill, 1989. **Military Serv:** USAF, 1951-54. **Home Addr:** 5106 Richview Rd, Mount Vernon, IL 62864, **Home Phone:** (618)244-3962. **Business Addr:** Chief Executive Officer, Kendrick Paper Stock Co, 1000 Salem Rd, PO Box 1385, Mount Vernon, IL 62864, **Business Phone:** (618)242-4527.

KENDRICK, TOMMY L.
School administrator. **Personal:** Born May 29, 1923, Sycamore, GA; son of George and Salbe; married Geneva Bhanton; children: Deborah Elane, Welchel, Diane H & Denise. **Educ:** Ft Valley State Col, BSA, 1948; Tuskegee Inst, MS, educ, 1958, MA, admin & Supv, 1969. **Career:** Ft Baptist Church, Sunday Sch, supt, 1955-85, clerk, 1961-85; elem sch prin; Chatto Valley Bible Col, Sch Theol, Edison, Ga, dean, 1989-93. **Orgs:** Worshipful master, Prince Hall Masons, 1950-85; Masonic Lodge, wishful master; GTA, 1970-85; Nat Asn Educr, 1970-85; Co Bd Comn, 1976-95; State Asn Co Community, 1976-95; Order Consery 32 Mason, 1979-95; Page Prof Org, 1983-; dep grand master, Prince Hall Masons, 1987-95. **Honors/Awds:** Man of the Year, 1988. **Special Achievements:** Citation from first Baptist Church of Georgetown, 1992. **Home Addr:** Rte 2, PO Box 234, Georgetown, GA 39854.

KENLAW, JESSIE
Basketball coach. **Personal:** Born in Guyton, CA. **Educ:** Savannah State, BS, health & phys educ, 1977. **Career:** Basketball player (retired), basketball coach; Houston Angels, 1979-82; Lamar Univ, asst coach, 1987-88; Univ Houston, women basketball head coach, 1990-98; Colorado Xplosion, 1998-99; Seattle Storm, asst coach, currently. **Business Phone:** (206)217-9622.

KENNARD, BILL. **See KENNARD, WILLIAM EARL.**

KENNARD, PATRICIA A.
Television news anchorperson, radio journalist, government official. **Personal:** Born in Canton, OH; divorced; children: Maya Khalilah. **Educ:** Cent State Univ, BS; Univ Akron Sch Grad Studies. **Career:** Hartford Jr High Sch, lang arts teacher; Canton Urban League; educ specialist (counr); WHBC, radio newscaster; tv reporter, TV-23, 1980-86; Rubber City Radio Group, mid-day news anchor; part-time fac, Univ Akron; WAKR-Radio, veteran news reporter & anchor; Ohio Dept Transp, Dist 4, spokeswoman & pub rels officer, 2007-. **Orgs:** Asn Black Prof Bus Women; Nat Asn Advan Colored People; Zeta Phi Beta Sorority; co-host, Nat Childrens Miracle Network; vol, Mentoring Mothers;House Lord. **Honors/Awds:** Black Women of Excellence Award, YWCA, 1998; Crystal Award for Community Service; Cleveland Press Club Award; National Broadcaster's Hall of Fame. **Business Addr:** Public Relations Officer, Spokeswoman, Ohio Department of Transportation, District 4, 2088 S Arlington Rd, Akron, OH 44306, **Business Phone:** (330)786-2209.

KENNARD, WILLIAM EARL (BILL KENNARD)
Government official. **Personal:** Born Jan 19, 1957, Los Angeles, CA; son of Robert A and Helen King; married Deborah D Kennedy, Apr 9, 1984. **Educ:** Stanford Univ, BA, commun, 1978; Yale Law Sch, JD, 1981. **Career:** Nat Asn Broadcasters, fel, 1981-82, asst gen coun, 1983-84; Verner, Liipfert, Bernhard, McPherson & Hand, assoc, 1982-83, partner, 1984-93; Fed Commun Comn, gen coun, 1993-97, comnr & chmn, 1997-2001; The Carlyle Group, managing dir, 2001-; The New York Times Co, bd dirs, 2001-; Nextel Corp, bd dirs, 2001-05; Dex Media, bd dirs, 2002-; Hawaiian Telcom, bd dirs, 2005-; Sprint Nextel Corp, bd dirs, 2005-07. **Orgs:** Fed Commun Bar Asn; Am Bar Asn; Nat Bar Asn; Phi Beta Kappa Soc; sr fel, Aspen Inst, 2001-. **Honors/Awds:** Congional Black Caucus Chair's Award, 2000; Honary degrees from Howard Univ, Long Island Univ & Gallaudet Univ. **Special Achievements:** First black chairman of United States Federal Communications Commission. **Business Addr:** Managing Director, The Carlyle Group, 1001 Pennsylvania Ave NW, Washington, DC 20004-2505, **Business Phone:** (202)729-5626.

KENNEDY, ADRIENNE LITA
Lecturer, playwright, educator. **Personal:** Born Sep 13, 1931, Pittsburgh, PA; daughter of Cornell Wallace Hawkins and Etta

Haugabook Hawkins; married Joseph C, May 15, 1953; children: Joseph Jr & Adam. **Educ:** Ohio State Univ, BA, 1953; Columbia Univ, grad study, 1956. **Career:** Yale Univ, lectr, 1972-74; Princeton Univ, lectr, 1977, prof, currently; Brown Univ, vis assoc prof, 1979-80; Univ Calif, Berkeley, fac; Univ Calif, Davis, fac; Plays: A Movie Star Has to Star in Black & White, 1976; A Lancashire Lad, 1980; Black Children's Day, 1980; Diary of Lights, 1987; She Talks to Beethoven, 1989; The Ohio State Murders, 1992; The Film Club, 1992; The Dramatic Circle, 1992; Motherhood 2000, 1994; June & Jean in Concert, 1995; Sleep Deprivation Chamber, 1996; Mom, How Did You Meet the Beatles, 2008. **Orgs:** PEN. **Honors/Awds:** Obie Award, 1964; Guggenheim Award, 1967; Rockefeller Grants, 1967-69, 1974, 1976; CBS Fellow, 1973; Manhattan Borough President Award, 1988; Stanley Award; The Lila Wallace Readers Digest Award; National Endowment for the Arts Award, 1993; Academy Award in literature, Am Acad Arts &Letters, 1994; American Book Award; Pierre Le comte du Novy Award, Lincoln Ctr, 1994; American Academy of Arts and Letters Award, 1994. **Home Addr:** 114-91 179th St, Jamaica, NY 11434. **Business Addr:** Professor, Princeton University, Department of Afro-American Studies, Princeton, NJ 08544, **Business Phone:** (609)258-3000.

KENNEDY, BERNICE ROBERTS
Educator, nurse. **Personal:** Born Sep 23, 1953, Eastover, SC; daughter of Samuel Roberts, Sr, Irene Jacobs Roberts; divorced; children: Chrishonda M & Kenard J. **Educ:** Univ SC, BSN, 1975, MS, 1988; Walden Univ, PhD, health services, 1998. **Career:** WBJD Veteran Med Ctr, advanced practice nurse, 1993-99; SC State Univ, assoc prof, 1999-; Amy V Cockcroft Leadership fel, Univ SC, 2003; psychiat nurse, pvt pract. **Orgs:** Sigma Theta Tau, Univ SC, 1998; Sister Care Inc, Women & Children Domestic Violence Bureau, 2000-03; Angel Nursing Inc, governing bd, 2001-03; Delta Sigma Theata, Columbia chap, 2002-03; Chi Eta Phi, Delta ETQ, SC State Univ, 2002-03; SC State Univ, Student Affairs Comm, chair, 2002-03. **Honors/Awds:** Living the Legacy honoree, Nat Coun Negro Women, 1996; Research Award Scholarship, Sigma Theta Tau, 2003. **Special Achievements:** Author: "Hallucinatory Experiences of Psychiatric Patients in Seclusion," 1994; "Mental Health Nursing Consultation in a Nursing Home," JCNR, 2000. **Business Phone:** (803)533-3356.

KENNEDY, BRENDA PICOLA
Judge. **Personal:** Born Jan 1, 1956?, Mexia, TX; daughter of Jimmie Vernon and Lois Bertha Hobbs; divorced; children: Mallore Kennedy Caldwell, Pilar Elise Caldwell. **Educ:** Univ Tex, Austin, BJ, 1978, Univ Tex Sch Law, JD, 1981. **Career:** City of Austin, asst city atty, 1981-82; Travis County, Dist Atty's Off, asst dist atty, 1982-87; State Tex, 403rd Dist Ct, dist judge, 1987-. **Orgs:** State Bar Tex; Travis County Bar Asn; Autsin Black Lawyers Asn; Links; Delta Sigma Theta Sorority Inc; Jack and Jill Inc; bd, Laguna Gloria Art Mus; Leadership Tex Alumnae Asn, bd, 1990-94; bd, Umlauf Sculpture Garden Mus, 1992-94. **Honors/Awds:** Thurgood Marshall Legal Soc, Virgil C Lott Alumni Award, 1993. **Business Addr:** District Judge, State Tex Dist Ct, 403rd Dist, Travis County Courthouse, 1000 Guadalupe St Rm 302, PO Box 1748, Austin, TX 78767-1748, **Business Phone:** (512)854-9808.*

KENNEDY, CALLAS FAYE
Educator. **Personal:** Born Oct 13, 1954, Lisman, AL. **Educ:** Sacramento City Col, AA (hons), 1975; Calif State Univ, Sacramento, BA, 1978. **Career:** Sacramento County Headstart Progs, teacher/dir, 1978-83; Children's Home Soc Calif, prog specialist, 1983-84; Pacific Oaks Col, instr, 1984; Yuba Comm Col, instr, 1985; Child-Human Develop specialist; Center CP, Health educr, currently. **Orgs:** Chairperson, Nat Black Child Develop Inst, 1978-; chairperson, Sacramento Area Black Caucus Inc, 1983-85; treas, Calif Child Passenger Safety Asn 1983-; consult/speaker Child Develop Inc, 1985; Marriage & Family Counsr Inc, 1986; conf speaker Sacramento Valley Asn Educ Young C; Sacramento Black Women's Network & Sacramento County C; Co-chair, Coalition of Sacramento Women's Orgn. **Honors/Awds:** Lewis Lamtier Award, Pac Bell, 1984; Black Female Educr Black Educs Action, 1985; Human Rights Awards, Sacramento City, 1985-86; Outstanding Women of the Year, YWCA, 1990. **Business Addr:** Health Educator, Center for CP, 6 Rancho Torre Ct, Sacramento, CA 95828, **Business Phone:** (916)383-5249.

KENNEDY, CORTEZ
Football player. **Personal:** Born Aug 23, 1968, Osceola, AR; son of Ruby; married; children: Courtney. **Educ:** Northwest Miss Community Col; Univ Miami, BA, criminal justice. **Career:** Football player (retired); Seattle Sea hawks, 1990-2002. **Honors/Awds:** First-team All-America choice, Sporting News, 1989; Pro Bowl, 1991-98; Marcus Nalley Trophy, 1992; Defensive Lineman of the Year, NFL Players Asn, 1992; NFL Defensive Player of the Year, 1992; Defensive Player of the Year, Asniated Pres, 1993; Steve Largent Award, 1996; inducted, Sea hawks Ring of Honor, 2006. **Special Achievements:** Semi-Finalist for the Pro Football Hall of Fame, 2008 & finalist, 2009.

KENNEDY, HENRY H., JR.
Judge. **Personal:** Born Feb 22, 1948, Columbia, SC; son of Henry H and Rachel Spann; married Altomease Rucker, Sep 20, 1980; children: Morgan Rucker, Alexandra Rucker. **Educ:** Princeton Univ, AB, 1970; Harvard Law Sch, JD, 1973. **Career:** Reavis, Pogue, Neal and Rose, 1973; US Atty Off, asst atty, 1973-76; US Dist Ct, US magistrate, 1976-79; Superior Ct DC, assoc judge, 1979-97; US Dist Ct, judge, 1997-. **Orgs:** Sigma Pi Phi; American Bar Found; trustee, Princeton Univ; Am Law IST Barristers. **Honors/Awds:** H Carl Mooltrie Award, Judicial Exellence, Trial Lawyers Asn Metrop, Wash, DC, 1997; Founders Award, Princeton Univ Community House, 1995. **Business Addr:** Judge, US District Court, 333 Const Ave NW, Washington, DC 20001, **Business Phone:** (202)354-3350.*

KENNEDY, HOWARD E.
Fashion designer. **Personal:** Born Nov 30, 1941, Fernandina Beach, FL; son of Charles Emmanuel and Cecil D Watson Williams; divorced. **Educ:** St Petersburg FL, Assoc, 1962; NY Inst Tech, New York, NY, 1980. **Career:** Revlon, Bronx NY, apprentice perfumer, 1965-70; Pfizer Consumer Products, chief perfumer, 1970-87; Royal Essence Ltd, New York New York, pres, 1987-; H K Enterprises, Union City, NJ, pres, 1990-. **Orgs:** Pres, Nat Advan Asn Colored People Youth Coun, 1961-62; Soc Cosmetics Chemists; dir, Am Soc Perfumers; Fragrance Found; Nat Bus Coun; bd dirs & trustees, United Methodist Home; pres, Am Soc Perfumers, 1997-98; African Scientific Inst. **Honors/Awds:** Black Achievers Industry, NY Chapter Greater YMCA, 1985; Outstanding Entrepreneur of the Year, Nat Black MBA Assn, 1989; Business Achievement Award, Black Retail Action Group, 1990; Ron Brown Award, Nat Black MBA Asn, 1998. **Military Serv:** AUS, pfc, 1962-65. **Business Addr:** President, HK Enterprises Inc, 654 Milton Ave, Lyndhurst, NJ 07071, **Business Phone:** (201)933-6001.*

KENNEDY, INGA D.
Business owner, executive. **Career:** Planners Environ Quality Inc, pres & owner, 1992-. **Business Addr:** President, Owner, Planners for Environmental Quality Inc, 6067 Roosevelt Hwy, Union City, GA 30291, **Business Phone:** (770)306-0100.

KENNEDY, JAMES E.
Educator. **Personal:** Born Sep 30, 1933, Jackson, MS; son of Tim and Esther Shelwood; divorced; children: Jia Lynette & Jason Edward. **Educ:** Ala State Univ, BS, 1954; IN Univ, MAT, 1964. **Career:** Mobile Co Pub Sch, instr, 1958-67; admin, 1967-68; Univ S Ala, from instr to prof art, 1968-97; chmn art dept, 1978-94; prof emer art, 1997-. **Orgs:** Col Art Asn; Nat Conf Artist; Kappa Alpha Psi; Adv Eta Nu Chap Univ S Ala;culture black & white mobile; bd mem, Mobile Museum Art; dir, curator Am Ethnic Art Slide Library. **Honors/Awds:** Recipient of 19 awards. **Special Achievements:** Exhibitor in innumerable shows. **Military Serv:** USAF, staff sgt, 1954-58. **Business Addr:** Professor Emeritus, University of South Alabama, Department Art & Art History, 307 N Univ Blvd Suite 2100 251460-6188, Mobile, AL 36608.

KENNEDY, REV. JAMES E
Manager, clergy. **Personal:** Born Jun 21, 1938, Weir, MS; son of Ethel and Girtha; married Thelma Brown, Sep 18, 1960; children: Sandra Kennedy, Sheri Kennedy & Stephon Kennedy. **Educ:** John Wesley Col, Owosso, MI, BA, 1976; Southern Seminary, Louisville, KY. **Career:** Manager (retired), Clergy; Gen Motors Corp, Flint, MI, supvr, 1956-87; Baptist State Convention, MI, family ministry consult; Mount Carmel Baptist Church, Flint, Mich, pastor, 1981-. **Orgs:** Bd dir, Genesee Baptist Asn; Genesee Baptist Asn; Sunday Sch; bd chair, Genesee County Comn Substance Abuse; adv coun, Gulf Coast Community Serv Asn; Nat chmn, Pro-Minority Action Coalition; bd, Urban League Flint; bd, Urban Co Boy Scouts Am; chaplain, Flint Police & Fire Dept; past pres, Interfaith Prevention Group; Big Bro, Big Sisters. **Honors/Awds:** Frederick Douglas Award, Nat Asn Bus & Prof Women, 1989. **Business Addr:** Pastor, Mount Carmel Baptist Church, 1610 W Pierson Rd, Flint, MI 48507, **Business Phone:** (810)785-4421.

KENNEDY, DR. JOYCE S.
Educator. **Personal:** Born Jun 15, 1943, St Louis, MO; divorced. **Educ:** Harris Teacher Col, BA, 1965; St Louis Univ, M.Ed, 1968; Mich State Univ, PhD, 1975. **Career:** Carver Elem Sch, teacher, 1966-68; St Louis Job Corps Ctr Women, counr,1968-69; Forest Park Jr Col, counr, 1969-71; Meramec Jr Col, counr, 1971-74; Mich State Univ, Nat Mental Health Inst, urban coun fel, 1972-74;Govs State Univ, Col Arts & Sci, occup educ coordr & univ prof commun, 1975-, distinguished prof, 1977, Div Liberal Arts, chair, 1999-2001. **Orgs:** Keynote speaker, Roseland Community Sch Grad, 1978; facilitator, Career Awareness Workshop, 1978; speaker, Harvey Pub Libr, 1978; Am Personnel & Guid Asn; Ill Asn Non-White Concerns; Ill Guid & Personnel Asn. **Honors/Awds:** Cert Recognition for Outstanding Service, Ill Guid & Personnel Asn, 1977; Outstanding Young Woman of America Award, 1978. **Business Addr:** University Professor of Communication, Governors State University College of Arts and Sciences, Div Liberal Arts, F Bldg 1 Univ Pkwy, University Park, IL 60466, **Business Phone:** (708)534-4085.

KENNEDY, DR. KAREL R
Educator, health services administrator. **Personal:** Born May 6, 1946, Greeleyville, SC; son of Ben and Susie. **Educ:** Howard Univ, BS, 1967, MD, 1971. **Career:** Greater Harlem Nursing Home, med dir; Mt Sinai Sch Med, asst clin prof; Karel Kennedy Med Ctr, currently. **Business Addr:** Physician, Karel Kennedy Medical Center, 137 Cedar Dr, Saint Stephen, SC 29479, **Business Phone:** (843)567-6237.

KENNEDY, LINCOLN (TAMERLANE KENNEDY, JR.)
Football player, broadcaster. **Personal:** Born Feb 12, 1971, York, PA; son of Tamerlane F Kennedy Sr and Carson Hope Brown; divorced 2003. **Educ:** Univ Wash, attended 1993. **Career:** Football player (retired), analyst; Atlanta Falcons, tackle, 1993-95; Oakland Raiders, offensive tackle, 1996-2004; NFL Total Access, NFL Network, studio anal, 2004-06; Fox Sports Radio, 2006-. **Orgs:** Am Red Cross; Reading is Fundamental; AFT; SAG. **Honors/Awds:** Pro Bowl player, 2000-02. **Business Phone:** (925)234-2046.

KENNEDY, MARVIN JAMES. See Obituaries section.

KENNEDY, PROF. MATTHEW W.
Educator, musician. **Personal:** Born Mar 10, 1921, Americus, GA; son of Royal Clement Kennedy and Mary Dowdell; married Anne Lucille Gamble; children: Nina Gamble. **Educ:** Fisk Univ, BA, 1946; Juilliard Sch Music, MS, 1950. **Career:** Musician (retired), Educator: Fisk Univ, assoc prof, 1947-48, 1954-84, acting dean music dept, 1975-78; piano soloist nat & intl; Fisk Jubilee Singers, dir, 1957-67, 1971-73, 1975-83, 1985-86; Fisk Univ, emer prof music, currently. **Orgs:** Music Teachers Nat Asn; Sigma Upsilon Pi; Omega Psi Phi; Nashville Fine Arts Club; First Baptist Church; Omega Psi Phi; TN Arts Comt, 1968-82; bd mem, John W Work Found, 1973-; prog chmn, Nashville Fine Arts Club,1967-69; bd mem, Nashville Symphony Asn, 1975-78. **Honors/Awds:** Gabriel Scholarship, Fisk Univ; Sigma Upsilon Pi Honor, Fisk Univ 1946; BM Fac Fel, United Negro Col Fund, 1969; Omega Man of Year, 1974; Distinguished Negro Georgians; W.E.B. DuBois Award, Asn Social & Behavioral Scientists, 2005. **Special Achievements:** Special Achievements solo recitals, Carnegie Hall recital; Nat Gallery Art; Town Hall Philadelphia 1958-60; Spirituals published Abingdon Press Nashville 1974. **Military Serv:** AUS m/sgt 1943-46. *

KENNEDY, NATHELYNE ARCHIE
Engineer, chief executive officer. **Personal:** Born Jun 1, 1938, Richards, TX; daughter of Nathaniel L and Ernestine Linton; married James D, Dec 27, 1961; children: Tracey A & David J. **Educ:** Prairie View A&M Univ, BS, Archit Engineering, 1959. **Career:** Alfred Benesch & Co, engr, 1960-72; Bernard Johnson Inc, engr, 1978-81; Nathelyne A Kennedy & Assocs, pres & chief exec officer, engr, 1981-. **Orgs:** Am Soc Civil Engrs, Am Soc Prof Engrs, Tex Good Roads Transportation Asn, Am Coun Engineering Cos, Houston Coun Engineering Cos. **Honors/Awds:** Toombs-Brown Prestige Award, Prof Black Womens Enterprise; Bus Develop Success Story, METRO Harris County; Outstanding MWBE Contractor Prof Servs, City Houston; Distinguished Service Award, 3yrs, City Houston Mentor-Protoge Prog; Entrepreneur of the Year, US Black Engr; Outstanding Alumi Award, Prairie View A&M Univ, Nat Alumni Asn. **Special Achievements:** First female engineering grad, Prairie View A & M Univ; first African-Am woman in the State to become registered as a Prof Engr. **Business Addr:** President, Cheif Executive Officer, Nathelyne A Kennedy & Associates Inc, 6100 Hillcroft Ave Suite 710, Houston, TX 77081, **Business Phone:** (713)988-0145.

KENNEDY, RANDALL
Educator, writer. **Personal:** Born Sep 10, 1954, Columbia, SC; married Yvedt Matory; children: William Henry. **Educ:** Princeton Univ, BA, 1977; Oxford Univ, grad studies, 1979; Yale Univ, JD, 1982. **Career:** US Ct Appeals, law clerk to Skelly Wright, 1982-83; US Supreme Ct, law clerk to Thurgood Marshall, 1983-84; Harvard Univ, asst prof law, 1984-85, assoc prof, 1985-89, prof, 1989-, Michael R Klein prof, 2005-. **Orgs:** Washington DC Bar, 1983; Am Law Inst; Am Acad Arts & Sci; Am Philosophical Asn. **Honors/Awds:** Nat Achievement scholarship, 1973-77; Rhodes scholarship, 1977-79; Earl Warren Legal Training scholarship, 1979-82; Robert F. Kennedy Book Award, 1998. **Special Achievements:** Author: Race, Crim, & the Law, 1997; Nigger: The Strange Career of a Troublesome Word, 2002; Interracial Intimacies: Sex. Marriage, Identity & Adoption, 2003. **Business Addr:** Michael R Klein professor of Law, Harvard Law School, Areeda 228, Cambridge, MA 02138, **Business Phone:** (617)495-0907.

KENNEDY, RAY C
President (Organization), chief executive officer. **Career:** Am Product Distribr, pres & chief exec officer, currently. **Orgs:** Bd dir, Found The Carolinas. **Business Addr:** Chief Executive Officer, President, American Product Distributors Inc, 8227 Arrow Ridge Blvd Suite E, Charlotte, NC 28273, **Business Phone:** (704)522-9411.*

KENNEDY, SANDRA DENISE
State government official, business owner, commissioner. **Personal:** Born Dec 25, 1957, Oklahoma City, OK; daughter of Leland W and Doll Baby Alford; children: Mahogany. **Educ:** Phoenix Col, attended 1975; Maricopa Community Col Dist, at-

tended 1986;Ariz State Univ, acct & bus admin, 1986. **Career:** State Ariz, House Reps, rep, 1986-92, Dist 23, sen, 1993-98; Kennedy & Assocs, consult, 1984-; Kennedy Restaurants LLC, owner, currently; Ariz Corp Comn, comnr, 2008-. **Orgs:** Off aide, Nat Youth Corps, 1974-75; tutor, Valle del Sol City Phoenixperformer, Black Theatre Troupe, 1981; Nat Asn Exec Women, 1983-; vol,Valley Christian Ctr, 1983-84; bd mem, Ariz Cactus Pine Girls Scout Coun,1987-; ex-officio mem, Phoenix Community Alliance, 1987; Phoenix Union High Sch Bd; City Phoenix, Surface Transp Adv Comt; Ariz Employ Training Coun; Nat Black Conf State Legislators. **Honors/Awds:** Outstanding Young Woman of America, 1984. **Business Phone:** (602)542-3625.

KENNEDY, TAMERLANE, JR. See KENNEDY, LINCOLN.

KENNEDY, TERESA KAY-ABA
President (Organization), founder (originator). **Personal:** Born in Ghana. **Educ:** Wellesley Col, BA; Harvard Univ, MBA. **Career:** MTV Networks, exec; Ta Life Inc, founder; Power Living Enterprises Inc, founder & pres, currently. **Orgs:** Bd dirs, Yoga Alliance. **Honors/Awds:** The Network Journal's 40 Under Forty Achievement Award. **Business Addr:** Founder, President, Power Living Enterprises Inc, 71 W 128th St 3rd Fl Suite B, New York, NY 10027-3102, **Business Phone:** (212)289-6363.*

KENNEDY, THEODORE REGINALD
Educator. **Personal:** Born Jan 4, 1936, Winter Haven, FL. **Educ:** Univ Wash, Seattle, BA, 1970; Princeton Univ, NJ, MA, 1972, PhD, 1974. **Career:** Boeing Co Seattle, 1961-69; State Univ NY, Stony Brook, asst prof, anthrop, 1974-80, assoc prof, antrhop, 1980-. **Orgs:** Nat Asn Advan Colored People, 1967; Asn Am Anthropologists, 1970-; Nat Hist Soc, 1974-; Consult, Howard Univ Press, 1980; adv group, Nat Endowment Humanities, 1980. **Special Achievements:** Recipient numerous fellowships & grants Afro-Am, Study Prof Univ Washington; Princeton Univ; Univ Pa; Ford Found; HEW; Research Found of NY, 1969-75; numerous research experiences Seattle New York City Philadelphia NJ Spain So US W & E Coasts US Vigin Islands; "Relations in a So Comm "Oxford Press 1979; pub "Black Argot assoc languistic analysis of black life style through verbal & non-Verbal communication" oxford u press; dissertation "you gotta deal With It the relationship in the black domestic unit". **Military Serv:** AUS, pfc, 1959-60. **Business Addr:** Assitant Professor, State University of New York, Department of Anthropology, Circle Rd Social Behav Sci Bldg 5th fl, Stony Brook, NY 11794.

KENNEDY, WILLIAM J., III
Executive. **Personal:** Born Oct 24, 1922, Durham, NC; son of William J Kennedy Jr. and Margaret Spaulding; married Alice C Copeland; children: William J IV. **Educ:** VA State Col, BS, 1942; Univ PA, MBA, 1946; NY Univ, MBA Finance & Investments, 1948; NY Univ, grad studies, 1950; Stanford Univ, exec pgm, 1971. **Career:** Retired: NC Mutual Life Ins Co, pres, ceo, chmn bd dirs. **Orgs:** Bd dir, Investors Title Co Chapel Hill NC; bd dir, The Quaker Oats Co Chicago; bd visitors, NC Central Univ Durham NC; charter mem, NC Soc Financial Analysts; Conf Bd NY; bd dir & vice chair, Mechanics & Farmers Bank; UNC Ventures Inc; NC Order Tar Heel One Hundred; bd visitors, Duke Univ, The Fuqua Sch Bus; bd dir, NC 4-H Develop Fund Inc; bd dirs, Mobil Corp NY; bd dir, Jones Group Inc Charlotte; bd dir, Pfizer Inc NY; chair, Pres Carter's Adv Comt Small & Minority Bus Ownership, 1980-81. **Honors/Awds:** 100 most influential Black Americans, Ebony Magazine, 1973-; annual award, prof achievement, Tribune Charities, 1974; annual achievement award, Black Enterprise magazine, 1975; Pathfinder Award, Opport Industrialization Ctrs Am, 1976; C C Spaulding Insurance Award, Nat Bus League, 1976; Twenty First Century Foundation Achievement Award, 1977; Alumnus of the Year, VA State Col, 1977; inducted, National Minority Business Hall of Fame, 1977; Achievement Award, NY Univ Grad School of Bus Admin Alumni Asn, 1980-81; Business & Professions Award, 1985; Ebony Magazine American Black Achievement Award, 1985; honorary Doctor Laws, NC Central Univ, 1986; J E Walker Humanitarian Award, Nat Bus League, 1987. **Military Serv:** AUS, lt, 1943-45. **Business Addr:** Durham, NC 27701.*

KENNEDY, HON. WILLIE B.
Government official. **Personal:** Born Nov 5, 1923, Terrell, TX; daughter of Abraham C Williams and Isa Bell Borders Williams; married Joseph G, Mar 1, 1954 (deceased); children: Paulette Marie Fobbs. **Educ:** San Francisco State Univ, BA, 1975. **Career:** Government official (retired); San Francisco Human Rights Comn, comnr, 1979-80; San Francisco Redevelopment Comn, comnr, 1980-81; City & County San Francisco, supvr; Bay Area Rapid Transit District, dir, 1996. **Orgs:** Regional dir, Gamma Phi Delta Sorority Far Western Region, 1974-82; Univ CA Vol Aux, 1978-90; Nat Asn Colored People, 1979-; pres, Methodist Federation Social Concern, 1979-86; Nat Coun Negro Women Golden Gate Section, 1981-; nat pres, Gamma Phi Delta Sorority; bd supvrs, City & County San Francisco, 1981-96; delegate, Asn Bay Area Govts, 1981-96; Nat Asn Black Co Officials, 1981-; Nat Forum Black Pub Admins, 1982-; Nat Black Caucus Local Elected Officials, 1982-96; N Coastal Co Supvrs Asn,1984-96; bd dirs, Co Supvrs Asn CA, 1986-; exec comt, Co Supvrs Asn CA,1986-96; City Dem Club San Francisco, Chinese Am Dem Club, Dem Women's Forum, CA Dem Black Caucus; African Am Agenda Coun, chairperson, 1981-95;Calif Coun Partnerships, 1984-92; Black Leadership Forum, 1981-. **Honors/Awds:** Woman of the Year, TX Col Alumni, 1976, 1981, 1984; Distinguished Service San Francisco Black Chamber Com, 1982; Community Service San Fran Bus &Prof Women Inc, 1982; Outstanding Service, Nat Coun Negro Women Golden Gate Section, 1983; Certificate of Merit, SF Mayor's Summer Youth Prog,1983; Outstanding Contributions Minority Bus Develop US Dept Com, 1984;Hon DL Urban Bible Col Sch Relig Studies Detroit MI; proclamation, Mayor Willie Bown, 1996; resolution, CA State Assembly, 1997; proclamation, San Francisco Community Col Dist, 1996; resolution, Golden Gate Bridge Dist,1996; Lifetime Achievement Award, Black Am Polit Asn Am.

KENNEDY, DR. YVONNE
State government official, school administrator. **Personal:** Born Jan 8, 1945, Mobile, AL. **Educ:** Bishop St Jr Col, AA, 1964; Ala State Univ, BS, 1966; Morgan St Col,MA, 1968; Columbia Univ, advanced study, 1972 & 1973; Univ Ala, PhD, 1979; AL Interdenominational Sem, LHD, 1986. **Career:** Southern Asn Col & Schs, assoc dir, cooper prog educ improvement prog; Bishop St Community Col, coordr higher educ achievement prog, 1971-74, eng instr, 1968-71, pres, 1981-2007, prof emer, currently; Morgan St Col, Baltimore, asst eng dept, 1966-68; St AL, Dist 103, Dist 97, st rep, currently. **Orgs:** Eng & Verbal Skills Comt, Educ Testing Serv, Princeton NJ, 1972; Human Rels Comn, Ala Educ Asn, 1972; adv comt mem, Southeastern Conf Eng 2-Year Col, 1972-74; bd dir, YMCA, 1973-; bd dir, Opportunities Industrialization Ctr, IOC, 1973-; Women's Missionary Correctional Coun, Christian Methodist Episcopal Church; chmn, Mobile County United Negro Col Fund Campaign, 1980; bd trustees, Miles Col, Birmingham; dir, Bd Christian Educ; NAACP; bd dirs, Am Asn Higher Educ, Am Asn Jr & Community Col; pres, Southern Region, Delta Sigma Theta Inc; chair, Ala Legis Black Caucus. **Honors/Awds:** Miss Alabama St University, 1965; Outstanding Community Service Award, Mobile AL, 1973; Queen of Mobile Area, Mardi Gras Asn, 1973; grant fel, Columbia Univ, NY, 1972 & 1973; President's Award, Ala St Univ, 1964 & 1966; Kermit Mathison Award, Univ Montevallo, 1985. **Business Addr:** State Representative, State of Alabama, 97th District, 11 S Union St Room 537-C, Montgomery, AL 36130, **Business Phone:** (334)242-7737.

KENNEDY FRANKLIN, LINDA CHERYL
Journalist. **Personal:** Born Oct 7, 1950, Brooklyn, NY; daughter of Adam C Falcon and Marjorie J Edwards; married Lonnie, Sep 20, 1982; children: Kennedy M. **Educ:** Univ NE, 1969; Macalester Col, BA, 1972. **Career:** KING-TV Seattle, news reporter, anchor, 1976-; KGW AM Portland, news reporter, anchor, 1974-76; WOW-AM Radio Omaha, news reporter, 1973-74; KOWH-AM Radio Omaha, pub affairs mgr, 1972-73; KOLN/KGIN-TV Lincoln, intern, 1968; KMTV Omaha, news intern, 1968. **Orgs:** AFTRA 1976-; NAACP 1980-91; local bd mem, 1988, nat bd mem, 1991, Am Fed TV & Radio Artists; Nat Asn Black Journalists, 1989-. **Honors/Awds:** Spot News Reporting Award, Sigma Delta Chi NW, 1979, 1983, 1988, 1990; Wash Educ Assn, Best Special Doc, 1990; Emmy Nomination, Outstanding Biog Doc, Natl Acad TV Arts & Sci, 1990. **Home Addr:** 403 8 45th Ave SW, Seattle, WA 98116. **Business Addr:** Reporter/Anchor, KING-TV, PO Box 24545, Seattle, WA 98124, **Business Phone:** (206)448-3875.

KENNEDY-OVERTON, JAYNE
Actor, fashion model, television show host. **Personal:** Born Oct 27, 1951, Washington, DC; married Bill Overton, Jan 1, 1985; children: 3; married Leon Issac Kennedy, Jan 1, 1970 (divorced 1928). **Career:** Show: "Speak Up, America", host, 1980; "Greatest Sports Legends", host, 1983; Happy 100th Birthday, Hollywood, host, 1987; Jackie Robinson: An American Journey, narrator, 1988; Films: Lady Sings the Blues, 1972; Group Marriage, 1973; Let's Do It Again, 1975; Big Time, 1977; Death Force, 1978; Body and Soul, 1981; Night Trap, 1993; TV Series: "Shaft", 1973; "Kojak", 1974;; "The NFL Today", 1975; "That's My Mama", 1975; "The Rockford Files", 1976; "Police Story", 1977; "Trapper John, M.D.", 1979; "CHiPs", 1981; "The Love Boat", 1983; "227", 1986; Coca Cola, rep. **Orgs:** Great Am Talk Festival, 1982; pub serv, The Nat Toll Free Number for finding lost c; Health Hotline Nat Coun Negro Women; Black Women Portrait of Dignity Black History Month, host; summer prog C Communication Bridge. **Honors/Awds:** Miss Ohio, 1970; Emmy Award, Image Award, 1982; Rose Bowl Parade; Belding Award, 1985. **Special Achievements:** First female host of CBS NFL.

KENNEY, WALTER T.
Mayor, vice president (organization). **Personal:** Born Dec 3, 1930, Richmond, VA; son of Jacob Kenney and Lois Moore Kenney; married Maime Mallory, 1962; children: Wilma Battle, Walter T & Marvette Denise. **Educ:** Old Dominion Col; Federal City Col; West Va Univ. **Career:** US Postal Serv, clerk, 1954-85; City Richmond, VA, city council member, 1977-94, mayor, 1990-94, councilman, 2003-04. **Orgs:** Nat vpres, Am Postal Workers, AFL-CIO, 1970-80; life mem, Nat Am Advan Colored People; Big Brothers Richmond. **Honors/Awds:** Outstanding Leadership, East view Civic League, 1970; Certificate of Appreciation, Richmond Crusade Voters, 1976; Outstanding Appreciation of Service, Black Awareness Asn, 1979. **Military Serv:** AUS, Sgt, 1948-52.

KENNISON, EDDIE JOSEPH, III
Football player. **Personal:** Born Jan 20, 1973, Lake Charles, LA. **Educ:** La State Univ. **Career:** St Louis Rams, wide receiver, 1996-98; New Orleans Saints, wide receiver, 1999; Chicago Bears, wide receiver, 2000; Denver Broncos, wide receiver, 2001; Kans City Chiefs, wide receiver, 2001-07; St. Louis Rams, wide receiver, 2008; free agent, currently. **Orgs:** Founder, Quick Start: The Eddie Kennison Found, 2003. **Honors/Awds:** Rams Rookie of the Year Award, 1995; St Louis Rams, Carroll Rosenbloom Memorial Award, 1996. **Special Achievements:** NFL Draft, First round pick, #18, 1996.

KENNON, ROZMOND H
Physician. **Personal:** Born Dec 12, 1935, Birmingham, AL; married Gloria Oliver; children: Shawn & Rozmond Jr. **Educ:** Talladega Col, BA, 1956; Univ Colo, cert, 1957. **Career:** St John's Hosp St Paul, asst chief phys therapist, 1957-58; Creighton Mem St Joseph's Hosp Omaha, asst chief phys therapist, 1958-61; Sis Kenny Inst Minn, asst chief & phys therapist, 1962; Sis Kenny Inst Minn, chief phys ther, 1962-64; Mt Sinai Hosp Minn, consult phys ther, 1963-70; Rozmond H Kennon RPT Inc, 1964; Physician's Phys Ther Serv, self-employ; Ebenezer Nurs Home Minn, chief phys therapist; Texa-tonka Nurs Home, consult physc ther; Cedar Pines Nurs Home; Villa Maria Nurs Home; all Minn; Midway Hosp, St. Paul; Daniel Kennon Jr & Verna Herron Kennon Found, pres, currently. **Orgs:** Am Phys Ther Asn; Am Reg Phys Therapist; Soc-ec Com; past chmn, Prof Prac Com; bd mem past secy, Minn Chap Am Physcl Ther Asn; patner, Phys Ther partner RKR Assoc; Minn Long-Term Care Physcl Thrpy Int & Grp Intntl Cong Physcl Thrpy; mem bd dir, Southdale YMCA; Edina Human Rights; Southside Med Ctr; bd trustees, Talladega Col. **Special Achievements:** Author various articles on phyical therpay. **Home Addr:** 5120 Lake Crest Circle, Hoover, AL 35226-5027.

KENNY, JAMES A
Association executive. **Career:** FleetBoston Financial, dir exec search & diversity recruiting.

KENOLY, BINGO
Singer, songwriter. **Personal:** Born Jan 18, 1977, Oakland, CA; son of Ronald and Tavita Kenoly; divorced; children: Deasia, Omari, Dezirae & Tre. **Career:** Next Generation Ministry Rec, owner & rec artist, 1999-; Who's There?God's There, Right hand Rec, 1998; All The Way, Next Generation Ministry Rec, 1999; No Distance, Next Generation Ministry Rec, 2002; No More Secrets; H.O,.G Life. **Special Achievements:** Grand Avenue, movie with Robert Redford, HBO, 1995. **Business Addr:** Recording Artist, Owner, Next Generation Ministry Records, 4904 Keeneland Cir, Orlando, FL 32819, **Business Phone:** (407)295-4451.*

KENOLY, RON
Gospel singer. **Personal:** Born Dec 6, 1944, Coffeyville, KS; son of Edith; married Tavita; children: Ron Jr, Samuel & Tony. **Educ:** Alameda Col, attended 1982; Friends Int, BS, 1983, PhD, 1997; Faith Bible Col, MDiv, 1985. **Career:** Album: Jesus is Alive, 1991; Lift Him Up with Ron Kenoly, 1992; God Is Able, 1994; Sing Out with One Voice, 1995; Welcome Home, 1996; Majesty, 1998; We Offer Praises, 1999; Dwell in the House, 2001; Ancient of Days; Mellow Fellows, singer; Alameda Col, instr, 1978-92; Jublee Christian Ctr, worship leader, 1985-87, minister music, 1987-99; Integrity Music, recording artist, 1991-; Faith World, minister music, 1999-; Praise Acad, founder, 1999-; Next Generation Ministry Rec, owner; Ron Kenoly Ministries Inc, founder, currently. **Honors/Awds:** Doctorate in Ministry, Sacred Music, 1966; Angel Awards, Lift Him Up, 1993; God Is Able, 1995; Dove Award, Gospel Music Association, 1997; Psalmist of the Century, Missionary Charismatic Int Church Bogota, 2000; Doctorate of Ministry, Friends Int Christian Univ. **Special Achievements:** Auth: Charisma, Ministries Today. **Military Serv:** USAF, 1965-68. **Business Addr:** Owner, Ron Kenoly Ministries Inc, PO Box 2200, Windermere, FL 34786, **Business Phone:** (407)352-7800.

KENOLY, SAMUEL
Singer, songwriter. **Personal:** Born Mar 14, 1979, Oakland, CA; son of Ronald and Tavita; married Vanessa Katzenberger, Jan 12, 2002. **Career:** NGMR LLC, recording artist, 1999-; Quick start Music Seminars, founder & ceo, 2001-. Albums: Who's There? God's There, 1998; All The Way, 1999; We Offer Praises, 1999; No Distance, 2002; Singles: "Eres Mi Gozo", 2000; "Forever You & I", 2000. **Business Addr:** Singer, c/o Capital Entertainment, 217 Seaton Pl NE, Washington, DC 20002, **Business Phone:** (202)636-7028.

KENT, DEBORAH STEWART
Automotive executive. **Personal:** Born Mar 10, 1953, St Louis, MO; daughter of Leodas and Earline; children: Jessica, Jordon & Wendell L Coleman Jr. **Educ:** Southern Ill Univ, BA, 1975; Wash Univ, MA, 1977. **Career:** Gen Motors, staff, 1977-87; Ford Motor Co, area mgr, 1987-92, asst plant mgr, 1992-94, plant mgr, 1994-96, quality dir, vehicle opers, 1996-, Assembly Plant, head, 1996-.

Orgs: Exec bd, Boy Scouts, 1992-94; bd dirs, Gov's State Univ, 1992-94; exec dir, Fla Trls Asn. **Special Achievements:** First woman to head a vehicle assembly plant at the Ford Motor Company; First African-American woman to run an assembly operation for an automaker as plant manager of Avon Lake (Ohio) Assembly Plant. **Business Phone:** (440)933-1200.

KENT, HERB
Radio broadcaster. **Personal:** Born Jan 1, 1929. **Career:** Radio host, 1949-; WVON, host; WVAZ-FM 102.7, host; Chicago State Univ, fac radio broadcasting. **Honors/Awds:** Inducted into the Radio Hall of Fame in 1995. **Special Achievements:** Became the first black deejay inducted into the Radio Hall of Fame in 1995; Author: The Cool Gent: The Nine Lives of Radio Legend Herb Kent. **Business Addr:** Faculty Radio Broadcasting, Chicago State University, 9501 South King Dr, Chicago, IL 60628-1598.*

KENT, MELVIN FLOYD
Manager, administrator. **Personal:** Born Oct 22, 1953, Panama City, FL; son of Floyd M Jr and Viletta McIntyre; married Donna Dunklin Kent, Sep 22, 1990; children: Preston J, Shante D & Shanice L. **Educ:** Gulf Coast Community Col, AA, 1974; Univ S Fla, BA, 1977. **Career:** Domestic Laundry & Cleaners, crew supvr, 1970-74; Int Paper Co, shop keeper, 1975; Sears Roebuck & Co, credit interviewer, 1978; Bay County Juv Detention Ctr, detention supvr, 1978-94; Fla Dept HRS, Foster Care Unit, c & families counr, 1994-99; Fla Dept C & Families, family serv specialist, 1999-2000; Fla Dept C & Families, Oper Prog Adminr, ESS, 2000-. **Orgs:** Vpres, secy, Xi Sigma Lambda Sphinx Club, 1985; secy, Xi Sigma Lambda Chap Alpha Phi Alpha, 1986. **Honors/Awds:** Outstanding American. **Home Addr:** 909 Bay Ave, Panama City, FL 32401, **Home Phone:** (850)784-0873.

KENYATTA, MARY
Educator. **Personal:** Born Aug 14, 1944, Greenville, SC; widowed; children: Malcolm Joseph Kenyatta, Asante Luana Kenyatta. **Educ:** Temple Univ, Philadelphia, BA, 1980; Harvard Grad Sch Educ, Cambridge, EdM, 1986. **Career:** United Presby Church, USA, Wayne, co-dir, WIL Proj, 1971-75; Williams Col, Williamstown, assoc dean, 1981-88; NJ Dept Higher Educ, Trenton, exec asst vice chancellor, 1988-89; Millard Fillmore Col, Buffalo, assoc dean, 1989-. **Orgs:** Vpres, Soc Organized Against Racism, 1985-88; chmn, nominations comt, Asn Continuing Higher Educ, 1990. **Home Addr:** 140 Linwood Ave C11, Buffalo, NY 14209, **Home Phone:** (716)883-3038. **Business Addr:** Associate Dean, State University of New York, Millard Fillmore College, 3435 Main St, 128 Parker Hall, Buffalo, NY 14214-3007, **Business Phone:** (716)829-3131.

KERNER, MARLON LAVELLE
Football player. **Personal:** Born Mar 18, 1973, Columbus, OH; married Nicole. **Educ:** Ohio State Univ, bus. **Career:** Football player (retired); Buffalo Bills, defensive back, 1995-99.

KERN-FOXWORTH, DR. MARILYN L.
Educator. **Personal:** Born Mar 4, 1954, Kosciusko, MS; daughter of Manella LouBertha Dickens-Kern (deceased) and Jimmie Kern (deceased); married Gregory Lamar, Jul 3, 1982; children: Lamar II. **Educ:** Jackson State Univ, BS, speech, 1974; Fla State Univ, MS, mass commun, 1976; Univ Wis-Madison, PhD, mass commun, 1982. **Career:** Fla State Univ, comm specialist, 1974-76; Gen Tel, personnel rep, 1976-78; Univ Tenn, asst prof, 1980-87; Aloca professional, PR fel, 1981; Michael Davis lectr; Tex A&M Univ, assoc prof, 1987; Poynter Inst fel, l988; Am Press Inst fel, l988; Agnes Harris AAUW Postdoctoral fel, 1991-92; Fla A&M Univ, Dept Jour, Media & Graphic Arts, Garth C Reeves Endowed chair, 1994, fac, 1994, prof; Kern-Foxworth International LLC, pres & chief executive officer, currently. **Orgs:** Exec comt, Asn Educ Jour, 1980-; Nat Coun Negro Women, 1980-; Asn Black Communicators 1980-; Nat Community Asn, 1982-; Int Platform Asn, 1982-; adv, Campus Practitioners, 1982; Pub Rels Soc Am, 1982-; consult & assoc, Nashville Banner, 1983; minister educ, Mt Calvary Baptist Church,1983; staff mem, Graduate Teaching Sem, 1983-; adv, Pub Rels Stud Soc Am1983-; Nat Fed Press Women, 1983-; Nat Asn Media Women, 1983-; Nat Fed Exec Women, 1983-; adv comt, YWCA, 1983-; Black Media Asn; newsletter ed, Black Faculty & Staff Asn. **Honors/Awds:** Readers Digest Travel Grant, 1979; First Prize, Alan Bussel Res Competition, 1980; Leadership Award, Asn Black Community, 1980; Kizzy Award, Black Women Hall of Fame Found, 1981; Amon Carter Evans Award Scholar, 1983; Women of Achievement, Univ Tenn, 1983; Unity Awards in Media, Lincoln Univ, 1984; Special Award Recognition of Excellence, PRSA Chap, Knoxville, TN, 1985; Pathfinder Award, Pub Rel Inst, 1988. **Special Achievements:** One of 12 outstanding African-American women in America; First African-American female president of the Association for Education in Journalism and Mass Communications; First & only black in the nation to receive a PhD in Mass communications with a concentration in advertising & public relations; Author of numerous publications. **Business Addr:** President, Chief Executive Officer, Kern Foxworth International LLC, 1713 Woodwell Rd, Silver Spring, FL 20906, **Business Phone:** (301)460-6004.

KERNISANT, DR. LESLY
Gynecologist, obstetrician. **Personal:** Born Aug 15, 1949, Port-au-Prince, Haiti; son of Claire Albert and Rene Kernisant; married Danielle Duclos; children: Lesly Jr & Natalie. **Educ:** Howard Univ Liberal Arts, BS, 1971; Howard Univ Sch Med, MD, 1975. **Career:** Harlem Hosp, exec chief resident, Ob & Gynec, 1978-79; Nat Health Serv Corps, physician 1979-81; Interfaith Hosp, clin instr, 1980-; Brookdale Hosp, assoc attending, 1981-; Mid-Brooklyn Health Asn, clin dir, 1981-86; Cent Med Group Brooklyn, Ob & Gynec partner 1983-89, chief Ob/Gyn dept, 1989-2003, vpres, med affairs, 2003-, chief med officer, currently. **Orgs:** Exec comt mem, Haitian Biomedical Found, 1987, Cent Med Group, 1987; trustee, CBMG Retirement Funds Prog; bd dir, Represent Action Haiti; AMA; Am Bd Obstetrics & Gynec, Clini Provident Soc; fel Asn Haitian Physicians Abroad. **Honors/Awds:** Best Chief Resident Certificate, Harlem Hosp Dept Ob/Gyn, 1979. **Home Addr:** 125 Ashland Pl Suite 4D, Brooklyn, NY 11201. **Business Addr:** President, Chief Medical Officer, Central Brooklyn Medical Group PC, 345 Schermerhorn St, Brooklyn, NY 11217, **Business Phone:** (718)828-6300.

KERR, BROOK
Actor. **Personal:** Born Nov 21, 1973, Indianapolis, IN; married Christopher Oneal Warren; children: Chris Warren Jr. **Career:** TV series: "The Wayans Bros.", 1996; "Moesha", 1996; "City Guys", 1998; "Smart Guy", 1998; "Hang Time", 1998; "The Steve Harvey Show", 1998; "Talent", 1998; "Passions", 1999-2007; "Shoe Shine Boys", 2000; "The Brother", 2001; "Special Unit 2", 2001; "Soap Talk", 2003-04; "McBrided:Dogged", 2006; "Cane", 2007; McBride: Dogged, 2007; "CSI: Miami", 2008; True Blood", 2008; Flower Girl, 2009; Films: Talent, 1998; Shoe Shine Boys, 2000. **Honors/Awds:** Nominee, Soap Opera Digest Award, 2005; Image Award, 2008. **Business Addr:** Actress, c/o William Morris Agency LLC, 151 El Camino Dr, Beverly Hills, CA 90212, **Business Phone:** (310)859-4000.

KERR, STANLEY MUNGER
Lawyer, judge. **Personal:** Born Sep 30, 1949, Des Moines, IA; son of Richard Dixon and Arlene Munger; married Myrna Hill, May 22, 1971; children: Mila, Tamara Aldridge. **Educ:** Christian Col SW, 1969; Univ Tex, 1971; Huston-19Tillotson Col, BA, 1975; Univ Tex Sch Law, JD, 1977. **Career:** Church Christ, preacher, 1966-71; Austin Ind Sch Dist, bus driver & maintenance, 1972-78; Austin State Sch, relief supvr mentally retarded, 1970-78; pvt Law Practice, 1977-87; Huston-Tillotson Col, govt dept head, 1978-81; City Austin, Tex, sr civil rights investigator, 1981-88; Travis County, Tex, Probate Court, ment health atty; City Austin, Municipal Ct Judge, Substitute Judge. **Orgs:** State Bar Tex; Austin Black Lawyers Asn; precinct chair, state & county convention del, Democratic Party; sr warden, stewardship chair, St James Episcopal Church; bd mem, Am Fed State, County & Municipal Employ Local 1624, 1983-; del, Austin Metrop Ministries, 1978-; partner, Trinity Broadcasting Network.

KERR, WALTER L.
Lawyer. **Personal:** Born Mar 26, 1928, Cleveland, OH; son of George H Sr; married Ruby Cowan Kerr; children: Diane. **Educ:** Kent State Univ, BBA, 1957; Cleveland Marshall Law Sch, JD, 1962. **Career:** Yellow Cab Co, taxicab driver, 1953-55; Postal Clerk, 1955-57; Internal Revenue Serv Cleveland, agent, 1957-83; atty at law, currently. **Orgs:** Admitted OH Bar 1963; mem Cleveland Bar Assn 1963, Cuyahoga Co Bar Assn 1963, OH Bar Assn 1963; mem John Harlan Law Club 1963; EEO counselor Cleveland Dist Internal Revenue Serv 1973-77; exec bd mem Chap 37 Natl Treas Emp Union 1974-83; assn exec E 147 St Club 1969-71; trustee Shiloh Baptist Church 1968-80; business mgr Shiloh Baptist Church Gospel Chor & Shiloh Male Church 1968-76; assn exec Shiloh Educ Bd 1971-72; chmn Supv Audit Comm Shiloh Credit Union 1973-86; assn exec The Metro Chorus 1974-89; pres Cleveland Chapter Amer Jr Bowling Cong 1974-78; trustee Forest City Hosp 1974-76. **Honors/Awds:** Fed Comm Serv Award Cleveland Program Exec Bd 1976; Cleveland Dist Equal Opportunity Program Commendation IRS 1976; Award Tax Inst Cleveland Public School System. **Military Serv:** AUS, sgt 1st class, 1947-53; Good Conduct Medal, 1950. *

KERRY, LEON G
Chief executive officer, commissioner. **Personal:** Born Jan 1, 1949, Hampton, VA; married Angela; children: Lisa & LeAnne. **Educ:** Norfolk State Univ, bus admin; Am Inst Banking, banking. **Career:** Sovran Bank, asst vpres; Atlantic Nat Bank, asst vpres; Syst Mgt Am, asst vpres; Cent Intercollegiate Athletic Asn, bus mgr, comnr & chief exec officer, 1990-. **Orgs:** NCAA Div II Comnrs Asn; NACDA John McLendon Minority Scholar Comt; Hampton Roads Comt 200 Men; Bus Adv Coun, Nat Repub Cong Comt. **Honors/Awds:** Leadership Award, NAACP, 1992; Distinguished Alumnus, NAFEO, 1996; Fellows Award, NCAA, 2002; Making Better Communities Award, MBC Network, 2003; Proclamation in the US House of Representatives, Randy J Forbes, VA, 2004; Meritorious Service Award, Livingstone Col, 2004. **Special Achievements:** listed in Who's Who Business Leaders, 1996-97; listed in Who's Who in Executives in Business, 1995, 2000-01, 2002-03; featured in the Bloomberg series, "Bloomberg History Makers", 2002; listed in Strathmore's Who's Who, 2002-03. **Military Serv:** AUS; USAR. **Business Addr:** Commissioner, Chief Executive Officer, Central Intercollegiate Athletic Association, 521 Butler Farm Rd Suite 210, PO Box 7349, Hampton, VA 23666, **Business Phone:** (757)865-0071.

KERSEY, B. FRANKLIN, IV
Lawyer. **Personal:** Born Oct 28, 1942, Richmond, VA. **Educ:** Tenn State Univ, BS, 1964; Howad Univ Sch Law, Wash, JD, 1968; George Washington Univ Nat Law Ctr, WA, attended 1971. **Career:** Howard Univ Sch Law Wash, Ford found fel, 1964-68; atty gen off, legal intern, 1966; George Washington Univ Nat Law Ctr, urban fel, 1969-71; Congressman Robert NC Nix D PA, legis analyst, 1968; US Dept Justice, admin justice spec community rels serv, 1969-71; Match Inst, sr legis analyst, 1971-72; Fed City Col Wash, Wash lectr, 1973-; Colston A Lewis EEO Comn Washington, spec asst, 1973; atty, currently. **Orgs:** Nat Bar Asn; Am Civil Lebierties Union; DC Bar Asn; bd dir DC ACLU; consult, Nat Bar Found Wash; Urban Law Inst Wash; The Urban Inst Wash; DC Bd Educ & Intensive Ed Develo Prog, Univ MD; reg dir, Young Lawyers; Nat Asn Advan Colored People; Nat Urban League; legal coun, Tenn State Alumni Asn; Nat Conf Black Lawyers; Big Brother Nat Capitol Big Brothers Inc. **Honors/Awds:** Citation of Appreciation, Univ Md Intensive Educ Develop Prog, 1972. **Home Addr:** 800 4th St SW, Washington, DC 20024. *

KERSEY, ELIZABETH T.
Administrator. **Personal:** Born Oct 30, 1956, Wadesboro, NC; married Marion W Kersey; children: Mario, Kinyotta, Fateana. **Educ:** Anson Tech Col, AAS, 1977. **Career:** Anson Tech Col, secy to dean instr, 1977; SPCC, Asst to VP Student Learning, currently. **Orgs:** Prof Secy Intl, 1983-; chairperson, Anson Cty Soc Serv Adolescent Parenting Prog, 1984-; secy, Parent Teacher Org, 1984-; pres, Anson Tech Col Alumni Assoc; Bd Dirs, Anson County. **Honors/Awds:** Outstanding Woman Young Women of America, 1983; Notary, 1983; Employee of Quarter Anson Tech College, 1983; Secretary of the Year, Anson Cty, 1985. **Business Addr:** Assistant to the V P of Student Learning, South Piedmont Community College, 4209 Old Charlotte Hwy, Monroe, NC 28110, **Business Phone:** (704)272-5436.

KERSEY, JEROME
Basketball player, executive, basketball coach. **Personal:** Born Jun 26, 1962, Clarksville, VA. **Educ:** Longwood Col, Farmville, VA, 1980. **Career:** Basketball player (retired), exec; Portland Trail Blazers, forward, 1984-95, dir player progs; Golden State Warriors, 1995-96; Los Angeles Lakers, 1996-97; Seattle Supersonics, 1997-98; San Antonio Spurs, 1998-2000; Milwaukee Bucks, 2000-01, asst coach, coach, 2005; Premiere Sports Inc, pres, currently. **Honors/Awds:** Longwoods Hall of Fame, 2005. **Business Phone:** 888-952-4368.

KEYES, ALAN L.
Talk show host, public speaker, writer. **Personal:** Born Aug 7, 1950, New York, NY; son of Allison and Gerthina; married Jocelyn Marcel, 1981; children: Francis, Maya & Andrew. **Educ:** Harvard Univ, BA, 1972, PhD, 1979. **Career:** US Dept State, foreign serv officer, 1978, consult officer, Bombay, India, 1979-80, desk officer, Zimbabwe, 1980-81, policy planning staff, 1981-83, US rep to UN Econ & Social Coun, 1983-85, asst secy int orgn affairs, Wash, DC, 1985-88; Am Enterprise Inst, resident scholar, 1987-89; US Sen Md, candidate, 1988; Scripps Howard, syndicated columnist, 1991-92; Ala A&M Univ, interim pres, 1991; Republican Party, pres, currently; WCBM radio, Owings Mills, MD, "America's Wake-Up Call," host; MSNBC, "AlanKeyes is Making Sense," host, 2002; Books: Masters of the Dream: The Strength & Betrayal of Black America, 1994; Our Character, Our Future: Reclaiming America's Moral Destiny, 1996; Leadership Defined: In-Depth Interviews with America's Top Leadership Experts, 2004; Judicial Tyranny, 2005. **Orgs:** Pres, Citizens Against Govt Waste, 1989-92; founder, Nat Tax payer Action Day, 1990; founder & chair, Declaration Found, 1996-; pres, Ronald Reagan Alumni Asn, 1998-. **Special Achievements:** Republican candidate for presidential race, 1996; appeared in the 2006 comedy "Borat: Cultural Learnings of America for Make Benefit Glorious Nation of Kazakhstan". **Business Addr:** President, Republican Party, 310 First St SE, Washington, DC 20003.

KEYES, GWENDOLYN R
Lawyer. **Personal:** Born Nov 2, 1968, Livingston, NJ; daughter of Andrew and Ursula. **Educ:** Douglass Col, Rutgers Univ, BS, finance, 1990; Emory Univ Sch Law, JD, 1993. **Career:** DeKalb County, sr asst solicitor gen, 1993-94; solicitor gen; Fulton County, sr asst dist atty, 1994-97; DeKalb County, dist atty, currently, solicitor gen, currently; Rotary Int, South DeKalb Chap, vpres. **Orgs:** State Bar Ga, 1993-; Ga Asn Black Women Attys; Leadership DeKalb, 1999-2000; Nat Asn Advan Colored People, DeKalb Chap; Nat Coun Negro Women, DeKalb Chap; pres Ga Asn Solicitors-Gen, 2003-04; chair, Admis Comt Emory Black Law Students Alumni Adv Bd; chair, DeKalb County Domestic Violence Task Force, Subcommittee DV Fatality Rev. **Honors/Awds:** Black Law Students Asn Distinguished Alumni Award, Emory Univ Sch Law, 1996; Communities of America Trail Blazer Award, 1998; Millennium Diva Award, 1999; Douglass Col Alumni Hall of Fame, inductee, 2001; Chief Justice Robert Benham Community Service Award, Ga Supreme Ct, 2001; Women Looking Ahead News Magazines' List of Georgia's 100 Most Powerful & Influential Women, 2001-02; Outstanding Atlanta, honoree, 2002-03; Award for distinguished service and leadership, DeKalb Rotary Coun, 2003. **Special Achievements:** DUI: Truth

& Consequence Prog, coordr; Faith-Based Domestic Violence Project, coordr; first African-American woman elected to the office of Solicitor-General in DeKalb County. **Business Addr:** Disrtrict Attorney, Solicitor-General, DeKalb County, 709 DeKalb Co Courthouse, Decatur, GA 30030, **Business Phone:** (404)371-2561.

KEYMAH, CRYSTAL T (T KEYMAH)
Actor, television producer, writer. **Personal:** Born Oct 13, 1962, Chicago, IL. **Educ:** Fla A&M Univ, BS, theater, 1984. **Career:** Chicago Public Sch, substitute teacher, 1984-89; TV Series: Half Baked, 2006; Hairy Christmas, 2006; Am Dragon: Jake Long, 2006; Actress, performance experience includes: Christmas Carol, Goodman Theatre, 1987-89; Call To Action Touring Co, member, 1989; Love Letters, stage play, 1991; Some of My Best Friends, theatrical tour, 1991-, Five Heartbeats Live 1994; Quantum Leap, NBC-TV, guest artist, 1992; ROC-Live, HBO-TV, special guest, 1993; In Living Color, Fox-TV, cast member, 1990-94; The Commish, ABC-TV, guest star, 1994; John Larroquette Show, NBC-TV, guest star, 1994-95; On Our Own, ABC-TV, cast member, 1995; One Last Time, executive producer/actress, 1995; Cosby, actress, 1996-2000; That's So Raven, actress, 2001-; Static Shock, 2003; Teen Titans, 2005; Wavelength, 2004; Crystal the Monkey, 2006; T'Keyah Keyman Inc, owner, currently. **Orgs:** Delta Sigma Theta Sorority Inc, 1983-; FAMU Alumni Asn, 1985-; vol, Ill Visually Handicapped Inst, 1986-87; vol, Citizens Comt Juv Ct, 1987-88; Nat Coun Negro Women, 1992-; Rainbow/Push Coalition; NAACP, 1991-; active vol, Inst Black Parenting, 1991-; celebrity partner, My Good Friend, 1993-; Nat Asn Brothers & Sisters In & Out, 1996; Chicago Urban League, 2002; Am Women Radio & TV, 2004. **Honors/Awds:** First Runner-Up, Miss Black America Pageant, 1985; Miss Black Illinois, 1985; T'Keyah Keymah Theatre Scholarship, Florida A&M Univ, 1990; Amazing Love, Inst Black Parenting, 1993; NAACP Theatre Award, Best Actress and Best Play for "Some of My Best Friends", 1994; Nat Black Theater Festival Award, 1999; RPI Vision Award, 1999; World Village Award for Art & Music, 2000; Special President's Award, Fla A&M Univ, 2001; Millennium Award, Fla A&M Univ, 2001; History Makers, 2004; Beverly Hills/Hollywood NAACP, Act-So Award for Sponsorship & Outstanding Support, 2004. **Special Achievements:** Author: Playboy of the West Indies, US Premiere, International Theatre Festival, 1988; panelist, Women in the Arts, w/Rosalind Cash and Trazana Beverly, 1991; Some of My Best Friends, 1992; author, Natural Women/Natural Hair, A Hair Journey, 2002. **Business Addr:** Owner, T, 10061 Riverside Dr Suite 714, Toluca Lake, CA 91602, **Business Phone:** (818)569-5456.

KEYMAH, T. See KEYMAH, CRYSTAL T.

KEYS, ALICIA
Singer, songwriter, pianist. **Personal:** Born Jan 25, 1980, New York, NY; daughter of Terri Augello and Craig Cook. **Educ:** Columbia Univ. **Career:** Albums: Songs in A Minor, 2001; Diary of Alicia Keys, 2004; Unplugged, 2005; As I Am, 2007; Film: Smokin' Aces, 2006; Songs: "Fallin'", 2001; "You Don't Know My Name", 2003; "Diary", 2004; "My Boo", 2004;"No One", 2007; "Like You'll Never See Me Again", 2007. **Orgs:** Hon mem, Alpha Kappa Alpha Sorority Inc, 2004-. **Honors/Awds:** Best New Artist, MTV Video Music Awards, 2001; 2 Am Music Awards, 2002; NAACP Image Award, 2002. **Special Achievements:** Books: Tears For Water, 2004; The Songbook, 2005; The Diary Of Alicia Keys, 2006; nominated for Grammy Awards, 2006; How Can I Keep from Singing?, 2006. **Business Addr:** Recording artist, J Recs, 745 5th Ave, New York, NY 10151, **Business Phone:** (646)840-5672.

KEYS, DORIS TURNER. See TURNER, DORIS.

KEYS, RANDOLPH
Basketball player. **Personal:** Born Apr 19, 1966, Collins, MS. **Educ:** Univ Southern Miss, Hattiesburg, MS, 1988. **Career:** Basketball player (retired); Cleveland Cavaliers, 1988-90; Charlotte Hornets, 1990-91; Los Angeles Lakers, 1994-95; Milwaukee Bucks, forward, 1995-96; Scaligera Basket Verona, 1998.

KEYSER, DR. GEORGE F
Engineer. **Personal:** Born Sep 27, 1932, Washington, DC. **Educ:** San Jose State Col, BS, 1965; Univ Md, MS, 1968; Wash Univ, St Louis, DSc, 1973. **Career:** Engineer (retired); US Army Ord Sch, philco field engr, 1957-60; Philco W Dev Labs, tech writer, 1960-65; Univ Md, grad teaching asst, 1966-68; McDonnell Astronautics St Louis, electronics design engr, 1968-70; Wash Univ, asst prof, 1973-74; Howard Univ, assoc prof, elec engineering dept, retired, 1989; Nat Sci Found, prog dir, Engineering directorate, 1992-93. **Orgs:** Mem Sigma Xi; Am Asn Adv Sci; Inst Elect & Electronic Engrs; Am Asn Artit Int, Asn for Computational Linguistics. **Honors/Awds:** Owens-Corning Fiberglas Scholar, 1965. **Military Serv:** USN, electronics tech fist class, 1953-57.

KHADAR, MOHAMED A
Engineer. **Personal:** Born Dec 17, 1946, Jimmi Bagbo, Sierra Leone; son of Haja Memunah and Achaj Yusuf; married Barbara, Jan 11, 1974; children: Rasheeda, Memunah, Mounrah, Rajheed & Zahra. **Educ:** Cairo Polytecnical Inst, 1968; North Va County Col, AS, 1979; Univ Md, BA, 1982. **Career:** Holy Cross Hosp, engr, 1980-; Metropol Condos Bldg, engr, 1990-. **Orgs:** Africa Cultural Ctr, dir & founder, 1983. **Home Addr:** 13815 Marianna Dr, Rockville, MD 20853, **Home Phone:** (301)871-1397.

KHALFANI, KING SALIM. See KHALFANI, SALIM.

KHALFANI, NYESHA. See BUCHANAN, SHONDA T.

KHALFANI, SALIM (KING SALIM KHALFANI)
Executive director, association executive. **Career:** Nat Asn Adv Colored People, Va, exec dir, pres, currently. **Orgs:** NAACP; African Am Adv Coun; adv bd, Virginians Alternatives Death Penalty. **Honors/Awds:** Richmond Peacemaker of the Year, Richmond Peace Educ Ctr, 2006. **Business Addr:** President, National Association for the Advancement of Colored People, 1214 W Graham Rd, PO Box 27212, Richmond, VA 23220, **Business Phone:** (804)321-5678.

KHALI, SIMBI (SIMBI KALI WILLIAMS)
Actor, screenwriter. **Personal:** Born Apr 28, 1971, Jackson, MS; married Cress Williams, Oct 14, 2000. **Educ:** Calif Inst Arts, BFA, actg. **Career:** TV series: "Martin", 1993-95; "The Sinbad Show", 1994; "Clifford the Big Red Dog"; "That '80s Show"; "She TV", 1994; "3rd Rock from the Sun", 1996; "Masquerade", 2000; "The Bernie Mac Show", 2004; "Sanctuary"; Films: Vampire in Brooklyn, 1995; A Thin Line Between Love and Hate, 1996; Plump Fiction, 1997; We Were Soldiers, 2002; Guild Wars Nightfall, 2006; The Inclidebile Hulk, 2008; Mississipi Damned, 2009. **Honors/Awds:** Nominee, Screen Actors Guild Award, 1998, 1999. **Business Addr:** Actress, CBS Studio Center, 4024 Redford Ave, Bldg 2 2nd Fl, Studio City, CA 91604, **Business Phone:** (818)760-5000.*

KHAN, AKBAR. See ELLIS, ERNEST W.

KHAN, CHAKA (YVETTE MARIE STEVENS)
Singer, music producer. **Personal:** Born Mar 23, 1953, Chicago, IL; daughter of Charles Stevens and Sandra Coleman; married Richard Holland, Aug 14, 1976 (divorced 1980); children: Damien; married Hassan, Jan 1, 1970 (divorced 1971); children: Milini; married Doug Rasheed, Jan 1, 2001. **Career:** Singer, music producer; Lyfe, musical group mem; The Babysitters, musical group mem; Rufus, musical group mem, 1972-78; solo singer, 1978; Earth Song record label, co-founder, 1996; Raeven Productions, co-founder, 1996; Albums: (with Rufus) Rufus, 1973; Chaka, 1978; Naughty, 1980; What Cha Gonna Do for M, 1981; Echoes of an Era, 1982; Chaka Khan, 1982; I Feel for You, 1984; Destiny, 1986; CK, 1988; Life is a Dance: The Remix Project, 1989; The Woman I Am, 1992; Epiphany: The Best of Chaka Khan, Vol. 1, 1996; Come 2 My House, 1998; Dance Classics of Chaka Khan, 1999; I m Every Woman: The Best of Chaka Khan, 1999; Classi Khan, 2004; The Platinum Collection, 2006; Chaka Khan Greatest Hits Live 2007; Funk This, 2007; Singles: "I'm Every Woman", 1978; "Life Is a Dance", 1979; "Clouds", 1980; "Papillon (Aka Hot Butterfly)", 1980; "Get Ready, Get Set", 1980; "What Cha' Gonna Do for Me", 1981; "We Can Work It Out", 1981; "Any Old Sunday", 1981; "Got To Be There", 1982; "Tearin It Up", 1983; "I Feel For You", 1984; "This Is My Night", 1985; "Eye To Eye", 1985; "Through the Fire", 1985; "(Krush Groove) Can't Stop the Street", 1985; "Own the Night", 1985; "The Other Side of the World", 1986; "Love of a Lifetime", 1986; "Tight Fit", 1986; "Higher Love", 1986; "Earth to Mickey", 1987; "It's My Party", 1988; "Soul Talkin'", 1988; "I'm Every Woman", 1989; "I Feel For You", 1989; "Baby Me", 1989; "I'll Be Good to You", 1990; "Love You All My Lifetime", 1992; "You Can Make the Story Right", 1992; "I Want", 1992; "Feels Like Heaven", 1993; "Don't Look At Me That Way", 1993; "Watch What You Say", 1995; "Missing You", 1996; "Never Miss The Water", 1996; "Spoon", 1998; "This Crazy Life of Mine", 1998; "I'll Never B Another Fool", 1998; "I Remember U", 1999; "All Good", 2000; "Disrespectful", 2007; "Angel", 2007; "You Belong To Me", 2007; "One For All Time", 2008; Films: The Blues Brothers, 1980; Globe hunters, 2000; TV series: Hunter, 1987; Malcolm & Eddie, 1999; "Friday Night with Jonathan Ross", 2008; The 40 Year Old Virgin, performer, 2005; Roll Bounce, writer, 2005; Get Rich or Die Tryin, performer, 2005; Madea's Family Reunion, 2006; I Now Pronounce You Chuck & Larry, 2007; 27 Dresses, 2008; Amongst Friends, 2009; Raeven Productions, owner &singer, currently. **Orgs:** Chaka Khan Found; Afro-Arts Theater. **Honors/Awds:** Numerous honors & awards including 10 Grammy Awards, 1975-2008; Lena HorneAward, 1998; Lifetime Achievement Award, Black Entertainment TV, 2006; Best R & B Award for "Funk This", 2008. **Special Achievements:** Ranked 17 on VH1's 100 Greatest Women of Rock N Roll; Co-author: Chaka!Through the Fire, 2003. **Business Phone:** (310)247-2400.*

KHAN, DR. RICARDO M
Artistic director. **Personal:** Born Nov 4, 1951, Washington, DC; son of Mustapha and Jacqueline; divorced. **Educ:** Rutgers Univ, Rutgers Col, BA, 1973; Mason Gross Sch Arts, MFA, 1977. **Career:** Crossroads Theatre Co, co-founder & artistic dir, currently; The World Theatre Lab, Johannesburg, London, currently; NYC, founder & dir currently; Univ Mo, Kansas City, grad theatre dept, vis prof; Lincoln Ctr Inst, resident artist; Plays Directed: The Darker Face Of the Earth; Fly!; Quindaro; The Amen Corner; Harriet's Return; Haarlem Nocturne; Flyin' West; Betsey Brown; Black Eagles; Yo Soy Latina!; Hot Feet, 2006; It Ain't Nothin' But the Blues, assoc producer, 1999; rep World Premiere's produced: Colored Museum, Spunk, Black Eagles, Sheila's Day. **Orgs:** Black Leadership Conf, 1993-; pres bd, Theatre Commun Group, 1994-98. **Honors/Awds:** Hall of Distinguished Alumni, Rutgers Univ, 1992; Visionary Leader Award, Middlesex & Camden City E, 1992; Hon Doctorate Fine Arts, Rutgers Univ, 1997; New Jersey Governor's Award, 1997; Tony Award. **Special Achievements:** NJ's 100 Most Influential, City News Publishing Co, Chap of NAACP, 1996. **Business Addr:** Artistic Director, Crossroads Theatre Company, 7 Livingston Ave, PO Box 238, New Brunswick, NJ 08901, **Business Phone:** (732)545-8100.

KHATIB, DR. SYED MALIK
Educator. **Personal:** Born May 7, 1940, Trenton, NJ; married 1965; children: Koren Clark & Adam Christopher. **Educ:** Trenton State Col, BA, 1962; UCLA, dipl African Studies, 1962; Mich State Univ, MA, 1966, PhD, 1968. **Career:** Educator(retired); Stanford Univ, asst prof, 1969-75; SF State Univ, assoc prof, 1978-82; Princeton Univ, vis lectr, 1984; Trenton State Prison MCC, instr, 1985; Rahway State Prison MCC, instr, 1985; Mercer Col, adjunct assoc prof; SUNY New Paltz, Dept African Studies, assoc prof, chmn, 1985-88; Marist Col, assoc prof commun, 1988. **Orgs:** Ed bd Asn Black Psychologists, 1970; consult, SRI 1970; SSRC, 1971; HEW, 1972. **Honors/Awds:** Dean's Honor List, Trenton State Univ, 1960; NDEA fel, Mich State Univ, 1965-67; post doctoral fel, Univ Pa, 1968; issue ed, J Social Issues vol 29, 1973; ed bd, J Black Psychol, 1974-76; recipient, Community Service Award, Bay Area, 1975. **Special Achievements:** Ten publications in the areas of methodology, philosophy & psychology. **Military Serv:** Peace Corps Vol Nigeria, 1962-64. **Home Addr:** 50 Dublin Rd, Pennington, NJ 08534, **Home Phone:** (914)473-1639.

KIDD, CHARLES C
School administrator. **Personal:** Born Aug 9, 1936, Washington, DC; son of Charles and Lorraine; married Mary A, Jun 12, 1959; children: Charles, Crayton, Chinyere, Cy, Change, Chekesha & Chaka. **Educ:** Case Inst Technol, BS, civil eng, 1958; State OH, PE, 1963; Univ Mich, MS, Sanitary & Indust Hygiene Eng, 1964, MS, Radiol Health Phys, 1967, PhD, environ health sci, 1970. **Career:** Sch administrator (retired); Olive-Harvey Col, pres, 1973-75; Chicago State Univ, vpres admin affairs, 1975-76; eng & educ consult, 1976-77; S Shore Nat Bank, vpres, 1977; Fla A&M Univ, dean & prof, 1977-92, assoc vpres & prof, 1993-96; York Col, pres, 1996-2002. **Orgs:** Alpha Phi Alpha Fraternity Inc; Health Physics Soc; Am Asn Blacks Energy; Tallahassee Chap, 100 Black Men Am. **Honors/Awds:** HBCU Fac fel, US Dept Energy, 1994-96. **Special Achievements:** The Role of 1890 Land-Grant Institutions in Meeting Long Term National Agricultural Research Needs, Sub-committee on National Resources, Agricultural Research and Technology, Committee on Science and Technology, US House of Representatives, 1982; Research and Other Strategies for Energy Conservation within Agricultural Communities in Florida, Sub-committee on Energy Dev and Applications, Committee on Science and Technology, US House of Representatives, 1983; A Center for Environmental Technology Transfer: A Model for Minority Involvement, HBCU/MI Consortium Regional Environment Technology Transfer Forum, 1992; Report of the Florida Commission on Environmental Equity and Justice, Florida Department of Environmental Protection, Florida A&M University, 1995. **Military Serv:** USAF, capt, 1960-66.

KIDD, HERBERT, JR.
Association executive. **Personal:** Married Grace Erby; children: 5. **Career:** Asn exec. **Orgs:** Pres, Bessemer Branch NAACP; Bristol Steel Corp; New Zion No 2 Choir; vpres, Choir Union; Bessemer Voters League; Bessemer Civic League; Bessemer Progress Asn; Citizens Comt Bessemer; Candidate Order Elks. **Military Serv:** US Navy.

KIDD, JASON FREDRICK
Basketball player. **Personal:** Born Mar 23, 1973, San Francisco, CA; son of Steve and Anne; married Joumana; children: Trey Jason, Miah & Jazelle. **Educ:** Univ Calif. **Career:** Dallas Mavericks, guard, 1994-96, 2007-; Phoenix Suns, 1996-2001: NJ Nets, 2001-. **Honors/Awds:** Co-Rookie of the Year, NBA, 1995; NBA All-Star Skills Challenge champion, 2003; USA Basketball's Male Athlete of the Year, 2007. **Business Addr:** Professional

Basketball Player, New Jersey Nets, 390 Murray Hill Pkwy, Brendan Byrne Arena, East Rutherford, NJ 07073, **Business Phone:** (201)935-8888.

KIDD, WARREN LYNN
Basketball player. **Personal:** Born Sep 9, 1970, Harpersville, AL. **Educ:** Mid Tenn State Univ. **Career:** Philadelphia 76ers, forward, 1993-2002; Armani Jeans Milano, 2002-03.

KIDD, WILLIE MAE. See ROBINSON, DR. KITTY KIDD.

KILCREASE, IRVIN HUGH, JR.
Judge. **Personal:** Born Nov 21, 1931, Nashville, TN; son of Irvin H Sr and Carrie E; married Kathleen Lacy, Aug 20, 1961; children: Irvin Hugh III. **Educ:** Nashville Sch Law, JD, 1966; Nat Judicial Col, cert, 1983. **Career:** Judge (retired); US Vet Admin Reg Off, claims examr, 1966-68; pvt pract law, atty, 1968-72; City Nashville, 1st asst pub defender, 1969-72; US Atty Off, asst atty, 1972-80; Tenn Ct Judiciary, presiding judge, 1989-91; State Tenn Judiciary Dept, chancellor ct judge. **Orgs:** Dist commdr, Am Legion Dept Tenn, 1961-62; dir, Nashville Chap, Urban League, 1971-72; vice chmn, Gov Comn Status Women, 1973; pres, Fed Bar Asn, 1975-76; Phi Beta Sigma, 1976-; pres, Frontiers, 1979; dir, Nashville Bar Asn, 1982-85; Napier-Looby Asn, 1984-89. **Honors/Awds:** Federal Employee of the Year, Fed Exec Asn, 1973; Presiding Judge Trial Judges of Nashville-Davidson Court, 1984-85. **Military Serv:** USY corp, 1952-54; Good Conduct Medal. **Home Addr:** 945 Inverness Ave, Nashville, TN 37204, **Home Phone:** (615)383-2594.

KILDARE, MICHEL WALTER ANDRE
Surgeon. **Personal:** Born Jan 15, 1935, Tunis, Tunisia; son of George Walter and Deay Andre; married Paula S Calahan, Aug 23, 1983. **Educ:** Univ Mass, BS, 1957; Meharry Med Col, MD, 1961. **Career:** Minneapolis Hennepin Gen Hosp, intern, 1961; Univ Iowa-Va Med Ctr, gen surg resident, 1966; New York Univ, resident neurol surg, 1969-74; Iowa Methodist Hosp, attending neurosurgeon, 1977-84; Robert Packer Hosp, attending neurosurgeon, 1984-85; United Communities Hosps, attending neurosurgeon. **Orgs:** Med serv comn, Iowa Med Soc, 1977-84; Am Med Asn, 1976-, Iowa Midwest Neurosurgical Soc, 1977-, Congress Neurol Surgeons, 1978-, Am Asn Neurol Surgeons, 1983-, Calif Asn Neurol Surgeons, 1987; Am Col Surgeons, 1989. **Honors/Awds:** Alpha Omega Alpha, 1960; Certification, Am Bd Surgery, 1969; Certification, Am Bd Neurol Surg, 1982, Fel, Am Col Surgeons, 1989. **Special Achievements:** "Annals of Neurology", Journal of Neurosurgery, 1980. **Military Serv:** US Med Corps, capt gen surgeon, 1966-68 Vietnam; Nat Serv, Vietnam Valor-Clusters. **Business Phone:** (916)741-1111.

KILGORE, TWANNA DEBBIE
Fashion model. **Personal:** Born Jan 1, 1954. **Career:** Immanuel Prod Inc, exec dir. **Honors/Awds:** Miss Black Washington DC, 1976; Miss Black America, 1976-77. **Special Achievements:** As title holder, traveled US & Europe, contracted with Avon as beauty consultant spokeswoman.

KILIMANJARO, JOHN MARSHALL
Educator. **Personal:** Born Jun 6, 1930, Little Rock, AR; married Culey Mae Vick. **Educ:** Univ Ariz, BA 1952; Univ AR, MA Ed D 1965; NC A&T State Univ. **Career:** Educator (retired); Carolina Newspapers Inc, publisher, pres; instr eng, 1955-58, 1962-69; State Univ IA, teaching fel, 1958-59; AR A M & N Col, prof eng, 1959-61; NC A & T State Univ, prof speech & theatre, 1969. **Orgs:** Exec dir, Richard B Harrison Players, 1969; pres, NC Black Pubs Asn; bd, Chome Soc Greensboro Arts Soc; mem, past pres, NADSA ATA; former second vpres, NCP; consult, Civil Rights; Comn Action Progs NC Fund; mem Guilford Co Young Dem; bd, NC Autism Soc. **Honors/Awds:** O Henry Award, 1973. **Military Serv:** USN 1949-50; USMC 1952-54. *

KILLENS, TERRY DELEON
Football player. **Personal:** Born Mar 24, 1974, Cincinnati, OH. **Educ:** Pa State Univ. **Career:** Football player (retired); Houston Oilers, linebacker, 1996; Tennessee Oilers, 1997-00; San Francisco49ers, linebacker, 2001; Seattle Seahawks, linebacker, 2002.

KILLINGSWORTH FINLEY, SANDRA JEAN
Consultant. **Personal:** Born Aug 14, 1950, Chicago, IL; daughter of Lee Hunter Killingsworth and Cleve Killingsworth; married Eddie Franklin, Aug 26, 1972; children: Bakari Khalid Ali. **Educ:** Loyola Univ, Chicago, IL, BA, 1972. **Career:** Chicago Bar Asn, Chicago, IL, dir pub rels, 1977-79; Chicago Econ Develop Corp, Chicago, IL, dir pub rels, 1978-79; 5100 Communs, Chicago, IL, pres, 1980-; Sandra Finley Co, pres, currently. **Orgs:** Fed Womens Prog, US Air Force, 1983; pres, League Black Women, 1987-89; bd mem, Brass Found, 1989-; bd mem, Chicago Chap, Nat Asn Advan Colored People, 1989-; bd mem, Chicago Youth Ctr, 1990-; Pub Prog Bd Comt, Field Mus Natural Hist, 1992; Chicago Bar Asn; Nat Black MBA Asn; Chicago Area Broadcast Pub Affairs Asn. **Honors/Awds:** Kizzy Award, Kizzy Scholar Fund, 1979; National Council Negro Women Award, 1986; Chicago's Up & Coming, Dollars & Sense Mag, 1985; Entrepreneur of the Year, PUSH, 1988; Meritorious Commission Citation, City Chicago, 1985; AT&T Synergy Award, 1999. **Home Phone:** (708)754-0825. **Business Addr:** President, The Sandra Finley Company, 254 Cove Dr, Flossmoor, IL 60422, **Business Phone:** (708)754-0825.

KILPATRICK, CAROLYN CHEEKS
Congressperson (u.s. federal government). **Personal:** Born Jun 25, 1945, Detroit, MI; daughter of Marvel Cheeks Jr and Willa Mae Cheeks; married Bernard (divorced); children: Kwame & Ayanna. **Educ:** Ferris State Col, AS, 1965; Western Mich Univ, BS, 1968; Univ Mich, MS, educ, 1977. **Career:** REA Express, secy, 1962-63; Detroit Pub Schs, teacher, 1971-78; Mich House Reps, state rep, 1978-96; US House Reps, Mich 13th Dist, rep, 1996-. **Orgs:** Bd Trustees New Detroit, 1983; Bd Trustees Henry Ford Hosp, 1984; Resource Comt, Your C Our C, 1984; Nat Org 100 Black Women; Nat Order Women Legis; vice chair, Intl Affairs Comt Nat Black Caucus State Legislators; chair, Mich Legis Black Caucus, 1983-84; Mich House Appropriations Comt, Dem chairperson the House Transp Budget Comt, 1993; co-chair, Cong Urban Caucus 107th Cong; House Appropriations Foreign Opers; USAF Acad Bd; chair, Cong Black Caucus, 2006-; Can-US Inter-Parliamentary Group. **Honors/Awds:** Anthony Wayne Award for Leadership, Wayne State Univ; Distinguished Legislator Award, Univ Mich; Burton Abercrombie Award; appointed by Gov James Blanchard to represent MI in first African Trade Mission, 1984; Woman of the Year Award, Gentlemen Wall St Inc; Dr, Ferris State Univ. **Special Achievements:** First African American woman to serve on the Michigan House Appropriations Committee. **Business Addr:** Congresswoman, US House of Representatives, Michigan's 13th Congressional District, 1274 Library Ave Suite 1-B, Detroit, MI 48226, **Business Phone:** (313)965-9004.

KILPATRICK, DR. GEORGE ROOSEVELT
Physician. **Personal:** Born Dec 9, 1938, New Bern, NC; son of George Sr and Priscilla Bryant; married Lillian Farrington; children: Michaux, Gregory, La Tonya. **Educ:** Meharry Med Col, Sch Med, 1968. **Career:** NC Textile Occupational Lung Dis Panel, physician; pvt practice; pulmonary diseases & internal med, currently. **Orgs:** Am Thoracic Soc; Greensboro Med Soc; Nat Med Soc; Am Med Asn; Am Bd Internal Med, 1973. **Honors/Awds:** Appreciation Award, Triad Sickle Cell Anemia Found, 1991. **Military Serv:** AUS Med Corps, colonel, 1970-95. **Business Addr:** Physician, 601 E Market St, Greensboro, NC 27401, **Business Phone:** (336)275-7658.*

KILPATRICK, HON. KWAME M (KWAME MALIK KILPATRICK)
Mayor, teacher, state government official. **Personal:** Born Jun 8, 1970, Detroit, MI; son of Bernard and Carolyn Cheeks; married Carlita Poles; children: Jalil, Jelani & Jonas. **Educ:** Florida Agr & Mech Univ, BS, polit sci; Detroit Col Law, Mich, State Univ, JD, 1999. **Career:** Rickards High Sch, Tallahassee, teacher; Marcus Garvey Acad, teacher & basketball coach, 1992; Detroit Pub Sch, teacher; State Mich House Reps, state rep, 1996-2001; City Detroit, mayor, 2002-05, 2006-. **Orgs:** Alpha Phi Alpha Fraternity; NAACP; Mount Pavan Lodge #2; Mich Bar Asn; Wolverine Bar Asn. **Special Achievements:** First African American and youngest rep to be elected to serve as Minority Floor Leader of House of Representatives; youngest mayor in the history of Detroit, as well as the third youngest current mayor of any major US city; First African American to hold a leadership position in the Michigan Legislature. **Business Addr:** Mayor, City Detroit, Executive Office Coleman A Young Municipal Center, 2 Woodward Ave Suite 1126, Detroit, MI 48226, **Business Phone:** (313)224-3400.

KILPATRICK, KWAME MALIK. See KILPATRICK, HON. KWAME M.

KILPATRICK, RICHARDO IVAN
Lawyer. **Personal:** Born Feb 14, 1952, Lakeworth, FL; son of George W and Winifred C; married Carole Camp Kilpatrick, Aug 10, 1985. **Educ:** Harvard Univ, BA, econs, 1973; Univ Mich Law Sch, JD, 1982. **Career:** Shermeta, Chimko & Kilpatrick PC, partner, 1987-00; Kilpatrick & Assoc, PC, founder & atty, 2000-. **Orgs:** Litigation comn, Am Bar Asn; Fed Bar Asn; Mich Bar Asn, 1983; US Dist Ct, Eastern & Western Dists Mich, 1984; US Ct Appeals, Sixth Circuit, 1988; US Supreme Ct, 1997; fed ct comn, Oakland County Bar Asn; Asn Trial Lawyers Am; bd mem, Am Bankruptcy Inst, various comts; ethics comn, Nat Asn Bankruptcy Trustees; chair, creditor's auxiliary, Nat Asn Chap 13 Trustees; Harvard Club Miami; Univ Mich Alumni Asn; co-founder & past pres, Consumer Bankruptcy Asn. **Business Phone:** (248)377-0700.*

KILPATRICK, ROBERT PAUL
Government official. **Personal:** Born Feb 9, 1945, Newton, GA; son of Delander and Julia Ann; married Mary Williams, Aug 5, 1981; children: Reginald J Williams, Robert Paul II & Nicole Kilpatrick. **Educ:** Morehouse Col, BA, 1967; Antioch Sch Law, MA, 1984; Howard Univ Sch Law, JD, 1987. **Career:** US Dept Educ, admin intern, 1968-71, prog mgt specialist, 1971-74, equal employ opportunity specialist, 1974-80, complaints analysis & conciliation unit chief, 1980-84, spec emphasis prog mgr, 1984-88, evaluation affirmative action & data anal unit chief, eeo specialist, currently. **Orgs:** Big brother, Big Brothers Am, 1974-79; charter mem, Blacks in Govt, Dept Educ; asst pack leader, Cub Scouts, 1991-92. **Honors/Awds:** Super Service Group Award, US Dept Health, Educ & Welfare, 1971. **Special Achievements:** One of the developers of Upward Mobility in the Fed Govt, 1971; speech, Dept of Educ, Health & Human Serv nationwide Black hist prog, C-PAN, 1992. **Business Addr:** EEO, US Department of Education, 400 Md Ave SW Bldg FOB-6 Rm 2W232, Washington, DC 20202, **Business Phone:** (202)401-3580.

KILSON, MARTIN LUTHER, JR.
Educator, consultant. **Personal:** Born Feb 14, 1931, E Rutherford, NJ; son of Martin Luther Sr and Louisa Laws; married Marion Dusser de Barenne; children: Jennifer Greene, Peter Dusser de Barenne & Hannah Laws. **Educ:** Lincoln Univ, BA, 1953 (valedictorian magna cum laude); Harvard Univ, MA, polit sci, 1958, PhD, Polit Sci, 1968. **Career:** Harvard Univ, Dept Govt, teaching fel, 1957-59, from tutor govt to prof, 1962-2003, Thomson Res Prof Govt Emer, 2003-; Harvard Ctr Int Affairs, res fel, 1961-72; Univ Ghana, vis prof, 1964-65. **Orgs:** Res fel, Ford Found Foreign Area Training Prog, 1959-61; Urban Politics, Int Politics, Afro-Am Politics, Ethnic Studies; Nat Asn Advan Colored People; fel, Am Acad Arts & Sci; founding fel, Black Acad Arts & Letters; bd dir, Am African Studies Asn, 1967-69; fel, Guggenheim Found, 1975-76; vis scholar, Un Chpts Phi Beta Kappa, 1974-75; consult, Fulbright-Hayes Int Exchange Prog, 1972. **Special Achievements:** First African-American to be granted full tenure at Harvard University; Aprolific writer who has authored numerous social and political articles on Black life in scholarly journals. **Business Addr:** Professor Emeritus, Harvard University, 2400 Sixth St NW, Washington, DC 20059, **Business Phone:** (202)806-6100.

KIMBLE, BETTYE DORRIS
School administrator, musician. **Personal:** Born Jun 21, 1936, Tulsa, OK; daughter of Ethel Kimble and J C Kimble; divorced; children: Jay Charles & Cheleste Kimble-Botts. **Educ:** Tulsa Univ, BME, 1959; Pepperdine Univ, MA, 1979, MS, 1980. **Career:** School administrator, Musician (retired); Sapulpa OK Bd Educ, music instr, 1959-61; Hamlin KS Sch Dist, coord Music, 1961-62; Kansas City, MO, Sch Dist, music instr, 1963-67; Willowbrook Jr High, choral dir & vocal music educ, 1967-79; Compton Unified Sch Dist, chairperson, performing & visual arts, teacher, choral dir, 1967-; Centennial High Sch, instr, 1979-90, supvr visual & performing arts, 1991-93; Broadcast Music Inc, composer, music publ; "Man Called Jesus;" music consult, Play Production, "Been In The Storm So Long". **Orgs:** Phi Delta Kappa Pepperdine Chap, 1983-; dist missionary dir, Southern CA Conf, 1985-; Performing Arts Coun; Am Choral Dir Asn; Chairperson, Compton NAACP Act-So Proj. **Honors/Awds:** Teacher of the Year, Centennial Sr High Sch, 1982; Honored for Music Serv City of Inglewood, CA, 1983; Commendation for Music Serv to Church & Comm, County of Los Angeles; Musical Tribute for Contributions to Music Industry, Kimble Comm Choir; founder & dir, internationally known "Kimble Community Choir"; Religious Musical Called "Revelation"; LHD, The London Inst Appl Res, 1992. **Home Addr:** 8013 Crenshaw Blvd, Inglewood, CA 90305. *

KIMBLE, BO (GREGORY KEVIN KIMBLE)
Basketball player. **Personal:** Born Apr 9, 1967, Philadelphia, PA. **Educ:** Univ Southern Calif, Los Angeles, CA, 1986; Loyola Mary mount Univ, Los Angeles, CA, 1990. **Career:** Basketball player (retired); Los Angeles Clippers, guard, 1990-92, New York Knicks, 1992-93. **Orgs:** Founder, Bo Kimble Found. **Honors/Awds:** Loyola Mary mount Hall of Fame. **Special Achievements:** Film: Heaven Is a Playground, actor, 1991; Author: For You, Hank: The Story of Hank Gathers and Bo Kimble.

KIMBLE, GREGORY KEVIN. See KIMBLE, BO.

KIMBREW, JOSEPH D.
Government official. **Personal:** Born May 31, 1929, Indianapolis, IN; married Carolyn; children: Joseph D Jr, Tracey. **Career:** Fort Benjamin Harrison Finance Ctr; Indianapolis Fire Dept, mem, 32 yrs, dep chief admin, 1985-87, fire chief, 1987. **Orgs:** bd dirs, Greater Indianapolis Fed Firefighters Credit Union, 10 yrs; Nat Asn Advan Colored People , 1968-. **Honors/Awds:** Firefighter of the Year, 1968; Overall Achievement Award, Ctr Leadership Develop, 1987; mem Red Cross Hall Fame; designated Distinguished Hoosier, gov IN; tribute paid to honor his service, 1992. **Special Achievements:** first black fire chief of Indianapolis Fire Dept. **Military Serv:** AUS, corpl, 2 yrs. *

KIMBRO, DENNIS PAUL
Educator, writer. **Personal:** Born Dec 29, 1950, Jersey City, NJ; son of Donald and Mary; married Patricia McCauley, Jan 14, 1972; children: Kelli, Kim, MacKenzie. **Educ:** Okla Univ, BA, 1972; Northwestern Univ, PhD, 1984. **Career:** Smithkline Beckman Corp, sales & mkt, 1978-87; ABC Mgt Consult Inc, consult, 1988-91; Ctr Entrepreneurship Clark Atlanta Univ Sch Bus & Admin, assoc prof & dir, 1992-96; P Kimbro Group, founder, currently. **Honors/Awds:** Personal Achievement Award, Dale Car-

negie, 1988; Dennis P Kimbro Day, City of Detroit, 1991; Dennis P Kimbro Day, City of Dayton, 1991; Parade of Stars, The United Negro Col Fund, 1992; Award of Excellence, Tex Asn Black Personnel in Higher Educ, 1992; City of Savannah Georgia, Keys to the City, 1992; Small Bus Dirs Asn, 1992; Keys to the City, City Macon Ga, 1992. **Special Achievements:** Author: Think and Grow Rich: A Black Choice, 1991; Daily Motivations for AFA Success, 1993; What Makes the Great Great: Strategies for Extraordinary Achievement, 1998; Wisdom of the Ages. **Home Addr:** 3806 Brandeis Ct, Decatur, GA 30034, **Home Phone:** (770)981-8166. *

KIMBROUGH, CHARLES EDWARD
Clergy, veterinarian. **Personal:** Born Jun 24, 1927, Prospect, TN; son of Sterling and Azie Smith; married Blondell M Strong; children: Adric L & Gwenell. **Educ:** Tenn State Univ, BS, 1956; Tuskegee Inst, DVM, 1960; Southern ill Col Bible, cert, 1965. **Career:** Veterinarian (retired); Sparta, area vet, 1960-69; Meat & Poultry Inspection Prog, supvr vet med officer, 1969-75; New Hope Missionary Baptist Church, Sparta, IL, pastor, 1964-69; Mt Zion Missionary Baptist Church, Watertown, TN, 1970-74; Bordeaux Realty Plus, broker, co-owner, currently. **Orgs:** Past pres, Nashville Branch, NAACP; life mem, Phi Beta Sigma Fraternity; Eta Beta Chap; Nashville-Tuskegee Alumni Club. **Honors/Awds:** Sigma Man of the Year, Phi Beta Sigma, Eta Beta Chapter, 1974; Citizen of the Year, Omega Psi Phi Fraternity, 1977. **Military Serv:** AUS, sgt, 1947-53; Purple Heart, Medical Combat Badge, Bronze Star. **Home Addr:** 3852 Augusta Dr, Nashville, TN 37207. **Business Phone:** (615)227-3898.

KIMBROUGH, DONNA L (DONNA L KIMBROUGH-THOMPSON)
Manager. **Personal:** Born Aug 26, 1948, Oklahoma City, OK; daughter of Irvin Rodger Kimbrough and Irene Betty Jones; children: Dawn Marie & Jason Leigh. **Educ:** Univ WA, BA, 1977, MBA, 1980; NFBPA-Exec Leadership Inst, 1993. **Career:** Dept Pub Welfare, Wash, DC, social serv caseworker, 1971-75; City Seattle Water Dept, personnel specialist, 1978-80; Seattle Pub Sch, classification admin, 1980-86; Pierce Transit, mgr personnel, 1986-89; City Seattle Water Dept, mgr human resources, 1989-94; Clover Park Sch Dist, dir human resources, 1994-97; King Co Solid Waste, asst dir, 1997-. **Orgs:** Delta Sigma Theta; pres, Urban League Metro Seattle Guild, 1995-98; NFBPA Seattle; King Co Womens Polit Caucus. **Honors/Awds:** Leadership Excellence Award, Seattle Water Dept, 1991; Advan Mgt, Prog Grad, City Seattle, 1991. **Home Addr:** 10233 66th Ave S, Seattle, WA 98178-2514, **Home Phone:** (206)723-1088. **Business Addr:** Assistant Director, King Co Solid Waste, 201 S Jackson, Seattle, WA 98104, **Business Phone:** (206)296-4388.

KIMBROUGH, KEN. See KIMBROUGH, KENNETH R.

KIMBROUGH, KENNETH R (KEN KIMBROUGH)
Government official. **Personal:** Born in Oklahoma; son of Irvin and Irene; married Juneanne; married Cheryl (divorced 1977); children: Karin. **Educ:** Okla State Univ, BA, indust engineering; Univ Rochester, MBA, finance. **Career:** Int Paper Co, 1980-87; Ameritech-IL Bell Telephone, gen mgr real estate serv, 1987-93; Gen Serv Admin, comnr pub buildings, 1993-; USAA Real Estate Co, Pub Sector Develop, managing dir, currently. **Orgs:** NACORE; civil Res, Engineering Res Found. **Honors/Awds:** Fel, Leadership Greater Chicago. **Special Achievements:** First black PBS commissioner. **Business Addr:** Director, USAA Real Estate Company, Public Sector Development, 9830 Colonnade Blvd Suite 600, San Antonio, TX 78230-2239, **Business Phone:** (210)498-6528.

KIMBROUGH, MARJORIE L.
Writer, educator. **Personal:** Born Jul 11, 1937, Brookhaven, MS; daughter of William T Lindsay and Louise P; married Walter L Kimbrough, Dec 20, 1964; children: Walter M, Wayne M. **Educ:** Univ Calif, BA, 1959; Interdenominational Theological ctr, MRE, 1965. **Career:** Lockheed Aircraft Corp, mathematical engr, 1959-63; Burroughs Corp, programming languages consult, 1963-66, systs rep, 1966-70; Advan Systs, Inc, video technical instr, 1970-72; Interdenominational Theological ctr, instr, 1972-73; MGT Sci AME, sales training specialist, 1973-87; Clark Atlanta Univ, asst prof, 1987-98. **Orgs:** Delta Sigma Theta, 1956-; Phi Beta Kappa, 1957-; lectr, Church Women United, 1987-; Grady Hosp, vol, 1987-02; United Methodist Clergy Spouses; GEO Coun Arts, 1988-91; Cascade United Meth Church. **Honors/Awds:** Woman of the Yr, H Ross Res, 1987; Fac Excellence Teaching, Clark Atlanta Univ, 1989-91; Ladies Distinction, Trailblazer-Enhancing Role & Status Women Educ, 1991; nonfiction author of the yr, 1991; Phenomenal Woman Award, Bennett Col, 1993; Woman of the 90s Award, Mirabella Mag, 1994. **Special Achievements:** Matthew Video Presentations, Methodist Publication House, 1990; Accept No Limitations, Abingdon Press, 1991; "Meditations for January," 365 More Meditations for Women, 1992; "Mark's Gospel," The Strong Son of God, 1992; Beyond Limitations, Abingdon Press, 1993; She is Worthy, Abingdon Press, 1994; "Thanksgiving & Praise," 365 Meditations for Mothers of Teens, Dimensions Press, 1996; Everyday Miracles, Dimensions Press, 1997; Coffee Breaks of Faith, Dimensions Press, 2002; Stories Between the Testaments, Abingdon Press, 2000. *

KIMBROUGH, ROBERT L.
Dentist. **Personal:** Born Aug 20, 1922, Birmingham, AL; married Luequster Murphy; children: Kernelia, Donna Lynn. **Educ:** Univ Ill, Col Dent, DDS, 1951. **Career:** Chicago, dent pvt prac. **Orgs:** Prog chmn, Chicago Dent Soc, 1975-76; pres, Kenwood Hyde Park Dent Soc; vpres, Med Asn Chicago; fel, Acad Gen Dent; treas, Legis Interest Comt Ill Dentist; chmn, Peer Review Comt Ill St Dent Soc; dir, Highland Community Bk Chicago; Am Dent Asn; Nat Dent Asn; Lincoln Dent Soc; Ill State Dent Soc; Am Soc Practice Childrens Dent; pres, Southside Community Arts Ctr; past exec comt, Chicago Br; life mem, Nat Asn Advan Colored People; Urban League. **Military Serv:** AUS, 1st lt, Dent Corps, 1951-53. **Business Addr:** 3233 King St, Chicago, IL 60616.*

KIMBROUGH, TED D.
Executive, school administrator, secretary general. **Personal:** Born in Chicago, IL. **Educ:** Northern Ill State Univ, BS; Calif State Univ, MS; Pepperdine Univ; Univ Calif; Univ Southern Calif. **Career:** Compton Unified Sch Dist, supt, 1982-90; Chicago Pub Sch Syst, supt, 1990-93; Sacramento Unified Sch, interim supt, 1996, supt, 1996-97; Multi-Kim & Assocs, pres, owner; Quadratech, dir, chmn, secy, currently. **Business Phone:** (626)401-2700.

KIMBROUGH, THOMAS J.
Educator, teacher. **Personal:** Born Apr 24, 1934, Morristown, NJ; son of Gladys; married Eva Harden; children: Jerome Joseph. **Educ:** Wilberforce Univ, BS, 1956; Xavier Univ, MEd, 1969. **Career:** Educator (retired); Middletown, OH, educr, 1963-90; Princeton Schs, adv staff on race relation, 1970-72; Princeton City Schs, asst prin, 1972-73; Educ OH Youth Comn, asst supt, 1974-76; guid couns, 1969-70; Student Servs Laurel Oaks Career Devel Ctr, supvr, 1976-79; Sch Creative & Performing Arts, teacher, currently. **Orgs:** Consult, Nat Equal Educ Inst Hartford, CN; consult, Equal Educ Office Ind; treas, Interracial Interaction Inc; pres, Funds for Legal Defense; chmn, Educ Com Middletown Coun for Human Dignity; exec comm, Middletown Br Nat Asn Advan Colored People; chmn, Educ Comm Nat Asn Advan Colored People; cofounder, Anti-Klan Network; chmn, polit action comt, Nat Asn Advan Colored People, 1991. **Military Serv:** AUS, Sp3, 1956-58. **Home Addr:** 6049 Todhunter Rd, Middletown, OH 45044. *

KIMBROUGH-THOMPSON, DONNA L. See KIMBROUGH, DONNA L.

KIMMONS, CARL EUGENE
Educator. **Personal:** Born Apr 10, 1920, Hamilton, OH; son of Posey Meadows and Mary Vanduren Whitaker; married Thelma Jean Lewis; children: Karen Toni West, Larry Carlton & Kimberly Ann Kimmons-Gilbert. **Educ:** Conn Col, BA, 1973; Univ Conn, MA, 1976; S Conn State Univ, Sixth Yr Cert, 1986. **Career:** Military, Educator (retired); Brd Educ Waterford CT, teacher, 1973; Waterford HS, teacher, 1973-95; Top secret control officer, USN, 1961-70; navy liason officer, bi-racial com City New London CT, 1965-66; pvt airplane pilot, 1965-97; Brd Educ Waterford CT, teacher, 1973; Waterford HS, teacher, 1973-95. **Orgs:** Fitness leader, YMCA New London CT, 1978-99; comnr, Waterford Sr Citizens Comn, 2000-; vol, AARP's 55 Alive Mature Driving Course. **Special Achievements:** First Black who had enlisted as a Mess Attendant to serve in every enlisted pay grade from E-1 to E-9 before becoming a Commissioned Officer. **Military Serv:** USN, mess attend third class, 1940, master chief yeoman, 1960, lt, 1963-70; WW II Victory Medal; Phillipine Liberation Ribbon; Submarine Combat Insignia w/5 Bronze Stars; enlisted Submarine Qualification Insignia; Navy Commendation Medal Combat Distinguished Device;Presidential Unit Citation; Navy Unit Commendation; Meritorious Unit Commendation; Good Conduct Medal w/1 Silver Star; Asiatic-Pacific Campaign medal w/1 Silver & 4 Bronze Stars; American Campaign Medal; Amer Defense Serv Medal w/Fleet Clasp; Navy Occupational Medal with Europe Clasp; Natl Defense Serv medal w/Bronze Star. **Home Addr:** 982 Hartford Tpke, Waterford, CT 06385, **Home Phone:** (860)443-5568.

KIMMONS, WILLIE JAMES
Educator, administrator, army officer. **Personal:** Born Apr 4, 1944, Hernando, MS; children: Tonia. **Educ:** Lincoln Univ, BS, health educ & psychol, 1966; Northern Ill Univ, MS, curric & Instr, 1970, PhD, educ admin & supv, 1974. **Career:** Sikeston HS, instr, 1966-67; Northern Ill Univ, instr, 1969-73; NC Cent Univ, asst vice chancellor, 1973-76; Shaw Univ, adj prof, 1974-76; Nat Lab Higher Educ, consult, 1973-74; Univ Dayton Grad Sch, lectr, 1976; Antioch Col, adj prof, 1976-; St Francis Col, dean, 1977-79; Cent State Univ, dir, 1976-77; Downtown Campus Wayne Community Col, dean, 1979; Lawson State Community Col, Birmingham, AL, vpres; Trenholm State Tech Col, Montgomery, AL, interim pres; Downtown Campus Wayne County Community Col, Detroit, MI, pres; Ivy Tech State Col, Bloomington, IN, chancellor; Pre-K-16 schs, educ consult, currently; Save Children Save Schs Inc, founder, 2005-. **Orgs:** Coun Black Am Affairs; Nat Alliance Black Educs; Kappa Alpha Psi Frat; Am Asn Higher Educ; Nat Univ Extensions Asn; Adult Educ Asn USA; Soc Ethnic & Spec Studies; Am Asn Jr & Comm Col; Phi Delta Kappa; Prof Educ Frat; Am Personnel Guide Asn; NEA Athletic schlrsp, 1962-66; teaching fel, 1969-70; post doc fel, Am Mgt Asn, 1975-76; Cont Educ Elderly OH Dominican Col, 1976; Black Adminrs Pub Comm & Col Carlton Press Inc, 1977; Volusia & Flagler Counties African Am Men's Prostate Cancer Bd Dir; African Am Men's Health Summit. **Honors/Awds:** Educator of Year, 1975-76; Distinguished Alumnus of his Alma Mater, Lincoln Univ, 2001; Furthering Rights, Investing in Equality and Nurturing Diversity Award, Fla Civil Rights & Human Rels Comn, 2003; Lifetime Achievement Award, Nat Alliance Black Sch Educr, 2006. **Special Achievements:** One of America's leading authorities on education, leadership, parental involvement, and health related issues; contributed more than 500 presentations and lectures. **Military Serv:** AUS, 1st lt, 1967-69. **Business Addr:** Founder, Save Children Save Schools Inc, 1653 Lawrence Circle, Daytona Beach, FL 32117.

KINCAID, BERNARD
Government official, mayor. **Personal:** Born Jun 5, 1945, Birmingham, AL; married Alfreda Harris; children: Amy. **Educ:** Miles Col, BA, 1970; Miami Univ, MA, 1971; Univ Ala, PhD, 1980; Birmingham Sch Law, JD, 1994. **Career:** Social Security Admin, Prog Ctr, youth counr, 1970-71; Univ Ala, Birmingham, Cult Diversity & Minority Affairs, Sch Health-Related Prof, asst prof & asst dean, 1971-95; Miles Col, contract dir develop, 1996-97; educ consult; Birmingham City Coun, 1997; City Birmingham, mayor, 1999-. **Orgs:** Bd dirs, Birmingham- Jefferson Co Conv Complex; Birmingham Racing Comn; Metrop Planning Orgn; vice chmn, Jefferson Co Mayors Asn; vice chair, Ala Conf Black Mayors; bd dirs, Ala League Munic; US Conf Mayors; chair, Elections Comn; US Conf Black Mayor; Am Legion; Am & Ala Educ Asn; UAB Retired Employees Asn; Miles Col Alumni Asn; Miles Col Booster Club; Jefferson Co Progressive Dem Coun Inc.; Omega Psi Phi Fraternity Inc; Sigma Pi Phi Fraternity Inc. **Military Serv:** USAF, 1962-66. **Business Addr:** Mayor, City of Birmingham, 3rd Fl City Hall 710 N 20th St, Birmingham, AL 35203-2216, **Business Phone:** (205)254-2277.

KINCAID, JAMAICA (ELAINE POTTER RICHARDSON)
Writer. **Personal:** Born May 25, 1949, St John, Antigua-Barbuda; daughter of Annie Richardson; married Allen Shawn; children: 2. **Educ:** New York Sch, photog; Franconia Col, attended. **Career:** Bennington Col, educr; writer; New Yorker, New York, NY, staff writer, 1976-; Harvard Univ, vis lectr, currently; Author: At the Bottom of the River (short stories), 1983; Annie John, 1985; Annie, Gwen, Lilly, Pam & Tulip, 1986; A Small Place, 1988; Lucy, 1991; At the bottom of the river, 1992; The Autobiography of My Mother, 1996; My brother, 1997; My garden, 1999; Talk stories, 2001; Mr. Potter, 2002; Among flowers: a walk in the Himalaya, 2005; Fantabulosos vuelos, 2005. **Honors/Awds:** Frequent contributor to periodicals, including the New Yorker; Morton Dauween Award, Am Acad & First of Arts & Letters.

KINCHEN, ARIF S.
Actor, chief executive officer. **Personal:** Born Feb 7, 1973, Los Angeles, CA. **Career:** Entertainment Partners, extra, 1990-96; Immortal Records, promoter, st mkt, 1993-94; Loud Records, Steven Rif kind Co, st mkt, video promotion,1995-96; Ed Weinberger Co, MTM, actor, 1996-99; A.S.K. Inc, ceo, dir promotions, 1996-; Films: Beverly Hood, 1999; Trippin', 1999; Clayton,2000; The Wash, 2001; Nikita Blues, 2001; The Trailer, 2003; Runaways,2004; One More Round, 2005; Holy Fit, 2006; TV series: "Hull High", 1990;"The Fresh Prince of Bel-Air", 1992; "Saved by the Bell: The New Class",1994; "Sparks", 1996-97; "For Your Love", 2002; "Family Guy", 2003-05; "Method & Red", 2004;"Talk Show with Spike Feresten", 2006; TV Commercials: "Coca Cola'; 'At & T "; "Dominos Pizza"; Album: "What' You Call Dis An Album?",2001. **Orgs:** Exec consult, Zera Found, 1997-; vol, Actors & Entertainers Kids, 1997-;Comics Kids, 1997-. **Honors/Awds:** Various city & state awards. **Business Addr:** Actor, c/o Jazzmyne Public Relations, 3727 Magnolia Blvd Suite 167, Burbank, CA 91510, **Business Phone:** (818)848-6056.

KINCHEN, DENNIS RAY
Law enforcement officer. **Personal:** Born Oct 11, 1946, Shreveport, LA; son of M B and Heareace; married Ruthie Douglas, Oct 24, 1988; children: Darrick Ray. **Educ:** Bossier Community Col, AS, 1990; La Techol, BS, 1992, MA. **Career:** Shreveport Police Dept, patrolman, 1969-78, corporal, 1978-80, sgt, 1980-82, lt, 1982-87, capt, 1987; Casino Asn La, assoc exec, currently. **Orgs:** Paradise Baptist Church; Nat Org Black Law Enforcement Execus; FBINA, La Chap; secy, Brothers & Sisters Shield; Woodlawns Mentor Prog; La Tech Alumni Asn; Bossier Parish Community Col Alumni Asn; Leadership Coun. **Honors/Awds:** Certificate of Training, San Antonio Police Dept, 1989; Distinguished 20 Years Service Award, 1989; Service Rendered Certificate, Proj ACCEPT Prog, 1992; Law Enforcement Certificate of Training, US Dept Justice, 1992. **Special Achievements:** The Detectives Nat Mag, 1974. **Military Serv:** AUS, sgt, 1963-67; Nat Defense Serv Medal, Vietnam Serv Medal, Repub Vietnam Campaign Medal. **Business Addr:** Association Executive, Casino Association of Louisiana, 700 N 10th St, Baton Rouge, LA 70821, **Business Phone:** (225)344-0037.

KINCHLOW, BEN
Clergy, writer, television journalist. **Personal:** Born Dec 27, 1936, Uvalde, TX; son of Harvey and Jewel; married Vivian Carolyn

Jordan, Jan 16, 1959; children: Nigel, Levi & Sean. **Educ:** SW Tex Jr Col, 1972; Univ Va, Darden Grad Sch Bus, 1984. **Career:** Minister, broadcaster, auth & businessman; African Methodist Episcopal Church, ordained; 700 Club, co-host, 1975-88, 1992-96, host int ed; Christian Broadcasting Network, vpres, 1982-85, pres; motivational speaker, currently; Christian Drug & Reha Ctr, exec dir; Front Page Jerusalem, co-host. **Orgs:** African Am Political Awareness Coalition; bd dir, Kids Against Hunger; Front Page Jerusalem; founder, Amns for Israel. **Honors/Awds:** Asniate Award, SW Texas Jr Col, 1972; American Legion Ward of Merit, 1972; Outstanding Alumni, Phi Theta Kappa, 1988. **Special Achievements:** Books: Plain Bread; You Don't Have To If You Don't Want To. **Military Serv:** USAF, 1955-68. **Business Addr:** Board of Director, Kids Against Hunger, 5401 Boone Ave N, New Hope, MN 55428, **Business Phone:** (763)257-0202.

KINDALL, DR. ALPHA S.
Business owner, consultant. **Personal:** Born Mar 5, 1944, Alamo, TN; daughter of B W Simmons and Kendall Associates; married Luther M, Jan 30, 1965; children: Kimberley & Katrina. **Educ:** Tenn State Univ, BA, 1964; George Peabody Col, MA, 1968; Univ Tenn, PhD, 1976. **Career:** Nashville Metro Sch BP, teacher, 1965-69; Knox Co Sch Bd, teacher, 1970-99; Kindall Assocs, chief exec officer, 1999-. **Orgs:** Alpha Kappa Alpha, 1962-; Phi Delta Kappa, 1975-; Gene Piaget Soc, 1975-99; Tenn Alliance Independent Voters, 1976-; Nat Edu Asn. **Business Addr:** Chief Executive Officer, Kindall Associates, 257 Newport Rd, Knoxville, TN 37922-1835, **Business Phone:** (865)386-5350.

KINDALL, DR. LUTHER MARTIN
Educator. **Personal:** Born Nov 1, 1942, Nashville, TN; son of Lucy Moore and Bruce; married Alpha J Simmons; children: Kimberly & Katrina. **Educ:** Tenn State Univ, BS, 1967, MS 1968, EdD, 1973. **Career:** Tenn State Univ, asst prof psychol, 1968-70; Brushy Mountain State Prison, instr psychol, 1972; Roane State Comm Col, asst prof psychol, 1972-73; Univ Tenn, prof educ psychol, 1973-2002, assoc prof emer, 2002-; Kindall & ASC Consult Co, pres. **Orgs:** Chmn, UT Commn Blacks; founding mem, Nat Asn Black Psychologists, 1968; state coord, Project Utilize Educ Talents, 1968; pres, TN Alliance Black Voters, 1979-; Omega Psi Phi Frat, 1973-; pres, Community Rels Coun Knoxville Job, 1986-95; comnr, Tenn Human Rights Comn, 1985-92; pres, Elk Develop Co, 1988-2001. **Honors/Awds:** Alpha Kappa Mu Honor Soc, 1966-; Outstanding Teacher of the Year, UT Panhellenic & Greek Org, 1978-79. **Special Achievements:** Candidate for the Democratic Primary for Governor of Tennessee in 1982. **Business Addr:** Associate Professor Emeritus, University of Tennessee, 1122 Volunteer Blvd A525 Claxton Complex, Knoxville, TN 37996-3452, **Business Phone:** (865)974-8145.

KINDLE, ARCHIE
Automotive executive. **Educ:** Davidson County Community Col. **Career:** Cloverdale Ford, sales mgr; Parkway Ford, sales mgr; Plz Ford Lincoln-Mercury Inc, owner & pres, 1987-2007; Plaza Auto Mart, owner, currently. **Business Addr:** Owner, President, Plaza Auto Mart, Lexington, NC 27292-2552.

KING, ALBERT
Basketball player. **Personal:** Born Dec 17, 1959, Brooklyn, NY. **Educ:** Univ Md, MD. **Career:** NJ Nets, forward, 1981-87; Philadelphia 76ers, forward, 1987-88; San Antonio Spurs, forward, 1988-89; Olimpia Milano, 1989; Wash Bullets, forward, 1991-92. **Honors/Awds:** All-Am First Team, The Sporting News, 1981; ACC Men's Basketball Player of the Year, 1989; inducted, Univ MD, 2002. **Special Achievements:** He appeared on the cover of Sports Illustrated twice during the 1980 season; He was rated the top prep player in the nation over Magic Johnson and Gene Banks during his senior year.

KING, ALONZO B
Choreographer. **Personal:** Born Dec 31, 1957, Albany, GA; son of Slater Hunter and Valencia LaVerne Benham Nelson. **Educ:** Sch Am Ballet; Am Ballet Theatre; Harkness House Ballet Arts; Calif Inst Art, choreography; Dominican Univ, hon doctorate. **Career:** NEA, Choreographers fel; Dancer: Honolulu City Ballet; Santa Barbara Ballet; Dance Theatre Harlem; teacher, master classes: Ballet Rambert, London; Nat Ballet Canada; Les Ballets de Monte Carlo; Ballet West; San Francisco Ballet; Alonzo Kings LINES Ballet, founder & artistic dir, 1982-. **Orgs:** Nat Endowment Arts; Calif Arts Coun; City Columbus Arts Coun; Lila Wallace-Readers Digest Arts Partners. **Honors/Awds:** Four Isadora Duncan Awards; Hero Award, Urban Bank; Excellence Award, KGO; Dominican Univ, hon Doctorate, 2005; prestigious Bessie Award, 2005; Community Leadership Award, San Francisco Found, 2007. **Business Addr:** Founder & Artistic Director, Choreographer, Alonzo Kings LINES Contemporary Ballet, 26 7th St, San Francisco, CA 94103, **Business Phone:** (415)863-3040.

KING, ANITA
Writer. **Personal:** Born Feb 3, 1931, Detroit, MI. **Educ:** Univ Detroit, BA, Music, 1956. **Career:** "Quotations in Black", author, 1981, 1997; "An Introduction to Candomble", 1987; "Samba! and other Afro-Brazilian Dance Expressions", 1989; Dance Herald: A Descriptive Index, Compiler, ed, publ, 2002. **Home Addr:** 10 E 138th St, New York, NY 10037. *

KING, DR. ARTHUR THOMAS
Educator. **Personal:** Born Feb 10, 1938, Greensboro, AL; son of Harvey James and Elizabeth Williams; married Rosa Marie Bryant, Jun 24, 1962; children: Donald & Kevin; married Rosa Marie Bryant, Jun 24, 1962; children: Donald & Kevin. **Educ:** Tuskegee Univ, BS, 1962; SDak State Univ, MS, 1971; Univ Colo, PhD, 1977. **Career:** Educator (retired); USAF Acad, asst prof econs, 1970-74; Air Force Inst Tech, assoc prof econs, 1979-82; Baylor Univ, prof econs, coordr minority affairs; Duke Univ, Am Coun Educ fel, 1993-94; Winston-Salem State Univ, tenured prof econs & dean sch bus, 1995, prof; Goodwill Indust Am Inc, bd dir. **Orgs:** Pres & bd dirs, EOAC, 1987-89; pres & bd dirs, Heart Tex Goodwill, 1986-88; pres, Nat Econ Asn; Am Econ Asn; bd dir, Tripath Imaging, 2003. **Special Achievements:** Numerous articles published on economics 1978-. **Military Serv:** USAF, lt col, 20 yrs; 2 Air Force Commendation Medals; 2 Meritorious Service Medals.

KING, B. B. (RILEY B KING)
Blues singer, guitarist. **Personal:** Born Sep 16, 1925, Itta Bena, MS; son of Albert and Nora Ella Pully; married Sue Carol Hall, Jun 4, 1958 (divorced 1966); children: 8; married Martha Lee Denton, Nov 11, 1944 (divorced 1952). **Career:** Singer, songwriter, guitarist; Albums: Anthology of the Blues; Better Than Ever; Boss of the Blues; Doing My Thing; From the; Incredible Soul of BB King; The Jungle; Let Me Love You; Live, BB King Onstage; Original Sweet 16; Pure Soul; Turn On With BB King; Underground Blues; Live at the Regal, 1965; Electric BB King, 1969; Completely Well, 1970; Indianola Mississippi Seeds, 1970; Live & Well, 1970; Live in Cook County Jail, 1971; Back in the Alley, 1973; Midnight Believer, 1978; Take It Home, 1979; Guitar Player; Love Me Tender, 1982; Deuces Wild, 1997; Live at the Regal, 1997; Blues on the Bayou, 1998; Riding With The King, 2000; Reflections, 2003; The Ultimate Collection, 2005; BB King & Friends: 80, 2005; Gold, 2006; Rhythm & Blues Christmas, 2006; One Kind Favor, 2008; Videos: Blues Summit Concert, 2005; Singles: "Why I Sing the Blues", 1992; "Got my Mojo Working", 1994; "In London", 2001. **Orgs:** Founding mem, John F Kennedy Performing Arts Ctr, 1971; co-founder, Found Advancement Inmate Rehab & Recreation. **Honors/Awds:** Golden Mike Award, Nat Asn TV & Radio Artists, 1969, 1974; Academie duJazz Award, France, 1969; Grammy Award for Best Rhythm & Blues Vocal Male for The Thrill Is Gone, 1970; Humanitarian Award, B nai B rith Music & Performance Lodge NY, 1973; honorary doctorate, Tongaloo Col, 1973; honorary doctorate, Yale Univ, 1977; Grammy Award for Best Traditional Blues Recording for My Guitar Sings the Blues, 1986; Lifetime Achievement Award, Nat Acad Recording Arts & Sci, 1987; Inducted to Rock & Roll Hall of Fame, 1987; Presidential Medal of the Arts, 1990; Nat Award of Distinction, Univ MS, 1992; Kennedy Center Honors, 1995; Trumpet Awards, spec honoree, 1997; Hollywood Walk of Fame; Grammy Lifetime Achievement Award, 1987; NAACP Image Awards Hall of Fame; Blues Foundation Hall of Fame; 15 Grammy Awards; A Christmas Celebration of Hope, Auld Lang Syne, 2003; 14th Grammy Award; honorary PhD, Univ Miss & Royal Swed Acad Music, 2004; Presidential Medal of Freedom, 2006; honorary doctorate in music, Brown Univ, 2007; presented with the keys to the city of Utica, New York, 2008; May 18, 2008, declared the day B B King Day in the city of Utica, 2008. **Special Achievements:** TV commercials for NW Airlines, Greyhound & Wendy's. **Military Serv:** AUS, 1943. **Business Addr:** Guitarist, Singer, William Morris Agency, 1325 Avenue of the Americas, New York, NY 10019, **Business Phone:** (212)586-5100.

KING, REV. BARBARA LEWIS
Clergy. **Personal:** Born Aug 26, 1930, Houston, TX; children: Michael Lewis. **Educ:** Tex Southern Univ, BA, 1955; Atlanta Univ, MSW, 1957, course work completed EdD; Univ Metaphysics, DD, 1978; Christian Church Universal Philos, DD, 1984. **Career:** South Chicago Comm Serv Asn, exec dir, 1966-68; Chicago City Col, Malcolm X Campus, dean, community rels, 1967-69; Atlanta Univ Sch Social Work, instr, 1970-71; S Cent comm Ment Health Ctr, dir, 1971-73; Spelman Col, Atlanta, dean stud, 1973-74; Barbara King Sch Ministry, founder/pres, 1977-; Hillside Chapel & Truth Ctr, founder & minister, 1971-; Nat & Int speaker, preacher, teacher. **Orgs:** Rules comt Democratic Nat Comt, 1984; bd mem, Christian Coun Metro Atlanta; bd treas, Int New Thought Alliance; captain & chaplain Fulton County Sheriff's Dept, Atlanta Sheriffs Servs; Fulton County Develop Authority Bd; Atlanta Bus League Bd. **Honors/Awds:** Achievement in Religion, numerous awards local, state, nat & int organizations 1974-; Zeta of the Year Award, Zeta Phi Beta Sorority Inc; 3 honarary degrees; Atlanta Gospel Choice Award, 1997; Hall of fame, 2000; Phenomenal Mother Of The Year, Alpha Kapha Sorority; Millennium Award, Hush Producaitons, 2000; Nobel Women Shining Star Award, Nat Orgn Black Elected Legislative Women, 2000; InterNat Hall of Fame, 2003. **Special Achievements:** Author of seven books; television show hostess "A New Thought, A New Life" weekly half-hour program, aired regionally. **Business Addr:** Minister, Founder, Hillside Chapel & Truth Center, 2450 Cascade Rd SW, PO Box 42909, Atlanta, GA 30311.

KING, BERNARD
Basketball player, sports manager. **Personal:** Born Dec 4, 1956, Brooklyn, NY; married Collette Caesar, Jan 1, 1981. **Educ:** Univ Tenn, attended 1977. **Career:** Basketball player (retired), sports speaker; NJ Nets, 1977-79, 1992-93; Utah Jazz, 1979-80; Golden State Warriors, 1980-82; NY Knickerbockers, 1982-85, 1987; Wash Bullets, 1988-93; Playing Field Promotions, sports speaker, currently. **Honors/Awds:** NBA Player of the Year, Sporting News; Player of the Month; Player of the Week; All-Am Team, 1976; NBA All-Rookie Team, 1978; NBA Comeback Player of the Year Award, 1980-81; All-Star, 1982, 1984, 1985, 1991. **Special Achievements:** Film appearance: Hustler, 1979; TV appearance: "Miami Vice", 1980; "The Fix"; nominee, Basketball Hall Of Fame, 2004; selected as one of the "Next 10", a list of 10 unofficial additions to the NBA's 50 greatest players list, 2006. **Business Phone:** (303)377-1109.

KING, REV. BERNICE ALBERTINE
Lawyer, minister (clergy). **Personal:** Born Mar 28, 1963, Atlanta, GA; daughter of Martin Luther Jr and Coretta Scott. **Educ:** Spelman Col, BA; Emory Univ, Theol & Law, 1990; Candler Sch Theol, Mdiv. **Career:** City Atty Off, internship; Ga Retardation Ctr, stud chaplain; Ga Baptist Hosp; atty, currently; Voice Communs Network, minister; Juv Ct Judge, clerk, 1990-92; Greater Rising Star Baptist Church, asst pastor, cur; New Birth Missionary Baptist Church, minister, elder, currently. **Orgs:** Bd dirs, King Ctr, Nat Black MBA; State Bar Ga; Alpha Kappa Alpha Sorority Inc. **Honors/Awds:** DDiv, Wesley Col. **Special Achievements:** Ten of Tomorrow future leaders of the black community, Ebony mag; Auth, Hard Questions, Heart Answers. **Business Addr:** Elder, New Birth Missionary Baptist Church, 6400 Woodrow Rd, Lithonia, GA 30038, **Business Phone:** (770)696-9600.

KING, BILLY
Manager, president (organization). **Personal:** Born Jan 23, 1966; married Melanie; children: Natane Alexandra. **Educ:** Duke Univ, polit sci. **Career:** Ill State Univ, asst coach; ESPN's basketball coverage, Ohio Valley Conf, color analyst; Ind Pacers, asst coach; USA Basketball, exec comn, athelete rep, 1997-2000, treas, 2001-04; Philadelphia 76ers, vpres basketball admin, 1997, gen mgr, 1998-, pres, 2003-. **Orgs:** USA Basketball Mens Sr Nat Team Prog Adv Panel; bd dirs, USA Basketballs; USA Basketball Mens Sr Nat Team Comn, 1997-00, treas, 2001-04. **Honors/Awds:** Henry Iba Corinthian Natl Defensive Player of the Year award; silver medal, USA World Univ Games, 1987; Sports Exec of the Yr, 2000; Forty under 40, St & Smiths Bus Jour, 2001; inducted, Duke Univ Hall of Hon, 2001; listed in 101 Most Influential Minorities in Sports, Sports Illustrated, 2003; Nat Basketball Asn Exec of the Yr, African-Am Ethnic Sports Hall of Fame, 2003. **Special Achievements:** TV & Radio appearnces: WBNQ-Radio, "Kings Clips". **Business Addr:** President, General Manager, Philadelphia 76ers, First Union Ctr, Philadelphia, PA 19102, **Business Phone:** (215)339-7676.*

KING, BRETT
Executive. **Educ:** Penn State, BFA. **Career:** WNYC-TV, prod asst, 1981-86; TV show Saturday Night Live, prod coorr, 1986-87, unit producer, 1987-90; Lost Planet Prod, music video & promo producer, 1990-91; Quincy Jones Entertainment, dir tv develop, 1991; Vibe mag, exec consult; Twentieth Century Fox TV, dir current programming, 1993-96; Paramount TV Group, vpres current progs, 1996-2003; Time Warner Inc, sr vpres, currently. **Business Addr:** Senior Vice President, Time Warner Inc, One Time Warner Ctr, New York, NY 10019-8016, **Business Phone:** (212)484-8000.

KING, CALVIN E.
Educator. **Personal:** Born Jun 5, 1928, Chicago, IL; son of David and Florence. **Educ:** Morehouse Col, AB, 1949; Atlanta Univ, MA, 1950; Ohio State Univ, PhD, 1959. **Career:** Educator (retired); Tenn State Univ, prof math & head dept physics & math, 1958-88; Dept Math Fed Adv Teachers Col, Lagos, Nigeria, spec math, 1962-64. **Orgs:** Math Asn Am; Nat Coun Teachers Math; Beta Kappa Chi Hon Scientific Soc; Omega Psi Phi; Alpha Kappa Mu Natl Hon Soc. **Military Serv:** AUS, corpl, 1951-53; Counter Intelligence Corps. *

KING, CEOLA
Government official. **Personal:** Born Jun 10, 1927, Macon, MS; children: Terasa. **Career:** Town of Old Memphis, council mem.

KING, CHARLES ABRAHAM
Lawyer. **Personal:** Born Feb 27, 1924, New York, NY; son of Charles Roy and Ruby Chaplin; married Nellie Alexander; children: Alexandra, Victoria. **Educ:** NY Univ Sch Bus, BS, 1949; Fordham Univ Sch Law, JD, 1952. **Career:** Deluxe Lab, sr acct, 1951-59; King & Jones Esqs, 1960-63; Nat Bur Casualty Underwriters, asst coun, 1964-68; Ins Rating Bd, coun, 1968-70; Ins Serv Off, coun, 1970-72; Metro Property & Liability Ins Co, vpres, gen coun, 1973-88; Arnelle & Hastie, Esqs, Coun; Cooper, Liebonitz, Royster & Wright Esqs Coun, atty; State IL Pollution Control Bd, atty, currently. **Orgs:** Chair bd dir, NY Motor Vehicle Accident Indemification Corp, 1985-88; chair, Legal Comt, Alliance Am Insurers, 1986-88; trustee, Barber-Scotia Col; Am Bar Asn, coun Tort & Ins Practice Sect, 1990-; NY State Bar Asn; RI Bar Asn; Nat Bar Asn; Ind adv com Recodification NY State Ins Law; Ins Com Am Arbitration Asn; past mem, Ind Adv Com implementation state no-fault auto ins law; vpres, Nat Urban League's Black Exec Exchange Prog. **Military Serv:** AUS,

second lt, 1943-46; USAR, second lt, 1946-50. **Home Addr:** 16 Midway Rd, White Plains, NY 10607-2109, **Home Phone:** (914)761-2863. **Business Addr:** Attorney, State of Illinois Pollution Control Board, 600 S 2nd St Suite 402, 3 W Main St Suite 2, Springfield, IL 62704-2542, **Business Phone:** (217)524-8512.

KING, REV. CHARLES E.
Singer, clergy. **Personal:** Born Jul 6, 1920, Cleveland, OH; married Helen Grieb; children: Oolissa & Darla. **Educ:** Heidelberg Col, Ohio, attended 1939; Juilliard Sch Music, NY, attended 1948. **Career:** Wings Over Jordan Choir CBS, dir & singer, 1941-48; Charles King Choir, NY, dir & founder, 1948-50; Karamu Theater Cleveland, Ohio, mgr, actor & voice teacher, 1950-53; Albums: Porgy & Bess; Showboat; The Medium; Kiss Me Kate; Lost in the Stars; Mikado; Carmen Jones; The Maid in & Mistress; Baritone singer & minister; Musical Church, pastor, 1988-. **Orgs:** Singer, all major concert stages, USA, 1941-70; song leader, speaker & leader, CFO Int, 1952-85; minister & founder, Awareness Ctr, 1965-; song leader-retreat dir, Unity Sch Practical Christianity, 1968-; pres, Charles King Orgn, 1971-; pres & owner, King Worm Ranch, 1975-79; pres & owner, King Tree Nursery, 1979-81. **Honors/Awds:** Invited by the Pentagon to entertain servicemen in Vietnam & Korea, 1970-71. **Home Phone:** (425)557-9595. **Business Addr:** Pastor, Musical Church, 24015 SE 30th St, Issaquah, WA 98075-9412, **Business Phone:** (425)557-9595.

KING, CLARENCE MAURICE
Executive. **Personal:** Born Jul 25, 1934, Greenwood, MS; son of C Maurice and Eddie Mae; divorced; children: Mark, Michael, Jeffrey, Cierra & Lydia. **Educ:** Detroit Inst Com, acct cert, 1961; Wayne State Univ, BS, 1974; Cent Mich Univ, MS, 1981. **Career:** Internal Revenue Serv, tax auditor, 1961-65, group mgr, 1965-68, branch & div chief, 1968-76, from asst dist dir to sidt dir, 1976-89; Langston Univ, Langston, OK, asst prof acct, 1989-90; Wichita Minority Supplier Coun Wichita Area Chamber Com, Wichita, KS, exec dir, 1990-92; Local 297 Wichita Musicians' Asn, secy & treas, 2000-; Wichita State Univ, lectr. **Orgs:** Alto saxophonist Clarence King Quartet; archon, Alpha Nu Boule Sigma Pi Phi, 1986-; life mem, NAACP; bd dirs, Nat Bus League; 32 degree Prince Hall Mason; IRS campus exec, Langston Univ & Wichita State Univ; Wichita Rotary; bd dirs, Goodwill Industs. **Honors/Awds:** Outstanding Community Activity Award, Sigma Gamma Rho, 1986; Corporate Achiever Award, Urban League Guild Wichita, 1988. **Military Serv:** AUS, sgt E-5, 5 yrs; Good Conduct Medal, European Occupation, Nat Defense & Marksman, 1954-59. **Home Addr:** 6526 ONeil St, Wichita, KS 67212, **Home Phone:** (316)945-2588. **Business Addr:** Secretary, Treasurer, Wichita Musicians, 530 E Harry St, Wichita, KS 67211, **Business Phone:** (316)265-6445.

KING, COLBERT I
Columnist, editor. **Personal:** Born Sep 20, 1939, Washington, DC; son of Isaiah and Amelia Colbert; married Gwendolyn Stewart, Jul 3, 1961; children: Robert, Stephen & Allison. **Educ:** Howard Univ, BA 1961, grad studies. **Career:** Riggs Nat Bank; US Dept St Foreign Serv Attache, 1964-70; HEW, special asst under sec, 1970-71; VISTA, dir prog & policy dir, 1971-72; Comn DC, US Senate, staff dir, 1972-76; re-election & campaign aid, 1974; Senator Mathias MD, legislative dir, 1974-; Govt Relations, Potomac Electric Power Co, dir, 1975-77; Treas Dept, dep asst sec, legis affairs, 1977-79; World Bank, exec dir, 1979-81; exec vpres, 1981-90; lectr, Foreign Serv Inst, 1982-86; lectr, JFK Inst Polit, Harvard Univ, 1983; The Wash Post, dep ed & columnist, 1990-. **Orgs:** Nat Am Advan Colored People, 1969; HEW Fel Prog, 1970-71; bd dir, Africare, 1987-89; Kappa Alpha Psi; trustee, Arena Stage Theatre, 1986-88. **Honors/Awds:** Distinguished Service Award, US Sec Treas, 1980; Distinguished Grad Award Bus, Bd Trustees, Howard Univ, 1987; Pulitzer Prize, 2003. **Special Achievements:** ASNE, Finalist, in Best Best Newspaper Writing, 1999. **Military Serv:** AUS, adj gen, 1961-63. **Business Addr:** Deputy Editor of Editorial Page and Columnist, The Washington Post, 1150 15th St NW, Washington, DC 20071, **Business Phone:** (202)334-6000.

KING, DELUTHA HAROLD
Physician. **Personal:** Born Jan 17, 1924, Weir City, KS; son of Delutha King Sr and Julia Banks; married Lois Weaver. **Educ:** Western Res, BS, 1952; Howard Univ, Col Med, 1956; Freedmen's Hosp, intern, 1957, resident, urology, 1961. **Career:** Physician, pvt prac, 1965-; VA Hosp, chf urology, 1961-65; Va Hosp, consult, 1966-72; SW Comm Hosp, chief staff, 1979; Hughes Spalding Pavilion, staff & mem; GA Bapt Hosp; Crawford W Long Memorial Hosp; Physician & Surgeons Hosp; St Joseph's Infirmary; Atlanta W Hosp; The Sickle Cell Found Ga Inc, founder, 1971-. **Orgs:** Amer Urol Asn; Am Col Surgeons; Atlanta Urol Soc; bd trustees, Nat Med Asn, 1979-; Ga State Med Asn; Metro-Atlanta Med Asn; bd trustees, SW Comm Hosp, 1979-80; pres, Atlanta Hlth Care Found, 1973-; chmn bd, Metro Atlanta Hlth Plan; sec, co-fndr, chmn bd, Sickle Cell Found, GA; pres, bd trustees, Atlanta Med Asn, 1974; bd mem, Cancer Network, GA State Com; bd mem, chmn, Physicians Com, GA Partners, 1976; Kappa Alpha Psi; Gov Task Force, HSA Devel, 1975; pres, N Ctr GA, Hlth Systems Agency; bd mem, Metro-Atlanta Counsel on Alcohol & Drug Abuse; 2nd vice pres, Nat Asn Sickle Cell Disease; bd mem, pres-elect, GA State Med Asn; bd mem, Amer Cancer Soc; nat pres, Howard Univ Alumni Asn, 1978-80; apptd Nat Council on HlthPlanning & Development; p pres, Atlanta Club, Howard Univ Alumni Asn. **Honors/Awds:** Outstanding achievement as Chief Resident in Urology, Assn of Former Interns & Residents, Freedmen's Hosp, 1961; spec award for service, Atlanta Med Assn; Alpha Omega Alpha. **Special Achievements:** Published article "Hyperparathyroidism" Journal of the Medical Assn of GA, 1966. **Military Serv:** AUS, tech, 1943-45. **Business Phone:** (404)755-1641.

KING, DEXTER
Association executive, chairperson, chief executive officer. **Personal:** Born Jan 1, 1961, Atlanta, GA; son of Martin Luther Jr and Coretta Scott. **Educ:** Morehouse Col, attended 1981. **Career:** Corrections officer, 1981-83; bus consult, music producer & music promoter, 1983-89; Martin Luther King Jr Ctr Nonviolent Social Change Inc, entertainment coordr, 1988-89, pres, 1989, chmn & chief exec officer, 1995-. **Special Achievements:** Author (with Ralph Wiley), Growing Up King: An Intimate Memoir, 2003. **Business Addr:** Chairman, Chief Executive Officer, Martin Luther King Jr Center Nonviolent Social Change Inc, 449 Auburn Ave NE, Atlanta, GA 30312, **Business Phone:** (404)524-1956.

KING, DON
Boxing promoter. **Personal:** Born Aug 20, 1931, Cleveland, OH; son of Clarence and Hattie; married Henrietta; children: Eric, Carl & Deborah. **Educ:** Kent State Univ; Case Western Res Univ. **Career:** Ernie Shavers, Larry Holmes, boxing mgr; George Foreman-Ken Norton, Ali-Foreman, Ali-Frazier, promoted prize fights; Don King Sports Entertainment Network, owner, pres; King Training Camp, owner; Don King Productions, pres, chmn & chief exec officer, 1974-. **Orgs:** United Negro Col Fund; Oper Push; Martin Luther King Ctr Social Change; Trans-Africa; Anti-Apartheid Asn; bd mem, President's Physical Fitness Coun; bd trustees, Shaw Univ; Don King Found. **Honors/Awds:** World Boxing Council Promoter of the Decade, 1974-84; Man of the Year Award, Nat Black Hall Fame, 1975; Urban Justice Award, Antioch Sch Law, 1976; Heritage Award, Edwin Gould Serv C, 1976; Minority Businessman of the Year, Greater WA Bus Ctr; Man of the Year, NAACP; US Olympic Community for Outstanding Support & Service, 1980; The Presidential Inaugural Comt George Herbert Walker Bush Award, 1981; Nat Black Caucus Awardee of the Year, 1981; Promoter of the Year, N Am Boxing Fedn, 1983-84; dedication & generous contribs, Nat Police Athletic League Unselfish, 1983; Humanitarian Award, World Boxing Coun, 1984; Merit Award, Black Entertainment & Sports Lawyers Asn, 1986; Freedom Award, Ind Black Expo, 1986; Only in America Can a Don King Hen Award, The Pigskin Club WA, 1986; Crack Buster of the Year Award, Natl Youth Movement, 1986; Dr Martin Luther King Jr Humanitarian Award, Jamaica Am Soc Asn, 1987; Guantes Mag Promoter of the Year Award; A True Champion of Humanitarian Causes, Ind State Br NAACP, 1987; Martin Luther King Humanitarian Award, E Chicago Chap, Ind Black Expo, 1987; Appreciation on Don King's Devotion to His Fellow Man, Minority Opportunity for Racial Equality More Inc, 1987; Inter Nat Boxing Hall of Fame, 1997. **Special Achievements:** Film appearance: producer, The Big Fight: Muhammad Ali - Joe Frazier, 1975; The Last Fight, 1983; Bicentennial Nigger, 2006. **Business Addr:** Chairman, Chief Executive Officer, Don King Productions, 501 Fairway Dr, Deerfield Beach, FL 33441, **Business Phone:** (954)418-5800.

KING, DONALD E.
Judge. **Personal:** Born Mar 24, 1934, Atlantic City, NJ; son of James E and Edna; married; children: 1. **Educ:** Lafayette Col, AB, 1956; St John's Univ Law Sch, LlB, 1960; St John's Univ Law Sch, JD, 1964. **Career:** Zashin & King, partner, 1962-70; City Newark, asst corp coun, 1970-73, corp coun, 1973-74; Juvenile & Dom Rel Ct, Essex County, NJ, judge, 1974-80; Rutgers Inst Cont Legal Educ Rutgers Law Sch, instr; Supereme Ct NJ, judge. **Orgs:** Pi Lambda Phi; PAD Legal Fraternity; Essex Co Bar Asn; NJ Bar Asn; Am Bar Asn; Nat Bar Asn; Urban League; Nat Advan Asn Colored People; Essex Co Ethics Comn; pres, Garden State Bar Assn. **Military Serv:** AUS, 1st lt. *

KING, EARL B.
Founder (Originator). **Personal:** Born Jan 5, 1953, Chicago, IL; son of John Barksdale and Mildred R; married Darryl S King, Jun 7, 1991; children: Earl B King II. **Educ:** North Tex State Univ, BA, spec ed, 1976. **Career:** NO DOPE EXPRESS FOUND, pres & chief exec officer, 1986-, founder, currently. **Orgs:** Continental Basketball League, 1977-78; San Diego Clippers, 1978-79, 1982-83; Western Basketball Asn, 1979-80; European Basketball League, 1980; Nat Asn Advan Colored People, 1994-. **Honors/Awds:** Outstanding Comm Serv & State, Secy of State, 1993; Man of the yr, Dollars & Sense, 1994; Bus & Prof, 1994; Nat Outstanding Comm Serv, Nat Asn Advan Colored People, 1994; Humanitarian of the Yr Black, Heritage Expo, 1994; DEA & Dept of Justice, Outstanding Contrib in Drug Law Enforcement. **Special Achievements:** First 4 yr letterman in twenty two years at North Tex State Univ, 1976. **Business Addr:** Founder, No Dope Express Foundation, 901 E 104th St, Chicago, IL 60628.*

KING, EDGAR LEE
Health services administrator. **Personal:** Born in Shellman, GA; son of J B and Bertha; married Georgia Roberta Chester; children: Laura Smith & Edgar Jr. **Educ:** Northwestern Univ; Ga State Col; Univ Ill, CPA, 1980. **Career:** Allied Radio Corp, sr acct, 1958-61; Schwab Rehab Hosp, bus mgr, 1961-63, controller, 1963-73, assoc adminr, 1980-88; Hosp Englewood, chief finance officer, 1973-79. **Orgs:** Am Inst CPAs; Ill Soc CPAs; Health Care Fin Mgt Asn; Am Hosp Asn; Ill Hosp Asn; serv exec, Nat Asn Hosp; Chicago Urban League. **Honors/Awds:** Delta Mu Delta, Beta Chap, Northwestern Univ.

KING, EMERY C
Journalist. **Personal:** Born Mar 30, 1948, Gary, IN; son of Natalie Harridy and Emery H; married. **Educ:** Indiana Univ, Bloomington, IN, 1966; Purdue Univ, Hammond, IN, 1971. **Career:** WJOB-Radio, Hammond, IN, reporter, 1970-72; WWCA-Radio, Gary, IN, reporter, 1972-73; WBBM-Radio, Chicago, IL, reporter, 1973-76; WBBM-TV, Chicago, IL, reporter, 1976-80; NBC News, Wash, DC, corresp, 1980-86; WDIV-TV, Detroit, MI, anchor & reporter; Detroit Med Ctr, dir commun, currently. **Orgs:** Bd dirs, Soc Yeager Scholars, Marshall Univ, 1986-91; bd dirs, Detroit Symphony Orchestra; Nat Asn TV Arts & Sci; bd mem, Michigan Multiple Sclerosis Soc; bd visitors, Wayne State Univ Sch Fine, Performing & Commun Arts, 2006. **Honors/Awds:** Emmy Award, Nat Asn TV Arts & Sci, 1977, 1979; 1st Place, Monte Carlo International Film Festival Award for NBC White Paper Documentary, "America Black and White," 1982. **Business Addr:** Director of Communications, Detroit Medical Center, Detroit, MI.

KING, FREDERICK L.
Government official. **Personal:** Born Nov 16, 1957, Washington, DC; married Teresa, Aug 18, 1979; children: Ryan & Erin. **Educ:** Cent State Univ, BS, 1980. **Career:** Pepsi Cola USA, regional sales mgr, 1987-90; Drackett Prod Co, bus develop mgr, 1990-92; Philip Morris USA, trade mkt dir, 1992-94, sales dir, 1994; M & M Mars Kal Kan, regional mgr, 1994-96; DC Lottery & Charitable Games Control Brd, exec dir, 1996-97, dir, 1998. **Orgs:** Bd mem, mem develop comt, Multi State Lottery; co-chair steering comt, mkt comt, Natl Assn State & Prov Lotteries; bd mem, CSU Bus Adv Coun; FOCUS, founder; Kappa Alpha Psi Fraternity Inc, pole march Cincinnati Alumni, 1999. **Honors/Awds:** Volunteer Award, United Negro Col Fund, 1989. **Military Serv:** AUS, capt, 1980-94; ARCOM, 1983.

KING, GAYLE
Television news anchorperson, talk show host. **Personal:** Born Dec 28, 1954, Chevy Chase, MD; daughter of Scott and Peggy; married Bill Bumpus, 1982 (divorced 1993); children: William & Kirby. **Educ:** Univ Md, BA, psychol. **Career:** WDAF-TV, reporter & weekend anchor; WFSB, news anchor, 1981-1998;Cover to Cover, cohost, 1991; The Gayle King Show, host, 1997; O, The Oprah Mag, ed, 1999, ed at large, currently. **Orgs:** WDAF-TV, Kans City, weekend anchor; WFSB-TV, Hartford, CT, even anchor, 1981-; O Mag, ed-at-large, 1991-; "Cover To Cover," co-host, 1992; Gayle King Show, host, 1997-98. **Honors/Awds:** Local Emmys. **Business Addr:** Editor at Large, O Magazine, 1 S Wacker Dr, Chicago, IL 60607, **Business Phone:** (212)903-5188.

KING, GERARD
Basketball player. **Personal:** Born Nov 25, 1972, New Orleans, LA. **Educ:** Nicholls State Univ. **Career:** CBA, Quad City, professional basketball player, 1995-96; Fontanafredda Siena, Italy, 1997-98; San Antonio Spurs, forward, beginning 1999; Washington Wizards, forward, 1999-2001. **Honors/Awds:** FIBA World Championships, bronze medal, 1998; inducted, Louisiana Basketball Hall of Fame, 2006. *

KING, GREG
Chief executive officer. **Educ:** Howard Univ, BA, Jour and Commun. **Career:** NBC, bus develop exec; Soundbreak.com, dir bus develop; The Big Balloon Communications, founder & chief exec officer, 2000-. **Orgs:** Nat Urban League Young Prof; Nat Asn Black Journalists; NABPR; VSED; EPPS. **Business Addr:** Chief Executive Officer, The Big Balloon Communications, 1968 W Adams Blvd Suite 203, Los Angeles, CA 90018-3510, **Business Phone:** (323)730-0029.*

KING, GWENDOLYN STEWART
Public utility executive. **Personal:** Born Jan 1, 1941, East Orange, NJ; married Colbert I; children: Robert, Stephen & Allison. **Educ:** Howard Univ, BA, 1962; George Washington Univ, 1974. **Career:** Public utility executive(retired); US Dept HEW, staff, 1971-76; US Dept HUD, dir div consumer complaints, 1976-78; US Sen John Heinz, sr legis asst, 1978-79; Lockheed Martin Corp,dir; Monsanto Co, dir; Marsh & Mc Lennan Cos Inc, dir; Common wealth PA, Dir, Wash Off, 1979-86; White House, dep asst to Pres & dir inter govt affairs, 1986-88; US Dept Health & Human Servs, Social Security Admin, comnr, 1989-92; PECO Energy Co, sr vpres corp & pub affairs; Podium Prose LLC, pres, 2000-; Monsanto Co, dir, currently. **Orgs:** Trustee, Coun Excellence Govt; adv mem, Nat Adoption Ctr & George Wash Univ Grad Sch Polit Mgt. **Honors/Awds:** Drum Major for Justice Award, SCLC, 1989; Annual Achievement Award, Xi Omega Chapter of Alpha Kappa Alpha, 1990; Ebony Black Achievement Award, 1992; honorary doctorates, Univ New Haven, Univ Maryland, Baltimore County.

KING, HERMAN
Entrepreneur. **Personal:** Born May 27, 1960. **Career:** VIP Exec Protection Inc, co-owner, currently. **Orgs:** Potter's House multiracial nondenominational church. **Business Phone:** (972)401-1172.

KING, HOWARD O., SR.
Government official. **Personal:** Born Aug 24, 1925, Pensacola, FL; son of Lula and Willie; married Lillie Marie Pollard; children: Howard O, Joanne K Carr & William C. **Educ:** Fla A&M Univ, BS, 1956; Fed Exec Inst, 1979. **Career:** Naval Air Sta Pensacola, supvr storekeeper & personnel staffing specialist, 1941-65; Wash Adult Sch Pensacola, adult educ, 1957-65; HO King Sales & Serv Pensacola, proprietor, 1958-65; Dept Defense, Atlanta, contract compliance officer, 1965-67; US Forest Serv, Atlanta, regional intergroup rels specialist, 1967-70; Off Civil Rights, FAA, Wash, DC, depdir, 1972-81; FAA, Atlanta, regional civil rights officer, 1970-72; Madison County, currently. **Orgs:** Bd dirs, MDTA Pensacola, 1963-65; secy, Bi-Racial Comm Pensacola, 1963-65; officer, Ebenezer Baptist Church, Atlanta, 1985-; Fla A&M Univ. **Honors/Awds:** Good Conduct Medal, USN, 1945; Business Award, SNEAD, 1956; Citizenship Award, NAACP, 1965; Citizenship Plaque, City Pensacola, 1965; Certificate of Achievement, Dept Transport, FAA, 1972; Outstanding Achievement Award, National Black Coalition FAA Employees, 1978; Key & Silver Beavers Awards, Scouters, 1992; The Livingston Ivy Award, for Making a Difference, Pensacola, FL, 1994; keys to cities, Tuskegee, AL, & Pensacola, FL; Distinguished Service Career Award, FAA. **Special Achievements:** Author of "You too can overcome". **Military Serv:** USN, petty officer, 1st class, 40 months.

KING, HULAS H
Executive. **Personal:** Born Oct 9, 1946, East St Louis, IL; son of Robert (deceased) and Willie Mae Patton; married Linda Bolton King, Dec 25, 1966; children: Gail & LaTasha. **Educ:** Southern Ill Univ, Edwardsville, BS, data processing, 1972, MBA, mkt, 1974, MS, int rel, 1975, MS, mgt sci & syst, 1978, SPC, 1979; Univ MSR, Columbia, MS, indust eng, 1983. **Career:** USA, Collinsville, IL, bagger, 1964-65; Dow Chem Co, scalper helper, 1965; Ford Motor Co, Hazelwood, body shop work, 1966; McDonnell Aircraft Co, St Louis, mfg eng positions, 1966-89; McDonnell Douglas Syst Integration Co, St Louis, project dir, Team Columbus, 1989-91; EDS-Unigraphics, St Louis, dir, indust mkt team, 1992, dir, indust operations team, 1993-; Southern Ill Univ, adj lectr; Unigraphics Solns, Global Strategic Partnership Prog, dir, currently. **Orgs:** Bd mem, Soc Mfg Eng; bd mem, Worldwide Youth Sci & Eng; bd mem, Am Inst Industl Eng; bd, Greater St Louis HTH Syst Agency, 1977-81; prog evalutor, Accreditation Bd Eng Technol, 1980-; reg coord, Numerical Control Soc, 1980-; adv bd, Child Assistance Prog, 1982-; bd mem, Prof Bus Leadership Coun bd, Jr Eng Technol Soc, 1985-; chair, Bus Adv Coun, Southern Ill Univ, 1989; adv coun, Lewis & Clark Community Col, 1988-; tech vpres, Asn Integrated Mfg-Tech, 1986-89; chair, Prof Bus Leadership Coun, 1992-; Int Fed Eng Educ Socs. **Honors/Awds:** Citizen of the Year Award, OMEGA's, 1978; Beta Gamma Sigma Scholastic Award, Southern Ill Univ, 1979; Engineer of the Year, 1989; St Louis Gateway Engineer's 1989; Salute to Excellence Award-Science, St Louis AMR, 1989; Distinguished Alumni Award, Southern Ill Univ, 1989; E St Louis Lincoln Sr High School Hall of Fame; PBLC, Outstanding Citizen Award, 1994; Charter Inductee to African-American Biographics Hall of Fame for Outstanding Contributions in Engineering, 1994; Black ENR of the Year Award, 1997. **Military Serv:** USY, spec sgt; Army Accommodation Medal, Vietnam Service Award. **Business Addr:** Director, UGS Corp, 13736 Riverport Dr, Maryland Heights, MO 63043, **Business Phone:** (314)334-8670.

KING, DR. JAMES, JR.
Manager. **Personal:** Born Apr 23, 1933, Columbus, GA; son of James (deceased) and Lucille Jameson Williams (deceased); married Jean H, Mar 23, 1966 (divorced 1986); children: Jennifer King Schlickbernd & Jeffrey. **Educ:** Morehouse Col, Atlanta, BS, chem, 1953; Calif Inst Technol, Pasadena, MS, chem, 1955, PhD, physics, 1958. **Career:** Manager (retired); Danforth Found, fel, 1953; Jet Propulsion Lab, mgr, 1969-74, prog mgr atmospheric sci, 1976-81, Space Sci & Appl, tech mgr, 1981-84, tech mgr, 1986-88, dep asst lab dir, Tech Div, 1988-93, asst lab dir, 1993-94; dir eng & sci, 1995; NASA, Wash DC, space shuttle environ effects, 1974-75, dir upper atmosp res off, 1975-76; Morehouse Col, Atlanta, chem prof, 1984-86. **Orgs:** Sigma Xi, 1958-; Am Phys Soc, 1960-; Am Chem Soc, 1960-; bd dir, Pasadena Child Guidance Clin, 1969-72, 1980-86; LA Air Pollution Control, 1971-74; bd dir, Caltech YMCA, 1972-74; Phi Beta Kappa, 1975; AAAS, 1976-; dir, Caltech Alumni Asn, 1977-80; Am Geophys Union, 1977-80; chmn, Pasadena Community Develop Comt, 1982-83; Pasadena Planning Comn, 1989-93; City Pasadena Planning Comn. **Honors/Awds:** Scholarship, Gen Educ Bd, 1953; Certificate of Merit, Nat Coun Negro Women, 1968; US Jaycee's Distinguished Service Award, 1966; Equal Opportunity Medal, NASA, 1986. **Special Achievements:** Author of 13 articles in professional journals. **Home Addr:** 1720 La Cresta Dr, Pasadena, CA 91103, **Home Phone:** (818)794-7932.

KING, JEANNE FAITH
Marriage counselor, manager, counselor. **Personal:** Born Sep 20, 1934, Philadelphia, PA; daughter of Julian Frederick and Minnie H Hines; divorced; children: Heather O Bond Bryant. **Educ:** Antioch Col LA, BA 1977, MA, clin psychol, 1987. **Career:** Performing Arts Soc La, TV producer, 1969-70; Watts Media Ctr, pr instr, 1972-74; WTTW-Chicago Pub TV, TV prod, 1975; Self Employed, free lance comm & pr, 1976-78; Central City Comm Ment Health Ctr, dir pub rel, 1978; In the Beginning Corp, pres, 1978; Jeanne King Enterprises, consult firm, 1984; Valley Cable LA, producer cable TV show Jazz n U, 1984; Local Jazz Clubs, free lance entertainment specialist, 1984; Julia Ann singer Ctr Family Stress Prog, intern, 1985-86, intern family therapy prog, 1986-87; Rosa Pks Sexual Assault Crisis Ctr, LA, counr 1987; Play It Safe SASA, consult & trainer focus consult teaching, 1987; MFCC pvt pract, 1988; Univ Calif Sch Med Doctoring Prog, instr; Marriage Family Child Counr, intern; consult New Horizons; Day of the Drum Festival Book, co-ed. **Orgs:** Exec dir, Performing Arts Soc, LA, 1973-74; cons, Contrib Black Art, An Int Quarterly, 1976-79; Black Womens Forum, 1978-80; bd dir, Ureaus Quarterly Mag, 1978-80; LA, Salvador Sister Cities Comt, 1978-80; Calif Asn Marriage, Family, Child Therapists, 1987; dirs, Centinela Child Guid Clinic, 1988-89; IRB-Human Subjects Protection comt, Univ Calif, 1995-97. **Honors/Awds:** Public Serv Award; Watts Summer Festival Award, 1969; Commt Contribution Head Start Award, 1970; Outstanding Serv Award, Compton Community Arts Acad, 1971; Outstanding Serv Award, 1975; Nat Conf Artists Award, 1975; Day Drum Fest Mistress Ceremonies, 1984; Marla Gibbs Commt Award, 1987.

KING, JIMMY HAL
Basketball player. **Personal:** Born Aug 9, 1973, South Bend, IN. **Educ:** Univ Mich. **Career:** Basketball player (retired); Toronto Raptors, guard, 1995-96; DallasMavericks; Denver Nuggets, guard, 1996-97; Continental Basketball Association, Europe, 1998; Tulsa 66er; Great Lakes Storm, guard; Merrill Lynch, Financial advisor, currently. **Honors/Awds:** Won Contintential Basketball Association MVP, 1998. *

KING, JOHN L
Executive. **Personal:** Born Apr 29, 1952, Detroit, MI; son of Johnnie L and Lillie Mae Hannah. **Educ:** Oakland Univ, Rochester, MI, BA, Human Resources, 1975. **Career:** Oakland County, Pontiac, MI, employ coordr, 1972-78; Visiting Nurses Asn, Detroit, MI, sr personnel rep, 1978-80; Rehab Inst, Detroit, MI, dir, human resources, 1980-88; The Detroit Med Ctr, Detroit, MI, compensation admin, 1988-89, mgr equal employ plan, 1989-92, dir equal employ planning, 1992-. **Orgs:** Nat Asn Advan Colored People, 1980-; Mich Develop Disabilities Coun, 1983-; Mayor's Handicapper Adv Coun, 1987-; treas, SW Detroit Community Mental Health Servs Group, 1987-; Nat Asn Advance Blacks Health, 1988-; prog develop chairperson, Healthcare Personnel Admin Asn, SE Michigan, 1988-90; spec proj chairperson, 1989-90, pres, Healthcare Personnel Admin Asn SE Mich, 1990-92; chmn, Southeastern Mich Indust Liaison Group. **Honors/Awds:** Testimonial Resolution, Detroit City Coun, 1983, State of Mich Senate, 1984.

KING, DR. JOHN Q. TAYLOR, SR.
School administrator. **Personal:** Born Sep 25, 1921, Memphis, TN; son of John Quill (deceased) and Alice Clinton Woodson (deceased); married Dr Marcet Alice Hines, Jun 28, 1942 (died 1995); children: John Q Jr, Clinton Allen, Marjon King Christopher & Stuart Hines. **Educ:** Fisk Univ, BA, 1941; Landig Col Mortuary Sci, Dipl, 1942; Huston-Tillotson Col, BS, 1947; DePaul Univ, MS, math, 1950; Univ Tex, Austin, PhD, 1957. **Career:** US Army, pvt capt, 1942-46; King Funeral Home, Austin, Tex, mortician, 1946-55; Kings-Tears Mortuary Inc, funeral dir & embalmer, pres; Huston-Tillotson Col, instr, 1947-52, asst prof, 1952-54, prof math,1954-88, acad dean, 1960-65, pres, 1965-88, chancellor, 1967-88, chancellor & pres emer, 1988, dir & chmn; Brigadier, Gen, 1974; Ctr Advan Sci, Engineering & Technol. **Orgs:** Gen secy, Nat Protestant Brotherhood, 1966-80; pres, Union Welfare & Burial Asn, 1941-85; sr vpres, Am Underwriters Life Ins Co, 1986-89; adv dir, Chase Bank Trust; trustee, Austin Col Sherman Tex; pres, King-Tears Mortuary Inc; life mem, Nat Advan Asn Colored People & Nat Urban League; Phi Beta Kappa; Alpha Phi Alpha Frat; Sigma Pi Phi Frat; Phi Delta Kappa; Philosophical Soc Tex; Austin Greater E Kiwanis Club, 1966-88; past chmn, Austin Civil Serv Comn; founder, Union Nat Bank; ch lay leader, United Methodist Ch; dir, secy, Found Ins Regulatory Studies. **Honors/Awds:** Alumni Awards, Huston-Tillotson Col & Fisk Univ; Roy Wilkins Meritorious Award, Nat Advan Asn Colored People; Distinguished Service Award, Tex Lutheran Col; Arthur B DeWitty Award, Austin Br Nat Advan Asn Coloerd People; Martin Luther King Humanitarian Award; Frederick D Patterson Award, Alpha Phi Alpha; Minority Advocate of the Year, Austin Chamber Com; Military & Education Award, San Antonio League, Nat Asn Bus & Prof Women's Clubs; Brotherhood Award, Nat Conf Christians & Jews; Distinguished Alumnus Award, Students' Assn, Univ of Texas-Austin, 1990; Meritorious Achievement in Education Award, Nat Sorority, Phi Delta Kappa, 1991; Philanthrophist of the Year, Austin Chap, Nat Soc Fund raisers, 1991; Man of the Year Award, Independent Funeral Dirs Tex Inc, 1994; George Washington Honor Medal, Freedoms Found Valley Forge, 1994. **Special Achievements:** Co-author: math texts; co-author, Stories of Twenty-Three Famous Negro Americans, Steck-Vaughan, 1967, Famous Black Americans, Steck-Vaughan, 1975; Booklet on Life of Mrs Mary McLeod Bethune. **Military Serv:** USY, maj gen, (WWII, 1942-46; USAR 1946-83); Tex State, Guard, lt gen,1985; received many combat & other military ribbons, decorations & awards. *

KING, JOHN THOMAS
Administrator. **Personal:** Born Dec 9, 1935, Detroit, MI; son of John and Frances Berry; married Joan Ardis King, Mar 18, 1955; children: Victoria D King, John K King & Pamela A King. **Educ:** Wayne State Univ, Detroit, MI. **Career:** Administrator (Retired); Detroit Police Dept, Detroit, MI, police cadet, 1954-57; Detroit Fire Dept, Detroit, MI, firefighter, 1957-72, Lt, 1972-77, fire marshal, 1977, from asst to fire commnr, 1978-87, chief adminir, 1987-93. **Orgs:** Pres, Phoenix Black Firefighters, 1970-80; CYO, 1973-; comt mem, New Detroit, 1974-; pres, Toastmasters, 1976-78; alternate, Detroit Police & Fire Pension, 1986-.

KING, JOSEPHINE
Insurance executive. **Career:** Chicago Metrop Assurance Co, chief exec officer. **Special Achievements:** Company is ranked No 5 on the Black Enterprise list of top Insurance Comopany, 1994.

KING, KELLEY A
Executive director. **Educ:** Wharton Sch, Univ Penn, BS, Econ. **Career:** Prof Women's Alliance, vpres; JB Polk Real Estate Develop Group, founding mem & partner; Am Express Co, dir strategic technol relationships, currently. **Orgs:** Co-chair, Career Develop Comm; Univ Penn Women's Track Alumni Asn; Black Employee Network's Career Comm. **Business Addr:** Director, American Express Inc, World Financial Center, 200 Vesey St, New York, NY 10285, **Business Phone:** (212)640-2000.*

KING, LAWRENCE C.
Executive. **Personal:** Born in Washington, DC; married Beulah; children: Larry & Craig. **Educ:** Howard Univ, BA, 1951. **Career:** Gen Foods Corp NY, regional sales mgr; Gen Foods Corp, former assoc marketers mgr, dist sales mgr & sales develop mgr. **Orgs:** Urban League; Kappa Alpha Psi.

KING, LAWRENCE PATRICK
Engineer, marketing executive. **Personal:** Born Feb 3, 1940, Detroit, MI; son of Samuel and Vivian; married Deborah Barrett, Dec 15, 1990; children: Dereck Jackson & Alexandria King. **Educ:** Univ Detroit, 1962; Cleveland State Univ, BSME, 1974; Univ Dayton, 1979; Univ Mich, 1990. **Career:** Gen Electric, sr market develop engr, 1977-79, mgr, mkt serv, 1979-80; Babcock-Wilcox, mkt specialist, 1980-81, sr mkt specialist, 1981-93; Edison Polymer Innovation Corp, dir mkt, currently. **Orgs:** Sales & Mkt Execs; past pres, Nat Tech Asn, 1986-87; Am Asn Blacks Energy; trustee, Nat Invention Ctr. **Honors/Awds:** Samuel Cheevers Distinguished Service Award, Nat Tech Asn, 1985. **Special Achievements:** Challenges ASOd with Increased Coal Consumption, 1992; Incineration in the Mgt of Hazardous Wastes, 1986; Outreach Strategy for Equity in Environmental Issues, 1995. **Home Phone:** (330)867-4879. **Business Addr:** Director of Marketing, Edison Polymer Innovation Corporation, 4040 Embassy Pkwy Suite 150, Akron, OH 44333, **Business Phone:** (330)668-9411.

KING, LEWIS HENRY
Consultant. **Personal:** Born in Birmingham, AL; son of Tony J and Lilly Bell Taylor; married Annie M Caster King, Sep 9, 1951; children: Debra, Cynthia, Lewis Jr, Marlon. **Educ:** Miles Col, Birmingham, AL; Lawson Community Col, Birmingham, AL; Samford Univ, Birmingham, AL, BS, 1978. **Career:** US Postal Serv, Birmingham, AL, postman, 1951-81; United Mgt Enterprises, vice chmn, owner & pres, currently. **Orgs:** Board mem, emer, National Coalition Title I, Chap I Parents, Meeting Planners Int; Am Soc Asn Exec; Religious Conf Mgt Asn; Nat Coalition Black Meeting Planners; bd dir, Birmingham Jefferson Civic Ctr Authority. **Military Serv:** AUS, Technician 4th Grade, 1944-46; Good Conduct, Expert Rifleman, 1944. **Business Addr:** 648 Center Way SW, Birmingham, AL 35211, **Business Phone:** (205)322-3219.*

KING, LEWIS M.
Scientist, college teacher. **Personal:** Born Oct 5, 1942, Trinidad and Tobago; son of Henry and Gladys; children: Eric. **Educ:** Howard Univ, BS, 1967; Univ Calif, Los Angeles, MA, 1968, PhD, 1971. **Career:** Univ Calif Los Angeles, psychol lectr, 1967-71; Martin Luther King Jr Hosp, chief psychol, 1971-73; Drew Med Sch, dir res, 1972-74; Drew Med Sch, prof psychiat, 1972-74; Drew Med Sch, Fanon Res & Devel Ctr, dir; Drew Med Sch, dean; Charles R Drew Univ Med & Sci, Dept Psychiat, prof, currently. **Orgs:** Dir, Trinidad Drama Guild, 1960-63; bd dir, Behavior Res & Develop, 1970-74; chmn, Community Res Review Com, LA, 1972-74. **Honors/Awds:** Howard Univ Scholarship, 1964-67; Outstanding contribution to Student Life, Howard Univ, 1966; Dean's honor role, 1964-67; UN Inst Int Educ Fel, 1965-67; Physics Honor Soc Howard Univ, 1965; Distinguished Teaching Award, Univ Calif Los Angeles, 1969-70. **Special Achievements:** First black PhD in Psychology from UCLA. **Business Addr:** Professor, Charles R Drew University of Medicine and Science, Department of Psychiatry, 1731 E 120 St, Los Angeles, CA 90059.*

KING, LLOYD
Educator. **Personal:** Born Sep 13, 1936, Zinnerman, LA; married Ann Adkins; children: Vicki & Eric. **Educ:** Grambling State Univ,

BS, 1960; La Tech Univ, MS, 1971. **Career:** Pinecrest HS, teacher vpres, coach, 1961-68; Winnfield Sr High Sch, teacher, 1968-75; Winnfield Middle Sch, teacher, math, 1985-. **Orgs:** Winn Educ Asn; adv comt, Title I prog Winn Parish; Nat Educ Asn; La Tech Alumni Asn; dir, Indoor Recreation Blacks; prog dir, Local Radio Prog Hobdy's Soul Sauce; publicity dir, Math Dept La Educ Asn; Nat Aerospace Educ Asn; pres, Grambling Alumni Asn; Winn Parish Voters League; counsr, Job Training Participation Act Summer Youth. **Honors/Awds:** Teacher of the Year, Winn Educ Asn, 1971; Citation for Outstanding Service, Educ & Comm, Winn Educ Asn, 1972; Teacher of the Year nominee, 1973-75; Honorary Secretary State, 1974; Cited for Outstanding Service,Winn Parish Voters League, 1975; Outstanding Service, Citation La Educ Asn, 1976; Teacher of the Year, Voters League, 1985. **Special Achievements:** Named To Who's Who Among Black Americans, 1977-78. **Military Serv:** Sgt, 1960-62.

KING, MARCELLUS, JR.
Marketing executive. **Personal:** Born Jun 14, 1943, Tampa, FL; married Romaine C Ruffin; children: Marcellus III. **Educ:** Hampton Inst, VA, BS (dean's list), 1965; Rutgers Univ, NJ, MBA, 1975; Am Col, CLU, 1978. **Career:** Prudential Investments, assoc mgr group pension, 1970-71, mgr group pensions, 1971-74, dir group pension serv, 1974-85, dir mkt, 1985-95, vpres mkt, 1995-. **Orgs:** Guest speaker Minority Interchange, 1978-80; pres Omega Phi Epsilon, 1961; mem allocations com United Way of Morris Co NJ, 1975-80; vice pres Urban League of Essex Co NJ, 1976-80. **Honors/Awds:** Designation CLU, Am Col, 1978; exec mgt prog Prudential Ins Co, 1980, registered representative, 1987. **Military Serv:** AUS, sp 6th class, 1966-72; Medic of the Year Award, 1971.

KING, MARTIN LUTHER, III
Government official. **Personal:** Born Oct 23, 1957, Montgomery, AL; son of Martin Luther Jr (deceased) and Coretta Scott. **Educ:** Morehouse Col, BA, polit sci & hist. **Career:** Fulton County Ga, comnr, 1986-93; Southern Christian Leadership Conf (SCLC), 1998-2004; King Ctr Nonviolent Social Change, pres & chief exec officer, 2004-. **Business Phone:** (404)522-1420.*

KING, MARY BOOKER
Educator. **Personal:** Born Jul 14, 1937, Quitman, GA; married Grady J; children: Felicia, Adriene & Karon. **Educ:** Morris Brown Col, BA, 1959; Atlanta Univ, MA, 1961; Nova Univ, MEd, 1975. **Career:** Miami Dade Comm Col, assoc prof eng, 1970-72, Dept Reading, chmn, 1973-75, prof lang & arts, 1975-, prof eng, 1979-97. **Orgs:** Commr, Dade Co Com Status of Women 1978-80; consult, Devel Col Progs Reading & Writing; Women Involved Comm Affairs, 1979-80; Educ Task Force Com, 1979-80. **Honors/Awds:** Outstanding Young Women Am, 1971; Community Leadership Award; Kappa Theta Delta, 1972. **Business Addr:** Professor, Miami Dade Community College, 300 N E 2nd Ave, Miami, FL 33132.

KING, ORA STERLING
Educational consultant. **Personal:** Born Oct 15, 1931, Delta, AL; daughter of William and Mary; married Lonnie; children: Sherri. **Educ:** Spelman Col, BA, 1954; Atlanta Univ, MA, 1969; Univ Md, PhD, 1982. **Career:** Atla Pub Sch, teacher instrnl coord, 1954-72; Fed City Col, reading dept chair, 1975-78; Univ DC, asst prof educ, 1978-81; Univ Md, Coppin State Col, prof & dept chair C&I, 1981-88, Div Educ, dean, 1988-90, Div Educ & Graduate Studies, interim dean, 1990-91, prof educ, coord Masters Arts teaching, 1991-99; MEd Cur & Inst Distance Learning, dir, 1999-2001, prof emer, 1999-. **Orgs:** First vpres, Nat Alumnae Asn Spelman Col, 1982-86, pres, 1986-88, 1990-95; ed adv bd, Innovative Learning Strategies Int Reading Asn, 1985-86; Alpha Kappa Alpha Lota Lambda Chap. **Honors/Awds:** Distinguished Alumni Award, Nat Asnr Equal Oppty, 1988. **Special Achievements:** twenty articles published in educational journals 1979-92; published textbook Reading & Study Skills for the Urban College Student, Kendall/Hunt Publ 1984, 1988. **Home Addr:** 9537 Kilamanjaro Rd, Columbia, MD 21045-3942.

KING, PATRICIA ANN
Educator. **Personal:** Born Jun 12, 1942, Norfolk, VA; daughter of Addison and Grayce; married Roger Wilkins, 1981; children: Elizabeth Wilkins. **Educ:** Wheaton Col, BA, 1963; Harvard Law Sch, JD, 1969. **Career:** Dept State, budget analyst, 1964-66; Equal Employment Opportunity Comn, spec asst chmn, 1969-71; Off Civil Rights, Dept Health Educ & Welfare, dept dir, 1971-73; Hastings Inst, NY, fel, 1977-; Civil Div Dept Justice, dept asst atty gen, 1980-81; Georgetown Univ, assoc prof law, 1974-88, prof law, 1988-, Carmack Waterhouse prof law, med, ethics & pub policy, currently. **Orgs:** Fel John Hay Whitney Found, 1968; Nat Comn Protection Human Subjects, 1974-78; chmn, Redevelop Land Agency, DC, 1976-79; US Circuit Judge Nomination Comn, 1977-79; Recombinant DNA Adv Comn, 1979-82; pres, Comn Study Ethical Probs Med & Res, 1980-81; bd, Russell Sage Found, 1981-91; bd, Womens Legal Defense Fund, 1987-; Am Law Inst, 1988-; bd trustees, Wheaton Col, 1989-; Nat Acad Sci. **Honors/Awds:** The Juridicial Status of the Fetus, Mich Law Review, 1647, 1979; Distinguished Service Award, HEW, 1973; Secretary's Special Citation, HEW, 1973; Senior Research Scholar, Kennedy Inst Ethics, 1977; Wheaton Clearing, LLD, 1992. **Special Achievements:** The first African-American woman to became a permanent member of the faculty in Georgetown University; co-author "Law Science and Medicine", 1984. **Home Addr:** 1253 4th St SW, Washington, DC 20024. **Business Addr:** Carmack Waterhouse Professor of Law, Medicine, Ethics, and Public Poli, Georgetown University, 600 New Jersey Ave NW 489 McDonough Hall, Washington, DC 20001, **Business Phone:** (202)662-9085.

KING, PATRICIA E.
Lawyer. **Personal:** Born Jan 16, 1943, Chester, SC. **Educ:** John C Smith Univ Charlotte, NC, BS, 1965; NC Cent Univ, JD. **Career:** Bell & King, atty; Jenkin Perry Pride, researcher, 1969-70; Pearson Malone Johnson & Dejermon, researcher, 1967-69; Chester, SC, sch tchr, 1965-66; Funeral, Directress & Atty; NC state, atty pvt pract, currently. **Orgs:** NC Bar Asn; Black Lawyers Asn; Am Bar Asn; NC Bar Found; NC State Bar Asn. **Honors/Awds:** OIC Award 1972. **Business Addr:** Attorney at Law, 4000 Beatties Ford Rd, Charlotte, NC 28216-3220.

KING, PRESTON
Educator. **Personal:** Born Mar 3, 1936, Albany, GA; son of Clennon Washington and Margaret; married Raewyn; children: Akasi Peter; married Murreil Hazel Stern (divorced); children: Oona & Slater. **Educ:** Fisk Univ, BA, 1956, MSC, econ; London Sch Econ, PhD, 1966; Univ Vienna; Univ Strasbourg; Univ Paris. **Career:** UNV Lancaster, Dept Polit & Inte Rel, chmn, 1986-; Univ E Anglia, Dept Philos, vis prof, currently; Lancaster Univ, prof emer, currently; Critical Rev Int Social & Polit Philos, ed; Emory Univ, Woodruff Prof Polit Philos, currently; Morehouse Col, Distinguished Prof Polit Philos, currently. **Special Achievements:** Author of 15 books, including: The History of Ideas, 1983; An African Winter, 1986; Hobbes: Critical Assessments, 1993. **Business Addr:** Woodruff Professor of Political Philosophy, Emory University, 201 Dowman Dr, Atlanta, GA 30322, **Business Phone:** (404)614-8565.

KING, RAY (RAYMOND KEITH KING)
Baseball player. **Personal:** Born Jan 15, 1974, Chicago, IL; married Charie; children: Tyrell & Brookelynn. **Educ:** Lambuth Univ, TN. **Career:** Chicago Cubs, pitcher, beginning, 1999; Milwaukee Brewers, 2000-02, 2007; Atlanta Braves, 2003; St Louis Cardinals, 2004-05; Colorado Rockies, 2006; Wash Nationals, 2007, 2008; Chicago White Sox, 2008; Houston Astros, 2008; Free Agent, Currently. *

KING, DR. REATHA CLARK
Association executive. **Personal:** Born Apr 11, 1938, Pavo, GA; daughter of Willie and Ola Watts Campbell; married N Judge King Jr, Jan 1, 1961; children: N Judge III & Scott Clark. **Educ:** Clark Col, BS, 1958; Univ Chicago, MS, 1960, PhD, chem, 1963; Columbia Univ, MBA, 1977. **Career:** Natural Bur Standards, res chemist, 1963-68; York Col, NY, asst prof chem, 1968-70, assoc prof chem & assoc dean natural sci & math div, 1970-74, chem prof & assoc dean acad affairs; Metrop State Univ, St Paul, MN, pres, 1977-88; Gen Mills Found, pres & exec dir, 1988-2002. **Orgs:** AAAS; Am Chem Soc; Nat Orgn Prof Advan Black Chemists & Chem Engrs; Sigma Xi; bd dirs, Exxon/Mobil Corp; bd dirs, H B Fuller Co Found; Hispanics In Philanthropy; Cong Black Caucus Found; chair, Gen Mills Found Trustees; life trustee, trustee emer, Univ Chicago. **Honors/Awds:** Educational Leadership Award, YMCA, St Paul, MN, 1984; Execeptional Black Scientist Award, CIBA-GEIGY Corp, 1984; Spurgeon Award for Community Work, Boy Scouts Am, Indian head Coun, 1985; Outstanding Publication Award, Nat Bur Standards; Honorary Doctorate, State Univ NY, Empire State Col, 1985; Civic Leader Award, League Women Voters, 2000; City Minneapolis Award, 2000. **Business Addr:** Trustee Emeriti, The University of Chicago, 5801 S Ellis Ave, Chicago, IL 60637, **Business Phone:** (773)702-1234.

KING, REGINA
Actor, movie producer. **Personal:** Born Jan 15, 1971, Los Angeles, CA; married Ian Desdune, 1998; children: 1. **Career:** Films: Boyz in the Hood, 1991; Poetic Justice, 1993; Higher Learning, 1994; Friday, 1995; A Thin Line Between Love & Hate, 1996; Jerry Maguire, 1998; How Stella Got Her Groove Back, 1998; Mighty Joe Young, 1998; Enemy of the State, 1998; Down to Earth, 2001; Final Breakdown, producer, 2002; Daddy Day Care, 2003; Legally Blond 2: Red, White & Blonde, 2003; A Cinderella Story, 2004; Miss Congeniality 2: Armed & Fabulous, 2005, Year of the Dog, 2007; This Christmas, 2007; Side by Side: The Story of the 50/50 Group of Sierra Leone, co-executive producer, 2007; TV: "Living Single"; "New York Undercover, Northern Exposure"; 227, 1985-90; "Silver Spoons"; "Frankly Female"; "Ira Joe Fisher"; "Leap of Faith", 2002; "Damaged Care", 2002; "The Boondocks", 2005-07; "Women in Law", 2006; "Framed", 2007; "Riley Wuz Here" (voice); Theatre: Wicked Ways; Seymour & Shirley; 227; A Rainy Afternoon; This Family; The Weirdo. **Honors/Awds:** BET Award, Best Actress, 2005; Image Award, Outstanding Supporting Actress, Ray, 2005. **Business Addr:** Actress, C/o Artists Investment Group, 1930 Century Pk W Suite 403, Los Angeles, CA 90067-4115, **Business Phone:** (310)552-1100.

KING, REGINALD F.
Engineer. **Personal:** Born Mar 11, 1935, Powellton, WV; son of Isaiah and Marie Fairfax; married Grace V Tipper; children: Reginald T, Thaxton E. **Educ:** Youngstown State Univ, BE, 1961; San Jose State Univ. **Career:** Reynolds Electronics, co owner & dir engr, 1968-70; NASA, res engr, 1961. **Orgs:** Inst Elec & Electronics Engrs; Nat Asn Advancement Colored people; KAY Frat; Int Studies Orgn. **Honors/Awds:** Technical Brief Award, NASA. **Special Achievements:** Patent in Field; Regis Prof Engr-Elec Engineering, State of Calif, 1975; Regis Prof Engr-Control Syst, State of Calif, 1978. **Military Serv:** USAF, 1954-58. **Home Addr:** 324 Gold Mine Dr, San Francisco, CA 94131. *

KING, RICHARD DEVOID
Psychiatrist. **Personal:** Born Nov 19, 1946, New Orleans, LA; children: Khent. **Educ:** Whittier Col, BA, 1968; Univ Calif San Francisco Med Ctr, MD, 1968; Univ S Calif Med Ctr, intern, 1973; Univ Calif Med Ctr, resident, 1976. **Career:** Los Angeles, teacher aide, 1965; Univ Calif, asst teacher, 1970; Neighbourhood Youth Cor, educ aide, 1969; lab tech, 1968; factory worker, 1967; Fanon Ment Health Res & Develop Ctr, develop scholar, 1976; San Francisco, psychotherapy res, 1974; Goddard Col, fac adv, 1975-76; Aquman Spiritual Ctr, prin, 1976-77; Univ Calif Los Angeles, lab asst, 1964; Palm Springs, lectr, 1977; Sch Ethnic Studies, Dept Black Studies SF State Univ, lectr, 1978; Pvt pract, psychiatrist, currently. **Orgs:** Nat Islam, 1969-71; Nat Inst Ment Health Ctr Develop Prog, 1973-; Black Psychiatrist Am, 1975-; Am Psychiat Asn, 1975-; Nat Med Asn; Asn Black Psychologist, 1977; Pan-Am Conf, 1977; lectr, Martin Luther King Hosp, 1977; Black Health Leadership Conf, 1977; Pres, Black Psychiatrists N Calif, 1978-80; pres, Black Psychiatrists Calif, 1980; Am Col Surgery; Fanon Adv Coun; Atlanta Med Asn; US Pub Health Serv. **Honors/Awds:** Bibliographymelannin, 1977; Pineal Gland Rev, 1977; Uracus, 1977-79. **Military Serv:** Lt com, 1973-78. **Business Phone:** (919)477-3885.

KING, RICHARD L.
Entrepreneur. **Personal:** Born Oct 17, 1942, Flint, MI; son of Richard and Johnnie E. **Educ:** Roosevelt Univ, BS, 1966; Harvard Bus Sch, MBE, 1972. **Career:** Richard King Sr Realtors, Property Mgt Dept, mgr, 1962-66; Chicago Bd Educ, admin asst to asst superintendent of schs, 1966-70; City of Flint, Econ Develop Div, adminr, 1972-94; Shape Future Habitats To Come Inc, pres, 1994-. **Orgs:** Nat Black MBA Asn; Nat Asn Homebuilders; Flint Community Develop Corp, 1982-94. **Honors/Awds:** Mich Municipal League First-Place, Annual Achievement Competition for the City of Flint, Genesee County Urban Investment Plan, 1994. **Business Addr:** President, Shape of Future Things To Come Inc, PO Box 1188, Flint, MI 48501-1188, **Business Phone:** (810)233-7483.*

KING, RILEY B. See KING, B. B.

KING, ROBERT SAMUEL
School administrator. **Personal:** Born Oct 16, 1921, Philadelphia, PA; married Rosalie Ernestine Ilivier; children: Gwendolyn Susan & Nancy Gail. **Educ:** WVa State Col, attended 1944; Univ PA, AB, physics, 1956; Temple Univ, attended 1959. **Career:** Veterans Admin, ins underwriter, 1950-55; Naval Air Engineering Ctr, Philadelphia, physicist, 1956-61; supr mech engr, 1961-74; Philadelphia Col Pharm & Sci, dir planning, affirmative action officer, 1975-80; dir, stud affairs, 1974-75. **Orgs:** Mem bd dirs, W Philadelphia Corp, 1964-80; mem bd dirs, Univ City Sci Ctr, 1970-80; bd trustees, Community Col Philadelphia, 1972-80; bd dirs, Magee Memorial Hosp, 1975-80; mem bd dirs, Berean Savings Asn, 1978-80; chmn west sub area coun, Health Systs Agency South east, PA, 1979-80; trustee emer, Community Col Philadelphia. **Honors/Awds:** ETO Central Phinel & Asia-pacific Award, AUS; Quality of Life Award, W Philadelphia Corp, 1965; Winner area dist speech contests ToastmastersInt, 1972-73. **Special Achievements:** Article "Identifying Urban Community Coll Needs" ACCT Trustee Quarterly,1978-79. **Military Serv:** AUS, tech sgt, 1943-46. **Business Addr:** Director, Philadelphia College of Pharmacy and Science, Kingsessing Mall 43rd St, Philadelphia, PA 19104.

KING, RONALD STACEY. See KING, STACEY.

KING, DR. ROSALYN CAIN
Pharmacist, health services administrator. **Personal:** Born Sep 10, 1938, New York, NY; daughter of Samuel and Ethel C Davis; married Sterling King Jr; children: Kristin & Aaron. **Educ:** Duquesne Univ, BS, 1962; Univ Calif-Los Angeles, MPH, 1972; Univ Southern Calif, PharmD, 1976. **Career:** Howard Univ, guest lectr, 1977, Continuing Educ Instruction, dir, currently; SECON Inc, vpres, 1977-80; Agency Int Develop, Charles R Drew, Univ Med & Sci, pub health adv to USAID, pharm & expert consult, 1980-85, assoc dir, office int health, 1985-86, dir, office int health, 1986-87, Dept Family Med, instr, 1984-87, assoc prof, 1987, Int Health Inst, dir, 1987; Florida A&M Univ, Col Pharm & Pharmaceut Scis, adjunct assoc prof, 1985; Xavier Univ, Col Pharm, adjunct assoc prof, 1987. **Orgs:** Chairperson, Ambulatory Care Comn, Am Pub Health Asn, 1979-; Am Pub Health Asn, Am Pharmaceut Asn, Nat Pharmaceut Found; deaconess, Mt Calvary Baptist Church, Rockville, MD. **Honors/Awds:** Elected to Rho Chi Nat Pharmaceutical Honor Soc, 1961; The Hildrus A Poindexter Award, Black Caucus of Health Workers, 1976; Certificate of Appreciation, Secy USD-HEW, 1978; 'Distinguished Service Award', Nat Pharmaceut

Found, 1982; Community Service Award, Nat Asn Black Hosp Pharmacists, 1986. **Home Addr:** 915 S Belgrade Rd, Silver Spring, MD 20902, **Home Phone:** (301)649-3517. **Business Phone:** (301)608-4100.

KING, RUBY E.
Consultant. **Personal:** Born Mar 3, 1931; married; children: Cynthia, Paul, Gayle & Carol. **Educ:** Mich Univ, BA, 1963; W Mich Univ, MA, 1968. **Career:** Nat Educ Asn, asst exec dir, pub affairs; elem sch educator, 1961-67; Mich Univ Campus Sch, supvr, 1967, educr, 1968-71; Minority Affairs Div Mich Educ Asn, consult, 1971-. **Orgs:** Chmn educ comt, Grand Rapids Model Cities Prog, 1969-71; group leader, NEA Urban Educ Conf, 1969; bd dir, YWCA 1970-71; Governor's Task Force Improving Educ, 1970; bd dir, Grand Rapids Legal Aid Soc, 1971; chmn, Personnel Com Grand Rapids, YWCA, 1971; Mayor's Adv Bd Housing, 1971; state adv bd, Migrant Educ, 1971; bd dir, Asn Supv & Curric Develop, 1971-74; Mich Educ Asn Prof Staff Asn; Lansing Urban League; Gen Educ Adv Comt. **Honors/Awds:** Nominee Teacher of Year, Grand Rapids, 1965.

KING, RUBY RYAN
Educator. **Personal:** Born Jan 26, 1934, Oktaha, OK; married Clifford; children: Diane, Gerald & LaDonna. **Educ:** BS, 1957; MS, 1975; Okla State Univ, attended 1975; Tex Tech Univ; Univ Central Okla. **Career:** Educator (retired); Okla Med Ctr, supvr, 1957-60; Morning side Hosp, Los Angeles, supvr, 1961-63; Langston Univ, Family Living Specialist Co op Extent Serv, 1972; asst dir, Coop Exten Prog, 1976; area prog agent, 1976. **Orgs:** Phi Upsilon Omicron; Langston Univ Alumni Asn; Upsilon Theta Omega Chap, Alpha Kappa Alpha Sor Inc; Order of the Eastern Star, Myra Chap 3; usher, Mount Olive Baptist Church. **Honors/Awds:** Outstanding Service Award, Langston Univ; Outstanding Service Award, Co op Exten Prog, Langston Univ.

KING, RUTH J. See PRATT, DR. RUTH JONES.

KING, SHAKA C
Fashion designer, executive, business owner. **Personal:** Born Mar 16, 1959, Miami, FL; son of Evelyn and Willie Jr. **Educ:** Pratt Institute, BFA, 1978-82. **Career:** Shaka King New York Mens Luxury Wear, owner, currently. **Orgs:** Black Alumni Pratt, 1992-; Founder, Black Fashion Collective, 1994-; Fashion Outreach, 1994-. **Honors/Awds:** TFA, Playboy New Talent Award, Absolut Subluxation Showcase. **Special Achievements:** First African to design a line of Hush Puppies, 1998; SKM customers include: Will Downing, Gregory Hines, Mayk Yoba; launched mail order catalog, 1997. **Business Addr:** Owner, Shaka King New York Fine Luxury Mens Wear, 825 Upsfaur St MW, Washington, DC 20111, **Business Phone:** (202)291-8700.

KING, SHAUN EARL
Football player. **Personal:** Born May 29, 1977, Saint Petersburg, FL; son of Sam and Carolyn. **Educ:** Tulane Univ, mkt, 1998. **Career:** Tampa Bay Buccaneers, quarterback, 1999-2003; Ariz Cardinals, quarterback,2004-05; Indianapolis Colts, quarterback, 2006; Arena Football League, Las Vegas Gladiators, quarterback, 2006; Candian Football League, Hamilton Tiger-Cats, 2007; ESPN, analyst, 2008-. **Orgs:** Founder, The Shaun King Found; mem, Kappa Alpha Psi Fraternity. **Business Addr:** Founder, The Shaun King Foundation, 1270 Orange Ave Suite E, Winter Park, FL 32789, **Business Phone:** (407)644-1600.

KING, SHAWN
Football player. **Personal:** Born Jun 24, 1972, West Monroe, LA; children: Charity. **Educ:** La State Univ; Northeast La Univ. **Career:** Carolina Panthers, defensive end, 1995-97; Indianapolis Colts, 1999-2000; Tampa Bay Storm, 2004.

KING, STACEY (RONALD STACEY KING)
Basketball player, basketball executive, basketball coach. **Personal:** Born Jan 29, 1967, Lawton, OK. **Educ:** Univ Okla, Norman, OK, attended 1989. **Career:** Basketball player (retired), basketball executive; Chicago Bulls, forward-ctr, 1989-94; Minn Timber wolves, forward-ctr, 1993-95; Miami Heat, 1995-96; Boston Celtics, 1996-97; Dallas Mavericks, 1996-97; CBA, Rockford Lightning, head coach & gen mgr; Comcast Sports Net, pre & post-game analyst; Chicago Bulls, game analyst, 2006-07; coach, currently. **Honors/Awds:** NBA All-Rookie Second Team, 1990.

KING, STANLEY OSCAR
Sports agent, vice president (organization). **Personal:** Born Mar 21, 1958, Bronx, NY; son of Ellridge and Alberta; divorced; children: Stanley O II & Stephanie N. **Educ:** Oglethorpe Univ, BA, 1981; Rutgers Univ, Sch Law, JD, 1994. **Career:** CIGNA Corp, course designer, 1981-85; Xerox Corp, major accounts sales mgr, 1985-89; Am Bus Alternatives, pres, 1989-92; First Round Sports Inc, exec vpres & chief operating officer, 1989-. **Orgs:** Nat Black MBA Asn, Philadelphia Chap, 1988; chmn, Negro Baseball League Celebrations, 1994; youth mentor, Philadelphia Youth Entrepreneurs Inst, 1994; bd mem, Philadelphia Sports Cong, 1994. **Honors/Awds:** Sponsor's Award, Concerned Black Men, 1994. **Home Addr:** 11 Del Sol Pl, Sicklerville, NJ 08081, **Home Phone:** (609)228-8105. **Business Addr:** Executive Vice President, Chief Operating Officer, First Round Sports Inc, 109 E Laurel Rd, Stratford, NJ 08084, **Business Phone:** (856)782-1113.

KING, DR. TALMADGE EVERETT
Physician, educator. **Personal:** Born Feb 24, 1948, Sumter, SC; son of Talmadge E Sr and Almetta; married Mozelle Davis; children: Consuelo & Malaika M. **Educ:** Gustavus Adolphus Col, BA 1970; Harvard Med Sch, MD 1974. **Career:** Emory Univ Affiliated Hosp, residency, 1974-77; Univ Colo Health Scis Ctr, pulmonary fellowship, 1977-79, prof med, 1991-97, vice chmn clin affairs, 1993-97; Nat Jewish Med & Res Ctr, sr fac mem, 1990-97, exec vpres clin affairs, 1992-96; San Francisco Gen Hosp, chief, med serv, currently; Univ Calif, San Francisco, Dept Med, Constance B Wofsy Distinguished prof & vice chair, Julius R Krevans Distinguished Professorship Internal Med, currently, Dept Med, chair, currently. **Orgs:** Bd dir, Am Lung Asn Colo, 1986-97; ALA Nat Coun, 1993-98; Gustavus Adolphus Col, 1993-2002; Glaxo-Welcome Pulmonary Fellowship, advisory bd, 1994-99, subspecialty bd pulmonary dis, 1995-2000; Am Thoracic Soc, pres, 1997-98; Am Col Chest Physicians; Am Col Physicians; Am Lung Asn; Nat Med Asn; Nat Inst Health, Lung Biol & Pathol Study Sect, 1997-2000; Calif Inst Med; Asn Am Physicians, 1998; Am Clin & Climatological Asn, 2002; Adv Bd Clin Res Nat Inst Health; San Francisco Regional Panel selection White House Fel, 2003, 2004; Bd Extramural Adv (BEA), Nat Heart Lung & Blood Inst, Nat Institutes Health; Am Bd Internal Med; Nat Acad Sci, Inst Med. **Honors/Awds:** First Decade Award for Early Achievement, Gustavus Adolphus Col Alumni Asn, 1980; Am Colof Chest Physicians Fel, Pulmonary Physicians of the Future, 1983, 1984; fel, Am Col Physicians, 1986; James J Waring Award Outstanding Leadership Treatment Lung Disease, Am Lung Asn Colo, 1992; elected mem, Western Asn Physicians, 1993; Constance B Wofsy Distinguished Professor, Univ CA, San Francisco; inducted Colo Pulmonary Hall of Fame, 1998; San Francisco's Top Doctors, San Francisco Mag, 2001-05; PAR Excellence Award. **Special Achievements:** Co-editor of eight medical textbooks; Author of over 200 articles. **Business Addr:** Julius R Krevans Distinguished Professorship in Internal Medicine, Chair, University of California, Department of Medicine, 505 Parnassus Ave, San Francisco, CA 94143, **Business Phone:** (415)476-0909.

KING, THOMAS LAWRENCE
Librarian. **Personal:** Born Feb 21, 1953, Medina, OH; son of Thomas and Mozella; married Toni; children: Maria Louise King. **Educ:** Univ Akron, Akron, Ohio, BA, geog, 1979; Univ Colo, Boulder, Colo, MA, geog, 1983; Univ Pittsburgh, Pittsburgh, Pa, MLS, 1986; Doctoral candidate, LIS; Simmons Col, Grad Sch Libr & Info Sci. **Career:** Libr Cong, Geog & Map Div, Wash, DC, ref librn, 1987-88; State Univ New York, Binghamton, NY, sci ref/maps librn, earth sci bibliogr, 1989-96; Marion Correctional Inst, librn, currently. **Orgs:** Asn Col & Res Lib; Bibliog Instr Sect, Black Caucus; Am Libr Asn, 1997. **Honors/Awds:** Grad Fel, Nat Sci Found, 1979. **Home Addr:** 608 Boulder Dr, Delaware, OH 43015. **Business Addr:** Librarian, Marion Correctional Institution, PO Box 57, Marion, OH 43302-0057.

KING, W JAMES
Executive. **Personal:** Born Aug 26, 1945, Evergreen, AL; son of John D and Vergie Smith; married Shirley (divorced 1984); children: Monica & Sean. **Educ:** Univ Cincinnati, OH, attended 1966. **Career:** Mutual New York, Cincinnati, OH, sales rep, 1970-74; Jaytag Inc, Cincinnati, OH, vpres, opers, 1974-78; J King Contractors, Cincinnati, OH, owner & pres, 1974-80; Avondale Redevelop Corp, Cincinnati, OH, exec dir, 1980; King & Assocs, pres & chief exec officer; Walnut Hills Redevelop Found, pres & chief exec officer, currently; Avondale Redevelopment Corp, exec dir; Calif Agr Labor Rels Bd, dir; Nat Farm Worker Serv Ctr,dir; Am Fedn Teachers, dir; Iniciativa Frontera, dir; Azteca Community Loan Fund, dir. **Orgs:** Exec bd, Hist Conserv Bd, 1980-; chairperson, Nat Cong Community Econ Develop, 1983-; exec bd, Boys & Girls Club Am, 1989-; chairperson, Xavier Community Adv Comt. **Honors/Awds:** Bi-Centennial Medal, 200 Greater Cincinnatians, 1990; Gonze L Twitty Award, Nat Cong Community Econ Develop; Xavier University Presidential Citation, Xavier Univ; 100 Black Portraits of Excellence, Bicentennial Celebration. **Military Serv:** USAF, staff sgt, 1970-74; Good Conduct Award. **Business Addr:** Executive Director, Walnut Hills Redevelopment Foundation, 2601 Melrose Ave Suite 100, Cincinnati, OH 45229.

KING, WARREN EARL
Management consultant. **Personal:** Born Jul 9, 1947, Durham, NC; son of Leroy Lesley and Alice Mae Umstead; married Hiawatha Mechall Jackson, Apr 8, 1972; children: Justin Christopher. **Educ:** Purdue Univ, BSE, 1976; Ind Univ, MBA, 1987. **Career:** US Postal Serv, distrib clerk, 1970-72; Delco Remy Div GMC, Anderson, eng proj mgr, 1976-87; Hewlett Packard Co, Sunnyvale, nat acct mgr, 1987-88; Crown Consult Group, Indianapolis, pres & owner; King & Assocs, pres, currently. **Orgs:** Life mem, Nat Asn Advan Colored People, 1984; chmn rules & bylaws comn, CASA/SME, 1984, 1985; Nat Black MBA Asn, 1985; bd dir, Indianapolis Prof Asn, 1990-. **Military Serv:** USMC, staff sgt, 1966-70; Avionics Commun, Navigation Meritorious Commendations; Vietnam Combat Air Crewman. **Business Addr:** President, King & Associates, 7934 N Richardt St, Indianapolis, IN 46256, **Business Phone:** (317)849-3019.

KING, DR. WESLEY A
Surgeon. **Personal:** Born Sep 25, 1923, Napoleonville, LA; son of Dr Wesley Sr; married Barbara Johnson; children: Robin, Wesley, Jan & Erik. **Educ:** Dillard Univ, AB, 1943; Howard Univ, MD, 1951. **Career:** Meharry Med Col Inst Surgery, surgeon, 1955-57; USC Med Sch, assoc prof, clin surg, 1974; LA County USC Med Ctr, attending surgeon, 1967-; pvt pract, currently. **Orgs:** LA County Med Asn; Am Med Asn; bd mgrs, Crenshaw YMCA, 1972; past jr warden Christ the Good Shepherd Episcopal Church; founding bd mem, The Good Shepherd Manor; Phi Beta Sigma; fellow Am Col Surgeons. **Honors/Awds:** Better Businessman's Award, 1962; Certified by Am Bd Surg, 1958. **Military Serv:** AUS, sgt, 1943-46. **Business Phone:** (818)385-1918.

KING, WILLIAM CARL
Dentist. **Personal:** Born Nov 29, 1930, Albany, GA; married Rosaria Thomas; children: Sarita, Sarmora. **Educ:** Paine Col, BA; Meharry Med Col, DT, DDS. **Career:** Val Comm Col, adv dent hyg, 1977; pvt pract, dentist, currently. **Orgs:** Cent Dist Dent Soc; Am Dent Asn; Nat Dent Asn; Fla Dent Asn; bd trustees, Valencia Community Col, 1971-75; treas, Goodwill Indust, FL; Handicap Advis Bd, FL; pres, Handicap Workshop. **Honors/Awds:** Acad Dentistry Award, Am Soc C, 1966; Excell scholarship, Alpha Omega Fraternity, 1966; Scholarship Award, Chi Delta Mu Fraternity 1966; Certificate of Appreciation Award, Fla Dept Educ, 1977. **Military Serv:** AUS, capt, 1960. **Home Addr:** 1137 Coretta Way, Orlando, FL 32805, **Home Phone:** (407)299-1908. **Business Addr:** Dentist, 809 S Goldwyn Ave, Orlando, FL 32805-4303.

KING, WILLIAM CHARLES
Lawyer. **Personal:** Born Sep 4, 1952, Pensacola, FL; son of Howard O King Sr; married Gayle Surles, Jan 12, 1973; children: W Charles & Kristen Noel. **Educ:** Lincoln Univ, Pa, BS, 1973; N Va Sch Law, JD, 1984; Antioch Sch Law. **Career:** DC Govt, retirement examr, 1973-82, personnel mgt specist, 1982-89, gen coun, 1989-91, asst crp coun, 1991-95; US Dept Housing & Urban Develop, ast gen coun, 1995, Off Dept Equal Employ Opportunity, dir, currently. **Orgs:** Shiloh Baptist Church, 1983-; Nat Bar Asn, 1984-; Wash Bar Asn, 1984-; DC Bar Asn, 1984-; Am Bar Asn, 1984-; bd trustees, chair, evaluations comt, Lincoln Univ, 1994-; Blacks Govt, 1995-. **Honors/Awds:** Employee of the Year, DC Govt, 1985. **Home Addr:** 10012 Tenbrook Dr, Silver Spring, MD 20901-2151, **Home Phone:** (301)681-6807. **Business Addr:** Director, US Department of Housing & Urban Development, Office of Departmental Equal Employment Opportunity, 451 7th St SW Suite 10170, Washington, DC 20410-3087, **Business Phone:** (202)708-3087.

KING, WILLIAM FRANK
Labor relations manager, chemist. **Personal:** Born Dec 13, 1938, Bluffton, GA; son of Eulalia Bankston King and Marcellus King; married S V Edwards Debourg (divorced 1971); children: William Jr & Kristina N; married Karen Aroyan King, Jul 5, 1977; children: Julian, Isaac & Jason (stepson). **Educ:** Lincoln Univ, BA, chem, 1961; Fisk Univ, MA, org chem, 1963; Utah State Univ, PhD, org chem, 1972. **Career:** Atomic Energy Comn, Oak Ridge TN, New Brunswick NJ, tech intern, chemist, 1963-67; Univ Utah, Salt Lake City, fac, intern, fel, 1972-73; Univ N Fla, Chem Dept, asst prof, 1973-75; Chevron Chemical Co, Richmond CA, sr res chemist, 1975-90; Chevron Res & Technol Co, Richmond CA, human resources rep, 1990; Chevron Corp, San Francisco CA, human resources rep, 1990-92; Chevron Chemical Co, Oronite Technol Division, Additive Synthesis & Processing, sr res chemist, 1992-; Col Marin, chem, instr, currently. **Orgs:** Bd trustee, Novato Community Hosp, 1993-; Nat Org Prof Advan Black Chemists & Chem Engrs; Am Chem Soc; NAACP; AABE; Am Asn Blacks Energy; ACLU, Marin County CA; Concerned Parents of Novato. **Honors/Awds:** Thirty US and foreign Patents, Chevron Corp, 1980-88. **Home Addr:** 1205 Lynwood Dr, Novato, CA 94947.

KING, REV. WILLIAM J
Clergy, educator. **Personal:** Born Jul 21, 1921, Selma, AL; son of Lillian and Joseph; married Clarice Robinson King, Aug 15, 1952; children: Judy Thornton, Eric King & James King. **Educ:** Talladega Col, BA, 1943; Howard Univ Sch Religion, 1946; Eden Theological Seminary, Howard Univ, 1946; Chapman Col Family Therapy Inst Marin. **Career:** Shiloh Baptist Church, pastor, private practice, licensed counr; Third Baptist Church, pastor 1946-51; Antioch Progressive Church, interim pastor; Trinity Missionary Baptist Church, interim pastor; Solano Comm Col, fac, currently. **Orgs:** Progressive Nat Baptist Conv; Am Asn Marriage & Family Counrs; CA State Asn Marriage Counrs; Nat Alliance Family Life Inc; Alpha Phi Alpha Fraterity; Nat Asn Advan Colored People. **Military Serv:** USAF, chaplain, 1951-73.

KING, WOODIE, JR.
Movie producer, administrator. **Personal:** Born Jul 27, 1937, Baldwin Springs, AL; son of Woodie King and Ruby; married Willie Mae, Nov 4, 1959; children: Michelle, Woodie Geoffrey, Michael. **Educ:** Will-O-Way Sch Theater; Lehman Col, BA; Brooklyn Col, MFA. **Career:** Ford Motor Co, arc welder; Detroit Tribune, drama critic, 1959-62; Concept E Theatre, Detroit, founder, mgr & dir, 1960-63; Mobiliz for Youth, cult arts dir,

1965-70; John Hay Whitney fel, 1965-66; Henry St New Fed Theatre NY, founder & dir, 1970-, pres, currently; Woodie King Asn, pres; Nat Black Touring Circuit, founder & producer; My One Good Nerve: A Visit With Ruby Dee, producer. **Orgs:** Nat Theatre Conf; Soc Stage Dirs & Choreographers; Audelco; Theatre Commun Group; Asn Study Negro Life & Hist; Black Filmmakers Found; Dirs Guild Am. **Honors/Awds:** Ford Found Grant; Theatre Award, Nat Asn Advan Colored People; Audelco Award; NAACP Image Award, 1987-88; Obie Award, 1996-97; Honorary Doctorate, Wayne State Univ, 2000. **Special Achievements:** Author of Black Theatre: Present Condition, 1982; author of feature articles in magazines; editor of 5 books of plays, short stories & poems. **Home Addr:** 790 Riverside Dr Apt 3E, New York, NY 10032, **Home Phone:** (212)283-0974. **Business Phone:** (212)353-1176.*

KINGDOM, ROGER NONA
Athlete, executive. **Personal:** Born Aug 26, 1962, Vienna, GA. **Educ:** Univ Pittsburgh, attended 2002. **Career:** Athlete (retired), executive; Pan American Games, Caracas, Venezuela,1983; Summer Olympics, Los Angeles, 1984, Seoul, South Korea, 1988; IAAF World Cup, Barcelona, Spain, 1989; IAAF World Indoor Championships,Budapest, Hungary, 1989; Goodwill Games, Seattle, USA, 1990; World Championships Athletics, Gothenburg, Sweden, gold medal, 1995; Calif Univ Pennsylvania, track & field coach, 2004, interim coach, 2005-, dir track &field & cross country, currently . **Orgs:** New Image Track Club; Omega Psi Phi Fraternity Inc. **Honors/Awds:** Pennsylvania Sports Hall Of Fame; Georgia Sports Hall of Fame; Gold Medal,Pan American Games, Caracas, Venezuela, 1983; Gold Medal, Summer Olympics,Los Angeles, 1984; Gold Medal, Seoul, South Korea, 1988; IAAF World Cup,Barcelona, Spain, gold medal, 1989; Gold Medal, IAAF World Indoor Championships, Budapest, Hungary, 1989; Gold Medal, Goodwill Games, Seattle, 1990; Gold Medal, World Championships Athletics, Gothenburg, Sweden, 1995; Natl Track & Field hall Of fame, 2005. **Special Achievements:** He set World rec of 12.92 in 110m highhurdles in zurich, switzerland, 1989 which lasted for four years. **Business Addr:** Director, Head Coach, California University of Pennsylvania, Department of Athletics, 250 Univ Ave, California, PA 15419, **Business Phone:** (724)938-4351.

KING-GAMBLE, MARCIA
Writer. **Personal:** Born in St Vincent, St. Vincent and the Grenadines. **Educ:** Elmira Col, BA, psychol & theater; MA, Communs, currently. **Career:** Novels: Remembrance, 1998; Eden's Dream, 1998; East of Eden, 1998; Under Your Spell, 1999; Illusions of Love, 2000; A Reason to Love, 2001; Change of Heart, 2001; Jade, 2002; Come Fall, 2003; This Way Home, 2003; Come Back to Me, 2004; A Taste of Paradise, 2005; Designed for You, 2006; Flamingo Place, 2006; Shattered Images, 2006; All About Me, 2007; Down & Out In Flamingo Beach, 2007; Sex On Flamingo Beach, 2007; Hook, Line & Single, 2008; More Than a Woman, 2008; The Way He Moves, 2008; Jack; Island Bliss; Island Book. **Orgs:** Exec bd, Soc Consumer Affairs Prof Bus; pres, Fla chap.

KING-HAMMOND, DR. LESLIE
Art historian, school administrator, art critic. **Personal:** Born Aug 4, 1944, Bronx, NY; daughter of Oliver and Evelyne Maxwell; divorced; children: Rassaan-Jamil. **Educ:** Queens Col, City Univ NY, BFA, 1969; Johns Hopkins Univ, MA 1973, PhD, 1975. **Career:** Performing Arts Workshops of Queens, New York, NY, Dept Art, chairperson, 1969-71; Horizon fel, 1969-73;Haryou-Act Inc, Harlem, NY, prog writer, 1971; Md Inst, Col Art, lectr, 1973-, dean grad studies, 1976-; John Hopkins Univ, Kress fel, 1974-75; Corcoran Sch Art, lectr, 1977, vis fac, 1982; Howard Univ, Dept African Studies, doctoral supvr, 1977-81; Civic Design Comn Baltimore City, comnr, 1983-87; Philip Morris Scholar Artists Color, proj dir, 1985-98; Afro-Am Hist & Cult Museum, art consult, 1990-96; Md Inst Col Art, dean grad studies, currently. **Orgs:** Panelist, Nat Endowment Humanities, 1978-80; guest cur, Montage Dreams Deferred, Baltimore Mus Art, 1979; panelist, Nat Endowment Arts, 1980-82; mem bd, Baltimore Sch Arts, 1984-; Nat Conf Artist; Col Art Asn; mem bd, Community Found Greater Baltimore, 1984-87; guest cur, The Intuitive Eye, MD Art Place, 1985; consult, Md Arts Coun, 1985-; mem bd, Art Comn, Baltimore City, Off Mayor, 1988; cur, 18 Visions/Divs, Eubie Blake Cult Ctr & Mus, 1988; co- curator, Art as a Verb: The Evolving Continuum, 1988; cur, Black Printmakers & the WPA, Lehman Gallery Art, 1989; bd, Alvin Ailey Dance Theatre Found Md, 1990-93; bd dirs, 1991-99, pres, 1996-98, CAA; bd overseers, Sch Arts, Baltimore, 1996-99; bd dirs, Int House Art Critics, 2000-; co-cur, Three Generations African-Am Women Sculptors, African-Am Hist & Cult Museum, Philadelphia, Equitable Gallery, NY; exhibiting artist, Artist-Scholar: In Search A Balance, Ctr African Am Hist & Cult; curator, Out the Shadows: the Photography Ed West, 2000; curator, Carl Clark: Photographer, 2000. **Honors/Awds:** Mellon Grant for Faculty Research, Md Inst, Col Art, 1984; Trustee Award for Excellence in Teaching, 1986; Woman of the Year, 1986; Womens Art Caucus, 1986; Mellon Grant for faculty research, 1987; The Smithsonian, 1997. **Special Achievements:** Published Celebrations: Myth & Ritual in Afro-American Art, Studio Museum in Harlem, 1982, coordinated Hale Woodruff Biennial, Studio Museum in Harlem, 1989, Masters, Makers and Inventors, Artscape, 1992, MCAC, 1992, Tom Miller Retrospective, Baltimore Museum of Art & Maryland Art Place, 1995, Hale Woodruff Biennale, Studio Museum in Harlem, 1994. **Business Addr:** Dean of Graduate Studies, Maryland Institute College of Arts, Rm B361 Bunting Ctr 1300 Mount Royal Ave, Baltimore, MD 21217, **Business Phone:** (410)225-2534.

KINGI, HENRY MASAO
Stunt performer, actor. **Personal:** Born Dec 2, 1943, Los Angeles, CA; son of Masao D and Henriella Dunn Wilkins-Washington; children (previous marriage): Henry Jr; married Lindsay Wagner, Jan 1, 1981 (divorced 1984); children: Dorian & Alex. **Career:** Films as actor: Halls of Anger, 1970; Black Girl, 1972; Black Belt Jones,1974; Truck Turner, 1974; Smoke in the Wind, 1975; The Ultimate Warrior,1975; Car Wash, 1976; Swashbuckler, 1976; Mr. Billion, 1977; Zero to Sixty, 1978; Stir Crazy, 1980; Charlie Chan & the Curse of the Dragon Queen, 1981; Scarface, 1983; Predator, 1987; Road House, 1989; Secret Agent OO Soul, 1990; Far Out Man, 1990; Parker Kane, 1990; Predator 2,1990; Grand Canyon, 1991; The Rapture, 1991; Batman Returns, 1992; Lethal Weapon 3, 1992; Conflict of Interest, 1993; Death Ring, 1993; Double Dragon, 1994; Out-of-Sync, 1995; Under Siege 2: Dark Territory, 1995; Barb Wire, 1996; Vampires, 1998; The Protector, 1998; Show time, 2002; The Sponge Bob Square Pants Movie, 2004; From Mexico with Love, 2008; Films asst stunt performer: Gun Shy, 2000; The Million Dollar Hotel, 2000; Here on Earth, 2000; Gone in Sixty Seconds, 2000; The Kid, 2000; Bless the Child,2000; Get Carter, 2000; Double Take, 2001; The Fast & the Furious, 2001;Ghosts of Mars, 2001; Soul Survivors, 2001; The Salton Sea, 2002; The First $20 Million Is Always the Hardest, 2002; Like Mike, 2002; Austin Powers in Gold member, 2002; xXx, 2002; Deliver Us from Eva, 2003; Daredevil, 2003; The Matrix Reloaded, 2003; The Italian Job, 2003; Bad Boys II, 2003; The Hard Easy, 2005; Constantine, 2005; The Island, 2005; The Fast & the Furious: Tokyo Drift, 2006; The Texas Chainsaw Massacre:The Beginning, 2006; Deja Vu, 2006; Mr. Brooks, 2007; Hell Ride, 2008; Street Kings, 2008; TV series: Daniel Boone, 1970; "Kung Fu", 1975; "The Bionic Woman", 1978; "T.J. Hooker", 1983; "Matt Houston", 1983; "V", 1985; Streets of Justice, 1985;Destination America, 1987; "Earth Star Voyager", 1988; "Disneyland", 1989; She Knows Too Much, 1989; "A Man Called Hawk", 1989; K-9000, 1991; In the Arms of a Killer?, 1992; Steel Justice, 1992; Sex, Love & Cold Hard Cash,1993; "Walker, Texas Ranger", 1993-98; "Renegade", 1996; "Profiler", 1999; "Soldier of Fortune Inc", 1999; "Angel", 1999; "The District", 2002;Franken fish, stunt performer, 2004; "Sleeper Cell", stunt performer, 2005. **Orgs:** Bd dirs, founder, Black Fashion Mag "Elegant", 1963; mgr, first major,Black Pvt Key Club Maverick's Flat, Calif; organizer, Coalition Black Stuntman's Asn Hollywood; sec mem, Soc 10th Cavalry Buffalo Soldiers; Nat Asn Advan Colored People; chmn, Labor & Industry Com; co-chmn, Motion Picture Com; PUSH; CORE Worked with Image; co-founder, Black Stuntmen's Asn. **Honors/Awds:** Awards to get Blacks in motion pictures; Image Award; 10th Cavalry Cowboy Hall Fame; Image Award; Stunt Award, Black Stuntmen's Asn; Stunt award, Most Spectacular Sequence, "To Live and Die in LA", Stuntmen Award Show, 1986; Taurus Award, 2004, 2005. **Business Addr:** Actor, Stunt Performer, c/o William Morris Agency Inc, 151 El Camino Dr, Beverly Hills, CA 90212, **Business Phone:** (310)859-4000.

KING-POYNTER, MARVA
Association executive. **Career:** Ministry Caring Inc, prog dir, currently. **Business Addr:** Program Director, Ministry of Caring Inc, 506 N Church St, Wilmington, DE 19801-4812, **Business Phone:** (302)652-1935.*

KINGTON, RAYNARD S
Association executive. **Educ:** Univ Mich, BS, MD; Univ Pa, MBA, PhD. **Career:** Nat Inst Aging Explor Minority Aging Ctr, Drew/RAND Ctr Health & Aging, co-dir; RAND Corp, sr scientist; Nat Health & Nutrit Exam Surv, dir; Nat Ctr Health Statist, Div Health Exam Statist, dir; NIH, Nat Inst Alcohol Abuse & Alcoholism, actg dir, 2002, Behav & Social Sci Res, assoc dir, 2000-03, prin dep dir, 2003-; Wharton Sch, Fontaine fel. **Business Addr:** Principal Deputy Director, National Institutes of Health, US Department of Health and Human Services, Office of Behavior & Social Science 9000 Rockville Pke, Bethesda, MD 20892, **Business Phone:** (301)496-4000.*

KINLOCH, JEROME. See Obituaries section.

KINNAIRD, MICHAEL LEON
School administrator. **Personal:** Born Jul 12, 1945, Indiana; son of David Renfroe and Thelma Renfroe; children: Eric Michael. **Educ:** Scottsbluff Col, AA, 1967; Chadron St Col, BS, Educ, 1969; Northern Ariz Univ, MA, 1973. **Career:** Educator (retired); Opportunity Sch Clark Co Sch Dist, prin, 1977-81; JimBridger Jr H Clark Co Sch Dist, teacher, 1970-71, dean 1971-72, admin asst, 1972-73, asst prin, 1973-77; Clark County Sch Dist, Las Vegas, Nev, Sec Prin, 1981; Brinley Miss, fac, 1981-92; Area Tech Trade Ctr, staff, 1993-94; Advan Technol Acad, prin, 1994-2002. **Orgs:** Nat Asn Sec Prin, 1973; Phi Delta Kappa Chap 1113, 1974; treas, ClarkCounty Sec Prin Asn, 1976-77; pres, Clark Co Asn Sch Admin, 1977-78; treas, PDK Chap 1113, 1979-80. **Honors/Awds:** Appreciation for Continued Support, Am Afro Unity Festival, Las Vegas, Nev, 1978; Nevada Secondary Principal of the Year, 1996; Distinguished Alumni Educator Award, Chadron State Col, 1998; Milken National Educator Award, 1998.

KINNEBREW, LARRY D.
Football player. **Personal:** Born Jun 11, 1960, Rome, GA. **Educ:** Tenn State Univ, attended. **Career:** Football player (retired); Cincinnati Bengals, 1983-87; Buffalo Bills, fullback, 1989-90.

KINNIEBREW, ROBERT LEE
Real estate executive. **Personal:** Born Feb 13, 1942, Manhattan, NY; son of Covton and Daisy Crawford Cobb; married Raymona D Radford, Nov 30, 1963; children: Robertina, Rolanzo. **Educ:** Acad Aeron NY; Commun School AUS; Non-Commiss Off Acad Bad Toelz W Ger; Off Cand Sch Commiss 2 Lt Artil Ft Sill OK; Ins Underwriter's Sch PA; MW Funk Sales Inst Real Estate NJ; S Jersey Realty Abstr Sales Sch NJ; Grad Realtors Inst NJ; Nat Assoc Independent Fee Appraisers NJ; Mgt Develop Course Wash DC. **Career:** Veterans Admin, mgt broker; Fed Housing Admin, mgt broker; Vet Admin, appraiser; Mutural NY Ins Co, dir sales underwriter; Protect A Life Burglar Alarm Co, dir sales; jewelry store chain, dir sales; Gen Sound Philadelphia, customer rel mgr; Westinghouse, mgr lighting dept; Fort Dix NJ, post signal, oper & commanding officer; Fort Bliss TX & Viet-Nam, battalion commun officer; AUS W Germany, pole lineman, fixed station transmitter repairman, 1963-65; Lockheed Aircraft Co Idlewild Airport, flight line mechanic; Century 21 Candid Realty Inc, pres, 1972-, broker; TREND, bd dir, currently. **Orgs:** Edgewater Park Jaycees, Burlington Cty Draft Bd, Burlington Cty Chamber Com, Masonic Lodge; Century 21 Brokers Coun SJ; Beverly Rotary Club; Boy Scouts Am; Make Am Better Comn; Nat Asn Realtors; bd mem, chap chmn, exec comm, chmn, Burlington Cty Red Cross; rep, Century 21 Nat Brokers Commun Congress; pres, dir Burlington Cty Bd Realtors; dir NJ State Bd Realtors; legal action comn; Nat Asn Realtors; nominating comn; equal opportunity comn; library comn; legal action comn, NJ Asn Realtors. **Honors/Awds:** Community Service Award, Burlington City Bd Realtors, 1983; Realtor of the Year Award, NJ State Assoc Realtors, 1983. **Military Serv:** Comn Chief, 101st Airbn Div 327th Battle Grp; 10th Spec Forces Bad Toelz, Germ, 1962; Comn, 2nd Lt Battal Comm Ofcr, 1st Battal 44th Artillery Ft Bliss. **Business Addr:** Board of Directors, TREND, 660 American Ave Suite 203, PO Box 7777 1090, King of Prussia, PA 19406, **Business Phone:** (610)783-4650.*

KINSEY, BERNARD W.
Executive, president (organization), founder (originator). **Personal:** Born Sep 20, 1943, W Palm Beach, FL; married Shirley; children: Khalil. **Educ:** Fla A&M Univ, attended 1967. **Career:** Humble Oil Co, sales rep, 1971; Xerox Corp, LA, field serv mgr, 1971, regional gen mgr, 1983, Voice Systs Div, vpres, 1991; Rebuild Los Angeles, chief operating officer & chmn; KBK Enterprise, pres & founder, currently. **Orgs:** Co-founder, Xerox Black Employees Asn; bd dir, Nat Underground Railroad Freedom Ctr, 2009. **Business Phone:** (813)874-3302.

KINSEY, JIM
Basketball executive. **Career:** NBA, referee, 2001-02. *

KIRBY, ANTHONY T
Fashion designer, entrepreneur. **Career:** Paris Europa, fashion designer; Anthony T NY, founder & owner, 1992-. **Business Addr:** Owner, Designer, Anthony T New York, 177 Madison St, Brooklyn, NY 11216, **Business Phone:** (718)783-2570.

KIRBY, JACQUELINE
Physician. **Personal:** Born Dec 17, 1946, Atlanta, GA; married Edward G Helm; children: Lisa. **Educ:** Spelman Col, BA, 1968; Meharry Med Col, MD, 1973. **Career:** Harvard Univ, res & fel, 1971; Emory Univ Affiliated Hosp, externship, 1972, med intern, 1973-74, internal med, 1974-76, rheumatology, 1977-; Crawford W Long Hosp, emergency room physician, 1976-77. **Orgs:** YWCA, 1973; assoc mem, Am Col Physicians. **Honors/Awds:** Res fel, Harvard Univ, 1971; honor, Dept Pharmcacol, 1971; fel Emory Univ, 1977.

KIRBY, MIZAN ROBERTA PATRICIA. See NUNES KIRBY, MIZAN ROBERTA PATRICIA.

KIRBY, NANCY J
College administrator. **Personal:** Born Apr 20, 1940, Haddonfield, NJ. **Educ:** Bennett Col, BA, psychol, 1960; Bryn Mawr Col, MSS, 1965. **Career:** Temple Univ Med Ctr, chief social worker outpatient med, 1966-69; Planned Parenthood SE Pa, dir social serv, 1969-71; Beaver Col, asst prof, 1971-79; Bryn Mawr Col, lectr, asst dean & dir admis, 1979-. **Orgs:** Bd dirs, Spectrum Health Serv, 1978-; trustee, Douty Found, 1993-; bd dirs, Inglis Innovative Serv, 1994-; bd dirs, Unitarian Universalist House, 1998-. **Business Addr:** Assistant Dean, Director, Bryn Mawr College, Graduate School of Social Work & Social Research, 101 N Merion Ave, Bryn Mawr, PA 19010-1697, **Business Phone:** (610)520-2608.

KIRBY-DAVIS, MONTANGES
Executive, manager. **Personal:** Born Jan 6, 1953, Wadesboro, NC; daughter of Archie William (deceased) and Minnie Allen. **Educ:**

Winston-Salem State Univ, Winston-Salem, BA, sociol, 1975. **Career:** Sara Lee, Winston-Salem, personnel specialist, 1978-83, mgr, mgt employment, 1983-88; Am Soc Personnel Admin, cert trainer, accredited personnel specialist recruiting; Sara Lee Products, Winston-Salem, NC, mgr, training & develop, 1988-91, dir workforce diversity, 1991-97; The Kirby Resource Group, founder & pres, 1997-. **Orgs:** Bd dir, Winston-Salem Personnel Asn, 1980-85; bd dir, Battered Women's Shelter, 1980-85; bd dirs, YWCA, 1980-85; pres, Forsyth County YWCA, 1982-83; Am Soc Training & Develop; co-chair, First Piedmont Triad Prof Develop Conf Women, 1990-; chmn, United Way Training & Develop Comt, 1990-91; NC Governor's Comn Workforce Preparedness, 1994; Winston Salem State Univ, bd trustees, 1994. **Honors/Awds:** Outstanding Woman Achiever Award, Prof Bus Women, 1982; Coop Ed Individual Leadership Award, Winston-Salem Univ, 1984; YWCA Volunteer Leadership Award, 1993; Leadership Am, 1996. **Special Achievements:** Published article: Minorities & Women Magazine, 1990. Women Who Make a Difference, 1991. **Business Addr:** President, Founder, The Kirby Resource Group, 535 N Pleasantburg Dr Suite 202, PO Box 25579, Greenville, SC 29616, **Business Phone:** (864)241-9900.

KIRCHHOFER, DR. WILMA ARDINE LYGHTNER
Consultant, executive director, founder (originator). **Personal:** Born Sep 30, 1940, Mason City, IA; daughter of William and Tressie Traylor; married Guy Marbury; married Kirk (divorced 1974); children: Gregory Luther & Douglas Bernard. **Educ:** Iowa State Univ, Ames, IA, BS, 1963; Emory Univ, Atlanta, GA, MPH, 1977; Univ Mo, Columbia, PhD, 1986. **Career:** Ga State Univ, Atlanta, GA, asst prof, 1977-81; Univ Mo, Columbia, MO, asst prof, 1984-86; Lincoln Univ, Jefferson City, MO, asst prof, 1982-86; Ross Labs, Columbus, OH, assoc dir med educ, 1986-87; Coca-Cola Co, Atlanta, GA, mgr, health prom, 1987-2000; Youth Leadership Global Health Inc, founder & dir, 2001-; WALK Assocs, health & productivity consult & prin, 2001-. **Orgs:** Bd mem, Ga Partners Americas, 1988-91; chair, Pub Rels Atlanta Dietetic Asn, 1989-91; ed, Newsletter Ga Nutrit Coun, 1989-91. **Business Addr:** Founder, Director, Youth Leadership for Global Health Inc, 2000 Filbert Lane Suite A, Atlanta, GA 30349, **Business Phone:** (404)559-9634.

KIRK, ORVILLE, SR.
Educator. **Personal:** Born Mar 5, 1936, St Louis, MO; married Joyce; children: Orville Jr, Gerald & Ronald. **Educ:** Wiley Col, BA, 1957; Harris Teachers Col, MO, attended 1965; St Louis Univ, MO, spec educ cert, 1967, MEd, 1970, post masters work educ specialist degree, 1972, resident student, 1973, supt cert, 1973. **Career:** St Louis Pub Sch Syst, teacher, 1961-72; St Louis Baby Study Proj CEMREL, res teacher, 1968-71; Univ Mo, res tech, 1971-72; Mo Dept Elem & Sec Educ, spec educ consult, 1972-76, supvr, 1976-; Urban Behav Res Assco, consult, 1973-77; Acad Urban Serv, consult, 1973-77. **Orgs:** Pres, Chap 103 Coun Except C, 1975-76; Coun Adminr Spec Educ; Coun C Behav Disorders; Coun Execpt C; bd dir, The Annie Malone Children's Home; Coun Mental Retardation CEC-MR. **Military Serv:** AUS, spec 4 c, 1959-61.

KIRK, RON
Lawyer, government official. **Personal:** Born in Austin, TX; married Matrice Ellis Kirk; children: Elizabeth Alexandra & Catherine Victoria. **Educ:** Austin Col, BA, polit sci & sociol, 1976; Univ Tex Sch Law, JD, 1979. **Career:** US Senator Lloyd Bentsen, legis asst, 1981-93; City Dallas, asst city atty & chief lobbyist, 1983-89; Johnson & Gibbs PC, shareholder, 1989-94; State Tex, 98th secy state, 1994-95; Gardere & Wynne LLP, partner; City Dallas, mayor, 1995-2000; Brinker Int, bd dirs; Dean Foods Co, bd dirs; PetSmart Inc, bd dirs; Vinson & Elkins LLP, partner, currently. **Orgs:** Leadership Dallas Alumni Asn, 1986-; Dallas Assembly, 1990-; Gen Serv Comn Tex, 1992-94, chmn, 1993; pres, Zool Soc, 1992-94; bd trustees, Austin Col, 1991-; Museum African Am Life and Culture, 1991-; Cotton Bowl Athletic Asn, 1991-; State Fair Tex Bd, 1993-; State Bar Tex; Am Bar Asn; Nat Bar Asn; J L Turner Legal Asn; chmn bd, Dallas Educ Found; bd trustees, March Dimes. **Honors/Awds:** Volunteer of the Year Award, Big Brothers/Big Sisters Metrop Dallas, 1992; Distinguished Alumni Award, Austin Col Alumni Asn, 1992; C B Bunkley Community Service Award, J L Turner Legal Asn, 1994; Citizen of the Year, Omega Psi Phi Frat, 1994; Mickey Leland Leadership Award; Woodrow Wilson Center Award, 2000; Jurisprudence Award, Anti-Defamation League, 2004; DHL, Austin Col, 2006. **Special Achievements:** First African American mayor of city of Dallas; First African American Mayor of any big city in Texas; One of the The Best Lawyers in America, 2007. **Business Addr:** Partner, Vinson & Elkins LLP, Trammell Crow Ctr, 2001 Ross Ave Suite 3700, Dallas, TX 75201-2975, **Business Phone:** (214)220-7968.

KIRK, DR. SARAH VIRGO
Educator, social worker. **Personal:** Born Oct 19, 1934, Kingston, Jamaica; daughter of David Clarke and Velmon Eaton; married Wyatt Douglass Kirk. **Educ:** St Augustines Col, Raleigh NC, BA, 1955; Atlanta Univ Sch Social Work, MSW, 1957; Univ Pittsburgh, Sch Pub Health, MPH, 1972, Sch Social Work, PhD Social Work, 1975. **Career:** Memorial Hosp Univ NC, med soc worker, 1957-60; Johns Hopkins Hosp, med soc worker, 1960-63; Pub Health Grant, res team mem, 1964-66; Dept Pub Welfare

Work Training Ctr, soc work supv, 1967, soc work supv, pub health adolescent prog, 1967, chief soc worker orthopedic prog, 1968; Howard Univ Sch Soc Work, asst prof, 1969-71; Sch Work Univ Pa, instr, 1972-74; Three Rivers Youth, res asst, 1975; Sch Soc Work Virginia Commonwealth Univ, asst prof, 1975-77; Western Mich Univ Sch Soc Work, asst prof, 1977-78; North Carolina Agri & Tech State Univ, assoc prof, field coordr, 1978-79, prof social work, chairperson, Dept of Sociology & Social Work 1982-. **Orgs:** Triad Asn Human Serv, 1978-84; chairperson, NC Coun Social Work Educ, 1983-84; Womens Prof Forum, 1986-; bd mem, Family Life Council, Greensboro, NC, 1986-87; Women Improving Race Relations, founder, 1990-; bd mem, Comn Status Women; chair, Guelford County DSS Bd. **Special Achievements:** Co-ed, "Student Athletes: Shattering The Myths and Sharing the Realities," with Dr. Wyatt Kirk,1993; co-auth "Counseling, Black Family Involvement," J Elem Sch Guidance & Counseling, with Dr. Wyatt Kirk, 1981; Inducted into Departments Hall of Fame, 1989. **Business Addr:** Professor, Chairperson, North Carolina Agri & Tech State University, Department of Sociology, 1601 E Market St, Greensboro, NC 27401-3209, **Business Phone:** (336)334-7903.

KIRK-DUGGAN, CHERYL ANN
Clergy, musician, educator. **Personal:** Born Jul 24, 1951, Lake Charles, LA; daughter of Rudolph Valentino (deceased) and Naomi Ruth Mosely (deceased); married Michael Allan Kirk-Duggan, Jan 1, 1983. **Educ:** Univ Southwestern LA, BA, 1973; Univ Tex, Austin, MM, 1977; Austin Presbyterian Theol Sem, MDiv, 1987; Baylor Univ, PhD, 1992. **Career:** Univ Tex, Austin, music Black Am coach accomp, 1974-77; Austin Community Col, music Black Ams, 1976-77; Prairie View A&M Univ, teacher, 1977-78; Williams Inst CME Church, organist, choir dir, 1979-83; The Actor's Inst, teacher, 1982-83; Self-employed, prof singer, voice teacher, vocal coach, 1980-85; Christian Methodist Church, ordained minister, deacons orders, 1984, elders orders, 1986; Baylor Univ, Inst Oral Hist, grad asst, 1987-89, Dept Relig, teaching asst, 1989-90; Meredith Col, asst prof, 1993-96; Ctr Women & Relig, dir, currently, Grad Theol Union, asst prof, 1997-; Ed Bd, Contagion: Jour Violence, Mimesis & Culture, 1994-; Asn Black Awareness, Meredith Col, adv, 1994-96. **Orgs:** Pi Kappa Lambda, 1976-; Omicron Delta Kappa, 1977-; assoc pastor, Trinity CME Church, 1985-86; pres, Racial Ethnic Faith Comm, Austin Sem, 1986-87; Golden Key Hon Soc, 1990; Colloquim On Violence & Religion; Soc Biblical Lit; Am Acad Relig; Ctr Black Music Res; Soc Chritian Ethics; Am Soc Aesthetics; Sigma Alpha Iota; Semeia, ed bd, 1999-. **Honors/Awds:** Univ Southwestern LA, Magna Cum Laude; Univ Tex, Austin, Univ Fellowship, 1975-77; Fund for Theol Educ, Fellowship for Doctoral Studies, 1987-88, 1988-89. **Special Achievements:** Carnegie Hall debut, 1981; featured: "Life, Black Tress, Das Goldene Blatte, Bunte," 1981, 1982; recording: "Third Duke Ellington Sacred Concert," Virgil Thompson's Four Saints in Three Acts, EMI Records, 1981-82; "African Spirituals: Exorcising Evil Through Song," A Troubling in My Soul: Womanist Perspectives on Evil and Suffering, Orbis Press, 1991; "Gender, Violence and Transformation," Curing Violence: The Thought of Rene Girard, Polebridge Press, 1991; author: Lily Teaching Fellow, 1995, 1996; Collidge Scholar with Assoc for Religion & Intellectual Life, 1996; African Special Days: 15 Complete Worship Services, Abingdon Press, 1996; It's In the Blood: A Trildgy of Poetry Harvested from a Family Tree, River Vision, 1996; Exorcizing Evil: A Womanist Perspective on the Spirituals, Orbis, 1997; Refiner's Fire, A Religious Engagement with Violence, Augsburg- Fortress, 2000; The Undivided Soul: Helping Congregations Connect Body and Spirit, Abingdon, 2001; Misbegotten Anguish: Theology and Ethics of Violence, Chalice, 2001. **Business Addr:** Director, Center for Women and Religion, Graduate Theological Union, 2400 Ridge Rd, Berkeley, CA 94705, **Business Phone:** (510)649-2490.*

KIRKLAND, GWENDOLYN V
Executive. **Personal:** Born Apr 24, 1951, Chicago, IL; daughter of Warren and Smith. **Educ:** Bradley Univ, BS, 1972; DePaul Univ, MEd, 1976; Chicago Theol Sem, MDiv, 2008. **Career:** Chicago Pub Schs, teacher primary grades, 1972-80; AJ Nystrom Inc, sales rep, 1980-82; Dean Witter Reynolds, assoc vpres investments, 1983-90; Chapman Co, Br Mgr, 1990-94; Am Investment Serv Inc, CFP/investment broker & Br Mgr, 1994-2002; Kirkland, Turnbo & Assoc, managing prin, 2002-. **Orgs:** Delta Sigma Theta, 1971-; vpres, Nat Asn Security Profs, 1985-; pres, Village W Growhomes Asn, 1987-92; bd dirs, S Suburban Family Shelter, 1989-91; speaker, Nat Black MBA. **Honors/Awds:** Harlem Black Achiever Award, Women Who Make A Difference, Clorox Corp, 2007. **Special Achievements:** People to People Ambassador to China, 2000, SAL Financial Services, Presidents Club, 2003. **Business Addr:** Managing Principal, Kirkland Turnbo & Associates, 4747 Lincoln Mall Dr, Suite 602, Matteson, IL 60443-3817, **Business Phone:** (708)481-8787.

KIRKLAND, PROF. JACK A.
Consultant, educator. **Personal:** Born Oct 28, 1931, Blythedale, PA; son of Aaron Kirkland and Anna Mae Kirkland; married Iris; children: Jack Jr, Adrianne & Kelly. **Educ:** Syracuse Univ, BA, 1959, MSW, 1961. **Career:** Peace Corps, Training Community Develop, Honduras, dir, 1964-67; St Louis Univ, Social Group Work Prog, chair, 1964-70; Wash Univ, assoc prof, social work,

1970-, dir & co-founder, African-Am studies, 1974-76, Econ Develop Concentration, Sch Social Work, founder, 1980-89; State Mo, dir transp, 1976-78; Shatil, Nat Israeli Community Develop Corp, Int Inst Educ, consult. **Orgs:** Phi Delta Kappa End Honorary Soc; Herbert Hoover Boy's Club; Mo State Dept Transp; consult, Int Inst Educ, S Africa. **Honors/Awds:** Educator of the Year, Omicron Eta Omega, 1992; Teaching Award, George Warren Brown Sch Social Work, 1995; Nat Service Award, Nat Asn Homes & Serv C, 1996; Spirit of Crazy Horse Award, Black Hills Seminars, 1997; prin invesr, Mo Head Start Tech Assistance & Training Grant; prin Consult grant writer, St Joseph's Children's Home; Proj Lifting Individual Vision Everyone. **Special Achievements:** National consultant in multicultural education; National/ International consultant in Economic Development; published numerous articles. **Business Addr:** Associate Professor of Social Work, Washington University, George Warren Brown School of Social Work, PO Box 1196, Saint Louis, MO 63130, **Business Phone:** (314)935-6601.

KIRKLAND, LEVON
Football player. **Personal:** Born Feb 16, 1969, Lamar, SC; married Keisha LeShun Tillman, 2002. **Educ:** Clemson Univ, sociol, 2004. **Career:** Football player (retired); Pittsburgh Steelers, linebacker, 1992-2000; Seattle Seahawks, 2001; Philadelphia Eagles, 2002; Educational Speaker, National Collegiate Scouting Asn, currently. **Honors/Awds:** Clemson Hall Fame, 2001; South Carolina Athletic Hall of Fame, 2008. *

KIRKLAND, SHARON ELAINE
Psychologist. **Personal:** Born Oct 19, 1957, Buffalo, NY; daughter of Theodore and Winona Kirkland. **Educ:** Spelman Col, BA, 1979; State Univ NY, Buffalo, MS, 1983, PhD, 1991. **Career:** City Buffalo Common Coun, legis asst, 1979-80; State Univ NY, Buffalo, Upward Bound Prog Counr, 1984-85, Sch Med, prog coord & res spec, 1985-88; Univ Md Coun Ctr, pre-doctoral intern, 1988-89, staff counr & psychologist, 1990-, dir internship training, 1998-. **Orgs:** Minority fel, Am Psychol Asn, 1986, Div 17 & 45, 1994-; Nat Asn Black Psychologists, 1991-94; Am Psychol Asn, Asn Coun Ctr Training Agencies, 1998-, bd dir, 2001-; Am Col Personnel Asn, 1998-. **Honors/Awds:** Outstanding Young Woman of the Year, 1977; Certificate of Appreciation, Govt Dominica, 1997; Certificate of Appreciation, Nat Weather Serv, 1998; Certificate of Appreciation, Am Psychologist Asn Minority Fel Prog, 2000. **Special Achievements:** Co-auth: "Univ Campus Consultation: Opportunities & Limitations", Jour Coun & Develop, 1993; "Organizational Racial Diversity Training", Racial Identity Theory: Applications to Individual, Group & Organizational Interventions, 1993. **Business Addr:** Training Director, Staff Counselor, University of Maryland, Counseling Center, 1203 Shoemaker Bldg, College Park, MD 20742, **Business Phone:** (301)314-7651.

KIRKLAND, THEODORE
Educator. **Personal:** Born Jan 1, 1934, Camden, SC; married Winona; children: Sharon, Adrianne & Cynthia. **Educ:** State Univ NY, Buffalo, BA, 1976, MS, 1984. **Career:** Buffalo Police Dept, police officer, 1962-78; WKBW-TV, Buffalo, "Kirkland & Co", TV host & producer, 1974-78; NY State Parole, bd comt, 1978-85; Hunter Col, Black & Puerto Rican Studies Dept, prof, currently. **Orgs:** Sr ed, Buffalo Black Newspaper, 1985; bd mem, Harlem Restoration Proj, 1985; bd mem, NY State Civil Liberties Union, 1985; Nat Asn Blacks Criminal Justice, 1985; pres & founder, Afro-Am Police Asn Buffalo,1969-71; Nat Black Police Asn, 1972; fel Buffalo State Col Comn, 1984; Nat Asn Advan Colored People. **Honors/Awds:** Presidential Citation for Exceptional Service, 1972; received numerous community awards and citations from community groups, Youth groups and prison inmate organizations including the NAACP, Operation PUSH, ACLU, Black Prof Women's Org Black Firefighters, Afro-American Police Asn. **Special Achievements:** Published an article "A Black Policeman's Perpective on Law Enforcement"in 1979 " which is used in numerous colleges and police training academies. His writings appears periodically in the Black Community newspaper. Hosts "Kirkland's Korner" on WUFO Fridays at 10pm. **Military Serv:** USAF, airman first class, 1952-56; United Nations Service Medal, NatDefense Medal, Good Conduct Medal, Korean Service Medal, 1952-56. **Home Addr:** 352 Pratt St, Buffalo, NY 14204. **Business Addr:** Professor, Hunter College, Department of Africana and Puerto Rican/Latino Studies, W Bldg 1711 695 Pk Ave, New York, NY 10021, **Business Phone:** (212)772-5035.

KIRKLAND-BRISCOE, GAIL ALICIA
Dentist. **Personal:** Born Apr 12, 1960, Tuskegee, AL; daughter of Mary L Pratt and Levi S Sr. **Educ:** Vanderbilt Univ, BS, 1982; Howard Univ Col Dent, DDS, 1986, Cert Orthod, 1988. **Career:** Pvt pract, Orthodontist, currently. **Orgs:** Alpha Kappa Alpha Sor; Alumni Asn Stud Clinicians Am Dent Asn; Omicron Kappa Upsilon; Nat Dent Asn; Am Asn Orthodontics; Nat Asn Female Exec. **Honors/Awds:** Deans Award, Alpha Omega Nat Soc, 1986; Int Col Dentists Award 1986; Harold S Fleming Memorial Award, 1986; Orthodontic Award, Howard Univ 1988. **Special Achievements:** author of Forensic Dentistry- Solving the mysteries of identification, General Dentistry, 1987; Featured on Working Woman Television Show. **Business Addr:** Dentist, Orthodontics, 3012 18th St NE, Washington, DC 20018, **Business Phone:** (202)526-4060.*

KIRKLAND-HOLMES, DR. GLORIA
Educator. **Personal:** Born Aug 29, 1952, Charleston, SC. **Educ:** Fisk Univ, BA, 1974; Ind State Univ, MS, 1975, PhD, 1978. **Career:** Margaret Ave Child Care Ctr, asst dir, parent coord, 1975-76; Maehling Terr Day Care Ctr, dir teacher, 1976; Ind State Univ, adj asst prof, 1976-78; Rose South side Child Care Ctr, dir, 1976-78; Ind State Lab Sch, nursery teacher, 1978; Malcolm Price Lab Sch, Univ Northern Iowa, 1978-98; Univ Northern Iowa, assoc prof, early childhood educ & dept curric & instr, prof, currently. **Orgs:** Nat Asn Educ Young C, 1975-; Iowa Asn Educ Young C, 1975-; Black Child Devel Inst, 1977; bd mem, Logandale Urban Housing Corp, 1979-; chairperson & secy, Iowa NE State Conf NAACP, 1979-; youth adv, Black Hawk Co, NAACP Youth Group, 1979-. **Honors/Awds:** Achievement of Knowledge, Afro-Am Cult Ctr & Black Student Union, Ind State Univ, 1977. Pi Chap, Alpha Kappa Alpha Sorority & Fisk Univ, 1971. **Special Achievements:** Top ten Min Women in Iowa appointed by Gov Ray 1980. **Business Addr:** Professor, University Northern Iowa, Department of Curriculum & Intstruction, schindler Educ Ctr 624, Cedar Falls, IA 50614-0606, **Business Phone:** (319)273-2007.

KIRKLIN, DR. PERRY WILLIAM (NANA KWAME BAFFOE, II)
President (organization), physical chemist, educator. **Personal:** Born Feb 28, 1935, Ellwood City, PA; son of Perry Kirklin and Martha Peek Kirklin; married Betty Jean Lampkins, Mar 25, 1956; children: Cheryl Hawkins, Perry Kirklin III & Pamela June. **Educ:** Westminster Col, New Wilmington, PA, BS, 1957; Univ Minn, Minneapolis, MN,PhD, 1964. **Career:** Pysical Chemist, Educator (retired): Rohm & Haas Co, analyst group leader, 1964-70; Mobil Res & Develop Corp, sr res chemist, 1970-78, assoc chemist,1978-91; Assoc Aviation Fuels Res; Bloomfield Col, assoc prof chem,1991-95; St Mary's Hall-Doane Acad, sub teacher, 1995-2001; Montgomery County Col, Summer Bridge, chem prof, 1995-2001; Cheyney Univ Pa, adj prof, 1996-97. **Orgs:** Dir, Bucks County Community Ctr, 1965-74; chmn, Buckes County Health Planning 1968-72; dir, PHILA Regional Health Planning 1968-74; Pa State Health Planning Coun, 1970-74; pres, vpres, asst treas, Salem Fed Credit Union, 1972-2001; chmn, ASTM Aviation Fuel Comn, 1977-91; Nat Org Black Chemists & Chem Engrs, 1979-; founder & pres, Kuntu Village (Ghana) Nkosohene Comt-USA, 2003-. **Honors/Awds:** PA Regional Introduction of Minorities to Engineering Award, 1988; ASTM Award of Appreciation, 1990; Distinguished Alumni Chemistry Lecturer,Westminster Col, 1997; Grandfather of the Year, Salem Baptist Church,1998; Meritorios Service Award, Nat Org Black Chemists & Chem Engrs, 2001& 2002; Man of Year, Nat Jesus, Salem Baptist Church, 2003. **Home Addr:** 5534 Grey Hawk Lane, Lakeland, FL 33810. **Business Addr:** President, Kuntu Village Nkosohen Committee-USA, 5534 Grey Hawk Lane, Lakeland, FL 33810-4001, **Business Phone:** (863)816-8285.

KIRKSEY, M JANETTE
Administrator. **Personal:** Born Apr 15, 1946, Brownsville, PA; daughter of George A Williamson (deceased) and Johnnie L (deceased); married Edward M Kirskey, Jun 8, 1966; children: Scott M (deceased) & Daniele B. **Educ:** Franklin Univ, BA, 1981. **Career:** Ross Labs, from assoc buyer to sr buyer, contact mgr, 1996-; Ross Products Div, packaging buyer, currently. **Orgs:** Delta Sigma Theta; Mt Herman Baptist Church, Usher Bd; proj bus vol counr; Jr Achievement. **Business Addr:** Contact Manager, Ross Products Division, 625 Cleveland Ave, Columbus, OH 43215, **Business Phone:** (614)624-7677.

KIRVEN, MYTHE YUVETTE
Government official. **Personal:** Born Jun 12, 1956, Dallas, TX. **Educ:** Tex Tech Univ, BS, 1977; Atlanta Univ, MPA, 1980. **Career:** City of Dallas, admin asst. **Orgs:** Nat Asn Advan Colored People; Conf of Minority Pub Admin, 1978-; recording secy, Delta Sigma Theta Dallas Chap, 1980-84; vpres, S Dallas Club Nat Asn Negro Bus & Prof Women's Clubs, 1985-; Urban Mgt Assts N TX, 1983-; TX City Mgt Asn, 1983-; Int City Mgt Assn, 1983-; dir, S Dallas Health Access, currently. **Business Addr:** Administrative Assistant, City of Dallas, 1500 Marilla St 2BS, Dallas, TX 75201.

KIRWAN, ROBERTA CLAIRE
Journalist. **Educ:** Manhattanville Col, Purchase, NY, BA, Russian; Fordham Univ Grad Sch Bus, NY, MBA, mkt, 1978. **Career:** Doyle Dane Bernbach, NY, personnel mgr, asst acct exec, 1978-80; freelance photogr & mkt res coordr, 1980-82; Merrill Lynch, NY, acct exec, 1982-83; freelance mkt res coordr, 1984-88; Time-Warner, Money Magazine, New York, NY, assoc ed, 1989-. **Orgs:** Nat Asn Black Journ, 1990. **Business Addr:** Associate Editor, MONEY Magazine, 1271 6th Ave 32nd Fl, New York, NY 10020, **Business Phone:** (212)522-3337.

KISPERT, DOROTHY LEE
Association executive, president (organization). **Personal:** Born Dec 10, 1928, Detroit, MI; daughter of Leo Priestley and Pearl Priestley; married Wilson G; children: Kimberly A & Cynthia L Kispert. **Educ:** Univ Mich, BA, 1950; Wayne State Univ, MA, 1971. **Career:** President, Association executive (retired); Merrill-Palmer Inst, fac, 1975-80; Parent Child Develop Ctr, dir, 1975-80; Parent Child Ctr, dir, 1980-81; Parents & C Together, dir, 1981-91; Detroit Family Proj, dir servs, coordr, 1991-94. **Orgs:** Lay rep Children's Hosp, Mich, 1978-88; consult, Spelman Col, 1979; tech, rev panel CDA Bank St Col, 1981; pres, Metro Detroit Day Care Asn. **Honors/Awds:** 4C Child/Family Advocate Award, 1989; Esther Dean Collard Award, Detroit Asn for Infant Mental Health, 1991; Citizen of the Year Award, WSU Sch Social Work Alumni Asn, 1993. **Special Achievements:** Pub: PACT, A Partnership with Parents, Contemporary Parenting, 1983, co-auth Teaming Social Services with Education Cooperative, Jour Coop Educ, 1986. **Home Addr:** 19310 Woodingham, Detroit, MI 48221.

KITCHEN, WAYNE LEROY
School administrator. **Personal:** Born Sep 7, 1948, Sedalia, MO; son of Imogene Nurse Kitchen and Edgar Roy Kitchen. **Educ:** Lincoln Univ, BS, bus educ, 1970; Univ MO, MEd, col admin, 1977. **Career:** Cogswell Col, Admis Dept, asst dir, 1978-80; St Mary's Col, Mkt Div, prog coord, 1980-82; Univ San Francisco, Mkt Div, assoc dir, 1982-84; Bay Area Urban League Training Ctr, dir, 1984-85; Peralta Comm Col Dist, educ consult; Mills Col, upward bound asst dir, 1986-90; Calif State Univ, Hayward, dir upward bound, 1990-. **Orgs:** Phi Delta Kappa, 1983-; bd dirs, Nat Alumni Asn, Lincoln Univ, 1984-88, pres, Mo Alumni Asn, 1984-88, nat vpres, Nat Alumni Asn; vpres, Phi Beta Sigma, 1984-86; chmn, Community Elect Lloyd Vann Sch Bd, 1985; bd dirs, Oakland Ensemble Theatre; United Negro Col Fund Inter-Alumni Coun; Western Asn Educ Opportunity Personnel. **Honors/Awds:** President's Service Award, Phi Beta Sigma Fraternity, Alpha Nu Sigma Chap, 1984; Distinguished Lincoln University Alumni Award, 1987; Distinguished Alumni Award, Local Chap, Lincoln Univ, 1989. **Military Serv:** AUS, E-4, 1970-72; Good Conduct Medal, Nat Defense Serv Medal, M-16SS Medal 1972. **Home Addr:** 44 Oak Hill Circle, Oakland, CA 94605. **Business Addr:** Director Upward Bound, Calif State University, Rm LI-2158 25800 Carlos Bee Blvd, Hayward, CA 94542.

KITCHEN-NEAL, MARY KIM
College administrator. **Personal:** Born Apr 18, 1961, Fort Riley, KS; daughter of John Morgan and Yuson Kim Williams; married Rickey Neal, Oct 21, 2000; children: Sandra, Raymond II, William, Michael, Sasha Neal, Tiffany Neal & Andrecia Wingfield. **Educ:** Kansas State Univ, BA, eng lit, 1996; Yale Univ, summer writing workshop, 1997. **Career:** Delta Airlines Inc, sales agent, 1988-96; Int Aviation & Travel Acad instr, 1996-98; Univ Tex, Arlington, Upward Bound Prog, acad coordr, 1997-. **Orgs:** Alpha Kappa Alpha Soroity, 1981; Work Advantage Youth Adv Coun, 1999-; adv, NACWC, 2003-. **Special Achievements:** Published Poetry Piece, "This Moment," Essence Magazine, April, 1994. **Business Addr:** Academic Coordinator, University of Texas at Arlington, Upward Bound Program, 503 W Third St Carlisle Hall Suite 706, Arlington, TX 76019, **Business Phone:** (817)272-2610.*

KITHCART, LARRY E
Legislator. **Personal:** Born Jul 25, 1939, Glasco, NY; married Audrey; children: Larry Jr. **Career:** Ulster Co, First Black legislator, exec dir, 1975, currently; Co Legislator, elected 4th consecutive term. **Orgs:** Pres, Kingston City Recreation Com, 1968-77; comnr recreation, 1977; past pres, Kingston Dem Men's Club, Sheriff's comm; pub health- Indus develop; taxbase & study; bridge & hwy; prog aged; conser Vation com Chmn Mayor's policy making bd Kingston Rondout Neighborhood Ctr; ward chmn; YMCA; United Way; Cancer com; Jaycees; NAACP; com pres, Ulster Cnty Community Action Adv Bd; Finance Com Co Legis; Audit & Ins Com, Legis, Finance Com Co Legis, Municipal Power Study Commn Co Legis. **Military Serv:** USAF, 4 yrs. **Business Phone:** (845)338-8750.

KITT, EARTHA MAE. See Obituaries section.

KITT, SANDRA ELAINE
Novelist. **Personal:** Born Jun 11, 1947, Bronx, NY; daughter of Archie and Ann; divorced. **Educ:** Bronx Community Col, AA, 1968; City Col NY, BA, 1970, MFA, 1975. **Career:** Am Museum Nat Hist, libr spec, Richard S Perkin Collection, 1973-2004; publ novelist, 1981-; graphic artist illusr; Novels: Rites of Spring, 1984; All Good Things, 1984; Adam & Eva, 1984; Perfect Combination, 1985; Only With the Heart, 1985; With Open Arms, 1986; An Innocent Man, 1988; This Way Home, 1989; Someone's Baby, 1991; Love Everlasting, 1993; Serenade, 1994; Sincerely, 1995; The Colour of Love, 1995; Suddenly, 1996; Significant Others, 1996; Between Friends, 1998; Family Affairs, 1999; Homecoming, 1999; Close Encounters, 2000; She's the One, 2001; Southern Comfort, 2004; The Next Best Thing, 2005; Celluloid Memories, 2007. **Orgs:** Int Astron Union Comn Astron Libr, 1986; New York chap pres, Special Librs Asn, 1999-2000; chair, Affirmative Action Comm, 1993-96, Prof development community, 1996-99; Am Libr asn, Black Caucus, 1995-2001; Romance Writers Am; Novelist Inc. **Honors/Awds:** NIA, Woman Excellence Award, 1993; Walden Books Award for "Sincerely," 1996; Romantic Times "Lifetime Achievement Award," 2001; Romance Writers of America Service Award, 2002; NAACP Image Award in Fiction, nominee for "Girlfriends," 2000; Lifetime Achievement Award, NY Chap, Romance Writers Am, 2004. **Special Achievements:** First African American to publish with Harlequin Enterprises. **Business Addr:** Writer, PO Box 403 Planetarium Sta, New York, NY 10024-0403.

KITTLES, KERRY
Basketball player. **Personal:** Born Jun 12, 1974, Dayton, OH. **Educ:** Villanova Univ, attended 1996. **Career:** NJ Nets, guard, 1996-2004, part-time scout, currently; Los Angeles Clippers, guard, 2004-05. **Orgs:** Kappa Alpha Psi Fraternity Inc. **Honors/Awds:** Gold Medal, World Univ Games, 1995. **Special Achievements:** NBA Draft, First round pick, No 8, 1996; NBA co-rookie of the Month, 1996.

KLAUSNER, WILLETTE MURPHY
Theatrical producer, business owner. **Personal:** Born Jun 21, 1939, Omaha, NE; daughter of William and Gertrude Jones; married Manuel S, Feb 1, 1969. **Educ:** Univ Calif, Los Angeles, BA, econs, 1961; Tobe-Coburn Sch Fashion Careers NY, hon cert, 1962. **Career:** Carnation Co, res analyst, 1965; Audience Studies Inc, res analyst, 1965-66, proj dir, 1966-88, res unit dir, 1968-72, res, 1972-74; MCA Universal Studios, Calif, vpres mkt res & mkt, 1974-81; Theatrical: "Hurlyburly," Westwood Playhouse, 1988-89; "The Apprentice," The Richard Pryor Theatre, Hollywood, 1991; Edgework Prod, producer, "Twist," Walnut St Theatre, 1992; "Twist," George Street Playhouse, 1996; "The Man in Room 304" Watermark Theatre, NY 1997; "To Take Arms," Tamarind Theatre, LA 1997; "Three Mo' Tenors," "Kat & the Kings," Cort Theatre, Broadway, 1999-2000; "Fully Committed," Coronet Theatre, Los Angeles, 2000; Edgework Productions, pres; WMK Productions Inc, owner, currently; Three Mo' Tenors, producer, currently. **Orgs:** Gold Shield, Univ Calif Los Angeles Alumni Asn, 1974-; founding mem, Am Inst Wine & Food, 1982-; mem bd dir, Const Rights Found, 1982; vpres, bd dir, Los Angeles Co Music Ctr Oper Co, 1987; mem bd dir, Audrey Skirball-Kenis Theatre Inc 1991-; mem bd dir, Individual Rights Found, 1994; bd dirs, Am Cinema Found, 1995. bd dirs, Los Angeles Music Ctr; bd trustees, Women Film Found; League Prof Theatre Women; Nat Women's Forum. **Honors/Awds:** Mehitabel Award for outstanding Professional Achievement, Tobe-Coburn Sch Fashion Careers, 1978. **Special Achievements:** First African American model to appear in a major fashion magazine (Mademoiselle) and she modeled in Copenhagen, Denmark and other major European cities; First African American woman in fashion merchandising at Bloomingdale's in New York; First female corporate VP at MCA Universal Studios. **Business Addr:** Owner, Producer, WMK Productions Inc, 601 W 5th St Suite 800, Los Angeles, CA 90071, **Business Phone:** (213)617-0414.

KLEVEN, THOMAS
College teacher. **Personal:** Born Aug 30, 1942, Cambridge, MA; married Ella Faye Marsh, Nov 24, 1971; children: Deborah & Aaron. **Educ:** Yale Univ, New Haven, CT, BA, 1964; Yale Law Sch, LLB, 1967. **Career:** Goulston & Storrs, Boston, MA, assoc, 1967-69; Boston Model Cities Prog, 1969-72; Univ Southern Calif, 1972-74; Univ San Diego, prof, 1975-79;Thurgood Marshall Sch Law, Houston, TX, prof, 1974-. **Orgs:** Conf Critical Legal Studies, 1988-. **Honors/Awds:** Third Year Class Favorite Prof, 1991-92; Outstanding Teacher of the Year Award, Texas Southern Univ, 1991- 92, 1995-96; CLSA Prof of the Yr, 1995-96; Faculty Member of the Year, 2002-03. **Special Achievements:** Several publications including Is Capital Punishment Immoral Even If It Deters Murder?, Santa Clara Law Review, 2006. **Home Addr:** 4914 N Braeswood Blvd, Houston, TX 77096. **Business Addr:** Professor, Thurgood Marshall School of Law, Texas Southern University, 3100 Cleburne St, Houston, TX 77004, **Business Phone:** (713)313-7355.

KLINE, JOSEPH N.
Government official, county court judge. **Personal:** Born Oct 8, 1948, Dale, SC; son of Frances and Eddie; married Audrey Annette Wheelwright, 1969; children: Marwin, Mikima, Miesha. **Educ:** Hartford Data Inst, comput operator & programmer, 1968. **Career:** Savannah-Chatham County Pub Sch, sr analyst programmer, 1984; Beaufort County, SC, councilman, 1979-98, judge, 1998-02. **Orgs:** Black Elected Off Beaufort County, bd mem, 1979-; Burton-Dale-Beaufort Br Nat Asn Advan Colored People, bd dirs, 1979; Mt Carmel Baptist Church, deacon, 1984; Dale-Lobeco Community Org, bd dirs, 1975; Beaufort Marine Inst, bd dirs, 1987; Beaufort Jasper EOC, bd dirs, 1984; Low County Coun Govt, bd dirs, 1979-94; Beaufort County Local Organizing Comn, coordr; SC Legis House. **Honors/Awds:** Most Outstanding Young Man, Black Arise, 1973; One of a Million Man Marcher; CT, Jaycee of the Year, Jaycees, 1973; Plaque of Appreciation, Beaufort County, 1977; Certificate of Appreciation, Beaufort Jasper Econ Opport Cmdr, 1991; Citizen of the Year, Omega Psi Phi Fraternity, 1992; Outstanding Contribution in Politics Award, Beaufort County Dr King Day Comn, 1993. **Home Addr:** 42 Kline Cir, Seabrook, SC 29940-3125. *

KLINE, WILLIAM M.
School administrator. **Personal:** Born Feb 24, 1933, Paterson, NJ; married Lillian Thomas; children: Wayne, Michelle, William Jr & Wesley. **Educ:** William Paterson Col, BS, 1954, MS, 1959. **Career:** School administrator (retired); Paterson Bd Educ, teacher, 1957-65; Neighborhood Youth Corp, dir, 1965-68, vice prin, 1968-71; East side High Sch, prin, 1971-79, dir curriculum & spl educ proj, 1979, asst supt; Paterson, NJ, council man-at large, 1998; City CNL, pres, 2000-01. **Orgs:** Bd Recreation, City Paterson, 1962-64; alderman, City Paterson, 1965-67; Nat Asn Advan

Colored People; Omega Psi Phi; Phi Delta Kappa; IBPOE WIntegrity Lodge; 4th Ward County Committeeman; Paterson Rotary Club; municipal chmn, Democratic Party; mem Bd Educ Paterson, NJ, 1996-97, chmn, 1997-98. **Honors/Awds:** Numerous honors & awards including Freedom Campaign Award, Nat Asn Advan Colored People, Paterson, 1963; Certificate of Merit, Passaic County Med Soc, 1964; Community Service Award, Nat Asn Advan Colores People, Paterson, 1967; Education Leadership Award, Lambda Kappa Mu Passaic County, 1971; Unity Service Award, 1982; Hinton Community Service Award, 1983; Community Bettermant Award, SECA, 1983; Morris County Service Award, NJ State, 1984; PH Grand Lodge Award, 1985; Appreciation Award, Am Indian Relief Coun, 1992; Education Award, Paterson Young Men's Asn, 1993; Appreceiation Award, Westend Warriors, 1994; Van Resalier Award, 1997; Board Education Award, 1998; In Memory of the Ancestors Award, 1998; Church Centennial Award, 1999; Million Family March Award, 2000. **Military Serv:** AUS, pfc 1955-57; Good Conduct Medal. **Home Addr:** 346 9th Ave, Paterson, NJ 07514. *

KLUGE, PAMELA HOLLIE
Administrator. **Personal:** Born Apr 17, 1948, Topeka, KS; daughter of Frances Hollie and Maurice Hollie; married P F Kluge, Feb 14, 1977. **Educ:** Washburn Univ, Topeka, Kans, BA, eng, 1970; Columbia Univ, New York, NY, MS Journ, 1971; Univ Hawaii, Honolulu, Hawaii, Asian Studies, 1977; Columbia Univ, Am Studies, 1987. **Career:** Wall Street Jour, staff, 1969-75; Honolulu Advertiser, Pac correspondent, Saipan, 1975-76; Trust Territory Pac Island, econs dept Micronesia, 1976; New York Times, nat correspondent Los Angeles, foreign correspondent Manilla, financial columnist New York, 1977-87; New York Stock Exchange, New York, NY, media consult, 1987-; Knight Bagenot Fel Econ & Bus Jour; Columbia Univ Grad sch Jour, dir, 1987-90; Poynter Inst, vis fac, 1989-; Kenyon Col, dir capital proj, 2005-, sr philanthropic advisor. **Orgs:** Dir, Newspaper Found, 1973-75; contribr, Encyclopdeia Americana, 1985-; adv bd, Kans Ctr Book, 1988-; consult, Paragon Group, 1989-. **Honors/Awds:** Distinguished Service Award, Washburn Univ, 1981; Best in the Business, Washington Journ Rev, 1985; Topeka High School Hall of Fame, 1988; Fulbright Fellow to Malaysia, 1988. **Special Achievements:** Editor, The Knight-Bagehot Guide to Business and Economics Journalism, Columbia Univ Press, 1990. **Business Addr:** Director of Capital Projects, Senior Philanthropic Advisor, Kenyon College, 101 Scott Lane, Gambier, OH 43022-9623.

KNABLE, BOBBIE MARGARET BROWN
School administrator. **Personal:** Born May 20, 1936, Knoxville, TN; daughter of Jacqueline Jordan (deceased) and Isaac (deceased); married Norman, Dec 21, 1963 (died 2007); children: Jacob. **Educ:** Oberlin Conserv, Oberlin Ohio, BA, music, 1958. **Career:** Tufts Univ, Medford, Mass, asst prof eng, 1970-76, dir continuing educ, 1974-78, dean freshmen, 1978-79, dean stud, 1979-99, dean emerita, 1999-; City on a Hill Public Charter High Sch, sch head, 2003-4; educ consult, currently. **Orgs:** New Eng Deans, 1978-; steering comn, New Eng Col Alcohol Network, 1980-; trustee, Vermont Acad, 1983-85; mem, Mass Asn Women Deans, Adminr & Counrs, 1986-, rec secy, 1988-89; Deans Round Table, 1988-; Stud Affairs Think Tank, 1988-; trustee, Pine Manor Col, 1989-; comnr, New Eng Asn Sch & Col, 1989-95; gov bd mem, Mass Inst Psychoanalysis, 1990-96 and 2007-; trustee, Bennington Col, 1997-; vice chair, bd trustees, City Hill, 2004-; Mass Charter Public School Asn, 2005-; Mass Ctr Public Charter Sch Excellence, 2008-. **Honors/Awds:** Doctor of Humanities, Oberlin Col, 2009. **Special Achievements:** Town Meeting Member, Town of Brookline, MA; Member of Advisory Committee, Town of Brookline, MA. *

KNIGHT, ATHELIA WILHELMENIA
Journalist. **Personal:** Born Oct 15, 1950, Portsmouth, VA; daughter of Daniel Dennis and Adell Virginia Savage. **Educ:** Norfolk State Univ, Norfolk, VA, BA, 1973; Ohio State Univ, Columbus, OH, MA, 1974; Harvard Univ, Cambridge, MA, Nieman Fel, 1986. **Career:** DC Cooperative Extension Serv, Wash, DC, summer aide, 1969-72; Portsmouth Pub Schs, Portsmouth, VA, substitute teacher, 1973; The Virginian-Pilot, Norfolk, VA, summer relief reporter, 1973; The Chicago Tribune, Chicago, IL, summer relief reporter, 1974; Washington Post, Wash, DC, metrop desk reporter, 1975-81, investigative reporter, 1981-94, sports reporter, 1994-, Scripps Howard, vis prof, 2001; staff writer, currently; Wash Posts Young Journalists Develop Project, form asst dir to dir, Hampton Univ, Sch Liberal Arts & Educ, staff mass media arts, currently. **Orgs:** Women in Communs; Nat Asn Black Journalists; Wash-Baltimore Newspaper Guild. **Honors/Awds:** Mark Twain Award, Asniated Press, 1982, 1987; 'Nat Award for Education', Nat Educ Writers Asn, 1987; Front Page Award, Wash/Baltimore Newspaper Guild, 1982; Nieman Fel Journalists, Harvard Univ, 1985-86; Ohio State Univ Fel, Ohio State Univ, 1973-74; Md, Delaware DC Press Asn, First Place, Pub Serv Award, 1990; Md/Delaware, DC Press Asn, First Place, Local Govt; Wash Chap Soc Prof Journalists, Dateline Award Gen News, 1993; MD-DE-DC Press Asn, First Place, Sport News, 1997. **Business Addr:** Writer, The Washington Post, 1150 15th St NW, Washington, DC 20071, **Business Phone:** (202)334-7132.

KNIGHT, BREVIN
Basketball player. **Personal:** Born Nov 8, 1975, Livingston, NJ; son of Melvin and Brenda. **Educ:** Stanford, BA, sociol, 1997. **Career:** Cleveland Cavaliers, guard, 1997-01; Atlanta Hawks, 2001; Memphis Grizzlies, guard, 2001-03; Wash Wizards, 2003; Phoenix Suns, 2003; Charlotte Bobcats, guard, 2004-07; Los Angeles Clippers, 2007-08. Utah Jazz, 2008-. **Honors/Awds:** Frances Pomeroy Naismith Award, 1997. **Business Addr:** Professional Basketball Player, Utah Jazz, 301 W South Temple, Salt Lake City, UT 84101, **Business Phone:** (801)325-2500.*

KNIGHT, BUBBA (MERALD KNIGHT)
Singer. **Personal:** Born Sep 4, 1942, Atlanta, GA. **Career:** Gladys Knight & the Pips, singer, 1952-; Shakeji Inc, mem; Albums: If I Were Your Woman, 1971; Neither One Of Us, 1973; Imagination, 1973; "I Feel a Song", 1974; 2nd Anniversary, 1975; The Best of Gladys Knight & the Pips, 1976; Visions, 1983; All Our Love, 1987. **Orgs:** Gladys Knight & the Pips.

KNIGHT, REV. CAROLYN ANN
Educator, clergy. **Personal:** Born in Denver, CO; daughter of Ed and Dorothy. **Educ:** Bishop Col, Dallas, TX, BA, 1977; Union Theological Sem, New York City, MDiv, 1980; United Theoligical Sem, Dayton, OH, DMin, 1995. **Career:** Canaan Baptist Church, NYC, asst pastor, 1978-87; Philadelphia Baptist Church, NYC, pastor, 1988-93; Union Theological Sem, NY, asst prof, 1989-93; ITC, Atlanta, asst prof, 1995-; Carolyn Ann Knight/Can Do Ministries Inc, pastor, currently. **Orgs:** Golden life mem, Delta Sigma Theta, 1982-; NAACP, 1980-. **Honors/Awds:** 15 Greatest Black Women Preachers, Ebony Mag, 1997; College of Preachers, Morehouse Col, 1996; Alumni Award, United Negro Col Fund, 1993; Bethune Award, Nat Coun Negro Women, 1991; Negro Professional Women Comt Serv, Laurelton Chap, 1987. **Special Achievements:** "If The Worst Should Come!," sermon, 1997; "When You Talk to Yourself!," sermon, 1997; "How To Deal With Failure," Sister to Sister, devotional, 1993. **Business Addr:** Pastor, Carolyn Ann Knight/Can Do Ministries Inc, 904 Walton Way SE, Smyrna, GA 30314-4143, **Business Phone:** (770)433-8644.

KNIGHT, FRANKLIN W.
Educator. **Personal:** Born Jan 10, 1942; son of Willis J and Irick M Sanderson; married Ingeborg Bauer; children: Michael, Brian & Nadine. **Educ:** Univ Col Wis, London, BA (honors), 1964; Univ Wis, Madison, MA, 1965, PhD, 1969. **Career:** SUNY Stony Brook, asst/assoc prof, 1968-73; Johns Hopkins Univ, assoc prof, 1973-77, prof, 1977-, Leonard & Helen R Stulman Prof Hist, 1991-, Undergrad Studies, dir, currently; Latin Am Studies Prog, dir, 1992-95; Howard Univ, vis prof, 1983, 1998-2000, 2002; Colgate Col, John D & Catherine T McArthur dist vis prof, 2000. **Orgs:** Bd dirs, Social Sci Res Coun, 1976-79; consult, NEH, 1977-85; vis prof Univ Tex, Austin, 1980; comm mem, Inter-Am Found, 1984-86; res comm., Am Hist Assn, 1984-86; chmn, Int Scholarly Rels Comm Conf Latin Am Historians,1983-86; exec comm., Assn Caribbean Hist, 1982-85; pres, Latin Am Studies Assn, 1998-2000. **Honors/Awds:** SUNY Res Found Grant, 1969, 1970; Stony Brook departmental Teaching Award, 1973; Am philosophical soc Grant, 1973; Fellow Nat Endowment for Humanities 1976-77; Fellow Center for Adv Studyin Behav Sciences 1977-78; Super Lion Award, 1979; Distinguished Grad Award Of the Council & senate Of the Univ westIndies, 1989; Distinguished Vis Lect Foreign Serv Inst Of the Dept Of state, 1993; Academia de Letras da Bahis, 2001. **Special Achievements:** First black faculty member to gain academic tenure, The Johns Hopkins Univ; author, "Slave Society in Cuba During 19th Century" 1970; "The Caribbean, Genesis of a Fragmented Nationalism" 1990. **Home Addr:** 2902 W Strathmore Ave, Baltimore, MD 21209. **Business Addr:** Leonard, Helen R Stulman Professor, Johns Hopkins University, Department History, Gilman Hall 320 3400 N Charles St, Baltimore, MD 21218, **Business Phone:** (410)516-7591.

KNIGHT, GLADYS MARIA
Executive, singer, actor. **Personal:** Born May 28, 1944, Atlanta, GA; daughter of Merald Knight Sr and Elizabeth Woods; married Barry Hankerson, Jan 1, 1974 (divorced 1979); children: 1; married Les Brown, Jan 1, 1994 (divorced 1997); married William McDowell, Apr 12, 2001. **Educ:** Morris Brown Col, DHL, 1990. **Career:** Morris Brown Choir, singer, 1950-53; Gladys Knight & The Pips, singer, 1953-90, solo artist, 1990-; concert appearances in England, 1967, 1972,1973, 1976, Australia, Japan, Hong Kong, Manila, 1976; Charlie & Company; Kenya's Cakes To The Stars, co-owner; Gladys & Ron's Chicken & Waffle Restaurant, co-owner, currently; Albums: Letter Full of Tears, 1961;Gladys Knight & the Pips, 1964; Everybody Needs Love, 1967; Feelin'Bluesy, 1968; Silk & Soul, 1968; Nitty Gritty, 1969; All in a Knight's Work, 1970; If I Were Your Woman, 1971; Standing Ovation, 1971;Imagination, 1973; Neither One of Us, 1973; All I Need Is Time, 1973; Help Me Make It Through the Night, 1973; Gladys Knight & the Pips Super-Pak,1973; It Hurt Me So Bad, 1973; Gladys Knight & the Pips, 1974; Knight Time, 1974; Claudine, 1974; I Feel a Song, 1974; A Little Knight Music, 1975; 2nd Anniversary, 1975; Bless This House, 1976; Pipe Dreams, 1976; Still Together, 1977; Love Is Always on Your Mind, 1977; Miss Gladys Knight, 1978; The One & Only, 1978; Gladys Knight, 1979; Memories, 1979; That Special Time of Year, 1980; About Love, 1980; Midnight Train to Georgia, 1980; Teen Anguish, Vol. 3, 1981; I Feel a Song, 1981; Touch, 1981; Visions, 1983; Life, 1985; All Our Love, 1988; Christmas Album,1989; Good Woman, 1991; Just for You, 1994; Lost Live Album, 1996; Many Different Roads, 1998; At Last, 2000; Many Different Roads, 2000; Midnight Train, 2001; Christmas Celebrations, 2002; The Best Thing That Ever Happened to Me, 2003; Every Beat of My Heart, 2003; TV: Never Can Say Goodbye, 1997; Always & Forever, 2001; Hollywood Homicide, 2003; Unbeatable Harold, Centennial, 2005. **Orgs:** Alpha Kappa Alpha Sorority Inc. **Honors/Awds:** Grand Prize, Ted Mack Amateur Hour, 1952; 1 Gold Album; 1 Platinum Album;Grammy Award, 1972, 1988; Top Female Vocalist, Blues & Soul Mag, 1972; 6 Gold Buddah Records; NAACP Image, Ebony Music, Cash box, Billboard, Record World Awards, 1975; Spec Award for Inspiration to Youth, WA City Coun; Rolling Stone Award; American Music Award, 1984, 1988; Rock & Roll Hall of Fame, 1996; Ladies Home Journal Award; Star, Hollywood Walk of Fame, 1995; Trumpet Awards, spec honoree, 1997; Grammy Award for Traditional R&B,2001; Heard It Through the Grapevine, Midnight Train to Georgia; Vocal Group Hall of Fame, 2001; Grammy for At Last, 2001; Grammy award, 2006. **Special Achievements:** Appeared in "Sisters in the Name of Love", HBO, 1986; Author, Between Each Line of Pain and Glory, 1997. **Business Phone:** (770)471-7556.

KNIGHT, JOHN F., JR.
School administrator, president (organization). **Personal:** Born Jun 7, 1945, Montgomery, AL; son of Johnnie F Knight Sr and Ruth Bateman; divorced; children: Tamara & Tehrik. **Educ:** Ala State Univ, BS, bus admin, 1974. **Career:** Ala State Univ, dir pub relations, 1976, dir of commun & pub affairs; Ala PSC, exec asst to pres; postal serv, clerk, 1969-74; Ala State Univ, spec asst to pres, 1993; State Ala, rep, currently. **Orgs:** Pres, adv coun Ala Dem Conf Young Dem, 1973; Studs Affairs Com, 1973;pres, Ala State Univ Student Govt Asn, 1972-73; State Dem Exec Comn, 1975; chmn, Montgomery County Dem Conf, 1979-; Montgomery County Democratic Exec Comt; comnr, Montgomery County Comn, 1980-; bd mem, Montgomery Housing Authority Bd, 1975-; bd dir, Kershaw YMCA; bd dir, Montgomery Improv Assoc, bd dir, Family Sunshine Ctr, bd dir, Southern Develop Coun Inc., bd dir, Retired Sr Volunteer Prog; bd dir, Cleveland Ave YMCA. **Honors/Awds:** Highest ranking black in AL State Govt, 1974; Presidential Citation, NAFEO, 1991; Man of the Year, Kappa Alpha Psi Fraternity, 1991. **Military Serv:** AUS 1967-69; Silver Star, 1964, Vietnam Service Medal, Nat Defense Medal, Vietnam Campaign Medal, Combat Infantryman Badge. **Home Addr:** 875 John Brown Ave, PO Box 6148, Montgomery, AL 36106. *

KNIGHT, LEONARD G.
Land speculator, consultant. **Personal:** Married; married Gail. **Educ:** Mount Saint Mary's College, BA; Baruch College at City University in New York, MPA; American University, International Relations post graduate work. **Career:** San Diego City Council, Executive Asst.; Protocol Communications Inc, Owner;. **Orgs:** President, 100 Black Men of Phoenix; National Strategic Planning Director and National Leadership Development Director, 100 Black Men of America; Distinguished Toastmaster, Toastmaster International; International Cities & County Management Association; National Civic League. **Honors/Awds:** Outstanding Young Man of America; National/Urban Rural Fellow in New York; Pi Alpha Alpha; W.K. Kellogg Foundation National Fellow. *

KNIGHT, LYNNON JACOB
Electronics engineer. **Personal:** Born Jan 13, 1920, Ernul, NC; married Louise Dixon. **Educ:** Lincoln Univ, BS, 1941; Univ Pa, postgrad, 1942-44; Univ Ariz, attended 1959-61; Univ Calif, Los Angeles, attended 1968-72. **Career:** Radar & Electronics Defense Dept, SE Asia, staff engr, 1946-58; Army Dept Ft Huachuca, Ariz, supvr electronics engr, 1958-62; Navy Dept Los Angeles, staff engr electronics, 1962-65; Def Supply Agency Pasadena, tech mgr chief engr, 1965-; Knight-dixon Co, Los Angeles, pres, 1971-. **Orgs:** Power Source Com Army Dept, 1961-62; AASS; IEEE; Armed Forces Communs & Elec Asn; Omega Psi Phi. **Home Addr:** 5300 Via Bernado Cir, Yorba Linda, CA 92887-2566. **Business Addr:** 125 S Grand, Pasadena, CA 91105.*

KNIGHT, MARION SUGE. See KNIGHT, SUGE.

KNIGHT, MERALD. See KNIGHT, BUBBA.

KNIGHT, DR. MURIEL BERNICE
Consultant, educator. **Personal:** Born Apr 21, 1922, Hartford, CT; daughter of Oscar Milton and Rosena Burnett Williams; widowed; children: Leo M (deceased), Philip A (deceased), Muriel Virginia,William & Sheila Eileen. **Educ:** Northeastern Univ, AS, 1970, BS, educ admin leadership & supv, 1972, EdD, 1988; Harvard Grad Sch Educ, EdM, sociol, 1973, PhD, educ mgt & leadership supv; Suffolk Univ, cert, consumer law, 1979. **Career:** Harvard Chap, Phi Delta Kappa, historian-elected, 1985-86; Beaver Co Day Sch, instr; Election dept Ward 5 Precinct 7, Warden, 1980-88; Northeastern Univ, Grad Sch Educ, teaching asst, 1977-78; Boston State Col, lectr, 1979-81; Mass Bay Comm Col, lectr, 1985; Audio Archeology Recordings: "Little Brown Jug", "America the Beautiful", "Nearer My God to Thee". **Orgs:** Northeastern Alumni, 1973-; Harvard Grad Alumni, 1974-; vpres, New England Woman's Press Asn, 1983-85; bd mem, Dimock St Health Ctr,

1983-85; warden, Election Dept City Boston, 1983-; Selective Serv Bd No 32; bd mem, S End Neighborhood Action Prog, 1985. **Honors/Awds:** Kennedy Federation Scholar; Martin Luther King Scholar, Northeastern Univ; Community Service Award; Professional Award, Educator's Award, Boston Chap, Negro Bus & Prof Women; Merit Media Award, Lambda Kappa Mu Sorority. **Home Addr:** 31-C Village Ct, PO Box 18366, Boston, MA 02118.

KNIGHT, NEGELE OSCAR
Basketball player. **Personal:** Born Mar 6, 1967, Detroit, MI. **Educ:** Dayton Univ, attended 1990. **Career:** Basketball player (retired); Phoenix Suns, guard, 1990-93; San Antonio Spurs, 1993-94; Detroit Pistons, 1994; Portland Trailblazers, 1995; Toronto Raptors, 1998-99. **Honors/Awds:** NBA Draft, 1990.

KNIGHT, RICHARD, JR.
Executive. **Personal:** Born May 31, 1945, Fort Valley, GA; son of Freddie Knight and Richard Knight; married Mavis Best; children: Richard L, Marcus E, Nolan C. **Educ:** Yale Univ, political sci, 1967; Fort Valley State Col, BA, political sci, 1968; Univ NC, MPA 1974. **Career:** Carrboro NC, town mgr, 1976-80; ICMA, vpres, 1980; Gainesville FL, dep city mgr, 1980-82; City Dallas, asst city mgr 1982-86, city mgr, 1986-90; city Dallas, asst city mgr, 1982-86, city mgr, 1986; Caltex Petrol Corp, dir total qual & envir mgt, 1990, gen mgr admin, 1993, gen mgr mkt, dir, 1995; Vista Stores, chmn bd dir, 1998; Knight Parking Co, owner, 1998-99; Knightco Oil Co, founder, currently. **Orgs:** Rotary Int; past comn, Cub Scout MAWAT Durham Dist Boy Scouts; int City Mgt Asn; chmn, Dallas Regional Minority Purchasing Coun, 1984-85; Chmn, Bd D & FW Minority Bus Develop Coun, 1984, 1985; v chmn, Dallas Alliance, 1985; Salesmanship Club Dallas, 1989; bd dirs, Comerica Bank, TX; bd dirs, Dallas Int Sports Comn; bd dirs, Dallas Zoological Soc; db dir, Comerica Bank; Bd Regents, Univ N Texas; Bd Trustees, Dallas Medical Resource; Bd Dirs, Arena Group; Chmn, Goodwill Industries; C Medical Ctr; JP Morgan Chase Bank; exec Bd mem, Circle Ten Coun Boy Scouts Am; mem Exec Comt State Fair Texas; mem Salesmanship Club Dallas and Dallas Citizens Coun; St. Paul United Methodist Ch. **Military Serv:** AUS, staff sgt, 1969-71. **Business Addr:** Founder, Knightco Oil, 3000 N Sylvania Ave, Fort Worth, TX 76111-3012, **Business Phone:** (817)831-6722.*

KNIGHT, DR. ROBERT S.
Educator, dentist, dean (education). **Personal:** Born Aug 10, 1929, Montgomery, AL; married Patricia Tyler; children: Lynn, Robert, Joan & Stephen. **Educ:** Talladega Col, BA, 1949; Meharry Med Col, DDS, 1954. **Career:** Bridgeport, CT, pvt pract, 1964; Howard Univ, Col Dent, asst prof, 1965-74, assoc dean stud affairs, 1975-77, prof, 1978-90, dean, 1991-95. **Orgs:** Am Dent Asn; Nat Dent Asn; DC Dent Soc; Robert T Freeman Dent Asn; Am Acad Oral Path; Am Asn Dent Sch; Soc Teacher Oral Path; Capital Order Oral Path; Nat Urban League; Am Cancer Soc fel oral path, NY Univ, 1963; com chmn, Explorer Scouts, BSA; Sigma Xi, 1971; Omicron Kappa Upsilon Hon Dent Soc, 1974, bd mem, Howard Univ, 2001-; fel Am Col Dent, 1981. **Military Serv:** AUS dent corps 1954-61; USAR Col. **Home Addr:** 609 Elm Ave, Takoma Park, MD 20912, **Home Phone:** (301)270-1480. **Business Addr:** Board Member, Howard University, College of Dentistry, 600 W St NW, Washington, DC 20059, **Business Phone:** (202)806-0440.

KNIGHT, SAMMY D., JR.
Football player. **Personal:** Born Sep 10, 1975, Fontana, CA; son of Sam Sr; married Freda; children: Shianne, Samone, Savannah & Aneka. **Educ:** Univ Southern Calif, commun. **Career:** New Orleans Saints, safty, 1997-2002; Miami Dolphins, safty, 2003-04; Kans City Chiefs, safety, 2005-06; Jacksonville Jaguars, 2007; New York Giants, safety, 2008. free agent, currently. **Orgs:** Founder, Sammy Knight Found, 2002. **Honors/Awds:** Trojans' Most Valuable Player, 1996. **Special Achievements:** Serves as a spokesperson for Kansas Citys Hooked on Books campaign. Anavid player of the EA Sports Madden Football video game .

KNIGHT, SUGE (MARION SUGE KNIGHT)
Executive. **Personal:** Born Apr 19, 1965, Los Angeles, CA; son of Marion and Maxine; married Sheritha; children: one. **Educ:** Attended Univ, Nevada, Las Vegas. **Career:** Death Row Records, co-founder & ceo, 1991-; Suge Knight Management, founder, 1994; Club 662, owner, 1994; Death Row Records, ceo, 200l-. **Honors/Awds:** VIBE Awards. **Special Achievements:** Started the Death Row Prisoner Appeal Fund. *

KNIGHT, THOMAS LORENZO
Football player. **Personal:** Born Dec 29, 1974, Marlton, NJ. **Educ:** Univ Iowa. **Career:** Ariz Cardinals, defensive back, 1997-2001; Baltimore Ravens, 2002-03; St Louis Rams, 2004.

KNIGHT, W H (W H JOE KNIGHT)
Educator. **Personal:** Born in Beckley, WV; son of W H Knight and Frances Knight; married; children: Michael Joseph Mask Knight & Lauren Louise Mask Knight. **Educ:** Univ NC, Chapel Hill, BA 1976; Columbia Univ Sch Law, JD, 1979. **Career:** Colonial Bancorp, assoc counsel & asst sec, 1979-83; Univ Bridgeport Sch Law, adj prof, 1981-83; Univ Iowa Col Law, assoc prof, 1983-88, prof, 1988-2001; Wake Forest Univ Law Sch, Winston-Salem, NC, guest prof, 1989; actg assoc dean, 1991-93; Duke Univ Law Sch, Durham, NC, visiting prof, 1991; Wash Univ, Sch Law, St Louis, MO, visiting prof, 1992; Univ Iowa, vice provost, 1997-2000; Univ Wash, Sch Law, Seattle, WA, dean & prof, 2001-; Univ Fla Law Sch, team chair, ABA AALS, site inspection team, 2003-. **Orgs:** Bd adv, Conn Econ Develop Authority, 1982-83; consult, Knight Financial Enterprises, 1982-; Lawyers Alliance Nuclear Arms Control, 1983-; Am & Iowa Civil Liberties Union, 1983-; pres, Iowa City, Nat Asn Advan Colored People, 1986-90; Nat Conf Black Lawyers; Soc Am Law Teachers, 1988-; Nat Bar Asn; Am Bar Asn; bd mem, Willowwind Sch, 1992-; bd mem, Mid-Eastern Coun Chem Abuse, 1992-; Am Law Inst, 1993-; bd mem, State Farm Fire & Casualty Co, 1995-; bd mem, State Farm Mutual Automobile Co, 1996-; bd mem, State Farm Life Ins, Co, 1998-; bd trustees, Law Sch Admis Coun, 2001-03. **Honors/Awds:** Nat Merit Scholar, 1972-76; Woodrow Wilson Administrative Fel, 1979; Distinguished Teaching Award, Duke Law Sch, 1990-91. **Special Achievements:** Co-auth, "Weep Not Little Ones: An Essay Our C About Affirmative Action," African Am & the Living Constitution, eds, JH Franlin, JR McNeil, Smithsonian Press, 1995; Co-Auth, Com Transactions Under Uniform Commercial Code, 5th edition, Matthew Bender, 1997; Auth, Iowa Bar Review Materials on Contracts 1985-89; Auth, book review "In Banks We Trust," P Lernoux Vol 10 IA J Corp Law 1095, 1985," International Debt & the Act State Doctrine: Judicial Abstention Reconsidered," 13 North Carolina J International Law & Commercial Regulation 35-72, 1988, book brief, "Black Robes, White Justice," Bruce Wright 10 UCLA Natl Black Law J 366-369, 1988," Loan Participation Agreements; Catching Up With Contract Law," 1987 Columbia Business Law Review 587-631," To Thine Own Self Be True," St. Louis Public Law Review, 1991, "Standing on the Corner Trying to Find Our Way", J Gender, Race & Justice, 1999. **Home Addr:** 3730 42nd Ave S, Seattle, WA 98144-7206. **Business Addr:** Dean, Professor, University of Washington Law School, William H Gates Hall, PO Box 353020, Seattle, WA 98195-3020, **Business Phone:** (206)685-3846.

KNIGHT, W H JOE. See KNIGHT, W H.

KNIGHT, WALTER R.
Government official, association executive. **Personal:** Born Aug 16, 1933, Camden, AR; married Sadie M Brown; children: Harriet, Vicki, Sabrena & Michelle. **Educ:** Univ Wis; Univ Minn. **Career:** City Councilman; USWA, vpres, 1969; UN Steelworkers Am Local 1533, pres, 1975-. **Orgs:** Bd dirs, Gr Beloit Asn Commerce; City Ambassadors Club; exec comn, Black Res Personnel; Beloit Improv Coalition; bd dirs, Wis Equal Employ Opportunity Asn; Rock Co Manpower Planning Coun, 1974. **Honors/Awds:** Service Award, Salvation Army, 1966. **Business Addr:** President, Un Steelworkers Am Local 1533, 614 Broad St, PO Box 1219, Beloit, WI 53511.*

KNIGHT-PULLIAM, KESHIA
Actor. **Personal:** Born Apr 9, 1979, Newark, NJ. **Educ:** Spelman Col, BA, sociol, 2001. **Career:** TV series: "Sesame Street", 1969; "The Cosby Show", 1984-92; "A Different World", 1987, 1988; TV Movies: The Little Match Girl, 1987; Polly, 1989; A Connecticut Yankee in King Aurthur's Court, 1989; What About Your Friends:Weekend Getaway, 2002; "Christmas at Water's Edge", 2004; "The Last Supper", 2008; "Party Over Here!", 2008; "Your Wife's a Payne", 2008; "Payneful News", 2008; "Back Where We Belong", 2009; "House of Payne" (7 episodes), 2007-09. films: The Last Dragon, 1985; Polly: Comin' Home, 1990; Motive, 2004; Christmas at Water's Edge, 2004; Beauty Shop, 2005;The Gospel, 2005; Cuttin Da Mustard, 2008; Death Toll, 2008; Madea Goes to Jail, 2009. **Orgs:** Delta Sigma Theta Sorority Inc. **Honors/Awds:** Emmy nomination for Outstanding Supporting Actress in a Comedy Series;Image Award for Outstanding Youth Actor & Actress, 1988, 2009; People's Choice Award, 1988; Young Artist Award for Best Young Actor & Actress Ensemble in a TV Comedy, Drama Seriesor Spec, 1989; Blimp Award, 1991. **Special Achievements:** Won a celebrity ed of the Weakest Link; Won a celebrity ed of Fear Factor,2003; Ranked No 19, VH1's list of the "100 Greatest Kid Stars"; Ranked #11on E! Television's "50 Cutest Child Stars All Grown Up" special, 2005. **Business Addr:** Actor, Carsey-Werner, 4024 Redford Ave Bldg 3, Studio City, CA 91604-2101, **Business Phone:** (818)655-5598.*

KNOTT, DR. ALBERT PAUL
Executive. **Personal:** Born Mar 23, 1935, Pittsburgh, PA; son of Albert Paul and Fannie Merideth Scott; married Lynda Steenberg; children: Albert Paul Knott III & Olivia Merideth Knott. **Educ:** Yale Col, BA, 1956; NJ Col Med, MD, 1960; DC Gen Hosp, internship, 1961; Michael Reese Hosp Chicago, Cardoiology fel, 1963; Va Hosp Hines IL, med res, 1965. **Career:** Tabernacle Community Hosp, med dir, 1972-77; Bethany/Garfield Park Hosp, med dir, 1977-81; Statevl Cortl Inst, med dir, 1981-83; Metrop Correctional Ctr, med dir, 1984-85; Luxury Yachts charaters, Miami, FL & Chicago, IL, pres, 1984-; CHA Ltd, Chicago Ill, pres, 1985-; Commun Equipment Consultants, pres, 1987-; Marine Cellular Specialists Chicago & Fort Lauderdale, vpres, 1988-; Knott Lock Corp, pres, 1988-. **Orgs:** Dir, Inner Cty Ind, 1967-; Am Col Phys, 1968-; dir, St Johns Entp, 1970-; dir, Kings Bay Ltd, 1972-; dir, Lux Yachts Ltd, 1980-; dir, Reg Ind 1980-. **Military Serv:** USN, lt cmndr, 1965-67. **Business Addr:** President, Knott Lock Corp, 800 S Wells Suite 532, Chicago, IL 60607, **Business Phone:** (312)939-9200.

KNOTT, MAY
Manager. **Personal:** Born in Montgomery, AL; daughter of Joseph Paige (both deceased) and Julia Kyle Alexander Mayberry; married Gerald Jordan (divorced 1995); children: Deborah L Jordan & Gerald Jordan Jr; married Harold Wynne; married William Edgar, Jul 29, 1970. **Educ:** Sinclair Col, Dayton, OH; Univ Dayton, OH. **Career:** Manager (retired); Wright Patterson AFB, Dayton, OH, reports control clerk, 1953-55; Gentile Air Force Depot, Dayton, OH, exec secy, 1959-72; Defense Electronic Supply Ctr, Dayton, OH, contract admin & negotiator, 1972-74, Columbus, OH, procurement analyst, 1974-77; Digital Equip Corp, Nashua, NH, buyer, 1977-80; Air Force Acquisition Ctr, Hanscom AFB, Lexington, MA, small bus specialist, 1982-91, Fed Womens Prog, mgr, 1989-93; Jazz Ensemble, May Knott, mgr. **Orgs:** Chair, YWCA Swim-In for Mentally Handicapped, 1980-82. **Honors/Awds:** Outstanding Performance, DLA, 1965, 1980; Letter of Commendation, DLA, 1974; Letter of Outstanding Fed Serv, AF. **Special Achievements:** Nominated for Nat Asn Advan Colored People Roy Wilkins Award, 1989.

KNOWLES, BEYONCE
Actor, singer, movie producer. **Personal:** Born Sep 4, 1981, Houston, TX; daughter of Mathew and Tina. **Career:** R&B group, Destiny's Child, lead singer; Albums with Destiny's Child: Destiny's Child, 1998; The Writing's On the Wall, 1999; Survivor, 2001; Albums: Romeo Must Die, 2000; Charlie's Angels, 2000; Osmosis Jones, 2001; Head of State, 2003; Soul Plane, 2004; White Chicks, 2004; Dangerously In Love, 2003; Live at Wembley, 2004; B'Day, 2006; Dreamgirls, 2006; Good Luck Chuck, 2007; TV: "Smart Guy", 1998; "Carmen: A Hip Hopera", MTV, 2001; "The 79th Annual Academy Awards", 2007; Films: Austin Powers in Goldmember, 2002; The Fighting Temptations, 2003; Bridget Jones: The Edge of Reason, 2004, Soul Plane, 2004; The Pink Panther, 2006; Dreamgirls, 2006. **Honors/Awds:** Image Award, Best Duo or Group, Nat Asn Advan Colored People, 2000; American Music Award, Favorite Soul/R&B Band, Duo, or Group, 2001; Grammy Award, Best R&B Performance By a Duo or Group, for "Say My Name," 2001; Pop Songwriter of the Year, Am Soc Composers, Authors & Publishers, 2001; MTV Video Music Award; Best R&B Video; Best Female Video; Best Choreography in a Video, all for "Crazy in Love," 2003; Grammy Award, four times; World Music Award. **Special Achievements:** First African-American woman to ever win the ASCAP Pop Songwriter of the Year Award, 2001; Endorsements and products: House of DerTon " her clothing line, Pepsi, L'oreal, Tommy Hilfiger, McDonald's, Ford, Samantha Thavasa. **Business Phone:** (212)833-8000.

KNOWLES, DR. EDDIE ADE
School administrator. **Personal:** Born May 3, 1946, New York, NY; son of Maggie and Ephraim; married; children: Alisa & Themba. **Educ:** Lincoln Univ, PA, BA, 1970; Columbia Univ Teachers Col, MA, 1973; State Univ NY, Rockefeller Col, PhD, 1998. **Career:** Bronx Community Col, from asst dir col discovery prog to dir col discovery prog, 1970-74; Hostos Community Col, asst prof, 1974-75; Rensselaer Polytech Inst, asst dean studs & foreign stud adv, 1977-79, dean minority affairs, 1979-82, dean studs, 1982-2000, interim vpres stud life, 2000-01, vpres stud life, 2001-, Arts Dept, adj assoc prof, currently; Black Col Mag, writer & consult, 1980-. **Orgs:** Bd dir, Sponsors Educ Opportunity, 1970-; consult, Exxon Educ Found, 1984; consult, NY Educ Opportunity Centers, 1984; bd dir, Edwin Gould Found C. **Honors/Awds:** Unity Award in Media, Lincoln Univ, MO, 1981; Service Award, Minority Stud Leader, Rensselaer Polytech Inst, 1982; Martin Luther King Award, Rensselaer Polytech Inst, 1983. **Home Addr:** 95 Brunswick Rd, Troy, NY 12180, **Home Phone:** (518)271-7919. **Business Addr:** Vice President for Student Life, Adjunct Associate Professor in Arts Department, Rensselaer Polytech Institute, Troy Bldg 3rd Fl 110 8th St, Troy, NY 12180-3590, **Business Phone:** (518)276-6201.

KNOWLES, DR. EM CLAIRE
School administrator. **Personal:** Born Jun 6, 1952, Sacramento, CA; daughter of Sidney S and Almeana Early. **Educ:** Univ Calif, Davis, BA, 1973; Univ Calif, Berkeley, MLS, 1974, cert mgt, 1975; Calif State Univ, Sacramento, MPA, 1986; Simmons Col, Boston, MA, Doctor Arts, 1988. **Career:** Univ Calif, Davis, ref librn, 1975-82, soc sci librn, 1982-85, coordr bib instr, 1985-88; Wentworth Inst Technol, fel, 1982; Wentworth Inst Tech, Boston, MA, archives librn, 1982; Simmons Col, Boston, MA, circulation librn, 1982, asst dean stud admin serv, 1988-, ALASC, fac adv, Libr Comnrs, chmn; freelance proof reader & reviewer, 1988-. **Orgs:** Calif Libr Asn, 1975-88, counr, 1978-90; Calif Gov's Conf Libr & Info Sci, 1979; Lambda Xi, 1980; Life mem, Am Libr Asn, 1984-; chmn, Librns Asn Univ Calif, Davis, CA, 1985-86; Mass Black Librns Network, 1988-; NAWE, AAHE, 1990; vpres, Greater Boston Inter-Univ Coun, 1998-99; comnr, Mass Bd Libr Comnrs, 2001-06; Delta Sigma Theta Sorority Inc. **Honors/Awds:** Outstanding Black Staff, Sacramento Observer, 1981; Outstanding Service, Ethnic Minority Stud, Delta Sigma Theta Sorority Inc. **Special Achievements:** Author of "How to Attract Ethnic Minorities to the Information Profession," Special Libraries; "Fulbright Scholars offered a Glimpse of American Academic Libraries," CA Clearinghouse of Library Instruction Newsletter, 7(2):1-2 May 1987; Dual Career Couple Relationships: An An-

notated Bibliography, Univ of CA, Women's Resources and Research Ctr, Working paper series No 7, April 20, 1980; Black Women in Science and Medicine: A Bio-Bibliography, with Mattie T Evans, Affirmative Action Council, 1977; co-author: "Recruiting the Underrepresented; Collaborative Efforts between Library Educators and Library Practitioners," Fall, 1991; "Recruiting the Underrepresented to Academic Libraries," College & Research Libraries, 1990; co-author, "Rethinking the Eurocentric Library Workplace," Reference Librarian, Winter 1996. **Business Addr:** Assistant Dean of Student Administration Service, Simmons College, Graduate School of Library and Information Science, 300 The Fenway, Boston, MA 02115-5898, **Business Phone:** (617)521-2798.

KNOWLES, SOLANGE PIAGET
Singer, actor. **Personal:** Born Jun 24, 1986, Houston, TX; daughter of Matthew and Tina Beyonce; married Daniel Smith, Feb 1, 2004 (divorced); children: Daniel Julez Smith Jr. **Career:** Albums: Solo Star, 2003; Films: Johnson Family Vacation, 2004; Bring It On: All or Nothing, 2006; Singles: "I Decided", 2008; "I Decided (Part2)", 2008; TV series: "The Proud Family," 2002; "Listen Up", 2005; "Ghost Whisperer", 2008. **Business Addr:** Recording Artist, c/o Columbia Records, Sony Music Entertainment Inc, 550 Madison Ave, New York, NY 10022-3211, **Business Phone:** (212)833-8000.*

KNOWLES, SUDANI
Executive. **Career:** City Detroit, Off Mayor, bd dirs. **Business Addr:** Board of Directors, City of Detroit, Office of the Mayor, 2 Woodward Ave Suite 1126, Detroit, MI 48226, **Business Phone:** (313)224-3400.

KNOWLING, ROBERT E, JR.
Executive. **Personal:** Born Jan 1, 1955?, Kokomo, IN; married; children: 4. **Educ:** Wabash Col, BA, theol, 1976; Northwestern Univ, MBA. **Career:** IN Bell, operator, engr, mkt exec, 1977-92; Ameritech, lead architect re-engineering corp transformation, 1992-94, vpres network opers, 1994-96; US West, exec vpres opers & tech, 1996-98; Covad Communications Group, pres & ceo, 1998-2000; Internet Access Tech, chair, ceo, 2001-03; Vercuity Inc, ceo, 2002-05; Heidrick & Struggles Int Inc, bd dir, currently; NYC Leadership Acad, ceo. **Orgs:** Ariba Inc, bd of dirs; Digital Divide, speaker; Juvenile Diabetes Fndn Intl, bd of dirs; Northwestern Univ, Kellog Grad School of Mgmt, adv bd; YMCA, volunteer, nat service group, chair. **Business Addr:** Board of Director, Heidrick & Struggles International Inc, 233 S Wacker Dr Sears Tower Suite 4200, Chicago, IL 60606-6303, **Business Phone:** (312)496-1200.*

KNOX, DOROTHY DEAN
Law enforcement officer, police chief. **Personal:** Born Mar 10, 1940, Jayess, MS; daughter of Robert Earl Brent and Juanita Jones; married Stanley R, Oct 23, 1960. **Educ:** Wayne State Univ, BS, criminal justice, 1975. **Career:** Detroit Police Dept, policewoman, 1969-74, sergeant, 1974-77, lt, 1977-80, inspector, 1980-86, comdr, 1986-93, dep chief, 1994-; Community Serv Div, head, 2000, currently; Wayne Co, prosecutor, chief investr, 1994-. **Orgs:** Bd mem, Black Family Develop, 1984-91; bd mem, Detroit Police Athletic League, 1985-91; bd secy, Children's Aid Soc, 1985-96; bd mem, Child Care Coord Coun, 1986-92; bd mem, Old Newsboys Good Fel Detroit, 1992-94; trustee, Leadership Detroit, 1994-99; Int Soc Poetry. **Honors/Awds:** Detroit Honoree, Women Police Mich, 1993; Honoree, Payne Pulliam Sch Trade & Com, 1993; Spirit of Detroit Award, Detroit City Coun, 1994; Woman of the Year, Boys Town Italy Inc, 1994. **Special Achievements:** First woman to be a commander in the Detroit Police Department in charge of the Community Services Division, 1986. **Business Addr:** Deputy Chief, Head of Community Service Division, Detroit Police Department, Rm 203 1300 Beaubien, Detroit, MI 48226, **Business Phone:** (313)596-2200.

KNOX, GEORGE F
Lawyer. **Personal:** Born Oct 17, 1943, Cleveland, TN; son of Iris Long and George; married Odette Curry, Oct 12, 1985. **Educ:** Mich State Univ, BS, zoology, 1966; Univ Miami Sch Law, JD, 1973. **Career:** Univ Miami Sch Bus Admin, lectr, 1973-74; City Miami, FL, asst city atty, 1974-75; Univ Ark, Fayetteville, asst prof law, 1975-76; City Miami, Fla, city att & dir law dept, 1976-82; Univ Miami Sch Law, lectr, 1978-80; Nova Univ Ctr Study Law, lectr, 1980-82; Paul, Landy Beiley & Harper Pa, partner, 1982-84; Long & Knox, partner, 1984; Kubicki Draper Gallagher, Miami, Fla, atty, 1990; pvt pract, lawyer, currently; Adorno & Zeder PA, vice chmn, currently. **Orgs:** Fla Bar Asn; Nat Bar Asn; Am Bar Asn; DC Bar Asn; Nat Inst Munic Law Officers; Asn Am Law Sch; Black Lawyers Asn; Fla League Cities; Asn Am Trial Lawyers; Acad Fla Trial Lawyers; US Dist Ct Southern Dist Fla, US Court Appeals Fifth Circuit, US Supreme Ct; Nat Asn Advan Colored People; bd dirs, Miami-Dade Community Col Found Inc; bd trustee, Greater Miami Chamber Com; bd trustee, Orange Bowl Comt; dir, Fla Wages Prog State Bd; Ctr Excellence; bd dirs, YMCA Greater Miami; Dade Co Blue Ribbon Comt; bd trustee, Fla Mem Col; bd dir, United Way; Miami Coalition Drug-Free Community. **Honors/Awds:** Jaycees Outstanding, Young Men Am, 1976; Miami-Dade Chamber Commerce Award of Outstand-

ing Contribution to Social and Economic Development, 1977; Virgil Hawkins Achievement Award, Black Lawyers' Asn, 1977; Alpha Phi Alpha Fraternity Achievement Award, 1977; Community Awareness Award, Fla Jr Col, Jacksonville; Community Service Award, Beta Beta Lambda Chap, Alpha Phi Alpha Fraternity, 1981; Appreciation Award, Nat Asn Advan Colored People, 1981; Jacksonville Achiever Award, Northwest Coun Jacksonville Chamber Comn, 1986. **Business Addr:** Vice Chairman, Adorno & Zeder PA, 2601 S Bayshore Dr, Miami, FL 33133, **Business Phone:** (305)858-5555.

KNOX, GEORGE L
Executive. **Personal:** Born Sep 6, 1943, Indianapolis, IN; son of George L II and Yvonne Nee Wright; married B Gail Reed, Jan 1, 1979; children: Reed & Gillian. **Educ:** Tuskegee Univ, Tuskegee, BS, 1967; Harvard Bus Sch, Boston, MBA, 1975; Am Univ, Wash DC. **Career:** Executive (retired); US Dept State, Wash, DC, Tokyo, foreign serv officer, 1968-73; McKinsey & Co, New York, NY, assoc, 1975-77; Philip Morris, NY, mgr internal mgt consult, 1977-79, mgr financial rels, 1979-83, dir financial rels & admin, 1983-85, dir corp Communs, 1985-87, vpres, pub affairs, 1987-95, vpres corporate affairs, 1995-2001. **Orgs:** Trustee, Studio Mus Harlem; dir, Franklin & Eleanor Roosevelt Inst; adv coun, Am Ballet Theatre; trustee, Afr Am Experience Fund; bd adv, Conn Can. **Military Serv:** USAF, 2nd lt, 1967.

KNOX, MARSHALL
Executive. **Career:** Retired teachers Asn Chicago, dir, currently. **Business Addr:** Director, The Retired Teachers Association of Chicago, 18621 Neal Cir, Country Club Hills, IL 60478, **Business Phone:** (708)647-1416.

KNOX, SIMMIE
Portrait painter. **Personal:** Born Aug 18, 1935, Aliceville, AL; married; children: 3. **Educ:** Univ Del, BA, 1967; Temple Univ, Tyler Sch Art, BFA, 1970, MFA, 1972. **Career:** Mus African Art, artist, Wash, DC, 1971; Simmie Knox Portraits Inc, portrait artist & still life artist, 1971-; portrait paintings: Frederick Douglas, 1975; Alex Haley, 1977; Justice Thurgood Marshall, 1989; Bill Cosby & family, 1983-91; Muhammad Ali, 1995; Bishop John T Walker, 1995; Henry Aaron, 1996. **Special Achievements:** First African American artist paint off presidential portrait; participant, Thirty Second Biennial Contemp Am Painting, The Corcoran Gallery Art, Wash, DC. **Military Serv:** US mil, 1950. **Business Addr:** Portrait Artist, Still Life Artist, Simmie Knox Portraits Inc, 13801 Ivywood Lane, Silver Spring, MD 20904, **Business Phone:** (301)879-1655.*

KNOX, STANLEY
Police chief. **Personal:** Born Jan 1, 1939?, Summerville, GA; son of Doris; married Dorothy Brent, 1960. **Educ:** Wayne State Univ, Detroit, MI, BA, criminal justice, 1976. **Career:** Detroit Police Dept, Detroit, MI, police officer, 1966, lt, 1977, inspector, 1978, head traffic sect, 1980, comdr, 1986, chief police, 1991-93. **Orgs:** Int Asn Chief Police; Mich Asn Chiefs Police. **Military Serv:** AUS sgt, 3 yrs.

KNOX, WAYNE D. P.
City planner, government official. **Personal:** Born Jun 19, 1947, West Reading, PA; son of John W and Mary V Peagram; children: Latina Marie. **Educ:** Cheyney State Col, BA, 1970; Penn State Univ, MA, 1984. **Career:** Bur Planning City Reading, urban planner, 1973-78; City Reading, dir orientation & training USAC proj, 1974-75; Neighborhood Housing Serv Reading, assoc dir, 1978-80, exec dir, 1980-82; Neighborhood Reinvestment Corp, field serv off, 1982-92; Martinsville Community Develop off, mgr, dir, currently. **Orgs:** Comt mem Reading Downtown Adv Comn, 1980-; dir, Old Bethel Cult Serv Ctr, 1985-91. **Honors/Awds:** Nat Col Poetry Publ, 1969-70; pres, Youth Employment Serv, 1970; Outstanding Serv Award, Cheyney State Col, 1970. **Military Serv:** AUS, E-5, 2 yrs; Letter of Commendation, 1st Infantry Div, 1971. **Business Addr:** Director, Manager, Martinsville Community Development Office, 55 W Church St Suite 217, PO Box 1112, Martinsville, VA 24114, **Business Phone:** (276)403-5169.*

KNOX, WAYNE HARRISON
Executive, president (organization), chief executive officer. **Personal:** Born Apr 26, 1942, Atlanta, GA; son of Nazareth Sr (deceased) and Lessie Heard; married Isabel Houston, Jun 14, 1968; children: Michelle, Vanessa & Meredith. **Educ:** Clark-Atlanta Univ, BS, physics; Geo Inst Technol, MS, nuclear eng, health physics. **Career:** Western Electric, elec engr, 1966-67; Clemson Univ, grad teaching asst, stud, 1971-72; Clark Col, instr, 1972-74; Westinghouse Hanford, operational health physics suv, 1974-77; Battelle Norhtwest, radiation safety auditor, res scientist, 1977-80; Inst Nuclear Power Operations, proj mgr, 1980-81; Advan Syst Technol Inc, pres, ceo, 1981-. **Orgs:** Health Physics Soc. **Honors/Awds:** MNY Service Firm of the Year, Atlanta MNY Bus Develop Ctr, 1991; Inc Magazine, No 195 privately held corpo US, 1991, No 108 fastest growing privately held corporations in US, 1992; ENT of the Year, Atlanta Pub Sch Syst, 1993. **Special Achievements:** First physics grad, Clark-Atlanta Univ. **Military Serv:** USF, capt; USY Reserve, major. **Business Phone:** (404)240-2930.

KNOX, WILLIAM ROBERT
Executive, football player. **Personal:** Born Jun 19, 1951, Elby, AL; son of Henry and Johnnie Finch; divorced; children: Jerett,

Rashard, Rachelle. **Educ:** Purdue Univ, BS, 1974. **Career:** Chicago Bears, defensive back, 1974-77; Correct Piping Co Inc, estimator, 1978-83; W R Knox Corp, pres, 1980-. **Orgs:** Pres, Purdue Club Lake Co, 1983. **Honors/Awds:** Member East Chicago Sports Hall of Fame; Red Macky Award, Purdue Univ. *

KNOX-BENTON, SHIRLEY
School administrator, philanthropist. **Personal:** Born Aug 8, 1937, Carthage, TX; daughter of Napoleon Byrdsong and Rhoberdia Goodwin Byrdsong; married Sammy L; children: Reginald Jerome Knox. **Educ:** Huston-Tillotson Col, BA, 1959; TX A&M Univ, summer study, 1965; TX Women's Univ, Masters, guid & coun, 1978, Masters, admin mgt, 1982; Harvard Univ, Ed Spec 1984-85. **Career:** School administrator, Philanthropist (retired); Southwest High Sch, asst prin, counselor, music teacher; Dunbar High Sch, prin, 1992-2004. **Orgs:** Pres, Neighborhood Club, 1971-; delegate NEA, TSTA, FWCTA 1974-; consult, High Sch Workshops, 1982-; vpres & pres, Ft Worth Counselors Assoc, 1983-85; consult, B&B Assocs, 1984-; consult, Links Sororities 1984-85; Nat Asn Advan Colored People; Zeta Phi Beta; Texas Asn Secondary Sch Prin, Ft Worth Admin Women, Phi Delta Kappa; bd dir, Camp Fire Girls; mem, FWASSP. **Honors/Awds:** Honorary Life Membership, PTA, 1975; Outstanding Teacher Award, H Ross Perot, 1975; Fellowship Harvard Univ, 1984; Outstanding Counselor of Year, N Tex Coun Orgn, 1985; TV Talk Shows KTVT Ch 11 1985; Texas Principal of the Year, 2001. **Home Addr:** 5901 Eisenhower Dr, Fort Worth, TX 76112.

KNUCKLES, FRANKIE (FRANCIS NICHOLLS)
Music producer, disc jockey. **Personal:** Born Jan 18, 1955, South Bronx, NY. **Career:** Disco jockey, record producer & remix artist; The Gallery, New York, dj, 1972-73; Continental Baths, New York, dj, 1973-76; SoHo Place, dj, New York, 1976-77; The Warehouse, dj, Chicago, 1977-82; Power Plant, Chicago, owner & dj, 1982-86; freelance dj & recording artist, 1986-; Albums: Beyond the Mix, 1991; Welcome to the Real World, 1995; Best of Frankie Knuckles, 1999; Choice: A Collection of Classics, 2000; The Godfather of House Music: Trax Classics; Out There: 2001 Mardi Gras; Motivation, 2002; Remixes: "This Time", "Happy"; "Let No Man Put Us Under"; "Ain't Nobody"; "Talking with Myself"; "Watcha Gonna Do With My Lovin'"; "The Pressure"; "Where Love Lives (Come On In)"; "I Want A Dog"; "Because of Love"; "Love Hangover"; "Bring Me Love"; "Rock With You"; "Closer Than Close"; "Unbreak My Heart"; "Sunshine"; "I'm Going to Go"; Blind ; "Rains Falls"; Singles: "You Can't Hide from Yourself"; "Tears"; "Your Love/Baby Wants To Ride". **Honors/ Awds:** Grammy Award, Remixer of the Year, Non-Classical, 1997; Dance Music Hall of Fame, 2005. **Business Addr:** Producer, Musician, Definity Records, 928 Broadway Suite 400, New York, NY 10010, **Business Phone:** (212)505-7728.*

KNUCKLES, KENNETH J
Vice president (Organization), government official. **Educ:** Univ Mich, BS, archit; Howard Univ Sch Law, JD. **Career:** Dep Bronx Borough pres, 1987-90; New York Dept Gen Serv, asst housing comnr; S Bronx Overall Econ Develop Corp, sr vpres econ develop, 1994-95; Columbia Univ, chief procurement officer; Columbia Univ, vpres support servs, 1996-2003; New York City Dept Gen Servs, comnr, 1990-93; New York City Planning Comn, vice chair, 2002-; Upper Manhattan Empowerment Zone Develop Corp, Bd Dirs, 2001-03, pres & chief exec officer, 2003-. **Orgs:** NY State Bar Asn; New York Planning Comn, 2002-. **Special Achievements:** First black commissioner of New York City's Department of General Services. **Business Addr:** President, Chief Executive Officer, Upper Manhattan Empowerment Zone Development Corporation, 290 Lenox Ave, New York, NY 10027, **Business Phone:** (212)410-0030.

KOCH, FRANCENA JONES
Counselor, educator. **Personal:** Born Dec 3, 1948, Bunnell, FL; daughter of Roosevelt Jones and Naomi Stafford; divorced; children: Ahmad Yussef Shaw. **Educ:** Fla Mem Col, BS, elem educ, 1972; Nova Southeastern Univ, MEd, 1984, specialist, early & middle childhood, 1994. **Career:** Miami Dade Co Pub Schs, intermediate instr, 1973-88, guid counr, 1988-; Fla Mem Col, adj prof, 1984-87; Dept Corrections, juvenile GED instr, 1994-97; Inmate to Inmate Tutoring, planner, 2000; Dorothy M Wallace Cope Ctr S, guid counr, currently. **Orgs:** Supt leadership cir, United Way, 1995-, ambassador, 1996-; Nat Asn Advan Colored People, Miami Br, 1997-; pres, Zeta Phi Beta, Beta Zeta Chap, 1997-99; Region 5 Steering Comt, Dade Co Schs, 1998-; Am Asn Univ Women, Miami Br, 2000-; pres-elect, Dade Co Coun Asn, 2001-02. **Honors/Awds:** Southeastern Leadership Award, Zeta Phi Beta Sorority Inc, 2001. **Business Addr:** GuidanceCounselor, Dorothy M Wallace COPE Center South, 10225 SW 147th Terr, Miami, FL 33176, **Business Phone:** (305)233-1044.

KODJOE, BORIS
Actor, fashion model. **Personal:** Born Mar 8, 1973, Vienna, Austria; son of Eric and Ursula; married Nicole Ari Parker, May 21, 2005; children: Sophie Tei Naaki Lee & Nicolas Neruda. **Educ:** Va Commonwealth Univ, Richmond, Va, mkt degree, 1996. **Career:** Films: Love & Basketball, 2000; Brown Sugar, 2002; The Gospel, 2005; Madea's Family Reunion, 2006; Alice Upside

Down, 2007; All About Us, 2007; Starship Troopers 3: Marauder, 2008; TV appearances: "Soul Food: The Series", 2000-04; "Street Time", 2003; Boston Public, 2003; "Second Time Around", 2004-05; If You Lived Here, You'd Be Home Now, 2006; "Crossing Jordan", 2007; "Women's Murder Club", 2007; Doing Hard Time, co-producer, 2004; "Nip Truck", 2007. **Orgs:** Eliminate Racism & Create Equality. **Honors/Awds:** Nominee, Image Award, 2002, 2003, 2004. **Special Achievements:** Named one of the "50 Most Beautiful People in the World 2002" by PeopleMagazine in 2002. **Business Addr:** Actor, Ujaama Talent Agency Inc, 501 Seventh Ave Suite 312, New York, NY 10018, **Business Phone:** (212)629-4454.

KODJOE, NIKKI. See PARKER KODJOE, NICOLE ARI.

KOGER, LINWOOD GRAVES, III
Physician. **Personal:** Born Feb 21, 1951, Baltimore, MD; son of Margaret Pigott and Linwood G Jr Esq; married Iantha Angela Hill Koger, Jul 4, 1987; children: Brian Anthony Koger, Kelsey Alexandria. **Educ:** Howard Univ Col Liberal Arts, BS, 1974, Col Med, MD, 1978. **Career:** Howard Univ, Dept Gen Surg, resident, 1983; pvt pract Baltimore, physician, 1983-85; Meharry Med Col, asst prof surg, 1985-89; Alvin C York Va Med Ctr, asst chief of surgery, 1985-; Morehouse Med Col, Atlanta, GA, prof surg, 1989-; pvt pract Baltimore, physician, currently. **Orgs:** Fel Am Col Surgeons; Asn Acad Surgeons; Soc Black Acad Surgeons. **Honors/Awds:** Diplomate, Am Bd Surg, 1984; Clinical Scis Fac Member of the Year, Meharry Med Col Pre-Alumni Coun, 1985-86; Mesenteric Ischemia; The York Va experience, presented Nat Med Asn Conv, 1989; Outstanding Surg Fac Mem, Morehouse Med Sch, Class 1994. *

KOGER, DR. MICHAEL PIGOTT, SR.
Physician. **Personal:** Born Jan 20, 1953, Baltimore, MD; son of Linwood and Margaret Pigott; children: Michael Pigott Jr. **Educ:** Fisk Univ; MIT; Meharry Med Col, MD, 1979. **Career:** Franklin Sq Hosp, resident physician, 1979-82; Provident Hosp, med staff, 1982-85; N Charles Gen Hosp, med staff, 1982-85; Jai Med Ctr, internist, 1982-84; Constant Care Med Ctr, internist 1984; Basil Health Systs, internist, 1985; St Joseph Hosp, physician 1985; Lutheran Hosp, house physician, 1985; Hancock Memorial Hosp, internist, 1985-86; Sparta Health Care Ctr, internist, 1986; Veterans Admin Med Ctr, internist, 1986-88; Cent State Hosp, med staff, 1988-92; Northwest Geog Regional Hosp, physician, 1992-96; S DeKalb Family Health Serv, 1997; Complete Wellness Med Ctr, 1997. **Orgs:** Certified in Basic Cardiac Life Support 1981, 1985, 1986, 1988-92; certified in Advanced Cardiac Life Support 1981, 1985; Baltimore City Medical Soc, 1983-, Med & Chirurgical Fac MD, 1983-; chmn, Hancock Co Bd Health Sparta GA, 1985-86; Med Asn GA, 1985-86; chmn, Dept Utilization Hancock Memorial Hosp Review & Qual Assurance, 1985-86; chmn physician's peer, Utilization Review Comm Hancock Memorial Hosp, 1985-86; vpres med staff, Hancock Memorial Hosp, 1986; Am Soc Internal Med, 1988-. **Honors/Awds:** Physician's Recognition Award, Am Med Asn, 1985; Physician's Recognition Award, Am Med Asn, 1988; Physician's Recognition Award, The Am Med Asn, 1991. **Special Achievements:** publication "Your Health," a weekly column in The Sparta Ishmaelite newspaper 1985-86.

KOMUNYAKAA, YUSEF (JAMES WILLIE BROWN, JR.)
Poet, educator. **Personal:** Born Apr 29, 1947, Bogalusa, LA; married Reetika Vazirani, Jan 1, 1990; children: Jahan; married Mandy Sayer, 1985 (divorced); children: 1. **Educ:** Univ Colo, BA, 1975; Colo State Univ, MA, 1979; Univ Calif, Irvine, MFA,creative writing, 1980. **Career:** Writer, poet, essayist, educator; New Orleans Pub Schs, elem teacher; Univ New Orleans, Lakefront, instr Eng & poetry; Colo State Univ, assoc instr Eng compos, 1976-78; Univ Calif, Irvine, teaching asst poetry, writing instr remedial Eng compos, 1980; Univ New Orleans, instr Eng compos & Am lit, 1982-84; poet-in-the-schools, New Orleans, 1984-85; Ind Univ,Bloomington, vis asst prof Eng, 1985-86, assoc prof Eng & African Am Studies, 1986-93, Ruth Lilly Prof, 1989-90, prof Eng & African Am Studies, 1993-98; Univ Calif, Berkeley, vis prof Eng, 1991, Holloway lectr, 1992; Princeton Univ, Coun Univ Ctr Creative & Performing Arts, prof, 1997-; Books: Dedications & Other Dark horses, 1977; Lost in the Bone wheel Factory, 1979; Copacetic, 1984; I Apologize for the Eyes in My Head, 1986; Toys in a Field, 1986; Dien Cai Dau, 1988; February in Sydney (chapbook), 1989; Magic City, 1992; Neon Vernacular: New & Selected Poems, 1993; The Insomnia of Fire by Nguyen Quang Thieu, 1995; Thieves of Paradise, 1998; Talking Dirty to the Gods, 2000; Blue Notes: Essays, Interviews, & Commentaries, 2000; Pleasure Dome: New & Collected Poems, 2001; Taboo: The Wishbone Trilogy, Part One, 2004; Gilgamesh: A Verse Play, 2006; co-ed: The Second Set: The Jazz Poetry Anthology, Vol 2, 1996; Best American Poetry 2003, 2003; auth essay: Covenant: Scenes from an African American Church, 2007; New York Univ, prof, currently. **Orgs:** Phi Beta Kappa; Alpha Iota Chap. **Honors/Awds:** Kenyon Review Award Literary Excellence, 1991; San Francisco Poetry Center Award; Nat Endowment for Arts, two creative writing fellowships; Claremont Grad Sch, Kingsley Tufts Poetry Award, 1994; Pulitzer Prize for Poetry, 1994; William Faulkner Prize, Univ Rennes, 1994; Thomas Forcade Award; Hanes Poetry Prize; Fellowships, Fine Arts Work Ctr Province town, La Arts Coun & Nat Endowment Arts; Shelley Memorial Award, Poetry Soc Am; Ruth Lily Prize for Poetry, 2001; Louisiana Writer Award, 2007. **Military Serv:** AUS, 1969; Awarded Bronze Star; "Southern Star" correspondent, ed. **Business Addr:** Professor, New York University, 70 Washington Square South, 1213 C, Bobst, NY 10012, **Business Phone:** (212)998-2415.

KONDWANI, KOFI ANUM
Consultant, educator. **Personal:** Born Mar 11, 1955, Dayton, OH. **Educ:** Maharishi Int Univ, Fairfield IA, PhD; Can Col Redwood City, Calif, attended 1979; Univ Calif, Davis, attended 1980. **Career:** AUS, admin asst Korea, 1972-75; Can Col, Redwood City, Calif, recruitment consult, 1976-78; TMC Inc, San Francisco, transcendental meditation teacher, 1977-; Univ Calif, Davis, recruitment consult, 1979-80; James ETolleson, public rel rep; Dayton & Calif, syndicated columnist; Univ Calif, affirmative action officer; Morehouse Sch Med, Atlanta, GA, Dept Community Health & Prev Med, asst prof, currently, Global Health Task Force, chair, 2007-; Nat Ctr Primary Care, Morehouse Sch Med, consult, currently. **Orgs:** Nat Asn Advan Colored People, 1978-; vpres, Black Health Sci, 1979-80. **Honors/Awds:** Award of Gratitude, Maharishi Int Univ, 1977; Eula Dyer Award, E Palo Alto, Calif, 1979; Citizens Against Racism Scholarship, Redwood City,Calif, 1979. **Military Serv:** AUS, E-4, 1972-75. **Business Addr:** Assistant Professor, Chair of Global Health Task Force, Morehouse School of Medicine, Department of Community Health and Preventive Medicine, 720 Westview Dr SW Suite 212, Atlanta, GA 30310.

KOONCE, GEORGE
Football player, football executive. **Personal:** Born Oct 15, 1968, New Bern, NC; married Tunisia; children: George & Jayla. **Educ:** E Carolina Univ, MS, sports mgt, 2006. **Career:** Football player (retired), Football executive; Green Bay Packers, linebacker, 1992-99; Seattle Seahawks, 2000; E Carolina Univ, special asst athletic dir, 2004-06; Green Bay Packers, dir player develop, 2006; Marquette Univ, sr assoc athletic dir; Univ Wisconsin-Milwaukee, dir Athletics . currently. **Orgs:** Founder, George Koonce Sr Found. **Honors/Awds:** Hall of Fame, Nat Junior Col, 2000; Athletic Hall of Fame, E carolina univ, 2002; Athletic Hall of Fame, Chowan Col, 2003, Hall of Fame, W Craven High Sch, 2005. *

KOONCE, NORMAN L.
Executive. **Educ:** La State Univ, attended 1956. **Career:** Executive (retired); Bogalusa City, city planning comn; Am Inst Architects, vpres, 1988-89, pres & chief exec officer, 1989-05. **Orgs:** pres, secy, treas, La Architects Asn, 1978-82; Am Archit Found, 1998; Nat Campfire Girls & Boys; St. Paul's Cathedral Trust; Boyer Ctr Advan Studies; Nat Ctr Preserv Technol & Training. **Honors/Awds:** Edward C Kemper Award, Am Inst Architects, 1998; Doctor of Humanities, Northwestern State Univ, 2001. *

KORNEGAY, DR. WADE M
Scientist. **Personal:** Born Jan 9, 1934, Mt Olive, NC; son of Gilbert and Estelle Williams; married Bettie Joyce Hunter; children: Melvin, Cynthia & Laura. **Educ:** NC Cent Univ, BS, 1956; Bonn Univ Ger, attemded 1957; Univ Calif, Berkeley, PhD, 1961; Mass Inst Technol Sloan Sch Mgt, attended 1979. **Career:** Scientist (retired); Univ Calif, postdoctoral fel, 1961-62, res assoc, 1962; Mass Inst Technol, tech staff mem, 1962-71, Radar Signature Studies, tech group leader, 1971-86, assoc div head, 1986-93, Radar Measurements, div head, 1993-2000, div fel. **Orgs:** Am Phys Soc, 1959-; Sigma Xi Sci Res Soc, 1960-; vpres, Humphrey's Task Force Youth Motivation, 1964-68; exec coun, United Church Christ, 1971-77; bd dir, Nat Consortium Black Prof Develop, 1976-80; Boston City Mission Soc, 1977-; YMCA MA & RI Camp Community, 1977-99; NYAS, 1984-99; AMR IST Aeronaut & Astronauts, 1986-; Alpha Phi Alpha; chmn, bd dirs, Two State YMCA, 1990-94; US Army Sci Bd, 1990-98; bd trustees, Andover Newton Theol Sch, 2001-. **Honors/Awds:** Fulbright Fellowship, US State Dept, 1956-57; Grad Fellowship, Danforth Found, 1956-61; Nat Science Found Postdoctoral Fellowship, 1961-62; Honor ScD, Lowell Univ, 1969; Black Achiever Award, Boston YMCA, 1979; ML King Jr Achievement Award, Mass Inst Technol, 1980; Scientist of the Year, Nat Soc Black Engrs, 1990. **Military Serv:** AUS, Outstanding Civilian Service Medal, 2000.

KORNEGAY, WILLIAM F
Labor relations manager. **Personal:** Born Mar 9, 1933, Apalachicola, FL; married Dorothy L Little; children: Bill Jr. **Educ:** Bethune-Cookman Col, BS 1954; Fla A&M Univ, MEd, 1961; Univ of Ill, PhD 1970. **Career:** Rosenwald HS FL, head sci dept, 1957-58; Univ HS FL, head sci dept 1958-61; Hampton Jr Col, instr sci & math, 1961-66; Bethune-Cookman Col FL, asst prof math, 1966-67, acad dean instr, 1970-74; Ford fel, 1967; Univ Ill, coord math teachers, 1967-70; Gen Motors Inst, dean stud affairs, 1974-79; Fisher Body Div, dir, Qual Work Life, 1979-82; Gen Motors Corp, Detroit, MI, dir, res & devt, 1982-85; Gen Motors Corp, Flint, MI, dir, personnel, 1985-. **Orgs:** Phi Delta Kappa Educ Frat, 1965; bd trustees, Jr Achievement, 1975-80; bd trustees, Flint Urban Leag, 1977-79; bd trustees, United Way Chpn Allocations Com; 1978-80; life mem, Alpha Phi Alpha Frat. **Military Serv:** AUS, 1954-56. **Home Addr:** 1486 Kennebec, Flint, MI 48507. **Business Addr:** Director of Personnel, General Motors Corporation, 6060 W Bristol Rd, Flint, MI 48554, **Business Phone:** (810)635-5612.

KOTTO, YAPHET
Television producer, actor, administrator. **Personal:** Born Nov 15, 1937, New York, NY; son of Yaphet Manga Bell and Gladys Maria; married Antoinette Pettyjohn, Jan 29, 1975; children: Natasha, Fredrick, Robert, Sarada, Mirabai & Salina; married Tessie Sinahon, 1997. **Career:** Appeared in Off-Broadway & Broadway productions including: Great White Hope, Blood Knot, Black Monday, In White America, A Good Place to Raise a Boy; Films: Nothing But a Man, 1964; Liberation of Lord Byron Jones, 1968;The Thomas Crown Affair, 1968; Man & Boy, 1972; Live & Let Die, 1973; Across 110th St, 1973; Report to the Commissioner, 1974; Sharks Treasure, 1975; Monkey Hustle, 1975; Drum, 1976; Blue Collar, 1978; Alien, 1979; Brubaker, 1980; Fighting Back, 1981; Hey Good Looking, 1982; Star Chamber, 1983; Eye of the Tiger, 1986; Pretty kill, 1987; Midnight Run, 1988; The Running Man, 1988; Extreme Justice, 1993; Out of Sync, 1994; The Puppet masters, 1994; Two If by Sea, 1996; Witless Protection, 2008; TV appearances: "Losers Weepers", 1967; "The Big Valley", 1967; "High Chaparral", 1968; "Daniel Boone", 1968; "Hawaii Five-O", 1969; "Mannix", 1969; "The Name of the Game", 1970; "Gunsmoke", 1970; "Night Chase", 1970; "Doctors Hosp", 1975; "Raid on Entebee", 1977; "Death in A Minor Key", 1979; "Women on San Quentin",1983; "For Love & Honor", 1983; "Rage", 1984; "Harem", 1986; "In Self Defense", 1987; "Badge of the Assassin"; "The Defenders: Payback", 1997; "Homicide: The Movie", 2000; "The Ride", 2000; "Stiletto Dance", 2001, "Witless Protection", 2008; TV series: "Homicide", 1993-99. **Special Achievements:** Author, Royalty; author, The Second Coming of Christ. **Business Phone:** (212)664-4444.

KOUNTZE, VALLERY J
Executive. **Personal:** Born in Cambridge, MA; daughter of Wallace H and Alberta M Yearwood Jackman. **Educ:** Chamberlain Sch Retailing, Boston, MA, 1975; USC Grad Sch Bus, Los Angeles, Calif, CME, 1986. **Career:** Mainstreet Commun, Los Angeles, Calif, vpres, 1981-83; RCA & Columbia Pictures Home Video, Los Angeles, Calif, vpres mkt, 1983-85, vpres, gen mgr mm & div, 1985-86; Repub Pictures Home Video, Los Angeles, Calif, vpres, mkt, 1986-87, sr vpres sales & mkt, 1987-89, pres, 1989-91; Main St Mkt, Los Angeles, Calif, pres, 1991-92; ITC Home Video, Los Angeles, Calif, exec vpres, gen mgr, 1992-; Films: The Film Phenomenon, exec producer, 2002, The High Octane Birth of a Superstar, exec producer, 2002. **Orgs:** Bd dir, AIDS Proj Los Angeles, 1990-; pres & steering comt, 1989-, bd dir, Entertainment AIDS Alliance, currently; Video Software Dealers Asn IAB, 1990-; founding mem, Video Industry AIDS Action Comt; chairperson, Break Cycle's Bd Dir. **Honors/Awds:** National Superior Achiever Award, RKO Gen Broadcasting, 1977; Bronze Merchandising Achievement Award, Point Purchase Advert Inst, 1984; Gold Merchandising Achievement Award, Point Purchase Advert Inst, 1985. **Business Phone:** (213)833-6694.

KRAFT, DR. BENJAMIN F.
School administrator. **Personal:** Born Jan 15, 1948, Baton Rouge, LA; son of Benjamin F Kraft and Frances H Simons; married Yanick Douyon; children: Benjamin Robeson, Phillip Fouchard & Guileine Frances. **Educ:** Rutgers Col, BA, 1970; Northeastern Univ, JD, 1973; Am Univ, MBA, 1978. **Career:** Nat Labor Rels Bd, staff atty, 1973-77; Caribsun Export-Import Inc, pres, 1977-79; Big Ben Hardware Haiti, owner/gen mgr, 1979-86; Fla Mem Col, assoc dir, ctr community change, 1986-87, chairperson, Div Bus Admin, 1988-89, 1990-91, assoc dean fac, 1989-90, dir, Govt Rels & Sponsored Progs, 1992-. **Orgs:** DC Bar Assoc, 1974-; credit community mem, NLRB Fed Credit Union, 1975-77; bd mem, treas, Haitian Am Chamber Com, 1984-86; Haitian Found Aid Women, 1985-86; bd mem Carib Am Enterprises Fla Inc, 1986-; bd mem, Ctr Family & Child Enrichment, 1988-90; Alpha Phi Alpha Frat Inc; Beta Beta Lambda 1989-; Nat Asn Advan Colored People; 100 Black Men S Fla Inc, 1990-. **Honors/Awds:** ACE fel, Am Coun Educ, 1991-92. **Military Serv:** USAF, Reserves capt, 4 yrs. **Home Addr:** 1430 Hawkins Mdw, San Antonio, TX 78248-1572. **Business Addr:** Director Government Relations, Sponsored Programs, Florida Memorial College, 15800 NW 42nd Ave, Miami, FL 33054, **Business Phone:** (305)626-3600.

KRAFT, KERRY. See JOHNSON, KERRY GERARD.

KRAVITZ, LENNY (LEONARD ALBERT KRAVITZ)
Singer. **Personal:** Born May 26, 1964, New York, NY; son of Seymour Kravitz (deceased) and Roxie Roker (deceased); married Lisa Bonet, 1987 (divorced 1993); children: Zoe Isabella. **Career:** Wrote "Justify My Love" for Madonna, 1990; Films: Coyote Ugly, performer, 2000; Blue Crush, writer, 2002; Bruce Almighty, writer, 2003; Peace One Day, writer, 2004; I'm Going to Tell You a Secret, writer, 2005; Precious: Based on the Novel Push by Sapphire, 2009; TV: "Alias", 2003; "One Tree Hill", 2004; "My Super

Sweet 16", 2005;"Ha-Shminiya", 2006; "60/90"; 2008; Albums: Let Love Rule, 1989; Mama Said, 1991; Are You Gonna Go My Way, 1993; Circus, 1995; 5, 1998; Greatest Hits, 2000; Lenny, 2001; Baptism, 2004; It Is Time for a Love Revolution, 2008; Singles: "Spirit of the Forest", 1989; "Let Love Rule", 1989; "I Built This Garden for Us", 1990; "Mr. Cab Driver", 1990; "Always on the Run", 1991; "It Ain't Over 'Til It's Over", 1991; "Fields of Joy", 1990; "Stand by My Woman", 1990; "What the Fuck Are We Saying?", 1990; "Stop Draggin' Around", 1990; "What Goes Around Comes Around", 1990; "Are You Gonna Go My Way", 1993; "Believe", 1993; "Heaven Help", 1993; "Is There Any Love in Your Heart", 1993; "Heaven Help", 1994; "Spinning Around Over You", 1994; "Deuce", 1994; "Rock & Roll Is Dead", 1995; "Circus", 1995; "Can't Get You Off My Mind", 1996; "The Resurrection", 1996; "I Belong to You", 1998; "If You Can't Say No", 1998; "Thinking of You", 1998; "Fly Away", 1999; "Black Velveteen", 1999; "American Woman", 1999; "Again", 2000; "Dig In", 2001;"Stillness of Heart", 2002; "Believe in Me", 2002; "If I Could Fall inLove", 2002; "Show Me Your Soul", 2004; "Where Are We Runnin'?", 2004; "California", 2004; "Storm", 2004; "Calling All Angels", 2005; "Lady",2005; "Breathe", 2005; "Bring It On", 2007; "I'll Be Waiting", 2007; "Love Love Love", 2008. **Honors/Awds:** Numerous awards and nominations including MTV Video Award, best male video, 1993; Grammy Award nominations, best rock song & best solo rock vocal performance, 1993; Best Male Rock Vocal Performance, 1999-02; VH1/Vogue Fashion Award, 1999; four Grammies, 1998, 1999, 2000, 2001; Am Music Award, 2002. **Business Addr:** Vocalist, Creative Artists Agency, 9830 Wilshire Blvd, Beverly Hills, CA 90212, **Business Phone:** (310)288-4545.*

KRIGGER, DR. MARILYN FRANCIS
Educator. **Personal:** Born Mar 27, 1940, St Thomas, Virgin Islands of the United States; daughter of Charles Adolphus and Mary Augusta Skelton; married Rudolph E Sr; children: Rudolph E Jr. **Educ:** Spelman Col, BA, social sci, 1959; Columbia Univ, MA, hist, 1960; Univ Del, PhD, hist, 1983. **Career:** Charlotte Amalie High Sch, St Thomas, soc stud teacher, 1960-66; Univ VI, St Thomas, hist prof, hist prof emer, currently. **Orgs:** VI Hist Soc; Assoc Caribbean Hist; Phi Alpha Theat; consult, VI; dept Ed; VI, Hum Coun; VI State Rev Bd hist; VI, 2000; VI Bd Ed, 1974-76; co-chair, VI Status Comm, 1988-93. **Honors/Awds:** John Hay Whitney Found Fel, 1959-60; African Am Inst Ed-to-Africa Prog, 1972; Natl Endowment Human, Summer Fels, 1976-88. **Home Addr:** Crown Mountain Rd, PO Box 4099, St Thomas, Virgin Islands of the United States 00803, **Home Phone:** (809)776-8342. **Business Addr:** Professor Emeritus, University of the Virgin Islands, 2 John Brewer, St Thomas, Virgin Islands of the United States 00802-9990, **Business Phone:** (340)693-1057.

KROON, MARC JASON
Baseball player. **Personal:** Born Apr 2, 1973, Bronx, NY. **Career:** San Diego Padres, pitcher, 1995, 1997-98; Memphis, 1996; Las Vegas, 1997; Indianapolis Indians, 1998; Cincinnati Reds, 1998; Azl Mariners, 1999;Tacoma Rainiers, 1999; Albuquerque Isotopes, 2000; Arkansas Travelers, 2003; Salt Lake Stingers, 2003; Colorado Springs Sky Sox, 2003; Colorado Rockies, relief pitcher, 2004-05; Yokohama Bay Stars, Japan's Central League, 2005-07; Yomiuri Giants, 2008-. *

KUMANYIKA, DR. SHIRIKI K
Nutritionist, educator. **Personal:** Born Mar 16, 1945, Baltimore, MD; daughter of Maurice Laphonso Adams and Catherine Victoria Williams; married Christiaan Morssink, Jun 19, 1986; children: Chenjerai. **Educ:** Syracuse Univ Col Arts & Sci, BA, psychol, 1965; Columbia Univ, MS, social work, 1969; Cornell Univ, PhD, human nutrit, 1978; Johns Hopkins Univ, Sch Hyg & Pub Health, MPH, epidemiol, 1984. **Career:** James Weldon Johnson Ment Health Clin; Bird S Coler Hosp; Windham Child Serv, caseworker, 1965-69; Nat Urban League, Family Planning Proj, dir, 1969-70; Addiction Res & Treat Corp, Dept Educ & Prevent, community organizer, 1970-71; Naomi Gray Assoc New York, proj dir, 1971-72; Cornel Univ, Ujamaa Residential Col, resident dir, 1973-74, Div Nutrit Sci, Gen Mills fel, 1974-76, Quaker Oats fel, 1976-77, asst prof, 1977-84; Johns Hopkins Univ Sch Hyg & Pub Health, asst prof, 1984-89, assoc prof, 1989; Pa State Univ, Univ Park, Pa, assoc prof, sr scholar epidemiol, currently, prof epidemiol, currently, Health Prom & Dis Prev, assoc dean, currently, Grad Prog Pub Health Studies, dir, currently, Inst Aging, sr fel, currently, Leonard Davis Inst Health Econ, sr fel, currently, Children's Hosp Philadelphia Dept Pediat, Sect Nutrit, prof epidemiol, currently; Ctr Pub Health Initiatives, sr adv, currently, Dept Biostatistics & Epidemiol, Sch Med, prof epidemiol, currently, Ctr Clin Epidemiol & Biostatistics, Sch Med, sr scholar, currently, Penn-Cheyney Export Ctr Inner City Health, dir, currently. **Orgs:** Am Public Health Asn, 1976-, chair, Food & Nutrit Sect, Equal Health Opportunity Comt; Asn Black Cardiologists; Black Caucus Health Workers; Soc Nutrit Educ; Soc Epidemiol Res; fel Am Col Nutrit; Am Dietetic Asn, 1979-; Am Inst Nutrit, 1990-; Am Soc Clin Nutrit, 1990-; bd dir, Health Prom Coun Southeastern Pa. **Honors/Awds:** Publ & abstr: "Towards a Lower Sodium Lifestyle in Black Communities," J Nat Med Asn, 1985; "Obesity in Black Women," Epidemiol Reviews, 1987; "Beliefs about High Blood Pressure Prevention in a Sample of Black and Hispanic Adults," Am J Preventive Med; "Designing Sodium Reduction Strategies: Problems and Solutions," Clin Nutrit, 1989; "Asn between Oity and Hypertension in Blacks," Clin Cardiol, 1989; "Diet and Chronic Disease Issues for Minority Populations," J Nutrit Educ, 1990; "Theoretical and Baseline Considerations for Diet and Weight Control of Diabetes among Blacks," Diabetes Care, 1990.

KUMBULA, DR. TENDAYI SENGERWE
Educator. **Personal:** Born Nov 3, 1947, Epworth, Harare, Zimbabwe; son of Isaac Sengerwe and Mandinema Edna Mungate; married Barbara Ann Jackson, May 8, 1971; children: Mandinema R, Runako T & Tendayi S Jr. **Educ:** San Diego State Univ, San Diego, BA (hon) jour, 1968; Univ Calif, Los Angeles, MA, jour, 1969, MA, polit sci, 1970; Univ SC, PhD, 1976. **Career:** Los Angeles Times, CA, reporter, 1968-82; Sunday Mail, Harare, Zimbabwe news ed, 1982-83; Herald, Harare, Zimbabwe, asst ed, 1984-86; Calif State Univ, Long Beach, CA, lectr, 1987-89; Ball State Univ, Muncie, Ind, asst prof jour & news ed seq crd, 1989-; Poynter Inst Media Studies fel, 2002; Am Press Inst fel, 2003; Am Soc Newspaper Ed fel, 2003. **Orgs:** Nat Asn Black Journalists, 1990-; founder, fac adv, Nat Asn Black Journalists Study Chap, Ball State Univ, 1990-; Soc Prof Journalists, 1989-; Asn Educ Jour & Mass Comm, 1990-; African Studies Asn, 1991-; bd trustees, Motivate Our Minds, 1992, bd, 1996-; Muncie Chap Ind Black Expo; Int Platform Asn; overseas dir, M'pisaunga, Mutandiro & Assocs, Harare, Zimbabwe; chair, Ball State Jour Dept, Multicult Affairs Adv Comt; Asn Third World Countries; Ind Consortium Int Prog; Nat Alliance Black Sch Educrs Minorities & Media. **Honors/Awds:** DuMont Scholarship, Univ Calif, Los Angeles, 1968-69; Top Student Reporter, San Diego State Univ, 1968; Sigma Delta Chi Golden Press Card, 1968; Phi Delta Kappa, Educ Honor Soc, 1976; Chief Munsee Award, City Muncie, Ind, 1994. **Special Achievements:** Research in Southern Africa on the drought, 1993; Publish articles: adviser The Muncie Times, newspapers; co-writer, The Muncie Times; contributor LA/Accent Newspapers; North American contributor to the Southern African Political of Economic Monthly, Harare, Zimbabwe; co-author of "The Process of Media Writing", 1997. **Home Phone:** (765)289-6930. **Business Addr:** Professor, Ball State University, Department of Journalism, Rm 300 Art & Jour Bldg 2000 W Univ Ave, Muncie, IN 47306, **Business Phone:** (765)285-1625.

KUNES, KEN R.
Insurance executive. **Personal:** Born Feb 7, 1932, Maywood, IL; son of Arthur F and Emily M; divorced; children: Ken, Leigh Ann, Jeff. **Educ:** Univ AZ, attended 1949; NE Univ, BS, 1955. **Career:** Phoenix-Am Inst Agency, fdr, 1965-85; Maricopa Co, assessor, 1968-81; Mid-City Glass & Mirror, owner, 1986; Security Reliable Inst, pres & chief exec officer. **Orgs:** Independent Ins Agents Asn; Phoenix Jaycees; vpres, Kiwanis; state rep, Int Asn Assessing Officers; past pres, Ariz Asn Assessing Officers; chmn, Maricopa Cty Sheriff's Religious Comn; licensed res, N Phoenix Baptist Church; Alpha Tau Omega Fraternity; Moon Valley Country Club; Phoenix Chamber Comn. **Honors/Awds:** Boss of year, Phoenix Midtowners Bus & Prof Women's Club, 1975; rec Cert Appraisal Evaluator prof design Int Asn Assessing Officers. **Military Serv:** AUS, sgt. *

KUNJUFU, JAWANZA
Writer, consultant. **Personal:** Born Jun 15, 1953, Chicago, IL; son of Mary Snyder Brown and Eddie Brown; married Rita Archer Kunjufu, Jun 1, 1985; children: Walker, Shik. **Educ:** Illinois State Univ, Normal, IL, BA, 1974; Union Graduate Institute, Cincinnati, OH, PhD, 1984. **Career:** African Am Images, Chicago, IL, pres, 1980-; Full feature film "Up Against The Wall," executive producer. **Orgs:** Founder, Unity; Living Word Christian Ctr. **Special Achievements:** Author of 18 books. **Business Addr:** President, African Am Images, 1909 W 95th St, Chicago, IL 60643, **Business Phone:** (312)445-0322.*

KUYKENDALL, DR. CRYSTAL ARLENE
Educator, lawyer. **Personal:** Born Dec 11, 1949, Chicago, IL; daughter of Cleophus Avant and Ellen Campbell Logan; married Roosevelt Kuykendall Jr, Apr 10, 1969 (deceased); children: Kahlil, Rasheki & Kashif. **Educ:** Southern Ill Univ, BA, 1970; Montclair State Univ, MA, 1972; Atlanta Univ, Ed.D, 1975; Georgetown Univ Law Ctr, JD, 1982. **Career:** Seton Hall US Orange NJ, Montclair State Univ, instr, 1971-73; DC Pub Sch, admin intern planning res & eval, 1974-75; Nat Comt Citizens Ed, dir,1975-77; Nat Sch Boards Assoc, Wash, DC, dir, urban & minority rel dept,1978-79; PSI Assoc Inc, Wash, DC, dir ed devel, 1979-80; Nat Alliance Black Sch Ed, exec dir, 1980-81; Roy Little john Assoc Inc, sr assoc,1982-; Kreative & Innovative Resources Kids, founder, pres & gen coun, 1989-. **Orgs:** Am Asn Sch Admin, 1974-; mem ed task force, Martin Luther King Jr Ctr Soc Change, 1977-; chmn, Nat Adv Coun Continuing Ed, 1978-81; consult, Nat Teachers Corp Proj, 1978-79; Black Am Law Students Asn, 1978-; cons, mem, Nat Transition Team Office Elem Sec Ed, 1980; Am Bar Asn, Nat Bar Asn, DCBar Asn, 1988, assoc supvr & curric developer, 1992-; bd dirs, HealthPower Inc, 1994-2002; bd dirs, Congressional Youth Leadership Coun, 1995-; bd dirs, Family Life Ctr, Shiloh Baptist Church, 1996-. **Honors/Awds:** Presidential Appointment to The Natl Advisory Council on Continuing Educ,US Pres, Jimmy Carter 1978-81, chairperson 1979-81; "50 Leaders of the Future" Ebony Mag 1978; Awd for Outstanding Comm Serv to Women &Minorities, Natl Coalition of Esea Title I Parents 1979; Hon Citizen New Orleans State of LA, Outstanding Serv Natl Caucus of Black School Bd Mems1979; Black Excellence Award, Black Alumni Asn of Southern IL Univ 1981;Urban League of Greater Muskegon, Service Award; Natl Assn of Blacks in Criminal Justice, Service Award; honarary Doctorate of Human Letters,Lewis & Clark Coll, 2002. **Special Achievements:** Auth, "Comm Serv & School Bd", Publ Cross Ref Jour Multicult Ed, 1979;You/Yours: Making the Most of this School Year, motivational calender,1987; booklets publ: "Improving Black Student Achievement Through Enhancing Self-Image", Am Univ Mid-Atlantic Equity Ctr, 1989; "From Rage to Hope: Strategies for Reclaiming Black & Hispanic Students", Nat Educ Serv Inc, 1992; auth, Dreaming of a PHAT Century, 2000. **Business Addr:** President, Kreative & Innovative Resources for Kids Inc, 8925 Harvest Sq Ct, Potomac, MD 20854, **Business Phone:** (301)299-2057.

KWAKU-DONGO, FRANCOIS
Chef. **Personal:** Married Ruth; children: Joseph-Paul & Christine-Elizabeth. **Educ:** Manhattan's Borough Col. **Career:** Alo Alo Restaurant, part-time prep cook; Antonucci, Remi, NY, sous chef; Marc Meneau L'Esperance; Bernard Loiseau Cote D'Or; Baumaniere Provence; Trois Gros Roasanne; Spago Chicago, executive chef & managing partner; L'Escale, exec chef, currently. **Orgs:** Meals On Wheels; Ronald McDonald Found; Rita Hayworth Alzheimer's Asn. **Business Addr:** Executive Chef, L'Escale, 500 Steamboat Rd, Greenwich, CT 06830, **Business Phone:** (203)661-4600.

KWEKU, BABAKUBWA. See DAVIS, DR. WILLIE.

KWELI, TALIB (TALIB KWELI GREENE)
Rap musician. **Personal:** Born Oct 3, 1975, Brooklyn, NY; son of Brenda Greene; married D J Eque. **Educ:** NY Univ, exp theatre. **Career:** Albums: Black Star, 1998; Reflection Eternal, 2000; Quality, 2002; The Beautiful Struggle, 2004; Right About Now, 2005; Liberation, 2006; Eardrum, 2007; Liberation, 2007; Hold it Down, 2008; MCA Rec, rec artist, currently. **Orgs:** Black August Benefit Concert . **Business Addr:** Recording Artist, c/o MCA Records Inc, 2220 Colorado Ave Suite 1, Santa Monica, CA 90404, **Business Phone:** (310)865-4500.*

KYLE, GENGHIS
Band musician, bandleader. **Personal:** Born Jun 7, 1923, Los Angeles, CA; married Dorothy F; children: Alfred C & Marie J. **Educ:** Los Angeles City Col; Univ SC, Ext. **Career:** Vultee Aircraft Co, sub assembler, 1942; City Los Angeles, Calif Dept Water & Power, storekeeper, 1954-82; Genghis Kyle Enterprises, bandleader, personal mgr. **Orgs:** Broadcast Music Inc; Local 47 Musicians Union; shop co-dir, Signature Music Pub Co Imperial Youth Theater Work; Coaches & Mgr Assoc LA. **Honors/Awds:** Salute to Stars Award, 1963. **Military Serv:** AUS, pfc, 1943-46; sgt ES, 1950. **Business Addr:** bandleader, Genghis Kyle Enterprises, 1544 W 93 St, Los Angeles, CA 90047.

KYLES, CEDRIC ANTONIO. See THE ENTERTAINER, CEDRIC.

KYLES, DWAIN JOHANN
Lawyer. **Personal:** Born Aug 25, 1954, Chicago, IL; son of Samuel Billy and Gwendolyn Kyles Griffin; married Theresa Cropper, Jun 19, 1988; children: Chad Joseph. **Educ:** Lake Forest Col, BA, econ urban study, 1976; Georgetown Univ, Law Ctr, JD, 1979. **Career:** Congressman Harold Ford 9th Dist TN, staff aide, 1976-78; Off Civil Rights Dept Health Educ & Welfare, law clerk, 1978-79; Johnson Prods Co, staff atty, 1979-83; Off Mayor Harold Wash, spec coun minority bus develop, 1983-84; McCormick Place Conv Ctr, house coun, mgt & intergovt liaison, 1984-88; Grill Inc, owner, 1987; Dept Econ Develop, spec coun comnr, 1989; Le Mirage Studio Ltd, pres & owner. **Orgs:** Am Bar Asn; Nat Bar Asn, 1979; Cook City Bar Asn, 1979; bd mem, Forum Evolution Progressive Arts, 1983-; founder & pres, New Chicago Comt; Operation PUSH, Nat Asn Advan Colored People. **Honors/Awds:** Mentor of the Year, Urban Focus, 1984.

L

LABAT, ERIC MARTIN
Oceanographer, scientist. **Personal:** Born May 8, 1962, Bay St Louis, MS; son of Rudolph H and Geraldine T; married Katrina R Lane, Jun 5, 1993; children: Arielle. **Educ:** Univ Southern Miss, BS, 1985; Naval Post Grad Sch, attended 1987; Faith Grant Col, Birmingham, AL, DLaw, 1994; Univ New Orleans. **Career:** Naval Oceanog Off, phys sci trainee, 1980-83, comput sci trainee, 1983-85; mathematician, 1986-91, oceanographer, 1991-. **Orgs:** Alpha Phi Alpha Fraternity; pres, Zeta Mu Lambda, 1991-94; vpres, St Rose de Lima Cath Church Pastoral Coun, 1991-93; chair, Magic's AYSE Prog, 1992-95; black employ prog coord, Naval Oceanog Off EEOC, 1990-; Marine Technol Soc, 1992-; NCP, 1990-; co-chair, GPS Enhancements VII, Joint Navig Conf, 2007; Blacks In Govt Stennis Chap. **Honors/Awds:** Walter "Duke" Wil-

liams Alumni Brother of the Year, Alpha Phi Alpha Fraternity, 1992; COT Service Award, N Gulfport Civic Club, 1991; Am Best & Brightest Bus & Prof Men, Dollars & Sense Mag, 1991. **Business Addr:** Oceanographer, Naval Oceanographic Office, 1002 Balch Blvd Code N333, Stennis Space Center, MS 39529-5001, **Business Phone:** (228)688-4389.

LABEACH, NICOLE ANN
Consultant, chief executive officer, public speaker. **Personal:** Married Calvin Thomas IV. **Educ:** Spelman Col, BA, psychol; St Louis Univ, MA, clin psychol, PhD, orgn psychol. **Career:** News Corp; Anheuser Busch Corp; Millenium Consulting, managing dir; Volition Enterprises Inc, chief exec officer, currently. **Orgs:** Founder, Prof Orgn Women (POW); founder, The Brightest Stars Found. **Special Achievements:** Auth, Choose Yourself A Journey Toward Personal Fulfillment for Women; auth, A Woman's True Purpose: Live Like You Matter. **Business Addr:** Chief Executive Officer, Volitions Enterprises Inc, 1740 SW St Lucie W Blvd Suite 159, Port St Lucie, FL 90036.

LABELLE, PATTI (PATRICIA LOUISE HOLTE)
Actor, singer. **Personal:** Born May 24, 1944, Philadelphia, PA; daughter of Henry Holte; married L Armstead Edwards, Jan 1, 1969 (divorced 2000); children: Stanley, Dodd & Zuri. **Career:** Ordettes, singer, 1960; The Blue Belles, singer, 1961-65; Patti LaBelle & the Blue Belles, lead singer, 1965-70; LaBelle, lead singer, 1970-77; solo artist, 1977-; Live AID Benefit Rock Concert; TV specials: PBS production, 1981; Your Arm's Too Short to Box with God, gospel musical, 1981-82; A Soldier's Story, 1985; "Unnatural Causes", 1986; "Sisters in the Name of Love", 1986, "Motown Returns to the Apollo"; "Out All Night", 1992-93; "Santa Baby!", 2001; "Living It Up with Patti LaBelle", exec producer, 2004; "All of Us", 2004; Tommy & Quadrophenia Live: The Who, voice, 2005; On the One, 2005; "Why I Wore Lipstick to My Mastectomy", 2006; Films:Idle wild, 2006; Cover, 2007; Semi-Pro, 2008; Mama, I Want To Sing, 2008; Albums: When A Woman Loves, 2000; Timeless Journey, 2004; Classic Moments, 2005; The Gospel According to Patti LaBelle, 2006; Miss Patti's Christmas, 2007. **Honors/Awds:** B'nai B'rith Creative Achievement Award; Image Award for Musical Excellence, NAACP; Congressional Black Caucus Medallion; Entertainer of the Year Award, NAACP, 1986; Platinum album, "Winner in You", 1986; Grammy Award, 1992; Career Achievement Award, 1996; Essence Award, 1998; Hon Doctor Music Degree, Berklee Col Music, 1996; Lifetime Achievement Award, Songwriters Hall of Fame, 2003. **Special Achievements:** Special Citation from President Ronald Reagan, 1986; Collaborated with Fiori Roberts Cosmetics to create a new line of lip and nail color products; author: Recipes to Sing About; Don't Block the Blessings, 1995; Patti's Pearls: Lessons on Living Genuinely, Joyfully, Generously, 2001; Eight Grammy nominations; three Emmy nominations. **Business Addr:** Singer, Owner, PattisButterflies.com, c/o Paid Inc., 4 Brussels St, Worcester, MA 01610, **Business Phone:** (508)791-6710.

LABODE, MODUPE GLORIA
Educator. **Educ:** Iowa State Univ, BS, hist, 1988, PhD, hist; Oxford Univ, DPhil, hist, 1992. **Career:** Iowa State Univ, Hist Dept, trainee, 1993-94, asst prof hist, 1994-2001; Rhodes Scholar; Colo Hist Soc, Colo Hist Mus, chief historian, dir, 2002-; Harvard Univ, WEB DuBois Inst Afro-Am Res, fel; Mary Ingraham Bunting Inst, Radcliffe Col, Berkshire Summer fel. **Orgs:** Am Asn State & Local Hist; Nat Coun Pub Hist; Orgn Am Historians; Western Hist Asn; Am Hist Asn; African Studies Asn; Coord Coun Women Hist; Rhodes Scholar Selection Comt. **Honors/Awds:** Nat Merit Scholarship, 1983; Truman Scholarship, 1985; Phi Beta Kappa, 1986; Rhodes Scholarship, 1988. **Special Achievements:** Author: A Native Knows A Native, 2000. **Business Phone:** (303)866-5784.

LABRIE, HARRINGTON
Executive. **Personal:** Born Oct 6, 1909, Lebeau, LA; married Ernestine (deceased); children: Dolores Fischer, Ann Marie McCune, Theron, Kenneth J, Willard, Doris Matthew & Janice Domechet. **Career:** St Landry Parish Sch Bd, sch bus driver, 1952-75; Cattle, Cotton, farmer, 1932-; Williams Progressive Life Ins Co, ins agent, 1951-; St Landry Parish Ward 4, justice peace, 1972-; Labrie Realty Corp, chmn bd, 1979-. **Orgs:** Grand knight, Knights Peter Claver, 1932-; NAACP 1956-; La Justice Peace Asn, 1972-; adv bd mem, First Nat Bank, 1978-. **Home Addr:** PO Box 395, Lebeau, LA 71345.

LACEY, BERNARDINE M.
Manager. **Personal:** Born Jul 28, 1932, Vicksburg, MS; daughter of Leroy Jackson and Katie; married Dr Wilbert Lacey, Apr 27, 1970; children: Amando Gomez, Elthon, Jacinta. **Educ:** Gilfoy School Nursing, Miss Bapt Hosp, Jackson, MS, Nursing Diploma, 1962; Georgetown Univ, School Nursing, BSN, 1968; Howard Univ, MA, sociol, 1985; Teachers Col, Columbia Univ, New York, NY, EdD, 1991. **Career:** Howard Univ, Nursing Grad Prog; Col Nursing, asst prof, 1986-94; W K Kellogg-Howard Univ, Col of Nursing, Homeless Project, proj dir, 1988-94; Univ VA, clinical asst, 1991-95; Johns Hopkins School Nursing, lecturer, 1991-93, adjunct asst prof, 1991-93; Howard Univ, Col Medicine, nurse dir, 1993-94; Western Mich Univ, dir school nursing, 1994-99; Prince George's Community Col, chair nursing dept, 2001-; Children's Nat Medical ctr, exec dir, 2002. **Orgs:** Am Academy Nursing; Am Nurses assn; DC Nurses assn; Nat Black Nurses assn; Sigma Theta Tau Int Nurses Honor Soc; Nat League Nursing; Soc Nursing Hist. **Honors/Awds:** Health Policy & Legislative Award, Univ Sch Educ, 1994; Pearl McIver Public Health Nurse Award, Am Nurses Assn, 1994; Community Serv Award, AKA Sorority Inc, Bowie State Univ, Bowie, MD, 1994; Distinguished Alumna Award, Sch Nursing, Goergetown Univ, 1993; Distinguished Scholar Lecturer, James Madison Univ, Dept Nursing, 1992; The Distinguished Scholars Award, W Mich Univ; Presidential Warrior Award, 2005-2006 . **Business Addr:** Chairman, Prince George's Community College, Department of Nursing, 301 Largo Rd, Largo, MD 20774-2199, **Business Phone:** (301)336-6000.*

LACEY, MARC STEVEN
Journalist. **Personal:** Born Nov 11, 1965, New York, NY; son of Earle Milton and Jean Lilian Moran; married Omaira Rivas, Feb 21, 1997. **Educ:** Cornell Univ, Ithaca, NY, BA, 1987; George Wash Univ, Wash, DC, MIPP, 2001. **Career:** Cornell Daily Sun, ed-in-chief; The Wash Post, Wash, DC, intern, summer, 1987; The Buffalo News, Buffalo, NY, journalist, 1987-89; The Los Angeles Times, Los Angeles, CA, suburban reporter, City Hall reporter & Wash corresp, 1989-99; The NY Times, New York, NY, White House corresp, 1999-2001, Nairobi Bureau Chief, Mexico Bureau corresp, currently. **Orgs:** Nal Asn Black Journalists, 1988-; Cornell Univ Alumni Asn, 1989-. **Honors/Awds:** Nat Merit Achievement Scholarship, 1983-87; Quill & Dagger Senior Honor Society, Cornell University, 1987; Cornell Tradition Academic Scholarship Cornell, 1983-85; Summer Research Exchange Program, Univ California, Berkeley Summer, 1985. **Business Addr:** Foreign Correspondent, Mexico City Bureau, New York Times, 1627 I St NW Suite 700, Washington, DC 20006-4007, **Business Phone:** (212)556-7415.

LACEY, DR. MARIAN GLOVER
School administrator. **Educ:** AM&N Col, BA, Eng, 1960; Ind Univ, MEd, 1967; Univ Ark, EdD, 1985, EDAS, 1999. **Career:** Elizabeth Miller Sch, Helena, Eng Dept, chmn & teacher, 1967-69; Dunbar Jr High Sch, Eng Dept, chmn & teacher, 1974-81, prin; Little Rock Cent High Sch, asst prin, 1981-86; Horace Mann Arts & Sci Magnet Jr High Sch, prin, 1988-; Little Rock Sch Dist, Little Rock, AR, asst supt, currently. **Honors/Awds:** Nat Educator Award, Milken Found, 1997. **Business Addr:** Assistant Superintendent, Little Rock School District, 6412 Shirley Dr, Little Rock, AR 72204, **Business Phone:** (501)664-7912.

LACEY, WILBERT
Psychiatrist, educator. **Personal:** Born Dec 1, 1936, Washington, DC; married Bernardine Jackson; children: 4. **Educ:** Howard Univ, BS, 1959, Col Med, MD, 1968; Am Bd Psychiat & Neurol, cert, 1977. **Career:** Howard Univ Col Med, Health Serv, univ psychiatrist, 1973-, clin asst prof, 1975-, internship prof staff, currently. **Orgs:** Fox Ridge Civic Asn, 1977; DC Mem Soc; Nat Med Asn; Am Inst Hypertension; Am Col Health Asn; Metro WA Soc Adolescent Psychiat; Joint Coun WA Psychiat Soc; life mem, Kappa Alpha Psi Frat. **Military Serv:** AUS, 1st lt, 1960-62. **Business Addr:** Psychiatrist, Internship Professional Staff, Howard University, University Counseling Service, 6th & Bryant St NW, Washington, DC 20059, **Business Phone:** (202)806-6870.

LACHMAN, DR. RALPH STEVEN
Physician, educator. **Personal:** Born May 12, 1935; married Rose Katz; children: Nicole & Monette. **Educ:** Temple Univ, BA, 1957; Meharry Med Col, MD, 1961. **Career:** Bronx-Lebanon Med Cntr NYC, rotating intern, 1961-62; AUS Hosp BadKreuznach, Ger, capt, 1964-66; Mt Sinai Hosp NYC, pres, 1962-64; radiol, 1966-68; Children's Hosp Boston, ped radiol, 1969-70; Univ Calif Los Angeles, from asst prof radiology to prof, 1970-99; assoc chair radiology, 1980-99; prof emer 1999-; Dept Pediatrics/Radiology, Stanford Univ, vis scholar, currently; Int Skeletal Dysplasia Registry, Cedars-Sinai Med Ctr, co-founder, currently. **Orgs:** Chmn, Equal Opportunity Acad Affirm Action Comn, Univ Calif Los Angeles,1981-83; Soc Pediatric Radiol; Am Col Radiol; Los Angeles Pediatric Soc; AAAS; Western Soc Pediat Res Am Fedn Clin Respresident; Pac Coast Pediatric Radiol Asn, 1985; mem, Gold Medal Committee, Society for Pediatric Radiology. **Honors/Awds:** Fel, Am Col Radiol, 1983. **Special Achievements:** Published 260 scientific articles, 4 books, 15 book chapters. **Military Serv:** AUS, capt med corps, 1964-66. **Business Addr:** Co-Director, International Skeletal Dysplasia Registry, Cedars-Sinai Medical Center, 8700 Beverly Blvd, Los Angeles, CA 90048.*

LACOUR, LOUIS BERNARD
Lawyer. **Personal:** Born Aug 12, 1926, Columbus, OH; son of Louis and Cleo Carter; married Jane McFarland; children: Lynne Denise, Avril R La Cour-Hartnagel, Cheryl Celeste La Cour-Belyn. **Educ:** Ohio State Univ, BA, 1951; Franklin Univ Law Sch, LLB, 1961; Capital Univ, JD, 1967. **Career:** City Columbus, OH, land acquisition officer, 1959-62; Capital Univ Law Sch, adjunct prof, 1975-80; pvt practice, atty; US Dist Ct, special master, 1981-84; GreenBern Mgt Inc, pres. **Orgs:** Past vpres, develop code adv comn United Comn Coun; Columbus Bar Asn, past pres, Columbus Urban League; past secy, Mid-Ohio Reg Planning Comn; past vpres, Columbus Area Int Prog; Columbus Leadership Conf, Selective Serv Appeals Bd, Fed Bar Exam Comn, Southern Dist, E Div; past vchmn, Columbus Civic Ctr Comn; steering comn, Develop Comt, Greater Columbus; adv bd, Bishop Hartley High Sch; adviser, Univ Area Civic Asn; Eastland Area Civic Asn; Kensington Pk Area Civic Asn; Blendon Meadows Civic Asn; Model Cities Neighborhood Rev Bd, Bethany Homes Develop Corp; Bide-A-Wee Pk Civic Asn; spec master US Dist Ct, 1975-80; fed bar examiner, US Dist Ct, 1980-84; spec coun, Columbus City Atty, 1984-91; trustee, Jazz Arts Group, 1984-85; trustee, Greater Columbus Arts Coun; trustee, Ohio Citizens Comt Arts; Am Planning Asn Task Force; The Capitol Club; New Albany Country Club. **Honors/Awds:** Most Influential Men in Columbus, 1972. **Military Serv:** US Air Corps, 1944-45. **Home Addr:** 1809 N Cassady Ave, Columbus, OH 43219. **Business Addr:** Attorney, 500 S Front St, Ste 1140, Columbus, OH 43215, **Business Phone:** (614)221-5373.*

LACOUR, NATHANIEL HAWTHORNE
School administrator. **Personal:** Born Feb 11, 1938, New Orleans, LA; married Josie Brown; children: Carey Renee, Carla Cenee & Charlette Jene. **Educ:** Southern Univ A&M Col, Baton Rouge, BS, 1960, MSTB 1965. **Career:** Carver Sr High Sch, biol teacher, 1961-70; United Teachers New Orleans, pres, 1970; Am Fedn Teachers, vpres, 1987-94, secy-treas, currently. **Orgs:** Nat bd mem, A Philip Randolph Inst; Nat Bd Prof Teaching Stand; chmn, New Orleans Manpower Adv Planning Coun; Am Inst Biologists; mem exec bd Greater New Orleans AFL-CIO; YMCA; Nat Asn Advan Colored People; exec bd, New Orleans Urban League; bd dirs, New Orleans Pub Libr; comnr, WhiteHouse Comn Presidential Scholars, 1993; bd dir, Amalgamated Bank Chicago; bd dir, Albert Shanker Inst; bd dir, Nat Dem Inst; bd dir, Coalition Black Trade Unionists; bd, Learning First Alliance; bd, Educ Qual Inst; bd dir, Thurgood Marshall Scholar Fund. **Honors/Awds:** Prestigious Ellis Island Medal of Honor, 2006. *

LACOUR, VANUE B.
Lawyer, educator. **Personal:** Born Sep 10, 1915, Natchez, LA; son of Ernestine Prudhomme and Ernest Lacour; married Arthemise Wilson; children: Vanue B Jr, Leonard J, Cynthia Marie, Bernard L, Elaine Theresa, Michael M & Anthony G. **Educ:** Xavier Univ, New Orleans, AB, 1938; Howard Univ, JD, 1941. **Career:** Lawyer, educator, (retired); Pvt Pract, Kansas City, MO, atty, 1942-47; Southern Univ Law Sch, Baton Rouge, LA, educr, 1947-70, dean law sch, 1970-71; Lacour & Calloway, atty. **Orgs:** Past chmn, LA Comn Govt Ethics; adv mem, Istrouma Area Boy Scout Coun; Alpha Phi Alpha; past mem, LA Comn Ethics Pub Employees; corresp secy, Greater New Orleans Louis A Martinet Soc Inc; past vpres, Nat Bar Asn; past secy, Nat Asn Advan Colored People. **Honors/Awds:** Alpha Eta Honor Soc; Silver Beaver Boy Scouts Am; Boss of the Year, Baton Rouge Legal Secretaries Asn, 1980-81; past bd mem, Blundon Home-Family Coun Serv; Br Chapter Am Red Cross. **Home Addr:** 2578 79th Ave, Baton Rouge, LA 70807. *

LACY, AUNDREA
Executive. **Personal:** Born in San Francisco, CA. **Educ:** San Jose State Univ, BS; Golden Gate Univ, MBA. **Career:** Hewlett Packard, 1990-2000; Luv's Brownies, owner & chief exec officer, 1996-; high technol consult, 2000-. **Orgs:** Mentor, Big Sisters Santa Clara County. **Honors/Awds:** Outstanding Academic Achievement, San Jose State Univ, 1993; People's Choice Best Dessert, Intl Hospitality Conv, 2004 & 2005; Outstanding Alumus Award, 2004-05. **Special Achievements:** Testimonial by Coach Ken Carter; Testimonial by Earl Graves Sr; author, Brownie Points - Seven Steps to Success for Women Entrepreneurs from One, Who Made It. **Business Addr:** Owner, Chief Executive Officer, Luv Brownies, 2910 Stevens Creek Blvd Suite 109, San Jose, CA 95128, **Business Phone:** (408)881-0759.*

LACY, DONALD E., JR.
Administrator, actor. **Personal:** Born Nov 26, 1958, Canton, OH; son of Donald and Mary; married Shaina, Aug 8, 1984; children: LoEshe (deceased), Donnie & Anwaar. **Educ:** San Francisco State Univ, BA, black studies, theater arts, 1984. **Career:** TV & Film: Metro; Bound By Honor; Jack; Catherine Crier Live; Hangin' with Mr. Cooper, 1997; Wolf; Comic View; LA Heart, 1999; Comedy Jam; Bay Sunday; Bay TV; Stage Shows: The Shelter; Ballard of Pancho & Lucy; Fists of Roses; Hairy Ape; Good Person of Szcezhuan; Jitney; Soul of a Whore; Wheel of Fortune; Hotel Angulo; Color Struck; Loeshe; Boogie Woogie Land Scapes; Evolution of Soul Brother; Streamers; The Loudest Scream; Boseman & Lena; Death of Bessie Smith; short films directed: Four & Romeo & Juliet Gettin' Busy; Recreation Ctr Handicapped, staff, 1983-88; KPFA Radio, host; KPOO Radio, pub affairs dir, show host, 1980-93, show host, 1997-; Harlem Globetrotters, announcer, 1995; actor, writer, comedian, 1984-2003; Kaleidovision Film works, exec dir, 1985-90; Explosion Comedy, host, currently; Martin & Glanz, conf organizer, 1999; Love life Found, founder & exec dir, 1997-. **Honors/Awds:** Black Filmmakers Hall Fame, 1999; Bay Area Cable Excellence award, 1999; Fade to Gold, 1999; PSA Award, Nat Pub Programming, 1999; Excellence Award, City Oakland, 1999; nominated, 10 Most Influential

African Americans in The Bay Area, 2002; Avanti Magic Award, 2003; Best Radio Talk Show Host, East Bay Express Newspaper, 2003; Healthy Oakland Father of the Year Award, 2003. **Special Achievements:** Helped reduce the murder rate in Oakland to a 25-year low in 1998, and a32-year low in 1999. **Business Addr:** Executive Director, Lovelife Foundation, PO Box 70351, Oakland, CA 94612.

LACY, HUGH GALE
Lawyer, educator. **Personal:** Born Mar 23, 1948, Huntsville, AL; son of Leo Marshuetz and Mary Crean Berry; married Paulette Nettles, Feb 12, 1977; children: Kenitra Irma, Hugh Shomari. **Educ:** Ala A & M Univ, BA, 1972, MEd, 1974; Miles Law Sch, JD, 1989. **Career:** Huntsville City Bd Educ, teacher corps intern, 1972-74; USY Ballistic Missle Defense Systems Command, supply mgt asst, 1974-75; USY Ordnance Missile & Munitions Ctr & Sch, educ spt, 1975-92; atty pvt practice, 1990-; USY Corps Engrs, educ spt. **Orgs:** Bldg & educ comt, St Bartley Primitive Baptist Church; area dir, associated ed Sphinx, APA Fraternity; Ala Lawyers Asn; Ala Trial Lawyers Asn; Am Bar Asn, 1990-; Nat Bar Asn, 1990-; NCP, 1972-; counr, Special Educ Action Com, 1989-; legislative comn, Huntsville & Madison County Bar Asn, 1990-. **Honors/Awds:** 4-H Club Leadership Award, 1974; Brother of the Year, APA Fraternity Inc, State Ala, 1990; Great American Family Award, 1990; Role Model of the Week, Speaking Out Newspaper, 1990; Brother of the Year, Delta Theta Lambda, 1991; Equal Employment Opportunity Counselor Appreciation Certificate, USY Missile Command, 1992. **Business Addr:** 300 E Clinton Ave Suite 2, PO Box 18341, Huntsville, AL 35804, **Business Phone:** (256)536-1849.*

LACY, VENUS
Basketball player, college administrator. **Personal:** Born Feb 9, 1967, Chattanooga, TN; children (previous marriage): 1; children: 1. **Educ:** La Tech Univ, BA, sociol. **Career:** Basketball player (retired): Japan, Italy & Greece, 1990-96; Seattle Reign, ABL, ctr, 1996-97; Long Beach Stingrays, WNBA, 1997-98; Nashville Noise, 1998-99; WNBA, NY Liberty, 1999-2000; Univ Tenn Chatanooga, stud develop specialist, currently. **Honors/Awds:** NCAA Championship, 1988-89; US Basketball Writers, Player of the Year, 1990; Bronze medal, Pan Am Games, 1991; European Championship, 1995-96; gold medal, Olympic Games, 1996; SGMA HEROES Award, 2000. **Special Achievements:** African-American to play on the U.S. Olympic Basketball Team, winning a gold medal in 1996. **Business Phone:** (423)425-4515.

LACY, VERSIA LINDSAY
Educator, lecturer. **Personal:** Born Mar 15, 1929, Houston, TX; married JW; children: Lindsay Keith, Elizabeth Juliene & Liz Mikel. **Educ:** Huston-Tillotson Col, BS, 1948; Atlanta Univ, MS, 1950; Univ Tex, attended1956; Univ Ore, attended 1958; Tex Womans Univ, PhD, 1973. **Career:** Paul Quinn Col, instr, dean women, 1950-55; Tyler Jr Col, asst prof, 1956-66; Tex Womans Univ, grad res asst, 1966-69; Bishop Col, assoc prof,1969-77; Tex So Univ, guest prof, 1971; Dallas ISD, sci & health coordr, 1977-82; Dallas Int Sch Dist Sci & Eng Magnet, prof, 1977; owner, Versia L Lacy Co. **Orgs:** Radiation Res Soc; AAAS; AIBS; NIS; SW Photobiol Group; TARR, TAS, NTBS, BBB Biol Soc; BKX Sci Hon Soc; TWU Club; Sigma Xi Soc; Third Nat Anti-Basileus Zeta Phi Beta Sor, 1952-54; gov S Cent Dist Nat Asn Negro Bus & Prof Womens Clubs Inc; second nat vpres, NANB & PH Clubs Inc, 1979-81; chmn, Am Heart Asn Spec Task Force; bd dir, Am Heart Asn Dallas Chapt; bd dir, YMCA Moorland Br; Nat ed of Crown; SME Comm Mustang Dist, Circle 10Counc, BSA, PTA, David W Carter & DA Huley Schs; founder, Dr V L Lacy Foudn, 2003. **Honors/Awds:** Outstanding Achievement Award, Top Ladies of Distinction, 1973; Outstanding Achievement Award, Zeta Phi Beta, 1974; Top Ladies of Distinction Inc; Woman of the Yr, Psi Chap Iota Phi Lambda Sor So Reg, 1976; 1st Runner-up Nat Liola P Parker Award; Woman of the Yr, United Action Dallas Black C C, 1976; Sojourner Truth Nat Meritorious Award, 1982; Total Images Award Mountain View C, 1983. **Business Addr:** Owner, Versia L Lacy Co, 7307 Ridge Park Lane, Dallas, TX 75232.*

LACY, WALTER
Manager. **Personal:** Born Nov 14, 1942, Huntsville, AL; son of Jessie Sr (deceased) and Lelia Acklin (deceased); married Julianne White, Sep 5, 1964; children: Lorraine Lacy Young, Walter Marcellus & Julian Crishon. **Educ:** Ala Agr & Mech Univ, BS, 1966, MS, 1972. **Career:** AUS Msl & Mun Cen & Sch, electronics instr, 1966-70; General Electric Co, equipment specialist, 1970-71; Safeguard Logistics Command, equipment specialist, 1971-73, equal opportunity specialist, 1973-74; AUS Missile Command, equipment specialist, 1974-85, logistics mgt specialist, 1985-92, int prg mgt specialist, 1992-. **Orgs:** Free & Accepted Masons, 1968-82; tutor, bd dir, Seminole Serv Ctr, 1989-; Am Poetry Asn, 1989, 1990; parliamentarian, vpres, Blacks Govt, 1990-93; various comn, Alpha Phi Alpha Fraternity, 1991-. **Honors/Awds:** Exceptional Performance Awards, AUS Missile Command, 1990-97; Honorable Mention, poem, Am Poetry Soc, 1991. **Special Achievements:** Poetry published: American Poetry Anthology, 1989. **Home Addr:** 1724 Millican Pl, Huntsville, AL 35816, **Home Phone:** (205)837-9034.

LACY-PENDLETON, STEVIE A
Journalist. **Personal:** Born Apr 19, 1956, Oklahoma City, OK; daughter of Robert and Bette J Lacy. **Educ:** John Jay Col Criminal Justice, attended; Case Western Reserve Univ, BA, 1974. **Career:** Cleveland Urban Learning Ctr, teacher, 1973-75; Xenia Daily Gazette, reporter, 1975-78; Cent State Univ, coord stud recruitment, 1978-79; Dayton J Herald, reporter, 1979-80; Staten Island Advance, columnist, 1980-, sunday prespective ed, 1995-2002, dep ed page ed & sr advance columnist, 2002-; NY 1 News & Staten Island Cable, In Focus, co-anchor, 1997-98. **Orgs:** Bd trustees & sec vice chair, Soc Children & Families; former bd mem, Polit Action Comt, former chair, Nat Coun Negro Women; governing bd mem, Friends Found; adv bd, Staten Island Univ Hosp, Univ Hospice; adv & former bd mem, Community Adv Bd, NY State Div Youth, Staten Island Community Residential Ctr; adv bd dir, Amethyst House Inc, Bayley Seton Hosp; adv, delivery volunteer, Meals Wheels, Staten Island Div; founder, pres, Ebony Elves; co-founder, Women's Health Initiative, Mary McLeod Bethune Ctr. **Honors/Awds:** Three Asniated Press Awards; Deadline Club Award; Front Page Award; Stevie Lacy-Pendleton Day, 1981; Leadership Award, United Negro Col Fund Inc, 1993; Front Page Award; Deadline Club Award, New York Deadline Club Soc Prof Journalists, 1996; Front Page Award, Newswomen's Club NY, 1997; Schools Chancellor Rudolph F Crew Caring Community Award Recognition of Excellence, Intergroup Relations Adv Coun, 1997; James Josey Memorial Community Harmony Award, 1997; Black American Achievement Award, State Island Borough Pres Guy V Molinari, 1997; Nat Asn of Black Journalists Award, 1998; Education Award, Port Richmond High Sch; Outstanding Young Women in America; First Place Columns, Nat Asn Black Journalist, 1999; Honorable Mention, Soc Silurians, 1999; 1st place, columns, NY State Asn Press, 2000; Community Service Award, Nat Coun Negro Women, Staten Island chap, 2001; Award of Excellence, NY Newspapers Eds & Publ, 2001; 1st place, columns, NY Asn Black Journalists, 2002; numerous community service awards. **Business Addr:** Deputy Editorial Page Editor, Advance Senior News Columnist, Staten Island Advance, 950 W Fingerboard Rd, Staten Island, NY 10305, **Business Phone:** (718)981-1234 Ext 2216.

LADAY, KERNEY
Executive, consultant. **Personal:** Born Mar 14, 1942, Ville Platte, LA; son of Lillius Laday and Sampson; married Floradese Thomas; children: Marucs K, Kerney Jr & Anthony D. **Educ:** Southern Univ, BS, 1965; La State Univ, MS, 1970; Southern Methodist Univ, MBA, 1982. **Career:** Southern Univ, asst placement dir, 1968-71; Xerox Corp, vpres & regional gen mgr, 1986-91, vpres, field operations, Southern Region, US Customer Oper, 1991-95; TXU Corp, dir, 1993-; The Laday Co, pres, 1995-. **Orgs:** Bd dirs, Eltrex Corp, 1982-86; United Way Dallas, 1987-; bd dir, N Tex Community; trustee, Shiloh Baptist Church, Plano Tex; assoc bd dirs, SMU; bd dir, African Am Mus; bd dirs, Dallas Chamber Com; bd dir, Dallas Citizens Coun; bd dirs, NC Nat Bank Texas; bd dirs, TD Industs Inc; bd dir, The Beck Group. **Honors/Awds:** Renowned Grad, Southern Univ; Presidential Citation, Nat Educ Equal Opportunities. **Military Serv:** Signal Corp, capt, 1965-68. **Home Addr:** 6001 Jericho Ct, Dallas, TX 75248. **Business Addr:** Director, TXU Corp, 1601 Bryan St Energy Plz, Dallas, TX 75201, **Business Phone:** (214)812-4600.

LADD, FLORENCE CAWTHORNE
Association executive, educator, executive director. **Personal:** Born Jun 16, 1932, Washington, DC; daughter of William and Eleanor Willis; married; children: Michael Cawthorne Ladd. **Educ:** Howard Univ, BS, 1953; Univ Rochester, PhD, 1958. **Career:** Age Ctr New England, res assoc, 1958-60; Simmons Col, asst prof, 1960-61; Robert Col, Istanbul, asst prof, 1962-63; Harvard Grad Sch Educ, lectr & res assoc, 1965-70; Radcliffe Inst, fel, 1970-72; Harvard Grad Sch Design, assoc prof, 1972-77; Sch Archit & Planning Mass Inst Techol, assoc dean, 1977-79; Wellesley Col, dean of students, 1979-84; S African Educ Prog, consult, 1984-85; WEB DuBois Inst, vis scholar; Oxfam Am, dir educ & outreach, 1985-87, assoc exec dir, 1987; Mary Ingraham Bunting Inst Radcliffe Col, Harvard Univ, dir, 1989-96, writer-in-residence, dir emer, currently. **Orgs:** Black Women Policy Action; TransAfrica; bd mem, Overseas Develop Network, United Nat Int Res & Training Inst Advan Women; Nat Coun South African Progs; Asn Women Develop; trustee, Bentley Col; bd mem, Inst Contemporary Art; bd mem, Overseer, WGBH; bd mem, Nat Coun Res Women. **Honors/Awds:** Hon mem, Am Inst Architects, Wellesley Alumnae Asn, Phi Beta Kappa, Sigma Xi; Best Fiction Award, Blk Caucus Am Libr Asn, 1997. **Special Achievements:** Author, Sarah's Psalm, Scribner, 1996; Cited by Mirabella magazine in 1994 in their selection of 100 Fearless Women. **Business Addr:** Emeritus Director, Mary Ingraham Bunting Institute, Radcliffe Institute for Advanced Study, 10 Garden St, Cambridge, MA 02138, **Business Phone:** (617)495-8601.*

LADNER, JOYCE A
School administrator, writer. **Personal:** Born Oct 12, 1943, Mississippi; married Walter Carrington. **Educ:** Tougaloo Coll, BA, 1964; Wash Univ, PhD, sociol, 1968. **Career:** S Ill Univ, asst prof & curriculum specist, 1968-69; Wesleyan Univ, 1969-70; Univ Dar es Salaam, Tanzania, res assoc, 1970-71; Hunter Col, CUNY, sociol fac, 1976-81; Brookings Inst, sr fel, govt studies, 1977-; Howard Univ, prof sociol, 1981-87; vp acad affairs, 1990-94, interim pres, 1994-95. Author: Tomorrow's Tomorrow: The Black Woman, 1971; Mixed Families: Adopting Across Racial Boundaries, 1977; The Ties That Bind: Timeless Values for Afr Amer Families, 1998; Co-Auth: Lives of Promise, Lives of Pain: Young Mothers After New Chance, 1994; Selected Papers from the Proceedings of the Conf on Ethics, Higher Educ, & Social Responsibility, 1996; The Ties That Bind: Timeless Values for African American Families, 1997; The New Urban Leaders, 2001. **Orgs:** Bd dirs, Am Sociol Asn; review comm & mem Minority Ctr, Nat Inst Ment Health; fel, Social Sci Res Coun; Soc for Study Social Problems; bd dirs, Caucus Black Sociologists; Asn for Study Afro-Am Life & Hist; bd dirs, 21st Century Found; Amn Sociological Asn. **Honors/Awds:** Russell Sage Found, grant, 1972-73; Cummings Engine Found, grant, 1972-73. **Special Achievements:** Named Washingtonian Magazine's Washingtonian of the Year, 1997. **Business Addr:** Senior Fellow, The Brookings Institution, 1775 Mass Ave NW, Washington, DC 20036, **Business Phone:** (202)797-6252.

LADSON, DR. LOUIS FITZGERALD
Pharmacist. **Personal:** Born Jan 3, 1951, Georgetown, SC; son of Henry and Susan Smith; married Sharon Harris; children: Eric & Tisha. **Educ:** St Olaf Col, BA, Hist, 1978; Creighton Univ, BS, Pharm, 1981; Cent Mich Univ, MA, Bus, 1982. **Career:** James A Haley Va Hosp, resident pharmacist, 1982-83; SuperX Univ, Sq Mall, pharm mgr, 1983-84; PCMC Pharm, consult, 1996; Lincourt Pharm, owner, 1984-. **Orgs:** Am Soc Hosp Pharm, 1979-, Kappa Psi Fraternity, 1980-, Nat Asn Retail Druggists, 1982-; Fla Pharm Asn, 1982-; pharm consult, Adult Care Living Facilities, 1984-; Chamber Com Clearwater, 1985-; Nat Asn Advan Colored Poeple, Clearwater Chap, 1985-; Alpha Phi Alpha Fraternity, 1988-; Prof Compounders Am; cub master, Boy Scouts, Pack #52, 1991; adv bd mem, care one, 1990; adv bd mem, Mt Zion AME Church, 1990; adv bd, Pharm Mag, Drug Topics; adv bd, CCH Homecare. **Honors/Awds:** Outstanding Leadership Certificate, Creighton Univ, 1981; Outstanding Service Award, Creighton Univ, Black Fac, 1982. **Military Serv:** AUS, Major; Certs Appreciation, 1977, 1980, Comn, 1981. **Business Addr:** Owner, Lincourt Professional Pharmacy, 501 S Lincoln Ave, Clearwater, FL 33756, **Business Phone:** (727)446-0302.

LAFAYETTE, BERNARD
School administrator. **Personal:** Born Jul 29, 1940, Tampa, FL; married Kate Bulls. **Educ:** Amer Baptist Theol Sem, BA, 1961; Harvard Univ, EdM, 1972, EdD, 1974. **Career:** SNCC AL Voters Regist Project, dir, 1962-63; Gustavus Adolphus Col, dirpr of, 1974-76; SCLC, nat prog admin, 1976; Lindenwood Col Four, dir; ExceInst, admin chief prog office, dep dir, PUSH, 1979-80; Ala State Univ Montgomery, fac, dean grad sch; Tuskegee Inst High Sch, Tuskegee, prin; Am Baptist Col, pres; Univ RI, dir ctr nonviolence & peace studies, currently, distinguished-scholar-in-residence, currently. **Orgs:** Nat coordr, Poor People's Campaign, 1968; founder, chmn exec bd, Inst Human Rights & Res, 1979-; nat chmn, Founder Nat Black Christian Stud Leadership Consult, 1979-; chmn, Consortium on Peace Res Educ & Develop, 1975; bd mem, Ministries Blacks Higher Educ, 1977; treas & past pres, Phi Delta Kappa; Am Friends Serv Comt; founder, Asn For Kingian Nonviolence Education and Training Works. **Honors/Awds:** Hon Prof Frat Harvard Chap; Underwood Fel Danforth Found; Full Fel Nat Coun Negro Women; Award for Settling School Strikes, The Group Concerned Studs, St Louis; Fact-finding Visit to Panama with Congressman Andrew Young, 1973; University's Diversity Award for Lifetime Achievement, Univ RI, 2005. **Special Achievements:** First of the leading southern civil rights activist, 1964; Appointed by Rhode Island Governor Donald Carcieri as the chairman for the Rhode Island Select Commission on Race and Police-Community Relations. **Business Addr:** Distinguished-Scholar-in-Residence, Director, University of Rhode Island, Centre for Nonviolence & Peace Studies, 74 Lower Col Rd, Kingston, RI 02881, **Business Phone:** (401)874-2875.

LAFAYETTE, EXCELL, JR.
Executive. **Career:** KTUL-TV Channel 8, oper supvr, electronic field prod producer, photographer & news photojournalist, 1983-89; Phillips Petroleum Co, video prod rep, 1990-93; Wal-Mart Stores Inc, TV Network, mgr, 1994-98, dir supplier develop, 1999-. **Orgs:** Chmn, Ark Minority Bus Adv Coun; bd mem, Women's Bus Enterprise Nat Coun; Nat Minority Supplier Develop Coun; bd trustee, Philander Smith Col; deacon, St James Missionary Baptist Church; bd mem, Rogers Community Support Ctr. **Honors/Awds:** Outstanding Men of Minority Business Development Award, Minority Bus News USA, 2000; Billion Dollar Round Table Award, Bus News USA, 2000, 2001; MBE Advocate of the Year, ARMSDC, 2001; Rising Star Award, African Am Bus Hall Fame & Mus, 2002; Corporate Partnership Award, ARMSDC, 2002; Commitment to Excellence Award, US Black Chamber Com, 2003. **Business Addr:** Director of Supplier Development, Wal-Mart Stores Inc, 702 SW 8th St, Bentonville, AR 72716, **Business Phone:** (501)273-4000.

LAFONTANT, DR. JULIEN J.
Educator. **Personal:** Born in Port-au-Prince, Haiti; married Blandine. **Educ:** SUNY Binghamton, MA, 1974, PhD, 1976. **Career:** Educator (retired); Exec Mansion Morovia Liberia, translator, 1961-63; Ivory Coast Embassy Monrovia Liberia, translator, 1963-66; Cuttington ColSuakoko Liberia, asst prof, 1966-72; SUNY Binghamton, teaching asst, 1972-76; Univ Nebr

Lincoln, asst prof, 1976-77; Acting Chair Black Studies UNO, asst prof, 1977-78, dept chair black studies, 1977-85; Univ Nebr, assoc prof, 1978-82, full prof French Chair Black Studies UNO 1983-85; full prof foreign lang & lit, 1986; Int Studies prog, faculty mem. **Orgs:** UNO's Third World Studies Conf. **Honors/Awds:** UNO Excellence in Teaching Award, 1981; Great Teacher Award, Univ Nebr Omaha, 1982. **Special Achievements:** Book on Montesquieu; book entitled Understanding A Culture; several articles dealing with the Black exper in general and the French encounter with Blacks. *

LAGARDE, REV. FREDERICK H
Clergy. **Personal:** Born Apr 10, 1928, Teaneck, NJ; son of Flovville Albert and Claudia; married Frances Frye; children: Frederica, Francine, Francella & Frederick Jr. **Educ:** Grand Music Acad, 1948; VA Union Univ & Sem, AB, MDiv, 1953-59. **Career:** First Baptist Church, pastor, 1956-58; Providence Baptist Church, pastor, 1958-66; Community Baptist Church Love, pastor, 1966-; Come-Unity & The Annual Greater Youth Crusade Paterson vicinity, pres & founder 1980; LaGarde Funeral Home Inc, vpres, currently. **Orgs:** Founder, United Neighborhood Indust Training & Econ Develop, 1967; Housing Opportunity Provided Everyone, 1969; House Action, 1970; Nat Asn Advan Colored People reg rep, SCLC; ASCAP; Alpha Phi Alpha; Paterson Community Sch, 1983; co-writer & producer, Martin Luther King video & song, 1986; New Jersey State Bd Educ, currently. **Honors/Awds:** Award IBPO Elks World, 1965; Black & Poor Citizens Award, 1966; Citizens Paterson Award, 1967; NJ Coun Churches Soc Ed & Action Award, 1969; Paterson Pastors Workshop Award, 1986; Outstanding Businessman of the Year, Modern Beauticians Association Unit 9; Service Man of Distinction Award, North Jersey Modern Beauticians Asn. **Special Achievements:** Co-writer Official Song Paterson, 1983. **Military Serv:** AUS, 1950-52. **Business Addr:** Member, New Jersey State Board of Education, PO Box 500, Trenton, NJ 08625-0500, **Business Phone:** (609)292-4469.

LAHR, DR. CHARLES DWIGHT
Educator, mathematician. **Personal:** Born Feb 6, 1945, Philadelphia, PA; married Beatriz Pastor; children: Elena, Maria, Emilio, Sonia & Katerina. **Educ:** Temple Univ, AB, magna cum laude, math, 1966; Syracuse Univ, MA, math, 1968, PhD, 1972. **Career:** Willow Grove Naval Air Sta; Bell Labs, mathematician, 1971-73; Savannah State Col, vis prof math, 1973-74; Amherst Col, vis prof math, 1974-75; Dartmouth Col, from asst to assoc prof math, 1975-84, assoc dean sci, dean grad studies, 1981-84, prof math & comput sci, 1984-, dean fac, 1984-89, prof math & comput sci, permanent fac, currently. **Orgs:** Consult, Alfred P Sloan Found, 1982-90; reviewer, Math Reviews; Am Math Soc; Math Asn Am; AAAS. **Special Achievements:** Book: Principles of Calculus Modeling An Interactive Approach; Articles: "Approximate identities for convolution measure algebras", 1973; "The trace class of an arbitrary Hilbert algebra", 1980; "Multipliers and derivations of Hilbert algebras", 1980; "Weak approximate identities and multipliers", 1982; First African American to get tenure in an Ivy League School department of mathematics. **Business Addr:** Professor of Mathematics & Computer Science, Dartmouth College, Department of Mathematics, 6188 Kemeny Hall, Hanover, NH 03755-3551.

LAINE, CLEO
Singer, actor. **Personal:** Born Oct 28, 1927, Middlesex, England; daughter of Alexander Campbell and Minnie Bullock; married John Philip William Dankworth, 1958; children: Stuart, Alec & Jacqueline. **Educ:** Open Univ, MA, 1975; Berkee Col, MusD, 1982. **Career:** John Dank worth's Jazz Band, popularized Gimme a Pig foot & It's a Pity to Say Goodnight, singer, 1952; Recordings: A Beautiful Theme; Pierrot Lunaire All About Me; Born on a Friday; Day by Day; That Old Feeling; Cleo Sings Sondheim; Woman to Woman; Feel the Warm; I'm a Song; Live at Melbourne; Best Friends; Sometimes When We Touch; actress, Seven Deadly Sins; Showboat; The Roman Spring of Mrs Stone, 1961; Colette, 1980; A Time to Laugh; Hedda Gabler; The Women of Troy; The Mystery of Edwin Drood, 1986; guest singer, One Man's Music; Marvelous Party; Talk of the Town; Not So Much a Programme; The Sammy Davis Show; Merv Griffin Show, 1974; Cotton Club, 1975; Dinah; Albums: Smilin' Through, 1982; Cleo at Carnegie: The 10th Anniversary, 1983; Let the Music Take You, 1983; Cleo Laine Sings Sondheim RCA, 1987; That Old Feeling, 1987; Woman to Woman, 1989; Jazz, 1991; One More Day, 1991; Blue & Sentimental, 1992; Solitude, 1994; Spotlight on Cleo Laine, 1995; The Very Best of Cleo Laine, 1997; Mad About the Boy, 1997; Ridin' High, 1998; Trav lin Light: The Johnny Mercer Songbook, 1998; Let's Be Frank, 1998; The Collection, 1998; Sondheim Tonight - Live From the Barbican, 1999; The Best of Cleo Laine, 1999; The Silver Anniversary Concert, 1999; Christmas at the Stables, 1999; Quintessential Cleo, 2001; Live in Manhattan, 2001; Films: The Last of the Blonde Bombshells, 2000; The Third Alibi, actor, 1961; "Kraft Mystery Theater", 1961; The Thief of Bagdad, 1940; TV: I Love Muppets, 2002; Victoria Wood: A BAFTA Tribute, 2005; "Sunday AM", 2006; "The Paul O'Grady Show", 2007; "Legends", 2007. **Honors/Awds:** Golden Feather Award, Los Angeles Times, 1973; Grammy Award for Best Female Jazz Vocalist, 1985; Singer of the Year, TV Times, 1978; Show Business Personality of the Year, Variety Club, 1977; Grammy Award for Jazz Female Vocal, 1985; Lifetime Achievement Award, 1991; Lifetime Achievement Award, Worshipful Co Musicians, 2002. **Special Achievements:** Ambassador for SOS Children's Villages UK in recognition of her support for the Cambridge based charity. **Business Phone:** (212)967-7350.

LAIRD, ALAN
Clergy, art museum director, artist. **Personal:** Born Dec 8, 1949, Oakland, CA; son of Levy and Sadie M; married Lorraine, Jan 26, 1997; children: Damon Alan, Aaron Jason, Mauryea, Chantalle & Rashaad. **Educ:** Laney Col, AA, 1976; Golden Gate Univ, 1980; Theol Union, MDiv, 1997. **Career:** AMR PRS Lines, 1980-92; Bethel AME Church, 1993-; Expressions Art Gallery, owner & artist, 1996-; Oakland Unified Sch, teacher, 1998. **Orgs:** Working Artist Coalition Oakland. **Honors/Awds:** African American Historical Society, art exhibition, 1998. **Special Achievements:** Part of Bethsaida Excavation team Northern Galilee. **Military Serv:** US Coast Guard, 1968-71. **Business Addr:** Gallery Owner/Painter, Expression Art Gallery, 3463 San Pablo Ave, Oakland, CA 94607, **Business Phone:** (510)547-6646.

LAIRET, DOLORES PERSON
Educator, lecturer. **Personal:** Born Dec 27, 1935, Cleveland; widowed; children: Christine & Evin. **Educ:** Wheaton Col, AB, 1957; Middlebury Col, AM, 1958; Univ Paris; Case Western Res Univ, PhD, 1972. **Career:** Southern Univ Baton Rouge, instr, 1959; Fox Lane Sch Bedford NY, educr, 1960-62; John Marshall HS, Fr teacher, 1963-65; Western Res Univ, teaching fel lectr, 1965-67; City of Cleveland, sr personnel asst, 1969-71; Cleveland State Univ, lectr, 1969-71, instr, 1971-72, assoc prof, 1972-77. **Orgs:** Secy & pres, Cleveland Chap Tots & Teens, 1963-73; Champs Inc, 1964-; Am Asn Teachers Fr, 1971-; Am Asn Univ Prof, 1971; Am Coun Teaching Foreign Lang, 1972-; NE Modern Lang Asn, 1974-; African Lit Asn; Music Critics Asn; OH Mod Lang Teachers Asn; bd mem, Glenville Health Asn, 1974-; Am Spec Lctr US Dept State Niger Mali Upper Volta Senegal & Togo. **Honors/Awds:** Published: The Francophone African Novel Perspectives for Critical Eval Presence Africaine; Various Art on Jazz Cleveland Press Showtime; Recipient of various Fellowships. **Business Addr:** E 24 St Euclid Ave, Cleveland, OH 44115.

LAISURE, SHARON EMILY GOODE
Government official. **Personal:** Born Sep 3, 1954, Wiesbaden, Germany; daughter of Robert A Goode; married W Floyd. **Educ:** Univ NC, Chapel Hill, BA, 1976, MPA, 1979. **Career:** Winston-Salem City, admin asst dep city mgr, 1977-78, admin asst asst city mgr, 1978-79, personnel analyst, 1979-80; Petersburg City, VA, personnel dir, 1980-85; Durham County, NC, personnel dir, 1985-86; Richmond County, VA, dir, human resources & employee rels, 1986-89, dep city mgr, 1990; Durham City, NC, asst mgr, currently. **Orgs:** Am Soc Pub Admin, 1979; mem bd dir, Southside Chap Am Red Cross, 1980; United Way Southside, VA, 1982, 1983; pres, elect, Southern Region, IPMA, 1984; Int City Mgt Asn; Nat Forum Black Public Adminr; NC City & County Mgt Asn. **Honors/Awds:** City Manager's Outstanding Achievement Award, 1987. **Business Addr:** Deputy City Manager, Durham County, 101 City Hall Pl, Durham, NC 27701-3328, **Business Phone:** (919)560-4122.

LAKE, ALFREEDA ELIZABETH (ALFREEDA LAKE MCKINNEY)
Educator. **Personal:** Born Jan 7, 1923, Hickory Valley, TN; divorced; children: Neeley Jr. **Educ:** LeMoyne Col, BA, 1943; Univ Tenn, MS, 1967; Memphis State Univ, 1970; Grambling State Univ, Pre-serv Training; Lane Col. **Career:** Bolivar Indust Sch, primary teacher, 1950-64; Prospect Sch, elem sch prin, 1945-50; Wash Sch, primary teacher, 1943-45; Hardeman County Schs, supvr instrs, 1964-. **Orgs:** St Paul Christian Meth Epis Ch; past pres, Delta Sigma Theta Sor Inc; Nat Asn Advan Colored People; Nat Counc Negro Women; exec bd dirs, W Tenn Health Improve Asn; Bolivar Housing Auth Bd; Prep Elem Sch Teachers, 1969; consult lectr, Num Cols Univs & Pub Sch Systs Civic & Religious Groups; volunteer, Western Ment Health Inst, 1970-. **Honors/Awds:** Publ, "A Study of 15 Black Students Enrolled in Formerly All White Schs inHardeman Co", 1965-66; Author, Handbook for Parents of Pre-Sch Children, 1974. **Business Addr:** Volunteer, Western Mental Health Institute, Courthouse 2nd Fl, Bolivar, TN 38008.

LAKE, CARNELL AUGUSTINO
Football player, football coach. **Personal:** Born Jul 15, 1967, Salt Lake City, UT; married Monica; children: Siena. **Educ:** Univ Calif Los Angeles, BA, polit sci, 1993. **Career:** Football player (retired); Pittsburgh Steelers, def back 1989-98; Jacksonville Jaguars, def back, 1999-2000; Baltimore Ravens, def back, 2001-02. **Orgs:** Alpha Phi Alpha. **Honors/Awds:** Pro Bowl, 1994-96; Natl Football Foundation Hall of Fame Scholar Athlete Award, 1988-89.

LAMAR, DR. HATTIE G
College administrator. **Career:** Miles Col, chief fiscal officer, dean acad affairs, currently. **Business Addr:** Dean of Academic Affairs, Miles College, Floor 2nd 5400 Myron Massey Rd, Birmingham, AL 35208, **Business Phone:** (205)929-1438.

LAMAR, JAKE V, SR.
Educator, writer. **Personal:** Born Mar 27, 1961, Bronx, NY; son of Jacob V Sr and Jouce Marie Doucette; married Dorli, Sep 11, 1999. **Educ:** Harvard Univ, BA, 1983. **Career:** Time Mag, staff writer, assoc ed, 1983-89; Univ Mich, adj lectr, Commun Dept, 1993; Paris Writers Workshop, lectr, currently. **Honors/Awds:** Lyndhurst Prize, Lyndhurst Found, 1992. **Special Achievements:** Author of a memoir Bourgeois Blues (Summit Books, 1991) and five novels: The Last Integrationist, translated into French as Nous avions un r?ve, (Random House, 1996), Close to the Bone (Crown, 1999), If 6 were 9, translated into French as Le Cam?leon Noir, (Crown, 2001), Rendezvous Eighteenth (St. Martin's Griffin, 2005), and Ghosts of St. Michel (St. Martin's Minotaur, 2006). **Business Addr:** Lecturer, Paris Writers Workshop, 20 bd du Montparnasse, **Business Phone:** (014)566-7550.

LAMAR, WILLIAM
Executive. **Personal:** Born Apr 25, 1952, Chicago, IL; son of William Sr and Jeanette Jarrett; married Kathy Amos Lamar, Aug 28, 1976; children: Brian & Andrew Marcus. **Educ:** Univ Ill, Chicago, IL, BS, 1973; Northwestern Univ, Kellogg Sch Mgmt, Evanston, IL, MBA, 1976. **Career:** Executive (retired); Quaker Oats Co, Chicago, IL, brand mgr, 1976-81; Burrell Advertising Co, Chicago, IL, vpres, acct supvr, 1981-82; United Airlines, Elk Grove Village, IL, mkt mgr, 1982-84; McDonald's Corp, Oakbrook, IL, dir mkt, Bloomfield NJ, dir opers, vpres, nat mkt, 1984-2000, sr vpres, chief mkt officer US, 2003-08. **Orgs:** Dir, Children's Memorial Med Ctr; Nat Caucus & Ctr Black Aged; Univ Ill Chicago Develop Comt; bd mem, Alliance Digital Equality. **Special Achievements:** First African-American senior vice president, chief marketing officer- US in charge of national marketing for McDonald's 13,000 US restaurants.

LAMARR, CATHERINE ELIZABETH
Lawyer. **Personal:** Born in Chicago, IL; daughter of Carl Leonard LaMarr and Sonya Frances Saxton LaMarr. **Educ:** Cornell Univ, Ithaca, NY, BA, 1982; Howard Univ, Sch Law, Washington, DC, JD, 1985. **Career:** Murtha, Cullina, Richter & Pinney, Hartford, CT, 1985-87; Levy & Droney LLP Farmington, CT, 1987-94; Bingham Dana & Gould, of f coun, 1994-98; Off State Treas, State Conn, gen coun, currently. **Orgs:** Treas's rep, Conn Lawyers Group; Nat Asn Pub Plan Attys; past pres, past bd mem, George W Crawford Law Asn; past bd dir, mem, Legal Aid Soc Hartford, 1989-. **Special Achievements:** Frequent lecturer to pension funds. **Business Phone:** (860)702-3018.

LAMAUTE, DENISE
Educator, lawyer. **Personal:** Born Mar 14, 1952, St Louis, MO; daughter of Josephine Carroll and Frederick Washington Sr; married Daniel, May 14, 1980. **Educ:** Brandeis Univ, Waltham, BA, 1973; Wash Univ, JD, 1977, LLM, tax, 1980. **Career:** Teachers Ins & Annuity Asn, sr tax attorney, 1978-82; Ernst & Whinney, supvr, 1982-85; Lamaute Tax & Financial Servs, owner, 1985-; Howard Univ Sch Bus, adj prof; Fla A&M Univ, assoc prof; Lamaute Capital Inc, pres; US Agency Int Develop, sr pension reform adv; Georgetown Univ Law Ctr, Social Security Admin, Off Policy, dir prog studies, currently. **Orgs:** US Tax Ct, 1981-; Nzingha Soc, 1987-88; co-chmn, Nat Bar Asn, 1988-89. **Special Achievements:** Auth, Tax Loopholes for Investors, Tab Books, NY, 1989; frequentcontributing writer to mags, newspapers on financial issues; her publishedwork has also appeared in numerous jour & mag articles. **Business Phone:** (202)358-6225.

LAMB, MONICA
Basketball player. **Personal:** Born Oct 11, 1964. **Educ:** Univ Southern Calif, attended 1987. **Career:** Basketball player (retired); Palermo, Italy, basketball player, 1986-87; Milan, 1987-88; Madrid, Spain, 1988-89; Catanzaro, 1989-90; Bari, 1991-94; Clermont, France, 1995-96; Parma, 1996-97; Houston Comets, ctr, 1997-2000. **Orgs:** Founder & pres, Monica Lamb Wellness Found, 1998-. **Business Addr:** Founder, President, Monica Lamb Wellness Foundation, 5330 Griggs Rd Suite B106, PO Box 14526, Houston, TX 77099, **Business Phone:** (713)504-7255.

LAMBERT, BENJAMIN FRANKLIN
Lawyer. **Personal:** Born Mar 6, 1933, Lowell, MA. **Educ:** Boston Univ, BA, chem, 1955; Brandeis Univ, MA, org chem, 1959; Seton Hall Univ Sch Law, JD, 1968. **Career:** Ciba Phar Co Inc, res chem, 1957-66; Ciba Ltd, res asst, 1962-63; Merck & Co Inc, atty, 1966-70; Fitzpatrick, Cella, Harper & Scinto, atty, 1970-72; Johnson & Johnson, patent atty, 1973-; Brandeis Univ, teaching fel. **Orgs:** Reg US Patent Off, 1968; US Dist Ct Dist NJ, 1969; Dist Ct So Dist NY, 1972; NY Bar Asn, 1972; Dist Ct Eastern Dist NY, 1972; NJ Patent Law Asn; Am Patent Law Asn; US Ct Customs & Patent Appeals, 1977; Nat Asn Advan Colored People, 1977; Delta Hon Soc; Scarlet Key Hon Soc. **Honors/Awds:** Augustus Howe Buck Scholar. **Military Serv:** AUS, Sgt, 1962. **Business Addr:** Patent Attorney, Johnson & Johnson, 1 Johnson & Johnson Plz, New Brunswick, NJ 08933, **Business Phone:** (732)524-0400.

LAMBERT, DR. BENJAMIN J., III
Government official, optometrist, senator (u.s. federal government). **Personal:** Born Jan 29, 1937, Richmond, VA; son of Benjamin T Jr and Mary Frances Warden; married Carolyn L Morris, May 14, 1966; children: Benjamin IV, David, Charles Justin & Ann Frances. **Educ:** Va Union Univ, BS, 1959; Mass Col

Optometry, attended 1962; Old Dominion Univ. **Career:** Pvt pract, optometrist, 1963-; Dominion Res, bd dir, 1994-; Consolidated Bank & Trust Co, dir; Va Gen Assembly, sen, 1986-2007. **Orgs:** Gen Assembly House Delegates, 1977-85; secy bd trustees, Va Union Univ, 1977-87; Corp Bd Va Power; chmn, Senate Sub Comt Higher Educ; Westwood Baptist Church; pres, Richmond Optom Soc; Va Optom Soc; Am Optom Asn; Nat Optom Asn; Richmond Med Soc; Omega Psi Phi Fraternity; pres Richmond Jackson Ward Civic Asn; dir, Richmond Jaycees. **Honors/Awds:** Most Outstanding Young Man for the City of Richmond, 1972; Optometrist of the Year, Nat Optom Asn, 1979; Optometrist of the Year, Va Optom Asn, 1980. **Home Addr:** 3109 Noble Ave, Richmond, VA 23222.

LAMBERT, JOSEPH C.
Executive. **Personal:** Born Jul 4, 1936, Vauxhall, NJ; married Joan E Cross; children: Kim, George & Joseph Jr. **Educ:** Va State Col. **Career:** St Bank Plainfield, NJ, teller trainee, 1961-64; Security Nat Bank Newark,NJ, chief clerk, 1964-66; Nat State Bank Linden, NJ, admin asst, 1966-68; Nat State Bank Elizabeth NJ, asst br mgr, 1968-70; Nat State Bank, Plainfield, NJ, asst cashier & br mgr, 1970-72; East Orange Comt Bank, vpres & treas, 1972; Deryfos Consumer Bank, sr vpres & treas. **Orgs:** Plainfield Area Urban Coalition; Plainfield Kiwanis; bd dir, S Second StYouth Ctr YMCA; finance chmn Plainfield Bd Educ. **Honors/Awds:** Apptd first Black Jury Comnr Union Co, 1974. **Military Serv:** AUS, 1958-60; USAAFR, 1960-62; discharge, 1966. **Business Addr:** Senior Vice President, Treasurer, Dreyfus Consumer Bank, 554 Central Ave, East Orange, NJ 07018.

LAMBERT, LECLAIR GRIER. See Obituaries section.

LAMBERT, LEONARD W.
Lawyer. **Personal:** Born Oct 27, 1938, Henrico Co, VA; married Sylvia Jeter; children: Leonard Jr, Ralph, Linda, Brice, Mark. **Educ:** Va Union Univ, BA, 1960; Howard Univ Sch Law, JD, 1963. **Career:** Lambert & Assoc, atty, currently. **Orgs:** Vpres bd, Metrop YMCA; Jewish Comn Ctr; C Home Soc; Travelers Aid Soc; Richmond Chap Am Red Cross; Neighborhood Legal Aid Soc; Old Dominion Bar Asn; Va Adv Coun Comn Youthful Offenders; Va State, Richmond Criminal Bar Asn; Va Trial Lawyers Asn; Nat Asn Defense Lawyers; Nat Bar Asn; Richmond Trial Lawyers Asn; Focus Club; Club 533; substitute Judge Juvenile & Domestic Rels Ct City Richmond Va; Omega Psi Phi Frat; selective appeal bd Eastern Dist Va; chmn trustee bd, Westwood Baptist Church; Nat Bd, YMCA; Nat Prog Chmn, YMCA; vpres, Va Ctr Performing Arts; vpres Federated Arts Coun. **Business Addr:** Attorney, Lambert & Associates, Corner 23rd Marshall St, Richmond, VA 23201, **Business Phone:** (804)648-3325.*

LAMBERT, SAMUEL FREDRICK
Engineer. **Personal:** Born Jul 8, 1928, Monroville, AL; son of Frederick and Nannie Howard; married Florence Mickings; children: Carla, Pamela Roberts, Samuel II, Michele & Wanda. **Educ:** Armstrong Sch Engineering, Marine Engrs License, 1953; Pace Univ, BS, 1978. **Career:** First Army Headquarters AUS, SP 3/C 1954-56; Military Sea Transport Service, marine engr, 1956-60; New York City Bd Educ, custodian engr, 1962-74, supvr custodian, engrs, 1974-. **Orgs:** Engr, consult, WEBB & Brooker Inc; past nat pres, Nat Assoc Power Eng, 1982; elected mem, Community Sch Bd 11, 1980-. **Honors/Awds:** Trinity Baptist Church, Community Service Award; Outstanding Custodial Admin, Morrisania Educ Counc; Certificate of Apppreciation, Bd Educ. **Military Serv:** AUS, spec 2nd class, 1954-56; USN, Reserve Lt jg, while serving as merchant marine engineering officer. **Home Addr:** 4071 Edson Ave, Bronx, NY 10466. **Business Phone:** (718)788-4707.

LAMOTTE, JEAN MOORE
Administrator. **Personal:** Born Sep 2, 1938, Shreveport, LA; divorced. **Educ:** Calif State Univ Sacramento; Am River Col, Sacramento; Central State Univ, Wilberforce, OH. **Career:** Campbell Soup Co, voc spec, 1966-70; Human Rights Comn, proj dir & Affirmative action prog, 1970-73; KXTV-10 Corinthian Broadcasting, host moderator daily pub serv talk show, 1973; Affirm Act Prog for underutilizing employers, writer. **Honors/Awds:** Comm Serv Award, Golden Empire Chap Am Heart Asn, 1977-80; Woman of Year, Sacramento Observer Newspaper, 1977; Sacramento's Most Influential Black Woman Sacramento Observer, 1978; Outstanding Community Serv Award, Women's Civic Improvement Ctr, 1980.

LAMPLEY, DR. EDWARD CHARLES
Physician, educator. **Personal:** Born Jun 21, 1931, Hattiesburg, MS; son of Willie Lee Lampley Sr and Elma Wilson Lampley; married Dr Norma Jean Mosley, Sep 11, 1959; children: Edward, Marguerite & Karl. **Educ:** Alcorn Col, 1954; Wayne Univ, AB, 1956; Howard Univ, MD, obstet & gynec, 1960; Stanford Univ, CA, attended; Univ Calif San Diego Med Sch, MD; Am Bd Observ & Gynec, dipl; Am Bd Obstet-19 Gynec, re-19cert, 1978. **Career:** Detroit Receiving Hosp, intern, 1960-61; Provident Hosp Chicago, resident, 1961-63; Harlem Hosp NY, resident, 1963-66; Pvt Pract Oakland, Calif, physician spec obstet & gynec, 1966-; Memorial Hosp, sr md, Dept Obstet & Gynec, chmn; Rosalind Franklin Univ Med & Sci, assoc prof, currently; mem staff, Highland Hosp; Herrick Memorial Hosp; Merrick Hosp; Univ Ill Chicago Med Ctr, residency obstet & gynec; Univ Pa, Maternal Fetal Med, fel. **Orgs:** Former clin med dir, E Oakland Planned Parenthood Clin; fel Am Col Obstet & Gynec; Am Chem Soc; AMA; Alameda County & Nat Med Asn; Golden State MedAsn; Sinkler-Miller Med Soc; Alameda County Gynec Soc; Am Fertility Soc; Am Asn Planned Parenthood Physicians; Alpha Psi; cofounder, E Oakland Med Ctr Oakland, Calif; chmn bd dir, Community Devel Inst East Palo Alto Calif, 1984-86; Kappa Alpha Psi; chmn, Scholarship Comt, Downs Memorial Church; chmn, Boy Scout Troup 33; Counman, Alameda Contra Costa Med Soc, 1985-; house deleg, Calif Med Asn, 1985-. **Honors/Awds:** Man of the Year Award, Ravenswood Sch Dist; Soloist Downs Memorial Church Chapel Choir. **Military Serv:** USAF s/sgt 1949-52. **Business Addr:** Associate Professor, Rosalind Franklin University of Medicine and Science, 3333 Green Bay Rd, North Chicago, IL 60064, **Business Phone:** (847)578-3000.

LAMPLEY, DR. PAUL CLARENCE
Educator, vice president (organization). **Personal:** Born Dec 12, 1945, Louisville, MS; married Fannie; children: Samantha. **Educ:** Tougaloo Col, BS, 1967; Atlanta Univ, MS, 1971; Howard Univ; Memphis State Univ; Univ Miss, PhD, 1981. **Career:** United Negro Col Fund, distinguished prof, 1985-86; Harris Jr Col, instr; NSF, grad trainee; Rust Col, asst develop dir, chair div social sci & acad dean, exec asst pres, SACS Reaffirmation Comt, chair, vpres assessment, currently. **Orgs:** Nat Asn Advan Colored People; Yacona Area Coun; Omega Psi Phi; Nat Asn Fed Rel Officers; Phi Delta Kappa; Sigma Pi Phi. **Honors/Awds:** Outstanding Young Man in American, 1972. **Business Addr:** Vice President for Assessment, Rust College, 150 Rust Ave, Holly Springs, MS 38635, **Business Phone:** (601)252-8000 Ext 4009.

LANCASTER, HON. GARY LEE
Judge. **Personal:** Born Aug 14, 1949, Brownsville, PA; son of Paul L and Ester Arabelle; children: Matthew. **Educ:** Slippery Rock State Col, BS, 1971; Univ Pittsburgh, JD, 1974. **Career:** Penn Human Rels Comn, 1974-76; Dist Atty Allegheny County, PA, 1976-78; pvt pract law, 1978-87; US Magistrate Judge, 1987-93; US Dist Ct Western Dist Penn, 1993-. **Orgs:** Allegheny County Bar Asn; Nat Bar Asn; Homer S. Brown Law Asn. **Business Phone:** (412)208-7400.

LANCASTER, HERMAN BURTRAM
Legal consultant, educator. **Personal:** Born Mar 6, 1942, Chicago, IL; son of Eddie and Louise; married Patricia L Malucci; children: Lauren E, Rachel J & Meredith E. **Educ:** Chicago State Univ, BS, 1965; Rosary Col, MA, 1968; De Paul Univ, JD, 1972. **Career:** Chicago Bd Ed, teacher, 1965-66; DePaul Univ Law Sch, asst dir law lib, 1966-70; Univ Chicago, psychiat dept dir info, 1970-72, legal coun, 1972-73; Glendale Univ Law Sch, prof law, dir res, 1973-; Legal Inst Law Consult, dir, 1976-; US Cent Dist Bankruptcy Ct, mediator. **Orgs:** Nat Asn Advan Colored People, 1975-; Glendale Law Rev, 1976-; advisor,Subcontractors Inst, 1984-; arbitrator, AAA, 1986-; arbitrator, Am Arbitration Asn. **Honors/Awds:** Omega Psi Phi Scholarship, 1963; Grad Fellowship 1966; Man of the Year, Omega Psi Phi, 1966.De Paul Law School Scholarship, 1968; Blue Key Law Hon Soc, 1968; De Paul Law Review Scholarship, 1969-72. **Special Achievements:** Published numerous articles. **Business Phone:** (818)247-0770.

LANCASTER, RONNY B.
College administrator. **Educ:** Catholic Univ, AB, econs, 1973; Univ Penn, Wharton Sch, MBA, 1975; Georgetown Univ, JD, 1984. **Career:** Blue Cross/Blue Shield Asn, sr wash rep; US Off Personnel Mgt, Div Fee-For-Serv Plans, chief, 1984-86; Hamilton Enterprises Inc, gen coun, 1988; Nat Inst Adv Studies, exec asst chmn; US Dept Health & Human Serv, exec asst secy & prin, dep asst secy planning & eval; Morehouse Sch Med, sr vpres & chief operating officer; US Dept Health & Human Servs, spec asst & dep dep under secy intergovernmental affairs, 1990, exec asst secy, currently. **Orgs:** Pres, Minority Health Profs Found; bd dirs, OraSure Technologies, 2003-; bars Commonwealth Pa; Dist Columbia Ct Appeals. *

LAND, DANIEL
Football player. **Personal:** Born Jul 3, 1965, Donalsonville, GA; married; children: 2. **Educ:** Albany State, GA. **Career:** Football player(retired), Tampa Bay Buccaneers, defensive back, 1987; Oakland Raiders, defensive back, 1989-97.

LANDER, C VICTOR
Lawyer, judge. **Personal:** Born Jun 29, 1954, Columbus, GA; son of Fred L Lander III and Agnes Levy. **Educ:** Morehouse Col, BA, hon, 1975; Univ Tex Sch Law, JD, 1978. **Career:** Tex Atty Gen Off, legal intern, law clerk, 1976-78; FDL Commun CMS, atty, 1978-86; Lander & Assocs, PC, atty, managing partner, 1986-; City Dallas Tex Munic Ct, assoc judge, 1991-96, munic judge, Ct 7, 1996-; City Balch Springs, Tex Munic Ct, munic judge, 1993-96. **Orgs:** Bd gov, Nat Bar Asn, gov lawyers div chair, 1977-89; chair, Legal Redress Comt, Nat Asn Advan Colored People, Nominations Comt, Election Supervising Comt, 1986-90, 1994-96; bd dirs, YMCA, 1989-; bd mem, Dallas Urban League, 1996-; atty, JL Turner Legal Asn, currently. **Honors/Awds:** Certificate of Achievement, Nat Judicial Col, Reno, NV, 1997. **Special Achievements:** Periodic writer, Dallas Weekly Newspaper, 1990-94; Frequent speaker on employment, legal, judicial issues, 1986-; Participant & co-founder, CAW Clark Legal Clin, 1989-; AMR Inns Court; Col State Bar Tex. **Home Addr:** 6521 Putting Green Dr, Dallas, TX 75241, **Home Phone:** (214)374-7740. **Business Phone:** (214)670-5573.

LANDER, CRESSWORTH CALEB
Government official, president (organization). **Personal:** Born May 15, 1925, Tucson, AZ; son of James Franklin and Julia Belle Watson; married Linda C Hill, Mar 3, 1979; children: Melodie Lynette & Rochelle Elaine. **Educ:** Univ Ariz Los Angeles State Col, BS, bus admin, 1958; MIT Sloan Bus Sch,summer course, 1975; Harvard Bus Sch & Kennedy Sch Govt, 1979. **Career:** Government Official (retired): real estate bus, 1959; City Tucson's Dept Human & Comm Dev, dir, 1974-78; Univ Aria Urban Planning Dept, lectr,1976-78; Civil Aeronautics Bd, managing dir, 1979-81; Comm Dev Training Inst, consult; Dept Housing City Tucson, dir. **Orgs:** Dep assessor, LA Co Assessor's Off Bus Div, 1958-59; dep dir, Pima-Santa Cruz Co CEO, 1968-69; dir, City Tucson's Dept Urban Resource Coord (Model Cities), 1969-74; bd trustees, Pub Housing Authority Dirs Asn; bd mem, Pima Coun Aging; bd mem, Tucson Airport Authority; vpres & bd mem, Tucson Urban League; bd, Ariz Multi bank Comm Develop Corp, 1992-; chairperson bd,Tucson Urban League, 1992-; pres, Community Develop Training Inst, 1992-;pres, Dunbar Coalition, currently. **Honors/Awds:** Senior Executive Service, US Govt Charter 1979; Meritorious Service, Civil Aeronautics Bd, 1981; Par Excellence Award, Ariz Black C of C, 1984; Comm Leadership Award, Jack & Jill Am Tucson Chap, 1985; Founders Award winner, 2006. **Military Serv:** USMC, gunnery sgt, 3 yrs. **Business Addr:** President, The Dunbar Coalition, Inc., PO Box 86132, Tucson, AZ 85754-6132.

LANDERS, NAAMAN GARNETT
Manager. **Personal:** Born Oct 23, 1938, Anderson, IN; married Stephanie E Cox; children: Naaman III. **Educ:** Purdue Univ, BS, CE, 1966; Univ Chicago, MBA, 1969. **Career:** manager (retired); Amoco Oil Co, engr, 1966-69, material mgr, 1972-76, proj dir, mgr, Bus & Financial Serv, 1980-91; Esso Chem Co, trans analyst 1969-71; Stand Oil Co, coord inventory control, 1977-79. **Honors/Awds:** Presidential Citation Reconnaissance over Cuba. **Military Serv:** USN, 1959-63. *

LAND-LATTA, THERESA E.
Municipal government official, law enforcement officer. **Career:** City NY, Dept Invest, dep inspector gen, currently. **Business Addr:** Deputy Inspector General, City of New York, Department of Investigation, 80 Maiden Lane 16th Fl, New York, NY 10038, **Business Phone:** (212)825-2467.*

LANDREAUX, KENNETH FRANCIS
Baseball player. **Personal:** Born Dec 22, 1954, Los Angeles, CA; divorced; children: Kenneth Antoine & Todd Xavier. **Educ:** Ariz State Univ; Ariz Sch Real Estate, attended 1992. **Career:** Baseball player (retired); Calif Angels, outfielder, 1977-78; Minn Twins, outfielder, 1979-80; Los Angeles Dodgers, outfielder, 1981-87; Sr ProfBaseball Asn, Orlando Juice, 1989, St. Petersburg Pelicans, 1989. **Orgs:** Community Affairs, Los Angeles Dodgers. **Honors/Awds:** Minor League Player of the Year, 1977; Am League All-Star Team, 1980; Wona World Series Ring with the Los Angeles Dodgers, 1981.

LANDRUM, TERRY LEE. See LANDRUM, TITO.

LANDRUM, TITO (TERRY LEE LANDRUM)
Baseball player. **Personal:** Born Oct 25, 1954, Joplin, MO; married Theresa; children: Melissa & Julie. **Educ:** Eastern Oklahoma State, Wilburton, OK. **Career:** Baseball player (retired), consultant; St Louis Cardinals, outfielder, 1980-83, 1984-87; Baltimore Orioles, outfielder, 1983; Los Angeles Dodgers, outfielder, 1987; Baltimore Orioles, outfielder, 1988; Hydro-Tone Sports & Med Equipment, dir res & develop 1992-94; Play It Again Ltd, team consultant, 1994. **Orgs:** Orioles. **Honors/Awds:** World Series Championship Team, 1983. **Special Achievements:** Participated in 1985 World Series.

LANDRY, DOLORES BRANCHE
Executive. **Personal:** Born Oct 9, 1928, Philadelphia, PA; daughter of Merwin Edward Branche (deceased) and Wilma Brown Branche (deceased); married Lawrence A Landry, Apr 16, 1966 (died 1997); children: Jennifer E, Michael H. **Educ:** Fisk Univ, BA, 1950; Denmark Int Hojskole Elsinore, Denmark, dipl, 1951; Univ Chicago, MA, 1960. **Career:** Executive (retired); Sci Res Assocs, ed & guid dir, 1954-60, proj dir res & develop, 1960-61; Chicago Community Youth Welfare, actg dir city-wide youth serv, 1961-63; Joint Youth Develop Community, youth employment consult, 1963-64; Horizons Employment Counr Inc, founder & pres, 1964-66; Chicago Community Urban Oppor, chief planner, 1964-65; private consult, 1965-71; Assoc Consults Inc, cofounder & pres, 1971. **Orgs:** Chicago Guid & Personnel Asn, 1955-66; mem bd dirs, Elliott Donnelly Youth Ctr, 1961-63; Asn Women Bus Owners, 1971-00; chmn, child guid comn vpres

Murch Home & Sch Asn, 1973-78; vpres, Howard Univ Faculty Wives Asn, 1974-75; vpres, mem bd dirs DC Asn C women & Learning Disabilities, 1974-87; Alpha Kappa Alpha; bd dirs, Glenbrook Found Exceptional C, Bethesda, MD, 1980-81; chair, budget & planning comt, DC Juvenile Justice Adv Group, 1987-90; Nat Fed Teaching Entrepreneurship, DC, adv bd, 1994-96; Int Network Women Bus Owners, 1990-00. **Honors/Awds:** Woman of the Year Award, Sigma Gamma Rho Sorority, Chicago, 1960; Outstanding Volunteer Award, DC Pub Schs, Wash, DC, 1979; Outstanding Commitment Fisk Univ, NE Regional Alumni Award, 1990. *

LANDRY, L. BARTHOLOMEW
Educator, sociologist. **Personal:** Born Apr 28, 1936, Milton, LA; married. **Educ:** St Mary's Col, BA, 1961; Xavier Univ, BA, 1966; Columbia Univ, PhD, 1971. **Career:** Columbia Univ, fac fel, 1966-67; New Sch Social Res, Instr, 1969-70; Purdue Univ, asst prof, 1971-73; Univ Md, from asst prof to assoc prof, 1973-2002, prof, 2002-, Currently. **Orgs:** African Studies Asn; Am Sociol Asn; Caucus Black Sociologists; Law Sociol Asn; Population Asn Am Publ field; Asn Black Sociologists. **Honors/Awds:** NIMH Fel, 1967-69; NIH Dissertation Fel, 1969-71; Research Contract 20th Century Fund, 1975-77; Curriculum Transformation Project Award, Univ Md, 1987; Curriculum Transformation Project Award, 1990; Graduate Research Board Semester Award, 1993; Distinguished Contribution to Scholarship Book Award, Am Sociol Asn, 2001; Excellence in Teaching Award, 2001; William J Goode Book Award, Am Sociol Asn, 2002. **Special Achievements:** Auth: The New Black Middle Class, 1987. **Business Addr:** Professor, Regular Member, University of Maryland, Department of Sociology, 3141 Art Sociol Bldg, College Park, MD 20742, **Business Phone:** (301)405-6416.

LANE, ALLAN C
City planner. **Personal:** Born Dec 21, 1948, Akron, OH; son of Sanford and Mable Farrior; married Nancy McClendon. **Educ:** Hiram Col, BA 1971; Univ Cin, MCP 1973. **Career:** City Cin, city planner 1972-73; Cin Comm Action Agency, asst proj dir 1972; Model Cities Housing Corp, dep planning dir 1973-75; City Dayton, sr city planner 1975-89; City Atlanta, urban planner 1989-92; GRASP Enterprises, dir cot develop, 1992-94, dir training, 1999-; Atlanta Community for Olympic Games, proj coordr, 1994-96; City Col Park GA, econ develop specialist, 2002-. **Orgs:** Founder/artistic advisor Creekside Players 1978-89; bd mem Dayton Contemporary Dance Co 1984-86; bd mem OH Theatre Alliance 1984-87; presenting/touring panelist 1984-86, theatre panel 1989-91, Ohio Arts Coun; Fulton County Arts Coun, theatre panel, 1993-95; Ballethnic Dance CPN, bdm, 1991-94; Proj Interconnections, bdm, 1996-98; Old Ntl Merchants Asn, bd mem, 2001-; Atlanta Airport Area Com, 2003-04. **Honors/Awds:** Employee Year Dayton Dept Planning 1981; Outstanding Service to Proj Alpha, Alpha Phi Alpha Frat 1985-86; Service to Gifted C Dayton Pub Schs 1986. **Home Addr:** 3150 Key Dr SW, Atlanta, GA 30311.

LANE, CHARLES (CHARLES ARTHUR LANE)
Movie director. **Personal:** Born Dec 26, 1953, New York, NY; son of Charles and Albertha; married Laura Lesser, Jul 8, 1984; children: Nicole Alysia & Julien Michael. **Educ:** State Univ NY, Purchase, BFA, 1980. **Career:** Filmmaker, 1976-; Films: A Place in Time, 1976; Sidewalk Stories, 1989; True Identity, 1991; Alma's Rainbow, 1994. **Orgs:** Nat Black Programming Consortium; Black Filmmakers Found; Acad Motion Pictures Arts & Sci; adv bd, Independent Film Prog; Actors Guild Am; Screen Actors Guild; Writers Guild. **Honors/Awds:** Prix du Publique award, Cannes Film Festival, 1989; Best Director and Best Film awards, Upsalla Film Festival, Sweden, 1989; Grand Prix and 2nd Prize, Journalise Jury, Chamrousse, France, 1989; Black Filmmakers Hall of Fame, 1990; CEBA Award, 1991; Nat Asn Advan Colored People, 1992; numerous other national & international awards. *

LANE, CHARLES ARTHUR. **See LANE, CHARLES.**

LANE, CURTIS
Executive, government official. **Career:** Hillsborough County Police, chief investgr; Tampa Police Dept, dep chief of police; City Tampa, exec asst to mayor, 1995-, dir code enforcement, currently. **Orgs:** Nat Forum of Black Pub Adminrs; Nat Asn Human Rights Workers; Int Asn of Police-Community Rels Officers Bd Dirs; Fed Bur Invest Nat Acad Assocs; Tampa Bay Area Police Chiefs Asn; Nat Asn of Black Law Enforcement Execs. **Business Addr:** Director, City of Tampa, Code Enforcement, 102 E 7th Ave, Tampa, FL 33602, **Business Phone:** (813)274-5545.*

LANE, DAPHENE CORBETT
Educator. **Personal:** Born Aug 24, 1964, Ivanhoe, NC; daughter of Billy and Laura; married Xavier, Sep 10, 1988; children: Brandon & Brandi. **Educ:** NC Cent Univ, BSN, 1986; E Carolina Univ, MSN, 1995. **Career:** Veterans Admin, staff nurse, 1986-87; Sampson Memorial Hosp, staff nurse, 1987-90; Sampson Community Col, nursing instr, cord pract nursing prog, 1990-. **Orgs:** NC Coun Practical Nurse Educr; Kenansville Eastern Missionary Baptist Youth Coun; NC Nurse's Assn; Community Outreach Mission; inductee, Sigma Theta Tau, 1994-95; co adv, Practical Nursing Student Assn. **Business Addr:** Nursing Instructor, Sampson Community College, 1801 Sunset Ave Hwy 24 W, PO Box 318, Clinton, NC 28328, **Business Phone:** (910)592-8081.

LANE, EDDIE BURGYONE
School administrator, clergy. **Personal:** Born Aug 8, 1939, Providence, LA; son of John and Cleo; married Betty Jo Washington; children: Felicia, Carla & Eddie II. **Educ:** Barber Col, M, 1960; S Bible Inst, Dallas, Theol Sem, ThM Bible Diploma, 1974; Univ Tex, Dallas, BA, 1980; Dallas Theological Seminary, ThM, 1980. **Career:** Bibleway Bible Church, founder, pastor, 1969-; Dallas Theol Sem, from admin asst to pres, 1975-80, assoc prof emer, currently; Dallas Bible Col, prof 1975-76; S Bible Inst, prof 1975-76; Dallas Seminary, asst dean studs, 1980-85, asst prof, pastoral ministry, 1980-90, assoc dean studs, am minorities, 1985-, assoc prof, pastoral ministry, 1990-. **Orgs:** Co-founder & vice pres, Black Evangelistic Enterprise, Dallas, 1974-; bd mem, Dallas Nat Black Evangelical Asn, 1974-; dir, Black Chr Lit Am Tract Soc, 1978-85; founder & pres, Inst Black Family Renewal. **Special Achievements:** Author: The African American Christian Single, 1995; The African American Christian Family, 1996; The African American Christian Parent, 1997; The African American Christian Man. **Business Addr:** Associate Professor Emeritus, Dallas Theological Seminary, Pastoral Ministry, 3909 Swiss Ave, Dallas, TX 75204, **Business Phone:** (214)824-3094.

LANE, ELEANOR TYSON
Educator. **Personal:** Born Feb 14, 1938, Hartford, CT; married James Perry Lane Jr; children: Randall P & Hollye Cherise. **Educ:** Howard Univ, attended 1958; St Joseph Col, BA, 1960; Univ Hartford, MEd, 1975. **Career:** Educator (retired); Hartford Bd Educ, teacher, 1960-72; Amistad House, actg dir, 1973-75; Univ Conn, asst dir, 1976-90; Manchester Cot Col, Assoc Prof Edu, 1990-97. **Orgs:** New Eng Minority Women Adminr Annual Conf Wellesley Col, 1985; panelist Assoc Social & Behav Scientists Inc, 1985; participant Successful Enrollment, Mgt Seminar sponsored by Consults Educ Resource & Res Inc, 1986; New England Minority Women Adminr, Assoc of Social & Behav Scientists, Urban League Greater Hartford, Nat League Bus & Prof Women, Delta Sigma Theta Sor Inc, Univ Conn, Prof Employees Asn, Conn Asn Col Admis Officers; Nat Asn Women Deans Adminr & Counr, Nat Asn Col Admis Counr, New Eng Asn Col Registr & Admis Officers. **Honors/Awds:** Eleanor Tyson Lane. **Home Addr:** 113 Vernwood Dr, Vernon, CT 06066. *

LANE, ERIC, III
Actor. **Personal:** Born in Chicago, IL. **Career:** Films: One Week, 2000; Novocaine, 2001; Love Relations, 2002; Barbershop, 2002; A Get2Gether, 2005; Subtle Seducation, 2008; TV series: "Soul Food", 2001; "The Parkers", 2004; "Prison Break", 2005. *

LANE, GEORGE S., JR.
Dentist. **Personal:** Born Dec 28, 1932, Norfolk, VA. **Educ:** BS, biol, 1958; BS, chem, 1959; MS, endocrinol, 1960; DDS, 1963; Cert Oral Surg, 1969; First Dist Dental Soc Ny Col; Albert Einstein Sch Med; Northwestern Univ; Roosevelt Hosp Ny Col; Walter Reed Army Hosp; Walter Reed Inst Dent Res. **Career:** Va State Den Health Prog, dent clinician; pvt pract, dentist, currently. **Orgs:** Am Dent Asn; Royal Soc Health London; Acad Gen Dentist; Va State Dent Soc; Va Tidewater Dent Asn; bd mem, YMCA; life mem, Nat Asn Advancemwnt Colored People; Alpha Phi Alpha; Shiloh Baptist Church; Norfolk C of C; diplomate, Nat Bd Dent Examiners. **Special Achievements:** Elected for fellowship confirmation Acad of Gen Dent. **Military Serv:** USAF capt. **Business Addr:** Dentist, 5428 Pine Grove Ave, Norfolk, VA 23502-4925.*

LANE, JANIS OLENE
Journalist. **Personal:** Born Jan 4, Kansas City, KS; daughter of Charles Thomas and Henrietta Perry. **Educ:** Univ Mo, Kans City. **Career:** KCPT-TV, Kans City, Mo, reporter/assoc producer, 1978-83; KBMT-TV 12, Beaumont, Tex, anchor/producer, 1984; KCMO 81 AM, Kans City, Mo, anchor/reporter, 1984-86; KCTV 5, Kans City, Mo, talk show host/reporter, 1985-88; Power 95 FM, Kans City, Mo, news dir & anchor, 1986-88; WTOL-TV 11, Toledo, Ohio, weekend anchor & reporter. **Orgs:** Nat Asn Broadcast Journalists, currently; Women Alive; prayer intecessor, Toledo Covenant Church, currently. **Honors/Awds:** Crystal Award, News Reporting, 1989. **Home Phone:** (419)472-0255. **Business Addr:** News Anchor, WTOL-TV - 11 News, 730 N Summit St, Toledo, OH 43604, **Business Phone:** (419)248-1107.

LANE, JEFFREY D
Airplane pilot. **Personal:** Born Oct 7, 1955, Chicago, IL; divorced. **Educ:** Wilberforce Univ, attended 1975; Marquette Univ, BS, bus admin, 1980. **Career:** Lockheed Support Syst, Black Hawk Helicopter Test Pilot, 1992-94; Pfizer Inc, Team Leader, 1995; Gulfstream Int Airlines, pilot, 1995-98; Northwest Airlines, pilot, 1998-, regional vpres midwest region, currently. **Orgs:** Alpha Phi Alpha Fraternity, 1974-; regional vpres, Orgn Black Airline Pilots, 2001-04; USAF; WVa Nat Guard. **Military Serv:** AUS, maj, 1990-92; Meritorious Service Medal; Joint Service Achievement Medal; Army Commendation Medal; National Defense Service Medal. **Business Addr:** Pilot, Regional Vice President, Northwest Airlines Corp., 2700 Lone Oak Pkwy, Eagan, MN 55121, **Business Phone:** (612)726-2111.

LANE, JEROME
Basketball player, manager. **Personal:** Born Dec 4, 1966, Akron, OH; married; children: 5. **Educ:** Univ Pittsburgh, Pittsburgh, PA, attended 1985. **Career:** Basketball player (retired), supvr; Denver Nuggets, forward, 1989-92; Ind Pacers, forward, 1992; Milwaukee Bucks, forward, 1992; Cleveland Cavaliers, forward, 1993; Amateur Athletic Union, Team Akron, coach; Summit Lake Community Ctr, supvr, 2002-08. **Honors/Awds:** Led NCAA Div I in rebounds per game (13.5), 1987.

LANE, JOHNNY LEE
Percussionist, educator. **Personal:** Born Dec 19, 1949, Vero Beach, FL; son of Alfred A and Anna Lee; married Claudia Hickerson, Aug 11, 1973; children: Latoya T, Maxine A & Johnny A. **Educ:** Southern Univ, attended 1971; Southern Ill Univ, MM, 1972; Univ Ill, advan study; Bobby Christian Sch Percussion, advan study. **Career:** Johnny Lane Percussion Sextet Ensemble, conductor, 1971-72; Accent on Music, percussion inr, 1971-72; Tenn State Univ, Univ Percussion Ensembles, dir, 1972-74, asst dir bands, 1972-74; Eastern Ill Univ, dir percussion studies, 1974-; Univ Baptist Church, dir music, 1978-; Johnny Lane Percussion Enterprises, pres, 1980-83; MIDCO Int, percussion consult, 1983; percussion clinics & workshops: Univ Central AK, 1996; Univ Mo-St Louis, 1997; UNLV, 1998; La State Univ, 1999; Univ Tenn-Knoxville, 1999; Clemson Univ, 1999; Music Fest Canada, 1999; Univ Miss, 2000; Remo Inc, dir educ, currently. **Orgs:** Ed, Percussive Notes Mag Percussive Arts Soc, 1978-86; bd, Percussive Arts Soc, Ill State Chap, 1979-85, int bd, 1979-88, 1991-92, second vpres, 1981-83, mem comt chair, 1986-90; Nat Asn Rudimental Drummers; Kappa Kappa Psi, Nat Band Fraternity; Phi Mu Alpha, Nat Music Fraternity; Pi Kappa Lambda, Nat Music Honors Soc; fac adv, Sigma Alpha Iota. **Honors/Awds:** Hon Artist Dipl, Musikschule, Bad Nauheim, Germany, 1986; EIU Faculty Excellence Award, 1988-89, 1994, 1996; Friend of the Arts Award, Sigma Alpha Iota, 1992; Lifetime Acheivement in Education Award, Percussive Arts Society, 2007. **Special Achievements:** Co-author with Samuel A Floyd, Four-Mallet Independence for Marimba, published the fall of 2006 by Hal Leonard Publications; author, Stick Control Exercises for Snare Drum; Rudiments in Slow Motion; My 30 Minute Workout; Have done many clinics and workshops all across America and also South Korea and Japan. **Business Addr:** Director of Education, Remo Inc., 8206 Rockville Rd Suite 283, Indianapolis, IN 46214, **Business Phone:** (661)510-1993.

LANE, NANCY L
Executive. **Personal:** Born in Boston, MA; daughter of Samuel M and Gladys Pitkin. **Educ:** Boston Univ, BS, pub rels, 1962; Univ Pittsburgh Grad Sch Pub & Int Affairs, MA, pub admin, 1967; Univ Oslo, Norway, undergrad studies; Harvard Univ Grad Sch Bus Admin, prog mgt devel, cert, 1975. **Career:** Vice president (retired); Chase Manhattan Bank, second vpres, 1972-73; Off-Track Betting Corp, New York City, vpres 1973-75; Johnson & Johnson Corp, corp personnel staff 1975-76; Ortho Diagnostic Systems Inc, Div Johnson & Johnson, dir personnel, 1976-78, vpres personnel & admin & mem bd dirs 1978-89; Johnson & Johnson Worldwide Headquarters, Govt Affairs Div, vpres, 1989-2000. **Orgs:** Bd trustees, Studio Mus Harlem, 1969-; adv bd, prog founder, Black Exec Exchange Prog, 1970; bd dir, exec comt, 1972-80, Catalyst; bd dir, Nat Black MBA Asn, 1972-75; trustee, Benedict Col, 1974-84; trustee, Wilson Col, 1975-78; Nat Comn Working Women, 1980-84; bd dir, vice chair, 1982-86, Better Chance; secy &treas, Harvard Bus Sch Alumni Asn, 1986-90; bd dir, Women's Forum, Woodrow Wilson Nat Fel, 1987-; chair bd trustees, Bennett Col, 1989-90; bd governors, Rutgers Univ, 1990-98; pres, 1990-92, bd dir, 1992-, Harvard Bus Sch, Club Greater New York; bd dir, Ronald McDonald House New York City, 1995-98; nat bd dir, NAACP, 1996-; Links Inc, 1998-; Bd Trustees, Freedom House Inc, currently; WARM2Kids Inc; Better Chance, CATALYST, Exp Int Living World Living; United Way Tri-State; Int Ctr Photog. **Honors/Awds:** Living Legends in Black, JE Bailey III, 1976; Twin Award, YWCA Int, 1978; Graduation Speaker, Univ Col, Rutgers Univ, 1992; Chairman's Award for Distinguished Service, Studio Mus Harlem, 1996; Leadership Award, New York City Support Group, 1996; Distinguished Alumni Award, Boston Univ, 1997; Distinguished Award, Harvard Bus Sch African Am, 1998. **Special Achievements:** Published numerous articles; profiled in The New York Times, Fortune, Black Enterprise, BusinessWeek, O, The Oprah Magazine. **Home Addr:** 37 W 12th St Apt 10J, New York, NY 10011.

LANE, DR. PINKIE GORDON
Educator, poet laureate. **Personal:** Born Jan 13, 1923, Philadelphia, PA; daughter of William A (deceased) and Inez Addie West (deceased); married Ulysses Simpson Lane, May 1948 (deceased); children: Gordon Edward. **Educ:** Spelman Col, Atlanta Ga, BA, 1949; Atlanta Univ, Atlanta Ga, MA, 1956; La State Univ, Baton Rouge La, PhD, 1967. **Career:** Educator, Poet laureate (retired); Southern Univ, instr, asst prof, assoc prof, 1959-86, prof, 1967-86, chief dept Eng, 1974-86, prof emerita, 1986; Books: Wind Thoughts. Fort Smith, Ark; South and West, 1972, A Quiet Poem; Broadside Press, 1974; I Never Scream, 1985; Girl at

the Window; Louisiana State Univ Press, 1991. **Orgs:** Poetry Soc Am; Nat Coun Teachers Eng; Modern Lang Asn; Col Lang Asn; contributing & adv ed, The Black Scholar; poetry ed, Black American Literature Forum; Delta Sigma Theta Sorority; Capita Area, Network Exec & Prof Women; YWCA. **Honors/Awds:** National Award, Achievement in Arts & Humanities, Spelman Col, Washington DC Alumnae Chap, 1983; National Award for Achievement in Poetry, Col Lang Asn, 1988; Louisiana State Poet Laureate, State Governor Roemer, 1989-92; Amistad Arts Award, 1998; numerous other honors & awards. *

LANE, TIFFANY. See BALTIMORE, CHARLI.

LANE, WILLIAM KEITH
Clergy, bishop. **Personal:** Born Dec 26, 1923, Knoxville, TN; son of George Alexander and Bertha Irvin; married Marion Keene Lane, Dec 28, 1948; children: Rhoda Lane Darling, William Keith Jr, Marcia Elizabeth (deceased), Brian Keith. **Educ:** Detroit Bible Col, attended 1952. **Career:** Eastside Church God, bishop, currently. **Honors/Awds:** Hon Doctorate, Faith Evangelistic Christian Sch, 1990. **Home Addr:** 15483 Fairfield St, Detroit, MI 48238-1445, **Home Phone:** (313)341-7743. **Business Addr:** Bishop, Eastside Church of God, 2900 Gratiot Ave, Detroit, MI 48207-2475.*

LANEUVILLE, ERIC GERARD
Actor, administrator, television producer. **Personal:** Born Jul 14, 1952, New Orleans, LA; son of Alexander and Mildred; married; children: Sean. **Educ:** Santa Monica City Col, attended 1973; Univ Calif, Los Angeles, attended 1974. **Career:** MTM Prod, actor & dir; PBS, producer; Lorimar Prod, dir & producer; Universal City, dir; 20 Century Fox, dir; Citadel Prod, dir; Warner Bros, co-executive producer & dir; Lan Ville Inc, pres; TV Series: "Head of the Class", 1986; "A Brand New Life", 1989; "Reasonable Doubts", 1991; "Goingto Extremes", 1992; "McKenna", 1994; "Rescue 77", 1999; Films: The Omega Man, 1971; Black Belt Jones, 1974; Death Wish, 1974; A Piece of the Action, 1977; Love at First Bite, 1979; The Baltimore Bullet, 1980; Fear of a Black Hat, 1994; Someone She Knows, 1994; ER: Summer Run, 1995; If Someone Had Known, 1995; A Case for Life, 1996; Twisted Desire, 1996; Pandora's Clock, 1996; Born into Exile, 1997; Trapped in a Purple Haze, 2000; Critical Assembly, 2003; America's Prince: The John F. Kennedy Jr. Story, 2003; Gilmore Girls: The Party's Over, 2004; Naughty or Nice, 2004; Monk: Mr. Monk and the Other Detective, 2005. TV series: Rescue 77, The WB, 1999. **Orgs:** Dirs Guild Am; Screen Actors Guild; Acad TV Arts & Sci; Dirs Guild Educ & Benevolent Found; Am Diabetes Asn. **Honors/Awds:** Outstanding Director, Dirs Guild Am, 1987, 1992; Christopher Award, The Christophers, 1987, 1996; Emmy Award, Acad TV Arts & Sci, 1992. **Special Achievements:** Nominated for Emmy for Drama and Comedy Series, 1993; On Ballot for Emmy, acting, 1968; Three nominations for Emmy for directing, 1989, 1992, 1993. **Home Addr:** 5140 W Slauson Ave, Los Angeles, CA 90056, **Home Phone:** (213)293-1277. *

LANG, ANDREW CHARLES
Basketball player. **Personal:** Born Jun 28, 1966, Pine Bluff, AR; married Bronwyn; children: 2. **Educ:** Univ Ark, Fayetteville, AR, 1988. **Career:** Basketball player (retired), chaplain; Phoenix Suns, ctr, 1988-92; Philadelphia 76ers, 1992-93; Atlanta Hawks, 1993-95, chaplain, currently; Minn Timberwolves, 1996; Milwaukee Bucks, 1996-98; Chicago Bulls, 1998-99; New York Knicks, 2000. **Honors/Awds:** NBA Man of the Year, Athletes Int Ministries, 1994; MetLife Community Assist Award, 2000. **Business Addr:** chaplain, Atlanta Hawks, 101 Marietta St NW Suite 1900, Atlanta, GA 30303, **Business Phone:** (404)827-3800.

LANG, ANTONIO
Basketball player, basketball coach. **Personal:** Born May 15, 1972, Mobile, AL. **Educ:** Duke Univ. **Career:** Phoenix Suns, 1994-95; Cleveland Cavaliers, 1995-97; Miami Heat, 1997-98; Cleveland Cavaliers, forward & guard, 1998-99; Toronto Raptors, forward & guard, 1999-2000; Philadelphia 76ers, forward & guard, 1999-2000; Mistubishi Melco Dolphins, Japan, 2001-06, asst coach, 2006-. **Business Phone:** (813)5468-6291.

LANG, KENARD
Football player, social worker. **Personal:** Born Jan 31, 1975, Orlando, FL. **Educ:** Univ Miami, Fla. **Career:** Wash Redskins, defensive end, 1997-2001; Cleveland Browns, linebacker, 2002-05; Denver Broncos, defensive end, 2006-07; NFL Denver Broncos, free agent, currently. **Orgs:** Founder, bd, Kenard Lang Found, 2002; Make-A-Wish Found. **Honors/Awds:** Big E Rookie of the Year; Defensive Player of the Week, Nat Football League, 1999; Defensive Player of the Week, AFC, 2004; Sportsman of the Year, Onyx. **Special Achievements:** First round pick, NFL Draft, No 17, 1997. **Business Addr:** Free Agent, NFL, 12 W 280 Park Ave, New York city, NY 10017, **Business Phone:** (212)450-2000.

LANG, MARK
Educator. **Career:** Wayne County Community Col Dist, Downtown Campus, vice chancellor admin & finance, Eastern Campus, Entrepreneurial Resource Admin, provost, currently.

Business Addr: Provost, Wayne County Community College District, Eastern Campus, 801 W Fort St, Detroit, MI 48226, **Business Phone:** (313)579-6996.*

LANG, DR. MARVEL
Educator. **Personal:** Born Apr 2, 1949, Bay Springs, MS; son of Rev Otha Lang Sr; married Mozell Pentecost, Sep 15, 1973; children: Martin & Maya. **Educ:** Jackson State Univ, BA, 1970; Univ Pittsburgh, MA, 1975; Mich State Univ, PhD, 1979. **Career:** Lansing Community Col, 1976-78; Jackson State Univ, assoc prof, 1978-84; US Census Bureau, res geographer, 1984-86; Mich State Univ, Ctr Urban Affairs, dir & prof; Contemporary Urban Am, ed, 1991; Walden Univ, fac, currently. **Orgs:** Gov's Coun Selective Serv (MS), 1969-70; Nat Youth Adv Coun Selective Ser, 1969-70; steering comt mem, Southeastern Asn Am Geographers, 1980-81; consult, Miss Inst Small Towns, 1980-84; bd mem, Catholic Social Servs-St Vincent's C's Home, 1986-89; Boys & Girls Clubs Lansing, 1986-89; adv bd mem, Mich Legis Black Caucus Found, 1987-90; gov bd mem, Urban Affairs Asn; ed bd mem, Jour Urban Affairs, Urban Affairs Quarterly. **Honors/Awds:** Candidate, US Air Force Acad, 1966; Meritorious Service Award, Mich Legis Black Caucus, 1988. **Special Achievements:** Black Student Retention in Higher Educ (book) co-editor, 1988. **Home Addr:** 3700 Colchester Rd, Lansing, MI 48906, **Home Phone:** (517)323-8204. **Business Addr:** Faculty, Walden University, 155 Fifth Ave, South Minneapolis, MN 55401.

LANGE, LAJUNE THOMAS
Judge, educator. **Personal:** Born Jan 29, 1946, Kansas City, MO; daughter of Thomas P; married. **Educ:** Augsburg Col, BA, psychology, 1975; Univ Minn Law Sch, JD, 1978; Minn Inst Criminal Justice, 1979; Harvard Law Sch, advan training prog, 1984, employment discrimination, 1985, Judicial Scholar's Prog, 1987; Nat Judicial Col, advan gen jurisdiction, 1985, drugs and the courts, 1989. **Career:** Judge (retired), Educator; Twin Cities Opportunities Industrialization Ctr, counr, 1967; Univ Minn, Dept Civil Rights, field rep, 1968-70; Harry Davis Mayoral Campaign, media & pub rel staff vol, 1971; Dorsey, Marquart, Windhorst, West & Halladay, legal asst, 1971-73; self-employed, civil litigation matters, 1973-74; Oppenheimer, Wolff, Foster, Shepard & Donnelly, legal asst litigation, 1974-75; Hennepin County Pub Defender's Off, law clerk, 1976-78, asst pub defender, 1978-85; Nat Inst Trial Advocacy, fac, 1980; William Mitchell Col Law, civil rights clin, adj prof, 1984-, trial advocacy, adj prof, 1983-; Hennepin County Munic Ct, judge, 1985-86; 4th Judicial Dist, judge. **Orgs:** Founding mem, Minn Minority Lawyers Asn, 1980-; bd dir, Minn Women Lawyers; co-chair, pub rel comt, Minn Women Lawyers, 1977-; comnr, Minn Civil Rights Comn, 1979-84, chair person, stand & procuedures comt; Nat Bar Asn; judicial coun, int law comt, criminal law & juv justice comt; impact of drugs on crime, educ & social welfare, Gov's Select Comt; chair person, Nat Asn Women Judges; minority affairs comt, nominating comt, Nat Bar Asn judicial Coun; bd dir, Penumbra Theatre Co; chancellor adv coun, Univ Minn; sr fel, Roy Wilkins Ctr Human Rel & Social Justice; chief exec, LaJune Thomas Lange Int Leadership Inst. **Business Addr:** Adjunct Professor, William Mitchell College of Law, 875 Summit Avenue, Saint Paul, MN 55105-3076, **Business Phone:** (651)227-9171.*

LANGE, TED W.
Administrator, actor. **Personal:** Born Jan 5, 1948, Oakland, CA; married Sherryl Thompson; children: Ted IV & Turner Wallace. **Educ:** San Francisco City Col; Merritt Jr Col. **Career:** San Francisco City Col, fac; Univ Calif, fac; George Washington Univ, fac; "Othello", producer, dir & actor; Plays: Love Boat segment "Starmaker"1981; Driving Miss Daisy, "Lemon Meringue Facade", 1998; "Family Matters"; Films: Wattstax; Trick Baby; Blade; Larry; Passing Through, writer, 1977; The Redemption, 2000; Is This Your Mother, 2002; Banana Moon, co-producer, 2003; Gang of Roses, 2003; Monster Movie, 2006; Dorm Daze 2, 2006; Uncle Tom's Apartment, 2006; Last of the Romantics, 2007; Senior Skip Day, 2008; Who Shot Mamba?, 2008; The Adventures of Umbweki, 2008; Phil Cobb's Dinner for Four, 2008; For Love of Amy, dir, 2008; TV specials: "The Big Buttingin Episode", 2003; "Guitar", 2004; "Mindy's Back", 2005, "All of Us", dir, 2005; "Eve", dir, 2003; "Bottoms Up", 2006; "TV L &: Myths & Legends", 2007; Maxim Mag, writer; Psych, dir (1 episode), 2008. **Orgs:** Am Film Inst, Musical Hair. **Honors/Awds:** Renaissance Man Theatre Award; The Heroes and Legends HAL Lifetime Achievement Award; The Dramalogue Award; James Cagney Directing Fellow Scholarship Award, Am Film Inst; Paul Robeson Awar, Oakland's Ensemble Theatre; Bartender of the Year, 1983; Certificate of Achievement, Black Film makers Hall of Fame, 1989.

LANGFORD, DR. ANNA RIGGS. See Obituaries section.

LANGFORD, DARIA
Executive. **Educ:** Univ Ill, Chicago. **Career:** Jr High Sch, teacher; RCA, regional promotions mgr; Virgin Records, promotions & sales; Mercury Records, promotions & sales; LaFace Records, sr vpres promotions & mkt, currently. **Business Phone:** (404)848-8050.

LANGFORD, DEBRA LYNN
Executive. **Personal:** Born Mar 27, 1963, Los Angeles, CA; daughter of Roland and Barbara Jean Wilkins. **Educ:** Univ

Southern Calif, BS, bus admin, 1984. **Career:** Golden Bird, dir mkt & advert, 1984-86; Hanna-Barbera Prod, dir develop, 1986-89; Warner Brothers TV, dir current prog, 1989-92, vpres current programming, 1992-93; Quincy Jones Entertainment, vpres TV, 1993; Warner Bros, senior vpres current programming, 2002; Time Warner, dir strategic sourcing, 2003, exec dir, currently. **Orgs:** Nat Asn Female Exec, 1988-; Nat Asn Advan Colored People, 1989-; African Am Film & TV Asn, 1989-; Kwanza, 1989-; steering cot, Black Entertainment Alliance, 1990-. **Business Phone:** (212)364-8200.*

LANGFORD, DENISE MORRIS
Judge. **Personal:** Born Jan 1, 1953?, Detroit, MI. **Educ:** Wayne State Univ, BA, guidance & coun, cum laude, 1976, MA, 1978; Univ Detroit, Sch Law, JD, 1982. **Career:** Child welfare worker; Oakland County, trial atty, asst prosecuting atty, bd mem child abuse & neglect coun; Sixth Judicial Circuit Ct Mich, US Atty's Office, asst US atty, judge, 1992-. **Orgs:** Fed Bar Asn; Nat Bar Asn; Nat Asn Women Judges; Am Bar Asn; bd dirs, Mich Judges Asn; Black Judges Asn; gov bd mem, Oakland-Livingston Human Servs Agency; bd mem, Salvation Army, William Booth Legal Aid Clinic; bd mem, St Joseph Mercy Hosp; Wolverine Bar Asn; bd dir, D Augustus Straker Bar Asn; Oakland County Bar Asn; Access Justice Group, Mich Supreme Ct. **Honors/Awds:** Certificate of Recognition, Judicial Admini Div, Am Bar Asn; United States Department of Agriculture Award, 1991; Certificate of Recognition, Southeastern Mich Asn Chiefs Police; Wonder Woman Award, Women's Survival Ctr, 1993; Break the Glass Ceiling Award, Pontiac Urban League; Judicial Award, Nat Asn Advan Colored People, 1994; Sprit of Detroit Award, 1998; Professor Award, Oakland County Bar Asn, 1998; Appreciation Award, Fed Bar Asn, 1998; Distinguished Alumni of the Year, Univ Detroit, 1998; Pontiac Urban League-Break the Glass Ceiling Award. **Special Achievements:** First African American judge to serve at Oakland County Circuit Court; First African American elected to a county government position; named one of Most Influention African-Am Women in Metro Detroit, 1998. **Business Addr:** Judge, 6th Judicial Circuit of Michigan, Bldg 12 E 1200 N Telegraph, Pontiac, MI 48341, **Business Phone:** (248)858-0363.

LANGFORD, JEVON
Boxer, football player. **Personal:** Born Feb 16, 1974, Washington, DC. **Educ:** Okla State Univ. **Career:** Football player (retired), Boxer; Cincinnati Bengals, defensive end, 1996-2001; prof boxer, 2001-; Functional Conditioning, coach, currently. **Business Addr:** Coach, Functional Conditioning, Bldg B 8120 Sheridan Blvd Suite 101, Westminster, CO 80003, **Business Phone:** (303)467-7954.

LANGFORD, VICTOR C., III
Clergy, army officer, president (organization). **Personal:** Born Aug 6, 1939, Detroit, MI; son of Victor Langford Jr and Charlotte; married Luana Calvert; children: Tanya, Natalie, Kineta, Victor IV. **Educ:** Seattle Pacific Col, BA, 1970; Concordia Theol Sem, BDiv, 1970, MDiv, 1975. **Career:** Bethel Lutheran Church New Orleans, founder & pastor, 1962-64; Holy Cross Lutheran Church Houston, pastor, 1965-68; Good Shepherd Lutheran Church, Seattle, pastor, 1968-76; St Mark's Lutheran Church, Seattle, minister, 1976-, Parish pastor, currently; Nu-Life Enterprises, pres, 1979-86. **Orgs:** Treas Black United Clergy Action, 1969-76; chmn exec com, Emerg Feeding Prog, Seattle, 1977-86; chmn, Proj People of Seattle, 1970-72; bd dir, Seattle Opportunities Indust Ctr, 1969-86; Nat Asn Advan Colored People, 1969-; exec bd, Asn for Black Lutherans, 1983-87; instr, Seattle Pacific Univ, 1978; instr, Seattle Univ, 1978, 1980; exec comt bd dir, Church Coun Greater Seattle, 1983-86; organizer & chmn, Filling the Gap Conf March 26 & 27, 1982; assoc educ, Lutheran Partners Mag, 1985-; exec bd, PNW Synod Lutheran Church Am, 1986-87; NW Wash Synod Coun, 1988-89; founding bd chmn, Emerald City Bank, Seattle, WA, 1988; pres, The African Am Luthern Asn, 1991-93; pres, Aid Asn Lutherans, 1983-; ed assoc, Lutheran Partners Mag, 1985-; dean, Cluster 8, NW Wash Synod, ELCA, 1994; pres, Faith Ministries, 1996-. **Honors/Awds:** Juneteenth Fathers Day Award, Future Prod Seattle, 1977. **Special Achievements:** The first African-American general appointed in the Washington National Guard. **Military Serv:** Army Nat Guard, special asst to the chief of chaplains, Dept of the Army, chaplain, 1972-, Brig Gen, 1998. **Business Addr:** Parish Pastor, St Mark's Lutheran Church, 6020 Beacon Ave S, Seattle, WA 98108, **Business Phone:** (206)722-5165.*

LANGHAM, ANTONIO (COLLIE ANTONIO LANGHAM)
Football player. **Personal:** Born Jul 31, 1972, Town Creek, AL; son of Willie and Deborah. **Educ:** Univ Ala. **Career:** Football player (retired); Cleveland Browns, defensive back, 1994-95, 1999; Baltimore Ravens, 1996-97; San Francisco 49ers, 1998; New Eng Patriots, cornerback, 2000. **Honors/Awds:** Jim Thorpe Award, 1993; Defensive Player of the Yr, Nat Football League Players Asn, 1994; Defensive Player of the Year, Football Digest, 1994.

LANGHAM, COLLIE ANTONIO. See LANGHAM, ANTONIO.

LANGHAM, JOHN M.
Executive. **Personal:** Married Carvine; children: John Jr, Jimmy. **Educ:** Alabama State Col, Alabama A&M; Univ Southern

Alabama, physical science. **Career:** Prichard Trading Post; self-employed. **Orgs:** pres, PTA Mobile Co; pres, Toulminville Recreation Ctr; pres, Prichard City Coun; Alabama & Am Teachers Asn; bd dir, Commonwealth Nat Bank; mem adv bd, Bishop State Jr Col; pres, Prichard NAACP; Supervisory Comn, Mobile Co Personnel Bd; Mobile United; Nat League Cities; Joint Ctr Political Action; Southern Black Caucus Elected Officials; Nat Democratic Party; Prichard Senior Citizen Org; ACT Educ Prog. **Honors/Awds:** pichard C Of C week; Kappa Citizen of the Year. **Military Serv:** AUS.

LANGHART COHEN, JANET (JANET FLOYD)
Television show host, television journalist. **Personal:** Born Dec 22, 1941, Indianapolis, IN; daughter of Sewell Bridges and Floyd Stamps; married Melvin Anthony Langhart (divorced); married Robert Kistner (divorced 1989); married William S Cohen, Feb 14, 1996. **Educ:** Butler Univ, attended 1962; Ind Univ. **Career:** New England's Good Day, ABC Affiliate, talk show host, 1981-85; nationally syndicated You Asked for It, overseas correspondent, 1985-86; The Boston Herald, columnist, 1986-88; Home Show, ABC, guest host, 1990; Entertainment Tonight, correspondent, 1990; Black Entertainment TV, commentator; Nationally Syndicated Am Black Forum, co-host, 1991-96; Personal Diary with Janet Langhart, host, 1993-94; On Capitol Hill with Janet Langhart, host, 1995-96; Media-Wise, gen partner, 1995-; Invest Am, creator, developer, 1996-; Langhart Communications, pres, 1996-; Special Assignment, host, 1997-2001; US News & World Repor, spokesperson; Avon Cosmetics, spokesperson. **Orgs:** US News & World Report; Digital Equipment Corp; US Senate Spouses; judge, New Eng White House Fel; judge, Miss Am Pageant; bd mem, United Negro Col Fund; bd mem, US Nat Arboretum. **Honors/Awds:** Outstanding Young Leader Award, Boston's Junior; Israel Cultural Award; The Casper Award, City of Indianapolis; One of Boston's Brights, Glamour Magazine; Emmy Nomination for writing, producing & hosting "Janet's Special People". **Special Achievements:** Featured in Francesco Scavullo's, Scavullo Women; Portrayed self in the movie adaptation of John Dean's "Blind Ambition," CBS-TV; acted in Haskell Wexler's movie, "Medium Cool"; author of 'My Life in Two Americas' & 'From Rage to Reason'. **Business Phone:** (202)393-5158.

LANG-JETER, LULA L
Government official. **Personal:** Born in Pickens Co, AL. **Educ:** Cent State Univ, BS, 1951, attended 1970; Wright State Univ Grad Sch, 1969. **Career:** Cent State Univ, supvr acct, 1968; Internal Revenue Servs, auditor & supvr, 1963-71, br chief, 1971-78, sr exec, 1979-; Imperial Ct Daughters Isis, imperial internal auditor, currently. **Orgs:** Co-chairperson, N VA Minority Task Force Am Cancer Soc; Am Inst Parliamentarians; participant, Nat Urban League's Black Exec Exchange Prog; Soc Women Accts; local pres & nat treas, Alpha Kappa Alpha Sor Inc; League Women Voters; life mem, Nat Coun Negro Women; bd dir, YM-YWCA, 1962-83; Nat Adv Bd Asn Improvement Minorities, 1981-; nat treas, Alpha Kappa Alpha Educ Advan Found, 1982-; Nat Adv Bd Federally Employed Women, 1983-; pub rels, Arlington Chap Links Inc, 1984-; nat treas, The Links, Inc. **Honors/Awds:** Fed Employee of the Year, Fed Exec Bd Cincinnati, 1971, Detroit, 1974, Indianapolis, 1982; Grad Leadership Award, Alpha Kappa Alpha, 1981; EEO Award, IRS Comn, IRS Wash, 1982; Outstanding Black Women in State of IN. **Special Achievements:** Top Ten Women, Dayton Daily newspaper, 1969. **Home Addr:** 1001 S Queen St, Arlington, VA 22204.

LANGSTON, DR. ESTHER J.
Educator. **Personal:** Born Jun 20, 1939, Shreveport, LA; daughter of Frank Jones and Daisy. **Educ:** Wiley Col, BA, bus educ, 1963; San Diego State Univ, MSW, 1970; Univ SCalif, 3rd Yr Cert Social Work/Geront, 1974; Univ Tex, PhD, human serv admin, 1982. **Career:** Nev State Welfare Dept, child specialist, 1965-70; Univ Nev Las Vegas, Emer Prof. of Social Work, Family Support Serv Div, Ctr Acad Advan & Enrichment, dir, currently. **Orgs:** Bd mem, Oper Life Community Develop Corp, 1977-79, 2003-06; proj dir,Minorities Pub Policies & Laws & Their Effect Serv Delivery, 1977; pres,LV Chap Nat Asn Black Social Workers, 1983-85; fac senate, Univ Nev LasVegas, 1984-85; pres, undergrad fac & assoc mem bd, Coun Social Work Educ,1984-85; vice chairperson, Gov's Comn Ment Health M/R, 1985-89; vpres & bd-dirs, Aids AIDS Nevada, 1988-90; pres, Nevada Chap, Nat Asn SocialWorkers, 1996-98, Legal Defense Comn, 1997-2000; pres, Les Femes Douze,1990-94, 1996-; bd dirs, BACC Prog Dirs, 1997-2000. **Honors/Awds:** Social Worker of the Year, Nat Asn Black Social Workers, 1982;Co-recipient, Univ Res Coun Grant, 1983; Fulbright Hays Scholar, USSR,1989; Social Worker of the Year, Nat Asn Social Workers, 1994. **Special Achievements:** Author of "The Family & Other Informal Supports," Campanile Press, 1983,"Care of the Terminally Ill, A Look at the Hospice Movement," IndianJournal of Social Services, 1986, "AIDS & the Black Church," 1990. **Home Addr:** 1943 Hobson Dr, Henderson, NV 89014-1002. **Business Addr:** Director, University of Nevada, CENTER FOR ACADEMIC ENRICHMENT AND OUTREACH EMBRACE PROGRAM, 4505 Md Pkwy CDC 10 Room 1026, PO Box 455032, Las Vegas, NV 89154-5032, **Business Phone:** (702)895-3311.

LANGSTON-JACKSON, WILMETTA ANN SMITH
Educator. **Personal:** Born Sep 16, 1935, Burlington, IA; daughter of William Amos Sr and Inez Jane Wallace; married Charles N Langston Jr (divorced 1966); children: Charles N III; married Robert Jackson (divorced); children: Robert Jackson Jr (stepson). **Educ:** Fort Valley State Col, Fort Valley, GA, BS, 1966; Atlanta Univ, Atlanta, GA, MLS, 1976. **Career:** Educator (retired); Fort Valley State Col, Div Vocational Home Econs, intermediate stenographer, 1960-64, Div Educ, secy, 1965-67; Houston County Bd Education, Perry, GA, media specialist, teacher, librn, 1967-88; Civil Serv, Warner Robins, GA, comput programmer asst, 1988-94; Fort Valley State Col UNIV, adjunct Eng & instr, 1988-00; libr, 2003-04. **Orgs:** Pres, Pink Ladies, Peach County Hosp; leadership team mem, Delta Sigma Theta Sorority, Inc, 1989-91; recording secy, GEO coun Auxiliaries, 1989-91, central district dir, 1996-98; Middle GEO Girl Scouts, 1968-03, bd, 1993-97; Fort Valley State Col NAT Alumni ASN, bd, asst secy & secy, hist, life mem, 1990-93, 1994-02; Peach County Pub Librs, bd trustees, 1992-04; bd mem, Peach County Unit, AM Heart ASN; Sunday sch supt, youth dir, Trinity Baptist Church, 1954-; Atlanta UNIV NAT Alumni ASN, Fort Valley Area Alumni Chap, charter mem, pres; life mem, NARFE; life mem, NAACP; life mem, Georgia TCRs Asn; life mem, GSUSA; life mem, Nat Educ Asn; life mem, GAE; Ft Valley Area Alumni Chap, secy; secy, Peach County health Educ & Wellness Coalition, 1990-; charter mem, Women Military Serv Am. **Honors/Awds:** Four Year Honors Convocation Awardee, Ft Valley State Col; One 75 Delta Diamonds, Delta Sigma Theta Sorority, Inc, 1988; Certificate Appreciation & Plaques, Middle Georgia Girl Scout Coun, 1986, 1990; 35 Years Service pin, US Girl Scouts Am, 2002; 9 Appreciation Plaques, Fort Valley State Col nat Alumni ASN, 1982, 1993-02; life mem, Alpha Kappa Mu NAT Honor SOC. **Special Achievements:** Editorial adv bd, "Col Writing Skills," Collegiate Press. **Military Serv:** USY, cpl, 1957-60; Proficiency P-1 Rating. *

LANIER, ANTHONY WAYNE
Editor. **Personal:** Born Aug 13, 1957, Louisville, KY; son of Austin and Ida Mae Smith; married Carlene Grace Foreman, Sep 13, 1997. **Educ:** Western Ky Univ, BFA, 1980; Univ Louisville, 1982. **Career:** The Courier-J, Louisville, KY, news artist, 1984-90; The Patriot Ledger, Quincy, MA, graphics ed, 1990-98; freelance photographer. **Orgs:** The Club, mentor, 1990-93; treas, Boston Asn Black Journalists, 1990-95; Soc Newspaper Design, 1990, bd, 1996; New England Soc Newspaper Eds, 1990; bd dirs, New England Press Asn, 1993-96; Region One treas, Nat Asn Black Journalists, 1993-96; middle adult ministry coordr, Concord Baptist Church, 1994-95. **Honors/Awds:** Newspaper Design Sem participant, Am Press Inst, 1985; Black Achiever Volunteer Service Award, YMCA, Chestnut St Branch, 1987; The Club, Outstanding Service Award, Mentor, 1991-93; Nat Asn Black Journalists, Inst Journalism Educ Fel, 1992. **Special Achievements:** The JB Speed Museum, 10th Annual Black Artists Exhibition, 1990.

LANIER, DOROTHY COPELAND
Educator. **Personal:** Born Aug 19, 1922, Pine City, AR; married Marshall Lee; children: Frederick Delano, Adrien Copeland & Vanessa King. **Educ:** Henderson State Teacher Col, BSE, 1965; E TX State Univ, MS, 1968, EdD, 1974. **Career:** Universal Life Ins Co, sec-cashier, 1952-54; Sparkman Training Sch, teacher, 1957-60; E Ariz Community Col, instr, 1975-77; Jarvis Christian Col, asst prof eng, pub rel assoc, 1960-75, chmn, Div Humanities, prof eng, 1977-87. **Orgs:** Zeta Phi Beta Sor, 1941-; exec comt mem, Linguistic Asn SW, 1974-77; talent file, Nat Coun Teacher Eng, 1974-; AR Philos Asn, 1976. **Honors/Awds:** Zeta of the Year, Zeta Phi Beta Sor, 1973; Outstanding Teacher, Jarvis Christian Col, 1974; publications: "Selected Grammar Patterns in the Language of Jarvis Students", "Sociolinguistics in the SW", 1974, "Black Dialect grammar in fact & fiction", Ariz Philos Asn Pub, 1976, "Textual Puzzle Technique", ERIC 1977; Outstanding Professional Service, Jarvis Christian Col, 1975; Outstanding Contributor to Education, Zeta Phi Beta Sor Inc, 1977.

LANIER, HORATIO AXEL
Association executive, president (organization). **Personal:** Born Feb 7, 1955, Augusta, GA. **Educ:** Univ Ga, AB, Jour, 1977; Georgetown Univ Law Ctr, JD, 1987. **Career:** Southern Bell Tel Co, bus off mgr, 1977-79; Xerox Corp, mkt rep, 1980-82; Sears Bus Syst Ctr, mkt rep, 1982-84; US Justice Dept Off Legal Coun, legal edl asst, 1984-85; H Lanier Small Bus Develop Consult, pres, 1985-86; Nat Black Alumni Asn, nat pres, 1986-. **Orgs:** Pres, Univ Ga Black Alumni Asn, 1980-82; Univ Ga Bicentennial Planning Comn, 1984-85; exec producer, UHURU Performing Arts Ensemble Georgetown Law Ctr, 1985-87; vice chmn, Black Law Stud Asn Georgetown Law Ctr, 1985-86; Am Bar Asn 1986-; Nat Bar Asn, 1987-; pres bd dir, Asn Conflict Resolution, 2006-. **Honors/Awds:** Distinguished Service Award, Black Law Stud Asn, 1985; WEB DuBois Award, Georgetown Law Ctr, 1987. **Business Phone:** (202)464-9700.

LANIER, JESSE M, SR.
Executive. **Personal:** Born May 2, 1941, Bath, NC; son of Daniel Sr and Beather O; married Barbara M, Nov 2, 1968; children: Audrey, Jesse Jr & Lucinda. **Educ:** NC A&T State Univ, BS, bus admin, 1968; Univ New Haven, MBA prog, 1971-73. **Career:** Lanier Trucking Co, partner & operator, 1959-69; C W Blakeslee & Sons Construct, acct, 1968-70; Southern New Eng Tel Co, staff acct, ade serv staff asst, cot rel mgr, purchasing mgr, 1970-83; Springfield Food Syst Inc, pres & chief exec officer, 1983-. **Orgs:** Life mem, NCP, 1972-; pres, NC A&T Alumni Asn, 1975-; Nat Asn Purchasing Mgr, 1980-; Asn Ky Fried Chicken Franchisee Inc, 1985-; officer, Urban League Springfield Inc, MA, 1987-, bd chairperson, 1997-; bd mem, Greater Springfield Chamber Com, 1988-92; bd mem, KFC Minority Franchisee Asn, 1989-; bd mem, Jr Achievement Western Mas Inc, 1992-; New England Chamber Com. **Honors/Awds:** Business Man of the Year, Greater New Haven Bus & Prof Asn, 1992; Business Man of the Year, Greater Springfield Bus Asn, 1991; Promise Pride Operator, KFC, 1996-98; Top Sales Award, Million Dollar Store Operator, 1985-98; Business Man of the Year, Conn Chap NC A&T Alumni, 1988. **Home Addr:** 310 Thompsonville Rd, Suffield, CT 06078, **Home Phone:** (203)668-2523. **Business Addr:** President, Chief Executive Officer, Springfield Food System Inc, 644 State St, Springfield, MA 01109, **Business Phone:** (413)733-4300.

LANIER, MARSHALL L.
Educator. **Personal:** Born Jan 12, 1920, Halifax Co, VA; son of Parish L and Mary S; married Dorothy Copeland; children: Frederick D, Adrien C & Vanessa C. **Educ:** Tuskegee Univ, AL, BSA, 1948, MSA, 1950; Tex A&M, PhD, 1971. **Career:** Marvell Independent Sch Dist, instr vets, 1950-51; Co Agr Agent, Texarkana, Ark, 1951-54; Sparkman Training Sch Sparkman AR, prin & teacher, 1957-60; E AR Community Col, dir spec serv, 1976-77; Jarvis Christian Col Hawkins, TX, dir student teaching, 1977-85. **Orgs:** Asn Supervision & Curriculum Develop; Kappa Delta Pi; Omega Psi Phi Frat. **Honors/Awds:** Recipient plaque Outstanding Adv, Jarvis Christian Col, 1975; Blue & Gold Plaque, Jarvis Christian Col, 1978. **Military Serv:** AUS, sgt, 1941-45. **Home Addr:** 18667 FM 2015, Tyler, TX 75706.

LANIER, ROB
Basketball coach, baseball player. **Personal:** Born Jul 24, 1968, Buffalo, NY; son of Bob Lanier; married Dayo; children: Emory & Kai. **Educ:** St Bonaventure Univ, psychol, 1990; Niagara Univ, MA, educ coun, 1993. **Career:** Basketball player(retired), basketball coach; St Bonaventure, 1990; Niagara Univ, grad asst & restricted earnings coach, 1990-91, 1991-92; St Bonaventure Univ, asst coach, 1992-93, 1996-97; Rutgers Univ, asst coach, 1997-99; Univ Tex, recruiter, 1999-01; Siena Col, head men's basketball coach, 2001-05; Univ Va, asst coach, 2005-07; Univ Fla, currently. **Honors/Awds:** Most Improved Player, 1988-89. **Business Addr:** Assistant Men's Basketball Coach, University of Florida, 1000 Legion Place Suite 1600, Orlando, FL 32801.*

LANIER, SHELBY, JR.
Police officer. **Personal:** Born Apr 20, 1936, Louisville, KY; son of Shelby and Florine Bridgeman; widowed; children: Michael, Ricardo, Stephanie, Rasheedah, Ciara. **Educ:** Central State Univ, Wilberforce, OH, 1956; Univ Louisville, Louisville, KY, BS, 1975. **Career:** Police officer (retired); Louisville Div Police, Louisville, KY, detective, 1961-92. **Orgs:** Comnr, Metro Junior Football Leaue, 1980-89; pres, Louisville Br Nat Asn Advan Colored People, 1988-92; Chmn, Nat Black Police Asn, 1990-92; pres, Louisville Black Police Officers Org, 1990-92. **Honors/Awds:** Equality Award, Louisville Urban League, 1972; Citizen of the Year, Omega Psi Phi Fraternity, 1984; Outstanding Community Involvement, World Community Islam, 1986; Renault Robinson Award, Nat Black Police Asn, 1989; Community Service Award, Louisville Defender Newspaper, 1989. **Military Serv:** USAF, Airman, 1956-60. *

LANIER, WILLIE
Football player. **Personal:** Born Aug 21, 1945, Clover, VA. **Educ:** Morgan State Univ, BS, bus admin. **Career:** Football player (retired), exec; Kansas City Chiefs, linebacker, 1967-77; Baltimore Colts, 1978; Wheat First Butcher & Singer, sr vpres; First Union Securities, stock broker, dir bus develop & vice-chmn; Wachovia Securities, sr vpres, currently. **Orgs:** Bd visitors, Va State Univ; United Way Greater Richmond; YMCA; The Garfield Childs Fund; WCVE Pub TV, Central Va; Indust Develop Authority Chesterfield City; bd dirs, Huddle House Inc; bd dir, Venture Richmond. **Honors/Awds:** NFL Man of the Year, 1972; NFL Players Asn, Linebacker of the Year, 1970-75; Chiefs Super Bowl IV, Defensive Star; All AFL & AFC, seven times; played in two AFL All Star Games; six Pro Bowls; elected to Kansas City Chiefs, Hall of Fame, 1985; Pro Football Hall of Fame, 1986; Virginia Sports Hall of Fame, 1986; Virginian of the Year, 1986; NFL 75thAnniversary Team, 1995. **Special Achievements:** First African-American to play at middle linebacker position.

LANKFORD, RAYMOND LEWIS
Baseball player. **Personal:** Born Jun 5, 1967, Los Angeles, CA; married Yolanda; children: Raquel & Danielle. **Career:** Baseball Player (retired); St Louis Cardinals, outfielder, 1990-2001, 2004; San Diego Padres, 2001-02. **Honors/Awds:** Texas League MVP, 1989; Nat League Player-of-the-Week September 4-10, 1995; Nat League outfield fielding champion, 1996; Nat League All-Star team, 1997; Baseball Man of the Year, St Louis Chap BBWAA, 1997.

LANSEY, YVONNE F.
Banker, executive. **Personal:** Born Sep 9, 1946, Baltimore, MD; daughter of E Gaines Sr and Priscilla. **Educ:** Morgan State Univ, Baltimore, MD, BS, 1969; Long Island Univ, Brooklyn, NY, MBA, 1974. **Career:** Fed Reserve Bank NY, credit analyst, 1969-74; Xerox Corp, Rochester, NY, financial analyst, 1974-76; Westinghouse Electric Corp, Hunt Valley, MD, financial analyst, 1976-79, proj dir, 1979-85; Ideal Fed Savings Bank, Baltimore, MD, vpres, 1985-88, pres & chief exec officer, 1988-; Real Estate Appraiser & Home Inspector Comn, Baltimore, MD, comnr, currently. **Orgs:** Trustee, Florence Crittenton Servs, 1986; trustee, Girl Scouts Cent Md, 1987; trustee, Combined Health Agencies Inc, 1987; financial secy, The Links Inc, Harbor City Chapter, 1987-89; bd dir & secy, Am League Financial Insts, Wash, DC, 1988; trustee, Baltimore Mus Art, 1989; Alpha Kappa Alpha Sorority; secy, Baltimore Community Lending. **Honors/Awds:** Women on the Move, Sigma Gamma Rho, 1986; Booker T Washington Business League of Baltimore, 1989. **Home Addr:** 3303 Glen Ave, Baltimore, MD 21215. **Business Addr:** President, Chief Executive Officer, Ideal Federal Savings Bank, 1629 Druid Hill Ave, Baltimore, MD 21217-0888.*

LAPOINT, VELMA
College teacher. **Educ:** Hartford Univ, BS, attended; Mich State Univ, MA, PhD, attended. **Career:** Howard Univ, assoc prof human develop, prof human develop prog, currently. **Business Addr:** Professor of Human Development, Howard University School of Education, Department of Human Development and Psychoeducational Studies, 2441 4th St NW, Acad Support A Rm 305, Washington, DC 20059, **Business Phone:** (202)806-6514.

LARA, EDISON R, SR.
Executive. **Personal:** Married Genevieve; children: Cecelia E, Valencia Ann, Edison Jr & Alysanne. **Career:** Co Club Malt Liquor, regional mgr; Westside Distributors, chief exec officer, 1974-. **Orgs:** Black Bus Asn; YMCA; adv bd, Calif State Univ; UNCF Leadership Coun; Los Angeles Urban League; 100 Black Men; Tee Masters Golf Club; CBBD; NBWA. **Honors/Awds:** Mind Fires Award, United Negro Col Fund, 1981; Frederick D Patterson Award; Good Scout Award, Los Angeles Area Coun Boy Scouts Am; 100 Black Men of America, Most Outstanding Black Businessman in the Nation, 1988. **Business Addr:** Chief Executive Officer, Westside Distributors, 2405 Southern Ave, South Gate, CA 90033-4219, **Business Phone:** (323)566-2304.

LARGE, JERRY D
Journalist. **Personal:** Born Jan 15, 1954, Clovis, NM; son of Viola Bailey; married Carey Gelernter, Jul 30, 1982. **Educ:** NMex State Univ, Las Cruces, NM, BA, 1976. **Career:** The Farmington Daily Times, Farmington, NM, reporter, 1976-77; The El Paso Times, El Paso, TX, reporter, 1977-80; The Oakland Tribune, Oakland, CA, copy ed, 1980-81; Seattle Times, WA, asst city ed, 1981-92, columnist, 1993-; Knight fel, Stanford Univ, 2000-01. **Orgs:** Soc Prof Journalists, 1977-; Nat Asn Black Journalists, 1983-; treas, Black Journalists Asn Seattle, 1989-90. **Business Addr:** Columnist, The Seattle Times, 1120 John St, PO Box 70, Seattle, WA 98109, **Business Phone:** (206)464-3346.

LARK, RAYMOND. See Obituaries section.

LARKE, CHARLES
School administrator. **Personal:** Son of Alvin and Staretha. **Educ:** Paine Col, BS, Math, 1969; Univ SC, MEd, 1979; Univ Ga, Educ Spec Voc Educ, 1983, DEd, 1987; Augusta Col, Bus Admin; Ga Tech, Environ Sci; Ga State Univ, Voc Curric Supv. **Career:** Westside High Sch, 1970-84, cordor, 1979-84, asst prin, 1984; Richmond County Pub Schs, dir sec voc educ, 1984-86, asst supt voc serv, 1986-95, interim supt, 1995-96, supt, 1996-. **Orgs:** Nat Educ Asn; Ga Asn Educr; Ga Sch Superintendents Asn; Ga Asn Educ Leaders; Richmond County Asn Educrs; Asn Career & Tech Educ; Educ Tech Consoritum Adv Comt; Kappa Delta Pi Hon Soc Educ; Beta Kappa, Univ Ga; Sigma Pi Phi Fraternity Alpha Mu Boule. **Honors/Awds:** Won several awards including: Distinguished Alumnus Award, Paine Col, 1996-97; BellSouth Quality Leadership Award, 1998; Administrator of the Year, Richmond County Bd Educ, 1998; Richmond County Neighborhood Asn Alliance Leadership Award, 2004; Citizen of the Year, Kappa Alpha Psi Fraternity, 2004. **Special Achievements:** First African American superintendent of the Richmond County Public Schools. **Business Phone:** (706)826-1000.

LARKEN HICKS, PATRICIA
Executive. **Educ:** Hampton Univ, BA; Mich State Univ, MA; Univ Memphis, PhD. **Career:** Clinician; Univ prof; clin supvr; researcher & corp exec; Am Speech-Lang Hearing Asn, Rockville, MD; NIH; Howard Univ; NovaCare Inc; Outcomes Mgt Group Ltd, founder & pres, currently. **Orgs:** Outcomes Advisory Comt, United Way Cent Ohio; Payne Theol Sem Bd; Payne Theol Sem Bd; Nat Governance Eval Comt, The Links Inc; chair, Orgn Effectiveness & Technol, Cent Area; chair, Serv Youth Facet, Columbus Chapter; Delta Sigma Theta Sorority Inc. **Honors/Awds:** Outstanding Alumnus of the Year, Mich State Univ; Outstanding Alumnus of the Year, Univ Memphis; Fellow, Am Speech-Language-Hearing Asn. **Special Achievements:** Has made over 250 presentations to both national and international audiences and has published two books, several book chapters and over 30 articles. **Business Addr:** Founder, President, Outcomes Management Group Ltd, 786 S Front St, Columbus, OH 43206.*

LARKIN, BARRY LOUIS
Baseball player, association executive. **Personal:** Born Apr 28, 1964, Cincinnati, OH; son of Bob and Shirley; married Lisa Davis, Jan 6, 1990; children: Brielle D'Shea, Cymber Nicole & DeShane Davis. **Career:** Baseball player (retired), executive; Cincinnati Reds, infielder, 1986-2004; Wash Nationals, spec asst to gen mgr, currently; Major League Baseball Int, Europ Baseball Acad, lead infield instr, 2008. **Honors/Awds:** Silver Slugger, 1988-92, 1995-96, 1998-99; Roberto Clemente Award, 1993; Lou Gehrig Memorial Award, 1994; Nat League Gold Glove-SS, 1994-96; MLB Most Valuable Player Award, 1995; Nat League All Star Team, 1988-91, 1993-97, 1999. **Business Addr:** Special Assistant to the General Manager, Washington Nationals, RFK Stadium, 2400 E Capitol St SE, Washington, DC 20003, **Business Phone:** (202)675-6287.

LARKIN, DR. BYRDIE A.
Educator, political scientist. **Personal:** Born in Tuskegee Inst, AL; daughter of Rev Charles Haile and Lula Berry; divorced; children: Seve & Mwangi Leonard. **Educ:** Ala State Univ, BS, 1973; Atlanta Univ, MA, 1975, PhD, 1983. **Career:** Ala State Univ, Dept Polit Sci, asst prof, 1977-82, actg chairperson, 1982-85, coordr polit sci prog & assoc prof, currently; Univ Miss, Ford Found fel, 1989. **Orgs:** Alpha Kappa Mu Nat Honor Soc; charter mem, Black Women Academicians; NatConf Black Polit Scientists; Ala Asn Polit Scientists; chair, Col Arts &Sci, Courtesy Comt; consult, Bd Dir, Local Govt Training Inst; Ala Comn Higher, pres, Ala Polit Sci Asn; adv coun, Ctr Leadership & Nat AsnAdvan Colored People, Ala State Univ. **Honors/Awds:** Outstanding Graduate Student Award, Dept Polit Sci, Atlanta Univ, 1975; Dept State Scholar, Diplomat Conf Europe, 1981; Outstanding Faculty Award, Col Arts & Sci, Ala State Univ, 1991; Outstanding Faculty Award, Ala State Univ Stud Govt, 1993; Outstanding Pike, Troy United Women's League, County Native, 1993. **Special Achievements:** Political commentator and analyst; participant: founding and structuring of the Consortium on National Voting Rights & Political Empowerment, 1991. **Home Addr:** 114 Mountain Laurel Rd, Prattville, AL 36066. **Business Addr:** Associate Professor of Political Science, Alabama State University, Department of Political Science, GW Trenholm Hall 211, 114 Mountain Laurel Road, Prattville, AL 36066, **Business Phone:** (334)229-4373.

LARKIN, MICHAEL TODD
Advertising executive. **Personal:** Born Mar 7, 1963, Cincinnati, OH; son of Robert L and Shirley J; married Sharon Denise Dean, May 23, 1992. **Educ:** Univ Notre Dame, BA, econ, 1985. **Career:** Cincinnati Reds Shortstop Barry Larkin, personal mgr; Hameroff, Milenthal Spence Inc, sports prom dir, currently. **Home Addr:** 1149 Vineyard Dr t, Gurnee, IL 60031-3103. **Business Addr:** Director Sports Promotion, Hameroff, Milenthal Spence Inc, 10 W Broad St, Columbus, OH 43215, **Business Phone:** (614)221-7667.

LARKINS, ELIJAH PAT
Mayor, executive. **Personal:** Born Jan 1, 1942?, Pompano Beach, FL. **Career:** Pompano Beach, FL, mayor, vice mayor; Minority Builders Asn, dir, currently. **Honors/Awds:** Ford Foundation Grant, Nat Housing Inst, Washington, 1970. **Business Addr:** Director, Minority Builders Association.

LARS, BYRON
Fashion designer. **Personal:** Born Jan 19, 1965, Oakland, CA. **Educ:** Brooks Col, AA, 1985; Fashion Inst Technol, attended 1986-87. **Career:** Freelance sketcher & pattern maker, Kevan Hall, Gary Gatyas, Ronaldus Shamask, Nancy Crystal Blouse Co. NY, 1986-91; showed first collection, 1991; Byron Lars Beauty Mark, fashion designer, 1991-; first full-scale New York show, 1992; En Vogue fashion collection, designer, 1993; Shirttails collection, 1995-97; Cinnabar Sensation Barbie, 1996; launched new collection, Green T, 1999. **Honors/Awds:** USA rep, Int Concours des Jeunes Creatures de Mode, 1986; Festival du Lin, 1989; Rookie of the Year, Women's Wear Daily, 1991. **Business Phone:** (212)764-7664.

LARTIGUE, ROLAND E
Engineer, executive. **Personal:** Born Mar 3, 1951, Beaumont, TX; son of Homer Lartigue Sr and Emily; married Dell Malone, Jul 12, 1980; children: Jason. **Educ:** Mich State Univ, BS, mech engr, 1973; Xavier Univ, advan bus studies, 1979-84. **Career:** Eastman Kodak, res engr; Rockwell Int, res engr, sales engr, purchasing mgr & commodity mgr; Columbus Auto Parts, vpres, materials; Stahl Mfg, exec vpres, gen mgr; United Technol, vpres, purchasing & logistics; Saturn Electronics, vpres, gen mgr, currently. **Home Addr:** 29222 Lancaster Dr Apt 206, Southfield, MI 48034-1445. **Business Addr:** Vice President, Saturn Electronics, 255 Rex Blvd, Auburn Hills, MI 48326-2954, **Business Phone:** (248)299-8529.*

LARVADAIN, EDWARD
Lawyer. **Personal:** Born Aug 18, 1941, Belle Rose, LA; son of Edward Sr and Maxine; married Patricia Dorsett, 1965; children: Edward III & Malcolm X. **Educ:** Southern Univ, BA, 1963, Law Sch, JD, 1966. **Career:** Ernest Morial, atty, 1966-67; Edward Larvadain Jr & Assoc, atty, currently. **Orgs:** Alexandria Br, NCP, 1968-; La State Bar Asn, 1968-; La Trial Lawyers Asn, 1970-; chair, State NCP Educ, 1985-; comt mem, YMCA Black Achiever, 1989-. **Honors/Awds:** Outstanding Contributions, Sickle Cell Anemia, 1984, 1992; Service Award, EDU, State NCP, 1984; Outstanding Service, 1988; Outstanding Service, Sickle Cell Anemia, 1990; Outstanding Contributions, Girl Scouts, 1992. **Business Addr:** Attorney, Edward Larvadain Jr & Associates, 626 8th St, Alexandria, LA 71301, **Business Phone:** (318)445-6717.

LASALLE, ERIQ
Actor, movie director, movie producer. **Personal:** Born Jul 23, 1962, Hartford, CT. **Educ:** NY Univ, BFA, 1984. **Career:** Films: Drop Squad, 1994; Coming to America, 1988; One Hour Photo, 2002; Crazy As Hell actor, producer & dir, 2002; Biker Boyz, 2003; Johnny Was, 2005; Inside Out, 2005; producer: The Salton Sea, 2002; TV series: "ER", 1994-2002; "The Twilight Zone", 2002-03; "Memphis", 2003; "Without a Trace", 2006; TV Movies: Rebound: The Legend of Earl 'The Goat' Manigault, 1996; Mind Prey, 1999, Conviction, 2005. **Honors/Awds:** The Actor Outstanding Performance, Ensemble in a Drama Series "ER", 1995, 1996, 1997, 1998; Nat Asn Advan Colored People Image Award Outstanding Lead Actor, 1998, 1999, 2000. **Business Addr:** Actor, c/o Allen Niprod, Gersh Agency, 232 N Cannon Dr, PO Box 5617, Beverly Hills, CA 90210.

LASANE, JOANNA EMMA
Theatrical director, consultant. **Personal:** Born Jul 24, 1935, Atlantic City, NJ; daughter of John Westley Foreman and Viona Marie Foreman; married Karlos Robert, Aug 29, 1955; children: Karlos Jr. **Educ:** Katherine Dunham Sch Dance, NY, attended 1953-55; Martha Graham Sch Modern Dance, NY, attended 1953-55; Am Sch Ballet & Int Sch Dance, attended 1957; Montclair St Col Theatre Arts & Speech, attended 1970; Negro EnsembleCo, NY, attended 1971; New Lafayette Theatre, NY, attended 1972-73. **Career:** Ebony Fashion Fair Johnson Publ, Chicago, high fashion model, 1965-66; Atlantic City Bd Educ, comm agent, 1972-75, drama consult, 1983-; Stockton Performing Arts Ctr, rep arts & lect series, 1983-85; Atlantic City Children's Theatre, dir, 1973-; Atlantic Human Resources, Atlantic City, NJ, drama consult, 1973-; Ctr Early Childhood Educ, Atlantic City, NJ, drama consult, 1983-; Atlantic City Bd Educ, drama consult, currently; Dr Martin Luther King Jr Complex, dir & consult, currently. **Orgs:** Allied Arts; Nat Asn Advan Colored People; Urban League; NJ Educ Asn; bd dirs, Atlantic City Educ Found, 1987; Nat Educ Asn; Stockton St Col Friends Asn; adv coun, Dr Martin Luther King Jr Sch Complex; NJ St Coun Arts; NJ Speech & Theatre Asn; comt chmn, Boy Scouts Am, 1988-89; comnr, NJ-Atlantic City Coord Coun, 1990-; bd dirs, Police Athletic League; Altantic Co Cult & Heritage Adv Bd; Atlantic City Fine Arts Comn; bd trustees, South Jersey Stage Co; Children's Cult Arts Found; bd dirs, Atlantic Co Womans Hall Fame; Atlantic City Arts Comn Bd. **Honors/Awds:** Numerous honors & awards including Cultural Arts Award, Atlantic City Mag 1981; Delta Sigma Theta Appreciation Award, 1983; Outstanding Citizen, Nat Asn Advan Colored People & Civic Betterment Asn, 1984; Theta Kappa Omega Arts Award, 1986; Community Service Award, Alpha Kappa Alpha, 1986; Omega Psi Phi Fraternity Upsilon Alpha Chapter Inspiration & Leadership Award, 1986; Role model Award, Sun Newspaper, 1989; People to Watch award, Atlantic City Mag, 1989; Mary Church Terrell Award, 1992; NJ St Legislature Superlative Accomplishment in the Arts Award, 1994; Atlantic County Women's Hall of Fame, 1996; The Omega Psi Phi Award for Arts Excellence, 1996; Educ Fund Achievement Award, 1997; Kiwanis Club Key Award, Excellence in the Arts, 1997. **Special Achievements:** First Black model to do an international advertisement for Pepsi Cola, 1967; First African American woman appointed to the New Jersey St Council on the Arts. **Business Addr:** Director, Drama Consultant, Atlantic City Public Schools, Dr Martin Luther King Jr School Complex Dr Martin Luther Kin, Atlantic City, NJ 08401, **Business Phone:** (609)343-7380.

LASLEY, PHELBERT QUINCY, III (PHIL LASLEY)
Musician, music arranger or orchestrator, composer. **Personal:** Born Mar 27, 1940, Detroit, MI; son of Phelbert Quincy and Josephine Wooldridge; married Trudy Diana Norresi, Oct 15, 1973; children: Felicia & Nagira. **Educ:** Inst Musical Arts, Detroit, MI, 1957-58. **Career:** Saxophonist, 1958-; Detroit Jazz Orchestra, alto saxophonist, 1983-;Greenpeace, 1986; Guerilla Jam Bank, alto saxophonist, 1987; composition:Nkenge?s Blues, Lady T Diana. **Orgs:** Jazz Heritage Soc, 1975-; Citizens Comt Save Jazz, 1975-. **Honors/Awds:** Best Alto Sax, Honorable Mention, Metro Times, Detroit, 1989-90; Jazz Hallof Fame, Graystone Jazz Mus, 1990.

LASLEY, PHIL. See LASLEY, PHELBERT QUINCY, III.

LASSITER, CHAD DION
Activist, educator, social worker. **Personal:** Born Oct 5, 1972, Philadelphia, PA; son of Marilyn Adele; married Wanda Jamilah Lassiter, Sep 18, 1999. **Educ:** Johnson C Smith Univ, BSW, 1995; Univ Pa Grad Sch Soc Work, MSW, 2001. **Career:** Gateway

Group Homes, coun, 1994-95; Palumbo Elem Sch, sch based lead therapist, 1995-96; Childrens Hosp Philadelphia, soc worker, 1996-99; Univ PA, soc worker & res fel, 1998-2001, health educ, 1993-2003, Sch Social Policy & Pract, adj prof, 2003-, Children's Hosp Pa, res, currently; co-founder, Respecting all Cult Essential, 2003-. **Orgs:** Founder, Bright Outstanding Young Scholars, 2001-; Triumph Baptist Church, Gideon 300 Mens Ministry, 2001-; bd dirs, Univ Pa Grad Sch Soc Work Alumni Asn, 2003-; bd mem, Leadership Learners Partners Charter Sch, 2003-; pres, Black Men Penn Sch Soc Work, 2003-. **Honors/Awds:** A Phillip Randolph Award Outstanding Leadership & Serv to Univ Community Univ Pa, 2001; Spotlighted as "One Us," Philadelphia Daily News, 2003. **Special Achievements:** Publications: Preventing Long-term Anger & Agression Youth, published Monograph Nat Mens Health, 2001; chp co auth: Playing with Anger: Teaching Coping Skills African Am Boys through Athletics & Cult, 2003; profiled in Ebony magazine as one of the "Young Leaders of the Future Under 30", February 2003; named 2005 Philadelphia's Most Influential African Americans "10 People Under 40 To Watch In 2005" by the Philadelphia Tribune. **Home Addr:** 6617 N 12th St, Philadelphia, PA 19126, **Home Phone:** (215)924-9291. **Business Addr:** Behavioral Interventionist/Researcher, Adjunct Professor, The Childrens Hospital Philadelphia, 34th St & Civic Ctr Blvd, Philadelphia, PA 19104.

LASSITER, JAMES EDWARD, JR.
Dentist. **Personal:** Born Feb 12, 1934, Newport News, VA; children: Teri, Tina, James III, Judi. **Educ:** Howard Univ Col Dent, BMus Ed, 1957, DDS, 1963. **Career:** Overlook Hosp Summit NJ, assoc attend; Martland Hosp, assoc attend, 1972; Col Med & Dent, assoc prof, 1972-73; Col Dentistry Fairleigh Dickenson, asst prof, 1974-78; Col Med & Dent, asst prof, 1982-84; pvt Practice, dentist. **Orgs:** Numerous lectures; consul Union Co Vocational Sch; adv comn Col Med & Dent, 1977-79; consul Piedmont Res Ctr, 1979; consul Dept Health Educ & Welfare, 1979; adv, comn Nat Health Prof Placement Network WK Kellogg Found, 1979; adv comn, Col Med & Dent Dent Sch, 1979; bd mem, Group Health Ins NY; Am Dent Asn; Nat Dent Asn; NJ Dent Asn; Commonwealth Dent Soc; Am Analgesia Soc; Acad Med NJ; NJ Dent Group PA; Morristown Dent Assoc, 1973-78; Paterson Dent assoc; Acad Gen Dent; Am Soc Dent C; Fellow, Acad Dent Int; Fellow, Am Col Dent; acting exec, Nat Dent Asn; sr consul, Nat Dent Asn; ADA's Special Comn "The Future of Dentistry", 1982; chmn & pres, Nat Dent Asn Found; life mem, Golden Heritage mem, Nat Advan Asn Colored People; Kappa Alpha Psi Frat; Wallace AME Chapel. **Honors/Awds:** Commission Service Award, Greater Newark Urban Coalition, 1975; Outstanding Service Award, Nat Dent Asn, 1976; President's Award, Nat Dent Asn, 1977; Citation Giant Excellence, Health Care Arena, 1979; Alumni Achievement Award, Howard Univ Col Dent, 1981; Bergen & Passaic Howard Univ Alumni Award, 1981; President's Award, Nat Dent Asn, 1982; Outstanding Achievement Award, Commonwealth Dental Soc NJ, 1983; Outstanding & Valuable Contrib Scientific Session, Nat Dent Asn Baltimore MD, 1983. **Business Addr:** President, Patient First Dentistry of Summit, 475 Springfield Ave Suite 210, Summit, NJ 07901.

LASSITER, KWAMIE
Football player. **Personal:** Born Dec 3, 1969, Newport News, VA. **Educ:** Univ Kans, BS, commun. **Career:** Football player (retired); Ariz Cardinals, free safety, 1995-2002; San Diego Chargers, free safety, 2003; St Louis Rams, free safety, 2004. **Honors/Awds:** Defensive Player of Week, Sports Illustrated; Defensive Player of Week, Nat Football League, 1998; Defensive Player of Month, Nat Football League, 2001; Defensive Player of Week, Pro Football Weekly, 2003.

LASSITER, DR. WRIGHT LOWENSTEIN
College president, college administrator. **Personal:** Born Mar 24, 1934, Vicksburg, MS; son of Wright L Lassiter Sr and Ethel F; married Bessie Loretta Ryan; children: Michele Denise & Wright Lowenstein III. **Educ:** Alcorn State Univ, BS, 1955; Tuskegee Inst, Cert, Inst Bus Mgmt, 1956; Ind Univ, MBA, 1962; Auburn Univ, EdD, 1975; Calif Western Univ, PhD, 1977. **Career:** Hampton Inst, investments acct, 1956; Tuskegee Inst, sr acct, 1958-61; Tuskegee Inst, dir aux Enterprises, 1962-76; asst prof mgmt, 1962; Ind Univ Bloomington, res assoc, 1961-62; Univ Ala, bus mgr; Morgan State Univ, vpres bus & fin, 1976-80; Schenectady County Community Col, pres, 1980-83; Bishop Col, pres, 1983-86; El Centro Col, pres; Seven-Col Dallas County Community Col Dist, chancellor, 2006-; Dallas Baptist Univ, distinguished adj prof mgt, currently. **Orgs:** Coun Educ Facility Planner, Soc Advan Mgt; bd dirs & sr dir, Dallas Urban League; bd dirs, United Way Metro Dallas; Dallas Black Chamber Com; bd dirs, Dallas Symphony Asn; Dallas County Youth Servs Comn; Dallas AIDS Educ Comn; bd dirs, Young Men Christian Asn Metropolitan Dallas; bd dirs, Dallas Urban League; bd govs, Dallas Model UN; Downtown Dallas Rotary Club; bd dirs & vpres, Dallas Black Chamber Comt; chmn, Bd Trustees African Am Mus; bd, Dallas Baptist Univ Found; db, Univ Tex Southwestern Med Sch Found; Nat Adv Coun; Ind Univ Acad Alumni Fel. **Honors/Awds:** Martin Luther King Disting Leadership Award, State Univ New York, 1981; Nat Asn Advan Colored People Leadership Award, 1982; Outstanding Conributions in Education Award, Alpha Phi Alpha 1983; Distinguished Service Award, Hamilton Hill Neighborhood Asn, 1983; Appreciation Award, State New York, 1983; Appreciation Award, Alpha Phi Alpha, 1984; Distinguished Achievement & Service Award, 1984; Meritorious Service Award, United Way Metro Dallas, 1984,85; Distinguished Service Award, Tex Baptist Conv, 1984; Distinguished Service Award, InterFirst Bank, 1984; Distinguished Service Award, InterdenomiNat Ministerial Alliance, 1984; Man of the Year Award, S Dallas Bus & Prof Women's Club Inc, 1984; Brotherhood Award, New Jersulaem Baptist Church, 1984; Certificate of Appreciation, Vet Admin Reg Med Ctr, 1985; Certificate of Special Congressional Recognition, US Congressman James Armey, 1985; Certificate of Appreciation, Dallas Reg Office US Agri, 1985; Appreciation Award in Education, Off Civil Rights Dallas Reg, 1985; Certificate of Recognition, Nat Republican Congressional Comn, 1985; Black Portfolio Excellence Award in Educ, 1985; Distinguished Service Award, New Birth Baptist Church, 1985; Distinguished Service Award in Education, Arlington Asn Concerned Citizens, 1985; Outstanding Service Award in Education, Most Worshipful St Joseph Grand Lodge, 1985; DHL, Dallas Baptist Univ; African Am Educators Hall of Fame. **Special Achievements:** First African American chairman of the board of the United Way of Dallas, 1989. **Military Serv:** AUS, lt col, 1956-62. **Business Addr:** Chancellor, Dallas County Community College District, 5001 N MacArthur Blvd, Irving, TX 75038.

LATEEF, DR. YUSEF (WILLIAM EMANUEL HUDDLESTON)
Composer, artist, musician. **Personal:** Born Oct 9, 1920, Chattanooga, TN. **Educ:** Manhattan Sch Music, BM, 1969 & MM, music educ, 1970; Univ Massachusetts, PhD, 1975. **Career:** TV & theater appearances; New York City, quartet leader, 1960; featured with Charles Mingus, 1960-61; Babatundi Olatunji, 1961-62; featured with Cannonball Adderley Combo on European tour; combo leader; Stan Kenton Summer Music Clin, saxaphone teacher, 1963; AFA Epic Suite, 1993; Borough Manhattan Community Col, assoc prof, music, 1971-76; musical compositions: Nocturne (Ballet), 1974; Ahmadu Bello Univ, sr res fel, 1981-85; Yusef's Mood; Univ Massachusetts, prof; Univ Massachusetts, Amherst, MA, vis prof; YAL Rec, owner, currently. **Orgs:** Local 802, NY; Local 5, MI. **Honors/Awds:** Grammy Award. **Special Achievements:** Author of Yusef Lateef's Flute Book of the Blues, Repository of Scales and Melodic Patterns, published a novella, "A Night in the Garden of Love," and two collections of short stories, "Spheres" and "Rain Shapes", composed symphony No 1, TAHIRA, 1980, performed by the Hamburg, Germany radio orchestra, performed with Atlanta, GEO symphony orchestra, 1998. **Business Addr:** Owner, FANA Music & YAL Records, PO Box 799, Amherst, MA 01004, **Business Phone:** (413)259-1501.

LATHAM, CHRISTOPHER JOSEPH
Baseball player. **Personal:** Born May 26, 1973, Coeur d'Alene, ID; married Sarah Cunningham; children: Christopher. **Career:** Minnesota Twins, outfielder, 1997-99; Colorado Rockies, 1999-2000; Toronto Blue Jays, outfielder, 2000-01; NY Yankees, outfielder, 2003; Yomiuri Giants, Japan, outfielder, 2003; Bridgeport Bluefish, Atlantic League, outfielder, 2005; World Cup Baseball, USA, 2005.

LATHAM, WELDON HURD
Lawyer. **Personal:** Born Jan 2, 1947, Brooklyn, NY; son of Avril Hurd and Aubrey G; married Constantia Beecher; children: Nicole Marie & Brett Weldon. **Educ:** Howard Univ, BA, bus admin, 1968; Georgetown Univ Law Ctr, JD, 1971; George Washington Univ Nat Law Ctr, advan legal courses, 1976; Brookings Inst, exec educ prog, 1981; Dartmouth Col, Amos Tuck Sch, Exec Bus cert, 1997. **Career:** Checchi & Co, mgt consult, 1968-71; Covington & Burling, atty, 1971-73; Howard Univ Sch Law, adj prof, 1972-82; The White House Off Mgt & Budget, asst gen coun, 1974-76; Hogan & Hartson, atty, 1976-79; Univ Va Law Sch, guest prof, 1976-91; US Dept Housing & Urban Develop, gen dep asst secy, 1979-81; Sterling Systs Inc, vpres & gen coun, 1981-83; Planning Res Corp, exec asst & coun chair & chief exec officer, 1983-86; Reed Smith Shaw & Mc Clay, managing partner, McLean VA off, 1986-92; Minority Bus Enterprise Mag, columnist, 1991-; Civilian Aide to the Secy Army, 1994-99; Shaw, Pittman, Potts & Trowbridge, Nat Law Firm, sr partner, 1992-2000; TeleCommun Syst Inc, bd dir, 1999-; Holland & Knight, sr partner, Corp Diversity Coun Group, pract group leader, 2000-04; Diversity Jour, columnist, 2002-; Davis Wright Tremaine LLP, sr partner, 2004-. **Orgs:** Legal Defense & Educ Fund, 1976-96; bd dir, Prof Serv Coun, 1984-88; ed adv bd, Wash Bus J, 1985-88; bd dir, Va Commonwealth Univ, 1986-89; bd dir, Wash Urban League, 1986-90; founding mem & gen coun, Nat Coalition Minority Bus, 1993-; Small Bus Admin Nat Adv Coun, 1994-2003; managing trustee, major sponsor, Dem Nat Comt, 1995-; Md Econ Develop Comn, 1996-98; Wash Hosp Ctr Found, 1996-97; Wash Hosp Ctr Found, 1996-97; Burger King Corp Diversity Action Coun, 1996-98; bd dir, Metrop Wash Airports Authority, 1997-; Joint Ctr Political & Econ Studies, 1998-; The Am Univ, 1999-2002; Coca-Cola Procurement Adv Coun, 2000-03; chair, Deloitte & Touche Diversity Adv Bd, 2002-; Georgetown Univ Law Bd Visitors, 2002-; Trustee, Fed City Coun, 2003-; Capital Area Adv Bd, bd dirs, Dem Nat Comn, DC; Nat Asn Advan Colored People. **Honors/Awds:** Nat Asn Equal Opportunity Higher Educ Achievement Award, 1987; Northern Va Min Bus & Prof Asn Award, 1990; Private Industry Advocate of the Year, Small Bus Admin, 1992; Advocate of the Year, Minority Enterprise Development Week, US Dept Com, 1996; Wash Bar Asn Hall of Fame, 2001; Ron Brown Legacy Award, Nat Black MBA Asn, 2002; Amtrak A. Philip Randolph Diversity Award; Outstanding Performance Award, US Dept HUD. **Business Addr:** Senior Partner, Davis Wright Tremaine LLP, 1919 Pa Ave NW Suite 200, Washington, DC 20006-3402, **Business Phone:** (202)973-4200.

LATHAN, SANAA
Actor. **Personal:** Born Sep 19, 1971, New York, NY. **Educ:** Univ Calif-Berkeley; Yale Sch Drama, MFA. **Career:** Films: Drive, 1996; Blade, 1998; Life, 1999; The Best Man, 1999; The Wood, 1999; Love & Basketball, 2000; Catfish in Black Bean Sauce, 2000; The Smoker, 2000; Brown Sugar, 2002; Out of Time, 2003; Nip/Tuck, 2006; A Raisin in the Sun, 2008; TV movies: "Disappearing Acts", 2000; "Brown Sugar", 2002; "Out of Time", 2003; "AVP: Alien Vs. Predator", 2004; "The Golden Blaze", 2005; "Something New", 2006. **Honors/Awds:** Acapulco Black Film Festival Rising Star Award, 2001; Black Entertainment Award, Best Actress, 2001; Black Reel Award for Theatrical, Best Actress, 2001, 2004; Image Award for Outstanding Actress in a Motion Picture, 2001; Theatre World Award, 2004. **Business Phone:** (310)859-4000.

LATHAN, DR. WILLIAM EDWARD
Physician. **Personal:** Born Apr 14, 1937, Philadelphia, PA; son of Stanley Edward and Julia Elizabeth Dunston; married Melvina Smith, Apr 12, 1969; children: William Earl, Robert Edward, Edward, Honey Bea & John Calvin. **Educ:** Pa State Univ, BS, 1959; Hahnemann Med Col, MD, 1963. **Career:** NY State Athletic Comn, med dir, 1996-2000; Westchester Med Ctr, asst attend, currently; pvt pract, currently. **Orgs:** Am Bd Family Pract, dipl; Am Acad Family Physicians; fel, NY Acad Med; fel, Philadelphia Col Physicians; consult, NY State Off Prof Med Conduct. **Honors/Awds:** Obie Award for Distinguished Direction, NY Off Broadway, 1973; Rocky Marciano Sports Medicine Doctor Award, 1999. **Special Achievements:** contributing auth, "The Medical Aspects of Boxing", CRC Press, 1993; contributing photogr, "The Family of Black America", Random House, 1996; "African American History & Culture Catalog", Barnes & Noble, 1999; photographs exhibited in "A History of Black Photographers", St Martin Press, 1999; stage dir, The Confessions of Stepin' Fetchit, So Nice They Name it Twice, The Sirens, What If It Had Turned Up Heads, The Fabulous Miss Marie. **Military Serv:** AUS, capt, 1966-68. **Home Phone:** (914)693-7795. **Business Addr:** Physician, 7 Dellwood Ln, PO Box 687, Ardsley, NY 10502, **Business Phone:** (914)693-7795.*

LATHEN, DEBORAH ANN
Lawyer. **Personal:** Born Mar 28, 1953, St Louis, MO; daughter of Olean and Levi. **Educ:** Cornell Univ, BA (magna cum laude), 1975; Harvard Law Sch, JD, 1978. **Career:** Foley & Lardner, atty; Keck, Mahin & Cate, atty, 1978-82; Quaker Oats Co, litigation atty, 1982-88; TRW Inc, sr coun, 1988-91; Nissan Motor Corp USA, managing coun, 1991-93, mgr, consumer affairs, dir consumer affairs; Fed Commun Comn, chief cable serv bur, 1998-2001; Lathen Consult, founder & pres, 2001-. **Orgs:** Bd dir, Nissan Found; bd dir, Leadership Calif; ABA; Black Women Lawyers Asn; Los Angeles Black Women Lawyers; bd mem, Remuneration Comt, Brit Telecommunications, currently. **Honors/Awds:** YWCA Women Leadership Award, 1987; Chairman's Award, Quaker Oats Co, 1988; Volunteer Award, Quaker Oats Co, 1992; Commendation from Mayor Thomas Bradley for Riot Relief Efforts, 1992; Americas Best & Brightest, 1993. **Special Achievements:** Selected by Dollars & Sense Magazine, Best & Brighest in America Issue, 1993. **Home Addr:** 19646 Stern Lane, Huntington Beach, CA 92648, **Home Phone:** (714)960-8996. **Business Addr:** Founder, President, Lathen Consulting, 4000 Mass Ave NW, Washington, DC 20016.

LATHON, LAMAR LAVANTHA
Football player. **Personal:** Born Dec 23, 1967, Wharton, TX; children: Octavia & Madison. **Educ:** Univ Houston, educ. **Career:** Football player (retired); Houston Oilers, linebacker, 1990-94; Carolina Panthers, linebacker, 1995-98. **Honors/Awds:** Pre-season First Team All-Southwest Conference; Pro Bowl, 1996.

LATIF, NAIMAH (DOREEN ALICIA CHARLES)
Newspaper publisher. **Personal:** Born Apr 15, 1960, Chicago, IL; married Sultan Abdul Latif. **Educ:** Univ Nebr Lincoln, BA, Jour, 1982. **Career:** oper PUSH, youth comt, 1982-84; Chicago Black United Comn, youth chmn, 1982-84; Black United Front, secy, 1982-83; Task Force Black Polit Empowerment, secy, 1982-83; Intl Commun Corp, pres, 1986-89; Int Bus Network, Managing Editor; Latif Commun Group Inc, vpres, 1989-. **Orgs:** PUSH Intl Trade Bur, 1984-; Int Black Writers, 1984-; NAACP, 1985-; Urban League, 1985-; deleg, Nat Small Bus Conf, 1985-86; Chicago Asn Black Journalists; Nat Asn Black Journalists. **Honors/Awds:** Outstanding Leadership Award, African People's Union, 1982; Certificate Achievement, Oper PUSH Polit Educ, 1983; published book, Til Victory is Won, 1984; wrote & acted one-woman show, "Sojourner Truth", 1986; co-author, Slavery: The African American Psychic Trauma, 1993. **Business Addr:** Vice President,

Latif Communications Group Inc, 8 S Mich Ave Suite 1510, Chicago, IL 60603, **Business Phone:** (312)849-3456.*

LATIFAH, QUEEN (DANA ELAINE OWENS)
Actor, singer. **Personal:** Born Mar 18, 1970, Newark, NJ; daughter of Lance Owens Sr and Rita Owens. **Educ:** Borough Manhattan Community Col, broadcasting. **Career:** Films: Jungle Fever, 1991; House Party 2, 1991; Juice, 1992; My Life, 1993; Set It Off, 1996; Hoodlum, 1997; Sphere, 1998; Living Out Loud, 1998; Bone Collector, 1999; Bringing Out Dead, 1999; The Country Bears, 2002; Brown Sugar, 2002; Chicago, 2002; Bringing Down the House, exec producer, 2003; Scary Movie 3, 2003; Barbershop 2: Back in Business, 2004; The Cookout, producer, 2004; Taxi, 2004; Beauty Shop, producer, 2005; Last Holiday, 2006; Stranger Than Fiction, 2006; Hairspray, 2007; Mad Money, 2008; What Happens in Vegas, The Secret Life of Bees, 2008; TV Series: Sisters in the Name of Rap, 1992; "Living Single", 1993-98; Mama Flora's Family, 1998; Spin City, 2001; Living with the Dead, 2002; Kung Faux, 2003; The Muppets' Wizard of Oz, 2005; Life Support, exec producer, 2007; Others: "Queen Latifah Show", host & exec producer, 1999; Who's Your Caddy?, 2007; Wifey, 2007; The Perfect Holiday, 2007; Albums: All Hail Queen, 1990; Nature a Sista, 1991; X-tra Naked, 1992; Black Reign, 1994; Order in Court, 1998; She's a Queen: A Collection of Hits, 2002; The Dana Owens Album, 2004; Trav'lin' Light, 2007; Flavor Unit Management, ceo, currently; Flavor Unit Records, owner, currently. **Honors/Awds:** Numerous honors & awards including Best New Artist, New Music Seminar, 1990; Best Female Rapper, Rolling Stone Readers' Poll, 1990; Grammy Award nominee, 1990; Soul Train Music Awards, Sammy Davis Jr Award, Entertainer of the Year, 1995; Golden Globe nomination, Actress in a Supporting Role for Chicago, 2003; Artist of the Year, Harvard Found, 2003; Nominated for Oscar Award, 2003; Image Award, 2004 & 2008; Satellite Award, 2008. **Special Achievements:** First female rapper to be nominated for an Academy Award. **Business Addr:** Chief Executive Officer, Flavor Unit Management, 155 Morgan St, Jersey City, NJ 07302, **Business Phone:** (201)333-4883.*

LATIMER, ALLIE B.
Lawyer. **Personal:** Born in Coraopolis, PA; daughter of Lawnye S and Bennie Comer. **Educ:** Hampton Inst, Hampton, VA, BS; Howard Univ, Wash, DC, JD; Cath Univ, Wash, DC, LLM; Am Univ, Study Towards Doctorate; Howard Univ, MDiv, DMin. **Career:** Lawyer (retired); Chief coun, atty, 1960-71; Gen Serv Admin, Wash, DC, asst gen coun, 1971-76; NASA, asst gen coun, 1976-77, gen coun, 1977-87, spec coun, 1987-96. **Orgs:** Vol work, Am Friends Serv Comn, Europe; secy, Nat Bar Asn, 1966-76; co-chmn & bd dirs, Presbyterian Econ Develop Corp, 1974-80; pres, Nat Bar Found, 1974-75; pres, DC Ment Health Asn, 1977-79; Supreme Ct US; US Ct Appeals DC; NC St Ct Appeals; Am Bar Asn; Fed Bar; Nat Bar; NC Bar; DC Bar; Wash Bar Asn; founder & first pres, Federally Employed Women, 1968-69; vpres, Links Inc, 1976-80; bd gov, Nat Coun Church, USA, 1978-84; Nat Asn Advan Colored People & Nat Asn Advan Colored People Legal Def Fund, DC Steering Comt. **Honors/Awds:** Public Service Award & Gen Serv Admin, 1971; Exceptional Service Awards, Gen Serv Admin, 1976-79; Humanitarian Award, Sigma Delta Tau Legal Fraternity, 1978; Outstanding Achievement Award; Kiwanis Club Award DC, 1978; Presidential Rank Award, 1983, 1995; Distinguished Service Award, Gen Serv Admin, 1984; Ollie May Cooper Award, Wash Bar Asn, 1998; Hall of Fame Award, Nat Bar Asn, 1999. **Home Addr:** 3050 Military Rd NW Suite 520, Washington, DC 20015-1364. *

LATIMER, CHRIS
Marketing executive. **Personal:** Born Dec 25, 1968, White Plains, NY; son of Benjamin and Sudie Hardy. **Educ:** Howard Univ, attended 1990. **Career:** The Source Magazine, tour coord, 1990-91; American Col Alliance Inc, promotions, 1990-91; NYA Area Entertainment Inc, pres & ceo, currently; Cancun All-Star Fiesta, founder, 1995, pres & ceo, currently; The Source Magazine, Designer & Co-Owner, 1997. **Honors/Awds:** Recognition Award, 1995; Mentor Award, Thomas H Slater Inc, 1997. **Business Phone:** (212)343-1700.*

LATIMER, FRANK EDWARD
Executive. **Personal:** Born Aug 28, 1947, Tulsa, OK; son of Frank Edward Sr and Wilda Dupree; married Connie Latimer-Smith (divorced 1989); children: Tomitra, Chelsea, Patrice, Tina & Ann; married Ava, 1991. **Educ:** Univ Md, College Park, BA, 1973; Harvard Univ, Cambridge, MA, MBA, 1976. **Career:** Brown & Williamson, Louisville, KY, prod mgr, 1976-77; Int Paper, New York, NY, plant controller, 1977-80; Atlantic Richfield, Louisville, KY, div controller, 1980-85; Regal Plastics, Roseville, MI, vpres & chief financial officer, 1986-93, pres, 1993-. **Honors/Awds:** Certified Management Accountant, Nat Asn Accts, 1985; YMCA Black Achiever's Award, YMCA, Louisville, 1983. **Home Addr:** 19280 Burlington St, Detroit, MI 48203, **Home Phone:** (313)368-5523. **Business Addr:** President, Chief Financial Officer, Regal Plastics Co, 655 Wabassee Dr, Owosso, MI 48867-9766, **Business Phone:** (989)723-6717.*

LATIMER, INA PEARL
Educator. **Personal:** Born Oct 19, 1934, Okeechobee, FL; married Harold A; children: Cynthia L. **Educ:** Tuskegee Inst, BS, nursing, 1956; N Ill Univ, MS, educ, 1979. **Career:** Univ Ill, staff nurse charge, 1958-60; St Mary Nazareth, Sch Nursing, instr med-surg nursing, 1960-70; Triton Col, instr, 1970-73, chair person prac nursing prog, 1973-. **Orgs:** Homemaker-Home Health Aide Comn; Ill Coun Home Health Servs; Nat League Nursing; Ill Voc Asn; Bd Review, Nat League Nursing Coun Prac Nursing Progs, 1979-84; eval, Dept Voc & Tech Educ, 1981; accreditation site visr, Nat League Nursing, 1978-; Lakeside Community Church. **Honors/Awds:** Award, Delta Sigma Theta Sororoty; Alpha Kappa Mu, Nat Honor Soc. **Business Addr:** Department Chairperson Practical Nursing, Triton College, 2000 5th Ave, River Grove, IL 60171.

LATIMER, JENNIFER ANN
School administrator. **Personal:** Born Apr 29, 1953, Gastonia, NC; daughter of Robert E Grier and Susie M Kithcart; children: Faith G. **Educ:** Univ RI, BA, 1975; RI Col, MA 1983; CAGS, 1990. **Career:** Atlanta Bd Educ, comt organizer, 1977-78; RI Educ Oppurtunity Ctr, follow-up counr, 1980; Community Col RI, counr access prog, 1981-83; RI Col, coord minority prog, 1983-86, asst dir student life/minority affairs, 1986-2001; Cornerstone Coun & Consult counr, 1989-93. **Orgs:** Vpres, URI Minority Alumni Coun, 1987-89; Providence Christian Outreach Ministries, 1988-90; Nat Asn Advan Colored People. **Special Achievements:** Wrote and directed gospel play, "Thy Will Be Done", 1985; co-wrote and directed gospel play, "Tis The Season", 1987. **Business Addr:** Staff, Ashbrook High School, 2222 S New Hope Rd, Gastonia, NC 28054.

LATIMORE, GAIL
Executive director. **Personal:** Married; children: 3. **Educ:** Columbia Univ, BS, archit; Boston Univ, MS, Urban Affairs. **Career:** Codman Sq Neighborhood Develop Corp, exec dir, 1998-. **Orgs:** Founding bd mem, Dudley Street Neighborhood Initiative; Metropolitan Boston Housing Partnership, Mass Asn Community Develop Corps; Four Corners Action Coalition; exec dir, Boston Found. **Business Phone:** (617)825-4224.

LATNEY, HARVEY, JR.
Lawyer. **Personal:** Born May 26, 1944, Caroline Co, VA. **Educ:** Va Union Univ, BA, 1966; Howard Univ, Sch Law, JD, 1969. **Career:** US Dept Transp, legal intern, 1969, 1971-72; Richmond Comn Sr Ctr, dir, 1972-73; Greene & Poindexter Inc, atty, 1973; Carolina County, VA, commonwealth atty, 1978-; Villa's Housing Bd, chair, currently. **Orgs:** Nat Bar Asn; Am Bar Asn; Va Bar & Asn; Va Trial Lawyer's Asn; Old Dominion Bar Asn. **Military Serv:** AUS, sgt, 1969-71. **Business Addr:** Attorney, Commonwealth Attorney, 521 523 N Adams St, PO Box 432, Richmond, VA 23220, **Business Phone:** (804)643-2097.*

LATTA, JUDI MOORE. See SMITH, DR. JUDITH MOORE.

LATTANY, KRISTIN HUNTER
Writer. **Personal:** Born Sep 12, 1931, Philadelphia, PA; daughter of George L Eggleston and Mabel M Eggleston; married John I Lattany Sr. **Educ:** Univ PA, BS, ed, 1951. **Career:** Pittsburgh Courier, columnist & feature writer, 1946-52; Lavenson Bur Advert, copywriter, 1952-59; Wermen & Schorr Philadelphia, advert copywriter, 1961-62; Univ PA, Sch Soc Work, res asst, 1962; City Philadelphia, info officer, 1963-65; freelance writer, novels, journ, fiction 1963-; Univ PA, sr lect, eng, 1972-95; One World Ballantine, Kinfolk, 1996; Do Unto Others, 2000; Breaking Away, 2003. **Orgs:** Dir, Walt Whitman Poetry Ctr, 1977-79; Alpha Kappa Alpha; authors guild, NAACP; chair, fiction bd, Shooting Star Rev, Pittsburgh, PA, 1989-92; Camden County Artists. **Honors/Awds:** Fund for the Republic TV Documentary prize, 1955; John Hay Whitney Opportunity fel, 1959-60; Philadelphia Athenaeum Literary Award, 1964; Bread Loaf Writers Conf Fel, 1965; Coun Interracial Books for Children Prize, 1968; Sigma Delta Chi Best Mag Reporting Award, 1969; Univ Wis Children's Book Conf Cheshire Cat Seal, 1970; Silver Slate-Pencil & Dolle Mina Awards, The Netherlands, 1973; Chicago Tribune Book World Prize, 1973; Christopher Award 1974; Nat Book Award Nom 1974; NJ State Council on the Arts Prose Fellowship, 1981-82, 1985-86; Netherlands 1973; Chicago Tribune Book World Prize, 1973; Christopher Award, 1974; Nat Book Award, Nom 1974; NJ State Coun on the Arts Prose Fellowship, 1981-82, 1985-86; Lifetime Achievement Award, Moontone Black Writing Celebration. **Special Achievements:** Retired; Pittsburgh Courier, columnist & feature writer, 1946-52; Lavenson Bur Advert, copywriter, 1952-59; Wermen & Schorr Philadelphia, advert copywriter, 1961-62; Univ PA, Sch Soc Work, res asst, 1962; City Philadelphia, info officer, 1963-65; freelance writer, novels, journ, fiction 1963-; Univ PA, sr lect, eng, 1972-95; Books: God Bless the Child, 1964; The Landlord, 1966; The Soul Brothers and Sister Lou, 1968; Boss Cat, 1971; Guests in the Promised Land, 1973; The Survivors, 1975; The Lakestown Rebellion, 1978; Lou in the Limelight, 1981; Kinfolks, 1996; One World Ballantine, Kinfolk, 1996; Do Unto Others, 2000, Breaking Away, 2003; television: "Minority of One," CBS TV, 1965. **Home Addr:** 721 Warwick Rd N, Magnolia, NJ 08049, **Home Phone:** (856)783-6190.

LATTIMER, DR. AGNES DOLORES
Physician. **Personal:** Born May 13, 1928, Memphis, TN; daughter of Arthur O and Hortense M Lewis; married Frank Bethel, Jan 1, 1971 (deceased); married Bernard Goss, Jan 10, 1952 (divorced 1961) (died 1984); children: Bernard C Goss Jr. **Educ:** Fisk Univ, BS (Magna Cum Laude), 1949; Chicago Med Sch, MD, 1954. **Career:** Michael Reese Hosp, dir amb peds, 1966-71; Cook County Hosp, dir amb peds, 1971-84, dir Fantus Clinic, 1984-85; Cook Co Hosp, med dir, 1986-95; Dept Pediatrics, Univ Health Sci/Chicago Med Sch, prof; Pvt Pract, physician, currently. **Orgs:** Fel Am Acad Pediatrics, 1960-; Ambulatory Ped Assoc, 1974-; pres, Ill Chap Am Acad Pediatrics, 1983-86; Physician's Task Force Hunger, 1984-86; Am Assoc Public Health; bd trustees, Childserv; bd trustees, Family Inst; Chicago Pediatric Soc. **Honors/Awds:** Outstanding Teaching, 1966; Outstanding Alumnus, 1971; Pediatrician of the Year Award, Ill, Chap AAP, 1985; Tsang Award; Outstanding Alumnus, Fisk Univ, 1990; Archibald Hoyne Award, Outstanding Service Children, Chicago Ped Soc, 1990; Community Service Award, 1992; Women Achievement Award, Consortium of Doctors, 1994; Distinguished Alumnus Award, Michael Reese Hosp, 1994.

LATTIMER, ROBERT L.
Lawyer. **Personal:** Born Jul 16, 1945; son of James and Mary-agnes; married Sarah, Apr 5, 1997; children: Ebony, Isoador, Hope, John. **Educ:** Rutgers Univ, BA, econs, 1973; Columbia Univ, Grad Sch Bus, Exec MBA Mgt Prog, Arden House, 1978. **Career:** J Walter Thompson Co, vpres, dir, 1976-81, CRE Operating Comn, 1976-81; Lattimer Group, chief exec officer, sr consult partner, 1981-90; Towers Perrin, global pract leader, 1990-96, managing partner; Andersen Consulting, assoc partner, 1996; City Atlanta, chief operating officer; Metrop Atlanta Rapid Transit Authority, dir, corp bus, currently. **Orgs:** Zoo Atlanta, vice chair, bd dirs, 1993-; Atlanta Neighborhood Develop Partnership, exec comn, chmn, Strategic Planning & Human Resources Comn, 1993; Cong Black Caucus Found, adv bd dirs, 1996; Am Soc Competitiveness. **Honors/Awds:** US Jaycees, One of the Ten Outstanding Young Men America, Honored with VP Albert Gore, Jr, 1987; Global Strategy Formulation & Execution, Am Soc Competitiveness, 1997. **Special Achievements:** Quoted in significant management books, journals, newspapers, and magazines such as: Fortune Magazine, Atlanta Journal Constitution, Atlanta Tribune; completed book chapter, "Redefining Diversity," in book Beyond Affirmative Action, 1996. **Military Serv:** US Marine Corp, recog off, 1968-70; Bronze Star Medal with Combat V, 1969; Purple Heart, 1969. **Home Addr:** 210 E Court Dr SW, Atlanta, GA 30331, **Home Phone:** (404)696-0837. *

LATTIMORE, DR. CAROLINE LOUISE
School administrator, college administrator. **Personal:** Born May 12, 1945, Winston-Salem, NC; daughter of Mary Rhodes Lattimore and Earl R Lattimore Sr. **Educ:** Hampton Inst, BS, 1967, MA, 1973; Duke Univ, PhD, 1978. **Career:** Richmond Pub Sch, Va, eng teacher, 1967-74; State Univ, coord sr citizens prog Winston-Salem, 1974; NTS Research Corp, Washington, coord, 1978; Duke Univ, psychol testing intern, 1974-75, educ consult & spec coun, 1978, dean minority affairs, asst provost, 1978-83, academic dean, 1987, asst dean, assoc acad dean & adj assoc prof, currently. **Orgs:** Pres, Coun Black Affairs, 1984-91; Reggie B Howard Scholar Selection Comn,1985-2001; Nat Asn Advan Colored People, 1985-; Defense Adv Comn Women Serv, 1999-2002; bd dir, AKA, 2002-06; WTVO-11 TV, 2003; bd dir, Duke Univ Federal Credit Union, 2003; NC Civil Rights Comn, 2003; Duke Resv Officer Training Corps, 2003; chair, Alpha Kappa Alpha, memship committee, 2009. **Honors/Awds:** Award of Merit for Outstanding Achievement, Winston Salem Jr C C, 1963; Nat Fel Ford Found, 1976-78; Regional Graduate Leadership Award, AKA,1986; JC Penny's Golden Rule Award, Durham, NC, 1990-91; Rockefeller Brothers Fund Mentor, 1997. **Home Addr:** 234 Overlook Ave, Durham, NC 27712, **Home Phone:** (919)471-3764. **Business Addr:** Associate Academic Dean, Adjunct Associate Professor, Duke University, Trinity College of Arts & Sciences, 213 West Duke Bldg Allen Bldg 011, PO Box 90041, Durham, NC 27708, **Business Phone:** (919)684-2096.

LATTIMORE, HENRY
Football coach. **Educ:** Jackson State Univ, attended 1957. **Career:** Morgan State Univ, head coach, 1976-77; NC Cent Univ, head coach, 1979-90. **Special Achievements:** Coached teams that earned two Southern Div CIAA championships, one CIAA championship & an appearance in the NCAA Div II playoffs.

LATTIMORE, KENNY
Singer. **Personal:** Born Apr 10, 1970, Washington, DC; married Chante Moore, Jan 1, 2002; children: 1. **Career:** Albums: Kenny Lattimore, 1996; From the Soul of Man, 1998; Weekend, 2001;The Essential, 2003; Things That Lovers Do, 2003; Things That Lovers Do,2003; Days Like This, 2004; Uncovered/Covered, 2006; TV: "Double Date",1997; "Moesha", 1997; "An Evening of Stars: A Celebration of Educational Excellence",2001; "To Love or Not to Love", 2002; "Abby", 2003; "The View", 2004; "The Tom Joyner Show", 2005; "Honors Reba", 2006; "In the Mix", 2006; "Black to the Future", 2009. **Honors/Awds:** Nat Asn Advan Colored People Image Award, Best New Artist, 1996. **Business Addr:** Singer, Arista Records, 6 W 57th St, New York, NY 10019.*

LAUDERBACK, BRENDA JOYCE
Executive. **Personal:** Born Apr 25, 1950, Pittsburgh, PA; daughter of Clayton Lauderback (deceased) and Dorothy Lauderback; mar-

ried Boyd Wright, Jul 5, 1980; children: Phallon & Adam. **Educ:** Robert Morris Col, BA, mkt, 1972; Univ Pittsburgh, grad studies, voc educ, 1972-73. **Career:** Gimbels, asst buyer, buyer; Dayton's Dept Store, asst buyer, 1975-76, buyer, 1976-79, mgr, 1979-82; Dayton-Hudson CRP, vpres, gen merchandise mgr, 1982; US Shoe Footwear, Wholesale Group, pres, 1993-95; Nine West Group Inc, Wholesale & Retail Group, pres, 1995-98; dir, Big Lots Inc, 1997-; Target Corp, vpres & gen mgr; Irwin Financial Corp, dir, currently; La-Pac Corp, dir, currently; Wolverine World Wide Inc, dir, 2003-. **Orgs:** NCP, 1975-; Urban League, 1989-; Comt 200, 1989-; Exec Leadership Coun, 1993; bd mem, Arthur Ashe Inst Urban Health, 1996-97; Irwin Fin, 1996; Consolidated Stores, 1997; Hord Found, 1997; For All Kids Found Adv Comn, 1998. **Honors/Awds:** Women's Leader, YWCA, 1977-79; Femme Award, Intimate Apparel Indust, 1987; Outstanding Retail Achievement Bragg Award, 1987; YWCA Career Woman of Achievement, 1995, Outstanding Young Women of America, 1995. **Home Addr:** 58 Good Hill Rd, Weston, CT 06883. **Business Phone:** (614)985-1103.

LAUDERDALE, PRIEST
Basketball player. **Personal:** Born Aug 31, 1973, Chicago, IL. **Educ:** Cent State Univ, OH, attended 1994. **Career:** Peristeri Nikas (Greece), 1995-96; Atlanta Hawks, ctr, 1996-97; Denver Nuggets, 1997-98; Lukoil Acad (Bulgaria), 2001. **Honors/Awds:** BulgarianBasket Center of the Year; BulgarianBasket MVP of the Playoffs, 2004.

LAUREN, GREEN
Television news anchorperson. **Personal:** Born Jun 30, 1963. **Educ:** Northwestern Univ, Medill Sch jour; Univ Minn. **Career:** WBBM-TV, news anchor, 1993-96; KSTP-TV, Minn, gen assignment reporter, 1988-93; FOX News Channel, news anchor, religion corresp, currently. **Honors/Awds:** Miss Minnesota, 1984. **Special Achievements:** In 2004, she released her debut CD, Classic Beauty; She was the third runner-up in the 1985 Miss America contest; state's first black Miss Minnesota. **Business Phone:** (310)369-1000.

LAVAILLE, MARTHA. See REEVES, MARTHA ROSE.

LAVALAIS, LESTER JOSEPH
Executive, vice president (organization), manager. **Personal:** Born Dec 16, 1959, Houston, TX; son of Tommie and Lois E Jones; married Sherry Edine, May 7, 1983; children: Lael E & Raziel J. **Educ:** McMurry Univ, BS, appl sociol & social svcs, 1984. **Career:** Woods Psychiat Inst, caseworker, 1983-85; Taylor County Detention Ctr, probation officer, 1985-88; Ment Health-Ment Retardation, Outpatient Servs, ment health prof, 1988-93; program mgr, Goodwill Industs, Residential Youth Treat Ctr, 1993, Electronic Monitoring, prog mgr, 1994-97; JEMS, vpres, currently. **Business Addr:** Vice President, JEMS, 117 W 9th St, PO Box 15630, Cheyenne, WY 82003, **Business Phone:** (307)634-7232.

LAVAN, ALTON
Football coach, football player. **Personal:** Born Sep 13, 1946, Pierce, FL; married Bessie Lavonia Jewell; children: Travis Alton, Douglas Milo & Maeleeke. **Educ:** Colo State Univ, Ft Colins, BA, Sociol, 1970. **Career:** Football player (retired), football coach; Philadelphia Eagles, defensive back, 1968; Atlanta Falcons, defensive back, 1969-70; Colo St Univ, asst coach, 1972; Louisville, asst coach, 1973; IA St Univ, asst coach, 1974; Atlanta Falcons, asst coach, 1975-76; Ga Tech, asst coach, 1977-78; Stanford Univ, asst coach, 1979; Dallas Cowboys, offensive backfield coach, 1980-88; San Francisco 49ers, asst coach, 1989-90; Univ Wash, asst coach, 1992-95; Baltimore Ravens, asst coach, 1996-98; Kansas City Chiefs, asst coach, 1999-2000; Eastern Mich Univ, asst coach, 2002-03, interim head coach, 2003; Del State Univ, 2004-. **Orgs:** Am Football Coaches Asn; Black Coaches Asn. **Special Achievements:** First Black Coach of Dallas Cowboys & Atlanta Falcons. **Military Serv:** AUS, sp 4, 1969-71. **Business Addr:** Head Coach, Delaware State University, 1200 N DuPont Hwy, Dover, DE 19901, **Business Phone:** (302)857-6060.*

LAVEIST, DR. THOMAS
Educator. **Educ:** Univ Md Eastern Shore, Princess Anne, MD, BA, 1984; Univ Mich, Ann Arbor, MI, MA, 1985, PhD, 1988, PDF, 1990. **Career:** Johns Hopkins Univ, Baltimore, MD, Prof & dir Hopkins Ctr Health Disparities Solutions, currently. **Orgs:** Bd dirs, Bon Secour Health Syst; assoc regional dir, Phi Beta Sigma Fraternity, 1983-84; health sub-comt, Md Comn Status Black Males, 1991-; Asn Black Sociologists, 1985-; Am Pub Health Asn, 1988-; Am Sociol Asn, 1984-. **Honors/Awds:** Alain Locke Presidential Futures Award, Phi Beta Sigma Educ Found, 1984; Nat Deans List, 1984; Best Dissertation Medical Sociol, Am Sociol Asn, 1989; Paul B Cornely Fel, Univ Mich, Sch Pub Health, 1988-90; Brookdale Nat Fel, Brookdale Found, 1991; Distinguished Alumni Award, Nat Asn Equal Opportunity Educ, 1994; Outstanding Young Alumnus Award, Univ Md Eastern Shore, 1994, Knowledge Award, DHHS Office Minority Health, Indicted Delta Omega. **Special Achievements:** Author: Minority Populations and Health; Race, Ethnicity and Health; 8 Steps to Help Black Families Pay for College; The Day Star College Guide for African American Students. **Business Addr:** Professor, Director, Johns Hopkins Bloomberg School of Public Health, Johns Hopkins University, 624 N Broadway 4th Fl Hampton House 441, Baltimore, MD 21205-1996, **Business Phone:** (410)955-3774.

LAVEIST, WILBERT FRANCISCO
Television producer. **Personal:** Born in Brooklyn, NY; son of William and Eudora; married Rita; children: Daniel, Joshua & Coryn. **Educ:** Lincoln Univ, BA, jour, 1988; Univ Ariz, MS, 1991. **Career:** Phoenix Gazette, copy ed, 1992-93; Ariz Republic, reporter, 1993-95; ArizonaCentral.com, online ed, 1995-97; Blackvoices.com, exec producer, proj mgr. **Orgs:** Nat Asn Black Journalists; pres, Ariz Asn Black Journalists; Md Inst Journ Ed; Nat Asn Minority Media Exec. **Honors/Awds:** Arizona Press Club Creative Writing, 1995. **Home Addr:** 18514 Dundee Ave, Homewood, IL 60430.

LAVELLE, AVIS
President (Organization), business owner, consultant. **Personal:** Born Mar 5, 1954, Chicago, IL; daughter of Adolph Eugene Sampson and Mai Evelyn Hicks; divorced. **Educ:** Univ Ill, BS, 1975; Keller Grad Sch Mgt, MBA. **Career:** WLTH Radio, news dir, 1978-79; WJJD/WJEZ, reporter, anchor, 1979-84; WGN-Radio/TV, chief polit reporter, 1984-88; Richard M Daley Mayor, campaign press secy, 1988-89; Off Mayor, Chicago, mayoral press secy, 1989-92; Clinton/Gore Campaign, nat press secy, 1992; Presidental Transition Team, spec asst chmn, 1992-93; US Dept Health & Human Serv, asst secy, pub affairs, 1993-95; Waste Mgt Inc, vpres commun & community rels; Chicago Bd Educ, vpres, 1997-2003; Foster Group, sr partner, 2003; A LaVelle Consult Serv, founder & pres, currently. **Orgs:** Delta Sigma Theta Pub Serv, 1973; Nat Comn Working Women, 1980; Black Adoption Task Force Ill, Steering Comt, 1987; bd mem, Proj Image Inc, 1988-89; bd mem, Human Resources Develop Inst, 1988. **Honors/Awds:** First Place Team Reporting Award, Asniated Press, 1984; African Am Bus/Prof Women, Dollars & Sense Mag, 1989. **Special Achievements:** Author: "Should Children Be Tried as Adults?", Essence Magazine, September 1994; Jet, July 31, 1995. **Business Phone:** (312)223-0581.

LAVELLE, ROBERT R.
Banker. **Personal:** Born Oct 4, 1915, Cleveland, TN; son of Franklin P and Mary Anderson; married Adah Moore Lavelle, Jul 25, 1942; children: Robert Moore, John Franklin. **Educ:** Univ Pittsburgh, Pittsburgh, PA, BS, 1951, MA, 1954. **Career:** Pittsburgh Courier, Pittsburgh, PA, asst auditor, 1935-56; Lavelle Real Estate Inc, pres, 1951-; Dwelling House savings & loan Asn, exec vpres, chief exec officer, dir, currently. **Orgs:** Elder, Grace Memorial Presbyterian Ch; life mem, Nat Advan Asn Colored People; certified property mgr, Inst RE Mgt. **Honors/Awds:** Honorary Doctor Laws, Geneva Col, PA, 1984, Gordon Col, MA, 1989; Robert R Lavelle Scholarship established, Univ Pittsburgh, Col Bus Admin, 1995. **Military Serv:** AUS, 1st Lt, 1943-46. **Business Addr:** Executive Vice President, Chief Executive Officer, Dwelling House Savings and Loan Association, 501 Herron Ave, Pittsburgh, PA 15219, **Business Phone:** (412)683-5116.*

LAVERGNE, LUKE ALDON
Judge, lawyer. **Personal:** Born May 7, 1938, Lawtell, LA; son of Adam Jr and Ida Nero; married Catherine A Malveaux, Oct 15, 1960; children: Lance A, Cynthia A. **Educ:** Univ Nebr, BS, 1969; Southern Ill Univ, MS, 1974; La State Univ Law Ctr, JD, 1982. **Career:** La State Univ, asst prof, aerospace studies, 1975-79; asst dist atty, 1982-84, asst parish atty, 1991-92; City Court, Judge Pro Tempore, 1988; State La E Baton Rouge Parish Family Ct, judge, currently. **Orgs:** state dir, Phi Beta Sigma Fraternity, 1984-88, regional legal coun, 1987-92; Pres, Louis A Martinet Legal Soc, 1989-92; bd dir, YMCA, 1989-96; La State Bar Asn; bd dir, Lions Club, 1989-96; bd dir, Baton Bar Asn, 1990-92; bd dir, Boy Scouts Am, 1990-96, scout show chair, 1992-94; 100 Black Men BR LTD; bd dirs, Our Lady of The Lake Col; Kiwanis Club; Phi Beta Sigma; Phi Delta Phi. **Military Serv:** USAF, capt, 1956-79; Good Conduct, 1959; Presidential Unit Citation, 1960; Air Force Commendation, 1972, Meritorious Service Award, 1979. **Home Addr:** 5956 Valley Forge Ave, Baton Rouge, LA 70808, **Home Phone:** (504)924-0590. **Business Addr:** Judge, State La Family Court Baton Rouge, 222 St Louis St Rm 989, Baton Rouge, LA 70802, **Business Phone:** (225)389-7657.*

LAVERGNEAU, RENE L.
Administrator, educator. **Personal:** Born Nov 4, 1933, New York, NY; son of Armando and Myrtle. **Educ:** Community Col New york, BA, 1958; MS, 1963; MA, 1974. **Career:** WNYE-TV, NY Ed TV, instr, 1965-67; Bur Audio-visual Instr NYC, writer & voice-over, 1966-68; NY City Bd Educ, bd examrs, 1968; Fair leigh Dickinson Univ PR, grad instr, 1969; Univ PR, Bayamon, instr, 1974; Hackensack Pub Schs, dir, bur foreign langs, bilingual ed & Eng second lang, 1986; coordr, foreign languages. **Orgs:** Consult, Princeton Conf Foreign Lang Curriculum Develop, 1967; chair, NE Conf Teaching Foreign Langs, 1974; chair, State wide Comt Bilingual &Teaching Eng Second Lang Ed Cert NJ, 1974; keynoter, Am Asn Teachers,1974; chair, NJ Bilingual Minimum Standards, 1978; Bergen City Health & Welfare Coun, 1980; chmn, bd dirs Teatro Duo, 1986-87; bd dir, Hackensack Pub Sch Historical Soc, 1986; sel comt, Am Coun Teaching Foreign Langs & Nat Textbook Co Award Bldg Community Interest Foreign Lang Educ, 1987. **Honors/Awds:** Careers Community and Public Awareness Award, NE Conf Rept Pub, 1974; National Award, Bldg Community Interest Foreign Lang Educ Am Coun Teaching Foreign Langs & Nat Textbook Co, 1983. **Special Achievements:** Actor "The Wiz" 1977.

LAVIZZO-MOUREY, RISA JUANITA
Physician, government official, chief executive officer. **Personal:** Born Sep 25, 1954, Nashville, TN; daughter of Philip V and Blanche Sellers; married Robert J Mourey, Jun 21, 1975; children: Rel & Max. **Educ:** Univ Wash, attended 1973; SUNY Stony Brook, attended 1975; Harvard Med Sch, MD, 1979; Wharton Sch, Univ Pa, MBA, 1986. **Career:** Brigham and Women's Hosp, medical resident, 1979-82; Temple Univ Med Sch, clin instr, 1982-84; Univ Pa, dir Inst Aging, chief div geriat med,Sylvan Eisman prof med & health Care systs; Philadelphia Veterans Admin Med Ctr, assoc chief of staff geriat; US Dept Health & Human Servs, depadminr agency health care policy & res; Robert Wood Johnson Found, vpres &dir health care group, pres & chief exec officer, 2003-. **Orgs:** Asn Acad Minority Physicians, 1990-; Nat Med Asn; White House Task Forceon Health Care Reform; consultm, White House Health policy. **Honors/Awds:** Fel Am Col Physicians; fel Am Geriat Soc. **Special Achievements:** Author: "Invasive Gynecologic Oncology," 1979; "Dehydration in the Elderly," 1987; "Amantad ine-related adverse reactions among African-American elderly nursing home residents," 1991; numerous others. **Business Addr:** President, Chief Executive Officer, The Robert Wood Johnson Found, College Rd E Rte 1, PO Box 2316, Princeton, NJ 08543.*

LAW, BOB. See LAW, ROBERT LOUIS.

LAW, M EPREVEL
Financial manager. **Personal:** Born Aug 19, 1943, Chicago, IL; married Marlene Ann; children: Martin Peter & Michelle Allison. **Educ:** NSF Fel, BS; Univ Minn, MS, 1969, PhD, 1970. **Career:** Minn Pub Schs & Univ Minn, teacher & res, 1966-88; Kenney Real, real est, 1971-74; H&R Block, tax consult, 1970-71; Pact Real Inc, pres, 1974-77; Law & Assoc Prof Fin & Tax Serv, 1974-; Archer & Law Inc, pres, 1976-77, owner; Southside Community Ctr Inc, owner; Three M Realty Co, broker, mgr 1977-; Twin City Property Mgmt Maintenance & Improvement Co, 1978-; Law & Assoc, owner; Lear Bus Connections, Ltd, pres & chief exec officer. **Orgs:** Kappa Alpha Psi Fraternity; Asn Afro-Am Educrs; Nat Asn Realtors; Nat Educ Asn; Am Fed Teachers; Citizens United Responsible Educ; bd mem, Southside Community Ctr; Minn Asn Retarded C; Minn Hist Soc; mayor's appointee, City Wide City-wide Adv Com; co-chmn, CW-CAC Phys Imp & Hous Asst Task Force; cap, Long-range Imp Comt Hum Dev Task Force; proj acct, St Minn Coun on Qual Educ; Cit Unit for Resp Educ Steer Comn; Minn Urban Leag; Citizen League; Nat Asn Advan Colored People; Nat Women's Polit Caucus; Minn DFL Feminist Causus; Minn Environ Educ Bd; S Minn Community Fed Credit Union; chair person, 60th Sen Dist, 1976; assoc chmn, 60th Sen Dist, 1974-76; The Stewards Club, bd mem; Lord's Table; Sunrise Creation Inc.

LAW, ROBERT LOUIS (BOB LAW)
Executive, radio host. **Personal:** Born Apr 6, 1939, Brooklyn, NY; son of John and Lucille; married Munty Doggett Law, Jan 19, 1985; children: Patrice Aisha & Abina Law Napier. **Career:** WWRL Radio, prog dir, Midday Magic Music, radio personality, Nat Black Network, producer & host, vpres; Namaskar, Bob Law's Health & Wellness Shop, owner; Bob Law's Seafood Cafe, owner, currently. **Orgs:** Founder, Nat Respect Yourself, Youth Orgn; chair, New York State Million Man March Orgn; founder & chair, Namaskar Community Assistance Prog; chair, Black Spectrum Theatre, currently. **Business Addr:** Owner, Bob Law's Seafood Cafe, 637 Vanderbilt Ave, Brooklyn, NY 11238, **Business Phone:** (718)789-4060.

LAW, TAJUAN E. (TY LAW)
Football player. **Personal:** Born Feb 10, 1974, Aliquippa, PA. **Educ:** Univ Mich. **Career:** New Eng Patriots, defensive back, 1995-2004; New York Jets, 2005, 2008; Kans City Chiefs, cornerback, 2006-07; free agent, currently. **Honors/Awds:** Alumni DB of the Year, Nat Football League, 1998; Nat Player of the Week, Sporting News & Sports Illustrated; Big Ten Conference Defensive Player of the Week; Two Times First Team All Pro Selection, 1998, 2003; Five Times Pro Bowl Selection, 1998, 2001, 2002, 2003, 2005; Three Times super bowl champion; Co-Pro Bowl MVP, 1998.

LAW, DR. THOMAS MELVIN
Educator, school administrator. **Personal:** Born Sep 23, 1925, Bristol, VA; son of Thomas K and Rebecca; married Katherine Tillar, Oct 14, 1954; children: Thomas Fenimore. **Educ:** St Pauls Col, BS, 1950, hon doctorate, 1982; NY Univ, MA, 1953; Cornell Univ, EdD, 1962. **Career:** Educr, sch adminr (retired); James Solomon Russell High Sch, instr, 1950-54; Hampton Inst, dir div bus, 1965-67; St Pauls Col, dean col & prof bus, 1967-69; Wash Tech

Inst, vpres acad affairs, 1969-71; Penn Valley Community Col, pres, 1971-76; Va State Univ, pres, 1976-82; State Univ NY, dep to chancellor spec progs, 1982-86, dep chancellor community col, 1986-87, assoc vice chancellor contracts & purchasing, 1987-89; St Pauls Col, Lawrenceville, VA, pres, 1989-2001. **Orgs:** Bd dir, Sch Human Ecol, Cornell Univ; VA A L Philpott Mfg Exten Partnership; bd dir, Coun Independent Col, VA; Am Coun Educ, Comn Leadership Develop; Va emissary, Va Chamber Com; Brunswick County, VA, Indust Develop Authority; adv bd, Essex Savings Bank, Emporia, VA; United Negro Col Fund, govt affairs comt, exec comt; bd dir, Nat Asn Equal Opportunity Higher Educ; lic lay reader, St Paul's Mem Chapel; Rotary Int; bd trustee, Am Voc Cooper Educ Asn; Southside VA Comn Bus & Educ; Nat Asn Advan Colored People; Nat Asn Independent Col & Univ, Comn Campus Concerns; bd dir, Brunswick County Mus; United Negro Col Fund; Nat Ctr Higher Educ Mgt Syst; Va State Fair; sire archon elect, Beta Psi Boule Sigma Pi Phi 1985-; bd dir, Living Resources Corp, Albany NY; bd dir, Child's Nursing Home, Albany NY. **Honors/Awds:** Cent Inter-Collegiate Athletic Asn Officials Hall of Fame; Board Resolution of Praise, Southeastern Univ Res Asn; Distinguished Trustee Award; Alpha Phi Alpha Fel; Community Service Award, Alpha Kappa Mu, Phi Delta Kappa, Sigma Gamma Rho; Distinguished Alumni Award, St Pauls Col, 1974; Distinguished Alumni Award, St Pauls Col Nat Alumni Asn, 1978; Martin Luther King Community Service Award, Southern Christian Leadership Coun, 1980; Academy Achievement Award, USA Today-NCAA Found, 2001; CIAA Officials Hall of Fame. **Special Achievements:** First graduate from St Pauls College to receive highest academic honors, summa cum laude; First 4-yr degree graduate to receive an earned doctorate degree from St Pauls College. **Military Serv:** AUS, sgt, veteran; Civilian Distinguished Service Award, 1979.

LAW, TY. See LAW, TAJUAN E.

LAWAL, KASE LUKMAN
Executive. **Personal:** Born Jan 1, 1954, Ibadan, Oyo, Nigeria; married Eileen. **Educ:** Tex Southern Univ, BS, 1976; Prairie View A&M Univ, MBA, finance & mkt, 1978; Fort Valley State Univ, PhD. **Career:** Shell Oil Refining Co, process engr, 1975-77; Dresser Indust, res chemist, 1977-79; Suncrest Investment Corp, vpres, 1980-82; Baker Investments, pres, 1982-86; CAMAC Holdings, pres, chmn & ceo, 1986-; Allied Energy Corp, chmn, 1991-; Port Houston Authority Bd Comnrs, comnr, 1999-2000, vice chmn, 2000-. **Orgs:** Vice chmn & bd dirs, Houston Airport Syst Develop Corp, 2001; bd dirs, Cape Investment Holdings; US Trade Adv Comt Africa; US Trade Rep Trade Policy Africa; dir, Cullen Eng Res Found. **Honors/Awds:** US Entrepreneur of the Year Award, 1994; US Africa Business Person of the Year, US Africa The Newspaper, 1997; Houston 100 Award. **Special Achievements:** listed in Black Enterprise 100s list, 2003; CAMACInternational Corporation, has been named as the '2006 company of the year' among African-American businesses. **Business Addr:** Chairman, Chief Executive Officer, CAMAC International Corporation, 1330 Post Oak Blvd Suite 2200, Houston, TX 77056, **Business Phone:** (713)965-5100.

LAWES, VERNA
Executive. **Personal:** Born in Philadelphia, PA; daughter of Thomas Jones and Jessie Lee Grier Jones; married Sylvester; children: Anthony & David. **Educ:** Temple Univ, BS. **Career:** Certified Data Services Inc, pres, 1970-; US Treas Dept, data coordr; IBM, libr; Sperry Univac Corp, res mgr; Nat Polit Cong Black Women, exec secy. **Orgs:** Howard County Housing Alliance; Howard County Drug & Alcohol Adv Bd; bd mem, Wilde Lake Village.

LAWHORN, JOHN B.
Educator, movie actor. **Personal:** Born Apr 2, 1925, Youngstown, OH; married Phyllis Jane; children: Michael John. **Educ:** Youngstown Univ, BS, 1950; Columbia Univ, MA, 1953. **Career:** Allen Univ, dept chmn & band dir, 1950-57; Albany St Col, acting chmn, dept music, band dir, 1957-62; Atlanta Pub Sch, band dir teacher, 1961-66; GA State Dept Edu, consult, 1966-73; Metro Coop Educ Serv Agency, music coodinator, 1973-74; Newton Co Sch, 1974-75; Basic Instrnl Concepts Inst Nat, concert pianist; Child & Leisure Com White House Conf C, chmn, 1970; Alliance Theatre prod, appeared; stage, film, television, actor, currently; Films: The Kudzu Christmas, actor, 2002; The Adventures of Ociee Nash, actor, 2003; Madea's Family Reunion, actor, 2006; TV Series: Fluke, 1995; The Price Heaven, 1997; Flash, 1997; The Wedding, 1998; Claudine's Return, 1998; Mama Flora's Family, 1998; Passing Glory, 1999. **Orgs:** Leadership Atlanta; Govs Adv Coun Arts; Atlanta Symphony Bd; St AdvComn, Correctional Recreation Publs Field. **Honors/Awds:** Mrs Fred W Petterson award. **Military Serv:** USN, 1943-46.

LAWHORN, ROBERT MARTIN
Military leader. **Personal:** Born Jan 8, 1943, Camden, SC; married Jacqueline Carter; children: Bridgett Tiffany, Brandon Tilman. **Educ:** NC A&T State Univ, BS, 1965; Nat Univ, MBA, 1985. **Career:** Aviation Officer Candidate Sch, officer cand, 1966; Basic Naval Aviation Training, aviation trainee, 1966; Advan NFO Training, 1967; VF-101 NAS Oceana VA & Key West FL, 1967; VF-41 Oceana VA, power plants div off & asst admin off, 1967-70; Navy Recruiting Dist St Louis, exec officer minor recruiting officer, 1970-72; VF-124 Miramar CA, 1972-73; VF1 NAS Miramar, info training officer admin officer, 1973-77; VF 124 Miramar, asst opers officer instr, 1977-79; VF 1 NAS Miramar CA, maintenance officer, safety office, 1980-81; USS Range CV 61 San Diego, weapons officer co-dept head, 1981-83; Commander Naval Base San Diego, asst chief staff admin, 1983-. **Orgs:** Nat Naval Officers Asn, 1972-. **Military Serv:** USN, comdr, 18 yrs; Nat Def Medal; Navy Expiditionary Medal; Meritorious Unit Commendation; Humanatrian Serv Medal; Sea Serv Ribbon; Armed Forces Exp Medal. **Home Addr:** 2106 Rancho Verde Dr, Escondido, CA 92025. *

LAWLAH, GLORIA GARY
State government official. **Personal:** Born Mar 12, 1939, Newberry, SC; married John Wesley Lawlah III; children: John Wesley IV, Gloria Gene & Gary McCarrell. **Educ:** Hampton Univ, BS, social studies, 1960; Trinity Col, MA, eng & admin, 1970. **Career:** McCormick Co SC Pub Schs, teacher, 1961; Prince George County Pub Schs, teacher, 1961-62; Wash DC Pub Sch, teacher & adminr, 1965-95; Md Gen Assembly, deleg, 26th dist, 1986-90, sen, 26th dist, 1991-; Women Legislators Md, pres, currently; Women Govt Inc, secy & treas, currently; Dept Aging, off secy, 2007-, currently. **Orgs:** Nat Asn Advan Colored People; bd dirs, Coalition Black Affairs, 1980-; Nat Coun Negro Women; Oxon Hill Dem; co-chair, PG Govt Review Task Force Pub Safety, 1982; Dem State Cent Comn, 1982-86; bd dirs, Hillcrest-Marlow Planning Bd, 1982-; bd dirs, Family Crisis Ctr, 1982-84; Alpha Kappa Alpha Sorority, 1984-; del, Dem Nat Conv, 1984; founder, Nat Polit Cong BlackWomen, 1984-; Black Dem Coun, 1985-; John Hanson Women's Dem Club, 1985-; bd, Ctr Aging Greater SE Comn Hosp, 1985-; St Md legis Comn, Econ &Environ Affairs Comn, Senate-House Joint Comn Invest; Child Care Admin Adv Coun; Educ Block Grants Adv Comn; adv bd, Transp Planning Bd Wash; incorporator & treas, Prince George's Co Alliance Black Elected Off Inc, 1986-; Am Bus Women Asn, 1990-; Nat Conf St Legis, Nat Black CaucusSt Legislators, 1991-; vchmn, Prince Georgeocos Co Senators, 1998-; bd dirs, Hospice Nat Capital Region, 1999-; treas, Nat Orgn Black Elected Legis Women Inc, 1999-; Regional Transp Comn VA & MD, 2000-; sen chair, Joint Comn Mgt Pub Funds, 2001-; Pierrians Inc, 2002-; vpres, Prince Georgeocos Chap, LINKS Inc; bd, Prince Georgeocos Southern Christian Leadership Conf, 2002-03; co-chair, Sen Protocol Comn, 2002-; pres, Prince George's County Chap, Links Inc, 2006-; chair & bd dir, Women Govt, 2006-. **Honors/Awds:** Hall of Fame inductee, Prince George's Co Women's, 1991; J Richard CrouseLegislator of the Year Award, 1998; Edgemeade Hon, 1999; Citizen of theYear Award, Prince Georges Co Bd Trade, 2000; Maryland Leadership Award, Md Greater Wash Bd Trade, 2001; Champion Against Oral Cancer, Univ Md MedSyst, 2001; Outstanding Transp Leader of the Year, MWBT, 2002; Award ofExcellence, Mothers Against Drunk Driving, 2002; Nat Coalition of 100Black Women, 2002; hon, Md State Bd Educ, 2002; Humanitarian Award, UnivMd Dent Sch, 2003; Legislator of the Year, Health Facilities Asn ofMaryland, 2006. **Home Addr:** 3801 24th Ave, Temple Hills, MD 20748. **Business Addr:** Senator, Secretary of Aging, Maryland Department of General Services, Department of Aging, Rm 1007 301 W Preston St, Baltimore, MD 21201, **Business Phone:** (410)767-1102.

LAWLESS, EARL
Administrator. **Personal:** Born Oct 10, 1947, Raceland, LA; married Otha M Lawless, Aug 27, 1977; children: Reneta Lawless, Sharmanice Lawless Bradley. **Educ:** Xavier Univ, attended 1967. **Career:** La Weekly Newspaper, asst ed, 1972-76; US Postal Serv, carrier, 1976-77, distribution clerk, 1984-86; Orleans Sheriff's Off criminal dept, deputy sheriff, 1977-81; Verona Police Dept, sergeant, 1982-84; Okolona Police Dept, sergeant, 1987-89; Tupelo Police Dept, patrolman, 1989-90; Tupelo Pub Sch Dist, security chief, 1990-96; Jackson Advocate, news correspondent. **Orgs:** Fed Commun Comn, 1974-02; Am Fedn Radio & TV Artists, 1976; chair, Adv Comt Legal Serv, 1982-90; Am Asn Retired Persons, 1997-02; pres, Vietnam Veterans Am, 1998-01; lay leader, NEMS Christian Methodist Episcopal Church, 1998-01; pub policy advocate, Arthritis Found, 1999-02; Int Soc Poets, 2001. **Honors/Awds:** Public Policy Advocacy Award, Arthritis Foundation, 1999-00; Merit Award, International Society of Poets, 2001. **Military Serv:** NEMS Daily Journal, 1-sec E, 2001. **Home Addr:** 2723 Lawndale Dr, Tupelo, MS 38801-6722. *

LAWRENCE, ANNIE L.
Educator, nurse. **Personal:** Born Feb 14, 1926, Virginia; widowed. **Educ:** Freedman's Hosp Nursing; Loyola Univ, cert pub health nursing; DePaul Univ, BS, MS; Sarsota Univ, EDd; Ill Stat Univ, EDd. **Career:** Div Nursing & Hosp Sci, chair; Govs State Univ, prof nursing; nursing educ coord; St Ill Dept Regist & Educ, asst nursing educ coord; Evangelical Sch Nursing, asst dir; Mt Sinai Hosp Sch Nursing, nursing educ; Provident Hosp Sch Nursing, sup instr & dir nursing educ. **Orgs:** Treas, Depaul Nursing Sch Alumni Asn; Northeastern League Nursing; chmn, Adv Stud Sect Am Nurses Asn; Nat League Nursing; parliamentarian N Asn Lawyers Wives; aux vice pres & immediate past pres, N Asn Lawyers Wives; N Ethical Guideline Community; United Church Christ; lay moderator, Park Manor Ongregational UCC; pres, Women's Fellowship Park Manor Cong Church; Am Inst Parliamentarians; corp mem bd, Homeland Ministries; pres, Sigma Gamma Rho Sorority; bd dir, Evangelical Hosp Asn Pub; site visitor & panel reviewer, Nat League of Nursing; vice chair & gov coun, Bethany Hosp; Ill Nurses Asn. **Honors/Awds:** Successful Blacks Award. **Special Achievements:** Author of "Can an Evaluation Tool be Meaningful to Studies & Teachers?".

LAWRENCE, ARCHIE
Lawyer. **Personal:** Born Jun 21, 1947, East St Louis, IL; son of Charlie and Addie; married Ernestine King; children: Chiestine, Crystal, Candace. **Educ:** Southern Ill Univ-Carbondale, BA, 1970; St Louis Univ, Sch Law, JD, 1975. **Career:** Legis Ref Bur, bill drafting agency, 1975-80; Internal Revenue Serv, estate tax atty, 1980-82; Ill Dept Revenue, staff atty, 1982-90; Ill Atty Gen's Off, asst atty gen, 1991-, atty gen, currently. **Orgs:** Ill State Bar Asn, 1982-; rep, County Bd, 20th Dist, Sangamm County, Ill, 1986-; bd dir, Nat Asn Advan Colored People, Springfield Br, 1996-, first vpres, 1990-92, bd, 1988-90, pres, 1984-88. **Honors/Awds:** Equal Opportunity Award, Sprinfield Ill Urban League, 1986; President's Award, Nat Asn Advan Colored People, Springfield Br, 1988, Political Action Award, 1989. **Special Achievements:** Elected rep, Sangamon County Bd, 1986-92; named plantiff, voter's rights lawsuit against city of Springfield, Ill, 1984-86. **Military Serv:** AUS, clerk spc4, 1971-73; Meritorious Service Award, 1973. **Business Addr:** Attorney General, State of Illinois, 500 S 2nd St, Springfield, IL 62706, **Business Phone:** (217)782-1090.*

LAWRENCE, AZAR MALCOLM
Jazz musician. **Personal:** Born Nov 3, 1953, Los Angeles, CA; children: Daneka, Azar Malcolm III & Aisha. **Educ:** W La Jr Col; Calif State Univ; USC. **Career:** McCoy Tyner's Quartet, jazz musician, 1973-77; Prestige Label Serv, leader, 1974-76; Azar Lawrence Quartet, saxist, currently; Albums: Bridge into the New Age, 1974; Summer Solstice, 1975; People Moving, 1976. **Orgs:** Sickle Cedd Fedn; Urban League Guild; Black Awareness Prog. **Special Achievements:** Featured in Downbeat Magazine, 1973 and Esq Magazine, 1975; Montreaux Jazz Festival, 1973.

LAWRENCE, DR. BARBARA ANN
School administrator. **Personal:** Born Feb 4, 1938, Indianapolis, IN; daughter of Harold and Norma Price; married Leonard E, Mar 3, 1962; children: Courtney N, Leonard M & David W. **Educ:** Mich State Univ, BA, 1959; Butler Univ, MS, 1967; Tex Agr & Mech Univ, PhD, 1994. **Career:** Indianapolis Public Sch, spec educ teacher, 1959-62; Sandia AFB, NMex, kindergarten teacher, 1964-65; Ind Univ Sch Med, psychometrist, 1967-69; Northside ISD San Antonio, spec educ teacher, 1969-70, Northeast ISD, dept head, special ed, 1976-84, lead teacher, pyschiatric hosp, 1984-91; Univ Tex, Inst Texan Cult, asst dir educ & technol initiative, 1994-. **Orgs:** Nat Med Asn, 1973-; past pres, Links, Inc, San Antonio Chap, 1983-; vpres, bd mem, Community Guidance Ctr, 1986-92; adv comn, Tex Cancer Coun, 1994-96; chair personnel comm, bd mem, San Antonio Child Advocates, 1994-99; Tex Agr & Mech Dev Bd, Col Educ, 1995-; chair dev comn, Merced Housing Tex, 1996-; dev bd mem, Univ Incarnate Word, 1998-. **Honors/Awds:** President's Award, San Antonio Child Guidance Ctr, 1995; Profiles Leadership, Mission City Bus & Prof Women, 1998; Leadership Texas, Found Women's Resources, 1999. **Special Achievements:** Dissertation (unpublished): Perceptions of First Year Medical Students at the Univ of Texas Health Science Center at San Antonio Toward the Delivery of Health Care to Ethnically Diverse Populations, 1994; San Antonio 100, Selected for Membership, 1998. **Home Addr:** 3107 Sable Creek, San Antonio, TX 78259-2636. **Business Addr:** Director of the Educational and Technology Initiative, The University of Texas Institute of Texan Cultures, 801 S Bowie St, San Antonio, TX 78205, **Business Phone:** (210)458-2300.

LAWRENCE, BRENDA L.
Mayor, school administrator. **Personal:** Born in Southfield, MI; married McArthur; children: Michael & Michelle. **Educ:** Cent Mich Univ, BA, pub admin. **Career:** Community advocate; Southfield City Coun, pres, 1999; Southfield City, mayor, 2001-. **Orgs:** Parent Youth Guid Comn; adv comn, Oakland Co United Way; Oakland Co Aids Coun; Oakland Co Chap, Nat Am Advan Colored People; adv bd, Mich Asn Mayor's; US Conf Mayors; Southfield-Lathrup Optimist Club; Women's Econ Club; bd dir, Women Off Network; adv bd, Birmingham YMCA; adv bd, Pepsi Community; bd gov, Renaissance & Skyline Club; bd mem, pres, vpres, secy, Southfield Sch Bd. **Honors/Awds:** Brotherhood Award, Jewish War Vet-State Mich; Challenging the Process Award, Leadership Detroit's; Woman of the Year Award, the ABWA Millennium Chap; Enterprising Women, Detroit Historical Soc; Distinguished Leadership& Future Leaders Award, Leadership Oakland, 2004; 95 Most Influential Women in Michigan; Black Women Achiever Award; Wand Award, 2004; Enterprising Women, Detroit Historical Soc, 2004. **Special Achievements:** First African American & first woman mayor of Southfield; initiated the following community programs: The Mayor's Walk community health prog; Mayor's Roundtable-a citizen driven forum; Southfield Reads!; Ann Flower Day; City-wide Blood Dr; Today's Woman-a cable show; named to the Women's Informal Network "List of the Most Influential Black Women in Metropolitan Detroit" and CORP Magazine's "95 Most Influential Women in

Michigan". **Business Addr:** Mayor, City of Southfield, 26000 Evergreen Rd, PO Box 2055, Southfield, MI 48034, **Business Phone:** (248)796-5100.

LAWRENCE, CHARLES
Lawyer, judge. **Personal:** Born Sep 27, 1955, Laurel, MS; son of Charels E and Mattie M; married Shirley Sutton Lawrence, Jun 5, 1977; children: Charles E CJ III & Chari E. **Educ:** Univ Southern Miss, BA, political sci, 1976; Howard Univ Sch Law, JD, 1979. **Career:** Southeast Miss Legal Serv, staff atty, 1979-84; Pvt Pract, atty, 1984-; City Hattiesburg, councilman ward 5, 1985-97, municipal ct judge, 1997-. **Orgs:** Omega Psi Phi Fraternity Inc, 1975-; Miss Bar & Magnolia Bar, 1979-; Hattiesburg Evening Optimist Club, 1987-; Nat Asn Advan Colored People; Hattiesburg Area Develop Partnership/Chamber Com, 1997-; Miss Municipal Judges Asn, 1997-; Am Trial Lawyers Asn, 1997-; United Way Southeast Miss, 1997-. **Honors/Awds:** Outstanding Service Award, SEMLS, 1979-84; Outstanding Service Award, Miss Headstart, 1985; Juneteenth Community, Black Excellence Award City Gov, 1992; Man of the Year, Omega Psi Phi Fraternity, 1998. **Business Addr:** Attorney, 1105 Edwards St, PO Box 1624, Hattiesburg, MS 39403-1624, **Business Phone:** (601)582-4157.

LAWRENCE, EDWARD
Actor. **Personal:** Born Jan 8, 1935, Gasden, AL; married Marion Winn; children: Rita, Edward Jr, Jill & Lawrence Jr. **Educ:** Empire State Col, BA, 1957; Studio Theatre Sch. **Career:** African-am Cultural Ctr, prof actor, exec dir; Film: Everybody's All-American (When I Fall in Love), 1988. **Orgs:** Actors Equity; Studio Arena Theatre, 1966-68; Buffalo Urban League; Community Action Orgn; Buffalo & Build Orgn. **Honors/Awds:** Community service award Black Harmony.

LAWRENCE, ELLIOTT
Association executive. **Personal:** Born May 27, 1947, Mt Vernon, NY; son of Muriel and Milford Brown; divorced. **Educ:** Albany State Univ, BA, 1973. **Career:** Events Plus, vpres sales, 1989-91; Themes & Schemes, dir sales & mkt, 1991-92; San Diego Conv & Visitors Bur, nat sales mgr, 1992, asst dir multicultural group sales, currently. **Orgs:** Nat Coalition Black Meeting Planners; Relig Conf Mgt Asn; Meeting Prof Int; bd mem, Jackie Robinson YMCA, San Diego; Nat Black MBA Asn; asst dir multicultural group sales, Int Asn Hispanic Meeting Planners. **Honors/Awds:** Multicultural Award, Nat Univ, 1997; Apex Award, Black Meeting & Tanesin Mag, 1999. **Special Achievements:** CMP Designation, Certified Meeting Planner, 1996; Former Broadway Singer/Dancer. **Military Serv:** USN, Third Class Petty Officer, 1966-68. **Business Addr:** Assistant Director for Multicultural Group Sales, San Diego Convention & Visitors Bureau, 2215 India St, San Diego, CA 92101, **Business Phone:** (619)232-3101.

LAWRENCE, JAMES FRANKLIN
Journalist. **Personal:** Born Aug 19, 1949, Orlando, FL; son of Ethel L and James; married Betty A (divorced 1986); children: Terrance, Jamil & Ebony. **Educ:** Howard Univ, Wash, DC, BA, 1971. **Career:** Cleveland Col & Post, Cleveland, OH, reporter, 1972-73; United Press Int, Denver, CO, reporter & ed, 1973-85; Orlando Sentinel, Orlando, FL, ed writer, 1985-87; Gannett Westchester Newspapers, White Plains, NY, assoc ed & ed; Rochester Democrat & Chronicle, ed, currently. **Orgs:** Treasurer, Alpha Phi Alpha (Eta Chi Lambda), 1989; Nat Asn Black Journalists. **Honors/Awds:** Second Place, Beat Commentary, The Orlando Sentinel, 1986; Mighty Pen, (4 first place, 2 second), Gannett Westchester Newspapers, 1987-91. **Special Achievements:** One of 15 Gannett Supervisors of the Year for 2004. **Business Addr:** Editor, The Rochester Democrat and Chronicle, 55 Exchange Blvd, Rochester, NY 14614, **Business Phone:** (585)232-7100.

LAWRENCE, JAMES H
Police officer. **Personal:** Born Apr 25, 1946, Harlem, NY; son of James and Alice; married Gail, Jun 7, 2002; children: James III. **Educ:** Fordham Univ, BA, Econs, 1978; CUNY Law Sch, JD, 1988; Columbia Univ, Police Mgt Inst, 1993. **Career:** Police officer (retired); New York Police Dept, 1970-2002; Nassau County Police Dept, comnr police, 2002-07. **Orgs:** Sigma Pi Phi; Nat Org Black Law Enforcement Execs; Am Acad Pro Law Enforcement; Guardian's Asn; NY State Asn Chiefs Police; Int Asn Chiefs Police; mem chair, Law Enforcement Employer's Prog; Sigma Pi Phi; bd dirs, Nassau County Munic Police Chief's Asn; bd dirs, Old Westbury Col Found; Major Cities Chiefs Asn; One Hundred Black Men Long Island Inc. **Honors/Awds:** Lloyd Sealy Award, NY Chap Nat Org Black Law Endorcement Execs, 2000; Man of the Year, NYPD Guardians Asn, 2001; Lifetime Achievement Award, Nubians Soc, 2001; Building Brick & Cornerstone Award, NY Chap, Urban League, 2002; Man of the Year, Police Self Support Group, 2002; 6th Criminal Justice Leadership Award, St. John's Univ, 2003; Man of the Year, Suffolk Minorities involved in Law Enforcement, 2004. **Special Achievements:** First African American police commissioner in Nassau County Police Dept. **Military Serv:** AUS, first lt, 1966-69, two Bronze Stars.

LAWRENCE, JOHN EDWARD
Educator. **Personal:** Born May 11, 1941, Durham, NC; son of Harry and Lucille; married Virginia Landers, Jun 12, 1945; children: John II & Jason. **Educ:** NC Cent Univ, BS; Fla A&M Univ, MS. **Career:** Lincoln High Sch, teacher, 1963-67; Godby High Sch, teacher, 1967-69, from asst prin to prin, 1969-78; Fla Dept Educ, bur adult & community educ, chief, 1979-. **Orgs:** Community Educr; Nat Commmunity Educ Asn; NAPCAE; FAEA; Leon Dist Adv Comn; Kappa Delta Pi; Phi Delta Kappa; Frontiers Int; bd dir, Capital City Tiger Bay Club; Tallahassee Urban League; life mem, Nat Asn Advan Colored People; bd mem, Leon Co Housing Finance Authority; Fla Lemon Law Bd; bd mem, Thurgood Marshall Achievers; chair, Nat dirs Adult Educ. **Honors/Awds:** Frontiersman of the Year Award, 1975 & 1998. **Business Addr:** Chief, Florida Department of Education, Bureau of Adult and Community Education, Rm 1244 FEC Bldg 325 W Gaines St, Tallahassee, FL 32399-0400, **Business Phone:** (850)487-4929.

LAWRENCE, DR. LEONARD E
Association executive. **Personal:** Born Jun 27, 1937, Indianapolis, IN; son of Leonard A and Elizabeth M; married Barbara Ann Price; children: Courtney, L Michae & David. **Educ:** Ind Univ, BA, MD 1962. **Career:** Ind Univ Sch Med, psych resident, 1965-68, chief psychol res, 1967-68, child psychol fellow, 1967-69; Child Psych Serv Wilford Hall USAF Med Ctr, chief, 1969-72; San Antonio C Ctr, assoc med dir; Univ Tex Health Sci Ctr, prof psych pediats, fam pract, assoc dean stud affairs, currently. **Orgs:** Cert Am Bd Psychol & Neurol, 1970-71; Tex Juvenile Corrections Master Plan Adv Coun, 1974-75; Coun C Adolesc & Their Families Am Psychol Asn, 1976, 1978-83; Nat Med Asn; Am Acad Child Psychol; Am Ortho Psychol Asn; Am Psychol Asn; Kappa Alpha Psi; ed bd, Jour Am Acad Child Psychol; pres-elect, pres, Nat Med Asn, 1992-93, 1993-94; Tex Youth Comn, 1992-, chmn, 1995. **Special Achievements:** Co-author with J Spurlock "The Black Child" Basic Handbook of Child Psych vol 1; JB Noshpitz Ed-in-Chief Basic Books Inc, NY, 1979. **Military Serv:** AUS, lt col, 1963-72. **Home Addr:** 3107 Sable Creek, San Antonio, TX 78259-2636, **Home Phone:** (210)260-5357. **Business Addr:** Associate Dean, Medical School - University of Texas Health Science Centre, Department Psychiat, 7703 Floyd Curl Dr MC 7792, San Antonio, TX 78229-3900, **Business Phone:** (210)567-5403.

LAWRENCE, LONNIE R
Manager. **Personal:** Born Jun 11, 1946, Miami, FL; married Carol Walker, Feb 14, 1987; children: Derek & Jonathan. **Educ:** Miami-Dade Community Col, attended 1972; St Thomas Univ, attended 1979; Barry Univ, Miami, Fla, prof studies, 1989; Harvard Univ, JFK Sch Gov, sr exec, 1990. **Career:** Manager (retired); Metro-Dade Police Dept, patrolman, 1968-80, sgt 1980, comdr, 1981-83, dist comdr, 1983-85, major, 1985-87; Metro-Dade HUD, asst dir, 1987-89; Metro-Dade Corrections, dir, 1989. **Orgs:** Bd dir, Leadership Miami Alumni Asn, Big Brothers & Big Sisters, Informed Families Dade; bd dir, treas, Miami-Dade Chamber Com; Fla Criminal Justice Exe Inst, 1990-; chmn, Youth Activities Dade County Asn Chiefs Police, 1984-; Am Correctional Asn, 1989-. **Honors/Awds:** Officer of the Year, Richmon-Porrine Jaycees, 1982; Public Serv US Dept Justice, 1984; Officer of the Year, MIK Develop Corp, 1985; Outstanding Participation Award, Hialeah-Miami Springs Co, 1991; Award of Honor, Alternatives Prog Inc, 1990; Cert Commendation, Bd County Comnr, 1991. **Military Serv:** USM, corporal, 1965-68. **Home Addr:** 831 NW 207th St, Miami, FL 33169, **Home Phone:** (305)652-2026.

LAWRENCE, DR. MARGARET MORGAN
Physician. **Personal:** Born Aug 19, 1914, New York, NY; daughter of Sandy Alonzo and Mary Elizabeth Smith; married Charles R II (deceased); children: Charles R III, Sara Lawrence-Lightfoot & Paula Wehmiller. **Educ:** Cornell Univ, AB 1936; Col Physicians & Surgeons Columbia Univ, MD/MS, pubhealth, 1943, cert psychoanalytic med, 1951. **Career:** Pediat Meharry Med Col, asso prof 1943-47; Pomona NY, practicing child psychiatrist psychoanalyst, 1951; Northside Child Develop Ctr, City Col Educ Clin, NYC, psychiatrist 1951-57; Child Develop Ctr, dir, 1969-74; Children's Ther, assoc dir, 1954-57; Sch Ment Health Unit, dir, 1957-63;Harlem Hosp Ctr, supv child psychiatrist & psychoanalyst, 1963-84; Col P& S Columbia, assoc clin prof psychiat, 1963-84; all Rockland Co Ctr Ment Health Pomona NY. **Orgs:** Fel, Rosenwald, 1942-43; fel, Nat Res Coun, 1947-48; fel, US Pub Health Serv, 1948-50; Licentiate Am Bd Pediat, 1948; Alpha Kappa Alpha Sorority,1990; life fel. Am Psychoanalytic Asn; life fel, Am Psychiat Asn; Am Acad Psychoanalysis; Am Orthopsychiat Asn; Nat Med Asn; Black Psychiatrists Am; Med Soc Co Rockland. **Honors/Awds:** Publ "Mental Health Team in the Schools" Human Sci Press 1971; publ "Young Inner City Families the Development of Ego Strength under Stress" Human Sci Press 1975; Joseph R Bernstein Mental Health Award Rockland Co NY1975; EY Williams MD Clinical Scholars of Distinction Award 1984;Outstanding Women Practioners in Medicine Award of the Susan Smith McKinney Steward Med Soc 1984; Honorary Doctor of Civil Law, University of the South, 1987; Honorary Doctor of Science, Connecticut Col, 1989; Honorary Doctor of Divinity, General Theological Seminary, 1990; Honorary Doctor of Humane Letters, Marymount Col, 1990; Honorary Doctor of Education,Wheelock Col, 1991; Cornell Black Alumni Award, 1992; Honorary Doctor ofHumane Letters, Berkeley Theological Seminary, 1998; Honorary Doctor of Science, Swarthmore Col, 2003; The 100 Most Notable Cornellians (Altschuler GC, Kramnick I, Moore RL, eds) Margaret Morgan Lawrence, class of 1936; Nevin Sayre Peace Award of the Episcopal Peace Fellowship, 2003. **Special Achievements:** First African -American psychoanalyst trained in the United States; First black female pediatrician certified by American Board of Pediatrics; Authored: The Mental Health Team in Schools, 1971; Young Inner City Families, 1975. **Home Addr:** 34 Dogwood Lane, Pomona, NY 10970, **Home Phone:** (845)354-2883.

LAWRENCE, MARTIN
Personal: Born Apr 16, 1965; son of John and Chlora; married Patricia Southall, Jan 7, 1995 (divorced 1996); children: Jasmine Page. **Career:** Actor, executive producer, writer & director; Films: Do the Right Thing, 1989; House Party, 1990; House Party II, 1991; Talkin' Dirty After Dark, 1991; Boomerang, 1992; You So Crazy!, 1994; Bad Boys, 1995; A Thin Line Between Love & Hate, exec producer & dir, 1996; Nothing to Lose, 1997; Life, 1999; Blue Streak, 1999; Big Mamma's House, exec producer, 2000; What's the Worst That Could Happen, 2001; Black Knight, exec producer, 2001; National Security, exec producer, 2003; Bad Boys II, 2003; Blue Streak II, 2003; Rebound, exec producer, 2005; Big Momma's House 2, exec producer, 2006; Wild Hogs, 2007; Welcome Home, Roscoe Jenkins, 2008; College Road Trip, 2008; Big Momma's House 3, 2009; TV serials: "What's Happening Now!", 1987-88; A Little Bit Strange, 1989; Private Times, 1991; Hammer, Slammer & Slade,1990; "Martin", 1992-97; "Saturday Night Live", 1994; Exec producer: You So Crazy, 1994; What's the Worst That Could Happen?, 2001; Martin Lawrence Live: Run teldat, 2002. **Honors/Awds:** Image Award, Nat Asn Asvan Colored People, 1995 & 1996; Male Star of Tomorrow, 1995; BET Icon Comedy Award, 2005. **Home Phone:** (212)586-5100. **Business Phone:** (310)859-4000.*

LAWRENCE, MERLISA EVELYN (MERLISA EVELYN LAWRENCE CORBETT)
Writer. **Personal:** Born Oct 14, 1965, Winter Haven, FL; daughter of Esther Mae Martin and Robinson Louis. **Educ:** Univ South Fla, Tampa, FL, BA, jour, 1987. **Career:** Tampa Tribune, Tampa, Fla, sports writer, 1987-88; Staten Island Advance, Staten Island, NY, sports writer, genl assignments, 1988-90; Pittsburgh Press, Pittsburgh, Pa, sports writer, 1990-92; Sports Illustrated, reporter, 1992-94; freelance writer, 1994-; Alexandria Coffee News, publ, 2005-. **Orgs:** Nat Asn Black Journalists, 1988-; Garden State Asn Black Journalists, 1992; ed, NABJ Sports Task Force Newsletter, 1990-. **Honors/Awds:** Outstanding Achievement on Brain Bowl Team, 1985; Public speaking to high school and college students, 1990-; Involved with local job fairs and workshops for minority high school and college students. **Home Addr:** 233 1/2 Summit Ave, Jersey City, NJ 07304, **Home Phone:** (201)451-1103. **Business Addr:** Publisher, Alexandria Coffee News, PO Box 22206, Alexandria, VA 22304, **Business Phone:** (703)966-7127.

LAWRENCE, OLLIE, JR.
Airline executive, founder (originator), vice president (organization). **Personal:** Born Aug 3, 1951, Chicago, IL; son of Ollie and Minnie; married Robin Warr-Lawrence, Dec 30, 1989 (deceased); children: Nicole. **Educ:** Univ Conn, BS, bus admin, 1973; Univ New Haven, attended 1978; George Wash Univ, attended 1990. **Career:** Pratt & Whitney Aircraft, compensation analyst, personnel counr, 1973-78; US Air Inc, Human Resources, vpres; Sodexho N Am, sr vpres, chief human resources officer; Lawrence Consult, founder, 2003-. **Orgs:** Wash Personnel Asn; Am Compensation Asn; bd mem, Black Human Resource Network; US Air Mgt Club; pub arbitrator, Nat Asn Securities Dealers Inc; pub arbitrator, Am Stock Exchange; chapter vpres, Soc Human Resources Mgt; Int Asn Bus Communicators; Capital Press Club; bd mem, VA Chamber Com; bd mem, Arlington Chamber Com. **Honors/Awds:** Mgt Achievement Award, US Air, 1990; Minority Human Resources Prof Award, Black Human Resources Network, 1992; Motivator of the Year Award, Elliot Group's, 2001; Pvt Sector Human Resources Prof Excellence Award, Black Human Resources Network, 2004. **Special Achievements:** Black Belt in Tae Kwon Do. **Business Addr:** Founder, Lawrence Consulting Inc, 3506 W 37th Ave, Vancouver, BC, Canada V6N 2V8.*

LAWRENCE, PHILIP MARTIN
Business owner. **Personal:** Born Nov 12, 1950, Evansville, IN; son of William H and Pilar; married Cheryl Darlene Moore, Jun 6, 1971; children: DeVonna Marcel, Philip M II & Shane Kiwan. **Educ:** ISUE, Evansville, IN. **Career:** People's Voice, Evansville, Ind, ed, Black Newspaper, 1969-71; WJPS, Evansville, Ind, radio announcer; City Evansville, Evansville, Ind, contract compliance officer (bus develop supvr); Tomorrow's Treasures, Calif, reg mgr; Heritage, NJ, regional mgr; Community Action Evansville, Evansville, Ind, sr aide dir; ATSCO Inc, Evansville, Ind, chief exec officer. owner, 1982-. **Orgs:** Treas, Nat Assn Advan Colored People, 1983-86; MIC chmn, IRMSDC,1984-85; bd mem, Coun Aging, 1984-87; Steering Comt Head, 1986-89; StateChamber Com, 1986-89; treas, 1987-89, Evansville Area Minority Supplies Develop Coun; Rotary Int, 1987-89; bd dir, Pvt Indust Coun, 1987-89; pres,Grace Lutheran Church, 1990-. **Honors/Awds:** Master of Ceremonies for Black History Talent, 1978-88; Certificate for Outstanding Business Achievement, Black Enterprise Mag, 1990; Freedom Award, Natl Assn Advan Colored

People, 1990; Leadership Award, Evansville Chamber Com, 1992; Natl Assn Advan Colored People, Minority Bus Leadership Award, 1992; Certificate of Appreciation, Downtown Master Plan Steering Comt, 1995. **Special Achievements:** Played the beast in "Beauty & the Beast" on local TV station, 1982. **Home Addr:** 907 E Gum St, Evansville, IN 47713. **Business Addr:** Chief Executive Officer, ATSCO Inc, PO Box 3912, Evansville, IN 47737, **Business Phone:** (812)423-0054.

LAWRENCE, PHILIP MARTIN
Executive, real estate developer, business owner. **Personal:** Born Nov 12, 1950, Evansville, IN; son of William H and Pilar; married Sandra Authur Robinson, Dec 31, 1963; children: Kevin & Rhonda. **Educ:** ISUE, Evansville, IN. **Career:** People's Voice, Evansville, Ind, ed, Black Newspaper, 1969-71; WJPS, Evansville, Ind, radio announcer; City Evansville, Evansville, Ind, contract compliance officer (bus develop supvr); Tomorrow's Treasures, Calif, regional mgr; Heritage, NJ, regional mgr; Community Action Evansville, Evansville, Ind, sr aide dir; ATSCO Inc, Evansville, Ind,chief exec officer. owner, 1982-. **Orgs:** Treas, Nat Asn Advan Colored People, 1983-86; MIC chmn, IRMSDC,1984-85; bd mem, Coun Aging, 1984-87; Steering Comt Head, 1986-89; State Chamber Com, 1986-89; treas, 1987-89, Evansville Area Minority Supplies Develop Coun; Rotary Int, 1987-89; bd dir, Pvt Indust Coun, 1987-89; pres,Grace Lutheran Church, 1990-. **Honors/Awds:** Master of Ceremonies for Black History Talent, 1978-88; Certificate for Outstanding Business Achievement, Black Enterprise Mag, 1990; Freedom Award, Nat Asn Advan Colored People, 1990; Leadership Award, Evansville Chamber Com, 1992; Nat Asn Advan Colored People, Minority Bus Leadership Award, 1992; Certificate of Appreciation, Downtown Master Plan Steering Comt, 1995. **Special Achievements:** Played the beast in "Beauty & the Beast" on local TV station, 1982. **Home Addr:** 907 E Gum St, Evansville, IN 47713. **Business Addr:** Chief Executive Officer, ATSCO Inc, PO Box 3912, Evansville, IN 47737, **Business Phone:** (812)423-0054.

LAWRENCE, PHILIP MARTIN
Executive, business owner. **Personal:** Born Nov 12, 1950, Evansville, IN; son of William H and Pilar; married Cheryl Darlene Moore, Jun 6, 1971; children: DeVonna Marcel, Philip M II & Shane Kiwan. **Educ:** ISUE, Evansville, IN. **Career:** People's Voice, Evansville, Ind, ed, Black Newspaper, 1969-71; WJPS, Evansville, Ind, radio announcer; City Evansville, Evansville, Ind, contract compliance officer (bus develop supvr); Tomorrow's Treasures, Calif, regional mgr; Heritage, NJ, regional mgr; Community Action Evansville, Evansville, Ind, sr aide dir; ATSCO Inc, Evansville, Ind, chief exec officer. owner, 1982-. **Orgs:** Treas, Nat Asn Advan Colored People, 1983-86; MIC chmn, IRMSDC, 1984-85; bd mem, Coun Aging, 1984-87; Steering Comt Head, 1986-89; State Chamber Com, 1986-89; treas, 1987-89, Evansville Area Minority Supplies Develop Coun; Rotary Int, 1987-89; bd dir, Pvt Indust Coun, 1987-89; pres, Grace Lutheran Church, 1990-. **Honors/Awds:** Master of Ceremonies for Black History Talent, 1978-88; Certificate for Outstanding Business Achievement, Black Enterprise Mag, 1990; Freedom Award, Nat Asn Advan Colored People, 1990; Leadership Award, Evansville Chamber Com, 1992; Nat Asn Advan Colored People, Minority Bus Leadership Award, 1992; Certificate of Appreciation, Downtown Master Plan Steering Comt, 1995. **Special Achievements:** Played the beast in "Beauty & the Beast" on local TV station, 1982. **Home Addr:** 907 E Gum St, Evansville, IN 47713. **Business Addr:** Chief Executive Officer, ATSCO Inc, PO Box 3912, Evansville, IN 47737, **Business Phone:** (812)423-0054.

LAWRENCE, RODELL
Executive. **Personal:** Born Feb 19, 1946, Apopka, FL; son of Adell and Estella Richardson; married Cedar Lavern Evans; children: Christopher, Debora, Biram, Raegena. **Educ:** SC State Col, BSEE, 1970. **Career:** N Am Rockwell Missile System Div, mem tech staff, 1970-73; Xerox Corp, test engr, sr field engr, regional prod serv mgr midwest region headquarters, project mgr I II III, multinat serv opers mgr, prod support mgr, prod serv mgr, Mgr, Multinat Configuration Mgt; Integrated Supply Chain, mgr, Off Document Systems Div; Stillman Col, from exec asst to pres; Meharry Med Col; Fort Valley State Univ, currently. **Orgs:** bd dirs, CARI, 1980-85; dean educ, Omega Psi Phi Frat, 1984, 1985, 1987; athletic dir, Irondequoit Football League, 1985-86; bd dir, Lewis St Settlement, 1986-87; bd visitor, Claflin Col; adv Coun, chmn engineering, SC State Col, 1991-94; vpres, Rochester Chap Nat Asn Advan Colored People, 1991-92; vpres, Dist Scholar Found, Omega Psi Phi, 1990-91. **Honors/Awds:** Distinguished Corp, Alumni Citation NAFEO, 1983; Houston Engineers Society Award, SC State Col, 1986; SC State Col, Benjamin E Mays Most Distinguished Grauate Award, 1989; Outstanding Performance Award, Xerox, 1989; Leadership through Quality Award, Xerox, 1989; hon doctor law degree, SC State Univ, 1992; President Award, Claflin Col, 1992. **Military Serv:** AUS; staff sgt E-6, 2 yrs; Bronze Star, Silver Star, Purple Heart, Army Accomodations. **Business Phone:** (478)825-6300.

LAWRENCE, SANDRA. See Obituaries section.

LAWRENCE, THOMAS R, JR.
Labor relations manager. **Personal:** Born Sep 2, 1929, Waycross, GA; son of Thomas Reid and Thelma Sue Williams; married Caroline Barbosa, Nov 16, 1952; children: Lisa Frazier, Dwayne, Damon & Rene. **Educ:** Suffolk Univ, BA, 1960, MA, 1962; Am Univ, grad study, 1964. **Career:** Labor relations manager (retired); Off Econ Opportunity, educ specialist, 1963-65; Urban League Springfield, exec dir, 1965-68; Info Syst, mgr EEO, N Am Oper, 1970-73; Honeywell Inc, Corp Employee Rel, mgr corp EEO prog, 1973-75, mgr univ rel & minority recruitment, 1983-92; Info Syst-Field Eng Div, Distrib & Priority Control, mgr, 1975-77, mgr nat accts, 1977-79; Avionics Div-Prod Support Logistics, mgr syst & procedures, 1979-80; Controls Syst-Honeywell Plaza, staff asst, 1980-82. **Orgs:** Nat Asn Advan Colored People, Minneapolis, 1972-, bd mem, Indust Adv Coun ACT-SO, 1985-; Minneapolis Urban League, 1972-; bd mem, Nat Consortium Minority Eng, 1985-; bd mem, Nat Soc Black Engs, 1988-. **Honors/Awds:** Meritorious Service Award, Fla A & M Univ, 1988; Honeywell Focus Award, 1988; Black Engineer of the Year Award, Affirmative Action, 1989; National Black Heritage Observance Council Award, 1990; Distinguished Service Award, NC A & T Univ, 1992; Awarded Honorary Doctrate of Laws, NC A&T Univ, 1993. **Military Serv:** U.S. Army, master sgt, 1948-52; received Bronze Star. **Home Addr:** 10541 Wyo Ave S, Bloomington, MN 55438, **Home Phone:** (952)942-1910. *

LAWRENCE, WILLIAM WESLEY
Educator, counselor. **Personal:** Born Jan 27, 1939, Whiteville, NC; son of Horace and Mary; married Queen E Wooten; children: William Wesley Jr, Lori Elecia. **Educ:** NC Col, BS, chem, 1962; St Josephs Sch Med Tech, Tacoma, WA, Cert Med Tech, 1967; NC Cen Univ, Durham, MA, coun, 1971; Univ NC Chapel Hill, PhD, coun psychol, 1974. **Career:** Liggett & Myers Inc, res chem, 1969-71; Univ NC Chapel Hill, counr, 1972-73; NC Cent Univ Durham, assoc dir inst res & eva,l 1973-74; NC A&T State Univ, Greensboro, chmn educ psychiat & guidance, 1974-78; Nat Inst Environ Health Sci coun psychiat & dir human resource devel, 1978-87; Fayetteville State Univ, prof educ, 1987-99; NC Cent Univ, chair, prof counr educ, prof educ, currently, consult & prog evaluator educ & educ related progs, currently. **Orgs:** Med lab consult, Hosps & Sci Labs, 1967-72; consult, Bus Educ Govt, 1975-85; pub notary Durham City, 198-85; real estate broker & instr, Century21 NC Comm Col, 1982-85. **Honors/Awds:** Ray Thompson Humanitarian Award, NC Personnel & Guidance Asn, 1973; Ed Leadership Award, Afro-Amer Soc Transit Employees NY, 1978; Outstanding Work Performance Award, US Dept of Health & Human Serv, 1983. **Military Serv:** AUS, E-4 lab spec, 2 yrs; Outstanding Recruit Award, Platoon Leader, 1963-65. **Home Addr:** 308 Wayne Cir, Durham, NC 27707. *

LAWRIE-GOODRICH, MADELINE
Vice president (Organization). **Career:** ABC Radio Networks, sr dir affil rels, prod specialist ABC news programming; Reach Media, vpres affil rels, 2003-. **Business Addr:** Vice President of Affiliate Relations, Reach Media Inc, 13760 Noel Rd Suite 750, Dallas, TX 75240, **Business Phone:** (972)789-1058.

LAWS, DR. RUTH M.
Educator. **Personal:** Born Jul 25, 1912, Gatesville, NC; married William J; children: Cherritta Matthews. **Educ:** Hampton Inst, BS, 1933; Cornell Univ, MS, 1943; New York Univ, EdD, 1956; Del Tech & Community Col, hon degree, 1994. **Career:** Educator (retired); Peabody Acad, teacher, 1933-34; Rural Soc, caseworker, 1934-36; Wilmington, adult educ supvr, 1936-37; Smyrna, teacher, 1937-41; State Dept Pub Instr Home Econ, dir asst supvr, 1942-68; Adult & Continuing Educ, state dir, 1968-71; Del Tech & Community Col, asst pres, 1971-78; L & M Educ Resources Ltd. **Orgs:** Mem & consult, numerous organizations; Nat Bd, YMCA, 1979-83. **Honors/Awds:** Education Award, Del Dept Pub Instr, 1972; Recognition, Adult Educ Asn, USA, 1974; Diamond State Award, Govt Del, 1974; Citizen of the Year, YMCA, 1980; Delaware Coun Women Hall of Fame, 1981; Philadelphia Freedom Day Award, 1981; Leadership in Education Award, Del Col Personnel Asn, 1981; Outstanding Achievers Award, Brandywine Prof Asn, 1982; Law Day Liberty Bell Award, Del State Bar Asn, 1983; Delaware Mother of the Year, 1986; Delaware Ecumenical Award, 1986. **Home Addr:** 844 Forest St, Dover, DE 19904, **Home Phone:** (302)734-3280.

LAWSON, ANTHONY EUGENE, SR.
Executive. **Personal:** Born Nov 15, 1954, Martinez, CA; son of Ardell Sr and Inez; married Gazelle Williams, Apr 27, 1979; children: Tony & Danielle. **Educ:** Univ Ariz, BS, pub admin, 1977; Univ LaVerne, MS, bus & organizational mgt, 1985. **Career:** Rockwell Int Space, supvr, quality, reliable assurance, test quality engr, 1980-85; Rockwell Int NAAO, supvr quality assurance, 1985; Northrop Corp B-2 Division, quality assurance mgr, prod inspector mgr, maj, final inspection operations mgr, vpres prod, vpres site operations; Northrop Grumman Corp, vpres, dep prog mgr, 1985-97; Burke Industs, vpres & gen mgr, 1998-2001; Everett Charles Technologies, gen mgr, 2001-02; Hitco Carbon Composites Inc, vpres prog mgt, 2003-. **Honors/Awds:** NCAA, All-Am, indoor track, 1975. **Business Phone:** (310)527-0700.

LAWSON, BRUCE B
Executive. **Personal:** Born Mar 30, 1948, New Orleans, LA; son of Henry and Josephine Hirsch; married Ruth Charles, Nov 15, 1969; children: Rachel & Roxanne. **Educ:** Southern Univ, Baton Rouge, LA, BSEE, 1969; Univ Chicago, Chicago, IL, 1974-76. **Career:** AT&T, Morristown, NJ, int mkt dir, 1969; Hearst-Argyle TV Inc, gen sales mgr, currently. **Orgs:** Chairperson, Comn Black Ministries, Diocese Paterson, NJ, 1988-91. **Home Addr:** 2 Thompson Way, Morris Plains, NJ 07950. **Business Addr:** General Sales Manager, Hearst-Argyle Television Inc., 300 W 57th St, New York, NY 10106, **Business Phone:** (212)887-6800.

LAWSON, CASSELL AVON
Educator. **Personal:** Born Mar 29, 1937, Little Rock, AR; married Amy Davison; children: Cassell, Cassandra, Roderick, Nikki & Joi. **Educ:** Langston Univ, BA, 1959; Ind Univ, MEd, 1970; Univ Notre Dame, PhD, 1974; Ind State Univ, postdoctoral, 1976. **Career:** Educator (retired); Grand Rapids Urban Leag, dir, 1956-68; S Bend UrbanLeague, exec dir, 1968-70; Off Campus Stud Activ & Min Stud Affairs UnivNotre Dame, dir, 1973-74; Univ Mass, asst prof & dir, 1974-75; Morgan State Univ, asst vpres dir, 1976-77; Erie Community Col, vpres city campus; Coppin State Col, vpres acad affairs; Gateway Tech Col, vpres & provost, 2005. **Orgs:** Kappa Alpha Psi Fraternity; Phi Delta Kappa; Nat Educ Asn, 1965; chair,Ind Coun Urban Leag Exec, 1967-68; chair, Midwestern Rep Urban Leag Exec,1968-69; chair, Black Student Affairs, 1973-74; chair, S Bend BlackCaucus, 1973-74; Am Personnel & Guid Asn, 1974-75; pres, Roxbury CommunityCol, 1974; Am Asn Higher Educ, 1975-76; Black Leadership Coun. **Honors/Awds:** Nat urban league scholarship, 1968; Community Service Award, Suburban Club, 1967; Community Service Award, Lamba Kappa Mu, 1968; Outstanding Man of the Year Award, 1968; Rockefeller fellow, Ind State Univ, 1975-76. **Military Serv:** USAF, a/1c, 1959-63.

LAWSON, CHARLES H, III
Association executive. **Personal:** Born Nov 20, 1931; married Marie; children: Kim & Linda. **Educ:** Tuskegee Inst, BS, 1954, advan study indust educ, 1955. **Career:** Manual Arts & Indust Therapy, Va hosp; Jefferson Barracks & John Cochran Div; St Louis, Mo, chief, 1967; Nat Asn Advan Colored People, Ill, prin corresp. **Orgs:** Kappa Alpha Psi Fraternity; Elks; past canister chmn, March Dimes, E St Louis & St Clair Co; Greater New Hope Bapt Church, E St Louis; Res Officers Asn, US; Am Fedn Govt Employees; E St Louis Model Cities Agency; Sigma Gamma Rho Soroity, Nat Asn Advan Colored People. **Military Serv:** USAFR lt col.

LAWSON, CHARLES J.
Airline executive. **Personal:** Born Jul 13, 1948, Jackson, GA; son of James and Eliza; married Jackie. **Educ:** Savannah State Col. **Career:** Delta Airlines, cargo service agent, Atlanta, 1971-73, passenger serv agent, Philadelphia, 1973-77, zone mgr, New York, 1977-81, sales mgr, Cleveland, 1981-87, sales mgr, Detroit, 1987-90, regional mgr, Atlanta, 1990-93, dir sales, Atlanta, 1994-95, Civic and Promotional Affairs, dir, 1996. **Orgs:** 100 Black Men of Atlanta; bd mem, Atlanta Convention & Visitors Bureau, 1994; bd mem, Atlanta Sports Council, 1994-; bd mem, French American Chamber, 1994-; bd mem, British American Chamber, 1994-; bd mem, Dekalb County Chamber, 1995-; bd mem, Cobb County Convention & Visitors Bureau, 1996-; bd mem, Atlanta Touchdown Club, 1996-; bd mem, Atlanta Tip-Off Club, 1996-. **Honors/Awds:** Crusade Award, American Cancer Society, 1983; United Negro Col Fund, Distinguished Leadership, 1983; UNCF Telethon, Appreciation Award, 1984; Corp Member of the Year, ACUB, 1997. **Military Serv:** AUS, surgent, 1968-71; Distinguished Serv Award, Army Commmendation. *

LAWSON, DAWN M
Computer engineer, technologist. **Personal:** Born May 1, 1963, Hamlet, NC; daughter of Leonard Sherwood and Mildred Gibson; divorced. **Educ:** George Mason Univ, MA, teleCommunications mgt, 1998, UNC-Greensboro, BS, clothing & textiles, 1986; Chicago State Univ, leadership sem, 1999; Leadership Develop Inst, 1999. **Career:** Dept Defense & Defense Info Syst Agency (DISA), telecommunications specialist, currently, mgr software prod, currently. **Orgs:** State legis coordr, Alpha Kappa Alpha Sorority, Inc, 1998-2002; Blacks Govt, nat corresp secy, 2000-01; Fairfax County Complete Count Comt, 2000; Nat SCY, 2001-02; League Women Voters; NAACP; Univ NC Greensboro Alumni Asn; Fairfax County Comn Organ & Tissue Donation & Transplantation; W Springfield Civic Asn; Antioch Baptist Church; Armed Forces Commun & Electronics Asn (AFCEA); Fairfax County Telecommunications Task Force. **Honors/Awds:** US Geological Survey Performance awards, 1993-96, 1998-99; AT&T FTS2000 award for management and administrative excellence, 1993; Spouse of the year, Joan Orr Air Force, 1995; Service Award, US Dept Interior, 1995; Outstanding mentor/community service award, 1996; Council involvement award, 1998; Certificate of Recognition, Alpha Phi Alpha Fraternity, 1998; Doris R. Asbury Connection award for legislative involvement, Alpha Kappa Alpha Sorority Inc, 1997, 1998; Meritorious Service Award, Blacks Govt, 1999; DISA special Action service Award, 2000; Women of Color Govt & Defense Awards Conf, Technology All Star, 2001; DISA Wall of Heroes, 2002. **Home Addr:** PO Box 523484, Springfield, VA 22152, **Home Phone:** (703)296-7466. **Business Addr:** Program Analyst, Defense Information System Agency, 5600 Columbia Pike Suite 900, Falls Church, VA 22041-2717, **Business Phone:** (703)681-2110.

LAWSON, DEBRA ANN
Executive. **Personal:** Born Oct 25, 1953, Detroit, MI; daughter of Purvis and Lois Marie Patterson; divorced; children: Christina Marie. **Educ:** Wayne State Univ, BFA, 1975. **Career:** WJBK-TV, Fox Television Stas Inc, part-time switchboard operator, 1972-76, typist clerk, acct, 1976-77, admin secy, acct & personnel, 1977-78, secy news dir, 1978-81, community affairs coordr, 1981-86, pub affairs dir, 1987-92; asst prog dir, 1993-96, pub rels dir, 1996-; news info coordr, currently. **Orgs:** Nat Acad TV, Arts & Sci- Mich Chap, 1979-; Detroit Chap, Nat Asn Advan Colored People, 1987-; bus contributions comn mem, Greater Det Chamber Com, 1988-92; corp leadership group, Boys & Girls Clubs Southeastern Mich, 1989-92; community adv bd, Substance Abuse Prev Coalition Southeast Mich, 1990-92; adv bd, MADD, 1991-92; affil bd dir, Am Heart Asn Mich, 1991-94; bd dir, Gleaners Comn Food Bank, 1991-92. **Honors/Awds:** Distinguished Service Award, United Negro Col Fund, 1987; Outstanding Woman in Televison, Am Women Radio & TV, Detroit Chap, Middle Mgt, 1991. **Business Addr:** News Information Coordinator, WJBK-TV2, Fox Television Stations Inc, 16550 W 9 Mile Rd, Southfield, MI 48075, **Business Phone:** (248)552-5218.

LAWSON, ELIZABETH HARRIS
Educator. **Personal:** Married Harris; children: Clyde H, Carol H Cuyjet & Leonard J. **Educ:** Ill Inst Technol, Chicago, BS; Chicago State Univ, MS, 1961; Univ Chicago, post grad, Hon PhD, 1974. **Career:** City Chicago, hs & univ counr, teacher; Chicago St Univ, dir intensive educ prog, 1968-72, asst dir admis & foreign stud adv, 1974-. **Orgs:** NAFSA; Nat Asn Women Deans Couns & Admins; Nat Guidance & Personnel Asn; Master Plan Com Chicago St Univ; chmn, CSU's 5th Div Univ Senator, 1968-74; Am Asn Sch Educr; Ill Guidance & Personnel Asn; res ch Delta Kappa Gamma Int Soc; Alpha Kappa Alpha Sorority; consult, SC Desegregation Ctr, 1968-69; N Cent Bd accreditation HS's, 1970-80; Ill del & co-chair White House Conf, Lib & Inf Serv Wash DC, 1979; bd gov's ICOLA, 1983-84; vol coordr, Nat Conf Christians & Jews, 1980-84. **Military Serv:** USAF; Citation 1965.

LAWSON, ERMA J.
Educator. **Educ:** Howard Univ, RN, nursing, 1976; Atlanta Univ, MA, sociol; Univ Ky, PhD, med social, 1990. **Career:** Univ Ky, Dept Behav Sci, asst res prof; Univ N Tex, Dept Behav Sci, from asst prof to assoc prof, prof, currently; dir, joint MPH/PhD prog, currently. **Orgs:** Am Sociol Asn; Asn Pub Health; Int Sociol Asn; Sociologists Women Soc; Southern Sociol Asn; Asn Black Social Behav Scientists. **Special Achievements:** Shattered Marriages: Black men and divorce (with A. Thompson), Love, Honor, Divorce: How Black women and children survive the breakup of families (forthcoming), Women's Health: Women's Lives (forthcoming), and more than 20 articles and book chapters. **Business Addr:** Professor, University of North Texas, Department of Sociology, 2336 Northway Lane, PO Box 311157, Denton, TX 76203-1157, **Business Phone:** (940)565-2296.

LAWSON, HERMAN A.
Consultant, state government official. **Personal:** Born Dec 25, 1920, Fowler, CA; son of Frances and Herman; married Pearl Lee Johnson; children: Betty, Patricia, Gloria, Yvonne, Thomas & Tracey. **Educ:** Fresno State Univ CA; Univ Pac; Sacramento State Univ; Chapman Col. **Career:** St Employ Develop Dept, minority employ rep & manpower consult, 1963-; Sacramento, councilman 2nd dist, 1973-75. **Orgs:** Del Paso Heights Libr Comm; col awareness Bd, Am River Col; adv, presidenton programs for the disadvantaged at Amer River Col; City Amendments Study Comm; adv coun, Sacramento Businessman's; 99th Fighter Squad Flight Leader Frt Pilot; bd dir, Tuskegee Airmen Inc, 1974-75, 1978-80; Nat Asn Advan Colored People; commodore Port Sacramento. **Honors/Awds:** Distinguished Flying Cross Air Medal, Commendation Medal, Unit Cit Medal, Award of Valor; campaign medals. **Military Serv:** USAF, major, 1942-63. **Business Addr:** Consultant, State Manpower Planning Office, 800 Capitol Mall, Sacramento, CA 95814.

LAWSON, JAMES M., JR.
Clergy, activist, college teacher. **Personal:** Born Sep 22, 1928, Uniontown, PA; married Dorothy Wood; children: John, Morris, Seth. **Educ:** Baldwin-Wallace Col, attended 1952; Boston Univ, STB, 1960; Vanderbilt Univ, Nashville, attended 1960. **Career:** Clergy (retired), visiting professor; Hislop Col, Hagpur, India, Dept Phys Educ, chmn, 1953-56; Fel Reconciliation Southern Region, field secy, 1957-69; Stud Nonviolent Coord Comt, adv, 1960-64; Nonviolent Educ Southern Christian Leadership Conf, dir, 1960-67; Centenary United Methodist Church, Memphis, pastor, 1962-74; Holman United Methodist Church, pastor; Vanderbilt Univ, vis prof, currently. **Orgs:** Nat Coun, 1960-66; chmn educ comt, Nat Asn Adv Colored People, Memphis, 1963-65 1974-; bd mem, Nat Asn Adv Colored People, Memphis Br, 1964-74; World Coun Church, 1966-; chmn, Black Methodist Church Renewal, 1968-71; Theol Comt Nat Comn Black Churchmen, 1969-; West TN ACLU, 1969-74; Phil Randolph Inst, 1971-; adv comt, Amnesty Prof, 1972-; bd mem, SCLC, 1973-. **Honors/Awds:** Elk Award, 1960; Nat Asn Adv Colored People Award, Memphis, 1965, 1974; Spec Award, AFSCME Int, 1968; Russwurm Award, 1969; Man of the Yr, Cath Interracial Coun, Memphis, 1969; Citation of the Yr, Prince Hall Lodge Tenn, 1969; Distinguished Alumnus Award, Boston, 1970; Outstanding Witness Christ Award, AME Nat Laymen's Asn, 1971; Civic Award, Mallory Knights Memphis, 1974. **Business Addr:** Visiting Professor, Vanderbilt University, 2201 W End Ave, Nashville, TN 37235.*

LAWSON, JASON
Basketball player. **Personal:** Born Sep 2, 1974, Philadelphia, PA. **Educ:** Villanova Univ, attended 1997. **Career:** Basketball player-(retired);Orlando Magic, ctr, 1997-98; Los Angeles Clippers, ctr, 2001-02; Pennsylvania Valley Dawgs, 2003. **Honors/Awds:** Big East Defensive Player of the Year; Big East Conference Defensive Player of the Yr, 1997. *

LAWSON, JENNIFER KAREN
Television producer, manager. **Personal:** Born Jun 8, 1946, fairfield, AL; daughter of William and Velma; married Anthony Gittens, Jan 1, 1982; children: 2. **Educ:** Tuskegee Univ; Columbia Univ, MFA, film making, 1974. **Career:** Stud Nonviolent Coord Comm, spec educ proj dir & staff mem, 1964-67; Nat Coun Negro Women, 1968-69; Quitman County, MS, dir adult educ prog; William Greaves Prods Film Co, ed, 1975; Film Fund, exec dir, 1977-80; Brooklyn Col, asst prof film, 1974-77; Corp Pub Broadcasting, TV fund dir, 1980-89; Pub Broadcasting Serv, exec vpres programming & promotional serv, 1989-95; Magic Box Mediaworks Inc, pres & exec producer, 1995-; Africa Series, exec prod, 2001-; Howard Univ Television, WHUT, gen mgr, 2004-; consult & producer, currently. **Orgs:** Bd mem, Am Pub TV, Boston, MA; community & friends bd, John F Kennedy Ctr Arts, Wash, DC; trustee, Sidwell Friends Sch, Wash, DC; hon bd mem, CINE. **Honors/Awds:** Dr, Teikyo Post Univ. & Med. **Special Achievements:** Named one of 101 Most Influential People in Entertainment Today, Entertainment Weekly, Nov 2, 1990; appeared on the Hollywood Reporter's list of the "Power 50," the 50 most influential women in entertainment. **Business Addr:** Producer, Consultant, Magic Box Mediaworks Inc, 1838 Ontario Pl NW, Washington, DC 20009, **Business Phone:** (202)232-7327.

LAWSON, JOHN C, II
Lawyer. **Personal:** Born Jul 17, 1961, Nashville, TN; son of James Jr and Dorothy. **Educ:** Oberlin Col, BS, 1983; Howard Univ Sch Law, JD, 1986. **Career:** Los Angeles County Public Defenders Off, atty, 1987-. **Orgs:** Los Angeles Black Pub Defenders Asn; John M Langston Bar Asn; Am Bar Asn. **Home Addr:** 4227 Mt Vernon Dr, Los Angeles, CA 90008, **Home Phone:** (213)291-6064. **Business Addr:** Attorney, Los Angeles County Public Defenders Office, Criminal Justice Center, Rm 19-513 Clara Shortridge Foltz 210 W Temple St, Los Angeles, CA 90012, **Business Phone:** (213)974-2811.

LAWSON, LAWYER
Government official. **Personal:** Born Aug 29, 1941, Cincinnati, OH; son of Lawyer and Fannie M Grant (deceased); married Mary Bates, Jun 25, 1989; children: Mary Adale Hall, Kenneth L, George & Robert. **Educ:** Ohio Col Applied Sci, attended; Pre-Med Xavier Univ, attended; Univ Cincinnati, attended. **Career:** Village of Woodlawn, mayor. **Orgs:** Ohio Mayors Asn, 1980-; Nat League Cities, 1980-; bd dirs, Nat Conf Black Mayors, 1984-; Trustee Hamilton County Develop Co, 1985-87; pres, Ohio Chap Black Mayors, 1985; second vpres, Nat Conf Black Mayors, 1990; pres, Hamilton County Munic League.

LAWSON, QUENTIN ROOSEVELT
Government official, educator. **Personal:** Born Jan 7, 1933; married Helen Louis Betts; children: Rosilend & Quentin II. **Educ:** WVa State Col, BA; Univ Md, MEd; Morgan State Col, MSc; Inst, NSF; Morgan State, 1958; Vassar Col, 1960; State Univ Col, 1962. **Career:** City Baltimore, human devel dir; Baltimore, former mayor; Baltimore City Schs, Md State Dept Edn, teacher unit head, unit prin, dir, dropout prev prog, 1958-71; Accountability Inner City, cons; Am psychol assn conf, 1971; Nat Alliance Black Sch Educrs, exec vpres, currently; Ohio, Fla,Ala, cons, dropout prev progs; Public Tech Inc, exec vpres. **Orgs:** PTA; Phi Delta Kappa; Gov Task Force State Sch Constrn; Mental Health Support System; Nat League Cities, mayor's rep; Cen MD Health Systems Agy; retail study Soc Serv Commn; John F Kennedy Inst Handicapped Children; Med Eye Bank; United Fund CICHA; Bay Col MD; Dept HEW; steering com Met Comms System Study; YMCA; Comm Orgn Notable Ams, 1976-77; Congressional Black Caucus Foundation, exec dir, 1992-. **Business Phone:** (202)226-7790.*

LAWSON, ROBERT L.
School administrator. **Personal:** Born Feb 24, 1950, Gallipolis, OH; children: Robert L Jr. **Educ:** Rio Grande Col, BS, 1973; Marshall Univ, MA, 1978; Nova Univ, D.Ed, 1988. **Career:** Gallia Acad HS, teacher, 1973-76; Marshall Univ, admin asst, 1977-83, dircontinuing ed, 1984-. **Orgs:** Consult, Continuing Ed & SUCCESS; speaker, SUCCESS; Community Col Coun; Comn Serv Round table; bd dir, Opportunity Indust Ctr; chmn, Affirmative Action Adv Comn. **Honors/Awds:** Trophy Oral Interpretation Poetry, Ohio Univ, 1969; Outstanding Col, Athletes Am Rio Grande Col, 1970. **Special Achievements:** Book:The Black Pursuit Study Guide;The Cutting Edge, A Study Guide for Achievers; tape published "The Power of Creative Genius". **Home Addr:** PO Box 5524, Huntington, WV 25703.

LAWSON, DR. WILLIAM DANIEL
Dean (Education), educator. **Personal:** Born Nov 5, 1948, Alpine, AL; married Nora Davenport; children: Sonya Danette & Nicole Danielle. **Educ:** Knoxville Col, BA, 1968; Atlanta Univ, MA, 1970; Iowa State Univ, PhD, 1978. **Career:** Ala State Univ, instr sociol, 1971-74; NC A&T State Univ, asst prof rural sociol, 1978-79; Ala State Univ, assoc prof sociol, 1979-85, chmn dept sociol, dean col arts & sci; consult, Ala Ctr Higher Educ, 1982-83; Tenn State Univ, dean col arts & sci, currently. **Orgs:** Fel Am Sociol Asn, 1977-78; licensure monitor, Am Sociol Asn, 1984-; polemarch, Montgomery Alumni Chap Kappa Alpha Psi, 1984-; pres, Tuskegee Area Knoxville Col Alumni Asn, 1984-; bd dirs, Montgomery Area Coun Aging, 1985. **Honors/Awds:** Kappa Man of the Year, Kappa Alpha Psi Frat, 1985. **Military Serv:** USAF, race relations spec, 1974-75. **Business Addr:** Dean, College of Arts & Sciences, Tennessee State University, 3500 John A Merritt Blvd, Nashville, TN 37209, **Business Phone:** (615)963-2164.

LAWSON, WILLIAM R
Architect. **Personal:** Born Mar 8, 1943, Washington, DC; son of Charlotte Hughes Lawson and LaMont Harris Lawson; married Carol Cloud, Aug 17, 1964; children: Derrick Mark & Leslye Michelle. **Educ:** Howard Univ, Wash, DC, BA, archit, 1966. **Career:** HTB Inc, Wash, DC, vpres; Gen Serv Admin, Region 3, Wash, DC, architect & proj mgr, 1966-70, US Postal Serv, Wash Region, Wash, DC, chief, design sect, 1970-71; asst comnr design & construct, Hq, 1971-87; McDevitt Street Bovis, vpres, 1987-93; PBS asst comn planning; ARA PBS, NCR, GSA, 1993-; Nat Capital Planning comn, actg exec dir; Trust Strategy Group, sr adv, currently. **Orgs:** Comt Pub Archit, Am Inst Architects, 1971-; Am Inst Architects, DC Chapter, 1987-; Nat Trust Hist Preserv, 1987-; Am Consult Engrs Coun, 1988-; Medals & Awards Comt, juror, Air Force Design Awards Prog, Soc Am Mil Engrs, 1988-; past pres, Soc Mkt Prof Servs, DC Chap, 1988-89; Greater Wash Bd Trade, 1988-; Nat Asn Indust & Office Parks, 1988-; past mem, exec Comt, Leukemia Soc Am Nat Capitol Area Chap, 1988; Urban Land Inst, 1988-; Consultative Coun, Nat Inst Bldg Sci, 1990-. **Honors/Awds:** Outstanding Performance Certificates, Gen Serv Admin, 1971-87; Alpha R Chi Medal, 1966; Gold Medal for Design, Howard University, 1966; Architect of the Year, DC Council of Engineers and Architects, 1972; Award for Exemplary Leadership, 1982. **Home Addr:** 11005 Saffold Way, Reston, VA 20190-3802, **Home Phone:** (703)437-5225.

LAWSON ROBY, KIMBERLA
Writer. **Personal:** Born May 3, 1965, Rockford, IL; daughter of LB Lawson and Arletha Stapleton; married Will M Roby Jr, Jan 1, 1990. **Educ:** Rock Valley Col, Bus Assoc, 1988; Cardinal Stritch Univ, BBA, 1993. **Career:** Sundstrand Corp, asst repair admin, 1985-89; State IL, welfare caseworker, 1989-91; Greenlee Textron, human resources admin, 1991-93; First Financial Bank, customer serv rep for loans, 1993-94; City Rockford, finance analyst housing, 1994-96; author/novelist, 1996-; Lenox Press, pres, currently. Author: Behind Closed Doors, 1997; Here & Now, 1999; Casting the First Stone, 2000; It's A Thin Line, 2001; Sin No More, 2008; Love & Lies; Changing Faces; The Best-Kept Secret; Too Much of a Good Thing; A Taste of Reality. **Orgs:** Adv bd, Womanspace, 1997-. **Honors/Awds:** 1st Time Author Award, Chicago Book Fair, 1997; Blackboard Book of the Year, Nominee, 1998. **Business Addr:** President, Lenox Press, PO Box 17016, Rockford, IL 61110-7016, **Business Phone:** (815)885-4053.

LAWTON, MATTHEW, III
Baseball player. **Personal:** Born Nov 3, 1971, Gulfport, MS; children: Chassity. **Educ:** Miss Gulf Coast Junior Col. **Career:** Minnesota Twins, outfielder, 1995-2001; New York Mets, outfielder, 2001; Cleveland Indians, outfielder, 2002-04; Pittsburgh Pirates, outfielder, 2005; Chicago Cubs, outfielder, 2005; New York Yankees, outfielder, 2005; Seattle Mariners, outfielder, 2006. **Honors/Awds:** Two times All-Star selection, 2000, 2004.

LAWYER, CYRUS J., III
Educator. **Personal:** Born Sep 21, 1943, Vicksburg, MS; married Vivian Moore; children: Lenaye Lynne & Sonya Denise. **Educ:** Tougaloo Col, BS, 1966; Bowling Green Univ, MS, 1969; Univ Toledo, PhD, 1974. **Career:** Bowling Green Univ, grad asst & teacher asst, 1967-69; Univ Toledo,1969-71, admin intern, 1971-72, asst dean adj instr, 1972-73, asst dean & housing dir 1973-75, sr prog assoc inst servs educ. **Orgs:** Am Chem Soc; Orgn Black Scientists; Am Asn Univ Professors; Phi Delta Kappa; Asn Col & Univ Housing Officers; Alpha Phi Alpha Frat; Nat Asn Advan Colored People. **Honors/Awds:** Outstanding Young Men of America, 1975. **Business Addr:** Educator, 2001 S St NW, Washington, DC 20009.

LAWYER, VIVIAN
School administrator. **Personal:** Born Jan 6, 1946, Cleveland, OH; married Cyrus J Lawyer III; children: Lenaye Lynne & Sonya Alyse. **Educ:** Bowling Green State Univ, BS, 1967; Green State Univ, MEd, 1968. **Career:** Nat Coun Teachers Eng, coord human

resources, 1967-68; Ohio Asn Women Deans & Counrs, 1968-; Bowling Green Sate Univ, asst dean stud, 1968-72. **Orgs:** Ohio Affirmative Action Officers Asn; Nat Asn Womens Deans, Admin & Counrs; Nat Coun Negro Women; Lucas Ct Health Serv Comn NW Ohio Health Planning Asn, 1971-72; Delta Sigma Theta Sor Toledo Alumnae; bd trustees, Toledo YWCA 1974-77. **Honors/Awds:** Distinguished Serv University Award, BGSU, 1967; Midwest Region's Advisory Award, Delta Sigma Theta, 1972.

LAY, CLORIUS L.
Lawyer. **Personal:** Born Sep 1, 1940, Mound Bayou, MS; son of Laddel and Arzzie; divorced; children: Rosmond M, Cloe R. **Educ:** Ind Univ, BS, 1966; Univ Chicago; Brunel Univ, Eng, 1973; Valparaiso Univ, JD, 1974; John M Marshall Grad Sch Law; Ind Continuing Legal Educ Forum's Prog, 1995; Harvard Univ, John F Kennedy Sch Govt, 1996. **Career:** Inland Steel Co, corp internal auditor & procedure designer; New Careers, project dir, 1968-69; E Chicago Hts Comn Ctr, exec dir, 1969; Black Ctr Strategy, vpres, 1969-71; Univ Nat Bank, vpres, 1971-72; Northwest Sickle Cell Found, exec dir, 1972-75; Clorius L Lay, atty & owner, 1975-. **Orgs:** Nat Fel, Woodrow Wilson Fel Found, 1972-74; Nat Alliance Black Sch Educrs; recruiter, Valparaiso Univ, Sch Law; Northwest Ind Alliance Black Sch Educrs; bd mem, Lake County Med Ctr; liaison, Ind Sch Bd Asn; honorary bd mem, Northwest Sickle Cell Found; sustaining mem, Urban League Northwest Ind Inc; Nat Asn Advan Colored People; Ind Univ Northwest Med Sch Scholar Comt; councilman-at-large, Gary City Coun, 1996-. **Honors/Awds:** Cleo Appointee, Coun Legal Educ Opport, 1973; US Top Master, Am Pool Checkers Asn; Service Award, Northwest Ind Sickle Cell Found Inc; Certificate of Appreciation, Kiwanis Int; Prog Sr Execs, State & Local Govt, Cambridge MA. **Military Serv:** USAF, sgt, 1958-62. **Home Phone:** (219)882-5243. **Business Phone:** (219)883-8538.*

LAYMON, HEATHER R
Banker. **Personal:** Born Nov 10, 1948; daughter of Beryl O Harris Sealy and Ellis W Sealy; married John, Dec 22, 1973; children: Shawn M Laymon & Nasya H Laymon. **Educ:** Northeastern Univ, MA, BA, 1972; Nat Sch Savings Banking, attended 1980; Cambridge Col, MA, MEd, 1983. **Career:** Suffolk Franklin Savings Bank, Boston, mgr, 1972-80; Mutual Bank Savings, Boston, asst treas, 1980-82; Bank Boston, asst vpres, 1982-87; Boston Bank Com, Boston, vpres, 1987-. **Orgs:** Boston Bankers Urban Forum, 1980-; trustee, Cambridge YWCA, 1983-87; pres, Boston & Vicinity Club Nat Asn Negro Bus & Prof Women, 1986-89; Plan Giving Comm, Andover Newton Theol Seminary, 1988-; treas, Roxbury Multi Serv Ctr; ber, 1988-; Mass Mortgage Bankers Asn, 1990-; Mass Young Mortage Bankers Asn, 1990-; pres, Beta Alpha Psi. **Honors/Awds:** Black Achiever's Award, YMCA, 1981; President Award, Nat Asn Negro Bus & Prof Women, 1988; Professional Award, Women Serv Club Boston, 1988. **Business Phone:** (617)423-1010.

LAYMON, JOE W.
Vice president (Organization). **Educ:** Jackson State Univ; Univ Wis. **Career:** Eastman Kodak Co, dir human resources, 1996-00; Ford Motor Co, group vpres corp human resources & labour affairs, 2003-. **Honors/Awds:** Alumni Leadership Award, Thurgood Marshall Scholar Fund, 2005. **Business Addr:** Group Vice President, Ford Motor Company, 1 American Rd, PO Box 1899, Dearborn, MI 48120, **Business Phone:** (313)322-3000.*

LAYNE, STEVEN
Clergy. **Career:** Reach Out & Touch Ministries Inc, pastor, currently. **Business Addr:** Pastor, Reach Out & Touch Ministers, 770 Brighton Ave, Staten Island, NY 10301, **Business Phone:** (718)448-1124.*

LAZARD, BETTY
Banker, chairperson. **Career:** WR Lazard, vice chmn, currently. **Business Addr:** Vice Chairperson, WR Lazard, 300 Garden City Plz, Garden City, NY 11530-3302, **Business Phone:** (212)406-2700.

LEACE, DONAL RICHARD
Educator. **Personal:** Born May 6, 1939, Huntington, WV; married Jakki Hazel Browner. **Educ:** Howard Univ, BFA, 1966; George Wash Univ, MFA, 1978; Georgetown Univ, MA, 1984. **Career:** Howard Univ Players, pres, 1965-66; Roanoke Va Total Action Against Poverty, dram & music consult, 1966-67; Duke Ellington Sch Arts, Theatre Dept, chair, 1979-86, 1990, teacher, currently; Georgetown Univ, adj fac, 1992. **Orgs:** Am Fed Music 161-710, 1960; Am Fed TV & Radio Artists, 1979; Tokama Theatre, bd dir, Wa, DC, 1983-85. **Honors/Awds:** Certificate of Excellence, Presidential Scholars Prog, Presidential Scholars Prog Comn, 1983; Judge Helen Hayse Awards, Wash Theatre Awards Soc, 1986-88; Atlantic Records Co, Gateway Records, Franc Records Co; Fulbright Memorial Fund Scholar to Japan, 1998; Washington Area Music Awards Hall of Fame, 2000; Washingtonian Magazine's Washington Music Hall of Fame, 2003. **Special Achievements:** 'A production analysis of Everyman', 1984; Conducted an Arts Assessment of the Federated Union of Black Arts Acad, Johannesburg, South Africa, 1991; proposed for a Fulbright Teacher Exchange, 1994-95; Recording, Leace on Life, JBL Records; fulbright memor to Japan, 1998. **Business Addr:** Teacher, Duke Ellington School of Arts, Theatre Department, 3500 R St NW, Washington, DC 20007, **Business Phone:** (202)298-1777.

LEACOCK, FERDINAND S., SR.
Physician, surgeon. **Personal:** Born Aug 8, 1934, New York, NY; married; children: 4. **Educ:** Columbia Col, BA, 1956; Howard Medical Col, MD, 1960. **Career:** Surgeon (retired); San Joaquin Hosp, rotating internship, 1961; Ft Howard VA Hosp, residency, 1961-65; Univ MD Hosp, thoracic surg residency, 1967-69; UCLA Sch Med, asst prof surg, 1972-76; Martin Luther King Jr Gen Hosp, chief div thoracic & cardiovasc surg, 1973-74; Charles R Drew Postgrad Med Sch, asst prof surg, 1972-76, vchmn dept surgery, 1974-75; CMA/CHA Educ Patient Care Audit Workshop Prog, 1974-76; pvt pract, thoracic & cardiovasc surg, 1975-; Bon Secours Hosp, chief thoracic & cardiovasc surg, 1987-; MD Gen Hosp, chief thoracic surg, 1987-92; Liberty Med Ctr, vpres med affairs, 1990-92, chmn, dept surg, 1992-99; Bon Secours Hosp, chrmn, dept surgery, 1998-. **Orgs:** Univ MD Surg Soc; Baltimore City Med Soc; Am Col Surgeons; Am Col Chest Physicians; The Baltimore Acad Surg. **Honors/Awds:** 3 publications; 1 abstract. **Military Serv:** AUS, 2 yrs. *

LEACOCK, PROF. STEPHEN JEROME
College teacher, educator. **Personal:** Born Oct 28, 1943; married Phyllis Otway; children: Natasha, Talitha & Baron. **Educ:** BA, 1970; Garnett Col, grad cert educ, 1971; King's Col, LLM, 1971; Guildhall Univ, MA; Middle Temple, barrister, 1972. **Career:** Univ West Indies, Barbados, fac law, 1972-75; Univ Cincinnati, Col Law, Ohio, fac, 1975-79; DePaul Univ, Col Law, Ill, fac, 1979-98; Univ Ind Sch Law, Bloomington, vis prof, 1992; Univ Ill Col Law, Chapaign-Urbana, vis adj prof, 1998; Barry Univ, prof law, currently. **Orgs:** Am Soc Int Law; hon mem, Brit Ins Securities Laws. **Special Achievements:** Publications: "Public Utility Regulation in a Developing Country", "Lawyer of the Americas", "Fundamental Breach of Contract & Exemption Clauses in the Commonwealth Caribbean", "Anglo-American Law Review". "Essentials of Investor Protection in Commonwealth Caribbean & US". **Business Addr:** Professor of Law, Barry University, 6441 E Colonial Dr, Orlando, FL 32807, **Business Phone:** (321)206-5656.

LEAGUE, CHERYL PERRY
Manager. **Personal:** Born Nov 29, 1945, New York, NY; daughter of Robert and Alberta; children: Anthony, Robeson & Assata. **Educ:** Merritt Col, AS, 1977; Univ Calif, bus planning cert; San Francisco State Univ, BA, 1979; Univ San Francisco. **Career:** Legal Aid Soc, Alameda County, CA, contract compliance officer, 1975; US Dept Com, Minority Bus Develop Agency, minority bus prog specialist, 1980; Mgt Prof Servs, Oakland, CA, prin partner, 1982; Port Oakland, CA, contract compliance officer, 1983-86, equal opport mgr, 1986-91, equal opportunity officer, 1991-, founding mem, Calif Affirmative Action Coun. **Orgs:** Nat Asn Adv Colored People; secy, treas, nat bd, Nat Forum Black Pub Admin; Calif Asn Affirmative Action Officers; pres, Bay Area Contract Compliance Officers Asn; bd mem, Bay Area Black United Fund; women's adv comn mem, Oakland Police Dept; bd mem, Northern Calif Minority Bus Opportunity Comn; steering comt mem, Calif Bus Coun Orgn Equal Opport. **Honors/Awds:** Minority Advocate of the Year Award, US Dept Com, San Francisco, CA, 1988; Special Recognition Award for the Port of Oakland for outstanding contribution to the minority business community, Minority Bus Develop Agency, San Francisco, CA, 1988; Outstanding Achievement Award on Behalf of Minority Entrepreneurs, Minority Enterprise Develop Week Comt, Oakland, CA, 1988; Community Service Award for outstanding service to the city of Oakland and for valuable service to the profession of public admin, Oakland/San Francisco Bay Area Chap Nat Forum Black Public Admin, 1989. **Business Addr:** Equal Opportunity Officer, Office of Equal Opportunity, Port of Oakland, 530 Water St, Oakland, CA 94604, **Business Phone:** (510)627-1417.

LEAK, PROF. LEE VIRN
Research scientist, educator. **Personal:** Born Jul 22, 1932, Chesterfield, SC; son of Robert Lincoln Leak and Lucille Elizabeth Moore Leak; married Eleanor C Merrick; children: Alice Elizabeth & Lee Virn Jr. **Educ:** SC State Col, BS 1954; Mich State Univ, MS, 1959, PhD, 1962. **Career:** Brookhaven Nat Lab, Dept Biol, res asst, 1960, collabor biol, 1968; Mich State Univ, Div Biol Sci, teaching asst cytol electron microscopist, res assoc biol sci 1961, asst prof biol sci, 1962; Harvard Med Sch, Mass, Gen Hosp, res fel surg, 1962-64, asst surg, 1964, asst biol surg, 1965, instr anat, 1965-67, asst prof anat, 1968-70, prof, chmn anat, 1971-81; Ernest E Just Lab Cellular Biol, founder, dir, 1972-; J Microvascular Res, ed bd, 1975-; Grad Sch Arts & Sci, prof, 1976-, res prof 1983-; J Microcirculation, ed bd, 1980-; Howard Univ, dir, cellular & molecular biol, 1985-90, res prof, currently; Marine Biol Lab; Microcirculatory Soc Inc. **Orgs:** Cancer biol & diag bd sci couns, Nat Cancer Inst, NIH, 1979-82, sr investr, 1982, adv bd lung dis, Nat Heart Lung & Blood Inst, 1982-86; vice pres, Howard Univ Chap, Sigma Xi 1974-75; chmn, Exec Comm Asn Anat, 1976-78; exec comn, Am Asn Anatomists 1980-84; panel basic biomed sci, Nat Res Coun; Nat Acad Sci, 1980-85; Am Physiol Soc; Am Soc Cell Biol, Am Soc Zoologists; Int Soc Lymphology; NY Acad Sci; NY Soc Electron Microscopy; Tissue Cult Asn; exec com, NA Soc Lympholgy; res comt, Am Heart Asn, Nat Capitol Affliation, 1989-91. **Honors/Awds:** Certificate, 1965, Microscopy Soc Am, Medal, 1968, Scientific Exhibit 23rd Annual Meeting of the Electron; Outstanding Faculty Research Award, Howard Univ 1976 & 1981; Outstanding Faculty Award, Grad Sch Arts & Sci, Howard Univ, 1979-80; Adelle Melbourne Award, Am Med Asn 1989. **Special Achievements:** Wrote chapters: Handbuch der Allgemeine Pathologie, 1972; Inflammatory Process, 1974; Respiratory Defense Mechanisms, 1977; Blood Vessels and Lymphatics in Organ Systems, 1984; The Lungs, Scientific Foundations, first ed, 1991, second, 1997. **Military Serv:** AUS 1st lt 1954-56. **Business Addr:** Research Professor, Howard University, College of Medicine, 520 W St NW, Washington, DC 20059, **Business Phone:** (202)806-6270.

LEAK, VIRGINIA NELL
School administrator, educator, administrator. **Personal:** Born Oct 18, 1950, Temple, TX; daughter of Frank and Doris Gregg; married William A Leak Jr, Oct 15, 1993; children: Volney Willis III & Vance Antoin Willis. **Educ:** Univ Mary Hardin-Baylor, BS, nursing, 1979; Tex Womans Univ, MS, nursing, 1984; Tex A&M Univ; Univ Tex Health Sci Ctr, San Antonio, attended 1991. **Career:** Scott & White Hosp, lic voc nurse, 1973-75; Olin E Teague VA Med Ctr, lic voc nurse, 1975-79; Kings Daughters Hosp, staff nurse, 1979-80; Temple Col, voc nursing instr, 1980-88, nursing dir, 1988-, chmn assoc deg prog & div dir, currently. **Orgs:** Secy, Tenoke Col, Fac Coun, 1980-; Temple Community Col Teachers Asn, 1980-; Pub Rels Comn, 1983-; bd mem, UMHB Consumer Adv Coun, 1993; Temple Educ Found Bd, 1993-; Stop Tobacco & Nicotine Damage Bell Co, 1994-; bd mem, King's Daughters Hosp Asn, 1994-; bd mem, Wilkerson Health Care Mgt, Prof Adv Comn, 1998-; Ebony Cult Soc, 1999-; chair, Nat Asn Advan Colored People, Membership Comn, 1999-; Univ Mary Hardin-Baylor, Alumni Bd, 1999; Am Nurses Asn; exec bd & sec, Tex Nurses Asn, Nominating Comn, chair. **Honors/Awds:** Outstanding Teacher of the Year, Temple Col, 1991; C L Neal Educator of the Year, Temple Kiwanis Club, 1992; Teaching Excellence Award, Nat Inst Staff & Orgn Develop, 1992; Educator of the Year, Workforce Develop, 1996; Crusader Alumna Award, Univ Mary Hardin-Baylor, 1997. **Special Achievements:** First Edition of Notable Women of Texas, 1984-85. **Home Addr:** 5120 Waterford, Temple, TX 76502. **Business Addr:** Division Director, Chairman, Temple College, 2600 S 1st St, Temple, TX 76504-7435, **Business Phone:** (254)298-8666.

LEAKS, EMANUEL, JR.
Association executive, basketball coach, basketball player. **Personal:** Born Nov 27, 1945, Cleveland, OH; son of Sadie and Emanuel; married Marna Hale, Oct 29, 1988; children: Richard W Leaks Hale Pace & DeAndre George. **Educ:** Niagara Univ, BA, 1968; Case Western Reserve UNiv, Mandell Sch Applied Social Sci, MSSA, 1994. **Career:** Basketball player (retired), basketball coach; New York Nets, center forward, 1968-72, 1972-74; City of Cleveland, community relations rep; Hough Area Develop Corp, public relations mgr; Somalian Nat Basketball Team, adv, coach; Ctr Families & Children, dir, currently. **Orgs:** Am Basketball Asn. **Business Addr:** Director, Center for Families & Children, 1117 E 105 St, Cleveland, OH 44108, **Business Phone:** (216)451-2559.

LEAKS, MARNA HALE. See HALE, MARNA AMORETTI.

LEAL, SHARON
Actor. **Personal:** Born Oct 17, 1972, Tucson, AZ; daughter of Jesse and Angelita. **Educ:** Diablo Valley Jr Col. **Career:** Films: Face the Music, 2000; What Are the Odds, 2004; Dreamgirls, 2006, Soul Men, 2008, Linewatch, 2008; tv series: "The Guiding Light", 1996-99; "Legacy", 1998; "Boston Public", 2000-04; "Chapter Forty-Five", 2002; "Las Vegas", 2003-; "The Longest Morning", 2004; "Thanksgiving", 2004; LAX, 2004-05; "Senator's Daughter", 2005; "Sperm Whales & Spearmint Rhinos", 2005; "CSI: Miami", 2007; "Internal Affairs", 2007. **Business Addr:** Actress, Boston Public, Manhattan Beach Studios, Bldg 4A 1600 Rosecrans Ave 3rd Fl, Manhattan Beach, CA 90266, **Business Phone:** (310)727-2700.

LEAPHART, ELDRIDGE
Engineer. **Personal:** Born Sep 2, 1927, Sims, NC; married Audra Lane; children: Eldridge jr & Eldon Gerrald. **Educ:** Howard Univ, BS 1953; Ohio State Univ, 1964; Univ Calif Los Angeles, 1967; Air Univ, 1965, 1966, 1973. **Career:** TN Valley Authority, elec engr, 1953-55; Air Force Logistics Command, 1955-58; Air Force Systems Command, electronics engr, 1958-. **Orgs:** Ass Old Crows; treas, Kitty hawk Toastmasters Club, 1974; supr com Bethel Bapt Fed Credit Union 1972-; supr Bethel Bapt Ch Sch, 1969-70. **Honors/Awds:** Air Force Systems Command Certificate Merit Award, 1974. **Military Serv:** USN 1945-47; USAR 2nd lt 1953-55. **Business Addr:** Member, Air Force Avionics Lab, Wright Patterson AFB, Dayton, OH 45433.*

LEATH, VERLYN FAYE
Educator, executive director. **Personal:** Born Jan 16, 1946, Burlington, NC; daughter of Ervin Isaiah Walker and Sallie Myrtle

Phillips; married; children: Andrienne Lynnette Weeks. **Educ:** NC A&T State Univ, BS, 1975, MS, 1982. **Career:** Alamance Burlington Sch Syst, teacher, 1975-; Harvey R Newlin Elem Sch, dir at-risk serv, currently. **Orgs:** Comt chair, Jack O'Kelley La Sertoma Club; secy, comt chair, Alamance Co Chap AT&T Alumni; NC Asn Educr; honors comt, chair, First Baptist Church; bd dir, Sunday Sch; bd mem, community comput comt, long range planning comt mem, Christian Educ. **Honors/Awds:** Teacher of the Year, Newlin Elem, 1983-84, 1987-88, 1997-98. **Home Addr:** 1031 Apple St, Burlington, NC 27217, **Home Phone:** (336)227-8256. **Business Addr:** Director of At-Risk Services, Harvey R Newlin Elementary School, Alamance Burlington School System, 316 Carden St, Burlington, NC 27215, **Business Phone:** (336)570-6125.

LEATHERWOOD, LARRY LEE
State government official. **Personal:** Born Sep 7, 1939, Peoria, IL; son of Larry and Helen Moody Brown; married Martha; children: Jeffrey & Stacy. **Educ:** Kellogg Community Col, AA, 1967; Western Mich Univ, BS, 1969, MPA, 1982; Harvard Univ, Boston, Sr Exec Fel, 1985. **Career:** Battle Creek Area Urban League, exec dir, 1970-73; Mich Dept Com, spec asst, 1973-77; Mich State Minority Bus Off, dir, 1977-83; Mich Dept Transp, liaison officer, 1983-85, dep dir admin, 1985-92; self employed, currently. **Orgs:** Vice chmn, Lansing Urban League, 1982-83; chmn, Minority Tech Coun Mich, 1983-; Midwest Rep, Howard Black Alumni Asn,1989-; pres, Lansing YMCA, 1991-92; pres, YMCA, 1992-93; Mich Dept Civil Serv, State Officers Compensation Comn, 2004-; exec dir, Citizens Coun Mich Pub Univ; vice chmn, State Adv Coun Voc Educ; Conf Minority Trans Officials, Am Pub Works Asn. **Honors/Awds:** Man of the Year, Nat Asn Black Women Entrepreneur, 1980; Presidential Small Bus Recognition, 1980; Mich Small Bus Advocate, 1985; Wall of Distinction, Western Mich Univ & Alumni Asn, 1986. **Special Achievements:** Recognition by Mich Coun NAACP Branches for Contributions to Black Economic Development, 1986. Public Servant of the Year, Capitol Chapter, ASPA 1990-; Partner In Community Service Award, Black Caucus Found Mich, Inc. **Military Serv:** USAF, sgt 4, yrs. **Business Addr:** Member, Michigan Department of Civil Service, State Officers Compensation Commission, Capitol Commons Ctr 400 S Pine St, Lansing, MI 48913, **Business Phone:** (517)373-3048.

LEAVELL, ALLEN FRAZIER
Basketball player. **Personal:** Born May 27, 1957, Muncie, IN; married Gwethalyn; children: Alex & Amanda. **Educ:** Okla City Univ, attended 1979. **Career:** Basketball player (retired); Houston Rockets, 1979-89; Tulsa Fast Breakers, 1989. **Honors/Awds:** All-Rookie.

LEAVELL, DOROTHY R.
Administrator, editor, newspaper publisher. **Personal:** Born Oct 23, 1944, Pine Bluff, AR; daughter of Sallie Gonder and Blane Gonder; married Balm L Leavell Jr (died 1968); children: Antonio, Genice. **Educ:** Roosevelt Univ, IL, attended 1962. **Career:** Holy Name Mary Sch Bd, pres; Chicago Crusader, off mgr, 1961-64, bus mgr, 1964-68, publ, 1968-; Gary Crusader, publ, 1968-; Amalgamated Publ Inc, chmn, 2002-. **Orgs:** Head, Nat Newspaper Publ Asn, 1995-97; bd dir, Wash Park YMCA, 1974; asst secy, 1976, treas, 1983-87, 89-95, pres, 1995-, Nat Newspaper Publ Asn; secy, PUSH; bd mem, Directions Scholar Found. **Honors/Awds:** YMCA Award; PUSH Award; Holy Name of Mary Award; Fourth District Community Improvement Association Award; Publishing Award, Nat Asn Negro Bus & Prof Womens Club; Dollars and Sense Award; Mary McLeod Bethune Award; Publisher of the Year, Nat Newspaper Publ Asn, 1989. **Special Achievements:** First female chief executive in the 40-year history of the nation's oldest African American placement firm; Second woman ever named to the position Of President Of Nat Newspaper Publ Asn. **Business Addr:** Editor, Publisher, Chicago Crusader, 6429 S King Dr, Chicago, IL 60637, **Business Phone:** (773)752-2500.*

LEAVELL, DR. WALTER F.
Educator. **Personal:** Born May 19, 1934, Chicago, IL; married Vivian; children: Pierce & Pierre. **Educ:** Univ Cincinnati Col Pharm, BS, 1957; Meharry Med Col, MD, 1964. **Career:** Univ Cincinnati Col Law, scholar-in-residence, 1981; St Univ NY, Upstate Med Ctr Col Med, assoc dean, 1971-75, vice dean & tenured assoc prof med, 1975-82; consult, EDUCOM, 1979-; Univ Cincinnati, Col Med, vice dean, 1975-82; Cincinnati Gen Hosp, assoc chief staff, 1977-79, prof affairs, assoc adminr, 1977-79; Hubbard Hosp, staff; Meharry Med Col, dean sch med & dir med affairs Hubbard Hosp, 1982-87; Charles R. Drew Univ Med & Sci, Los Angeles, CA, pres; Howard Univ, WA DC, sr vpres health affair, consult & health adv, currently. **Orgs:** AAMC/GSA Steering Comt, 1974-; nat chairperson, AAMC/GSA Minority Affairs Sect, 1976-; Coun Deans, 1982-; adv bd Nat Fund Med Educ, 1983-; AAMC AdHoc MCAT Review Comt, 1985; AAMC Spring Meeting Prog Comt, 1985-; LCME Accreditation Review Team; Am Nat Cincinnati Med Asn; Nat Asn Med Minority Educr; Am Asn Med Cols; Acad Educ Develop. **Honors/Awds:** AAMC Serv Recognition Award, 1979; NAMME Presidential Citation, 1985. **Military Serv:** USAF, major. **Business Addr:** Advisor and Consultant, Howard Univ, 2400 Sixth St NW, Washington, DC 20059.

LEAVY, WALTER
Editor. **Career:** Ebony Mag, managing ed, currently. **Orgs:** Am Foun Blind. **Business Addr:** Managing Editor, Ebony Magazine, 800 S Michigan Ave, Chicago, IL 60605, **Business Phone:** (312)322-9200.*

LECESNE, ALVAREZ
Executive director, lawyer. **Personal:** Born Aug 31, 1942, New Orleans, LA; son of Alvarez Louis LeCesne Jr and Garnet Latisha Barra; married Brenda Irons; children: Craig & R Dyane. **Educ:** Calif State Univ, Los Angeles, BS bus admin & acct; Loyola Univ Sch Law, Los Angeles, Calif, JD; Stanford Univ, pub mgrs. **Career:** United States Dept Justice, former sr trial atty, tax div; U.S. Internal Rev Serv, mgr & auditor; Community Resource Unlimited, vpres, tax consult, Emerging Scholars Prog, exec dir, currently. **Orgs:** Former Pres, Optimist Club Reston; Former chair, Reston Community Coalition; Former exec comt, NAACP; Calif Bar Asn; Dist Columbia Bar Asn. **Honors/Awds:** Best of Reston Award; Making A Difference Award, NAACP. **Business Addr:** Executive Director, Emerging Scholars Program, 3320 Jermantown Rd, Oakton, VA 22124, **Business Phone:** (703)584-2307.

LECESNE, TERREL M
School administrator, government official. **Personal:** Born Apr 13, 1939, New Orleans, LA; married Gale H; children: Terrel jr & Haydel. **Educ:** Xavier Univ, BA, 1961; Eastern Mich Univ, MA, 1967, EdS, 1973; Univ Mich, PhD, 1979. **Career:** City Inkster, MI, former mayor, coun mem, teacher, 1961-66; Jr high sch counr, 1966-68; Willow Run/Romulus Sch, elem prin, 1968-79; Romulus Sch, asst supt, 1979-95; Inkster Schs, supt, 1995-; Ypsilanti Pub Sch, exec dir opers & labor rels, currently; City Inkster, bd mem, Housing Comn, Currently. **Orgs:** Pres Romulus Asn Sch Bldg Adminr; past pres, Inkster Jaycees; Dearborn-Inkster Human Rel Coun. **Honors/Awds:** Named outstanding young man of year, Inkster Jaycees, 1970. **Business Addr:** Board Member, City Inkster, 2121 Inkster Rd, Inkster, MI 48141, **Business Phone:** (313)563-9770.

LECHEBO, DR. SEMIE
School administrator. **Personal:** Born Apr 5, 1935, Addis Ababa, Ethiopia; divorced; children: Monique Thomas, Shena Thomas & Meskeram. **Educ:** Univ Wis, BS, 1964, MS, 1967; Southern Univ NY, Albany, EdS, 1975, EdD, 1975; Harvard Univ, MLE, 1982. **Career:** Haile Selassie I Day Sch, Addis Ababa, Sch adminr, 1956-60; Ministry Educ, Addis Ababa, dir, 1964-66; Milwaukee Pub Sch, teacher, 1967-68; UNESCO fel, 1967-68; Jimma Teacher Training, dir, 1968-69; Col Teacher Educ, Addis Ababa, vice prin, 1969-71; AFGRAD fel, 1971-75; Comm Agency Albany, res fel, 1975; NY State Educ Dept, res assoc, 1976-77; Southern Univ NY, Albany, coord tutorial prog, 1976; Southern Univ NY, Col Brockport, coord acad affairs; Baden Street Settlement Inc, dir educ develop. **Orgs:** Consult, NY Educ Dept, 1975-76; Rochester City Sch Dist, 1978-82; Faculty Senate Southern Univ NY, Brockport, 1980-86; Col Affirmative Action Bd, Southern Univ NY, Brockport, 1982-83; chair, Rochester Inst Tech Adv Bd Minority & Female Recruitment, 1984-86; chair, Educ Comt, County Monroe Human Rels Comn, 1985-; supv interns Southern Univ NY, Brockport, 1986; chair, mentoring prog Urban League Rochester, 1986; Col Acad Coun, Southern Univ NY, Brockport, 1986-; Youth Serv Qual Coun, 1996-98; Black Leadership Comn AIDS Rochester, 1996-; bd pres, Montgomery Neighborhood Ctr, 1998-2006; Int Soc Poets. **Honors/Awds:** Outstanding Award for Service, Urban League of Rochester, 1984-85; Black Scholars Sponsor Award, Urban League of Rochester, 1985; Naturalized United States Citizen, 1985; Outstanding Professional Service Award, Southern Univ NY, Brockport, 1992; Cert of Appreciation for Service, Monroe County, Human Relations Commission, 1991-94. **Special Achievements:** Published: "Do More Than," "Peace," "Letting Go", "You," "Whatever," "What Could It Be," "Being An American," Hilltop Records; You Can Be The Boss: Business Start-Up Kit, 1999; Editor's Choice Awd for Outstanding Achievement in Poetry, Intl Library Poetry, 1998, 2001, 2003, 2004, 2005; The Book of The Best Selected Success Quotes for Every Occasions, 2003. **Home Addr:** 420 Audino Lane Apt B, Rochester, NY 14624, **Home Phone:** (585)889-9444.

LECOMPTE, PEGGY LEWIS
School administrator, television show host. **Personal:** Born Oct 7, 1938, St Louis, MO; daughter of Obadiah Sr and Winnie Penguite; married Larry Ferdinand LeCompte Sr, Nov 22, 1962; children: Larry F Jr. **Educ:** Lincoln Univ, BS, 1960; Sangamon State, MS, 1985; Nat Col Educ, Evanston,Ill, MS, 1990. **Career:** E St Louis Sch Dist 189, educr, 1962; USAF, librn, 1968; E St Louis Sch Dist 189, educr, 1970; Channel 13 E St Louis, TV host, 1983; Language Arts High Sch Dept Head, Dist 189, 1998-; Time Network; Limelight Mag, columnist; E St Louis News Jour. **Orgs:** Bd pres, Boys Club E St Louis, 1978-86; cent regional dir, Alpha Kappa Alpha Sorority, 1978-82 & 1997-98; pres, E St Louis Fedn Teachers, Local 1220; vpres, Ill Fedn Teachers, 1985-90; pres, Area III dir & organizer, Top Ladies Distinction; nat workshop chmn & nat parliamentarian, 1987-91; secy bd dir, Girl Scouts Am, 1990-97; pres & bd dirs, GEMM, 1990; nat vpres, Top Ladies Dist Inc, 1999; pres, Comp Ment Health Ctr; pres, St Clair County, SWAC; YMCA; Nat YWCA bd, Nat Policy Comm, Nat Const & Bylaws Comm; bd, Racial Harmony; int mem chmn & nat secy, Alpha Kappa Alpha Sorority. **Honors/Awds:** Teacher of the Year Award, Zeta Phi Beta Sorority, 1977; Outstanding Service Award, Nat Asn Advan Colored People E St Louis, 1978; Key to the City, E St Louis, 1978-79; Most Outstanding Jill Past Pres Award, Jack & Jill Am E St Louis, 1980; Most Outstanding Speaker Toastmasters, Metro St Louis, 1982; Media Award, Shriners Aahmes Temple 112, 1983; Leadership, Alpha Kappa Alpha Sorority, 1983; Boys Club Medallion, Boys Clubs Am, 1984; Youth Award, YMCA, 1984; YMCA Communications Award, 1986; Boys Clubs of America Nat Serv Medallion; Top Lady of Distinction of Area III, 1986; Master Teacher, Sch Dist 198, 1988; Volunteer of the Year, YWCA, 1990; Carol Kimmel Community Service Leadership Award, 1991; Key to City, Waterloo, Iowa, 1992; Suburban Journal Woman of Achievement, 1995; Women of Achievement in Leadership, Alpha Kappa Alpha Sorority, 1997; American Express Leadership Award, 1998; Trailblazer Award, 1998; Omega Purple &Gold Leadership Award, 1998; NCNW, 1999; AIP, 1999; Dist No 189 Fine Arts Award, 1999; Community Service Award, Black Family Life Inc, 2000; Labor Woman of the Year, 2000; Service Award, Phi Delta Kappa. **Home Addr:** 212 Bunker Hill Rd, Belleville, IL 62221. *

LEDAY, JOHN AUSTIN
Executive, president (organization), business owner. **Personal:** Born Sep 11, 1931, Basile, LA; son of Alsay and Edna Papillian; married Christine Sandoval; children: Anna & Angela. **Career:** Warehouseman, 1948-52; People Chem Co, sales mgr, 1954-61; Southend Janitorial Supply Inc, owner & pres, 1961-. **Orgs:** Pres, Am Enterprises Inc; Govt Brown Adv Coun Econ Bus Develop State Calif, 1978; pres, MTM Corp; Nat Asn Black Manufacturers; Sanitary Supply Asn Southern Calif; Los Angeles C C; bd dir, Black Businessmen's Asn Los Angeles; exec comt, Los Angeles Off Urban Develop; dir, Equip Bank; bd dir, Pickett Enterprises; Nat Community Bus Develop. **Honors/Awds:** Businessman of Year Award, BBA, 1977. **Military Serv:** AUS, 1952-54. **Business Addr:** President, Owner, Southend Janitorial Supply Inc, 11422 S Broadway, Los Angeles, CA 90061-1833.

LEDBETTER, CHARLES TED
Educator. **Personal:** Born Dec 29, 1949, Muskogee, OK; son of Jerome and Dora Ledbetter; married Eva Blake, Jul 4, 1964; children: Vicki Ann. **Educ:** Lincoln Univ, BA, 1963; Golden Gate Univ, MPA, 1969; Univ MO-Columbia, 1975; Kent State Univ, PhD, 1991. **Career:** Univ Mo, assoc prof, 1972-75; WVa State Coll, chair, ROTC, 1979-83, vpres stud affairs, 1983-88, exec asst to the pres & adj prof, 1988-97, dean prof studies & prof educ, 1997-2000, prof educ, 2000-. **Orgs:** Dunbar Torary Club, 1980-; public ed comm, Am Cancer Soc, 1985-87; Charleston Job Corps, 1988-96; Charleston Regional Chamber Comm, 1989-92; Consortium WVa State Coll, 1992-95; bd dir, Family Services Kanawua Valley, 1992-; bd dir, Red Cross, Central Chp, 1992-; vice chmn, WVa Archives & Hist Comn. **Honors/Awds:** Lincoln Univ, ROTC Hall of Fame, 1980; WVSC, Outstanding Admin Awd, 1995. **Special Achievements:** Publications: Black Student Departure & Patterns of Social & Academic Integration in Historically Black Coll & Univ with Different Proportional Rates of Blacks Enrolled: A Test of a Conceptual Model, 1991; "Practical Advice for Gaining & Maintaining Active Involvement in the Self Study Process," 1995; "The West VA State Coll Aviation Program," 1995. **Military Serv:** AUS, Lt Col, 1963-83; Bronze Star; Joint Services Commendation Medal; Natl Defense Service Medal; Army Service Medal; Presidential Service Medal; Vietnam Cross of Gallantry; Vietnam Service Medal. **Business Addr:** Professor, West Virginia State College, PO Box 1000, Institute, WV 25112, **Business Phone:** (304)766-5160.

LEDE, NAOMI W
School administrator, educator. **Personal:** Born Mar 22, 1934, Huntsville, TX; married; children: Susan & Paul. **Educ:** Mary Allen Col, Crockett, Tex, BA, Social Sci & Eng; Tex S Univ, Houston, MA, Sociol &Political Sci; Univ Tex, Arlington, MA, Urban Affairs & Transportation; Univ Houston, Tex, EdD, Multicultural Studies, 1979. **Career:** Lifson Wilson & Ferguson Houston; Survey Res Ctr Ann Arbor; Juvenile Delinquency Survey Univ Houston; Race Relations Inst Survey Fisk Univ Nashville; Reg Transportation Study Arlington TX; Consumer Opinion Inst NY; SRDS DATA Inc NY; Batten Barton Drustine & Orborne NY; Louis Harris & Asso; Inst for Social Res Univ SC; Natl Urban League St Louis; St Louis Urban League, dir research; St Louis Univ; lectr; Washington Univ; Urban Intern Arlington Tex; City of St Louis, program analyst & res cons; Bishop Coll Dallas Tex, asst prof & dir res; Texas Southern Univ, prof transportation & urban planning, dean & dir, Ctr for Urban Progs, vpres for instnl advan, distinguished Prof, Dept Transp Studies, exec dir emer, Ctr Transp Training & Res, currently; chair bd, Samuel Walker Houston Mus & Cultural Ctr, Huntsville, TX. **Orgs:** Am Asn Univ Profs; Nat Coun Univ Res Admins; Assoc Study Negro Life & Hist; Tex Asn Col Teachrs; Nat Asn Social Sci Teachrs; Am Sociol Soc; Res & Consult Dallas Urban League & Dallas Negro C C; Soc Study Negro in Dentistry; Delta Sigma Theta Sor; Iota Phi Lambda Bus Sor; World Future Soc; Soc Res Admins; Counc Univ Inst Urban Affairs; bd mem, Urban Affairs Corp; Transportation Res Bd; Nat Acad Political & Social Sci; Smithsonian Inst; asso mem, AIP; State Educ Comm AIP; Mayor's Manpower Adv Coun; Am Planning Asn; Univ Aviation Asn.

Honors/Awds: Received spec recognition for participation in prog 'Operation Champ from Vice Pres Hubert Humphrey'. **Special Achievements:** "Extensive Research in Transportation Planning & Citizen Participation/Mental Health Services/Feasibility of Housing". **Business Addr:** Executive Director Emeritus, Texas Southern Univerity, Center for Transportation Training & Research, 3100 Cleburne Ave, Houston, TX 77004, **Business Phone:** (713)313-1841.

LEDEE, ROBERT
Consultant. **Personal:** Born Aug 20, 1927, Brooklyn, NY; son of Reginald and Mary Godfrey; married Victoria Marzan; children: Yvonne Alvarez, Robert Jr, Reginald & Anthony. **Educ:** Fed Bur Narcotics Training Sch, 1967; FBI Nat Acad, 1968; John Jay Col, criminal justice, AS, 1971; BA, 1973; MPA, 1976. **Career:** New York City Housing Police Dept, apptd, 1955; sgt, 1958-60; lt, 1960-64; capt, 1964-67; dep insp, 1967-70; insp, 1970; dep chief, 1970-78; Sea Gate NY Harbor Police Dept, chief, 1979-81; Fed Funded Comm Serv Officer Prgm, adminstr; Hispanic Law Enforcement Training Inst Justice, cons; New York City Dept Personnel, cons. **Orgs:** Guest lectr, FBI Nat Acad; rep Housing Pol Dept; first Nat Symposium Law Enforcement Tech, 1967; 13th Annual Inst on Polic & Comm MI St Univ, 1967; Crive Prevention Sem, 1968; Insterst Conf Delinq Control, 1965; adminstr Model Cities Comm Serv Officer Program. **Honors/Awds:** First black mem to hold rank of lt, capt, dep insp, dep chief New YorkCity Housing Police Dept; dept commendations for outst police work; Awards from, Upper Pk Ave Bapt Ch, 1963; Fed Negro Civil Serv Orgs, 1964; BronxDective Unit, 1965; Counc of Police Orgns, 1966; Hispanic Soc, 1966, 1970; Anti-Crime Com, 1969; Grand Counc of Hispanic Soc, 1971; Nat Police Ofcrs Asn, 1972; Comm Rel Unit, 1973; NY Club, 1974; John Jay Coll Alumni Asn, 1976; Nat Conf of Christians & Jews, 1977; author article FBI Bull, 1975; manual High Rise Policing Tech US Merchant Marine, 1945-55. **Military Serv:** US Merchant Marine, AB, 1945-55; Atlantic War Zone, Pacific War Zone Bars & Victory Medal. **Business Addr:** Consultant, PO Box 657, Jamaica, NY 11434.*

LEDOUX, JEROME G
Theologian. **Personal:** Born Feb 26, 1930, Lake Charles, LA. **Educ:** Divine Word Sem, Ordained, 1957; Ponitifical Gregorian Univ Rome, Italy, MST, 1961, Dr, church law, 1961. **Career:** Divine Word Theol Bay, St Louis, MS, prof moral theol & canon law, 1961-67; Miss Hist Divine Word HS Sem, instr eng & civics, 1967-69; Xavier Univ, New Orleans, 1st black chaplain, 1969-71, assoc prof theol, 1971-80; St Augustine Church, pastor, 1990-2006. **Special Achievements:** Author, Weekly Synd Column, 6 Cath Diocesan Papers & 3 Black Weeklies; author, Monthly Column, Nat Cath Paper. **Home Addr:** 1210 Governor Nicholls St, New Orleans, LA 70116.

LEE, AARON
Executive. **Personal:** Born Aug 29, 1948, Hinds Co, MS; married Frances Jackson; children: Aaron Brennan. **Educ:** Utica Jr Col, AA, 1970; Jackson State Univ, BS, 1975, MS, 1976. **Career:** Major Assoc Construct Co, estimator, 1975-77; Nat Bus League, construct mgr, 1977-80; Town of Edwards, alderman, 1977-, fed prog coord, 1982; Jackson State Univ, super building serv, 1981-83; asst dir physical plant, 1983. **Orgs:** Phi Beta Sigma Frat, 1976; mem bd dirs, NAACP Bolton-Edwards Branch, 1981-; Am Mgt Asn, 1984. **Honors/Awds:** Outstanding Achievement Pub Serv, MS Valley State Univ, 1977; Outstanding Dedicated Serv Nat Bus League, 1980; Outstanding Young Men Am, 1984. **Military Serv:** AUS, sgt, 1st class 14 yrs; Meritorial Serv Award, USAR, 1978.

LEE, DR. ALLEN FRANCIS, JR. (WILLIAM FRANCIS LEE, JR.)
Educator, scientist. **Personal:** Born Apr 12, 1943, Notasulga, AL; married Lula M Wheat; children: Allen F III & Aryanna F. **Educ:** Tuskegee Inst, AL, DVM, 1967; Univ Ga, Athens, PhD, 1978. **Career:** Univ Ga, res asst, 1967-69, res assoc, 1969-71; Emory Univ, NIH spec fel, 1971-72; Univ Ga, instr, 1972-73; La St Univ, assoc prof Vet Neurophysiology, 1973-. **Orgs:** Am Vet Med Asn, 1967-; Am Soc Vet Physiologists & Pharmacologists, 1969-; AAAS; Kappa Alpha Psi Fraternity, 1965-; Am Radio Relay League, 1977-; bd dir, Campus Fed Credit Union, 1978-; bd dir, Kenilworth Civic Asn, 1980-. **Honors/Awds:** Scholar in Veterinary Medicine, Tuskegee Inst, 1965; Outstanding Service, Vet Stud Womens Aux AVMA, 1967; NIH Post Doctoral Fellowship, Emory Univ, 1971; res nerve/muscle physiol EMG. **Special Achievements:** Author, "Evaluation of Ulnar Nerve Conductio Velocity in the Dog", Univ Ga, 1978. **Business Addr:** Associate Professor of Veterinary Neurophysiology, Louisiana State University, School of Veterinary Medicine Department of Physiology Pharmacy &Toxicology, 114 David Boyd Hall, Baton Rouge, LA 70803.

LEE, AMP (ANTHONIA WAYNE LEE)
Football player. **Personal:** Born Oct 1, 1971, Chipley, FL; married Natalie; children: Saben. **Educ:** Fla State Univ. **Career:** Football player (retired); San Francisco 49ers, running back, 1992-93; Minn Vikings, 1994-96; St Louis Rams, 1997-99; Philadelphia Eagles, 2000. **Honors/Awds:** First Team All-American, 1991; Rookie of the Year, 1992; Daniel F Reeves Memorial Award, St Louis Rams, 1997; Most Valuable Player, St Louis Rams, 1997; Twelveth Man Award, 1998.

LEE, DR. ANDRE L
Health services administrator, school administrator. **Personal:** Born Aug 14, 1943, Detroit, MI; son of Laura Lee and Clyde Lee; married Katrina (divorced); children: Andre, Bryan, Tracey & Robin. **Educ:** Mich State Univ, BS 1966; Cornell Univ, MPA, 1972; Nova Univ, DPA 1978. **Career:** Highland Park Gen Hosp, Mich, dir, 1972-76; Sidney Sumby Hosp, Mich, dir, 1976-78; St Joseph Hosp, Ft Wayne, Ind, asst dir, 1978-81; Hubbard Hosp, Tenn, dir, 1981-88; Urban Health Assoc Inc, pres; Friendship Hospice of Nashville Inc, pres, currently; United Community Hosp, pres & chief exec officer, currently. **Orgs:** Tech Sinai Hosp Detroit 1966-67; state dir, Am Acad Med Admin Ind & Tenn, 1983-85; pres, Nat Assoc Health Serv Exec, 1985-87; chmn, Mgt Housing Scholar Comt; Alpha Phi Alpha; NAACP; proper Health Care Fin System; Am Professional Mgt Ltd; Am Col Hosp Admin; Am Pub Health Assoc; Am Acad Med Admin, Mich; Pub Health Assoc; bd mem, Comprehensive Health Ctr; Model Neighborhood Health Ctr; Resd Manpower Ctr; MI C of C Ed Sub-Com; Reg Emergency Room Task Force; City Emergency Room Task Force. **Honors/Awds:** COGME Fellowship Award, 1970-72; Whitney Young Award, Boy Scouts Am, 1989; Silver Beaver Award, Boy Scouts Am, 1991. **Special Achievements:** Published over 60 articles. **Military Serv:** AUS, capt 2 yrs active, 4 yrs reserve. **Home Addr:** 317 E Crescent Lane, Detroit, MI 48207. **Business Addr:** President, Friendship Hospice Nashville Inc, 293 Plus Pk Blvd Suite 140, Nashville, TN 37217-1064, **Business Phone:** (615)365-0220.

LEE, ANDREA
Writer, novelist. **Personal:** Born Jan 1, 1953?, Philadelphia, PA. **Educ:** Harvard Univ, BA, MA. **Career:** New Yorker mag, NY, staff writer; books: Russian Journal, 1981; Sarah Phillips, 1984; Interesting Women; Lost Hearts in Italy. **Honors/Awds:** American Book Award Nomination, Russian Journal, 1981; Jean Stein Award, Am Acad & Inst Arts & Letters, 1984. *

LEE, ANTHONIA WAYNE. See LEE, AMP.

LEE, AUBREY WALTER, SR.
Banker, president (organization), chief executive officer. **Personal:** Born Oct 26, 1934, Huntington, WV; married Jeane F Lee, Apr 13, 1956; children: Aubrey Jr, David & Mark. **Educ:** Morehouse Col, 1951-52; WV State Col, BA, polit sci, econ, 1955; Marshall Univ, MA polit sci, econ, 1956; Univ Wis Grad Sch Banking, dipl, 1969. **Career:** Banker, President, Chief executive officer (retired); NBD Bank, teller trainee, 1957, asst mgr, br mgr, 1966, asst vpres, regional mgr, vpres, head minority & commercial lending, 1971, first vpres, regional banking ctr dir, 1983-96, sr vpres, 1997-99; NBD Troy Bank, chmn, ceo, pres, 1980-83; Bank one, Munic banking group, sr vpres, 1999. **Orgs:** Dir, vice chmn, treas, chmn finance comt, William Beaumont Hosp,; bd trustees, Walsh Col, chmn orgn & compensation comt; Bloomfield Hills Country Club; pres, chmn & ceo, Troy; Econ Club of Detroit; Nat Asn Advan Colored People; past pres, Outer Dr Faith Lutheran Church. **Honors/Awds:** Pi Sigma Alpha Honor Fraternity, Nat Honor Society; YMCA Minority Achiever Award in Industry; City of Detroit, Medallion; Urban Bankers Forum, Distinguished Banker's Award; Marshall Univ, Distinguished Graduate Student Alumnus Award; Distingushed Warriors, Urban League, 2001. received over 20 awards and honors from local, state and national organizations, including the Trailblazer Award, Nat Bankers Asn, Distinguished Warrior Award, Detroit Urban League; Crain's Detroit Business Black Business Leader Award, Distinguish Graduate Student Alumnus Award, Marshall Univ. **Military Serv:** AUS, Reserves, capt, 1957-65.

LEE, AUBREY WALTER, JR.
Financial manager. **Personal:** Born Oct 14, 1956, Ashland, KY; son of Aubrey W Lee Sr and Jeane F; married Janice D, Dec 2, 1989; children: Aubrey Bejamin, Lauren Nicole, Natalie Ann Booker & Nathan Alexander McGhee. **Educ:** Univ Mich Dearborn, attended 1976; Univ Mich Ann Arbor, attended 1978. **Career:** Booth Am Co, radio announcer, 1978-81, 1987-90; Manufacturers Nat Bank Detroit, br asst mgr, 1980-87; Inner City Broadcasting, radio announcer, 1981-83; Amaturo Group Inc, radio announcer, 1983-85; Merrill Lynch, resident dir, Wealth Mgt Adv, vpres, 1987-; Evergreen Media, radio announcer, 1990-; CBS Radio, WVMV-FM, radio announcer, 1997-. **Orgs:** Nat Asn Securities Prof, Detroit Chap, 1996; asst minister, Men Faith, Outer Dr Faith Lutheran Church, 1996; internship comt, Go lightly Vocational Sch, 1996-97; Promise keepers, 1996; corp liaison, Mich Minority Bus Develop Coun, Merrill Lynch, 1996; Penn Ctr-Mich Support Group, 1996; Detroit Discovery Mus; bd trustees, Leadership Detroit; bd mem, Detroit Urban League; Diversity Adv Coun Mgt, Merrill Lynch, 2005-06. **Honors/Awds:** Father & Son Footsteps Award, YMCA, 1985; Guild Community Service Award, Detroit Urban League, 2003; Leadership in Diversity & Inclusion Award, Merrill Lynch 2007. **Business Addr:** Resident Director, Vice President - Wealth Management Advisor, Merrill Lynch & Co, 26200 Town Ctr Dr Suite 200, Novi, MI 48375, **Business Phone:** (248)348-3990.

LEE, BARBARA JEAN
Politician. **Personal:** Born Jul 16, 1946, El Paso, TX; children: Tony & Craig. **Educ:** Mills Col, BA, 1973; Univ Calif, Berkeley, MSW, 1975. **Career:** Congressman Ronald V Dellums, Cong aide advisor & sr advisor chief staff, 1975-87; Bus owner, 1987-98; Calif State Assembly, 1990-96; Calif State Senate, 1996-98; 1987-98; US House Rep, congresswoman, 1998-. **Orgs:** Chair, CBC Task Force Global HIV/AIDS; Co-Chair, CBC Haiti Task Force. **Honors/Awds:** Received numerous awards including: Honorary doctorate Calif Sch Prof Psychiat; Mills Col, 1999; Virtuous Woman Community Award, Muhsana Center for Health, 2006; 2006 Urban Education Leadership Award, Catapault Online, 2006; MLK Freedom Award, Progressive Nat Baptist Convention, 2006; Nat Achievement Award, Nat Asn Negro Bus & Professional Women's Clubs, 2006; Outstanding Woman Award, Black Expo, 2006; Peacemaker of the Year Award, Baptist Peace Fellowship of N Am Conv, 2006; Leadership In Advocacy Award, AIDS Alliance, 2006. **Special Achievements:** First woman to represent California's 9th congressional district. **Business Addr:** Congresswoman, Oakland District Office, 1301 Clays St Suite 1000 N, Oakland, CA 94612, **Business Phone:** (510)763-0370.

LEE, BILL. See LEE, WILLIAM JAMES EDWARDS, III.

LEE, CARL
Football player, football coach. **Personal:** Born Apr 6, 1961, South Charleston, WV. **Educ:** Marshall Univ. **Career:** Football player (retired), football coach; Minn Vikings, cornerback, 1983-94; New Orleans Saints, 1994; W Va State Univ, yellow jacket, head coach, 1996-2005; State's admin, currently. **Honors/Awds:** Sporting News NFL All-Star Team, 1988; post-season play: NFC Championship Game, 1987, Pro Bowl, 1988, 1989.

LEE, CHANDLER BANCROFT
Automotive executive. **Educ:** Western Mich Univ, polit sci, 1974; Central Mich Univ, bus admin, 1982; Gen Motors Univ, degree in dealership mgt, 1985. **Career:** Gen Motors Corp, Fisher Body Div, staff; Chandler Lee Motors Inc, Southern Pines, NC, chief exec officer, 1986; Classic Pontiac-Buick-GMC Inc, pres, 1991-. **Orgs:** Southern Pines Rotary Club; Southern Pines Chamber Com; NC Real Estate Comn; Nat Automobile Dealers Asn; Sandhills Community Col; Moore Count Sch. **Business Addr:** CEO, Classic Pontiac Buick GMC, 8800 Ridge Rd, Ellicott City, MD 21043-4122, **Business Phone:** (410)465-9100.*

LEE, CHARLES GARY, SR.
Construction manager, business owner, president (organization). **Personal:** Born Sep 29, 1948, Jacksonville, FL; married Claudia Pittman; children: Charles, Marcus & Cedric. **Educ:** H Coun Trenholm Jr Col, A Masonry, 1969; Westfield State Col, Cert Occ Educ, 1974; Univ Mass, BA, Occupational Educ, 1984. **Career:** Springfield Sch System, adult educ instr, 1973-80; Lee-Hamilton Construction Co, pres, gen mgr, 1974-78; Neighborhood Housing Servs, asst dir, 1978-80; Charles Gary Lee Inc, owner & pres, 1980-. **Orgs:** Third Degree Master Mason FAM Ala Prince Hall, 1967-; dir, corp mem, Springfield Girl's Club Family Ctr Inc, 1979-; pres, Big Will Express Athletic Club, 1983-; certified mem, Minority Bus Enterprise, 1983-; affil mem, Western Mass Contractor's Asn, 1985-; consult, shareholder Lee-Brantley Inc, 1986-. **Honors/Awds:** Man of the Year Award, Big Will Express, 1984; Outstanding Citizen Award, Mass Black Caucus, 1986; Letter of Recognition, Mayor City of Boston, 1986. **Home Addr:** 32 Briarwood Ave, Springfield, MA 01118. **Business Addr:** President, Charles Gary Lee Inc, PO Box 90953, Springfield, MA 01139, **Business Phone:** (413)732-2339.

LEE, CHARLIE
Football executive. **Career:** Denver Broncos, dir player & community rels. **Honors/Awds:** Summit Award.

LEE, DR. CHARLOTTE O.
Educator. **Personal:** Born Jul 13, 1930, Boligee, AL; married Ralph Hewitt; children: Krystal, Karla, Rachel & Rosalind. **Educ:** Knoxville Col, BS, 1953; Tuskegee Inst, MS, 1955; Univ Kans, PhD, 1959. **Career:** Am Asn Univ Women, res fel, 1958-59; Univ Kans, asst prof nutrit, 1963; Ala A&M Univ, prof chem, 1964-69; Nassau Community Col, asst prof chem, 1970-71; St Louis Univ, res assoc, 1971-72; Southern Ill Univ, Edwardsville, assoc prof, 1972-78; City Univ, parks comnr, 1976-78; Triton Col, instr, 1979-; Oak Park River Forest Community Chest, dir, 1982. **Orgs:** Am Asn Univ Women, 1958-59; Women in Science Proj, NSF, 1977-78; proposal review panelist, NSF, 1978 & 1979. **Home Addr:** 333 N Cuyler, Oak Park, IL 60302. **Business Addr:** Instructor, Triton College, 2000 Fifth Ave, River Grove, IL 60171, **Business Phone:** (708)456-0300.

LEE, CLARA MARSHALL
Educator. **Personal:** Born Feb 14, 1946, Mobile, AL; daughter of Edward J Sr and Clara Mae; married Marion Sidney Lee Jr, Jul 10, 1971; children: LaToia Ejuan Marius Sidward. **Educ:** Ala State Univ, Montgomery Al, BS, 1967; Nat Col Educ, Chicago IL, MA, 1983. **Career:** Harvey Park Dist, comnr, 1981; Delta Sigma Theta Sor Inc Joliet Area Alumni Chapter, finance secy, 1984; Harvey Pub Schs Dist 152, hist teacher, asst prin, currently. **Orgs:** Bd

mem, People Organized Secure Election Equalities, 1982; IEA, NEA, NPRA, IPRA, The Nat Sor Phi Delta Kappa Inc. **Business Addr:** Assistant Principal, Harvey Public Schools District 152, 147th and Main, Harvey, IL 60426, **Business Phone:** (708)331-1390.*

LEE, CLIFTON VALJEAN
Physician. **Personal:** Born Jan 21, 1929, New York, NY; married Irene Warner; children: Marquetta C, Michele C, Jeanine C. **Educ:** Howard Univ, Wash, DC, BS, 1951, MD 1955; Am Bd Obstetrics & Gynec, dipl. **Career:** Western Res Med Sch, Cleveland OH, demonstr obstetrics & gynec, 1962-63; Calif Col Med, Los Angeles, clin instr obstetrics & gynec; Univ Southern Calif Med Sch, Los Angeles, physician/asst clinical prof obstetrics & gynec. **Orgs:** Nat Med Fel, 1960-63. **Military Serv:** USAF, capt, 1956-58. **Business Addr:** Gynecologist, 4361 S Western Ave, Los Angeles, CA 90062.*

LEE, CONSELLA ALMETTER
Journalist. **Educ:** Wayne State Univ, Detroit, MI, journalism, 1989. **Career:** Mich Chronicle, Detroit, MI, staff writer, 1990; Dow Jones Newswires, currently. **Business Addr:** Staff Writer, Dow Jones Newswires, 1 World Financial Ctr 200 Liberty St, New York, NY 10281, **Business Phone:** (212)416-2000.

LEE, DAMON
President (Organization), movie producer. **Personal:** Born Jan 8, 1969, Washington, DC. **Educ:** Brandeis Univ, BA; Univ Southern Calif, attended 1994. **Career:** Flims: Higher Learning, prod asst; There Goes The Nation; My Babies Mamas; Hustlin' Hank; Undercover Brother; Disturbing Behavior; American Coffee, 2001; One Flight Stand, 2003; This Christmas, 2007; Who's Your Caddy?, 2007; Whisper, 2007; Silver Pictures, vpres prod; MGM, vpres prod; Urban Entertainment, pres; Deacon Entertainment's, founder & pres, currently; Our Stories Films, exec vpres prod, currently. **Orgs:** Teacher For America; BDADS.

LEE, DR. DANIEL
Physician. **Personal:** Born Apr 28, 1918, Pinehurst, GA; son of Amos Jr and Leila; married Thelma Ragin (deceased); children: Daniel Jr, Kenneth & Sharon. **Educ:** Lincoln Univ, BA, 1940; Howard Univ Col Med, MD, 1945; Harlem Hosp, internship, 1946. **Career:** Lincoln Univ Col, sch physician & asst prof, 1946-48; Pine Forge Inst, sch physician, 1948-55; Coatesville Hosp, med staff, 1960-; Coatesville Area Schs, sch physician, 1968-; Coatesville Sr High Sch, varsity football, 1968-; physician, pvt prac. **Orgs:** Pres, Club XV, 1972-; Nat Asn Advan Colored People, 1976-; grand asst med dir, IBPOE W 1983-; coord coun, Southeastern PA High Blood Pressure Control Prog, 1983-; charter mem, US Defense Comm, 1983-; bd dirs, United Cerebral Palsy Asn Chester Co, 1985-; Health & Welfare Coun; dir, Health Dept, Improved Develop Protective Order 1988; bd dir, Atkinson Memorial community Ctr 1989-; Paul Harris fel, Rotary Int, 1989; life mem, Am Acad Family Pract, 1989; pres, Western Chester County; bd dir, W Chester ColIndust Develop Corp & Auth; Coatesville Red Cross; AMA; Fel Comm,Philadelphia, PA; comn admiss & allocations United Way; bd dir, Chester CoOIC Inc; NMA; Boy Scout Coun; Philadelphia Urban League; Kappa Alpha Psi. **Honors/Awds:** Fel, Acad Family Physicians, 1975; Coatesville Hall of Fame, 1976; Man of Year Award, S Eastern Business & Prof Women of Chester Co, 1979; 50 Year Membership Award, 1989; Community Service Award, Veterans of Foreign Wars, 1989; Elks Diamond Ebony Award, Penn State Asn, 1991. **Military Serv:** AUS, Maj, 1959.

LEE, DEBRA LOUISE
Lawyer. **Personal:** Born Aug 8, 1954, Columbia, SC; daughter of Richard M and Delma L; married Randall Spencer Coleman; children: Quinn Spencer Coleman Ava Coleman. **Educ:** Brown Univ, AB 1976; Harvard Law Sch, JD 1980; Harvard Kennedy Sch Govt, MPP 1980. **Career:** US Dist Ct Judge Barrington Parker, law clerk, 1980-81; Steptoe & Johnson, atty, 1981-86; Black Entertainment TV, vpres, gen coun, 1986-92, exec vip, gen coun & secy, 1992-96, pres & chief oper officer, currently; Publisher, Young Sisters & Brothers Mag, pres. **Orgs:** Minority Recruitment Comn Federal Comn Bar Asn, 1982-; Pub Serv Activities Comn DC Bar, 1983-; bd dirs, Legal Aid Soc DC, 1986-. **Honors/Awds:** Eva A Mooar Award, Brown Univ, 1976; Nat Achievement Award, Wash DC Area Chap Nat Alumnae Asn Spel Col, 1992. **Business Addr:** President, Chief Operating Officier, Black Entertainment TV, 1900 W Pl NE, 1 BET Plz, Washington, DC 20018-1211.*

LEE, DERREK LEON
Baseball player. **Personal:** Born Sep 6, 1975, Chicago, IL; son of Leon Lee and Pamela; married Christina. **Career:** San Diego Padres, infielder, 1997; Florida Marlins, infielder, 1998-2003; Chicago Cubs, infielder, 2004-. **Orgs:** Co owner, 1st Touch Foundation/Project 3000. **Honors/Awds:** Gold Glove Award, 2003, 2005, 2007; Player of the Month, Nat League, 2005; Louisville Slugger Silver Bat Award, 2005. **Business Addr:** Professional Baseball Player, Chicago Cubs, Wrigley Field 1060 W Addison, Chicago, IL 60613-4397, **Business Phone:** (773)404-2827.

LEE, DON LUTHER. See MADHUBUTI, HAKI R.

LEE, DOROTHY A H
Educator. **Personal:** Born Jan 22, 1925, Columbia, MO; daughter of Victor Hicks and Helen Lee; married George E, Jun 18, 1950 (deceased); children: George V & Helen Elaine. **Educ:** Wayne State Univ, BA, 1945, MA, 1947; Radciiffe Col, MA, 1948; Radcliffe Col & Harvard Univ, PhD, 1955. **Career:** Wayne State Univ, asst prof, 1952-62; Henry Ford Community Col, instr, 1963-72; Univ Mich-Dearborn, prof, 1972-93, prof emer. **Honors/Awds:** Susan B Anthony Award, Univ MI-Dearborn, 1985; Distinguished Teaching Award, 1985; Distinguished Facility Award, Mich Asn Governing Boards Cols & Universities, 1987; F Cousens Retired Person Award, Univ Mich-Dearborn, 1993. **Special Achievements:** Essays published in Michigan Quarterly Review, Black Women Writers; Callaloo Black American Literary Forum; College Language Assn Journal; Journal of Spanish Studies-Twentieth Century; Critique; Modern Drama. **Home Addr:** 939 Green Hills Dr, Ann Arbor, MI 48105-2721, **Home Phone:** (734)213-6015.

LEE, E JACQUES
Executive, manager, vice president (organization). **Personal:** Born Sep 5, 1953, Atlanta, GA. **Educ:** Simmons Col, BS, math & econ. **Career:** Fulton Fed Savings & Loan, mgt assoc, br mgr; First Union Nat Bank, br mgr; First Southern Bank Lithonia, regional br mgr; Citizens Trust Bank, div mgr retail banking, consumer banking div mgr & sr vpres retail banking, currently. **Orgs:** Ga Environ Facilities Authority; United Way African Am Partnership. **Special Achievements:** Oone of the 100 most influential women in banking & finance, Women Looking Ahead Magazine. **Business Addr:** Senior Vice President of Retail Banking, Consumer Banking Division Manager, Citizens Trust Bank, 75 Piedmont Ave, Atlanta, GA 30303, **Business Phone:** (404)575-8400.

LEE, EDWARD S.
Government official. **Personal:** Born May 12, 1935, Philadelphia, PA; married Fay E Jones; children: Michael & Eric. **Educ:** Cheyney State Col, BA, polit sci, 1968; Univ Pa, Fels Inst & State Govt, 1970. **Career:** US Post Off; HELP Inc, exec dir, 1967-69; Philadelphia Urban Coalition,exec staff mem, task force coordr & chmn, 1969-71; City Philadelphia, elected clerk quarter sessions, 1971-; Nat Asn Postal & Fed Employees,former union rep; Regional & Community Treatment Ctrs Women, appointed attys, 1967, elected ward leader, 1970; Black Political Forum, exec dir, 1968-70; Cheyney State Col, adjunct prof, 1974; Pa Gov's Justice Comn; Cernitian Am Inc, producer; Hall Realty Inc, agent, currently. **Orgs:** Bd mem, Nat Asn Ct Adminrs; Ile-Fe Black Humanitarian Ctr; Greater German town Youth Corps; bd trustees, Canaan Baptist Church; Ralph Bunche Club Philadelphia; Nat Asn Advan Colored People; Urban League Philadelphia; elected delegate, Democ Nat Mini Conv, 1974; exec asst chmn, Second World & Conf Arts & Culture; bd dir, Police Athletic League; bd dir, Community Servs & Develop Corp; chmn & bd trustees, Cheyney State Col, 1974. **Honors/Awds:** Outstanding achievement award, Inter Urban League Pa; "top ten" producer, Cernitian Am Inc; light weight boxing champion, 1956. **Military Serv:** USAF, 1952-56. **Business Addr:** Agent, Hall Realty Inc, 442 Linden Ave, PO Box 30, Pocomoke City, MD 21851, **Business Phone:** (443)783-1623.

LEE, FELICIA R.
Journalist. **Personal:** Born Nov 11, 1956, Chicago, IL; daughter of Felix and Sarah Crawford. **Educ:** Northwestern Univ, Evanston, IL, BSJ, 1978. **Career:** Fort Worth Star-Telegram, Fort Worth, TX, reporter, 1978-79; Cincinnati Enquirer, reporter, 1979-82; USA Today, Wash, DC, reporter, 1982-85; Cincinnati Enquirer, Cincinnati, OH, asst metro ed, 1985-86; Miami Herald, Miami, FL, reporter, 1986-88; NY Times, New York, reporter, 1988-. **Orgs:** Nat Asn Black Journalists, 1982-; Nieman fel, Harvard Univ, 1996. **Business Addr:** Reporter, The New York Times, 229 W 43rd St 3rd Fl, New York, NY 10036.*

LEE, FORREST A, SR.
Executive. **Personal:** Born Nov 19, 1937, Boley, OK; son of Maurice W Sr and Harriett Anderson; married Joyce A Kirksey; children: Forrest, Carole, Catherine, Brian, Gregory, Michael, Rachael, Reginald & Crystal, Lee Otis. **Educ:** Okla City Univ, BA, 1961. **Career:** Liberty Tower Co, Ok City, draftsman, 1959; Cent State Hosp Norman, OK, psychiat aide, 1960-61; MW Lee Mfg Co, plant supvr, 1961-68; Leefac Inc, Boley, OK, pres 1963-70; Farmers Home Adm Okemah, FHA loan committeeman 1970-73, chmn, 1973; Smokaroma Inc, vpres 1974; Capitol Chamber Com, exec dir; Privileged Info Inc, pres, currently. **Orgs:** Exec comm mem, Cent Okla Criminal Comm, 1970-73; pub Chap Boley Chamber Com, 1962; councilman, Town Boley, 1961-73; Nat Asn Black Mfgrs, 1972, bd dir, 1972-76; comm State Okla Human Rights Comm, 1973; bd trustees, treas, Ward Chapel AME Church Boley; Nat restaurant asn, 1977.Wewoka Alumni Chap Kappa Alpha Psi Fraternity; nat assoc food equipment mfgrs, 1980. **Business Addr:** President, Privileged Information Inc, Oklahoma, OK.

LEE, FRED D, JR.
Automotive executive. **Personal:** Born Apr 26, 1947, Tallahassee, FL; son of Fred Douglas Mosley Sr and Maude Sneed; married Patricia Mosley Lee, Aug 26, 1971; children: Ronald, Adrienne Dionne & Fred Douglas III. **Educ:** Fla A&M Univ, Tallahassee, Fla, BS, music, 1969, guid coun, 1971. **Career:** Ford Motor Co, Jacksonville, FL, market analyst, 1971-74, Memphis, TN, dist sales rep, 1974-78, bus mgt mgr, 1978-79, truck merchandising, 1979, fleet/leasing/rental mgr, 1979-82, vehicle dist mgr, 1982-84; Shoals Ford Inc, Muscle Shoals, AL, pres & owner, 1986-. **Orgs:** Black Ford Lincoln Mercury Dealer Asn, 1986-; vice chmn, Area New Car Dealers Asn, 1988-89; bd dir, Am Heart Asn, 1988-; Exec Comt, United Way Shoals, 1988-; Sheffield, Ala, Rotary Club, 1988-; chair, Ala Comn Higher Educ, 1988-: Sheffield Rotary Club; vice chmn, Ala Comn Higher Educ, 1992-. **Honors/Awds:** Distinguished Achievement Award, Ford Motor Co, 1988; Small Business Person of the Year Award, Retail Category, COC Shoals, 1992. **Special Achievements:** Top 100 Auto Dealers in the Nation, Black Enterprise Mag, 1988; Performed a musical variety show to benefit the Tennessee Valley Art Association, 1992; Recorded an album during Operation Desert Shield for USF.

LEE, GERALD BRUCE
Chief executive officer. **Personal:** Born Jan 1, 1952?, Washington, DC. **Educ:** Am Univ, BA; Wash Col Law. **Career:** Fairfax County, Va, pvt practice; Eastern Dist Va, judge, currently. **Orgs:** Active mem, Va Judges Judicial Conf; Chmn, Judicial Educ Comt; Bench Book Comt; legal community; Va State Bar; Va State Bar Coun; Pres, Northern Va Black Attorneys Asn; Chmn, Judicial Selection Comt Alexandria Bar Asn; Bd Dirs, Metropolitan Wash Airports Authority. **Business Addr:** Judge, Eastern District Virginia, US Courthouse, 401 Courthouse Sq, Alexandria, VA 22314-5798, **Business Phone:** (703)299-2100.*

LEE, GERALD E.
School administrator. **Personal:** Born Jan 11, 1958, Los Angeles, CA; son of Eugene and Erma Willis; married Tonya Marie Durley, Jul 22, 1978; children: Dawn Racquel, Gerald Eugene II, Darryl Eugene, Dennis Edward. **Educ:** Southwestern Christian Col, AS, 1978; Okla Christian Col, BS, 1980; Amber Univ, Garland, MA, prof develop, 1992, MA, coun psycholo, 1997. **Career:** First & Euclid Church Christ, minister, 1976-78; Eastside Church Christ, minister, 1978-81; Florence St Church Christ, minister, 1981-84; Metropolitan Church Christ, minister, 1984-87; Southern Christian Col, dir admis & recruitment, asst pres develop, 1992-, assoc prof, currently. **Orgs:** Am Coun Asn; Am Col Coun Asn; Asn Humanistic Educ & Develop; Asn Spiritual, Ethical & Religious Values & Coun; Int Asn Marriage & Family Counrs; Nat Career Develop Asn. **Honors/Awds:** GP Bowser Bible Award, Southwestern Christian Col, 1978; Outstanding Young Men Am, 1981, 1982, 1983, 1987, 1998. **Business Addr:** Assistant, Southwestern Christian College, 200 Bowser Cir, PO Box 10, Terrell, TX 75160.*

LEE, DR. GUY MILICON, JR.
Educator. **Personal:** Born May 24, 1928, East Chicago, IN; married Trevor J; children: Kim Valerie, Rodney & L Smith. **Educ:** Roosevelt Univ, BA, 1954; Ind Univ, MS, 1959; Ball State Univ, EdD, 1969. **Career:** Educator (retired); Gary Community Schs, IN, pub sch teacher, 1956-64, adminr, 1964-70; Saginaw Valley State Col, dir stud teaching, 1970-73, assoc dean sch educ prof, 1973-75, admin asst to pres, 1975-78, asst to pres, 1978-82, dean sch educ, 1982-86, prof educ 1986-95, prof emer, 1995. **Orgs:** Asn Supv & Curric Develop; Nat Orgn Legal Problem Educ; Am Asn Sch Admin; rep, United Way Saginaw Co; Asn Teach Educ; Am Asn Higher Educ; bd dir, League United Latin Am Citizens, 1982-95; Metro Fayette Kiwanis Club,1998-; Fayette County Sr Servs Bd, 1999-. **Honors/Awds:** High Scholastic Achievement Award, Ind Univ, Bloomington, 1953; Doctoral Fellowship, Ball State Univ, Muncie, IN, 1968-69; Citizen of the Age of Enlightenment Award, Am Found Sci Creative Intelligence, 1976; Keyman Award, United Way, Saginaw County, MI, 1979. **Military Serv:** AUS technician 1946-48. **Home Addr:** 165 Hampstead Mnr, Fayetteville, GA 30214-3465. *

LEE, DR. GWENDOLYN B
Educator. **Personal:** Born Feb 3, 1950, Gary, IN; daughter of Willie and Emma Byrd; married Ronald Warren, Aug 21, 1971; children: Michelle Victoria. **Educ:** Ball State Univ, BS, 1971; Purdue Univ, MS, 1975, MS, 1985; Loyola Univ, PhD, 1998. **Career:** Thornridge High Sch, teacher, 1971-81, dean stud, 1981-85, asst prin, 1985-92, prin, 1994-; Hillcrest High Sch, prin, 1992-94. **Orgs:** Alpha Kappa Alpha Sorority, 1969-; pres, S Suburban Chap, 1978-82, chairperson, Nat Trends & Serv, 1998-99, nat rec secy, 1998-, nat pres, currently; The Links Inc; Nat Asn Sec Schs Prins, 1985-; Asn Supvn & Curric Develop, 1985-; bd dir, S Suburban Family Shelter, 1994-; Nat Coun Negro Women; state dir, Ill Prins Asn, 1997-2000. **Special Achievements:** "The Study of Protege's Perceptions of Mentoring Relations in Secondary Schools and the Implications of Their Findings for Future Mentorship Projects," doctoral disseration, 1998. **Business Addr:** Principal, Thornridge High School, 15000 Cottage Grove, Dolton, IL 60419, **Business Phone:** (708)841-5180.

LEE, HELEN ELAINE
Educator, novelist. **Personal:** Born Mar 13, 1959, Detroit, MI; daughter of George Ernest and Dorothy Ann Hicks. **Educ:** Harvard Col, BA, 1981; Harvard Law Sch, JD, 1985. **Career:** Univ Mich, Dearborn, adj lectr, 1995; Mass Inst Technol, asst prof writing, assoc prof, writing & humanistic studies, currently; novelist.

Orgs: Phi Beta Kappa. **Honors/Awds:** First Novel Award, Am Libr Asn, Black Caucus, 1994-95. **Special Achievements:** Author: The Serpent's Gift, Atheneum Publishers, 1994, London Headline Press, 1994; Marriage Bones, The African Diaspora in Short Fiction, ed; Charles Rowell West view Press, 1995; Silences, The Best Short Stories by Black Writers vol II, ed, Gloria Naylor, Little, Brown and Co, 1995; Novel Water Marked, Scribner, 1999; Life Without about the lives of inmates in American prisons, currently. **Business Addr:** Associate Professor, Massachusetts Institute of Technology, Program for Writing & Humanistic Studies, Rm 14E-303, Cambridge, MA 02139-4307, **Business Phone:** (617)253-7894.

LEE, HOWARD N.
Government official. **Personal:** Born Jul 28, 1934, Lithonia, GA; married Lillian Wesley; children: Angela, Ricky & Karin Alexis Lou Tempie. **Educ:** Clark Col, 1956; St Col Ft Valley, BA, sociol, 1959; Univ NC, MSW, 1966; Acad Cert Social Workers, 1968; Shaw Univ, LLD, 1971. **Career:** Juvenile Comestic Rel Ct Savannah, prob off, 1961-64; Youth Prog Duke Univ, dir, 1966-68; NC Cent Univ, vis asst prof, 1967-68; Employee Rel Duke Univ, dir, 1968-69; Chapel Hill, Mayor, 1969-75; Lark Cinemas Inc, pres; Lee Dist & Mfg Co; Lark Entertainment Enter, pres & chmn bd; Plastiwood Prod Inc, pres; Shaw Univ adj prof; off human develop duke Univ, dir; chapel hill NC, mayor, 1969-75; State Bd Educ, chmn; Jim Hunt Inst, sr adv, currently; NC Utilities Comn, comnr, 2005-. **Orgs:** Numerous professional mem; NC State Bd Education, 2008. **Honors/Awds:** Recip Ga St Teachers Hon Student's Award; honor student's Award, St Col; hunt fel Award Ft Valley St Col; achievement Award, Atlanta Br Nat Asn Advan Colored People; Achievement Award Phi Beta Sigma Fraternity, 1969; Nat Urban Leag Equal Oppor Day Award, 1970; publs field; William Richardson Davie Award, UNC; Distinguished Service Medal, UNC. **Special Achievements:** After graduate school he made history by becoming the youngest and mostrecent graduate to be elected President of the NC Chapter of TheProfessional Association of Social Work. **Military Serv:** AUS 1959-61. *

LEE, IVIN B
Police chief, executive. **Personal:** Born in Beard, WV; divorced; children: Carlene, Carlett, Carla, Carl & Carlton. **Educ:** BS, criminal justice. **Career:** Police Chief (retired), Executive; Charleston WV Police Dept, sgt; Dunbar Police Dept, police chief; WV Human Rights Comn, exec dir, currently. **Orgs:** Mt Zion Baptist Church; WV Human Rights Comn, exec dir Hate Crimes Taskforce; WV BLEU; KCNC; NOBLE; WV Chiefs Police Asn; Bus & Prof Women's Club USA; Fraternal Order Police-Capitol City Lodge; Dunbar, WV Women's Club; Nat Asn Advan Colored People, Charleston, adv coun Salvation Army, Boys' & Girls' Club; exec bd Job Corps; Task force to study perceived racial disparity In the juvenile justice syst. **Honors/Awds:** Community Reflection Award, Nat Asn Advan Colored People, 1995; Lifetime Achievement Award, Optimist Club, 1995; Community Service Award, Charleston Black Ministerial Alliance, 1996; Woman of the Decade 1986-96, NAACP, 1996; 100-year Anniversary Community Award, Charleston Women's Improvement League, Inc; Appalachian Women of WV, Smithsonian Inst, 1996; Outstanding Law Enforcement Award, WV Trial Lawyers, 1997; Women of Achievement in Government, YWCA, 1998. **Special Achievements:** First woman and the only African American to be appointed chief of the Dunbar Police Dept. **Business Addr:** Executive Director, West Virginia Human Rights Commission, 1321 Plz E Rm 108A, Charleston, WV 25301-1400, **Business Phone:** (304)558-2616.

LEE, DR. JAMES E
Dentist. **Personal:** Born Mar 5, 1940, Conway, SC; son of Richard Allen and Ophelia Buck; married Patricia Ponds, Apr 21, 1973; children: James E Jr, Allen Earlington & Arrington Patrick. **Educ:** SC State Col, 1963; Howard Univ, Col Dent, DDS, 1971. **Career:** Pvt pract, dent, 1973-; Appalachian Reg Health Policy & Planning Coun Anderson, SC, staff dentist, 1971-72; Dent Serv, Howard Univ Upward Bound Prog, dir, summer 1971; Franklin C Fetter Comprehensive Health Care Clin Charleston, staff dentist, 1972-74. **Orgs:** Chmn, Salvation Army Adv Bd, 1980; chmn, Conway Housing Authority, 1980-81; chmn, 1992-93, past pres, coun pres, Palmetto Med Dent & Pharmaceut Asn, 1984-; vpres, State Bd Dent, 1994; Int Col Dent, 1993; Col Dents, 1993; Palmetto Med Dent & Pharm Asn; Pee Dee Dist Dent Soc; SC Dent Soc; Am Dent Asn; Nat Dent Asn; Conway Alumni Chap; Kappa Alpha Psi; Bethel AME Church Young Adult Choir; exec comt, Palmetto Med Dent & Pharm Asn; Grand Strand Dent Soc; pres, Pee Dee Med Dent & Pharmaceut Asn; health adv comn, Waccamaw Econ Opptunity Coun; Ment Health Asn Horry County; steward Bd, Bethel AME Church. **Honors/Awds:** Dental Award, Howard Univ, 1958; Doctor of the Year, Palmetto Med Dent & Pharmaceut Asn, 1989. **Military Serv:** AUS, sp5, 1964-67. **Business Addr:** Dentist, James E Lee, 611 Church St, Conway, SC 29527.

LEE, JEFFERI K
Executive. **Career:** WDVM-TV, Wash DC, freelance producer, 1979-81; Black Entertainment TV, Network Opers, exec vpres, 1982-98.

LEE, JOHN C, III
Executive. **Career:** John C Lee Construction & Supply Co, chief exec officer, 1977-. **Business Addr:** C, John C Lee Construction and Supply Co Inc, RR 1 PO Box 216A, Petrolia, PA 16050-9312.

LEE, JOHN M
Banker, president (organization). **Career:** Standard Savings Bank, chmn & pres; East West Bank, vice chmn, currently. *

LEE, JOHN ROBERT E.
Executive, president (organization). **Personal:** Born Jul 11, 1935, Tallahassee, FL; children: John Robert E Lee IV. **Educ:** FL A&M Univ, BA, 1959; Boston Univ, MA, 1961; Univ KS, Doctorate, 1973. **Career:** Commun Transportation & Real Estate Develop, pres, owner, entrepreneur; Silver Star Commun Corp, pres. **Orgs:** Dir, athletics TN State Univ, 1985; Nat Assoc Broadcasters, 1985; pres, Nat Assoc Black Owned Broadcasters; chmn, fund raising YMCA, 1985; comt mem, Boy Scouts Am, 1985; Nat Col Athletic Assoc, 1985, ford Mercury Lincoln Minority Auto Assoc, 1985. **Honors/Awds:** Outstanding Service Award, Albany State, 1970; Humanitarian of the Year, NAACP, 1977; Broadcaster of the Year, HABOB, 1983; Outstanding Community Service, Hella Temple 105, 1984.

LEE, JOIE (JOY LEE)
Actor, movie director, movie producer. **Personal:** Born Jun 22, 1962, Brooklyn, NY; daughter of William James Edwards lee III and Jacquelyn Shelton (deceased). **Educ:** St Ann's Sch, Brooklyn; Sarah Lawrence Col, music, writing, dance. **Career:** Films: She's Gotta Have It, 1986; School Daze, 1988; Do the Right Thing,1989; Mo' Better Blues, 1990; Bail Jumper, 1990; A Kiss Before Dying,1991; Fathers & Sons, 1992; Crooklyn, 1994; Losing Isaiah, 1995; Girl 6,1996; Get on the Bus, 1996; Nowhere Fast, 1997; Personals, 1999; Summer of Sam, 1999; Coffee and Cigarettes, 2003; She Hate Me, 2004; Full Grown Men, 2006; Starting Out in the Evening, 2007; Screenwriter & assoc producer: Crooklyn, 1994; Nowhere Fast, 1997;Snapped, dir, 2001; Jesus Children of America, 2005; All the Invisible Children, exec producer, 2005; TV: "Making 'Do the Right Thing'", 1989;"The Cosby Show", 1989; "100 Centre St", 2002; "Zero Tolerance", 2002; "Rotten", 2003; "Law & Order: Special Victims Unit", 2003. **Business Addr:** Actress, co 40 Acres and a Mule Filmworks, 124 DeKalb Ave 2, Brooklyn, NY 11217, **Business Phone:** (718)624-3703.*

LEE, JOY. See LEE, JOIE.

LEE, KERMIT J., JR.
Architect, educator. **Personal:** Born Mar 27, 1934, Springfield, MA; son of Lillian B Jackson and Kermit James Sr; married Lore Leipelt; children: Karin Justine, Jason Anthony. **Educ:** Syracuse Univ, BArch, 1957; Technische Hochschule Braunschweig Ger, Fulbright, 1958, 1959. **Career:** Afex, Wiesbaden Ger, chief architect, 1960-63; P Zoelly Arch Zurich Switz, assoc architect, 1963-66; Skoler & Lee Architect, vpres arch,1969; Syracuse Univ, prof architect 1973, prof emer, currently; SU Inst Energy Res, fac assoc, 1978; Chimaera Energy Tech Corp, prin & chief exec officer, 1979; Syracuse Univ Pre-Col Prog, appoint dir, 1986; Energenesis Develop Corp, vpres, 1983; Kermit J Lee Jr, AIA architect & prin, 1989-. **Orgs:** Medary fel, Am Inst Archit, 1959-60; consult, Urban Designer Model Cities, Springfield, MA, 1969-75; dir, Campus Plan Group Syracuse Univ, 1970; bldg code bd appeal, 1970-; Am Inst Architect; mayors comm Revise City Charter, 1972-74; adj assoc prof, urban design, Columbia Univ, 1974; NY Coalition Black Architect, 1977; graphic exhibit Proj Energy Syracuse Univ Sch Architect, 1979; tech consult Onondaga County Citizens Energy Comm, 1979-; NY Bd Architect, 1979-, Gov Cultural Adv Comm Time Square, Nat Coun Architect Regional Bd ARE, 1985; Citizen's Cult Adv Comt, Times Square Develop, 1985-;chmn, NY Bd Architect, 1986-87. **Honors/Awds:** Honor Diploma Swiss Nat Exposition, 1964; Research Grant, Nat Endowment Arts, 1980; School Medal, Am Inst Architects, 1957; Luther Gifford Prize Design, 1967; Class Marshal, 1957; Phi Kappa Phi Hon, 1957; Alpha Rho Chi Medal, 1957; NY State Soc Architect Medal, 1957; Appt AIA Nat Comm Design; Black Pioneer Award, Syracuse Black Leadership Coun, 1986; Elected College of Fellows, Am Inst Architects, 1990; Dean's Outstanding Alumni Award, Syracuse Univ, 1997. **Military Serv:** USAF, exchange gs12, 2 yrs. **Home Addr:** 301 Houston Ave, Syracuse, NY 13224-1755. **Business Phone:** (315)443-3518.

LEE, KEVIN BRIAN
Executive. **Personal:** Born Aug 15, 1967, Philadelphia, PA; son of William Keith and Grenthian Lee. **Educ:** Pa State Univ, BS, 1990, MEd, 1995. **Career:** Pa State Univ, admis asst, 1990-91, human resources asst, 1991-92, staff develop & training coordr, 1992-96; TRW Syst Integration Goup, mgr human resources, 1997-. **Orgs:** Nat Asn Advan Colored Peopel, Educ Comt, 1988-90; pres, Groove Phi Groove Social Fel Inc, Penn State, 1990-91, adv, 1991-92; exec asst, Univ Libr Diversity Coun, 1991-96; Am Col Personnel Asn, 1994-; Pa Col Personnel Asn, 1994-95; Penn State Univ, Black Grad Stud Asn, 1994-96; Grad Stud Asn, 1994-96. **Honors/Awds:** Community Service Award, 1989; Homecoming King, 1989-90; Black Caucus, Penn State Univ. **Home Addr:** 4421 Fairstone Dr, Fairfax, VA 22033. **Business Addr:** Human Resources Manager, TRW Systems & Information Technology Group, 1 Fed Syst Dr, Fairfax, VA 22033, **Business Phone:** (703)803-5759.

LEE, LARRY DWAYNE
Sports manager, football player, musician. **Personal:** Born Sep 10, 1959, Dayton, OH; son of Charles V and Evolia; married Daphne Y, Jan 16, 1982; children: Dayna & Danielle. **Educ:** Univ Calif, Los Angeles, BS, 1981. **Career:** Football Player (retired), football staff, Musician; Detroit Lions,player, 1981-85; Denver Broncos, player, 1987-89; Mel Farr Ford, mgr,1987-91; Miami Dolphins, player, 1991-93; While Allen Honda, gen mgr, 1991-93; Detroit Lions, football adm, vpres, 1993-2001; Larry Lee & Back In The Day, founder, 2002-. **Orgs:** Kappa Alpha Psi; bdm, Dayton Pro Stars Football Camp, 1981-. **Honors/Awds:** Kappa Alpha Psi, Man of the Year, 1981. **Home Addr:** 3397 Sawgrass Ct, Rochester Hills, MI 48309, **Home Phone:** (810)852-1984. **Business Addr:** Founder, Larry Lee And Back In The Day, 2826 Tall Oaks Ct Suite 12, Auburn Hills, MI 48326, **Business Phone:** (248)852-1984.

LEE, LAVERNE C.
Educator. **Personal:** Born Dec 19, 1933, Bayonne, NJ; daughter of Charles H Churn and Violet M Grayson Churn; widowed; children: Juvia A. **Educ:** Morgan St Col, BS, 1955; Loyola Col, MEd, 1969; Johns Hopkins Univ. **Career:** Baltimore Co Bd Educ, instr reading spl; teacher physically handicapped; Battle Monumental Sch Eastwood Ctr, prin; Baltimore County Pub Schs, coord recruitment. **Orgs:** Treas, 1970-74, vpres, 1974-75, CEC; sec, Teacher Asn Baltimore Co, 1973-; pres, Baltimore Co Chap Coun Excep C, 1974-76; del, NEA Conv; del, CEC Conv; Orton Soc; PTA; exec bd, TABCO; Phi Delta Kappa; Delta Kappa Gamma; Phi Delta Kappa, 1988-. **Honors/Awds:** Teacher of the Year Award. **Business Addr:** Coordinator of Recruitment Personnel, Baltimore County Public Schools, 6901 N Charles St, Towson, MD 21204.

LEE, LERON
Executive, baseball player. **Personal:** Born Mar 4, 1948, Bakersfield, CA; son of Leon and Jewel Williams; married Vicquie Tanaka, Oct 31, 1982; children: Juliet M & Vivian Y. **Career:** Football player (retired), football coach; St Louis Cardinals, St Louis,MO, player, 1969-71; San Diego Padres, San Diego, CA, player, 1971-73;Cleveland Indians, Cleveland, OH, player, 1974-75; Los Angeles Dodgers,Los Angeles, CA, player, 1975-76; Lotte Orions Baseball Club, Tokoyo,Japan, player, 1977-88; Oakland Athletics, Oakland, CA, coach, 1989-90;Pro-Elite Sports Inc, pres; Bold Tech Corp, owner; Cincinnati Reds,advising batting coach, currently. **Business Addr:** Advising batting coach, Cincinnati Reds, Great American Ball Pk 100 Main St, Cincinnati, OH 45202, **Business Phone:** (513)765-7000.

LEE, M DAVID, JR.
Educator, architect. **Personal:** Born Aug 31, 1943, Chicago, IL; son of M David Sr and Mae Thomas; married Celeste E Reid, Apr 27, 1991; children: M David III, Aron Ford & Raquel Yvette. **Educ:** Univ Ill, BA, 1967; Harvard Univ, MA, 1971. **Career:** Candeub Flessig & ASC, planning draftsman, 1962-64; Roy D Murphy Architect, draftsman, 1965-67; David A Crane Architects, urban design draftsman, 1967-69; Stull ASC Inc, architects, arch & urban designer, 1969-83; Stull & Lee Architects, partner, 1983-; Harvard Univ, adj prof, 1988-; Rhode Island Sch Design, fac; Mass Inst Technol, fac. **Orgs:** Pres, Boston Soc Architects, 1992; fel, Inst Urban Design; mayor's inst fac, Nat Endowment Arts; Boston Coc; Boys & Girls Clubs; vis comt, Mass Inst Tech Sch Arch; trustee, Berklee Col Music; fel, John Hay Whitney Found, 1970; fel, Am Inst Architects, 1992. **Honors/Awds:** Presidential Design Award, Nat Endowment Arts, 1988; Regional & Statewide Governor's Design Award, Mass Coun Arts & Humanities, 1986; Von Moltke Urban Design Award, Boston Soc Architects, 1988; Boston Historic Neighborhoods Foundation Award for Excellence, 1990; New England Council Design Award, Am Inst Architects, 1991; Social Advocacy Award, Am Planning Asn, 1996; Boston Society of Architects Year 2000 Award, 2000. **Special Achievements:** Featured in Pub Broadcast Service (PBS) documentary Divided Highways. **Business Addr:** Partner, Stull and Lee Incorporated, 38 Chauncy St, Boston, MA 02111, **Business Phone:** (617)426-0406.

LEE, MALCOLM D
Movie director, writer. **Personal:** Born Jan 11, 1970. **Educ:** Georgetown Univ; Packer Col Inst, Brooklyn, NY. **Career:** Malcolm X, post-prod asst, 1992; Clockers, asst to Spike Lee, 1995; Undercover Brother, dir, 2002; The Best Man, writer, dir, 1999; "Everybody Hates Chris", dir, 2006; Roll Bounce, tv series, 2005; The Music Makers, actor, 2005; Everybody Hates the Lottery, tv series, 2006; Welcome Home, Roscoe Jenkins,dir, 2008; Welcome Home, Roscoe Jenkins, writer, 2008. **Business Phone:** (310)859-4000.

LEE, DR. MARGARET CAROL
Educator. **Personal:** Born Oct 3, 1955; daughter of Charles Henry Lee Sr and Carol Rae Carruthers. **Educ:** Spelman Col, Atlanta, BA, polit sci, 1976; Univ Pittsburgh, PA, MA, 1981, PhD, pub & int affairs, 1985. **Career:** Lake Forest Col, Lake Forest, IL, lectr polit, 1986; Harry Frank Guggenheim proj, adv; Tenn Tech Univ, Cookeville, assoc prof, polit sci, 1986-; Spelman Col, assoc prof, polit sci, 1994-; Univ NC, assoc prof African studies, currently. **Orgs:** African Studies Asn, 1988-. **Honors/Awds:** SADCC, The Political Economy of Development in Southern Africa, Winston-Derek, 1989; Resource Guide to Information on Southern Africa, Winston-Derek, 1988; Black Faculty of the Year, Black Stud Orgn,

Tenn Tech, 1990. **Special Achievements:** Publications: The State and Democracy in Africa, co-editor (1997, 1998); SADCC: The Political Economy of Development in Southern Africa (1989); The Political Economy of Regionalism in Southern Africa, 2003); Unfinished Business: The Land Crisis in Southern Africa, co-editor (2003); Over two dozen other publications, including journal articles, chapters in books, occasional papers, etc.; Research support from the Harry Frank Guggenheim Foundation.

LEE, MARGARET S
Association executive. **Personal:** Born Mar 31, 1936, Ocean City, NJ; daughter of Theodore Scott and Mary Roberta Outen. **Educ:** Temple Univ, Philadelphia, Pa, 1957; Taylor Bus Inst, New York, NY, 1970. **Career:** Association executive (retired);City Philadelphia, Philadelphia, Pa, zoning clerk, 1954-60; Bankers Trust Co, New York, NY, credit clerk, 1964-68; Leitner & Goodman, Esqs, Brooklyn, NY, legal secy, 1969-74; Nat Bowling Asn, New York, NY, exec secy, 1974-2006. **Orgs:** Nat Coalition Black Meeting Planners, 1989-; trustee, Nat Bowling Hall of Fame & Mus, 1990-; Nat Asn Female Execs, 1991. **Honors/Awds:** Received the NBA Mary L Wilkes Award, Outstanding Service, 1974; received numerous local, regional and national NBA Awards and citations for outstanding service from 1974-; Inducted into Local Chapter Hall of Fame, 1990. **Special Achievements:** First all female Executive Cabinet of TNBA.

LEE, MARK ANTHONY
Football player. **Personal:** Born Mar 20, 1958, Hanford, CA. **Educ:** Univ Wash. **Career:** Green Bay Packers, cornerback, 1980-90; New Orleans Saints, 1991; SanFrancisco 49ers, 1991.

LEE, DR. MILDRED KIMBLE
Educator. **Personal:** Born Jan 2, 1919, New York, NY; daughter of Ernestine Scott (deceased) and Ural (deceased); married Granville Wheeler Sr, Nov 9, 1940; children: Granville Wheeler Jr. **Educ:** Hunter Col, New York, NY, AB, cum laude, 1938, attended 1960; City Col, New York, NY, MBA, 1943, attended 64; State Univ Humanistic Educ Ctr, Albany, NY, 1971-72; Fordham Univ, New York, NY, EdD, 1977. **Career:** Morris High Sch Bd Educ, New York, NY, teacher, guid counr & AP guid, 1949-66; Dist 8 Bd Educ, New York, NY, supvr guid, 1966-77; City Univ New York Grad Ctr, Ctr Advan Study Educ, New York, NY, proj dir, 1984-97; Adelphi Univ Urban Ctr, adj prof, 1966-77; City Col New York, adj prof, 1966-77; Teachers Col Columbia Univ, adj prof, 1966-77; Fordham Univ, Lincoln Ctr Campus, New York, NY, asst & assoc prof, 1977-84; Lee & Lee Financial Mgt, partner, 1982-97; Fordham Univ, Day Care Coun, evaluator, 1984-95; Adult Basic Educ, NYC Bd Educ, consult, 1984-94. **Orgs:** Hunter Col Alumni, 1938-; Retired Sch Supvrs & Admin; NYC Bd Educ, 1977-; Asn Black Women Higher Educ, 1979-84; Nat Urban Educ Asn, 1981-85; contrib, Nat Asn Advan Colored People; contribr, Nat Urban League; contribr, United Negro Col Fund; membership chairperson, Wistarians Hunter Col, 1980-94; Fordham Univ Alumni Asn, 1977-; MENSA, 1985. **Honors/Awds:** Hunter College Hall of Fame, 1983. **Special Achievements:** Author of articles published in periodicals, including Forum, Educ Technology, Journal of Black Studies, and Educ Forum, poems published in International Library of Poetry in 2000. **Home Addr:** 2 Fordham Hill Oval Suite 8EF, Bronx, NY 10468.

LEE, MILTON B
Executive. **Educ:** Univ Tex, Austin. **Career:** Gen Elec Co, staff, 1976; Pub Utility Comn Tex; Austin Energy; Lower Colo River Authority; City Pub Serv, gen mgr, chief exec officer; CPS Energy, San Antonio, TX, gen mgr & chief exec officer, 2002-. **Orgs:** Past pres, TPPA; Elect Reliability Coun Tex; Tex Pub Power & Am Pub Power Asns; Univ Tex Austin Engineering Found Adv Bd; Univ Tex San Antonio's Develop Bd; bd dir, Greater San Antonio Chamber Com.

LEE, MINNIE JOYCELYN. See ELDERS, DR. M. JOYCELYN.

LEE, NATHANIEL
Lawyer. **Educ:** Morehead State Univ, BA, 1977, MA, 1978; Univ Ga, JD, 1982. **Career:** Wilson, Coleman Roberts, 1981-83; Nathaniel Lee & Assocs, 1983-86; Watkins & Lee, partner, 1986-91; Lee, Cossell, Kuehn & Love, LLP, sr partner, 1991-. **Orgs:** Vpres, NCP, Indianapolis Br, 1986-88; life mem, chair bd dir, Marion Co Bar Asn, 1987-91 & 1993-2003; bd mem, Ronald McDonald House, 1987-2000; golf chmn, Indianapolis Urban League, 1992-94; bd mem, Police Athletic League, 1993-96; mem litigation sect, Indianapolis Bar Asn, 1993-2002, grievance comt, 1999-, Judicial Evaluation Comt, co-chair, 2002-; life mem, spec asst pres, Nat Bar Asn, 2001, Am Inns Ct, 2002, Legal Educ Comt, 2002; Am Trial Lawyers Asn; Ind Trial Lawyers Asn. **Honors/Awds:** COT Service Award, Marion County Bar Asn, 1992; Special Contributor Award, Wheelers Boys Club; COT Service Award, Nat Bar Asn, 1992; Distinguished Fellow Award, Indianapolis Bar Asn, 2002; Presidential Award, Nat Bar Asn, 2002; Service to Organization Award, In Ronald McDonald House; Indiana Super Lawyer, 2006, 2007 & 2008. **Business Addr:** Senior Partner, Lee, Burns, Cossell, & Kuehn, LLP, 127 E Mich St, Indianapolis, IN 46204, **Business Phone:** (317)631-5151.

LEE, OLIVER B.
Educator. **Personal:** Born Sep 27, 1926, Cleveland, OH; married Isis Edna; children: Brenda, Linda, Jacquelyn & John. **Educ:** Springfield Col, Springfield, Mass, BS, 1953, MS, 1957. **Career:** Cleveland YMCA, dir, 1954-59; Cleveland, Vocational Rehab Cleveland, counr supr, 1959-64; Ohio Bur Voc Rehab, Cleveland, 1964-66; Rehab Serv Cleveland Soc Blind Cleveland, dir, 1966-67; Coun & Placement Aim-Jobs Cleveland, dir, 1967-69; Comn Extension Prog Cleveland State Univ, dir, 1969-73; Cleveland State Univ, asso dean, 1973-; Youth Prog Dir, Salvation Army, Superior Corps, Cleveland, 1963-. **Honors/Awds:** United Area Citizens Agency Leadership Devel Award 1972; Lincoln HS Football Hall of Fame Hinton, WV, 1972; Youth Award, Kiwanis Club Service, 1973. **Military Serv:** USAF, sgt, 1946-48. **Business Addr:** Director, Cleveland State University, Division of Continuing Edition, Cleveland, OH 44115.

LEE, OTIS K (OTIS KNAPP LEE)
Restaurateur. **Personal:** Born in Detroit, MI. **Career:** Mr FoFo's Deli & Restaurant, owner, 1973-. **Special Achievements:** Commissioned by Kentucky Fried Chicken to create a sweet potato pie for mass marketing, beginning 1993. **Business Addr:** Owner, Mr FoFo's Deli, 8902 2nd Ave, Detroit, MI 48202, **Business Phone:** (313)873-4450.*

LEE, OTIS KNAPP. See LEE, OTIS K.

LEE, PAULINE W.
Librarian. **Personal:** Born Nov 6, 1933, Simsboro, LA; daughter of Clinton Willis and Mionia Williams Willis; married Melvin Lee, Oct 3, 1963. **Educ:** Southern Univ, Baton Rouge, LA, BA, social studies/libr sci, 1955; Univ Mich, Ann Arbor, MI, MALS, 1961; Calif State Col, La, CA, 1966; La Tech Univ, Ruston, LA, 1972. **Career:** Librarian (retired). St Tammy High Sch, LA, sch librn, 1955-58; Grambling State Univ, Grambling, LA, circulation librn, 1958-62, educ librn, 1962-76, coordr pub serv, 1975-77, acting dir, 1977-78, assoc prof, dir libr AC Lewis Memorial Libr, 1978-99; Staff Develop Workshop, SUSBO, consult, 1980; J Int libr Loan & Info Supply, consult ed, 1989. **Orgs:** Acad Libr Adminrs La; Am Libr Asn; Libr Develop Comt La; Grambling State Univ Alumni Asn; La Libr Asn; Trail Blazer Libr Syst; Ruston-Grambling League Women Voters; Black Caucus Am Libr Asn. **Honors/Awds:** Certificate of Recognition, Lewis Temple CME Church, 1972; Certificate of Appreciation, Future Bus Leaders Am, 1973; Awards of Recognition, Alpha Kappa Alpha Sorority, 1976; Certificate of Merit, Gov Edwin Edwards, 1978; Task Force on Academic Libraries/Library Master Plan, 1980; Service Award, New Rocky Valley Baptist Church, 1981; author, Courage Through Love: A Story of a Family, Ruston Daily Leader, 1982. **Home Addr:** 1229 Martin Luther King Jr Ave, PO Box 456, Grambling, LA 71245. *

LEE, RITTEN EDWARD
Executive. **Personal:** Born Jun 25, 1925, Brighton, AL; son of Mattie Hogue (deceased) and Ritten (deceased); married Betty Allen; children: Anthony Edward & Juliana Hogue. **Educ:** Earlham Col, BA 1950; Univ CT Sch Social Work, MA, 1953. **Career:** Rutgers Univ, Newark, NJ, adj prof, 1965-81; Hudson Guild NYC, exec dir, 1972-77; adj lectr, Hunter Col Sch Social Work, 1977-78; United Neighborhood House NYC, dir manpower, 1977-80; Nat Info Bur NYC, asst dir, 1980-81; WCVI, WENY, WHRC, disc jockey, 1981-84; NYC Dept Law, consult, 1981; Seneca Ctr, exec dir, 1982-93; BLACFAX Jour, publ, 1982-98; Col New Rochelle, adj prof, 1997-98. **Orgs:** Trustee, Comm Church NY, 1973-77; founder & bd mem, RENA-COA Multi-Serv Ctr; trustee, Earlham Col, 1970-79. **Honors/Awds:** Sarah Addington Award, Earlham Col, 1950; Hon Mention Poetry Mag, 1950-51; Comn NCNCR Appt Newark Comm for Neighborhood Conserv, 1968; Certificate of Appreciation, RENA-COA Multi Serv Ctr, 1979; Henry McNeal Turner Community Service Award, 1993. **Special Achievements:** Poetry Published in Span, Botteghe Oscure Crisis, Flame, Crucible, Pittsburgh Courier, Chicago Defender, Michigan Chronicle, Ebony Rhythm (an anthology) & others. **Military Serv:** AAF, sgt, 2 yrs 4 mo; Good Conduct; Am Theatre Victory, 1943-46. **Home Addr:** 214 W 138th St, New York, NY 10030.

LEE, ROBERT EMILE
Executive, manager. **Personal:** Born Aug 19, 1948, New Orleans, LA; son of Robert Emile Sr and Mae Louise; married Glendarene Beck; children: Joseph. **Educ:** Tulane Univ, BS, 1970; Univ Chicago, MBA, 1973. **Career:** Martin Marietta Aerospace, eng admin specialist, 1973-75; Tenneco Oil, planning analyst, 1976-78, supply coord, 1978-80, mgr prod distrib, 1980-84, mgr mkt & planning, 1984-86, sr crude oil rep, 1986-87. **Orgs:** NBMBA Asn Houston Chapter, 1986-. **Home Addr:** 2318 Sugarline Dr, Sugar Land, TX 77479. **Business Addr:** Sr Crude Oil Rep, Tenneco Oil Co, PO Box 2511, Houston, TX 77001, **Business Phone:** (713)757-3104.

LEE, ROBINNE
Artist. **Personal:** Born Jul 16, 1974, Mount Vernon, NY. **Educ:** Columbia Law Sch, law degree; Yale Univ, BA, psychol. **Career:** Films: National Security, 2003; 13 Going On 30, 2004; Deliver Us from Eva, 2004; Hitch, 2005; TV series: "Tyler Perry's House of Payne". **Business Addr:** Actress, c/o Paradigm, 10100 Santa Monica Blvd 25th Fl, Los Angeles, CA 90067, **Business Phone:** (310)277-4400.*

LEE, SHALON D
Chief executive officer. **Educ:** Univ Mich, Sch Social Work, MSW. **Career:** PATH; Soka Serv LLC, pres & chief exec officer, currently. **Business Addr:** President, Chief Executive Officer, Soka Services LLC, 28 N Saginaw Suite 813, Pontiac, MI 48342, **Business Phone:** (248)451-0540.*

LEE, SHAWN SWABODA
Football player. **Personal:** Born Oct 24, 1966, Brooklyn, NY. **Educ:** Univ N Ala, Westchester Comm Col,communs major. **Career:** Football player (retired); Tampa Bay Buccaneers, defensive tackle, 1988-89; Miami Dolphins, 1990-91; San Diego Chargers, 1992-97; Chicago Bears, 1998; Oakland Raiders, 2000. **Orgs:** Co-founder, Players Community Resource Ctr.

LEE, SHEILA JACKSON
Congressperson (U.S. federal government). **Career:** Congressperson. **Orgs:** Congressional Black Caucus; Congressional Caucus for Women's Issues; Congressional Caucus for Women's Issues; Congressional Caucus on the Judicial Branch. **Special Achievements:** Senior Whip, Democratic Caucus. **Business Addr:** 2435 Rayburn Building, Washington, DC 20515, **Business Phone:** (202)225-3816.*

LEE, SHEILA JACKSON
Congressperson (u.s. federal government). **Personal:** Born Jan 12, 1950, Queens, NY; married Elwyn Cornelius; children: Erica Shelwyn & Jason Cornelius Bennett. **Educ:** Yale Univ, BA (honors), polit sci, 1972; Univ Va, Sch Law, JD, 1975. **Career:** John Courtney Murray Traveling & Res fel, Mudge Rose Guthrie & Alexander assoc, summer, 1974; Wld Harkrader & Ross, atty, 1975-78; Municipal Court for the city of Houston, assoc judge; US House Reps & Select Comm Assassinations, staff coun, 1977-78; Fulbright & Jaworski, atty, 1978-80; United Energy Resources, atty, 1980-87; Brodsky & Ketchand, partner, 1987-; City Houston, assoc judge, 1987-90; pvt practice, atty,1988-; Homeland Security Subcommittee on Transportation Security and Infrastructure Protection, chwmn; Houston City Coun, Position Number Four, cnm at large, 1990-94; Human relations Commt, Chwmn; Airport & Cables commt; US House Reps, congresswoman, 1994-. **Orgs:** Bd dirs, John Courtney Murray Found, Yale Univ, New Haven, 1972-73; Episcopal Ctr Children, 1976-78; Wash Coun Lawyers, 1976-78; Houston Area Urban League, 1979-; State Bar Tex, Bar Jour Comm, 1980; brd dir, Am Assn Blacks Energy, 1980; chairperson, Black Women Lawyers Assn, 1980; pres, Houston Lawyers Assc, 1983-84; pres, Houston Metro Ministries, 1984-85; dir, Children's Museum, 1985-; dir, Tex Young Lawyers Assc, 1986; dir, Sam Houston Area Coun Boy Scouts Am, 1987-; Alpha Kappa Omega Chap, Houston, TX, 1988-; Congressional Children's Caucus, the Afghan Caucus; founder & co-chairperson, Pakistan Caucus; founder & co chairperson, Algerian Caucus; mem, Alpha Kappa Alpha Sorority Inc. **Honors/Awds:** Outstanding Young Lawyer, Pampered Lady Boutique Awards, Luncheon NY,1977; Womens Day Speaker Award, Linden Blvd Seventh Day Adven Chap, NY, 1978; Rising Star of Texas Award, Tex Bus Mag, 1983; Outstanding Young Houstonian Award, C of C, 1984; Outstanding Service Award, Houston Lawyers Assn, 1984; Outstanding Young Lawyer of Houston, 1985; Outstanding History Maker (Legal), Riverside Gen Hosp Awards Prog, 1987; 2006 Award for Policy, 16th Annual Phillip Burton Immigration & Civil Rights Awards,2006; Revelation Urban Dev Inst, drum Major Award; Natl Mental Health Assn, Legislator Of the Year Award. **Special Achievements:** Named one of Houston's 20 Most Influential Black Women 1984; the only female to serve as a Ranking Member of a Judiciary Subcommittee, has been hailed by "Congressional Quarterly" as one of the 50 most effective members of Congress and by "U.S. News and World Report" as one of the 10 most influential legislators in the House of Representatives. Introduced legislation to enhance federal enforcement of hate crimes with H.R. 254, the David Ray Hate Crimes Prevention of 2007; played a significant role in the recent renewal and reauthorization of the Voting Rights Act; contributed an amendment to the NASA reauthorization bill. **Business Addr:** Congresswoman, US House of Representatives, Houston Office, 1919 Smith St Suite 1180, Houston, TX 77002, **Business Phone:** (713)655-0050.

LEE, SHIRLEY FREEMAN
Association executive. **Personal:** Born May 6, 1928, Cleveland, OH; daughter of Marvin and Vivian Salvant; married Douglas F Lee (deceased); children: Vivian & Durriyya (deceased). **Educ:** Notre Dame Col, BA, 1950; Boston Col, Sch Social Work, MSW, 1952; Case Western Res Univ, 1980-. **Career:** Association Executive (retired); Com Mass Div Child Guardianship, foster home, 1954-58; Head Start, supvr, 1965; Boston Redevelopment Authority, relocation spec, 1968-71; De Paul Infant Home, admin, 1981-83; Ohio Licensed Independent Social Worker, 1986; Catholic Soc Serv, Cuyahoga City, Adminr Day Care Ctr, counsel outpatient mental health, 1997. **Orgs:** Delta Sigma Theta; bd dir, Long Beach & Van Nuys Sch Bus, 1977-89. **Home Addr:** 14221 Kingsford Ave, Cleveland, OH 44128.

LEE, DR. SILAS, III
Educator. **Personal:** Born Jul 24, 1954, New Orleans, LA; son of Henrietta Johnson and Silas Jr; divorced. **Educ:** Loyola Univ, BA, 1976; Univ New Orleans, MA, 1979, PhD(urban studies), 1999. **Career:** Silas Lee & Assoc, pres, 1982-; Consult, Ed Found,

1984-; Xavier Univ, New Orleans, LA, sociol instr, 1988; Pub opinion pollster & analyst local & nat media; asst prof sociol; Dept Sociol Xavier Univ, prof, currently. **Orgs:** Vice chmn, Nat Black Tourism Asn, 1989. **Honors/Awds:** Honorary Secy State, LA 1984; Court Certified Expert, Social & Econ Status Blacks & Pub Opinion Res, Eastern Dist La Court & Fed District Court. **Special Achievements:** First Black Opinion Pollster in New Orleans; Published the Economic Profile Blacks & Whites New Orleans. **Business Addr:** Assistant Professor, Xavier University, Department Sociol, 1 Drexel Dr 500 Xavier S Bldg, PO Box 32 B, New Orleans, LA 70125-1098.*

LEE, SPIKE
Movie director, actor, writer. **Personal:** Born Mar 20, 1957, Atlanta, GA; son of William James Edwards III and Jacquelyn Shelton; married Tonya Lynette Lewis, Jan 1, 1993; children: Satchel Lewis & Jackson. **Educ:** Clark Atlanta Univ, Morehouse Col, BA, mass commun; New York Univ, Sch Arts, MFA, film & TV, 1979. **Career:** Forty Acres & A Mule Film works, owner, 1986-; Spikes Joint, owner, 1990-; Spike DDB, pres & chief exec owner, currently; Films: Shes Gotta Have It, dir, producer & writer, 1986; Sch Daze, dir, producer & writer, 1988; Dothe Right Thing, dir, writer & producer, 1989; Mo Better Blues, dir, writer & producer, 1990; Jungle Fever, dir, writer & producer, 1991; Malcolm X, dir & producer, 1992; Crooklyn, dir, writer & producer, 1994; Clockers, dir, writer & producer, 1995; Get on the Bus, dir & producer, 1996; 4 Little Girls, dir & producer, 1997; The Original Kings of Comedy, dir & producer, 2000; Bamboozled, dir, writer & producer, 2000; Come Rainor Come Shine, dir, 2001; Jim Brown: All American, dir & producer, 2002; The 25th Hour, dir & producer, 2002; She Hate Me, dir, writer & producer, 2004; Sucker Free City, dir & producer, 2004; Jesus Children of America, dir, 2005; All the Invisible Children, dir & producer, 2005; Inside Man, dir, 2006; Lovers & Haters, dir, 2007; Harvard Univ, instructor; New YorkUniv, Kanbar Inst of Film & Television, artistic dir, 2002-; co-author childrens book, Please Baby Please, 2002; TV Progs: "Pavarotti & Friends for the Children of Liberia", 1998; "A Huey P. Newton Story", 2001; "The Concert for New York City", 2001; "Jim Brown: All American", 2002; "Sucker Free City", 2004; "Miracles Boys", 2005; "When the Levees Broke", 2006;"Shark", 2006; "Chapelles Show", 2006; "M.O.N.Y", 2008; Music Videos:"Sunless Saturday", 1991; "White Lines (Dont Do It)", 1993;"Breakfast at Dennys", 1994; "They Dont Care About Us", 1996. **Honors/Awds:** Student Academy Award, Acad Motion Picture Arts & Sci, 1982; New Generation Award, LA Film Critics; Prix de Jeunesse, Cannes Film Festival, 1986; Special Mention, 1996; Honorary French Academy of Cinema Award, 2002; Filmmaker Trumpet Award, 2003; Innovator Award, 2004; Black Movie Award, 2006; Human Rights Film Network Award, 2006; Venice Horizons Documentary Award, 2006; Black Reel, 2006; Image Award, 2007; Emmy Award, 2007. **Special Achievements:** Nominated Oscar, 1990 & 1998; Nominated Emmy, 1998. **Business Addr:** President, Chief Executive Officer, Spike DDB, 437 Madison Ave, New York, NY 10022, **Business Phone:** (212)415-3100.

LEE, TAMELA JEAN
Executive. **Personal:** Born Feb 9, 1959, Denver, CO; daughter of Gentry and Patsy Burks; married Kyle Robert, Jan 27, 1982; children: Taja & Blaine. **Educ:** Howard Univ, finance, 1982. **Career:** Wells Fargo (formerly First Interstate Bank Denver), credit analyst, 1982-83; Bank One (formerly Denver Nat Bank), corp loan Officer, 1983-89; Fedn Deposit Ins Corp, bank examr, liquidation specialist, 1989-93; Pvt consult bus, 1993-94; Small Bus Develop Ctr, circuit rider, 1994-95, dir, 1995-. **Orgs:** Leadership Denver Alumni Asn, 1996-; bd mem, Human Servs Inc, 1997-; Colo Lending Source, 1997-; Am Coc Execs, 1998-; bd mem, Colo Enterprise Fund, 1998-; Denver Urban Econ Develop Corp, 2002-; Better Bus Bur, 2002-; Rocky Mountain Minority Supplier Develop Coun, 2002. **Honors/Awds:** ASBDC Star Performer, Asn Small Bus Develop Ctrs, 1997; Diamond Award, US Small Bus Admin, Col Dist Off Dist Dir's, 2000. **Business Addr:** Director, Small Business Development Center, 1445 Market St, Denver, CO 80202, **Business Phone:** (303)620-8086.

LEE, VIVIAN BOOKER
Government official. **Personal:** Born Jan 28, 1938, Spring, TX; daughter of Alvirita Wells Little; children: Anthony. **Educ:** Registered Nurse Cert, 1958; Pub Health Cert, 1959; Univ Wash, BS, 1959, Master's Degree Nursing Admin, 1961; Sch Nurse Cert, 1967; Univ Puget Sound, M Pub Admin, 1980. **Career:** Government official (retired); Va Hosp, Seattle, psychiat nurse, 1959-60; Group Health Corp Puget Sound, outpatient clinic nurse, 1961-66; Seattle Pub Sch, sch nurse, 1966-68; Renton Sch, supvr group health hosp & title I health supvr, 1968-72; Health Care Consult & Community Volunteer, 1994;Off Women's Health, Off Regional Health Admin, US Pub Health Serv, Region X, Seattle, founding dir, 1993-94, Regional Mgr Title X Family Planning Prog, 1980; Title X Family Planning Prog, US PHS, Region X, Seattle, reg mgr, 1980-93, Regional Women's Health Coordr, 1984-93; Region X Family Planning & Maternal & Child Health Progs, pub health adv, 1975-80, Region X Adolescent Health Coordr, 1975-91, first PHS Region X Minority Health Coordr, 1987-92, PHS EEO investr; US PHS, Region X, PHS EEO Officer, prog mgt officer, 1972-75; Emer Rm Nursing, Va Mason & Univ Hosp; Psychiat Nursing, Vet Admin Hosp; Pub Health Nursing, Seattle/King Co DPH; Sch Nursing Seattle & Renton Sch Dists; relief supvr, Outpatient Clin Servs; Hosp Nursing Supvr Group Health Cooperative, Puget Sound; Nurse instr, 50th Gen Hosp Army Reserve Corp, 1960-64. **Orgs:** Univ Wash Nurses Alumnae Asn; Found Int Understanding through Studs; Delta Sigma Theta; Girls Clubs Inc; participant, White House Conf Civil Rights, 1966; Food Nutrit Health & C, 1969-70; Nat Family Planning & Reproductive Health Asn, Wash State Family Planning Coun; Wash Alliance Concerned With Sch Age Pregnancy; Univ Wash Minority Community Advy Comn; Rainier Beach United Methodist Church, Univ Wash Alumni Asn, bd, Multicultural Alumni partnership Club, Univ Wash Alumni Asn; Univ Wash Diversity Coalition; Univ Wash Diversity coun; Mary Mahoney Prof Nurses Orgn, Nat Family Planning & Reproductive Health Asn; Wash State Asn Black Health Profs; Alan Guttmacher Inst. **Honors/Awds:** Outstanding Performance Award for Promoting Women's Equality, Dept HEW, 1975; DHHS Sustained Superior Performance Awards, 1973-90; HRSA Award for Excellence, 1982; Nurse of the Year, Wash Sch, 1972; Outstanding Dedication Award Wash State Coun Family Planning, 1978; Annual Award of Family Planning Advocates of Oregon State, 1983, 1987 & 1990; Region X Clinician Award is named "The Vivian O Lee Clinician of the Year Award", 1987; WACSAP Award, 1988; NFPRHA Award, 1991; Chief Nurse Officer's Award, US Pub Health Serv, 1993; Certificate of Recognition, Mary Mahoney Prof Nurses Orgn, 1995; Irving Kushner Award, Nat Family Planning & Reproductive Health Asn, 1995; Certificate of Appreciation, US PHS, Region X, African-American Women's Health Care, 1994; Exemplary Service Award, Surgeon Gen US, Dr Joycelyn Elders, 24 yrs pub serv, 1994; Distinguished Service Award, US PHS Dep Asst Secy, Population Affairs, Wash, DC, 1994; Special Honors, nationwide group RPC's for FPS; Dep Asst Secy, Women's Health &the Dir of the PHS Office on Women's Health, US PHS, DHHS, 1994; PHS Region X Office Women's Health Annual Award, 1996; UWAA Volunteer of the Year, 1996; University Washington Annual Charles E Ode guard Award, 2000; Nordstrom Community Service Award, 2001; WWAA Distinguished Alumnus Award, 2003. **Special Achievements:** Co-author of eight publications; Family Planning Services for Southeast Asians, Chlamydia, 1990 Health Objectives for the Nation, Title X Family Planning Prog, Pap Smear quality assurance; Region X Women's Health. **Military Serv:** Fiftieth Gen Hosp Reserve Corps, 1959-63. **Home Addr:** 6323 Sand Point Way NE, Seattle, WA 98115, **Home Phone:** (206)524-1312. *

LEE, VIVIAN O
Government official. **Educ:** Univ Wash Sch Nursing, BSN, 1959. **Career:** Government official (retired); US Pub Health Serv, regional prog mgr, Off Women's Health, dir, 1995. **Honors/Awds:** Distinguished Alumna, Univ Wash Sch Nursing, 1993; Vivian O Lee Women's Health Award, named in honor, 1995; Charles E. Odegaard Award, 2000. *

LEE, W. RANDOLPH
Administrator, business owner. **Career:** Anheuser-Busch Company Inc, mgr; Raven Transp, pres & owner, 1985-. **Orgs:** Jacksonville Minority Bus Develop Coun. **Special Achievements:** Transport Company which is ranked No 1 on The Business Journal's list of the top 50 minority-owned businesses in Northeast Florida. **Business Addr:** President, Owner, Raven Transport Company, 6800 Broadway Ave, Jacksonville, FL 32254, **Business Phone:** (904)880-1515.*

LEE, WILLIAM FRANCIS, JR. See LEE, DR. ALLEN FRANCIS, JR.

LEE, WILLIAM H
Publisher. **Personal:** Born May 29, 1936, Austin, TX; son of Rev Charles R; married Kathryn Charles; children: Roderick Joseph, William Hanford Jr & Lawrence Charles. **Educ:** Univ Calif, BA, 1957; Sacramento State Col, attended 1953-55. **Career:** Lee Sacramento Observer, pres, publ, currently; Lee Publ Co, pres. **Orgs:** Secy, bd dir, Nat Newspaper Publs Asn, 1970-73; pres, W Coast Black Publs Asn, 1974-; Delta Sigma Chi Journalism Frat; comnr, Sacramento County Welfare Commn; founder, past pres, Men's Civil League Sacramento; bd dir, Sacramento Nat Asn Advan Colored People Credit Union; United Christian Ctr; dir, Sacramento Cent YMCA; Sacramento Urban League; United Way; Sacramento County, Am Cancer Soc; bd chmn, Sacramento Bus Coordinating Coun; co-founder, Sacramento Area Black Caucus; vice-chmn, Cancer Fund Drive; Sacramento Comm Urban Renewal; Statewide Comm Voter Regist. **Honors/Awds:** Sacramento's Outstanding Young Man of Year, 1965; Distinguished Serv Award, Sacramento C of C; John B Russwurm Trophy, 1973, 1975; Media Award, Western Regional Conf Black Elected Officials, 1973; United Negro Col Fund, 1975; Nat Media Appreciation Award; Exemplary Leader Award Dinner, 2004; Numerous nat & local newspaper awards; other civic leadership citations. **Military Serv:** USAFR, 1959-65. **Business Addr:** Founder, Publisher, The OBSERVER Newspapers, 2330 Alhambra Blvd, Sacramento, CA 95817, **Business Phone:** (916)452-4781.

LEE, WILLIAM JAMES EDWARDS, III (BILL LEE)
Musician, writer. **Personal:** Born Jul 23, 1928, Snow Hill, AL; son of Arnold W III and Alberta Grace Edwards; married Jacquelyn Shelton, Jun 7, 1954 (deceased); children: Shelton, Chris, David, Joie & Cinque; married Susan Kaplan, Aug 9, 1985; children: Arnold Tone Kaplan-Lee VI. **Educ:** Morehouse Col, BA, 1951. **Career:** Self-employed jazz musician, 1950-; Folk Jazz Opera, Village Vanguard, 1968; Theatre in the St, Youth In Action, Children's Folk Jazz Opera, Little Johnny, dir & writer, 1971; Folk Jazz Opera, Alice Tully Hall, 1972; Folk Jazz Opera, Hampton Univ, 1973; Folk Jazz Opera, various Col campuses, 1975; Essex County Community Col, bass violin & ARO literature teacher, 1979-80; 29-B-Folk Jazz Opera, 1981; Colored Col Folk Jazz Opera,1986; She's Gotta Have It, 1991; West chester Community Col, Lectr, Movie Music, 1992; Opera: The Depot, One Mile East, Baby Sweets, The Quarter, The Rabbi, Monica, Juan Valdez. **Orgs:** Founder, pres, musical dir, The NYK Bass Violin Choir, 1968-; Co-founder, co-musical dir, The Brass Co, 1970; founder, musical dir, The Desendents Mike & Phoebe, 1971-77; founder, dir, The Natural Spiritual Orchestra, 1982-; co-founder, musical dir, Noah's Ark, 1989-; Bill Lee & Mo' Betta' Quartet, 1990; founder, Jacobs Ladder, children's chorus, 1991; musical dir, His Wonders to Perform, umbrella group, 1991; The Family Tree Singers; Tone as Is. **Honors/Awds:** Composing Grant, The Natioanal Endowment Arts, 1979, 1982; The LA Critics Awards, Best Movie Picture Score, Do the Right Thing, 1988; Columbia Records Citation, 300000 record sales, Mo' Better Blues, 1990; Borough of Brooklyn, Howard Golden Citation Service, 1991; has written numerous folk-jazz operas. **Business Addr:** President, New Version Music, 165 Washington Pk, Brooklyn, NY 11201, **Business Phone:** (718)522-5802.*

LEE, WILLIAM THOMAS
Labor activist, executive director. **Personal:** Born Mar 27, 1942, Philadelphia, PA; son of Walter and Thelma Harper; married Celestine Tolbert Lee, Mar 25, 1978; children: Marie, Thomas & Melissa Cora. **Educ:** Temple Univ, Philadelphia, PA, BA, acct, 1966. **Career:** Budd Co, Philadelphia, PA, cost acct, 1966-67; Philadelphia Dress Joint Bd Street, Philadelphia, PA, asst mgr, bus agent, organizer, 1967-85; Local 132-98-102, ILGWU, New York, NY, mgr/secy, 1985-96; New York-New Jersey Regional Joint Bd, mgr, 1996-2001; UNITE HERE CLC, exec dir, 2001-. **Orgs:** Bd dirs, Empire Blue Cross/Blue Shield, 1988-; Nat Asn Advan Colored People, 1988-; Jewish Labor Comt, 1978-; Temple Varsity Club, 1966-; bd mem, A Philip Randolph Inst, 1988-. **Honors/Awds:** Achievement Award, Nat Asn Advan Colored People, 1988; Achievement Award, Philadelphia S Jersey Dist Coun, 1985; "Spirit of Life Award", City Hope Med Ctr, 1991. **Business Addr:** Executive Director, UNITE HERE CLC, 275 7th Ave, New York, NY 10001-6708, **Business Phone:** (212)265-7000.

LEE-EDDIE, DEBORAH
Executive. **Educ:** Univ Michi, Ann Arbor, BA, psychology, MA, health services admin; American Col Healthcare Execs. **Career:** Brackenridge Hosp, Texas, chief exec officer, chief operating officer, 1991-94; Univ Miami & Jackson Memorial Hosp, sr v pres, chief admin officer, 1995-98; Nat Assoc Health Serv executives, past pres, 1997-99; Kaiser Permanente Hospitals and Health Plans, sr v pres, serv area mgr, 1998-2000; Catholic Health Initiatives, sr vpres, CIO, currently. **Honors/Awds:** Senior Healthcare executive Award, 2002; Nat Quality Award, Judges Panel Malcolm Baldrige, 2003. **Business Addr:** Senior Vice President, Catholic Health Initiatives, 1999 Broadway Suite 2600, Denver, CO 80202, **Business Phone:** (303)298-9100.*

LEEK, SANDRA D
Lawyer. **Personal:** Born Oct 8, 1954, Durham, NC; daughter of J Donald and Inez Rempson Anderson. **Educ:** Tufts Univ, Medford, MA, BA, polit sci, 1976; Ind Univ, Bloomington, IN, JD, 1979. **Career:** Legal Serv Orgn Ind Inc, Indianapolis, IN, staff atty, 1979-81, managing atty, 1986-90; Ind Legal Serv Support Ctr, dir, 1981-86; Ind Dept Employment & Training Serv, chairperson review bd mem, unemployment ins, 1990-92; Baker & Daniels LLP, of coun, currently. **Orgs:** Delta Sigma Theta Sorority Inc, 1979-; Am Bar Asn, 1979-; Ind State Bar Asn, 1979-; Indianapolis Bar Asn, 1979-; Civil Comt Rep, Nat Legal Aid & Defender Asn, 1981-89; Nat Bar Asn, 1982-; chmn, Pub Affairs Indy YWCA, 1983-86; chmn, Polit Action, Coalition 100 Black Women, 1986-88; second vpres, bd mgrs, Fall Creek YMCA, 1987-88; pres, Marion City Bar Asn, 1987-88; exec comt, NAACP, Indianapolis Br, 1988-; Links, Inc, 1988-; corp atty, Ind Black Expo, Inc, 1988-; Racial Diversity Legal Profession Comt; Comt Character & Fitness; Ind Bd Law Examrs; Race Rels Leadership Network Indianapolis. **Honors/Awds:** Woman of Achievement, Indy YWCA, 1985; Outstanding Contribution, Legal Serv Orgn Ind Inc, 1986, Outstanding Communnity Service, Marion County Bar Asn, 1989; Ind highest honor of Sagamore of the Wabash Award; Dr. Andrew J Brown Award for Leadership in Civil Rights; Legacy & Leadership Award, Thurgood Marshall Scholar Fund; Spirit of Justice Award, Dr. Martin Luther King Jr Ind Holiday Comn. **Special Achievements:** exec ed, "You and the Law," 1983, 1985, 1992; moderator, Law for Laymen TV series, 1983, 1984, 1985. **Home Addr:** 2323 W 66th St, Indianapolis, IN 46260, **Home Phone:** (317)255-5892. **Business Addr:** Of Counsel, Baker & Daniels LLP, 300 N Meridian St Suite 2700, Indianapolis, IN 46204, **Business Phone:** (317)237-0300.

LEEKE, JOHN F.
Educator, president (organization). **Personal:** Born May 19, 1939, Indianapolis, IN; married Therese Gartin; children: Michael,

Madelyn, Mark & Matthew. **Educ:** Ind State Univ, BS, 1961; Univ Mich, MS, 1966; Union Grad Sch, PhD, 1977. **Career:** Ind State & Penal Farm, counsr, 1962; DC Pub Sch, teacher, 1962-63; Flint Community Schs, teacher, 1963-68; NEA, instr, prof, develop spec, 1968-85; John F Leeke Assoc Inc, orgn develop consult, 1985-, pres, currently; Nat Training Lab App Behav Sci, consult; Johnson & Johnson Pharmaceut Core States, staff; US Dept Agr Grad Sch, staff; Corning Inc, staff; Kodak, staff; Nat Inst Drug Abuse, consult; Consumer Product Safety Comn, consult; Bell Labs, consult; GS USA, consult; Ind State Dept Inst, fac. **Orgs:** St Joseph Churh, Landover, MD; Neighborhood Civic Orgn; Pi Lambda Phi; Nat Schs Brd Assn. **Honors/Awds:** Acheivement Recognition, Pi Lambda Phi. **Business Addr:** President, Consultant, John F Leeke Associates Inc, 11305 Indian Wells Lane, Mitchellville, MD 20721, **Business Phone:** (301)350-0925.

LEEKE, MADELYN CHERYL
Artist, writer, consultant. **Personal:** Born Dec 18, 1964, Flint, MI; daughter of John and Therese Leeke. **Educ:** Morgan State Univ, BA, 1986; Howard Univ Sch Law, JD, 1989; Georgetown Univ Law Ctr, LLM, 1991. **Career:** Commodities Futures Trading Comn, legal adv, 1989-90; John F Leeke Assocs Inc, res policy analyst, 1990-93; DC Off Treas, debt mgr, 1993-95; The Hamilton Securities Group, Inc, mgr, 1996-97; Kiamsha.com, found, pres, artist, author & bus consult, 1997-. **Orgs:** A Salon Ltd; Women's Caucus Art; bus volunteer, Cultural Alliance Greater WASH; Yoga Alliance; Soc Arts Healthcare; Cultural Alliance Greater Washington's Bus Volunteer Prog; Sigma Gamma Rho Sorority, Inc; All Souls Unitarian Church. **Business Addr:** Founder, President, Kiamsha.com, PO Box 4444, Washington, DC 20010, **Business Phone:** (202)444-4444.*

LEEPER, RONALD JAMES
Government official. **Personal:** Born Dec 14, 1944, Charlotte, NC; married Phyllis Mack; children: Rhonda & Atiba. **Career:** LRT & Assoc Consult Firm, pres; L&S Housing Corp, pres; Charlotte City Coun, former coun mem; RJ Leeper Construct Co Inc, pres, currently. **Orgs:** Chmn city coun, Community Develop Comm, 1979-87; past pres, NC Black Elected Munic Off Assoc, 1982; former mem bd dir, Urban League, 1983; chmn, Charlotte-Meck Lenburg Black Elected Off, 1984-85; organizer, Westpark Youth Athletic Asn; organizer, Colony Acres Home Owners Asn; former bd dir, Nat Conf Christians & Jews; bd mem, Visitors Boys Town NC; organizer, Vote Task Force; past pres, St Mark's United Methodist Church; bd mem, Habitat for Humanities; past chmn, bd dirs, C W Williams Health Ctr; former bd mem, Z Smith Reynolds; organizer, Save the Seed; former bd mem, Metrop YMCA. **Honors/Awds:** Certificate of Appreciation, St Mark's United Methodist Church, 1978 & 1980; Sr Citizen United Serv Christian Social Concern, 1980; Certificate of Appreciation, Black Polit Awareness League, Winston-Salem, NC, 1984; Meritorious Award, Nat Asn Advan Colored People, Outstanding Community Serv, 1984; Selected as one of ten Outstanding Men in America, 1979-81; Award of Appreciation for Service to Senior Citizens & the Handicapped, Sr Citizens United, 1981; Outstanding Community Service Award, Alpha Kappa Alpha Sorority, 1980; Recognized as Chart Pres, NC-BEMCO, 1982; YMCA Outstanding Service Award, Community Serv Prog, 1987; Hon Neighbor of the Year Award, Charlotte Organizing Prog, 1987; Award of Appreciation, Charlotte Civic League Leadership, 1987; Award of Appreciation, Nat Asn Negro Bus & Prof Women's Club, 1987; Martin Luther King Gold Medallion,Charlotte-Mecklenburg Community Rels Comn, 1991; Citizen of the Year, Community Pride Mazina, 1994; Honorary Doctor of Laws, Livingston Col, 2004. **Business Addr:** President, Ronald J Leeper Company Inc, 601 Morris St, Charlotte, NC 28202-1317, **Business Phone:** (704)522-8700.

LEE SANG, SHARON NOLAN
Judge, lawyer. **Personal:** Born Mar 26, 1946, Kansas City, KS; daughter of James Dewitt and Mary Louise Davis; divorced; children: David Lee Nolan. **Educ:** Metropolitan Jr Col, AA, 1966; Univ Mo Kans City, BA, 1968; Howard Univ, Sch Law, JD, 1972. **Career:** US Virgin Islands & US, pvt law pract, 1973-86; law clerk NYK Supreme Ct justice, 1986; NYC Bd Educ, impartial hearing officer, 1987; Abyssinian Baptist Church, New York City, lawyer, coun, 1987-89; NY State Dept Motor Vehicles, 1989-. **Orgs:** Secy, assoc dir, Nat Bar Asn, Region II, 1984; Metropolitan Black Bar Asn, 1986-98; panel mem, Ny State Supreme Ct, Med Malpractice Bd, 1986-89; Metrop Black Bar Scholarship Fund, 1986-; NY Civil Ct Arbritrator, 1986-; pres, Asn Ade Law Judges NY State Dept Motor Vehicles, 1992-; trustee, Brooklyn Bar Asn, 1995-98; lay mem, Am Diabetes Asn, Harlem Coalition, 1996-; soloist, Abyssinian Baptist Church, Chancel Choir; coun leader, Ny State Pub Employees Fed, Afl-Cio, 1996-. **Honors/Awds:** Award, Nat Asn Negro Bus & Pressional Women, 1999. **Special Achievements:** Carole King's background singer; Saundra Reeves's background singer, 1995-; soloist, City Bar Choir, Asn of the Bar of the City of NY, gospel singer since age 5. **Business Addr:** Administrative Law Judge, New York State Department of Motor Vehicles, 6 Empire State Plz, Albany, NY 12228, **Business Phone:** (518)473-5595.

LEFEBVRE, DALE
Executive. **Personal:** Born Jan 1, 1971, Beaumont, TX. **Educ:** Mass Inst Technol, BS, elec eng; Harvard Law Sch, JD; Harvard Bus Sch, MBA. **Career:** Testa, Hurwitz & Thibeault LLP, law consult; McKinsey & Co, mgt consult; Morgan Stanley Capital Partners, consult; Blue Capital, consult; First Union Pvt Equity Group, consult; etang.com, US Oper, head, chief financial officer; McKinney & Co, founder; AIC Ltd, managing partner; Converge Global Trading, chmn; Pharos Capital Group LLC, chmn, ceo & managing partner, currently. **Orgs:** Bd mem, Smart Direct Inc; bd mem, Atherotech Inc; Nat Urban League Inc; African Am Stud Union. **Special Achievements:** Named as 10th largest African American-owned US business by Black Enterprise magazine in 2004. **Business Addr:** Managing Partner, Pharos Capital Group LLC, 100 Crescent Ct Suite 1740, Dallas, TX 75201, **Business Phone:** (214)855-0194.*

LEFEBVRE, DALE
Executive. **Personal:** Born Jan 1, 1971, Beaumont, TX. **Educ:** Massachusetts Inst Technol, BS, Elec Eng Dept; Harvard Law Sch, JD; Harvard Bus Sch, MBA. **Career:** Bell Laboratories, res; Converge Global Trading, chmn; AIC Caribbean Pvt Equity Fund, managing patner; McKinsey & Co, strategy, pricing & corp restructuring; Morgan Stanley Capital Partners, Morgan Stanley MBA; First Union Pvt Equity Group; Testa Hurwitz & Thibeault LLP, Boston; MacFarlanes, London; Pharos Capital Group LLC, managing partner, currently. **Orgs:** Bd mem, Nat Urban League. **Honors/Awds:** The Henry Crown Fellows, 2006. **Special Achievements:** Black Enterprise magazine named Dale one of "America's Most Powerful Players Under 40". **Business Addr:** Managing Partner, AIC PRivate Equity, E&Y Corporate Centre, Bush Hill & Bay St, St Michael, Barbados, West Indies, **Business Phone:** 888-710-4242.

LEFFALL, LASALLE D
Administrator, president (organization). **Educ:** Harvard Univ, BA, JD, & MBA. **Career:** Lockhart Companies Inc, bd dirs, currently; NHP Found, pres, adv & chief operating officer, currently. **Business Phone:** (202)789-5300.*

LEFFALL, DR. LASALLE DOHENY, JR.
Oncologist, educator. **Personal:** Born May 22, 1930, Tallahassee, FL; son of LaSalle D, Sr and Martha Leffall; married Ruth McWilliams, Aug 18, 1956; children: LaSalle III. **Educ:** Fla A&M Col, BS, summa cum laude, 1948; Howard Univ, MD, 1952. **Career:** Homer G. Phillips Hosp, St. Louis, med training, 1953-54; Freed mans Hosp, from asst resident surg to chief resident surg, 1953-57; DC Gen Hosp, asst resident surg, 1954-55; Memorial Sloan-Kettering Hosp, sr fel, cancer surg, 1957-59; US Army Hosp, Munich, Ger, 1960-61; Howard Univ, fac, 1962, asst prof, 1970, chmn, dept surg; Howard Univ Col Med, asst dean, 1964-70, acting dean, 1970, prof chmn dept surg, 1970-95, prof surg, 1995-. **Orgs:** Nat Med Asn, 1962; SE Surg Congress, 1970; Soc Surg Chmn, 1970; Alpha Omega Alpha, 1972; Inst Med Nat Acad Sci, 1973; Amer Surg Asn, 1976; pres, Am Cancer Soc, 1979; pres, Soc Surgical Oncology, 1978-79; Nat Urban League; NAACP; YMCA; Alpha Phi Alpha; Sigma Pi Phi; Nat Cancer Adv Bd, 1980; Am Bd Surg, 1981; Cosmos Club; Comm Calif; Am Col Surg, 1983; pres, Soc Surg Chairmen, 1988-90; exec comt chmn, United Way of Am, 1989-92; Am Col Surgs, pres, 1995-96. **Honors/Awds:** First prize, Charles R Drew Fundamental Forum, 1954; Outstanding Young Man of Year, 1965; Outstanding Educator in Am, Fla A&M 1971, 1974; William H Sinkler Memorial Award, 1972; Star Surgeon Newsletter NMA, 1973; St George Medal & Citation, Amer Cancer Soc, 1977. **Special Achievements:** First African-American president of the American Cancer Society. First African-American president of the American College of Surgeons. Heauthored or coathored over 130 articles and chapters. To honor him in Quincy, Florida and a hospital surgical wing has been given his name in1989. **Military Serv:** AUS, capt, 1960-61. **Business Addr:** Professor, Howard University Hospital, Department of Surgery, 520 W St NW, Washington, DC 20059, **Business Phone:** (202)806-6270.

LEFLORE, DR. LARRY
Government official, educator, counselor. **Personal:** Born Oct 1, 1949, Cuba, AL; married Amanda L Collins. **Educ:** William Carey Col, BA, sociol, 1971; Univ Southern Miss, MS, community coun, 1974, MS, family life studies/psychol, 1980; Fla State Univ, PhD, sociol, 1984. **Career:** Columbia Training Sch, inst social worker, 1971-72; Miss Dept Youth Serv Forrest City, Youth Ct, youth ct counr, 1972-74, intake counr, 1974-76, regional supvr, 1976-77; Univ Southern Miss, from instr to prof, 1977-99; pvt pract, marriage & family therapist, 1982-; US Dept Health & Human Serv, Ctr Substance Abuse Prev, grant reviewer, 1989-; US Dept Justice, Off Juvenile Justice & Delinquency, grant reviewer, 1990-; Miss C Justice Act Prog, adminr, 1991-; Forrest Gen Hosps, Pine Grove, Life Focus Ctr, marriage & family therapist, 1992-; W Va Univ, Dept Family & Consumer Sci, adj prof, 1999-, Ctr 4-H & Youth, Family & Adult Develop, exten prof & ctr dir, 1999-; Substance Abuse Ment Health Serv Admin, 2001-; Univ S Miss, adj prof, 2001-; Tex Women's Univ, Dept Family Sci, prof & chair, currently. **Orgs:** Nat Col Juvenile Ct Judges; comnr, Gov Comn Standards & Goals Criminal Justice; bd dir, Spel Serv Prog, William Carey Col; Opportunity House; curric comn mem, Miss Judicial Col, 1984-; adv comn, Governor's Miss Juvenile Justice, 1984-; consult, Jackson County Dept Pub Welfare, 1987-; bd dir, Hattiesburg Miss Main St Proj, 1987-88; adv bd mem, Grad Sch Social Work, Univ Southern Miss, 1987-89; chair, Youth Coun, Workforce Investment Bd, Region Six, WVa Univ, 2001-. **Honors/Awds:** Faculty Excellence in Service Award, 1989; Harding Faculty Leadership Award, 1992; Heritage Award for Community Service, William Carey Col, 1992; Outstanding Alumus Award, 1992. **Special Achievements:** First African-American elected President, University of Southern Mississippi Faculty Senate, 1990-91; First African American assistant vice president for academic affairs at University of Southern Missisipi, 1994; First African American extension professor and center director at West Virginia University. **Business Addr:** Professor, Chair, Texas Woman's University, College of Professional Education, Dept Family Sci, PO Box 425769, Denton, TX 76204, **Business Phone:** (940)898-2685.

LEFLORE, LYAH B
Writer, television producer, administrator. **Personal:** Born Jan 1, 1970, St Louis, MO. **Educ:** Stephens Col, BA, commun media, 1991. **Career:** Writer, Media Executive: Nickelodeon, asst vpres programming, 1991-93; Uptown Entertainment/Universal Tv, dir develop, 1993; Dick Wolf/Wolf Films, assoc producer; Alan Haymon Productions Inc, vpres production & develop; "Midnight Mac", HBO, consult; "New York Undercover", assoc producer; "Between Brothers", Fox, develop exec; "Lawless", Fox, "Grown-Ups", "Off Limits", UPN, producer; Books: Cosmopolitan Girls, co-author, 2004; Last Night a DJ Saved My Life, author, 2006. **Orgs:** Alpha Kappa Alpha Sorority Inc; bd trustees, Stephens Col, 2005-. **Honors/Awds:** Fel, Nat Asn Black Journalists; "25 To Watch Under 25", Essence Magazine's 25th Anniversary issue, 1995; "What 35 Looks Like", Essence Magazine's monumental 35th Anniversary issue, 2005. **Special Achievements:** Second African American to be appointed to the Board of Stephens College. **Business Addr:** Board Member, Stephens College, 1200 E Broadway, Columbia, MO 65215.

LEFLORE, DR. WILLIAM B. **See Obituaries section.**

LEFLORES, GEORGE O., JR.
School administrator. **Personal:** Born Jul 2, 1921, Mobile, AL; children: Victoria Gray, Willie J, George Jr & Claira. **Educ:** Vernon Sch Real Estate, AA, 1962. **Career:** Faith Deliverance Ctr, bd mem, 1972-; Delpaso Hts Sch Dist, clerk sch bd; Project Area Comn, elected bd mem, 1974-82; Sacramento Black Alcohol Ctr, bd mem, 1979-82; Delpaso Heights Sch Dist, elected bd mem, 1981-. **Orgs:** Trustee bd mem, Elks Lodge 587, 1948-85; bd mem, Faith Deliverance Serv, 1972-85; trustee bd mem, Coop Group, 1977-81. **Honors/Awds:** Recognition & Outstanding Valuable Service to the Young People, Search for Solution Award, 1973; Outstanding Service & Board Member Award, SCARE, 1973; Community Service Award, Delpaso Heights Proj Area Comn, 1974; Community Involvement Award, City Sacramento Parks & Recreation Dept, 1981.

LEFTWICH, BYRON ANTRON
Football player. **Personal:** Born Jan 14, 1980, Washington, DC; son of Brenda. **Educ:** Marshall Univ, WVA, bus. **Career:** Jacksonville Jaguars, quarterback, 2003-06; Atlanta Falcons, 2007; Pittsburgh Steelers, 2008; Tampa Bay Buccaneers, 2009-. **Honors/Awds:** MAC's Vern Smith Leadership Award; Walter Camp Nat Offensive Player of the Year Award; Motor City Bowl, 2000. **Special Achievements:** First repeat winner of conf's Offensive Player of the Year in a decade; featured on "Hey Rookie, Welcome to the NFL", 2003. **Business Addr:** Professional Football Player, Tampa Bay Buccaneers, One Buccaneer Place, Tampa, FL 33607, **Business Phone:** (813)870-2700.

LEFTWICH, NORMA BOGUES
Lawyer. **Personal:** Born Aug 8, 1948, New York, NY; married Willie L Jr; children: Curtis. **Educ:** Univ Pittsburgh, BA, 1969; Harvard-Kennedy Sch Govt, Sr Govt Mgrs Prog, 1982; Georgetown Univ, Law Ctr, JD, 1992. **Career:** Boone Young & Assoc, sr consult, 1977; Dept Com, spec asst, 1978-79; Dept Defense, dir; Howard Univ, gen coun, 1995-. **Orgs:** Delta Sigma Theta Sorority, 1968. **Honors/Awds:** Outstanding Achievement, Black Bus Asn LA, 1982, 1986; SBA Award of Excellence, 1984; Special Achievement Award, Dept Defense, 1985; The Roy Wilkins Meritorious Service Award, Nat Asn Advan Colored People, 1985; Governor's Award Commonwealth of Puerto Rico, 1985. **Home Addr:** 1732 Shepherd St NW, Washington, DC 20011, **Home Phone:** (202)882-0807. **Business Addr:** General Counsel, Howard University, Office of the General Counsel, 2400 6th St NW Suite 321, Washington, DC 20059, **Business Phone:** (202)806-2650.

LEFTWICH, WILLIE L.
Lawyer. **Personal:** Born Jun 28, 1937, Washington, DC; married Norma. **Educ:** Howard Univ, BSEE, 1960; George Wash Univ, Sch Law, JD, 1967, LLM, 1972. **Career:** Fed Aviation Admin, patent atty; Hudson Leftwich & Davenport, founding partner; Ga Wash Univ Sch Law, prof; Tech Media Sys Inc, vpres & gen counsel; Dept Transportation FAA, patent atty; Naval Air Systs Command, adv, res engr, res electro-optical engr; NASA, res aero instrumentation engr; dir, Pa Ave Develop Corp; DC Redevelopment Land Agency, dir; Neighborhood Legal Servs Prog, dir; Nat

Inst Trial Advocacy, dir; First Cavalry Div, ordnance officer, 1961-62; Leftwich Moore & Douglas, managing partner, 1985-96; Potomac Surety Ins Co Inc, pres, chief exec officer; Willie's Pots, owner, currently. **Orgs:** DC Bar Asn; DC Redevelop Land Agency; Com Tech Adv Bd DC Judicial Nomination Comn; life mem, Nat Asn Advan Colored People; life mem, Am Bar Asn. **Military Serv:** AUS, lt, 1960-62. **Business Addr:** Owner, Willie's Pots, 12380 Yeawood Dr, Boston, VA 22713, **Business Phone:** (703)330-1173.*

LEGENDRE, HENRI A
Executive, vice president (organization). **Personal:** Born Jul 11, 1924, New York, NY; married Ruth E Mills; children: Renee, Laurette & Jacques. **Educ:** Howard Univ, civil eng ASTP, 1943; City Col NY, liberal arts, 1949; Pratt Inst, dipl arch, 1952. **Career:** Designs for Bus, designer, 1962; Ifill & Johnson Arch, partner, 1963-67; LeGendre Johnson McNeil Arch & Planners, private arch pract, 1978; LeGendre, Purse Architects, PC, vpres, currently. **Orgs:** US Gen Serv Admin Adv Panel A/E Selections, 1977; Am Inst Arch; NY State Asn Arch; NY Soc Arch; Nat Orgn Minority Arch; Am Arbitration Asn; 100 Black Men Inc; Bd Educ Valhalla; Alpha Phi Alpha; Promeatheans Inc; Rotary Int; St George Asn B&P Chap DAV; Order St Vincent, Euclid Lodge 70 F&AM; Arch State NY; Nat Asn Advan Colored People; Westchester Coalition; 9th & 10th Cavalry Horse Asn. **Honors/Awds:** Concrete Indiana Award of Merit, Riverside Park Com & IS, 1977; World Service Award, YMCA Housing Develop, 1979; Certificate of Merit, 139th St Playground NY Asn Arch. **Military Serv:** AUS, 9th cavalry buffalo soldier. **Business Addr:** Vice President, LeGendre Purse Architects PC, 7218 Bevington Woods Lane, Charlotte, NC 28277, **Business Phone:** (704)542-6977.

LEGETTE, TYRONE
Football player. **Personal:** Born Feb 15, 1970, Columbia, SC; married Reginene. **Educ:** Univ Nebr. **Career:** Football player (retired), New Orleans Saints, corner back, 1992-95; Tampa Bay Buccaneers, corner back, 1996-98; San Francisco 49ers, corner back, 1998; Carolina Panthers. 1998.

LEGGETT, CHRISTOPHER J W B
Cardiologist. **Personal:** Born Nov 8, 1960, Cleveland, OH; son of Willie Leggett and Ethel Leggett; married Denise. **Educ:** Princeton Univ, BA, 1982; Case Western Reserve Sch Med, MD. **Career:** John Hopkins Hosp, intern, 1986-89; Emory Univ Sch Med, fel, beginning 1989; Cardiovascular Lab Vet Admin Hosp, Dept Med & Cardiol, physician, 1992-93; Birmingham Sch Med, Dept Cardiol, interventional Cardiol fel, beginning 1993; Nat Practicing Physician Adv Coun, cardiologist, 2002-06; Med Assoc N GA, dir cardiol, currently; Saint Joseph's Hosp, cardiologist, currently. **Business Addr:** Cardiologist, Medical Associates Of North Georgia, 320 Hospital Rd, Canton, GA 30114.

LEGGETT, RENEE
Manager, executive. **Personal:** Born Oct 7, 1949, Cleveland, OH. **Educ:** Fisk Univ, BA, 1972; Northwestern Univ, MA, 1973; NY Univ, MBA, 1980. **Career:** Cleveland State Univ, instr, 1973; Lincoln First Bank, mkt analyst, 1973-76; Fortune Mag, reporter, 1976-79; Mobil Corp, mkt analyst, 1979-81; NY Times, mkt analyst, 1981-82, planning mgr, 1982-83, circulation mkt mgr, 1983-86, advert mkt & prom mgr. **Orgs:** NY Univ Black Alumni Asn; Nat Black MBA Asn; Black Reps Adv NY; tutor, First World Alliance C Ctr; vol fund raiser, Boy Choir Harlem; speaker, New Alliance Pub Schs. **Honors/Awds:** Wall St Journal Student Achievement Award, 1972.

LEGGETTE, VIOLET OLEVIA BROWN
Educator, mayor. **Personal:** Born in Tallula, MS; daughter of Alfred Rufus and Theresa Gary Bowman; married Clyde Lamar Sr, Jul 21, 1957 (divorced); children: Clyde, Melanye, Eric & Terrell. **Educ:** Natchez Jr Col, AA 1955; Tougaloo Col, BS elem educ 1957; Univ Ill, MLS, 1974; Educ Admin, 1996. **Career:** Bob Woods Elem Sch, teacher 1957-74; West Bolivar Sch Dist, Rosedale, MS, media specialist, 1957-78, 1989-96; Bolivar Co Sit, elem libr supr, 1974-78; Town Gunnison, mayor, 1977-97; Delta Pace Presch, dir, 1978-79; Bolivar County Head Start, educ dir 1979-89; W Bolivar Sch Dist, curric staff develop coordr, 1996-2000; Miss Dept Educ, Writing Instrnl Intervention Suppl, Creative Arts Work Group, 2002. **Orgs:** Vice chairperson, MS Democratic Party; chairperson, Bolivar Co Democratic Comn; pres Bolivar Co Sch Dist I Teacher Asn, 1977; vpres, Miss Conf Black Mayors, 1978-88; NAACP; chmn Legis Com MCBM 1978-88; chmn, Miss Inst Small Towns Bd, 1980-2000; Miss Asn Educrs; NEA, Alpha Kappa Alpha Sor; Nat Coun Negro Women. **Honors/Awds:** Outstanding Achievement Award Alcorn Col Chap/Negro Bus & Prof Women Club 1978; Community Serv Award, MS Valley St Univ, 1978; Leadership Award Black Genesis Found, 1979; Mother of theYear, 1988, First Baptist Church.

LEGGON, HERMAN W.
Systems analyst, mathematician. **Personal:** Born Sep 20, 1930, Cleveland, OH; married Zara M. **Educ:** BS, chem, 1953; MS, chem, 1966. **Career:** Union Carbide Corp, systs analyst & mathematician; Dyke Col, part-time instr, bus math, comput sci & applied quantitative techniques; Systs & Comput Techol Corp, supvr tech support micro comput. **Orgs:** Life mem, Alpha Phi Alpha Frat; Juvenile Delinquency ACLD; bd chmn, Am Sickle Cell Anemia Asn; chmn, Am Soc Testing & Mat Comt E31 01; scoutmaster, Troop 370; Nat Asn Advancement Colored People; Urban League; former serv dir, coun man & pres, Coun Oakwood Village. **Home Addr:** 3470 Belvoir, Beachwood, OH 44122.

LEGRAND, BOB SNAKE
Business owner, educator, basketball coach. **Personal:** Born Aug 28, 1943, Nashville, TN; son of Sarah H Joyner; married Gloria Jean Young; children: Lisa, Robert III, Christopher, Brianna & Brian. **Educ:** St Mary's Univ, San Antonio, TX, BA, 1970; Southwest Tex State Univ, MA1973, Professional Cert, Guid & Coun, 1974. **Career:** Jefferson High Sch, San Antonio, TX, head coach, 1970-75; Univ Tex, Arlington, from asst coach to head coach, 1975-87, Irving High Sch, Irving,TX, 1988; Nichols Jr High Sch, counr; Lamar High Sch, counr, currently; Sport 'n' Goods 4 U, owner, currently. **Orgs:** Chmn, Dist 6 Ed Community, Nat Asn Basketball Coaches; chmn, Dist 6memship Community, Nat Asn Basketball Coaches; chmn, United Way Campaign, Univ Tex Arlington 1980; bd dir Arlington Boys Club 1978-82; Arlington Noon Optimist Club; Tex Asn Basketball Coaches. **Honors/Awds:** Man of the Year, Omega Psi Phi, 1980; Honorary Commissioner, Tarrant County Comnrs, 1980; Award for Outstanding Achievement, Omega Psi Phi, 1977; Coach of the Year, Southland Conf, 1981; News Maker of the Year, Fort Worth Press Club, 1981. **Military Serv:** USAF, E-4, 4 yrs. **Home Addr:** 3112 Westwood Dr, Arlington, TX 76012. **Business Addr:** Owner, Sport N Goods 4 U, 3112 Westwood Dr, Arlington, TX 76012, **Business Phone:** (817)919-0750.

LEGRAND, YVETTE MARIE
Management consultant, executive. **Personal:** Born Nov 8, 1950, Chicago, IL. **Educ:** Loyola Univ Chicago, BA, hist, 1971; Univ Chicago, MBA, 1975. **Career:** First Nat Bank, first scholar mgt trainee, 1972-75, acct mgr, 1975-77; Int Mgt Asst United Way Met Chicago, dir, 1977-; First Nat Bank Chicago, loan officer, 1977; Nat Housing Trust, Enterprise Preserv Corp, Chicago Regional Off, dir, currently. **Orgs:** Nat Black MBA Asn, Chicago Chap, 1974-77; vpres, Chicago Jr Asn Com & Indust Found, 1979-80; first black pres, Chicago Jaycees, 1980-81 Vol; Lois R Lowe Women's Div, United Negro Col Fund, 1972-79; vpres pub rel, Chicago Jaycees, 1977-78; dir, Chicago Jazz Gallery, 1978-80; adv comt, Mid-S Planning & Develop Comn; bd mem, Landmarks Preserv Coun Ill; chair, United Way Chicago Priority Grants Comt; First Cong Dist Housing Task Force. **Honors/Awds:** President Award, Honor Chicago Jaycees, 1975-76; Outstanding Chaper Officer, Chicago Jaycees, 1978; Outstanding Young Woman of America, 1979. **Business Addr:** Director Chicago Regional Office, National Housing Trust, Enterprise Preservation Corporation, 1101 30th St NW Suite 400, Washington, DC 20007, **Business Phone:** (202)333-8931.

LEHMAN, DR. CHRISTOPHER PAUL
Educator. **Personal:** Born Oct 14, 1973, Philadelphia, PA; son of Paul Lehman and Marion; married Yolanda K Denson, Jul 11, 1998; children: Imani Karlyn Denson & Erik Paul Denson. **Educ:** Oklahoma State Univ, BA, 1995; Univ Mass-Amherst, MA, hist, 1997, PhD, Afro-Amer studies, 2002. **Career:** Bay Path Col, adj prof, 2000-01; Western New England Col, adj prof, 2000-02; Eastern CT State Univ, adj prof, 2001-02; St Cloud State Univ, asst prof, 2002-07, assoc prof, 2007-. **Orgs:** Phi Eta Sigma, 1992-; Phi Kappa Phi, 1995-; Nat Asn Ethnic Studies, 2000-; Am Historical Asn, 2001-. **Honors/Awds:** Homer L Knight Undergrad Award, Oklahoma State Univ, 1994; Professor of the Year, Multicultural Student Serv, St Cloud State Univ, 2005; Scholarship & Social Justice Award, Minnesota Governor's Comn Statewide Celebration of Rev. Dr. Martin Luther King, Jr. Holiday and the Council on Black Minnesotans, 2008; CHOICE Outstanding Academic Title award for book THE COLORED CARTOON, 2008. **Special Achievements:** Presenter: "Black Images in Disney's Animated Short Films," Rethinking Disney Conference, Florida, 2000; publication: "The New Black Animated Images of 1946," Journal of Popular Film and Television, 2001; "Civil Rights in Twilight: The End of The Civil Rights Movement Era in 1973,"Journal of Black Studies, 2006; American Animated Cartoons Of The Vietnam Era, McFarland & Company, Inc, 2006; The Colored Cartoon, University of Massachusetts Press, 2007; dissertation: "Black Images in American Animated Short Films, 1928-54," 2002; book review? Doing Their Bit: Wartime American Animated Short Films by Michael S. Shull and David E.Wilt, Historical Journal of Film, Radio, and Television, 2005; A CRITICAL HISTORY OF SOUL TRAIN ON TELEVISION, McFarland & Company, Inc., 2008. **Business Addr:** Associate Professor, Saint Cloud State University, Ethnic Studies Department, 51 Building Room 205, 720 4th Ave S, St Cloud, MN 56301-4498, **Business Phone:** (320)308-5127.

LEHMAN, DR. PAUL ROBERT
Educator. **Personal:** Born Apr 18, 1941, Mansura, LA; son of Frances Revare and Kermit; married Marion W White; children: Christopher Paul, Karlyn Elizabeth (deceased) & Jeffrey Robert. **Educ:** La City Col, AA, 1966; Cent State Col, BA, 1969; Cent State Univ, ME, 1971; Lehigh Univ, PhD, 1976. **Career:** Western Electric Co, tester insptct, 1963-66; Stand Oil Calif, credit dept, 1966-67; KOFM radio, music newsman, 1968-69; KWTV, newsman, reporter, writer, ed, photogr, producer & weekend anchorman, 1968-70; CSU, lectr, 1969-71, instr, 1971-73; NCACC, adj prof, 1974-76; Northampton Co Area Community Col, develop co-ordinated col orientation wkshp minority stud, 1975; Cent State Univ, from assoc prof dept eng to prof dept Eng, 1977-88, dean grad col, 1985-88; Blk Am Lit, vol lectr col pub pvt sch churches Radio/TV News, 1974-75; Univ Cent Okla, dean studies, Prof Dept Eng, 1988-; Edmond Arts & Humanities, 1991-. **Orgs:** Nat Jay-Cees; Nat Asn Advan Colored People; Urban League; Heart Asn Nat Asn Press Photogr; stud exec officer, LACC 1966; NEA, OEA, CSEA, NCTE, CEA; vice chmn, Okla Found Humanities, 1988-89; treas, Okla Alliance Arts Educ, 1988-; Okla Folklife Coun; Edmond Community Housing Resource Bd; Afro-Am Southern Asn; Edmond Arts & Humanities; Okla Arthritis Found. **Honors/Awds:** Best actor in minor role, CSC, 1968; dean's honor roll, CSC1968; listed in Contemporary Authors, 1977-78; Lehigh Univ Fel, 1973-76; first dissertation John Oliver Killens, 1976; Award for Service to Urban League Greater Okla City, 1984; Award for Service to Boy Scouts of Am, 1985; Fulbright Senior Specialist, 2004. **Special Achievements:** First black American to teach at CSU, 1969; first black in Oklahoma to anchor weekend TV news, 1969; first black American to receive PhD in English from Lehigh, 1976; Author: The Making of the Negro in Early American Lit, 2003, The Development of A Black Psych in the Works of John Oliver Killens, 2003; book reviewer, The Oklahoman, The Making of the Negro in Early American Lit, second edition, 2006. **Military Serv:** USN, 3rd cl petty off, 1959-63. **Business Addr:** Professor, University of Central Oklahoma, Department of English, 100 Univ Dr, Edmond, OK 73034, **Business Phone:** (405)974-5608.

LEIGH, FREDRIC H
Association executive. **Personal:** Born Mar 29, 1940, Columbus, OH; son of William F Leigh Sr and Cathrine A; married Karyn; children: Tracey, William & Jade Moore. **Educ:** Cent State Univ, BA, hist, 1963; Syracuse Univ, MS, jour & pub relations, 1972; USY, Command & Staff Col, MMS, 1973; Nat War Col, grad, 1982; Univ Chicago, Exec Develop Prog, cert, 1986; Ctr for Creative Leadership, Eckerd Col, FL, cert, 1990; Harvard Univ, JFK Sch Govern Sr Exec in govern prog, cert, 1993. **Career:** Off secy USY, sr military asst, 1982-83; Off Chief Staff, USY, dep dir army staff, 1983-85; 19th Support Command, 8th USY, Korea, chief staff, 1985-87; 1st Brigade, 101st Airborne Division (Air Assault), Fort Campbell, KY, commander, 1987-89; Senior Leadership Res, Army War Col, dir, 1989-90; 7th Infantry Division (Light), Fort Ord, CA, asst div commr (support), 1990-91; Nat Military Command Ctr, dep dir, 1991-93; Chief of Staff, Army Office, dir mgt, 1993; Joint Ctr for Polit & Econ Studies, exec vpres, 1994-98; Intl Trust Co, exec vpres & gen mgr, Monrovia, Liberia; Karyn Trader & Assoc Global Partners, exec vpres & chief operating officer, currently. **Orgs:** Past pres, Rocks Inc; The New Initiatives Comt for Historically Black Col ROTC Assistance, chr; Korean-Am Friendship Asn, bd mem, 1985-87; Big Brothers Inc, Clarksville, TN, 1977-78; Boy Scouts, Syracuse, NY, leader, 1971-72. **Honors/Awds:** Central State Univ, Hall of Achievement, 1991; Korean-Am Friendship Society, Outstanding Friendship Award, 1987; Taegu Korea Labor Union, Labor Development Award, 1987; Command & Staff Col, Commandant's List Graduate, 1973; Northern New York Public Relations Society of Am, Outstanding Graduate in Public Relations 1972; Newhouse School of Communications, Syracuse Univ, Faculty Award to Most Outstanding Graduate Student, 1972. **Military Serv:** USY, Major General, 1963-94; Army Distinguished Service medal, Defense Superior Service Medal; Legion of Merit (with 3 oak leaf clusters), Bronze Star Medal (with 4 oak leaf clusters), Bronze Star Medal with V Device, Meritorious Service Medal (with 2 oak leaf clusters), Army Commendation Medal (with oak leaf cluster); numerous others; Natl Military Command Ctr, deputy dir, 1991-93; Office Chief of Staff, dir of management, 1993. **Business Addr:** Executive Vice President, Chief Operating Officer, Karyn Trader & Associates Global Partners LLC, 7768 Glade Ct, Manassas, VA 20112, **Business Phone:** (703)794-8682.

LEIGH, WILLIAM A
Contractor, entrepreneur. **Personal:** Born Sep 12, 1929, Dayton, OH; children: William, Cornell & Bernard. **Educ:** Miami Jacobs Bus Col; Sinclair Comn Col. **Career:** Fleetline Cab Co, owner, 1950-61; Main Auto Parts & Glass Co, sales rep, 1960-68; Madden Inc, pres, currently. **Orgs:** Bd mem, Newfields Comn Authority; treas, bd mem, Am Bus Coun; chmn, Black Contractors & Bus Asn; Adv Bd, Dayton Housing; bd mem, Miami Valley Coun Boy Scouts; United Fund Agency; Miami Valley Child Develop; vpres, Dayton Fund Home Rehab; bd mem, Southern Christian Leadership Conf; pres, Ohio Real Estate Investors Asn; bd mem, Montgomery Co Child Develop Corp; bd mem, Unity State Bank; past pres, Greater Dayton Real Estate Investor Asn; facilitator, Barbara Jordan Comt Race Unity; Dayton City Sch Adv Bd. **Honors/Awds:** Frontiersman of the Year, 1972; Outstanding Land Use & Design, Professional Builders Magazine, 1972; Outstanding Black Businessmen, Jimmy Carter, 1978; WS McIntosh Achievement Award, 1980. **Business Addr:** Chairman, President,

Madden Investment Inc, 2305 Heartsoul Dr, Dayton, OH 45408, **Business Phone:** (937)268-1314.*

LEIGHTON, GEORGE NEVES
Judge, lawyer. **Personal:** Born Oct 22, 1912, New Bedford, MA; son of Antonio Leitao and Annay Sylvia Garcia Leitao; married Virginia Berry Quivers, Jun 21, 1942 (deceased); children: Virginia Anne & Barbara Elaine. **Educ:** Howard Univ, AB, 1940; Harvard Univ, LLB, 1946. **Career:** Judge (retired); Moore, Ming & Leighton, Chicago, IL, partner, 1951-59; McCoy, Ming & Leighton, Chicago, IL, partner, 1959-64; Circuit Ct Cook Co, IL, judge, 1964-69, appellate ct, First Dist, judge, 1969-76; US Dist Ct, Northern Dist Ill, judge, dist judge, 1976-89, sr dist judge, 1986-87; Earl L Neal & Assocs, coun. **Orgs:** Mass Bar Asn, 1946; Ill Bar Asn, 1947; Chicago Bar Asn; US Supreme Ct Bar, 1958; Am Bar Asn; comnr, 1955-63, chmn, 1959-63, Character & Fitness Comt, First Appellate Dist Supreme Ct Ill; Joint Comt Revision Ill Criminal Code, 1964; life mem, Nat Asn Advan Colored People, 1964; bd dirs, United Church Bd Homeland Ministries; United Church Christ; Grant Hosp; Am Bar Found; Howard Univ Chicago Alumni Club; chmn, Legal Redress Comt, Nat Asn Advan Colored People, Chicago Chap; coun, Nat Harvard Law Sch Asn; Phi Beta Kappa; trustee, 1979-83, trustee emer, Univ Notre Dame, 1983; bd overseers, Harvard Col, 1983; Hon degrees: LLD, Elmhurst Col, 1964; LLD, John Marshall Law Sch, 1973; LLD, South eastern Mass Univ, 1975; LLD, New England Univ Sch Law, 1978; LLD, Loyola Univ, 1989. **Honors/Awds:** Civil Liberties Award, Ill Div Am Civil Liberties Union, 1961; Chicagoan of the Year in Law & Judiciary, Jr Asn Com & Indust, 1964; Laureate of the ISBA, Acad Ill Lawyers, 2001; American Inns of Court Professionalism Award, 2003. **Special Achievements:** Author of numerous articles on the law; first African-American lawyer to sit on the Board of Managers of the Chicago Bar Association; first African-American judge to serve as a Chancellor in the Circuit Court of Cook County; first African-American judge to sit on the Illinois Appellate Court. **Military Serv:** AUS, capt, 1942-45; Bronze Star.

LELAIND, DETRA LYNETTE
Chief executive officer. **Personal:** Born Jul 26, 1967, San Francisco, CA; daughter of Richard Lelaind and Dorthy Matthews; children: Ayron Joseph & Laron Walker. **Educ:** Laney Col, AA, 1988; San Francisco State Univ, BA, 1990. **Career:** AF Evans Property Mgt, property mgr, 1992-95; Insignia Corp, property mgr,1995-97; Brick Housing Mgt Inc, chief exec officer, 1997-, Currently. **Orgs:** Nat Ctr Housing Mgt, 1997; Womens Initiative Self Employ, 1998; Nat Apt Asn, 1999; Asn Housing Mgt Agents, 2001. **Honors/Awds:** Certificate of Recognition, CA State Assembly 12th Dist, 2001. **Special Achievements:** Publications: Black Business Listings; Bayarea Career Women; AEO Conference City of Oakland Mayor's Conference, 2001; Redbook, 2001. **Home Addr:** 21 Shetland Ct, Oakland, CA 94605, **Home Phone:** (510)638-7555. **Business Phone:** (510)568-2227.

LELAND, JOYCE F.
Police chief. **Personal:** Born Sep 8, 1941, Washington, DC; married John Watkins. **Educ:** Howard Univ, BA, sociol, 1965; Union Inst, PhD, clin psychol, 1998. **Career:** Metrop Police Dept, lt, 1975-78, capt, 1978-83, eeo inspr, 1983-85, deputy chief, 1985. **Orgs:** Bd dirs, MPDC Boys & Girls Club, Police Mgt Asn; consult, Police Found, Ctr Youth Serv. **Honors/Awds:** Crime Reduction Awards; Numerous awards from citizens, law enforcement agencies, churches, business establishments. **Business Addr:** Deputy Chief of Police, Metropolitan Police Department, 1324 Miss Ave SE, Washington, DC 20032.*

LEMELLE, IVAN
Judge. **Personal:** Born Jun 29, 1950, Opelousas, LA; son of Clifford J and Cecilia Comeaux; married Patricia Waddell Lemelle, Apr 28, 1973; children: Christopher, Marc & Tricia. **Educ:** Xavier Univ La, BS, 1971; Loyola Univ Sch Law, JD, 1974. **Career:** Orleans Parish Criminal Dist Ct, law clerk, 1972-74; New Orleans Legal Assistance Corp, law clerk, 1972; Judge Robert Collins, law clerk, 1973-74; District Atty Office, asst district atty, 1974-77; pvt pract, 1977-81; City Atty Office, asst city atty, 1977-79; Douglas, Nabonne & Wilkerson, law partner, 1977-84; La Dept Justice, asst state atty gen, 1981-84; US District Ct, US magistrate judge, 1984-98, dist judge, 1998-. **Orgs:** Co chair, Fed Bar Asn, 1992-; pres comm on bench & bar rels, La Bar Asn, 1994-, comm community involvement, 1995-; Loyola Univ Sch Law, 1994-; Tulane Univ Med Sch, chancellor's comm, 1988-; pres advsior comm, Martinet Legal Soc, 1978-; adv bd mem, DeLille Inn Sr Citizen Ctr, 1986-98; Fed Judge's Asn; treas, Amistad Research Ctr, 1990-95. **Honors/Awds:** AP Tureaud Award, 1991; Ernest Dutch Morial Judicial Pacesetters' Award, 1998; Legal Defense Fund Scholar, Nat Asn Advan Colored People, 1971-74; William H Mitchell Award, Xavier Univ, 1971; Service Award, Fed Bar Asn, 1995. **Special Achievements:** First African American appointed US Magistrate Judge in LA. **Business Addr:** Federal Judge, US District Court- East Dist of Louisiana, 500 Camp St, Chambers C525, New Orleans, LA 70130, **Business Phone:** (504)589-7555.

LEMELLE, TILDEN J.
School administrator. **Personal:** Born Feb 6, 1929, New Iberia, LA; son of Eloi Sabas and Therese Marie; married Margaret Guillion, Aug 12, 1959; children: Joyce Marie, Stephanie Marie & Therese Marie. **Educ:** Xavier Univ, New Orleans, BA, 1953, MA, 1957; Univ Colorado, Denver, PhD, 1965. **Career:** Grambling Col, LA, asst prof, 1957-63; Fordham Univ, NY, assoc prof, 1966-69; Ctr Int Race Rel Univ, Denver, prof, dir, 1969-71; Hunter Col, NY, prof & acting dean, from asst provost to provost, vpres, vice-chancellor, Dept Black & Puerto Rican Studies, prof & chair, Dept Acad Skills & SEEK Prog, chmn & dir; New York Tech Col, actg pres, 1988-90; Univ DC, pres, 1991-96; City Univ New York, comnmr, currently. **Orgs:** John Hay Whitney Fel, NY, 1963-65; trustee, Africa Today Asn Inc, 1967-; ed & pub, Africa Today, 1967-; bd office pres, Am Community Africa, 1973-; trustee, New Rochelle Bd Educ, 1976-; Coun Foreign Rel, 1978-; trustee, Social Sci Found, 1979-; trustee, Africa Found, 1979-; trustee, Int Leaguer Human Rights, 1980-; trustee, Nurses Educ Fund, 1984-; Coun Int Exchange Scholars, Fulbright, 1991-; bd trustees, City Univ NY, 1997-; Coun Foreign Rels, currently; reviewer & consult, Nat Sci Found; African Heritage Studies Asn. **Honors/Awds:** The Black Col Praeger, NY, 1969; Hon Consul-Senegal, Denver, CO, 1969-71; Race Among Nations Heath-Lexington, 1971; New York Urban League BuildingBrick Award, 1991. **Military Serv:** AUS, sp4 1953-56; Special Agent Counterintelligence. **Business Phone:** (212)817-7000.

LEMMIE, VALERIE A
Government official, commissioner. **Personal:** Married Olan Strozier. **Educ:** Univ Mo, BS; Wash Univ, MS. **Career:** Mgr, City of Dayton (OH), 1996; Cincinnati city, city mgr; Pub Utilities Comn Ohio, comnr, 2006-. **Orgs:** Cincinnati Zoo; Cincinnati Fine Arts Coun; Nat Civic League Coun Adv. **Special Achievements:** First African American city manager in Dayton; First woman city manager in Dayton. **Business Addr:** Commissioner, The Public Utilities Commission of Ohio, 180 E Broad St, Columbus, OH 45202, **Business Phone:** 800-686-7826.

LEMMONS, HERBERT MICHAEL
Clergy, executive director. **Personal:** Born Sep 25, 1952, Little Rock, AR; son of Herbert G and Deliah A Herron; married Karenga Rashida Hill, Aug 31, 1974; children: H Michael II, Malcolm R. **Educ:** Univ Detroit, MI, BA, 1973; Interdenominational Theol Ctr, Atlanta, GA, MDiv, l976; Howard Univ Sch Law, WA DC, Juris Doctor, l979. **Career:** Seaton Mem AME Church, Lanham, MD, pastor, 1977-84; US Small Bus Admin, WA DC, atty adv, 1979-81; Univ MD, Col Park, chaplain, 1982-84; Cong Nat Black Churches, WA DC, dep dir, 1984-85; Mount Moriah AME Church, Annapolis, MD, pastor, l984-89; Cong Nat Black Churches, Washington, DC, exec dir, currentlyl; Hist Ebenezer AME Church, pastor, currently. **Orgs:** Human Relations Comn, Annapolis, MD, 1986-88; Mayor's Task Force on Substance Abuse, 1987-89; Bd Commrs, Annapolis Housing Authority, 1988-. **Honors/Awds:** Walder G Mueller Student Lectureship in Social Ethics, Interdenominational Theol Ctr, 1976; Clergy Award, Annual Kunte Kinte Celebration, 1990. *

LEMMONS, KAREN. See LEMMONS, KASI.

LEMMONS, KASI (KAREN LEMMONS)
Movie director, writer, actor. **Personal:** Born Feb 24, 1961, St. Louis, MO; married Vondie Curtis-Hall, Jan 1, 1995; children: Hunter & Zora. **Educ:** NY Univ, UCLA, New Sch Social Res. **Career:** Director, writer, actor; Films: School Daze, 1988; Vampire's Kiss, 1989; The Five Heartbeats, 1991; The Silence of the Lambs, 1991; Candyman, 1992; Hard Target, 1993; Fear of a Black Hat, 1994; Drop Squad, 1994; Gridlock'd, 1997; Til There Was You, 1997; Eve's Bayou, dir & writer, 1997; Dr. Hugo, dir & writer, 1998; Liars' Dice, 1998; The Caveman's Valentine, dir, 2001; Waist Deep, 2006; Talk to Me, dir, 2007; TV (acting): "11th Victim", 1979; "A Man Called Hawk", 1989; "The Court-Martial of Jackie Robinson", 1990; "The Big One; The Great Los Angeles Earthquake", 1990; "Under Cover",1991; "After burn", 1992; "Override", 1994; "Zooman", 1995; "Er", 2002. **Honors/Awds:** Best Debut Director Award, Nat Bd Rev, 1997; Independent Spirit Award, Best First Feature, 1998; Black Film Award, 1998; Image Award, 2008. **Business Phone:** (310)314-2000.*

LEMON, ANN
Executive. **Career:** PaineWebber Inc, vpres investments, UBS PaineWebber, vpres investments. **Orgs:** Nat Black MBA Asn; Financial Women's Asn; treas, Smith Col Alumnae Asn; Nat Structured Settlement Trade Asn; Smith Col Club. **Honors/Awds:** Member of the Year, Conn Westchester Chap, 1994.

LEMON, MEADOWLARK
Athlete, preacher, actor. **Personal:** Born Apr 25, 1932, Wilmington, NC; married Willie Maultsby (divorced); children: George, Beverly, Donna, Robin & Jonathan. **Educ:** Vision Intl Univ, DDiv. **Career:** Basketball player (retired), speaker, preacher; Harlem Globetrotters, 1957-79, 1994; The Bucketeers, basketball group, 1980-83; Shooting Stars, 1984-87; Meadowlark Lemon's Harlem All Stars, 1998; Films: The Fish That Saved Pittsburgh, 1979; TV Series: "Harlem Globe Trotters", voice, 1970; "Hello Larry", 1979; Sweepstakes; ordained minister, 2005; preacher, currently; Meadowlark Lemon OnLine Acad, founder, currently; Meadowlark Lemon Ministries, founder, currently. **Honors/Awds:** North Carolina Hall of Fame; John Bunn Award, Basketball Hall of Fame, 2000; Naismith Memorial Basketball Hall of Fame, 2003. **Military Serv:** AUS, 1952-54. **Business Phone:** (480)951-0030.

LEMON, MICHAEL WAYNE, SR.
Police officer. **Personal:** Born Nov 2, 1953, Detroit, MI; son of Primus and Mary Strong; married Valerie Mennifee Lemon, Apr 2, 1978; children: Michael Wayne Lemon Jr, Ashlee Michelle Lemon. **Educ:** Wayne County Community Col, attended 1988; Wayne State Univ. **Career:** Police officer (retired); Mich Bell Tel, consult, 1987-; Detroit Police Dept, Narcotics Div, police officer, 2001, sergent. **Orgs:** Bd mem, Community Vol, 1986-; Task Force Drug Abuse, Detroit Strategic Plan, 1987-91. **Honors/Awds:** Appreciation Award, Mich Bell Tel, 1986; Community Serv Award, Detroit Chamber Com, 1988; Man of the Year Award, Minority Women Network, 1988; Spirit of Detroit, Detroit Common Coun, 1989, Heart of Gold Award, United Found, 1989. *

LEMUWA, IKE EMMANUEL
Executive. **Personal:** Born Oct 1, 1961, Mband, Nigeria; son of Ononiwu and Cyrina Adim; married Chioma N, Apr 7, 1997. **Educ:** Univ DC, BA, econ, 1993. **Career:** Dickinson & Co, stockbroker, 1995-96; RAF Financial Corp, investment exec; Nat Hubzone Incubator Mgmt, owner, currently. **Orgs:** The Int Asn Friends Africa Inc, IAFA, pres, founder.

LENARD, VOSHON KELAN
Basketball player. **Personal:** Born May 14, 1973, Detroit, MI; married; children: Tayler, Tyler & Tae Shon. **Educ:** Univ Minn, pre-speech commun. **Career:** Okla City Calvalry, CBA, 1995; Miami Heat, guard, 1995-2000; Denver Nuggets, 2000-02, 2004-05; Toronto Raptors, 2002; Portland Trail Blazers, guard, 2005-06; free agent, currently. **Orgs:** Continental Basketball Asn.

LENIX-HOOKER, CATHERINE JEANETTE
Administrator. **Personal:** Born May 10, 1947, Camden, SC; daughter of Frank and Annie Lenix; divorced; children: Frank R Jr. **Educ:** Univ MD, MLS, 1970; Howard Univ, BA, 1968; Victorian Soc Am Summer Sch, 1999. **Career:** Wash DC Pub Libr, chief, black studies div, 1970-77; Anaheim Calif Pub Libr, dir public servs, 1977-81; Schomburg Ctr Research Black Culture, asst chief, 1981-90; Krueger-Scott Mansion Cult Ctr, exec dir, dir, Mkt & Develop, Newark Performing Arts Corp, 2000-; Newark Symphony Hall, actg mgr, 2000-. **Orgs:** Am Libr Asn, 1970-; Black Caucus, 1970-; chairperson, S CA Chap Howard Univ Alumni Scholar, 1980-81; Chmn, Harlem Hosp Ctr Comm Adv Bd, 1981-90; Victorian Soc Northern NJ; vol, Habitat Humanity, Newark, NJ Chap; Harlem Tourism Asn. **Honors/Awds:** HEW Title II Fellowship, Univ MD, 1969-70; Community Service Award, NY Chap Negro Bus & Prof Women's Club, 1985; Community Service Award, Aka Sorority, Beta Alpha Omega Chap, 1992. **Business Addr:** Acting Manager, Newark Symphony Hall, 1020 Broad St, Newark, NJ 07102, **Business Phone:** (973)643-8468.

LENNON, PATRICK ORLANDO
Baseball player, automotive mechanic. **Personal:** Born Apr 27, 1968, Whiteville, NC. **Career:** Baseball player (retired), baseball coach; Seattle Mariners, outfielder, 1991-92; Kansas City Royals, 1996; Oakland Athletics, 1997; Toronto Blue Jays, 1998-99; Matt Guiliano's Play Like A Pro, coach, currently. **Honors/Awds:** 2-Time Minor League Player Of The Month, 1994, 1998; 300 Career Minor League Hitter. **Business Phone:** (631)342-9033.

LENNOX, BETTY
Basketball player. **Personal:** Born Dec 4, 1976, Hugo, OK; daughter of Bernice Lennox. **Educ:** Trinity Valley Community Col, KS; La Tech Univ, attended 2000. **Career:** Minn Lynx, guard, 2000-01, 2002; Miami Sol, guard, 2002; Cleveland Rockers, guard, 2003; Seattle Storm, guard, 2004-08; Atlanta Dream, 2008-. **Orgs:** Founder, The Lennox Found 22. **Honors/Awds:** Conf Player of the Yr, Sun Belt, 2000; Rookie of the Yr, WNBA, 2000; Most Valuable Player, 2004. **Business Addr:** Professional Basketball Player, Atlanta Dream, 83 Walton St NW Suite 500, Atlanta, GA 30303, **Business Phone:** (404)954-6645.

LENOIR, KIP
Lawyer. **Personal:** Born Apr 27, 1943, Knoxville, TN; son of Henry and Teri Adkins; married Richelle Guilmenot, Jun 8, 1967. **Educ:** Howard Univ, Wash, BS, 1966, JD, 1969; NY Univ, Grad Sch Law, criminal justice. **Career:** Legal Aid Soc Crim, NY, 1971-73; Mayor's Off, supv atty, NY, 1973-75; NY State Atty Gen Off, NY, asst atty gen, 1975-77; Lenoir & Bogan, PC, NY, partner, 1977-85; Malcolm King Col, law instr, 1980; Bronx Community Col, City Univ NY, adj prof, crim law, 1987-88; Kip Lenoir, Prof Corp, NY, pres, 1985; pvt pract atty, currently. **Orgs:** Mayor's Graffiti Comt, NY, 1974-75; Coun Harlem Interfaith Coun Serv Inc, 1980-; NY State Bar Asn, 1975-; NY Co Lawyers Asn, 1975-; bd mem, Metrop Black Bar Asn, 1987-88. **Honors/Awds:** Outstanding Achievement, Harlem Interfaith Coun Serv Inc, 1984. **Home Addr:** 19 W 122nd St, New York, NY 10027. **Business Phone:** (212)333-2225.

LENOIR, MICHAEL A
Pediatrician. **Personal:** Born Feb 22, 1942; married; children: 4. **Educ:** Univ TX, Austin, BA, sci, 1965; Univ TX, Galveston, Med

Degree, 1967; William Beaumont Army Hosp, El Paso, TX, Residency Pediats, 1970; Los Angeles County Hosp, CA, Rotating Internship, 1968; Am Bd Allergy & Immunol, cert, 1973. **Career:** Letterman Army Hosp San Francisco, chief pediat serv, 1972-75; KCBS Radio, med ed, 1981-89; KPFA Pacifica Radio, med ed, 1996-; Ethnic Health Am, chief exec officer, currently; Univ Calif, assoc clin pr, pediats, currently; Ethnic Health Am Network, chief exec officer, currently; Bay Area Multicultural Clin Res & Prev Ctr, dir & chief operating officer, currently; Ethnic Health Inst, Summit Med Ctr, pres, currently; Comprehensive Allergy Servs, med dir, currently; Bay Area Pediats, med dir, currently; Alta Bates Med Group, allergist & pediatrician, currently. **Orgs:** Am Bd Pediats, 1972; chair, Allergy & Asthma initiative; Nat Med Asn; fel Am Acad Pediatrics; fel Am Acad Allergy & Immunol; fel Am Acad Cert Allergist & Immunol; fel Am Col Allergy; Nat Med Asn; pres, Nat Asn Physician Broadcasters; pres, Clin Fac Asn, Univ Calif; pres, Northern Calif Allergy Asn; pres, Region VI, Nat Med Asn; pres, Sinkler Miller Med Asn; bd, E Bay Regional Ctr; chmn bd, Bay Area Black United Fund; Bd Calif Spec Olympics; bd, Int Visitors Ctr. **Honors/Awds:** Citizen of the Year, Oakland; Burbridge Award Community Service, Univ Calif; Positive Profiles Award, Am Med Asn; Lyda Smiley Award, Calif Sch Nurses Asn; John B. Jackson Community Service Award, Inst Alta Bates Summit Med Ctr. **Special Achievements:** Over 50 Publ and Presentations on Asthma & Allergy; distinguished honor, one of the 50 most positive physicians in Am; one of the Nations Top 100 Black Physicians, 2001, ed of Black Enterprise mag. **Military Serv:** Army Commend Medal. **Business Addr:** Allergist, Pediatrician, Alta Bates Medical Group, 401 29th St Suite 201, Oakland, CA 94609, **Business Phone:** (510)834-4897.

LEON, JEAN G
Executive, nurse. **Personal:** Born in Trinidad, Trinidad and Tobago; daughter of Vida Barrington; divorced. **Educ:** San Fernando Gen Hosp, Sch Nursing, dipl; Sch Midwifery, dipl; St Joseph's Col, BSC, MPA; New York Univ, public admin. **Career:** San Fernando Gen Hosp, staff nurse, 1968-71; Cumberland Hosp, staff nurse, 1971-73; Brooklyn Jewish Hosp, staff nurse, 1973-80; Interfaith Med Ctr, Q A coordr, 1980-85; Woodhull Med Ctr, assoc dir nursing, 1985-89; Metrop Med Ctr, assoc exec dir, 1989-92; Harlem Hosp, chief operating officer, 1992-94; Kings County Hosp Ctr, exec dir; Cent Brooklyn Family Health Network, sr vpres, 1994-. **Orgs:** Nat Asn Health Care Qual, 1981-; bd mem, NY Asn, 1984-94; pres, Caribbean Am Nurses Asn, 1990-94; Am Col Healthcare Exec, 1993-; New York City Health & Hospitals Corp, bd mem. **Honors/Awds:** Community Award, Nat Asn Prof Women, 1997; Quality Healthcare Award, NY Asn Healthcare Qual, 1995; Foundation Award for Leadership, Dolores E Jackson, 1996. **Special Achievements:** First in KCHC history to receive JACHO Accreditation with Commendation. **Business Addr:** Executive Director, Kings County Hospital Center, 451 Clarkson Ave, B Bldg, Brooklyn, NY 11236, **Business Phone:** (718)245-3901.

LEON, ROBERT. See HUSKEY, BUTCH.

LEON, DR. TANIA JUSTINA
Composer, conductor (music), educator. **Personal:** Born May 14, 1943, La Habana, Cuba; daughter of Oscar Leon de Los Mederos and Dora Ferran; married Francisco Javier Perez (divorced 1985). **Educ:** Nat Conserv, La Habana, CU, MA, music educ, 1965; NY Univ, BS, music educ,1973; NY Univ, MA, compos, 1975. **Career:** Dance Theatre Harlem,co founder & music dir, 1969-78; conductor, 1971-; Brooklyn Col, prof, 1985-; Kurt Masur, music adv, 1993-97; NY Philharmonic, revson composer, 1993-; Yale Univ, vis prof, 1993; Harvard Univ, vis lectr, 1994; Univ Mich, vis lectr; Musik schule, Hamburg, vis lectr; Brooklyn Col, Claire & Leonard Tow prof, 2000; Concorso Int di Composizione, pres, 2002; Ithaca Col Sch Music, Karel Husa vis prof composition; Conductor & Composer: Beethoven halle Orchestra; Gewandhaus orchester; Santa Cecilia Orchestra; Natl Symphony Orchestra South Africa; Netherlands Wind Ensemble; NY Philharmonic, 1969-; Alvin Ailey Am Dance Theatre, Madrid Symphony Orchestra, 2002; Symphony Orchestra Marseille, 2003; Orquesta de la Comunidad de Madrid, 2004; MOSAIC Chamber ensemble, 2004; NY Univ Symphony Orchestra, 2004; Symphony Orchestra Marseille, 2005; Shangri La" Opera by Susie Ibarra, The Kitchen,2005; Fargo Moorhead Symphony, 2005. **Orgs:** Byrd Hoffman Found, 1981; Queens Coun Arts, 1983; Manhattan Arts, 1985; ASCAP; Am Music Ctr Inc; Composers Forum Inc, NY, Local 802, AFL CIO; bd mem, NY Found Arts; bd mem, Am Composers Orchestra; bd mem, Meet Composer; bd mem, Am Acad Poets; Fromm Music Found, Harvard Univ. **Honors/Awds:** Natl Endowment Arts Comn, 1975; CINTAS Award, 1976, 1979; ASCAP Composer's Awards, 1978-89; Natl Coun Women US Achievement Award, 1980; Key to the City, Detroit, 1982; Dean Dixon Achievement Award, 1985; NY State Coun Arts, 1988; Acad Inst Award, Am Acad & Inst Arts & Letters, 1991; Ann Residency Artists, Yaddo, John D & Catherine T MacArthur Found, 1991; Meet Composer & Reader's Digest Comn Award, 1992; Natl Endowment Arts Rec Award, 1993; Distinguished Alumni Award, NY Univ, 1994; BMW Music Theater Prize, Munich Biennale, 1994; NY Gov's Lifetime Achievement Award, 1998; Hon Doctorate, Colgate Univ & Oberlin Col; received numerous awards from various organization including: Chamber Music Am; NYSCA; Lila Wallace & Reader's Digest Fund; ASCAP; Koussevitzky Found; Fromm Music Found. **Special Achievements:** Publications: "Ritual" for solo piano, Southern Music Publ Co, 1991; "Parajota Delate" for mixed quintet, Southern Music Publ Co, 1992; recordings: "De Orishas The Western Wind" Newport Classic; piano solo, Leonarda Records, Momentum; Chamber works by Tania Leon, Composers Recordings Inc, Indigena; The Western Wind, Western Wind Records, Batey; Ana Maria Rosado, Albany Records, Paisanos Semos; Louisville Orchestra, First Edition Records, Bata, Carabali; TV appearances: Univision, "Orgullo Hispano"; Two of her piano works, Ritua & Mistica were featured in the Chicago Symphony's Music Now Pierre Boulez's 80th Birthday Celebration. **Business Addr:** Professor, Brooklyn College, Brooklyn, NY 11210.

LEON, WILMER J., JR.
Consultant. **Personal:** Born Mar 6, 1920, Louisiana; married Edwina T Devore; children: Valerie & Wilmer III. **Educ:** S Univ, BS, 1949; Univ Calif Berkeley, MA, 1954. **Career:** Calif Adult Auth, admin officer; Calif Dept Educ, Bur Intergroup Rels, Sacramento, consult; Calif Dept Corrections, parole agent; asst dist parole supr; State Dir Corrections, consult; Calif State Univ Sacramento, lectr Criminal Justice. **Orgs:** Calif Probation & Parole Asn; Proj Safer Calif, Off Criminal Justice Planning; Sacramento Reg Area Planning Comn, Calif Coun Criminal Justice; Am Sociol Soc; bd dir, Cath Welfare Bur; exec bd, Catholic Youth Orgn; Golden Gate Psychotherapy Soc; Nat Asn Advan Colored People; Sacramento Comt Fair Housing; Sacramento Unified Sch Dist Adult Educ Group; Urban League Formation Comt, educ coordr.

LEONARD, CAROLYN MARIE
School administrator. **Personal:** Born Nov 20, 1943, Portland, OR; daughter of Kelly Miller Probasco (deceased) and Grace Ruth Searcie Probasco (deceased); divorced; children: Cherice M & Chandra M. **Educ:** Portland State Univ, BS, bus admin, 1976, MS, educ, 1979; Stand Admin cert, 1988. **Career:** Ore Assembly Black Affairs, vpres, 1979-86; re Comn Black Affairs, 1986-; Ore Coun Excellence Educ, sec, 1987-99; Portland Pub Sch, Portland, OR, evaluator, 1979-85, coordr multicult educ, 1985-, Acad Stands Reform Unit, admin, currently, Multicultural & Multiethnic Educ Off, coord; Jefferson Comm Cluster, Stud Achiev, dir, 2000-01; Compliance, Diversity & State Fed Progs, dir, 2003-; Univ Portland, adj prof. **Orgs:** Treas, Alpha Kappa Alpha, 1982-86; Nat Alliance Black Sch Educ; sec, BlackUnited Fund Ore, 1987-90; bd mem, Ore Comn Black Affairs, 1984-94, bd mem,Nat Coun Black Studies, 1984-; Metro Human Rels Community, 1987-91, chair,1990-91; bd mem, Portland State Univ Alum, 1997-; bd, McCoy Acad, 1997-00;bd, Multicult Resource Ctr, 1997-00; bd, Hyalite, 1997-00; bd, MoralRe-Armament, 2000-; bd mem, Initiatives Change, 2000-. **Honors/Awds:** President's Award, Ore Assembly Black Affairs, 1984; Community Leadership Award, Skanner Newspaper, 1987; Merit Award, Skanner Newspaper, 1987; Cheik Anta Diop Award, Outstanding Scholarly Achievement Multicultural Educ, 1988; Education Award, Delta Sigma Theta Sorority, 1988; Ancient Free & Accepted Masons OR, Recognition Outstanding Service, 1989; Certificate of Appreciation, Commercial Club Portland, 1989; Woman of Excellence Award Education, Delta Sigma Theta Sorority, 1989; Outstanding Community Service Award, Ore Black Resource Ctr Found, 1990; Alma "Nomsa"John Inspiration Award, Int Black Women's Congress, 1991; NABRLE Community Service Award, Nat Asn Black Reading & Language Educrs, 1991; Mary McLeod Bethune-Carter G Woodson Award, Nat Coun Black Studies, 1992; Joseph J. Malone fellow, 1995; Community Service Award, Muslim Educ Trust, 1996; Community Harmony Award, Metro Human Rels Ctr, 1998; Outreach Award, Mrs. J.M. Gates, 1998; Mrs JM Gates "Coming Out" Award, 1999. **Special Achievements:** Editor, AFA Baseline Essays, 1987; Hispanic-Am Women, 1988; chair, Martin Luther King Jr Street Renaming Comn, 1989. **Home Addr:** 311 NE Jessup St, Portland, OR 97211. **Business Addr:** Coordinator, Portland Public Schools, Multicultural & Multiethnic Education Office, 501 N Dixon St, Portland, OR 97227, **Business Phone:** (503)916-3183.

LEONARD, CURTIS ALLEN
School administrator. **Personal:** Born Aug 18, 1939, Philadelphia, PA; son of Henry and Rhebena Castteberry; married Jacqueline, Jun 20, 1964; children: Laurent C. **Educ:** Temple Univ, BS, educ, 1961, PhD, 1979; Univ Pa, MSW, 1963. **Career:** NIMH, fel, 1961-63; Va Family Care Prog, dir, 1965-68; Temple Univ, prof, 1968-90, prof & dean, 1990-2002, prof emer, 2002-. **Orgs:** Nat Asn Social Work, 1965-; Nat Asn Black Social Work, 1965-; Coun Social Work Educ, 1968-; Am Polit Sci Asn, 1979-; Nat Asn Deans & Dirs, 1990-. **Special Achievements:** The BLK Male in Amer J Soc Issue, 1977, Race, Class, Bureaucracy BLK Caucus J, 1978, Perspectives on African American Soc Work, Housing, Support, and Comm, Families in Soc, 1994, Admin Appointment at the Academy, chapter, 1995. **Home Phone:** (215)763-1379. **Business Addr:** Professor Emeritus, Temple University, School Of Social Work, Ritter Annex Fifth fl 1301 W Cecil B Moore Ave, Philadelphia, PA 19122-6091, **Business Phone:** (215)204-8623.

LEONARD, DONIS
Administrator, educator. **Educ:** Prairie View A&M Univ, BA, theatre arts; Wayne State Univ, MFA, acting. **Career:** Calif State Univ, dir speech forensics prog & assoc prof theater arts, currently. **Special Achievements:** Founder & director "New African Grove" Black Theatre Prog Univ; directing credits include: August Wilsons "The Piano Lesson", "The Shadow Box","Miss Evers Boys", & Pearl Cleage's "Flyin West" recognized as "Best Drama South Bay in 2000". **Business Phone:** (310)243-2847.

LEONARD, GLORIA JEAN
Library administrator. **Personal:** Born Jan 12, 1947, Seattle, WA; daughter of Charles Ratliff Jr and Katie Mae Stratman Ashford; children (previous marriage): Melanie Renee Smith; married James Leonard, Apr 11, 1981; children: James Oliver Leonard Jr. **Educ:** Fisk Univ, Nashville, TN, 1967; Univ Wash, Seattle, WA, BA, 1971, MLS, 1973; City Univ, Seattle, WA, MBA, 1985. **Career:** Univ Wash, Seattle, WA, reference & outreach librn, 1973-79; Seattle Pub Libr, Seattle, WA, south region servs develop librn, 1979, mobile servs & bookmobile dept head, 1981, special asst city librn, 1989, south region mgr, 1990, advocate & dir, neighborhood libr serv, 1990-. **Orgs:** past pres, Seattle Chapter, Jack & Jill Am, Inc, 1981-; Am Libr Asn, 1973-; exec bd, Black Caucus Am Libr Asn, 1975-; Wash Libr Asn, 1973; memship comt mem, Pub Libr Asn, 1990-. **Honors/Awds:** Reading Aloud: A Good Idea Getting Better by Tom Watson, Wilson Library Bulletin, volume 61, February, 1987, p 20-22; Articles: "Bias Busting: Valuing Diversity Work Place," Library Administration & Management, Vol 5, No 4, Fall 1991; "Learning to Get Along with Each Other," Library Personnel News, Vol 5, No 2, March-April, 1991. **Business Addr:** Advocate, Director, Seattle Public Library, 1000 4th Ave, Seattle, WA 98104-1109, **Business Phone:** (206)386-4144.*

LEONARD, JEFFREY
Baseball player, manager. **Personal:** Born Sep 22, 1955, Philadelphia, PA. **Career:** Baseball Player (retired), Manager; Los Angeles Dodgers, outfielder, 1977; Houston Astros, outfielder 1978-81; San Francisco Giants, outfielder, 1981-88; Milwaukee Brewers, outfielder, 1988; Seattle Mariners, outfielder, 1989-90; Oakland Athletics farm system, coach; Montreal Expos, hitting coach; Independent Western League, mgr; Golden Baseball League, Reno Silver Sox, mgr, currently. **Orgs:** Golden Baseball League. **Honors/Awds:** Most Valuable Player, Nat League Championship Series, 1987; All-Star team,Nat League, 1987; All-Star team, Am League, 1989; only player in baseball history to hit home run in four straight playoff games. **Business Addr:** Manager, Golden Baseball League, Reno Silver Sox, 7080 Donlon Way Suite 109, Dublin, CA 94568, **Business Phone:** (925)226-2889.

LEONARD, JOHN. See DAVIS, JOHN.

LEONARD, RAY CHARLES. See LEONARD, SUGAR RAY.

LEONARD, SUGAR RAY (RAY CHARLES LEONARD)
Boxer, actor. **Personal:** Born May 17, 1956, Wilmington, NC; married Bernadette Robi; married Juanita Wilkinson, Aug 20, 1993 (divorced); children: Sugar Ray Jr & Jarrel. **Career:** Boxer (retired), actor; Amateur Fights Olympics, team capt, boxer, 1976; prof boxer, 1988; HBO, commentator, Sugar Ray Leonard Boxing Inc, chmn & founder; Films: Riot, 1997; I Spy, 2002; Boxin Buddies: Knockout Juvenile Diabetes, 2006; TV Series: "Tales from the Crypt", 1992; "Vault of HorrorI", 1994; "Half & Half", 2003; NBC, "The Contender", 2005; Miss USA 2005, celebrity judge, 2005. **Honors/Awds:** Nat Golden Gloves Lightweight Champion, 1972, 1973, 1974; Nat AAU LightWelter weight Champion, 1974, 1975; Light Welterweight Gold Medal, Pan Am Games, 1975; Light Welterweight Gold Medal, Olympics, Montreal, 1976; WBC Welterweight Champion, 1980; US Olympic Hall of Fame, 1985; Middle weight Crown, 1987; Future of America Award, DARE Am, 1997; Inter Nat Boxing Hall of Fame. **Business Addr:** Actor, NBC, The Contender, 30 Rockefeller Plz, New York, NY 10112, **Business Phone:** (212)315-9016.

LEONARD, DR. WALTER J.
Educator, scholar, college president. **Personal:** Born Oct 3, 1929, Alma, GA; married Betty E Singleton; children: Anthony Carlton & Angela Michele. **Educ:** Savannah State Col, attended 1947; Morehouse Col Atlanta, attended 1959-60; Atlanta Univ Grad Schl Bus, attended 1961-62; Howard Univ Sch Law, JD, 1968, Inst Educ Mgt,1974, AMP, 1977. **Career:** Ivan Allen Jr Atlanta, asst campaign mgr, 1961; Leonard Land Co Atlanta, owner/operator, 1962-65; Sam Phillips McKenzie, campaign asst, 1963; Dean Clarence Clyde Ferguson Jr Sch Law, Howard Univ, legal res asst, 1966-67; Washington Tech Inst, admin asst to pres, 1967-68; Howard Univ Sch Law, asst dean & lectr, 1968-69; Harvard Univ Law Sch, asst dean/asst dir admin & fin aid, 1969-71; US Office of Econ Opportunity, hearing examiner, 1969-70; Univ Calif, visit prof summers, 1969-72; Univ Va, visit prof summers, 1969-72; Harvard Univ, asst to pres 1971-77; Fisk Univ, pres, 1977-84, pres emer, 1984-; Howard Univ, distinguished sr fellow, 1984-86; US Virgin Islands, executive asst to governor, 1987-89; private consulting, 1989-90; Cities in Schs, Inc. (National/International), executive director, 1990-94; Oxford Univ, Ctr Socio-Legal Studies, vis scholar, 1995-. **Orgs:** Asn Am Law Schs; Coun Legal Educ

Opportunity; Law Sch Admissions Coun; Am Asn Univ Prof; Howard Univ Law Sch Alumni Asn; bd visitors, USN Acad; bd trustees, Nat Urban League; bd trustees, Nat Pub Radio; Int Asn Y'sMen's Club Inc; Nat Asn Advan Colored People; pres, Nat Bar Asn; consult, The Ford Found NY, 1969-71; Omega Psi Phi Fraternity; Sigma Pi Phi Fraternity; bd trustees, US Naval Acad FND; bd dir, Cities Schs Inc; Mem, Asn Am Law Sch. **Honors/Awds:** Appreciation Award, Harvard Black Students' Asn, 1971; Distinguished Serv Award, Asn & Office Pres, 1972; Exemplary Achieve Award, Fac Resolution Grad Sch Educ, Harvard Univ, 1976; First Annual Melnea A Cass Community Award, Boston YWCA, 1977; Paul Robeston Award, Black Am Law Students Asn, 1977; Frederick Douglass Pub Serv Award, Greater Boston YMCA, 1977; Alumni Achievement Award, Morehouse Alumni Club New England, 1977; Appreciation Dinner & Award, Urban League Eastern MA, 1977; Service Award & Appreciation Citation, Governor US Virgin Islands. **Special Achievements:** Two books & more than two dozen published articles; numerous published works l, "Our Struggle Continues-Our Cause is Just" The Crisis, 1978; "Reflecting on Black Admissions in White Colleges" The Morning After A Retrospective View, 1974; articles in, The Boston Globe, USA Today, The Harvard Law Sch Bulletin; Holder of more than 300 awards & honors in education. **Military Serv:** USCG, 1945-46. **Business Addr:** Visiting Scholar, University of Oxford, Centre for Socio-Legal Studies, Manor Rd, Oxford OX1 3UQ, United Kingdom, **Business Phone:** (441)86528-4220.

LEONEY, ANTOINETTE E M
Lawyer. **Personal:** Born Jul 22, 1950, Boston, MA; daughter of Calvin and Marie E Cardoza; children: Dasan C. **Educ:** Lesley Col, Cambridge, MA, BS, 1980; New England Sch Law, Boston, MA, JD, 1984. **Career:** Commonwealth Mass, Dept Social Serv, Legal Coun, Boston, MA, 1984-86; Dept Atty Gen, Boston, Ma, asst atty gen, 1986-87; Gov Michael S Dukakis, Boston, MA, dep chief coun, 1987-90; Brandeis Univ, Waltham, MA, dir off govt regulation compliance, 1990-91; McKenzie & Edwards PC, sr assoc, 1991; US Attys Off, asst US atty, currently. **Orgs:** Trustee, Lesley Col, Cambridge, MA, 1989-; vpres, Mass Black Women Atty Asn, 1990-; dir, Mass Pension Res Investment Mgt Bd, 1990-92; dir, Mass Crime & Justice Found, 1990-92; exec bd mem, Mass Black Lawyers Asn, 1990-; Mass Bar Asn, 1991-; Boston Bar Asn, 1991-; deleg, MBA's House Deleg, 1998-2001; Nat Black Prosecutors Asn; adv bd, Mass Trial Court's Gender Equality, 1999-2002. **Honors/Awds:** Young Alumni Award, Lesley Col, 1990; Outstanding Achievement Award, New England Sch Law, Women's Law Caucus. **Special Achievements:** pres, Women's Bar Asn, 1999-2000; pres, Women's Bar Found, 2002-03. **Home Addr:** 1 Winter Island Rd, Salem, MA 01970. **Business Addr:** Assistant United States Attorney, United States Attorney Office, US Department of Justice, 1 Courthouse Way, Boston, MA 02210, **Business Phone:** (617)748-3139.

LEROY, GARY LEWIS
Physician, administrator. **Personal:** Born Jun 30, 1956, Dayton, OH; son of Abraham and Flora; married Sherlynn, Jun 14, 1980; children: Julia & Ciara. **Educ:** Wright State Univ, Sch Med, BS, 1984, MD, 1988; Mich State Univ, fel training, 1992. **Career:** Dayton Daily News, Customer Serv, supvr, 1976-81; Miami Valley Hosp, Dayton, Ohio, Med technologist, 1982-84, East Dayton Health Ctr, Med doctor, 1992, med dir, currently; Miami Valley Hosp, inpatient attending, currently; Wright State Univ, asst dean minority & stud affairs, currently. **Orgs:** Alpha Phi Alpha Fraternity Inc, 1987-; Ohio Acad Family Physicians, 1988-; AMA, 1988-; Am Acad Family Physicians, 1988-; bd trustees, Miami Valley Hosp, 1997-2000; bd dir, Mary Scott Nursing Home, 1998-2001; bd dir, United Health Servs, 1998-2001; Sigma Pi Phi Fraternity, 1999-; bd dir, Am Red Cross, Dayton Chap, 1999-2002; Community Adv Bd. **Honors/Awds:** Dean's Award to Outstanding Graduate, Wright State Univ, Sch Med, 1988; Outstanding Grad Recognition Award, Dayton Schs MGT Asn, 1997; fel, Am Acad Family Physicians, 1998; Outstanding Grad Achievement Award, Wright State Univ, 1998; Dayton's Top Ten African Am Male Award, Parity 2000, 1998; Alumni Achievement, Alpha Omega Alpha, Med Hon Soc, 1999. **Special Achievements:** One of the 50 Most Positive Doctors in America, Philadelphia-based Positive Medicine project. **Business Addr:** Associate Dean for Student Affairs and Admissions, Wright State University, Boonshoft School of Medicine, 210 Med Sci Bldg 3640 Colonel Glenn Hwy, Dayton, OH 45435, **Business Phone:** (937)775-2934.

LESLIE, LISA DESHAUN
Basketball player, fashion model. **Personal:** Born Jul 7, 1972, Gardena, CA; daughter of Christine Leslie-Espinoza; married Michael Lockwood, Nov 1, 2005; children: Lauren. **Educ:** USC, attended. **Career:** Atlanta Glory, center, 1996-97; Wilhelmina Models, model, 1996; Los Angeles Sparks, 1997-. **Honors/Awds:** USA Basketball Player of the Year, 1993; National Player of the Year,1994; US Women's Olympic Basketball Team, Gold Medal, 1996, 2000, 2004. 2008; All-WNBA First Team, 1997; WNBA All-Star Game Most Valuable Player, 1999-03, 2004, 2006, 2009; WNBA Most Valuable Player, 2001, 2004, 2006. **Special Achievements:** First player to dunk in a WNBA game; Guest appearances on the television shows "Hangtime," "Moesha," "NBA Inside Stuff" and "The Simpsons". **Business Phone:** (310)341-1000.

LESLIE, MARSHA R
Editor, journalist. **Personal:** Born Apr 16, 1948, Lexington, MS; children: Michaela Leslie-Rule. **Educ:** Univ Mo, BJ, jour, 1970; Columbia Univ, MS, jour, 1974. **Career:** Journalist, 1970-; KMOX Radio; The Associated Press; The Houston Chronicle; The Seattle Times; KCTS-TV; The Rochester Democrat & Chronicle; The Single Woman's Companion, Seal Press, ed, 1994. **Home Phone:** (206)527-5409. **Business Addr:** Editor, c/o Seal Press, The Single Mother, 3131 Wern Ave Suite 410, Seattle, WA 98121, **Business Phone:** (206)283-7844.

LESTER, BETTY J.
Judge. **Personal:** Born Oct 14, 1945, Bristol, PA; daughter of John and Ollie Kimbrough; married Althear; children: Alyse Renee. **Educ:** Howard Univ, BBA, 1968; Rutgers Univ, JD, 1971; Marymount Manhattan, LLD, 1983. **Career:** Pub Defenders Off, asst dep pub def, 1972-74; Pub Advocates Off, asst dep pub advocate, 1974-76; Supermkts Gen, staff atty, 1976-77; Newark Munic Ct, judge, 1977-80, presiding judge, 1980-85; Super Ct NJ, super ct judge, 1985-; State NJ, Super Ct, 5th Vicinage, criminal div, 1996-99, presiding judge, currently. **Orgs:** EC Bar Asn, 1971-, Nat Bar Asn, 1971-; Nat Asn Negro Bus & Prof Women's Club, 1977; bd dir, Joint Connection, 1978; bd dir, gov NJ State Bar Asn, 1978-80; treas, EC Mun Ct Judges Asn, 1982-; Nat Asn Women Judges, 1982-, NJ Coalition 100 Black Women, 1983-. **Honors/Awds:** Outstanding Achievement, Asn Black Women Lawyers, 1980; Mary Philbrook Award, Rutgers Law Sch, 1986; Woman of the Year, Zonta Club Int, 1986. **Business Addr:** Presiding Judge, State of New Jersey Superior Court 5th Vicinage, 50 W Market St Rm 514 NCB, Newark, NJ 07102.*

LESTER, BILL (WILLIAM ALEXANDER LESTER, III)
Race car driver. **Personal:** Born Feb 6, 1961, Washington, DC; married Cheryl; children: William Alexander IV. **Educ:** Univ CA, Berkeley, BS, elec engineering & comput sci. **Career:** Hewlett-Packard, software engr & proj mgr, 1982-98; pro racecar driver, 1998; Bill Davis Racing Inc, driver, 2004; NASCAR Craftsman Truck Series, driver; Rolex Sports Car Series, driver, 2008-. **Orgs:** NASCAR Diversity Council; Int Motor Sports Asns (IMSA). **Honors/Awds:** Rookie of the Year, SCCA N CA Region, 1985; Regional Road Racing Championship, SCCA GT-3, 1986; Four-Hour Endurance Race Championship, RDC, 1989, 1991. **Special Achievements:** Filming his first TV commercial to advertise the NASCAR Craftsman Truck Series; First African American to drive in NASCAR Nextel Cup debut in 20 years. **Business Addr:** Professional Racecar Driver, Rolex Sports Car Series, 1801 W Int Speedway Blvd, Daytona Beach, FL 32114-1243, **Business Phone:** (386)947-6681.*

LESTER, DONALD
Educator. **Personal:** Born Sep 20, 1944, Detroit, MI; married; children: Tarik. **Educ:** Wayne State Univ, BS, 1967; Western Mich Univ, EdM, 1972. **Career:** Detroit Pub Sch Syst, teacher; Wayne County Community Col, instr; Univ Detroit, instr; Western Mich Univ, instr; Shaw Col, assoc prof. **Orgs:** Nat dir Basic Training, Black Christian Nationalist Church; vice chmn Reg 1; bd ed, Detroit Schs; southern reg bishop, Shrines of the Black Madonna of the Pan-African Orthodox Christian Church; chmn, Atlanta Housing Auth; Kappa Alpha Psi Fraternity.

LESTER, ELTON J.
Lawyer. **Personal:** Born Sep 28, 1944, Bronx, NY; married Sandra Hight; children: Eric, Shawne. **Educ:** Atlantic Union Col, BA, 1966; Howard Univ, JD, 1969. **Career:** Off Mgt & Budget, examr; US Dept Housing & Urban Develop, atty & adv, Asst Gen Coun, currently. **Orgs:** Fed Bar Asn; DC Bar Asn; Nat Bar Asn; Omega Psi Phi; Urban League; Concerned Black Fathers. **Honors/Awds:** Recipient, Ford Found Scholar, 1966. **Business Addr:** Assistant General Counsel, US Dept Housing & Urban Develop, Off of Assisted Housing & Community Develop, 451 Seventh St SW, Room 8158, Washington, DC 20410.*

LESTER, GEORGE LAWRENCE
Writer, executive, historian. **Personal:** Born Dec 11, 1949, Charleston, AR; son of George and Casteline Williams; married Valcinia Marie Boyd, Jul 3, 1976; children: Tiffany, Marisa & Erica Joi. **Educ:** Columbia Col, BA, 1978. **Career:** Negro Leagues Base Ball Mus, co-founder & res dir, 1990-95; Negro Leagues Comt, co-chmn, currently. **Orgs:** NAACP; Asn Study Afro Am Life & Hist; Soc Am Baseball Res; Am First Day Cover Soc; Am Topical Asn; Black Am Philatelic Soc; vpres, Midwest Afro Am Genealogy Interest Coalition, 1995; African Am Mus Asn; Am Jazz Mus; Asn Prof Basketball Res; Ebony Soc Philatelic Events & Reflections; Nat Asn Black Sch Educr; Nat Baseball Hall of Fame & Mus; Negro Leagues Baseball Mus; N Am Soc Sports History; Prof Football Res Asn. **Honors/Awds:** Black Collectors Hall of Fame, 1992; Chairman Award, Negro Baseball Leagues Celebrations Inc, 1995. **Special Achievements:** The Negro Leagues Book, 1994; Silhouettes Newsletter, 1992-95; Discover Greatness Yearbook, 1993-95; Programmer & Creator of DataBall; National Baseball Hall of Fame, Blue Ribbon Committee; guest curator at Dallas African Am Mus exhibit: Triumph over Adversity: Black Baseball in Chicago, 2000; Black Baseball in Detroit, 2000; Black Baseball in Kan City, 2000; Black Baseball in Pittsburgh, 2001; Black Baseball's National Showcase: the East-West All-Star Game, 1933-53, 2002. **Home Addr:** PO Box 380146, Kansas City, MO 64138, **Home Phone:** (816)358-0475.

LESTER, ISAAC
Association executive. **Personal:** Son of Isaac Lester Sr. **Career:** The Education Hwy Found, pres, currently. **Business Addr:** President, The Education Highway Foundation, National Sales Office, 96 Linwood Plz Suite 325, Fort Lee, NJ 07024, **Business Phone:** (201)862-0206.

LESTER, JULIUS
Educator, writer. **Personal:** Born Jan 27, 1939, St Louis, MO; son of Woodie Daniel and Julia B Smith; married Alida Carolyn Fechner, Mar 21, 1979; children: Elena Milad & David Julius (Step Daughter); children: Jody Simone & Malcolm Coltrane. **Educ:** Fisk Univ, Nashville, TN, BA, 1960. **Career:** Look Out, Whitey! Black Power's Gon' Get Your Mama, Dial Press, 1968; To Be A Slave, Dial Press, 1968, author of fiction, including Black Folktales, Baron, 1969; Revolutionary Notes, 1969; The Thought & Writings of W E B Dubois, 2 vols, Random House, 1971; Search for the New Land, 1969; Two Love Stories, 1972; The Knee High Man & Other Tales, 1972 The Seventh Son, All Is Well: An Autobiography, Morrow, 1976, Lovesong: Becoming A Jew, Holt, 1988; Long Journey Home: Stories from Black History, Dial Press, 1972; author of poems, Who I Am, Dial Press, 1974; This Strange New Feeling, Dial Press, 1982; The Tales of Uncle Remus: The Adventures of Brer Rabbit, Dial Press, 1987, More Tales of Uncle Remus: The Further Adventures of Brer Rabbit, Dial Press, 1988, Do Lord Remember Me, Dial Press, 1984; How Many Spots Does a Leopard Have, Dial Press, 1989; Falling Pieces of the Broken Sky, Arcade Publications, 1990; The Last Tales of Uncle Remus, 1994; All Our Wounds Forgiven, 1994; John Henry, 1994; The Man Who Knew Too Much, 1994; Othello: A Novel!, 1995; Caldecott Honor Book, 1996; Sam & The Tigers, 1996; From Slaveship to Freedom Road, 1998; Black Cowboy, Wild Horses, 1998; What a Truly Cool World, 1999; When the Began, 1999. Pharaoh's Daughter, Harcourt/Silver Whistle, 2000; Albidaro & the Mischievous Dream, Phyllis Fogelman Books, 2000; Ackamarackus: Julius Lester's Sumptuously Silly Fabulously Funny Fables, Scholastic, 2001; When Dad Killed Mom, 2001, The Blues Singers: Ten Who Shook the World, Hyperiod/Jump At The Sun, 2001; Why Heaven is Far Away, Scholastic, 2001; Shining, Harcourt/Silver Whistle, 2003; Let's Talk about Race, 2003, The Autobiography of God, 2003; Univ Massachusetts, Amherst, MA, prof, 1971-2003, vis prof, prof emer, currently. **Honors/Awds:** Newbery Honor Award, Am Libr Asn, 1969; Nat Book Award finalist, Am Publ Asn, 1972; Massachusetts State Professor of the Year, 1986; Nat Jewish Book Award Finalist, 1988; Boston Globe, Horn Book Award, 1995; 2006 Coretta Scott King Book Award. **Special Achievements:** First faculty member to have been awarded all three of the university's most prestigious faculty awards. **Business Addr:** Professor Emeritus, University Massachusetts, Herter 7th fl, Amherst, MA 01003-9312, **Business Phone:** (413)545-5871.

LESTER, NINA MACK
Journalist, consultant. **Personal:** Born in Fort Davis, AL; married Eugene A (deceased); children: Rev Adlai, Valinda & Regina. **Career:** WGPR TV, variety show hostess, 1976; Consumer Guardian Newspaper,co organizers, 1972; Detroit Courier, adv & gen mgr; L & T Advert Specialties Gifts, founder. **Orgs:** Samaritan Hosp Div Brd Qual Assurance; adv brd, Women Comn, United Negro Col Fund; League Women Voters; Adv Comm Exp Negro Hist & Educ; Deaconess emer, Plymouth United Church Christ; Nat & Area Publicist; pres, Top Ladies Distinction; trustee, Met Assn United Church Christ; bd mem, Booker T Washington Bus Asn; Urban League Guild; Chamber Comn; pres, Eta Phi Beta; life mem, Nat Assn Advan Colored People; Million Dollar Club, 1991; Women's Assn Detroit Symphony Orchestra. **Honors/Awds:** Service Award March of Dimes, 1966; Recognition Certificate, Un Comn NegroHist, 1967; Woman of the Year, 1971; Town Crier Bell Award & Citizen ofYear Award, Ford Motor Co; Honorary Doctorate Humanities, Shaw Col, 1983;Top Lady of the Year, 1983; Outstanding Mother of the Year, Highland ParkYMCA, 1983; Detroit Urban League Guild Initiative Award, 1985; DetroitCity Council Testimonial Resolution, 1985; National Top Lady of the Year,1991-93; Spirit of Detroit Award, 1992; Budweiser Community Award, 1993;Edith Gamble Award, Outstanding Community Service; UNCF, 1993-95;Meritorius Service Award, United Negro Col Fund Inc, 1994; PresidentAward, Eta Phi Beta, 1995; Volunteer Recognition Award, UNCF. **Special Achievements:** First black to work for Ford World in Dearborn.

LESTER, TIM LEE (TIMOTHY LEE LESTER)
Football player, football coach, advocate. **Personal:** Born Jun 15, 1968, Miami, FL; son of Johnny and Robbie; married Kendra; children: Brandi & Breanna. **Educ:** Eastern Kent Univ, graduated Criminol & Pshycol. **Career:** Football player (retired), Football coach,partner: Los Angeles Rams, 1992-94; Pittsburgh Steelers, running back, 1995-98; Dallas Cowboys, running back, 1999; Melbourne Cent Catholic High Sch, asst head football coach & offensive cord; Chamimade Madonna High Sch, volunt coach team couns, recrut cord & run backs coach,2001; Scottish Claymores, coaching asst, 2004, Lovells, leader capital market & securitization team;AAR, partner corp & fin,2007-. **Orgs:** Founder, Tim

Lester Cares Inc, 2000-. **Honors/Awds:** Unsung Hero Award, Nat Football League, 1995,1996; ALB Japan Law Awards, Intl Deal Maker of the Year Award. **Business Addr:** Partner, Allens Arthur Robinson, Level 37 QV 1 250 St Georges Terrace, Perth, WA G2 5QD, Australia, **Business Phone:** (618)9488-3841.

LESTER, TIMOTHY LEE. See LESTER, TIM LEE.

LESTER, WILLIAM ALEXANDER, III. See LESTER, BILL.

LESTER, DR. WILLIAM ALEXANDER
Chemist, educator. **Personal:** Born Apr 24, 1937, Chicago, IL; son of William Alexander and Elizabeth Frances Clark; married Rochelle Diane Reed; children: William Alexander III & Allison Kimberleigh. **Educ:** Univ Chicago, BS, 1958, MS, 1959; Cath Univ Am, PhD, 1964. **Career:** Nat Bur Standards, phys chemist, 1961-64; Univ Wis-Madison, Theoret Chem Inst, from res assoc to asst dir, 1964-68; Univ Wis-Madison, Dept Chem, lectr, 1966-68; Int Bus Mach, San Jose Res Lab, from res staff mem to mgr, 1968-78; IBM TJ Watson Res Lab, technol planning staff, 1975-76; Lawrence Berkeley Lab, assoc dir, 1978-81; Nat Resource Comput Chem, dir, 1978-81; Univ Calif, Berkeley, prof chem, 1981-, assoc dean, Col Chem, 1991-95; NSF, Human Resource Develop, sr fel for sci & eng, asst dir, 1995-96. **Orgs:** Vol Instr Proj, Spec Elem Educ Disadvantaged, 1970-72; chmn, Black Liason Comn, San Jose Unified Sch Dist, 1971-72; Chem Eval Panel, Air Force Off Sci Res, 1974-78; US Nat Community Int Union Pure & Appl Chem, 1976-79; coun mem, Gordon Res Conf, 1977-2000; chmn, Div Phys Chem, Am Chem Soc, 1979; Nat Res Coun Panel Chem Physics, Nat Bur Stand, 1980-83; Chem Adv Panel NSF, 1980-83; Community Survey Chem Scis, Nat Acad Scis, 1982-84; bd mem, Marcus Foster Educ Inst, 1982-86; Community Recommendations AUS Basic Res, 1984-87; chmn, Div Chem Physics, Am Phys Soc, 1986-87; adv bd, World Book Inc, 1989-93; fel AAAS, 1991; mem, adv bd, Model Inst Excellence, Spelman Col, 1991-; Fed Networking Coun Adv Comt, 1991-95; fel Calif Acad Sciences, 1994; Army Res Lab Tech Assessment Bd, 1996-99; External Vis Comt, Nat Partnership Advan Computational Infrastructure, 1999-2002; Selection & Scheduling Comt, 2000-; pres's comt mem, Nat Medal Sci, 2000-02; Dept Energy Adv Comt, Advan Computational Comput, 2000-04; bd mem, Chem Sci & Technol, Nat Res Coun, 2003-. **Honors/Awds:** Outstanding Contribution Award, Int Buis Mach Corp, 1974; Percy L Julian Award, Nat Orgn Black Chemists & Chem Engrs, 1979; Alumni Award in Science, Catholic Univ Am, 1983; Outstanding Teacher Award, Nat Orgn Black Chemists & Chem Engrs, 1986; Professorial Achievement Award, Northern CA Coun Black Prof Engrs, 1989; Outstanding Service Award, NSF, 1996. **Business Addr:** Professor of Chemistry, University of California Berkeley, Department of Chemistry, Rm 8 & 13 Gilman Hall, Berkeley, CA 94720-1460, **Business Phone:** (510)643-9590.

LESURE, JAMES
Actor. **Personal:** Born Sep 21, 1975, Los Angeles, CA. **Educ:** Univ Southern Calif, BFA, theater; Univ Kent. **Career:** Films: Giving It Up, 1999; The Package, 2005; The Ring Two, 2005; Love less in Los Angeles, 2007; TV: "Macbeth"; "Martin", 1992-96; "Space: Above & Beyond", 1995; "Mad About You", 1996; "Pacific Blue", 1996; "Diagnosis Murder", 1996; "Dangerous Minds", 1996; "Seinfeld", 1996; "Saved by the Bell: The New Class", 1997; "The Burning Zone", 1997; "The Drew Carey Show", 1997; "Getting Personal", 1998; "For Your Love", 1998-2003; "Alias"; "Suddenly Susan", 2000; "What Wouldn't Jesus Do?", 2002; "The Johnny Chronicles", 2002; "The Division", 2003; "Las Vegas", 2003-08; "Monk", 2008; "Lipstick Jungle", 2009; "The New Adventures of Old Christine", 2009; "Studio 60 On The Sunset Strip", guest appearance; "Seinfeld", guest appearance; "NYPD Blue", guest appearance; "The Drew Carey Show", guest appearance; "Lost", guest appearance. **Honors/Awds:** Most Valuable Player, NBA Entertainment League, 2006; Distinguished Support Award, Sickle Cell Disease Found; Outstanding Male Actor, MIB Prism Awards. **Military Serv:** Air Force Academy. **Business Addr:** Actor, Kyle Avery Public Relations, 1107 Fair Oaks Ave Suite 321, Pasadena, CA 91030.*

LETSON, AL. See LETSON, ALFRED, JR.

LETSON, ALFRED, JR. (AL LETSON)
Poet, playwright, actor. **Personal:** Born Aug 8, 1972, Plainsfield, NJ; son of Alfred Sr and Ruth; children: Brooklyn, Greg & Syrus. **Career:** Poet, 1998-; playwright, 2001-; radio host; Author: Stoplights, short film, 1999; Essential Personal, play, 2001; Theatre Project, Griot: He who Speaks the Sweet Word, poetry slammer. **Honors/Awds:** Atlanta Grand Slam, 2000; 3rd rank Nat Poetry Slam 2000; Individual Artist Fellowship, State Fla, 2005. **Special Achievements:** Film: Sign Language, On the Lot; One of the three finalists out of more than 1,500 applicants to win the Public Radio Talent Quest. **Business Addr:** Playwright, Poetry Slammer, Theatre Project, 45 W Preston St, Baltimore, MD 21201.

LETT, GERALD WILLIAM
Entrepreneur. **Personal:** Born Sep 28, 1926, Lansing, MI; married Ruby Truitt; children: William, Gerald & Debra. **Career:** Lett's Bridal Inc, owner & pres, 1952-. **Orgs:** Mich Retailers Asn; YWCA; Lansing Econ Develop Corp; Lansing Sexton HS PTA; Nat Asn Advan Colored People; Urban League. **Honors/Awds:** Sales & Idea Book Citation Award, Int Newspaper Advert Exec; Boss of Year, Prof Women's Club; Man of Year, Negro Prof & Bus Women's Club. **Special Achievements:** First black retail owner to have story written on him Women's Wear Daily. **Business Addr:** President, Lett's Bridal Inc, 2225 E Grand River Ave, Lansing, MI 48912-3292, **Business Phone:** (517)484-0944.

LEVELL, EDWARD, JR.
Manager, military leader. **Personal:** Born Apr 2, 1931, Jacksonville, AL; son of Edward A Sr (deceased) and Gabrella Williams (deceased); married Rosa M Casellas, Aug 3, 1951; children: Edward A III (deceased), Ruben C, Kenneth W (deceased), Raymond C (deceased), Randy C, Cheryl D Levell Rivera & Michael K. **Educ:** Tuskegee Inst, BS, 1953; USAF, Bryan AFB, USAF Pilot Training, 1953-54; Univ Northern Co, Greeley, MA, Urban Sociol, 1972; Air War Col, Maxwell AFB, AL, leadership, mgt, 1973-74; Indust Col Armed Forces, MA, mgt, 1973. **Career:** Military leader, Manager (retired); USAF, col, 1953-83, Acad Comdr, Colo Springs, Cadet Group l, 1970-72, dep commandant Cadets, 1972-73, Hurlburt AFB, comdr 1st Spec Opers WG Wing, 1976-77, USAF, Luke, AFB, comdr 58th Tactical Training Wing, 1977-78, Langley AFB, comdr 20th Air Div, 1978-83; Chicago, dir aviation, 1984-89; New Orleans Airport, dep dir aviation, 1989-92, dir aviation, 1992. **Orgs:** Life mem, Kappa Alpha Psi Fraternity; life mem, The Retired Officers Asn (TROA); life mem, The Daedalian Found; life mem, The Tuskegee Airman Inc (TAI). **Honors/Awds:** Top Gun Award, USAFE, 1961; Top Gun, Tactical Air Command (TAC), 1961, 1965, 1969; Vietnam Campaign Medals, 1965-69; Distinguished Flying Cross, 1969; Air Force Commendation Medal, 1966; Air Medal (eight awards) 1970; Meritorious Service Medal, 1970; Distinguished Service Award, Jacksonville, 1974; Air Force Asn Special Citation of Merit, State Fla, 1977; State Fla Comn Human Relations Award Special Recognition, 1977; Legion of Merit Award, 1983; Hall of Fame, Tuskegee Univ, 1991. **Special Achievements:** First & only African-American commander of the 1st Special Operations Wing at Hurlburt Field; first Air Force pilot to log 3,000 flying hours in the F-100 Super Sabre aircraft. **Military Serv:** USAF, 1953-83.

LEVENS, DORSEY
Football player. **Personal:** Born May 21, 1970, Syracuse, NY; son of Herbert and Patricia; children: Amaya. **Educ:** Ga Tech, mgt. **Career:** Football player (retired); Green Bay Packers, 1994-2001; Philadelphia Eagles, 2002, 2004-05; New York Giants, 2003; NFL analyst, currently. **Orgs:** Founder & chief exec officer, Dorsey Levens Found. **Honors/Awds:** Pro Bowl selection, 1997; All-Pro selection, 1997. *

LEVER, LAFAYETTE
Basketball player, basketball executive. **Personal:** Born Aug 18, 1960, Pine Bluff, AR. **Educ:** Ariz State Univ, BA, educ, 1982. **Career:** Basketball player (Retired), basketball exec; Portland Trail Blazers, 1982-84; Denver Nuggets, 1984-90; Dallas Mavericks, 1990-94; Sacramento Kings, dir player develop, 2007-. **Orgs:** NBPA, vpres, 1987; Nat Basketball Asn. **Honors/Awds:** All-NBA Second Team, 1987; NBA All-Defensive Second Team, 1988; All Star, 1988, 1990. **Business Addr:** Director of Player Development, Sacramento Kings, 1 Sports Pkwy, Sacramento, CA 95834, **Business Phone:** (916)928-0000.

LEVERETTE, DR. MICHELLE A
Administrator, health services administrator. **Personal:** Born Oct 27, 1962, Washington, DC; daughter of James and Gloria Abram; widowed; children: Kristin M & James A. **Educ:** Tougaloo Col, BS, 1984; Johns Hopkins Sch Med, MD, 1988. **Career:** Bienville Med Group, pediatrician, 1991-93; pvt pract, pediatrician, 1991-93; Johns Hopkins Med Serv, pediatrician, 1993-95; Johns Hopkins Hosp, Dept Pediat, instr, 1995-99; Baltimore Co Dept Health, dir & health off, 1995. **Orgs:** Friends C MS, Med Adv Bd, Baltimore Co Med Asn; Md Med & Chirurgical Asn; Md Asn Co Health Offrs; Nat Asn Co & City Health Offs; Am Pub Health Asn; adv comn, Johns Hopkins Comnunity Health Workers; res & adv panel, Inst Racial & Ethnic Health Studies, Univ Md; Md Sch-Based Heatlh Ctr Policy Adv Coun; State Interagency Coord Coun Infants & Toddlers; Md Partnership C & Families; Gov Task Force Emerging Med & Surg Treatments; US Congman Ben Cardin's Health Adv Comn; chair, Baltimore Co Local Mgt Bd. **Honors/Awds:** Civil Service Award, Baltimore Co Chap, Nat Asn Advan Colored People, 1997; Distinguished Woman in Health, Alliance Black Attys Md, 1997; Glass Ceiling Award, Nat Coalition 100 Black Women, 1997; Renaissance Award, Fullwood Found, 1998; Award for outstanding contributions to church & community, Bethel AME Church, 1998; Outstanding Community Service Award, Baltimore Drifters Inc, 1998; Special Recognition Award, Essex-Middle River-White Marsh Chamber Com, 2000; Top 100 Women, Daily Register, Md, 2001. **Special Achievements:** Created Partners for Health Improvement Plan (PARTNERSHIP), which provides health care to Baltimore County's working poor; annual publication, "Health Profile Update"; first African American and youngest person to head the Baltimore County Department of Health. **Business Addr:** Director, Health officer, Baltimore County Department of Health, 400 Washington Ave, Towson, MD 21204, **Business Phone:** (410)887-3196.*

LEVERMORE, CLAUDETTE MADGE
School administrator. **Personal:** Born Feb 28, 1939, St Andrew, Jamaica; daughter of Herbert Willacy; married Oswald Burchell; children: Monique Althea & Jacqueline Maureen. **Educ:** McGill Univ, cert, 1968; Univ Miami, BBA, 1978; Wharton Univ, cert, 1981; Nova Univ, MBA, 1984. **Career:** Govt Jamaica, civil servant, 1958-64; Geigy Pharmaceut, admin asst, 1964-68; McGill Univ, admin asst, 1968-71; Univ Miami, dir admin serv, 1971-; Miami Dade South Campus, instr, 1984-. **Orgs:** Woodson Williams Marshall Asn, 1978-; Nat Black MBA Asn; bd mem, Black Cult Art Ctr, Black S Fla Coalition Econ Develop; Nursing Sch Bus Officers Asn; bd mem & treas, United Nations Fla Chapter. **Honors/Awds:** Outstanding Achievement Acct, Univ Miami; Outstanding Achievement Bus Consult, Univ Miami. **Home Addr:** 14865 SW 166th St, Miami, FL 33187. **Business Phone:** (305)995-1000.

LEVERMORE, JACQUELINE MAUREEN
Publisher. **Personal:** Born Oct 10, 1968, Montreal, Canada;daughter of Oswald and Claudette. **Educ:** Univ Miami, BA, 1990; Univ Iowa, Col Law, JD, 1993. **Career:** Mustered Seed Publishing Worldwide Inc, chief exec officer, 1993-. **Honors/Awds:** Gold Drum Award, 1986; Iron Arrow Hon Soc, 1990; Bowman Ashe Scholar. **Business Addr:** Chief Executive Officer, Mustered Seed Publishing Worldwide Inc., PO Box 192011, Dallas, TX 75219, **Business Phone:** (214)252-9704.

LEVERMORE, DR. MONIQUE A
Psychologist. **Personal:** Born Oct 29, 1966, Montreal, Canada;daughter of Claudette and Oswald; married Mark Bartolone, Oct 17, 1998; children: Nino & Kai. **Educ:** Univ Miami, BA, psychol, 1988, MSEd, psychol, 1990; Howard Univ, MS, clin psychol, 1990, PhD, clin psychol, 1995. **Career:** Johns Hopkins Med Inst, psychol extern, 1993-94; Harvard Med Sch, psychol intern, 1994-95; Eckerd Youth Develop Ctr, resident psychologist, 1995-96; Palm Beach Atlantic Col, asst prof, dir couns ctr, 1996-97; Levermore Psychol Servs, pres, psychologist, 1997-; Fla Inst Technol, asst prof, 1998-2004; Miami Teaching Fel, 2006-08; Carlos Albizu Univ, assoc prof, 2008-. **Orgs:** Am Psychological Asn, 1995-; founder, dir, GIRLS, 1998-2003; co-founder, Adolescent Behav Inst; Links Inc, 2003-; adv bd mem, Salvation Army. **Honors/Awds:** Outstanding Young Women Am Award, 2000; Woman of Distinction, Education & Govt, Girl Scouts Citrus Coun. **Business Addr:** President, Licensed Clinical Psychologist, Levermore Psychological Services, PA, Palmetto Bay Ctr 15715 S Dixie Hwy Suite 334, Palmetto Bay, FL 33157, **Business Phone:** (305)763-9095.

LEVERT, EDDIE
Actor, singer. **Personal:** Born Jun 16, 1942, Bessemer, AL; married Raquel Capelton; married Martha, Jan 1, 1966 (divorced); children: Gerald & Sean. **Career:** The O'Jays, singer, currently; Albums: Comin' Through, 1965; Back on Top, 1968; Back Stabbers, 1972; Peace, 1975; So Full of Love, 1978; My Favorite Person, 1982; Love Fever, 1984; Serious, 1989; Heartbreaker, 1993; Love You to Tears, 1997; For the Love, 2001; TV Series: "Tavis Smiley", 2004-07; "The Apprentice", 2004; "The View", 2005; "Jimmy Kimmel Live!", 2005; Films: Coming to America, 1988; The Fighting Temptations, 2003; An Evening of Stars: 25th Anniversary Tribute to Lou Rawls, 2004; TV Movies: "Rock & Roll Hall of Fame Induction Ceremony", 2005; "An Evening with Quincy Jones", 2008.

LEVERT, FRANCIS E.
Engineer. **Personal:** Born Mar 28, 1940, Tusculoosa, AL; married Faye Burnett, 1965; children: Francis, Gerald, Lisa. **Educ:** Tuskegee Inst, BS, 1964; Univ Mich, MS, 1966; Pa State Univ, PhD, nuclear engineering, 1971. **Career:** Tuskegee Inst, Sch Engr, actg head mech engineering, 1972-73; Commonwealth Edison Co, prin engr, 1973-74; Argonne Nat Lab, nuclear engr appl physics div, 1974-79; Tech Energy Corp, chief scientist, 1979-85; Trans-Africa Gas & Elec, tech adv, 1999-; KEMP Corp, pres, currently. **Orgs:** Am Nuclear Soc; exec comt, Plant Maintenance Div; Am Soc Mech Engrs; Phi Kappa Phi; Pi Tau Sigma; Beta Kappa Chi; Nat Soc Prof Engrs; fel, Atomic Energy Comn, Univ Mich; Am Soc Engineering Educ; fel, Ford Found; fel, Pa State Univ. **Special Achievements:** Inventor: 23 US Patents; author of two books & 63 technical journals, articles. **Business Addr:** President, Kemp Corporation, 1909 Matthew Lane, Knoxville, TN 37923, **Business Phone:** (865)691-0860.*

LEVINGSTON, BASHIR
Football player. **Personal:** Born Oct 2, 1976, Seaside, CA. **Educ:** Eastern Wash Univ, admin justice. **Career:** New York Giants, defensive back, 1999-2000; Amsterdam Admirals, 2000; Toronto Argonauts, 2002-07; Montreal Alouettes, 2007; free agent, currently. **Honors/Awds:** All-NFL Europe honors; Outstanding Special Teams Player & East Division Special Teams Player of the Year, 2003; Grey Cup, 2004. **Special Achievements:** CFL record when he returned a missed field goal by Paul Mc Callum for a 129 yard touchdown.

LEVINGSTON, CLIFFORD EUGENE
Basketball player, basketball coach. **Personal:** Born Jan 4, 1961 San Diego, CA. **Educ:** Wichita State Univ, Wichita, KS, 1979-82

Career: Basketball player (retired), basketball coach; Detroit Pistons, 1982-84; Atlanta Hawks, 1984-90; Chicago Bulls, 1990-92; Denver Nuggets, 1994-95; Fort Wayne Furhead coachy, asst coach, 2000; Dodge City Legend, asst coach, 2001, head coach, 2002; Harlem Globetrotters, asst coach; St. Louis Flight, coach, 2004; Gary Steel heads, asst coach, 2005; Kansas Cagerz, asst coach, 2006; Gary Steel heads, head coach, 2005-07; Kansas Cagerz, 2006; Oklahoma Cavalry, 2007. *

LEVISTER, DR. ERNEST CLAYTON
Physician. **Personal:** Born Feb 4, 1946, New York, NY; son of Ernest Clayton Sr and Ruth Amos; married Chris; children: E Clay & Michelle Nicole. **Educ:** Lincoln Univ, AB, chem, 1958; Lafayette Col, BS, chem engr, 1958; Howard Univ Col Med, MD, 1964. Am Col Prev Med, Fel, 1991. **Career:** Norfolk VA, internal medicine & cardiology pvt pract, 1974-78; Embassy USA Lagos Nigeria, med attache, 1978-79; Eastern Virginia Med Sch, asst prof; George Wash Sch Med, prof; Tuskegee Inst, Sch Engineering, instr; Pvt Pract, internal & occup med San Bernardino CA, 1979-; Univ Calif-Irvine, clinical prof internal & occup med 2002-. **Orgs:** Inst Sch Engr Tuskegee Inst, 1958-59; asst prof med George Wash Med Sch 1973-74; asst prof med Eastern VA Med Sch, 1974-81; fel Am Col Physicians, 1977; asst clinical prof internal & occup med, 1986-2001; radio host Medical Talk Show Norfolk, 1980-81; mem Los Angeles Coun Black Prof Engrs 1982-; comnr, Environ Protection Comn, Riverside CA, 1989-91; mem bd trustees, Lincoln Univ; pres, JW Vines Med Soc, 1994-2001; nat adv bd, Sci Edu New Civic Engagements & Responsibilites; Calif Sco Indust med & Surgery. **Honors/Awds:** Media Award, Asn Black Women Entrepreneurs, 1995; Dr Rosemary Schraer Humanitarian Award, 1999; Leadership Award, Calif Med Asn; Black Rose Award, San Bernardino Black Cult Found, 2000; Silver Scalpel Award, Calif Sco Indust med & Surgery, 2000; Outstanding Contribution to the Community Award, San Bernardino County Med Soc, 2003; Robert D. Sparks Leadership Achievement Award, 2004. **Military Serv:** AUS, Med Corps major, 1969-72; Vietnam, Unit Citation. **Business Addr:** Owner, Medical Practice, 1738 N Waterman Ave St 1, San Bernardino, CA 92404, **Business Phone:** (909)883-8683.

LEVISTER, WENDELL P.
Judge. **Personal:** Born May 14, 1928, Rocky Mount, NC; divorced; children: Degna P, Drew F. **Educ:** Hampton Inst, BS, 1950; NY Univ, MBA, 1951; NY Univ Law Sch, JD, 1958; Stanford Univ, cert Stanford Exec Prog, 1973. **Career:** Greenup Golar & Levister Esqs, co-founder, 1960-63; NY City Law Dept, asst corp counsel, 1963-67; Borough Brooklyn NYC, dir off spec proj city planning comm, 1970-74; fel, Merrill Found; Dept Parks & Recreation, deputy comnr revenue develop & park policy, 1979-; NY City Civil Court , judge. **Orgs:** Chief Internal Rev DAC HQ Ft Wadsworth USARADCOM SI, NY; assoc, Am Inst Planners 1973; Bedford Stuyvesant Lawyers Asn; Brooklyn Bar Asn; Omega Psi Phi; bd dir, Stuyvesant Community Ctr Brooklyn, 1964-65; Nat Asn Advan Colored People; exec bd United People's Com Brooklyn UPC, 1973-. **Military Serv:** USAF 1946-47.

LEVY, VALERIE LOWE
Government official. **Personal:** Born in New York, NY; married Edward J Levy Jr; children: Vanessa Lynn & Edward Joseph III. **Educ:** NY Univ, BA; City Col NY, grad studies; New Sch Social Res, masters candidate. **Career:** New York City, Dept Aging, dir, Manhatten field off, 1969-79, dir minority affairs, 1990. **Orgs:** Geront Soc Am, 1973-; Bd mem, Nat Caucus & Ctr Black Aged, Wash, DC,1974-05; Am Pub Health Asn, 1979-; Delta Sigma Theta Sorority. **Honors/Awds:** Has written and presented many papers on aging and the elderly in the US; also a recognized authority on the minority elderly. **Special Achievements:** One of original organizers & coordinator of the Harlem Interagency Council on Aging. **Business Addr:** Director of Minority Affairs, New York City Department for the Aging, 2 Lafayette St, New York, NY 10007.

LEVY, VICTOR MILES, JR.
Television news anchorperson. **Personal:** Born Nov 7, 1931, Philadelphia, PA; divorced; children: 3. **Career:** KDKA-TV, corresp; NBC monitor-Radio press internat, voice am, 1966-71; WHOA radio, prog news dir; WCBS-TV repoter anchorman, 1995. **Orgs:** The Inner Circle. **Honors/Awds:** Numerous honors & awards including Community Service Award; Pittsburgh Guardian Soc, 1970; Black Achiever Award, Harlem YMCA, 1972; Ministerial Interfaith Association Media Award, 1977; WCBS-TV, 3 Emmy Awards, 1976, 1991 & 1993; Several nominations; Deadline Feature Award, WY Soc Prof Journalists; Women in Communications, "Clarion Award;" AP & UPT Awards. **Special Achievements:** First Black to Anchor Sched News Prog in Pittsburgh. **Military Serv:** USAF, 1950-54.

LEVYCHIN, RICHARD
Accountant. **Personal:** Born Feb 13, 1959, London, England; son of Cosmo Levychin and Mary; married Belinda, Aug 20, 1988; children: Richard Jr. **Educ:** Bernard M Baruch, CUNY, BBA, 1982. **Career:** Deloitte Touche, sr acct, 1982-85; Adler & Topal, supvr, 1985-87; Backer, Berson & Adler, supvr, 1987-88; Richard Levychin, CPA, pres, 1988-93; Kahn, Boyd, Levychin, Co, partner, 1993-; KBL Eisner LLP, managing patner, currently; RFM Broadcasting Inc, chief financial officer, currently. **Orgs:** Am Inst Certified Public Accts, 1982-; NY State Soc Certified Public Accts, 1982-; 100 Black Men, 1985-; treas, 100 Black Men Inc; Nat Asn Black Accts Inc; Nat Asn Tax Prof; Nat Asn Black Accts Inc. **Honors/Awds:** 40 Under 40, Network Jour, 1998. **Business Phone:** (212)843-4100.

LEWELLEN, MICHAEL ELLIOTT
Public relations executive, administrator. **Personal:** Born Jan 16, 1960, Marianna, AR; son of Mildred King and Herman L; married Merle Williams, Aug 6, 1983; children: Elliott. **Educ:** Ark State Univ, Jonesboro, Ark, BS, jour, 1982. **Career:** Pine Bluff Com, Pine Bluff, Ark, sports reporter, 1982-85; Bloom Tennis Ctr, Pine Bluff, Ark, tennis pro, 1983-85; Southwestern Bell Tel, St Louis, Mo, pub rel mgr, 1985-91; Nike Inc, urban & minority affairs dir; Black Entertainment TV, vpres corp commun, sr vpres corp commun, currently. **Orgs:** Treas, St Louis Asn Black Journalists, 1987-88; bd dir, nat adv coun, Nat Asn Partners Educ, 1989-; bd dir, St Louis Jour Found, 1990; pres, Int Asn Bus Communicators, St Louis Chap, 1990. **Honors/Awds:** Yes I Can Role Model for Minority Youth, St Louis Metro Sentinel Newspaper, 1986; Cert Prof, US Prof Tennis Asn, 1986-; Accredited Bus Communicator, Int Asn Bus Communicators, 1989; Corporate Volunteer Award, St Louis Affiliate Nat Black Child Development Institute, 1990; Accredited Pub Rel Prof, Pub Rel Soc Am, 1991. **Business Phone:** (202)608-2003.

LEWIS, AISHA
Engineer. **Personal:** Born Oct 30, 1971, Indianapolis, IN; daughter of Cleveland A Lewis and Betty F Lewis. **Educ:** Purdue Univ, AS-EET 1995, BS-EET, 1997. **Career:** IBM Corp, electronic assembly mfg engr, 1997-99, mfg test engr, 1999-2003, mfg engineering proj mgr, 2003-. **Orgs:** Nat Soc Black Engrs, 1990-; exec bd sec, Region IV, 1994-97, adv bd, 1999-; Ctr Leadership Develop Alumni, 1998. **Honors/Awds:** Engineering Technology Student Service Award, Purdue Univ Indianapolis, 1993; IBM Women in Technology Award, 2002; U.S. Women of Color in Science and Technology Award, 2002; Multicultural Women in Leadership Institute Alumni, 2003; IBM Bravo Award, 2004. **Special Achievements:** "Nightmare" (poem) published in Tomorrow's Dream, Natl Library of Poetry, 1996; Proficient in the Japanese language; musician (piano, organ, cello, taiko drum, drum kit, tenor guitar, tenor mandola, handbells). **Business Addr:** Manufacturing Engineering Project Manager, Lenovo International, Global Supply Chain Division, 3039 Cornwallis Rd, Research Triangle Park, NC 27709, **Business Phone:** (919)254-8098.

LEWIS, ALBERT RAY
Football player. **Personal:** Born Oct 6, 1960, Mansfield, LA. **Educ:** Grambling State Univ. **Career:** Football player (retired), football coach; Kans City Chiefs, corner back, 1983-93; Los Angeles Raiders, 1994; Oakland Raiders, 1995-98; San Diego Chargers, asst sec coach, 2006. **Honors/Awds:** Pro Bowl, 1987-90; NFL All-Star Team, Sporting News, 1989; AFC Top Defensive Back, Nat Football League Players Asn, 1989; Kansas City Chiefs Hall of Fame, 2007.

LEWIS, HON. ALEXIS OTIS
Judge. **Career:** State Ill, Circuit Ct, 20th Judicial Circuit, assoc judge, currently. **Orgs:** Ill Bar Asn, 1985-. **Business Addr:** Associate Judge, State of Illinois Circuit Court 20th Judicial Circuit, 10 Pub Sq, St Clair County Courthouse, Belleville, IL 62220, **Business Phone:** (618)277-7325.*

LEWIS, ALMERA P.
Educator, social worker. **Personal:** Born Oct 23, 1935, Chicago, IL; married Thomas P; children: Tracy & Todd. **Educ:** Univ Wis, BS, 1957; Loyola Univ, MSW, 1959. **Career:** Day Care Ctrs & Sch, counr; Ment Health Ctr, psychiatric & social worker, 1959-65; Crittenton Comprehensive Care Ctr, supvr prof staff, 1966-68; Park Forest Sch Syst, social worker, 1968-69; Chicago Circle-jane Adams Sch Social Work, work prest; Univ Ill, prof/dean studs, social work, acting dean, 1990-91. **Orgs:** Natl bd dir, Nat Asn Social Workers; Ill Asn Sch Social Workers; Acad Cert Social Workers; Am Asn Univ Prof Bd; Women's Community United Cerebral Palsy Greater Chicago; Chicago Urban League PUSH; Art Inst Chicago.

LEWIS, ALONZO TODD
Health services administrator. **Personal:** Born Jun 29, 1969, Detroit, MI; son of Alonzo and Vera Lewis. **Educ:** Univ Mich, BA, sociol, 1991, MHSA, 1993. **Career:** Mercy Health Serv, mgt fel, 1993-94; Mercy Hosp, dir sr servs, 1994-; Henry Ford Hosp. **Orgs:** Alpha Phi Alpha, Fraternity Inc, 1989-; assoc, Am Col Healthcare Exec, 1991-; Nat Asn Health Serv Exec, 1991-; bd mem, Adult Well-Being Serv. **Business Phone:** (313)579-4000.

LEWIS, DR. ALVIN
Executive. **Personal:** Born Oct 1, 1935, Chicago, IL; married Dr Juanita L; children: Alvin, Lydia & Lystrelle. **Educ:** Northern Bapt Sem, theol studies, 1962; KS State Univ, MS, 1970, PhD, 1975; Garrett Evangelicol Theol Sem, MDiv, 1993. **Career:** First Ch God, pastor, prof, dir; Minorities Res Ctr, family consult, 1966-74; Kans State Univ, from instr to asst prof, 1970-75; Minor Res & Res Ctr, dir, 1973-75; Bd Christian Educ Ch God, assoc secy, 1975-89; Nat Asn, Church God, chief exec officer, 1989-92; Vernon Park Church God, minister admin & spec programmer, 1992-. **Orgs:** Nat Coun Family Rel; dir, Nat Met Black Family Conf; Am Asn Univ Prof; vice chmn & comnr, Family Life Nat Coun Church; supvr & clin mem, Nat Acad Counr & Family Therapists Inc; cert leader marriage enrichment, Asn Couples Marriage Enrichment; former pres, Junction Manhattan Nat Asn Advan Colored People, 1967-71; vice chmn, Madison County Urban League, 1985-86; Phi Alpha Theta, 1969-71; Beverly Nat Bank; served as educ consult in Africa Caribbean & Europe. **Honors/Awds:** Omicron Hon Soc, 1968. **Business Addr:** Central Community Church of God, 2305 St Charles St, Jackson, MS 39209, **Business Phone:** (601)353-8678.

LEWIS, ANDRE
Banker, president (organization). **Personal:** Born May 4, 1960, Walterboro, SC; son of Clara Lee Martino and William; married Queen E Govan, Oct 15, 1983; children: Shana Nicole & William Andre. **Educ:** SC State Col, Orangeburg, BS, acct, 1982. **Career:** First Union National Bank, Columbia, SC, branch mgt, 1983-87; SC Nat Bank, Columbia, SC, assoc vpres corp banking, 1987-88; Victory Savings Bank, Columbia, SC, pres, 1988-92; Richland Teachers Coun FCU, pres, ceo, 1992-99; TLC Real Estate Holdings, pres, 1997-. **Orgs:** Bd mem, Comt 100, 1990-92; comt mem, United Way Midlands, 1989-90; bd mem, Greater Columbia Chamber Com, 1989-90. **Honors/Awds:** Outstanding Bus Achievement, Black Enterprise Magazine, 1990; Outstanding Alumnus, Upper Dorchester Alumni SC State Col, 1989; Business Person of the Year, Phi Beta Lambda, 1988. **Business Addr:** President, TLC Real Estate Holdings, PO Box 7432, Cola, SC 29202-7432, **Business Phone:** (803)799-6045.

LEWIS, DR. ANGELA K.
Educator. **Educ:** Univ Ala, BA, polit sci, regional & urban planning, master pub adminis; Univ Tenn, PhD. **Career:** Univ Ala, Birmingham, asst prof, currently. **Orgs:** Delta Sigma Theta Sorority Inc; Am Polit Sci Assn; Natl Coun Black Studies;Natl Conf Black Polit Scientists; Southwest Polit Sci Assn; Ala Black Fac Assn; UAB Black Fac Assn; Pi Sigma Alpha; Pi Alpha Alpha; Omicron Delta Kappa. **Special Achievements:** Published in the American Review of Politics. **Business Phone:** (205)934-9679.*

LEWIS, ARTHUR A., JR.
Accountant, auditor. **Personal:** Born Nov 4, 1925, Los Angeles, CA; son of Arthur and Verna Deckard Williams; married Elizabeth, Aug 1, 1970; children: Ivy, Derek, Cornell, Arthur III, Jeffrey, Jason. **Educ:** Univ Calif Los Angeles, BS, 1947. **Career:** Auditor (retired), accountant; Dept Energy, audit investr; Defense Contract Audit Agency; Golden State Mutual Life Ins Co, 1947-52; Vending Mach Bus La, owner, 1954-; Lewis Tax Serv, La, owner, currently. **Orgs:** Bd dirs, Southeast Symphony Asn; Fed Govt Accountants Asn; Nat Asn Advan Colored People; Urban League; Alpha Phi Alpha Frat; trustee, Lincoln Memorial Cong Church, Los Angeles. **Honors/Awds:** Cert, Cert Internal Auditor. **Military Serv:** AUS, e-5, 1952-54. **Home Addr:** 1749 Virginia Rd, Los Angeles, CA 90019. **Business Addr:** Owner, Lewis Tax Serv, 2415 W Martin Luther King Blvd, Los Angeles, CA 90008, **Business Phone:** (323)295-2258.*

LEWIS, ARTHUR W
Consultant. **Personal:** Born Jul 1, 1926, New York, NY; son of Arthur and Marlon. **Educ:** Dartmouth Col, BA, 1966, MA, 1969; Foreign Serv Inst, Postgrad 1970. **Career:** USIA, foreign serv, US Embassy, cult affairs officer Bucharest, 1970-72, counr pub affairs Lusaka, 1972-74, Addis Ababa, 1974-77, Lagos 1977-79, dir African Affairs 1979-; US ambassador, Repub Sierre Leone, 1983-86; Fletcher Sch Law & Diplomacy, Edward R Murrow fel, 1986-87; Nord Resources Corp, sr consult, currently. **Military Serv:** USN, 1943-45, 1950-. **Business Phone:** (520)292-0266.

LEWIS, DR. BETTYE DAVIS
Association executive, president (organization). **Educ:** Univ Houston, psychol; Prairie View A&M Univ Col Nursing, BS, nursing, 1959; Univ Houston, BA, 1972; Tex Southern Univ, MA, EdD, 1982. **Career:** Allen Health Care Inc, dir nurses; Diversified Health Care Syst Inc, adminr & supv nurse, ceo; Tex Southern Univ, adj prof; Nat Black Nurses Asn, pres, currently. **Orgs:** Ethnic Coalition Minority Nurse Asn; Black Nurses Asn Greater Houston; Jessie Jackson Acad; Negro Coun Black Women; Nat Cong Black Women; United Negro Col Fund; Am Cancer Soc; Alzheimer's & Related Diseases, State TX; State Bar Grievance Comt; Nat Heartburn Alliance; sr fel, Am Leadership Forum; fel, Int Soc Hypertension Blacks. **Honors/Awds:** Edith Irby Jones Leadership Award, 2000; Lifetime Achievement Award, Black Nurses Asn, 2000; Distinguished Leadership Award, Nat Cong Black Women, 2003; Leadership Achievement Award, Zeta Phi Beta Sorority, 2003; One of Ebony magazine's 100 Most Influential Black Americans and Organization Leaders, 2005. **Special Achievements:** First African American selected as a Leadership Extern in Sigma Theta Tau International Honor Society. **Business Addr:** President, National Black Nurses As-

sociation, 8630 Fenton St Suite 330, Silver Spring, MD 20910-3803, **Business Phone:** (301)589-3200.*

LEWIS, BILLIE JEAN
Librarian. **Personal:** Born Dec 6, 1947, Eden, NC; daughter of William Manns and Darnella Blackstock Worthington; married Jerome M Lewis Jr, Aug 6, 1966; children: Jerome V & Jill Renee. **Educ:** Corning Community Col, AAS, 1983; Cornell Univ, cert, indust rels & human serv, 1984; Fla A&M Univ, BS, 1988; Univ Mich, MS, 1989. **Career:** Corning Glass Works, quality, ade aide, 1984-85; Fla State Univ, ade aide, 1985-88; Mich State Univ, GEAC operator, 1988; Wayne State Univ, res asst, 1989; Detroit Pub Libr, C librn, 1989-92, asst mgr, C librn, 1992-. **Orgs:** Am Libr Asn, 1989-94; chap, AFA C Book C chap, Fund-Raising Community, C Book Community, 1990-; Asn AFA Librns, 1992-; Detroit Pub Libr C Servs. **Business Addr:** Librarian, Detroit Public Library, Bowen Branch, 3648 W Vernor Hwy, Detroit, MI 48216-1441, **Business Phone:** (313)297-9381.

LEWIS, DR. BRENDA NEUMON
Educator, college administrator. **Personal:** Born in New Jersey; daughter of Jacob and Mari Neumon; married Woodrow Lewis Jr, Aug 19, 1972; children: Kayin, Kimani & Killian. **Educ:** Univ Copenhagen, attended 1969; Doane Col, BA, 1970; Atlanta Univ, MA,1974; Ohio State Univ, PhD, 1985. **Career:** Ohio State Univ, coordr, 1975-79; Univ Md, assoc dir coop educ, 1981-84; Old Dominion Univ, acting assoc dean, 1995-96, dir, interdisciplinary studs, 1985-99, asst vpres grad studies, 2004-; Norfolk State Univ, special assist to vpres, 1999-2000, assoc vpres acad affairs, 2000-04. **Orgs:** Bd mem, 1993-99, bd pres, 1995-97, YWCA; bd mem, Places C, 1994-97; bd mem, 1994-2000, chair, nominating comt, 1996, 1998, Old Dominion Univ Credit Union; Va Symphony Edu Comm, 1997-98; personnel comt, UWCA South Hampton Roads, 1999-. **Honors/Awds:** Leila Robinson Volunteer Award, YWCA, South Hampton Rds, 1995-97; Visionary Award, Old Dominion Univ, 1996; Outstanding Professor Award, ODU/Delta Sigma Lamda, 1997. **Special Achievements:** Publications: "Breaking Away" in Baby Care Magazine, 1983; "Qualitative Analysis: An Alternative to Traditional Research Methodology" in Benjamin E Mays Monograph, 1987. **Business Addr:** Assistant Vice President for Graduate Studies, Old Dominion University, 212 Koch Admin Bldg, Norfolk, VA 23529-0082, **Business Phone:** (757)683-4885.

LEWIS, BYRON E
Executive. **Personal:** Born Dec 25, 1931, Newark, NJ; son of Thomas Eugene and Myrtle Evelyn Allen; divorced; children: Byron Eugene Lewis Jr. **Educ:** Long Island Univ, BA, 1953; NY Univ, grad study; City Col NY; King Meml Col, hon DHL. **Career:** Urbanite Magazine, co-founder, 1961; Amalgamated Publs, asst advert mgr, 1963-64; Tuesday Magazine, vpres & advert dir, 1964-68; Uniworld Group Inc, chmn & chief exec officer; Afro Mkt Co, pres, 1968-69; Sounds City, exec producer, 1974-75. **Orgs:** Lectr, Black Col; Black Exec Exch Prog Nat Urban League; Am Inst Pub Serv; Phoenix House Found. **Honors/Awds:** Minority Bus Man of the Year, Interracial Coun Bus Opportunity, New York City, 1980. **Special Achievements:** ranked #2, Black Enterprise's list of Top Advertising Agencies, 1999, #1, 2000. **Military Serv:** AUS, pfc, 1953-55. **Business Addr:** Founder, UniWorld Group Inc., Fl 16 100 Ave of the Americas, New York, NY 10013, **Business Phone:** (212)219-1600.*

LEWIS, CARL (FREDERICK CARLTON LEWIS)
Track and field athlete, actor. **Personal:** Born Jul 1, 1961, Birmingham, AL; son of William Mckinley Lewis Jr(deceased) and Evelyn Lawler. **Educ:** Univ Houston, communs, 1979. **Career:** Track & field athlete (retired), actor; track & field athlete, 1984-96; Films: Atomic Twister, 2002; Alien Hunter, 2003; The Last Adam, 2005; Tournament of Dreams, 2006; Material Girls, 2006; F*ck You Pay Me!, 2007; Tournament of Dreams, 2007; Carl Lewis Found, founder, currently. **Honors/Awds:** World Championships: Helsinki, gold medal, 100m, 4x100 m, Long Jump, 1983; Rome, gold medal, 100 m, 4x100 m, Long Jump, 1987; Tokyo, gold medal, 100m, 4x100 m, Long Jump, 1991; Stuttgart, gold medal, 200 m, 1993; Olympic Games: Los Angeles, gold medal, 100m, 200m, 4x100m, long jump, 1984; Seoul, gold medal,100 m, Long Jump, 1988, silver medal, 1998; Barcelona, gold medal, 4x100 m, Long Jump, 1992; Atlanta, gold medal, Long Jump; Sportsman of the Century, Int Olympic Comt; Olympian of the Century, Am sports mag. **Special Achievements:** World athlete of the year, 1982-86; Olympic Athlete of the Century. **Business Addr:** Actor, Cleve Lewis Management, 10940 S Parker Rd Suite 526, Parker, CO 80134, **Business Phone:** (303)531-4469.

LEWIS, CARMEN CORTEZ
Educator. **Personal:** Born in Detroit, MI; daughter of John E Farris and Maggie M Farris; married Thomas J, Jan 17, 1975. **Educ:** Univ Detroit, BA, 1973; Wayne State univ, MEd, 1987. **Career:** Detroit Bd Educ, Ruddiman Mid Sch, teacher, 1974-2001; Univ Pub Sch, teacher, 2001-. **Orgs:** Vpres, Zeta Phi Beta; treas, State Mich; NCP, Women's Community, Detroit Br; March Dimes Orgn; Retirement Community, Detroit Br; pres, Greater Ebenezer Baptist Church, Usher Bd 2; comt mem, Ladies Distinction; comt mem, Nat Asn Bus Women; Greeters Ministry Greater Ebenezer Church. **Honors/Awds:** Nominated Zeta of the Year, Zeta Phi Beta; March of Dimes Award. **Home Addr:** 9190 Dale St, Redford, MI 48239, **Home Phone:** (313)532-0462. **Business Addr:** Teacher, University Public School, 2001 Martin Luther King Jr Blvd, Detroit, MI 48208, **Business Phone:** (313)596-3780.

LEWIS, CHARLES GRANT. See Obituaries section.

LEWIS, CHARLES HENRY
Consultant, business owner. **Personal:** Born Nov 22, 1930, Bessemer, AL; son of Charles M Lewis (deceased) and Erline Mills Carter; married Joyce Jean Hale Lewis, May 25, 1952; children: Joyce Rene Rich, Donna Kay (deceased), Charles Michael. **Educ:** Langston Univ, BS, 1953; Wayne State Univ, MA, 1967; Mich State Univ, MBA, 1974. **Career:** Consultant (retired); City Detroit Recreation Dept, recreation instr, ctr supvr, 1956-64; Detroit Pub Sch, sch-community agt, 1964-66; City Detroit Comn C & Youth, proj dir, 1966-69; City Detroit Recreation Dept, recreation instr, 1969-71; Blvd Gen Hosp, dir, personnel serv, 1971-74; Wayne State Univ, assoc prof & chair, rec & parks serv, 1974-83; Mich Coun Humanities grant, Urban Recreation Conf, 1975; City Detroit Recreation Dept, supt recreation div, 1983-93; Creative Holistic Leisure Serv, leisure consult & owner. **Orgs:** Mich Recreation & Park Asn, 1974-; Nat Recreation & Park Asn, 1974-; pres, Nat Recreation & Park Ethnic Minority Soc, 1981-83; fel Am Acad Park & Recreation Admin, 1991-; chmn, Detroit Recreation Adv Comt, 2002-03; World Future Soc; pres, treas, Prof Recreation Employees, Detroit Local 836 AFSCME; Alpha Phi Alpha Fraternity; Langston Univ Alumni Asn. **Honors/Awds:** Ernest T Atwell Award, Nat Recreation & Park Ethnic Minority Soc, 1991; Citation Award, 1978, 1984; Fel Award, Mich Recreation & Park Asn, 1985; State Mich 84th Legis, Spec Tribute, 1988; Various Awards from local community groups and organization. **Special Achievements:** First African Am Chmn, Wayne State Univ Recreation & Park Services Dept; First African Am Superintendant, Rec Div, Detroit Rec Dept; Established Leisure Resource Center & Charles H Lewis Collection, Detroit Gray Branch Library, 1992; Co-Chair, Community Analysis Committee UCS Report, "Looking At Leisure: A Study of the Negative Aspects"; numerous articles, papers and proposals written. **Military Serv:** AUS, spec-5, 1953-56; grad, Guided Missile School, All-Star Baseball. **Home Addr:** 3202 Waverly, Detroit, MI 48238, **Home Phone:** (313)868-1592. *

LEWIS, CHARLES MCARTHUR
Manager, librarian. **Personal:** Born May 29, 1949, Fitzgerald, GA; married Katrinda McQueen. **Educ:** Fort Valley State Col, BS, math, 1971; Univ Ga, MA, math, 1973; Ga State Univ, MBA, 1984. **Career:** Southern Bell Tel & Tel, engr, 1973-78, mgt skills assessor, 1978-80, staff engr, 1980-86; BellSouth Serv Inc, info systs planner, 1986-, staff mgr. **Orgs:** Alpha Kappa Mu Hon, Soc Fort Valley State Col, 1970; Church Affiliated Orgns, 1983-87; Nat Black MBA Asn, 1986-87. **Honors/Awds:** Speakers Award, 1986. **Home Addr:** 3424 Boring Rd, Decatur, GA 30034. **Business Addr:** Staff Manager, BellSouth Service Inc, 675 W Peachtree St NE, 37F57 SBC, Atlanta, GA 30375, **Business Phone:** (404)927-2047.

LEWIS, CHARLES MICHAEL
Manager. **Personal:** Born Jul 17, 1949, Columbus, OH; son of Charles W Lewis and Irene V Lewis Fisher (deceased); married Anita Graham, Feb 25, 1978; children: Michael Jr, Christopher Morgan & Anicca. **Educ:** Central State Univ, Wilberforce, OH, BS, bus, 1971. **Career:** Wilmington Col, Wilmington, OH, admis counr, 1972-74; Bliss Bus Col, Columbus, OH, instr, 1974-78; Huntington Bank, Columbus, OH, Br Load Serv, 1978-79; Anheuser Busch Cos, Columbus, OH, area mgr, 1979-82, dist mgr, 1982-87l; Anheuser Busch Cos, Houston, TX, regional mgr corp affairs, 1987-. **Orgs:** Bd mem, Houston Area Urban League, 1988-; bd mem, Houston Sun Literacy Acad, 1988-; Alpha Phi Alpha Fraternity Inc; Nat Asn Advan Colored People; New Orleans Urban League, Oakland, CA. **Honors/Awds:** Black Achievers in Business & Indsutry, Harlem Branch YMCA, 1983; 2nd Degree Black Belt Karate,1971-. **Business Phone:** (713)367-1183.

LEWIS, CLARENCE K
Automotive executive, business owner. **Career:** Pryor Ford Lincoln-Mercury Inc, owner; Cloverleaf Chevrolet Oldsmobile, owner & ceo. **Special Achievements:** Pryor Ford Lincoln-Mercury ranked #95 on Black Enterprise's list of Top 100 Auto Dealers, 1992; Cloverleaf Chevrolet Oldsmobile ranked #99 on BE Top 100 Auto Dealers, 2000. *

LEWIS, CLEVELAND ARTHUR
Engineer, clergy. **Personal:** Born Apr 21, 1942, Selma, AL; son of Elsie and Levi; married Betty Faye Harris; children: Aisha & Jahmilla. **Educ:** Purdue Univ, AAS, 1972, BS, indust engineering technol, 1976; Ind Wesleyan Univ, Marion, IN, MS, 1991. **Career:** Chrysler Corp, indust engr, 1972-76; Clevetech Work Systems Inc, pres & chief exec officer, 1975-; Allison Transmission Div, sr product engineer, sr industrial engineer, currently; Indiana Univ; Purdue Univ Indianapolis, mech engineering dept, instr; US Food Serv. **Orgs:** Inst Indust Eng, 1970-; bd regents Concordia Col, 1986-; bd dir, Purdue Univ, Bd Alumni. **Honors/Awds:** Outstanding Achievement, General Motors, 1984; Distinguished Alumni Purdue Univ, 1986; Maynard K Hine Award, IUPUI, 1998. **Military Serv:** USAF, airman 2nd class, 4 yrs; Outstanding Performance Award. **Business Addr:** President, Chief Executive Officer, Clevetech Work Systems Inc, PO Box 88424, Indianapolis, IN 46208, **Business Phone:** (317)257-6383.

LEWIS, DANIEL
Judge. **Personal:** Born Apr 22, 1946, New York, NY; son of Matthew Gray and Anna Copeland; married Vernice Jackson-Lewis, Aug 15, 1982; children: Sharon Elaine, Morgan Nicole. **Educ:** New Lincoln Sch, acad deg, 1963; Brown Univ, BA, 1967; Pa Law Sch, JD, 1970. **Career:** State Dept Bur African Affairs, Wash, DC, intern, 1966; Am Emb Rome, intern 1967; Nat CORE, researcher 1968; Harlem Commonwealth Coun New York, writer, 1969; Dist Atty Off, asst dist atty, 1970-75; NY State, Appellate Div, First Dept, 1971; NY State Dept Law, Harlem Off, asst atty-gen-in-charge, 1975; NY State, Div Criminal Justice Servs, civil rights comp officer, 1975-77; NY K State Supreme Ct, prin law clerk, Justice Browne, 1977-91; New York Criminal Ct, judge, 1992-95; NY Supreme Ct, Queens County judge, 1996-. **Orgs:** Vol SCLC SCOPE Project, AL, 1966; One Hundred Black Men; Am Civil Lib Union; former trustee, Prof C's Sch; pres, Asn Law Secretaries, 1988-91; arbitrator, Small Claims Ct, 1986-91; parliamentarian, Epsilon Sigma Chap, Phi Beta Sigma, 1982-. **Honors/Awds:** Citation for Excellence, Mayor Wagner, 1960; Outstanding Young American Award, 1975; Certificate of Recognition, Small Claims Ct, 1990; Brandies Association Award, 1992; Association of Law Secretary's Award, 1992. **Business Addr:** Judge, Supreme Court Queens County, 88 11 Sutphin Blvd, Jamaica, NY 11435.*

LEWIS, DARREN JOEL
Baseball player, athletic coach. **Personal:** Born Aug 28, 1967, Berkeley, CA. **Career:** Baseball player (retired), athletic coach; Oakland Athletics, 1990; San Francisco Giants, outfielder, 1991-95; Cincinnati Reds, 1995; Chicago White Sox, 1996-97; Los Angeles Dodgers, 1997; Boston Red Sox, 1998-2001; Chicago Cubs, 2002; Dougherty Valley High Sch, coach, currently. **Honors/Awds:** NL Gold Glove, 1994.

LEWIS, DAVID BAKER
Lawyer, educator, administrator. **Personal:** Born Jun 9, 1944, Detroit, MI; son of Walton Adams and Dorothy Florence Baker; married Kathleen McCree (deceased) (deceased); children: Aaron McCree Lewis & Sarah Susan. **Educ:** Oakland Univ, BA, 1965; Univ Chicago Grad Sch Bus, MBA, 1967; Univ Mich, JD, 1970. **Career:** Northern Trust Co, admin dept, 1966; Morgan Guaranty Trust Co, corp res analyst, 1967; Lewis & Thompson Agency Inc, 1968; Miller Canfield Paddock & Stone, law clerk, 1969; Univ Mich, Afro-Am & African Studies Dept, lectr, 1970; Hon Theodore Levin US Dist Ct, law clerk, 1970-71; Patmon Young & Kirk, assoc atty, 1971-72; Detroit Col Law, assoc prof, 1972-78;Lewis & Munday PC, pres, 1972-82, bd chmn, 1982-; Atty Law, sole practitioner, 1972; Lewis & Munday's Corporate Services Practice Group, Chair & Chief Exec officer, currently. **Orgs:** State Bar Mich, 1970-; Wolverine Bar Asn, 1970-; Detroit Bar Asn, 1970-;Am Bar Asn, 1970-; Nat Asn Bond Lawyers, 1979-; bd trustees, Mich Opera Theatre, 1982-99; bd dirs, Music Hall Ctr for the Performing Arts,1983-94; bd dirs, Ctr Creative Studies, 1983-96; bd dirs, Detroit Symphony Orchestra Inc, 1983-; bd dirs, Metropolitan Affairs Corp, 1984-90; exec comt, bd dirs Inst Am Bus, 1985-; Nat Asn Securities Prof, 1985-; 1985-, chmn, 1998-2000, Oakland Univ Found; bd trustees, Am Bar Found, 1987-;Client Security Fund, 1988-89; bd dirs, Booker T Business Assoc, 1988-91; bd dirs, Nat Conf Community & Justice, 1990-99; SEMCOG-Regional DevelopInitiative Oversight Comt, 1990-92; bd dirs, Greater Detroit & WindsorJapan-Am Soc, 1990-93 bd dirs, Arts Comn City Detroit, 1992-99; mem,1992-2000, chmn 1996-2000, LG & E Energy Corp; mem1992-, bd dir, chmn,2001-, Paradies Metro-Ventures; life mem, Judicial Conf US Ct Appeals forthe Sixth Circuit; mem comt visitors, Univ Mich Law Sch; life mem, Nat Bar Asn; NAACP; bd dir, Commerical Bank, 1995-2000; bd dir, TRW Inc, 1995-; bd dir, MA Hanna Co, 1997-2000; bd Mgrs, Fife Electric LLC, 1998-2000; bd dir, Lakefront Capital Adv Inc, 1999-; chmn, Consolidated Rail Corp, 2000-; bd mgrs Detroit Edison Securitization Funding, 2001-; life mem, Nat Asn Advan Colored People. **Honors/Awds:** LHD, Univ Detroit Mercy 1991; Learned Hand Award, Am Jewish Comt, 1995; Honrary Degree: Central Michigan University, Doctor of Public Service 2008. **Business Addr:** Chairman, Lewis & Munday PC, 1300 First Nat Bldg, 660 Woodward Ave, Detroit, MI 48226, **Business Phone:** (313)961-2550.

LEWIS, DAVID LEVERING
Educator, writer. **Personal:** Born May 25, 1936, Little Rock, AR son of John Henry Sr. **Educ:** Fisk Univ, BA, 1956; Columbia Univ, MA, hist, 1958; London Sch Econs & Polit Sci, PhD, 1962 **Career:** US Army, Landstuhl, Ger, psychiat technician, 1961-62 Univ Md, lectr, 1961-62; Univ Ghana, lectr, 1963-64; Howard Univ, lectr, 1964-65; Univ Notre Dame, asst prof, 1965-66 Morgan State Univ, from asst prof to assoc prof, 1966-70; Univ DC, from assoc prof to prof, 1970-80; Univ Calif, San Diego, prof 1981-85; Rutgers State Univ NJ, Martin Luther King Jr prof 1985-94, Martin Luther King Jr univ prof, 1994-; Univ NY, Gra

Ctr, vis prof, 1995-96; NY Univ, Julius Silver univ prof & prof hist, 2003-; writer; District of Columbia: A Bicentennial History, 1976; W E B Du Bois:The Fight for Equality & the American Century 1919-63, 2001. **Honors/Awds:** Pulitzer Prize, two times; Phi Beta Kappa Ralph Waldo Emerson Award, 1994; Francis Parkman Prize, 1994; Bancroft Prize American History & Diplomacy Anisfield, 1994; Wolf Book Award, 1994; English Speaking Union Book Award, 1994; Horace Mann Bond Book Award, Harvard Univ, 2000; Anisfield-Wolf Book Award, 2001; Medal for Distinguished Service to Education, Columbia Teachers Col, 2002; Inaugural Medalist, John Hope Franklin Award, 2004. **Special Achievements:** First author to win two Pulitzer Prizes for biography for back-to-back volumes; Author of seven books and editor of two more. **Military Serv:** AUS, psychiat technician, 1961-62. **Business Addr:** Professor of History, New York University, Department of History, King Juan Carlos I Ctr, 53 Wash Sq S, New York, NY 10012-1098, **Business Phone:** (212)998-8619.

LEWIS, DAWNN
Musician, actor. **Personal:** Born Aug 13, 1961, Brooklyn, NY; daughter of Carl and Joyce; married Johnny Newman, Jan 1, 2004 (divorced 2006). **Educ:** Univ Miami, BA (magna cum laude), 1982. **Career:** Television appearances: "Stompin' at the Savoy"; "Kid-N-Play Cartoon";"voice of Lela"; "A Different World"; "series regular"; "Hangin with Mr.Cooper"; feature films: I'm Gonna Git U Sucka; Your Love, co-writer; A Different World, theme song, singer; HBO's Dream On; Other works: The Cherokee Kid; Bad Day on the Block, 1997; How to Succeed in Business Without Really Trying; voices for several animated TV series: C Bear &Jamal; Mortal Kombat; Bruno the Kid; Wayne's Head; Spider Man; Black Jaq, 1998; The Poof Point, 2001; "A Leela of Her Own", "The Route of All Evil",2002; "Bend Her", The Sting", 2003; "Medical Investigation"- Little Girl True Crime: New York City, "The Boondocks", 2005; The Adventures of BrerRabbit, 2006; Marvel: Ultimate Alliance, 2006; Holly Hobbie & Friends:Christmas Wishes, 2006; Dream girls, 2006; "Hell on Earth", 2006; "Grim &Evil", 2007; "Handy Manny", 2007; "One Tree Hill", 2008-09; Spider-Man 3, 2007; The Last Sentinel, 2007; Futurama:Bender's Big Score, 2007; Morning Jewel Inc, pres, currently. **Orgs:** Bd dirs & spokesperson, Campfire Boys & Girls; spokesperson, Nat 4H Club;spokesperson, Planned Parenthood; spokesperson, UNICEF; spokesperson, Inst Black Parenting; dir speakers bur, Arnold Schwarzenegger's Inner City Games. **Honors/Awds:** Illustrious Alumni Award, Univ Miami, 1991; Outstanding Service, Am Lung Asn, 1991; Act-So Award, NAACP; Smile of the Year, Am Dent Asn; Outstanding Service Award, 1988, 1990, 1991, UNCF; Excellence in Achievement, Howard University, 1992; ASCAP Award & four BMI Honors for Best Song; Grammy, Handel's Messiah: A Soulful Celebration; Gold Record,on the Take 6 Album, So Much To Say; BMI TV Music Award, 1990, 1991, 1992. **Special Achievements:** First graduate to receive musical theatre degree in the University of Miami. **Business Addr:** President, Morning Jewel Inc, PO Box 56718, Sherman Oaks, CA 91413, **Business Phone:** (310)315-4150.

LEWIS, DR. DELANO EUGENE
Government official, executive, executive director. **Personal:** Born Nov 12, 1938, Arkansas City, KS; son of Raymond E and Enna W; married Gayle Jones; children: Delano Jr, Geoffrey, Brian & Phillip. **Educ:** Univ Kans, BA, 1960; Washburn Sch Law, Topeka, KS, JD, 1963. **Career:** US Dept Justice, gen atty, 1963-65; US Equal Employment Opportunity Comn, staff anal & advice, 1965-66; US Peace Corps, Nigeria & Uganda, assoc dir & country dir, 1966-69; Off Sen Edward W Brooke, legis asst, 1969-71; Off Rep Walter E Fauntroy, admin asst, 1971-73; Chesapeake & Potomac Telephone Co, vpres, 1973-88, pres, 1988-93, chief exec officer, 1990-93; Nat Pub Radio, pres, 1994-98; Repub S Africa, US ambassador, 1999-2001; Lewis Assocs, consult pract, 2001; Colgate-Palmolive Co, bd dir, 1991-99, 2001-;New Mexico State Univ, sr fel, 2006-; Hallburton Co, dir; Guest Serv, dir; Apple Comput, dir; BET, dir; Eastman Kodak Co, dir, currently. **Orgs:** Bd dir, Comt Found Greater Wash, 1978-; pres, Greater Wash Bd Trade, 1987; Mil Order Knights Malta, 1987-; chmn, Pro Clef Culinary Concepts; mem. Alpha Phi Alpha Fraternity. **Honors/Awds:** Washingtonian of the Year, Wash Mag, 1978; President Medal, Catholic Univ Am, 1978; Honorary Degree, Marymount Univ, 1988; Distinguished Community Service Award, Washburn Univ, 1989; Distinguished Alumnae Award, Washburn Univ, 1990; Citizenship Award, Nat Coun Christians & Jews, 1989; Cultural Alliance of Washington Community Service Award, 1991; Honorary Degree, Loyola Col; Honorary Degree, Barry Univ Miami. **Special Achievements:** First African-American president of National Public Radio, 1993. **Business Addr:** Director, Colgate-Palmolive Company, 300 Pk Ave, New York, NY 10022-7499, **Business Phone:** (212)310-2000.

LEWIS, DIANE
Administrator, lawyer. **Personal:** Born in New York, NY; daughter of George A and Alyce Morris; divorced. **Educ:** Beaver Col, Glenside Pa, BA, 1969; Columbia Univ, New York NY, MS, 1977; Hastings Col Law, JD, 1995. **Career:** Nat Urban League, New York NY, proj dir, 1970-73; Ctr Urban Educ, New York NY, liaison, 1970-71; Trans Urban East, New York NY, consult, 1972-73; Jamaica Urban Develop Corp, Kingston, Jamaica, West Indies, social planner, 1974-76; City Oakland, Oakland Calif, sr urban econ analyst, 1977-82, div mgr, 1982-92; Oakland city, dep city atty, currently. **Orgs:** Consult, Trans Urban East Orgn, 1972-73; vpres, Progressive Black Bus & Prof Women, 1983-86; assoc mem, Urban Land Inst, 1984-; chmn, Econ Develop Comn, BA-PAC, 1984-86; past vpres & secy, chmn, nominations comn, Citicentre Dance Theatre, 1985-89; Niagara Movement Democratic Club; Nat Asn Planners; Black Women Organized Polit Action; Nat Forum Black Pub Admin, 1985-; Am Soc Pub Admin, 1988-; mem chmn, Asn Black Families, 1989-92; loan comt mem, Womens Initiative Self Employ, 1990-93; Asn Symposium ed, W Northwest Environ Law J; staff, Hastings Law News; Charles Houston Bar Asn; Am Bar Asn; Am Inns Ct; 2nd yr rep Hastings BLSA; Phi Alpha Delta. **Honors/Awds:** William F Kinne Fel, Columbia Univ, 1972, 1977; Int Fel, Columbia Univ, 1972-73; Int Intern, Ford Found, 1973-74; Wiley F Manuel Law Found Scholar, 1994. **Home Addr:** 1106 Trestle Glen Rd, Oakland, CA 94610. **Business Addr:** Deputy City Attorney, Oakland City Attorney, City Hall 6th Fl 1 Frank Ogawa Plz, Oakland, CA 94612, **Business Phone:** (510)238-2338.

LEWIS, DUANE
Executive. **Educ:** Southern Univ, attended 1995. **Career:** New Orleans Times- Picayune, sports corres; Baton Rouge Advocate, sports corres; Rams, St. Louis, staff, 1997-2003, pub rels dir, 2003-05, dir news media, 2006-07; Allstate Sugar Bowl, dir Commun, 2007-. **Orgs:** Football Writers Asn Am.

LEWIS, EARL
College administrator, educator. **Educ:** Concordia Col, BA, hist & psychol, magna cum laude, 1978; Univ Minn, MA, am hist, PhD, hist, 1984. **Career:** Univ Calif, Afro-Am Studies Dept, asst prof, 1985-89; Univ Mich, Dept Hist & Ctr for Afro-Am & African Studies, assoc prof, 1989-95, interim dir, 1990-91, dir, 1991-93, prof, 1995-, Horace H Rackham Sch Grad Studies, from interim dean to dean, 1997-2004, vice provost acad affairs & grad studies, 1998-2004; Emory Univ, provost & exec vpres acad affairs, 2004-, Asa Griggs Candler prof hist, 2004-. **Orgs:** Am Antiquarian Soc; prin investr, Nat Sci Found. **Honors/Awds:** Harold R. Johnson Diversity Service Award, Univ Mich, 1999; Distinguished Achievement Award, Univ Minn, 2001; hon degree, Doctor Humanities, Honoris Causa, Concordia Col, 2002; Elsa Barkley Brown & Robin DG Kelley Collegiate Prof Hist & African Am & African Studies designate, 2003. **Special Achievements:** Published numerous articles. **Business Addr:** Provost, Executive Vice President Academic Affairs, Emory University, 201 Dowman Dr, Atlanta, GA 30322, **Business Phone:** (404)727-6123.*

LEWIS, EDWARD
Chief executive officer, publisher. **Personal:** Born May 15, 1940. **Educ:** Univ NMex, BA, 1964, MA, 1966. **Career:** City Mgr's Off, Albuquerque, NM, admin analyst, 1964-65; First Nat City Bank, financial analyst, 1966-69; Essence Commun Inc, chmn, 1968-; stalwart advocate; Essence Commun Partners, founder, 1968-; Black Coun Africa, bd dirs; Rheeland Found, bd dirs; Negro Ensemble New York City, bd dirs. **Orgs:** trustee, Tuskegee Univ; trustee; Leadership Coun Tanenbaum Ctr Interreligious Understanding; trustee, Teachers Col Columbia Univ; chmn, Mag Publ Am; chmn, TransAfrica Forum. **Honors/Awds:** Entrepreneur of the Year Award, Ernst & Young, 1994; National Association of Black Journalists Award, 1995; President's Award, One Hundred Black Men of America Inc., 1995; Frederick Douglass Award, New York Urban League, 1995; A.G. Gaston Lifetime Achievement Award, Black Enterprise/Nationsbank Entrepreneurs Conf, 1997 ; Media-Bridge-Builder Award, Tanenbaum Ctr Interreligious Understanding, 1998; Lifetime Achievement Award, United Negro Col Fund; Diversity Achievement Award, Am Advert Fedn; The Men Who Dare Award, Black Women's Forum, Los Angeles; Henry Johnson Fisher Award, 2002; Robert C Maynard Legend Award, 2003; Lifetime Achievement Award, Mag Publ Am; hon DHL, Univ NMex. **Special Achievements:** Ranked seventh on Advertising Age's 2003 "A-List"; first African American to lead the 700-magazine trade group; first African American to receive the Media-Bridge-Builder Award from the Tannenbaum Center for Interreligious Understanding. **Business Phone:** (212)522-1866.*

LEWIS, EDWARD T.
Publisher. **Personal:** Born May 15, 1940, Bronx, NY; married Carolyn Wright, Jan 1, 1991. **Educ:** Univ NMex, BA, 1964, MA, 1966, DHL, 2003; NY Univ, attended 1969; Harvard Bus Sch. **Career:** Peace Corps Univ NM, lectr, 1963; City Mgr's Off Albuquerque, admin analyst, 1964-65; First Nat City Bank New York City, fin analyst, 1966-69; Essence Commun Inc, founder & chmn, 1968-; Great Atlantic & Pacific Tea Co, bd dir, 2000; Latina Media Ventures LLC, chmn bd, 2008-. **Orgs:** Bd dir, Vol Urban Consult Group; Black Coun Africa; Fund New Horizons Retarded Inc; 21st Century Found; Rheeland Found; Negro Ensemble; Sch Vol Prog; trustee, Coty; 100 Black Men Inc; Uptown C C; New York City Com & Indust; chmn, Mag Publ Am, 1997-; Trans Africa Forum; trustee, Columbia Univ; NY Partnership; Times Sq Bus Improvement Dist; Lincoln Ctr Performing Arts; Jazz Comt; Int Peace Comt; Greater Harlem Chamber Com; bd mem, Howard Univ Sch Publishing. **Honors/Awds:** Decision Maker Award, Nat Asn Media Women, 1974; Businessman of the Year, Black Africa Promotions Inc, 1974; Nat IGBO Award, 1979; Ellis Island Medal of Honor; Good Scout Award, Boy Scouts Am; Lifetime Achievement Award, United Negro Col Fund; Our World News Award, Dow Jones; Good Guy Award, Dem Womens' Polit Caucus; FL Yates Ruffin Ridley Award, NY's Asn Black Charities; The Men Who Dare Award, Black Women's Forum; Entrepreneur of the Year Award, Ernst & Young, 1994; Award Honor, Nat Asn Black Journalists, 1995; AG Gaston Lifetime Achievement Award, Black Enterprise Mag, 1997; Diversity Achievement Role Model Award, Am Advert Fedn, 1997; Henry Johnson Fisher Award, Mag Publ Am, 2002. **Special Achievements:** Featured with other prominent businessmen on the cover of Black Enterprise Magazine as one of the "Marathon Men" for 25 yrs of Entrepreneurial Excellence, June 1997; first African American to chair Magazine Publishers of America; ESSENCE ranked seventh on Advertising Age's 2003 "A-List,"which is the first time that an African-American targeted publication has received this honor. **Business Addr:** Chairman, Founder, Essence Communications Inc, 135 W 50th St Fl 4, New York, NY 10020, **Business Phone:** (212)642-0600.

LEWIS, EMMANUEL
Actor. **Personal:** Born Mar 9, 1971, Brooklyn, NY; son of Margaret. **Educ:** Clark Atlanta Univ, BA, theatre arts, 1997. **Career:** Film: Frank McKlusky, C.I., 2002; Dickie Roberts: Former Child Star, 2003; Kickin It Old Skool, 2007; TV Series: A Midsummer Night's Dream, 1982; Webster, 1983-89; The Love Boat, 1984; A Celebration of Life: A Tribute to Martin Luther King, Jr, 1984; Circus of the Stars #9, 1984; Night of 100 Stars II, 1985; The ABC All-Star Spectacular, 1985; "Lost in London", 1985; "The Tonight Show"; "The Phil Donahue Show"; "The World's Funniest Commercial Goofs, host", 1983-85; "Salute to Lady Liberty", 1984; "Mr T & Emmanuel Lewis in a Christmas Dream", 1984; "Secret World of the Very Young", 1984; "Life's Most Embarassing Moments", 1986; "Candid Camera: The First Forty Years", 1987; "Emmanuel Lewis: My Own Show", 1987; "The New Adventures of Mother Goose", 1995; "Moesha", 1998; "Tripping the Rift", 2004; "I Love the 80's 3-D", 2005; "100 Greatest Kid Stars", 2005; "Child Star Confidential", 2006; "The Surreal Life: Fame Games", 2007. Emmanuel Lewis Entertainment Enterprises Inc, owner. **Orgs:** Am Fedn TV & Radio Artists; Screen Actors Guild; Actors Equity Asn. **Honors/Awds:** People Choice Awards, 1984, 1985, 1986 & 1987. **Special Achievements:** Ranked 6 in VH1's list of the "100 Greatest Kid Stars", 2005. **Business Addr:** Actor, c/o Schuller Talent Agency, 276 5th Ave Suite 207, New York, NY 10001, **Business Phone:** (212)532-6005.

LEWIS, EPHRON H.
Executive, business owner, president (organization). **Personal:** Son of Jasper Lewis (deceased) and Adline Mathis Lewis (deceased); married Doris; children: Ephron Lewis Jr. **Educ:** Ark AM&N Col, Grad. **Career:** Lewis & Son Rice Processing Co, owner. **Orgs:** Pres, AR Land & Farm Develop Corp, 1980-92; former mem, Nat Rice Adv Comm. **Honors/Awds:** Distinguished Alumni of Year, Univ Arkansas, Pine Bluff Nat Asn Equal Opportunity Higher Educ, 1986; Persistence of the Spirit, Univ AR Pine Bluff, 1987; Minority Contractor of the Year, US Dept Agr, ASCS, 1989. **Military Serv:** AUS, PFC, 1956-58. **Business Addr:** President, Lewis & Son Rice Processing Corp, 1127 CR 1005, Earle, AR 72331, **Business Phone:** (501)775-2727.

LEWIS, DR. FELTON EDWIN
School administrator. **Personal:** Born Oct 2, 1923, New Orleans, LA; son of Felton B Lewis (deceased) and Ethel Martin Lewis (deceased); children: Ronald, Anthony, Felton III, Marita & Karen. **Educ:** Xavier Univ, BA, cum laude, 1955; Univ Wis, Madison, MA, 1956; Univd Aix-Marseille France, dipl, 1956-58; Univ Interamericana Mexico, PhD, 1970. **Career:** New York City Bd Educ, teacher 1958-66; Foreign Lang Dept JHS, acting chmn, 1963-66; Jr High Spec Serv Sch, acting asst prin 1966-67; Title I New York City Bd Educ, ESEA coordr, 1967-68; New York City Bd Educ, intern educ admin & super prin intern, 1968-69, Dist 12, dep dist supt, 1969-71, District 12, acting comm supt, 1971-72, Dist 12, comm supt, 1972-78; Dist 16, community supt, 1978-82; New York State Dept Educ, Albany, New York, asst comnr educ, 1985-86. **Orgs:** Phi Delta Kappa; Am Asn Sch Adminr; New York City Asn Supt; Doctoral Asn New York Educr; Int Reading Asn; Asn Supervision & Curric Develop, NAACP; Nat Urban League, Bronx Boys Clubs. **Honors/Awds:** Alpha Epsilon Partial Grad Scholar, Middlebury Col, 1955; French Teaching Assistantship, Univ Wis, 1955-56; Maison Francaise Scholar, Univ Wis, 1956; Fulbright Scholar, 1956-57; Fulbright Grant, 1957-58; Ford Found Fel, Fordham Univ, 1968-69; numerous awards & testimonials including SBronx NAACP, WIN Adult Council, JFK Library for Minorities, Bronx NAACP, Fairmount Sch, Prin of Dist 12, CSA of Dist 12, Bronx Boys Club, Behav ResLab, Drug Abuse Prevention Proj, Dr Martin Luther King Comn, numerous certifications in teaching & admin. **Military Serv:** AUS, Sgt, 1942-45, Bronze Star.

LEWIS, FLOYD EDWARD
Manager. **Personal:** Born Nov 23, 1938; married Ruth M. **Educ:** S Ill Univ, BS, 1961; M Urban Affairs Bus St Univ, 1972. **Career:** United Way St Louis, agency rel asn, 1970-72; Urban League St

Louis, dir personnel, 1972-74; Monsanto Co, mgr equal oppor, 1974-75; Anheuser-Busch Co Inc, dir equal oppor affairs, 1975, dir corp affairs, consult, 2003-; AOL Time Warner Inc, dir corp affairs, 2003. **Orgs:** Bd mem, Carver House Asn, 1977; bd mem, Asn Black Psychologist, 1977; bd mem, Annie Malone C Home, 1978, St Louis Minority Coun. **Home Addr:** 11954 Sackston Ridge, Saint Louis, MO 63141. **Business Phone:** (314)577-2000.

LEWIS, FREDERICK CARLTON. See LEWIS, CARL.

LEWIS, GEORGE E.
Educator. **Personal:** Born Jan 1, 1952, Chicago, IL; married Miya Masaoka; children: 1. **Educ:** Yale Univ, BA, philos, 1974. **Career:** Univ Calif, San Diego, asst to prof music, 1991-2004; McArthur fel, 2002; Columbia Univ, Edwin H Case prof music, 2004-, dir, Ctr Jazz Studies, dir grad studies, 2008-09; Sch Art Inst Chicago, prof music; Simon Fraser Univ's Contemporary Arts Summer Inst, prof music. **Orgs:** Asn Advan Creative Musicians, 1971-. **Honors/Awds:** Cal Arts/Alpert Award, 1999. **Special Achievements:** Numerous fellowships from the National Endowment for the Arts including winner. **Business Addr:** Edwin H Case Professor of Music, Columbia University, Department Music Columbia University, 615 Dodge Hall MC 1814, 2960 Broadway, New York, NY 10027, **Business Phone:** (212)854-5837.

LEWIS, GEORGE RALPH
Executive. **Personal:** Born Mar 7, 1941, Burgess, VA; son of Spencer Harcum and Edith Pauline Toulson; married Lillian Glenn; children: Tonya, Tracey. **Educ:** Hampton Univ, BS, 1963; Iona Col, MBA, 1968. **Career:** Retired: Gen Foods Corp, sales analyst, 1963-64, profit planning analyst, 1964-65, prod analyst, 1965-66; WR Grace Co, financial analyst, 1966-67; Philip Morris Inc, corp analyst, 1967-68, sr planning analyst, 1968-70, mgr investor rels, 1970-72, mgr financial serv, 1972-73, asst treas, 1973-74, vpres financial & planning & treas, 1975-82; Seven Up Co, vpres finance, 1982-84; Philip Morris Cos Inc, vpres, treas, 1984-97; Philips Morris Capital Corp, pres & Chief Exec Officer, 2001. **Orgs:** Bd mem, Wachovia Bank, 1998; Nat Urban League, 1986, Hampton Univ, 1985, Kemper Nat Ins Co, 1993, Ceridian Corp, 1994; bd The Professional Golfers Asn Am, 1995. **Honors/Awds:** Arthur A Loftus Achievement Award, Iona Col, 1980; Outstanding Twenty Year Alumnus Award, Hampton Inst, 1982. *

LEWIS, GREEN PRYOR, JR.
Labor activist. **Personal:** Born Apr 27, 1945, Columbus, GA; son of Green Pryor Sr and Minnie Jones; married Christine McGhee, Dec 22, 1967; children: Raquel, Green III & LeKeisha. **Educ:** Fort Valley State Col, Fort Valley, Ga, BS, 1967; Am Univ Fort Benning, 1969. **Career:** Buckner Construct Co, Columbus, Ga, bricklayer apprentice, stud, 1963-64; Am Toy Co, Columbus, Ga, asst dept Mgr, 1965-67; Muscogee County Sch Syst, Columbus, Ga, teacher, coach, 1967-69; Am Fedn Labor & Cong Indust Orgns, asst dir, 1969-, dir, currently. **Orgs:** Keeper rec, Columbus Alumni Chap, Kappa Alpha Psi, 1968-69; pres, Proud Neighbors South De Kalb, 1973-75; first vpres, Field Rep Fedn AFL-CIO, 1979-84; vice-chair, fourth dist, Dem Party De Kalb County Ga, 1982-84; exec comt, A Philip Randolph Inst, 1985-; United Way Am Bd Gov, 1997. **Honors/Awds:** High Achievement Award, Kappa Alpha Psi, 1963; Distinguished Serv, Houston Organizing Proj, 1984; Distinguished Serv, Field Rep Fedn, 1985; Labor Award Outstanding Serv, Serv Employees Local 579, 1987; High Achievement Award, Lewis Family Reunion, 1988; Histadrut Menorah Award, 1989; A Philip Randolph Achievement Award, 1992; Keeper Flame Award Nat Asn Advan Colored People, 1992. **Business Addr:** Assistant Director, AFL-CIO, Department of Field Mobilization, 815 16th St NW Suite 509, Washington, DC 20006, **Business Phone:** (202)637-5189.

LEWIS, HANK. See LEWIS, WILLIAM HENRY.

LEWIS, HAROLD T
Educator, clergy. **Personal:** Born Feb 21, 1947, Brooklyn, NY; son of Frank Walston and Muriel Kathleen Worrell; married Claudette Richards, Feb 7, 1970; children: Justin Craig. **Educ:** McGill Univ, BA, 1967; Yale Divinity Sch, M Div, 1971; Cambridge Univ, res fel, 1973; Univ Birmingham, Eng, PhD, 1994. **Career:** NY City Dept Social Serv, social worker, 1967-68; Overseas Missionary, Honduras, staff, 1971-72; St Monica's Church, rector, 1973-82; Episcopal Church Foundation, res fel, 1978; St Luke's Episcopal Church, assoc priest, 1983-96; Episcopal Church Cent, staff officer, 1983-94; Mercer Sch Theol, prof homiletics, 1988-96; Yale Univ, res fel, 1990; NY Theol Sem, prof homiletics, 1995-96; Calvary Episcopal Church, Pittsburgh, PA, rector, 1996-; Pittsburgh Theol Sem, adj prof, 1996-. **Orgs:** Racial Justice Working Group, Nat Coun Churches, 1986-96; exec comt, Prophetic Justice Unit, Nat Coun Churches, 1988-96; Sigma Pi Phi, 1991-. **Honors/Awds:** Distinguished Alumnus Award, Oper Crossroads Off, 1985; Doctor of Divinity, Berkeley Divinity Sch Yale, 1991; Doctor of Canon Law, Seabury-Western Theol Sem, 2001; Yale Tercentanary For God Award, 2001. **Special Achievements:** Author, In Season, Out of Season, A Collection of Sermons, 1993; Yet With a Steady Beat: The Afro-Amer Struggle for Recognition in the Episcopal Church, 1996; Elijah's Mantle: Pilgrimage, Politics & Proclaimation, 2001; Christian Social Witness, 2001. **Business Addr:** Rector, Calvary Episcopal Church, 315 Shady Ave, Pittsburgh, PA 15206, **Business Phone:** (412)661-0120.

LEWIS, DR. HENRY L., III
Educator, school administrator. **Personal:** Born Jan 22, 1950, Tallahassee, FL; son of Henry Lewis Sr and Evelyn P Lewis; married Marisa Ann Smith, Dec 1, 1990. **Educ:** Fla A&M Univ, BS, 1972; Mercer Univ, PharmD, 1978. **Career:** Florida A&M Univ, asst dean, 1974-90; Tex Southern Univ, dean & prof,1990-94; Fla A&M Univ, Col Pharm Pharmaceut Sci, dean, 1994-2001, prof,1994-, interim pres, 2002-02, dir, dean, currently. **Orgs:** Am Asn Col Pharm, 1974-; Rho Chi Honor Soc, 1975-; ASHP, 1978-; Am Pub Health Asn, 1980-; Alpha Phi Alpha, 1985-; Bd County Comnr, Leon County,1986-90; pres, NPHA, 1988-90; Tex Pharm Asn, 1990-; bd adv, Nat Inst GenMed Sci, 1992-96; pres, AMHPS, 1992-95; pres, MHPF, 1994-; bd dirs, Fla Educ Fund Chair, 1999-. **Honors/Awds:** Pharmacist of the Year, Nat Pharmaceut Asn, 1988; Outstanding Young Black Houstonian, HELP Inc, 1990; Merck, Sharpe, Dohme, Leadership Achievement Award, 1990; Meritorious Achievement Award, Fla A&M Univ, 1992; Meritorius Service Award, Tex Sen, 1994; Richards Award, Fla Pharmacy Asn, 2000; Famuan of the Century, 2000; Administrator of the Year, NFBPA, 2001;Wendell T Hill Award, Asn Black Health Systs Pharmacist, 2001; Hugo H. Schaefer Award; Statewide Onyx Award, 2008; American Pharmacists Association's, 2009. **Special Achievements:** Numerous publications. **Business Addr:** Professor, Dean, Florida A&M University, 333 New Pharm Bldg, Tallahassee, FL 32307, **Business Phone:** (850)599-3301.

LEWIS, HENRY S., JR.
Counselor, clergy. **Personal:** Born Sep 26, 1935, Chester County, SC; son of Henry S Sr and Marie S; married Savannah D Winstead; children: Robin Anita, Kenneth W, Jonathan H, Karen E. **Educ:** Winston Salem State Univ, BS, 1957; Wake Forest Univ, further study; Sch Pastoral Care Boston City Hosp, 1959; Andover Newton Theol Sch, MDiv, 1961; Sch Pastoral Care North Carolina Baptist Hosp, 1977; Univ Kentucky Col Med RBT Ctr, 1977. **Career:** Shiloh Bapt Church, student asst, 1957-59; Wentz Mem United Church Christ, summer minister, 1958-; Zion Bapt Church, 1959; Winston Salem State Univ, Univ chaplain & James A Gray asst prof religion & sociol, 1960-77; Mt Pleasant Bapt Church, pastor, 1966-77; Winston Salem Forsyth Cty Schs Urban Affairs Inst, human rels consult, 1967, 1969; Wake Forest Univ, part time instr dept religion, 1970-72; RJ Reynolds Tabacco Co, Winston Salem NC, senior employ counr 1977-00; Wentz Mem Congregational Church, pastor, currently. **Orgs:** Clinical mem, Am Asn Marriage & Family Therapy, Nat Inst Bus & Indust Chaplains, North Carolina Chaplains Asn; Phi Beta Sigma, Winston Salem Chap NAACP; North Carolina Licensed Marital & Family Therapist; bd dir, pres, soc Study AFA Hist; North Carolina Asn Marital & Family Therapy; Employ Prof Asn; Simon G Atkins CDC, WSSU. **Business Addr:** Pastor, Wentz Memorial Congregational Church, 3435 Carver School Rd, Winston-Salem, NC 27105-4756, **Business Phone:** (336)722-0430.*

LEWIS, DR. HOUSTON A.
Dentist. **Personal:** Born May 4, 1920, Bonham, TX; married Clara; children: Ruth Ann Collins & Pamela Brinkley. **Educ:** Xavier Univ, attended 1942; Fish Univ, attended 1947; Meharry Med Col Sch Dent, DDS, 1951. **Career:** Girl Scouts, dir, 1958-67; Gtr Wheeling Coun Chs, dir, 1955-64; C & Family Serv Asn, dir, 1956-62; United Way, dir, 1967-60; pvt practice, dentist, currently; Houston A. Lewis DDS Inc, dentist, currently. **Orgs:** Am Soc Endodntics; Acad Gen Dent Memorial Civitan Club Wheeling, 1963; dir, Moundsville Wheeling Chap Am Red Cross, 1963-66; dir, Urban Renewal Auth, 1966-71; ran WVA House Del, 1968; dir, Wheeling Area Blue Cross-Blue Shield, 1969; Int Plat Asn; Nat Dent Asn; Am Dent Asn; pres, WVa Med Soc Inc, 1977-78. **Honors/Awds:** One Outstanding W Virginians, 1965-66. **Military Serv:** AUS, enlisted man, 1942-45, comdr duty Den Corps, 1951-53; col active res. **Business Addr:** Dentist, Houston A Lewis DDS Inc, 1118 Main St, Wheeling, WV 26003.*

LEWIS, IDA ELIZABETH
Educator, college teacher, publisher. **Personal:** Born Sep 22, 1935, Malverne, PA. **Educ:** Boston Univ Sch Pub Commun, BA, jour, 1956. **Career:** NY Amsterdam News, financial & bus writer, 1957-60; NY Age, financial ed, 1959-61; Life Mag, writer, 1964-65; BBC, writer & broadcaster, 1967; Jeune Afrique Mag, corresp, 1968-71; Essence Mag, ed-in-chief, 1970-71; Tanner Publ Co, pres, 1972; Encore: Am & Worldwide News, founder, publ & ed-in-chief; Nat Asn Advan Colored People, Crisis, ed-in-chief, 1998; Boston Univ Sch Pub Commun, Dept Jour, adj prof, lectr jour, currently. **Orgs:** Trustee Tougaloo Col; bd dir, Am Com Africa; Comn Inquiry Into High Sch Journ; Nat Coun Negro Women; Alpha Kappa Alpha Soc; Am Mgt Asn; founder, Ida E Lewis Scholarship Fund; Boston Univ Alumni Coun; Boston Univ Commun, Deans Exec Adv Bd. **Honors/Awds:** Scarlet Key, Boston Univ, 1956; Journalism Award, Asn Study Afro-Am Life & Hist, 1974; Citizen of the Year, Omega Psi Phi, 1975; Bicentennial Award, 1975; Int Benih Award, 1975; Media Executive Award, Nat Youth Movement, 1975; Distinguished Alumni Award, Boston Univ, 1999; Woman of Distinction Award, Kingsborough Col, City Univ NY. **Special Achievements:** First black woman in the US to publish a magazine; first woman editor-in-chief of Crisis, the magazine of the NAACP, 1998. **Business Addr:** Lecturer in Journalism, Boston University, 1 Sherborn St, Boston, MA 02215, **Business Phone:** (617)353-2000.

LEWIS, J B, JR.
Funeral director. **Personal:** Born Oct 22, 1929, Clifton Forge, VA; son of J B Lewis Sr (deceased) and Mattie E Douglas (deceased); married Mary Louise Colbert; children: Aaron. **Educ:** Eckels Col Mortuary Sci, grad, 1957. **Career:** Ins underwriterm 1958-63; Greyhound Lines, optr, 1964-65; Mt View Terr Apts, mgr & agent, 1970-; JB Lewis Funeral Serv, owner. **Orgs:** VA Mortic Asn, 1959; pres, Lylburn Downing PTA, 1962-63; treas, sec Cub Scouts 1963; vpres, Rockbridge Area Housing Corp, 1967-70; vpres, Human Rel Coun, 1968; councilman City Lexington, 1969; Adv bd, Coreast Savings Bank, 1972; VA Funeral Dir Asn, 1976; Nat Funeral Dir Asn, 1976; Nat Asn Advan Colored People; Am Legion Post 291. **Honors/Awds:** Eye Enucleat Cert, 1976. **Military Serv:** AUS, 1954-56. **Home Phone:** (540)463-5101. **Business Addr:** Owner, JB Lewis Funeral Service, 112 N Randolph St, Lexington, VA 24450.

LEWIS, JAMES. See LEWIS, JIM.

LEWIS, JAMES, JR.
Educator, writer. **Personal:** Born Mar 7, 1930, Newark, NJ; married Valdmir M; children: Michael, Patricia & Terrence. **Educ:** Hampton Inst, BS, 1953; Columbia Univ, MS, 1957; Union Grad Sch, PhD, 1972. **Career:** Wyandanch Sch Dist, teacher act asst, high sch prin, 1957-66, elem prin, 1966-67, dist prin, 1967-72; Harvard Univ, Alfred North Whitehead fel, 1970; Villanova Univ, assoc prof, 1972-73; City Univ NY, prof educ & chmn div teacher educ, 1972-74; Cent Berkshire Regional Sch Dist, supt schs, 1974-; Educ Improvement Ctr, NE, exec dir, 1974-; Educ Ctr Prostate Cancer Patients, exec dir & founder, 1996-; Books: A Contemporary Approach to Nongraded Education, 1971; Appraising Teacher Performance, 1973; Updated Guidelines for Surviving Prostate Cancer, 2003. **Orgs:** Am Asn Univ Professors; Am Asn Sch Adminr; Nat Educ Asn; Nat Alliance Black Sch Educr; Mass Asn Sch Supervisors; Asn Supv & Curric Develop; NJ Asn Sch Adminr; Am Soc Training & Develop; Am Mgt Asn; Nat Soc Corp Planners. **Honors/Awds:** Outstanding Leadership Award, Sch Dist, 1968. **Military Serv:** AUSR, major, 1955-67. **Business Addr:** Writer, EICNE 2 Babcock Pl, West Orange, NJ 07052.*

LEWIS, JAMES B.
Government official, commissioner, administrator. **Personal:** Born Nov 30, 1947, Roswell, NM; son of William Reagor and Dorris; married Armandie Lillie Johnson; children: Teri Seaton, James Jr, Shedra, LaRon. **Educ:** Bishop Col, BS, educ, 1970; Univ NM, MPA, 1977; Nat Col Bus, AS, bus, 1980, BS, bus, 1981; Duke Univ, chief staff cert; Univ Va, minority leadership cert. **Career:** Chief Administrative Officer (retired); Univ Albuquerque, Afro-studies admin/instr, 1974-77; Dist Atty Off, investr/purchasing dir, 1977-83; Bernalillo Co, treas, 1983-85; NMex State Govt, state treas, 1985-91; Chief Staff Governor Bruce King, 1991-94; NM State Land Off, Oil Gas & Minerals Div, dir, 1995-99; US Dept Energy, Off Econ Impact & Diversity, dir, 1999-01; City Albuquerque, chief opers officer, 2001-04, chief admin officer 2004-05. **Orgs:** state housing chair, Nat Asn Advan Colored People, 1980-; bd mem finance comn, Victims Domestic Violence, 1983-; treas, Am Soc Pub Admin, 1983-; Nat State Treas, 1985-; bd mem, State Investment Coun, NM, 1985, Pub Employee Retirement Bd, 1985, Educ Retirement Bd, 1985; Am Legion PC 99, 1985; pres, NMex Chap, Am Soc Pub Admin, 1989; commencement speaker, Zuni High Sch, Zuni, NM 1989; Ad-Hoc Comt, State Investment Coun, 1989; hon mem, Beta Alpha Psi CPA Hon Soc, 1989; PRS Bill Clinton Transition Team, 1992-; commencement speaker, Univ NMex, Dept Pub Admin, 1992; Kiwanis Club Albuquerque; Am GI Forum; Int Alumni Asn, Bishop Col; Taylor Ranch Neighborhood Asn; Omega Psi Phi Fraternity NMex State Bd Finance; Educ Found Assistance Bd; Mid Rio Grande Coun Govts, Metrop Transp & Exec Bd; Albuquerque Armed Forces Adv Asn; Univ NMex Sch Eng, Diversity Coun Metrop Criminal Justice Coord Coun; bd dirs, United Way; bd dirs, Albuquerque Hall of Fame; bd dirs, St Joseph Community Health Serv; First State Bank, Metro Community Adv Bd; bd trustees, W Mesa Med Ctr; bd dirs, Albuquerque Conv & Visitors Bur. **Honors/Awds:** Outstanding Young Men in Am, Nat Jaycees 1980; Citizen of Year, Omega Psi Phi, 1983; Outstanding County Treasurer, County Treasurer's Asn, 1984; Inductee, Nat Asn Advan Colored People Hall of Fame, 2003; Inductee, NMex African Am Hall of Fame, 2004; Distinguished Alumni, Leadership NMex, 2004; 100 Influential Power Brokers in the City Albuquerque, NMex Bus J; Distinguished Honoree Papers Filed Univ NMex Libr. **Military Serv:** AUS E-4 2 yrs; Hon Base Comdr, Kirtland AFB. *

LEWIS, JAMES D
Publisher, president (organization). **Career:** Minority Bus J Inc pres & publ, currently; James D Lewis Enterprises, currently. **Business Addr:** President, Publisher, Minority Business Journal 511 Junilla St, PO Box 3543, Pittsburgh, PA 15219-4837, **Business Phone:** (412)682-4386.*

LEWIS, JAMES R.
Dentist. **Personal:** Born Aug 3, 1938, Asheboro, NC; married Barbara Walker; children: Krista, Erica. **Educ:** Chem NC Central Univ, BS, 1963; Howard Univ, DDS, 1968. **Career:** McGill Univ, Montreal, Can, rotating dent internship; VA Hosp, Albany, 1968-69; Univ NC Sch Dent, asst prof, 1969-71; Lincoln Health Cent Durham NC, dental dir, 1971-75; Univ NC Dent, adj assoc prof dent ecol, 2002. **Orgs:** Am Dent Asn; Acad Cent Dent; NC Dent Soc; Am Endodontic Soc; Chi Delta Mu Med & Dent Frat Bd NC Health Plan Agency; Highest Order Mystic Shrine 32nd deg Mason; health prof Coun Black Students Int Dent;admin comt, Sch Dent Univ NC, 1969-71. **Special Achievements:** First black as mem Adm Comm for Sch of Dent UNC 1969-71. **Military Serv:** USN, HM3 3rd class hosp man, 1956-59. **Business Addr:** University North Carolina, School of Dentistry, CB 7450, Chapel Hill, NC 27599-7450.*

LEWIS, JAMES R.
Administrator. **Personal:** Born Jan 1, 1950?. **Educ:** Berea Col, Ky. **Career:** Aetna Life & Casualty; CIGNA; St Paul Cos, sr vpres US field opers, reg pres northeast reg; sr vpres, personal lines; pres small com; CNA Ins Co, pres & ceo, currently. **Orgs:** Bd mem, BoardSource; bd mem, Metrop Family Servs; bd mem, Young Men's Christian Asn Metrop Chicago; bd mem, C[b4]s Home & Aid Soc. **Business Phone:** (312)822-5000.*

LEWIS, JANICE LYNN
Executive. **Personal:** Born Dec 11, 1958, Magnolia, MS; daughter of Joe and Ruth Robertson; divorced; children: Kerrington Lavern Howard. **Educ:** Southern Univ, BS, journ, 1980; Barry Univ, theol. **Career:** Wash Post, journalist, off mgr, circulation, 1981; The Miami Herald, circulation mgr, 1989; WPLG, TV-10, sales asst, 1990; John S & James L Knight Found, jour prog asst, 1990-. **Orgs:** Bd dir, Miami Mega City Spec Olympics, 1995-; bd dir, exec forum, James K Batten Black, 1995. **Honors/Awds:** James K Batten Black Executive; Miami Black Executive, 1995. **Home Phone:** (305)653-4842. **Business Addr:** Program Assistant, John S & James L Knight Foundation, 200 S Biscayne Blvd Suite 3300, Miami, FL 33131-2349, **Business Phone:** (305)908-2600.

LEWIS, HON. JANNIE (JANNIE M LEWIS)
Judge. **Personal:** Born Jan 1, 1958. **Educ:** Univ Iowa Col, attended. **Career:** Legal Servs Corp, atty; Pvt Pract, atty; State Miss Circuit Ct 21st Circuit Ct Dist, judge, currently. **Special Achievements:** First African Am judge in two of the counties in the district. **Business Addr:** Judge, State of Mississippi Circuit Court, 21st District, Holmes County 1 Court Sq N Entrance, PO Box 718, Lexington, MS 39095-0718, **Business Phone:** (662)834-1452.

LEWIS, JANNIE M. See **LEWIS, HON. JANNIE.**

LEWIS, JEFFREY MARK
Executive. **Personal:** Married; children: two. **Educ:** Rutgers Univ, BS, econs, BA, bus admin, 1980; Northwestern Univ, JL Kellogg Grad Sch Mgt, masters mgt, 1981. **Career:** Sands Hotel & Casino, acct, 1980; Anheuser-Busch, Spec Proj & Corp Investments, mgr, 1985; SmithKline Beckman, Financial Planning & Analysis, mgr, 1981-85; Bus Improv Forum, exec dir, 1986; Mars Inc, 1986-91; Northwest Airlines Inc, Int Treas, dir, 1991-93; World Trade Inst Int Finance Prog, chmn, lectr; Ark State Univ; Lewis & Co Inc, pres, 1993-. **Orgs:** Rotary Int. **Honors/Awds:** Omicron Delta Epsilon, Int Economics Honor Soc, 1981; fel, Chase Manhattan Bank, 1981. **Special Achievements:** Language Proficiency: Spanish, French, Japanese, Chinese; Professional Speaking Engagements: Int Treasury Mgt Principles, US Dept of Commerce, Int Opportunities for Women & Minorities in Bus; Professional Papers: Foreign Trade & Investment Review, Intl Trade Considerations in European Russia, 1995 Edition; Trade & Culture, South Africa: How to Use Investment & Trade Incentives; Treasury Mgt Asn, Derivatives Rick Mgt Compendium; numerous others. **Business Addr:** President, Lewis & Company Inc, 3432 Denmark Ave Suite 136, St Paul, MN 55123-1088, **Business Phone:** (612)707-8571.

LEWIS, JENIFER JEANETTE
Actor, singer. **Personal:** Born Jan 25, 1957, Kinloch, MO. **Educ:** Webster Univ, attended. **Career:** Films: Sister Act, 1992; Poetic Justice, 1993; Renaissance Man, 1994;Corrina, Corrina, 1994; Dead press, 1995; The Preacher's Wife, 1996; The Mighty, 1998; Mystery Men, 1999; Partners, 2000; Dancing in September, 2000; Cast Away, 2000; The Brothers, 2001; Juwanna Man, 2002; The Cookout,2004; Dirty Laundry, 2006; Redrum, 2007; Who's Your Caddy?, 2007; Redrum, 2007; Meet the Browns, 2008; Prop 8: The Musical, 2008; Not Easily Broken, 2009; tv movies: Deconstructing Sarah, 1994; Temptaions, 1998; Little Richard, 2000; The Ponder Heart, 2001; tv guest appearances: "For Your Love", 1998; "Fresh Prince of Bel-Air", 1990; "Murphy Brown", 1988; "Cosby", 1996;"Grown Ups", 1999; "Time of Your Life", 1999; "Girlfriends", 2002-06; "Family Affair", 2002; "The Proud Family", 2003; "Strong Medicine", 2000-06; "The PJs", 1999-2008; "Boston Legal", 2007-08. **Honors/Awds:** Two National Association Advanced Colored People Theater Awards; Nominated, Image Award, 1997. **Business Addr:** Actress, William Morris Agency, 1325 Avenue of the Americas, New York, NY 10019, **Business Phone:** (212)586-5100.*

LEWIS, JERMAINE EDWARD
Football player. **Personal:** Born Oct 16, 1974, Lanham, MD; married Imara; children: JJ & Ali. **Educ:** Univ Md. **Career:** Football player(retired); Baltimore Ravens, wide receiver, 1996-2001; Houston Texans, 2002; Jacksonville Jaguars, 2003-04. **Orgs:** Geronimo Lewis Found. **Honors/Awds:** Two time Pro Bowl selection, 1998, 2001.

LEWIS, JESSE CORNELIUS
School administrator. **Personal:** Born Jun 26, 1929, Vaughan, MS; son of Jefferson Lewis; married Emma Goldman; children: Valerie. **Educ:** Tougaloo Col, BS, 1949; Univ Ill, MS, 1955, MA, 1959; Syracuse Univ, PhD, 1966. **Career:** Southern Univ, Baton Rouge, instr math, 1955-57; Prairie View Col, 1957-58; Syracuse Univ, res asst comput ctr, 1963-66; Jackson State Col,prof math, dir, comput ctr, 1966-84; Norfolk State Univ, Norfolk, VA, vpres, acad affairs, 1984-. **Orgs:** Fel, Nat Sci Found Sci Fac, 1958 & 1961; lectr, Am Math Asn, 1971; proj dir, Nat Sci Found Comput Network, 1973-; chmn, fac Senate, Jackson State Col, 1970-73; Am Asn Comput Mach; Math Soc; Alpha Phi Alpha. **Honors/Awds:** Administrators of the Year, 1990. **Business Addr:** Vice President of Academic Affairs, Norfolk State University, 700 Pk Ave, Norfolk, VA 23504, **Business Phone:** (757)823-8768.

LEWIS, JESSE J.
Executive. **Personal:** Born Jan 3, 1925, Tuscaloosa, AL; married Helen Merriweather; children: James, Jesse Jr. **Educ:** Miles Col, Birmingham, AL, BA, 1955; Troy State Univ, Montgomery, AL, MS, 1977. **Career:** The Birmingham Times Newspaper, pres, 1963-64; Office Hwy Traffic Safety Montgomery, dir, 1974-78; Lawson State Community Col, pres, 1978-87. **Orgs:** Law Enforcement Planning Agency; Birmingham Urban League; life mem, Alpha Phi Alpha. **Honors/Awds:** Citation for Outstanding Service, Gov AL, 1975; Outstanding Acadamy Excellence Award, Miles Col, 1975.

LEWIS, JIM (JAMES LEWIS)
Administrator, vice president (organization), certified public accountant. **Personal:** Born in Hammond, IN; married LaFaye Floyd. **Educ:** Ind State Univ, acct, 1984; Krannert Sch Bus, Purdue Univ, MBA. **Career:** PepsiCo, Frito-Lay, controller, dir invest rels, vpres, gen mgr; Price Waterhouse Cooper, cert pub acct; PepsiCo; Walt Disney World, sr vpres pub affairs; Disney Vacation Develop, The Walt Disney Co, dir planning, vpres bus develop & vpres finance, pres, currently. **Orgs:** Chmn, Orlando Regional Chamber Com. **Honors/Awds:** Distinguished Alumni Award, Krannert Bus Sch. **Business Addr:** President, Disney Vacation Development Inc, The Walt Disney Company, 200 Celebration Pl, Celebration, FL 34747, **Business Phone:** (407)824-4321.*

LEWIS, JIMMY
Manager. **Personal:** Born Sep 3, 1952, Elizabethtown, NC; son of Gaston Lewis and Martha; married Hsieh Lewis, Aug 30, 1978; children: Sandra, Dexter & Tiffany. **Educ:** Univ NY, BS, 1990; Cent Mich Univ, MSA, 1992. **Career:** USN, tele commun opers mgr, 1987-90, tele commun mgr, 1990-93, dir Commun, 1993-96, Communs network mgr, 1996-99; Ai Metrix Inc, opers mgr, dir opers, 1999-. **Orgs:** Arm Forces Commun Asn, 1990-93; pres, Makakilo Housing Asn, 1998-99; mentor, Hawaii Youth Challenge, 1996-99; supporter, advisor, Fishing Sch, 1990-. **Military Serv:** USN, lt comdr, 1972-99; 2 Navy Achievement Medals; 2 Joint Service Achievements; 3 Defense Meritorous Service Medals; 2 Navy Commendations Medals. **Home Addr:** 2156 Capstone Circle, Herndon, VA 20170, **Home Phone:** (703)742-4268.

LEWIS, JOHN R.
Congressperson (u.s. federal government). **Personal:** Born Feb 21, 1940, Troy, AL; married Lillian Miles; children: John Miles. **Educ:** Fisk Univ, BS, relig & philos. **Career:** Congressperson, United States Congress, 2006. **Orgs:** President, Student Non-Violent Coordinating Committee (SNCC), 1963-66; Field Foundation, Associate Director; Voter Education Project (VEP), Director; mem, Congressional Black Caucus Foundation, Inc. **Honors/Awds:** Academy of Excellence's Golden Plate Award; National Trust for Historic Preservation, Preservation Hero Award; Capital Award of the National Council of La Raza; Martin Luther King, Jr. Non-Violent Peace Prize; President's Medal of Georgetown University; NAACP Spingarn Medal; JFK Profile in Courage Award; The Timberland Company created the John Lewis Award honoring humanitarian service. **Special Achievements:** Co-authored a biography "Walking with the Wind: A Memoir of the Movement". **Business Addr:** Congressmen, Academy of Acheivement, 1222 16 St NW, Washington, DC 20036.*

LEWIS, JOHN ROBERT
Congressperson (u.s. federal government). **Personal:** Born Feb 21, 1940, Troy, AL; son of Meline Thas and Willie Mae Carter; married Lillian Miles. **Educ:** Am Baptist Theol Sem, BA, 1961; Fisk Univ, BA, 1967. **Career:** Nonviolent Coord Comm, chmn stud, 1963-66; Field Found, assoc dir, 1966-67; Southern Regional Coun, comm orgn proj dir, 1967-70; Voter Educ Proj Inc, exec dir, 1970-77; Atlanta City Councilman-At-Large, Congressman, 1986-. **Orgs:** Leadership Atlanta, 1974-75; Am Civil Liberties Union; Afro-Am Inst; adv comm, Biracial Com Atlanta Bd Educ; adv bd, Black Enterprises; Martin Luther King Jr Ctr Social Change; life mem, Nat Asn Advan Colored People; SCLC; leading speaker, organizer & worker, Civil Rights Movement; Speaker's Bur during Sen Robert Kennedy's campaign. **Honors/Awds:** Martin Luther King Jr Peace Prize, 1975. **Special Achievements:** Appointed by President Johnson to White House Conference "To Fulfill These Rights" 1966, named "One of Nation's Most Influential Black" Ebony Magazine, 1971-72, "One of America's 200 Rising Leaders" by Time Mag, 1974, author of Walking with the Wind, 1998. **Business Addr:** Congressman, U.S. House of Representatives, 343 Cannon House Office Bldg, Washington, DC 20515, **Business Phone:** (202)225-3801.*

LEWIS, KAREN A
Marketing executive. **Personal:** Born Mar 9, 1962, Philadelphia, PA; daughter of Wallace and Anita Lewis. **Educ:** La Salle Univ, BS, bus, 1985, media rels, cert prog, 1999; Univ Pa, fund raising, cert prog, 1996. **Career:** Greater Philadelphia Chamber Com, prog develop specialist, 1990-91; USN Int Logistics Control Off, mgt analyst, 1985-91; Mayor's Off, asst dep mayor, 1992-94; City Philadelphia, dep city rep, 1994-96; Greater Philadelphia Tourism Mkt Corp, vpres, 1996-99; Greater Philadelphia Cultural Alliance, vpres; Ave Arts Inc, exec dir, currently. **Orgs:** Nat Asn Female Execs, 1997-99; Travel Indust Am, 1996-99; bd mem, Optum Inc, 1999-2001; bd mem, Cult Fund, Nominating Comm chair, 1999-2003; bd mem, Welcome Am, 1999-2001; bd mem, Multucultural Affairs Cong, 1999-2001. **Special Achievements:** Appointed by Governor Ridge to Quebec/Pennsylvania Task Force, 1998; appointed by Mayor Rendell to President Clinton's Summit, 1997. **Business Addr:** Executive Director, Avenue of the Arts Inc, 123 S Broad St Suite 1240, Philadelphia, PA 19109, **Business Phone:** (215)731-9668.

LEWIS, KENNETH DWIGHT
Engineer, clergy, college administrator. **Personal:** Born Aug 11, 1949, Newark, NJ; son of Joseph Lewis Sr and Carrie Attles; married Pamela Josephine Masingale, May 27, 1978; children: Caleb & Sarah. **Educ:** Rutgers Univ, AB, physics, 1971; Lehigh Univ, MS, physics, 1972; Stanford Univ, MSE, Nuclear Engineering, 1974; Univ Ill-Urbana Champaign, AM (applied Math), 1979, PhD, Nuclear Engineering, 1982; Trinity Theol Seminary, Newburgh Ind, ThD, 1986; Moody Bible Inst Chicago, cert Biblical Studies, 1992; Anderson Baptist Seminary, Camilla, GA, Ministry degree prog. **Career:** Lockheed Martin Energy Systs, sr engr, 1982-88, dev staff mem I, 1988-90, engr specialist, 1990-95, sect mgr, nuclear calculations sect, 1994-98, sr staff engr, 1995-, cre nuclear criticality safety mgr, 1995-97; Knoxville Col, adj prof physics, 2000-; Master Ministry, Andersonville Baptist Seminary, Camilla, GA, 2001-; BWXT Y-12, LLC Oak Ridge, Tenn, sr staff engr II; SC State Univ, Col Sci, Math & Engineering Technol, dean, currently. **Orgs:** Sigma Xi Honorary Soc; Pi Mu Epsilon Math Honor Soc; Licensed Prof Engr; assoc pastor & youth dir, Little Leaf Baptist Church, TN, 1993-; assoc pastor, Second Baptist Church, Stockton CA, 1988-90; asst pastor, trustee, First Baptist Church, Chillicothe, OH, 1983-87; deacon, Salem Baptist Church, Champaign Il, 1979-82; Dept Adv Bd, Univ Ill, NUCE, 2000-; fel Am Nuclear Soc. **Honors/Awds:** Certificate of Merit, Ohio Soc Prof Engr, 1983; Outstanding Achievement Award, Univ Ill, Black Alumni Asn, 1992; Lockheed Martin Cash Awards, Technical Achievement, 1992, 1994, 1998, 2000, 2003; Certificate of Recognition, Ohio House Reps, 1983; Grad Col Fel, Univ Ill, 1977-78; Letter of Appreciation, Pres Clinton, 1995; Black Engineer of the Year President's Award, 1998; Engineer of the Year, Lockheed Martin Energy Systems, 1998; Lockheed Martin Corp NOVA Award; DOE Award for Excellence, 2000, 2001. **Special Achievements:** Delegate to People's Republic of China Radiation Protection Conference, 1987; Session Chair, Am Nuclear Soc Annual Meeting, PA, 1995; Over 20 Technical Publications; Visiting Prof Math, Univ the Pacific, 1989-90; Authored over two dozen journal articles and technical reports, including works presented in Germany and in Shanghai, China, before China's largest nuclear science association. **Home Addr:** 128 Capital Circle, Oak Ridge, TN 37830. **Business Addr:** Dean, South Carolina State University, College of Science, Mathematics & Engineering Technology, 300 College Ave NE, PO Box 8083, Orangeburg, SC 29117, **Business Phone:** (803)536-7132.

LEWIS, KERI
Singer. **Personal:** Married Toni Braxton, Apr 21, 2001; children: Denham Cole & Diezel Ky. **Career:** Mint Condition, mem, 1991-99; Writer: Mo' Money, 1992; Albums: Meant to Be Mint, 1991; From the Mint Factory, 1993; Definition of a Band, 1996; The Collection, 1998; Life's Aquarium, 1999; Snowflakes, producer & composer, 2001; TV appearances: "New York Undercover", 1997; "Intimate Portrait", 2002; "Soul Train", 2005. **Business Addr:** Singer, c/o Atlantic Records Inc, 1290 Avenue of the Americas, New York, NY 10104, **Business Phone:** (212)707-2000.*

LEWIS, KIRK
Administrator. **Educ:** Wayne State Univ, MBA, finance, 1993. **Career:** Bing Assembly Systs, chief financial officer, currently. **Business Addr:** Chief Financial Officer, Bing Assembly Systems, 11500 Oakland Ave, Detroit, MI 48211, **Business Phone:** (313)867-3700.

LEWIS, LAURETTA FIELDS
Educator. **Personal:** Born in Chattanooga, TN; daughter of Mark Sr and Lula Ballard Hogue; divorced; children: Jeffrey L & Mark

F (divorced). **Educ:** Univ Tenn, Chattanooga, BSW, 1971, MSW, 1974; Univ Mich Inst Geron, certaging, 1982; NC A&T State Univ, Summer Inst Aging, 1986. **Career:** Educator (retired); Family Serv Agency, social worker aide, 1966-68; Community Action Prog, out reach soc worker, 1968-70; Neighborhood Youth Corp, youth counsr, 1972; Clover Bottom Dev Ctr Nashville TN, social worker, 1973; Florence Crittenton Home TN, social worker aide, 1973-74; E Carolina Univ, assoc prof, social work, instr, Univ Geroutol Ctr. **Orgs:** Consult Long Term Care, 1976-; vice chmn, treas, 1980-82, chmn, 1983 NC Coun Social Work Ed; pres, exec bd, Pitt Coounty Ment Health Asn, 1983-92; chmn bd, Pitt County Coun Aging, 1983-85; exec comm & chap rep state bd Pitt County Ment Health Asn, 1987; exec bd, Creative Living Ctr Day Prog Geriatric Patients; grants & res comt mem, Southern Gerontol Soc, 1990-92; chair, personnel action, Pitt County Coun Aging, 1989-92; scholarshipliaison, Sch Social Work & Pitt County Ment Health Asn, 1985-93; Greenville/Pitt County Habitat Humanity, PORT Adolescent Substance AbuseProg, MH/Pitt County, bd mem; Pitt County Coalition Adolescent Pregnancy Prevention Inc, comt mem; East Carolina Organization Black Fac & Staff, prog comt mem; Hospice Volunteer, Home Health & Hospice Care Inc; Certified Clin Practitioner, recertified CCSW, 1994; Chi Zeta - Phi AlphaECU - Sch Social Work Chapter Phi Alpha Nat Social Work Hon Soc, fac adv. **Honors/Awds:** Alumni Upper Classman Award, 1971; Danforth Assoc Danforth Found, 1980; Awards Appreciaiton NC Dept Human Serv MR, 1981; Teacher of the Year, Student Assoc Social Work Dept, 1983; Outstanding Service Mental Health Assoc, 1984-85; Appointee Reg Faculty Liaison Nat Assoc Soc Works; Minority Leadership Develop Fellowship Award Sch Pub Health Univ NC Chapel Hill, 1985; Certificate of Appreciation from Undergrad Stud Org, 1987; Training Assistantship Geriatric Educ & Leadership Dev Univ NC, Chapel Hill Sch Social Work & Geriatric Educ Ctr Summer Inst, 1987; Merit Award Ment Health Assoc Pitt County, 1987; inducted into "The Carolinas Assoc "Excellence in Higher Educ as Charter Mem, 1987; Reviewer for Educational Gerontol Int Jour; Pitt County habitat Humanity Family Selection COM; Faculty Liaison Service Award, Nat Asn Social Workers, 1995. **Special Achievements:** Book Review Published in International Journal: Educational Gerontology: v18 No 5 Jul-Aug, 1992, Serving the Elderly: Skills for Practice, edited byPaul K H Kim, NY: Aldine de Gruyter Inc, 1991. **Home Addr:** PO Box 21061, Greenville, NC 27858.

LEWIS, LEMUEL E.
Chief financial officer. **Educ:** Darden Grad Sch. **Career:** Chief financial officer (retired); Landmark Commun, exec vpres & chief financial officer. *

LEWIS, LEO E
Athletic director, football player, consultant. **Personal:** Born in Columbia, MO; son of Leo and Doris. **Educ:** Univ Mo; Univ Tenn; Univ Minn, PhD, kinesiol, 1997. **Career:** Football player (retired), consultant; Minn vikings, wide receiver, 1981-91, dir player develop; Univ Minn, Dept Kinesiology & Leisure Studies, instr, 1986-94, assoc athletic dir, currently; St Cloud State Univ, Dept Health Phys Educ, adj instr, 1999-2000; Athletic Serv LLC, cert consult, currently. **Orgs:** Sigma Pi Phi; AAASP; NASSS; founder & pres, Lewis Sports Found, 1993-. **Honors/Awds:** Played in NFC Championship Game; Univ Mo All-Century Team, Hall of Fame. **Business Addr:** Certified Consultant, Athletic Services LLC, PO Box 46451, Eden Prairie, MN 55347, **Business Phone:** (612)625-5444.

LEWIS, LILLIAN J.
Social worker. **Personal:** Born Apr 20, 1926, Chicago, IL; widowed; children: Robert, Gloria, Benjamin & Vivian. **Career:** US Naval Hosp, 1955-63; DeWitt Army Hosp, nurs div 1963-65; Group Health Assoc, clin asst, 1966-70; Manpower Admin, chief support serv, 1971-. **Orgs:** Nat Org for Women, Nat Polit Womens Caucus, Mass State Dem Steering Comt,1976, Nat Women's Polit Caucus Affirm Action Task Force; vpres, Nat Asn Advan Colored People; Community Rel Deseg Task Force; adv bd, Model Cities Fel, League Women Voters, Prince Georges Pol Womens Caucus & Affirm Action Coord, Prince George County Pub Sch ESAP, 1971, Prince George Ment Health Asn; comn elect, Marvin Mandel; chmn, Community Affairs 1970-72; bd dir, SChristian Leadership Conf Md Chap, Prince Georges County Md Black Dem Coun. **Honors/Awds:** Certificate of Appreciation for Meritiroius Assistance, US Dept Com, 1970; Certificate of Merit, Nat Asn Advan Colored People, 1973; Delegation At Large, Dem Conv State Md, 1976. **Business Addr:** Chief Support Service, Manpower Administration.

LEWIS, DR. LLOYD ALEXANDER
Educator, clergy. **Personal:** Born Nov 12, 1947, Washington, DC; son of Lloyd Alexander and Alice Christine Bell. **Educ:** Trinity Col, AB, 1969; Va Theol Seminary, MDiv, 1972; Yale Univ, MA, 1975, MPhil, 1981, PhD, 1985. **Career:** St George's Church, cur, 1972-74; Gen Theol Seminary, tutor, 1977, vis prof, 1989; Va Theol Seminary, asst prof, New Testament, 1978-86, assoc prof, New Testament, 1986-91; Molly Laird Downs prof New Testament, currently; George Mercer Sch Theol, dean, 1991; General Theological Seminary, vis prof. **Orgs:** Soc Study Black Relig; Soc Biblical Lit; Prog Theol Educ, World Coun Churches, comnr; Union Black Episcopalians; consult, Standing Liturgical Comn, The Episcopal Church. **Honors/Awds:** Rockefeller Doctoral Fellowship, 1974-76; Canon Theologian, Cathedral of the Incarnation, 1991; Honorary Doctorate in Divinity, Va Theol Seminary, 1992. **Special Achievements:** Author of "An AFA Appraisal of the Philemon Paul Onesimus Triangle," Stony the Road We Trod, 1991; "The Law Courts at Corinth: An Experiment in the Power of Baptism," Christ and His Communities, 1990. **Home Addr:** 200-16 Hilton Ave, Hempstead, NY 11550, **Home Phone:** (703)461-0977. **Business Addr:** Professor, Virginia Theological Seminary, 3737 Seminary Rd, Alexandria, VA 22304, **Business Phone:** (703)461-1713.

LEWIS, LOIDA NICOLAS
Executive, lawyer. **Personal:** Born Dec 7, 1942, Sorsogon, Philippines; married Reginald F, 1969 (died 1993); children: Leslie & Christina. **Educ:** St Theresas Col, Manila; Univ Philippines. **Career:** Immigration atty, 1979-90; TLC Beatrice Int Holdings Inc, chmn & chief exec officer, 1993-99; TLC Beatrice, China, chmn & chief exec officer; TLC Beatrice Foods, Philippines, chmn & chief exec officer. **Orgs:** Nat chair, Nat Fedn Filipino Am Asn. **Special Achievements:** No 1 among the Top 50 Women Business Owners in America by Working Woman Mag, 1994.

LEWIS, DR. LONZY JAMES
Educator, scientist. **Personal:** Born Aug 29, 1949, Sharon, GA; son of Joseph Lewis and Lillian (Seals) Lewis; married Cynthia Patterson Lewis, Jun 30, 1972; children: Lillianne Marie, Brianna Nicole & Adrianne Zanetta. **Educ:** Morehouse Col, BS, 1971; Ga Inst Technol, MS, physics, 1973; State Univ NY, Albany, PhD, 1980. **Career:** Deutsches Elektronen-Synchrotron, work study fel, 1970; Ga Inst Technol, EPA trainee, physics dept, Chem dept, 1972-73, Sch Geophys Sci, res sci II, 1980-83; Atmos Sci Res Ctr, res asst, 1974-80; Col St Rose, HCOP prog, math instr, 1979-80; State Univ NY, Albany, res fel; State Miss, Dept Environ, Air Quality Control Off, consult, 1983-93; Jackson State Univ, Dept Physics & Atmos Sci, chmn, 1983-87, assoc prof, 1983-93; Clark Atlanta Univ, Dept Physics, chmn, 1993-98, assoc prof, 1993-. **Orgs:** Mem bd, meteor & ocean ed in univ, 1983-87, mem 1978-, Am Meteorol Soc; treas, finance comt chmn, 1990-95; conf chmn, 1991-92, 1994-95, 1998-99; Proj Kalleidoscope, 1994-; fac assoc, curric supv, mentor, sci res agt, 1994-2000, Ronald E McNair Found; pres-elect, vice chmn, 1995-96; pres, chmn, 1996-98; sci ambassador, Nat Soc Black Physicists, NSBP, 1997-99. **Honors/Awds:** Charter Fellow, Nat Soc Black Physicists, 1992; Fellow, Sigma Pi Sigma, 1993; Teaching Excellence Award, Vulcan Materials Co, 2003; Aldridge-McMillan Achievement Award, Clark Atlanta Univ, 2003; Vulcan Teaching Excellence Award, Clark Atlanta Univ, 2003. **Special Achievements:** Auth: Multiple Excitation of Neon by Photon & Electron Impact, Phys Lctr, 1970; Terrestrial Solar Spectra Data Sets, Solar Energy, 1983; Proceedings of the XIX Day of Scientific Lectures and 15th Annual Meeting of NSBP, 1993; Proceedings of the XXII Day of Scientific Lectures and 18th Annual Meeting of NSBP, 1996; Certificate of Proficiency in the German Language, Zeugnis, 1970; Certificate of Proficiency in Air Pollution Control Technology, 1973. **Business Addr:** Associate Professor, Clark Atlanta University, Department of Physics, McPheeters Dennis Hall Rm 102, 223 James P Brawley Dr SW, Atlanta, GA 30314, **Business Phone:** (404)880-8798.

LEWIS, LYN ETTA
School administrator, educator. **Personal:** Born Oct 1, 1947, Monroe, LA; daughter of Rufus and Onita Lewis. **Educ:** Grambling State Univ, BA, 1965-68; Univ Tenn, MA, 1968-70; Wayne State Univ, PhD, 1972-78. **Career:** Spelman Col, inst sociol, 1969-72; Univ Detroit, assoc prof, 1973-90; Univ Detroit-Mercy, chair & assoc prof, 1990-. **Orgs:** Boysville Mich; pres, Detroit Advisory Coun, 1993-. **Honors/Awds:** Distinguished Alumnae Award, Wayne State Univ, Ctr Black Studies, 1981; Distinguished Alumnae Award, Grambling State Univ, 1990; Faculty Award Excellence. **Special Achievements:** Publ: Book review in publ Mich Psychol Asn. **Home Addr:** 14368 Warwick, Detroit, MI 48223, **Home Phone:** (313)836-1877. **Business Addr:** Associate Professor, Chair of Sociology, University of Detroit-Mercy, 4001 W McNichols Rd, PO Box 19900, Detroit, MI 48221-3038, **Business Phone:** (313)993-1094.

LEWIS, DR. MARGARET W
Educator, administrator. **Personal:** Born in Oviedo, FL; daughter of Morris T Williams and Margaret Ellis Williams; married Howard E Lewis, May 15, 1959. **Educ:** Fla A&M Univ, Tallahassee, FL, BSN, 1958, PhD, 1977; Ohio State Univ, Columbus, OH, MSN, 1968. **Career:** Fla A&M Univ Hosp, Tallahassee, FL, staff nurse, 1958-59, Fla A&M Univ, Tallahassee, FL, instr, 1959-61, asst prof, 1966-78, dean, sch nursing, dean emer, currently; Ctr County Hosp, Belafonte, PA, supvr, 1961-66; Albany State Col, Albany, GA, assoc prof, 1978-79; Winston-Salem State Univ, Winston-Salem, NC, dir, div nursing, 1979-82; Brevard Pub Sch, Off Career & Tech Educ, dir, currently. **Orgs:** Bd mem, Fla League Nursing, 1983-84, 1991; bd mem, Big Bend Deaf Ctr, 1989-; Am Nurses asn, 1958-; mem, Nat League Nursing, 1975-; Fla League Nursing, pres, 1992-. **Honors/Awds:** Outstanding Alumnus Award Administration, Fla A&M Univ Sch Nursing Alumni Asn, 1990; Outstanding Dean Award, Florida A&M Univ, 1988. **Military Serv:** AUS, cpt, 1951-54. **Business Phone:** (321)633-1000.

LEWIS, MARTIN
Basketball player. **Personal:** Born Apr 28, 1975, Liberal, KS. **Educ:** Butler Co Comm Col; Seward Co Comm Col. **Career:** Toronto Raptors, 1995-97.

LEWIS, MARVIN
Basketball coach. **Personal:** Born Sep 23, 1958, McDonald, PA. **Educ:** Id St, BA, phys educ, 1981, MA, athletic admini, 1982. **Career:** Id State Univ, linebackers coach, 1981-84; Long Beach State, linebackers coach, 1985-86; Univ New Mex, linebackers coach, 1987-89; Univ Pittsburgh, linebackers coach, 1990-91; Pittsburgh Steelers, linebackers coach, 1992-95; Baltimore Ravens, defensive coordr, 1996-01; Wash Redskins, defensive coordr, 2002; Cincinnati Bengals, head coach, 2003-. **Special Achievements:** Only head coach in Bengals history; Idaho State's Hall of Fame 2001. **Business Phone:** (513)621-3550.*

LEWIS, MATTHEW
Photographer, editor. **Personal:** Born Mar 8, 1930, McDonald, PA; son of Alzenia Heath and Matthew; married Jeannine Wells; children: Charlene, Matthew & Kevin. **Career:** Photographer, Editor (retired); The Washington Post, asst mgr, ed & photographer; Morgan State Col, instr, 1957-65; The Thomasville Times, photographer, 1994-2001. **Orgs:** White House New Photograph Asn; Nat Press Photograph Asn; Nat Asn Black Journalists. **Honors/Awds:** Pulitzer Prize for Feature Photograph, 1975; 1st prize, Nat Newspaper Publ Asn, 1964; White House News Photograph Asn, 1968 & 71; Bill Pryor Award, Washington-Baltimoer Newspaper Guild, 1971-72; Hall of Fame, 1990. **Military Serv:** USN, 1949-52. **Home Phone:** (910)472-6683.

LEWIS, MAURICE
Journalist, television news anchorperson. **Personal:** Born Aug 23, 1943, Chicago, IL; children: Stephanie, Kevin. **Career:** AF Radio, reporter & commentator; Boston TV, reporter; CNL Radio, mgr, 1965-67; WBZ Radio News, reporter, 1969-74; WHDH TV, anchor, 1972-79; WNAC-TV, anchorman& reporter, 1974-76; WNAC-TV, co-anchorman, 1975-76; WHYY, guest journalist, 1976-77; WBZ-TV 4, news anchorman & reporter, 1976; Marlborough Pub Libr, host prog, 2007. **Orgs:** Chmn & co-founder, The Afro Am Media Asn, 1975-; bd dir, Elma Lewis Sch Fine Art, 1977; bd dir, Family Serv Ctr, 1976; Nat Asn Advancement Colored People;bd dir, Urban League, 1976; bd trustees, Graham Jr Col, 1977. **Honors/Awds:** Outstanding Service to Community Award, Jan Matzlinger, 1974; News Reporter of the year, Afro Am Patrolman's Asn, 1977; Outstanding Acheivement Award, Mass Sec State Paul Guzzi, 1976; Outstanding Citizen of the Year, Mass State Sen, 1976; Outstanding Citizen of the Year, Congrsnsl Record, 1976; Outstanding Minute Broadcaster, Mass House Rep, 1976; Black Acheiver Business Award, Grtr Boston YMCA, 1976; Man Of The Year, Nat Asn Negro Bus & Professional Women's Club; Black Acheiver Of The Year, Boston 200's Victorian Exhib & Gilette Co; Outstanding Service to Community Award In Media, Boston Chap, Nat Asn Advancement Colored People. **Special Achievements:** Who's Who Boston's 100 Influential Black Citizens 1976-77; 10 outst yg ldrs Boston Jaycees 1975. **Military Serv:** USNR, seaman, 1960-62, 1965-67. **Business Addr:** 1170 Soldiers Field Rd, Boston, MA 02134.

LEWIS, DR. MEHARRY HUBBARD
Educator. **Personal:** Born Aug 2, 1936, Nashville, TN; son of Felix E and Helen M; divorced 2005; children: Karen Anita & Arlan David. **Educ:** Tenn State Univ, BS, 1959, MS, 1961; Ind Univ, Bloomington, PhD, 1971. **Career:** Ind Univ, NDEA fel, 1966-67; Sch City Gary, bio teacher, 1966-91; Stud Activ Off, Ind Univ, frat affairs adv, 1967-69, lectr, 1970, vis asst prof, 1970-72; Bullock County Bd Ed, coordr res & eval, 1972-73; Nat Alliance Black Sch Educrs, dir res proj, 1973-74; Tuskegee Inst, Sch Educ, prof educ, asst dean, dir inst res & planning, 1974-84; MGMT Inc, pres, dir 1984-91; Bullock County, Bd Educ, sr counr, 1992-2000; Tuskegee Inst Relig & Sacred Music, pres & founder, 2000-01; Church of the Living God, the Pillar & Ground of the Truth Inc, pres, chief Overseer, 2001-. **Orgs:** Nat Alliance Black Sch Ed; Kappa Delta Pi; Phi Delta Kappa Int; Alpha Kappa Mu Nat Honor Soc; Am Personnel & Guid Assoc; ACES Div & Assoc for Non-White Concerns; gen sec, trustee, Church the Living God, the Pillar & Ground the Truth Inc; youth community, YMCA, 1963-66; Beta Kappa Chi; Chi Sigma Iota Hon Coun & personal servs; Nat & Ala Educ Asn. **Honors/Awds:** President Award, Nat Alliance Black Sch Educrs, 1974. **Special Achievements:** Publ several poems & articles; publ seven in a series of books on the life of Mary Lena Lewis Tate & org she founded, 1903, The Church of the Living God, the Pillar and Ground of the Truth Inc. (The New and Living Way Publishing Compan0y, Nashville, TN). **Business Addr:** President, Chief Overseer, Church of the Living God, the Pillar & Ground of the Truth Inc., PO Box 12236, Durham, NC 27709, **Business Phone:** (919)596-7598.

LEWIS, MELANIE
Journalist. **Personal:** Born Dec 19, 1964, Wilmington, DE; daughter of F Pearle Saulsberry and Leurhman Saulsberry. **Educ:** Univ Del, Newark, DE, BA, 1986. **Career:** Univ Del, Newark, DE, resident asst, 1983-84, hall dir, 1984-86; WILM-AM, Wilmington, DE, pub affairs reporter, 1984, 1985, traffic reporter, 1986; Des Moines Register, Des Moines, IA, staff writer, 1986-90; Da

las Morning News, Dallas, TX, staff writer, 1990-94. **Orgs:** Nat Asn Black Journalists, 1990-; Delta Sigma Theta, 1990-; Dallas-Fort Worth Asn Black Communicators, 1990-; Educ Writers Asn. **Honors/Awds:** Omicron Delta Kappa, 1985-; Mortar Bd, 1985. **Home Phone:** (214)559-0559.

LEWIS, MICHAEL W
Executive. **Personal:** Born Sep 15, 1949, Detroit, MI; married Jacqueline Lewis, May 5, 1973; children: Kamilah & Neamen. **Educ:** Western Mich Univ, 1971; Ind Univ, MBA, 1976. **Career:** Harris Bank, com banking officer, 1979, asst vpres, 1981, vpres, 1983, team leader, 1987, svp & mkt exec, 1994, exec vpres com banking, 1998, city region, pres, currently. **Orgs:** Prin & bd Chair, Chicago United; bd mem, Local Initiatives Support Corp; adv bd, WMU Haworth Col; Exec Club Chicago; Union League Club; Ill Govt Finance Officers Asn; Black MBA; zoning bd, Village Olympia Fields; adv bd, Urban Fin Serv Forum; Kappa Alpha Psi Fraternity. **Honors/Awds:** fel, Consortium Grad Study in Mgmt, 1974; Chicago United Business Leaders Color awardee. **Business Addr:** City Region President, Harris Bank, 111 W Monroe St 3E, Chicago, IL 60603, **Business Phone:** (312)461-2121.

LEWIS, MICHELE
Business owner. **Educ:** Southern Univ, New Orleans, bus admin, attended. **Career:** Afro Am Book Stop, owner, 1992-2005, 2008, currently. **Business Addr:** Owner, Afro-American Book Stop, 3951 Magazine St, New Orleans, LA 70115, **Business Phone:** (504)896-9190.

LEWIS, MO (MORRIS LEWIS)
Football player. **Personal:** Born Oct 21, 1969, Atlanta, GA; married Christy; children: Mo. **Educ:** Univ Ga. **Career:** Football player (retired); New York Jets, linebacker, 1991-2003, 2005. **Honors/Awds:** Miller Lite Player of the Year, 1994, Three Pro Bowls, 1998-2000; A.F.C.'s defensive player of the week, 2000.

LEWIS, MORRIS. See LEWIS, MO.

LEWIS, NATHAN L
Investment banker. **Personal:** Born in Georgia; married. **Educ:** Univ Ga, BBA; Clark Atlanta Univ, MBA. **Career:** Jackson Securities Inc, equity res analyst, investment banker, currently.

LEWIS, NICOLE
Executive, vice president (organization). **Career:** Kelly Serv, sr dir corp accts, vpres corp accts, vpres, supplier diversity develop, currently. **Business Addr:** Vice President of Supplier Diversity Development, Kelly Services, 999 W Big Beaver Rd, Troy, MI 48084, **Business Phone:** (248)362-4444.*

LEWIS, ORA LEE
Executive. **Personal:** Born Apr 27, 1930, Port Huron, MI; married Cornelius W; children: 5. **Educ:** Erie Comn Col. **Career:** Exec (retired); United Mutual Life Ins Co, sec, 1947-51; Buffalo Criterion, pres, rptr clmnst, 1947-65; Frienship House, prog asst, 1947-49; Mrs Sims, sec atty, 1951-54; Ora-Lee's Sec Serv, owner; YWCA, chaperone, 1956-67; Westminster Comn House, adminr asst, 1967-71; Comn Youths Boys Town, coun; Arts, exec dir; NY State Div Youth, supvr coun; Langston Hughes Inst, admin asst, exec dir, 1975-96; Memories In Time, author. **Orgs:** Human Serv Asn; E Side Coalition; bd, Review & Referral, 1972-74; vpres, Embassy Educ Culture Com Model Cities, 1972-74; Consortium Human Serv, 1975-77; Westminster Comn House, 1972-74; Buffalo Sister City Ghana, 1974-77; rep, City Buffalo, 1975. **Honors/Awds:** Honor member award, vol serv Friendship House, 1949; community service award, Westminster Comn House, 1975; certificate of completion, Erie Comn Col, 1976; outstanding achivement, Arts Comn Univ, 1976; certificate of award, Victoria ch Reporting, 1976; exhib, Buffalo Savings Bank, 1976.

LEWIS, PATRICIA
Administrator. **Career:** Los Angeles SW Col, dept chair, currently. **Orgs:** Chair, Arts Patricia McCollum. **Business Addr:** Chair, Los Angeles Southwest College, 1600 W Imperial Hwy, Los Angeles, CA 90047-4899, **Business Phone:** (323)241-5320.*

LEWIS, PEGGY
Government official. **Educ:** Trinity Col, 1977. **Career:** TV reporter/anchor; The White House, spec asst pres, media affairs; 's Defense Fund, commun dir, 1999; Alliance Retired Am, dir commun, currently; Howard Univ, teacher journ, currently. **Orgs:** pres, Alumnae Asn Bd Dirs, Trinity Col. **Business Addr:** Director of Communications, Alliance for Retired Americans, 815 16th NW 4th Floor, Washington, DC 20006, **Business Phone:** (202)637-5399.*

LEWIS, POLLY MERIWETHER
Administrator, executive. **Personal:** Born Aug 16, 1949, Clarksville, TN; daughter of Virgil Meriwether and Viola Elliot Meriwether; children: J Barry & Justin L. **Educ:** Austin Peay State Univ, 1967-69; Ga State Univ, BS, 1973, MPA, 1991. **Career:** DeKalb Co Comn Develop Dept, prog monitor, 1975-79; Ga Dept Comn Affairs, prog mgt consult, 1979-80; DeKalb Comm Rels Comn, exec dir, 1981-94; Fulton-DeKalb Hosp Authority, exec liaison, 1995-, corp secy, currently. **Orgs:** Organizer, Lambda Epilion Omega Chap; basileus, Alpha Kappa Alpha, 1973-; chairperson, bd dir, DeKalb EOA Inc, 1980-; Leadership Atlanta, 1981-82; bd dir, YWCA Greater Atlanta, 1984-; Jr League DeKalb Co Inc; steering comt chair, Leadership DeKalb, 1987-88; bd dirs, Black Women's Coalition Atlanta, 1986-; bd dirs, Decatur/DeKalb Coalition100 Black Women, 1989-; bd dirs, Citizens S DeKalb, 1986-; chair, bd dirs, Greater Travelers Rest Baptist Church; chair, bd dirs, S DeKalb YMCA; chair, bd dirs, Atlanta Labor Day Football Classic; Regional Leadership Inst, 1992; Jr League DeKalb; bd dirs, DeKalb Coun Arts. **Honors/Awds:** Woman of the Week, DeKalb News Sun, 1984; Woman of Achievement, Atlanta Urban BPW; Women of the Year, DeKalb EOA; Outstanding Service Award, Toney Gardens Civic Asn, 1988; Volunteer Service Award, DeKalb Br, YWCA Greater Atlanta Inc, 1989; Volunteer of the Year, S DeKalb YMCA, 1992. **Business Addr:** Executive Liaison, Corporate Secretary, The Fulton-DeKalb Hospital Authority, Grady Memorial Hospital, 80 Jesse Hill Dr SE, PO Box 26135, Atlanta, GA 30303-3050, **Business Phone:** (404)616-6813.

LEWIS, RAMSEY EMANUEL
Musician. **Personal:** Born May 27, 1935, Chicago, IL; son of Ramsey Emanuel and Pauline Richards; married Geraldine Taylor (divorced); married Janet Tamillow, Jun 1990; children: Vita Denise, Ramsey Emanuel III, Marcus Kevin, Dawn, Kendall, Frayne &Robert. **Educ:** Chicago Music Col, attended 1954; Univ Ill, 1954; De Paul Univ, 1955; pvt music study. **Career:** Hudson-Ross Inc Chicago, mgr rec dept, 1954-56; Ramsey Lewis Trio, organizer & mem, 1956-; prof appearance, 1957; Randalls Island Jazz Fest, New York, 1959; Saugatuck, Mich Jazz Fest, 1960; Newport Jazz Fest, 1961, 1963; Argo-Cadet recs, rec artist; CBS Recs, 1971-90; Black Entertainment TV, BET Jazz, co-host, 1990-; WNUA-FM Jazz, Ramsey & Yvonne, co-host, 1990-97, Ramsey Lewis Morning show, host, 1997-; lectr music, 1990-; Legends Jazz, co-host, 1990-; Ravinia Festival "Jazz at Ravinia" series, Chicago, IL, artistic dir, 1992-; albums: Gentlemen of Swing, 1956; Gentlemen of Jazz, 1958; Down to Earth (Music From the Soil), 1959; An Hour With the Ramsey Lewis Trio, 1959; Stretching Out, 1960; More Music From the Soil, 1961; Sound of Christmas, 1961; Bossa Nova, 1962; The Sound of Spring, 1962; Pot Luck, 1963; Barefoot Sunday Blues, 1963; Bach to the Blues, 1964; More Sounds of Christmas, 1964; At the Bohemian Caverns, 1964; Country Meets the Blues, 1964; The In Crowd, 1965; Choice! The Best of Ramsey Lewis Trio, 1962-64; Hang On Ramsey, 1965; Wade in the Water, 1966; The Movie Album, 1966; The Groover, 1966; Goin' Latin, 1967; Dancing in the Street, 1967; Up Pops Ramsey Lewis, 1967; Maiden Voyage, 1968; Mother Nature's Son, 1968; Live in Toyko, 1968; Another Voyage, 1969; The Piano Player, 1969; Them Chas, 1970; Back to the Roots, 1971; Upendo Ni Pamoja, 1972; Funky Serenity, 1973; Solar Wind, 1974; Sun Goddess, 1974; Don't It Feel Good, 1975; Salongo, 1976; Love Notes, 1977; Tequila Mockingbird, 1977; Legacy, 1978; Ramsey, 1979; Routes, 1980; Blues for the Night Owl, 1981; Three Piece Suite, 1981; Live At the Savoy, 1982; Chance Encounter, 1982; Les Fleurs, 1983; Reunion, 1983; The Two of Us (with Nancy Wilson), 1984; Fantasy, 1985; Keys to the City, 1987; A Classic Encounter, 1988; Urban Renewal, 1989; We Meet Again, 1989; Ivory Pyramid, 1992; Sky Island, 1993; Urban Knights, 1995; Between the Keys, 1996; Urban Knights II, 1997; Dance of the Soul, 1998; Appassionata, 1999; Time Flies, 2004; With One Voice, 2005; The Best of Urban Knights, 2005; The Very Best of Ramsey Lewis, 2006; Mother Nature's Son, 2007. **Orgs:** Bd dirs, Merit, 1986-; bd dirs, CYCLE, 1987-; bd dirs, Gateway Found, 1990-; bd dirs, Ravinia Mentor Prog, 1995-; bd dirs, Cares Kids Found, 1997-. **Honors/Awds:** Grammy Award, 1965, 1966, 1973; ACE Awards; Nominee, Jazz Cent, BET, 1991,1992; honorary doctorate, De Paul Univ, 1993; honorary doctorate of arts degree, Univ Ill Chicago, 1995; Man of the Week, ABC Nightly News, 1995; "Laureate", Prestigious Lincoln Acad Ill, 1997; numerous gold records; NAACP Image Award, Outstanding Jazz Artist, 2004. **Special Achievements:** Numerous TV appearances, Person White House Performance, 1995, CBS Sunday Morning, Billy Taylor Jazz Segment, 1997. **Business Addr:** Composer, Pianist & Jazz Legend, Ted Kurland Agency, 173 Brighten Ave, Boston, MA 01234.

LEWIS, RASHARD QUOVON
Basketball player. **Personal:** Born Aug 8, 1979, Pineville, LA. **Career:** Seattle Supersonics, forward, 1998-07; Orlando Magic, currently. **Honors/Awds:** Most Valuable Player, Magic Johnson Round ball Classic, 1998; mem, Good will Games gold medal-winning Team. **Special Achievements:** Selected for Radio Shack Shooting Stars competition, 2004; Youngest player in Sonics hist to start a game. *

LEWIS, RAYMOND ANTHONY
Football player. **Personal:** Born May 15, 1975, Lakeland, FL; son of Ray Anthony Lewis Sr and Sunseria Keith; children: Ray Anthony III. **Educ:** Univ Miami. **Career:** Baltimore Ravens, linebacker, 1996-. **Orgs:** Founder, Ray Lewis Found; Vietnam Veterans Am Found. **Honors/Awds:** Super Bowl Most Valuable Player Award, 1971; John Mackey Award, 1997; Most Valuable Player, Super Bowl XXXV, 2001; Defensive Player of the Year, Nat Football League, 2001; NFL Defensive Player of the Year, 2000, 2003. **Special Achievements:** Actor,"Rome Is Burning". **Business Addr:** Professional Football Player, Baltimore Ravens, 11001 Owings Mills Blvd, Owings Mills, MD 21117, **Business Phone:** (410)654-6200.

LEWIS, RETA JO
U.S. attorney. **Personal:** Born Sep 22, 1953, Statesboro, GA; daughter of Charlie and Aleathia; married Carlton, Sep 11, 1993. **Educ:** Univ Ga, BA, 1975; Am Univ, MSAJ, 1978; Emory Univ, JD, 1989. **Career:** Democracy S Africa, Nelson Mandela USA Tour, trip dir, 1991; Verner Liipfert Bernhard McPherson & Hand, atty, 1989-91; DC Govt, DC Dept Pub Works, chief staff, 1992-93; Exec Off Pres, The White House, special asst pres, polit affairs, 1996-97; Arter & Hadden, counsel, 1996-97; Greenberg Traurig, partner, 1997-; US Chamber Com, atty, currently; Vanderbilt Consulting LLC, founding partner, managing prin, currently. **Orgs:** Delta Sigma Theta, 1997; Broader Image Inc, 1997; adv coun, Women's Info Network, 1997; Emory Law Sch Coun, 1998; Outreach Prog head, US Chamber Com, 2002-, vpres & counr chamber pres, 2002-. **Home Addr:** 2030 16th St NW, Washington, DC 20009, **Home Phone:** (202)328-9355. **Business Phone:** (202)349-0880.

LEWIS, RICHARD ALLEN
Administrator. **Career:** African Methodist Episcopal Church, treas & chief financial officer, 1996-, Connectional Lay Econ Develop Corp (CLEDC), consult. **Business Addr:** Treasurer, Chief Financial Officer, African Methodist Episcopal Church, 1134 11th St NW, Washington, DC 20001, **Business Phone:** (202)371-8700.

LEWIS, RICHARD JOHN, SR.
Government official. **Personal:** Born Jun 7, 1936, Manheim, WV; son of Thomas Ellington (deceased) and Ida McLane Carroll; children: Richard Jr, Thomas. **Educ:** Numerous Govt, Com Insts & Comput Manufacture Sponsored Training, 1983; Liberty Univ, Lynchburg, VA, 1991. **Career:** Government official (retired); Dept Health & Human Servs, Wash, DC, from clerk/typist to comput programmer, 1964-70, sr comput systs programmer, 1970-80, chief, software mgt div, 1980-84; Adv Mgt Inc, McLean, VA, comput security consult, 1984-91. **Orgs:** Past chmn, Audit Comt, Pittsburghers Wash, DC Inc, 1985-90; Am Legion, 1972-; Marine Corps Asn. **Honors/Awds:** Lifesaving Bronze/Medal, Carnegie Hero Fund Comn, 1968; Secretary's Special Citation, Dept Health & Human Servs, 1968; many other awards for superior government service performance. **Military Serv:** US Marine Corps, sergeant (E5), 1953-63. **Home Addr:** 3214 SE Quay St, Port St Lucie, FL 34984. *

LEWIS, ROBERT ALVIN
Airline executive. **Personal:** Born Jul 10, 1945, Henderson, NC; son of Robert A Sr and Dorothy A; married Joanne Mangum, Sep 2, 1967; children: Derek Robert. **Educ:** NCA State Univ, BS, aero space engineering, 1966; Univ Conn, MS, aerospace engineering, 1969, MBA, 1975. **Career:** Pratt & Whitney, dir, int sales & serv, 1995-. **Orgs:** Am Inst Aeronaut & Astronaut, 1966. **Honors/Awds:** Outstanding Contributor to Corporation, UTC, 1992. **Special Achievements:** "Propfan Power," Asn Singapore Licensed Aircraft Engrs, 1988; "Choosing Propulsion Technology," Alfred Wegener Inst, Germany, 1988; "Advances in Commercial Aviation," Indian Aeronautical Soc, 1990; "High Thrust Engines for Middle East," Abu Dhabi, 1994. **Home Addr:** 197 Fairview Dr, South Windsor, CT 06074, **Home Phone:** (860)644-8780. **Business Addr:** Director of International Sales & Services, Pratt & Whitney, 400 Main St, PO Box 131-16, East Hartford, CT 06108, **Business Phone:** (860)565-4321.

LEWIS, ROBERT LOUIS
Clergy, government official. **Personal:** Born Mar 10, 1936, Gilbert, LA; married Lendy Mae Neal; children: Gregory B, Keith A, Steven J, Christine M, Gerald W, Pamela V. **Educ:** Southern Ill Univ, BA, 1980. **Career:** Sears, salesman, 1978-83; Pulaski Cty Spec Sch Dist, sub teacher, 1975-; Mt Pisgah Baptist Church, asst pastor, Interim Pastor, 1980-00; City Jacksonville, alderman. **Orgs:** Scout master Boy Scouts Am, 1956-60; short order cook Grand Forks AFB Exchange, 1967-70; eoa rep, USAF, 1972-74; minister Base Chapel, 1973-74; childrens church minister, Mt Pisgah Baptist Church, 1982-. **Military Serv:** USAF, tsgt, E-6, 1955-75; AFM, 900 3; AF & SA W & 4; AFM 900 3; AFGCM W & 40LC, 1973.

LEWIS, RODERICK ALBERT
Football player. **Personal:** Born Jun 9, 1971, Washington, DC; married Becky. **Educ:** Univ Ariz. **Career:** Houston Oilers, tight end, 1994-96; Tenn Oilers, 1997.

LEWIS, RONALD ALEXANDER
Football player. **Personal:** Born Mar 25, 1968, Jacksonville, FL. **Educ:** Fla State Univ, commun, 1989. **Career:** Football player (retired); San Francisco 49ers, wide receiver, 1990, 1992; Green Bay Packers, wide receiver, 1992, 1993-94.

LEWIS, RONALD C.
Government official. **Personal:** Born Jun 15, 1934, Philadelphia, PA; married Leslie Annette Williams; children: Terri Anne, Anita

Marie Lewis & Audrey Yvonne. **Career:** Government Official (retired); Philadelphia Fire Dept, fire fighter, firelt & fire capt, 1956-78, fire battalion chief, 1974-78; Valiants Incl ABPFF Local, pres, 1970-74; Int Asn Black Prof Firefighters, regional v pres, 1974-77, affirm action officer, 1978-82; City Richmond, dir dept fire & emergency serv, 1978-95. **Orgs:** Life mem, Nat Asn Advan Colored People, 1960-; Int Asn Black Prof Fire Fighters, 1970-; Int Asn Fire Chiefs, 1978-; bd dir, Offenders Aid &Restoration, 1979-81; Muscular Dystrophy Asn, 1979-81; Bldg Officials &Code Admin, 1979-; Alcohol & Drug Abuse Prev & Treat Serv, 1984-90; bd,Rich Chap Am Red Cross, 1989-. **Honors/Awds:** S Singleton Award of Excellence, Valiants IA BPFF Philadelphia, 1977;Outstanding Serv Award, NE Reg IABPFF, 1978; Outstanding Achievement Award, Nat Asn Advan Colored People Richmond Chap, 1978; Outstanding Firefighter, Phoenix Soc Hartford, CT, 1979; Person of Year, State Va EEO,1991; Freedom Award, Nat Asn Advan Colored People, 1994. **Special Achievements:** Was Richmond's first black fire chief, from 1978 until 1995.

LEWIS, RONALD N
Executive. **Career:** Greater Orlando Aviation Authority, staff, 1992-, dir airport oper, currently. **Business Addr:** Director Terminal Operations, Greater Orlando Aviation Authority, 1 Airport Blvd, Orlando, FL 32827-4399, **Business Phone:** (407)825-2095.

LEWIS, RONALD STEPHEN
Counselor, television producer. **Personal:** Born Sep 3, 1950, Raleigh, NC; son of Thomas J and Beatrice H; married Veronica Nichols Lewis, Jul 29, 1978; children: N'Zinga Monique, Preston Stanford-Hashim. **Educ:** NC Cent Univ, BA, sociol, 1973. **Career:** Wake County Opportunities Inc, social servs coordr, 1973-78; Rhodes Furniture, collection Officer, credit counr, 1978-81; K-Mart, mgt, 1981-82; Va CARES, pre/post release counr, 1982-83; Small Bus Broadcasting Serv, studio supvr, 1983-89; St Augustine's Col, WAUG-TV, producer, host, 1990-; Drug Action Inc, Awareness Ctr, coordr, substance abuse counr, 1990-; Shaw Univ, NC Cent Univ, radio progr, 1990-; Chapel Hill & Carrboro Sch Syst, dir fam resource ctr, 1994-. **Special Achievements:** Produced a four-part television series on substance abuse recovery, 1992; co-produced additional progming for local base origination such as: Black Male, Are we an Endangered Species?.

LEWIS, SAMELLA SANDERS
Educator, artist, writer. **Personal:** Born Feb 27, 1924, New Orleans, LA; daughter of Rachel Taylor and Samuel Sanders; married Paul G, Dec 22, 1948; children: Alan & Claude. **Educ:** Hampton Univ, BA, 1945; Ohio State Univ, MA, 1948, PhD, fine arts, 1951. **Career:** Artist, educator & author; Hampton Inst, instr, 1946-47; Morgan State Univ, assoc prof, 1948-53; Fla A&M Univ, prof & chair, 1953-58; State Univ NY, Plattsburgh, prof, 1958-68; Fulbright fel, 1962; Nat Defense Act fel, 1964; Ford Found fel, 1965; Calif State Univ, assoc prof, 1966-67; Los Angeles Co Mus Art, coordr educ, 1968-69; Scripps Col, prof art hist, 1970-84, prof emer, 1984-; Nat Conf Artists, nat co-chairperson, 1972-74; Clark Humanities Mus, dir, 1976-84; Int Review African Am Art, ed, 1976-; Mus African Am Art, Los Angeles, founder, 1976; Nat Endowment Arts, proj dir, 1980-; Nat Res Coun/Ford Found fel, 1981; Col Art Asn Am, adminr, 1990-94; Books: Black Artists on Art, 2 vols, 1976; Art: African American, 1978; The Art of Elizabeth Catlett, 1984; African American Art & Artists, 1990; African American Art for Young People, 1991. **Orgs:** Expansion Arts Panel, NEA, 1975-78; dir & founder, Mus African Am Art, 1976-80; pres, Contemp Crafts Inc; bd mem, Museum African Am Art; Art Educ Black Art Int Quarterly Nat Conf Artists; Col Art Asn Am; pres, Oxum Int. **Honors/Awds:** Hon doctorate, Chapman Col, 1976; Who's Who in Black America Award, 1982; Senate of California Special Award, 1983; Vesta Award, 1984; Scripps College Faculty Recognition Award, 1985; Los Angeles Achievement in the Visual Arts Award, 1985; Citation for Distinguished Alumnae, Ohio State Univ, 1986; National Conference of Artists Achievement Award, 1988; Legend in Our Time Tribute, Essence, 1990; Hon doctorate, Hampton Univ, 1990; Lifetime Achievement Award, Brandywine Workshop, 1992; Charles White Lifetime Achievement Award, 1993; Hon doctorate, Univ Cincinnati, 1993; UNICEF Award, 1995; Hon doctorate, Bennett Col, 1996; Distinguished Scholar Award, Getty Ctr Hist Art & Humanities, 1996. **Home Addr:** 1237 S Masselin Ave, Los Angeles, CA 90019, **Home Phone:** (213)573-2343. **Business Addr:** Professor Emeritus, Scripps College, 1030 Columbia Ave, Claremont, CA 91711-3948, **Business Phone:** (909)621-8000.

LEWIS, DR. SAMUEL, JR.
Transport worker. **Personal:** Born Jul 19, 1953, Philadelphia, PA; son of Samuel Lewis Sr and Georgianna Johnson. **Educ:** Penn State Univ, BA, 1976; Community Col Philadelphia, AS, Mgt, 1986; MS, Admin Info Resource Mgt, 1998. **Career:** Transport worker (retired); WPHL-TV Philadelphia, broadcast dir, 1976-77; Consolidated Rail Corp, opers mgr, 1977-83; New Jersey Transit Rail Opers, revenue analyst, 1983-85, sr opers planner, 1985. **Orgs:** Conf Minority Transportation Officials, Am Pub Transit Asn Minority Affairs Comn, Omega Psi Phi Frat, F&AM, The Brain Trust, Penn State Alumni Asn, Concerned Black Men Philadelphia, Nat Asn Watch & Clock Collectors, Black Music Asn; HBCU Transportation Consortium; transportation res bd, Nat Acad Scis; Columbia Univ MBA Conf; Wharton Sch Black MBA Conf. **Honors/Awds:** 'Outstanding Young Men of America', 1984, 1986, 1987; Honorary Doctorate of Humane Letters, Faith Grant Col, 1995. **Home Addr:** 1643 Cobbs Creek Pkwy, Philadelphia, PA 19143.

LEWIS, SARASVATI ANANDA
Television show host, executive. **Personal:** Born Mar 21, 1973, San Diego, CA; daughter of Stanley and Yvonne. **Educ:** Howard Univ, BA, hist, 1995. **Career:** Black Entertainment TV, "Teen Summit", host, "1st Annual BET Awards", host, "Politically Incorrect", host, "The View", host, "The Chris Rock Show", host, "The Late Late Show with Craig Kilborn", host; MTV, video jockey, 1997, "Total Request Live", host; "Wanna Be a VJ Too", host; "Hot Zone", host; "The Ananda Lewis Show", 2001; A&E, "America's Top Dog", co-host; ABC, "Celebrity Mole: Yucatan", contestant; Radio Show, "The John Salley Block Party", co-host; TV Series: "Method & Red", 2004; "Pilot", 2004; "America's Top Dog", 2004; The Insider, chief corresp, 2004-; L.A. Radio Station 100.3, "The Beat's Morning Show", co-host, 2005. **Orgs:** Nat spokesperson, Nat Reading Is Fundamental. **Honors/Awds:** NAACP Image Award, 1996. **Special Achievements:** Featured in People magazine's "50 Most Beautiful People"; Cable Ace nomination; Nominee, Teen Choice Award, 2000, 2002. **Business Addr:** Chief Correspondent, The Insider, Paramount Domestic Television, 5555 Melrose Ave, Hollywood, CA 90038.*

LEWIS, SHERMAN
Football coach. **Personal:** Born Jun 29, 1942, Louisville, KY; married Toni; children: Kip & Eric. **Educ:** Mich State Univ, educ admin, 1974. **Career:** Football coach (retired); Mich State Univ, asst head coach & defensive coord 1969-82; San Francisco 49ers', running back coach, 1983-88, receiver coach, 1989-91; Green Bay Packers, offensive coordinator, 1992-99; Minnesota Vikings, offensive coordinator, 2000-01; Detroit Lions, offensive coordr, 2002-04. **Honors/Awds:** Col Player of the Yr, 1963. *

LEWIS, DR. SHIRLEY A R
Executive, school administrator. **Personal:** Born in West Virginia; married Dr Ronald Lewis; children: Mendi. **Educ:** Univ Calif Berkeley, Spanish & speech, social work; Stanford Univ, doctorate, 1979; Ghana & Univ London, cert, African studies. **Career:** Educational administrator (retired); Gen Bd Higher Educ & Ministry United Methodist Church, educ exec; Paine Col, pres, 1994-2007. **Orgs:** Bd dirs, UNCF; Augusta United Way; GA Bank & Trust; Assoc Governing Bds; Zeta Phi Beta Sorority Inc. **Honors/Awds:** Citizen of the Year, Zeta Phi Beta Sorority Inc; hon doctorate, Bethune Cookman Col; Georgia's 50 Most Influential Women for 2007. **Special Achievements:** First woman president of Paine College.

LEWIS, STEPHEN CHRISTOPHER
Executive. **Personal:** Born Aug 19, 1950, Chicago, IL; son of Robert Lewis and Elizabeth Stewart Lewis; married Stefanie Woolridge. **Educ:** Bradley Univ, BSIE, 1972; Marquette Univ, MBA, 1975, EMBA, 1995; Duke Univ, Exec MBA. **Career:** Jos Schlitz Brewing Co, supt prod scheduling, 1974-78; Ford Motor Co, Escort/Lynx, planning analyst, 1978-82, Taurus/Sable, planning analyst, 1982-83, small car import mgr 1983-86, Dearborn, MI, advanced prod mgr, 1988-91, assoc dir; New Market Develop, dir mfg, 2000-.; Auto Alliance, Inc, gen mgr, 1998-; Success Guide, Cleveland, OH, regional dir, 1990-. **Orgs:** Omega Psi Phi, baselius, 1971-72; Nat Asn Advan Colored People, 1978-; Nat-Tech Asn, 1983-85; pres, Nat Black MBA, detroit chap, 1984; Nat Black MBA-Detroit Chap, 1984; chairperson, Nat Scholar, 1984-, nat vpres, 1985-; Asn MBA Exec; Detroit Econ Club, 1989-; Engineering Soc Detroit, 1989-; nat pres, Nat Black MBA, 1994-98; Black Achievers Industry, YMCA-Detroit, 1996; chair, Ford Employees African Ancestry Network, 2001-; Am Bar Asn. **Honors/Awds:** Omega Man of the Year, Omega Psi Phi, 1971; Black Achievers Industry, YMCA Greater New York, 1976; President's Award, 1984; Outstanding MBA of the Year, 1990; Best in Business, Success Guides, 2000. **Business Addr:** Board of Director, National Black MBA Association, 108 N Mich Ave Suite 1400, Chicago, IL 60601, **Business Phone:** (312)236-2622.

LEWIS, STEVE EARL
Track and field athlete. **Personal:** Born May 16, 1969, Los Angeles, CA; son of Stella. **Educ:** Univ Calif, Los Angeles, BA (with honors), hist, 1992. **Career:** Track & field athlete. **Orgs:** Santa Monica Track Club, 1987-93. **Honors/Awds:** Gold Medal, 1988, 1992 & Silver Medal, 1992, Olympic Games; Hall of Fame, Univ Calif, Los Angeles, 2004.

LEWIS, TERRY
Songwriter, music producer, business owner. **Personal:** Born Nov 21, 1956, Omaha, NE; married Indira Singh; children: Talin & Tierra; married Karyn White, Jan 1, 1991 (divorced); children: Ashley Nicole. **Career:** Producer, business owner; Flyte Tyme Prod, owner, 1982-; Perspective Records, owner, 1991-; Albums With Jimmy Jam: "On the Rise", 1983; "Just the Way You Like It", 1984; "Fragile", 1984; "High Priority", 1985; Cherrelle & Alexander O'Neil, 1985; (Alexander O'Neal; "Tender Love, 1985; Force MD's;"Control", 1986; "Rythm Nation",1989; janet, 1993; "The Velvet Rope", 1997(Janet Jackson); Rainbow, 1999 (Mariah Carey); Mountain High, Valley Low,1999 (Yolanda Adams); When A Women Loves, 2000 (Patti Labelle); Own Label Artists: Sounds of Blackness, Mint Condition, Lo-Key, Raja-Nee, Ann Nesby. **Honors/Awds:** Grammy Award, Producer of the Year, 1986; Essence Award & Grammy Award,2002. **Business Addr:** Owner, Flyte Tyme Productions Inc, 4100 W 76th St, PO Box 398045, Edina, MN 55435, **Business Phone:** (952)897-3901.

LEWIS, REV. THEODORE RADFORD
Clergy. **Personal:** Born Jul 23, 1946, Galveston, TX; son of Theodore Radford Sr and Carrie Ann Eaton; married Martha Fox, Nov 29, 1968; children: Geoffrey Bernard & Carrie Elizabeth. **Educ:** Univ Houston, BA, 1970; Sam Houston State Univ Grad Sch, 1974; Univ Houston Continuing Educ Ctr, attended 1977; Episcopal Theol Sem, MDiv, 1982. **Career:** Fed Pre-Release Ctr, asst counr, 1970-71; Harris County Adult Probation Dept, probation officer, 1971-75; US Probation & Parole Off, probation & parole officer, 1975-79; St James Episcopal Church, asst rector, 1982-83; St Luke Episcopal Church, rector, 1983-91; Tex Southern Univ, Episcopal chaplain, 1983-91; Calvary Episcopal Church, rector & pastor, 1992-; Charleston Youth Leadership League, elder, 1997-. **Orgs:** Union Black Episcopalians, 1982-; chaplain, dean educ, record & seal keeper, membership comt chair, Nu Phi Chapter, Omega Psi Phi Fraternity, 1987-91; Bd Edu Redirection, 1995-98; chaplain, Mu Alpha Chapter, Omega Psi Phi Fraternity, 1992-; Bd Crisis Ministries, Inc, 1997-2003; chaplain, vol, Homeless Shelter Crisis Ministries, 1997-; gov bd, Charlestown Acad, 1997-98; Charleston County Sch Bd, 1998-2003. **Honors/Awds:** Omega Man of the Year, Nu Phi Chapter, Omega Psi Phi Fraternity, 1990; Scroll of Honor, Mu Alpha Chapter, Omega Psi Phi Fraternity, 1992; Omega Man of the Year, Mu Alpha Chapter, Omega Psi Phi, 1999; Delta Sigma Theta, Merit Award for Service, N Charleston Alumnae Chapter, 1999; Scroll of Honor, NCP, Mu Alpha Chapter, 2002; honoree in the field of religion, MOJA Arts Festival, Charleston, SC, 2003. **Business Addr:** Rector, Calvary Episcopal Church, 106 Line St, Charleston, SC 29403-5305, **Business Phone:** (803)723-3878.

LEWIS, THERTHENIA WILLIAMS
Educator. **Personal:** Born Mar 1, 1947, Dayton, OH; daughter of Alexander Williams and Mattie Williams; married Dr Jerry J Lewis. **Educ:** Sinclair Community Col, A Liberal Arts, A Early Childhood Educ, 1974; Univ Dayton, BS, 1975; Ohio State Univ, MS, 1978; Atlanta Univ, MSW, 1986; Univ Pittsburgh, MPH, 1992. **Career:** Ohio State Univ, grad admin asst, 1976-78; Wernle Residential Ctr, adolescent therapist, 1978-81; Ga State Univ, Col Arts & Sci, asst dir, 1982-84; Bureau Planning City Atlanta, HUD fellow intern, 1984-85; Univ pittsburgh, grad stud asst, 1986-87; C Hosp, Family Intervention Ctr, Pittsburgh, PA, 1988-92; Clark Atlanta Univ, Sch Social Work, Kellogg Proj, 1992-94, asst prof, 1994-, dir stud affairs, instr social work, currently; Southeast Ark Behavioral Healthcare Syst, DASEP proj dir, currently. **Orgs:** Adv community mem, Big Sisters/Big Brothers Adv Bd, 1977-78; Am Soc Pub Admin, 1984-; Nat Assoc Black Social Workers, 1987; Am Home Econs Assoc, 1987; Black Child Develop Inst, 1987; Coun Social Work Educ, 1988; Am Pub Health Asn, 1988; Am Asn Univ Prof, 1994; Am Asn Ment Retardation, 1994. **Honors/Awds:** Outstanding Young Women of America, 1978; HUD Fel, Atlanta Univ, 1984-86; Hon Soc Alpha Kappa Delta Int Soc, 1985; Maternal & Child Health Fel, Grad Sch Pub Health, Univ Pittsburgh, 1986-88; Child Abuse & Neglect Fel, Univ Pittsburgh Grad Sch Pub Health, 1989. **Business Addr:** Project Director, Southeast Arkansas Behavioral Healthcare System Inc, 2500 Rike Dr, PO Box 1019, Pine Bluff, AR 71613, **Business Phone:** (870)534-2206.

LEWIS, THOMAS
Football player, athletic director. **Personal:** Born Jan 10, 1972, Akron, OH. **Educ:** Ind Univ. **Career:** Football player (retired), Athletic Director; New York Giants, wide receiver, 1994-97;Chicago Bears, wide receiver, 1998; MONY sports,exec; Syndicated Capital Inc, dir athletic mgt div,2002-.

LEWIS, THOMAS P.
Executive, educator. **Personal:** Born Mar 17, 1936, Chicago, IL; married Almera P; children: Tracy & Todd. **Educ:** Kentucky St Col, BS, bus admin, 1959. **Career:** Horner Sch Chicago, teacher 1959-61; Chicago Housing Authority, 1961-63; Commonwealth Edison Co, mkt res & sales rep, 1963-65; Mgt Opportunity Inc Northfield, pres, 1968-69; Prof Opportunity Inc, pres, 1969-70; Independence Bank Chicago, vpres, 1970-72, sr vpres, 1972; S Side Bank Chicago, pres & chief exec officer, 1973-. **Orgs:** Chmnm Com Div Oper, PUSH; mem bd dir, YMCA Hotel Chicago Urban League; Chicago Forum; Chicago Asn Com & Indust. **Business Addr:** President, Chief Executive Officer, South Side Bank, 4659 S Cottage Grove Ave, Chicago, IL 60653.

LEWIS, TOM
Activist, president (organization), school administrator. **Personal:** Born Aug 7, 1939, Chadborn, NC; son of Gaston and Martha; married Lucille, Aug 22, 1970; children: Jason, Patrick & Tisha. **Educ:** Am Univ, BS, 1975. **Career:** Metrop Police Dept, DC

police officer, 1965-86; Hope Village Community Treatment Ctr, voc counr, 1986; Lutheran Social Serv, counr, 1987-89; For Love Children, coordr, child & family serv, 1989-93; The Fishing Sch, founder, exec dir & chief exec officer, 1990-2005, pres emer, 2005-. **Orgs:** Coun mem, Lifers Lorton, 1970; pres, chair safety comn, PTA, 1974-86; chief steward, Fraternal Order Police, 1978-86; Leadership Wash; chairperson, Juv Justice Adv Group, 1988-97; steering comm governance, Mid NE Collab, 1996-97; Hands Across DC. **Honors/Awds:** Youth Sports Director Award, Nat Baptist Convention, 1983; The Doll League Award, 1986; One & Only 9 Award, 1995; Jefferson Award, Inst Pub Serv, 1995; Public Service Award, Noble Nat Orgn Black Law Enforcement Exec, 1997; Washingtonian of the Year, Washingtonian, 1997. **Special Achievements:** Recorded 5 Gospel Albums, 1982, wrote article in Channel 32 Magazine in 1994, Philanthropic work has been highlighted on CBS This Morning, Hard Copy & several news channels. **Military Serv:** AUS, sp/4, 1963-65. **Home Addr:** 7017 16th St NW, Washington, DC 20012. **Business Addr:** President Emeritus, The Fishing School, 1240 Wylie St NE, Washington, DC 20002, **Business Phone:** (202)399-3618.

LEWIS, VICKIE J
Chief executive officer. **Career:** Acct mgr; independent contractor; VMX Int LLC, pres & chief exec officer, currently. **Orgs:** Bd mem, Environ Mgt Asn. **Business Phone:** (586)291-7778.*

LEWIS, VINCENT V
Executive, consultant, president (organization). **Personal:** Born Oct 1, 1938, Wilmington, DE; son of Vincent and Matilda Janet; married Babirette Babineaux (divorced 1974); children: Dawn C & Duane A. **Educ:** Upper Iowa Univ, Fayette, IA, BA, 1980, Loyola Col, Baltimore, MD, MBA, 1983. **Career:** Wilmington Housing Authority, Wilmington, DE, vpres & exec dir, 1972-77; Nat Ctr Community Develop, Wash, DC, 1978-79; HUD Headquarters, Wash, DC, housing mgt officer, 1979-85; Coopers & Lybrand, Wash, DC, mgr, 1982-85; Vinelle Assocs Inc, Wash, DC, pres, 1985-. **Orgs:** Am Soc Pub Admin; Am Mgt Asn; Asn MBA Execs; NAHRO. **Military Serv:** US Marine Corps, 1956-59. **Business Phone:** (202)659-4466.

LEWIS, VIOLA GAMBRILL
Educator, psychologist. **Personal:** Born Feb 5, 1939, Baltimore, MD; divorced; children: Robin & Van Allen. **Educ:** Morgan State Col, BS, 1959; Loyola Col, MA, 1978. **Career:** Educator (retired); Psychohormonal Unit Johns Hopkins Sch Med, res asst, 1960-62, asst med psychol, 1962-74, instr, 1974.

LEWIS, VIRGINIA HILL
Quality control inspector. **Personal:** Born Feb 13, 1948, Berria Co, GA; daughter of H B Hill and Mary Hill; married Robert Lewis; children: Michael, Roslyn. **Educ:** Albany State Col GA, BS, chem, 1970; UOP Stockton CA, MS 1972. **Career:** Grad Sch Univ Pac, lab asst 1972; Albany State Col, advanced chemist; 3M Co, qual mgr, 1973-, Dyneon, qual mgr, 1998-. **Orgs:** Summer training prog Argonne Nat Lab Argonne IL 1969; Sunday Sch Teacher, Mt Olivet Bapt Ch St Paul MN 1973 & 1975-76; social affairs, 3M & community; Step Program, 3M; Visiting Tech Women, 3M; Delta Sigma Theta Sor 1969. **Honors/Awds:** Alpha Kappa Mu Honor Soc Albany State Coll GA 1967-70; Affiliate ACS 1968-70; "This Is Your Life" Award. **Business Addr:** Quality Manager, Dyneon, 6744 33rd St N, Oakdale, MN 55128.*

LEWIS, DR. VIVIAN M
Physician. **Personal:** Born in Pensacola, FL; daughter of Edward and Vivian L Crawley (deceased); married Billie; children: Vivian V Sanford MD, William P & Beverly Gooden. **Educ:** Fisk Univ, BA, 1952; Univ Okla, Sch Med, MD, 1959; Hurley Hosp, rotating intern, 1959-60, pediatric residency, 1961-63. **Career:** Mott Childrens Health Ctr, pediatric staff, 1963-69; Dept Maternal & Infant Health Mott Childrens Health Ctr, chairperson, 1967-69; Hurley Med Ctr & St Joseph Hosp, mem teaching staff; McLaren Hosp, courtesy staff; Mich State Univ, Dept Human Med, asst prof clinical pediatrics; Univ Mich, Med Sch, preceptor for the inter-ex prog; Lewis Med Servs, pediatric practice, 1970-. **Orgs:** Life mem, Alpha Kappa Alpha Sor Inc; bd dirs, Girl Scouts Am; bd dirs, Flint Inst Arts; Flint Women Bus Owners' Coun; Mich State Med Soc; Am Med Asn; Nat Med Asn; Am Acad Pediatrics; Genesee Valley March Dimes Med Adv Comn; med adv, Flint Easter Seal Soc; bd mem, Genesee Valley Chap Am Lung Asn, 1969-78; chairperson, Genesee Co March Dimes Campaign, 1971; Flint Acad Med; co-chair, 1975 Flint United Negro Col Fund Dr; adv comn, Univ Mich-Flint; pres, Flint Chap Links Inc, 1983-; citizens adv comn, Univ Mich-Flint; pres, Greater Flint Pediatric Asn; pres, Prof Med Corp Hurley Med Ctr; Genesee County Med Soc, 1963-; Family Servs Bd, 1990-; Whaley Children's Community Bd, 1993-; Univ Mich Corp, adv bd, 1986-; Mich Nat Bank, Flint, adv bd, 1976-; bd treas, Hurley Found, 1993-; vpres, Flint Inst Arts Bd. **Honors/Awds:** Community Serv Award, Flint Chap Negro Bus & Prof Women's Club, 1973; Liberty Bell Award Genesee Co Bar Asn, 1975; Pan Hellenic Woman of the Year, 1978; Woman of the Year, Zeta Beta Omega Chap Alpha Kappa Alpha Sor Inc, 1978; Nana Mills Award, YWCA, 1985; Outstanding Citizen Award, Gamma Delta Boule, Sigma Pi Phi Fraternity, 1985; Behold the Woman Award, Top Ladies Distinction, 1987; Urban Coalition Service Award, 1989; Paul Harris Award, Rotary Club of Flint, 1994. **Special Achievements:** Recognized as an Outstanding African American Woman Physician in publication, Alpha Kappa Alpha Sorority, Heritage Series, 1993; First black woman graduate from University of Oklahoma Medical School; First woman president, Genesee County Medical. **Home Addr:** 1618 Kensington, Flint, MI 48503, **Home Phone:** (313)233-0539. **Business Addr:** Physician, Lewis Medical Service, 1910 Robert T Longway Blvd, PO Box 28, Flint, MI 48503, **Business Phone:** (810)239-0011.

LEWIS, W ARTHUR
Housing developer, clergy. **Personal:** Born Dec 13, 1930, Princeton, NJ; son of George Peter Lewis Sr and Blanche E Taylor Chase; married Rose Marie Dais, Jun 20, 1970; children: Adrienne Richardson & Andrea Lewis. **Educ:** Trenton Jr Col, AA 1957; Rider Col, BS, 1959, MA, 1977; Harvard Univ John F Kennedy Sch Govt, Cert, 1982; Lutheran Theol Sem, MAR 1985; Luthern Sch Theol, DMin, 1992. **Career:** United Progress Inc, personnel dir, 1966-68; OIL Int, prog adv, 1968-69; Economic & Manpower Corp, project mgr 1969-71; NJ Dept Comm Affairs, div dir & asst comnr, 1972-82; Philadelphia OIC, exec dir 1982-85; Lutheran Children & Family Svcs, clergy/administrator 1985-; Evangelical Lutheran Church Am, 1988; NJ Dept Comm Affairs, housing adminr, 1990-; Calvary Lutheran Church, Philadelphia, PA, pastor, 1990-; Office Gov, dir, currently. **Orgs:** Consult, Nat Urban Coalition, 1974; chmn, Nat State Econ Opportunity Off Dir Asn, 1976-77; bd trustee, Glassboro State Col, 1979-; vpres, NJ Chap ASPA, 1980-82; bd mem, Evesham Twp Sch Dist, 1981-; Alpha Phi Alpha, 1983-; Philadelphia Liberty Bell City Philadelphia 1984; consult, NJ Synod Lutheran Church Am, 1985; bd trustees, NJ Prison Complex, 1991-. **Honors/Awds:** Man of the Year, Somerset County Community Action, 1976; Man of the Year, Burlington County Nat Asn Advan Colored People, 1977. **Military Serv:** USAF, Airman 2nd class 1951-54; Nat Defense Medal, Good Conduct Medal, European Defense Medal. **Business Addr:** Director Office of African-American Affairs, Office of the Governor, CN 001, Trenton, NJ 08625, **Business Phone:** (609)777-0991.

LEWIS, W HOWARD
Automotive executive. **Career:** Daimler Chrysler, Advance Quality Planning, sr mgr, currently. **Orgs:** Automotive Serv Asn; chmn, Cong Automotive Repair & Serv, 2006. **Business Phone:** (248)576-5741.

LEWIS, WENDELL J.
Government official. **Personal:** Born Mar 22, 1949, Topeka, KS; son of Bryon and Bonnie. **Educ:** Kans State Teachers Col, BS Ed, 1972, MS, 1973. **Career:** Disability Determination Serv, disability examnr, I 1974-80, disability examnr II, 1980-85, quality assurance speciality, 1985-88; unit mgr, 1989-91, sect adminr, 1991-. **Orgs:** Exec secy, Great Plan Wheelchair Athletic Conf, 1974-76; adv bd, Vocational Rehab, 1978-79; Shawnee County Affirmative Action Prog, 1979-80; Kans Coun Develop Disabilities, 1982-; chairperson, Kans Coun Develop Disabilities, 1991; chmn, Adv Bd, Accessible Transp, 1992; bd dirs, NADDC, 1993-94, vpres, 1994-. **Honors/Awds:** Inductee, Nat Stud Reg, 1970-72; 2nd Place 100 yard dash Rocky Mountain Wheelchair Games, 1975; 1st Place table tennis Rocky Mountain Wheelchair Games, 1975; Del, White House Conf Handicapped, 1977; Leadership Award, Kans Advocacy & Protective Serv, 1980; John Peter Loux Award, Cerebral Palsy Res Found, 1993; Personal Achievement Award, Muscular Dystrophy Asn, 1994. **Home Addr:** 1619 SW 28th Terr, Topeka, KS 66611. **Business Addr:** Section Administrator, Disability Determination Service, 915 Harrision St 10th Fl, D50B, Topeka, KS 66612.*

LEWIS, WENDY
Manager, vice president (government). **Career:** Chicago Cubs, dir human resources, 1989-95; Major League Baseball, exec dir human resources, 1995, vpres strategic planning recruitment & diversity, currently, sr vpres diversity & strategic alliances, currently. **Business Addr:** Vice President of Strategic Planning for Recruitment and Diversity, Senior Vice President Diversity and Strategic Alliances, Major League Baseball, Office of the Commissioner, 245 Pk Ave, New York, NY 10167, **Business Phone:** (212)931-7800.

LEWIS, WILLARD C
Banker. **Personal:** Born Apr 9, 1961, LaGrange, GA; son of Willard (deceased) and Dora Lewis; married Patricia, Dec 31, 1986; children: Charles & Camille. **Educ:** Morehouse Col, BA, banking & fin, 1983. **Career:** Citizens Trust Bank, controller, 1983-91; First Southern Bank, exec vpres & COO, 1991-; Citizens Trust Bank, sr exec vpres & coo, currently. **Orgs:** Chmn bd, Eastlake YMCA, 1992-94, 2000-; AUBA, 1995; Dekalb Med Ctr Found Bd, 1997-; exec bd mem, Berry Col Campbell Sch Bus; bd chmn, Sweet Auburn Bus & Improv Asn, 1998; Leadership, Atlanta Grad, 1999; treas bd, Nat Bankers Asn, 2000-; treas, co-founder, New Century Forum Bd, 2001-; bd dir, Ga Coun Econ Edu, 2002; bd,Com Club Operating, 2002; Morehouse Col Nat Alumni Asn. **Honors/Awds:** Spec Recognition, Nat Bankers Asn, 2000; Richard Wright Founders Award, Nat Bankers Asn, 2002. **Special Achievements:** Guest ed columnist, Atlanta Bus J & Columbus Times; Top 40 Exec Under 40 Ga,Ga Trend Mag, 1997. **Business Addr:** Senoir Executive Vice President, Chief Operating Officer, Citizens Trust Bank, 75 Piedmont Ave, Atlanta, GA 30303, **Business Phone:** (404)653-2840.

LEWIS, WILLIAM A
Lawyer. **Personal:** Born Aug 15, 1946, Philadelphia, PA; son of William A and Constance Merritt; married Deborah Cover; children: Ryan. **Educ:** Am Univ, 1968; Susquehanna Univ, BA, 1968; Boston Univ Law Sch, JD, 1972. **Career:** City Philadelphia, PA, asst dist atty, 1972-75; US Civil Rights Comn, atty, 1975-80, dir cong lia div, 1980-85, dir congressional & community rels div, 1985-86, actg asst staff dir, congressional & pub affairs, 1987, coun senate judiciary comt, 1987-; Senate Judiciary Comt, Wash, DC, coun, 1987-89; Equal Employ Opportunity Comn, Wash, DC, supervisory atty, 1989-92; Off Admin & Mgt, US Dept Energy, exec asst dir, 1992-94, Off Sci Educ Progs, dir, 1994-96, Off Employee Concerns, dir, 1996, nat ombudsman, Employee Worklifr Ctr, currently. **Orgs:** Del, Legal Rights & Justice Task Force White House Conf Youth Estes Park County, 1970; Pa Bar Assoc, 1972-; Eastern Dist Ct Pa, 1974-; pres, Blacks Govt US Civil Rights Comn, 1977-80; exec comt, 1980-83, sec vpres, 1987, pres, 1988-91, Susquehanna Univ Alumni Assoc; bd dirs, Susquehanna Univ, 1988-. **Honors/Awds:** Legal Defense Fund Scholarship, NAACP, 1971-72; publ: "Black Lawyer in Private Practice", Harvard Law Sch Bulletin, 1971. **Military Serv:** UASF, sgt e-5, 1968-75. **Business Addr:** Director, United States Department of Energy, Office of Employee Concerns, Rm 5B 140 1000 Independence Ave SW, Washington, DC 20585, **Business Phone:** (202)586-6530.

LEWIS, WILLIAM HENRY (HANK LEWIS)
Writer, educator. **Personal:** Born in Denver, CO. **Educ:** Trinity Col, BA, 1989; Univ Va, MFA, 1994. **Career:** McCallie Sch, eng teacher, 1989-92; Univ Va Fall, Instr Creative Writing, 1993; Denison Univ, asst prof, Eng, 1994-95; Mary Wash Col, asst prof, Eng, 1995-97; Trinity Col, asst prof creative writing 1997-2000; Col Bahamas, lectr creative writing, 2000-03; Centre Col, vis prof, 2004-05; Colgate Univ, assoc prof, Eng, currently. **Honors/Awds:** Balch Prize for Best Short Story; honorable mention for the Prize for Short Fiction, Zora Neale Hurston/Richard Wright Found. **Special Achievements:** Author: I Got Somebody in Staunton, 2005. **Business Phone:** (315)228-7101.*

LEWIS, WILLIAM M., JR.
Consultant, executive. **Personal:** Born Apr 30, 1956, Richmond, VA; son of William M Sr and Essie. **Educ:** Harvard Univ, BA, econ, 1978; Harvard Bus Sch, MBA, 1982. **Career:** Morgan Stanley Group Inc, Mergers & Acquisitions Dept, financial analyst, 1978-80, Midwest M&A Dept, Chicago, head, 1988, managing dir, 1989-91, NY City, managing dir, 1992-, Worldwide Real Estate Dept, head, Morgan Stanley Estate Funds, pres & Chief Oper Officer, Worldwide Mergers, Acquisitions & Restructuring Dept, head, 1999, Global Banking, co-managing dir, 2001-04; Lazard, co-chair investment banking, 2004-. **Orgs:** Morgan Stanley Group Inc, task force mem, examining recruiting techniques better retaining African Am talent; NAACP Legal Defense & Educ Fund, bd mem; A Better Chance Inc, chair, bd trustees; Nat Urban League, treas, bd trustees. **Honors/Awds:** Ranked among Most Powerful Black Executives, Fortune, 2002; named one of Top 50 African Americans Wall St, Black Enterprise, 2002. **Business Addr:** Managing Director, Co Chair, Lazard Limited, 3414 peachtree Rd NE Suite 705, Atlanta, GA 30326, **Business Phone:** (404)422-2144.*

LEWIS, WILLIAM SYLVESTER
Educator. **Personal:** Born Aug 31, 1952, Manhattan, NY. **Educ:** Columbia Univ Col, BA, Sociol, 1974; Columbia Grad Sch Jour, MS, 1976. **Career:** Columbia Univ Grad Sch Jour, CBS Fel, 1976; Black Sports Mag, contrib ed,1977-78; Encore Mag, sports ed, 1979-80; Good Living Mag, sr ed, 1979-80; Black Agenda Reports, producer, writer, 1979-81; Touro Col, instr lang & lit, currently. **Orgs:** Legacy Int Inc; Morrisania Educ Coun; Columbia Univ Club NY; Am Athletic Union Distance Running Div. **Honors/Awds:** Bennett Cert Award Writing, Columbia Univ, 1974; Loyal & Outstanding Service Award, Morrisania Educ coun, Bronx NY, 1978; Presidential Citation for Excellence Dist nine Comm School Bd 1983, 1984. **Home Addr:** 348 W 123rd St, New York, NY 10027. **Business Addr:** Instructor, Touro College, 27-33 W 23 St, New York, NY 10010, **Business Phone:** (212)463-0400.*

LEWIS, WILMA A
Educator, business owner, u.s. attorney. **Personal:** Born Jan 1, 1956. **Educ:** Swarthmore Col, BA, 1978; Harvard Law Sch, JD, 1981. **Career:** Steptoe & Johnson, Gen Litigation Group, assoc, 1981-86; DC, asst US atty, 1986-93; lectr & instr employ discrimination law, 1987-98; US Dept Interior, Civil Div, dep chief; US Dept Interior, Div Gen Law, assoc solicitor, 1993-95; George Wash Univ, Nat Law Ctr, adj fac mem, 1993, prof lectr law, currently; DC, US atty; US Dept Interior, inspector gen, 1995-98; US Dist Ct, DC, practr, 1998-2001; US Ct Appeals, DC, practr; Supreme Ct US, practr; Crowell & Moring, partner, currently. **Orgs:** DC Bar Asn; US Dist Ct, Civil Justice Reform Act Adv

Group, DC, 1992-93; fel, Am Bar Found; chmn, DC Bd Elections & Ethics; DC Judicial Nomination Comn; adv comm, US Dist Ct, DC; bd dirs, Wash Lawyers Comn Civil Rights & Urban Affairs; bd mgr, Swarthmore Coll; bd visitors, Howard Univ Sch Law; bd trustees, Moravian Theol Sem; bd adv, Nat Youth Leadership Forum Law; Phi Beta Kappa; bd dir, Am Arbitration Asn. **Honors/ Awds:** Founders Award, Natl Black Prosecutors Asn, 1999; Dr Martin Luther King Jr Dream Keepers Award, Martin Luther King Jr Celebration Day Community Inc, 2001;; Wilma A Lewis Award, named in hon, 2001; Charlotte E Ray Award, Nat Bar Asn, Greater Wash Area Chap Women Lawyers Div & GWAC Found Inc, 2001; Bethune-Dubois Inst Award, 2001; Janet Reno Torchbearer Award, Women's Bar Asn, 2001; Excellence in Leadership Award, US Atty Off Drug Educ Youth Prog, 2001; bd dirs, Am Arbitration Asn's, 2007-. **Special Achievements:** First African-American woman to hold the position of US Atty for the DC; first African-American served as inspector gen for the US Dept of the Interior; first presidentially app woman. **Business Addr:** Partner, Crowell & Moring LLP, 1001 Pa Ave NW, Washington, DC 20004-2595, **Business Phone:** (202)624-2860.

LEWIS-KEMP, JACQUELINE
Manager, president (organization). **Personal:** Daughter of James O Lewis. **Career:** Lewis Metal Stamping & Mfg Co, prod control mgr, 1985-93, pres & chief exec officer, 1993. **Orgs:** Bd visitors, Sch Bus Admin, Oakland Univ. **Honors/Awds:** Rising Star Award, Enterprise Mag, 1996.

LEWIS-LANGSTON, DEBORAH
Judge. **Personal:** Born in Detroit, MI. **Educ:** Univ Mich, BA, 1978; Univ Mich Law Sch, JD, 1982. **Career:** Macomb Co, asst prosecutor; Detroit City, asst corp coun; Mich State Senate, assoc senate gen coun; 36th Dist Ct, judge, 1988-. **Special Achievements:** First African American individual to be hired as Assistant Prosecutor for Macomb County. **Business Addr:** Judge, 36th District Court, 421 Madison Ave, Detroit, MI 48226, **Business Phone:** (313)965-8717.

LEWIS-THORNTON, RAE
Clergy, aids activist. **Personal:** Born May 22, 1962; daughter of Alfred Henry Lewis Jr and Judith. **Educ:** Southern Ill Univ; NE Ill Univ, Chicago, hon degree, magna cum laude, 1991; McCormick Theol Sem; Mdiv, 2003; Univ Ill, Chicago, grad studies. **Career:** Jesse Jackson Presidential Campaign, dep nat youth dir, 1984, nat youth dir, 1988; AIDS advocate & motivational speaker, 1993-; Rae Lewis-Thornton Inc, founder & pres, currently; Barbara Mikulski & Carol Mosley Braun, staff. **Orgs:** Delta Sigma Theta Sorority; Leadership Bd Core Ctr. **Honors/Awds:** Chicago Emmy Award, 1995. **Special Achievements:** Featured on the cover of the December 1994 Essence magazine as well as in numerous feature stories in Ebony and Emerge magazines, Chicago Tribune newspaper, Chicago Sun-Times newspaper, Washington Post, Dayton Daily News, and on several national television documentaries, news shows, and television specials. Rae was featured on NIGHTLINE WITH Ted Koppel in a news article entitled "Rae's Story". The Oprah Winfrey Show had her on to share her story. Rae uses all forms of media to convey her message. She served as a contributing editor for WBBM-TV, a CBS-owned and operated television station for an ongoing series of first person stories on living with AIDS. **Business Addr:** Founder, President, Rae Lewis-Thornton Inc, 1507 E 53rd St Suite 315, Chicago, IL 60615, **Business Phone:** (773)643-4316.

LEWTER, ANDY C, SR.
Clergy. **Personal:** Born Oct 6, 1929, Sebring, FL; son of Rufus Cleveland Sr (deceased) and Mary Lee; married Ruth Fuller; children: Rita Olivia Davis, Cleo Yvette, Veda Ann Pennyman, Andy C Jr, Rosalyn Aaron & Tonya Marie. **Educ:** Morris Brown Col, BA, 1954; Friendship Col, Hon DD, 1962; Atlanta Univ; Biblical Sem, New York; James Teamer's Sch Religion, BD, 1964; T Sch Religion, LLD, 1975; New York Theol Sem, MDiv, 1985. **Career:** St John Baptist Church, Ft Myers, asst minister, 1951-52; Morris Brown Col, asst col pastor, 1953-54; Zion Grove Baptist Church, Atlanta, asst minister, 1953-54; Stitt Jr HS, teacher, 1954-60; First Baptist Church, Rockaway, asst minister, 1954-59; Hollywood Baptist Church Christ Amityville, pastor, 1959, pastor emer, currently; AC Lewter Interdenom Sch Religion, founder pres, 1975; Pilgrim State Psychiatric Hosp, chaplain. **Orgs:** Pres, N Amityville Ministerial Alliance & Vicinity, 1989-; vice moderator, Eastern Baptist Asn, 1990-; Past vpres, Nat Asn Advan Colored People; past chmn mem, Interfaith Health Asn; Bd Gov Interfaith Hosp Queens; pres, Inter-denominational Ministerial fel, Amityville; trustee, Long Island Health & Hosp Planning Coun; vpres, Lewter-Scott Travel Asn; supvr, Ushers Nat Baptist Conv, USA; adv bd, Suffolk County Office Aging; Amityville Taxpayers Asn; adv bd, Suffolk Co Office Aging; pres, New Millennium Develop Servs, currently. **Business Addr:** President, New Millennium Development Services Inc., 1274 Straight Path, Wyandanch, NY 11798, **Business Phone:** (631)803-2846.

LIAUTAUD, GEORGE. See LIAUTAUD, JAMES.

LIAUTAUD, JAMES (GEORGE LIAUTAUD)
Educator, chairperson. **Educ:** Univ Ill, BS, mech eng, 1963. **Career:** Univ Ill, Chicago, clin res prof; Gabriel Inc, Elgin, IL, founder, chmn bd, 1968-; Entrepreneurship Inst, dir & trustee; Univ Ill Family Bus Coun, dir & trustee; Blue Rhino Corp, dir; Capsonic Group Inc, chief exec officer, currently. **Honors/Awds:** Design of the Year Award, Ill Am Soc Prof Engrs, 1994; Alumni Award for Distinguished Service, Col Eng, Univ Ill. **Special Achievements:** Black Enterprise's Top 100 Co list, ranked No 31, 1994; No 56, 1999. **Business Addr:** Chief Executive Officer, Capsonic Group Inc, Fleetwd Dr & II, Elgin, IL 60120, **Business Phone:** (847)888-7300.

LIDE, DR. WILLIAM ERNEST
School administrator. **Personal:** Born Feb 14, 1950, Darlington, SC; married Cheryl Anita Leverett-Lide, Dec 22, 1980; children: Desiree Danielle, Amber Nicole, Lindsey Koren & Kristin Regina. **Educ:** Johnson C Smith Univ, Charlotte, NC, BS, 1973; Univ NC, Charlotte, NC, MEd, 1976; Ohio Univ, Columbus, OH, PhD, 1980. **Career:** Johnson C Smith Univ, Charlotte, NC, phys educ, 1975-78, 1980-84; Winston-Salem State Univ, Winston-Salem, NC, chair, phys educ, 1984-87; NC Central Univ, dir athletics, 2000-; Salisbury State Univ, Salisbury, Md, dir athletics, chair phys educ & recreation. **Orgs:** Nat secy, The Nat Roundtable Parks, Conserv & Recreation, 1982-; bd dirs, NCAA Coun, 1989-; NACDA Postgrad Scholar Comt, 1993-; pres, Easterm State Athletic Conf, 1989; Division III Steering Committee, NCAA, 1990; pres, The Roundtable Asn, 1994; chair, NCAA Cou Postgrad Scholar Comt. **Honors/Awds:** All Pro-Countdown Team, Calgary Stampeders, 1974; Awards of Tenure, Johnson C Smith Univ, 1977; Award of Achievement, Am Bus Women's Asn, 1980; Awards of Tenure, Salisbury State Univ, 1990. **Business Addr:** Director of Athletics, North Carolina Central University, 1801 Fayetteville St, Durham, NC 27707, **Business Phone:** (919)530-6100.

LIGGINS, ALFRED, III
Chief executive officer, president (organization). **Personal:** Born Jan 1, 1965?, Omaha, NE; son of Alfred Jr and Catherine Hughes. **Educ:** Univ Calif, Los Angeles; Univ DC; Univ Pa, MBA, 1995; Wharton SchBus/Exec, MBA. **Career:** Light Records, sales exec, 1984; CBS Records, production asst, 1984-85; Radio One Inc, acct mgr, 1985-87, gen sales mgr, 1987, gen mgr opers, 1988, pres, treas & dir, 1989-, chief exec officer, 1997-. **Honors/Awds:** Golden Mike Award (with Cathy Hughes), Broadcasters Foundation, 2002; Entrepreneur of the Year, Ernst and Young, 2003; Outstanding Communicator of the Year, National Black MBA Asn, 2003; 30 Most Influential African Americans in Radio. **Business Addr:** Chief Executive Officer, President, Radio One Inc, 5900 Princess Garden Pkwy 7th Fl, Lanham, MD 20706, **Business Phone:** (301)306-1111.

LIGGINS, W ANTHONY
Fashion designer. **Personal:** Born Jul 4, 1965, Hampton, VA; son of Wilbert A; married Kym Liggins, Feb 1, 1998. **Educ:** Del State Univ, Am Col Appl Arts, AA, fashion design, 1989; Am Intercontinental Univ, Atlanta, London, AA, fashion merchandising, 1990. **Career:** Future Mode LLC dba Anthony Liggins, pres & fashion dir, currently. **Honors/Awds:** Alumni Hall of Fame, Am Inter-Continental Univ, 1998. **Special Achievements:** Annual 10 Best Man List, guest ed, Jezebel Mag, 50 Best Dressed Women In Atlanta, guest ed, Today's Atlanta Woman Mag, been featured on VH-1, E Entertainment, F-TV, Frankfurt, Ger, 1996, featured in Atlanta Bus Chronicle, 1995, Atlanta Mag, 1995, 1998, 1996, Atlanta J Const, 1995, 1996, 1997, 1998, 1999, Essence, 1997, Black Enterprise Mag, 1997, Swissotel OCo Spellbound, Atlanta, GA, 2000, Gallery Sklo, Red & Loaded, 2001, Sacred Ground, 2002, Shanghai Dreams, 2003, Sacred Language, 1000 Kisses from Shanghai, 2004. **Business Phone:** (404)842-0621.

LIGHT, ALAN
Executive. **Educ:** Yale Univ, BA, 1988. **Career:** Rolling Stone Mag, sr writer, 1989-93; VIBE Mag, ed in chief, 1994-97; SPIN Mag, ed in chief, 1999-02; Tracks Mag, ed in chief, currently. **Honors/Awds:** Deems Taylor Award, Am Soc Composers Authors & Publishers. **Special Achievements:** Auth: The Skills to Pay the Bills: The Story of the Beastie Boys, 2006. *

LIGHTFOOT, JEAN DREW
Government official. **Personal:** Born in Hartford, CT. **Educ:** Howard Univ, BA, 1947; Univ Mich, MPA, 1950. **Career:** Government official (retired); Coca Cola, WA, pub rels, 1954-55, asst dir, 1959-61; Community Rel Conf S Calif, Los Angeles, dir, 1961-62; Dept State, foreign serv res officer, 1962-69; Consumer Protection & Environ Health Serv HEW, chief consumer spec sect, 1969-70, asst dir pub affairs, 1970-71; EPA, int affairs officer, 1971, spec asst Training & Upward Mobility, dep dir, 1978. **Orgs:** Women's Auxiliary Bd NW Settlement House; former bd mem, W Coast Reg Nat Negro Col Fund; Nat Asn Advan Colored People; Urban Laeague; Fred Douglass Mus African Art; Legal Def Fund; Int Club Wash Inc; Indian Spring Country Club; Univ Mich Club; Circle-Lets Inc; Neighbors Inc. **Honors/Awds:** Good Citizenship Award, Daughters of the Am Revolution, 1940; Ideal Girl Award, Hartford Pub High Sch, 1940; Nat Council Negro Women Mary McLeod Bethune Award, 1962; Community Service Award, Community Rels Conf S Calif, 1962; Community Service Award, Nat Asn Advan Colored People, 1975. **Home Addr:** 2000 Trumbull Terr NW, Washington, DC 20011. *

LIGHTFOOT, JEAN HARVEY
Educator. **Personal:** Born Nov 29, 1935, Chicago, IL; divorced; children: Jaronda. **Educ:** Fisk Univ, BA, 1957; Univ Chicago, MA, 1969; Northwestern Univ, Evanston, PhD, 1974. **Career:** Chicago Pub Schs, Eng teacher, 1957-69; Kennedy King Campus, Chicago City Col, prof Eng, 1969-; Citizens Comn Pub Educ, exec dir, 1975-76; Comn Urban Affair Spec Projects, AME Church, exec dir, 1978-80; Neighborhood Inst, educ coordr, 1979; Univ Chicago, dir Educ Assistance Prog, 2002-. **Orgs:** Counr, Hillcrest Ctr C, NY, 1958-61; featured soloist Park Manor Cong Church, 1958-, John W Work Chorale, 1959-; asst prof educ, Northeastern Univ, Chicago, 1974-76; consult, Prescription Learning Inc, 1977-; staff dir, convener, S Shore Schs Alliance, 1979-80; Nat Asn Col Admission Coun. **Honors/Awds:** Outstanding Young Women of America, 1968; Ford Fel, Univ Chicago, 1968-69; TTT Fel, Northwestern Univ, 1972-73. **Business Addr:** Director for the Educational Assistance Program, University of Chicago, 5801 S Ellis Ave, Chicago, IL 60637.

LIGHTFOOT, DR. SARA LAWRENCE
Socialist, educator, writer. **Personal:** Daughter of Charles Radford and Margaret. **Educ:** Harvard Univ, EdD. **Career:** Educator, sociologist, writer; Harvard Grad Sch Educ, Emily Hargroves Fisher Prof Educ, currently; writer, currently; Books: Balm in Gilead:Journey of a Healer, 1988; The Good High Sch: Portraits of Character &Culture; "Portraits of Exemplary Secondary Schs: Highland Park," Daedalus, Fall 1981, p. 59; "Portraits of Exemplary Secondary Schs: George Washington Carver Comprehensive High Sch," Daedalus, Fall 1981, p. 17; "Portraits of Exemplary Secondary Schs: St Paul's Sch," Daedalus, Fall 1981, p. 97; I've Known Rivers: Lives of Loss & Liberation, 1994; The Essential Conversation: What Parents & Teachers Can Learn From Each Other, 2003; The Third Chapter: Passion, Risk, and Adventure in the 25 Years After 50, 2009. **Orgs:** Chair bd, MacArthur Found; Nat Acad Educ; Bright Horizons Family Solutions; Boston Globe; Berklee Col Music. **Honors/Awds:** Mac Arthur Prize fellowship, 1984; Harvards George Ledlie prize, 1993; endowed professorship, Swarthmore Col; Sara Lawrence-Lightfoot endowed chair; Emily Hargroves Fisher endowed chair, Harvard Univ, 1998; Candace Award, Nat Coalition 100 Black Women. **Special Achievements:** Featured on the 2006 Documentary on PBS, African American Lives; First African-American woman in Harvard's history to have an endowed professorship named in her honor. **Business Addr:** Emily Hargroves Fisher Professor of Education, Harvard Graduate School of Education, Appian Way, Cambridge, MA 02138, **Business Phone:** (617)496-4837.

LIGHTFOOT, SIMONE DANIELLE
Association executive. **Personal:** Born Oct 22, 1967, Detroit, MI daughter of Henry and Mary Ann Patterson; married Phillip, 1996 children: Jaydaka & Jaydan. **Educ:** Eastern Mich Univ, BS, 2003 **Career:** USAF, Air Transp Specialist, 1986-90; US EPA, mech engineering tech, 1990-91; Bus owner, proprietor, 1991-96; Mich House Rep, legis asst, 1996-98, dep chief staff, 1998-; African Am Health Inst, state health conf dir, 1999; NAACP, Mich State dir 2001-; Mallory Campaign for Cincinnati, campaign mgr currently. **Orgs:** NAACP, Detroit br, 1987-; Tuskegee Airman 1992-; Nat Coun Negro Women, 1998-. **Honors/Awds:** Dr Martin Luther King Humanitarian Award, Huron High Sch, 1985 Distinguished Citizen Award, Cent Delaware Chamber Com 1989; Minority Business Owner of the Yr, Minority Bus Owne Washtenaw County, 1995; Best of Award, Craine Bus Mag, 1995 Annette Rainwater Political Award, Mich State Dem Party, 2001 **Military Serv:** AUS, E-4, 1986-90. **Home Addr:** 2356 Arrowwood, Ann Arbor, MI 48105, **Home Phone:** (734)996-8230. **Business Addr:** Campaign Manager, NAACP Voter Empowerment 5846 Hamilton Ave Col Hill, Cincinnati, OH 45224, **Business Phone:** (513)591-1100.

LIGHTFOOT, DR. WILLIAM P.
Physician. **Personal:** Born Sep 12, 1920, Pittsburgh, PA; married Edith Wingate; children: William & Philip. **Educ:** Lincoln Univ AB, 1943; Howard Univ Med Col, MD, 1946. **Career:** John F Kennedy Memorial Hosp, Philadelphia, attending surgeon Temple Univ Hosp & Med Sch Fac, prof surgery. **Orgs:** Am Col Surgeons; Philadelphia Acad Surgery; Philadelphia Col Physician s;AMA, Nat Med Asn, Philadelphia Co Med Soc; Am So Abdominal Surgeons. **Military Serv:** AUS, capt, 1953-55. **Home Addr:** 6 Old Fort Way, Hilton Head Island, SC 29926-2697 **Home Phone:** (803)681-5915.

LIGON, DORIS HILLIAN
Museum director. **Personal:** Born Apr 28, 1936, Baltimore, MD married Dr Claude M Ligon; children: Claude M Jr & Carole Ann **Educ:** Morgan State Univ, BA social, 1978, MA Art Hist, Museo 1979; Howard Univ, PhD, courses African Hist. **Career:** Nat Mus African Art Smithsonian Inst, docent (tour guide) 1976-88 Morgan State Univ, art gallery res asst 1978-79; Howard Count Md Sch Syst, consult African art & cult; Md Mus African Ar founder & exec dir, 1980-. **Orgs:** Asn Black Women His African-Am Museums Asn; charter Columbia Chap Pierians In 1983; charter Eubie Blake Cult Ctr 1984; Morgan State Uni Alumni; Nat Asn Advan Colored People; Urban League; Ar Coun African Studies Asn; Phi Alpha Theta (Nat Hist Hon Soc

Alpha Kappa Mu. **Honors/Awds:** Goldseeker Fellowship, Grade Studies MSU, 1978-79; Nirmaj K Sinha Award highest honors Sociol, 1978. **Business Addr:** Founder, Executive Director, African Art Museum of Maryland, 5430 Vantage Pt Rd, PO Box 1105, Columbia, MD 21044-0105, **Business Phone:** (410)730-7106.

LILES, KEVIN
Executive. **Personal:** Born Jan 1, 1968?, Maryland. **Educ:** engineering. **Career:** Numarx, founder & contrib, 1989-90; Marx Bros Records, founder & pres, 1991-92; Def Jam Recs, internship, 1992-94, Mid-Atlantic Region, mgr, 1994, W Coast, gen mgr prom, 1994-96, gen mgr & vpres prom, 1996-98, pres, 1998-2002; Island Def Jam, exec vpres, 2002-04; Warner Music Group, exec vpres, currently. **Orgs:** Bd mem, Hip-Hop Summit Action Network. **Honors/Awds:** Diversity Award, Found Ethnic Understanding, 2002; Music Visionary of the Year, UJA-Fed NY & Music Youth Found, 2003. **Business Addr:** Executive Vice President, Warner Music Group, 75 Rockefeller Plz Suite 7, New York, NY 10019, **Business Phone:** (212)275-2000.*

LILLARD, KWAME LEO (LEO LILLARD, II)
Activist, industrial engineer. **Personal:** Born Sep 16, 1939, Tampa, FL; son of Leo I and Louise Taylor; married Evelyn Downing Lillard, Mar 11, 1970; children: Leo III, Jessica, Joshua, Nyleve, Troy, Chiffonda & Edward. **Educ:** Tenn State Univ, Nashville, TN, BS, mech engineering, 1961; City Col New York, MS, mech engineering, 1965; Hunter Col, NY, MS, urban ulanning, 1971. **Career:** Malcolm X Univ, Greensboro, NC, engineering instr, 1972; Weyerhaeuser, Plymouth, NC, indust engineer, 1972-76; Nashville City Planning Dept, Nashville, TN, sr planner, 1976-80; Textron, Nashville, TN, indust engineer, 1981-91; C21 Architect Engineers, planning analyst, Tenn Dept environ & conservation, environ specialist, currently. **Orgs:** Pres, African Am Cult Alliance, 1984-; co-founder, Men Distinction Youth Develop, 1989-; prog coordr, Nashville Peace Coalition, 1990-; exec bd, Nashville NCP Chap; exec bd, Coun COT Serv. **Honors/Awds:** Black Expo Education Innovator, Black Expo Inc, 1980; Martin Luther King Award, Nashville Martin Luther King Celebration, 1989. **Home Addr:** 2814 Buena Vista Pke, Nashville, TN 37218. **Business Addr:** President, African American Cultural Alliance, 1215 9th Ave N Suite 210, PO Box 22173, Nashville, TN 37208, **Business Phone:** (615)210-6963.

LILLARD, LEO, II. See LILLARD, KWAME LEO.

LILLIE, VERNELL A
Theatrical director, educator. **Personal:** Born May 11, 1931, Hempstead, TX; married Richard L Jr (deceased); children: Charisse Lillie McGill & Hisani Lillie Blanton. **Educ:** Dillard Univ, BA, 1952; Carnegie-Mellon Univ, MA 1970, DA 1972; Seton Hill Univ, PhD, 2005. **Career:** Julius C Hester House Settlement Asn, group work spec, 1952-56; Houston Indep Sch Dist Phillis Wheatley HS, chmn & teacher speech, drama & debate 1956-59; Tex So Univ Project Upward Bound, instr eng, curriculum developer & drama specialist, 1965-69; Carnegie-Mellon Univ Proj Upward Bound, dir student affairs, 1969-71; Kuntu Repertory Theatre, founder & dir, 1974-; Feasibility Study Black Sch, dapt project dir; Univ Pittsburgh, Dept Africana Studies, chair & assoc prof, assoc prof emer, currently; Plays: The Buffalo Soldiers Plus One,She'll Find Her Way Home, dir; Difficult Days Ahead in a Blaze, dir; Ashes to Africa, dir; Whispers Want to Holler, dir; Mahalia Jackson: Standing On Holy Ground, dir; The Crawford Grill Presents Billie Holiday, dir; Zora: The Dark Town Strutter, dir; Papa's Blues, dir; Over Forty, dir; Little Willie Armstrong Jones, dir; Two Can Play, dir; Blues for an Alabama Sky, dir; Pittsburgh Crawfords & the Homestead Grays, dir; Hester House Exper Theatre, dir & founder. **Orgs:** Am Soc Group Psychotherapy & Psychodrama; Nat & PA Counc Teachers Eng; Speech Assoc Am; Nat Adult Day Servs Assoc; Assoc Theatre Higher Educ; Afro-Am Educrs; bd dir, Julius C Hester House Houston, 1965-69; Earnest T Williams Mem Ctr, Pittsburgh Ctr Alterntive Ed, 1972-78; Women Urban Crisis, 1973-80; coord curriculum & staff devel mem, Hope Devel Houston; Black Theatre Network. **Honors/Awds:** Award for Outstanding Contribution to Arts, Delta Sigma Theta, 1969; Award for Editorial Achievements, Carnegie-Mellon Univ Proj Upward Bound, 1972; Pittsburgh Outstanding Editor Black Cath Ministries, 1973; Distinguish Teacher Award, Univ Pittsburgh, 1986; Arts & Letter Award, Alpha Kappa Alpha Sorority, 1987; Women of Color Caucus, 1985; Performances, Fringe Festival, Edinburgh Univ, Scotland, 1989, 1994; Dillard Vernell Andrew Watson Lillie Scholarship, Smith Col. **Business Addr:** Associate Professor Emeritus, University of Pittsburgh, Department of Africana Studies, 230 S Bouquet St, Pittsburgh, PA 15260, **Business Phone:** (412)648-7547.

LIMA, GEORGE SILVA
Government official. **Personal:** Born Apr 4, 1919, Fall River, MA; son of Manuel Duarte Lima and Anna Morais Silva; married Elma Elizabeth Boone; children: Anna Maria Lima Bowling, George II & Robert. **Educ:** Brown Univ, AB, 1948; Harvard Bus Sch, Trade Union Labor Rels Mgt, 1958. **Career:** Am Fedn State County & Municipal Employees New Eng, regional dir, 1950-64; US Govt Action Dept Vista, Older Am Vol Progs, dir 1979-84; State RI, state rep; 1986-87. **Orgs:** Vice chmn, E Providence Community Develop Corp, 1978-82; Nat bd mem, Nat Blacks Govt, 1980-84; chmn, Steering Comm New Eng Gerontology, 1984-85;bd mem, RI AFL-CIO; chmn, E Providence Coalition Human Rights; RI State Employees Retirement Comn; Am Asn Retired Persons; Int Sr Citizens Org; chmn steering comn, SENE Gerontology Ctr, Brown Univ; RI Black Caucus State Legislators; Comm to Study State RI Affirmative Action; vice chmn RI Comn Needs Cape Verdean Community; mem House Labor Comm; exec dir, RI Black Caucus State Legislators. **Honors/Awds:** NAACP Membership Enrollment Award, 1961; Delta Sigma Theta Comm Service Award, 1978; Achievement Award, 274 Business Club, 1986; Omega Man of the Year Sigma Nu Chap, 1987; NAACP, Joseph Lecourt Medal, Distinguished Service & Achievement, 1989; Nation Builder Award, Nat Black Caucus of State Legislators, 1991. **Military Serv:** AUS Air Corps first lt, 4 yrs; Tuskegee Army Air Base, 477th Bom B Gp.

LINCOLN, ABBEY. See MOSEKA, AMINATA.

LINCOLN, JEREMY ARLO
Football player, consultant. **Personal:** Born Apr 7, 1969, Toledo, OH; married Lisa. **Educ:** Univ Tenn, attended 1991. **Career:** Football player (retired); Chicago Bears, defensive back, 1993-95; St Louis Rams, 1996; Seattle Seahawks, 1997; New York Giants, 1998-99; Detroit Lions, 2000-01; CB Richard Ellis, assoc; Legacy growth partners, consult & owner currently. **Orgs:** Founder, Jeremy Lincoln Found; CB Richard Ellis African-Am Network Group. **Business Phone:** (212)647-8940.

LINDO, DELROY
Actor. **Personal:** Born Nov 18, 1952, London, Greater London, England; married Neshormeh; children: 1; married Kathi Coaston (divorced). **Career:** Films: Find the Lady, 1976; Malcolm X, 1992; Crooklyn, 1994; Congo, 1995; Clockers, 1995; Get Shorty, 1995; Broken Arrow, 1996; Ramsom, 1996; The Devil's Advocate, 1997; A Life Less Ordinary, 1997; Cider House Rules, 1999; Romeo Must Die, 2000; Gone in 60 Seconds, 2000; The Book of Stars, 2001; Heist, 2001; The Last Castle, 2001; The One, 2001; The Core, 2003; Wondrous Oblivion, 2003; This Christmas, 2007; TV movies: "Soul Of The Game", 1996; "Glory & Honor", 1998; "Strange Justice", 1999; "Profoundly Normal", 2003; "The Core", 2003; "Wondrous Oblivion", 2003; "Lackawanna Blues", 2005; "The Exonerated", 2005; "Sahara", 2005; "Domino", 2005; "Kidnapped", 2006-07; "Law & Order: Special Victims Unit", 2009. **Honors/Awds:** Golden Satellite Award, 1999. **Special Achievements:** Was nominated for Broadway's 1988 Tony Award as Best Actor. **Business Addr:** Actor, William Morris Agency, 151 S El Camino Dr, Beverly Hills, CA 90212-2775, **Business Phone:** (310)274-7451.*

LINDSAY, DR. ARTURO
Educator, artist. **Personal:** Born Sep 29, 1946, Colon, Panama; son of Arthur and Louise; married Melanie Pavich-Lindsay, Jun 30, 1985; children: Urraca, Joaquin & Javier. **Educ:** Cent Conn State Univ, BA, 1970; Univ Mass, MFA, 1975; New York Univ, DA, 1990. **Career:** Royal Athena Galleries, asst dir, 1984-89; Franklin & Marshall Col, scholar-in-residence, 1989-90; NY Univ, scholar-in-residence, 1993; Spelman Col, assoc prof, prof art & art hist, currently; Rockefeller Found, Bellagio fel, 2003; Davidson Col, Kemp distinguished vis prof, 2005. **Orgs:** Founding mem, Taller Portobelo, 1995-; bd dir, Col Art Asn, 1996-2000. **Honors/Awds:** First Prize Sculpture, Second Annual Atlanta Life Ins Co Nat Art Competition & Exhib, 1981; Fulbright, Senior Scholar Award, 1998-99; Lila Wallace-Reader's Digest InterNat Artist Award, 1994; Presidential Award for Scholarship, Spelman Col, 1997; Fulbright Senior Scholar Award, J William Fulbright Foreign Scholar Bd, 1999; Merrill InterNat Travel Grant, Spelman Col, 2000. **Special Achievements:** Publication: Santeria Aesthetics in Contemporary Latin American Art, 1996; Exhibition: El Retorno De Las A'nimas - LimaBienal, 1999. **Home Addr:** 4026 Birchwood Cove, Decatur, GA 30034. **Business Addr:** Professor of Art and Art History, Spelman College, Department of Art, 350 Spelman Lane SW, Atlanta, GA 30314-4399, **Business Phone:** (404)270-5452.

LINDSAY, EDDIE H S
Executive. **Personal:** Born Oct 23, 1931; married Joyce McCrae; children: Paul & Lisa. **Educ:** London Polytechnic Col, London; Queens Col, NY; Am Inst Banking NY, Hofstra Univ. **Career:** Ins Salesman, 1968; Mfrs Hanover Trust Co, credit officer; Broadway Bank & Trust Co, dir urban affairs, loan officer com minority econ develop, br mgr main off & asst vpres; Priority Chem Co, pres, currently. **Orgs:** Nat Bankers Asn; NJ Bankers Urban Affairs Comn; EDGES NY Prof Asn; dir, Cath Diocese Comm Human Develop; dir, Planned Parenthood Passaic Co; finance chmn mem, Boys Club Paterson-Passaic; Legal Aid Soc; YMCA; United Way. **Business Phone:** (201)345-7010.*

LINDSAY, GWENDOLYN ANN BURNS
Federal government official. **Personal:** Born Nov 13, 1947, Baltimore, MD; daughter of Lucinda Bowman Burns (deceased) and Robert Burns (deceased); divorced; children: Brock A. **Educ:** Coppin State Col, BA, summa cum laude, 1975; Univ Baltimore, MPA, 1977. **Career:** Bur Prog Operation Prospective Reimbursement Br, social sci res analyst, 1975-77; Bur Prog Operation Prog Iniatives Br, prog analyst, 1977-79; Off Executive Operation Prog Liaison Br, prog liaison specialist, 1979-82; Dept Health & Human Serv Health Care Financing Admin, Off Regulations, health ins specialist, 1993-97, Off Commun & Operations Support, 1997-2002, Ctr Med & Medicaid Serv, sr tech health ins specialist, 2002-. **Orgs:** Baltimore Alumnae Chapter, 1995, first vpres, second vpres, third vpres, fin secy, Ebony, budget & finance, 1977-91; Nat Coun Negro Women, 1980-; bd mem & personnel comt, YWCA Greater Baltimore, 1986-92; bd mem, Md State Bd Dietetic Practices, 1988-92; bd mem, Towson Catholic Adv Bd, 1989-94; pres, Delta Sigma Theta Sorority Inc, 1991-93; Baltimore Metrop Chap Nat Black Women's Health Proj, workshop facilatator, 1993-00, regional journalist, 1997-; corresponding secy, 1994-99, vpres, 1999-, Baltimore Chap Continental Socs Inc; regional journalist, Delta Sigma Theta Inc, 1997-01. **Honors/Awds:** Outstanding Public Service Award, Delta Sigma Theta, 1983; Presidential Continued Service Award, Md Coun Deltas, 1986; Award for Volunteerism, Associated Black Charities, 1988; Mayor's Citation, Mayor Baltimore, 1988, 1990, 1993, 1994-96 & 1999-02; Helen Clapp Service Award, YWCA Greater Baltimore, 1992; Governor Citation, Gov Md, 1992, 1994-03; "The Valued Hours Award", Fullwood Found Inc, 1994; National Service Project Award, Continental Socs, 2002. **Home Addr:** 12 Garobe Ct, Baltimore, MD 21207.

LINDSAY, HORACE AUGUSTIN
Executive. **Personal:** Born Mar 1, 1938, New York, NY; son of Horace A Sr and Cecelia T Mitchell; married Donna McDade; children: Gloria & Horace. **Educ:** Prairie View A&M Univ, BS, 1959; Calif State Univ, MS, 1969. **Career:** Executive (retired); Boeing Co, res engr, 1961-63; Martin Co, sr engr, 1963-64; Bunker Ramo, prog mgr, 1964-68, mkt dir, 1969-73, prog dir, 1973-77, mkt vpres, 1977-84; Eaton Corp, plans & bus develop vpres, 1984-89; Contel Corp, vpres & gen mgr, 1989-91; GTE Govt Systs, IIPO, vpres & gen mgr, 1991-93; GTE Airfone, pres, 1993-96; GTE Corp, vpres technol mkt, 1996-2000; pvt investor. **Orgs:** Armed Forces Commun & Electronics Asn. **Military Serv:** AUS, first lt, 1959-61. **Home Addr:** 5620 N Harbor Village Dr, Vero Beach, FL 32967, **Home Phone:** (772)569-9865.

LINDSAY, REGINALD CARL
Judge. **Personal:** Born Mar 19, 1945, Birmingham, AL; son of Richard and Louise; married Cheryl Elizabeth Hartgrove, Aug 15, 1970. **Educ:** Univ Valencia Spain, Cert, 1966; Morehouse Coll, BA, Hon, 1967; Harvard Law Sch, JD, 1970. **Career:** Hill & Barlow, atty, 1970-75, partner, 1978-93; pvt pract, Boston, Mass, 1970-75 & 1977-93; Mass Pub Utilities Dept, comnr, 1975-77; US Dist Ct Mass, US dist judge, 1993-. **Orgs:** Bd dir, Morgan Mem Goodwill Indust Inc; trustee, Newton-Wellesley Hosp; bd dir, Partners Youth Disabilities; bd gov, Downtown Club; bd trustees, Thompson Island Educ Ctr, 1975-86; bd dir, Mass Bay United Way, 1981-85; Mass Comn Judicial Conduct, 1983-89; Com Arbit Panel, Am Arbit Asn; bd dir, Disability Law Ctr. **Honors/Awds:** Ruffin-Fenwick Trailblazer Award, Harvard Black Law Students Asn, 1994; Amanda V Houston Community Service Award, Boston Col, 1998; Citation of Judicial Excellence, Boston Bar Asn, 1999; Frederick E Berry Expanding Independence Award, Easter Seals Mass, 1999; Heroes Among US Award, Boston Celtics, 2001; Leadership Award, New England Black Law Students Asn, 2001. **Business Addr:** District Judge, United States District Court Massachusetts, John Joseph Moakley US Courthouse, 1 Courthouse Way Suite 2300, Boston, MA 02210, **Business Phone:** (617)748-9152.

LINDSAY, SAM A.
Judge. **Personal:** Born Oct 16, 1951?, San Antonio, TX. **Educ:** St Marys Univ, San Antonio, BA, 1974; Univ Tex Sch Law, JD, 1977. **Career:** Tex Aeronaut Comn, 1977-79; Dallas City Attorneys Off, 1979-92; Dallas City, atty, 1992-98; Northern Dist Texas, fed judge, 1998-. **Orgs:** State Bar Tex; Dallas Legal Asn; Dallas Inn Ct; JL Turner Legal Asn; City Dallas Judicial Nominating Comn; Int Municipal Lawyers Asn; Southwestern Legal Found; Leadership Dallas Class; fed Judiciary adv comt, Northern Dist Tex; adv comt, Dallas Bus Jour; trustee, Ctr Am & Int Law. **Honors/Awds:** Trailblazers Award, 1993; CB Bunkley Award, JL Turner Legal Asn, 1996. **Special Achievements:** First African American to serve on the District Court in Dallas. *

LINDSEY, JEROME W.
Educator, planner. **Personal:** Born Apr 7, 1932, Phoenix City, AL; son of Jerome W II and Willie Mae Harper Swinton. **Educ:** Howard Univ, BArch, 1956; Mass Inst Technol, March, 1960, MCity Planning, attended 1961. **Career:** Harold M Lewis, planner, 1955-56; John Hans Graham, planner, 1956-58; Samuel Glaser, planner, 1958-59; Jose Luis Sert, planner, 1959-61; Providence Redevelopment Agency, sr planner, 1961-62; Howard Univ, assoc prof, 1962-68, chmn, 1969-70, assoc dean, 1970-71, dean, 1971-79, prof, 1971-; Wash DC, dir planning, 1964-68; Yale Univ, vis prof, 1967-68. **Orgs:** Regional architect; Am Inst Architects; Bd Educ; consult, World Bank Urban Devel Proj. **Honors/Awds:** NCARB Certificate. **Home Addr:** 501 Aspen St NW, Washington, DC 20012. **Business Phone:** (202)806-6100.

LINDSEY, PATRICK O
Executive. **Career:** DaimlerChrysler Group, sr mgr state rels, external affairs & pub policy, currently. **Orgs:** Bd mem, Warren/

Conner Develop Coalition; FutureGen Ill Task Force; speaker, Growth Dimensions; bus mem, Eight Mile Blvd Asn; bd dir, Black Family Develop Inc. **Business Addr:** Senior Manager State Relations, External Affairs, Public Policy, DaimlerChrysler Group, 1000 Chrysler Dr, Auburn Hills, MI 48326-2766, **Business Phone:** (248)512-3358.

LINDSEY, S. L.
Government official, clergy. **Personal:** Born Aug 23, 1909, Swiftwater, MS; widowed. **Educ:** Miss Baptist Sem, Jackson, MS, B Theol. **Career:** Ordained minister, 37 yrs; Town of Metcalfe, mayor. **Orgs:** Pres Metcalfe Devel Assoc 1975-; mem South Delta Planning 1977-; bd mem Washington Cty Oppty 1978-; mem Black Mayors Conf 1978-; pres Metcalfe Indust Dev Found 1981-; pastor at 4 churches. **Honors/Awds:** Outstanding Achievements, Delta Coun Aging 60, 1980. **Home Addr:** PO Box 250, Metcalfe, MS 38760.

LINK, JOYCE BATTLE
Lawyer. **Personal:** Born Dec 24, 1956, Columbus, OH; daughter of William R and Dorothy L; married Michael D Link, Mar 21, 1981. **Educ:** Wash Univ, St Louis, BA, educ & psychol, 1978; Ohio State Univ, Col Law, JD, 1983. **Career:** Asst city prosecutor, 1983-85; asst atty gen, 1985-89; Bricker & Eckler LLP, assoc, 1989-95, partner, litigation dept, 1995; Central State Univ, Ohio Atty Gen, spec coun, 1996-2004; Ohio Supreme Ct Chief Justice Moyer, ohio supreme ct's civil rules comt, 2002-04; Montgomery, McCracken, Walker & Rhoads LLP, atty, currently. **Orgs:** Columbus Bar Asn, former chair judiciary comt, 1998; Ohio State Bar Asn; Am Bar Asn; Nat Bar Asn; Nat Asn Col & Univ Atty; Nat Coun Ohio State Univ Col Law Alumni Asn; vchmn, Community Shelter Bd, 2001-04. **Honors/Awds:** Women of Achievement Award, Ypung Women Christian Asn, 2003; Columbus Communitys Black Women of Courage Award. **Business Addr:** Attorney, Montgomery, McCracken, Walker & Rhoads, LLP, 123 S Broad St, Philadelphia, PA 19109, **Business Phone:** (215)772-7692.

LINTON, GORDON J.
State government official, executive. **Personal:** Born Feb 26, 1948, Philadelphia, PA; son of James and Alberta James; married Jacqueline Flynn; children: Sharifah & Sabriya. **Educ:** Peirce Jr Col, AS, 1967; Lincoln Univ, PA, BA, economics, 1970; Antioch Univ, MEd, coun psycol, 1973. **Career:** Sch Dist Philadelphia, comn consult, 1971-74; Baptist Children's House, educ dir, 1974-78; Philadelphia Child Guid Ctr, psych-ed spec, 1978-80; Dept Auditor Gen, reg dir, 1980-82; Pa House Rep, state rep, 1982-93; fed transit adminr, 1993-99; Hagler Bailly Inc, senior adv, 2000-04; Wage Works Inc, sr adv & vpres, currently; Wash Metrop Area Transit Authority, alternate dir, bd dirs, currently. **Orgs:** Nat Black Caucus State Legislators, 1982-, Minority Bus Enterprise Coun, 1982-; trustee, Lincoln Univ, 1982-; Philadelphia Econ Round table, 1983-;pres, Conf Minority Transp Officials, 1984. **Honors/Awds:** Community Service Award, Hill Youth Asn, 1982; Community Service Award, Leeds Middle Sch, 1982; Community Service Award, Crisis Intervention Network, 1984; Appreciation Award, New Pa Del Minority Purchasing Coun, 1985; Appreciation Award, Independent Minority Businessmen Cent Pa, 1985; Outstanding Civic Leadership Award, Entrepreneurial Club-Bus & Technol Ctr, 1985; Dedicated Service to Higher Education Award, Lincoln Univ,1986; Pride Peirce, Peirce Jr Col, 1989; Adviser of the Year Award, Nat Asn Women Bus Owners, 1989. **Business Addr:** Alternate Director, Washington Metropolitan Area Transit Authority, 600 Fifth St NW, Washington, DC 20001, **Business Phone:** (202)962-1234.

LINTON, JONATHAN C.
Football player. **Personal:** Born Nov 7, 1974, Catasauqua, PA. **Educ:** NC State Univ, sociol. **Career:** Football player (retired); Buffalo Bills, running back, 1998-2000. **Honors/Awds:** Rookie of the Year, 1998.

LINTON, SHEILA LORRAINE
Educator. **Personal:** Born Dec 19, 1950, Philadelphia, PA; daughter of Harold Louis (deceased) and Elvera Linton Boyd (deceased). **Educ:** Pa State Univ, BS, 1972; Drexel Univ, MS, 1976. **Career:** Sch Dist Philadelphia, teacher, 1972-78; Pew Charitable Trusts, prog officer, 1979-87; Sch Dist Philadelphia, teacher 1988-. **Orgs:** Alpha Kappa Alpha, 1970-; Nat Sec Bullock Family Reunions, 1978-85; adv comt, Jack & Jill Am Found, 1981-87, bd dir, 1989-2001; vol, United Negro Col Fund, 1982-87; Women Philanthropy, 1983-87; bd dir, Asn Black Found Exec, 1984-87; Friends Free Libr Philadelphia, 1989-96; bd dir, Family Reunion Inst, Temple Univ, 1990; bd, Kearsley Retirement, 1992-2003; Nat Coalition 100 Black Women. **Honors/Awds:** Presidential Award for Distinguished Service, Jack & Jill Am Found, 1984; Teacher of the Year, Audenried Cluster, Sch Dist Philadelphia, 2000; National Board Certified Teacher, 2002. **Home Addr:** 1030 Harbour Dr, Palmyra, NJ 08065, **Home Phone:** (856)303-2286. **Business Addr:** Teacher, School District of Philadelphia, 4909 Chestnut St, Philadelphia, PA 19139, **Business Phone:** (215)471-2271.

LINTZ, FRANK D E
Landscape architect. **Personal:** Born Feb 5, 1951, Ottumwa, IA; son of Franklyn and Margaret; married Lisa M Campos, Jun 27, 1992. **Career:** Mid-Continent Meats, union leader, 1972-79; Circle C Beef Co, union leader, 1979-83; Swift & Co, lead butcher, 1983-86; Nebraska Turf Co, co-owner, 1994-98; Farmland Foods Co, Warehouse & Transportation, coordr, 1998-. **Orgs:** Amalgamated Meat Cutters & Butcher Workmen, 1972-79, chief steward, 1979-83; United Food & Com Workers, 1983-86. **Special Achievements:** BET News Network, Drought in Midwest, television Interview in 1989, Des Moines Register, farming article in 1968. **Military Serv:** AUS, spec-7, 1969-71; basic service awards, campaign Medals. **Home Addr:** 4915 N 61st St, Omaha, NE 68104, **Home Phone:** (402)571-3251.

LINYARD, RICHARD
Banker. **Personal:** Born Nov 16, 1930, Maywood, IL; married Maggie; children: Linda, Lance, Timothy. **Educ:** Northwestern Univ; Am Inst Banking standard & advan cert; grad sch banking Univ Wis, dipl. **Career:** Oak Pk Trust & Savs Bank, janitor, elevator Oper, savs bookkeeper, teller, gen bookkeeper, savs dept, asst mgr, asst cashier, 1950-64; Seaway Nat Bank Chicago, exec vpres, bd dir cashier, 1964-72, pres & chief exec officer. **Orgs:** Pres, Chicago Chap Am Inst Banking.

LIPPETT, RONNIE LEON
Football player. **Personal:** Born Dec 10, 1960, Melbourne, FL. **Educ:** Univ Miami. **Career:** New England Patriots, corner back, 1983-88, 1990-91. **Orgs:** Patriot, Nat Alliance Dedicated Patriots, 2003-. **Honors/Awds:** Post-season play, 1985: AFC Championship Game, NFL Championship Game.

LIPPS, LOUIS ADAM
Football player, talk show host, manager. **Personal:** Born Aug 9, 1962, New Orleans, LA. **Educ:** Univ Southern Miss. **Career:** Football Player (retired); Pittsburgh Steelers, wide receiver, 1984-91; New Orleans Saints, wide receiver, 1992; Steel City Mortgage Services, mgr, currently; ESPN radio, co-host, currently. **Orgs:** Hon chmn, Big Bros & Sisters Bowl Kids; chmn, MS Readathon; chmn, Variety Club Golf Tournament, Ronald McDonald House; owner, Halls Mortuary; Drug & Alcohol Educ Prog, Blue Cross Western Pa, 1986-. **Honors/Awds:** Rookie of the Year, Nat Football League, 1984; Pro Bowl, 1984, 1985; Professional Athlete of the Year; Joe Greene Great Performance Award, 1984; Steeler Most Valuable Player, 1985; Pittsburgh's Man of the Year in Sports; Louisiana Prof Athlete of the Year, Sugar Bowl's Sports Awards Community, 1985. **Special Achievements:** First Steeler rookie since Franco Harris to be named to AFC Pro Bowl. **Business Phone:** (412)784-8808.*

LIPSCOMB, CURTIS ALEXANDER
Publishing executive. **Personal:** Born Mar 23, 1965, Detroit, MI; son of Lester Lewis and Mary Salley. **Educ:** Parsons Sch Design, BFA, 1987. **Career:** Dagger Group, knitwear designer, 1987-89; Bonaventure, knitwear designer, 1989-90; Chelsea Young, knitwear designer, 1990; Ruff Hewn, knitwear designer, 1990-91; Banana Repub, knitwear designer, 1991-92; Kick Mag, pres & chief exec officer, exec dir, currently. **Orgs:** Men Color Motivational Group, Detroit, 1992-; co-chair, Mich Clinton & Gore Lesbian Gay Leadership Counre-elect Pres Clinton, 1996;ed bd, Between The Lines; ed bd, Mich Community News Lesbians, Gays, Bisexuals & Friends. **Honors/Awds:** Adolf Klein Scholarship Award, 1986; Roz & Sherm Fashion Award, 1983; SBC Magazine, Brother of the Year Award, Community Servicee, 1996. **Special Achievements:** Traveled to Europe/UK, 1990; Traveled to Far East, 1990; Publications: Kick! Magazine, The Motivator, Detroit Pride Guide, The Official Resouce Guide to Hotter Than July 1996 & 1997. **Business Addr:** Executive Director, Kick Publishing Company, PO Box 2222, Detroit, MI 48231, **Business Phone:** (313)438-2222.

LIPSCOMB, DARRYL L.
Government official. **Personal:** Born Jan 18, 1953, Chicago, IL. **Educ:** Univ Wis-La Crosse, BS, jour, 1977, MS, educ, 1979. **Career:** Univ Wis, admis counr, 1979-82; COE Col, asst dir admis, 1982-83, assoc dean admis, 1983-87; Cedar Ridge Publ, dir mkt, 1986-89; City Cedar Rapids, chief civil rights compliance off, 1989-; HUD, syst admin; Lipscomb & Assocs, pres & chief exec officer, 1995-; comnr, Iowa Comn Status African-Am, 1996-2000; Kirkwood Community Col, Stud Develop, adj counr, dir admis, part time counr, ICCSSA, web master, 2004-08. **Orgs:** Adv comt, Kirkwood Community Col, 1991-; bd dirs, Friends Unity Inc, 1996-; Equal Opportunity Prog Personnel, 1985-89; Kappa Alpha Psi Frat; IC/CR Alumni Chap Kappa Alpha Psi; NAACP; bd mem, Equal Employ Opportunity Affirmative Action. Nat Assoc Human Rights Workers; Nat Assoc Black Pub Officals. **Honors/Awds:** Keeper of Records, Kappa Alpha Psi IC/CR Alumni Chap, 1988-94, Keeper of Ex checquer, 1996-. Pole march, 2003-07. **Business Addr:** President, Chief Executive Officer, Lipscomb & Associates, PO Box 102, Cedar Rapids, IA 52406, **Business Phone:** (319)431-4788.

LIPSCOMB, DR. WANDA DEAN
Administrator. **Personal:** Born Jan 29, 1953, Richmond, VA; married Keith N Lipscomb; children: Nicholas K & Victoria N. **Educ:** Lincoln Univ, BA, 1974; Wash Univ, MA, 1975; Mich State Univ, PhD, 1978. **Career:** Mich State Univ, Col Human Med, assoc chairperson educ prog, 1994, dir ctr excellence, currently, assoc prof psychol, currently, asst dean stud affairs, currently; HCOP, dir, currently. **Orgs:** Bd dirs, Asn Multiculture Coun & Develop, 1980-88; bd dirs, Am Asn Coun & Develop 1982-85; Asn Black Psychologists, 1984-; bd dirs, Nat Bd Cert Counselors, 1985-90; pres, Lansing Alumnae Chap Delta Sigma Theta Sorority Inc; Nat Prog Planning Comn Delta Sigma Theta Sorority Inc; bd dirs, Mich State Univ Black Alumni Asn. **Honors/Awds:** Numerous honors & awards including John L Lennon Award for Distinguished Professional Service, Asn Multicultural Coun, 1984; Sisterwood Award, Delta Sigma Theta, 1985; Professional Service Award, 1992; O'Hana Award for Multiculturalism, 1994; Diversity Award, Mich State Univ, 1995. **Home Addr:** 3422 Penrose Dr, Lansing, MI 48911. **Business Addr:** Assistant Dean & Associate Professor, Director, Michigan State University, College Of Human Medicine, A-234 Life Sci Bldg, East Lansing, MI 48824.

LIPSCOMBE, MARGARET ANN
Educator. **Personal:** Born Dec 12, 1939, Alabama. **Educ:** NY Univ, MA, 1960; Univ Minn, BS, 1957; Columbia Univ, attended 1968; Conn Col, attended 1967; Juilliard, attended 1970; New York City Studios, attended 1975. **Career:** Valmar Dance Co, performer, 1958-59; Hunter Col HS, instr, 1959-60; Spelman Col, instr, 1959-64; Women's Dance Proj Henry St Play house NY,performer, 1960; City Col NY, instr, 1964-67; Vassar NY, choreographyperformance under Mary Jean Corvele 1965-68; Dance W Conn State Col, profdance workshops, instr, 1967-; Dancers of Faith, performer, 1971-72. **Orgs:** Asn Ment Health; Am Asn Health Phys Educ & Recreation; Nat Teachers Asn; Univ Prof Women; Music Fedn Inc.

LIPSCOMBE, DR. WENDELL R. See Obituaries section.

LISTER, ALTON LAVELLE
Basketball coach, basketball player. **Personal:** Born Oct 1, 1958, Dallas, TX; married Elaine; children: J Ross & Alton. **Educ:** Ariz State Univ, attended 1981. **Career:** Basketball player (retired), basketball coach; USA Olympic Basketball team, 1980; Milwaukee Bucks, ctr-forward, 1981-86, 1994-95; Seattle Super Sonics, 1987-89; Golden State Warriors, 1990-93; Boston Celtics,1995-97; Portland Trailblazers, 1997-98; Mesa Community Col, mens basketball coach, ABCD Reebok camp, coach, 2006; Coach, San Miguel Beermen, 2008-. **Special Achievements:** First round pick, 21, NBA Draft, 1981. **Business Addr:** Skills Coach, San Miguel Beermen.

LISTER, DAVID ALFRED
School administrator, educator. **Personal:** Born Oct 19, 1939, Somerset, NJ; son of James Lister and Etoile Johnson Lister; married Anita Louise Browne, Dec 29, 1962; children: Mimi & Gigi **Educ:** Cent State Univ, BA, 1962; Stetson Univ Col Law, JD, 1977. **Career:** Johns Hopkins Med Inst, dir affirmative action 1978-79; Univ Mass Med Ctr, assoc vice chancellor, 1979-82; Ins Int Educ, dir personnel, 1982-86; Fairleigh Dickinson Univ, univ dir & human resources, 1986-87, asst vpres admin, 1987-88; Univ Med & Dent NJ, vpres, human resources, 1988-94; Jersey City Med Ctr, vpres human resources, 1994-99; vpres human resources St Peter's Univ Hosp, 1999-2001; Detroit (Mich) Pub Schs, dep chief exec officer human resources, 2001-. **Orgs:** President's adv Comn, Morgan State Univ, 1978; Nat Asn Advan Colored People Soc Human Resources Adminr; Col & Univ Personnel Asn; Alpha Phi Alpha Fraternity Inc; bd mem, chmn Program Comm, mem Exec Comm, Community Newark Pvt Indust Coun; Am Asn Affirmative Action; Int Personnel Mgt Asn; Am Mgt Asn; Am Hospital Asn; Am Compensation Asn; Asn Hosp Personnel Adminr; NJ Col & Univ Personnel Asn; NJ Asn Hosp Personnel Adminr; Greater Newark Chamber Com; Urban League; Cent State Univ Alumni Asn. **Business Phone:** (313)494-1810.

LISTER, VALERIE LYNN
Writer. **Personal:** Born Jun 21, 1961, Niagara Falls, NY; daughter of Espinetta Griffin Dorsey and Valentine Jonathan Dorsey. **Educ:** Univ Texas at El Paso, El Paso, TX, BA, 1983. **Career:** Athens Daily News, Athens, GA, sports writer, 1984; Pensacola News Journal, Pensacola, FL, sports writer, 1984-88; USA Today, Arlington, VA, sports writer, 1988-. **Orgs:** Member, Natl Assn of Black Journalists, 1987-; steering committee, NABJ Sports Task Force, 1989-; regional director, Assn of Women in Sports Media 1990-; mem, Delta Sigma Theta Sorority Inc, 1982-. *

LISTER, WILLA M
Executive. **Personal:** Born Jan 16, 1940, Charleston, SC; daughter of Willie Coaxum Sr (deceased) and Beatrice Coaxum; married Venice. **Educ:** Dillard Univ, BA, 1962; N Tex State Univ, MEd 1978; E Tex State A & M Com TX; Kennedy-Western Univ **Career:** New Orleans Sch, phys educ teacher, 1962-63; Ft Worth Sch, teacher, 1964-73; Highland Park YWCA, ballet & modern dance instr, 1964-71; Community Action Agency, activities dir 1967-70; Episcopal Found Youth, dir Top Teens Tune, 1968-7[illegible] City Ft Worth, personnel analyst training div HRD, 1986-88, asst city mgr, 1989-90, human serv admin, 1990-91; Lone Star Auctioners Inc, onsite mgr & assets shipping staff, currently. **Orgs:** Pres, Delta Sigma Theta Sor Ft Worth Chapter, 1966-67; Astr

Rangers Riding Club, 1980-; Nat Forum Black Pub Admin, 1990-; secy, Tarrant County Youth Collaboration, 1991-93; bd mem, Am Heart Asn, 1991-94; pres, US Conf Human Serv Officials; Tex Asn Comm Action Agencies; bd dir, Meals Wheels; policy adv bd, State Tex Weatherization; Ft Worth Comm Develop Fund. **Honors/Awds:** Henry Armstrong Award, Col Sr Dillard Univ, 1962. **Home Addr:** 4008 Freshfield Rd, Fort Worth, TX 76119. **Business Addr:** Onsite Auctions Office Manager, Assets Shipping Staff, Lone Star Auctioneers Inc, 4629 Mark IV Pkwy, Fort Worth, TX 76106, **Business Phone:** (817)740-9400.

LITTLE, BENILDE ELEASE
Writer. **Personal:** Born Jan 1, 1958?, Newark, NJ; daughter of Matthew Little and Clara; married Clifford Virgin III, Jun 13, 1992; children: Baldwin & Ford. **Educ:** Howard Univ, BA, Jour, 1981; Northwestern Univ, Grad Sch, 1982. **Career:** The Star Ledger, reporter, 1982-85; People Magazine, reporter, 1985-89; Essence Magazine, sr editor, 1989-91; author: Book Good Hair, National Bestseller, 75,000 copies; Los Angeles Times, One of 10 Best Books, Good Hair, 1996; The Itch, Simon & Schuster, 1998, Acting Out, 2003; Who Does She Think She Is?, 2005. **Honors/Awds:** Go On Girl Book Club, National Best New Author, 1996; NAACP Image Award, Finalist, 1996.

LITTLE, BRYAN
Physician. **Personal:** Married. **Educ:** Univ of Michigan, BS, 1994; Wayne State Univ, MD, 1998; a resident orthopedic surgeon from Northwestern Univ. **Career:** Senior attending staff surgeon of the Department of Orthopedics at Henry Ford Hospital, 2004-09, Orthopedic surgeon, DMC Detroit Receiving Hospital, 2009-. **Special Achievements:** Minority Peer Advisor to 1500 students at the Univ of MI; won full tuition scholarships for both his undergraduate and medical school education; made presentations to the Am Assoc of Hip and Knee Surgeons; published research. **Business Addr:** Detroit Receiving Hospital, 4201 St. Antoine, Detroit, MI 48201.*

LITTLE, GENERAL T.
Physician. **Personal:** Born Sep 10, 1946, Wadesboro, NC; married Barbara McConnell; children: Christopher, Adrienne, Kimberly. **Educ:** NC A&T State Univ, BS, 1967; Meharry Med Col, MD, 1971; Walter Reed Gen Hosp, attended 1975. **Career:** Cardio-Pulmonary Assoc Charleston, md; Kimbrough AUS Hosp, chief internal med, 1975-76; Am Bd Internal Med, dipl, Pvt Pratice, currently. **Orgs:** Nat Med Assoc; consult, internal med Sea Island Health Care Corp, 1976-77; Am Soc Internal Med; bd trustees, Charleston Co Hosp; bd trustees, Charleston Area Ment Health Bd; Omega Psi Phi Frat Inc. **Military Serv:** USMC, major, 1971-76. **Business Addr:** 280 Rutledge Ave, Charleston, SC, **Business Phone:** (843)722-6336.*

LITTLE, HANNAH. See BERRY, HALLE M.

LITTLE, HERMAN KERNEL
School administrator, county government official. **Personal:** Born Jan 25, 1951, Wadesboro, NC; son of Margie and Bryant; married H Patricia; children: Kentrell & Karlton. **Educ:** Anson Tech Col, AAS, acct, 1980, AAS, retailing & mkt, 1980; Wingate Col, BA, Bus Admin Mgt, 1984. **Career:** Anson Tech Col, asst proj dir 1977-83, proj dir 1983-, ed admin; Anson County Govt, Bd Commissioners, chmn, currently. **Orgs:** Bd dir Morven Area Med Ctr, 1978-, Anson City Red Cross, 1978-; NC Community Col Adult Ed Assoc, 1978-; bd dir, Anson County, Bd Adjustment, 1980; Anson County Waste Mgt Bd, 1981-; Savannah AME Zion Church, 1982-; Am Soc Personnel Admin, 1982-; pres, Polit Action Community Concerned Citizens, 1982-; Anson County Young Dem Party, 1982-83; Phi Beta Lambda Wingate Col, 1982-; Grace Sr Ctr Adv Coun 1983-; Anson County Personnel Assoc, 1983-; bd dir, Anson County Art's Coun, 1984-; PDCOG Emergency Med Serv Adv, 1984-; elected first black Anson County Comnr 1986; Anson Counnty Health Bd, 1987; bd mem, NC United Way, 1991; bd mem, Sandhills Ctr Area, 2003-. **Honors/Awds:** Governor's Vol Award, State NC, 1983; Outstanding Service Award, 1991; President's Award, Anson County United Way, 1991; Outstanding American Award. **Military Serv:** USAF, E-4, 1972-77; NDSM, AFOUA, AFLSA, AFGCM, AFM 900-3. **Home Phone:** (704)848-8165. **Business Addr:** Chairman, Anson County Government, Board Of Commissioners, 114 N Greene St, Wadesboro, NC 28170, **Business Phone:** (704)994-2676.

LITTLE, IRENE PRUITT
Government official. **Personal:** Born Feb 9, 1946, Aliceville, AL; daughter of Bill and Ruth Wade; widowed; children: Christopher Sean Little & Shana Nicole Little Dawson. **Educ:** Wellesley Col, 1965; Stillman Col, BA, educ, 1967; Univ Md, MS, pub admin, 2000. **Career:** Government official (retired); Social Security Admin, personnel mgt specialist, 1972-77; US Customs, sr labor rels specialist, 1977-80;Environ Protection Agency, Off Civil Rights, dir, 1980-82, asst toregional admin, 1982-87; US Nuclear Regulatory Comn (NRC), regional personnel dir, 1987-89, dir resource mgt & admin, 1989-96, Off Small Bus & Civil Rights, dir, 1997-2003. **Orgs:** Chicago Fed Recruitment Coun, 1972-90; vpres, 1986-89, mem, 1998-, Blacks Govt; NAACP; pres, 1998-99, treas, 2000-, DC Metro Chap, Stillman Col Alumni; trustee, 1999-2000, pastoral search comm, 2000-, Resurrection Baptist Church; Nat Alumni Asn Stillman Col, Souther Region vpres, currently. **Honors/Awds:** Meritorious Service Award for Equal Employment Opportunity, NRC, 1989;Outstanding Contribution to Higher Education, NAFEO, 1990; Outstanding Client Award, GSA, 1994; Outstanding Alumnus, Stillman Col, 2000; Presidential Meritorious Executive Rank Award, 2003.

LITTLE, LEONARD ANTONIO
Football player. **Personal:** Born Oct 19, 1974, Asheville, NC. **Educ:** Univ Tenn, psy chol. **Career:** St Louis Rams, linebacker, 1998-. **Honors/Awds:** Super Bowl champion (XXXIV), All-Pro selection, 2003; Pro Bowl selection, 2003, 2006. **Business Addr:** Defensive End, St Louis Rams, 1 Rams Way, Saint Louis, MO 63045, **Business Phone:** (314)982-7267.

LITTLE, MONROE HENRY
Educator. **Personal:** Born Jun 30, 1950, St Louis, MO; married Shelia Maria Josephine Parks; children: Alexander. **Educ:** Denison Univ, BA, 1971; Princeton Univ, MA, 1973, PhD, 1977. **Career:** Mass Inst Technol, instr, 1976-77, asst prof, 1977-80; Ind Univ-Purdue Univ, Indianapolis, from asst prof to assoc prof, 1980-81, dir african am studies prog, 1981-, Sch Liberal Arts, assoc prof hist, currently; US Dept Labor, CSR Inc, consult, 1981. **Orgs:** Fel Rockefeller Fel Afro-Am Studies, 1972-75; Am Hist Asn; Orgn Am Historians; Nat Urban League; Study Afro-Am Life & Hist; consult, Educ Develop Ctr, 1980; consult, Black Women Mid-West Proj, Purdue Univ, 1983. **Honors/Awds:** Elected Omicron Delta Kappa Men's Leadership Hon, 1971. **Business Addr:** Associate Professor, Indiana University School of Liberal Arts, Department of History, 425 Univ Blgd Cavanaugh Hall 441 CA 503C, Indianapolis, IN 46202, **Business Phone:** (317)274-0098.

LITTLE, REUBEN R.
Manager, teacher. **Personal:** Born Sep 1, 1933; married Margaret Jean Davis. **Educ:** Alabama A&M, BS, 1957; Univ Texas, grad study 1963; Kansas State Univ, attended 1964; Western Il Univ, attended 1965; Indiana Univ, MSS, 1966. **Career:** Retired: DHHS & SSA, Meridian MS, oper supvr, cur; DHEW & SSA, Tuscaloosa AL, mgt trainee, 1974-75; tchr admin, jr high sch level; Neighborhood Youth Corp Prog, dir; Bonita EDUc Ctr, tchr, social studies, 1995-. **Orgs:** Nat Bus League 1970; NAACP, 1968; Nat Coun Geography Tchrs, 1964; Nat Assoc New York City Dirs, 1970; vol Youth Court Coun, 1972; EEO Assoc, 1970; lay minister trustee chmn Bd of Elders Good Shepherd Luthern Ch Meridan MS; Kappa Alpha Psi, 1954; Rescue Lodge 439 3rd Deg Mason, 1958; IBPO Elk W, 1960; charter mem, Cloverleaf Toastmaster Club, 1967; past pres & area gov, Toastmasters Intl, 1973-74; Choctaw Area Coun BSA, 1965; div chmn, Lauderdale Co March of Dimes 1968-70; Central Meridian Optimist Club, pres, charter mem, 1984, past pres, 1990-91; past pres, bod, retired sr volunteer program, 1990-; pres, Meridian Area Toastmasters, 1989-93, Area VI Governor, 1985-86-; Zoning Bd, City Meridian, 1978-92; past chmn, Lauderdale Coun Planning & Airport Zoning CMS, 1992-; life mem, NAACP; pres, Sandwedge Golfers Asn, Meridian, 1982-92-; finance com Meridale Girl Scouts; AL and MS Dist, past lt governor; pub Official, elected Election Comn, Dist 4, 1994-. **Honors/Awds:** Recipient, Leadership Award, Outstanding Achievement Toastmasters, 1969; Hall of Fame Award, 1973; Keyman Toastmasters, 1974; Able Toastmaster, 1974; Recipient, NAACP, Man of the Year Award, 1990; Distinguished Service Award, RSVP, 1989; Superior Performance Award, SSA, 1988-91; Outstanding Club Award, PRS, optimist, 1990. **Business Addr:** Teacher, Bonita Educ Ctr, 730 Oak Dr, Meridian, MS 39301, **Business Phone:** (601)484-5696.*

LITTLE, ROBERT BENJAMIN
Physician. **Personal:** Born Apr 25, 1955, Dublin, GA; son of William Albert and Druzy Perry. **Educ:** Morehouse Col, BS, 1977; Meharry Med Col, MD, 1982. **Career:** Harlem Hosp, internship & residency, gen surg, 1983-85; US Navy, gen med officer, 1986-89; Morehouse Med Sch, Atlanta, Ga, family med intern, resident, 1989-92, chief resident, 1991-92; Family Med & Emergency Med, independent contractor, 1992-. **Orgs:** Am Acad Family Physicians; Am Med Asn; Am Col Emergency Physicians; Asn Emergency Physicians; Am Med Stud Asn; Atlanta Med Asn; Ga State Med Asn; Am Asn Physician Specialists. **Honors/Awds:** Bd Certification, Family Med, 1992. **Military Serv:** USN, lt cmdr, 1986-89; Sharp Shooters Medal 1988. **Business Addr:** Physician, 225 Canaan Glen Way SW, Atlanta, GA 30331.*

LITTLE, ROBERT E
President (Organization), public speaker. **Career:** Relde Publ LLC, founder; Solutions Training & Develop LLC, pres, currently. **Orgs:** Bd dirs, Toastmasters Intl; Am Soc Training & Develop; Nat Speakers Asn. **Honors/Awds:** Cert Pub Speaker, Nat Speakers Asn. **Special Achievements:** Auth: Spoken Success: Understanding The Art Of Public Speaking. **Business Addr:** President, Solutions Training & Development LLC, 931 Hwy 80 W Suite 218-C, PO Box 21304, Jackson, MS 39289, **Business Phone:** (601)968-9052.

LITTLE, RONALD EUGENE
Surgeon, educator. **Personal:** Born Jun 29, 1937, Chicago, IL; married Jane Mclemore; children: Ronald Jr, Kevin, Bryan & Jennifer. **Educ:** Wayne State Univ, BS 1965; Howard Univ Col Med, MD 1970. **Career:** Wayne State Univ, orthoped Surgeon clinical instr, 1975-. **Orgs:** Am Acad Orthop Surgeons, 1977; AMA; Nat Med Asn; Mich State Med Soc; Wayne County Med Soc; Detroit Med Soc; Am Bd Orthop Surgeon; Detroit Acad Orthoped Surgeons; Alpha Omega Alpha Hon Med Frat. **Military Serv:** AUS, spec 4, 1955-58. **Business Addr:** Physician, Wayne State University, 5700 Cass Ave 3100 Acad Admin Bldg, Detroit, MI 48202.

LITTLEJOHN, BILL C.
Judge, business owner. **Personal:** Born Jan 25, 1944, Gaffney, SC; son of Elviry Geter; married Gail A Hodge; children: Erica A, Shai A & Eric. **Educ:** Cent State Univ, BS, acct, 1969; Ohio Northern Law Univ, JD, 1972; Payne Theol Sem. **Career:** Montgomery County Pub Defender, criminal defense atty, 1974-75; City Dayton, prosecutor, 1975-76, traffic court referee, 1978-80, actg judge, 1978-91; Austin, Jones, Little john & Owens, trial atty, 1980-85; Littlejohn & Littlejohn, pres, 1985-91; State Ohio Munic Ct Dayton Municipality, judge, 1991-; North River Coffee House & Eatery LLC, owner, currently. **Orgs:** Nat Bus League, bd mem, 1985-, regional vpres, 1986, treas, 1990-93; bd mem, Pvt Indust Coun, 1985; chmn bd, Cent State Univ, Gleksto Inc, 1986; pres, Neighborhoods USA, 1986; 32 Degree Prince Hall Mason; distinguished pres, Optimist Int; bd mem, United Cerebral Palsy Found. **Honors/Awds:** Wrote a column for media on entertainment law; Young Republican of the Year, State of Ohio, 1978; Over 100 awards & certificates. **Military Serv:** AUS, First lt, 1966-75. **Home Phone:** (937)275-8825. **Business Addr:** Owner, North River Coffee House & Eatery LLC, 323 Salem Ave, Dayton, OH 45402, **Business Phone:** (937)226-1532.

LITTLEJOHN, DONNA M.
Association executive. **Career:** Women Color Found & Health Ministries Inc, founder, 2001-. **Business Phone:** (248)569-3532.

LITTLEJOHN, DR. EDWARD J.
Educator, lawyer. **Personal:** Born May 5, 1935, Pittsburgh, PA; son of Chester W Littlejohn and Crystal; divorced; children: Martin & Victor. **Educ:** Wayne State Univ, BA, 1965; Detroit Col Law, JD (cum laude), 1970; Columbia Univ Law Sch, LLM, 1974, JSD, 1982. **Career:** City Detroit, varied govt serv, 1959-70; Detroit Col Law, asst prof,1970-72; Wayne State Law Sch, assoc prof & asst dean, 1972-76, assoc dean& prof law, 1976-78, prof law 1972-96, prof emer law, 1996-; Univ UtrechtNeth, vis prof, 1974; Wayne State Ctr Black Studies, fac res assoc; DamonJ Keith Law Collection & Archive, founder. **Orgs:** Chmn, Bd Police Comners Detroit, 1977-78; Mich Bar Asn; NBA; ABA; Wolverine Bar Asn; Alpha Phi Alpha; ed bd, Urban Educr & the Compleat Lawyer; hearing officer, Mich Dept Civil Rights; consult, Police Civil Liability & Citizen Complaints; reporter, Am Bar Assoc; Mich Comt Juvenile Justice, 1987-90; Task force Minorities Legal Prof; Mich Correctional Officers, training coun, 1990-93; trustee, Kurdish Mus & Library NY, 1990-96; chmn, City Detroit Bd Ethics, 1994-97; Arts Comn, City Detroit, 2000-01. **Honors/Awds:** Charles Evans Hughes Fellow, Columbia Univ Law Sch, 1973-74; WEB Dubois Scholarship Award, Phylon Soc, Wayne State Univ, 1986; Special Alumni Award, Wolverine Student Bar Asn, Detroit Col Law, 1986; Trailblazer Award, Wolverine Bar Asn, 1988; Black Educator of 1991 (MI & Ohio), Detroit Peace Corps; Alumni Faculty Service Award, Wayne State Univ AlumniAsn, 1991; DH Gordon Excellence in Teaching Award, Alumni & Friends Law Sch, 1994; Champion of Justice Award, State Bar Mich, 1995; Dr Alain Locke Award, Detroit Inst Arts Founders Soc, Friends African-Am Art, 1997. **Military Serv:** AUS, 1957-59. **Business Addr:** Professor of Law Emeritus, Wayne State University, Law School, 471 W Palmer St, Detroit, MI 48202, **Business Phone:** (313)577-2424.

LITTLEJOHN, JOHN B.
Government official. **Personal:** Born Mar 17, 1942, Chicoda, TX; son of Hattie Brown and J B Littlejohn; divorced; children: Cheryl Ann & David Alan. **Educ:** Dodge City Col, AA, 1958; Kans State Univ, BS, 1961; Kans Univ, MSW Cand. **Career:** Marin Tractor Co, dir pub affairs, 1973-78; urban renewal negotiator1972-74; Topeka Corrugated Container Corp, owner, vpres, gen mgr 1970-73;Greater Topeka C of C, div mgr 1969-70; Juvenile Ct, chief counr, 1964-69;Topeka Upward Bound, guidance dir, 1968-69; State Banking Bd, dir,1976-81; Blue Cross/Blue Shield, adv bd; Mental Health Prog Kans, advcoun; Topeka Club, dir; Greenbay Packers, player, 1961; 52nd Dist, staterep, 1976-81. **Orgs:** Chmn bd, Topeka Boy's Club, 1976-; dir, YMCA; co-founder, Big Bro/ Big Sister; co-founder, The Villages Inc; dir, Topeka United Way. **Honors/Awds:** Football All-Am, 1957-58; all big 8 hon mention, 1959; outstanding young man of America, 1970-71. **Military Serv:** AUS, sp 5, 1961-64. **Home Addr:** 2730 SW Logito Dr, Topeka, KS 66614, **Home Phone:** (785)478-9124. **Business Addr:** Senior Specialist, US Department of Housing & Urban Development, 400 State Ave Gateway Tower II Room 400, Kansas City, KS 66101-2406, **Business Phone:** (913)551-5594.

LITTLEJOHN, JOSEPH PHILLIP
School administrator. **Personal:** Born Aug 31, 1937, Hackensack, NJ; divorced; children: Mavis & Marc. **Educ:** Rutgers Univ, BS,

sociol, 1960; NY Univ, MPA, 1972; Lancaster Ctr Mediation, Lancaster, Pa, cert. **Career:** Sch Administrator (retired); Steward AFB, NY, equal employ office, officer & fed women prog coord, 1968-70; Nat Asn Advan Colored People, NY, asst dir housing prog, 1970; Inter-religious Found for Comm Organ Amilcar Cabral Inst, asst dir for admins, 1972-73; Nat Coun Churches, coord, 1973; NY Human Resources Admin, prog mgr, 1973-75; Jersey City State Col, dir affirmative action, 1975-78; Fairleigh Dickinson Univ, dir affirmative action, 1978-87; NJ Dept Trasp, Trenton, dir civil rights compliance, 1987-88; Shawnee Develop Corp, PA, sales, owner rep, 1988-92; Pa Legal Servs, Harrisburg, dir, human resources & cultural div, 1992-96; Hudson Valley Community Col, Troy, NY, asst to pres affirmative action & human resources develop. **Orgs:** Bd dirs, Orange County United Fund, 1968-71; bd dirs, Jersey City Br Nat Asn Advan Colored People, 1977-83; bd dirs, Hudson Co Opportunities Indust Ctr, 1978-82; vpres, Am Asn Affirmative Action, 1984-; consult, Nat Urban League, NY; consult, Newburgh Community Action Agency; consult, United Church Christ, NY; consult, Nat Asn advan Colored People, NY; consult, Seton Hall Univ, Orange, NJ; consult, AT & T Bell Lab, Whippany, NJ; consult, Southern Col Technol, Marietta, GA; consult, Ron Jackson Assoc, Harrisburg, PA; One Hundred Black Men Albany; adv comt, Greater Harrisburg United Negro Col Fund; Unity Coalition Poconos. **Honors/Awds:** Student Council, Rutgers Univ, 1958-60; Martin Luther King Scholarship NY Univ, 1969. **Military Serv:** AUS, signal corps, 1960-68. **Home Addr:** 66 Madison Ave, Jersey City, NJ 07304.

LITTLEJOHN, SAMUEL GLEASON
School administrator, school principal. **Personal:** Born Sep 4, 1921, Gaffney, SC; son of Cleo and Mamie Gleason; married Juanita Price, Aug 6, 1946 (died 2008); children: Samuel G Jr. **Educ:** A&T State Univ, Greensboro, NC, BS, MS, 1942; Appalachian State Univ, Educ Specialist Degree, 1974. **Career:** School principal (retired); Richmond Co Sch, prin; city coun, 1972-77; pro-tem, mayor, 1973-74. **Orgs:** Past master Masonic Order; Nat Asn Advan Colored People; dir, NC Teachers Asn; NC Educ Asn; NC Prins Asn; dir, Scotland Mem Hosp; dir, Laurinburg-Maxton Airport; dir, United Way; NEA; chmn, Scotland Co Br Nat Asn Advan Colored People, 1959-69; pres, Richmond County Teachers Asn, 1959-65, 1967-69; dist pres, Dist 8 NC Educ Asn, 1972-74. **Home Addr:** 218 Ctr St, Laurinburg, NC 28352, **Home Phone:** (910)276-0393. *

LITTLEPAGE, CRAIG
Administrator, athletic coach. **Personal:** Born Aug 5, 1951, LaMott, PA; married Margaret Murray; children: Erica, Murray & Erin. **Educ:** Univ Pa, Wharton Bus Sch, BA, econs, 1973. **Career:** Univ Va, asst coach, 1967-82, asst coach, 1976-82, asst basketball coach, 1988-90; asst athletic dir, 1990-91; assoc athletic dir progs, 1991-95; sr assoc dir athletics, 1995-2001; athletic dir, 2001-; Villanova Univ, asst coach, 1973-75; Yale Univ, asst coach, 1975-76; Univ Pa, head coach, 1982-85; Rutgers Univ, head coach, 1985-88. **Orgs:** Univ Va Athletics Admin, 1990-; NCAA Div I Infractions Comn; Reinstatement Subcomt, 1999-2000; head, NCAA Men's Div I Basketball Comt, 2006. **Honors/Awds:** Athletics Administrator of the Year, Black Coaches Asn, 2003. **Special Achievements:** The first African-American athletics director in Atlantic Coast Conference history; 101 most influential minorities in sports in 2003 & 2004; Named as one of Black Enterprise Magazine's Most Powerful African-Americans in Sports. **Business Addr:** Athletic Director, University of Virginia, McCue Ctr, PO Box 400846, Charlottesville, VA 22904-4835, **Business Phone:** (434)982-5106.

LITTLE RICHARD (RICHARD WAYNE PENNIMAN)
Entertainer, singer. **Personal:** Born Dec 5, 1932, Macon, GA; son of Bud Penniman and Leva Mae Penniman; married Ernestine Campbell, 1959 (divorced 1961). **Educ:** Oakwood Col, Huntsville, AL. **Career:** Performing & recording artist, 1948-57, 1960-76, 1986-; albums: Here'sv Little Richard, 1958; The Fabulous Little Richard, 1959; Little Richard Sings Freedom Songs, 1964; King of Gospel Songs, 1965; Little Richard's Greatest Hits, 1972; Shut Up!: A Collection of Rare Tracks, 1951-64, 1988; Little Richard: Specialty Sessions, 1990; TV: "Merv Griffin"; "The Tonight Show"; "Midnight Special, Rock 'n' Roll Revival", 1975; "Night Dreams", 1975; "Dinah", 1976; "Tomorrow", 1976; "Mother Goose Rock 'n' Rhyme", 1990; "Las Vegas", 2004; Arsenio Hall Show; appeared at Radio City Music Hall, 1975; church soloist; Black Heritage Bible, salesman, 1977; Universal Remnant Church of God, minister; performer in traveling medicine show; films: Rock Around the Clock, 1956; The Girl Can't Help It, 1956; MrRock 'n' Roll, 1974; Down & Out in Beverly Hills, 1986; Last Action Hero, 1993; The Trumpet of the Swan, voice, 2001; Hit Singles include"Tutti-Frutti", 1955; "Long Tall Sally," 1956; "Slippin' & Slidin', " 1956; "Rip It Up, " 1956; "The Girl Can't Help It, " 1957; "Lucille, " 1957; "Jenny, Jenny," 1957; "Keep a Knockin', " 1957; "Good Golly, Miss Molly,"1958; Celebrity Duets, judge, 2007. **Honors/Awds:** Charter mem, Rock & Roll Hall Of Fame; received star Hollywood Walk of Fame, 1990; Little Richard Day recognition from Mayor Tom Bradley, Los Angeles, 1990; Grammy Lifetime Achievement Award, 1993; Am Soc Young Musicians, Rock & Roll Pioneer Award; Song writers Hall of Fame, 2003.inducted in to Apollo Theater Legends Hall of Fame, 2006, "Tutti Frutti" topped Mojo's The Top 100 Records, 2007. **Special Achievements:** Rock and Roll Hall of Fame, 1986; Macon Convention & Visitors Bureau,named goodwill abassador to hometown, 2000; inducted into the National Association for the Advancement of Colored People Hall of Fame, 2002; inducted into the Song writers Hall of Fame, 2003; 100 Greatest Artists of All Time, Rolling Stone Magazine, 2004; Apollo Theater Legends Hall of Fame, 2007. **Business Addr:** Entertainer, c/o William Morris Agency, 151 El Camino Dr, Beverly Hills, CA 32767, **Business Phone:** (310)859-4000.

LITTLES, EUGENE SCAPE. See LITTLES, GENE.

LITTLES, GENE (EUGENE SCAPE LITTLES)
Basketball coach, basketball player. **Personal:** Born Mar 6, 2006, Washington, DC; married Loredana; children: Darren, Travis & Gino. **Educ:** High Point Col, 1969. **Career:** Basketball player (retired), Basketball Coach; ABA, player, six years; Appalachian State, asst player, 1975-77; NC A&T, head coach, 1977-79; Utah Jazz, asst coach, 1979-82; Cleveland Cavaliers, asst coach, 1982-86; Chicago Bulls, asst coach, 1986-87; Charlotte Hornets, asst coach, 1987; Denver Nuggets, asst head coach, interim coach, 1994-95; coach, currently. **Orgs:** Bd trustees, High Point Univ.

LITTLES, DR. JAMES FREDERICK, JR.
Physician. **Personal:** Born Nov 7, 1960, Florence, SC; son of James and Ella; married Barbara Moultrie, Jun 15, 1985; children: Jessica & Elena. **Educ:** SC State Univ, BS, 1982; Howard Univ, MD, 1986. **Career:** Univ Mich, Med Sch, clinic instr, 1990-; Veterans Affairs Med Ctr, chief, radiation oncol serv, 1991; Midland Bay Radiation Oncol Assocs, chief, radiation oncol dept, currently. **Orgs:** One Hundred Black Men of Greater Detroit; Dipl Am Bd Radiology; NAACP; South Carolina State Univ Alumni Asn; MI Soc Therapeutic Radiol; Straight Gate Church, deacon. **Special Achievements:** The First African-American Faculty Member, Dept Radiation Oncol, Univ Mich, Med Sch; The First African-American Clinical Service Chief, Veterans Affairs Med Ctr, Ann Arbor, MI. **Home Addr:** 170 Camelot Dr Suite P7, Saginaw, MI 48603-6426. **Business Addr:** Chief, Radiation Oncology Service, Midland Bay Radiation Oncology Associates, P.C., 3180 E Midland Rd, Bay City, MI 48706, **Business Phone:** (989)667-6670.*

LITTLETON, DR. ARTHUR C.
Psychologist. **Personal:** Born Sep 25, 1942, St Louis, MO; married Paula; children: Stephen, David, Jeffrey & Dennis. **Educ:** Univ Mo, BA, 1962, MEd, 1963; St Louis Univ, PhD, 1969. **Career:** Univ Mo, St Louis, instr, 1968-69, asst prof ed, res psychol, 1969-71; Urban Behavioral Res Assoc, pres, currently; Littleton & Assoc, pres, currently. **Orgs:** Chmn, Black Caucus Am Ed Res Assoc, 1972; bd mem, Bi State Transit Agency. **Honors/Awds:** Co-author "Black Viewpoints"; contrib articles in various scholarly jour. **Business Addr:** President, Littleton & Associates, 1900 Locust St Suite101, St Louis, MO 63103, **Business Phone:** (314)421-4470.

LIVELY, IRA J.
Real estate agent. **Personal:** Born Apr 18, 1926, Memphis, TN; children: Illona D Threadgill Jones. **Educ:** Monterey Peninsula Col, AS, 1970; Golden Gate Univ, attended 1974, MA, 1978. **Career:** Seaside Police Dept, juvenile officer, 1956-82; MPC & Gavilan Col, instr, 1972-; Bell's Real Estate, realtor assoc, 1984-; Seaside City Coun, coun mem, mayor proterm, 1986-88; Monterey Peninsula Unified Sch Dist, sch bd mem, realtor asn; Univ Nev, Las Vegas, fac. **Orgs:** Pres, Monterey Peninsula Unified Sch Dist, 1982-84; notary public Bell's Real Estate 1984-. **Honors/Awds:** Officer of the Year, Seaside Amer Legion, 1971. **Special Achievements:** First black female officer in the Seaside Police Department 1956.

LIVERPOOL, CHARLES ERIC
Financial manager. **Personal:** Born Mar 14, 1946, Ann's Grove Village, Guyana; son of Ivy Thomas (deceased) and Eric C (deceased); married Joan Ann Paddy; children: Charles Jr, Dionne, Euisi & Jamal. **Educ:** Bronx Community Col, AA, 1978; Bernard M Baruch Col, BBA, 1982; LongIsland Univ, attended 1988; Cent Mich Univ, MSA, 1995. **Career:** Navy Resale Serv Support Off, acct/liab ins asst, 1974-83, prog analyst,1980-86; HQ 77th US Army Res Command, budget analyst, 1986-89; Fulton County Govt, Atlanta, GA, financial budget eval specialist, 1990-. **Orgs:** Educ vpres & secy, Navresso Toastmasters #2285, 1978-82; vice chmn & supv comn, 1980-85, mem bd dirs, 1985-89, CGA Fed Credit Union Brooklyn, NY;literacy vol tutor, Queens Boro Pub Lib, 1984-89; mem, NY Urban League,1985-89; mem, Nat Black MBA Asn, 1986-; prog comt mem/tutor support coordr, Literacy Vol Am, 1990-; mem, Am Asn Budget & Prog Anal, 1994-. **Special Achievements:** Author/Publisher: A Brother's Soul: Writings of a Country Boy-Poetry, 1992; Another Days Journey-Poetry, 1996. **Military Serv:** AUS, res master sgt, 17 yrs; Army Res Components Achievement Medal, 1979; Meritorious Service Medal, 1988, 1989. **Home Addr:** 424 Orchards Walk, Stone Mountain, GA 30087. **Business Addr:** Financial Budget Evaluation Specialist, Fulton County Government, 141 Pryor St, Atlanta, GA 30303-3453, **Business Phone:** (404)730-4000.*

LIVERPOOL, HERMAN OSWALD
Clergy. **Personal:** Born Feb 12, 1925, Georgetown, Guyana; son of Joseph Nathaniel and Hilda Beatrice Hinds; married Lucille Joycelyn Cleaver, Jun 1, 1953; children: Lorraine Janet, James Nathaniel, Lynda Alethea. **Educ:** Univ London, Avery Hill Col, teacher's cert, educ, 1971; Univ West Indies, BA, theol, 1977; Intl Sem, ThM, 1985, DMin, 1990. **Career:** Clergy (retired); The Inner London Educ Authority, teacher, 1971-73; The Bishop, Anglican Diocese Guyana, clergyman, 1977-80; The Bishop, The Episcopal Diocese FLA, vicar, 1983; St Cyprian's & St Mary's Episcopal Church, vicar, 1983-96. **Orgs:** Vestry mem, St Hilda's Anglican Church, Brockley Rise, England, 1971; exec mem, COT Rels Coun, London, England, 1971-73; founder, Holy Redeemer Boy Scouts, Guyana, 1977-80; initiator, East Coast Musical Church Festival, Diocese Guyana, 1980; founder, St Cyprian's Annual Church Festival, 1984-; founder, Friends St Cyprian's, 1984; St Augustine Ministerial Alliance, 1983, pres, 1987-88; bd mem, Vicar's Landing, Life Pastoral Care Servs, 1988-91; Brotherhood St Andrews, 2000. **Honors/Awds:** Awarded symbolic gavel, St Augustine Ministerial Alliance, 1986; plaque & letter appreciation, Vicar's Landing, 1991. **Special Achievements:** A Brief History of the Anglican Church in Guyana, unpublished, 1826-70; Collection Poems, unpublished; Contributed to "Theatre of the Mind," Noble House Publishers-Poetry Division, 2003. *

LIVINGSTON, JOYCE
Librarian, educator. **Personal:** Born in Houston, TX; daughter of C W Gunnells and Jessie M McKelvey; married Ulysses (divorced); children: Deanne, Ronald & Kevin. **Educ:** Univ Southern Calif, BA, 1974, MLS, 1975. **Career:** Los Angeles County Pub Libr, Los Angeles, CA, librarian-in-charge, 1980-81; Los Angeles Trade Tech Community Col, CA, ref librn, 1980-91, Dept Libr, chairperson, 1991-, co-maker, currently. **Orgs:** Calif Black Fac & Staff Asn, 1981-; Black caucus, Calif Libr Asn, 1985-; elected mem exec bd, Am Fedn Teachers Los Angeles Community Col Dist, 1988-; Black caucus, Am Libr Asn, 1989-90; Am Libr Asn, 1989-90. **Honors/Awds:** Ford Foundation Honoree, Los Angeles Community Col Dist, Southwest Col, 1972. **Business Addr:** Co-Maker, Chairperson, Los Angeles Trade-Technical College, Department of Library Services, 400 W Washington Blvd, Los Angeles, CA 90015, **Business Phone:** (213)763-3960.

LIVINGSTON, RANDY ANTHONY
Basketball player. **Personal:** Born Apr 2, 1975, New Orleans, LA; married Tameka. **Educ:** La State Univ. **Career:** Houston Rockets, guard, 1996-97; Atlanta Hawks, free agent, 1997-98; CBA, Sioux Falls Skyforce, 1998; Phoenix Suns, 1998-2000; Golden State Warriors, 2001; Seattle Supersonics, 2002, 2007; New Orleans Hornets, 2003; Los Angeles Clippers, 2004; Utah Jazz, 2005-06; Turkish League, Galatasaray, 2005-06; Chicago Bulls, 2006; NBA Develop League, Idaho Stampede, point guard, currently. **Business Addr:** Point Guard, NBA Development League, Idaho Stampede, 233 S Capital Blvd Suite 100, PO Box 6525, Boise, ID 83702.

LIVINGSTON-WHITE, DR. DEBORAH J H (DEBI STARR-WHITE)
Educator, fashion model, consultant. **Personal:** Born Nov 21, 1947, DuQuoin, IL; daughter of Jetson Edgar and Tressie May Gaston; married Dr William Tyrone. **Educ:** Southern Ill Univ, BS, educ, 1968, MS, educ, 1971; Northern Ill Univ, EdD, admin, 1975; Mich State Univ, post-19 doctoral studies, 1982; Univ Mich, post-19doctoral studies, 1984. **Career:** Dansville Ag Schs, teacher & consult, 1976-78; Mgt Recruiters, acct exec, 1976-78; Mich Dept Educ, spec educ consult, 1978-; Mich State Univ, asst prof; Yale Univ, guest lectr, 1984-2001; Affiliated Models & Talent Agency, Full-Figure, model & actress, 1987-; Talent Shop, Oak Park Sch Dist, dir spec educ, 1987-96; E Detroit Pub Schs, dir spec educ, 1996-2000; Int Consults, People's Network's "Success Channel," pub rels, personal develop & mkt consult, motivational keynote speaker, travel agent; Inkster-Edison Pub Schs, asst supt, chief acad officer, 2000. **Orgs:** Consult & evaluator, US Dept Educ, 1979-; adv comm mem, Black Notes MSU Media Prod, 1980-83; Mich EPFP Alumni, 1980-84; pres & exec dir, Int Consult, 1981-; voc chairperson, Altrusa Int, 1982-83; regional coordr, Vols Spec Educ, 1982-; trainer, Proj Outreach MDE, 1984; founder & pres, Tressie Found; Mich Asn Artists & Songwriters, 1989-; Int Photographers Asn, 1990-; Nat Asn Black Journalists, 1990-; secy, vpres, Self-Esteem Inst, 1990-, Musicians', Entertainers', Composers' Creative ASN, 1992-; Ment Health Educ Exhibit Treas; pers, Alternative Living Positive Handicapped Adults, 1992-; Habitat Humanity fund raising comm, Detroit; chair, Archer, McNamara, Pub & Media Rels, 1995. **Honors/Awds:** Illinois Congress of Parents & Teachers Scholarship, 1968; Fresh Start Award, Self Magazine-Chrysler, 1986; International Model & Talent Award, 1987; Kids Are Special PTA Service Award, 1991. **Special Achievements:** Published "The Vicky Caruso Story, A Miracle in Process" 1979, "Use of the Optacon by Visually Impaired Persons in MI", 1980, Follow-up Study of Visually Impaired Students of the Michigan School for the Blind "Journal of Visual Impairment & Blindness", 1985, poem "Black Glass" in World's Most Cherished Poems 1985, poem "White Pearl Satin, Pink Orchid Lace" in World's Best Poets 1985, author of Lyrics From Life by Livingston-White, The Early Years 1969-89, 1991, author of Transition Life Planning: A Handbook, Oakland Schools, 1991, Transition Planning: A Manual for Students & Parents, 1995-96.

LIVINGSTON-WILSON, KAREN E
Insurance executive, lawyer. **Personal:** Married Mark Wilson. **Educ:** Univ Mich, BA, polit sci, 1979; Wayne State Univ, JD, 1983. **Career:** Citizens Ins Co Am, gen coun, 1996-98, vpres & secy; Butler, Snow, O'Mara, Stevens & Cannada, PLLC, atty, currently. **Orgs:** Am Bar Asn; Am Health Lawyers Asn; Nat Bar Asn; Nat Asn Women Lawyers; Women Lawyers Asn; Mich Bar Asn; Ohio Bar Asn; Miss Bar; Magnolia Bar Asn; Hinds County Bar Asn; mem bd dirs & exec comt, YMCA Metrop Jackson; bd trustees, Miss Mus Art; bd dirs, Bethany Christian Serv. **Special Achievements:** First woman and first African American to hold the posts of vice president, general counsel and secretary of Citizens Insurance Company of America in Howell, MI; one of 50 Leading Business Women, Mississippi Business Journal, 2007. **Business Addr:** Attorney, Butler, Snow, O'Mara, Stevens & Cannada, PLLC, 210 E Capitol St Suite 1700, Jackson, MS 39201, **Business Phone:** (601)985-4593.

LLEWELLYN, JAMES BRUCE
Executive. **Personal:** Born Jul 16, 1927, New York, NY; son of Charles and Vanessa Llewellyn; married Shahara; children: Kristen Lisa, Alexandra & JayLaan. **Educ:** City Univ New York, BS; New York Law Sch, JD, 1960; Columbia Univ, MBA; New York Univ, MPA. **Career:** Harlem Liquor Store, owner, 1952-56; New York County Dist Atty Off, stud asst, 1958-60; Evans Berger & Llewellyn, 1962-65; Housing & Redevelop Bd New York City, 1964-65; Small Bus Develop Corp, reg dir, 1965-68; New York City Housing & Develop Admin, dep comnr housing, 1967-69; Fedco Food Stoes, pres, 1969-84; Overseas Pvt Investment Corp, Wash, DC, 1978-80; Dickstein Shapiro & Marin, partner, 1982-; Philadelphia Coca-Cola Bottling Co, founder, chmn & ceo, 1985-. **Orgs:** Harlem Lawyers Asn; NY State Food Merchants; Pres, 100 Black Men Inc; past pres, Riverpoint Towers Coop; chmn bd, Freedom Nat Bank; past co-chmn, NY Interracial Coun Bus Opportunity; vpres, bd mem, Bd Fed Protestant Welfare Agencies; chmn, Bd New York Urban Coalition Venture Capital Corp; Bd New York Urban Coalition; bd dir, Flower 5th Ave Hosp; bd trustees, City Col; bd trustees, Grad Ctr City Univ, New York; dir, Am Can Co; Am Capital Mgt Res. **Honors/Awds:** Hon PhD, Wagner Col Staten Island; Hon PhD, City Univ New York; Hon PhD, Atlanta Univ. Top Black Business Owner, Black Enterprise Mag, 2001; Inducted to National African-Am Business Hall of Fame, 2003; Presidents Medal of Honor, New York Univ, 2004. **Military Serv:** US Corp Engrs, first Lt, 1944-48. **Home Phone:** (212)721-1187. **Business Addr:** Chairman, Chief Executive Officer, The Philadelphia Coca-Cola Bottling Co, 725 E Erie Ave, Pennsylvania, PA 10112, **Business Phone:** (215)427-4500.

LLEWELLYN-TRAVIS, CHANDRA
Association executive. **Personal:** Born Jun 11, 1960, New York, NY; daughter of Gilbert Metcalfe Llewellyn Sr and Jenny Cody; married Jack Travis, Sep 28, 1996; children: Sojourner Joy. **Educ:** City Univ NY-Lehman Col, BA, 1986; Norwich Univ-Vermont Col, MA, 1992; City Univ NYk-Grad Ctr, PhD cand. **Career:** NY Dept Health, health resource coord, 1984-86; Canaan Baptish Church, project dir, living consortium, 1986-89; Colonial Park Community Servs, family counr, 1986-89; Malcolm King Col, adj prof, 1989; NY Urban League, assoc & dir educ, 1989-91; The Nat Urban League, dir youth serv, 1991-95; Korea Soc, dir, intercultural outreach, 1994-97; Col New Rochelle, adj, 1997; Intercultural Outreach Korea Soc, exec dir, currently. **Orgs:** Com chair, NY Bd Educ Multicultural Task Force, 1989-91; downstate adv mem, NY State Bd Regents, 1989-91; Educ Priorities Panel, 1989-91; Tri-State Parent Adv Coun, 1992-94; bd mem, White Wave Rising, 1995-; comt mem, Intercultural Alliance, 1995-; Meml Baptist Church-AIDS Ministry, pr com chair, 1996-; Walks of Life, prof vol, 1996-; bd mem, NY Med Col, Westchester County Med Ctr. **Honors/Awds:** Awardee, Outstanding Young Women Am, 1987; Community Serv Award, Countee Cullen Sch Parent Asn, 1988; NY Bd Educ, Partner in Educ 1990; Miss Black Am, Judge, 1994; Mentorship Recognition, Walks of Life, 1998. **Special Achievements:** "The AFA Male: A Second Emancipation," co-editor, 1992; "AFA Male Immersion School: Segregation? Separation? or Innovation," proj dir, 1992; "Rap: Good? Bad? or Both?," exec producer, 1994.

LLOYD, DR. BARBARA ANN
Educator. **Personal:** Born Sep 21, 1943, Fairfield, AL; daughter of Arthur Lee (deceased) and Alberta Salley (deceased). **Educ:** Tuskegee Inst AL, BS, nursing, 1965; Univ Ala, Birmingham AL, MS, community health nursing, 1975, Tuscaloosa, AL, EdD, admin higher educ, 1986. **Career:** Educator (retired); Univ Ala Hosp, Birmingham, AL, staff nurse, 1965; Veterans Admin Hosp, Birmingham, AL, staff nurse, 1966-68; Tuskegee Inst, Tuskegee, AL, instr, 1968-70; Jefferson St Jr Col, Birmingham, AL, instr, 1970-72, Lawson State Jr Col, instr, 1972-74; Univ Ala, Birmingham, AL, instr/asst prof/assoc prof, 1975-95, Western Mental Health Ctr, Birmingham, AL, 1984-88; Fairfield City Sch, Fairfield Bd Educ, pres bd, 2004-. **Orgs:** Pres, Tuskegee Univ; Nat Nursing Alumni Asn; Kappa Delta Pi Hon Soc Educ, 1982; Sigma Theta Tau Int; Hon Soc Nursing; Chi Eta Phi Sorority Inc; Order Eastern Stars, 1983-; bd educ, Fairfield City Sch Syst, AL, 1992-97; life mem, Chi Eta Phi Sorority Inc. **Special Achievements:** Author: Articles, Journal of Gerontological Nursing, 1979; The Glowing Lamp (journal), 1980, 1989; Association of Black Nursing Faculty Journal, 1994. **Home Addr:** 204 Westmoreland Cir, Fairfield, AL 35064, **Home Phone:** (205)923-3848. **Business Addr:** President of the Board, Fairfield City Schools, Fairfield Board of Education, 6405 Ave D Fairfield, Fairfield, AL 35064, **Business Phone:** (205)783-6850.*

LLOYD, EARL FRANCIS
Basketball player, basketball coach. **Personal:** Born Apr 3, 1928, Alexandria, VA. **Educ:** WVa State Col, attended 1950. **Career:** Basketball player (retired), basketball coach; Wash Capitols, 1950-51; Syracuse Nat, 1952-58; Detroit Pistons, 1958-59, asst coach, 1968-70, head coach, 1971-73; Detroit Public Schs, job-placement adminr; Bing Steel, Detroit, community liaison work. **Honors/Awds:** All-Time CIAA All-Tournament team; CIAA Hall of Fame; CIAA's 50 Greatest Players; Player of the Decade, CIAA, 1947-56; NAIA Golden AnniversaryTeam; inducted, Basketball Hall of Fame, 2003; named to the NAIA Silver and Golden Anniversary Teams. **Special Achievements:** First African American to play in an NBA game, 1950; first African-Am towin an NBA championship, 1955; first African-Am Assitant Coach with Detroit Pistons, 1968-70; first African-Am bench coach with Detroit Pistons, 1970-71; first African-American head coach in American pro sports. **Military Serv:** AUS, 1951-52.

LLOYD, GREGORY LENARD
Football player. **Personal:** Born May 26, 1965, Miami, FL; married Rhonda; children: Gregory Lenard II, Tiana Cassandra & Jhames Isaac. **Educ:** Fort Valley State Univ. **Career:** Football player (retired); Pittsburgh Steelers, linebacker, 1988-97; Carolina Panthers, 1998. **Honors/Awds:** Pittsburgh Steelers, Ed Block Courage Award, 1988; Man of the Year Award, Pittsburgh YMCA, 1994; Defensive Player of the Year, UPI, 1994; Defensive Player of the Year, Kans City 101 Club, 1994; Five Times Pro Bowler, 1991-95; First All Team Pro Thrice, 1993-95.

LLOYD, REV. DR. J ANTHONY
Clergy, college teacher. **Personal:** Born Aug 22, 1955, Philadelphia, PA; son of James and Ruth. **Educ:** Houghton Col, BS, 1979; Gordon Conwill Theol Sem, MDiv, 1982; United Theol Sem, DMin, 1996. **Career:** Camp Ladorol, staff prog coordr, 1980; The Hillar Sch, consult, 1989-90; 12th Baptist Church, ministerial staff, 1985-92; Gordon Conwill Theol Sem, adj prof, 1990-, assoc dean students, 1982-; Greater Framingham Community Church, pastor, 1992-. **Orgs:** Alumni chapter pres, 1986-89, trustee, 1993-, Houghton Col; bd trustees, Bittnaz Hill Sch, 1995-98; bd dir, United Way, 1996-; MA/NH/RI chair comn ministry, United Baptist Conv, 1996-; conf comt, Vision NE, 1997; life time mem, NAACP, 1997; mgr search comt, Framingham Town, 1998-99. **Honors/Awds:** MLK Award in Preaching, Gordon Conwill Theol, 1982; Benjamin E Mays fellow, Benjamin E Mays Found, 1980-82; License to Preach, 12th Baptist Church, 1992; Community Award, PFI, ALPA, PSY, 1996. **Special Achievements:** Gordon Conwill, certified supervisor of ministry, 1979; Evangelical Teaching Training Research, teaching diploma, 1979; Govt of Zaire, fact finding teacher, 1989; Seminar on Evangelism, CO, instructor of Evangelism, 1981; St Thomas, Virgin Islands, missionary, 1981. **Business Addr:** Pastor, Greater Framingham Community Church, 44 Franklin St, PO Box 629, Framingham, MA 01702, **Business Phone:** (508)626-2118.

LLOYD, HON. LEONIA JANNETTA
Manager, lawyer, judge. **Personal:** Born Aug 6, 1949, Detroit, MI; daughter of Leon and Naomi. **Educ:** Wayne State Univ, BS, Education, 1971, JD, 1979. **Career:** Lloyd & Lloyd, sr law partner; Double L Mgt, partner; State Mich 36th Dist Ct, judge, currently. **Orgs:** Nat Conf Black Lawyers, 1975-79; Friends Afro-Am Museum, 1983-; Am Bar Asn; Wolverine Bar Asn; Mary McLeod Bethune Asn; Nat Asn Negro Bus & Prof Women; Asn Black Judges Mich; Nat Judicial Coun; 36th District Court's Handgun Intervention Prog. **Honors/Awds:** Scholar Bd Govs Scholar, Wayne State Univ, 1970, 1975; Cert Appreciation bestowed Mayor Coleman Young, 1977; Kizzy Image Award, 1985; Fred Hampton Image Award, 1984; IL Black Womans Hall of Fame; Black Women MI Exhibit, 1985; Nat Coalition of 100 Black Women Award, 1986; ABBS Minority Business of the Year, 1986; Wayne County Exec Community Serv Award, bestowed by William Lucas, 1986; Keep The Dream Alive Award, 1995; BNAI BRITH Award, 1993; Special Tribute, State Mich Sen Michael J OBrien, 1995; Recognition Award, Nat Assoc Drug Ct Professionals; Women of Wayne Headliner Award; Wayne County Commissioners Recognition Award; Ray of Hope Award, Guiding Light Sober Living; Spirit of Detroit Award; Allen Bray Dedication Award, Det Recovery Project, 2006; Lamplighter of the Year Award, 2007; Sojourner Truth Award, 2008; Making a Difference For Woman Award, 2009; Transformation Award, Nat Assoc Drug Ct Professionals, 2009. **Special Achievements:** The Second Best Drug Court in the Nation; negotiated recording contracts for, Arista's recording artist, "KIARA" & MCAs recording artist, "Ready for the World" & RCAs recording artists, "David Ruffin" & "Eddie Kendricks". **Business Addr:** Judge, State of Michigan District Court 36th District, 421 Madison Ave Suite 3066, Detroit, MI 48226-2358.

LLOYD, LEWIS KEVIN
Basketball player. **Personal:** Born Feb 22, 1959, Philadelphia, PA. **Educ:** Drake Univ, attended 1981. **Career:** Basketball Player (retired); Golden State Warriors, guard, 1981-83; Houston Rockets, 1984-86, 1990; Cedar Rapids, 1988-89; Philadelphia 76ers, 1989-90.

LLOYD, MARCEA BLAND
Lawyer. **Personal:** Born Oct 12, 1948, Chicago, IL; daughter of Ralph and Beatriz; children: Randy Jr, Shomari & Malaika. **Educ:** Knox Col, BS, BA, 1968; Northwestern Univ, JD, 1971. **Career:** Montgomery Wards Co, sr antitrust coun, 1974-77; Pillsbury Co, coun; Univ Minn Bus Law, asst atty, 1977-78; Medtronic Inc, int coun, 1978-83, sr legal coun, 1983-91, asst gen coun, 1991-99, vpres, 1993-99; VHA Inc, gen coun & secy, 1999-2004, group vpres, chief admin officer, gen coun, 2005-07; Amylin Pharmaceut Inc, sr vpres govt & corp affairs & gen coun, 2007-. **Orgs:** Jack & Jill Am Inc; Links Inc; dir, NBA, 1971-; Turning Point Inc Found; dir, chairperson, Exec Leadership Found; assoc, Women Bus Leaders, US Health Care Indust Found. **Home Phone:** (972)991-2508. **Business Addr:** Senior Vice President, Government & Corporate Affairs, General Counsel, Amylin Pharmaceuticals Inc, 9360 Towne Ctr Dr, San Diego, CA 92121, **Business Phone:** (858)552-2200.

LLOYD, PHIL ANDREW
Automotive executive. **Personal:** Born Jun 24, 1952, Buffalo, NY; son of Otis and Mable Spivey; divorced; children: Phil A Lloyd Jr. **Educ:** Erie Community, Buffalo, NY, AAS, 1972; Buffalo State, Buffalo, NY, BS, 1975. **Career:** Mfr Trader Trusts, Buffalo, NY, collector, 1975; Wicks Lumber, Orchard Pk, NY, sales mgr, 1976-80; Ed Mullinax Ford, Amherst, OH, salesman, 1981-86; Western Ford-Mercury, Clyde, OH, pres, 1987-. **Orgs:** Phi Beta-Lamba, 1971-73; Environ Pollution Control, 1972-73; Clyde Bus Asn, 1987-; pres, Twin City Kiwanis, 1980-81; trustee, Clyde Kiwanis, 1988-89. **Honors/Awds:** Distinguished Serv, Ford Motor, 1981-86; Salesman of the Year, Mullinas Ford, 1985; Sales Quality & Servi, Lincoln-Mercury Div, 1988; Marketshare Pacesetter, Black Ford-Lincoln Mercury Asn, 1988; Quality Commitment, Black Ford-Lincoln Mercury Asn, 1988.

LLOYD, RAYMOND ANTHONY
Physician, educator. **Personal:** Born Nov 25, 1941; married Eveline Moore; children: Raymond, Rhea & Ryan. **Educ:** Jamaica Col, 1958; Howard Univ, BS, 1962; Howard Univ Col Med, MD, 1966. **Career:** Vet Affairs Med Ctr, resident; Freedmen's Hosp, resident, 1968; Va Hosp, Children's Hosp & Nat Inst Health, fel, 1971; Howard Univ Col Med, asst prof med, 1971-; Comm Group Health Found, consult, 1971-76; Narcotics Treatment Admin, assoc admin treatment, 1972-73; Div Prevention, Nat Inst Alcoholism & Alcohol Abuse, initial rev comn, 1972. **Orgs:** DC Med Soc; Caribbean Am Intercultural Org; Nat Asn Intern & Residents; Am Med Asn; Nat Capital Med Found Inc; Am Heart Asn; Am Fedn Clinical Res; Am Prof Practice Asn; fel, Int Col Angiol; Wash Heart Asn; sub-comt, Cardiopulmonary Resuscitation; Nat Capital Med Found; sub-comt, Cardiovascular Diseases; pres, L&L Health Care Asn; adv bd, Hemisphere Nat Bank; Bata Kappa Chi, 1962; Phi Beta Kappa, 1962; Cent Tex Med Found. **Honors/Awds:** BKX Award in Chemistry, 1961; Honors in chemistry, 1962; honors in pediatrics, 1966; Daniel Hale & Williams Award. **Business Addr:** Physician, 1160 Varnum St NE Suite 117, Washington, DC 20017.

LLOYD, WANDA
Editor. **Personal:** Born Jul 12, 1949, Columbus, OH; married Willie Burk; children: Shelby Renee. **Educ:** Spelman Col, BA, 1971. **Career:** The Providence Evening Bulletin, copy ed, 1971-73; Columbia Univ, instr, 1972; The Miami Herald, copy ed, 1973-74; The Atlanta Jour, copy ed, 1974-75; The Wash Post, copy ed, 1975-76; Univ MD, instr, 1978; Los Angeles Times-WA Post News Serv, dep ed; USA Today, dep managing ed, cover stories, managing ed, Admin, sr ed & admin, sr ed/days & admin, 1986-96; The Greenville News, managing ed, 1996-2000; Freedom Forum Diversity Inst, Vanderbilt Univ, founding exec dir, 2001-04; Montgomery Advertiser, exec ed, 2004-. **Orgs:** Am Soc Newspaper Ed; Nat Asn Black Journalists; Delta Sigma Theta Sorority. **Honors/Awds:** Career Achievement Award, Columbia Univ, 2006; Robert McGruder Award for Media Diversity, 2007; Ida B Wells Award for Media Diversity; Nat Asn of Black Journalists Southeast Region Hall of Fame, 2007; Honorary Doctorate of Laws, Briarwood Col, Southington, CT. **Business Addr:** Executive Editor, Montgomery Advertiser, 425 Molton St, Montgomery, AL 36104, **Business Phone:** (334)261-1509.

LOCKARD, JON ONYE
Artist, educator, lecturer. **Personal:** Born Jan 25, 1932, Detroit, MI; son of Cecil E and Lilian Jones; divorced; children: John C, Carlton E. **Educ:** Wayne Univ, attended 1950; Fields' Sch Art, cert, 1952; Meinzinger Art Sch, cert, 1952. **Career:** Univ Mich Ctr Afro-American & African Studies, artist & asst prof art & afro-am hist; Acad Creative Thought, dir; Nat Conf Artists, pres, exec bd, 1972-83; Washtenaw Community Col, fac, 1979-; "The State of Black America" channel, consult; 56 PBS Detroit, consult, 1983-84; Asubuhi Cult Ctr, Univ Mich, artist & curator, 1984; Washtenaw Community Col, fac mem, currently; Univ Mich, adj fac, currently; Visions of Destiny, founder. **Orgs:** Exhibiting artist, Suriname Festival Diaspora, 1980-81; sponsor, Sandy Sanders Basketball League, Ann Arbor, 1983-85; pres, Nat Conf Artists;

assoc dir, Soc Study African Am Cult & Aesthetics. **Honors/Awds:** 3 Emmy Awards; African American Mural "Continium", Wayne State Univ, Detroit, 1979; City Detroit Proclamation, Detroit City Coun, 1980; mural "Tallest Tree in the Forest", Cent State Univ, Wilberforce, OH, 1981; NCA Distinguished Award of Honor, Nat Conf Artists Dakar, Seneyal, 1985. **Special Achievements:** Numerous art exhibitions throughout the country & abroad - Africa, Brazil, Suriname. **Home Addr:** 2649 Wayside Dr, Ann Arbor, MI 48103.

LOCKE, DR. DON C.
Educator. **Personal:** Born Apr 30, 1943, Macon, MS; son of Willie and Carlene; married Marjorie; children: Tonya E & Regina C. **Educ:** Tenn A&I State Univ, BS, 1963, MEd 1964; Ball State Univ, EdD, 1974. **Career:** South Side HS, social studies teacher, 1964-70; Wayne HS, sch counsr, 1971-73; Ball State Univ European Prog, asst prof, 1974-75; NC State Univ, from asst prof, to prof, 1975-89, dept head 1987-93; NCSU Doctoral Prog,dir, Asheville Grad Ctr, 1993-2005, dir, diversity & multicult Affairs, 2005-; alumni distinguished grad prof, Univ NC, 2003-05. **Orgs:** Alpha Phi Alpha Fraternity Inc; New Bern Ave Day Care Ctr Bd, 1978-86; pres, NC CounAssoc, 1979-80; chairperson, S Region Br ACA, 1983-84; chairperson, NC Bd Registered Practicing Counsrs, 1984-87; sec, Asn Counsr Educ & Supervision, 1985-86; pres, Southern Asn counsr Educ & Supervision,1988-89, bd dir, Asheville -Buncombe United Way, 1997-; Asheville Citizen-Times Ed Bd, 1998-2000; pres, Chi Sigma Iota Int Hon Soc, 1999-2000; pres, Asn Counsr Edu & Supervision, 2000-01; mem, Phi Delta Kappa; life mem, Am CounAsn; mem, Am Mental Health Counselors Asn. **Honors/Awds:** Summer Fellow Center Advanced Study, Behav Sci, 1979, 1992; ACA Prof Develop Award, 1996; Ray Thompson Multicultural Counseling Award, North Carolina. **Special Achievements:** Co-author of "Psychological Techniques for Teachers", "Cultural and Diversity Issues in Counseling"; Author of "Increasing Multicultural Understanding"; Co-editor of "The Handbook of Counseling"; Author or Co-author of more than 50 articles in professional journals. **Business Addr:** Director, Doctoral Program in ACCE, Asheville Graduate Center, 252 Phillips Hall, PO Box 1400, Asheville, NC 28804.

LOCKE, DONALD
Artist, educator. **Personal:** Born Sep 17, 1930, Stewartville, Demerara, Guyana; son of Donald and Ivy Mae; married Leila Locke Nee Chaplin (deceased); children: Hew, Jonathan & Corinne Rogers; married Brenda Stephenson, May 23, 1981. **Educ:** Bath Acad Art, Eng, certi educ, 1956, cert visual arts, music & drama, 1957; Edinburgh Univ, Scotland, MA, hon, fine art, 1964, ceramic res, 1969-70. **Career:** Educator (Retired), artist; Ariz State Univ, artist-in-residence, 1979-80; Univ Calif, Santa Cruz, asst prof, fine art, 1987; Aljira Arts, critic-in-residence, 1988; Augusta Col, asst prof, fine art dept, 1990-91; Ga State Univ, fine art dept, interim asst prof, 1991-92, asst prof. **Special Achievements:** Received many honrs & awards including: Travelling Grant USA, 1977; British Coun, Exhibition Grant, 1978;, Pathway to Excellence: 20 Year Retrospective," 2001, Aljira Arts Center, Newark, NJ, 2001; Southern Mansions, Mary Pauline Gallery, Augusta, GA, 2000; "Amarna Sphinx," Kubatana Gallery, Atlanta, GA, 2000; "From the Altars of El Dorado," Solomon Projects, Atlanta, GA, 2002. **Home Addr:** 97 Mobile Ave NE, Atlanta, GA 30305, **Home Phone:** (404)262-2249.

LOCKE, HENRY DANIEL JR.
Government official, journalist. **Personal:** Born Nov 16, 1936, Greenville, SC; son of Henry Locke Sr and Josephine; married Audrey Marie Harris; children: Daniel Leroy, Tara Yvonne & Henry III. **Educ:** Univ Md, attended 1958; Univ Buffalo, NY, attended 1961; Am Press Inst, Reston, VA, completed ed sch, 1979. **Career:** MI Ave YMCA Buffalo, weekend exec, 1959-63; Buffalo Courier-Express, dist mgr 1960-72; Buffalo, youth counr, 1964-78; Black Enterprise Mag NYC, contrib, 1979-; Buffalo Courier-Express, columnist/reporter, 1972-82; The Nat Leader Phila, columnist/reporter, 1982-83; Chicago Defender, nat reporter, 1983-89, managing ed, 1988-92; Mayor's Off, City Chicago, Dept Human Serv, dir public affairs, freedom of info officer, 1992-2000; Chicago Dept Human Serv, Comm Relations Div, coordr Spec Proj, Chicago Dept Family & Support Serv, spec proj coordr, United Negro Col Fund (UNCF) DFSS, coordr, photographer for DFSS, Dir Veterans Affairs for City of Chicago, currently. **Orgs:** Comm Asn Black Journalists; bd dir, MI Ave YMCA 1960-64; bd trustees, Lloyd's Memorial United Church Christ, 1962-63; state pr dir, NAACP Conf Br, 1976-77; Alpha Phi Alpha Frat, NAACP, Buffalo Urban League, Operation PUSH; Black Commun Asn; Black Social Workers/No Region Black Polit Caucus; NY State Affirmative Action Com; BUILD; vice chmn, Local 26 Am Newspaper Guild, 1975-; CABJ; Headlines Club; Marycrest Homeowners Asn. **Honors/Awds:** Nominee Pulitzer Prize, 1977; 6 awards, page-one competition, newspaper articles; first place On the Spot Newspaper Reporting, AP Wire Serv, 1977; 61 Awards Outstanding Comm Serv various orgns; Pulitzer Prize nominee,1978, 1986, 1987; Man of the Year Award, Chicago, IL, 1988. **Special Achievements:** As a journalist, covered (investigative) stories in five continents—Africa, Asia, Europe, North America, and South America. Also interviewed five sitting U.S. presidents and most national political and elected leaders across the U.S. **Military Serv:** USAF A/1c 1954-58; Good Conduct Medal; Occupation of France; Germany Occupation; Nat Defense Medal. **Business Addr:** Coordinator of Special Projects, Director of Veterans Affairs, City of Chicago, Chicago Department of Family & Support Services, 1615 W Chicago Ave Suite 3 East, Chicago, IL 60622.

LOCKE, DR. HUBERT G.
Educator, school administrator. **Personal:** Born Apr 30, 1934, Detroit, MI; son of Hubert H and Willa; married; children: Gayle & Lauren. **Educ:** Wayne Univ, BA, 1955; Univ Chicago, BD, 1959; Univ Mich, MA, 1961; Payne Theol Sem, DDiv, 1968; Chicago Theol Sem, DDiv ChC, 1971; Univ Nebr, D.Litt, 1992. **Career:** Detroit Police Dept, admin asst to comnr, 1966-67; Wayne State Univ, asst prof, ed soc, 1967-72; Univ Nebr, Omaha, dean pub affairs, 1972-76; Univ Wash, assoc dean arts & sci, 1976-77, vice provost acad affairs, 1977-82, dean, 1982-88, prof pub affairs, dean emer, 1988-, Marguerite Corbally prof pub serv emer, currently; Richard Stockton Col, New Jersey, vis prof, 2001; Pac Sch Relig, actg pres, 2003; Whitman Col, vis prof relig, 2004; Antioch Univ, Seattle, distinguished vis fel, 2005-06. **Orgs:** Exec dir, Citizens Community Equal Opportunity, 1962-65; bd dir, Police Found, 1970-71; dir, Wm O Douglas Inst, 1972-; exec vpres, Inst Study Contemp Soc Problems, 1972-; Bullitt Found, Seattle; Disciples Divinity House, Chicago; Disciples Sem Found, Claremont; Comt Educ & Church Rels; US Holocaust Mem Mus, Wash, DC; Nat Coun Crime & Delinquency, Oakland; Seattle Police Found; Seattle Symphony Orchestra; Inst Int Educ, Chicago; Lakeside Sch, Seattle; chair, Ethics Bd, King Co; co-chair, Wash State Comn Ethics & Political Accountability; chair, Wash State Sentencing Guidelines Comn; Wash State Comn Judicial Conduct. **Honors/Awds:** Liberty Bell Award, Mich Bar Asn, 1966; Doctor of Divinity, Payne Theol Sem; Doctor of Divinity, Chicago Theol Sem; DHL, Univ Akron; DHL, Univ Bridgeport. **Special Achievements:** Author: Publ "The Detroit Riot of 1967", Wayne State Univ; press; 1969; "The Care & Feeding of White Liberals" Paulist; Press, 1970, "The Church Confronts the Nazis", 1984, "Exile in the Fatherland", 1986; The Black Antisemitism Controversy, 1994; Learning From History, 2000; Searching for God in God-Forsaken Times & Places, 2003. **Home Addr:** 2801 1st Ave Suite 609, Seattle, WA 98121. **Business Addr:** Marguerite Corbally Professor of Public Service Emeritus, Dean Emeritus, University of Washington, Daniel J Evans School of Public Affairs, PO Box 353055, Seattle, WA 98195-3055, **Business Phone:** (206)543-4900.

LOCKE, DR. MAMIE EVELYN
School administrator, government official. **Personal:** Born Mar 19, 1954, Brandon, MS; daughter of Ennis and Amanda McMahon. **Educ:** Tougaloo Col, Tougaloo, BA, 1976; Atlanta Univ, Atlanta, MA, 1978, PhD, 1984. **Career:** Dept Archives & Hist, Jackson, archivist, 1977-79; Atlanta Hist Soc, Atlanta, archivist, 1979-81; Hampton Univ, assoc prof, 1981-97, prof, 1997-, asst dean, 1991-96, dean, 1996-; Hampton, Va, mayor, 2000-04; City Hampton, Coun Mem, 1996-98; Legislature Va, state sen, 2004-. **Orgs:** Alpha Kappa Alpha Sorority, Inc, 1973-; Nat Conf Black Polit Scientists, 1976-, exec coun, 1989-92, pres elect, 1992-93, pres, 1993-94; Am Political Sci asn, 1981-97; Alpha Kappa Alpha Sorority Inc; Am Polit Sci Asn, 1990-; Southeastern Women's Studies Asn, 1987-; adv, Alpha Kappa Mu Nat Honor Soc, 1990-; ed bd, PS: Polit & Polit Sci, 1992-95; pres, Nat Conference Black Political Scientists, 1997; ed bd, Nat Polit Sci Rev, 1994-; Hampton Democratic Comm, 1994-; Hampton City Coun; former comnr, Hampton Planning CMS; Hampton Redevelopment & Housing Authority; VA Municipal League, Gov Affairs Comn; Nat Black Caucus Local Elected Officials; Hampton Chapter, Links, Inc, 1997-; bd mem, Women in Municipal Gov, 1998-99; United Way Va Pa, 2000-02; Downtown Hampton Child Develop Ctr, 2001-; Towne Bank, 2003-; Transitions Family Violence Ctr, 2006-; Start Strong Coun, 2006-07; Nat Asn for the Advan Colored People; Roman Catholic Church. **Honors/Awds:** NEH fellowship, Nat Endowment Humanities, 1985; Fulbright-Hays Award, Dept Educ, 1986; Rodney Higgins Award, Nat Conf Black Polit Scientists, 1986; Ford Found Grant, Duke Univ, 1987; Ford Found Grant, Col William & Mary, 1988; Lindback Award Distinguished Teaching, Hampton Univ, 1990. **Special Achievements:** First African American mayor of Hampton, Va. **Home Phone:** (757)846-1085. **Business Addr:** Dean, State Senator, Hampton University, School of Liberal Arts & Education, 119 Armstrong Hall, Hampton, VA 23668, **Business Phone:** (804)727-5400.

LOCKE-MATTOX, BERNADETTE
Basketball coach. **Personal:** Born Dec 31, 1958, Rockwood, TN; daughter of Alfred M Locke; married Vince; children: Vincent. **Educ:** Roane State Community Col, Harriman, TN, 1977-79; Univ Ga, Athens, GA, BS,1979-82. **Career:** Univ Ga, Athens, GA, acad adv, 1982-83; Xerox Corp, Atlanta, GA, customerserv rep, 1984-85; Univ Ga, Athens, GA, asst coach, 1985-90; Univ Ky, Lexington, KY, asst coach, 1990-94, asst athletics dir, 1994-95, Head Women's Basketball Coach, 1995-03; Connecticut Sun, asst coach, 2003-. **Honors/Awds:** Academic Award, Univ Ga, 1980; Acad All-Am, Univ Ga, 1981; Nat Hon Soc,Univ Ga, 1981. **Special Achievements:** First Black woman to head coach the woman's basketball team at Univ of Ky; First Female to Serve as a Division I Assistant for a Men's Team. **Home Addr:** 4529 Pentlalla, Lexington, KY 40517, **Home Phone:** (606)272-5598. **Business Addr:** Assistant Coach, Connecticut Sun, One Mohegan Sun Blvd, Uncasville, CT 06382, **Business Phone:** (860)862-4000.

LOCKET, ARNOLD, JR.
Clergy, counselor. **Personal:** Born Oct 6, 1929, Bethel, NC; married Jeffie Bernadine; children: Gwendolyn E. **Educ:** Northern Ariz Univ, Flagstaff, BA, 1971, MA 1975. **Career:** Coconino Co & Flagstaff Nat Asn Advan Colored People Br, rev, 1977-; Coconino Comm Guidance Ctr Inc, prog dir, 1974-77; Ariz State Dept Econ Security, vocat rehab counsr, 1973-74; Ariz State Dept Econ Security, correctional rehab counsr, 1971-73. **Orgs:** Nat Asn Vocational Couns, 1971-; adv coun mem, Ariz State Dept Econ security, 1977-; chmn plan devel com, Northern Ariz Health Systs Agency, 1979; br pres, Flagstaff Nat Asn Advan Colored People Br, 1976-; chmn, Mayor's Human Rel Com City of Flagstaff, 1976-80; Disbursing Real Educational Acad Minority Scholarships. **Honors/Awds:** 1st Worshipful Master F&AM Prince Hall Lodge Killeen TX, 1963; Ust Black Dept Head Coconion Co Flagstaff, AZ, 1977. **Military Serv:** AUS, sfc-e7, 1948-68, Bronze Star & Army Commendation Medal. **Business Addr:** Disbursing Real Educational Academic Minority Scholarships, 1804 N Meadow Lark Dr, Flagstaff, AZ 86001.*

LOCKETT, ALICE FAYE
Nutritionist. **Personal:** Born Sep 6, 1944, Linden, TX; daughter of Bernice Fisher and Eddie. **Educ:** Prairie View A&M Univ, BS, 1968; Univ Iowa, cert, 1972; Col State Univ, MS, 1974; Montreal Diet Dispensary, cert, 1975. **Career:** Denver Dept Health & Hosps, pub health nutritionist, 1969-73; L&L Health Care Asn, community nutritionist, 1974-76; Community Col Denver, nutrition instr, 1973; Dept Human Serv, pub health nutritionist, 1976-81; DC Gen Hosp, Maternal & Child Nutrition, chief, 1981-94; USDA, Food & Nutrition Serv, nutritionist, currently. **Orgs:** Am Dietetic Asn, 1969-; DC Metropolitan Dietetic Asn, 1974-; health adv bd, March Dimes, 1978-; Soc Nutrition Educ, 1990-. **Honors/Awds:** Outstanding Performance Award, 1983-94, Outstanding Woman of Div, 1984, Employee of the Month, 1985, nominee, Outstanding Woman of Col, 1972, DC Gen Hosps; Certificate of Merit, 1997-02; Outstanding performance Awards, Food & Nutrition Serv, 1999-02; SCY's Honor Award, 2002. **Special Achievements:** Presentation, "The Impact of Drug Abusers on Prenatal and the Unborn," 1991, author of Preliminary Results from a Study to Examine the Effects of Breastfeeding on Neonatal Intensive Care Cost, 1991, Prenatal Nutrition for Substance Abusing Women: Reaching the Unreachable, 1991, Perspectives on Breastfeeding for the High Risk Neonate, 1992, Nutrition Offset Drugs, 1993, coordinated USDA's WIC Natl Breastfeeding Promotion Loving Support Campaign, represented USDA'S under secretary for Food and Nutrition Service (FNS) in "People to People Ambassador Program", Breastfeeding and Human Lactation delegation to Israel and Egypt. **Home Addr:** 4914B Barbour Dr, Alexandria, VA 22304. **Business Phone:** (703)305-2478.

LOCKETT, BRADFORD R.
Designer, tailor. **Personal:** Born Sep 26, 1945, Norfolk, VA; married Brendale Joyce; children: Belinda Joyce. **Educ:** Nat Sch Dress Design, 1966; Tex Southern Univ, BS, clothing & textiles, 1968; EW Kyles Sch Voc Tailoring, Houston, TX, master cert tailoring. **Career:** JC Penney Co Tucson, AZ, head tailor, 1970-71; Brotherhood Asn Mil Airmen Tucson, vpres, 1971-72; Tucson, master mason, 1971-72; Res & Anal DMAFB Tucson, AZ, clothing counr USAF, 1970-72; Joe Frank Houston, asst fashion designer, 1973; Mr Creations Inc & Battlesteins, fashion designer & master tailor; Lockett Oshins Collection, pres, currently. **Orgs:** Gulf Coast Fashion Asn; Small Bus Admin; Basilus Omega Psi Phi Frat, 1966-67; master mason 11th Degree Pima Lodge No 10 Tucson. **Honors/Awds:** Award to study fashion design under Italian Designer Emilio Pucci, 1966; Man of Year Award, Omega Psi Phi, 1967; Outstanding Clothing Design Award, Yardley Co, 1969; Spec Air Force Doc (AFN Series No 38-ON Preparatory Mgt) Film Fashion Entertainment Brad Lockett, 1972; Creative Garment Design award, 1991; American Designers and Tailor's Guild Award for Outstanding Celebrity Service Achievement, 1997 & 1999; American Designers and Tailor's Guild award for master tailoring and wardrobe design work; Special Support Award, 1997 & 1999; Yardley Fashion Award for Construction Merit. **Military Serv:** USAF, e-5 staff sgt; Outstanding Military Achievements, 1972. **Business Addr:** President, Lockett Oshins Collection, Houston, TX.

LOCKETT, JAMES D.
Educator. **Personal:** Son of Elvie Thomas Lockett and J D Lockett. **Educ:** Morehouse Col, BA, polit sci; Atlanta Univ, MLS, DA, hist, humanities;Case Western Reserve Univ, MA, polit sci. **Career:** Allen Univ, nat teaching fel, 1966-67; Tenn State Univ, asst prof, polit sci & hist, 1967-69; Tuskegee Inst, asst prof, 1969-70; St Augustine Col, acting chmn, Dept hist, polit sci, black studies, social sci, 1970-72;Miss Valley State Univ, asst prof TCCP, 1972-74; Opportunities Industrialization Ctr, staff; Stillman Col, assoc prof, hist, polit sci & geog, 1977-91, prof, 1991-. **Orgs:** Pres, West AL Chap, Asn Study Afro-Am Life & Hist, 1983; app mem, Econ Adv Coun, Ala Conf Black Mayors Inc, 1984; chmn bd, Ala Afro-Am Black Hall Fame, 1985; app mem, Econ Devt Comn, Ala Conf Black Mayors Inc, 1985; appmem, adv bd, Ala

Hist Comn, 1985; NEA; Am Libr Asn; Asn Higher Educ; AmHisl Asn; Southern Hist Asn; Orgn Am Historians; Asn Study Afro-Am Life &Hist; Birmingham Astronomical Soc; adv bd, Ala Hist Comn; assoc comnr, AlaElection Comn; Exec Comn, W Ala Oral Hist Asn; campus coordr Kettering Pub Leadership; coordr, SREB; ed adv bd, Col Press, 1993-94; fnd bd, Murphy African Am Mus; campus coordr, Exxon Kettering Pub Leadership; adv comn, Govs Salute Great Black Alabamians. **Honors/Awds:** Cert Appreciation, Atlanta-Fulton Co Dist Social Sci Fair, 1983; one of principal founders & first pres, West Ala Chap, Asn Study Afro-Am Life &Hist; one of principal founders Ala Afro-Am Black Hall of Fame; first chmnbd dir, Ala Afro-Am Hall of Fame; articles pub US Black & News, Negro Hist Bullet, Presby Surv, Aerospace Historian; compiled bibliog works by &about Dr Martin Luther King Jr & Civil Rights Movement, Dr Martin LutherKing Jr Ctr Social Chg, Atlanta, Ga; nominated for NAFEO Achievement Award; books: James A Garfield & Chester A Arthur vols 1 & 2 of a fivevolume work, ed Frank N Magill, Great Lives from History, A BiographicalSurvey Pasadena CA, Salem Press Inc, 1987; saluted as Great BlackAlabamian by Gov's Ala Reunion; nominated, Stillman Col Faculty MeritIncentive Award, 1988, 1989, 1990; fel, Royal Geog Soc, 1991; NEH fel,1994, 1995; Special Recognition Award, Stillman Col Alumni Asn, 1994;selected rep, Rhodes Scholar Trust, 1995. **Special Achievements:** The Negro & the Presbyterian Church of the South from the Antebellum Through the Postbellum Period, The Griot, 1992; Authored: A Historical Portrait of the Leaders And Missionaries of Stillman College And the Southern Presbyterian Church, 2006; The Deportation of the Maroons of Trelawny Town to Nova Scotia, then Back to Africa. **Business Addr:** Professor, Stillman College, Department of Social Sciences, PO Box 1430, Tuscaloosa, AL 35403.

LOCKETT, KEVIN
Football player, manager. **Personal:** Born Sep 8, 1974, Tulsa, OK. **Educ:** Kans State Univ, BAcc. **Career:** Football player (retired); Kans City Chiefs, wide receiver, 1997-2000; Wash Redskins, 2001-02; Jacksonville Jaguars, 2002; New York Jets, wide receiver, 2003; Free agent, 2004; Kauffman Found, mgr res & policy, currently. **Orgs:** Exec Comt Bd of Trustees, KSU. **Honors/Awds:** Rookie of the year, 1997.

LOCKETT, SANDRA BOKAMBA
Librarian. **Personal:** Born Nov 18, 1946, Hutchinson, KS; daughter of Herbert Wales Johnson and Dorothy Bernice Harrison; married Eyamba G Bokamba, 1969 (divorced 1972); children: Eyenga M Bokamba; married James C, 1979 (divorced 1983); children: Madeline B. **Educ:** Univ Kans, Lawrence, BS, educ, 1968; Ind Univ, Bloomington, IN, MLS, 1973. **Career:** Hutchinson Community Jr Col, Hutchinson, KS, assoc arts, 1966; Gary Pub Libr, Gary, IN, Alcott Br, librn, 1973-76, asst dir pub rels & programming, 1976-78, head exten serv, 1978-79; Univ Iowa Law Libr, Iowa City, IA, head gov docs dept, 1979-84; Milwaukee Pub Libr Syst, Milwaukee, WI, br mgr, 1984-88, exten serv coordr, 1988-91, asst city librn, 1991, dep city librn, 2006-. **Orgs:** Alpha Kappa Alpha Sorority, 1967-; Greater Milwaukee Literacy Coalition, 1986-; comt mem, Pub Libr Asn, Am Libr Asn, 1988-; bd mem, Links Inc, 1996-. **Honors/Awds:** Librarian of the Year, Bookfellows, Milwaukee Pub Libr, 1987; Management Merit Award, Milwaukee Pub Libr, City Milwaukee, 1988. **Special Achievements:** Author, "Adult Programming.", The Bottom Line, 1989. **Business Addr:** Deputy City Librarian, Milwaukee Public Library System, 814 W Wis Ave, Milwaukee, WI 53233, **Business Phone:** (414)286-3023.

LOCKETTE, DR. AGNES LOUISE
Educator. **Personal:** Born Apr 21, 1927, Albany, GA; daughter of Wessie McIntee Pollard (deceased) and Fred Pollard (deceased); married Emory W Sr; children: Sharon Anita, Emory W Jr & Robert P (deceased). **Educ:** Albany State Col, Albany, GA, BS (hons), 1948; Univ Nev, Las Vegas, MEd,1967; Univ Ariz, Tucson, EdD, 1972; Albany State Col, dipl. **Career:** Carver High Sch Dawson, GA, teacher, 1948-49; Clark County Sch Dist, Las Vegas, NV, teacher, 1952-70; Univ Nev, Las Vegas, prof educ, 1972-84; Univ Nev, Las Vegas, Dept Curric & Instr, assoc prof, 1971-84, assoc prof emer, 1984-. **Orgs:** Church coun, fin sect, Grace Community Church, Boulder City, NV, 1989-; Kappa Delta Pi; Delta Kappa Gamma Soc; Nat Coun Teachers Eng; Am Asn Univ Women; Phi Kappa Phi; Asn Childhood Educ Int; Nat Soc Profs; Nat Educ Asn; chairperson, Clark Co Air Pollution Hearing Bd, Las Vegas, NV. **Honors/Awds:** Distinction Teaching Award, Col Educ, Univ Nev, Las Vegas, 1984; Outstanding Service Award, W side Sch Alumni Asn, 1988. **Special Achievements:** First woman appointed to Clark County Air Pollution Hearing Bd, 1972-; Recipient of one of Univ Nev, Las Vegas First Master's Degrees, Elementary Education, MEd, 1967. **Business Addr:** Emeritus Associate Professor, University of Nevada, Department Curriculum & Instruction, 4505 Maryland Pkwy, PO Box 453005, Las Vegas, NV 89154-3005, **Business Phone:** (702)895-1540.

LOCKHART, BARBARA H
Executive, consultant. **Personal:** Born Apr 1, 1948, Cleveland, OH; daughter of Willie and Estelle. **Educ:** Cleveland State Univ, BS, 1972; Cent Mich State Univ, MSA, 1987. **Career:** Aetna Casualty & Surety Ins, sr underwriter, 1972-77; Blue Cross NE Ohio, underwriting specialist, mkt res analyst, 1977-80; Mead Corp, HMO & cost control coordr, 1980-83; Ohio Dept Health, health care cost analyst, 1983-84; Physicians Health Plan Ohio, vpres, gov progs, 1984-94; Medimetrix Group Inc, sr consult, currently. **Orgs:** Past chair, 1986-89, bd of trustees, 1991-, Ohio HMO Asn Human Services Comt; Ohio Med Care Adv Comt, 1990-; Nat Acad State Health Policy, 1992-; Am Managed Care Asn Medicaid Adv Comt, 1992-; HCFA Medicaid Coordication Care Indust Group, 1992-; Asn Black Ins Professionals, 1992-. **Honors/Awds:** Ohio House Representatives, Community Service Proclamation, 1992. **Special Achievements:** Appointed, Governor's Comn, Ohio Health Care Costs, 1983; Appointed, State Legislators Medicaid Oversight Comt, 1986. **Business Addr:** Senior Consultant, Medimetrix Group Inc, 25 W Prospect Ave Suite 1100, Cleveland, OH 44115-1073.*

LOCKHART, EUGENE
Football player, restaurateur. **Personal:** Born Mar 8, 1961, Crockett, TX; married Sharon; children: Bryan, Brandon & Eugene III. **Educ:** Univ Houston, BA, mkt, 1983. **Career:** Football player (retired), restaurant owner; Dallas Cowboys, linebacker, 1984-91; New England Patriots, linebacker, 1991-94; Lockhart One-Hour Photo, Dallas, TX, co-owner, currently; Cowboys Sports Cafe, Irving, TX, partner, currently; Lockhart Custom Pools, partner, currently. **Honors/Awds:** NFL All-Star Team, Sporting News, 1989; Nat Cancer Soc Golf Tournament.

LOCKHART, JAMES ALEXANDER BLAKELY
Lawyer. **Personal:** Born May 27, 1936, New York, NY; son of Edgar and Margaret; married Ruth Yvonne Douglas, Oct 30, 1976; children: Marc Blakely & Diallo Henry. **Educ:** Palmer Mem Inst, 1954; Boston Univ Col, BS, bus admin, 1957; Boston Univ Sch Law, JD, 1959. **Career:** Lawyer (retired); Off Chief Coun US Treas Dept, atty adv, 1963-65; City Chicago, asst corp coun, 1965-67; Rivers Lockhart Clayter & Lawrence Attys Law Chicago, partner, 1967-71; Budget Rent A Car Corp, sr vpres, 1971-79; Transamerica Corp, vpres pub affairs, 1979-98. **Orgs:** Bd dirs, Pub Affairs Coun; dep, Calif Bus Roundtable; Ill & SC Bar Asns; Sigma Pi Phi Boule Fraternity Inc; Kappa Alpha Psi Fraternity Inc; Episcopalian; bd dir & vice chmn, Legal Legis Comt, Int Franchise Asn; Car & Truck Rental & Leasing Asn; bd trustee & exec comn, Episcopal Charities Diocese Chicago; Standing Comt Episcopal Diocese Chicago; Comn Legis Conv Episcopal Diocese Chicago; life trustee, vpres & exec comt, Lawrence Hall Sch Boys; pres, Downtown Asn San Francisco; chair, Bay Area Urban League; dir & vice chairperson, Pub Broadcasting Serv; dir, Oakland Pvt Indust Coun; Bohemian Club; dir, founding chairperson, City Club San Francisco; Sequoyah Co Club; pres, bd port comnrs, Port Oakland; trustee emer, Fine Arts Mus San Francisco, 1986-; bd govs, San Francisco Tennis Club, 1988-91; bd trustees, Alta Bates Med Ctr & Hosp San Francisco; chmn, Social Action Comt, Sigma Pi Phi Fraternity Inc; vice chair, Boule Found; chair, City Club San Francisco. **Honors/Awds:** San Francisco Planning & Urban Research Associates Award, 1988; Good Scouts Award, San Francisco Bay Area Boy Scouts, 1997; Champion for Equality, Nat Asn Advan Colored People Legal Defense Fund, 1998. **Special Achievements:** Outstanding contributions to the CHI comm WBEE (Radio) Community Service Citation, 1973. **Military Serv:** AUS, capt & asst army staff judge advocate, 1960-63.

LOCKHART, KEITH E
President (Organization), advertising executive. **Career:** Lockhart & Pettus Inc, advertising exec, pres, currently. **Business Phone:** (212)633-2800.

LOCKHART, DR. ROBERT W
Dentist. **Personal:** Born Jul 19, 1941, Houston, TX; married Betty J Moore; children: Robert III, Chris & Lisa. **Educ:** Univ Tex, BA, 1962, DDS, 1966, MPH, 1973. **Career:** Harris Co Hosp Sunnyside Clinic, dir dept serv, 1973-74; Calif George Dental Soc, vpres, 1974-76; pvt pract, dentist, 1968-. **Orgs:** Amer & Nat Dental Assoc, Acad Gen Dent, Amer Assoc Publ Health Dentists, Alpha Phi Alpha, NAACP, Urban League. **Military Serv:** AUS Dental Corps, capt, 1966-68. **Home Addr:** 9285 S Main St, Houston, TX 77205, **Home Phone:** (713)666-1116. **Business Addr:** Dentist, 9285 S Main St, Houston, TX 77205, **Business Phone:** (713)666-1116.

LOCKHART, DR. VERDREE, SR.
Educator. **Personal:** Born Oct 19, 1923, Louisville, GA; son of Fred D and Minnie B Roberson; married Louise Howard, Aug 5, 1950; children: Verdree II, Vera Louise, Fernandez & Abigail. **Educ:** Tuskegee Univ, BS, 1949; Atlanta Univ, MA, 1957, PhD, 1975; George Peabody Col, attended 1960. **Career:** Educator (retired); Jefferson County High Sch, teacher, 1949-58, counr, 1958-63; GA Dept Educ, educ consult, 1963-80; Atlanta Univ, vpres, 1981-82; Phillips Col, dean educ, 1984-85; Regional Asbestos Inspector, 1985-86; N Fulton High Sch, counr, 1986-92; W Fulton Middle Sch, counr, 1992-2000; candidate, US Congress, 1992, 1998. **Orgs:** Alpha Phi Alpha Fraternity, 1949-; Former state pres, Asn Coun & Devel, 1963-65; mem exec bd, Atlanta Area Coun, Boy Scouts Am, 1965-; treas, Atlanta Br Nat Asn Advan Colored People, 1972-90; trustee, Atlanta Univ, 1975-81; Tuskegee Univ Forest Resource Coun, 1978-88, 1995-; Tuskegee Univ Nat Alumni Asn, 1980-84; Parlimentarian, Eta Lambda Chapter; Am Coun Asn, 1960-; Phi Delta Kappa, 1981-; mem bd dir, Econ Opportunity Atlanta Inc, 1985-88; Am Voc Asn; Ga Adult Educ Asn; Ga Educ Artic Com; Nat Educ Asn; former mem, Youth Employ & Planning Coun, Atlanta CETA Office; Mayor'sTask Force on Public Educ, 1986-92; pres, Atlanta Univ Consortion Chapter, Phi Delta Kappa, 1988-89; asst parlimentarian, Tuskegee Univ Nat Alumn Asn, 1990-92; bd mem, Atlanta Asn Eucators, 1990-95; Zion Hill Baptist, 1996-; exec bd mem, Clark Atlanta Univ Nat Alumni Asn; Am Sch Counr Asn; treas, exec bd mem, Fulton Atlanta Community Action Authority Inc, 1995-01; pres, Tuskegee Univ, Col Agr, Environ & Nat Scis Alumni Asn, 1997-; chmn, Eminent Assoc Prog, Tuskegee Univ, 1998-, chmn exec bd, Fulton-Atlanta Community Action Authority, 2002-; Eminent Presidential Assocs chmn, Tuskegee Nat Alumni Asn Exec Bd. **Honors/Awds:** Alumni Merit Award, Atlanta Univ Alumni Asn, 1972; Silver Beaver Award, Atlanta Area Coun, Boy Scouts Am, 1968; Ga Gov Medallions, Gov State GA, 1967-68; Alumni Brother of the Year, Alpha Phi Alpha Fraternity, 1980; Presidential Award, Atlanta Univ Consortium Chapter of Phi Delta Kappa, 1989; George Washington Carver Outstanding Alumni Award, Tuskegee Univ Agr, Environ & Nat Scis Alumni Asn; A Heritage of Leadership Plaque, Atlanta Area Coun, Boy Scouts Am; Presidential Citation, Nat Asn Equal Opportunity Higher Educ; Alumni Merit Award, Tuskegee Univ. **Military Serv:** AUS, M/sgt, 20 years; WW II Victory Medal; Good Conduct Medal, 1943-45; Am Serv Medal; Asiatic Pacific Serv Medal w/2 Bronze Stars; Am Campaign Medal; Army Occup Medal; Nat Defense Serv Medal, Armed Forces Res Medal; Expert Badge w/Rifle & Carbine Bars. **Home Addr:** 2964 Peek Rd NW, Atlanta, GA 30318. *

LOCKHART, ZELDA
Writer. **Educ:** BS, Norfolk State Univ; MS Old Dominion Univ. **Career:** Author: "PRESENT TENSE", 1997; "SOJOURNER", 2002; "HIS HANDS, HIS TOOLS, HIS SEX, HIS DRESS", 2002; "FIFTH BORN", 2003; "COLD RUNNING CREEK", 2006; "TRACKING LOVE," THE HONEYMOON'S OVER, 2006; "WITHOUT A WORD," WHEN I WAS A LOSER", 2007. **Honors/Awds:** Zora Neale Hurston/Richard Wright Legacy Foundation Award; Honor Fiction Award, 2008.

LOCKLEY, CLYDE WILLIAM
Law enforcement officer. **Personal:** Born Jul 14, 1938, Jacksonville, FL; married Mary Frances Jordan; children: Rhonda M, Karen P, Larry K, Brian K, Darrell W, Rodney A. **Educ:** Liberal Arts Los Angeles SW Col, AA, 1971; Calif State Univ, BA, polit sci, 1974; Univ SC, MS, pub adminr, 1976; Calif Highway Patrol Acad, attended 1965; Calif Specialized Inst, cert, 1976; Univ Va, cert Criminal Justice, 1978; FBI Acad Quantico, VA, attended 1978. **Career:** Law enforcement officer (retired); Calif Highway Patrol, capt; Compton Community Col, part-time instr criminal justice. **Orgs:** Vice chmn, Environ Commn City Cars Calif; FBI Nat Acad Asn; Calif Asn Hwy Patrolman; Los Angeles County Peace Officers Asn; life mem, Univ Southern Calif Alumni Asn; Calif State Employees Asn. **Honors/Awds:** Outstanding Airman-Special Honor Guard VIP Guard March AFB, CA, 1959. **Military Serv:** USAF, airman 2nd, 1956-60.

LOCKLEY-MYLES, BARBARA J
Librarian. **Educ:** Fla A&M Univ, BS, 1996; Fla State Univ, MSLS, 1999. **Career:** Fla A&M Univ, fac, 1974, instr & librn, currently. **Business Phone:** (850)599-3393.

LOCKLIN, JAMES R.
Marketing executive. **Personal:** Born Jan 20, 1958, Monroe, GA; son of Orell and Geneva Malcolm; married Sherry Jackson-Locklin, Nov 23, 1981; children: Jacques, Kimberly. **Educ:** Clark Col, BA, 1980. **Career:** WCLK-FM, announcer, reporter, prog mgr, 1978-80; WAOK-AM, admin asst, 1979-80; WORL-AM, news, pub affairs dir, 1980; Clarke City, GA, probation officer, 1980-82; WXAG-AM, gen mgr, 1982-83; Leon Farmer & Co, vpres mkt, 1983-; First Class Mkt Ltd, pres, 1984-. **Orgs:** Athens Ad Club 1983-; bd mem, Morton Theatre Corp, 1984; bd mem, Hope Haven Sch, 1985; bd mem, Athens Tutorial Prog, 1985; exec comt, Athens Area Human Rel Coun; Zeta Beta Beta Chap Omega Psi Phi Frat Inc; Athens Bus Coun; Huntington Park Homeowners Asn; Ga Planning Asn; Am Planning Asn; Greater Athens Jazz Asn; Nat Asn Advan Colored People; Northeast Ga Bus League; Athens Area Chamber Com; comn mem, Athens Clarke County Planning Comn; comn mem, Athens Clarke County Clean & Beautiful Comn. **Honors/Awds:** Leadership Athens Participant, 1985; Man of the Year, Omega Psi Phi Fraternity, 1989; Local Business Person of the Year, Nat Asn Advan Colored People, 1990. **Home Addr:** 151 Chesterfield Rd, Bogart, GA 30622. **Business Addr:** Vice President Marketing, Leon Farmer & Co, PO Box 249, Athens, GA 30603.

LOCKWOOD, JAMES CLINTON
Educator. **Personal:** Born May 22, 1946, Philadelphia, PA; son of William and Signora; married Carolyn Francina McGowan, Sep 22, 1979; children: Jason Perry & James Andrew. **Educ:** West Chester Univ, BS, 1968; Salisbury State Univ, 1976; Univ Md, College Park, MA, sociol. **Career:** Oxford Area Sch Dist PA, fifth

grade teacher, 1968-70; Lincoln Univ, PA, asst financial aid, 1970-71; Salisbury State, MD, dir financial aid, 1971-77; Coppin State Col, MD, dir financial aid, 1977-78; Univ MD, Eastern Shore, dir financial aid, 1979-89; Sociol Univ, MD Eastern Shore, instr, 1983, 1985-89; Montgomery Col, MD, dir financial aid, 1989-97. **Orgs:** Nat Appeals Panel, US Dept Educ, 1981; stud fin aid trainer, Nat Asn Stud Fin Aid ADM & US Dept Educ, 1981, 1983, 1989, 1993; chairperson, FED Relations Com, 1981-82; Middles States Sociol, Univ MD Eastern Shore, 1983, 1985-89; Asn Stud Fin Aid ADM Inc; Moton Consortium Admissions & Fin Aid, instr, 1986; Nat Regional Assembly, 1994-96; trainer, exec coun, Eastern Asn Stud Fin Aid ADM, 1996; life mem, US Chess Fedn. **Home Addr:** 1404 Timberwolf Dr, Frederick, MD 21703, **Home Phone:** (301)696-1893.

LOFTON, ANDREW JAMES
Government official. **Personal:** Born Oct 16, 1950, Longstreet, LA; son of Junius E and Ethel M Peyton; married Verda J Minnix, May 30, 1970; children: Junius & Lamar. **Educ:** Univ of Puget Sound, Tacoma, WA, BA, 1972; Univ of Washington, Seattle, WA, MUP, 1974. **Career:** City Seattle, WA, Off Policy Planning, human resource planner, 1974-76, capital improv planner, 1976-78, Dept Community Develop, block grant adv, 1978-80, dep dir, 1980-87, Dept Lic & Consumer Affairs, dir, 1987-89, Off Mgt & Budget, dir, 1990-92, dep chief staff, mayor's off, 1992-94, deputy dir, Dept Community Trade & Econ Develop, 1994-95; Seattle City Light, Customer Serv, dep supt, 1995-; Seattle Housing Authority, dep exec dir finance & admin, 2004-. **Orgs:** Nat Forum Black Pub Admin, 1983-90; Region X Coun Mem, Blacks Govt, 1983-87; pres, Seattle Chap, Blacks Govt, 1983-86; bd mem, Seattle Mgt Asn, 1986-87; bd mem, Rainier High Boys & Girls Club, 1987-; region IX rep, Conf Minority Pub Adminr, 1989-91. **Business Addr:** Deputy Executive Director for Finance & Administration, Seattle Housing Authority, 120 6th Ave N, PO Box 19028, Seattle, WA 98109-5003, **Business Phone:** (206)615-3300.

LOFTON, DR. BARBARA
Administrator. **Personal:** Born May 2, 1954, Jackson, MS; daughter of Fred Alexander Jr and Alberta Alexander; married Jon C, Jul 10, 1987; children: Torri A Irving, Norman W Irving & Anastasia A. **Educ:** Jackson State Univ, BS, 1975; Univ Iowa, MA, 1977; Grambling State Univ, EdD, 1993. **Career:** Chicago Asn Retarded Citizens, activities specialist, 1981-82; Children's Haven, recreations specialist, 1982-83; Grambling State Univ, asst prof, 1983-93; Univ Ark, from visiting asst prof to asst prof, 1993-95, dir diversity programs, 1996-. **Orgs:** Nat Asn Academics; Am Asn Univ Women; Am Asn Black in Higher Education. **Honors/Awds:** Faculty of the Year, Nat Asn Black Accountants, 1997; Dr Martin L King Faculty/Staff Leadership, 1998, Outstanding Faculty Mem, 2001, Univ Ark; The Civil Rights Project, Harvard Law Sch, 2000; High Performance Award, Walton Col Bus, 2001. **Business Addr:** Director of Diversity Programs, University of Arkansas, Sam M Walton College of Business, Fayetteville, AR 72701, **Business Phone:** (479)575-4557.

LOFTON, DOROTHY W.
Educator. **Personal:** Born Jun 22, 1925, Marlin, TX; married Donald D; children: Ronald & Deanne Michelle. **Educ:** Baylor Univ, BA, 1971. **Career:** Marlin Independent Sch Dist, teacher. **Orgs:** Tex Classroom Teachers Asn; Falls County Teachers Asn; Tex St Teacher Asn; pres, City Fedn Women's Clubs; vpres, Strivette Club; secy, Falconerstamps Comn Ctr; secy & treas, Marlin Parents Orgn; treas, Carrie Adams Dist Tex Women & Girls' Clubs. **Honors/Awds:** Adult leader certificate, 4H Coun, 1974.

LOFTON, ERNEST
Labor activist, vice president (organization). **Personal:** Born Feb 25, 1932, Detroit, MI; children: Terry & Penny Holloway. **Career:** Labor activist (retired); Dearborn Iron Foundry, water tester, 1950; Ford Motor Co, Specty Foundry Unit, bargaining comt man, pres, 1967-76; UAW Local 600, second vpres, 1976-81, first vpres, 1981-82; UAW Int Exec Bd, Region 1A dir, 1983-89, int vpres, 1989; UAW Mich Community Action Prog Dept, dir, 1989-99. **Orgs:** Bd dirs, Blue Cross & Blue Shield Mich; bd dirs, United Found; New Detroit Inc; bd dirs, Detroit Police Athletic League; Transafrica; bd, Save Our Sons & Daughters; bd dirs, Metropolitan Realty Corp; bd mem, Detroit Econ Growth Corp; adv bd, Detroit Repertory Theatre; Econ Policy Coun United Nations Asn USA; nat secy, Coalition Black Trade Unionists; vpres, Nat Asn Advan Colored People, Detroit chap. **Military Serv:** AUS, staff sgt, 1950-52.

LOFTON, JAMES
Football player, football coach. **Personal:** Born Jul 5, 1956, Fort Ord, CA; married Beverly Fanning, 1980; children: David, Daniel & Rachel. **Educ:** Stanford Univ, BA, engineering, 1978. **Career:** Football player (retired), coach; Green Bay Packers, wide receiver, 1978-86; Los Angeles Raiders, 1987-88; Buffalo Bills, 1989-92; Los Angeles Rams, 1993; Philadelphia Eagles, 1993; sports commentator, 1990; San Diego Chargers, wide receiver coach, 2002-08; Oakland Raiders, wide receiver coach, 2008-09; Oakland Raiders, asst coach, 2009-. **Honors/Awds:** All-Rookie Team, 1978; Pro Football Hall of Fame, 2003. **Business Addr:** Wide Receiver Assistant Coach, Oakland Raiders, 1220 Harbor Bay Pkwy, Alameda, CA 94502, **Business Phone:** (510)864-5000.*

LOFTON, KENNETH (KENNY LOFTON)
Baseball player. **Personal:** Born May 31, 1967, East Chicago, IN. **Career:** Houston Astros, outfielder, 1991; Cleveland Indians, 1992-96, 1998-2001, 2007; Atlanta Braves, 1997; Chicago White Sox, 2002; San Francisco Giants, 2002; Pittsburgh Pirates, 2003; Chicago Cubs, 2003; NY Yankees, 2004; Philadelphia Phillies, 2005; Los Angeles Dodgers, 2005; Tex Rangers, 2007; free agent currently; post-prod co, Hollywood, co-owner, currently. **Honors/Awds:** AL Gold Glove-CF, 1993-96; AL All Star Team, 1994-96, 1998-99; NL All Star Team, 1997. **Business Addr:** Professional Baseball Player, Texas Rangers, PO Box 90111, Arlington, TX 76004-3111, **Business Phone:** (817)273-5100.

LOFTON, KENNY. See LOFTON, KENNETH.

LOFTON, MELLANESE S
Lawyer. **Personal:** Born Aug 24, 1941, Houston, TX; children: Frederick Douglas & Robin Mellanese. **Educ:** Univ Tex, BA, 1962; Univ Calif, Boalt Hall Sch Law, JD, 1974. **Career:** Univ Tex, photog teacher, 1961-62; Alameda & Co, soc worker employ counslt, 1963-69; Contra Costa Co, social worker, 1969-73; Jacobs Sills & Coblentz, law clerk, 1973-74; US Steel Corp, atty, 1974-82; Siemens Corp, Tel Plus Commun, 1984-92; Lofton & Lofton, partner & atty, 1991-. **Orgs:** Pa Bar; Calif State Bar; Alpha Kappa Alpha Sorority; Pub Project Future. **Special Achievements:** Auth: The Medi-Cal Advantage: How to Save the Family Home from the Cost of Nursing Home Care. **Business Addr:** Attorney, Partner, Lofton & Lofton, 836 Southampton Rd Suite B360, Benicia, CA 94510-1960, **Business Phone:** (707)280-6388.

LOFTON, MICHAEL (MIKA'IL SANKOFA)
Athlete, public relations executive. **Personal:** Born Dec 10, 1963, Montgomery, AL; son of Inez. **Educ:** NY Univ, BA, econ, 1988; Semmelweis Univ, Budapest, Hungary, Maestro hon, 2006. **Career:** Shearson Lehman Hutton, broker, 1988-90; Ernst & Young, public relations assoc, 1990-; Grey Advertising; Kirshenbaum; Bond & Partners and Shandwick International; Peter Westbrook Foundation, dir athletics & fencing coach, 1990-; United Nations Int Sch, head fencing coach; NBC Sports, analyst; Ross Schs summer prog, East Hampton, NY, head sabre coach; Stevens Institute of Technology Men's fencing team, head coach, currently. **Orgs:** Dir bus affairs, Peter Westbrook Foundation, 1990-. **Honors/Awds:** Chancellors Award for Leadership, 1988, Chancellors Award for Volunteerism, 1987; NY Univ; Sid Tanenbaum Award, NYU Varsity Club, 1989; New York University Sports Hall of Fame, 1994; United States Fencing Association Hall of Fame, 2005. **Special Achievements:** Olympian, 1984, 1988, 1992; Pan Am team member, 1987 won silver medal,1991 won silver medal & bronze medal; National sabre champ, 1991, 1992;NCAA sabre champ, 1984, 1985, 1986, 1987.

LOFTON, STEVEN LYNN
Football player. **Personal:** Born Nov 26, 1968, Jacksonville, FL; married Tarita; children: Christian & Courtney. **Educ:** Tex A&M Univ. **Career:** Football player (retired); Phoenix Cardinals, defensive back, 1991-93; Carolina Panthers, 1995-96, 1998-99; New England Patriots, 1997-98.

LOGAN, BARBARA
Educator, executive. **Educ:** Bronx Community Col, AA; Loyola Univ, BSN; Univ Ill, MS; Northwestern Univ, MA & PhD, sociol. **Career:** Clemson Univ, Sch Nursing, dir, 1993-2003, prof emer, currently, EXPORT Ctr, res core dir, 2007-, Ctr Res Health Disparities, assoc dir, currently. **Orgs:** Fel, Am Acad Nurses; fel, Am Nurses Asn Minority Fel Prog. **Honors/Awds:** Excellent in Nursing Education Award, SC League Nursing, 2002.

LOGAN, BENJAMIN HENRY
Lawyer, judge. **Personal:** Born Jun 25, 1943, Dayton, OH; son of Jeanne Ross and Ben H Logan Sr; married Creola, Nov 14, 1987 (divorced); children: Fonda, Benjamin M & Barry; married Denice M; children: Bradford & Benjamin W. **Educ:** Ohio Northern Univ, Ada, Ohio, BA, 1968; Ohio Northern Law Sch, Ada, Ohio, JD, 1972. **Career:** Ben's Enterprise, Dayton, Ohio, mgr, 1960-68; Dayton Tire & Rubber, Dayton, Ohio, cost acct, 1968-69; Dayton Bd Educ, Dayton, Ohio, sub teacher, 1969-70; G R Legal Aid, Grand Rapids, Mich, staff atty, 1972-74; Davenport Col, instr, 1973-75; Grand Valley State Univ, instr, 1975-77; Logan & Beason, Grand Rapids, Mich, partner, 1974-88; 61st Dist, Grand Rapids, Mich, judge, 1988-94, chief judge, 1994-. **Orgs:** Am Bar Asn, 1974-, judicial admin div, 1992-, task force opportunities minorities & ABA Standing Committee Judicial Selection, Tenure Compensation, 1995-96, & Comn on Minorities, 1997-; co-chair; Nat Bar Asn, 1974-, bd dir, 1989-92, judicial coun chair, 1994-95, bd dir, 1991-94; Grand Rapids Bar Asn, 1973-, bd mem, 1991-94; Grand Rapids Urban League, 1973-; Press Club, 1975-; bd dir, mem, A Philip Randolph, 1978-; WolverineBar Asn, 1980-; Grand Rapids Junior Col President's Comt, 1984-; Mich Supreme Ct Hist Soc, 1989-; founding mem, exec bd, vice chmn, Citizens RepGovt, 1985-88; Boy Scouts Western Shores, 1983-, vpres, bd mem, 1986; Lions Club, 1986-, bd mem, 1991-94; Dispute Resolution, 1990-; Fair Housing Bd, 1992-; Leadership Grand Rapids, 1993-; Economic Club, 1990-; Arkon City Club, 1994-; US Supreme Court History Soc, 1992-; Fel State BarMich, 1995; YWCA Tribute Comn, 1993-; Nat Asn Advan Colored People, Grand Rapids Chapter, bd mem, 1972, life mem, 1985; YMCA, gen coun, 1980-88, bd dir, 1993-; Sigma Pi Phi Fraternity, charter mem, 1982-, pres, 1986-87, 1993-95; nat bd mem, Kappa Alpha Psi Found, gen coun, 1996-; nat bd mem, Pan Hellenic Coun, 1996-; Kappa Alpha Psi; founder, Floyd Skinner Bar Asn. United Negro College Fund Chair, 2003. **Honors/Awds:** Role Model of the Year, NAACP, 1989; Distinguished Citizen, Muskegon, Mich, 1989; Donald R Black Civic Award, Grand Rapids Jr Col, 1989; Lawyer of the Year, Floyd Skinner Bar Asn, 1987; Kappa Distinguished Member, Kappa Alpha Psi, 1990; Boys Scouts Am, Whitney Young Award, 1991; Ohio Northern Law, Honorary Doctorate Degree, 1992; Giant of Giants Award, 1996; UNCF, Col Fund Distinguished Award, 1997; Roastee Award, Grand Rapids Community Col, 1994; Judge Benjamin Logan Day, Grand Rapids, Mich,1994; Trailblazer Award, 1994; Renaissance Group Vol of the Year Award, 1995; NAACP, nominated for Spingarn Medal, 1995; William Ming Award, NatAsn Advan Colored People, 1997; Judge Benjamin Logan Day, Baltimore, Md,1995; Judge Benjamin Logan Day, Milwaukee, Wis, 1995; Awarded keys tofollowing cities: Dayton, OH; Las Vegas, Nev; Huntington, WVa; Bay City, Mich; Muskegon, Mich; Muskegon Heights, Mich; Baltimore, Md; Seattle, Wash; Saginaw, MI; Dowagiac, Mich; Cincinnati, OH; Kan City, MO; Milwaukee, Wisc; inducted into Distinguished Hall of Fame, Alumni Chaminade High Sch, 1995. **Business Addr:** Chief Judge, State of Michigan 61st District Court, 333 Monroe Ave NW, Grand Rapids, MI 49503-2211, **Business Phone:** (616)456-3278.

LOGAN, BILL. See LOGAN, WILLIS HUBERT.

LOGAN, CAROLYN GREEN
Law enforcement officer. **Personal:** Born Jul 5, 1957, Asheville, NC; daughter of Mack and Gladys; married Karl, Sep 20, 1987 (divorced); children: Christopher Green, Morgan & Taelor. **Career:** Asheville Police Dept, police officer, 1977-84; NC State Hwy Patrol, master trooper, 1984-. **Orgs:** Onyx Optimist Club, friendship chmn, 1995-96; First Mayfield Mem Baptist Church, infant & toddler counr, 1995-96. **Honors/Awds:** Dedicated Services, Central Asheville Optimist, 1983; Dedicated Services Award, Asheville Police Dept, 1984, 1985; Law Enforcement Award, Hidden Valley Optimist, 1985; Certificate, Advan Law Enforcement, 1992; HP Trooper of the Year, Meck Co Rotary/Boy Scouts Am, 1995; First Black Female Pioneer Trooper, Northstate Law Enforcement, 1996. **Special Achievements:** General Instructor, 1996; Radar-Vascar Instructor, First African-American female to join North Carolina State Highway Patrol, 1984. First African-American female to join the Asheville Police. **Business Addr:** Master Trooper, North Carolina State Highway Patrol, 2206 Fowler Secrest Rd, Monroe, NC 28262, **Business Phone:** (704)283-8559.

LOGAN, EDDIE. See LOGAN, JAMES.

LOGAN, ERNEST EDWARD, II
Football player. **Personal:** Born May 18, 1968, Fort Bragg, NC; married Diana; children: Ernest III. **Educ:** East Carolina Univ. **Career:** Football player(retired), football coach, Cleveland Browns, 1991-92; Atlanta Falcons, defensive tackle, 1993-94; Jacksonville Jaguars, 1995-96; New York Jets, 1997-2000. Jackvili Univ, defensive coach, currently.

LOGAN, GEORGE, III
Lawyer. **Personal:** Born Dec 23, 1942, Elizabeth, NJ; married Sheila Jacqueline Miller; children: Natalie, Camille, George Spencer. **Educ:** Rutgers Col, BA, 1964; Rutgers Sch Law, JD, 1967. **Career:** Ctr Const Rights, staff atty, 1967-68; USAF, asst staff judge advoc, 1968-72; Deprima Aranda & de Leon, 1972-73; Karl & N Stewart, 1973-74; Lindauer & Goldberg, assoc atty, 1975; Lindauer & Logan, 1975-76; atty, self-emp, 1976-78; Logan Marton Halladay & Hall, atty, 1978-99; Ariz Dept Econ Security, chief admin law judge & asst dir, 1980-91; Arizona Supreme Ct, project mgr, 1992-97; Phoenix Munic Ct, ltd jurisdiction judge, 1999-06; Surprise City Coun, AZ, presiding judge, 2006-. **Orgs:** Pres, Ariz Black Lawyers Asn; Phoenix Urban League; Nat Bar Asn; Am Civil Liberties Union; bd dir, Casa Linda Lodge; former pres, Community Legal Serv; City Phoenix, Comn Aging; Joint Legis Comn Conflict Interest. **Military Serv:** USAF, capt, 1968-72. **Business Addr:** Presiding Judge, Surprise City Council of Arizona, 12425 W Bell Rd, Surprise, AZ 85374.*

LOGAN, HAROLD JAMES
Publishing executive. **Personal:** Born Feb 27, 1951, Washington, DC; son of Jean Rhodes and Harold Green; married Etienne Gabrielle Randall, Sep 10, 1988; children: Justin & Gabrielle Randall. **Educ:** Harvard Univ, Cambridge, AB, econ, 1973; Stanford Univ, MBA, 1980. **Career:** Wash Post, Wash, reporter, 1973-78, mgr, electronic publ, 1980-84; Dow Jones & Co, Princeton, dep dir bus dev, 1984-88; Pac Bell diry, San Francisco, dir, bus dev, 1988; Vicinity Corp, chief exec officer; Third Set Partners, mgr; Manheim, sr vpres mkt, sr vpres strategic planning, currently, Man-

heim Interactive Inc, pres & chief exec officer. **Orgs:** Nat Black MBA Asn, 1980-; founding mem, Black Harvard Alumni, Wash, 1982-84; bd dir, Crossroads Theatre, 1986-88; bd dir, Princeton Nursery Sch, 1986-88; Minority caucus, New Oakland Comn, 1991-; dir, WEB Du Bois Soc. **Business Addr:** Senior Vice President of Strategic Planning, Manheim, 6205 Peachtree Dunwoody Rd NE, Atlanta, GA 30328, **Business Phone:** (678)645-0000.

LOGAN, JAMES (EDDIE LOGAN)
Football player. **Personal:** Born Dec 6, 1972, Opp, AL. **Educ:** Univ Memphis. **Career:** Houston Oilers, linebacker, 1995; Cincinnati Bengals, linebacker, 1995; Seattle Seahawks, linebacker, 1996-2000.

LOGAN, DR. JOHN C.
Executive, educator. **Personal:** Born Nov 23, 1948, Dayton, OH; son of John and Harleen; married Tracy, Sep 19, 1994; children: Tina & Marquetta Walker. **Educ:** The Union Inst, PhD, 1997. **Career:** WDAO-FM, program dir/announcer, 1970-83; Acad Broadcasting, owner, pres, 1983-86; Cent St Univ, WCSU-FM, gen mgr, 1986-, Cosby Mass Commun Ctr, dir, 1989-; Logan Commun, pres & gen mgr, 1991-. **Orgs:** Unity Lodge 115, 1983; Nat chair, Logan Family Reunion, 1984; St JamesCath Church; United Negro Col Fund, chair; chair, Sickle Cell AnemiaDrive; local hostm Jerry Lewis Muscular Dystrophy Telethon. **Honors/Awds:** Black Col Radio/Station of the Year, WCSU-FM, 1994; Dayton Ohio Music Hallof Fame, 1999; over 300 honors and awards. **Special Achievements:** Published: The Logan Report, newsletter; The Reality of a Fantasy; Rap, Ritual and Reality; The Academy of Broadcasting; Stranded; released: TheReality of a Fantasy, CD; The Reality of Fantasy, screenplay. **Military Serv:** Army, pfc, 1969-70. **Business Addr:** General Manager, WCSM FM, Central State University, Cosby Mass Communication Center, 1400 Brush Row Rd, Wiberforce, OH 45384, **Business Phone:** (937)376-6261.

LOGAN, JUAN LEON
Artist. **Personal:** Born Aug 16, 1946, Nashville, TN; married Geraldine Johnson; children: Sidney & Jonathan; married Lorna Hosein (divorced 1970); children: Kim. **Educ:** Howard Univ, attended 1964-65; Clark Col, attended 1965-67; Md Inst, MFA, 1996. **Career:** Exhibitions: Jefferson Gallery, 1969; Charlotte Arts & Cult Soc, 1970; Davidson Col Art Gallery, 1973; Winthrop Gallery Winthrop Col, 1974; SC State Col, 1976; Winston-Salem Univ Art Gallery, 1979; Nat Mus African Art Wash, DC 1980; Rowe Gallery, Univ NC, Charlotte, 1983; Selected Juried & Invit Exhib, Drawing Invitational Somerhill Gallery, 1984; Six NC Artists Pfeiffer Col Gallery, 1984; Afro-Am Artists NC Ctr/Gallery, 1984; La Watercolor Soc 14th Annual Int Exhibit 1984; 1984 Invitational/Black & White Spirit Square Arts Ctr, 1984; Spirit Sq Ctr Art & Educ, 1985; Deborah Peverall Gallery, 1985; Portsmouth Mus, 1986; Mus Sci & Indust, 1986; Hickory Mus Art, 1986; Gaston City Mus Art & Hist, 1986; Afro-Am Cultural Ctr, 1986; NC Cent Univ, 1987; Green Hill Ctr NC Art, 1987; Waterworks Visual Arts Ctr, 1988; Johnson C Smith Univ, 1988; Hodges Taylor Gallery, 1989; Lawton Gallery Univ Wis Green Bay, 1990; NC State Univ, 1990; Marita Gilliam Gallery, 1990; Greenville Mus Art, 1991; VA Polytechnic Inst & State Univ, 1991; Tubman Mus, 1992; Lincoln Cultural Ctr, 1992; Gainesville Col, 1992; Univ Ill, Chicago, 1992; Asheville Art Mus, 1993; Ga Southern Mus, 1993; Southeast Ark Arts & Sci Ctr, 1993; Wilmer Jennings Gallery, Kenkeleba, 1993; Isobel Neal Gallery, 1993; McIntosh Gallery, 1993; Potsdam Col State Univ, NY, 1993; St John's Mus Art, 1994; Mint Mus Art, 1994; Jerald Melberg Gallery, 1994; Montgomery Mus Art, 1994; Diggs Gallery Winston-Salem State Univ, 1994; Southeastern Ctr Contemporary Art, 1995; Cleveland Ctr Contemporary Art, 1995; June Kelly Gallery, 1996; Anderson Gallery, Va Commonwealth Univ, 1996; Howard Univ Art Gallery, 1997; Asheville Art Mus, 1997; Budapest Galeria, 1997; Corcoran Gallery, 1997; Litografiska Akademin, 1998; Waterloo Mus Art, 1998; Landmark Gallery, Tex Tech Univ, 1998; Print Ctr 2000, Gomez Gallery, 1999; John Hopkins Univ, 1999, Md Art Place, 1999; Sande Webster Gallery, 2000; James E Lewis Mus, 2000; Philadelphia Mus Art, 2000, San Francisco Craft & Folk Art Mus, 2000; World Bank 2000; Arts Coun Artist fel, 1991-92; Phillips Morris fel, 1996-98; Carolina Minority fel, 1999-2001; Tryon Ctr Visual Arts, artist-in-residence, 2000; Collections: Afro-Am Cultural Ctr; Asheville Art Mus; Atlanta Fulton Pub Libr; Bell South; Blue Cross Greater Philadelphia; Davidson Col; Glaxo Inc; Hammonds House Galleries; Lincoln Nat Ins; Mint Mus Art; Mint Mus Craft & Design; Mus African Am Art; NC A&T State Univ; NC Mus Art; Northwestern Univ; Philadelphia Mus Art; Sch Law, Univ NC, Chapel Hill; SE Ark Arts & Sci Ctr; St John's Mus Art; Tubman African Am Mus; Winston-Salem State Univ; artist, currently. **Honors/Awds:** The Romare Bearden Award for Creativity/Innovation, Medium Carnegie Inst, 1972; Honorable Mention-PIC Award/Nonprocess Educ, Posters Assoc Printing Co, Charlotte, NC 1974; First Place Award, La Watercolor Soc 14 Annual Int Exhib, New Orleans, 1984; Artist as Catalyst, Mid Atlantic Arts Found, 2000. **Military Serv:** USAF, 1967-69. **Home Addr:** 14 Brandon Rd, Chapel Hill, NC 27514-5601. **Business Addr:** Artist, c/o June Kelly, June Kelly Gallery, 591 Broadway Suite 3C, New York, NY 10012, **Business Phone:** (212)226-1660.

LOGAN, LEWIS E
Executive, executive director. **Career:** Md State Treas Off, dir, currently. **Business Addr:** Director, Maryland State Treasurer Office, Rm 108 Treas Bldg 80 Calvert St, Annapolis, MD 21401-1991, **Business Phone:** (410)260-7920.

LOGAN, LLOYD
Pharmacist. **Personal:** Born Dec 27, 1932, Columbia, MO; married Lottie A Pecot; children: Terri, Connie, Gerald, Michael & Kevin. **Educ:** Purdue Univ, 1952; Belleville Jr Col, 1954; St Louis Col Pharmacy, BS, 1958. **Career:** Pharmacist (retired); Daughter Charity Nat Health Syst, asst vp contracts, 1970-95, consult; Rhodes Med Supply Inc, 1968-72; Mound City Pharmacy, owner; Dome Pharmacy, owner; St Louis Univ Hosp, staff pharmacist, 1958-59, chief pharmacist, 1959-67; dir pharmacy & purchasing, 1966-69. **Orgs:** Am Hosp Asn; pres, People Inc; Chi Delta Mu Med Frat; YMCA; Help Inc; treas Page Community Develop Corp; Lindell Hosp; Am Pharmaceut Asn; Nat Pharmaceut Asn; Mound City Pharmaceut Asn; Nat Asn Retail Druggists; St Engelbert Sch Bd; St Louis Archdiocesan Sch Bd; St Louis Urban League. **Military Serv:** USAF, 1952-56. **Home Addr:** 6055 Lindell Blvd, St Louis, MO 63112, **Home Phone:** (314)726-0427. *

LOGAN, THOMAS W S, SR.
Clergy. **Personal:** Born Mar 19, 1912, Philadelphia, PA; son of John Richard Logan Sr and Mary Harbison Logan; married Hermione Hill, Sep 3, 1938; children: Thomas Jr. **Educ:** Johnson C Smith Univ, 1930-33; Lincoln Univ, AB, 1935, LLD, 1985; Gen Theol Sem, cert, 1935-38; Philadelphia Div Sch, STM, 1941; Mansfield Col, Oxford, Eng, cert, 1974; St Augustine's Col, Raleigh, NC, LHD, 1984; Durham Col, Durham, NC, DD, 1984. **Career:** St Augustine, New York, vicar, 1938-39; St Philips, New York, curate 1938-39; St Michaels, vicar, 1940-45, rector, 1945; Philadelphia police, chaplain, 1968; Calvary Episcopal Church, Philadelphia, PA, rector & canon, 1945-84, Rector, emer, 1984; First Colonel Wesley Church, Philadelphia, PA, intern, 1984-86; Historic St Thomas Church, Philadelphia, PA, intern, 1990-92; Annunciation Church, Philadelphia, PA, intern, 1993-94; Calvary Episcopal Church, Wash, rector emer, currently. **Orgs:** Past pres, Tribune charters, 1945-69; founder, past pres, chaplain, Philadelphia Chap Frontier, 1945, 1965-67; founder, Parkside YMCA, 1945; past pres, Philadelphia YMCA, 1946-47; past pres, Nat Church Workers conf, 1951-61; past pres, Hampton Min conf, 1960-61; asst chaplain, IBPOEW, 1968; past grand master, Prince Hall Masons, 1968-69; trustee, Haverford St Hosp, 1970-84; life mem, Alpha Phi Alpha; past chaplain, Imperial Coun, Shrinedon, 1970-71, 1982-84, 1996-97; past grand chaplain Frontiers Int, 1971; life mem, Central HS; life mem, Lincoln Univ; life mem, Nat Asn Advan Colored People; bd mem, Darby Nat Asn Advan Colored People; dean, summer sch St Paul, Laurenceville, VA; pub dir, Black Clergy Dir Episcopal Church; 33rd degree Mason. **Honors/Awds:** Afro-American Award, 1944; hon mem Cornish Post 292, 1944; bd Eme, Philadelphia USO, 1944; Demolay consult Award, 1966; Philadelphia Tribune Char Award, 1968; LHL, St Augustine's College, Raliegh, NC, 1982; LLD,Lincoln Univ, Chester Cty, PA, 1985; VA Seminary, 1989; LLD, Lynchburg,VA; ThD, Episcopal Seminary, Cambridge, Mass, 1994; General Theological Seminary, STD, 1995. auth, chapter, Voices of Experiences, M L King Fellow Press, 1985. **Home Addr:** 46 Lincoln Ave, Yeadon, PA 19050. **Business Addr:** Rector Emeritus, Calvary Episcopal Church, 509 Eye St NE, Washington, DC 20002, **Business Phone:** (202)546-8011.

LOGAN, WARREN E
President (Government). **Educ:** BS. **Career:** Off Minority Bus Enterprise, Statewide Bus Develop Ctr, Chattanooga, Memphis & Nashville, exec dir; Tenn Valley Authority, Div Power; Tenn Urban League Affiliates, Knoxville, Memphis & Nashville, chief operating officer, 1998; Urban League Greater Chattanooga, pres & chief exec officer, currently. **Orgs:** Nat Urban League. **Business Phone:** (423)756-1762.

LOGAN, WILLIE FRANK
State government official. **Personal:** Born Feb 16, 1957, Miami, FL; son of Willie and Ruth; married Lyra Blizzard, Jan 23, 1993. **Educ:** Miami Dade Community Col, AA, 1976; Univ Miami, BBA, 1977. **Career:** Opa-locka Mayor, comnr, 1980-82; Opa Locka Community Develop CRP, consult; Fla House Rep, state rep, currently; Performing Arts Ctr Trust Inc. **Orgs:** Nat Asn Advan Colored People; Urban League; Nat CNF State Legislators; pres, Phi Beta Sigma; Alpha Kappa Psi; Alpha Phi Omega; vpres, UBS. **Honors/Awds:** Opa-locka Community Development Corporation Appreciation Award; Greater Miami Chamber of Commerce Legislative Appreciation Award; FEA/UTD Award; Dade County Park Legislative Service Award; Metro-Dade Legislative Appreciation Award; Legislative Service Award, Locktown Community Health Ctr; United Teachers of Dade TIGER Award; Florida Conference of Black State Legislators Award; Dade County Legislative Delegation Service Award; Florida Federation of CDC's Recognition Award; Dade County League of Cities Good Government Award; ACTSO Award; Bethune-Cookman Col Outstanding Contribution Award; Distinction Legislative Service Award, Univ Miami. **Business Addr:** State Representative, House Representatives, 513 The Capitol 402 S Monroe St, Tallahassee, FL 32399-1300, **Business Phone:** (850)488-1157.

LOGAN, WILLIS HUBERT (BILL LOGAN)
Social worker. **Personal:** Born Nov 23, 1943, Springfield, IL; married Joyce A Day; children: Gennea & Andre. **Educ:** Western Ill Univ, attended 1943; Sangamon State Univ, BA, 1972. **Career:** Springfield Recreation Commn, youth supvr, 1962; Allis Chalmers, mach operator, 1963; Ill Nat Bank, bank teller, 1967; Dept Conser, employ coordr, 1979; Dept Community Develop & Progs, Springfield, Ill, exec dir; Springfield Housing Authority, bd dirs, 1984-89; dir Housing Progs, Dept Com & Community Affairs, 1991-97, exec dir, 1997-2005; Springfield Pk Dist, Comnr, currently; Ill Asn pk Districts, treas, vchair, currently. **Orgs:** Frontiers Int, 1976; vchmn, Springfield Planning Comn, 1979; bd mem, United Fund, 1976; pres, Springfield E Asn, 1977; sec Alpha Phi Alpha Mu Delta Lambda, 1980; chmn, Springfield Sangamon Co Reg Planning Comn, 1980; presidential adv comt, Univ Ill; Springfield Golf Club. **Honors/Awds:** Community Service Award, NAACP, 1977; Community Service Award, United Way, 1978. **Military Serv:** AUS, sgt e-4, 1965-67. **Home Addr:** 5017 Blackwolf Rd, Springfield, IL 62707. **Business Addr:** Vice Chair, Illinois Association of Park Districts, 211 E Monroe St, Springfield, IL 62701-1186.

LOGANS, RENEE
Consultant, chief executive officer. **Educ:** Univ Fla, BA. **Career:** Smith Inc, financial consult; Fenner, financial consult; Pierce, financial consult; Merrill Lynch, financial consult; Xerox Corp, sales & mkt, sales exec; Control Data, sales & mkt, acct rep; Access Data Supply, pres & chief exec officer, currently. **Orgs:** Houston Minority Bus Coun; bd the Houston Area Women's Ctr; Da Camera Houston; Ensemble Theatre. **Honors/Awds:** Who's Who US Execs, 1991; Woman Entrepreneur of the Year, Asn Urban Women Entrepreneurs, 1992; Individual Technical Achiever Award, Nat & Greater Houston Area Tech Achievers Acad, 1992; Administrator's Award for Excellence, US Small Bus Admin, 1993. **Business Addr:** President, Chief Executive Officer, Access Data Supply Inc, 2425 W Loop S Suite 855, PO Box 56002, Houston, TX 77256, **Business Phone:** (713)439-0370.

LOGAN-TOOSON, LINDA ANN
Executive. **Personal:** Born Aug 7, 1950, Cincinnati, OH; daughter of Harold John and Amelia Edna. **Educ:** Fisk Univ, BA, 1972; Xavier Univ, MBA, 1975. **Career:** Frigidaire Gen Motors, mkt analyst, 1972-75; IBM, mkt trainee, 1975-76; Drackett Co Bristol Myers, proj dir, 1977-82, mgr consumer res, 1982-84, sr mgr consumer res, 1984-92; W Shell Coldwell Banker, realtor, 1993-; Tucson Limousine Service Inc, vpres, 1991. **Orgs:** Life mem, Alpha Kappa Alpha Sorority Inc, 1970-, chap vpres, 1996-97, pres, 1998-2000; Nat Urban League Black Exec Exchange Prog, 1978-; Nat Asn Female Execs, 1982-; youth prog chairperson, YMCA Black Achievers Prog, 1983-84; bd mem, Gross Br YMCA, 1984-85; vpres, Am Mkt Asn, mem bd dirs, 1985-86, exec adv bd, 1986-89; Nat Black MBA Asn, 1986-; acct mgr, United Way Campaign 1987, 1989, 1990; exec secy, Cincinnati Scholar Found, bd dirs, 1986-88, pres, 1990-91; bd realtors, Nat Asn Realtors, 1993-; vpres, Greater Cincinnati Limousine Asn, 1994-96. **Honors/Awds:** Black Achiever Award, YMCA, 1981; Outstanding Alumni Black Achiever, YMCA, 1982. **Home Addr:** 7624 Castleton Pl, Cincinnati, OH 45237, **Home Phone:** (513)821-4514. **Business Addr:** Vice President, Tucson Limousine Service Inc, 7624 Castleton Pl, Cincinnati, OH 45237-2636, **Business Phone:** (513)821-4515.

LOGUE-KINDER, JOAN
Executive. **Personal:** Born Oct 26, 1943, Richmond, VA; daughter of John Thomas and Helen Harvey; married Lowell A Henry Jr, Oct 6, 1963 (divorced 1981); children: Lowell A Henry III, Catherine Dionne Henry & Christopher Logue Henry; married Randolph S, Dec 13, 1986 (divorced 1995). **Educ:** Wheaton Col, 1959-62; Adelphi Univ, BA, 1964; NY Univ, Mercy Col, cert educ, 1971. **Career:** TWA NYC, ticket agt, 1964-65; US Census Bur, admin asst to dist mgr, 1970; Bd Educ Yonkers, social studies teacher & admin, 1971-75; Nat Black Network, dir pub rels, 1976-83; World Inst Black Commun Inc, co-dir, co-founder, 1978-90; NBN Broadcasting Inc, vpres, 1984-90; Mingo Group Plus Inc, sr vpres, 1990-91; Edelman Pub Rels Worldwide, vpres, 1991-93; US Dept Treasury, Wash, dep asst sec pub affairs, 1993-95; Seagram Co, NY, dir corp comn prog, 1995-96; Save C, Westport, Conn, vpres, 1997-98; Lynch Jones & Ryan Inc, sr vpres mkt & communs, 1998-99; Govt DC, commun dir; Overseas Pvt Investment Corp, Wash, vpres investment devel, 1999-2001; Greater Jamaica Devel Corp, consult, 2001-; Sari Katz Mayor, consult, 2001-; Philadelphia Acad Fine Arts, consult, 2001-; Off Mayor DC, dir comn, 2001. **Orgs:** Asst coord, Howard Samuels Gov NY, 1974; adv pers rep, Morris Udall, 1976; consult, KLM Royal Dutch Airlines, 1976; consult, Ky Fried Chicken, 1976; consult, ATESTA Spanish Nat Tourist Bd, 1977; coord, Nat Asn Black Owned Broadcasters 1977-; bd dirs, NY Chap PUSH, 1983; bd dirs, Girl Scout Coun Greater NY, 1985-; bd dirs, Nat PUSH, 1985; bd dirs, Nigerian-Am Friendship Soc; 100 Black Women; del, White House Conf Small Bus; consult, Sony Corp; sr black media advisor, Dukakis-Bentsen. **Honors/Awds:** Co-publ, "Communications Excellence to Black Audiences" CEBA Exhibit Awards Jour, 1978-90; creator & developer, Action Woman Radio Prog, 1979-; Excellence in Media Award, Inst New Cinema Artists Inc, 1984. **Home Addr:** 1800 7th Ave 9B, New York, NY 10026, **Home Phone:** (212)864-7152. **Business Phone:** (718)291-0282.

LOKEMAN, JOSEPH R
Accountant. **Personal:** Born Jul 24, 1935, Baltimore, MD; son of Joseph Miles and Beulah V; married Shirley M Morse; children: Pamela, Kimberly, Sherre & Shereen. **Educ:** AS, 1967; BS, 1969. **Career:** Bur Pub Debt Treas, auditor, 1968-70; Bur Acct Treas, staff acct, 1971-73; Bur Govt Fin Opers Treas, syst acct, 1973-84, chief gen ledger br, treas, 1984-90; pub acct, enrolled agent, pvt pract, 1967-. **Orgs:** Fed Govt Accts Asn; Nat Soc Pub Accts; Nat Soc Black Accts; Nat Soc Enrolled Agents; Md Soc Accts, Notary Pub; White Oak Civic Asn Silver Spring. **Honors/Awds:** Gallatin Award, 1990. **Military Serv:** AUS, 1957-59. **Home Phone:** (301)622-2695. **Business Addr:** Public Accountant, 4022 Edmondson Ave, Baltimore, MD 21229, **Business Phone:** (410)362-6500.

LOMAS, DR. RONALD LEROY
Educator. **Personal:** Born May 21, 1942, Rock Island, IL. **Educ:** Western Illl Univ, BA, 1965, MA, 1967; Bowling Green State Univ, PhD, 1976. **Career:** Western Ill Univ, grad asst dept speech, 1965-66; Bowling Green State Univ, grad asst dept speech, 1969-70; Lorain City Comm Col, instr speech & dir forensics, reg adv, 1969; Bowling Green State Univ, instr speech & ethnic studies, 1970-, asst dir ethenic studies 1970-75; Univ of Cincinnati Med Sch, coord supportive serv 1975-76; Tex Southern Univ, Houston, assoc prof, speech comm, currently. **Orgs:** Chmn fac eval comt, Lorain County Community Col, 1968-69; chmn, Minority Affairs Comt, 1968-69; adv, Black Progressives, 1968-69; producer, "Black Perspectives", WBGU Channel 70, 1971; consult & lectr, Black Culture St Pauls Episcopal Church Maumee, Ohio, 1972-73; leadership consult B'nai B'rith Youth Org, S Euclid, OH, 1972-73; Lorain Coun, 1970-71; Mich Coun, 1973; Int Commun Assoc; Speech Commun Assoc; producer, host & writer prog WBGU Channel 57, 1973; commun consult, Title I Grant Toledo Minority Businessmen, 1974-75. **Honors/Awds:** Foreign Serv Scholar, 1964; Omicron Delta Kappa, 1973; Distinguish Faculty Award, 1974; Outstanding Instructor, Texas Souther University, 1980. **Business Addr:** Associate Professor Speech Communication, Texas Southern Univ, 3100 Cleborne St, Houston, TX 77004, **Business Phone:** (713)313-7757.

LOMAX, DERVEY A.
Engineer, mayor. **Personal:** Married. **Career:** Naval Electronic Syst Command, electronic specialist; City Coun Col Park, elected, 1957-65; City Coun, re-elected, 1967-73; Col Park Md, elected mayor, 1973; Charles Lomax Dory Estate, rep, 2003; Prince Georges County, Md, Citizens Complaint Oversight Panel, 2002-2006. **Orgs:** Mat Wash Coun Govt Policy Com Pub Safety; City Univ Liason Com; Lakeland Civic Asn, founder; Lakeland Boy Scout Troop, founder; Am Legion; bd dir, Col Park Boys Club; vpres Col Park Boys Club; Prince George's Boys Club; basketball coach for Boys Club of Col Park 7 yrs; Local Civil Air Patrol Unit. **Business Addr:** Off Mayor, 4500 Knox Rd, College Park, MD 20740.*

LOMAX, JANET E
Television journalist. **Personal:** Born Jan 18, 1955, Louisville, KY; daughter of James A and Sedalia M; married Charles V Smith, Aug 31, 1986; children: Erica Claire Smith & Charles Lomax Smith. **Educ:** Murray State Univ, BS, jour & radio/TV prod, 1976. **Career:** WAVE-TV, journalist, 1976-80; WHEC-TV, anchor, 1980; NEWS 10NBC, reporter, co-anchor, curretly. **Orgs:** Nat Asn Black Journalists, 1978-; founding pres, Rochester Asn Black Communicators, 1982; Delta Sigma Theta, 1975-; bd dirs, Community Heating Fund; Jack & Jill Am Inc. **Honors/Awds:** Numerous awards, Louisville, KY, 1976-80; Communications Award, Delta Sigma Theta, 1987; Communicator of the Year, Rochester Advert Asn, 1989. **Business Addr:** Co-Anchor, NEWS 10NBC, 191 E Ave, Rochester, NY 14604, **Business Phone:** (585)546-5670.

LOMAX, MICHAEL L.
School administrator, chief executive officer, president (organization). **Personal:** Married Cheryl Ferguson Lomax; children: 3 daughters. **Educ:** Columbia Univ, MA; Emory Univ, Phd, am & african am lit; Atlanta's Morehouse Col. **Career:** Asst to Maynard Jackson, African Am Mayor; Morehouse Col, prof; Spelman Col, prof; Dillard Univ, pres; United Negro Col Fund, pres & chief exec officer, currently. **Orgs:** Bd chair, Bd Comnr Fulton County, 1980-93; pres, Nat Fac, 1994-97; United Way Am, bd gov; head, Atlanta's Bur Cult Affairs; trustee, Emory Univ; mem founding coun, Smithsonian Insts Nat Mus African Am Hist & Cult; bd dirs, Teach for Am; KIPP Found; Carter Ctr; High Mus Art Atlanta; Studio Mus, Harlem; Bill T Jones Dance Co; founding chair, Nat Black Arts Festival; pres bd adv, Hist Black Cols & Univs. **Honors/Awds:** Laurel Crowned Circle Award, Omicron Delta Kappa, 2006; Distinguished Emory Medal; Candle in the Dark Award, Morehouse Col; received numerous honorary degrees from institutions, including Allen University, Florida Memorial University, Livingstone College, Tuskegee University, University of Vermont, and Virginia Union University. **Business Addr:** President, Chief Executive Officer, United Negro College Fund, 8260 Willow Oaks Corp Dr, PO Box 10444, Fairfax, VA 22031-8044.*

LOMAX, MICHAEL WILKINS
Executive. **Personal:** Born in Philadelphia, PA; married Dr A Faye Rogers; children: Lauren. **Educ:** St Josephs Univ, BS, Soc, 1973; Ins Inst Am. **Career:** Allstate Insurance Co, dist claim mgr, 1977, div claim mgr, 1978-79, asst reg claim mgr, 1979-83, reg claim mgr, 1983-84. **Orgs:** Ins Ed Dir Soc, 1982; Black Exec Exchange Prog Urban League, 1982; bd dir, Brockport Found, 1983-84.

LOMAX, PEARL. See CLEAGE, PEARL MICHELLE.

LOMAX, WALTER P.
Physician. **Personal:** Born Jul 31, 1932, Philadelphia; married; children: 3 girls, boys. **Educ:** Lasalle Col, AB, 1953; Hahnemann Med Col, attened 1957. **Career:** Pvt pract, physician, 1958-90; Univ Pa Sch Med, fac; Lomax Health Systems Inc, founder, 1982-00; Lomax Co, chmn, currently. **Orgs:** Med Soc E Pa; Am Med Asn; Philadelphia County Med Soc; trustee, col alma mater, LaSalle Univ; trustee, Philadelphia Orchestra; trustee, WHYY Public radio & TV sta; Cent Bucks Chamber Com. **Honors/Awds:** Excellence Award, Lincoln Univ, 2003; Fatherhood Award, Nat Fatherhood Initiative. **Business Addr:** Chairman, The Lomax Companies, 200 Highpoint Dr Suite 215, Chalfont, PA 18914.*

LOMBARD, GEORGE PAUL
Baseball player. **Personal:** Born Sep 14, 1975, Atlanta, GA. **Career:** Atlanta Braves, 1994, 1998-2000; Eugene Emeralds, 1995; Macon Braves, 1995-96; Durham Bulls, 1997, 2003; Greenville Braves, 1998, 2002; Richmond Braves, 1999- 2001, 2002; Detroit Tigers, 2002; Tampa Bay Devil Rays, 2003; Boston Red Sox, outfielder, 2004; Portland Sea Dogs, 2004; Pawtucket Red Sox, 2004-05; Wash Nationals, 2006, 2007; New Orleans Zephyrs, 2006; Columbus Clippers, 2007, 2009; Las Vegas 51s, 2008; Albuquerque Isotopes, 2008; Marlins, 2008; Cleveland Indians, 2009. *

LOMBARD, KEN
Executive. **Educ:** Univ Wash, BS, commun. **Career:** Johnson Dev Corp, pres, 1992-04; Starbucks Entertainment, pres, 2004-; Starbucks Coffee Co, pres, 2004-. **Orgs:** Bd dir, Timberland. **Honors/Awds:** City of Angels Corporate Award; Los Angeles Business Journal Corporate Leadership Award. *

LONDON, DR. CLEMENT B G
Educator. **Personal:** Born Sep 12, 1928; son of John London and Henrietta Myrtle Simmons; married Pearl Cynthia Knight, Jun 3, 1962; children: Al Mu. **Educ:** City Col, City Univ New York, BA, 1967, MA, 1969; Teachers Col, Columbia Univ, NY, EdM, 1972, EdD, 1973. **Career:** Toco & Morvant EC Elem Schs, Trinidad-Tobago Sch System, Trinidad, WIndies, asst prin, 1953-60; St Augustine Parochial Sch, Brooklyn, NY, teacher, 1960-61; Harlem Hosp Sch Nursing, New York, sec/registrar, 1963-66; Develop & Training Ctr, Dist rb tv Trades Inc, NYC, instr math & eng, 1967-70; Crossroads Alternative HS, asst prin & dean, 1970-71; Teachers Col, Columbia Univ, New York, grad asst & instr, 1971-73; Intermediate Sch, substitute teacher math, 1974; Fordham Univ, Lincoln Center, Grad Sch Educ, from asst prof educ to assoc prof educ 1974-91, prof emer educ, currently. **Orgs:** Nat Alliance Black Sch Educr, 1975; Ed Bd, Col Stud Jour; ed Curric Career, Ed & Dev Demonstration Proj Youth, 1978; ed consult, Nat Coun Negro Women, 1978; Asn Teacher Educr, 1979; summer chmn, Div Curric & Teaching, 1979; bd elders, Coun Mwamko Wa Siasa Educ Inst, 1980; Nat Sch Bd Asn, 1980-; Org Am Historians, 1980; Asn Caribbean Studies 1980-; Am Asn Advan Humanities, 1980; Am Acad Polit & Social Sci 1980-; reporter & bd dirs, Kappa Alpha Psi 1980-; fac & sec, Sch Educ, Fordham Univ 1981; Salem Cot Serv Coun New York, 1981; Jour Curic Theorizing, 1982-; dir,Project Real, 1984; bd dir Solidaridad Humana 1984; bd mem, Schomburg Corp, Ctr Res Black Cult, 1992-; bd mem, ALL Bereavement Ctr Ltd, 1996-; fac adv, exec comt, Phi Delta Kappa; Kappa Delta Pi; adv bd, curric consult, La Nueva Raza Half House prog; bd mem, African Heritage Studies Asn. **Honors/Awds:** Clement London Day, Celebrant, Toco Anglican Elem Sch, 1977; Spec Recognition Award, Outstanding Quality, Proj Real, 1983. **Special Achievements:** Author, numerous research publications & professional activities including: "Black Women of Valor," African Heritage Studies Association Newsletter, p 9, 1976; 2 video-taped TV appearances: Natl TV Trinidad, WIndies, featuring emotionally oriented issues, 1976-77; "Conf Call, The Caribbean & Latin America", WABC Radio, 3 hour broadcast, 1979-80; "Career& Emplymnt, Critical Factors in Ed Plng," African American Journal for Research & Education, 1981; "Crucibles of Caribbean Conditions, Factors of Understanding for Teaching & Learning Caribbean Students American Editorial Settings" Journal of Caribbean Studies, 2&3, p 182-188, Autumn/Winter 1982; Through Caribbean Eyes, 1989; Test-taking Skills:Guidelines for Curricular & Instructional Practices, 1989; A Piagetian Construct vist Perspective on Curriculum, 1989; On Wings of Changes, 1991; "Multicultural Curriculum Thought: A Perspective," 1992; "Multicultural Education and Curriculum Thought: One Perspective," 1992; "Curriculum as Transformation: A Case for the Inclusion of Multi culturality", 1992; "ARO Catholic School NYC", Black Educator in the Univ Role as Moral Authority Clg Stdnt Jrnl Monograph 18(1 Pt 2), Career Ed for Educational Ldrs, A Focus on Decision Making 1983, Parents and Schools: A sourcebook, Garland Publishings, Inc, 1993; A critical perspective of multi culturality as a philosophy for educational change, Education, 114(3), p 368-383, 1994; Three Turtle Stories, New Mind Productions, Inc, 1994; Linking cultures through literacy. A perspective for the future, In NJ Ellsworth, CN Hedleyand AN Baratta (Eds), Literacy: A redefinition, Lawrence Erlbaum Associates, 1994; Queens Public Access Television, discussing Fordham University Graduate School of Education and its leadership role in Language, Literacy, and Learning, 1994; Enchanted Village & Other Stories, 2000; Crossing Boundaries, 2000; Spring Poems for Children Everywhere, 2000; Beyond the Beaches: On an Archipelago of Words, 2000; Caribbean Visions in Folktales, 2001. **Business Addr:** Professor Emeritus of Education, Fordham University, Lincoln Ctr Campus, New York, NY 10023, **Business Phone:** (212)636-6000.

LONDON, DENISE
Marketing executive. **Educ:** Glassboro State Col; Tex A&M Univ; Univ Cambridge, Eng. **Career:** Patrol officer; Broadcast sta, acct exec; Ford Motor Co, zone mgr; Tex State Aquarium, dir mkt; Nat Aquarium Baltimore, vpres mkt, sr mkt dir. **Orgs:** Am Mkt Asn; Am Zool Aquarium Asn; Am Asn Mus; Pub Rels Soc Am. **Honors/Awds:** Best of Tex & Silver Spur Award,Tex Pub Rels Soc; Hon, YWCA Am; Gold Key Award, Ford Motor Co; Comm Serv, Mayor's Baltimore Citation; Torchbearers Award, 100 Black Women. **Special Achievements:** First African-American to be named senior director of marketing, The Nat Aquarium, Baltimore; First female patrol officer, Camden co, NJ. *

LONDON, EDDIE
Executive. **Personal:** Born Nov 25, 1934, Morgan City, LA; children: Lori B. **Educ:** AA; BA; MBA. **Career:** Design technician, 1965-70; Navy, mgt analyst, 1970-71, oper res analyst 1971-73; Pac Missile Ctr Div Head, analyst, 1974-90; London Enterprise Info Syst, pres, 1990-; Lifestyles Recovery Ctr, chmn & ceo, currently. **Orgs:** Pres, Oxnard-Ventura NAACP; bd Prof Employees; past chmn, Grass Roots Poverty Prog; pres, San Luis Obispo County NAACP, 1992-. **Honors/Awds:** Fed Exe Bd Outstanding Mgt, 1983. **Military Serv:** AUS, Sgt, 1953-56. **Home Addr:** 2655 Campo Rd, Atascadero, CA 93422, **Home Phone:** (805)461-3841. **Business Addr:** Chairman, CFO, Lifestyles Recovery Center Inc, 715 24th st Suite B, Paso Robles, CA 93446, **Business Phone:** (805)238-2290.

LONDON, DR. EDWARD CHARLES
Real estate executive. **Personal:** Born Aug 18, 1944, Memphis, TN; son of James London Sr and Juanita S; married Nell R London; children: Edwin C & Torrick. **Educ:** LeMoyne-Owen Col, BA, econ, 1967; Atlanta Univ, MBA, 1972; John Marshall Law Sch, JD, 1975. **Career:** Metrop Atlanta Rapid Transit Authority, fed grants/sr acct, 1973-75, sr contracts admin, 1975-79, mgr contracts, 1979-81; Edward C London & Assocs Real Estate & Mgt Consult, pres, 1981-, chmn, prin & chief exec officer, currently; Real Estate Mgmt Brokers Inst/Nat Asn Real Estate Brokers, nat dir, 1984-; Cornelius King & Son Inc, Atlanta, GA, chief exec officer, managing broker, 1988-94; Empire Real Estate Bd Inc, pres & chief exec officer, 1989-90; Empire Real Estate Bd Inc, chmn, 1993-95; Harold A. Dawson Co Inc, exec vpres. **Orgs:** Chmn bd dirs, Reach-Out Inc, 1979-84; comt mem, Ga Real Estate Comn Educ Adv Comt, 1983-87; coordr, Pastor's Higher Ground Task Force Antioch Baptist Church 1984-86; bd mem, GA Chap Nat Soc Real Estate Appraisers, 1986-87; Real Estate Educators Asn, 1987; mem bd dirs, 1st vpres Empire Real Estate Bd Inc, 1987; Alpha Phi Alpha, Nat Asn Advan Colored People Atlanta Bus League, Atlanta Exchange, Progressive Alliance, Minority Purchasing Coun, Atlanta Chamber Com; sr mem & cert real estate appraiser Nat Asn Real Estate Appraisers, 1987; cert sr mem, Nat Soc Real Estate Appraisers 1989-; Bd Zoning Appeals, Fulton County GA, 1987-; bd dirs, Community Housing Resources Bd Atlanta, 1987-; chmn, bd trustees, Antioch Baptist Church N; US Dept HUD, Reg Adv Bd, 1991-95; Geo Real Estate Comn Task Force on Brokerage Indust; bd dirs, Atlanta Urban Residential Finance Authority/Atlanta Develop Authority, 1993-; Nat pres/CEO, Nat Asn Real Estate Brokers, 2001-03; former mem, Bd Comnrs, Ga Equal Employ Opp Comm; Atlanta Com Club; Metro Atlanta Lions Club; Fannie Mae Nat Adv Coun Nat Housing Impact Coun, 2001-03; Chase Home Finance Corp Adv Bd, 2003-04. **Honors/Awds:** Outstanding Leadership Award, Reach-Out Inc, 1981; Asn Partner Award; Century Club Award, Butler St YMCA, 1986; Outstanding & Dedicated Service Award, Empire Real Estate Bd Inc, 1986; Basic Budgeting & Accounting for Property Management, 1986; Real Estate Broker of the Year, Empire Real Estate Board Inc 1988; Local Board President of the Year, Nat Asn Real Estate Brokers, 1989; Ga Real Estate Comn Task Force on Brokerage Indus; Realtist of the Year, Nat Asn Real Estate Brokers Inc, 1992; Realtist of the Year, Empire Real Estate Bd Inc, 1994; Outstanding Alumnus Award, United Negro Col Fund (UNCF), 1995. (UNCF), 1995; Presidential Citation, Nat Asn Equal Opportunity HIS HER Educ, 1997. **Special Achievements:** Publications Principles of Apartment Management, 1983. **Military Serv:** AUS, E-5 2 yrs; Superior Cadet Award, Expert Rifleman Badge, Bronze Star, USRVN Serv Medal, Good Conduct Medal, 1968-70. **Business Addr:** Principal & Chairman, Chief Executive Officer, EC London & Associates, 101 Marietta St NW Suite 3310, Atlanta, GA 30303, **Business Phone:** (404)688-6607.

LONDON, GLORIA D.
Banker, executive director. **Personal:** Born Jul 24, 1949, Clinton, LA; daughter of London Hampton and Georgia Lee; children:

Kena Elizabeth. **Educ:** Southern Univ, A&M Col, BS, bus mgt, 1971, MPA, 1993. **Career:** Premier Bank NA, staff, 1971-91; Life Savings Bank, chief opers officer, 1991-92, chief admin officer, 1992; Southern Univ A&M Col, bus develop specialist, 1994-97; Los Angeles County Develop Capital Fund, exec dir, 1997-; Ctr Rural & Small Bus Develop, dir, currently. **Orgs:** Philacter, Alpha Kappa Alpha Sorority Inc; Pi Gamma Mu Honor Soc; Phi Beta Lambda Honor Soc; Beech Grove Baptist Church; NCP; Community Develop Initiative Comt State La. **Honors/Awds:** Outstanding Soror, Alpha Kappa Alpha Sorority Inc, 1985; Black Achievers Award, Young Men's Christian Asn, 1992. *

LONDON, DR. HARLAN
Executive. **Educ:** PhD. **Career:** Syracuse Univ, Human Develop, prof & chair dept, child & family studies, adv to vice chancellor & provost, 1997-. **Business Addr:** Adviser to Vice Chancellor, Provost, Syracuse University, 900 S Crouse Ave, Syracuse, NY 13244-4100, **Business Phone:** (315)443-4291.

LONDON, ROBERTA LEVY
Executive. **Personal:** Born in New York, NY; daughter of Carrie Belle Calier Levy and Henry Edward Levy; married Lester London Jr, Jul 30, 1955. **Educ:** Nassau Community Col, Garden City, NY, AA, 1972; Hunter Coll, New York, NY, BA, 1977; Queens Col, Flushing, NY, educ credits, 1978; Adelphi Univ, Garden City, NY, Grad Cert, 1988. **Career:** Presbyterian Church, New York NY, mgr Human Resources, Prog Agency, 1981-89; Turner/Santa Fe Construction Co, Brooklyn, NY, coordr Local Laws 49/50; Delta Minerva Life Develop Ctr Inc, chmn currently. **Orgs:** Lakeview Pub Libr; One Hundred Black Women Long Island, 1979-83; gov, NE Dist, Nat Asn Negro Bus & Prof Women's Clubs Inc, 1987-91; Delta Sigma Theta Sorority Inc; bd trustees, Union Baptist Church, Hempstead, NY. **Honors/Awds:** Community Service Award, Long Island Black Hist Comt, 1981; Finalist, Long Island Woman of the Year, 1986; Sojourner Truth Award for Meritorious Service, Brooklyn Club, Nat Asn Negro Bus & Prof Women's Clubs Inc, 1989. **Home Addr:** 425 Columbia Ave, Rockville Centre, NY 11570.

LONEY, CAROLYN PATRICIA
Banker. **Personal:** Born Jun 16, 1944, New York, NY; daughter of Daniel and Edna. **Educ:** Morgan State Univ, BS, 1969; Columbia Univ, MBA, 1971. **Career:** Royal Globe Ins Co, rater, 1962-65; NY Nat Asn Advan Colored People, br mgr, 1965; Human Resources Admin, field auditor, 1967; NY State Senate, res worker, 1967; Citibank, corp lending officer, 1969-77, vpres; Fed Res Bank NY, spec asst. **Orgs:** Bd dir, New Harlem YWCA, 1975-76; mem, 100 Black Women, 1977-; adv bd, Columbia Univ Alumni, 1971-; Urban Bankers Coalition, 1973-80; Nat Asn Accts, 1973; Nat Credit & Financial Women's Orgn, 1972-74; founder, Carolyn P Loney Scholarship Award, Morgan State Univ; Am Mgt Asn, 1977-; Uptown C C, 1977-. **Honors/Awds:** Outstanding Instructor of the Year, ICBO, 1974; Black Achiever Award, Harlem YMCA, 1973. **Home Addr:** 363 Murray Ave, Englewood, NJ 07631.

LONG, DR. CHARLES H.
Educator. **Personal:** Born Aug 23, 1926, Little Rock, AR; son of Samuel Preston Long and Geneva Diamond Thompson; married Alice M Freeman, 1952; children: John, Carolyn, Christopher, & David. **Educ:** Dunbar Jr Col, dipl, 1946; Univ Chicago, BD, 1953, PhD, hist relig, 1962. **Career:** Univ Chicago, instr, hist religs, 1956-59, asst prof, 1960-62, from assoc prof to prof, 1963-74; Duke Univ, prof, hist relig, 1974-87; Univ NC, Chapel Hill, Wm Rand Kenan, jr prof, hist relig, 1974-88; Princeton Univ, vis prof, 1961-62; St Xavier's Col, vis prof, Chicago, Ill, 1969; Carleton Col, vis prof, Northfield, Minn, 1970; Univ Tenn, Dept Relig, vis prof, 1980; Univ Pittsburgh, vis prof, 1983-87; Univ Calif, Dept Relig Studies, Ctr Black Studies, Santa Barbara, prof & dir hist relig, 1992-96, prof emer, 1996-; Syracuse Univ, vis prof; Univ Queensland, vis prof, Brisbane, Australia; Tsukuba Univ, Inst Philos, Tsukuba, Japan, vis prof; Univ SC, vis prof, 2003; Univ Mich, vis prof, 2004; Univ Mo, vis prof, 2005. **Orgs:** Am Acad Relig; Soc Relig Higher Edn; Int Asn Historians Relig; Soc Stud Black Relig; Am Soc Stud Relig; bd govs, Univ NC; Press Nat Humanities Fac. **Honors/Awds:** Alumni Yr, Divinty Sch Univ Chicago, 1985; Distinguished Alumni Award, Univ Chicago, 1991; DHL, Dickinson Col, 1971; DHL, Claremont Grad Univ, 2009. **Special Achievements:** Author: Myth, Culture and History in West Africa, 1960; Alpha, The Myths of Creation, 1963; The History of Religions: Essays in Understanding, 1967; Significations: Signs, Symbols and Images in the Interpretation of Religion, 1986. **Military Serv:** USAAF Sgt 1944-46. **Home Addr:** 405 Wesley Dr, Chapel Hill, NC 27516.

LONG, EDDIE L.
Clergy, bishop. **Personal:** Born Jan 1, 1953?, Charlotte, NC; son of Floyd and Hattie; married Vanessa; children: Eric, Edward, Jared, Taylor. **Educ:** Charlotte Pub Sch Syst; NC Cent Univ, BS, bus admin, 1976, hon doctorate; Atlanta Interdenominational Theol Ctr, divinity, 1986; Beulah Heights Bible Col, Atlanta, hon doctorate; Morehouse Sch Relig. **Career:** Atlanta's Morning Star Baptist Church, pastor, 1981; New Birth Missionary Baptist Church, pastor, 1987-; Full Gospel Baptist Conv, bishop; Ford Co; Faith Acad, founder & chief exec officer. **Orgs:** Co-chair, Hosea Feed Hungry Proj, 2001; bd trustees, NC Cent Univ, 2002; vice-chair, Morehouse Sch Relig. **Honors/Awds:** Legacy Award, Big Brothers & Big Sisters Metro Atlanta, 1999; Faith/Community Leadership Award, 100 Black Men Am, 2003; Trumpet Awards, 2005; Relig Contemporary Award, IRC; Champion Award; New York Festival's Silver World Medal; World Media Festival's Intermedia Golden Globe. **Special Achievements:** America's 125 most influential leaders; one of the Most Influential Leaders in Black America, Savoy Magazine; One of first among Baptist clergy appointed to office of Bishop in the newly formed Full Gospel Baptist Convention; nation's best-known and most influential black clergy to craft a new role for US; Book: Taking Over. **Business Addr:** Bishop, New Birth Missionary Baptist Church, 6400 Woodrow Rd, Lithonia, GA 30038.*

LONG, GERALD BERNARD
Accountant. **Personal:** Born Oct 19, 1956, Bessemer, AL; son of Edward Beckon Sr and Ruby Stein; married Darlene Gillon Long, Oct 20, 1980; children: Claudia Miranda. **Educ:** Bessemer Tech Col, aso, 1978; Univ Ala, Birmingham, BS, 1983; Mich State Univ Grad Sch Bus Admin, attended 1989. **Career:** Peat Marwick Main, asst acct, 1983-84, staff acct, 1984-85, sr acct, 1985-86, level 1 suv, 1986-87, level 2 suv, 1987-88; Booker T Wash Ins Co, dir internal audit, 1988; State Ala Pub Serv Cms, adv staff cpa, 1988-93, dir telecommunications div, 1993-96; Gerald B Long & Co, owner, 1995-. **Orgs:** Am Inst CPA's, 1988-; Ala Soc CPA's, 1985-. **Honors/Awds:** Goldstein Fund, Goldstein Scholar, 1982; Ala State Univ, Scholastic Achievement Award, 1978. **Home Phone:** (334)284-5241. **Business Addr:** Owner, Gerald B Long & Co, 2400 Presidents Dr Suite 200, PO Box 231447, Montgomery, AL 36123-1447, **Business Phone:** (334)279-5768.*

LONG, GRANT ANDREW
Basketball player. **Personal:** Born Mar 12, 1966, Wayne, MI; married Nikki; children: Garvis, Gavar, Abagayl & Amiala. **Educ:** Eastern Mich Univ, Ypsilanti, MI, 1988. **Career:** Basketball player (retired); Miami Heat, forward, 1988-94; Atlanta Hawks, 1994-96; Detroit Pistons, 1996-98; Atlanta Hawks, 1998-99; Vancouver Grizzlies, 1999-2001; Memphis Grizzlies, 2001-02; Boston Celtics, 2002-03. **Orgs:** Lorenzo Benz Youth Detention Ctr.

LONG, DR. IRENE
Physician. **Personal:** Born Nov 16, 1951, Cleveland, OH; daughter of Andrew Duhart and Heloweise Davis Duhart. **Educ:** Northwestern Univ Evanston Ill, BA, 1973; St Louis Univ Sch Med, MD, 1977; Wright State Univ Sch Med, MS. **Career:** Cleveland Clinic, internship gen surgery; Mt Sinai Hosp, resident gen surg; Wright State Univ, Dayton, OH, resident aerospace med; NASA, Kennedy Space Ctr, chief med officer & assoc dir, 2000-. **Honors/Awds:** Women of the Year, Kennedy Space Ctr, 1986; Women in Aerospace Outstanding Achievement Award, 1998; Soc NASA Flight Surgeons President's Award, 1995; NASA Outstanding Leadership Medal, 1997; NASA Exceptional Serv Medal, 2000; Ohio Women' Hall of Fame, 2001; Women of Color Technology Awards Conference Lifetime Achievement Award, 2005. **Special Achievements:** First black woman chief of med at Kennedy Space Ctr. **Business Addr:** Chief of Medical Operations, Associate Director Support Services, NASA, Kennedy Space Center Office, MD-MED, Orlando, FL 32899, **Business Phone:** (321)867-5000.

LONG, JAMES, JR.
Executive. **Personal:** Born Apr 26, 1931, St Francis County, AR; son of James Sr and Almamie Gray; married Patricia Hardiman, Apr 18, 1954; children: Karen R Long, Kathryn C Long, Kaye Patrice H Long Allen & James III. **Educ:** Lincoln Univ Mo, BS, educ/commun ROTC Corp Engineers, 1954; Northeastern Univ, Boston, Mass, Grad Sch, MBA, 1976. **Career:** US Govt Army, Ft Belvoir, officer & US Army, 1954-57, Ft Riley, Kans, officer & US Army Corp Engr, 1954-57; Lincoln Univ Jefferson City, Mo, asst instr & dir stud union, 1957-61; Lincoln Sr High Sch, Kans City, Mo, teacher & coach, 1961-64; Western Elec Co, Lee's Summit, Mo, supvr mfg & safety dir, 1964-69; Gen Electric Co, Lynn, Mass, mgr mfg manpower develop, mgr personnel practices, 1970-74, mgr employee rels LUO, 1974-81, mgr equal opportunity & compliance, 1982-. **Orgs:** Chmn, Lynn Corp Adv Bd Salvation Army, 1982-86; dir, Pvt Indust Coun, 1983-; dir, Action Boston Community Develop, 1984-; dir, vpres, Indust Rels Mass Pre-Engineering Prog, 1985-; dir, Lynn, Mass Hist Soc, 1986-. **Honors/Awds:** Omega Man of the Year, Beta Omega Grad Chapters, 1967; co-founder, The Henry Buckner Sch, St Paul, AME Church, Cambridge, Mass, 1973; Hall of Fame ROTC, Lincoln Univ Mo, 1975; Others Award, Salvation Army, 1986; Past Basileus Award, Beta Omega Chapter Omega Psi Phi Frat Inc, 1988; Gen Electric Managerial Award, 1989. **Special Achievements:** Developed a group of black square dancers for TV, 1957; No 1 Safety Prog, Western Electric's Parent Body, 1964; organized "The Soulful Squares" during black history month, 1988; co-organized Minority Mentor's Program at Gen Electric, 1989. **Military Serv:** AUS Corp Engineers, First Lt, 1954-57; No 1 Student, Ft Riley, Kans, Fifty Army Physical Training Instructors Acad, 1955. **Home Addr:** 149 Adams St, Lexington, MA 02420. **Business Addr:** Manager Equal Opportunity, Compliance, Gen Electric Co, General Electric Co, Aircraft Engines & Turbine Business Ope, 1000 Wern Ave Suite 14512, Lynn, MA 01910, **Business Phone:** (617)594-2687.

LONG, JAMES ALEXANDER
Executive. **Personal:** Born Dec 26, 1926, Jacksonville, FL; son of Willie James and Ruby Hawkins; married Ruth Beatrice Mitchell; children: John Alexander. **Educ:** NC A&T State Univ, BS, 1950; Univ Mich, MA, 1962; Wayne State Univ, post grad study. **Career:** Executive (retired); NC A&T State Univ, instr Eng & jour, 1950-52; St Paul's Col, instr Eng & jour, 1952-57; Foch Jr High Sch, teacher Eng & soc studies, 1957-62, Eng dept head, 1962-65; Cooley High Sch, guidance counr, 1965-67, asst prin, 1967-70; Northwestern High Sch, prin, 1970-72; Storer Broadcasting Co, gen exec & coordr training progs, 1972-74, mgr personnel develop, 1974-80; Storer Communs Inc, corp vpres personnel develop, 1980-87; Am Civil Liberties Union Fla, exec dir, 1987-88; Am Civil Liberties Union Fla, exec dir, 1987-88; Dade County Public Schs, educ specialist, 1988-99. **Orgs:** Am Mgmt Asn, 1973-; Am Soc Personnel Admin, 1975-; Admin Mgmt Soc, Phi Delta Kappa Educ Frat; Ind Labor Coun Human Resources Ctr Albertson NY; Dade's Employ Handicapped Community; exec bd, Goodwill Ind Miami; Lafayette Park Kiwanis Club; Church Open Door United Church Christ; Alpha Phi Alpha Frat Inc; Alpha Rho Boule Sigma Pi Phi Frat Inc; bd dirs, Family Coun Serv Miami; chairperson employment comn, Pvt Ind Coun, Miami. **Honors/Awds:** NC A&T State Univ Gate City Alumni Chap Award; Achiever's Award Family Christian Asn Am Inc, Miami, 1986; Presidential Citation Nat Asn for Equal Opportunity in Higher Educ, Wash, DC, 1986. **Military Serv:** USAAF. **Home Addr:** 20 NW 89th St, Miami, FL 33150-2432.

LONG, JAMES L.
Judge, lawyer. **Personal:** Born Dec 7, 1937, Wintergarden, FL; son of James J and Susie L. **Educ:** San Jose State Col, BA, 1960; Howard Univ Law Sch, JD, 1967. **Career:** Legislative Coun Bur Calif State Legislature, grad legal asst; Legal Aid Soc Sacramento Co, grad legal asst; pvt pract atty; Super Court Bar Asn Liaison Comt, mem; Supreme Ct, judge; Calif State Univ, Sacremento, CA, asst prof criminal justice; Sacramento Co Super Ct, judge, currently. **Orgs:** Hon mem, Wiley W Manual Bar Asn, Sacramento, CA; Appellate Dept Super Ct Sacramento Co, 1987; Sacramento City/Co Comn Bicentennial US Constitution; spec coun, Nat Asn Advan Colored People Western Region. **Honors/Awds:** Law & Justice Award, Sacramento Br, Nat Asn Advan Colored People; Outstanding Contribution Award, Riverside Br, Nat Asn Advan Colored People; Pro Tem Justice Supreme Ct, 1985; Justice Pro Tem, Ct Appeal Third Appellate Dist, 1987; Judge of the Year Award, Sacramento Co Bar Asn, 1998. **Special Achievements:** Co-author "Amer Minorities, The Justice Issue," Prentice Hall Inc, 1975. **Military Serv:** AUS Reserve Corps, 2nd lt. **Business Addr:** Judge, Sacramento County Superior Court, 720 9th St, Sacramento, CA 95814.*

LONG, JERRY WAYNE
Computer executive, president (organization). **Personal:** Born Jun 6, 1951, Murfreesboro, TN; son of Delois and Ernest; married Marjorie E Russell, Aug 1, 1987; children: Julian, Jamaal & Khalilah. **Educ:** Middle Tenn State Univ, BS, 1972; Univ Tenn, MBA, 1980. **Career:** Gen Elec, prog mgr; CG Aetna, proj mgr; Hartford Ins Group, mgr data archit planning; PC Consult, founder & owner; PCC Technol Group LLC, founder, pres & chief exec officer, 1994-. **Orgs:** Pres, Black Data Processing Asn, Bloomfield Chamber Com; Bus Leadership Circle, 1998; bd dir, Conn Bus & Indust Asn; Kappa Alpha Psi Fraternity; Metro Hartford Chamber Com, currently. **Honors/Awds:** Metro Hartford Bus Leader Year Technol, 2000. **Home Addr:** 17 Avery Rd, Bloomfield, CT 06002-4318. **Business Addr:** President, Chief Executive Officer, PCC Technology Group, 2 Barnard Lane, Bloomfield, CT 06002, **Business Phone:** (860)242-3299 Ext 225.

LONG, JOHN EDDIE
Basketball player. **Personal:** Born Aug 28, 1956, Romulus, MI. **Educ:** Univ Detroit Mercy. **Career:** Basket Ball Player (retired); Detroit Pistons; Atlanta Hawks; Toronto Raptors.

LONG, JOHN EDWARD
Educator. **Personal:** Born Mar 16, 1941, Philadelphia, PA; married Carolyn Yvonne Wakefield. **Educ:** Temple Univ, BA, 1963; Theol Sem Reformed Episcopal Ch, BD, 1966; Westminister Theol Sem, attended 1970; Tunisia N African Ctr, Fellowship Arabic Studies, 1972; Brandeis Univ, MA, PhD, 1978. **Career:** Western Ky Univ, dept head, assoc prof religious studies, currently. **Orgs:** Fulbright-Hays Res Fellow, Algeria, 1974-75; Middle E & Studies Asn, 1975;Middle E Inst, 1975; Am Asn Teachers Arabic, 1979. **Business Addr:** Associate Professor, Western Kentucky University, Department of Philosophy & Religion, 1906 College Heights Blvd, 1 Big Red Way Cherry Hall Room 318B, Bowling Green, KY 42101, **Business Phone:** (270)745-5753.

LONG, LEONARD
Executive. **Educ:** Univ Tex, MSSW. **Career:** W Dallas Community Ctr, chief exec officer, currently. **Business Addr:** Chief

Executive Officer, West Dallas Community Center, 8200 Brookriver Dr Suite N704, Dallas, TX 75247.*

LONG, MONTI M
Automotive executive. **Personal:** Born Sep 24, 1957, Chicago, IL; son of Curtis and Edna Phillips Carlson; married Dana L Lucas, Nov 22, 1980; children: Tiffany Nicole & Tonya Renee. **Educ:** Glen Oaks Community Col, attended 1975-77; Ford Dealer Training, 1988; Chrysler Dealer Seminar attended 1989; Chrysler Financial Seminar, 1990. **Career:** Clark Equipment, qual control, 1979-82; Monti Long's Automobile Referral Serv, pres, owner, 1980-81; M & M Dodge-Honda Inc, salesman, 1982-85; Dick Loehr's Auto Mart, bus mgr, 1985-87; Brighton Ford-Mercury Inc, vpres, gen mgr, 1988-90; Vicksburg Chrysler-Plymouth-Dodge Inc, pres, gen mgr, dealer prin, 1989-. **Orgs:** Vpres, Jeep Eagle Div, Chrysler Minority Dealers Asn; pvt capitol dealers chmn, 1982-; Chamber Com, 1988-; Nat Asn Minority Auto Dealers, 1988-; Better Bus Bur, 1988-; Mich Automobile Dealers Asn, 1988-; Ford Black Dealers Asn, 1988-; Chrysler Advert Asn, 1989-; Chrysler Dealer Adv Coun, 1992-. **Honors/Awds:** Chrysler, Pentastar Club, 1990, 1991, 1992, 1993; Just the Best Award, 1990, 1991, 1993, 1994, Sales Profs, 1983, 1984; Hall of Fame Award, Marcellus High Sch, 1991. **Home Addr:** 5727 Briarhill Dr, Kalamazoo, MI 49009-9536. **Business Phone:** (269)649-2000.

LONG, NIA (NITARA CARLYNN LONG)
Actor. **Personal:** Born Oct 30, 1970, Brooklyn, NY; daughter of Doc and Talita Long; married Massai Dorsey; children: Massai Dorsey II. **Career:** Films: Boyz N The Hood, 1991; Made in America, 1993; Friday, 1995; Love Jones, 1997; Soul Food, 1997; The Best Man, 1999; Stigmata, 1999; Held Up, 1999; The Secret Laughter of Women, 1999; The Broken Hearts Club, 2000; Boiler Room, 2000; Big Momma's House, 2000; How to Get the Man's Foot Outta Your Ass, 2003; Big Momma's House 2, 2006; Premonition, 2007; Are We Done Yet?, 2007; Gospel Hill, 2008; TV Films: "The BRAT Patrol", 1986; "Fresh Prince of Bel-Air", 1996; "Butter", 1998; "Judging Amy", 2001-02; "Sightings: Heartland Ghost", 2002; "Alfie", 2004; "Are We There Yet", 2005; TV Series: "The Guiding Light"; "Live Shot", 1995; "Third Watch", 2003-05; "Big Shots", 2007; "Boston Legal", 2007; Big shots, 2007-08. **Honors/Awds:** Black Star Award for Star of the Year, 2000; Black Reel Award, 2000; Image Award for Outstanding Actress in a Motion Picture, 2000; Image Award, 2004, 2005; BET Comedy Award, 2005; Nominated for Blockbuster Entertainment Award, 2001. **Special Achievements:** Image Award Nomination, Guiding Light, 1993. **Business Phone:** (310)277-4400.*

LONG, NITARA CARLYNN. See LONG, NIA.

LONG, PROF. RICHARD A.
Educator. **Personal:** Born Feb 9, 1927, Philadelphia, PA; son of Leila Washington Long and Thaddeus. **Educ:** Temple Univ, BA, 1947; MA, 1948; Univ Pa, 1948-49; Oxford Univ, 1950; Univ Paris, 1954; Fulbright Scholar, 1957-58; Univ Poitiers, PhD, 1965. **Career:** Morgan State Col, instr, assoc prof, 1951-66; Univ Poitiers, lectr,1964-65; Hampton Inst, prof, mus dir, 1966-68; Atlanta Univ, Afro-Am studies, instr, 1968-87; Atlanta Univ, prof, 1968-87; Harvard Univ, lectr, 1969-71; Univ NC, vis prof, 1972; Emory Univ, atticus haygood emer prof, interdisciplinary studies, 1973-. **Orgs:** Pres, Col Lang Assoc, SE Conf Ling; ed bd, Phylon. **Special Achievements:** Published books like: Black Americana (cult hist) 1985; African American Writing (anthology) 1985; The Black Tradition American Dance; Conducted numerous symposiums, exhibition, conferences. **Business Addr:** Atticus Haygood Professor Emeritus, Emory University, 201 Dowman Dr, Atlanta, GA 30322, **Business Phone:** (404)727-6123.

LONG, STEFFAN
Executive. **Personal:** Born Oct 6, 1929, Philadelphia, PA. **Educ:** Howard U; Univ Mex; Univ Bridgeport; Am Inst Banking. **Career:** CT Nat Bank, vpres & mgr. **Orgs:** Past treas, Family Serv SE Fairfield Co; Gtr Bridgeport Heart Asn; bd mgrs, YMCA; exec bd mem, Gtr Bridgeport-Stratford NAACP; treas, Hall Neighborhood House; bd mem, St Marks Day Care Center; UNA; Nat Negro Col Fund; 2nd pres, UNA Fairfield Co; pres, Japanese Scholarship Comt Univ Bridgeport; treas, Gr Bridgeport Opera Co; treas, Gr Bridgeport Vis Nurses Asn; bd mem, Italian Community Center Guild. **Honors/Awds:** Barnum Festival Society Award, 1968; Rotary Club of Newtown, 1952; Bureau of Naval Personnel Award, 1946; Spec Guest & Soloist Chap England; formalinvitation to White House; citations Mayor Bridgeport NAACP & Nat Negro Business Women.

LONG, TERRENCE DEON
Baseball player. **Personal:** Born Feb 29, 1976, Montgomery, AL. **Career:** Baseball Player (retired); New York Mets, 1999; Oakland A's, 1999-2003; San Diego Padres, 2004; Kansas City Royals, outfielder, 2005; New York Yankees, 2006. *

LONG, WILLIAM H, JR.
Judge. **Personal:** Born Jun 7, 1947, Daytona Beach, FL; children: William III & Cherylen. **Educ:** Univ Miami, BA, 1968; Univ Miami Law Sch, JD, 1971. **Career:** Univ Miami Law Sch, instr, 1970; Opa Locka Mun Ct, assoc judge, 1972; Long & Smith Pa, partner; Long Knox Mays, Pa; Coun Legal Educ Oppor. **Orgs:** Founder, United Black Students Univ Miami, 1968; pres, Black Am Law Students Asn, 1971; chmn, adv comn, Dade Co Comprehensive Offender Rehab Prog Inc; Phi Alpha Delta; Colo Bar Asn. **Honors/Awds:** James E Scott Community Service Award, 1973.

LOPES, DAVID EARL
Athletic coach, baseball player. **Personal:** Born May 3, 1945, East Providence, RI; married Linda Bandover. **Educ:** Washburn Univ, BS, educ, 1969. **Career:** Baseball player (retired), baseball coach; Los Angeles Dodgers, infielder & outfielder, 1972-81; Oakland Athletics, infielder, outfielder & designated hitter, 1982-84; Chicago Cubs, infielder & outfielder, 1984-86; Houston Astros, outfielder & infielder, 1986-87; Rangers, first base coach, 1988-91; Tex Rangers, coach; Baltimore Orioles, first base coach,1992; Orioles, first base coach, 1992-94; Padres, first base coach,1995-99; Brewers, mgr, 2000-02; San Diego Padres, first base coach, 2003-05; Wash Nationals, first base coach, 2006; Philadelphia Phillies, first base coach, currently. **Honors/Awds:** All-Star team; Gold Glove winner; Nat League All-Star Team, 1978-81. *

LOPEZ, D JACQUELINE
Psychologist, educator. **Personal:** Born Mar 4, 1922, New York, NY; daughter of Sydney A and Hilda Gabay; divorced. **Educ:** New York Univ, BA, 1944, MA, 1955, PhD, 1970, postdoctoral cert, 1985. **Career:** Chicago Defender, writer, reporter, 1945-48; Ebony Mag, writer, reporter, 1945-48; Univ Chicago, Test Admin Office, asst dir, 1948-53; City Col New York, instr, 1970-75; Pvt Practice Psychoanalytically Oriented Psychotherapy, 1965-93; NYU Testing & Advisement Ctr, sr psychologist, 1960-69; Univ Coun Servs, clinic psychologist, 1975-98, Dept Applied Psychol, adjunct assoc prof, 1975-. **Orgs:** Am Psychological Asn, 1955-; Psychoanalytic Soc, NYU Postdotoral Prog, 1985-. **Special Achievements:** Written Race, Ethnicity and the Psychoanalytic Contact, Psychoanalytic Society Conference, Feb 1, 1992 NYU; "The Sexually Promiscuous Adolescent" Manhattan College Conference, 1976. **Business Addr:** Adjunct Associate Professor, New York University, Department of Applied Psychology, 239 Greene St E Bldg 4th Fl, New York, NY 10003, **Business Phone:** (212)998-5555.

LORD, CLYDE ORMOND
Physician. **Personal:** Born Aug 10, 1937, Brooklyn, NY; son of Mildred Agatha and F Levi; married Barbara; children: Sharon, Clyde Jr, David. **Educ:** Univ VT, BA, 1959; Meharry Med Col, MD, 1963. **Career:** Kings County Hosp, internship, 1963-64; Columbia Presbyterian Med Ctr, resident, 1964-66, fel pharmacol, 1966-67; AUS Hosp, chief anesthesia, 1967-69, asst prof dept anesthesia, 1969-70; SW Community Hosp, staff physician, 1970-; Westside Anesthesia Asn, anesthesiologist; pvt pract, physican, currently. **Orgs:** Elder Westend Presbyterian Church, 1973-; Am Med Asn; Nat Med Asn; Am Soc Anesthesiologist; Alpha Omega Alpha Hon Med Soc; Am Bd Anesthesiology; fel Am Col Anesthesiol; diplomate, Am Acad Pain Mgt; pres, W Side Anesthesia Assocs . **Honors/Awds:** AUS, maj, 1967-69. **Business Addr:** Anesthesiologist, 501 Fairburn Rd SW, Atlanta, GA 30311.*

LORENZO, IRVING DOMINGO, JR. See GOTTI, IRV.

LORTHRIDGE, DR. JAMES E.
School administrator, school superintendent. **Educ:** Prairie View A&M Univ, BS, 1964; Calif State Univ Long Beach, MA, 1970; Claremont Grad Sch, PhD, 1974; Rockefeller Found, Post Doctoral, 1978. **Career:** School Superintendent (retired), school administrator; Mt Pleasant Sch Dist, asst supt, 1978, supt, 1978-79; W Valley Community Col, dir personnel, 1979-83; Stockton Unified Sch Dist, supt, 1983-86; Ithaca City Sch Dist, supt. **Orgs:** Bd mem, Mt Pleasant Sch Bd; Calif Asn Sec Sch Admin, Am Asn Sec Sch Admin, Asn Calif Sch Admin; Phi Delta Kappa, Nat Asn Advan Colored People; hon life mem, PTA; panel mem, Am Arbit Asn. **Honors/Awds:** Hon Serv PTA. **Home Addr:** 5609 Pintail Ct, Stockton, CA 95207.

LOTT, GAY LLOYD
Lawyer. **Personal:** Born Mar 12, 1937, Chicago, IL; children: Gay Lloyd, Jr. **Educ:** Univ Ill; Roosevelt Univ, attended 1962; John Marshall Law Sch, attended 1964. **Career:** IRS, 1960-65; Peterson Johnson & Harris, 1965; Chicago, asst corp coun, 1965-67; Ill Judicial Coun, judge & chmn, 2001. **Orgs:** Pres, chmn, Civil Serv Comn Met Sanitary Dist, 1967; Weston Lott & William, 1969-70; atty Lott, Powell & Williams, 1970-78; Alpha Phi Alpha; Phi Alpha Delta Law Frat; Am Bar Asn; regional dir, Nat Bar Asn; bd governors, Ill State Bar Asn; past pres, Cook County Bar Asn; speakers, bureau Chicago Bar Asn; Defense Lawyers Asn; Trial Lawyers Asn. **Business Addr:** Judge, Chairmam, Circuit Court Cook County Judicial Circuit, Richard J Daley Ctr, 50 Wash St Rm 1001, Chicago, IL 60602.*

LOTT, RONALD M
Chief executive officer. **Career:** Tracy Toyota, chief exec officer, currently. **Business Addr:** Chief Executive Officer, Tracy Toyota, 2895 N Naglee Rd, Tracy, CA 95304, **Business Phone:** (209)834-1111.*

LOTT, RONNIE
Football player. **Personal:** Born May 8, 1959, Albuquerque, NM; son of Roy Lott; married; children: Ryan Nece. **Educ:** Univ Southern Calif, BA, public admin, 1981. **Career:** Football player (retired); San Francisco 49ers, corner back, 1981-84, free safety, 1985-90; All Stars Helping Kids, owner, founder & pres, 1989-; Los Angeles Raiders, strong safety, 1991-93; NY Jets, 1993-94; Kansas City Chiefs, 1995. **Orgs:** Bd dir, Positive Coaching Alliance. **Honors/Awds:** Pro Bowl, 1981- 91; Defensive Back of the Year, NFL Alumni Asn, 1983; runner-up, NFL Rookie of the Year; All-Pac 10 performer; Pro Football Hall of Fame, 2000; Pro Hall of Fame, 2001; Inducted, Col Hall of Fame, 2002; Defensive IMPACT Player of the Year, 2006.

LOTTIER, PAT. See LOTTIER, PATRICIA ANN.

LOTTIER, PATRICIA ANN (PAT LOTTIER)
Publisher. **Personal:** Born in Ironton, OH; daughter of Ruth Franklin and Melvin Franklin; married George. **Educ:** Western Conn State Univ, BS, 1980; Emory Univ, MPH, 1984. **Career:** Baxter Int, operations mgr, 1982-86; Atlanta Tribune, publisher, 1987-. **Orgs:** Jack & Jill, 1984-97; Coalition of 100 Black Women, 1990; Links, 1995-; Ga Asn Minority Entrepreneurs; Atlanta Chamber Com; Atlanta Bus League; adv bd, Clark All Bus SCh; Nat Newspaper Asn; Ga Minority Supplier Develop Coun; Atlanta Asn Black Journalist; Atlanta Asn Media Women; Nat Asn Market Developers; NAACP; bd visitors, CDC Found; bd mem, Atlanta AD Club; bd mem, Atlanta Women Network; bd mem, Atlanta Press Club; adv bd, Emory Univ Pub Health. **Honors/Awds:** 100 Atlanta Women of Power, 1992, Diamond Award, 1993, Trailblazer Award, 1993; Atlanta Bus League Nontraditional Bus Owner, 1998; Female Eentrepreneur of the Year, US Dept Com Minority Develop Agency; Founders Award, GMSDC; Women of Achievement, YWCA. **Special Achievements:** Selected as attache for the 1996 Olympic games by Cayman Island. **Business Addr:** Publisher, Atlanta Tribune: The Magazine, 875 Old Roswell Rd Suite C-100, Roswell, GA 30076-1660, **Business Phone:** (770)587-0501.

LOUARD, AGNES ANTHONY
Educator. **Personal:** Born Mar 10, 1922, Savannah, GA; daughter of Joseph Anthony and Agnes Anthony; married V Benjamin, Sep 2, 1950 (deceased); children: Rita, Diane & Kenneth. **Educ:** Univ Pa, BA, 1944; Fisk Univ, MA, 1945; Columbia Univ, MS, 1948; NY Univ, add studies. **Career:** Educator (retired); The Manhattanville Neighborhood Ctr, C Div, supvr,1948-52; Union Settlement Asn, dir rec & educ, 1952-57; The E Harlem Proj, dir, 1958-59; Speedwell Serv for C NYC, sr caseworker, 1959-61; Leake & Watts C's Home, sr caseworker, 1962-63; Patterson Home for Aged, supvr, 1964-65; Columbia Univ, asst prof, 1965-72, assoc prof, 1972, prof(retired), 1992. **Orgs:** Bd mem, Harriet Tubman Comt Ctr, 1965-; vpres, Pleasant Ave Day Care Ctr, 1971-; bd mem, 1972-, pres, 1985-88 Peninsula Couning Ctr; consult Spence Chapin Service for Families & Children, 1974-; exec comt, State Manpower Servcs Coun, 1977; NY State Employment & Training Coun, 1977-82; consult, Harlem Teams, 1979-82; Alumni Asn Columbia Univ; adv bd, JW Jr Comm Mental Health Bd, 1982-84; panel chmn, staff mediation comm Columbia Univ, 1984-89; consult, Brooklyn Bur Community Servs, 1988-; bd mem, Schomburg Corp, 1988-; NY Coalition of hundred Black Women, 1988-; ACLU, Nat Asn Advan Colored People, Common Cause, Urban League, The Cottagers; trustee, Union Chapel Marthas Vineyard; NASW; hon comm, Schs centennial, Columbia Univ; founder, V Benjamin & Agnes Louard Scholar; Co-chair, 50th Class Reunion, Alumni Asn Bd conf planning & intl comt, Columbia Univ; Ivy stone Soc. **Honors/Awds:** Class of 1968; Award for dedicated Serv, Peninsula Coun Ctr & Town of Hempstead, NY, 1988; Outstanding Teacher Award, Columbia Univ Sch of Social Work, 1993; Alumini Medal, Columbia Univ, 1998. **Home Addr:** 560 Riverside Dr, New York, NY 10027. *

LOUCHIEY, COREY
Football player. **Personal:** Born Oct 10, 1971, Greenville, SC; married Nicole. **Educ:** Univ SC, retiling. **Career:** Football player (retired); Buffalo Bills, tackle, 1995-97; Atlanta Falcons, tackle, 1998-2000.

LOUD, KAMIL KASSAN
Football player. **Personal:** Born Jun 25, 1976, Richmond, CA. **Educ:** Calif Poly-San Luis Obispo. **Career:** Football player (retired); Buffalo Bills, wide receiver, 1998-99; pittsburgh steelers, 2000. **Honors/Awds:** Rookie of the year, 1998.

LOUIS, CONAN N.
Executive. **Educ:** Georgetown Univ, BS, Appl Linguistics, MS, Sociolinguistics; Georgetown Univ Law Ctr, JD. **Career:** Pvt Law Pract, Wash Off; Wash, social sci res; Georgetown Univ, assoc vpres alumni rel & assoc vpres ext rels; Howard Univ, vpres adv; Nat Asn Adv Colored People, Legal Defense & Educ Fund, dir develop; Bentz Whaley Flessner, sr consult; Coun Adv & Support Educ, Int J Educ Adv, ed bd; SEED Found, chief develop officer, currently. **Orgs:** Nat Asn Adv Colored People; Coun Adv & Support Educ; Nat Col Athletic Asn. **Honors/Awds:** John Carroll Award, 2002. *

LOUIS, JOSEPH
Manager. **Personal:** Born Apr 4, 1948, Vacherie, LA; son of Albertha Davis and Marshal; divorced 1992; children: Crystal

Michelle, Jeremy Allen, Jennifer Ann, Pernell Joseph & David Wayne. **Educ:** Southern Univ, attended 1970; Lamar Univ, environ mgt. **Career:** Manager (retired); BMC Holdings, shift prod mgr; Terminal technician. **Orgs:** NAACP, 1964-; Southern Univ Alumni Fedn, 1970-; Hiram Lodge No 12 Free & Accepted Masons, 1974-. **Special Achievements:** Stratford Business School Achieved an "A' in Business Management, 2008. **Military Serv:** ROTC, E-5, 1966-68. **Home Addr:** 3046 29th St, Port Arthur, TX 77642.

LOUIS, DR. SUCHET LESPERANCE
School administrator. **Personal:** Born Dec 23, 1935, Port-au-Prince, Haiti; son of Joseph and Anaida; married Mathilde Clerge, Aug 31, 1965. **Educ:** Fac Agron & Vet Med, Damien, Haiti, BS, 1963; Interamerican Inst Agri Fural Scis, Turrialba, Costa Rica, MS, 1967; Univ Calif, Davis, CA, PhD, 1973; Univ Calif, Berkeley, CA, post doctoral studies, 1974-75. **Career:** Univ Calif, Berkeley, CA, res assoc, 1974-75; Tuskegee Univ, Tuskegee, AL, asst prof & assoc prof, 1975-83, prof & assoc dir int progs, 1986-89, assoc provost & dir int progs, 1989-, Centennial Planning Comt, OIP, currently, assoc vice pres & dir; Tufts Univ, N Grafton, MA, vis assoc prof, 1983-86. **Orgs:** Am Asn Animal Sci, 1970-; liaison officer, Nat Asn Equal Opportunity, 1986-; trustee, S E Consortium Int Develop, 1989-; Int Adv Coun & Int, 1986-89; chairperson, Interdisciplinary Working Comt & Int, 1989-. **Honors/Awds:** Best Student Agricultural Award, Fac Agronomy, 1962; Fellow, Orgn Am States, 1965; Permanent Membership, Sigma Xi Scientific Asn, 1977; Outstanding Teacher Award, Tuskegee Univ, 1978; Outstanding Faculty Performance Award, Tuskegee Univ, 1988. **Business Addr:** OIP, Tuskegee University, Centennial Planning Committee, 1200 W Montgomery Rd, Tuskegee Institute, AL 36088, **Business Phone:** (334)727-8953.

LOURY, DR. GLENN CARTMAN
Educator. **Personal:** Born Sep 3, 1948, Chicago, IL; married Charlene (divorced); married Linda Datcher, Jun 11, 1983; children: Lisa, Tamara, Alden, Glenn II & Nehemiah. **Educ:** Northwestern Univ, BA, math, 1972; Mass Inst Technol, PhD, econ, 1976. **Career:** Northwestern Univ, asst prof econ, 1976-79; Univ Mich, from assoc profe con to prof econ, 1979-82; Harvard Univ, John F Kennedy Sch Govt, profecon & afro-am studies, 1982-84, prof political econ, 1984-91; Boston Univ, prof econ, 1991-, univ prof, 1994-2005, Inst Race & Social Div, founder & dir, 1997-2003, Merton P Stoltz prof social sci, 2005-. **Orgs:** Coun Foreign Rels; AAAS; Pub Interest; First Things, Ed Adv Bd; vpres, Am Econ Asn, 1997; ed bd, Am Interest. **Honors/Awds:** John Simon Guggenheim fel, 1985-86; Leavey Award for Excellence in Free Enterprise Education, 1986; Econ Soc fel, 1994; American Book Award, 1996; Christianity Today Book Award, 1996; Templeton Honor Roll for Education in a Free Society, 1997-98; John von Neumann Award, 2005. **Special Achievements:** Listed in 150 Who Are Making a Difference by National Journal, 1986; listed in Men and Women Under 40 Who Are Changing the Nation, Esquire Register, 1986, 1987; Published numerous articles including: "Inter generational Transfers and the Distribution of Earnings,"Econometric a, 1981; "Self-Censorship in Public Discourse: A Theory of'Political Correctness' and Related Phenomena," Rationality and Society, 1994; One By One, From the Inside Out: Essays and Reviews on Race and Responsibility in America, The Free Press, 1995; Boston Univ, University Lecturer, 1996; "Will Affirmative Action Policies Eliminate Negative Stereotypes," American Economic Review, 1993; Harvard Univ, Dubois Lecturer, 2000; author of The Anatomy of Racial Inequality, Harvard UnivPress, 2002; Princeton Univ, Moffett '29 Lecturer on Ethics; Ethnicity, Social Mobility and Public Policy, harvard univ press, 2005; Race, Incarceration, and American Values, 2008. **Business Addr:** Merton P Stoltz Professor of the Social Sciences, Professor of Economics, Brown University, Department of Economics, 64 Waterman St, Providence, RI 02912.

LOVE, DR. BARBARA J.
Educator. **Personal:** Born Apr 13, 1946, Dumas, AR. **Educ:** Ark AM & N, BA, 1965; Univ Ark, MA, 1967; Univ Massachusetts, PhD, EdD, 1972. **Career:** Univ Massachusetts, Am herst Campus, assoc prof, currently; Fel House, exec dir; Kans City, teacher, 1969-70; Ctr Urban Educ, grad asst, 1970-71, instr, 1971-72. **Orgs:** Panel Am Women, 1968-70; Urban Coalition Task Force Educ,1968-70; comm rep, Nat Teachers Corps, 1969-70;; task force, Nat Alternative Schs Prog, 1971-73; Nat Alliance Black Sch Educr, 1973; Phi Delta Kappa, 1974; Am Educ Studies Asn, 1974. **Honors/Awds:** Leadership Found Scholar, 1965-66; Junior League Award, 1967; Outstanding Teacher Award, 2004-05. **Special Achievements:** Has written on issues of equity in education, social justice facilitator self-awareness, factors affecting the organizational participation of women and people of color, and internalized oppression among African Americans. **Business Addr:** Associate Professor, University of Massachusetts, Rm 385 159 Hills S, Amherst, MA 01002, **Business Phone:** (413)545-0013.

LOVE, BOB
Basketball player, basketball executive. **Personal:** Born Dec 8, 1942, Bastrop, LA; married Rachel Dixon. **Educ:** Southern Univ, attended. **Career:** Basketball player (retired), dir; Chicago Bulls, 1969-70; Chicago Bulls,dir of community rels, 1993, dir of community, affairs, currently. **Honors/Awds:** NBA All-Defensive Second Team, 1973-74; NBA All-Star, 1971-73. **Special Achievements:** Wrote a book The Bob Love Story: If It's Gonna Be, It's Up to Me, 1999. **Business Addr:** Director of Community Affairs, Chicago Bulls, United Ctr 1901 W Madison St, Chicago, IL 60612-2459, **Business Phone:** (312)455-4000.

LOVE, CAROLYN DIANE
Executive director. **Personal:** Born Dec 30, 1950, Gary, IN; daughter of James and Catherine Ross; married David R Love; children: Leslie N Holloway. **Educ:** Ind State Univ, BS, 1971; Denver County Leadership Forum, 1992; Leadership Denver, 1994; Col Inst for Leadership Training, 1998. **Career:** Conn Nat Bank, Product mgr, 1981-91; Denver Metro COC, Small Bus Develop Ctr (Denver SBDC), exec dir, 1991-95, Vpres County Develop, Chamber Found, exec dir, 1995-97; Rocky Mountain Minority Supplier Develop Coun, exec dir, 1998-. **Orgs:** Conn Housing & Fin Authority (CHFA), bd mem, 1997-; Platte River Industries, Bd Mem, 1995-; Asian Pacific Ctr for Human Develop, Bd Pres, 1993-95; Shorter AME Church Scholar Comt, 1993-; Junior League Denver Citizen's Adv Comt, 1995-; Mile High United Way, Diversity In Giving Campain, Chair, 1999; Key Bank Conn Adv Bd, Mem, 1999; Conn Small Bus Develop Ctr, Adv Bd, 1999. **Honors/Awds:** Denver Bus J, 1994, Who's Who in Minority Bus, 1994; Ernst & Young, Small Bus Advocate of the Year, Regional Finalist, 1993. **Business Addr:** Executive Director, Minority Enterprises Inc, Rocky Mountain Minority Supplier Development Council, 1445 Market St Suite 310, Denver, CO 80202-1797, **Business Phone:** (303)623-3037.

LOVE, DARLENE (DARLENE WRIGHT)
Entertainer. **Personal:** Born Jul 26, 1941, Los Angeles, CA; daughter of Joseph Wright and Ellen Wright; married Alton A Allison, Jun 28, 1984; children: Marcus Peete, Chawn Peete & Jason Mitchell. **Career:** Songs: "White Christmas", "Winter Wonderland", "Marshmallow World", "(Today I Met) The Boy I'm Going to Marry," 1963; "Wait Til My Bobby Comes Home," 1963; "Christmas (Baby Please Come Home)," 1963; Albums: Darlene Love Live, 1985; Paint Another Picture, 1988; The Best of Darlene Love, 1992; Bringing it Home, 1992; Grease is the Word, 1998; Its Christmas Of Course, 2007; Film: Leathal Weapon, 1987; Leathal Weapon 2, 1989; Leathal Weapon 3, 1992; Leathal Weapon 4, 1998; Christmas with the Kranks, 2004; The Holiday, 2006; Talent Consult Int, actor, currently. **Orgs:** Make a Wish. **Honors/Awds:** Image Award, NCP, 1972; Honorary Citizen, City of Atlanta, 1985; Darlene Love Day delcared, Tocca, Ga, Aug 3, 1991; Rythm & Blues Pioneer Award, 1995. **Special Achievements:** Published: My Name is Love: The Darlene Love Story, 1998. **Business Addr:** Actor, Talent Consultants International, 1560 Broadway Suite 1308, New York, NY 10036, **Business Phone:** (212)730-2701.

LOVE, EDWARD TYRONE
Educator. **Personal:** Born Dec 8, 1954, Philadelphia, PA; children: Danielle J Floyd & Keith T Morris. **Career:** Sch Dist Philadelphia, prog dir, 1997-; Electric Factory Concerts,security dir, 1998. **Orgs:** Omega Psi Phi Fraternity, 1975-; Prince Hall Masons, 1977-. **Honors/Awds:** Droupout Prevention Award, Sch Dist Philadelphia, 1999. **Home Addr:** 5801 Rodman St, Philadelphia, PA 19143, **Home Phone:** (215)748-1134.

LOVE, DR. ERIC
Manager, educator. **Educ:** Brown Univ, BA; Idaho State Univ, attended; Univ Vermont, MA; Univ Princeton, MA, PhD. **Career:** Ind Univ, proj cord; Univ Colo, undergrad dir, Dept Hist, assoc prof, currently. **Orgs:** Am Hist Asn. **Special Achievements:** Author: 'Race Over Empire: Racism and U.S. Imperialism", 1865-1900 (2004); "The Way of All Flesh". **Business Addr:** Associate Professor, University of Colorado, Department of History, 234 UCB Hellems Room 204, Boulder, CO 80309, **Business Phone:** (303)492-5729.

LOVE, FAIZON (LANGSTON FAIZON SANTISIMA)
Actor. **Personal:** Born Jun 14, 1968, Santiago de Cuba, Cuba. **Career:** Films: Bebe's Kids, 1992; The Meteor Man, 1993; Fear of a Black Hat, 1994; Friday, 1995; Don't Be A Menice, 1996; A Thin Line Between Love & Hate, 1996; BAPS, 1997; The Players Club, 1998; The Replacements, 2000; Made, 2001; Mr Bones, 2001; Blue Crush, 2002; Wonderland, 2003; Elf, 2003; TheFighting Temptations, 2003; Torque, 2004; Rumble, 2006; Who's Your Caddy?,2007; A Day In my life, 2009; TV series: "The Parent Hood", 1995-98; TV films: "Play'd: A Hip Hop Story", 2002; "Just My Luck", 2005; "Animal", 2005. **Honors/Awds:** Action on the Film Award, 2007. **Business Addr:** Comedian, Actor, The Artists Group, Talent & Literary Agency, 10100 Santa Monica Blvd Suite 2490, Los Angeles, CA 90067-4144, **Business Phone:** (310)552-1100.*

LOVE, DR. GEORGE HAYWARD
Educator. **Personal:** Born Oct 15, 1924, Philadelphia, PA; son of Samuel H and Daisy Gripper; married Hettie Simmons, Jun 10, 1948; children: George Hayward Jr & Karen. **Educ:** Univ Penn, BA, 1948, MS, Educ, 1950, EdD, 1973. **Career:** Philadelphia Sch Dist, teacher, admin, 1952-71; Penns Dept Educ, asst comnr, 1971-75; Appalachia Educ Lab, assoc dir, 1975-81; Harrisburg Sch Dist, biology teacher, 1981-84; dir personnel, 1984-88; dir, div spec proj, 1988-92; educ consult, 1992-. **Orgs:** Consult, Penn Dept Educ, 1981-; bd mem, Allison Hill Community Ctr; founder past sire archon, Beta Pi Boule, Sigma Pi Phi, 1983; chmn, Dept Christian Educ Diocese Penn, 1984-; pres, Greater Harrisburg Area Br, NAACP, 1986-; pres, Harrisburg Bridge Club, 1989; bd mem, Penn State Conf Branches, NAACP; chmn, Cities Schs, 1992; lay reader & vestryman, St Paul Episcopal Church; Dauphin County Area Aging Bd; Central Regional Council Aging; bd dir, Dauphin County Coop extension. **Honors/Awds:** Service Award, Frontiers Int, 1973; Outstanding Citizenship Award, Omega Psi Phi Frat 1981; Judge Award, Penn Jr Acad Sci, 1987; YMCA Award, 1988; Omega Man of the Yr, Kappa Omega Chap, Omega Psi Phi Frat, 2002. **Military Serv:** USAF, pvt, 1943-45. **Home Addr:** 3757 Chambers Hill Rd, Harrisburg, PA 17111. *

LOVE, J. GREGORY
Firefighter, commissioner. **Educ:** Wayne County Community Col, AS; Univ Detroit-Mercy, BA; Wayne State Univ, ME. **Career:** City Detroit, Detroit Fire Acad, firefighter, capt-instr, 1971-95; Royal Oak Township Pub Safety Dept, fire chief, 1995-96; Jackson Fire Dept, fire chief, 1996-; Buffalo Fire Dept, dep comnr, currently. **Honors/Awds:** Numerous citations for bravery & rescue. **Special Achievements:** First African American fire chief in Jackson, MI. *

LOVE, JAMES O, SR.
Law enforcement officer. **Personal:** Born Jan 12, 1957, Chicago, IL; son of Jerry L and Henrietta; divorced; children: James O Jr & Jerry L II. **Career:** Chicago Police Dept, police officer, 1985-. **Orgs:** Fraternal Order Police; Carter Harrison/Lambert Tree Soc; Ill Police Asn; Ill Drug Enforcement Officers Asn. **Honors/Awds:** Chicago Police DPT, 53 Honorable Mentions, 1985-91, Dept Commendation, 1987, 1995; Carter Harrison Award, City Chicago, 1991; Blue Star, City Chicago, 1991, Life Saver Award, City Chicago, 1991; Unit Meritorious Award, 1996; Certificate of Appreciation, US Dept Justice, 1997; Letter of Recognition, US Atty, 1997. **Special Achievements:** Author: Bleeding Blue, The James Love Story; profiled in "Sacred Bond," by Keith Brown, Little Brown & Co Publishing. **Business Phone:** (312)791-4650.

LOVE, JAMES RALPH
Executive, president (organization), chief executive officer. **Personal:** Born Apr 2, 1937, Hahira, GA; married Bernice Grant; children: Rhita V, James R II, Gerald K & Reginald. **Educ:** Ky State Col, BS, 1958; Tuskegee Inst, MS, 1968. **Career:** Proj MARK Jackson MS, job developer, 1968; Nat Alliance Bus Denver C of C,mgr, 1968-71; Mt Bell, pub relations, 1971-74; Mutual Benefit Life, thsagt, 1974-79; James R Love & Assocs Inc, pres, 1980-86; Pyramid Financial & Insurance Services Inc, pres, ceo, 1986-. **Orgs:** Pres, Delta Psi Lambda, 1971-74; treas, Denver Bd Mentally Retarded & Physically Handicapped, 1972-78; vpres, Park Hill Br Nat Asn Advan Colored People, 1979-80; adv Gov Love Govt, 1969-71; dir, UNCF Co, 1971-72; ethics comm Denver Area Life Under writers, 1978-79. **Honors/Awds:** Agent of the Yr, Mutual Benefit, 1974-75; Man of the Yr, AA, 1975-76. **Special Achievements:** Article published "Prospecting Through My Board of Directors" Life Insurance Selling. 1978. **Business Addr:** President, Chief Executive Officer, Pyramid Financial & Insurance Services Inc, 1901 Peoria St Suite 200, Aurora, CO 80010-2236, **Business Phone:** (303)367-5577.

LOVE, JON
Executive. **Personal:** Born Jul 3, 1961, Washington, DC; son of Charles James and Anne Lucinda; married Jeanette Victoria Dorsey, Jul 6, 1985; children: Ryan Michael & Jonee Denise. **Educ:** Knoxville Coll, attended, 1981; Bowie State Univ, BS, 1983; Rutgers Univ Advan Mgt Prog; Columbia Univ Exec Educ Prog, mkt mgt. **Career:** Lucent Technologies, Large Bus Prod Div, gen mgr sales, 1996; Robbins-Gioia LLC, commercial opers, sr vpres, 2004-, Bus Develop & Mkt, exec vpres, 2005-; AT&T, sales specialist; Network Opers, engr, fed systs div, mgr, gen bus systs, mgr, fed govt sales, br mgr; Access Financial Mgt, engr. **Orgs:** Steering comt mem, Mayor's Scholarship Ball; United Way Int; Lau Rawls Telethon; Habitat Humanity; United Negro Col Fund. **Special Achievements:** Forty under 40, most influential business leaders in Detroit, 1998. **Business Addr:** Executive vice President, Robbins-Gioia LLC, 11 Canal Ctr Plz, Alexandria, VA 22314, **Business Phone:** (703)548-7006.

LOVE, KAREN ALLYCE (KAREN A WISE-LOVE)
Newspaper executive. **Personal:** Born May 22, 1946, River Rouge, MI; daughter of Ruth Lee McIlwain and Joseph William Wise; married John L, Nov 5, 1975; children: Schari Alana Dixon & Lloryn Ruth. **Educ:** Ferris State Col, 1964-65; Col DuPage, 1973-75; Los Angeles City Col, 1976-78; Wayne Co Community Col, 1990-91. **Career:** Commonwealth Edison Co, Syst Security Div, 1972-76; Los Angeles Times Co, acct exec, 1976-78; Western States Asn Los Angeles, regional acct exec, 1978-79; Chicago Tribune Co, acct exec, 1979-86; Security Bank & Trust, acct dept, 1986; Asod Newspapers, retail mgr, 1986-89; Mich Chronicle Newspaper, exec admin asst, 1989, chief operating officer, currently; Mich Frontpage, publ, currently. **Orgs:** Grand officer,

Order Eastern Star, 1975-; officer, Heroines Jericho, 1984-; life mem, Publicity Comn, Nat Asn Advan Colored People, 1990-; Ladies Cir Perfection, 1990-; Life Directions, publicity comn, 1992-; Urban League, publicity comn, 1992-; Nat Newspaper Publ Asn. **Honors/Awds:** Black Achievement Award, City Chicago, 1981; Benjamin Hooks Outstanding Black Leader, 1991; Woman of the Year, Nat Polit Congr Black Women, 1992. **Business Addr:** Chief Operating Officer, Michigan Chronicle Newspaper, 479 Ledyard St, Detroit, MI 48201, **Business Phone:** (313)963-5522.

LOVE, LAMAR VINCENT
Executive, business owner. **Personal:** Born Oct 20, 1964, Columbus, OH; son of Lamar E Love and Marie C Love. **Educ:** Ohio State Univ, BA, BS, 1989. **Career:** Banc Ohio, crt operator, 1981-83, group leader, 1983-86; Lamar Love Co, owner, 1988-2002; Foster & Assoc, sales rep, 1989-90, sales & opers mgr, 1991-92, vpres, 1993-95; CML Group, pres & ceo, 2002-; Action Int, owner, currently. **Orgs:** Vpres, Ohio State Entrepreneur Network, 1988-89. **Military Serv:** UAS, Reserves, AUS, Nat Guard, sgt, 1982-92; Army Achievement Medal, 1989. **Business Addr:** Owner, Action International, 2459 Dorset Rd, Columbus, OH 43221, **Business Phone:** (614)486-4970.*

LOVE, LYNNETTE ALICIA
Athletic coach, educator. **Personal:** Born Sep 21, 1957, Chicago, IL; daughter of Dolores Merritt. **Educ:** Wayne State Univ, BFA, 1983. **Career:** Maryland Federal Savings, asst mgr, 1986-89; City Alexandria, recreation supvr, 1993-94; Love's Taekwondo Acad, pres, 1994-. **Orgs:** Women's Sports Found, 1988-; vice chairperson, United States Taekwondo Union, 1988-96, vpres, 2001-. **Honors/Awds:** Outstanding Female Player, United States Taekwondo Union, 1984, 1988; Alumni Award, Cass Technical High Sch, 1988; Sullivan Award Outstanding Sports Performance, Nominated AAU, 1988. **Special Achievements:** Female Coach, World Championships, 1993; Female Coach, Pan American Games, 1995; Ten-Time National Champion, 1979-87, 1990; Five-Time Pan American Champion, 1982, 1984, 1986, 1988 & 1990; Two-Time Olympic Medalist, Gold, 1988, Bronze, 1992; Team Captain, 1989-92; Three-Time World Champion, 1985, 1987 & 1991. **Business Addr:** President, Owner, Love, 7605 Barbara Ln C, PO Box 1620, Clinton, MD 20735-1429, **Business Phone:** (301)645-9125.

LOVE, MILDRED L.
Administrator. **Personal:** Born Oct 25, 1941, Ringgold, LA. **Educ:** So Univ, BA, 1963; Univ Pittsburgh, MA, 1969; Columbia Univ, MBA 24 credits, 1979. **Career:** NY City Dept Soc Svc, case worker, 1964-65; Harlem Teams Self Help, instr & counr, 1965-72; Cowles Pub Co, editorial consult, 1971-72; Manhattan State Hosp, rehab counr, 1970; Nat Urban League Inc, asst dir eastern reg office, 1973-76; Nat Urban League Inc, dir Eastern reg office, 1976-79; Nat Urban League Inc, dir career trng & econ resources, 1979; NAT URBAN LEAGUE, SENIOR VPRES OPER; Nat Urban League, consult, 2002-. **Orgs:** Volunteer, ATC Domestic Peace Corps, 1963-64; comr Nat Comn Unemployment Compensation, 1980-82. **Honors/Awds:** Ford Foundation Fellowship Award, 1968-69; League's Ann Tanneyhill Award. **Business Addr:** Consultant, National Urban League Inc, 120 Wall St 8th Fl, New York, NY 10005, **Business Phone:** (212)558-5300.

LOVE, PRISCILLA WINANS. See WINANS, CECE.

LOVE, ROOSEVELT SAM
Executive. **Personal:** Born Jun 11, 1933, Bulloch Co, GA; widowed; children: Katheleen, Patricia, Bonnie, Julia & Sandra. **Career:** Love's Fina Serv St, operator; JP Stevens, cement mixer; Gulf Inc, serv sta attend. **Orgs:** Comn Rels Counc, 1975-77; DUSO develop Unique Serv Ourselves; Comn Action Club; SCWC; Negotiations Com Textiles Workers Union, 1974; rep, JP Stevens Employ Twisting Dept, 1971; pres, Bulloch Co Br NAACP; Bethel Primitive Bapt Ch. **Honors/Awds:** Outstanding service award, NAACP, 1977.

LOVE, RUTH BURNETT
School administrator, newspaper publisher. **Personal:** Born Apr 22, 1939, Lawton, OK; daughter of Alvin E and Burnett C. **Educ:** San Jose State Univ, BA, 1954; San Francisco State Univ, MA, 1961; US Int Univ, Cal Western, PhD, 1969. **Career:** Oakland Unified Sch Dist, ford found, consult, supt; Calif State Dept Educ, bur chief; US Off Educ, Wash, DC, dir, Right Read; Chicago Bd Educ, gen supt; Oper Crossroads Africa, Ghana, proj dir; Calif Voice, publisher, currently; San Francisco State Univ, distintuished prof; Ex-publisher of 9 weekly Black Newspapers; RBL Enterprises LTD, founder & pres, currently. **Orgs:** Am Asn Sch ADR, 1974-; bd trustee, Morehouse Med Sch, 1976-; vice chair, PRS Mental Health Comn, 1976-79; bd dir, Cities In Schs, 1977-; bd dir, NUL, 1977-82; Asn Suv & Counr Develop, 1979-; chair, scholar comt, Links Inc; bd dir, Nat Newspaper Publishers Asn, 1988-; PRSial Con HBUC, 1989-92. **Honors/Awds:** Honorary Doctorate, Marquette Univ; Library named in honor; Certificate of Recognition, Dept of Health, Educ & Welfare. **Special Achievements:** First African and First woman superintendent in Chicago school district; Author: Hello World, Field Publications, 1975; Strengthening Counseling Sevices for Disadvantaged Youth, 1966; Johnny Can Read, So Can Jane, Addison Wesley, 1982; The Paideia Proposal: An Educ Manifesto, w/Moeriwe Adler, MacMillan, 1982; The Paideia Proposal: Questions and Answers, MacMillan, 1983; numerous articles; traveled & lectured extensively around the world; Motivational Speaker. **Business Phone:** (510)622-7707.*

LOVE, THOMAS CLIFFORD
Editor, college teacher. **Personal:** Born Jul 23, 1947, New Rochelle, NY. **Educ:** Howard Univ, BA, 1969. **Career:** WRC-TV AM-FM, Wash, employ spec, pub serv dir, 1969-71; WABC-AM Radio, New York, pub serv dir, 1971-72, dir comm affairs, 1972-73; WABC AM-Radio NY, ed, community affairs dir, 1973-79; St Johns Univ, adj prof, 1976-78; Montclair St Col, vis prof, 1978-; WABC-TV, ed dir, 1979. **Orgs:** Nat & Int Radio & TV Soc; Nat Broadcast Ed Asn; Alpha Phi Alpha. **Honors/Awds:** NY State Broadcasters Award, 1979, 84; Black Achievers Industry Award, YMCA, 1974; UPI & AP Award, 1974; Andy Award, Merit Ad Club NY, 1978; NY Emmy Award, 1980.

LOVELACE, DEAN ALAN
Government official. **Personal:** Born Jan 31, 1946, Ford City, PA; married Phyllis Jean Rutland; children: Leslie Denise, Laeina Deandra & Dean Nyerere. **Educ:** Sinclair Community Col, AS, bus, 1971; Univ Dayton, BSBA, 1972; Wright State Univ, MS, appl & social econs, 1981. **Career:** Nat Cash Register, lathe operator, 1965-71; Community Leadership Consult,1970-; City Dayton, Dept Planning, neighborhood planner, 1973-79, NW Off Neighborhood Affairs, community serv adv, 1977-79, coordr & dir, 1979-80;Univ Dayton, dir neighborhood develop, Strategies Responsible Develop Off,1983, dir, Dayton Civic Scholars Prog, currently; City Dayton, OH, comnr, 1993-. **Orgs:** Citizens adv coun, Model Neighborhood Community Ctr, 1977-; EconsResources Comt, Miami Valley Regional Planning Coun, 1977-; chmn, DaytonOhio Black Polit Assembly, 1977-; trustee, Housing Justice Fund Inc,1978-; pres, Edgemont Neighborhood Coalition Inc, 1980-; first vpres,Dayton Urban League, 1982-; adv bd, Dayton Found Neighbor Neighbor, 1983-;coun mem, Montgomery County Human Serv Levy, 1984-; chmn,Dayton-Montgomery County Rainbow Coaltion, 1984-; Dayton Anti-ApartheidComn, 1985-. **Honors/Awds:** Community Service Award, Concerned Citizens Dayton View, 1977; Employee ofthe Year, City Dayton, Div Neighborhood Affairs, 1978; Distinguished Service Award, Ohio State Leg, 1979; Outstanding Young Man of America, US Jaycees, 1979; NAACP Freedom Fund Dinner Civil Rights Award, 1985. **Special Achievements:** Participated in Race Relations Conferences in Caux, Switzerland and Durban, South Africa. **Business Addr:** Commissioner, City Commissioner Office, City Hall 2nd Fl 101 W Third St, Dayton, OH 45402.

LOVELACE, JOHN C.
Executive. **Personal:** Born Mar 4, 1926, West Point, GA; married Mary Jean Roebuck; children: Juan Carlos, Carlita Joy. **Career:** Pittsburgh Plate Glass Industrial Inc; Nat Asn Advan Colored People, pres; Allegheny-Kiski Valley, pres. **Orgs:** Drug & Alcoholic Comn; NAACP; mgr, Valley Choraliers Leechburg, 1960-75; Youth Comn, 1968; planning comn Gilpin Township, 1973-75; bd dirs, Kiski Valley Med Facilities Inc, 1974-75. **Honors/Awds:** Thalheimer Award, NAACP, 1970. **Military Serv:** USN, 1944-46.

LOVELESS, THERESA E
Association executive. **Career:** Girl Scout Coun Greater St Louis, exec dir, 1996, chief exec officer, currently. **Orgs:** Missouri Bot Garden Subs Dist Comn; Regional Arts Comn. **Honors/Awds:** Woman of Achievement, 1992. **Special Achievements:** First African American to take helm of Girl Scout Council in St Louis. **Business Addr:** Chief Executive Officer, Girl Scout Council of Greater St. Louis, 2130 Kratky Rd, Saint Louis, MO 63114, **Business Phone:** (314)890-9569.

LOVETT, LEONARD
Clergy, consultant, executive director. **Personal:** Born Dec 5, 1939, Pompano Beach, FL; son of Charles and Cassie; married Marie Bush; children: Laion, Lamont, Lamar, Mandon. **Educ:** Saints Jr Col, AA, 1959; Morehouse Col, BA, 1962; Crozer Theol Sem, MDiv, 1965; St Jr Col, DLaw, 1972; Emory Univ, PhD, ethics & soc, 1979; Univ Ghana, cert, 1994. **Career:** Memorial Church God Christ, pastor, 1962-70, ecumenical officer urban affairs; Health & Welfare Coun, Philadelphia, NY City Proj, coordr, 1965-67; Stephen Smith Towers 202 Sr Citizens, proj mgr, 1967-70; Church Mason Theol Sem, pioneer pres, 1970-74; Grad Theol Union, Berkeley, visit prof, 1975; Fuller Theol Sem, Black Ministries, assoc dir , 1977-81, Seminex Ministries, chief exec officer & consult; Ecumenical Ctr Black Church Studies, prof ethics & theol, 1978-; Am Baptist Sem W, prof ethics & theol, 1984; Black Perspective, Ministries Today Mag, columnist, 1988-; C H Mason Sem, dean emer; Church God Christ Inc, Off Ecumenical Rels, exec dir, currently. **Orgs:** Soc Study Black Relig, 1972-; reactor, Vatican-Pentecostal Dialogue W Ger, 1974; pres, Soc Pentecostal Studies, 1975; vis fel Human Behavior Am Inst Family Rels, 1982-85; bd mem, Watts Health Found, United Health Plan, 1985-. **Special Achievements:** Conditional Liberation Spirit Journal 1977; What Charismatics Can Learn from Black Pentecostals Logos Journal 1980; Tribute to Martin Luther King in Outstanding Black Sermons Vol 2 Judson Press 1982; contrib Aspects of the Spiritual Legacy of the Church of God in Christ in Mid-Stream An Ecumenical Journal Vol XXIV No 4 1985, Black Witness to the Apostolic Faith Eardmans 1988; Black Holiness-Pentecostalism, Black Theology, Positive Confession Theology, Dictionary of the Pentecostal Charismatic Movement, Zondervan 1988. **Business Addr:** Executive Director, Church of God in Christ Inc, Off Ecumenical Rels, 107 S W St Suite 422, Alexandria, VA 22314.*

LOVETT, MACK, JR.
Educator. **Personal:** Born Aug 31, 1931, Shreveport, LA; married Marlene; children: Alice, Pamela, Michelle & Albert. **Educ:** Oakland City Col, AA, 1959; Calif State Univ, BA, 1965, MPA, 1970. **Career:** Municipal Court, ct clerk, 1956-65; Litton Indus, instr, 1965-66, admin, 1966-68; Calif State Univ, asst pres, 1968-72, dir instruct serv, 1972, asst vpres instruct serv, 1978-2000. **Orgs:** Chmn, Polit Actn Com Nat Advan Asn Colored People So Alameda Co Chap, 1958-64; bd dir, So Alameda Co Econ Opportunity Orgn, 1965-67; Consult, Hayward Univ Sch Dist, 1966-73; dir, Plnd & Appl Res Inc, 1967-68; consult, Calif Employ Serv, 1968; consult, Chabot Comm Col, 1969; dir & treas, Ebony Constr Co, 1972-73; Gr Hayward Kiwanis Serv Club; pres, Nat Advan Asn Colored People, 1964-68; bd dir, New Lady mag, 1965-70; Reg Adult, Voca Educ Advis Com; bd mgrs, YMCA Eden area. **Special Achievements:** Publ "How to File Your Income Tax" Litton Indus Educ Sys Div. **Military Serv:** AUS, 1954-56. **Business Addr:** Assistant Vice President, Instructional Service, California State University, 25800 Carlos Bee Blvd, Hayward, CA 94542.

LOVICK, CALVIN L
Publisher. **Personal:** Born Aug 6, 1950, Belhaven, NC; son of Nathan; divorced; children: Scott, Christian & Jeannie. **Educ:** Kean Col, BS, 1974. **Career:** CL Lovick & Assocs, ceo, publ, 1979-. **Military Serv:** USAF, sgt, 1968-71. **Business Phone:** (310)410-7220.

LOVILLE, DEREK KEVIN
Football player. **Personal:** Born Jul 4, 1968, San Francisco, CA; married Nina, Mar 14, 1998; children: Derek II. **Educ:** Univ Ore, am studies. **Career:** Football player (retired); Seattle Seahawks, running back, 1990-91; San Francisco 49ers, 1994-96; Denver Broncos, 1997-98; St Louis Rams, runningback, 1999-2000.

LOVING, JAMES LESLIE
Executive. **Personal:** Born Aug 14, 1944, Boston, MA; son of James Leslie and Wauneta Barbour; married Leebertha Beauford, Jul 1, 1967; children: Robyn Leslie. **Educ:** Boston Bus Sch, Dipl, 1964; Harvard Univ, EdM, 1974, CAS, 1975; Aenon Bible Col, D. D. **Career:** City Boston, spec asst mayor, 1972-77; US Dept HHS, spec asst, 1977-81; Stud Nat Med Asn, exec admin, 1981-83; Data Processing Inst, vpres 1983-86; Career Bus Acad, pres, 1986-90. **Orgs:** Treas, Boston Br NAACP, 1972; dir, Boston Legal Asst Proj, 1972; chmn, Roxbury Cancer Crusade, 1974; hew fel, US Dept Health Ed & Welfare, 1977; trustee, Emmanuel Temple Church, 1977;nat coord, Dr King 51st Celebration, 1980. **Honors/Awds:** Finalist White House Fellows Prog, 1977; Outstanding Leader, JC's Boston Chap, 1978; Outstanding Young Men of America, 1976; 100 Black Influentials, 1976; United Student Oakwood Col Huntsville, 1975. **Home Addr:** 8717 Baskerville Pl, Upper Marlboro, MD 20772, **Home Phone:** (301)627-5267. **Business Phone:** (301)441-3740.

LOWE, DR. AUBREY F.
Executive. **Personal:** Born Jul 7, 1940, Suffolk, VA; married Anne L Pulley; children: Gary & Brandon. **Educ:** NC Cent Univ, BS, acct, 1960, S.J.D, 1963. **Career:** Fed Housing & Admin, staff atty, 1963-67; Eli Lilly Co, financial analyst, 1967-71, 1973; Indianapolis Bus Investment Corp, pres, 1971-73; Citizens Health Corp, comptroller, 1994-. **Orgs:** Nat Asn Advan Colored People; Omega Psi Phi; St Paul's PE Church, Indianapolis Urban League. **Home Addr:** 1620 W 63rd St, Indianapolis, IN 46260.

LOWE, EUGENE YERBY
Clergy, school administrator. **Personal:** Born Aug 18, 1949, Staten Island, NY; son of Eugene Y Sr and Miriam V; married Jane Pataky Henderson, Nov 4, 1989; children: Benjamin & Sarah. **Educ:** Princeton Univ, AB, 1971; Union Theol Sem, MDiv, 1978, PhD, 1987. **Career:** Northwestern Univ, assoc provost fac affairs, sr lectr relig; Princeton Univ, dean studs, 1983-93; Union Theol Sem, tutor, 1979-82; Gen Theol Sem, tutor, 1978-80; Parish Calvary & St George's, asst minister, 1978-82; Chase Manhattan Bank, vpres, 1973-76; St Agatha Home C, soc work asst, 1971-73; Northwestern Univ, asst to pres, 1995-. **Orgs:** Trustee, Princeton Univ, 1971-83; trustee, Elizabeth Seton Col, 1972-83; Comn Soc Responsibility & Investments, Exec Coun Episcopal Church, 1976-81; dir, Forum Corp Responsibility, 1976-80; Coun Foreign Rels, 1977-81; trustee, Berea Col, 1995-; trustee, Seabury-Western Sem, 1996-. **Honors/Awds:** The Harold Willis Dodds Prize, Princeton Univ, 1971; Phi Beta Kappa, Princeton Univ, 1971; fellow, Fund for Theol Educ, 1976-77; fellow, Episcopal Ch Found, 1978-80. **Business Addr:** Assistant to the President,

Senior Lecturer, Northwestern University, Department of Religion, Crowe Hall 1860 Campus Dr, Evanston, IL 60208-2164, **Business Phone:** (847)491-5255.

LOWE, HAZEL MARIE
Government official. **Personal:** Born Aug 4, 1936, La Grange, NC; daughter of George Rouse (deceased) and Musetter Gardner (deceased); married Earl C Lowe; children: Katrina E Lombre & Cassandra Eileen. **Educ:** Barnes Business Col, dipl, 1955; US Agr Dept Sch Bus, attended 1963-64, Univ DC, attended 1982-83. **Career:** Government official (retired); Interstate Com Comn, secy/stenographer, 1977-78, secy/admin asst, 1978-79, secy/admin officer, 1982-84, confidential asst, 1995. **Orgs:** Frink High Sch Alumna, 1982-; Lake Arbor Civic Asn, 1989-; Disabled Am Veterans Auxiliary, 1996-. **Honors/Awds:** Outstanding Performance Award, Interstate Com Comn, 1965, 1977, 1978, 1981 & 1983-95. **Home Addr:** 10334 Sea Pines Dr, Mitchellville, MD 20721.

LOWE, JACK, JR.
Law enforcement officer. **Personal:** Born Sep 5, 1936, Gadsden, AL; son of Jack Sr. **Career:** Law enforcement officer (retired); Baptist Hosp, staff; Calhoun County; dir nursing; Etowah County Sheriff's Dept, chief investr. **Orgs:** Ala New South Coalition. **Honors/Awds:** Doctorate, Calhoun County. **Special Achievements:** First African American police chief in Etowah County; highest ranking African American official in Etowah County; First African American to run for sheriff in Etowah County; One of the first two black deputies in the Etowah County Sheriff's Department.

LOWE, JACKIE
Actor. **Personal:** Born in Bamberg, SC. **Educ:** Rider Col, 1973. **Career:** TV: "The Guiding Light"; "Edge of Night"; "Ryan's Hope"; "The Merv Griffin Show"; "Easter Seals Telethon"; Films: The Wiz; Daddy Daddy; The First; Ain't Misbehavin; Eubie; Best Little Whorehouse in TX; Story ville, Selma;West Side Story; Sweet Charity; The Tap Dance Kid; Pippin; J Walter Thompson Advertising, prod asst, 1973-76; Wind in the Willows, 1985; Ain't Misbehavin, 1988-89; performer, currently. **Orgs:** Cord Mothers March March of Dimes, 1972; mem, AFTRA, SAG, AGVA, Equity Unions. **Honors/Awds:** Nominated Best Supporting Actress Santa Monica Theatre Guild, 1977; First recipient of Capitol City Dance Award in Recognition for accomplishments in dance fine arts Trenton NJ, 1985. **Business Addr:** Actor, Minskoff Theater, 200 W 45th St, New York, NY 10036, **Business Phone:** (212)869-0550.*

LOWE, JAMES EDWARD, JR.
Physician. **Personal:** Born Dec 5, 1950, Warsaw, NC; son of James Edward and Alice Mae Gavins; married Philamina Lucy Lozado Lowe, Oct 7, 1989; children: James Edward Lowe III, Joseph Alexander Lowe, Jesse J Carattini. **Educ:** Harvard Univ, Health Careers Prog, 1970; Livingstone Col, BS, 1971; Univ NC, Chapel Hill, Health Careers Prog, 1971; Meharry Medical Col, MD, 1975. **Career:** Downstate Med Ctr, resident surg, 1975-78; Lutheran Med Ctr, resident & chief resident, 1978-81, teaching fel, gen surg, 1981-82, assoc attending plastic & reconstructive surg; Lenox Hill Hosp, plastic surg residency, 1982-84, asst attending plastic & reconstructive surg, 1985-. **Orgs:** Phi Beta Sigma Fraternity, 1968-, Nat Asn Advan Colored People, 1985-; CORE, 1985-; NY County Med Soc 1985-; Nat Med Asn, 1986-; Am Soc Plastic & Reconstructive Surgeons, 1986-. **Honors/Awds:** Physician Recognition Award, Am Med Asn, 1998-01; spec lectr, Non-Caucasian Rhinoplasty, Keloid & Hypertrophic Scans; spec lectr, Breast reconstruction with Auto Genous Tissue Lenox Hill Hosp. **Special Achievements:** Publications: "Adriamycin Extravasation Ulcers," Ame Soc Plastic & Reconstructive Surg Meeting, 1983; "Non-Caucasian Rhinoplasty," "Common Pressure Ulcers and Treatment", "History of the Carter-Morestin Society", presented at Nat Med Assoc Convention, New Orleans, LA, 1987; "Autologous Secondary Breast Augmentation with Pedicled Transverse Rectus Abdominus Musculocutaneous Flaps," Annals Plastic Surg, 1995. *

LOWE, MARTHA P.
Business owner. **Personal:** Born Mar 17, 1945, Pocahontas, VA; daughter of Nathaniel Fitzgerald and Josephine Fitzgerald; married Arthur F Lowe, Nov 12, 1969; children: Patrice White, Cherri Latta, Timothy, Arthur, Jr. **Educ:** Ohio State Univ; Wilberforce Univ, attended 1995; Cent Mich Univ, MSA, 1998. **Career:** Ohio State Univ, develop assoc, 1978-97; Accountants Assoc, vpres, 1997-98; ADT/US Alert, Inc, dist mgr, 1998-99; Shekinah Grande Salon & Day Spa, 1999-. **Orgs:** Pres & bd mem, Nat Asn Working Women Inc, 1987-97; event planning & fundraising comt, Alpha Kappa Alpha Sorority, 1996-; Victory Matrons Club Inc, 1996-; steering comt, Nat Black Women's Health Proj, 1997-99; scholar comt, Northeasterners Inc, 1997-; bd mem, Hannah Neil Ctr C, 1997-; fundraising comt, Jack & Jill Am Inc, 1997-; vol, Am Cancer Found, 2004-. **Honors/Awds:** Outstanding Teacher, Bible Way Church of Our Lord Jesus Christ Inc, 1997; Outstanding Mentor, Bible Way Church of Our Lord Jesus Christ Inc, 1998; #1 sales nationally, ADR/US Alert Inc, 1998. *

LOWE, SCOTT MILLER
Physician. **Personal:** Born Sep 2, 1942, Charlottesville, VA; married Sharon Brewer. **Educ:** VA Unoin Univ, BS, 1964; Meharry Med Col, MD, 1970. **Career:** Richmond Dept Health, insp, 1964-66; Harlem Hosp Ctr, intern, 1970-71; obstetrics & gynec jr resd, 1971-73; Albany Med Ctr, obstetrics & gynec sr resd, 1973-74; obstetrics & gynec chief resd physician, 1974-75. **Orgs:** Bd dir, Tidewater Area Bus & Contractors Asn, 1975; physician, Norforlk Comn Hosp; Norfolk Gen Hosp; Bayside Hosp; Leigh Meml Hosp; Norfolk Med Soc; Norfolk Acad Med; VA obstetrics & gynec Soc; jr fellow, Am Col obstetrics & gynec; Med Soc VA Omega Psi Phi; Zeta Chap Busileus, 1963-64; Delta Chap Basileus, 1969-70; VA Unoin Univ Alumni Asn; Meharry Med Col Alumni Asn, 19720. **Business Addr:** 400 W Brambleton Ave Suite 103, Norfolk, VA 23510, **Business Phone:** (757)622-3339.

LOWE, SIDNEY ROCHELL
Basketball coach, basketball player. **Personal:** Born Jan 21, 1960; children: Sidney II. **Educ:** NC State Univ. **Career:** Basketball player (retired), basketball coach; Ind Pacers, prof basketball player, 1983-84; Detroit Pistons, Atlanta Hawks, prof basketball player, 1984-85; Charlotte Hornets, prof basketball player, 1988-89; Minn Timberwolves, prof basketball player, 1989-90, asst coach, 1990-93, interim/head coach, 1993-94, asst coach, 1999-2000; Cleveland Cavaliers, asst coach, 1994-99; Memphis Grizzlies, head coach, 2000-02; Minn Timberwolves, asst coach, 2003-05; Detroit Pistons, asst coach, 2005-06; NC State Univ, head coach, 2006-. **Special Achievements:** Nat Basketball Assn's youngest head coach, 1993. **Business Addr:** Head Coach, North Carolina State University, Rabbit Box Circle, Raleigh, NC 27610, **Business Phone:** (919)513-4896.

LOWE, VICTORIA
President (Organization), chief executive officer. **Personal:** Born in St Louis. **Educ:** Univ Mo, BS, mktg & bus admin, 1983. **Career:** Alert Staffing, founder, pres & ceo. Victoria Lowe Enterprises, pres & ceo, currently. **Honors/Awds:** Women in Color; Small Bus Admin Entrepreneurial Success Award, 2000; Southwestern Bell Commun Bronze Supplier of the Year, 2000; Black Bus Asn, Black Bus in Los Angeles, 2001. **Special Achievements:** US Department of Defense, National Business Woman of the Year. First African American woman to serve on a national school accreditation team.First National Association Women Business Owners President. 5 of Top 25 Minority Businesses in Los Angeles 2001. **Business Phone:** (310)665-9380.*

LOWE, WALTER EDWARD, JR.
Executive. **Personal:** Born Aug 20, 1951, Milford, VA; son of Walter E Sr and Fraulein C; married Sheryl Ferguson, Oct 28, 1978; children: Ashley Patrice & Walter Edward III. **Educ:** Univ Va, BA, 1976. **Career:** Ford Motor Co, buyer, 1976-83; Gen Dynamics, buyer spt, 1983, chief procurement, 1983-85, mgr procurement, 1985-90, dir procurement, 1990-93, dir mat acquisition, 1994-. **Orgs:** Am Mgt Asn, 1983-; Cert mgr, Inst Cert Prof Mgr, 1985-; NCP, 1988-; chair, United Way Allocation Panel, 1990-; bd trustees, Henry Ford HTH Syst, 1992-; mat steering comt, Electronic Indust Asn, 1995-; Automotive Indust Action Group. **Honors/Awds:** America's Best & Brightest Young Business & Professional Man Award, Dollars & Sense Mag, 1988. **Special Achievements:** Feature article, "Buying More Bank for the Buck," Electronics Purchasing Magazine, 1992. **Military Serv:** USY, spec 4, 1972-74. **Home Addr:** 4899 Peggy St, West Bloomfield, MI 48322, **Home Phone:** (810)737-6942. **Business Addr:** Director, General Dynamics, Land Systems Division, 38500 Mound Rd, PO Box 2074, Warren, MI 48310, **Business Phone:** (586)825-4000.

LOWERY, DR. BIRL
Educator. **Personal:** Born Dec 24, 1950, Starkville, MS; son of Clem and Katie Collins; married Ester Hamblin, Feb 24, 1973; children: Ramona C & Tyson B. **Educ:** Alcorn Univ, Lorman, BS, agr educ, 1973; Miss State Univ, Starkville, MA, agr Engineering technol, 1975; Ore State Univ, Corvallis, PhD, soil physics, 1980. **Career:** Univ Wis, Madison, WI, asst prof, 1980-86, assoc prof, 1986-92; prof, 1992-, Dept Soil Science at UW-Madison, chair, 1999-2004; Jour Soil & Water Conserv, assoc. **Orgs:** Soil Sci Soc Am; Int Soil Tillage Res Org; Soil & Water Conservation Soc; Am Society of Agronomy, 1977-; The Scientific Research Society, Sigma Xi, 1980-96; Soil Water Conservation Society, 1981-; Am Society of Agricultural Engineers, 1984-94; InterNatSoil Science Society, 1986-98; InterNatUnion of Soil Science, 1998-; InterNat-Soil Tillage Research Organization, 1987-; Gamma Sigma Delta, 1984-; Vilas Research Assoc, 1998-2000. **Honors/Awds:** The ASAE Blue Ribbon Award for an outstanding entry in the 1987 Educational Aids Competition. **Special Achievements:** Published more than 100 articles. **Business Addr:** Professor, University of Wisconsin-Madison, Department of Soil Science, 263 Soils Bldg, 1525 Observatory Dr, Madison, WI 53706-1299, **Business Phone:** (608)262-2752.

LOWERY, BOBBY G
Executive. **Personal:** Born Nov 26, 1932, Blacksburg, SC; son of Eliza Morgan and Garance Lee; married Betty Mason, Oct 16, 1955; children: Regina Jones, Reginald, Revonsia Dozier & Robert. **Educ:** Carver Col, lib arts, 1957. **Career:** US Post Off, lett carrier, 1957-70; Better Cleaning, pres, 1970-. **Orgs:** Vice chmn, Nat Minority Supplier Develop Counl, Minority Input Comt, 1978-79; pres, Charlotte Bus League, 1981-82; bd deacons, St Paul Baptist Church, chmn, 1982-; dir, Bldg Serv Contractors Asn Int, 1985-88; exec comt, Charlotte Chamber Com, 1985-86; trustee, Univ NCA Charlotte, 1987-95. **Honors/Awds:** Outstanding Citizen Award, Sigma Gamma Rho Sorority, 1978; Minority Business Enterpriser of the Year, Charlotte Chamber Com, 1985. **Military Serv:** USY, cpl, 1951-54; USY Occupation, Germany, 1952. **Home Addr:** 5930 Sierra Dr, Charlotte, NC 28216, **Home Phone:** (704)392-2377. **Business Addr:** President, Better Cleaning Maintenance Supply Inc, 500 W 32nd St, Charlotte, NC 28206-2215, **Business Phone:** (704)372-9242.

LOWERY, CAROLYN T
Association executive. **Personal:** Born Jul 7, 1940, New Iberia, LA; daughter of Genivie Thomas Davis and Eldridge Thomas; divorced; children: Donald Jr, Valencia, Michael, Peter & Donald Wayne. **Educ:** Maricopa Tech Col, AA, 1978; Ariz State Univ, Sch Social Work. **Career:** Palmade Sch, teacher's aide; Motorola Plant, assembly worker; Ebony House rehab prog men, 1977-81; Wesley United Methodist Church, black community developer, 1981-85; Kid's Place, founder & dir, 1989; Ariz Black United Fund Inc, exec dir, 1985-. **Orgs:** Co-chairwoman, Ariz New Alliance Party, 1985-; co-chairwoman, Westside Neighborhood Community Ctr, 1988-; bd mem, Ariz Future Forum Prog, Phoenix, Ariz; bd mem, Ariz Regional Pub Transp Authority; co-founder, Ariz Black Cult Mus, 1981-; co-founder, Ariz Stop Police Brutality Orgn, 1981-; co-founder, Ariz New Alliance Party, 1986; founder, Moms Moms Orgn, 1998; founder, Pennies Heaven Found, 1999; Ariz Repub Champion C. **Honors/Awds:** Outstanding community service citations: Masons, 1982, Nation Islam, 1983, City Phoenix, 1984, Black Engineers & Scientists, 1986, Black Community, 1988; Leadership Award, Black Women Task Force, 1995; As They Grow Awards, Parents Magazine, Ceremony White House, 1997; Foot Soldier Award, Ariz Nat Asn Blacks Criminal Justice, 1997; Nat Freedoms Foundation at Valley Forge award, 2005; Hon Kachina Volunteer Award, 2006. **Business Addr:** Executive Director, Arizona Black United Fund, PO Box 24457, Phoenix, AZ 85074, **Business Phone:** (602)268-0666.

LOWERY, DONALD ELLIOTT
Investment banker. **Personal:** Born Jan 6, 1956, Chicago, IL; son of R D Lowery and Annie. **Educ:** Wesleyan Univ, Middletown, CT, BA, econ, 1977. **Career:** Landmark Newspapers, reporter, 1977-79; Ariz Rep, Phoenix, reporter, 1979-80; The Boston Globe, MA, reporter, 1980-82; WHDH-TV, Boston, MA, dir, pub affairs & ed, 1982-91; Lazard Freres & Co, investment banker, 1992. **Orgs:** Nat Asn Black Journalist, 1980-; past pres, Nat Broadcast Ed Asn, 1982-; Bus Assocs Club, 1984-; bd dirs, Bay State Games, 1990-. **Honors/Awds:** Emmy, Nat Acad TV Arts & Scis, 1985, 1986; UPS Tom Phillips Award, 1985; Lincoln University Unity Award, 1988, 1989, 1991. *

LOWERY, REV. DR. JOSEPH E.
Association executive, president (organization), chief executive officer. **Personal:** Born Oct 6, 1921, Huntsville, AL; married Evelyn Gibson; children: Yvonne, Karen & Cheryl. **Educ:** Clark Col, AB, BD, DO, DD, 1975; Chicago Ecumenical Inst, Garrett Theol Sem; Payne Theol Sem; Knoxville Col; Payne Col; Wayne Univ; Morehouse Univ, DD; Atlanta Univ, LLD; Dillard Univ, LittD. **Career:** Warren St Church, Birmingham, AL, pastor, 1952-61; Bishop Golden, admin asst, 1961-64; St Paul Church, pastor, 1964-68; Southern Christian Leadership Conf, founder, vpres, 1967, nat chmn, bd dir, 1967-77, nat pres, 1977-97, pres emer, 1997-; Cent United Methodist Church, minister,1968-86; Emory Univ, Candler Sch Theol & Nursery Sch, instr, 1970-71;Cascade United Methodist Church, minister, 1986-92; Enterprises Now Inc, pres. **Orgs:** Gen Bd Pub Housing, 1960-72; Comt Race Rels, United Methodist Church, 1968-76; bd dir, MARTA, 1975-78; bd dir, Comt Relief, Global Ministry,1976; Mayors Comt Human Rels; chmn, Civil Rights Coord Comt; pres, InterdenomiNat Ministry All, Nashville, TN; pres, OEO Comt Act Agency; bd dir, United Way; Martin Luther King Jr Ctr Social Change; bd dir, Urban Act Inc; Nat Leadership Coun Civil Rights; bd trustees, Paine Col; founder& pres, Cascade First Comt Asn; Ga Coalition Peoples Agenda; co-founder&pres, Black Leadership Forum; vice chmn, Atlanta Community Rels Comt. **Honors/Awds:** Medal of Honor, Moscow Theol Sem, 1971; Citizen of the Year OEO Award, Atlanta Urban League, 1975; Humanitarian Award, Kappa Alpha Psi, 1983; Justice Award, Alpha Kappa Alpha, 1985; Religion Award, 1985; Martin Luther King Award, Progressive Nat Baptist Conv, 1986; Black Achievement Award, Ebony Mag, 1989, 1990; President's Achievement Award, Nat Asn Advan Colored People, 1997; Martin Luther King Jr Award, Boston Univ, 1992; Justice Award, United Methodist Church, Coun Bishops, 1993; Civil Rights Award, United Auto Workers, 1994, 1995, 1998; Tribute to a Black American, Nat Conf Black Mayors, 1997; North Star Award, Nat Black Publ, 2002; Lifetime Achievement Award, Black Leadership Forum, 2002; Lifetime Achievement Award, Concerned Black Clergy, 2002; Whitney M Young Jr Lifetime Achievement Award, 2004; Urban League Equal Opportunity Award;Nation of Islam Inter Nat Affairs Award; OIC Clergy of the Year; Martin Luther King Center Peace Award; Outstanding Community Service Contributor; Committee to Abolish Death Penalty Award; Martin Luther King Award, George Washington Univ; Presidential Medal of Freedom, 2009. **Special**

Achievements: Fifteen Greatest Black Preachers, 1984, 1994. **Business Addr:** President Emeritus, Southern Christian Leadership Conference, 334 Auburn Ave NE, Atlanta, GA 30303-2604, **Business Phone:** (404)522-1420.

LOWERY, MICHAEL
Football player. **Personal:** Born Feb 14, 1974, McComb, MS. **Educ:** Univ Miss. **Career:** Chicago Bears, linebacker, 1996-97.

LOWERY, MICHAEL DOUGLAS
Educator. **Personal:** Born Feb 21, 1950, Madisonville, KY; son of Hendrix and Lila. **Educ:** BORE, 1980; BS, hist political sci, 1992; MA, 1993. **Career:** City Recreation, dir; Elliott Mortuary, general asst; State Highway Dept; Library, special worker; paralegal, Gifted Educr, teacher, gifted dir, 1999-2000. **Orgs:** Pres, Nat Asn Advan Colored People; HCEA, Vic II; KEA; NEA; Nat Funeral Dirs; OPP, founder, Murray State Univ Chap; Nat Baptist, Progressive Baptist, Ky Bapt. **Honors/Awds:** Teacher of the Year, Hopkins County Bd; Smith Wilson Award, KY Educ Asn; Omega Man, Omega Psi Phi, Alpha Beta Chap; Baptist Man of Year; Leadership Award, Nat Asn Advan Colored Peopel. **Special Achievements:** Published: Gifted Hand Book. **Home Addr:** 343 N Church St, Madisonville, KY 42431, **Home Phone:** (270)821-7803. **Business Addr:** Teacher, Browning Springs Middle School, 357 W Arch St, Madisonville, KY 42431, **Business Phone:** (502)825-6006.

LOWERY, TERRELL
Baseball player. **Personal:** Born Oct 25, 1970, Oakland, CA; married Denise; children: 3. **Educ:** Loyola Marymount Univ. **Career:** Chicago Cubs, outfielder, 1997-98; Tampa Bay Devil Rays, outfielder, 1999; San Francisco Giants, outfielder, 2000. *

LOWERY-JETER, RENECIA YVONNE
Association executive. **Personal:** Born Jul 2, 1954, Detroit, MI; daughter of Harold and Sarah; married Darrell, Sep 3, 1993. **Educ:** Wayne State Univ, BA, 1976; Marygrove Col, MA, 1991, MEd, 2005. **Career:** Genesis Training & Develop, 2000-; Detroit Pub Sch, dir benefits, 2004-07; Pretty Products LLC, vpres human resources, 2007-; United Way Servs, dir human resources. **Orgs:** Bd mem, Spaulding C, 1993-96; pres, Am Soc Training & Develop, 1997-98; vol, Jr Achievement; Soc Human Resource Mgt; Am Soc Training & Develop; Nat Asn Women Bus Owners. **Home Phone:** (313)531-2509. **Business Phone:** (706)884-1711.

LOWMAN, CARL D
Executive, vice president (organization). **Personal:** Born Dec 1, 1962, Philadelphia, PA; son of Carl N and Delores Guy-Lowman; divorced. **Educ:** Univ Mass, Amherst, BBA, 1984; Colo State Univ, MBA. **Career:** The Gillette Co, budget analyst asst, 1984-85, ade & controls analyst, 1985-86, budget analyst, 1986-87; Continental Airlines Inc, financial analyst, 1987-89, sr financial analyst, 1989-91, mgr budget & forecasting, 1991-95; Western Pac Airlines Inc, dir financial serv, 1995-96, treas, 1995-97; MWH Global Inc, vpres & dir global financial planning & analysis, currently. **Honors/Awds:** Outstanding Young Men of America Award, 1987; YMCA of the Pikes Peak Region, Multicultral Achievers in Business & Industry Award, 1996. **Business Addr:** Director, Vice President, MWH Global Inc, 380 Interlocken Crescent Suite 200, Broomfield, CO 80021, **Business Phone:** (303)533-1900.

LOWMAN, ISOM
Physician, commander. **Personal:** Born Jun 3, 1946, Hopkins, SC; married Irma Jean Smith; children: Joye Katrese, Isom Batrone, Robin Patrese. **Educ:** SC State Col, BS, chem, 1968; Meharry Med Col, MD, 1972; Wm Beaumont Army Med Ctr, Bd Internship, 1975, Bd Residency, 1980. **Career:** Ft Benning, chief med, 1975-78; Wm Beaumont Army Med Ctr, nuclear fel, 1978-80; Moncrief Army Hosp, Ft Jackson, SC, chief nuclear med, 1980-82, dep comdr, chief nuclear med & med, 1983-. **Orgs:** Alpha Phi Alpha Fraternity, 1965-, Palmetto Med Soc; pres, Cong Med Soc; fel Am Col Physicians; Soc Nuclear Med, Am Med Asn; Nat Asn Advan Colored People. **Honors/Awds:** Outstanding Alpha Alpha Phi Alpha Fraternity; Distinguished Grad Hopkins High Sch, 1984. **Military Serv:** AUS, col; military medal of merit award. **Home Addr:** 51 Running Fox Rd, Columbia, SC 29223. *

LOWNES-JACKSON, DR. MILLICENT GRAY
School administrator. **Personal:** Born Dec 24, 1951, Philadelphia, PA; daughter of James Gray and Mildred Gray; married Arthur Jackson, Sep 1, 1995; children: Robert Jr & Monique. **Educ:** Fisk Univ, BA, admin, 1972; Vanderbilt Univ, MBA, mgt, 1975, PhD, 1981. **Career:** Tenn State Univ, Col Bus, Dept Bus Admin, prof, 1976-, assoc dean, 1995-. **Orgs:** Founder, InterdenomiNat Serv Orgn Am, 1990-; 100 Black Women, 1994-; Links Inc, 1994-; Jack & Jill Am; Phi Kappa Phi Hon Soc, 1995-; Beta Gamma Sigma Hon Bus Frat, 1995-; founder, Bus Exchange Entrepreneurially Minded, 1995-; founder, Women's Inst Success Entrep, 1995-. **Honors/Awds:** JC Penney, Golden Rule Award, Community Service, 1993, Golden Rule Award for Educators, 1994; Distinguished Service Award, Nashville Jaycees, 1994; Distinguished Professionalism, Nat Asn Negro, 1994; Business Leader of Nashville Award, Black Expo, 1995. **Special Achievements:** Author of 13 entrepreneurial books; conducted over 200 workshops & seminars, entrepreneurial empowerment; impacted lives of over 4,000 youth and 1,000 women, through non-profit organization; established ISOA to economically & entrepreneurially empower youth & women, 1990. **Home Addr:** 205 Augusta Nat Ct, Franklin, TN 37069, **Home Phone:** (615)646-8881. **Business Addr:** Professor, Associate Dean, Tennessee State University, College of Business, Department of Business Administration, 330 10th Ave N, Nashville, TN 37203-3401, **Business Phone:** (615)963-7127.

LOWRY, DONNA SHIRLYNN (REID)
Television journalist. **Personal:** Born May 19, 1957, Pittsburgh, PA; daughter of Walter J S and Alma M; married Bennet W Reid Jr; children: Nicole Fuller, Lakisha Reid, Sparkle Reid. **Educ:** Chatham Col, BA, Commun & Admin & Mgt, 1979; Northwestern Univ, MSJ, 1981. **Career:** WEEK-TV, news anchor, reporter, 1981-83; WESH-TV, news anchor, reporter, 1983-86; WXIA-TV, educ ed, 1986-. **Orgs:** Save The Children, adv bd, 1991-; Bd, West End Boys & Girls Clubs, 1992-; bd dirs, Old Nat Christian Acad, 1994-; honorary chaplian, South Fulton PTA, 1991; Atlanta Asn Black Journalists, 1987-; Alpha Kappa Alpha Sorority Inc; Magnolia Chaplian, Links Inc, 1994-; Statewide Safety Belt Task Force, 1994-; adv bd, Georgia Asn Family Daycare, 1994; bd dirs, Georgia Asn Sch Age Care, 1996-; The Sheltering Arms Child Care Ctrs; Beulah Baptist Church Dollars for Scholars; Black Women Film Preservation Proj; Educ Writers Asn; Nat Acad Television Arts & Scis; Magnolia Chapter LINKS Inc; Atlanta Asn Black Journalists. **Honors/Awds:** Outstanding Business & Professional Award, Dollars & Sense Mag, 1992; Positive Image Award, The Minority Recruiter Newspapers, 1993; Media Award, GEO Psychological Asn, 1992; various Child Care Media Awards, 1991; Salute to Women of Achievement, YWCA, 1987, 1990. **Business Addr:** Education Editor, WXIA-TV, 11Alive News, 1611 W Peachtree St NE, Atlanta, GA 30309, **Business Phone:** (404)892-1611.*

LOWRY, JAMES E.
Executive. **Personal:** Born Jul 8, 1942, Wyoming, OH; son of Henry and Mamie. **Educ:** Xavier Univ Cincinnati, BS, bus admin, 1975. **Career:** Gen Elect Co, equal opportunity minority relations, adminr, 1970-71, mgt trainee, 1975-78, buyer machined parts, 1978-79, mgr specialty parts, 1979-84, materials adminr, 1984-89, mgr sourcing advanced tech, 1989-93; Lincoln Heights OH, mayor, 1972-74; Indirect Materials & Serv, mgr, 1993-95; Bus Practices, mgr, 1995. **Orgs:** Bd dir, Community Action Comn Cincinnati, 1972-74; bd dir, Lincoln Heights Health Clin, 1972-74; consult, Community Chest Cincinnati, 1972-74; bd dir, People United Save Humanity, 1972-74; bd dir, Freedom Farm Ruleville MS, 1972-74; bd dir, Ohio Black Polit Assembly, 1972-74; bd dirs, Gen Elec Credit Union, 1984; Union Experimenting Col & Univ, 1986; City Forest Park Civil Serv Comn, 1989-94; AECU Credit Union, chmn, 1993; chmn, Forest Park Civil Serv Community, 1994. **Honors/Awds:** Key to City Cincinnati, 1972; Award of Appreciation, City Fayette, 1973; Outstanding Political Service to the Community, Ohio Black Polit Assembly, 1973; Extra Step Award, Gen Elec Co, 1980; Extra Step Award, Gen Elec Corp, 1980; GE Purchasing Gold Cup Award, 1982.

LOWRY, JAMES HAMILTON
Executive. **Personal:** Born May 28, 1939, Chicago, IL; son of Wlliam E and Camille; married Doris Davenport; children: Aisha. **Educ:** Grinnell Col, BA, 1961; Univ Pittsburgh, MPIA, 1965; Harvard Univ, prog mgt develop (PMD), 1973. **Career:** Grinnell Col, Travel fel, 1961-62; Univ Pittsburgh, John Hay-Whitney fel, 1963-65; Bedford-Stuyvesant Restoration Corp Brooklyn, from spec asst to pres proj mgr, 1967-68; Peace Corps Lima, Peru, assoc dir, 1965-67; McKinsey & Co Chicago, sr assoc, 1968-75; James H Lowry & Assoc, pres, 1975-2000; Boston Consulting Group, vpres, 2000, sr vpres, currently. **Orgs:** Inst Mgt Consult, 1980-85; Nat Black MBA Asn, 1981-85; prin, Chicago United, 1982-85; Harvard Alumni Asn, 1980-85; pres, Chicago Publ Library Bd, 1981-85; bd trustees, Northwestern Mem Hosp, 1980-85; bd trustees, Grinnell Col, 1971-85; bd dirs, Independence Bank, Chicago, 1983-85; bd dirs, Johnson Product; chair, Chicago-Durban Sister City Prog. **Honors/Awds:** President of class, Harvard Bus Sch, 1973. **Special Achievements:** Co-author of "The New Agenda for Minority Business Development. First African American recruit. **Business Addr:** Senior Vice President, Boston Consulting Group, 200 S Wacker Blvd, Chicago, IL 60606, **Business Phone:** (312)715-2211.

LOWRY, WILLIAM E, JR.
Executive. **Personal:** Born Feb 16, 1935, Chicago, IL; son of Camille and William; married Teri; children: Kim Maria & William Andre. **Educ:** Kenyon Col, AB, 1956; Loyola Univ, Chicago, MSIR, 1969. **Career:** Francis W Parker Sch, athletic dir, coach, 1960-62; Inland Steel Co, supvr, 1962-65; Inland Steel Container Co, personnel mgr, 1965, 1968-76; Opportunity Line WBBM TV, host TV ser, 1967-82; Objective Jobs WBBM TV, host TV ser, 1982-; Jos T Ryerson & Son Inc, mgr human resource, 1976-86; Personnel Admin dir, 1986-88; Inland Steel Indust, dir personnel & recruitment, 1988-93; John D & Catherine T MacArthur Found, vpres human resources, 1994-2005, sr advisor pres, currently; James H Lowry & Assoc, chief operating officer. **Orgs:** Human Resources Asn, Chicago, 1965-; secy, Midwest Col Placement Asn, 1967-68; bd dir, Children 's Home & Aid Soc Ill; vpres, bd dir, Chicago Boys & Girls Clubs, 1967-92; bd dir trustees Kenyon Col; Chicago United, 1975-93; bd dir trustees, Lake Forest Col, 1984-88; bd dir, Rehab Inst Chicago, 1988-; chmn, Chicago Pvt Indust Coun, 1990-; bd dir, United Way Crusade Mercy, 1996-; bd dir, Donor's Forum Chicago, 1996; bd dir, Ill Issues, 1998-; Chicago Workforce Bd; chair, City/Co Task Force Welfare Reform. **Honors/Awds:** George Foster Peabody Award, 1968; Emmy Award, Nat Acad TV Arts & Sci, 1968-69; Human Rel Mass Media Award, Am Jewish Comn, 1968; 10 Outstanding Men of Chicago, 1969; Blackbook's Black Business Man of the Year, 1981; Distinguished Jour Award, AICS, 1984. **Military Serv:** USAF, 1st lt, 3 yrs. **Home Addr:** 1023 W Vernon Pk Pl, Chicago, IL 60607. **Business Addr:** Senior Advisor to the President, John D & Catherine T MacArthur Foundation, 140 S Dearborn St, Chicago, IL 60603-5285, **Business Phone:** (312)726-8000.

LOYD, WALTER
Manager. **Personal:** Born Dec 23, 1951, Tampa, FL; children: Stacey, Tracey, Symon & Samuel. **Educ:** Univ Ariz-Pine Bluff, BS, 1974. **Career:** Ark Power & Light, sales rep, 1974-77, adm rate analyst, 1977-78, procedures analyst, 1974-78, contracts adminr, 1979-84, mgr, 1984-; Entergy Servs Inc, mgr, 1991-97, dir, supplier diversity, 1997-. **Orgs:** Treas, Am Asn Blacks Energy; century club & leadership mem, Quapaw Area Boy Scouts Am; chair bd dirs, Ark Regional Minority Supplier Develop Coun; bd dirs, Ouachita Girl Scout Coun; chair, Little Rock Bd Housing & Appeals; bd mem, Ariz Regional Minority Purchasing Coun; bd dir, Nat Minority Supplier Develop Coun; Greater Little Rock COC, Small Bus Coun; NCP, Econo Develop Coun; SBA. **Honors/Awds:** Treas, Am Asn Blacks Energy; century club & leadership mem, Quapaw Area Boy Scouts Am; chair bd dirs, Ark Regional Minority Supplier Develop Coun; bd dirs, Ouachita Girl Scout Coun; chair, Little Rock Bd Housing & Appeals; bd mem, Ariz Regional Minority Purchasing Coun; bd dir, Nat Minority Supplier Develop Coun; Greater Little Rock COC, Small Bus Coun; NCP, Econo Develop Coun; SBA; leadership mem, Boy Scouts Am, 1984; century mem, Boy Scouts Am, 1987-90; Exceptional Leadership & Dedication EEI Minority Bus Develop Comt, Edison Electric Inst,1996. **Special Achievements:** Publication: Enlightened Interest, Minority Business Enterprise, 1993. **Business Addr:** Director of Supplier Diversity, Entergy Services Inc, 639 Loyola Ave, PO Box 61000, New Orleans, LA 70113, **Business Phone:** (504)576-2036.

LOZADA, DE JUANA
Business owner. **Personal:** Born May 20, 1970, Raleigh, NC; daughter of Clarence Boone Jr and Dorothy Jeffries; married Victor, Nov 13, 1995; children: Deryian & Jhaylen. **Educ:** Univ NC, FSU campus, BA, commun, 1991; Univ Md, European campus, MA, commun, 1996; Defense Info Sch, advan pub affairs officer course, 1998. **Career:** Dept Defense, US Army Europe, pub affairs officer, 1991-99; Copydesk, pub rels firm, founder & ceo, 1999-. **Orgs:** Am Women Radio & TV; Pub Rels Soc Am; Nat Asn Advan Colored People; Am Civil Liberties Union; Urban League. **Honors/Awds:** Keith L Ware Military Awards Journal; Civilian Journalist of the Year, 1997. **Business Phone:** (719)633-6765.

LUCAS, DR. C PAYNE
Association executive. **Personal:** Born Sep 14, 1933, Spring Hope, NC; son of Minnie Hendricks and James Russel; married Freddie Emily Myra Hill, Aug 29, 1964; children: Therese Raymonde, C Payne Jr & Hillary Hendricks. **Educ:** Md State Col, Princess Anne, MD, 1953, BA, 1959; Am Univ, Wash, DC, MA, 1961. **Career:** Peace Corps, Wash, DC, Togo, asst dir, 1964, Niger, dir, 1964-66, Africa Region, dir, 1967-69, dir, off/returned vol, 1969-71; Africare, Wash, DC, exec dir, 1971-2002; Lodestar LLC, ceo, currently. **Orgs:** Bd dir, Overseas Develop Coun, 1977-; Int Develop Conf; bd mem, Environ Energy Inst, 1986-; bd dirs, Interaction; adv bd, Nat Peace Corps Asn; adv bd, Discovery Channel Global Educ Fund; Coun Foreign Rels, 1983-; bd mem, Pop Action Int, 1990-; Nat Asn Advan Colored People; Africa Soc; Modern Africa Fund Mgrs; Constituency Africa; Kennedy Ctr Community & Friends Bd; Univ Md Found; chmn & founding mem, US Comt United Nations Develop Programme; Comn Post-Conflict Reconstruction; founding mem, Corp Coun Africa; and the Andrew Young Ctr Int Affairs, Morehouse Col; US Africa Trade & Aid Link Corp; DC Campaign Prevent Teenage Pregnancy; bd dir, US Comt United Nations Develop Prog; Helping Enhance Livelihood People Comn, currently. **Honors/Awds:** President's Award for Distinguished Federal Civilian Service 1967; Distinguished Federal Service Award Peace Corps, 1967; Honorary Doctorate of Law, Univ Md, 1975; Capitol Press Club's Humanitarian of the Year, 1980; Presidential Hunger Award Outstanding Achievement, 1984; Phelps-Stokes Fund Aggrey Medal, 1986; Officers of the Order of Distinguished Service Award, 1986; Recognition from the National Order of the Republics of Niger, Zambia & Ivory Coast, 1988; Land Grant Colleges Distinguished Bicentennial Award, 1990; Nation Order of Merit Award, Govt Senegal, 1990; Hubert H Humphrey Public Service Award, Am Polit Sci Asn. **Special Achievements:** First Black Recipient of the American Political Science Association's Hubert H Humphrey Public Service Award. **Military Serv:** USAF airman first class, 1954-58. **Home Addr:** 4241 Mathewson Dr

NW, Washington, DC 20011, **Home Phone:** (202)722-0061. **Business Addr:** Board of Directors, United States Committee for the United Nations Development Program, PO Box 65345, Washington, WA 20035, **Business Phone:** (202)558-7104.

LUCAS, DAVID EUGENE
State government official. **Personal:** Born Apr 23, 1950, Byron, GA; son of David and Beatrice; married Elaine Huckabee; children: David Jr, Leonard, Aris & Albert. **Educ:** Tuskegee Inst, BS, polit sci, 1972; Mercer Univ Med Sch, JD; Atlanta Law Sch, attended. **Career:** Lucas Supply Co, owner; Northeast High Sch, Macon GA, social studies teacher & coach, 1972-73; Bibb Tech High Sch, Macon, GA, social studies teacher & varsity girls basketball, 1973-74; Barney A Smith Motors, Macon,GA, car salesman, 1974-75; State Ga, state rep, dist 139, 1975-; independent ins agt, 1980-86; Horace Mann Co, ins agt, 1986-88; TBL Inc, pres, 1988-. **Orgs:** Vpres, Macon Chfs Amtr football team; Black Eagles Motorcycle Club; C CMacon; fel, Christian Athletes; GA Asn Black Elected Offs; Nat Conf Black State Elected Offs; bd mem, Boys Club Macon; Coalition Polit Awareness; bdmem, Small & Minority Bus Coun, City Macon; bd gov, appointed Mercer Univ Sch Med, 1994. **Honors/Awds:** Distinguished Service Award, Columbia Univ, 1979; Community Service Award, Macon Courier Newspaper, 1986; Inducted into the Tuskegee Univ Athletic Hall of Fame, 1993. **Special Achievements:** Youngest African-Am to be elected to the GA Gen Assembly at age 24, 1974. **Business Addr:** Representative, Georgia House Representatives, Coverdell Legislative Office Bldg Room 509, Atlanta, GA 30334, **Business Phone:** (404)656-0220.

LUCAS, DOROTHY J.
Physician, teacher, community activist. **Personal:** Born Nov 27, 1949, Lambert, MS; daughter of Garvie Lucas Sr and Elizabeth Killebrew; divorced 1981. **Educ:** Kennedy-King Col, AA (Hons), 1971; Roosevelt Univ, BS, 1973; UHS Chicago Med Sch, MD, 1977; Univ Ill, MPH, 1993. **Career:** Mercy Hosp Med Ctr, asst attending physician, 1986-87; Columbus Cuneo Cabrini, resident, 1977-81, assoc attending physician, 1981-; Catholic Health Partners, sr attending physician, 1986-; instr, Roosevelt Univ; Greater Bethesda Baptist Church, health ed; pvt pract, physician, currently; Cook Co Dept Pub Health, med dir, currently. **Orgs:** pres, Nat Asn Advan Colored People, Southside Chicago Br; Alpha Kappa Alpha, 1986-; CMC, AMA, ISMA; dipl Am Bd Ob-Gyn; fel Am Col Ob-Gyn; Am Med Asn; Am Soc Addiction Med; Chicago Med Soc, Health Care Economics Comt, consult, currently. **Honors/Awds:** ACOG, Am Coll Ob-Gyn, 1985; AMA Physician recognition Am Med Asn, 1985; Chicago Jaycees Ten Outstanding Young Citizens, 1987; Distinguished Alumni City Cols Trustee Award, 1987; Push-Andrew Thomas Health Award, 1987; Urban League Women in Health Award, 1999. **Business Addr:** Medical Director, Cook County Department of Public Health, 1010 Lake St Suite 104, Oak Park, IL 60301-1133, **Business Phone:** (708)492-2000.*

LUCAS, EARL S.
Government official. **Personal:** Born Jan 1, 1938, Renova, MS; married Marilee Lewis; children: Eric, Vicki, Carla, Tina, Mark & Kendric. **Educ:** Dillard Univ, BA, 1957; De Pauw Univ; Beloit Col. **Career:** Bolivar County Sch Syst, teacher, 1958-65; Star Inc, exec dir, 1965-73; City Mound Bayou, mayor, 1969; Nat Conf Black Mayors, founder, currently. **Orgs:** Treas, So Conf Black Mayors; dir, Mound Bayou Develop Corp; dir, Fund Educ& Community Develop; Com Delta Ministry Nat Coun Church; dir, Delta Found; Alpha Phi Alpha Fraternity; Conf Black Mayors. **Business Addr:** Founder, Nat Conf Black Mayors, 1151 Cleveland Ave Bldg D, East Point, GA 30344.*

LUCAS, GERALD ROBERT
Government official, social worker. **Personal:** Born Sep 18, 1942, Washington, DC; son of Mack and Sylvia Coats Jiles; married Patricia Selena Jones, Jan 19, 1975; children: Gerald R Jr, Kenya & Kimberlee. **Educ:** Brandeis Univ, 1971; State Univ, NY Stoney Brook, MSW, 1973; Univ Minnesota, PhD, 1976. **Career:** US Dept Health, Educ & Wealth, personnel mgt specialist, 1969-71; Wash Urban League, prog dir, 1967-69; Minneapolis Urban League, proj dir, 1974-76; Univ Cincinnati, assoc prof, 1976-78; US Dept Comn, spec asst secy admin, 1978-; US Dept Com, dir off civil rights, 1982-; US Dept Com, Eastern Admin Support Ctr, dir; Econ Develop Admin, dep cfo, 2002; Dir Civil Rights, Dept Com, sr adv, currently. **Orgs:** Bd dirs, Minneapolis Zion Group Home, 1975-76; Nat Asn Black Social Workers Minneapolis Chap, 1973-76; Am Soc Pub Adminr, Nat Capital Area Chap, 1979-80; Cincinnati Title XX Adv Comn, 1975-76; Barnaby Manor Civic Asn, 1978-80; Conf Minority Pub Admin, 1979-80. **Honors/Awds:** Commendation award, AUS. **Military Serv:** AUS, specialist, 1964-66. **Business Addr:** Senior Advisor, US Department of Commerce, Director Of Civil Rights, 1401 Const Ave NW, Washington, DC 20230, **Business Phone:** (202)482-2000.*

LUCAS, JOHN HARDING, II
Executive, basketball coach, president (organization). **Personal:** Born Oct 31, 1953, Durham, NC; son of John and Blondola; married Debbie; children: Tarvia, John Jr & Jai. **Educ:** Univ Md, BS, bus admin, 1976; Univ San Francisco, MA, educ. **Career:** Houston Rockets, 1976-78, 1985-86, 1989-90; Golden Gaters World Tennis Team, 1977; New Orleans Nets World Tennis Team, 1978; Golden State Warriors, 1978-81; Wash Bullets; 1981-83, San Antonio Spurs, 1983-84; Milwaukee Bucks, 1987-88, Seattle Super Sonics, 1989; Basketball player (retired); tennis player (retired); head coach; San Antonio Spurs,coach, 1993-94; Philadelphia 76er's, coach & gen mgr, 1994-96; Denver Nuggets, asst coach, 1998-2001; Cleveland Cavaliers, head coach, 2001-04; head coach, Houston Wranglers, 2004; coach, Lori McNeil, 2006; John Lucas Enterprises, founder & pres, 1990-. **Orgs:** Bd of dirs, Nat Coun Alcoholism & Drug Dependence Inc. **Honors/Awds:** ACC Athlete of the Year, 1976; NBA All Rookie Team, 1977; All-Am Tennis Player; Atlantic Coastal Conf Singles Title (Tennis); Man of the Year, USBL, 1992; NC Sports Hall of Fame, inductee, 1995. **Special Achievements:** Author: Winning A Day At A Time, Hazelden Publishing Group, 1994.

LUCAS, DR. JOHN HARDING
Educator, founder (originator). **Personal:** Born Nov 7, 1920, Rocky Mount, NC; son of John William and Rebecca Bowles; married Blondola O Powell; children: Cheryl & John Harding, Jr. **Educ:** Shaw Univ NC, BS, 1940; NC Central Univ, MA, 1951; NYU, certificate advanced study educ; NYU, Univ NC, Duke Univ; Appalachian State Univ; Durham Technical Community Col. **Career:** Adkin HS NC, sci teacher, 1940-44, guidance dir coordr diversified occupations coack admin asst, 1946-52; Orange St Elem Sch Oxford NC, prin, 1952-57; Mary Potter HS Oxford NC, prin, 1957-62; Hillside Sr HS Durham NC, prin, 1962-86; Shaw Univ, pres, 1986-87; Durham City Bd Educ, 1987-; Durham Pub Schs, Bd Educ, 1992-96; Durham Pub Educ Network, founder, 1997-. **Orgs:** Pres, NC Asn Educs, 1974-75; pres, Kinston Teacher Asn, 1942-44; adv com,Gov Commn on Study Pub Sch NC, 1967-68; bd dir, NC Asn Educrs, 1970-72; dir, NC Nat Educ Asn, 1961-72; Liaison Com NC Tchr Asn NC Edn Asn; US Delegate to World Assembly of World Confederation of Orgn of Tchr Profession in Africa, Asia British Columbia & Ireland, 1965-73; consult, Race Relations; contr, Educational & Professional Jours; chmn, NC Delegationsto Annual Conv NC Asn Educrs at Nat Educ Asn Nat Rep Assemblies; editor, Beta Phi Chap Omega Psi Phi Frat Inc; deacon trustee, White Rock Bapt Ch Durham NC; Task Force on NC Mental Health Ctr, 1970; Nat Commn for TX Educ Asn Evaluation, 1970; adv com, White House Conf on Children & Youth, 1970; chmn, Durham Human Relations Comn, 1973; bir, Learning Inst of NC, 1971-; bd dir, Nat Found for Improvement of Educ, 1970-; NC Cit Com on Sch; Durham Civic Conv Cntr Comn, 1972-; honorary mem bd dir, NEA, 1973; Boy's Adv Coun Salvat; chair, bd deacons, White Rock Baptist Church, 1990-; bd dirs, NC Public Sch Forum; bd dirs, Durham Pub Sch Fund; bd trustees, Shaw Univ, 1978-; Nat Asn Advan Colored People; Governors Adv CNL on Aging. **Honors/Awds:** Man of the Year Award, Citizen's Welfare League NC, 1951; Distinguished Service Award, NC Teachers Assn, 1968; Meritorious Award, NC Resource Use Educ, 1969; Honor Award, NC State Fair, 1969; Distinguished Service Award, Durham City Assn of Educrs, 1971-72; Durham's Father of Year, 1972; Honorary Citizen, Durham NC, 1974; Hall of Distinction, Shaw Univ, 1990; Martin Luther King, Jr Meritorious Award, General Baptist Convention of North Carolina, 1987; Citizen of the Year, Omega Phi Psi Fraternity, 1988; Wachovia Principal of the Year, 1984; Above & Beyond Award, NCAE, 1986; NCAE Lobby named Lucas-Radar Lobby, NCAE Equity Award, 1995; DHL, Shaw Univ. **Military Serv:** WWII veteran, 1944-46. **Business Addr:** Founder, Durham Public Schools, PO Box 30002, Durham, NC 27702, **Business Phone:** (919)560-2000.

LUCAS, L LOUISE
Government official. **Personal:** Born Jan 22, 1944, Portsmouth, VA; daughter of Joseph Boone and Lillie Boone; married Charlie C Trotter, Oct 28, 1997; children: Jeffrey Lucas, Lisa Lucas Burke & Theresa. **Educ:** Norfolk State Univ, BS, 1976, MA, 1982. **Career:** Norfolk Naval Shipyard, from apprentice shipfitter to shipfitter, 1967-75, Engineering draftsman, 1975-76, naval archit technician, 1976-79; SE Tidewater Opportunity Proj, 1985-86, exec dir, 1986-92; Old Dominion Univ, congional liaison sponsored progs, 1992-94; Virginia State Senate, senator, 1992-; Norfolk State Univ, asst prof, 1994-98, spec asst, vpres univ advan, 1998-; Southside Direct Care Provider, pres & admin, 1998-; Lucas Lodge, pres & exec dir, 1998-. **Orgs:** Golden life mem, Delta Sigma Theta Sorority Inc; Portsmouth Naval Civilian Adminr's Asn; bd mem large, Portsmouth Torch Club; Order Eastern Star, Brighton Light Chap, No 118; African Methodist Episcopal Church; Nat Asn Advan Colored People; Nat Coun Christians & Jews. **Honors/Awds:** Woman of the Year, Zeta Phi Beta, 1985; Alumnae of the Year, Norfolk State Univ Sch Tech, Stud Adv Comt, 1992; Appreciation Award, Wash DC Service Corps, 1994; Child Advocate Award, Places & Programs C Inc, 1995; Paul A Askew Community Service Awd, 1996; VA Water Project Community Service Awd, 1997; Committment to Health Care Legislation Award, Chesapeake Hosp Auth, 1998. **Business Addr:** State Senator, Virginia State, 1819 Elm Ave, PO Box 700, Portsmouth, VA 23705-0700, **Business Phone:** (757)397-8209.

LUCAS, LINDA GAIL
Counselor, president (organization). **Personal:** Born Jul 18, 1947, Charleston, SC; married Henry Lucas Jr (deceased); children: Ayoka L. **Educ:** Herbert Lehman Col, BA, 1969; The Citadel, MEd, 1984. **Career:** Rockland C Psych Ctr, sr speech pathologist, 1972-80; Dorchester Co Schs III, speech correctionist, 1980; Chas Co Sch Dist, speech correctionist, 1980-84; Hunley Pk Elem, guid counr 1984-85; Buist Acad, guid counr 1985; Wands High Sch, guid counr, 1988-90; Septima P Clark, guidance dir, 1990; Charleston Southern Univ, adjunct cour, 1992-99. **Orgs:** Sec Tri-County Foster Parents Assoc, 1982; adjunct staff mem Dorchester Ment Health Ctr 1984; guardian ad litem GAL Prog, 1985; delegate Alice Birney Sch Bd, 1986-87; Womens Aglow Int, 1988; pres, Tri-County Counr Develop Asn, 1991-92. **Honors/Awds:** News & courier article single parent survival, 1985; Licensed prof counr State SC, 1986; Counselor of the Year, 1987-88.

LUCAS, MAURICE
Basketball player, basketball coach. **Personal:** Born Feb 18, 1952, Pittsburgh, PA; son of Bill Walton; married Rita; children: Maurice II, David & Kristin Nicole. **Educ:** Marquette Univ, attended 1974. **Career:** Basketball player (retired), Basketball Coach; Carolina Saint Louis ABA, 1974-75, Kentucky Colonels ABA, 1975; Portland Trail Blazers, 1976-80; New Jersey Nets, 1980-81; New York Knicks, 1981-82; Phoenix Suns, 1982-85; Los Angeles Lakers, 1985-86; Seattle SuperSonics, 1986-87; Portland Trail Blazers, 1987-88; Lucas Investment Properties, Travel Planners Inc, owner; ML Sports, owner; Portland Trail Blazers, asst coach, 1988, 2005-. **Orgs:** Bd mem, NBA Retired Players Asn; vpres, NBA Players Asn; found mem, UNICRU Inc; found mem, EID Passport Inc. **Honors/Awds:** Portland's World Championship Team, 1977; NBA All-Star, 1977, 1978, 1979,1983; All-NBA Second Team, 1978; All-NBA-Defense First Team, 1978; All-NBA-Defense Second Team, 1979; Named one of the 30 Greatest Players in ABA History, 1997; Inducted into the Oregon Sports Hall of Fame in 2000. **Business Phone:** (503)234-9291.

LUCAS, MAURICE F
Government official, mayor. **Personal:** Born Oct 10, 1944, Mound Bayou, MS; son of Glady Collins and Julius; married Carolyn Cousin, Feb 3, 1968; children: Maurice F Lucas Jr. **Educ:** Delta State Univ, Cleveland, MS, BBA, 1971. **Career:** Cleveland Sch Dist, secy & trustee, 1987-; Town Renova, Renova, MS, mayor, 1978-. **Orgs:** Dep grand master, PH Masons Miss, 1984-; dir, Indust Develop Found, 1985-; dir, Chamber Com, 1985-; dir, United Way, 1985-. **Special Achievements:** First Black President of Cleveland Chamber of Commerce. **Military Serv:** AUS, sgt, 1962-65. **Business Addr:** Mayor, Town of Renova, 5 Second St, Cleveland, MS 38732, **Business Phone:** (662)843-8233.

LUCAS, RAYMOND J.
Football player, television game show host. **Personal:** Born Aug 6, 1972, Harrison, NJ. **Educ:** Rutgers Univ. **Career:** Football player (retired), Television game show host; New Eng Patriots, quarterback, 1996; New York Jets, 1997-2000; Miami Dolphins, 2001-02; Baltimore Ravens, quaterback, 2003; SportsNet, Jets Nation, NY, studio analyst, 2006-. **Honors/Awds:** Hudson County Sports Hall of Fame, 2008. **Business Addr:** Studio Analyst, SportsNet New York, 75 Rockefeller Plz, New York, NY 10019, **Business Phone:** (212)485-4800.

LUCAS, RENDELLA
Social worker. **Personal:** Born Oct 30, 1910, Cheriton, VA; widowed. **Educ:** Va Union Univ, BA, 1932; Hampton Inst, MA, 1943; Va Sem, doctor humane letters, 1982. **Career:** Fauquier High Sch, teacher, 1932-36; Pa Dept Pub Welfare, retired case worker supvr admin asst, 1945-73. **Orgs:** Youth leader, Salem Baptist Church, 1937-55; supvr, Youth Dept Northern Baptist Missionary Union, 1940-55; pres, Bapt Ministers' Wives Union, 1943-45; vpres, Woman's Aux Eastern Baptist Keystone Asn, 1945-48; vpres, Woman's Aux Sub Baptist Church Asn, 1951-53; corrs sec, Nat Asn Ministers Wives Inc, 1943-55; pres, Nat Asn Ministers' Wives Inc, 1957-78; pres, Int Asn Ministers' Wives & Ministers' Widows, 1957-78; fed first ed Newsletter, 1965; Philadelpha Nat Asn Advan Colored People; exec secy, Nat Asn Ministers' Wives Inc, 1970-74; Salem Baptist Church; Church Women United; life mem, Nat Asn Ministers' Wives Inc; exec bd, Northern Baptist Missionary Union & Woman's Aux Suburban Baptist Church Asn; scholar secy, Northern Baptist Missionary Union; recording sec Inter denom Ministers Wives Fel Philadelphia; vpres, Pa Baptist Bus & Prof Women; vpres Baptist& Women's Ctr Philadelphia; communist Ministers' Wives Herald; ML Chepard Chap Va Union Univ Alumni; Comn Disadvantaged Students Eastern Sem & Col; vol, Leukemia Soc Am; adv coun, Rose Butler Brown Fund, RI Col Educ. **Honors/Awds:** Testimonial & Distinguished Achievement Award, Philadelphia Chap Comn, 1957; cert merit, Va Union Univ, 1958; Distinguished Service Award,Philadelphia Nat Asn Advan Colored People, 1961; Distinguished Service Award, Bapt Ministers' Wives Philadelphia, 1961; Elizabeth Coles Beueymem Leadership Trophy, Nat Asn Ministers' Wives, 1962; National Achievement Award, Salem Baptist Church, 1965; Certificate of Achievement, Baptist Ministers' Wives Union, 1967; Certificate of Award, Pa Baptist Asn, 1968;Community Service Award, Chapel 4 Chaplains, 1968; Outstanding Award, Plaque Baptist Ministers' Philadelphia Conf, 1967; Outstanding Service Award, Plaques New York & Rose City Portland Ministers' Wives. 1969; Outstanding Service Citation, Pa Dept Welfare, 1973; Shriner's Woman ofthe Year Award, 1970.

LUCAS, RUBYE
Executive, vice president (organization). **Personal:** Born Sep 26, 1935, Fort Myers, FL; daughter of Viola Hendley and Booker T Mims; married William, Apr 27, 1958 (deceased); children: William Jr, Wonya & Andrea. **Educ:** Fla A&M Univ, social sci degree; Atlanta Univ, MEd. **Career:** Turner Broadcasting Syst, Inc, human resources admin/mgmt training, 1990-91, mem bd, vpres community rels, 1999; The Atlanta Proj, dir community rels, 1991-96; Fla Pub Sch Syst, teacher; Atlanta Pub Sch Syst, teacher. **Orgs:** Atlanta Braves Nat Leagues Baseball Club, bd dir; Bill Lucas Scholarship Found, bd dirs; bd dirs, Bill Lucas Br Butler St YMCA; bd dir, Alliance Theatre; Hank Aaron Rookie League, co-founder; sect, GA World Congress Ctr Authority; Fulton County Comn Children & Youth; bd dir, Turner Broadcasting Syst Inc. **Honors/Awds:** Humanitarian Award, AKA Sorority Inc, 1994; Outstanding Achievement Award, 20th Judicial Circuit, Florida, 1994; Youth Foundation Award, Butler St YMCA, 1994; Serv Award, 1994; Award of Appreciation, The Atlanta Proj, 1994. **Special Achievements:** Fine & Performing Arts and Talent Center, 1993; first black women to sit on the bd of dir of Turner Broadcasting Syst Inc.

LUCAS, VICTORIA
Public relations executive. **Personal:** Born in Chicago, IL. **Educ:** Malcolm-King Col; Chicago Ill, liberal arts; Univ NY, bus admin. **Career:** Am Mus Immigration, pub rels asst, 1955-57; Nat Coun Alcoholism, mgr publ dept, 1957-63; Norman Craig & Kummel, copywriter & acct exec, 1964-66; Cannon Advert, pub rels dir & copywriter, 1966-67; Victoria Lucas Assoc, pres & owner. **Orgs:** Bd dir, Publicity NY; Nat Assoc Media Women; pub rel, New Sch Social Res NY, 1977-; Pub Rel Soc Am, NY Chap Comt Minorities, 1985. **Honors/Awds:** Woman of the Year Award, Nat Asn Media Women Media; Outstanding Mentor Award, D Parke Gibson. **Business Phone:** (212)489-8008.

LUCAS, DR. WILLIAM
Judge. **Personal:** Born Jan 15, 1928, New York, NY; son of George and Charlette Hazel; married Evelyn Daniel. **Educ:** Wayne State Univ. **Career:** Teacher, social worker, policeman, civil rights investigator, & FBI agt;lawyer; Wayne County Mich, 1st Wayne County, sheriff, 1969-82, county exec, 1983-87; US Govt, Wash, DC, dir off liaison servs, 1989-93; Recorder's Court, judge,1993-94; US Justice Dept, dir community rel servs; Circuit Ct Three, Wayne Co, judge, 1997-2001. **Orgs:** Sports Hall Fame; Jr Achievement Vol Am; Nat Asn Advan Colored People; bd dir, Hutzel Hosp; bd govs, Manhattan Col. **Honors/Awds:** Michigan Man of the Year, 1986; Honorary doctorate, Manhattan Col.

LUCAS, WILLIE LEE
Chairperson, librarian, college teacher. **Personal:** Born Dec 17, 1924, Jacksonville, FL; daughter of William Lavert Joyner and Maude Roberts; married Elcee R Lucas, Jul 23, 1948 (divorced 1980); children: Kim. **Educ:** Tenn A&I Univ, BS, 1944; Univ Mich, AMLS, 1952; Univ FL, EdS, 1977, EdD, 1982. **Career:** Professor (retired); Off Price Admin, stenographer, 1944-45; Afro-Am Life Inst Co, stenographer, 1945-46; McGill & McGill Law Firm, stenographer, 1946-47; Duval Co Bd Pub Instr, teacher & librn, 1947-74; Fla Community Col, librn, dept chmn, 1974, prof libr sci. **Orgs:** Charter mem, Jacksonville Alumnae Chap, Delta Sigma Theta Sorority, 1947; Kappa Delta Pi, 1977; Am Libr Asn; Jacksonville Bd Realtors; adv comt, Educ & Res Found; Fla Real Estate Comn; Altar/Rosary Soc, St Pius V Cath Church; Alpha Kappa Mu. **Honors/Awds:** Outstanding Fac Award, Fla Community Col, 1990. **Home Addr:** 1774 Shore View, PO Box 28274, Jacksonville, FL 32220-6274.

LUCAS DARBY, DR. EMMA TURNER
School administrator, educator. **Personal:** Born Feb 5, 1949, Meridian, MS; children: Kamilah Aisha. **Educ:** Tougaloo Col, BA, 1970; Purdue Univ, MA, 1972; Univ Pittsburgh, MSW, 1978,PhD, 1986. **Career:** Planned Parenthood, counr, 1973-75; St Francis Hosp, rehab specialist,1975-76; Chatham Col, dir black studies, 1976-79, assoc vpres acad affairs, 1979-84; Presbyterian Home C, consult, 1982-90; Carlow Univ, assoc prof, 1984-, prof social work & polit sci, currently, Carlow Hill Educ Ctr, prog cord, currently, Sch Social Chg, interim chair, currently; Community Col Allegheny Co, brd dirs, 1998. **Orgs:** Bd dirs, YWCA Pittsburgh, 1982-86; pres, Pittsburgh Chap, Asn StudyAfro-Am Life & Hist, 1983; bd dirs, Training Wheels C Ctr, 1984-88; PABlacks Higher Educ, 1987-; bd secy, Pittsburgh Coun Pub Educ; Girl ScoutsSW PA, 1988-90; Youth Build Pittsburgh, 1998-2000. **Honors/Awds:** Pittsburgh Professor Award, Talk Mag, 1982; TV prod, Career Trends for the80's, 1983; Meritorious Service Award, Juvenile Ct Judges Comn & the PACoun; NIH Grant. **Business Addr:** Professor & Chair of the School for Social Change, Program Coordinator, Carlow University, Division of Social Sciences, Rm 503 Antonian Hall 3333 Fifth Ave, Pittsburgh, PA 15213.

LUCK, DR. CLYDE ALEXANDER, JR.
Surgeon. **Personal:** Born Mar 3, 1929, Danville, VA; son of Clyde Sr; children: Kelli. **Educ:** Howard Univ, BS, 1950; New York Univ, MA, 1952; Howard Univ, MD, 1959. **Career:** St Joseph Mercy Hosp & Detroit Receiving Hosp, resident gen surg, 1960-64; Kaiser Found Hosp, La, fel, 1964-65; Crenshaw Hosp, chmn dept surg, 1974-78; Clyde A Luck Inc, owner & surgeon, currently. **Orgs:** Omega Psi Phi; NAACP; Urban League; Los Angeles City Med Soc; fel, Am Col Surgeons; Int Col Surgeons. **Military Serv:** USAF, First lt, 1952-54. **Home Addr:** PO Box 34877, Los Angeles, CA 90034. **Business Addr:** Surgeon, Owner, Clyde A Luck Inc, 6200 Wilshire Blvd Suite 1012, PO Box 34877, Los Angeles, CA 90048, **Business Phone:** (323)937-6182.

LUCKEY, DR. EVELYN F.
Educator. **Personal:** Born Apr 30, 1926, Bellefonte, PA; daughter of Arthur R Foreman and Agnes A Haywood Foreman; divorced; children: Jennifer & Carolyn. **Educ:** Wilberforce Univ, attended 1945; Ohio State Univ, BA, BsEd, Eng, Psychol, 1947, MA, Eng, 1950, PhD, Ed, 1970. **Career:** Educator (retired); Columbus Pub Sch, Fair Avenue, Title I teacher, special educ, 1957-59; Beatty Pk teacher, 1959-62; Ohio State Univ, asst prof, 1971-72; Columbus Pub Schs, exec dir, 1972-77, asst supt, 1977-90; Otterbein Col, Westerville, Ohio, asst prof, 1990-98. **Orgs:** Am Assoc Sch Admin; Assoc Suprv, trustee, pres, Bd Pub, Libr Columbus & Franklin City, 1973-89; Links Inc; trustee, pres, bd, Columbus Metrop Libr, 1973-89; Curriculum Develop, 1972-93; Nat Alliance Black Sch Ed;Cent Ohio Mkt Coun, 1984-89; trustee, Cent Ohio Mkt Coun, 1984-89; Bd, Planned Parenthood Cent Ohio, 1984-87; Adv Bd, Urban Network Northern Cent Reg Ed Lab, 1985-90. **Honors/Awds:** Outstanding Educator Award, Alpha Kappa Alpha, 1978; Woman of the Year, Omega Psi Phi, 1980; Distinguished Kappan Award, Phi Delta Kappa, 1981; Distinguished Alumnae Award, Ohio State Univ, 1982; Cert Honor City Columbus, 1984; Woman of Achievement Award, YWCA, 1987, 1991; United Negro Col Fund Eminent Scholar, 1990. *

LUCKEY, DR. IRENE
Administrator, educator. **Personal:** Born May 29, 1949, New York, NY. **Educ:** NC Agric & Tech State Univ, BA, 1971; Univ Chicago, MA, Sch Soc Serv Admin, 1973; City Univ New York, Grad Sch, DSW, 1982. **Career:** Metrop Hosp, New York, med social worker, 1973-76; NC Agri & Tech St Univ, asst prof social work, 1976-78; Brookdale Ctr Aging-Hunter Col, dir educ prg, 1979-81; LeMoyne Owen Col, vis prof, 1981-82; Clark Col, asst prof, 1982-84; Univ West Fla, asst prof soc work, assoc dir ctr on aging, 1985-89; Univ Mich, Ann Arbor, res fel, 1987-89; St Univ New York, Albany, asst prof, 1989-90; Rutgers Univ; St Univ New Jersey, asst prof, 1990; Univ SC, Inst Family & Soc, res assoc prof soc work, currently. **Orgs:** Consult, Admin Aging, 1981; Atlanta Reg Comn Aging, 1984; Clark Col SocWork Prog, 1985-86; chair educ prog, Nat Asn Black Soc Workers, 1985-; adv mem, Ment Health Asn, Escambia County, 1985-; State Fla Long Term Care Coun, 1986-; bd dir, Northwest Fl Area Agen Aging, 1986; Geriatric Residential & Treatment Northwest Fl, 1986-; Phi Alpha; Kappa Alpha Kappa; Alpha Kappa; adv bd, Rutgers Univ, Undergrad Soc Work Prog; Geronotological Task Force, Gerontological Soc Soc Res, Planning & Pract; Task Force Minority Issues, Sub comt Policy & Serv Pract; referee & reviewer, Nat Soc Sci J Gerontological Soc. **Honors/Awds:** Appreciation Award, Asn Minority Affairs, Sch Soc Welfare, State Univ NewYork; Kappa Alpha Psi Scholastic Achievement Award; Phi Alpha Nat Soc WorkHonor. **Special Achievements:** Author: The Black Aged: Understanding Diversity and Service Needs, Calif,Sage Publications, Inc, 1969-81; "Impact of Race on Student Evaluations of Faculty", article pub 1986; "Evaluation from the Start". **Business Phone:** (803)777-2919.

LUCY, WILLIAM
Engineer. **Personal:** Born Nov 26, 1933, Memphis, TN; son of Joseph and Susie B Gibbs; married Dorotheria; children: Benita Ann, Phyllis Kay. **Educ:** Univ Calif, Berkeley, CA, civil eng, 1950; Contra Costa Jr Col, Richmond. **Career:** Contra Costa Co, CA, asst mat & res eng, 13 yrs; Am Fedn State County Munic Employs Local 1675 union Contra Costa employs , staff, 1956, pres, 1965; Am Fedn State County Munic Employs Dept Legislation & Community Affairs, assoc dir,1966, secy & treas, 1972 & 2004; Am Fedn State, County & Munic Employs, int secy & treas, currently; Am Fedn State, County & Munic Employs, Dept Prof Employs, vpres, currently. **Orgs:** bd trustees, African Am Inst; bd trustees, Transafrica; vpres, Indust Union Dept Am Fedn Labor & Cong Indust Orgn; vpres, Maritime Trades Dept Am Fedn Labor & Cong Indust Orgn; bd dir, Am Dem Action; bd dir, Nat Laws Black Aged; pres & founder, Coalition Black Trade Unionists; Judicial Nomination Comn, Wash, DC; bd trustee, Martin Luther King Ctr Social Change; past pres, Local 1675; Employs Asn Contra Costa Co, Calif; vpres, Pub Serv Int. **Honors/Awds:** DHL, Bowie State Col. **Special Achievements:** One of the founders of the Free South Africa Movement; highest-ranking African American in the Labor movement; Ebony, named one of "The 100 Most Influential Black Americans". **Business Addr:** American Federation of State County & Municipal Employees, 1625 L St NW, Washington, DC 20036-5687.

LUCY FOSTER, AUTHERINE
Educator. **Personal:** Born Oct 5, 1929, Shiloh, AL; daughter of Milton Cornelius and Minnie; married Hugh Lawrence, Apr 22, 1956; children: Hugh, Anglea, Grazia & Chrystal. **Educ:** Selma Univ, teaching cert; Miles Mem Col, BA, eng, 1952; Univ Ala, MA, elem educ, 1992. **Career:** English teacher & substitute teacher, 1952-; pub speaker. **Orgs:** Bd mem, Birmingham Civil Rights Inst. **Honors/Awds:** Scholarship, Univ Ala, 1992. **Special Achievements:** First African American student enrolled, Univ of Alabama, 1956. **Business Addr:** Board Member, Birmingham Civil Rights Institute, 520 16th St N, Birmingham, AL 35203.

LUDACRIS (CHRISTOPHER BRIAN BRIDGES)
Rap musician. **Personal:** Born Sep 11, 1977, Champaign, IL; son of Wayne and Roberta Shields; children: Karma. **Educ:** Ga State Univ. **Career:** Hot 107.9 FM, disc jockey; Disturbing Tha Peace Rec, chief exec officer; Albums: Incognegro, 2000; Back for the First Time, 2000; Word of Mouf, 2001; Chicken-N-Beer, 2003; The Red Light Dist, 2004; Release Therapy, 2006; Theater of the Mind, 2007; Films: The Wash, 2001; The Bros, 2002; 2 Fast 2 Furious, 2003; Crash, 2005; The Heart of the Game, 2005; The Bros, 2006; Gamer, 2009. **Honors/Awds:** Black Reel Award, 2006; Screen Actors Guild Award, 2006. **Special Achievements:** Nominated for numerous awards. **Business Addr:** Recording Artist, Def Jam Records, 825 8th Ave, New York, NY 10019, **Business Phone:** (212)333-8000.*

LUE, TYRONN JAMAR
Basketball player. **Personal:** Born May 3, 1977, Mexico, MO; son of Kim Miller and Kim Jones. **Educ:** Univ Nebr, sociol. **Career:** Los Angeles Lakers, guard, 1998-2001; Wash Wizards, 2001-03; Orlando Magic, 2003-04; Houston Rockets, 2004-05; Atlanta Hawks, 2005-; Sacramento Kings, 2008-. **Honors/Awds:** Rookie Year, NBA, 1998. **Business Addr:** Professional Basketball Player, Atlanta Hawks, Centennial Twr, 101 Marietta St NW Suite 1900, Atlanta, GA 30303, **Business Phone:** (404)878-3800.

LUE-HING, CECIL
Engineer. **Personal:** Born Nov 3, 1930, Jamaica; married 1952; children: Cecil Barrington & Robert James. **Educ:** Marquette Univ, BS, civil engineering, 1961; Case Western Reserve Univ, MS, sanitary engineering, 1963; Wash Univ, St Louis, doctorate, environ & sanitary engineering, 1966. **Career:** Univ Wis, Col Med, chief technician, 1950-55; Mt Sinai Hosp, sch med tech, Wis, instr histol & cytol chem & lab suv, 1955-61; Huron Rd Hosp, Wis, res assoc clin biochem, 1961-63; Wash Univ, res assoc, environ engr, 1963-65, asst prof, 1965-66; Gov bd Environ & Water Resources Inst Am Soc Civil Engrs, pres; Nat Asn Clean Water Agencies, pres; Ryckman, Edgerley, Tomlinson & Assoc, 1966-68, sr assoc, 1968-77; Metrop Water Reclamation Dist Greater Chicago, dir res & develop, 1977; Ill Inst Technol, prof; Cecil Lue-Hing & Assocs Inc, pres, currently. **Orgs:** AAAS; Nat Acad Scis Task Force; Water Pollution Control Fed; Am Water Works Asn; Am Pub Works Asn; Sigma Si, hon mem, Nat Eng Soc; Hon Mem, Am Soc Civil Engrs. **Honors/Awds:** Fel, Wash Univ; Nat Government Civil Engineer Award, Simon W Freese Environmental Engineering Award, Gordon Maskew Fair Award, Am Acad Environ Engrs' Kappe; President's Award, Environmental Award, Asn Metrop Sewerage Agencies AMSA; Charles Alvin Emerson Medal, Water Environ Fed; Appointed by the mayor of Atlanta to a nine-member independent council on the city's Clean Water Plan; Professional Achievement Award, Marquette Univ Alumni Asn, Col Engineering, 2006; Sustained Achievement Award, Renewable Natural Resources Found, 2007. **Special Achievements:** Published numerous industry-recognized books and reference materials, and has contributed more than 30 chapters to various other publications; Metrop Water Reclamation Dist Greater Chicago's res facility renamed the 'Dr. Cecil Lue-Hing Research and Development Complex', 2005. **Home Addr:** 6101 N Sheridan St 40B E, Chicago, IL 60660. **Business Addr:** President, Cecil Lue-Hing & Associates Inc, 6815 County Line Lane, Burr Ridge, IL 60527-5724, **Business Phone:** (630)986-5751.

LUIS, DR. WILLIAM
Educator. **Personal:** Born Jul 12, 1948, New York, NY; son of Petra Diluvina Santos and Domingo; married Linda Garceau; children: Gabriel, Diego, Tammie & Stephanie. **Educ:** State Univ NY, Binghamton, BA, 1971; Univ Wis, Madison, MA, 1973; Cornell Univ, MA, 1979, PhD, 1980. **Career:** Bd Educ, NY City, teacher, 1971-72, 1973-74; Dartmouth Col, asst prof latin Am & Caribbean, 1980-85, assoc prof, 1985-88, fac fel, 1983; Handbook Latin Am Studies, contrib ed & consult, 1981-91;Latin Am Lit Review, mem ed bd, 1985-; Nat Endowment Humanities, reader, 1985; Nat Res Coun, Ford Found Fel Panel, staff, 1986; Wash Univ, vis assoc, 1988, Latin Am & Caribbean Area Studies Prog, assoc prof & dir, 1988-91; Vanderbilt Univ, assoc prof Spanish, 1991-96, prof Spanish & Portuguese, 1996-, prof eng, 2001; Robert Penn Warren Ctr Humanities, Vanderbilt Univ, fel, 1991-94; Am Coun Learned Soc, fel, 1993-94; Yale Univ, vis prof, 1998. **Orgs:** Vpres, Asn Caribbean Studies, 1985-86; speakers bur, Tenn Coun Humanities, 1992-93; ed bd, J Afro-Latin, Am Res Asn, 1996; ed bd, Afro-Hispanic Rev, 1987-; Exec comt, Afro-Latin Am Res Asn, 2000-; Modern Lang Asn; Asn Caribbean Studies; Am Asn Teachers Spanish & Portuguese; adv bd, Comt Spec Educ Proj; Ad Hoc Comt Study Hisp Admis & Recruitment; Minority Educ Coun; Black Caucus; African Afro-Am Studies Steering Comt; Lit Criticism Sem; Latin Am Lit Sem; co-dir, Latin Am Lit Sem; fac adv, Phi Sigma Psi; African & Afro-Am Studies Sem; Exec Comt, Asn Caribbean Studies; dir, Screening Comt; adj curator, Film DC; Native Am Studies Steering Comt; Exec Comt Fac DC; Agenda Subcomt Exec Comt Fac DC; Libr Search Comt Humanities Bibliographer. **Honors/Awds:** Editorial Board Award,

State Univ NY, Off Spec Prog, 1989 & 1994; Certificates of Recognition & 13th Annual Affirmative Action and Diversity Initiatives Award, 1999. **Special Achievements:** Luis has written more than one hundred scholarly articles, has delivered numerous talks, and is a sought after speaker; Published: Literary Bondage: Slavery in Cuban Narrative, University of Texas Press, 1990; Dance Between Two Cultures: Latino-Caribbean Literature Written in the United States, Vanderbilt University Press, 1997; Culture and Customs of Cuba, Greenwood Press, 2001; Lunes de Revolucion: Literatura y cultura en los Primeros Anos de la Revolucion Cubana, Editorial Verbum, 2003; Autobiografia del esclavo Juan Francisco Manzano y Otros Escritos, Iberoamericana-Vervuert Verlag, 2005; Edited with Edmundo Desnoes, Los dispositivos en la flor, Ediciones del Norte, 1981; Edited Voices from Under: Black Narrative in Latin America and the Caribbean, Greenwood Press, 1984; edited with Julio Rodriguez-Luis, Translating Latin America: Culture as Text and Translation Perspectives VI, State University of New York at Binghamton, 1991; edited Modern Latin American Fiction Writers, First Series, Gale Press, 1992; edited with Ann Gonzalez, Modern Latin American Fiction Writers, Second Series, Gale Press, 1994; edited "Antologia: Poesia hispano-caribena escrita en los Estados Unidos," Boletin de la Fundacion Federico Garcia Lorca, 1995; Bibliografia y antologia critica de las vanguardias literarias: El Caribe, Iberoamericana, 2005. **Business Addr:** Professor of Spanish and Portuguese, Vanderbilt University, Department of Spanish and Portuguese, HB 1617 Sta B Furman Hall, Nashville, TN 37235, **Business Phone:** (615)322-6862.

LUKE, DR. LEARIE B
Educator. **Educ:** MA, PhD. **Career:** SC State Univ, Dept Social Sci, asst prof hist & interim chair, currently. **Orgs:** Fel, Sasakawa Young Leaders Fel Fund, Howard Univ, 1998-2001; Adv Comt Acad Progs, SC Comn Higher Educ. **Business Addr:** Assistant Professor, Chairperson, South Carolina State University, Department of Social Sciences, 300 Col St NE, PO Box 7768, Orangeburg, SC 29117, **Business Phone:** (803)536-7127.

LUKE, SHERRILL DAVID
Judge. **Personal:** Born Sep 19, 1928, Los Angeles, CA; son of Mordecai and Venye Luke Corporal; divorced; children: David & Melana. **Educ:** Univ Calif, Los Angeles, BA 1950; Univ Calif, Berkeley, MA, 1954; Golden Gate Univ, JD, 1960. **Career:** Judge (retired), mediator; Dist Columbia Govt, dir prog dev, 1967-69; Aetna Life & Casualty, dirurban affairs, 1969-71; Conn Val Dev Corp, pres & dir, 1971-73, Pacht Ross Coun, 1973-76; Jacobs Kane Luke, partner, 1976-78; Los Angeles County,chief dep assessor, 1978-81; Los Angeles Munic Ct, judge, 1981-88; super ct judge, 1989; Am Arbit Asn, arbit & mediator, currently. **Orgs:** Cabinet Sec CA Governor's Office, 1964-65; consult, Ford Found, 1966-67;pres, LA City Planning Comn, 1975-76; bd govs, Univ Calif LA Found, 1976-;adj prof, Loyola Law Sch, 1979-81; pres, Univ Calif LA Alumni Assoc,1988-90; regent, Univ Calif, 1988-90; bd vis, Univ Calif LA,1991-94; Calif Judges Asn; Judicial Div Langston Bar Asn; Judicial Coun Calif Asn; bd dirs, UCLA Stephens House Scholarship Asn; adv bd, Southeast Symphony Asn; adv bd, UCLA Chancellor's Community Adv Comn. **Honors/Awds:** Outstanding Senior Award, Univ Calif LA Alumni Asn, 1950; Outstanding Achievement Award, Kappa Alpha Psi, 1963-; Justice Pro Tem CA Ct Appeal, 1985-86, 1995; University Service Award, Univ Calif LA Alumni Asn, 1994; Hall of Fame Award, John M. Langston Bar Asn, 1999. **Special Achievements:** First African-American to be elected president of undergraduate student government at UCLA. **Military Serv:** USAF, 1st lt, 1954-56. **Business Addr:** Arbitrator, Mediator, American Arbitration Association, 335 Madison Ave Fl 10, New York, NY 10017-4605.

LUKE, HON. SHERRILL DAVID
Judge. **Personal:** Born Sep 19, 1928, Los Angeles, CA; son of Mordecai and Venye Luke Corporal; divorced; children: David & Melana. **Educ:** Univ Calif, Los Angeles, BA, 1950; Univ Calif, Berkeley, MA, 1954; Golden Gate Univ, JD, 1960. **Career:** Dist Columbia Govt, dir prog dev, 1967-69; Aetna Life & Casualty, dir, urban affairs, 1969-71; Conn Val Dev Corp, pres & dir, 1971-73, Pacht Ross Coun, 1973-76; Jacobs Kane Luke, partner, 1976-78; Los Angeles County, chief dep assessor, 1978-81; Los Angeles Munic Ct, judge, 1981-88; superct judge, 1989; Am Arbit Asn, arbit & mediator, currently. **Orgs:** Cabinet Sec CA Governor's Office, 1964-65; consult, Ford Found, 1966-67; pres, LA City Planning Comn, 1975-76; bd govs, Univ Calif LA Found, 1976-; adj prof, Loyola Law Sch, 1979-81; pres, Univ Calif LA Alumni Assoc,1988-90; regent, Univ Calif, 1988-90; bd vis, Univ Calif LA, 1991-94; Calif Judges Asn; Judicial Div Langston Bar Asn; Judicial Coun Calif Asn; bd dirs, UCLA Stephens House Scholarship Asn; adv bd, Southeast Symphony Asn; adv bd, UCLA Chancellor's Community Adv Comn. **Honors/Awds:** Outstanding Senior Award, Univ Calif LA Alumni Asn, 1950; Outstanding Achievement Award, Kappa Alpha Psi, 1963-; Justice Pro Tem CA Ct Appeal, 1985-86, 1995; University Service Award, Univ Calif LA Alumni Asn, 1994; Hall of Fame Award, John M Langston Bar Asn, 1999. **Special Achievements:** First African-American to be elected president of undergraduate student government at University of California, Los Angeles. **Military Serv:** USAF, 1st lt, 1954-56. **Business Addr:** Arbitrator, Mediator, American Arbitration Association, 335 Madison Ave Fl 10, New York, NY 10017-4605.

LUMBLY, CARL
Actor. **Personal:** Born Aug 14, 1952, Minneapolis, MN. **Educ:** Macalester Col, St. Paul, eng. **Career:** Assoc Press, journalist; Films: Caveman, 1981; The Adventures of Buckaroo Banzai, 1984; The Bedroom Window, 1987; Everybody's All-American, 1988; To Sleep With Anger, 1990; Pacific Heights, 1990; Brother Future, 1991; South Central, 1992; How Stella Got Her Groove Back, 1998; Men of Honor, 2000; Just A Dream, 2002;Nat Turner: A Troublesome Property, 2003; Namibia: The Struggle for Liberation, 2007; The Alphabet Killer, 2008; TV Series: "Cagney and Lacey", 1982-88; "Conspiracy: The Trial of the Chicago 8", 1987; "M.A.N.T.I.S", 1994; "On Promised Land", 1994; "Night john", 1996; "The Ditch digger's Daughters", 1997;"Buffalo Soldiers", 1997; "The Wedding", 1998; "The West Wing", 2000; "The Color of Friendship", 2000; "Little Richard", 2000; "Justice League", 2001-04; "Alias", 2001-06; "Static Shock", 2003; "Sounder", 2003; "Justice League Unlimited", 2004-06; "Battlestar Galactica", 2006; "Cold Case", 2008; "Grey's Anatomy", 2008; "Black Panther", 2009; "Batman: The Brave and the Bold", 2009. **Special Achievements:** Nominated for Image Awards, Cable ACE Awards and Black Reel Awards. **Business Addr:** Actor, 1033 Miller Ave, Berkeley, CA 94708.*

LUMPKIN, ADRIENNE KELLY (ADRIENNE LORRAINE KELLY)
Business owner. **Personal:** Born Apr 12, 1957, Bronx, NY; daughter of James and Lorraine; married Kelly M, Aug 9, 1986; children: Amelia Janine & Samantha Moriah. **Educ:** Wesleyan Univ, BA, 1979; Harvard Univ, MBA, 1983. **Career:** IBM, systs engr, 1979-81; Hewlett-Packard, mkt mgr, 1983-92; Alt Access, fonder & pres, 1993-; Wake County Public Sch Bus Alliance, chair. **Orgs:** Vpres, Raleigh/Durham Chap, 1994-96, bd dirs, 1997-2002, Nat Black MBA Asn; Nat Asn Women Bus Owners, 1995-; Coun Entrepreneurial Develop, 1993-;bus adv bd, Meredith Col, 1999-; NAWBO Nat Nominating Comm. **Honors/Awds:** MBA of the Year Award, Raleigh/Durham Chap, Nat Black MBA Asn, 1993, 1997;Outstanding MBA Award, 1997; Future 30 Award, 1997, Pinnacle Award, 1998,1999, Greater Raleigh Chamber Com, 1997; Super Gazelle, southeast region,Entrepreneurial Educ Found, 1997; North Carolina Tech 50 Award, 1998-00; Triangle Women in Business Award, 1998; Forbes ASAP Fast 500 Award, 1999;H. Naylor Fitzhugh Award of Relevance, 1999; 2005 Entrepreneur inductee,YWCA Acad Women; Women Extraordinaire Award & Women in Business Award,Triangle Bus Jour. **Business Addr:** President, Director of Marketing, Alternate Access Inc, The Glenwood Ctr, 5623 Duraleigh Rd Suite 111, Raleigh, NC 27612-2700, **Business Phone:** (919)831-1860.

LUMPKIN, ELGIN. See GINUWINE.

LUNDIN-HUGHES, DONNA
Public relations executive. **Personal:** Born Nov 25, 1949, Chicago, IL; daughter of Donald and Estella Walker Madden; married Michael Dean Hughes, Sep 3, 1972; children: Lyn, Natalie & Melissa. **Educ:** Wesleyan Col, BA, 1971. **Career:** S Cook County Girl Scout Coun, field exec, 1971-72; Girl Scouts-Seal Ohio Coun Inc, field exec, 1972-76, dir commun, 1976-84, field supvr, 1984-86, pub rels dir, 1986-90, asst dir, resource develop & serv, pub rels dir, currently. **Orgs:** Alpha Kappa Alpha; Pub Rels Soc Am, 1990-; Jack & Jill Am; Nat Coalition 100 Black Women, 1991-92. **Home Phone:** (614)459-0333. **Business Addr:** Public Relations Director, Girl Scouts-Seal of Ohio Council Inc, 1700 WaterMark Dr, Columbus, OH 43215-1097, **Business Phone:** (614)487-8101.

LUNDY, DR. HAROLD W
President (Organization), school administrator, founder (originator). **Career:** Grambling State Univ, vpres admin & strategic planning, 1991, pres, 1991-2001; Lundy Enterprises LLC, founder & pres, currently. **Business Addr:** Founder, President, Lundy Enterprises LLC, 4505 N Sherwood Forest Dr, Baton Rouge, LA 70814, **Business Phone:** (225)275-1773.

LUNDY, LARRY
Executive. **Personal:** Born in New Orleans, LA; married; children: 3. **Educ:** Dillard Univ, bachelor's degree, acct; Pepperdine Univ, master's degree, bus admin. **Career:** Peat, Marc & Mitchell, staff; Alexander Grant & Co, staff; Pizza Hut, controller, 1983, vpres/controller, vpres, restaurant develop, 1988; Lundy Enterprises Inc, pres & chief exec officer, currently. **Honors/Awds:** Gambit Newspaper, New Orleanian of the Year, 1993. **Special Achievements:** Controller of the largest minority owned fast food franchise in America; Company is ranked #69 on the Black Enterprise list of Top 100 businesses, 1994. **Business Addr:** President, Chief Executive Officer, Lundy Enterprises Inc, 10555 Lake Forest Blvd Suite 1J, New Orleans, LA 70127, **Business Phone:** (504)241-6658.

LUNEY, PERCY R
Educator, vice president (organization). **Personal:** Born Jan 13, 1949, Hopkinsville, KY; son of Percy R Luney; married Beverly Marshall, Nov 24, 2001; children: Jamille & Robyn. **Educ:** Hamilton Col, AB, 1970; Harvard Law Sch, JD, 1974. **Career:** US Dept Interior, Off Solicitor, atty, adv, 1975-77; Fisk Univ, univ legal coun spec asst to pres, 1977-79; Birch, Horton, Brittner, Monroe, Pestinger & Anderson, assoc, 1979-80; NC Cent Univ Sch Law, asst dean, prof, dean, 1980-98; Duke Univ, adj prof law, 1984-98; Nat Judicial Col, pres, 1998-2001; Fla A&M Univ Sch Law, dean & prof law, 2001-05; Space Florida, vpres, educ res & develop & workforce, 2008-. **Orgs:** Fel, Thomas J Watson Found, 1970; Hamilton Col, Alumni Asn, 1970-; Harvard Law Sch, Alumni Asn, 1974-; Dist Columbia Bar, 1975-; Am Bar Asn, 1983-; fel, NC Japan Ctr Fac, 1983; NC Bar Asn, 1983-; Nat Bar Asn,1994-; fel, Am Bar Found, 1996-; Univ NC Chapel Hill, Parents Coun, 1999-. **Honors/Awds:** Fulbright Program Award, Japan, 1986, 1991. **Special Achievements:** Published: Sum & Substance Quick Review: Professional Responsibility, Second Edition, 1996; North Carolina Discovery, 1992, Supplement, 1995; Japanese Constitutional Law, 1993; Careers in Natural Resources and Environmental Law, 1987; numerous articles.

LUPER, CLARA M.
Social worker, educator. **Personal:** Born May 3, 1923, Okfuskee County, OK; daughter of Ezell Shepard and Isabell; married Charles P Wilson; children: Calvin, Marilyn Luper Hildreth & Chelle Marie. **Educ:** Langston Univ, Langston, OK, BA, math, 1944; Okla Univ, Norman, MA, hist, attended 1951. **Career:** Amigos Club Grayhoff & Woods Neighborhood Club, co-founder, 1949-; consult, var col & univ, 1959-80; Okla City Bd Educ, teacher hist, 1959-79; Choctaw Bd Educ, teacher hist, 1961-78; Soul Bazaar, founder, 1970-93; Miss Black Okla, state promoter, 1970-93; Talent USA, pres, dir, 1974-80; Dunjee High Sch, teacher hist & pub rels; John Marshall & Classen High Sch, teacher. **Orgs:** Youth adv, Nat Asn Advan Colored People, 1957-80; past basileus, Zeta Phi Beta Sor; Chi Zeta Chap, 1962-; pres, Freedom Ctr Inc, 1968-93, Fifth St Baptist Church; Okla Educ Asn; Nat Educ Asn; Okla Hist Soc. **Honors/Awds:** Received Honors & Awards more than 472. Langston Alumni Award; Phi Beta Sigma Service Award; Robert A. Taft Scholarship; Phi Beta Sigma Service Award; Oklahoma Federated Women's Club Service Award; Woman of the Year, Zeta Phi Beta Sorority; NAACP Regional Voter Registration Award; National Advisor of the Year Award, Nat Asn Advan Colored People; National Service Citation, Nat Asn Advan Colored People; Pioneer Woman Award. **Special Achievements:** First African American Vice President of the Oklahoma City Social Science Teachers Association, First African American Vice President of the Oklahoma County Teacher's Association and First African American student to enroll in the History Department at the University of Oklahoma. Authored a book named "Behold The Walls", 1979. **Home Addr:** 1111 N E 43rd St, Oklahoma City, OK 73111, **Home Phone:** (405)424-3027. **Business Addr:** 2401 N Laird Ave, Oklahoma City, OK 73105, **Business Phone:** (405)521-2491.

LUSTER, JORY
Executive. **Educ:** Bradley Univ, BS, bus admin; Kellogg Grad Sch Mgt, MBA. **Career:** Luster Prod Inc, pres, currently. **Special Achievements:** Ranked 20 on Black Enterprise magazine's list of top 100 idl/service companies, 1992. **Business Addr:** President, Luster Products Inc, 1104 W 43rd St, Chicago, IL 60609, **Business Phone:** (773)579-1800.*

LUSTER, ROBERT
Executive, president (organization), chief executive officer. **Educ:** US Military Acad, BS; Long Island Univ, MBA, finance. **Career:** Luster Group, pres & chief exec officer, currently. **Orgs:** Bd dir, Bay Planning Coalition, San Francisco, CA; bd dirs, W Point Soc San Francisco; bd dir, Golden Gate Bank; founding trustee, Univ Calif. **Business Addr:** President, Chief Executive Officer, Luster Group Inc, 2123 C St, Bakersfield, CA 93301, **Business Phone:** (661)869-0157.

LUTEN, THOMAS DEE
Educator, administrator. **Personal:** Born Mar 12, 1950, Youngstown, OH; son of Ernest D and Christine Motley; married Nedra Farrar Luten, Jun 18, 1983; children: Thomas David & Christian Douglas. **Educ:** Kenyon Col, Gambier, 1969; Ohio State Univ, MA, 1974; Mich State Univ, East Lansing, 1982; Univ NC, attended 1984. **Career:** Mich Dept Com, admin analyst, 1977-78; Mich Dept Mental Health, personnel specialist, 1978-80; Univ NC, assoc dir, univ career planning & placement, 1980-83; GTE the South, organizational effectiveness spec, 1984; NC Cent Univ, dir, career coun, placement & coop educ, 1984-88; Mich State Univ, dir, career devt & placement, 1988-91; self-employed, edu & human resource consult; Wayne County Community Col, vpres stud develop, 1993-95; Hampton Univ Career Ctr, dir; Univ NC, Sch Dent, dir stud serv & asst prof dent ecol, 2000-. **Orgs:** AACD, ACPA, 1972-81, 1984-92; SCPA, 1984-91; MCPA, 1988-91; ASCUS, 1985-86, 1988-91; IMPA, 1978-81, 1985-88; Nat Coun Stud Dev, 1993-; Southeastern Asn Stud Personnel Admin, 1993-96. **Special Achievements:** Presentations: Building a Global Workforce for a Competitive Edge, fall conference, Midwest College Placement Association, 1990; The Employment Outlook for Physical Science Professionals in the 1990's, American Institute of Physics, 1990; Making a College Relations Program Work, EDS Corporation, 1990; numerous others, articles published in Black Enterprise, 1985, 1991. **Home Addr:** 1511 Edgeside Ct, Raleigh, NC 27609.

LUTHER, LUCIUS CALVIN
Clergy, religious educator. **Personal:** Born Feb 19, 1929, Mound Bayou, MS; divorced; children: Shirl Taylor, Elaine Taylor, Carol

K, Lucius C Jr, Jacqueline F, Rev Byron E. **Educ:** Boliver County Training Sch, JL Campbell Sch Religion, Religious Law; Brewster Sch Theol, TN Reg Bapt Sch Rel, B Theol, LLD, M Theol. **Career:** Brewster's Sch Theol, teacher, assoc dean; Nat Bapt Conv USA Inc, Dept Christian Educ, instr stewardship; EC Morris Inst of AR Bapt Col, instr christian educ; Thomas Chapel MB Church, pastor, 1963-65; New Wrights Chapel MB Church, pastor, 1963-65; Mt Zion MB Church, pastor, 1965-68; Greater First Baptist MB Church, pastor, 1967-68; First Baptist Church, pastor, 1968-95; First Fellowship Baptist Church, pastor, currently. **Orgs:** Vchmn Stewardship Bd, 1976-, Nat Bapt Conv USA Inc; bd dirs, Chicago Baptist Inst; moderator, New Fellowship Baptist Dist Asn; bd mem evangelism,Nat Bapt Conv USA Inc; vpres, United Baptist State Conv Ill; vchmn bd, EC Morris Inst at AR Baptist Col, Little Rock; chmn loan dept, chmn fed housing dept, Nat Bapt Conv USA Inc; bd mem, Nat Bapt Convention USA Inc. **Honors/Awds:** Mayor's Key to the City for Soul Saving Citywide Revival Tacoma, WA; Mayor's Key to the City Gary IN, Baton Rouge LA; Hon Dist Atty, Baton Rouge, LA; Hon Coun Mem of Baton Rouge, Hon Mayor of Baton Rouge; Hon Degrees, Brewster's Sch Theol, DD, JL Campbell Sch Religion DD, TN Regular Baptist Sch Religion DL. **Military Serv:** AUS, 1954-56. **Home Addr:** 2526 25th St, North Chicago, IL 60064. **Business Addr:** Pastor, First Fellowship Baptist Church, 124 S Utica, Waukegan, IL 60085.*

LYDE, JEANETTE S
Educator. **Personal:** Born Apr 23, 1946, Paterson, NJ; daughter of William Smith and Delphine Williams; married Ray, Aug 19, 1967; children: Ray Jr & Jalyn Elizabeth. **Educ:** William Paterson Coll, BA, 1969; Montclair State Coll, MA, 1982; Seton Hall Univ, doctoral candidate, cur. **Career:** Paterson Pub Sch, high sch guidance dir, 1986-92, high sch vice prin, 1988-89, elem sch vice prin, 1992-93, elem school prin, 1993-94, high sch prin, 1994-98, high sch coordr, 1998-. **Orgs:** Kappa Delta Pi, 1997-; Nat Asn Soc Sch Prin, 1994-; NJ Prin & Supvr Asn, 1993-; Paterson Prin Asn, pres, 1994-98; Asn Supvr & Curriculum Devel, 1993-; NAACP, life mem, local exec bd mem; Delta Sigma Theta Sorority, Paterson Alumnae Chap, 1974-. **Honors/Awds:** NJ equity Hall of Fame, Honorary Equity Award, 1998; Delta Woman of the Year, 1998; NJ Arts Alliance Award Principal of the Year, 1998; Mayoralty Recognition Award for Community Service; NJ General Assembly Resolution. **Business Addr:** District High School Coordinator, Paterson Public School District, 35 Church St, Paterson, NJ 07505, **Business Phone:** (973)321-0790.

LYGHT, TODD WILLIAM
Football player. **Personal:** Born Feb 9, 1969, Kwajalein, Marshall Islands; son of William. **Educ:** Univ Notre Dame. **Career:** Football player (retired); Los Angeles Rams, defensive back, 1991-94; St Louis Rams, 1995-2000; Detroit Lions, defensive back, 2001-02. **Honors/Awds:** Two time All American, 1988-89; Kris Samons Trophy.

LYLE, FREDDRENNA M
Lawyer. **Personal:** Born Jun 1, 1951, Chicago, IL; daughter of Delores Murphy Harris and Fred. **Educ:** Univ Ill-Chicago, BA, 1973; The John Marshall Law Sch, Chicago, Ill, JD, 1980. **Career:** Cornelius E Toole & Assocs, Chicago, Ill, assoc, 1980-83; F Lyle & Assocs, Chicago, Ill, partner, 1983-85; Smith & Lyle, Chicago, Ill, partner, 1985; City Chicago, alderman, currently. **Orgs:** Pres, Cook County Bar asn, 1980-; bd mem, Nat Bar asn, 1981-; bd mem, Constitutional Rights Found, 1985-; mem, Nat Black Child Devt Inst, 1989-. **Honors/Awds:** William Ming Award, Cook County Bar Assn, 1987. **Business Addr:** Alderman, City Chicago 6th Ward, 406 E 75th St, Chicago, IL 60619, **Business Phone:** (773)846-7006.

LYLE, KEITH ALLEN
Football player. **Personal:** Born Apr 17, 1972, Washington, DC; son of Garry. **Educ:** Univ Va, psychol. **Career:** Football player (retired); St Louis Rams, defensive back, 1994-2000; Wash Redskins, defensive back, 2001; San Diego Chargers, defensive back, 2002. **Honors/Awds:** All-Rookie Team, Pro Football Weekly, 1994.

LYLE, PERCY H., JR.
Salesperson. **Personal:** Born Oct 15, 1947, Detroit, MI; married Glenda Wilhelma (divorced); children: Kipp E, Jennifer B, Anthony S. **Educ:** Commun Univ Colo, BA, 1970; Webster Univ, MA, 1972; Univ Denver, Phd, 1997. **Career:** Int Bus Machines, systems mkt rep; Community Col Aurora, instr, dir diversity, adv, Black Stud Allicance; Red Rocks Community Col, instr; Community Col Denver, instr; Radio Talk Show Host. **Orgs:** Park Hill Bus Asn; Optimist Club; Mt Gilead Baptist Ch; Comnr, Elect George Brown Lt Gov; exec bd, Malcolm X Mental Health Ctr; YMCA; Park Hill Improvement Asn. *

LYLE, ROBERTA BRANCHE BLACKE
Teacher. **Personal:** Born Jul 20, 1929, Glasgow, VA; widowed; children: Valerie, Robert Jr & Carl. **Educ:** Va State Col, BS, 1966; Univ Va, MEd, 1972. **Career:** Teacher (retired); Rockbridge City Sch Bd, teacher; Town Glasgow, towncoun, Budget & Finance Parks & Recreation Comt, 1974-. **Orgs:** Past mem, bd dir Stonewall Jackson Hosp, 1972-78; scholarship comt Burlington Indust Glasgow, 1976-77; Grand Worthy Matron Grand Chap OES VA,1998-00; REA, VEA, NEA, 1958, Order Eastern Star, 1952, past secy, NAACP, PTA, Ann Ellen Early 209 OEA; usher bd, sr choir, past teacher Sunday Sch, Union Bapt Church; past secy, Mt Olivet Cemetary Comn; secy, Concerned Citizens Inc, Glasgow; chaor, Parks & Recreation Comn; Lylburn Downing Asn; Concern Citizens Glasgow. **Honors/Awds:** Teacher of the Year Award, 1975. **Business Addr:** Town council, Town of Glasgow, 1100 BlueRidge Rd, PO Box 326, Glasgow, VA 24555, **Business Phone:** (540)258-2246.*

LYLE, RON (RONALD DAVID LYLE)
Boxer. **Personal:** Born Feb 12, 1941, Denver, CO. **Career:** Prof boxer (retired), boxer coach, currently. **Orgs:** US Boxing Team. **Honors/Awds:** Nat AAU Title; N Am Title Int Boxing League; fight of the year award. **Home Addr:** 2801 E 120th Ave, Denver, CO 80233, **Home Phone:** (303)255-5518. *

LYLE, RONALD DAVID. See LYLE, RON.

LYLES, DEWAYNE
School administrator. **Personal:** Born Mar 8, 1947, Clanton, AL; married Michelle Billups; children: Raquel Lynn, Ryan Milton & Roderic. **Educ:** Miles Col, sociol & ed, 1969; Univ Ala, Birmingham, coun & guidance, 1975; Marshall Univ, mgt, 1981. **Career:** Miles Col Spec Prog, counr, 1971-75, instr, 1975; Emergency Sch Aide Act Prog Miles Col, asst dir, 1975-76; Miles Col, dir admiss, 1976-77; Marshall Univ, dir minority stud affairs. **Orgs:** Nat Assessment Stud; consult, WV Sch Osteop Med, 1983; Fairfield W Community Ctr Jobs, 1983-84; Progressive Black Men's Asn, 1983-; treas, Omega Psi Phi; vpres, Men's Asn Church. **Honors/Awds:** Volunteer Service Award, Joint Action Community Serv, 1973; Certificate of Appreciation Outstanding & Dedicated Service, Miles Col Stud Govt Asn, 1974-77; 1st Place Winner, 1st Award Miles College Alumni Tennis Tournament, 1977; Certificate of Appreciation, OIC Help Youth Week Tri-State Opportunity Indust Ctr, 1979; Certificate of Appreciation for Outstanding Service Student Activities. **Military Serv:** AUS, E-4, 1969-71; Commendation Medal, w/2 OLC, 1970-71. **Business Addr:** Assistant Dean for Educational Services, Dentson University, Granville, OH 43023, **Business Phone:** (614)587-6666.

LYLES, LESTER EVERETT
Football player. **Personal:** Born Dec 27, 1962, Washington, DC. **Educ:** Univ Va, attended. **Career:** Football player (retired); NY Jets, defensive back, 1985-87; Phoenix Cardinals, cornerback, 1988; San Diego Chargers, defensive back, 1989-90.

LYLES, MARIE CLARK
Government official, educator. **Personal:** Born Oct 12, 1952, Sledge, MS; daughter of Dave Clark and Mary McCoy Clark; married Eugene D, Oct 1977; children: Jamaal Ventral Lyles, Justin Eugene Lyles & Jessica Marie Lyles. **Educ:** Coahoma Jr Col, AA, 1972; Miss Valley State Univ, BS, 1974. **Career:** Quitman Caenties Sch, Marks, MS, teacher, 1970-89; Town Crenshaw, Crenshaw, MS, mayor, 1987-; Southside Jr High Sch, teacher. **Orgs:** Nat Teacher Org, 1970-89; treas, Crenshaw Community Builders, 1985; troop leader, Brownie Troop (Girl Scouts,) 1986; vpres, Ebonette, 1988. **Honors/Awds:** Outstanding Religion Leader, Quitman Co, 1978; Outstanding Young Women, 1988. **Business Addr:** Teacher, Southside Junior High School, PO Box 175, Lambert, MS 38643, **Business Phone:** (601)382-5272.

LYLES, WILLIAM K.
Educator, psychologist. **Personal:** Born in Winston-Salem, NC; children: Don L. **Educ:** Univ NC, BS, 1939; New York Univ, MS, 1947, PhD, 1958. **Career:** Queens Col, assoc dean stud, 1972-73; W Harlem-Inwood Mental Health Ctr, exec dir, 1973-74; Children Aid Soc, coordr ment health, 1974-79; Bronx-Lebanon Hosp, assoc chief psychologist, 1978-83; Harlem-Dowling Children Serv, coordr ment health serv, 1984; Vet Acad, Bronx, NY, consult, 1993; psychologist, currently. **Orgs:** Pres, Richmond Co Psychol Asn, 1974; NY Urban League Adv Bd, 1980-83; pres, Nat Asn Black Psychol, 1983; pres, NY Asn Black Psychol, 1983; Nat Black Leadership Round Table, 1983; Nat Task Force Black Race Homicide, 1984; exec comt, Nat Asn Advan Colored People, 1998; bd dir, Addie Mae Collins Early Childhood Prog, 1993. **Honors/Awds:** President's Award, Nat Asn Black Psychol, 1984. **Business Addr:** Psychologist, 1000 Clove Rd Apt 60, Staten Island, NY 10301, **Business Phone:** (718)556-0595.

LYMAN, WEBSTER S. See Obituaries section.

LYNCH, ERIC
Football player. **Personal:** Born May 16, 1970, Woodhaven, MI. **Educ:** Grand Valley State Univ. **Career:** Football player (retired); Detroit Lions, running back, 1993-96; Scottish Claymores, running back, 1998.

LYNCH, GEORGE DEWITT
Basketball player, basketball coach. **Personal:** Born Sep 3, 1970, Roanoke, VA. **Educ:** Univ NC, BA, arts & sci. **Career:** Basketball player (retired), basketball coach; Los Angeles Lakers, forward, 1994-96; Vancouver Grizzlies, 1996-98; Philadelphia 76ers, 1998-2001; Charlotte Hornets, 2001-02; New Orleans Hornets, forward, 2002-05; Southern Methodist Univ, admin asst & graduate mgr, 2006-. **Orgs:** Nat Basketball Asn. **Honors/Awds:** First round pick, NBA Draft, 1993; Citizen of the Year, Police Athletic League; NBA Community Hero of the Month, 2001.

LYNCH, HOLLIS R.
Educator. **Personal:** Born Apr 21, 1935, Port-of-Spain, Trinidad and Tobago; divorced; children: Shola Ayn, Nnenna Jean, Ashale Herman & John Benjamin. **Educ:** Univ British Columbia, BA (with honors), 1960; MA, 1961; Univ London, PhD, 1964. **Career:** Educator (retired); Univ IFE Nigeria, lect, 1964-66; Roosevelt Univ Chicago, from asst prof to assoc prof, 1966-68; State Univ NY, assoc prof, 1968-69; Columbia Univ, prof, 1969-, Inst African Studies, dir, 1971-74, 1985-90; Am Coun Learned Soc, fel, 1978-79. **Orgs:** African Studies Asn; Asn Study Afro-Am Life & History; Am Hist Asn,1971-73; Caribbean Studies Asn. **Honors/Awds:** Recipient Commonwealth Fellow, London Univ, 1961-64; Hoover National Fellow, Stanford Univ, 1973-74; Fellow, Woodrow Wilson Int Ctr Scholars, 1976. **Special Achievements:** Author of Edward Wilmot Blyden Pan Negro Patriot 1967 & The Black Urban Condition 1973. Author of many books and articles. The Foundation of American-Nigerian Ties: Nigerian Students in the United States, 1939-48, Black Ivory, The Pan-African Magazine, 1989. **Home Addr:** 100 La Salle St Suite 69, New York, NY 10027.

LYNCH, LEON
Vice president (Organization). **Personal:** Born Jun 4, 1935, Edwards, MS; married Doris Tyndall; children: Tina, Sheila, Tammy & Maxine. **Educ:** Ind Univ; Purdue Univ; Roosevelt Univ, Chicago, BS, 1967. **Career:** Vice pres (retired); Youngstown Sheet & Tube Co, loader, 1956; United Steelworkers Am, staff rep, 1968, int rep, 1973, int vpres human affairs, 2001-06. **Orgs:** USWA Int Civil Rights Comn, chair, Const Comn, chair, Polit Action Comn; Am Fedn Labor & Cong Indust Orgs Civil Rights, Exec Coun; chmn, Nat Philip Randolph Inst, Workers Defense League, Indust Rels Res Asn; Nat Planning Asn; life mem, Nat Asn Advan Colored People, 1981; Dem Nat Comn; Dem Party Comn Pres Nominations; nat exec comt, Am Dem Action, NBCSL Labor Roundtable; President's Adv Coun Unemploy Comp; chair, Steelworkers Health & Welfare Fund; appointed by pres Clinton, bd dir, Air Traffic Orgn Sub-Comt, Fed Aviation Admin; adv bd, Am Income Lige Ins Co. **Honors/Awds:** A Philip Randolph Achievement Award, A Philip Randolph Inst, 1977; A Philip Randolph Labor Award, Negro Trade Union Leadership Coun, 1977; Chicago Conference for Brotherhood Award, 1979; Appreciation Award, APRI Chattanooga Chap, Nat Asn Advan Colored People Perth Amboy Br, 1980; Local Union 1011 Award of Gratitude & APRI Calumet Chap Grateful Recognition Award, 1981; Henry Harrison Award, APRI Chicago Chap; Certificate of Appreciation, Voc Rehab Ctr; Indiana State Award for Outstanding Contributions to the Labor Movement, Nat Asn Advan Colored People, 1982; ADA 35th Annual Roosevelt Day Dinner Award & Dist 29 Cert Appreciation Award for Outstanding & Dedicated Service in Saving Jobs at McLouth Steel, 1983; APRI Youngstown Chapter Award for Dedicated Service to Mankind Careers Inc; Humanitarian Award Local Union 1011 Award in Recognition for Outstanding Service & Achievements in USWA; Man of the Year, Vectors/Pittsburgh, 1995; Hall of Fame, Gary, IN, 1998; Nation Builder Award, Nat Black Caucus State Legislators, 2002. **Military Serv:** AUS, sgt, 1 yr. **Business Addr:** International Vice President, United Steelworkers of America, 5 Gateway Ctr, Pittsburgh, PA 15222, **Business Phone:** (412)562-2400.

LYNCH, DR. LILLIE RIDDICK. See Obituaries section.

LYNCH, REV. LORENZO A, SR.
Clergy. **Personal:** Born in Oak City, NC; married Lorine Harris; children: Lorenzo A Jr, Loretta E & Leonzo D. **Educ:** Shaw Univ, BA, 1955, Divinity Sch, BD, 1957; Boston Univ, grad stud, 1958, 1968; Univ NC, Chapel Hill, 1957; Duke Univ, Divinity Sch, 1965; Southeastern Theol Sem, 1959; Shaw Divinity Sch, hon DD, 1982. **Career:** White Rock Baptist Church Durham, pastor, 1965-; Davis Chapel Wash; Endstreet Baptist Church, Scotland Neck; Mt Zion, Arapahoe; St Delight, Nashville; Reid's Chapel, Fountain; Mt Olive, Ayden; Bazzel Creek, Fuquay Springs; Providence Baptist Church, Greensboro, former pastor; Lynch Chapel, Oak City; Jones Chapel, Palmyra; Peoples Baptist Church, Boston, past asst pastor; Religious Educ Prog, sponsored Boston Coun Weekday Religous Educ, former teacher; Baptist Student Union, A&T Col, former adv; Palmer Memorial Inst, Sedalia, preacher; former counr. **Orgs:** Pres, Durham Minister's Asn, 1967-68; bd dir, Edgemont Community Ctr, 1968-71; adv bd, Durham Co Mental Health Ctr, 1968-74; unsuccessful candidate Durham's Mayor 1973; critic Interdenominational Minister's Alliance, 1975; bd dir Triangle Kidney Found, 1975-; Gen Baptist Conv NC Inc; exec bd, Durham Nat Asn Advan Colored People; chmn, Comn Econ Develop; Durham's Com Affairs Black People; Durham's Clergy Hosp Chaplain's Asn; Greensboro Br Nat Asn Advan Colored People; bd dir, United Southern A&T Col; bd dir, Cumberland C Inc. **Business Addr:** Pastor, White Rock Baptist Church, 3400 Fayetteville St, Durham, NC 27707, **Business Phone:** (919)688-8136.

YNCH, LORETTA E
.S. attorney. **Educ:** Harvard Col, AB, 1981; Harvard Law Sch, D, 1984. **Career:** St John Univ Sch Law, adj prof; US Dept ustice, Criminal Trial Advocacy Prog, frequent instr; NY firm, itigation assoc; St John's Univ Sch Law, adj prof; Long Island Off, dep chief, chief, 1994-98; Eastern Dist NY, chief asst US atty, 999-2001; Hogan & Hartson LLP, partner, currently. **Orgs:** Bd ir, Fed Res Bank NY; bd dir, The Legal Aid Soc; bd adv, Brennan Ctr Justice, NY Univ Sch Law; Eastern Dist Comt Civil Litigaion; Fed Bar Coun; Judicial Screening Panel, Senator Charles chumer; Magistrate Judge Selection Panel, Eastern Dist, NY; bd ir, Nat Inst Trial Advocacy; bd dir, Off Appellate Defender; bd ir, Nat Inst Law & Equity; chmn, Fed Bar Found; vpres, NY City ar Asn. **Business Addr:** Partner, Hogan & Hartson LLP, 26th Fl 75 3rd Ave, New York, NY 10601, **Business Phone:** (212)918-544.

YNCH, ROBERT D.
ducator. **Personal:** Born Sep 4, 1933, Greensburg, PA; son of Robert E Lynch and Martha Dickson Lynch; married Dolores Cruse, Apr 16, 1960. **Educ:** Ind Univ Pa, BS, 1956, MEd, 1965; Duquesne Univ, MME, 1966; Pa State Univ, DEd. **Career:** Hempeld Area Sch Syst, dept head, 1958-65; Duquesne Sch Music, intr, 1965-66; Pa St Univ, grad asst dept chmn, 1966-67; Fine Arts Component, asst proj dir & coordr; Pa Reg J Title III, 1967-69; Upward Bound, proj dir; Lock Haven Univ, assoc prof, 1969-71, dir supr coordr, 1971-, dir develop & spec prog, 1974-83, asst pres admin & develop, affirmative action officer, 1983-, asst pres dmin, 1989-, mgr emer, currently. **Orgs:** Life mem, Music Educ Nat Conf; Pa Music Educ Asn; Nat Sch Orchestra Asn; Pa Black Higher Educ Conf; Asn Inst Res; Nat Coun Univ Res Admin; Am Asn Univ Admin; Am Col Pub Relat Asn; Pa Asn Trio Prog Adnin; Phi Beta Mu; Phi Delta Kappa; Phi Mu Alpha; pres, Phi Delta Kappa, 1973-81; pres, Phi Beta Mu, 1980-82; conductor, Lock Haven Univ Symphony Orchestra & Chorus, pres, 1983-94, bd dir, 984-95; pres, Pa Black Conf Higher Educ, 1984-90; gov, Rotary nt Dist 737, 1985-86. **Honors/Awds:** Lock Haven Citizen of the Year; TV Station WFBG "People Are Great Awd "Rotary Int Paul Harris Fel; Mary Davis Baltimore Awd, Pa BCOHE State & Community Serv; Hon Lt Colonel Aide-De-Camp to the Gov State of AL; Distinguished Educr, Phi Delta Kappa, Lock Haven, 1990; Frank D O'Reilly Jr Memorial Award, Bcohe Stud Leadership Dev nst. **Military Serv:** AUS, 1956-62. **Home Addr:** RR 4 Box 848 Cedar Heights, Mill Hall, PA 17751-9737, **Home Phone:** 717)726-6270. **Business Addr:** Assistant to President for Administration, Director of Social Equity, Lock Haven University f Pennsylvania, N Fairview St 301 Sullivan Hall, Lock Haven, A 17745, **Business Phone:** (570)484-2011.

YNCH, DR. RUFUS SYLVESTER
ocial worker, educator. **Personal:** Born Nov 30, 1946, Baltimore, MD; son of Rufus and Marie; married VeRita Amelia Barnette; hildren: Marie Rachel & Kirkland Alexander. **Educ:** Morgan State Univ, BA, sociol, 1968; Univ Pittsburgh Sch Social Work, MSW, 1970; Univ Pa Sch Social Work, advan cert, social work adnin, 1971, DSW, social work admin & policy, 1973; Nat Gerontoogical Soc, res fel, 1978; Nat Ctr State Courts, Inst Court Mgt, rad fel, 1990. **Career:** Westinghouse Defense & Space Ctr, urban oc scientist, 1967-68; Catholic Diocese Pittsburgh, prog dir & onsult, 1969; Ford Motor Co, staff coordr, 1969; Philadelphia Health Mgt Corp, res develop & outreach specialist, 1973-74; Community Col Philadelphia, dir serv aging, 1975-76; Off Lt Gov PA, sr human serv policy adv, 1975-76; Off Majority Leader PA H R, exec asst chief staff, 1976-77; Off Speaker Pa H R, exec asst hief staff, 1977-78; MLB Inc, pres, 1978-84; Temple Univ, sr exec mgt, cons, spec asst exec vpres univ admin, 1984-85; Admin Off Supreme Ct Pa, asst ct admin, 1986-87, dir ct mgt, 1987-94; Univ Pen Sch Social Work, adj fac; Cheyney Univ Pa, prof, 1994-97; Ctr Studying Social Welfare & Community Develop, Philadelphia, Pa, pres, 1994-; Lincoln Univ Multidisciplinary Ctr Aging, assoc prof; Chestnut Hill Col, adj criminal justice fac; Ctr Studying Social Welfare & Community Develop, pres, 1994-; Fresh Start Community Develop Corp, founder, pres, 1997-99; Pvt ndust Coun Philadelphia, vpres, Transitional Workforce Dept, 999-2000; Philadelphia Workforce Develop Corp, sr vpres, 2000-; Inst Advan Working Families, pres & prin investigator, 2001; Whitney M Young Jr, Sch Social Work, Clark Atlanta Univ, prof & dean, 2004-. **Orgs:** The Justice System Jour ed bd; Nat Asn Court Mgt; Am Bar Asn, Judicial Admin Div; Asn Black Social Workers; Am Bar Asn, Criminal Justice Div; Coun Social Work Educ; Nat Ctr State Courts; Ctr Studying Social Welfare & Community Develop, 1979; congressional delegate, White House Conf Aging, 1981; Bicentennial Comn US Const, 1985; Nat Ctr Social Policy & Pract, founding mem, 1986; Black Caucus/African Am Network, NASW, convenor, 1990; Nat Community Inquiry, NASW; 1991-94; Pa Rep Nat Delegate Assembly, 1992-95; Continuing Ed Comn, Pa Chap NASW, 1992-94; Adjudication Prog Issues Advy Group, 1993-95; pres, Pa Chap Nat Asn Social Workers (NASW), 1994-98; proj dir, Philadelphia Juvenile Ctr nc, 1995-; pres, Fresh Start Community Develop Corp, 1995-; bd dirs, Blacks Educating Blacks Sexual Health Issues, 1996-; bd dirs, W Philadelphia YMCA & Family Ctr, 1996-. **Honors/Awds:** Social Worker of the Year, NASW PA, 1978; Certificate of Appreciation, City Philadelphia Personnel Dept, 1980; Alumni of Year Award, Univ Pittsburgh Sch Social Work, 1981; Pa Asn Spec Courts Spec Award, 1988; President's Friendship Award, Pa State Constable's Asn, 1988; Distinguished Service Award, Nat Constable's Asn, 1989; Distinguished Minority Scholars in Residents Prog, Pa State Univ, 1991; Man of the Year Award, Pa State Constables Asn, 1991; President's Award, Nat Asn Ct Mgt, 1991; Summit Award, City Charleston, SC, 1994. **Special Achievements:** First African American elected President of Pennsylvania Chapter of National Assoc of Social Workers, 1995. **Military Serv:** AUS. **Home Addr:** 1013 S St Bernard Pl, Philadelphia, PA 19143-3312. **Business Addr:** Dean and Professor, Clark Atlanta University, School of Social Work, 223 James P Brawley Dr SW, Atlanta, GA 30314, **Business Phone:** (404)880-8863.

LYNN, ANTHONY RAY
Football player, football coach. **Personal:** Born Dec 21, 1968, McKinney, TX; married; children: D'Anton & Danielle. **Educ:** Tex Tech. **Career:** Football player (retired), Football coach; Denver Broncos, running back, 1993, 1997-99; SanFrancisco 49ers, 1995-96; Jacksonville Jaguars, running backs coach, 2003-04; Dallas Cowboys, running back coach, 2005-06; Cleveland Browns,running backs coach, 2007-. **Business Phone:** (440)891-5000.*

LYNN, LONNIE RASHID
Rap musician, actor. **Personal:** Born Mar 13, 1972, Chicago, IL; son of Lonnie Lynn and Mahalia Ann Hines; children: Omoye Assata Lynn. **Educ:** Fla A&M Univ. **Career:** Albums: Can I Borrow A Dollar?, 1992; Resurrection, 1994; One Day It'll All Make Sense, 1997; Like Water for Chocolate, 2000; Electric Circus, 2003; Be, 2005; Films: "Girlfriends," 2003; "Chappelle's Show," 2004; "One on One," 2004; Smokin' Aces, 2006; "Thisisme Then", 2007; The Believer, 2008; Actor: Brown Sugar, 2002; Dave Chapelle's Block Party, 2006; Smokin' Aces, 2007; American Gangster, 2007; Street Kings, 2008; Wanted, 2008. **Honors/ Awds:** Grammy Awards: Best Rap Solo Performance ("The Light"), Nominated, 2001; Best Urban/Alternative Performance ("Love of My Life (Ode to Hip-Hop)"), Nominated, 2003; Best R&B Song ("Love of My Life (An Ode to Hip-Hop)"), Won, 2003; Best Song Written for a Motion Picture/Television Movie ("Love of My Life (An Ode to Hip-Hop)"), Nominated, 2003; Best Rap Solo Performance ("Testify"), Nominated, 2006; Best Rap Album (Be), Nominated, 2006; Best Rap/Sung Collaboration ("They Say"), Nominated, 2006; Best Rap Performance by a Duo or Group ("The Corner"), Nominated, 2006; Best Rap Solo Performance ("The People"), Nominated, 2008; Best Rap Album (Finding Forever), Nominated, 2008; Best Rap Performance by Duo or Group ("Southside"), Won, 2008; BET Awards: Best Male Hip-Hop Artist, Nominated, 2006; BET Hip Hop Awards: Hip-Hop Video of the Year ("Testify"), Nominated, 2006; Element Award- Lyricist of the Year, Won, 2006; Lyricist of the Year, Won, 2007; CD of the Year: "Finding Forever", Won, 2007; Best Hip Hop Video: "The People", Nominated, 2007; Best Live Performance, Nominated, 2007; MVP Of The Year, Nominated, 2007; MTV Video Music Awards: Best Hip-Hop Video ("Testify"), Nominated, 2006; Best Hip-Hop Video ("Go"), Nominated, 2005. **Special Achievements:** album Be nominated for Grammy Awards, 2006. **Business Addr:** Artist, MCA Records, 2220 Colorado Ave, Santa Monica, CA 90404, **Business Phone:** (310)865-4500.

LYNN, LOUIS B.
Research scientist, president (organization), horticulturist. **Personal:** Born Mar 8, 1949, Bishopville, SC; son of Lawton and Dorothy Evans; married Audrey Johnson; children: Adrienne, Krystal, Bryan. **Educ:** Clemson Univ, BS, hort (honors), 1970, MS, hort, 1972; Univ MD, PhD, hort, 1975. **Career:** Elanco Product Co, field res scientist, 1976-80; Monsanto Agr Co, prod mgr, 1980-83, sr scientist, 1983-88; Environ Affairs, mgr, 1988-90; Environ Agr Sci Inc, pres & chief hort, 1985-; Univ SC, adj prof pub health; Benedict Col, adj prof biol; Clemson Univ, adj prof hort; SC Dept Agr, crop prod consult; Atlanta Parks Dept, hort consult; Laidlaw Environ Serv, agrichem waste consult; US Dept Energy, conserv tillage consult; Agr Ministry Bahamas, crop consult; Trinidad & Tabago Govts, crop consult. **Orgs:** Clemson Black Alumni Coun, 1986-88; Clemson Univ Alumni Asn; SC Hort Soc, 1987-88; Am Soc Hort Sci; SC Agr Study Comt; bd trustees, Clemson Univ; bd dir, BB&T Bank; President's Club; Major Gifts Club; vchmn, Clemson Univ Bd Trustees. **Honors/ Awds:** Alumni Distinguished Service Award, Clemson Univ, 2001. **Military Serv:** AUS, Capt, 5 yrs. **Business Addr:** President, Chief Horticulturist, Environmental Agrscience Inc, PO Box 23285, Columbia, SC 29229, **Business Phone:** (803)714-7290.*

LYONS, A BATES
State government official, consultant. **Personal:** Born Nov 20, 1944, Philadelphia, PA; son of Archie and Irma; divorced; children: Joanna, Daniel & Ashley. **Educ:** Central State Univ, Wilberforce, OH, BS, 1966; Columbia Univ, New York, NY, MBA, 1972; Mass Inst Technol, cert. **Career:** Atlantic Richfield, Philadelphia, PA, mgr, 1969-72; Philip Morris, New York, NY, mgr, 1972-79; Heublein, Farmington, CT, mgr, 1977-78; Office Policy Mgt, Hartford, CT, under secy, 1978-87; State Technical Col, Hartford, CT, dep exec dir, 1987-92; consult, 1992-; Torrington pub sch, staff, 1999-, elected vice chair, currently; staff develop consult, pvt pract, currently; Univ Conn Sch Bus, adj prof, currently; Capital Community Tech Col, adj prof. **Orgs:** Pres, Fedn Black Democrats, 1982-84; polemarch, Kappa Alpha Psi Fraternity, 1982-84; State Retirement Comn, 1985-; Conn Asn Bd Educ. **Military Serv:** AUS, capt, 1966-69. **Home Addr:** 212 Carriage Lane, Torrington, CT 06790. **Business Addr:** Vice Chair, Torrington Public Schools, 212 Carriage Lane, Torrington, CT 06790, **Business Phone:** (860)614-0893.

LYONS, CHARLOTTE
Editor, writer. **Educ:** Morris Brown Col, Atlanta. **Career:** Ebony Mag, food ed, author, currently. **Business Addr:** Food Editor, Author, Ebony magazine, 820 S Michigan Ave, Chicago, IL 60605-2190, **Business Phone:** (312)322-9250.*

LYONS, DONALD WALLACE
Athletic director. **Personal:** Born Dec 11, 1945, Lexington, KY; son of Joseph Bailey and Sam Ella; married Myra Briggs, Jun 28, 1969; children: Donald Wallace & Reginald. **Educ:** Ky State Univ, AB, 1968; Univ KY, MSLS, 1971. **Career:** Athletic Director (retired); KY State Univ, athletic dir, dir libr, asstlibrn, teacher, supvr adult educ; Am Libr Asn, teacher; Am Asn Univ, prof; KY Libr Asn, KSU Foundation Executiv, currently. **Orgs:** NEA Alpha Phi Alpha frat. **Honors/Awds:** Pub African & African Am History & Cult a bibliography; follow-up of on the job training placements"; blazer bugle. **Home Phone:** (859)299-6420. *

LYONS, GEORGE, JR.
Executive, vice president (organization). **Educ:** Univ NC, BA, econ, MBA, JD. **Career:** Parke-Davis, state govt regional mgr; Peco Energy, vpres regulatory commun & external affairs; Exelon Corp, vpres, govt & pub affairs; Pepco, DC region vpres govt affairs & pub policy issues, 2006-; Pfizer Inc, govt rels; Am Gas Asn, govt rels. **Orgs:** DC Bar; Fed Energy Bar; Nat Health Lawyers Asn; Nat Bar Asn; bd, World Affairs Coun; bd, Greater Philadelphia Urban Affairs Coalition; bd, Philadelphia Urban League; bd, WYBE Pub TV Arts & Bus Coun. **Business Addr:** Region Vice President, PEPCO, 701 Ninth St NW, Washington, DC 20068.*

LYONS, DR. JAMES E.
College president. **Educ:** Univ Conn, BA, Spanish, 1965, MA, stud personnel, 1971, PhD, prof higher educ admin, 1973; Harvard Univ Inst Educ Mgt, attended 1976. **Career:** Ky State Univ, assoc prof educ, 1973-74; Fayetteville State Univ, prof educ, 1974-75; Barber Scotia Col, vpres acad affairs, 1975-78; Del State Col, vpres & dean acad affairs, 1978-83, prof educ, 1978-83; Bowie State Univ, pres, 1983-92, prof educ, 1983-92; Jackson State Univ, pres, 1992-99; Calif State Univ, Dominguez Hills pres, 1999-. **Orgs:** Comt Diversity & Social Change, Am Asn State Cols & Univs, 1996-99; US Air Force Bd Advisors Hist Black Cols & Univs & Minority Inst, 1997; bd dir, Nat Asn Equal Opportunity Higher Educ, 1997-99; bd trustee, Citizens Scholar Found Am, 1998; bd dir, Golden Eagle Educ & Training, Int Youth Inst, 1998; evaluator, Vis Comt, Southern Asn Cols & Schs, Comn Cols, 1998; Coun Educ & Human Resources, Miss Econ Coun, 1998-99; Alcohol Abuse & Misuse Col Campuses Comt, Nat Inst Alcohol Abuse & Alcoholism, Dept Health & Human Servs, 1998; Comt Standing Rules, Miss Conf, United Methodist Church, 1998; Nominating Comt, Comn Cols, 1998-2000; Coun Exec Bd, Andrew Jackson Coun Boy Scouts Am, 1998; pres, Calif Coliate Athletic Asn, 2001-02; comnr, Am Coun Educ, Comn Minorities Higher Educ, 2001-04; Nat Coliate Athletic Asn, Division II, Pres Coun, 2003-07; Am Asn Cols Teacher Educ; Am Asn State Cols & Univs; Am Coun Educ; Hispanic Asn Cols & Univs; CSU Comt Alcohol Policies & Progs; CSU Comn Extended Univ; CSU Archives; chair, Accreditation Team, Middle States Comn Higher Educ; S Bay Econ & Develop Partnership; S Bay Work force Investment Bd; S Bay Bus Round table; Citizens Scholar Found Americas Scholar Mgt Servs Sub comt & Dollars Scholars Sub comt. **Honors/Awds:** Distinguished Alumni Award, Neag Sch Educ, Univ Conn, 2000; Named Regional Citizen Year, Omega Psi Phi Fraternity, 2001; Franklin H Williams Award, Peace Corps, 2001. **Special Achievements:** Published numerous articles. **Business Phone:** 877-634-6361.

LYONS, LAMAR ANDREW
Chief executive officer, banker. **Educ:** Univ Calif, Los Angeles, BA, philos & math; Howard Univ, Sch Law, JD. **Career:** Morgan Stanley Inc, staff; L F Rothschild & Co Inc, staff; Rideau Lyons & Co Inc, chief exec officer & exec managing dir, currently. **Business Phone:** (323)965-1710.

LYONS, DR. LAURA BROWN
Public speaker. **Personal:** Born Jul 15, 1942, Birmingham, AL; daughter of Jesse and Annie M; married Edward, May 16, 1970 (died 1995); children: Kobie. **Educ:** Dillard Univ, New Orleans, LA, BA 1963; NYK Univ, MSW. **Career:** Kaiser Corp, asst personnel mgr, 1975-80; BVI Govt, Road Town, Tortola, BVI, asst cot develop off, 1980-81; Career Dynamics Int, Tortola, BVI, pres, chief exec officer, currently; WBNB-TV, CBS Affiliate, former TV talk show hostess; Ann Wigmore Health Inst, marketing & promotions, currently. **Orgs:** Caribbean Exec Woman's Network, 1985-; Am Soc Training & Develop, 1985-; Int Prof Pract Asn, 1989-. **Honors/Awds:** Multi-Cultural Trainer Year Award, ASTD, 1990;

Outstanding Bus Person, Virgin Islands Bus Journal, 1988 Outstanding Female Exec, CEWN, 1990, 1997; Educator Year, US Virgin Islands Bus Jour, 1988; Am Express Recognition Award, Excellence Motivational Training, 1989; Business Person Year, nominee, British Virgin Islands Hotel & Com Asn, 1990; Black Career Women's Asn, "Legacy Messenger," Cincinnati, OH, 1997; nominee, Avon/US Small Bus Women Year Award. **Special Achievements:** Author: Lyon's Guide to the Career Jungle, Odenwald Connection Publishing, 1989. **Business Addr:** Chief Executive Officer, President, Career Dynamics International, 6363 Curistis Ave Suite 1412, Emeryville, CA 94605, **Business Phone:** (510)658-8133.

LYONS, PATRICK ALAN
Financial manager, consultant, business owner. **Personal:** Born Feb 18, 1972, Ft Belvoir, VA; son of Gwendolyn A and Charlie J; married Kelly. **Educ:** Fla A&M Univ, BS, 1994; NC State Univ, MSM, 2001. **Career:** Wake Tech Community Col; NCM Capital Mgt Group, sr res analyst, 1995-2001, assoc portfolio mgr, portfolio mgr, 2001-; Lyons Den Press, owner, currently; Lyons Den Capital LLC, pres, currently. **Orgs:** Prince Hall Masons; Nat Black MBA Asn; Alpha Phi Alpha Frat Inc, 1993-; Mkt Technician Asn. **Honors/Awds:** Featured inBlack Enterprise magazine and on Bloomberg Radio. **Special Achievements:** Author, Map Your Financial Future: Starting on the Right Path in Your Teens and Twenties; numerous publications and shows including in Black Enterprise magazine, WHUR 96.3, Washington, DC, Bev Smith Show, WJZ, CBS Affiliate, WNCN, NBC Affiliate & Bloomberg Radio. **Business Addr:** President, Lyons Den Capital LLC, PO Box 1341, Durham, NC 27702.

LYONS, ROBERT P.
Executive. **Personal:** Born Nov 18, 1912, Kansas City, MO; married Claudia Mae Hopkins. **Educ:** Univ Kans. **Career:** Retired: Universal Life Ins, dist mgr Kansas City, 1949-55; Crusader Life Ins Co, agency dir, 1957-69; AMR Woodmen's Life Insurance Co, past bd chmn. **Orgs:** Past pres, Millionaires Club Nat Ins Asn; Beta Lambda chap Alpha Phi Alpha; past chmn, Agency Sect Nat Ins Asn; past chmn, pro-tem, Bethel AME Trustee Bd; Bethel AME Ch; co-incorporator, Bethel AME Ch Not-For-Profit Found; pres & founder, Soft & Sweet Music Club; past dir, Region 2 Nat Ins Asn; past mem, Bd Mgt Paseo-Linwood YMCA; past mem, KS City Area C C; life mem, Alpha Phi Alpha. **Honors/Awds:** Certificate of Achievement, Millionaires Club Nat Ins Asn, 1958-71; elected, Midwestern Hall of Fame. **Special Achievements:** Author "The Life of a Black Salesman from Selling Newspapers to Serving as Chairman of a Board of Directors". *

LYTHCOTT, JANICE LOGUE
Executive. **Personal:** Born Jun 19, 1950, St Albans, NY; daughter of John Thomas and Helen Harvey; married Michael, Jun 1983; children: Omi & Shade. **Educ:** Simmons Col, Boston, MA, 1968-69; Lehman Col, Bronx, NY, 1969-71; Howard Univ, Wash, DC, BA, 1975. **Career:** WHUR, Wash, DC, spec asst to gen mgr, 1976; Gil Scott Heron, New York, NY, mgr, 1977-78; CBS Records, New York, NY, mgr, admin, 1978-80, assoc dir progs & proj develop, 1980-88; Sony Music & CBS Records, New York, NY, dir, proj develop, 1988; Lincoln Theatre, exec dir, 2006-. **Orgs:** Comt chair, Jackie Robinson Found, 1982-89; bd mem, Alvin Ailey Am Found, 1987-; bd mem, Jamison Proj, 1988-89. **Honors/Awds:** Award for Excellence, Am Women Radio & TV, 1975; Black Achiever, YMCA, 1983; Award of Excellence, CEBA Award, 1984; Award for Distrinction, CEBA Award, 1987; Volunteer of the Year, Jackie Robinson Found, 1990. **Business Phone:** (202)328-6000.

LYTLE, ALICE A
Judge. **Personal:** Born in Jersey City, NJ; divorced. **Educ:** Hunter Col, AB, physiol & pub health; Hastings Col Law, JD, 1973. **Career:** Judge (retired); Albert Einstein Col Med, med res tech, 1961-70; Univ Calif, San Francisco Cardiovascular Res Inst; Gov Edmund G Brown Jr, dep legal affairs sec, 1975-77; Dept Indust Rels Div Fair Employee Pract, chief, 1977-79; State & Consumer Serv Agency, Cabinet Off Admin Gov Brown, secy, 1979-82; Sacramento Munic Sup Ct, judge. **Orgs:** Legal Defense Fund, Nat Asn Advan Colored People. **Honors/Awds:** Hall of Fame, Hunter Col, New York City; Rose Bird Memorial Award, 2005.

LYTLE, MARILYN MERCEDES
Association executive, educator. **Personal:** Born May 10, 1948, Mound Bayou, MS; daughter of C Preston Holmes and Pauline J Thompson; married Erskine Lytle III, Jun 26, 1971; children: Brandon Kyle & Kiera Danine. **Educ:** Fisk Univ, Nashville, TN, BS, 1969; Stanford Univ, Palo Alto, CA, MAT, 1970. **Career:** Wash High Sch, San Francisco, CA, music teacher, 1970-71; Jordan High Sch, Durham, NC, choral music teacher, 1972-78; INROADS Inc, Nashville, TN, coordr, asst dir, 1979-83, dir, 1983-86, regional dir, 1986-88, regional vpres, 1988-93, vpres, 1994-95, exec vp, 1995-99, pres affiliate org; Univ Tenn, Knoxville, exec-in-residence, 1997. **Orgs:** Bd mem, United Way, 1987-94; head, Allocations Comt, United Way, 1984-86; bd mem, St Mary's Villa, 1984-87; Selection Comt, Bootstraps Scholars, 1988; Leadership Nashville, 1986-; Alpha Kappa Alpha Sorority Inc; bd mem, exec comt mem, Nashville CARES, 1994-2001; exec comt mem, YWCA, 1995-97; bd mem, Community Found Middle Tennessee, 1999-. **Honors/Awds:** Community Role Model Award, St Peters AME Church, 1994; Outstanding Community Leadership and Service Award, Alpha Delta Omega Chap, Alpha Kappa Alpha Sorority; Project Cherish Honoree, Delta Sigma Theta Sorority Inc, 1995; President's Citation for Excellence, INROADS Inc, 1995; Inductee, Acad Women Achievement, YWCA, 2002. **Special Achievements:** Selected to 100 Top African-American Business & Professional Women, Dollars and Sense Magazine, 1989; selected, Phelps Stokes West Africa Heritage Tour, Phelps Stokes Fund, 1978.

M

MABEN, HAYWARD C., JR.
Physician. **Personal:** Born Jun 3, 1922, Augusta, GA; son of Hayward Sr and Ethel Marie; married Carrie M Harris; children: Hayward III, Burton, Michael. **Educ:** Wayne State Univ, BS, 1942; Meharry Med Col, MD, 1945. **Career:** Harper Hosp, 1967; Highland Park Gen, 1969; surg staff, Blv Gen; surg staff, Burton Mercy; surg staff, Sumby Memorial Hosps; Wayne State Univ Sch Med, clin asst prof; pvt pract, cardiovasc & thoracic surgeon, currently. **Orgs:** Fel, Am Col Chest Physicians; Soc Thoracic Surgeons; life mem, Nat Asn Advan Colored People; emer mem, Nat Med Asn; emer mem, Detroit Med Soc; Detroit Cotillion Club; Wayne County Med Soc; Mich State Med Soc; Mich Thoracic Surgeons Soc. **Honors/Awds:** First black thoracic surgeon in state of MI; one of the first three blacks to be accepted into the Wayne State University School of Medicine's surgery residency training program; certified in general surgery in 1964 and in thoracic-cardiovascular surgery in 1965 following a residency in Chicago. At that time, Dr. Maben was the fifth African American in the country to achieve such certification. **Military Serv:** AUS, 1943-45. **Home Addr:** 3011 W Grand Blvd Suite 868, Detroit, MI 48201. **Business Addr:** Cardiovascular & Thoracic Surgeon, Fisher Bldg 3011 W Grand Blvd Suite 868, Detroit, MI 48202.*

MABIN, JOSEPH E
Executive. **Career:** Mabin Construct Co, Inc, Kansas City, MO, exec dir, 1980-. **Orgs:** Pres, Black Chamber Com Greater Kans City; exec dir, Minority Contractors Asn; pres, exec dir, Nat Asn Minority Contractors. **Business Addr:** Executive Director, Minority Contractors Association of Greater Kansas City, 3200 Wayne Ave, Kansas City, MO 64108, **Business Phone:** (816)924-4441.*

MABREY, ERNEST L
Executive. **Personal:** Born Oct 1, 1937, Bristow, OK; son of Ernest and Jemima House; married Emma L Nixon, Jun 15, 1965 (divorced 1978); children: Ernest T Mabrey III. **Educ:** George Wash Univ, BS, math, 1968, MS, engineering, 1978, Appl Sci degree, 1982. **Career:** USN, mathematician, 1963-70; Nat Oceanic & Atmospheric Dept Com, oper res analyst, 1970-77; Bur Census, supv math statistician, 1977-78; Dept Energy, supv math statistician, 1978-82; Bowie State Univ, asst prof of math & comput sci, 1982-87; LOGI-TECH Engineering Resources Inc, pres & chief exec officer, currently. **Orgs:** George Wash Univ, Pi Mu Epsilon, Nat Math Honors Soc, 1968; Reg vice chair, Math Asn Am, 1980-82; bd dir, Northern Va Minority Bus Asn, 1989-92; Inst Elec Electronics Engrs, 1990; Joe Gibbs Charities, 1991-; Northern Va Technol Coun, 1992-; bd govs, Tower Club, 1992-95; Armed Forces Commun Electronics Asn, 1993-; bd mem, Northern Va Community Col Educ Found. **Honors/Awds:** Faculty Summer Internship, Nat Aeoronaut & Space Adm, 1981; Entrepreneur of the Year Nominee, KPMG Peat Marwick, 1991, 1992. **Special Achievements:** "General Purpose Programs for CAL/COMP Platters," IR No 69-65, 1969; "Participation in Marine Recreational Fishing, SE US, Current Fishery Statistics," No 733, 1977; "Applied Analysis Model Summaries," TR DOE/EIA 018316, 1979; Copernicus Software/Final Report, SPAWAR Contract, 1991. **Military Serv:** USN, SP4, 1959-62. **Business Phone:** (703)824-8213.

MABREY, HAROLD LEON
Military leader. **Personal:** Born May 24, 1933, Pittsburg, TX; son of Horace L and Ethelyn E Brown; married Barbara J Johnson; children: Vicki Lynn, Lesley Harold, Kevin Frank. **Educ:** Lincoln Univ, BS, Bus Admin, 1955; George Wash Univ, MBA, 1971; Indus Col, the Armed Forces, attended 1978; Harvard Univ, dipl, Nat & int security affairs, 1987. **Career:** Military leader (retired); USY Avn Res & Develop Cmdr, GM-15 suprv contract specialist & chief proc div, 1977-83, GS-14 supv contr spec, 1973-77, GS-13 supv contr spec, 1969-73, GS-12 supv contr spec, 1966-69, GS-11 supv contr spec, 1964-66, aviation systems command, 1983-86, GM-15 supv cont sp; US Army, troop sup comd, sr exec serv-04, SES-04, 1986-91, Avn Sys Cmd, GM-15, supr cont sp & div chief, 1983-86, dir proc and prod, 1985-91; Mabrey & Asn. **Orgs:** NB-MBAA; Nat Contract Mgt Asn; Minority Bus Oppor Comn; vchmn, EEO Working Group AUS, 1980; Omega Psi Phi Frat; Lincoln Univ Alumni Asn; Berea Presbyterian Church. **Honors/Awds:** Good Conduct Medal, Marksman, USY, 1955-57; Stained Sperior Prformance Award, USY Transp Cmd, 1962; Meritorous Civilian Serv Award, USY, 1970, 1976, 1977, 1980, 1991 Outstanding performance award, USY, 1971, 1977 & 1980; hono grad def adv proc mgt, USY, 1973; Cert Achievement, USY 1977 Distinguished Alumni Award, 1986; Secy Defense Superior Mg Award, 1989; Prsial Rank Meritorious Service Award, 1989 Exceptional Civilian Service Award, US Army, 1990. **Militar Serv:** USY, corpl, 1955-57. *

MABREY, PROF. MARSHA EVE
Educator, conductor (music). **Personal:** Born Nov 7, 1949 Pittsburgh, PA; daughter of Theodore R and Ella Jones. **Educ** Univ Mich Sch Music, BM, 1971, MM, 1972; Univ Cincinnati Co Conservatory Music. **Career:** Sch Music & Cincinnati Conservatory Music, asst conductor, 1973-76; Winona State Uni Symphony Orch, instr music, 1978-80; Grand Rapids Symphony Orch, asst conductor, 1980-81; Grand Valley State Col Symphony Orch, asst prof music, 1980-82; Interlochen All State Music Prog conductor All State Orchestra Concer Prog, 1982; Eugen Chamber Orch, music dir, conductor comn orchestra, 1984-91 Univ Ore Symphony Orch, asst prof music, 1982-89; Univ Or Sch Music, asst dean, 1989-91; Detroit Symphony Orchestra Hall vpres educ affairs; Philadelphia Orchestra, interim dir educ; Interlochen Nat Music Camp Mich & Encore Music Camp Pa; Detroi Symphonys African-Am Composer Forum & Symposium; Seattl Philharmonic Orchestra, music dir & conductor, 1996-2002 **Orgs:** Guest conducting Mich Youth Symphony Orch, 1977; co ordr dir, W Coast Women Conductor & Composer Symposium 1984-85; orchestra chmn, Ore Music Ed Assoc, 1984-86; keynot speaker, Ore String Teacher Assoc, 1984; guest conducting, Musi Ed Assoc All-Star Orchestras; Nat Sch Band & Orchestra Assoc Col Music Soc; Am Symphony Orchestra League; The Conductors Guild; MENC; OMEA; guest conductor, Utah All-Stat Orchestra, 1990; Savannah Symphony Orchestra, 1991; Aller Park Symphony, 1992; guest conductor, Ore Symphony, 1988 Sinfonietta Frankfort, Germany, 1988; Women's Philharmonic Vancouver Symphony (WA); San Jose Symphony (CA) Wash New World Symphony, Fla; Duke University. *

MABREY, VICKI L
Journalist. **Personal:** Born Apr 3, 1956, St Louis, MO; daughte of Harold Mabrey and Barbara; divorced. **Educ:** Howard Univ BA, Polit Sci, 1977. **Career:** WUSA-TV, Wash, DC, reporte trainee, 1982-83; WBAL-TV, Baltimore, MD, reporter, 1983-92 CBS News, corresp, 1992-95, foreign corresp, 1995-98, 6(Minutes II, corresp, 1999-05; ABC News, corresp, 2005-. **Orgs** Am Fedn TV & Radio Artists (AFTRA), 1984-. **Honors/Awds** Four Emmy Awards, 1996, 1997; Gracie Allen Award, Am Wome Radio & TV. **Business Addr:** News Correspondent, ABC news, 7 W 66th St, New York, NY 10023, **Business Phone:** (212)456-4060.*

MABRIE, HERMAN JAMES, III
Physician. **Personal:** Born Jul 10, 1948, Houston, TX; marrie Linda; children: David, Herman IV, Brent. **Educ:** Howard Univ BS 1969; Meharry Med Col, MD 1973. **Career:** Baylor Affiliate Hosp, otolaryngol, res, 1975-78, gen surg res, 1973-75; Pvt pract Otolaryngologist, currently. **Orgs:** Houston Med Forum; Alpha Phi Omega Serv Frat; The Deafness Res Found; AMA; Nat Me Asn; Harris Co Med Asn; Tex Med Asn; Am Coun Otolaryngol Houston Otolaryngol Asn. **Special Achievements:** First black otolaryngol res, Baylor Affiliated Hosp, 1975-78; One of the first 1(Nat Achievement Scholarship, 1965. **Business Addr:** Physician Herman J Mabrie III MD, 1313 Herman Dr, Houston, TX 77004.*

MABRY, EDWARD L
Educator. **Personal:** Born Nov 21, 1936, Brownsville, TN; son o Charlie and Mary Palmer. **Educ:** Millikin Univ, BA, 1966; Princeton Theol Sem, MDiv, 1969; Princeton Theol Sem, PhD, 1982 **Career:** Princeton Theol Sem, Rockerfeller fel, 1967-69; Millikir Univ, dir religious activ, 1969-70, vis prof, 1988; Princeton Theo Sem, master residence, 1970-73; NJ State Home Girls, chaplain 1971-72; Talladega Col, dir religious action & asst prof religion 1973-75; Morning Star Baptist Church Tulsa, minister educ 1975-, organist, 1975; Okla Sch Religion, dean; Richard Community Col, instr & evening coordr, 1988-90; Augustana Col, as soc prof, 1990-, chmn religion dept, 1995-, prof church hist currently. **Orgs:** Am Asn Univ Prof, 1973-; dir, Christian Edu Okla Baptist State Conv, 1975-; lifetime mem Nat Asn Advar Colored People; assoc minister, Second Baptist Church, Roc Island, IL. **Honors/Awds:** Student Senate Appreciation Award Talladega Col, 1974; Swank Prize in Homiletics, Princeton Theo Sem. **Military Serv:** AUS, sp4, 1960-63. **Business Addr:** Professor of Church History, Augustana College, 639 38th St, Roc Island, IL 61201.

MABRY, MATTIE
Association executive. **Career:** Haven Acres Neighborhood Asn vpres, pres, currently; Tupelo Neighborhood Asn Coun, past pres vpres, currently. **Orgs:**. **Business Addr:** Vice President, Tupel Neighborhood Association Council, Department Of Planning & Community Development, 71 E Troy St, PO Box 1485, Tupelo MS 38802, **Business Phone:** (662)841-6510.*

MABSON, GLENN T
Manager. **Personal:** Born Feb 23, 1940, Tulsa, OK; son of Lowel and Ozella; married; children: Athena, Darvell, Kimberly &

Daniel. **Educ:** Calif Inst Technol, BEE, 1966; Nat Tech Sch, MS, 1968. **Career:** MGM/Sony Studios, prod sound mixer, 1968-75; Burbank Studios, prod sound mixer; 20th Cent Fox, West La, prod sound mixer; Paramount Studios, prod sound mixer; NBC News, prod sound mixer; CBS News, prod sound mixer; ABC News, prod sound mixer; Universal Studios, prod sound mixer; Mabson Audio Eng, Hawaii, prod sound mixer, currently. **Orgs:** Epileptic Found Maui, pres & exec dir. **Honors/Awds:** Community Leader of Achievement of Volunteers. **Special Achievements:** First African American to be in charge of production sound for a motion picture TV series; First African American to be hired as a Production Audio Engineer in the TV industry; First African American to produce a perfect sound track for a TV series; Emmy Winner "Reflections," 1981; First person to produce a perfect sound track for a motion picture "Car Wash," 1981; "The Greatest, Muhammed Ali Story," 1982. **Business Addr:** Prod Sound Mixer, Mabson Audio Engineering, Kihei, HI 96753, **Business Phone:** (808)879-8999.

MAC, BERNIE (BERNARD JEFFREY MCCOLLOUGH)
Actor, comedian. **Personal:** Born Oct 5, 1958, Chicago, IL; married Rhonda McCullough; children: J. **Career:** Live performance: Original Kings of Comedy, comedian; Films: Mo' Money; Above the Rim, 1994; House Party 3, 1994; Friday, 1995; The Player's Club, 1998; Life, 1999; The Original Kings of Comedy, actor, writer, 2000; What's the Worst That Could Happen?, 2001; Oceans 11, 2001; Head of State, 2003; Charlies Angels 2, 2003; Lil' Pimp, 2003; Bad Santa, 2003; Mr 3000, 2004; Ocean's Twelve, 2004; The Dinner Party, 2005; Inspector Gadget's Biggest Caper Ever, 2005; Pride, 2007; Ocean's Thirteen, 2007; Transformers, 2007; Television: Moesha, recurring role, 1996-2001; HBO, Don King: Only In America, 1997; Def Comedy Jam, comedian, host; The Bernie Mac Show, producer, 2005-06; Hall of Fame, 2002; Racist Dawg, 2003; Episode #28.16, 2003; Bar Mitzvah Crashers, 2006; The Whole Truth, Nothing But the Truth, So Help Me Mac, writer, producer, 2008. **Honors/Awds:** Screen Actors Guild Award, Best TV Actor-Comedy, 2002; Golden Globe Award, Best Actor in a TV Series-Musical or Comedy, 2003; Golden Globe Award, Best Actor-Musical or Comedy, 2003; Peabody Award; TV Critics Assn Award; Nat Asn Advan Colored People Image Award, 2003. **Special Achievements:** Auth: I Ain't Scared of You, MTV/Pocket Books, 2001; Maybe You Never Cry Again, Regan Books/HarperCollins, 2003. **Business Phone:** (310)273-6700.

MACK, ALLY FAYE
School administrator, college administrator. **Personal:** Born Apr , 1943, Marthaville, LA; married Robert; children: Robert III, Ryan, Renfred & Jessica. **Educ:** Grambling State Univ, BA, 1963; Atlanta Univ, MA, 1964; Tex A&M Univ, further study, 1971; Univ So, MS, PhD, 1979. **Career:** Prairie View A&M Univ, asst prof, 1968-69; Tex A&M Univ, instr, 1969-71; Langston Univ, asst prof, 1971-74; Jackson State Univ, acting chairperson, chair & dir int progs, 1993-, dept polit sci, prof, currently. **Orgs:** Hinds Co Dem Exec Domm, 1975-; MS Health Systems Agency State Brd, 1978-79;Consult, Tenn Valley Authority, 1979-; trainer, Nat Womens Educ Fund,1980-; dist chair, Dem Women, 1982-. **Honors/Awds:** Citizen Participation Award, Plaque Nat Assn Advan Colored People, 1977;Public Service Award, Fannie Lou Hamer Award, 1980. **Business Addr:** Professor, Director of International Programs, Jackson State University, Office of International Programs, 1400 J R Lynch St, PO Box 17103, Jackson, MS 39217-0103, **Business Phone:** (601)979-3791.

MACK, DR. ASTRID KARONA
Educator, colonial administrator. **Personal:** Born Aug 21, 1935, Daytona Beach, FL; son of Meta Marietta Mack; divorced; children: Astrid Kyle & Kristen Nichole. **Educ:** Bethune-Cookman Col, BS, magna cum laude, 1960; Univ Minn, MS, zoology, 1965; Mich State Univ, PhD, human genetics, 1974. **Career:** Dade Co Fla Pub Schs, teacher, biol & chem, 1960-66; Miami-Dade Community Col, instr asst prof, 1966-73; Univ Miami Sch Med, Miller Sch Med, asst assoc prof, res assoc prof, currently, Sickle Cell Clin Ctr, assoc dean minority affairs, currently. **Orgs:** Am Soc Human Genetics, 1969-; AAAS, 1974-; Am Genetics Asn, 1978-; exec dir, Dade Co Sickle Cell Found, 1978-; first five dist rep, Omega Psi Phi Fraternity Inc, 1982-85; dist rep, Omega Psi Phi Fraternity Inc, 1985-89. **Honors/Awds:** Clay Hamilton Memorial Hope Award, Human Services Coalition Miami. **Military Serv:** AUS, sp5, 1955-58. **Business Addr:** Associate Dean of Minority Affairs, Research Associate Professor, University of Miami, Sickle Cell Clinical Center, 2010B Zanetti Bldg 794 NW 18th St, Miami, FL 33136, **Business Phone:** (305)243-6924.

MACK, C.
Banker, vice president (organization), manager. **Personal:** Born Mar 8, 1959, Canton, OH; son of Henry Mack; married Tenetia, Sep 21, 1985; children: Lauren, Sean, Ryan. **Educ:** Univ Cincinnati, BA, 1982; Ind Univ, MBA, 1984. **Career:** Consortium Grad Study Mgt fel, 1983; Procter & Gamble, brand mgr, 1984-91; Ryder Syst Inc, dir consumer trade rental mkt, 1991-92, group dir consumer truck mkt & mkt serv, 1992-93, vpres consumer truck rental mkt, 1994, vpres worldwide, 1994-96; Citibank FSB, sr vpres branch sales & opers, 1986-97; Citibank FSB, pres & chief exec officer, 1997-03; JP Morgan Chase & Co, exec vpres & retail banking exec, 2003-; Retail Bank, PNC Financial Serv Group, exec vpres & dep mgr. **Orgs:** Bd dirs, Nat Black MBA Asn, 1987-95; co-chair, Super Bowl Mkt Comt, 1995; prin & co-chair, Chicago United, Econ Develop Comt, 1997-; bus advisory coun, Chicago Urban League, 1997-; Lincoln Found Bus Excellence, bd trustees, 1997-; Neighborhood Housing Serv Chicago, Leadership Comt, 1997-; bd mem, Steppenwolf Theatre, 1997-; advisory coun, DePaul Univ, Col Com, 1997-; fel Indiana Univ, Kelley Sch Bus, 1998. **Honors/Awds:** Keepers of the Flame, Black Enterprise Mag, 1997. **Special Achievements:** Speaks fluent German and Portuguese. **Business Addr:** Executive Vice President, Retail Banking Executive, JP Morgan Chase Bank, 270 Park Ave, New York, NY 10017, **Business Phone:** (212)270-6000.*

MACK, CHARLES RICHARD
Educator. **Personal:** Born Oct 2, 1942, Clarke County, GA; married Joan Jacqueline Thomas. **Educ:** Univ Ga, BS, MEd. **Career:** Clarke County Sch Syst, teacher, asst prin; Macedonia Baptist Church, Athens, GA, Baptist minister; City Athens, ward alderman. **Orgs:** Vpres, Clarke Chap Nat Asn Advan Colored People; CCAE; GEA; Nat Educ Asn; secy, NE Ga Baptist Ministerial Union; vpres, 8 Dist Gen Missionary Baptist Conv Ga; secy, 8th Dist Layman Group; pres elect, Clarke County Asn Educators; Phi Beta Kappa. **Special Achievements:** First African-American elected to Athens City Council in 1974.

MACK, CLEVELAND J., SR.
Chief executive officer. **Personal:** Born Dec 5, 1912, Alabama; married Mary Holly; children: Cleveland Jr, Mary & Clarence. **Career:** Detroit, MI, contractor; C J Mack Improvement Co, owner. **Orgs:** Asn Gen Contractors Am; Met Contract Asn; BTWBA; Urban League; Prince Hall Masons. **Honors/Awds:** MCA Award, Contractor of Year, 1973; laid out & poured found, The Renaissance Ctr, 1974; businessman of year, BTWBA, 1975; man of year Award, State MI Dept Com, 1976; listed, Top 100 Business of Nation, 1977. **Business Phone:** (313)931-0624.

MACK, DANIEL J
Executive. **Career:** Mutual Benefit Life Insurance Co Inc, Richmond, VA, chief exec.

MACK, DR. DEBORAH L
Consultant, administrator. **Educ:** Univ Chicago, BS, geog; Northwestern Univ, MA, PhD, anthrop. **Career:** Schomburg Ctr Res Black Cult, New York, consult; Nat Mus Am Hist, consult; Nat Mus Natural Hist, consult; Smithsonian Inst, Wash, consult; Chicago Hist Soc, consult; Ill State Bd Educ, consult; Mus Int Folk Art, Santa Fe, NM, consult; UNESCO, Paris, consult; His Mus, Senegal, consult; Palace Mus, Cameroon, consult; Orgn Mundo Afro, Uruguay; Nat Underground RR Freedom Ctr, Cincinnati, OH, mgr, 2003; Northwestern Univ, res assoc & curator; Terranova Pictures, chief sci consult, currently. **Orgs:** Asn African Am Mus; McIntosh Sustainable Environ & Econ Develop; Smithsonian Coun.

MACK, DR. DEBORAH LYNN
Consultant, curator. **Educ:** Univ Chicago, BA, geog, 1976; Northwestrn Univ, MA, anthrop, 1977, PhD, anthrop, 1986. **Career:** Sociol & Anthrop, Lake Forest Col, asst prof, 1986-88; Northwestern Univ, vis scholar, 1988-89; Sch Art Inst Chicago, vis asst prof, 1989-90; Field Mus Natural Hist, proj dir, sr exhibit developer, 1990-95; Field Mus, resassoc, dept anthrop; Northwestern Univ, res assoc & curator, 1996-; Mus Acad Consult, currently; Terranova Pictures, chief sci consult, currently. **Orgs:** AFA Mus Asn; African Studies Asn; Am Anthrop Asn; Asn Am Mus; US Comt, Int Comt Mus; Mus Group; adv coun, McIntosh Sustainable Environ & Econ Develop, Ga; adv bd, Smithsonian Coun; adv bd, McIntosh SEED. **Honors/Awds:** Illinois State Scholarship, 1970-74; Fellowship, Univ Chicago, 1970-74;Ralph Bunche Fellow, United Nations Asn, 1974-75; Fellowship, North westernUniv, 1976-77; Fulbright-Hays, US Dept Educ, Group Proj Abroad, 1988; Nat Endowment for the Humanities, Field Mus Africa Exhibit, 1992. **Special Achievements:** The Beni Amer," Greenwood Press, 1984; Film Review of "The South-East Nuba," Am Anthropologist, 1986.

MACK, DONALD J
Publisher. **Personal:** Born Jun 1, 1937, Port Arthor, TX; married Gussie L Vinson; children: Todd. **Educ:** Lamar State Col, BS, 1963. **Career:** Tex Univ, teacher, 1964-66; Galveston Co, Calif, asst dir, 1966-67; Neighborhood Action Inc, dir, 1967-72; Community Action Agency, dir, 1972-74; Ft Worth Ctr Ex-offenders Inc, exec dir; Ebony Mart, publisher. **Orgs:** Chmn, Neighborhood Action Apts, 1973-; bd mem, Conf Christians & Jews, 1974-; Leadership Ft Worth, 1974-. **Honors/Awds:** Certificate of Merit, Community Action Agency; Certificate of Accomplishment, Criminal Justice Syst; Certificate of Completion, Leadership Inst Community Develop. **Military Serv:** USN.

MACK, FAITE
Military leader. **Personal:** Born Jan 8, 1919, Stratham, GA; married Katie; children: Faite Jr, Phillip & Gregory. **Educ:** Wilson Jr Col, 1951; Aircraft & Engine Mech Course, grad, 1942 & 48; Army Helicopter Mech Course, 1956; Multi-engine Single-rotor Helicopter Mech Course, 1966; Air Frame Repair Extension Course, 1962; Shop-Foreman Sch, 1971; Leadership & Personnel Mgt Extensions Course, 1971; UH1 Extension Course, 1971; Radiol Monitoring Course, 1971; Command & Gen Staff Col, 1973; numerous other mil courses. **Career:** AUS, master sgt, 1942-; Ill Army Nat Guard, 1947; Sr Aircraft Mech; Communs Chief; Sec Leader; Platoon Sgt; Tech Inspector; Sr Flight Ops Chief; Battalion Sgt Major; Command Sgt Major, current assign, Nov, 1975; Gov Dan Walker, selected as aide promoted to Bird Col; Gov James RT hompson Gov, Ill Mil Aide, personal staff, 1977; Army Aviation Maintenance Shop, civilian aircraft maintenance supvr, 25 yrs; Ill & Army Aviation Support Facility; Midway Airport; Ill Army Nat Guard, racial relat recruiting & retention specialist, charge minority affairs mil, recruiting & human rels. **Orgs:** Pres, Ill Nat Guard Non-Command Officer Asn; Bd Elimination Racial Imbalance, Ill Nat Guard. **Honors/Awds:** Recipent, Am Theatre Ribbon; European, African, Middle Eastern Theatre Ribbon with 4 Bronze Stars; Good Conduct Medal; Victory Medal WW II;Rome-Arno Campaign; N Appennines Campaign; PO Valley Campaign; State of ILLong & Hon Serv Medal; State Active Duty Ribbon 9th Award; Sr Air Crewman Badge.

MACK, FRED CLARENCE
Financial manager. **Personal:** Born Sep 1, 1940, Elloree, SC; married Mildred Elaine Oliver; children: Lennie B, Keith O, Erika L & Fred S. **Educ:** SC state Col, BS, 1973. **Career:** Utica Tool Co, leadman, 1968-72; NC Mutual Insurance Co, debit mgr, 1970-73; Family Health Center, Inc, assoc dir, 1973-85; Orangeburg County Council, vice-chmn. **Orgs:** Exec bd, Nat Asn Advan Colored Peopel Bowman Br, 1960-85; Antioch Baptist Church, Treasurer, 1970-85, chmn & Deacon, 1983-85; Political Action Concerned Citizen Dist 94, 1972-85; Chamber of Commerce, 1980; OCAAB Community Service Agency, 1983-85; Advisor bd, Orangeburg-Calhoun Tec Col, 1983-85. **Business Addr:** Vice Chairman, Orangeburg County Council, PO Box 1125, Orangeburg, SC 29115.

MACK, GLADYS WALKER
Government official. **Personal:** Born Feb 26, 1934, Rock Hill, SC; daughter of Zenith Walker and Henrietta Alexander; married Julius Mack, Jan 25, 1958; children: Geofrey, Kenneth & Johnathan. **Educ:** Morgan State Univ, Baltimore MD, BS, 1955; Catholic Univ Am, Washington DC, 1958. **Career:** Urban Renewal Admin Housing & Home Finance Agency, Wash, DC, budget analyst, 1955-65; Off Econ Opportunity, VISTA Prog, Wash, DC, budget analyst, 1965-67, prog anal officer, 1967-69; Exec Off Mayor, Wash, DC, sr budget analyst, 1969-72; Wash Tech Inst, Wash, DC, dir budget & finance, 1972-75; Exec Off Mayor, Wash, DC, dep budget dir, 1975-78, actg dir, 1978-79, asst city admin, 1979-82, dir Off Policy & Prog Evaluation, 1983-85, gen asst mayor, 1985-86; DC Bd Parole, Wash, DC, chairperson, 1986-91; Wash Metrop Area Transit Authority, chmn bd, currently. **Orgs:** Pres, Asn Paroling Authorities Int; dep exec dir, United Planning Orgn; Am Pub Transp Asn; Am Correctional Asn; Mid Atlantic States Correctional Asn; Delta Sigma Theta. **Business Phone:** (202)962-1234.

MACK, GORDON H. See Obituaries section.

MACK, JAMES KEVIN. See MACK, KEVIN.

MACK, JOAN
Journalist, association executive. **Personal:** Born Nov 23, 1943, Charleston, SC; daughter of Alonzo Gladden and Harriet Robinson Gladden; married Charles Henry; children: Dandria, Charles & Kashauna. **Educ:** SC State Univ, BS, biol, 1964; City Col NY, cert, 1965. **Career:** Manpower Training & Devel Ctr, teacher, 1970-72; WCSC TV-5 Charleston SC, pub serv dir/TV hostess, 1972-77; WCBD-TV Channel 2, Charleston SC, news reporter, 1977-84; Col Charleston, media resources coord, adj prof, asst dir col rel & media commun, dir admin & host/producer, currently. **Orgs:** Am Women Radio & TV, 1972-80; bd mem, Mayor's Comm Handicapped, 1976-80; March Dimes, 1976-80; Charles Webb Ctr Crippled C, 1977-80; Gov Comm Phys Fitness, 1980; Nat Fed Press Women, 1983-85; ITVA, 1986-87; Charleston County Heart Asn, 1986-87; speakers bureau, YWCA; Charleston County Substance Abuse Comn, 1987-; pub relations comn, YMCA Auxiliary, 1988-. **Honors/Awds:** Communications Award, Omega Psi Phi Fraternity, 1974; Voluntary Service Award, United Negro Col Fund, 1974; Sch Bell Awards, SC Educ Asn, 1975-76 & 1979; Outstanding Young Woman of America, 1977, 1978; YWCA Tribute to Women in Industry Award, 1981; Women Broadcast Award, SC Comn, 1981; Nat Federation of Press Women Award, 1983; Silver Reel Awards, Int TV Asn, 1986, Merit Award, 1988; Communicators Award, Carolina Asn Bus, 1987; Papal Award, "Pro Ecelesia Pontifice", 1999; Southern Regional EMMY Award, 2001. **Business Addr:** Director of Administration, Host/Producer, College of Charleston, College Relations and Media Communications, Rm 210 25 St Philip St, Charleston, SC 29401, **Business Phone:** (843)953-8168.

MACK, JOHN L.
Educator, government official. **Personal:** Born Jul 25, 1942, Philadelphia, PA; son of Norman Mack and Catherine Mack; mar-

ried Bettie Taylor; children: Monica, Michael, Mark & Gwendolyn. **Educ:** Mass Inst Technol, BS, 1973; Suffolk Univ, MBA, 1978; Univ Tex, postgrad, int finance, 1980. **Career:** Personel staff rec, 1974-75; Mass Inst Technol, assoc dir admin, 1975-78; Univ Providence RI, assoc dir admin, 1978-79; Sonicraft, Chicago, dept prog mgr control, 1980-82; US State Dept Wash Dc, admin officer, 1982-83;US Embassy Abidjan Ivory Coast, admin officer, 1983-85; US Embassy Paris France, mgt officer, 1985-87; US State Dept, Wash Dc, Regional Admin Mgt Ctrs, coordr, 1987-; Mass Inst Technol, fel; House Foreign Affairs Comt, staff consult. **Orgs:** Election consult, Fed Dearborn Proj; bd dir & pres, Cambridge Community Ctr; Mass Inst Technol Community Serv Fund; chmn, Mass Inst Technol Urban Act Comn; Mass Inst Technol Res Training Adv Comn; bd dir, Hope Housing; co-chmn, Mass Inst Technol Black Stud Union; Mass Inst Technol Task Force Educ Opportunity; Int Asn Fin Planners; Int Asn Black Prof Foreign Affairs. **Honors/Awds:** American Spirit Medal of Honor. **Special Achievements:** Selected as Outstanding Young American, Jaycees, 1977. **Military Serv:** USN elec, petty off, 1961-66.

MACK, JOHN W.
Civil rights activist. **Personal:** Born Jan 6, 1937, Kingstree, SC; married Harriett Johnson; children: Anthony, Deborah, Andria. **Educ:** NC A&T Univ, BS, appl sociol; Atlanta Univ, MSW. **Career:** Camarillo St Hosp, P SW, 1960-64; Urban League Flint, MI, exec dir, 1964-69; Los Angeles Urban League, pres, 1969-. **Orgs:** Leader, Atlanta Stud Civil Rights Protest, 1960; co-founder/vice chmn, Comt Appeal Human Rights, 1960; co-founder & Co-chair, La Black Leadership Coalt educ, 1977; bd mem, KCET-TV-CHANNEL 28, 1975-; vpres, United Way Corp Coun Execs, 1984; bd mem, La County & County Pvt Ind Coun, 1983. **Honors/Awds:** Mary McCleod Bethune, Nat Coun Negro Women, 1984; Outstanding Public Service Award, Asn Black Law Enforcement Exec, 1984; La Basin Equal Opport League, 1984; La Bd Zoning Applications, 1984; Calif's Atty Gen John Van DeCamp's Racila, Ethnic, Rel & Minority Violence Comt. **Business Addr:** President, Los Angeles Urban League, 3450 Mount Vernon Dr, Los Angeles, CA 90008.

MACK, JULIA COOPER
Judge. **Personal:** Born in Fayetteville, NC; widowed; children: Cheryl. **Educ:** Hampton Inst, BS, 1940; Howard Univ, LLB, 1951. **Career:** Dept Justice, trial atty appellate sect criminal div, 1954-58; EEO Comm, assoc gen coun, 1968-73, dep gen coun, 1973-75; DC Ct Appeals, assoc judge, sr judge, currently. **Orgs:** Women's Law Soc. **Honors/Awds:** Nominee Fed Women's Award, 1969; EEOC Award for Distinguished Service, 1971; Outstanding Fed Career Lawyer Justice Tom C Clark Award, 1974; Alumnus of Yr Howard Univ, Law Alumni Asn, 1975; Distinguished Alumnus Award, Hampton Inst, 1976; Hon Mem AKA Sorority; Nat Bar Asn Distinguished Jurist Award, 1980; Howard Univ Award, Distinguished Postgraduate Achievement, 1981. **Business Addr:** Senior Judge, DC Court Appeals, 500 Indiana Ave NW, Washington, DC 20001.*

MACK, KEVIN (JAMES KEVIN MACK)
Football player. **Personal:** Born Aug 9, 1962, Kings Mountain, NC; son of Calvin and Mary Francis; married Ava Bassett, May 31, 1986. **Educ:** Clemson Univ. **Career:** Football player (retired); USFL, Los Angeles Express, running back, 1984; Cleveland Browns, running back, 1985-93. **Honors/Awds:** Co-Most Valuable Player of Year, Akron Browns' Backers; named in hon, Kevin Mack Day, Hometown Kings Mountain; NFL Offensive Rookie of Year, Football Digest; AFC Rookie of Year, UPI; first team, UPI NFL All-Rookie squad; first team, Football Digest All Star team; Most Valuable Player, Cleveland TD Club; PFWA All Rookie team; AFC Offensive Player of the Week, 1985; broke Jim Brown's rookie rushing rec; Pro Bowl team, 1986, 1988. **Special Achievements:** Drafted by the Cleveland Browns in the 1st round (11th overall) of the 1984 Supplemental Draft. *

MACK, LEVORN
Government official. **Career:** Town McBee, SC, town councilman, mayor, currently. **Orgs:** Nat Conf Black Mayors. **Special Achievements:** First African American mayor in Chesterfield County, SC. **Business Addr:** Mayor, Town McBee, PO Box 248, McBee, SC 20101, **Business Phone:** (803)335-8474.*

MACK, LURENE KIRKLAND
School administrator. **Personal:** Born May 20, 1948, Graceville, FL; married Robert Eastmon Mack; children: Uhura Jamal & Niesha Rochet. **Educ:** Miami Dade Community Col, AA, 1970; Barry Col, BS, 1982. **Career:** Dade County, consumer protection agent, 1970-74; Dade County Schs, investr, 1974-79, area supvr, 1980-; Early Advantage Kindergarden Inc, Miami, FL, pres, 1980-. **Orgs:** Nat Asn Advan Colored People, 1979-; Youth Crime Watch Adv Bd, 1982-; Black Pub Admin Asn, 1983-; exec bd, YEW, 1984-; vpres, NOBLE-FL Chap Sect 6, 1984-. **Military Serv:** AUS, sp4, 4 yrs. **Home Addr:** 18635 NW 38th Ave, Opa Locka, FL 33055. **Business Addr:** Area Supervisor, Dade County School Board, 2210 SW 3rd St, Miami, FL 33135.

MACK, LUTHER W, JR.
Restaurateur. **Personal:** Born May 7, 1939, Sun Flower, MS; son of Luther and Frances Mack; married Eugeni Mack, Aug 26, 1978; children: Janelle Mack. **Educ:** Univ Nevada, Reno; LaSalle Univ. **Career:** State Nev, dept employ security, 1968, job coordr, 1969, dept hwy, equal opportunity coordr, 1970; US Small Bus Admin, dep contract compliance officer, 1971; McDonald's, owner, operator of 11 franchises, 1974-; Boyd Gaming corp, dir, 2003-; Washoe Med Hosp Health Plan, bd dir, currently; Nev Cancer Inst, bd dir, currently; Wells Fargo Bank Nev, Community Bd, currently. **Orgs:** Bd trustees, chmn affirmative action comn, chmn archit rev comn, Airport Authority Washoe County; comnr, chmn, 2001-03, Nev State Athletic Comn; bd dir, budget comn, found comn, chmn, 1997-98, Univ Nev, Reno. **Honors/Awds:** Civic Leader of the Year, Raymond I Smith, 1990; Appreciation Award, Reno Police Dept; Ronald McDonald Awards, San Francisco Region McDonald's; Humanitarian Award, Nat Conf Christians & Jews, 1984; Distinguished Nevadan Award, Univ Nev, Reno; Honorary Doctorate Degree, Univ Nev, Reno, 1998. **Home Addr:** 35 Cassas Ct, Reno, NV 89502. **Business Addr:** Director, Boyd Gaming Corporate Office, 2950 Indust Rd, Las Vegas, NV 89109, **Business Phone:** (702)792-7200.

MACK, MELVIN
Government official, mayor. **Personal:** Born May 28, 1949, Laurel, MS; son of Roger and Lennie; married Doneater Mack, Feb 19, 1972; children: Trina. **Educ:** Meridian County Col, AA, 1970; MS Valley State Univ, BS, 1972; Jackson State Univ, MS, 1979. **Career:** Cent State Univ, Univ Ctr, dir; MS Valley State Univ, asst basketball coach; Ellisville State Sch, staff develop dir; Laurel City, coun; Jones County, supvr; City Laurel, mayor, currently. **Orgs:** Omega Psi Phi Fraternity; MS Asn Supervisors; pres, Laurel High Sch Booster Club. **Honors/Awds:** Omega Man of the Year, twice; Outstanding Young Man of the Year. **Special Achievements:** First African American mayor of Laurel in 2005. **Home Addr:** 2059 Airport Dr, Laurel, MS 39440, **Home Phone:** (601)649-4359. **Business Phone:** (601)428-6401.*

MACK, NATE
Association executive. **Personal:** Born Oct 15, 1956, Detroit, MI; son of Uler Mack and Dorothy; married Jamie Baker; children: Ramone. **Educ:** Wayne State Univ, Detroit, MI, BS, Mgt. **Career:** Syntex Labs, Palo Alto, CA, sales rep, 1979-84; Glaxo Inc, Res Triangle Park, NC, sales, 1984-89; Coalesce, co-founder; Centrifuge, pres, currently. **Home Addr:** 337 Kimberly Ct, Atlanta, GA 30311. **Business Addr:** President, Centrifuge, Atlanta, GA.

MACK, PEARL WILLIE
Educator. **Personal:** Born Aug 16, 1941, Laurel, MS; daughter of Sammie Gilmer and Delia Ann Jones Moncrief; married Tommie Lee; children: Dwayne. **Educ:** Ill State Univ, BA, 1962; Roosevelt Univ, attented; Governor's State Univ, MA, 1975. **Career:** Teacher (retired); Harvey Educ Asn, teacher, 1962-71, treas, 1971-75,chair grievance comn; Ill Educ Asn, resolutions comn, 1972-74; Ill Educ Asn & Nat Educ Asn, teacher; Women's Caucus, planning comn; MinorityCaucus, chairperson 1974-75; Nat Educ Asn, exec comn, 1987-87, chairelections comn, 1987-89, chairperson special community black concerns. **Orgs:** Pol Action Comn Ill Educ Asn, 1975-; bd mem, Nat Educ Asn, 1975-; Pol Action Comn, Nat Educ Asn, 1976-; bd dir, World Confederation Org Teaching Prof, 1976, 1978, 1984, 1986; Grievance Com Harvey Educ Asn, 1977-; PUSH,Nat Asn Advan Colored People, Gov State Univ Alumni Asn, 1977; deleg, Dem Nat Conv, 1980; Coalition Labor Union Women, 1980-; Women Arts, 1984-; Citizens Utility Bd, 1984-; del rep, Nat Educ Asn. **Special Achievements:** Top 100 Outstanding Women in Education, Nat Educ Asn, 1975; co-writer Mini-grant Proposal for Cultural Studies Program, 1974-75; Intl Bus & Prof Women, Dollars & Sense Magazine 1987.

MACK, PHYLLIS GREEN
Librarian. **Personal:** Born Jul 1, 1941, Charleston, WV; daughter of Leroy Stanley Green and Gladys Webster Green; married Arnold Rudolph Mack (died 1989); children: Stephanie Michele Mack & Nicole Renee Mack. **Educ:** WVa State Col, BS, educ, 1963; Pratt Inst Grad Sch Libr Sci, MLS, 1967; Columbia Univ Sch Libr Serv, cert advan librarianship, 1985; NY Univ, NY real estate salesperson cert, 2003. **Career:** Librarian (retired); NY Pub Libr, clerk, 1963-65, librn trainee & librn, 1966-68, sr br librn & sr first asst, 1968-73, supv br librn, 1973-83, Cent Harlem Region, regional librn, 1984-2002; Hunter Col Libr, jr libr asst, 1965-66; Columbia Univ, doctoral fel, 1983-84. **Orgs:** St Marks United Methodist Church, 1963-; Black Caucus-Am Libr Asn, 1980-; Upper Manhattan Rotary Club Int, 1988-; first vpres, Delta Sigma Theta Inc, N Manhattan Alumnae Chap, 1989-93; chair, Community Bd 10 Manhattan, 1989-90; trustee, Sch Bd, Dist 5, NY, 1997-98; NY Black Librn Caucus. **Honors/Awds:** Special Performance Award, NY Pub Lib, 1988; Citation for Community Service, New York City Coun, 1990; Dr Charles A Wahlburg Service Award, Cent Harlem Meals Wheels, 2001. **Home Addr:** 1901 Madison Ave, New York, NY 10035, **Home Phone:** (212)426-6961.

MACK, RODERICK O
Manager. **Personal:** Born Jul 30, 1955, Birmingham, AL; son of Edward and Irene; married Votura E Hendeson; children: Amrette, Shanta, Roderick Jr & Tamarka. **Educ:** Miles Col, Birmingham, AL, BS, acct, 1977; Jefferson St Jr Col, Birmingham, AL, AAS finance, 1981; Samford Univ, Birmingham, AL, MBA, 1981 **Career:** Liberty Nat Life Ins Co, acct intern, 1975-76; Emergenc Sch Aid Act, tutor, 1976-77; Am S Bank NA Birmingham, cor acct officer 1977-85; Am Inst Banking, instr, 1982-83; Mack & Assoc, sr managing owner, 1982-; Southern Junior Col Bus, inst 1986; Miles Col, Birmingham AL, instr, 1991. **Orgs:** Treas, Na Black MBA Asn, Birmingham Chap, 1985-87, pres 1988-89; treas Family & Child Servs A United Way Agency, 1985-87; pres Birmingham Minority Bus Adv Community, 1986-88; co-chai Youth Leadership Forum Birmingham, 1987; Edward Lee Norton Bd Adv Mgt & Prof Educ, Birmingham-Southern Col, 1990-93 adv comt, Birmingham Pub Schs Bus Educ, 1992-95; assoc di Nat Asn Accts Birmingham Vulcan Chap; Inst Mgt Accts Birmingham Inter Prof Asn; Nat Soc Tax Prof; Birmingham As Urban Planners. **Honors/Awds:** Outstanding Member Award, Na Asn Accts, 1983, 1985; Member of the Year, Nat Black MBA As Birmingham Chap, 1987; Presidents Award, Birmingham Ass Urban Bankers, 1993. **Home Addr:** 801 Graymont Ave W Birmingham, AL 35204. **Business Addr:** Senior Managin Owner, Mack & Associates, 801 Graymont Ave W, Birminghan AL 35204-3923, **Business Phone:** (205)787-2870.

MACK, RUDY EUGENE
Airplane pilot. **Personal:** Born Feb 9, 1941, Miami, FL; son c Flossie M Mack; married Denise, Jan 13, 2000; children: Rudy J Derek, Maurice & Jason; married; children: Angie & Brandon **Educ:** Tenn A&I, BS, 1967. **Career:** Airplane Pilot (retired) Prudential, inst agt 1967-71; Burnside OTT, flight instr, 1968-71 Northwest Airlines, capt; TAB Express Airline Inc, Turbine & Sir Instr. **Orgs:** Airline Pilot Asn; co-chmn com rel com, The Airlin Pilot Union; aeromed chmn Orgn Black Airline Pilot. **Honors Awds:** Orgn Black Airline Pilot ACE Camps Dirs Award, 1999 01; Parent Appreciation Award, 1999-01. **Home Addr:** 642 Chestnut Hill Rd, Flowery Branch, GA 30542, **Home Phone** (770)967-2645.

MACK, SHANE LEE
Baseball player. **Personal:** Born Dec 7, 1963, Los Angeles, CA **Career:** Baseball player (retired); San Diego Padres, outfielde 1987-88; Minn Twins, 1990-94; Yomiuri Giants, 1994-97; Bosto Red Sox, 1997; Oakland Athletics, 1998; Kans City Royals outfielder, 1998. **Honors/Awds:** American League Pennant, 1991 World Series Champion, 1991; UCLA Athletic Hall of Fame 2002.

MACK, SYLVIA JENKINS
School administrator. **Personal:** Born Dec 22, 1931, Deal Island MD; daughter of Violet Armstrong Jenkins and William E Jenkins; widowed; children: Alphonso L, Michael L, Don Frederick Thomas Everett & Anthony Charles. **Educ:** Newman Col, BS prof educ; Certified Trade & Indust Inst, Del State Bd Educ; S Joseph Univ Philadelphia PA, MS, prof educ. **Career:** Del Stat Bd Cosmetology, licensed cosmetologist, licensed cosmetol inst New Castle Co Sch Dist, voc instr, 1970-93; Mas Aivlis Acad Cosmetol & Barbering, owner & curator, currently. **Orgs:** Brandywine Prof Asn; bd mem, Brandywine Sch Dist Del, 1981-89; b mem, Nat Asn Black Sch; vpres, Brandywine Sch Dist Bd Educ Nat Asn Univ Women; life mem, Nat Asn Advan Colored People Nat Polit Cong Black Women; pres, Moss-Robertson Auxiliary vol, Del Veterans Nursing Ctr. **Business Addr:** Owner, Mas Aivli Academy of Cosmetology & Barbering, 216 E 22nd St, Wilmington, DE 19802, **Business Phone:** (302)652-7370.

MACK, TREMAIN
Football player. **Personal:** Born Nov 21, 1974, Tyler, TX. **Educ** Univ Fla, Miami. **Career:** Football player (retired); Cincinna Bengals, defensive back, 1997-2000. **Honors/Awds:** Pro Bowl 1999.

MACK, WILBUR OLLIO
Educator. **Personal:** Born Aug 11, 1919, Seward, OK; son of Addie Lowe Mack and Collister Mack; married Julia Hobb (deceased); children: Ronald Wilbur, Waymond Ollio, Larr Wayne, Wilma Denise & Meltonia; married Martha Griffin, Au 11, 1970 (deceased). **Educ:** Langston Univ, BS, 1947; Okla Stat Univ, MS, 1954. **Career:** Educator (retired); Prairie View Col, assoc prof, 1953-57; Southern Univ Baton Rouge, assoc prof, 1957-62; Fla Agr & Mech Univ, Tallahassee, asst prof engineering 1962-89. **Orgs:** Agri engr, ASAE, 1955-; Soil & Crop Society 1970-; regist prof engr, Tex; Am Soc Engrs; Nat Safety Cour Kappa Alpha Psi; Mason 32 degree. **Military Serv:** AUS 1st 1941-45. **Home Addr:** 7033 Swamflower Dr N, Jacksonville, F 32244.

MACK, WILHELMENA
Hospital administrator, chief executive officer, presiden (organization). **Personal:** Born Oct 1, 1951, Kendall, FL; daughte of Eugene and Gladys Terry; divorced; children: Shanno Lynnette. **Educ:** Univ Miami, BA, 1972, MEd, 1973; Fla Atlanti Univ, EdS, 1983, Ed.D, 1988. **Career:** Dade County, personnel officer, 1973-74; Jackson Memorial Health care Syst,personnel officer, 1974-75, educ coordr, 1975-78; Memorial Healthcare Sys asst dir for mgmt training, 1978-79, training & develop dir, 197

ight Mgmt Consults, vpres consulting Servs; N Broward Hosp ist, vpres, chief human resource officer; W Mack & Assocs Inc, o & pres, 2004-. **Orgs:** Am Asn Univ Women, 1991-; Am Soc ealth Educrs & Trainers, 1989-; Broward Econ Develop Counc; xec comt, 1993-; Educ Comt, 1994-; Dania Chamber Com; bd, 988-91, exec comt, 1989-91; Greater Ft Lauderdale Chamber om; bd,1994-, Exec Comt, 1995-97; Leadership Hollywood, 994; Hollywood Chamber Com, Phi Delta Kappa, 1991-; BAND Business Against Narcotics and Drugs)bd, 1994-; Browards ounty Sch Bds Blu Ribbon Comt, Bus Coalition Educ Excel-nce; World Class Schs. **Honors/Awds:** Nat Asn Negro Bus & rof Women, Ft Lauderdale chap, Woman of the Year,1986; Nat Jr chievement, Bronze Leadership Award, 1987; Price Waterhou-,Up and Comers Award, 1989; Outstanding Service Award, 990; Dania Chamber Com, President's Award for Outstanding ervice, 1990; Council for Black Economic Develop, Apprecia-on Award, 1990; Dollars and Sense Magazine,America's Up and oming Business and Professional Women Award, 1991;Greater Lauderdale Chamber Com, Abraham S Fischler Award ducation),1992. **Special Achievements:** Appointed, Council for lack Econo Develop. **Business Phone:** (954)741-8138.

IACKAY, LEO S, JR.
hief executive officer. **Career:** State Ga, Medicaid adminr; Af-iated Comput Serv State Healthcare Solutions, Atlanta, Ga, chief perating officer & sr vpres, currently. **Business Addr:** Senior ice President, Chief Operating Officer, Affiliated Computer ervices State Healthcare Solutions, 3 Ravinia Dr Suite P750, tlanta, GA 30350, **Business Phone:** (678)441-0359.*

IACKEL, DR. AUDLEY MAURICE
urgeon. **Personal:** Born Dec 3, 1955, Natchez, MS; son of Aud-y M Jr and Nannie Love Blassingame; married Sharon White, ug 14, 1982; children: Ashley Monique & Audley Maurice. **duc:** Morehouse Col, BS, 1977; Meharry Med Col, MD, 1981. **areer:** Northwestern Univ Med Ctr, intern, 1981-82, orthop esident, 1982-86; Kerlan Jobe Orthop Clin, orthop surgeon, thritis, joint implant fel, 1986-87; Charles Drew Med Sch, Los ngeles, Calif orthop surgeon, 1987-88; Assocs Orthop, leveland, Ohio, orthop surgeon, 1988-. **Orgs:** Nat Med Asn, 982-; Cleveland Orthop Club, 1989-; fel Am Acad Orthop urgeons, 1991-; Am Asn Hip & Knee Surgeons. **Honors/Awds:** lpha Omega Alpha Med Hon Soc, 1981; Outstanding Young len of America, 1983; Anatomy Award, Dept Orthop Surgery, 984; Physician Recognition Award, Am Med Asn. **Home Addr:** 201 Shaker Blvd Suite 328, Cleveland, OH 44122. **Business ddr:** Orthopaedic Surgeon, Associates in Orthopaedics Inc., 5 everance Circle Suite 304, Cleveland, OH 44118, **Business hone:** (216)691-9000.

IACKEY, JOHN
pokesperson, football player. **Personal:** Born Sep 24, 1941, New ork, NY. **Educ:** Syracuse Univ. **Career:** Football player (retired), pokesperson; Baltimore Colts, tight end &offensive end, 1963-1, San Diego Chargers, tight end & offensive end,1972; Nat ootball League, Coaching Am Family, speaker, currently. **Orgs:** d adv, Leukemia Soc Am & Syracuse Univ Bus Sch; bd dirs, yracuse Univ Alumni Asn; bd mem, Overcoming Obstacles Prog, ommunity Educ Found, currently. **Honors/Awds:** Paul Robeson ward, NCP; John Mackey Award in the name of honor, 2000; assau County Sports Hall of Fame, 2000. **Business Phone:** 12)406-7488.

IACKEY, MALCOLM
asketball player. **Personal:** Born Jul 11, 1970, Chattanooga, TN. **duc:** Ga Inst Technol. **Career:** Phoenix Suns, 1993-94; Dallas Iavericks, 1997; Sacramento Kings, 1999; Quad City Thunder, 999-2000; Giallorosso Basket Messina, 2000-01; FIBA Europe, aos Jda Dijon Bourgogne, 2002; ABA, Z Chattanooga, power rward; Media Broker Messina, 2000-01; SIG Strasbourg, 2003-4; Chattanooga Steamers, 2005-06. **Honors/Awds:** Ga Tech Hall f Fame, 2005.

IACKIE, DR. CALVIN
ollege teacher, business owner, consultant. **Personal:** Born Jan , 1969?, New Orleans, LA; married Tracy; children: Myles Ah-ad & Mason Amir. **Educ:** Morehouse Col, BS, 1990; Ga Inst echnol, BME, 1990, MS, 1992, Phd, mech engineering, 1996. **areer:** Morehouse Col, instr; Channel ZerO, founder & pres, 992-; Tulane Univ, Dept Mech Engineering, fac, 1996-2002, nured assoc prof, 2002-07; Univ Mich, Dept Chem Engineering, s prof, 2004-05; Prof, Speaker, Author, Inventor & Entrepreneur. **rgs:** Phi Beta Kappa; Pi Tau Sigma; Tau Beta Pi; bd mem, La ecovery Authority, currently; Nat Speaker Asn; 100 Black Men letro New Orleans. **Honors/Awds:** Excellence in Teaching ward in Mechanical Engineering, Pi Tau Sigma, Am Soc Mech ng, 2000 & 2002; Black Engineer of the Year Award, 2002; railblazer Award, New Orleans Data News Weekly, 2002; Nat itle One Distinguished Graduate for Louisiana, 2003; residential Award for Excellence in Science, Mathematics & ngineering Mentoring in a White House Ceremony, 2003. **pecial Achievements:** Numerous publications including, "Effect f Environmental Phase Characteristics on the Discharge of a hermal Storage System", 2001; "Inward Solidification of Couette Flow in an Annulus with Translating Cylinder", 2001; "Solidification of Couette Flow in an Annulus with Inner Cylinder Rotation", 2002; "A View from the Roof: Lessons for Life and Business"; Welcome to Manhood, 2007. **Business Addr:** President, Channel ZerO, PO Box 312, Harvey, LA 70058, **Business Phone:** (504)391-0730.

MACKIE, TIMOTHY
Vice president (Organization). **Educ:** Southern Univ. **Career:** AXA Advisors LLC, div exec vpres, currently. **Orgs:** Booker T Washington Bus Asn; Nat Asn Black Accountants; The Double OO Riders Asn; 102nd United States Colored Troops Civil War Re-Enactors. **Business Addr:** Divisional Executive Vice President, AXA Advisors LLC, 1155 Brewery Pk Suite 100, Detroit, MI 48207, **Business Phone:** (313)259-9044.

MACKLIN, JOHN W
Chemist, educator. **Personal:** Born Dec 11, 1939, Fort Worth, TX; son of Vera L Macklin; children: Marcus E. **Educ:** Linfield Col McMinnville, BA, 1962; Cornell Univ, PhD, inorganic, 1968. **Career:** Univ Wash, from asst prof to prof, prof emer, currently. **Orgs:** Am Chem Soc, 1966-; AAAS, 1978-; NOBCCHE, 1986-; ISSOL, 1984-. **Honors/Awds:** Stanford, NASA-ASEE Summer Res fel. **Special Achievements:** Published books like: Spectrochemica Acta, 1985; J. Phys. Chem, 1989; Raman Spec, 1995; Chemistry of Materials, 1999. **Business Addr:** Professor Emeritus, University of Washington, Department of chemistry, Bagley Hall 225 PO Box 351700, Seattle, WA 98195, **Business Phone:** (206)543-7199.

MACLACHLAN, JANET A.
Actor, educator, television producer. **Personal:** Born Aug 8, 1933, Harlem, NY; daughter of James M (deceased) and Ruby Iris South (deceased); children: Samantha. **Educ:** Hunter Col, BS (psychol), 1955. **Career:** TV Series: "Spy", 1967; "The FBI", 1966; "Star Trek", 1967; "The Fugitive", 1966; "The Name of the Game", 1969-70; "The Rockford Files",1975; "Good Times", 1978; "Archie Bunker's Place", 1980; "Cagney and Lacey", 1982-83; "Amen", 1988; "Murder She Wrote", 1985; "Murder One", 1986; "Family Law", 2000; "Alias", 2002; TV movies: "Louis Armstrong -Chicago Style", 1976; "Roll of Thunder Hear My Cry", 1978; "The Sophisticated Gents", 1981; "For Us the Living: The Medgar Evers Story", 1983; "The Tuskegee Airmen", 1995; Doctor in the House, 1995; "Home Improvement", "Murder One", (3episodes) 1996-97; "My Last Love", 1999; "The Thirteenth Floor " 1999; "A Private Affair", 2000; "Affairs of the State", 2000, "The Gay Divorcee", 2001; "Family Law", 200-01; "Cipher", 2002; "Alias", 2002. Films: Up Tight, 1968; tick.tick. tick, 1970; The Man, 1972; Sounder, 1972; Tightrope, 1984; Black Listed, 2003. **Orgs:** Bd dirs, Screen Actors Guild, 1976-81; bd dir, MagaLink Inc, 1982-88;treas, Media Forum Inc, 1984-88; bd govrs, 1986-88, chmn, 1989-94, Acad TV Arts & Sci; chmn, 1992-95, Acad Scholar & Grants Comm, Acad Motion Picture Arts & Sci, 1997-99. **Honors/Awds:** Emmy Award for Best Performance, Los Angeles area Acad TV Arts & Sci,1982; NAACP Theatre Award: Best Actress in "Eyes of The American,"1986-87. **Home Addr:** 2018 Griffith Park Blvd, PO Box 27593, Los Angeles, CA 90039. *

MACLEAN, ANITA
Executive. **Business Addr:** President, Chief Executive Officer, Broome County Urban League Inc, 43 45 Carroll St, Binghamton, NY 13901, **Business Phone:** (607)723-7303.

MACON, MARK L
Basketball player, basketball coach. **Personal:** Born Apr 19, 1969, Saginaw, MI. **Educ:** Temple Univ, BS, 1991. **Career:** Basketball player (retired) basketball coach; Denver Nuggets, guard, 1991-93; Detroit Pistons, guard, 1993-99; Temple Owls, Temple Univ, asst coach, 2004; Ga State Univ, asst coach; Binghamton Univ, asst coach, 2007. **Orgs:** Founder, Mark Macon Found, 1991. **Honors/Awds:** NBA All-Rookie second team, 1992; Athletics Hall of Fame, Temple Univ, 2004; Silver Anniversary Team, ESPN, 2006. **Business Addr:** Assistant Coach, Binghamton University, PO Box 6000, Binghamton, NY 13902-6000, **Business Phone:** (607)777-4255.

MADDOX, ELTON PRESTON, JR.
Dentist, educator. **Personal:** Born Nov 17, 1946, Kingston, MD; son of Virginia and Elton; married. **Educ:** Morgan State Col, BS, 1968; Univ Md, Dent Sch, DDS, 1972. **Career:** Univ Md Dent Sch, instr, 1973-75, asst prof, 1975-77, clin asst prof, 1977-82; pvt pract, 1977-; Team Clin, clin dir & actg dir, 1976-77. **Orgs:** Chmn, Minority Recruitment Comt, 1974-77; Univ Md Dent Sch, Admis Comt, 1974-77; Clin Competency Comt, 1975-76; Alpha Phi Alpha Fraternity Inc; Jr C of C; Md State Dent Asn; Eastern Shore Dent Asn; pres, Community Awareness Comt. **Special Achievements:** Publications namely "A Guide to Clinical Competency," Journal of Dental Education, 1976; "Why Not?" University of Maryland, 1976. **Home Phone:** (410)546-4418. **Business Addr:** Dentist, 1229 Mt Hermon Rd, Salisbury, MD 21801, **Business Phone:** (410)749-1155.

MADDOX, GARRY LEE
Baseball player. **Personal:** Born Sep 1, 1949, Cincinnati, OH; married Sondra; children: Garry & Derrick. **Educ:** Harbor Col. **Career:** Baseball player (Retired); San Francisco Giants, outfielder, 1972-75; Philadelphia Phillies, outfielder, 1975-86; A Pomerantz & Co, ceo, 1995-. **Orgs:** Philadelphia Child Guidance Clinic, bd dir; Federal Reserve Bank, Bddir, currently; investor, Washington Philadelphia, Foxwoods. **Honors/Awds:** NL All-Star Fielding Team 1975-79; Young Leaders of Philadelphia Award, 1984; shares LCS record for most consecutive games with one or more RBI's total series w/4; 8 Gold Glove Awards. **Military Serv:** AUS 1968-70. **Business Addr:** Chief Executive Officer, A Pomerantz & Co, 701 Market St suite 7000, Philadelphia, PA 19106, **Business Phone:** (215)408-2100.*

MADDOX, JACK H.
Real estate agent. **Personal:** Born Jul 17, 1927, Detroit, MI; son of John (deceased) and Wylma (deceased); divorced; children: 1 daughter. **Educ:** Wayne State Univ, BS; Univ MI, Cert; MI State Univ, Cert. **Career:** Real estate & rel subj teacher; Assoc Ins Agency, pres & gen agent; Past Brokers Invest Co, past vpres; JH Maddox & Co, proprietor real estate, currently. **Orgs:** Past secy & dir, Ebony Dist County; Real Estate Alumni, MI; chmn fund raising comt local state, Nat Police Candidates; chmn, Alpha Phi alpha; guardsman, Jaycees; past dir, Nat Asn Advancement Colored People Freedom Fund Dinner Comt; chmn, Housing Comn; Detroit Real Estate Brokers Asn; Police Action Comt; Million Dollar Club,Nat Asn Advancement Colored People1975-88; dir, Housing Owners US Exchange; original chmn, 1300 Lafayette E Co-op Bd Dir; Detroit Bd Realtors; chmn, Govt Affairs Comt, 1988-95. **Special Achievements:** Named as representative of City of Acapulco, Mexico to the City of Detroit by El Pres Municipal De Acapulco, 1994. **Military Serv:** USN, SK3, 1946-48; Victory Medal. **Business Addr:** Real Estate Broker &, Owner, J H Maddox & Company, 1300 Lafayette E Suite 2603, Detroit, MI 48207.

MADDOX, JULIUS A
Association executive. **Personal:** Born Oct 9, 1942, Philadelphia, PA; son of Fannie; married; children: Marcus & Christopher. **Educ:** Wayne State Univ, BS; Oakland Univ, MA; Wayne State Univ, spec collectioncialist. **Career:** Highland Pk Schs, educr, 1974-76; Pontiac Schs, educr, 1976-91; Mich Educ Asn, pres, 1991-. **Orgs:** Prof Standards Comn Teachers; Mich Dept, Educ Periodic Rev Coun; life mem Nat Asn Advan Colored People; bd dirs, Delta Dent Mich; Phi Delta Kappa. **Honors/Awds:** Man of the Year, MEA Women's Caucus, 1980; Apple Award, Jefferson Co Ky Teachers Asn. **Special Achievements:** One Detroit's Fifteen Top Educrs, Success Guide. **Military Serv:** AUS, spc 5, 1966-68; Usaryis Soldier Month, 1967. **Business Addr:** President, Michigan Education Association, 1216 Kendale Blvd, PO Box 2573, East Lansing, MI 48826-2573, **Business Phone:** (517)332-6551.

MADDOX, MARK ANTHONY
Football player. **Personal:** Born Mar 23, 1968, Milwaukee, WI. **Educ:** Northern Mich Univ. **Career:** Football player(retired); Buffalo Bills, linebacker, 1992-97; Ariz Cardinals, linebacker, 1998-2000.

MADDOX-SIMMS, MARGARET JOHNNETTA
Educator, executive. **Personal:** Born Aug 31, 1952, Clio, SC; married Rev Odinga Lawrence Maddox. **Educ:** Livingstone Col, BA, 1973; Ohio State Univ, MA, 1975, PhD, 1991. **Career:** TRW Marlin-Rockwell Div, syst analyst, 1977-78; Fla A&M Univ, fac, 1978-80; Sen Wm F Bowen OH, admin asst, 1980-83; MJ Simms & Assocs Inc, chief exec officer, pres, 1983-; Wilberforce Univ, Wilberforce prof, polit sci, 1991-; Livingstone Col, assoc prof polit sci, currently. **Orgs:** Columbus Area C C 1983-; Am Mkt Assoc Cent OH, 1984-; Pub Rel Soc Am, 1986-; Livingston Col Alumni Asn, vpres local chap, pres. **Honors/Awds:** Outstanding Young Women of America, 1983; Certificate of Commendation, Ohio Senate, 1983. **Business Phone:** 800-835-3435 Ext 6147.

MADGETT, DR. NAOMI LONG (NAOMI WITHERSPOON)
Publisher, college teacher, editor. **Personal:** Born Jul 5, 1923, Norfolk, VA; daughter of Maude Selena Hilton Long and Clarence Marcellus Long Sr; married Leonard P Andrews, Mar 31, 1972 (deceased); married William Harold Sr, 1954 (divorced 1960); married Julian F Witherspoon, Mar 31, 1946 (divorced 1949) (died 1996); children: Jill Witherspoon Boyer. **Educ:** VA State Col, BA 1945; Wayne State Univ, MEd 1955; Int Inst Advanced Studies (Greenwich Univ), PhD 1980. **Career:** Poet & author, 1941-; MI Chronicle, staff writer, 1946-47; MI Bell Tel Co, serv rep, 1948-54; Detroit Pub Sch, teacher, 1955-65, 1966-68; public speaker, poetry readings only, 1956-; Oakland Univ, res assoc, 1965-66; Eastern MI Univ, assoc prof eng, 1968-73; Univ MI, lectr, 1970; Eastern Mich Univ, prof, 1973-84, prof emer, 1984-; Lotus Press, publ & ed, 1974-; poetry ed, Mich State Univ Press, 1993-98. **Orgs:** Col Lang Asn; Alpha Kappa Alpha Soc; Nat Asn Advan Colored People; Detroit Women Writers; Southern Poverty Law Ctr; Langston Hughes Soc; Charles H Wright Mus African Am Hist; Detroit Inst Arts; Fred Hart Williams Geneological Soc; Plymouth United Church Christ. **Honors/Awds:** Distinguished English Teacher of the Year, Met Detroit; first recipient Mott Fel eng, 1965; Disting Soror Award, Alpha Rho Omega Chap, Alpha Kappa Alpha Sor, 1969; Key to the City of Detroit 1980; Resolu-

tions from Detroit City Coun, 1982 & MI State Legis, 1982 & 1984; Recognition by Black Caucus Nat Coun Teachers Eng, 1984; Nat Coalition 100 Black Women, 1984; Induction into Stylus Soc Howard Univ, 1984; Distinguished Artist Award, Wayne State Univ, 1985; Robert Hayden Runagate Award, 1985; Creative Achievement Award, MI Coun arts, 1987; Creative Achievement Award, Col Lang Asn, 1988; "In Her Lifetime" Award, Afrikan Poets Theatre Inc, 1989; Literature Award, Arts Found Mich, 1990; Honorary Degrees: Siena Hgts Coll, 1991; Recognition by Black Caucus of American Library Assn, 1992; Loyola University, Chicago, 1993; MI Artist Award, 1993; Am Book Award, 1993; Honorary Degree: MI State Univ, 1994; Sumner HS Hall of Fame, 1997; Nat Literary Hall of Fame for Writers of African Descent, 1999; City of Detroit, poet laureate, 2001-; MI Women's Hall of Fame, 2002; Alain Locke Award, DIA Friends of African Am Art, 2003; lifesize bronze bust created by sculptor Artis Lane part of the permanent collection of the Charles H Wright Mus of African Am Hist, 2005; Naomi Long Madgett/Lotus Press Papers in the Special Collection Library, Univ Mich, Ann Arbor. **Special Achievements:** Ed two anthologies including: Adam of Ife: Black Women in Praise of Black Men, 1992; nine books published including: Star by Star, 1965, 1970; Pink Ladies in the Afternoon, 1972, 1990; Exits & Entrances, 1978; Octavia and Other Poems, 1988; Remembrances of Spring: Collected Early Poems, 1993; Octavia: Guthrie and Beyond, 2003; poems widely anthologized & translated; poem: Octavia: Guthrie and Beyond, 2002; Connected Islands: New and Selected Poems, 2004. **Home Addr:** 18080 Santa Barbara Dr, Detroit, MI 48221, **Home Phone:** (313)342-9174. **Business Phone:** (313)861-1280.

MADHUBUTI, HAKI R (DON LUTHER LEE)
Association executive, editor. **Personal:** Born Feb 23, 1942, Little Rock, AR; son of Jimmy L Lee and Maxine Graves Lee (deceased); married Johari Amini; children: 2. **Educ:** Wilson Jr Col, Roosevelt Univ, Univ Illinois, Chicago Circle; Univ Iowa, MFA, 1984. **Career:** DuSable Mus African Am Hist, Chicago Ill, apprentice cur, 1963-67; Montgomery Ward, Chicago Ill, stock dept clerk, 1963-64; US Post Off, Chicago Ill, clerk, 1964-65; Spiegels, Chicago Ill, jr exec, 1965-66; Cornel Univ, Ithaca NY, writer-in-residence, 1968-69; Northeastern Ill State Col, Chicago Ill, poet-in-residence, 1969-70; Univ Ill, Chicago Ill, lectr, 1969-71; Howard Univ, Wash DC, writer-in-residence, 1970-71; Morgan State Col, Baltimore Md, 1972-73; Chicago State Univ, Chicago Ill, assoc prof Eng, 1984-; Third World Press, Chicago Ill, publ & ed, 1967-; Inst Positive Educ, Chicago Ill, dir, 1969-. **Orgs:** Founding mem, Orgn Black Am Cult, Writers Workshop, 1967-75; past exec coun, Cong African People; vice-chmn, African Liberation Day Support Comn, 1972-73; pres, African-Am Publ, Booksellers', & Writers' Asn, 1990-. **Honors/Awds:** Published works include Think Black, Broadside Press, 1967; Black Pride, Broadside Press, 1967; For Black People (and Negroes Too), Third World Press, 1968; Don't Cry, Scream, Broadside Press, 1969; We Walk the Way of the New World, Broadside Press, 1970; Dynamite Voices I: Black Poets of the 1960s, Broadside Press, 1971; Directionscore: Selected and New Poems, Broadside Press, 1971; From Plan to Planet-Life Studies: The Need for Afrikan Minds & Institutions, Broadside Press, 1973; Book of Life, Broadside Press, 1973; Earthquakes and Sunrise Missions: Poetry and Essays of Black Renewal, 1793-1983, Third World Press, 1984; Say That the River Turns: The Impact of Gwendolyn Brooks, Third World Press, 1987; Black Men: Obsolete, Single, Dangerous; Claiming Earth: Race, Rage, Rape, Redempti Blacks Seeking A Culture of Enlightened Empowerment, 1994. **Business Addr:** Editor, Third World Press, 7822 S Dobson Ave, PO Box 19730, Chicago, IL 60619, **Business Phone:** (773)651-0700.

MADISON, EDDIE L, JR.
Writer, publicist, editor. **Personal:** Born Sep 8, 1930, Tulsa, OK; son of Laverta Pyle and Eddie L Madison Sr; married Davetta Jayn Cooksey, Nov 17, 1956; children: Eddie III, Karyn Devette & David. **Educ:** Lincoln Univ Mo, Jefferson City, BJ, 1952; Univ Tulsa, MA, mass commun, 1959. **Career:** The Chicago Tribune, sect ed, 1963-65; Info Div US Dept Com, info spec, 1965; Off Publ & Info for Domestic & Intl Bus, dept dir, publ div, 1965-69; Wash Star Station Group, mgr comm serv, 1969-77; Wash Star Comm Inc Broadcast Div, mgr admin serv, 1977-78; US Indsl Outlook, 1979, chief ed, 1978-79; US Dept Com Bus Am Mag, asst ed, 1979-81; Congressman Gus Savage Ill, chief press asst, 1981-82; Three Elms & Assocs, founder/pres; US Dept Health & Human Serv, writer/ed/public affairs coord, 1982-92, mgr, 1991-92; Lincoln Univ, asst prof & dept chmn, 1992-99; Three Elms & Assoc Inc, pres & chief exec officer, 2001-. **Orgs:** Nat Broadcast Asn Community Affairs, 1974-76; public relations dir, Alpha Phi Alpha Fraternity; Int Bus Serv; US Dept Com; Nat Asn Educ Broadcasters, 1978-79; Industrialization Ctr, 1971-78; mem, Commn on Human Rights, DC, 1970-75; dir, DC United Way, 1970-78; bd trustees, Children's Hosp Nat Med Ctr, 1975-78; mem & officer, numerous organizations & committees. **Honors/Awds:** Outstanding Young Men Am, 1966; Outstanding Performance, Jour, Lincoln Univ, Mo; Spl Citation Presidential Classroom Young Am, 1973; Plaque/Appreciation/Thanks Natl Broadcast Assn Com Affairs Columbus, OH, 1977. **Military Serv:** AUS, 1952-54; UN Defense Medal; Good Conduct Medal. **Home Addr:** 1120 Netherlands Ct, Silver Spring, MD 20905, **Home Phone:** (301)236-9511. **Business Addr:** President,

Chief Executive Officer, Three Elms & Assocs, PO Box 90603, Washington, DC 20090, **Business Phone:** (202)436-8586.

MADISON, JACQUELINE EDWINA
Manager, librarian, entrepreneur. **Personal:** Born Jul 16, 1951, Darlington, SC; daughter of John Brown and Lula Mack McLeod; married Calvin Lee, Aug 18, 1975; children: Jaquenette & Calexandria. **Educ:** Fayetteville State Univ, BS, 1972; Baylor Univ, Waco, cert, 1974; Kans State Univ, attended 1986; Emporia State Univ, MLS, 1991. **Career:** FDA, Orlando, FL, food & drug inspector, 1972-73; US Army, Nurnberg, Ger, sanitary engr, 1974-77, sup appt clerk, 1977-79; Cent Tex Col, Fort Lewis, WA, substitute teacher, 1980-82; Fort Riley Libr, Fort Riley, KS, libr tech, 1987-90; Youth Serv, Fort Riley, KS, secy & personal admin asst, 1990-; Jaqcal's Infophone, parent, teacher, stud commun line; Wyeth Ayerst Res Lab, prin info scientist, currently. **Orgs:** Delta Sigma Theta, 1971-; Parent Teacher Asn, 1988-; Kan Library Asn, 1989-; Black Caucus Ala, 1989-; SLA, 1989-; North Country Girls Scouts; Phi Beta Kappa, Phi Kapa Phi. **Honors/Awds:** Golden Poet Awards, World Poetry, 1990-91; Science Awards, Phi Beta Kappa, 1971-72; Scholarship, E Stroudsburg Univ, 1989; Gold Poet Awards, World of Poetry, 1992, Phi Kapa Phi, 1991; Woman of the Year, Nominee & Finalist, 1996. **Military Serv:** AUS, capt, 1974-77; Nat Defense Service Medal, 1977, Army Commendation Medal, 1977, Good Conduct Medal, 1979; Certificates of Appreciation. **Business Addr:** Principal Information Scientist, Wyeth Ayerst Research Laboratory, Drug Safety Information Center, 641 Ridge Rd, Chazy, NY 12921, **Business Phone:** (518)846-6394.

MADISON, KRISTEN DOROTHY
Lawyer. **Personal:** Born Jun 13, 1972, Rochester, NY; daughter of William and Barbara. **Educ:** Univ Va, BA, 1994; Univ Conn Sch Law, JD, 1997. **Career:** US Dept Labor-OECCP, junior officer, 1998-2000; Jackson Lewis LLP, assoc atty, currently. **Honors/Awds:** Sr Compliance Off, OFCCP, 1998-2000. **Business Addr:** Associate Attorney, Jackson Lewis LLP, 58 S Serv Rd Suite 410, Melville, NY 11747, **Business Phone:** (631)247-4655.

MADISON, LEATRICE BRANCH
Educator. **Personal:** Born Sep 5, 1922, Washington, DC; daughter of Hayes Louis and Julia Bailey; married Robert P; children: Jeanne M Anderson & Juliette M Little. **Educ:** Miner Teachers Col, BS, cum laude, 1943; Univ Chicago, MA, guidance & personnel, 1947. **Career:** Educator (Retired); Syphax Elem Sch, teacher, 1943-49; Miles Standish Elem Sch, Cleveland, Ohio, teacher, 1949-51; Harvard Univ, Grad Sch Design, asst librn, 1951-52; George Washington Carver Sch, teacher, 1954-57; Case Elem Sch, teacher, 1958-59; Miles Standish, 1959-60. **Orgs:** Welfare Fund, 1964-70; Fedn Community Planning, 1972-82; United Way Servs, 1970-76; bd overseers 7 vis comts, Case Western Reserve Univ, 1973-86; Blue Cross NE Ohio, 1974-84; pres & founding mem, HARAMBEE, 1979-85; Greater Cleveland Girl Scouts; Shaker Lake Regional Nature Ctr; Cleveland Child Guidance Ctr; Western Reserve Historical Soc; YWCA; Planned Parenthood; alumni bd dirs, Univ Chicago; Cleveland Symphony Orchestra Adv Coun; Nat Asn Advan Colored People Freedom Fund Dinner; youth servs adv bd, Juvenile Ct; Cleveland Heights Adv Comn HUD Block Grants; Cleveland Symphony Orchestra Women's com; bd pres, Cleveland Heights Univ, Heights Library; Severance Gala Reopening Comm; Severance Organ Gala Comm; Pi Lambda Theta Hon Educ Sorority. **Honors/Awds:** Distinguished Serv Award, Blue Cross, 1984; Distinguished Serv Award, HARAMBEE, 1985; Citation, Cuyahoga County Commissioners, 1993-94; Citation, Ohio State House Representatives, 1994; Univ Chicago Public Service Citation, 1994; Cleveland Opera Award, Special & Unique Contributions Cleveland Opera, 2004; President's Award, Fedn Community Planning. **Special Achievements:** First African American President to Cleveland Heights, University Heights, PTA Unit, 1971; First Black Woman to serve as VIP, Federation of COT Planning, 1977; vchair of United Way Services Capital Campaign, 1974; first black woman to serve as chair of Federation of COT Planning Annual Health and Human Services Institute, 1981. **Home Addr:** 13600 Shaker Blvd, Shaker Heights, OH 44120, **Home Phone:** (216)991-4347.

MADISON, PAULA
Executive, president (organization). **Personal:** Born Jan 1, 1952?, Harlem, NY; married Roosevelt Madison; children: Imani. **Educ:** Vassar Col, BA, 1974; Syracuse Univ, Newhouse Sch Communs. **Career:** Syracuse Herald Jour, reporter, 1974-80; Ft Worth Star-Telegram, reporter, 1980-82; Dallas Times Herald, asst city ed, 1982; WFAA-TV, community affairs dir, 1982-84, news mgr, 1984-86; KOTV-TV, news dir, 1986; KHOU-TV, exec news dir, 1987-89; WNBC, asst news dir, 1989-96, news dir, 1996-99; NBC, vpres, sr vpres diversity, 2000-02; KNBC, pres & gen mgr, 2000-; KNBC, KVEA, KWHY, regional gen mgr, 2002-. **Orgs:** Nat Asn Black Journalists; Chinatown Serv Ctr; bd mem, Nat Med Fel; bd mem, Ctr Pub Integrity; bd mem, Poynter Inst; bd mem, Maynard Inst; NY Vassar Club; NY Press Club. **Honors/Awds:** Ida B Wells Award, NABJ, 1998; Ellis Island Medal Honor, Nat Ethnic Coalition Orgns, 1999; President Award, NAACP, LA br, 2001; Frederick D Patterson Award, UNCF, 2001; Catlyst Award, Nat Asn Minority Media Execs, 2002; Outstanding Women Mkt & Communs Award, Ebony, 2002; Woman of the Yr, LA Co Comn

Women, 2002; Deborah Award, Anti-Defamation League, 200?; Citizen of the Yr Award, LA Marathon, 2004; 75 Most Powerful Af Am Corp Am, Black Enterprise Mag, 2005; included Ho lywood Reporter's Power 100 the mag's list most powerful femal execs Hollywood; Corporate Impact Award, Asian Pacific A Legal Ctr; NY's 100 Top Minority Executives. **Special Achieve ments:** first African Am woman to become gen mgr at a network owned station in a top-five mkt. **Business Addr:** Presiden General Manager, NBC4, 3000 W Alameda Ave, Burbank, C 91523, **Business Phone:** (818)840-3379.

MADISON, RICHARD. See Obituaries section.

MADISON, ROBERT P
Architect. **Personal:** Born Jul 28, 1923, Cleveland, OH; son o Robert James and Nettie Josephine Brown; married Leatrice Luc lle Branch, Apr 16, 1949; children: Jeanne M Anderson & Juliett M Little. **Educ:** Western Reserve Univ, BA 1948; Harvard Uni MA 1952; Ecole Des Beaux Arts Paris, 1953. **Career:** Robert Little Architects, designer, 1948-51; Howard Univ, asst pro 1952-54; Robert P Madison Int, prest, chmn, chief exec office currently. **Orgs:** Case Western Reserve Univ, 1969-81; truste Univ Circle, Inc, 1974-; dir, Industrial Bank WA, 1975-81; truste Cuyahoga Metrop Gen Hosp, 1982-; trustee, Midtown Corrido Inc, 1982-; OH Bd Bldg Standards State OH, 1984-; chmn Ju Fel Nat AIA, 1985; trustee, Cleveland Chap Am Red Cross, 1986 trustee, OH Motorists Asn, 1986-; Cleveland Downtown Pla Steering Comm, 1986; City Planning Commn Cleveland Height OH, 1987-;, Alpha Phi Alpha, Sigma Pi Phi; trustee, Clevelan Opera, 1990-. **Honors/Awds:** Architect US Embassy Dakar Sene gal 1965-77; Architect's delegation Peoples Republic of Chin 1974; Fellow Amer Inst of Architects 1974; Distinguished Servic Award BEDO State of Ohio; President's Award Cleveland Cha AIA; Distinguished Firm Award, Howard Univ, 198 Distinguished Serv Award, Case Western Reserve Univ, 198 Honorary Doctor of Humane Letters, Howard University, 198 AIA Ohio, Gold Medal Firm Award, 1994, Gold Medal Architec Award, 1997; Cleveland Opera honors, Robert P Madison an Leatrice Madison, 1999. **Military Serv:** AUS, 1st Lt, 1942-4(Purple Heart, 1944. **Home Addr:** 18975 Van Aken Apt 41(Shaker Heights, OH 44122. **Business Addr:** President, Chairma Robert P. Madison International, 2930 Euclid Ave, Cleveland, O 44115, **Business Phone:** (216)861-8195.

MADISON, DR. ROMELL J
Dentist. **Personal:** Born May 25, 1942, Nagoya, Japan; marrie Grace Perkins, Jul 8, 1972; children: Romell Jarrod & Lesli Educ:** Xavier Univ, BS, pharmacol, 1975; Meharry Med Co DDS, 1984. **Career:** Pvt pract, dentist, currently. **Orgs:** Pres, N Dent Asn; bd mem, La State Bd Dent; La Healthcare Comn; Ne Orleans Dent Soc; Pelican State Dent Asn. **Business Add** Dentist, 743 Terry Pkwy, Gretna, LA 70056, **Business Phone** (504)394-9907.

MADISON, SAM. See MADISON, SAMUEL ADOLFUS, JR.

MADISON, SAMUEL ADOLFUS, JR. (SAM MADISON)
Football player. **Personal:** Born Apr 23, 1974, Thomasville, GA married Saskia; children: Kellen & Kennedy. **Educ:** Uni Louisville. **Career:** Miami Dolphins, defensive back, 1997-200 New York Giants, cornerback, 2006-08; free agent, currentl **Orgs:** Founder, Madison Ave Kids, 2000-. **Honors/Awds:** Pr Bowl, 1999-02; Nat Moore Community Serv Award, 2004; Sup Bowl champion.

MADISON, SAMUEL C.
Clergy. **Personal:** Born Feb 24, 1922, Greenville, SC; son of Sa uel and Rosa Lee; married Elizabeth D Madison, Jun 12, 197 **Career:** United House Prayer People, pastor, 1969-91, judg 1973-91, sr minister, 1986-91, chief exec officer, bishop, 1991 **Orgs:** Nat Asn Advan Colored People; Urban League; Unite Supreme Coun, AASR 33rd Degree; exec dir, McCollou Scholar Col Fund; Nationwide Madison Bldg Prog. **Honor Awds:** DHL, Washington Saturday Col, 1998; DHL, Bowie Sta Univ, 1999; African American Male IMAGE Award, Phi Be Sigma Fraternity; Mayor of Jerusalem, Israel, JERUSALE PILGRIM; Greater Wash Urban League, honoree, 22nd Annu Whitney M Young Dinner. **Special Achievements:** Annual Tru & Facts of the United House of Prayer, 2000; McColloug Magazine (periodical), 2000; Are You Aware? annual publicatio 2000; Advice & Precepts, 2000.

MADISON, SHANNON L
Engineer. **Personal:** Born Jun 21, 1927, Texas; married Ruth Jea children: Earl Wayne, Michael Denard, Stephanie Annett, Share & Maria. **Educ:** Howard Univ, BS. **Career:** York Div Bo Warner Corp, develop engr, 1954-59; Emerson Radio Phonograph Co, chief test engr, 1959-61; Delco Appliance Di GM, sr proj engr, 1961-65; Whirlpool Corp, sr mfg res eng 1965-. **Orgs:** Human Resources Coun; Tri-Co Comn Action Con munity; Soc Mfg Engrs; NTA; Am Soc Heating, Refrig & Ai Conditioning Engrs; Sigma Xi; SPE; Homes Berrien Co Familie Inc; State Adv Bd Gov Mich; Comprehen State Health Plannin

dv Coun, 1971-74; Community Twin City Area Human Rels oun; Twin Cities Community Forum; Model Cities; Nat Asn Adan Colored People. **Business Addr:** Senior Manufacturer esearch Engineer, Whirlpool Corp, Monte Rd Rm 2050, Benton arbor, MI 49022.

MADISON, WILLIAM EDWARD
xecutive. **Personal:** Born Jan 31, 1947, Rochester, NY; son of Williams E White and Addie D Adkins; married Barbara D, Mar 7, 1970; children: Kristen D & William E Jr. **Educ:** City col New ork, BS, 1970. **Career:** Xerox Corp, region personnel mgr, 1981-4, div human resources mgr, 1984-87, employee resources, dir, 989-91, hr Americas vpres, 1991-94, hr US customer operations, pres, 1995-97; E I DuPont de Nemours & Co, human resources S, vpres, 1988-2000; US Region, pres, 1997-98; AVIS Group oldings Inc, sr vpres & chief human resources officer, 2000-01; ntergy, Human Resources & Admin, sr vpres, 2001-07, Gatestne Group, chief exec officer, curently. **Orgs:** Omega Psi Phi raternity, 1966-; dir, Boy Scouts Am, 1992-; dir, Talents Alliance nc, 1998-00, pres, US Region; dir, Urban Park Housing, 1984-97; r, Boys & Girls Club Rochester, 1984-87; Nat Action comt inority Engrs, 1998-00. **Honors/Awds:** Omega Man of the Year, mega Psi Phi Fraternity, 1978. **Special Achievements:** Harvard us Sch, exec develop prog, 1991. **Business Addr:** Chief Execuve Officer, Gatestone Group, Atlanta, GA.

MADISON, YVONNE REED (YVONNE REED MATHEWS)
ducator. **Personal:** Born Feb 22, 1954, Mobile, AL; daughter of red and Leila Roberts; divorced; children: Henry Clay Scott, ucy Yvette Hillery & Sonya Williams. **Educ:** Univ S Ala, BM, 976, ME, 1982. **Career:** St Joseph Baptist Church, minister usic, 1972-; Mobile County Bd SchComnr, teacher, 1982-; Leore Magnet Sch, chorus & piano instr, currently. **Orgs:** Music oordr, Alpha Kappa Alpha Sorority, Undergrad Chapter, 1974-5; music dir, asst rep, Port City United Voices, 1981-; Ala Vocal sn, 1982-; Nat Educ Asn; Mobile County Educ Asn; Music Edu-s Nat Conf; Ala Music Educrs Asn; pres, Nu Image, 1990-; em,music coordinator, Nazaree Full Gospel Church. **Honors/wds:** Career Women of the Year, Gayfers, 1996; Coalition of 100 lack Women Coral Award nominee, 1998; Outstanding Citizen ward, Alpha Alpha Fraternity, Beta Lambda Omicron Chapter, 999. **Special Achievements:** Black Nativity/Blues City Cultural enter of Memphis, TN, 1994; Nat Governors Conference, erformance, 1994; Nat Baptist Convention, Inc, Mid Winter oard Meeting Musical, 1996; Church Music Workshop, Jackson ate Univ, AME Churches, 1998; Youth on the Winning Side, ummer Youth Program, 1998. **Home Addr:** PO Box 40042, obile, AL 36640-0042, **Home Phone:** (334)432-3516.

MADISON POLK, SHARON L
rchitect, business owner. **Personal:** Born Aug 17, 1953, leveland, OH; daughter of Julian C and Mildred R Madison; arried Robert G, Sep 28, 1991. **Educ:** Univ Mich, BA, 1975, A, Urban Planning, 1994. **Career:** Madison Madison Int, chmn, 978-; M2 Int, chmn, 1987-. **Orgs:** Bd, Nat Women's Bus Coun, 998-99; pres, Bus Women's Alliance, 1999-; trustee, Detroit Inst rt, 1999-; chair, Friends African & African Am Art, 1999-; ustee, Detroit Downtown Develop Authority, 2000-; Am Planng Asn. **Honors/Awds:** Lifetime Achievement Award, NAACP; mall Business Female Entrepreneur Award, Detroit Chamber om; Economic Achievement Award, SCLC; Alain Locke Award, AAAA. **Business Addr:** Chairperson, Chief Executive Officer, adison Madison International, The Julian C Madison Bldg 1420 ashington Blvd, Detroit, MI 48226.

MADLOCK, BILL, JR.
aseball player. **Personal:** Born Jan 12, 1951, Memphis, TN; mared Cynthia; children: Sarah, Stephen, William Douglas & Jeremy oseph. **Educ:** Southwestern Community Col, Keokuk, IA. **Career:** Baseball player (retired); Texas Rangers, infielder, 1973; hicago Cubs, infielder, 1974-76; San Francisco Giants, infielder 977-79; PittsburghPirates, infielder 1979-85; Los Angeles Dodgs, infielder, 1985-87; Detroit Tigers, infielder, 1987. **Orgs:** ystic Fibrosis "65 Roses" Campaign. **Honors/Awds:** All-Star eam, The Sporting News, 1975; All-Star Team, National League, 975, 1981, 1983; World Series champion, 1979; 4 NL batting les, 1983; 11th player, win crown 4 times, 1983. *

MADU, ANTHONY CHISARAOKWU
ducator, research scientist. **Personal:** Born Jun 10, 1956, Ulwo, Nigeria; son of John and Pricilla Madu; married Mary Ellis, n 14, 1986; children: Geoffrey, Theandra. **Educ:** Benedict Col, S, 1979; Meharry Med Col, PhD, 1985; Univ MI, Postdoc, 1990. **Career:** Univ MI, lect, 1989, Dept Biol, res fel, 1985-89, sr assoc, 89-90; Emory Univ, Dept Biol, sr assoc, 1990-91; VA Union niv, Dept Biol, assoc prof, 1991-; Med Col VA, Dept Surg, fac soc, 1992-; Va Union Univ, Dept Natural Scis, MARC, prog dir, 92-. **Orgs:** Coun Undergrad Res, 1994-; Am Soc Microbiol, 83-; Am Asn Advancement Sci, 1985-; Alpha Kappa Mu Honor oc, Kappa Pi Chapter, 1988-. **Honors/Awds:** Teaching Excelnce Award, VA Union Univ, 1992-93; Am Soc Microbiol, Visitg Scientist; Minority Faculty Supplement Research Award, NIH, 92-95; VUU, Beneficiary Mobil Found Institutional Award, 91; Post-Doctoral Fellowship Research Award, NIH, 1987-89. **Special Achievements:** Numerous publications, 1981-91. **Business Addr:** Associate Professor, Program Director, Virginia Union University, Department Natural Science, 1500 N Lombardy St, Ellison Hall Rm 205, Richmond, VA 23220, **Business Phone:** (804)257-5614.*

MAGEE, ROBERT WALTER
Physician. **Personal:** Born Apr 23, 1951, New Orleans, LA; married Deborah Ketcheus. **Educ:** Southern Univ, BS, 1973; Meharry Medical Col, MD, 1977. **Career:** Plasma Alliance, staff physician, 1979-82; Mathew Walker Health Ctr, staff physician, 1980-82; Meharry FP Prog, asst prof, 1980-82; New Orleans Health Corp, med dir, 1982-85; HMO, staff physician; pvt pract, currently. **Orgs:** Staff Physician Health Am, 1985-.

MAGEE, WENDELL ERROL, JR.
Baseball player. **Personal:** Born Aug 3, 1972, Hattiesburg, MS; children: Joshua. **Educ:** Pearl River Jr Col, Samford. **Career:** Philadelphia Phillies, outfielder, 1996-98; detroit tigers, 2000-02; Colo Rockies, outfielder, 2002; Long Island Ducks, 2004-05. **Special Achievements:** Trans America Conference All-Star, 1994; Florida State League All-Star, 1995. *

MAHAL, TAJ (HENRY SAINT CLAIRE FREDERICKS)
Musician. **Personal:** Born May 17, 1942, New York City, NY; son of Henry Saint Claire Fredericks and Mildred Shields; married Inshirah Geter, Jan 23, 1976; children: Aya, Taj, Gahmelah, Ahmen, Deva & Nani. **Educ:** Univ Mass, BA, agr & animal Husb, 1964. **Career:** Performing & recording artist, 1964-; Taj Mahal & Elektras, group mem; Albums: Taj Mahal, 1968; The Natch'l Blues, 1968; Giant Step, 1969; The Real Thing, 1971; Happy Just to Be Like I Am, 1971; Recycling The Blues & Other Related Stuff, 1972; Oooh So Good 'n Blues, 1973; Mo' Roots, 1974; Music Keeps Me Together, 1975; Satisfied 'N Tickled Too, 1976; Music Fa'Ya, 1976; Brothers, 1977; Evolution, 1977; Take A Giant Step, 1983; Taj, 1987; Shake Sugaree, 1988; Mule Bone, 1991; Like Never Before, 1991; VolPour Sidney, 1991; Taj's Blues, 1992; Dancing The Blues, 1993; An Evening of Acoustic Music, 1993; The Source by Ali Farka Toure, 1993; MumtazMahal, 1995; Phantom Blues, 1996; Senor Blues, 1997; Sacred Island, 1998; In Progress & in Motion: 1965-98, 1998; Kulanjan, 1999; houtin' In Key, 2000; Hanapepe Dream, 2003; Blue Light Boogie, 1999; Shoutin' In Key, 2000; Hanapepe Dream, 2003; Martin Scorsese Presents The Blues - Taj Mahal, 2003; Blues with Feeling, 2003; Musicmakers with Taj Mahal, 2004; Etta Baker with Taj Mahal (Music Maker 50), 2004; Mkutano Meets The Culture Musical Club Of Zanzibar, 2005; The Essential Taj Mahal, 2005; Maestro, 2008. **Honors/Awds:** Grammy Award, 1997 & 2000; Grammy Award, Shoutin In Key, 2000; Blues Music Award, 2006; Honorary Doctorate, Fine Arts, Univ Mass, 2006. *

MAHAN-POWELL, LENA. **See Obituaries section.**

MAHOMES, PATRICK LAVON
Baseball player. **Personal:** Born Aug 9, 1970, Bryan, TX. **Career:** Minn Twins, pitcher, 1992-96; Boston Red Sox, 1996-97; NY Mets, 1999-2000; Texas Rangers, 2001; Chicago Cubs, 2002; Pittsburgh Pirates, 2003-04; Los Angeles Dodgers, 2005; Long Island Ducks, 2006; Toronto Blue Jays, 2007; Sioux Falls Canaries, 2008-. **Business Phone:** (605)333-0179.*

MAHONE, BARBARA J.
Automotive executive. **Personal:** Born in Notasulga, AL; daughter of Freddie Sr and Sarah L Simpson. **Educ:** Ohio State Univ, Columbus, OH, BS, 1968; Univ Mich, Ann Arbor, MI, MBA, 1972; Harvard Bus Sch, Boston, MA, cert, 1981. **Career:** Gen Motors Corp Hq, Detroit, MI, 1968-79; Gen Motors Rochester Prod, Rochester, NY, dir personnel admin, 1979-82; Gen Motors Packard Elec, Warren, OH, mgr labor rels & safety, 1982-83; Fed Govt, Wash, DC, chmn, fed labor rels auth, 1983-84; Gen Motors C-P-C Group, Warren, MI, dir, HRM, 1984-86; Gen Motors Corp, Warren, MI, gen dir, employee benefits, personnel, 1986-93; GM Truck Group, group dir human resources; Shiloh Community Restoration Found, exec dir, Human Resources Global Product Develop, currently. **Orgs:** Ad bd mem, Univ Mich Bus Sch, 1986-; bd dirs, Urban League Detroit, 1990-; bd dirs, Merrill-Palmer Inst, 1990-; adv bd mem, Nat Black MBA Asn, 1985-; adv bd mem, Cong Assistance Prog, 1989-; bd mem, Charter One Bank; Am Soc Employers; bd dirs, William Beaumont Hosp; life mem, Nat Asn Advan Colored People. **Honors/Awds:** Mary McLeod Bethune Award, Nat Coun Negro Women, 1977; Young Woman of the Year, Nat Asn Negro Bus & Prof Women, 1978; Distinguished Bus Award, Univ Mich, Black Bus Students Asn, 1978; Outstanding Member of the Year, Nat Black MBA Asn, 1981. **Special Achievements:** One of eleven Women "Making It Happen in MI", Redbook Magazine, 1978; One of Crain's Detroit Business Most Influential Women, Ebony, 2001. *

MAHONE, DR. CHARLIE EDWARD
Educator, school administrator. **Personal:** Born Aug 26, 1945, Washington, DC; married. **Educ:** Wayne State Univ, BBS, 1976; Univ Mich, MBA, 1978, PhD, 1981. **Career:** Prof Training Prog, 1979-; Univ Mich, lectr, 1979-81; Ga State Univ, asst prof int bus, 1981-83, dir res, 1981-83; Florida A&M Univ, assoc prof int bus, 1985-89; Howard Univ, Sch Bus, assoc prof, 1989, dept chmn, 1994-98, assoc dean, 1998-2000, dir grad progs, 2000-03, prof int bus, 2000, dept finance int bus & ins, prof, currently. **Orgs:** Chmn social action comt, 1990-94, asst keeper records, 1991-92, WashingtonDC Alumni Chap, Kappa Alpha Psi, Inc; bd dirs, Japan-Am Stud Conf, 1996; Kappa Scholarship Endowment Fund Inc, chmn bd, 1996-98, bd dirs, 1991-95, 1999-, vpres, 1991-95, 1999-; Acad Int Bus Studies; Book ReviewerSouthwestern Publ Co; ed comt, Competitiveness Rev; Int Acad Bus Disciplines; Int Jour Com & Mgt, reviewer; Nat Econ Asn; Soc Int Bus Fel. **Honors/Awds:** Delta Sigma Pi Fraternity; Kappa Alpha Psi Fraternity, Outstanding Educator Award, Outstanding Service to the Fraternity; Melville DiamondScholars Program, Outstanding Service & Dedicated Services; Certificate of Appreciation, Small Bus Develop Ctr; Certificate of Appreciation, Japan-AmStud Conf; Certification of Appreciation, Md Div Corrections; OutstandingAlumnus of the Year, Univ Mich, Black Bus Studs Asn; Exxon Corp Fellow (twice); Chrysler Corp Academic Scholarship (three). **Military Serv:** USAF, airman first class, 1964-68. **Business Addr:** Professor, Howard University School of Business, Department Finance, International Business & Insurance, Rm 519 2600 6th St NW, Washington, DC 20059-0001, **Business Phone:** (202)806-1585.

MAHONE, JEANINE
Marketing executive, buyer. **Personal:** Married Derell Stinson. **Educ:** Tenn State Univ. **Career:** Ericson Mkt Communication, media buyer; Bohan Advert & Mkt, media planner & buyer, currenlty. **Business Addr:** Media Planner, Buyer, Bohan Advertising & Marketing, 124 12th Ave S, Nashville, TN 37203, **Business Phone:** (615)327-1189.

MAHONEY, DWAYNE
Executive. **Career:** Boys & Girls Club Rochester, exec dir & chief prof officer.

MAHONEY, KEITH WESTON
Mental health counselor. **Personal:** Born Jan 12, 1939, Montego Bay, Jamaica. **Educ:** Brooklyn Col, BA, sociol, 1968, MA, polit sci, 1975, MSc, educ, 1982. **Career:** Counselor (retired); Dept Welfare, caseworker, 1968-72; Sch Dist 22 Drug Prev Prog, specialist, 1972-99; consult. **Orgs:** Comt organiser, Vanderveer Park Actions Coun, 1973-79; bd dirs, Amersfort Flatlands Dev elop Corp, 1980-; mediator, C Aid Soc, 1982-; mediator, Brooklyn Col Dispute Resolution Ctr, 1982-; health coordr, Caribbean Action Lobby, 1983-; comt organiser, Amersfort Junction Anti Drug Task Force, 1983-; comn bd mem, Community Bd 14, 1985-; Nat Asn Black Counr, 1985-; Nat Asn Jamaican & Supportive Orgn, (NAJASO); vpres, E Region; co-founder, vpres, Howard Educ & Cult Inst. **Honors/Awds:** Service to Community, Amersfort Flatlands Develop Corp, 1980-83; Excellence & Service to Community, Brooklyn Col Grad Guidance & Counseling Student Orgns, 1982-83; Outstanding Effort to Prevent Drug Abuse, Sch Dist 22 Drug Prev Prog, 1972-. **Military Serv:** AUS, Med Corps, PFC, 2 yrs. *

MAHORN, RICK
Basketball player, basketball coach. **Personal:** Born Sep 21, 1958, Hartford, CT; married Donyale; children: 6. **Educ:** Hampton Univ, BS, bus admin, 1980. **Career:** Basketball player (retired), basketball coach; Washington Bullets, forward, 1980-85; Detroit Pistons, forward, 1986-89, 1996-98; Philadelphia 76ers, forward, 1989-91, 1999; Il Messaggero, forward, 1991-92; Virtus Roma, forward, 1991-92; New Jersey Nets, forward, 1992-96; Detroit Pistons, forward, 1996-98; Detroit Shock, asst coach, 2005-; NBA TV, Tuesday Night with Ahmad, co-host. **Orgs:** Active in numerous charities. **Honors/Awds:** NBA Champion, Detroit Pistons, 1989; CIAA John B McLendon, Jr, Hall of Fame, 2003. **Special Achievements:** NBA All-Defensive Second Team, 1990. **Business Addr:** Assistant Coach, Detroit Shock, 5 Championship Dr, Auburn Hills, MI 48326, **Business Phone:** (248)377-0100.

MAITH, SHEILA FRANCINE
Lawyer. **Personal:** Born Sep 9, 1961, Baltimore, MD; daughter of Warren Edward and Georgia Vinau Haddon; married David Lloyd Douglass, Aug 17, 1985. **Educ:** Duke Univ, Durham, NC, AB, 1983; Harvard Law Sch, Cambridge MA, JD, 1987; Kennedy Sch Govt, Cambridge, MA, MPP, 1987. **Career:** Hill & Barlow, Boston, MA, assoc, 1987-89; Boston Redevelop Authority, Boston, MA, spec asst, 1989; Fannie Mae Found, vpres, 2002; Div Consumer & Community Affairs, asst dir, currently. **Orgs:** Bd dirs, Tent City, 1987-; dir, United South End Settlements, 1987-; Boston Bar Asn & Young Lawyers Div, 1987-89; alumni adv admis comt, Duke Univ, 1989-. **Business Phone:** (202)872-4984.*

MAITLAND, DR. CONRAD CUTHBERT
Physician. **Personal:** Born Jan 17, 1947, St Georges, Grenada; son of Denis and Mavis; children: Nicholas. **Educ:** Univ Detroit, BS, 1973; Wayne State Univ, Sch Med, MD, 1978. **Career:** Self-employed, med dr, pvt practice, 1984-. **Orgs:** Am Med Asn; Mich State Med Soc; Wayne County Med Soc Legislation/Community Affairs; Southeastern Med Soc; Wayne State Univ, Medical Alumni; Wayne County Med Soc Project HOW Volunteer Physi-

cian; Black Medical Alumni Asn. **Honors/Awds:** WCMS-Project HOW, Certificate of Appreciation, 1991; US member of Congress, Certificate of Appreciation, 1991. **Home Addr:** 2106 Hyde Pk Dr, Detroit, MI 48207, **Home Phone:** (313)393-1371. **Business Phone:** (313)864-4452.

MAITLAND, TRACEY
Banker. **Personal:** Born in New York, NY. **Educ:** Columbia Univ, BA, econ, 1982. **Career:** Merrill Lynch & Co Inc, corp intern, NY, corp finance, securities res, Wash, DC, equities sales, Detroit, vpres, sales, dir, convertible bond sales, New York, currently. **Special Achievements:** Listed as one of 25 "Hottest Blacks on Wall Street," Black Enterprise, 1992. **Business Addr:** Director, Convertible Securities, Trading, Merrill Lynch & Co, World Financial Ctr, N Tower 5th Fl, New York, NY 10281, **Business Phone:** (212)449-4040.*

MAJETE, DR. CLAYTON AARON
Educator. **Personal:** Born Apr 19, 1941, Woodland, NC; son of Doreather Jefferson Majete (deceased) and Barnabas Majete (deceased); divorced; children: Lisa & Kim. **Educ:** Morgan State Univ, BA, 1964; New York Univ, MA, 1965, PhD 1984; Univ Pa, Warton Sch, attended 1970. **Career:** City Univ New York, John Jay Col, instr, 1970-72; City Univ New York, Baruch Col, instr 1972-75, dept sociol & anthrop, lectr, 1975-, researcher, currently; New York Times & WCBS-TV, consult & researcher, 1985; Gov State MAR, consult, 1986; State Univ New York, Stonybrook, summer prog med careers, dir. **Orgs:** Am Asn Univ Profs, 1975-; Soc Field Experience Educ, 1978-; chmn bd dirs, Inst Urban Affairs, 1978-; Nat Assoc Black Social Workers, 1980-; Am Sociol Assoc 1981-; Alpha Kappa Delta. **Honors/Awds:** Fel, Johns Hopkins Sch Med. **Special Achievements:** Published "Black Voting Behavior: The Effect of Locus of Control and Socio-economic Status," The Western Journal of Black Studies Vol II, No 3,1987; "Bias on the Study of Interracial Relationships," round table, 1996; Presentation of Annual Lecture Series, Interrace Magazine, ASA AnnualConvention; Appeared on PBS, Tony Brown's Journal, in a discussion onracial categories. **Home Addr:** 35 Hampton Pl, Brooklyn, NY 11213-2612. **Business Addr:** Lecturer, Researcher, City University of New York, Baruch College, Department of Sociology and Anthropology, Rm 260 4th Fl Vertical Campus, New York, NY 10010, **Business Phone:** (646)312-4460.

MAJETTE, DENISE
Politician, lawyer. **Personal:** Born May 18, 1955, Brooklyn, NY; son of Voyd and Olivia; married Roger J Mitchell Jr; children: two sons. **Educ:** Yale Univ, BA, 1976; Duke Univ, JD, 1979. **Career:** Legal Aid Soc Winston-Salem, NC, attny, 1981-83; GA Ct Appeals, law asst, 1984-89; Jenkins, Nelson & Welch, partner, 1989-92; GA Attny Gen's off, spec asst, 1991-92; GA State Bd Worker's Comp, admin law judge, 1992-93; State Ct DeKaulb County, judge, 1993-02; US House Reps, rep, 2003-05; Pvt pract, atty; Ga State, Politician. **Honors/Awds:** You Go Girl Award, GA Asn Black Women Attnys, 1998, 2003; Judge's Community Recognition Award, Black Law Stud Asn, GA State Univ Col Law, 2001. **Business Addr:** Congresswoman, US House Representatives, 1517 Longworth House Off Bldg, Washington, DC 20515-1004.*

MAJOR, DR. CLARENCE
Poet, educator, novelist. **Personal:** Born Dec 31, 1936, Atlanta, GA; son of Inez Huff and Clarence; married Pamela Jane Ritter, 1980. **Educ:** State Univ NY, Albany, BS; Union Inst, PhD. **Career:** Sarah Lawrence Col, Bronxville, NY, lectr, 1972-75; Howard Univ, Wash, DC, lectr, 1975-76; Univ Wash, Seattle, WA, asst prof, 1976-77; Univ Colo,Boulder, CO, from assoc prof to prof, 1977-89; Univ Calif, Davis, profeng, 1989-; Novels: All-Night Visitors, 1969; No, 1973; Reflex & Bone Structure, 1979; Emergency Exit, 1979; My Amputations: A Novel, 1986; Painted Turtle: Woman with Guitar, 1988; New Version of All-Night Visitors, 1998; Dirty Bird Blues, 1996; Poems: Swallow the Lake, 1970;Symptoms & Madness, 1971; Private Line, 1971; The Cotton Club: New Poems,1972; The Syncopated Cakewalk, 1974; Inside Diameter: The France Poems,1985; Surfaces & Masks, 1987; Some Observations of a Stranger at Zuni in the Latter Part of the Century, 1988; Configurations: New & Selected Poems: 1958-98; Dictionary of Afro-American Slang, 1970; The Dark &Feeling: Black American Writers & Their Work (essays), 1974; Such Was the Season: A Novel, 1987; Juba to Jive: A Dictionary of African-American Slang, Penguin, 1994; Calling the Wind, Anthology, 1993; The Garden Thrives, Anthology, 1996; Necessary Distance: Essays & Criticism, 2001;Come by Here: My Mother's Life; Waiting for Sweet Betty, 2002; author of numerous articles, reviews & anthologies; editor; Publication: Waiting for Sweet Betty, 2002; Come by Here: My Mother's Life, 2002; One Flesh, 2003; Such Was The Season, (poetry) 2003; Myself Painting, 2008. **Honors/Awds:** Nat Coun Arts Award, Asn Univ Presses, 1970; Pushcart prize for poem"Funeral," 1976; Fulbright-Hays Inter-Univ Exchange Award, Franco-Amer Comn Educ Exchange, 1981-83; Grant, I.R.E.X. (Poland) 1984-85; Grant, US Info Serv, Am Embassy, Paris, France, 1985; PEN-Faulkner Award; Western State Book Award for Fiction (My Amputations), 1986; Bronze Medal Finalist, Nat Book Award, 1999. **Military Serv:** USAAF, Airman, 1955-57. **Business Addr:** Professor, University of California, Department of English, Davis, CA 95616.

MAJOR, HENRYMAE M.
Counselor. **Personal:** Born Mar 9, 1935, Earle, AR; daughter of Andrew and Clara Sims; married Isadore; children: Kelly Dianne. **Educ:** Lincoln Univ, BS, 1956; Wayne State Univ, MA, Guid & Coun, 1963. **Career:** St IL, recreational therapist, 1957; Cent High Sch Detroit, health, phys educ teacher, bd & educ teacher, 1958-65; guid counr, 1965-70, guid dept head 1970-. **Orgs:** Nat Bd Cert Counr, 1979-; Am Asn Coun Develop, 1980-; Mich Asn Coun Develop, 1980-; Phi Delta Kappa, 1988-; Detroit Counrs Asn; Guild Asn Metro Detroit; Orgn Sch Admin & Supvr; Asn Black Admin; Future Teachers Am Sponsor; Lincoln Univ Alumni Asn; Delta Sigma Theta Alum Chap; Women Wayne St Univ Alumni Chap; established Coord Health Clinic, Spain Middle Sch health coun socio-econ areas; Nat Asn Advan Colored People; Hartford Mem Baptist Church; Mich Asn Col Admis Counr. **Special Achievements:** Co-author, Role of the Counselor. **Home Addr:** 19410 Stratford Rd, Detroit, MI 48221. **Business Addr:** Department Head Guidance, Counseling, 2425 Tuxedo, Detroit, MI 48206, **Business Phone:** (313)252-3017.

MAJORS, ANTHONY Y (TONY MAJORS)
Business owner, automotive executive. **Career:** Varsity Ford Lincoln Mercury Inc, owner & pres, currently. **Special Achievements:** Co is ranked No 29, Black Enterprise mag's list of top 100 auto dealers, 1992. **Business Addr:** Owner, President, Varsity Ford Lincoln Mercury Inc, 1351 Earl Rudder Freeway, College Station, TX 77845, **Business Phone:** (979)694-2022.

MAJORS, JEFF
Musician, media executive. **Personal:** Born Nov 3, 1960?, Washington, DC; son of Major Graham and Annie Pauline Fitzgerald. **Career:** Radio One, Magic 102.3, announcer, 1991-92; WWIN-AM, announcer, 1992-93, asst prog dir & music dir, 1993-95, host, 1994, prog dir, 1995-98; WXCB-AM, prog dir, 1997-98, vpres gospel programming, 1998-; WMAL-TV, Grace & Glory show, host; Tv One, host, 2004-; Albums: Sacred, Universal Music, 1998; Sacred Holidays, 2000; Sacred 2000, 2001; Sacred 2001, 2001; Sacred 4 You, 2002. **Honors/Awds:** Nominated, Stellar Award, 2000; Outstanding Gospel Instrumentalist, Gospel Truth Mag Music Awards, 2002. **Business Addr:** Host, TV One, 5900 Princess Garden Pkwy Suite 400, Lanham, MD 20706, **Business Phone:** (301)429-3270.*

MAJORS, MATTIE CAROLYN
Public relations executive. **Personal:** Born Jan 16, 1945, Waynesboro, GA; daughter of Carrie L Skinner and Willis Van; children: Brandon Matthew Quentin Van. **Educ:** Cent State Univ, BA, chemistry, 1970. **Career:** CWRU Cleveland, rsch lab tech, 1970-72; WABQ Radio Cleveland, newsreporter, 1970; WJMO Radio Cleveland, news reporter, acting news dir, 1970-72; WKBN Radio-TV, Youngstown OH, minority affairs coord, 1972-77; WJKW-TV, reporter, 1977-82; WJBK-TV, news reporter, PM Magazine, 1982-88; Simons Michelson Zieve Advertising, 1991; Ambrose Associates Inc, dir public relations, currently. **Orgs:** Pres mem, Youngstown Sickle Cell Anemia Found, 1973-76; MENSA, Cleveland Press Club, 1980; Negro Bus & Professional Women's Club, 1980; Young Black Businessmen, 1979; Youngstown Fedn Women's Clubs; Freedom Inc; United Negro Improvement Asn; Omega Psi Phi Frat; hon co-chmn, 1986, hon chair, 1987; Black United Fund Campaign, 1986; local AFTRA Chap. **Honors/Awds:** American Cancer Society, 1990; Volunteer Award, State of Mich, 1987. **Business Addr:** Director of Public Relations, Ambrose Assocs Incoporated, 429 Livernois, Ferndale, MI 48220, **Business Phone:** (313)547-4100.*

MAJORS, RICHARD G
Psychologist, educator. **Personal:** Born in Ithaca, NY; son of Richard Majors II and Fannie Sue Majors. **Educ:** Auburn Community Col, AA, humanities, 1974; Plattsburgh State Col, BA, hist, 1977; Univ Ill, Urbana, PhD, educ psychol, 1987. **Career:** Univ Kans, postdoctoral fel, 1987-89; Harvard Med Sch, postdoctoral fel & clin fel, 1989-90; Univ Wis, syst, asst prof, 1990-93; Urban Inst, Wash DC, sr res assoc, 1993-95; Mich State Univ, David Walker Research Inst, fel & scholar, 1996-; Georgetown Univ, Social Policy Prog, hon vis scholar, 1996-97; Univ Manchester, Eng, Leverhulme fel & hon sr scholar, 1996-; Glasgow Univ, Ctr Learning & Support, head, currently. **Orgs:** Greenpeace, 1988; Nat Coun African Am Men, chmn, 1990-92, bd dir, co-founder, 1990-, pres, CEO, 1995-; Am Psychol Asn, 1987; Soc Psycholl Study Ethnic Minority Issues, 1989; Am Orthopsychiatric Asn, 1990; J African Am Men, founder, dep ed; Initiative African Amn Males, co-chmn, 1996. **Honors/Awds:** Outstanding Col Poet Award, Int Publ, 1979; chosen delegate to US Student Lobbyist Asn, Univ Ill Stud Govt Asn, 1981; Am Psychol A, elected fel, Pre-Doctoral Minority Fel, 1984; Presidential Congressional District Delegate, State Kans, 1988; Distinguished EOP Alumni Award, Plattsburg State Col, 1992; Recipient, Arturo Schomburgh Distinguished Service Award & Fred Hampton Image Award, 1994; Minority Achievement Award for Research in Psychology, Am Psychol Asn, 1995; selected one of 2,000 people of the 20th Century, Int Biog Ctr, 1998. **Special Achievements:** Author: "Non-verbal Behaviors and Communication Styles among Black Americans," Black Psychology, Cobb & Henry, 1991; Co-auth, Cool Pose: The Dilemmas of Black Manhood in America, Lexington Bk, 1992; co-ed, The American Black Male: His Present Status & Future, Nelson Hall, 1994; "Black Men," J Men' Studies, 1993, "Cultural Value Differences: Implications for th Experiences of African Am Males," J Men's Studies, 1993 founder, dep ed, J African Am Men, 1992; appointee Rep Ma Owens' exec comt Nat Citizens Comn African Am Educ, 1991 **Home Addr:** N44023 Lee Rd, Strum, WI 54770, **Home Phone** (715)695-3476. **Business Phone:** (014)1330-3420.

MAJORS, SHEENA L
U.S. attorney. **Career:** Wayne Co Neighborhood Legal Serv AID Law Ctr, managing atty, currently. **Business Addr:** Managing A torney, Wayne County Neighborhood Legal Services AIDS Lav Center, Rm 345 51 W Hancock Ave, Detroit, MI 48226, **Busines Phone:** (313)832-8730.

MAJORS, TONY. See MAJORS, ANTHONY Y.

MAJOZO, ESTELLA CONWILL
Educator, poet. **Personal:** Born Jan 1, 1949?, Louisville, KY **Educ:** Univ Louisville, BA, 1975, MA, 1976; Univ Iowa, PhD 1984. **Career:** Blackaliedoscope Cult Ctr Inc, founder & di 1975-77; Ky State Univ, asst prof, 1986-88; City Univ NY, Hunte Col, prof, 1988-2000; Univ Louisville, Dept Eng, distinguishe alumni fel, 1999, prof creative writing, 2000-. **Honors/Awds:** J Stewart Literary Award, Hedgebrook, 2000; Salute to Seve Sisters award, 2006. **Special Achievements:** Autho Metamorphosis, 1975; Darkness Knows, 1975; Jiva Telling Rite 1991; Libation: A Literary Pilgrimage through the African American Soul, 1991; Come Out The Wilderness, 1999; Come O Up to Bright Glory, 2001; Middle Passage: 105 Days, 2002. **Business Addr:** Professor of Creative Writing, University c Louisville, Department of English, Room 319D Humanities Bld 2211 S Brook, Louisville, KY 40292, **Business Phone:** (502)852 3052.

MAKAU, ELENA K
Lawyer. **Personal:** Born Jun 20, 1966, New York, NY; daughte of Marjorie Ann Mathias and Peter M Makau. **Educ:** Hamilto Col, BA, 1988; Albany Law Sch JD, 1991. **Career:** King's Count Dist Atty's Off, atty, 1991-95; Dienst & Serrins LLP, atty, 1995 98; pvt pract, atty, 1998-. **Orgs:** Metrop Black Bar Asn, 1991-; Na Bar Asn, 1991-; New York County Lawyers Asn, 1991-; Brookly Bar Asn, 1991-; AKA Sorority Inc, 1987-. **Business Addr:** At torney, Private practice, 16 Court St Suite 1112, Brooklyn, N 11241, **Business Phone:** (718)643-1922.

MAKOKHA, JAMES A N
Educator, government official. **Personal:** Born Jun 20, 195 Kakamega, Kenya; son of Ali N and Anjema Mitungu; married Pa tricia Brown, Dec 26, 1977; children: Audrey, Jarrett & Justi **Educ:** Albany State Col, Albany, Ga, BBA, 1975-78; Aubur Univ, Auburn, Ala, MSc, 1978-79; Century Univ, Los Angele Calif, PhD, 1985-87. **Career:** Genesee County, Flint, Mich, d elections, 1979-83, dep county clerk, 1984-87; State Mich Lansing, Mich, economist, 1987-88; City Flint, Flint, Mich, d parks & recreation, 1988-90, dir policy & interGovt rels, 1991 Detroit Col Bus, Flint, Mich, exec dir community rels, 1990-9 **Business Addr:** Director, Policy and Intergovernmental Rela tions, 1101 S Saginaw St, Flint, MI 48502, **Business Phone** (313)766-7346.

MAKUPSON, AMYRE ANN PORTER
Television news anchorperson. **Personal:** Born Sep 30, 194 River Rouge, MI; daughter of Rudolph and Amyre Porter; marrie Walter H, Nov 1, 1975; children: Rudolph Porter & Amyre Nis **Educ:** Fisk Univ, BA, dramatics & speech, 1970; Am Univ, MA speech arts commun theory, 1972. **Career:** WSM-TV, Mic Health Maintenance Orgn Plans, pub rels dir, 1973-75; UPN 5 news anchor & pub affairs mgr, 1975-2002; CBS Eyewitne News, news anchor; WSM-TV, anchor; WKBD-TV, news anch & dir pub affairs. **Orgs:** Bd mem, March Dimes, 1983-; bd mer Alzheimers Asn, 1985-; bd mem, Merrill Palmer Inst, 1985-; b mem, Sickle Cell Asn, 1990-; bd mem, Providence Hosp Foun 1995-; bd mem, Skillman Found, 2001; bd mem, Covenant Hous Mich; bd mem, AAA Mich; bd mem, Home Fed Savings Ban **Honors/Awds:** Media Person of the Year, Southern Christia Leadership Conf, 1995; Bishop Harrington Award, Providen Hosp, 1999; Hon Nat Hon Soc, Howard Univ, 2001; 6 Emm Awards: Best Anchor, Best Interview Prog, Best Commentar Michean Year, 2002; Distinguished Woman of theYear, GM Wor ens Club; Exemplary Volunteer Service Award, Mich Govt, 200 **Special Achievements:** March of Dimes, telethon host, 1980-8 C Miracle Network, telethon host, 1986-, UNCF, telethon hos 2001-02, author of So.What's Next, AuthorHouse, honered b City Detroit, City Pontiac, Nat Acad TV Arts & Sci, March Dime Oakland Co Bar Asn, Allstate Ins, Ment Illness Res Asn; Wome In Communs. **Home Addr:** 23475 Coventry Woods, Southfiel MI 48034, **Home Phone:** (248)357-4544.

MALBROUE, JOSEPH, JR.
Executive. **Personal:** Born Aug 24, 1949, Grand Coteau, LA; sc of Joseph Sr and Earline Key; married Joretta Leauntine Tyso **Educ:** Univ Southwestern La, BS, chem, 1966-70. **Caree** Executive (retired); Union Carbide Corp, prod engr, 1970-73, te

sales rep, 1973-76, asst customer serv mgr, 1976-78, dist planner, 1978-84, LPG supply mgr, 1984-2001; SAP Proj Implementation Team, 1997-98. **Orgs:** Dir & coun, Union Carbide Corp, 1975; Gas Processors Asn. **Honors/Awds:** Chairman's Award Union Carbide, 1993; E I Dupont scholarship, Univ Southwestern LA, 1968. **Military Serv:** USMCR, sgt, 1970-76. **Home Addr:** 17114 Canyon Stream Ct, Houston, TX 77095.

MALCOLM, CATHERINE
Restaurateur. **Personal:** Born in Jamaica. **Career:** Jerk Mach Inc, co-owner, 1983-. **Orgs:** Founder, It Takes a Village. **Honors/Awds:** Caribbean Business Women of the Year 2000 Award, Nat Asn Carribean Women, S Fla; Excalibur Awards, Sun-Sentinel Co, 2005. *

MALCOLM, DESMOND
Restaurateur. **Personal:** Born in Jamaica. **Career:** Jerk Mach Inc, co-owner, 1989-. **Business Addr:** Co Owner, Jerk Machine Inc, 111 NW 2nd St, Fort Lauderdale, FL 33301, **Business Phone:** (954)467-8332.*

MALCOM, DR. SHIRLEY MAHALEY
Association executive. **Personal:** Born Sep 6, 1946, Birmingham, AL; daughter of Ben Lee Mahaley and Lillie Mae Funderburg; married Horace, May 31, 1975; children: Kelly Alicia & Lindsey Ellen. **Educ:** Univ Wash, Seattle, Wash, BS, zool, 1967; Univ Calif, Los Angeles, Calif, MA, 1968; Pa State Univ, Univ Park, Pa, PhD, ecol, 1974; Col St Catherine, DHL, 1990; NJ Inst Technol, ScD, 1991; St Joseph Col, DHL, 1992; Knox Col, attended 1993; Bennett Col, attended 1993; Hood Col, attended 1994. **Career:** Univ NC, Wilmington, NC, asst prof, 1974-75; AAAS, Wash, DC, res assoc, staff assoc, proj dir, 1975-77, head, off opportunities sci, 1979-89, head, dirate educ & human resources prog, 1989-; Nat Sci Found, Wash, DC, prog officer, 1977-79. **Orgs:** Am Mus Nat Hist; Nat Sci Bd, 1994-; Bd mem, Nat Ctr Educ & Econ; bd mem, Sci Serv; trustee, Carnegie Corp New York; President's Comt Adv Sci & Technol; bd dir, Howard Heinz Endowment; Sigma Xi. **Honors/Awds:** Black Women Who Make It Happen, Nat Coun Negro Women, 1987; Humanitarian of Year Award, Nat Coalition Title I/Chap I Parents, 1989; Scroll of Honor, Nat Med Asn, 1989. **Business Phone:** (202)326-6400.

MALDON, ALPHONSO, JR.
Executive. **Educ:** Fla A&M Univ; Univ Okla, MA. **Career:** Fleet Boston Financial Corp, Wash, DC, head; Fed Govt Banking, exec vpres; PNC Bank, Corp Banking, sr vpres; dep asst to pres legis affairs; US Senate & House Reps, white house cong liaison; Force Management Policy, asst secy defense, 1999; Lerner Group, partner, currently; Wash Nationals, founding partner & sr vpres external affairs, 2006-. **Orgs:** Am Legion Veterans Asn; Boston Col Club; Boston Partnership; Nat Minority Supplier Develop Coun Inc; Nat Retired Mil Officers Asn; Nat Urban League Inc; Prince Hall Masons Asn. **Honors/Awds:** Civilian Distinguished Public Service Award; Congressional Award. **Special Achievements:** In 1999 he held the highest ranking African-American in the Department of Defense. **Military Serv:** AUS, lt col. **Business Addr:** Senior Vice President External Affairs, Founding Partner, Washington Nationals, RFK Stadium 2400 E Capitol St SE, Washington, DC 20003, **Business Phone:** (202)675-6287.

MALLEBAY-VACQUEUR DEM, JEAN PASCAL
Automotive executive. **Personal:** Born Apr 3, 1953, Paris, France; son of Raymonde and Oumar; married Mada Dao, Sep 7, 1982; children: Alain Moussa, Nelhai Adama, Sara Macora & Alexandre Sega Oumar. **Educ:** Ivory Coast Univ, BA, 1969; ESME, Sch Mech & Electronical Eng, BSME, MSME, 1973-74; INSEAD, European Sch Bus Admis, MBA, 1978; Pantheon Sorbonne, Paris Univ, postgraduate, 1978. **Career:** Mauritania Sch Syst, tech asst, 1974-76; Regie Renault, mfg eng, 1978, mfg plant mgr, 1981-84, eng opers gen mgr, 1985-87, int opers proj exec, 1988; RUSA, asst to exec vpres, 1979-80; Chrysler Corp, spec proj eng gen mgr, 1989-93, Environ Testing Labs, exec eng, environ & emissions testing, exec eng, currently. **Orgs:** INSEAD Alumni, 1978-; Eng Soc Detroit, 1990-; Chrysler African Am Network, 1995. **Military Serv:** Foreign Technical Assistance, VSNA, 1974-76. **Business Addr:** Environmental & Emissions Testing Executive Engineer, Chrysler Corporation, 800 Chrysler Dr E, Auburn Hills, MI 48326-2757, **Business Phone:** (810)576-2769.

MALLETT, CONRAD L
Judge. **Personal:** Born Oct 12, 1953, Detroit, MI; son of Conrad L Mallett Sr; married Barbara Straughn Mallett; children: 3. **Educ:** Univ Calif, Los Angeles, BA, 1975; Univ Southern Calif, MPA, 1979, JD, 1979. **Career:** Judge (retired); State Mich, Lansing, MI, gov, legal adv, dir legis affairs, 1983-84; City Detroit, Detroit, MI, mayor, polit dir, exec asst, 1985-86; Jaffe, Raitt, Heuer & Weiss PC, Detroit, MI, atty, 1986-90; Mich Supreme Ct, Detroit, MI, assoc judge, 1990, chief judge, 1998. **Orgs:** Am Bar Asn; Mich State Bar Asn; Detroit Bar Asn; Wolverine Bar Asn; Genesee County Bar Asn; Nat Asn Advan Colored People; Nat Asn Bond Lawyers; Mich Supreme Ct Hist Soc. **Special Achievements:** The third African American jurist to sit on Michigan Supreme Court; one of only five African American chief justices in the country; first African American to serve as Chief Justice on the Michigan Supreme Court.

MALLETTE, CAROL L
Educator. **Personal:** Born in Philadelphia, PA; daughter of Lewis Moore and Florence Evans Moore; married Kenneth (divorced); children: Tashia & Sydney. **Educ:** Morgan State Univ, Baltimore, MD, BS, 1963; Kean Col New Jersey, Union, NJ, MA, 1971. **Career:** Bd Educ, Pleasantville, NJ, teacher, 1963-65; Dist Columbia Pub Schs, Wash, DC, teacher, 1966-70; Kean Col New Jersey, Union, NJ, coordr col projs, 1971-79; Harristown Develop Corp, Harrisburg, PA, coordr community events, 1981-85; Penn State Univ, Middletown, PA, asst provost/dean, spec events coordr; Southern Jersey Family Med Ctrs, Prog Dir, currently. **Orgs:** Jack & Jill Inc; Delta Sigma Theta Sorority; Pa Legis Black Caucus Found; Atlantic County Human Servs Adv Coun; Atlantic City Chap Links Inc. **Honors/Awds:** Numerous community service awards. **Special Achievements:** Patriot newspaper recognition for carrier judging panel. **Home Phone:** (717)652-7535. **Business Addr:** Director of the Diabetes Outreach and Education System, Southern Jersey Family Medical Centers Inc., 1301 Atlantic Ave, Atlantic City, NJ 08401, **Business Phone:** (609)572-0000.

MALLIET, SCHONE
Executive, president (organization), chief executive officer. **Personal:** Born in South Bronx, NY. **Educ:** Holy Cross, MA, BA, Econ, 1974; Pepperdine Univ, MBA, 1983. **Career:** Applied Data; Comput Assoc; Ziff Davis, vpres sales; Unisys, dir new prod; Western Region Sales Info Resources, vpres; Max Madison Group, managing partner; Citadon Inc, Senior VPres, 2000-01; alyxsys, chmn & chief exec officer, currently; ViaNovus, pres, chief exec officer & founder, currently. **Orgs:** bd dir, The Valley; nat youth competition dir, Nat Brotherhood Skiers; Coaches Educ Comn, US Skiing & Snowboard Asn. **Honors/Awds:** Building Brick Award, NY Urban League; Olympic Torchbearer, Olympic Games Torch Relay, 2002. **Special Achievements:** conducted workshops & presentations to small & large groups in the US & abroad. **Military Serv:** Marine Corps, pilot, 1973-80. **Business Addr:** Presient, Chief Executive Officer, ViaNovus, 1001 Marina Village Pkwy Suite 401, Alameda, CA 94501, **Business Phone:** (510)337-1930.

MALLISHAM, JOSEPH W.
Executive, advocate. **Personal:** Born Jun 14, 1928, Tuscaloosa, AL; married Sadie B Townsend; children: Sheila, Ivy, Darlene. **Educ:** Tuscaloosa County Tech, Trade Sch, 1954. **Career:** advocate, individual rights & social justice; Gulf Serv Station, owner; commissioner, 1984; W Ala Regional Planning Commission, chmn; UA's Presidents Advisory Board; Tuscaloosa Transit Authority; W Ala Health Center. **Orgs:** pres, Druid HS PTSA, 1974; chmn, Tuscaloosa Opportunity Prog, 1968-71; chmn, Tuscaloosa Community Relations Adv Bd, 1969; bd mgmt, YMCA, 1969; Human Rights Com for Bryce Hosp, 1972; NAACP; hon, ODK; pres, Tuscaloosa Citizens for Action; Christ Lutheran Church; Southern Christian Leadership Conference; Ala Democratic Conference. **Honors/Awds:** Citizen of Yr, W Ala Unit, Nat Asn; Man of Yr, Tuscaloosa Community Alpha Phi Alpha Frat, 1974; hon staff, State of Ala, 1972; DavidCochrane Award. **Military Serv:** Corp AUS 1950-51.

MALLORY, GEORGE L, JR.
Lawyer. **Personal:** Born Apr 13, 1952, Washington, DC; son of George L and Anna P. **Educ:** Occidental Col, BA, polit sci, 1974; Western State Univ Law Sch, JD, 1977. **Career:** Los Angeles City Atty, dep city atty, 1979-86; George L Mallory & Assoc, atty, 1986-. **Orgs:** Langston Bar Asn, 1982-; Ncp Los Angeles Br, 1982-; Ctr Early Educ, 1988-; pres, John M Langston Bar Asn, 1991. **Honors/Awds:** Recognition of Service, USS Congressional Records, 1991; Calif State Legislature, Recognition of Service, 1991; Los Angeles District Atty, Recognition of Service, 1990-91; City of Inglewood, Recognition of Service, 1991. **Special Achievements:** Roy Wilkins Dinner; 1986, 1987, 1991. **Business Addr:** Partner, George L Mallory & Associates, 1925 Century Pk E Suite 2000 10th Fl, Los Angeles, CA 90067-2701, **Business Phone:** (310)788-5555.

MALLORY, GLENN OLIVER, JR.
Executive. **Personal:** Born May 2, 1927, Colorado Springs, CO; son of Ruth B and Glenn Mallory; divorced; children: Stephen V, Kim F. **Educ:** Univ Calif, Los Angles, BS, 1951; Calif State Univ, MS, 1975. **Career:** Witco, Allied-Kelite Div, res & develop, 1966-85; Electroless Technologies Corp, pres & owner. **Orgs:** Am Electroplaters Soc, 1953; Electrochemical Soc, 1970; ASTM, 1974; NACE, 1979. **Honors/Awds:** Fel Inst Metal Finishing, UK, 1974. **Special Achievements:** 29 published papers & one book; 15 US patents. **Military Serv:** USN, Pharmicist Male 3rd class, 1944.

MALLORY, JAMES A
Journalist. **Personal:** Born Aug 1, 1955, Detroit, MI; son of Gertrude P Mallory; married Frances, Nov 5, 1977; children: Allison & Allen. **Educ:** Western Mich Univ, BBA, 1977; Mich State Univ, MA, 1982. **Career:** Lansing State J, reporter, 1981-83; Grand Rapids Press, reporter, 1983-84; Detroit News, reporter, 1984-86, asst bus ed, 1986-88; Atlanta J & Constitution, reporter, 1988-89, asst bus ed, 1989-93, news personnel mgr, 1993-96, asst managing ed/nights, 1996-99, managing ed, Initiatives & Opers, sr managing ed & vpres, currently. **Orgs:** Nat Asn Black Journalists, 1993-; Nat Asn Minority Media Execs, 1993-; Atlanta Asn Black Journalists, 1988-97; bd visitors, Sch Journ, Mass Media & Graphic Arts, Fla A&M Univ, 1994-; Western Mich Univ, Alumni Asn, 1994-. **Honors/Awds:** First Place Bus Reporting, Ga Asniated Press, 1992; First Place Bus Reporting, Nat Asn Black Journalists, 1992. **Home Addr:** 2626 Twin Lakes Way, Marietta, GA 30062. **Business Addr:** Senior Managing Editor, Vice President, The Atlanta Journal & Constitution, 72 Marietta St NW, Atlanta, GA 30302, **Business Phone:** (404)526-5325.

MALLORY, WILLIAM L.
State government official. **Personal:** Born Jan 1, 1931?, Cincinnati, OH; married Fannie, Jan 1, 1955; children: William Mallory Jr, Mark, Joe, Dwane, Dale & Leslie Denise. **Educ:** Cent State Univ, elem educ, 1954; Univ Cincinnati. **Career:** Newspaper salesman; bus boy; junkman; iceman; camp counr; porter; bowlingalley attendant; unit leader juv ct; Hamilton County Welfare Dept, casworker & hwy inspector; Cincinnati Pub Sch teacher; Univ Cincinnati, adj prof polit sci, 1969-94; State OH, state rep, 1966-94; OH Elections Comn, mem, 2003-. **Orgs:** Pres, W End Community Coun, 1965; Nat Fedn Settlement Housing; founder, Mallory Ctr Community Develop; founder, African Am Historical Ball. **Honors/Awds:** Pioneer Award, Hamilton OH Comt Aging; Outstanding Citizen Award, City Cinn. **Special Achievements:** The record of being the longest service majority leader in Ohio's hist & the longest service Ohio rep Hamilton Co; First African-American elected as majority floor leader; one of the 50 most influential African Americans, survey by WCIN. **Business Addr:** Member, Ohio Elections Commission, 21 W Broad St Suite 600, Columbus, OH 43215, **Business Phone:** (614)466-3205.

MALONE, AMANDA ELLA
Government official. **Personal:** Born May 30, 1929, Lafayette County, MS; daughter of Jerry Ingrom and Leona; married James; children: Lawrence, Malcolm L, Kenneth Leon, Kelsey LeeSheila Elaine, Cheryl Leona,Travis & James Roland (deceased). **Educ:** Rust Coll Holly Springs MS, AS. **Career:** Marshall County Bd Educ, vice chmn, currently; Elem Sch, sub teacher; Head Start, teacher, parent involvement coord, social serv dir; Marshall & Lafayette County, Social Serv Orgn, pres. **Orgs:** Counr, Sunrise Chap Order Eastern Star, 1989-91; Nat Asn Advan Colored People; sunday sch teacher, New Hope MB Church; Marshall City Bd Educ; Marshall County Hosp Adv Bd; Holly Springs Baptist Asn Banking Comt. **Honors/Awds:** Outstanding Community Service Award, Galena Elem Sch, 1980; Citation, Inst Community Serv Head Start Agency, 1980; Cert Recognition for Outstanding African Am Elected Official Chulahoma MB Church. **Business Addr:** Vice Chairman, Marshall County Board of Education, 2217 Lawshill Rd, Holly Springs, MS 38635.

MALONE, CHARLES A
Lawyer. **Personal:** Children: Tony, Charles, Vicki, Keith, Kevin & Julian. **Educ:** Detroit Col, JD. **Career:** Sura & Malone, Inkster, Mich, atty law; Mobil Oil Corp, anal chemist, 1966-72. **Orgs:** Mich Bar Asn; Detroit Bar Asn; charter mem, Mich State Bar Crim Law Sect, Nat Asn Advan Colored People; chmn, Inkster & Elected Officers Compensation Bd; co-chmn, Westwood Community Sch Dist Ad Hoc Comn; Elks; Golden Gate Lodge; IBPOE W; Lions.

MALONE, CLAUDINE BERKELEY
Executive. **Personal:** Born in Louisville, KY. **Educ:** Wellesley Col, BA; Harvard Bus Sch, MBA. **Career:** IBM Corp, systs engr, 1963-65; Raleigh Stores, controller, mgr dp, 1966-70; Crane Co, sr systs engr, 1966; Harvard Bus Sch Bus Admin, assoc prof, 1972-81; Fin & Mgt Consult Inc, pres & chief exec officer, 1982-; Sch Bus Admin, Georgetown Univ, adj prof, 1982-84; Colgate-Darden Bus Sch, Univ Va, vis prof, 1984-87; Fed Res Bank Richmond, chmn bd, 1996-99; Hasbro Inc, dir; Novell Inc, dir; viva Life Ins Co, dir. **Orgs:** Trustee, Dana Hall Sch, 1974-77; treas, Wellesley Col Alumni Asn. 1977-80; trustee, Wellesley Col, 1982-; dir, cott Paper Co, Campbell Soup Co, MTV Networks, The Limited, Dart Drug, Supermarkets Gen Corp, Houghton Mifflin Corp, Penn Mutual Life, The Boston Co. **Honors/Awds:** Candace Award, Nat Coalition Black Women, 1982. **Business Addr:** President, Chief Executive Officer, Financial Management Consulting Inc, 7570 Potomoc Fall Rd, McLean, VA 22102.

MALONE, DR. CLEO
Health services administrator, executive director. **Personal:** Born Mar 2, 1934, Athens, AL; son of Phillip Sr and Estelle Hereford; married Judy Sue Lower, Aug 31, 1974; children: Pamela McKinley, Daniel, Karen Wade, Donald & Kaya Malone. **Educ:** Cleveland Col Case Western Res Univ, psychol, social, 1963-66; Urban Training Inst Chicago, theol training, 1967-68; Cleveland State Univ, Group Dynamics, 1970-71; Union Inst, Health Planning, PhD, philosophy, 1981. **Career:** United Church Christ, Community Org, United Area Citizens Agency, consult & expeditor, 1969-71; UCSD Muir Col, LaJolla, assoc dean students, 1971-75; Univ Hosp, asst dir, comm liaison officer, 1975-80; S San Diego Health Educ Ctr, exec dir, 1980-84; The Palavra Tree Inc, San Diego, exec dir, 1984-. **Orgs:** Campus minister Case Western Res Univ, 1969-71; Calif Coun Alcohol Problems; adv bd, San Diego County Alcohol; sec San Diego Asn Black Health Serv Exec; orgn, Protestant Ministry Poverty, 1961-64; assoc minister, E Cleveland Cong Church, 1961-64; vpres, San Diego Interdn-

mntnl Ministerial Alliance, 1985; bd dir, San Diego Urban League; bd dir, Calif Coun Alcohol Policy, 1984-; bd dir, Nat Black Alcoholism Coun, 1988-. **Honors/Awds:** Black Fellowship Award; UCSD Black Faculty & Staff; Outstanding Achievement Award, 1985-88; Outstanding Drug Service Provider Award, San Diego County, 1987-90; Outstanding Achievement Award, Asn Drug & Alcohol Admin Calif, 1992; Outstanding Community Service Award, San Diego Police Dept, 1992; Citizen Recognition Award, County of San Diego, 1992; Eureka Fellowship, 1995. **Special Achievements:** Publication "Minority Participation in Health Planning" 1981. **Home Addr:** 6659 Thornwood St, San Diego, CA 92111. **Business Addr:** Executive Director, Palavra Tree Inc, 1212 S 43rd St, San Diego, CA 92113, **Business Phone:** (619)263-7768.

MALONE, EUGENE WILLIAM
Educator. **Personal:** Born Aug 8, 1930, Washington, PA; married Roberta Joanne Miller; children: Gina Dawn. **Educ:** Cent State Univ, AB, sociol, 1957, BS, educ, 1958; Ky State Univ, MEd, guid & couns, 1962; Nova Univ, EdD, 1976. **Career:** Canton Pub Schs, teachr, 1958-59; Cleveland Pub Schs, teacher, 1959-64, guidance counr, 1965-67, group discussion leader, 1966-67; Community Action Youth, guidance counr, 1964-65; Cent State Univ, dean men, 1967-68; Curber Assoc, consult, 1968-71; Shaker Heights Pub Schs, consult, 1969-70; Cleveland State Univ, coordr stud develop proj, 1968-70, dir stud develop prog, 1970-72; Cuyahoga Community Col, dean stud servs, 1975-, dir coun admin & recs, 1972-75. **Orgs:** Vocational Educ Adv Bd, 1979; Ohio Asn Staff Prog & Orgn Develop, 1979; Nat & Asn Stud Pers Adminr; Am Pers & Guidance Asn; Ohio Pers & Guidance Asn. **Honors/Awds:** Good Conduct Medal. **Military Serv:** USAF, airman, 1949-53. **Business Addr:** Dean, Cuyahoga Community College, 25444 Harvard Rd, Cleveland, OH 44122.

MALONE, DR. GLORIA S.
Educator. **Personal:** Born May 12, 1928, Pittsburgh, PA; daughter of John H Snodgrass and Doris Harris Snodgrass; married Arthur A; children: Merrick, Deanna & Myrna. **Educ:** Cent State Col, OH, BS, 1949; Kent State Univ, MEd, 1956, MA, 1969, PhD, 1979. **Career:** Alliance OH Pub Schs, elem teacher, 1949-53, high sch teacher, 1953-69; Mt Union Col, prof eng, 1969-90, prof emer, 1991-; Ohio Northern Univ, vis prof, 1990-91; Stark Co Head Start Prog, educ coordr, 1991-93; SCCPA, employ develop officer, currently. **Orgs:** Nat Asn Advan Colored People; Second Baptist Church; Nat Educ Asn; Am Asn Univ Prof; Delta Kappa Gamma Soc; grand worthy matron, Amaranth Grand Chapter OES PHA, 1972-74; bd dir, Alliance United Way; bd dir, Alliance Salvation Army; Alpha Kappa Alpha Sorority; bd dir, Alliance YWCA; bd dir, Church Women United. **Honors/Awds:** State Scholarship Awards, Delta Kappa Gamma, 1967, 1974; Teacher of theYear, Alliance High Sch, 1969; Outstanding Member, Al Kaf Ct Dts Isis Akron, 1970; Citizen of the Year, 1986; Martin Luther King Award, 1996. **Home Addr:** 323 E Main St, Alliance, OH 44601. **Business Addr:** Professor Emeritus, Mount Union College, 1972 Clark Ave, Alliance, OH 44601.

MALONE, DR. J. DEOTHA
School administrator, educator, government official. **Personal:** Born May 27, 1932, Sumner County, TN; daughter of Sadie Malone and Harvey Malone. **Educ:** Fisk Univ, Nashville, BA, 1950, MA, 1955; Tenn State Univ, MA, adult educ,1973; Ala State Univ, Montgomery, EdD, 1974; Univ Ala, Tuscaloosa, PhD, 1981. **Career:** School administrator, educator (retired), government official; Sumner Co Sch Syst, teacher & librn, 1950-70; suprv elem educ, 1969-81; suprv adult educ, instr & supvr sec educ, supvr int stud, 1986-2004; City Gallatin, TN, vice-mayor, 1969-; State Community Col, instr, 1976-80; Tenn State Univ, instr, 1982-83. **Orgs:** Dept Elec Power Adv Bd, 1990-; Nat Asn Advan Colored People; Gallatin Voter's League; Beacon Civic Club; Econ Dev Prog; vpres, Dem Women's Club Sumner Co; Notary Pub; Nat Educ Asn; adv bd, Tenn Educ Asn; Mid Tenn Educ Asn; Sumner Co Educ Asn; Tenn Asn Pub Sch Adult Educ; Austin Peay Area Supvr Coun; Tenn Asn Adult Educrs; Phi Delta Kappa; Tenn Asn Supvr & Admin; adv, Gallatin Day Care Ctr; Human Serv Career Educ Adv Comm Vol, State Community Col; adv bd, Tenn Asn Lic Practical Nurses; bd dir, Tenn Educ Asn; adv bd, First & Peoples Bank Gallatin; Gov Mgt Team; Tenn Master Teacher Prog; First Baptist Church; Rotary Club; Rotarian chmn, Community Drug Awareness Prog; Gallatin Planning Comn; Kappa Delta Pi Nat Hon Soc. **Special Achievements:** First African-American female notary public Sumner Co. **Home Addr:** 229 S Pardue Ave, Gallatin, TN 37066, **Home Phone:** (615)452-5546. **Business Phone:** (615)451-5961.

MALONE, JAMES HIRAM
Graphic artist, writer, painter (artist). **Personal:** Born Mar 24, 1930, Winterville, GA; son of Ralph Sr and Sarah Lena Echols; married Mary Louise Liebaert (divorced 1982); children: Andrew Ralph & Matthew Martin. **Educ:** Morehouse Col, Atlanta, GA, AA, 1951; Ctr Creative Studies Col Art & Design, Detroit, MI, AA, 1962. **Career:** Graphic Artist (retired), Writer, Painter: Feds Dept Stores, Detroit, MI, graphic artist designer, 1964-69; Northgate Art Agency, Detroit, MI, graphic artist designer, 1969-75; Montgomery Ward, Southfield, MI, graphic artist designer, 1975-80; K-Mart Int Hq, Troy, MI, sr graphic artist designer, 1980-83; Atlanta J Const Newspapers, Atlanta, GA, advert graphic artist, sr graphic designer, 1983-90; graphic artist & writer, currently; Atlanta News Leader, Street Beat, columnist, 1991-; Laughing Trees, Inc, chief exec officer, currently; Metrop Col Art, graphic designer, 2002; Self-illustrated books: Here There Poetry, Blues poetry, 1954; Grandma Sarah's Closet, 1960; Brother Cartoons, 1970; Malone's Atlanta cartoon panel, 1986; Simply Apply Yourself (say) literacy Guide, 1988; Y All Come Back, 1988; The Democrats are coming, 1988; No-Job Dad juvenile book, 1992; Urban History: Buttermilk Bottom RepoHistory Art Markers, 1995-97; Jones' Family Cart, 1997; Black Movie Theatres Markers, 1996; April Mae Jones' Coloring Book, Ralph's Post syndicated comic strip, 1998; Living Longer cartoon strip, 1999; If I live novel, 1999; Artistic Trees, Craftsman Guide, 2000; Song Lyrics: "Married to This World", 1973; "Talk to Your Child", 1986; "Willie Lives in the Streets", 1986; "Homeless Hope", 1987; "The Atlanta Project (Tap)", 1995; June Mundy, song tribute, 2006. **Orgs:** Ctr Creative Studies, Col Alumni Asn, 1963-; Ad Hoc Comt, Atlanta Art Coun, 1990-; writer & contrib, Asn Am Cults, 1980-; promotions & gallery assoc, Visual Vanguard Art Group, 1988-; bd mem, Atlanta/Fulton County Neighborhood Planning Unit J, 1984-; bd mem, Grasp: Bankhead Hwy Revitalization Proj, Atlanta, 1990-; bd mem, First World Writers, Inc, 1985-; Atlanta Mayor Jackson's Arts Task Force Comm, consult, 1990-; publicity, Lit Inc, 1988-; consult, Gas Artists Registry, Atlanta Col Art, 1989-; publicity consult, Pres Carters Atlanta Cluster Proj, 1992-; vpres, 1993, pres, 1997, Int Black Writers Asn, Inc; arts consult, Atlanta Olympic Comm, 1993; NPU-J area chairperson, Atlanta Mayors Bicycle Planning Comm, 1995; arts consult, Douglass Cluster, 1995, arts chairperson, W Fulton Cluster, 1995, Atlanta Proj; bd mem, 1984, pub safety comm, 1996, Atlanta/Fulton County Neighborhood Planning Unit J; vpres, 1993, pres, 1997, Int Black Writers Asn, Inc, Local 22; bd mem, Atlanta/Fulton County Action Authority, Inc, 1996; pres, Buttermilk Bottom Comm Asn, Inc, 1996; bd mem, Individual Visual Artists Coalition Asn, 1996; bd mem, Keep Atlanta Beautiful, 2004; chief exec officer, Grove Park Arts Alliance, 2005; Southern Poverty Law Ctr; RepoHistory Asn. **Honors/Awds:** Atlanta University Nat Art Award, 1949; Nat Scholastic Art Award, 1949; Bronze Jubilee Community Art Award, Atlants, 1986; Center For Creative Studies Alumuni Art Honor, 1987; Art with a Southern Drawl Art Award, Mobile Col, 1993; Top prize, Atlanta Olympic Wall Art contest, 1995; First Place, Centennial Olympic park Fence Art Contest, 1995; Atlanta Olympic Art Award, 1996; Boone Express, Bus Tour Laughing Trees, Inc., 1998; Together Atlanta Community Award, 1999; First Place, Motion Through Art Chrysler Calendar Contest, 2001; Perfect Lawn Contest, 2001; Georgia Artist for Gallery, Green Puzzle Art, 2002; Daimler Chrysler Art Award, 2002. **Special Achievements:** First person of color to hold the Fort Jackson post of Art Coordinator NCO and an instructor of the 3431 Army Services Unit Craft Shop; Featured in Disney Movie, 2002. **Military Serv:** AUS, Spec Serv, chief illusr, sfc, 1951-59. **Home Addr:** 1796 North Ave NW, Atlanta, GA 30318-6441, **Home Phone:** (404)794-0948. **Business Addr:** Chief Executive Officer, Laughing Trees Inc, 1796 N Ave NW, Atlanta, GA 30318-6441, **Business Phone:** (404)794-0948.

MALONE, JEFFREY NIGEL
Basketball coach, basketball player. **Personal:** Born Jun 28, 1961, Mobile, AL; children: Joshua Malone & 2 children. **Educ:** Miss State Univ, BS, polit sci, 1983. **Career:** Basketball player (retired), basketball coach; Wash Bullets, 1983-90; Utah Jazz, 1990-93; Philadelphia 76ers, 1993-95; Miami Heat, 1995-96; Yakima Sun Kings, asst coach, 1998; Columbus River dragons, head coach; Florida Flame, head coach, 2006. **Honors/Awds:** All-Southeastern Conf; SEC Player of the Year; All-Am, The Sporting News; All Rookie Team, 1984.

MALONE, KARL ANTHONY
Basketball player, basketball coach. **Personal:** Born Jul 24, 1963, Summerfield, LA; son of Shirley Turner and J P Malone; married Kay; children: Kadee Lynn, Kaylee Ann & Karl Jr. **Educ:** La Tech Univ, Ruston, LA, 1985. **Career:** Basketball player (retired); Utah Jazz, forward, 1985-2003; Los Angeles Lakers, forward, 2003-04; La Tech Univ, Ruston, dir basketball promotion & asst strength & conditioning, 2007-. **Honors/Awds:** NBA All-Star, 1988-97; NBA All-Rookie Team, 1986; All-NBA First Team, 1989 & 1990; Most Valuable Player, NBA All Star Team, 1989, 1993, 1997; Olympic gold medalist, 1992, 1996; Utahn of the Year, Salt Lake Tribune, 1997; IBM Award, 1997-98; Number Retired, Utah Jazz, 2005. **Special Achievements:** US Olympic Basketball Team, 1992, 1996; Selected as one of the 50 Greatest Players in NBA Hist, 1996; NBA All-Star Game, top vote getter in Western Conf, 1998; first player in league hist to be named to 11 All-NBA first teams; holds third place on the NBA career scoring list; broke NBA free-throw record, 2001. **Business Addr:** Director, La Tech University, PO Box 3178, Ruston, LA 71272, **Business Phone:** (318)257-3555.

MALONE, MAURICE
Fashion designer, business owner. **Personal:** Born 1965, Detroit, MI. **Career:** Hardware Maurice Malone, founder, 1984; Label X, founder, 1988; Maurice Malone Designs Blue Jeans Your A-, founder, 1990; Hostile Takeover Records, founder, 1999; Maurice Malone Designs, pres & ceo, currently; MM Licensing Group LLC, owner & designer, currently. **Orgs:** Coun Fashion Designers Am. **Honors/Awds:** Nominee, Perry Ellis Menswear Designer of the Year award, 1998. **Business Addr:** Owner, Designer, MM Licensing Group LLC, 89 Grand St, Brooklyn, NY 11211, **Business Phone:** (718)486-0088.

MALONE, MICHAEL GREGORY
Administrator. **Personal:** Born Oct 27, 1942, Evansville, IN; son of Eugene Malone, Jr and Norma Louise; children: Malik LeRoi & Stephanie Nicole. **Educ:** Butler Univ, attended 1961; IN State Univ Evansville, 1971; Univ Evansville, BS, Pol Sci, 1974. **Career:** Iglehart Opers, qual control tech, 1966-68; CAPE, dir youth prog, 1968-71, dir commun serv, 1971-72, exec dir; Malone Assoc Inc, pres, mgr. **Orgs:** Nat Assoc Social Workers; charter mem, bd dirs, Nat Council Transp Disadvantaged; bd mem, Govs Coun Addictions; Downtown Civitans; Lakeview Optimist; exec bd mem, Boy Scouts Am Buffalo Trace Coun; Southern IN Soccer Officials Assoc. **Honors/Awds:** Community Service Award, Gov IN, 1976; Outstanding Man Award, Commun Affairs Evansville Black Expo, 1978. **Home Addr:** 2607 Belize Dr, Evansville, IN 47725.

MALONE, MOSES EUGENE
Basketball player. **Personal:** Born Mar 23, 1955, Petersburg, VA; married Alfreda (divorced); children: Moses & Michael. **Career:** Basketball player (retired); Utah Stars, ABA, ctr, 1974-75; St Louis Spirits, ABA, ctr, 1975-76; Buffalo Braves, 1976-77; Houston Rockets, 1976-82; Philadelphia 76ers, 1982-86, 1993-94; Wash Bullets, 1987-88; Atlanta Hawks, 1989-91; Milwaukee Bucks, 1991-93; San Antonio Spurs, Ctr, 1994-95. **Honors/Awds:** NBA Most Valuable Player, 1979, 1982, 1983; NBA Playoff MVP, 1983; Virginia Sports Hall of Fame, 1999; NBA Hall of Fame, 2001; Naismith Basketball Hall of Fame, 2001. **Special Achievements:** First basketball player to jump straight from high school into the professional leagues; named one of the NBA's 50 greatest players, 1997.

MALONE, ROSEMARY C
Law enforcement officer. **Personal:** Born Jun 23, 1954, Detroit, MI; daughter of Jesse James (deceased) and Rosetta M Cook; divorced; children: LaNetha P. **Educ:** Univ Detroit, MA, 1990; Univ Detroit-Mercy, doctoral cand, clin psychol. **Career:** Detroit Police Dept, police officer, 1974; Family Investment Admin, chief, currently. **Orgs:** Co-dir, Adopt-A-Cop, 1992-; Nat Asn Advan Colored People; World Prophetic Outreach Ministries. **Honors/Awds:** Twenty Letters of Appreciation, 1979-90; 15 Citations, 1979-90; Chiefs Unit Award, 1989; Officer of Year, Detroit Police Dept, 1993. **Business Addr:** Chief, Family Investment Administration, 311 W Saratoga St, Baltimore, MD 21201, **Business Phone:** (410)767-7974.

MALONE, SANDRA DORSEY
Educator, executive. **Personal:** Born in Mexia, TX; married Joseph L. **Educ:** MEd, 1972; BS. **Career:** Team Teaching Sch Chattanooga, team leader, 1961-65; Guaranteed Performance Proj Dallas, educ analyst, 1970-71; Accountability, asst dir, 1972-74; Dallas Independent Sch Dist, asst dir, 1974-75; The Links Inc,Western Area dir, 2003-07. **Orgs:** Dallas Sch Adminr & Asn; Am Asn Sch Adminr; Am Educ Res Asn State; organizer, Nat Coun Negro Women, 1973-75; pres, Dallas Alumnae Chap Delta Sigma Theta, 1973-75; pres, RL Thornton PTA, 1973-74; vpres, Hulcy Middle Sch PTA, 1975-76. **Honors/Awds:** President Award, Pan Hellenic Coun, 1973; President Award, RL Thornton PTA, 1974; Community Service Award, United Action Dallas Negro Chamber Com, 1975; Service Award, Delta Omega Chap Delta Sigma Theta, 1975. **Business Addr:** Western Area Director, The Links Inc, 1200 Mass Ave NW, Washington, DC 20005.

MALONE, THOMAS ELLIS
Scientist. **Personal:** Born Jun 3, 1926, Henderson, NC; married Dolores; children: Shana & Thomas Jr. **Educ:** NC Ctrl Univ, BS, 1948; MD; Harvard Univ, PhD, 1952. **Career:** Professor (retired), NC Ctrl Univ, Durham, prof zoology, 1952-58; Argonne Nat Lab, resident res assoc, 1958-59; Loyola Univ, Chicago, fac mem, 1959-62; Nat Inst Dental Res, NIH, asst chief res grants sec, 1963-64, dep chief extramural progs, 1964-66, chief periodont dis & soft tissue studies, 1966-67; Am Univ Beirut, Lebanon, Biol Dept, pro & chmn, 1967-69, assoc dir extramural progs, Nat Inst Dental Res, 1969-72, assoc dir extramural res & training, dep dir, NIH, act dir, 1972-86; Univ Md, Baltimore, assoc vice chancellor res, 1986-88; Asn Am Med Cols, vpres biomed res, 1988-93. **Orgs:** Ins Med-Nat Acad Sci. **Honors/Awds:** Harvard Fellow, 1950-52; NAS-NRC Research Fellow, 1958-59; Superior Service Award, Dept Health, Educ & Welfare, 1971; Distinguished Service Award, 1974; Certificate of Merit, Am Col Dentists, 1975; Presidential Merit Award, Sr Exec Serv, 1980; Distinguished Exec Ran Award, 1983; DHHS, Secretary's Recognition Award, 198 **Military Serv:** AUS 1945-46. **Home Addr:** 8512 Post Oak R Potomac, MD 20854.

MALONEY, CHARLES CALVIN
Physician. **Personal:** Born May 24, 1930, W Palm Beach, FL; married Ethel Pearl Covington; children: Charda Corrie, Charl

ılvin, III. **Educ:** FL A&M Univ, BS, 1951;Franklin Sch, Med ·c, 1956. **Career:** N Dist Hosp Inc, chief med tech; Christian ɔsp Miami, Chief Tech 1956-58; Provident Hosp, 1958-62; Broırd Gen Med Ctr, 1962-75; Gen Diagnostics Sci Prod, clinical ·ecialist. **Orgs:** Am Med Tech; Omega Psi Phi; Boys Club; Jacs c; vpres & secy, Broward Med Ctr Credit Univ, 1971; Jack & ıl Am Inc; secy, Omega Psi Phi, 1962-65; Connecting Link; All ·n Tackle FL Agr & Mech Univ, 1950-55; Basilus, 1970-71. **onors/Awds:** Man of Year, Omega Psi Phi, 1960-62. **Military ·rv:** USAF, sgt, 1951-54. *

IALRY, LENTON
ıucator, government official. **Personal:** Born Sep 30, 1931, ıreveport, LA; married Joy. **Educ:** Grambling State Univ, BS, ·52; Tex Col, MEd, 1957; Univ NMex, PhD, 1968. **Career:** buquerque Sch Syst, jr high sch teacher & prin; Albuquerque ·b Sch, teacher, human resources eeo dir, dir cultural awarness, un & advisor; La Mesa Elem Sch, prin, equal opportunity of- ·er, 1975; John Marshall Elem Sch, prin; Univ NMex, adj prof; Mex House of Representatives, rep, 1968-78; NMex Legis, Ber- ·lillo County Bd County Comnrs, comnr, 1980-83, chmn, 1983- ·, 1987-88; Malry & Assocs, pres; Albuquerque, co-comnr; Ber- ·lillo County govt, neighborhood prog coordr, currently. **Orgs:** ıiv NMex African Am Studies Prog. **Special Achievements:** buquerque's first Negro school principal, 1964; The first black ·ected to the New Mexico House Representatives, 1968; The first frican American to be elected as Bernalillo County Commis- ·ner, 1980. **Business Phone:** (505)768-2500.

'ALVEAUX, ANTOINETTE MARIE
ssociation executive. **Personal:** Born Mar 19, 1958, San Fran- ·o, CA; daughter of Warren and Proteone. **Educ:** Wharton Sch; ıiv San Francisco, MBA, 1981; Univ Pennsylvania, MBA, 1985. **areer:** Am Express Bank, planner, 1985-86; sr planner, 1986-88, ·, strategic planning, 1988-90, dir, strategic planning & global ·kt, 1990-91; Nat Black MBA Asn, dir opers, 1991-93, exec dir, ·94-00, pres & ceo, 2000-. **Orgs:** bd mem, Girl Scouts Am, ·98-99; bd mem, Better Bus Bur, 1998-; bd mem, Mgt Asn Ill, ·96-99; chair, Mamott Customer Diversity Leadership Forum, ·93-; bd mem, Behav Res & Action Social Sci Found, 1993-97; · mem, chap pres, Nat Black MBA Asn, 1987; Nat Urban ·ague, Black Exchange Prog, 1989; Alumni Admissions rep, ·harton Sch, Univ Pennsylvania, 1985-; Alumni Adv Comt, Delta ·gma Theta Sororities Inc, 1986. **Honors/Awds:** Outstanding ·ung Women of America, 1987; Black Achievers Award, Harlem ·ung Men's Christian Asn, 1989; Today's Chicago Women, 100 ·omen Making a Difference, 1995, 1999. **Special Achievements:** ·ople to People Ambassador Programs, Delegation Leader to ·uth Africa, 1998. **Business Addr:** President, National Black ·BA Association, 180 N Michigan Ave Suite 1400, Chicago, IL ·601, **Business Phone:** (312)236-2622.*

ALVEAUX, FLOYD JOSEPH
ımunologist, executive director. **Personal:** Born Jan 11, 1940, ·pelousas, LA; son of Delton and Inez Lemelle; married Myrna ·iiz Malveaux, Dec 27, 1965; children: Suzette, Suzanne, Court- ·y, Gregory. **Educ:** Creighton Univ, Omaha, NE, BS, 1961; ·yola Univ, New Orleans, MS, 1964; Mich State Univ, East ·nsing, PhD, 1968; Howard Univ Col Med, MD, 1974. **Career:** ·oward Univ Col Med, asst prof microbial, 1968-70, assoc prof ·d, 1978-84, assoc prof microbiol & med & chair, Dept Micro- ·l, 1989-94, prof microbiol & med & dean, 1995-05, interim ·res Health Affairs, 1996, vice provost health affairs, 2000-03; ·hns Hopkins Univ, assoc prof med, 1984-89; Urban Asthma & ·lergy Ctr, Baltimore, founder & pres, 1986-89; Merck Child- ·od Asthma Network Inc, exec dir, 2005-. **Orgs:** Am Col Physi- ·ans; Am Acad Allergy Asthma & Immunol; bd dir, Am Lung ·sn; bd dir, Nat Allergy & Infectious Diseases Adv Coun; comt ·mn, Underrepresented Minorities, Am Acad Allergy Asthma & ·munol; bd trustee, Asthma & Allergy Found Am; Nat Asthma ·uc & Prev Prog, Nat Heart Lung Blood Inst, NIH; founder & ·s, Urban Asthma & Allegory Ctr, Baltimore, MD, 1986-89; bd ·ıstee, Nat med Asn, 1988-84; Alpha Omega Alpha Hon Med ·c; elected mem, Inst Med, Nat Acad Scis; Nat Asn Advan ·lored People; Sigma Xi Sci Res Soc. **Honors/Awds:** Medical ·rvice Award, Nat Med Asn, 1986; National Research Service ·ward, NIH; Clemens von Pirquet Research Award, Georgetown ·h Med; Outstanding Faculty Research Award, Howard Univ; ·gacy of Leadership Award, Howard Univ Hosp. *

ALVEAUX, JULIANNE
·onomist, writer. **Personal:** Born Sep 22, 1953, San Francisco, ·; daughter of Proteone and Paul Warren. **Educ:** Boston Col, ·, 1974, MA, 1975; Mass Inst Technol, PhD, 1980. **Career:** ·onomist, author & commentator; Books: Wall Street, Main ·reet & the Side Street: A Mad Economist Takes a Stroll, Pines ·e Publications, 1999; What is Robeson's Legacy?; Paul Robe- ·n: Artist & Citizen, contributor, 1998; Minister Farrakhan's ·onomic Rhetoric & Reality; The Farrakhan Factor, 1998; Sex, ·s & Sterotypes: Perspectives of a Mad Economist, 1994; Slip- ·ng Through the Crack: The Status of Black Women, contributor, ·89; San Francisco State Univ, asst prof, 1981-85; Univ Calif- ·rkeley, vis scholar, vis faculty, 1985-92; Pacifica Radio ·twork, The Julianne Malveaux Show, host, exec producer, ·94-96; Nat Coun Negro Women, Voice of Vision: African-Am Women on the Issues, editor-in-chief, 1996; WLIB, Julianne Malveaux's Capitol Report, radio host, 1997-98; Black Issues in Higher Education, columnist, 1993-; Last Word Productions, pres & chief exec officer, 1995-; USA Today, guest columnist, currently; Bennett Col, pres, currently. **Orgs:** Pres, Nat Asn Negro Bus & Prof Women's Club Inc, 1995-; chair, bd dir, Nat Child Labor Comm, 1996-; mem numerous Bds and committees. **Honors/Awds:** Honarary Doctorate, Sojourner Douglas Col. **Business Phone:** (202)298-9490.

MAN, METHOD. See SMITH, CLIFFORD.

MANAGER, VADA O.
Presidential aide. **Personal:** Born Nov 26, 1961, East St Louis, IL; son of Ethel; married Charlene; children: 5. **Educ:** Ariz State Univ, BS, Polit Sci, 1983; London Sch Econ, Grad work. **Career:** Ariz Dept Com, special asst, 1984-86; Office Gov, special asst, 1986-87, pres secy, special asst, 1988-91; Babbit PRS, polit adv, special asst pres, 1987-88; Young Smith Res, vpres pub finance, 1988; Off Mayor, pres secy, 1991; Nike Inc, dir global issues mgt, Ashland's bd dirs, Finance and Personnel & Compensation comm, 2008-; independent global consultant, currently. **Orgs:** Ariz Bd Regents, 1982-83; NCP; Am Coun Germany, 1990; pres, CMS Presial Debates, 1992; Coun USS & Italy, 1992. **Honors/Awds:** Young Alumni Achievement, Ariz State Univ Alumni Asn, 1989. **Home Addr:** 1304 R St NW, Washington, DC 20009, **Home Phone:** (202)387-6513.

MANCE, JOHN J.
Consultant. **Personal:** Born Mar 18, 1926, Chicago, IL; son of S J and Anna; married Eleanore Edson, Oct 9, 1949; children: Richard & David. **Educ:** Calif-AERO Tech Inst, AeroE, 1949; UCLA, Indust Rel, 1969; Univ So CA, Exec Progs, 1972. **Career:** Consultant (retired); Frank Mayer Engr Co, tool designer, 1950-52; So CA Coop, Wind Tunnel Tech, 1952-56; Marquardt Aircraft Co, wind tunnel engr, 1956-59; Don Baxter Inc, engr designer, 1959-63; San Fernando Valley Lutheran Hosp Asn Credit Union, asst treas & mgr, 1963-66; Lockheed Watts Willowbrook Plant, indust rel dept mgr, 1970-72, asst indust rel dir, 1973-79, employee transp mgr, 1980-85, personnel rel rep, 1986-88, human rel consult, 1988-90; Employ Interviewer, 1969; Aerospace Engr, 1966-68; Lockheed Aeronautical Systems Co, 1966-90. **Orgs:** Nat bd dirs, pres, Nat Advan Asn Colored People Golden Heritage, 1967-76; pres, Nev Housing Develop Corp; Nat Mgt Asn Lockheed Mgt Club; pres, CA Credit Union League, San Fernando Valley Chap, 1968; Dominguez Hills Black Alumni Asn, 1981. **Honors/Awds:** Man of the Month, Lockheed Mgt Club, 1970; Cert Appreciation, Indust Col Armed Forces, 1972; Distinguished Black American; Civil Rights Award; Outstanding Service Award, Nat Advan Asn Colored People, 1985; Roy Wilkins Award, 1985; Honor Mem, Sme Education Foundation. **Military Serv:** USN, aviation metal smith 3rd class, 1944-46. **Home Addr:** 16257 Marilyn Dr, Granada Hills, CA 91344. *

MANDLE, PAULA R.
President (Organization), chief executive officer. **Educ:** Susquehanna Univ, BS physics, Chartered Property Casualty Underwriter. **Career:** Gov of PA, 26th Senate Dist, Pub Employees Retirement Comn, comnr; The Swarthmore Group, pres & chief exec officer, 1995-. **Business Phone:** (610)918-7200.*

MANDULO, RHEA
Editor, writer, educator. **Personal:** Born Jun 6, 1950, Brooklyn, NY; daughter of William H Wilkins Sr and Martha Benson; children: AmTchaas Nera Adea, Tais Seshua, Sihmen & Kaitu Maat. **Educ:** Marymount Manhattan Col, BA, 1973; Teachers Col, Columbia Univ, attended 1975; Brooklyn Col, MA, Engineering & teaching, 2005. **Career:** USVI, Dept Educ, chair, reading teacher, Title I prog, St Thomas USVI, 1979-80; United Press Int, city desk ed, reporter, 1983-92; The New York Law J, feature writer, 1992-93; City Sun Newspaper, exec ed, 1993; NYC Bd Educ, eng teacher, elem teacher, 1979-2003; Daily Challenge, freelance writer, 1999-2001; A&B Books, freelance ed, 2000-01. **Orgs:** Ausar Auset Soc, 1980-. **Honors/Awds:** Outstanding Contribution Col Community, Marymount Manhattan Col, 1973. **Special Achievements:** Publ in worldwide newspapers, 1987-92; publ in Black Enterprise, Essence & NY Newsday. **Home Addr:** 301 Jefferson Ave, Brooklyn, NY 11216, **Home Phone:** (718)623-6042.

MANGUM, ERNESTINE BREWER
Educator. **Personal:** Born Aug 7, 1936, Durham, NC; daughter of Patti Brewer (deceased) and Robert Brewer (deceased); married Billy Lee, Jul 25, 1969. **Educ:** NC Cent Univ, BA, Spanish, Libr Sci, 1957; Rutgers Univ, MLS, 1965; Fairleigh Dickinson Univ, MA, Human Develop, 1982. **Career:** Educator (retired); Civil Rights & Human Rights Comn, officer, 1963; sch teacher & librn. **Orgs:** NJ Educ Asn, 1957; Nat Educ Asn, 1957; NJ Hist Soc, 1960; NJ Media Asn, NC Cent Univ Alumni Asn, 1960-; Rutherford Educ Asn, 1962-; Elmwood Presbyterian Church, 1964-74; mem & officer, Mt Ararat Women's Club,1974-; Mt Ararat Baptist Church, 1975; vol counr, various self-help groups, 1980; vol, Rutherford Child Care Ctr, 1999-; deaconess, Mt. Ararat Baptist Church; outreach vol; mem, Civil Rights Comn. **Honors/Awds:** Publ article NJEA Rev, 1970, 1994; interviewed three editors during Black History Month, 1984; Gov's Teachers Recognition Prog, 1986; Lifetime Achievement Award, Stud Aide & Coun Comt Rutherford & E Rutherford NJ, 1996; Civil Rights Commission Recognition Award, Keri Bennett Multicultural Festival Comt. **Home Addr:** 80 W Erie Ave, Rutherford, NJ 07070.

MANGUM, ROBERT J.
Judge. **Personal:** Born Jun 15, 1921, Petersburgh, VA; married; children: one. **Educ:** City Col NY, BS, 1942, DL, 1977; Brooklyn Law Sch, LLB, 1949, JD, 1967; NY Univ, MPA, 1957; Adm Med Columbia, MS, 1964; St John Univ, DHL, 1969. **Career:** Judge (retired); NY Police Dept, 1942-54; 7th Dept Police, patrolman; Licensing Youth, dep comnr, 1954-58; Dept Hosp NYC, 1st dep commr, 1958-66; OEO, NE reg dir, 1966-67; NY State Div Human Rights, comnr, 1967-71; Ct Claims NY, state judge, 1971-78; Beth Israel Med Ctr, legal coun, 1978. **Orgs:** Chmn steering comt, Interdept Health Coun NY; bd trust past, NY Univ; chmn bd trust, Harlem Preparatory Sch; bd trust legal couns, Beth Israel Med Ctr; Guardians Asn Police Dept NYC; 100 Blackmen NY City. **Honors/Awds:** Frederick Douglass Award, NY Urban League; Man of the Year, NY Bd Trade; Certificate of Merit, Hosp Admin Asn Dept Hosp NYC. **Military Serv:** AUS, 1st lt, 1946.

MANIGO, GEORGE F, JR.
Clergy. **Personal:** Born Nov 10, 1934, Bamberg, SC; son of George F Sr and Ertha M Ramsey; married Rosa L Lewis; children: Marcia B & George F III. **Educ:** Claflin Col, BS, 1959; Gammon Theol Sem, BD, 1962. **Career:** Hurst Memorial United Methodist Church, 1960-62; Market St United Methodist Church, 1962-65; Wesley Church St James, 1965-70; St Mark & St Matthew Chs Taylors SC, minister, 1970-; Camden First United Methodist Church, pastor, 1977-86; United Methodist Church, Walterboro Dist, dist supt, 1986; Trinity United Methodist Church, pastor. **Orgs:** SC Conf Merger Comt, 1973-; trustee, Columbia Col, Columbia, SC, 1978-; chmn, bd dirs, Greenville CAP Ageny; Nat Asn Advan Colored People; secy, Greenville Urban Ministry; Phi Beta Sigma. **Military Serv:** AUS, sp/3, 1953-56.

MANLEY, DR. AUDREY FORBES
Physician, college administrator. **Personal:** Born Mar 25, 1934, Jackson, MS; daughter of Ora Buckhalter and Jesse Lee; married Albert E, Apr 3, 1970 (deceased). **Educ:** Spelman Col, AB, 1955; Meharry Med Col, MD, 1959; Cook County Hosp,resident, 1963; Abraham Lincoln Sch Med, fel, 1965; Johns Hopkins Univ Sch Hygiene & Pub Health, MPH, 1987. **Career:** Educator (retired); Spelman Col, med dir, family plan prog, chmn healthcareers adv comn, 1972-76, orgn prog consult family plan program & inst,1972-76; Emory Univ, Family Planning Prog Grady Memorial Hosp, chief medserv, 1972-76; USPHS, comn officer, med dir, chief family health & prevserv, 1976-78, comn officer, chief sickle cell dis, 1978-83; Howard UnivDept Pediat, clin asst prof, 1981; Nat Naval Med Ctr, Dept Peds, CourtClin attend, 1981; NIH Inter-Inst Genetics Clin, guest attending, 1981;USPHS, capt 06, med dir, assoc admin clin affairs, 1983-85; Nat HealthServ Corps, dir, 1987-89; US Pub Health Serv, asst surgeon gen, 1988-97; USPHS, Dept HHS, Wash, DC, dep asst secy health, 1989-93; Dep Surgeon Gen& Acting Dep Asst Ser minority health, 1993-95; Acting Surgeon Gen,1995-97; Spelman Col, alumna pres, 1997-2002. **Orgs:** Fel Am Acad Pediat; Nat Med Asn; Am Pub Health Asn; Am Asn Univ Women; Inst Med, Nat Acad Sci; AAAS; Comned Officers Asn; Am Soc Human Genetics; Nat Soc Genetic Counr; NY Acad Sci; Nat Coun Negro Women; Asn Mil Surgeons US; UNICEF, WHO, comt health policy, 1990-92; bd dir: March Dimes, COC Found, Am Cancer Soc Found, FDA adv ctm Vaccines & Biologies; Quelcty Educ Minorities; Spelman Col Alumni Asn; Meharry Med Col Alumni Asn. **Honors/Awds:** Woman of the Year, Zeta Phi Beta Sorority, 1962; NIH Fel, 1963-65; Mary McLeod Bethune Achievement in Government Award, Nat Coun Negro Women,1979; Meritorious Service Medal, 1981, Commendation Medals, 1986, Unit Commendation Award, 1989, Distinguished Service Medal, 1992, PHS; invited for launch of Space Shuttle Challenger Mission no 7, 1985; Community Health Awareness Award, Nat Med Asn, 1988; Outstanding Contribution Award,Minority Women Sci, 1989; Achievement Award, Coalition 100 Black Women,1989; elected Hon Mem, Delta Sigma Theta Sorortity, 1989; DHL, Tougaloo Col, 1990; Hon Doctor Laws, Spelman Col, 1991; LHD, Meharry Med Col, 1991; LHD, Morehouse Col, 2002; LHD, Univ Del, 2002. **Special Achievements:** First African American woman to be appointed chief resident at Cook County Children's Hospital, Chicago; First African American woman appointed Principal Deputy Assistant Secretary for Health in the United States Public Health Service; First African-American woman to achieve rank of asst surgeon gen, USPHS, 1988. **Military Serv:** PHS, RAdm.

MANLEY, BILL
Banker. **Personal:** Born Jul 18, 1944, New Bern, NC; son of Robert and Bernice; married Gloria Myers, Apr 19, 1967; children: Christi, Stewart, Lorin, David. **Educ:** NC A&T State Univ, BS, 1966; Vanderbilt Bus Sch, MBA, 1972. **Career:** Vanderbilt Bus Sch, dir admis, 1972-75; Nat Bank, mgr, Bank LPO, 1984-88, sr vpres, 1988-. **Orgs:** Bd mem, YMCA, Matthews, NC, 1992-; corp bd mem, United Negro Col Fund, 1992-. **Special Achievements:** Commencement speaker at Owen School, Vanderbilt's Bus Sch, 1990. **Military Serv:** AUS, captain, 1966-70. *

MANLEY, JOHN RUFFIN
Clergy. **Personal:** Born Oct 15, 1925, Murfreesboro, NC; married Gloria Roysler. **Educ:** Shaw Univ, AB, BD, 1949; Duke Univ Durham NC, ThM, 1967; Shaw Univ, DA, 1955. **Career:** First Bapt Ch Chapel Hill NC, pastor, 27 yrs; Hickory Bapt Ch, 23 yrs; New Hope Asn, moderator. **Orgs:** Vp & chmn Political Action Comn Gen Baptist Conv & NC Inc; Chapel Hill-caraboro Sch Bd; Chapel Hill Planning Bd; NAACP; 2nd Masonic Lodge; vice chmn, Governor's Coun Sickle Cell Syndrone; chmn, Proj Area Comn Redevelop Comt; Task Force Community Develop Act Chapel Hill; Manley john ruffin trustee. **Honors/Awds:** Man of Year, Shaws Theol Alumni; delegate to World, Baptist Alliance.

MANLOVE, BENSON
Executive. **Personal:** Born Jan 1, 1943; married. **Educ:** Wayne State Univ, BBA, 1969. **Career:** Wayne State Univ, asst to pres, 1968-70; Amtask Inc, dir mktg, 1970-71; L&M Off Prod, co-owner, 1970-79; Mich Consol Gas Co, exec asst to pres, 1979-81, exec dir, int support serv, 1981-83, vpres admin, 1983, co-dir; Detroit Econ Growth Corp, acting pres, 1995. **Orgs:** Chmn & bd dir, Detroit Urban League, 1989-.

MANN, CHARLES
Television show host, football player. **Personal:** Born Apr 12, 1961, Sacramento, CA; married Tyrena; children: 3. **Educ:** Univ Nevada, Reno, attended. **Career:** Football player (Retired), TV Host; Wash Redskins, defensive end, 1983-93; San Francisco 49ers, defensive line, 1994; WJFK, host, currently; WUSA-TV, host, currently. **Orgs:** Co-founder, Good Samaritan Found; Nat Serv Initiative Community; Nat Kidney Found; United Way; Ronald McDonald C Charities; Border Babies Found; Lever Bros; Why Sch Cool prog; Metrop Police Boys & Girls Clubs; C Hosp; C's Cancer Found. **Honors/Awds:** Most Valuable Defensive Lineman, Big Sky Conf, 1981-82; Washingtonian of the Year Award, 1994. **Business Addr:** Host, WUSA-TV, 4100 Wisconsin Ave NW, Washington, DC 20016, **Business Phone:** (202)895-5999.

MANN, DR. MARION
Educator. **Personal:** Born Mar 29, 1920, Atlanta, GA; son of Levi J and Cora Casey; married Ruth R, Jan 16, 1943; children: Marion Jr & Judith R. **Educ:** Tuskegee Inst, BS, 1940; Howard Univ Col Med, MD, 1954; Georgetown Univ Med Ctr, PhD, 1961. **Career:** Educator (retired); Howard Univ col med, dean, 1970-79, assoc vpres & res, 1988-91. **Orgs:** Sigma Pi Phi Fraternity, 1997; Nat Med Asn; Inst Med; Nat Acad Sci; Am Bd Path; Sigma Pi Phi. **Honors/Awds:** DSc Honoris Causa, Georgetown Univ, 1979; DSc Honoris Causa, Univ Mass, 1984; DSC Honoris Causa, Tuskegee Univ, 1998. **Military Serv:** AUS, 1942-50; USAR, 1950-54, 1958-80, brigadier gen, 1975-80. **Home Addr:** 1453 Whittier Pl NW, Washington, DC 20012.

MANN, RICHARD
Football coach. **Personal:** Born Apr 20, 1947, Aliquippa, PA; son of Broadies Hughes; married Karen; children: Deven, Richard II, Mario & Brittany. **Educ:** Ariz State Univ, BS, elem educ. **Career:** Aliquippa High Sch, teacher & coach, 1970-73; Ariz State Univ, widereceivers coach, 1974-79; Univ Louisville, wide receivers coach, 1980-81; Indianapolis Colts, wide receivers coach, 1982-84; Cleveland Browns, widereceivers coach, 1985-93; NY Jets, wide receivers coach, 1994-96; Baltimore Ravens, wide receivers coach, 1997-98; Kansas City Chiefs, widereceivers coach, 1999-2000; Wash Redskins, wide receivers coach, 2001; Tampa Bay Buccaneers, wide receivers coach, 2002-. **Orgs:** Chmn, Charlotte Housing Authority Scholar Fund, 1990. **Honors/Awds:** Aliquippa Sports Hall of Fame, 1982; Black Image Achievement Award, 1989. **Business Addr:** Wide Receivers Coach, Tampa Bay Buccaneers, One Buccaneer Pl, Tampa, FL 33607, **Business Phone:** (813)870-2700.

MANN, THOMAS J.
Lawyer, state government official. **Personal:** Born Dec 15, 1949, Brownsville, TN; son of Thomas and Flossie; married Leala Ann Salter, 1976; children: Nari & Kari. **Educ:** Tenn State Univ, BS, polit sci, 1971; Univ IA Law Sch, JD, 1974. **Career:** St IA, asst atty gen, 1974-76, 1980-82, st sen, 1983-91; IA CivilRights Comn, exec dir, 1976-79; Mann & Mann Law Off, partner, 1983-92, 1995; Tex Comn Alcohol & Drug Abuse, gen coun, 1993-95. **Orgs:** IA St Bar Asn; Polk Co Bar Asn; bd mem, Des Moines Br NAACP; Omega Psi Phi; Tex Bar Asn. **Honors/Awds:** Community Appreciation Award, Omega Psi Phi, 1978; Civil Libertarian of the Year Award, The IA Civil Liberties Union, 1990.

MANNEY, WILLIAM A.
Executive. **Personal:** Born Jul 12, 1931, Springfield, AR; married Alice. **Educ:** Philander Smith Col, Little Rock, BA. **Career:** WENN Radio, gen mgr; WBEE Radio, Chicago, acct exec, 1966-70, gen mgr, 1970-. **Orgs:** Nat Asn Mkt Developers; black media rep, bd dir, Cosmopolitan C C Chicago; second vpres, Jane Dent Home Aged.

MANNING, BLANCHE MARIE
Educator, judge. **Personal:** Born Dec 12, 1934, Chicago, IL; daughter of Julius L Porter and Marguerite Anderson Porter; married William. **Educ:** Chicago Teachers Col, BE, 1961; John Marshall Law Sch, Chicago, JD, 1967; Roosevelt Univ, Chicago, MA, 1972; Univ NV, gen jurisdiction cert, 1982; Univ Va, Charlottesville, VA, LLM, 1992. **Career:** Chicago Bd Educ, sch teacher, 1961-67; Cook Co State Attys Off, asst states atty, 1968-73; Malcolm X Community Col, lect, 1970-71; Equal Employment Opportunity Comn, supvry trialatty, 1973-77; United Airlines, gen atty, 1977-78; US Attys Off, asst US atty, 1978-79; NCBL Community Col Law, adj prof, 1978-79; Circuit Ct Cook Co, assoc judge, 1979-86; Dept Justice, Atty Gen Adv Inst, adj fac mem, 1979; IL Judicial Conf New Judges Sem, Prof Develop Prog New Asn Judges, IL Judicial Conf Asn Judges Sem, lectr, 1982-86; First Munic Dist Circuit Ct Cook Co, supv judge, 1984-86, supv circuit judge, 1986-87; Justice Ill Appellate Ct, First Dist, 1987-94; Harvard Law Sch, Univ Chicago Law Sch, Trial Advocacy Workshops, teaching team mem, 1991-; De Paul Univ Col Law, adj prof, 1992-; US Dist Ct, ND IL, judge, 1994-. **Orgs:** Nat Asn Women Judges; Cook County Bar Asn; Ill Judicial Coun; New Judges Sem; Chicago Bar Asn; Symphony Orchestra; Chicago State Univ Community Concert Band & Jazz Band. **Honors/Awds:** Edith Sampson Memorial Award, 1985; Award of Appreciation, Int Asn Pupil Personnel Workers, 1985; IL Judicial Coun; Kenneth E Wilson Judge of the Year Award, Cook County Bar Asn; Distinguished Alumna Award, Chicago State Univ, 1986; Award of Excellence in Judicial Admin, Women Bar Asn, 1986; Black Rose Award, League Black Women, 1987; We Care Role Model Award, Chicago Police Dept, 1987-94; Thurgood Marshall Award, IIT Kent Law Sch BALSA, 1988; Professional Achievement Award, Roosevelt Univ, 1988; Distinguished Service Award, John Marshall Law Sch, 1989; Distinguished Service Award, Guardians Police Orgn, 1991; Citizen's Award, The Guardians Police Orgn, 1991; We Care Outstanding Role Model Award, Chicago Pub Schs & Chicago Police Dept, 1992-94; Honorary Doctor of Humane Letters Degree, Chicago State Univ, 1998. **Business Addr:** Judge, United States District Court, Northern District of Illinois, Everett McKinley Dirksen Bldg, 219 S Dearborn St Fl 20, Chicago, IL 60604, **Business Phone:** (312)435-7608.

MANNING, BRIAN
Counselor, research scientist. **Personal:** Born Apr 22, 1975; son of Ray and Marvelyn; married Roxanne M, May 23, 1998; children: Micah & Caleb. **Educ:** Stanford Univ, BS, sociol; Univ KS Med Ctr, MPH. **Career:** Miami Dolphins, wide receiver, 1997-98; Green Bay Packers, wide receiver, 1998-99; Univ KS Med Ctr, researcher & counr, 1999-. **Orgs:** Stanford Alumni Asn; Nat Football League Players Asn; Lenexa Christian Ctr; Am Pub Health Asn. **Honors/Awds:** Overall Best Student Entry, Univ KS Med Ctr, 2000. **Home Addr:** 2612C S Peck Ct, Independence, MO 64055. **Business Addr:** Counselor, KU Med Ctr, 3901 Rainbow Blvd Suite 3001S, Kansas City, KS 66160-7313, **Business Phone:** (913)588-2775.

MANNING, DANIEL RICARDO
Basketball coach, basketball player. **Personal:** Born May 17, 1966, Hattiesburg, MS; son of Edward and Darnelle; married Julie; children: Elizabeth & Evan. **Educ:** Univ Kans, communs. **Career:** Basketball player (retired), dir; Los Angeles Clippers, forward-ctr, 1988-94; Atlanta Hawks, forward-ctr, 1994; Phoenix Suns, forward-ctr, 1994-99; Milwaukee Bucks, forward-ctr, 1999-2000; Utah Jazz, forward-ctr, 2000-01; Dallas Mavericks, forward-ctr, 2001-02; Detroit Pistons, forward-ctr, 2002-03; Univ Kans, dir stud-athlete develop & team mgr, 2003-07, asst coach, 2007-. **Orgs:** Kappa Alpha Psi Fraternity Inc. **Honors/Awds:** Bronze medal, Seoul Olympics, 1988; Silver Medal, Pan-American Games, 1987; Col Basketball Player Year, 1988; NBA All-Star, 1993, 1994. **Business Addr:** Assistant Coach, Director of Student-Athlete Development & Team Manager, University of Kansas, 1000 Sunnyside Ave, Lawrence, KS 66045, **Business Phone:** (785)864-2700.

MANNING, DR. EDDIE JAMES
Administrator. **Personal:** Born Mar 19, 1952, Philadelphia, PA; married Carolyn; children: Eddie Jr & C Jamal. **Educ:** Cheyney Univ, BS, 1974; Temple Univ, MEd, 1976, DEd, 1984. **Career:** Chester Upland Sch Dist, teacher & guid counsr; Ashbourne Sch, teacher; Temple Univ Spec Recruitment & Admis Prog, counr & acad adv, 1977-79; Act 101 Prog Temple Univ, coord, 1979-80, dir 1975-86; actg assoc dean, 1998; Acad Support Progs Rutgers Univ, actg dir, 1999; Rutgers Univ, Educ Opport Fund Prog, assoc dean & interim exec dir, currently. **Orgs:** Am Asn Couns & Develop; Pa Coun Asn; Am Asn Multi-Cult Coun & Develop; Pa Asn Multi-Cult Coun & Develop; treas, Pa Chap Am Asn Non-White Concerns Personnel & Guid, 1982-; chmn, Act 101 Eastern Reg Exec Comt, 1982-83; chmn, State Chapts Div Am Asn Multi-Cult Couns & Develop, 1983-85; Temple Univ Sub-Comm Acad Excellence Athletics, 1985-; Temple Univ Resid Review Bd, 1985-. **Home Addr:** 7834 Williams Ave, Philadelphia, PA 19150. **Business Phone:** (732)932-7067.

MANNING, EVELYN. See HALL, EVELYN ALICE.

MANNING, JANE A.
School administrator. **Personal:** Born Mar 22, 1947, Wichita Falls, TX. **Educ:** Tex Southern Univ, Houston, BA, Jour, 1969; Columbia Univ NY, MA, Jour, 1970. **Career:** Press Enterpise, ci reporter, 1971-74; Tex Southern Univ, instr jour, 1974-7 Riverside City Col, dir info serv, 1979-84; Media Methods, own & gen mgr, 1981-; Truckee Meadows Community Col, part-tir jour inst; Univ Nev Reno, dir off pub info. **Orgs:** Asn Calif C Admin, 1979-85; Nat Coun Community Rels, 1980-84; dir, O portunity Indust Ctr Inland Counties, 1980-82, Friends Inla Counties Legal Serv, 1981-83; bd mem, Pub Rels Soc Am, 198 83; Soc Prof Jour, Sigma Delta Chi; Coun, Advan & Support E Silver State Chap Int Assoc Bus Comn; Nev State Press Assc WIN; Am Asn Health Educ; bd mem & Univ Nev Reno Rep, A Asn Univ Women; bd dir, Nev Women's Fund; Nat Assoc Adv Colored People; Alliance Racial Minorities; Reno & Sparks Neg Bus & Prof Women's Club; bd dir, Am Red Cross. **Honors/Awd** Valuable & Distinguished Service Award, City Riverside, 198 Inspirational Award, Univ Nev, Reno Black Stud Orgn, 1985.

MANNING, DR. JEAN BELL
Educator. **Personal:** Born Aug 14, 1937, LaMarque, TX; marri Reuben D. **Educ:** Bishop Col, BA (hon stud Valedictoria Schol 1958; N Tex State Univ, MEd, 1964, EDd, 1970. **Career:** Dougl High Sch, Ardmore, OK, instr, 1958-60, 1964-65; Reading L Jarvis Col, Hawkins, TX, instr & dir, 1961-64; Southern Tex Uni Houston, TX, vis prof, 1964-65; Paul Quinn Col, Waco, TX; chn dept educ, 1970-73, 1974-78; Univ Liberia, Liberia, W Afric prof Eng, 1973-74; Okla City Chap, prog coordr & facet dir Langston Univ, OK, assoc prof & dir resources, 1978-86; vpre acad affairs 1987-2007; vpres, emer acad affairs, 2007-. **Org** Educ for Leadership in Black Ch Lilly Found Sponsored Houst TX, 1975-77; curriculum devel Wiley Col Marshall TX, 197 competency based educ Dallas Independent S Dist, 1979; me Alpha Kappa Alpha Sor, 1956-; mem Links Inc,1974-; mem F Delta Kappa Sor, 1956-. **Honors/Awds:** Doctoral Grant, Fo Found, 1969; Outstanding Sorority, SW Phi Delta Kappa Sorori 1978; Hall of Fame Inductee, Okla Higher Educ Heritage Sc 2007. **Business Addr:** Vice President Emeritus, Langst University, Off Acad Affairs, 201 Univ Women, PO Box 12C Langston, OK 20005, **Business Phone:** (405)466-3207.

MANNING, DR. RANDOLPH H
Educator, school administrator. **Personal:** Born Dec 18, 194 New York, NY; son of Ruthfoy and Gertrude Webber; marri Monica S McEvilley; children: Randolph, Craig C & Corey **Educ:** Suffolk Co Community Col, AA, 1969; State Univ Ne York Stony Brook, BA, 1971, MA, 1975, PhD, 1998. **Career:** H Manning Enterprises, owner & operator, 1973-; Suffolk C Community Col, counr, 1971-80, prof psycol & sociol, 1980-8 assoc dean, 1985-. **Orgs:** Educ consult, BOCES; adv bd mem, R Rout Dept Labor, BOCES, SOCC, SC Correction; bd dirs, Sickle Cell; bd dir, Gordon Heights Fed Credit Union; Past Pr NY State Spec Prog Personnel Asn; Suffolk City Youth Bd; a community, Brookhaven Social Serv; Long Island Asn Bla Counr; Long Island Minority Educrs; E End Guidance Asn; pr emeritus, former chmn, Supvry & Publicity Community; Gord Hgts Fed Credit Union; treas, Long Island Sickle Cell Project; c dir, Coun Int Prog; Am Sociol Asn; State Univ NY Asn; steeri comm, Suffolk City Probation Dept, Day Reporting Ctr; nat pr Community Col Gen Educ Asn; NY State bd Prof Med Conduc United Way steering comm, Proj Blueprint; restoration adv bd, U Navy; Alpha Beta Gamma Nat Bus Honor Soc, 1986. **Honor Awds:** Outstanding Young Men Am, 1981; State University New York Distinguished Alumni Chancellor Award, State Ur NY, 1983; Proclamation Serv, County Suffolk, 1986; Cert A preciation, 1970; Certificate of Appreciation, Special Prog Perso nel Asn, 1980; NCP Award; Recognition of Service Award, Halp County Exec, 1991; Outstanding Young Men of America Awar Prof & Comm Serv, 1981; SUNY Distinguished Alumni Chance lors Award, 1983; Recognition of Service Award, Sunrise Fir County exec Gaffney, 1995; Cert Special Recognition, US Hou Reps, 1997. **Special Achievements:** Book: A World Apa Viewpoints, Newsday series, 1990; Eastern Campus Researc Project article for ERIC, 1992. **Business Addr:** Associate Dea State University of New York, Suffolk County Community Cc lege, Crooked Hill Rd, Brentwood, NY 11717, **Business Phon** (631)451-4588.

MANNING, SHARON (SHARON MANNING BEVERLY
Basketball player. **Personal:** Born Mar 20, 1969. **Educ:** Quee Col, BA, MA; Capella Univ, PhD. **Career:** Basketball Playe Charollete Swing, 1997-99; Miami Sol, 2000; Women Basketball Open Division, state chair; U.S. Olympic Festiv North Team, asst coach, 1994; Charlotte Sting, center-forwa 1997-99; Miami Sol, 2000; New Jersey Institute Technol, 200 02; Vassar Col Athletics, assoc dir of athletics & sr woman a minr, 2002-04, interim dir of athletics, 2004, dir of athletics phys educ, 2005-; New Jersey State Coaches Assn, pres; New Yo Metropolitan Coaches Assn. **Orgs:** NCAA Div III Nominati Comm; NCAA Div III Conv Planning Subcomt. **Honors/Awd** National Achievement Award, National Pro-Am City Leag Assn; Queens College's Distinguished Service Award, 1990. **Bu ness Addr:** Director of Athletics, Physical Education, Vassar Cc lege Athletics, 124 Raymond Ave, PO Box 750, Poughkeepsie, N 12604-0750, **Business Phone:** (845)437-7450.*

MANSFIELD, ANDREW K.
Government official. **Personal:** Born Feb 17, 1931, Morehou Parish, LA; married Mae. **Educ:** Grambling St, BS; Atlanta Uni

d; Southern Univ. **Career:** Grambling, LA, mayor, 1977; New ion Learning Acad, exec dir, 1998-. **Orgs:** Lincoln Parish ice Jury, 1972-; Am Personnell & Guid Asn; NEA; LEA. **Busis Addr:** Executive Director, New Vision Learning Academy, 3 Cherokee St, St Louis, MO 63118, **Business Phone:** 4)771-7933.

NSFIELD, DR. CARL MAJOR
sician, educator. **Personal:** Born Dec 24, 1928, Philadelphia, ; married Sarah Lynne; children: Joel & Kara. **Educ:** Lincoln v, AB, 1951; Temple Univ, attended 1952; Howard Univ, MD, 6. **Career:** Physician, educator (retired); Episcopal Hosp, dent intern, 1956-58, resident, 1960; USAF, radiologist, 1958- Jefferson Med Col Hosp, assoc radiologist, chief div, cherni- fel, instr radiologist, NIH post doct fellow, resident, 1960-67; erson Med Col, adv clin fel, 1965-68, asst prof, 1967-69; Univ Sch Med, lectr, 1967-73; Thomas Jefferson Univ Hosp, from oc prof to prof, 1970-76; Hahnemann Med Col Hosp, vis prof, 1; Univ Kans Med Ctr, prof chmn dept radiation, 1976-83; omas Jefferson Univ Hosp, prof & chmn dept radiation thermo uclear med, 1983-94; Univ Md Sch Med, chmn, dept radiation ol, 1998. **Orgs:** Am Bd Radiol, 1962; Mt Carmel Baptist urch, 1965-73; adv bd, Boys Scout Am, 1965-66; Pharmacy n, 1965-66; Admis Com, 1968-72; Stud Affairs Com, 1968-71; Judiciary Com 1971-72; Am Bd Nuclear Med, 1972; Am Col clear Med; Am Col Radiol; Am Med Asn; Am Soc Therapeut liologists; Asn Univ Radiologists; British Inst Radiol; Am Col clear Physicians; Nat Med Asn; Radiol Soc N Am; Royal Soc d; Soc Nuc Med Gardens Bd; Hall-Mercer Comm Mental alth & Mental Retardation Ctr Pa Hosp, 1973-74; Philadelphia levelop Authority, 1973-75; Stud Promotion Com, 1973-75; rma & Therapeut Comn, 1974-76; Radiation Safety Comn, 4-76; Comput Comn, 1974-76; bd trustees, Peter's Sch, 1975- nat bd, Am Cancer Soc; pres,Am Radium Soc, 1988-89; pres, ladelpia Am Cancer Soc, 1989-90. **Honors/Awds:** Over 150 lications, exhibits, presentations; Natl & Intl meetings; doctor cience, Lincoln Univ, 1991; fel, Am Col Radiol, 1976; fel, Am Nuclear Med, 1989; fel, Philadelphia Col Physicians, 1984; nze Medal, Am Cancer Soc, 1990. **Military Serv:** USAF, t, 1958-60. *

NSFIELD, W. ED
nsultant. **Personal:** Born May 7, 1937, Clifton Forge, VA; mar- Maxine L; children: Amy & Yolanda. **Educ:** Defense Inf Sch, 4; Univ Denver, 1970. **Career:** Radio Sta KTLN, moderator, nmentator, newscaster, 1966-67; Lincoln Nat Life Ins Co, spec nt, 1966-69; Pub Rels, dir, 1967-68; Univ Denver, asst to ncellor, 1969-71; Colo Asn Indust Cols & Univs, exec dir, 9-71; Nat Urban Coalition, asst dir field opers, 1971; mkt & ollment, dir, 1971-72; Gen Mills Inc, from consult to chmn of & pres, 1972; Affirmative Action Progs Dept, leader, 1972-75; ernative Mgt, consult, 1975-76; Minority Affairs Corp Pub adcasting, dir, 1976;Equal Employ Opportunities Comn, St is Dist Office, dist dir. **Orgs:** Consult, EEO Laws Affirmative ion; Gen Mills Inc; Nat Asn Cos; Nat Civil Serv League; Int sonnel Mgt Asn; Minn League Cities; N Dak League Cities; Compliance Soc & Inc; Int Asn Off Human Rights Orgn; City ounty Denver; Affirmative Action Asn; chmn Hennep in Co entennial Planning Comn; Affirmative Action Adv Comt; 1st chmn, Minnea polisUrban Coalition; mem Minn State Bd sing; Abbot-Northwestern Hosp; Minneapolis Citizens Cond Pub Educ; Am Soc Personnel Admin; Nat Orgn Women; Nat Adv Colored People; Nat Urban League. **Military Serv:** AF, 1954-66.

NSON, RICHARD
wyer. **Career:** Manson Jones & Whitted, Pvt Pract, atty, ently. **Business Addr:** Attorney, Private Practice, 1314 5th N Suite 300, Nashville, TN 37208-2726, **Business Phone:** 5)254-1600.*

NUEL, JERRY
eball manager, baseball player. **Personal:** Born Dec 23, 1953, nira, GA; married Renette Caldwell; children: 4. **Career:** eball player (retired), baseball manager; Detroit Tigers, prof eball player, 1975-76; Montreal Expos, prof baseball player, 0-81, instructor, 1987, field coordr, 1988-89, third base coach, 1-96; San Diego Padres, prof baseball player, 1982; Fla rlins, bench coach, 1997; Chicago White Sox, scout, 1985, r, 1998-2003; New York Mets, base coach, 2005, bench coach, 6-. **Honors/Awds:** Southern League Co-Manager of the Year, 0; California Black Sports Hall of Fame, 2000; C.I. Taylor ard, Manager of the Year, Am League, 2000. **Special Achievents:** First permanent African American manager in Chicago ite Sox history.

NUEL, LIONEL
otball player, football coach. **Personal:** Born Apr 13, 1962, ncho Cucamonga, CA. **Educ:** Citrus Col, attended; Univ Pac, nded. **Career:** Football Player (retired); Football coach; NY nts, wide receiver, 1984-91; Fontana High Sch, coach; Univ Verne, coach; Citrus Col, coach; NJ High Sch, coach; Riverside nmunity Col, wide receiver coach, currently. **Honors/Awds:** st-season play, 1986: NFC Championship Game, NFL ampionship Game.

MANUEL, LOUIS CALVIN
Physician. **Personal:** Born Jun 13, 1937, Cleveland, OH; married Idabelle Todd; children: Donna L, April D, Erika L, Louis C. **Educ:** Bowling Green State Univ, BA, 1960; Meharry Med Col, MD, 1965. **Career:** Louis C Manuel MD Eye Serv Inc, ophthalmologist. **Orgs:** Secy, Kansas City Med Soc; pres & secy, Mo Pan Med; House Delegates; Nat Med Soc; AMA; Mo State Med; Jackson Co Med; SW Med Asn; APPA KC Oph & Otol; Roman Barnes Soc; Castroviejo Soc; Am Soc Con Oph; life mem, Nat Advan Asn Colored People; consult, ophthal Model Cities Health Orgn KC Mo, 1971-80; fellow, Royal Soc Medicine, 1973; deacon Covenant Presbyterian Ch KC Mo; youth coun, career develop United Presbyterian Ch; bd dir, Civic Plaza Nat Bk KC Mo; Alpha Phi Alpha; YMCA; Univ Mo Assoc; Midwesterners Greater KC Med Serv. **Honors/Awds:** commendation Medal; vietnamese serv ribbon AUS. **Military Serv:** AUS, capt, 1966-68. **Business Addr:** Opthalmologist, 1734 E 63rd St Suite 501, Kansas City, MO 64110, **Business Phone:** (816)363-4700.*

MAPP, CALVIN R.
Judge. **Personal:** Born Sep 10, 1924, Miami, FL; son of Herschel and Edna; married Catherine Nelson Mapp; children: Calvin Jr, Corey Ramon. **Educ:** Morris Brown Col, BA; Howard Law Sch, LLB; N Dade Jr Col; Bethune Cookman Col; Nat Judicial Col; Univ Fla. **Career:** Judge (retired); Teacher, Math & Chem, 1951-52; City Miami, police officer, 1952-60; Community Rels Bd, 1963-66; All State Courts, State Fla, atty, 1965; State Atty's Off, 1966-68; Matthews Braynon & Mapp, atty, 1968-73; Co Dade, county ct, judge. **Orgs:** Fla, Am, Nat Bar Asn; Bar State FL; Fla Supreme Ct; US Supreme Ct; S Dist Fla, 1965; Kappa Alpha Psi Fraternity; Milton Littman Memorial Found. **Honors/Awds:** Morris Brown Col Hon Dr Laws degree, 1974; included in the Black Archives photo section of Dade Co, 1976; Cert Appreciation Supreme Ct, 1980; selected as a delegate by People to People Org, 1981; Judge of the Month Award Spotlight Club, 1983; City Opa Locka Commendation, 1983; Commendation City Hialeah Gardens Fla, 1983; Gwen Cherry Political Award, Sigma Gamma Rho Sorority, 1983-84; Outstanding Commitment to Mankind & Continuous Support of Shrine Progs Award, 1984; Cert Appreciation Black Hist Month Lillie C Evens Elem Sch, 1984; Distinguished Leadership Award, Conf County Court Judges Fla; Cert partic, 1981 F Judicial Col Instr Fla Supreme Ct; inventor, holds patents disposable syringe, 1977, electra hoop, 1978, sliding glass door dustpan; Rotary Int. **Special Achievements:** written books entitled, Traffic, A Compilation of Florida Case Law. **Military Serv:** AUS, s/sgt, 1943-46. *

MAPP, DAVID KENNETH, JR.
Law enforcement officer. **Personal:** Born Nov 15, 1951, Norfolk, VA; married Cynthia Gaines; children: Shomarr, Patrice. **Educ:** Norfolk State Univ, BA, sociol, 1973. **Career:** Norfolk Sheriff's Dept, recreation dir, 1973-75, classification officer, 1975-78, dir classification & rehabilitative progs, 1978-80, sheriff, 1981-93. **Orgs:** Officer Norfolk State Univ Alumni Asn, 1973; officer, Eureka Lodge, 1973; officer, Norfolk Jaycees; Nat Sheriff's Asn, 1981; VA State Sheriff's Asn, 1981; VA Asn Law Enforce Const Officers, 1981; JJDP State Advisory Council 1982. **Honors/Awds:** Citizen of the Year, Alpha Phi Omega Frat, 1983; chmn, Norfolk United Way, 1983; Cardiac Arrest Award, Norfolk Heart Asn, 1984. *

MAPP, DR. EDWARD C.
School administrator, writer. **Personal:** Born Aug 17, 1929, New York, NY; son of Edward Cameron and Estelle Sampson; children: Andrew, Elmer & Everett. **Educ:** City Col NY, BA, 1953; Columbia Univ, MS, 1956; NY Univ, PhD, mass commun, 1970. **Career:** School administrator (retired), writer; books: Blacks in American Films, 1972; Puerto Rican Perspectives, 1974; Blacks in Performing Arts, 1978, 2nd edition, 1990; A Separate Cinema, 1992; African Americans and the Oscar, 2003; New York City Bd Educ, teacher, 1957-64; New York City Tech Col, dir Libr Learning Resources Ctr, 1964-77; Borough Manhattan Community Col, dean fac, 1977-82, prof, 1983-92; Movie & TV Mkt, feature columnist, 1979-91; City Col Chicago, vchancellor, 1982-83; New York City Comn Human Rights, Comnr, 1987-94; prof emer, 1994; Univ New York, prof speech & commun, 1998. **Orgs:** Treas, City Univ New York Fac Senate, 1972-77; bd dir, United Nat Assoc New York, 1975-78; 100 Black Men Inc, 1975-85; bd mem, Brooklyn Region, Nat Conf Christians & Jews, 1975-81; bd trustees, New York Metro Ref & Res Agency, 1980-81; Brooklyn Borough Pres, Ed Adv Panel, 1981; dir, Nat ServCorp, 1984-87; comnr, vchair, New York City Human Rights Comn, 1988-94; bdmem, Friends Thirteen. **Honors/Awds:** Founders Day Award for Outstanding Scholarship, New York Univ, 1970; Distinguished Service Award, Borough Manhattan Community Col, The City Univ New York, 1982; Black Collectors Hall of Fame, 1992; Community Service Award, Knoxville Col Alumni Asn, 1993. **Special Achievements:** Curator: Edward Mapp African-American Film Poster Collection, presented to Center for Motion Picture Study of the Academy of Motion Picture Arts and Sciences, 1996; "Close Up in Black": A Smithsonian Touring Exhibition from the Mapp Collection, 2003-05. **Home Addr:** 155 W 68th St, New York, NY 10023. *

MAPP, JOHN ROBERT
Physician. **Personal:** Born Jan 26, 1950, Springfield, MA; son of Alexander B and Edna Royster; married Maria Mejia, Nov 13, 1981; children: Alexandra, Lorean. **Educ:** Hillsdale Col, Hillsdale, MI, BA, 1971; Meharry Med Col, Nashville, TN, MD, 1975; Calif State Univ, San Diego, MPH, 1987. **Career:** Med Col, PA, residence Pediat, 1975-77; Univ Southern Calif, Los Angeles County Med Sch, neonatal pathologist, 1979-80; Univ Southern Calif Med Sch, clin instr pediat, 1977-79; Pediat Los Angeles, Calif, symp re neonatol, 1978; Hosp Italiano Rosario S Am, guest lectr neonatologist, consult neonatol, 1979; Glendale Adventist Med Ctr, co chief neonatol dept, 1979-. **Orgs:** Co founder & pres, Blacks United Hillsdale Col, 1969-71; Am Asn Pediat, 1976-. **Special Achievements:** Nat TV Prog "Lifeline" segment filmed at USC newborn/neonatology unit of Med Center at Los Angeles 1978; Organized unit of Buffalo Soldiers, circa 1866-1890, cavalry unit in LA CA, which appeared in TV show, Geronimo, 1993 and an episode of Dr Quinn, Medicine Woman, 1993; appeared in tv servies, The District, 2003; rides in Rose Bowl Parade, 1995-. **Home Addr:** 135 Thompson St, Springfield, MA 01109. *

MAPP, RHONDA
Basketball player. **Personal:** Born Oct 13, 1969. **Educ:** NC State Univ, attended 1992. **Career:** Charlotte Sting, center-forward, 1997-2000; Los Angeles Sparks, 2001-03. *

MAPP, ROBERT P
Executive. **Career:** RPM Supply Co Inc, chief exec officer, currently. **Business Addr:** Chief Executive Officer, RPM Supply Co Inc, 5301 Tacony St, PO Box 203, Philadelphia, PA 19137-2309.

MAPP, DR. YOLANDA INEZ
College teacher, physician. **Personal:** Born Jun 26, 1930, New York, NY; daughter of Edward Jones and Viola Jefferson Jones; divorced; children: Donald, David, Douglas, Daniel, Dorothy & Darryl. **Educ:** Monmouth Jr Col, AA, 1951; NJ Col Women Rutgers Univ, BS, Chemistry & Bacteriology, 1953; Howard Univ Col Med, MD, 1957. **Career:** Physician, college teacher (retired); DC Gen Hosp, internship, 1957-58, residency, 1960-61; Freedman's Hosp, Wash DC, residency, 1958-60; Hahnemann Med Col & Hosp Philadelphia, instr med & dir alcoholic clin, 1961-64; Temple Univ Hosp, fel hemat oncol, 1964-66, physician, 1967-84; Emory Univ Col Med Atlanta, assoc prof of med & internist, 1969-70; Temple Univ, acting dir univ health serv, 1984-93. **Orgs:** Med adv, Leukemia Soc Am Greater Atlanta Chap, 1970; vol physician, Thaler Memorial Hosp, Bilwaskarma, Nicaragua, 1972; med adv, Am Cancer Soc, Philadelphia, 1976-; Am Col Physicians, 1977; bd trustees, Rutgers Univ, 1979-91; mem, Keys to Living volunteers; life mem, Nat Asn Advan Colored People. **Honors/Awds:** Howard Whitfield Found Med Scholar, 1952-57; Corporate Honorary Award, Schering Pharma, 1957; speaker "Honors & Awards Day", Howard Univ Col Med, 1965; Distinguished Achievement Award, Rutgers Univ, New Brunswick, NJ, 1973; Award for Free Flight Soaring Entry Nordic A-2 Glider Aero Crafts Exhibit Civic Ctr, Philadelphia, 1974; The Four Chaplains Legion of Hon Membership, Chapel of Four Chaplains Philadelphia, 1973; Courage Award, Am Cancer Soc, 1988; Distinguished Alumnus Rutgers Univ, 1992. **Special Achievements:** Third degree black belt in Judo, 1989. *

MARABLE, HERMAN, JR.
Judge. **Personal:** Born Oct 4, 1962, Flint, MI; son of Herman Sr and Iris Butler. **Educ:** MI State Univ, James Madison Col, BA, 1984; Ohio State Univ, Col Law, JD, 1987. **Career:** NAACP, Wash Bur, intern, 1983; 68th Dist Judge Lee Vera Loyd, law clerk, 1983-84; UAW-GM Legal Serv, law clerk, 1985; Garan, Lucow, Miller, Seward, Cooper & Becker, summer assoc, 1986; Riegle Senate Comt, regional coord, 1987-88; atty Kathie Dones-Carson, dir res, 1988-91; County Allegheny, asst dist atty, 1991-93; County Genesee, asst prosecuting atty; 1993-00; 68th Dist Ct, judge, 2001-. **Orgs:** Vpres, Flint Br, NAACP, 1988-94; state cent comt mem, Mich Dem Party, 1989-93, 1995-98; 9th Congressional Dist Dem Exec Comt, 1995-97; treas, Genesee County Black Caucus, 1989-91; exec bd mem, Genesee County Black Caucus, 1995-00; vice chair, Genesee County Black Caucus, 1997-98; sec & nominating comt chair, Urban Coalition Greater Flint, 1987-91; bd dir, MSU James Madison Col Alumni Asn, 1987-89, 1990-94; adv bd chair, United Way Genesee & Lapeer Counties, 1988-91; vice chmn admin, Boy Scouts Am, 1989-91; Homer S Brown Law Asn, 1990-93; Nat Bar Asn, 1985-; Nat Bar Asn Judicial Coun, 2001-; Pa Bar Asn; Pa Dist Atty's Asn, 1991-93; Nat Black Prosecutor's Asn, 1993-00; vice pres, Mich Chap Nat Black Prosecutors Asn, 1993-00; 1994-95; Prosecuting Atty's Asn Mich, 1993-00; Prosecution Diversity Comt, 1997-00; Allegheny County Bar Asn, 1990-93; Mallory-Scott-Van Dyne Bar Asn, 1987-; Genesee County Bar Asn, 1993-; Mich Dist Judges Asn, 2001-; Asn Black Judges Mich, 2000-; Am Judges Asn, 2001-; co-chmn, Legal Redress, Mich NAACP, 1994-00; Urban League Flint, 1991-; bd dir, Flint Neighborhood Coalition, 1997-; vpres, Flint Neighborhood Coalition, 1998-00; Genesee County Dem Party, officer-at-large, 1988-91, 1994-00; Cent Flint Optimist Club, 1996-; Flint City Wide Hate Crimes Task Force, Human Relations Comn, 1993-98; Int F & A M Masons, 1994-; Evergreen Valley Block Club; Southeast Crime Watch. **Honors/Awds:** Outstanding Service Award, Nat NAACP Radiothon, 1994; Flint NAACP Service Award, 1992; Olive R Beasley Volunteer Award, Urban League Flint, 1989; Stud Leadership Award, Housing Programs

Office, MSU, 1983; Outstanding Black Student Scholarship, Kappa Alpha Psi, MSU, 1983; Honorary Page, State Senate of Tenn, 1980; Best Petitioner's Brief Award, Frederick Douglass-Midwest Regional Moot Court Competition, Black Law Students Asn, 1986; Outstanding Young Men of America, 1986, 1988, 1989, 1996, 1998; Who's Who in American Law; Who's Who Among African-Americans. **Business Addr:** Judge, 68th District Court, 630 S Saginaw St, Flint, MI 48502, **Business Phone:** (810)766-8985.

MARABLE, REV. DR. JUNE MOREHEAD
School administrator, clergy. **Personal:** Born Jun 8, 1924, Columbus, OH; daughter of Rev J W (deceased) and Minnie Martin (deceased); married; children: Dr James Marable Jr (deceased), Dr Manning Marable & Madonna Howard. **Educ:** Cent State Univ, Wilberforce, Ohio, BS, educ, 1948; Univ Dayton, MS, educ, 1965; Miami Univ, Oxford, Ohio, PhD, educ, 1974; United Theol Seminary, Dayton, OH, MDiv, 1989. **Career:** Wright Patterson AFB Dayton, cartographic draftsman & clerk-typist, 1948-52; Kans City Bd Educ, Kans City, Mo, teacher 1952-54; Dayton Bd Educ, teacher, reading consult, 1954-72; Wright State Univ, Dayton, asst prof, 1972-77; Miami Univ, Oxford, Ohio, vis assoc prof, 1978-80; Payne Seminary, Wilberforce, OH, Alternative Theol Educ Prog, exec dir, 1989-; AME Church, elder, minister, 1989. **Orgs:** Sen Mer Rek Honor Soc, Wilberforce Univ, Wilberforce, Ohio, 1948; Alpha Kappa Mu, Wilberforce Univ, Wilberforce, Ohio, 1948; educ dir, Marable Early Childhood Educ Ctr, Dayton 1960-77; Ohio State Right Read Community, State Dept Educ Ohio, 1970-80; educ consult & lectr Pub Schs Univs, Community Civic Organisation Churches, 1970-; crd, Reading Improvement Prog, Alpha Kappa Alpha Sorority, 1974-78; admin asst, Black Res Asn, Dayton, 1979-85; pres, Delta Kappa Gamma Int Sorority, Dayton chap. **Honors/Awds:** Outstanding Citizen Award, Optimist Club, Dayton, 1978; Alumni Hall of Fame, Cent State Univ, 1988; Annie Webb Blanton Award. **Home Addr:** 5145 Dayton Liberty Rd, Dayton, OH 45418. **Business Addr:** Executive Director, Payne Theological Seminary, Alternative Theological Education Program, 1230 Wilberforce Clifton Rd, Wilberforce, OH 45384-0474, **Business Phone:** (937)376-2946.

MARBURY, DONALD LEE
Broadcaster. **Personal:** Born Nov 26, 1949, Pittsburgh, PA; son of Sherrill and Susie Burroughs; married Sheila JoAnn King, Mar 24, 1973; children: Cara Jean & Evan Lee. **Educ:** Univ Pittsburgh, BA, 1971. **Career:** Pittsburgh Post Gazette, gen assignment reporter, 1969-71; WQED-TV, exec prod, 1973-80, prod, 1977-80, co-producer, 1977, prod & broadcast host, 1973-77, prod, 1976-77, instr, 1978-79, exec prod & coordr local programming, 1978-80; KQED-TV, Scriptwriter, 1979; Chatham Col, Commun Dept, instr, 1976-80; Television Program Fund, Cultural & Children's Programs, assoc dir, 1980-89, dir, 1989-95; Univ DC, Black Film Inst, instr screenplay writing, 198-85; Corp Pub Broadcasting, Dept Educ & Programming, vpres programming, 1995-97; Under One Sky Media, Pres, 1997-; Howard Univ, Sch Commun, Dept Radio, Television, Film, instr, 2002-; St John African Methodist Episcopal Church, pastor; Ebenezer African Methodist Episcopal Church, pastor, currently, ordained African Methodist Episcopal Church elder, currenlty. **Orgs:** Bd dirs, Intercultural House, 1971-; mem & bd dirs, Pittsburgh Black Media Coalition, 1971-74; bd dirs, WYEP-FM, 1974-75; steering comm., Producers Coun, 1976-80; mem & bd dirs, Nat Black Prog Consortium, 1978-80; mem & exec steering comm, Producers Coun Nat Asn Educ Broadcasters, 1978-80; Task Force Pub Participation, 1978; bd dirs, Louise Child Care Ctr; bd dir, Children's Advocacy Newspaper, 1989. **Honors/Awds:** Golden Quill Western Pa Journalism Honorary, 1973; Pittsburgh Goodwill Ambassador, Pittsburgh Goodwill, 1975; Black Achiever of the Year, Talk Mag, 1975; Founders Award, Nat Black Programming Consortium, 1983; Certificate of Appreciation, Nat Black Programming Consortium, 1988; Leokoeberlein Distinguished Alumnus Award in Journalism, Univ Pittsburgh, 1990. **Home Addr:** 1 Tupelo Ct, Rockville, MD 20855, **Home Phone:** (301)963-9380. **Business Phone:** (301)248-8833.

MARBURY, MARTHA G.
Administrator. **Personal:** Born Nov 22, 1946, Morgantown, WV; daughter of John Dobbs Jr (deceased) and Georgia Johnson Dobbs (deceased); children: Anthony Vaughn. **Educ:** Univ Md, Col Park, MD, BS, 1980. **Career:** USDA Soil Conserv Serv, Morgantown, WV, clerk steno, 1967-73; USDA Soil Conserv, Ser Col Park, MD, personnel clerk, 1973-75, personnel asst, 1975-76, personnel mgt specialist, 1976-78, personnel officer, 1978-83; USDA Soil Conserv Serv, Wash, DC, classification specialist, 1983-85, chief, employ br, 1985-88, chief, EEO br, 1988-92; Human Resources Mgmt Serv, assoc dir, 1992-94; USDA, Natural Resources Conserv Serv, admin off, SE Region, 1994-. **Orgs:** Nat Orgn Prof NRCS Employees; Int Personnel Mgt Asn. **Honors/Awds:** Outstanding Performance Award, USDA Soil Conserv Serv, 1975, 1978, 1980, 1983, 1985, 1986, 1989, 1990, 1994, 1997; Honorable Mention Blue Pencil Award, Blue Pencil Asn, 1989; Reinventing Govt: Group Winner Award, USDA Soil Conserv Serv, Natural Resources Conserv Serv, 1998; The first black personnel officer and the first black branch chief in the personnel division of Soil Conservation Service's national headquarters. **Business Addr:** Administrative Officer Southeast Region, USDA Natural Resources Conservation Services, 1720 Peachtree Rd NW Suite 446N, Atlanta, GA 30309.*

MARBURY, STEPHON (STEPHON XAVIER MARBURY)
Basketball player. **Personal:** Born Feb 20, 1977, Brooklyn, NY; son of Don and Mabel; children: Stephanie, Xaviera & Stephon Jr. **Educ:** Ga Tech Univ. **Career:** Minn Timberwolves, guard, 1996-98; NJ Nets, guard, 1999-2001; Phoenix Suns, 2001-03; NY Knicks, point guard, 2003-. **Honors/Awds:** All Rookie team, NBA, 1997; Hometown Hero Award, 2001; NBA's most underrated player, 2003-04; NBA Community Assist of the Month Award, 2004; Nat High School Player of the Year, Parade Mag. **Special Achievements:** First round pick, No 4, NBA Draft, 1996; listed in "Good Guys in Sports," Sporting News, 2005. **Business Addr:** Professional Basketball Player, New York Knicks, 2 Pennsylvania Plz, New York, NY 10121-0091, **Business Phone:** (212)465-6471.

MARBURY, STEPHON XAVIER. See MARBURY, STEPHON.

MARCHAND, INGA (FOXY BROWN)
Rap musician. **Personal:** Born Sep 6, 1979, Brooklyn, NY. **Career:** Solo Albums: Ill Na Na, 1996; Chyna Doll, 1998; Broken Silence, 2001; Black Roses, 2005; Group Albums: The Firm, 1997; Songs: "Get Me Home", 1996; "I'll Be", 1997; "Hot Spot", 1999; "B.K. Anthem", 2001; "Too Much For Me", 2003; "I Need a Man", 2003; "Come Fly With Me", 2005; Films: Rush Hour 2, 2001; Marci X, 2003; Cradle 2 the Grave, 2003; The 40 Year Old Virgin, 2005; The Firm, group mem; Universal Music Group, currently; Def Jam Rec, currently. **Special Achievements:** Rapped on "I Shot Ya", with LL Cool J; "Touch Me, Tease Me", with Case; "No One Else", with Total, lil' Kim, and Da Brat; "You're Makin' Me High", with Toni Braxton. **Business Addr:** Rapper, Universal Music Group, 1755 Broadway Lobby, New York, NY 10019-3743, **Business Phone:** (212)841-8000.*

MARCHAND, MELANIE ANNETTE
Chemical engineer, chief executive officer. **Personal:** Born Mar 12, 1962, New Orleans, LA; daughter of Edward Janvier and Sandra Baker. **Educ:** Tulane Univ, New Orleans, LA, BS, Chem Engineering, 1980-84; Wharton Sch Bus Univ Pa, MBA, 1991. **Career:** Union Carbide Corp, Taft, La, production eng, 1984-86; Air Prods & Chem, Inc, New Orleans, La, process eng, 1986-87; Air Prods & Chem Inc, Allentown, PA, process eng; corporate planning, prod mgt, tech sales & mkt mgt; Sisters In Shape Inc, pres & chief exec officer, currently. **Orgs:** La Engineering Soc; Soc Women Engineers, 1988-90; Asn Integrated Mgt; Minority Community Adv Bd Muhlenberg Col, 1989; consult, Philadelphia Black Women's Health Project Black Men. **Honors/Awds:** Appreciation Award for Leadership and Dedication, Union Carbide Corp Family Safety & Health Comm, 1985; Quality Recognition Variable Compensation Award, Air Products & Chem Inc, 1989. **Business Addr:** President, Chief Executive Officer, Sisters In Shape Inc, 1320 Somerville Ave, Philadelphia, PA 19141, **Business Phone:** (215)457-8663.*

MARCHANT, ANN WALKER
Government official, chief executive officer. **Educ:** Sarah Lawrence Col, attended. **Career:** Burson Marsteller, staff commun; White House, spec asst pres; Shandwick Int, exec vpres & dir global bus develop; Walker Marchant Group, founder, ceo, currently. **Orgs:** Bd dir, Washington Ballet; bd dir, The Decatur House Nat Hist Trust & Preservation; bd visitors, Howard Univ. **Business Phone:** (202)466-6040.

MARCUS, ANTONIO. See CARTER, TONY A.

MARDENBOROUGH, LESLIE A.
Consultant, executive. **Personal:** Born Mar 25, 1948, Bronx, NY; daughter of Victor E and Dorothy Richards; children: Adina N, Keith A Clark & Kevin A Clark. **Educ:** Albright Col, AB, 1968; Simmons Col Grad Sch Mgt, prog develop execs,1989. **Career:** Brooklyn Col, career counr, 1969-73; Wildcat Serv Corp, vpres opers, 1978; New Life Group Inc, consult, Career Ctr, exec dir, 1979-81; NY Times Co, proj mgr, human resources, 1981-84, dir employee rels, 1984-86, dir personnel, 1986-87, dir corp personnel, 1987-90, vpres human resources, 1990; Mardenborough Assoc, mgt consult & prin, currently. **Orgs:** Bd mem, Human Resource Planners Assn, 1982-, 1991; bd mem & mem officer, NY Human Resource Planners, 1986-88; NAA Employee Rels Comn, 1988-; Newspape rPersonnel Rels Assn, 1988-; brd dir, NY Brd Trade, 1989-92; brd dirs, Westchester Residential Opportunities, 1989-; brd dirs, Westchester Housing Fund, 1991-94; brd dirs, United Neighborhood Houses, 1991-; pres, Brd Dirs Sch Alumnae Assn, 1996-; Gen Mgt Adv Brd, Am Press Inst. **Honors/Awds:** Black Achievers in Industries, YMCA, Harlem, 1986; Hon Doctorate, Albright Col, 1990; Rappaport Alumni Achievement Award, Simmons Col GSM, 1992. **Special Achievements:** Hundred of the Best and Brightest Black Women in Corporate America, Ebony Mag, 1990. **Business Addr:** Principal, Managemaent Consultant, Mardenborough Associates, 256 Hamilton Ave, New Rochelle, NY 10801, **Business Phone:** (914)632-0589.

MARIA, DONNA. See O'BANNO, DONNA EDWARDS.

MARIEL, SERAFIN
Banker, chief executive officer, president (organization). **Care** New York Nat Bank, pres & ceo, currently. **Business Pho** (212)589-5000.*

MARINER, JONATHAN
Executive. **Personal:** Born Jan 1, 1954?; married Mildr children: Brian, Matthew & Phillip. **Educ:** Univ Va, BS, acct; H vard Bus Sch, MBA. **Career:** MCI Communs, Wash, DC, financial analyst; Fla Marlins Baseball Club, Miami, exec vpres chief financial officer, 1992-2000; Charter Schs USA, exec vp & chief operating officer, 2000-02; Major League Baseball, N York, NY, chief operating officer, sr vpres & chief financial offi 2002-, exec vpres finance, currently; Baseball Assistance Te Inc, treas; BankAtlantic Bancorp, dir; Ryan, Beck & Co, bd **Orgs:** Chmn, Broward Community Col Found Bd; adv bd, U Va McIntire Sch Com; adv bd, Stanford Parents' Adv Bd; adv Pine Crest Sch Ft Lauderdale; mem exec comt, Exec Comt Gre Miami Chamber Com; bd dirs, United Way Greater Mia Beacon Coun. **Special Achievements:** Featured on the cover CFO Magazine; Top 10 in Sports Illustrated's annual listing of 101 Most Influential Minorities in Sports. **Business Addr:** Ser Vice President and Cheif Financial Officer, Executive V President Finance, Major League Baseball, 75 Ninth Ave 5th New York, NY 10011, **Business Phone:** (212)485-3444.*

MARION, BROCK ELLIOT
Football player. **Personal:** Born Jun 11, 1970, Bakersfield, C son of Jerry; married Keri; children: Brianna, Olivia & Brock **Educ:** Univ Nev, Reno. **Career:** Football player (retired); Da Cowboys, defensive back, 1993-97; Miami Dolphins, 1998-20 Detroit Lions, safety, 2004-05. **Orgs:** Founder, Brock Mar Found; Cystic Fibrosis Found. **Honors/Awds:** Spec Teams Pla of the Week, Nat Football League, 1994; 1st Team All-Conf, 20 Defensive Player of the Month, Asian Football Confederati 2002. **Special Achievements:** Ranked fourth on the Dolphins w 100 tackles and had three interceptions, eight passes defensed, two forced fumbles in 2003; Participated in various social s prog.

MARION, FRED D
Football player. **Personal:** Born Jan 2, 1959, Gainesville, FL; m ried Anne; children: Monica Nicole, Natasha Monigue, Aly Dinita & Fred Donald. **Educ:** Univ Miami, Fl, Bus Mgt. **Care** Football player (retired); New Eng Patriots, safety, 1982-91; I mons franchise restaurants, owner, currently. **Honors/Awds:** P season play, 1985: AFC Championship Game, NFL Champi ship Game, Pro Bowl; Ed Block Courage Award. **Business Ad** Owner, Damon's franchise restaurants, Gainesville, FL.

MARION, DR. PHILLIP JORDAN
Physician. **Personal:** Born May 14, 1958, Albany, NY; son o W and Marie; married Tanya C Lumpkins, May 21, 1990. **Ed** SUNY Purchase, BA, 1981; New Yoyk Univ Sch Med, MD, 19 New York Univ, MS, 1989; George Wash Univ, MPH, 19 **Career:** Rusk Ist Rehabilitation Med, chief resident, 19 Howard Univ Sch Med, asst prof; Nat Rehabilitation Hospl, med dir, 1990-95, Ambulatory Serv, med dir, 1990-95; He Policy Fellow, Off Senator Orrin G Hatch; Senate Judiciary C Health Policy Fellow. **Orgs:** Am Col Physician exes; fellow, Acad Physical Med & Rehab, 1990; Concerned blk Men, 19 95; Nat Mentorship Prog; Am ment asn; Asn Acad Physiatri Health Policy Fellow, Robert Wood Johnson, 1994-95. **Busin Addr:** 102 Irving St NW, Washington, DC 20010, **Busin Phone:** (202)966-1615.*

MARIUS, KENNETH ANTHONY
Physician. **Personal:** Born Feb 22, 1937, New York, NY; so Edwin and Aldith; married Esther Bailey; children: Kenneth Robert. **Educ:** Howard Univ, BSEE, 1960; NJ Inst Technol, M 1965; Howard Univ Col Med, MD, 1970. **Career:** Commu Coop Corp, pres, 1972; Tricities Progress Women, consult, 19 NJ Col Med & Dent, clinical prof, 1976-. **Orgs:** Essex Co M Soc; Consult City Newark; Orange Bd Educ, med dir, team ph cian Weeguanic HS; speaker, Essex Co Heart Asn; Alpha Om Alpha Med Hon Soc; Tau Beta Pi Eng Hon Soc; pres, N Je Med Soc, NJ Med Soc, 1984; delegate, Nat Med Asn, 1981-; Bd, Sickle Cell Found, 1983-. **Honors/Awds:** Distinguis Service Award, Sports Physician, Weequahic, 1983- Distinguished Service Award, Tricities Chamber Com, 19 Board Of Concerned Citizens Award, 1986; Award, Col Me Dent NJ, 1992. **Military Serv:** USAF, 1952-56; USAR, med ficer, 1984-86. **Business Addr:** 202 Clinton Ave, Newark, 07108.*

MARK, RICHARD
Chief executive officer. **Educ:** Iowa State Univ, BS, 1977, MS, mgt. **Career:** Collinsville, high sch football coach & spec e teacher; State Ill, asst to Mayor, customer serv Ill Power; St. C County Intergovernmental Grants Dept, exec dir; St Mary's H sr vpres & chief oper officer, pres & chief exec officer, 1994-2 Ancilla Syst, sr vpres; Ameren Serv, vpres customer serv, 20

03, vpres govt policy, econ develop & community rels, 2003-)05; Ameren UE, sr vpres, 2002-. **Orgs:** Chmn Financial versight Panel, East St. Louis School District 189, 1994; bd dirs, ıst St. Louis Nat Asn Advan Colored People; bd dirs, Major Case quad; bd dirs, Belleville Dioceses Cath Community Found; bd rs, St. Louis, 2004; St Clair County Sheriff's Dept Merit Comn. **onors/Awds:** St. Louis Univ, hon Doctorate Pub Serv; Quincy niv, hon Doctorate Law; Nat Louis Univ, DHL. *

ARKHAM, HOUSTON, JR.
lucator, football coach. **Personal:** Born Dec 20, 1942, rookhaven, MS; son of Ethel Tanner Markham and Houston arkham Sr; married Annie Davis, Jan 14, 1968; children: olanda & Houston III. **Educ:** Alcorn State Univ, Lorman, Miss, S, physical ed, 1965; Tenn State Univ, Nashville, TN, MS, 1971. **areer:** Educator, Football coach (retired); Vicksburg High Sch, icksburg, Miss, head football coach, 1967-75; Jackson State niv, Jackson, Miss, asst football coach, 1975-87; Ala State Univ, ontgomery, Ala, head football coach, 1987. **Honors/Awds:** oach of the Year, Sheridan Poll, 1987; SWAC Coach of the Year, uthwestern Athletic Coach, 1990-91; Coach of the Year, Pigskin ub of America, 1990-91; Coach of the Year, 100% Wrong Club, 90-91.

ARKS, JOHN
ayor, educator. **Educ:** Fla State Univ Sch Bus, BS, 1969; Fla ate Univ Col Law, JD, 1972. **Career:** Katz, Kutter PA; Knowles, arks & Randolph, PA; Tallahassee Off Adorno & Yoss, manag- g partner; Fla State Univ Col Law, adj prof; City Tallahassee, ayor, 2003-. **Orgs:** Chmn, admin Law Judge, Fla Pub Serv omn; trustee, Collins Ctr Bd, Fla State Univ; fac mem, Nat Asn egulatory Utility Comnrs; Am, Nat, Fla & Tallahassee Bar; Tal- hassee Barristers Asn; Am Law Inst; Fla Bars Local Gov & Ad- in Law Sect; bd dirs, Fringe Benefits Mgt Co; bd dirs, Fla eague Cities; bd dirs, Tallahassee Econ Develop Coun;bd dirs, llahassee & Leon County Civic Ctr Authority; bd dirs, Sunshine ate Gov Financing Comn; bd dirs, Econ Club Fla; Energy & Arts Cult Comt; life mem, Nat Asn Advan Colored People; bd dirs, llahassee Urban League. **Special Achievements:** Co-host on the cal TV show. **Military Serv:** USAF, judge advocate, 4 yrs. **Busi- ss Addr:** Mayor, City of Tallahassee, 300 S Adams St, City ıll, Tallahassee, FL 32301, **Business Phone:** (850)891-0000.

ARKS, KENNETH HICKS
wyer. **Personal:** Born Sep 15, 1951, Lawrenceville, VA; son of enneth H Sr and Nethel H; married Fe Morales, Jan 13, 1979; ildren: Kenisha Maria Morales. **Educ:** Columbia Col, BA, 74; Columbia Univ Sch Law, JD, 1977. **Career:** Shearman & erling, assoc, 1977-80; Webster & Sheffield, assoc, 1980-84; ickwire, Gavin & Gibbs PC, partner, 1984-89; Ginsburg, Feld- ın & Bress, partner, 1989-91; Alexander, Bearden, Hairstonetal, 91-97; Reid & Priest LLP, coun, 1997-98; Columbia Energy oup, asst gen coun, 1998-2000; Exostar LLC, secy & gen coun, 01-. **Orgs:** Am Bar Asn; chair pub rels comt, Hispanic Bar Asn C, 1983-85, bd dir, 1984-85; bd dir, Ayuda Inc, 1984-89; pub bitrator, Munic Securities Rulemaking Bd, 1986-89; planning & ning comt, Reston Community Asn, 1986-91; bd dir, Turn- idge Cluster Asn, 1987-90, pres, 1989-90; DC Bar Asn Elec- ns Comt, 1988-91; co-vice chair, Pub Finance Comt Sect Urban, ate & Local Govt Law, 1993-96; fel, Am Bar Found, 1993-; Nat r Asn; Hispanic Nat Bar Asn; NY Bar Asn; Nat Asn Bond wyers; Japan Soc. **Business Addr:** General Counsel, Exostar, 530 Dulles Technol Dr Suite 200, Herndon, VA 20171, **Busi- ss Phone:** (703)793-7713.

ARKS, LEE OTIS
ucator. **Personal:** Born Nov 17, 1944, Carthage, AR; married ren Vaughn; children: Cynthia Lynne, Valerie Jeanne & Allison rie. **Educ:** Sioux Falls Col, BA, 1966; Univ ill, Champaign- bana, MS, 1974. **Career:** Co-capt, MVP football Sioux Falls l, 1965; Rockford Guilford High Sch, Phys Educ teacher, head ck coach, asst football coach, 1967-; Lincoln Park Elem Sch, cher, 1966-67; Madison Mustang, football player, 1966-67; ckford Rams, football player, 1969-70. **Orgs:** SFC Letterman ub Sioux Falls Col Alumni Asn, 1966; prog dir, BT Wash Comm nt, 1966-70; exec bd dir, Rockford Educ Asn, 1971-73; Ill Hu- ın Relations Commn, 1971-73; bd dir, Rockford Black Educrs n, 1971-73; deleg, Nat Educ Asn Conv, 1971; bd dir, Central rrace Co-op, 1972; Rockford Educ Asn; Ill Educ Asn; Nat Educ n; Ill Health Phys Educ & Recreation Asn; Ill Coaches Asn; Nat tterman Asn; Rockford Coaches Asn; Nat Educ Asn Black ucus; Allen Chapel AME Church. **Honors/Awds:** Teacher of ır, Guilford High Sch Stud Body, 1971.

ARKS, ROSE M.
orarian. **Personal:** Born Mar 17, 1938, Chicago, IL; children: borah, Charles. **Educ:** Sacramento City Col, attended 1958; cramento State Univ. **Career:** Sacramento City-Co Libr, libr rk, 1961-77; Martin luther king jr libr; Oak Pk Br Libr, br supvr. **gs:** Past bd dir, KVIE Educ TV; past bd dir, Sacramento Reg s Coun; past secy, Oak Pk Comn Theatre; mgr Band & co-mgr ging group, Sacramento Black Women's United Front; past es, Sacramento City Employ Asn; past pres, Sacramento City or Asn.

ARQUEZ, CAMILO RAOUL
ysician. **Personal:** Born Feb 25, 1942, New York, NY; son of cil and Gloria. **Educ:** Colby Col, AB, 1963; Howard Univ Sch Med, MD, 1976. **Career:** St Vincent's Hosp, resident psychiat, 1977-79, chief resident, 1978-79; Manhattan Psychiat Ctr, res psychiatrist, 1979-80; Harlem Hosp, staff psychiatrist, 1980-82, attend physician div child & adolescent psychiat, 1988-92; N Gen Hosp, dir inpatient psychiat, 1982-84; State Univ NY, Health Sci Ctr, Brooklyn, asst instr; Columbia Univ, Col Physicians & Surgeons, asst clinical prof psychiat, 1988-92. **Orgs:** Am Psychiat Asn, 1978-; Black Psychiatrists Am, 1979-; bd trustees, Wooster Sch, 1986-92; Am Acad Child & Adolescent Psychiat, 1986-; co-chmn, Black Health Professionals Sch Based Health & Sex Educ Progs, 1986-88; bd trustees, The Children's Annex, 1998-. **Honors/Awds:** Falk Fel, Am Psychiat Asn, 1978-79. **Special Achievements:** Diagnosis of Manic Depressive Illness in Blacks, Comprehensive Psychiatry, Vol 26, No 4 1985. **Military Serv:** AUS, 1963-70. **Home Addr:** Fawn Hill Rd, PO Box 361, Phoenicia, NY 12464-0361. *

MARR, CARMEL CARRINGTON
Lawyer, consultant. **Personal:** Born Jun 23, 1921, Brooklyn, NY; daughter of William P Carrington (deceased) and Gertrude C Lewis Carrington (deceased); married Warren II; children: Charles & Warren III. **Educ:** Hunter Col, BA (Cum Laude), political sci, 1945; Columbia Univ Law Sch, JD, 1948. **Career:** Lawyer, consultant (retired); Dyer & Stevens Esqs, law asst, 1948-49; Pvt Pract, atty law, 1949-53; US Mission United Nations, adv legal affairs, 1953-67; United Nations Secretariat, sr legal officer, 1967-68; NY State Human Rights Appeal Bd, 1968-71; NY State Pub Serv Comn, commdr, 1971-86; Amistad Res Ctr, co founder, 1976; US Dept Transp Tech Pipeline Safety Stand Comn, chair, 1979-85; Gas Res Inst, chair adv coun, 1979-86; Consult, energy, 1987-90. **Orgs:** Amistad Res Ctr, Tulane Univ, 1970-, chmn & pres, 1982-95; exec comt, Brooklyn Soc Prevent Cruelty C, 1972; Prospect Park Alliance, 1983-97; Nat Coun UN Asn US, 1983-94; chairperson, Nat Asn Regulatory Utility Comns, Gas Comt, 1984-86, pres, Great Lakes Conf Pub Utility Comn; Nat Arts Stabilization Fund, 1984-93; Nat Coun Hampshire Col; President's Coun, Tulane Univ, 1989-96; Alpha Kappa Alpha Sorority. **Honors/Awds:** Outstanding Community Service, Brooklyn Urban League; Hall of Fame, Hunter Col; Honorary Citizen, New Orleans; Sojourner Truth Award, Jamaica Club Nat Bus & Prof Women's Clubs; Distinguished Alumni Award, Columbia Univ Law Sch, 1998. **Home Addr:** 831 Sherry Dr, Valley Cottage, NY 10989, **Home Phone:** (914)268-5811.

MARR, WARREN, II
Editor. **Personal:** Born Jul 31, 1916, Pittsburgh, PA; son of Warren Quincy and Cecelia Antoinette McGee; married Carmel Carrington, Apr 11, 1948; children: Charles Carrington & Warren Quincy III. **Educ:** Wilberforce Univ, Jour & Printing. **Career:** Editor (retired); St Louis Argus, linotype oper, 1938-39; Plaindealer KCKS, lino type oper, shop foreman, asst ed, 1939-42; Concert Mgt, 1942-48; James Lassiter & Sons Madison NJ, drapery maker & asst decorator, 1948-52; House Marr Inc, proprietor, 1952-60; United Church Bd Homeland Ministries, NY Div Higher Educ & Am Missionary Assoc, Am Med Asn, Col Centennials,secy, 1961-68; Amistad Awards, founder & dir, 1961-; Nat Asn Advan Colored People, Crisis Mag, ed, 1968-80; co-ed, "Minorities & Am Bicentennial Perspective" NY Arno Press, 1977; co-ed, "Negro Almanac" 3rd ed NY Bellwether Publ Co, 1977. **Orgs:** Founder & pres, Amistad Affiliates Inc, 1989; founder & exec dir, Friends Amistad; bd mem, S NY Div, UN Asn USA, Brooklyn Arts & Cultural Asn, Brooklyn Boys Club, Medgar Evers Col Community Coun; past hon, Nat Chmn Pan-African Found Art Shows, photography exhibits, pvt art collections; comnr, Art Comn NYC; chmn, Community Art Comn, York Col; co-founder with Clifton H Johnson, Amistad Res Ctr, New Orleans, 1966; NY City Community Board No 9; trustee, Nat maritime Hist Soc, 1992-00; Brooklyn Culture Asn,1993; bd mem, Amistad Am Inc, 1998; builder, 130-foot schooner, Amistad, 2000. **Honors/Awds:** Awards: Am Asn United Nations Eleanor Roosevelt, 1955, Testimonial Luncheon, Waltann School for Creative Arts, 1967, JFK Award, JFK Lib Minorities, 1972; International Key Women of America, 1974; Pan-African Found, 1974; Frederick Douglass Award, Afro-Am Hist Asn, 1975; Third Army ROTC Reg, 1974; Black Heritage Asn, 1974; Achievement Award, Detroit Friends Amistad, 1976; UCC Partners Ill, 1998; Friends of Education Leadership Award, 1999; American Ship Trust Award, Nat Maritime Hist Soc, 1995; United Church Partners Ill, 1998; City of Cleveland, 1998; Leadership Award, Friends Educ, 1999; Builders Award, Amistad Am, 2000. **Home Addr:** 831 Sherry Dr, Valley Cottage, NY 10989. *

MARRETT, DR. CORA B.
Educator. **Personal:** Born Jun 15, 1942, Richmond, VA; daughter of Horace S Bagley and Clorann Boswell Bagley; married Louis E. **Educ:** Va Union Univ, BA, sociol, 1963; Univ Wis, MA, sociol, 1965, PhD, sociol,1968. **Career:** Univ NC, Chapel Hill, asst prof, 1968-69; Western Mich Univ, asst toassoc, 1969-74; Ctr Advan Study, fel, 1976-77; Univ Massachusetts,provost, 1997-2001; Univ Wis, assoc prof to full prof, sr vpres acad affairs, 2001-; NSFs Educ& Human Resources Directorate, asst Dir, 2006. **Orgs:** Nat Acad Sci, 1973-74; Bd govs, Argonne Nat Lab, 1982-89, 1996-; bdtrustees, Ctr Adv Study Behavioral Sci, 1983-89; Nat-Science Found, 2007. **Honors/Awds:** Distinguished Teaching Award, Univ Wis, 1989; Inductee, African Am Portrait Gallery, Nat Acad Sci, 1996; honorary doctorate, Wake Forest Univ, 1996; Erich Bloch Distinguished Service Award, Quality Education for Minorities Network, 2005. **Special Achievements:** Editor of "Research of Race & Ethnic Relation" (JAI Press), 1985. **Business Addr:** Senior Vice President for Academic Affairs, University of Wisconsin System, 1624 Van Hise Hall 1220 Linden Dr, Madison, WI 53706-1559, **Business Phone:** (608)262-3826.

MARRIOTT, MICHEL
Writer. **Personal:** Born Mar 8, 1954. **Educ:** Morehead State Univ, BA, 1976; Northwestern Univ, Medill Sch Jour, MA, 1978. **Career:** Columbia Univ Grad Sch Jour, adj prof; City Col, New York, prof jour; Marion Chronicle-Tribune, reporter; The New York Times, reporter, 1987-94; Newsweek Mag, New York, gen ed, 1994; Film: New Jersey Drive, co-writer, 1995; New York Times, Style Dept, writer, 1995, staff writer, currently; The Frederick Douglass Creative Arts Center, head workshop. **Honors/Awds:** Nieman fel, 2002. *

MARRIOTT, DR. SALIMA SILER
Legislator. **Personal:** Born Dec 5, 1940, Baltimore, MD; daughter of Cordie Ayers Siler and Jesse James Siler; married David Small Marriott (divorced 1972); children: Terrez Siler Marriott Thompson & Patrice Kenyatta Siler Marriott. **Educ:** Morgan State Univ, BS, 1964; Univ Md, MSW, 1972; Howard Univ, DSW, 1988. **Career:** Baltimore City Pub Schs, teacher, 1964-65; Dept Social Serv, NY, social worker, 1965-68; Dept Social Serv, Baltimore, social worker, 1968-72; Morgan State Univ, Baltimore, MD, instr, 1972-90, chairperson, 1981-87, asst prof, 1990-96; Md Gen Assembly, delegate, 1991-; Cantonsville Community Col, adj fac, 1998-99; Hood Col, 1999-2000; Bowie State Col, vis lectr, 2001-03. **Orgs:** Chair, Park Heights Develop Corp, 1988-92; founding mem/vpres, African-Am Women Caucus, 1982-85; vice chmn, Md Chap Nat Rainbow Coalition, 1988-89; Delta Sigma Theta Sorority Inc, 1989-, chair, 1993-95; chair, Nat Black Women's Health Proj, 1993; secy, Nat Rainbow Coalition, 1994-95; Nat Am Advan Colored People; vice chair, Md Legis Black Caucus, 1994-95; Women Legislators; regional chair, Nat Black Caucus State Legislators, 1994-; trustee, Bethel AME Church, 1997-; vice chair, Baltimore Substance Abuse Systems Bd, 1998-. **Honors/Awds:** Workshop Convener, United Nation's Decade Women Conf, 1985; Outstanding Teacher, Dept Social Work & Ment Health, Morgan State Univ, 1988; Baltimore's Black Women of Courage Exhibit, 1988; African American Humanitarian Award, 1991; Senator Verda Welcome Political Award, 1992; Delegate of the Year, Mid Atlantic Div Am Asn Marriage & Family Therapist, 1993; Sarah's Circle Award, Col Notre Dame, MD, 1994; Nat Legacy Award, Delta Sigma Theta Sorority, 1994; Fleming Fel, 1995; Nat Black Caucus of State Legislators Labor Roundtable Award, 1999; Maryland Legislative Black Caucus Chairman's Meritorious Award, 2000; Ctr Women Policy Studies Foreign Policy Inst, 2001; Bold Dreamer Award, Quixote Ctr Justice USA, 2002; Women Legislator's Lobby Pacesetters Award, 2003; Nat Coalition Abolish Death Penalty's Abolition Year, 2003. **Special Achievements:** Editor of US Policy Toward Southern Africa, 1984; Convener and Organizer of National Conference: Women of African Diaspora, 1984; Jesse Jackson Delegate, Democratic National Convention, 1988; Maryland Democratic Central Committee; deputy state dir, Dukakis/Bentsen Campaign, 1988; elected to Maryland General Assembly; Chair International Health Conference, Women of African Diaspora, 1995; Maryland General Assembly: Chair of the Baltimore City Delegation, 1998-; Chair of Way's and Means Committee on Children and Youth, 2003; House Chair of Joint Committee on Children, Youth and Families, 2003. **Business Addr:** State Delegate, Maryland General Assembly, Lowe House Off Bldg, 84 College Ave, Annapolis, MD 21401-1991, **Business Phone:** (410)841-3255.

MARROW, TARA CENTEIO (TARA CENTEIO MORROW)
Administrator, editor. **Personal:** Daughter of Marlene. **Educ:** Spellman Col, Ga. **Career:** Mahogany card line, writer, currently; Hallmark Cards Inc, writer, ed dir, currently. **Special Achievements:** "Fish in the Water", The Standard-Times. *

MARROW-MOORING, BARBARA A
Government official, executive director. **Personal:** Born May 4, 1945, Trenton, NJ; married Kelly Daniel, Oct 29, 1988; children: Carla, Paula, Connie, Venessa Culbreth, Kelly D Mooring Jr, Anthony Mooring & Shawn Mooring. **Educ:** Mercer County Community Col, AA (cum laude), social sci & humanities, 1973; Trenton State Col, BS (magna cum laude), elem educ, 1975. **Career:** Government official, Executive director (retired); Educ Testing Serv, Princeton, NJ, div mgr, 1982-83, asst vpres, 1983-86, field serv rep, 1982-89; Trenton Bd Educ, teacher, 1983-88; NJ Gen Assembly, Trenton, NJ, clerk, 1986-87; NJ Lottery, Trenton, NJ, exec dir, 1987. **Orgs:** Pres, Nat Asn Univ Women, 1977-79; vpres, mem, Lawrence Township Sch Bd, 1978-87; founder, past pres, Coalition 100 Black Republicans; treas, mem, Mercer County Improv Authority, 1983-88; trustee, Rider Col, 1987-; Capital City Redevelopment Corp, 1987-; NJ Job Training Coord Coun, 1987-89; trustee, Urban League Metrop Trenton Inc, 1988-. **Honors/Awds:** Outstanding Achievement Award, NJ State Fedn Colored Women's Clubs Inc, 1986; Community Service Award, BAC Publ Co, 1988; Women of Achievement Award, NJ Fedn Bus & Prof Women Inc, 1989.

MARRS, DR. STELLA
Writer, activist, singer. **Personal:** Born Mar 22, 1932; daughter of Theodore and Mary; divorced; children: Lynda, Joseph, Walter, Maria-Tita, Jude & Nellie. **Educ:** CCNY, RCC, Hunter Col. **Career:** Lional Hampton Orchestra, vocalist, 1969-73; TV spec Toots Thielmans, 1977; recorded album Belgium Dicovers Stella Marrs, 1977; toured US, Australia, Europe, jazz artist; Stella Marrs Cable TV Show, hosted; WRVR Radio, jazz DJ; WNJR, bright moments in jazz; Jazz Festivals Belgium, France, Amsterdam, Holland; Martin Luther King Multi-Purpose Ctr Inc, exec dir; Leadership Rockland Inc, bd dir, currently. **Orgs:** Int Jazz Fed; contributing ed, African Am Classical Music/Jazz Publ; Jazz at Home Club, 1972, Westchester Jazz Soc, 1975, Bi-Centennial Jazz Citation Manhattan Boro Pres, 1976; Rockland County Womens Issues, 1986; adv comn, Cooperative Extension 4H Club, 1986; Crystal Run Environ Ctr Adv Bd, 1986; Spring Valley NAACP Educ Comn, 1987; adv coun, Village Spring Valley Community Develop Adv Coun, 1987; Rotary Int, 1989; bd mem, Ramapo Housing Authority, 1988; Jazz Fed Am Coalition Jazz Musicians Health & Welfare; Jazz Interactions Audience Develop; treas, People to People; bd dirs, Leadership Rockland Inc. **Honors/Awds:** Woman of the Year, Kennedy Ctr, Harlem, 1976; Consortium of Jazz Artists Award of Excellence, 1981; Certificate of Excellence, A proud Heritage; St Paul Honorary Black Belt; Certificate of Appreciation, 1989; Certificate of Appreciation, Rockland County Dept Soc Serv, 1989; Distinguished Service Award, County Rockland, 1992; Distinguished Service Award, Senator Joseph R Holland, 1993; Citation, NY State Assembly, 1994; Positive Image Award, Delta Sigma Theta, Rockland County Alumni chap, 1997; Al Dykstra Memorial Award, 1998; Jan 19, 1999, declared Dr Stella Marrs Day, Rockland County; Outstanding Female Advocate Activist, Spring Valley NAACP, 2000; Joseph R Bernstein Memorial Award, Mental Health Asn Rockland County, 2000; Humanitarian Award, Rockland Co Ladies & Mens Club, 2000; Dr Stella Mars scholar prog established, 2000; Certificate of Recognition, Town Orangetown, 2000; Certificate of Merit, NY State Assembly, 2000; Cert Spec Congressional Recognition, 2000; Image Award, NAACP, Nyack chap, 2003. **Home Phone:** (845)352-9865. **Business Addr:** Board of Directors, Leadership Rockland Inc, 2 New Hempstead Road Suite 208, New City, NY 10956, **Business Phone:** (845)708-7258.

MARSALIS, BRANFORD
Jazz musician, saxophonist. **Personal:** Born Aug 26, 1960, Breaux Bridge, LA; son of Ellis II and Dolores Ferdinand; married Nicole; children: Peyton; married Teresa Reese, May 31, 1985 (divorced 1994); children: Reese Ellis. **Educ:** Southern Univ, 1979; Berkeley Col Music, 1981. **Career:** Lionel Hampton Orchestra, musician, 1980; Clark Terry Band, musician,1981, Art Blakey & the Jazz Messengers, musician, 1981, Herbie Hancock Quartet, musician, 1981 & 1986; Wynton Marsalis Quintet, musician, 1982-85; Sting, musician, 1985-89, English Chamber Orchestra, musician, 1986; Buckshot LeFonque, musician, 1995-97; The Tonight Show, music dir, 1992-95; Films: Bring on the Night, recording artist, 1985, Sch Daze, recording artist, 1987, Throw Momma from the Train, recording artist, 1987; Mich State Univ & San Francisco State Univ, music prof, 2000-; Marsalis Music, head & owner, 2002-; Nat Pub Radio, host; Albums: Scenesin the City, 1983; Royal Garden Blues, 1986; Renaissance, 1986; Romances-for Saxophone, 1986; Random Abstract, 1987; Trio Jeepy, 1988; Crazy People Music, 1990; The Beautiful Ones Are Not Yet Born, 1991; Bloomington, 1991; I Heard You Twice the First Time, 1992; Dark Keys, 1996; Requiem, 1999; Contemporary Jazz, 2000; Creation, 2001; Footsteps of Our Fathers, 2002; Romare Bearden Revealed, 2003; Steep Anthology, 2004; Eternal, 2004; A Love Supreme Live, 2004; Braggtown, 2006; Metamorphosen, 2009; TV appearences Wait Wait.. Don't Tell Me!; Shanice's, 1992; Space Ghost Coast to Coast, 1994; The Fresh Prince of Bel-Air, 1994; Top Chef (Season 5). **Honors/Awds:** Grammy Award, 1993; Grammy Award Best Pop Instrumental Performance, 1994; Grammy Award Best Jazz Instrumental Album, 2001; Am Soc Composers, Authors & Publ Film & Tv Music Awards, 2001-06. **Special Achievements:** Grammy Award nominations, 1987. **Business Addr:** Jazz musician, Wilkins Management, 323 Broadway St, Cambridge, MA 02139, **Business Phone:** (617)354-2736.

MARSALIS, DELFEAYO
Musician, composer, trombonist. **Personal:** Born Jul 28, 1965, New Orleans, LA; son of Ellis and Dolores. **Educ:** Tanglewood Inst; Berklee Col Music, BA, performance & audio prod, 1989;Univ New Orleans, grad studies, eng; Univ Louisville, MA, jazz performance, 2005. **Career:** La Div Arts, artistic fel, 1998; Three Fifths Prod, founder & producer, currently; Uptown Music Theatre, founder; Minnesota Orchestra, concerts, currently; Blues in C, producer, 1994; Albums: The List, 1986; Crystal Stair, 1987; Truth is Spoken Here, 1988; Vision's Tale, 1989; Jazzy Wonderland, 1990; Mo' Better Blues, 1990; The Beautiful Ones Are Not Yet Born, 1991; As Serenity Approaches, 1991; Citi Movement, 1992; I Heard You Twice the First Time, 1992; It Don't Mean a Thing, 1993; Series, 1993; Joe Cool's Blues, 1994; Loved Ones, 1995; Musashi, 1996; Dark Keys, 1996; Jazz Machine, 1997; Irvin Mayfield, 1998; Citizen Tain, 1999; Blessed, 2000; Late Night at the Blue Note, 2000; How Passion Falls, 2001; Half Past Autumn Suite, 2003; Steep Anthology, 2004; Grey Mayfield, 2005; Minions Dominion, 2006; King Bolden, 2007. **Orgs:** Dir summer prog, Found Artistic & Musical Excellence, 1998-. **Honors/Awds:** Outstanding Performance Award, Jefferson Performing Arts Soc, 1983; 3 MVisionary Award, 1996; hon doctorate, New England Col, Henniker. **Special Achievements:** Earned a cover article for the industry source, Mix magazine in 1997. **Business Addr:** Musician, Braithwaite & Katz Communications, 248 S Great Rd, Lincoln, MA 01773, **Business Phone:** (781)259-9600.*

MARSALIS, ELLIS, JR.
Pianist, composer, educator. **Personal:** Born Nov 14, 1934, New Orleans, LA; married Dolores Ferdinand, 1958; children: Branford, Wynton, Ellis III, Delfeayo, Miboya & Jason. **Educ:** Dillard Univ, BA, 1955; Loyola Univ, MA, music educ, 1986. **Career:** Musician, educator, host, tenor saxophonist; Am Jazz Quartet, pianist, mid-1950s; Marine Corps TV, "Dress Blues", pianist, 1956-58; New Orleans High Sch, music teacher, 1960; "Leatherneck Song book", radio show, pianist; played with Al Hirt's band, 1967-70; French brothers' Storyville Jazz Band, 1971; ELM Rec, founder, owner, 1972-; New Orleans Ctr Creative Arts, head, 1974-86; Va Commonwealth Univ, Jazz Studies Prog, head, 1986-89; Univ New Orleans, Jazz Studies Prog, head, 1990; Xavier Univ, adj prof; Va Commonwealth Univ, commonwealth prof; Univ New Orleans, CocaCola endowed chair, Jazz studies, dir; Albums: Monkey Puzzle, 1963; The Monkey Puzzle, 1963; Gumbo, 1976; Fathers & Sons, 1982; Syndrome, 1984; Homecoming, 1986; The New New Orleans Music: Vocal Jazz, 1989; The Vision's Tale, 1989; Piano in E, 1991; Ellis Marsalis Trio, 1991; The Classic, 1992; Heart of Gold, 1993; Whistle Stop, 1994; Joe Cool's Blue, 1995; A night At Snug Harbour, 1995; Duke In Blue, 1999; Jazz At Christmas in New Orleans, 2002; Ruminations in New York, 2005. **Orgs:** Nat Endowment Arts; bd mem, Southern Arts Fedn. **Honors/Awds:** ACE award for musical performance on cable TV, 1984; Hon Doctorate, Dillard Univ, 1989; Hon Doctorate, Ball State Univ, 1997; Lousiana Music Hall of Fame, 2008. **Special Achievements:** The Ellis Marsalis Center for Music at Musicians' Village in New Orleans is named in honor of Ellis Marsalis. **Military Serv:** USMC, 1956-58.

MARSALIS, JASON
Musician. **Personal:** Born Jun 4, 1977, New Orleans, LA; son of Ellis and Dolores. **Educ:** Loyola Univ. **Career:** Los Hombres Calientes, co-founder; Album: The Year Of The Drummer; Music In Motion; You Don't Have To See It To Believe It; Roots, Branches & Leaves; A Jazz Celebration; Twelve's It; Live At The Blue Note; Los Hombres Calientes; In Honor Of Duke. **Business Addr:** Jazz Drumer, Basin Street Rec, 4130 Canal St, New Orleans, LA 70119, **Business Phone:** (504)483-0002.

MARSALIS, WYNTON
Jazz musician. **Personal:** Born Oct 18, 1961, New Orleans, LA; son of Ellis and Dolores; children: 2; children: Jasper Armstrong. **Educ:** New Orleans Ctr Performing Arts; Berkshire Music Ctr, Juilliard Sch Music, attended 1981. **Career:** Trumpet soloist, New Orleans Philharmonic Orchestra, 1975; recitalist, New Orleans Orchestra; Art Blakey's Jazz Messengers, mem, 1980; HerbieHancock's VSOP quartet; formed own group, 1981; Albums include: Father & Sons, 1982; Wynton Marsalis; Think of One, 1983; Trumpet Concertos, 1983; Hot House Flowers, 1984; Black Codes from the Underground, 1985; Joe Cool's Blues, 1994; CITI Movement; Blood on the Fields, jazz oratorio, 1997; The Marciac Suite, 1999; Big Train, 1999; Immortal Concerts: Jody,2000; All Rise, 2002; Angel Eyes-PRISM, 2002; Angel Eyes-SWEDEN IMPORT, 2003; Unforgivable Blackness: The Rise & Fall of Jack Johnson, 2004; The Magic Hour, 2004; Live at the House of Tribes, 2005; From the Plantation to the Penitentiary, 2007; Jazz at Lincoln Ctr, artistic dir; Colorblind, composer, 2006. **Honors/Awds:** Named Jazz Musician of the Year, Downbeat readers' poll, 1982, 1984, 1985; Wynton Marsalis album named best jazz recorded, Downbeat readers poll, 1982; best trumpet player Downbeat critics' poll, 1984; Acoustic Jazz Group of Year Award, 1984; Grammy Awards for solo jazz instrumental, 1984,1986, classical soloist orchestra, 1984, best trumpet player, 1985, Group Award, 1986; Hon Degrees: Manhattan Col, Yale Univ, Princeton Univ, Hunter Col; inducted into Big Band & Jazz Hall of Fame, 1996; Pulitzer Prize, 1997; Young STAR Award, 1998. **Special Achievements:** First jazz musician to win the Pulitzer Prize in music, 1997; UN, named cult ambassador, 2001. **Business Addr:** Trumpeter, Sony Music Entertainment Inc, 550 Madison Ave, New York, NY 10022, **Business Phone:** (212)833-8000.

MARSH, ALPHONSO HOWARD
Manager. **Personal:** Born Sep 22, 1938, Mobile, AL; son of Alphonso Howard and Augusta Barney; married June E Peterson (deceased); children: Preston Howard & Alphonso Van. **Educ:** Howard Univ, BSEE, 1961. **Career:** Radio Corp Am, elec engr, 1961-63; General Dynamics, elec engr, 1963-66; Rochester Inst Syst, elec engr, 1966-67; Raytheon Co, sr engr, 1967-73; Digital Equip Corp, proj engr, 1973-77; LFE Corp, eng mgr, 1977-87; Honeywell-EOD, engr supvr, 1987-90; EG&G, Rocky Flats Inc, develop assoc engr, 1990. **Orgs:** Inst Elec & Electronic Engrs, 1960; Tau Beta Pi Honor Soc, 1960; elected Town Medway Planning Bd, 1979-90, chmn, 1986-87; Nat Soc Prof Engrs, 1984-86; nat dir, Nat Soc Prof Engrs, 1984-86; state pres, Mass Soc Prof Engrs, 1983-84; st PEI chmn, MA Soc Prof Engrs, 1984-86; chap pres, MSPE Western Middlesex Chap, 1978-79; elected Tow Medway Sch Comt, 1984-89, vchmn, 1987-88; chmn, MA Eng Week Comt Proclamation, 1984-90; Constitution & Bylaws Co Nat Soc Prof Engrs, 1986-88; Minuteman Nat Soc Prof Eng 1988; Prof Engrs Co, 1990. **Honors/Awds:** Reg Prof Engr St MA, 1972; Pres Award MA Soc Prof Engrs, 1984; Serv Award M Soc Prof Engrs, 1982, 1984; Design Awards Prof Jour, Raythe Co, 1969; 12 articles pub prof jour, 1968; Govt Citations Gov M & House Reps, 1983; Town Medway Sch Comt Serv Award, 198 *

MARSH, BEN FRANKLIN
Government official, manager. **Personal:** Born Feb 17, 194 Holly Springs, MS; son of Willie (deceased) and Lizzie Dawkir married Jessie Floyd, Sep 30, 1967 (divorced); childre Kimberly; married Gloria, Aug 4, 1993. **Educ:** Ohio State Un Columbus, OH, BS, 1963; Boston Univ, Heidelberg, Germar MET, 1980. **Career:** Clayton County Bd Educ; Third Army, McPherson, GA, progs/plans officer; Parking Co Am, shift mg 1995-. **Orgs:** Pres, Clayton County Br, NAACP, 1990-92; c chair, Clayton United Negro Col Fund, 1985-; div lt gov, (Toastmasters Int; bd mem, Clayton County Water Authority; co muns comn, Clayton United Way, 1991; adv comt, Clayton Coun Rainbow House; Ga Agr Exposition Authority, 1992. **Hono Awds:** Distinguished Toastmaster, Toastmaster's Int, 5 y Certificate of Appreciation, United Negro Col Fund, 5 y **Military Serv:** USA, major, 1963-83, Meritorious Service Awa (20 years), Army Commendation (10 years). **Home Phon** (770)808-7911. **Business Addr:** Shift Manager, Atlanta Airp Parking, PO Box 20786, Atlanta, GA 30320.

MARSH, DONALD GENE
Health services administrator. **Personal:** Born Oct 12, 1936, Madison, IA; married Rose E Guy; children: David, Diann Donna. **Educ:** Parsons Col, BS, 1958; Univ Minn, radiol, 196 Univ Iowa, MD, 1962. **Career:** Univ Minn, asst prof radiol, 196 78; St Croix Valley Memorial Hosp, chief radiol, 1978-; NW W Med Imaging, pres, 1980-. **Special Achievements:** Publicati Traumatic Rupture of the Aorta, 1977. **Home Addr:** 6810 Kin ston Cir, Golden Valley, MN 55427. *

MARSH, DOUG
Football player. **Personal:** Born Jun 18, 1958, Akron, OH. **Edu** Univ Mich. **Career:** Football player (retired); St Louis Cardina tight end, 1980-86. **Special Achievements:** Listed in Top 10 Mi Football Players, 1969-00.

MARSH, SEN. HENRY L., III
Lawyer, government official. **Personal:** Born Dec 10, 193 Richmond, VA; married Diane Harris; children: Nadine, Sonya Dwayne. **Educ:** Va Union Univ, BA, socio, 1956; Howard Un LL.B; Howard Univ, JD, 1959. **Career:** Hill Tucker & Mars partner, atty; City Richmond, former mayor, 1977-82; Ci Richmond Va, councilman; 1966-77, 1982-92; Senate Va, se currently. **Orgs:** US Conf Mayors Spec Comn Decennial Censu chmn, subcom urban hwy system US Conf Mayors; adv bd, N League Cities; past pres, Nat Black Caucus Local Elected C ficials; Youth Task Force, Nat League Cities; chmn, Incor Security Comn Nat League Cities; Human Resources Steeri Policy Comn, US Conf Mayors; chmn, Effective Govt Poli Comn, Va Municipal League; Judicial Coun Nat Dem Party; me adv, State Dem party; Judicial Selection Comn US Ct Appeals 4 Circuit, Alpha Phi Alpha; bd dir, Voter Ed Project; Lawyers Cor Civil Rights Under Law; founder, NatBlack Caucus of Elect Officials. **Honors/Awds:** Outstanding Man of the Year Kap Alpha Psi; Outstanding Mason of the Year VA; Man of the Ye Alpha Phi Alpha. **Special Achievements:** First African Americ Mayor of Richmond, 1977. **Business Addr:** Senator, Senate Virginia, 600 E Broad St Suite 201, PO Box 396, Richmond, 23218, **Business Phone:** (804)698-7516.*

MARSH, MCAFEE
Insurance executive. **Personal:** Born Aug 29, 1939, Meridi MS; married Ruby Putmon; children: Marcellus G. **Educ:** Wils Col; LIAMA Mgrs Sch. **Career:** Chicago Metrop Mutual Ass ance Co, 1960-72; Supreme Life Ins Co, assoc agency dir, vpr 1972-79; Cosmopolitan Chamber Com Sch Bus Mgt, instr; Johnson Cadillac, 1979-80; United Ins Co, 1980-82; McAf Marsh Ins Agency & Mutual Funds, pres, owner, 1982-. **Or** Secy, Chicago Ins Asn, 1975; pres, grad class LUTC, 1969; vpr Nat Ins Asn; Oper PUSH; Christ Universal Temple; pres, M CUC Christ Universal Temple, Chicago Ill, 1987-89. **Hono Awds:** President Award, Hong Kong & Tokyo, 1987, Haw 1990; Excellence Award, Time Ins Co, 1989; Leader's Circ Time Ins Co, 1991; Fortes Investors Excellence Award, 19 Certificate of Merit, Chicago Asn Com. **Military Serv:** AU 1962-64. **Home Addr:** 2952 Polly Lane, Flossmoor, IL 6042 **Home Phone:** (708)798-5746. **Business Addr:** President, Mc fee Marsh Insurance and Mutual Funds, 2952 Polly Lane, Flo moor, IL 60422, **Business Phone:** (708)798-5746.

MARSH, MICHAEL LAWRENCE
Track and field athlete. **Personal:** Born Aug 4, 1967, Los Angel CA; son of Jonnie Brown and Thamas Brown. **Educ:** Univ Ca

Los Angeles, hist, bus, 1989. **Career:** Track & field athlete (retired); US Summer Olympic Team, track & field team, athlete. **Honors/Awds:** Gold Medal Track & Field, Olympic Games, Barcelona, 1992; Silver Medal, Olympic Games, 1996.

MARSH, DR. PEARL-ALICE
Political scientist. **Personal:** Born Sep 6, 1946, La Grande, OR; daughter of Amos Sr and Mary Patterson. **Educ:** Sacramento State Col, Sacramento, CA, BA, 1968; Univ Calif, Berkeley, CA, MPH, 1970, PhD, 1984. **Career:** Neighborhood Health Ctr Sem Prog, Berkeley, CA, coordr, 1970-73; Alameda County Mental Health Servs, Oakland, CA, assoc dir planning, 1973-76; Asn Bay Area Govt, Oakland, CA, researcher, 1984-85; Univ Calif, Berkeley, CA, assoc dir African studies, 1986-93; Joint Ctr Polit & Econ Studies, Wash, DC, sr res fel, 1993-97; Africa Policy Info Ctr, actg exec dir, 1997; Rep Juanita Millender-McDonald, sr policy adv, 1999-2000; House Representatives, staff, currently. **Orgs:** Comnr, Berkeley Rent Stabilization Prog, 1989-92; elected officer, bd mem, Asn Concerned African Scholars, 1989-; African Studies Asn, 1984-; Polit Sci Asn, 1989-; Afro-Am General & Hist Soc, AAGHS; Afri Geneas; The online African-Am geneal Asn; Northern La Geneal Soc. **Business Phone:** (202)224-3121.

MARSH, SANDRA M
Lawyer. **Personal:** Born Jan 14, 1943, Charleston, SC; daughter of William Baker and Ethel Baker; divorced; children: David. **Educ:** Brooklyn Col, City Univ NY, BA, 1977; NY Univ Sch Law, JD, 1981; NY Univ Wagner Grad Sch, MS, 1995. **Career:** Public Educ Asn, staff atty, 1981-82; NY State Educ Dept, Off Prof Discipline, prosecuting atty, 1982-85; NY Police Dept, asst trial commnr, 1985-88, dep police commnr, exec dir, 1988-93; US Equal Employ Opportunity, dept commnr, 1998-99; Admin Law Judge Environ Control Bd, 1999-2001; The Family Ctr Inc, sr atty, 2001-. **Orgs:** Vpres, NY Univ Law Sch Alumni Asn, 1993-; Asn Black Women Attys, 1981-; Nat Asn Black Law Enforcement Execs, 1986-; mentor, Black Law Stud Asn, 1981-; Metropolitan Black Bar Asn, 1993-; bd mem, NY Univ Alumni Asn; Asn Bd City NY. **Honors/Awds:** Alumna Award for Excellence, NY Univ Law Sch, 1996. **Special Achievements:** First African-Am female appointed trial commnr, NYPD, 1985; First African-Am female to head NYPD Civilian Complaint Review Bd, 1988; first African-Am to head NYPD OEEO, 1993; launched EEO/ Diversity Consulting Firm, SMMARSH Associates, 9/1998; Appointment to NYC, Equal Employment Practices Adv Comm. **Business Addr:** Attorney, The Family Center Inc., 315 W 36th St 4th Fl, New York, NY 10007, **Business Phone:** (212)766-4522.

MARSH, WILLIAM A., JR.
Lawyer. **Personal:** Born Jan 31, 1927, Durham, NC; married Bernice Sawyer; children: William A, Jewel Lynn. **Educ:** NC Cent Univ, BS, 1949; NC Cent Univ, LLB, 1953; NC Cent Univ, JD, 1970. **Career:** Self-employed, atty; Mechanics & Farmers Bank, gen coun; Mutual Community Savings Bank, gen coun; UDI-CDC Garrett Sullivan Davenport Bowie & Grant CPA's, atty; Marsh & Marsh Attorneys, managing partner, currently. **Orgs:** Urban Develop Inst Comn Develop Corp; Found, Community Develop; Durham Opportunities Found; chmn, Legal Redress Comn; Am Bar Asn; Nat Bar Asn; Durham Comn Negro Affairs; Durham Chap, Nat Advan Asn Colored People; Beta Phi Chap; Ontario Provincial Police; Durham C C; NC Cent Alumni Asn; Masonic Lodge; Shriners; historian, NC Asn Black Lawyers; chmn, NC State Bd Elections. **Military Serv:** WWII, veteran. **Business Addr:** Managing Partner, Marsh & Marsh, 120 E Parrish St, Durham, NC 27701-3346.*

MARSH, WILLIAM ANDREW, III
Lawyer. **Personal:** Born Mar 6, 1958, Durham, NC; son of William A Jr and Bernice S; married Sonja Denalli, Jul 20, 1991; children: William Andrew IV, Kylie Alexandra & Nicholas Emerson. **Educ:** Hampton Inst, Hampton Univ, BA, 1979; Univ NCA, Chapel Hill, Sch Law, JD, 1982. **Career:** Marsh & Banks, assoc, 1982-83, 1985-86; Off Gov NCA, asst legal coun, 1983-85; Dist Off Corp Coun, Juv Div, prosecuting atty, 1987-92; Marsh & Marsh, atty & gen partner, 1993-. **Orgs:** Kappa Alpha Psi Fraternity, 1978-; Am Bar Asn, 1983-; Dist Bar Asn, 1983-; NCA State Bar, 1984-; NCA Asn Black Lawyers, 1984-; pres, Durham Co Bar Asn, 1998-99; pres, 14th Judicial Dist Bar NC, 1998-99; trustee, St Joseph's Am Church; Ancient & Accepted Scottish Rite Free Masons Prince Hall Affiliation; African Methodist Episcopal Church. **Honors/Awds:** General Counsel AME Church. **Business Addr:** Attorney, Partner, Marsh & Marsh, 120 E Parrish St Suite 310, PO Box 125, Durham, NC 27701-3346, **Business Phone:** (919)688-2374.

MARSHALL, AMEILA
Fashion model, actor. **Personal:** Born Apr 2, 1958, Albany, GA; married Kent Schaffer (divorced 2001); children: 1; married Daryl Waters (divorced 1995). **Educ:** Univ Tex, Austin, bus admin. **Career:** Films: Stuart Little, 2002; According to Spenser, 2001; Actress: Big Deal; Harrigan & Hart; Porgy & Bess; TV show: "Guiding Light"; "One Life to Live"; Houston Jazz Ballet Co, mem; NBC soap opera Passions, actress, currently. **Honors/Awds:** Nominee, Image Award, 1998, 1999, 2000; Nominee, Soap Opera Digest Award, 2005. **Business Addr:** Actress, Passions NBC, GE Bldg, 30 Rockefeller Plz, New York, NY 10112, **Business Phone:** (212)664-7174.

MARSHALL, ANITA
Librarian. **Personal:** Born May 30, 1938, Newark, NJ; daughter of Noah Willis and Estelle Mitchell; children: Harry Vaughn Bims. **Educ:** Newark State Col, Newark, NJ, BS, educ, 1959; Chicago State Univ, Chicago, IL, MS, educ, 1974; Univ Chicago, attended 1986; Mich State Univ, East Lansing, attended 1989; Garrett Evangelical Theol Sem, MCE, 1999. **Career:** Newark Bd Educ, Newark, NJ, teacher, 1959-62; Peace Corps, Philippine Islands, TESL, Sci & ESL, teacher, 1969-82; Chicago Bd Educ, Chicago, media specialist, ESEA, coordr, workshop facilitator, 1964-82, 1995-2004; Chicago State Univ, Chicago, lectr libr sci, HEW proj dir, 1976-77; Mich State Univ, head, gift unit, ethnic studies & sociol bibliographer, 1982-95; Chicago Conf Am Church, S Dist, consult, 1999-2002; Christian Educ Workshop, presenter; Am Church, Sunday Sch, curric writer; Chicago Bd Educ, librn; Bethel African Methodist Episcopal Church, ministerial team mem, currently; African Methodist Episcopal Church, Dept Christian Educ, Writers Guild coordr, currently. **Orgs:** Pres, Gamma Zeta Chap, Alpha Kappa Alpha Sorority, 1957-59; Am Libr Asn, 1968-95; Phi Delta Kappa, 1981-; chair, Tech Servs Caucus, Mich Libr Asn, 1988-92; Women's Adv Comt to Provost, Mich State Univ, 1988-91; Planning comt, Black Caucus Am Libr Asn, First Nat Conf, 1990-92; Mission & Ethics Comt, St Lawrence Hosp Exec Bd, 1991-95; Mich State Univ Mus Assocs Bd, 1992-96, co-chair, 1995-95; Kresge Art Mus Docent, Lansing Pub Libr Adv Bd, 1995-96; Womens Missionary Soc, Am Church, 1999-2004; secy & vpres, Mich State Univ, Black Fac & Adminrs Asn; Women's Missionary Soc, Chicago Conf Committe Chair & Fourth Dist Worship Leader & Comt Chair; Comt Uniform Series, Nat Coun Churches. **Honors/Awds:** State Acad Scholar, New Jersey, 1955-59; Archibald Carey Scholar, 1997-98; Outstanding Christian Educator, Chicago Cult Found, 1999; Am Bible Soc Award for Christian Educ, Garrett Theol Sem, 1999; Dedicated Teacher Award, Dusable High Sch, Chicago, IL. **Special Achievements:** Contributor, Liberation & Unity Lenten Meditation Guide, 1993-98, 2000; Quilting Bibliography in "African-Am Quilting in Mich," 1998. **Home Addr:** 4358 Ind Ave, Chicago, IL 60653-3216. **Business Addr:** Writers Guild Coordinator, African Methodist Episcopal Church, Christian Education Department, 500 8th Ave S, Nashville, TN 37203, **Business Phone:** 800-525-7282.

MARSHALL, ANTHONY DEWAYNE
Football player. **Personal:** Born Sep 16, 1970, Mobile, AL. **Educ:** La State, Univ. **Career:** Football player(retired;)Chicago Bears, defensive back, 1994-97; Philadelphia Eagles, 1998.

MARSHALL, BETTY J
Executive, vice president (organization), manager. **Personal:** Born Oct 15, 1950, Youngstown, OH; daughter of L V Sharpe Mitchell and Grant Mitchell; married Richard H Young; children: Melanie D. **Educ:** Youngstown State Univ, Youngstown, OH, attended. **Career:** Arbys Inc, Atlanta, GA, dir purchasing, 1975-89; Rax Restaurants Inc, Columbus OH, dir purchasing & distrib, 1989-90; Shoney's Inc, Nashville, TN, dir purchasing, 1990, dir corp & community affairs, 1990, vpres corp & community affairs, 1996, sr vpres, corp communs; Phoenix Restaurant Group Inc, srvpres, chief admin officer, 2001; Sams Club, vpres & div merchandise mgr, regional gen mgr & vpres purchasing, currently. **Orgs:** Treas & steering comt mem, Nat Restaurant Asn, 1987-; Hospitality Mgt Adv Bd mem, Eastern Mich Univ, 1990-; Tourism Task Force mem, Nashville Area Chamber Com, 1990-; vice chair, Health & Rehabilitative Servs Community Initiatives Steering Comt, United Way, 1990-; bd dirs, Tenn Minority Purchasing Coun, 1991; YWCA; Union Planters Community Bank Bd; Tenn Minority Supplier Develop Coun; Nashville Airport Authority. **Honors/Awds:** Minority Business Advocate of the Year, Minority Enterprise Develop Ctr, Nashville Chap, 1993; Apollo Award, PRSA, Nashville Chap, 1994. **Special Achievements:** Selected as 1 of 15 women that make a difference, Minorities-Women in Business, Jan/Feb 1991; Economic Development Advocate of the Year, NCP, Nashville Chap, 1992. **Business Phone:** (615)231-2889.

MARSHALL, REV. CALVIN BROMLEY
Clergy. **Personal:** Born Jun 13, 1932, Brooklyn, NY; son of Evans B and Edith Best; married Delma Mann; children: Sharon Wallinger, Smitn, Edythe & Chad. **Educ:** Anderson Col, Anderson, IN, BA, 1955; Anderson Theol Sem, BD, 1958; Teamer Sch Relig, NC, DD, 1972, LHD, 1973; Grasslands Hosp, Valhalla, NY, CPC, 1965. **Career:** Park St AME Zion Church, Peekskill, NY, pastor, 1960-68; Cumberland Hosp, dir Pastoral care, 1972-83; Varick Mem AME Zion Church, pastor, 1968-; Woodhull Med & Ment Health Ctr, dir Pastoral Care. **Orgs:** Chief Protocol, AME Zion Church; vchair, Nat Action Network; Am Asn Christian Counrs US Chaplains Asn; Am Asn Pastoral Counrs; Asn Clinical Pastoral Educ. **Special Achievements:** Articles: "Living on the Left Hand of God," Theol Today, 1968; "The Black Church-Its Mission Is Liberation," Black Scholar, 1970. **Military Serv:** USAF, first lt, 1951-53. **Home Addr:** 125 Fairway, Hempstead, NY 11550. **Business Addr:** Pastor, Varick Memorial AME Zion Church, 120 Atlantic St, Hackensack, NJ 07601, **Business Phone:** (201)343-8240.

MARSHALL, CHARLENE JENNINGS
State government official. **Personal:** Born Sep 17, 1933, Osage, WV; married Roger Leon; children: Gwendolyn, Roger Jr & Larry. **Career:** Rockwell Intl, machine operator & stores attend, 1963-78; United Steel workers Am Local 6214, recording secy, 1976; Mon Preston Labor & Coun, 1968-78; W Va Dept Labor, state insp; W Va mayor,1991-97; W Va House Del, v chMonongalia Countymn political sub-div; St House, currently. **Orgs:** Dir, W Va Women's Bowling Asn; chmn, Morgantown Human Rights Comn, 1974-79;past vpres, Natl Advan Assn Colored People, Morgantown Br, 1973-76; St. Paul African Methodist Episcopal; president's Visiting Comt Stud Affairs &Social Justice, W Va Univ; mem, Boys & Girls Club of am; former mem, Leadership Monongalians First Class; former rec sec, Monongalia Preston Labor Coun; former Pres, Morgantown Natl Assn for the Advanc of Colored People (NAACP);bd mem, Morgantown Theater Company; former exec bd mem, Red Cross; former mem;, Steelworks Local 6214; mem, Valley Health Care; mem, W Virginia Bar Assn; former mem, W Virginia Univ Local 814; mem, W Virginia Univ Pres Visiting Commt Stud Affairs; former mem, W Virginia Univ Sch of Nursing Adv Brd; mem, Energy, Industry & Labor/Economic Development & Small Business; mem, Finance; mem, Health & Hum Res; mem, Rules; mem, Senior Citizen Issues. **Honors/Awds:** Exceptional Service in the Public Interest Award, FBI; Mayor of The Year, 1994. **Special Achievements:** First African American Mayor Of Virginia.

MARSHALL, CONSUELO B.
Judge. **Personal:** Born Sep 28, 1936, Knoxville, TN; married George E Marshall Jr; children: Michael, Laurie. **Educ:** Los Angeles City Col, AA, 1956; Pepperdine Univ, attended 1957; Howard Univ, BA, 1958, LLB, 1961; Univ Southern Calif Law Ctr, attended 1971. **Career:** City of Los Angeles, dep city atty, 1962-67; Cochran & Atkins, pvt pract, 1968-70; City of Los Angeles, super ct comnr, 1971-76; Inglewood Munic Ct, judge, 1976-77; Los Angeles Super Ct, judge, 1977-80; US Dist Ct, Cent Dist CA, judge, 1980-, sr dist judge, 2005-. **Orgs:** Black Women Laywers Asn; Calif Women Lawyers Asn; Calif Judges Asn; State Bar Calif; Los Angeles City Bar Asn; Nat Asn Advan Colored People; Urban League; Beta Phi Sigma; Los Angeles Women Lawyers' Asn; Asn Black Lawyers; Nat Asn Women Judges; bd mem, Legal Aid Found; YMCA; Beverly Hills WestLinks Inc; mem bd dir, Antioch Sch Law Wash, DC; 9th Circuit Ct Appeals Educ Comn, 1984-86; fac mem, Trial Advocacy Workshop Harvard Law Sch, 1984-85; 9th Circuit Ct Appeals Libr Comn, 1985-86. **Honors/Awds:** Honoree Black Women Laywers Asn, 1976; Woman of the Year, Zeta Phi Beta, 1977; Honoree Angeles Mesa, YWCA 1977; Honoree Nat Bus & Professional Women's Club of Los Angeles, 1978; Graduate of the Year, Howard Univ, 1981; Woman of the Year, The Los Angeles Sentinal, 1983; Presidential Award, Alpha Phi Alpha 1984; Honoree, Black Am Law Students Asn, UCLA 1985; Honoree Verbum Dei Catholic Boys High Sch Los Angeles, 1986; Honoree Econ Equal Opportunity Prog Black History Month, 1986; Ernestine Stahlhut Award, Women Lawyers Asn Los Angeles; CWL's Joan Dempsey Klein Award. **Business Addr:** Judge, United States District Court Central California, 312 N Spring St Rm G 8, 826 US Courthouse, Los Angeles, CA 90012.*

MARSHALL, DAVID
Manager. **Personal:** Born Aug 27, 1960, Orange, NJ; son of Ruth; married Shirley Ann, Jun 28, 1997. **Educ:** Upsala Col, BA, bus admin, 1982. **Career:** Macy's Corp, sales mgr, 1982-84; Park Tower Assoc, acct exec, 1985-90; Super Personnel, sr acct exec, 1990-92; Krow Assoc, exec recruiter, 1992-93; Solvay Pharmaceut, sales prof, 1993-94; Target Pros Inc, pres, 1994-. **Orgs:** Nat Sales Network, 1992-. **Business Addr:** President, Target Pros Inc, 80 Main St, West Orange, NJ 07052-3034, **Business Phone:** (973)324-0900.

MARSHALL, DR. DON A, SR.
Physician. **Personal:** Born Mar 4, 1929, Frankfort, KY; married Roumania Mason; children: Donna Marya (deceased), Don A Jr & C Angela. **Educ:** Ky St Univ, BS, 1951, MA, 1954; Meharry Med Col, MD, 1967. **Career:** Delco Prods (GM), med dir, 1974-; Ky St Univ, phys educ instr, 1961-63; USPHS (Narcotic Farm Lexton KY), physchiatric aide, 1950-56; pvt pract, currently. **Orgs:** Mem Alpha Kappa Mu, Ky St Univ, 1948; Phi Delta Kappa, Univ Ky, 1955; pres, Gem City Med Dental & Pharm Soc, 1976. **Home Addr:** 3769 Wales Dr, Dayton, OH 45405. **Business Addr:** Physician, 9000 N Main St G-35, Dayton, OH 45415, **Business Phone:** (937)836-7211.

MARSHALL, DONALD JAMES
Actor. **Personal:** Born May 2, 1936, San Diego, CA; son of Ernest and Alma; married Diane (divorced). **Educ:** San Diego City Col, eng, 1956-57; La City Col, theater arts, 1958-60. **Career:** DJM Productions Inc, past actor, 1970-73; Bob Gist Group, Frank Silvera Theater Being, Theater E Workshop, Richard Boone Repertory Co, 1960-67; Land of the Giants ABC-TV, co-star, 1967-71; JoCo Int Enterprises Inc,dist ribr, licensing agent, 1984; Stage Work: Of Mice & Men, A Cat Called Jesus; Films: The Interns, 1962; Shock Treatment, 1964; Sergeant Ryker, 1968; The Thing with Two Heads, 1972; Terminal Island, 1973; Uptown Saturday Night, 1974; TV series: "Kraft Suspense Theatre", 1963; "The Alfred Hitchcock Hour", 1963-65; Great Gettin' Up Mornin', 1964; "Rawhide", 1964; "Bob Hope Presents the Chrysler Theatre", 1964-65; "Daktari", 1966; "Ironside", 1967; "Dragnet 1967",

1967-68; Braddock, 1968; Julia, 1968; "Land of the Giants", 1968-70; The Reluctant Heroes,1971; "Police Story", 1974-75; Benny & Barney: Las Vegas Undercover, 1977; "The Incredible Hulk", 1978-80; Rescue from Gilligan's Island, 1978;Capitol", 1982; Highway Heart breaker, 1992. **Orgs:** Mem equity, Am Fedn TV & Radio Artists; Screen Actors Guild; Nat Acad TV Arts & Sci; nat mem, Am Film Inst; charter mem, Fedn Negro Actors Action; vpres & nat mem, Nat Asn Advan Colored People. **Honors/Awds:** Actor's Achievement Award, African Meth Epis Church, 1970; Black Achiever Award, 1976. **Military Serv:** AUS, PFC, 1954-56. **Business Phone:** (323)935-1700.

MARSHALL, DONYELL LAMAR
Basketball player. **Personal:** Born May 18, 1973, Reading, PA; son of Alonzo Cook Jr and Stephanie; children: Marquis Lamar, Paryss, Donyell Jr & Devynn. **Educ:** Univ Conn. **Career:** Minn Timberwolves, forward, 1994-95; Golden State Warriors, 1995-2000; Utah Jazz, 2000-02; Chicago Bulls, 2002-03; Toronto Raptors, 2003-05; Cleveland Cavaliers, forward, 2005-08; Seattle Supersonics, forward, 2008-. **Honors/Awds:** Good Guys, Sporting News, 2003. **Special Achievements:** First round, fourth pick, NBA Draft, 1994. **Business Addr:** Professional Basketball Player, Seattle Supersonics, 351 Elliott Ave W Suite 500, Seattle, WA 98119, **Business Phone:** (206)281-5800.

MARSHALL, DR. EDWIN COCHRAN
School administrator, optometrist. **Personal:** Born Mar 31, 1946, Albany, GA; children: Erin C & Erika H. **Educ:** Ind Univ, BA, 1968, BS, 1970, OD, 1971, MS, 1979; Univ NC, MPH, 1982. **Career:** Ind Univ Sch Optom, assoc prof, 1977-92, chmn dept clin sci, 1983-92, assoc dean acad affairs, 1992-, prof, 1992-; Cebu Drs Col Optom Philippines, consult, 1980-87; Inter Am Univ PR, consult, 1982; Nat Optom Asn, exec dir, 1981-89, 1993-; Nat HBP Educ Prog, coord comn mem, 1984-; Nat Univ Malaysia, consult, 1992; 1995-; Ind Univ Sch Med, adj prof pub health, 1998-. **Orgs:** Life mem, Kappa Alpha Psi Fraternity; pres, Nat Optom Asn, 1979-81; pub health exam comn, Nat Bd Examrs Optom, 1983-94; coun acad affairs, Asn Schs & Cols Optom, 1983-84; secy, Black Cong Health Law & Econ, 1985-87; pres, Eye Ski Inc, 1986-94; Nat Adv Coun Health Prof Educ, 1987-91; dipl Pub Health, Am Acad Optom, 1987; vice chmn, Black Cong Health, Law & Econ, 1987-92; chmn, Vision Care Sect, Am Pub Health Asn, 1988-90; chair, Dipl Prog, Pub Health Am Acad Optom, 1990-93; chair, Task Force Health Policy, Asn Schs & Cols Optom, 1991-92; Ind Health Care & Develop Comt, 1995-; exec bd, Am Pub Health Asn, 2000-. **Honors/Awds:** Optometrist of the Year, Nat Optom Asn, 1976; Delta Omega Nat Public Health Honor Soc, 1982; Founders Award, Nat Optom Asn, 1987; Distinguished Service to Optometry, Ind Optom Asn, 1998; Tony & Mary Hulman Health Achievement Award in Public Health & Preventive Medicine, Ind Pub Health Found, 1999; Optometrist of the Year, Am Optom Asn, 2007. **Special Achievements:** National Academies of Practice, 2007; Co-Editor: Pub Health & Community Optom, Second Edition, 1990. **Business Addr:** Vice President for Diversity, Equity, & Multicultural Affairs, Indiana University, Bryan Hall 115, 107 S Ind Ave, Bloomington, IN 47405.

MARSHALL, ERIC A
Executive. **Personal:** Born Oct 16, 1963, Marion, IN; son of Frank and Alice. **Educ:** Ind Univ, BA, jour, psychol, 1987. **Career:** Clique Creative Services, founder, owner, 1987-. **Orgs:** Am Soc Media Photographers; Ind pres, Am Soc Media Photographers; Ind Univ Sch Jour Alumni Bd; bd dirs, Marion Gen Hosp; bd dirs, Main St Marion. **Business Addr:** Owner, Clique Creative Services, 422 E 4th, Marion, IN 46952, **Business Phone:** (765)664-2300.

MARSHALL, GLORIA A. See SUDARKASA, NIARA.

MARSHALL, H JEAN
Executive. **Personal:** Born Jun 7, 1945, Lake Providence, LA; daughter of William L and Thelma Jones Harden; divorced; children: Lyndon E & Tangie F. **Educ:** Univ Cincinnati, BS, psychol, 1972. **Career:** St Leo Sch, teacher, 1976-78; Cincinnati Pub Schs, work training coor, 1978-82; Ohio Lottery, regional mgr & field coodr, 1983-87, dep dir sales, 1990-92; British Am Banknote, acct mgr, 1987-89; Ohio Dept Rehab, consult, 1989-90; Interlott, vpres, dir retailer rels, 1992-93, 1993-97, consult, 1997-; Ohio Civil Rights Comn, regional dir, currently. **Orgs:** Harriett Beecher Stowe Historical Cultural Asn, 1981-; vpres, bd trustee, Arts Consortium of Cincinnati, 1993-; United Way, commun chest-field of service, 1993-; secy, bd dir, Cincinnati Minority Bus Develop Ctr, 1994-; vice chair, Children & Youth Field Serv; adv bd, WCPO TV; Boys Scout Am. **Honors/Awds:** Ohio House of Representatives, Outstanding Leadership, 1993; Women of the Year, The Cincinnati Enquirer, 1994; Women of Distinction, Cincinnati Herald, 1999; Listed in 'Who's Who Among African-Americans, 1996; Leading Woman in Ministry, by Leading Women Inc, 2001; Keeping the Dream Alive Award, Ohio Civil Rights Comn, 2001; Profiles in Courage award, 5/3 Bank, WCPO TV & Urban League of Greater Cincinnati, 2004. **Special Achievements:** First African-American Executive for the U.S. Division of British American Banknote, a Canadian Manufacturing Company; first African-American appointed to the Board of Directors, Interlott Technologies, Inc; "Developing Positive Retail Relations," Public Gaming Ins, 1991; "Let's Talk Job Search," Series of Articles, Cinti Herald, 1989; Author/Poet, "Beautiful Words, Hearts of Love". **Home Phone:** (513)729-2935. **Business Phone:** (513)852-3344.

MARSHALL, HENRY H.
Football player. **Personal:** Born Aug 9, 1954, Broxton, GA. **Educ:** Univ Mo. **Career:** Football player (retired); Kansas City Chiefs, wide receiver, 1976-87. **Honors/Awds:** Chiefs 25 Year All-time Team, 1987.

MARSHALL, JOHN W (JOHN WILLIAM MARSHALL)
Government official. **Personal:** Son of Thurgood Marshall (deceased); married Jean Marie. **Educ:** Georgetown Univ, BA, 1988; Va Commonwealth Univ, attended 1998. **Career:** E Dist Va, US Marshal, 1994-99; US Marshals Serv, dir, 1999-. **Special Achievements:** First African American app dir of US Marshal's Service. **Business Phone:** (202)353-0600.

MARSHALL, JOHN WILLIAM. See MARSHALL, JOHN W.

MARSHALL, JONNIE CLANTON
Social worker. **Personal:** Born Jul 24, 1932, Memphis, TN; married Kenneth Evans Marshall (deceased); children: James Kwame, Evan Keith Marshall. **Educ:** Morgan State Col, BA, 1956; Columbia Univ Sch Social Work, MSW, 1963; Fashion Inst Tech, attended 1986. **Career:** Social worker (retired); Retreat Living Hartford, psych aide, 1958-59; YWCA NY, group leader, 1959-61; Grant Houses Community Ctr, supvr & dir, 1964-67; Designer Fine Millinery, 1980; Bd Educ Community Special Educ NY, sch social worker, 1967-91. **Orgs:** Alpha Kappa Alpha Sor Inc, Tau Omega Chap, 1954-; bd, Friend Children's Art Carnival, 1968-; bd dirs, Harlem Community Council Inc, 1971-; Commonwealth Holding Co Inc, 1971-; vpres, Nat Asn Milliners Dressmakers, 1983-; Harlem Fashion Inst New York, 1983-; mem fashion show coord, pres, Cottagers Martha's Vineyard MA, 1985-86; life mem, Morgan State Univ Alumni Asn. **Honors/Awds:** Fashions have appeared in numerous fashion shows at the Black Fashion Museum, Howard Univ Alumni Fashion Show, Cottagers, Salem United Methodist Church Affairs. **Home Addr:** 470 Malcolm X Blvd, New York, NY 10037. *

MARSHALL, JOSEPH EARL, JR.
Association executive. **Personal:** Born May 12, 1947, Saint Louis, MO; son of Joseph E Sr and Odessa; married; children: Malcolm, Sydney, Cassie. **Educ:** Univ San Francisco, BA, polit sci & sociol San Francisco State Univ, MA, educ; Wright Inst, PhD, psychol. **Career:** San Francisco Unified Sch Dist, teacher, adminr; Omega Boys Club, pres & founder, 1987-; host of syndicated radio show "Street Soldiers" currently. **Orgs:** Adv bd, Harvard Univ, Community Violence Prevention Program; pres, Street Soldiers Nat Consortium; trustee emer, Univ San Francisco; planning bd mem, Surgeon General's Report on Youth Violence. **Honors/Awds:** Received numerous awards including: Spotlight on Crime Award, Nat Crime Prevention Coun; Certificate of Recognition, Calif State Assembly; Fel MacArthur Found, 1994; Leadership Award, Children's Defense Fund, 1994; Essence Award, Essence Mag, 1994; Martin Luther King Jr Memorial Award, Nat Educ Asn, 1996; Congressional Freedom Works Award, 1997; Candle in Community Serv Award, Morehouse Col, 1998; Alumni Educators Award, Univ San Francisco, 2003; Human Rights Leadership Award, Harvard Univ Alumni San Francisco, 2003; Living History Makers Award, Turning point Mag, 2004; Angel Award, Take Wing Found, 2006; Community Leadership Award, San Francisco Found, 2006; Jefferson Award, 2006. **Special Achievements:** Author of Street Soldier: One Man's Struggle to Save a Generation, One Life at a Time, 1996. **Business Addr:** Executive Director, Co-founder, Omega Boys Club, 1060 Tennessee St, PO Box 884463, San Francisco, CA 94188-4463, **Business Phone:** (415)826-8664.*

MARSHALL, JULYETTE MATTHEWS
Association executive. **Personal:** Born Oct 26, 1942, Port Arthur, TX; daughter of Dr J B Matthews (deceased); married Robert James, Aug 17, 1966 (divorced); children: Nicole Yvette. **Educ:** Fisk Univ, BA, 1964. **Career:** Mayor's Off, asst dir spec events, 1970-73; Gov's EEO Off, compliance officer, 1973-75; Univ Tex, personnel officer, 1975-77; Houston Community Col, personnel officer, 1977-78; Career Planning Ctr, counr, 1978-80; Concepts Unlimited, dir, founder, 1980-90; Zamaani, cult designer, owner, dir, 1990-. **Orgs:** Actor writer, PBS, Channel 8, 1969-70; Tex Harlem Ren Comn, 1973-74; Twz African Art Gallery, 1990-; Tex Writer's Guild, 1995-; Houston Black Doll Asn, 1995-; Houston Culinary Hist Asn, 1995-. **Honors/Awds:** Special Series for Texas Newspaper, Tex Writers Asn, 1980; Community Involvement Award, 1983; Special Arts Award, Arts Comn Austin, 1985; Contribution to the Arts, Friends of the Phoenix, 1987; Outstanding Alumni for 25 Years, Fisk Univ, 1989; Excellence Community Service Award, NAACP, 1989. **Special Achievements:** Created a series of "Black History in Port Arthur Texas", 1980; assisted in an 18 part TV series on "Black History in Pt Arthur, Texas", 1980-81; created and produced, "Tribute to Twenty-Eight Black Women in Pa," 1981-82; created and produced "Tribute to Twenty-Eight Black Women in Austin", 1984; developed and produced seminars for disabled persons in state of Texas, 1985; developed and designed 25th class reunion, Fisk Univ, 1989. **Business Phone:** (713)790-0012.

MARSHALL, LEONARD ALLEN, JR.
Executive, football player, capitalist or financier. **Personal:** Born Oct 22, 1961, Franklin, LA; son of L Marshall Sr; married Maryann; children: Erika Christina & Arianna Nicole. **Educ:** La State Univ, BA, bus finance; Fairleigh Dickerson Univ, Teaneck, NJ, BS. **Career:** Football player (retired), mortage lender, exec residence; New York Giants, 1983-93; New York Jets, 1993; Wash Redskins, 1994; Pro Star Athletic, chmn & chief exec officer; Promise Healthcare, dir corp diversity, 2004; Pro Star Athletic, founder; Capital Source Mortgage, lic corresp mortgage lender, currently; Seton Hall Univ, exec residence, currently. **Orgs:** Nat sports chmn, Leukemia Soc, Westchester & Putnam Valley, NY; NY City Bd; March Dimes; NAACP. **Honors/Awds:** Most Valuable Person, La State Univ, 1983; All-NFL, 1985 & 1986; United Way Lifetime Achievement Award, 1986; NFC Defensive Lineman of the Year, NFLPA, 1986; Pro Bowl, 1986 & 1987; Byron Whizzer White Award, 1990. **Business Addr:** Executive in Residence, Seton Hall University, Stillman School of Business, Center for Sport Management, Jubilee Hall 547/5th Fl, South Orange, NJ 07079, **Business Phone:** (973)275-2485.

MARSHALL, MARVIN
Football player, football coach. **Personal:** Born Jun 21, 1972, Aschaffenburg, Germany; married LaScotia; children: Marvin Jr & Matlin. **Educ:** SC State Univ. **Career:** Football player (retired), Football coach; Barcelona Dragons, wide receiver; Tampa Bay Buccaneers, wide receiver, 1996; Carolina Cobras, arena football league; Hephzibah High Sch, defensive backs coach, 1997-2001; Josey High Sch, offensive coordr, 2001; NFL Europe, coach, 2005; San Diego Chargers, offensive asst; coach, Augusta Spartans, 2006; coach, San Diego Chargers, 2007; coach, Miami Dolphins, 2008; coach, Detroit Lions, 2008.

MARSHALL, PATRICIA PRESCOTT
Educator, school administrator. **Personal:** Born Apr 4, 1933, Houston, TX; daughter of Willie Mae and St Elmo Leonidas; married Cornelius, Aug 26, 1969. **Educ:** Calif State Univ, BA, 1955, MA, 1960; Univ Southern Calif, EdD, 1980. **Career:** Educator, School Administrator (retired); Los Angeles Unified Sch Dist, teacher, 1955-60; Berkeley Unified Sch Dist, teacher, 1960-63; Los Angeles Unified Sch Dist, training teacher, 1963-66, prin, 1966-79; Mount St Mary's Col, instr, part-time, 1972-76; Los Angeles Unified Sch Dist, prog dir acad, 1979-86; KCLS, sta mgr, asst supt, 1986. **Orgs:** Bd, Nat Mus Women Arts; bd, Educ Adv Los Angeles Co Mus Art; bd, YWCA Greater Los Angeles; UNICEF; Acad TV Arts & Sci; Am Women Radio & TV; Women Target; Pub Broadcasting Serv Adv Comn; ESEA. **Honors/Awds:** Emmy Award, Acad TV Arts & Sci, 1985, 1988; Ida B Wells Achievement for Female Executives, Phi Delta Kapa, Los Angeles BLK Media Coalition, 1986; Children's Television International, William E Fagan, 1989; Model Excellence Award, 1991; Black Women of Achievement, NCP Legal Defense Fund, 1992.

MARSHALL, REV. PAUL M
Executive director, clergy. **Personal:** Born Aug 17, 1947, Cleveland, OH. **Educ:** Univ Dayton, BA, arts, 1969; Univ St Michael's Col, Toronto Sch Theol, Canada, MD, 1976; Case Western Univ, pastoral psychol cert; Catholic Theological Union, PhD, ministry, 2000. **Career:** Dayton Urban Corps, City Dayton, dir, 1970-73; Formation Prog, Cincinnati Prov, Soc Mary, regional coordr, 1972-74; Nat Urban Corps Asn, regional coordr, 1972-73; high sch teacher & chaplain, 1977-80; pastor, 1980-97; Soc Mary, relig bro; Nat Black Cath Cong, exec dir, currently; Univ Dayton, rector. **Orgs:** Bd dir, Nat Black Cath Clergy Caucus, 1970-75, 1972; Bd dir, Nat Urban Corps Asn, 1971-73; vice chmn, Social Action Comn, Archdiocese Cincinnati, 1971-73, 1973; chmn, Dayton Black Cath Caucus, 1971-73; bd dir, Pub Serv Internship Prog, 1972-73; dir, bd youth, Screen Printing Co, 1972-73; vice chmn, Archdiocese Cincinnati Black Cath Caucus, 1972-73; Nat Community Urban Ministry, Notre Dame. **Business Addr:** Executive Director, National Black Catholic Congress, 320 Cathedral St, Baltimore, MD 21201, **Business Phone:** (410)547-5330.

MARSHALL, PAULE BURKE
Writer. **Personal:** Born Apr 9, 1929, Brooklyn, NY; daughter of Samuel and Ada Clement; married Nourry Menard, Jul 30, 1970 (divorced); children: Evan; married. **Educ:** Brooklyn Col, BA, 1953; Hunter Col, 1955. **Career:** Our World Mag, staff writer, 1953-56; Guugenheim fel, 1960; Yale Univ, lectr creative writing, 1970; Va Commonwealth Univ, prof Eng; New York Univ, Helen Gould Sheppard prof, currently; Author: Brown Girl, Brownstones, Random House, 1959; Brown Girl, Brownstones, 1960; Soul Clap Hands & Sing, Atheneum, 1961; The Chosen Place, The Timeless People, Harcourt, 1969; Praisesong for the Widow, Putnam, 1983; Reena & Other Stories, Feminist Press, 1983; The Fisher King, Scribner, 2000. **Honors/Awds:** Guggenheim fel, 1961; Rosen Award, Nat Inst Arts & Letts, 1962; Ford

grant, for drama, 1964; Nat Endowment for the Arts grant, 1966, 1977; Creative Artists Public Service fellowship, 1974; Before Columbus Foundation American Book Award, 1984; Honoree, PEN/Faulkner Found, 1990.

MARSHALL, PLURIA W.
Publisher, association executive, photographer. **Personal:** Born Oct 19, 1937, Houston, TX; married Corbin Carmen; children: Pluria Jr, Mishka, Jason, Natalie & Christopher. **Educ:** Tex Southern Univ. **Career:** Nat Black Media Coalition, nat organizer, treas, chmn, 1975, sr chmn & chief exec officer; Nat Asn Black Journalists, co-founder & freelancer, 1975-; prof photographer; Oper Breadbasket TX, exec dir; Los Angeles Wave, publ, currently. **Orgs:** Tex State Adv Comn, US Comn Civil Rights. **Honors/Awds:** Community Service Award, Nat Asn Mkt Developers, 1973; Community Service Award, Omega Psi Phi, Houston Chap, 1973; Outstanding Ex-Student Award, Tex Southern Univ, 1974; Marketeer of Year Award, Houston Chap, NAMD, 1974. **Military Serv:** USAF, E-3, 1956-60. **Business Addr:** Co-Founder, Freelancer, National Association of Black Journalists, 8701-A Adelphi Rd, Adelphi, MD 20783-1716, **Business Phone:** (301)445-7100.

MARSHALL, PLURIA WILLIAM, JR.
Executive, radio broadcaster. **Personal:** Born Jan 17, 1962; son of Pluria W Sr and Olivia F. **Educ:** Clark Col, Atlanta, Ga, BS, 1984. **Career:** KTRE-TV, Lufkin, Tex, sales & mkt, 1982, sales & acct exec, 1983; WTBS/Turner Broadcasting, Atlanta, Ga, res, 1982-83; WLBT-TV, Jackson, Miss, mgt develop sales, 1983-84; WLBM-TV30, Meridan, Miss, sta mgr & sales mgr, 1985-86, vpres/gen mgr, 1986; KHRN-FM, genl mgr, owner, currently; Marshall Media Group, pres, currently. **Orgs:** Nat Black Media Coalition; Nat Asn Broadcaster; Nat Asn TV Programming Execs. **Honors/Awds:** Outstanding Young Men Am, 1985. **Business Phone:** (219)884-1370.

MARSHALL, REESE
Lawyer. **Personal:** Born Sep 3, 1942, Fort Lauderdale, FL; married Leonora Griffin; children: Dara Isabelle, Kemba Lee, Reese Evans. **Educ:** Morgan State Col, BA, 1963; Howard Univ, LLB, 1966. **Career:** Jacksonville Urban League, chmn; Fla Comn Human Rels, chmn; Fla Chap NBA, pres; Regional Bd Dir-MBA ; Johnson & Marshall, partner, 1971-79; Reese Marshall Law Off, atty, 1979-. **Orgs:** Kappa Alpha Psi Frat Inc. **Home Addr:** 9100 Westlake Cir, Jacksonville, FL 32208. **Business Addr:** Attorney, 214 E Ashley St, Jacksonville, FL 32202, **Business Phone:** (904)354-8429.*

MARSHALL, THURGOOD
Government official, lawyer. **Personal:** Born Aug 12, 1956, New York, NY; son of Thurgood Marshall and Cecilia S; married Colleen P Mahoney, Sep 24, 1983; children: Thurgood William III & Edward Patrick. **Educ:** Univ Va, BA, 1978; Univ Va Sch Law, JD, 1981. **Career:** Judge Barrington D Parker, law clerk, 1981-83; Kaye Scholer Fierman Hays & Handler, atty, 1983-85; Sen Albert Gore Jr, coun & staff dir, 1985-87, dep campaign mgr, 1987-88; Sen Judiciary Comt, Sen Edward M Kennedy, coun, 1988-92; Clinton-Gore Campaign, Sen Al Gore Traveling Staff, sr policy adv, 1992; Off vpres, dep coun, dir legis affairs, 1993-97; White House, asst to pres Clinton, Cabinet secy, 1997-2001; Bingham McCutchen LLP, partner, 2001-; Bingham Consulting Group, prin, currently; Swidler Berlin's Harbor Group, dir, 2005. **Orgs:** Am Bar Asn; Dist Columbia Bar Asn; Bars US Dist Ct Dist Columbia Second Circuit Ct Appeals; Comn Advan Policy Affecting Disadvantaed, 1978-80; bd mem, Fed Bar Asn, DC Chap, 1984-86; bd mem, Am Coun Young Polit Leaders, 1993; bd trustees, Supreme Ct Hist Soc; Interagency Task Force US. Coast Guard Roles & Missions. **Honors/Awds:** Secretary of Transportation's Award for Outstanding Public Service; United States Coast Guard Distinguished Public Service Award; Meritorious Service Medal, Federal Govt; One of Washington's top lawyers (Campaigns & Elections), Washingtonian; One of the 100 people to watch in the new century, Newsweek; Leading lawyer in government relations law, Best Lawyers Am, 2008; "Best Lawyers List", Wash Post Mag, 2008. **Special Achievements:** Co-author: The Sony Betamax Case, Computers & The Law, 1984; contributing editor, The Nicaragua Elections: A Challenge of Democracy, 1989. **Business Addr:** Partner, Principal, Bingham McCutchen LLP, Bingham Consulting Group, 3000 K St NW, Washington, DC 20007, **Business Phone:** (202)373-6598.

MARSHALL, TIMOTHY H.
Consultant, musicologist. **Personal:** Born Dec 8, 1949, Aiken County, SC. **Educ:** Lone Mtn Col San Francisco, BA, 1974; Lone Mtn Col San Francisco. **Career:** Nat United Comn free Angela Davis & all Pol Prisoners Commun Fund raising, nat staff mem, 1971-72; The Black Scholar Speakers Bureau, nat dir; Black World Found The Black Scholar, promotional dir, 1973-74; Comn Lieson Cinema Lone Mountain Col San Francisco, promotional coord. **Orgs:** In Concert for Angela, Creator & dir, 1972; Black Expo Concert Prod Staff, 1972; prof, musician Episcopal Diocese Augusta, GA 1970-71; "Jr League Follies", musical dir Extravaganza, 1970; Black World Found; Afro-Am Music Opportunites Asn; Nat Alliance Against Racist & Pol Repression; Inst BlackWorld; African-Am Historical & Cultural Soc; founder & pres Black Stud Union, Agusta Col, 1968-69; Nat Coordr Elayne Jones Defense Com; founding mem pres & min affairs Progressive Black Orgn, 1967-70. **Honors/Awds:** Silver Ring, Loatian Delegation; fraternal pin deleg Guinea Bissau Africa, 1973; outstanding service trophy Laney HS Agusta, GA, 1968; Omega Psi Phi Scholarship, 1967; Augusta Chronical Newspaper Gold Plaque, 1966-67. **Business Addr:** Co-ordinator, KEAL, PO Box 6285, San Francisco, CA 94101.

MARSHALL, WILBER BUDDYHIA
Football player. **Personal:** Born Apr 18, 1962, Titusville, FL. **Educ:** Univ Fla. **Career:** Football player (retired); Chicago Bears, linebacker, 1984-87; Wash Redskins, linebacker, 1988-92; Houston Oilers, linebacker, 1993; Ariz Cardinals, linebacker, 1994; New York Jets, linebacker, 1995. **Honors/Awds:** Lombardi Award Finalist; Nat Defensive Player of the Year, ABC Sports, 1983; All-Southern Player-of-the-Year & Acad All-Am sr; Team Century, Univ Fla, 1999.

MARSHBURN, EVERETT LEE
Executive. **Personal:** Born Jan 4, 1948, Baltimore, MD; son of William A Hall and Theresa G. **Educ:** Morgan State Univ, Baltimore, Md, BA, 1976. **Career:** Md Pub TV, Owings Mills, Md, dir regional prod, 1993, vpres broadcast prod, exec producer, vpres, currently. **Orgs:** Charter mem, Beta Omega Epsilon Frat Inc, 1965-; Md Humanities Coun, 1987-92; Black Ment Health Alliance, 1990-92; Nat Asn Black Journalists. **Honors/Awds:** Emmy Awards, 1975 & 1996; Iris Award, 1986; Alfred I Dupont Award, Columbia Sch Jour, 1989; Frederick Douglass Award, Nat Asn Black Journalists, 1990; John R Haney Award, SECA Award, 1990; EEN Award, 1996. **Business Addr:** Vice President, Maryland Public Television, 11767 Owings Mills Blvd, Owings Mills, MD 21117, **Business Phone:** (410)356-5600.

MARTIN, AL. See MARTIN, ALBERT LEE.

MARTIN, ALBERT LEE (AL MARTIN)
Baseball player. **Personal:** Born Nov 24, 1967, West Covina, CA; married Cathy; children: Brandon. **Career:** Baseball player (retired); Pittsburgh Pirates, outfielder, 1992-99; San Diego Padres, 2000; Seattle Mariners, 2001; Tampa Bay Devil Rays, outfielder, 2003; LG Twins, outfielder, 2004. *

MARTIN, AMON ACHILLES, JR.
Dentist. **Personal:** Born May 21, 1940, Anderson, SC; married Brenda Watts; children: Jocelyn, Amon III, Theodore. **Educ:** Fisk Univ, BA; Howard Univ, Col Dent, DDS, 1966. **Career:** labor licensing & regulation, Bd Dent, vpres, 1999-05, chmn, 2004-05; Dent, Seneca, currently. **Orgs:** Am Dent Asn; Nat Dent Asn; Palmetto Med Dent & Pharmaceut Asn; fel Int Col Dentists; Omega Psi Phi; past pres, Anderson Dent Soc; Seneca Adv Bd; mem bd visitors, Clemson Univ 1984-86; Sigma Pi Phi Frat; SC State Bd Dent; mem comn, pres comn, Clemson Univ, currently. **Military Serv:** USF, lt colonel, retired; Primary Duty LO of the Year, 1991. **Business Addr:** Dentist, 208 N Walnut St, Seneca, SC 29678.*

MARTIN, DR. ANNIE B.
Association executive. **Personal:** Born Dec 20, 1925, South Carolina. **Educ:** Allen Univ, Columbia, MA, social science, Guidance Counseling; NY Univ, MSW; Cornell Rutgers PA State Univ, Cert Labor Educ. **Career:** NY State Dept Labor, asst indust comnr; Cornell Univ, sr extension assoc; Fordham Univniv, asst adj prof; ER Squibb & Sons Brooklyn, chem; NY Chap NAACP, pres, currently. **Orgs:** Int Asn Personnel Employ Security; NY City Guidance Adv Coun; Am Asn Univ Women; chmn, NY State Advisory Coun Voc Educ; Soroptimist; charter mem, vpres, Black Trade Unionists Leadership Com; exec bd, NY City Central Labor Coun; AFL-CIO; bd dir, NY Lung Asn; exec bd, NY City Central Labor Coun AFL-CIO; Nat Coun Negro Women; NAACP; Bethel AME Ch; golden heritage, diamond mem, NAACP; Dir, Labor Participation; Am Red Cross; Episcopal ch. **Honors/Awds:** Community service award, NY City Central Labor Coun, 1961; district service award, 1971; woman of year, NY Br NAACP, 1976; award of merit, Black Trade Unionists Leadersihp Com, 1977; awards in Black, NY City Central Labor Coun AFL-CIO, 1973; woman of year award, Pvt Voc Sch, 1973; hon doctorate, Humane Letter, Claflin Col, Orangeburg, SC; Nat Ellis Island Medal of Honor; named "Who's Who in Black America"; Medal of Honor, coveted national Ellis Island; honor, Udumeze Ohafia. *

MARTIN, ARNOLD LEE, JR.
Health services administrator. **Personal:** Born Jan 10, 1939, Hartford, CT; married Ramona Garner; children: Zena Monique & Arnold Lee III. **Educ:** FBI Nat Acad, attended 1981; New Hampshire Col, BS, 1983. **Career:** Hartford Police Dept, chief's adv, 1962-83; WTIC 1080 Corp, chmn adv comn, 1974-82; Am Red Cross Hartford, bd dirs, 1975-84, exec dir 1986-. **Orgs:** Chmn, Proj 90 USN Recruiting Team, 1974-75; bd dir, Nat Asn Advan Colored People, 1975; first vpres, Conn Asn Police Community Rel Off, 1979-81; Hartford Hosp Pub Rels Bd, 1981-83; first vpres, W Hartford Lions Club, 1982; Urban League, 1982; rhetoricos, Sigma Pi Phi Fraternity, 1985-; pres, Alpha Phi Alpha Fraternity, 1986-. **Honors/Awds:** Hartford Man of the Month, Conn Mutual Life Ins Co, 1974; Outstanding Service Award, March Dimes, 1977; USAF Commendation Medal Westover AFB, 1980; Lions International District Governor Service Award, 1980; Director's Award, FBI Nat Academy, 1981; Chairman's Award, Am Red Cross, 1984; Hartford Guardians Outstanding Community Service Award, 1985. **Military Serv:** AUS, res sgt; Non-Commissioned Officers Achievement Ribbon, 1987. **Business Addr:** Executive Director, American Red Cross, 75 Pearl St, Hartford, CT 06103, **Business Phone:** (860)249-9000.

MARTIN, BARBARA ANITA. See BLACKMON, BARBARA MARTIN.

MARTIN, BARON H
Judge. **Personal:** Born Sep 14, 1926, Boston, MA; married. **Educ:** Suffolk Univ, AA, BA, 1951, JD, 1957; Univ Chicago, exec mgt training, 1972. **Career:** MA Bay Transit Authority, clerk, 1951, atty, 1958, sr atty, 1970, Comn MA, spl asst atty gen, 1972, asst gen coun, 1976, dir, 2001; Roxbury Dist Ct, Spec Justice, 1973-80; Wareham Dist Ct, presiding justice, 1981-85; Appellate Div Dist Cts, Southern Dist, presiding justice, 1985-95; Southern New Eng Sch Law, sr adj prof law, bd trustee, currently. **Orgs:** MA Bar Asn; Am Bar Asn; MA Trial Lawyers; chmn, Dem Ward Comt, 1950-64; Am Judges Asn; US Dist Ct, 1959; US Supreme Ct, 1966; Am Jud Soc; Int Acad Law & Sci; Urban League; Nat Asn Advan Colored People; alt deleg, Dem Nat Conv, 1968; dir, Southern ME Law sch; gen coun & chmn, Exec Bd Unity Bank & Trust, 1990-. **Honors/Awds:** Outstanding Achievement, Alpha Phi Alpha Sigma Chap, 1948; Honarary Doctorate, William Penn Saints Jr Col; Brass Gavel Award, Plymouth Co Bar; Plymouth County Prosecutors Award; Outstanding Performance Award, Comn MA Probation Dept; Honarary Doctorate, Bridgewater State Col, 2001. **Business Addr:** Board of Trustee, Southern New England School of Law, 333 Faunce Corner Rd, North Dartmouth, MA 02571-2112, **Business Phone:** (508)998-9600.

MARTIN, DR. BERTHA M
Dentist. **Personal:** Born Apr 5, 1926, Pulaski, TN; daughter of Fannie Martin Jones (deceased); married May 19, 1962 (divorced 1964); children: Beryl (deceased). **Educ:** Howard Univ, BS, 1947, DDS, 1951; Holyoke Hosp, Internship, 1951-52; Univ MI, Cert, Pediatric Dentistry, 1955-56. **Career:** Pvt pract, Berkley, CA,1959-62; Los Angeles, CA, dent consult, 1963-66; pediatric dentist, Wash, DC, 1966-97; Howard Univ Dent Sch, clin prof, 1977, assoc prof, currently. **Orgs:** Am Dental Asn; Am Acad Pediat Dent; Alpha Kappa Alpha Sor; DC Dent Soc; Robert T Freeman Dent Soc; Am Soc Dent C; St Mark's Church Vestry; bd trustees, Dean Jr Col, Franklin Mass; bd adv, Burgundy Farm Country Day Sch, Alexandria, Va, 1987-93. **Home Addr:** 3547 Texas Ave SE, Washington, DC 20020, **Home Phone:** (202)575-0418. **Business Addr:** Associate Professor, Howard University, Department of Pediatric Dentistry, 600 W St NW, Washington, DC 20059, **Business Phone:** (202)806-0440.

MARTIN, BLANCHE
Dentist. **Personal:** Born Jan 16, 1937, Millhaven, GA; widowed; children: Gary, Steven, Michael, Gunnar, Skye, Koffar, Rane & Hantar. **Educ:** MI St Univ, BS, 1959; Univ Detroit, DDS, 1967. **Career:** Dentist, pvt pract, currently. **Orgs:** Cent Dist Dent Asn, 1967-; Omicron Kappa Upsilon Nat Den Hon, 1967; bd trustee, Mich St Univ, 1969-76, 1977-84; chmn bd, 1975-76; Am Dent Asn; Mich Dent Asn; SPP; A&A Fraternities; Golden Heritage; NCP. **Honors/Awds:** Academic All American Football player, 1957, 1958; Recipient award for excel in General Dental. **Special Achievements:** First African American member of the Michigan State University Board of Trustees. **Business Addr:** Dentist, Blanche Martin, 201 1/2 E Grand River, East Lansing, MI 48823.

MARTIN, CARL E.
Government official. **Personal:** Born Feb 14, 1931, Birmingham, AL; married Patricia; children: Ennis, Joel, Carla & Dana. **Educ:** Miles Col, BA, 1953; Pepperdine Univ, MPA, 1973; La Col Law, JD, 1978. **Career:** La County Human Rel Comn, exec dir; Calif Youth Auth, group supvr; Calif Youth Auth, parole agt; La County Probation Dept, sr dep prof officer; La Inglewood Culver City Duarte Sch Dist, coun; Univ S Calif & Univ Calif, Los Angeles, Calif State Univ Sys, coun. **Orgs:** Bd dirs, Econ & Youth Opport Agency; pres, Fedn Black Hist & Arts Inc; bd dir, HELM Scholar Found; bd dir, RAKESTRAW Educ & Community Ctr Wesley United Methodist Church; Employ Develop Comn, La Urban League; bd dir, Westminster Neighborhood Asn. **Honors/Awds:** Number of awards from organisations in Greater Louisiana areas. **Military Serv:** AUS, sp-4, 1953-55. **Business Addr:** 320 W Temple St 1184 Hall of Records, Los Angeles, CA 90012.

MARTIN, CAROL (FRANCES MARTIN)
Journalist, vice president (organization). **Personal:** Born Jul 15, 1948, Detroit, MI; daughter of Daniel (deceased) and Idessa. **Educ:** Wayne State Univ, BA, 1970. **Career:** Journalist, executive; WWJ-TV, Detroit, dept asst pub affairs, 1970-71; Detroit Free Press, ed features dept, feature writer, 1971-73; WMAL-TV, Wash, DC, gen assignment reporter, 1973-75; WCBS-TV, NY, gen assignment news corresp, 1975-95; Making Hist Ltd, sr vpres &

Founder, 2001-. **Orgs:** Am Fed TV & Radio Artists; US Sen & House of Representatives Radio TV Gallery; adv bd, Nat Child Day Care Asn, 1974-75. **Honors/Awds:** Wayne State Univ Scholarship, 1966-70.

MARTIN, PROF. CAROLYN ANN
Educator. **Personal:** Born Aug 14, 1943, Versailles, MO. **Educ:** Lincoln Univ, Miss, BS, phys edus & psychol, 1968; Calif State Poly Univ Pomona, MS, 1974; Univ Calif, Riverside, grad courses, 1972; Pepperdine Univ, Los Angeles, CA, attended 1984. **Career:** Lincoln Univ Miss, Dept Phys Educ, teaching asst, 1964-68; Perris High Sch Dist, instr phys ed, 1968-78, phys educ teacher, nursing women's athletic dir, 1968-74; Perris Jr High Sch, chmn phys educ, 1970-74; Calif St Univ Summer Upward Bound, recreation cord, 1976; San Bernardino High Sch, head coach womens varsity softball, 1981-84; Calif St Univ, assoc prof phys educ, 1974, prof phys educ, prof emer, currently. **Orgs:** Calif Assn Health Phys Educ Recreation & Dance, 1973-74, 1979-80; St Sch Supt Wilson Riles, St Task Force Athletic Injuries, 1976-77; bd mem, 3 Sports Inc, 1977; Am Alliance Health Phys Educ Recreation & Dance, 1979; Natl Girls & Womens Speed ball Guide Comt, 1980-84; San Bernardino Sexual Assault Serv Ctr, 1983-84; Joint Comn Am Assn Leisure & Recreation, Am Alliance Health Phys Educ, Recreation & Dance, Natl Assessment Elem Sch Playgrounds, 1985; Am Alliance Health; Calif Teachers Assn; Calif Fac Assn;Natl Bowling Coun; Natl Assn Sport & Phys Educ; Natl Assn Girls & Womens Sports; Calif Assn Black Fac & Staff; Delta Kappa Gamma. **Honors/Awds:** Softball Coach of the Year, Perris High Sch, 1970; Teacher of the Year, Perris High Sch, 1973, Perris Jr High School Teacher of the Year, 1973; Teacher's Advocate Award, San Bernardino Teachers Assn, 1974; Certif of Appreciation, Kiwanis Intl San Bernardino 1976; San Bernardino Affirm Action Faculty Development Award, State Univ, 1981. **Special Achievements:** Published Workbook, Fundamentals of Basketball Officiating, 1978; Games Contests & Relays, 1981; Teaching Softball, 1985. **Business Addr:** Professor Emeritus, California State University, 5500 Univ Pkwy, San Bernardino, CA 92407, **Business Phone:** (909)537-5358.

MARTIN, CHARLES HOWARD
Lawyer. **Personal:** Born Nov 13, 1952, Washington, DC; son of John and Hestlene. **Educ:** Harvard Univ, BA, 1974; Univ Calif, Berkeley, Boalt Hall Sch Law, JD, 1977; Columbia Bus Sch, MBA. **Career:** Hogan & Hartson, law pract; US Dep Navy, law pract; DC Off, Corp Coun, law pract; Off Legal Affairs Fla, law pract; State Fla, asst atty gen, 1982-84; Fla State Univ, asst prof law, 1984-85; Villanova Univ, asst prof law, 1985-87; Sallie Mae, asst gen coun, 1987; Civic Educ Proj, vis fac fel; UDC David A ClarkeSch Law, vis assoc prof, 2005-. **Business Addr:** Visiting Associate Professor of Law, UDC David A. Clarke School of Law, 4200 Conn Ave NW, Washington, DC 20008, **Business Phone:** (202)274-7400.*

MARTIN, CHARLES WESLEY
Insurance executive. **Personal:** Born Apr 23, 1937, Middlesboro, KY; son of Allen and Cora; married Ella K, May 1, 1972; children: Tracy M Cargo, Charla M Sturdivant, Katheryn & Angela. **Educ:** Ky State Univ, attended 1960. **Career:** Proctor & Gamble Co, sales rep, 1970-71; Eastern Life Zone, vpres, 1981-82; Allstate Ins Co, sales agent, 1971-72, sales mgt, 1972-80, reg vpres, Denver, Colo, 1982-86, reg vpres southern calif, 1986-94, vpres sales corp off, 1995-. **Orgs:** First vpres, Nat Asn Advan Colored People, Waukegan, Ill chap, 1967; bd trustees, Shaker Heights Community Church Christ, Ohio, 1980-81; bd trustees, Second Baptist Church, Santa Ana, Calif, 1988-91; bd trustees, bd deacons, Zion Baptist, Denver, Co, 1984-86; bd mem, Urban League, Orange County, Ca, 1991-94; Prison Fel Ministry, Inland Empire, Orange City, Ca, 1992-94; Calif Ins Commissioners, anti discrimination task force, 1993-94; Kappa Alpha Psi Fraternity. **Honors/Awds:** Black Achievers of Industry, YMCA Metrop Chicago, 1976. **Military Serv:** USN, E6, 1960-70; Navy Unit Commendation Award, Navy Achievement Award. **Home Addr:** 4486 Normandy Ct, Long Grove, IL 60047.

MARTIN, CHERYL
Television news anchorperson. **Career:** Black Entertainment TV, anchor. *

MARTIN, CHRISTOPHER
Singer, actor, business owner. **Personal:** Born Jul 10, 1962, New York, NY; married Shari Headley (divorced); children: Skyler. **Career:** Actor, singer, producer, dir, business owner; Film: House Party, 1990; House Party 2, 1991; Class Act, 1992; House Party 3, 1994; Rising to the Top, 1999; Singer: Traveling Companion, 1998; TV Show: "Sealab 2021", 2002; Kid n Play; Amen Films, exec dir, currently; HP4 Digital Works & Solutions, founder & chief exec officer, currently. **Honors/Awds:** New York Inter Nat Film Festival Award, 2007. **Business Phone:** (205)781-4411.

MARTIN, CLARA SYLVIA COOKE. See MARTIN, SYLVIA COOKE.

MARTIN, CLARENCE L.
Lawyer. **Personal:** Born in Baxley, GA; married Annie D; children: Anthony L, Bernard E. **Educ:** Savannah St Col, BS, 1970; Emory Univ, Notre Dame Law Sch, 1973. **Career:** City Savannah, asst city atty, judge pro temporo recorders ct; C & S Bank; SS Kresge Co; Hill, Jones & Farrington; Whitcomb & Keller Mortgage Co; Martin, Thomas & Bass PC, atty; Clarence L Martin PC, atty, currently. **Orgs:** Savannah Bar Asn; Ga Bar Asn; Am Bar Asn; Nat Asn Advan Colored People; Oper Push; Martin Luther King Fel, Woodrow Wilson Found. **Military Serv:** USAF, staff sgt, 1962-67. **Business Addr:** Attorney, Clarence L. Martin PC, 109 W Liberty St, Savannah, GA 31412.*

MARTIN, CURTIS
Football player. **Personal:** Born May 1, 1973, Pittsburgh, PA; children: Diamond. **Educ:** Univ Pittsburgh, pub admin. **Career:** Football player (retired); New Eng Patriots, running back, 1995-97; New York Jets, 1998-2006. **Honors/Awds:** City League Player of the Year, Pittsburgh Post-Gazette & Pittsburgh Press, 1990; Pro Bowl, 1995, 1996; Rookie of the Year, 1995; Dennis Byrd Award, 2001, 2002; Fourth Team Most Valuable Player Award, 2004.

MARTIN, CURTIS JEROME
Educator. **Personal:** Born Nov 16, 1949, Kansas City, MO; married Valerie Joy Smith. **Educ:** USAF Acad, BS, humanities, 1971; Mich State Univ, MA, Eng, 1976. **Career:** USAF Acad CO, asst ftbll coach, 1971-72; Lowry Air Force Base Denver, dir drug/alcohol abuse prgm, 1972-75; USAF Acad, asst prof of Eng, 1976-80; USAF Acad Activties Grp, chief congr liaison br, 1980-. **Orgs:** Nat Coun Teachers Eng, 1975-; course dir, Black Lit, Minority Lit, African Lit USAF Acad Eng Dept, 1978-80; acad liaison officer mem, USAF Acad Way of Life Com, 1976-80; alcohol abuse rehab coun SW Denver Ment Health Ctr,1973-74; parliamentarian Lowry AFB Chap Brthrhd Asn Black Serv cmn & Svc wmn, 1973-75; Aurora CO Drug Alcohol Abuse Coun, 1973-75; Spkrs BurLowry AFB, 1973-75; Spkrs Bur USAF Acad, 1976-80. **Honors/Awds:** Outstanding young man of Am US Jaycees, 1977; dist grad Squadron Officer Sch Maxwell AFB, 1978; jr ofcr of yr, USAF Acad Facu, 1979; Clements award "Mil Educator of Year" USAF Acad 1980. **Military Serv:** USAF, capt 1971-, Commendation Medal, 1975. **Business Addr:** HQ USA MPPA Pentagon, Washington, DC 20330.

MARTIN, DANIEL E
Judge. **Personal:** Born Apr 14, 1932, Bluffton, SC; son of John Henry and Rena Johnson; married Ruby Nesbitt, 1960; children: Daniel E Jr & Max Maurice. **Educ:** Allen Univ, BS, Health & Phys Educ, 1954; SC State Col, JD, 1966. **Career:** Judge (retired); Wallace HS, phys educ dept, 1959-62; Gresham Meggett HS, math teacher, 1962-63; Neighborhood Legal Asst Prog, dir, 1968-72; 9th Jud Circuit, asst solicitor first black; SC House Rep, vchair, judicial comt; Ninth Judicial Circuit SC, presiding judge, 1992-2001. **Orgs:** Am Bar Asn; SC Bar Asn; Charleston Co Bar Asn; Judges Selection Comt State SC Black Lawyer; Gov Energy Comn; State Bd Voc Rehab; US Tax Ct; US Ct Customs & Patent Appeals; Fed Dist Ct, Dist SC; US Supreme Ct; trustee, Emanuel AME Church; trust bd, Allen Univ; charter mem, Choraliers Music Club; life mem, Alpha Phi Alpha; Downtown Charleston Rotary Int Club; Charleston Bus & Prof Asn. **Honors/Awds:** Scroll of Honor, Alpha Phi Alpha Fraternity, Omega Psi Phi Fraternity, 1969; Certificate of Achievement, Alpha Phi Alpha Fraternity, 1970; Certificate of Appreciation, Charleston Sym Asn, 1970; District Service Award, Alpha Phi Alpha Fraternity, 1973; Appreciation Award, Clara D Hill Mission Club, 1974; Appreciation Award, BSA, 1974; Juris Prudence Achieve Award, Omega Psi Phi Fraternity, 1974; Man of the Year, Charleston Bus & Prof Asn, 1975; Recognition Award for Social Action, Phi Beta Sigma Fraternity,1976; Certificate of Appreciation, Selective Service System, 1976; Certificate from Gov James B Edwards, SC Vocational Rehab Asn, 1976; Certificate of Achievement, Alpha Phi Alpha Fraternity, 1979; Appreciation Award, Arabian Temple #139, 1979; Thelma F Murray Appreciation Award; Mary Ford Sch Award, Black History Contribution, 1987; AKA Debutante Award-Distinguished Service, 1988; American Education Award, Burke High Sch, 1988; Resolution of Honor, Benedicat Col, 1989; DHL, Univ Charleston, 1992. **Military Serv:** AUS, corpl, 1955-57. **Home Addr:** 117 Gordon St, Charleston, SC 29403, **Home Phone:** (843)723-3046.

MARTIN, DANIEL EZEKIEL
Lawyer, judge. **Personal:** Born Jan 21, 1963, Charleston, SC; son of Daniel E Jr and Ruby N; married Reba Hough, Apr 29, 1989. **Educ:** Howard Univ, Wash, DC, BA, 1985; Univ SC Sch Law, Columbia, SC, JD, 1988. **Career:** House Rep, Columbia, SC, law clerk, 1986-88; Martin, Gailliard & Martin, Charleston, SC, atty/partner, 1988-; Charleston Co, Charleston, SC, magistrate, 1989-93; Martin Law Off, atty & partner, currently. **Orgs:** Pres, Network Charleston, 1989-; treas, SC Black Lawyer Asn, 1990-; corresp secy, Beta Kappa Lambda Chap, Alpha Phi Alpha, 1990-; bd trustees, Emmanuel AME Church, 1990-; exec bd, Charleston, Nat Asn Advan Colored People, 1991-; exec bd,Cannon St YMCA; Mayor's Comt 12; Charleston Comm C; Masonic Lodge No 51; George Washington Carver Consistory No 162; Arabian Temple No 139; Owl's Whist Club; 100 Black Men Charleston. **Honors/Awds:** Community Service, Charleston Chap, 1990; Celebrity Reader, Charleston Co Lib Asn, 1990. **Home Phone:** (843)766-9280. **Business Addr:** Attorney, Partner, Martin Law Offices, 61 Morris St, Charleston, SC 29403-6038, **Business Phone:** (843)723-1686.

MARTIN, DANYEL CECIL
Football player. **Personal:** Born Jul 8, 1975, Chicago, IL; son of Diana. **Educ:** Univ Wis, madison. **Career:** Football player (retired); Philadelphia Eagles, running back, 1999-2002; Tampa Bay Buccaneers, running back, 2003; Oakland Raiders, running back, 2003; Nat Collegiate Scouting Assoc, Educ Speaker, currently; Sky Sports, studio analyst, currently.

MARTIN, DARNELL
Movie director. **Personal:** Born Jan 7, 1964, Bronx, NY; daughter of Marilyn; married Giuseppe Ducrot. **Educ:** Sarah Lawrence Co; NY Univ. **Career:** Deadly Obsession, actress, 1989; Nowhere Fast, Actress, 1997; Prison Song, exec producer, 2001; Circulo vicioso, El, assoc producer, 2003; Filmmaker, currently. **Special Achievements:** Film: "I Like It Like That"; songs: "Prison Song", 2001; "I Like It Like That", 2004. **Business Phone:** (310)244-4000.*

MARTIN, DARRICK
Basketball player. **Personal:** Born Mar 6, 1971, Denver, CO; son of Pam Martin and Jesse. **Educ:** Univ Calif-Los Angeles, attended 1992. **Career:** Sioux Falls Skyforce (CBA), guard, 1994-95; Minn Timberwolves, 1995-96, 2003-04; Los Angeles Clippers, 1996-99, 2004-05; Sacramento Kings, 1999-2001; Dallas Mavericks, 2001-02; Toronto Raptors, guard, 2005-. **Honors/Awds:** Newcomer of the Year, CBA, 1995; Most Valuable Player, CBA, 2003. **Business Phone:** (416)815-5600.

MARTIN, DEWAYNE
Government official. **Personal:** Born Oct 18, 1967, Chicago, IL; son of DeWitt N Jr and Anne. **Educ:** Morehouse Col, BA, 1989; Ga State Univ Col Law, JD, 1994. **Career:** US Census Bur, mgr field opers, 1989-90; City Atlanta, legislative aide, 1991-94, dep chief staff, 1994-97, chief staff, 1997-. **Orgs:** Butler St YMCA, 1975-; bd mem, Greater Atlanta Community Corps, 1996-; State Bar Asn, 1996-; bd mem, Nat Black Arts Festival, 1997-; bd adv, Metro Atlanta Super Bowl XXXIV, 1998-. **Special Achievements:** 30 Young Leaders of the Future, Ebony Magazine, 1997. **Business Addr:** Chief of Staff, City Atlanta, 55 Trinity Ave SW Suite 2400, Atlanta, GA 30303, **Business Phone:** (404)330-6809.

MARTIN, DUANE
Actor. **Personal:** Born Aug 11, 1965, Brooklyn, NY; married Tisha Campbell, Aug 17, 1996. **Educ:** NY Univ. **Career:** Impact Sports, owner, currently; TV series: "Out All Night", 1992; "Getting Personal", 1998; "Sugar Hill", 1999; "All of Us", 2003; TV movies: "Different Worlds: A Story of Interracial Love", 1992; "Mutiny", 1999; Films: White Men Can't Jump, 1992; Above the Rim, 1994; The Ink well, 1994; Down Periscope, 1996; Scream 2, 1997; Fakin' Da Funk, 1997; Woo, 1998; The Faculty, 1998; Any Given Sunday, 1999; The Groomsmen, 2001; Ride or Die, 2003; Al Of Us, 2003; The Seat Filler, 2004; Killer Movie, 2007. **Honors/Awds:** Nominated for Image Award, 2007; Nominated for BET Comedy Award, 2004; Nominated for Day Time Emmy Award, 1993. **Special Achievements:** Nominee, BET Comedy Award, 2004, 2005, 2007. **Business Addr:** Actor, c/o Stan Rosenfield & Associates, 2029 Century Pk E Suite 1190, Los Angeles, CA 90067.*

MARTIN, EDWARD
Clergy. **Personal:** Born Jun 30, 1936, Grove Hill, AL; divorced. **Educ:** Ala State Univ, BS, 1969; Carver Bible Inst, BTh; Interdenom Theol Ctr & Horehouse Sch Rel Atlanta, mDiv (honor roll), 1973. **Career:** Bethel Baptist Church Montgomery, AL, pastor, 1967-; Union Acad Bapt Ch; Selma Univ Sch Rel, instr. **Orgs:** Nat Asn Advan Colored People, 1958-; YMCA, 1966-; Montgomery Improvement Asn Inc, 1967-; Phi Beta Sigma, 1969-; Pres Montgomery-Antioch Dist SS & Bapt Training Union Cong, 1970; Nat Bapt Conv USA Inc; Am Beatury Lodge 858; Charlie Garrett Chap Royal Arch No 78a; United Supreme Coun, 32; Prince Hall Affil Grand Orient Wash, DC. **Honors/Awds:** Nat Found March of Dimes award, 1971.

MARTIN, EDWARD ANTHONY
Podiatrist. **Personal:** Born Dec 25, 1935, Mason City, IA; married Barbara C Payne; children: Gail Ingrid, Edward Brian & Stephen Vincent. **Educ:** Mason City Jr Col, 1954; Ill Col Podiatric Med, DPM, 1958. **Career:** Podiatrist, 1958-; podiatry examr, Ill Dept Registration/Educ, 1978. **Orgs:** Pres, Acad Ambulatory Foot Surg, 1973-74; Nat Podiatry Asn; Am Podiatry Asn. **Honors/Awds:** Henri L DuVries Award, Proficiency Clin Surg, 1958. **Special Achievements:** First National President of Academy of Ambulatory Foot Surgery, 1973-74; Private pilot Single Engine-land, 1974; "Podiatry A Step Toward Healthy Happy Feet", Ebony Article, 1978; Instructor in surgery-instructional movie on ambulatory surgery, 1979. **Business Addr:** Podiatrist, 637 E Homestead Rd, San Jose, CA 94087, **Business Phone:** (408)733-5510.

MARTIN, DR. EDWARD WILLIFORD
Dean (Education), administrator, educator. **Personal:** Born Nov 29, 1929, Sumter, SC; son of Eddie and Frances; married Pearl Evelyn Sewell; children: Andrea Michelle, Debra Yvette & Christopher Edward. **Educ:** Fisk Univ, BA, 1950; Univ Ind, MA,

1952; Univ IA, PhD, 1962. **Career:** Prairie View A&M Univ, instr biol, 1952-56, asst prof biol, 1956-59, chmn, div nat sci, 1968-81; Prairie View A&M Univ, Coll Arts & Sci, interim dean, 2003-; Prairie View A&M Univ, Biol Dept, Chair, dean, dean emer, prof, currently. **Orgs:** Am Soc Zoologists; Soc Sigma Xi; Am Men Sci; adv bd, Baylor Col Med; Omega Psi Phi Fraternity; Sigma Pi Phi Fraternity Nu Boule; Beta Kappa Chi Scientific Honor Soc; Beta Beta Beta Biol Honor Soc; Alpha Kappa Mu Nat Honor Soc. **Honors/Awds:** Nat Sci Fac Fel, Nat Sci Found, 1961-62; Beta Kappa Chi Distinguished Awd, Beta Kappa Chi Sci Hon Soc, 1965; Minnie Stevens Piper Professor Award, 1979. **Business Addr:** Dean Emeritus, Professor, Prairie View A&M University, Department of Biology, PO Box 277, Prairie View, TX 77446-0519, **Business Phone:** (936)857-3911.

MARTIN, EMANUEL C.
Football player. **Personal:** Born Jul 31, 1969, Miami, FL; married Kimarya; children: Emanuel, Tyree & Kimar. **Educ:** Ala State Univ. **Career:** Football player(retired), Houston Oilers, 1993; Canadian Football League, Ottawa Rough Riders,1994-95; Buffalo Bills, defensive back, 1997-99.

MARTIN, FRANCES. See MARTIN, CAROL.

MARTIN, FRANK C
Curator, educator. **Personal:** Born Aug 17, 1954, Sumter, SC; son of Frank C and Leola Glisson; married Shirley Fields, Jun 19, 1989. **Educ:** Yale Univ, BA, 1976; City Univ New York, Hunter Col, MA, 1990; New York Univ, Inst Fine Arts. **Career:** Metorp Mus Art, curatorial asst, educ assoc, 1979-87, Off Educ Servs, asst mgr, 1988-89, assoc mgr, 1989-91; IP Stanback Mus & Planetarium, SC State Univ, instr, 1991-; Univ SC, Salkehatchie, instr. **Orgs:** Artists Color, SC; Renaissance Soc Am, 1988-91; Col Art Asn, 1988-91; exe bd, Eboni Dance Theatre; Orangeburg Arts Coun; Grants in Aid Panel, SC Arts Comn, visual arts chair, 1992; Orangeburg Arts League. **Honors/Awds:** Honorable Mention, Scholastic Arts Awards Comt, 1970; Nat Achievement Commended Scholar, Educ Testing Service, 1972; Kiwanis of America, Key Club Scholar Award, 1972; Yale Nat Scholar, Yale Univ, 1976; City Univ New York; William Graf Grant Travel & Study Abroad, Hunter Col, 1986. **Special Achievements:** Auth: The Museum as an Artists' Resource, Am Artist Mag, 1991; Cultural Pluralism: A Challenge for the Arts in SC, Triennial Exhibition Catalogue, 1992; The Acacia Historical Collection, Am Visions Mag, 1992; Art, Race, and Culture: Context & Interpretive Bias in Contemporary Africa Art in Transcendence and Conflict: Africa Art in SC 1700-Present, 1992. **Business Addr:** Instructor, South Carolina State University, Visual & Performing Arts Campus, 300 Col St NE, PO Box 7505, Orangeburg, SC 29117, **Business Phone:** (803)536-8388.

MARTIN, FRANK T
Executive. **Personal:** Born Jul 24, 1950, Nashville, TN; son of William Henry and Maureen Kimbrough; married Pamela Johnson, Nov 1, 1980; children: Jessica Maureen. **Educ:** Tenn State Univ, BS, bus admin, 1973; Fisk Univ, MURP, 1974. **Career:** N Cent Fla Region Planning Coun, local assistance & mass transit planner, 1974-77; Greater Richmond Transit Co, operation planning dir, 1978-80; Birmingham Jefferson County Transit Authority, from asst gen mgr to general mgr, 1980-84; ATE, Ryder Systs Inc, Transit Mgt SE La, vpres, gen mgr, 1984-87; Metro-Dade County Transit Agency, dep dir, 1987-89, rail operations asst dir, 1989-. **Orgs:** Nat Forum Black Pub Admin, 1987-; pres, Tenn State Univ, Alumni Asn, Miami Chap, 1990-93, 1997-; bd mem, Am Pub Transit Found, 1991-97; bd mem, New Miami Group, 1991-97; bd mem, Conf Many Transp Officials, 1992-. **Honors/Awds:** President's Special Achievement Award, ATE, Ryder, 1982; Administrator of the Year, Am Soc Pub Admin, Ala, 1983. **Business Addr:** Assistant Director Rail Operations, Metro-Dade Transit Agency, 7701 NW 79th Ave, Miami, FL 33166, **Business Phone:** (305)884-7520.

MARTIN, GEORGE ALEXANDER, JR.
Administrator. **Personal:** Born May 4, 1943, New York, NY. **Educ:** Parsons Col, BS, 1966; City Univ NY, MPA, 1977. **Career:** Univ Year ACTION Proj, New York City & Urban Corps, dir, 1972-73; New York Univ Grad Sch Pub Admin, clinical asst prof pub admin, 1972-73; Bedford-Stuyvesant Alcoholism Treatment Ctr, special asst to admin; Marlin Enterprises, pres, 1973-. **Orgs:** Am Soc Public Admin; Amer Soc Political Sci; Conf Minority Pub Admin; dir, Pub Mgt Sys Inc; consult, VISTA Region III, 1971; ATAC Inc 1972; Williamsbridge NAACP; Williamsburg Taxpayers Asn; Citizens Comn Children; Brooklyn Comn Alcholism; co-chmn, Achievement Week Comn, Omega Psi Phi Frat; adv bd, New York City Urban Corps & Acad Credit Internship Prog, 1973; dir, Independent House Inc, Pub Prof Studies pub Mgt NYC & Compa Forum, 1975.

MARTIN, GEORGE DWIGHT
Football player. **Personal:** Born Feb 16, 1953, Greenville, SC; married Diane; children: Teresa Michelle, George Dwight II, Benjmain Dean & Aaron. **Educ:** Univ Ore. **Career:** Football player (retired); New York Giants, defensive end, 1975-88. **Orgs:** Former rep, United Way Pub Serv TV Community. **Honors/Awds:** Byron Whizzer White Award; Sports Hall of Fame of New Jersey, 2004.

MARTIN, GERTRUDE S
Public relations executive. **Personal:** Born in Savannah, GA; daughter of Walter S (deceased) and Laura McDowell (deceased); married Louis Emanuel, 1937 (deceased); children: Trudy Hatter, Anita Martin, Toni Martin, Linda Purkiss & Lisa Martin. **Educ:** Ohio State Univ, Columbus, BA, 1934, MA, 1936. **Career:** United Planning Orgn, Washington, educ coord, 1963-66; Willmart Services, Washington, coordinator, 1966-68; Univ Chicago, Dept Educ, ed, 1970-74; Integrated Educ Assoc, Evanston, ed, 1974-78; Calmar Commun, Chicago, vpres, 1978-88; free-lance ed, 1988-. **Orgs:** Bd mem, Ill Child Care Soc, 1955-58; bd gov, Am Red Cross, 1966-72; comt, A Better Chance, Wash, 1983-85; bd mem, Black Women's Agenda, Wash, 1989-92; life mem, Nat Coun Negro Women. **Honors/Awds:** Nat Coun Negro Women; New Horizons, George Washington Univ.

MARTIN, GWENDOLYN ROSE
Labor activist, vice president (organization). **Personal:** Born Dec 12, 1926, Cleveland, OH; daughter of Monroe (deceased) and Rosa M Johnson (deceased); married Aaron; children: Jeffrey A. **Educ:** Ohio State Univ, 1946-48; Case Western Reserve Univ, real estate, 1952; George Wash Univ, Ext Course, 1976. **Career:** Labor activist, Vice president (retired); Commun Workers Am, CWA rep, 1972, dir, 1975, admin asst to vpres, 1976-87; State Ill, Dept Labor, dir, 1987-91; Communs Workers, Itasca, Ill, CWA rep, 1991-92. **Orgs:** Delegate Dem Nat Conv, 1976, 1978, 1982, 1984; vpres, Leadership Coun Comn, 1978-81; vpres, Ill AFL-CIO, 1978-87; chmn, United Way New Appl, 1980-81; Dem Nat Comn; vchmn, Dem Nat Comn Women's Caucus, 1980-84; bd dir, Am Red Cross, 1982-84; exec bd mem, Nal Asn Govt Labor Officials, 1988-91; exec bd mem, Women Execs State-Govt, 1987-88. **Honors/Awds:** Sojourner Truth Awd, Mich Women Trial Lawyers Assoc, 1974; Harriet Tubman Awd, Coalition Black Trade Unionist, 1975; Resolution #1161 Ill, House of Rep, 1978; Florence Criley Award, Coalition Labor Union Women, 1980. **Home Addr:** 219 Hickory, Arlington Heights, IL 60004.

MARTIN, HAROLD B.
Dentist, college teacher. **Personal:** Born Oct 26, 1928, Petersburg, VA; married Dolores H; children: Harold, Lisa & Gregory. **Educ:** Lincoln Univ, AB, 1950; Howard Univ, DDS, 1957; John Hopkins Univ, MPH, 1971. **Career:** College teacher (retired), Dentist; Pvt pract, dentist, 1959; Howard Univ Col Dent, Dept Comm Dent, prof, 1959-87, assoc dean advanced educ & res, 1987-96; Dept Corrections, DC, 1960-70; Am Col Dentist, fel, 1978; Int Col Dent, fel, 1985; founder, Century Ltd Inc; Pvt Pract, dentist, currently. **Orgs:** Vpres, Nat Dent Asn; bd dir, E River Health Asn; Am Dent Asn; Nat Dent Asn; DC Med Care Adv Comt; Nat Review Comn Guidelines Expanded Function Training Prog; Midway Civic Asn; US Youth Games Community; Nat Asn Advancement Colored People; Urban League; Omega Psi Phi; past pres, Huntsmen; bd dir, Ionia Whipper Home Unwed Mothers; bd dir, Pigskin Club, Wash; Am Pub Health Asn; Sigma Xi, 1975; Omicron Kappa Upsilon, 1976; pres, Howard Univ Chap, 1984-85. **Military Serv:** AUS, Med Corp, Dent Sec, 1951-53. *

MARTIN, HOSEA L
Marketing executive. **Personal:** Born Aug 10, 1937, Montezuma, GA; son of Marion Cannon and H L. **Educ:** Univ Chicago, BA, 1960; Univ Chicago, Grad Sch Bus, attended 1965-66. **Career:** Prudential Ins Co, advert specialist, 1966-67; Coca-Cola Co, nat prom mgr, 1967-75; Safeway Stores Inc, mkt progs mgr, 1975-86; Univ Calif, ed specialist, 1986-89; United Way San Francisco, assoc vpres, vpres, 1989-2000; Int Asn Bus Communicators, media rels dir, 2000-01. **Orgs:** San Francisco Media Alliance, 1986-. **Honors/Awds:** First Place, Am Advert Fedn, Direct Mail Develop, 1968. **Special Achievements:** Articles: Wall Street Journal, 1991; Essence, 1992; Author: The Wrong Place to Die, 2002. **Military Serv:** AUS, Spec 4, 1960-63; Soldier of the Month, 1962. **Home Addr:** 6 Greenbank Ave, Piedmont, CA 94611, **Home Phone:** (510)652-4233.

MARTIN, HOYLE HENRY
Government official, college teacher. **Personal:** Born Oct 21, 1927, Brooklyn, NY; son of Mattie Garrett and Jesse T (deceased); married Mary Campbell Martin, Jun 28, 1951; children: Hoyle Jr, Michael C, David E, Cheryl L. **Educ:** Benedict Col, BA, 1957; Syracuse Univ, MA, 1961; New Life Theol Sem, DCSM, 1999. **Career:** NC & SC, col educr, teaching, 1958-66; Charlotte Concentrated Employ Prog, chief exec officer, exec dir, 1967-71; Univ NC, Urban Inst, Charlotte, assoc dir, 1972-76; Charlotte Post, NC, chief ed writer, 1974-89; City Charlotte, NC, housing develop admin, 1977-88, city coun mem, 1989-95; Mecklenburg County, comnr, 1996-98; New Life Theol Sem, prof, dept head, currently. **Orgs:** Adv mem, WBTV Black Adv Comt, 1983-89; adv bd mem, Habitat Humanity, 1987-94; bd mem, Charlotte Civilian Club, 1989-98; bd mem, Reachline Inc, 1989-92; bd mem, W Charlotte Bus Incubator, 1990-. **Honors/Awds:** Meritorious Serv Award, Charlotte Concentrated Employ Prog, 1967-71; Devoted Serv Award, Univ NC, Col Bus, Charlotte, 1969-77; Vol Serv Award, Joint Action Community Serv, 1970; Dedicated Serv Award, Southern Piedmont Health Syst Agency, 1977-78; Meritorious Serv Award, Nat Alliance Businessmen, 1978; Sr Urban Ministry Award, 2006-07. **Military Serv:** AUS, staff sergent, 1950-51; US Merchant Marines, 1945-49, 1952-53. **Home Phone:** (704)392-4623. **Business Addr:** Department Head, Professor, New Life Theological Seminary, PO Box 790106, Charlotte, NC 28206-7901, **Business Phone:** (704)334-6882.*

MARTIN, I MAXIMILLIAN
Executive. **Career:** Berean Savings Asn, Philadelphia, PA, chief exec officer, pres; Eden Cemetery Co, treas. **Orgs:** Life Heritage mem, Nat Asn Advan Colored People. **Business Addr:** Chief Executive Officer, Berean Savings Association, 5228 Chestnut St, Philadelphia, PA 19139, **Business Phone:** (215)472-4545.

MARTIN, IONIS BRACY
Artist, educator, painter (artist). **Personal:** Born Aug 27, 1936, Chicago, IL; daughter of Francis Wright Bracy and Hattie O Robinson Bracy; married Allyn A; children: Allyn B. **Educ:** Fisk Univ, BA, 1957; Univ Hartford, MEd, 1968; Pratt Inst, MFA, 1987. **Career:** YWCA Y-Teen Assoc, dir, 1957-59; Hartford Bloomfield Pub Schs, sec art teacher, 1961-2001; Artist's Collective Inc, artist & educr, 1970-73; WFSB-TV/Wadsworth Atheneum, produced art segments children's prog, 1972-75; Northwestern Conn Community Col, lectr, 1985-90; Cent Conn State Univ, instr & lectr, 1985-; Hartford Courant, illusr, 1986-90; Skidmore Col, art fel, 1987; Getty Ctr Educ Arts, Los Angeles, CA, consult, 1990-93; Gale Res, consult, 1992; Harvard's WEB Dubois Inst, fel, 1994; Univ Hartford, Hartford Art Sch, co-founder, currently. **Orgs:** Comnr, Hartford Fine Arts Comn; dir, Greater Hartford Arts Coun, Charter Oak Temple Cult Ctr & Hartford Stage Co; co-founder, vpres & dir, Artists Collective, 1970-; trustee, Wadsworth Atheneum, 1977-85, 1986-96; The Links Inc, 1985-, pres, Greater Hartford Chap, 1998-02, secy, 1994-98; mem adv comn Conn Bd Educ, 1986-87; NAEA, CAEA, Delta Sigme Theta; pres, Artworks Gallery, 1986-87; Romare Bearden/Jackie McLean "Sound Collages & Visual Improvizations" 1986; cur/producer, Cotra Gallery "Five From CT", 1987; JP Getty Trust Curric Devel Inst, 1988-; co-trustee, Burr McManus Trust, 1990-2001; Capital Comn Col, 2000. **Honors/Awds:** Outstanding Community Service Award, Univ Hartford, 1974; 200 Years of Achievement Against the Odds Black Women of CT; One Woman Show, Christ Church Cathedral, Hartford, 1990; Best in Show, Pump House Gallery, 1990; One Woman Show, Lindgren Gallery, Manchester, 1990; One Woman Show Northampton Arts Center, Northampton MA, 1990; One Woman Show, Wethersfield Hist Soc, 1991; Jubilee, One Woman Show, Fisk Univ, 1992; Solo exhibit, Univ Vt, 1993; Group shows: Artworks Gallery, The CRT Gallery and Pump House Galley, 1993-94; Secondary Art Educator of the Year, Conn Art Ed Asn, 1993-94; One Woman Show, First Church of Christ Art Gallery, New Britain, CT, 2003. **Home Addr:** 1234 Prospect Ave, Hartford, CT 06105-1123. **Business Addr:** Co-Founder, University of Hartford, Hartford Art School, 200 Bloomfield Ave, West Hartford, CT 06117, **Business Phone:** (860)768-4100.

MARTIN, JAMES LARENCE
Dentist. **Personal:** Born Sep 3, 1940, Dubuque, IA; son of James Martin and Ada Martin; married Willie Mae; children: Linda, James Larence III, John Lance. **Educ:** Loras Col, BS 1959; Tenn State Univ, MS 1960; Meharry Med Col Sch Dent, DDS 1966; Univ MI, MPH 1975; DLitt, Loras Col 1982. **Career:** Meharry Med Col, instr 1960-62, instr 1967-69, dental dir 1967-72, assoc prof 1969-72; Comprehensive Health Care Prog C & Youth Prom, proj dir 1972-73; Meharry Med Col, asst prof, dept pediatrics 1972-, dir 1973-75, asst prof dept operative 1974-75, coord, 1975-, assoc prof, 1977-, prof, 1981-, Dept Dent Pub Health, 1999-. **Orgs:** Am Dent Asn; Nat Dent Asn; Am Pub Health Asn; Int Asn Dent Res; Am Asn Dent Res; Am Acad Oral Med; Am Acad Gold Foil Operators; AAAS; Am Asn Dent Schs; Am Asn Med Schs; Tenn Pub Health Asn; Capitol City Dent Soc; Human Rights Comn; Alpha Phi Alpha; St Vincent DePaul Men's Club; Boy Scouts Am; Meharry Century Club; Nashville Area Chamber Com; 50 Critics Orgn; Civitan Int St Vincent DePaul Church Coun. **Honors/Awds:** Numerous awards, honors, and recognitions; numerous manuscripts & publications. **Business Addr:** Professor, Chair, Meharry Med College, Dept Dent Pub Health, 1005 18th Ave N, Nashville, TN 37208.*

MARTIN, JAMES TYRONE
Physician, clergy. **Personal:** Born Aug 17, 1942, Elkhorn, WV; son of Henry. **Educ:** Bluefield St Col, Bluefield, WV, BS, 1966; Meharry Med Col, Nashville TN, MD, 1973. **Career:** Tri-Dist Community Health Serv, med dir; McDowell Col, teacher, 1966-69; Community Health Serv, Raleigh County, Beckley, WV, med dir, 1988-95; Emmanuel Tabernacle Baptist Church, asst pastor, 1965-88, pastor, 1992-; Pvt Pract, physician, currently. **Orgs:** Beta Kappa Chi Hon Sci Fraternity; F&AAY; Royal Arch Masons; Am Acad Family Physicians; WVa Acad Family Physicians. **Military Serv:** AUS, major, 1980-88; Army Serv Medal, 1980; Army Commendation Medal, 1986; Army Achievement Medal, 1988. **Home Addr:** 211 Leon Sullivan Way, Charleston, WV 25301. **Business Addr:** Physician, 211 Leon Sullivan Way, Charleston, WV 25301, **Business Phone:** (304)252-8551.*

MARTIN, JANICE R.
Judge. **Personal:** Married Paul Porter; children: 2. **Educ:** Univ Louisville, BA, polit sci, 1977; Univ Louisville Law Sch, JD, 1980. **Career:** Univ Louisville, instr; Pvt pract, atty; Jefferson County Atty's Office, Juvenile Div, Jefferson Dist Ct, judge, 1992-. **Orgs:** Women's Lawyers Assn; bd mem, Lousiville Bar Assn; bd mem, Jewish Hosp; bd mem, NAWJ; bd mem, Ky Bar Assn. **Honors/Awds:** Distinguished Law School Alumni Award, 1992; Continuing Legal Education Award, 1994, 1996; Kentucky

Women's Leadership Class, 1994; Order of Merit, Univ Louisville Alumni Assn, 1997; Jeff Co Office for Women Hall of Fame, 1999; Trailblazer Award, Louisville Bar Assn 2002; Most Admired Woman, Today's Woman Magazine 2004; Mary K Bonsteel Award Gender Equity Award, 2006. **Special Achievements:** First African American female to serve on the Judiciary in the Common wealth of Kentucky. **Business Addr:** Judge, Jefferson District Court, 600 W Jefferson St, Louisville, KY 40202, **Business Phone:** (502)595-4999.

MARTIN, JESSE LAMONT
Actor. **Personal:** Born Jan 18, 1969, Rocky Mountain, VA; son of Virginia Price and Jesse Reed Watkins. **Educ:** NY Univ, theatre. **Career:** Actor; Stage: Rent, original cast, 1996; TV series: New York Undercover, 1992; 413 Hope St, 1997; Ally McBeal, 1997; The X-Files, 1999; Law & Order, 1999-2008; Deep in My Heart, 1999; A Christmas Carol, 2004; Films: Restaurant, 1998; Burning House of Love, 2002; Season of Youth, 2003; Rent, 2005; The CORPS, 2007; The Cake Eaters, 2007. **Orgs:** John Houseman's The Acting Co; The Robinhood Found. **Honors/Awds:** Obie Award, Best Ensemble, Rent; Critics Choice Award, 2008. **Business Addr:** Actor, Law & Order Production Office, W 23rd St & Hudson River Pier 62, New York, NY 10011.

MARTIN, DR. JOANNE MITCHELL
Educator. **Personal:** Born Jun 12, 1947, Yulee, FL; daughter of Jeremiah Mitchell and Bessie Russell Mitchell; married Elmer P, Jul 29, 1972 (deceased). **Educ:** Fla Agri & Mech, Tallahassee, FL, BA, french, 1969; Atlanta Univ, Atlanta, GA, MA, french, 1971; Case Western Reserve Univ, Cleveland OH, MA, reading, 1976; Howard Univ, Wash DC, PhD, Educ Psych, 1985. **Career:** Nassau County Bd Educ, Fernandina Beach, FL, teacher, 1969-70; Coppin State Col, Baltimore MD, dir & coordr, learning skills ctr, 1977-92; Nat Great Blacks Wax Mus, exec dir, founder & chief exec officer, 1983-. **Orgs:** Bd dir, Great Blacks Wax Mus, 1985-; African Am Heritage Tour Asn, 1987-. **Honors/Awds:** Teacher of the Year, Coppin State Coll, 1984; Community Service Award, Lambda Kappa Mu Sorority; Distinguished Black Women Award; Nat Asn of Negro Women Business & Professional Club Award; Delta Sigma Theta Community Service Award. **Special Achievements:** Co-auth four books: The Black Extended Family, Univ of Chicago Press, 1978; The Helping Tradition in the Black Family & Community; The Black Woman: Perspectives on Her Role in the Family in Ethnicity & Women, Univ of Wisconsin, 1986; The Effects of a Cooperative, Competitive & Combination Goal Structure on the Math Performance of Black Children from Extended Families, 1985; "Social Work & the Black Experience," National Asn Social Workers Press, 1996. **Business Addr:** Co-Founder & President, Chief Executive Officer, The National Great Blacks In Wax Museum, 1601 03 E N Ave, Baltimore, MD 21213, **Business Phone:** (410)563-7809.

MARTIN, JOSHUA WESLEY
Judge, president (organization), executive. **Personal:** Born Sep 14, 1944, Columbia, SC; son of Joshua W Jr and Bernice Baxter; married Lloyd E Overton; children: Victoria & Alexis. **Educ:** Case Inst Tech, BS, 1966; Drexel Univ, 1973; Rutgers Univ Sch Law, JD, 1974; Wharton Sch Exec Develop Prog. **Career:** EI DuPont De Nemours & Co, sr physicist, 1966-71; Hercules Inc, sr patent atty, 1974-82; DE Pub Serv Comm, chmn, 1978-82; Del Law Sch, adj prof, 1988-89; Wilmington Col, adj prof, 1984-89; Bell Atlantic, DE, vpres, gen coun & secy, 1990-96; Verizon, DE, pres & chief exec officer, 1996-2005; Potter Anderson & Corroon LLP, partner & diversity comt chair, currently; dir, PNC Bank, DE, currently; dir, Nuclear Electric Insurance Ltd, currently; dir, Southwest Power Pool Inc, currently; trustee & dir, Christiana Care Corp, curently. **Orgs:** Del Bar Asn, 1975-, pres; Nat Bar Asn, 1975-; Philadelphia Patent Law Asn, 1976-82; trustee, Goldey Beacom Col, 1982-; Better Bus Bur Del, 1978-82; adv comn, Univ Del Legal Asst Prog, 1982; chmn, Wilmington Renaissance Corp; chmn, United Way Del; trustee, Del Community Found; trustee, Wilmington Friends Sch; New Castle County Vo-Tech Sch Bd; chmn, YMCA Black Achievers Prog; trustee, Del Community Found, 1988-; fel Am Bar Found; trustee, Case Western Reserve Univ; trustee, Winterthur Mus; life trustee, Goldey Beacom Col. **Honors/Awds:** Community Service Award, Rutgers Univ-Camden, BLSU Camden, NJ, 1974; Alpha Man of the Year, Alphi Phi Alpha Frat Wilmington, DE, 1978; Citizen of the Year, Omega Psi Phi Frat, Wilmington, DE, 1982; Outstanding Achievement, Sigma Pi Phi, Wilmington, DE, 1983. **Business Addr:** Partner, Potter Anderson & Corroon LLP, Hercules Plz, 1313 N Market St 6th Fl, Wilmington, DE 19801, **Business Phone:** (302)984-6010.

MARTIN, DR. JUANITA K
Psychologist, educator. **Personal:** Born Mar 22, 1955, Mt Vernon, NY; daughter of Willie C Martin and Irene G. **Educ:** Brown Univ, AB, psychol, 1977; Univ Hartford, MEd, 1979; Kent State Univ, PhD, clin psychol, 1990. **Career:** Massilon State Hosp, psychology assist, 1989-88; Univ Akron, Coun Testing & Career Ctr, dir, 1988-; Minority Behav Health. **Orgs:** Western Reserve Girl Scouts, 1997-; African Am Bd YWCA Rape & Sexual Assault Servs, 1997-. **Honors/Awds:** Gardner Award, Univ Akron, 1999. **Special Achievements:** "Thinking Black Thinking Internal, Thinking Feminist", Jour of Coun Psychol, 1992. **Business Addr:** Director, Psychologist, University of Akron, Coun, Testing & Career Ctr, Akron, OH 44301.

MARTIN, KEVIN
Aeronautical engineer. **Personal:** Born in Sylmar, CA; son of Juanita Roberson Acker; children: Kameron. **Career:** JMR Electronics, qual control supvr, currently. **Business Addr:** Quality Control Supervisor, JMR Electronics, 20400 Plummer St, Chatsworth, CA 91311, **Business Phone:** (818)993-4801.

MARTIN, KIMBERLY LYNETTE
Activist, college administrator. **Personal:** Born Sep 5, 1963, Detroit, MI; daughter of Eldon and Linda. **Educ:** Univ Mich, BA, mkg mgt, 1985; Atlanta Univ, MBA, mkg/info systs, 1988; Wayne State Univ, PhD, higher educ. **Career:** Highland Park Bd Educ, adult educ instr, 1990-; Wayne State Univ, comm serv dir, 1992-2003; Purdue Univ, asst dean stud community engagement & involvement, 2003-. **Orgs:** Grad adv, Alpha Kappa Alpha Sorority Inc, 1982-84; Univ Mich Alumni Asn, 1985-; Nat Black MBA Asn, 1986-; Atlanta Univ Alumni Asn, 1988-; Am Asn Univ Prof, 1992-; Nat Asn Student Personnel Adminr. **Honors/Awds:** Nominee, State Community Service Award, State Mich Gov's Off, 1993; Outstanding Contributor Award, Wayne State Univ, 1994; Outstanding Graduate Advisor for Great Lakes Region, Alpha Kappa Alpha Sorority, Inc, 1994; Distinguished Service Award, Wayne State Univ; Ron Fausnaugh Faculty Fellow Award, Purdue Univ. **Business Addr:** Assistant dean, Purdue University, Community engagement and involvement, Stewart Center Rm G4, West Lafayette, IN 47907, **Business Phone:** (765)496-2450.

MARTIN, DR. REV. LAWRENCE RAYMOND
Clergy, president (organization), teacher. **Personal:** Born Sep 4, 1935, Archie, LA; married Barbara Thompson; children: Lawrence II, Perry & Chantel. **Educ:** Grambling State Univ, BS, 1959; United Theol Sem, BTh, 1973; Interdenom Theol Ctr & Morehouse Sch Relig, MDiv, 1973. **Career:** Tenth Dist Asn, bible instr, 1970-; Monroe City Edu Asn, pres, 1971-; Nat Asn Adv Colored People, Monroe, LA, pres, 1973-74; Trenton Baptist Church, pastor, currently; Union Theol Sem, instr, currently; Am Baptist Exten Classes, teacher. **Orgs:** Monroe City Educ Asn; La Educ Asn; Nat Educ Asn; La Baptist Conv; Nat Baptist Conv Inc; La Bicentennial Comn; bd mem, Drug Abuse & Alcoholism Co, Gov Edwin Edwards. **Business Addr:** Pastor, Trenton Baptist Church, 2117 Cypress St, West Monroe, LA 71291, **Business Phone:** (318)325-8840.

MARTIN, LEE
Educator. **Personal:** Born Aug 4, 1938, Birmingham, AL; married Nora White; children: Lee Jr, Kristi & Dia. **Educ:** Eastern Mich Univ, BS, 1963, MA, 1965; Univ MI, PhD. **Career:** Univ Detroit, instr, 1973-74; Romulus Sch, dir, 1974-; Metro Learning & Mental Health Clin, co-dir, 1974-; Detroit Pub Schs, Stud Support Serv, exec dir, 2000. **Orgs:** Task Force 1977; MI Dept Mental Health, 1976; Coun Exceptional C, 1975-; MI Soc Mental Health, 1976-; mgt bd, Western Wayne County, YMCA; trustee, Peoples Comt, 1975; bd dir, NW Guidance Clin, 1975-; trustee, Inkster Sch Bd, 1973-; pres, Annapolis Park Home owner's Asn, 1965-67; aiding fel-minorities, MI Asn Retarded Citizens. **Honors/Awds:** Achvmt Spec Educ. **Business Addr:** 36540 Grant Rd, Romulus, MI 48174.

MARTIN, LEROY
Government official. **Personal:** Born Jan 29, 1929, Chicago, IL; son of Henry Lee and Lela Burts; married Constance Bertha Martin, Jun 20, 1954; children: Ronald, LeRoy, Dawn. **Educ:** Northwestern Univ, Chicago, IL, police supv, 1965; Univ Ill, police supv, 1968; Roosevelt Univ, Chicago, IL, BA, psychol, 1972, collective bargaining & personnel admin, 1975, MPA, 1976; Ill State Police Acad, dimensional mgt II, 1986. **Career:** Chicago Police Dept, patrolman, 1955-64, sergeant, vice control & gambling, 1965-67, sergeant, internal affairs, 1967-70, patrol sergeant, 1970-71, supv sergeant, 1971-75, lt, 1975, inspector, 1976-79, comdr, 1979-81, capt, 1981, dir pub & internal info, 1981-82, comdr detectives, 1982-83, dep chief patrol, 1983-87, supt police, 1987-92; State Ill, chief police cent mgt serv, 1994-. **Orgs:** Nat Orgn Black Law Enforcement Exec; adv bd, Ill Criminal Justice Info Authority, 1988; adv bd, YMCA, 1989-; chmn adv bd, Chicago City-Wide Cols, 1990-; adv bd mem, Boy Scouts Am, Chicago Chapter, 1989-; Nat Asn Juv Officers; Roosevelt Univ Alumni Asn; United Negro Col Fund; Ill Police Asn; Int Asn Chiefs Police; Northwestern Traffic Inst; Chicago Asn Com & Indust; Major City Chiefs; Nat Exec Inst; Salvation Army; Chicago Cluster Initiative; trustee, Chicago Clergy Asn; Abraham Lincoln Ctr; Guardian Police Asn. **Honors/Awds:** Distinguished Service Award, Chicago Asn Com & Indust, 1990; Outstanding Contribution to the Law Enforcement; Recognition Award for Support & Assistance, Chicago Housing Authority, 1990; City of Chicago Recognition Award, Mayor Richard Daley, 1990; We Care Role Model, Chicago Bd Educ, 1986, 1987, 1988, 1989, 1990; Law Enforcement Man of the Year, Chicago Area Coun, Boy Scouts Am, 1988. **Special Achievements:** Author, "Chicago Drug Enforcement Administration Task Force," Int Asn of Chiefs of Police Mag, 1984. Featured in the Int Asn of Chiefs of Police magazine for his work on the Chicago Drug Enforcement Task Force. Pofiled in Law Enforcement News and N'digo magazines. **Business Addr:** Chief of Police, State Ill, Central Management Services, Chicago, IL 60653-1020.*

MARTIN, MAXINE SMITH
School administrator. **Personal:** Born Aug 9, 1944, Charleston, SC; daughter of Emily Simmons and Henry W; married Montez C Jr, Mar 8, 1974; children: Emily Elise & Montez C III. **Educ:** Hampton Inst Hampton, VA, BS, 1966; Atlanta Univ, MA, 1973. **Career:** School administrator(retired); Suppl Educ Ctr, pub specialist, 1970-71; Atlanta Univ, pub rels asst, 1971-72; Morehouse Col, fedn rels coord, 1972-73; Col Charleston, pub info specialist, 1973-79, dir col rels, 1979-80; Charleston Co Sch Dist & Trident Tech Col, eng instr, 1980-85; Col Charleston, stud prog coord & advisor, Ctr Continuing Educ, 1985-; Charleston Co Sch Dist, reading consult, 1988-89; Trident Urban League Inc, dir, pres & ceo, 1998. **Orgs:** Charleston Chap Hampton, Univ Alumni Asn, 1966-; Delta Sigma Theta Sorority, 1969-; YWCA, 1971-; Coun Advan & Support Educ, 1973-80; Col News Asn, 1973-80; comn chmn, SC Chap Links Inc, 1974-; bd mem, Charleston Area Ment Health Asn, 1976-80; Univ & Col Designers, 1977-80; bd mem-,Charleston Civic Ballet, 1983-85; Florence Crittenton Home, 1983-85, SC Asn Higher Continuing Educ, 1985-; bd dirs, Young Charleston Theatre Co,1988-. **Honors/Awds:** Certificate for Public Relations Service, Delta Sigma Theta, 1975; Certificate for Public Relations Service, YWCA, 1975; Certificate for Public Relations Service, Am Freedom Train Found, 1977; Public Relations Award, YWCA, 1984; Twin Women Award, YWCA, 1985; Radio Community Service Award, WPAL, 1986.

MARTIN, DR. MCKINLEY C.
School administrator. **Personal:** Born Dec 2, 1936, Clarksdale, MS; married Willie Beatrice Burns; children: McKinley C II, Myron Craig & Marcia Corteze. **Educ:** Coahoma Jr Col, AA, magna cum laude; Jackson State Univ, BS, cum laude, 1961; Delta State Univ, ME, 1967; Fla State Univ, PhD, summa cum laude, 1972. **Career:** Sandy Bayou Elem Sch, prin, 1962-65; Coahoma Jr Col, registr, 1965-66; FlaState Univ, instr, admin asst, 1970-72; Coahoma Jr Col, dir continuing educ, 1973-80, pres, 1980-92; Northside High Sch, counsr; LeMoyne-OwenColl, Memphis, TN, prof, Grad Div, asst to the pres & dean. **Orgs:** Exec bd mem, Coahoma City Chamber Com; planning com, Gov's Office Job Develop & Training; spec steering comg, US Dept Interior Historically Black Col & Univ; state chmn, Child Develop Asn, Delta Agency Progress; Coahoma County Port Community; Prince Hall Mason; Alpha Phi Alpha Fraternity; planning comn, US Dept Educ, Off Student Fin Assistance; US Dept Interior's Nat Parks Servs; Coahoma Co Comt Lower MS Delta Develop Act; bd dir, Leadership Clarksdale; MS Jr & Community Col Econ Coun; vpres, MS Asn Community & Jr Col; vice chmn, MS Asn Community & Junior Col Legis Comm; M Univ MS Minority Adv Bd; Black Bus Asn Memphis; pres, MS Asn Community & Jr Col; pres, guidance div, TN Vocational Asn. **Honors/Awds:** Citizen of the Year, Clarksdale Coahoma Co, 1990. **Military Serv:** AUS, 1955-58.

MARTIN, MONTEZ CORNELIUS
Government official, construction engineer. **Personal:** Born Jun 11, 1940, Columbia, SC; married E Maxine Smith; children: Tanya Elayne, Terrie Lanita, Emily Elise & Montez Cornelius III. **Educ:** Hampton Inst, BS, 1963; Polytech Inst Brooklyn, grad studies, 1967. **Career:** WSB-TV, acct exec, 1970; WSOK Radio, dir opers, 1973-74; Col Charleston, dir construct, 1974-80; Montez Real Estate, broker-in-charge 1976-92; Charleston County Housing & Redevelop Authority, exec dir, vpres, 1992-. **Orgs:** SC Chap Nat Asn Real Estate Brokers, 1977-; Greater Charleston Bd Realtors, 1979-; pres, Charleston Citywide Local Develop Corp; Nat Asn Community Col Trustees; pres, SC Asn Tech Col Comnr; chmn, Trident Tech Col, Area Comn; dir, SC Coun Econ Ed; bus ed subcomt, SC Comt Excellence Ed; City Charleston Hqs Comt; Trident Urban League Formation Comt; Leadership SC Alumni Asn. **Honors/Awds:** Marketeer of the Year, Atlanta Chap Nat Asn Market Developers 1972; Certificate, Am Freedom Train Found 1977; Certificate of Achievement, Beta Kappa Lambda Chap Alpha Phi Alpha Frat Inc 1978; Living the Legacy Award, Columbia Sect Nat Coun Negro Women, 1980; Leadership SC, Class of 1982; Community Involvement Award, Charleston Bus & Prof Asn, 1985. **Special Achievements:** Business Education Partnerships, South Carolina Business Journal, South Carolina Chamber of Commerce, 1989; Contributing editor, The Business Roundtable Participation Guide: A Primer for Business on Education, 1990. **Military Serv:** AUS, major, 1963-70; Presidental Unit Citation, 1967; Army Commendation w/Oak Leaf Cluster, 1967, 1969; Meritorious Service Medal, 1970. **Business Addr:** Executive Director, Vice President, Charleston County Housing & Redevelopment Authority, 2106 Mt Pleasant St, Charleston, SC 29403, **Business Phone:** (843)722-1942.

MARTIN, MYRON C
Consultant. **Personal:** Born Oct 4, 1969, Clarksdale, MS; son of McKinley C Sr and Willie B. **Educ:** Coahoma Community Col, AA, 1989; Univ Va, BS, 1991. **Career:** Coopers & Lybrand LLC, assoc, 1991-95; Price Waterhouse LLP, sr consult, 1995-97; Perot Systems Inc, sr consult, 1997-. **Orgs:** Victory Apostolic Church, Chicago Heights, IL; Country Club Hills Youth Baseball, Country Club Hills, IL. **Home Addr:** 22382 Karlov Ave, Richton Park, IL 60471. **Business Addr:** Senior Consultant, Perot Systems Inc, 370 Southpointe Blvd, Pittsburgh, PA 15317, **Business Phone:** (724)514-5000.

MARTIN, PATRICIA ELIZABETH
Law enforcement officer. **Personal:** Born May 29, 1951, Brooklyn, NY; daughter of Malverse Sr and Helen Elizabeth

Smith; children: Linese Antoinette Martin. **Educ:** NY Community Col, Brooklyn, AAS, nursing, 1972; City Col, NY, BS, nursing, 1990; NY City Technical Col, AAS hospitality, 1995, BTech, hospitality mgt, 2000. **Career:** St Vincent's Hosp, NY, regist nurse, 1973-81; NY City Police Dept, NY, sgt, 1981-91; lt, 1991-. **Orgs:** Guardians Asn, 1982-; Nat Org Black Law Enforcement Exec, 1989-; Police Women Endowment, 1984-; NOBLWE, 1985-; Int Asn Women Police, 1986-; St George Asn, 1987; church usher, Bentel Tabernacle Am Church; Northeast Asn Women Police, 1988; usher, Bridge St AWME Church. **Honors/Awds:** Centurion Found Award, 2000. **Home Addr:** 204-04 45th Rd, Bayside, NY 11361. **Business Addr:** Lieutenant, Employee Relation Section, 127 Utica Ave, Brooklyn, NY 11213, **Business Phone:** (718)735-0616.

MARTIN, DR. PATRICK M
Research scientist. **Educ:** Univ Va, PhD, cell biol. **Career:** Univ Va, Dept Path, res scientist, postdoctoral fel, currently. **Honors/Awds:** UNCF/Merck Award, 2004. **Business Addr:** Postdoctoral Fellow, University of Virginia, Department of Pathology, PO Box 800904, Charlottesville, VA 22908-0214, **Business Phone:** (434)924-1946.*

MARTIN, PAUL W.
Dentist. **Personal:** Born Dec 4, 1940, Columbus, OH; son of Emmeal and Pauline Locke; married Barbara Burts, Jun 30, 1973; children: Todd Christopher Emmeal. **Educ:** Ind Univ Sch Dent, BS, DDS, 1962. **Career:** Ind State Teachers Col, 1955-58; Ind Univ Sch Dent, instr, 1965-69; Harlem Hosp, oral surg residency, 1969-72; Prison Health Serv, dir, 1973-75; Hostos Community Col, asst prof, 1975-76; pvt pract, oral surg, 1976; NY Univ Col Dent, 1978; Govt Hosp, staff oral surg; 223 W 80th St Corp, pres, 1983-; N Gen Hosp, actg chief oral surg, 1985; Harlem Hosp Ctr, attend surgery, 1986-; Mt Sinai Sch Med, clinical instr, 1986-; attend oral surg, dir clinics, 1998-. **Orgs:** Am Dent Asn, 1962-; Frontiers Int, 1963-; Nat Dent Asn, 1963-; co-founder & mem exec comt, Nat Dent Acupuncture Soc, 1984-; Am Col Oral & Maxillofacial Surgeons, 1989-; Nat Soc Oral & Maxillofacial Surgeons, 1990-; Int Soc Plastic Aesthetic & Reconstructive Surgery, 1990-; Am Acad Pediat Dent. **Honors/Awds:** Fel, Royal Soc Health, 1962; Topical Antibiotic Maintenance Oral Health, 1968; Supraorbital Emphysema, 1972; Phencyclidine PCP Abuse, 1986; Crack Abuse, 1987; Fel, Am Col Dentists, 1990; Fel, Am Col Acupuncture, 1991. **Military Serv:** USNR, lt, 1963-69. *

MARTIN, RALPH C
Government official, lawyer. **Educ:** Brandeis Univ, BA, 1974; Northeastern Univ Sch Law, JD, 1978. **Career:** Chief law enforcement officer, 1992-2002; Suffolk County, dist atty, 1992-2002; Bingham Consult Group, managing prin, currently; Bingham McCutchen LLP, partner, currently. **Orgs:** Nat Bar Asn; life mem, Mass Black Lawyers Asn; Boston Bar Asn; Mass Bar Asn; trustee, Boston Children's Hosp, 1994?2004; chmn, Judicial Nominating Comt, 2003?05; Greater Boston Chamber Com, dir & vice chair, 2002?06; Greater Boston Chamber Com, chmn, 2006?. **Honors/Awds:** Hon doctorate, New Eng Sch Law, 1994; Brandeis University Alumni Achievement Award, 1996; Outstanding Alumni Award in Public Service, Northeastern Univ Alumni Asn, 1997; Anti-Defamation League's Civil Rights Award, 1998; President's Award of Excellence, Nat Black Prosecutors Asn, 2000; Pro Bono Award for "Prosecutor of the Year", Mass Bar Asn, 2002; hon doctorates, Northeastern Univ, 2003; Selected as one of the 35 most influential judges and lawyers of the past 35 years, Mass Lawyers Weekly; Massachusetts Super Lawyer, Boston mag, 2005 & 2006. **Special Achievements:** First African American district attorney named to Suffolk County. **Business Phone:** (617)951-8844.

MARTIN, RAYFUS
Educator, politician. **Personal:** Born Jan 12, 1930, Franklinton, LA; married Elnora Lowe; children: Mechelle Denise. **Educ:** Leland Col, BA 1956; Southern Univ, attended 1973; S eastern La Univ, MEd 1974. **Career:** Educator, politician (retired); St Tammary High Sch, teacher, eng, 1957; Wash Parish High Sch, hist teacher, 1962-90; Franklinton High Sch, eng teacher, 1969-90; Franklinton County, city council man, 1975-96. **Orgs:** Bd dir, Good Samaritan Living Ctr. **Honors/Awds:** Received a Plaque, Mayor of Franklinton for having served on the Council for 20 Years, 1996. **Special Achievements:** Poems: A Readers Creed, 1995; Twenty Frogs, 1995; First African American council member Town of Franklinton in 1975. **Military Serv:** AUS, corpl 1951-54. **Home Addr:** 2020 Williams St, Franklinton, LA 70438. *

MARTIN, REDDRICK LINWOOD
Real estate agent. **Personal:** Born Jul 20, 1934, Anderson, SC; son of Reddrick B and Mamie Lee; married Ernestine Heath. **Educ:** Allen Univ, BS, 1962. **Career:** Winnsboro SC Pub Schs, teacher, 1962-63; Lancaster SC Pub Schs, teacher, 1963; Columbia Coca-Cola Bottling Co, Columbia SC, sales & Mkt rep, 1963-73; Miami Coca-Cola Bottling Co, reg mkt mgr, 1973-76; Coca Cola USA,area mkt mgr, 1976-82, market develop mgr 1982-83; Martin Real Estate Invest Co, pres, currently; real estate agent, 1989-. **Orgs:** Palmetta Bus Asn, 1970-73; OIC Columbia, SC, 1972-73; adv, Bus Dept Ft Valley State Col, 1980; Indust Cluster A&T State Univ, 1980; Nat Asn Advan Colored People; Urban League; Nat Asn Mkt. **Honors/Awds:** Outstanding Serv Award Community Affairs, Save Our Community Club Columbia, SC 1970; Meritorious Service Award, S Reg Press Inst Savannah State Col, 1980; Community Service Award, Richmond Perrine Optimist Club, 1974; Serv Award, MEAC Conf, 1981; Service Award, Business Department, Ft Valley State Col, 1987. **Military Serv:** USAF, airman first class, 1954-57. **Home Addr:** 1123 Braemar Ave SW, Atlanta, GA 30311, **Home Phone:** (404)696-0069. **Business Addr:** President, Martin Real Estate Investment Company, 1123 Braemar Ave SW, Atlanta, GA 30311, **Business Phone:** (404)696-0069.

MARTIN, DR. RICHARD CORNISH
Clergy. **Personal:** Born Oct 15, 1936, Philadelphia, PA; son of Leon Freeman and Virginia Lorette Bullock. **Educ:** Pennsylvania State Univ, BA Sci, 1958; Episcopal Theol Sem VA, MDiv, 1961; St Augustine's Col, Canterbury; Howard Univ, Wash DC, DMin, 1988. **Career:** Penn State Univ, chaplain, 1961-64; St Andrew's Church State Col, PA, assoc rector 1961-64; George Wash Univ, Wash DC, chaplain, 1964-66; St Paul's Parish, Wash DC, assoc rector, 1966-73, rector, 1989-96; St George's Parish, Wash DC, rector, 1973-89; The Church Advent, interim rector, 1996-99; St. Mark's Church, interim rector, 2000-01; Grace Church, interim rector, 2001. **Orgs:** Superior Soc Mary Am Region, 1966-; pres, Prev Blindness Soc, 1982-84; Studia Liturgica; dir, Community Outreach Ministry; Inter-Church Club; bd, Hospice DC; chair, Ams Friends Anglican Ctr Rome; Anglican Int Liturgical Consult; bd trustees, Nashotah House Seminary; founder, Anglo-Catholic Rectors, coordr; Soc Holy Cross; bd, Guild All Souls. **Special Achievements:** Editor Studies & Commentaries I & IV; editor The Dragon; composer Liturgical Music; Venerable Order of St John. **Home Addr:** 2926 Saint Paul St, Baltimore, MD 21218.

MARTIN, ROBERT E. (BOB MARTIN)
Television journalist, television producer, educator. **Personal:** Born Dec 17, 1948, Bronx, NY; son of Robert and Mary; divorced; children: LeRonne. **Educ:** RCA Inst, 1973. **Career:** WABC-TV, assoc producer, 1971-72; Capital Formation Inc, dir commun, 1972-75; WNEW-TV, producer, 1976-83; WNBC-TV, producer, 1983-88; Fox-TV, reporter & producer, "A Current Affair", 1988-93; MSNBC, currently; Unified Force Zujitsu-Ryu Martial Arts, founder & chief instr, currently. **Orgs:** Writers Guild Am E; Coun Concerned Black Exec; YMCA; dir, Male Echoes 1stUnion Bapt Church; Am Fedn TV & Radio Artists; NYAJB; Nat Asn Black Journalists; Am Chi Kung Int Asn; founding mem, Zujitsu Fedn. **Honors/Awds:** Emmy Award, 1972; Special Award, NY Jaycees, 1973; Service Award, Salvation Army, 1977; CEBA Award, 1988; World Karate Union Hall of Fame Master Instructor Zujitsu-Ryu, 2003; Outstanding Contributions to the Martial Arts, Action Martial Arts Mag, 2004; Legends Champion Martial Arts Hall of Fame Master of the Year, 2004; WKU Hall of Fame Golden Lifetime Achievement, 2005. **Special Achievements:** Has conducted Women's Self Defense/Self Protection Seminars for major corporations including NBC, Pain Webber, CNBC, MSNBC and Reed Travel Group; inducted by the World Head of Family Sokeship Council Hall of Fame Millennium Master Instructor, 2000. **Military Serv:** AUS, sgt-E5, 1969-71. **Home Addr:** 1 Pegasus Pl, Hackettstown, NJ 07840, **Home Phone:** (908)850-9289. *

MARTIN, DR. ROSALEE RUTH
Educator. **Personal:** Born Mar 10, 1944, New York, NY; daughter of Lucille; children: Deshon, Tishana & Yvette. **Educ:** Univ TX El Paso, BA, 1967; Univ TX Austin, MSSW, 1970, PhD, 1979. **Career:** Meridell Achievement Ctr, social worker & adminr, 1969-73; Mental Health-Mental Retardation, caseworker, 1981-88; Huston-Tillotson Univ, Sociol Dept, prof social, 1973, head social sci div; outreach dir proj reach (AIDS Project,) 1988-95; pvt therapist, 1987-; Licensed Chem Dependency, counr, 1993-. **Orgs:** Social work cert State TX, 1983-; licensed prof counr, TX Bd Examiner, 1983-; vpres, Black Arts Alliance, 1985-94; teacher, Vocation Bible Sch Belize, Cent Am, 1985, 1986, 1988-95. **Honors/Awds:** Leadership Austin Chamber of Commerce 1981; Black Author's Award, l984, Rishon Lodge #l Community Serv Award, l988; H-TC President's Faculty Achievement Award, l989; John Seabrook Professorship in Social Science, l989-; PRO of the Year, 1998; author of book "l Like Myself" (children's book), l977; article, "Feeling Secure in A Single Parent Home," l986; article, "Empowering Black Youths: AIDS Prevention," l989; God's Master Plan, 1993, (poetry); History: Falling Up A Down Escalator, 1997, (poetry); and many other poetry books. **Special Achievements:** Author of book: l Like Myself (children's book), l977; article: "Feeling Secure in A Single Parent Home," l986; "Empowering Black Youths: AIDS Prevention," l989; God's Master Plan, 1993, (poetry); History: Falling Up A Down Escalator, 1997, (poetry); & many other poetry & books. **Home Addr:** 2105 Teakwood Dr, Austin, TX 78757. **Business Addr:** Professor of Sociology, Huston-Tillotson University, 900 Chicon St, Austin, TX 78702-2753, **Business Phone:** (512)505-3000.

MARTIN, ROSETTA P
Librarian. **Personal:** Born Jun 20, 1930, Charleston, SC; daughter of Phoenix Poaches Sr and Della Scott Poaches; married George E. **Educ:** Morgan State Col, BA, 1953; Boston Univ, adv grad work educ, 1957; Simmon Col, MS, 1962. **Career:** Manning HS, teacher, 1954-55; Boston Pub Lib, C librn, 1958-63; Tufts Univ, ref libr, 1970-78, supr curric lab, 1965-, asst ref librn, 1963-70; Trident Tech Col, Main Campus, Charleston, librn, 1978-95. **Orgs:** Am Libr Asn; Spec Libr Asn; New Eng Libr Asn; Am Asn Univ Prs; Librns Educ & Res The NE; NAACP; Civic Asn; Black Bibliographer; Asn Study Negro Life & Hist; S Carolina Libr Asn; Charleston Libr Consortium; Bibliographic Instruction Sect. **Special Achievements:** Author: Inherited Beliefs: Concepts of White Racism-A Subjective Bibliograhical Essay, Dorrance Publishing Co, 2003. **Home Addr:** 851 Bent Hickory Rd, Charleston, SC 29414-9071, **Home Phone:** (843)766-5475. *

MARTIN, RUSSELL F.
Dentist, consultant. **Personal:** Born Aug 18, 1929, Hartford, CT; married Jean E Procope. **Educ:** Howard Univ, BS, 1950, DDS, 1955; Yale Univ, MPH, 1970. **Career:** Pvt Practice Hartford, 1957-68; St Dept Health, oper Mobile Dent Trailer Unit Rural CT, 1957-58; Hartford Dispensary; staff dentist 1958-68; Univ Conn Health Ctr, staff dentist, 1968-69; Univ Conn, Health Ctr, res assoc,1969-70; Health Action Survey, proj dir, 1969-70; City Health Action Coun HEW, proj dir, 1971-72; Health Planning Coun Inc, assoc dir, 1972-74; Pvt Practice; Dept Corrections, staff dentist; Aetna Ins Co, dent cons; Dept Comm Dent Univ Conn, clin assoc, 1974-. **Orgs:** Am Dent Asn; Conn State Dent Asn; Hartford Dent Soc; Am Pub Health Asn; Conn State Pub Health Asn; bd dir, Community Health Serv Inc, Hartford, pres bd; Pub health & welfare comm Urban League Greater Hartford; Sickle-Cell Anemia & Com Bloomfield, CT; adv com Occup Ther, Manchester Community Col; Ambulatory Health Care Coun Inc; chairperson, NW Hartford Health Care Task Force; bd dir Urban League of Greater Hartford; Minority Involvement Higher Educ Com Hew Haven, Ct. **Special Achievements:** Co-author "Health & Health Care in Hartfords N End" 1974. **Military Serv:** AUS, Dent Corps capt, 1955-57.

MARTIN, SHEDRICK M., JR.
Government official, real estate developer. **Personal:** Born Jan 5, 1927, Savannah, GA; son of Shedrick and Hattie Mew; married Laura B Randolph, Jan 10, 1956; children: Beverly Anne & Brenda Annette. **Educ:** Savannah State Col, BS, biol, 1951; FBI Nat Acad, 1970. **Career:** US Postal Serv, Atlanta, GA, railway postal clerk, 1951-52; Chatham Co Bd Educ Savannah, teacher, 1952-57; Savannah GA, Police Dept, detective,1957-70; Savannah, personnel asst training, 1971-72; City Savannah, Savannah, GA, dept pub, serv adminr, 1972, dir code enforcement, 1988-94; spec Dept, US Marshall, city security officer, 1994-; City Savannah, dir code enforcement, currently. **Orgs:** Am Pub Works Asn; Fraternal Order Police; Nat Asn Advan Colored People; Cath Holy Name Soc; Wolves Social Club; Chatham S Lions Club, vpres, 1988-. **Military Serv:** AUS, 1945-46. **Home Addr:** PO Box 60626, Savannah, GA 31420-0626. **Business Addr:** Director of Code Enforcement, City Savannah, PO Box 1027, Savannah, GA 31402, **Business Phone:** (912)651-6579.*

MARTIN, SHIRLEY
Administrator. **Personal:** Born Nov 21, 1948, Kosciusko, MS; daughter of Henry and Leora Beamon; married Wisdom Martin, May 10, 1970; children: Wisdom T & Timothy D. **Educ:** Jackson State Univ, BS, 1973; Miss State Univ, MA, 1993. **Career:** Leake County Schs, eng teacher, 1974-91; Attala County Sch, guidance counr, 1991-92; Miss dept educ, prog supvr, 1992-96, prog specialist, 1996-98, div dir, 1998-. **Orgs:** Awards chmn, Miss Teacher asn, 1980-82; adv, Miss Asn Needy Students, 1998-. **Honors/Awds:** Star Teachers Award, 1979; FFA Award, 1979, 1982, 1983; Star Teacher Award, 1980; Professional Development Award, 1990; Excellence in Leadership Award, 1998. **Business Addr:** Division Director, Mississippi Department of Education, 500 Greymont Bldg Suite H, PO Box 771, Jackson, MS 39205-0771, **Business Phone:** (601)354-7792.

MARTIN, STEVEN ALBERT
Football player. **Personal:** Born May 31, 1974, St Paul, MN; married Catherine; children: Evan & Emanuel. **Educ:** Univ Mo. **Career:** Football player (retired); Indianapolis Colts, defensive tackle, 1996-98; Philadelphia Eagles,1998-99; Kans City Chiefs, 2000; New York Jets, 2001; New England Patriots, 2002; Houston Texans, 2003; Minn Vikings, 2004-05.

MARTIN, SYLVIA COOKE (CLARA SYLVIA COOKE MARTIN)
Government official, manager. **Personal:** Born May 2, 1938, Baltimore, MD; daughter of Emanuel Levi and Clara M Evans; children: Donald E K Martin & Marcia Lauren Martin. **Educ:** Univ Md, Col Park, MD, BA, 1972, MPS, 1978; Univ Va, Charlottesville, VA, cert, 1975; Bowie State Univ, cert, 1987. **Career:** Soc Security Admin, Baltimore, MD, file clerk, 1963-66, health ins analyst, 1966, mgt intern, 1968-70; Soc Security Admin & Health Care Financing Admin, Baltimore, MD, career develop specialist, 1970-78; Bowie State Col, Bowie, MD, instr, 1986-89, lectr; Libr Cong, Wash, DC, chief staff training & develop, 1978-93; self-employed mgt consult, 1979-; Univ Md Baltimore County, McNair Scholar Program Coord, 1994-99; Friends Ellicott City Sch dist, pres & chief exec officer, 2000-. **Orgs:**

Historian, Nat Asn Negro Bus & Prof Women's Clubs, Inc, 1978-89; Md Historical Soc, 1980-89; Oral History Asn, 1984-89; pres, Daniel Murray AFA Culture Asn, 1984-85, 1987-88; historian, AFA Historical & Geneal Soc, 1984-85, parliamentarian, 1985-88, pres, 1988-90; parlimentarian, Nat Pierians Inc, 1985-89, recording secy, 1989-91, 1999-2001, pres, 2001-03; Nat Coun Negro Women; life mem, Nat Am Advan Colored People; life mem, Delta Sigma Theta; Omicron Delta Kappa 1997; Md Geneal Soc, 1980-91; Coalition 100 Black Women, 1999; pres, Am Soc Freedmen's Descendants. **Honors/Awds:** Commissioner's Citation, Soc Security Admin, 1972; DRR's Citation, Health Care Financing Admin, 1978; Distinguished Achievement Award, Conf Minority Pub Adminr, 1980; Distinguished Service Award, 1983; Sojourner Truth Award, Nat Asn Negro Bus & Prof Women's Clubs Inc, 1985; Special Achievement Awards, Libr Cong, 1987 & 1988, Superior Service Award, 1993; Dedication And Leadership Award, ARO Historical & Geneal Soc, 1989; Distinguished MAR AFA, Towson Univ, 2002; Outstanding COT Achievement, Eastern Panhellenic Region, 2002. **Special Achievements:** Author: Another Cook Book, A Family History, 1989; editor, Just For You Cook Book, 1986; developer/designer, AFA history month exhibits; lecturer and public speaker, African-Am genealogy, history and culture. **Home Addr:** 6375 Shadowshape Pl, Columbia, MD 21045. **Business Addr:** President, Chief Executive Officer, Ellicott City Colored School Restoration Project, PO Box 6595, Columbia, MD 21045.

MARTIN, DR. TONY
Educator. **Personal:** Born Feb 21, 1942, Port-of-Spain, Trinidad and Tobago; son of Claude G and Vida B Scope. **Educ:** Hon Soc Grays Inn, Barrister-at-Law, 1965; Univ Hull, Eng, BSc, econs, 1968; Mich State Univ, MA, hist, 1970, PhD, hist, 1973. **Career:** St Marys Col, Trinidad, teacher, 1962-63; Univ Mich Flint, asst prof, 1971-73; Wellesley Col, assoc prof, 1973-79, full prof, prof emer, currently; Brandeirs Univ, visiting prof; Co Col, visiting prof; Univ Minnesota, visiting prof; Brown Univ, visiting prof. **Orgs:** Negro Hist Asn Colo Springs; vpres, Nat Coun Black Studies New Eng, 1984-86; exec bd mem, African Heritage Studies Asn, 1982-88; exec bd, Asn Caribbean Historians; Asn Study Afro-Am Life Hist; Asn Study Classical African Civilizations. **Honors/Awds:** Hon res fel, Univ WI, Trindad, 1986-87; Research Award, Am Philos Soc, 1990; John Henrik Clarke Award, John Henrik Clarke Award, Asn Study Classical African Civilizations, 2000; one of the principal speakers at the First Conference of Intellectuals of Africa and the Diaspora, 2004. **Special Achievements:** Numerous publications including "Race First: The Ideological and Organizational Struggles of Marcus Garvey and the Universal Negro Improvement Association" 1976, Literary Garveyism: Garvey, Black Arts andthe Harlem Renaissance, 1983, African Fundamentalism: A Literary &Cultural Anthology of Garvey's Harlem Renaissance, 1991, Numerous scholarly articles and reviews in such places as the Journal of Negro History, Journal of Caribbean History, Journal of American History, etc,reviewer of proposals for National endowment for the Humanities, Austrian Science Fund; reviewer of submissions to professional journals, expert witness, Congressional hearings, contribution to the reference books,including: Oxford Dictionary of National Bio, Encyclopedia of African-American Business History, Black Women in America: A History Ency. **Business Addr:** Professor Emeritus, Wellesley College, Department Africana Studies, 106 Cent St, Wellesley, MA 02481, **Business Phone:** (781)283-2564.

MARTIN, TONY DERRICK
Football player. **Personal:** Born Sep 5, 1965, Miami, FL. **Educ:** Bishop Col; Mesa Col, MBA. **Career:** Football player (retired); Miami Dolphins, wide receiver, 1990-93; San Diego Chargers, 1994-97; Atlanta Falcons, 1998, 2001; Miami Dolphins,1999-2000. *

MARTIN, WALTER L
Manager. **Personal:** Born Apr 15, 1951, New York, NY; son of Robert and Elizabeth Monterio Brito; married Regina Marvel Montgomery; children: Shalya Mekeela Kelly & Merissa Tarla Mekeshia. **Educ:** Northeastern Univ, BS, 1975; Atlanta Univ, MBA, 1977. **Career:** Pyramidwest Develop Corp, financial analyst & acct, 1979-82; Mobil Chem Co, financial analyst, 1982-83; Fed Express Corp, sr financial analyst, 1983-86, station oper mgt, 1986-. **Orgs:** Dir, Changes Full Arts Prod Co, 1977-82; chmn allocation comt, Youth Servs United Way Atlanta, 1985-; dir, Nat Black MBA Asn Atlanta, 1985-86; dir stud affairs, Nat Black MBA Asn Atlanta, 1987; partner, East Coast mgt Group. **Business Addr:** Station Operations Manager, Federal Express Corp, 2441 Cheshire Bridge Rd, Atlanta, GA 30324.

MARTIN, WANDA C.
Manager. **Personal:** Born Mar 10, 1953, Gratham, NC; daughter of Nathaniel Cogdell; married Louis Martin, Aug 21, 1976; children: David Durand, Louis Demar. **Educ:** NC A&T State Univ, BS, 1975; Univ NC-Chapel Hill, MPH, 1992. **Career:** Manager (retired); Guilford Co, Dept Pub Health, staff nurse, 1975, team leader, 1976, nursing supvr, 1980, health prom & dis prev mgr, 1994. **Orgs:** Community assignments prog, Sigma Theta Tau, Mu-Tau, 1992; exec bd, Nat Asn Advan Colored People, 1999; treas, Guilford County AIDS Partnership Bd. **Honors/Awds:** Service Award, Guilford County, 1981; Volunteer Award, Project Head Start, 1991; Dr Joseph Holiday Scholarship Award, NAPHA, 1992; Outstanding Service, HIV/STD Prev & Care Sect, 1997. *

MARTIN, WAYNE. See Obituaries section.

MARTIN, WAYNE
Football player, real estate executive. **Personal:** Born Oct 26, 1965, Forrest City, AR; married Gladys; children: Wayne Jr, Whitley & Wishawn. **Educ:** Univ Ark, criminal justice, 1990. **Career:** Football player (retired); New Orleans Saints, defensive tackle, 1989-99; Real Estate bus, currently. **Honors/Awds:** Ed Block Courage Award, 1991.

MARTIN, WILLIAM R.
Chemist. **Personal:** Born Dec 19, 1926, Washington, DC; married Mildred Dixon; children: William R jr & Janice Y. **Educ:** Morgan St Col, BS, 1951; Southeastern Pa Univ, MBA, 1976. **Career:** NIH, biologist, 1952-55; Walter Reed Ins, res biochem, 1955-60; NIMH res, neurochemist, 1960-62; Howard Univ, res proj, 1962-63; Food & Drug Admin, chemist drug mfg controls, 1963-. **Orgs:** Am Soc Qual Control 1972-; Plymouth Cong United Church Christ; Bowie St Col; Prince George Co; Nat Asn Advan Colored People, 1979; Chillum-ray Citizens Asn; Morgan St Univ Nat Alumni Asn; DC Metro Chap, Nat Conf Community & Justice; Org Black Sci; Omega Psi Phi Frat. **Military Serv:** USN, 1944-46. **Business Addr:** 5600 Fishers Lane, Rockville, MD 20852.*

MARTIN, WISDOM T
Television journalist, television news anchorperson. **Personal:** Born Sep 25, 1970, Kosciusko, MS; son of Wisdom D, Sr and Shirley; married Monifa Alexander; children: Anaya Martin. **Educ:** Jackson State Univ, BA, broadcast jour, 1993. **Career:** WAPT TV News, photorapher & reporter, 1991-95; KNDO TV News, reporter & sports anchor, 1995-97; KSEE TV News, reporter, 1997-98; WRAL TV News, reporter, 1998-99; CNN, anchor & reporter, 1999; WKRN News, anchor & reporter, 1999-2002; WTTG TV News, gen assignment reporter, tv news anchor & reporter, currently. **Orgs:** Lake Providence Baptist Ch. **Honors/Awds:** Outstanding Reporting, TN State Univ Nat Asn Broadcastors, 2001; School Bell Award, Tenn Edu Asn, 2001; Kenya Hale Communication Award, Nat Broadcasting Soc, 2001; Outstanding Journalism. **Business Addr:** TV News Reporter, Anchor, WTTG Fox 5 News, 5151 Wisconsin Ave NW, Washington, DC 20016, **Business Phone:** (202)895-3000.

MARTIN CHASE, DEBRA
Executive, television producer. **Personal:** Born Oct 11, 1956, Greater Lakes, IL; daughter of Robert Douglas and Beverly M Barber; married Anthony (divorced). **Educ:** Mount Holyoke Col, AB, 1977; Harvard Law Sch, JD, 1981. **Career:** Butler & Binion, assoc, 1981-82; Mayor, Day & Caldwell, assoc, 1982-83; Tenneco Inc, atty, 1984-85; Columbia Pictures, motion picture dept, atty; Mundy Lane Entertainment, sr vpres; BrownHouse Productions, exec vpres, producing partner, 2000-; TV Series: Cinderella, 1997; The Cheetah Girls, 2003; "1-800-Missing", 2006; The Cheetah Girls 2, 2006; The Cheetah Girls: One World, 2008; Films: Hank Aaron: Chasing the Dream, 1995; Courage Under Fire, 1996; The Preacher's Wife, 1996; Cinderella, 1997; The Princess Diaries, 2001; The Princess Diaries 2: Royal Engagement, 2004; The Sisterhood of the Traveling Pants, 2005. **Honors/Awds:** Peabody Award, 2 Emmy nominations. **Special Achievements:** Produced Devil In A Blue Dress; Courage Under Fire; "Hank Aaron: Chasing The Dream;" The Preacher's Wife; "Rodgers & Hammerstein's Cinderella," 1997. **Business Addr:** Executive Vice President, BrownHouse Productions, 566 Buena Vista St, Burbank, CA 91521-0001, **Business Phone:** (323)650-2670.

MARTINEZ, RALPH
Executive, chief executive officer. **Personal:** Born in New York, NY. **Career:** Town & Country Chrysler-Plymouth Inc, Milwaukie, OR, chief exec officer; Town and country Ford Body Shop, 1985-. **Orgs:** Bd dir, SAIF Corp, 2006-08; mem, Brand Oregon advisory. past vpres, Chrysler Minority Dealership. **Business Phone:** (503)288-5211.

MARTINEZ, RAMON JAIME
Baseball player. **Personal:** Born Mar 22, 1968, Santo Domingo, Dominican Republic. **Career:** Baseball player (retired); Los Angeles Dodgers, pitcher, 1988-98; Boston Red Sox, 1999-2000; Pittsburgh Pirates, 2001. **Honors/Awds:** Dominican Republic Olympic baseball team, 1984; Nat League All-Star Team, 1990; Pitched no-hitter, 1995.

MARTIN-OGUNSOLA, DELLITA LILLIAN
Educator. **Personal:** Born Oct 27, 1946, New Orleans, LA; daughter of Ret Sgt Wellie Martin (deceased) and Wilma M Martin (deceased); married David Olajire, Aug 22, 1979; children: Oludare Ajayi-Martin Ogunsola & Oladimeji Ade-Olu Ogunsola. **Educ:** La State Univ, New Orleans, BA, 1968; Ohio State Univ, MA, 1971, PhD, 1975. **Career:** St Mathias High Sch, instr Span & Fr, 1975-76; Univ Ala-Birmingham, from asst prof spanish to assoc prof Span, 1976-99; prof spanish, 1999-; chair dept foreign lang, 1993-; Univ Ala-Birmingham, African-Am Studies, interim dir. **Orgs:** Mod Lang Asn, 1976-, secy, 1977-78, chair Afro-Am Exec Comt, 1979; Ala Asn Teachers Spanish, 1977-; Col Lang Asn, 1977-, foreign language rep, 1996-98, from vpres to pres, 1998-2002; South Atlantic Mod Lang Asn, 1979-; secy exec subcomt, Ala Humanities Found, 1978-80, chair nominations subcomt, 1979; liaison secy, Asn Caribbean Studies, 1979, 1982-84; Hisp Conf Greater Birmingham, 1984-89; dir, Am Scholars Listings, 1978, 1982. **Honors/Awds:** Ingalls Finalist for Teaching Excellence, Univ Ala Birmingham, 1979-80, 1983, 1989; Honarary Society International Scholars, Phi Beta Delta, Beta Nu Chap, 1992; Honarary Fac Mem, Alpha Lambda Delta, Univ Ala Birmingham, 1992; Fac Rep, Univ Ala Syst, 1994-95; Presidential Award for Excellence in Teaching, 1997. **Special Achievements:** Selected Poems of Langston Hughes and Nicolas Guillen, Doctoral Dissertation, Ohio State Univ, 1975; "West African & Hispanic Elements in NG's La cancion del bongo," South Atlantic Bulletin, 45:1, p 47-63, 1980; "Langston Hughes & the Musico-Poetry of the African Diaspora," in Langston Hughes Review, 5:1, p 1-17, 1986; "Translation as a Poetic Experience/Experiment: Short Fiction of Quince Duncan," Afro-Hispanic Review, 10:3, p 42-50, 1991; Las mejores historias de Quince Duncan/The Best Short Stories of Quince Duncan editorial, San Jose, Costa Rica, 1995; Female Calibans in the Fiction of Quince Duncan, forthcoming; editor, Collected Works of Langston Hughes, vol 14 Translations, Univ of MO Press, forthcoming; Outstanding Faculty-UAB Honors Program, 1998. **Business Addr:** Professor of Spanish, Chair of Department Foreign Language, University of Alabama at Birmingham, 900 S 13th St Arts & Humanities Bldg Rm 407-B, Birmingham, AL 35294-1260, **Business Phone:** (205)934-1834.

MARTS, LONNIE, JR.
Football player, athletic coach. **Personal:** Born Nov 10, 1968, New Orleans, LA; married Gionne; children: Gilone & Lonnie III. **Educ:** Tulane Univ, BA, sociol. **Career:** Football player (retired), Athletic coach: Kansas City Chiefs, linebacker, 1991-93; Tampa Bay Buccaneers, 1994-96; Tennessee Oilers, 1997-98; Jacksonville Jaguars, 1999-2000; Godspeed Sports Performance, owner, founder, coach, currently. **Orgs:** Life Athletes. **Special Achievements:** Radio appearance. **Business Phone:** (190)480-9991.

MARVE, EUGENE RAYMOND
Football player. **Personal:** Born Aug 14, 1960, Flint, MI; children: Robert. **Educ:** Sagina WVAlley State Col. **Career:** Football player (retired); Buffalo Bills, linebacker, 1982-87; Tampa Bay Buccaneers, linebacker, 1988-91; San Diego Chargers, linebacker, 1992. **Honors/Awds:** All-Rookie teams; AP Defensive Rookie-of-the-Year; Most Valuable Player; Man of the Year, Nat Football League, 1984-85.

MARYLAND, MARY ANGELA
Nurse, educator. **Personal:** Born Sep 27, 1953, Cincinnati, OH; daughter of Christine Nero and James Pearl. **Educ:** Elmhurst Col, Elmhurst, Ill, BA, psychol, 1975; Malcolm X Col, Chicago, Ill, AAS, nursing, 1977; Chicago State Univ, Chicago, Ill, BSN, 1980; Govs State Univ, Univ Park, Ill, MSN, nursing admin, 1983. **Career:** Mount Sinai Hosp Med Ctr, Chicago, Ill, staff nurse II, 1977-83; Evangelical Health Systs, Oak Brook, Ill, mgt Engr, 1983-85; City Cols Chicago, Chicago, Ill, nursing fac, 1985-87; Univ Ill Chicago Col Nursing, Chicago, Ill, coord, urban health prog recruiter, admis counr, 1987-90, res asst, 1990; Jackson Park Hosp & Med Ctr, nurses practitioner, currently. **Orgs:** Am Asn Critical Care Nurses, 1980-; Asn Black Nursing Fac, 1988-; People People Int, 1988-; Nominating Comt, Med Surg Nursing, 1989-92, bd dirs, Am Nurses Asn, currently; steering comt, Ill Nurses Asn, 1989-91. **Honors/Awds:** Cert Med Surg Nurse, Am Nurses Asn, 1981-; Outstanding & Dedicated Serv Award, Chicago Pub Schs, 1989; Serv Award, Ill Coun Col Attendance, 1990; Co-Investr, I'm Ready Minority Recruitment Prog, Robert Wood Johnson Found, 1990; Prin Investr, HTH Behavior AFA Eighth Graders, Sigma Theta Tau INT, 1992. **Military Serv:** USF Reserve, capt, 1986-. **Home Addr:** 420 Home Ave Apt 307-N, Oak Park, IL 60302-3716. **Business Addr:** Nurses Practitioner, Jackson Park Hospital and Medical Center, 7531 S Stony Island Ave, Chicago, IL 60649, **Business Phone:** (773)947-7500.

MASERU, DR. NOBLE AW
Government official. **Educ:** Wayne State Univ, BS; Emory Univ Sch Med, MPH; Atlanta Univ, PhD. **Career:** Accrediting Comn Health Educ, fel; Clark Atlanta Univ Sch Social Work, fac; Ga Dept Human Resources, state dir, 1986-88; Ga Dept Human Resources, Family Health Section, asst dir; Women Infants & C Suppl Food & Nutrit Prog, dir; Atlanta Pub Schs, coordr, 1990-94; Pub Health Sci Inst, Morehouse Col, acad & pub health policy scientist; Morehouse Sch Med, Master Pub Health Prog, founding dir, 1994; USAID, consult; City Detroit Dept Health & Wellness Prom, dir & health officer, 2003-06; Cincinnati Health Dept, health comnr, 2006-. **Orgs:** Cong Black Caucus Found; African Am Acads Pub Health Progs; vpres, Health Coun, Div Community Health, Greater Detroit Area, 1998-2000; bd trustees, Wayne State Univ; bd mem, St Georges Univ; Grenada West Indies; Detroit Receiving Hosp & Detroit Brownfield Redevelop. **Business Addr:** Health Commissioner, City of Cincinnati, Cincinnati

Health Department, 3101 Burnett Ave Suite 201, Cincinnati, OH 45229, **Business Phone:** (513)357-7281.

MASHBURN, JAMAL
Basketball player, television show host. **Personal:** Born Nov 29, 1972, New York, NY; son of Bobby; married Michelle; children: Taylor. **Educ:** Univ Ky. **Career:** Basketball player (retired), television show host; Dallas Mavericks, forward, 1993-97; Miami Heat, 1997-2000; Charlotte Hornets, 2000-02; New Orleans Hornets, forward, 2002-04; Philadelphia 76ers, forward, 2005-06; ESPN, NBA Fastbreak, host, currently. **Orgs:** Spokesperson, Boys & Girls Club. **Honors/Awds:** Col Player of the Year, Basketball Times, 1993; Player of the Week, NBA, 1994; NBA All-Rookie First Team, 1994. **Business Addr:** Host, ESPN, ESPN Plaza 935 Middle St, Bristol, CT 06010, **Business Phone:** (860)766-2000.

MASK, SUSAN L
School administrator, lawyer. **Personal:** Born in New York, NY; daughter of Joseph C and Eleanor G; married W H Knight, Jun 6, 1981; children: Michael Joseph Mask Knight & Lauren Louise Mask Knight. **Educ:** City Univ NY, BA, 1975; New York Univ, JD, 1978. **Career:** Univ Iowa, Off Affirmative Action, asst pres & dir, currently. **Orgs:** Nat Bar Asn; bd dir, Salvation Army. **Honors/Awds:** Vanderbilt Medal, NY Univ, 1978; State Board of Regents Staff Excellence Awards, Univ Iowa, 2001. **Business Addr:** Assistant to the President, Director, University of Iowa, Office of Affirmative Action, 202 Jessup Hall, Iowa City, IA 52242, **Business Phone:** (319)335-0705.

MASON, ANTHONY
Basketball player. **Personal:** Born Dec 14, 1966, Miami, FL; married Mary; children: Anthony Jr. **Educ:** Tenn State Univ, criminal justice, 1988. **Career:** Basketball player (retired); NJ Nets, 1989-90; Denver Nuggets, 1990; NY Knicks, 1991-96; Tulsa Fast Breakers, CBA, 1990-91; Long Island Surf, 1991; Charlotte Hornets, 1996-2000; Miami Heat, 2000-01; Milwaukee Bucks, forward, 2001-03. **Honors/Awds:** Miller Genuine Draft NBA 6th Man award, 1995.

MASON, DR. CHERYL ANNETTE
Physician. **Personal:** Born Jul 2, 1954, McAlester, OK; daughter of Lucious C Mason III and Helen M Stuart; married Mack Henderson, Feb 14, 1988; children: Alisha Dixon & Samuel Dixon. **Educ:** Univ CA, San Diego, BA, 1977; Howard Univ Col Med, MD, 1981. **Career:** San Pedro & Peninsula Hosp, family pract intern, 1983; Georgetown Univ Hosp, resident Ob-Gyn, 1983-87; The Memorial Hosp Danville, VA, staff physician, 1987-89; Pvt Pract, physician, currently. **Orgs:** Am Bus Women's Asn, 1988-90; Pittsylvania County Med Soc, 1988-; bd mem, Am Cancer Soc.

MASON, CLIFFORD L.
Playwright, writer. **Personal:** Born Mar 5, 1932, Brooklyn, NY; married. **Educ:** BA, 1958. **Career:** Manhattanville Col, teacher; Rutgers Univ, NEH Grant Theatre, resident, 1978; Playwright: Captain At Cricket, 1982; Boxing Day Parade, 1983; Books: When Love Was Not Enough, 1980; The African-American Bookshelf, 2003. **Honors/Awds:** Grant for Playwriting, NEH Grant, 1979. **Special Achievements:** Published article on Black Theatre, NY Times Mag, 1979; penned a remarkable series of essays on the fifty greatest books ever written by and about African-Americans.

MASON, DR. DONNA S.
Educator. **Personal:** Born Jan 15, 1947, Mount Vernon, NY; daughter of Alexander and Olga Spence; married Charles L Mason Sr, Jun 30, 1973; children: Charles L Mason Jr. **Educ:** Howard Univ, BA, 1969, MEd, 1972; Univ Maryland, College Park, AGS, 1975, PhD,1987. **Career:** District Columbia Pub Schs, classroom teacher, bldg resource teacher, comput camp teacher, comput curric writer, comput teacher trainer, comput educ instr/lab cord, 1969-; US Off Educ, Christa McAuliffe fel, 1988,1994; Cafritz Found, teacher fel, 1988; Alice Deal Jr High Sch, comp instr & comp lab cord, currently. **Orgs:** Md Instrnl Comp Cordr Assn; Univ Md Alumni Asn; Int Soc Tech Educ; Spec Interest Group Comp Cords;mem, NCSSM Foundn. **Honors/Awds:** Washington Post Mini-Grant Award, Wash Post, 1986, Agnes Meyer Out standingTeacher Award, 1991; Teacher of the Year for the District of Columbia,IBM/Classroom Comp Learning, 1988; Thanks to Teachers Award, Apple Comput, 1990; Award for Innovative Teaching, Bus Week, 1990; 10 Who Made A Difference Award, Electronic Learning's, Educr Decade, 1991; Professional Best Teacher Excellence Award, Learning Magazine/Oldsmobile, 1991;Distinguished Alumni Award, Univ Md, 1995; Christa McAuliffe Fellowship Grant Award, 1995; Forge Award, Freedom Found Valley, 1995; Goals 2000Competitive Teacher Mini-Grant, 1998; Junior High/Middle Sch Teacher of the Year, Career & Tech Educ, 2001. **Special Achievements:** Auth: "A Teacher's Place To Work and Learn", Teaching & Computers, 1986;"Display Word Processing Terms" The Computing Teacher, 1986; "Ten Computers-One Thousand Students" Sigcc Bulletin for Computing Coordinators, 1987; "Factors that Influence Computer Laboratory Use in Exemplary Junior High/Middle schools in the District of Columbia" UMI's Dissertation Abstracts, 1988; "Multimedia Applications in the Curriculum:Are Schools Preparing Students for the Twenty First Century?" NASSP Curriculum Report, 1997; Intel-ACE master teacher, 1999; Microsoft Office use specialist, 2000. **Business Addr:** Computer Instructor/Lab Coordinator, Alice Deal Junior High School, 3815 Ft Dr NW, Washington, DC 20016, **Business Phone:** (202)282-0100.

MASON, EDDIE LEE
Football player. **Personal:** Born Jan 9, 1972, Siler City, NC. **Educ:** NC State Univ. **Career:** Football Playe (Retired); New York Jets, linebacker, 1995; Jacksonville Jaguars, 1998; Washington Redskins, 1999-2002. **Honors/Awds:** Rookie of the Year, 1995.

MASON, FELICIA LENDONIA
Journalist, writer. **Personal:** Born May 8, 1962, Pittsburgh, PA; daughter of Rev William L Sr and G Bernice. **Educ:** Hampton Inst, BA, 1984; Thomas Nelson Community Col, paralegal course work; Ohio State Univ, MA, 1986; Poynter Inst Media Studies, media mgt fel, 1988. **Career:** Pittsburgh Post Gazette, reporter, 1984-85; Hampton Univ, asst prof, 1986-90; Daily Press, copy ed, 1989-90, assoc ed, 1990-92, asst metro ed, 1992-94, columnist, metro ed, 1994-; United Way, loaned exec, 1991; Novels: Body and Soul, 1995; For the Love of You, 1995; Seduction, 1996; Rhapsody, 1997; Foolish Heart, 1998; Forbidden Heart, 2000; Testimony, 2002; Sweet Accord, 2003; Enchanted Heart, 2004; Sweet Devotion, 2004; Sweet Harmony, 2004; Gabriel's Discovery, 2004; Seductive Hearts, 2005; What Ana Mae Left Behind, 2005. **Orgs:** Nat Asn Black Journalists; Romance Writers Am; Chesapeake Romance Writers; Va Romance Writers. **Honors/Awds:** Print Alumni Award, Hampton Univ, 1991; Leadership Award, WICI, 1983; Emma Award; Reviewer's Choice Award, Career Achievement Award, Romantic Times, 1999. **Special Achievements:** Top 10 Romance Writer, Affaire de Coeur, 2002; two best of 2002 listings from Black Issues Book Review; a two-time winner of the Best-Selling Multicultural Title Award from Waldenbooks for Body and Soul and Seduction. **Home Addr:** PO Box 1438, Yorktown, VA 23692. **Business Addr:** Metro Editor, Daily Press Inc, 7505 Warwick Blvd, Newport News, VA 23607, **Business Phone:** (757)247-7860.*

MASON, GILBERT RUTLEDGE
Physician. **Personal:** Born Oct 7, 1928, Jackson, MS; married Natalie Lorraine Hamlar. **Educ:** TN State Univ, BS, 1947; Howard Univ, MD, 1954. **Career:** Homer G Phillips Hosp St Louis, intern, 1954-55; Harrison Co Head Start, med dir, 1969; Biloxi, gen prac med, 1955-. **Orgs:** chmn, USO 1959-60; Scoutmaster BSA, 1959-72; pres, Biloxi Civil League 1960-69; chmn Comn, Action Prog 1966-69; tissue & drug consult, Howard Mem Hosp Biloxi, 1967; Harrison Co Dem Exec Com 1968-72; chief family prac secy, 1971; vchmn, Harrison Co Regl Econ Comn, 1973; Fellow, NY Res Found; dipl, Am Bd Family Prac; fellow, Am Acad Family Phys; AMA; Nat Med Assoc; vchmn bd, Greater Gulf Coast Sand Develop Corp; dir MS Indsl Spl Serv Inc; pres, Nat Advan Asn Colored People Biloxi; city planning comn; state adv comt, Div Comprehensive Health Planning; Alpha Phi Alpha; Elk Mason 32 Deg. **Honors/Awds:** Citizen of Year, 1959, 1964; outstanding Alumnus citation, Semi-Centennial Celebration TN State Univ, 1962; Sivler Beaver Award, BSA 1963; Outstanding Citizen, 1970. **Business Addr:** 670 Div St, Biloxi, MS 39530.

MASON, REV. HERMAN SKIP
School administrator, writer. **Personal:** Born Jul 14, 1962, Atlanta, GA; son of Herman Mason Sr and Deloris Harris Hughes. **Educ:** Morris Brown Col, Atlanta, GA, BA, mass commun, 1984; Jimmy Carter Presidential Libr, Atlanta, GA, archival mgt, 1989; Atlanta Univ, Atlanta, GA, MS, libr sci, 1989. **Career:** The Herndon Home Mus, Atlanta, GA, historian, interpreter, 1983-86; The Martin Luther King Nat Historic Site, Atlanta, GA, historian, 1986; Atlanta-Fulton Pub Lib, Atlanta, GA, archivist, historian; Morris Brown Col, dean, 2003; Morehouse Col Archives, dean, archivist; Apex Museum, consultant, "Music Masters", currently. **Orgs:** Pres, African-Am Family History Asn, 1988-91; chmn, Southern Region Historical Comn; historian, Eta Lambda Chap Alpha Phi Alpha Fraternity,1985-90; bd mem, Ga Asn Museums & Galleries, 1988-91; Outstanding Atlanta; founder, corr secy, African-Am Male Study Group; pres, WestSide Community CME Church Sr Usher Bd, 1988-91. **Honors/Awds:** Nat Alumni Brother of the Year, Alpha Phi Alpha Fraternity Inc, 1989;Volunteer Service Award, United Negro Col Fund, 1988-91; Distinguished Alumni Citation, Nat Coun Negro Women, 1987-89; Distinguished Alumni Citation, NAEFEO, 1989. **Special Achievements:** Books: Hidden Treasures: African-American Photographers in Atlanta,1870-70; Alpha In Atlanta: A Legacy Remembered, 1920-87. **Business Addr:** Archivist, Morris Brown College, 643 Martin Luther King Jr Dr, Atlanta, GA 30314, **Business Phone:** (404)681-2800.

MASON, JOHN
Radio host. **Career:** WJLB-FM, disc jockey; WDMK-FM, air personality, 2001-06; Detroit Pistons, pub add announcer, currently. **Honors/Awds:** Emmy Awards. **Special Achievements:** Consistently ranked the number one African-American morning show in Detroit; was honored for his community service or cheering the Detroit Pistons to victory; was chosen to serve as the PA announcer at the 2007 NBA All-Star Game in Las Vegas. **Business Addr:** Public Address Announcer, Detroit Pistons, 5 Championship Dr, Auburn Hills, MI 48326, **Business Phone:** (248)377-0100.*

MASON, LUTHER ROSCOE
Government official, association executive, association executive. **Personal:** Born Feb 21, 1927, Georgetown, KY; married Anne Nutter; children: Gregory K, Kurt D. **Educ:** Ed Davis High Sch, 1945. **Career:** Am Red Cross, dir, 1975-; Ky Sch Bds, dir 1979-; Scott Co Sch, chmn, 1983-84, bd mem, 1976-. **Orgs:** Council mem, Scott City Agr Exten Serv, 1981-; Burley Tobacco Adv Comn. **Honors/Awds:** Treas Scott City, Nat Asn Advan Colored People, 1984-85. **Military Serv:** AUS, corpl, 1947-49. **Business Addr:** Board Member, Scott County Schools, 2168 Frankfort Pk, PO Box 578, Georgetown, KY 40324, **Business Phone:** (502)863-3663.

MASON, MAJOR ALBERT
Consultant. **Personal:** Born Jul 15, 1940, McKeesport, PA; married Ann Mathilde Floberg; children: Major Albert IV & Arianna Melany. **Educ:** Univ Pittsburgh, MEd, 1976, PhD, 1984. **Career:** NOW Enterprises Inc, exec dir, 1968-73; Comm Col Allegheny Co, res planning consult, 1974-75, res assoc, 1974-96; Infor MASON & Assoc, founder& pres, 1995-. **Orgs:** Bd mem, Allegheny OIC, 1972-76; bd mem, United Mental Health Inc, 1973-75;radio show host, WEDO Radio, 1973-75; Community Col African-Am Caucus, 1990-97; Convener, 1995-97; Prog to Aid Citizen Enterprise (PACE), bd mem, secy, 1990-96; Comm Media, pres, bd dir, 1998-; Black Men Solidarity Day Mobilization Endorsements. **Honors/Awds:** Outstanding Young Men of America, 1971. **Special Achievements:** Co-ed, The State of Black Youth in Pittsburgh, 1999. **Military Serv:** USN, musician first class, 1960-66. **Home Addr:** 1409 Bailey Ave, McKeesport, PA 15132, **Home Phone:** (412)672-1519. **Business Addr:** President, InforMason and Associates, 1409 BaileyAve, McKeesport, PA 15132, **Business Phone:** (412)672-1519.

MASON, RONALD EDWARD
Executive, vice president (organization). **Personal:** Born Aug 22, 1948, New York, NY; son of Thurman and Eleanor Pierce; married Louise Orazio, Aug 10, 1980; children: Brian & Jonathan. **Educ:** Utica Col, BA, 1974; Long Island Inst Ment Health, cert, 1976; City Col NY, MEd, 1978; Baruch Col, NY, cert, 1979. **Career:** State Univ NY, Brooklyn, placement dir, 1974-76, dean stud, 1979-80; Fordham Univ, NY, HEOP, dir, 1976-79; SCM Corp, NY, asst mgr, AA/EEO, 1980-81; NBC, NY, dir, personnel, 1981-89; Reader's Digest, Pleasantville, human resources dir, 1989-92; BBDO Worldwide, NY, human resources exec vpres, bd dir, 1992-2000; Empire Blue Cross Blue Shield, human resources sr vpres; Platform Learning, Human Resources, human resources sr vpres, 2004-. **Orgs:** Nat Urban Affairs Coun, 1974-; bd mem, La Guardia Community Col, 1978-; Am Asn Personnel Admin, 1979-; bd mem, NY, Metro Asn Develop Educ, 1989-; coun mem, Westchester Acad, 1990-; NYC Technical Col Found, bd mem, 1993-; NY Urban League, bd mem, 1993-; exec bd mem, Edges Group, 1993-; bd mem, Am Red Cross, Rockland Cty Chap, 1993-; bd mem, Am Advertising Found, EEO/AA Community, 1994-; bd mem, Rockland Community Col Found, 1995-; Am Asn Affirmative Action Prof; Soc Human Resources Mgt; Black Human Resources Network; Nat Urban Affairs Coun Human Resources Forum. **Honors/Awds:** Outstanding Young Men of America, Nat Jaycee, 1983; Black Achiever Award, Harlem YMCA, 1984; Presidential Award, NBC, 1988, 1989; Outstanding Minority Human Resources Professor of the Year, Black Human Resources Network, 1994. **Business Addr:** Senior Vice President Hhuman Resources, Platform Learning, 25th Fl 55 Broad St, New York, NY 10004, **Business Phone:** (646)442-2500.

MASON, DR. TERRY
Physician, surgeon. **Personal:** Born Sep 13, 1951, Washington, DC; divorced; children: Terry Jr & Shaakira. **Educ:** Loyola Univ, BS, 1974; Univ Ill, MD, 1978, gen surg residency, 1978-80; Michael Russels Med Ctr, urol residency, 1980-83. **Career:** Comprehensive Urol SC, pres, 1986-; Prairie Med Asn, pres, 1994-; Mercy Hosp-Chicago, Dept Urol, chmn, currently; Univ Ill, Sch Med, asst prof, currently; Pub Health Comnr, Chicago, currently; pvt pract, currently. **Orgs:** Am Col Surgeons, fel; Am Urological Asn; Chicago Urological Asn, exec comt mem; Chicago Med Soc; Am Med Asn; Nat Med Asn; R Frank Jones Urological Soc Nat Med Asn; Ill State Med Asn; N Central Section Am Urological Asn; Cook County Physicians Asn; Impotence Inst Am, regional dir; NAACP, life mem. **Honors/Awds:** Human Resources Develop Inst, On the Move In Med, 1988; Chicago Health & Med Careers Prog, Ill Inst Technol Award, 1981; City of Chicago, Teen Opportunity Award; Dollars & Sense, Men In Med; Monarch Awards Foundation, Men in Med, 1988. **Special Achievements:** Surveillance Study of Diltiazem Use in Black & Non-Black Patients, Journal of Natl Med Assn, 1988; Making Love Again, Renewing Intimacy & Helping Your Man Overcome Impotence, Valarie Contemporary Books, 1988. **Business Phone:** (312)842-4400.

MASON, WILLIAM E.
Government official. **Personal:** Born Mar 12, 1934, Shuqualak, MS; married Catheryn; children: Terry & William Jr. **Educ:** Tenn

State Univ, BS, 1952; Southern Ill Univ, MS; Univ St Louis, PhD, 1975. **Career:** Instnl Res & Assoc, pres; Dist 189, teacher, prin, personnel dir, dist supt; E St Louis, IL, mayor, precinct committee man; State Ill, human rights specialist. **Orgs:** E St Louis Chamber Com; first pres, exec bd Comprehensive Educ Comn; Model Cities Planning Comn; mem bd dir Madison, St Clair Urban League; Phi Delta Kappa; Alpha Phi Alpha; Friendship Baptist Church. **Home Addr:** 1800 Tudor Ave, East Saint Louis, IL 62207. **Business Addr:** President, Institutional Research & Associate, 1800 Tudor Ave, East St Louis, IL 62207.

MASON, WILLIAM THOMAS, JR.
Lawyer. **Personal:** Born Jul 27, 1926, Norfolk, VA; son of William T and Vivian Carter. **Educ:** Colby Col, BA, 1947; Howard Univ, LLB, 1950. **Career:** William T Mason, jr atty, pvt pract, 1951-63; Justice Dept, ED, VA, asst US atty, 1963-72; Mason & Robinson Atty, partner, 1972-79; Robinson Eichler Zaleski & Mason, partner, 1980-87; Robinson, Zaleski & Lindsey, coun, 1987-92; Robinson, Madison, Fulton & Anderson, coun, 1992-95; Robinson, Banks & Anderson, coun, 1995-97; Robinson, Shelton & Anderson, coun, 1997-98; Robinson & Anderson, coun, 1998-2000; Robinson, Neeley & Anderson, coun, 2000-. **Orgs:** Secy bd, Visitors Norfolk State Univ, 1969-73; secy, Old Dominion Bar Asn, vpres, pres, 1969-90, exec comt, newsletter ed; vice chmn, Norfolk Community Hosp, 1975-98, chmn bd dir; bd mem, Planning Coun, 1976-; secy, Norfolk State Univ Found, vpres & pres bd dirs, 1980-; overseer, Colby Col, 1982-94; Va State Bar Asn. **Honors/Awds:** Award for Devoted Service, Old Dominion Bar Asn, 1983. **Home Addr:** 2113 Carriage Lane, Norfolk, VA 23518, **Home Phone:** (804)853-3005. **Business Addr:** Counsel, Robinson Neeley & Anderson, 256 W Freemason St, Norfolk, VA 23510, **Business Phone:** (757)622-4686.

MASS, EDNA ELAINE
Executive. **Personal:** Born Mar 17, 1954, Escatawpa, MS; children: Edward Juwan. **Educ:** Tougaloo Col, BS, 1976; Jackson State Univ, MEd, 1978. **Career:** AT&T Network Systems, supvr software tools develop. **Home Addr:** 1251 Folkstone Ct, Wheaton, IL 60187. **Business Addr:** Supervisor Software Tools Dev, AT&T Network Systems, 2600 Warrenville Rd, Lisle, IL 60532, **Business Phone:** (312)510-6498.

MASSAQUOI, HANS JURGEN
Editor. **Personal:** Born Jan 19, 1926, Hamburg, Germany; son of Al-Haj and Bertha; married Joan DeBerry, Oct 20, 1956 (divorced 1971); children: Steve & Hans, Jr. **Educ:** Univ Ill, BS 1957; Northwestern Univ Medill Sch Jour, grad studies, 1958. **Career:** Brit Occup Forces Ger, interpreter, 1945-47; Nat Asn Educ Broadcasters, ed, 1947; W Africa, travel, 1948-50; Jet Mag, assoc ed, 1958-59; Ebony Mag, from asst managing ed to assoc managing ed, 1959-64, managing ed, 1967. **Honors/Awds:** Outstanding Immigrant Award, Travellers Aid Soc & Immigrant Serv League, 1970. **Special Achievements:** Author: "Destined to Witness: Growing Up Black in Nazi Germany," 1999. **Military Serv:** Paratrooper, 1951-53.

MASSENBURG, KEDAR
President (Organization), executive. **Personal:** Born Jan 1, 1964?, California. **Educ:** Univ NC, Chapel Hill, law degree. **Career:** Pepsico Corp, dist mgr; SmithKline Beecham Clin Labs Pharmaceut, sales work, 1980; Motown Records, pres, 1997-04; Universal Records, sr vpres, 1999; Kedar Entertainment, pres & chief exec officer, currently. *

MASSENBURG, TONY ARNEL
Basketball player. **Personal:** Born Jul 13, 1967, Sussex, VA; children: Tony James. **Educ:** Univ Md, human ecol. **Career:** San Antonio Spurs, forward, 1990-91; Charlotte Hornets, 1991-92; Boston Celtics, 1992; Golden State Warriors, 1992; Unicaja-Mayoral, Spain, 1992-93; FC Barcelona, Spain, 1993-94; Los Angeles Clippers, 1994-95; Toronto Raptors, 1995-96; Philadelphia 76ers, 1996; NJ Nets, 1996-97; Vancouver Grizzlies, 1997-99, 2000-02; Houston Rockets, 1999-2000; Memphis Grizzlies, 2000-02; Utah Jazz, 2002-03; Sacramento Kings, 2003-04; San Antonio Spurs, forward, 2004-05; Washington wizards, 2007-.

MASSEY, ARDREY YVONNE
Administrator. **Personal:** Born Feb 18, 1951, Charlotte, NC; daughter of LeRoy and VeElla; divorced. **Educ:** Nat Univ, BBA, mkt, comput, bus, 1988; Strayer Univ, MPA, 2007-. **Career:** Royal Globe Ins Co, asst underwriter, 1975-78; Nat Univ, acad adv, 1984-86, asst educ coordr, 1986-88; CMSDC field coordr, 1989-94; Roots & Wings Unlimited, owner, 1994-2006; Barber Scotia Col, Pub Rels/Alumni Affairs dir, 1999; Charlotte Mecklenburg Urban League, placement specialist, spec employ serv; Cent Piedmont Community Col, Northeast Campus, eve dir; Strayer Univ S Charlotte Campus, Learning Resources Ctr, mgr, currently. **Orgs:** New Birth Charlotte Mem, Carolinas Minority Supplier Develop Coun Inc, 1991-94; chairperson, Bus Opportunity Conf, Educ & Regist Comn, 1991-94; chairperson, Rockwell AME Zion, Youth Develop Prog, 1992-94; vpres, Hemphill Heights Community Orgn; Diversity Coun Carolinas, 1995-; mgr, One Accord Charlotte Gospel Group, 1995; Boy Scouts Am Nominating Comn, 1996. **Honors/Awds:** Certificate of Excellence - Library and Technical Support, Strayer Univ S Charlotte; Fruit of the Spirit Award, Rockwell AME Zion Church, 1990; Most Outstanding Woman of the Year Award, Rockwell A.M.E. Zion Church, 1994; Ordained Deaconess-New Birth Charlotte, 2008. **Special Achievements:** Writer, "The Way Things are Now Won't Always Be", Am Poetry Anthology, volume II, number 1-2, p 16, Spring/Summer 1983. **Business Phone:** (704)499-9229.

MASSEY, BRANDON
Writer. **Personal:** Born Jun 9, 1973, Waukegan, IL. **Career:** Computer systs admin, 1990-; Author: Thunderland, Kensington Publ Corp, 2002; Dark Corner, 2004; contributed short stories: Tomorrow: Speculative Fiction mag; After Hours anthology, Dark Dreams, 2004, Within The Shadows, Kensington, 2005; Voices From The Other Side: Dark Dreams II; Thunderland; Twisted Tales; The Other Brother, 2006; Don't Ever Tell, 2008. **Honors/Awds:** Gold Pen Award.

MASSEY, JACQUELENE SHARP
School administrator. **Personal:** Born Oct 8, 1947, Jackson, MS; married James; children: Jermane Edward & Jamie Patrice. **Educ:** DC Teacher Col, Wash, cert, 1970; Knoxville Col, Tenn, BA, sociol, 1979;Col Notre Dame, Baltimore, MS, gen mgt courses. **Career:** US Dept Housing & Urban Develop, Wash, DC, summer coordr, 1970; Delta Sigma Theta Inc/Pub Serv Sorority, mem off, 1970-71; Fed Educ Prog/Direct Search Talent, Md, admin prog coordr, 1973-77; Baltimore City Pub Sch, 1977-78; Univ Md, Baltimore, assoc dir, spec prog, 1978-; US Dept Labor, Job Corps, voc specialist, 1994-97; DC Pub Sch, teacher; Off Employ Develop, Sch-To-Work Educ Alternative Learning prog, mgr, 1997-; Career Acad, Baltimore City Mayors Off Employ Develop, prog mgr, currently, Community Partnership & Resource Develop, dir, currently. **Orgs:** Second vpres, Delta Sigma Theta Inc, Pub Serv Sorority, 1965-67; cons/decision making prog Col Entrance Exam Bd, New York, 1976; vpres, Girl Scouts Cent Md, 1977-; Speakers Bur, United Fund Cent, Md, 1977-78; cons/cosmetic Bus Fashion Two-Twenty Co, 1978-; chmn, Hebbville Elem Sch PTA, 1979-; Echo House Multi-Svc Ctr, 1995-; Svc Acad Rev Bd, 7th Cong Dist, 1996; Gov Comn Serv, 1996; bd mem, Elijah Cummings Youth Pro, 1997-. **Honors/Awds:** Leadership Award, White House Nat Youth Conf Nat Beauty & Conserv, 1965; Mayoral Award, Mayor City Coun, Baltimore, 1978; Thanks Badge Management Leadership Award, Girl Scouts Cent Md, 1979. **Business Addr:** Director of Community Partnership & Resource Development, Program Manager, Baltimore City Office of Employment Development, Academy for College and Career Exploration, 101 W 24th St, Baltimore, MD 21218.

MASSEY, JAMES EARL
Clergy, school administrator. **Personal:** Born Jan 4, 1930, Ferndale, MI; married Gwendolyn Inez Kilpatrick. **Educ:** Detroit Bible Col, BRE, BTh, 1961; Oberlin Grad Sch Theol, AM, 1964; Asbury Theol Seminary, DD, 1972; Pacific Sch Religion, addit study, 1972; Univ Mich; Boston Col Grad Sch; Ashland Theological Seminary, DD, 1991; Huntington Col, DD, 1994; Tuskegee Univ, Hum D, 1995; Warner Pacific Col, DD, 1995; Anderson Univ, Litt D, 1995; Wash & Jefferson Col, DD, 1997; N Pk Theological Seminary, DD, 1999. **Career:** Ch God Detroit, assoc minister, 1949-51, 1953-54; Metro Ch God, sr pastor, 1954-76; Anderson Col, Sch Theol, campus minister, prof religious studies, 1969-77; Christian Brotherhood, speaker, 1977-82; Anderson Univ, Sch Theol, prof new testament, 1981-84; Tuskegee Univ Chapel & Univ Prof Religion, dean, 1984-90; Anderson Univ, Sch Theol, dean, prof preaching & Biblical studies, 1990-95, dean emer & prof large, currently; Pk Pl Ch God, Anderson, Ind, Preacher Residence, 1994-95. **Orgs:** Lecturer Gautschi Lectures Fuller Theol Sem, 1975-86; Freitas Lectures Asbury Theol Sem, 1977, Rall Co-Lecturer Garrett-Evangelical Sem, 1980, Mullins Lectures So Bapt Sem, 1981, Swartley Lectures Eastern Baptist Sem, 1982, Jameson Jones Lecturer Iliff Sch Theol, 1983, Rom Lectures Trinity Evangelical Div Sch, 1984; northcutt lectures, Southwestern Bapt Theol Sem, 1986; bd dir, Detroit Coun Chs; theol study commiss, Detroit Coun Ch; corp mem, Inter-Varsity Christian Fellowship; matl comn Black Churchmen; Wesleyan Theol Soc; ed bd, Christian Scholars Review; bd dir, Warner Press Inc; vchmn, Pub Bd Ch God; ed adv, Tyndale House Publ, 1968-69; comn chmn, Christian Unity; Nat Assoc Col & Univ Chaplains; bd dir, Nat Black Evangelical; Nat Advan Asn Colored People; Lausanne Continuation Comn; Underwood Fellow, Danforth Found, 1972-73; pres, Anderson Civil Serv Merit Commiss, 1975-81; ed bd, Leadership Mag; bd dir, Nat Religious Broadcasteers; ed bd, Preaching Mag, 1987; Resource Scholar, Christianity Today Inst, 1985; sr editor, Christanity Today, 1993-95. **Honors/Awds:** Staley Distinguished Christian Scholar, Staley Found, 1977; Lifetime Achievement Award, Wesleyan Theological Soc, 1995. **Military Serv:** AUS, corpl, 1951-53. **Business Phone:** 800-428-6414.*

MASSEY, JANELLE RENEE
Lawyer. **Personal:** Born Dec 7, 1976, New Orleans, LA; daughter of Johnny and June. **Educ:** Southern Univ & A&M Col, BS, psychol, 1998; Southern Univ Law Ctr, JD, 2001. **Career:** Orleans Parish Sch Bd, teacher, 2001-02; Orleans Parish Criminal Ct, law clerk, 2003-. **Orgs:** Golden Key Nat Hon Soc, 1996-; Nat Psychol Hon Soc, 1996-; Delta Sigma Theta Sorority Inc, 1997-; Delta Theta Phi Legal Fraternity, 2000-. **Special Achievements:** Trombonist, Pinettes Brass Band (world's only all female brass band). **Business Addr:** Law Clerk, Criminal District Court of Orleans Parish, Rm 114 2700 Tulane Ave 7th Fl, New Orleans, LA 70119, **Business Phone:** (504)658-9000.

MASSEY, REV. REGINALD HAROLD
Clergy. **Personal:** Born Jun 23, 1946, Rowan County, NC; married Arletta Bingham; children: Angela, Marc & Reginald, Jr. **Educ:** Livingstone Col, BS, Sociol; Hood Theol Sem, Livingstone Col, MDiv; Rowan Tech Col, Cert Crisis Counseling; Baptist Hosp, Winston Salem, CPE certi. **Career:** Town E Spencer Police Dept, police officer, 1971-73; Town E Spencer, mayor, 1973-81; Salisbury Rowan Community Serv Coun Inc, asst planner, 1976-78, asst dir 1978; Herndon Chapel AME Zion Church, pastor, 1979-81; Ezekiel AME Zion Church, 1979-83; Ctr Grove AME Zion Church, 1983-89; VA Med Center Salisbury, chaplain 1984-; Hood Memorial AME Zion Church, pastor, 1989-. **Orgs:** E Spencer Planning bd; Aux Policeb 1971-73; water quality policy adv comn, Gov's Appointment, 1980; intergovt rels comn, NC League Municipalities 1980; C of C; Southern Conf Black Mayors; comn chmn, NC League Municipalities Com; Boy Scout Troup 383; Am Legion Post 107; E Spencer Civic League; Salisbury-Rowan Civic League; Livingston Col Alumni Asn; bd trustees, Southern City AME Zion Ch; Nat League Cities; Nat Conf Black Mayors; exec comt, Durham Col; vpres, NC Conf Black Mayors; Masonic Lodge Western Star #9. **Honors/Awds:** Martin Luther King Jr Humanitarian Award. **Military Serv:** AUS, sgt, 1966-69; Cert of Accomplishment at General Supply Ft Bragg. **Home Addr:** 3275 Jake Alexander Blvd, Salisbury, NC 28144. **Business Addr:** Pastor, Hood Memorial AME Zion Church, 45 Sacco St, Belmont, NC 28012, **Business Phone:** (704)638-3330.

MASSEY, SELMA REDD
Association executive. **Personal:** Born Sep 8, 1953, Fort Campbell, KY; daughter of Redd and Gaynelle; divorced. **Educ:** Univ Detroit, BA, 1974, MA, educ, 1975; Western Mich Univ, EdD, orgn & leadership, 1993. **Career:** C's Aid Soc, social worker, 1974-75; State Mich, social worker, 1975-79; Wayne Co Community Col, instr, 1977-; Detroit's Most Wanted, producer/host, 1986, chief exec officer, 1995; Proj Start Inc, chief exec officer & exec dir, 1981-; Whosoever Ministry, pres, currently; Proj BAIT (Black Awareness in Tv), host, 1994-; For My People, host, 1994. **Orgs:** Univ Detroit Alumni Asn, 1974; Am Correctional Asn, 1983-; WDTR Educ Broadcasting, 1986-; Urban League, Detroit, 1994-; Mich Asn Community Corrections Advan, 1987-; Western Mich Univ Alumni Asn, 1993. **Honors/Awds:** Leadership Commitment, IBM Leadership Develop, 1992; Excellence Recognition, Detroit Pub Schs, 1993, Certificate of Participation, 1994; Teen Violence Accomplishment, Urban League, 1994. **Special Achievements:** "Continue the Fight Against Crime," Mich Chronicle, 1994; "We Cannot Afford Short-Sightedness," Mich Chronicle, 1994; "A Study Needed to Understand Behavior," Mich Chronicle, 1994; "I Don't Care," 1994; "Hurry Up! Bring it Back Home," 1995. **Business Addr:** President, Whosoever Ministry, 1411 E Jefferson Ave, Detroit, MI 48207, **Business Phone:** (313)259-9922.

MASSEY, WALTER EUGENE
Scientist, school administrator, educator. **Personal:** Born Apr 5, 1938, Hattiesburg, MS; son of Chester Massey and Essie Massey; married Shirley Anne, Oct 29, 1969; children: Keith & Eric. **Educ:** Morehouse Col, BS, math & physics, 1958; Wash Univ, MS, PhD, physics,1966. **Career:** Scientist, school administrator, educator (retired); NDEA, fel, 1959-60; Nat Sci Found, fel, 1961; Argonne Nat Lab, post doctoral fel, 1966-68, staff physicist, 1966-68, dir, 1979-84; Univ Ill, asst prof, 1968-70; Brown Univ, assoc prof, 1970-75, prof, dean, 1971-79; Am Coun Educ, fel, 1974; Univ Chicago, prof, 1979-93; vpres res, 1984-91; Nat Sci Found, dir, 1991-93; Univ Calif-System wide, provost & sr vpres of academic affairs, 1993-95; Morehouse Col, pres, 1995-2007. **Orgs:** Rev comt, Nat Sci Found, 1971; rev comt, Nat Acad Sci, 1973; Nat Sci Bd, 1978-84; fel, bd dir, 1981-85, pres elect, 1987, pres, 1988; Am Asn Advan Sci; Am Nuclear Soc; Am Phys Soc; NY Acad Sci; Ill Gov Comn Sci & Technol; Ill Gov Sci Adv Comt; Sigma Xi; bd dirs, BP Amoco; bd dirs, Argonne-Chicago Develop Corp; bd dirs, Motorola; bd dirs, Chicago Tribune Co; bd dirs; Continental Materials Corp; bd dirs, First Nat Bank Chicago; bd dirs, Bank of Amer; bd dirs; Hewlett Found Commonwealth Fund; bd fels, Brown Univ; bd trustees, Rand Corp; Museum of Science & Industry; Chicago Orchestral Asn; bd gov, JF Symphony; bd dirs, Mellon Found; bd dirs, McDonalds; bd, Atlanta Symphony Orchestra, Woodruff Arts Ctr; Am Asn Physics Teachers; pres, AAAS. **Honors/Awds:** Distinguished Service Citation, Am Asn Phys Teachers, 1975; Archie Lacey Memorial Award, NY Acad Sci, 1992; Bennie Trailblazer Award, Morehouse Col, 1992; Morgan State Univ, Distinguished Achievement Award, 1992; Golden Plate Award, 1992. **Special Achievements:** Numerous science publications; recipient of 25 honorary Doctor of Science

degrees. **Business Addr:** President, Morehouse College, 830 Wview Dr, Atlanta, GA 30314-3773, **Business Phone:** (404)681-2800.

MATCHETT, JOHNSON
Executive. **Personal:** Born Oct 17, 1942, Mobile, AL; son of Johnson Matchett Sr. **Educ:** Alabama State Univ, BS, 1963; Univ Ala, MA, 1969; Univ Southern, MissS, EdS, 1975. **Career:** Anniston Pub Schs, teacher, 1963-64; Mobile Pub Schs, teacher, 1964-69; Miles Col, dir teacher educ, 1969-73; Ala State Univ, part-time instr, 1972-75; Univ S Ala, curric consult, 1974; BellSouth Services Inc, mgr training, 1974-. **Orgs:** Am Soc Training & Develop, 1975-, Phi Delta Kappa Hon Educ Fraternity, 1975-, Nat Soc Performance & Instr, 1982-; Nat Asn Advan Colored People, 1983-; exec bd, Ala State Univ Gen Alumni Asn, 1985-89; Nat Black MBA Asn, 1986-, Ala Initiative Black Col Recruitment & Retention Birmingham Chapt, 1987-89, Holy Family HS bd dirs, 1987; Acad Affairs Com, Nat Soc perf & instr, 1992-; PRS Birmingham Chapter Nat Black MBA Asn, 1992-. **Home Addr:** PO Box 752, Birmingham, AL 35201. **Business Phone:** (205)945-2165.

MATEEN, MALIK ABDUL
Association executive, firefighter. **Personal:** Born Oct 19, 1949, Hialeah, FL; son of Rubbie L Laughlin and Zula M Jackson; married Fern Troupe, Sep 19, 1977; children: Africa & Clifford. **Career:** Life Geo Ins Co, ins agt, 1973-73; Dade County Solid Waste Dept, truck driver, 1973-81; Metro Fire Rescue, firefighter, 1981-. **Orgs:** Pres, Progressive Firefighters Asn, 1989-. **Military Serv:** Army, sgt, 1969-72. **Business Addr:** President, Progressive Firefighters Association, 926 Rutland Britton St, Opa Locka, FL 33054, **Business Phone:** (305)688-3473.

MATHABANE, MARK JOHANNES
Writer, lecturer. **Personal:** Born Oct 18, 1960, Alexandra Township, Republic of South Africa; son of Jackson and Geli Mabaso; married Gail Ernsberger, Aug 1, 1987; children: Bianca Ellen, Nathan Phillip & Stanley Arthur. **Educ:** Limestone Col, 1978; St Louis Univ, 1979; Quincy Col, 1981; Dowling Col, BA, econ, 1983; Columbia Univ, 1984. **Career:** Author, lecturer, 1985-; Books: Kaffir Boy: The True Story of a Black Youth's Coming of Age in Apartheid S Africa, 1986; Kaffir Boy in America, 1989; Love in Black & White, co-auth with Gail Ernsberger, 1992; African Women: Three Generations, 1994; Ubuntu, 1999; Miriam's Song, 2000; Deadly Memory; The Last Liberal; black ed, Dowling Col. **Orgs:** Authors Guild; PEN Am Ctr. **Honors/Awds:** Christopher Award, 1986; White House fel, Dept Educ, 1996-97; Robert Kennedy Memorial Award, finalist. **Home Addr:** 341 Barrington Pk Lane, Kernersville, NC 27284, **Home Phone:** (336)996-1703. **Business Addr:** Author, Lecturer, Mathabane Books & Lectures, 1320 NW Frazier Ct, Portland, OR 97229, **Business Phone:** (503)758-9024.

MATHEW, KNOWLES
Executive. **Personal:** Married Tina; children: Beyonce & Solange. **Educ:** Fisk Univ. **Career:** Destiny's Child, mgr, currently; Music World Entertainment, founder & owner, currently. **Orgs:** Grammy Comt; Recording Indust Asn Am; Omega Psi Phi Fraternity. **Business Addr:** Founder, Owner, Music World Entertainment, 2202 Crawford St, Houston, TX 77002, **Business Phone:** (713)772-5175.*

MATHEWS, GARY C
Chief executive officer. **Career:** Afro-Am Newspapers Group Inc & Nat Newspaper Pubs Asn, consult; Educ Communicate, pres; ETC Info Inc, chief exec officer, currently. **Orgs:** Bd mem, Brown's Community Outreach. **Business Addr:** Chief Executive Officer, ETC Information Inc, PO Box 41078, Baltimore, MD 21203, **Business Phone:** (410)788-6471.*

MATHEWS, GEORGE
Executive. **Career:** WGPR Inc, Detroit, MI, chief exec officer & pres, currently. **Orgs:** Int Free & Accepted Modern Masons Inc. **Honors/Awds:** Honorary LHD. **Business Addr:** President, Chief Executive Officer, WGPR Inc, 3146 E Jefferson, Detroit, MI 48207, **Business Phone:** (313)259-8862.

MATHEWS, DR. K KENDALL (K KENDALL STEVENS)
Army officer, social worker. **Personal:** Born in Detroit, MI. **Educ:** Greenville Col. **Career:** Pontiac Pub Sch Syst, mentor; Oakland Univ, supvr; Greenville Col, admis assoc; Salvation Army, officer, 1991, corps officer, capt, secy & Detroit city comdr, currently; Nat Network Social Work Mgr, social work mgr, 1998-. **Orgs:** Founder, Booth Acad; Stud Asn, Social Life Comt; dipl, Am Psychotherapy Asn. **Honors/Awds:** Honor, Former Mich Gov John Engler; Who's Who Among Outstanding Corporate Executives, The Salvation Army. **Special Achievements:** Finalist for the George Romney lifetime achievement award. **Military Serv:** Salvation Army. **Business Addr:** Detroit City Commander, Regional Coordinator, Salvation Army, 150 W Grand Blvd, Detroit, MI 48216, **Business Phone:** (248)443-5500.

MATHEWS, KEITH E
Judge. **Personal:** Born Mar 2, 1944, Steubenville, OH. **Educ:** Morgan State Univ, BS, chem, 1966; Univ Baltimore, JD, 1972. **Career:** Police Dept, Baltimore City, police officer, 1968-69; Water Dept, Baltimore City, chemist, 1969; Community Col Baltimore, instr, 1971-72; Legal Aid Bur Inc, Baltimore, staff atty, 1972-73; Congressman Parren Mitchell, legis asst, 1973-74; US Dept Justice, Antitrust Div, atty, 1974-75; Foster Mathews & Hill, atty, 1975-82; States Atty Off Baltimore, asst states atty, 1978-83; Dist Court Md, assoc judge, 1983-, admin judge 1999-. **Orgs:** Bd govs, Univ Baltimore Alumni Asn, 1973; vice chmn, Consumer Affairs Adb Bd Howard Co, 1978; Monumental Bar Asn; Nat Bar Asn; founding mem, Univ Baltimore Law Rev; Admin Judges Comt, Dist Ct Md, 1999-; Criminal Law & Procedure Comt, 2000-01; Judicial Coun, 2000-03; Monumental City Bar Asn; Drug & Alcohol Abuse Coun, Baltimore City, 2004-. **Honors/Awds:** Validictorian, Police Acad Baltimore City, 1968. **Special Achievements:** Editorial Staff Law Review in University of Baltimore, 1972. **Military Serv:** USAF, 1966-68. **Business Addr:** Administrative Judge, District Court of Maryland, Borgerding Dist Ct Bldg 5800 Wabash Ave, Baltimore, MD 21215-3330, **Business Phone:** (410)764-8714.

MATHEWS, LAWRENCE TALBERT
Executive, financial manager, executive director. **Personal:** Born Oct 12, 1947, Michigan City, IN; married Beverly Ann Hoze; children: Gerald. **Educ:** Univ Mich, Flint, AB, 1969; Univ Detroit, MBA, 1975. **Career:** Arthur Young & Co, sr auditor, 1972-75; Comn Credit/Mc Cullagn Lsng, controller & treas, 1975-78; Mich Peninsula Airways, vpres finance, 1978-80; Clipper Int Mfg, vpres finance, 1980-82; Comprehensive Health Serv Detroit, dir finance oper; Wellness Plan, vpres, chief financial officer, currently; Mich Asn Ceritified Pub Acct, dir, currently. **Orgs:** Asst exec dir, Detroit Area Agency Aging, 1984; pres, Nat Asn Black Acct, 1992-94; Mich Asn Health Maintenance Org Finance Comn. **Honors/Awds:** Distinguished Service, Nat Asn Black Accts, 1985. **Military Serv:** AUS, 1st lt, 3 yrs; Distinguished Mil Grad & Off Cand Sch, 1973. **Business Phone:** (248)267-3700.

MATHEWS, YVONNE REED. See MADISON, YVONNE REED.

MATHEY, JORGE ANTONIO BELL. See BELL, GEORGE ANTONIO.

MATHIS, DAVID L
Executive. **Personal:** Born Sep 16, 1947, Riverhead, NY; son of Freddie Mae Thompson; married Dorothy; children: David, Denise & Doreen. **Educ:** Mohawk Valley Community Col, AAS, 1970; Syracuse Univ, Uitca Col, BS, 1972. **Career:** Mohawk Valley Opportunity Indus Ctr, dir training, 1972-73, exec dir, 1973-74; Career Develop Ctr, dir manpower serv, 1974-79, dir job develop, 1979-80; Oneida Co Employment & Training, dep dir, 1980-86, dir, 1986-, Off Workforce Develop, currently. **Orgs:** Bd dirs, Cosmopolitan Community Ctr; bd trustees, Hope Chapel AME Zion Church; adv bd, Oneida Co Youth Bur; bd trustees, Mohawk Valley Community Col, bd dirs, Alumni Asn, 1990, vpres; bd dir, Asn Governing Bds NY State Comm Cols; chmn, Utica Col Ed Bass Black Stud Scholar Fund; bd dirs, Ferre Inst, l988; bd dirs, Neighborhood Ctr Utica, l988; bd trustees, Munson-Williams-Proctor Inst, l988; Rotary Club Utica, 1989; bd dirs, Utica Found, 1989; bd dirs, Asn Community Col Trustees, 1990; Commit, 1991; bd dir, Utica Neighborhood Housing Serv; bd pres, Utica Head Start; bd dir, ARC Oneida & Lewis Counties, 1993; adv bd, Fleet Bank New York, CRA, 1993; Am Red Cross, Northeast Reg Com, 1994; bd dir, State Univ NY Alumni Confederation, 1995; pres, New York State Affirmative Action Officers, 1995; bd dir, Ct St Family Health Ctr, 1996; bd dir, Am Lung Asn Mid NY, 2000-03; bd dir, House Good Shepard, 2000; pres, NY Asn TRG & Employment Prof, 2002. **Honors/Awds:** Outstanding Commission Service Award, Mohawk Valley Frontiersman, 1977; Man of the Year Award, St Time, 1978; Outstanding Alumnus, Mohawk Valley Community Minority Union 1981; Citizen of the Year Award, League Women Voters Utica/Rome, 1984; Hero Award, United Way Greater Utica; Outstanding Alumnus, Utica Col; Len Wilbur Award, Utica Kiwanis Club, l986; Outstanding Service Award, Lambda Kappa MU, 1987; Outstanding Community Service Award, Utica Salvation Army, 1987; Achievement Award, Oneida Co Nat Asn Advan Colored People, 1987; Community Achievement Award, Aleppo No 140, 1988; Martin Luther King Jr Humanitarian Award, Mohawk Valley Psychiatric Ctr, 1990; Alumni of Merit, Mohawk Valley Community Col, 1990; COT Service Award, Utica-Rome Black Ministerial Alliance, 1992; AFAs of Distinction Award, New York State Govs Off, 1994; PRSs Fund Award for Cultural Diversity, AME Red Cross, 1996; Distinguished Service Award, Fac Coun Community CLGs NY, 2001; Distinguished Service Award, NY Community Col trustees Marvin A Rapp, 2002; Senate James A Donovan Award, BOCES Consortium Continuing Educ, 2001. **Home Phone:** (315)797-8069. **Business Addr:** Director, Oneida County Office of Employment & Training, Office of Workforce Development, 209 Elizabeth St, Utica, NY 13501, **Business Phone:** (315)798-5908.

MATHIS, DEBORAH F
Journalist. **Personal:** Born Aug 24, 1953, Little Rock, AR; daughter of Rachel A and Lloyd H; divorced; children: Meredith Mathis, Allison Mathis & Joseph Mathis. **Educ:** Univ Ark, Little Rock, 1972. **Career:** KTHV-TV, gen assignment reporter, 1973-74; WTTG-TV, weekend anchor, 1974-76; KARK-TV, asst news dir, 1976-82; KATV-TV, "Live at Five," anchor, 1983-88; Ark Gazette, ed, 1988-91; The Clarion-Ledger, columnist, 1992-93; Tribune Media Services, syndicated columnist, 1992-; Gannett News Serv, White House correspondent, 1993-; Northwestern Univ Medill Sch Jour Wash Prog, asst prof; Medill News Service Wash Bur, Managing ed, currently; freelance writer, 2001-. **Home Addr:** 6702 Kenwood Forest Lane, Chevy Chase, MD 20815, **Home Phone:** (301)913-9553. **Business Phone:** (202)347-8700.

MATHIS, DEDRIC
Football player. **Personal:** Born Sep 26, 1973, Cuero, TX. **Educ:** Univ Houston. **Career:** Football player(retired); Indianapolis Colts, defensive back, 1996-98; Chicago Bears, 1997-98; Seattle Seahawks, 1999; Chicago Enforcers, Xtreme Football League, Chicago Enforcers, 2000; Orlando, Arena Football League, 2000; Hamilton Tiger Cats, 2001-05.

MATHIS, GREGORY
Judge, broadcaster. **Personal:** Born Apr 5, 1960, Detroit, MI; son of Alice Mathis; married Linda Mathis, Jun 1, 1985; children: Camara, Gregory & Amir. **Educ:** Eastern Mich Univ, BS, 1984; Univ Detroit, JD, 1988. **Career:** Judge (retired), Broadcaster; Detroit City Coun, admin asst councilman Clyde Cleveland, 1984-88; Off Mayor, City Detroit, mgr, neighborhood city hall, 1989-93, lawyer pvt pract, 1993-95; State Mich, 36th Dist Ct, judge, 1995-98; TV courtroom show, Judge Mathis, host, 1999-. **Orgs:** Chmn, Reclaim our Youth Crusade, 1993-; founder & chmn, Young Adults Asserting Themselves, 1986-; special asst Rev Jesse Jackson, Nat Rainbow Coalition, 1994-; life mem, NAACP. **Honors/Awds:** Has recieved more than 100 awards including Man of the Year, Southern Christian Leadership Conf, 1995; Detroit City Coun, Testimonial Resolution, 1995; Proclaimation from Mayor, Off Mayor, City Detroit, 1995; Spec Tribute Proclamation, Mich Legis, 1995. **Special Achievements:** Co-author, play, Inner City Miracle, 1995. **Home Addr:** 14455 Stahelin, Detroit, MI 48223, **Home Phone:** (313)836-5682. **Business Addr:** Television Show Judge, Warner Brothers Domestic Television, 4000 Warner Blvd, Burbank, CA 91522.

MATHIS, JOHN ROYCE. See MATHIS, JOHNNY.

MATHIS, JOHNNY (JOHN ROYCE MATHIS)
Singer. **Personal:** Born Sep 30, 1935, Gilmer, TX; son of Clement and Mildred. **Educ:** San Francisco St Col. **Career:** San Francisco Night Clubs, singer; Albums include: Chances Are; It's Notfor Me to Say; Twelfth of Never; Too Much, Too Little, Too Late; Small World; In a Sentimental Mood: Tribute to Duke Ellington, 1990; In ASentimental Mood - Mathis Sings Ellington, 1990; Better Together, 1991; How Do You Keep the Music Playing, 1993; The Christmas Music Of Johnny Mathis, 1993; How Do You Keep The Music Playing, 1993; This Heart of Mine, 1994; All About Love, 1996; Johnny Mathis - 40th Anniversary Edition, 1996; The Global Masters, 1997; Because You Loved Me: Songs of Diane Warren, 1998; The Ultimate Hits Collection, 1998; Because You Loved Me, 1998; For Christmas, 1998; Christmas Is, 1999; Mathis on Broadway, 2000; Christmas Album, 2002; That's What Friends Are For, 2003; Merry Christmas, 2003; 20 Grandes Exitos, 2003; Over the Rainbow, 2004; The Essential Johnny Mathis, 2004; Isn't It Romantic: The Standards Album, 2005; Winter Wonderland; 2005; Isn't It Romantic - The Standards Album, 2005; Great Johnny Mathis, 2006; Gold: A 50th Anniversary Christmas Celebration, 2006; A 50th Anniversary Christmas, 2006; A Night To Remember, 2008. **Orgs:** Founder, The Shell & Johnny Mathis Golf Classic. **Honors/Awds:** Hollywood Walk of Fame, 1972; Lifetime Achievement Award, Acad Rec Arts & Sci, 2003; Grammy Hall of Fame. **Special Achievements:** Nominated for a Grammy, 1961, 1992; one of only five recording artists to have Top 40 Hits spanning each of the four decades since 1955; listed in Guinness Book, 490 continuous weeks (almost ten years) on the BILLBOARD Top Albums Chart. **Business Addr:** Singer, Richard De La Font Agency, 4845 S Sheridan Rd Suite 505, Tulsa, OK 74145, **Business Phone:** (918)665-6200.

MATHIS, KEVIN
Football player, president (organization). **Personal:** Born Apr 29, 1974, Gainesville, TX; married Kimberly; children: Kennedy & Kaleb. **Educ:** Tex A&M Univ. **Career:** Dallas Cowboys, defensive back, 1997-99; New Orleans Saints, 2000-01; Atlanta Falcons, 2002-06; Another Chance Properties LLC, pres, currently. **Orgs:** Founder, Kevin Mathis Found. **Special Achievements:** Instituited Kevin Maths "Stay Focused " scholarship awards for college-bound Gainesville High School seniors who have shown determination, commitment & focus in achieving their goals.

MATHIS, ROBERT LEE, JR.
Health services administrator. **Personal:** Born Apr 21, 1934, Concord, NC; son of Minnie V; married Margaret Miller; children: Calven, Rodney, Jeffery, Kim West. **Educ:** US Navy, Cooks & Bakers Sch, 1956; Central Piedmont Comm Col, AS, polit sci, 1976; NC State Univ, Personnel Mgt Dipl, 1978; St Louis Univ, Food Serv Dipl, 1978. **Career:** Health services administrator

(retired); Cabarras Memorial Hosp, cook spec diets, 1958, cook & baker supvr 1965, asst food serv dir, 1979-94; Concord, NC, mayor pro-team, 1995. **Orgs:** Dir, Cabarrus City Boys Club, 1979-; Mt Zion Lodge 26 Concord NC, 1980-, NC Chap Am Soc Hosp; Food Serv, 1980; adv bd, Salvation Army, 1981-; leader Boy Scouts, 1983; dir, Cab County United Way, 1983; mem bd visitor, Barber-Scotia Col, Concord NC, 1984; delegate for the city NC Centralina Coun Gov; elder First Christian Church; bd dir, Life Ctr & Logan Day Care; Bd Corrections, 1994; chmn, Cabarrus Cty, elected offical assoc, 1994. **Honors/Awds:** Represented the largest ward in NC, 1980; first black elected Bd of Alderman Concord Bd of Alderman, 1980-; Outstanding Citizen of the Yr, Kannpolis Daily Independence, 1981; co-founder, Fourth Word Develop Corp, 1982; Citizen of the Yr, Phi Chi, 1985. **Military Serv:** USN, third class, commissaryman, 5 1/2 yrs; Nat Defense, Korean Serv, 1951-56. **Home Addr:** 2676 RocK Hill Church Rd, Concord, NC 28027, **Home Phone:** (704)782-9757. *

MATHIS, SHARON BELL
Writer, educator. **Personal:** Born Feb 26, 1937, Atlantic City, NJ; daughter of John Willie Bell and Alice Mary Frazier Bell; married Leroy Franklin, Jul 11, 1957 (divorced 1979); children: Sherie, Stacy & Stephanie. **Educ:** Morgan State Col, BA, 1958; Cath Univ Am, MLS, 1975. **Career:** C Hosp DC, Wash DC, interviewer, 1958-59; Holy Redeemer Elem Sch, Washington DC, teacher, 1959-65; Stuart Jr High Sch, Wash DC, spec educ teacher, 1974-75; Chas Hart Junior High Sch, fac, 1966-74; DC Black Writers Workshop, founder & writer-in-charge C lit div; Howard Univ, Wash DC, writer-in-residence, 1972-73; Benning Elem Sch, Wash DC, librn, 1975-76; Patricia Roberts Harris Educ Ctr, librn, 1976-95; Author: Brooklyn Story, 1969; Sidewalk Story, 1971; Teacup Full of Roses, 1972; Ray Charles, 1973, 2001; Listen for the Fig Tree, 1974; The Hundred Penny Box, 1975; Cartwheels, 1977; Red Dog & Blue Fly: Football Poems, 1991; Running Girl, 1997; Hundred penny box, 2006. **Orgs:** Bd adv lawyers comt, DC Comn Arts, 1972; Black Womens Community Develop Found, 1973; Am Libr Asn, 1995-. **Honors/Awds:** Award, Coun Interracial Books C, 1970; Author Award, 1974; Coretta Scott King Award, 1974; Newbery Honor, Book Am Libr Asn, 1976; Arts & Humanities Award, Archdiocese Wash, 1978; Wallace Johnson Memorial Award, 1984; Arts & Letters Award, Delta Sigma Theta Sorority, 1985; Outstanding Writer Award, Writing-to-Read Prog, 1986.

MATHIS, DR. THADDEUS P.
Educator. **Personal:** Born Sep 8, 1942, Americus, GA; married Deborah Moore; children: Latanya, Evan & Talani; married Deborah Moore-Stewart. **Educ:** Bluefield State Col, BS, Sec Educ, 1965; Bryn Mawr Col, MSS, Social Service, 1968; Temple Univ, MA, African American Studies, PhD, Political Sci, 1985. **Career:** Dept Pub Welfare, group leader, 1965-66; Child Study Ctr Philadelphia Temple Univ Hosp, social work intern, 1966-68; Dept Pub Welfare, social worker, 1968; Philadelphia Model Cities Prog, planning coordr, 1968-70; Temple Univ, prof social admin, 1970-, Adjunct Prof, African Am Studies Dept, assoc dean, 1999-. **Orgs:** Exec comt, Philadelphia Congress Racial Equality, 1971-75; chairperson, Philadelphia Black Political Convention, 1971-80; presiding officer, Nat Black Independent Political Party, 1981-83; chairperson Sch Soc Admin Grad Dept, 1981-84; pres, Philadelphia Alliance Black Soc Workers; bd mem, Housing Asn Delaware Valley; Philadelphia Alliance Black Social Workers; bd Housing ASN DEL Valley; chairperson, IST AFA Develop; dir, IST African Social Work. **Honors/Awds:** Shapp Found Scholar Shapp Foundation Philadelphia, 1961-65; PEP Fellow State PA Off Children & Youth, 1966-68; Fellow, Urban Affairs Inst Am Univ, 1971; Bernard C Watson Award, 1985. **Business Addr:** Professor, Adjunct Professor, Temple University, School of Social Administration, Ritter Annex 5th fl 1301 W, Cecil B Moore Ave, Philadelphia, PA 19122-6091, **Business Phone:** (215)204-8621.*

MATHIS, WALTER LEE
Government official. **Personal:** Born Feb 2, 1940, Columbus, MI; married Patricia E Grier; children: Walter, Tracy, Daryl & Melissa. **Educ:** Davenport Col, MI, ceret acct. **Career:** Meijer Inc, shipping clerk, mgr trainee; Mathis Tax Serv, owner; Party Store, owner; Take Pride, Community Mag, founder; Oper Resources Inc, chmn bd & chief exec officer, 1991-. **Orgs:** Past mem, Grand Rapids Housing Bd Appeals; past bd mem, Freedom Homes Inc; Nat Asn Advan Colored People; Kent-CAP Gob Bd; Take Pride! Community. **Honors/Awds:** Named VIP of Grand Rapids Press, 1972. **Military Serv:** AUS, pfc, 1959-62. **Business Addr:** Chairman, Chief Executive Officer, Operation Resources Inc, 1014 Franklin St SE, Grand Rapids, MI 49507-1327, **Business Phone:** (616)243-1919.

MATSON, OLLIE GENOA
Football player. **Personal:** Born May 1, 1930, Trinity, TX; married Mary Louise, May 1, 1952; children: Lisa, Lewis, Ollie III, Bruce & Barbara. **Educ:** San Francisco City Col, 1948; Univ San Francisco, BS, 1952. **Career:** Chicago Cardinals, Halfback(Retired), 1952-58; Los Angeles Rams, 1959-62; Detroit Loins, 1963; Philadelphia Eagles, 1964-66; professional scout, 1966-68; Swinger Golf Club, pres. **Honors/Awds:** U.S. Olympic medal winner, 1952; silver & bronze, 1952; Professional Football Hall of Fame, 1972; College Hall of Fame, 1976; All-NFL honors; Bay Area Sports Hall of Fame, 1983. **Military Serv:** AUS, Cpl, 1953-54. *

MATTHEW, CLIFTON, JR.
Educator. **Personal:** Born Sep 25, 1943, Brooklyn, NY; married Claraleata Cutler; children: Darryl & Adrian. **Educ:** NC A&T State Univ, BS, 1966; Rutgers Univ, MEd, 1973. **Career:** Baltimore Orioles, prof baseball player, 1966-71; Camden Sch Syst, teacher, 1966-71; Trenton State Col, baseball coach, 1974; Upward Bound, dir; Educ Opportunity Fund Trenton St Col, asst dir, 1971-74; Camden City Bd Edn, supr recreation, 1974-79; Pleasantville Pub Sch, dir comm educ, 1979-83; Lower Camden County Bd Ed, asst principal, 1983; Edgewood Jr High Sch, 1990. **Orgs:** Kappa Alpha Psi; Nat Assoc Sec Sch Prins; NJ Princs & Supervisor's Assoc; Phi Delta Kappa Fraternity.

MATTHEWS, ALBERT D
Judge. **Personal:** Born Feb 19, 1923, Oklahoma City, OK; son of Samuel Matthews and Della Matthews; married Mildred; children: Angela M. **Educ:** Howard Univ Sch Law, LLB 1954; Howard Univ, attended, 1941-43 & 1950-51. **Career:** Judge (retired); pvt pract, 1955-58; Los Angeles Co, dep dist atty, 1958-60; Dept Employ, state referee hearing officer, 1960-62; munic ct judge, 1968-73; Pro Tempr, super ct comnr, 1962-68; State Calif, super ct judge, 1973-89; Los Angeles Co Super Ct, judge, 1989-2004. **Orgs:** Los Angeles Bar Asn; Langston Law Club; Nat Conf Trial Ct Judges; Am Bar Asn; bd dirs, Henderson Community Ctr, S Los Angeles; bd mgrs, Am Baptist Pac SW; chmn, MATE; deacon, Church Sch Admin, second Baptist Church, Los Angeles; exec bd, Am Baptist Churches, USA Valley Forge, Pa; christian educr, Sunday Sch Teacher. **Military Serv:** AUS, sgt 1943-45.

MATTHEWS, CANDACE S
Businessperson. **Personal:** Born in New Brighton, PA; children: 3. **Educ:** Carnegie-Mellon Univ, BS, metall eng, admin & mgt sci; Stanford Grad Sch Bus, MBA. **Career:** Bausch & Lomb Oral Care Div, mkt; Proctor & Gamble, Cosmetics & Fragrance Div, sr mkt; Gen Mills, sr mkt; CIBA Vision Corp, sr mkt; Coca-Cola Co, man dir non-cola brands; New Prod & Package Innovation, vp; Soft Sheen-Carson, pres, 2001-. **Orgs:** Bd trustee, Carnegie Mellon Univ, Stanford Grad Sch Bus Adv Coun; bd trustee, Peggy Notebaert Nature Mus; bd trustee, Cosmetic Exec Women & Figure Skating Harlem. **Honors/Awds:** Women of Color iBusiness Person Year Award; Alumni Merit Award, Carnegie Mellon, 2003; Technology Business Person of the Year Award, Oper Push, 2004; United Cerebral Palsy Women Who Care Award, 2005; HELP USA Leadership Award, 2005; Advertising Working Mother of the Year Award, 2005; Outstanding Women in Marketing & Communications Award, Ebony, 2006; Power Award, Essence, 2006. **Special Achievements:** Has been featured in major publications, such as Ebony, Essence, Black Enterprise, Glamour, Salon Sense, and the Wall Street Journal. **Business Addr:** President, Soft Sheen/Carson Inc, 575 5th Ave, New York, NY 10017, **Business Phone:** (212)818-1500.

MATTHEWS, CHRISTY
Executive. **Personal:** Born May 1, 1964, Orlando, FL. **Educ:** Hampton Univ, BA, multidisciplinary studies, 1992, MA, mus studies, 1996. **Career:** Baltimore City Life Mus, asst educ & asst dir educ prog, 1986-89; Colonial Williamsburg Found, character interpreter, 1982-86, dir prog & interpretive prog develop, 1989-99. **Orgs:** IMTAL; CDR; AAAM; AAM. *

MATTHEWS, CLAUDE LANKFORD, JR.
Television producer, u.s. attorney. **Personal:** Born Jun 18, 1941, High Point, NC; son of Claude and Georgianna; married Cynthia C Clark; children: Georgeanne N. **Educ:** Howard Univ, BA, 1963; Georgetown Univ Law Ctr, JD, 1978. **Career:** WTOP-TV, reporter, 1968-70, "Harambee", talk show host, 1970-74; NBC News, ed network radio, 1976-77, ed network TV, 1977-80, Wash producer weekend nightly news, 1980; Pvt Pract, atty, currently. **Orgs:** Pa Bar Asn; Am Bar Asn; DC Bar Asn. **Home Addr:** 2805 31st Pl NE, Washington, DC 20018. **Business Addr:** Attorney, 2805 31st St Pl NE, Washington, DC 20018-1603, **Business Phone:** (202)637-8883.

MATTHEWS, CYNTHIA CLARK
Lawyer. **Personal:** Born Aug 27, 1941, Nashville, TN; married Claude Lankford. **Educ:** Wellesley Col, attended 1961; Howard Univ, BA, 1965; George Wash Univ Nat Law Ctr, JD, 1973. **Career:** Lawyer (retired); Hon John Conyers US Cong, legislative & press asst, 1965-69; United Planning Orgn, pub info officer, 1970-72; US Comm Civil Rights, equal opportunity specialist, 1973-75; Onyx Corp, vpres mkt & contract mgr, 1975-76; Housing Com Coun DC, exec asst to coun mem & atty, 1976-79; US Equal Employ Opportunity Comn, atty advisor dir, chair, mgt dir, 1980-92, dir. **Orgs:** DC Bar 1975; Supreme Ct Bar, 1980; US Dist Ct DC Bar, 1980; Nat Asn Black Women Atty; Am Bar Asn; Anacostia Mus Bd Dir. *

MATTHEWS, REV. DAVID
Clergy, president (organization). **Personal:** Born Jan 29, 1920, Indianola, MS; son of Albert and Bertha Henderson; married Lillian Pearl Banks; children: Denise D. **Educ:** Morehouse Col, BA, 1950; Atlanta Univ; Memphis Theol Sem; Delta State Univ; Reformed Sem. **Career:** Ordained Baptist minister, 1946-; Sunflower City & Ind Pub Schs, teacher, 1950-83; Mt Heroden Baptist Church, Vicksburg MS, pastor, 1951-53; St Paul Baptist Church, pastor, 1953-58; Bell Grove Baptist Church, pastor, currently; Strangers Home Baptist Church, pastor, currently. **Orgs:** Indianola Community Rels Comt; Phi Delta Kappa; Miss State Dept Educ Task Force; moderator, Sunflower County Baptist Asn; vpres, oratorical contest supvr, Nat Baptist Conv USA Inc, 1971-94; pres, Gen Missionary Baptist State Conv Miss, 1974-98. **Honors/Awds:** Honorary Doctor of Divinity, Natchez Junior Col, 1973, Mississippi Industrial Col, 1977, Morris Booker Memorial Col, 1988. **Military Serv:** AUS, pfc, 1942-45; Good Conduct Medal, APTO Medal 1945. **Home Addr:** PO Box 627, Indianola, MS 38751. **Business Addr:** Pastor, Bell Grove Baptist Church, 1301 Bb King Rd, Indianola, MO 38751, **Business Phone:** (662)887-9165.

MATTHEWS, DENISE (VANITY MATTHEWS)
Singer, actor, clergy. **Personal:** Born Jan 4, 1959?, Ontario;married Anthony Smith, 1995. **Career:** Vanity 6, lead singer; Works: Nasty Girls, single; Wild Animal, Skin On Skin, Motown; Film: The Last Dragon, 1985; Never Too Young To Die, 1986; 52 Pickup, 1986; Love You To Death; Deadly Illusion, 1987; Action Jackson, 1988; Neon City, 1991; Da Vinci's War, 1993; South Beach, 1993; Kiss of Death, 1995; TV Series: "The Late Show", 1987; "The New Mike Hammer", 1987; "Miami Vice", 1987; "Ebony/Jet Showcase", 1988; "Memories of Murder", 1990; "Lady Boss", 1992; "Counterstrike", 1992; "Highlander", 1992; Pure Heart Ministries, evangelist & head, currently. **Honors/Awds:** Gold Single, Nasty Girls. **Business Addr:** Evangelist, Head, Pure Heart Ministries, 39270 Paseo Padre Pkwy Suite 214, Fremont, CA 94538, **Business Phone:** (510)744-9822.

MATTHEWS, DOLORES EVELYN
School administrator. **Personal:** Born Jul 23, 1938, DuBois, PA; daughter of George Daniel and Evelyn Goodrich. **Educ:** NY City Community Col, AA&S, assoc, 1961. **Career:** School administrator (Retired); Columbia Univ Col, Physicians & Surgeons Dept Psychiat, prog coordr, postgrad educ officer, 1979-2001. **Orgs:** Nat past pres, Continental Socs Inc, 1993-97; past exec comt, NCNW; moderator, Presbytery New York City, 2000-02; chair, Gen coun, Presbytery New York City, 2002-03; Vice Moderator, Presbyterian women, 2005. **Honors/Awds:** Merit Award, Presbyterian Hosp Comt Adv Coun, 1978; Community Adv Council Award, Columbia Presbyterian Med Ctr, 1979; The Presbyterian Hosp Community Adv Council Award, 1979; President's Award, Continental Societies Inc, 1982, 1984; Distinguished Music Alumnus Award, Du Bois Area High Sch Musical Dept, 1985; Harlem Hosp Pastoral Care Service Award, 1986-93; Psychiatric Residents Award, Columbia Univ Col Physicians & Surgeons, 1988. **Home Addr:** 790 Riverside Dr, New York, NY 10032.

MATTHEWS, DOROTHY
Advertising executive. **Personal:** Born Jan 21, 1962, St Louis, MO. **Educ:** Maryville Col, BA, 1983. **Career:** NY Ins, salesperson, 1983; Channel 4 Newsroom, res person, 1984; Sch Bd Dist 188, secy. **Orgs:** Elks Purple Temple 126; Black Media Coalition; St Louis First Freewell Baptist Church; United Parcel Holiday Club. **Honors/Awds:** Best Essay, First Freewill Bapt Church, 1979. **Business Addr:** Secretary, Lovejoy School District 188, 800 Madison St, Lovejoy, IL 62059.

MATTHEWS, GARY NATHANIEL, JR.
Baseball player. **Personal:** Born Aug 25, 1974, San Francisco, CA; son of Gary Sr. **Career:** San Diego Padres, outfielder, 1999, 2003; Chicago Cubs, 2000-01;Pittsburgh Pirates, 2001; New York Mets, 2002; Baltimore Orioles, 2002-03;San Diego Padres, 2003; Texas Rangers, 2004-06; Los Angeles Angels of Anaheim, 2007-. **Business Addr:** Professional Baseball Player, Los Angeles Angels of Anaheim, 2000 Gene Autry Way, Anaheim, CA 92806, **Business Phone:** 888-796-4256.*

MATTHEWS, DR. GERALD EUGENE
Educator. **Personal:** Born Oct 25, 1943, Michigan City, IN; son of Andrew and Cassie; married Carolyn, Oct 31, 1965; children: Gregory, Corwin & McKenzie Sproul. **Educ:** Univ Mich-Flint, BA, 1978; Univ Mich, MSW, 1980, EdS, 1983, PhD, 1985. **Career:** CS MOH Community Col, adj instr, 1985-; Hamilton Family Health Ctr, exec dir, 1986-92; Wayne State Univ, lectr, 1993-94; Eastern Mich Univ, lectr, 1995-97; Univ Mich, Flint, adj instr Africana studies, 1998-2006; Ferris State Univ, tenured, assoc prof social work, prof social work, currently. **Orgs:** Nat Asn Soc Workers, 1980 & 1992-; planning comnr, Genesee Co, 1984-91; bd dirs, Mich Primary Care Asn, 1985-91; bd governors, Univ Mich, Flint, 1990-93; chair, Ferris State Univ, PAC Subcomt, 1998-; adv bd mem, Mich State Univ Kinship Care Prog, 2000-; Phi Alpha Kappa, 2000. **Special Achievements:** Author: A Declaration of Cultural Independence for Black Americans, 1995; Journey Toward Nationalism: The Implications of Race & Racism, 1999, 2nd Edition, 2001. **Military Serv:** AUS, airborne E-3, 1962-65. **Business Addr:** Professor of Social Work, Ferris State University, ASC 2106 820 Campus Dr, Big Rapids, MI 49307-2225, **Business Phone:** (231)591-2752.

MATTHEWS, GREGORY J.
Administrator. **Personal:** Born Oct 25, 1947, Baltimore, MD; married Paula Allen. **Educ:** Morgan State Univ, BA, socio, 1970; Cop-

pin St Col, MA, Counseling, 1973. **Career:** Adult Ed Economic Manpower develop, instr, 1970; Conciliation & Compliance-MD Comn on Human Rel, dir, 1970-75; Int Asn Offical Human Rights Agencies, EEO consult, 1975; Affirmative Action-Great Atlantic Pacific Tea Co, dir, 1975-78; GJ Matthews & Assoc, managing partner; Staffing & Equal Opp Prog, dir, 1978-85; Am Express Travel Related Serv Co Inc, dir employee rels, 1985-. **Orgs:** Chmn, Nat Urban Affairs Coun; chmn, Fed Corporate Prof; bd mem, Assoc Black Charities; life mem, NAACP; bd mem, Nat Assoc Mkt develop; Edges Group. **Honors/Awds:** Herbert H Weight Award, 1985; distinguished service citation, Nat Black MBA Assoc, 1984. **Business Addr:** Director Employee Relations, American Express Travel, World Financial Center, New York, NY 10285.

MATTHEWS, HARRY BRADSHAW
College administrator. **Personal:** Born Mar 1, 1952, Denmark, SC; son of James Edgar and Lucretia Killingsworth Parler; married Pamela Davis. **Educ:** SUNY Col Oneonta, BA, 1974; Carnegie Mellon Univ, attended 1979; Northern MIch Univ, MA 1981. **Career:** NYS Minority Ways & Means Res Div, trainee, intern, 1973-74; SUNY Col Oneonta, asst dean res, 1974-78; Northern Mich Univ, dir black student serv, 1978-81; Hobart & William Smith Col, asst dean, 1981-85; Gettysburg Col, dean intercultural advancement 1985-93; Hartwick Col, assoc dean, 1993-, US Pluralism Prog, dir & USCT Inst Local Hist & Family Res, pres, currently. **Orgs:** Mich Gov & Bd Educ Task Force, 1980-82; Human Rights Comn, Geneva NY, 1983-85; Penn Hist & Mus Comns Black Hist Adv Comn, 1989; dir & founder, Minority Youth Educ Inst, 1988-; co-chmn, Ann Conf, Afro-Am Hist & Geneal Soc, 1991. **Honors/Awds:** Presidential Classroom for Young Americans, 1970; American Legion Leadership Award, SUNY Oneonta 1974; Distinguished Visitor US 8th Air Force, 1979; WEB DuBois, Dist Lecturer Hobart & William Smith Col, 1986; Certificate of Merit, AAHGS, 1989. **Home Addr:** 140 W Broadway, Gettysburg, PA 17325. **Business Addr:** Associate Dean, Director of US Pluralism Programs, Hartwick College, Bresee Hall 205, Oneonta, NY 13820.

MATTHEWS, DR. HEWITT W.
Educator, school administrator, vice president (organization). **Personal:** Born Dec 1, 1944, Pensacola, FL; son of Hewitt and Jestine; married Marlene Mouzon; children: Derrick & David. **Educ:** Clark Atlanta Univ, BS, pharm, 1966; Mercer Univ Sch Pharm, MS, pharmaceut biochem, 1968; Univ Wis Madison, PhD, pharmaceut biochem, 1973. **Career:** Center for Disease Control, res chemist, 1976; TX Southern Univ, visiting assoc prof 1979; Mercer Univ Sch Pharmacy, asst dean 1980-83; visiting scientist-,summer 1987, 1988; Mercer Univ Atlanta, prof & asst provost; Mercer Univ Sch Pharmacy, prof, assoc dean 1985-89; Mercer Univ Atlanta, Sch Pharmacy, Hood-Meyer Alumni prof, dean, 1990, vpres health sci, Currently. **Orgs:** AACP, NPhA; ASHP; AphA; Rho Chi; Sigma Xi; Phi Kappa Phi; bd dirs, Geo Pharm Asn; chmn, Comn Pharmaceut Care; gov adv coun, Sci & Technol Dev;Nat Asn Chain Drug stores, educ comt; Nat Community Pharmacist Asn. **Honors/Awds:** Fel, Am Found Pharmaceut Educ, 1968; Nat Inst Health, predoctoral fel,1970-76; Prof of the Year, Mercer Univ Sch Pharm, 1980; Hood-Myers Alumni Chair, Mercer Univ Sch Pharm, 1983-; Teacher of the Year, 1991; Outstanding Teacher Award, Southern Sch Pharm; Rennebohm Teaching Asst Award, Univ Wis. **Business Addr:** Dean, Vice President, Mercer University, School of Pharmacy, 3001 Mercer Univ Dr, PAC-106, Atlanta, GA 30341-4155.*

MATTHEWS, IRVING J.
Executive. **Educ:** Southern Univ, BS, eng; A&M Col, MS, eng. **Career:** Daytona Lincoln Mercury, owner; Matthews Automotive Group (Advantage Ford,Prestige Ford & Daytona Lincoln Mercury), pres & chief exec officer, currently; Bd Dirs, Volusia County Advanced Technology Center. **Orgs:** Daytona Beach Symphony Soc; Bd trustees, Bethune-Cookman Col; Beta Xi Boule; Advanced Technol Ctr Williamson Blvd. **Business Addr:** Chief Executive Officer, Prestige Ford Inc, 17701 US Hwy 441, Mount Dora, FL 32757-6743, **Business Phone:** (352)357-5522.

MATTHEWS, REV. JAMES VERNON, II
Clergy. **Personal:** Born Oct 25, 1948, Berkeley, CA; son of James Vernon and Yvonne Feast. **Educ:** St Patrick's Col, Mountain View, CA, BA, Humanities, 1970; St Patrick's Sem, Menlo Park CA, MDiv, 1973; Jesuit Sch Theo, Berkeley CA, DMin, cand, 1979. **Career:** St Louis Bertrand Church, Oakland, CA, assoc pastor, 1974-78; All Saints Church, Hayward, CA, admin, 1978-80; St Cyril Church, Oakland, CA, admin, 1980-83; Oakland Diocese, Oakland, CA, vicar Black Catholics, 1983-87; St Cornelius Church, Richmond, CA, admin, 1987-89; St Benedict Church, Oakland CA, pastor, 1989-. **Orgs:** Knights St Peter Claver Third & Fourth Degrees, 1971-; past bd mem, Nat Black Catholic Clergy Caucus, 1973-; rev bd, Alameda County Revenue Sharing, 1975-76; bd dir, Campaign Human Develop, 1979-84; comnr, Oakland Sch Dist, Comn Educ & Career Develop, 1982-83; Bay Area Black United Fund Relig Task Force, 1982-; bd dir, Catholic Charities Parish Outreach Prog, 1983-87; adv bd, Oakland Mayor's Task Force Hunger, 1984-87; adv bd, Oakland Mayor's Task Force Black & Jewish Rels, 1984-87; diocesan coordr, Nat Conf Interracial Justice, 1984-; chaplain, African-Am Catholic Pastoral Ctr, 1990-; Oakland Mayor's Adv Coun, 1991-; Oakland Strategic Planning, 1991-; bd mem, Alameda County Health Care Found. **Honors/Awds:** Outstanding Black Sermons, Judson Press, Publishers, 1975; Rose Casanave Serv Award, Black Catholic Vicariate, Oakland CA, 1982; Martin Luther King Jr Award, United East Oakland Clergy, 1984; Marcus Foster Distinguished Alumni Award, Marcus Foster Educ Inst, 1984; Religion Award, Alameda/Contra Costa Chapter Links Inc, 1985; Service Award, Xavier Univ Alumni Asn, 1985. **Special Achievements:** Father James Vernon Matthews, II was ordained as the first Black Catholic Priest in northern California on May 3, 1974. **Home Addr:** 2245 82nd Ave, Oakland, CA 94605. **Business Addr:** Pastor, Saint Benedict Catholic Church, 2245 82nd Ave, Oakland, CA 94605, **Business Phone:** (510)632-1847.

MATTHEWS, LEONARD LOUIS
Educator. **Personal:** Born Dec 4, 1930, New Orleans, LA; son of Alex and Angie Bell; married Dolores, Dec 29, 1952; children: Mallory Louis & Cassandra Duere. **Educ:** Southern Univ, BS, BA, 1952-59; Calif State Univ, credential psychol, 1964-65; Univ Calif, Los Angeles, credential psychol, 1970-72; Calif State Univ, MA, 1972-74; Pepperdine Univ, Los Angeles, credential educ, 1973-74. **Career:** Educator (retired), Director; St John School Dist, elem prin, 1952-59; La Unified Sch Dist, drama spec, master teacher, 1959-70, counsr, 1970-74; Inglewood Unified Sch Dist, sec prin, 1974-; Youth Positive Alternatives, organizer, educ dir, currently; Atherton Christian Sch, prin, 2000-02. **Orgs:** Secy, Alpha Phi Alpha, 1963-64; chmn, YMCA, 1981-85; Organizer Citizens Against Prostitution, 1982-84; Dr Martin L King Jr Mem, 1983-86; Citizens Against Crime & Drugs, 1984-86; vpres, Parents Teachers Asn, 1985-86; vpres, Inglewood Mgt Asn, 1986; Calif Continuation Educ Asn; City Inglewood, Leadership Coun, chmn, Educ Award Youth Comt; pres, Block Club; educ chmn, City Inglewood Leadership Coun. **Honors/Awds:** Award of Recognition Project Investment, 1978; Proclamation City Inglewood, 1980, 1982; Service Award, Asn Calif Adminrs, 1982; Commendation, City Inglewood, 1985. **Military Serv:** AUS, act sgt, 1976-78. **Home Addr:** 9626 5th Ave, Inglewood, CA 90305, **Home Phone:** (213)777-0856. **Business Addr:** Principal, Inglewood Unified School District, 401 S Inglewood Ave, Inglewood, CA 90301, **Business Phone:** (310)419-2700.

MATTHEWS, MARY JOAN
Educator, mayor. **Personal:** Born Dec 19, 1945, Boley, OK; divorced. **Educ:** Langston Univ, BS, elem educ, 1967; Calif State Col Dominguez Hills, MA, Learning Disabilities 1976; Univ Okla, cert psychometry, 1980. **Career:** Paramount Unified Sch Dist, teacher, 1968-70; Sapulpa City Sch, teacher, 1971-74; Boley Public Sch, teacher, 1976-79; Okla State Dept Educ, psychometrist, 1979; mayor, Boley, OK, 1999-. **Orgs:** Secy, Greater Boley Area Nat Asn Advan Colored People Br, 1981; Okla Coun Voc Educ, 1982-97; secy, Boley Chamber Com, 1983-96; bd dir, CREOKS Mental Health, 1983-00; Grammateus, Epsilon Rho Omega Chapter Alpha Kappa Alpha Sorority, 1989; secy, Self Culture Club Okla Federated Colored Women's Club. **Home Addr:** PO Box 352, Boley, OK 74829. **Business Addr:** Mayor, PO Box 158, Boley, OK 78429, **Business Phone:** (918)667-9790.

MATTHEWS, DR. MERRITT STEWART
Physician. **Personal:** Born Jul 8, 1939, Atlantic City, NJ; son of George and Bessie; married Patricia Anne Delgado; children: Shari, Luis, Merritt Jr, Michael & Marguerite. **Educ:** Howard Univ, BS, Liberal Arts, 1961, Sch Med, MD, 1965. **Career:** St Joseph's Hosp, intern, 1965-66, resident, 1966-68, chief resident family practice, 1967-68; Otay Med Clinic SD, CA, 1971-74; USAF Med Corps, 1968-70; San Diego Acad Family Physicians, pres, 1984-85; Family Practice Community Paradise Valley Hosp, chairperson, 1983-86, 1993-96; Skilled Nursing Facility, San Diego Physicians & Surgeons Hosp, med dir, 1983-87; pvt practice, physician. **Orgs:** Physician, San Diego County Jails, 1976-92; bd dir, San Diego Acad Family Physicians, 1982-, Jackie Robinson YMCA San Diego, bd dirs, 1983-85; co-dir, Western Med Group Lab, 1982-87; Task Force SD Police Dept, 1983; dir, 1988-95, Calif Acad Family Physicians; alternate delegate, Calif Med Asn, 1987-93; Comn on Minority Health Affairs AAFP, 1992-95, chair, 1995; bd, San Diego AIDS Found, 1992-94. **Honors/Awds:** Certified, Am Bd Family Physicians, 1970, recertified 1976, 1982, 1988, 1995, 2001; Delegate, Calif Med Asn, 1994-; fel, Am Acad Family Physicians, 1974; Spec Achievement Award, Jackie Robinson YMCA, 1985; Competitive Award for Practicing Phys, Fam Practice, NMA, 1993, 1994. **Special Achievements:** publ article "Cholelithiasis: A Differential Diagnosis in Abdominal Crisis of Sickle Cell Anemia," J of NMA, 1981. **Military Serv:** USAF, capt, 1968-70. **Home Addr:** 383 Winewood St, San Diego, CA 92114. **Business Addr:** Physician, 752 med Ctr Suite 210, Chula Vista, CA 91911, **Business Phone:** (619)656-0206.

MATTHEWS, ROBERT L. (BOB MATTHEWS)
School administrator, consultant. **Personal:** Born Jun 2, 1930, Tonganoxie, KS; son of Suzie Jane Brown Matthews and Mark Hanna Matthews; married Ardelle Marie Dunlap, Aug 26, 1952; children: Mark Douglas, Brian Louis & Scott Wallace. **Educ:** Kans State Teachers Col, Emporia, Kans, BS, 1952; Columbia Univ, MA, 1955; US Int Univ, PhD, 1971. **Career:** San Diego City Sch, teacher, 1955-64, prin, 1965-72, dir elem educ, 1972-83, prin, 1983-84; US Govt, NDEA fel, 1965; Rockefeller Found fel, 1971-72; Humanities fel, Nat Endowment Humanities, 1976; Educ Cult Complex, pres, 1984-86; Continuing Educ Centers San Diego Community Col Dist, pres, 1986-92; self-employed, educ consult. **Orgs:** Officer, San Diego Urban League, 1965-; Educ Comt, San Diego Zool Soc, 1973-; pres, Elem Inst Sci, 1983-84; pres, Zeta Sigma Lambda Alpha Phi Alpha, 1984-85; bd dir, Mus Nat Hist, 1984-; Nat Asn Advan Colored People. **Military Serv:** AUS, cpl; Peace Medal, Marksmanship, 1952-54. **Home Addr:** 4931 Dassco Court, San Diego, CA 92102-3717.

MATTHEWS, ROBERT L
Law enforcement officer. **Personal:** Born Oct 8, 1947, Wilmington, DE; married Elsie Nichols, Aug 26, 1972; children: Miel & Amne. **Educ:** Fla A&M Univ, BA, (magna cum laude), sociol, 1972; Ind State Univ, MS, criminol, 1973. **Career:** Bur Prisons, USP Leavenworth, assoc warden, 1980, warden, 1981, FCI Ashland, warden, 1981, FCI Lexington, warden, 1985, USP Atlanta, warden, 1990, regional dir, 1991-94, asst dir, Southeast Region, regional dir; US Marshals Serv, Dist Columbia, US marshal, 1983; Correctional Serv Corp, Adult Div, sr vpres, 2001-. **Orgs:** Am Correctional Asn, 1981-; Nat Asn Blacks Criminal Justice, 1982-; FDL Exec Bd, Atlanta, 1990-91; FDL Exec Bd, San Francisco, 1991-; exec mem, Correctional Employees Comt ACA, 1992. **Honors/Awds:** Attorney General's Award, Distinguished Service, 1983; Bureau Prisons Director's Award, Pub Serv, 1989; Correctional Service Award, Nat Asn Blacks Crimininal Justice, 1990; Senior Executive Service Meritorious Service, Dept Justice, 1990-92; Distinguished Service Award, Am Fedn Gov Employees, Labor Mgt, 1991. **Special Achievements:** Appointment to Leavenworth Civil Service Commission, 1990; Dept Justice, Sr Exec Service Outstanding Performance Rating, 1990-92. **Military Serv:** USF, sgt, 1965-69. **Home Addr:** 705 Birkdale Dr, Fayetteville, GA 30215. **Business Phone:** (941)953-9199.

MATTHEWS, VANITY. See MATTHEWS, DENISE.

MATTHEWS, VINCENT EDWARD
Athlete. **Personal:** Born Dec 16, 1947, Queens, NY. **Educ:** Johnson C Smith Col. **Career:** Athlete (retired); Olympic Track Runner. **Orgs:** Mem Olympic Teams 1968, 1972. **Honors/Awds:** Won Silver Medal Pan-Am Games 1967; AAU 1968; gold medals, Summer Olympics, 1968 & 1972.

MATTHEWS, VIRGIL E.
Scientist, politician. **Personal:** Born Oct 5, 1928, Lafayette, AL; son of Virgil (deceased) and Izetta Roberta Ware (deceased); married Shirley McFatridge Matthews, Jan 23, 1960 (divorced); children: Brian Keith, Michael Andre, Deborah Michelle. **Educ:** Univ Ill, BS, chem, 1951; Univ Chicago, SM, chem, 1952, PhD, chem, 1955. **Career:** Scientist (retired); Univ Chicago, teaching asst, 1951-52; Union Carbide Corp, res chemist, 1954-67, proj scientist, 1967-75, develop scientist chem & plastics div, 1975-86; W Va State Col, instr part time chem, 1955-60, prof part-time chem, 1960-70, Dept Chem, prof & chmn, 1986-94. **Orgs:** Vpres, Nat Asn Advan Colored Pres, Charleston Br, 1964-72; pres, Charleston Bus & Prof Men Club, 1965-66; councilman-at-Large Charleston, 1967-83; mem, Alpha Phi Alpha Frat, 1967-; Dem Nat Conv W Va, 1968; Dem nominee for state senate 8th Dist of W Va, 1970; Munic Planning Comn, Charleston, 1971-83; chmn Planning Comn City Coun Charleston, 1971-83; Am Chem Soc; elected mem, W Va State Dem Exec Comn, 1978-82; Fel Am Inst Chemists; Fel AAAS; Sigma Xi; Phi Lambda Upsilon; Am Men Sci; alternate delegate, Dem Nat Conv W Va, 1980; Dem Nominee for City Treas, Charleston, WV 1983. **Special Achievements:** First African American chemist to be employed by Carbide at South Charleston; first African American elected to a Council-at-Large seat in Charleston. **Home Addr:** 835 Carroll Rd, Charleston, WV 25314, **Home Phone:** (304)343-0724. *

MATTHIS, JAMES L., III
Marketing executive, business owner, executive director. **Personal:** Born Mar 21, 1955, Chicago, IL; son of James L and Doris Buckley; married Michelle Englander; children: Jordan. **Educ:** Ala A&M Univ, Huntsville, BS, acct, 1977; Univ Chicago, MBA, 1994. **Career:** Miller Brewing Co, Chicago, IL, merchandiser, 1977-78, Miller Brewing Co, Bloominton, IN, area sales mgr, 1978-81, Miller Brewing Co, St Louis, MO, area sales mgr, 1981-85, Miller Brewing Co, Milwaukee, WI, talent & video mkt mgr, 1985-96; Educ Innovations, owner, 1995-2006; Community Econ Develop Corp Inc, exec dir, 2007-. **Orgs:** Am Mkt Asn, 1984-; Nat Asn Advan Colored People, 1978-; World Tae Kwon Do Fedn, 1980-; exec dir, Proj Equality Wis, 2001-03. **Home Addr:** 2227 N First St, Milwaukee, WI 53212, **Home Phone:** (414)264-5356. **Business Addr:** Executive Director, Community Economic Development Corporation Inc, 718 N Mem Dr, Racine, WI 53404, **Business Phone:** (262)635-8908.

MAULDIN, JERMAINE DUPRI. See DUPRI, JERMAINE.

MAULTSBY, DR. PORTIA K
Educator. **Personal:** Born Jun 11, 1947, Orlando, FL; daughter of Valdee C Maultsby and Maxie Clarence Maultsby Sr. **Educ:** Mt St

Scholastica Col, Atchison, KS, BM, piano & theory compos, 1968; Univ Wis, Madison, Wis, MM, musicol, 1969, PhD, ethnomusicology, 1974. **Career:** Ind Univ, Bloomington, Ind, vis asst prof, 1971-74, asst prof, 1975, assoc prof, 1981, assoc chmn, afro-am studies, 1981-84, dept chmn, afro-am studies, 1985-91, prof, 1992, dir, archives African Am music & cul, 1991-; Swarthmore Col, Music Dept, vis prof, 1982; Seattle Pac Univ, Music Dept, vis prof, 1983; Mus Am Hist Smithsonian Inst, Wash, DC, sr vis scholar, 1984-85; Indiana Music Educators Asn, bd dir, 1993-95; Colorado Col, Music Dept, vis prof, 1994; Utrecht Univ, Neth, Musicol Dept, Belle van Zuylen, Prof African Am Music, 1998; Ctr Advan Study Behavioral Sci, Stanford, Calif, vis prof, 1999-2000. **Orgs:** Exec bd, Int Asn Study Popular Music, Am Br, 1987-95, ed bd, 1989-; coun mem, Soc ethnomusicology, 1973-76, 1977-80, 1988-91; Asn African Am Museums; Am Music Soc. **Honors/Awds:** Portia K Maultsby Day proclaimed by the Mayor of Orlando, FL, 1975; Course Development Grant Learning Resources, Ind Univ, 1981-82; InterNat Travel Overseas Conference Fund for travel to Oxford, Eng-Ind Univ, 1981; Ind Comt Humanities Summer Res Fel, 1984; Ford Senior Postdoctoral Fel, Nat Res Coun, 1984-85; Awarded Hon Doctor Music Deg, Benedictine Col, Kans, 1985; Research Grant, Found Nat Res Coun, 1985-86; selected as one of 6 American ethnomusicologists to participate in an American-Soviet Research Conference in the Soviet Union, 1988; selected as one of 8 American performers & scholars to participate in workshop & conference on African American Sacred Music in Havana, Cuba, 1990; Utrecht Univ, Netherlands, apptd prof, "Belle van Zuylen" Chair, Distinguished Vis Prof, 1998; Research Grant, Pres's Coun Int Prog, 1998; IU Ameritech Grant, "Multicultural Multimedia on the Web: From Spirituals to Hip-Hop, the Music and Culture of Black America", 2000-01. **Special Achievements:** Delivered keynote address for GATT Conference on the exchange of culture between America and Europe in Tilburg, Neth, 1994; fel, Ctr Advan study Behavioral Sci, Stanford, Calif, 1999-00. **Home Addr:** 537 Plymouth Rd, Bloomington, IN 47408, **Home Phone:** (812)333-2544. **Business Addr:** Professor, Indiana University, Department of Folklore and Ethnomusicology, 504 N Fess St, Bloomington, IN 47405, **Business Phone:** (812)855-2708.

MAULTSBY, REV. DR. SYLVESTER
Government official. **Personal:** Born Oct 24, 1935, Whiteville, NC; son of Reather; married Mildred Baldwin; children: Jerome, Hilda & Thimothy. **Educ:** Atlanta Col, Mortuary Sci, grad, 1959; Penn Univ, 1973; Hampton Inst, CT Sch Rel, Cert, 1978; Liberty Univ, attended 1985; Liberty Bible Col, Lynchburg, Va Th G, 1989-; Conn Inst Christian Relig, Sch Theol Va Union Univ, bd, 1981; Wheaton Col, Sch Evangelism, 1992; Shaw Divinity Sch, DDiv, 1990; Liberty Univ, PhD, 1995. **Career:** Edwards Co, expediter, 1960-62; Norwalk Police Dept, patrolman, 1962-68; Norwalk Area Ministry, youth dir, 1968-70; New York Life Ins Co, underwriter, 1970-75; Gen Motors, Finance Div, 1973-75; Conn State Police, chaplain, 1985-; Prudential Life Ins Co Am, dist agent, 1975-; State Conn, justice peace, 1993-. **Orgs:** Assoc minister, Calvary Baptist Church, Norwalk, CT, 1976-; Nat Black Caucus Local Elected Officials 1976; Hampton Univ Minister Conf, 1976; vpres, Greater Norwalk Black Democratic Club, 1976-; city sheriff, Norwalk City,1977-80; Counman, City Norwalk, 1981-; exec bd, NAACP; 32 degree Prince Hall Masonic Order; William Moore Lodge #1533, Elks IBPOEW; past patron, Eastern Star PHA; founding bd dir, PIVOT, alcoholic & drug rehab center; founder & dir, Norwalk InterdenomiNat Youth Movement; CT Baptist Missionary Conv; chmn Political Affairs Conn Missionary Baptist Convention 1987-; The Baptist Ministers Conf, Greater New York & Vicinity 1986-; The Am Asn Christian Counr, 1992-; Int Conf Police Chaplains, 1993; comnr, Second Taxing Dist Norwalk City, CT. **Honors/Awds:** Distinguished Achievement Greater Norwalk Black Dem Club; Outstanding Citizen Norwalk Area Improvement League; US Jaycees Spoke Award Junior Chamber Commerce; Service Award, United Way; Holy Order of Past High Priesthood Award, 1974; Man of the Year Award, The Norwalk Youth Comm Concert Choir, 1983; CT Gen Assembly Official Citation for Presidential Campaign of Jesse Jackson, 1984; Realities of Empowerment Award CT State Fed of Black Dems, 1985. **Special Achievements:** First Black Democrat for State Senator from Fairfield County, CT 1980. **Military Serv:** AUS paratrooper Cp Jumpmaster 1953-56; Sr Jumper; Good Conduct; Serv Medal; Leadership Medal Korean War.

MAUNEY, DONALD WALLACE, JR.
Executive. **Personal:** Born Oct 16, 1942, New Castle, PA; divorced; children: Michael A, Dawnya M & Donovan T. **Educ:** New Castle High Sch, attended 1960. **Career:** State Dept Fed Govt, budget analyst, 1962-69; Robert Hall Store, asst mgr, 1969-70; Gen Acct Br DC Land Agency, chief, 1970-75; Tenant Ledger Br DC Dept Housing & Comn, chief, 1988; Diversified Payments & Loan Servicing Br, chief, 1985; The DM Products Corp, CEO; D W M Enterprises Inc, pres, currently; Awards & Things, pres, currently. **Orgs:** Pres, Tri-State Enterprises Inc; proprietor, Tri-State Engraving Co, 1969-70; state pres, DC Jaycees, 1975-76; vpres, US Jaycees, 1976-77; treas, Commerce Dept Toastmasters, 1976-77; AFA, USA Elected Jaycess Int World V Pres Johannesburg S Africa, 1977; AFA mem, US Jaycees Exec Com; NE & SE Regional Bd Dirs, Greater Wash Boys & Girls Clubs, 1994-95; chmn bd, DC Coun Clothing Kids Inc; exec com, DC Vol Clearing House; bd dir, DC Jacyee Youth develop Trust; trustee, Plymouth Congregational United Ch Christ; pres, Jaycee Int Senate, Wash DC; secy, Assoc Renewal Educ Inc. **Honors/Awds:** Spl DC City Council Community Award Resolution, 1976; Jaycee of Year, 1973; Hon Citizen Baton Rouge LA. **Military Serv:** AUS, 1965-67, Reserves, 1967-76; DC, NG, 1977-94. **Business Addr:** President, Awards & Things, 2811 12 St NE, Washington, DC 20017, **Business Phone:** (202)635-3555.*

MAUPIN, DR. JOHN E
Dentist, school administrator, educator. **Personal:** Born Oct 28, 1946, Los Angeles, CA; married Eilene; children: Deanne, Henry & Virgil. **Educ:** San Jose State Col, pre-19dentistry & bus admin, 1968; Meharry Med Col, DDS, 1972; Loyola Col, MBA, 1979. **Career:** Mitary service (retired), educator, dentist; US Army Dental Corps, capt, 1972-81; West Baltimore Community Health Care Corp, dental dir, 1976-81; Baltimore City Health Dept, assist commnr health servs, 1981-84, dep commnr med servs, 1984-87; Southside Healthcare Inc, chief execut officer, 1987-89; Morehouse Sch Med, execu vpres, 1989-94, pres, currently; Meharry Med Col, pres & chief exec officer, 1994; Health South Corp, dir, 2004. **Orgs:** Nat Dental Asn; Am Asn Higher Educ; Asn Am Med Cols; Nat Asn Health Serv Execs; Nat Asn Community Health Centers; Am Dental Asn; N Ga Dental Asn; Nat Inst Health. **Honors/Awds:** N Ga Dental Soc, Dentist of the Year; President's Award, Nat Dental Asn; City Baltimore, Mayors Citation; City Coun Baltimore, Presidents Citation; Hon Doctor Laws Degree, Va Union Univ; Hon Doctor Sci Degree, Morehouse Sch Med. **Military Serv:** AUS Dental Corps Active Reserve, lt col; The Army Commendation Medal; The Army Achievement Medal; Meritorious Service Medal. **Business Addr:** President, Chief Executive Officer, Morehouse School of Medicine, 720 Westview Dr SW, Atlanta, GA 37208-3599, **Business Phone:** (404)752-1500.

MAUSI, SHAHIDA ANDREA
Artistic director. **Personal:** Born Dec 27, 1954, Detroit, MI; daughter of Nathan T Garrett and Joyce Finley Garrett; divorced; children: Dorian, Sulaiman, Rashid, Malik. **Educ:** Univ Detroit, Detroit, MI, BA, 1976. **Career:** Arts in Pub Places, Detroit, coordr & dir, 1976-78; Detroit Pub Libr, prog specialist, 1978-81; Capricorn Enterprises, producer, 1979-80; Detroit Coun Arts, Detroit, MI, exec dir, 1982-93; Greater Detroit YWCA, exec dir, 1993-; The Right Prods Inc, owner & pres, currently; Producer: "Amen Corner", 1980; "Nina Simone in Concert", 1985; "Fela in Concert", 1986; "Debut of Jamison Project", 1988. **Orgs:** New Detroit Art Comt, 1982-; bd mem, Mus African Am Hist, 1984-; Mich Dem Party, 1985-; panel mem, Nat Endowment Arts, 1985-; Detroit People Mover Art Comn, 1986-; bd mem, Jamison Proj, Repertory Dance Am Found, 1989-. **Business Addr:** Owner, President, The Right Productions Inc, PO Box 32778, Detroit, MI 48232, **Business Phone:** (313)869-1367.*

MAXEY, MARLON LEE
Basketball player. **Personal:** Born Feb 19, 1969, Chicago, IL. **Educ:** Univ Minn; Univ Tex-El Paso. **Career:** Minn Timberwolves, forward, 1992-94; Breogan, 1994-95; Larissa, Greece, 1995-96; Peristeri, Greece, 1996-97; Iraklis Salonique, Greece, 1997-98; Peristeri, 1998-99; Villeurbanne, France, forward, 1999-2000.

MAXEY, DR. RANDALL W
Educator, physician. **Personal:** Born Dec 1, 1941, Cincinnati, OH; married Gem L, 1979; children: 5. **Educ:** Univ Cincinnati, Col Pharm, BS, 1966; Howard Univ Grad Sch, PhD; Howard Univ, Col Med, MD, 1972. **Career:** Howard Univ, chmn & founder, 1969-72, instr, 1969-72, dir, 1969-71, chair, 1970-71; Univ Hosp, Downstate Med Ctr, dir, 1976-78; State Univ Ny, clin asst prof, 1977-78, asst prof, 1977-78; Kings County Hosp, asst dir, 1977-78; Daniel Freeman Mem Hosp, attend physician, 1978-, dir, 1983-88; Centinela Hosp Med Ctr, attend physician, 1978-; Robert F Kennedy Med Ctr, attend physician, 1978-2004, dir, 1983-96; Brotman Med Ctr, attend physician, 1978-2000; Cedars Sinai Med Ctr, attend physician, 1978-2000; Charles R. Drew Univ, Dept Med & Sci, Los Angeles, CA, clin asst prof, 1980-88; Pacific Coast Dialysis Ctr, med dir, 1986-98; Church Health Network, CA, founder & pres, 1990-; Guam Mem Hosp, attend physician, 1992-2000; Los Angeles Dialysis Ctr, supv med dir, 1993-98; Pacific Dialysis Ctr, supv med dir, 1993-98; Associated Primary Care Physicians Med Group, Inglewood, pres, 1994; Guam Renal Care, supv med dir, 1996-98; pvt practice, currently. **Orgs:** Am Soc Pharmacol & Exp Therapeut, 1960-75; Am Soc Nephrology, 1975-; International Soc Artificial Internal Organs, 1975-80; Am Soc Artificial Internal Organs, 1975-80;founding pres & mem bd, Asn Minority Nephrologists, 1986-; pres, Charles R Drew Med Soc, 1992-94, exec db, 1992-95, bd dir, 1992-2000; pres, Golden State Med Asn, 1994-95; chmn, Integrated Health & Managed Care Task Force, 1996-99; bd trustee, Nat Med Asn, 1996-, secy, 1999-2001, chmn, 2001-02, pres, 2002-04, immediate past pres, 2004-05; pres, Alliance Minority Med Asn, 2004-; Res Found Ethnic-Related Dis; Nati Asn Patients on Hemodialysis & Transplantation; t Unity One- Anti-Gang Advocacy Prog Adv Bd. **Honors/Awds:** Dolly Cohen Award, Univ Cincinnati, Outstanding Service to Univ, 1966; First place, Student Res Presentation, Student Nat Med Asn, 1969; President's Service to Howard Award, Howard Univ, 1972; Award for "Academic Excellence," Cincinnati Chapter, Operation P.U.S.H, 1972; Physicians Award Inglewood Physicians, 1990; Minority Nephrologists Presidents Award; Minority Health Inst Award for Serv, 1991; Presidents Award, Charles R. Drew Medical Soc, 1992 Dean's Special Service Award, Howard Univ, 2000. **Home Phone:** (310)680-1810. **Business Phone:** (310)680-1810.*

MAXIE, PEGGY JOAN
Executive, consultant. **Personal:** Born Aug 18, 1936, Amarillo, TX; daughter of Cleveland Maxie and Reba Harris M Jackson. **Educ:** Seattle Univ, BA, 1970; Univ Wash, MSW, 1972. **Career:** Off Atty Gen; Seattle Univ; Seattle Urban League, housing counr; State Wash, state rep, 1971-83; House Higher Educ Comm, chair, 1972-76; Joint Comn Higher Educ, officer, 1972-76; Cent Area Coun Alcoholism, exec dir & consult; Peggy Maxie & Assoc, pres, 1978-; Permanent Prof Staff Employment Comn & Session Staff Employment Comn, 1979-84. **Orgs:** Nat Asn Social Workers; Employee Assistance Prof Asn; US Tennis Asn; Nat Rehab Coun-Asn; League Women Voters; bd mem, Capital Hill Chamber Co-m;Alpha Kappa Alpha; Delta Epsilon Sorority; Ladies Auxiliary, Knights Peter Claver; Iota Phi Lambda Sorority Inc; Munic League; Madrona Community Coun; Seattle Chamber Com; Seattle Exec Asn; Self-Insured Org. **Honors/Awds:** Hon LLD, St Martin's Col, 1975; Elder of Distinction Award; Certificate, Seattle Univ. **Special Achievements:** First black Woman Ever Elected in Washington Legislature; Featured in The Washington Story' a History of Our State, published by the Board of Directors of Seattle Public Schools. **Business Addr:** President, Peggy Maxie & Associates, 1441 Madrona Dr, Seattle, WA 98122-3519, **Business Phone:** (206)325-6088.

MAXWELL, ANITA
Basketball player. **Personal:** Born Apr 7, 1974, Dallas, TX. **Educ:** NMex State Univ, BA, intl bus, 1996. **Career:** Basketball player (retired); Asa Jerusalem, Israeli Pro League, basketballplayer; Cleveland Rockers, forward, 1997. **Honors/Awds:** Big West Conference Player of the Year.

MAXWELL, BERTHA LYONS
Educator. **Personal:** Born in Seneca, SC. **Educ:** Johnson C Smith Univ, BA, 1954; UNC Greensboro, MEd, 1966; Union Grad Sch, PhD, 1974; Cath Univ; Howard Univ; Univ SC. **Career:** Alexander State Sch, teacher, 1954-60, corrective reading teacher, 1960-67; Villa Heights Elem Sch, ast prin, 1967; Morgan Elem Sch, prin, 1967-68; Albemarle Rd Elem Sch, prin, 1968-70; Univ NC Charlotte, assoc prof educ, dir black studies prog, 1970-. **Orgs:** Organizer & coordr, Charlotte's first Volunteer Teacher Corps; cons Head, Start Winthrop Col Rock Hill SC, 1965; visiting comn, Southern Asn Accreditation Gastonia City Sch System, 1967; local consult, ACE Workshop UNCC, 1969; mem bd dir, Int Reading Asn, 1969-72; African Heritage Study Asn; Resolutions Comn, 1970; chmn, Resolutions Comn, 1971; consult, So Regional Educ Bd Regional Conf, 1971; chmn, visiting comn Harrisburg Sch; So Asn Accreditation Cabarrus Co Sch, 1972; chmn, visiting comn Greensboro City Sch, 1973; NEA; Nat Asn Elem Sch Prin; Afro-Am Study Asn; secy, Charlotte-Mecklenburg Elem Pring Unit; Greater Charlotte Coun Int Reading Asn; Int Platform Asn; League Women Votes; chmn, Charlotte-Mecklenburg Human Resources Comn League Women Voters; bd dir, Johnston Memorial YMCA; Jack & Jill Inc; past pres, Merry Makers Inc. **Honors/Awds:** Outstanding Community Services Award, Las Amagis Inc, 1967; outstanding leadership, Sigma Gamma Rho Sorority, 1969; outstanding community leader, 1971; outstanding educator, Las Amagis Inc, 1973.

MAXWELL, DR. MARCELLA J.
Government official, educator. **Personal:** Born Nov 6, 1927, Asbury Park, NJ; daughter of William B Redwood and Ethel Click; married Edward C, Apr 10, 1968 (deceased); children: Deborah Young. **Educ:** Long Island Univ, Brooklyn NY, BS, 1956, MS, 1958; Fordham Univ, NY, EdD, 1972. **Career:** New York City Comm Status Women, asst acad dean; Pub Sch Dist 20, elem sch teacher & teacher trainer, 1958-63; Puerto Rico Sch Dist, exchange teacher, 1963; Bank State Col, curric coordr; Bd Higher Educ Medgar Evers Col, 1971-84; Medgar Evers Col, City Univ, dean, 1972-; NY City Comn Human Rights, chairperson, 1984-88, comnr. **Orgs:** Bd mem, Women's Forum; vpres Nat Coun Women, 1989-; treas & pres, Nat Comn Status Women; chairperson, New York City Commn Status Women, Comn Human Rights, 1978-84, 1988-; trustee. Brooklyn Hosp Ctr, currently; Governance Coun Links Inc., currently; secy, Carver Bank Scholar Fund, currently; BdDirs, Am Heart Asn, currently; Vice Chairperson, Special Contribution Fund NAACP, currently; dir, New York Found Senior Citizens, currently. **Honors/Awds:** Nat Achievement Award, Nat Asn Negro Bus & Prof Women's Clubs; Exxon Scholarship, Harvard Bus School; Keynote Speaker, Older Women's League; Human Relations Award, NCCJ; Doctor Law Pratt Inst Brooklyn NY, 1985; Doctor Humane Letters Marymount Manhattan Col, 1984; Frederick Douglass Award, May 2006. **Home Addr:** 35 Prospect Pk W, Brooklyn, NY 11215. **Business Phone:** (212)481-4100.

MAXWELL, ROGER ALLAN
Government official, composer. **Personal:** Born Jul 31, 1932, Marshalltown, IA; married Arenda; children: Jennifer, Courtney,

David & Matthew. **Educ:** Univ N Iowa, BA, music educ, 1954. **Career:** Iowa State Bd Regents, field rep, 1968, affirmative action off, 1969-. **Orgs:** Nat pres, Nat Asn Affirmative Act Officers, 1979-80. **Special Achievements:** Composer, "Mass in Honor of the Uganda Martyrs", 1964; composer, "Fourteen Weeks to a Better Band", Books I & II publ, CL Barnhouse Co, 1973-74; composer, "Twelve Weeks to a Better Jazz Ensemble", publ, CL Barnhouse Co, 1978. **Military Serv:** AUS, asst counductor, AUS, Band Pacific Honolulu, HI, 1956-58. **Business Addr:** Staff, Affirmative Act Office, Lucas State Off Bldg, Des Moines, IA 50319.*

MAXWELL, STEPHEN LLOYD
Judge. **Personal:** Born Jan 12, 1921, St Paul, MN; son of Paul barber; married Betty Rodney. **Educ:** Morehouse Col, BA BSL, 1951; St Paul Col Law, JD, 1953. **Career:** Judge (retired); IRS, auditor, 1945-48; St Paul Auditorium, acct, 1948-51; OPS, investr, 1951-53; pvt pract, 1953-59; Ramsey Ct, asst atty, 1959-66; City St Paul, corp coun, 1964-66; US Cong Rep Cand, 1966; Munic Ct, judge, 1967-68; Ramsey Co Dist Ct, judge, 1968-87. **Orgs:** Bd trustees & treas, Minn State Cols & Univs, 1998. **Special Achievements:** First African American to serve as a district court judge in Minnesota. **Military Serv:** USCG, WWII; USNR, capt, retired. **Home Addr:** 882 Carroll Ave, St Paul, MN 55104, **Home Phone:** (612)222-7600.

MAXWELL, VERNON
Basketball player. **Personal:** Born Sep 12, 1965, Gainesville, FL; married Shell; children: Vernon Jr, Brandon & Ariel. **Educ:** Univ Fla, attended 1988. **Career:** Basketball Player (retired); San Antonio Spurs, guard, 1988-90, 1996-97; Houston Rockets, 1989-95; Philadelphia 76ers, free agent, 1995-96; Charlotte Hornets, 1997-98; Orlando Magic, 1998; Sacramento Kings, 1998-99; Seattle Supersonics, free agent, 1999-2000; Dallas Mavericks, free agent, 2000-01; Philadelphia 76ers, guard, 2000-01. **Honors/Awds:** Mr. Basketball, Fla; NBA Champions, Houston Rockets, 1994 & 1995.

MAY, DERRICK
Musician. **Personal:** Born Apr 6, 1963, Detroit, MI. **Career:** Deep Space Sound works, dj, 1980; Transmat Rec, founder, 1986-; albums: Let's Go, 1986; Nude Photo, 1987; Strings Of Life, 1987; It Is What It Is, 1988; Beyond The Dance, 1989; The Beginning, 1990; Icon / Kao-tic Harmony, 1993; Mayday Mix, 1997; Innovator, 1997; I Travel EP, 2009; films: High Tech Soul, 2006; Mastercuts Life Style Summer House, 2007; Things To Be Frickled, 2008; Balance 014, 2009; Remix: Truck On Road, 2009. **Business Addr:** Founder, Transmat Records, 1492 Gratiot Ave, Detroit, MI 48207.*

MAY, DERRICK BRANT
Athletic coach, baseball player. **Personal:** Born Jul 14, 1968, Rochester, NY. **Career:** Baseball player (retired), Athletic coach; Chicago Cubs, outfielder, 1990-94; Milwaukee Brewers, 1995; Houston Astros, 1995-96; Philadelphia Phillies, 1997; Montreal Expos, 1998; Baltimore Orioles, outfielder, 1999-2000; Japan, Chiba Lotte, 2003; St Louis orgn, Palm Beach Cardinals, Fla State League, hitting coach, 2005-06; Springfield Cardinals AA. hitting coach, currently. *

MAY, DICKEY R.
Administrator. **Personal:** Born Dec 14, 1950, Dublin, GA; son of Clarence W Sr and Zelma Smith; married L Yvonne Fambrough, Jul 3; children: Andrea Lynette May, Ronald Maurice May. **Educ:** Fort Valley State Col, Fort Valley GA, BBA, 1972. **Career:** Ch's Fried Chicken, Atlanta GA, exec mgr candid, 1972-73, mgr area mgr, 1973-75, San Antonio TX, auditor, 1975-80, regional liason, 1980-84, dir corp planning, 1986-89, dir oper acct, 1989-; Ron's Krispy Fried Chicken, Houston TX, regional controller, corp controller, 1984-86. **Orgs:** Inst Internal Auditors, 1975-; Long Range Planning Comn; Northminister Presbyterian Ch, 1988-. **Business Addr:** Director Of operational accounting, Church's Fried Chicken Inc, 355 Spencer Lane, San Antonio, TX 78250, **Business Phone:** (210)737-5805.*

MAY, FLOYD O
Government official. **Personal:** Born Dec 2, 1946, Kansas City, MO; married Connie S Brown; children: Cheriss Dachelle & Floyd O. **Educ:** Kansas State Col, Pittsburg, BS, 1970, MS, 1971. **Career:** Miss Dept Voc Rehab, counr 1971-75; US Dept HUD, investigator, 1975-77, mgt liaison officer, 1977-85, dept dir & dir comp, 1985, regional dir office Fair Housing & Equal Opportunity. **Orgs:** Lee's Summit Chamber Com; Urban League KC; pres, Channel, 19 Public TV Comm; adv bd, Heart Am Pop Warner Football Asn; Urban League; bd mem, Nat Asn Advan Colored People, Kans City, MO, Chap; KC Civil Rights Consortium. **Honors/Awds:** Outstanding Performance Award, US Dept of HUD, 1977, 1985; Pride in Public Service Award, 1991; Distinguished Service Award, 1992; Outstanding Performance Award, 1991, 1992. **Military Serv:** AUS, capt, 7 yrs; Outstanding Military Graduate. **Home Addr:** 2072 Westchester Dr, Silver Spring, MD 20902-3557. *

MAY, DR. GARY STEPHEN
Educator. **Personal:** Born May 17, 1964, St Louis, MO; son of Warren and Gloria; married LeShelle, Jun 11, 1994; children: Simone & Jordan. **Educ:** Ga Inst Technol, BEE, 1985; Univ Calif, Berkeley, MS, elect engr & comput sci, 1987, PhD, elect engr & comput sci, 1991. **Career:** GA Inst Technol, res asst, 1985, from asst prof to prof, 1991-2000, Motoral Found prof, 2001-02, exec chair, 2002, exec asst to the pres, 2002-05, prof, Steve W Chaddick Sch Chair, 2005-; AT&T Bell Lab, tech staff, 1985-86; Univ Calif, Berkeley, res asst, 1986-91, grad student instr, 1988-90, workshop coord, 1990-91; ed-in-chief, IEEE Transactions, 1997-2001. **Orgs:** Amer Soc Engr Educ, 1995-; fel Inst Elec & Electronics Engrs; Int Microelectronics & Packaging Soc; Int Soc Optical Engr; Nat Sci Found; Nat Soc Black Engrs; Soc Mfg Engrs; fel, AT&T Bell Labs. **Honors/Awds:** Nat Young Investigator, NSF, 1993-98; Outstanding Faculty Mem Award, Afr Amer Student Union, 1993; Outstanding Young Alumni, GA Tech, 1993; Outstanding Community Service Award, Ralph Bunche Middle Sch, 1998; Outstanding Service Award, GA Tech, 1999; Giant Sci Award, Quality Edu Minorities Ntwk, 2002; Outstanding Fac Res Author, GA Tech Sch ECE, 2002; Wickenden Award for Outstanding Paper, 2003; Georgia Tech Outstanding Undergraduate Research Mentor Award, 2004; American Asn for the Advancement of Science Mentor Award, 2006; NSBE Golden Torch Award: Janice A. Lumpkin Educator of the Year, 2006. **Special Achievements:** Numerous scholarly publications & presentations. **Home Addr:** 1310 Regency Ctr Dr SW, Atlanta, GA 30331.

MAY, JAMES F.
Educator, mayor. **Personal:** Born Feb 10, 1938, Millry, AL; married Bessie Hill; children: Keita & Katrice. **Educ:** Ala A&M Univ, BS, 1962; Tuskegee Inst, MEd, 1968. **Career:** May's Plumbing & Elec Serv, owner; Union town Al, mayor; Perry County Bd Educ, teacher; former city coun man. **Orgs:** Union town Civic League; keeper recs, Omega Chi Chap, Omego Psi Phi; AVATA Perry Co Teacher Asn; AEA; NEA; Pride AL Elks No 1170, Perry County Chamber Com. **Honors/Awds:** First Black Councilman Award, 1972. **Military Serv:** AUS, pfc, 1956-58.

MAY, LEE ANDREW
Baseball player, athletic coach. **Personal:** Born Mar 23, 1943, Birmingham, AL; children: Lee May Jr & 2 children. **Educ:** Miles Col. **Career:** Baseball player(retired), baseball coach; Cincinnati Reds, infielder/outfielder, 1965-71; Houston Astros, 1st baseman 1972-74; Baltimore Orioles, infielder, 1975-80; Kansas City Royals, infielder, 1981-82; Kansas City Royals, base & hitting coach, 1984-86, 1992-94; Cinti Reds, base coach, 1988, 1989; Tampa Devil Rays, base coach. **Honors/Awds:** Nat League Rookie Player of Yr 1967. *

MAY, MARK ERIC
Football player, television sportscaster. **Personal:** Born Nov 2, 1959, Oneonta, NY; married Kathy; children: Abra. **Educ:** Univ Pittsburgh, attended 1980. **Career:** Football player (retired), sportscaster; Wash Redskins, guard, offensive tackle, 1981-90; San Diego Chargers, 1991; Phoenix Cardinals, 1992-93; TNT, " Sunday Night Football," studio analyst, 1995-96, game analyst, 1997; CBS Sports, game analyst, 1998-2000; ESPN, football analyst & commentator, 2001-, "Col GameDay," analyst, currently. **Orgs:** C's Hosp; chmn, Ams Helping Am prog, Christian Relief Serv, 1989; Juvenile Diabetes Asn. **Honors/Awds:** Outland Trophy, 1980; Pro Bowl, 1988; offensive Most Valuable Player, DC Touchdown Club, 1988; Pro Bowler, 1988; Col Football Hall of Fame, 2005. **Special Achievements:** Author, Mark May's Tales from the Washington Redskins, 2005. **Business Phone:** (860)766-2000.

MAYBERRY, ANTHONY. **See MAYBERRY, TONY.**

MAYBERRY, CLAUDE A., JR.
Publisher, entrepreneur. **Personal:** Born Feb 17, 1933, Detroit, MI; son of Claude Sr. and Anna Johnson Riley; divorced; children: Lawrence, Karen, Cheryl, Claude III, Eric. **Educ:** Purdue Univ, West Lafayette, IN, BS, 1965, MS, 1968; Columbia Univ, Teachers Col New York, NY, PhD, 1973. **Career:** Univ Pa, Philadelphia, dean stud, 1973-76; Colgate Univ, Hamilton, NY, provost, 1976-81; US Dept Educ, Wash, DC, spec asst secy math & sci, 1981-84; Sci Weekly Inc, Silver Spring, MD, pres & chief exec officer, 1984-. **Orgs:** Alumni Asn, Purdue Univ, 1965-; Alumni Asn, Columbia Univ, 1973-; Nat Alliance Black Sch Educr, 1975-; chair, Black Entrepreneurs Educ Publishers, 1984-; chair, Minority Entrepreneurs Comt, 1987-; pres, alumni adv comt, Teachers Col, Columbia Univ, 1990-93; Nat chairperson, Nat Conf Educating Black Child, 1990-92; pres, Nat Citizens Comn African American Educ, 1994-; bd mem, Reading Is Fundamental Inc. **Honors/Awds:** Teacher of the Year Award, Ind State Jr Chamber Com, 1968; Marcus Foster Distinguished Black Educator Award, Nat Alliance Black Sch Educr, 1988; African-American Businessman Award, Montgomery County, MD, 1990; School of Science Distinguished Alumni Award, Purdue Univ, 1991; Hammond Achievement Award, 1992. **Military Serv:** USAF, airman first, 1952-56. **Business Addr:** President, Science Weekly Inc, 2141 Indust Parkway Suite 202, Silver Spring, MD 20904, **Business Phone:** (301)680-8804.*

MAYBERRY, JERMANE TIMOTHY
Football player. **Personal:** Born Aug 29, 1973, Floresville, TX; married Danielle; children: Jermane. **Educ:** Univ Tex A&M, Kingsville. **Career:** Football player (retired); Philadelphia Eagles, tackle, 1996-2004; New Orleans Saints, tackle, 2005-06. **Honors/Awds:** Extra Effort Award, Nat Football League, 1996. **Special Achievements:** NFL Draft, First round pick, #25, 1996.

MAYBERRY, PATRICIA MARIE
Social worker, judge. **Personal:** Born Aug 25, 1951, St Louis, MO; daughter of Samuel and Shirley Hawkins; divorced. **Educ:** Univ Mo, BA, 1973; Univ Houston, MSW, 1976; Tex Southern Univ, Thurgood Marshall Sch Law, JD, 1979. **Career:** USAF, atty/asst staff judge advocate, 1980-84; Alvin Dillings, PC, atty, 1984-87; pvt pract, atty, 1987-89; Immigration & Naturalization Serv, trial atty, 1989-93; Calif Unemployment Ins Appeals Bd, admin law judge, 1993-96; Dept Air Force, labor law atty, 1996-; Judicial Coun AMEC, pres, currently. **Orgs:** Delta Sigma Theta Sorority, 1973-; Phi Alpha Delta, 1977; State Bar Tex, 1979; Colo Bar, 1985; Top Ladies Distinction, 1990; exec bd, Nat Asn Advan Colored People, 1990; trustee, Calif Conf, 1991-; judicial coun mem & pres, AME Church, 1992-; bd dirs, Fel Manor, 1992-97. **Special Achievements:** 100 Outstanding African Americans, Dollars & Sense Mag, 1991. **Military Serv:** USAF, lt col, 1980-84, reserves, 1984-; Commendation Medal, 1981, 1984 & 1996; Achievement Medal, 1984 & 1990; Meritorious Service Medal, 1998. **Business Addr:** President, Judicial Council AMEC, 17887 Balsam Ct, Carson, CA 90746, **Business Phone:** (310)653-3168.

MAYBERRY, TONY (ANTHONY MAYBERRY)
Football player. **Personal:** Born Dec 8, 1967, Wurzburg, Germany; married Rachel; children: Joshua & Briana. **Educ:** Wake Forest, BA, sociol. **Career:** Football player (retired); Tampa Bay Buccaneers, Offensive Line man, 1990-99. **Honors/Awds:** Most Valuable Player, Tampa Sports Club, 1997; Athletics Hall of Fame, 2002; TJR Hall of Fame, 2005. **Special Achievements:** First Buccaneer offensive lineman ever selected for the Pro Bowl in 1997.

MAYBERRY-STEWART, MELODIE IRENE
Health services administrator. **Personal:** Born Sep 4, 1948, Cleveland, OH; daughter of Marie Hague; divorced; children: George, Jay. **Educ:** Union Col, BS, bus admin & sociol; Univ Nebraska, MA, sociological res & statistics; Pepperdine Univ, MBA; Claremont Grad Sch, MA, exec mgt, PhD, philos. **Career:** IBM Corporation, various positions, ended career western area telecommuns mkt mgr; Saint Thomas Hosp, vpres & chief info officer; Beth Israel Hosp, vpres, chief info officer; Black Diamond IT Consult Group LLC; BP Amoco Oil Corp, gen mgr & vpres, info technol corp & shared servs; City Cleveland, chief technol officer, currently. **Orgs:** Bd dirs & treas, Tennessee Sportsfest; bd mem, Limited Way Middle Tennessee; exec comt mem, Nashville NAACP; bd mem, SunTrust Bank; finance comt chmn, Cumberland Valley Girl Scout Coun; Nat Asn Female Execs; Nat Black MBA Asn; Nat Coun Negro Women; Healthcare Info & Mgt Systs Soc; Am Hosp Asn; Col Healthcare Execs; Nat Asn Healthcare Execs; bd chairwoman, Nat Black MBA Asn. **Honors/Awds:** Women of Achievement Award, Legal Defense Fund NAACP; Alumni Award for Extraordinary Service, Peter F Drucker Mgt Ctr; 100 Most Promising Corporate Women. **Special Achievements:** Co-authored two publications network mgt & network design; first African Am vpres & chief info officer Beth Israel Hosp; first African Am vpres St Thomas Hosp. **Business Addr:** Chief Technology Officer, City Cleveland, 601 Lakeside Ave Rm 202, Cleveland, OH 44114, **Business Phone:** (216)664-2220.*

MAYDEN, RUTH WYATT
Educator. **Personal:** Born Dec 20, 1946, Baltimore, MD; daughter of John Clifton Jr and Wilhelmenia Outerbridge. **Educ:** Morgan State Univ, Baltimore, MD, BA, 1968; Bryn Mawr Col, Bryn Mawr, PA, MSS, 1970. **Career:** Educator (retired); Day Care Asn Montgomery County, Blue Bell, PA, social serv coordr, 1970-72, exec dir, 1972-79; Bryn Mawr Col Grad Sch Social Work & Social Res, Bryn Mawr, PA, asst dean, 1979-81, assoc dean, 1981-86, dean, 1986-2001. **Orgs:** Chair, Child Welfare Adv Bd, 1985-91; bd exec comt, United Way Southeastern PA, 1986-91; Nat Asn Deans & Directors Sch & Social Work, 1987-; treas, PA Chap, Nat Asn Social Workers, 1989-91; Am Asn Black Women Higher Educ, 1989-91; bd mem, Nat Asn Social Workers; pres, Nat Asn Social Workers, 1999-2001; bd dir, Coun Social Work Educ, 2006-. **Honors/Awds:** Service Appreciation Award, Montgomery County Mental Health, Mental Retardation Bd, 1974-84; Service Appreciation Award, Community Serv Planning Coun, 1978-84; Social Worker of the Year, PA Chap, Nat Asn Social Workers, 1999, 1987-89. **Business Addr:** Board of Director, Council on Social Work Education, 1725 Duke St Suite 500, Alexandria, VA 22314-3457, **Business Phone:** (703)683-8080.

MAYE, BEATRICE CARR JONES
Librarian, educator. **Personal:** Born in Warren County, NC; daughter of James S and Ellen Brown; married John W Maye Sr, Jul 13, 1938 (deceased); children: John Walter Jr & Mamie Ellene Maye-Bryan. **Educ:** NC A&T State Univ, BS, English, French; NC Central Durham, BS, MS, librsci; E Carolina Univ, post grad study. **Career:** WH Robinson Sch, librn, 1947-68; EB Aycock Jr High Sch, media specialist, 1968-81; Greenville City Bd Sheppard Mem Public Libr, 1972-74, dept librsci, libr sci consult, 1972;

Pittsburgh & Greenville Media Soc, pres,1981-82; Carolinian, columnist; "M" Voice, columnist; Pittsburgh Community Col, teacher, resource person. **Orgs:** Delta Sigma Theta Aux, 1937; Am Asn Retired Persons, 1981-; Elections Study Comn by mayor, 1981; NC Asn Educrs, 1981; Golden Key Nat Honor Soc, E Carolina Univ, 2001. **Honors/Awds:** SE Black Librarian, 1976; 25 Most Influential Black Women in Greenville/Pittsburgh City, 1983; Greenville Pre-Release, 'Volunteer-of-the Year', 1983; 'Citizen of the Year' Award for Community Serv 1984; 'Citizen of the Year', Mu Alpha Chapter, Omega Psi Phi Fraternity, 1984; 'Outstanding Senior Citizen', Greenville-Jaycees, 1988; Co-host, "M" Voices of Eastern NC Acad, Wisn Univ, Channel 7, TV Station; Plaque for over 50 years in Delta Sigma Thega Sorority, 1998; Soc Golden Eagles, 54th Annual Founder's Day Convocation NC Central Univ, 2001; Golden Key Nat Honor Society, East Carolina Univ, 2001; John G Clark Jr Memorial Awd, sheppard Memorial Library, 2002. **Special Achievements:** Author: Personalities in Progress, Biographies of Black North Carolinians, Treasure Bits, An Anthology of Quotes, 1984; Editorials: The Minority Voice, We The People, The Daily Reflector, The News & Observer, The Wilson Library Bulletin, NC Libraries, Greenville Dispatch, The Carolinian; host,"Talk Show," WOOW Radio, Greenville Pre-Release & After-Care Center; UBE Publishing, "The Wit and Wisdom of Beatrice Maye"; City Greenville, NC, The Beatrice Maye Garden Park, 2002. **Home Addr:** 1225 Davenport St, Greenville, NC 27834, **Home Phone:** (919)752-5478.

MAYE, RICHARD

Clergy. **Personal:** Born Oct 26, 1933, Uniontown, AL; married Rose Owens; children: Darryl Kermit, Byron Keith. **Educ:** Sangamon State Univ, BA & MA, 1972; Ohio State Univ, BS; Univ IA, PhD, Intl Theol Sem. **Career:** Pleasant Grove Baptist Church Springfield, IL, pastor, 1970-; IL State Univ Normal, lect political sci, 1973-77; IL Dept Corrections Springifield, admin asst, 1970-72; Chicago Baptist Inst IL, fac, 1968-70; City Springfield, comnr civil serv, 1979-72, MacMurray Col, Instr Sociol, 2004. **Orgs:** grad dean fellow, Soc Ill Univ Carbondl, 1975-76; bd dir, Morgan Wash Sch Girls, 1977; Sch Integration Comn Springfield, 1977-79; bd dir, Lincoln Libr; Mayor's Complete Count Comn Springfield, 1980. **Honors/Awds:** Citizen of the Year Award, NAACP Springfield, 1976; Grad Fellow, Univ IA, 1977-80; Public Service Award, US Dist Ct Springfield, IL, 1978. **Military Serv:** AUS, spec & 3, 1954-56. **Business Addr:** Instructor Sociology, MacMurray College, 447 East Col Ave, Jacksonville, IL 62650, **Business Phone:** (217)479-7000.*

MAYERS, JAMAL DAVID

Hockey player. **Personal:** Born Oct 24, 1974, Ontario;son of Doreen Mayers; married Natalie. **Educ:** W Mich Univ, BA, mkt, 1996. **Career:** Jam & Sal's Comm Stars, developer; Hockey Acad of St Louis, designer &instr; Thornhill MTJHL, 1990-92; Western Mich CCHA, 1992-96; WorcesterAHL,1996-98, 1998-99; St Louis Blues, right wing, 1996-97, 1998-99, 1999-00, 2000-04, 2005-08; Canada WC-A, 1999-00; Hammarby Sweden-2, 2004-05; Missouri UHL, 2004-05; Toronto Maple Leafs, 2008-. **Orgs:** Ice Hockey Harlem. **Honors/Awds:** World Championships, gold medal, 2007; World Championships, silver medal, 2008. *

MAYERS, ONIDA COWARD. See COWARD, ONIDA LAVONEIA.

MAYES, ALONZO (ALONZO LEWIS MAYES, JR.)

Football player. **Personal:** Born Jun 4, 1975, Oklahoma City, OK. **Educ:** Okla State Univ. **Career:** Football player (retired); Chicago Bears, tight end, 1998-2000; Miami Dolphins, 2001-02.

MAYES, ALONZO LEWIS, JR. See MAYES, ALONZO.

MAYES, CLINTON, JR.

Executive. **Career:** State Mutual Federal Savings and Loan Asn, Jackson, MS, chief exec. **Business Addr:** First American Bank, PO Box 23518, Jackson, MS 39225-3518.

MAYES, DERRICK

Football player, chief executive officer. **Personal:** Born Jan 28, 1974, Indianapolis, IN. **Educ:** Univ Notre Dame, BA, commun. **Career:** Football player (retired); Green Bay Packers, wide receiver, 1996-98; Seattle Seahawks, wide receiver, 1999-2000; CEO and Dir Exec Action Sports and Entertainment, currently. **Honors/Awds:** Rookie of the Year, 1996; Super Bowl champion XXXI.

MAYES, DORIS MIRIAM

Educator, musician, opera singer. **Personal:** Born Dec 10, 1928, Philadelphia, PA; daughter of James and Evelyn Bulter; married Jurgen Ploog, Jun 21, 1960; children: Flavia Miriam. **Educ:** Philadelphia Conserv Music, Philadelphia, PA, BM, teaching cert; Hochshule Fur Musik, Munich, Ger; Juilliard Sch Music, New York, NY. **Career:** Fulbright fels; Syracuse Univ, Syracuse, NY, assoc prof, 1966-68; Oberlin Col, Oberlin, OH, asst prof, 1968-74; Western Reserve Univ, Hudson, OH, voice technician, 1974-80; Univ Arts, Philadelphia, PA, teacher conserv div, 1982-; Lincoln Univ, Lincoln, PA, artist in residence & asst prof voice &

opera, 1988-. **Orgs:** Scholar chairperson, Pro Arts Soc, 1983-. **Honors/Awds:** Key to city of Philadelphia, PA, 1961; Presidential Commendation, Lincoln Univ, 1989; Citation, Philadelphia City Coun, 1989; Congressional citation, 1989; Philadelphia Orchestra Award; Bell Isle Award, Detroit Sym; John Hay Whitney award; Winner, Munich Int Competition & Geneva Int Competition; Winner, Grande Prix Toulouse Int Competition; Lindback Award, Lincoln Univ, 1994. **Special Achievements:** Performances with Philadelphia and Cleveland orchestras and Detroit, Wiesbaden, Paris, Delaware, and Akron symphonies, opera performances in Europe and the United States. **Home Phone:** (215)849-3137.

MAYES, HELEN M.

College administrator. **Personal:** Born May 28, 1918, Waycross, GA; daughter of Oscar Moody (deceased) and Mary Woodson Moody (deceased); married Nathaniel H (deceased); children: Nathaniel H Mayes Jr. **Educ:** Savannah State Col, BS, 1938; New York Univ, MA, 1961. **Career:** College administrator (retired); Albany State Col, GA, emer dir admis & rec, 1976. **Orgs:** Exec secy, Nat Asn Col Deans Registr & Admis Officers, 1963-; first black pres, GA Asn Collegiate Registr & Admis Officers, 1971-72; GA Teachers & Educ Asn; Nat Educ Asn; Alpha Kappa Alpha; Am Asn Col Registr & Admis Officers; selection comt, Nat Merit Achievement Scholarship Prog; United Way Dougherty County Bd; bd dirs, Albany Symphony Asn; dir finance, SemperFidelis Club, 1980-; steward, Bethel AME Church. **Honors/Awds:** Hon mem, GA Asn Collegiate Registrs & Admis Officers & Nat Asn Col Deans, Registrs & Admis Officers; Top Leadership Award, Alpha Kappa Alpha Sor; Women of Distinction; Community Service Award, Iota Phi Lambda Sor. **Business Addr:** Albany, GA 31701.*

MAYES, MCKINLEY

Government official. **Personal:** Born Oct 7, 1930, Oxford, NC; son of Henry and Julia; married Mattie Louise Dupree, Aug 22, 1959; children: Byron Christopher Mayes. **Educ:** NC A&T State Univ, BS, 1953, MS, 1956; Rutgers Univ, PhD, 1959. **Career:** Government official (retired); Southern Univ, Baton Rouge LA, prof, 1959-76; US Dept Agr, Coop State Res Serv, Wash, DC, 1976. **Orgs:** Fel Am Soc Agron; Sigma Xi; Global ministries; VA Conf; United Methodist Church; vice chair, admin bd, Roberts United Methodist Church, 1987; USDA Task Force. **Military Serv:** AUS corporal, 1953-55. **Business Addr:** Washington, DC 20250-2209.*

MAYES, NATHANIEL H., JR.

Consultant, educator. **Personal:** Born Aug 22, 1941, Waycross, GA; married Constantina; children: Nathaniel III & Muriel. **Educ:** Howard Univ, BS, 1962, MS, 1966. **Career:** Clark Col, Atlanta, instr psychol, 1966-68; Orgn Develop, consult, 1968-70; Greater Boston Area Pub Schs; Soc Dynamics Inc, Boston, prog mgr, 1970-71; Univ Mass, Inst Learning & Teaching, consult trainer, 1971; Sloan Schl Mgt, dir, International Prog and Resource Development. **Orgs:** Co-founder, Inter-Culture Inc, Cambridge; Soc Inter cultural Educ Training & Res. **Honors/Awds:** Outstanding Teaching Certificate, Clark Col, 1965. **Special Achievements:** Co-author booklet on Multi-Cultural Tchr Training 1974.

MAYFIELD, JOANN H O

Government official. **Personal:** Born Jul 1, 1932, Jackson, AL; divorced; children: Joyce, Barbara & Theresa. **Educ:** Louise Beauty Col. **Career:** Cosmetology. **Orgs:** Dist pres Am Legion Aux, 1963-64; unit pres, Am Legion Aux, 1963-64; dist pres, Am Legion Aux, 1965-66; chmn Cit Training Dist A B C, 1966-67; unit Pres, Am Legion Aux, 1967-68; usher bd sec Am Legion Aux, 1972; chmn Ed & Scholar 9th Dists; Celebrity Club; Counwoman City Comn GA. **Business Addr:** 324 S Elm St, Commerce, GA 30529.

MAYFIELD, DR. WILLIAM S.

Lawyer, educator. **Personal:** Born Mar 2, 1919, Gary, IN; son of William H Mayfield Sr and Elnora E Williams-Mayfield (deceased); married Octavia Smith (deceased); children: Pamela L, William E & Stephanie K; married Mildred Harris, May 25, 1991. **Educ:** Detroit Inst Technol, AB, 1946; Detroit Col Law, JD, 1949. **Career:** Lewis Rowlette Brown Wanzo & Bell Detroit, atty pvt law pract, 1949-51; US Off Price Stabilization, atty, 1951-53; Friend Ct Detroit, referee, 1953-72; Southern Univ Sch Law, prof law; La St Univ Law Ctr, Baton Rouge, La, vis prof, 1979. **Orgs:** Nat Bar Asn; St Bar Mich; Am Bar Asn; Wolverine Bar Asn; Louis A Martinet Legal Soc; World Asn Law Prof World Peace Law Ctr; Detroit Col Law Alumni Asn; Retired Officers Asn; former vpres, Cotillion Club, Detroit; Asn Henri Capitant; Delta Theta Phi Law Frat; former pres, Krainz Woods Prop Owners Asn; former mem, Regional Bd Boy Scouts Am. **Honors/Awds:** Outstanding Professor Awd, Delta Theta Phi Law Frat, 1982-83; Hall of Fame, Nat Bar Asn, 1989; Hall of Fame, La State Univ Law Ctr, 1988. **Military Serv:** AUS, lt col, ret. *

MAYHEW, RICHARD

Artist, educator. **Personal:** Born Apr 3, 1924, Amityville, NY. **Educ:** Art Stud League; Brooklyn Museum Art Sch, 1951; Columbia Univ. **Career:** Freelance med, illusr & singer, 1945-50; MacDowell Colony Fel, 1958; John Hay Whitney Fel, 1959;

Brooklyn Mus Art Sch, instr, 1963-68; Art Students League, instr, 1965-71; Smith Col, instr, 1971-75; Pa State Univ, prof art, 1977-91, prof emer art, 1991-. **Orgs:** Founder, Spiral Group, 1963-; academician, Nat Acad Design; founding dir, Creative Ctr Arts & Sci; Nat Acad Design. **Honors/Awds:** Ingram Merrill Foundation Award, 1960; Purchase Award, Ford Found, 1962; Tiffany Foundation Award, 1963; grant, Nat Inst Arts & Letters, 1965; Childe Hassam Purchase Award, 1963-64; Henry Ward Ranger Purchase Prize, 1964; Benjamin Altman Award, 1970; Merit Award, Nat Acad Design, 1977; Grumbacher Gold Medal, 1983. **Home Addr:** PO Box 7720, Santa Cruz, CA 95061, **Home Phone:** (831)476-3388. **Business Addr:** Professor Emeritus of Art, Penn State School of Visual Arts, Pennsylvania State University, 210 Patterson Bldg, University Park, PA 16802, **Business Phone:** (814)865-0444.*

MAYNARD, DR. EDWARD SAMUEL

Educator, psychologist. **Personal:** Born Jul 16, 1930, Brooklyn, NY; son of Robertine Maynard and Samuel Maynard; married Ernestine Gaskin; children: Jeanne & Charles. **Educ:** Brooklyn Col, BA, cum Laude, 1958; Columbia Univ, MA, 1967; New York Univ, PhD, 1972; Grad Ctr, City Univ New York PhD 1984. **Career:** New York City Bd Educ, teacher, 1958-67; Brooklyn Col, lectr, 1967-69; Medgar Evers Col, dir pub rels, 1970-71; Hostos Community Col, prof, 1971-; psychologist, pvt practice, 1980-. **Orgs:** Nat Asn Advan Colored People, 1980-; Am Psychol Assoc, 1984-; minister couns, Howells Congregational Church. **Honors/Awds:** Founders Day Award, New York Univ, 1972; New York Acad Sci, 1983. **Military Serv:** USMC corpl 2 yrs; Nat Defense Serv Medal, 1951-53. **Home Addr:** 52 Mine Rd, Monroe, NY 10950. **Business Addr:** Professor, Hostos Community College, 500 Grand Concourse, Bronx, NY 10451, **Business Phone:** (718)518-4444.

MAYNARD, VALERIE J

Educator, artist, curator. **Personal:** Born Aug 22, 1937, New York, NY; daughter of William Austin Maynard Sr and Willie-Fred Pratt Maynard. **Educ:** Mus Mod Art, New York, Drawing & Painting, 1954-55; Elaine Journet Art Sch, New Rochelle, New York, apprentice, 1955-60; The New Sch, New York, printmaking, 1968-69; Goddard Col Plainfield, VT, MA, sculpture, 1977. **Career:** Studio Mus, New York,instr printmaking, artist-in-residence, 1969-74; Langston Hughes Lib, New York, instr sculpture, 1971-72; Howard Univ, Wash, DC, instr sculpture, 1974-76; Jersey City State Col, NJ, instr sculpture, 1977-78; Baltimore Sch Arts, instr sculpture, 1980-81; Col Virgin Islands, St Thomas, instr sculpture, 1984-85; Northeastern Univ, Boston, MA, Goddard Coll, Plainfield VT, Rutgers Univ, NJ, Harlem State Office Bldg NY, St Thomas, Col Virgin Islands, St Thomas, lectr, 1979-85; Univ Virgin Islands, St Thomas, sculpture instr & artist-in-residence, 1984-88; Women's Studio Workshop, 1986-87; Blue Mouin ctr, 1987-91; McDowell Colony, 1991; Mass Inst Tech, 1992; Brandywine Workshop, 1992; Bob Blackburn Printing Workshop, 1992-93; Univ Rochester, Susan B Anthony Ctr Women's Studies, Rockefeller Humanities fel, currently; self employed, currently. **Honors/Awds:** Travel Grant FESTAC, Lagos Nigeria, 1977; CEBA Design Award, World Inst Black Commun, New York, 1978; Citation of Merit Seward Park Alumni, New York, 1979; Living History Award, New York Urban League Westchester, 1980; Bedford-Stuyvesant Arts Award, Brooklyn, NY, 1980; Finalist Nat Sculpture Competition, Columbus, OH, 1980; Finalist Independence Monument Antigua, West Indies, 1981; Pub Sch 181, Brooklyn, New York; Womens Studio Workshops, residency, 1989-; Sculpture Award, Atlanta Life Insurance CPN, 1990; New England Fund Artists Grant, 1992; randywine workshop, artist-in-residence grant, 1992; LifeAmerica, MacDowell Colony, fel, 1991; Nat Endowment Arts; grant, for a stage set for play, "Nz-inga", 1992. **Special Achievements:** One woman exhibitions: creator/designer: Communications Excellence to Black Audiences Award, statuette, 1978; Two person exhibit, "Works in Progress," Valerie Maynard & Carol Byard Gallery, 1978; Travelling xhibits "Impressions/Expressions" Black Am Graphics Studio Mus, New York, 1979-84; "Tradition & Conflict, Images of a Turbulent Decade 1963-73", Studio Museum, NY, 1985-87; Reichhold Ctr Arts, St Thomas, US Virgin Islands, 1983; First PA Bank, St Thomas, US Virgin Islands, 1984;"Orie's Potpourri" St Thomas Cable TV, "Newscenter 10," WBNB-TV St Thomas, "AMVI," WBNB-TV St Thomas, "Sunday Morning," CBS-TV NY, films & videos 1985-86; Caribbean Ctr, New York, 1989; New York COT Col, 1989; "No Apartheid Anywhere", Compton Gallery, MIT, 1992. **Home Addr:** 2116 E Madison St, Baltimore, MD 21205.

MAYNOR, KEVIN ELLIOTT

Opera singer. **Personal:** Born Jul 24, 1954, Mt Vernon, NY. **Educ:** Manhattan Sch Music, Diploma, 1972; Bradley Univ, BME, 1976; NW Univ, MM, 1978; Moscow Conserv, MMV, 1980; Ind Univ, DM, 1987; Ind Univ, doctoral candidate, currently. **Career:** Chicago Lyric Opera, soloist, 1978; Sante Fe Opera, soloist, 1979; Bolshoi Opera, soloist, 1980; VA Opera, soloist, 1984; New York City Opera,soloist, 1986; Alice Tully Hall, soloist, 1985; Avery Fischer Hall, soloist, 1985; Carnegie Hall, 1986; Nashville Opera, soloist, 1986; Long Beach Opera, soloist, 1986; Mobile Opera, soloist, 1986; NYC Opera, 1985-98; Orlando Opera, soloist, 1986; Metropolitan Opera-Netherlands Dance Theatre, soloist, 1986-87; Triangle Music Theatre Asn,

Durham, NC, soloist, 1987; Metropolitan Opera House, 1987; Opera Co Boston, soloist,1988; Alice Tully Hall, New York, NY, soloist, 1988; Valparaiso Univ, soloist & recitalist, 1988; Fort Worth Symphony, soloist, 1988; Knoxville Symphony, soloist, 1988; Music Under The Stars Festival, soloist, 1988; Opera Music Theatre Int, soloist, 1989-90; Skylight Opera Theatre, 1990-91; Scottish Opera, 1991-92; Connecticut Opera, 1992-93; Cincinnati Opera, 1992-93; Chattanooga Symphony, 1993-94; Greensboro Opera, 1994-95;Opera Pacific, 1996; Edmonton Opera, 1996; Market Theatre, Johannesburg S Africa, 1997; Lyric Opera Chicago, 1997-98; Sacramento Opera, 1998; Dallas Opera, 1998; Milwaukee Symphony, 1998; Lyric Opera Boston, 1999; Saraton Opera, Russia, 2000; Flint Symphony, 2000; Knoxville Opera, 2000; Friends of the Roanoke Symphony, 2000; Lyric Opera Austin, 2000-01; Pacific Opera Victoria, 2001; National du Rhin Opera, Strasbourg, France, currently & Sacramento Opera, currently. **Orgs:** NCP, 1983-85; bd mem, Edler G Hawkins Fund Inc, 1989; bd, Univ Heights Sci Park; deacon bd, Bethany Baptist Church; bd, Greater Newark Conservacy; bd, Neward Comm Sch Arts. **Honors/Awds:** Fulbright Award, Fulbright-Hays Act Const, 1979; Sullivan Award, William M Sullivan Found, 1983; Recitalist Award, Nat Endowment Arts, 1984; Winner First Prize, Int Singing Competition S Africa, 1984; Singing Award, Nat Asn Teachers, 1984; Richard Tucker Award, 1985; George London Award, NIMT, 1986; Tito Gobbi Award, 1986. **Home Addr:** 32 Howard Ct, Newark, NJ 07103. **Business Phone:** (916)737-1000.

MAYNOR, VERNON PERRY
Entrepreneur, accountant. **Personal:** Born Feb 8, 1966, Mount Vernon, NJ; son of Godfrey and Josephine; married Shevella Brown Maynor, Dec 28, 1992. **Educ:** Hampton UNIV, BS, finance, 1988. **Career:** Johnson & Johnson Consumer Products Inc, Cooperative Educ Prog, 1987-88; Johnson & Johnson Corporate, acct mgt trainee, 1988-90, financial acct, 1990-, Me 2 You Inc, pres, currently. **Orgs:** OPP Fraternity, editor; NAT ASN BLK Accts. **Special Achievements:** Urban Profile Magazine, 1992 Top 30 Under 30 Black Professionals, 1992. **Business Addr:** President, Me 2 You Inc, PO Box 394, Dayton, NJ 08810, **Business Phone:** (732)940-3000.*

MAYO, BARRY ALAN
Executive, president (organization). **Personal:** Born Jun 30, 1952, Bronx, NY; son of Charles C Mayo and Anne Lewis Mayo; divorced 1992; children: Barry A II, Alana Aisha & Alexander. **Educ:** Howard Univ, radiol, 1974-76. **Career:** WRAP, Norfolk, prog dir, 1978; WMAK, Nashville, prog dir, 1978; WGCI-FM, Chicago, prog dir, 1978-81; WJLB-FM, Detroit, prog consult, 1981-84; WDMT-Cleveland, prog consult, 1984; WRKS-FM, New York, vice pres, gen mgr, 1984-88; Broadcasting Partners Inc, presid, 1988-; WVAZ-FM, pres, gen mgr, 1988-95; Emmis Boradcasting, gen mgr, mkt mgr, sr vpres, 2003-06; Radio One Inc, consult, 2006, pres, 2007-. **Orgs:** Bd dir, secy, NY Mkt Broadcasters; bd, Providence St Mel High Sch, 1990-; bd dir, Black United Fund. **Honors/Awds:** Black Achiever Award, NY Harlem YMCA, 1983; Radio Award, Nat Black Media Coalition, 1985. **Business Addr:** President, Radio One Inc, Radio Division, 5900 Princess Garden Pkwy 7th Fl, Lanham, MD 20706, **Business Phone:** (301)306-1111.

MAYO, BLANCHE IRENE
School administrator. **Personal:** Born Jan 24, 1946, Woodstock, OH; daughter of Gertrude E (deceased) and William E; married Terry, Dec 30, 1965; children: Terry Jr. **Educ:** Cent State Univ, BS, 1976, MBA, 1980, CMI diploma, 1989. **Career:** Cent State Univ, fed credit union treas & mgr, 1976-78, asst vpres acad affairs, asst title III, 1978-85, asst vpres acad affairs, title III coordr, 1980-85, exec asst pres, title III coordr, 1985-87, vpres admin support serv, currently. **Orgs:** Comnr, Ohio Stud Loan Comn, 1987; steering comn, CACUBO Mgt Inst, 1990-93; chaplain & sr usher bd, Middle Run Baptist Church, 1991-92; bus officer, Exec Comm Cent Asn Col & Univ, 1991-93; consult & evaluator, N Cent Asn Col & Schs, 1992-93. **Honors/Awds:** Special Recognition, YWCA Salute Career Women, 1980; Award of Scholarship, Winning Team CACUBO, 1987; Distinguished Alumni of the Year, Nat Asn Equal Opportunity, 1992. **Business Addr:** Vice President, Central State University, Administrative Support Services, 1400 Brush Row Rd Rm 211, PO Box 1004, Wilberforce, OH 45384-1004, **Business Phone:** (937)376-6011.

MAYO, HARRY D., III
Financial manager, educator. **Personal:** Born Aug 28, 1939, Brooklyn, NY; son of Harry D Jr and Lillie Mae Clark; married Joan Etta Bradley. **Educ:** Pace Univ, BBA, finance, 1968, MBA Exec Mgt, 1978; Harvard Univ, Cert Exec Educ Prog, Harvard Business Sch, 1978; various other mgt, comput & commun courses, cert. **Career:** Sperry & Hutchinson Co Inc, stand admin, Sr Syst Analyst, sr programmer, oper, 1958-68; Facts Inc, JP Morgan & Co, mgr financial serv, 1968-69, dir mkt, 1969-70; Borden's Inc, proj mgr, 1970-73; Arthur Young & Co, mgr, 1973-76; Int Paper Co, mgr syst develop, 1976-80; Merrill Lynch & Co Inc, dir MIS, 1980-82; Peters, Mayo & Co, pres & ceo, 1983-85; SRI Int, mgr info serv & syst div NY, 1985-86; HD Mayo & Assoc, founder & chmn, 1982-; Passaic Valley Sewerage Comnr, dir human resources, currently; instr, Fairleigh-Dickinson Univ. **Orgs:** Sem chmn, guest spkr Am Mgt Asn; prin mem, Am Nat Stand Inst, 1967-70; Asn Syst Mgt guest spkr, Data Process Mgt Asn, IBM Process Indust Users Grp NY Univ; MENSA; asst vpres, Eastern Rgn, Chap pres, Pledge Line pres Alpha Phi Alpha Frat NC, 1963-66; pres & dir, Parker Imperial Asn Inc, 1975-; secy & mem Planning Bd Township North Bergen, 1979-87, vice chmn, 1988-; chmn & guest spkr, Nat Inst Mgt Res, 1986-87; trustee and chmn, Investment Comn, St Lukes Found, 1994-; dir & mem, Develop, Strategic Planning & Search Comn, Youth Consult Serv, 1995-; chmn, Planned Giving Comn, St Luke's Episcopal Church, 1996-. **Honors/Awds:** Designated info syst expert Am Nat Stand Inst, 1967, Am Mgt Asn, 1967; chmn, Stonehenge Tenants Comn, 1969-72; pres, first vpres, treas, dir, Pace Univ Alumni Asn, 1977-80; mem, pres, adv comn, Pace Univ 1981-. **Military Serv:** AUS, Nat Guard pvt e2; Grad Trainee Leadership Schl, 1962; Squad Ldr, Platoon Guide, 1962. **Home Addr:** 7855 Blvd E, North Bergen, NJ 07047. **Business Addr:** Chairman, HD Mayo & Associates, 7855 Blvd E, North Bergen, NJ 07047, **Business Phone:** (201)861-6173.

MAYO, JAMES WELLINGTON
Administrator, educator. **Personal:** Born Mar 2, 1930, Atlanta, GA; married Sandra Bratton; children: Joanna, Janell & Jamila. **Educ:** Morehouse, BS, 1951; Howard Univ, SM 1953; MIT, PhD, 1964, MS, 1961. **Career:** Morehouse clearing, prof chmn, 1964-72; Dept Sci Educ Res, NSF, dept dir, 1975-77, sec head, 1973-75, prg dir, 1971-73; Mass Inst Tech, tutor, 1961-63, res asst, 1957-63; Howard Univ, instr, 1955-57, res asst,1951-52; National Bur Stand, physicist, 1952-53; Dept Energy, Energy Storage Syst, div dir, 1978-81, consult, 1981-82; AMAF, res group, mkt mgr, 1982-83; Sonicraft, mgr, 1983-88; Pailen-Johnson Assoc, dir, techserv, 1988-89; Comp Tech Group, vpres, mkt, 1989-90; Catholic Univ Am, asst acad vpres res, 1990-2005, assoc provost; chair, Byte Back Inc. **Orgs:** NatRes Coun, CHR, 1975-; Sloan Found, 1975; BEEP Nat Urban League, 1972-; pres, Brown Station Sch, PTA, 1971; NSF, 1969-71; Ctr Res, 1969-71; consult, Atlanta Sci Cong, 1969-71; comr Comt Clearing Physics, 1968-71; Beta Kappa Chi; Sigma Pi Sigma; Sigma XI; Phi Beta Kappa; Am Phy Soc; Am Assc Physics Teachers; AAAS; Ga Acad Sci; Nat Inst Sci. **Honors/Awds:** DOE, Achievement Award; dept Army, Outstanding Service Award.

MAYO, DR. JULIA A (JULIA MAYO JOHNSTON)
Sociologist, psychiatrist. **Personal:** Born Aug 16, 1926, Philadelphia, PA; daughter of Mamie Clark and Henry Mayo; married William E Johnston, Dec 28, 1958 (deceased); children: Wilvena. **Educ:** Univ PA, BA, 1947; Bryn Mawr Col, MS, 1949; Univ PA, PhD, 1958. **Career:** St Vincents Hosp & Med Ctr NY, chief clncl stds & evaluation 1966-, prof emer, 1991-; NIMH St Elizabeth Hosp Wash DC, chief psychosocial stds 1960-66; Mental Hygiene Clinic VA Hosp Wilmington, DE, asst chief 1953-60; Psychotherapy, indiv/group part time pvt prac 1966-; DHew Ofc of Ed, consult 1975-; South Beach Psycho Ctr NY, consult rsrch 1978-; Medical Coll, New York, NY, assoc prof clinical psychiatry, 1989-91; New York Medical Col, clin prof emer, psychiat, 1991-. **Orgs:** Am Sociol Asn; APPA; Am Acad Pediat; Am Asn Marriage and Family Ther; Nat Asn Social Workers; Am Group Psychotherapy Asn. **Special Achievements:** Numerous scientific publ. **Business Addr:** Professor Emeritus, New York Medical College, Department Psychiatry & Behavioral Sciences, Admin Bldg, Valhalla, NY 10595, **Business Phone:** (914)594-4000.

MAY-PITTMAN, INEVA
Educator. **Personal:** Born Jul 6, 1934, Jayess, MS; married Joe; children: Albert Jefferson & Davion Jamaal. **Educ:** Jackson State Col, BS, elem educ, 1956; Jackson State Univ, MS, 1973; AA, 1974. **Career:** Nat Asn Advan Colored People, vpres, 1965; Nat Coun Negro Women, pres, 1974; Bus & Prof Women's Club, vpres; CSA, bd mem, poverty prog; Jackson Missionary Baptist Dist Asn, asst teacher; Jackson Sch Syst, first grade teacher, exec bd mem, currently. **Orgs:** Pleasant Hill Missionary Baptist Church; vpres, N Jackson Community Boy's Club; chmn, trustee bd, NCNW; bd mem, Jackson Golden Heritage; Nat Asn Advan Colored People; life mem, Jackson State Univ Nat Alumni Asn; MS Teachers Asn; Nat Coun Negro Women; Bus & Prof Women's Club; life mem, Nat Educ Asn. **Honors/Awds:** Teacher of Year, 1959; President of the Year, Jackson Dist Missionary, 1970; Nat Asn Advan Colored People Fight for Freedom Cert of Merit, 1973; John W Dixon Outstanding Community Service Award, Nat Asn Advan Colored People, 1977; Finer Womanhood Award, Jackson Sect NCNW, 1978; Distinguished Service Award, Jackson Pub Schs, 1986; Dedicated Service Award, Jackson Asn Educr, 1987; Dedicated Service Award, City Usher Bd, 1989; Exceptional Achievement Award, Black Women's Polit Action, 1989. **Business Addr:** Executive Board Member, Jackson School System, 5110 Inwood Dr, Jackson, MS 39206, **Business Phone:** (601)497-4360.

MAYS, DAVID
Dentist, football player. **Personal:** Born Jun 20, 1949, Pine Bluff, AR. **Educ:** Tex Sothern Univ, BA, 1971; Univ Sothern Calif, DDS, 1976. **Career:** Football player (retired), Dentist; Houston Texans & Shreveport Streamer, 1974; The Hawaiians, 1975; Los Angeles, pvt prac, dentist, 1978-; Community Dent Dept & Pedodontic Dent Dept Univ Calif, clin prof, 1978; Cleveland Browns, 1976-77; Buffalo Bills, 1978. **Orgs:** Western Dental Soc; Angel City Dental Soc; Am Dent Asn; Alpha Phi Alpha Frat. **Home Addr:** 7427 S Figueroa St, Los Angeles, CA 90003, **Home Phone:** (323)751-2395.

MAYS, DR. JAMES ARTHUR
Physician, educator. **Personal:** Born May 1, 1939, Pine Bluff, AR; son of Talmadge and Edna Mays; children: James Arthur Jr, James Anthony, James Ornett & James Eddie. **Educ:** Univ Ark, BS, MD, 1960; Univ Calif Sch Med, intern, 1965; Univ Calif, Los Angeles, cardiology. **Career:** Stud Gov Univ Ark Pine Bluff, vpres, 1960; Merrill High Sch, stud counr, 1965; Los Angeles & Chap Alumni Asn, pres, 1972-73; United High Blood Pressure Found, med dir, 1974; Martin Luther King Hosp, cardiologist self congestive heart failure comt ed; Charles R. Drew Med Sch, cardiologist & asst prof; Medical Clin, Los Angeles, owner. **Orgs:** Publ ed, Los Angeles Times, 1974; State Coun Hypertension Control, CA,1975; Washington Human Rels Comt, 1977; chmn, PUSH LA, 1981; founder, Adopt-a-Family; creator, Black Super Heroes Radian and Radiance; chmn, NewYork Pub Serv Found; Philantropee Asn; bd dir, Watt & Health Found; Steering Comt, Pres Reagan's Comn Tax Reform; fel, African Sci Inst. **Honors/Awds:** News Maker, Nat Asn Media, 1975; ANA Award, 1975; Citation Calif State Senate, 1976; Senator Nat Holder 50 Award; George Washington Medal,Freedom Found Valley Forge. **Special Achievements:** Written songs "Baby Coy", 1977, "Resing Wright", 1977, "Disco Bill Happy Birthday", 1977; Appeared on Donahue, Today Show; Publications such as "Methods to Make Ethnic Foods Safer" 1976, "Monogram on High Blood Pressure" 1976, "Chameleon Released" 1977, "Circle of Five", "Blink of an Eye", "Doctor Dan-Man of Steel"; write-ups in Washington Post, Jet, Ebony,LA Times, LA Harold, Life, Look, Newsweek, CBS News, CNW News, ABC News,USA Today, AMA News, Christian Serv Monitor; spoke before Commissioner of US Senate and House of Reps. **Military Serv:** AUS, capt, 1966-68; Bronze Star, Combat Medic's Badge. **Business Addr:** Owner, Mays Medical Clinic, 8915 S Broadway, Los Angeles, CA 90003, **Business Phone:** (323)778-7697.

MAYS, KIVUUSAMA
Football player. **Personal:** Born Jan 7, 1975, Anniston, AL. **Educ:** Univ NC. **Career:** Minn Vikings, linebacker, 1998-99; Green Bay Packers, 1999; Orlando Rage, 2001.

MAYS, LESLIE A
Executive, president (organization), vice president (organization). **Personal:** Born in Houston, TX. **Educ:** Texas Southern Univ, BA, Commun. **Career:** Tex Air, flight attend, human resources mgr, 1970; Redbook Int, human resources dir, 1989-94; Gen Mills, diversity dept, 1994-96; Shell Oil Co, exec dir diversity, 1996-99, vpres group global diversity, 1999; Pfizer, vpres global diversity, 2005-; Peoples Express Airline, personnel dir, city mgr; Am Works, recruitment officer; Jane C Edmonds & Assoc, consult. **Orgs:** Bd mem, Nat Coalition 100 Black Women, 1997-2001, pres, 2001-. **Business Addr:** Vice President of Global Diversity, Pfizer Inc, 235 E 42nd St, New York, NY 10017, **Business Phone:** (212)733-2323.*

MAYS, TRAVIS CORTEZ
Basketball coach, basketball player. **Personal:** Born Jun 19, 1968, Ocala, FL; married Mirella; children: Cherrell & Trevor. **Educ:** Univ Tex, BA, psychol, 1990. **Career:** Basketball player (retired), basketball coach; Sacramento Kings, guard, 1990-91; Atlanta Hawks, guard, 1992-93; Panionios BC Athens, FIBA Europe, guard, 2001; WNBA San Antonio Silver Stars, asst coach, 2002-03, head scout, 2003-04; Univ Tex, asst basketball coach, 2004-07; Louisiana State Univ, asst coach, 2007-. **Honors/Awds:** Southwest Conference Player of the Year, 1988-89 & 1989-90; European All-Star Game, 1994 & 1995; First Team All-Star, 1999-01; Men's Athletics Hall of Honor, Univ Tex, 2002. **Business Phone:** (225)578-8001.

MAYS, DR. VICKIE M
Educator. **Personal:** Born Jan 30, 1952, Chicago, IL; daughter of Leonard and Ruth. **Educ:** Loyola Univ Chicago, IL, BA, psychol & philos, 1973, MA, clin psychol, 1979; Univ Massachusetts, Amherst, MA, PhD, clin psychol, 1979. **Career:** Loyola Univ, Dept Psychol, Chicago, IL, res asst, 1972; Univ Massachusetts, Amherst, MA, teaching asst, 1973-74, instr & dorm counr, 1974, lectr, 1974, teaching asst & clin supvr, 1976-77, acting intake coordr & clin supvr, 1977, res asst, 1978; George Wash Univ, Wash, DC, instr, 1975-76; Univ Calif Los Angeles, asst to prof clin psychol, 1979-; UCLA Acad Senate, vice chairperson, chairperson, 1997-99; consult & adv to govt & educ insts; Nat Comm Vital & Health Studies, 2000-, chairperson subcomm pop; UCLA, Ctr Res Educ Training & Strategic Commun, dir, currently, Col Letters & Sci, Dept Health Sci, prof, currently, Dept Psychol, prof, currently. **Orgs:** Am Psychol Asn, 1970-; Western Psychol Asn, 1981-; Am Pub Health Asn, 1986-, Black Caucus Health Workers Prog Comm, 1991-; chairperson minority affairs comm, Am Col Epidemiol, 1996-; ed bd mem, Clin Psychol Women, AIDS Educ & Prev & Jour Homosexuality; Jour Cult Diversity & Ment Health. **Honors/Awds:** Outstanding Woman of the Year, Bd Outstanding Young Women, 1984, 1986; Women and Psychotherapy Research

Award, Div Psychol Women, Am Psychol Asn, 1985; Master Lecture, 1997, Leadership Award, Am Psychol Asn. **Special Achievements:** Author: The Impact of Racial and Feminist Attitudes on the Educational Achievement and Occupational Aspirations of College Level Black Women," UCLA Center for Afro-American Studies Newsletter, May, 1980; co-author of "Educating Community Gatekeepers About Alcohol Abuse in Women: Changing Attitudes, Knowledge and Referral Practices," Journal of Drug Education, 15 (4), 1985, "Introduction to the Special Issues: Psychology and AIDS," American Psychologist, 43 (11), 1988, author of numerous other research reports, review articles, abstracts, book chapters, and articles on behavioral science and AIDS. **Business Addr:** Professor, University of California-Los Angeles, Department of Psychology, 405 Hilgard Ave 1283 Franz Hall, PO Box 951563, Los Angeles, CA 90095-1563, **Business Phone:** (310)206-5159.

MAYS, WILLIAM, JR.
Executive director, president (organization). **Personal:** Born Oct 12, 1929, Detroit, MI; married Marilouise; children: Elisabeth & Adrienne. **Educ:** Eastern Mich Univ, BA, 1954; Univ Mich, MA, 1958. **Career:** Ann Arbor Pub Schs, speech therapist, 1958-66, elem prin, 1966-72, asst supt, 1972-74, dir elem educ, 1974-75; Mich Elem & Mid Sch Prin Asn, exec dir, 1975-97; E Mich Univ Alumni Asn, pres, currently. **Orgs:** Bd trustees, Washtenaw Community Col, 1974; E Mich Univ Alumni Asn. **Honors/Awds:** Churchmanship Award, First United Methodist Church, 1969. **Special Achievements:** Article published in Mich Asn Sch Bds J, 1976. **Business Phone:** (734)487-0250.

MAYS, WILLIAM G
Executive, president (organization), chief executive officer. **Personal:** Born Dec 4, 1945, Indiana; married Rose Cole; children: Kristin & Heather. **Educ:** Ind Univ, BA, chem, MBA. **Career:** Mays Chem Co Inc, Linkbelt Facil, Indianapolis, test chemist, 1967; Proctor & Gamble, acct mgr, 1967; Mays Chem Co Inc, pres & chief exec officer, 1980-; Anthem Ins, dir, 1993-2003; WellPoint Inc, dir, 2001-; Eli Lilly & Co, mkt planning; Cummins Engine Co, asst to pres; Specty Chems, pres. **Orgs:** Chair, Consortium Grad Study Mgt; bd dir, Anthem Ins Inc; Bank One, IN; Ind St Chamber Comn; Ind Univ Found; Ind Univ Pres's Coun; Indianapolis Chamber Com; Nat Urban League & United Way Cent, IN; dir, Chem Educ Found; dir, Indianapolis Conv & Visitors Asn; dir, Nat Minority Supplier Develop Coun. **Honors/Awds:** B'Nai B'Rith Isidora Feibleman Award, 1990; Indiana Minority Small Business Advocate of the Year, 1991; Distinguished Hoosier, 1992; President's Award, Black President's Roundtable Asn, 1992; Anti-Defamation League Americanism Award, 1993; Charles Whistler Award, 1993; Human Rights Award, Ind Ed Asn, 1994; Labor and Industry Award, Ind St Conf Nat Asn Advan Colored People, 1994; Herman B Wells Visionary Award, 2000; Honorary Doctorate, Univ Evansville; Honorary Doctorate, Marlin Univ; Honorary Doctorate, Ind Univ; Gen Motors Outstanding Supplier of the Year Award; Man of the Year Award. **Special Achievements:** Carried Olympic Flame during trip through Indianapolis, 1995. **Business Addr:** Chief Executive Officer, President, Mays Chemical Company Inc, 5611 E 71st St, Indianapolis, IN 46220, **Business Phone:** (317)842-8722.

MAYS, DR. WILLIAM O
Executive, physician. **Personal:** Born Dec 21, 1934, Little Rock, AR; married Deborah Easter; children: William III, Ryan Easter & Eric Easter. **Educ:** Howard Univ, BS, 1956; Univ Ariz, MD, 1960. **Career:** Wayne County Gen Hosp, internshp, 1960, residency, 1965; Southwest Medical Plaza, physician, currently; Mays Chem Co, founder, 1980. **Orgs:** Pres & chmn bd, Mich Health Maint Org Plans Inc; pres chmn bd, Detroit Med Found; vpres, Harris Mays & Assocs PC; NMA; AMA; Detroit Med Soc; Wayne Co Med Soc; Mich State Med Soc; Wolverine Med Soc; bd dir & exec com & tres CHPC, SEM; bd dir, Blue Shield Mich; pres, Detroit Med Soc, 1972-74; Am Col Physician Execs. **Military Serv:** AUS, Med Corps, 1962-63. **Business Addr:** Physician, Southwest Medical Plaza, 2401 20th St, Detroit, MI 48216, **Business Phone:** (313)961-8450.

MAYS, WILLIE HOWARD
Baseball executive, baseball player. **Personal:** Born May 6, 1931, Westfield, AL; son of William Howard Mays Sr and Anna Sattlewhite; married Margherite Wendell Chapman, Feb 14, 1956 (divorced 1961); children: Michael; married Mae Louise Allen, Nov 27, 1971. **Career:** Baseball player (retired), baseball executive; Birmingham Black Barons Baseball Team, 1948-50; Trenton Team, 1950-51; Minneapolis Millers, 1951; NY Giants, 1951-57; San Francisco Girants, 1958-72, spec asst to pres, currently; NY Mets, 1972-73; Bally Park Place Atlantic City, asst to pres; Ogden Corp & Gruntal & Co, pub rels; Health Spring, spokesperson, currently. **Orgs:** Pres, Say Hey Found; Giants Community Fund; San Francisco Food Bank; Whitney Young Child Develop Ctr. **Honors/Awds:** Rookie of Year, 1951; Male Athlete of Year, AD, 1954; Hickock Belt, 1954; Nat League's Most Valuable Player, 1954, 1965; Player of Year, Sporting News, 1954; League's Stolen Bases Champion, 1956-59; Gold Glove Award, 1957-68; Baseball Player of Decade, 1970; First Commissioner's Award, 1970; Black Hall of Fame, 1974; Nat Baseball Hall of Fame, 1979; San Francisco Bay Area Hall of Fame, 1980; George Moscone Memorial Award, Big Bros, 1980; A Phillip Randolph Award, 1980; DHL, Yale Univ, 2004; Lifetime Achievement Award, Bobby Bragan Youth Found, 2005; Honorary Doctorate,Dartmouth Col, 2007; California Hall of Fame, 2007.Doctor of Humane Letters degree from San Francisco State University, 2009. **Special Achievements:** Author, Willie Mays, My Life In and Out of Baseball, 1966; ranks second among the 100 greatest baseball players of the century, The Sporting News;ranks eighth among the top 50 athletes of the century, ESPN. **Military Serv:** AUS, 1952-54. **Business Addr:** Special Assistant to the President, San Francisco Giants, 24 Willie Mays Plz, Pac Bell Pk, San Francisco, CA 94107, **Business Phone:** (415)972-1800.

MAYWEATHER, FLOYD
Athlete. **Personal:** Born Feb 24, 1977, Grand Rapids, MI; son of Floyd Mayweather, Sr. **Orgs:** Founded the Floyd Mayweather Foundation; Bronze medal winner, 1996 Olympics; junior lightweight, WBC world title, 1999. **Honors/Awds:** Won six world boxing championships in five different weight class. **Special Achievements:** Total fights, 40; total wins, 40; wins by knock out, 25; losses, 0. **Business Addr:** Mayweather Promotions, LLC, 1001 S. Rancho Dr., Las Vegas, NV 89106, **Business Phone:** (702)386-8009.*

MAZON, LARRI WAYNE
Educator, college administrator. **Personal:** Born Dec 6, 1945, Roanoke, AL; son of Dewey and Fannie; married Dorothy Antrum Mazon, May 21, 1982; children: Jeffrey (stepson) & Nikki. **Educ:** Univ New Haven, West Haven, Conn, BS, criminal justice Admin, 1976; State Univ New York-Stony Brook, MSW, 1983; Nova-Southeastern Univ, doctoral grad. **Career:** Fairfield Hills Hosp, rehabilitation counr, 1968-72; Regional Network Progs, Bridgeport, Conn, dir, rehabilition servs, 1972-78; Conntac-Wesleyan, Middletown, Conn, counr & coordr, 1978-84; Fairfield Univ, dir, Multicultural Rels & Stud Acad Support Serv, dir, 1984-2007, Inst Diversity Initiatives, dir, 2007-. **Orgs:** Inst Afro-Am Scholar, 1984-91; steering com mem, African-Am in Higher Educn Conn, 1988-90; chmn, Minority Advisory Coun, Hamden Bd Educ & Suptd Schs, 1989-90, 1990-91; chmn, Asn Jesuit Cols & Univs, Conference on Minority Affairs, 1990-91; bd dir, Greater Bridgeport Coun Churches Inc. **Home Addr:** 15 Jayne Lane, Hamden, CT 06514, **Home Phone:** (203)281-7749. **Business Addr:** Director of Institutional Diversity Initiatives, Fairfield University, 1073 N Benson Rd Loyola Hall Rm 4, Fairfield, CT 06430, **Business Phone:** (203)254-4000.

MCADOO, BOB
Basketball player, athletic coach. **Personal:** Born Sep 25, 1951, Greensboro, NC; married Patrizia; children: Rita, Robert III, Ross, Russell, Ryan & Rasheeda. **Educ:** NC Univ, 1972. **Career:** Basketball player (retired), asst coach; Buffalo Braves, 1972-76; NY Knicks, 1976-79; Boston Celtics, 1979; Detroit Pistons, 1980; New Jersey Nets, 1980; Los Angeles Lakers, 1981-84; Philadelphia 76ers, 1985-86; Forli, Milan, Italy; Miami Heat, asst coach, 1996-. **Honors/Awds:** Rookie of the Year 1973; leading scorer in the NBA (130); NBA Rookie of the Year, 1973; MVP & 2nd team All-League Honors 1974-75; All Star Team, 1974-77; Basketball Hall of Fame, 2000. **Special Achievements:** Ranks 20th on NBA's all-time scoring list with 17,803 career points. **Business Phone:** (305)577-4328.

MCADOO, DR. HARRIETTE P
School administrator. **Personal:** Born Mar 15, 1940, Fort Valley, GA; daughter of William and Ann; married John; children: Michael, John, Julia & David. **Educ:** Mich State Univ, BA, 1961, MA, 1963; Univ Mich, PhD, 1970; Harvard Univ, Post-doctoral, 1974; Univ Mich, Post-doctoral, 1982. **Career:** Milan & Ypsilanti HS, teacher, 1964-67; Univ Mich, Sch Educ, teaching asst & res adv, 1968-70; Univ Md, Baltimore, proj dir, 1976-78; Howard Univ, Sch Social Work, from assoc to prof, 1970-91, acting dean, 1984-85; George Washington Univ Medical Center, res prof, 1988-97; Mich State Univ, Col Human Ecol, Dept Family & Child Ecol, prof, 1991-, fac, African Studies Ctr, Ctr Advan Study Int Develop, 1993-; univ distinguished prof, 1996-; vis prof, summer, Smith Col, Washington Univ, Mich State Univ, Univ Minn. **Orgs:** Bd dirs, Nat Coun on Family Relations, 1979-82; publs com, Soc for Res in Child Develop, 1979-85; gov coun Soc for Res in Child Develop, 1979-85; bd dirs, Groves Conf on Marriage & Family, 1983-88; dir conf VIII, XI, XII Empirical Conf on Black Psych, 1985, 1987, 1988; prog vpres, Nat Coun on Family Rel, 1985; mem at large AERA Spec Interest Group in Early Educ & Child Devel 1985-87; Am Sociol Asn; Nat Asn Educ Young Children; Nat Asn Black Psychologists; Nat Asn Social Workers; Nat Coun Family Relations; Soc Human Ecol; Soc Res Child Develop. **Honors/Awds:** Nat Adv Comm White House Conf on Families 1979-81; Outstanding Com Award, Howard Co Found for Black Educ, 1980; Outstanding Soror Alpha Kappa Alpha Iota Lambda Omega Chap, 1981; Marie Peters Award, Nat Coun on Family Relations, 1984; Nat Acad Sci Comm on Status Black Ams Demography & Health Panel; 'Researcher of the Year', 1982, 1987; Outstanding Researcher of the Year, Nat Ason Black Psychologists, 1978, 1991; Janet Helms Award, Columbia Univ, 1993; Award for Distinguished Contributions to Family Systems Research, Am Family Therapy Acad, 1995; Golden Key Research Award, 1996; Michigan State University Faculty Award, 1996; Human Ecology Excellence Awards, 1997; Ernest Burgess Award, Nat Coun Family Relations, 2004. **Special Achievements:** Published, 'The nationally-acclaimed Black Families (Third Edition, Thousand Oaks, CA: Sage, 1997)', 'Family Ethnicity: Strength in Diversity (Second Edition, Sage, 1999)', 'Black Children: Social, Educational and Parental Environments (Sage, 1985)'. **Business Addr:** University Distinguished Professor, Michigan State University, Department of Child & Family Ecology, 442 Berkey Hall, East Lansing, MI 48824-1111, **Business Phone:** (517)432-3321.

MCADOO, HENRY ALLEN
Government official. **Personal:** Born Feb 9, 1951, Murfreesboro, TN; son of John Allen and Doris Ann Wade; married Gayle Elizabeth Howse McAdoo, Dec 3; children: Carol, Allen Jr, Lauren. **Educ:** Middle Tenn State Univ, Murfreesboro, TN, BS, 1975; Univ Tenn Space Inst, Tullahoma, TN, attended 1977; Middle Tenn State Univ, Murfreesboro, TN, attended 1979. **Career:** Scales & Son Funeral Home Inc; Sedrulp Technologies, appln programmer, 1972-82; NISSAN, sr analyst, 1982-86, sr systs analyst, 1986-; Rutherford County Comn, comnr 18th Dist, 1978-. **Orgs:** Chmn, Law Enforcement Rutherford County, 1978-79; chmn, Econ Comt Rutherford County, 1983-84; Mason Murfreesboro Lodge No 12; Elks EA Davis Lodge No 1138; Kappa Alpha Psi Fraternity, Murfreesboro Alumni Chapter; chmn pro term, Rutherford County Comn, 1998-02. **Honors/Awds:** Nominated & appointed Rutherford County Bd Gov Mid-Cumberland, 1978-79, Bd Zoning Appeals, 1979-. **Home Addr:** 1111 SE Broad St, Murfreesboro, TN 37130. **Business Addr:** Commissioner, Rutherford County 18th District, PO Box 3132, Murfreesboro, TN 37133-3132.

MCAFEE, CARRIE R.
Educator. **Personal:** Born Dec 20, 1931, Galveston, TX; married Joshua. **Educ:** Lincoln Univ, BA, 1951; Columbia Univ, MA, 1963; Univ Calif, Berkeley, TSU. **Career:** New York Col, teacher 1955-64, coun, 1965-68, asst prin, 1968-73, coun & coord, 1969-72; Houston Independent Sch Dist, prin, 1974-89. **Orgs:** TASSP; NASSP; ASCD; TSCD; HSCD; Nat Asn Women Exec; Nat Asn Sex Educ & Coun; TS&A Hon Prin Asn Bd Dirs; Am Bridge Asn; YWCA; MacGregor Orioles Little League; Am Lung Asn; San Jacinto Lung Asn; Nat Coalition 100 Black Women; chmn, Am Lung Asn Tex; Greater Houston Found, Houston Fedn Prof Women; Zeta Phi Beta; VIL State Exec Comt; Tex Democratic Women Harris County. **Honors/Awds:** Lady of the Year, 1951; Outstanding Journ Teacher, 1962; Newspaper Fund Fellow, 1964; Outstanding Master Bridge Player, 1969; ABA Lady, 1974; Achieve in Educ TSU, 1974; Professional Award, Nat Asn Bus & Prof Women, 1975; Outstanding Women YWCA, 1977; Big E Award, Boy Scouts Am, 1989;Outstanding Women, Houston Woman Newspaper, 1989; Carrie Rochon McAfee Library, 1995; Sojourner Truth Award, 1996. **Special Achievements:** First black female principal of a Senior High School established a precedent for the Houston Independent School District and the state of Texas.

MCAFEE, CHARLES FRANCIS
Architect. **Personal:** Born Dec 25, 1932, Los Angeles, CA; son of Arthur James McAfee Sr and Willie Anna McAfee; married Gloria Myrth Winston; children: Cheryl Lynn, Pamela Anita & Charyl Frena Duncan. **Educ:** Univ Nebr, BArch, 1958. **Career:** Charles F McAfee FAIA NOMA PA, pres & chief exec officer, currently. **Orgs:** Fel, AMR Inst Architects, 1963; sr vpres, Nat Bus League; Wichita Urban League; Wichita Chamber Com; Phyllis Wheatley C Home; Excelsior Club; Kappa Alpha Psi Fraternity; Sigma Pi Phi Fraternity; fed past pres, Nat Asn Minority Architects. **Honors/Awds:** Numerous Design Awards, Am Inst Architects, 1964-96; Design Awards, Fed Housing Admin, 1964; Design Awards, Nat Orgn Minority Architects, 1983; Alumni Achievement Award, Univ Nebr; Distinguished Alumni Award, Col Archit. **Special Achievements:** Joint Venture selected for program, construction and design Management, Olympic Games facilities, Atlanta, 1996; developer, architect: Richmond Health Dept; McAfee Manufacturing Modular Housing Systems, pres. **Military Serv:** AUS, cpl, 1953-55. **Business Addr:** President, Chief Executive Officer, Charles F McAfee FAIA NOMA PA, Architects Planners, 2600 N Grove St, Wichita, KS 67219, **Business Phone:** (316)686-2138.

MCAFEE, FLO
Government official. **Career:** The White House, Office of Public Liaison, spec asst pres; Wisdom Works Inc, develop & mkt adv, currently. **Orgs:** Bd mem, Alethos Found, currently. **Business Phone:** (202)456-2930.

MCAFEE, FRED LEE
Football player, football executive. **Personal:** Born Jun 20, 1968, Philadelphia, MS; children: Jaela & Frederick. **Educ:** Miss Col, BS, mass commun; Stanford Univ, Exec Educ Grad Sch Bus, NFL mgrs prog. **Career:** Football player (retired), Football executive; New Orleans Saints, runningback, 1991-93, 2000-06, dir player, 2007-; Ariz Cardinals, 1994; Pittsburgh Steelers, 1994-98; Kansas City Chiefs, 1999; Tampa Bay Buccaneers, 1999. **Business Phone:** (504)731-1804.*

MCAFEE, LEO C
Educator. **Personal:** Born Dec 15, 1945, Marshall, TX; married Sandra Wray; children: Leo III, LaRuth & Lawrence. **Educ:**

Prairie View A&M Univ, BS, 1966; Univ Mich, MSE, 1967, PhD, 1970. **Career:** Bell Telephone Labs, tech Staff, 1968; Univ Mich, IBM Thomas J Watson Res Labs NY, fac, 1971-78; Semiconductor Group Electronics, Dept Gen Motors Res Labs Mich, assoc sr res engr, 1973-74; Univ Mich, from assoc prof to prof, elect & comput engr, Ctr Wireless Integrated Microsystems, assoc dir educ & outreach, currently. **Orgs:** Inst Elect & Electronics Engr Inc; Eta Kappa Nu; Tau Beta Pi; Sigma Xi; Phi Kappa Phi; Alpha Kappa Mu. **Honors/Awds:** Outstanding Engineering Student, Prairie View A&M Univ, 1956-66; Nat Sci Found Trainee Univ Mich, 1966-68; EECS Faculty Service Award, Univ Mich, 1992. **Special Achievements:** Published and co-author for books like: Data Knowl. Eng. 6: 421-443, 1991. **Business Addr:** Associate Director of Education & Outreach, University of Michigan, Wireless Integrated Microsystems, 2316B EECS 1301 Beal Ave, Ann Arbor, MI 48109-2122.

MCALLISTER, SINGLETON BERYL
Lawyer. **Personal:** Born Mar 25, 1952, Baltimore, MD; daughter of James Winfred and Ann Hughes. **Educ:** Univ Md, BA, 1975; Howard Univ, Sch Law, JD, 1984. **Career:** Parren J Mitchell, legis assist, 1975-78; TransAfrica, Inc, asst dir, 1978-79; Congressman William H Gray, III, legis dir, 1979-81; Congressman Mickey Leland, spec asst, 1981-83; US Fed Dist Ct, law clerk, 1984-85; US House Reps, budget comt coun, 1986-88; Reed, Smith, Shaw & McClay, partner, 1988-92; Shaw, Pittman, Potts & Trowbridge, coun, 1992-96; Agency Inst Develop, gen coun, 1996-01; Patton Boggs LLP, partner, 2001-. **Orgs:** Bd mem adv bd, AFR Develop Found, 1987; Capitol Ballet Guild Inc, board member, 1988; bd mem, Vir Local Anti-Trust Fund Drug Authority, 1990; VIR Small Bus Financing Authority, 1990; gen coun & bd mem, Women Govt Rels Inc, 1991; adv bd mem, Congressional Black Caucus Found, 1991; Northern VIR Minority Bus & Prof Asn, gen coun, 1992; Pres, Women Govt Rels Inc, 1994; Democratic Nat Comt Women Leadership Forum, 1994; Health Policy Adv Comt, Joint Ctr Political Studies, 1994; Fed Affairs Comt, Greater Wa Bd Trade, 1994. **Honors/Awds:** AMR Federation Government Employees Award, Local 1733, 1978; Recognition Award, Am Lung Asn Dist Columbia, 1992; Minority Business Award. **Special Achievements:** WA Tech, Commentary, 1992; Nat Med Asn News, Articles, 1991; Asn Black Cardiol News, Articles, 1992. **Business Addr:** Partner, Patton Boggs LLP, 2550 M St NW, Washington, DC 20037-1350, **Business Phone:** (202)457-6000.*

MCALPINE, ROBERT
Association executive. **Personal:** Born Jul 13, 1937, New Haven, CT; son of Rachel Thomas Simpson; married Carole J Robinson; children: Monique, Angie. **Educ:** Southern CT State Col, BS, 1960, MS, 1969; Yale Univ, Cert Urban Studies, 1969; Occidental Col, MA, 1970. **Career:** Guilford Pub Sch, tchr, 1960-67; New Haven Pub Sch, admin, 1967-69; US Conf Mayors, prog analyst, 1970-74; Nat Urban League Inc, congressional liaison, 1974-1989, director of policy & govt rels, l989-. **Orgs:** NAACP; Washington Urban League. **Honors/Awds:** National Urban Fellows, 1969-70; New Haven Jaycees Key Man of the Year, 1969-. **Business Addr:** National Urban League Inc, 500 E 62nd St, Ste 600, New York, NY 10021, **Business Phone:** (212)310-9000.*

MCANDREW, ANNE E BATTLE
Educator. **Personal:** Born May 28, 1951, Philadelphia, PA; daughter of Turner Charles Battle III and Marian Louise Chester Battle; married John, Dec 3, 1983 (divorced 1998); children: Allison & Christina. **Educ:** Moore Col Art & Design, Philadelphia, Pa, BFA, BS, 1972; Visual Studies Workshop, Rochester, NY, photog, 1974; Rochester Inst Technol, Rochester,NY, MFA, 1983. **Career:** Panther Publ House, New York, NY, researcher, 1971; Univ Rochester, Rochester, NY, mus video asst, 1974-75; Rochester City Sch Dist, Rochester, NY, art teacher, 1974-, lead teacher, 1988-; Rochester Inst Technol, Rochester, NY, grad asst, 1982-83; Wedge Newspaper, Rochester, NY, managing ed, 1985-86; Theodore Roosevelt Sch No 43, prin, currently. **Orgs:** Designer, Prof Teaching Portfolio Format, Rochester City Sch Dist, 1989-; curric comn dir, Prof Pract Sch Design Team, Am Fed Teachers, 1990-; Sch Based Planning Team, 1990-. **Honors/Awds:** Outstanding Teacher Award, 1993; Nat Excellence Teaching Award, Shell Oil Co & Nat Coun Negro Women, 1994; Teacher of the Year, Rochester City Sch, 1995; Most Outstanding Educr, Urban League Rochester, 1996; Mayor's Award COT Achievement, 1997. **Home Addr:** 72 Penn Lane, Rochester, NY 14625-2218. **Business Addr:** Principal, Theodore Roosevelt School No 43, 1305 Lyell Ave, Rochester, NY 14606, **Business Phone:** (585)458-4200.*

MCARTHUR, DR. BARBARA JEAN
Educator, epidemiologist. **Personal:** Born Jul 1, 1929?, Dubuque, IA; daughter of James Laurence Martin and Ada Boone Martin; divorced; children: Michele Jean & William Michael. **Educ:** Provident Hosp & Training Sch, dipl, nursing; DePaul Univ, BSN, MS; Univ Wash, MS, PhD, 1976. **Career:** Educator (retired); Knoxville Col, nurse & asst prof Biol & Sci Educ; Wayne State Univ, assoc prof, 1976-78, grad prog inst epidemiol, 1976-84, assoc dept Immunol & Microbiol Med Sch, 1976, adj prof biol & liberal arts, 1980-88, prof nursing, 1978-96. **Orgs:** Prin investr, Wayne State Univ, Med Sch, 1976-83; consult, Plymouth Ctr Human Develop, 1978; bd mem, Wayne State Univ, Phylon Soc, 1979-, co-chair, 1980-82, 1990-92; bd mem, United Condo Owners Mich, 1979-81; bd mem, Planned Parenthood League Inc, 1982-88; bd mem, Wayne State Univ, Minority Biomed Support Prog, 1979-81; consult, CURN Proj Self Catheterization Rehab Care, 1979; dir, Mich Soc Infection Control, 1979-81; bd mem, ed advy bd, Infection Control, 1979-87; Oral Assessment Bd Higher Educ; consult, Mich Civil Serv Comn, 1980; bd mem, Total Health Care Inc, 1981-84; Task Force, Nat Coun Alcoholism & Chem Dependence, 1983-84; New Detroit Inc Health Comn, 1984-90; Founder's Soc Detroit Inst Arts, 1984-86; Womens' Economic Club, 1984-85; chair, Pub Rels Comt, Southfield Alumnae Chap Delta Sigma Theta Inc, 1984-86; keynote speaker, SW Hosp Nurses Day, 1985; Wayne State Univ, Grad Coun, 1985-93; expert witness malpractice suites, 1984-; first assembly secy, govr, bd regents, gen comn, Nightingale Soc, 1988-91; Coalition Health Care, 1988-89; Friends SW Hosp, 1988-91; bd mem, Conn Health Awareness Group, 1992-93; dir, Consortium Doctors Ltd, 1993-94; Life Style Comn, Southfield, 1998. **Honors/Awds:** A Wilberforce Williams Award, Provident Hosp; Student Research Grant, Sigma Theta Tau, 1974; Nurse Traineeships, DePaul Univ & Univ Wash; Am Acad Nursing, 1978; Sigma Theta Tau Nursing Honor Soc, 1980; NY Acad Sci, 1980; AIDS presentation at second int conf & exhibition on infection control, Eng, 1988; First Ed Review Bd, ABNF J, 1990-95; presenter, First Res Workshop, Michigan Nurses Va, 1989; Key Note Address, Health Care Crisis in Black Community, Univ Wis, 1990; key note address, seventeenth annual state meeting, Ala Dent Soc, 1990; honoree, Consortium Doctors, Ltd, 1993. **Special Achievements:** Numerous publications, chapters in books, journal articles, abstracts; biography in Dr Elizabeth Carnegie's History of Black Nursing 1986; first African Amer faculty to win salary discrimination lawsuit against a predominantly white univ, 1987. **Home Addr:** 26500 Summerdale Dr, Southfield, MI 48034-2235, **Home Phone:** (248)357-1161. *

MCBEAN, CLEAVE A
Military leader. **Educ:** Col VI, BA, bus admin, 1976. **Career:** Command & Control HQS, VIARNG, St Thomas, VI, oper & training officer, 1978-81; 666th MP BN, VIARNG, St Thomas, C-E officer, 1981-83, BN S-3, 1983-84; HQ TARC-VI, Det 1 (Trp Cmd), VIARNG, St Thomas, BN S-1, 1984-85; HQS TARC-VI, Det 2 (VIMA), VIARNG, St Thomas, asst commandant sr instr, 1985-88; 666th MP BN & 786th S&S BN, VIARNG, St Thomas, exec off, 1988-90; 786th S&S BN VIARNG, St Thomas, battalion commdr, 1990-92; HQS TARC-VI, VIARNG, St Croix, VI, training officer, 1992-94, POMSO, 1994-95, deputy TERARC commdr, 1995-96, POTO, 1996-97, deputy TERARC commdr, 1997; retired reserve, 1997-2000; HQS TARC-VI, VI Nat Guard, the adj gen, 2000-. **Military Serv:** Republic Vietnam Campaign Medal; Vietnam Serv Medal; Army Reserves Component Overseas Training Ribbon; Armed Forces Reserve Medal; Nat Defense Serv Medal; Humanitarian Serv Medal; Army Reserve Component Achievement Medal; Army Achievement Medal; Army Commendation Medal; Meritorious Serv Medal. **Business Addr:** The Adjutant General, VI National Guard, 4031 La Grande Princesse, Lot IB, Christiansted, Virgin Islands of the United States 00820-4353, **Business Phone:** (340)712-7710.

MCBEE, VINCENT CLERMONT
Criminologist. **Personal:** Born Nov 4, 1946, Greenville, SC; son of Bozie C and Scotia Marion Henderson; married Virginia Daniels (divorced); children: Vanessa Latasha & Victoria Simone. **Educ:** Johnson C Smith Univ, BS, 1971; Florida Int Univ, 1971; Univ Miami, 1976. **Career:** Nat Brewing Co, Southern Div, qual control chem dir, 1971-75; Southland Corp Velda Farms, qual control supvr, 1975-76; Metro-Dade Police Dept, Miami, FL, criminalist II, 1976-. **Orgs:** Southern Asn Forensic Sci, Prince Hall Masons, Omega Psi Phi Frat Inc, Ordained Elder New Covenant Presbyterian Church; Nat Asn Fire Investrs; Am Acad Forensic Scis; Int Asn Arson Investrs. **Home Addr:** 8625 Claridge Dr, Miramar, FL 33025, **Home Phone:** (954)704-2293. **Business Addr:** Criminalist II, Metro-Dade Police Dept, 9105 NW 25th St Rm 2149, Miami, FL 33172-1505, **Business Phone:** (305)471-3012.

MCBETH, HON. VERONICA SIMMONS
Judge. **Personal:** Born Feb 23, 1947, San Diego, CA; daughter of Lemuel Jackson and Judith LaBrie Jackson; divorced; children: Ashley & Alison. **Educ:** Calif State Univ, BS, 1972; Univ Calif, JD, 1975. **Career:** Judge (retired); Off Los Angeles City Atty, trial dep, 1975-76, coordr-domestic violence prog, 1976-78, spec coun city atty, 1978-79, supvatty, 1979-81; Los Angeles Muni Ct, asst presiding judge, 1996-98, presiding judge, 1999; Los Angeles Super Ct, judge. **Orgs:** Pres, Black Women Lawyers Asn CA, 1979-80; Nat Bar Asn, 1975-; bd mem, LA-NAACP, 1979-80; Nat Asn Women Judges, 1981-; dir, UCLA Law Sch Exec Comt, 1981-; exec comt, LA Muni Ct, 1982-, chair, comt, 1985, 1987; sec, Judicial Div CA Asn Black Lawyers, 1984-85, vpres, 1986-; dir, Harriet Buhai Ctr Family Law; bd dir, judicial coun, Nat Bar Asn, 1985-; bd dir, Coalition 100 Black Women, 1985-; lectr, Nat Judges Col, PA Trial Judges Conf, ABA Appelate Judges Sem; pres, judicial div CABL, 1988-89; Pres Munic Ct Judges Asn, 1988-89; chair elect, 1989-90, chair, 1990-91, judicial coun, Nat Bar Asn; bd dirs, Jack & Jill Am, 1987-91. **Honors/Awds:** UCLA Law Review, 1973-74; Ed, Chief Black Law Jour, 1974-75; Bernard Jefferson Jurist of the Year Award, John Langston Bar Asn, 1991; Raymond Pace Alexander Award, Judicial Coun, Nat Bar Asn, 1989; Presidential Award, Nat Bar Asn, 1987; NAACP Thomas Griffith Award, 1991; Cal Asn Black Lawyers, Judge of the Year, 1991; Calif State Bar Pub Law Sec, Pub Law Award, 1992; Nat Ctr State Ct, Distinguished Service Award, 1996; Century City Bar Asn, Munic Ct Judge of the Year, 1996; Nat Ctr State Ct, WmRehnquist Award for Judicial Excellence, 1998; Margaret Bahai Ctr Family Law, Community Service Award, 1998; Am Bar Asn Judge R Flashner Award for Judicial Excellence, 1999; Gertrude Rush Award, Nat Bar Asn, 1999. **Special Achievements:** Became the first woman & the first African Am to receive the William H Rehnquist Award for Judicial Excellence.

MCBETH-REYNOLDS, SANDRA KAY
Banker, president (organization). **Personal:** Born May 7, 1950, Loma Linda, CA; daughter of Timothy L Woods and Velma A Woods; married James L; children: Brandon Lincoln. **Educ:** Ind Univ, Bloomington, IN, BA, psychol, 1970; Pepperdine Univ, Malibu, CA, MA, urban planning & develop, 1972, MA, sci, pub admin, 1973; Univ W Los Angeles, Sch Law, JD, 1981. **Career:** Loyola Marymount Univ, Westchester, CA, dean student serv, 1976-79; United Int Mortgage, pres, 1980-; Tobin & Assocs Inc, staff. **Orgs:** Jack & Jill Am, 1986-; Alpha Kappa Alpha Sorority, 1969-; Nat Asn Female Execs, 1987-; Coalition 100 Black Women, 1988-. **Honors/Awds:** Top 50 Bus Executives, LA Chamber Com, 1985; Black Women of Achievement, Legal Defense Fund, 1988; Top 100 Black & Professional Women, Dollars & Sense Mag, 1989. **Business Addr:** President, United International Mortgage, 5 Wilshire Blvd 21st Fl, Los Angeles, CA 90302, **Business Phone:** (310)207-5060.

MCBRIDE, BRYANT
Executive. **Personal:** Born May 30, 1965, Chicago, IL; son of William and Julia; married Tina McBride; children: Taylor Jake. **Career:** Nat Hockey League, Bus Develop, Diversity Task Force, vpres bus develop; Vision Sports & Entertainment Partners, pres & chief exec officer, 2005; Active Network, vpres & group dir, currently. **Orgs:** Nat Sports Mkt Networking; NY Road Runners Club; All Hallows High Sch; vice chmn, Tevhniques Effective Alcohol Mgt; Citizens Sports Alliance. **Business Addr:** Vice President, Group Director, The Active Network, 300 5th Ave 6th Fl, Waltham, MA 02451.

MCBRIDE, CHI
Actor. **Personal:** Born Sep 23, 1961, Chicago, IL. **Career:** MCI, tel oper; Films: What's Love Got to Do With It?, 1993; The Frighteners, 1996; Hoodlum, 1997; Mercury Rising, 1998; Dancing in Sept, 2000; Gone in 60 Seconds, 2000; The Kid, 2000; Undercover Brother, 2002; Paid in Full, 2002; Narc, 2003; The N-Word, 2004; Roll Bounce, 2005; Annapolis, 2006; Let's Go to Prison, 2006; Brothers Solomon 2007; Pushing Daisies, 2007; TV movies: King of the World, 2000, Squarepants, 2004; Inside 'The Terminal', 2004; Killer Instinct, 2005; Annapolis, 2006; Let's Go to Prison, 2006; Brothers Solomon, 2007; American Son, 2008; Still Waiting, 2009; Human Target, 2010; tv series: "Max Steel," 2000; "God, the Deviland Bob", 2000; "Boston Public", 2000; "Jimmy Kimmel Live", 2005; "Ellen: The Ellen DeGeneres Show", 2005; "The Late Late Show with Craig Ferguson", 2005. **Business Addr:** Actor, c/o Fox Broadcasting Co, 10201 W Pico Blvd, Los Angeles, CA 90035, **Business Phone:** (310)369-3553.*

MCBRIDE, FRANCES E.
Educator. **Personal:** Born in Athens, GA; married Willie; children: Reginald. **Educ:** Savannah State Col, BS, 1945; Atlanta Univ, MA, 1953. **Career:** Alps Rd Elem Sch Clarke Co, teacher, 1954-83; Polk Co, 1949-53; Lagrange, GA, 1946-47; Jones Co, 1945-46; Univ Ga, supporter, currently. **Orgs:** Resolution Comm NEA, 1973-74; Ebenezer Bapt Ch; Am Asn Univ Women Athens Br; Nat Asn Advan Colored People; Delta Sigma Theta Sor; Savannah St Col Alumni Asn, 1976-77; Atlanta Univ Alumni Asn, 1976-77; Eval Team Southern Asn Schs Habersham Co Sch, 1977; past pres, Silhouette Club Athens; chmn, Kappa Alpha Psi Frat Clarke Co; state prs, GEO CRs, ASN, 1988-89; Clarke Co Asn Educr; Ga Asn Edn; Nat Asn Educs. **Honors/Awds:** Teacher of the Year, 1970; Teacher of the Year, Ga St C, 1970; Teacher of Year, 1970; Teacher of Year, Asn Classroom Teachers, 1975-76. **Special Achievements:** First black female pres of local Clarke Co Assn of Educ 1971; First blackfemale pres of GA Assn of Classroom Teachers, 1972-73; First black female dir tenth dist GAE, 1974-78. **Home Addr:** 284 Plaza St, Athens, GA 30606. **Business Addr:** Supporter, The University of Georgia, 999 Brumby Hall, Athens, GA 30602, **Business Phone:** (706)542-3000.

MCBRIDE, JAMES
Writer. **Personal:** Born Jan 1, 1957, New York, NY; son of Andrew McBride and Ruth McBride Jordan; married; children: 3. **Educ:** Oberlin Col, Ohio; Columbia Univ, Ma, jour, NY, 1979. **Career:** Jazz saxophonist, composer, producer; Wash Post, journalist; Boston Globe, journalist; People Mag, journalist; freelance writer; Author: The Color of Water: A Black Man's Tribute to His White Mother, 1996; Miracle of St Anna, 2003; NY Univ, distinguished writer-in-residence, currently. **Honors/Awds:** Stephen Sondheim Award, Am Music Fest 1993; Am Arts & Let-

ters Richard Rogers Award, for work in musical theater, 1996; Anisfield-Wolf Book Award. **Special Achievements:** Featured in People, Newsweek, Savoy & USA Today; Appeared on several national radio and television shows including The Rosie O'Donnell Show, NPR's All Things Considered, Fresh Air, Morning Edition, and in major news outlets in Australia, New Zealand, and across Europe.

MCBRIDE, SHELIA ANN
Registered nurse. **Personal:** Born Aug 27, 1947, Albany, GA; married Mathis; children: William Alexander Corbett & Erica Monique Corbett. **Educ:** Albany St Col, BS, 1971. **Career:** Orthopedics & Newborn Nursery, Pheobe Putney Mem Hosp, 1971-74; Albany Urban League Fam Planning Prgm, proj dir, nurse 1974-75; ICU, PheobePutney Meml Hosp, charge nurse 1975-76; ICU, Coatesville Vet Adminstrn Hosp, staff nurse 1976-77.

MCBRIDE, TOD ANTHONY
Football player. **Personal:** Born Jan 26, 1976, Los Angeles, CA. **Educ:** Univ Calif, Los Angeles. **Career:** Football player (retired); Green Bay Packers, defensive back, 1999-2002; Atlanta Falcons, 2003; St Louis Rams, corner back, 2004; Seattle Seahawks, 2004; Indianapolis Colts, free agt. *

MCBRIDE, ULLYSSES
Educator. **Personal:** Born Nov 27, 1938, Atmore, AL; son of George and Mamie; married Mabel Copridge; children: Valeri. **Educ:** Knoxville Col, BA, 1959; Ind Univ, Masters Degree; Auburn Univ, Doctoral Degree, 1974; Alabama State Univ, Montgomery, AL, Doctoral Degree, Law, 1990; Univ NY, Stony Brook, Coe fel; Troy State Univ, Post-Doctoral Studies. **Career:** James H Faulkner Col, prof, secondary social sci, dean, 1988-; Escambia Cty Training Sch, Atmore AL, teacher, coach; No Norman HS Brewton AL, dir. **Orgs:** Pres, Kappa Alpha Psi Fraternity, 1989-; past pres, Escambia City Teachers Asn; pres, Faulkner State Col Educ Asn; dist dir, Ala Coun Social Studies;Polemarch S Province KAY; Kappa Delta Pi; Alpha Kappa Mu; dir, United Fund; bd mem, Ala Libr; mem grand bd dir, Kappa Alpha Psi; Pensions &Security bd Escambia County; chmn bd dir, Ala Dem Conf; reader, Fed Grants Washington DC; dir, Self Study Southern Asn Col & Schs Faulkner State Col. **Honors/Awds:** Achievement Awards; Teacher of the Year, Faulkner State Col, 1974. **Special Achievements:** The 100 Most Influential Black Americans, Johnson Publishers 1989. **Home Addr:** PO Box 1026, Atmore, AL 36504. **Business Addr:** Grand Polemarch, Kappa Alpha Psi Fraternity Inc., 2322-24 N Broad St, Philadelphia, PA 19132, **Business Phone:** (215)228-7184.

MCBURROWS, GERALD
Football player. **Personal:** Born Oct 7, 1973, Detroit, MI. **Educ:** Univ Kans. **Career:** St Louis Rams, defensive back, 1995-98; Atlanta Falcons, 1999-2003; free agent, currently. *

MCCAA, JOHN K
Television journalist, naval officer. **Personal:** Born Feb 24, 1954, Rantoul, IL; son of Johnnie and Margaret Britt; married Michele Moore, Oct 30, 1982; children: Collin. **Educ:** Creighton Univ, Omaha, NE, BA, jour & mass commun, 1972-76; Univ Dallas, masters polit. **Career:** WOWT-TV, Omaha, Nebr, reporter & anchor, 1976-84; WFAA-TV, Dallas, Tex, reporter, anchor & mgr, 1984-. **Orgs:** Pres, Dallas-Fort Worth Asn Black Communicators, 1984-; Nat Asn Black Journalists, 1987-; pres, Press Club Dallas. **Business Addr:** News Manager, WFAA-TV, 606 Young St, Dallas, TX 75202, **Business Phone:** (214)977-6213.

MCCABE, JEWELL JACKSON
Association executive, consultant. **Personal:** Born Aug 2, 1945, Washington, DC; daughter of Hal Jackson and julia jackson; married Frederick Ward (divorced); married Eugene L McCabe Jr (divorced). **Educ:** Bard Col, lib arts, 1966. **Career:** NY Urban Coalition, dir pub affairs, 1970-73; Spec Serv C, pub rel officer, 1973-75; Women's Div Off Gov, NY, assoc dir pub info, 1975-77; WNET-TV/Thirteen, dir gov comt affairs, 1977-82; NCBW/ Community Serv Fund, pres; Nat Coalition 100 Black Women, founder & chair, 1978-; Jewell Jackson McCabe Assoc Inc, pres, currently. **Orgs:** Bd dir, Bus Mkt Corp; NY Urban League; New York City Planned Parenthood; Lenox Hill Hosp; Settlement Housing Fund Inc; Community Planning Bd four; Exec Comt, Asn Better NY; bd dir, Women's Forum; co-chair, Women United NY, Planned Parenthood New York City Pub Issues & Answers; Edges; bd dir, Harlem Interfaith Coun Serv, Comt Coun Gr NY; David Rockefeller chmn, Policy Planning Comt, NY Partnership, founding mem, 1981-2000; New York City Comn Status Women, 1982-2002; Reliance Group Holdings Inc; Alight.Com; New York City Investment Fund LIC, founding mem, 1996-2001; Wharton Sch Bus; Bard Col; Nat Alliance Bus; Res Am; Nat Assoc Advan Colored People. **Honors/Awds:** E Region Urban League Guild Award, 1979; Seagrams Civic Award, 1980; Links Civic Award, 1980; Dep Grand Marshal, Annual Martin Luther King Jr Parade, New York City, 1980; Outstanding Community Leadership Award, Malcolm King Col, 1980; The Jewell Jackson McCabe Emerging Leaders Institute, Inc, named in honor, 2003. **Special Achievements:** Publications: Give A Damn, 1970-73; Women New York, 1975-77. **Business Phone:** (212)947-2196.

MCCAIN, ELLA BYRD
Librarian, educator. **Personal:** Born Mar 8, 1925, Dothan, AL; daughter of Olivia Claudia Woods Byrd and Erskine Byrd; married John McCain, Jun 17, 1947. **Educ:** Ala A&M Univ, Normal, BS, 1945; Univ Mich, Ann Arbor, MLS. **Career:** Educator, librarian (retired); Opelika Bd Educ, AL, teacher, 1945-47; Jefferson County Bd Educ, teacher, 1947-52, librn, 1952-72; SC State Col, vis instr, 1953; Atlanta Univ Sch Libr & Scis, Atlanta, GA, asst prof, 1956-82; Rogers Area Voc Ctr, librn, 1972-87. **Orgs:** Ala State Dept Educ Accreditation Comt, 1954-67; pres, Ala Asn Sch Librarians, 1956-58; bd dirs, Birmingham Int Educ Film Festival, 1985-; vol, Am Red Cross, 1986-; 2nd vpres, Birmingham Urban League Guild, 1989-; parliamentarian, Ala Instrnl Media Asn, 1989; vpres, Progressive Action Club Birmingham, AL; Jefferson County Retired Teachers Asn; Ala Retired Teachers Asn; pres, Ala Instrnl Media Asn; Am Asn Retired Persons; Am Voc Asn; Am Asn Sch Librarians; Asn Educ Commun & Technoly; Phi Delta Kappa Fraternity; Friends Ala Libr; Univ Mich Alumni Asn; Ala A&M Univ Alumni Asn; Seasoned Performers; vol, McWane Ctr. **Honors/Awds:** Leadership Award, Phi Delta Kappa Chapter, Univ Mich; Alabama Instructional Media Association Award; Library Service Plaque, Atlanta Univ; Rogers Area Voc Ctr Serv Plaque; Alumni Plaque of the Year, Alabama A&M Univ; American Red Cross Volunteer of Year Award; Red Cross Service Medal. **Home Addr:** 1 Green Springs Ave SW, Birmingham, AL 35211. *

MCCALL, BARBARA COLLINS
Educator. **Personal:** Born Nov 17, 1942, Norfolk, VA; daughter of Gladys George Collins and Joseph Collins, Sr; children: Monsita McCall Allen, Monique Lavitia & Clifton III. **Educ:** Norfolk State Univ, BS, 1965, MA 1982. **Career:** Norfolk State Univ, confidential secy & pres, 1966-75, instr eve Col, 1970, asst dir couns upward bound, 1975-76, dir asst instr irc, 1976-81, instr, Engl Lang skills ctr, 1981-91, asst dir writing ctr & Eng instr, 1991-, asst prof, currently. **Orgs:** Secty & treas, Nat Sorority Phi Delta Kappa Alpha Lambda Chap, 1985-87; The Natl Coun Negro Women, The Natl Assn Negro Bus & Prof Women's Club Norfolk; charter mem, Metropolitan Club; Sigma Tau Delta Nat Eng Hon Soc,1987-; Delta Sigma Theta Sorority, Chesapeake-VA Beach Alumnae Chapter, 1990-; Citizens Drug Adv Comn, app Chesepeake, VA mayor Dr William Ward,1991-. **Home Addr:** 3032 Sunrise Ave, Chesapeake, VA 23324, **Home Phone:** (804)545-6695. **Business Addr:** Assistant Professor, Norfolk State University, Department of English, 700 Pk Ave, Norfolk, VA 23504, **Business Phone:** (757)823-2371.

MCCALL, REV. EMMANUEL LEMUEL, SR.
Clergy. **Personal:** Born Feb 4, 1936, Sharon, PA; son of George and Myra Mae Preston; married Emma Marie Johnson; children: Emmanuel Jr & Evalya Lynette. **Educ:** Univ Louisville, BA, 1958; Southern Baptist Theol Sem, BD, 1962, MRE, 1963, MDiv, 1967; Emory Univ, DMinistry, 1976. **Career:** Simmons Bible Col, Louisville, prof, 1958-68; Twenty-eighth St Baptist Church, Louisville, pastor, 1960-68; Coop Ministries Nat Baptist, Southern Baptist Conv, assoc dir, 1968-74; Southern Baptist Theol Sem Louisville, adj prof, 1970-96; Southern Baptist Conv, dir dept black church rels home missions bd, 1974-88; Black Church Extension Div, Home Mission Bd, SBC, dir, 1989-91; Christian Fel Baptist Church, Col Park, GA, pastor, 1991; Mercer Univ Sch Theol, adj prof, 1996-; Emory Univ, vis prof Baptist Studies; McAfee Sch Theol, Mercer Univ, adj prof, currently. **Orgs:** Bd dir Morehouse Sch Religion, 1972-85; Am Soc Missionology, 1975-80; bd trustees, Interdenominational Theol Ctr, 1978-91, from co-chmn to chmn, 1990-96; pres, Nat Alumni Asn; pres, SBTS, 1991-92; trustee, Atlanta Univ Ctr, 1993-96; trustee, Truett McConnell Col, 1994-98; chair, Ethics Baptist World Alliance, 1995-2000. **Honors/Awds:** Hon DD Simmons Bible Coll, 1965; Ambassador of Goodwill, City of Louisville, 1967; Hon DD United Theol Sem, 1977; Victor T Glass Awd Home Mission Bd So Bapt Conv, 1979; E Y Mullins Denominational Service Award, Southern Bapt Theological Seminary, 1990, E Y Mullins Humanitarian Award; American Baptist College, 1990. **Business Addr:** Adjunct Professor, Mercer University, McAfee School of Theology, 3001 Mercer Univ Dr, Atlanta, GA 30341-4155, **Business Phone:** (678)547-6000.

MCCALL, H. CARL
Executive, government official, chairperson. **Personal:** Born Oct 17, 1935, Boston, MA; married Joyce Brown; children: Marci. **Educ:** Dartmouth Col, Grad, 1958; Univ Edinburgh; Andover-Newton Theol Sem, MDiv. **Career:** spec polit affair, ambassador; UN under Pres Jimmy Carter; NY State Div Human Right, comnr; State NY, senator, 1974-79; WNET-TV, sr vpres, 1981; NY State, cand for lt gov, 1982; Citicorp, vpres, 1985-93; NY City Bd Educ, pres, 1991-93; State of NY, comptroller, 1994-03; NYSE, chmn bd Audit & Finance comt, 1999-03; Bd Comt Corp Accountability, co-chair, 1999-03; bd mem, Tyco Intl, 2003-; HealthPoint, vice chmn, currently. **Orgs:** dir, Blue Hill Protestant Ctr, 1961-63; dir, church comt serv NY City Missionary Soc, 1964-; proj dir, Taconic Found Inc, 1964-66; Founder, past pres, Inner City Broadcasting Corp; past chmn, ed bd NY Amsterdam news; dep admin, NY City Human Resources Admin; chmn, NY City Coun Against Poverty, 1966-69; ordained minister, United Church Christ; preaching minister, Met Comt Methodist Church in Harlem; trustee, NY Med Col; vchmn, bd Ctr NY Affairs New Sch; Gamma Delta Chi; Alpha Phi Alpha; bd dirs, NYSE. **Honors/Awds:** Nelson A Rockefeller Award, 1997; Hon Canon of Cathedral of St John the Divine; Torchbearer Award, Rainbow PUSH Coalition, 2001. **Special Achievements:** 1st African-Am elected to a statewide off in NY; broken down longstanding racial & cultural barriers; doubled the State Pension Fund's value to more than $100 billion - the nation's 2nd largest; implemented policy for largest sch system in the nation. **Business Addr:** Vice Chairman, Healthpoint Ltd, 3909 Hulen St, Fort Worth, TX, **Business Phone:** 800-441-8227.

MCCALL, NATHAN
Journalist, writer. **Personal:** Born Jan 1, 1955; divorced; children: Monroe, Ian & Maya. **Educ:** Norfolk State Univ, BA, jour, 1981. **Career:** Va Pilot & Ledger Star, reporter; Atlanta Const, rep; Wash Post, rep, 1989, writer; Emory Univ, Dept African Am Studies, Jour Prog, instr, currently. **Honors/Awds:** Blackboard Book of the Year, 1955. **Special Achievements:** Has written autobiography Makes Me Wanna Holler: A Young Black Man in America, 1994; What's Going On, 1997; numerous articles and essays. **Business Addr:** Instructor, Emory University, Department of African American Studies, 201 Dowman Dr, Callaway S106E, Atlanta, GA 30322, **Business Phone:** (404)727-6123.

MCCALL, PATRICIA
State government official. **Personal:** Born Jul 29, 1948, Columbus, OH; daughter of Theodore Hollingsworth Sr (deceased) and Mildred L (deceased); married Jun 1, 1970 (divorced); children: Stacie R. **Educ:** Franklin Univ, attended 1979-81. **Career:** State Ohio Civil Rights Comn, secy, typist, 1973-74, admin asst, clerk staff supvr, 1974-80, civil rights compliance coordr, compliance Officer, 1980-99; spec enforcement Officer, 1999-; Mary Kay Cosmetics, beauty consult, 1996-; MCS Properties, owner. **Orgs:** Nat Asn for Human Rights Workers, 1989-, Hosp chap; spec communion minister, Christ King Cath Church, 1986-, women's club, 1980-; tutor, math, reading, Eastgate Elem Sch, 1991-; steward secy, treas, OCSEA-AFSCME CHA 2540, 1986-, lead educ advocate, 1997-; secy, Christ King Cath Sch Bd, 1983-86, combined charitable co-coord, 1992-98; secy, Bishop Hartley Athletic Bd, 1986-89; Nat Nominating Com, Outstanding Young Ams, 1996-; Christ King Church Coun, 2000-03. **Honors/Awds:** San Kuy Ninjabudo Martial Arts, 3rd Degree Brown Belt, 1972; Model of the Year, D&W Alinatha Estello Modeling Agency, 1977; Outstanding Young Woman of America, 1984. **Home Addr:** 3469 Liv-Moor Dr, Columbus, OH 43227, **Home Phone:** (614)235-0099. **Business Addr:** Special Enforcement Officer, State of Ohio Civil Rights Commission, 1111 E Broad St Suite 301, Columbus, OH 43215, **Business Phone:** (614)466-7384.

MCCALLA, ERWIN STANLEY
Executive. **Personal:** Born Dec 10, 1928, New York, NY; son of Isma I Levy; married Ruth Elizabeth Thomas, Apr 1, 1956; children: Kim, Ruth, Christopher, Richard. **Educ:** Elec Tech Acad Aerontics NY, AAS, 1958; Engr Sci CW Post Col Brookville NY, BS, 1971. **Career:** Retired: Grumman Aerospace Corp, Bethpage, NY, test engr, 1958, proj test engr, 1966, lab mgr, 1970, grp head, 1972, mgr affirm act progs, 1973, engr test opers, 1976-85, vice pres facilities mgt, 1986-90, dir. **Orgs:** Assoc fellow, 1985-, AIAA 1975; Toastmasters Intl, 1975; ITEA 1980; NY Pioneer Track Club 1947; 5th AF & FEC Champ Track Team, 1950; Urban League LI, 1973; chmn, Long Island Section AIAA, 1983-85. **Honors/Awds:** Honoree Black Achievers Ind YMCA NY, 1979; Occuptn Medal, 5 Bronze Stars AUS, 1948-52; Basil Staros Memorial Award, AIAA-LI Section, 1985-86. **Military Serv:** AUS, e6, 1948-52. *

MCCALLUM, LEO. See SALAAM, DR. ABDUL.

MCCAMMON, MARQUES
Executive. **Educ:** NC A&T State Univ, BS, mech eng. **Career:** DaimlerChrysler's Chrysler Group, Product Strategy Team, mem; Am Specialty Cars Inc, dir product & bus, gen mgr w coast opers, 2006-. **Orgs:** X Prize Found. **Business Addr:** General Manager, West Coast Operations, American Specialty Cars Inc, One ASC Ctr, Southgate, MI 48195, **Business Phone:** (734)246-0098.*

MCCAMPBELL, RAY IRVIN
Songwriter, singer. **Personal:** Born Jun 22, 1959, Flint, MI; son of Victoria and Ellsworth. **Educ:** Olivet Col, Olivet MI, Music, 1979; Tex Southern Univ, Houston TX, BA, commn, 1982. **Career:** Self Employed, saxophonist, 1975-77, singer, 1977-82, singer/ songwriter 1983-87; MCA Records, Los Angeles, Calif, singer/ songwriter, 1987; Lorimar Productions, Los Angeles CA, actor, 1988; Albums: The Mac Band, 1988; Love U 2 the Limit, 1990; The Real Deal, 1991; Singles: "Jealous", 1989; "Roses are Red", 1989; "Stalemate", 1989; "That's the Way I Look at Love", 1989; "Love U 2 the Limit", 1990; "Someone to Love", 1990; "Everything", 1992. **Orgs:** Kappa Alpha Psi Fraternity, 1980-; Oak Cliff Bible Fellowship, 1983-. **Honors/Awds:** Symphonic Award, Flint Northwestern High Sch, 1977; NBA Pre Game Song, Dallas Mavericks, 1988; Appearance, Lorimar Productions, 1988; NBA Legend's All star Pre Game Song, NBA, 1989; Soul Train Performance, 1988; McDonald's Commercial, 1989; Dallas City Proclamation, 1989; Houston City Proclamation, 1989; Arsenio Hall Show Performance, 1989.

MCCANE, CHARLOTTE ANTOINETTE
Educator. **Personal:** Born in Washington, DC; daughter of Charles A (deceased) and Margaret Perea (deceased). **Educ:** Albright Col,

BA, hist; Univ Mysore, India, Fullbright Grant, 1964; N western Univ, NDEA Grant, 1968; Fairleigh-Dickinson Univ, MA, hist. **Career:** Educator (retired); New London CT Bd Ed, educr, 1957; Red Bank NJ Bd Ed, educr, 1957-69; Ridgewood NJ Bd Ed, educr, 1969-94. **Orgs:** Group leader World Youth Forum Tour of Europe, 1965; Oper Cross roads Africa Liberia, 1966; mem eval comt, Middle State Asn Sec Sch; mem eval comt, Yorkers & Hempstead Sch; NASDTEC Eval Comn, Princeton Univ, Glassboro State; assoc inst, adv comm Racism & Social Justice Nat Coun Social Studies; sec & treas, Multicultural Ed SIG; mem, Life Assoc Study Afro-Am Life & Hist; mem, Am Asn Univ Women; Nat Asn Advan Colored People; life mem, Nat Coun Negro Women; Falmouth Woman's Club; AARP; Falmouth Sr Ctr; Anti-Racism Task Force; sec, Falmouth Women's Club; secy, Cape CodHollyberry Quilter's Guild, 2000-02. **Honors/Awds:** Falmouth Year of the Reader Comn, 2002-. **Home Addr:** 493 Old Meeting House Rd, East Falmouth, MA 02536.

MCCANNON, DINDGA FATIMA
Writer, educator, artist. **Personal:** Born Jan 1, 1947, Harlem, NY; daughter of Ralph Miller and Lottie Porter; married Percival E McCannon, Jan 1, 1967; children: Afrodesia (Zumhagen) & Harmarkhis. **Educ:** Bob Blackburn Workshop, Nyumba Ya Sanaa Galleries. **Career:** Artist, auth, illusr, painter, printmaker fashion designer, quiltmaker, teacher, fiber artist, currently. **Orgs:** Where We At, Black Women Artists; New York Found Arts. **Home Addr:** 800 Riverside Dr, New York, NY 10032. **Business Addr:** 800 Riverside Dr, New York, NY 10032.

MCCANTS, JENNIFER BARNES, DR.
Educator. **Educ:** Tenn State Univ, BS; Ind Univ, MDS; Meharry Med Col, DDS. **Career:** Univ Louisville Sch Dent, Diag Sci Prosthodontics & Restorative Dent, asst prof, currently. **Business Phone:** (502)852-5661.*

MCCANTS, DR. JESSE LEE, SR.
Executive, president (organization). **Personal:** Born Feb 13, 1936, Fairfax, AL; son of Gabe and Rosie; married Hettie Jane Lindsay; children: Sheree Yvonne, Jesse Jr, Jacinta Lariece, Jerel Lindsay & Janella Larose. **Educ:** Ala State Univ, BS, 1958; Tenn State Univ, admin, 1966; Columbia Pacific Univ, San Rafael, PhD 1990. **Career:** City Chattanooga, teacher, 1961-68; City Govt, admin, 1969-72; Security Fed Savings & Loan Asn, bd chmn, pres, founder, 1971-74; Peoples Bk Chattanooga, chmn, organizer 1972-76; Allstate Loan & Inv Co, pres, founder, 1985. **Orgs:** Bd dir, Chatta Chap Nat Bus League; Am Diabetes Asn; Chatta Area Vo Tech Sch; Chatta E 5th St Day Care Ctr; bd chmn, dir Allstate Loan & Inv Co Inc; chmn, bd dir McCants Dev Co Inc; Kappa Alpha Psi Frat; active Corps Execs; NAACP; Big Bros Asn; Better Bus Bur Chatta. **Honors/Awds:** Black Businessman of Yr Award, 1975; Distinguished Service Award, Jaycees, 1972; Commissioned Gov Winfield Dunn Tenn rank of college, 1972. **Military Serv:** USY, sp4, 1959-61. **Business Addr:** President, Allstate Investment Co, PO Box 16214, Chattanooga, TN 37416, **Business Phone:** (615)894-4873.

MCCANTS, KEITH
Football player. **Personal:** Born Nov 19, 1968, Mobile, AL. **Educ:** Univ Ala, gen studies. **Career:** Football player (retired); Tampa Bay Buccaneers, linebacker, 1990-92; Houston Oilers, 1993-94; Ariz Cardinals, linebacker, 1994-95. **Honors/Awds:** Defensive Player of the Year, CBS-TV, 1989; first-team choice on all three All-SEC Teams, AP, UPI, football coaches, 1989; All-Am selection, AP, UPI, football coaches, 1989; Sports Illustrated Defensive Player of the Week.

MCCANTS, DR. ODELL
Physician. **Personal:** Born Sep 5, 1942, Winnsboro, SC; married Laura; children: Odell Jr. **Educ:** Howard Univ, BS, 1965, MD, 1970. **Career:** Howard Univ Hosp, resident; Automobiles Int, ceo; Greater SE Comm Hosp, pres & designate; Automobiles Int, broker & founder; pvt pract, 1975-. **Orgs:** Fel, Am Col Obstetricians & Gynecologists; Int Col Surgeons; mayor's task force Adolescent Health City Alexandria, VA; instr, Howard Univ Col Med; house specialist, Alexandria Hosp & Dept Health Commonwealth, VA, 1982; dir, United Black Fund, WA; bd dir, Northern VA, 1978-79; mem & bd dir, Am Cancer Soc. **Honors/Awds:** Daniel Hale Williams Award, Asn Former Residents & Interns Freedmen's Hosp. **Business Addr:** Physician, 1600 Crystal Square Arc Suite K, Arlington, VA 22202, **Business Phone:** (703)412-7100.

MCCARRELL, CLARK GABRIEL
Mechanical engineer. **Personal:** Born Apr 13, 1958, Chicago, IL; son of Clark G Sr and Melva Lee Washington; married Errika "Ricca" Grace-McCarrell, Oct 27, 2001; children: Clayton Gabriel McCarrell. **Educ:** Wright Col, Chicago Ill, AA, 1984; Wash Col, Chicago Ill, Dipl Comput Sci, 1986; Univ Nevada, Las Vegas NV, BS, Mech Engineering, 1991, MS, Engineering Mgt, 1999. **Career:** Donohue & Assocs, Milwaukee, Wis, engineering aide, 1978-80; Consult Consortium, Chicago, Ill, engineering apprentice, 1980-82; Dunham & Assocs, Las Vegas, NV, mech designer, 1986-87; Sci Appln Inter Corp, Santa Barbara, Calif, CAE Designer, 1987-88; Clark County Sch Dist, Las Vegas, NV, CAD designer, 1989-90; Southwest Gas Corp, Las Vegas, NV, 1990-2002; Univ Phoenix, Las Vegas, instr; Nevada Power Co, Las Vegas, NV, Sr Proj Mgr & sr engr, 2002-. **Orgs:** Am Soc Mech Engineering, 1977-, Nat Soc Black Engrs, 1979-; asst prog coordr, Ray Col Design, 1983-86; Diaconate Bd, Congional Church Park Manor United Church Christ, 1984-86; Nat Fire Protection Asn; Procurement consult, Nevada Econ Develop Co, 1986; Am Nuclear Soc, 1987-88, Am Soc Plumbing Engineering, 1987, Nat Soc Prof Engineering; pres, Am Soc Heating, Vent & Air Conditioning Engrs, 1989; Stud Adv Comt, Univ Nev Las Vegas, 1990; pres, TNBA Mixed Bowling League, Las Vegas, 1994-; deacon, 1994-96, ecclesiastical dir, 2001-, Mountain Top Faith Ministries, Las Vegas; Opers & Maintenance Aux, Toastmasters Int, 1993; dir, treas, Daybreak Christian Fel, 1998-2000; bd chair, Howard R Hughes Col Engineering; bd dir alumni, Univ Nev Las Vegas. **Honors/Awds:** Outstanding Alumni Award, Hales Franciscan High Sch, Chicago Ill, 1994; Outstanding Alumnus award, Univ Nev, Las Vegas, 1997; Faculty Member of the Year award, Univ Phoenix, 2007. **Business Addr:** Senior Project Manager, Generation Planning and Engineering, Nevada Power Company, 6226 W Sahara Ave, PO Box 98910 Mailcode 25, Las Vegas, NV 89193, **Business Phone:** (702)367-5381.

MCCARTHY, GREGORY O'NEIL
Baseball player. **Personal:** Born Oct 30, 1968, Norwalk, CT. **Career:** Baseball player (retired); Baseball coach; Seattle Mariners, pitcher, 1996-98; Atlantic City, pitcher, 2004; Austrian Baseball League, mosquito athletics attnang-puchhnim head coach, 2009-. *

MCCARTNEY, JOHN
Educator. **Educ:** Univ Iowa, PhD. **Career:** Bahamian Parliament, 1977-82; Vanguard Party, pres, 1979-85; Struggle for Freedom in the Bahamas, co-ed; Lafayette Col, Easton PA, dept head & assoc prof govt & law, prof & co-chair, africana studies prog, currently. **Honors/Awds:** Black Power in the 1990s; Bahamian Parliament Jones Lecture Award; Marquis Distinguished Teaching Award. **Special Achievements:** Author: Black Power Ideologies: An essay on African American Political Thought. **Business Addr:** Professor, Co-chair of Africana Studies Program, Lafayette College, 17 Watson Hall, Easton, PA 18042, **Business Phone:** (610)330-5100.

MCCARTY, WALTER LEE
Basketball player, basketball coach. **Personal:** Born Feb 1, 1974, Evansville, IN. **Educ:** Univ Ky, commun, 1996. **Career:** Basketball Player (retired), basketball coach; NY Knicks, forward, 1996-97; Boston Celtics, 1997-2005; Phoenix Suns, forward, 2005; Los Angeles clippers, forward, 2005-06; Univ Louisville, asst coach, 2007-. **Honors/Awds:** NCAA Championship, 1996. **Business Addr:** Assistant Coach, University of Louisville, 501 S Preston St, Louisville, KY 40292, **Business Phone:** (502)852-5555.

MCCAULEY, JAMES R.
Government official. **Personal:** Born Nov 6, 1952, Rochester, NY; son of James and Virginia; married Carolyn, May 9, 1982; children: James, John & Kelli. **Educ:** St John Fisher Col, BA, 1975. **Career:** Monroe County, Off Employ & Training, mgr emp serv, Child Support Enforcement, asst admin, Child Support, court liaison, investr, regional dir. **Orgs:** Vpres, bd dirs, Monroe County, Fed Credit Union; bd dir, Camp Good Days &Spec Times; adv bd, Boces I; adv bd, United Way, human resources; usherbd, Mt Oliver Bapt Church, men's chorus; adv bd, Baden St Settlement. **Honors/Awds:** Coordinator of the Year, United Way, 1998; Outstanding Service, Urban League, 1998. **Special Achievements:** Renegotiated all county contracts for a cost savings to County approximatley $5300/month, 1992.

MCCLAIN, ANDRE
Circus performer, singer. **Personal:** Born in Kansas City, MO. **Career:** Ringling Bros & Barnum & Bailey, singer, trick roper, rodeo cowboy, ringmaster, horse & camel trainer, currently. **Business Addr:** Cowboy, Ringling Bros & Barnum & Bailey, 8607 Westwood Ct, Vienna, VA 22182.*

MCCLAIN, ANDREW BRADLEY
School administrator, lawyer. **Personal:** Born Nov 12, 1948, Akron, OH; son of Andrew H and Margaret L Greene; children: Andrew & Peter. **Educ:** Univ Akron, Akron, OH, BA, 1970, JD, 1988; Kent State Univ, Kent, OH, Med, 1978. **Career:** Akron Bd Educ, eng teacher, 1970-73; Western Reserve Acad, Upward Bound, dir, 1973-87; Univ Akron, Upward Bound, dir, 1987, Pre Col Progs, dir, 1988, Acad Achievement Progs, dir, currently; pvt pract, atty, currently. **Orgs:** Consult A Better Chance, 1975-86; dir, Sch Scholar Serv, 1979-84; consult, Mid-South Assoc Independent Schs, 1981-83, Marquette Univ, 1984; former dir & pres state chap, Mid-Am Asn Educ Opportunity Prog Personnel, treas, 1992-95; Nat Asn Advan Colored People; consult, Nat Coun Educ Opportunity Asn; parlamentarian, Nat Coun Educ Opportunity Asns, 1993-94; African Am Male Community, 1989-. **Honors/Awds:** James Rankin Award, Ohio Asn Educ Opportunity Prog Personnel, 1990. **Business Addr:** Director of Academic Achievement Program, The University of Akron, Gallucci Hall 112, Akron, OH 44325-7908, **Business Phone:** (330)972-6804.

MCCLAIN, DR. PAULA DENICE
Educator. **Personal:** Born Jan 3, 1950, Louisville, KY; daughter of Robert Landis and Mabel T Molock; married Paul Crane Jacobson, Jan 30, 1988; children: Kristina L Jacobson Ragland & Jessica A Jacobson. **Educ:** Howard Univ, Washington, DC, BA, 1972, MA, 1974, PhD, 1977. **Career:** Univ Wis-Milwaukee, Milwaukee, WI, asst prof, 1977-82; Ariz State Univ, Tempe, AZ, from assoc prof to prof, 1982-91; Univ Va, prof, 1991-2000; Univ Va, dept chair, 1994-97; Duke Univ, Dept Polit Sci, prof, 2000-; Duke Univ, prof law, pub policy & african am studies, currently; Duke Univ, co-dir, Ctr Study Race, Ethnic & Gender, currently. **Orgs:** Pres, Nat Conf Black Polit Scientists, 1989-90; Am Polit Sci Asn; Exec Coun, Western Polit Sci Asn, 1989-92; Southern Polit Sci Asn. **Honors/Awds:** Distinguished PhD Alumni Award, Grad Sch Arts & Sci, Howard, Univ, 1993; Miriam Mills Award, Policy Studies Org, 1994; Aaron Wildavsky Award for the Best Book in Public Policy, Policy Studies Orgn, 1997; Frank Goodnow Award, 2007, Am Polit Sci Asn; Meta-Mentor Award, 2007. **Business Addr:** Professor, Duke University, Department of Political Science, PO Box 90204, Durham, NC 27708-0204, **Business Phone:** (919)660-4303.

MCCLAIN, WILLIAM ANDREW
Lawyer. **Personal:** Born Jan 11, 1913, Sandford, NC; son of Frank and Blanche Leslie (deceased); married Roberta White. **Educ:** Wittenburg Univ, AB, 1934, Univ Mich, JD, 1937; Wilberforce Univ, LLD, 1963; Univ Cincinnati, LLD, 1971. **Career:** Lawyer (retired); City Cincinnati, asst city solicitor, 1942-57; Berry & McClain, 1938-58; City Cincinnati, dep city solicitor, 1957-63, city solicitor, 1963-72, actg city mgr, 1968, 1972; Keating, Muething & Klekamp, 1972-73; Cincinnati Br Small Bus Admin, gen counsel, 1973-75; Hamilton County Common Pleas Court, judge, 1975-77; Hamilton County Munic Court, judge, 1977-80; Manley Burke, counr, 1980. **Orgs:** Bd dir Cincinnati Chapter Red Cross, 1975-; Nat Conf Christians & Jews Cincinnati, 1975; Cincinnati Bar Asn; Am Bar Asn & Nat Bar Asn; Am Judicature Soc; Am Bar Found; Cincinnati Bar Found; Fed Bar Asn; Prince Hall Mason 33 Degree; Alpha Phi Alpha; pres & bd dir, Wittenberg Alumni Asn; mem comt visitors, Univ Mich Law Sch; Sigma Pi Phi Fraternity; Alpha Delta Boule. **Honors/Awds:** Wilberforce Univ, LLD, 1963; Univ Cincinnati, LLD, 1971; Wittenberg Univ, LHD, 1972; Ellis Island Gold Medal Honor, 1997; Univ Mich, hon degree, 2002. **Military Serv:** Judge Advocate General USA 1st lt 1943-46; Army Commendation Award 1945. **Home Addr:** 2101 Grandin Rd Apt 904, Cincinnati, OH 45208. *

MCCLAIN, WILLIAM L
Automotive executive. **Personal:** Born Apr 25, 1958, Bronx, NY; son of Willie Lee and Jacqueline Francis Jackson Winters; married Pamela Kay Johnson, May 18, 1985. **Educ:** Oregon State Univ, Corvallis, OR, BS, Bus Admin, 1981. **Career:** Westside Timber Inc, vpres, 1985-; Stayton Motors Inc, dealer, owner, 1985-; Jackies Ribs Inc, vpres, 1985-; Reedsport Motors Inc, dealer, owner, 1988-; Stayton Motorsports, pres, 1996-; Zale Corp, Salem, OR, mgr. **Business Addr:** President, Stayton Motors Inc, PO Box 536, Stayton, OR 97383, **Business Phone:** (503)769-6666.

MCCLAIN-THOMAS, DOROTHY MAE
Government official. **Personal:** Born Jun 17, 1931, Hartsville, SC; daughter of Eloise Eltridge Hunter and Chester Hunter; married Thurman McClain, Mar 31, 1950 (died 1987); children: Thurman Jr, Roxcella McClain Brown & Vaness McClain Smith; married Donald, Jun 6, 1998. **Educ:** Wash Tech Inst, cert, 1972; Howard Univ, Univ Without Walls, 1980; Morgan State Univ. **Career:** Government Official (retired); DC Govt, clerk-typist, 1962-79; DC Govt Newspaper Recycling, prog coordr, 1979-81; DC Govt Environ Serv, off supvr, 1975-79; DC Govt Dept Pub Works Mayor's Beautification Community, exec dir, 1984-89; McClain & Assocs. **Orgs:** Counwoman, Town Cheverly, MD, 1974-86; bd dir, Combine Communities Action, 1975-; bd dir, Md Municipal League, 1977-78; pres, Iota Phi Lambda Sor Epsilon Delta Chap, 1979-81; Dir, Ander-Mac Video Prod, 1983-84; Prince George's County Voluntary Action Ctr, S County rep, 1989-91; Prince George's County Pub Schs, Group Activ Leader for Gladys Noon Spellman Elem Sch (Before & After Sch Prog), 1991-; bd mem, Prince George's County Housing Develop Corp. **Honors/Awds:** Outstanding Job Performance, Dept Environ Serv, 1974, 1975, 1979, 1980; Outstanding Community Service, Los Amigos Serv Club, 1976; plaque, 25thLegis Distinguished Alliance Club, 1976; Sorority of the Year, Iota Phi Lambda Sorority, 1984; Certificate of Appreciation, Dept Environ Serv Women's Prog, Adams-Morgan Comm, 1984. **Business Addr:** Staff, D. T. Enterprises, 6547 Bock Rd, Oxon Hill, MD 20745-3002.

MCCLAMMY, DR. THAD C
College president, state government official, real estate agent. **Personal:** Born Oct 22, 1942, Evergreen, AL; son of Ukla Maye and T C McClammy; married Patricia Larkins, Jun 5, 1966; children: Christopher & Patrice. **Educ:** Ala State Univ, Montgomery, AL, BA, 1966; Auburn Univ, Montgomery AL, MS, voc & adult educ, 1977; Selma Univ, LLD, 1982. **Career:** City Montgomery, AL, real estate officer & broker, 1967-68, developer, 1968-72; Lomax-Hannon Jr Col, Greenville, AL, develop officer, 1974; Trenholm State Technical Col, Montgomery AL, instr, 1974-77, coordr community serv, 1977-81, pres, 1981-95; Capitol Realty, owner; State Ala, House Rep, 76th Dist, rep, currently; Tots & Teens Inc, nat financial secy, currently. **Orgs:** Omega Psi

Phi Frat, 1963-, Phi Delta Kappa Prof Coun; Pres's Club, Nat Democratic Party, 1976-80; Bd Dirs, Montgomery Area United Way, 1982; Lion's Club, 1987-; Ala & Montgomery Democratic Confs; Montgomery Dem Club; Ala & Nat Educ Asns; Southern Placement Coun; Iota Lambda Sigma Frat; chmn, House Public Safety Comt; St Matthews Baptist Church. **Home Addr:** 3035 Rosa Parks Ave, Montgomery, AL 36105, **Home Phone:** (334)264-6767. **Business Addr:** Representative, State of Alabama, House of Representatives, 11 S Union St Rm 525 D, PO Box 250776, Montgomery, AL 36125-0776, **Business Phone:** (334)284-1769.

MCCLANE, PROF. KENNETH ANDERSON, JR.
Educator, poet. **Personal:** Born Feb 19, 1951, New York, NY; son of Kenneth A and Genevieve Dora Greene; married Rochelle Evette Woods. **Educ:** Cornell Univ, AB (with distinction), 1973, MA, 1975, MFA, 1976. **Career:** Colby Col, instr Eng, 1974-75; City Univ New York, asst dir SEEK, 1977-78; Williams Col, Luce, visiting prof Eng, 1983-84; Cornell Univ, asst prof Eng, 1976-83, assoc prof Eng, 1983-89, prof Eng, 1989-, WEB DuBois, Prof Eng, currently; Poems: A Tree Beyond Telling, 1983; Take Five, 1987; Essays: "A Death in the Family", 1985; "The School", 1985; Walls, 1991. **Orgs:** Cornell Univ, Dir, Creative Writing Prog, 1983-86; Salton Stall Found, bd dir; Epoch Mag, ed, 1984-86; "The Bluest Eye", script consult, 1984; Cornell Univ, col scholar adv bd, 1984-; Human Affairs Training Prog, bd dir, 1986-; Modern Lang Asn, 1989-; Adelphi Univ, bd trustees, 2002; Stephen H Weiss Presidential Fel, 2004. **Honors/Awds:** Clark Distinguished Teaching Award, 1983; Wayne State Univ Press, 1991; Henry Adams Medal, Collegiate Sch 2000; Presidential Medal, Adelphi Univ, 2001; Robert & Donna P Paul Award, 2001; elected bd trustees, Adelphi Univ, 2002; Distinguised Prose Prize, Antioch Review, 2002. **Home Addr:** 114 Glenside Rd, Ithaca, NY 14850. **Business Addr:** Professor, Cornell University, Department of English, 278 Goldwin Smith Hall, Ithaca, NY 14853, **Business Phone:** (607)255-9314.

MCCLEAN, VERNON E
Educator. **Personal:** Born Sep 17, 1941, St Thomas, Virgin Islands of the United States; married Freda; children: Malaika, Maliki & Macheo. **Educ:** St Augustine's Col, BA, 1965; Atlanta Univ, MA, 1967; Columbia Univ, EdD, 1975; Johns Hopkins Univ; Yale Univ; Univ Mich. **Career:** Paine Col, teacher, 1966-67; William Paterson Col, NJ, prof, chair, dept African Am & Caribbean Studies, 1969-. **Orgs:** Life mem, S Hist Asn; Asn Study Negro Life & Hist; Asn Soc & Behav Scientists; nat pres, Sigma Rho Sigma Hon Soc; founder, BASE; Nat Orgn Men Against Sexism; fel Danforth Found. **Honors/Awds:** Establishment Vernon E McClean Award, 1972. **Special Achievements:** Auth: Solutions to Problems of Race, Class, & Gender, with Lois Lyles, Kendall/Hunt Publishing Company, Dubuque, Iowa, 1993; author, Solutions For The New Millennium, Kendall/Hunt Publishing Company, Dubuque, Iowa, 1999; editor, Brother: The Newsjournal of the National Organization for Men Against Sexism; Published articles in The New York Times, The City Sun, Brooklyn NY, The GlenRidge paper, Glen-Ridge, NJ, The Nutley Journal, Nutley, NJ, The Irvington Herald, Irvington, NJ, Dawn Magazine, Washington, DC. **Business Addr:** Professor, African-American & Caribbean Studies, William Paterson University, 300 Pompton Rd, Wayne, NJ 07470.

MCCLEARN, BILLIE
Activist, clergy. **Personal:** Born Aug 6, 1937, Cushing, TX; daughter of Charlie Smith and Ida G Smith; married Sylvester, Nov 30, 1957; children: Richard Kyle, Michael Anthony, Sylvester Darnell, Billy Cathel & Alex Bernard. **Career:** Black Community Develop Inc, exec dir; First United Methodist Church, Newburgh, NY, community developer, currently. **Orgs:** Dir, Community Outreach. **Honors/Awds:** Humanitarian Award, Newburgh Free Acad, 1987; Sojourner Truth Youth Community Serv Award, Newburgh City Sch Dist, 1987; Distinguished Serv Award, Nat Asn Advan Colored People, 1989; Distinguished Serv Award, Black Ministerial Asn, 1989; Recognition Award, Coalition People's Rights, 1991; Milton Ash McQuade Found, 1996; Glenn Hines Community Spirit Award, 1996; NY Culturist Award, 1997; Cong Recognition Serv Award, 1998; Orange Co Human Rights Award, 1998; Cert Merit, NY State Assembly, 1998. **Home Addr:** 48 Hy-Vue Dr, Newburgh, NY 12550, **Home Phone:** (914)561-6517. **Business Addr:** Community Developer, First United Methodist Church, 241 Liberty St, Newburgh, NY 12550, **Business Phone:** (845)565-4267.*

MCCLEAVE, MANSEL PHILIP
Clergy. **Personal:** Born Aug 7, 1926, Rock Hill, SC. **Educ:** NC Agr & Tech Col, BS, 1950, MS, 1959; NY Sch Floral Design, Grad, 1953; NC St Univ; Univ NC; Friendship Col Rock Hill SC, DD, 1970. **Career:** First Baptist Church Siler City NC, pastor, 1957-70; Edwards Grove Church Liberty NC, pastor, 1958-81. **Orgs:** Pres, Deep River Baptist Training Union, 1943-66; instr horticulture, NC Agr & Tech St Univ, 1953-; pastor, Edwards Grove Missionary Baptist Church, Liberty NC, 1958-; moderator Deep River Missionary Baptist Asn, 1959-; Am Asn Univ Prof; gen bd Gen Baptist St Conv NC; adv bd, Human Health Serv, RandolphCo Health Dept; Intl Black Writers Conf, Greensboro Pulpit Forum; Liberty Ministerial Asn; Greensboro Ministers Fellowship; Am Horticultural Soc; org, found Liberty Improvement Asn; committeeman BS Am; Phi Beta Sigma Frat; Hayes Taylor YMCA; Hampton Inst Alumni Asn. **Honors/Awds:** Honorary DD, Friendship Col Rock Hill SC; Gamma Sigma Delta Honor, Soc Agriculture; author publs, Murmurs Heart A Collection Poems Vantage Press, 1976, The Story Deep River Missionary Asn NC & Auxiliaries, Deep River Missionary Baptist Assoc Ushers' Hist & Resource Manual. **Military Serv:** WW II, staff sgt.

MCCLELLAN, FRANK MADISON
Lawyer, educator. **Personal:** Born Feb 5, 1945, Marion, SC; married Linda J Hughey; children: Malik & Toussaint. **Educ:** Rutgers Univ, AB, 1967; Duquesne Univ, JD, 1970; Yale Univ, LLM, 1974. **Career:** Chief Judge William H Hastie, US Ct Appeals, law clerk, 1970-71; Wilmer Cutler & Pickering, assoc atty, 1971-72; Duquesne Univ, asst prof law,1972-74, assoc prof law, 1974-76, prof law, 1981; Temple Univ, I HermanStern prof law, currently, Sch Med, lectr. **Orgs:** Pa Bar Asn; DC Bar Asn; bd dir, House Crossroads; law rev ed, United Way Rev Comn. **Honors/Awds:** Merit Award; Felix S Cohen Prize; Lindback Award for Distinguished Teaching, Temple Univ, 1986; Friel-Scanlon Prize for Outstanding scholarship, Temple Univ, 1995; George D Harris Memorial Award, 1999. **Special Achievements:** First recipient of the Dr. George D. Harris Memorial Award, in recognition of his service as a founder and the first president of the Black Students Union at the university; Author: "Medical Malpractice: Law, Tactics & Ethics",Co author: "Torts: Cases, Problems & Materials". **Business Addr:** I Herman Stern Professor of Law, Temple University, Beasley School of Law, 1719 N Broad St, Philadelphia, PA 19122, **Business Phone:** (215)204-7861.

MCCLELLAND, MARGUERITE MARIE
Educator. **Personal:** Born Dec 6, 1919, St Louis, MO; daughter of Brooks Manuel Sr and Minnie Mae Marshall; married John Clyde, Sep 2, 1972. **Educ:** Sch Art Inst Chicago, Chicago, IL, BA, 1943; Wayne State Univ, Detroit, MI, MA, 1949; Temple Univ, Philadelphia, PA, attended 1963, Univ Mich, Ann Arbor, MI, attended 1975; Wayne State Univ. **Career:** Educator (retired); Chicago Pub Schs, Chicago, IL, art teacher, 1943-47; Detroit Pub Schs, Detroit, stud teacher & supvr; Wayne State Univ, teacher art educ, 1948-78, guid counr, 1963-78, guid dept head, 1978-83. **Orgs:** Alpha Kappa Alpha Sorority Inc, 1949; Am Guidance Asn; Nat Coun Negro Women; Nat Assault Literacy; life mem, Nat Asn Advan Colored People; Nat Asn Univ Women; Org Sch Admins; Mich Personnel & Guid Asn; Mich Asn Career Educ; Detroit Sch Women's Asn; United Methodist Women; Top Ladies Distinction; supreme basileus, Nat Sorority Phi Delta Kappa, 1989-. **Honors/Awds:** Teachers Medal, Valley Forge Freedom Found; Teacher of the Year Award, Detroit Educ Asn; Industrial Arts Award, Ford Motor Co; Assault on Illiteracy Service Award; Alpha Rho Chapter Service Award; Outstanding Service Award; Aide De Camp Award; Certificate of Appreciation; Spirit of Detroit Award; Exceptional Achievement, Outstanding Leadership, Dorcas Soc Detroit; DHL, Nat Theol Seminary Commonwealth Univ. **Special Achievements:** Co-author: Art Education Guide, Grades 7-8-9 for Detroit Public Schools; Author: The Language of Child Art, Art of Education in Spain: A Comparative Report, A Handbook for Art Education Student Teachers. **Business Addr:** President, Phi Delta Kappa Inc, 8233 S Martin Luther King Dr, Chicago, IL 60619, **Business Phone:** (312)783-7379.

MCCLENDON, CLARENCE E.
Clergy, educator, executive. **Personal:** Born Jun 7, 1965, Decatur, IL; son of Miriah and Rev Howell Levi; married. **Educ:** Friends Intl Christian Univ, PhD, 2001. **Career:** Harvest Fire Media Inc, chief exec officer; Clarence E McClendon Ministries, founder; Siloam Bible Col, founder & pres; Clarence E McClendon Leadership Inst, founder & pres; Church Full Harvest Intl, sr pastor, currently. **Orgs:** Bishop's Coun, Full Gospel Baptist Church Fel, Overseer Fel Rels; Intl Communion Charismatic Churches, Col Bishops; bd mem, Do Something Found; Calif Regent, Pres Bush's Faith Based Initiative Nat Ctr. **Honors/Awds:** nominated, Stellar Award; Dove Award, Best New Gospel Artist Nominee, 2000. **Special Achievements:** Auth: The X Blessing and When You Pray: The Key to Accessing the Presence of God; TV appearance: "Evening News", CBS; Nightline, ABC & Black Entertainment TV. **Business Addr:** Senior Pastor, Church Full Harvest Intl, 18355 South Figueroa St, Gardena, CA 90248, **Business Phone:** (310)323-2600.*

MCCLENDON, KELLEN
Lawyer, educator. **Personal:** Born May 7, 1944, New Castle, PA; son of Leroy and Sylest Butler; married Michele. **Educ:** Westminster Col, BA, 1966; Duquesne Univ Sch Law, 1974. **Career:** Pa Dept Justice, asst atty gen, 1974-79; Pvt Pract, sole practitioner, atty, 1979-82; City Pittsburgh, asst city solicitor, 1982-89; Robert Morris Col Legal Asst Prog, instr, 1985-89; Duquesne Univ Sch Law, adj prof, 1987-89, vis prof, 1989-90, asst prof, 1990-96; assoc prof, prof law, currently. **Orgs:** Allegheny County Bar Asn, 1974-; minority bus enterprise rev comn, City Pittsburgh, 1982-; bd dirs, Housing Authority City Pittsburgh, 1990-. **Military Serv:** USAF, intelligence officer, 1967-71; Bronze Star; Vietnam Serv Medal. **Business Addr:** Professor of Law, Duquesne University, School of Law, 600 Forbes Ave, Pittsburgh, PA 15282, **Business Phone:** (412)396-6307.

MCCLENDON, LLOYD GLENN
Baseball executive, baseball player. **Personal:** Born Jan 11, 1959, Gary, IN; son of Grant and Hattie; married Ingrid Scott, Feb 14, 1981; children: Schenell & Beaudillio. **Educ:** Valparaiso Univ, attended 1981. **Career:** Baseball player (retired), athletic coach, baseball executive; Appalachian League, baseball player; Cincinnati Reds, 1987-88; Chicago Cubs, 1989-90; Pittsburgh Pirates, 1990-94, hitting coordr, 1996, hitting coach, 1997-2000, mgr, 2001-05; Detroit Tigers, bullpen coach, 2006, hitting coach, 2007-. **Orgs:** Kappa Alpha Psi Fraternity. **Honors/Awds:** Alumni Achievement Award, Valparaiso Univ, 1993; Little League Hall of Fame. **Special Achievements:** Batted 1000, all home runs, for first all Black Team in Little League World Series, 1971; first African Am mgr of Pittsburgh Pirates; founded, McClendon's Atheletes Against Crime, MAAC. **Business Addr:** Hitting Coach, Detroit Tigers, 2100 Woodward Ave, Detroit, MI 48201.

MCCLENDON, MOSES C.
Engineer. **Personal:** Born Dec 11, 1934, Graceville, FL; son of Harry and Virginia; married Grace Jones McClendon, Jun 24, 1962; children: Chantelle M, Michelle R, Moses C II. **Educ:** Edward Waters Col, Jacksonville FL, AA, 1954; Morris Brown Col, Atlanta GA, BA, 1957; NC A&T State Univ, Greensboro NC, MS, 1967. **Career:** Engineer (retired) Wash Bd Educ, Chipley FL, asst prin, math & sci teacher, 1960-66; Bell Telephone Labs, Winston-Salem NC, assoc mem of tech staff, 1967-70; Western Elect, Greensboro NC, mat engr, 1971-80; AT&T Technol, Richmond VA, dept chief, Mat Eng, 1980-88; AT&T Microelectronics, Richmond VA, sr mat engr, 1988. **Orgs:** The Soc of Plastic Engrs, 1975-87; Am Chemical Soc, 1980-86; instr, Richmond Area Prog Minorities Eng, 1984-86; YMCA, 1985-87; Am Mgt Asn, 1987-88; Nat Asn Advan Colored People, 1987-; Black Exec Exchange Program, 1988; nat pres, Phi Beta Sigma. **Honors/Awds:** Beta Kappa Chi, Nat Sci Soc, 1956; Reaction Selected Hydrazino Phosphonate, Phrosphorium Bromides & Phosphorane, 1967; Eval One Component Silicone Encapsulant, 1967; Cost Reduction of Power Transformers by Plastics Encapsulants, 1968; Differential Scanning Calorimetric Eval B-Staged Epoxy Resin, 1972; Sigma Man of the Yr, Phi Beta Sigma Frat Inc, 1980; Morris Brown Coll Athletic Hall of Fame, Morris Brown Col, 1988. **Military Serv:** AUS, E4, 1957-60. *

MCCLENDON, RAYMOND
Investment banker, chief executive officer, chairperson. **Personal:** Married Ryland Needom; children: 4. **Educ:** Morehouse Col, BA; Ga State Univ, MBA. **Career:** City Atlanta, dir financial anal & auditing; Fed Nat Mortgage Asn, Mutli-Family Activities, vpres; R L McClendon Capital Corp, founder; Pryor, McClendon, Counts & Co, vice chmn & chief exec officer, 1993-97. **Orgs:** Atlanta Community.

MCCLENDON, RUTH JONES
Government official. **Personal:** Born Oct 5, 1943, Houston, TX; married Denver, Jul 3, 1987; children: Four Children. **Educ:** Tex Southern Univ, bachelor, poli sci & hist; Webster Univ, masters, mgt; Guadalupe Col, attended. **Career:** Worked with dysfunctional youth in the juvenile justice system, 17 yrs; San Antonio city councilwoman & mayor pro tempore, 1993-96; Community Crime Prev Network Inc, founder; RJMcClendon & Co, pres & chief exec officer, currently; Tex House Representatives, rep, 1996-. **Honors/Awds:** Hon Doctrate, Guadalupe Theol Sem, 1993; Friend of Youth Award, San Antonio Downtown Youth Ctr; Fleming Fel, Nat Ctr Policy Alternatives; Who's Who Am Polit; Who's Who Am Women; World's Who's Who Women; Int Who's Who Prof & Bus Women; Who's Who Tex Hist; Legislator of the Year, Texas Coun Child Welfare Bds; Texas Advocacy Award, Am Cancer Soc. **Special Achievements:** First African American woman elected to San Antonio City Council, 1993. **Business Addr:** State Representative, Texas House of Representatives, 403 S WW White Rd Suite 210, San Antonio, TX 78219, **Business Phone:** (210)225-2107.

MCCLENIC, PATRICIA DICKSON
Administrator. **Personal:** Born Nov 13, 1947, Akron, OH; children: Richard L Jr; Dennis K & Nicole M. **Educ:** Akron Univ, BA, 1978. **Career:** WSLR Radio, dir pub affairs, 1970-75; United Way Summit City, dir comn, 1975-79; United Way S Hampton, dir comn, 1979-83; Am Cancer Soc, state pub info dir, 1983-84; United Way Am, assoc dir, 1984-. **Orgs:** Pub Rels Soc Am; Int Asn Bus Comn; Nat Press Club, 1985.

MCCLEON, DEXTER KEITH
Football player. **Personal:** Born Oct 9, 1973, Meridian, MS. **Educ:** Clemson Univ, mgt, 1996. **Career:** St Louis Rams, defenseiveback, 1997-2002; Kansas City Chiefs, defensiveback, 2003-05; Houston Texans, defensiveback, 2006; free agent, currently.

MCCLESKEY, J. J. (TOMMY JOE MCCLESKEY)
Football player. **Personal:** Born Apr 10, 1970, Knoxville, TN; married Susan; children: Jalen Austin. **Educ:** Univ Tenn, BA, political sci. **Career:** Football player (retired); New Orleans Saints, defensive back, 1994-96; Ariz Cardinals, 1996-99.

MCCLESKEY, TOMMY JOE. See MCCLESKEY, J. J.

MCCLINTON, CURTIS R., JR.
Investment banker. **Personal:** Born in Muskogee, OK; married Devonne French MD; children: Tobi, Margot. **Educ:** Univ KS,

BS; Univ NE, sch banking; Cent Mich Univ, MPA; Univ MO, Real Est Law; Am Inst Banking; Weaver Sch Real Est Pract Franklin Fin Serv Inst; Real Est Bd Inst; Wharton Sch, Univ Pa. **Career:** Univ Kans, asst football coach & recruiter, 1962-63; Franklin Life Ins Co, ins salesman, 1963-; Interstate Securities, loan officer & collector, 1964-65; KPRS, tv, radio broadcaster, 1965-66; Douglass St Bank, community loan officer & asst cashier, 1965-67; Swope Pky Nat Bank, founder & exec vpres, 1969-; Tech Fab Inc, gen mgr & pres, 1972-; Midwest Prog Serv, lectr, 1974-; Franklin Fin Servs, reg securities broker & dealer, 1974-; Black Econ Union Gr KC, pres, founder & exec dir, 1985; McClinton Develop Co, owner, currently; Dept Com, Wash, nat exec dir; Black Econ Union, nat exec dir; Valdes & Moreno Inc, invest banker; Real Estate Partnerships, developer & gen partner; Govt Leased Facil Dep Mayor Econ Develop, Wash, DC; Amtraks Real Estate Mgt & Mkt, nat dir, currently. **Orgs:** Am Mgt Asn; Black Econ Union Gr KC; C of C KC; Nat Asn Mkt Develop; Nat Brokers Asn; Nat Security Dealers Asn; past pres, Comm Econ Develop Cong; Counr, Urban Econ Develop; Mid-Am Reg Coun; Planned Ind Expansion Comn City; Univ Mo Ext Prog Adv Coun; Fel Christian Athlets; Kappa Alpha Psi Frat; Nat Asn Advancement Colored People; Urban League; YMCA; bd dir, Who's Who Outstanding Young Men Am; St Mary's Hosp; United Negro Col Fund; Selec Counl Sch Med Univ Mo; Prof Football Club, 1962-70; Inst Brokers & Invest Bankers; comr & vice chmn, Jackson County Tax Increment Finance Comn; pres, Black Econ Union, Kans; Mo Kan Minority Contractors Asn;Prof Athletes Fed Credit Union; comr,Kans Keys Inner City Football League. **Honors/Awds:** DHL, Miles Col; C of C Leader of the Month, 1970; Outstanding Young American, 1971; Boss of the Year, C of C, 1975. **Special Achievements:** Prof Concert Singer; runner-up to MrKS Cit Annual C of C Hon 1970; Outst Cit Award, Presby Interracial Cncl; A Writer and lecturer of economic and sports development, and inte~ational singer of the songs of the renowned Paul Robeson, Esq. **Military Serv:** AUS. **Business Addr:** Owner, McClinton Development Co, 11714 Jefferson St, Kansas City, MO 64114.*

MCCLOMB, GEORGE E.
College administrator, educator. **Personal:** Born Apr 24, 1940, Long Island, NY; married Audrey Hamilton; children: George Jr. **Educ:** Colgate Univ, BA, 1962; Univ Pittsburgh, MSW, 1964, MA, polit sci, 1974, PhD, polit sci, 1984. **Career:** Homewood Brushton Health Ctr, asst proj dir, 1967-68, proj dir, 1968-71,Community Orgn & Soc Admin; Univ Pittsburgh, adj asst prof, 1969, guest lectr, 1970, assoc prof 1973-, health care consult, 1971-72, chair; Health Syst, asst dir, 1971-73. **Orgs:** Pres & bd dir, Lemington Home Aged, 1971-83; bd dir, W Pa Comprehensive Health Planning Ageny; W Pa Reg Med Prog; Vis Nurses Asn; Pittsburgh Model Cities Health Task Force; Urban League Health Comn; Comprehensive Care Task Force, Sickle Cell Anemia; comnr, Pub Parking Auth City Pittsburgh;comnr, Prog Aid Citizen Enterprise; deleg, White House Conf Aging, 1981;Pa State Conf Aging, 1984; Nat Asn Social Workers; Asn Community Orgn & Social Admin; Am Polit Sci Asn; Hill House Asn, Pittsburgh, PA. **Honors/Awds:** Outstanding Volunteer Award, Allegheny County United Way; Outstanding Citizens Award, Allegheny Co Med Soc, 1981; Black History Award, Pittsburgh Fed Exec Bd, 1983; Chancellors Award, 2000. **Military Serv:** USAF, lt, 1964-67.

MCCLOUD, AARON C.
Educator. **Personal:** Born Oct 28, 1933, Saginaw, MI; married Doris Jean Godbee; children: Sylvia Lynn & Monica Delis. **Educ:** AA, 1954; BA, pub admin, 1957; MA, 1967; EdD, 1973. **Career:** Eng & soc studies teacher, 1960-68; eve adult ed, 1967-69; counr, 1968. **Orgs:** Exec bd, Winter halter PTA, 1966-67; Concerned Cit for Action, 1966-70; pres, Mumford Constel Cit Group, 1968-71; pres, Mich Asn Supv Curr Develop, 1969; pres exec bd, Hampton PTA, 1971-72; Phi Delta Kappa, 1972; Messiah Baptist Church. **Honors/Awds:** Outstanding Community Contribution, WJR Radio, 1970; Recipient Whitney Young, Outstanding Contribution Black Culture, 1971. **Military Serv:** AUS, 1958-59. **Business Addr:** 2470 Collingwood, Detroit, MI 48206.

MCCLOUD, ANECE FAISON
School administrator. **Personal:** Born May 29, 1937, Dudley, NC; daughter of J D Faison and Nancy Simmons Cole; married Verable L, Jun 1, 1959; children: Aja Siobhan & Carla D. **Educ:** Bennett Col, BS, 1959; Univ Nebr, MA, 1989. **Career:** Lincoln Jr High Sch, teacher, 1959-60; Univ NE Med Ctr, asst registr, 1972-76, dir minority affairs, 1976-85, asst instr med juris prudence & humanities, 1980-85; Wash & Lee Univ, assoc dean stud, 1985-99. **Orgs:** Peer reviewer, Health Career Opportunity Prog Grant, 1982-84; Div Disadvantaged Assist Bur Health Prof HHS; consult, Life & Career Planning Workshop Urban League, NE, 1985; bd dirs, Rockbridge Comm Unit Am Cancer Soc, Va Div, 1986; Nat Asn Women Deans Admins & Counr; Am Asn Coun & Develop; Asn Multicult Coun & Develop; Nat Asn Foreign Stud Adv; Asn Am Med Col. **Honors/Awds:** Certificate Black Hist Month Prog Speaker Veterans Admin Med Ctr, 1984; Certificate Acknowledgement of Contrib, Educ Omaha Pub Sch, 1984; Plaquein Appreciation, Minority Health Career Opportunity, 1984; Plaque in Appreciation, Stud Nat Med Asn, UNMC Chap, 1985; Excellence in Diversity Award, named in hon. **Business Addr:** Associate Dean, Washington and Lee University, Lexington, VA 24450, **Business Phone:** (540)458-8400.

MCCLOUD, GEORGE AARON
Basketball player. **Personal:** Born May 27, 1967, Daytona Beach, FL; son of George McCloud; children: Travis. **Educ:** Fla State Univ, criminol, 1989. **Career:** Ind Pacers, forward, 1989-93; Scavolini Pesaro, Italy, 1993-94; Rapid City Thrillers, CBA, 1994-95; Dallas Mavericks, 1994-97; Los Angeles Lakers, 1996-97; Phoenix Suns, 1997-99; Denver Nuggets, 1999-2002; Golden State Warriors, forward, 2000. **Honors/Awds:** NBA Most Improved Player Award, 1995-96.

MCCLOUD, REV. J OSCAR
Clergy. **Personal:** Born Apr 10, 1936, Waynesboro, GA; married Robbie J Foster; children: Ann Michelle, Cassandra Anita & Tony Delancy. **Educ:** Warren Wilson Col, Swannanoa, NC, AA, 1956; Berea Col, Berea, KY, BA 1958; Union Theol Sem NY, MDiv, 1961; Mary Holmes Col, Hon DD, W Point, MS, 1974; Whitworth Col, Spokane, WA, DHL. **Career:** Clergy (Retired); Davis St United Presby Ch, Raleigh NC, pastor, 1961-64; United Presby Ch, Atlanta, GA, field rep, bd christian educ, 1964-67; Div Church & Race Bd Nat Missions, 1968-69; United Pres Church New York, 1969-71; Gen Sec Comm Ecumcl Mission & Rel, asso gen secy, 1971-72; The Prog Agency United Presby Church, gen dir, 1972-86; The Fund Theol Educ New York, exec dir, 1986-95; Fifth Ave Presby Church, assoc pastor. **Orgs:** Proj coordr, Am Forum Int Study Tour W Africa, 1971; bd trustee, Berea Col, 1990-; Bd dir Southern Christian Leadership Conf, Ga Coun Churches; black pres united, Nat Conf Black; vice-chairperson, Div Overseas Ministries, Nat Coun Churches; Comn World Mission & Evangelism; World Coun Churches; NE Community Org C, Teaneck; Proj Equality Inc Nat; mem exec comt, central comm World Coun Churches; mem exec comn, governing bd, Nat Coun Churches USA;; bd dir, Independent Sector; chair, adv bd, Comun Rels, Teaneck, NJ; pres, The Presby Ctr Holmes Camp & Conf Ctr. **Honors/Awds:** Community Service Award, Black Cong Caucus, 1978. **Special Achievements:** First alumnus to receive Berea College Community Service Award in 1981.

MCCLOUD, THOMAS HENRY
Association executive. **Personal:** Born Jul 29, 1948, Jersey City, NJ; son of Robert Sr and Pearline; married Georgia. **Educ:** Rutgers Univ, BA, 1974, MPA, 1977; Georgetown Univ Law Ctr, JD, 1989. **Career:** Rutgers Univ, counr, spec progs, 1974-76; City Newark, dep dir, PSE, 1977, acting dir, 1977-78; Nat League Cities Wash, DC, dir, employment & training proj, 1978-81, dir, Urban Noise Progs, 1981-82; Wash Convention Ctr, dir, human resources & bus servs, 1982-86, asst gen mgr, 1986-87; Nat League Cities, dir membership serv, 1987-91, dir, pub affairs, 1991-; Network Fighting Back Partnership, exec dir, 1993-96; 18th Congressional Dist, chief staff, 1996; Pub Technol Inst, vp, 1996-, dep/interim exec dir, chief operating officer, currently. **Orgs:** Chmn, EOF Comt Adv Bd, 1972; treas, Rutgers Univ Alumni Asn, NCAS 1976; pres, MPA Alumni Asn, 1976-77; trustee, Leaguers Inc, 1977-78; Am Soc Pub Admin, 1978-; Nat Bar Asn; bd mem, Nat Forum Black Pub Adminrs. **Honors/Awds:** Strauss Human Rels Scholar, 1972, Robert A Wynn Mem Award 1974 Rutgers Univ; Pub Serv Educ Fel, Dept HEW Wash, DC, 1974; Mgr of the Year, Wash Convention Ctr, 1984. **Military Serv:** USMC, sgt, 1966-70. **Home Addr:** 1310 Merganser Ct, Upper Marlboro, MD 20774. **Business Addr:** Chief Operating Officer, Public Technolog Inc, 1301 Pennsylvania Ave NW Suite 800, Washington, DC 20004, **Business Phone:** (202)626-2414.

MCCLOUD, TYRUS KAMALL
Football player. **Personal:** Born Nov 23, 1974, Pompano Beach, FL; son of Armie. **Educ:** Univ Louisville. **Career:** Baltimore Ravens, linebacker, 1997-98; Wash Redskins, linebacker; Miami Dolphins, linebacker, 2001; Ga Force, Arena Football League, linebacker, 2002-03. **Honors/Awds:** Defensive Player of the Yr, Conference USA, 1995, 1996.

MCCLUNG, WILLIE DAVID
Clergy. **Personal:** Born Apr 3, 1939, Aliceville, AL; married Mary Jean Shamery; children: David, Rosemary, Bonita LaDawn, Rashawn. **Educ:** Wayne Co Community Col, AA, 1970; Wayne St Univ, BS, 1971, PhD, 1975; Univ Detroit, MA, 1972. **Career:** Detroit Counc Bapt Pastors, secy, 1966-67; Comm Human Relatiom, Highland Park, 1969-73; New Grace & Univ Detroit, minister. **Business Addr:** 25 Ford, Highland Park, MI 48203.

MCCLURE, BRYTON ERIC
Actor, singer. **Personal:** Born Aug 17, 1986, Lakewood, CA; son of Eric and Bette. **Educ:** Studies dance instr, choreographer, Michael Chambers, currently. **Career:** TV appearances: "Family Matters", 1990-97, "Thirty Something"; "The Kids From Room 402", 1999; "The Young & the Restless", 2004-08; Film: The Jungle Book: Rhythm 'n Groove, 2001; The Intruders, 2009. **Orgs:** Screen Actors Guild AME; AFTRA Union. **Honors/Awds:** Youth in Films Award, 1992; Michael Landon Award, 1998; Daytime Emmy Award, 2007; NAACP Image Award, 2009. **Business Addr:** Actor, Barbara Cameron & Associates, 8369 Squsalito Ave Suite A, Canoga Park, CA 91304, **Business Phone:** (818)888-6107.*

MCCLURE, DONALD LEON, SR.
School administrator. **Personal:** Born Nov 10, 1952, San Antonio, TX; son of Edmond and Vera James. **Educ:** Prairie View A&M Univ, Prairie View, TX, BS, educ, 1974, MS, coun, 1975; Our Lady Lake Univ, San Antonio, TX, MS, admin, 1982. **Career:** San Antonio Independent Sch Dist, San Antonio, TX, J T Brackenridge Elem, teacher, 1975-79; Tafolla Middle Sch, counr, 1979-82; Douglass Elem Sch, prin, 1982-86; S H Gates Elem Sch, prin, 1986-90; M L King Middle Sch, prin, 1990-; Cleto L Rodriguez Elem Sch, prin, currently. **Orgs:** Tex Elem Prins & Supvr Asn, 1983-; founder, SAISD Black Hist Month Fine Arts Festival Scholar Fund, 1983-; trustee, I Have A Dream Scholarship Found, 1988-; founder, People Against Corruption, Anti-Drug/Crime Community Coalition, 1988-; trustee, Alamo Community Col Dist Bd Educ, 1989-; bd chair, Alamo Co Col Dist; Gov State Prins Incentive Bd, 1996-97. **Honors/Awds:** Luby Prize for Educational Leadership San Antonio, 1988; Texas PTA Community Life Membership Award, 1989; TEPSAN of the Year-Region 20, 1989, 1990; Citizen of the Year Award, Omega Psi Phi Fraternity Inc, 1990-91, 1994-95; Texas Gov's Community Service Award, Sen Frank Tejeda, 1990; San Antonio Mind Science Award. **Special Achievements:** First African American Chair, Alamo County Col Dist, trustee bd, 1994, re-elected, 1996. **Business Addr:** Principal, Cleto L Rodriguez Elementary School, San Antonio Independent School District, 3626 W Durango Blvd, San Antonio, TX 78207, **Business Phone:** (210)433-4251.

MCCLURE, EXAL, JR.
Executive. **Personal:** Born Mar 24, 1941, Proctor, AR; son of Exal and Dorothy; married Bertha, 1962; children: Marlon, Marilyn & Cheryl. **Career:** Action Printing Co, pressman & owner, 1972-. **Home Addr:** 110 Marsala Ct, Florissant, MO 63031, **Home Phone:** (314)837-2724. **Business Addr:** Owner, Action Printing Co, 7232 W Florissant Ave, Saint Louis, MO 63136, **Business Phone:** (314)381-2433.

MCCLURE, FREDERICK DONALD
Investment banker. **Personal:** Born Feb 2, 1954, Fort Worth, TX; son of Foster and Mayme Barnett; married Harriet Jackson, Dec 17, 1977; children: Lauren Elizabeth & Frederick Donald Jr. **Educ:** Texas A&M Univ, Col Sta, Tex, BS (summa cum laude), Agr Econ, 1976; Baylor Univ, Waco, Tex, JD, 1981. **Career:** Reynolds, Allen & Cook, Houston, Tex, trial atty, 1981-83; Senator John Tower, Wash, DC, legis dir, legal coun, 1983-84; Dept Justice, Wash, DC, assoc deputy atty gen, 1984-85; The White House, Wash, DC, spec asst to pres, legis affairs, 1985-86; Tex Air Corp, Wash, DC, staff vpres, 1986-89; The White House, Wash, DC, asst to pres, legis affairs, 1989-92; First Southwest Co, Dallas Tex, managing dir, 1992-; partner, Sonnenschein Nath & Rosenthal LLP, 2001-07, managing patner, 2007-. **Orgs:** Pres, Nat Capital A&M Club, Texas A&M Univ Asn Former Studs, 1990-92; bd dirs, Texas Lyceum, 1986-; bd dirs, Nat Fraternity Alpha Zeta, 1985-; int vpres, Texas A&M Univ Asn Former Studs, 1984-88; 1993-; bd, Childrens Med Ctr Dallas, 1992-; bd, United States Naval Acad, 1992-; mem, Am Coun Germany, 1988-. **Honors/Awds:** Nat FFA Hall of Achievers, Nat FFA Org, 1990; Distinguished Alumnus, Texas A&M Univ, 1991; Outstanding Young Alumnus, Baylor Univ, 1991; Jon Ben Sheppard Outstanding Texas Leader, 1992. **Special Achievements:** First Black ever to head a presidential congressional liaison team. **Home Addr:** 6722 Lakehurst Ave, Dallas, TX 75230. **Business Phone:** (202)408-3235.

MCCLURE, FREDRICK H L
Lawyer. **Personal:** Born Oct 21, 1962, Chattanooga, TN; son of Howard McClure Jr and Carrie M Green. **Educ:** Earlham Col, BA, 1984; Univ Cincinnati, Col Law, JD, 1987. **Career:** Univ Cincinnati, instr, 1986-87; Grant, Konvalinka & Grubbs PC, assoc & partner, 1987-98; Holland & Knight, LLP, partner, 1998-2002; Piper Rudnick LLP, partner, 2002-. **Orgs:** Pres, Chattanooga Bar Asn, Young Lawyers Div, 1987-; Tenn Bar Asn, Young Lawyers Div, 1987-; Am Bar Asn, career issues comt, minorities in the profession commt nat conf team, 1991-; Alpha Phi Alpha, 1988-; justice, Phi Alpha Delta Legal Fraternity, 1986; Hillsborough County Bar Asn; fel, Am Bar Found; George Edgecomb Bar Asn. **Honors/Awds:** Man of the Year, Alpha Phi Alpha, 1990; Service Award, Tenn Young Lawyers Conference, 1989; Young Leader of the Future, Ebony Magazine, 1991. **Home Addr:** 1020 Talley Rd, Chattanooga, TN 37411, **Home Phone:** (615)629-9980. **Business Addr:** Attorney, Partner, Piper Rudnick LLP, 101 E Kennedy Blvd Suite 2000, Tampa, FL 33602-5149, **Business Phone:** (813)222-5908.

MCCLURE, DR. WESLEY CORNELIOUS
College administrator, college president, chancellor (education). **Personal:** Married Mary Bradley; children: Wesley II (Karla), Carter Bradley (Marsha) & Dessalines McLeod Pieh (Hinga). **Educ:** Lane Col, BA, math, 1964; Univ Va, MA, doctorate math & educ res, 1968 &1970; Harvard Univ, dipl, 1971. **Career:** Lane Col, asst to pres & title III coordr, 1970-78, pres & trustee, 1992-; Clark Col, dean of fac & instr, 1978-79; St Augustines Col, exec asst to pres, 1979-81; Southern Univ Baton Rouge, vice chancellor acad affairs, 1981-85, chancellor, 1985-88; Va State Univ, Petersburg, VA, pres, 1988-92. **Orgs:** Exec comt mem, Tenn Independent Cols & Univ; Comn Pub Affairs, Nat Asn Independent Cols & Univ; chmn, Nat Asn Equal Opportunity Higher Educ; Comn Gov Rels, Am Coun Educ; Nat Urban League. **Business Addr:** President, Trustee, Lane College, 545 Lane Ave, Jackson, TN 38301-4598, **Business Phone:** (731)426-7500.

MCCLURKIN, DONNIE
Gospel singer. **Personal:** Born Nov 9, 1959, Amilyville, NY. **Career:** Albums: Donnie McClurkin, 1996; 'Tis So Sweet, 2000; Live in London & More, 2000; Donnie McClurkin. Again, 2003; Films: The Fighting Temptations, 2003; Apollo at 70: A Hot Night in Harlem, 2004; The Donnie McClurkin Story: From Darkness to Light, 2004; 25 Strong: The BET Silver Anniversary Special; The Prince of Egypt, 1998; Diary of a Mad Black Woman, 2005; The Gospel, 2005; Valley Of God, 2008; We All Are One: Live in Detroit, 2009; Tv Series: Girlfriends, 2001; An Evening of Stars: A Celebration of Educational Excellence, 2001; The Parkers, 2002; An Evening of Stars: Tribute to Stevie Wonder, 2006. **Orgs:** Founder, New York Restoration Choir. **Honors/Awds:** Seven Stellar Gospel Awards, 2002-05; Grammy Award, Best Contemporary Soul Gospel Album for Again, 2004; NAACP Image Award; BET Award; Soul Train Award; Dove & Steller Awards. **Special Achievements:** Author of "Eternal victim/Eternal victor", has appeared in numerous television shows. **Business Addr:** Gospel Vocalist, Sierra Management, 1035 Bates Ct, Hendersonville, TN 37075, **Business Phone:** (615)822-5308.

MCCLURKIN, JOHNSON THOMAS
Executive. **Personal:** Born Sep 25, 1929, Chester, SC; married Evelyn Rudd; children: Gary. **Educ:** Morgan State Univ, BS, 1958. **Career:** Retired: Nat Asn Real Estate Brokers Inc, exec dir; Nat Corp Housing, asst dir; Wash, DC, partner 1972-73; The Rouse Co, asst to dir property mgt, 1970-72; City Balto Mayor's office, asst opers, 1987-96. **Orgs:** Bd dir, Nat Asn Real Estate Brokers Inc; life mem, NAACP; Leadership Conf Civil Rights; Nat Bus League; St John Bapt Ch Columbia Interfaith Ctr; Columbia Asn; Am Soc Asn Execs. **Honors/Awds:** President's Award, 1974, 1977; Lang & Speech Merit Award, Morgan State Col. **Military Serv:** AUS, 1951-53. *

MCCLUSKEY, AUDREY THOMAS
Educator. **Personal:** Born Aug 30, 1947, Valdosta, GA; daughter of Paul and Eva; married John McCluskey Jr, Dec 24, 1969; children: Malik, Jerome & Toure. **Educ:** Clark Col, BA, 1967; Howard Univ, MA, 1969; Ind Univ, PhD, 1991. **Career:** Ford Found, post grad fel, 1994; Ind Univ, Univ Div, asst to the dean; Cleveland State Univ, asst prof womens studies & African Am studies, assoc dir womens studies, assoc dir, Black Film Ctr Archive, assoc prof African Am studies, currently. **Orgs:** Life mem Nat Asn Advan Colored People; Monroe Co Chap Educ Comn Chair; pres, Alpha Kappa Alpha; Kappa Tau Omega, Grad Chap; Asn Study African Am Life; Nat Womens Studies Asn. **Honors/Awds:** Martin Luther King Jr Image Award, 1996. **Special Achievements:** Co-editor, McLeod Bethune: Building A Better World, Indiana Univ Press, 2000; editor, Frame by Frame III; Filmography of the African American Image, 1994-03, Indiana Univ Press, 2004. **Business Addr:** Associate Professor of African American Studies, Indiana University, Smith Research Center, 10th & Bypass Suite 180, Bloomington, IN 47415, **Business Phone:** (812)855-6041.

MCCLUSKEY, JOHN A
Educator. **Personal:** Born Oct 25, 1944, Middletown, OH; son of John A and Helen Harris; married Audrey Louise T, Dec 24, 1969; children: Malik Douglass, Jerome Patrice & John Toure. **Educ:** Harvard Univ, BA, 1966; Stanford Univ, MA, 1972. **Career:** Miles Col, Birmingham, AL, instr eng, 1967-68; Valparaiso Univ, IN, lectr humanities, 1968-69; Case Western Reserve Univ, from coordr to lectr, Afro-Am Studies, 1969-72, asst prof am studies, 1972-74, asst prof eng, 1974-77; Ind Univ, assoc prof, Afro-Am Studies, 1977-85, adjunct prof eng, 1983-, dir, CIC Minorities Fels Prog, 1983-88, fac am studies, 1983-, assoc dean grad sch, 1984-88, assoc dean, Grad Sch, 1984-88, founding co-ed, Blacks Diaspora Series, 1985-2000, prof, Afro-Am Studies, 1985-, chair, Afro-Am Studies, 1994-2000. **Orgs:** Am Studies Asn; Modern Lang Asn; Am Asn Univ Prof; Asn African-Am Life & Hist; Nat Coun Black Studies; Midwest Modern Lang Asn; Nat Soc Arts & Letters. **Honors/Awds:** Yaddo Fel, Yaddo Corp, 1984, 1986; Distinguished Service Award, 1998. **Special Achievements:** Author, "Look What They Done to My Song", 1974, "Blacks in History Nine Stories", 1975, Best Amer Short Stories, 1976, Blacks in Ohio History, 1976, "Mr America's Last Season Blues" 1983, "City of Refuge, Collected Stories of Rudolph Fisher", 1987; co-ed with Charles Johnson, "Black Men Speaking," 1997. **Business Addr:** Professor, Indiana University, Department of Afro-American Studies, Mem Hall East M28, Bloomington, IN 47405, **Business Phone:** (812)855-9539.

MCCOLLOUGH, BERNARD JEFFREY. See MAC, BERNIE.

MCCOLLUM, JUDGE ALICE ODESSA
Judge. **Personal:** Born Feb 15, 1947, Oklahoma City, OK; daughter of Irving A and Maryland G. **Educ:** Univ NC Greensboro, BA, 1969; Univ Cincinnati Sch Law, JD, 1972. **Career:** Reginald Heber Smith Community Lawyer, fel, 1972-74; Legal Aid Soc Dayton, co-dir, 1974-75; Wilberforce Univ, dir, prelaw, 1975-76; Univ Dayton Sch Law, asst prof, asst dir clin legal, 1976-79; Dayton Munic Ct, judge, 1979-2003; Montgomery County Ohio, Common Pleas Probate judge, 2003-. **Orgs:** Bd mem, United Theological Sem, 1980-95; United Way, 1980-84; Dayton Contemp Dance Co, 1980-84; Am Judges Asn; Nat Bar Asn; Ohio State Bar Asn; Am Bar Asn; Thurgood Marshall Law Soc; bd trustees, Victoria Theatre, 1987-93; Ohio Criminal Sentencing Comn, 1991-2002; bd trustees, Children's Med Ctr, 1993-99; pres, Dayton Bar Asn, 2006-07. **Honors/Awds:** Marks of Excellence Award, Nat Forum Black Pub Admin Dayton Chap, 2000; Woman of Influence, YWCA, 2002; Community Service Award, Dayton Chap NAACP, 2002. **Special Achievements:** First Woman Dayton Municipal Court Judge; first Woman & African Am Probate Judge in Montgomery County; Ten Top African-Am Women, African-Ame CEO, 2002. **Business Addr:** Judge, Montgomery County Court of Common Pleas, Probate Division, PO Box 972, Dayton, OH 45422, **Business Phone:** (937)225-4552.

MCCOLLUM, ANITA LAVERNE
Executive. **Personal:** Born Aug 20, 1960, Cleveland, OH. **Educ:** Kentucky State Univ, BS, 1983; Atlanta Univ, MBA, 1985. **Career:** IBM, admin asst, 1981; NASA Lewis Res Ctr, procurement coordr Summers, 1981-83; IBM, sales asst, 1984; Atlanta Exchange, asst to the exec vpres, 1984-; AT&T Communs, supvr Residence Mkt. **Orgs:** Undergraduate mem, Nat Bd Dirs Alpha Kappa Alpha, 1982-84; Toastmaster's Intl, 1983-85; student mem, Nat Black MBA Asn, 1985; NAACP. **Honors/Awds:** Soror of the Year, Alpha Kappa Alpha, 1982; Nat Dean's List, KY State Univ, 1981-83; Executive Management Scholarship, AUGSBA, 1983. **Business Addr:** Staff Supvr Residence Mktg, AT&T Communications, 295 N Maple Ave., Basking Ridge, NJ 07920.

MCCOMBS, ANTONIAS ORLANDO. See MCCOMBS, TONY.

MCCOMBS, TONY (ANTONIAS ORLANDO MCCOMBS)
Football player. **Personal:** Born Aug 24, 1974, Hopkinsville, KY. **Educ:** Eastern Ky Univ. **Career:** Football player (Retired); Ariz Cardinals, linebacker, 1997-98.

MCCONNELL, CONRAD
Editor. **Personal:** Born Sep 2, 1952, Denver, CO; son of Geraldine Blanche Christian and Conrad N. **Educ:** Univ Ore, Eugene, BS, jour, 1974. **Career:** Ore Jour, Portland, reporter, 1975-82; Portland Ore, Portland, reporter, 1982-83; Seattle Post-Intelligencer, Seattle, ed, reporter, 1983-. **Orgs:** Nat Asn Black Journalists, 1983-; Seattle Asn Black Journalists, 1983-; Seattle Youth-at-Risk, 1989-; Amnesty Int, 1989-. **Honors/Awds:** C B Blethen Memorial Award, Blethen, 1985; Pacific Northwest Excellence Journalism, Soc Prof Journalists, 1986; St Matthew Award, Northwest Harvest, 1986; Fair Housing Award, Seattle Bd Realtist, 1987; Challenge of Excellence, Wash Press Asn, 1987. **Home Phone:** (206)938-2037. **Business Addr:** Night Assistant City Editor, Seattle Post-Intelligencer, 101 Elliott Ave W, Seattle, WA 98119, **Business Phone:** (206)448-8048.

MCCONNELL, DOROTHY HUGHES
Educator. **Personal:** Born in Cleveland, OH; daughter of Harry and Genevieve Harris; children: Jan Yvette Evans. **Educ:** Ohio State Univ, BS, 1946; Western Reserve Univ, MA, 1956. **Career:** Specialist (retired), consult; Los Angeles Unified Sch Dist, training teacher, 1960-79, sch improvement coordr, 1979-80, integration coordr, 1980-81, lang arts specialist, 1982-90; Black Studies, specialist, consult, 1990. **Orgs:** Los Angeles Alumnae; Delta Sigma Theta Sor; life mem, Nat Asn Advan Colored People, Los Angeles Br, 1995; pres, Nat Asn Univ Women, Los Angeles Br, 1996-98; deacon, Park Hills Reformed Church, 1998-2001. **Honors/Awds:** Recognition Special Certificate Outstanding Teacher of the Year, Human Rel City Los Angeles, Human Rel Comt, 1979; Woman of the Year, Nat Asn Univ Women, Los Angeles Br, 1995; Honoree, Nat Asn Univ Women, 1997; Honoree, WCoast Cities Br, Nat Asn Univ Women, 1998. **Special Achievements:** Selected by USC & Dept Educ, Washington, DC as Research Participant in Egypt, 1980. **Home Addr:** 5547 Secrest Dr, Los Angeles, CA 90043.

MCCOO, MARILYN
Singer, actor. **Personal:** Born Sep 30, 1943, Jersey City, NJ; daughter of Wayman Glenn and Mary Ellen Holloway; married Billy Davis Jr. **Educ:** Univ Calif, BS, bus admin; Talladega Col, doctorate. **Career:** Art Link letters Talent Scout, singer; The Hi-Fi's, singer; The Fifth Dimension formerly the Versatiles, mem, 1965-75; Solid Gold, host; Road Tour with Billy Davis Jr, Duke Ellington Review, 1999; Broadway Performedas "Julie" in "Showboat", 1995; Chicago, Role of "Julie" in "Showboat", 1996; Los Angeles Role of "Aldonza" in "Man of LA Mancha", Miami, Role of "Reno Sweeny" in "Anything Goes"; Grizzly Adams & the Legend of Dark Mountain, 1999; "The Jamie Foxx Show", 2001; Miss Rising, 2005; Albums: The Me Nobody Knows, 1991; White Christmas, 1996. **Orgs:** Bd gov, C Miracle Network; Los Angeles Mission Bd; Meharry Med Col Bd; Cancer Res Found Bd. **Honors/Awds:** Grammy Award for "You Don't Have to be a Star", 1977; 4 Grammy Awards for Up, Up & Away; 2 Grammy Awards for Aquaris & Let The Sun Shine; Prestigious Grand Prize, Tokyo Music Fest; 14 Gold Recs & Albums with the 5th Dimension; One Gold Rec & Albums with husband Billy Davis Jr; Grammynominee for The Me Nobody Knows, 1992; Harvard Found Award, Harvard Univ; 14 Gold Recs & Albums with the fifth Dimension; 3 Platinum Recs with theFifth Dimension. **Special Achievements:** First to record Whitney Houston's "Saving All My Love For You", 1978. **Home Addr:** PO Box 7905, Beverly Hills, CA 90212. **Business Addr:** Singer, Actress, The Sterling Winters Co, 10877 Wilshire Blvd Suite 1550, Los Angeles, CA 90024, **Business Phone:** (310)557-2700.

MCCORD, LANISSA RENEE
Executive. **Personal:** Born May 4, 1969, Kansas City, MO; daughter of Ingrid and Derrick. **Educ:** Rutgers Univ, Mason Cross Sch Arts, 1990; Univ Mo, Kans City Conservatory, 1992. **Career:** DANCE, choreographer, 1991-2000; Le Ballet Ivoire Spectacle, mgt, 1997-2000; Orlando Sch Cult Dance, 1998-99; Cent Fla YMCA System, 1998-2000; Nu Look Performers, 1999-2000. **Orgs:** Arts Complete Educ; United Arts Cent Fla; Orlando Sch Cult Dance, coun elders, 1998. **Special Achievements:** Performances: Walt Disney's MGM Studio, 1999-00; Universal Studios Citywalk, 2000; BET Sound Stage, 1998; Universal Studio-Island of Adventure. **Home Phone:** (407)298-7688.

MCCORMACK, HURVIN (HURVIN MICHAEL MCCORMACK)
Football player. **Personal:** Born Apr 6, 1972, Brooklyn, NY. **Educ:** Ind Univ. **Career:** Dallas Cowboys, defensive tackle, 1994-98; Cleveland Browns, 1999.

MCCORMACK, HURVIN MICHAEL. See MCCORMACK, HURVIN.

MCCORVEY, DR. EVERETT D.
Educator. **Personal:** Born Dec 3, 1957, Montgomery, AL; son of David McCorvey and Olga; married Alicia Helm; children: Elizabeth, Julia & David. **Educ:** Univ Ala, BM, 1979, MM, 1981, DMA, 1989. **Career:** Newtown High Sch, Queens, NY, music instr, 1983-84; Knoxville Col, prof voice, 1984-85; Univ Ky, prof voice, dir opera theatre, 1991-; artistic dir, founder, Am Spiritual Ensemble, 1995-; Lexington Opera Soc Endowed Chair, currently. **Orgs:** Opera Cent Ky, 1992-; Lexington Ballet, 1994-97; UK Athletics Asn, 1996-; chair, Univ Ky, visit by Archbishop Desmond Tutu, Convocation Comn, 1999; Ky Arts Coun, 1999-; Ky Advocates for Higher Educ, 1999; chair, Lexington Opera Soc; dir, Nat Assembly State Arts Agencies; bd trustees, Univ Kentucky, 2008-. **Honors/Awds:** Eagle Award, Lyman T Johnson Alumni Group, 1998; Acorn Award, Ky Advocates for Higher Educ, 1999; Alumnus Arts Award, Univ Ala, 1999; Ancient Hellenic Ideals Program Award, 2002. **Business Addr:** Professor of Music, University of Kentucky, College of Fine Arts, 105 Fine Arts Bldg, Lexington, KY 40506-0022, **Business Phone:** (606)257-9331.

MCCORVEY, KEZ (KEZARRICK MONTINES MCCORVEY)
Football player. **Personal:** Born Jan 23, 1972, Gautier, MS; married Loris; children: Imoni. **Educ:** Fla State Univ, BA, sociol, 1995. **Career:** Football player(retired); Fla State Univ, 1990-94; Detroit Lions, wide receiver, 1995-97; Carolina Panthers, wide receiver; Rhein Fire; Edmonton Eskimo.

MCCORVEY, KEZARRICK MONTINES. See MCCORVEY, KEZ.

MCCOVEY, WILLIE LEE
Businessperson, baseball player. **Personal:** Born Jan 10, 1938, Mobile, AL. **Career:** Baseball player (retired), restaurateur; San Francisco Giants, 1959-73, 1977-80, gen mgr, spec asst to pres; San Diego Padres, 1974-76; Oakland Athletics, 1976; Mc Covey's Restaurant, partner, 2003-. **Orgs:** Chmn, Willie McCovey March Dimes Ann Charity Golf Tournament. **Honors/Awds:** Nat League Rookie of the Year, 1959; Nat League All Star Game, 1963, 1966, 1968-71; Nat League Comeback Player of the Year; Nat League MVP, 1969; Hutch Award, 1977; Willie Mc Covey Day Candlestick Park, 1977; Nat Baseball Hall of Fame, 1986; Mc Covey Point park at Giants' Pacific Bell Park, named in his honor, 2003. **Special Achievements:** Ranks 9th on baseball's all-time list of HR & first among active players; only player in baseball hist to hit two HR in same inning twice in career; ranked No 56 on The Sporting News' list of the 100 Greatest Baseball Players, 1999. **Business Addr:** Partner, McCovey's Restaurant, 1444 N California Blvd, Walnut Creek, CA 94596, **Business Phone:** (925)944-9444.

MCCOY, ANTHONY BERNARD (TONY MCCOY)
Football player. **Personal:** Born Jun 10, 1969, Orlando, FL; married Jodie; children: Anthony Bernard Jr. **Educ:** Univ Fla. **Career:** Indianapolis Colts, defensive tackle, 1992-99; Ariz Cardinals, 2000; Hope International Church, Groveland, Fla, sr pastor, currently. **Honors/Awds:** Noble Max Award, 1994; Ed Block Courage Award, 1994.

MCCOY, GEORGE H. See Obituaries section.

MCCOY, JAMES F.
Librarian. **Personal:** Born Aug 1, 1925, Clarkton, NC; son of Gertrude Smith and Frank. **Educ:** Lincoln Univ, AB, 1952; Rutgers

Univ, MLS, 1956; Univ Denver, advanced cert, 1973; Appalachian State Univ, HEW Inst. **Career:** NJ State Libr, ref librn, 1956; Elizabeth Pub Libr, ref librn, 1956; Mercer County Community Col, Libr Dept, chmn, 1956-74; Hudson Valley Community Col, dir learn resources, 1974-84, dir emer, currently. **Orgs:** Pres, Alumni Asn GSLS Rutgers, 1958 & 1975; Adv Comt, Grad Sch Libr Serv Rutgers, 1958-59; secy, NJ Jr Col Asn, 1960 & 1965; Books Jr Col Libr, 1963; pres, Col & Univ Sect, 1964-65; Trenton Hist Soc, 1965-74; chmn, Scholar Comt, 1966-67; contrib Biblio of Negro in NJ 1967; Adv Comt Trenton Urban Renewal, 1966-68; Mayor's Adv Comt, Trenton Model Cities, 1968-73; NJ Libr Asn Exec Bd, 1968-70; vpres, 1969-70; secy, NJ Exec Bd, 1970-72; Nominating Comt, ALA-ACRL, 1971-72; pres, Trenton Neighborhood Health Ctr, 1971-72; Ad Hoc Comt Interns, 1972-77; Ed Bd, CHOICE, 1974; AV Comt, 1975; pres, Am Asn Univ Prof Mercer Co Col; Am Asn Univ Prof; Adv Comt, Grad Sch Libr Serv Rutgers, 1975-76; secy, Coun Head Librn, State Univ New York,1977; chmn, Adv Asn, GLIS Rutgers Univ, 1979; pres, Alumni Asn, Sch Libr & Info Mgt, Univ Denver, 1979; chmn, Intellectual Freedom & Due Process, New York Libr Asn, 1979; Basic Kappa Alphsi Frat; ALA; New York Libr Asn; NJ Libr Asn; NAACP; chair, State Univ New York Coun Head Librn, 1984; chair, Membership Comt, Am Libr Asn, 1985; chair, Comt & Jr Col Lib Sect, 1986; trustee, Elder Pres Scholar Comt, Berean Presbyterian Church. **Honors/Awds:** Colleges & Universities Section Award Distinguished Service, NJ Librn Asn; Distinguished Alumni Award, Lincoln Univ; Certificate of Achievement Trenton Model Cities; Founders Award, Black & Hispanic Fac & Admin Asn, 1984; Sire Archon Beta Psi Boule Sigma Pi Phi Frat, 1984; 50th Anniversary Award of Appreciation, 1985; Appreciation Award, Beta Psi Boule, Sigma Beta Psi Fraternity, 1986; Outstanding Contribution, Comt Org 1986. **Military Serv:** USY, sergeant 4th grade; 1944-46. **Home Addr:** 317 N Broad St Apt 604, Philadelphia, PA 19107. **Business Addr:** Director Emeritus, Hudson Valley Community College, 80 Vandenburgh Ave, Troy, NY 12180, **Business Phone:** (518)629-7358.

MCCOY, JELANI MARWAN
Basketball player. **Personal:** Born Dec 6, 1977, Oakland, CA; son of Frederick and Bettie. **Educ:** Univ Calif, attended 1999. **Career:** Seattle Supersonics, ctr, 1998-01; Los Angeles Lakers, 2001-02; Toronto Raptors, 2002-03; Atlanta Hawks, ctr & forward, 2004-05; Viola Reggio Calabria, Italian club, 2006; Menorca Basquet, Spanish club, 2007; Denver Nuggets, 2007; Los Angeles D-Fenders, 2007-08; Los Angeles Clippers, 2008. *

MCCOY, JESSIE HAYNES
School administrator. **Personal:** Born Nov 17, 1955, Mound Bayou, MS; divorced; children: Raven & Tameka. **Educ:** Coahoma Jr Col, AA, eng, 1975; Univ S Miss, BA, jour, 1976; Miss State Univ, 1984; Bloomsburg Univ, 1985. **Career:** Hattiesburg Am Newspaper, part-time reporter, 1976; Delta Democrat-Times Newspaper, news reporter, 1976-79; MS Valley State Univ, dir univ rels, 1979-84; freelancer various print media; Bloomsburg Univ, univ rels dir, 1984-86; J & R Enterprises, co-owner, 1987-; Bloomsburg Univ, asst city mgr, pub info officer, 1986-. **Orgs:** PTA pres, Fulwiler & LS Roger Elem Schs, 1978-82; dist chairwoman, MS Press Women, 1981-83; pres, Col Pub Rels Asn MS, 1982-83; pub rels officer, Am Asn Univ Women, 1983; mgt intern comn, Bloomsburg Univ, 1984-85; Columbia-Montour Tourist Promotion Agency, 1984-85, Black Coun Higher Educ, 1984-85; telecommun coun, pres coun, Bloomsburg Univ; mayorstask force, War on Drugs; mayors bicentennial constitution comn, Jubilee Comn, C C PR Comn, city hall grand opening comn, road bond referendumcomn, mayors youth day comn; curricullum adv bd comn, Tidewater Community Col; Nat Asn Advan Colored People Chesapeake VA, Nat Forum for Black Public Admin, Int City Mgrs Asn, Pub Rels Soc Am, Am soc Pub Admin, Am Mkt Asn, Va Munic League, Conf Minority Pub Admin, PTA. **Honors/Awds:** Journalism Scholarship, Univ S Miss, 1976; Ford Fellow in Journalism, Ford Found Wash, 1979; CASE Fellow, Coun Adv & Support Educ, 1981; Exec Coun, Miss Valley State Univ, 1982-84; Outstanding Young Woman of America, 1983; Regional Finalist President's Commission on White House Fellows. **Special Achievements:** Only Black non-academic mgr, Bloomsburg Univ, 1984-86.

MCCOY, TONY. See MCCOY, ANTHONY BERNARD.

MCCOY, DR. WALTER D.
Administrator, educator, military leader. **Personal:** Born Mar 17, 1930, Damascus, GA; married Toni Moynihan (divorced); children: Jonathan D & Wanda D Noble. **Educ:** Fla A&M Univ, BS, 1951; Univ Tex, El Paso, MS, 1971; NMex State Univ, ABD, 1974; Univ Tex, Arlington, PhD, admin, 1980. **Career:** Military leader, educator, administrator (retired); AUS, col, 1950-70; Univ Tex, El Paso, vpres, stud affairs, 1970-74; Univ Tex, Arlington, dir stud serv, 1974-76; Corpus Christi State Univ, assoc prof mgt, 1975-85, dir pub admin; Mich Technol Univ, Sch Bus, dean, asst provost. **Orgs:** Acad Mgt, 1981-; chmn allocation comn, United Way Corpus Christi, 1981-83; pres bd, Women's Shelter Corpus Christi, 1984-; Fed Mediator & Mediation Serv, 1989-. **Honors/Awds:** Leadership Award, United Way Coastal Bend, 1970-80; Honor, Soc Phi Kappa Phi, 1974; Honor, Soc Order Omega, 1974. **Special Achievements:** Pres Unit Citation, Rep Korea. **Military Serv:** AUS Col; Meritorious Service Medal, Bronze Star w/Devices, Commendation Medal w/4 OLC.

MCCRACKEN, QUINTON ANTOINE
Baseball player. **Personal:** Born Mar 16, 1970, Wilmington, NC; son of Saundra; married Maggie Moskel, Jan 29, 2005. **Educ:** Duke Univ. **Career:** Colorado Rockies, outfielder, 1995-97; Tampa Bay Devil Rays, 1998-00; Minnesota Twins, 2001; Ariz Diamond backs, outfielder, 2002-05; Seattle Mariners, 2004; Cincinnati Reds, 2006; Rochester Red Wings, 2006; Bridgeport Bluefish, 2007; Leones del Escogido, currently. *

MCCRACKIN, OLYMPIA H
Teacher, librarian. **Personal:** Born Jun 8, 1950, Tuscaloosa, AL; daughter of Oliver G Hines Sr and Susie Seltz Hines; divorced. **Educ:** Stillman Col, BA, 1972; Univ Ala, MLS, 1990. **Career:** Social Security Admin, Tuscaloosa, AL, claims rep, 1973-85; FBI, Birmingham, AL, rotor clerk, 1985-88; Tuscaloosa Pub Libr, librn, 1988-90; Bryce Hosp, librn, 1991-2001; Tuscaloosa City Schs, teacher, 2001-. **Orgs:** Bd dirs, Hospice West Ala, 1985-87; Ment Health Asn Tuscaloosa County, 1988-99; anti basileus, Eta Xi Omega Chap, Alpha Kappa Alpha Sorority, Inc, 1989-90; Am Libr Asn, 1989-2001; Ala Pub Libr Asn, 1989-2001; dep registrar, Tuscaloosa County Bd Registrars; secy, Eta Xi Omega Chap, Alpha Kappa Alpha Sorority; co-moderator, Presbyterian Women, Brown Memorial Presbyterian Church, 1990-91, moderator, Presbyterian Women, 1991-95; pres, Eta Xi Omega Chap, AKA Sorority, Inc, 1993-94; bd mem, bd chmn, ALA Adv CNL on Libraries, 1995; mentor, Big Brothers Big Sisters, 1997-99; pres, Lucy Sheppard Art Federated Club, 1997-98; Tuscaloosa Asn Women's Clubs, Inc; Challenge 21 Vision Coun, area rep, 1998-; Westside Community Develop Corp, Stillman Col; comt on voc develop, Presbytery Sheppards & Lapsley; Tuscaloosa City Sch BRD EDU, 1999-2001; Nat Middle Sch Asn, 2001-04; Nat Coun Teachers Eng, 2003 -; Asn Supv & Curric Develop, 2004-; AEA & NEA 2001-; Delta Kappa Gamma Soc Int, 2003-. **Honors/Awds:** Alabama Public Library Asn Scholarship, Ala Pub Libr Asn, Montgomery, AL, 1989; Louise Giles Minority Scholar, Am Libr Asn, Chicago, IL, 1989; AEA Emerging Leader, 2003; grad, Tuscaloosa City Schs, Sch Leadership Prog, 2003. **Home Addr:** 3 Greenbriar, Tuscaloosa, AL 35405. **Business Phone:** (205)759-3673.

MCCRAE, LARRY C
Chief executive officer. **Career:** Larry C McCrae Inc, pres & chief exec officer, currently. **Orgs:** Greater Philadelphia Chamber Com. **Special Achievements:** Top Black Technol Entrepreneurs, US Black Engr & Info Technol Magazine, 2004. **Business Addr:** President, Chief Executive Officer, Larry C McCrae Inc, 3333 W Hunting Pk Ave, Philadelphia, PA 19132, **Business Phone:** (215)227-5060.*

MCCRARY, FRED DEMETRIUS
Football player. **Personal:** Born Sep 19, 1972, Naples, FL. **Educ:** Miss State Univ. **Career:** Philadelphia Eagles, fullback, 1995-96; New Orleans Saints, fullback, 1997-98; San Diego Chargers, fullback, 1999-2002; New England Patriots, fullback, 2003; Atlanta Falcons, fullback, 2004-06; Seattle Seahawks, 2007; free agent, currently.

MCCRARY, MICHAEL
Singer, actor, actor. **Personal:** Born Dec 16, 1971?, Philadelphia, PA; son of Robert McCary Sr and Omarnetta Thomas. **Career:** Boys II Men; Albums with Boys II Men: Cooley high harmony, 1991; II, 1994; Evolution, 1997; Full Circle, 2002; The Mannsfield 12, 2007; Beyond the Pretty Door, 2007. **Business Addr:** Recording Artist, Arista Records, 6 W 57th St, New York, NY 10019.

MCCRARY-SIMMONS, SHIRLEY DENISE
Lawyer. **Personal:** Born Nov 7, 1956, Boston, MA; daughter of Eupha McCrary and Earlie McCrary; married Nathaniel O; children: Charity Denise Simmons. **Educ:** Brown Univ, AB, 1978; Boston Univ Sch Law, JD, 1982. **Career:** Ga Legal Serv, law intern, 1982; Internal Revenue Serv, tax rep/revenue officer, 1983-84, atty estate tax, 1984-90; atty, 1990-93; Arrington & Hollowell, PC, atty, 1993. **Orgs:** Pres, Black Am Law Student Asn, 1980-81; JD Curric Comn, 1981-82; Nat Bar Asn, 1983; dep registr, Fulton Co, Ga, 1983; State Bar Ga 1983-; Gate City Bar Asn, 1985 & 1987; union steward, Nat Treas Employees Union 1985-88; legal adv, Africare Atlanta Inc, 1985-89; Ga Asn Black Women Attorneys; Metrop Atlanta Chap 100 Black Woman; bd dirs, Joseph E Mertz Memorial Educ Found; Antioch Urban Ministries Inc; Walton Mgt Inc. **Honors/Awds:** Superior Performance Award, IRS 1988, 1989. **Special Achievements:** First African American female to be hired as an estate tax attorney in the Atlanta District.

MCCRAVEN, CARL CLARKE
Executive. **Personal:** Born May 27, 1926, Des Moines, IA; son of Marcus H McCraven (deceased) and Buena Vista Rollins Alexander (deceased); married Eva Louise Stewart; children: Carl Bruce, David, Larry & Maria. **Educ:** Howard Univ, BS, elec engr, 1950; Calif State Univ, Northridge, MS, health serv admin, 1976. **Career:** Nat Bur Stand, Wash DC, radiation physicist, 1950-55; Lockheed Calif Co, Burbank, CA, sr res engr, 1955-63; TRW Systems Inc, Space Elec Power Engr Dept, mem tech staff, 1963-72; Pacoima Mem Hosp Inc, Lake View Terr, CA, assoc admin vpres, 1972-73; Hillview Mental Health Ctr, Lake View Terr, CA, founder, pres, 1973-; Calif State Univ Northridge, asst prof, 1974-76; Hillview Village Housing, gen mgr, 1992-, pres & chief exec officer, currently, mental health adminr, currently. **Orgs:** Pres, Nat Asn Advan Colored People Southern Area, Calif Conf, 1967-71, nat bd dir, 1970-76; bd dir, regent Casa Loma Col, 1970-85; Am Pub Health Asn, 1976-90; Nat Asn Health Serv Exec, 1976-85; Am Mgt Asn, 1978-85; bd dir, San Fernando Valley Girl Scout Coun, 1980-82; pres, North San Fernando Valley Rotary, 1981-85; Sigma Phi Xi Boule, 1984-; Asn Mental Health Admin, 1984-90; pres, Los Angeles Co Asn Mental Health Agencies, 1996-2000; Community Health Facilities Fund. **Honors/Awds:** Citation, CA Senate, 1971; Certificate of Appreciation Councilman, Bob Ronka first Dist, 1979; Certificate of Appreciation, Los Angeles Co Bd Supvrs. **Military Serv:** AUS, 1945-46. **Home Addr:** 17109 Nanette St, Granada Hills, CA 91344. **Business Addr:** President & Chief Executive Officer, Mental Health Administrator, Hillview Mental Health Center Inc, 12450 Van Nuys Blvd Suite 200, Pacoima, CA 91331, **Business Phone:** (818)896-1161.

MCCRAVEN, MARCUS R.
Executive. **Personal:** Born Dec 27, 1923, Des Moines, IA; son of Marcus H and Buena Rollins; married Marguerite Mills; children: Carol J, Stephen A, Paul A. **Educ:** Howard Univ, BSEE; Univ MD; Univ CA. **Career:** exec (retired); Naval Res Lab, engr; Lawrence Radiation Lab, engr group leader nuclear test; Phelps Dodge Community Co, chief engr; Bridgeport Elec Co, vpres; United Illuminating Co, vpres. **Orgs:** Dir, First Constitution Financial Corp; pres, Middletown Ave Asn Real Est; dir, Metrodata Inc Okla City; bd trustees, CT State Cols; chmn bd, So Central CT Am Red Cross; Sigma Pi Phi Fraternity; exec comn, EPA Science Adv Bd; bd trustees, Quinnipiac Univ, The Graduates Club, Jr Achievement; chmn bd, So Central Ct Health Planning; pres, Yale Univ Peabody Museum Assoc; Quinnipiack Club; Golden Heritage Life Member, NAACP; State Conn Statewide Grievance co; aso fellow, Yale univ; Quinnipiack Club; pres, N Haven CT Rotary; Urban League; United Way. **Honors/Awds:** Most Notable Citizen Award, Hamden CT; IRA Hiscock Award; New Haven Chamber of Commerce Award; Junior Achievement, Free Enterprise & Spirit of Achievement Hall of Fame; Quinnipiac Univ, honorary doctorate, 2003. **Military Serv:** AUS. *

MCCRAW, TOM
Baseball player, athletic coach. **Personal:** Born Nov 21, 1940, Malvern, AR; children: Bryan & Marla. **Career:** Baseball player (retired), Athletic coach; White Sox, first baseman, 1963-70; Washington Senators, 1971; Cleveland indians, 1972, infielder, 1974-75; California Angels, 1973; Cleveland Indians, coach, 1975, minor league hitting instr, 1976-79, first-base coach, 1980-82; Calif Angels, 1973-74; San Francisco Giants, hitting instr, 1983; New York Mets, first-base coach, 1992-96; Montreal Expos, hitting coach, 2002; Wash Nat, hitting coach; Wash Senators, hitting coach, 2005; Gulf Coast Mets, hitting instr & mgr, 2006-. **Honors/Awds:** All-Star Team, 1962. **Military Serv:** USNG. **Business Addr:** Hitting coach and instructor, Manager, Gulf Coast League Mets, Tradition Field 525 NW Peacock Blvd, Port Saint Lucie, FL 34986, **Business Phone:** (772)871-2132.

MCCRAY, ALMATOR FELECIA
Art museum director. **Personal:** Born Sep 16, 1956, Charlotte, NC; daughter of Robert Lee and Alma O; children: Ryan Lamar. **Educ:** Queens Col, BA, hist, 1992. **Career:** Belk Stores Serv, cre buyer, 1975-88; Ubiquitous Art Space, dir. **Orgs:** Nat Asn Negro Bus & Prof Women's Asn; adv bd, NC Museums Art, AFA; art adv bd, UNCC, Nat Black Child Dev Inst; Nat Asn Female Execs. **Honors/Awds:** Arts Award, Focus Leadership, 1992; Speaker's Award, Optimist Club, 1991; Emerging Artist Grant, Arts & Sci Coun. **Home Addr:** 2120 Aberdeen St, Charlotte, NC 28208.

MCCRAY, BILLY QUINCY
County government official. **Personal:** Born Oct 29, 1927, Geary, OK; son of Ivory B and John J; married Wyvette M Williams, Oct 12, 1952 (deceased); children: Frankielieen Conley, Anthony, Melody Miller & Kent. **Educ:** Langston Univ, Langston, OK, 1947; Colo Univ Boulder, 1950. **Career:** Boeing Co, Wichita, KS, indust photographer, 1952-77; Govt KS, Topeka, KS, st rep, 1967-72, st senator, 1973-84; KS Dept Econ Develop, Topeka, KS, dir, 1984-86; Sedgwick County, comnr, 1987-93; McCray's Publ Inc, consult. **Orgs:** Pres, Wichita Ach Club, 1953-55; Wichita Human Rels Comm, 1963-66; KS Drug Abuse Coun, 1972-74; dir, Wichita A Phillip Randolph Inst, 1976-78; adv coun, US Small Bus, 1977-80. **Honors/Awds:** Outstanding Legislator, KS Asn Pub Employees, 1977; plaque Outstanding Award, KS Credit Union League, 1975; Outstanding State Senator, KS Asn Pub Employees, 1983; President Award, Langston Univ Regional Alumni, 1982; Outstanding Service, Nat Adv Coun Small Bus, Pres Jimmy Carter; Honoree, Howard and Jeanne Johnson Global Citizen Award, 2004. **Special Achievements:** Published Song of Autumn, 1948 and A Tree by the Highway, 1956, has also published two books "My View from the Bridge" a collection of poems and prose published in 1997 and "Between These Walls: Working for the People" a political autobiography. **Military Serv:**

USAF, s/sgt, 1947-51. **Business Addr:** PO Box 8682, Wichita, KS 67208, **Business Phone:** (316)612-2455.

MCCRAY, CHRISTOPHER COLUMBUS
Government official. **Personal:** Born Sep 16, 1925, Waycross, GA; son of Pompey (deceased) and Rosa Lee (deceased); married Jewel Hollis; children: Cynthia, Linda Bacon & Christi. **Career:** Government official (retired); CSX Railroad Co, equip operator, 1943-92; Waycross/Ware Co, co-chmn bi-racial comm, 1966-71; Waycross GA, sch bdmem, 1967-71; City Waycross, mayor pro-tem. **Orgs:** Waycross Community Concert Asn; John Sutton Am Legion Post No 517; Keystone Voters League; Nat Asn Advan Colored People, Waycross Chap; hon life mem, Future Bus Leaders Am; Supreme Grand Lodge Ancient & Accepted Scottish Rites Free Masons. **Honors/Awds:** Kiwanis Club Miller Medal Award, 1976; Martin Luther King Jr Commission Award, 1994; Citizen of the Year, Woodmen of the World, Way cross Chap,1994; Gaines Chapel Merit Award of Civics; Silver Bowl Award, Waycross City Sch Bd; Waycross College Appreciation Award; Certificate of Appreciation, Keystone Voters & Civic League; Certificate of Appreciation, Nat Law Enforcement Community; Certificate of Appreciation, Jacksonville Fla Urban League; Certificate of Appreciation, CSX Transp; Merit Award of Civics, Greater Mt Zion AME Church; Delta Zeta Chapter Public School Award, Phi Delta Kappa Sorority; Public Service Award of Achievement in Community Service, Groveland Park Community Club; Sunday School Award for Civic & Christian Leadership, Mt Zion AME Church; Morris Jacobson Award; Certificate of Merit for Outstanding Service, SE Ga Area Planning &Develop Comn; E E Moore Membership Award for Outstanding Solicitation of Members, Nat Asn Advan Colored People; Distinguished Service Award for Service Rendered, Nat Guard Ga; Honorary Life Member, Future Bus Leaders Am; Award for Outstanding Service to the Community, Northside Community Club. **Special Achievements:** First African American mayor of the city of Waycross. **Military Serv:** USN, petty officer 2/c, 1943-46. **Home Addr:** 1217 Toomer St, Waycross, GA 31501.

MCCRAY, DARRYL K
Fashion designer. **Personal:** Born Oct 3, 1963, Bronx, NY; children: Akira, D'Andra, Darryl II & D'Yon. **Career:** IBEW LU no 3, purchasing agent, 1985-90; Midtown Electric Supply, purchasing agent, 1987-90; House Nubian Inc, pres & chief exec officer, 1989-. **Military Serv:** USMC, cpl, 1981-85. **Business Addr:** Chief Executive Officer, President, House of Nubian Inc, 35 W 8th St, New York, NY 10011-9029, **Business Phone:** (201)547-3553.

MCCRAY, MELVIN
Manager. **Personal:** Born Aug 9, 1946, Ft Benning, GA; married Rosie M Thompson; children: Kimya Nicole, Keisha Michelle, Cora Danielle, Diedra Marie. **Educ:** GA State Univ, BS, 1972. **Career:** Atlanta City Aviation, admin asst II, 1975-76, admin asst III, 1976-77, project coordr, 1977-80, dir maintenance, 1980-. **Orgs:** Fin field City Atlanta City Hall, 1972-; collector dep marshal, 1975; Am Assoc Airport Exec, Southeastern Airport Mgrs Assoc, Conf Minority Pub Admin, Nat Forum Black Pub Admin; bd dir Cty Atlanta Credit Union. **Honors/Awds:** Cert of Appreciation, ASPA, 1982; Cert of Recognition, GA Engg Found, 1982; Pres City of Atlanta Employees Club, 1982; Certificate of Merit, Cty Atlanta & Andrew Young, 1983; Certificate of Appreciation, COMPA, 1983; Christmas Fundraiser, 1983.

MCCRAY, NIKKI
Basketball player. **Personal:** Born Dec 17, 1971, Collierville, TN; married Thomas Penson. **Educ:** Univ Tenn, BA, sports mkt, 1995. **Career:** Basketball player (retired), basketball coach; Am Basketball League, Columbus Quest, 1996-97; Wash Mystics, 1998-01; Ind Fever, 2002-03; launched Cubby Bear Daycare Ctr, Knoxville, TN, 2003; Phoenix Mercury, guard, 2004-06; Western Ky, asst coach, 2006-08; South Carolina, 2008-. **Honors/Awds:** US Olympic Basketball Team, Gold Medal, 1996, 2000; Most Valuable Player, Am Basketball League, 1997; All-Star team, 1999-01. **Special Achievements:** Two-time Olympic gold medal winner . *

MCCRAY, DR. ROY HOWARD
Dentist. **Personal:** Born Mar 14, 1946, Birmingham, AL; son of Maceo Cleggett and Annie Cleggett; children: Kenja, Kendyl & Kennethia. **Educ:** Ala A&M Univ, BS, 1972; Meharry Med Col, DDS, 1978. **Career:** Meharry Med Col, instr oper dent, 1978-81; Ala Dent Soc, parliamentarian, 1985-86; Pvt Practice, dentist, currently. **Orgs:** Huntsville Madison Co Dent Soc, 1980-86; vpres, No Ala Med Asn, 1985-; NAFEO, 1985. **Honors/Awds:** CV Mosby III Award, Dr Martin Luther King Award, Meharry Dent Sch, 1977; Int Col Dentists, 1978; Am Asn Endodontists & Orthodontists, 1978. **Military Serv:** AUS, e-4/sp4 infantry, 1967-69; Vietnam Overseas, Combat Infantryman, Unit Citation, 1968. **Business Addr:** President, Roy H Mccray Dds, 2510 Pulaski Pike NW, Huntsville, AL 35810, **Business Phone:** (205)852-6954.

MCCREARY, BILL
Journalist. **Personal:** Born Aug 18, 1933, Manhattan, NY; married O. **Educ:** Baruch Col; City Col NYC; New York Univ Sch Commun. **Career:** Radio Sta WWRL Woodside Queens, staff anchor eng, 1960, co-producer, 1961; Night Prog, mgr, 1962; Radio Sta WLIB, newscaster, 1963; News Dir, 1965; Metro Media Broadcasting Inc, TV newscaster, 1967; WNEW & TV'S 10 O'Clock News, co-anchorman; 1 Hour TV Newscast, anchorman; Black News, anchorman, 1970, managing ed & exec dir, 1971; Gen Assignment reporter; Fox Broadcasting Co, exec producer "McCreary Report" & vpres, 1987-2000; Quest Media Entertainment, Spec Ed, co-producer & co-host, vpres, media consult & host, currently. **Orgs:** Cambria Hghts Civic Asn Queens; vpres, Royal Crusdrs Bowling Club; bd mem, New York Urban League; lifetime mem, NAACP. **Honors/Awds:** Emmy Award, New York Chap Nat Acad TV Arts & Sci, 1969-70; Citation of Merit, 1971-72; Achievement Award, Berkeley Chap Nat Assoc Negro Bus & Prof Women's Club Inc; Cambria Heights Service Award, 1975; Achievement Award, NAACP LI Chap, 1975; Emmy Award for co-anchoring 10 o'clock news, 1980-81; Public Service Award, FDA. **Special Achievements:** Special Citation from the Commissioner, voted Most Watched and Belived Black Correspondent in Metro Area. **Military Serv:** AUS, corpl, 1953-55. **Business Addr:** Vice President, Media Consultant & Host, Quest Media Entertainment Inc, 1000 Richmond Ter, Staten Island, NY 10301, **Business Phone:** (718)727-3777.

MCCREE, EDWARD L.
Clergy. **Personal:** Born Feb 24, 1942, Quitman, MS; married Mae Lois Heath; children: Anita, Edward, Michele. **Educ:** Univ Detroit, 1963; Detroit Bible Col, 1962; Am Baptist Theo Sem, BA, 1972. **Career:** Creeball Ice Cream Co, founder, 1961-62; Shell Oil Sta, Co-owner, 1962; Cedar Grove Miss Baptist Church Mt Juliet, TN, pastor, 1968; Macedonia Baptist Church, Pontiac, MI, pastor, currently. **Orgs:** Hoi Adelpos Frat; Ministerial Fel; Gen Mtr Truck & Coach; Chapel Pontiac Gen Hosp; adv bd, United Brotherhood; bd dirs, Christians Tomorrow; pres, Boy Hope Club; Lectr, coun, adv. **Honors/Awds:** Recipient Most Progressive Young Business Man, Royal Oak Township, 1962; most outstanding young man, Ferndale, 1963; big brother award, Royal Oak Township, 1963; activities award, 1964. **Business Addr:** Pastor, Macedonia Missionary Baptist Church, 512 Pearsall Blvd, Pontiac, MI 48342, **Business Phone:** (248)335-2298.*

MCCRIMMON, NICKY
Basketball player. **Personal:** Born Mar 22, 1972, Harlem, NY. **Educ:** Univ Southern Calif. **Career:** Seattle Reign, guard, 1997; Atlanta Glory, 1997; Los Angeles Sparks,2000-03; Houston Comets, guard, 2005; Lubbock Hawks, guard, 2005. **Honors/Awds:** All Am, Basketball Times; First Team All-Pac 10, 1994. *

MCCRIMON, AUDREY L.
Government official, secretary (government). **Personal:** Born Oct 21, 1954, Covington, KY; daughter of Arthur and Letha Lewis Patrick. **Educ:** Northern Ill Univ, BS, educ, 1974, MS, educ, 1975; City Chicago, Exec Develop Symposium, Harvard Univ, Boston, MA, 1993. **Career:** Jewish Voc Serv, Chicago, IL, counr, 1975-77; City Cols Chicago, coordr, 1977-84; Chicago Dept Aging & Disability, dep comnr, 1984-90; Dept Rehab Serv, Chicago, IL, assoc dir, 1990-91, dir, 1991-97; Ill Dept Human Serv, asst secy, 1997-, asst compliance access & workplace safety, asst secy, currently. **Orgs:** Ill Asn Deaf, 1978-; Coalition Citizens Disabilities, 1985; Renaissance Women, 1990-; Nat Coun Disability, 1994-; bd men, United Way Chicago Coun, 1994-; bd trustees, Comn Accreditation Rehab Facil, 1995-; Res Agenda Steering Comt, Nat Inst Disability & Rehab Res, 1995-. **Honors/Awds:** August Christmann, City Chicago-Advocacy, 1990-94; Nominated by Pres Clinton, Nat Coun Disability, 1995. **Business Addr:** Assistant Secretary, Illinois Department of Human Services, 401 S Clinton 7th Fl, Chicago, IL 60607.*

MCCROOM, EDDIE WINTHER
Lawyer. **Personal:** Born Sep 11, 1932, Memphis, TN; married Shirley Kathryn Lewis; children: Darren Winther, Audrey Jay & Sandra Marguerite. **Educ:** Univ Ark, BS, 1955; Case Western Res Univ, LLB, 1961. **Career:** OH Civil Rights Comn, field rep, 1961-63; US Dept Justice, asst US atty, 1964-69; Univ Cincinnati, lectr bus law, 1971-72; State OH Dept Admin Serv, state EEO coordr, 1972-74; E Winther McCroom & Assoc, pvt law pract, 1976-. **Orgs:** Exec vpres, Indust Fed S & L Assocs, 1969-70; legal coun Jaycee, 1970-; Ohio Legal Adv; NCP, 1970-; IBPOE W Elks, 1980. **Military Serv:** USN, seaman II, 1955-57. **Business Addr:** Attorney, E Winther McCroom & Associates, 402 Legal Arts Ctr 101 Mkt St, Youngstown, OH 44503, **Business Phone:** (330)747-1163.

MCCROREY, DR. H LAWRENCE
Educator. **Personal:** Born Mar 13, 1927, Philadelphia, PA; son of Henry Lawrence Jr and Marian Dawley; married Constance Gilliam; children: Desiree, Lauren, Leslie & Larry. **Educ:** Univ Mich, BS, biol, 1949, MS, 1950; Univ Ill, MS, 1958, PhD 1963. **Career:** Sharp & Dohme pharmaceut, res assoc, 1951-55; Univ Ill, asst prof physiol, 1966-63; Univ Vt, dept physiol & biophysics, asst prof, 1966, Sch Alied Health Sci, dean, 1981, assoc vpres, Acad Affairs, 1973-77, prof emer, currently; Statist Walter Reed Army Inst Res, vis prof 1967-70; Univ Co Med Col, vis prof 1978-79; Howard Univ, vis prof; Tuskegee Inst, vis prof; Goddard Col, vis prof; Univ Calif, vis prof; Charles Drew Med Sch, vis prof; Col VI Fla A&M, vis prof; Dillard Univ, vis prof. **Orgs:** Surgeon Gen Ad Hoc Comt Health Am, 1968-69; bd trustee, VT-NY Proj, 1968-70; bd dirs, Am Civil Liberties Union, 1971-75; Gen Res Support Prog Adv Comt, NIH, 1973-78 & 1980-84; corporator, Burlington Savings Bank, 1976-; bd dir Burlington YMCA 1976-. **Honors/Awds:** Outstanding Teaching Award, Col Nursing, 1960 & 1964; Outstanding Teaching Award, Col Pharm, 1965; Outstanding Teaching Award, Col Med, 1970, 1971 & 1984; Teacher of the year, Col Med, 1970 & 1984; Karl Jefferson Thompson MD Teaching Scholar Award, 1971; Outstanding Teaching Award, Univ Vt, 1988; Kroepsch-Maurice University Professor Teaching Award, 1988; Golden Apple Teaching Award, Sch Nursing. **Military Serv:** AUS nco 1944-46. **Business Addr:** Professor Emeritus, University of Vermont, Dept Physiol, 85 S Prospect St, Burlington, VT 05405, **Business Phone:** (802)656-2540.

MCCUISTON, FREDERICK DOUGLASS, JR.
Automotive executive. **Personal:** Born Nov 27, 1940, Wynne, AR; son of Frederick McCuiston Sr and Erma; married Norma P; children: Frederick III, Marcus, Maia. **Educ:** TN State Univ, BS, 1961; Univ Cincinnati, MS, 1970, PhD, 1976. **Career:** Gen Motors, develop systs mgr. **Orgs:** Am Soc Mech Engrs, 1962; Soc Automotive Engrs, 1968; mem, NBCDI, 1981; pres, Ann Arbor NAACP Br, 1982-92. **Honors/Awds:** Omega Psi Phi Comm Service Award, 1984; Alpha Phi Alpha Man of the Year, 1985; Region III NAACP Leadership Award, 1986, 1990. **Military Serv:** USAF, capt, 5 yrs. *

MCCUISTON, DR. STONEWALL, JR.
Physician. **Personal:** Born Feb 23, 1959, Chicago, IL; son of Stonewall and Annie M. **Educ:** Grinnell Col, BA, 1981; Meharry Med Col, MD, 1985. **Career:** Cook County Hosp, resident physician; pvt med pract, internal med & pediat, currently. **Orgs:** Pres, Cook County Hosp House Staff Asn, 1988; pres, Cook County Hosp Black Physicians Asn, 1987-88; Cook County Hosp Union Coalition, 1988; Cook County Hosp Exec Med Staff, 1988; AMA; Chicago Med Soc; Ill State Med Soc. **Honors/Awds:** Research grant March of Dimes 1982-83; First place Research Day, Med Div Meharry Med Col, 1983. **Home Addr:** 7810 S Ridgeland, Chicago, IL 60649, **Home Phone:** (312)731-3717. **Business Addr:** Physician, 375 N Wall St Suite P520, Kankakee, IL 60901, **Business Phone:** (815)933-0194.

MCCULLERS, EUGENE
Executive. **Personal:** Born Jan 30, 1941, Garner, NC. **Educ:** Shaw Univ, BA 1962; Univ Wisconsin & Univ Puerto Rico, additional study. **Career:** Retired: US Peace Corps, volunteer, 1963-65; Capitol Coca-Cola Bottling Co, Raleigh, NC, special markets rep, 1965-67; Coca-Cola Bottling Co, Thomas, TN, acct exec, 1968-76; Coca-Cola USA, Atlanta, GA, marketing mgr, 1976-81, mgr community affairs, 1981-96; Almirante Consulting, principal. **Orgs:** Bd dirs, trustee, Shaw University; bd dirs, Grambling State Univ Athletic Found; bd dirs, Nat Black Col Hall of Fame Found; bd dirs, The Jacquelyn McClure Lupus Ctr; bd dirs, Nat Asn Market Develop; life mem, NAACP; Elks; Kappa Alpha Psi. **Honors/Awds:** Distinguished Alumni Award, Shaw Univ; Marketer of the Year Award, Nat Asn Market Develop; Inductee, Hall of Fame, Grambling Univ, 1986; inductee, Hall of Fame, Central Intercollegiate Athletic Asn, 1987; Honorary Doctor of Humane Letters, Shaw UNIV, 1992. *

MCCULLERS JOHNSON, ALTHEA. See RENE, ALTHEA.

MCCULLOUGH, GERALDINE
Sculptor, high school teacher, college administrator. **Personal:** Born Dec 1, 1922, Kingston, AR; daughter of Hugh and Esther Hamilton; married Lester McCullough, Sr. (deceased) (deceased); children: Lester Jr. **Educ:** The Art Inst Chicago, BA, 1948, MA, art educ, 1955; Univ Chicago, acad course work towards, 1958. **Career:** Teacher (retired), Sculptor; Chicago Pub Schs, teacher, art educ; Dominican Univ, prof, 1968-88, chair, art dept, 1976-89; John D Standecker Scholar; Studio Geraldine Mccullough, artist. **Orgs:** The Links Inc, W Towers Chap, 1975-; Arts Club Chicago, Chicago, Ill; Delta Sigma Theta Sority; Pub Arts Comn, Village, Oak Park, 2002-. **Honors/Awds:** George D Widener Gold Medal for Sculpture, PA Acad Fine Arts, 1965; Hard Hat Award, Monumental Sculpture, IL Arts Coun, 1985; Osceola Award, Delta Black Arts Excellence, 1987; hon doc, Dominican Univ, 1990; Joseph Randall Shapiro Award, Oak Park Area Coun, 2000; distinguished guest artist, Russian govt. **Special Achievements:** Numerous exhibitions & commissions; works included in many collections, such as the Johnson Publishing Cp, Chicago State univ and others. *

MCCULLOUGH, REV. JACQUELINE (JACKIE MC-CULLOUGH)
Gospel singer, chief executive officer. **Personal:** Born in Kingston, Jamaica. **Educ:** Drew Theol Sem, Doctor Ministry; NY Univ, MA philos; Jewish Theol Sem, postgraduate study. **Career:** Harlem Hosp, registered nurse pediat, nurse practr; Gospel vocalist; reverend; Beth Rapha Church, sr pastor & founder, currently. **Orgs:** Pres & chief exec officer, Daughters of Rizpah. **Special**

Achievements: "The Most Influential African-American Ministers In The Nation", 1996; Discography: This If For You Lord, 1998; Auth: "Daily Moments With God: In Quietness and Confidence". **Business Addr:** Senior Pastor, Beth Rapha Church, 1540 Rte 202 Suite 4, Pomona, NY 10970.*

MCCUMMINGS, DR. LEVERNE
School administrator. **Personal:** Born Oct 28, 1932, Marion, SC; son of Henry and Mamie; married Dr Betty L Hall; children: Gregory, Gary & Ahada. **Educ:** St Augustine's, BA, 1960; Univ Pa, MSW, 1966; Ohio State Univ, PhD, 1975. **Career:** Competency Cert Bd, Bd of Health & Human Servs, Futures Think Tank, chmn, 1981-82; Natl Conf of Grad Deans/Dirs & Off Soc Work Progs, pres, 1982-85; Cheyney Univ Pa, pres, 1985-91. **Honors/Awds:** Outstanding Educrs Award, Univ Ky, 1971; Recognition Award NASW Sixth Biennial Prof Symposium, 1980; Distinguished Alumni Award, Univ Pa, 1980; Recognition Award Coun Intl Prog, 1981; Inst Edu Mgt, Harvard Univ, 1989; Distinguished Career Award, Ohio St Univ, 2008. **Military Serv:** AUS, 1955-57.

MCCURDY, DR. BRENDA WRIGHT
Microbiologist. **Educ:** Va Union Univ, BS (Magna Cum Laude), 1968; Va Commonwealth Univ, Sch Med, MS, 1970; Wayne State Univ, Sch Med, PhD, 1980. **Career:** Henry Ford Hosp Detroit, microbiologist III, 1970-72; Wayne State Univ, res asst, 1972-75; Wayne State Univ, adj asst prof immunol & microbiol, 1980-; Veterans Admin Med Ctr, section chief microbiol, 1979; US Food & Drug Admin, dir, currently. **Orgs:** Am Soc for Microbiol, 1970-; South Central Asn for Clinic Microbiol, 1978-; chairperson, Med Ctr Adv Comn for Equal Employment Opportunities, 1983-; pres, Windsor Black Coalition (Canada), 1983-85; Delta Sigma Theta; Clinic Lab Improv Adv Comt, 1992. **Honors/Awds:** Graduate Professional Scholarship, Wayne State Univ, 1976-77; 'National Fellowship Award', 1977-78; Augusta T Calloway Fellowship Award, 1979. **Business Phone:** (313)393-8203.

MCCUTCHEON, LAWRENCE
Scout, executive director, football player. **Personal:** Born Jun 2, 1950, Plainview, TX; son of Roland and Leanna Bell; married Myra Emerson, Dec 9, 1983; children: Adrian Campbell & Marcus McCutcheon. **Educ:** Colo State Univ, attended, 1972. **Career:** Football (retired), Scout; Los Angeles Rams, running back, 1972-79; Denver Broncos, running back, 1980; Buffalo Bills, running back, 1981; Los Angeles Rams, dir player personnel, 2003-06; St Louis Rams, dir player personnel, 2006-. **Honors/Awds:** NEA'S Third Down Award; Second team ALL-NFC, UPI; Pro Bowl for 4th Staight Time; Outstanding Offensive Back, 1974; Daniel F Reeves Mem Award; Most Valuable Player; All-Rookie Team, UPI; All-Western Athletic Conf; CO State Univ; NFC All Star Team, Sporting News, 1974; Inducted into the Tex Panhandle Hall of Fame, 2005. **Home Addr:** 19981 Weems Lane, Huntington Beach, CA 92646. **Business Addr:** Director player personnel, St Louis Rams, 1 Rams Way, St Louis, MO 63045, **Business Phone:** (314)982-7267.

MCDADE, JOE BILLY
Judge. **Personal:** Born Jan 1, 1937; married Mary Evelyn. **Educ:** Bradley Univ, BS, 1959, MA, 1960; Mich Univ, JD, 1963. **Career:** US Dept Justice, staff atty antitrust div, 1963-65; First Fed Savs & Loan Asn, exec trainee, 1965; Hafele & McDade, Peoria, Ill, partner, 1968-77; pvt pract, Peoria, 1977-82; Peoria COC Leadership Sch, guest lectr, 1977; Ill State, Peoria, assoc circuit judge, 1982-98, ciruit judge, 1988-91; US Dist Ct, Cent Dist Ill, judge, currently. **Orgs:** Greater Peoria Ill Legal Aid Soc, exec dir, 1965-69; Bd dir, Ill Judges Asn; chmn, Legal Action Comn, Peoria Chap, Nat Asn Advan Colored People, 1966-67; bd dir, Ct Counselors Prog Inc, 1968-75 & 1983-86; bd dir, Tri-Co Peoria Urban League, 1970-72; panel mem, Heart Ill United Fund, 1974-77; bd dir, Peoria YMCA, 1975-77 & 1985-92, prog comn, 1989-92; bd dir, Ill Cent Health Systs Agency, 1975-82, pres, 1978-80; adv bd, Comprehensive Work & Training Prog, 1975-83; Creve Coeur Club, 1978-82; bd dir, Greater Peoria Sports Hall Fame Inc, 1980-82; trustee, St Peter's Catholic Church, 1980-85; bd dir, Cent Ill Bradley Alumni Club, 1982-83; bd dir, Upgrade Non-Profit Housing Corp, 1983-89; exec bd, Boy Scouts Am, WD Boyce, 1984-86; chmn, House Prayer Comn, 1987-89; bd dir, SHARE Foods Inc, 1987-92; Ill Eagle Scouts, Citizenship Prom Comn, 1988-94; bd dir, Amateur Musical Club Peoria, 1988-92; bd dir, Peoria Tri-Centennial, 1990-92; bd dir, Am Red Cross Central Ill Chap, 1991-94; Ill State Bar Asn; Peoria Co Bar Asn. **Honors/Awds:** NIT Championship Team, Bradley Univ, 1957; All NIT Team, Bradley University, 1959; Shriner's East/West All-Star Basketball Team, Bradley Univ, 1959; Outstanding Academic Athlete, Bradley Univ, 1959; Watonga Award, Bradley Univ, 1959; Highest Student Award, Bradley Univ, 1959; Bradley University Hall of Fame, Bradley Univ, 1961; Leadership Award, First Presbyterian Church Youth Retreat, 1966; Bradley Honorary Coach Award, Bradley Univ, 1980; Citizen of the Year Award, Omega Psi Phi Fraternity, 1983; IBPO Elms of the World Achievement Award, Bethel United Meth Men's Club, 1989; Distinguished Alumnus Award for 1990, Bradley Univ, 1990; Bradley University Centurion, Bradley Univ, 1990; Certificate of Appreciation, Ill Dept C & Family Serv, 1991; Recognition Award, African Hall Fame Mus, 1991; Award of Appreciation, Share Food Prog Cent IL, 1992; Certificate of Recognition, Peoria Christian Leadership Coun, 1992; Certificate of Recognition, Peoria Christian Leadership Coun, 1992; Award of Appreciation, Share Food Prog Cent Ill Inc, 1992; Award of Recognition, Houston Area Urban League, 1994. **Business Addr:** US District Judge, US District Court, Fedral Bldg 100 NE Monroe St Suite 122, Peoria, IL 61602, **Business Phone:** (309)671-7821.

MCDANIEL, DR. ADAM THEODORE
Dentist. **Personal:** Born Jun 8, 1925, Rock Hill, SC; married Lois Butler; children: Jenita & Frederic. **Educ:** NC Central Univ, BS, 1946; Howard Univ, DDS, 1951; Jersey City Med Ctr, Internship, 1951-52; Friendship Jr Col, attended. **Career:** Pvt pract, dentist, currently; Rahway Geriatric Ctr, dental consultant. **Orgs:** Rahway Rotary Club; pres, Rahway Mun Coun Caucus Elected Black Officials, 1960-72; Union Co & NJ Dental Soc; 100 Black Men NJ; Omega Psi Phi Fraternity; NJ Chap Nat Guardsmen Inc; state rep, Rahway Housing Auth, 1959-70; Correctional Health Serv Invest Comm NJ State Prisons; Lay Comm Pub Sch Systems; Urban League. **Honors/Awds:** Beta Kappa Chi Hon SJI Soc Honoree; Testimonial Dinner 1961, 1973. **Military Serv:** USF, capt, 1953-54. **Business Addr:** Dentist, 97 E Milton Ave, Rahway, NJ 07065, **Business Phone:** (732)381-9005.

MCDANIEL, CHARLES WILLIAM
Government official, clergy. **Personal:** Born Mar 17, 1927, Fairfield, AL; son of Charles Andrew and Willie V Seldon; married Rose L Bowen; children: Deborah Roberts, Charles F & Reginael. **Educ:** Miles Col, attended 1946; Civil Serv Comm, attended 1978; Coast Guard Acad, attended 1982; GA State Univ, attended 1981; AUS Logistics Mgt Ctr, 1970-81. **Career:** AUS, Warren MI, system analyst, 1967-70, budget analyst, 1970-76; AUS, Wash, DC, budget analyst, 1976-80; AUS HQ FORSCOM, suprv budget analyst, 1980-89; Log Mgmt Div, deputy dir, 1989; Ind Ave Baptist Church, admin asst pastor, 1990-. **Orgs:** Pres, Am FED Musicians 286, 1965-73; church organist, Ind Baptist Church, 1966-76; band leader, Detroit MI, 1968-76; NAACP, 1970; Am Fed Musician 15/286, 1973-75; Am Military Comptrollers, 1981-; church organist, Shiloh Baptist Church, 1982-, treas, 1987-; staff union negotiator, AUS HQ FORSCOM, Ft McPherson, 1983; Mayor's Com Substance Abuse, 1990; organist, New Hope Baptist Church, 1990. **Honors/Awds:** Outstanding Award, AUS, 1973-75; Special Act, AUS, 1975; Letter from Pres Ford Cost Reduction, AUS, 1976; Outstanding Award, AUS Pentagon, 1980; Outstanding Award AUS, Ft McPherson 1980; Outstanding Achievement, AUS, Ft McPherson, 1983; Exceptional Performance, HQ FORSCOM, Ft McPherson, GA, 1986; Outstanding Chief Award Program & Budget Branch, HQ FORSCOM, 1987; Dept of Army, Commander's Award for Civilian Service. **Military Serv:** USN stewards mate III 2 yrs. **Home Addr:** 2412 Valley Brook Rd, Toledo, OH 43615-2956. **Business Addr:** Assistant Pastor, Indiana Avenue Baptist Church, 640 Indiana Ave, Toledo, OH 43602, **Business Phone:** (419)246-3850.

MCDANIEL, EDWARD
Football player. **Personal:** Born Feb 23, 1969, Batesburg, SC. **Educ:** Clemson Univ, BA, human resources & develop. **Career:** Minn Vikings, defensive back, 1992-2001; co-owner, D1 Sports Training, Greenville, currently.

MCDANIEL, ELIZABETH
Health services administrator. **Personal:** Born May 3, 1952, St Louis, MO; children: Paul. **Educ:** Forest Park, BA, arts, 1981. **Career:** Forest Park Admin Bldg, work study, 1978; Forest Park Community Col, work study, 1981, student asst, 1982; Coalition Sch Desegration, secy, 1982; St Louis Comp N Health Ctr, secy & clerk 1982; Vis Nurse Assn, billing clerk, 1984; St Louis Univ Hosp, lead clerk, 1986; St Louis Regional Physician's Billing, 1987. **Orgs:** vpres, Wellston Sch Bd. **Home Addr:** 6562 Jesse Jackson Ave, Saint Louis, MO 63121.

MCDANIEL, EMMANUEL
Football player, football coach. **Personal:** Born Jul 27, 1972, Griffin, GA; married Lynn Viehmeyer; children: Jaylen. **Educ:** East Carolina Univ. **Career:** Football player (retired), Football coach; Carolina Panthers, defensive back, 1996, 2002; Indianapolis Colts, 1997; New York Giants, 1999-2001; Ariz Cardinals, 2003; Univ Akron, asst coach, 2007-. **Honors/Awds:** East Carolina Rookie Year, 1996. **Business Phone:** (330)972-6245.

MCDANIEL, JAMES BERKLEY, JR.
Physician. **Personal:** Born Aug 8, 1925, Pittsburgh, PA; son of James McDaniel Sr; widowed; children: James B III & Nancy Alben Lloyd. **Educ:** Howard Univ, Wash, DC, BS, 1950; Howard Univ, MD, 1957. **Career:** Physician Obest & Gynec, prv practice, 1962; State Univ NY, asst clinical prof, Buffalo, 1974; Geneva B Scruggs Community Health Care Ctr Inc, head, Obest & Gynec dept; pvt pract, currently. **Honors/Awds:** First achiever award, Stud Nat Med Asn & Buffalo, 1972; achiever award, Buffalo Youth Bd; Chief Executive Officer's Lifetime Achievement Award, Geneva B Scruggs Ctr, 1989. **Military Serv:** USN, musician 3/c, 1944-46. **Home Addr:** 180 N Pearl St, Buffalo, NY 14202-1108, **Home Phone:** (716)885-1885. **Business Addr:** Physician, 180 N Pearl S, Buffalo, NY 14202-1108, **Business Phone:** (716)885-1885.

MCDANIEL, KAREN COTTON
Librarian, college administrator. **Personal:** Born Nov 16, 1950, Newark, NJ; daughter of Alphonso C Jr and Maude Smoot Bledsoe; married Rodney McDaniel Sr, Aug 25, 1971; children: Rodney Jr, Kimberly Renee & Jason Bradley. **Educ:** Berea Col, BS, 1973; Univ Ky, MSLS, 1975. **Career:** KY State Univ, asst librn, 1975-83, dir libraries, 1989-2005, Carter G Woodson lectr, 2001-02, prof emer, currently; KY Dept Pub Advocacy, law librn, 1983-85; KY Dept Librs & Archives, prog coord, 1985-89. **Orgs:** Delta Sigma Theta Sorority, 1976-; KY Coun Archives, 1987-; Am Libr Asn, 1989-; Asn Col & Res Librs, 1989-; sect secy, KY Libr Asn, 1990-91, 1975-; Black Caucus Am Libr Asn, 1991-; State Assisted Acad Libr Coun KY, chair, 1992-93, secy, 1991-92, 1989-; chair, Land Grant Lib Dir's Asn, 1994-98, vice chair, 1992-94, 1989-; bd dirs, treas, SOLINET, 1995-96, secy, 1996-97, 1994-97; chair, Asn Agricultural Admin, 1996-98, 1989-; chair, Womens Hist Coalition KY, 1997-98, 1993-2004; HBCU Libr Alliance, 2002-, treas, 2004-; Asn Black Women Historians. **Honors/Awds:** Outstanding Young Women in America, 1979-81; Honorary Sorority for Women Educators, Alpha Delta Kappa, 1991-; Distinguished Alumna Award, Univ Ky Sch Libr & Info Sci, 1999. **Special Achievements:** Author of numerous essays published in encyclopedias. **Business Addr:** Professor Emeritus, Kentucky State University, Paul G Blazer Library, 400 E Main St, Frankfort, KY 40601, **Business Phone:** (502)597-6852.

MCDANIEL, MYRA ATWELL
Lawyer. **Personal:** Born Dec 13, 1932, Philadelphia, PA; daughter of Toronto C Jr and Eva Yores; married Dr Reuben Jr, Feb 2, 1955; children: Diane & Reuben III. **Educ:** Univ Pa, Eng, 1954; Univ Tex Law Sch, JD, 1975. **Career:** Aviation Supply Off Philadelphia, mgt analyst; Baldwin-Wallace Col Berea Ohio, Ind Univ Bloomington, admin asst jobs; Railrod Commiss Tex, asst spec coun, asst atty gen in charge taxation div; Gov Mark White, gen coun; State Tex, secy state, 1984-87; Bickerstaff Heath & Smiley, partner, 1987-96; Bickerstaff, Heath, Smiley, Pollan, Kever & McDaniel, managing partner, 1996-, atty, currently; State & Gen Coun, Gov Tex, secy; Off Gov Tex, gen coun; Railroad Comn Tex, asst spec coun; Taxation Div, Off Atty Gen Tex, chief. **Orgs:** Tex Bar Asn; Am Bar Asn; Travis County Bar Asn; Austin Black Laweyrs' Asn; Travis County Women Lawyers' Asn; fel Tex Bar Found; fel Am Bar Found; admitted pract, State Tex, US Supreme Ct, US Fifth Circuit Ct Appeals, US Dist Cts Eastern Western Southern & Northern Dist Tex; Prof Efficiency & Econ Res, 1978-84, Asset Mgt Adv Comn State Treas 1984-86, Hobby-Lewis Joint Select Comm Fiscal Policy 1984-86, Criminal Justice Policy Coun State TEX 1984-86, Nat Asn Secretaries State 1984-86; chmn, atty, secy, Nat Asn Tax Admins, 1980-81; mem bd dir Austin Consulting Group Inc 1983-86; mem bd trustees, St Edward's Univ Austin 1986-, TEX Bar Found 1986-89, Episcopal Found Houston TEX 1986-90; Lay Eucharistic Minister, St James Episcopal Church, vestry bd, 1988-91, sr warden, 1990-91, newsletter ed, 1991-; adv bd, Longhorn Asn, Excellence Women's Athletics, 1988-91; co-chair, TEX Ex-studs Athletics Comm, 1988-89; Black Alumni Adv Comm, Univ TEX, Ex-studs Asn, 1989-; bd trustees, Episcopal Sem Southwest, 1989-96; bd dirs, Asn Govering Bd Cols & Universities, 1992-96; dir, Law Alumni Asn, Univ TEX, 1992-94; trustee, Leadership Educ Arts Prog, 1995-; adv bd mem, Women Basketball Coaches Asn, 1996-; trustee, Episcopal Health Charities, 1997-; bd dirs, Found Ins Regulatory Studies, Tex; mem & chair, bd trustees, St Edward's Univ; bd trustees, Bishop Quin Found, Episcopal Diocese Tex; adv bd, Tex Asn Counties Leadership Found; bd trustees, Austin Pub Edu Found. **Honors/Awds:** Citizen Of the year, Mega Psi Phi Fraternity, Epsilon Iona Chap, Austin, 1985; Woman of the year, Int Training Commun, Austin Chap, 1985; Woman of the year, Longview Metro Chamber Com, Longview, 1985; Hon Doctorate Deg, Jarvis Christian Col, Hawkins, 1986; Woman of the year, Tex Nat Orgn Women, 1993; Hendrick Arnold Lifetime Achievement Award, Tex African-Am Heritage Orgn, 1993; Women Distinction, Lone Star Girl Scouts Coun, 1997. **Business Addr:** Managing Partner, Bickerstaff, Heath, Smiley, Pollan, Kever & McDaniel LLP, 1700 Frost Bank Plz 816 Congress Ave, Austin, TX 78701-1443, **Business Phone:** (512)472-8021.

MCDANIEL, REV. PAUL ANDERSON
Clergy. **Personal:** Born Jul 5, 1930, Rock Hill, SC; married Edna Carolyn Phillips (deceased); children: Paul Jr, Pamela Anita, Patricia Ann & Peter Adam; married Linda Isadora. **Educ:** Morehouse Col, Atlanta, BA, hist polit sci, 1951; Colgate Rochester Div Sch, MDiv, 1955; Univ Rochester, MA, 1959. **Career:** Second Baptist Church Mumford, pastor, 1952-56; Second Baptist Church, Rahway, NJ, pastor 1956-66; Second Missionary Bapt Ch Chattanooga, pastor, 1966; National Baptist Congress of Christian Educ, instr. **Orgs:** Tenn Const Conv, 29th Dist Nashville, 1977; chmn, Ga-Tenn Regional Health Comn, 1978-80; chmn & past vice chmn, Hamilton Co Comn, Chattanooga, 1979; Chattanooga African Am Black Chamber Com, currently; former pres, Clergy Asn Greater Chattanooga; past pres, Tenn Leadership Educ Congress. **Honors/Awds:** DD Friendship Jr Coll Rock Hill SC, 1975; various serv awds comm orgs. **Business Addr:** Member, Chattanooga African American Chamber of Commerce, 535 Chestnut St Suite 200, Chattanooga, TN 37402, **Business Phone:** (423)265-0021.

MCDANIEL, RANDALL CORNELL
Football player. **Personal:** Born Dec 19, 1964, Phoenix, AZ; married Marianne. **Educ:** Ariz State Univ, BS, physical educ. **Career:**

Football player (retired); Minn Vikings, guard, 1988-99; Tampa Bay Buccaneers, 2000-01. **Honors/Awds:** Most Inspirational Man of the Year, NFL 1990s All-Decade Team, Midwest Sports Channel, 1996; Unsung Hero Award, Nat Football League Players Asn, 1997; Minnesota Vikings "Ring of Honor", 2006; Pro Football Hall of Fame, 2009.

MCDANIEL, PROF. REUBEN R
Educator. **Personal:** Born Jan 6, 1936, Petersburg, VA; son of Reuben R and Nannie Finney; married Myra Yores Atwell; children: Diane & Reuben R III. **Educ:** Drexel Univ, BS, mech eng, 1964; Univ Akron, MS, guid coun, 1968; Ind Univ, EdD, higher educ, 1971. **Career:** Claremont Grad Sch; Baldwin-Wallace Col, asst dean, asst prof educ, & dir div educ serv, 1965-69; Ind Univ, assoc instr, 1969-71; Fla State Univ, asst prof, 1971-72; Helsinki Sch Econ & Bus Admin; Univ Tex, Austin, Jesse H Jones prof, 1983-89, Tom E. Nelson, Jr. Regents prof, 1989-91, Charles & Elizabeth Prothro Regents chair heath care mgt, 1991-; bd dirs, USA Inst Managed Care Inc, 1995-98. **Orgs:** Actg dep comnr, Tex Dept Human Resources, 1979; consult, Seton Med Ctr, Austin, 1980-; bd trustees, Seton Med Ctr, Austin, 1985-91; Fac Senate Univ Tex, Austin, chmn, 1985-87; Adv Comt, Banaker Honors Col, Prairie View A&M Univ, 1987-91; Priority Schs Comt, Austin Ind School Dist, 1989-91; Sci Adv Comt, Plexus Inst. **Honors/Awds:** J D Beasley Graduate Teaching Award, 1982; Key D Award, Outstanding Alumni, Drexel Univ, 1988; Myron D Fottler Exceptional Service Award, Health Care Mgt Div, Acad Mgt, Univ Tex, 2001; Elective Fac Honor Role, McCombs Sch Bus, 2000-02; Civitatis Award, Univ Tex, Austin, 2004. **Special Achievements:** Numerous publications. **Home Addr:** 3910 Knollwood Dr, Austin, TX 78731, **Home Phone:** (512)345-0006. **Business Addr:** Professor of Management, The University of Texas at Austin, Department of Information, Risk, and Operations Management, CBA 6 454 One Univ Sta, Austin, TX 78712, **Business Phone:** (512)471-9451.

MCDANIEL, ROBERT ANTHONY
Writer, journalist. **Personal:** Born Aug 2, 1952, Arden, NC; son of Mary Alice Spain McDaniel and Theodore Roosevelt McDaniel; divorced; children: Demayne Z Ginyard, Marc A McDaniel, Tristan S McDaniel. **Educ:** Univ North Carolina, Asheville, NC, BA, English, 1974. **Career:** Asheville Citizen-Times, Asheville, NC, sports writer, 1974-75; Life of Georgia Ins Co, Asheville, NC, insurance agent, 1975-78; Piedmont Airlines, Asheville, NC, ticket agent trainee 1978-79; Times-News, Hendersonville, NC, sports writer, 1979-82, sports editor, 1982-93; Golf World Magazine, Trumbull, CT, sr writer, 1993-97; Golf Digest, 1997-. **Orgs:** Member, National Association of Black Journalists, 1989-; mem, Associated Press Sports Editors, 1982-93; mem, Golf Writers of America Assn, 1993-. **Honors/Awds:** Spot Sports News, 3rd Pl, NC Press Assn, 1981; Sports Feature, 2nd Pl, NC Press Assn, 1984; Sports Feature, 2nd Pl, NC Press Assn, 1985; 1st Place, Sports Reporting, NC Press Association, 1992; Black Achiever in Bus/Industry Award, 1997. **Special Achievements:** Co-Author of best-selling book "Training A Tiger"; author, Uneven Lies: The Heroic Story of African Americans in Golf. *

MCDANIEL, SHARON A.
Arts administrator, music critic. **Personal:** Born Jan 3, 1950, Hampton, VA; daughter of James Cornelius and Mae Hallie Payne. **Educ:** Paris Am Acad Music, Paris, France, cert piano & cert French, 1967; Col-Conservatory Music, Cincinnati, OH, BA, music theory, 1971; Eastman Schc Music, Rochester, NY, 1974, 1988. **Career:** Gen Tel & Electronics, Los Angeles, CA, regional sales mgr, 1974-78; Oakland Symphony Orchestra, Oakland, CA, orchestra mgr, 1978-79; Dayton Contemporary Dance Co, Dayton, OH, gen mgr, 1982-84; Springfield Symphony, Springfield, OH, gen mgr, 1984-86; Hochstein Music Sch, Rochester, NY, dir commun, 1988-; About Time Mag, Rochester, NY, ed asst, 1991. **Orgs:** Classical music announcer/host WRUR-FM, Rochester, NY, 1986-; singer, Rochester Bach Festival Choir, Rochester, NY, 1972-74 & 1987-; Rochester Asn Black Communicators, Rochester, NY, 1987-; bd dirs, publicity, Madrigalia Ltd, Rochester, NY, 1987-; fund raising comts, IBM-PC Club Rochester, NY, 1988; Music Critics Asn, 1984, 1991. **Honors/Awds:** National Merit Scholar, 1967; Outstanding Junior Woman; Daisy Chain, Univ Cincinnati, 1970; Educational Institute Fellow, Music Critics Asn, 1991. **Business Addr:** Director, Hochstein Music School, 50 N Plymouth Ave, Rochester, NY 14614.*

MCDANIEL, TERRENCE LEE
Football player. **Personal:** Born Feb 8, 1965, Saginaw, MI; married. **Educ:** Univ Tenn. **Career:** Los Angeles Raiders, defensive back, 1988-94; Oakland Raiders, cornerback, 1995-97; Seattle Seahawks, defensive back, 1998.

MCDANIEL, WILLIAM T., JR.
Educator, jazz musician. **Personal:** Born Sep 24, 1945, Memphis, TN; married Bernice Dowdy; children: William Theodore III. **Educ:** Morehouse Col, BA, 1967; Univ IA, MA, 1968, PhD, 1974. **Career:** Sch Music, Ohio St Univ, prof; NC A&T St Univ, prof, chmn dept music; Morehouse Col, dir bands, 1968-72, chmn dept Music, dir bands, 1974-77; Univ IA, instr black music, 1973-74. **Orgs:** Mus Ed, Nat Conf; Am Musicological Soc; Col Mus Soc; Col Band Dir Nat Asn; Nat Asn Col Wind & Percsn Instrs; Nat Band Asn; Alpha Phi Alpha. **Honors/Awds:** Distinguished Teaching Award; Distinguished Scholar Award, 1994. **Business Addr:** Professor, Ohio State University, School of Music, Room 313A, 1866 College Rd, Columbus, OH 43210, **Business Phone:** (614)292-6571.

MCDANIEL, XAVIER MAURICE
Basketball player, executive. **Personal:** Born Jun 4, 1963, Columbia, SC. **Educ:** Wichita State Univ, attended 1985. **Career:** Basketball player (retired), executive; Seattle Super Sonics, forward, 1985-91; Phoenix Suns, forward, 1991; NY Knicks, forward, 1991-92; Boston Celtics, forward, 1992-96; Irak lis BC, 1995-96; NJ Nets, forward, 1996-98; 34 X-man, owner, currently. **Honors/Awds:** NBA All-Rookie Team, 1986. **Business Addr:** Owner, 34 X-man.

MCDANIELS, ALFRED F.
Athletic coach, educator. **Personal:** Born Sep 21, 1940, Muskogee, OK; son of Alvin; married Cheryl McDaniels Kieser, Jun 11, 1971; children: Alfred Jr & Debbie. **Educ:** Bakersfield Jr Coll, AA, 1961; Univ NV, Reno, BS, 1965, Univ NV, Las Vegas, MED, 1971; Univ NV, BS, 1965, MEd, 1972. **Career:** PE Health Educ, teacher, 1965-70; Varsity Football, asst varsity head jr varsity asst track coach, 1965-67; Merced HS, head track coach, 1968-80;Univ NV, asst football coach, 1970-72, asst track coach, 1971-74, asst prof phys educ head track coach, 1975-92, Dept Kinesiology, teacher, PE Activities, teacher, currently. **Orgs:** Nat Educ Asn; NSEA; NAHPER; AAHPER; United Teaching Prof; US Track & Field Coaches Asn; Women's Track & Field Coaches Asn; designed & developed, USA Youth Track & Field Prog Nev, 1980-93; trained & organized, Southern Nev Track & Field Off Asn, 1975-92. **Honors/Awds:** Most Outstanding in Track, 1963; Most Outstanding in Football, 1964; Most Outstanding Senior Athlete, Univ NV Reno, 1965; Outstanding Athlete, Bakersfield Col, 1959, Bakersfield HS, 1960, Univ NV, 1965; Women's PCAA Team Champion Track & Field, 1984-86 & 1989; Women's PCAA Coach of the Year Track & Field, 1984-86 & 1989; big west coach of year, PCAA, 1989; District Eight Coach of the Year, Nat Col Athletic Asn, 1989 & 1991; Las Vegas Black Sports Hall of Fame, 1991; Bakersfield Col Track & Field Hall of Fame, 1993; USA Track & Field President's Award, 1993; Big West Coach of the Year, 1984-86 & 1989; publication in athletic journal, speaker at numerous clinics. **Special Achievements:** Wrote a chapter on track and field in "Sports & Recreational Activities for Men and Women," January 1994. **Business Addr:** Teacher, University of Nevada, Depttartment of Physical Education, 4505 S Maryland Pkwy, Las Vegas, NV 89154, **Business Phone:** (702)895-4179.

MCDANIELS, JEANEEN J
Lawyer. **Personal:** Born Mar 29, 1960, Canton, OH; daughter of Albert H (deceased) and Nadine Williams. **Educ:** Cent State Univ, Wilberforce, OH, 1981; Univ Akron, Akron, OH, JD, 1984. **Career:** Co Prosecutor's Off, Canton, OH, asst prosecuting atty, 1985-86; City Prosecutor's Off, Canton, OH, asst prosecuting atty, 1986-90; Timken Co, Canton, OH, sr personnel & logistics analyst, 1990-91, indust rels rep, 1992-, Gam Roller Plant, mgr hr, 1992-; We'll Do It For You Inc, owner; pvt pract atty, currently. **Orgs:** Legal adv, Indian River Sch, 1987-92; vpres, 1988-90, pres, 1990-92; Stark Co Delta Sigma Theta Inc; pres, Mahogany Asn, 1988-90, treas, 1990-92; secy, Canton City Sch Found, 1990-92; secy, Canton Urban League, 1990-92. **Home Addr:** 2328 Raintree St NE, Canton, OH 44705, **Home Phone:** (330)492-4733. **Business Addr:** Industrial Relations Representative, Manager of human resources, Timken Company, 1835 Dueber Ave SW, Canton, OH 44706, **Business Phone:** (330)471-4131.

MCDANIELS, WARREN E
Firefighter, president (organization). **Educ:** Harvard Univ, John F Kennedy Sch of Government, fellow. **Career:** President, Firefighter (retired); New Orleans Fire Dept, firefighter, 1969-, superintendent, 1993-2002. **Orgs:** Chair, Nat Fire Protection Asn; Nat Fire Acad; Black Chief Officers Comt Int Black Prof Firefighters; past pres, Metropolitan Chiefs Comt. **Honors/Awds:** Metropolitan Fire Chief of the Year. **Special Achievements:** First African American Fire Chief in New Orleans. **Business Addr:** Chair, National Fire Protection Association, 1 Batterymarch Pk, Quincy, MA 02169-7471, **Business Phone:** (617)770-3000.

MCDEMMOND, DR. MARIE V
School administrator. **Educ:** Xavier Univ; Univ New Orleans; Univ Mass Amherst, PhD. **Career:** Fla Atlantic Univ, vpres, finance & COO, chief finance officer; Norfolk State Univ, pres, 1997-. **Orgs:** Pres, Southern Asn Col & Univ Bus Officers; bd mem, United Way & Urban League Hampton Rd; AAAS. **Honors/Awds:** Pioneer Award, Outstanding Prof Women Hampton Rd; Administrator of the Year, Va Asn Educ Off Prof; adv bd, Historically Black Col & Univ. **Special Achievements:** First African-American woman president of SACUBO. **Business Addr:** President, Norfolk State University, Office of the President, 700 Pk Ave, Norfolk, VA 23504, **Business Phone:** (757)823-8670.

MCDONALD, ALDEN J
Banker. **Personal:** Married Rhesa Ortique; children: 3. **Educ:** La State Univ Sch Banking, grad, attended; Columbia Univ, com banking mgt prog, attended. **Career:** Liberty Bank & Trust Co, New Orleans, LA, pres & chief exec officer, 1972-. **Orgs:** Chmn, New Orleans Chamber Com; FannieMae; Am Bankers Asn; Nat Bankers Asn, La Bankers Asn; bd mem, Stewart Enterprises Inc; bd mem, Entergy New Orleans Adv Bd; chmn, Lindy Boggs Med Ctr; Minority Alliance Capital; Ernest N Morial Convention Ctr; Port Authority New Orleans. **Honors/Awds:** R R Wright Presidential Award, Nat Banker's Asn; Whitney Young Award, Urban League Greater New Orleans; Civil Rights Award, Nat Dent Asn; Minority Suppliers Award, JC Penney; Business Hall of Fame, J Achievement; Loving Cup, Times Picayune, 2001; A G Gaston Lifetime Achievement Award, Black Enterprise, 2005. **Business Phone:** (504)240-5115.

MCDONALD, ANITA DUNLOP
Social worker. **Personal:** Born May 11, 1929, Morgantown, WV; daughter of William J (deceased) and LaFronia Chloe (deceased); married James J, Dec 27, 1950; children: Janice-Marie McDonald. **Educ:** WV State Col, BA 1951; WV Univ, MSW, 1953. **Career:** Social worker (retired); Syracuse Memorial Hosp, med soc worker, 1954-56; Family Serv Jamestown, social worker, 1975-79; Chautauqua Co Ment Health-Jamestown, psychiat social worker, 1980-94. **Orgs:** AAUW Jamestown Branch, 1968-; sec bd trustees, Jamestown Comm Col, 1969-78; pres bd dirs, YWCA, 1973-75; chmn pub affairs bd dirs, YWCA, 1984-85; Ebony Task Force, 1986-; Sch Community Rels Coun, 1989-91; adult leader, Emmanuel Baptist Church Youth Group, 1990-; pres, Chaut Co Am Baptist Women, 1990-; nominating comt, Girl Scouts, Jamestown, 1991-94; Jamestown Chapter, Links, Inc, 1993-, pres, 1998-; bd mgrs, Am Baptist NY State, 1994-; NY State American Baptist Church, 1994-00; pres, Ebony Task Force, 1995; pres, Ebony Task Force, 1995-02; vpres, Girl Scouts, 1996-01; treas, Emmanuel Baptist Church, 1996-; pres, Int Chap Links Inc, 1998-00; adv bd, Jamestown Community Learning Coun, 1998-03; adv bd, Safe House of Chautauqua County, 2000-02; fin secy & chmn trustee bd Emmanuel Bapt Church. **Honors/Awds:** Lifetime Achievement Award, Western Division New York State Chapter NASW, 1994; 3rd VP, Girl Scouts, Jamestown, 1996; Jamestown Woman of the Year, 1997. **Home Addr:** 40 W 22nd St, Jamestown, NY 14701.

MCDONALD, AUDRA ANN
Actor. **Personal:** Born Jul 3, 1970, Berlin, Germany; daughter of Stanley Jr (deceased) and Anna; married Peter Donovan, Sep 10, 2000; children: Zoe Madeline Donovan. **Educ:** Juilliard Sch, BM, 1993. **Career:** Films: Seven Servants, 1996; The Object of My Affection, 1998; Cradle Will Rock, 1999; It Runs in the Family, 2003; Tea Time with Roy & Sylvia, 2003; The Best Thief in the World, 2004; TV series include: "Great Performances", PBS, 1998; "Homicide: Life on the Street", 1999; "Having Our Say: The Delany Sisters' First 100 Years", 1999; "Annie", 1999; "Law & Order: Special Victims Unit", 2000; "Wit", 2001; "The Last Debate", 2000; "Mister Sterling", 2003; Partners & Crime, 2003; "Live from Lincoln Center", 2005; "The Bedford Diaries", 2006; "Kidnapped", 2006-07; A Raisin in the Sun, 2008; "Grey's Anatomy", 2009; "Private Practice", 2007-09; Narration: The Music Instinct: Science and Song, 2009. **Honors/Awds:** American Theater Wing, Tony Antoinette Perry, Best Featured Actress, 1994; Outer Critics Circle, Outer Critics Circle Award, Best Actress, 1994; Drama Desk, Best Supporting Actress, 1994; Theater World, Outstanding New Talent in a Musical; Tony Award for Best Supporting Actress in a Play, 1996; La Ovation Award, 1996; Ragtime, Tony Award, 1998; Tony Award for Portrayal of Ruth Younger in "A Raisin in the Sun", 2004; Nominated for Tony award for playing Lizzie Curry in "110 in the Shade", 2007; Nominated for Emmy Award, 2008; Grammys Award, 2009; Nominated for Image Award, 2008, 2009. **Business Addr:** Actress, c/o William Morris Agency LLC, 151 El Camino Dr, Beverly Hills, CA 90212, **Business Phone:** (310)859-4000.*

MCDONALD, DR. CHARLES J.
Physician, educator. **Personal:** Born Dec 6, 1931, Tampa, FL; married Maureen; children: Marc, Norman & Eric. **Educ:** NC A&T Univ, BS, 1951; Univ Mich, MS, 1952; Howard Univ, MD, 1960. **Career:** Hosp St Raphael New Haven, intern, 1960-61, asst resident, 1961-63; Yale Univ, Sch Med, asst resident dermat, 1963-65; US Pub Health Serv, Spec Res Fel, Yale Univ Sch Med, fel & chief resident dermat, 1965-66; Yale Univ Sch Med, Yale-New Haven Med Ctr, instr, assoc physician, 1966-67, asst prof, asst attending physician med & pharm, 1967-68; Brown Univ Providence, RI, asst prof med sci, 1968-69, assoc prof, 1969-74; Roger William Hosp, head dermat, assoc chief med, 1968-97; Brown Univ, dermat prog dir, 1970, prof med sci, head subsect dermat, 1974-96, chmn, dept dermat, 1996-; RI Hosp, Dept Dermat, physician chief, 1997-. **Orgs:** New Eng Dermat Soc, Soc Investigative Dermat, Am Fed Clinical Res, Am Acad Dermat, Nat Med Asn; chmn, AAAS, secy dermat, 1973-75; RI Dermat Soc, Noah Worcester Dermat Soc, Am Soc Clinical Oncol, Dermat Found; Assoc Profs Dermatol; consult, Nat Inst Arthritis Metab & Digestive Dis; consult, RI State Dept Health; consult, Providence Health Ctrs Inc; former chmn, Health Task Force, RI Urban Coalition; former mem, Govs Conf Health Care Cost; mem & bd dir, vpres, pres, RI Div Am Cancer Soc, 1969-80; bd, Nat Am Cancer Soc, 1983-; vpres & pres elect, Nat ACS, 1997-98, pres, 1998-99; mem bd trustees, Citizens Bank Providence, RI; Alpha Omega

Alpha, Med Soc; vpres & pres, New Eng Dermat Soc, 83-85; mem & bd dirs, Am Acad Dermat, 1986-90; Nat Inst Gen Med Scis, Pharmaeological Scis Review Comt, 1978-82; FDA Dermat Adv Comt, 1970-75; Nat Inst Arthrites, Musculoskeletal & Skin Disease, Nat Adv Bd, 1992-95; Noah Worcester Dermat Soc, bd dirs, 1983-86; Providence Pub Library, bd dirs, 1987-, secy, 1990-96, chair nominating comt, 1990-96; residency review comn, Accreditation Coun Grad Med Educ,1991-97, vice chair, 1995-97; Assoc Prof, bd dirs, 1991-95; Howard Univ, bd trustees, 1993-, chair, Med Affairs, 1994-98; chair, bd advisors, 1997-; Rhode Island Commodores, 1990-; pres elect, Am Dermat Asn, 2002-03; Sigma Xi; Dermat Soc, New England. **Honors/Awds:** Highest Academic Achievement Award, Col Med, Howard Univ; First Annual Distinguished Service Award, Hosp Assoc RI; Distinguished Alumni Award, Col Med, Howard Univ, 1983; Honorary MS, Brown Univ, 1970; Certified Am bd Dermat, 1966; National Division Award, Am Cancer Soc; St. George Medal, Am Cancer Soc, 1992; The Best Doctors in America, 1992, 1994, 1997, 2001, 2002; Eric Zwerling Memorial Lecturer & Outstanding Dermatology Professor, Nat Med Asn, 1987; WW Keen Award, Brown Sch Med, 2002; RI Black Heritage Soc Award, Med & Community Affairs, 2005. **Special Achievements:** Published more than 100 articles on Dermitology. **Military Serv:** USAF, major, 4 yrs. **Business Addr:** Chief Dermatologist, Rhode Island Hospital, Department of Dermatology, 593 Eddy St, Providence, RI 02903.*

MCDONALD, DR. CURTIS W. See Obituaries section.

MCDONALD, DARNELL ALI
Football player. **Personal:** Born May 26, 1976, Fairfax, VA. **Educ:** Kans State Univ. **Career:** Tampa Bay Buccaneers, wide receiver, 1999; Xtreme Football League, Los Angeles Xtreme, 2001; Xtreme Football League, BC Lions, 2001-02; Miami Dolphins, wide receiver, 2002; Calgary Stampeders, 2003-04, 2006; Winnipeg Blue Bombers, 2005. **Honors/Awds:** Rookie of the Year, 1999.

MCDONALD, DONZELL
Baseball player. **Personal:** Born Feb 20, 1975, Long Beach, CA. **Educ:** Trinidad Community Col; Yavapai Community Col. **Career:** NY Yankees, 2001; Kans City Royals, 2002; Acereros de Monclova, ctrfield, currently. **Honors/Awds:** All-Star Team, New York-Penn League, 1996.

MCDONALD, ELLA SEABROOK
Administrator. **Personal:** Born in Adel, GA. **Career:** Health & human serv specialist, currently; Richard Allen Ctr Life, exec dir, currently. **Orgs:** Black Agency Execs; Nat Asn Univ Women; The Schomung Corp; Black Adminr Child Welfare. **Honors/Awds:** Oni Award, Int Black Woman Cong, 1991; Woman of the Year, Black Health Res Found, 1992. **Business Addr:** Executive Director, Richard Allen Center on Life, 1872 Amsterdam Ave, New York, NY 10031, **Business Phone:** (212)862-7160.*

MCDONALD, GABRIELLE KIRK
Judge. **Personal:** Born Apr 12, 1942, St Paul, MN; married Mark T (divorced); children: Michael & Stacy. **Educ:** Boston Univ; Manhattan's Hunter Col; Howard Univ Law Sch, LLB, 1966. **Career:** Legal Def Fund NYC, staff atty, 1966-69; McDonald & McDonald, Houston, partner, 1969-79; Tex Southern Univ Houston, asst prof, 1970, adj prof, 1975-77; Univ Tex Houston, lectr, 1977-78; US Dist Ct, Houston, judge; Mathews Branscomb, atty; UN Gen Assembly, Int War Crimes, Trial Chamber II, fed judge, chief judge, currently. **Orgs:** Bd dir, Commun Serv Option Prog, Alley Theatre Houston; Nat Coalition 100 Black Women, ARC; trustee, Howard Univ, 1983-; bd visitors, Thurgood Marshall Sch Law Houston; Am Bar Asn; Nat Bar Asn; Houston Bar Asn; Houston Lawyers Asn; Black Women Lawyers Asn; Nat Asn Advan Colored People. **Special Achievements:** First African American appointed to a federal court in Texas.

MCDONALD, HERBERT G
Architect. **Personal:** Born Feb 11, 1929, Jamaica, NY; son of Priscilla A Young and Herbert C; married Debra H; children: Gail Louise & Cathy Allison. **Educ:** Howard Univ, BArch, 1953. **Career:** Gitlin & Cantor Architects, Wash, DC, assoc, 1959-60; Edwin Weihe, architect, 1960-62; Herbert G McDonald & Assoc, architect, 1962-65; McDonald & Williams AIA, architect, partner, 1965-90; McDonald Williams Banks Architects, architect, 1990-. **Orgs:** Dir, Lawrence Johnson Assocs, Wash, DC; vpres, dir, Barkingside Develop Inc, Bahamas; dir, secy, Davis Construct Co; adv, Independence Fed Savings & Loan, Wash, DC; Am Inst Archit; DC Coun Black Archit; Aircraft Owners & Pilots Asn; Omega Psi Phi Archit Clifton Ter Apts, 1969; DC Correctional Detention Facility, 1974; archit NECIP 1977; Lincoln Westmoreland Apts, 1972; DC Legis Comn Housing; dir, Nat Housing Rehab Assoc; vpres, dir, chief exec officer, H Bear Enterprises Inc. **Military Serv:** AUS Corps of Enginners, first lt, 1954-56. **Home Addr:** 4243 Blagden Ave NW, Washington, DC 20011, **Home Phone:** (202)829-2343. **Business Addr:** Architect, McDonald Williams Banks Architects, 7705 Georgia Ave NW, Washington, DC 20012, **Business Phone:** (202)291-5103.

MCDONALD, JASON ADAM
Baseball player. **Personal:** Born Mar 20, 1972, Modesto, CA. **Educ:** Univ Houston; Sacramento City Col. **Career:** Oakland Athletics, outfielder, 1997-99; Texas Rangers, 2000. *

MCDONALD, JEFFREY BERNARD
Executive. **Personal:** Born Oct 12, 1952, Benham, KY; son of Nathan and Orya Jr; children: R Malik. **Educ:** Ky State Univ, BSBA, 1976; Boston Univ, MBA, 1978. **Career:** Monsanto, supvr, internal audit, 1977-87; Ralston Purina, dir, financial serv, 1987. **Orgs:** Nat Asn Black Accountants; MBA Asn; Internal Audit Asn; Cash Mgt. **Special Achievements:** Fluent in Spanish. **Military Serv:** US Marine Corps, sgt, 1970-72.

MCDONALD, JON FRANKLIN
Educator. **Personal:** Born Jun 28, 1946, Jackson, MS; son of Ruby Tripplet and Charles; married Mary Ann Davies, Jan 18, 1972; children: Gabriel Charles & Beau Richards. **Educ:** Kendall Sch Design, cert, 1969; San Francisco Art Inst, MFA, 1972. **Career:** Spung buggy Works, asst animator, 1974-75; Every woman's Village, teacher, 1977-79; Kendall Col Art & Design, Grand Rapids, MI, prof, 1980-. **Orgs:** Visual arts adv Frauenthal Ctr Performing Arts, Muskegon, MI, 1986-89; comm mem, Mayor's Adv Comm Art/Grand Rapids, 1989-90; artist-in-residence, Grand Haven Pub Sch, 1989-90. **Honors/Awds:** Ellen Hart Bransten Scholarship, San Francisco Art Inst, 1970-72; One Man Show in Congressional Offices, Washington, DC, 1986; Best of Show in the Festival of the Arts, Grand Rapids, 1997; Docents Award, W Mich Reg, Muskegon Mus Art, 2002. **Special Achievements:** Moscow/Manhattan Connection, 48 paintings travelled in USSR & USA 1989-91. **Business Addr:** Professor of Visual Communication, Kendall School of Design, 17 Fountain St, Grand Rapids, MI 49503-3102, **Business Phone:** (616)451-2787.

MCDONALD, KATRINA BELL
Educator. **Personal:** Born Nov 5, 1961, Denison, TX; daughter of Gladys Murrel Bell; married Arnold Ray McDonald, Aug 6, 1994; children: Jordan Ray Bell-McDonald. **Educ:** Mills Col, Oakland, CA, BA, written commun, 1983; Stanford Univ, MA, applied commun res, 1984; Univ Calif, MA, 1990, PhD, sociol, 1995. **Career:** San Francisco Newspaper Agency, mkt res analyst, 1984-85; Calif State Univ, res analyst, 1985-88; Univ Calif, res asst, 1988-90, 1992, teaching asst, 1991-93, assoc instr, 1990-94, 1996, 1998, 2000; Johns Hopkins Univ, from instr to asst prof, 1994-2000, assoc prof, 2000-; Johns Hopkins Population Ctr, new prog develop grant, 2000-01. **Orgs:** Minority fel, Am Sociol Asn, 1989-92, dissertation fel, 1992-93; Am Sociol Asn; Population Asn Am; Asn Black Sociologists; Nat Asn Advan Colored People; Hopkins Black Fac & Staff Asn. **Honors/Awds:** William E Johnson Award, Univ Calif, 1993; Distinguished Faculty Award, Stud Coun Schs Arts, Sci & Engineering, Johns Hopkins Univ, 1999. **Special Achievements:** Thesis: "Sister-Friends: Re-Creating Maternal Support in the African-American Community" Primary Teaching and Research Areas: African American families; African-American women; intersections of race, class, and gender; sociology of the family; women's psychosocial health; qualitative research methods; introductory social statistics & numerous publications. **Business Addr:** Assistant Professor, The Johns Hopkins University, Department of Sociology, 3400 N Charles St 540 Mergenthaler Hall, Baltimore, MD 21218, **Business Phone:** (410)516-7624.

MCDONALD, LARRY MARVIN
Executive, association executive. **Personal:** Born Mar 12, 1952, Louisville, KY; son of Charles S and Angie V; married Denise Harker (divorced 1989); children: Angie M, Ebeni M & Denisha I. **Educ:** Univ Ky, Lexington, Ky, BBA, 1974; Univ Louisville, Louisville, Ky, MBA, 1992. **Career:** Humana Inc, Louisville, Ky, equipment specifier/buyer, 1982-85, mgt develop intern, 1985-87, personnel mgr, 1987-89, dir equal employ opportunity, affirmative action, 1989; The Lincoln Foundation Inc, pres, currently. **Orgs:** Vice chmn, trustee bd, First Congregational Methodist Church, 1981-; Steering Comt, Black Achievers Orgn, 1983-89, 1992-; pres, Steering Comt, Proj BUILD, 1985-; bus consult, Proj Bus, Jr Achievement, 1986-88; bd mem, BETA Adv Bd, Univ Louisville Speed Scientific Sch, 1986-; bd mem, Classical Roots, 1990; bd mem, Louisville Urban League, 1990-; bd mem, Louisville Orchestra, 1992-. **Honors/Awds:** Black Achiever, Chestnut St YMCA, 1983; Outstanding Volunteer of the Year, YMCA Greater Louisville, 1986; honoree, Leadership Louisville, 1987; Golden Apple Award, Jefferson County Pub Sch, 1988; Hon Vol, Spirit Louisville Found Inc, 1989; Citizen of the Month, Louisville Jaycees, 1989; Night of 1,000 Stars, Cathedral Heritage Found, 1995; Whitney M Young, Jr. Equal Employment Opportunities Awards, 1997; Diversity Role Model, Humana Inc, 1999; Appreciation Award, Whitney M Young Job Corp Ctr, 2002; Honorary Award, Lincoln Inst Kentucky Alumni Asn, Inc, 2003. **Business Addr:** President, The Lincoln Foundation Inc., 200 W Broadway Suite 500, Louisville, KY 40202, **Business Phone:** (502)585-4733.

MCDONALD, MARK T.
Lawyer. **Personal:** Born Jun 20, 1935, Henderson, TX; married Babrielle Kirk; children: Mark T, Jr, Micheal K, Stacy Frances. **Educ:** Prairie View A & M Col, BA, hon, 1956; Tex Southern Univ, LlB, 1962. **Career:** McDonald & McDonald Atty Law, atty, 1962; Legal Serv Div OEO, consult, 1965; Tex Southern Univ, asst prof law, 1964-70; Prarie View A & M Col, asso prof Polit sci, 1963-64. **Orgs:** State Bar Tex; Am Bar Asn; Asn Trial Lawyers Am; Nat Bar Asn; Am Judicature Soc; Nat Asn Criminal Def Attys; Tex Trial Lawyers Asn; Houston Bar Asn; Houston Trial Lawyers Asn; Nat Advan Asn Colored People; Houston Bus & Prof Men's Club; Am Civil Liberties Union, Houston; YMCA Century Club.

MCDONALD, MIKE
Football coach, football player. **Personal:** Born Jun 22, 1958, North Hollywood, CA. **Educ:** Univ Southern Calif. **Career:** Univ Southern Calif, grad asst coach, 1980, 1981; Burroughs (CA) High Sch, asst coach, 1982, 1983, 1985; Los Angeles Rams, linebacker, 1984, 1986-91; Detroit Lions, 1992. **Honors/Awds:** NFC Championship Game, post-1989 season.

MCDONALD, DR. R. TIMOTHY
School administrator. **Personal:** Born Sep 29, 1940, Pittsburgh, PA; married Beverly Clark; children: Lawana, Monica, Lanita & Patrick. **Educ:** Oakwood Col, BS, elementary educ, 1963; Atlanta Univ, MS, educ admin, 1968; Univ Miami, EdD, 1972. **Career:** School administrator(retired); AL A&M Univ, prof educ, 1972-78; Oakwood Col, vpres develop, 1975-78; Barber Scotia Col, vpres acad affairs, 1978-79; OH State Univ, develop officer, 1979-83; Seventh-day Adventist Church, dir educ; oakwood col, vpres; univ east africa, baraton, kenya, pres, currently. **Orgs:** Bd mem, Columbus Mental Health Asn, 1980-83; consult, Higher Educ Asns, 1975-; proposal writer-reader Fed Govt, 1975-; bd mem, Columbia Union Col, 1983-. **Honors/Awds:** Higher Education Fellowship, Fed Govt, 1969-72; Title III Grant, Fed Govt, 1972-78; Special Service Award, OH State Univ, 1981.

MCDONALD, RAMOS
Football player. **Personal:** Born Apr 30, 1976, Dallas, TX. **Educ:** Univ NMex, Phys educ. **Career:** Minn Vikings, defensive back, 1998-99; San Francisco 49ers, 1999; NY Giants, 2000; Oakland Raiders, corner back, 2001; Seattle Seahawks, corner back, 2002. *

MCDONALD, RICARDO MILTON
Football player. **Personal:** Born Nov 8, 1969, Kingston, Jamaica. **Educ:** Univ Pittsburgh. **Career:** Football player (retired); Cincinnati Bengals, linebacker, 1992-97; Chicago Bears, 1998-99.

MCDONALD, TIMOTHY
Football player, football coach, executive. **Personal:** Born Jan 26, 1965, Fresno, CA; married Alycia; children: Timothy Jr, Tevin & Taryn. **Educ:** Univ SC, bus admin. **Career:** Football player (retired), Football coach, owner; St Louis Cardinals, defensive back, 1987; Phoenix Cardinals, 1988-92; San Francisco 49ers, 1993-99; Edison high sch, coach; World Sports Cafe, owner, currently; Malloch Elem Sch, 2001-03. **Business Phone:** (559)650-4949.

MCDONALD, WILLIAM EMORY
Engineer, air force officer. **Personal:** Born Mar 9, 1924, Detroit, MI; son of Emory S and Willie Mae Burrill; widowed; children: Varnell, William, Jeannette. **Educ:** Univ Mich, BS, 1950. **Career:** Air Force officer; engineer (retired); Pub Lighting Comn, jr engr, 1950-54; Detroit Arsenal, electronic scientist, 1954-57; Farrara Inc, chief proj engr, 1957-58; Chrysler Missile, design engr, 1958-59; Rockwell Int, sr proj engr, 1959-72; NC Cent Univ, phys plant dir, 1972-91. **Orgs:** Pres bd, Urban Ministries, 1970-71; Alpha Phi Alpha Fraternity; secy & treas, S Eastern Reg Asn Phys Plant Admin, 1980-89; mem bd adjustment, City Durham, NC, 1981-91; NC Synod Coun, Evangelical Lutheran Church Am, 1988-; secy, treas, Asn Phys Plant Admin, 1989-91; Congressional Gold Medal, US Congress, 2007. **Honors/Awds:** Meritorious Serv Award SE Reg Assn of Physical Plant Admin 1987. **Special Achievements:** First black officer Southeastern Regional Association of Physical Plant Administration. **Military Serv:** USAF, 1944-46. *

MCDOUGALL, GAY J
Lawyer. **Educ:** Bennington Col, BA, 1969; Yale Univ Law Sch, JD, 1972; London Sch Econs & Polit Sci, LLM, pub int law, 1978. **Career:** Debevoise, Plimpton, Lyons & Gates Law Firm, New York, assoc, 1972-74; Bd Corrections, Minimum Stand Unit, New York, staff atty, 1976-77; Off Dep Mayor Criminal Justice, New York, assoc coun, 1979-80; Southern Africa Proj Lawyer's Comt Civil Rights Under Law, dir, 1980-94; Comn Independence Namibia, 1989; UN Human Rights Bodies, independent expert, 1997-2001; Int Human Rights Law Group, Global Rights Headquarters, DC, exec dir, 1994-2006; Wash Col Law, Am Univ, Wash, DC, distinguished scholar residence, 2006-. **Orgs:** Gen coun, Nat Conf Black Lawyers, New York, 1975-76; UN Comn Human Rights, 1996-2000; DC Bar Asn; South Africa's 16-mem Independent Electoral Comn; CARE Int, 1994-2003; fel, MacArthur Found, 1999; chair, UN Comt Elimination Racial Discrimination; Am Soc Int Law, 2003-; Robert F. Kennedy Memorial Found, 2004-; UN Independent Expert Minority Issues, 2005-; Global Fund Women, 2005-; AfriCare, 2005-; Equal Rights Trust, 2006-; Open Soc Inst Sub-Bd Women's Rights, 2006-. **Honors/Awds:** MacArthur Fellows Award, 1999; Hon Degree, City Univ NY Law Sch, 2000; Lamplighter Award Human Rights, 2003; Hon Degree, Univ Georgetown Law Ctr, 2006. **Special Achievements:** First black student to integrate Agnes Scott College in Decatur, Georgia; first United Nations Independent Expert

on Minority Issues. **Business Addr:** Distinguished Scholar in Residence, American University, Washington Collage of Law, 4910 Bldg Suite 125, Washington, DC 20016, **Business Phone:** (202)274-4387.

MCDUFFIE, DEBORAH
Composer, music producer. **Personal:** Born Aug 8, 1950, New York, NY; daughter of Thomas and Nan Wood; children: Kijana Saunders & Kemal Gasper. **Educ:** Western Col Women, Oxford, OH, BA, music, 1971. **Career:** McCann-Erickson Advert, New York, NY, music producer & composer, 1971-81;Mingo Group, New York, NY, music dir, 1981-90; Strachan McDuffie CommunsInc, New York, NY, exec vpres & creative dir, 1990-92; Jana Prods Inc, NewYork, NY, pres & chief exec officer, 1981-; Ritz Theatre & Lavilla Mus,ritz voices, prod mgr, artistic dir, currently, Ritz Voices, founder; Jacksonville Mass Choir, Art dir, currently. **Orgs:** Bd dir, NY Urban League, 1990-; Am Soc Composers, Authors & Publ, 1980; AmFedn Musicians, 1978; Screen Actors Guild, 1982; Am Fedn TV-Radio Artists,1977-; chairperson, Fine Arts Dept Paxon Sch Adv Studies, 2001-; exec dir,NE Fla Found Arts Inc, Jacksonville, FL, 2004-; Jacksonville Sch Music. **Honors/Awds:** Clio Award, 1981; Ceba Awards, Advertising Black Consumer Mkt, 1982-90;Telly Awards, 1986; Award Music & Entertainment, Onyx Mag, 2004. **Business Phone:** (904)504-2763.

MCDYESS, ANTONIO KEITHFLEN
Basketball player. **Personal:** Born Sep 7, 1974, Quitman, MS. **Educ:** Univ Ala, attended 1997. **Career:** Denver Nuggets, forward-center, 1995-97, 1998-02; Phoenix Suns, 1997-98, 2004; New York Knicks, forward, 2003-04; Detroit Pistons, forward, 2004-09.San Antonio Spurs, 2009-. **Honors/Awds:** NBA All-Rookie First Team, 1996; All-NBA Third Team, 1999. *

MCEACHERN, D HECTOR
Banker. **Personal:** Born in Fayetteville, GY; married Brenda Britt; children: Todd, Natashia, Dorian & Brandon. **Educ:** Fayetteville State Univ, BA, Eng, 1969; NC State Univ, grad study psychol, 1971; mgt study, supvry mgt, Am Mgt Asn, 1977; Interaction Mgt Instr Cert; Duke Univ, Mgr Develop. **Career:** Fayetteville Observer Newspaper, news reporter, 1968-70; Cumberland County Ment Health Ctr, social worker, 1970-72; Mt Vernon Psychiat Clin, psychiat social worker, 1972-74; Texfi Indust Inc, plant personnel mgr, 1974-78, group personnel dir, 1978-90; Wachovia Bank & Trust Co, sr vpres, mgr personnel serv, 1980-87; Wachovia Bank NC, dir personnel, sr vpres, group exec, chief diversity officer, 2001-. **Orgs:** Bd mem, United Way NC, 1992; bd mem, Work Family Resource Ctr, 1992; bd mem, Leadership Winston-Salem; former chmn, Bank Admin Inst, Human Resources Comn; bd trustees, Fayetteville State Univ; bd dir, Winston-Salem Urban League; Leadership Winston-Salem, Bi-Racial Comt; found bd mem, Fayetteville State Univ Alumni Asn; former chmn, C Home Soc. **Home Phone:** (336)287-1988. **Business Addr:** Executive Vice President, Chief Diversity Officer, Wachovia Corporation, Wachovia Bankl, PO Box 3099, Winston-Salem, NC 27150, **Business Phone:** (336)732-5654.

MCEACHERN-ULMER, SYLVIA L
Government official. **Personal:** Born Mar 24, 1934, New York, NY; married Joseph Ulmer; children: Patricia McEachern & Brian McEachern. **Educ:** Rutgers Extension Sch, cert regist municipal clerk, 1977. **Career:** Government Official (retired); City Paterson, city clerk, 1971-89; Bd Educ Passaic Co Voc & Tech Sch, comnr, pres, 1986-87; Cecile Dickey Ctr, human resource mgr. **Orgs:** NJ State Municipal Clerk's Asn, 1972-; Int Municipal Clerk's Asn, 1980-; Nat Black Caucus Sch Bd, 1980-; pres, Passaic Co Municipal Clerk's Asn, 1984; vpres, 1984-86, pres, 1986-87, NJ County Voc Sch Bd. **Honors/Awds:** Testimonial Dinner, 1975; Honored Mother, Women Active Comm Affairs, 1983; Salute to Black Men & Women spec award, Comm Black Hist Month, 1984; Christian Service Award, Calvary Baptist Church, 1983, Canaan Baptist Church, 1983; plaques from various comm groups. **Special Achievements:** First African American Municipal Clerk in the State of New Jersey.

MCEACHIN, JAMES
Novelist, actor, playwright. **Personal:** Born May 20, 1930, Rennert, NC; married Lois Davis; children: Felechia McEachin & 2 children. **Career:** Actor, Author, Director, Producer; Films: Uptight!, 1968; If He Hollers, Let Him Go!, 1968; True Grit, 1969; Hello Dolly!, 1969; The Undefeated, 1969; Play Misty for Me, 1971; Buck & the Preacher, 1972; The Ground star Conspiracy, 1972; Short Walk to Daylight, 1972; Fuzz, 1972; Every Which Way But Loose,1978; Sudden Impact, 1983; 2010, 1984; Double Exposure, 1993; Reveille, 2004; TV Series: "Mannix", 1968; "Hawaii Five-O", 1968; "That Certain Summer", 1972; "Escape", 1972-73; "Tenafly", 1973-74; "Murder, She Wrote", 1984-85; "Matlock", 1986-95; "Perry Mason: The Case of the Poisoned Pen", 1990; "Perry Mason: The Case of the Silenced Singer", 1990; "Perry Mason: The Case of the Glass Coffin", 1991; "Perry Mason: The Case of the Maligned Mobster", 1991; "Perry Mason: The Case of the Ruthless Reporter",1991; "I'll Fly Away", 1991-92; "Perry Mason: The Case of the Fatal Framing", 1992; "Perry Mason: The Case of the Heartbroken Bride", 1992;"Perry Mason: The Case of the Reckless Romeo", 1992; "Perry Mason: The Case of the Wicked Wives", 1993; "Perry Mason: The Case of the Killer Kiss", 1993; "Perry Mason: The Case of the Skin-Deep Scandal", 1993; "Perry Mason: The Case of the Telltale Talk Show Host", 1993; "Willie, Sworn To Vengeance", 1993; "Diagnosis Murder", 1993-94; "Perry Mason: The Case of the Lethal Lifestyle", 1994; "Perry Mason: The Case of the Jealous Jokester", 1995; "City of Angels", 2000; "First Monday", 2002; Novels: Tell Me a Tale: A Novel of the Old South, 1996; Farewell to the Mockingbirds, 1997; The Heroin Factor, 1999; Say Goodnight to the Boys in Blue, 2000; The Great Canis Lupus, 2001; Pebbles in the Roadway: Tales & Essays, Bits & Pieces, 2003; USAR, army res ambassador, 2005-08; ambassador emir, currently; VOICES: A Tribute to the American Veteran 2005; Old Glory DVD 2007; Above the Call; Beyond the Duty, A one-man, two-act play, 2008. **Orgs:** Military Order of the Purple Heart, Am Legion. **Honors/Awds:** Benjamin Franklin Award, Publishers Mkt Asn, 1998; Best Fiction Award, Farewell to the Mockingbirds; Distinguished Achievement Award, Morgan State Univ, 2001; honored by the Maryland House Delegates, 2001; Benjamin Franklin Award, 2005; Best Audio for VOICES: A Tribute to the American Veteran, 2003; Audio Book of the Year for Pebbles in the Roadway: Essays and Tales, Bits and Pieces, Foreword Magazine, 2007; Best Film Short for Old Glory, GI Film Festival; American Airlines Honorary Captain of the Flagship Liberty; Military Order of the Purple Heart; George Washington Medal of Merit, 2007; Veterans Brain Trust Award, 2008. **Special Achievements:** Silver Star, multiple-wound Purple Heart Veteran of the Korean War. USAR Ambassador Emeritus. **Military Serv:** AUS, 1947-53; Silver Star; Purple Heart. **Business Addr:** Actor, C/o Rharl Publishing Group, 16161 Ventura Blvd PMB Suite 550, Enconia, CA 91436, **Business Phone:** (818)519-5453.

MCELRATH-FRAZIER, WANDA FAITH
Security guard, musician, artist. **Personal:** Born Jan 11, 1959, Sylacauga, AL; daughter of Danfort McElrath (deceased) and Josephine L McElrath; married James, Apr 28, 2000. **Educ:** Troy State Univ, BME, 1983. **Career:** Anchor Club, sr dir, 1976; Avondale Mills, winder operator, 1977-82; Troy State Univ, stud secretarial asst dean fine arts & arts & sci, 1977-82; self-employed, pvt trumpet instr & performer, 1983-, karate instr, cert, 1988-, airbrusher, 1988-; security officer, 1994-; Ala Sports Festival, co-tournament dir, currently; Sylacauga Parks & Recreation, instr, currently. **Orgs:** Prin's Adv Comt, 1971-72; Sr Scholastic Soc, 1976, 1977; US Yoshukai Karate Asn, 1976; founding pres, The Troy State Karate Club-Dojo, 1978-82; Women Band Dir's Nat Asn, 1979; pres, Music Educrs Nat Conf, 1980-81; elected regional secy, Tau Beta Sigma Nat Honorary Band Sorority, 1981-83; pledge class pres, Alpha Phi Omega Nat Serv Fraternity, 1981, social chair, 1981; Tau Beta Sigma, 1983; Alpha Phi Omega, 1983-; secy, Nat Asn Advan Colored People, 1991-; secy, S Talladega County Amateur Radio Soc, 2002-04; Sylacuga Alliance Family Enhancement; Am Radio Relay League; Talladega Radio Amateur Club; bd mem, Troy State Alumni Band Asn. **Honors/Awds:** All American Music Hall of Fame, 1976; Band Scholarship, Troy State Univ, 1977; Security Officer of the Month, 1995; Outstanding Musician Award, Nat Asn Advan Colored People; Appreciation Award, Troy State Alumni Band. **Special Achievements:** First African-Am voted in Anchor Club, 1976; Miss Sylacauga Pageant, first black to enroll, 1976; first African-Am president-elect of the Troy State Alumni Band Asn, 1991, pres, 1993-95. **Home Addr:** PO Box 462, Sylacauga, AL 35150, **Home Phone:** (205)249-0508. **Business Addr:** Instructor, Sylacauga Parks & Recreation, 2 W 8th St J Craig Smith Community Ctr, PO Box 1245, Sylacauga, AL 35150, **Business Phone:** (256)249-8561.

MCELROY, CHARLES DWAYNE, SR.
Baseball player. **Personal:** Born Oct 1, 1967, Port Arthur, TX; son of Herman C and Elizabeth Simmons Mayfield; married Shari Lannette Cooper, Jan 19, 1991. **Career:** Baseball player (retired); Philadelphia Phillies, pitcher, 1989-90; Chicago Cubs, 1991-93; Cincinnati Reds, 1994-96; Anaheim Angels, 1996-97; Chicago White Sox, 1997; Colorado Rockies, 1998-99; New York Mets, 1999; Baltimore Orioles, 2000-01; San Diego Padres, 2001; Houston Astros, pitcher, 2004. **Orgs:** Professional Baseball Players Asn, 1986-. *

MCELROY, COLLEEN J.
Educator, writer. **Personal:** Born Oct 30, 1935, St Louis, MO; daughter of Ruth C Long and Jesse D; divorced; children: Kevin D, Vanessa C. **Educ:** Kansas State Univ, Manhattan KS, BS, 1958, MS, 1963; Univ Wash, Seattle WA, PhD, 1973. **Career:** Rehabilitation Inst, Kansas City MO, chief, Speech & Hearing Serv, 1963-66; Western Washington Univ, Bellingham WA, asst prof speech, 1966-74; Univ Wash, Seattle, WA, supvr, EOP Composition, 1972-83, dir, Creative Writing, 1984-87, prof Eng, 1983-. **Orgs:** Writers Guild Am E, 1978-, Dramatists Guild, 1986-, PEN Writers, 1989-; Auth's Guild, 1989-; Writer's Union, 1989-. **Honors/Awds:** NEA Creative Writing Fellowship for Poetry, 1978; Fiction 1st place, Callalvo Mag, 1981; Poetry 1st place, Cincinnati Poetry R, 1983; Creative Writing Residency, MacDowell Colony, New Hampshire, 1984, 1986; Before Columbus American Book Award, 1985; Women of Achievement, Theta Sigma Phi, 1985; Creative Writing Residency Yugoslavia, Fulbright Fellowship, 1988; Washington State Governor's Award for Fiction and Poetry, 1988; NEA Creative Writing Fellowship for Fiction, 1991; Rockefeller Fellowship to Bellagio Inst, Lake Como, Italy, 1991; DuPont Distinguished Scholar in Residence, Hollins Col Va, 1992; Fulbright Research Fellowship, Madagascar, 1993; Arts Am, Jordan & Morocco, 1996. **Special Achievements:** The Wild Gardens of the Loup Garou, 1983; Queen of the Ebony Isles, 1984; Jesus and Fat Tuesday, 1987; Follow the Drinking Gourd, 1987; Driving Under the Cardboard Pines, 1990; What Madness Brought Me Here, 1990; A Long Way from St Louie, 1997; Travelling Music, 1998; Over the Lip of the World: Among the Storytellers of Madagascar, 1999. **Business Addr:** Professor, University of Washington, Dept Eng, A101 Padelford Hall, PO Box 354330, Seattle, WA 98109.*

MCELROY, GEORGE A.
Journalist. **Personal:** Born May 25, 1922, Houston, TX; son of Hugh G and Philomena Woodley; married Lucinda Martin McElroy, Nov 27, 1951 (deceased); children: Madeline Johnson, Toni, Linda, Kathleen, Sherri. **Educ:** Tex Southern Univ, BA, 1956; USAF Systs Command, Hon Doc, 1966; Univ MO-Columbia, MA, 1970. **Career:** Houston Independent Sch Dist, jour teacher, 1957-69; Univ Houston, asst prof commun, 1970-76; Houston Post, columnist, 1971-78; Tex Southern Univ, assoc prof jour, 1976-89; Houston Informer, publ & ed. **Orgs:** Chap adv, Soc Prof Journalists, 1979; publicist 9th & 10th Cavalry Asn; lay adv, Tenn State Univ Catholic Newman Ctr; publicity chair United Negro Col Fund & Houston; Nat Asn Black Journalists; Nat Newspaper Publ Asn; Tex Press Asn; Omega Psi Phi; Press Club Houston; pres, Houston Breakfast Club, 1990. **Honors/Awds:** Amigo de Guatemala Award, govt Guatemala, 1977; Lynn C Eusan Serv Award, Prof Amateur Boxing Asn, 1979; Cert Recognition Tenn State Univ, Ex-Students Asn, 1985; Tenn State Univ Relays Serv Award, Tex Southern Univ, 1985. **Military Serv:** USN, steward 1st class, 1940-46; USAF, Information Specialist, 1950-52. *

MCELROY, DR. LEE A
Executive, educator. **Personal:** Born Mar 19, 1948; son of Lee A Sr and Ada Mae Ford. **Educ:** Univ Calif, Los Angeles, BA, 1970; Univ Southern Calif, MS, 1974; Univ Houston, TX, PhD, 1984. **Career:** Santa Monica Schs, Santa Monica, CA, coach & teacher, 1971-76; S Parks High Sch, Beaumont, TX, vice prin, 1976-81; Univ Houston, TX, assoc athletic dir, 1981-88; Univ Dist Columbia, athletic dir, vpres & stud affairs, 1988-89; Calif State Univ, Sacramento, dir inter athletics, 1989-; Bd Dirs, Sacramento Sports Med, 1989-; Bd Dirs, Comstock Mag, 1990; Univ Albany, Dept Athletics & Recreation, vpres athletic admin & dir, currently. **Orgs:** Pub Rels, Rotary, 1989-; Bd Dirs, Doug Williams Found, 1988-; pres, Nat Asn Acad Advs, 1986; consult, Am Inst Res, 1987. **Honors/Awds:** Pub Rels, Rotary, 1989-; bd dirs, Doug Williams Found, 1988-; pres, Nat Asn Acad Adv, 1986; consult, Am Inst Res, 1987; Nat Asn Collegiate Directors Athletics, vpres, 2005-06, pres, 2006-07. **Special Achievements:** An Analysis of the Relationships among Control Variables, Orgn Climate, Job Satisfaction & Turnover/Absenteeism in the Pub Schs, Univ of Houston, 1984. **Business Addr:** Vice President for Athletic Administration & Director, University at Albany, Department of Athletics and Recreation, 1400 Wash Ave, Albany, NY 12222, **Business Phone:** (518)442-2562.

MCELROY, LEELAND
Football player. **Personal:** Born Jun 25, 1974, Beaumont, TX; married Vinita. **Educ:** Tex A&M Univ. **Career:** Football player (retired); Ariz Cardinals, running back, 1996-97; Tampa Bay Buccaneers, 1998; Denver Broncos, 1999; Indianapolis Colts, running back, 1999.

MCELROY, DR. NJOKI
Executive, educator, writer. **Personal:** Born in Sherman, TX; daughter of J D Hampton and Marion Hampton; married Clenan C McElroy, Mar 1946 (deceased); children: Ronald, Phillip, David, Marian, Harry & Larry. **Educ:** Xavier Univ, BS, 1945; Northwestern Univ, MA, 1969, PhD, 1973. **Career:** Northwestern Univ, adj prof, 1970-; Black Fox Enterprises Ltd, pres, 1972-; storyteller, performer, 1980-; Southern Methodist Univ, adj lit, 1987-, prof master Lib arts, currently; DFW Int Community Alliance, story teller, currently; Author: "Black Journey," play on African-American history, 1975; "The Gods Were Watching Them," play, Northwestern Univ, 1991; Common Bond, 1991; "La Bakaire," play, Northwestern Univ, 1992; Spiritual Walks, 1993. **Honors/Awds:** Travel Grant, Ford Found, 1972; Cultural Affairs, City Dallas, 1992 & 1993. **Business Addr:** Adjunct in Literature, Professor of the Master of Liberal Arts, Southern Methodist University, 6425 Boaz Lane, PO Box 750181, Dallas, TX 75205, **Business Phone:** (214)768-2000.

MCELROY, RAYMOND EDWARD
Football player. **Personal:** Born Jul 31, 1972, Bellwood, IL; married Michelle; children: Miray, Ramiah, Jamaria & Janae. **Educ:** Eastern Ill Univ. **Career:** Indianapolis Colts, defensive back, 1995-98; Chicago Bears, 2000; Detroit Lions, 2001-02; Chicago Bears, team chaplain, currently.

MCELVANE, PAMELA ANNE
Insurance executive, publisher, chief executive officer. **Personal:** Born Sep 4, 1958, Stockton, CA; daughter of Charlene Penny.

Educ: Univ Calif, Berkeley, BA, Social Welfare & Sociol, 1981, MBA, 1983, MA,public policy. **Career:** US Dept Labor, contract mgr, 1980-82; Gelco-Cti Leasing Co, lease admin &sys supervisor, 1982-84; Allstate Ins Co, market mgr, 1984-88; Chubb Groupof Ins Cos, dept mgr & off, 1988-92; Hanover Ins Co, dir personal lines, 1992-; P & L Group Ltd, ceo, cur; DRi, ceo, cur; P & L Publ Group, ceo &publ, cur. **Orgs:** Newsletter editor, 1984-86, exec bd mem, 1984-87, co-chair std affrs,1987, mgr editor, SFMBA, 1987; coordr Bay Blk Profiles 1984-; bd mem,newsletter editor, vpres, UCB Alumni Assoc, 1985-; recruiter Big Bros,1985-86; organizer March of Dimes, 1986; pres, UCB Alumni Asn, 1988-89;Cinti MBA, 1989-90; chapter commun dir, Mentor, 1989-91; InsProfessionals, 1990-95; MBA, Boston Chapter, vpres opers, 1995; NBMBAA,conference pub rels dir, 1995. **Honors/Awds:** Coach of the Year, Madeliene Sch, 1984-86; Merit Award, Big Brothers,1984; Rosalie Stern Outstanding Comm Achiev UC Berkeley, 1986; Community Serv Award, March of Dimes, 1986; Mentor Award, Cincinnati Public Schools, 1989-90; Outstanding MBA, Unti Chapter, 1992; Media Ambassador Award,Board room bound, 2005. *

MCEWEN, MARK
Television show host. **Personal:** Born Sep 16, 1954, San Antonio, TX; son of Alfred and Dolores; married Judith Lonsdale; children: Maya Alexis. **Educ:** Univ Md, Col Park, attended 1976. **Career:** WWWW-FM Radio, Detroit, MI, music dir & disc jockey, 1978-80; WLUP-FM Radio, Chicago, IL, res dir & disc jockey, 1980-82; WAPP-FM Radio, New York, NY, disc jockey, 1982; WNEW-FM Radio, New York, NY, disc jockey, 1982-86; CBS, Morning Prog, weatherman, 1987, CBS This Morning, weatherman, music ed, 1987-92, entertainment ed, 1992-96, co-anchor, 1996, Early Show, weather & entertainment reporter, 2000-02; WKMG Local 6, First News, News at Noon, anchor, currently. **Orgs:** Nat Asn Black Journalists. **Honors/Awds:** Electronic Media Journalist of the Year, Country Music Asn, 1992. **Special Achievements:** Listed as one of the 10 Most Trusted Newspeople in TV Guide, Feb 1995, has covered almost every imaginable television event including the Oscars, the Cannes Film Festival, the Golden Globe awards, the Grammy awards, and the Country Music Association awards. **Business Addr:** Anchor, WKMG-TV, 4466 John Young Pkwy, Orlando, FL 32804, **Business Phone:** (407)521-1200.

MCEWING, MITCHELL DALTON
School administrator. **Personal:** Born May 16, 1935, Jacksonville, TX; married Verta Lee Ellis; children: Andre R & Veronica Lee. **Educ:** Wiley Col Marshall, Tx, BS, 1958; Tex Southern Univ, degree credits summers, 1964; N Tex State Univ, MEd, 1973, degree credits, 1975; Tex State Bd Examiners Prof Counrs, Licensure Prof Counr, 1982. **Career:** School administrator (retired); Bethlehem United Comn Ctr, athletic dir, 1958-63; IM Terrell Jr & Sr High Sch, teacher & asst coach, 1963-67, teacher & head coach, 1968-69; Tarrant Cty Jr Col, counr & instr, 1971-75, dean of students develop serv. **Orgs:** Soc worker Bethlehem United Comt Ctr, 1971; vpres, United Com Ctrs, Ft Worth, 1971-73; bd mem, Adv Coun Coun Stud N Tex State Univ, 1981-82; Phi Delta Kappa; Coun Black Am Affairs; secy & treas, E St Paul Bapt Church. **Honors/Awds:** Coach of the Year, IM Terrell High Sch, 1959-69; Dedicated Serv, The Dukes, 1975-76; Serv Awd Phi Theta Kappa, 1984. **Military Serv:** AUS, Spec 4, 3 years; Berlin Serv Award, Second Team Army Quarterback, 1959; Hon discharge from the Army, 1960. **Home Addr:** 3445 Denbury Dr, Fort Worth, TX 76133, **Home Phone:** (817)292-0941. *

MCFADDEN, REV. ARTHUR B.
Clergy, religious educator. **Personal:** Born Jan 5, 1940, Jacksonville, FL; married Marjesta Sanders; children: Anntoinette, Renee. **Educ:** Stillman Col, BA, 1962; Johnson C Smith Univ, BD, 1965; Eden Theol Sem, STM; D Min, 1970, 1973; St Louis Univ, attended 1971; Southern Ill Univ, attended 1984. **Career:** Calvary Presbyterian Church, Detroit, MI, asst minister, 1965-66; Butler Mem Church, Youngstown, OH, minister, 1966-68; Third United Presbyterian Church, St Louis MO, minister, 1968-; McKendre Col, adj prof, 2000-. **Orgs:** Alumni bd dir, Stillman Col, 1973-79; adj prof, St Louis Univ, 1974-82; bd consult, Black Clergy Eden Theol Sem, 1976-80; Omega Psi Phi Frat; bd dir, King Fanow Ment Health Ctr, 1985-; clergy support comm St Louis OIC; Men Organized Against Juvenile Crime. **Honors/Awds:** Community Serv, St Louis Univ; 25th Anniversary of Ordination to the Christian Ministry, 1990; Distinguished Alumnus of Johnson C Smith Theol Sem, 1996. **Special Achievements:** Co-author: "Together. A Biblically based Evangelism Resource with Particular Focus on African-American Youth in the Presbyterian Church and Community," 1993; Moderator of Presbytery of Giddings-LoveJoy, 1995. **Home Addr:** 7223 Ravinia Dr, St Louis, MO 63121. **Business Addr:** Minister, 3rd United Presbyterian Church, 2426 Union Blvd, St Louis, MO 63113.*

MCFADDEN, BERNICE L
Writer. **Personal:** Born Sep 26, 1965, Brooklyn, NY; daughter of Robert Lewis McFadden and Vivian Hawkins-McFadden; children: R'yane, Azsa. **Educ:** Lab Inst Merchandising, NY; Fordham Univ. **Career:** Books: Sugar, 2000; The Warmest December, 2001; This Bitter Earth, 2002; Loving Donovan, 2003; Camilla's Roses 2004; Nowhere Is A Place, 2006; As Geneva Holliday:Groove 2005; Fever 2006; Heat 2007; Seduction 2008. **Honors/Awds:** Honor Award, Black Caucus, AL, 2000; Best New Author of the Year, Go On Girl Book Club, 2000; Best Mainstream Fiction Award, Golden Pen Award, 2001; Best New Author Award, Golden Pen Award, 2001; Zora Neale Hurston Award, 2002. Black Caucus, AL 2004; MacDowell Colony Fel, 2005. **Special Achievements:** Pulitzer Prize nominations & Hurston Wright Award Nominations: The Warmest, 2001; Nowhere is a Place, 2006. **Business Addr:** Writer, Plume Books, 375 Hudson St 3rd Fl, New York, NY 10014.

MCFADDEN, CORA (CORA COLE-MCFADDEN)
Government official, city council member. **Personal:** Born Oct 3, 1945, Durham, NC; divorced; children: Lori Yvette & Larry Everette. **Educ:** NC Cent Univ, BA, MA; NC Chapel Hill Univ, post grad. **Career:** City council member, Government official (retired); Durham Co Dept Social Serv, social worker, 1969-76, foster care supvr, 1976-78; City Durham, community serv, supvr, 1978-81, affirmative action dir, 1981-; Durham city coun mem, 2001-. **Orgs:** NC Asn Black Social Workers, 1972; bd mem, Volunteer Servs Bur, 1980-83; bd mem, YWCA, 1983-84; state coordr, Am Asn Affirmative Action, 1985; Durham County Coun Women, 1985; pres, Ebonettes Serv Club, 1985; past bd dir, Durham Chapter, NC Symphony; past bd dir, Vol Serv Bur; chair, past chairwoman, Durham Community Martin Luther King Steering Comt; past secy, vice chairwoman & chair, Durham County Dem Party State Exec Comt, NC Dem Party; Zeta, Eastern Star, Golden Circle; vice chair, Nat Asn Advan Colored People, Durham Br; human develop comt, Nat League Cities; youth comt, NC League Cities; People's Alliance; Old Farm Neighborhood Asn; Durham Community Martin Luther King Steering Comt; polit comt, Durham Comt Affairs Black People. **Honors/Awds:** Founders Award, NC Asn Black Social Workers 1984. **Business Addr:** City Council Member, City Durham, 101 City Hall Plz, Durham, NC 27701.

MCFADDEN, ERNEST
Philanthropist. **Personal:** Married Patricia McFadden. **Educ:** Marist College, Bachelor of Science. **Career:** Heineken USA Inc., Industry Government Affairs Manager; New York Department of Labor. **Orgs:** National Blacks in Government; NAACP; Congressional Black Caucus Foundation. **Home Addr:** 000150. *

MCFADDEN, GREGORY L.
Physician. **Personal:** Born Jun 18, 1958, Tallahassee, FL; son of Robert L and Alma L Johnson; married Cynthia Williams, Dec 12, 1987; children: Desiree. **Educ:** Florida A&M Univ, BS, 1980; Howard Univ Col Med, MD, 1984. **Career:** Orlando Regional Med Ctr, resident physician, 1984-87; Cigna Health Plan, staff physician, 1988-. **Orgs:** Am Col Physicians; Am Med Asn; Alpha Phi Alpha Fraternity Inc; diplomate Nat Bd Med Examiners. **Honors/Awds:** Nat Dean's List 1980; Physicians Recognition Award, Am Medical Asn, 1987. **Home Addr:** 4308 Ellenville Pl, Valrico, FL 33594. *

MCFADDEN, JAMES L.
Educator. **Personal:** Born Nov 9, 1929, Darlington, SC; married Gertha Moore; children: Dionne Jametta. **Educ:** Claflin Col, AB, 1954; NY Univ, MA. **Career:** Morris Col, Art instr, 1954-56; Orangeburg City Sch chair person Jr High Sch, art teacher, 1954-70; Art & Music Texts, 1969; SC State Col, Orangeburg, prof art, 1970-. **Orgs:** SC Educ Asn; Nat Educ Asn; Nat Art Educ Asn; NY Univ Alumni Asn; Am Legion Post No 210, 1954; Edisto Masonic Lodge No 39 AF & M, 1966; Shriner Jeddah Temple No 160, 1966; treas, SC Art Educ Asn, 1971-75; Orbg Alumni Chapter KAY; adv, Alpha Lambda Chapter KAY; Attend William Chapel AME Church; Nat Asn Advan Colored People. **Honors/Awds:** South eastern Province Achievement Award, Kappa Alpha Psi Fraternity, 1950; Outstanding Leadership & Dedication Award, Alpha Lambda Chap Kappa Alpha Psi Fraternity, 1976. **Military Serv:** AUS, 1951-55. **Business Addr:** Professor, South Carolina State College, PO Box 1962, Orangeburg, SC 29115.

MCFADDEN, NATHANIEL JAMES
School administrator, government official, senator (u.s. federal government). **Personal:** Born Aug 3, 1946, Philadelphia, PA; married Rachel Tift; children: Nathaniel Jr, Byron & Devon Dodson. **Educ:** Morgan State Col, BA, 1968; Morgan State Univ, MS, 1972. **Career:** Baltimore City Pub Schs, teacher, 1968-75, dept head, 1975-82, 1987-88, prin, 1979-82, coordr, 1988-94, work-based learning mgr, 1997-; Sojourner-Douglass Col, coordr community affairs, 1985-88; City Coun Baltimore, coun mem, 1982-87; State Md, senator, 1995-; Pro Tem, pres, 2007-; Spec Joint Comt Pensions, Senate Chair, 2008-. **Orgs:** Asn Study Negro Life & Hist Baltimore City Chap, 1980-82; Eastern Dist Police Community Rels Coun Baltimore, 1982-; adv bd, Johns Hopkins Med Plan, 1985-; Optimist Club East Baltimore, 1985-; asst record keeper, Baltimore Alumni Chap, Kappa Alpha Psi Fraternity, 1989-; bd mem, Eastside Democratic Org, 1975-; Urban League; NAACP; Alpha Kappa Mu, 1968-; Kappa Delta Pi, 1968-; Phi Alpha Theta, 1967-; Gamma Theta Upsilon, 1963-; Alpha Phi Omega, Nat Serv Fraternity, Baltimore Area Alumni; RAIDE-EOP Inc, bd dirs; 100 Black Men Md Inc; 1 to 1 The Baltimore Mentoring Partnership, bd dir, 1997-; Youth Fair Chance, adv bd, 1994-; Juvenile Justice, adv bd, Baltimore City, 1994-; Comt 100 Associated Black Charities, 1994-; Lakewood Chase Improvement Asn, 1982-; Eastside Neighborhood Asn, 1983-; Eastern Dist Police Community Rel Coun, 1982-; E Baltimore Women's League, 1974-; Governor's Task Force on Afr Am Entrepreneurship Baltimore City, 1996-99; Task Force on Charitable Giving, 1996-; Small Bus Develop Ctr Netwok, adv bd, 1997; Privatization Adv Panel, Mass Transit Admin, 1997-98; Partnership Policy Coun Block Grants, 1998; Task force End Smoking MD, vchair, 1999; Joseph Fund Bd, 1999-; Coun Mgmt & Productivity, 2000-; State Coun Cancer Control, 2001-. **Honors/Awds:** Legislator Recognition Award, Maryland Asn of Counties, 2002. **Home Addr:** 3224 Belair Rd, Baltimore, MD 21213-1228. **Business Addr:** Senator, Miller Senate Office, Miller Senate Office Bldg Rm 422 11 Bladen St, Annapolis, MD 21401.

MCFADDEN, SAMUEL WILTON
Physician. **Personal:** Born Jun 17, 1935, Newark, NJ; married Nancy A Peters; children: Jonathan, Jesse. **Educ:** NY Univ Col, BA, 1956; Univ Basel, Switzerland, MD, 1964. **Career:** BU Sch Med, pediatric radiologist/asst prof, 1971-77; Child Abuse & Neglect Unit, chief, 1973-75; Roxbury Comprehensive Comm Hlth Ctr, pediatrician, 1973-77, chief radiol, 1974-77; Eunice Kennedy Shriver Med Ctr, chief radiol, 1974-83; Tobry Hosp, radiologist, 1977-80, chief radiol, 1980-; Wareham Radiol Assoc Inc, pres. **Orgs:** Pres New Eng Med Soc, 1975-77; Bay State Peer Standards Rev Orgn, 1976; treas, New Eng Med Soc, 1977-78; Am Col Radiol, Nat Med Asn; bd dir, Mass Radiol Soc; sch comn, Ore Reg HS, 1981-; pres, M & L Staff Toby Gen Hosp, 1981-83; med advr, Registry Motor Vehicles, 1983-; nat secy, Syst Radiol Nat Med Assoc, 1987; med advr, Marion UNA; Am Acad Pediatrics. **Business Addr:** President, Wareham Radiology Associates Inc, 295 Delano Rd, Marion, MA 02738.*

MCFADDIN, THERESA GARRISON
Teacher, counselor. **Personal:** Born Jul 23, 1943, Philadelphia, PA; daughter of Alvin Prunty and Barbara Campbell Prunty; widowed; children: Roslyn Ballard & Theresa McFaddin. **Educ:** Fuller Theol Sem, MA. **Career:** Motown Records, Los Angeles, CA, writer, producer; Christian Broadcasting Network, Va Beach VA, writer, producer; Terri McFaddin & Friends, Pasadena, CA, teacher & counr. **Honors/Awds:** Grammy Award, 1986; Citizen of the Year, Zeta Phi Beta Sorority, 1989. **Business Phone:** (626)794-5402.

MCFALL, MARY
School administrator, president (organization). **Personal:** Born Aug 30, 1938, San Angelo, TX; children: Jeannette & Owen III. **Educ:** San Angelo Jr Col, Honor Grad, 1955; Univ Tex, BA Honor Grad, 1957; Univ Tex, JD 1979. **Career:** Soc Security Adm, serv rep, 1965-66; Comm Action Agy, asst nghbr hd servs dir, 1967-69; Intercultural Devel S Meth Univ, dir, 1971-; Tarrant Co YWCA, br exec, 1969-71; Soc of Ethnic & Spec Studies, sec, 1975-; Tex Asn Black Personnel Higher Educ, co-founder 1st vpres conf coord, 1973-79; Tex Asn Black Personnel Higher Educ, pres, 1979-81. **Orgs:** Bd dirs, Family Guidance Asn, 1979-; Coalition Educ Black C; Tex Asn Col; Univ Stu Personnel Adm Goals Black Dallas Com, 1976-77; vpres, Minority Cultural Arts Asn, 1970-71; chmn, Am Civil Liberties Union Ft Worth Chap, 1968-70; Citizen's Planning Com Ft Worth, 1971; co-fdr Students for Direct Action Univ Tex; del Nat Students Asn, 1961; Alpha Kappa Alpha Sor. **Honors/Awds:** First Black Student Admitted to San Angelo Col; 1st Black Student to Receive BA from Univ of TX Austin; Listed Golden Profiles of Dallas Ft Worth, 1980.

MCFARLAND, ANTHONY DARELLE
Football player. **Personal:** Born Dec 18, 1977, Winnsboro, LA. **Educ:** La State, BS, bus mgt. **Career:** Tampa Bay Buccaneers, defensive tackle, 1999-2006; Indianapolis Colts, 2006-07; free agent, currently. **Honors/Awds:** Super Bowl champion (XXXVII, XLI).

MCFARLAND, ARTHUR C
Lawyer. **Personal:** Born Feb 5, 1947, Charleston, SC; married E Elise Davis; children: Kira Jihan & William Joseph. **Educ:** Univ Notre Dame, BA, Govt, 1970; Univ Va, JD, 1973. **Career:** Pvt Pract, atty, 1974-; City Charleston SC, munic judge, 1976-78, chief munic judge, 1978-; McFarland & Assoc, atty, currently; Knights Peter Claver, Inc, chief exec officer, currently. **Orgs:** Nat Am Bar Asn, 1974-; Nat Conf Black Lawyers, 1974-; Am Judges Asn; NBA Judiciary Coun, 1976-; bd dir, Trident United Way, 1977-; pres, Robert Gould Shaw Boys Club, 1978-; Chas SC NAACP Exec Com, 1978-; pres, Charleston Bus & Prof Asn, 1983-85; Charleston Waterfront Park Comt, 1983-; Charleston Neighborhood Legal Assistance Prog Bd Dir, 1984-86; Nat advocate, Knights Peter Claver, 1994-; SC Bar; Am Bar Asn. **Honors/Awds:** Earl Warren Fel NAACP Legal Defense Fund, 1973-74; Earl Warren Fel NAACP Legal Defense & Educ Fund, 1973-77. **Business Addr:** Chief Executive Officer, Knights of Peter Claver, Inc, 1825 Orleans Ave, New Orleans, LA 70116, **Business Phone:** (504)821-4225.

MCFARLAND, OLLIE FRANKLIN. **See Obituaries section.**

MCFARLAND, ROLAND C
Executive, television producer. **Personal:** Born Aug 13, 1940, Devern, TX; son of Booker and Ada McFarland; married Paulette,

Dec 4, 1982; children: Curtis McFarland & Roselyn Daniels. **Educ:** San Diego State Univ, BA, 1961. **Career:** ABC, sr ed, mgr broadcast standards; FOX Broadcasting Co, dir broadcast standards, 1993, vprea broadcast standards & practices, sr vpres, 1993-. **Orgs:** Chair, Image Award, NAACP, 1988-90; vpres & advisor, Nat Comt Youth Opportunity; adv, C Now; adv, Media Scope; adv, Ctr Commun Police, UCLA; adv, SAG, media awareness committee; Chrysalis Found Homeless; CA Dance Ctr; Boys & Girls Club Am; San Diego Nat & IntlFilm Fest; dir's coun pub rep, NIH. **Special Achievements:** OH Asn Broadcasters, keynote speaker; Mich Advertising Council, keynote speaker; Business for Social Responsibility, 5th Annual Conf, discussion panel moderator. **Business Addr:** Senior Vice President, FOX Broadcasting Company, 10201 W Pico Blvd, Los Angeles, CA 90035, **Business Phone:** (310)369-1000.

MCFARLIN, EMMA DANIELS
Government official. **Personal:** Born Nov 14, 1921, Camden, AR. **Educ:** Philander-Smith Col, Little Rock, BA, 1950; Univ Wis-Madison, MS, 1961; US Int Univ San Diego, PhD, 1975. **Career:** Low Rent Housing Proj Little Rock Redevelop & Housing Authority, mgr, 1952-64; San Francisco Unified Sch Dist, teacher, 1964-65; US Dept HUD, spec rep, 1965-70; US Dept HEW, regional rep, 1970-73; Menlo Park, CA, asst city mgr, 1973-74; Off Mayor Los Angeles, spec asst, 1974-75; Univ Calif, Los Angeles, asso prof, 1975-77; US Dept HUD, regional adminr, 1977; HUD, consult, currently. **Orgs:** Omicron Nu Nat Honor Soc, 1961. **Honors/Awds:** Emma McFarlin Day Award, City of Menlo Park, CA, 1974; Newsmaker Award,Nat Asn Media Women, 1975; Outstanding Serv & Achievement City Council Los Angeles, 1975. **Home Addr:** 4207 Enoro Dr, Los Angeles, CA 90009. **Business Addr:** Consultant, HUD, 4207 Enoro Dr, Los Angeles, CA 90008.*

MCFERRIN, BOBBY
Singer, actor, songwriter. **Personal:** Born Mar 11, 1950, New York, NY; son of Robert K Sr and Sara; married Debbie Lynn Green, 1975; children: Taylor John & Jevon Chase. **Educ:** Sacramento State Univ; Cerritos Col. **Career:** Singer, 1977-; Solo: Bobby Mc Ferrin, 1982; The Voice, 1984; Spontaneous Inventions, 1985; Elephant's Child, 1987; Simple Pleasures, 1988; How the Rhino Got His Skin/How the Camel Got His Hump, 1990; Medicine Music, 1990; Many Faces of Bird, 1991; Sorrow Is Not Forever, 1994; Paper Music, 1995; Bang! Zoom, 1997; Circle songs, 1997; Mouth Music, 2001; Beyond Words,2003; collaborations: The Just So Stories, 1987; Play, 1990; Hush, 1991; The Mozart Sessions, 1996; TV Series:, "For Our Children: The Concert ", 1993; "Sessions at West 54th", 1997; "In My Life", 1998; "VH-1 Where Are They Now?", 2000; "Great Performances", 2003. **Honors/Awds:** Best Jazz Vocal Performance, 1985; Best Vocal Arrangement for two or more voices, 1985; Best Jazz Vocal Performance, 1986; Best Jazz Vocal Performance, 1987; Best Recording for Children, 1987; Song of the year, Best Pop Vocal Performance, 1988; Best Jazz Vocal Performance, 1988; Best Jazz Vocal Performance, 1992. **Business Addr:** Singer, EMI-Manhatten, CEMA, 1750 N Vine St, Hollywood, CA 90028, **Business Phone:** (323)462-6252.

MCFERRIN, SARA ELIZABETH COPPER
School administrator, musician, educator. **Personal:** Born Sep 10, 1924, Washington, DC; daughter of Charles and Elizabeth; divorced; children: Robert & Brenda. **Educ:** Howard Univ, attended 1942; Univ Southern Calif, attended; California State Univ, Los Angeles, attended. **Career:** CBS-TV, Christmas specials; solo recitalist & oratorio soloist throughout USA; symphony soloist; New York City Ctr, Opera Chorus, soloist; Hollywood Greek Theatre Opera Chorus, soloist; Calif State Univ, Long Beach/ Nelson Sch Fine Arts, Canada, Pasadena City Col, Cerritos Col, teacher; Fullerton Col Music Dept, chmn voice dept, 1973-90; chmn, 1990-93; prof emer, currently; Univ Okla, Norman, Okla, vis prof voice, 1986. **Orgs:** Nat Asn Teachers Singing; Adjudicator Met Opera Western Region Auditions Calif, Ariz, Nev; Adjudicating Panels Vocal comp Southern Calif; San Francisco Opera, South California Opera Guild; bd assoc, Los Angeles Master Chorale Assoc; bd dirs, Pacific Chorale, Costa Mesa Coeducational comm. **Honors/Awds:** Staff of Distinction Award, Fullerton Col, 1993. **Special Achievements:** Appeared in films: Porgy & Bess, Elmer Gantry; Appeared in Television shows, "Lost in the Stars", "Troubled Island". **Business Addr:** Professor Emeritus, Fullerton College, 321 E Chapman Ave, Fullerton, CA 92832-2095, **Business Phone:** (714)992-7000.

MCGARITY, WANE
Football player. **Personal:** Born Sep 30, 1976, San Antonio, TX. **Educ:** Univ Tex. **Career:** Football player (retired); Dallas Cowboys, wide receiver, 1999-2001; New Orleans Saints, 2001; Calgary Stampeders, 2002-04; Winnipeg Blue Bombers, 2005.

MCGATHON, CARRIE M
Nurse. **Personal:** Born Feb 3, 1936, Mendenhall, MS; daughter of Lena Hays Smith (deceased) and James Smith Sr; married John A, 1954; children: Berlinda, Brenda & John Reginald. **Educ:** Dillard Univ, BSN, 1964; Col Holy Names, PHN, 1970; Jackson State Univ, MEd, 1978. **Career:** Naval Regional Med Ctr Oakland, Calif, clin supvr Ob/Gyn, 1975-80; Health Care Serv Inc, dir/ adminr; Alameda Community Hosp, Alameda, Calif, RN, labor & delivery, 1980-; COGIOC, lic, evangelist, 1980-; Healthforce, case mgr, nursing dept; Corp Regist Nurses, staff ltd; pvt pract, nursing, currently. **Orgs:** Calif Nurses Asn, 1964-; Dillard Alumnus, 1964-; NAACOG, 1970-; Biblesway CIGOGC, 1975-; Black Nurses Asn Greater E Bay; Coun Black Women Female Executives; Order Eastern Star 49A; Heroines Jericho. **Honors/Awds:** Commendation, Juris Doctoral Bishop EE, Cleveland, COGIOC; JD Bishop Larry J McEathon, Woman of Boldness Award. **Special Achievements:** Certified herbalist, nutritional consultant, iridologist, 1994. **Military Serv:** USN, nurse rep, 1967-80; Merit Award, 1975. **Home Addr:** 2653 76th Ave, Oakland, CA 94605. **Business Addr:** Nurse, 2653 76th Ave, Oakland, CA 94605, **Business Phone:** (510)569-8790.

MCGAUGHY, WILL
Government official, administrator. **Personal:** Born Feb 23, 1933, Plantervills, MS; divorced; children: Felix Xavier. **Educ:** Mildred Louis Bus Col, attended 1954. **Career:** Citizen Participation, dir, 1969-72, 1973-75; Will McGaughy Health Ctr, dir, 1972-73; Health Educ & Welfare, dir, 1975-78; E St Louis Township Citizen Prog, 1978-81; East St Louis Township, asst town super, 1981-89, supvr, 1989-; bd comnr, 2000. **Orgs:** Dir, Dawson Manor Housing, 1954-; Adv, Nat Asn Advan Colored People Youth Coun, 1966; pres, Metro E Health Serv, 1970-72; dir, Proj Life, 1970-73; precinct comt man, 1971-86; chmn, E St Louis Transit Bd, 1975-; vpres, City Cent Dem, 1978-; city bd mem, Spec Asst to Mayor, E St Louis, 1978-; pres, Southend Neighborhood Improvement Asn, 1982-; taxation comt chmn, St Clair County Bd, 1991; Am Red Cross. **Honors/Awds:** Outstanding Leadership Award, E St Louis, 1975; Politician of the Yr, 1976; Citizen Participation Workshop, 1977; Resolution Commendation, Mayor E St Louis, 1980; Arson Awareness, 1981; Man of the Yr, E St Louis Monitor Newspaper, 1982; Dr Martin Luther King Jr Drum Major Award, GEMM Ctr, 1991. **Military Serv:** AUS, corp, 3 yrs. **Home Addr:** 1402 S H St, East St Louis, IL 62207. **Business Addr:** Supervisor, East St Louis Township, 1210 State, East St Louis, IL 62201.*

MCGEE, ADOLPHUS STEWART
School administrator. **Personal:** Born Jan 29, 1941, Dos Palos, CA. **Educ:** Coalinga Col, BA, 1960; CA State Univ, BA, 1963; CA State Univ, MA, 1970; CA State Univ, MA, 1972. **Career:** Union High Sch Dist Sacramento, teacher math, head track football coach, 1963-66; Luther Burbank High Sch Sacramento, teacher math sci, track & football coach, 1966-68; Sacramento City Unified Sch Dist, asst, supt, 1968-70; inter-group relations adv, 1969-70; Sacramento Sr High Sch, prin, 1970-. **Orgs:** Jount Legislative Comn Educ Goals & Evaluations; Joint Task Force Goals & Evaluation State CA, 1972-; pres, Sacramento Sr High Sch Mem Scholar Fund, 1970-; Asn CA Sch Adminstrs; chmn, Minority News Media Joint Task Force Urban Coalition, 1969-71; YMCA; NAACP; Blue Key; Phi Delta Kappa; Omega Chi Delta. **Business Addr:** 2315 34 St, Sacramento, CA 95817.

MCGEE, BENJAMIN LELON
Executive. **Personal:** Born Feb 18, 1943, Booneville, MS; married Rose M Jackson; children: Ivy, Ben II, Brian, Holly. **Educ:** AR AM&N Col Pine Bluff AR, Agronomy Sci, 1967; Memphis State Univ, 20 hrs, 1975. **Career:** Dept of Agr ASCS, compliance supr, 1967-75; GMAC, credit rep, 1976-77; Liquor Ctr, owner, 1977-. **Orgs:** Bd mem, Marion Sch Dist, 1975-; vice chmn, bd trustees AR State Univ, 1977-; state comt man Dem Party, 1979-; bd trustees, AR State Univ Jonesboro. 1980; bd trustees, AME Ch. **Business Addr:** Owner, The Liquor Center, 3107 E BROADWAY, West Memphis, AR 72301.

MCGEE, BUFORD LAMAR
Football player. **Personal:** Born Apr 16, 1960, Durant, MS. **Educ:** Univ Miss, BS, bus, 1984. **Career:** Football player (retired); San Diego Chargers, 1984-86; Los Angeles Rams,running back, 1987-91; Green Bay Packers, fullback & running back, 1992. *

MCGEE, COL. CHARLES EDWARD
Military pilot, executive. **Personal:** Born Dec 7, 1919, Cleveland, OH; married Frances E Nelson (deceased); children: Charlene McGee Smith, Ronald A & Yvonne G. **Educ:** Columbia Coll, MO, BA, 1978. **Career:** Military Pilot, Executive (retired): Army Air Corps/US Air Force, colonel, 1942-73, 44th Fighter Bomber Squadron, Philippines, comdr, 1951-53, 7230th Support Squadron, Italy, 1961-63, 16th TRS, 1967-68, Richard-Gebaur ARB, Mo, 1972; ISC Financial Corp, dir of real estate & purchasing, 1973-78, vice pres real estate, 1974-78; City of Prairie Village, asst dir of administration, 1979; City of Kansas City, Downtown Airport, mgr, 1980-82. **Orgs:** Life mem, Tuskegee Airmen Inc, 1972-; life mem, Military Order World Wars; life mem, Air Force Asn; life mem, Alpha Phi Alpha; life mem, NAACP; Boy Scouts Am; Boy's & Girls Clubs Greater Kans; Christian Church; Aviation Adv Comn, Kans City; dir, Municipal Assistance Corp, Kans City. **Honors/Awds:** Elder Statesman of Aviation, Nat Aeronaut Asn, 1998; Brig Gen Noel F Parrish Award, Tuskegee Airmen Inc, 1988; Boy Scouts of America, Silver Beaver Award. **Military Serv:** Highest Legion of Merit, 1968, 1973; Army Commendation Medal, Air Force Commendation Medal with cluster, Presidential Unit Citation, Korean Presidential Unit Citation, the Hellenic Republic WWII Commemorative Medal, the French Legion of Honor; Distinguished Flying Cross, three times; Bronze Star; numerous air medals.

MCGEE, EVA M
Educator. **Personal:** Born Jun 13, 1942, Nashville, AR. **Educ:** AM & N Col, BS, 1963; Univ Ark Fayetteville, MEd, 1971. **Career:** AM & N Col Pine Bluff, Ark, educ secy, 1963-69; Univ Ark, instr, dir instnl advan, 1969-86; Broadcast Media, dir; Univ Ark Pine Bluff, Assoc Vice Chancellor, Planning & Instnl Res, Interim Media Rel dir, currently. **Orgs:** Treas, Nat Bus Educ Asn, 1970-72, pres, 1972-74, st coordr, 1974-; secy, Ark Bus Ed Asn, 1972-73, pres, 1973-74; Ark Col Tchrs Educ & Bus; Sthrn Bus Educ Asn; Pine Bluff Alum Chap Delta Sigma Theta; bd dir, Pine Bluff OIC, 1973-74; Nat Coun Negro Wmn; Jeff County Adv Comn, Blk Adptn, 1973-74. **Honors/Awds:** Listed Leaders Black Am, 1973-74; named Outstanding Educator Am, 1974-75; Leadership Award, Pine Bluff Alum Chap Delta Sigma Theta, 1973; Delta of the Year, 1974. **Business Addr:** Interim Media Relations Director, University of Arkansas Pine Bluff, 1200 N Univ Dr, Mail Slot 4789, Pine Bluff, AR 71601.

MCGEE, GLORIA KESSELLE
Nurse, psychotherapist. **Personal:** Born Jul 12, 1954, Monrovia, Liberia; daughter of Andrew Belton and Izola Lewis; married Waddell, Feb 16, 1992. **Educ:** Wayne State Univ, BS, 1977; Univ Mich, MS, 1981. **Career:** Lafayette Clin, clin nurse specialist, 1981-87; Va Med Ctr, Oklahoma City, head nurse, 1987-90; Va Med Ctr, Lincoln, NE, assoc chief nurse, 1990-; Inner Visions Coun Ctr Inc, bd pres, 1990-. **Orgs:** Sigma Theta Tau Int, 1980-; bd, Nat Asn Advan Colored People, 1980-; Am Nurses Asn, 1980-; Univ Mich Alumni Asn, 1981-; Lincoln Human Rights Comn, comnr, 1991-; bd, Am Red Cross, 1991-; Altrusa Int, 1992-; secy & treas, Am Veterans Alliance Auxiliary Inc. **Honors/Awds:** Special Advancement for Achievement, Va Med Ctr, 1988, Special Advancement for Performance, 1991; Woman of the Year, Inner Visions Counseling CTR Inc, 1991. **Special Achievements:** "Reducing and Controling Absenteeism in Nursing," 1991. **Business Addr:** Associate Chief Nurse, Veterans Affairs Medical Center, 600 S 70th Mail Symbol 118, Lincoln, NE 68506, **Business Phone:** (402)489-3802.

MCGEE, HENRY W
Educator. **Personal:** Born Dec 31, 1932, Chicago, IL; son of Henry W and Attye Belle Truesdale; married Victoria; married Alice (divorced); children: Henry III, Kevin, Byron, Gregory & Erik. **Educ:** NW Univ, BS, 1954; DePaul Univ, JD, 1957; Columbia Univ, LLM, 1970. **Career:** Gottlieb & Schwartz, law clerk, 1955-56; Ming & Leighton Moore, law clerk, 1957-58; Cook County, asst state atty, 1958-62; Jesmer & Harris, Chicago, Ill, atty, 1962-66; US Off Econ Opportunity, Great Lakes Region, Regional Legal Serv dir, 1966-67; Univ Chicago, Law Sch Ctr, Studies Criminal Justice Legal Serv, Youth Action Res Proj, legal dir, 1967-68; Univ Calif, Los Angeles Sch of Law, from asst prof to prof, 1969-94, Grad Prog, dir, prof emer law, 1994-; Fordham Univ Sch Law, vis prof law, 1992, 1993 & 1994; Seattle Univ Sch Law, prof law, 1994-, Mexico & Latin Am Initiatives, dir, currently. **Orgs:** Nat Bar Asn; Nat Hispanic Bar Asn; consult, City Poverty Comn, London, Eng, 1973; draftsman, Nat Conf Bar Examiners, 1974-95; consult & lectr, Urban Planning USIS Italy, 1976; US Equal Employment Opportunity Comn; Am Arbitration Asn; Asn Am Law Sch Teaching Clin. **Honors/Awds:** Blue Key Nat Honor Frat, 1957; Fulbright professor, Univ Madrid, 1982; Pub numerous articles. **Business Addr:** Professor of Law, Mexico/ Latin American Initiatives Director, Seattle University School of Law, 900 Broadway 12th Ave, Seattle, WA 98122.

MCGEE, HENRY WADSWORTH
Executive, president (organization). **Personal:** Born Jan 22, 1953, Chicago, IL; married Celia; children: 1. **Educ:** Harvard Univ, Cambridge, MA, BA, 1974; Harvard Bus Sch, Cambridge, MA, MBA, 1979. **Career:** News week Mag, NY & Wash, reporter, 1974-77; HBO, NY, mgr film acquisition, 1979-80, Family Programming Dept, mgr, 1982-83, Enterprises, dir, 1983-85, Home Video, vpres, 1985-88, sr vpres programming, 1988-95, Home Video, pres, 1995-; Time-Life TV, dir prog acquisitions, 1980-81; Cine max, dir budgeting & planning, 1981-82. **Orgs:** Bd dirs, New 42nd St Inc, 1990-; pres, Film Soc Lincoln Ctr; dir, Black Filmmaker Found; pres, Alvin Ailey Dance Theater Found. **Honors/Awds:** Professional Achievement Award, Harvard Business School African-American Alumni Assn, 2004. **Special Achievements:** One of New Yorks Top 100 minority executives by Crains New York Business, 1998; Black Enterprise Magazine named him one of the 50 most powerful African-Americans in the entertainment business, 2002,2007. **Business Addr:** President, HBO Home Video, 1100 Avenue of the Americas, New York, NY 10036, **Business Phone:** (212)512-1000.

MCGEE, JAMES M
Association executive, president (organization). **Career:** Nat Alliance Postal & Fed Employees, pres, currently; credit union, chmn, currenly. **Business Addr:** President, National Alliance of Postal and Federal Employees, 1628 11th St NW, Washington, DC 20001, **Business Phone:** (202)939-6325.

MCGEE, JAMES MADISON
Association executive. **Personal:** Born Dec 22, 1940, Nashville, TN; married Mary Francis Wilkins; children: Andrea, LaSandra, James Jr. **Educ:** Fisk Univ, attended 1960; Mid S Sch Electronics Nashville, 1970. **Career:** Nat Alliance Postal & Federal Employees, Treas, 1968-72, vice pres, 1976-89, pres, currently; US Postal Service, clerk, 1965, LSM operator, 1967, LSM instr trainer, 1973-76. **Orgs:** TN Voters Counc, 1967-80; NAACP, 1968-80; Benevolent Protective Order Elks TN, 1970-80. **Honors/Awds:** HJ Johnson Honor Soc, 1955-59. **Military Serv:** USMC, PFC, 1961-65. **Business Addr:** President, National Alliance of Postal and Federal Employee, 1628 11th St NW, Washington, DC 20001, **Business Phone:** (202)939-6325.*

MCGEE, DR. JOANN
Counselor, executive director, educator. **Personal:** Born in Buffalo, NY; daughter of Rev Cephus Jr and Verlene Freeman. **Educ:** Elmira Col, NY, BA, MS, reading educ, 1992; Univ Scranton, MS, couns, 1987; Columbia Univ Teachers Col, MA, EdD, adult & continuing educ, 1987-92; Bank St Col Edu, MEd, special educ, 1992. **Career:** SUNY, Binghamton, NY, instr, 1980-81; Arnot Art Mus, traveling artist, instr, 1982-85; Southern Tier fice Social Ministry, community residence counsr, 1985-86; Elmira Correctional Facility, suv volunteer tutors, 1984-94; Elmira City Sch District & Corning City Sch District, home teacher, 1994-; MG Ed Serv, exec dir, currently; Art/Reading Educ, instr, Mansfield Univ, 1998-2000; Johnson City Sch District, special ed teacher, currently. **Orgs:** Reading Reform Found, NY, 1999-00. **Honors/Awds:** MNY Group Scholarship, Teachers Col, 1989-92. **Business Addr:** Child Life Consultant, Johnson City School District, 811 W Water St, Elmira, NY 14905, **Business Phone:** (607)737-6777.

MCGEE, PAMELA
Basketball coach. **Personal:** Born Dec 1, 1962; children: Javale & Imani. **Educ:** Univ SC, econ & commun. **Career:** Basketball coach (retired); Sacramento Monarchs, center, 1997-98; LosAngeles Sparks; Detroit Shock, asst coach. **Honors/Awds:** US Olympic Basketball Team, Gold Medal, 1984. *

MCGEE, REV. PAULA L.
Basketball player, preacher, president (organization). **Personal:** Born Jan 1, 1963?, Flint, MI. **Educ:** Univ Southern Calif; Inter denominational Theol Ctr, Atlanta, GA, MDiv; Vanderbilt Univ, MA, relig; Claremont Grad Univ, Claremont, CA, PhD, womens studies. **Career:** Basketball player (retired), preacher, motivational speaker; WNBA, Harlem Globetrotters, basketball player; WNBA, Dallas Diamonds, basketball player; Europe League, Italy, basketball player; Europe League, Spain, basketball player; Fisk Univ, dean chapel, ordained minister, currently; Christian Bus Success Network, co-founder. **Orgs:** Pres & minister, Paula McGee Ministries, currently. **Honors/Awds:** Nat Championships, Univ Southern Calif, 1983 & 1984. **Special Achievements:** Author: Accepting Your Greatness; featured in various magazines; published numerous articles. **Business Addr:** President, Minister, Paula McGee Ministries, 1325 N Col Ave D-225, PO Box 1265, Claremont, CA 91711, **Business Phone:** (909)476-3207.

MCGEE, ROSE N. See Obituaries section.

MCGEE, SHERRY
Business owner, educator. **Personal:** Born Nov 16, 1957, Honolulu, HI; daughter of Winnie R Johnson; children: Michael L. **Educ:** Wayne State Univ, BS, 1987, MBA, 1991. **Career:** CDI Corp, div sales mgr, 1978-89; McGee & Co, sales training consult, 1990-92; Bartech Inc, dir mkt, 1992-97; Apple Book Ctr, founder & pres; AppleKids LLC, founding pres & consult, currently. **Orgs:** Vol, Jr Achievement, Nat Black MBA Asn. **Special Achievements:** Author of Anatomy of a Business Failure: The Incredible Story of the Beloved, Multi-Million Dollar Apple Book Center, 2003. **Business Phone:** (313)268-7156.

MCGEE, SYLVIA WILLIAMS
School administrator. **Personal:** Born Aug 5, 1952, Macon, GA; daughter of John Paul and Nora Cunningham; married Terry D Sr, Mar 19, 1977; children: Terese Lynette & T Dwight Jr. **Educ:** Tift Col, BA, 1974; Univ Ga, MSW, 1976. **Career:** Mercer Univ, Proj Upward Bound, counr, 1976-77; Bibb County Pub Schs, Sch Social Serv, dir, admin, dep supt, currently. **Orgs:** Regional dir, Jack & Jill Am Inc, 1991-93, nat vpres & bd trustees, 1996-00; exec comm, Ga Indust Home C, 1994-97; corresp secy, Jr League Macon, 1996; chmn progs, Youth Leadership Bibb County, 1996-97; chmn eval comm, United Way Cent GEO, 1997-; bd dirs, Family Coun Ctr, 1998-; Macon 2000, comm chmn resource serv; fin secy, New Hope Missionary Bapt Church. **Honors/Awds:** Leadership Georgia, 1989; Volunteer of the Year, Jr League Macon, 1995; Hatcher Leadership Award, Leadership Macon, 1997; Distinguished Mother, Jack & Jill Am, Macon Chap, 1997; Social Worker of the Year, Sch Social Workers Asn Ga, Leadership Ga, 1998. **Business Addr:** Deputy superintendent administration, Bibb County Public Schools, 484 Mulberry St Suite 390, Macon, GA 31204, **Business Phone:** (912)765-8605.

MCGEE, TIMOTHY DWAYNE
Football player. **Personal:** Born Aug 7, 1964, Cleveland, OH. **Educ:** Univ Tenn. **Career:** Football player (retired); Cincinnati Bengals, wide receiver, 1986-93, 1994; Wash Redskins, wide receiver, 1993. **Honors/Awds:** Post-season play, 1988: AFC Championship Game, NFL Championship Game.

MCGEE, TONY (TONY LAMONT MCGEE)
Football player. **Personal:** Born Apr 21, 1971, Terre Haute, IN. **Educ:** Univ Mich, communications. **Career:** Football player (retired); Cincinnati Bengals, tight end, 1993-2001; Dallas Cowboys, tight end, 2002-03; New York Giants, tight end, 2003.

MCGEE, TONY LAMONT. See MCGEE, TONY.

MCGEE, VONETTA
Actor. **Personal:** Born Jan 14, 1940, San Francisco, CA; daughter of Lawrence and Alma Irene Scott; married Carl Lumbly, May 29, 1987; children: 1. **Career:** Films: Faustina, 1968; Grande silenzio, 1968; The Lost Man, 1969; The Kremlin Letter, 1970; Blacula, 1972; Melinda, 1972; Hammer, 1972; Shaft in Africa, 1973; Detroit 9000, 1973; Thomasine & Bushrod, 1974; The Eiger Sanction, 1975; Brothers, 1977; Woo fook, 1977; Repo Man, 1984; To Sleep With Anger, 1990; Brother Future, 1991; Johnny B Good, 1998; Stormy Weathers, 1992; Perry Mason: The Case of the Reckless Romeo, 1992; You Must Remember This, 1992; Cagney & Lacey: The Return, 1994; The Man Next Door, 1996; Johnny B Good, 1998; Amen; TV series: "The Norliss Tapes", 1973; "Superdome", 1978; "Scruples", 1981; "Hell Town", 1985; "Bustin' Loose", 1987; "L.A. Law", 1989-90. **Business Addr:** Actress, Writers & Artists Agency, 8383 Wilshire Blvd, Beverly Hills, CA 90211, **Business Phone:** (323)866-0900.*

MCGEE, WADDELL
Consultant. **Personal:** Born Dec 13, 1946, Hattiesburg, MS; son of Ovell and Corine; married Gloria Kesselle, Feb 16, 1990. **Educ:** Alcorn State Univ, BS, 1968; Southern Univ, LLB, 1976; Am Univ, Sch Environ Studies, MS, 1980, PhD, 1985. **Career:** US, nuclear & environ engr, 1968-73; Oil Field Environ Safety, consult, dir opers, 1977-86; asst mayor, law dir, 1986-87; Calif Environ Waste Mgt, consult, vipres opers, 1987-88; Mid-Am Environ Consultants Engineers, chief exec officer, 1988-; Mid-Am Archit Design & Engrs, owner & mgr, 1999. **Orgs:** Soc Am Military Engrs; Am Bar Asn, 1975-; chair, Clean in Am, 1989-; chair, NEB Energy CMS, 1991-; bd dir, Goodwill Industries, 1991-; pres, Int Soc Environ Professionals, 1991-; pres, Nat Asn Advan Colored People, 1992-; bd dir, Am Red Cross, 1992-; NEB Environ CMS, 1992-; bd dir, Ky Pollution Prev Ctr. **Honors/Awds:** Senatorial Citation, 1989; Man of the Year, Clean Am Inc, 1990; Professional Award, Int Soc Environ Professionals, 1991. **Special Achievements:** Author, Blacks and the Environment, 1992. **Military Serv:** AUS, sgt, 1969-73. **Business Addr:** Owner, Manager, Mid-America Architectural Design & Engineers, 1613 Farnam St Suite 625, Omaha, NE 68102, **Business Phone:** (402)345-8797.*

MCGEE, WILLIAM TORRE
Journalist, editor, editor, writer. **Personal:** Born Sep 3, 1966, Miami, FL; son of William (deceased) and Betty Jean. **Educ:** Northwestern Univ, BS, jour, 1988. **Career:** Miami Times, copy ed, reporter, 1988-90; Miami Herald, copy ed, 1990-92, reporter action line, 1992-94, reporter, 1994-99, staff writer, copy ed, 1999-. **Orgs:** S Fla, Black Journalists Asn, 1988-; NAACP; Am Copy Ed Soc. **Home Addr:** 2423 NW 179th St, Opa Locka, FL 33056-3623, **Home Phone:** (305)626-8837. **Business Phone:** (305)376-3569.*

MCGEE, WILLIE DEAN
Baseball executive, baseball player. **Personal:** Born Nov 2, 1958, San Francisco, CA. **Educ:** Diablo Valley Jr Coll, attended. **Career:** Baseball player, baseball coach (retired); St Louis Cardinals, outfielder 1982-90, 1996-99; Oakland Athletics, outfielder, 1990; San Francisco Giants, outfielder, 1991-94; Boston Red Sox, outfielder, 1995; Contra Costa Col, asst baseball coach, 1999. **Orgs:** Founder & co-chairperson, Willie McGee Found; involved in numerous community organizations including the Police Activities League, Greater Richmond Souper Kitchen, ACORN Track Club. **Honors/Awds:** Named to Howe News Bureau post-season All Star team, 1981; Topps Chewing Gum All-Rookie team, 1982; mem, All Star Teams,1983, 1985; St Louis BBWAA Rookie of the Year; 3 Gold Glove Awards; Nat League MVP, 1985; named to The Sporting News & UPI NL All Star teams 1985; Sporting News NL Player of the Year, 1985; BBWAA Nat League MVP, 1985; voted to first Silver Slugger Team 1985; Player of the Week, Sports Illustrated & Nat League, 1985; Nat League Player of the Month, 1985. **Special Achievements:** 17 consecutive steals; tied World Series record for outfielders with 24 putouts in the Series; set record for highest fielding average in 7 game series with most chances accepted.

MCGEHEE, NAN E
School administrator, psychologist. **Personal:** Born Mar 9, 1928, Chicago, IL; daughter of Ethel Davis and Winston T. **Educ:** Univ Chicago, BA, 1947; Northwestern Univ, BSE, 1958, MS, 1959, PhD, 1962; Harvard Univ, IEM Cert, 1972. **Career:** School administrator (retired), psychologist; Northwestern Univ Eve Div, instr, 1960-61; Univ Ill, Chicago Circle, from instr to asst prof, 1961-66, assoc prof, 1966-, dir, univ hons progs, 1967-70, dean faculties, 1970-72, assoc chancellor, 1972-79. **Orgs:** Secy & treas, Ill Psychol Asn, 1968-70; consult, US Civil Serv Comn; EEOC; FWP Reg & Training, 1970-72; bd mem, Ill Reg Libr Coun, 1973; policy bd mem, Nat Ctr Study Ed Policy Alternatives, 1972; Sigma Xi, Alpha Kappa Alpha; Am Psy Asn; Ill Psychol Asn; Midwest Psychol Asn; Am Asn Univ Profs; Alpha Lambda Delta; Phi Eta Sigma. **Special Achievements:** Co-author several articles. **Home Addr:** 14214 Glen Acres Rd SW, Vashon, WA 98070.

MCGHEE, GEORGIA MAE
Executive, association executive. **Personal:** Born Dec 9, 1934, Joiner, AR; daughter of Webb Young and Marge; divorced; children: Curits L, Steven Alan, Garry Lynn, Cheryl Denise Johnson, Rita Lorain & Kenneth G. **Educ:** Davenport Bus Col, 1958-59; Jr Col, Data Processing, eng, 1973. **Career:** Executive, association executive (Retired); AFSCME AFL-CIO, vpres coun 07, 1972-76, coun vpres 1977-79; Coalition Labor Union Women, pres local 261, 1973-77, convenor, 1974, chap pres, 1975; Coalition Labor Union Women Nat Officers Coun, second vpres, 1977-86; AFSCME AFL-CIO, int vpres, 1977-84, AFSCME Int, vpres two terms; Mich Women's Comn, comnr, 1977-84. **Orgs:** Pres, Block Club, 1969-70; int vpres, AFSCME AFL-CIO, 1977-84; vpres, Coalition Labor Union Women Nat Officers Coun, 1977-80; Mich Women's Comn, 1977; AFL-CIO Community Serv Comt, 1978-86; audit & rev comt, Kent City, United Way Comt, 1978-81; pres, AFSCME AFL-CIO local 261; exec bd mem, United Way Kent Co, 1978-82; coalition Labor Union Women term, 1984-86. **Honors/Awds:** Rosalyn Carter's Community Plan Cert, 1979; Kenneth W Robinson Community Serv Award, Kent City United Way, 1982; Mary McLeod Bethune Award, Nat Coun Negro Women, 1984; Michigan Women's Commn Distinguished Serv Award, Mich Women's Comn, 1984; GR Giants Award 1984; Martha Reynolds Labor Award; Coalition Black Trade Unionist Trail Blazer Award, 1990. **Home Addr:** 612 Worden SE, Grand Rapids, MI 49507.

MCGHEE, JAMES LEON
Executive. **Personal:** Born Mar 3, 1948, Wayne, IN. **Educ:** Univ Puget Sound, BA, 1974. **Career:** City Planning Comn Tacoma WA, asst planner, 1972-73; US Treasury Dept, asst bank examiner, 1973-76; Housing & Devel Seattle, DC, dir, 1977-78; Northwest Tech Inc, pres, chmn, 1983-; Medsco Inc Med Supply Corp, pres, chmn, 1983-85; greater telecommunication syst Inc, pres & chief exec officer, 1985-88; McGhee & Assocs, pres & chief exec officer, 1989-93; Am Automotive distribr, 1989-96; Global Automotive distribr, pres & chief exec officer, 1996-99; JLM Mgt Group, pres & chief exec officer, 1998-. **Orgs:** Pres, Alpha Phi Alpha & Sphinx OH State, 1968; Fin treas NW Black Elected Official Assoc, 1973-85; founder, United Trade Worker Assoc, 1975; cofounder, Seattle Central Comm Col Found, 1978; pres, chmn bd, WA State Bus League, 1980-85; bd dir, NW Tech Inc, 1981-85; planning comn, City of Seattle, 1981-85; asst reg vice pres, Nat Bus League, 1983-85; bd dir, Medsco Inc, 1983-85; bd dir, UnitedNegro Col Fund, 1985; Pub mem, bd of psychology, 2003. **Honors/Awds:** Honors for Serv, EFP Rhomania, 1979; Community Black Leader, 1980 NW Conf Black Public Official, 1980. **Military Serv:** AUS, sgt, E-5, 3 yrs; Hon Discharge; Viet Nam Medal; Serv Citation, 1971. **Business Addr:** President, chief executive officer, J L M Management Group, 200 Warren Dr, San Francisco, CA 94131-1032, **Business Phone:** (415)665-5940.

MCGHEE, MALESA OWENS
Executive. **Career:** Wayne Co Community Col Dist, pub rels consult; Detroit Acad Arts & Sci, dir commun, currently. **Business Phone:** (313)923-0281.*

MCGHEE, SAMUEL T
Educator. **Personal:** Born May 29, 1940, Jersey City, NJ; son of Samuel T and Lucile Bitten; children: Darren, Elissa, Samuel III & Jeffrey. **Educ:** Jersey City State Col, BA, 1962; Seton Hall Univ, MA, 1965. **Career:** Educator (retired); Jersey City State Col, from asst dir admis to dir admis, 1971-98, asst dean stud affairs, 1998-2001; Hillside, NJ Finance Comnr, 1987; Hillside Township, Hillside NJ, mayor, 1988, police comnr, 1989-90, 1993-94, mayor, 1991, public works comnr 1992, 1996, fire comnr, 1995-96, mayor, 1997-98, coun mem, 1999. **Orgs:** Omega Psi Phi Fraternity, 1988-; Nat Conf Black Mayors, 1988-; Local Adv Comt Alcoholism & Drug Abuse, 2001-03. **Honors/Awds:** Black Merit Acad E St Louis, 1973; Distinguished Alumni Award, Jersey City State Col, 1981; Phi Delta Kappa, 1990; Omega Psi Phi Superior Service Award, 1991. **Home Addr:** 1548 Maple Ave, Hillside, NJ 07205.

MCGILL, LENNY
Football player, football coach. **Personal:** Born May 31, 1971, Long Beach, CA. **Educ:** Ariz State Univ, BA, criminal justice, 1994. **Career:** Football player (retired), college scout; Green Bay Packers, defensive back, 1994-95; Atlanta Falcons, 1996-97; Carolina Panthers, defensive back, 1998; Seattle Seahawks, 1999; Green Bay Packers, col scout, 2000-09; asst dir coll scouting, Denver Broncos, currently. **Honors/Awds:** Hall of Fame, San Diego High Sch Sports, 2002; Most Improved Defensive Player, Sun Devils. **Business Addr:** Assistant Director of College Scouting, Denver Broncos Football Club, 13655 Broncos Pkwy, Englewood, CO 80112, **Business Phone:** (303)649-9000.

MCGILL, MICHAEL
Singer. **Personal:** Born Feb 17, 1937. **Career:** Albums; There Is, 1968; On Their Corner, 1992; I Salute You, 1992; Dreams of Contentment, 1993; Bring Back the Love; Classic Dells, 1996; I Touch aDream/Whatever Turns., 1998; (With Michael Ross); We Finally Meet, 1995; Last Love Letter, 1996; The Dells, mem, currently. **Business Addr:** Singer, The Original Dells, Inc, PO Box 1133, Harvey, IL 60426-7133.

MCGILL, MICHELE NICOLE JOHNSON
Writer. **Personal:** Born Jul 14, 1966, San Diego, CA; daughter of Leonard and Dianne Campbell. **Educ:** Univ Fla, Gainesville, FL, BS, Journ 1988; Univ N Fla, Jacksonville, FL, currently. **Career:** Independent Fla Alligator, Gainesville, FL, layout ed, 1987-88; Fla Times-Union, Jacksonville, FL, copy ed, 1988-90, columnist, 1990-, asst reader advocate, cur. **Orgs:** Nat Asn Black Journalists, 1987-90; past pres, Univ Fla Asn Black Communicators, 1987-88; pres, Jacksonville Asn Black Communicators, 1991-93; pres, Soul Autonomy Inc, 1991-; newsletter dir, Jacksonville Urban League Auxiliary, 1991-92; First Baptist Church Mandarin Youth Group. **Business Addr:** Assistant Reader Advocate, Florida Times-Union, Reader Serv, 1 Riverside Ave, PO Box 1949, Jacksonville, FL 32231.

MCGILL, THOMAS L
Lawyer. **Personal:** Born Aug 13, 1946, Martinsburg, WV; son of Thomas L McGill Sr and Dorthy Kathryn Baylor; married Charisse R Lillie, Dec 4, 1982; children: Leslie Janelle, Thomas L III & Alison Charisse. **Educ:** Lincoln Univ, BA, 1968; Occidental Col, MA, 1972; Notre Dame Law Sch, JD, 1975. **Career:** Olney HS, teacher, 1968-71; Hon Kenneth Gibson Mayor, mayor's aide, 1971-72; Hon Paul Dandridge Judge, law clerk, 1975-82; Pa Human Relations Comn, comnr, 1981-90, chairperson, 1986-90; McGill & Seay, atty, 1975-90; Clark, McGill, Newkirk & Seary, 1990; Clark & McGill P C, managing partner, currently. **Orgs:** Philadelphia Bar Asn, 1975-, Am Bar Asn, 1975-; Nat Bar Asn, 1977-; Recording Sec Barristers Asn, 1977-78; pres, Barristers Asn, 1980-81; bd mem, Veritas Inc, 1980-83, Germantown Boys Club, 1982-84; bd dirs, West Mount Airy Neighbors, 1986-87; bd dirs, Friends Neighborhood Guild, 1995; Pa Asn Criminal Defense lawyers. **Honors/Awds:** All Conf Baseball Team Lincoln Univ, 1967; Sr Class Award for Creative Writing Lincoln Univ, 1968; Nat Urban Fel, Nat Conf Mayors, Yale Univ, 1971-72. **Home Addr:** 7000 Emlen St, Philadelphia, PA 19119-2556. **Business Addr:** Attorney, Managing Partner, Clark & McGill PC, 230 S Broad St 2nd Fl, Philadelphia, PA 19102, **Business Phone:** (215)735-5300.

MCGINEST, WILLIE
Football player. **Personal:** Born Dec 11, 1971, Long Beach, CA; son of Willie and Joyce; children: Riley & Halie. **Educ:** Univ Southern Calif, pub admin, 1994. **Career:** New Eng Patriots, defensive end, 1994-2005; Cleveland Browns, linebacker, 2006-; 55 Entertainment, owner, currently. **Orgs:** Founder, Willie Mc Ginest Freedom Sch. **Honors/Awds:** Rookie of the Year, 1776; Quarterback Club New Eng, 1994; Player of the Game, Staples Star, 1995; Pro Bowl, 1996; Defensive Player of the Month,Asian Football Confederation, 1996; Defensive Player of the Week, Asian Football Confederation, 1996, 1999, 2003; Miller Lite Player of the Game, 2001; Levitra Play of the Week, Nat Football League, 2003; Super Bowl XXXVI; All-Conf hons; All-Pac-10 conf hons; Defensive Player of the Year, Southern Calif; Willie was voted as one of the twenty hottest influencers by Urban Influence Magazine, 2009. **Special Achievements:** Lombardi Award finalist; appeared in various TV shows; City Council of Long Beach declared May 3rd of every year will be recognized as Willie McGinest Day. **Business Addr:** Linebacker, Cleveland Browns, 76 Lou Groza Blvd, Berea, OH 44017, **Business Phone:** (440)891-5000.

MCGINNIS, JAMES W.
Educator, lawyer. **Personal:** Born Jul 8, 1940, Fairfield, AL; son of James and Reatha Saunders Felton; married Debra Hughes, Mar 16, 1988; children: Ayana Marie. **Educ:** Wayne State Univ, BS, 1963; San Francisco State Univ, MA, 1965; Yeshiva Univ, PhD, 1976; Wayne State Univ Law Sch, JD, 1977. **Career:** Col Entrance Exam Bd, asst dir, 1967-69; Univ Calif, Berkeley, instr, 1970-72; Far West Lab Educ Res, res assoc, 1972-73; Oakland Univ, asst prof, 1976-81; Private Practice, lawyer, currently. **Orgs:** Pres, Kappa Alpha Psi Frat Wayne State Univ, 1961-62; Asn Black Psychologists, 1963-73; researcher Black Studies Inst Wayne St Univ,1975-76; off coun Hall & Andary Law Firm, 1982-84; chmn, PAC, 1982-85, 1982-, Nat Conf Black Lawyers, Nat Bar Asn, 1989-. **Business Addr:** Attorney, 660 Woodward Ave, Detroit, MI 48226, **Business Phone:** (313)963-2910.

MCGINNIS, ROBERT LAWRENCE
Insurance executive. **Personal:** Born Oct 1, 1966, Minneapolis, MN; son of Ronald and Judy; married Jennifer Latwesen, Dec 7, 1991; children: Lauren & Nathan. **Educ:** Univ Wis-Madison, BA, 1990. **Career:** Prudential Insurance, group mgr, 1990-95; United Healthcare, COO, small business, 1995-2001; CNA Insurance Co, group oper, exec vpres, life & group opers, pres & chief exec officer, 2003-. **Orgs:** Dir, AAHP/HIAA, 2001-04; dir, ACLI, 2004-; adv bd mem, Univ Wis, 2005-06. **Honors/Awds:** Crain's Chicago Business, 40 Under 40, 2002.

MCGLOCKTON, CHESTER
Football player, football coach. **Personal:** Born Sep 16, 1969, Whiteville, NC; married Xena. **Educ:** Clemson Univ. **Career:** Football player (retired), Football coach; Oakland Raiders, defensivetackle, 1992-97; Kans City Chiefs, 1998-2000, Denver Broncos, 2001-02; New York jets, defensive tackle, 2003; D1 Sports Training, co-owner; Amsterdam Admirals, intern coach. **Honors/Awds:** Four times Pro Bowl selection, 1994, 1995, 1996, 1997; Three times All-Pro selection, 1994, 1995, 1996. **Business Addr:** Co-Owner, D1 Sports Training, 1334 Miller Rd, Greenville, SC, SC 29607, **Business Phone:** (864)288-3868.

MCGLOTHAN, EARNEST. See MCGLOTHAN, ERNEST.

MCGLOTHAN, ERNEST (EARNEST MCGLOTHAN)
Executive. **Personal:** Born Oct 25, 1937, Tuscaloosa, AL; married Willa Rean May; children: Wilma, Kecia, Corey. **Educ:** Tuskegee Inst Sch Arch, 1971; Tuskegee Inst Sch Arch, BS, 1971. **Career:** Mac-Pon Co Gen Contractors, pres & owner; Gaillard Construct Co, Birmingham; A H Smith Construct Co, Birmingham; Steel City Serv, Birmingham, AL. **Orgs:** Alpha Phi Alpha Frat; Mayor's Adv Com; Nat Asn Minority Contractors; Birmingham Zoining Bd Adjustments; bd dir BSA, Omicron Lambda; chmn, Cooper Green Golf Course Comt. **Honors/Awds:** Outstanding business men of year, Omega Psi Phi, 1973; business of the year award, Dr Herman H Long, 1977; licensed Minority General Contractor AL. **Military Serv:** AUS, 1971-73. **Business Addr:** President, Owner, Steel City Service, 1820 Seventh Ave, N Suite 207, Birmingham, AL 35203, **Business Phone:** (205)324-3249.

MCGLOTHEN, GOREE
Government official, electrician. **Personal:** Born Aug 17, 1915, Huntsville, TX; married Allie Mae Hightower; children: Goree Jr & Mattie Grant. **Educ:** Indust Educ Tuskegee Inst, BS, 1937. **Career:** United Gas Corp, master gas meter repair, 1941-45; State Tex, master electrical, 1942-77, master plumber, 1944-55; McGlothen Elect Co, owner; City Huntsville, City Councilman, 1975. **Orgs:** Secy Walker Co Negro C C, 1941-44; pres, Cood gellows Club, 1942-43; adult educ bd, Huntsville High Sch, 1975-76; chmn, Janes Found, 1976-77; deacon teacher, First Mission Bapt Ch; pres, Cent Mission Baptist Asn Tex; Nat Asn Advanc Colored People; Int Bus Fellowship. **Honors/Awds:** Golden Eagle Award, Small Bus Asn, 1967; Leader Celeb Bicent Year, 1976; Plaque Trinity River Authority, 1978; Black History Award, Pres Jimmy-Carter, 1979; Hon Fine Lighter of the Year, 1980; Outstanding Male Alpha Phi Alpha, 1984; Plaque Huntsville Housing Authority, 1985; Outstanding Achievement Award, Nat Coun Orgn, 1986. **Special Achievements:** First black to defeat a white political opponent since Reconstruct Days Huntsville, 1975.

MCGLOTTEN, ROBERT
Lobbyist. **Personal:** Married Cheryl Goode McGlotten. **Educ:** University of Pennsylvania; St. Joseph's College for Industrial and Labor Management. **Career:** AFL-CIO, Executive Director of the Human Resources Dept. Institute, 1970-1972; U.S. Dept. of Labor, Special Asst. to the Secretary, 1973; AFL-CIO, Legislative Representative, 1974-1980; AFL-CIO, Asst. Director, 1980-1986; AFL-CIO, Legislative Director, 1986; McGlotten & Jarvis, Partner. **Orgs:** Member, Transport Workers Union; Consultant and Lobbyist, Office & Professional Employees International Union; Member, Congressional Black Caucus Foundation, Inc. **Military Serv:** U.S. Army. *

MCGLOVER, STEPHEN LEDELL
Executive, president (organization). **Personal:** Born Nov 8, 1950, Los Angeles, CA; son of Theo and Octavia Bell; married. **Educ:** Woodbury Col, Int bus mgt, BS, 1978; Univ Md, int Bus Mgt, 1980; Black Businessmen Asn, BS, bus, 1981; Ohio State Univ, NOPA Dealer Mgt Inst, 1984; Nat Office Products Asn, IBM sales course, 1984; Southern Methodist Univ, Edwin Cox Sch bus, 1984; Minister Training inst, CCC, 1995; Golden Gate Baptist Sem, attended 1996; Amos Tuck exec, met Course, 1996. **Career:** Occidental Ins, salesman, 1974-76; Inventory Data Supplies, shipping mgr, 1975, dir & collections, 1976, gen mgr, 1977-78; McGlover Enterprises, salesman, 1977-79; Oasis Office Supplies, pres & partner, 1979-83; Oasis Office Prods Inc, pres & ceo, 1983-. **Orgs:** Black Bus Asn, 1980-; Mayors Small Bus Adv Bd, 1988-; Nat Office Prods Asn; LAMBOC Comt, GSA Small bus Coun; chair, BBA, Church & Comt Rels; minister asst, pastor. **Honors/Awds:** BBA Member of the Year Award, Black Business Asn, 1987; Man of the Year, Mid-City Chamber Community, 1987; Small business of the Year Award, 1996; Exceptional Performance Award, The Boeing Co, 1998. **Military Serv:** USF. **Business Addr:** President, Chief Executive Officer, Oasis Office Products Inc, 4600 W Washington Blvd, Los Angeles, CA 90016-1728, **Business Phone:** (323)938-6211.*

MCGLOWAN, ANGELA
Public relations executive, television talk show host. **Personal:** Born in Oxford, MS. **Educ:** Univ Miss, pub admin. **Career:** Ole Miss, ambassador; DC, goodwill ambassador, 1994; Sen John Ensign, legis corresp asst, 1996; Roscoe Bartlett, press staff asst cong man, 1996; Rupert Murdoch's News Corp, dir govt affairs & diversity develop, 1999-2005; Polit Strategies & Insights, ceo & founder, currently; Fox 5 WNYW, pub & polit affairs show, host, currently; FOX News Channel, polit analyst, 1999-. **Orgs:** Independent Women's Forum; Miss Soc; pres, Carter's Habitat Humanity; dir, Better Am Found; mgr legis affairs & policy res enhancement, Am Trucking Asn. **Honors/Awds:** Top Ten Ole Miss Beauty. **Special Achievements:** Spokesperson, Am Cancer Soc; speaker at numerous sch on the Just Say No prog. **Business Addr:** Political News Analyst, FOX News Channel, 400 N Capitol St NW Suite 550, Washington, DC 20001, **Business Phone:** (202)824-0001.*

MCGOODWIN, DR. ROLAND C
Dentist. **Personal:** Born Jul 15, 1933, Evansville, IN; married Lillian Pollard; children: Nina Marie & Roland Jr. **Educ:** Cent State Col, BS, 1955; Meharry Med Col Sch Dent, DDS, 1963. **Career:** Hubbard Hosp, intern, 1964; Albert Einstein Med Ctr, resident, 1965; Lincoln Heights Health Ctr, staff; Bethesda Hosp; Cincinnati OH, pvt pract, currently. **Orgs:** Dentist Crippled C; bd educ, Am Dent Asn; Nat Dent Asn; OH State Dent Asn; OH Valley Dent Soc; Cincinnati Dent Soc; Acad Gen Dentists Bd Mt Auburn Health Ctr; adv coun, Walnut Hill Area; Health Manpower Linkage Sys; OH Dept Health; bd mem, Dent Care Plus Ins Co; pres, Union Found. **Honors/Awds:** Dr Martin L King Jr Award, St Mark Catholic Church, 2007. **Military Serv:** AUS, 1st lt 1956-59; col dc USAR. **Business Addr:** Dentist, Roland C McGoodwin, 645 E Mc Millan St, Cincinnati, OH 45206.

MCGOUGH, ROBYN LATRESE
Health services administrator, manager. **Personal:** Born Sep 15, 1961, Spokane, WA; daughter of Harold McGough (deceased) and Eva McGough. **Educ:** Clark County Community Col, cert completion, LPN, 1983; Univ Nev, Las Vegas, BSW, 1986, MSW, 1993. **Career:** Sunrise Hosp, food serv worker, 1978-79, diet clerk, 1979-86, med social worker, 1986-93; THC Las Vegas, social serv dir, 1993-97; Vencor Hosp, Las Vegas, soc serv dir; Kindred Healthcare Inc, mgr social serv, currently. **Orgs:** Nat Asn Social Workers, 1986-98; Progressive Nat Baptist Conv, Southwest Region, asst youth dir, 1989-91; Delta Sigma Theta Sorority Inc, 1986-, financial secy, 1988-90; debutante adv, 1994-, Les Femmes Douze, 1996-. **Honors/Awds:** Outstanding Young Women of Am, 1985; Outstanding Achievement for Black Stud, Univ Nev, Las Vegas, 1986; Woman of the Yr, Vegas Stars Chap, Am Bus Women's Asn, 1990; Distinguished Women in Southern Nev, 1990-91. **Business Addr:** Manager of social services, Kindred Healthcare Inc, Kindred Hospital, Flamingo Campus, 2250 East Flamingo Rd, Las Vegas, NV 89119, **Business Phone:** (702)784-4300 Ext 4353.*

MCGOWAN, ANNA-MARIA
Scientist. **Educ:** Purdue Univ, BS, aeronaut & astronaut engineering; Old Dominion Univ, MS, aerospace engineering. **Career:** NASA, Langley Res Ctr, Air & Space Conf & Technol Exposition, proj mgr morphing proj, currently. **Orgs:** Air Force Asn. **Honors/Awds:** Space Day spokesperson, Langley Res Ctr, NASA, 2003. **Business Phone:** (757)864-5800.

MCGOWAN, CLARENCE
Lawyer. **Personal:** Born Oct 20, 1921, Bryan, TX; son of Elihu and Ollie Mae; married Gloria Helen, Nov 19, 1958; children: Valorie. **Educ:** Prairie View Univ, BS, 1943; Iowa State Col, MS, 1950; St Mary Univ, JD, 1958. **Career:** San Antonio Sch Dist, math & sci teacher, 1945-60, sch prin, 1960-63; City San Antonio, City Water Utility Syst, vpres; self employed, atty, 1963-99. **Orgs:** Bd dir, United Way, 1950-55; Phi Delta Kappa Scholar Fraternity, 1965-99; coun, Nat Asn Advan Colored People, 1965-99; basileus,Omega Psi Phi Fraternity, 1973-75; Nat Bar Asn, 1990-99; founder, San Antonio Black Lawyers Asn. **Honors/Awds:** Achievement, Nat Asn Advan Colored People, 1965; MLK Distinguished Achievement Award, Martin Luther King Comn, 2004. **Special Achievements:** First African American black man to graduate from St Mary's Univ, Law Sch, 1963; first African Am Judge San Antonio, Bexan County, TX, 1974. **Home Addr:** 102 Wyndale Dr, San Antonio, TX 78209, **Home Phone:** (210)822-5956.

MCGOWAN, ELSIE HENDERSON
Executive director. **Personal:** Born Jul 3, 1947, Pell City, AL; daughter of Rannie Collins and Franklin; married James Oliver, Jan 3, 1970; children: Kenneth Eugene & LaCindra DeNae. **Educ:** Knoxville Col, Knoxville, Tenn, BS, 1969; Univ Ala Birmingham, Ala, MA, 1982, EdS, 1989. **Career:** St Clair County Bd Edu, Ashville, Ala, bus edu teacher, 1969-83, asst prin (elem), 1983-94, dir migrant edu prog, 1986-94; Headstart Prog, exec dir; John Pope Eden Career Tech Ctr, teacher; St. Clair County Head Start, exec dir, currently. **Orgs:** Pres, St Clair County Educ asn, 1979; coordr, Substitute Teachers' Workshop, 1987. **Honors/Awds:** Mem, Kappa Delta Pi Honor Soc, Univ Ala, Birmingham, Ala, 1980; Outstanding Woman of the Year, 1979; mem, Nat State, Local Education Asns in Ala, 1969-; Nat Alumni Soc, Univ Alab, 1981; Delta Sigma Theta Sorority, Anniston Alumnae Chapter; Administrator of the Year, Community Asn of Alabama. **Business Addr:** Executive director, St Clair County Head Start Inc, 21685 US Hwy 231 Coal City Sch, PO Box 641, Pell City, AL 35125, **Business Phone:** (205)338-9694.

MCGOWAN, THOMAS RANDOLPH
Manager. **Personal:** Born Apr 19, 1926, Baltimore, MD; son of Robert and Mary; married Roedean Olivia Oden; children: James, Karen White, Terry V Stevens, Kevin & Kurt. **Educ:** Oakland City Col, AA, 1964; San Francisco State Col, attended 1966; Univ Calif, Berkeley, attended 1967; Univ Md, BS, 1978. **Career:** San Francisco Procurement Agency, contract specialist, 1963-68; AUS Harry Diamond Labs, branch chief, 1972-79; AUS Yuma Proving Ground, dir proc dirate, 1979-81; Roman Catholic Diocese, Oakland, dir ecumenism, 1983-96; St John Baptist Church, deacon, currently. **Orgs:** Chmn bd, Columbia Found, 1978-79; dir, Youth Serv, 1985-; deacon, Diocese Oakland, 1995-; bd dirs, St Mary's Ctr. **Honors/Awds:** James Fitzgerald Award for Ecumenism, 1999. **Military Serv:** AUS, pfc, 1944-46. **Home Addr:** 139 Pinto Dr, Vallejo, CA 94591. **Business Addr:** Deacon, St John Baptist Church, 11150 San Pablo Ave, El Cerrito, CA 94530, **Business Phone:** (510)232-5659.

MCGRADY, EDDIE JAMES
Manager. **Personal:** Born Mar 6, 1928, Americus, GA; son of Ola Scott and Will; married Alice, Dec 26, 1952 (deceased); children: Broderick, Rodney, Valery McGrady Trice, Tonika, Shanika. **Educ:** US Army Admin School Germany, Admin, 1951; US Const NCO Acad, Sr NCO, 1951. **Career:** Retired: US Army 555th Parachute Infantry, sgt 1946-66; Americus & Police Dept, one of first black patrolmen 1966-71; Only Black Star Security Patrol, owner, mgr 1971; Campus Safety, lt, 1st black shift suprv, 1973, captain campus safety and asst dir, 1st black, 1985-90. **Orgs:** Bd mem, Americus City School Bd 1967-80, Natl Amer Council Amer Legion; chmn Seventh Dist Title 20 Council 1967-80; post commander CB Dowdell Amer Legion Post 558 1971-76; jr commander 3rd Dist Amer Legion Dept of GA 1976-80; adv Boy Scouts of Amer 1977; v chmn 3rd Dist of GA Assn of Black Elected Officials 1978; com mem GA Sch Bd Assn 1979; bd mem W Central GA Comm Act Councl 1979; commander The Amer Legion Third Dist Dept of GA 1979-80; Nat Membership Comm Amer Legion 1983; appt Patriotic Observance of Flag Etiquette Amer Legion State of GA 1984; chmn bd of directors of West Central GA Community Action Council, 1985-94; served on Americus-Sumter County Bi-Centennial Commission, 1987-88; chairman, board of trustees Flint Services Inc, 1988. **Honors/Awds:** Outstanding Dist Commander, 1979-80; Mr legionnaire of the Year, CB Dowdell Amer Legion 558, 1976; Barnum Dosey-Comm Serv Awd, Elks & Lodge 691 & BSAT 226, 1977; Cert Black Youth in Action, 1979; Awd Support of Delta Sigma Theta GA, SW Col 1980, Support of Kappa Alpha Kappa, 1980, Asn of Women Students, 1980, Support of SABU, 1980, 3rd Dit of Amer Legion Aux, 1980, CB Dowdell Amer Legion Post 558, 1980, CB Dowdell Amer Legion Ladies Aux 558, 1980; Proclamation from Gov George Busbee State of GA, 1981; Resolution from GA House of Reps, 1981; Lt Col Aide De Campfrom gov JoeFrank Harris State of GA, 1984; Comm SV and Region VI of Noble, 1987; Outsting Leadership Award, West Central Georgia Community Action Council, 1987; Community Service Award, United Holiness Church 1987; Life Achievement Award, Boy Scout Troup 226, 1988; Distinguished Service Award, Georgia Southwestern College, Campus Safety Dept 1973-90; Cert of Appreciation, Fraternal Order of Police Lodge 72, 1990; Cert of Achievement, Alpha Kappa Alpha Sorority, Inc 1991; West Central GA CAC Inc, Appreciation for Devoted Leadership, 1996; Men Standing in the Gap; Certif of Achievement, Sumter County. **Military Serv:** AUS 1st sgt E-8 20 yrs active 24 retired reserve; Sr Parachutist Army Commendation Ribbon, 1946; Commendation Ribbon with Metal Pendant; 3 Awards by Sec of the Army, 1957-66. **Home Addr:** 112 Ashby St, PO Box 1305, Americus, GA 31709. *

MCGRADY, TRACY
Basketball player. **Personal:** Born May 24, 1979, Bartow, FL; children: Layla Clarice & Laymen. **Career:** Toronto Raptors, forward-guard, 1997-2000; Orlando Magic, 2000-04; Houston Rockets, guard, 2004-. **Orgs:** Founder, Tracy McGrady Found. **Honors/Awds:** Player of the Year, USA Today; NC State Player of the Yr, Assoc Press; Most Improved Player Award, 2001-02; Rich & Helen DeVos Community Enrichment Award, 2003; Player of the Week, Nat Basketball Asn Conf; Player of the Month; Western Conf Player of the Week, 2004-05. **Business Addr:** Professional Basketball Player, Houston Rockets, 2 E Greenway Plz Suite 400, Houston, TX 77046, **Business Phone:** (713)627-3865.*

MCGREGOR, EDNA M.
School administrator. **Personal:** Born in Ontario;daughter of Charlotte Maud Jackson McGruder and Walter Jay McGruder; married Albert (deceased). **Educ:** Howard Univ, BS, 1945; Univ Michigan, MA 1950; Mich State Univ, attended; Univ Detroit, attended. **Career:** School administrator (retired); Detroit Schs, health & phys educ teacher, 1945-52, sci teacher, 1952-66; Butzel Jr High Sch, guid counr, 1966-68; Northeastern High Sch, guid counr, 1968-82; Osborn High Sch, guid counr, 1982-85; Ivery's Professional Travel Agency, travel agent, 1985. **Orgs:** Exec comm counr Detroit Fed Teachers, 1970-; House Delegates, Detroit Asn Black Orgn; delegate Mich Senate, 1980; Metro Detroit Guid Asn; Am Asn Univ Women; bd dir Detroit Asn Univ Mich Women Alumnae; life mem NAACP; pres, Detroit Urban League Guild; Alpha Kappa Alpha; Alpha Rho Omega; bd mgt, YWCA; Howard Univ, Alumni Club; exec comt, Nat Howard Univ Alumni Coun; Women's Day chairperson Second Baptist Church 1984; proj coordr Health-O-Rama, 1984; vol Southwest Detroit Hosp 1984; regist staff, Metro Detroit Convention & Visitors Bur, 1985; Women's Comn NAACP, 1985; pres, Howard Univ Alumni Club Detroit, 1986-88; prog chmn, Detroit Asn, Univ Michigan Alumnae; bd dir, Univ Michigan, 1989-; Mus African Hist, milliondollar club, 1988; Operation Big Vote, vice chair; Alpha Rho Omega Chap; Health Care Comn, chap; life mem, AKA Sorority. **Honors/Awds:** Human Relations Award, Detroit Round table Protestants, Catholics & Jews, 1955; Guilder of the Year, Detroit Urban League, 1972; Alumni Meritorious Award, Detroit Howard Univ Alumni, 1975; Top Ladies of Distinction, 1984; Five-Year Pin for Volunteerism, SW Detroit Hosp, 1983; 10 Service Awd Pin, Metro Detroit Convention & Visitors, 1995; NUL, Living Legends Award, 1996; 15 Yr Svc Pen, Metro Detroit Convention & Visitor Bur, 2000; 50 Yr Alumni Grad Pin, Univ Mich. **Special Achievements:** NCP, Fight for Freedom Dinner, Million Dollar Club MBR, 1990, 1991, 1992; held two children's health fairs at elementary schools, 265 were screened by professionals, follow-up in dental and nutritional areas. *

MCGREW, REGGIE (REGINALD GERARD MCGREW)
Football player. **Personal:** Born Dec 16, 1976, Mayo, FL. **Educ:** Univ Fla. **Career:** San Francisco 49ers, defensive tackle, 1999-2001; Atlanta Falcons, 2002. *

MCGRIER, JERRY, SR.
District attorney. **Personal:** Born Apr 4, 1955, Dallas, TX; son of Joseph and Irve Leen Bass Looney; married Diane Jones, Aug 21, 1982; children: Jerry McGrier Jr. **Educ:** Col Wooster, Wooster, OH, BA, polit sci, 1977; State Univ NY, Buffalo, NY, JD, 1980. **Career:** Neighborhood Legal Serv, Buffalo, NY, staff atty, 1980-82; Erie County Dist Atty, Buffalo, NY, asst dist atty, 1982; State NY, Law Dept, asst atty gen, currently. **Orgs:** Erie County Bar Asn, 1980-; Nat Dist Atty's Asn, 1982-; Nat Bar Asn, 1984-; NY State Bar Asn, 1984-; chmn, Minority Bar Asn Western NY, 1986-88; bd dir, Grace Manor Nursing Home, 1987-; bd dirs secy, Buffalo Fedn Neighborhood Ctrs Inc; NY State Defenders Asn; chair, Young Men's Christian Asn Bd Mgr; Grace Manor; Bd, Community Action Info Ctr. **Honors/Awds:** Lawyer's Service Award, Minority Bar Asn Western NY, 1988; Special Faculty Award, State Univ NY, Buffalo Law Sch, 1989. **Business Addr:** Assistant Attorney General, State of New York Law Department, Statler Towers 107 Delaware Ave, Buffalo, NY 14202-3473, **Business Phone:** (716)855-2424.*

MCGRIFF, DR. DEBORAH M.
School administrator. **Personal:** Born Jun 6, 1949, Portsmouth, VA; daughter of Everlena Madkins and Ernest Boyd Madkins; married Howard Fuller, Nov 16, 1995; children: Jacqueline Denise. **Educ:** Norfolk State Col, BS, 1970; Queens Col, MS, 1975; Fordham Univ, PhD, 1985. **Career:** NY Pub Sch, exec asst supt, 1983-85; Ctr Educ Leadership, NY, proj mgr, 1985-86; Cambridge Pub Sch, Mass, asst supt, 1986-88; Milwaukee Pub Sch, exec asst supt, 1988-89, dep supt, 1989-91; Detroit Pub Sch, gen supt, 1991-93; Edison Proj, 1993; Edison Sch, exec vpres & chief Relationship officer, currently. **Orgs:** Adv Panel, Harvard Urban Supt Prog; Nat Urban Alliance; Educ Testing Serv Bd Trustees; C Defense Fund Educ Task Force; bd trustee, United Am Health care Found; pres, bd dirs, Edison Sch Inc; ED Ventures planning comn; pres, Educ Indust Asn, currently; bd mem, Prog Educ Policy; adv bd, Nat Coun Teacher Qual, currently. **Honors/Awds:** Excellence in Education, Career Youth Development, 1989-90; Woman of the Year, Pulaski High Sch, 1991; News maker of the Year, Crains Detroit Bus, 1992. **Special Achievements:** First female gen supt in the hist of the Detroit Pub Sch; first woman asst supt, Cambridge, Mass; first female dep supt, Milwaukee, Wis. **Business Phone:** (212)419-1600.

MCGRIFF, FREDERICK STANLEY
Baseball player, athletic coach, broadcaster. **Personal:** Born Oct 31, 1963, Tampa, FL; married Veronica; children: Erick & Ericka. **Career:** Baseball player (retired); athletic coach, broadcaster; Toronto Blue Jays, infielder, 1986-90; San Diego Padres, 1991-93; Atlanta Braves, 1993-97; Tampa Bay Devil Rays, 1998-2001, 2004; Chicago Cubs, 2001-02; Los Angeles Dodgers, 2003; front office adv, currently; Catch 47, co-host, currently; radio show, co-host, currently; Jesuit High Sch Tampa, asst baseball coach, currently. **Honors/Awds:** AL Home Run Champion, 1989-90; NL Home Run Champion, 1992; NL All-Star Team, 1992-93, 1995-96; NL Silver Slugger Award, 1993; All-Star Game MVP, 1994; Hall of Fame eligible, 2009. **Special Achievements:** Has appeared in commercials for Tom Emanski Baseball Training videos on ESPN since 1991. **Business Addr:** Assistant Baseball coach, Jesuit High School of Tampa, 4701 N Himes Ave, Tampa, FL 33614.

MCGRIGGS-JAMISON, IMOGENE
Lawyer. **Personal:** Born Jan 1, 1965, Frankfurt, Germany. **Educ:** Alcorn State Univ, BA (summa cum laude), 1986; Bowling Green State Univ, MA, Eng, 1987; Univ Miss Col Law, JD, 1991. **Career:** AUS, Judge Advocate Gen Corps, capt, prosecutor, defense atty, currently. **Orgs:** Miss Bar Asn, 1991; DC Bar Asn, 1991; Delta Sigma Theta Sorority Inc. **Honors/Awds:** Outstanding Young Military Service Lawyer Award, nominee, Am Bar Asn, 1996. **Business Addr:** Trial Defense Attorney, US Army, Usa Armor Center & Fort Knox, Fort Knox, KY 40121-5000.

MCGRUDER, AARON (AARON VINCENT MCGRUDER)
Cartoonist or animator, writer. **Personal:** Born May 29, 1974, Chicago, IL; son of Bill and Elaine. **Educ:** Univ Md, attended 1997. **Career:** Writer, artist, public speaker; writer & cartoonist, currently; Creator of "The Boondocks", syndicated cartoon strip, 1996-; Books: The Boondocks: Because I Know You Don't Read the Newspapers, 2000; Fresh for '01—You Suckas!: A Boondocks Collection, 2001; A Right to Be Hostile: The Boondocks Treasury, 2003; Birth of a Nation: A Comic Novel, 2004; Public Enemy Number 2: An All-New Boondocks Collection, 2005. **Honors/Awds:** Chairmans Award, Nat Asn Advan Colored People Image Awards, 2002. **Business Addr:** Cartoonist, c/o Universal Press Syndicate, 4520 Main St Suite 500, Kansas City, MO 64111, **Business Phone:** (816)932-6600.

MCGRUDER, AARON VINCENT. **See MCGRUDER, AARON.**

MCGRUDER, DR. CHARLES E.
Physician, educator. **Personal:** Born Jul 25, 1925, Alabama; married Curlie Haslip; children: Charles II & Jeffery. **Educ:** Ala A&M Col; Xavier Univ; Meharry Med Col, MD, 1952. **Career:** Meharry Med Col, assc prof; Fel Am Col, Obstet & Gynec, physician, 1956-; Am Bd Obstet & Gynec, diplomate. **Orgs:** Asst Scoutmaster Troop 77; Middle TN Coun, BSA. **Honors/Awds:** Woodbadge Beads in Scouting; Long Rifle; Silver Beaver. **Home Addr:** 1524 22nd Ave N, Nashville, TN 37208, **Home Phone:** (615)327-1628. **Business Addr:** 1005 18th Ave N, Nashville, TN 37208.

MCGUFFIN, DOROTHY BROWN
Counselor, educator. **Personal:** Born Jul 27, 1944, Metropolis, IL; daughter of Lester Brown and Mary Brown; married Robert; children: Denise & Toni Greathouse. **Educ:** Southern Ill Univ, Carbondale, Ill, BS, Home Econ Educ, 1965, MS, Educ, 1968; Drake Univ, MS, Coun & stud personnel serv, 1985. **Career:** Lawrence Adult Ctr, adult educr, 1977-81; Des Moines Area Community Col, adult educr, 1981-84; Young Women's Resource Ctr, community outreach counr, 1984-86; St Louis Community Col Forest Park, assessment specialist, 1986-87; St Louis Community Col Florissant Valley, coun, assoc prof, prof, scholar coordr, career counr, currently. **Orgs:** Prog chmn, secy, treas, Black Women's Coalition, 1976-80; bd mem, Continuing Educ Comn, St Louis Asn Coun & Develop; lic teacher & counr 4 states; Am Couns Asn; troop leader, consult, bd rep, Girl Scouts Coun; past pres, St Louis Coun Asn; past pres, MO Multicultural Coun Asn; bd mem, Licensing PRO Counr Mo; adv, Florissant Valley Chap Nat Soc Black Engr; co-chmn, Dist Diversity Comt; co-chmn, Florissant Valley Martin Luther King Celebration; bd mem, Spanish Lake Community Asn. **Honors/Awds:** Distinguished Service Award, Mo vocational Spec Needs Asn, 1990; Parent of the Year, INROADS, St Louis Inc, 1992, 1998, 2004; recipient, David L. Underwood Memorial Lect Award, St Louis Community Col Florissant Valley, 2004; A World of Difference Institute Community Serv Award, 2004; Distinguished Legislative Award, Am Coun Asn, 1995. **Special Achievements:** Workshop presenter, Drake Univ Career Develop; Conf presenter, English as a Second Language, Kans City Mo. **Home Addr:** 1821 Lakemont Lane, Saint Louis, MO 63138, **Home Phone:** (314)355-8071. **Business Addr:** Career Counselor, St Louis Community College at Florissant Valley, 300 S Broadway, Saint Louis, MO 63102-2800, **Business Phone:** (314)513-4269.

MCGUIRE, ALFRED D
Educator. **Personal:** Born Dec 7, 1981, Decatur, GA; son of Al and Dorothy. **Educ:** Savannah State Univ, BA, hist, 2003. **Career:** Coastal Heritage Soc, intern & interpreter, 2001-; Savannah Chatham County Pub Schs, substitute teacher, 2003. **Orgs:** Pres, Stud Govt Asn, 2001-03; Alpha Phi Alpha, Delta Eta Chaplain, 2001-; adv bd mem, St Joseph's Candler Afr Am Health Ctr, 2001; pub relations chair, Nat Asn Advan Colored People, 2001-; tutor, May Street Young Men Christian Asn, 2001; stud activities coordr, Savannah Black Heritage Festival, 2001-; basketball coach, May Street Young Men Christian Asn, 2002-; bd dirs, Achievers Today & Tomorrow Inc, 2002-; Ga Bd Regents, Task Force Enhancing Access Afr Am Males, 2003-. **Honors/Awds:** SGA Rookie of the Year, Savannah State Univ, 2000; Image Award, Savannah State Univ, 2001; Man of the Year Award, Achievers Today & Tomorrow Inc, 2001.

MCGUIRE, DR. CHESTER C., JR.
Educator. **Personal:** Born Oct 29, 1936, Gary, IN; married Julieivory; children: Michael, Angela & Gail. **Educ:** Dartmouth Col, BA, 1958; Univ Chicago, MBA, 1964; Grad Sch Bus, PhD, 1974. **Career:** Inland Steel Co, financial analyst, 1962-64; Real Estate Res Corp,economist, 1965-68; Wington A Burnett Const Co, vpres, gen mgr, 1968-70; Univ Calif, Berkeley, Dept City & Regional Planning, fac, 1970; prof, currently. **Orgs:** Am Inst Plan-

ner; Am Econ Asn; bd dirs, Acameda-contra Costa Co Transit Dist; vice chairperson, Berkely, Master Plan Revision Com; BCDC Adv Comt. **Military Serv:** USN, lt, 1959-62. **Business Addr:** Professor, University of California, Department of City & Regional Planning, 228 Wurster Hall, Berkeley, CA 94720-1850, **Business Phone:** (510)642-3256.

MCGUIRE, CYRIL A.
Labor activist. **Personal:** Born Apr 9, 1926, Lansing, MI; married Mary Jane Haithco; children: Cyril, Terence, Pamela. **Educ:** Lansing Bus Univ, attended 1956; Mich State Univ, attended 1957. **Career:** UAW Int Union, educ rep; Gen Motors, employee. **Orgs:** Dist committeeman, 1956-59; shop & committeeman, 1959-69; chmn, shop com, 1965-69; dE UAW Int Convs, 1966, 1968, 1970, 1972, 1974, 1977; vpres, 1969-72; vpres, Lansing Labor News Bd, 1971-75, pres, 1975-77; pres, UAW Local 652, 1972-77, com secy, Int Credentials, 1974, comt chmn, 1977; instr, Labor Rel Studies Lansing Comn Col, 1976-77; rec sec Capitol Area Comm Action Progs; Genesee Co Comm Action Progs Coun; pres, vpres, treas, secy, PTA; bd mem, Gtr Lansing Urban League; Gtr Lansing Coun Against Alcoholism; treas, Dem Bus & Prof Org; Salvation Army; Boy Scouts Am; Big Bros Inc; Vol Action Ctr; Health Contorl; Gtr Lansing Safety Coun; Model Cities & Woldumar Nature Ctr; treas, Dem 6th Cong Dist; precinct del Ingham Co Dem Exec Comn; NAACP; Dem Party; Urban League; Mich Labor Hist; Labor Adv Comt Lansing Comn, Mich State Univ; liaison consult Region 1-C Big Bros Lansing; state pres, Mich Chap A Philip Randolph Inst; Mich Democrate State Central Comt, 8th Dist. **Honors/Awds:** Outstanding Serv award, Lansing Model Cities; Man of yr, Nat Asn Negro Bus & Prof Women, 1976-77; Distinguished Service Award, Flint Chap, A Philip Randolph Inst, 1990; Distinguished Service Award, Nat Off, APRI, 1991; Distinguished Service Award, Ingham County; Edward Taylor Memorial Lifetime Achievement Award, 1991; State Mich, Special Tribute, 1991; US House Rep Cong Record, 1991. **Military Serv:** AUS, sgt, 1950-52. *

MCGUIRE, JEAN MITCHELL
Association executive. **Personal:** Born Apr 11, 1931, Canton, MA; married Clinton; children: Johanna, David & Clinton Jr. **Educ:** Howard Univ, attended 1951; Boston State Col, BS, 1961; Tufts Univ, MEd, 1963. **Career:** Boston Pub Schs, pupil adjust counr, 1963-73; Simmons Col, instr, 1971-74; Metrop Coun Educ Opportunity, exec dir, 1973-; Boston Sch Comn, staff, 1982-. **Orgs:** Boston Teachers Union, 1962; Black Educ Alliance Mass; Negro Air Masns Int; Nat All Black Sch Educ; adv bd, Mass Womens Polit Caucus; corporator, Homes Savings Bank; mem bd, Mass Conf United Church Christ; trustee, Boston C Mus; Negro Airmen's Int New Eng Chap; Delta Sigma Theta Sorority, Boston Alumnae Chap; Mass Black Polit Task Force; life mem Nat Asn Advan Colored People; Eta Phi Chapter; Omega Psi Phi Fraternity Inc. **Honors/Awds:** Alice K Pollitzer Award, Encampment Citizenship, 1978; Zeta Phi Beta Sorority Award, 1980; Black Achievers Award, Boston, 1982; Fred Douglass Publication Service, YMCA, 1982; DHL, Salem State Col, 1983; WGBH Community Achievement Award; Bristol Co Juvenile Court Award; Big Brothers Asn Award; Founders Award, Omega Psi Phi Fraternity Inc; Mass Teachers Asn Award. **Business Addr:** Executive Director, Metropolitan Council for Educational Opportunity Inc, 40 Dimock St, Roxbury, MA 02119, **Business Phone:** (617)427-1545.

MCGUIRE, RAYMOND J.
Banker. **Educ:** The Hotchkiss Sch, Harvard Col, AB, 1979; Harvard Bus Sch, MBA, 1984; Harvard Law Sch, JD, 1984; Univ Nice, France. **Career:** First Boston Corp, assoc, 1984-88; Wasserstein Perella & Co, partner, 1988-94; Wasserstein Perella & Company Inc, managing partner, 1991-; Merrill Lynch, Mergers & Acquistions, managing dir, 1994-; Patterson, Belknap, Webb & Tyler, assoc; Skadden, Arps, assoc; Morgan Stanley Global Co-Head Mergers & Acquisitions; Citigroup, managing dir & co-head global Invest banking, currently. **Orgs:** Chmn bd, De La Salle Acad; pres bd, Int Ctr Photog; trustee, Lincoln Ctr; trustee, NY Presbyterian Hosp; trustee, NY Pub Libr; pres bd, San Remo Tenants Corp; chmn bd, Studio Museum in Harlem; trustee, Alex Hillman Family Found; vpres, Whitney Mus Am Art; trustee, New Mus Contemporary Art; bd mem, Wyeth, 2006-; Overseers & Dirs Nominating Comt; bd mem, Joseph & Claire Flom Found; bd mem, Howard Gilman Found; bd mem, Hotchkiss Sch. **Honors/Awds:** Rotary Fel, 1980; Black Enterprise, one of the 25 Hottest Blacks on Wall Street, 1992-97; Make-A-Wish Found & Art for Life Found; Distinguished Alumni Award & Distinguished Alumni Speaker Series, Harvard Bus Sch; Patron of the Arts, Pratt Inst. **Special Achievements:** First African managing dir at Wasserstein Perella; specialist in mergers & acquisitions; Distinguished Alumni Speaker Series. **Business Addr:** Managing Director, Co Head of Global Investment Banking, Citi Markets & Banking, 399 Park Ave, New York, NY 10043, **Business Phone:** (212)559-1000.*

MCGUIRT, MILFORD W
Certified public accountant. **Personal:** Born Aug 15, 1956, Niles, MI; son of Milton and Vhuaness; married Carolyn J Sconiers; children: Shavonne, Andrea & Brittany. **Educ:** Western Mich Univ, BBA, cum laude, 1978. **Career:** Coopers & Lybrand, audit mgr, 1978-85; Peat Marwick Mitchell & Co, sr audit mgr, 1985-90; KPMG Peat Marwick, partner, 1990-; KPMG LLP, partner, currently. **Orgs:** Bd mem, South Bend Ind Chap Urban League, 1981-82; Am Inst CPA's, 1980; Mich Asn CPA's, 1980; Ga Soc CPA's, 1986; Nat Asn Black Acct, 1986; Fin Mgr's Soc, 1986; Atlanta Chamber Com Pres Comn, 1986; bd mem, Atlanta West End Rotary Club, 1986; bd mem, West End Boys & Girls Club, 1995; bd mem, UNICEF Atlanta, 1997; Atlanta Steering Comt, 2005-06; bd advisor, Ga Found Independent Col Inc. **Honors/Awds:** Outstanding Alumni Award, Beta Alpha Psi, Western Mich Univ, 1995; Best Mentor, KPMG Peat Marwick, 1997. **Home Addr:** 4234 Nobleman Pt, Duluth, GA 30097, **Home Phone:** (404)987-1941. **Business Addr:** Audit Partner, KPMG LLP, 303 Peachtree St NE Suite 2000, Atlanta, GA 30303, **Business Phone:** (404)222-3000.

MCHENRY, DONALD F.
Executive, ambassador, educator. **Personal:** Born Oct 13, 1936, East St Louis, IL; divorced; children: Michael Stephen, Christina Ann, Elizabeth Ann. **Educ:** IL State Univ, BS, 1957; So IL Univ, MS, 1959; Georgetown Univ, post grad studies, 1962. **Career:** Howard Univ Wash, instr, 1959-62; US State Dept, various positions, 1963-73; Brookings Inst, guest scholar, 1971-73; Coun Foreign Rels, intl affairs fellow, 1971-73; Sch Foreign Serv Georgetown Univ, lect, 1971-72; Carnegie Endowment INTL Peace, humanitarin policy studies, project dir, 1973; Am Univ Wash, lect, 1975; US State Dept, Pres Jimmy Carter's transition staff, 1976; UN Security CNL, appointed US deputy rep, 1977-79; United Nations, US permanent rep, 1979-81; Georgetown Univ, Distinguished Prof Diplomacy & Int Affairs, 1981-; Coca-Cola co, dir, 1981-; Ambassador, United Nations; IRC Group, pres, currently. **Orgs:** UN Western Five Contact Group; dir: Intl Paper Co, Coca-Cola Co, SmithKline Beecham Corp, AT&T, Fleet Boston Financial Corp; Am Stock Exchange, former gov; Coun Foreign Rels, dir; editorial bd mem, Foreign Policy Magazine; Am Acad Diplomacy; Ctr Transitional Justice; Alpha Phi Alpha. **Honors/Awds:** Superior Honor Award, Dept of State, 1966; Family of Man Award, NY Coun Churches, 1980; fellow, AM ACAD Arts & Sci. **Special Achievements:** US negotiator on question of Namibia; author, Micronesia: Trust Betrayed, 1975. **Business Addr:** President, IRC Group, 1320 19th St, N W Suite 410, Washington, DC 20036, **Business Phone:** 800-306-2653.*

MCHENRY, DOUG. **See MCHENRY, DOUGLAS.**

MCHENRY, DOUGLAS (DOUG MCHENRY)
Administrator, movie producer, movie director. **Educ:** Stanford Univ, BA, econs, 1973; Harvard Bus Sch, MBA, 1977; Harvard Law Sch, JD, 1977. **Career:** Producer, dir, Actor, Business Owner; Krush Groove, 1985; Disorderlies, 1987; House Party 2, 1991; New Jack City, 1991; Private Times, 1991; Jason's Lyric, 1994; House Party 3, 1994; The Walking Dead, 1995; Scenes for the Soul, 1995; A Thin Line Between Love & Hate, 1996; Body Count, 1998; Two Can Play That Game, 2001; The Brothers, 2001; Double Tap, 2006; Direcor: House Party 2, 1991; Jason's Lyric, 1994; Kingdom Come, 2001; "Keep the Faith, Baby", 2002; Actor: Fear of a Black Hat, 1994; Road to 'New Jack City', 2005; Casablanca Rec & Filmworks, dir bus affairs; Avco Embassy Pictures, dir legal & bus affairs, TV exec; Solar Rec, vpres film entertainment; Quincy Jones Entertainment, prod exec; Jackson/McHenry Entertainment, pres & partner; Elephant Walk Entertainment, partner, chief exec officer & pres, currently. **Honors/Awds:** Numerous honors and awards including Award for outstanding drama, HUGHIE, ACE; Nat Asn Advan Colored People Image Award; CSTA Leadership Award; Western Film Archive Award; National Association of Advertisers Award for excellence in film; Urban League Leadership Award, Los Angeles Br; CEBA Award, Pioneers of Excellence, World Inst Black Commun Inc, 1991. **Special Achievements:** Landmark three-year production deal with Savoy Pictures. **Business Phone:** (310)887-3977.*

MCHENRY, EMMIT J
Executive, founder (originator), consultant. **Personal:** Born Jul 12, 1943, Forrest City, AR. **Educ:** Univ Denver, BS, commun, 1966; Northwestern Univ, MS, commun, 1979. **Career:** Int Bus Mach; Conn Gen, mgr; Union Mutual & Allstate Ins, staff; Network Solutions Inc, co founder, 1979; NetCom Solutions Int Inc, founder, chmn & chief exec officer, 1995-. **Orgs:** Exec comt, bd dirs, NetCom Solutions Int Ltd, UK; chair, Governance Comt, Phelps Stokes Fund; adv bd, DECIS Technol; chmn bd, LearnCity Inc; Fairfax Co Econ Develop Authority; State Va Econ Develop Authority; bd dirs, James Martin Govt Intelligence; chair bd dirs, NeCom Solutions S Africa. **Honors/Awds:** Vendor Award for Quality Service Provider, IBM; Subcontractor Quality Service Provider Award, NASA; Highest Vendor Quality Award, AT&T; Partner in Excellence Award, Lucent Technologies. **Military Serv:** USMC, Lt. **Business Addr:** Chairman, Chief Executive Officer, NetCom Solutions International Inc, 14360 Sullyfield Circle, Chantilly, VA 20151, **Business Phone:** (703)736-0700.*

MCHENRY, DR. JAMES O
Administrator. **Personal:** Born Nov 11, 1940, Sterlington, LA; son of S O McHenry and Rebecca; married Esther C Johnson; children: Stephanie Diane & Ali Kenyatta. **Educ:** Grambling State Univ, BS, 1963; Wayne State Univ, MEd, 1970, DEd 1979. **Career:** Monroe Los Angels Bd Educ, music teacher, 1962-63; AUS Educ Ctr, Europe, GED teacher, 1965; Mich Bd Educ, res teacher, 1966-67; Wayne City Recorders Ct, probation officer, 1967-73; Recorders Ct Probation Dept, asst supvr, 1973-78; Mich Dept Licensing & Reg, cert marriage counr, 1975-80; Recorders Ct Drug Prog, dir, 1978-80; Recorders Ct Pretrial Serv, dir, 1980-82; Oakland Univ, lectr, 1984-; US Pretrial Serv Agency, Detroit, Mich, chief pretrial serv officer, currently. **Orgs:** Omega Psi Phi Frat, 1960-; Restoration Comt; Formal Dance Comt; Assault Illiteracy Comt; block chmn, San Juan Pennington Block Club; vpres-Recording Partner, Fifteen Investors Group. **Honors/Awds:** Special Award, NARCO, 1983; Leadership Award, Recorders Ct Probation Dept, 1983; President's Award, Grambling State Univ, 1983. **Military Serv:** AUS, E-4. **Home Addr:** 17191 Pennington Dr, Detroit, MI 48221. **Business Addr:** Chief Pretrial Services Officer, US District Court, Pretrial Services Agency, 231 W Lafayette St, Detroit, MI 48226, **Business Phone:** (313)226-4962.

MCHENRY, MARY WILLIAMSON
Educator. **Personal:** Born Jan 23, 1933, Washington, DC; children: Michael S, Christina A & Elizabeth A. **Educ:** Mt Holyoke Col, AB, 1950-54; Columbia Univ, MA, 1955-60; George Washington Univ, 1962-65. **Career:** Howard Univ, instr eng, 1960-62; George Washington Univ, asst prof eng, 1964-69; DC Teachers Col, guest lectr eng, 1967-68; Fed City Col, asst prof eng, 1969-74; Mt Holyoke Col, assoc prof eng, assoc dean studies, prof eng, 1974-97, prof emer eng, 1998-. **Orgs:** Phi Beta Kappa MHC Chap, 1954; fel, John Jay Whitney Opportunity, 1954-55, 1957-58; Danforth Found fel, 1961-62; instr, Am Studies Peace Corps Training Prog, 1962-63; consult ed, Univ Mass Press, 1978-79; adv bd, Radcliffe Seminars Forum Continuing Ed, 1980. **Honors/Awds:** Nat Endowment for the Humanities, 1972-73. **Home Addr:** 3001 Veazey Terr NW, Washington, DC 20008. **Business Addr:** Professor Emeritus of English, Mount Holyoke College, Deptartment of English, 111 Shattuck Hall 50 Col St, South Hadley, MA 01075, **Business Phone:** (413)538-2146.

MCILWAIN, NADINE WILLIAMS
School administrator. **Personal:** Born Jul 29, 1943, Canton, OH; daughter of Willie J and Mabel W; married Albert H (divorced); children: Jeaneen & Floyd; married William P Massey, Jul 4, 2002. **Educ:** Malone Col, BA, 1970; Univ Akron, MA, 1978; Ashland Univ, MA, 1990. **Career:** Canton City Health Dept, lab asst, 1962-65; Ohio Bell Telephone Co, opr & consult, 1967-70; Timken Sr High Sch, teacher, 1971-90; Canton City Sch, teacher, curric specialist, bd & pres, currently; Nefertiti Nuptials, owner, operator, 1984-; Canton City Coun, ward council person, 1984-86; Alliance City Sch, prin; Allen Elem Sch, Dayton, OH, prin; Sisters Charity Found, Canton, prog officer, 2001-05. **Orgs:** Pres, Frontiers Intl Aux, 1971; dir, Canton City Sch, 1975-82; pres, LeilaGreen Educrs Coun, 1978; sec, Am Bus Womens Assoc, 1980; st parliamentarian, Nat Black Womens Leadership Caucus, 1983-84; ward Counwoman, Canton City Coun, 1984-; owner & operator, Nadine's Nuptials, 1984-; elected mem, Canton City Bd Educ, 2002-06. **Honors/Awds:** Woman of the Year, Canton Negro Oldtimers Athletic Asn, 1979; Political Award, Black Women's Leadership Caucus, 1981; Woman of the Year, Greater Canton Am Bus Women's Assoc 1982; Nat Educ Award, Milken Family Found; Ohio Humanitarian Award, Educ Martin L King Jr Holiday Comn, State Ohio. **Home Addr:** 3409 Tradewinds Cove NW, Canton, OH 44708. **Business Addr:** Board, President, Canton City Schools, 617 McKinley Ave SW, Canton, OH 44707, **Business Phone:** (330)438-2500.

MCILWAIN, TONI
Executive. **Personal:** Born Jan 26, 1948, Akron, OH; daughter of Julius and Dorothy; married Roger, Apr 21, 1974; children: Luther, Lance, Lashon & Lanette. **Career:** Wayne State Univ, Harmony Proj, dir; Metro E, coun; Twin Sisters, Same Spirit, co-founder; Ravendale Community Inc, founder & pres, currently. **Orgs:** Secy, Detroit Revitilization Inc; co-chair, Metro E; Lakewood Manor. **Honors/Awds:** Found Sharing Award, Tiger Woods Found, 1998; Block Builder; Triumphs Josephs, Detroit News. **Business Phone:** (313)527-1603.

MCINNIS, JEFF LEMANS
Basketball player. **Personal:** Born Oct 22, 1974, Charlotte, NC. **Educ:** Univ NC, Chapel Hill, psychol, 1996. **Career:** Panionios, Greece, prof basketball player, 1996-97; Denver Nuggets, 1996; CBA, Quad City; Wash Wizards, guard, 1999; Los Angeles Clippers, 2000-02; Portland Trailblazers, 2002-04; Cleveland Cavaliers, guard, 2004-05; NJ Nets, guard, 2005-07; Charlotte Bobcats, guard, 2007-08. **Honors/Awds:** Most Valuable Player of the CBA, 1999-00; Most Improved Player Award, Nat Basketball Asn, 2000-01. *

MCINTOSH, DR. FRANKIE L.
School administrator, educator. **Personal:** Born Dec 15, 1949, Quitman, GA; daughter of Frank and Ida Hardy. **Educ:** NC Cent Univ, Durham, NC, BA, 1972; Atlanta Univ, Atlanta, GA, 1973; Univ Ga, Athens, GA, MPA, 1981; Ga State Univ, Atlanta, GA, PhD, 2000. **Career:** Social Security Admin, Atlanta, GA, claims rep, 1974-78; Social Security Admin, Atlanta, GA, supvr, 1978-

80; Social Security Admin, Atlanta, GA, mgr, 1980-86; Ga Perimeter Col, Clarkston, GA, prof polit sci, 1986-, dept chair, 1988-2002, Acad Adv Comt Polit Sci, mem, currently. **Orgs:** Alpha Kappa Alpha Sorority, 1970-; NC Cent Univ Alumni Asn, Atlanta Chap, 1972-; Am Bus Women's Asn, 1980-86; SSA Southern Regional Mgt Asn,1980-87; Ga Polit Sci Asn, 1986-; Nat Conf Black Polit Scientists, 1986-; Nat Educ Asn/GAE/DCFA, 1987-; Ga Asn Women Deans, Administrators, & Counsr, 1988-91; Southern Polit Sci Asn, 1989-; Am Bus Women's Asn, 1999-. **Honors/Awds:** Superior Performance Award, Social Security Admin, 1976 & 1980; Woman of the Year, Am Bus Women's Asn, Mableton Chap, 1983; Outstanding Public Service Award, Social Security Admin, 1986-; Teaching Excellence Award, Dekalb Col, 1995; Outstanding Faculty Award, 1996; NISOD Teaching Excellence Award, 1996. **Business Addr:** Professor Political Science, Georgia Perimeter College, 555 N Indian Creek Dr, CB-2250, Clarkston, GA 30021, **Business Phone:** (678)891-3284.

MCINTOSH, HELEN YOUNG
Chief executive officer. **Career:** Kirkland Chrysler Jeep, chief exec officer, currently. **Orgs:** Premier mem, Nat Asn Minority Automobile Dealers. **Business Addr:** Chief Executive Officer, Kirkland Chrysler Jeep, 12828 NE 124th St, Kirkland, WA 98034, **Business Phone:** (866)435-2999.*

MCINTOSH, JAMES E.
Dentist, educator. **Personal:** Born Jul 15, 1942, St Louis, MO. **Educ:** Univ Mo, BA, 1965; Meharry Col, DDS, 1969; Columbia Univ, MPH, 1975. **Career:** Fed Food & Drug Div, inspector, 1965; Univ Mo, fel, 1963-65; Nashville Health Dept, researcher, 1968-69; Cloverbottom Mental Health Inst, 1969; Sydenham Hosp, rotating internship 1970, periodentics residency, 1971; Pvt Practice, 1971-; Dental Clin Sydenham Hosp, adminr, 1971-; Tri State Eval Accident Ins, consult, 1974-; Asn NY Neighborhood & Health Ctrs, consult, 1974-; Columbia Univ, asst prof 1974-; Sydenham Hosp, dir, 1975-. **Orgs:** Nat Student Dent Asn, 1956-69; Rose Hill Baptist Church, 1958-; rep, Nat Conclave Kappa Alpha Psi, 1964; Nat Asn Advancement Colored People, 1965-; Ewell Neal Dent Soc, 1965-69; class pres, Dental Sch 1967-69; Proctor & Gamble Res Symp, 1968; pres, Student Faculty Rels Com Meharry Med Col, 1968-69; Black Am Med & Dent Asn Students, 1969-; diplomate, Nat Dent Bd , 1969-; Nat Dent Asn, 1969-; Ny State Dent Soc, 1970-; First Dist Dent Soc, 1970-; Mo Dent Soc, 1972-; Am Pub Health Asn, 1974-; bd, Eligible Am Acad Pub Health & Prev Dent, 1974-; pres, Sydenham Hosp Med Bd, 1976-; exec comt, Sydenham Hosp Med Bd, 1976-; Na Omicron Sigma Nat Hon Ldrshp Frat 1976-. **Honors/Awds:** Award, Table Clin Presentation, 1969. **Business Addr:** Professor, Columbia University College Of Dental Medicine, Community DentCare Network, 630 W 168th St, PO Box 20, New York, NY 10032.*

MCINTOSH, LEVI H., JR.
Educational consultant. **Educ:** New Mexico State University, Bachelor of Science; San Francisco State University, Masters in Educational Administration; Nova Southeastern University, Doctor of Philosophy. **Career:** President and CEO of McIntosh and Asociates, LLC Consultant Group. **Orgs:** Executive Committee Member, 100 Black Men of America; Association for Supervisor and Curriculum Development; Florida Association School Administrators; National Alliance of Black School Educators; Duval County Association of School Administrators; American Association of School Administrations; National Association for Multi-Cultural Education (NAME). **Honors/Awds:** Florida PTA Life Membership; African-American Achievers Special Recognition Award. *

MCINTOSH, MARC
Executive, vice president (organization). **Personal:** Born in Chicago, IL. **Educ:** De Paul Univ; Harvard Bus Sch. **Career:** Goldman, Sachs & Co, finance, vpres, 1989; PaineWebber Group Inc, managing dir, Telecommunications Group, head, 1989-, Latin Am group, head, 1991-. **Orgs:** Bd dir, Greater New York, Coun Boys Scouts Am. **Honors/Awds:** Black Enterprise, one of the 25 Hottest Black Wall Street, 1992. *

MCINTOSH, RHODINA COVINGTON
Lawyer. **Personal:** Born May 26, 1947, Chicago Heights, IL; daughter of William George and Cora Jean Cain; married Gerald Alfred, Dec 14, 1970; children: Gary Allen, Garvey Anthony & Ayana Kai. **Educ:** Mich State Univ, BA (Cum Laude), 1969; Univ Detroit, JD, 1978. **Career:** Mich State Univ Off Equal Opportunity, asst dir, 1969-70; Bell & Hudson PC Detroit, law clerk, 1977-79; Covington McIntosh & Assocs Int, pres, Detroit MI, Wash, DC & Mbabane, Swaziland, 1980-83; Univ Swaziland & Botswana Kwaluseni Swaziland, lectr, 1981-83; US AID Off Pvt & Vol Coop, chief info & tech assistance, 1983-87, chief info & prog support, 1987-88; Automation Res Systs Ltd, corp coun, 1988-93; Konsider It Done Mgt Corp, 1993-, pres, 2000-. **Orgs:** NCP, 1960-70; founding bd mem, Women's Justice Ctr Detroit, 1975-77; Phi Alpha Delta Law Fraternity, 1977-; coord, Women's Leadership Conf Wayne State Univ Detroit, 1979; bd mem & counr, Awareness Inc Detroit, 1979-80; consult, Polit Educ Workshops Detroit, Flint, Lansing, Saginaw, Grand Rapids MI, 1979-80; bd mem, Detroit Urban League, 1980-; founding bd mem, Wayne Co Chap MI Republican Women's Task Force Detroit, 1980; Detroit Urban League, 1980; main rapporteur, First All Africa Law Conf Univ, Swaziland & Botswana Kwaluseni Swaziland, 1981; charter mem, Nat Asn Female Execs, 1983-; chairperson foreign rels subcom, Nat Black Women's Polit Caucus Wash, 1984; bd mem, Am Opportunity Found Wash, 1984-87; Mich State Univ Alumni Asn, 1985-; GOP Women's Network, 1986-87; Teacher Asn Springbrook High Sch, 1986-90; Naval Acad Athletic Asn, 1987-90; St Teresa Avila Roman Catholic Church, 1987-89; Nat Bar Asn, 1989-; Am Bar Asn, 1989-; Univ Calif, Berkeley Booster Club Track, 1990-93; vice chair, Small Bus Community ABA, 1991-92; chair bd, Christian Vision Ctr Homeless Shelter, 1995-, Far South Suburban Cook Co; prog chair, Goodwill Charity Club, 1995-; adv bd mem, Suburban Recovery Ctr Inc, 1996-2000; ed, Union Banner, Union Evangelistic Baptist Church, 1996-99; City Chicago Heights Beautification Comn, 1998; City Chicago Heights Cable Comn, 2000; Delta Sigma Theta. **Honors/Awds:** National Achievement Scholar Finalist National Merit, 1965; Scholar, Martin Luther King Jr Ctr Social Change Atlanta, 1976; Award, Detroit Women's Justice Ctr, 1978; Award, Goodwill Charity Club, Chicago Heights, IL, 1978; Award Outstanding Volunteer Service Reagan/Bush Campaign, 1980; Award Detroit Edison, 1980; Award, Wayne Co Chap Republican Women's Task Force, 1980; Distinguished Leadership Award, ABI, 1987; Activist of the Year Award, Far So Sub Cook Co, Nat Asn Advan Colored People, 1999; Certificate of Achievement, Welfare Work Initiative, Chicago Heights Ministerial Alliance, 1999; Pioneer Award, Frederick Douglas Soc, Detroit, MI, 1994; Woman of the Decade Award, Bloom Township High Sch Centennial Celebration, 2000. **Home Phone:** (708)757-5732. **Business Addr:** President, Konsider It Done Management, 1508 Hanover St, Chicago Heights, IL 60441, **Business Phone:** (708)715-5685.

MCINTYRE, DIANNE RUTH
Choreographer. **Personal:** Born Jul 18, 1946, Cleveland, OH; daughter of Francis Benjamin and Dorothy Layne. **Educ:** Ohio State Univ, Columbus, OH, BFA, dance. **Career:** Choreographer, 1972-; Sounds in Motion, New York, NY, choreorapher & founder, 1972-88; tv progs, choreographer; Nat Endowment Arts, choreographers fels, 1990-93; Theatre/Dance Pieces: In Living Color: a Gullah Story; Blues Rooms; I Could Stop on a Dime & Get Ten Cents Change; Open the Door, Virginia!; Dance: Mule Bone; King Hedley II; Spell #7; Miss Evers? Boys, Polk County; Crowns. **Orgs:** Soc Stage Dirs & Choreographers; Am Fedn Tv & Radio Artists; Nat Endowment Arts & New York State Coun Arts; Soc Stage Dir Choreographers. **Honors/Awds:** AUDELCO Black Theatre Awards, United Black Artists Cornell Univ, choreography, 1979; Bessie Award, 1989; Performance Award, 1989; Helen Hayes Award; Thelma Hill Award; Woodie Award; AUDELCO Pioneer Award. **Home Phone:** (216)337-1376. **Business Phone:** (216)337-1376.

MCINTYRE, NATALIE. See GRAY, MACY.

MCIVER, EVERETT
Football player. **Personal:** Born Aug 5, 1970, Cumberland, NC; children: Everett, Eric & Briallen Dutches Lynn. **Educ:** Elizabeth City State Univ. **Career:** Football player (retired); New York Jets, guard, 1994-95; Miami Dolphins, 1996-97; Dallas Cowboys, 1998-99; Atlanta Falcons, guard, 2000; free agent, currently.

MCIVER, JOHN DOUGLAS
Mayor, paper industry worker. **Personal:** Born Nov 7, 1941, Savannah, GA; son of James and Hagar Norman; married Gloria Grant, Mar 26, 1966; children: Andrea, Timothy, Anthony, Pamelia & Cassandra. **Educ:** Liberty County High Sch. **Career:** Interstate Paper Corp, Riceboro, GA, paper maker first asst, 1968-99; City Riceboro, mayor, 2001; Co Comn, chmn, 2003-. **Orgs:** Liberty County Ind Authority, 1980; vice chmn, Riceboro Community Found, 1982; chmn, New Zion Baptist Church, 1977, vice-chmn, 1989; pres, Ga Conf Black Mayors, 1989; bd mem, Coastal Ga Community Action Agency Inc, 1988-91, vpres, 1991-92; chmn, Liberty County Joint Planning Comn; bd dirs, Ga Regional Develop Ctr. **Honors/Awds:** First Black Dorchester Credit Union, 1978; community leader, Riceboro Community Found, 1983; Outstanding Achievement Award, Omega Psi Phi Fraternity Inc, 1992. **Military Serv:** AUS, spec-4. **Home Addr:** PO Box 246, Riceboro, GA 31323. *

MCIVER, MARGARET HILL
Educator. **Personal:** Born Jun 3, 1925, High Point, NC; married Conerlious W; children: Conerlious W Jr & Deborah Ann. **Educ:** Bennett Col, Greensboro, NC, BA, 1944; Atlanta Univ, Sch Social Work, MSW, 1946; Harvard Univ, EdM, 1967. **Career:** Clark Col Atlanta, teacher counr, 1946-49; Fla A&M Univ, counr women,1949-51; Morris Brown Col, dean women, 1951-53; Douglass High Sch, GA,teacher guidance counr, 1953-69; Proj Upward Bound Norman Park Col, GA,counr, 1968-70; Douglass Middle Sch, guidance counr, 1969-; Ga Gov Honors Prog Gifted Wesleyan Col Macon, GA, guidance counr, 1972-74 & 1979. **Orgs:** Pres, Ga br Am Personnel & Guidance Asn, 1968; pres, Ga Sch Counrs Asn, 1973-74; dir, dist 2 Ga Asn Educrs, 1974-77. **Honors/Awds:** Alpha Kapa Mu Honor Soc, Bennett Col, Greensboro, NC, 1943; Teacher of theYear, Thomasville, Ga Teachers Asn, 1962; Counselor of the Year, Dist 2 Ga Sch Counrs Asn, 1972; Women of the Year, Thomasville, GA C C, 1975. **Business Addr:** Guidance Counselor, Douglass Middle School, Forrest St, Thomasville, GA 31792.

MCKANDERS, JULIUS A., II
Lawyer, clergy. **Personal:** Born Jun 21, 1941, Jackson, MS; married Yvonne Mclittle. **Educ:** Wayne State Univ, JD, 1971; Henry Ford Comm Col, attended 1962; Detroit Inst Tech, attended 1962; Eastern Mich , BS, 1964; Univ Mich Med Sch, attended 1966; Morehouse Sch Religion, ITC, 1976. **Career:** Univ Mich Med Sch, res asst, 1964-66; City Detroit, syst analyst-progmr, 1966-67; IRS Detroit, sys analyst, 1967-69; Price Waterhouse, sr mgt, 1969-70; Detroit Bd Ed, mgr, 1970-71; Coun Leg Ed Opp, deputy dir oper, 1971-72; Ebenezer Bapt Ch, assoc minister; Metro Atlanta Rapid Transit & Auth, dir contracts & procur 1972-; Mich Bar, admitted 1972; Ga Bar, 1974. **Orgs:** Am Bar Asn; Detroit Bar Asn; Atlanta Bar Asn; Phi Alpha Delta; Purch Mgt Asn GA; Atlanta Jr C C; bd dirs, Martin L King Jr Child Develop Ctr; bd dirs, Nat Asn Advan Colored People Atlanta Br Prog Comn; Am Pub Transit Asn; adv coun, Martin L King, Jr Handicapped Child Proj; bd mem, Ebenezer Bapt Ch Charitable Found & life mem, Nat Asn Advan Colored People; ordained Bapt min. **Business Addr:** 101 Prof Bldg, 2192 Campbellton Rd SW, Atlanta, GA 30311.

MCKANDERS, KENNETH ANDRE
Lawyer. **Personal:** Born Nov 18, 1950, Inkster, MI; son of Julius Aaron and Addye N Norwood Smith; married Carolyn M Welch McKanders, Aug 4, 1973; children: Kimberly, Karla, Kristal & Kenneth. **Educ:** Mich State Univ, E Lansing, MI, BA, 1972; Wayne State Univ, Detroit, MI, JD, 1977. **Career:** Recorder's Ct, Detroit, MI, probation officer, 1973-78; Wayne State Univ, Detroit, MI, asst gen coun, 1978-86; Wayne County Community Col, Detroit, MI, gen coun, 1986-87; Eastern Mich Univ, Ypsilanti, MI, gen coun, 1987-. **Orgs:** Mich State Bar Asn, 1978-; Am Bar Asn, 1980-; bd mem, past pres, Wayne State Univ Campus Ministry, 1984-; bd mem, past vchair, Hartford Agape Inc, 1984-90; bd mem, past pres, Renaissance Optimist Club, 1986-. **Business Addr:** General Counsel, Eastern Michigan University, Office of Legal Affairs, 11 Welch Hall, Ypsilanti, MI 48197, **Business Phone:** (734)487-1055.

MCKANDES, DARNELL DAMON
Educator. **Personal:** Born Aug 26, 1966, Honolulu, HI; son of Robert Henry Sr and Dorothy Clark. **Educ:** SC State Col, 1984-88. **Career:** Gen Motors Corp, Saginaw Div, security officer, 1986; Maple Hill Golf Club, asst prof, 1991; Jackson State Univ, golf coach, girls golf team, 1992; PGA, prof golf player, currently. **Orgs:** Kappa Youth Leadership League; Saginaw Alumnae Chapter Kappa Alpha Psi Fraternity Inc, 1983-84; Bethel AME Church, vol; Frontiers Annual Christmas Shopping Spree Underpriviledged C, 1982-84. **Honors/Awds:** Frontiers Int, Community Leadership & Service Youth Award, 1983; Golf Scholarship, SC State Col, 1984; Alpha Phi Alpha Fraternity Inc, Iota Chi Lambda Chapter Annual Golf Tournament, First place, 1989, 1990; medalist honors, Saginaw Dist Invitational Golf Tournament, 1989; Scholarship Recipient, Tri-City Chapter, The Links Inc, 1984; Black Honors Convocation, 1980-82; A Anton Pieritz Scholarship, nominee, 1984; runner-up, Saginaw Valley League's All Conf Golf Team, 1983; First Place, First Annual Nat Col Minority Golf Championship Tournament, 1987; Second Annual South Carolina State Golf Team, First Place, 1988; Saginaw Valley All League Golf Honors; Lee Elder Golf Invitational, golf participant, Myrtle Beach, 1988; First Place, Hawaii Golf Tournament Players Asn, Hawaii Prince Course, 1994; First Place, 51st Vehichle City Open, Pro Div, Flint MI, 2000. **Home Phone:** (517)752-9961. **Business Addr:** Professional Golf Player, The PGA of America, 100 Ave of the Champions, Palm Beach Gardens, FL 33418, **Business Phone:** (561)624-8400.

MCKANDES, DOROTHY DELL
Educator. **Personal:** Born Jul 5, 1937, Saginaw, MI; daughter of William Henry Clark and Katherine Halliday Clark; married Robert Henry, Jan 16, 1961; children: Robert Henry Jr & Darnell Damon. **Educ:** Leeward Community Col, Pearl City, Hawaii, AA, 1974; Cent Mich Univ, Mt Pleasant, MI, BA, 1975, MA, 1977; Delta Col, Cert, Adult Lit, 1986. **Career:** Leeward Community Col, Pearl City, Hawaii, asst instr, 1975; Pub Schs Saginaw, Saginaw, MI, elem teacher, 1977-84; Stud Task Force Prog, job shadow coordr, 1982; Mich Child Care Ctr, asst dir, 1986-89; Kiddie Kingdom Pre-Sch Ctr, Saginaw, MI, dir, 1990-. **Orgs:** Cofounder, Tri-City Chap, Links Inc, 1980-; bd mem, Bethel African Methodist Episcopal Church; United Way Saginaw County; fund distrib comt, Lit Task Force, 1991; life mem, Cent MI Univ; bd mem, Saginaw County Foster Care, 1988-89; former co-owner, Cosmopolitan Roller Arena, 1978-83; bd dirs, READ Asn, 1997; bd dirs, Mitten Bay Girl Scout Coun, 1997-98. **Honors/Awds:** Dedicated Service & Distinguished Service Awards, Tri-City Links Inc, 1990; State Scholarship, Hawaii Fedn Bus & Prof Women's Club, 1977; Nominee, 1990; Kool Achiever Awards, Brown & Williamson Tobacco Corp, Ky, Cert Recognition; Community Service Award, Nestle USA Inc, 1992; Certificate of Appreciation, Int Revenue Serv, 1992; J. C. Penney Golden Rule Nominee, 1995; Woman of Distinction, Mitten Bay Girl Scout Coun, 1997.

MCKAYLE, DONALD COHEN
Educator, writer, choreographer. **Personal:** Born Jul 6, 1930, New York, NY; son of Philip Augustus and Eva Wilhelmina Cohen; married Leah Levin, 1965; married Lea Vivante, 1965; children: Gabrielle, Liane & Guy. **Educ:** Col City NY, attended 1949. **Career:** Dance instr: Juilliard Sch Music, Sarah Lawrence Col, Bennington Col, Neighborhood Playhouse, New Dance Group, Martha Graham Sch; Cult Prog Tunisia, adv, 1964; choreographer: Donald McKayle Dance Co, Alvin Ailey Am Dance Theater, Batsheva Dance Co, Israel; Repertory Dance Theater; Dayton Contemp Dance Co; Cleo Parker Robinson Dance Ensemble; Los Angeles Contemp Dance Theatre, artistic mentor & resident choregrapher; Limon Dance Co;choreographer of films: Bedknobs & Broomsticks, 1970; The Minstrel Man,1975-76; The Jazz Singer, 1980; choreographer of Broadway plays: GoldenBoy, 1964; The Last Minstrel Show, 1974, Raisin, 1974; Dr Jazz, 1975; Sophisticated Ladies, 1981; It Ain't Nothin' But the Blues, 1999; dir/choreographer: Hollywood Palace, 1969; Good Times, 1974; Free to Be You & Me, 1974; Komedy Tonite, 1977; The Richard Pryor Special, 1977; choreographer & creator: Regional Theatre, Denver Ctr Theatre Co, Mark Taper Forum, dir, choreographer & fac: Inner City Cult Ctr; Univ Wash; Portland State Univ; Fla State Univ; Alvin Ailey Dance Ctr; Calif Inst, Sch Dance, dean; Univ Calif, Irvine, prof finearts, dance, artistic dir, currently. **Orgs:** Bd dirs, Am Dance Festival, Durham, NC, New Dance Group, New York; Clarke Ctr Performance Arts, NYC; Soc Stage Dir & Choreographers, NYC; Modern Dance Found; Dance Circle Boston, MA; Nat Ctr Afro-Am Artists Rox bury, MA; Irvine Barclay Theatre, St Joseph Ballet; Nat Endowment Arts Dance Panel; bd trustees, Nat Found Advan Arts; Asn Am Dance Co; ASCAP; AEA; AGMA; AFTRA; AGVA; fel, Black Acad Arts & Letters; fel, Dir Guild Am. **Honors/Awds:** Capezio Award, 1963; The 43rd Annual Academy Awards, 1973; Emmy Nomination Choreography, The Minstrel Man, 1977; The 49th Annul Academy Awards, 1977; The Annual Emmy Awards, 1979; Nominee, Tony Award; Drama League Critics Award Choreography, Evolution Blues, 1978; NAACP Image Award, 1981; Outer Circle Critics Award Choreography, Sophisticated Ladies, 1981; American Dance Festival Award, Samuel H Scripps,1992; Living Legend Award, Nat Black Arts Festival, 1994; American Dance Guild Award, 1994; UCI Distinguished Faculty Lectureship Award for Research, 1997-98; Balasaraswati/Joy Ann Dewey Beineck Chair for Distinguished Teaching, 1997; Martin Luther King, Caesar Chavez, Rosa Parks Scholar Western Mich Univ, 1998; De La Torre Bueno Prize. **Special Achievements:** Numerous articles & publications including The Dance Has Many Faces, Columbia Univ Press, Modern Dance: Seven Points of View, Wesleyan Univ Press, Transcending Boundaries: My Dancing Life, autobiography, 1999, has been named by the Dance Heritage Coalition "one of America's Irreplaceable Dance Treasures. **Business Addr:** Professor of Dance, University of California, Irvine Campus Dance, 1001 Presidio Sq, Costa Mesa, CA 92626, **Business Phone:** (949)824-6798.

MCKEE, ADAM E
Veterinarian. **Personal:** Born Apr 12, 1932, Fairfield, AL; married Barbara Nance; children: Adam III, Eric & Brett. **Educ:** Dillar Univ New Orleans, AB, 1954; Tuskegee Inst, DVM, 1958. **Career:** Vet Path Armed Forces Inst Path, res, 1963-66; Lackland AFB, TX, chief altitude chamber unit aerospace path, 1966-67, sentry dog clinian, 1960-63; Istanbul, Turkey, vet, 1958-60; Naval Med Res Inst Nat, Naval Med Ctr, Bethesda, MD, chmn Qqqexptl path dept, 1969-; Biol & Med Scis Div Naval Radiol Defense Lab San Francisco, chief vet & path, 1967-69. **Orgs:** USAF Distinguished Unit, 1960-64; chmn, Naval Med Res Inst Policy Adv Coun sci & Managerial bd, 1975-; pres, Tuskegee Vet Med Alumni Asn, 1975-; Am Vet Med Asn; Int Acad Path; Wash So Scanning Electron Micros; Am Soc MicroBiol; Post Doctoral Res Asso Prog Com; 76; Am Asn Lab Animal Sci; Omega Psi Phi. **Honors/Awds:** Commendation medal, USAF, 1963; keynote speaker 6th Annual Intl Scanning Electron Microscopy Symposium Chicago, 1973; Special Merit Award, Naval Med Res Inst, 1976; chmn, Scanning Electron Cicroscopy Application in Med Microbiology 10th Annual Interna Scanning Electron Microsocpy Symposium Chicago, 1977. **Military Serv:** USAF, 1975. **Business Addr:** Member, Tuskegee Veterinary Medical Alumni Association, PO Box 1303, Bethesda, MD 20814.

MCKEE, CLARENCE VANZANT
Executive, lawyer. **Personal:** Born Nov 16, 1942, Buffalo, NY. **Educ:** Hobart Col, BA, 1965; Howard Univ Sch Law, JD, 1972. **Career:** Dept HEW, civil rights compliance officer, 1966-67; Senator Jacob Javits, legal asst, 1969-71; Senator Charles MacMathias, legal asst, 1971-72; Off Cong Rel US Civil & Aeronaut Bd, acting dir, 1972; Indust EEO Unit Off Gen Coun FCC, dep chief, 1973-76; FDL Commun CMS, legal asst; Comnr Ben Hooks FCC, legal asst, 1976-77; Law, Murphy & McKee, atty, 1978-79; Pepper & Corazzini, coun, 1977-87; Nat Union Total Independence Angola, coun, 1985-87; WTVT, Channel 13, co-own, chief exec officer, chmn, pres, 1987-92; McKee Commun, McKee Holdings, McKee Acquistion Corp, chmn, chief exec officer, pres, 1992-2005; Ruden McClosky Consult, prin, 2007-. **Orgs:** Bd mem, DC United Way; Am Bar Asn; Nat Conf Black Lawyers; Fed Bar Asn; Unified Bar DC; NY, PA, DC Bars; Wash commentator, FOX Broadcasting Co; Fla Progress Corp; Fla Power Corp; Am Heritage Life Ins Co; Checkers Dr In Restaurants Inc; Fla Asn Broadcasters; sr fel Broward Chamber Commerce, chmn Broward Republican Party; Destination Florida Comn. **Honors/Awds:** Outstanding Alumni Public Service Award, Hobart Col; John Mercer Langston Award, Outstanding Achievement Law & Pub Serv, Howard Univ Sch Law; inductee, Hall of Fame, Tampa Bay Bus, 1998. **Home Addr:** 2525 Bayshore Blvd, Tampa, FL 33629. **Business Addr:** Principal, Ruden McClosky Consulting, 200 E Broward Blvd, PO Box 1900, Ft Lauderdale, FL 33301, **Business Phone:** (954)527-6263.

MCKEE, EVELYN PALFREY
Judge. **Personal:** Born Jun 24, 1950, Texarkana, AR; daughter of John and Lois; married Darwin Mckee, Dec 30, 1978; children: 2. **Educ:** Southern Methodist Univ, BA, 1971; Univ Tex, Law Sch, JD, 1981. **Career:** State Tex, City Austin Munic Ct, presiding judge, 1989-; novelist, 1995-; Austin Pub Libr Found, bd dir; Travis County Lawyer Referral Serv, bd dir; Travis County Women Lawyers, govt serv, 2002. **Orgs:** State Bar Tex, mem, 1982-, bd mem, 1994; Austin Community Radio, 1987-; Travis County Bar Asn, 1989-; Writers League Tex, 1996-; Austin Romance Writers Am, 1998-. **Honors/Awds:** Distinguished Judge of the Year, Tex Munic Cts Asn, 2000. **Special Achievements:** Author: Three Perfect Men, 1996; The Price of Passion, 1997; Dangerous Dilemmas, 1999; Everything In Its Place, 2002; Nominated for Career Achievement Award, Romantic Times Magazine. **Home Addr:** PO Box 142495, Austin, TX 78701, **Home Phone:** (512)773-8776. **Business Addr:** Judge, State of Texas Municipal Court Austin Municipality, 700 E 7th St, PO Box 2135, Austin, TX 78768-2135, **Business Phone:** (512)477-0925.

MCKEE, LONETTE
Writer, singer, television producer. **Personal:** Born Jul 22, 1954, Detroit, MI; daughter of Lonnie and Dorothy McKee; married Leo Compton, Jan 1, 1983 (divorced 1990). **Career:** Actress, Soundtrack, Director, Writer, Producer, Composer, Self; Actress: Sparkle, 1976; Which Way Is Up", 1977; Cuba, 1979; The Cotton Club, 1984; Brewster's Millions, 1985; 'Round Midnight, 1986; Gardens of Stone, 1987; The Women of Brewster Place; Jungle Fever, 1990; Malcolm X, 1992; Fast Food Fast Women, 2000; Men of Honor, 2000; Lift, 2001; The Paper Mache Chase, 2003; Honey, 2003; She Hate Me, 2004; Dream Street, 2005; ATL, 2006; TV Series: "The Tys That Bind", 2000; "32 Bullets & a Broken Heart", 2000; "This Band of Brothers", 2000; "For Love of Olivia", 2001; "Chameleon", 2002; "Law & Order: Special Victims Unit", 1 Episode, 2001;"My Opening Farewell", 2003; "Superheroes: Part 2", 2002; "Half & Half",2004; "The Big Thanks for Nothing Episode ", 2004; "Tonya, Spencer's Mother", 1 Episode, 2004, "Exposure", 2006, "It's Hard Being Kelly Pitts", 2007; Director, producer, Writer & Composer: Dream Street, 2009; Lonette Productions Ltd, owner, currently. **Orgs:** Actors' Equity Asn; Am Fedn Tv & Radio Artists. **Honors/Awds:** Tony nomination, Julie, pre-Broadway revival of Showboat, 1983; NAACP nomination, CBS soap opera As The World Turns; Tony Award. **Special Achievements:** First and only African Amercian female to star in the role of Julie on Broadway, Show Boat; Image Award, 1998, 1999; Black Reel Award, 2003.

MCKEE, THEODORE A
Judge. **Personal:** Born Jun 5, 1947, Rochester, NY; son of Clarence V and Etta V; married Ana Pujols; children: 2. **Educ:** State Univ NY, Cortland, BA, 1965; Syracuse Univ, Col Law, JD (magna cum laude), 1975. **Career:** State Univ NY, Binghamton, dir minority recruitment & admis; Wolf Block Schorr & Solis-Cohen, assoc, 1975-77; Eastern Dist PA, asst US atty, 1977-80; Law Dept, City Philadelphia, dep city solicitor, 1980-83; Rutgers Univ Sch Law, Camden, trial advocacy, 1980-91; Ct Common Pleas Commonwealth PA, judge; US Ct Appeals, circuit judge, 1994-; Am Law Inst Proj, advisor. **Orgs:** Bd dirs, Crises Intervention Network; Crime Prevention Asn; Concerned Black Men; New Directions for Women; bd dir, Fox Chase Cancer Ctr, Temple Univ; bd dir, City Year Greater Philadelphia; Crime Prev Asn; Edna McConnell Clark Found; bd trustees, Temple Univ, 2002, vice chmn, Stud Affairs Comt. **Honors/Awds:** Order of the Coif, Syracuse Univ, 1975. **Business Addr:** Circuit Judge, US Court of Appeals, Third Circuit, 20614 US Courthouse 601 Mkt St Suite 21400, Philadelphia, PA 19106, **Business Phone:** (215)597-9601.

MCKELLER, THOMAS LEE
Educator, law enforcement officer, clergy. **Personal:** Born Dec 31, 1940, Middletown, OH; children: Yolanda M, Monica L, Julia L & Angie H. **Educ:** Monmouth Col, AA, bus law, 1962-64; Univ Toledo, BA, bus & educ, 1969-73; MI State Correctional Spl Sch, cert, 1977; MI Constr Training Coun, cert, 1979. **Career:** Berrien City State Correction Ctr, counr, 1978-81; Benton Harbor Elem Sch Adv Comm, chmn, 1982-83; Church Our Lord & Savior, minister, 1982-; Benton Harbor Area Sch Bd Educ, trustee, 1983-84; Educ instr; Benton Harbor High Sch, pub serv, 1984-. **Orgs:** Sergeant major, OH Explorer Scouts Drill Coun, 1964-65; coordr, OH Model Cities Signing Comm, 1965-67; corner back Cincinatti Bengals Prof Football Team, 1966-67; chmn, OH Hi-Y Council 1971; pres, Chosen Few Literary Soc, 1974; pres, Silver Tax & Bookkeeping Serv, 1978-80; chmn, finance supt Educ Task Force, 1983; dir, Brotherhood Christian Ministers, 1983; assoc dir, BH Marriage Counrs Asn, 1984; bd dir, Full Gospel Businessmans Asn, 1984; pres appointee, Local Selective Serv Bd No 11, 1992; African & Am 32nd Degree Scottish Rite Masons; Most Worshipful Master, New Bethel Lodge No 2, 1998-; grand lectr & sr warden, King Darius Grand Lodge Mensa Int, 1973-; chair, DAW. **Special Achievements:** Published "I Am God's Child" Oh Methodist Youth Dept, 1960, "Black Is" US Black Legion of Scholars in 1967. **Military Serv:** USAF, tech sgt, 6 yrs; USMC, 2 yrs sgt Pres Citation, 1958; pres citation, Special Merit Award, Special Service Medal, 1960-66. **Business Addr:** Public Service, Benton Harbor High School, 870 Colfax Ave, Benton Harbor, MI 49022, **Business Phone:** (269)927-0616.*

MCKELPIN, JOSEPH P.
Educator. **Personal:** Born May 6, 1914, Leflore County, MS; married Peggy A Jones; children: Joseph P Jr & Emmett O. **Educ:** SU, AB, 1943; Univ Wis, MS, 1948, PhD, 1952. **Career:** Southern Univ, prof ed, 1952-62; S Asn Cols & Schs, dir res & eval, 1967-73; Morris Brown Col, dean, 1973-74; Fed City Col, prof ed, 1974. **Orgs:** Phi Delta Kappa; Kappa Delta Pi; Kappa Phi Kappa; Omega Psi Phi. **Military Serv:** AUS, 2nd lt, 1943-46.

MCKELVEY, DR FELDER. See FELDER, LORETTA KAY.

MCKENNA, DR. GEORGE J.
School administrator. **Personal:** Born Sep 6, 1940, New Orleans, LA; son of George Jr and Leah. **Educ:** Xavier Univ, New Orleans, LA, BS, 1961, EdD; Loyola Univ, Chicago, IL, MA, 1962. **Career:** Los Angeles Unified Sch Dist, Los Angeles, CA, teacher, 1962-70, prin, admin, 1970-88; Inglewood Unified Sch Dist, Inglewood, CA, supt, 1988; Compton Unified Sch Dist, dep supt; Pasadena Unified Sch Dist, asst supt sch opers & support, currently. **Orgs:** Bd mem, Los Angeles Southern Christian Leadership Conf, 1978-; pres, Los Angeles Unified Schs, Coun Black Adminrs, 1981-82, 1986-87; comn mem, Nat Drug Free Schs Comn, 1989-90. **Honors/Awds:** UNCF Achievement Award, 1988; Congressional Black Caucus CHR's Award, 1989. **Special Achievements:** Subject CBS television movie, "The George McKenna Story," starring Denzel Wash; Great Black Educs Calendar, 1988. **Business Addr:** Assistant Superintendent of School Operations & Support, Pasadena Unified School District, Division of School Operations & Support, 351 S Hudson Ave, Pasadena, CA 91109, **Business Phone:** (626)568-4517.

MCKENZIE, ELI, JR.
Executive. **Personal:** Born Dec 28, 1947, Byromville, GA; married Vera Lee Thomas; children: Jatun Kreatson, Eli III & Jennifer Ashley. **Educ:** Ft Valley State Col, BS, 1969; Univ Ill, MS, 1971, PhD, 1975. **Career:** Univ Ill, res asst 1969-74; Ft Valley State Col, res sci 1975; Prairie View A&M Univ, dept head soil sci, 1976-78; M&M products Co, dir R&D 1978-83; EAR Enterprise, pres, ceo, currently. **Orgs:** Soc Cosmetic Chemist, 1978; Am Soc Quality Control, 1979. **Honors/Awds:** Research Grant Univ Ill, 1969. **Special Achievements:** "Effect of Pretreatment of Loss of Nitrogen", Soil Sci Soc Am Proc, 1976; "15-Labelled Fertilizer N from Waterlogged Soil During Incubation", "Phosphorus Fertility of Some Tropical Soils in Sierra Leone" Soil Sci Soc Amer Proc 1977. **Business Phone:** (770)484-2411.

MCKENZIE, FLORETTA D
Consultant, school administrator. **Personal:** Born Aug 19, 1935, Lakeland, FL; daughter of Martin W Sr (deceased) and Ruth J; children: Dona R & Kevin. **Educ:** DC Teachers Col, BS, hist, 1956, postgrad, 1967-69; Howard Univ, MEd, 1957; George Wash Univ, Am Univ, Catholic Univ Am, Union Grad Sch Baltimore, postgrad; George Wash Univ, EdD, 1984. **Career:** Baltimore & Wash Sch, teacher, 1957-67; DC Pub Sch, asst supt charge secondary sch dep supt educ prog & servs; Montgomery County Pub Schs, area asst supt, 1974-77, dep supt sch, 1978-79; State MD, asst dep supt sch, 1977-78; US Dept Educ, 1979-81; Off Sch Improv, dep asst sec, 1980-81; Ford Found, educ consult, 1981; Wash Off Col Entrance Exam Bd, adv com, 1970-; Educ Products Info Exchange, trustee, 1970; DC Pub Schs, supt, 1981-89; The McKenzie Group, pres, 1988-, chairperson, ceo, 1997-2004; Harvard Univ, Kennedy Sch Educ, vis scholar, 1989-91; Am Univ Grad Sch Educ, prof, 1991-; Marriott Int Inc, dir, 1992, bd, trustee, currently; Howard Univ, chairwoman emer, currently; Am Inst Res, sr advr, currently. **Orgs:** Am Asn Sch Admin, Urban League, Gamma Theta Upsilon, Phi Alpha Theta, Phi Delta Kappa; hon life mem MD PTA; bd trustees George Wash Univ; bd dirs, Nat Geog Soc, Potomac Electric Power Co, World Book, Acacia Life Insurance; Delta Sigma Theta Inc; bd dirs, Riggs Nat Bank; bd mem, Marriott Hotels. **Honors/Awds:** Honorary doctorates: Catholic Univ, 1985, Georgetown Univ, 1986, Columbia Univ Teacher's Col, 1987. **Special Achievements:** First African American and female elected to the Marriott Hotels board, 1992. **Business Addr:** Chairwoman, Chief Executive Officer, The McKenzie Group, 555 13th St NW Suite 700 E Tower, Washington, DC 20001, **Business Phone:** (202)637-6800.*

MCKENZIE, KEITH (KEITH DERRICK)
Football player, football coach. **Personal:** Born Oct 17, 1973, Detroit, MI; married Tamiko; children: Keith Jr. **Educ:** Ball State Univ, BS, hist. **Career:** Football player (retired), Football coach; Green Bay Packers, defensiveend, 1996-99, 2002; Miami

Dolphins 1999; Cleveland Browns, 2000-01; Chicago Bears, 2002 Buffalo Bills, 2003; Wayne State Univ, Dept Athletics, defensive line coach, 2008, linebackers coach, 2009. **Honors/Awds:** Inducted in BSU Athletic Hall of Fame, 2006. **Business Phone:** (313)577-4280.*

MCKENZIE, MICHAEL (MICHAEL TERRANCE MCKENZIE)
Football player, executive. **Personal:** Born Apr 26, 1976, Miami, FL. **Educ:** Univ Memphis, bus mgt, 1998. **Career:** Green Bay Packers, defensive back, 1999-2004; New Orleans Saints, cornerback, 2004-; 34 Ways Entertainment, owner, currently. **Honors/Awds:** All-Rookie Team, Football News, 1999; All-Rookie Team, Football Digest, 1999; All-Madden Team, 2001; NFL Play of the Week, 2003; Man of the Year Award, New Orleans Saints, 2007. **Business Addr:** Cornerback, New Orleans Saints, 5800 Airline Dr, Metairie, LA 70003, **Business Phone:** (504)731-1804.

MCKENZIE, MICHAEL TERRANCE. See MCKENZIE, MICHAEL.

MCKENZIE, MIRANDA MACK
Executive. **Personal:** Born Jun 21, 1955, Atlanta, GA; daughter of Dennis Mack and Jewel Hillman Mack; married Therman, Feb 15, 1992. **Educ:** Morris Brown Col, BA, 1977. **Career:** WAOK Radio, copy writer, 1977-79, acct exec, 1979-80; City Beverage Co, dir mkt develop, 1980-84; Coors Brewing Co, asst mgr, spec mkt, 1984-85, field mgr, 1985-86, comm rel regional mgr, 1986-93; Atlanta Comt, Olympic Games, dir commun, 1993-; Anheuser-Busch Co, corp affairs, dir, 1994-, regional mgr, currently. **Orgs:** Bd mem, Atlanta Nat Asn Advan Colored People, 1977-95; bd mem, Nat Asn Advan Colored People, 1983-; bd mem, Atlanta Urban League, secy, 1987-; bd mem, Ga Asn Minority Entrepreneurs, 1988-; founding bd mem, Coalition 100 Black Women, 1988; bd mem, Atlanta Bus League, 1989-91; Morris Brown Col Athletic Found, 1989-95; nat pres, Nat Asn Mkt Developers, 1991-92; Albany State Univ Found Bd, 1998-; found bd, Atlanta Area Tech Sch, 1999-; bd trustees, Morris Brown Col, 2003-04. **Honors/Awds:** Media Woman of the Year, Nat Asn Media Women, 1986; Leadership Atlanta, 1986; Leadership Award, Coun Nat Alumni, 1986; C L Harper Award, Nat Asn Advan Colored People, 1986; Marketer of the Year, NAMD, 1987; Athletic Hall of Fame, Morris Brown Col, 1987; Top African Am Bus & Prof Women, Dollars & Sense Mag, 1987, 1992; Leadership Am, 1989, 1992; Bronze Woman of the Year, Iota Phi Lambda, 1989; Leadership Ga, 1992. **Special Achievements:** Named 1 of 10 Outstanding Atlantans, Outstanding Young People Atlanta, 1986; 100 of the Best & Brightest Black Women Corp Am, Ebony Mag, 1990. **Home Addr:** 1257 Weston Dr, Decatur, GA 30032. **Business Addr:** Director Corporate Affairs, Regional Manager, Anheuser-Busch Companies, One Busch Pl, St Louis, MO 63118, **Business Phone:** (314)577-2000.

MCKENZIE, REGINALD
Football player, association executive. **Personal:** Born Jul 27, 1950, Detroit, MI; son of Hazel and Henry; married Ethellean Hicks (divorced). **Educ:** Univ Mich, BS, 1972. **Career:** Football player (retired), association executive; Buffalo Bills, offensive guard, 1972-82; Seattle Seahawks, offensive guard, 1983-84; Seattle Seahawks, dir mkt & sales, offensive line coach; Reggie McKenzie Found, founder & pres, currently. **Orgs:** Comm Proj, Spec Olympics, United Way, Boys Clubs Am; Cent Area Youth Assoc Seattle; bd dirs, King County Boys & Girls Club. **Honors/Awds:** Unsung Hero Award, Detroit Sports Media 1986; Sportsman of the Year, Detroit March Dimes, 1986; Brotherhood Award, BTWBA, 1988; Outstanding Young Citizen, Wash State Jaycees, 1989; Michigan Sports Hall of Fame, 1994; College Football Hall of Fame, 2002. **Business Phone:** (313)869-8081.

MCKENZIE, REV. VASHTI
Clergy. **Personal:** Born May 28, 1947; married Stanley McKenzie; children: Jon-Mikael, Vashti-Jasmine & Joi-Marie. **Educ:** Univ Md, BA, jour; Howard Univ, MDiv; United Sch Divinity, DMin; Howard Univ, honorary degree; Goucher Col, honorary degree; Wilberforce Univ, honorary degree; Cent State Univ, honorary degrees; Morgan State Univ, honorary degree. **Career:** Payne Memorial African Methodist Episcopal Church, pastor; 18th Episcopal Dist, SE Africa, chief pastor, 2000-04; African Methodist Episcopal Church, bishop, 13th Episcopal Dist, presiding prelate, currently; Cong Black Caucus Prayer Breakfast, preacher, 2006; Hampton Minister's Conf, preacher, 2007. **Orgs:** African Methodist Episcopal Sch Ann Conf, Lesotho & Swaziland; former pres, Coun Bishops; chairperson, Gen Conf Comn; chairperson, Bd Ministers Retirement Prog; chair, Quadrennial Theme Comt; nat chaplain Delta Sigma Theta Sorority. **Honors/Awds:** Honor Roll of Great African American Preachers, Ebony Mag, 1993, 1997. **Special Achievements:** One of the first women to be ordained as pastor in the African Methodist Episcopal Church; First woman elected as an African Methodist Episcopal Church bishop, 2000; First female president of the Council of Bishops of the African Methodist Episcopal Church, 2005; Author of three books: Not Without a Struggle; Strength in the Struggle; Journey to the Well; editor of the book, The Anvil, Coun Bishops; listed in 15 Greatest African American Female Preachers by Ebony Mag. **Business Addr:** Presiding Prelate, African Methodist Episcopal Church, Thirteenth Episcopal District, 500 8th Ave S, South Nashville, TN 37203, **Business Phone:** (615)242-6814.

MCKERSON, EFFIE M.
Educator. **Personal:** Born Mar 16, 1924, Henderson, TX; married Hayward Cornelious; children: Hayward Alton. **Educ:** Tex Col, BA, 1948; Univ Wis, MS, 1957; Boston Univ, Post Grad Study, 1949; Sonoma St Col, attended 1965; US Int Univ, attended 1972; LaVern Col Ctr, attended 1972; IGSE, attended 1973; Univ MN, attended 1973; Univ VA, attended 1974. **Career:** Longview, Tex, teacher, 1948-59; Gary, IN, teacher, 1959-68; Manilla Phillippine, teacher, 1968; Minn, MN, teacher, 1968-69; Edina Pub Sch, teacher, 1969-; Creek Valley Sch, teacher. **Orgs:** Pres, Nat Adv Vo Rehab; Nat Coun Soc Studies; Nat Educ Asn; Am Acad Polit & Social Sci; Int Asn Childhood Educ; Edina Hist Soc; rep, Nat Coun Social Studies, 1967, 1970, 1973-74; Nat Coun Negro Women; vice chmn, MN Rep; Minneapolis Girls Club Aux; pres, St Stephen Luth Ch Women. **Honors/Awds:** Certificate of Appreciation, Sec Casper Weinberger.

MCKERSON, MAZOLA
Manager. **Personal:** Born Jan 10, 1921, Bluff, OK; married Alfred; children: 4. **Career:** Gourmet resturantt, mgr & owner, 1962-97; Ardmore City comn, City Comn, 1977-79, mayor, chmn, 1979, pres, 1992-93; Murray State Col; AHEC. **Orgs:** Chmn, Gov Comn St Women; municipal bd St OK; comn, ed St OK; chmn, Ardmore's 100th Birthday Centennial, 1887-87, adv bd, Higher Educ Center; Ardmore YWCA; Greater SW Historical Museum bd. **Honors/Awds:** Lady of Year, Zeta Phi Beta Sor, 1976-77; Hon Serving chmn C of C Bicentennial Com, 1976; Woman of the Year, YMCA, 1980; hon mem Sigma Gamma Rho, 1986. *

MCKEY, DERRICK WAYNE
Basketball player. **Personal:** Born Oct 10, 1966, Meridian, MS; married; children: Mackenzie & Austin. **Educ:** Univ Ala, attended 1988. **Career:** Basketball player (retired); Seattle Supersonics, forward, 1987-93; Ind Pacers, 1993-2001; Philadelphia 76ers, forward, 2001-02. **Honors/Awds:** Gold medal, US basketball team, World Games, 1986; NBA All-Rookie Team, 1988.

MCKIE, AARON FITZGERALD
Basketball player, basketball coach. **Personal:** Born Oct 2, 1972, Philadelphia, PA. **Educ:** Temple Univ. **Career:** Portland Trail-Blazers, guard, 1995-97; Detroit Pistons, 1997-98; Philadelphia 76ers, 1998-2005; Los Angeles Lakers, guard, 2005-07; Philadelphia 76ers, asst coach, 2007-08; Memphis Grizzlies, 2008-. **Honors/Awds:** NBA Community Assist Award, 2003. **Special Achievements:** First round pick, No 17, NBA Draft, 1994. **Business Addr:** Professional Basketball Player, Memphis Grizzlies, 191 Beale St, Memphis, TN 38103, **Business Phone:** (901)888-4667.

MCKINES, CHARLOTTE
Marketing executive, executive director. **Career:** Merck & Co, mkt dir, Integrated Mkt Commun, exec dir, currently. **Orgs:** Healthcare Businesswomen's Asn. **Honors/Awds:** Outstanding Woman in Marketing & Communications Award. **Business Addr:** Executive Director of Integrated Marketing Communications, Merck & Co, 1 Merck Dr, PO Box 100, Whitehouse Station, NJ 08889-0100, **Business Phone:** (908)423-1000.

MCKINNEY, ALFREEDA LAKE. See LAKE, ALFREEDA ELIZABETH.

MCKINNEY, ALMA SWILLEY
Educator. **Personal:** Born Mar 4, 1930, Lamont, FL; children: Matthew M. **Educ:** Fla A&M Univ, Tallahassee, BA, 1951; Fla State Univ, MS, 1966; Univ Minn, attended. **Career:** Madison City Sch Bd, Madison, Fla, teacher, 1951-60; Greenville Training Sch, Greenville, Fla, math instr, 1960-63; Suwannee River Jr Col, Madison, Fla, head math dept, 1963-67; N Fla Jr Col, assoc prof math, 1967-73, cordr learning lab, 1976-80; Univ Minn, teaching asst, 1973-76; chmn regional adv coun, Dept Corrections, 1977-79; corp dir, ACTT Inc, Madison, 1978-80; State Dept Educ, Tallahassee, consult. **Orgs:** Bd dir, Madison City Mem Hosp, 1981-84; pol action comt, Nat Asn Advan Colored People; Zeta Phi Beta Sor; voters League, RECS Serv Club. **Honors/Awds:** Teacher of the Year, Suwannee River Jr Col, 1964; Citizen of the Year, Iota Alpha Zeta Chap Zeta Phi Beta, 1979.

MCKINNEY, BILLY
Sports manager, radio broadcaster. **Personal:** Born Jun 5, 1955. **Educ:** Northwestern Univ, BS, educ, 1955. **Career:** Chicago Bulls, asst vpres basketball opers, 1985-87; Minnesota Timberwolves, dir player personnel, 1988-90, radio analyst, currently; Detroit Pistons, vpres basketball opers, 1991-93; Billy McKinney Enterprises Inc, pres; Seattle Sonics & Storm, vpres basketball opers, exec vpres. **Orgs:** Harlem Globetrotters; Bellevue; Wash Boys & Girls Club; Big Brothers & Big Sisters; Jr Achievement; Seattle-King County Sports & Events Coun. **Honors/Awds:** Northwestern Hall of Fame; Hall of Fame, Ill Basketball Coaches. **Business Addr:** Radio Analyst, Minnesota Timberwolves, 600 1st Ave N, Minneapolis, MN 55403, **Business Phone:** (612)280-3165.

MCKINNEY, CYNTHIA ANN
Congressperson (U.S. federal government). **Personal:** Born Mar 17, 1955, Atlanta, GA; daughter of Leola and Billy; divorced; children: Coy Grandison Jr. **Educ:** Univ Southern Calif, BA, 1978; Tufts Univ, Fletcher Scho Law & Diplomacy, MA, PhD, candidate, 1993. **Career:** Spelman Col, diplomatic fel, 1984; Clark Atlanta Univ, instr polit sci; Agnes State Col, educr; State Ga, House Reps, rep, 1988-92; US House Reps, congresswoman, 1992-2003, 2005-. **Orgs:** Bd mem, Metro Atlanta, HIV Health Serv Planning Coun; Nat Coun Negro Women; NAACP; Sierra Club; Agr Comt; Cong Black Caucus; Women's Caucus; Progressive Caucus; secy, 103rd Congress Freshman Class; Intl Relations Comt. **Special Achievements:** first African-Am woman elected to Congress from Georgia, 1992; only father-daughter team ever to serve in country, Ga State House, 1988-92. **Business Phone:** (202)225-1605.

MCKINNEY, ERNEST LEE, SR.
Educator. **Personal:** Born Nov 26, 1923, Chesnee, SC; son of Jaffer N and Corrie C Dodd; married Marion L Birdwell; children: Ernest Jr & Kevin. **Educ:** Tenn State Univ, BS, 1947; E Tenn State Univ, MA, 1964; Swift Mem Jr Col, cert, 1945. **Career:** Educator (retired); Swift Jr Col, teacher, 1947-49; Rogersville Ala, teacher, 1949-53; Booker T Wash, prin, 1953-56; Langston HS, teacher, 1956-65; Sci Hill HS, teacher, 1965-70; So Jr HS, guid, 1970-76; Sci Hill HS, asst prin, 1976-85; Wash County Bd Educ, elected 1988, 1992, 1996 & 2000; Headstart Policy Coun, 1991-94. **Orgs:** Alderman Town Jonesborough, 1968-73, 1976-84; pres, Jonesborough Kiwanis Club, 1980; Omega Psi Phi Frat; First Tenn Develop Dist; secy, Pro-ToClub, 1986-; All Tenn Sch Bd, 1996; bd mem, Master Sch, Tenn, 1999; elder, Bethel Christian Church; chmn, Upper E Human Develop Inc, 2001. **Honors/Awds:** Omega Man of the Year, Iota Alpha Chap, 1968, other chaps, 1973, 1974, 1977, 1978, 1983, 5th dist, 1989; 50 years Omega pen, Grand Conclave, Los Angeles, 1996. **Special Achievements:** A follow-up study of the 1959-63 graduates of Langston High School, Johnson City, Tennessee, 1964. **Home Addr:** 119 N Lincoln Ave, Jonesborough, TN 37659. *

MCKINNEY, GENE C
Military leader. **Personal:** Born Nov 3, 1950, Monticello, FL; married Wilhemina Hall; children: Zuberi. **Educ:** El Paso Community Col, assoc sci degree gen mg; Park Col, BS, mgt human resources. **Career:** AUS Europe, command sergeant major; AUS, sergeant major, 1995-97. **Honors/Awds:** Bronze Star, Meritorious Service Medal; Republic of Vietnam Campaign Medal; Vietnam Service Medal; Army Service Ribbon; Overseas Service Ribbon; Combat Infantryman Badge; The Parachutist Badge. **Special Achievements:** First African American sergeant major.

MCKINNEY, GEORGE DALLAS
Clergy. **Personal:** Born Aug 9, 1932, Jonesboro, AR; married Jean Brown; children: George, Grant, Gregory, Gordon & Glenn. **Educ:** Ark State AM & N Col, Pine Bluff, BA, magna cum laude, 1954; Oberlin Col, MA, 1956; Univ Mich, attended 1958; Calif Grad Sch Theol, PhD, 1974. **Career:** Chargin Falls Park Comm Ctr, dir, 1955-56; Toledo State Mental Hosp, prot chaplain, 1956-57; Family Ct Toledo, counr, 1957-59; San Diego Co Probation Dept, sr probation officer, 1959-65; St Stephen's Cathedral Church God Christ, pastor, 1962-, founder & chief exec officer, currently; Econ Opportunity Comn, asst dir, 1965-71; Community Welfare Coun, consult, 1968-71; Pvt Prac, marriage family & child counr, 1971-; St Stephan's Day Care Ctr, founder; Southeast Counseling & Consulting Serv, founder; St Stephan's Christian Sch, founder; St Stephen's Retirement Ctr, founder; Am Urban Univ, founder; San Diego Monitor Newspaper, publ. **Orgs:** Calif Probation Parole & Correctional Asn; founder & chmn bd dirs, St Stephen's Group Home; Sandiego Co Coun Churches; bd trustees, InterdenomiNat Theol Ctr Atlanta; bd dirs, C H Mason Theol Sem, Atlanta; bd dirs, Bob Harrison Ministries; bd elders, Morris Cerillo, World Evangelism; Sigma Rho Sigma Social Sci Frat; San Diego Rotary Club; Alpha Kappa Mu Nat Hon Soc; Oper Push; vol chaplain, summer camp BSA; San Diego Mental Health Asn; Nat Asn Advan Colored People; Young Men Christian Asn; San Diego Urban League; bd advs Black Comun Ctr SanDiego State Univ; Calif Mental Health Asn; sr ed, African Am Devotional Bible. **Honors/Awds:** JF Kennedy Award; Outstanding Pastor Award, San Diego State Univ Black Stud; Award For Services To Youth, Black Bus & Prof Women San Diego; listed in Contemporary Authors; Social worker of the year Award, San Diego County, 1963; Outstanding Man of the Year Award, Int Asn Aerospace Workers Dist 50, 1969; Outstanding contributions to the San Diego Community in Field of Religious Activities, Nat Asn Advan Colored People, 1975; Achievement Award, So CA Church God Christ; honorary DD, Geneva Col, Beaver Falls; Racial Reconciliation Man of the Year Award. **Special Achievements:** African American Devotional Bible, sr editor, 1997; author of numerous books. **Business Addr:** Founder, Pastor, St. Stephen's Cathedral Church of God in Christ, 5825 Imperial Ave, San Diego, CA 92114, **Business Phone:** (619)262-2671.

MCKINNEY, JACOB K.
Publicist. **Personal:** Born Jun 10, 1920, Columbus, OH; married Marjorie Weiss; children: Jacquelyn Kyle. **Educ:** Ohio State Univ; La City Col, 1955. **Career:** Kyle Leader Mus variety act, 1940-50; UAW-CIO Local No 927, pub dir, 1950-53; La Sentinel, adv mgr, 1953-56; Bronze Am Mag, ed pub, 1957-65; Columbia-Screen Gems, asst dir pub, 1968-71; Am Int Pictures Inc, pub-

commrel dir, 1972-80; Knott's Berry Farm, asst mgr pub rel; Mc Kinney & Asso PR, pres. **Orgs:** Nat Safety Coun, 1950-52; bd dir, Pub Guild Local 818; Elder Presby Church, 1963; bd dir, Watts Community Ctr, 1969-70. **Special Achievements:** First black pub, Nat TV network, 1965-68. **Military Serv:** USAAF, pvt, 1943-44. **Business Addr:** President, McKinney & Assoc PR, 6515 Sunset Blvd, Los Angeles, CA 90028.

MCKINNEY, REV. JESSE DOYLE
Clergy. **Personal:** Born Oct 9, 1934, Jonesboro, AR; son of George D Sr (deceased) and Osie L (deceased); married Mary Francis Keys, Aug 5, 1978; children: Antoinette, Patrick, Bruce, Gloria & Carla. **Educ:** Univ Ariz, BA, 1957; San Diego State Univ, MSW, 1972. **Career:** San Diego State Univ, Grossmont Community Col, teacher, lectr, 1972-74; Southeast Counseling & Consult Servs, counr & dir, 1974-76; San Bernardino Co Mental Health Dept, mental health clinician II, 1977-79; Pleasant Place Group Home, dir, 1979-82; licensed clinical social worker; St Stephen's COGIC, pastor, social serv dir, currently; Samaritan Counseling Ctr. **Orgs:** Bd mem, Home Neighborly Serv, 1985-; mem, adv bd, Grad Sch Social Work, 1989-; Nat Asn Social Workers; founder, pastor, St Stephen's Church Samaritan Shelter; psychiatric social worker, Mental Health Dept, San Bernardino City; San Diego County Health Adv Bd; Calif Personnel & Guidance Asn; Asn Black Social Workers; bd dirs, San Diego Oper PUSH. **Special Achievements:** Fellowship Grant National Institute of Mental Health. **Home Addr:** 1883 Myrtlewood St, Colton, CA 92324. **Business Addr:** Pastor & Counselor, Director, St. Stephen Church of God in Christ, 12219 W 3rd Ave, San Bernardino, CA 92407, **Business Phone:** (909)881-1693.

MCKINNEY, LEWIS L., JR.
Legal consultant. **Educ:** St. Louis University, BA in Communications; University of St. Etienne, French. **Career:** Anheuser-Busch, Inc., Group Director of Government Strategies in the Industry and Government Affairs division. **Orgs:** Vice Chairman of the Board of Commissioners, Metro; Member, Congressional Black Caucus Foundation; Board Member, St. Louis University's School of Arts and Sciences Advisory Board; Member, Leadership Missouri Alumni Association. *

MCKINNEY, NORMA J.
Banker. **Personal:** Born Dec 30, 1941, Banks, AR; daughter of Jesse Marks and Lorene Fry Bizzell; married Herman McKinney, Aug 16, 1959; children: Kristal, Kevin, Kent. **Educ:** Northwest Intermediate Banking Sch, 1986; Babson Col Human Resource Sch, 1989; Univ Wash Sch Bus Admin Mgt Sch, attended 1990. **Career:** Security Pacific Bank, Seattle, WA, 1968-78, vpres & human resource specialist, 1978-89, vpres & human resource mgr, 1987-89, first vpres & human resource mgr, 1989-. **Orgs:** Bd dir, United Negro Col Fund; bd dir, First AME Headstart Prog; Nat Urban Bankers Assocs; facilitator, Diversity Training, Security Pacific Bank; Seattle Human Rights Comn, 1990. **Honors/Awds:** National Urban Bank Award, 1988. *

MCKINNEY, RUFUS WILLIAM
Executive. **Personal:** Born Aug 6, 1930, Jonesboro, AR; son of GD McKinney Sr.; married Glendonia Smith; children: Rufus Jr, Frederick Warren, Ann Marie, Paula Elaine. **Educ:** AM&N Col, AK, BS, 1953; Indiana Univ Sch Law, JD, 1956. **Career:** exec (retired); US Dept Labour, atty, 1956-69; Pacific Lighting Corp, atty, 1969-71, sr atty, 1971-72, asst vpres, special counsel, 1972; nat public affairs Southern CA Gas Co, asst v pres, 1975, v pres . **Orgs:** vice pres, bd dir, WA Chapter NAACP 1963-69; Nat Urban League; pres, Gas Men's Roundtable, 1975; chmn, Amer Assn Blacks Energy, 1980-82; CA & IN Bar Asn; Kappa Alpha Psi; Sigma Pi Phi Frat; mem, MD Comn Human Rel, 1996-03. **Special Achievements:** Beating the Odds, publisher. *

MCKINNEY, SAMUEL BERRY
Clergy, banker. **Personal:** Born Dec 28, 1926, Flint, MI; son of Wade Hampton and Ruth Berry; married Louise Jones; children: Lora Ellen, Rhoda Eileen. **Educ:** Morehouse Col, BA, 1949; Colgate-Rochester Div Sch, MDiv, 1952, D Ministry, 1975. **Career:** Clergy (retired); Aenon Bapt Church, stud asst, 1950-52, asst to pastor, 1952-54; Olney St Bapt Church, pastor, 1954-58; Mt Zion Baptist Church, pastor, 1958-98. **Orgs:** Life mem, Nat Asn Advan Colored People; Alpha Phi Alpha; Sigma Pi Phi Alpha Omicron Boule; Princehall Mason 33rd deg; Wash State Voc Educ Comn; pres, N Pacific Bapt State Conv; pres, Black Am Bapts; pres, Seattle Coun Churchs; bd exec comt mem, Am Bapt Bd Natl Ministries; bd exec com mem, Am Bapt Gen Bd ; fedr Seattle OIC; 2nd nat vpres, OIC Am; fdr past bd mem, Liberty Bank of Seattle; former mem bd trustee, Wash Mutual Savings Bank. **Special Achievements:** Co Authour: "Church Administration in the Black Perspective"; The first black-owned bank in Seattle and was the first black president of the Church Council of Greater Seattle. *

MCKINNEY, VENORA WARE
Library administrator. **Personal:** Born Jun 16, 1937, Meridian, OK; daughter of Odess and Hazel Parrish; married Lafayette; children: Carole Louise & James Christopher. **Educ:** Langston Univ, Langston, OK, BS, 1959; Univ Ill, Urbana, IL, libr sci, 1965; Univ Wis-Milwaukee, Milwaukee, WI, 1974; Marquette Univ, Milwaukee, WI, 1980, 1982. **Career:** Library administrator (retired); Milwaukee Pub Libr, Milwaukee, Wis, librn, 1963-69; Peoria Pub Schs, Peoria, Ill, librn, 1970-71; Milwaukee Pub Schs, Milwaukee, Wis, librn, 1972-79, br mgr, 1979-83, dep city librn, 1983-97. **Orgs:** Delta Sigma Theta Sorority; Links Inc, NCP; 1990-97; Wis Libr Asn, pres, 1995; co-founder, High Point, 1997; Langston Univ Nat Alumni Asn, secy, currently; Am Libr Asn. **Home Addr:** 1717 W Green Tree Rd Suite 207, Glendalee, WI 53209-2960, **Home Phone:** (414)352-7259.

MCKINNEY, WADE H
Administrator. **Personal:** Born Sep 6, 1925, Flint, MI; married Sylvia Lawrence (died 1993); children: Wade Hampton IV. **Educ:** Western Reserve Univ, BA, 1948. **Career:** Administrator (retired); Cleveland Press, copy ed & reporter, 1949-53; Urban League, Ft Wayne, indust rels secy, 1953-56; Denver, indust rels secy, 1956-59; Milwaukee, indust rels dir, 1959-61; Chicago, youth guid proj dir, 1961-63, employ & guid dir, 1963-68, prog dir, 1968-71; Nat Urban League Skills Bank, midwest rep, 1963-66; Econ Develop Corp, vpres, 1965-68; Northwestern Univ Bus Sch, Mgt Assistance Class, dir, 1971-72; US Postal Serv Headquarters, Wash, DC, staff, 1972-92. **Military Serv:** USAAF, staff, 1943-46; USAFR, capt, 1946-67.

MCKINNEY-JOHNSON, ELOISE
Writer, lecturer. **Personal:** Born Dec 7, 1926, Greensboro, NC; divorced; children: Myron H Johnson Jr. **Educ:** Spelman Col, AB, 1947; Boston Univ, Col Lib Arts, AM, 1948; Univ WI,1950-51; Univ Colo, 1953; Univ Calif, 1966-67, 1970; San Fran State Univ,1976, 1998; Stanford Univ, cert publ course, 1986. **Career:** Winston Salem St Col, instr, 1948-52; Morehouse Col, instr, asst prof,1953-61; NC Agr Tech St Univ, assoc prof, 1961-65; SF Unified Sch Dist,eng reader, 1965-67; San Fran Comm Col, teacher, 1966-71; N Peralta Col,instr, chairperson, 1971-73; Laney Col, instr eng, 1973-89; Praisesinger,ed, currently; freelance writer & lectr, currently. **Orgs:** San Francisco Chap, United Nations Asn; bd dirs, San Francisco Acad World Studies; Nat Asn Advan Colored People; essay contest judge, San Francisco Chap Eng-Speaking Union; Asn Study Afro-Am Life & Hist; Col Lang Asn; Am Asn Univ Women; Friends Johnson C Smith Univ; Spelman Col Nat Alumnae Asn; Sanderson Trustee Bd San Francisco African-Am Hist & Cult Soc; San Francisco Bay Area Chap, Asn Study Classical African Civilizations; adv bd, Langston Hughes Soc; AAAS; adv bd, Charlotte Hawkins Brown Mem State Historic Site; Alpha Kappa Alpha Sorority; Junos & Junos W; ed-,Praise singer, San Francisco African Am Hist & Cult Soc, 1998-2000. **Honors/Awds:** Study Abroad Certificate, Nat Coun Teachers Eng, 1959. **Special Achievements:** Has written articles that have appeared in: Black Art: An International Quarterly; Langston Hughes Review; Journal of Negro History; CLA Journal;Black Women in Antiquity; Nat Asn Advan Colored People Crisis; Black Women Stirring the Waters; Gumbo Yaya: Anthology of Contemporary African-American Women Artists, From Blues to Rap: A Special Issue of Black Sacred Music, among others; eponym for a special collection of books, journals, articles, programs, and monographs at the African American Historical Society; 25th Anniversary Luncheon Speaker, Committee on Multicultural Concerns (COMC), Nat Art Educ Asn, 1996. **Home Addr:** 1280 Ellis St Suite 10, San Francisco, CA 94109.

MCKINNEY-WHETSTONE, DIANE
Educator, writer. **Personal:** Born Jan 1, 1954, Philadelphia, PA; daughter of Paul McKinney and Bessie; married Gregory, 1978; children: Taiwo & Kehinde. **Educ:** Univ Pa, BA, eng, 1975. **Career:** USDA Forest Serv, pub affairs officer; writer, currently; Univ Pa, writing instr, currently; auth: Tumbling, 1996; Tempest Rising, 1998; Blues Dancing, 1999; Leaving Cecil Street, 2004. **Honors/Awds:** Atheneum of Philadelphia, citation, for portrayal of Philadelphia in novel, Tumbling; Award for Creative Contribution to literature, Zora Neal Hurston Soc; Author of the Year, Go On Girl Book Club; Black Caucus of the American Library Asn Award for fiction, 2005. **Special Achievements:** Appeared in Philadelphia Mag, Essence, the Sunday Philadelphia Inquirer Mag, anthologies Bluelight Corner & Mending the World. **Business Addr:** Writer, Pam Bernstein & Associates Inc, 790 Madison Ave Suite 310, New York, NY 10065, **Business Phone:** (212)288-1700.

MCKINNON, DARLENE LORRAINE
Government official. **Personal:** Born Jul 28, 1943, Baltimore, MD; daughter of Percy Otto McClaine Jr and Ruth Estelle Thurston McClaine; divorced. **Educ:** Morgan State Univ, attended; Univ Redlands, BA (summa cum laude), bus mgt, 1985. **Career:** Rouse Co, new projs, spec asst to dir, 1973-75; Baltimore Coun Equal Bus Opportunity, Procurement Servs, dir, 1975-79; US Small Bus Admin, dir, Score Prog, women's rep, 1983-92, dep dist dir, 1992-, actg dir, currently. **Orgs:** Bd mem, YWCA, 1990; Scripps Hosp Women's Health Source, 1990-; adv bd, San Diego Community Col Dist, 1992-; adv bd, San Diego Housing Comn, 1992-. **Honors/Awds:** Women's Bus Representative Year, 1988; Wonder Woman in Bus, Women's Times, 1990; Regional & District Employee Year, Small Bus Admin, 1991, 1986; Soroptomist Inter Nat, Woman Distinction, 1992; Woman of Achievement Awards. **Special Achievements:** Founding member, Nat Asn Women Bus Owner, San Diego, 1990; One San Diego 100 Bus & Community Leaders, San Diego Bus Jour, 1992. **Business Addr:** Deputy District Director, US Small Business Administration, 455 Market St 6th Fl, San Francisco, CA 94105-2420, **Business Phone:** (415)744-8475.

MCKINNON, ISAIAH
Police chief, educator, public speaker. **Personal:** Born Jun 21, 1943, Mongomery, AL; son of Cota and Lula; married Patrice, Oct 18, 1975; children: Jeffrey & Jason. **Educ:** Mercy Col Detroit, BA, hist & law enforcement, 1976; Univ Detroit, MA, criminal justice, 1978; Mich State Univ, PhD, admin higher ed, 1981; FBI Acad, police mgt & procedures, 1987. **Career:** Detroit Police Dept, inspector, 1965-84; Univ Detroit, dir pub safety, 1984-89; Renaissance Ctr, dir security, 1989-93; Detroit Police Dept, chief police, 1994-98; Univ Detroit Mercy, assoc prof, 1998-; speaker. **Orgs:** Mgt Adv Bd; FBI Nat Acad Grads Orgn; Int Asn Chiefs Police; Am Soc Indust Security; pres, Citizens Crime Watch; Detroit Police Officers Asn; Lt & Sergeants Asn; Mich Trial Lawyers Asn; dom violence, Ala State Univ; dom violence, Nat Orgn Black Law Enforcement Officers. **Special Achievements:** Author of North Between The Houses, In the Line of Duty, Stand Tall. **Military Serv:** USAF, sgt, 1961-65. **Business Addr:** Associate Professor, University of Detroit Mercy, 4001 W McNichols Rd, PO Box 19900, Detroit, MI 48219-0900, **Business Phone:** (313)993-1000.

MCKINNON, PATRICE
Government official. **Personal:** Married Isaiah McKinnon; children: Jeffrey, Jason. **Career:** Wayne County GIS, dir budget, currently. **Business Addr:** Director, M&B Budget, Wayne County GIS, 415 Clifford 2nd Fl, Detroit, MI 48226, **Business Phone:** (313)224-5061.*

MCKINNON, RONALD
Football player. **Personal:** Born Sep 20, 1973, Fort Rucker, AL; married; children: 2. **Educ:** Univ N Ala. **Career:** New Orleans Saints, linebacker, 1994-96, 2005; Ariz Cardinals, linebacker, 1996-2004; free agent, currently. **Honors/Awds:** Hill Trophy, 1995; College Football Hall of Fame, 2008.

MCKINZIE, BARBARA A
Association executive, certified public accountant. **Personal:** Born Jan 2, 1954, Ada, OK; daughter of Leonard T and Johnnie M Moses Watson. **Educ:** East Central OK Univ, BS (Cum Laude) 1976; Northwestern Univ, MBA, 1997. **Career:** Touche Ross & Co, supvr & health care coordr, 1976-83; DeLoitte Haskins & Sells, mgr, 1983-85; Alpha Kappa Alpha Sor Inc, exec dir, 1985-87, Int pres, 2006-; Coopers & Lybrand, mgr 1987-94; Whitman Corp, Internal Audit, dir, 1994-96; Ill Toll Authority, chief internal audit, 1996; Hollywood Casino, chief fin officer, 2000-02; Cook County Forest Preserve, chief fin officer, 2002-05. **Orgs:** Am Inst Cert Pub Accts, 1978; Nat Assoc Black Accts, 1980; minority recruitment subcomm IL Soc CPA's 1983; Am Womens Soc CPAs, 1986. **Honors/Awds:** Outstanding Alumnae, E Cent Okla Univ, 1976; Valuable Contrib Award, Okla City, 1983; Outstanding Young Woman Am, 1980, 1985; hon Doctorate Humane Letters, 2006, Stillman Col; Keys and Proclamations from over 50 cities. **Business Addr:** International President, Alpha Kappa Alpha Sorority Inc, 5656 S Stony Island Ave, Chicago, IL 60637, **Business Phone:** (773)684-1282.

MCKISSACK, CHERYL MAYBERRY
Business owner, educator. **Personal:** Married Eric. **Educ:** Seattle Univ, BS; Northwestern Univ, Kellogg Sch Mgt, MBA. **Career:** IBM Corp; Open Port Technol, sr vpres & gen mgr; 3Com, Network Systems Div, vpres; Nia Enterprises LLC, founder, pres & chief exec officer, 2000-; Kellogg Sch Mgt, adj asst prof entrepreneurship, 2005-; Deluxe Corp, bd dir; Deluxe Corp, dir. **Orgs:** Info Technol Resource Ctr; bd mem, LINK Unlimited, Chicago, IL. **Special Achievements:** Co-editor: The Nia Guide for Black Women; One of the 25 Influential Black Women in Business by the Network Journal Magazine, 2006; one of the 2005 Business Leaders of Color by the Chicago United Organization. **Business Phone:** (312)222-0943.*

MCKISSACK, FREDRICK LEM, SR.
Writer. **Personal:** Born Aug 12, 1939, Nashville, TN; son of Lewis Winter and Bessye Fiser; married Patricia C McKissack, Dec 12, 1964; children: Fredrick L II, Robert Lewis, John Patrick. **Educ:** Tenn State Univ, Nashville, BS, engineering, 1964. **Career:** US Corp Engrs, civil engr, 1964-90; Nimrod Corp, owner, 1972-80; All-Writing Serv, co-owner, currently; Books: Rookie Readers; Messy Bessey; Who is Coming?; Who is Who?; Bugs and Constance; Stumbles; Let my People Go!; Old Testament Bible Stories; A Long Hard Journey: The Story of the Pullman Porter; Sojourner Truth: Ain't I a Woman; Young, Black and Determined: A Biography of Lorraine Hansberry; Jesse Owens: Olympic Star; Paul Robeson: A Voice to Remember; Black Hands, White Sails: The Story of African-American Whalers; Red-Tail Angels: The Story of the Tuskegee Airmen of World War II. **Orgs:** Nat Storytelling Network; Nat C's Book & Literacy Alliance; trustee, Olive Chapel AME Church; St Louis Hist Soc; Kirkwood Hist Soc; Nat Writers Union. **Honors/Awds:** Honorary doctorate, Univ Mo; C S Lewis Silver Medals, 1985; Image Award, Nat Asn Advan Colored People, 1994. **Special Achievements:** A Long Hard Journey—

The Story of Pullman Porter won the Coretta Scott King Award for Text and the Jane Addams Peace Award; Ain't I a Woman won the Coretta Scott King Honor book, an ALA Notable title, a NCSS Notable title, and winner of the Boston Globe-Horn Book Award for Nonfiction. **Military Serv:** US Marine Corps, sgt, 1957-59. **Home Addr:** 14629 Timberlake Manor Ct, PO Box 967, Chesterfield, MO 63017. **Business Phone:** (636)519-0726.*

MCKISSACK, LEATRICE BUCHANAN
Executive. **Personal:** Born Jul 27, 1930, Keytesville, MO; daughter of Archie and Catherine Brummell; married William DeBerry, Oct 31, 1949 (deceased); children: Andrea McKissack Krupski, Cheryl & Deryl. **Educ:** Fisk Univ, BS, math, 1951; Tenn State Univ, MS, psychol, 1957. **Career:** Executive (retired); Metropolitan Bd educ, teacher, 1952-69; McKissack & McKissack, ceo, 1983. **Orgs:** Federal Reserve Bank Bd, 1990-95; adv bd mem, State Tenn Employ Sec, 1991-; Commissioner-Metro Planning Comn, 1989-95; Nashville Chamber Com, 1983-; United Way, 1983; Nat Conf Christians & Jews, 1995-; Cheekwood Fine Arts ctr, 1991-; Nashville Symphony Guild, 1975; Nashville Symphony Bd, 1997-; Tenn Bd Econ Growth, governor's appointee, 1995-; bd trustees, Fisk Univ, 1995-; bd governors, 1995-; YMCA adv bd, 1994-. **Honors/Awds:** Nat Female Entrepreneur, Dept Comm, PRS Bush, 1990; Business Award, Howard Univ, 1993; Distinguished Alumni Award, NAFEO, 1991; Business Woman of the Year, State Tenn, 1990, Women Owned Business of the Year, 1990. **Home Addr:** 6666 Brookmont Terr, Nashville, TN 37205, **Home Phone:** (615)352-8546.

MCKISSACK, PATRICIA CARWELL
Writer. **Personal:** Born Aug 9, 1944, Smyrna, TN; daughter of Robert and Erma Carwell; married Fredrick L McKissack Sr, Dec 12, 1964 (divorced); children: Fredrick L II, Robert & John. **Educ:** Tenn State Univ, BS, eng, 1964; Webster Univ, MA, early childhood lit & media programming, 1975. **Career:** Concordia Publ Co, ed, 1975-81; Nipher Jr High Sch, teacher, 1969-75; Forest Park Col, instr, 1977-84; Univ Mo, instr, Eng, 1979-84; Lindenwood Col, instr, Eng, 1977-80; All-Writing Servs, co-owner, 1978-; Inst Children's Lit, 1884-; educ consult, currently; Auth: A Long Hard Journey: The Story of the Pullman Porter; Sojourner Truth: Ain't I a Woman?; A Long Hard Journey: The Story of the Pullman Porter; Black Diamond; Black Hands, White Sails; Christmas in the Big House, Christmas in the Quarters; Color Me Dark: The Diary of Nellie Lee Love, The Great Migration North, Chicago, Illinois, 1919; Days of Jubilee: The End of Slavery in the United States; Dear America: Look to the Hills; The Honest-to-Goodness Truth; Tippy Lemmey; To Establish Justice : Citizenship & the Constitution; Where Crocodiles Have Wings; Loved Best; Abby Takes a Stand; Precious & the Boo Hag; Amistad : Station Stop 3; Away West; A Song for Harlem : 1928. **Orgs:** Ark Sorority; AME Church Olive Chapel; MO Arts & Educ Coun. **Honors/Awds:** Hon doctorate; Univ Mo, C S Lewis Silver Medals 2, 1985; A Long Hard Journey—The Story of Pullman Porter won the Coretta Scott King Award, Jane Addams Peace Award; Ain't I A Woman won the Coretta Scott King Honor book, an ALA Notable title, a NCSS Notable title & winner of the Boston Globe—Horn Book Award for Nonfiction; NAACP, Image Award, for work in children's literature, 1994; Newberry Honor, ALA, for The Dirty Thirty: Southern Tales of the Supernatural, 1994; Regina Medal, Catholic Library Assn, 1998; NAACP Image Award, for Let My People Go: Old Testament Bible Stories; numerous others. **Business Phone:** (314)725-6218.

MCKISSACK, PERRI ALETTE
Executive, singer, social worker. **Personal:** Born Nov 6, 1966, Oakland, CA; married Antonio Reid, 1989 (divorced 1995); children: Aaron; married Otis Nixon, 2001 (divorced 2004); married George Smith (divorced); children: Ashley. **Career:** Social Worker, Singer, Entertainment Industry (retired); Albums: Pebbles, 1987; Always, 1990; Straight from the Heart, 1995; Greatest Hits, 2000; Savvy Records, pres, 1993-97; Women of God Changing Lives Through Christ, founder & owner, currently. **Special Achievements:** Two platinum albums: Always, Pebbles. **Business Phone:** (404)815-7788.*

MCKISSICK, EVELYN WILLIAMS
Commissioner. **Personal:** Born Aug 19, 1923, Asheville, NC; married Floyd Bixler; children: Joycelyn, Andree, Floyd Jr. **Career:** Soul City Sanitary Dist, comnr chmn; Educ Enrichment Prog, dir, 1970-72; Pre Sch Educ & Rec Bd , dir. **Orgs:** Soul City Cultural Arts & Hist Soc; bd mem, Soul City Pks & Rec Asn; bd mem, Interfaith Comn Soul City; Durham Comn Negro Affairs; CORE; Durham Rec Dept; Union Baptist Ch Youth Prog; Nat Asn Advan Colored People; vchmn, Warren County Rep Party; Black Elected Officials.

MCKISSICK, FLOYD B
Lawyer. **Personal:** Born Nov 21, 1952, Durham, NC; son of Floyd B Sr and Evelyn Williams; married Cynthia Heath McKissick, Jun 29, 1990; children: Alicia Michelle, Floyd B III, & Graison Heath. **Educ:** Clark Univ, AB, 1974; Univ NC Chapel Hill, Sch City & Regional Planning, MRP, 1975; Harvard Univ, Kennedy Sch Gov, MPA, 1979; Duke Univ Sch Law, JD, 1983. **Career:** Floyd B McKissick Enterprises, asst planner, 1972-74; Soul City Com, dir planning, 1974-79; Peat, Marwick & Mitchell, mgt consult, 1980-81; Dickstein, Shapiro & Morin, atty, 1984-87; Faison & Brown, atty, 1987-88; Spaulding & Williams, atty, 1988-89; McKissick & McKissick, atty, 1989-; NC Senate, senator, 2007-. **Orgs:** Durham City Coun, 1994-; pres, NC Ctr Study Black Hist; past chmn, Land Loss Prev Proj; Durham City-Coun Planning Comn; St Joseph's Hist Soc; Mus Life & Sci; Durham City Adjustments; Rural Advancement Found Int. **Special Achievements:** Co-author of Guidebook on Attracting Foreign Investment to the US, 1981; Author of books like: When an Owner can Terminate a Contract Due to Delay, 1984; Mighty Warrior, Floyd B McKissick, Sr, 1995. **Business Phone:** (919)490-5373.

MCKISSICK, MABEL F. RICE
Librarian. **Personal:** Born Jun 12, 1921, Union, SC; daughter of Phillip H and Charity M; married Wallace T McKissick; children: Wallace T Jr. **Educ:** Knoxville Col, AB, 1943; SC State Col, summer courses libr sci, 1950; Teachrs Col, Columbia Univ, MA, 1954; Sch Libr Serv, Columbia Univ, MSLS, 1966. **Career:** Librarian (retired); Sims HS, teachr/librarian, 1943-48, librarian, 1948-68; New London Jr HS, librarian/media specialist, 1968-79; New London HS, librarian/media specialist, 1979-90. **Orgs:** Nom comt, Nat Coun Negro Women, 1979-, Am Asn Univ Women, 1978-; second vpres, 1969-, pres, 1988-90, Delta Kappa Gamma, Eta Chap, 1969-; Delta Sigma Theta Sor, 1943-; founding mem, County Coun Comn, 1985-; New Eng Asn Schs & Col Evaluation Comt, 1986-. **Honors/Awds:** First black pres, Conn Sch Libr Asn, 1973-74; "Black Women of Connecticut, Achievements Against the Odds" Exhibit Hartford Conn Historical Soc, 1984; Outstanding Woman of the Year Award, Conn Div Am Asn Univ Womenn 1982; Rheta A Clark Award, Conn Educ Media Asn, 1980; Outstanding Library Media Services; Coretta Scott King Award, 1974; Dr Martin Luther King Jr Community Service Award 1981; New Haven Alumnae Chap Delta Sigma Theta Educ Devel Award, 1985; Citation Office of the Mayor City of New London for Outstanding Educational Achievements in Education, 1985; State of Connecticut General Assembly Official Citation in Educ Achievements 1985; Community Service Award as an Educator Miracle Temple Church, 1985; Certificate of Appreciation, 1986; Service Award, Conn Educationaldia Asn, 1988. **Special Achievements:** First black president in the Connecticut School Library Association. **Home Addr:** 201 Hempstead St, PO Box 1122, New London, CT 06320. *

MCKITT, WILLIE, JR.
Law enforcement officer. **Educ:** Troy State Univ, criminal justice, psychol, sociol. **Career:** Law enforcement officer (retired); Montgomery County Sheriff's Dept, jailer, 1968-70, Civil Div, 1970-77, asst jail adminr, 1977-81; Montgomery County Detention Facility, adminr, 1981-92. **Orgs:** FOP; Air Force Memorial Found. **Special Achievements:** First African-American to be employed by the Montgomery County Sheriff's Department, 1968. **Military Serv:** USF, twenty years. *

MCKNIGHT, ALBERT J.
Financial manager, clergy. **Personal:** Born in Brooklyn, NY. **Educ:** St Mary's Sem, BA, BT; Holy Ghost Fathers PA & CT. **Career:** clergy (retired); So Cooperative Develop Fund Lafayette, LA, pres, 1970-84; Southern Develop Found, novice dir. **Orgs:** LA econ develop task forces; So Consumers' Coop; LA Task Force; US Off Econ Opportunity Task Force; People's Enterprise Inc; diocesan dir, Credit Unions, 1963; former assoc, Lady Lourdes; Immaculate Heart Mary & St Martin de Porres Chs LA; bd mem, Nat Consumer Coop Bank; chmn, Consumer Coop Develop Corp; pastor, Holy Ghost Catholic Ch Opelousas, LA.

MCKNIGHT, BRIAN
Singer, songwriter, musician. **Personal:** Born Jun 5, 1969, Buffalo, NY; married; children: 2. **Career:** Albums: Brian McKnight, 1991; I Remember You, 1995; Anytime, 1997; Bethlehem, 1998; Back at One, 1999; Superhero, 2001; From There to Here: 1989-2002, 2002; U-Turn, 2003; Gemini, 2005; Ten, 2006; Songs: "The Way Love Goes", 1992; "Goodbye My Love", 1992; "One Last Cry", 1993; "After the Love", 1993; "Love Is", 1993; "Crazy Love", 1995; "On the Down Low", 1995; "Still in Love", 1995; "You Should Be Mine (Don't Waste Your Time)",1997; "Anytime", 1998; "Hold Me", 1998; "The Only One for Me", 1998; "Back at One", 1999; "6, 8, 12", 2000; "Stay or Let It Go", 2000; "Win", 2000; "Love of My Life", 2001; "Still", 2001; "What's It Gonna Be", 2002; "All Night Long (With Nelly)", 2003; "Shoulda, Woulda, Coulda", 2003; "What We Do Here", 2005; "Everytime You Go Away", 2005; "Find Myself In You", 2006; "Used To Be My Girl", 2006; "I Il be Home for Christmas", 2008; Brian McKnight Live from Fifteen", 2009; Where house Music, singer, currently. **Honors/Awds:** Soul Train Award, Best R&B/Soul Male Album, 1999; American Music Award, Favorite Soul/R&B Male Artist, 2000; Image Award, Outstanding Male Artist, Nat Asn Advan Colored People, 2000; Blockbuster Awards; BillBoard Songwriter of the Year. **Special Achievements:** A few Grammy nominations; worked with Sean "P Diddy" Combs, Justin Timberlake of NSync, Mary J Blige, Boyz II Men, and Take 6. **Business Addr:** Singer, Wherehouse Music, 100 N La Cienega, Los Angeles, CA 90048.*

MCKNIGHT, CLAUDE V., III
Singer. **Personal:** Born Oct 2, 1962, Brooklyn, NY; son of Claude Jr and Elaine; children: Jessica. **Educ:** Oakwood Col. **Career:** The Gentlemen's Estate Quartet, founder & mem, 1985-87; Take 6, founder & mem, 1987-; Do the Right Thing, music, lyrics, performer, 1989; Albums: Take 6, 1988; So Much 2 Say, 1990; He Is Christmas, 1991; Join the Band, 1994; Brothers, 1996; So Cool, 1996; The Greatest Hits, 1999; We Wish You a Merry Christmas, 1999; Tonight: Live, 2000; Live, 2000; Beautiful World, 2002; Feels Good, 2006; singer, ICM, currently. **Business Addr:** Singer, International Creative Management, 825 Eighth Ave, New York, NY 10019, **Business Phone:** (212)556-5600.

MCKNIGHT, JAMES (JAMES EDWARD MCKNIGHT)
Football player, football coach. **Personal:** Born Jun 17, 1972, Orlando, FL; married Mikki; children: David. **Educ:** Liberty Univ, criminal justice. **Career:** Football player (retired), Football coach; Seattle Seahawks, wide receiver, 1994-98; Dallas Cowboys, 1999-2000; Miami Dolphins, 2001-03; New York Giants, 2004; Cypress Bay High Sch, wide receivers & track team coach, currently. **Business Addr:** Wide Receivers & Track Team Coach, Cypress Bay High School, 18600 Vista Pk Blvd, Weston, FL 33332, **Business Phone:** (754)323-0350.

MCKNIGHT, JAMES EDWARD. See MCKNIGHT, JAMES.

MCKNIGHT, REGINALD
Educator, writer. **Personal:** Born Feb 26, 1956, Furstenfeldbruck, Germany; son of Frank and Pearl M Anderson; married Julie Scott Buchness, 1999; children: Eve; married Michele Davis, Aug 25, 1985 (divorced 1993); children: Rachae. **Educ:** Pikes Peak Community Col, Colorado Springs, CO, AA, gen studies, 1978; CO Col, Colorado Springs, CO, BA, African Lit, 1981; Univ Denver, Denver, CO, MA, Eng, 1984. **Career:** Univ Pittsburgh, Pittsburgh, PA, asst prof, Eng, 1988-91; Carnegie Mellon Univ, Pittsburgh, PA, assoc prof, Eng, 1991; Univ Md, prof, Eng creative writing prog, 1994-2000; Univ Mich, prof, Eng, 2000-; Univ Ga, Hamilton Holmes prof eng, currently; Novel: I Get on the Bus, 1990; The Kind of Light That Shines on Texas, 1992; African American Wisdom, 1994; Wisdom of the African World, 1996; Moustapha's Eclipse, 1998; White Boys & Other Stories, 1998; He Sleeps, 2001. **Orgs:** PEN Am, 1989-; African Lit Asn, 1989-; Thomas J Watson Found Fel, 1981; Phi Beta Kappa, 1981. **Honors/Awds:** Bernice M Slate Award for Fiction, Univ Nebraska, 1985; Drue Heinz Prize for Literature, Univ Pittsburgh, 1988; Drue Heinz Prize for Literature, Univ Pittsburgh, 1988; O Henry Prize, 1990; Doctor of Humane Letters, Colo Col, 1990. **Military Serv:** USMC, corporal E-4, 1973-76. **Business Addr:** Hamilton Holmes Professor, University of Georgia, The Department of English, 133 Pk Hall, Athens, GA 30602-6205, **Business Phone:** (706)542-2233.*

MCLAREN, DOUGLAS EARL
Management consultant, lawyer. **Personal:** Born Nov 3, 1948, Wilmington, NC; son of Huldah E and Austen E; married Rosemarie P Pagon; children: Damion Earl & Kaili Elizabeth. **Educ:** Univ W Indies, BSc, eng, 1970; McGill Univ, MBA, 1974; Harvard Law Sch, JD, 1984. **Career:** Hue Lyew Chin, engr, 1970-72; Peat Marwick Mitchell, mgt consult, 1974-76; Jamaica Nat Investment Co, proj officer, 1976-78; Exxon Int Co, planning analyst, 1979-84; ICF Kaiser Engrs, proj mgr, 1984; Bechtel SAIC Co LLC, co-ordinator, currently. **Orgs:** Admitted to NY & DC Bars, 1985; Am Bar Asn, 1985; Panel Com Arbitrators Am Arbitration Asn; past Chair, DC Bar Int Law Sect; bd dirs, Wash Foreign Law Soc; coordr, DC Bar, currently. **Home Addr:** 1825 Tulip St NW, Washington, DC 20012, **Home Phone:** (202)291-5383. **Business Addr:** Coordinator, Bechtel SAIC Company LLC, 955 LEnfant Plz SW Suite 8000, Washington, DC 20024-2108.

MCLAUGHLIN, DR. ANDREE NICOLA
Poet, educator. **Personal:** Born Feb 12, 1948, White Plains, NY; daughter of Willie Mae Newman and Joseph Lee. **Educ:** Cornell Univ, BS, 1970; Univ Mass, Amherst, Med, 1971, EdD, 1974. **Career:** Medgar Evers Col, City Univ NY, asst prof & project dir, 1974-77, chairperson, 1977-79, dean admin & assoc prof, 1979-82, planning coord Women's Studies Res & Devel, 1984-89, prof lang, lit & philos prof interdisciplinary studies, 1992-, Off Int Women's Affairs, dir, 1996-, Dr Betty Shabazz Distinguished Chair Social Justice, 2001-; Nat Endowment Humanities fel, 1976, 1979, 1984, 1989, 1993; Univ London Inst Educ, distinguished vis scholar, 1986; Hamilton Col, Jane Watson Irwin, vis prof Women's Studies, 1989-91. **Orgs:** Bd mem, Where We At, Black Women Artists, 1979-87; Nat Women's Studies Asn, 1980-84; Am Asn Univ Profs, 1982-; founding int coord, Int Resource Network Women African Descent, 1982-85, founding mem, Sisterhood Support Sisters SAfrica 1984-; adv bd mem, Sisterhood Black Single Mothers, 1984-86; founding int coord, Cross-Cult Black Women's Studies Inst, 1987-; chair, Ed Bd, Network: Pan African Women's Forum (J), 1987-91; Policy & Publication Comn, The Feminist Press, City Univ NY, 1988-99; Am Coun Educ. **Honors/Awds:** Susan Koppelman Book Award, AmCult Studies, 1990. **Special Achievements:** Author & editor of many books. **Business Addr:** Professor, Medgar Evers College, City University of New York 1650 Bedford Ave, Brooklyn, NY 11225, **Business Phone:** (718)270-5051.

MCLAUGHLIN, BENJAMIN WAYNE
Manager. **Personal:** Born Feb 24, 1947, Danville, VA; son of Lucy S and Daniel S; married Gwen Stafford; children: LaShandra &

Sonya. **Educ:** Johnson C Smith Univ, Charlotte NC, attended 1969. **Career:** Lockheed Martin, buyer, 1969-70, maintenance engineering tech asst, 1970-76, ORGDP affirmative action coordr, 1975-79, wage & salary assoc, 1979, ORGDP employ dept supvr, 1979-81, barrier mfg div supt, 1981-82, maintenance engrg dept supt, 1982-83, ORGDP wage & salary dept head, 1983-84, energy syst dir minority prog develop, 1984-86, personnel mgr Portsmouth OH gaseous diffusion plant, 1986-95; admin support mgr, 1995-. **Orgs:** Mem pres circle, United Way of Ross County; Comnr, Chillicothe, Ohio, Civil Serv Comn; Omega Psi Phi; Ionic Lodge no 6, F & AM. **Honors/Awds:** Distinguished Service Award, State Tenn, 1980; Martin Marietta Energy Syst Community Service Award, 1985; Omega Man of the Year Award, Zeta Gamma Gamma Chap Omega Psi Phi Frat, 1985; Light From the Hill Award, Knoxville Col, 1985; Jefferson Award for Community Service, 1986. **Home Addr:** 1055 Edgewood Dr, Chillicothe, OH 45601. **Business Addr:** Member of President, United Way of Ross County, 53 E 2nd St, Chillicothe, OH 45601, **Business Phone:** (740)773-3280.

MCLAUGHLIN, BRIAN P
Government official. **Personal:** Born Jan 1, 1974. **Educ:** Duke Univ, cum laude; Massachusetts Inst Technol, MCP; Am Univ, MS. **Career:** Crispus Attuacks Community Develop Corp, dir; Fannie Mae, American Communities Fund, sr asset mgr; CyberCorps, co-founder, currently; Md Dept Housing & Community Develop, Div Neighborhood Revitalization, Community Revitalization Subcomt, vice chair, asst secy, currently. **Orgs:** Rural Md Coun. **Honors/Awds:** Unsung Hero Award, Md Small Bus Admin. **Business Addr:** Assistant Secretary of Neighborhood Revitalization, Vice Chair of Community Revitalization Subcommittee, Maryland Department of Housing & Community Development, 100 Community Pl, Crownsville, MD 21032-2023, **Business Phone:** (410)514-7014.

MCLAUGHLIN, EURPHAN
Government official. **Personal:** Born Jun 2, 1936, Charlotte, NC. **Educ:** Univ Md, Baltimore Col Com, 1958; Univ Baltimore, AA, 1963, LLB, 1969, BS,1972, MBA (23 credits completed). **Career:** Baltimore City Police Dept, intelligence div officer, 1959-73; MD Comn Human Rels, intergroup rels rep, 1973-75; State MD Dept Health & Ment Hygiene, EEO supr, 1975-76; MD Comn Human Rels, dep dir, 1976-79; State MD Dept Personnel, asst sec for employee serv, 1979-; Otis Warren & Co,currently. **Orgs:** Real estate assoc & bd mem Century 21/Otis Warren & Co, 1971-; Nat Asn Advan Colored People; Nat Asn Human Rights Workers; MD Asn Equal Opportunity Personnel; Nat & MD Asn Real estate Brokers; Baltimore Bd Realtors. **Honors/Awds:** Nine accommendations commendations, City Police Dept, 1959-73; Award Merit, MD Comn Human Rels, 1978; Award Merit, Staff MD Comn Human Rels,1978. **Military Serv:** USAF, a/2c, 39 years. **Business Addr:** Realotr, Otis Warren & Co, 10 S Howard St Suite 110, Baltimore, MD 21201.

MCLAUGHLIN, DR. GEORGE W.
Educator. **Personal:** Born Feb 14, 1932, Petersburg, VA; married Sadie Thurston; children: Wesley, George Jr & Avis. **Educ:** St Paul's Col, BS, educ, 1957; Va State Col, 1958; Univ Va, MEd, EdD, 1970; Bank St Col, Univ Pa; Am Bible Inst, DD, 1974. **Career:** Del State Col, dir stud teaching, 1966-72, chmn educ, 1972-75; St Paul's Col, chmn educ & psych; Mecklenburg Co Pub Schs, coordr gifted educ. **Orgs:** Asn Blvd Cab Co, 1962-; pastor, Wayland Baptist Church, 1974-; pres, L&M Const Co, 1976-; vice chmn, Alberta Child-Care Ctr, 1978-; Los Angeles City Law Enforcement Comt, 1980; pres, Epsilon Omicron Lambda, Alpha Phi Alpha, 1980-85; vpres, Lawrenceville Optimist Int, 1982-84. **Honors/Awards:** Outstanding Citizen Award, Los Angeles Emancipation Orgn, 1979; Faculty of the Year, St Paul's Col, 1979; Alpha Man of the Year, Alpha Phi Alpha Fraternity, 1982; Distinguished Service Award, Optimist Int, 1983. **Military Serv:** AUS, maj, 1952-72. **Business Addr:** Coordinator of Gifted Education, Mecklenburg County Public Schools, PO Box 190, Boydton, VA 23917, **Business Phone:** (804)738-6111.

MCLAUGHLIN, JACQUELYN SNOW
School administrator. **Personal:** Born Aug 12, 1943, Camden, NJ; daughter of Arlington Reynolds Sr; married Herman; children: Jevon & Jacques. **Educ:** Shaw Univ, Raleigh NC, BA, sociol, 1965; Univ Bridgeport, CT, couns cert, 1965; Glassboro St Col, NJ, MA, couns, 1972; Rutgers Univ, NJ, DEd, 1976. **Career:** Div NJ Employ Serv, counr, 1965-66; Wash Elem Sch, teacher, 1966-70; Camden Co Col, counr, 1970-71, dir, EOF prog, 1971-75, dean student affairs, 1975-. **Orgs:** Mid St Accreditation Asn, 1980-; pres, NJ St Deans Stud, 1980-; Juv Resource Ctr, staff, 1986-89; ad comn mem, Affirmative Action, 1989; YWCA, bd dirs, 1990-93; Asn Col Admin, 1990-93; New England Accreditation Asn, 1992; Nat Asn Foreign Studs; Asn Col Adminr; Alpha Kappa Alpha Sorority; bd dirs, Nat Coun Black Am Affairs. **Honors/Awds:** Plaque of Outstanding Service to Education Opportunity Fund Program, Camden Co Col, 1976; Certification Cited in Bicentennial Vol, Comm Leaders & Noteworthy Am, 1976; Delta Kappa Pi Hon Soc; Exec Leadership Inst, League for Innovations in the Community Col; Leaders for the 80s Inst for Leadership Develop; Honorary Mem of Phi Theta Kappa Honor Fraternity.

MCLAUGHLIN, KATYE H
Chief executive officer. **Personal:** Born Jan 31, 1943, Richland Parish, LA; daughter of Johnnie Sr and Etta Stephens; married Joseph C, Aug 27, 1955 (died 1984); children: Brian David & Bridget Diane. **Educ:** DC Teachers Col, WA, DC, BS, 1963; Antioch Grad Sch Educ, Wash, DC, MA, 1975; Kensington Univ, Glendale, CA, PhD, 1983. **Career:** DC Bd Educ, Wash, DC, teacher, 1976-89; McLaughlin Oldsmobile Inc, pres & chief exec officer; Penguin Unity Enterprises Inc, Penguin Greeting Cards, Wash, DC, pres & chief exec officer. **Orgs:** Phi Delta Kappa Sorority, 1980-; chairperson, United Negro Col Fund Telethon, Wash Metrop Area, 1985 & 1986; Int Club, 1991; bd dir, Langston Univ, 1992; Nat Polit Cong Black Women, 1992. **Honors/Awds:** Women's Achievement Award, Ertha M M White, Nat Bus League, 1985. Business Woman of the Year, Prince Georges Minority Develop Off, 1986; Outstanding Black Business Leader in Maryland, Baltimore Sun Newspaper, 1987-89; Outstanding Service Award, Prince Georges Ed Support Adv Coun, Langston, Okla, 1989.

MCLAUGHLIN, LAVERNE LANEY
Educator, librarian. **Personal:** Born Jul 29, 1952, Ft Valley, GA; daughter of John and Gladys Slappy; married Frederick; children: Frederick Laney. **Educ:** Spelman Col, BA, polit sci, 1974; Altanta Univ, MSLS, libr & info sci, 1975. **Career:** Atlanta Univ, Andrew Mellon fel, 1974-75; Byron Elem Sch, Bryon, Ga, teacher, 1975-76; Ga Southwestern State Univ, Americus, Ga, James Earl Carter Libr, assoc prof/librn/head tech serv, 1975-98; Albany State Univ, James Pendergrast Memorial Libr, libr dir, assoc prof, 1998-. **Orgs:** Pianist, St John Baptist Church, 1968-; Organist Allen Chapel AME Church, 1977-81; bd dir, Am Cancer Soc; Am Libr Asn; Ga Libr Asn; Southeastern Libr Asn; Ga Pub TV Adv Bd, 1980-85; Data Base Qual Control Comt Southeastern Libr Network, 1981-87; Sumter Co Chamber Com/Educ Comt, 1989; Martin Luther King Jr State Holiday Comn Ga, 1991-; organist, Bethesda Baptist Church, 1992-; commencement comt, Albany State Univ, 1998-99, acad leadership comt, 1998 " 2004, technol steering comt, 1999-2000, vpres acad affairs search comt, 2000 " 2001, aaron brown acad,2005 " 2006; HBCU Libr Allianc; Beta Phi Mu; Phi Delta Kappa; Spelman Col Nat Alumnae Asn; Clark Atlanta Univ Nat Alumni Asn; Alpha Kappa Alpha Sorority Inc. **Honors/Awds:** Cum laude, Spelman Col, 1974; Beta Phi Mu, Atlanta Univ, 1975; Outstanding Young Women America, 1983. **Home Addr:** 536 E Jefferson St, Americus, GA 31709. **Business Addr:** Associate Professor/Director of Library, Albany State University, James Pendergrast Memorial Library, 536 E Jefferson St, Albany, GA 31705, **Business Phone:** (229)924-9426.

MCLAUGHLIN, MEGAN E.
Social worker. **Personal:** Children: Afiya McLaughlin-White. **Educ:** Howard Univ, BA, 1966, MSW, 1968; The Graduate Ctr CUNY, Doctoral work Cultural Anthropology, 1972; Columbia Univ Sch Social Work, Cert Advan Social Welfare, 1976, DSW, 1981. **Career:** Social worker (retired); Columbia Univ Sch Social Work, lectr, 1975-78; The New York Community Trust, prog officer, 1978-83, sr prog officer, 1983-86; Fed Protestant Welfare Agencies Inc, exec dir & Chief Exec Officer, 1986-02. **Orgs:** Adv coun Columbia Univ Sch Social Work; Caribbean Women's Health Asn; Dept Social Serv Adv Comt, Health Syst Agency; Neighborhood Family Serv Continuing Crisis Implementation, Task Force Human Servs; Agenda Children Tomorrow; Black Leadership Comn AIDS; Interagency Task Force Food & Hunger Policy; chair, New York State Assembly Braintrust Children & Families; adv comt, Human Resources Admin; adv comt, New York Dept Aging; New York City Partnership; co-chair, Human Servs Coun. **Honors/Awds:** 8 publications including "West Indian Immigrants, Their Social Network & Ethnic Identification" Distribution Columbia Univ, 1981. *

MCLAURIN, DANIEL WASHINGTON
Executive, real estate executive. **Personal:** Born Nov 24, 1940, Philadelphia, PA; son of Abraham and Dorothy E Foster; married Delores E White, Sep 9, 1961; children: Craig Blair & Brian Keith. **Educ:** LaSalle Col, BS, Mkt, 1981. **Career:** Gulf Oil Corp, retail marketer, 1970-73, coordr, 1973-76, dir admin serv, 1976-83; Chevron Gulf Oil Corp, dir security & safety 1983-85, supv buildings mgt, 1985-; Chevron Real Estate Mgt Co, rep, bldg proj, 1994-. **Orgs:** Am Soc Indust Security; Soc Real Prop Admin; Bldg Owners & Mgr Inst Int. **Honors/Awds:** Chaplin of Four chaplins, 1973; Black Am Indust, 1974.

MCLAURIN, JASPER ETIENNE
Physician. **Personal:** Born Dec 12, 1927, Braxton, MS; son of Jasper and Magdeline Hicks; married Doris Williams McLaurin, Nov 24, 1956; children: Karen, Pamela, Toni. **Educ:** Wayne State Univ, BA, 1954; Meharry Med Col, MD, 1958; Harvard Med Sch, basic sci neurol, 1962; Univ Mich, MS, 1964; Mt Carmel Mercy Hosp, intern, 1959. **Career:** Va Hosp, resident, 1962; Pvt Med pract, 1964-90; Univ Mich Med Ctr, assoc neurologist, 1962-65; Univ Mich Med Sch, instr; chief neurol, 1963-64; VA Hosp, asst chief neurol, 1962; Wayne State Univ, asst prof; Mt Carmel Mercy Hosp, staff mem; Samaritan Med Ctr; Family Rehab Clin, neurologist, 1992-93; New Ctr Hosp, dir neurol serv, 1990-92; McLaurin Neurodiagnostic PC, chief exec officer, 1993-. **Orgs:** Wayne Co Med Soc; Mich State Med Soc; Am Med Asn; Detroit Med Soc; Nat Med Asn; MI Neurol Asn; Am Acad Neurol; Am Neurol Asn; fel, Am Col Angiol; Am Geriatrics Soc; Am Heart Asn; bd dir, Epileptic Ctr, MI; World Med Relief 1970, 1972; consult, Mich State Dept Educ; Detroit Bd Educ; Mich Cripple Children's Soc; Mich Neuromuscular Inst; Soc Security Admin; life mem, Nat Asn Advan Colored People; Urban League; Omega Psi Phi Fraternity; Nat Yacht Racing Union; bd dir, Huron River Heights Property Owners Asn; Knights Columbus. **Military Serv:** USN, lt comdr, 1946-50. **Business Addr:** Physician, 29425 Ryan Rd, Warren, MI 48092, **Business Phone:** (586)751-3060.*

MCLAWHORN, JAMES THOMAS
Association executive. **Personal:** Born Apr 27, 1947, Greenville, NC; son of James T McLawhorn; married Barbara Campbell; children: Karla, James III & Mark. **Educ:** NC A&T State Univ, BS, polit sci, 1969; Univ NC Chapel Hill, MA, city & regional planning, 1971; Univ Miami, MBA, 1977. **Career:** Model Cities, prog planning coord, 1971-74; City Charlotte, prog mgt coord, 1974-76; First Union Bank, loan develop analyst, 1977-78; Dem Nat Community Cong Black Caucus, admin asst, 1978-79; Columbia Urban League Inc, pres, chief exec officer, 1979-. **Orgs:** City Columbia Community Minority & Small Bus; Seven Thirty Breakfast Club; Govs Vol Awards Selection Comt; Crime Stoppers; Indian Waters Boy Scouts Am Exec Coun; chmn, Govs Primary Health Care Task Force Richland Co; Nat Black Family Summit; MNY Prof Develop Prog; Black Male Workshop, Midland; Sanders Mid Sch Improv Coun; bd visitors, Columbia Col; Richland Co Pvt Indust Coun; CHOICE, Study Community; Alliance Carolina's C; SC Equal Policy Coun. **Honors/Awds:** Mayor of Columbia, JT McLawhorn Day Honoree, Nov 28, 1989; Governor of South Carolina, Order Palmetto, 1992. **Special Achievements:** Publication: The State of Black SC: An Agenda for the Future; Ten for the Future Columbia Record; one of 60 civilian leaders in the nation invited to participate in the Joint Civilian Orientation Conf Sec of Defense 1985; assisted in bringing national attention to the plight of the rural poor and small farmers who were devastated by Hurrican Hugo, 1989. **Business Addr:** President, Chief Executive Officer, Columbia Urban League Inc, 1400 Barnwell St, PO Box 50125, Columbia, SC 29250, **Business Phone:** (803)799-8150.

MCLEAN, DENNIS RAY
Executive. **Personal:** Born Dec 8, 1951, Fuquay, NC; son of Mathew McLean Jr and Minnie Mae; married Hyesuk McLean Ohm, Jun 24, 1985; children: Louis, Enoch & Tiffany. **Educ:** Midlands Tech Col, AA, 1978; Benedict Col, BS, 1980. **Career:** SC Youth Serv, family counr, 1975-82; SKM3/Transax Inc, founder & pres, 1982-. **Orgs:** Greater Columbia Chamber Com, 1982-; co-founder & pub rels officer, Greater Columbia Tennis Asn, 1983-86. **Honors/Awds:** Private Pilot Certificate, Midlands Aviation, 1984; Dr King Living the Dream, Prof Black Women Asn, 1986; Academic Small Business Man of the Year, Gen Dynamics, 1989; Top Supplier of the Year, Gen Dynamics, 1992. **Military Serv:** USAF, sgt, 1970-75. **Home Addr:** 1800 Broadview Ct, Columbia, SC 29212. **Business Addr:** President & Chief Executive Officer, Transax Inc, 108F White Oak Lane, Lexington, SC 29072, **Business Phone:** (803)739-2253.

MCLEAN, DOLLIE CLARICE H
Executive. **Personal:** Born in New York, NY; daughter of Cleveland Robert and Gladys T Hamilton; married Jackie McLean (John L); children: Rene, Vernone & Melonae. **Educ:** Fashion Inst, fashion design, 1958; Univ Hartford, TV production & creative writing, 1985. **Career:** Negro Ensemble Co, dancer, actress; Arnold Originals, showroom & design asst; NY Eye & Ear Infirmary, ENO Laboratory, secy, 1960-71; Wadsworth Antheneum Mus, community liaison; Artists Collective Inc, founder, exec dir, currently. **Honors/Awds:** Omega Ohi Exelon, Comm Service Trailblazer Awd, 1977; Upper Albany Merchants Assn, Leadership Comm Service Awd, 1986; Hartford Coll, Pioneer's Awd, 1995; CREN, Hartford Hero Awd, 1998; Smith-Whiley Trailblazer Awd, 1999; Girl Scouts of Amer, Comm Service Awd, 1999; Trinity Coll, honorary doctorate, 1999; Citizen Club of Hartford, Citizen of the Year, 2000; Ancient Buriel Ground, Thomas Hooker Awd, 2002. **Business Addr:** Founding Executive Director, The Artists Collective, 1200 Albany Ave, Hartford, CT 06112, **Business Phone:** (860)527-3205.

MCLEAN, DR. HELEN VIRGINIA
School administrator, educator. **Personal:** Born Jul 23, 1933, Southern Pines, NC; daughter of Nora Jackson and Mitchell. **Educ:** NC Cent Univ, BA, 1954; Univ Pa, MA, 1956; Univ Fla, EdD, 1974. **Career:** Educator (retired); Wilberforce Univ, assoc prof lang, 1956-58; Gibbs Junior Col, chair person commun dept, 1958-64; St Petersburg Junior Col,chairperson directed studies dept, 1964-75, dir div commun, 1975; Tangley Oaks Educ, fel, 1972-73; Univ Fla, EDDA-E, grad fel, 1972-74. **Orgs:** Am Assn Univ Women; Modern Lang Assn; Col Eng Assn; Fla Eng Assn; Coun Black Am Affairs Southern Region; YWCA; secy exec comt mem, Pinellas Co Dist Ment Health Brd; Nat Assn Advan Colored People; brd, United Negro Col Fund St Petersburg Fla; Greater St Petersburg Coun Human Rel. **Special Achievements:** Published "Reading-A Total Faculty Commitment," "Career Educ and Gen Edn,""Every Tchr a Reading Tchr," "Teaching Strategies for a Developmental Studies Curriculum"; various other publications. **Home Addr:** 1583 McAuliffe Lane, Palm Harbor, FL 34683-7209, **Home Phone:** (727)736-5143.

MCLEAN, DR. JOHN ALFRED, JR.
Educator. **Personal:** Born Nov 8, 1926, Chapel Hill, TN; son of John Alfred Sr and Anna Belle Sheffield; married Esther Ann

Bush; children: Jeffery, David & Linda. **Educ:** Tenn A & I State Univ, BS, 1948; Univ Ill, MS, 1956, PhD, 1959. **Career:** Educator (retired); State Bd Pub Community & Jr Col, chmn 1965-81; Univ Detroit Mercy, prof chem, chmn dept chem & chem engineering, 1959-94. **Orgs:** Phi Delta Kappa; Phi Lambda Upsilon; Sigma Xi; bd dirs, Am Heart Asn,1988-. **Honors/Awds:** Community Service Award, Wayne County Community Col, 1977; Certificate for Outstanding Leadership of Detroit, Am Chem Soc, 1982; Annual Distinguished Service Award, Detroit Sect Am Chem Soc, 1985; President's Award Excellence Teaching & Research, Univ Detroit, 1986. **Military Serv:** AUS, sgt, 1953-55.

MCLEAN, DR. MABLE PARKER
Educator. **Personal:** Born in Cameron, NC; widowed; children: Randall P. **Educ:** Harvard Univ, Inst Educ Mgmt, 1972; Johnson C Smith Univ, LHD, 1976; Rust Col, LHS, 1976; Col Granada, LlD; Barber-Scotia, Pedu. **Career:** Barber-Scotia Col, prof educ & psychology, coordr stud teaching, 1969-71; chmn, dept elementary educ, 1970-7; dean col, 1971-74; interim pres, pres, 1974-88 & 1994-96. **Orgs:** Asn Childhood Educ; Asn Stud Teaching; Nat & St NC Asn Supr & Curriculum Develop; St Coun Early Childhood Educ; Delta Kappa Gamma Soc Women Educ; NC Admin Women Educ; Am Asn Univ Admin; Nat Coun Admin Women Educ; Metrolina Lang Asn; Dem Women's Org Cabarrus Co; Alpha Kappa Alpha Sorority Inc; Children's Home Soc NC; United Pres Women's Org John Hall United Press Ch; Presidents Round table UPC USA; NAFEO; United Bd Col Develop; United Way Cabarrus Co; NC Asn Independent Cols & Univs; NC Asn-Cols & Univs. **Honors/Awds:** Honorary Degrees 7; Johnson C Smith Alumni Outstanding Achievement Award, 1977; Distinguished Alumna Award, 1977; Alumna Yr, Johnson C Smith Univ, 1980; Dedicated Serv Citation-Consortium Res Training, 1982; Distinguished Serv Award, Grambling State Univ, 1984. **Special Achievements:** First woman pres Barber-Scotia Col & first woman chair UNCF Member Col & Univ Pres. **Business Addr:** Interim President, Barber Scotia College, Concord, NC 28025, **Business Phone:** (704)789-2900.

MCLEAN, MARQUITA SHEILA MCLARTY
Environmental scientist, manager, consultant. **Personal:** Born Aug 5, 1933, Richmond, VA; daughter of William C and Daisey B; married Cecil P. **Educ:** Va State Univ, BA, 1953; Ohio State Univ, MA, 1956; Univ Cincinnati, post grad, 1957-69. **Career:** Delaware Ohio, teacher 1954-57; Robert A Taft High Sch, Cincinnati, teacher, 1957-62; Sawyer Jr High Sch, Cincinnati, counr, 1962-65; Withrow High Sch, Cincinnati, counr, 1965-67; Cincinnati Pub Sch, assoc guid serv div, 1968-73; Off Univ Commitment Human Resources, Univ Cincinnati, dir, 1973-77; Univ Personnel Serv Univ Cincinnati, assoc sr vpres, 1978-83; Ohio Environ Protection Agency, dep admin 1983-85; McLean Olohan & Associates, prin-in-charge, currently. **Orgs:** Alumni Adv Coun, Ohio St Univ, 1971-; vice chairperson, Ohio Water Adv Coun, Gov appointee, 1985-89; Leadership Steering Comt, Cincinnati, 1986-87; pub mgr, State & Local Govt Coun, 1988-92; Cincinnati Environ Adv Coun 1988-; charter mem, Withrow Dollars Scholars, 1988; past trustee, Cincinnati Tech Col; Ohio Educ Asn; Cincinnati Personnel & Guid Asn; Am Sch Counr Asn; Ohio Sch Counr Asn; Nat Asn Sch Counselors; Delta SigmaTheta; Ohio St Alumni Club; Nat & Cincinnati Women Polit Caucus; Citizens Scholar Found Am Inc; Nat Bd Governors. **Home Addr:** 5324 Kenwood Rd, Cincinnati, OH 45227. **Business Addr:** Principal, McLean Olohan & Associates, 5324 Kenwood Rd, Cincinnati, OH 45227, **Business Phone:** (513)271-3351.

MCLEAN, RENE (RENE PROFIT-MCLEAN)
Educator, musician, composer. **Personal:** Born Dec 16, 1946, New York, NY; son of Jackie and Dollie; married Thandine January; children: Rene Jr, Sharif, Thandine-Naima & Nozipho-Jamila. **Educ:** NY Col Music; Univ Mass. **Career:** EDR, band leader, 1965-; New York State Narcotic Control Comm, Melrose Community Ctr, band master, 1970-73; Univ Hartford, Dept African Am Music, artist in residence, 1984-85; MMABANA Cultural Ctr, Safrica, consult, music dept head, 1987-90; Triloka Records, recording artist, producer, 1988-; New Sch Jazz, New York, vis mem, 1991-92; Univ Capetown, lectr Jazz studies, 1994-98; McLean Entertainment Group, founder & ceo, 1997-; Artists Collective, Hartford, Conn, master artist/dir-in-residence music, currently; Jackie McLean Inst, Univ Hartford, prof African-Am music, currently; Broadcast Music Inc, writer, publ; Harry Fox Agency, publ; Nordisk Copyright, publ. **Orgs:** AFM 802. **Honors/Awds:** Scholar, Outward Bound Mountaineering Sch, 1963; Cultural Medallion, presented by Mayor Karlstad, Sweden, 1977; Survival Black Artist Award, Howard Univ Fine Arts Festival, 1983; Creative Artist Fel Award, Japan-US Friendship Comn, Nat Endowment Arts, 1986-87. **Business Addr:** Professor, Jackie McLean Institute of Jazz, University of Hartford, 200 Bloomfield Ave, West Hartford, CT 06117, **Business Phone:** (860)768-4371.

MCLEAN, ZARAH GEAN
Physician, pediatrician. **Personal:** Born Aug 28, 1942, Tallulah, LA; married Russell; children: Paul, Crystal, Grant. **Educ:** Fisk Univ, BA, 1964; Howard Univ Col Med, MD, 1968. **Career:** Med Col Wis, assoc prof pediat, 1972-86; pvt pract, pediatrician, currently. **Orgs:** bd dirs, Emma Murry Child Care Ctr, 1982-86. **Honors/Awds:** Physician of Yr, Cream City Med Soc, 1989; Outstanding Community Serv, St Mary's Col Women of Color Alliance, 1990. **Business Addr:** Physician, 2040 W Wisconsin Ave, Milwaukee, WI 53233.*

MCLEMORE, ANDREW G
Executive, founder (originator), president (organization). **Personal:** Born Dec 13, 1931, Memphis, TN; son of Benjamine and Belle; married Dorothy Ellison, 1954; children: Andrew Jr & Raymond S. **Educ:** WVA State Col, BS, 1953. **Career:** A-MAC Sales & Builders Co, pres, currently. **Orgs:** Asn Black Gen Contractors. **Military Serv:** USY, 1st lt, 1953-56. **Business Phone:** (313)837-4690.

MCLEMORE, LESLIE BURL
Educator. **Personal:** Born Aug 17, 1940, Walls, MS; son of Christine Williams and Burl; divorced; children: Leslie Burl McLemore II. **Educ:** Rust Col, BA, 1964; Atlanta Univ, MA, 1965; Univ Mass, Amherst, PhD, 1970. **Career:** Atlanta Univ, res asst, 1960-65; Southern Univ, 1965-66; Univ Mass Amherst, teaching asst, 1966-69; Johns Hopkins Univ, post-doctoral fel,1970, Dept Polit Sci, prof, 1976-; Miss State Univ, Dept polit sci, vis prof, 1979-80; Harvard Univ, res assoc, 1982-83; Rockefeller Found, resfel, 1982-83, dean grad sch, dir res & admin, 1984-90, acting dir, 1990-; Univ Ctr Jackson, actg dir; Hammer Inst, fac, currently. **Orgs:** Am Asn Higher Studies, 1992; pres, Rust Col Nat Alumni Asn; past vpres, S Polit Sci Asn; former pres, Nat Conf Black Polit Scientist; Jackson League Task Force Local Gov; exec comt, Black Miss Coun Higher Educ; chair, Liaison Community NCEA; chair, Task Force Minorities Grad Educ; Pi Sigma Alpha Polit Sci; pres, City Coun Jackson; chair, Miss Humanities Coun; vice chair, Bd Fedn State Humanities Coun; pres, Coun Historically Black Grad Sch. **Honors/Awds:** Spotlight on Scholars Award, Jackson State Univ, 1980-81; Chancellor's Medal, Univ Mass, Amherst, 1986; Certificate of Commendation for Outstanding Service, US Secy Energy, 1990; Certificate of Appreciation, Miss Ctr Technol, 1992; Award of Appreciation, Sci & Eng Alliance, 1992; Hon Woodrow Wilson Fel, Rust Col; Travel Grant Awards, Jackson State Univ, 2005. **Special Achievements:** Hundred Black Men of Jackson, 1991; Appointed to the Commission on the Status of Black Americans. **Home Addr:** 746 Windward Rd, Jackson, MS 39206. **Business Addr:** Professor Political Science, Jackson State University, 1400 John Roy Lynch St, PO Box 17091, Jackson, MS 39217, **Business Phone:** (601)979-1564.

MCLEMORE, MARK TREMELL
Baseball player, baseball executive. **Personal:** Born Oct 4, 1964, San Diego, CA. **Career:** Baseball player (retired), baseball executive; Calif Angels, infielder, 1986-90; Cleveland Indians, 1990; Houston Astros, 1991; Baltimore Orioles, 1992-94; Tex Rangers, 1995-99; Seattle Mariners, 2000-03; Oakland Athletics, second baseman, 2004; ESPN baseball, color commentator; Mark McLemore Sports Complex, owner, currently. **Business Addr:** Owner, Mark McLemore Sports Complex, 2020 Industrial Blvd, Rockwall, TX 76087.

MCLEMORE, NELSON, JR.
Government official. **Personal:** Born Jan 29, 1934, Chicago, IL; married Ollie Stokes; children: Nelson III. **Educ:** Tenn A&M State Univ, BS, 1955; Gov State Univ, MA, 1978; Chicago Teachers Col & John Marshall Law Sch, add study. **Career:** Government official (retired); Chicago Pub Elem & Sec Sch, teacher,1955-65; Chicago Comn Youth Welfare, community unit dir, 1965-69; Chicago Dept Human Resources, asst comnr, coordr community serv, 1972-74;Planning-Human Serv, asst dir, 1978-79; chief-of-staff; Human Serv, dir personnel & training, 1979-80; Human Serv, dep comnr, 1980; Dept Pub Works, dir prog, 1985-90; Kennedy King Col, Chicago, coordr, transfer ctr, 1990. **Orgs:** Nat Asn Comm Develop; pres & mem, 2nd ard Reg Dem Orgn Boosters Club; Kappa Alpha Psi; cert, social worker. **Military Serv:** AUS, pfc, 1956-58. **Home Phone:** (312)225-7668. *

MCLEOD, GEORGIANNA R.
Social worker. **Personal:** Born Oct 6, 1937, New York, NY; daughter of George and Annie Coles. **Educ:** NY Univ, BS, 1959; Inst Appl Res, London, England, PhD, humanities. **Career:** Social Worker (retired); Morningside Community Ctr Camp 41, group work & recreation, 1952; Rusk Inst, recreation therap, 1957-58; Neighborhood House, 1959; New York City Dept Soc Serv Emer Asst Unit/Bronx, dir & social worker, 1984-89; Willow Star II, Womens Shelter for Substance Abusers, dir, social serv; Social Servs 68 Lex Womens Shelter, dir, 1996. **Orgs:** Am Pub Works Asn; Nat Charter Sch Watch; Nat Asn Black Social Workers; Am Chama Soc; Am Soc Prof Exec Women; trustee & grand secy, Eureka Grand Chap, PhOES; past matron, Alpha Chap; past pres, exec bd mem & life mem, founder & dir, New York City; Nat Asn Advancement Colored People, 1960-; master activist, secy, deacon, trustee, corp pres & admin asst, Church Master, 1947-; vpres, Nat Black Presbyterian Caucus, Ny Col; founder & dir, Proj THRESH, Nat Asn Advancement Colored People, 1967-; chap, Consumer Educ Econ Develop, New York City; Nat Asn Advancement Colored People, 1966-; under Gov Rockefeller served on Migrant Workers Comm; dir, Westchester County; voter rep dir, St Compt Carl McCall; vpres, Black Dems Westchester, 1968-. **Honors/Awds:** Woman of the Year, Interboro Civic 5, 1980; Community Service Award, Nat Asn Advancement Colored People, 1983; Outstanding Service, Church Master, 1983; Employee of the Year, Willow Star II, 1993; Certificate of Appreciation, Nat Park Trust. **Home Addr:** 28 University Ave, Yonkers, NY 10704.

MCLEOD, DR. GUSTAVUS A.
Business owner, airplane pilot. **Personal:** Born Jan 1, 1955?, Corinth, MS; married Mary Alice Lockmuller, 1976; children: 3. **Educ:** Catholic Univ Am, BA, chem, 1976; Univ Md, MS, chem engineering, 1977; Fla Atlantic Univ, Hon Doctorate, 2002. **Career:** CIA, chemist; Raytheon Corp, chemist; surgical supply co, owner; Beerdistrib co, owner; 3 Roads Commun Inc, aviator, currently. **Honors/Awds:** Distinguished Achievement Award, Air Force Asn; Distinguished Flying Cross, Distinguished Flying Cross Soc, 2004; Hon Researcher, Korea Aerospace Res Inst, 2005. **Special Achievements:** First person to fly the first open cockpit aircraft over the magnetic North Pole, 1999; First person to fly an open cockpit aircraft over the Geographic North Pole, 2000; first person to cross the treacherous Drake Passage at night in an experimental aircraft; Author: Solo to the Top ofthe World: Gus McLeod's Daring Record Flight. **Business Addr:** Aviator, 3 Roads Communications Inc, 241 E 4th St Suite 202, Frederick, MD 21701, **Business Phone:** (301)662-4121.

MCLEOD, JAMES S.
Funeral director. **Personal:** Born Oct 14, 1939, Bennettsville, SC; married Shirley J Jeffries; children: Tracey, Maymia, Erica. **Educ:** A&T State Univ; NC Cent Univ Durham NC, Eckels Col Mortuary Sci Philadelphia. **Career:** Morris Funeral Home Bennettsville SC, mgr, 1964-72, owner 1972-. **Orgs:** 6 Dist Morticians Asn; SC State & Nat Morticians Asn; exec bd, Pee Dee Reg Planning & Develop Coun Marlboro Co Betterment League; 6th Dist VEP; Carolina Messenger Inc Shiloh Baptist Church; Landmark Masonic Lodge; F & AM; CC Johnson Consistory Cairo; Am Legion Post; Theta Phi Lambda Chap; Alpha Phi Alpha; Nat Asn Advan Colored People. **Honors/Awds:** Cert merit, United Supreme Coun, 1970; Distinguished serv Award, Alpha Phi Alpha, 1971; Cert achievement, Omega Psi Phi Frat, 1971; Certificate, Pub serv Mayor Bennettsville SC; dean's Award Eckels Col Mortuary Sci. **Special Achievements:** First black since Reconstruction to be appointed to a Boardin Marlboro Co Social Services 1968 & to be elected to Bennettsville City Coun 1971 presently serving 2 terms. **Military Serv:** AUS signal corp 1962-64. **Business Addr:** Owner, Morris Funeral Home, PO Box 551, Bennettsville, SC 29512.

MCLEOD, KEVIN
Football player, football coach. **Personal:** Born Oct 17, 1974, Montego Bay, Jamaica; married Sharon. **Educ:** Auburn Univ. **Career:** Football player (retired), football coach; Jacksonville Jaguars, 1998; Tampa Bay Buccaneers, fullback, 1999; Cleveland Browns, fullback, 2003; Inlet Grove High Sch, coach, 2007. **Honors/Awds:** Rookie of the Year, 1999.

MCLEOD, DR. MICHAEL PRESTON
Dentist. **Personal:** Born Aug 16, 1954, Tulsa, OK; son of Jeanne and Wallace B; married Corlis Clay; children: Lauren Micah & Kathleen Blake. **Educ:** Howard Univ, BS (Cum Laude), 1976; Univ Okla, DDS, 1980; Martin Luther King Genl Hosp, GPR, 1981. **Career:** Pvt pract, dentist; Univ Okla, Col Dent, Okla City, OK, part-time faculty, 1984-. **Orgs:** Kappa Alpha Psi, 1975-; Oklahoma City Med Dental-Phar, 1982-; Citizen's Advisory Comm, Capital-Medical Ctr Improvement & Zoning Commn, 1984-. **Honors/Awds:** Amer Acad of Periodontology Award, 1980; Amer Soc Dentistry for Children Award, 1980; Div Comm Dent Award, 1980; Univ Okla Assoc Black Personnel Award, 1980. **Home Addr:** 2216 N Martin Luther King A Suite A, Oklahoma City, OK 73111, **Home Phone:** (405)427-0237. **Business Addr:** Physician, 2216 N Martin Luther King A Suite A, Oklahoma City, OK 73111, **Business Phone:** (405)427-0237.

MCLEOD, ROSHOWN
Basketball player, basketball coach. **Personal:** Born Nov 17, 1975, Jersey City, NJ. **Educ:** Duke Univ. **Career:** Basketball player (retired), basketball coach; Atlanta Hawks, 1998-2000, 2000-01; Philadelphia 76ers, 2000; Fairfield Univ, asst coach, 2002-03; Coach K Acad, coach. **Honors/Awds:** Swett Memorial Trophy, Duke MVP, 1998.

MCLIN, LENA JOHNSON
Educator, composer. **Personal:** Born Sep 5, 1928, Atlanta, GA; daughter of Benjamin and Bernice Dorsey; married Nathaniel; children: Nathaniel G & Beverly. **Educ:** Spelman Col, AB, 1951, BM, piano & violin, Spelman Col, Atlanta, Georgia;Roosevelt Univ, Chicago State Col, electronic music & voice; Am Conservatory, Mm, 1954. **Career:** Singer; composer numerous works; clinician; Kenwood High Sch, Chicago,teacher, dir, head music dept; small opera co "Mclin Ensemble", founder, dir; Trinity Congregational Church, founder. **Orgs:** Chicago Bd Educ; TCI Educ Film Co MENC; Nat Asn Negro Musicians; NJE; Inst Black Am Music; founder & pastor; holy Vessel Christian Ctr, Chicago. **Honors/Awds:** Outstanding composer Award, Va Union Univ, 1973; Best teacher of the year, 1983; Critics Association Outstand-

ing Composer, 1971; outstanding musician, Nat Advan Asn Colored People; hon degree, HHD VA Union Univ,1975. **Special Achievements:** Publisher: Pulse: A History of Music, 1977.

MCLURKIN, JAMES
Consultant, scientist. **Personal:** Born Jan 1, 1972?. **Educ:** Mass Inst Technol, SB, elec engineering minor mechanical engineering,1995; Univ Calif, Berkeley, MS, elec engineering, 1999; Mass Inst Technol,SM, 2004, Comput Sci, PhD, comput Sci, 2008. **Career:** Walt Disney Imagineering, Sensable Technologies & Micro Display Corp,consult; iRobot, lead res scientist & mgr swarm project, currently. **Honors/Awds:** Guest speaker, Interval Res Inc, Dartmouth Col, LEGO Advanced Design Ctr,Asn Sci-Tech Ctrs; Lemelson MIT prize, Mass Inst Technol, 2003. **Special Achievements:** Recognized by Time Magazine as one of five leading robotics engineers in their "Rise of the Machines" feature, and by Black Enterprise magazine asa "Best and Brightest Under 40". "Distributed Coverage Control with Sensory Feedback for Networked Robots", 2006; "Protoswarm: A Language for Programming Multi-Robot Systems Using the Amorphous Medium Abstraction", 2008; "Analysis and Implementation of Distributed Algorithms for Multi-Robot Systems", 2008; From Theory to Practice: Distributed Coverage Control Experiments with Groups of Robots", 2008; "Measuring the Accuracy of Distributed Algorithms on Multi-Robot Systems with Dynamic Network Topologies", 2008; "A Distributed Boundary Detection Algorithm for Multi-Robot Systems", 2009. **Business Addr:** Manager, MIT Computer Science & Artificial Intelligence Lab, 32 Vassar St 32-G430, Cambridge, MA 02139, **Business Phone:** (617)253-5223.*

MC LYTE (LANA MICHELE MOORER)
Rap musician. **Personal:** Born Oct 11, 1971, Queens, NY. **Career:** Rap singer, currently; began rapping at age 12; released first single, "I Cram to Understand U (Sam)", 1987; single: "Cha Cha Cha" reached number one on rap charts; signed to Electra, 1996; Albums: The Lion & The Cobra, 1988; Lyte as a Rock, 1988; Eyes on This, 1989; The First Priority Music Family: Basement Flavor, 1989; Act Like You Know; 1991; Mo' Money, 2002; Ain't No Other, 1993; Panther, soundtrack, 1994; Sunset Park, soundtrack, 1996; Bad as I Wanna B, 1997; Badder Than B-Fore, 1998; Seven & Seven, 1998; TV: I Cram to Understand You, 1988; Cha Cha Cha, 1989; Ruffneck, 1993; janet, 1994; Brandy, 1994; Lyte of a Decade, 1996; Keep on Keeping On, 1997; I Can't Make A Mistake, 1998; 1993, 1999; Everyday, 1999; Da Undaground Heat Vol One, 2003; Shit I Never Dropped, 2003; "Half & Half", 2004-06; Girlfriend's Story, 2004; Da Jammies, 2006; "The Big Hide & Sneak Episode", 2006; "The Big Diva Down Episode", 2006. **Honors/Awds:** Nominated, Grammy award for Best Rap Single for "Ruffneck"; earned first-ever gold cert for record sales by a female rap artist; Soul Train Lady of Soul Music Award, 1996. **Special Achievements:** First rapper to perform at Carnegie Hall; acted on TV's: Moesha; In the House; New York Undercover; For Your Love; in the film A Luv Tale, 1999; Train Ride, 2000; Civil Brand, 2002; Holla, 2002; Playas Ball, 2003; began doing voice-overs; founded own management co, Duke Da Moon Productions; signed three-year deal with Sirius Satellite Radio. **Business Addr:** Rap Singer, Elektra Records, 75 Rockefeller Plz, New York, NY 10019, **Business Phone:** (212)275-4000.

MCMICHAEL, EARLENE CLARISSE
Journalist. **Personal:** Born Sep 29, 1963, New York, NY; daughter of Norma Krieger and Earl McMichael. **Educ:** Cornell Univ, Ithaca, NY, BS, 1984; Columbia Univ Grad Sch Jour, New York, MS, 1987. **Career:** The Oakland Press, Pontiac, MI, reporter, 1987; Kansas City Times, Kansas City, MO, reporter, 1987; Shoreline Newspapers, Guilford, CT, reporter, 1988; The Jersey J, Jersey City, NJ, reporter, 1988-. **Orgs:** Vpres, Brooklyn chapter, Zeta Phi Beta Sorority, 1986-87; sec, New Jersey chapter, Nat Asn Black Journalists, 1988-90. **Honors/Awds:** WNBC-TV Minority Fellow Scholarship, 1986-87; participant in the Capital Cities/ABC Inc Minority Training Program, 1987-88. **Home Addr:** 163 Eastern Pkwy Suite D4, Brooklyn, NY 11238, **Home Phone:** (718)857-7290. **Business Addr:** Reporter, The Jersey Journal, 30 Journal Square, Jersey City, NJ 07306, **Business Phone:** (201)795-6147.

MCMILLAN, DOUGLAS JAMES
Clergy, educator. **Personal:** Born Feb 8, 1947, New York, NY; son of James and Irene Wilson. **Educ:** Community Col, Allegeny Co, AA, Eng, 1975; Univ Pittsburgh, BA, Lang Comm, 1977; Xavier Univ La, New Orleans, LA, ThM, 1990. **Career:** Canevin High Sch, Pittsburgh, PA, teacher, 1973-80; Assum Acad NY, teacher, 1980-81; Bishop Grimes High Sch, NY, Eng Dept, teacher, 1981-89, 1997-, asst prin, 1989-90, chair, 1999-; Diocese Syracuse, Syracuse, NY, dir, off Black Cath Ministry, 1990-97; Archbishop Curley High Sch, Eng Dept, teacher, 2005-. **Orgs:** Order Friars Minor Conventuals, 1968-; Nat Black Cath Clergy Caucus, 1984-; bd mem, Off Black Cath Ministry Diocese Syracuse; Nat Asn Black Cath Adminr, 1990-; Conventual Franciscan Province Immaculate Conception. **Military Serv:** AUS, spec-5, 1966-68. **Home Addr:** 4220 Erdman Ave, Baltimore, MD 21213. **Business Addr:** Teacher, Archbishop Curley High School, 3701 Sinclaire Lane, Baltimore, MD 21213, **Business Phone:** (410)485-5000.

MCMILLAN, JACQUELINE MARIE
Educator, management consultant. **Personal:** Born Dec 15, 1966, Jamaica, NY; daughter of Vincent Savage and Margaret; married LeMorris Neil (divorced); children: De Morris Jourdan Baity. **Educ:** Col Holy Cross, BA, 1989; Kent State Univ, MPA, 1993, PhD, 1998. **Career:** Stud Progs Urban Develop, co-dir, 1986-89; Col Holy Cross, resident asst, 1987-89; NY City Child Welfare Admin, case mgr, 1990-92; Kent State Univ, acad adv, 1992-95, res asst, 1995-. **Orgs:** Nat Forum Pub Adminrs, 1992-; Women's Network, 1993-; mentor, C's Serv Bd, 1994-; prog adv, Black Grad Stud Asn, 1994-; Am Asn Higher Educ, 1994-95; bd mem, Phi Delta Kappa, 1995-; fel, World Bible Way, 1995; Kappa Delta Pi, 1996-; Nat Asn Women Educ, 1996-. **Honors/Awds:** World Bibleway fel, 1991; Leadership Award, Future Bus Leaders Am Inc, 1994; Service Award, Col Educ, 1995; Phi Delta Kappa Dissertation Award, 1996. **Special Achievements:** Financial Analysis of the City of Kent, Ohio, 1993; Dealing with Fiscal Stress in the Twentieth Century, 1993; Health Care Admin & the Budget Crunch, 1994; A Review of the Prospective Health Care Plans, 1995; Total Quality Mgt in Ohio Inst, 1997. **Home Addr:** 325 Beechwood Dr, Akron, OH 44320. **Business Addr:** Research Assistant, Kent State University, 404 White Hall, Kent, OH 44242, **Business Phone:** (330)672-2580.

MCMILLAN, JAMES C.
Educator. **Personal:** Born Dec 23, 1925, Sanford, NC; son of J E; divorced; children: Eric Wesley & Frances Lynne. **Educ:** Howard Univ, BA, art, 1947; Fresco Mural Skowhegan Sch Art ME, fel, 1947; Acad Julian (Paris France), cert, 1951; Catholic Univ Am, Wash DC, MFA, sculpture, 1952; Syracuse Univ NY, fel (adv study), 1958, 1961. **Career:** US Naval Air Station, art instr & illustrator, 1945-46; Bennett Col, Greensboro NC, prof & chmn art dept, 1947-50, 1952-53, 1956-69, prof emer,currently; Syracuse Univ, Bennett Col, NY, Danforth teacher fel, 1960-61; Guilford Col, prof art, 1966-88, dir London/European arts sem, 1968-72, painter, sculptor, prof art emer, 1988-; Va State Univ, Petersburg, eminent scholar fine arts, 1990. **Orgs:** Dir cult enrichment, EPDA Bennett Col, 1969-70; dir, NY Art Sem, Guilford Col, 1971-75; Col Art Asn, 1984-85; Nat Conf Artists, 1984-85; DC Art Asn, 1985; pres, Afro-Am Atelier Inc Gallery, Greensboro, NC, 1990-91. **Honors/Awds:** Mural Providence Baptist Church Greensboro, NC, 1977. **Special Achievements:** Became the first African-American to receive a fellowship at the Skowhegan School of Painting and Sculpture in Maine in 1947. **Military Serv:** USN, aviation mach mate 2nd class, 1944-46; Pac Theatre Oiper, WWII, 1946. **Business Addr:** Professor Emeritus, Guilford College, Art Department, 5800 W Friendly Ave, Greensboro, NC 27410, **Business Phone:** (336)316-2249.

MCMILLAN, DR. JOSEPH TURNER
College administrator. **Personal:** Born Jul 19, 1944, Valdosta, GA; son of Rev J T McMillan and Olivia Cooper McMillan. **Educ:** Howard Univ, BS, psychol, 1965, MA, stud personnel admin, 1970; Teachers Col; Columbia Univ, doctorate, higher educ admin, 1986; Harvard Univ, cert, educal mgt, 1990. **Career:** United Church Bd Homeland Ministries, secy higher educ relships, exec secy coun higher educ, 1970-88; Huston-Tillotson Col, Austin, TX, pres, 1988-2000, pres emer, 2000-; Tex Col Traditional Chinese Med, acad dean, currently. **Orgs:** Chmn, bd trustees, Tex Asn Developing Cols, 1993-97; bd trustees, Pension Bds United Church Christ; bd dirs, Amistad Res Ctr; bd dirs, United Negro Col Fund, 1990-99; Congregational Church Austin; chair, Coun Higher Educ United Church Christ, 1996-99; Austin Regional Adv Bd, Chase Bank Tex. **Honors/Awds:** Educator of the Year Award, Nat Alliance Black Sch Educr, 1990; Outstanding Texan Award for Educator, Texas Legis Black Caucus, 1993; Whitney M Young Jr Award, Austin Area Urban League, 1995; DHL, Yankton Col, 1978; Doctor Laws, Huston-Tillotson Col, 1984; Austin Area Affiliates. **Business Addr:** Academic Dean, Texas College of Traditional Chinese Medicine, 4005 Manchaca Rd, Austin, TX 78704, **Business Phone:** (512)444-8082.

MCMILLAN, DR. MAE F.
Physician, psychiatrist. **Personal:** Born May 12, 1936, Austin, TX; daughter of Ben S Sr and Annie M Walker. **Educ:** Wiley Col Marshall TX, BS, BA, 1955; Meharry Med Col, MD, 1959; Wayne Co Gen Hosp Mich, internship, 1960; Baylor Univ Col Med Houston, affiliated hosp residency, 1963 1965; Hampstead Child Therapy Course & Clinic London, post-19doctoral Fellowship, 1967. **Career:** Baylor Col Med Depts Psychiat & Child Psychiat, asst prof, 1966; pvt practice, part time child psychiatry specialty pre-schoolers; Tex Res Inst Mental Sci, asst dir div child Psychiat, 1968-72, dir div child Psychiat, 1972-74, dir early childhood therapy course & clinic; Univ Tex Med Sch Houston, clinical assoc prof; Faculty Advanced Studies Univ Tex Sch Biomedical Science, asst prof, 1975; Univ Tex Health Sci Ctr Houston, clinical assoc prof, 1976; Tex Woman's Univ Child Develop & Family Living, adjunct prof; Baylor Col Med Depts Psychiat & Child Psych, clinical assoc prof. **Orgs:** Bd mem, CAN DO IT, 1973-80; bd dirs, Girls Clubs Houston Sect; Nat Coun Negro Women; Delta Sigma Theta; Mental Health Asn; coord, Child Care Coun Houston Harris Co; United Methodist Women; treas, Tex Community Corp; chmn, Child Advocacy com, Houston Psychiatric soc, 1992; Am Psychiat Asn; Tex Soc Psych Physicians; bd trust, vchmn, Harris county Mental Health & Mental Retardation Authority; distinguished life fellow, Am Psychiat Asn, 2002; vchmn, bd mental health, Mental Retardation Authority Harris County, 1999. **Honors/Awds:** Criminal Justice Award, Delta Sigma Theta; One Amer Proj, 1973; Distinction of Merit; Nat Coun Negro Women, 1977; Woman of Distinction Award, YWCA Houston Sect, 1980; Notable Women of Texas Award, Gov's Comn, 1983. **Special Achievements:** Certified Lay Speaker, United Methodist Church, 1992; consultant, Depelchin Children's Services, Florence Crittenton Services. **Business Addr:** Board of Trustee, Mental Health Mental Retardation Authority of Harris County, 7011 Southwest Freeway, Houston, TX 77074, **Business Phone:** (713)970-7000.*

MCMILLAN, NAOMI. See GRIMES, NIKKI.

MCMILLAN, NATE
Basketball player, basketball coach. **Personal:** Born Aug 3, 1964, Raleigh, NC; married Michelle; children: Jamelle & Brittany. **Educ:** Chowan Coll, attended 1984; NC State Univ, attended 1986. **Career:** Basketball player (retired), basketball coach; Seattle Supersonics, guard-forward, 1986-98, asst coach, 1998-2000, interim head coach, 2000-01, head coach, 2001-05; Portland Trailblazers, head coach, 2005-. **Honors/Awds:** Nat Junior Col Basketball Hall of Fame; Bronze Medal, FIBA World Championship, 2006. **Business Addr:** Head Coach, Portland Trailblazers, 1 Center Ct Suite 200, Portland, OR 97227, **Business Phone:** (503)234-9291.

MCMILLAN, REGINA ELLIS
Lawyer. **Personal:** Born Mar 27, 1964, Louisville, KY; daughter of Geoffrey S and Mary A; married Antonio B, 1993. **Educ:** Univ Louisville, summer, 1981; Fisk Univ, BA, 1985; London Sch Econ, England, summer, 1985; Georgetown Univ Law Ctr, JD, 1988. **Career:** Brown-Forman Distillers Corp, summer intern, 1984-85; Georgetown Univ Law Ctr, res asst, 1987; Perpetual Savings Bank, law clerk, 1987; Wyatt, Tarrant & Combs, assoc atty, 1988-89; Thomas, Kennedy, Sampson & Patterson, assoc atty, 1989-95; Atlanta Tech Col, paralegal instr, 1994-2000, coord staff support/ grievance coord, 2000-01; Danley & Assoc, assoc atty, 1995-96; Regina Ellis McMillan, PC, solo pract, 1996-97, 2001-. **Orgs:** Pres, Mortar Bd, 1984-85; Phi Beta Kappa, 1985; Nat Bar Asn, 1987; Geo Asn Black Women Attys, 1990-; State Bar Ga, 1992-; Nat Asn Female Execs, 1993-; Atlanta Vol Lawyers Found, truancy proj, 1993-; GA High Sch Mock Trial Competition, coach & evaluator, 1995-; Nat Asn Advan Colored People. **Honors/Awds:** Youth Achiever of the Year, YMCA, 1981; National Dean's List, Fisk Univ, 1982-85; Rhodes Scholar State Finalist, 1984-85; Adult Black Achievers Awards, YMCA, 1989; TRIO Achiever Award, Nat Coun Educ Opportunity Asn, 1991. **Home Addr:** 11235 Chelsea Lane, Hampton, GA 30228, **Home Phone:** (770)472-5988. **Business Addr:** Attorney, McMillan Regina Ellis PC, 1575 Phoenix Blvd Suite 5, College Park, GA 30349-5532, **Business Phone:** (770)994-1558.

MCMILLAN, ROBERT FRANK, JR.
Executive. **Personal:** Born Jul 8, 1946, Glassboro, NJ; son of Kurt Yvonne (deceased) and Robert F Sr; divorced; children: Ayisha Nell & Marcia Akillah. **Educ:** Temple Univ, BS, Civil Engineering, 1972; Northwestern Univ, MBA. **Career:** Turner Construct, field engr, supt, 1972-76; Hudson Corp, proj mgr, 1976-80; Urban Investment & Develop Co, develop mgr, 1980-85; Joseph J Freed & Assocs Inc, dir develop, 1985-87; Wil-Freds Develop Inc, develop officer, 1988; McMillan Garbe Structures Inc, owner & pres. **Orgs:** Charter mem, Rotary Int, 1984-; bd mem, Greater Aurora Chamber Com; bd mem, Aurora Crime Stoppers; bd mem, Merchants Bank. **Military Serv:** AUS, 1st lt, 3 yrs; Bronze Star; Meritorious Achievement Vietnam, 1969. **Home Addr:** 31 W Downer Plz, Aurora, IL 60506-5123, **Home Phone:** (708)844-3052.

MCMILLAN, ROSALYN A.
Writer. **Personal:** Born Oct 14, 1953, Port Huron, MI; daughter of Edward and Madeline Washington; married John D Smith, Mar 2, 1984; children: Vester Jr, Shannon, Ashley, Jasmine. **Career:** Ford Motor Co, seamstress; Books: Knowing, 1996; Once Better, 1997; Blue Collar Blues, 1998; The Flip Side of Sin: A Novel, 2000; This Side of Eternity, 2001. **Orgs:** Toastmasters; 100 Black Women; exec adv bd, Memphis Black Writers Conf; ed bd, VIP Memphis Mag. **Honors/Awds:** Rosalyn McMillan Day, Southfield, MI, named in honor, 1996; Black Board Fiction Novel of the Year, 1998. **Business Addr:** Author, Warner Books, 1271 Ave of The Americas, New York, NY 10020, **Business Phone:** (212)522-7200.*

MCMILLAN, TERRY L.
Educator, novelist. **Personal:** Born Oct 18, 1951, Port Huron, MI; daughter of Edward and Madeline Washington Tillman; married Jonathan Plummer, Jan 1, 1998; children: Solomon Welch. **Educ:** Univ Calif, Berkeley, BA, 1977; Columbia Univ, MFA, 1979. **Career:** NY Times, HERS Column, guest columnist, Book Review, Atlanta Const, Philadelphia Inquirer, book reviewer; NY Found Arts, fel, 1986; Univ Wyoming, Laramie, WY, vis prof, 1987-90; Univ Ariz, Tucson, AZ, assoc prof, 1990-92; Stanford Univ, vis prof; Doubleday Columbia Univ, lit fel; Editor: Breaking Ice, Viking Penguin, 1990; Novels: Mama, Houghton Mifflin, 1987; Disappearing Acts, Viking Penguin, 1989; Waiting to Exhale,Viking Penguin, 1992; How Stella Got Her Groove Back, 1996;

A Day Late & A Dollar Short, 2001; Interruption Everything, 2005; The Black Nation's Cry, 2007. **Orgs:** PEN; Authors League; Harlem Writer's Guild. **Honors/Awds:** Nat Book Award, Before Columbus Found, 1987. **Business Addr:** Author, c/o Viking Penguin, 375 Hudson St, New York, NY 10014.

MCMILLAN, DR. WILLIAM ASBURY. See Obituaries section.

MCMILLAN, WILTON VERNON
Educator. **Personal:** Born Jun 5, 1943, Hope Mills, NC; son of Eunice E; married Lenora W, Apr 13, 1974; children: Valerie Kay. **Educ:** St Paul's Col, BS, 1973; George Mason Univ, MEd, 1979. **Career:** Fairfax Co Pub Schs, teacher, 1972-. **Orgs:** Founder & chair, Phi Delta Kappa, 1995-; baseluis, Omega Psi Phi Fraternity, 1995-; master, Prince Hall Mason, 1980-; Fairfax Educ Asn; Va Educ Asn; Nat Educ Asn. **Honors/Awds:** Omega Man of the Year, 1989; Doctor of Humanities, Eastern NC Theol Inst, 1995. **Military Serv:** AUS, Sp 4, 1966-69. **Home Addr:** 3208 Norwich Ter, Alexandria, VA 22309, **Home Phone:** (703)780-1679. **Business Addr:** Teacher, Woodlawn Elementary School, 8505 Highland Lane, Alexandria, VA 22309, **Business Phone:** (703)780-5310.

MCMILLIAN, FRANK L.
Chemist. **Personal:** Born Jun 9, 1934, Mobile, AL; son of Walter J and Roberta E; married Ruby A Curry; children: Franetta L, Kecia L. **Educ:** Dillard Univ, BA 1954; Tuskegee Univ, MS 1956; Univ KS, PhD 1965. **Career:** Chemist (retired); Ft Valley State Col, instr, 1956-58; NC Cent Univ, instr chem, 1959-60; Norfolk State Col, asst prof chem, 1960-62; E I du Pont de Nemours & Co, res chemist sr technical specialist, 1965-99; Dillard Univ, vis assoc prof chem, 1968-69. **Orgs:** Omega Psi Phi Frat, 1954-; Phi Lambda Upsilon Chem Soc, 1964-; Sigma Xi, 1967-. **Honors/Awds:** Fel NSF, 1963. **Home Addr:** 66 Bay Rd, Rehoboth Beach, DE 19971. *

MCMILLIAN, JOSIE
Executive. **Personal:** Born Oct 21, 1940, Childersberg, AL; divorced; children: 1 son, 2 daughters. **Educ:** Cornell Univ, Trade Union Study & George Meany Labor & Women Studies, 1977. **Career:** Retired: NY Metro Area Postal Union, sector aide, chief steward, shop steward, 1969, ex dir clerk, 1975, org'l vice pres, 1976, exec vice pres, 1979, pres. **Orgs:** Labor adv coun, NY Nat Urban League; Coalition Labor Union Women; Nat Org Women; mem, NY Cty Black Trade Leadership Comt; adv bd mem, Cornells Sch Indust & Labor Rels; bd dirs United Way NY Cty; bd mem, NY City & NJ combined Federal Campaign; life mem, NAACP; clerk craft rep NYS Am Postal Workers Union; adv mem, NY Cty Central Labor Coun; bd of dirs NYC Arthritis Found. **Honors/Awds:** Hispanic Labor Committee Award, NY Cty Central Labor Coun, 1978; Outstanding Achievement Award, New York City Chap Coalition Labor Union Women, 1981; Mary McLeod Bethune Award, Nat Coun Negro Women, 1981; Achievement Award, NY Cty Br NAACP, 1981; Distinguished Service Award, NY Cty Central Labor Coun, 1981; Sojourner Truth Loyalty Award, NY Chap Blk Trade Unionist, 1982; Hoey Ecumenical Award, NY Catholic Interracial Coun, 1982; Appted Admiral, Great Navy NE, 1982; Award of Appreciation, NY Chap Arthritis Found, 1983; Pacific Group Home Award, Little Flower Children's Serv, 1983; Outstanding Labor Leader Award, Nat Asn Negro Bus & Prof Women's Clubs, 1984; Citation of Appreciation, Am Legion Dan Tallon Post 678; Appreciation Award, Women Racial & Econ Equality, 1985; Citan of Appreciation, Brooklyn Borough Pres H Golden, 1984; Labor Leaders' Award, NY Cty Arthritis Found, 1988; Women's Achievement Award, YWCA, 1985; Leadership Award, Borough Manhattan Community Col, 1989; Ellis Island Medal of Honor Award, 1998. *

MCMILLIAN, MARCO W
Executive, executive director. **Educ:** Jackson State Univ; St Marys Univ. **Career:** Jackson State Univ, asst vpres & assoc dir develop; Ala A&M Univ, exec asst to pres, currently; Phi Beta Sigma Fraternity, coo & int exec dir, currently. **Orgs:** Phi Beta Sigma Fraternity. **Business Addr:** Executive Assistant to the President, Alabama A&M University, 4900 Meridian St, PO Box 1357, Normal, AL 35762, **Business Phone:** (256)372-5000.*

MCMILLIAN, MARK (MIGHTY MOUSE)
Football player. **Personal:** Born Apr 29, 1970, Los Angeles, CA. **Educ:** Glendale JC, Ala. **Career:** Football player (retired); Philadelphia Eagles, defensive back, 1992-95; New Orleans Saints, 1996; Kans City Chiefs, 1997-98; San Francisco 49ers, 1999; Wash Redskins, defensive back, 1999.

MCMILLON, BILLY (WILLIAM EDWARD MCMILLON)
Personal: Born Nov 17, 1971, Otero, NM. **Educ:** Clemson Col. **Career:** Fla Marlins, outfielder, 1996-97; Philadelphia Phillies, 1997; Detroit Tigers, outfielder, 2000-01; Columbus Clippers, outfielder, 2001; Oakland Athletics, outfielder, 2003; Triple-A Sacramento, outfielder, 2004; Oakland Raiders, outfielder, 2004; Boston Red Sox, outfielder, 2005; Class A Greenville, hitting coach, 2007-. **Honors/Awds:** First-Team NCBWA All-American honors, 1993. *

MCMILLON, WILLIAM EDWARD. See MCMILLON, BILLY.

MCMORRIS, JACQUELINE WILLIAMS
Government official. **Personal:** Born Mar 18, 1936, Washington, DC; daughter of John D; married James Oliver McMorris. **Educ:** Temple Univ, AB, 1958; Howard Univ Col Med, MD, 1962. **Career:** Off Econ Opportunities, med consult, 1965; DC Pub Health Dept, med officer child health & sch health servs, 1965-69; Health Servs Children Spec Needs, clinic dir, 1969-95, supvr med officer, Chief med officer, 1999-. **Orgs:** Church choir dir, 1962-82; Howard Univ Med Alumni, 1962-87; bd dirs, DC Spec Olympics, 1978-79; chairperson, Mamie D Lee Neighborhood Sch Coun, 1982-86; Mayor's Develop Disabilities Coun, 1984-87, secy, St Anthony's Grade Sch PTA, 1984-86; Mayor's Developmental Disabilities & Planning Coun, 1980-; Med Adv Rehab Serv, 1985-87, Mayor's Community Handicapped, 1985-87, Am Med Women's Asn, 1985-86; Howard Univ Transgenerational Proj Children Learning Disabilities, 1986-87; Mayor's Comt Early Child Develop, 1990-; DC Early Intervention Consortium Providers, 1990-98; Missies Diabetes adv, 1998-. **Honors/Awds:** Appreciation Award, Inst Integration Handicapped Children Early Educ Progs, 1974; Award for Outstanding Service to Mentally Retarded Citizens, DC Spec Olympics, 1978; Silver Lily Membership Club Award, Easter Seals Soc, 1986; The Second Roland J Queene Sr Memorial Award, Information, Protection & Advocacy Ctr Handicapped Individuals, 1987; Angels with Tears Award, 1998. **Business Phone:** (202)675-5214.*

MCMORRIS, LAMELL
Political consultant, chief executive officer. **Educ:** Morehouse Col, BA, religion & soc, 1995; Princeton Theol Seminary, MDiv, Social Ethics & Pub Policy, 1998. **Career:** Fulton County Comnr, Ga, asst Tom Lowe, 1996; Democratic Nat Convention, Chicago, Ill, press asst, 1996; New Jersey Mayor Sharpe James, Aide, Newark; Youth Develop Initiative, Chicago Urban League, dir; Southern Christian Leadership Conf, exec dir; Perennial Strategy Group & Perennial Law Group, founder & chief exec officer, prin, currently. **Orgs:** Wash Govt Rels Group; Wash Bd Trade; US Chamber Com; Rainbow PUSH Trade Bureau Chicago & Wash; DC Urban Leagues; Nat Advan Asn Colored People; Morehouse Col Nat Alumni Asn; Young Democratic Candidates Network; Unity Parenting & Coun; bd mem, Democratic Nat Comt Bus Coun; dir, chief exec officer, Southern Christian Leadership Conf. **Honors/Awds:** 30 Leaders of the Future 30 and under, Ebony Mag, 1998; Kelly Miller Smith Interfaith Award; Kelly Miller Smith Interfaith Award, Stud Empowerment Connection; Morehouse College Award, Nat Black Caucus Local Elected Officials. **Business Phone:** (202)638-5090.*

MCMORRIS, MICHAEL ANTHONY
Writer, educator. **Personal:** Born in Highland Park, MI; children: Montina L McMorris. **Educ:** Saginaw Valley State Univ, BA, criminal justice, 1985, MA, polit sci & criminal justice, 1988; Capella Univ, PhD, educ, 2001. **Career:** Saginaw Police Dept, police officer, 1985-89; Saginaw Sch Dist, criminal justice coordr, 1989-93; US Treas Dept, spec agent, 1993-95; Ocean County Col, instr criminal justice, 1995-96; Ferris State Univ, assoc prof, 1996; NC Central univ, dept criminal justice, assoc prof, currently. Author: Perceptions of Criminality, 2003; Hostile Corridors, 2003; Criminal Justice Scenarios, 2004. **Orgs:** Horizons Upward Bound Alumni Asn, 1981-; Acad Criminal Justice Scis, 1996-; Midwestern Criminal Justice Asn, 1996-; Nat Educ Asn, 1996-; Nat Asn African Am Studies, 1999-. **Honors/Awds:** Distinguished Service Award, City Saginaw Police Dept, 1987; Sharp Shooter Award, US Dept Treasury, 1993; Dean's Faculty Recognition Award, Ferris State Univ, 2003. **Special Achievements:** international scholar: Beijing Polytechnic Univ, China. **Home Addr:** PO Box 32, Comstock Park, MI 49321. **Business Addr:** Associate Professor, North Carolina Central University, Department of Criminal Justice, 309 Whiting 1801 Fayetteville St, Durham, NC 27707, **Business Phone:** (919)530-5206.

MCMULLINS, TOMMY
Executive. **Personal:** Born Sep 15, 1942, Macon, GA; son of Ulysses Anderson and Alummer McMullins; married Gwendolyn Williams, 1966; children: Tommy, Tyrone & Timothy. **Educ:** Ft Valley State Col, BS Social Sci, 1964; Am Inst Banking, Var Bank Courses, 1975; Pepperdine Univ, 1972; Pacif Coast Banking Sch, grad cert, 1980. **Career:** Bank Executive (retired); Ylwstn Nat Pk, seasonal pk rgr, 1963-64; First Int Bank, mgr reg sales mgr vpres, 1965-82; Crocker Nat Bank, vpres, 1982-85; Wells Fargo Bank, 1985-94; vpres, Citibank, 1994-2001; pres, chief exec officer, Bank Whittier, NA, 2002. **Orgs:** Co-chairperson, Emerg Hispanic Mjty 1978-80; bd mem, Pasadena Nat Asn Advan Colored People, 1979-82; bd mem, Comm Bell Gdns Rotary, 1981-85; bd mem, Monrovia Kiwanis; pres, Pasadena Chap Alpha Phi Alpha; chmn, Int Visitors Coun Los Angeles; pres, Pasadena Unified Sch Dist Bd Educ, 2001-02. **Honors/Awds:** Crusader Award, Am Cncr svcs 1973-74; Special LARIBA Award for Community, 2001. **Military Serv:** USM corpl 2 yrs; Expert Riflmn 1967. **Home Addr:** 1245 Rubio Vista Rd, Altadena, CA 91001.

MCMURRY, DR. KERMIT ROOSEVELT, JR.
School administrator. **Personal:** Born Jul 31, 1945, Kansas City, KS; married Valerie M; children: James Patrick, Chris, Nikii, Kermetria & Justin. **Educ:** Univ Colo, BS, 1968, MS, 1970; Univ Nebr, PhD, 1975; Harvard Univ, Post-Doctoral Study, 1979. **Career:** Dept Admin Serv Exec Br State Govt State Nebr, asst dir, 1974-75; Nebr Coord Comt Post Sec Educ, exec dir, 1975-77; Grambling State Univ, exec vpres, 1977; Nebr Dept Social Serv, dir, 1986-90; Okla State Regents Higher Educ, assoc vice chancellor acad affairs, 1990, Student Serv, vice chancellor, currently; Governor's Transformation, adv bd, currently. **Orgs:** Asst dir, Leisure Serv, Univ Nebr, 1970-74; vice chmn, United Campus Ministers; Lincoln Total Com Action Prog. **Honors/Awds:** Outstanding Young Man, Nebr Jaycees, 1971; Pioneering Coord Award, Nebr Coord Comn Post Sec Educ, 1977. **Home Addr:** 23391 Hunters Spring Dr, Edmond, OK 73003. **Business Addr:** Vice Chancellor for Student Services, Oklahoma State Regents for Higher Education, 655 Res Pkwy Suite 200, Oklahoma City, OK 73104, **Business Phone:** (405)225-9100.

MCMURRY, MERLEY LEE
Government official. **Personal:** Born Aug 20, 1949, Kansas City, MO; daughter of Andrew Jackson Owens III; married Murvell McMurry, Jul 1, 1989; children: Steven Andrew, Courtney Michelle. **Educ:** Univ Mi, Columbia, MO, BA, 1971; Central Mich Univ, Mt Pleasant, MI, MA, 1974. **Career:** Mi Employ Security, Kans City, MO, employ counr, 1972-74; Metro Community Cols, Kans City, MO, counr, 1974-78, proj coordr, 1978-83, tutorial coordr, 1983-85; Am Nurses' Asn, Kans City, MO, educ consult, 1985-86; Greater Kans City Chamber Com, Kans City, MO, vpres; Kansas City Power & Light, community bus mgr, currently. **Orgs:** Small & Minority Bus Networking Comt, vice chair, 1986-; Univ Mi Jackson County Extension Bd, 1988-; Teenage Parent Ctr Adv Bd, secy, 1989-; Pres's Adv Univ Mi Extension Bd, 1989-; Univ Mi Small Bus Develop Adv Bd, 1990-. **Honors/Awds:** Women Who Make A Difference Award, Minorities & Women's Mag, 1990; US Small Bus Admin, Minority Bus Advocate, District, State, Region, 1991. **Business Phone:** (816)556-2809.*

MCNABB, DONOVAN
Football player. **Personal:** Born Nov 25, 1976, Chicago, IL; son of Samuel and Wilma; married Raquel-Ann Nurse, Jun 1, 2003; children: Alexis. **Educ:** Syracuse Univ, BA, speech commun, 1998. **Career:** Philadelphia Eagles, quarterback, 1999-; Mem Bd Trustees, Syracuse Univ; Super Five, owner, currently; McNabb Unlimited, founder, currently. **Orgs:** Nat spokesperson, Am Diabetes asn; Pinnacy Soc Am Diabetes asn; founder, Donovan McNabb Golden Arm Scholar, 2000. **Honors/Awds:** NFL Player of the Year, CBS Radio, 2000; Terry Bradshaw Awards, Fox Sports, 2000; All-Madden team, 2000; Wanamaker Award, 2002; Horse Trailer Player of the Game hons, Monday Night Football, 2002; Big East Rookie of the Year; Most Caring Athlete,USA WEEKEND Mag, 2003; NFC Offensive MVP, 2004; Pudding Pie Award winner, 2008; FedEx Air Player of the Week, 2008. **Special Achievements:** Youngest person to be named to the Syracuse University Board of Trustees. **Business Addr:** Professional Football Player, Philadelphia Eagles, 1 NovaCare Way, Philadelphia, PA 19145, **Business Phone:** (215)463-2500.

MCNAIR, CHRIS
Government official, judge, photographer. **Personal:** Born Nov 22, 1925, Fordyce, AR; son of Jewel and Lilliebelle. **Educ:** Tuskegee Univ, Bachelor in Agriculture, 1942. **Career:** Commissioner (retired), photographer, ceo; Jefferson County Courthouse, county commissioner, 1994-95, judge; Chris McNair Studio & Art Gallery, ceo, currently. **Special Achievements:** First African Americans to serve in the Alabama Legislature. **Business Addr:** Chief Executive Officer, Chris McNair Studio and Art Gallery, 45 6th Ave S, Birmingham, AL 35263.*

MCNAIR, STEVE LATREAL. See Obituaries section.

MCNAIRY, DR. FRANCINE G.
School administrator, president (organization). **Personal:** Born Nov 13, 1946, Pittsburgh, PA; daughter of F E McNairy and Gladys. **Educ:** Univ Pittsburgh, BA, sociol, 1968, MSW, 1970, PhD, com, 1978. **Career:** Allegheny Co Child Welfare Servs, supvr & soc worker, 1970-72; Comm Action Regional training, tech asst specialist, 1972; Clarion Univ PA, assoc prof& coun, 1973-82, coord acad devel & retention, 1983, dean acad support serv & asst to the acad vpres, 1983-88; West Chester Univ, Assoc Provost, 1988; Millersville Univ PA, pres, 2004-. **Orgs:** Adv, Clarion Univ Black Student Union, 1973-; Presenter, Nat Conf Freshmen Yr Experience Univ SC, 1982-86; Wesleyan Col, 1983; St Lawrence Col, 1984; vchmn, Clarion Co Human Resources Devel Comm, 1983-86; presenter, Int Conf First Year Exp England, 1986; Creative Mgt Higher Educ, Boston, 1986; consult, Univ NE, Briar Cliff Col, Marshall Univ, 1986; PA Adv Bd to ACT; AAHE; Nat Asn Black Women Higher Educ; mem, Pennsylvania State Bd of Educ; mem, Lancaster County comm. **Honors/Awds:** Publs "Clarion Univ Increases Black Student Retention"; co-authored "Taking the Library to Freshman Students via Freshman Seminar Concept", 1986; "The Minority Student on Campus" 1985; named Outstanding First-Year Advocate by the National Resource Center. **Special Achievements:** First female, African American university president in the state system of higher education. **Business Addr:** President, Millersville University, 1 S George St, PO Box 1002, Millersville, PA 17551.*

MCNARY, OSCAR LEE
Artist, educator. **Personal:** Born Mar 23, 1944, San Antonio, TX; married Maudene J; children: Omar. **Educ:** San Antonio Jr Col, attended 1965; Tex Southern Univ; Southern Methodist Univ; Hunters Sch Art, attended 1974. **Career:** Internet Art Resources, dir, currently. **Orgs:** Dallas Mus Fine Arts; Nat Conf Artists, 1975-81; adv bd mem, Phoenix Cult Arts Ctr, 1975-81; Tex Arts Alliance; state & local mem, Tex Fine Arts Asn, 1975-81; assoc mem, Am Watercolor Soc, 1976-81; nat mem, Artists Equity Asn, 1977-81; elect mem, Int Platform Asn, 1978-81; vpres & bd mem, Artists Coalition Tex, 1979; bd trustees & pres, Richardson Civic Art Soc, 1979-81; Schomberg Soc; Af Am Museum; Studio Mus Harlem; Irving Black Arts Coun; guest curator, Artist & Elaine Thornton Found Arts Dallas Mus Art, 2000. **Honors/Awds:** Man Exhibit, Phoenix Cult Arts Ctr, 1979. **Special Achievements:** Numerous Group exhibs, 1965-80; first Black vice president & first Black board member of Artists Coalition of Texas, 1979; first Black president of Richardson Civic Art Soc, 1979-81. **Business Addr:** Director, PO Box 832627, Richardson, TX 75083-2627, **Business Phone:** (214)250-0548.*

MCNEAL, DON
Religious leader, public speaker, football player. **Personal:** Born May 6, 1958, Atmore, AL; married Rhonda. **Educ:** Univ Ala, BS, social welfare. **Career:** Football player (retired), public speaker, pastor; Miami Dolphins, corner back, 1980-89; New Testament Baptist Church, children's pastor,currently. **Honors/Awds:** NFL all rookie; Tommy Fitzgerald Member Award Outstanding Rookie, 1980; Dolphins' Player of the Year, 1982, 1984; Dolphins' Silver Anniversary team, 1982; Alabama Sports Hall of Fame, 2008. **Business Phone:** (305)558-4930.

MCNEAL, REV. JOHN ALEX
School administrator. **Personal:** Born Jun 18, 1932, Metter, GA; married Earlene Hazel; children: Lydia Tryphenia & Kezia Ruth. **Educ:** Fort Valley State Col, BS, 1961; Grace Theol Sem, BRE, 1964; GA State Univ, Med, 1975; Carver Bible Col, doctor divinity, 1986. **Career:** Fundamentalist Baptist Asn, publicity chmn, 1964, pres, 1975-77, vpres, 1977-80, pres, 1996-2000; Carver Bible Inst & Col, rev & dean students, 1964-87; Evangel Baptist Mission N Am, ethnic rep, 1985; Atlanta Bible Baptist Church, sr pastor & founder, currently. **Orgs:** Evangel Baptist Mission; Fundamental Baptist; Asn Regular Baptist Churches. **Honors/Awds:** Outstanding Educators of America, 1972; Award for Dedicated Serv, Carver Alumni Asn, 1972; Carver Bible Inst & Col Founder's Award, 1999; Pastor of the Year Award, Moody Bible Inst & Col, 1999. **Military Serv:** USAF, airman 1st class 1952-56; Good Conduct Medal; Service Awd. **Business Addr:** Founder, Senior Pastor, Atlanta Bible Baptist Church, 1663 Boulder Crest Rd, Atlanta, GA 30316, **Business Phone:** (404)241-1176.

MCNEAL, TIMOTHY KYLE
Executive. **Personal:** Born Jun 27, 1960, Sacramento, CA; son of Carol and Homer. **Educ:** Univ Calif, Los Angeles, BA, polit sci. **Career:** WB Network, vpres drama develop, currently. **Home Addr:** 800 S Shanandoah St, Los Angeles, CA 90035. **Business Addr:** Vice President of Drama Development, The WB Network, 4000 Warner Blvd Bldg 34R, Burbank, CA 91522, **Business Phone:** (818)977-5000.

MCNEAL, WILLIAM R.
School superintendent. **Personal:** Born Jan 1, 1948. **Educ:** NC Cent Univ, BA, 1971, MA, 1976. **Career:** Teacher (retired), school superintendent (retired), executive dir; Danbury, CT, teacher, 1971-74; Wake County Schs Syst, Carroll Jr High Sch, teacher social studies, 1974-76, asst prin, 1976-78, E Garner Middle Sch, prin, 1978, from asst supt to assoc supt, 1979-2000, nat supt, 2000-06; NC Asn Sch Adminrs, exec dir, 2006-. **Orgs:** Wake Med Found; Everybody's Bus Coalition; Lightner Found. **Honors/Awds:** National Superintendent of the Year, American Association of School Administrators, 2004; Bill McNeal Day named in honor, Wake County Schs, June 9, 2006. **Business Addr:** Executive Director, North Carolina Association of School Administrators, PO Box 27711, Raleigh, NC 27611, **Business Phone:** (919)828-1426.*

MCNEELY, CAROL J.
Dentist, consultant. **Personal:** Born Jul 17, 1954, Chicago, IL; daughter of Lewis W and Jessie O Woodfin; divorced; children: Matthew Allan Ivy. **Educ:** Univ IL Col Dentistry, DDS, 1979; Kellogg Sch Mgt Northwestern Univ, MM, 1995. **Career:** Tyrone Holiday DDS, assoc dentist, 1979-80; Dr Carol McNeely & Assocs, owner, 1979-; Provident Dental Assocs, owner, 1984-; Soulful Expressions, owner, 1987; Dental Network Am, Consult, 1988-. **Orgs:** Speaker, Am Asn Women Dentists, 1982; treas, Lincoln Dental Soc Nat Dental Soc, 1982-83; assoc bd mem, Chicago Child Care Soc, 1982-85, Am Acad Cosmetic Dentistry, 1988; Am Dental Asn; Nat Dental Asn; co-chairperson, Chicago Urban League Sholarship Comt, 1989; Taskforce Women & Minorities, AM Dental ASN, 1992; pres, Chicago Metro ASN Black Women Dentists, 1992; Am Asn Dental Consult; Am Asn Healthcare Execs. **Honors/Awds:** Partners, Comt Nat Bar Asn Chicago Chap, 1985. **Business Phone:** (765)622-7646.*

MCNEELY, CHARLES E
Government official. **Personal:** Born Jun 24, 1951; son of Louise Johnson and Aubrey; married Rosalind Gulley McNeely, May 21, 1974; children: Leslie, Brian & Brandon. **Educ:** Univ Kans, Lawrence, BA, polit sci, 1973, Masters, pub admin, 1975. **Career:** City San Diego, int rels intern, 1971; City Palo Alto, admin analyst, budget & staff servs, 1974-75, personnel adminr, 1975-76, mgt asst, 1976-78, asst city mgr, 1978-83; City Seaside, city mgr, 1983-93; instr, Golden Gate Univ, 1991; Reno City, mgr, 1996-. **Orgs:** Bd mem, CRA, 1990; chairperson, Coalition African Am Men, 1990-91; comt mem, League Calif Cities Advan Minorities & Women, 1990-91; comt mem, League Calif Cities Housing & Community & Econ Develop, 1991. **Honors/Awds:** Managerial Award for Excellence; Stene Award, Univ Kans. **Business Addr:** City Manager, City of Reno, 1 E 1st St, PO Box 1900, Reno, NV 89501, **Business Phone:** (775)334-2020.

MCNEIL, DEEDEE
Poet, singer, playwright. **Personal:** Born in Detroit, MI; daughter of Frank Lawton and Mary Virginia; divorced; children: Maricea Lynn McNeil, Harry Lawrence McNeil III & William A Chappell Jr. **Educ:** Pasadena City Col; Los Angeles City Col, music & jour. **Career:** Jobete Publ Co, Motown Rec Co, Detroit, contract songwriter, 1968-71; Ala Rec Co, Los Angeles, rec artist, 1971; Watts Prophets, col campus lectr & traveling poet, 1971-77; songwriter, singer, freelance jour & publ, 1971-; A&M Rec Co, Hollywood, publicist, 1972-73; United Artist Recs, Hollywood, Nat Press & Media Coord, 1973-74; contrib writer: various newspapers & mag in US & Canada, 1974-75; Soul & Jazz Rec Mag, contrib ed, assoc ed & co-publ, 1975-77; Great Legends & Great Music Co, pres, currently; Double Dee Production & Publ Co, founder. **Orgs:** Asst, David Gest & Assoc PR Firm, Hollywood; col speaker, sem promotional publ & publicity & co-establisher, Al-Bait Haram Publ Co, CA, 1971; co-publ & operator, House Haram Publ Found; co-producer, Ar-Tee/Double Dee Prod Co; consult & pub rels specialist, KWANZA Orgn; Eddie Beal Scholar Fund Creative Youth; bd dir & lifetime mem, prog coordr, free prog C, Jazz & You, Jazz Heritage Found; Clifford Brown Found; founder, Great Legends & Great Music Co, Detroit; pres, Great Legends & Great Music Co. **Honors/Awds:** The Outreach Award, Pasadena, 1976; Shreveport Regional Bicentennial Comm Award, KWANZA Org, 1976; named Director of Publicity, NATRA, 1976-77; dean's honor list, Pasadena City Col Music Dept, Los Angeles City Col; Certificate of Merit, Am Song Festival, 1977; nominee, Best Spoken Word Image Award, NAACP, 1972; winner, BET Jazz Nationwide Jazz Discovery Contest, 2001; Vocal Coach and Artist Develop Coach, Pasadena Int Music Acad, 2002-04. **Special Achievements:** Numerous articles published in Black Stars Magazine, Essence, Soul & Jazz Record Mag, numerous poems, wrote numerous songs for Kiki Dee, Gladys Knight, Diana Ross Nancy Wilson, performed various coll concerts with Watts Prophets, various TV appearances, featured vocalist, recordings & concerts, listed as west coast rap originator in "The Black Music History Los Angeles, It's Roots," 1992, wrote jazz column, Michigan Chronicle, 2000-04, was the first female, African-American Publicist for a major record label in Hollywood to establish a premiere comprehensive press list to service African-American newspapers and magazines across the country. **Business Addr:** Founder, Double Dee Productions & Publishing Company, 132 N El Camino Real Suite 154, Encinitas, CA 92024, **Business Phone:** (248)262-6877.

MCNEIL, ERNEST DUKE
Lawyer. **Personal:** Born Oct 9, 1936, Memphis, TN; married Sandra; children: 2. **Educ:** Tenn State Univ, BS; Fisk Univ, BA, 1957; Depaul Univ, JD, 1965. **Career:** law clerk & defense atty Leo Gilfoy Attorneys;McNeil E Duke & Assoc, atty, currently. **Orgs:** Pres, The woodlawn Orgn; pres, TWO Enterprises; pres, woodlawn Redevel Asn; vpres Cook County Bar Asn; Health Comnr Cook Co Governing Comn; weekly columnist Chicago Defender Cook Co Dept Pub Aid; chmn, speaker, Bureau Am Negro Emancipation Centennial Authority; adv, youth div Chicago Urban League; co-founder & treas, Orgn Black Am Culture; co-founder & treas, Legal Found; Phi Alpha Delta; Kappa Alpha Psi; bd dir; Mandel Legal Aid Clinic; bd dir, Mid S Health Planning Coun; bd dir, Gateway House Ill Drug Abuse Prog; Jackson Park-Woodlawn Bus Asn; co-chmn, Civil Rights Com; chmn, Woodlawn Comm. *

MCNEIL, FRANK
Government official. **Personal:** Born Jan 6, 1937, St Louis, MO; married Annetta Cropp; children: Frank, Anita Louise, Patricia Ann, Betty Marie & Scott Kevin. **Career:** Wellston Mo, city treasurer; Block Mothers, dir, 1973-. **Orgs:** Treasurer, Wellston Youth League Boys; Nat Roster Black Elected Officials, 1974. **Military Serv:** AUS, sp/4 hon discharge, 1963.

MCNEIL, FRANK WILLIAM
Lobbyist. **Personal:** Born Dec 12, 1948, High Point, NC; son of Walter H and Madge Holmes; married Barbara Jean Curtain McNeil, Mar 17, 1977; children: Kwahme & Kofi. **Educ:** NC Cent Univ, Durham NC, BA, 1971; JD, 1974. **Career:** Ill Law Enforcement Comm, Springfield Il, legis specialist, 1974-76; State Bd Ethnics, Springfield Il, admin asst, 1976-77; Secy State Corp Div, Springfield Il, corp specialist, 1978-79, admin asst, 1979-81; Senate Democratic Staff Parliamentarian, Springfield IL, 1981-86; Chicago Urban League, govt rel coordr, 1986-87; consult & lobbyist, Springfield Il, 1987-; Ill Dept Transportation, Off Bus & Workforce Diversity, dir. **Orgs:** Springfield Urban League Guild; Springfield Br NAACP; bd dirs, Family Serv Ctr Sangamon County; bd dirs, Boy's Club; City Coun, City Springfield. **Honors/Awds:** Political Action Award, NAACP, 1986; Man of the Year, Omega Psi Phi, 1986, 1987; Webster Plaque, NAACP, 1987; Plaintiff in successful voting rights suit, McNeil vs City Springfield; Elected Alderman Ward 2 City of Springfield, 1987. **Home Addr:** 2010 E Brown St, Springfield, IL 62703. **Business Addr:** Director, Office of Business and Workforce Diversity, Illinois Department of Transportation, Springfield, IL.

MCNEIL, FREEMAN
Football player, manager. **Personal:** Born Apr 22, 1959, Jackson, MS. **Educ:** Univ Calif, Los Angeles. **Career:** Football player (retired), Computer executive; New York Jets, runningback, 1981-92; , mgr, currently. **Honors/Awds:** Most Valuable Player, New York Jets, 1981-84; Mackiey Award, 1981; AFC Offensive Player of the Month, 1986. **Business Addr:** Manager, Advance Digital Data & Technology Inc., 1490 N Clinton Ave, Bay Shore, NY 11706, **Business Phone:** (631)969-2600.

MCNEIL, LORI MICHELLE
Association executive, tennis player. **Personal:** Born Dec 18, 1963, San Diego, CA; daughter of Charlie and Doris. **Educ:** Okla State Univ, attended 1983. **Career:** Prof tennis player (retired), tennis coach; tennis player, 1984-2002; Jr Tennis Champions Ctr, sr tennis prof, Col Park, MD; Coached Amanda Coetzer, 2001-04; US Olympic Team, asst coach, 2004; US Tennis Asn, high performance coach, nat high performance coach, currently. **Orgs:** Women Tennis Asn, 1983-; Wightman Cup Team, 1989; founder & chmn, Lori McNeil Tennis Found. **Special Achievements:** First African-American Woman to receive a scholarship to the University of Miami. **Business Phone:** (305)365-8782.

MCNEIL, DR. OGRETTA V.
Educator, politician. **Personal:** Born Sep 2, 1932, Savannah, GA; married Kingsley R; children: John & Robert Vaughn. **Educ:** Howard Univ, BS, magna cum Laude, 1954; Clark Univ, MA, 1959; PhD, 1967. **Career:** Educator (retired), Politician; Worcester Youth Guidance Ctr, psychologist, 1967-68; Worcester Pub Schs, clin psychologist, 1968-70; Assumption Col, asst prof, 1968-71; Clark Univ, visit lectr, 1972; Anna Maria Col, consult clin psychologist, 1968-78; Holy Cross Col, assoc prof psychol, 1971-97, adv, dean. **Orgs:** Danforth assoc, 1971-77; NSF, 1971; Am Psychol Asn; pres, New England Psychol Asn, 1988-89; AAUW corp laison; bd trustees, Univ Mass, 1976-81, 1992-97; Sigma Xi; bd trustees, LeMoyne Col, 1977-82; exec com, Asn Soc & Behav Sci, 1978-; AAUP Phi Beta Kappa; Worcester Sch Comt.

MCNEIL, RANDY
Association executive. **Career:** Youth Sports & Recreation Comn, exec dir, pres, 2004-. **Business Addr:** President, Youth Sports and Recreation Commission, 1274 Library Suite 201, Detroit, MI 48226, **Business Phone:** (313)963-8916.*

MCNEIL, ROBERT LAWRENCE
Business owner, consultant. **Personal:** Born Oct 3, 1969, Atlanta, GA; son of Robert L and Yvonne Sr; married Stacey R. **Educ:** Ga State Univ, exec, MBA; Nat Minority Supplier Develop Coun, grad. Kellogg Grad Sch Mgt, Advan Mgt Educ Prog; Tuck Sch Bus, advan MBE. **Career:** Images USA, pres & chief exec officer, 1989-, Currently. **Orgs:** Am Mkt Asn; Atlanta Ad Club; Ga Minority Supplier Develop, Coun, AID Atlanta; Alpha Phi Alpha; Big Brothers Big Sisters; bd mem, Nat Conf Community & Justice; bd mem, Am Inst Managing Diversity; bd mem, Nat Black Arts Festival. **Business Addr:** President, Chief Executive Officer, Images USA, 1320 Ellsworth Industrial Blvd, Atlanta, GA 30318, **Business Phone:** (404)892-2931.

MCNEIL, RYAN DARRELL
Football player. **Personal:** Born Oct 4, 1970, Fort Pierce, FL. **Educ:** Miami Univ, Fl. **Career:** Football player (retired), Detroit Lions, defensive back, 1993-96; St Louis Rams, defensive back, 1997-98; Cleveland Browns, defensive back, 1999; Dallas Cowboys, defensive back, 2000; San Diego Chargers, defensive back, 2001-02; Denver Broncos, defensive back, 2003. OverTime Magazine pre, currentently. **Honors/Awds:** Pro Bowl selection, 2001; Led NFL in interceptions, 1997.

MCNEILL, CERVES TODD
Artist, advertising executive. **Personal:** Born Jun 20, 1950, Jamaica, NY; son of Todd Cerves and Ella Mae; married Elizabeth Straka, Aug 15, 1972; children: Nigel Isaiah. **Educ:** NY Univ, undergrad, 1971; Univ Calif, LA, screenwriting, 1981, film prod, 1985; pvt study with Bess Bonnier, Jazz Piano Improvisation, 1990; Continental Cable Public Access, prod cert, 1993. **Career:** Freelance bassist, guitarist, vocalist, composer, actor, 1965-; Young & Rubicam Inc, NY copywriter, 1976-79; Benton & Bowles Inc, NY, sr copywriter, 1980; SSC&B Inc, Los Angeles, sr copywriter, 1980-81; Dancer Fitzgerald Sample Inc, Los Angeles, sr copywriter, 1982-84; self-employed, freelance copywriter & screenwriter, 1984-; Campbell-Ewald Advertising, sr vip, assoc creative dir, 1986-98; O'Neal McClure, Detroit, exec, creative dir, 1998-99; Asher/Gal & Partners, Los Angeles, African Am Smok-

ing Cessesion Proj, freelance copywriter, composer & producer, 1999-; Freelancealot Productions, owner, writer, dir, prod, composer, 1999-; Veriad, Brea, Calif, copywriter, web content writer, 2000-; Others: "Chaffed Elbows", bass player, 1965; Putney Swope, actor, 1969; "The White Whore & the 2 Bit Player", bass player, 1970; "My Heart & I Don't Believe," co-writer, bass player, 1972; "Plantation", writer, co-producer, actor, 1979; "The Great Steal," co-writer, co-producer, co-dir, music dir, 1991. **Orgs:** Am Fed Musicians, 1965-93; writer, publisher affiliate, Broadcast Music Inc, 1972-; Christians In Advertising, 1985-86; evangelist, Raulerson Evangelistic Asn, 1987-90; First & Second Annual Am Adv Fed, Top 25 Minority Adv Students Roundtables, 1997-98; music minister, Arise Christian Ctr, 1999-. **Honors/Awds:** CEBA Award, World Inst Black Commun Inc, United Negro Col Fund, 1979; CEBA Award, UNCF/Poster, 1980; ANDY Merit Award, Interagency Coun Child Abuse & Neglect, 1983; Merit Award, Art Dirs Club NY, Chevrolet, 1987; NY Festival Bronze Award, Int Film & TV Festival, 1990; Caddy Award of Merit, Detroit Creative Dirs Coun, GMAC Financing/TV, United Way/TV, 1990; Caddy Silver Award, Delta Faucet/TV, 1991; ADDY Award, Delta Faucet/TV, 1992; Continental Cable Access Award, 1993; O'Toole Award, Chevrolet Diversity/African Am, 1998. **Business Addr:** Freelance Bassist, 4900 Overland Ave Apt 329, Culver City, CA 90230, **Business Phone:** (310)836-8271.

MCNEILL, SUSAN PATRICIA
Military leader. **Personal:** Born Oct 3, 1947, Washington, DC; daughter of Lula M and Robert H. **Educ:** Wilson Col, BA, 1969; Creighton Univ, JD, 1978; Pepperdine Univ, MBA, 1980. **Career:** Military leader (retired); USF, Edwards AFB, Asst Staff Judge Advocate, contract atty, 1978-81; Norton AFB, Ballistic Missile Off, Asst Staff Judge Advocate, staff atty, 1981-84; Lindsey Air Sta, Ger, Staff Judge Advocate, chief legal officer, 1984-87; Dept Justice, Defense Procurement Fraud Unit, trial atty, 1987-89; Pentagon, Air Force Contract Law Div, trial atty, 1989-91, Air Force Gen Coun Off, staff atty, 1991-92; Defense Systs Mgt Col, Acquisition Law Task Force, assoc dir, sr atty, 1992-93; AF Gen Couns Off, civilian staff atty, 1993-95. **Orgs:** Big Sisters Omaha, 1977-78; Nebraska Bar Asn, 1978-; chap pres, Nat Contract Mgt Asn, Wiesbaden, Ger, 1985-87; exec bd mem, Air Force Cadet Off Mentor Prog, 1991-; Am Bar Asn, Gov Contracts Sect, 1991-; pres, Md Citizen Planners Asn, 2002-03; vice chair, St Mary's County Bd Zoning Appeals. **Honors/Awds:** Big Sister of the Year, Judge Advocate, Big Sisters Omaha, 1978; Serv Award, Nat Coalition, 100 Black Women, VA Commonwealth Chapter, 1993. **Special Achievements:** Highest ranking AFA female Judge Advocate in all branches of the Armed Forces, 1993. **Military Serv:** USF, col, 1970-93; Air Force Meritorious Serv Medal, 1981, 1984, 1987; Air Force Commendation Medal, 1982; Legion of Merit, 1993; Defense Meritorious Serv Medal, 1993. *

MCNEILL-HUNTLEY, ESTHER MAE
Government official, educator. **Personal:** Born May 7, 1921, Fayetteville, NC; daughter of Margaret; widowed; children: Micheline E, Karen D & Frances M. **Educ:** NC A&T State Univ, BS, home econ, 1944; Bank St Col NYC, teachers cert; NY Univ, admin, attended 1953; Fayetteville State Univ, small bus mgt, attended 1977. **Career:** Educator (retired); NY, postal clerk; day care teacher; Headstart teacher; Wash Ave Day Care Ctr, first dir; Rainbow Nursery Sch, proprietor & dir, curently. **Orgs:** Girl Scout Leader, NY, 1970-72; Third Dist Chairwoman, Women in Municipal Govt, 1982-85; found bd, Bladen Tech Col; NC Black Leadership Caucus; Nat Black Caucus Local Elected Officials; vpres, NC Minority Pub Officials; Bladen Co Improvement Asn; charter & former mem, Bladen Co Arts Coun; Mt Zion AME Zion Church; Rainbow Nursery Parent Club, Sch Parent Teach Asn. **Honors/Awds:** County Chmn, LINC Children's 100, 1974; represented, City of Elizabethtown Nat League of Cities; First woman to be elected to City Coun; Lobbyist in Wash DC for Newtown Comn Block Grant awarded, 1983; Outstanding Community Serv, Zeta Phi Beta, 1983; Cert of Appreciation, Holshouser Jr; appointed by Gov James G Martin, serve Local Govt Advocacy Coun, 1985 (2 yr term); State of NC Human Relations Comn, Gov Jim B Hunt, Certificate of Appreciation, 1994; Outstanding Service to Family & Community, Rainbow Nursery Sch, 1994; Nat Asn Advan Colored People, W Bladen Br, 50 Years Service to Children, 1945-95, Humanitarian Award, 1996. **Special Achievements:** First Black elected to Elizabethtown's City Council in 1979. **Home Addr:** PO Box 2391, Elizabethtown, NC 28337-2391. *

MCNORRIELL, MOZELL M.
Executive. **Personal:** Born Oct 20, 1922, Marshall, TX; divorced; children: Robert, Jr. **Educ:** Wayne State Univ Labor Sch, 1971. **Career:** AFL-CIO, int vpres; Wayne Co Local 409 AFSCME, pres; Metro Cist Council 23, sec. **Orgs:** Life mem, NAACP; Elliottirian Bus Women's Club; Plymouth United Ch Christ; nat coordinating com mem Coalition Labor Union Women; dir, Civil-Rights Trade Union Leadership Coun; Coalition Blak Trade Unionists.

MCNORTON, BRUCE EDWARD
Football player, football executive. **Personal:** Born Feb 28, 1959, Daytona Beach, FL. **Educ:** Georgetown (KY) Col, BA, social work, 1982. **Career:** Football player (retired), football executive; Detroit Lions, cornerback & safety, 1982-90; Pittsburgh Steelers, Football Opers, col scout, currently. **Honors/Awds:** Georgetown Col Athletic Hall of Fame, 2000. **Business Phone:** (412)323-1200.

MCPHAIL, DR. CHRISTINE JOHNSON
Administrator, educator. **Personal:** Born Feb 1, 1946, Tyler, TX; children: Ralph Bessard & Roderic Bessard. **Educ:** Fresno City Col, BA, 1967; Calif State Univ, MA, 1972; Univ Southern Calif, Berkeley, PhD. **Career:** Fresno County Econ Opportunities Comn, counr job develop, 1968-69; Fresno State Univ, Live & Learn Ctr, coordr, 1969-70; Fresno State Univ, asst prof, 1971-74; Contra Costa Col, chair person counseling-instrs, 1974-76; Col Alameda, asst dean, 1976-78; Col Alameda, dean stud serv; Kings River Community Col, Reedley, CA, dean stud; Cypress Col, pres & chief instrnl officer; Morgan State Univ, Community Col Leadership Doctoral Prog, Baltimore, MD, prof & coordr; bd dir, adv coun, Am Assoc Community Cols, Currently. **Orgs:** Consult Regional Off Health & Welfare Head Start San Francisco; Calif-State Univ Law Enforcement Training Prog; com on status of women Univ ofCA Berkeley; mem Am Personnel & Guidance Assn; mem Am Assn of Univ Women;mem Coun on Black Am Affaris; Coun for the Study of CommunityColleges and the Am Educational Research Asn. **Honors/Awds:** White house fellows finalist Commn on White House Fellows, 1972; Golden Educator's Award, Fresno state Col, 1973; Outstanding young women of America, 1976; Summer institute fellow, Bryn Mawr Summer Inst, 1979; Research Award, Am Asn Univ; Outstanding Alumini of the Year, Fresno City Community Col, 1990; Outstanding Alumini of the Year, Calif State Univ, Fresno, 1998. **Special Achievements:** Co-author of "Transforming Classroom Practice for African American Learners: Implications for the Learning Paradigm", Books such as "Walkthe Rainbow: When You Get Tired of Waiting to Exhale" and "A Pocket Bookof Mother Wit: Leadership Principles for the New Millennium". Guest columnist and featured writer for newspapers in California and Texas; State Center Community College Educator's Hall of Fame. **Business Addr:** Professor & Co-ordinator, Coll of Alameda, 555 Atlantic Ave, Alameda, CA 94501.

MCPHAIL, IRVING P.
School administrator, chancellor (education). **Personal:** Born Mar 27, 1949, New York City, NY; married Carolyn Jean Carver; children: Kamilah Carole. **Educ:** Cornell Univ, BS, 1970; Harvard Univ, MAT, 1971; Univ PA, EdD, doctor of educ, sch educ, 1976. **Career:** Morgan State Univ Baltimore, coord freshman reading prog, 1971-73, assocprof ed, chmn dept curr & instr, 1977-80; The Johns Hopkins UnivBaltimroe, spec asst to pres & provost, 1978-79; Univ MD Col Park, asstprovost div human & comm res, assoc prof curriculum & instr; BaltimoreCity Pub Sch, chief operating officer, 1984-85; Kamilah Educ EnterprisesInc, pres, prin cons; Del State Col, vpres, dean acad affairs, prof educ,1985; Lemoyne-Owen Col, pres, 1993-95; St. Louis Community Col Florissant Valley, pres, 1995-98; Community Col Baltimore Co, Chancellor, Currently. **Orgs:** Antioch Univ, 1975-76,82-; co-found & pres, Nat Asn Black Reading & LangEd; Nat Alliance Black Sch Educrs; Int Reading Asn; Am Asn Higher Ed; Nat Coun Teachers Eng; Phi Delta Kappa; Col Reading Asn; consult, AID Prog Staff Devel Sch Dist Philadelphia, 1976; consult off Right to Read Baltimore City Publ Sch, 1977; auth over 25 articles chaps & meno graphs inprof lit; Alpha Phi Alpha, ZetaRho Lambda; vchmn Del Coalition Literacy. **Honors/Awds:** Am Counc Ed Fel Acad Admin, 1978-79; Nat Fel Fund Doctoral Fel Phi Delta Kappa Univ of PA; Certs Outstanding Contribs & Servs, Morgan State Univ,1973; MD Reading Inst, 1977,81,85; Baltimore City Pub Sch, 1977,85; IRA, 1978,81,82,85; Teacher Corps, 1979; DC Public Schs 1983; Copping State Col 1984; MD State Dept of Educ 1985; Concord Black Parents Hartford City,1986; listed in Men of Achievement 1977; selected as Eminent Scholar Norfolk State Univ, 1981. **Special Achievements:** One of Americass Ten Outstanding Youn Men, US Jaycees, 1982. **Business Addr:** Chancellor, Community College Baltimore Co, College Syst Office, 800 South Rolling Rd Grossely Hall, Baltimore, MD 21228.

MCPHAIL, JERRIS
Football player. **Personal:** Born Jun 26, 1972, Clinton, NC. **Educ:** E Carolina Univ. **Career:** Football player (retired); Miami Dolphins, running back, 1996-97; Detroit Lions, 1998; Cleveland Browns, 1999.

MCPHAIL, SHARON M
Government official, lawyer. **Personal:** Born Nov 6, 1948, Cambridge, MA; daughter of Robson Bacchus and Natalie Fowler; married David Snead, May 27, 1995 (divorced); children: Angela & Erika. **Educ:** Coe Col, Cedar Rapids, IA, 1968; Northeastern Univ, Boston, MA, BA, 1972; Univ Mich Law Sch, 1976; Northeastern Univ Law Sch, JD, 1976. **Career:** Ford Motor Co, staff atty, 1976-80; asst US atty, 1980-82; spec asst US atty, 1982-83; Dickinson, Wright, Moon, Van Dusen & Freeman, assoc, 1982-84; Bushnell, Gage, Doctoroff & Reizen, assoc, 1984-86; Wayne Co Corp Coun, prin atty, 1986-87; Wayne Co Prosecutors Off, chief screening & dist cts, 1987-94; Feikens, Vander Male, Stevens, Bellamy, & Gilchrist, partner, 1995-; Detroit City Coun, councilwoman, 2002-06. **Orgs:** Pres, 1992, vpres, 1986-89; Nat Bar Asn; dir, Nat Coun Northeastern Univ, 1988-; chairperson, Detroit Bd Police Comnrs, 1985-90; vice chair, State Officers Compensation Comn, 1988; vice chair, Wayne County Neighborhood Legal Servs, 1987-; dir, Kirwood Mental Health Ctr, 1990; Sixth Circuit Judicial Conf, US Ct Appeals; member, bd dirs, Fed Bar Asn, 1988; bd dirs, Music Hall Center for the Performing Arts, 1988; secy & treas, bd dirs, Detroit Br, NAACP; pres, Wolverine Bar Asn, 1985-86; Women Lawyers Asn Mich; Asn Defense Trial Coun; fel, Mich State Bar Found, 1988; Nat Asn Adv Colored People. **Honors/Awds:** Ladies Lit, Soc Poetry, 1968; Nat Poetry, Press Poetry, 1968; Acad Honors, Northeastern Univ, 1972; Phi Kappa Phi, Northeastern Univ, 1972; Member of the Year, Wolverine Bar Asn, 1987; Cora T Walker Award, Nat Bar Asn, 1988; NAACP Unsung Heroine, 1989-90; Women of Excellence Award, Renaissance Chapter of the Links Inc, 1991. **Special Achievements:** First Woman in History to Win Primary for Mayor of Detroit, 1993.

MCPHATTER, THOMAS H.
Association executive. **Personal:** Born Oct 8, 1923, Lumberton, NC; married Genevieve R Bryant; children: Thomas, Doretha, Mary Elizabeth, Joseph, Neil. **Educ:** Johnson C Smith Univ Charlotte, NC, BA, 1948, MDiv, 1951; Prog Human Behavior Urban Develop, PhD. **Career:** Newport News Shipyard, ship rigger 1941-43; Clothing Store, clk & mgr 1946-51; St Paul Presb Ch KC, MO, pastor 1951-58; navy chaplain 1958-69; LCDR Consult Religions & Race No CA 1969-70; Golden Hill Presb Ch, assoc pastor, hon ret Presbyterian Mini, 1970-71. **Orgs:** Pres, Omega Housing & Develop Co; project dir, MDTA; Dept Labor; dep equal Employ Opportunity Officer, Dept Def, 1974-75; comnr, United Presb Ch Gen Assembly, 1968; comn Synod MO, 1953, 1955; Moderator, Presbytery KC, 1957-58; v pres, Coun Ch Greater KC, 1956-57; MO Synod Coun; rep, Omega Psi Phi Frat; vpres, MO State Conf NAACP, 1969-70; bd mem, YMCA, 1954-55; pres, Eisenhowers Minority Adv Com, 1954-58; Urban League Bd, 1957-58; pres, Any Boy Can, 1968-69; SD Dist Chaplain & Post Chaplain Am Legion KC MO, 1955-58; Life mem, Urban League Omega Psi Phi; fed Tan Yanks Defenders Freedom; dedication speaker, Vietnam Monument, El Camino Park, San Diego, 2001. **Honors/Awds:** Key to City of San Diego, 1963; District of citizen of year, Omega Psi Phi Frat; Honorary Thomas H McPhatter (DD), Doctor of Divinity, Interdenomination Theological Ctr. **Special Achievements:** Caught in the Middle, A Dychotomy of An African-American Man, Author; They Called Him Troublemaker, Author. **Military Serv:** USMC, sgt, 1943-46; USN, chaplain Capt, 1958-83, Iwo Jima, Japan; chaplain, Vietnam, 1996-98. *

MCPHERSON, DAVID
Executive. **Personal:** Born Jan 1, 1968?, St Louis, MO; married Virginia. **Educ:** William Patterson Univ. **Career:** Elecktra Rec, intern; Mercury Rec, intern, mkt dept, A&R mgr; Jive Rec, A&R dir; Epic Rec, sr vpres urban music, 1998-2000, exec vpres A&R, 2000-, exec vpres urban music, 2000-. **Business Addr:** Exec Vice President, Epic Records Group, 550 Madison Ave, New York, NY 10022, **Business Phone:** (212)833-8000.

MCPHERSON, JAMES ALAN
Educator, writer. **Personal:** Born Sep 16, 1943, Savannah, GA; son of James Allen and Mable Smalls; divorced; children: Rachel Alice. **Educ:** Morris Brown Col, BA, eng/hist, 1965; Harvard Law Sch, LLB, 1968; Univ Iowa, MFA, 1972. **Career:** Atlantic Monthly, contrib ed, 1969-; Univ Calif, teacher, 1969-72; Morgan State Univ, Baltimore, MD, asst prof, 1975-76; Univ Va, Charlottes ville, assoc prof, 1976-81; Univ Iowa, Iowa City, prof, 1981-, Writers' Workshop, fac, currently. **Orgs:** Nat Asn Advan Colored People; Writers Guild; panel mem, Giles Whiting Found, 1986; lit panel, McDowell Colony, 1988-89; planning panel, Dewitt Wallace Found, 1989; fiction judge, Pulitzer Prize Panel, 1990; fiction judge, Nat Book Awards Panel, 1993; Am Acad Arts & Scis. **Honors/Awds:** Guggenheim Fellowship, 1973; Pulitzer Prize, 1978; Yale Law Sch, visiting scholar, 1978; LLB Honorary, Morris Brown Col, 1979; MacArthur Prize Fellowship, 1981; Award for Excellence in Teaching, Univ Iowa, 1991; Green Eyeshades Award for Excellence in Print Commentary, Soc Southern Journalists, 1994; fel, Stanford Univ, Ctr for Advanced Studies, 1997-98, 2002-03. **Special Achievements:** Author: Hue and Cry, 1969, Railroad, 1976, Elbow Room, 1977, Crabcakes, 1998; A Region Not Home, 2000; essays, stories and reviews published innumerous journals, magazines and authologies including Atlantic, New York Times Magazine, Reader's Digest, The Nation, The Best Amer Short Stories, O'Henry Prize Stories and Best Amer Short Stories of the 20th Century. **Business Addr:** Professor, University of Iowa, 102 Dey House, Iowa City, IA 52240.*

MCPHERSON, JAMES R
Lawyer, manager. **Personal:** Born Mar 26, 1953, Fayetteville, NC; son of Willie D Wright and Annie R Wright; married Michelle Bagley McPherson, Jul 3, 1982. **Educ:** Fayetteville State Univ, BS, bus admin, 1975; Univ Wis, Madison, MBA, 1980; Georgetown Univ Law Ctr, JD, 1985. **Career:** Scott Paper CPN, personnel ast, 1981-82; SUU DPT Lab, prog analyst, 1983-84; US Claims Ct, legal intern, 1983-84; Int Brotherhood Teamsters, law clerk, 1984-85; Clark, Klein & Beaumont, asoc, 1985-88; Carolina Power & Light CPN, asoc gen coun, 1988-92; human resource projs mgr,

asst vpres, employee rels dept, area employee servs mgr, 1992-94; Area Human Resources, mgr, 1994, asst Northern Region vpres, 1994-95; Sanford, dist mgr, 1995-96; Sanford, Southern Pines, dist mgr, 1996-.; Triangle Orgn Develop Network, orgn leadership consult, dir, currently. **Orgs:** Charter mem, Fayetteville State Univ, Delta Mu Delta Nat Honor Soc Bus Admin, 1976; fel, Consortium Grad Study Mgt, 1979-80; NCA Bar Asn, Labor & Employ Sec, 1989-91; Am Asn Blacks Energy, 1989-; Am Cre Coun Asn, 1989-92; Wake County Bar Asn, 1989-92; chair, Bar Exam Stipend Sub Community, Minorities Prof Community, 1989-92; Nat Bar Asn, 1989-92; NCA Asn Black Lawyers, 1989-92; Soc Human Resource Mgt, 1992-95. **Honors/Awds:** Advanced Opportunity Fellowship, Univ Wis, 1980; Earl Warren Legal Scholar, 1982. **Military Serv:** USF Reserves, capt & First lt, 1979-90; USF, First lt, 1975-79; Air Force Commendation Medal; Air Force ROTC Most Outstanding Cadet, Mid-Atlantic Region; Exceptional Performance Citation, NCA Air Force ASN; Comdr, Detachment 607th Air Force Reserve Officer Training Corp. **Business Addr:** Director, Triangle Organisation Development Network, Southern Region Department, 5200 Paramount Pkwy, Morrisville, NC 27560, **Business Phone:** (919)380-6178.

MCPHERSON, ROOSEVELT
Educator, clergy, writer. **Personal:** Born Nov 27, 1948, Fayetteville, NC; son of Clara Mae Hill McPherson and Arthur McPherson; married Carrie Lee Ratliff McPherson, Mar 5, 1977; children: Phillip Ratliff, Kenyatta Troy, Tameka McGilvary. **Educ:** Fayetteville State Univ, Fayetteville, NC, BA, 1969, 1974; Lafayette Col, Fayetteville, NC, 1977; Fayetteville Technical Institute, Fayetteville, NC, 1980; Appalachian State Univ, Boone, NC, 1990; Fayetteville State Univ, Fayetteville NC, MA, Educational Leadership Program, 1997. **Career:** Burlington Industries, Raeford, NC, production supervisor, 1974-76; Kane-Miller, Fayetteville, NC, administrative assistant, 1976-78; Sears Roebuck, Fayetteville, NC, credit correspondent, 1978-81; General Productions, Inc, Raeford, NC, publisher & ed, 1981-; Sandhills Community Col, Raeford, NC, instructor, 1984-92, ERA Fowler Realtors, Fayetteville, NC, realtor, 1987-88; Fayetteville Tech Community Col, Fayetteville, NC, instructor, 1988-90; West Hoke Middle Sch, Raeford, NC, teacher, 1992-97, assoc prin, currently. **Orgs:** Board of directors, Sanctuary Deliverance Churches, Inc, 1986-89; associate minister, Mt Sinai Sanctuary Deliverance Church, 1985-88; minister/deacon, Mt Carmel Holy Church of God, 1978-83; mem, Hoke County Black Caucus, 1985; mem, Hoke County Branch, NAACP, 1981; mem, Hoke County Civic League, 1981; mem, National Newspaper Publishers Assn, 1985-; mem, North Carolina Black Publishers, 1985-. **Honors/Awds:** Sunday School Superintendent of the Year, Holy Church of God, Inc, 1978-79; Top Salesman/lister, ERA Realtor, 1988; Special Awards of Recognition, Miss Black Teenage Pageants, 1982-85; Asst Principal's Executive Prog, School Improvement Awd, 1998. **Military Serv:** AUS, E-5, 1969-71; North Carolina Army National Guard, 1985-; received Academic Achievement Award, 1990. **Home Addr:** 190 Major Evans Rd, Raeford, NC 28376, **Home Phone:** (919)875-5845. **Business Addr:** Associate Principal, West Hoke Middle Sch, 201 Aberdeen Rd, Raeford, NC 28376.*

MCPHERSON, ROSALYN J
Publishing executive, writer. **Personal:** Born Mar 27, 1953, New Orleans, LA; daughter of James and Lillie; divorced; children: Jackie Robert Kelley II, Monique Cheri Kelley & Jasmin Renee Andrews. **Educ:** Southern Univ, A & M Col, BS, sec ed, 1973; Fairleigh Dickinson Univ, MBA, mkt, 1982. **Career:** Roosevelt Pub Schs, teacher, 1975-76; CBS Inc, ed, 1976-79; McGraw-Hill, ed, 1979-80; Time Warner Educ Task Force, NY, chair; Scholastic Inc, prod mgr, 1980-83; Time Inc, source mgr, circulation, 1983-85; McPherson Andrews Mkt Inc, pres, 1985-92; Time Life Inc, sr vp & publ, 1992; Franklin Inst, sr vpres; RJM Consult Group Inc, pres, currently; The ROZ Group, pres, currently. Author: Milestones in Science & Mathematics, Facts-on-File, 1996; African Americans: Voices of Triumph. **Orgs:** Nat Asn Black Sch Educ; Int Reading Asn; Nat Coun Social Studies; bd mem, Northern Va Urban League; bd mem, Models in Excellence, NASA, NSF; bd mem, Women's Proj & Prod; Col Bd, Task Force mem. **Home Addr:** 2808 Holland Ct, Alexandria, VA 22306, **Home Phone:** (703)360-5921. **Business Addr:** President, The ROZ Group Inc, 2032 Arch St Suite1, Philadelphia, PA 19103, **Business Phone:** (215)563-6042.

MCPHERSON, VANZETTA PENN
Judge. **Personal:** Born May 26, 1947, Montgomery, AL; daughter of Luther L and Sadie G; married Thomas McPherson Jr, Nov 16, 1985; children: Reagan Winston Durant. **Educ:** Howard Univ, BA, 1969; Columbia Univ, MA, speech path, 1971; Columbia Law Sch, JD, 1974. **Career:** Judge (retired); NMSC, nat achievement scholar, 1965-69; Legal Serv Elderly Poor, summer assoc, 1972; Thatcher, Proffit & Wood, summer assoc, 1973; Hughes, Hubbard & Reed, assoc, 1974-75; State Ala, asst atty gen, 1975-78; pvt pract, atty, 1978-92; US Govt, US Dist Ct, Mid Dist Ala, judge, 1992-06. **Orgs:** Fel Am Asn Univ Women, 1974-85; pres, Ala Lawyers Asn, 1980-81; Am Bar Asn, 1981-; bd mem, Ala Shakespeare Festival, 1987-; Leadership Montgomery; master bencher, Montgomery County Inn Ct, 1990-; Nat Coun Negro Women; pres, Fed Bar Asn, 1997-99; Montgomery Symphony Orchestra; Nat Bar Asn; co-owner, Roots & Wings. **Honors/Awds:** Legacy of the Dreamer Award, SCLC, 1981; Law Off Design Award, Am Bar Asn, 1985; Women of Achievement, Montgomery Advertiser, 1989. **Special Achievements:** Introduction of Blood Tests in Paternity Litigation, ABA, 1986. *

MCPHERSON, WILLIAM H.
Editor, technical writer. **Personal:** Born May 18, 1927, Ft Worth, TX; married Olivia T Denmon; children: Valencia D, Olivette R. **Educ:** Morehouse Col, BS, 1948. **Career:** Editor (retired); N Am Aviation Space & Info Systems Div, tech writer, 1963-67; N Am Rockwell Corp Autonetics Div, tech writer, 1967-68; The Aerospace Corp El Segundo, CA, publ ed, supvr. **Business Addr:** El Segundo, CA 90245.*

MCQUARTERS, ROBERT WILLIAM, II
Football player. **Personal:** Born Dec 21, 1976, Tulsa, OK; married; children: Robert III, Rylan & Reagan. **Educ:** Okla State Univ. **Career:** San Francisco 49ers, defensive back, 1998-99; Chicago Bears, 2000-04; Detroit Lions, 2005; New York Giants, cornerback, 2006-08. **Honors/Awds:** Super Bowl XLII, New York Giants, 2007. **Business Addr:** Cornerback, New York Giants, Giants Stadium, East Rutherford, NJ 07073, **Business Phone:** (201)935-8111.

MCQUATER, PATRICIA A
Lawyer. **Personal:** Born Sep 25, 1951, Washington, DC; daughter of Matthew and Margaret Jackson. **Educ:** Boston Univ, Col Bus Admin, BS, 1973; Univ San Diego Sch Law, JD, 1978. **Career:** San Diego City Coun, admin intern, 1976-78; US Supremem Ct, intern, 1977; Country San Diego, admin asst, 1979-82; Foodmaker Inc, corp coun, 1982-84; Solar Turbines Inc, sr corp atty, 1984-. **Orgs:** Nat Bar Asn, 1981-; bd govs, Earl B Gellium Bar Asn, 1982-; Am Bar Asn; Calif Asn Bulk Lawyers; San Diego Country Bar Asn; Am Arbitration Asn; sec, San Diego Urban League, bd dir, 1982-, chairperson, bd chair, 1988-89, nat delegate, 1986-89, chair, budget & finance comn, 1986-88; EO-Chr Country San Diego Affirm Action Comn, 1983-; Girl Scouts, San Diego-Imperial Coun Inc, 1985-90, nat deleg, 1986-89, exec dir search comm, coun nominating comt, 1990-92; San Diego Conv Ctr Corp, pres, 1989-95, chair, 1992-93; vpres, San Diego Convention Ctr, corp bd dir, 1990-; bd dir, Univ San Diego Sch Law Admin, 1990-; Calif Bar Asn; Am Immigration Lawyers Asn; Am Corp Coun Asn; USD Sch Law Alumni Asn, 1991-, pres, 1995-96; exec comn, Children's Hosp & Health Ctr, 1992-94; port/airport comnr, San Diego Unified Port Dist, 1994-, vice chair, 1998; Port San Diego, bb port Commissioners, chair. **Honors/Awds:** California Women Governor Award, 1992; TWIN Award, Solar Honoree, 1992; San Diego Mus Art, Songs My People: 100 Role Models, 1994; San Diego Hotel-Motel Assn, Gold Key Award, 1994; Outstanding Alumni Award,USD Women's Law Caucus, 1997; Tribute to a Living History, Palavra Tree Inc, 1998; Distinguished Alumni Award, Univ San Diego Sch Law, 1999; Career Achievement Award, 2000. **Business Addr:** Senior Corporate Attorney, Solar Turbines Inc, 2200 Pac Hwy, San Diego, CA 92101, **Business Phone:** (619)544-5000.*

MCQUAY, JAMES PHILLIP
Business owner. **Personal:** Born Nov 15, 1924, Baltimore, MD; married Doris; children: James Jr, Kevin & Jamal. **Educ:** New York Fashion Sch Design. **Career:** Fur Bus, owner; James McQuay Furs, NY, owner, currently; James McQuay Furnitures Inc, owner, currently. **Honors/Awds:** Fur Design Award, 1972, 1975, 1976; spec furniture showing for congressional black caucus Wash, 1977; first place award for design Century Furniture Trade Show, 1980; Madame C J Walker Award, 2008; Featured in Alpha Kappa Alpha Sorority. **Special Achievements:** First black furrier in the US; featured in Essence, Ebony, Jet and The New York Times and has appeared on David Letterman and Today. **Military Serv:** AUS, tech sgt. **Business Addr:** President, James McQuay Furnitures Inc., 151 W 30th St, New York, NY 10001.

MCQUEEN, ANJETTA
Public relations executive, administrator, senator (u.s. federal government). **Personal:** Born Sep 12, 1966, Brooklyn, NY. **Educ:** Univ NC, Chapel Hill, NC, BA, jour, polit sci, 1988. **Career:** News & Observer, Raleigh, NC, part-time copy editor, 1986-88; Philadelphia Inquirer, Philadelphia, PA, copy ed, 1988; Nat Educ Asn, sr press officer, spokeswoman, currently; Brookings Inst, sr commun adv, currently. **Orgs:** Fleisher Art Memorial, 1988-; Int Soc Gen Semantics, 1989-; Nat Asn Black Journalists, 1989-; Urban League, 1990-; Carolina Alumni Asn, currently; Wash Col Law Student Bar Asn. **Business Addr:** Senior Press Officer, Spokeswoman, National Education Association, 1201 16th St NW, Washington, DC 20036-3290.

MCQUEEN, KEVIN PAIGE
Banker, president (organization), manager. **Personal:** Born Jul 8, 1958, Brooklyn, NY; son of Robert Paige and Constance Marie Jackson. **Educ:** Brown Univ, Providence, RI, AB, 1976-80. **Career:** Nat Westminster Bank, USA, New York, NY, banking officer, 1980-82; Citibank, NA, New York, NY, relationship mgr, 1982-85; Nat Congress Community Econ Develop, Wash, DC, prog dirr, 1985-88; Nat Coop Bank Develop Corp, Wash, DC, vpres, 1988; Brody Weiser Burns, partner, 1996-. **Orgs:** Pres, Wash Area Community Investment Fund; chair, bd dirs, Dance Place; treas, Enterprising Staffing Servs; bd, Wash DC Local Develop Corp; Nat Neighborhood Coalition; Metropolitan Delta Adult Literacy Coun; Bd mem, Nat Neighborhood Coalition, 1987-88; pres, Brown Univ Club Wash, DC, 1988-90; steering comt coordr, Third World Alumni Network Brown Univ, 1990-. **Business Phone:** (203)481-4199.

MCRAE, EMMETT N
Restaurateur, government official. **Personal:** Born Feb 12, 1943, Rennert, NC; son of Donnie and Katie Smith; married Helen McLean, Aug 5, 1962; children: David, Linda F & Lori A McRae Strickland. **Career:** CS&X Transp Railroad, Florence, cook, 1968-90; E & H BBQ Hut, Rennert, owner, operator, 1984-; City Rennert, mayor, currently. **Orgs:** Deacon, 2nd St Matthew Baptist Church, 1970-; Carpenters Consistory No 164, 1975-; worship master, St Pauls Masonic Lodge, No 354, 1979-87; pres, Sunday Sch Conv, 1986; past master, St Pauls Masonic Lodge No 354, 1987-; bd mem, Lumber River Coun Govt, currently. **Honors/Awds:** Hon Attorney General, Rufus L Edmisten Atty Gen NC, 1984; Certificate of Appreciation, James B Hunt Govr NC, 1984; Service Award, St Matthew Baptist Church, 1985; Jefferson Award, Jefferson Broadcasting Co Channel 11 Durham, NC, 1986; Man of the Year, Carpenters Consistory No 164, 1986; Service Award, Rennert Volunteer Fire Dept, 1990. **Business Addr:** Owner, Mayor, Town of Rennert, 62 Pk St Rte 1, PO Box 42, Shannon, NC 28386, **Business Phone:** (910)843-2162.

MCRAE, HAROLD ABRAHAM
Baseball manager, baseball player. **Personal:** Born Jul 10, 1945, Avon Park, FL; son of Willie James and Virginia Foster; married Johncyna Williams; children: Brian, Cullen & Leah. **Educ:** Fla A&M Univ, Tallahassee, FL, attended 1966. **Career:** Baseball player (retired), baseball coach; Minor Leagues, baseball player, 1965-68; Cincinnati Reds, baseball player, 1968-72; World Series, 1970, 1972, 1985; League Championship Series, 1970, 1972, 1976-78, 1985; Kansas City Royals, baseball player, 1973-87, hitting instr, 1987; Pittsburgh Pirates, minor league hitting instr, 1987-89; Montreal Expos, Montreal, Canada, hitting instr, 1990-91; Kansas City Royals, mgr, 1991-94; Cincinnati Reds, hitting instr, 1995-96; Philadelphia Phillies, hitting instr, 1997-2000; Tampa Bay Devil Rays, mgr, 2001-02, asst to gen mgr, 2002; St Louis Cardinals, hitting coach, 2004-. **Honors/Awds:** Royals Player of the Year, 1974; All-Star Games, 1975-76; Designated Hitter of the Year, Sporting News, 1976, 1980, 1982; Silver Slugger Award, 1982; Royals Hall of Fame, 1989; Missouri Sports Hall of Fame, 2004. **Business Addr:** Hitting Coach, St Louis Cardinals, Busch Stadium, 250 Stadium Plz, St Louis, MO 63102, **Business Phone:** (314)421-3060.

MCRAE, RONALD EDWARD
Salesperson. **Personal:** Born Feb 7, 1955, Dillon, SC; son of Dudley and Betty. **Educ:** Macalester Col, BA, 1976; Northwestern Univ Sch Mgt, MBA, 1978; DePaul Univ Sch Law, JD, 1986. **Career:** The Toro Co, mkt internship, 1976; Federal Savings & Loan Ins Corp, res asst, 1977; Searle Pharmaceut Inc, asst prod mgr, 1978-79, prod mgr, 1979-84, key acct hosp consult 1984-88; Westwood Pharmaceuticals Inc, mgr, new bus develop, 1988-93; Bristol-Myers Squibb, sr dir, Lic, 1993-. **Orgs:** Am Mgt Asn, Am Bar Asn, Nat Black MBA Asn, Midwest pharmaceut Advert Club, Asn MBA Execs, Chicago Vol Legal Servs, Lic Exec Soc. **Business Addr:** Senior Director, Licensing, Bristol Myers Squibb Co, PO Box 4000, Princeton, NJ 08543-4000, **Business Phone:** (609)252-3830.

MCREYNOLDS, ELAINE A.
Government official, executive. **Personal:** Born Feb 5, 1948, Louisville, KY; married George R McReynolds; children: Jennifer, Jason, Julie. **Educ:** Univ Montpellier, France, attended 1965; Centre Col, Ky, 1968; Univ Tenn, BS, 1975. **Career:** Nat Life & Accident Ins Co, comput programmer, 1970-73, programmer analyst, 1974-75, expense mgt analyst, 1975-76, admin asst, 1976-78, asst sec & mgr, 1978-83; trustee, Univ Tenn Bd Trustees, 1975-84; bd dirs, Dir Crisis Intervention, 1977-78; bd dir, Cumberland Mus, 1978-81; bd dir, Citizens Bank; bd dir, St Bernard Acad; bd dir, Harpeth Hall Middle Sch; Am Gen Life & Accident Ins Co, asst vpres, 1983-85; real estate, 1985-87; Tenn Dept Com & Ins, 1987-94; Fed Ins Admin, 1994-96; Am Gen Life & Accident Ins Co, sr vpres ins servs, 1996-. **Orgs:** LINKS. **Honors/Awds:** Woman of Achievement Award, 1993; Person of the Year, March Dimes, 1994; Insurance Person of the Year, Md Asn Independent Insurors, 1996. **Special Achievements:** Top Ten Outstanding Grads Nashville Mag, 1976. **Business Addr:** Senior Vice President of Insurance Services, American General Life and Accident Insurance Company, 3011 Armory Dr, Nashville, TN 37204, **Business Phone:** (615)242-0546.*

MCRIPLEY, G. WHITNEY
Government official, lawyer. **Personal:** Born Nov 29, 1957, Detroit, MI; married Sandie Cameron; children: Marlena L; Gil Whitney McRipley Jr. **Educ:** Univ Detroit, BA, 1979; Univ MI, MA, 1983; Thomas M Cooley Law Sch, JD, 1984. **Career:** Detroit Pub Schs, teacher, 1980-81; Waverly Pub Sch, teacher,

1981-83; City Lansing, dir div dept, 1983-84; Charter Twp Royal Oak, supvr; Pvt Pract, currently. **Orgs:** Pi Sigma Alpha; Dem Party; pres, Royal Oak Twp Bus Asn, Royal Oak Twp Mainstream; secy, MI Conf Black Mayors. **Business Addr:** Lawyer, Private Practitioner, 20848 Garden Lane, Ferndale, MI 48220-2236, **Business Phone:** (248)546-7477.

MCROY, DR. RUTH GAIL
Educator. **Personal:** Born Oct 6, 1947, Vicksburg, MS; daughter of Lucille A McKinney Murdock and Horace David Murdock; children: Myra Louise & Melissa Lynn. **Educ:** Univ Kans, BA, 1968, MSW, 1970; Univ Tex, Austin, PhD, 1981. **Career:** Family Consult Serv, social worker, 1970-71; KS C's Serv League, adoption worker, 1971-73; Univ Kans, asst prof, 1973-77; Prairie View A&M Univ, asst prof, 1977-78; Danforth fel, 1978; Black Anal fel, 1978; Univ Tex, from asst prof to assoc prof, 1981-90, Ruby Lee Piester Centennial Prof Serv C & Families, Ctr African & African Am Studies & Sci Social Work, prof, assoc dean res, res prof & Ruby Lee Piester Centennial prof emer, currently; Serv C & Families, Ruby Lee Piester fel, 1985; Ctr Social Work Res, dir, 1994-. **Orgs:** Bd pres, Black Adoption Prog & Serv, 1975-77; Coun Social Work Educ, 1977-; Nat Asn Social Workers, 1977-; Phi Kappa Phi, 1979; bd pres, Carver Mus, 1983-86; Nat Asn Social Workers Steering Comn, Austin, 1986-90; bd mem, Carver Mus, 1987-90; Casey Family Adv Comn, 1989-; Adoptive Families Am Adv Comn, 1989-92; Marywood BOD, 1991-94. **Honors/Awds:** Outstanding Dissertation Award, Univ Tex, 1981; Lora Lee Pederson Teaching Excellence Award, 1984; Phi Kappa Phi Scholar Award, 1985; Rishon Lodge Wilhemina Delco Award for Excellence in Educ, 1987; Texas Excellence Teaching Award, 1990, Leadership Tex, 1995. **Special Achievements:** Author: Transracial and Inracial Adoptees: The Adolescent Years, 1983; Emotional Disturbance in Adopted Adolescents, 1988; Openness in Adoption, 1988; Social Practice with Black Families, 1990. **Home Addr:** 5705 Sam Houston Circle, Austin, TX 78731. **Business Addr:** Research Professor, Ruby Lee Piester Centennial Professor Emerita, University of Texas at Austin, School of Social Work, Rm 3208A 1 Univ Sta D3510, Austin, TX 78712-0359, **Business Phone:** (512)471-0551.

MCSWAIN, MICHAEL CRITTENDEN
Military leader. **Personal:** Born Jun 11, 1956, Detroit, MI; son of Louis and Theda; married Sherelyn, Aug 15, 1992; children: Michael Jr. **Educ:** Columbia Col, AA, 1977, BS, 1997. **Career:** Advisor (retired); AUS, first line supr, 1986, sr personnel supr, 1990-95, sr operations adv, 1996-97, chief sr adv, 1997-99, chief sr adv, 1999-2002. **Honors/Awds:** Army Commendation Medal, 1986, 1992, 1995; Meritorious Service Medal, 1997, 1999; Humanitarian Service Award, 1998; Legion of Merit, 2002. **Military Serv:** AUS, Command sgt Maj, 1974-02. **Home Addr:** 5705 Montrose Dr, Killeen, TX 76542, **Home Phone:** (254)699-9707.

MCSWAIN, RODNEY
Football player. **Personal:** Born Jan 28, 1962, Caroleen, NC. **Educ:** Clemson Univ. **Career:** Atlanta Falcons, defensive back, 1984; New Eng Patriots, cornerback, 1984-90; AFL Detroit Dr, 1992-93.

MCSWEEN, CIRILO A.
Executive. **Personal:** Born Jul 8, 1929, Panama City, Panama; married Gwendolyn Amacker; children: Esperanza, Veronica, Cirilo Jr. **Educ:** Univ IL, BA 1954, MA. **Career:** McSween Ins Counselors & Brokers, 1957-; McDonalds, bus exec. **Orgs:** Vchmn Independence Bank of Chicago; owner, oper Cirilo's Inc McDonald Franchise; vp, nat treas So Christian Leadership Conf; IL Adv Bd tothe Dept Ins; IL State Prop Ins Study Comn; nat treas, bd mem PUSH; vpres Chicago Econ Develop Corp; bd King Ctr Nonviolent Soc Change Atlanta; Univ IL Athletic Bd; rep, Panama Olympic Games in Track & Field. **Honors/Awds:** McDonalds Golden Arch Award, 1984; 1st Black Elected State St Coun, 1984; Life & Qualifying member, Million Dollar Round Table, 1958-. **Special Achievements:** 1st black history to sell over $1,000,000 of life ins in 1 month. **Business Addr:** Agent broker insurance, McSween Cirilo A Insurance Agency, 20 E Jackson Blvd, Chicago, IL 60604, **Business Phone:** (312)786-1857.

MCTEER, GEORGE CALVIN
Dentist. **Personal:** Born Mar 9, 1938, Barnwell, SC; son of Henry A (deceased) and Janie Elizabeth Williams (deceased); married Norma Jean Eaddy McTeer, Aug 17, 1963; children: Sonja Nichelle, Arlene Veronica, George Calvin Jr. **Educ:** SC State Univ, BS, 1960, MEd, 1968; Med Univ SC Col Dent Med, DMD, 1974. **Career:** Fairfield Co Schs, math & sci teacher, 1960-63; Charleston Co Schs, math teacher & adult sch teacher, 1963-69; Franklin C Fetter Family Health Ctr Inc, chief dent serv, 1974-76; pvt pract, 1976-; Sea Island Health Care Nursing Home, former dent consult. **Orgs:** Alpha Phi Alpha Frat 1958-; Psi Omega Dental frat 1974-; former chmn ad hoc comt health, Charleston Bus & Prof Asn, 1981-; former pres, Charleston County Med Asn, 1982-86; former mem bd dirs, Sea Island Health Care Corp, 1984-90; former mem bd chmn, Personnel Comn Cannon St YMCA, 1986-87; past state pres, Palmetto Med Dent & Pharmaceut Asn; SC Dental Asn; Coastal Dist Dent Soc, Am Dent Asn; bd deacons, Cent Baptist Church; Charleston Dental Soc; Acad Gen Dent; Charleston Mules; Nat Asn Advan Colored People; Jack & Jill Am Inc; Owl's Whist Club; former secy & pres, CBC Men Club, 1991-. **Honors/Awds:** Management Development Award, Franklin C Fetter Family Health Ctr, 1976; Certificate of Achievement, Alpha Phi Alpha Frat, 1982; Appreciation for Outstanding Leadership, Charleston County Med Asn, 1984; Volunteer Award, Coming St YWCA, 1985; Volunteer Award, Stono Park Elem Sch, Parent Teachers Asn, 1986; Merit Award, Nat Dental Asn, 1987; Recognition of Service in Dentistry, Sigma Gamma Rho Sorority, 1987; Distinguished & Exemplary Service, Delta Sigma Theta Sorority, 1988. **Special Achievements:** First black graduate College of dental Medicine, Medical University of South Carolina in 1974. *

MCTYRE, ROBERT EARL, SR.
Journalist. **Personal:** Born Aug 2, 1955, Detroit, MI; son of Earl Melvin and Barbara Jean; married Carmela, Sep 22, 1990; children: Tamika Baldwin, DuJuan Robinson, Cornelius Fortune & Rob Jr; married Dianne Denise Ball, Nov 1, 1978 (divorced 1982); married Earn Diane Fortune, Mar 1, 1975 (divorced 1977). **Educ:** Wayne County Commun, cert, training emergency med tech, 1976; Highland Park Commun, liberal arts; Wayne State Univ, jour scholar, 1989. **Career:** Ambro Ambulance, Detroit, MI, attend/driver, 1973-75; Detroit Gen Hosp, Detroit, MI, emergency room attend, 1975-77; Detroit Fire, EMS, Detroit, MI, EMT, 1977-85; Metro Times, Detroit, MI, classified salesman, freelance writer, 1984-86; Citizen News, Detroit, MI, managing ed, gen mgr, 1985-87; Mich Chronicle, Detroit, MI, reporter, assoc exec ed, 1987-93, exec ed, 1993-. **Orgs:** Detroit Chapter, Nat Asn Black Journalists, 1985; Investigative Reporters & Editors Inc, 1990; Soc Environ Journalist, 1991. **Honors/Awds:** Licensed Baptist Minister, New Resurrection MB Church. **Home Addr:** 93 Elmhurst, Highland Park, MI 48203, **Home Phone:** (313)869-0305. **Business Addr:** Associate Executive Editor, Michigan Chronicle, 479 Ledyard, Detroit, MI 48201, **Business Phone:** (313)963-5522.

MCWHORTER, ABNER, III
Personal: Born in Detroit, MI. **Career:** The Frame Up, owner; real estate developer; McWhorter Properties, owner, 1997-; Xpression Publ, publ & chief exec officer, currently; OurPC mag, publ & chief exec officer, currently. **Honors/Awds:** Rising Star Award; African American Business Hall of Fame. **Business Addr:** Publisher, Chief Executive Officer, Xpression Publishing, 453 ML King Jr Blvd Suite 101J, Detroit, MI 48201.*

MCWHORTER, GRACE AGEE
Agricultural engineer. **Personal:** Born Jan 15, 1948, Mobile, AL; married George R McWhorter MD; children: Kenya, Lia. **Educ:** Tuskegee Inst, BS, 1970, MS, 1972; Univ Fla, PhD, 1978; Besson Divinity Sch, Samford Univ, MDiv, 1992. **Career:** Univ Fla, res assoc, 1973-75; Univ Mo, vis prof biol, 1976-77; Talladega Col, asst prof biol, 1980; Jacksonville State Univ, asst prof of biol, 1980-81; Univ Tex, San Antonio, lectr biol, 1981-82; Fla Agr & Mech Univ, assoc prof agr, 1982-86; LaFontain Floral Design, owner, 1984-; Farmers Home Admin USOA, vis prof, 1984-85; State Univ Syst Fla Bd Regents, prog rev assoc, 1986; Lawson State Community Col, chairperson, Natural Sci Dept, 1993. **Orgs:** Delta Sigma Theta Sor; Jack & Jill; Am Assoc Higher Educ Black Caucus; United Fac Fla Polit Action Chmn; bd volunteers, Tallahassee Memorial Hosp; Toastmasters Int; Tuskegee Alumni Club; Am Asn Univ Women; bd mem, George Wash Carver Soc; Ala Acad Sci; Nat Asn Biol Teachers. **Honors/Awds:** BOR Res Fel, 1977; Distinguished Service Award, Fla A&M Univ; Outstanding Alumnus Award, Tuskegee Univ; Chancellor's Award, Ala Col Syst. **Special Achievements:** Several publications on small farm issues and concerns 1977. **Home Addr:** 2421 Tempest Dr, Birmingham, AL 35211.

MCWHORTER, ROSALYND D
Manager. **Personal:** Born Dec 19, 1960, Chicago, IL; daughter of Edward H and Earnestine Pollard; married Anthony Michael, May 28, 1988. **Educ:** Univ Ill, Urbana, IL, BA, eng, 1982. **Career:** R J Dale Advert, Chicago, IL, acct exec, 1984-88; Burrell Pub Rels, Chicago, IL, acct group supvr, 1988-. **Orgs:** Black Pub Rels Soc, 1988; Publicity Club Chicago, 1990-; Nat Coalition 100 Black Women, Chicago Chap, 1991. **Honors/Awds:** Certificate, McDonald's Corp Media Rels Training Prog; Certificate, Publicity Club Chicago. **Business Addr:** Account Group Supervisor, 20 N Michigan Ave Fl 2, Chicago, IL 60602, **Business Phone:** (312)443-8700.

MCWHORTER, SHARON LOUISE
Executive, president (organization), chief executive officer. **Personal:** Born Feb 22, 1951, Detroit, MI; daughter of Leroy B Harris Jr and Josie Azeez; divorced; children: Abner McWhorter III. **Educ:** Wayne State Univ, BA, 1988. **Career:** Galactic Concepts & Designs Inc, pres, 1976-81; Wayne County Community Col, acct tech, 1977-93; Am Resource Training Syst, pres & chief exec officer, 1983-; Idea Corp, facilitator, 1988-89; McWhorter Devel Co, pres, 1999-. **Orgs:** Bd dirs, Inventor's Coun Mich, 1979-80; MADD, pres, Wayne County Chap, 1985-87; Citizen's Review Comt, appointee, 1990-94; bd chair, Neighborhood Family Initiative, 1991-93; bd dirs, Detroit Empowerment Zone Develop Corp, 1994-, bd sec, 1996-99, bd chair, 2000-; Detroit Grand Prix Asn; Citizen Band Patrol; South Cass Business Asn; Nat Asn Adv Colored People. **Honors/Awds:** Spirit of Detroit, Detroit City Coun, 2000, 2003; Certificate of Appreciation, Detroit City Clerk, 2003. **Special Achievements:** United States Patent 4256281, 1981; Canadian Patent 125242, 1982; Sound Board Engr Level 1, 1982; Intl Bd Cert Trainers, 1995; writer, OURPC Mag, currently. **Business Addr:** President, Chief EXecutive Officer, American Resource Training System Incorporated, 453 Martin Luther King Jr Blvd Suite 101H, Detroit, MI 48201-2311, **Business Phone:** (313)832-2787.

MCWILLIAMS, DR. ALFRED E.
Educator. **Personal:** Born Feb 3, 1938, Wewoka, OK; son of Alfred E Sr and Elvira M Bowles McWilliams; married Wilmer Jean Bible; children: Kimberly Beatrice, Esther Gabriel Moten, Cassandra Gabriel, KennethGabriel, Fredericka Gabriel Rice & Keith Gabriel. **Educ:** Colo State Col, BA, 1959, MA, 1960; Univ Northern Colo, PhD, 1970. **Career:** Denver Pub Sch Colo, teacher, counsr & admin asst, 1960-68; Proj Upward Bound Univ Northern Colo, dir, 1968-70; Univ Northern Colo, asst dean-spec educ & rehab, 1970-72; Univ Northern Colo, asst prof, 1970-72, assoc prof educ 1976-82; Fed Rocky Mt States Inc, consult & career educ content coord, 1972-76; Univ Northern Colo, dir personnel AA/EEO, 1976-79, asst vpres, admin serv personnel, 1979-82; Univ Colo, vpres admin, 1982-84;Atlanta Univ, vpres admin, 1984-85; Atlanta Univ, dean, sch educ, 1985-87; Ga State Univ, prof, educ policy studies, 1987-09, coord, educa leadership prog, 1995-, Prof Educ Coun, chair; Emeriti Prof, Georgia State Univ, currently. **Orgs:** Chmn, co-founder, Black Educrs United, 1967-68; bd mem, Colo Christian Home Denver 1977-; sec, Aurora Colo Career Serv Comn, 1977-, chmn,1980-84; bd mem, Nat Brotherhood Skiers, 1978-79, 1980-85, coun mem, 1978-; Am Asn Univ Admin; Colo Merit Syst Coun; Col & Univ Personnel Asn;Am Soc Personnel Admin, 1979-; consult & trainer, Nat Ctr Leadership Develop Atlanta Univ, 1979-80; consult & trainer, Leadership Develop Training Prog, Howard Univ, 1981-82; chmn elect, EEO, 1981-82; Rotary Club West End Atlanta, 1984-87, 1989-; army committeeman, Greater Atlanta Chapter Res Officers Asn US, 1985-; chmn bd dir, APPLE Corps, 1986; Prof Jour Comt, Asn Teacher Educrs, 1987-; Am Asn Higher Educ, 1989-; Asn Supervision & Curric Develop, 1989-; Am Asn Univ Profs, 1995-. **Honors/Awds:** Appreciation Award, Nat Brotherhood Skiers, 1979; Leadership Styles &Management Strategies Award of Management Education, Atlanta Univ, 1986. **Special Achievements:** Published articles like: Review of KA Heller, et al Placing Children in Special Education: A Strategy for Equity, National Academy Press, 1987. **Military Serv:** AUS, col, 1961-68, 1977-93; Army Res Component Medal; Army Achievement Medal; Army Commendation Medal; Meritorious Serv Medal. **Home Addr:** 1221 Ashley Lake Dr, Marietta, GA 30062. **Business Addr:** Emeriti Professor, Georgia State University, Univ Plaza, Atlanta, GA 30033-3083, **Business Phone:** (404)651-3330.

MCWILLIAMS, JAMES D
Lawyer. **Personal:** Born Dec 25, 1932, Fairfield, AL; son of James and Minnie; married Anne; children: Laura, Susan & Diana. **Educ:** Talladega Col, Talladega, AL, BA, 1954; Univ Wis Law Sch, Madison, WI, JD, 1962. **Career:** US Dept Interior, att adv, 1962-66; United Planning Organ, Wash, DC CAP, asst gen coun, 1966-67; US Virgin Islands, asst att gen, 1967-72; US Virgin Islands Port Authority, gen coun, 1969-72; Coop Assistance Fund, asst sec; Opp Funding Corp, gen coun sec, 1973-77; Pvt Pract, atty, currently; DC Govt Dept Transp, asst dir, 1979-91. **Orgs:** Nat Bar Asn; Am Bar Asn; State Bar Wis, 1962-; DC Bar Asn, 1972. **Honors/Awds:** Drafted legislation which establshed US Virgin Islands Port Authority. **Military Serv:** AUS, 1955-58. **Business Addr:** Attorney, 5604 MacArthur Blvd NW, Washington, DC 20016, **Business Phone:** (202)537-0544.

MCWILLIAMS, JOHNNY
Football player. **Personal:** Born Dec 14, 1972, Pomona, CA; married Elizabeth; children: Johnny Jr. **Educ:** Univ Southern Calif, pub admin. **Career:** Ariz Cardinals, tight end, 1996-99; Minn Vikings, tight end, 2000-01; New England Patriots, tight end, 2001.

MCWILLIAMS-FRANKLIN, TAJ
Basketball player. **Personal:** Born Oct 20, 1970, El Paso, TX; daughter of Marvin McWilliams and Stephanie Wiggins; married Reggie; children: Rashundra Michele. **Educ:** Ga State Univ, attended 1989; St Edwards Univ, rhetoric. **Career:** Wolfenbuettel, Germany, 1993-94; Contern, Luxembourg, 1994-95; Galilee,Israel, 1995-96; Philadelphia Rage, ctr, 1996; Orlando Miracle, 1999-2003;Connecticut Sun, 2003; Los Angeles Sparks, 2007; Washington Mystics, 2008; Detroit Shock, 2009-. **Honors/Awds:** NAIA National Player of the Year, 1993; All-Am team, 1993; Kim Perrot Sportsmanship Award, 2005. **Business Addr:** Professional Basketball Player, Detroit Shock, 4 Championship Dr, Auburn Hills, MI 48326, **Business Phone:** (248)377-0100.*

MCWRIGHT, CARTER C
Executive. **Personal:** Born Feb 7, 1950; children: Carter II. **Educ:** Southern Univ, BA, 1972. **Career:** Music Planet, owner, currently.

Orgs: Saginaw Black Bus Asn, vpres, 1982-84; vpres, Saginaw E Side Lions Club, 1983-84; bd mem, E Cent Mich Planners, 1984-87; Nat Asn Advan Colored People; Joy Baptist Church. **Honors/Awds:** Businessman of the year, Saginaw Frontiers Club, 1983; Lion of the year, Saginaw Eastside Lions, 1983; Businessman of the year, Saginaw Black Bus Asn, 1984. **Business Addr:** Owner, Music Planet, 517 W Carpenter Rd, Flint, MI 48505-2034, **Business Phone:** (810)787-0099.*

MCZEAL, ALFRED, SR.
Executive, chief executive officer. **Personal:** Born Mar 6, 1931, Ridge, LA; son of Alzfall and Olivia; married Virgis Mary Sampay, Jan 5, 1952; children: Olivia Figaro-McZeal, Myra Holmes, Alfred Jr & Janet Lynn. **Career:** Morgan & Lindsey, janitor, 1948-64; Southern Consumers Coop Inc, vol, 1962-64, gen mgr & ceo, 1964-. **Orgs:** Nat Asn Advan Colored People, 1955; supvr, St Pauls Credit Union, 1961; Better Business Bur, 1986; MLK Holiday Comt, 1991; Inst Karamic Guid, Holy Family African Tour, 1992; secy, Black Alliance Prog; La Black Assembly; Nat Black Assembly. **Honors/Awds:** Black Citizen Award, Southern Consumers Educ Found, 1975; LA Beautician Asn, Achieving Civic & Relig Improv, 1985; Dedicated Service Award, Fed Southern Coop, 1987; support, Immaculate Heart of Mary, 1988; Lifetime Achievement Award, Southern Consumers Educ Found, 1991; Outstanding Citizen Award, Acadiana Kiwanis, 1990; Serv Award, KJCB Radio Sta, 1990. **Special Achievements:** Traveled to Geneva Switzerland to speak on Human Development to the third world countries, 1975. **Business Addr:** Chief Executive Officer, General Manager, Southern Consumers Coop Inc, 1006 Surrey St, Lafayette, LA 70501, **Business Phone:** (318)232-1126.

MCZIER, ARTHUR
Management consultant, president (organization). **Personal:** Born May 4, 1935, Atlanta, GA; married Ruby Burrows; children: Sandra, Jennifer Rose. **Educ:** Loyola Univ, BS, 1959, study towards M, 1961. **Career:** Seeburg Corp, intl sales & mktg rep, 1962-66; Ford Motor Co, mktg analyst, 1966-67; US Dept Com Off Foreign Direct Investments, 1968; US Small Bus Admin, asst adminr minority enterprise, 1969-73; Gen Bahamian Co, bus exec, 1973-74; Resources Inc, mgt consult, 1974-; Nat Bus Serv Enterprise, pres, 1998. **Orgs:** Adv Bd, Inst Minority Bus Educ Howard Univ; Wash Bd Coun Fed City Col. **Honors/Awds:** Who's Who in Am Adv Bd; Robert Russo Moton Leadership Award, Nat Bus League, 1971; hon dr laws degree Daniel Payne Col, 1971; gold medal disngshed serv USSmall Bus Admin, 1969; award of merit, Nat Econ Develop Admin, 1971; speciall achievement award, US Small Bus Admin, 1969; recognition award, outst contrib minority econ develop Black Businessmen's Prof Asn, 1971; recognition award, outst serv minority bus TX & USA Pylon Salesmanshp Club, 1971; hall of fame, Loyola Univ, 1972; certified outstanding perform, Small Bus Admin, 1972; city economical developement center award, Miami, 1972; public service award, Houston Citizens C C, 1973; Arthur S Fleming award, nominee Small Bus Admin, 1972; key award, Natl Asn Black Manufacturer's, 1974. **Business Phone:** (202)332-6600.*

MEACHAM, ROBERT B.
Educator, administrator. **Personal:** Born Mar 21, 1933, Tuscaloosa, AL; son of Manarah and Armond; married Grace A; children: Anthony & Alexander. **Educ:** AB, EdM, 1973; doctoral cand 1975. **Career:** Univ Cincinnati, lectr psychol, counr, 1970-73, Col Appl Sci, asst dir, 1973-74, dir stud life & coun, 1974-, assoc vice provost minority prog & serv & int serv, assoc vice provost, stud serv, 1978-89, assoc athletic dir, 1989-, transfer coordr, currently. **Orgs:** Paddock Hills Assembly Inc, 1970-; United Black Fac Asn, 1973; Am Personnel & Guid Asn; Asn Non-White Concerns; treas, Asn Coun Educ & Supervision Comn Develop Adv Coun, Cincinnati. **Honors/Awds:** Affirmative action plan, Ohio Col Appl Sci, 1973. **Military Serv:** USAF A/1C 1952-56. **Home Addr:** 1228 Westminster Dr, Cincinnati, OH 45229. **Business Addr:** Transfer Coordinator, University of Cincinnati, College of Applied Science, 2220 Victory Pkwy, Cincinnati, OH 45206-2839, **Business Phone:** (513)556-1039.

MEADE, ALSTON B., SR.
Research scientist, biologist. **Personal:** Born Jun 28, 1930, Jamaica, West Indies; son of Frank I R and Hepsy Condell; divorced; children: Alston B Jr, Allison D, Jule Anne, Brandon D, Fred A. **Educ:** Fisk Univ, BA, 1956; Univ Minn, MS, 1959, PhD, 1962. **Career:** Research scientist & Biologist (retired); EI du Pont de Nemours Co, res biologist, 1964, sr res biologist, 1971, res assoc, 1992. **Orgs:** Pres, Nat Asn Advancement Colored People, Southern Chester County Br, 1965-75; Bd Educ W Chester Area Sch Dist, 1970-80; chmn, Joint Community Spec Educ Chester County, Pa, 1974-80; Inter Unit Chester County, Pa, 1974-80; vpres, Bd Educ W Chester Area Sch Dist 1975-77; fel African Scientific Inst; pres, Int Soc African Scientists, 1988-90; pres, Nat Asn Jamaican & Supportive Orgn, 1993-98; pres, Nat Coalition Caribbean Affairs, 1998-. **Home Addr:** 2014 Valley Dr, West Chester, PA 19382. *

MEADE-TOLLIN, DR. LINDA C
Biochemist, educator. **Personal:** Born in London, WV; daughter of Robert A and Virginia; married Gordon Tollin; children: Amina Rebecca. **Educ:** WVa State Col, BS, 1964; Hunter Col, MA, 1969; City Univ NY, PhD, 1972. **Career:** Col Old Westbury, asst prof, 1972-75; Rockefeller Univ, vis asst prof, 1973-74; Univ Ariz, NIH postdoctoral fel, 1975-77, res assoc, 1978-80; Coord Women Sci & Engrg Off, staff, 1980-82, vis asst prof, 1982-85; Morehouse Sch Med, fac develop fel, 1985-86; Univ Ariz, sr lect & asst res sci, 1987-91, NIH minority spec investr, 1987-89, 1990-93, Ariz Health Scis Ctr, Dept Surg, res asst prof surg, 1987-. **Orgs:** Alpha Kappa Alpha Sorority, 1962-; Nat Orgn Prof Advan Black Chemists & Chem Engrs, 1973-85, 1987-, chair exec bd, 1981; consult, Am Med Womens Asn, 1977-85; bd dir, Ododo Theatre Found, 1977-85; Am Med Womens Asn, 1979; Jack & Jill Inc, 1987-89. **Honors/Awds:** Award for Excellence in Medicine, Scimitar Temple 108, 1981; Scientist of the Year, Ariz Coun Black Engrs & Scis, 1983; NIH-N HLBI Minority Faculty Career Developmen Award, 1996-2001. **Business Addr:** Research Assistant Professor of Surgery, Arizona Health Sciences Center, Department of Surgery, PO Box 245084, Tucson, AZ 85724-5084, **Business Phone:** (520)626-7019.

MEADOWS, CHERYL R
Government official, executive director. **Personal:** Born Sep 7, 1948, Cincinnati, OH; daughter of Ruth Pulliam and Jack Pulliam; children: Jerry L Wilkerson Jr. **Educ:** Tenn State Univ, BA, 1970; Univ Cincinnati, MS, 1975. **Career:** City Cincinnati, planner, 1971-76, prog mgr, 1976-82, asst city mgr, dir, Dept Neighborhood Serv, employ & training dir, exec dir, Cincinnati Human Relations Comn, currently. **Orgs:** AS Conf Mayor/City Human Serv, 1976-; Nat Forum Black Pub Admin, 1986-; Am Soc Pub Admin, 1989. **Honors/Awds:** Fel, Aspo Ford Found, 1975; Univ Scholar, 1975; Outstanding Young Women of America, 1982; Community Chest's President Award, 1983; Community Action Commission Award, 1986; Community Service Award, 1987; Career Women of Achievement, 1992; Outstanding Manager Award, City Cincinnati Managers Asn, 1992. **Business Addr:** Executive Director, Cincinnati Human Relations Commission, 801 Plum St City Hall Rm 158, Cincinnati, OH 45202-5407, **Business Phone:** (513)352-3237.

MEADOWS, RICHARD H.
Dentist. **Personal:** Born Dec 7, 1928, Roanoke, VA; married Dorothy M Magee; children: William C. **Educ:** VA Union Univ, BS, 1951; Howard Univ Sch Dent, DDS, 1955; Freedman' Hosp, intern, 1956. **Career:** Dentist, pvt prac. **Orgs:** Pres, PBR Dent Soc, 1961-68; pres, Old Dominion Dent Soc, 1968-71; Nat Dent Soc; Int Endodontic Soc; Aircraft Owners & Pilots Asn; Omega Psi Frat; Nat Advan Asn Colored People. **Honors/Awds:** award oral surgeon, Beta Kappa Chi Nat Sci Soc Howard Univ, 1955. **Business Addr:** 215 W Clay St, Richmond, VA 23220.

MEADOWS, TIM
Actor, comedian. **Personal:** Born Feb 5, 1961, Highland Park, MI; married Michelle, 1997; children: 1. **Educ:** Wayne State Univ. **Career:** Actor, currently; Second City, improv comedy troupe; TV: "Saturday Night Live", 1991-2000; "The Michael Richards Show", 2000; "Leap of Faith", NBC, 2001; "Leap of Faith", 2002; 'You Don't Have to Go Home", 2004; 'The Ex Factor", 2005; "Perserverance", 2006; " Pink Freud", 2006; "According to Jim", 2007; films: Coneheads, 1993; Wayne's World 2, 1993; It's Pat, 1994; The Ladies Man, 2000; Olive the Other Reindeer, 2000; 3 Days, 2001; The Stevens Get Even, Disney, 2002; Wasabi Tuna, 2003; The Cookout, 2004; The Benchwarmers, 2006; TV episodes: "Everybody Hates Corleone", 2006; "Everybody Hates Chris", 2006; "The Sperminator", 2006; "Lovespring International", 2006; "The Colbert Report", 2006; "Help Me Help You", 2006; "According to Jim", 2007; "Shredderman Rules", 2007; "Have You Seen My Muffins, Man?", 2007; "The Bill Engvall Show", 2007; "Curb Your Enthusiasm", 2007; "Walk Hard: The Dewey Cox Story", 2007; "Semi-Pro", 2008. **Business Addr:** Actor, Brillstein-Grey, 9150 Wilshire Blvd Suite 350, Beverly Hills, CA 90212, **Business Phone:** (310)275-6135.

MEANS, BERTHA E
Educator, government official. **Personal:** Born May 1, 1920, Valley Mills, TX; married James H; children: Joan, Janet, James Jr, Patricia & Ronald. **Educ:** Huston-Tillotson Col, AB, 1945; Univ Tex, MEd, 1955; Univ Tex, Austin. **Career:** Prairie View A&M Univ, vis instr, 1959-68; Austin Independent Sch Dist, dir head start, 1969-70; Univ Tex, Austin, instr, 1971-72; Austin-Maseru Comt, chair, currently; Austin Independent Sch Dist, instr coord sec reading, currently. **Orgs:** Pres, Austin Chap Jack & Jill Am Inc, 1956-58; Women Ed Area Church, United Fund, Austin & Travis Ctr, 1965-67; pres, Episcopal Women St James, 1966-67; City Coun appointee, Park & Recreation Adv Bd, 1967-74; vpres, Austin Nat Asn Advan Colored People, 1970-74; Citizens Comt A More Beautiful Town Lake, 1972-75; Local Citizens Adv Comt & Tex Constitutional Adv Comt, 1973; Int Reading Asn; past pres, Capitol Area Coun; Tex State Teachers Asn; charter mem, Ad Hoc Com Enactment Human Rels Comt City Austin; bd mem, YWCA; Epsilon Kappa Chap Delta Kappa Gamma Soc; Alpha Kappa Alpha Sorority, St James Episcopal Chap. **Honors/Awds:** Woman of the Year Award, Zeta Phi Beta Sorority, 1965; DeWitty Civil Rights Award, Austin Br Nat Asn Advan Colored People, 1966; Committee Leadership Certificate of Appreciation, Capital City Lions & Optimist Clubs, 1972; Austin Amer Statesman; Special Award for Service to Parks & Recreation Dept, Nat Asn Advan Colored People, 1975; Committee Service Award, Zeta Phi Beta, 1976. **Special Achievements:** Selected one of Austins Outstanding Women of 1975. **Business Addr:** Chair, Austin-Maseru Committee, 7400 Valburn Dr, Austin, TX 78731, **Business Phone:** (512)478-2222.

MEANS, DR. CRAIG R. See Obituaries section.

MEANS, DONALD FITZGERALD
Government official. **Personal:** Born Dec 29, 1966, Tuscaloosa, AL; son of Harry L and Mary Turner. **Educ:** Univ Ala, Tuscaloosa, AL, mkt mgt, 1989. **Career:** Greene County Racing Comn, Eutaw, AL, chmn comn, 1989-, financial mgtanalyst, 1989-90; District 4, Ala, comnr, currently. **Orgs:** Chmn, Greene County Water Authority, 1990-; pres, Community Fire Dept, 1990; Extension Serv Adv Bd, 1990-; chmn, Agr Adv Bd, 1991-. **Business Addr:** Commissioner, Greene County, District 4, 400 Morrow Ave, PO Box 656, Eutaw, AL 35462, **Business Phone:** (205)372-3349.

MEANS, ELBERT LEE
Government official. **Personal:** Born Feb 3, 1945, Sandy Ridge, AL; married Harriet Ivory; children: Madelene, Jennifer & Kristen. **Educ:** Selma Univ, attended 1964; AL State Univ, attended 1966 & 1969. **Career:** Station Help Inc, supvr, 1969-73; Gen Motors, shipping clerk, 1973-75; Brockway Glass, laborer, 1975-79; Lowndes County, tax assessor; Fort Deposit, Ala, coun mem, currently. **Orgs:** State exec mem, Alabama Democratic Conf; county coord, Lowndes County Dem Party; mem adv bd, Lowndes County Community Org; vpres, Selma Univ Alumni-Chap. **Military Serv:** AUS E-5 sergant 1966-68; hon lt col, aide-de-camp, Ala State Militia; Bronze Star Vietnam Veteran. **Business Addr:** Council Member, Fort Deposit, Lowndes County, 205a E Tuskeena St, Hayneville, AL 36040-0065.*

MEANS, DR. FRED E.
School administrator. **Personal:** Born in Pacolet, SC; son of Fred Means Sr and Lemor Tucker; married Helen Pryor; children: Chad, Marc & Vincent. **Educ:** NY Univ, BS, 1959; Trenton State Col, MA, 1963; Rutgers Univ, EdM, 1973, EdD, 1975. **Career:** New York City Schs, teacher, 1959-60; Newark Sch System, teacher, adminr, 1960-70; Rutgers Univ, lectr & dir, 1970-75; NJ City Univ, dir, 1975-78, from asst dean to dean 1978-94, adj prof, 1994, prof emer, 2000-. **Orgs:** Trustee, UCC Newark Anti Poverty Agency, 1965-66; Orgn Newark Educr, Newark, 1967-70; Newark Bd Educ, 1973-76; trustee, Action Sickle Cell Anemia Hudson County, 1982-88; bd dirs, Res Better Schs, 1983-94; pres, AACTE; Am Educ Res Asn; Nat Alliance Black Sch; Phi Delta Kappa; Am Asn Col Teacher Educ. **Special Achievements:** Proj PRIME; paper presented, Norfolk State Univ, 1988; "The Process and Product of Restructuring an Urban Teacher Education Program," paper presented, Asn Teacher Educr Conf, New Orleans, 1991. **Military Serv:** AUS, Spec 3, 1953-56. **Business Addr:** Professor Emeritus, New Jersey City University, 2039 Kennedy Blvd, Jersey City, NJ 07305-1597, **Business Phone:** (201)200-2552.

MEANS, NATRONE JERMAINE
Football player, football coach. **Personal:** Born Apr 26, 1972, Harrisburg, NC. **Educ:** Univ NC. **Career:** Football player (retired), coach; San Diego Chargers, running back, 1993-95, 1998-99; Jacksonville Jaguars, 1996-97; Carolina Panthers, running back, 2000; Livingston Col, asst coach, running backs coach, offensive coordr; W Charlotte High Sch, offensive coordr, currently. **Honors/Awds:** Pro Bowl, 1994. **Business Addr:** Offensive Coordinator, West Charlotte High School, 2219 Senior Dr, Charlotte, NC 28216, **Business Phone:** (980)343-6060.

MEASE, QUENTIN R.
Association executive. **Personal:** Born Oct 25, 1908, Buxton, IA; son of Charles Henry and Cornelia Frances; married Jewell Mary Chenault (deceased), Sep 25, 1950; children: Barbara Ann Ransom. **Educ:** Des Moines Univ, BS, 1939; George Williams Col, MS, 1948. **Career:** Crocker Br YMCA, exec dir, 1939-42; Metro YMCA Chgo, asst prog sec,1946-49; Bagby Br YMCA Houston, exec dir, 1950-55; S Cent YMCA, exc dir,1955-75; Human Enrichment Life Progs Inc, pres, 1975-. **Orgs:** Houston Bus & Prof Men's Club, exec sect, 1950-75; Houston Area Urban League, founder & pres, 1967-69; Harris County Hosp Dist, chmn bd mgrs, 1970-75; bd mem, Baylor Col Med, 1971-; bd mem, Lockwood Nat Bank, 1984-; Sheltering Arms, bd mem, 1987-89; bd mem, Rotary Club Houston, 1987-89; bd mem, Inst Int Educ, 1988-; life bd mem, S Cent YMCA; chmn bd, Hosp Dist Found, 1993-; Rotary Club Houston; bd mem Tex Med Ctr; bd mem, Alley Theater; Star Hope Mission. **Honors/Awds:** Distinguished Service Award, Tex Peace Officers Asn, 1983; Distinguished Service Award, Baylor Col Med, 1985; First Annual Sheriff Johnny Klevenhagen Award, 1986; Community Service Award, Houston Area Urban League, 1989; Distinguished Service Award, 152nd Anniversary, City Houston, 1989; Distinguished Service Award, Black United Fund, 1989; Distinguished Citizens Award, Metrop Transit Authority, 1991; Life Trustee Award, Tex Med Ctr, 1991. **Military Serv:** USAF, capt, 1942-46. **Home Addr:** 3321 Calumet Dr, Houston, TX 77004, **Home Phone:** (713)746-6005.

MEAUX, RONALD
Artist, educator. **Personal:** Born Feb 15, 1942, Louisville, KY. **Educ:** Univ Ky, BA, art, 1965. **Career:** Cleveland Pub Schs, art

instr. **Orgs:** Nat Conf Artists; Nat Asn Advan Colored People; Metro Opera Guild. **Special Achievements:** One man art show, Karamu, 1974. **Business Addr:** Art Instructor, East Technical High School, 2439 E 55th St, Cleveland, OH 44105.

MEDEARIS, VICTOR L
Clergy. **Personal:** Born Apr 3, 1921, Austin, TX; son of James Ever and Pearl B Edgar; married Gladys Lonell Alexander, Apr 3, 1943; children: Victor L, Pamela Faye & Charlotte Briana. **Educ:** San Francisco Baptist Bible Col, Std Theol, 1948-53; City Col San Fran, AA, 1958; San Francisco Univ, Std Soc Sci, 1961. **Career:** Double Rock Baptist Church, San Francisco, pastor, 1948-; Fed Employ, mechanic helper, warehouse foreman, heavy duty driver trainer, driver examiner, mech inspector, equal employ spec, 1949. **Orgs:** Chmn, San Francisco Humn Rights Comn, 1971; secy bd, Fel Bible Inst; chmn, Civic Comn Bay view Baptist Min Fel; Bay Area Dist Asn; bd mem, San Francisco Chap, Nat Asn Advan Colored People; bd mem, Sickle Cell Anemia; West Bay Clergy Rep Northern CA; adv bd, United Negro Col Fund Bay Area Int Alumni Com; Org Calif State Baptist Conv. **Honors/Awds:** Highest Award of Merit, City San Francisco, 1971; Honorary Award Quartett Singers Asn Am, 1972; Honorary Award, Pelton Jr High School, 1973; Outstanding Community Achievement Award, San Francisco Bayview Hunters Point Multi-purpose Senior Serv, 1989; 40th Pastoral Anniversary Commemoration, Senator Quentin Kopp, 1989. **Business Addr:** Pastor, Double Rock Baptist Church, 1595 Shafter Ave, San Francisco, CA 94124, **Business Phone:** (415)822-4566.

MEDFORD, ISABEL
Lawyer. **Personal:** Born in Louisiana; children: Richard Kevin. **Educ:** Univ Calif, Berkley, BA, psych & polit sci, 1972; Univ Calif, Boalt Hall Sch Law, JD, 1975; Univ Calif, MCrim, 1976. **Career:** Robert T Cresswell Inc, atty, 1974-78; Nat Asn Advan Colored People Legal Def Fund, law clerk, 1974-75; Isabel Medford Law Firm, atty, 1978-. **Orgs:** Chmn, Mem Com Niagra Movement Dem Club, 1974-; Bd dir, A Safe Place, 1979-; vpres, UC Black Alumni Asn, 1979-; legal adv Oakland E Bay Chap Delta Sigma Theta, 1979-.

MEDINA, BENNY
Television producer, executive. **Personal:** Born Jan 24, 1958. **Career:** Apollo. vocalist; Warner Brothers Records, artists & repertoire, vpres; Handprint Entertainment, talent agent & partner, currently; Producer: The Fresh Prince of Bel-Air", co-producer, 1990-94; Above the Rim, writer & music supvr, 1994; "Getting Personal", exec producer, 1998; 3 Strikes, 2000; Jennifer Lopez in Concert, 2001; Maid in Manhattan, exec producer, 2002; Anything Else, exec producer, 2003; The Fighting Temptations, 2003; In the Game, exec producer, 2004; In the Game, exec producer, 2005; The Tyra Banks Show, exec producer, 2005; Celebrity Autobiography: In Their Own Words, 2005; The Adventures of Mimi, exec producer, 2007; Lovers & Haters, exec producer, 2007. **Honors/Awds:** Daytime Emmy Award, 2008. **Business Phone:** (310)481-4400.*

MEE, LAFARRELL DARNELL
Basketball player. **Personal:** Born Feb 11, 1971, Cleveland, TN. **Educ:** Western Ky Univ, attended. **Career:** Denver Nuggets, 1994-95; NBL: Canberra Cannons, 1996; Adelaide 36ers, 1998-2000, 2001; Cairns Taipans, 2002-03; Wollongong Hawks, 2003-05; Cairns Taipans, guard, 2005-. **Orgs:** Nat Basketball Asn. **Honors/Awds:** NBL Championships, 1998, 1999; All-NBL third team, 2004; NBL All-Star, World Team, 2005. **Business Phone:** (074)030-7555.

MEEK, CARRIE P
Congressperson (U.S. federal government), administrator, government official. **Personal:** Born Apr 29, 1926, Tallahassee, FL; daughter of William and Carrie; divorced; children: Lucia Raiford, Sheila Davis Kinui & Kendrick Meek. **Educ:** Fla A&M Univ, Tallahassee, FL, BS, Biol & Physical Educ, 1946; Univ Mich, MS, pub health, physical educ, 1948; Fla Atlantic Univ; Univ Indiana. **Career:** Miami-Dade Community Col, prof, 1961; Fla Legislature, seat, house reps, 1979-83; Fla State Senate, senator, 1983-93; US House Reps, congresswoman, 1993-2003; Bethune Cookman Col, physical educ, health instr; Fla A&M Univ, asst prof, health-physical educ. **Honors/Awds:** Morris W Milton Sr Polit Achievement Award, Democratic Black Caucus, Fla, 1988; Distinguished Serv Award, Frontiers Int Miami Club, 1988. **Special Achievements:** First African-American elected to the US Congress from Florida this century, 1992; one of the 50 Most Effective Members of Congress, Congressional Quarterly Mag.

MEEK, KENDRICK B
Government official, senator (u.s. federal government). **Personal:** Born Sep 6, 1966, Miami, FL; son of Carrie Meek; married Leslie Dixon; children: Lauren & Kendrick B Jr. **Educ:** Fla A&M Univ, BS, criminol, 1989. **Career:** Fla Hwy Patrol, capt; Wackenhut Corp, develop rep; Dem Cong Campaign Comn, vice chair; Fla House Representatives, state rep, 1994-98; Fla State Senate, senator, 1998-2002; US House Representatives, Fla 17th Cong dist, congressman, 2002-. **Orgs:** Numerous memberships including life mem, NAACP; 100 Black Men; powerful House Armed Serv Comn; chair, bd dirs, Cong Black Caucus Found; bd dirs, Dem Nat Community Comn; hon co-chair, Col Dem Am; co-founder, Fla A&M Univ Col Dem. **Honors/Awds:** Outstanding Service Award, MADD, 1990; One of 50 Leaders of Tomorrow, Ebony Mag, 1995; Gwen Sawyer Cherry Memorial Award, Fla Conf NAACP Branches, 1997. **Business Addr:** Congressman, 17th Congressional District of Florida, 111 NW 183rd St Suite 325, Miami, FL 33169, **Business Phone:** (305)655-3213.*

MEEK, DR. RUSSELL CHARLES
Educator, consultant, movie director. **Personal:** Born Sep 9, 1937, Springfield, IL; son of Albert Jackson and Josephine Snowden; divorced; children: 4. **Educ:** Milliken Univ Nat Col LaSalle Univ, 1960; Hwa Rang Do Martial Arts Acad, 1970, Universal Life Ch, DD 1975; Natl Col Chiropractic Med, Doctor Religious Humanities; Temple Univ; CLC, comput programming, 1991; Chicago Access Corp, TV producer. **Career:** Cook Co Dept Corrections, 1966-; Search for Truth Inc, pres, 1966-; Westside Art & Karate Center Inc, dir, 1968-; Univ Ill, instr radio TV prod Psycholinguistics & Philology; CETA V, Devel Educ & Employ Prog, proj dir; Malcolm X Coll, instr 1970-72; Radio Sta WVON, prod host, 1970-; Natl Black Writer's Workshop, lecturer, 1973-75; Northeastern Ill Univ, rehab educ specialist 1974-75; Study Commn Residential Schs Ill, hearing coord, 1974; Investigative Jour & Historical Rsch, writer; Malcolm X Col, bd dir; Parents Without Partners, comm adv commn. **Orgs:** Instr Martial Arts; pres Black Karate Fed; Black United Front, Black Enpowerment Comm; Search for Truth Inc; radio commentator, talk show host WBEE Radio; Dr Russ Meek's Jazz AllSTARS; bd of dir African Am Clergy for Action, 1988-. **Honors/Awds:** Songs "My Love," "You," and "Shadows of the Night,", 1969; Blue Ribbon Panel Citizens for Police Reform, 1973-75; received 10 humanitarian, community, integrity, merit & special awards, 1972-75; Westside Citizen of Year, 1972-76; starred in 2 documentary films, "Crisis in the Cities" (EmmyAward winner) and "A Letter to Martin"; produced and directed TV & radioshows since 1966, Search for Truth News, editor; Comm Integrity Award, 1973; doctoral candidate, Univ the Pacific; publicist, co-sponsor, African-Amer Culture Center Imo State; The Can Do It Awd, 1973; Champion of Imprisoned Award, 1974; The Get It Done Award, 1973; Special Commendation Award for Community Interest & Support, El Centro de La Causa, 1975; Nat Community Leaders; Gentlemen Distinction; Master of the MartialArts; Outstanding Serv to the Martial Arts & Community; playwright, "TheMessage," 1976; co-author "Our Songs"; Image Makers Award, 1977; co-producer, actor, The Sinister Reign, Anna Lucasta, and Blues for MrCharlie; author, Poems for Peace, Justice and Freedom, 1966; co-director"Mfundishi," Pan African Martial Ars Federation Inc. **Special Achievements:** First black to produce & direct TV, radio shows since 1966 in the country. **Home Phone:** (312)995-8679. **Business Addr:** President, Search for Truth Inc., 10937 S Lowe Ave, Chicago, IL 60628, **Business Phone:** (773)264-1691.

MEEKS, CORDELL DAVID
Judge. **Personal:** Born Dec 17, 1942, Kansas City, KS; son of Cordell D Sr (deceased) and Cellastine D Brown; married Mary Ann Sutherland, Jul 15, 1967; children: Cordell III. **Educ:** Univ KS, BA, polit sci, 1964; Univ Kans Law Sch, JD, 1967; Harvard Law Sch, Practicalities Judging, 1978; Nat Judicial Col, Grad Gen Jrs 1981. **Career:** Wyandotte Cty Legal Aid Soc, staff coun, 1968-70; Univ PA Law Sch, Smith fel, 1968; Meeks Sutherland McIntosh Law Firm, sr partner, 1968-81; State Kans, spec asst atty gen, 1975; Kans City KS, municipal judge, 1976-81; 29th Judicial Dist Kans, dist ct judge, 1981-; Nat Inst Trial Advocacy, fac, 1986-. **Orgs:** Pres, Kansas Municipal Judges Asn, 1980-81; Gov Comm Crime Prev, 1982-91; Comniv Law Sch, 1984-85; pres, Substance Abuse Ctr Eastern KS, 1985-87; KS Comn Bicentennial US Const, 1987-91; pres, Am Lung Asn Kansas, 1988-89; bd ed, Kans Bar Jour Kans Bar Asn, 1989-97; pres, Vis Nurses Asn, Greater Kansas City, 1989-91; Nat bd trustees, 1990-94; chmn, United Way Wy&otte County, 1991-92; co-chair, Nat Conf Christians & Jews, Greater Kansas City Region, 1993-97; chmn, Kaw Dist, Heart Am Boy Scouts Am, 1994-95, BSA cnl vp opers, 1996-99; chmn, Midwest Bioethics Ctr, 1995-97; chmn, El Centro, Inc, 1996-97; bd dirs, Children's Mercy Hosp, 1997-; chmn, Univ Kans Alumni Asn, 1997-98; vice chair, Youth Friends, 1999-; pres, Nat bd, Am Lung Asn, 2001-02; trustee, Harry S Truman Library, 2001-; Midwest Research IST, bd dir, 2003-. **Honors/Awds:** Outstanding Services Award, United Way, 1979; Men of Distinction Award, Yates Br, 1982; Distinguished Service, Kansas City Chap, Nat Asn Advan Colored People, 1986; Distinguished Service Award, Blacks Govt Greater Kansas City, 1989; President's Award, Southern Christian Leadership Conf, 1990; Distinguished Service, Kansas City Asn Ment Health, 1990; Kansas City Spirit Award, 1994; Kansas Citizen of the Year, Chap Nat Asn Social Workers, 1994; Distinguished Service Award, Park Col, 1995; Sire Archon Pres, Theta Boule Chap, Sigma Pi Phi Fraternity, 1995-97; Distinguished Service Citation, Univ Kans, 1995; Silver Beaver Award, Boy Scouts Am, 1996; Most Influential Black Man in Kansas, KC GLOBE, 1997-; Distinguished Alumnus Award, Kans Univ Law Sch, 2001; Distinguished Service Award, Nat Conf COT & Justice, 2001; Legion of Merit Medal, 2001; Mid-America Education Hall of Fame Inductee, 2001; Ellsworth Medallion, Kans Univ, 2002; Distinguished Civic Leadership Award, Baker Univ, 2003. **Military Serv:** AUS, NG COL; US Army, active duty, 1968-70,War College Class, 1997, vpres, Army Commendation Medal, 1969; Meritorious Service Medal, 1995; US Army Command & Gen Staff Col, grad, 1980; US Army War Col, grad, 1997; 35th Infantry Div KS Nat Guard, staff judge advocate, 1983-89, state judge advocate gen, 1989-90, sr military judge, 1991-01. **Home Addr:** 7915 Walker Ave, Kansas City, KS 66112, **Home Phone:** (913)334-1879. **Business Addr:** District Court Judge, 29th Judicial Dist of Kansas, Wyandotte County Courthouse, 710 N 7th St, Kansas City, KS 66101, **Business Phone:** (913)573-2926.

MEEKS, GREGORY WELDON
Government official, legislator. **Personal:** Born Sep 25, 1953, New York, NY; son of James and Mary; married Simone-Marie, Jul 18, 1997; children: Ebony, Aja & Nia-Aiyana. **Educ:** Adelphi Univ, BA, 1975; Howard Univ, JD, 1978. **Career:** Queens Dist Atty Off, asst DA; Off Special Narcotics Prosecutor, asst prosecutor; State Investigation Comn, counr; NJS Workers Compensation Bd, supervising judge; New York State Assembly; US Congress, New York Sixth Cong Dist, rep, currently. **Orgs:** Alpha Phi Alpha; Nat Asn Advan Colored People; 100 Black Men; Nat Bar Asn; Meacon B Allen Black Bar Asn; New Democrats Caucus; Dem Leadership Coun. **Honors/Awds:** Thurgood Marshall Award, Howard Sch Law. **Business Addr:** US Congressman, US House of Representatives, 2342 Rayburn House Off Bldg, Washington, DC 20515, **Business Phone:** (202)225-3461.*

MEEKS, LARRY GILLETTE
Writer. **Personal:** Born Apr 11, 1944, Bakersfield, CA; son of Henrietta Meeks and Reuben Meeks; married Dinnie Jean Williams, Feb 6, 1966; children: Kimerley & Corey. **Educ:** Bakersfield Jr Col, AA, 1963; Univ Calif Davis, BS, 1970; Golden Gate Univ, MPA, 1973; Nat Univ, MA, 1995; Angeles Univ, Hons Docorate Humanity, 1989. **Career:** State Calif Office Health Planning & Develop, dir, 1983-92; Syndicated Columnist Ethnically Speaking, 1991-; Radio, talk show host, 1991-93; Los Rios Community Col, col prof, 1995-. **Orgs:** Bd mem, Univ Southern Calif, 1983-92; Natomas Sch Bd, 1985-00; bd mem, Golden Gate Univ 1989-; bd mem, Mercy Hosp Bd, 1992-94; Women Escaping a Violent Environ; Japanese Am Civil Liberties; League Women Voters; Prof Golden Gate Univ; Am Health Planers; chmn, Williams Memorial Church God Christ; life mem, Nat Urban League; NAACP. **Honors/Awds:** Certificate of Appreciation, Los Angeles County, 1990. **Military Serv:** AUS, 1st lt 1966-69; Army Cmndtn, Combat Inftrymn, Vietnam Serv Medals. **Home Phone:** (916)920-8203.

MEEKS, PERKER L., JR.
Judge, lawyer, educator. **Personal:** Born Aug 6, 1943, Tallahassee, FL; married Patricia E Evans MD; children: Perker III & Alicia Nicole. **Educ:** Fla A&M Univ, BS, 1965, JD, 1968. **Career:** Judge (retired); Gov State Fla, admin aide, 1968-69; San Francisco Sch Dist, teacher, 1970-72; San Francisco Pub Defender's Off, trial lawyer, 1972-80; San Francisco Munic Ct, judge, 2004-07. **Orgs:** Secy & bd mem, Charles Houston Bar Asn, 1977-80; pres & bd mem, OMI Comn Asn, 1970-80; bd mem, San Francisco Chap Nat Advan Asn Colored People, 1978-79. *

MEEKS, REGINALD KLINE
Government official. **Personal:** Born Mar 21, 1954, Louisville, KY; son of Florian and Eloise M; divorced; children: Nilaja Nurajehan. **Educ:** Wabash Col, BA, hist, 1976; Univ Iowa Col Law, JD, 1979; Univ Louisville, PhD. **Career:** Legal Aid Soc, community devel unit, 1981-82; Christian & Bynum Atty, law clerk, 1982-83; Bleidt, Barnett & Shanks Atty, law clerk, 1983-88; City Louisville, 11th ward alderman, 1982-; Jefferson County Pub Schs, Louisville KY, career developer, 1988-91; Univ Louisville, assoc dir admis, 1991-; Ky Legis, state rep, 2001-; Univ La, Col Arts & Sci, dir external prog; McKendree Col, instr. **Orgs:** Nat Black Caucus Local Elected Officials, 1982-; secy bd dirs, Seven Counties Servs, 1983-88; bd dirs, Stage One, Louisville Children's Theater, 1983-87; chmn, Shawnee Dist Old KY Home Coun Boy Scouts, 1984-87; Nat Asn Advan Colored People; Nat League Cities; KY Munic League; Nat Bar Asn; chmn, Mus Develop Comt KY African Am Mus, 1987-; bd dirs, Farm & Wilderness Camps Plymouth, VT, 1987-90; adv coun, Salvation Army Boy's & Girl's Clubs, 1987-; bd dirs, Neighborhood Housing Servs, 1991-; KY Polar Bear Club. **Honors/Awds:** Dean's List Wabash Col; Black Achievers Award, YMCA, 1983; Numerous local awards. **Special Achievements:** One of Fifty Young Future Leaders, Ebony Mag, 1983. **Home Addr:** 2301 Osage Ave, Louisville, KY 40210. **Business Addr:** State Representative, Kentucky Legislation, PO Box 757, Louisville, KY 40201, **Business Phone:** (502)564-8100 Ext 653.

MEEKS, STEPHEN ABAYOMI OBADELE
Educator, physician. **Personal:** Born Aug 31, 1958, Philadelphia, PA; son of Clyde R Meeks and Pearl A Moore; divorced; children: Oji K, Kumasi D O & Adeyemi O. **Educ:** Howard Univ, BS, 1982; Inst TCM NYC, dipl Acupuncture, 1986; Inst Int D'Acupuncture et Medecine Chinois, Doctor Acupuncture, 1988. **Career:** Pro Martial Arts, 1968-; Family Planning Coun, health educr, 1983-84; MIC-FPP, Inc, Health Educ, asst dir, 1984-89; prof musician, percussionist, vocalist, 1983-; prof speaker, health & cult confs, 1984-; Moyo Nguvu CAC, Inc, fed dir, 1990-97; Moyo Health Assoc Inc, pres, doctor Asian Med, 1988-. **Orgs:** Qamata Int Martial

Arts Asn, 1989-; Acupuncture Asn Colo, 1990-; Nat Black Child Develop, 1994-97; Denver Black United Fund, 1994-96; Nat Comn Cert Acupuncturist. **Honors/Awds:** Outstanding Young Man of the Year, NYC, 1987. **Special Achievements:** Music DRR, "Moyo Arts Ensemble," 1990-97; Ikhalipha: Black Belt 6th Degree, 1993; principal res/co-author, Am Pub Health Asn, published "The Role & Needs of the Male Partner in Reproductive Health Care: A Survey of Low Income, Inner City Males," 1985; Recorded "Afrikans in Amerika," as producer, writer, performer, 1996.

MEEKS, WILLIS GENE
Executive, vice president (organization). **Personal:** Born Jan 19, 1938, Harlan, KY; son of Maceo and Thelma; married Magalene Powell, Aug 3, 1991; children: Larry, Pamela Moore, Eric & Shauna. **Educ:** Hancock col, AA, 1964; Calif State Univ, BS, 1975, MBA, 1977. **Career:** Jet Propulsion Lab, Helios Proj engr, 1972-75, seasat chief, mission operations, 1975-78, mission operations mgr, 1978-83, Ulysess Project mgr, 1983; OAO Corp, Corp Strategic Planning, sr vpres. **Orgs:** Am Geophys Union, 1990-; Urban League; LA Sickle Cell Found; Nat Asn Advan Colored People; LA Coun Black Prof Engrs; Calif Tech Mgt Asn. **Honors/Awds:** EEO Medal, NASA, 1984; Outstanding Leadership Medal, 1992; dir, Europ Space Agency, 1990; Prof Award & Human Relations, City Pasadena, 1991; Commendation, County Los Angeles, 1991. **Military Serv:** USF, sgt, 1956-64.

MEGGETT, DAVE. See MEGGETT, DAVID LEE.

MEGGETT, DAVID LEE (DAVE MEGGETT)
Football coach, football player, executive. **Personal:** Born Apr 30, 1966, Charleston, SC; children: Davin. **Educ:** Morgan State Univ; Towson Univ. **Career:** Football player (retired), football coach, executive; NY Giants, running back, 1989-94; New Eng Patriots, 1995-97; NY Jets, running back, 1998; Am Int Col, asst coach; Robersonville, NC, parks & recreation dir. **Honors/Awds:** Walter Payton Award, 1988; Pro Bowl, 1989, 1996.

MEHLINGER, KERMIT THORPE. See Obituaries section.

MEHRETEAB, GHEBRE-SELASSIE
Executive. **Personal:** Born Jun 29, 1949, Asmara; married Sarah Brill Jones; children: Two Step Daughters. **Educ:** Haverford Col, BA 1972; Haverford Col, LLD, 2007. **Career:** Health & Welfare Coun, staff assoc 1972-73; E Mt Airy Neighbors, dir 1974-76; YMCA of Germantown, assoc dir 1976-78; New World Found, assoc dir 1978-81; The Ford Found, prog officer 1981-87; Nat Corp Housing Partnerships, vpres, pres, chief exec officer; NHP Found, pres, chief exec officer, exec vpres, 1987-. **Orgs:** JP Morgan Chase Community Adv Bd; Comsos Club; City Club; Sigma Pi Phi; Coun Foreign Rels; bd dir, Na Housing Conference and Douglas Emmett Inc. **Honors/Awds:** Citation Senate of Pennsylvania, 1979; Key to the City Savannah GA, 1987. **Business Addr:** Co-Chairman, Chief Executive Officer, The NHP Foundation, 1090 Vermont Ave NW Suite 400, Washington, DC 20005, **Business Phone:** (202)789-5300.

MELANCON, NORMAN
Educator. **Personal:** Born Nov 6, 1939, Paincourtville, LA; son of Alphage Melancon Sr and Alice; married Joyce Carr; children: Norman Jr, LaTisha & Marlon. **Educ:** Dillard Univ, BA, 1962; Nicholls State Univ, M.Ed, 1969; Loyola Univ, M.Sc, 1972. **Career:** Assumption Parish, asst prin, 1964-85; Ward 6, police juror, 1976-85; Belle Rose Primary & Middle Schs, asst prin, currently. **Orgs:** Sponsor 4-H Club; Boy Scout coordr; St Charles Bapt Ch Sunday Sch, supt. **Business Addr:** Assistant Principal, Belle Rose Middle School, 7177 Hwy 1, Belle Rose, LA 70341.*

MELENDEZ-RHINEHART, CARMEN M.
Real estate agent, teacher, chief executive officer. **Personal:** Born Jan 1, 0718?, Chicago, IL; daughter of Stanis S and Mae Hodge; married Vernon, Oct 1, 1983 (died 2002). **Educ:** Southern Ill Univ, BA, history, 1968; Nat Louis Univ, M.Ed, 1977. **Career:** Teacher (retired), real estate agent, chief executive officer; Chicago PubSchs, hist dept, chair; Oscar C. Brown Real Estate, real estate assoc,broker, 1974-85; State IL, real estate lic, assoc, 1974, broker, 1983;Melendez Realty Group Ltd, pres & chief exec officer, 1986-. **Orgs:** Phi Delta Kappa Fraternity, 1979; Dearborn Real Estate Bd, 1983; formersecy, Links Inc, Windy City Chap, 1986; Delta Sigma Theta Sorority,Chicago Alumnae Chap, 1986; Nat Smart Set Inc, Chicago Chap, 1987; ArtInst Chicago, 1993; pres, Nat Sorority Phi Delta Kappa, Mu Chap, Krinonclub, 1999; Harris Young Women Christian Asn; Mikva Challenge. **Honors/Awds:** Citizens Award, Mayor Harold Wash, City Chicago, 1984; Achievement Award,Delta Sigma Theta Sorority, 1991; Quality Teacher of the Year, TeslaAlternative Sch, 1997; Armonk Institute Scholar, 1999; Citizen Award,Young Women Christian Asn. **Special Achievements:** Japan Project, participant, Chicago Public Sch, 1995; Univ Mass, FiveCollege Center for Asian Studies, 1997; Rocky Mountain Project, Japan,Univ CO-Boulder, 1997.

MELL, PATRICIA
Educator. **Personal:** Born Dec 15, 1953, Cleveland, OH; daughter of Julian Cooper and Thelma Webb; married Michael Steven Ragland. **Educ:** Wellesley Col, BA, 1975; Case Western Reserve Univ Law Sch, JD, 1978. **Career:** Ohio Atty Gen Off, asst atty, 1975-82; Ohio Secy State Off, corp coun, 1982-84; Capital Univ Law Sch, Columbus Oh, 1984-86; Toledo Univ, Law Col, vis asst prof; Widener Univ Sch Law, DE, 1986-91; Lewis White & Clay; MichState Univ, Detroit Law Col, prof, 1996-98, assoc dean acad affaris, 1998-2001; Univ Memphis, Cecil C Humphreys Sch Law, vis prof, 2002; John Marshall Law Sch, dean, 2003-. **Honors/Awds:** International Associated Corps of Administrators, award, 1983; Crain's Chicago Business, Chicago's 100 Most Influential Women, 2004. **Special Achievements:** First woman and first African American dean in the John Marshall Law school; Auth: Criminal Law: Cases, Commentary and Questions, 2005. *

MELTON, BRYANT
State government official, manager. **Personal:** Born May 9, 1940, Marion, AL; son of Bryant Melton Sr and Bertha Dobyne; married Emma Jean Holmes, 1962; children: Tony, Delisa & Emily. **Educ:** Ala A&M Univ, 1958; Stillman Col, Tuscaloosa, AL, BS, 1965; Univ Ala, 1968. **Career:** US Post Off, Tuscaloosa, AL, postman, 1965-69; Hale Co Bd Educ, Greensboro, AL, teacher, 1969-72; Protective Ins Co, Tuscaloosa, AL, mgr, 1972-75; BF Goodrich, quality control mgr, 1976; Ala State House Reps, state rep. **Orgs:** Nat Asn Advan Colored People, Tuscaloosa Co Chap; Boy Scouts; Stillman Col Alumni Asn; Alpha Phi Alpha; Masons. **Honors/Awds:** Man of the Year & Charlie Green Award, Alpha Phi Alpha, 1977; Man of the Year, Nat Asn Advan Colored People, 1978. **Military Serv:** AUS, Sgt, 1960-63; USAR.

MELTON, FRANK E
Executive. **Personal:** Children: Matthew & Lauren. **Educ:** Stephen F Austin State Univ Tex, BS, Educ. **Career:** Tex Dept Ment Health & Ment Retardation, 1969-74; Angelina Col Lufkin Tex, part-time teacher, 1974-85; KTRE-TV Lufkin, weekend news anchor, 1974; KLTV-TV Tyler Tex, exec vpres & gen mgr, 1976-81; WLBT-TV-3 Inc, Jackson Miss, chief exec officer, 1984-2002; TV-3 Found, Jackson, chmn & ceo, currently; City Jackson, Miss, mayor, currently; Jackson State Univ, Sch Bus, Mass Commun Dept, vol instr, swimming instr; Tougaloo Col, guest lectr; Millsaps Col, guest lectr; Belhaven Col, guest lectr; Miss Col, guest lectr. **Orgs:** Pres, Broadcast Div, Buford TV Inc Tyler; Gov Mark White; Tex Bd Ment Health & Ment Retardation, 1985; dir, Miss Bur Narcotics, 2002; chmn, Criminal Justice Task Force; bd dir, Miss State Dept Educ; nat bd dir, Broadcast Music Indust; bd dir, Liberty Broadcasting; bd dir, Wave; bd dir, Miss Dept Human Serv; chmn, Miss Dept Youth Serv. **Honors/Awds:** Distinguished Leadership Award, Univ Miss; Distinguished Alumnus Award, Stephen F Austin State Univ. **Business Addr:** Mayor, City of Jackson, 219 S Pres St, PO Box 17, Jackson, MS 39205-0017, **Business Phone:** (601)960-1084.

MENCER, DR. ERNEST JAMES
Surgeon. **Personal:** Born Apr 24, 1945, Baton Rouge, LA; son of George E Jr and Maudra E; married Thomasine Haskins; children: Melanie Lynn, Marcus Kinnard. **Educ:** Morehouse Col, BS, 1967; Meharry Med Col, MD, 1972; Am Bd Surgery, dipl, 1983. **Career:** Our Lady Lake Regional Med Ctr, chief surgery, 1983; Earl K Long Hosp LSU Med Sch, asst prof surgery; Baton Rouge Gen Med Ctr, vchief surgery; pvt practice, gen surgeon, currently. **Orgs:** bd dir, Baton Rouge Gen Med Ctr; fellow, Am Col Surgeons, 1985; bd dir, E Baton Rouge Parish Am Cancer Soc. **Business Addr:** Physician, 7777 Hennessy Blvd Suite 306, Baton Rouge, LA 70808, **Business Phone:** (225)769-1300.*

MENDENHALL, JOHN RUFUS
Football player. **Personal:** Born Dec 3, 1948, Cullen, LA. **Educ:** Grambling Col. **Career:** Green Bay Packers, prof football player; New York Giants, football player, 1972-79; Detroit Lions, 1980.

MENDES, DR. DONNA M
Surgeon. **Personal:** Born Oct 25, 1951, Oceanside, NY; daughter of Benjamin and Bernice Smith; married Ronald E LaMotte, May 4, 1986. **Educ:** Hofstra Univ, Hempstead, NY, BA, 1973; Columbia Univ, Col Physicians & Surgeons, NY, MD, 1977. **Career:** Self-employed surgeon, 1984-; Columbia Univ, clin asst prof, 1990-93; St Luke's Hosp, chief vascular surg, 1993-98; North Gen Hosp, chief vascular surg, 2002-05; St Luke's-Roosevelt Hosp Ctr, fac, 2003-. **Orgs:** Peripheral Vascular Surg Soc, 1984-; Manhattan Chapter NMA, 1986-; Peripheral Surg Soc, 1986-; NY County Med Soc, 1986-2004; Soc Clin Vascular Surg, 1986-; Am Col Surgeons, 1987-; adv bd mem, Urban League, 1988-91; Am Med Women's Asn, 1988-; NY Cardiovasc Soc, 1989-; Susan Smith McKinney, 1989-91; adv panel, Vascular Surg, Am Bd Surg; Am Asn Vascular Surgeons, 1992-2003; Soc Clin Vascular Surgeons 1992-; Int Soc Endovascular Surgery, 1993-; Asn Black Cardiologists, 1998-2005; Soc Black Acad Surgeons, 1999-; Am Bd Vascular Surg; Leukemia & Lymphoma Soc, 2002-; chair minority comt, Soc Vascular Surgeons; Soc Vascular Surgeons 2003-; Bergen County Urban League, 2005-. **Honors/Awds:** Outstanding Women of the Year, 1990; Teacher of the Year Award, St Luke's-Roosevelt Hosp Ctr Dept of Surgery, 1992; Student Nat Med Asn Award, 1995; Phenomenal Woman, KISS/FM, 2005; Hofstra University Alumnus of the Year 2005. **Special Achievements:** 1st board certified black female vascular surgeon in USA. **Business Addr:** Vascular Surgeon, St. Luke's Roosevelt Hospital Center, 1090 Amsterdam Ave, New York, NY 10025, **Business Phone:** (212)636-4990.

MENDES, DR. HELEN ALTHIA
President (organization), social worker, consultant. **Personal:** Born May 20, 1935, New York, NY; daughter of Arthur Davenport and Louise Davenport; married Gregory R Love, Dec 20, 1980; children: Sheila & Leon. **Educ:** Queens Col, BA Music, 1957; Columbia Univ, MSW, 1964; Univ Calif, Los Angeles,CA, DSW, 1975; Fuller Theol Sem, 1989. **Career:** Jewish Family Serv, social worker, 1964-67; Big Brothers Res Treatment Ctr, acting dir 1967-69; Albert Einstein Col Med, ment health consult,1969; Hunter Col Sch Soc Work, lectr, 1970-72; UCLA, assoc, 1972-75; Univ Southern Calif, assoc prof, 1975-86; Mendes Consult Serv, founder & pres, 1976-; Pepperdine Univ, social work minor prog, dir, 2001- 05. **Orgs:** Chairperson, Pastor Parish Rels Comt Wilshire UM Church, 1981-87; Alt Pvt Indus Coun LA, 1984-86; Distrib Success Motivation Inst, 1985-89; bd dir, Jenesse Ctr Inc, 1985-86; Nat Assoc Black Soc Workers; Black Womens Network; mem bd dir, House Ruth, 1985-89; vpres, Prof Develop NASW, CA,1986-88; vpres NASW, CA, 1988-90; bd dirs, SISCA; Hollygrove Children'sHome, 1987-2004, vpres, 2000-04; bd dirs, W Angeles Church God Christ;Acad Certified Soc Workers; Nat Asn Soc Workers. **Honors/Awds:** Outstanding Service Award, LA Community Col, 1974; Outstanding Educator,Zeta Phi Beta Sor Altadena Pasadena Chap, 1985; Diplomate in Clin Social Work; Award of Merit for Outstanding Service, USC Sch Social Work, 1986; Women of Religious Achievement Award, 1995; Zeta Phi Beta Sorority Woman of the Year Award; Outstanding People of the Twentieth Century, Whos Who Among Black Americans. **Special Achievements:** Publ: Stress Management; The Africian Heritage Cookbook, MacMillan Publ Prof Jour, 1971; "Single Parent Families", Religion/Therapy, Black Families 1976-; God's Stress Management Plan, Vicstone Publishing Co,2004. Bd Certified Diplomate. **Business Addr:** President, Mendes Consultation Services, 3660 Wilshire Blvd Suite 907, Los Angeles, CA 90010, **Business Phone:** (213)388-6668.

MENDEZ, HUGH B.
Athletic coach, educator. **Personal:** Born Dec 16, 1933, E Orange, NJ; married Dorothy L; children: Robert Hugh. **Educ:** Springfield Col, BS, 1958; Whittier Col, MEd, 1975; Newark St Col; Montclair St Col; CA St Col; UCLA. **Career:** Whittier Col CA, instr afro-Am history & varsity baseball coach; Milwaukee Braves Baseball Asn, 1958-60; Long Br NJ, supvr elem phys educ, 1960-66; Long Beach, teacher baseball coach, 1968-70. **Orgs:** Capt Springfield Col Baseball Team, 1958. **Honors/Awds:** Led NCAA in stolen bases; signed bonus contract with Milwaukee Braves, 1958. **Special Achievements:** First black coach maj sport Whittier College. **Military Serv:** USN.

MENDOZA, GRACE. See JONES, GRACE.

MENEFEE, JUAN F.
Executive, consultant. **Personal:** Born Jan 24, 1961, Chillicothe, OH. **Educ:** Univ Cincinnati, BBA, 1984. **Career:** Procter & Gamble, sales mgt; Johnson & Johnson, mgr; Frito Lay, regional sales mgr; Juan Menefee & Assocs, founder & pres, 1988-. **Orgs:** Omega Psi Phi Frat; Nat Black MBA Asn; pres, Nat Asn Black Sales Prof. **Business Phone:** (708)848-7722.

MENKITI, BO
Real estate developer. **Career:** The Menkiti Group, Founder & CEO, 2008. **Business Addr:** Founder, Chief Executive Officer, Menkiti Group, 2701 12th St NE, Washington, DC 20018.*

MENOGAN, ANNITA M
Executive, lawyer, vice president (organization). **Educ:** Acad Art Col, BFA; Univ Denver, JD. **Career:** Pvt pract law, 1983-99; Coors Brewing Co, vpres, secy & gen coun, 1999-2005; Red Robin Intl Inc, vpres, chief legal officer & secy, 2006-. **Orgs:** Colo Lawyer Trust Acct Found; Colo Bar Asn. **Business Addr:** Vice President, Chief Legal Officer & Secretary, Red Robin International Inc, 8585 E Arapahoe Rd, Greenwood Village, CO 80112, **Business Phone:** (303)771-3350.

MENSAH, E. KWAKU
Executive, president (organization). **Personal:** Born Nov 1, 1945, Accra, Ghana; son of Mensah Amuzu and Bertha Mensah-Amuzu; married Linda May Mensah, Jul 27, 1974; children: Sidney, Sylvester, Tonyo, Asanvi, Delali. **Educ:** St Joseph's Univ, Philadelphia, PA, BS, bus admin, 1974. **Career:** Hilton Hotels Corp, comptroller, area dir finance, 1979-; Gold Coast Financial Corp, pres, currently. **Honors/Awds:** Career Achievement Award, Hilton Hotels Corp. **Business Addr:** President, Gold Coast Financial Corporation, 14919 Carry Back Dr, North Potomac, MD 20878-3712, **Business Phone:** (301)990-2600.*

MENZIES, DR. BARBARA A
Physician. **Personal:** Born Oct 24, 1950, Memphis, TN; daughter of Simon Ledbetter; divorced; children: Simone Benai Williams. **Educ:** Mich State Univ, BS, 1972; Wayne State Univ, MS, 1974, Med Sch, MD, 1978; Univ Wisconsin-Madison, MS, 1996.

Career: Self-employed, physician, currently; Harper Hosp, chief int med; Blue Cross Blue Shield Mich, med dir, currently. **Special Achievements:** Took part in the American College of Physician's Executive Delegation visit to China; Representative of the People to People International Ambassador program. **Home Addr:** PO Box 04390, Detroit, MI 48204, **Home Phone:** (313)896-0935. **Business Addr:** Medical Director, Blue Cross Blue Shield of Michigan, 600 E Lafayette Blvd Suite 2022, Detroit, MI 48226, **Business Phone:** (313)225-0452.

MERCADO-VALDES, FRANK MARCELINO
Executive, president (organization), founder (originator). **Personal:** Born May 18, 1962, New York, NY; son of Frank Mercado and Lidia Valdes. **Educ:** Miami-Dade Col, AA, 1983; Univ Miami, BA, 1985. **Career:** Bush Quayle, media asst, 1988; Alto-Marc Commun, African Heritage Movie Network, pres, 1985, founder. **Orgs:** Kappa Alpha Psi Fraternity, 1983-; Golden Gloves Fla Benefit Comn, 1987; Kappa Alpha Psi Scholar Found, 1989-92; Dancer's Alliance; African-Am Anti-Defamation Asn, 1991-; African-Am Film & Tv Asn; Nat Asn Tv Prog Exec. **Honors/Awds:** Golden Gloves Lightweight Champion Fla, 1979; Jr Olympic Boxing Champion Fla, 1978. **Special Achievements:** Quarter finalist 1980 Olympic trials, lightweight; Urban Profile "Under Thirty Entrepreneur of Excellence Award"; creator of Miss Collegiate African-Am Pageant/Creator of "Stomp" tv spec; youngest black exec producer in tv hist. **Military Serv:** USMC, corporal, 1980-82. **Home Addr:** 10 W 135 St Suite 6T, New York, NY 10037, **Home Phone:** (212)281-1141.

MERCER, ARTHUR, SR. See Obituaries section.

MERCER, RONALD EUGENE
Basketball player. **Personal:** Born May 18, 1976, Nashville, TN. **Educ:** Univ Ky, attended 1999. **Career:** Basketball player (retired); Boston Celtics, 1997-99; Denver Nuggets, guard, 1999-00; Orlando Magic, 2000; chicago bulls, 2001-02; Indiana Pacers, guard, 2002-03; San Antonio Spurs, guard,2003-04; New Jersey Nets, guard, 2004-05. *

MERCER, VALERIE JUNE
Curator. **Personal:** Born Jun 5, 1947, Philadelphia, PA; daughter of William J and Helen Kono. **Educ:** Sch Visual Arts, New York, NY, attended 1974; NY Univ, NY, BA, art hist, 1979; Harvard Univ, Cambridge, MA, art hist, 1982. **Career:** Harvard Univ fel, 1982-86; Studio Museum, Harlem, sr curator, 1992-99; NY Times, New York, NY, freelance art writer, 1988-91; The Brooklyn Paper, Brooklyn, NY, freelance art writer, 1990-91; Am Visions, New York, NY, Wash, DC, 1991; Detroit Inst Art, cur African Am art & head Gen Motors Ctr African Am Art, 2001-. **Orgs:** Nat Asn Black Journalists, 1989-; Col Art Asn, 1985-. **Honors/Awds:** Woman of the Year Award, NY Asn Prof Black Women, 1996. **Special Achievements:** First curator of the African American art. **Business Addr:** Curator of African American Art, The Detroit Institute of Arts, 5200 Woodward Ave, Detroit, MI 48202, **Business Phone:** (313)833-4249.

MERCER-PRYOR, DIANA
Executive director. **Personal:** Born Dec 4, 1950, Detroit, MI; daughter of Elisha and Dessie Hogan; married Donald Pryor; children: Eleasha De Ann Mercer, Jason Thomas Mercer. **Educ:** Univ Mich, Ann Arbor, BBA, 1972; Univ Detroit, Detroit, MI, MBA, finance, 1975. **Career:** Executive director (retired); Chrysler Corp, Highland Park, Mich, gen purchasing agt, 1972; DaimlerChrysler African Am Network, bd mem; Chrysler Corp, dir. **Orgs:** Bd mem, Univ Detroit Alumni Bd, 1989; assoc bd mem, Franklin Wright Settlement Bd, 1989; past mem, Detroit Urban League; Alpha Kappa Alpha Sorority Inc; Faith Christian Ctr. **Honors/Awds:** YMCA Achievement Award, YMCA, 1988; Americas Top Black Business & Professional Women, Dollars & Sense Mag, 1988; 100 Most Promising Black Women in America, Ebony Mag, 1990, 1991; High Profile Style, Essence Mag, 1991; Women of Color Technol Corp Responsibility Award; Bus Assoc Award, Am Bus Women's Assn; Corp Female Trailblazer Award; Procurement Award. **Special Achievements:** The first African-Am woman to become a director at DaimlerChrysler; TV appearance: "Success Through Education", ABC.

MERCHANT, JAMES S, JR.
Executive. **Personal:** Born Apr 28, 1954, Clarksburg, WV; son of Millie A and James S; married Joyce A Walton, Sep 27, 1975; children: Linel, Shelita & Ebony. **Educ:** WVa Univ, BS, bus admin, 1976. **Career:** Bob Evans Farms Inc, mgr trainee, 1977-78, from second asst mgr to first asst mgr, 1978-79, gen mgr, 1979-83, area dir, 1983-94, vpres & regional dir, restaurant operations, 1994, sr vpres restaurant operations, currently. **Orgs:** Omega Psi Phi, 1974-; adv bd, Touchston Cafe, 1988-. **Honors/Awds:** Cent Zone Mgr of the Year, Bob Evans Farms Inc, 1982; King Year, WV Black Heritage Festival, 2006. **Special Achievements:** Blue Chip Award, nominated, 1991. **Business Addr:** Senior Vice President, Bob Evans Farms Inc, 3776 S High St, Columbus, OH 43207, **Business Phone:** (614)491-2225.

MERCHANT, JOHN CRUSE
Lawyer. **Personal:** Born Apr 1, 1957, Lexington, KY; son of John and Thelma; married Debra Spotts, Aug 15, 1981; children: Leah Cruse. **Educ:** Morehead State Univ, BA, 1979; Univ Ky, JD, 1982. **Career:** Shirley A Cunningham, law assoc, 1982-83; Off Lt Gov, admin asst, 1983-87; Wilkinson Govr Campaign, staff worker, 1987; Off Legal Serv, finance cabinet, staff atty, 1988-91; Peck, Shaffer & Williams, assoc, 1991-94, partner, 1994-. **Orgs:** Ky Bar Asn, 1982-; Nat Bar Asn, 1985-. Nat Asn Securities Pressionals, 1991-; Cincinnati Bar Asn, 1991-; Nat Forum Black Pub Adminrs, 1985-; Black Male Coalition, 1992-; exec bd, Jr Achievement Cincinnati, 1992-; mentor, Cincinnati Youth Collaborative, 1992-; Ohio Bar Asn, 1992-. **Honors/Awds:** Alumni Award, Morehead State Univ, 1989; Black Business Award, Quinn Chapel AME Church, 1995. **Home Addr:** 4156 Allenhurst Close, Cincinnati, OH 45241, **Home Phone:** (513)769-5088. **Business Addr:** Partner, Peck, Shaffer & Williams LLP, 201 E 5th St Suite 900, Cincinnati, OH 45202, **Business Phone:** (513)639-9224.

MERCHANT, JOHN F
Lawyer. **Personal:** Born Feb 2, 1933, Greenwich, CT; son of Essie L Nowlin and Garrett M; divorced; children: Susan Beth. **Educ:** Va Union Univ, BA, 1955; Univ Va, LLB, 1958. **Career:** State Conn, atty, 1962-; ABCD Inc, dep dir, 1965-67; State Dept Community Affairs, dep comnr, 1967-71; Fairfield Univ, vis lectr, 1970-75; Gen Elec Corp & Candeub Fleissig Asn, consult; Peoples Bank, dir, mem loan & Trust Comt, 1969-; Consumer Coun, State Conn, 1991-96; Nat Minority Golf Found Inc, pres, chief exec officer, 1996; Jomer & Asn, partner, 1998. **Orgs:** Trustee, Univ Bridgeport; partner, Merchant & Rosenblum Attorneys Law; Nat Asn Advan Colored People; pres, Child Guidance Clin; dir, Regional Plan Asn; pres, Hartcom Inc; chmn, Conn Coun Human Rights, 1964-65; pres, Brideport Area Ment Health Asn, 1968; dir, Bridgeport Hosp 1968-79; dir, Child Welfare League Am, chmn, Public Policy Comt, 1986-92, pres, 1993-96; trustee, St Vincent's Col Nursing; trustee, Fairfield Univ. **Honors/Awds:** First black graduate, Univ Va Law Sch, 1958; Citizen of the Year, Omega Psi Phi, 1983; Community Service Award, Sacred Heart Univ, 1982; First black member, US Golf Asn Exec Comt; Tree of Life Award, Jewish Nat Fund; First Black President, Child Welfare League Am Inc. **Military Serv:** USN, lt comdr, 1958-61. **Home Addr:** 289 Agawam Dr, Stratford, CT 06614, **Home Phone:** (203)386-1480. **Business Addr:** Attorney General, State of Connecticut, Office of the Attorney General, 490 Riders Lane, Fairfield, CT 06430, **Business Phone:** (860)808-5318.

MEREDAY, RICHARD F.
Government official. **Personal:** Born Dec 18, 1929, Hempstead, NY; son of Charles Mereday and Melta; married Emma (divorced); children: Philip, Richard & Meta. **Educ:** Hofstra Univ, BA, 1951; Brooklyn Law Sch, LLB, 1958. **Career:** Government official(retired); Charles Mereday Trucking Corp, v pres; Tri County Truck Owners Assn, sec scribe, 1956-63; licensed NY Ins Broker,1961; Town Hemp stead, probation officer supvr, 1964-65; Dept Pub Works, admin, 1965-70; Nassau County, Bur Career Planning & Develop, Dep Gen Servs, former dir, 1971-75; Off Manpower Progs, cord educ serv, nassau county govt, 1975-02; Nassau County Met Regional Coun TV classes, speaker; Nassau County, Off Affil Action, exec dir. **Orgs:** Rep exec, Town Leader; former vpres, Uptopia Comm Civic Assn; past chmn, Roosevelt United Fund; former inst rep, Natl Boy Scouts Coun; past pres, Lions Club; adv brd, Salvation Army. **Honors/Awds:** Plaque Unselfish Service to the Community of Roosevelt, 1969; Recipient good neighbor award, Nassau County Press Assn, 1973; recognition cert, Dist 20 K 2 Lions Intl, 1973; active participant, Rep Leadership Conf, 1975. **Military Serv:** USN, med corps, 1951-53. *

MERENIVITCH, JARROW
Executive. **Personal:** Born Jun 1, 1942, Alexandria, LA; son of Audrey Merenivitch Sr and Georgia N Merenivitch; married Hazel R Wilmer; children: Jarrow Jr, Marion E & Jonathan R. **Educ:** Grambling State Univ, BA, polit sci, 1964; Inst Appl Mgt & Law, cert, 1985. **Career:** Grambling State Univ, stud govt pres, 1963, 1964, alumni pres; Procter & Gamble Co, Green Bay, WI, team mgr, 1969-72, Albany, GA, plant personnel relations mgr, 1972-75, Cincinnati corp personnel develop consult, 1975-78, employee/employer relations mgr, 1978-80, personnel mgr, Macon, GA Plant, 1980-83, mgr industrial relations, 1983-85, food mfg div human resources mgr, 1985-90, assoc dir, food & beverage personnel sector, 1990-93; Human Resources Customer Serv, Global, assoc dir, 1993-2001; Creative Marketing Consult, LLC, pres, chief exec officer, currently; Visions Inc, bd mem, currently. **Orgs:** Vpres, Grambling Univ Alumni, 1990; Omega Psi Phi Fraternity; Nat Asn Advan Colored People; bd dir, Quinn Chapel AMG Church. **Honors/Awds:** Outstanding Service, Eta Omicron Chap, Psi Phi Omega, 1975; publication: "Toward a Multicultural Organization," 1979; Citation Outstanding Contribution to Procter & Gamble Beverage Div, 1984; John Feldmann Diversity Leadership Award, 1988; Outstanding Contribution to Food PSS in the Diversity Area, 1989; Rosa Parks Award, Leadership Diversity & Multiculturalism; Diversity Planning Initiative Award, 1996; Diversity Globe Award, 1996. **Military Serv:** USAF, staff sgt, 1964-68. **Home Addr:** 1817 Forester Dr, Cincinnati, OH 45240. **Business Addr:** Board Member, VISIONS Inc, 48 Juniper St, Roxbury, MA 02119.

MERIDETH, CHARLES WAYMOND
Educator. **Personal:** Born Nov 2, 1940, Atlanta, GA; son of Charlie Merideth and Ruth Wilson Merideth; married Rebecca Little; children: Kelli & Cheryl. **Educ:** Morehouse Col, BS, 1961; Univ Calif, Berkeley, PhD, phys chem, 1965. **Career:** Educator (retired); Lockheed Georgia Co, res scientist; Univ Ill, fel, 1956-66; Morehouse Col, prof, 1965; Atlanta Univ, dir eng, 1969, provost, 1976, chancellor, 1978-90; Harvard Univ Inst Educ Mgt; New York City Tech Col, pres, 1990-96; sci consult, NSF; sci consult, NIH; sci consult, Jet Propulsion Lab. **Orgs:** Phi Beta Kappa; Soc Sigma Xi; Beta Kappa Chi Sci Soc; Am Chem Soc; Am Phys Soc; AAAS; NY Acad Sci; bd dir, Blayton Bus Col, 1971; vpres, 100 Black Men Atlanta Inc, 1988-90; mem, President Jimmy Carter s Sci Advisory Comt; mem, Comt Minorities, Nat Acad Eng. **Honors/Awds:** Woodrow Wilson National fel, 1961; Charles E Merrill Early Admission Scholar, Magna Cum Laude, 1961; Danforth Fac Asn 167; Fresman Achievement Award Chem, 1957. **Special Achievements:** Noted as one of the top ten Outstanding Young People of Atlanta by TOYPAin 1956. **Home Phone:** (212)486-2455.

MERIDITH, DENISE PATRICIA
Consultant, executive. **Personal:** Born Apr 14, 1952, Brooklyn, NY; daughter of Glenarva and Dorothy Sawyer. **Educ:** Cornell Univ, Ithaca, NY, BS, 1973; USC, Sacramento, Calif, MPA, 1993. **Career:** Bur Land Mgt, Las Vegas, Nev, wildlife bio & env spec, 1973-77, SilverSpring, Md, environ spec, 1977-79, Wash, DC, wild life biologist, 1979-80, Alexandria, Va, deputy state dir, 1980-86, Santa Fe, NM, deputy state dir,1986-89, Sacramento, Calif, assoc state dir, 1989-91, Alexandria, Va, state dir, 1991-93, deputy dir, Wash, DC, 1993-95, Ariz state dir, 1995-2002; Denise Meridith Consults Inc, pres & chief exec officer, currently. **Orgs:** Bd dir, Ariz Cactus-Pine Coun Girl Scouts, 1996-2002; bd dir, Ariz Black, 1996-; pres, Phoenix Federal Exec Assoc, 1996; Bd, Soc Air Foresters, Forest Sci & Technol, 1998-2001; bd trustees, Cornell Univ, 2000-; ceo, The Leadership Consortium; mem, Girl Scouts (AZ Cactus Pine Coun Board); mem, The Society for Am Foresters, Partners Outdoors. **Honors/Awds:** Meritorious Award, Dept Interior, 1987; Senior Executive Service Cert, 1990; BLM Legend Award, 2002. **Business Addr:** President, Chief Executive Officer, Denise Meridith Consults Inc, 5515 N 7th St Suite 5, Phoenix, AZ 85014, **Business Phone:** (602)763-9900.

MERIWEATHER, MELVIN, JR.
Government official. **Personal:** Born Oct 22, 1937, Hernando, MS; son of Melvin and Virgie; married Juliet Ilene Thomas; children: Kristel, Douglas & Dana. **Educ:** Isaac E Elston, grad 12th, 1957. **Career:** Riley Sch PTA, pres, 1968-79; Eastport Improv Asn, pres, 1971-73; Mich City PTA Coun, pres, 1974-75; N Cent Comn Action Aency, pres, 1979-84; Mich City Sch Bd, pres; Mich City Area Sch, bd pres, 1987-88; secy, 1988-89; Midwest Steel, Portage IN, crew coordr, 1989; Mr. America contest. **Orgs:** Treas & deacon New Hope Baptist Church, 1963-85; parents adv bd, Rogers HS, 1978-79; health & safety chmn, 1980-82, 2nd vpres, 1982-84; Ind Cong Parents & Teachers; Daniel C Slocum Mem Found, 1982-85; vol fireman, Fire Brigade Midwest Steel, 1970-85; Ind Dept Educ "Parent/Community Involvement" task force. **Honors/Awds:** Mr Ind, Ind AAU Amateur Body building, 1966; Mr Most Muscular, AAU Mid States Competition, 1966; state life mem, Ind Cong PTA, 1974; vpres, Mich City Area Sch Bd, 1982-86; Sch Bd Pres, 1986-87; cert merit, Ind Dept Educ. **Home Addr:** 616 Monroe St, Michigan City, IN 46360. *

MERIWETHER, LOUISE
Writer, educator. **Personal:** Born May 8, 1923, Haverstraw, NY; daughter of Lloyd and Julia Golphin; married Earl Howe; married Angelo (divorced). **Educ:** NY Univ, BA, eng; Univ Calif, Los Angeles, MS, jour, 1965. **Career:** Los Angeles Sentinel, Los Angeles, CA, newspaperwoman, 1961-64; Universal Studios, N Hollywood, CA, story analyst, 1965-67; City Col, New York, NY, Black studies teacher, 1979; Sarah Lawrence Col, Bronxville, NY, creative writing teacher undergrad & grad, 1979-88; Univ Houston, Houston, TX, creative writing teacher undergrads & grads, 1985; Author: Daddy Was A Number Runner, 1970; The Freedom Ship of Robert Small, 1971; The Heart Man: The Story of Daniel Hale Williams, 1972; Don't Ride the Bus on Monday: The Rosa Parks Story, 1973; Fragments of the ARK, 1994; Daddy Was a Number Runner, 2002; Shadow Dancing, 2000; Incidents in the Life of a Slave Girl : The Givens Collection Classics, 2003; Contributor in: Black Review No 2, Morrow, 1972; Black-Eyed Susans, Anchor Press, 1975, confirmation: An Anthology of African-American Women, Morrow, 1983; Daughters of Africa, Pantheon, 1992; Shadow Dancing, 2000; Incidents in the Life of a Slave Girl, 2003; freelance writer, currently. **Orgs:** PEN. **Honors/Awds:** Fiction Grant, Rabinowitz Found, 1968; Fiction Grant, NY State Found Arts,1973, 1977, 1992, 1996; Fiction Grant, Nat Endowment Arts, 1973; Mellon Research Grant, Sarah Lawrence Col, 1983. **Business Addr:** Author, Ellen Levine Literary Agency, 15 E 26th St Suite 1801, New York, NY 10010, **Business Phone:** (212)725-4501.

MERIWETHER, ROY DENNIS
Pianist, composer, music arranger or orchestrator. **Personal:** Born Feb 24, 1943, Dayton, OH; children: Tammi & Cyd. **Career:** Columbia-Capitol-Gambit-Stinger-Faharenheit Rec Co, pianist, composer & rec artist, 1966; Howard Roberts Chorale & Dayton Contemp Dance Co, Composer & arranger, 1976; Dayton Philharmonic Orchestra, guest artist, 1980; Thomas A Edison St

Col, composer lyricist col alma mater, 1984; Gemini Rec, producer, arranger, composer & rec artist, 1985; Albums: Live!4 Queens; Twilight Blues; This One's On Me; Opening Night; Soup and Onions; Popcorn and Soul; The Stone Truth; Soul Knight; Jesus Christ Superstar; Nubian Lady. **Orgs:** Am Fedn Musicians Local 802, 1966-; Am Soc Composers, Authors & Publishers, 1966-. **Honors/Awds:** Jazz Composition Fellowship Grant, Nat Endowment Arts, 1973; proclamation to honor Black Snow, Mayor, City Dayton, OH, 1976; Significant Achievement Award, Black Snow Powell & Assocs, 1976; Outstanding Jazz Instrumentalist, Manhattan Asn Cabarets, 1987; Lifetime Achievement honoree, Dayton Ohio Music Award, 1999; Man of the Year Award, Thessolonian Missionary Baptist Church, 1999; Jazz Community Award, Jamaica Queens, NY; Lifetime Achievement to Music Award. **Special Achievements:** Nominated for a Grammy Award. **Home Addr:** 7 W 87th St Suite 4D, New York, NY 10024. *

MERKERSON, SHARON EPATHA
Actor. **Personal:** Born Nov 28, 1952, Detroit, MI; daughter of Ann Merkerson; married Toussaint L Jones, Jan 1, 1994. **Educ:** Wayne State Univ, BFA. **Career:** Broadway plays: The Piano Lesson; I'm Not Stupid; Three Ways Home; films: She's Gotta Have It, 1986; Navy Seals, 1990; Loose Cannons, 1990; Jacob'sLadder, 1990; Terminator 2, 1991; Random Hearts, 1999; Law & Order: Deadon the Money, voice, 2002; The Rising Place, 2003; Law & Order II: Double or Nothing, voice, 2003; Radio, 2003; Jersey Girl, 2004; Black Snake Moan, 2006; Slipstream, 2007; TV movies: Christmas Special, 1988; Moe's World, 1990; Equal Justice, 1990; It's Nothing Personal, 1993; A Place for Annie, 1994; A Mother's Prayer, 1995; Breaking Through, 1996; An Unexpected Life, 1998; Exiled, 1998; A Girl Thing, 2001; The Rising Place, 2001; Inside TV Land: Cops on Camera, 2002; Lackawanna Blues, 2005; Girl, Positive, 2007; TV series: "Pee-wee's Playhouse", 1987; "The Cosby Show", 1988; "The More You Know", 1989; "CBS Summer Playhouse", 1989; "The 44th Annual Tony Awards", 1990; "Here and Now", 1992; "Mann and Machine", 1992; "Here and Now", 1992; "ABC Afterschool Specials", 1992; "South Beach", 1993; "Law & Order", 1993; "Fifth Annual Screen Actors Guild Awards", 1999; "Late Night with Conan O'Brien", 1999; "Larry King Live", 2000; "Frasier", 2000;"Hollywood Squares", 2001; "Law & Order: Criminal Intent", 2002; "Life & Style", 2005; "The WIN Awards", 2005; "Ellen: The Ellen DeGeneres Show", 2005-06; "Tavis Smiley", 2005-07; "Law & Order: Trial by Jury", 2005; "The Sixty third Annual Golden Globe Awards", 2006; "Live with Regis and Kathie Lee", 2006; "2006 Independent Spirit Awards", 2006; "Inside the Actors Studio",2006; "The Sixtyth Annual Tony Awards", 2006; "Comic Relief 2006", 2006; "The View", 2007; "The Late Late Show with Craig Ferguson", 2007; "The Closer", 2007. **Honors/Awds:** Obie Award, 1992; Helen Hayes Award, 1999; Regulus Award, 2002; Emmy Award, 2005; SunDeis Film Festival at Brandeis University Entertainer of the Year Award, 2006; Screen Actors Guild Award, 2006; PRISM Award, 2006; Obie Award, 2006; NAACP Image Award, 2006; Gracie Allen Award, 2006; Golden Globe Award, 2006; Black Reel Award, 2006. **Special Achievements:** Nominations for many awards including Tony Award Nomination, Drama Desk Award, Vision Award etc. *

MERRICK-FAIRWEATHER, NORMA. See SKLAREK, NORMA MERRICK.

MERRITT, ANTHONY LEWIS
Automotive executive. **Personal:** Born Sep 15, 1940, New Haven, CT; son of Bernadine Merritt; married Ann Sarver; children: Eric & Heather. **Educ:** Dodge City Jr Col, AA, 1958; Westminister Col, BS, 1964; Univ Utah, MBAh 1966; Univ Detroit, Post, MBA, 1968-70. **Career:** Pomona Unified Sch Dist, biol & bus teacher, 1966-67; Ford Motor Co, numerous mgt assignments, 1968-77, reg sales planning & distrib, 1977-78, gen field mgr, 1978-81; Toyota Motor Sales USA, national merchandising mgr, 1981; San Francisco Region Toyota Motor Distribtr, gen mgr; Superstition Springs Auto Group, owner, currently. **Orgs:** Westminster Col Alumnus & bd. **Honors/Awds:** Special recognition for group for exceeding assigned task United Way Coordinator Ford Motor Co, 1972-73. **Military Serv:** AUS, pfc, 1961-63. **Home Addr:** 415 Shirlee Dr, Danville, CA 94526. **Business Addr:** Owner, Superstition Springs Auto Group, 6136 E Auto Loop Ave, Mesa, AZ 85206, **Business Phone:** (480)324-8900.

MERRITT, ELEANOR L
Community activist, educator, artist. **Personal:** Born Aug 17, 1933, New York City, NY; daughter of Wilbert and Lynette Lipsett; married WH Chris Darlington, Sep 26, 1980; children: Lori Ellen & Lisa Ann. **Educ:** Brooklyn Col, BA, 1955, MA, 1958; Hofstra Univ, attended 1972. **Career:** NYC Sch Syst, art teacher, 1955-58; Westbury Sch Dist, art teacher, 1959-70; chairperson art dept dist wide, 1970-82; artist, currently. **Orgs:** Charter mem, Women's Mus Art; bd mem, vpres, Women's Caucus for Art, 1989-99; bd, Sarasota Visual Arts Ctr, 1992-98; Fla Artists Group, 1996-; vpres, Sarasota County Arts Coun, 1996-; chair, Arts Pub Places, 1996-; pres, Venice Arts Ctr, 1999-2000. **Honors/Awds:** Women Impact Award, Sarasota County Comn, 1992; Sarasota Artist Year, Sarasota Visual Arts Ctr, 1994; Nat Presidential Award, Women's Caucus for Art, 1996. **Special Achievements:** Curated Exhibitions: "Minority Artists," Boston Fed Reserve Bank, 1996; first "Women Color Slide Inventory," Universal Color Slide Co, 1997-99; "Abstract Invitational," Manatee Art League, 1998; "Twenty Treass," Women's Resource Ctr, 1999.

MERRITT, JOSEPH, JR.
Executive. **Personal:** Born May 24, 1934, Tunica, MS; divorced; children: Joseph III. **Career:** Fillmore Taxi Svc, proprietor pres, 1968-. **Orgs:** YMCA, 1950; St John Bapt Ch, 1961; Black Men's Devel Found, 1963; NAACP,1963; Buffalo C of C, 1973; Buffalo Metro Bus Asn, 1974; Better Bus Bur,1974; Jefferson-Fillmore Revital Asn, 1975; vpres, Dem Party, 1976; apptdCivil Serv Commr Buffalo, 1977; Local Devel Corp. **Honors/Awds:** Black Achievement Award, 1976. **Business Addr:** Manager, Fillmore Taxi Service, 1000 E Ferry St, Buffalo, NY 14211.

MERRITT, WENDY WARREN
Interior designer. **Personal:** Born Mar 4, 1953, Shelby, NC; daughter of Nevada and Lucy Buggs. **Educ:** North CA Central UNIV, BS, 1974. **Career:** Montaldo's & Night Gallery, buyer, mgr couture retail, 1974-80; Games Production, Inc, D.C. instant lottery sales exec, 1980-84; Condominium Rentals, Ltd, buyer & int design & sales, 1984-87; TBS Inc Turner Properties, interior serv coordr, 1990-; Speakers Forum & Lotus, PSS, chief exec officer, speakers bureau & int design, 1980-. **Orgs:** S Phi S, Inc; Sisters Interest Never Gone, proj mgr; Atlanta Grad Chapter; United Negro COL Fund, special events fundraiser, 1992-; Apex Mus, spec events coordr, 1995; BLK Adults Action Section NAT COUN Negro Women, prog chair, 1985-88. **Honors/Awds:** UNCF Star Volunteer Award, Atlanta Chapter, 1992-00; UNCF Legacy Award, 2001. *

MERRITT, WILLETTE T.
Association executive. **Personal:** Born in Reidsville, NC; married Bishop (deceased); children: Bishetta D. **Educ:** VA State Col, BS, 1935; Univ NC; A&T State Univ; Univ VA. **Career:** VA Polytechnic Inst & State U, extension agent home economist; Pittsylvania Co, VA VPI & SU Extension Div Blacksburg, extension agent; A&T State Univ, dist supvr; A&T Univ, sub matter spec; Rockingham Co NC, extension agent; Reidsville NC, teacher pub sch, 1935-37. **Orgs:** Epsilon Sigma Phi Extension hon frat; Am Asn Univ Women; Am Home Econ Asn; pres Danville Chap Delta Sigma Theta Sor; organized Jack & Jill Inc; Danville Chap Links; mem exec bd, Mental Health Asn, 1974-75; past mem, exec bd Heart Asn, 1973-74; past mem exec bd, Cancer Asn, 1973-74; past pres, Western Dist Home Econ Asn, 1969; pres, VA Home Econ Asn first black, 1975; first vpres Nat Asn Extension Home Econ, 1974-75; deacon Holbrook St Pres Chap. **Honors/Awds:** Distinct Service Award, 1968; Danville Woman of the Day, 1975; first black Virginian elected, 1974-75; nat officer, Nat Asn extension Home Econ.

MERRITT, WILLIAM T
Association executive, president (organization). **Educ:** NC Central Univ; Rutgers Univ, Grad Sch Social Work. **Career:** National Black United Fund Inc, Newark, NJ, pres & ceo. **Orgs:** Dir, Girls Ctr Essex County; dir, Victory Home; dir, Janet Memorial Home; bd mem, Nat Black Leadership Roundtable; Model Child Abuse Reporting Law; Governor's Committee on Youth; pres, Nat Asn Black Social Workers, 1982-86; bd dir, Vol Consult Group; bd dir, Nat Ctr Black Philanthropy; pres, NJ Asn Children's Residential Facilities. **Business Phone:** (202)530-9770.*

MERRITT CUMMINGS, ANNETTE (ANNETTE MERRITT JONES)
Marketing executive, public relations executive, advertising executive. **Personal:** Born May 14, 1946, Grady, AL; daughter of Henry W and Virgie Mathews Dowdell; married Iran Cummings, Aug 31, 1985; children: Michael O & Angela J. **Educ:** Cuyahoga Community Col, AA, 1975; Cleveland State Univ, BA (magna cum laude), 1977; Univ Detroit, MBA, 1993. **Career:** EI DuPont de Numours, Wilmington DE; Occidental Petrol, Madison Heights, MI, sr sales rep, 1979-81; Publs Rep, Detroit MI, independent contractor, 1981-82; NW Ayer Inc, sr acct exec, 1982-88; Nat Bd Prof Teaching, dir develop & mkt; Nat Bd Prof Teaching, 1988-92; Campbell & Co, vp, 1992-94; Courier-Jour Newspaper, mkt Communs mgr; Paul Werth Assocs, vpres, 1996; Bernard Hodes Group, vpres & nat dir diversity servs div, currently. **Orgs:** Adcraft Club Detroit, 1985-; Literacy Volunteers Am, 1986-; Women's Econ Club Detroit, 1987-; Nat Soc Fund-Raising Execs, 1988-; Detroit Rotary Club Int, 1989-; Nat Black MBA Asn, 1992; Pub Rels Soc Am; bd mem, Strategies Against Violence Everywhere. **Honors/Awds:** PRSA, Bronze Anvil, 1992. **Special Achievements:** Contributing Author: "The Census 2000 Toolkit". **Home Addr:** 209 Mallet Hill Rd, Columbia, SC 29223-3203. **Business Addr:** Vice President, National Director, Bernard Hodes Group, 220 E 42nd St, New York, NY 10017, **Business Phone:** 888-438-9911.

MERRIWEATHER, BARBARA CHRISTINE
Educator. **Personal:** Born May 11, 1948, Philadelphia, PA; daughter of Robert C and Elizabeth Livingston; married Frank Washington. **Educ:** Cheyney State Univ, BS, 1969; Beaver Col, MA, humanities, 1989; Cheyney Univ, cert prin, 1998. **Career:** Philadelphia Sch Dist, teacher, coordr, supvr, 1969-2002; Holy Family Univ, prof; Cheyney Univ, prof. **Orgs:** Mem chair, Black Women's Ed Alliance, 1981-83; bd dir, Minority Asn Stud Support, 1981-; co-chair, public rel, Salem Baptist Church 100 Anniversary, 1983-84; chair pub rel, 1984-87, pres, Philadelphia Fed Black Bus & Prof Orgn; recruiter, Am Fed Teachers, 1985; task force mem, Youth Serv Coord, Comn, 1986-; pres, Philadelphia Fed Black Bus & Prof Orgn, 1987-90; mem, planning comm AFNA Educ & Res Fund, 1987; exec dir, Frank Wash Scholar Fund, 1990-; charter mem, Phi Beta Omega Chap Alpha Kappa Alpha Sorority, 1998; Second Anti-Basileus, 1998. **Honors/Awds:** Chapel of Four Chaplins, 1970; Achievement Award, BWEA, 1984, Women in Education, 1985; City Council Citation, City of Philadelphia, 1985; Outstanding Achievement, BWEA, 1986; Outstanding Service Citation, Commonwealth Pa House Reps, 1987; Teacher of the Year Award, Rose Lindenbaum Commt, 1990; Distinguished Educator Award. **Home Addr:** 514 Greenhill Lane, Philadelphia, PA 19128.

MERRIWEATHER, MICHAEL LAMAR
Football player, football coach, business owner. **Personal:** Born Nov 26, 1960, Albans, NY; son of John (deceased); married Djuna Mitchell. **Educ:** Univ Pac, BA, hist, 1982. **Career:** Football player (retired), Football coach, Business owner; Pittsburgh Steelers, linebacker, 1982-87; Minn Vikings, linebacker, 1989-92; New York Jets, linebacker, 1993; St Patrick-St Vincent, asst coach, 1990; StanfordUniv, East-West Shrine Game, defensive coach, 2005; Mike Merriweather, owner, currently; motivational speaker, currently. **Orgs:** Alpha Phi Alpha, 1980-; Big Brothers Bowling Kids, 1986-87; founder, John Merriweather Athletic Scholar. **Honors/Awds:** Olympia Gold Bowl; Vallejo Sports Hall of Fame, 2004. **Business Addr:** Owner, Mike Merriweather, PO Box 8351, Stockton, CA 95208.

MERRIWEATHER, ROBERT EUGENE
Consultant, manager. **Personal:** Born Sep 1, 1948, Cincinnati, OH; son of Andrew J and Ruth Hawkins; married Augustine Pryor, Sep 19, 1970; children: Tinia, Andre & Tarani. **Educ:** Univ Cincinnati, BA, math, 1970. **Career:** Procter & Gamble Co, math consult, 1970-78, statist analyst, 1978-81, affirmative action mgr, 1981-83, sr syst analyst, 1983-89, personnel servs mgr, 1989-. **Orgs:** Bd mem, Mt Zion Federal Credit Union 1980-88; trustee Mt Zion Baptist Church, 1986-; Community Adv Bd, Univ Cincinnati, 1988-; Project Alpha, chairperson Alpha Phi Alpha Fraternity, 1989-91; Nat Asn Advan Colored People, Cincinnati Br. **Honors/Awds:** Black Achiever, YMCA, 1983; Black Networking Award, Procter & Gamble, 1986; Diversity Award, Procter & Gamble, 1988; Unsung Hero Award, Procter & Gamble, 1990. **Home Addr:** 9580 Heather Ct, Cincinnati, OH 45242. **Business Addr:** Personnel Services Manager, Procter & Gamble Co, 1 Procter & Gamble Plz, Cincinnati, OH 45202, **Business Phone:** (513)983-1100.

MESA, MAYRA L
Educator, dentist. **Personal:** Born Jul 20, 1949, Cuba. **Educ:** Univ Puerto Rico, BS, 1968; Univ Puerto Rico Dent Sch, DMD, 1972; Boston Univ Sch Grad Dent, MSc, 1974. **Career:** Univ Med & Dent NJ, NJ Dent Sch, asst prof oral path, 1974-77, assoc prof oral path, prof oral path, biol & Diag Sci, currently; Commonwealth Dent Soc, secy, 1977-79. **Orgs:** Bd dirs, Act Boston Community Develop, 1973; bd dirs, Act Boston Community Develop, 1973; Nat Dent Asn, 1975-; supvr, Black Coalition Health Law Fair, 1977-79; Table Clinics Nat Dental Asn, 1977-79. **Honors/Awds:** Outstanding Young Women of America, 1978. **Special Achievements:** Published numerous articles. **Business Addr:** Professor of Oral Pathology, Biology & Diagnostic Sciences, University of Medicine & Dentistry New Jersy, New Jersey Dental School, Rm C-829 110 Bergen St, Newark, NJ 07103-2400, **Business Phone:** (973)972-4506.

MESIAH, RAYMOND N.
Manager, consultant. **Personal:** Born Sep 1, 1932, Buffalo, NY; son of Nicklos and Marie; married; children: 2. **Educ:** Canisius Col, BS, 1954; MS, 1960. **Career:** FMC Corp, Philadelphia, PA, sr environ engr, 1977-90, eastern reg environ mgr, 1991-93, environ mgr, 1993-95; pvt environ consult, 1995. **Orgs:** Franklin Twp Jaycees, 1963-68; chmn, Franklin Twp Civil Rights Comn, 1967-68; treas, Franklin Twp Pub Libr, 1967-69; treas, Frederick Douglass Liberation Libr, 1969-70; Am Chem Soc; brd educ, Franklen town, 1969-75; Presenting team Worldwide Marriage Encounter, 1977-; Alpha Phi Alpha; cord, Camden diocese, NJ, 1985-87; cord, sect 3, 1992-95. **Honors/Awds:** One of Five Outstanding Men of Year, NJ Jaycees, 1967. **Military Serv:** Cpl, 1954-56.

MESSIAH-JILES, SONCERIA
Publisher. **Personal:** Born in Baytown, TX; married Jodie Lee; children: 2. **Educ:** Univ Houston, jour, 1974; Tex Southern Univ, MBA. **Career:** KYOK-AM Radio, news reporter; KMJQ-FM, adv acct exec; KHOU-TV, talk show host; KRIV-TV, talk show host; Houston Defender Newspaper, owner & publ, 1981-. **Orgs:** Secy & bd mem, United Way Tex Gulf Coast; secy & bd mem, March Dimes Tex Gulf Coast Chap; pres, Nat Newspaper Publ Asn. **Honors/Awds:** The Phenomenal Woman Award; American Civil

Liberties Freedom of Speech Award; Outstanding Woman of the Year, YWCA; Houston Women on the Move Award; Outstanding Texan, Jaycees; Publisher of the Year, Nat Newspaper Publ Asn; Civil Rights Award, Nat Dent Asn. **Business Addr:** Publisher, Houston Defender Newspaper, PO Box 8005, Houston, TX 77288, **Business Phone:** (713)663-6996.*

METCALF, ANDREW LEE, JR.
Government official. **Personal:** Born Feb 21, 1944, Muskegon, MI; married Elizabeth Jane Lamb; children: Andrea & Andrew III. **Educ:** Muskegon Community Col, AA, police sci tech, 1971; Grand Valley State Univ, BS, pub serv, 1972; Thomas M Cooley Law Sch, JD, 1987. **Career:** Muskegon Heights Police Dept, patrolman & juvenile officer, 1967-71; Mc Croskey, Libner, Van Leuven, Cochcrane, Kortering & Brock Law Firm, legal investigator, 1971-78; US Dept Justice, US marshal, 1978-81; Mich Dept Com, Liquor Control CMS, hearings comnr, 1982-83, Finance Sect, dirinternal audit, 1983-84; Mich Dept Licensing & Regulation, Bur Com Serv, div dir enforcement, 1987-89, Bur Occup Prof Regulation, Off Com Serv, dir, 1989-. **Orgs:** Asst regional dir, Nat Asn Legal Investigators, 1973-78; W Mich Law Enforcement Officer Asn, 1978; charter mem, Muskegon Heights Lions Club, 1975; treas, Iota Phi Lambda Chap Alpha Phi Alpha Fraternity, 1973-; exec bd mem, Nat Asn Advan Colored People, Grand Rapids Mich Chap, 1980;Freedom Fund Chair, 1987; pres, Grand Rapids Gentry Club, 1987-88; Citizens Responsible Govt, 1986. **Honors/Awds:** Academic scholarship (3.75 gpa), Ford Found, NY, 1971. **Military Serv:** USAF, sgt, 1962-66. **Business Addr:** Director, State of Michigan Department of Commerce, Bureau of Commercial Services, 611 N Ottawa, Lansing, MI 48909, **Business Phone:** (517)373-9879.

METCALF, DAVINCI CARVER
Librarian. **Personal:** Born Jul 1, 1955, Dayton, OH; son of Zubie West Metcalf Jr and Maggie Lee Blake Metcalf. **Educ:** Auburn Univ, BS, polit sci, 1977; E Carolina Univ, MS, community health, 1982; Univ NC, MLS, 1985; Fla State Univ, MLS, 1988; NE Fla Reg Libr Network, attended 1999; Fla State Univ, cert, 2000; Fla A&M Univ Media Ctr, attended 2001. **Career:** Libr Cong, Wash, intern, 1984; W Va Univ, Main Libr, gen ref librn, col instr, 1985-86; Jacksonville Pub Libr, bus, sci, doc ref librn, 1989-2000; Jacksonville Jaguars Booster Club News, reporter, 1995-; Coleman Libr, Fla A&M Univ, asst univ librn, 2000-. **Orgs:** Am Libr Asn, 1985-; Fla Libr Asn, 1985-; NAACP, 1988-; Black Caucus, Jacksonville Jaycees, 1992-94; Am Libr Asn; Panhandle Lib Access Network. **Honors/Awds:** McKnight Fellowship Scholar, McKnight Found, 1987-88; Pi Sigma Alpha Polit Sci Honor Soc, Pi Sigma Alpha Soc, 1981-83; Nat Catholic Scholarship Negroes, Nat Catholic Scholarship Found, 1973-82; Volunteer Service Award, Tuskegee Veteran's Admin Hosp, 1975-76; Certificate of Recognition, Outstanding Community Serv, Delta Sigma Theta, 1987. **Home Addr:** 1900 Centre Pointe Blvd, Paddock Club Apts Suite 296 Bldg 19, Tallahassee, FL 32308, **Home Phone:** (850)656-9510.

METCALF, ERIC QUINN
Football player. **Personal:** Born Jan 23, 1968, Seattle, WA; son of Terry; married Lori; children: 3. **Educ:** Univ Tex, libr arts, 1990. **Career:** Football Player (Retired), football coach; Cleveland Browns, wide receiver, 1989-94; Atlanta Falcons, 1995-96; San Diego Chargers, wide receiver, 1997; Ariz Cardinals, 1998; Carolina Panthers, 1999; Wash Redskins, 2001; Green Bay Packers, wide receiver, 2002; Rainier Beach Vikings, coach, currently. **Honors/Awds:** Played in AFC Championship Game, post-1989 season; Pro Bowl, 1993, 1994, 1997; Wash DC area prep Player of the Year.

METCALF, DR. MICHAEL RICHARD
Physician. **Personal:** Born Jan 4, 1956, Detroit, MI; son of Adele C; married Ruth Chantell Holloman; children: Michael Jr, Leah, Jonathan & Christina. **Educ:** Dartmouth Col, BA, 1978; Howard Univ Col Med, MD, 1982. **Career:** DC Gen Hosp, internship, 1982-83, resident, 1983-85, chief resident, 1984; CW Williams Health Ctr, internist, 1985-94, health servs dir, 1991-94; Meridian Med Group, chief internal med, 1996-2003; Carolinas Med Ctr, assoc div, active staff, dept internal med, 1987-; pvt pract, currently. **Orgs:** Charlotte Med Soc, 1986-; Mecklenburg Med Soc, 1991. **Honors/Awds:** Dipl, Am Bd Internal Med, 1985. **Home Addr:** 6622 Harrison Rd, Charlotte, NC 28270. **Business Addr:** Physician, Metrolina Comprehensive Health Center, 1918 Randolph Rd Suite 670, PO Box 668093, Charlotte, NC 28207, **Business Phone:** (704)393-7720.

METCALF, DR. ZUBIE WEST, JR.
School administrator. **Personal:** Born Jul 4, 1930, Ft Deposit, AL; son of Zubie West Metcalf Sr and Ella Louise Reasor; married Maggie L Blake; children: DaVinci C & Caroletta A. **Educ:** Univ Dayton, BS, 1957; Miami Univ, MAT, 1961; State Univ NY Buffalo, EdD, 1972. **Career:** School administrator (retired); Ball State Univ, dir acad opportunity prog, 1971-73; Tuskegee Inst, asst vpres acad affairs & dean grad prog, 1973-76; East Carolina Univ Sch Med, asst vice chancellor, assoc dean, dir med center student opportunity & minority affairs, 1976-92. **Orgs:** Dir, Nat Sci Found Summer Inst, Fla A&M Univ, 1966-69; coordr, Teacher Educ Prog State Univ, NY, Buffalo, 1969-70; consult, US Dept of Health & Human Serv Div of Disadvantaged Asst, 1983-84; bd mem, Pitt-Greenville Cof C, 1983-87; chairperson, Southern Region Minority Affairs Sect of Asn Am Med, 1984-86; bd Centura Nat Bank, 1986-92; vpres, Nat Asn Med Minority Educrs, 1987-89; bd dir, Am Lung Asn Fla, Big Bend Region, 2001-03. **Honors/Awds:** Hon Soc in Ed Univ of Dayton, OH, 1957; fel Nat Sci Found, Wash DC, 1960-61; fel Ford Found, NY, 1970-71; Distinguished Serv Award, Nat Asn Med Minority Educrs, 1992; Merit Award, 16 Institutions Health Sci Consortium, 1993; Outstanding Leadership Award, 1992; Health & Human Serv Bd, Dist 2, State Fla, 1999. **Special Achievements:** Author, Career Planning Guide in the Allied Health Professions, 1997. **Home Addr:** 3518 Colonnade Dr, Tallahassee, FL 32309, **Home Phone:** (850)668-1681. *

METOYER, CARL B.
Lawyer. **Personal:** Born Aug 8, 1925, Oakland; married Coline Apperson; children: Carl, Ronald, Monique. **Educ:** Univ CA; Hastings Col, attended 1952. **Career:** Firm Fracois & Metoyer, partner, 1953-55; pvt pract law sole practr, 1955-59; firm Metoyer & Sweeney, sr practr, 1959-68; pvt pract law sole practr, 1968-. **Orgs:** Vchmn, exec comt, CA State Bar Conf Del; State Bar CA; Alameda County Bar Asn; Lawyers Club Alameda County; Thurston soc Hastings Col Law Hon Soc; founding mem, Chalres Houston Bar Asn; Alameda County Super Ct Arbitration Panel; vpres & mem bd dirs, CA Lawyers Serv; past vpres, Hastings Col Law Alumni Asn; past judge, Oakland Mun Ct; past mem, bd govs, Alameda County Community Found; CA State Univ, Hayward Adv Bd; vpres & mem bd dirs, Family Serv Bur, Alameda County; NAACP; UrbanLeague; Sigma Pi Phi Frat; past chmn, Manpower Comn City Oakland; Past mem, Oakland Econ Develop Coun; past mem, bd dirs C Home Soc CA; past pres, Sen Div Hayward Little League; past mem, exec bd, San Fran Coun Boy Scouts Am. **Honors/Awds:** Recipient, Order of the Coif, Hastings Col Law, 1952. **Military Serv:** USNR 1943-46. **Business Addr:** Attorney, 6014 Market St, Oakland, CA 94608.

METOYER, ROSIA G
Librarian. **Personal:** Born Mar 2, 1930, Boyce, LA; daughter of Eloise Pannell Washington and Horace Gilbert; married Granvel G; children: Renwick, Keith, Karlette & Toni Rosette. **Educ:** Grambling Col, BS, 1951; Webster Col, MA; Northwestern State Univ, attended 1964. **Career:** Acadian Elem Sch, libr; Lincoln Rd Elem Sch Rapides Parish Sch Bd, former sch librn; Rapides Parish Libr, selections librn; Sickle Cell Anemia Res Found Inc, founder & exec dir, currently. **Orgs:** Pres, La Classroom Teacher Asn, 1977-78; Exec Coun La Asn Educators, 1978-80; United Teaching Prof La Libr Asn; SW Libr Asn; Alexandria Zoning Bd Adjustment & Appeals; Asn Classroom Teachers; La Libr Asn; YWCA; Nat Asn Advan Colored People; secy, La Asn Sickle Cell Disease, 1986-; secy, Rapides Parish Democratic Exec Comt, 1988-92; chairperson, Nat Polit Congress Black Women, Alexandria Chap, 1990-92; Alapha Kappa Alpha Sorority, Zeta Lambda Omega Chapr, Basileus; Alexandria Chap Jack & Jill Am, 1990-92; dist coordr, La Fedn Dem Women, 1990-91; second vpres, La Fedn Democratic Women, 1991-93; gov bd, Huey P Long Med Ctr; La Develop Disabilities Coun. **Honors/Awds:** James R Hovall Award; Service Award, La Asn; La Beauticians Service Award; La Asn Educators Outstanding Service to Teachers Award Zeta Lambda Omega; Alpha Kappa Alpha Sor Community Service Award; SE Kiwanis Community Service Award. **Home Addr:** 910 Papin St, Alexandria, LA 71302. **Business Addr:** Executive Director, Sickle Cell Anemia Research Foundation Inc, 910 Papin St, PO Box 206, Alexandria, LA 71309.

METTERS, DR. SAMUEL
Executive, chief executive officer, engineer. **Personal:** Born Jan 1, 1934?. **Educ:** Prairie View A&M Univ, BS, archit eng; Univ Calif, Berkeley, BA, archit & urban planning; Univ Southern Calif, MS, systs mgt, MS, pub admin, PhD, pub admin; AUS Command & Gen Staff Col; Harvard Grad Sch Bus Admin, Cambridge, MA, Owner/Pres Mgt Corp Exec Prog. **Career:** Hughes, Bendix & Holmes & Narver Eng, prog mgr & mgt info syst coordr; Metters Industs Inc, founder, chmn & chief exec officer, 1981-; NASA Career Explor Prog, co-founder; NASA Advisory Council; Nat Capital Area Coun Boy Scouts Am, pres & chief exec officer; bd dirs, Granville Acad. **Orgs:** Dulles Corridor Metrorail Asn; bd trustees, Fairfax Bus Partnership; Northern Va Prof Serv Coun; Northern Va Urban League; Prairie View A&M Univ Found; Rosslyn Renaissance Urban Design Comt Arlington, Va; Shiloh Econ & Community Develop Corp; Shiloh Bd Trustees; United Black Col Fund; US Black Engr Year Award Prog; S E Conf Minority Engrs; Kappa Alpha PSI Fraternity; pres & founder, Prairie View A&M Univ Nat Alumni Found; State Va, Vet Strategic Policy Bd; Northeast Region Bd Dirs, Boy Scouts Am; cofounder, NASA Career Explor Prog; Armed Forces Commun & Electronics Asn. **Honors/Awds:** Distinguished Graduate Award, Prairie View A&M Univ; NASA Special Services Award, 1997; National Baptist Convention (PNBC) Community Service Award, 1998; Community Service Award, Northern Va Urban League; Community Service Award, Progressive Nat Baptist Conv, 1998; NASA Public Service Medal, 2001. **Special Achievements:** Co ranked #43 on BE's Top 100 Industrial/Service Companies, 1992; published numerous papers & articles; Howard Univ's recognition of "50 Most Important Black Owned Cos in Am"; listed in Who's Who in Am; Who's Who in the S & Southwest; Who's Who Among Black Am; inducted into the State of Tex Football Hall of Fame & Black Coll Hall of Fame, Atlanta, Ga; First African Am to be elected to the office of Pres & CEO of the NCAC/BSA; First varsity football player to graduate from the Col Eng PVAMU. **Military Serv:** AUS, comdr, sr instr & lt col; Vietnam, S-3 artillery officer observer; HAWK Missile Brigade, Ger, logistics officer; Mare Island Naval Shipyard, naval archit & struct engr; Air Medal; 3 Bronze Stars; 3 Army Commendation Medals; Meritorious Serv Medal; Purple Heart. **Business Addr:** President, Chief Executive Officer, Metters Industries Inc, 8200 Greensboro Dr, McLean, VA 22102, **Business Phone:** (703)821-3300.

MEYER, ALTON J
Automotive executive. **Career:** Meyer Acquisition Corp, pres; Al Meyer Ford Inc, pres, currently. **Business Addr:** President, Al Meyer Ford Inc, 800 N Medford Dr, Lufkin, TX 75901-5222, **Business Phone:** (936)632-6611.*

MEYERS, ISHMAEL ALEXANDER
Judge. **Personal:** Born Feb 3, 1939, St Thomas, Virgin Islands of the United States; son of Elvera L and H Alexander; married Gwendolyn Lorraine Pate; children: Ishmael Jr, Micheline & Michael. **Educ:** Morgan State Univ, BS, 1962; Am Univ, MBA, 1964; George Wash Univ, JD, 1972. **Career:** Interstate Com Comn, acct & auditor, 1963-64; VI Dept Housing & Comm Renewal, 1964-69; VI Dept Law, asst atty gen, 1973; US Dept Justice, asst US atty, 1973-78, US atty, 1978-82; Territorial Ct VI, from assoc judge to judge, 1982-2002; Superior Ct VI, sr sitting judge, 2004-. **Orgs:** Bar Supreme Ct US, 1980-; DC Bar Asn, 1973-; VI Bar Asn, 1973-; Am Bar Asn, 1973-; charter mem, St Thomas Lions Club, 1968-; vpres, historian, Theta Epsilon Lambda Chap, Alpha Phi Alpha Frat Inc. **Honors/Awds:** Alpha Kappa Mu Nat Honor Soc, Morgan State Univ, 1960-62; John Hay Whitney Found Fel, 1962-64; US Atty Gen Spec Achievement Award, US Dept Justice, 1976; Spec Achievement Award, Nat Alumni Asn Morgan State Univ, 1984. **Business Addr:** Senior Sitting Judge, Superior Court of the Virgin Islands, Alexander A Farrelly Justice Ctr 5400 Veterans Dr, PO Box 70, St Thomas, Virgin Islands of the United States 00802, **Business Phone:** (340)774-6680.

MEYERS, LISA ANNE-MARIE
Publicist, executive. **Personal:** Born Feb 22, 1973, Atlanta, GA; daughter of Tim and Carolyn; divorced. **Educ:** Univ Va, BA, 1995. **Career:** Ketchum Pub Rels, assoc, 1995-96; BET Holdings, publicist, 1996-97; Magic Johnson Enterprises, publicist; exec vpres, Commun & Branding, currently. **Orgs:** Alpha Kappa Alpha Sorority, 1993-95; Am Cancer Soc. **Honors/Awds:** Class Community Service Award, Univ Va Deans List, 1995; PRSA, Silver Anvil, 1996; Distinguished PR Professional, PRAME, 1998. **Business Phone:** (310)247-2033.

MEYERS, DR. ROSE M.
Research scientist. **Personal:** Born Aug 18, 1945, Mt Pleasant, SC. **Educ:** Bennett Col, Greensboro, BS, chem, 1966; NY Univ, MS, bio chem, 1972, PhD, biochem, 1976. **Career:** Howard High Sch, Georgetown, SC, math teacher, 1966-67; Yeshiva Univ NY,res teacher chem, 1967-68; NY Univ Med Sch, res teacher I cancer res, 1968-72, res teacher II cancer res, 1972-76; Univ Louisville Med Sch, resfel, 1976-78; Philip Morris Res Ctr, res scientist, 1978-. **Orgs:** Sister Cities Int, 1978-; Nat Asn Black Chem; Bennett Col; Bus & Prof Women's Club; Mus African Art. **Special Achievements:** Published article "Studies on Nucleoside Deaminase" J Biol Chem 24850901973; published "sialyltransferase in lympocytes" federation proceedings 351441 1976; Louis villecitz awd Mayor Harvey Sloane Louisville 1976-77; published "Immuno supprsn & Tobacco Smoke" federation proceedings 3612301977.

MFUME, KWEISI (FRIZZELL GERARD GRAY)
Association executive, government official. **Personal:** Born Oct 24, 1948, Baltimore, MD; son of Rufus Tate and Mary Elizabeth Willis; divorced; children: Ronald T Gray, Donald, Kevin, Keith & Michael. **Educ:** Morgan State Univ, BA, 1976; Johns Hopkins Univ, MA, liberal arts, 1984. **Career:** Radio Sta, prog dir; Baltimore City Coun, mem; US House Rep, State Md, congressman, 1987-96; Nat Asn Advan Colored People, pres & chief exec officer, 1996-2004; US Senate, cand, 2006-. **Orgs:** Chmn, Cong Black Caucus; Caucus Women's Issues; Cong Arts Caucus; Fed Govt Serv Task Force; bd trustees, Baltimore Mus Art; Sr Adv Comt, Harvard Univ John F Kennedy Sch Gov; Meyerhoff Nat Adv Bd, Univ Md; bd trustee, Enterprise Found; Big Brothers & Big Sisters; hon chair, Ctr Stage, Theater New Generation Advocacy; Morgan State Univ Bd Regents. **Honors/Awds:** Drum Major for Justice Award, SCLC, 1997; Inter generational Award, Sister 2 Sister Mag, 2000. **Special Achievements:** Author: No Free Ride: From the Mean Streets to the Mainstream, 1996; Coauthor: Harry Truman & Civil Rights: Moral Courage & Political Risk, 2002. **Business Phone:** (410)468-3338.

MICHAEL, B
Fashion designer. **Personal:** Divorced; children: 2. **Educ:** Univ Conn, grad. **Career:** Wall St Firm, acct exec; Oscar de la Renta,

apprentice; AbApparel Group, Jazz Lincoln Ctr, fashion partner; DM Fashion Group Inc, fashion designer & partnership, 1999-; Fashion Inst Technol, guest lectr, currently. **Orgs:** Coun Fashion Designers Am, 1998; New Yorkers C; Styleworks; adv bd mem, Fashion Target Breast Cancer campaign. **Business Addr:** Fashion Designer, DM Fashion Group Inc, 202 W 40th St 4th Fl, New York, NY 10018, **Business Phone:** (212)703-9494.

MICHAEL, DR. CHARLENE BELTON
Manager. **Personal:** Born in Heath Springs, SC; daughter of Charles Belton and Cherryane Powe; married Joseph Michael Sr, Jul 29, 1941; children: Joseph M Jr & Charles B. **Educ:** Knoxville Col, BA, 1939; Teachers Col, Columbia Univ, MA, 1955; Univ Tenn, MS, 1958; Univ Tenn, PhD, 1976. **Career:** Knoxville City Schs, teacher, 1950-75; Knoxville City Sch & Univ Tenn, speech pathologist 1958-75; Knoxville & Knox Co Proj Headstart, dep dir, 1965-66; Knoxville Col-Upward Bound, assoc dir, 1968-69; Educ & Training Adaption Serv Inc, ed dir, 1971-75; MAARDAC & Univ Tenn, assoc dir, 1974-; Univ Assoc, Johns Hopkins Univ, consult, 1979, 82-83; Mid Atlantic & Appalachian Race Desegregation Asst Ctr, actg dir, 1987. **Orgs:** Pres, Phi Delta Kappa Univ Tenn, 1979-80; bd trustees, Knoxville Col, 1984; pres, Knoxville Col Nat Alumni Assoc Inc; pres, Knoxville Educ Assoc; Delta Sigma Theta Sor Alumnae Chapt; bd dirs, Knoxville Women's Ctr, Matrix, C Ctr; Metropolitan Planning Commn. **Honors/Awds:** Cert Rec Knoxville Col SE Reg & Nat Alumni Assoc, 1977; Citizen of the Year Award, For Serv & Contrib Humanity, 1984; Selwyn Award, Knoxville Women's Ctr, 1985; YWCA Award Tribute Outstanding Women, 1986. **Special Achievements:** Pub: Why I Teach, The Effect of Parental Involment on the Learning Process, "Advantages of Lang-Experience Approach in the Teaching of Reading, Coping with Stresses in the Classroom, Student Team Learning, An Educational Equity Tool, Workshop Participants Perception Rankings Second General School Desegregation Issues; lic speech pathologist State Tenn.

MICHAUX, ERIC COATES
Lawyer. **Personal:** Born Sep 23, 1941, Durham, NC; married Della Dafford. **Educ:** Univ NC, 1959; NC Cent Univ, Sch Law, 1965; Boston Univ, BS, bus admin, 1963; Duke Univ, Sch Law, 1966; Univ Denver, 1968. **Career:** Durham Col Durham, NC, teacher bus law, 1965; W G Pearson, atty, 1967; Perason Malone Johnson & DeJormon, atty, 1971-73; 14th Solicitoral Dist, asst dist atty, 1973-75; Eric C Michauz Law Firm, pres. **Orgs:** Vis prof, NC Cent Univ, 1971-73; adj asst prof, Dept Health Educ, Univ NC, Chapel Hill, 1972-73; Cong aide Congressman Nick Galifianakis, 1971-72; pres, Unoin Ins & Reality Co; vpres, Glenview Mem Park Wash Terr Apts Inc; bd dir, Harrison Constrn Realty Co; vice chmn & bd dir, Cardinal Savs & Loan; Am Bar Asn; Nat Asn Advan Colored People; S Christian Leadership Conf; Omega Psi Phi Fraternity; Phi Alpha Delta Legal Fraternity; Nat Soc Perishing Rifles; Durham Comt Affairs Black People; United Citizens Against Drug Abuse; steward trustee treas, St Joseph's African Methodist Episcopal Church; NC Bar Asn; bd dirs, Durham Chap, Am Nat Red Cross; mem bd trustees, NC Cent Univ. **Honors/Awds:** Recipient of Nat Defence Service Medal; Vietnam Service Medal; Vietnam Campaign Medal. **Military Serv:** USAF, 1967-69, Bronze Star. **Business Addr:** Attorney, Eric C Michauz Law Firm, PO Box 2152, Durham, NC 27702.

MICHAUX, HENRY M
State government official, real estate executive. **Personal:** Born Sep 4, 1930, Durham, NC; son of Henry M and Isadore C; children: Jocelyn. **Educ:** NC Central Univ, BS, 1952; Rutgers Univ, attended 1955; NC Cent Univ Law Sch, JD, 1952, 1964. **Career:** Real estate agent, government official, buiness exec; Union Ins & Realty Co, vpres, 1955-; Durham Co, chief asst dist atty, 1969-72; Michaux & Michaux, sr partner, 1970-; real estate broker; NC Gen Assembly & House Rep, 1972-76; Middle Judicial Dist NC, US atty, 1977-81; NC State House Reps, rep, 1973-77, Dist 31, rep currently. **Orgs:** Trustee, NC Cent Univ; exec comt mem, 14th Judicial Dist Bar; N State Bar; NC Bar Asn; George H White Bar Asn; Black Lawyers NC; Am Bar Asn; Judicature Soc; Criminal Code Comn State NC, 1973-77; Steering Comt Caucus Black Dem; NC Comn Human Skills & Resources; NC Com Law Focused Educ; NC Cent Alumni Asn; bd dir, NC Cent Univ Found Inc; Durham Bus & Prof Chain; Durham C C; Durham Merchants Asn; Nat Asn Advan Colored People; NC Med Soc. **Honors/Awds:** Hon Doctorate, Durham Col & NC Central Univ; Realist of Year; Public Affairs & Political Achievement Award, 1973-74 & 1976; Annual Award, Triad Sickle Cell Anemia Found, 1973; Citizen Com Sickle Cell Syndrome Award, 1976; Political Achievement Award, NAACP 1975; Service Award, Phi Alpha Delta Law Frat; Achievement Award, Calif Real Estate Brokers, 1974; Service Award, 14th Judicial Dist Bar, 1972; Triangle "J" Coun Govt, 1973; NC Bar Asn, 1975; Public Service Award, NC Chiropractic Asn, 1977; NC Black Dem Leadership Caucus, 1977. **Special Achievements:** Longest-serving African American member of the North Carolina General Assembly. **Military Serv:** AUS, 1952-54; USAR, 1954-60. **Business Addr:** Representative, North Carolina State House of Representatives, District 31, 16 W Jones St Rm 1227, 1227 Legisl Bldg, Raleigh, NC 27601-1096, **Business Phone:** (919)715-2528.

MICHEL, HARRIET RICHARDSON
Association executive. **Personal:** Born Jul 5, 1942, Pittsburgh, PA; daughter of John Robert and Vida Harmony; married Yves; children: Christoper & Gregory. **Educ:** Juniata Col, Huntingdon, PA, BA, sociol & criminol. **Career:** Nat Scholarship Serv & Fund Negro Students, prog officer, 1965-70; Off Mayor New York, asst, 1971-72; New York Found, exec dir, 1972-77; US Dept Labor, Washington, DC, dir youth employment, 1977-79; John Jay Col, New York, NY, 1981; US Dept Housing & Urban Development, Washington, DC, consult, 1982-83; New York Urban League, New York, NY, pres, 1983-88; Harvard Univ, Kennedy Sch Gov, Inst Polit, resident fel, 1988; Nat Minority Supplier Develop Coun, New York, NY, pres & chief exec officer, 1988-. **Orgs:** Bd mem, African Am Inst; bd mem, Juniata Col; bd mem, NY Nat Bank; bd mem, TransAfrica Forum. **Honors/Awds:** First Nonprofit Leadership Award, New Sch, 1988; First Women on the Move Award, B Nai B rith, 1990; Ethnic New Yorker Award, 1985; Black Entrepreneurial Award, Wall St J, 1994; Building Bridges Award, Rainbow/PUSH Coalition, 2002; Legacy Award, Minority Bus Develop Agency, Ronald H. Brown Leadership Award, Dept Com, 2003; Champion Award, Black Enterprise Entrepreneurs Conf, 2003; Enterprising Woman of the Year Award, 2004; Executive Leadership Councils Achievement Award; Pioneer Award, Minority Business News USA. **Business Phone:** (212)944-2430.

MICHEL, PRAKAZREL SAMUEL. See MICHEL, SAMUEL PRAKAZREL.

MICHEL, SAMUEL PRAKAZREL (PRAKAZREL SAMUEL MICHEL)
Rap musician. **Personal:** Born Oct 19, 1972, South Orange, NJ. **Educ:** Rutgers Col; Yale Univ. **Career:** Tranzlator Crew, founder, 1990-; Ruffhouse/Columbia Rec, rap artist, 1993-; Fugees, founder, 1993-; Albums: Blunted on Reality, 1994; The Score, 1996; Refugee Camp - Bootleg Versions, 1996; Ghetto Supastar, 1998; Fugees Greatest Hits, 2003; Win Lose or Draw, 2005; Experience, 2009; Fugees Besides, 2007; Films: Mystery Men, 1999; Turn It Up, 2000; HigherEd, 2001; Go For Broke, 2002; Nora's Hair Salon, 2004; Careful What You Wish For, 2004; Feel the Noise, 2007; Reggaeton, 2007; First Night, 2006; Skid Row, 2007; The Mutant Chronicles, 2007. **Orgs:** PrAsperity Proj. **Honors/Awds:** Best Rap Album, The Score, 1997. **Special Achievements:** Launching a line of urban sportswear called Refugee Camp; author of Ghetto Superstar; Winner, Grammy Award Winner.

MICKELBURY, PENNY
Novelist, playwright. **Personal:** Born May 31, 1948, Atlanta, GA; daughter of Arthur Jennings and Mexico. **Educ:** Univ Ga, BA, 1971. **Career:** Novelist, writer, currently; Atlanta Voice, newspaper, 1968-69; Banner-Herald, reporter, 1970-71; Wash Post, reporter, 1971-72; Nat Caucus & Ctr on Black Aged, pub rels dir, 1972-75; WHUR-FM, news reporter, 1975-78; WJLA-TV, ABC, news reporter, 1978-84; asst news dir, 1984-87; City Kids Reperatory Co, teacher, 1988-89; Alchemy: Theatre Change, cofounder & managing dir, 1990-93; writing teacher, 1994-; Author: Keeping Secrets, 1994; Night Songs, 1995; Where to Choose: A Carol Ann Gibson Mystery, 1999; One Must Wait, 1999; Paradise Interrupted, 2001; Night Songs; Love Notes, 2002; Keeping Secrets; Darkness Descending, 2005; Two Graves Dug, 2005. **Honors/Awds:** Lambda Literary Award, Nightsongs. **Business Addr:** Writer, Novelist, clo Lisa A Jones, 1200 G St NW Suite 370, Washington, DC 20005.

MICKELL, DARREN
Football player. **Personal:** Born Aug 3, 1970, Miami, FL. **Educ:** Univ Fla. **Career:** Football player(retired), Kans City Chiefs, defensive end, 1992-95; New Orleans Saints, 1996-99; San Diego Chargers, 2000; Oakland Raiders, defensive end, 2001; free agent, currently. **Honors/Awds:** Rookie of the Year, 1992.

MICKENS, MAXINE
Executive. **Personal:** Born Dec 3, 1948, Clarksdale, MS; married Caesar Jr; children: Leonora. **Educ:** Univ Mich, AB, 1974; Comm Film Workshop Chicago, cert, 1976; ICBIF Small Bus mgmt Detroit, cert, 1978; Univ Phoenix, MBA, global mgt, 2001. **Career:** Max Belle & Assoc, vpres, 1977-; Simpson's Wholesale Detroit, adv mgr, 1977; WJLB Radio Detroit, merchandising & promotion dir, 1976-77; Detroit Bd Educ, voc & adult educ teacher, 1974-80; Detroit High Sch Fine & Performing Arts, govt & econ teacher. **Orgs:** WXYZ-TC Women's Adv Com Detroit Mich, 1974-76; Black Communicators Asn Detroit, 1979-; Nat Asn Media Women Detroit; communs chairperson, Triedstone Baptist Church, 1972-73; communs chairperson, Jeffersn Chalmers Com Asn, 1974-75. **Home Phone:** (313)894-0204. **Business Addr:** Vice president, Max Belle & Associates, 1308 Broadway Suite 206, Detroit, MI 48226.

MICKENS, DR. RONALD ELBERT
Research scientist, educator, mathematician. **Personal:** Born Feb 7, 1943, Petersburg, VA; son of Joseph P and Daisy; married Maria Kelker; children: Leah & James. **Educ:** Fisk Univ, BA, 1964; Vanderbilt Univ, PhD, 1968. **Career:** MIT Ctr for Theoret Physics, post doctoral res, 1968-70; Fisk Univ, Dept Physics, asst prof, 1970-81; MIT Dept Physics, vis prof physics, 1973-74; Morehouse Col/Atlanta Univ, vis prof, physics, 1979-80; Vanderbilt Univ Dept Physics, vis scholar, 1980-81; Joint Inst Lab astrophys Boulder, CO, res fel, 1981-82; Clark Atlanta Univ, chairperson 1984-86, distinguished Fuller E Callaway prof physics, 1985-. **Orgs:** Consult, Nat Acad Sci; Los Alamos Sci Lab; Col Old Westburg; Nat Sci Found, Dept Energy; Nat Insts Health; Am Asn Physics Teachers; Am Phys Soc; AAAS; Sigma Xi; Beta Kappa Chi; Am Math Asn; London Math Soc; Soc Math Biologists; Soc Indust & Appl Math; Am Math Soc; Nat Soc Black Physicists; Soc Math Biol. **Honors/Awds:** Phi Beta Kappa, Fisk Univ Chap elect, 1964; Woodrow Wilson Fellowship, 1964-65; Danforth Fellowship, 1965-68; Postdoctoral Fellowship, Nat Sci Found, 1968-70; Postdoctoral Fellowship, Ford Found, 1980-81; Fellowship, Joint Inst Lab Astrophys, 1981-82; research grants from Dept Energy, NASA, Nat Sci Found, GTE Found, Army Res Off; UNCF Distinguished Faculty Fellowship, 1984-85; Distinguished Lecturer for Sigma Xi, Res Soc, 2000-02. **Business Addr:** Distinguished Fuller E Callaway Professor, Clark Atlanta University, Department Physics, Rm 102 McPheeters-Dennis Hall 223 James P Brawley Dr SW, PO Box 1744, Atlanta, GA 30314, **Business Phone:** (404)880-6923.

MICKENS, WILLIAM RAY
Football player. **Personal:** Born Jan 4, 1973, Frankfurt, Germany; married Nicole; children: Kamray, Ray Jr & Preston. **Educ:** Tex A&M Univ. **Career:** New York Jets, defensive back, 1996-2004; Cleveland Browns, cornerback, 2005; New England Patriots, 2006; free agency, currently. **Honors/Awds:** All-American, 1994 & 1995; All-Southwest, 1994 & 1995.

MICKEY, DR. GORDON EUGENE
School administrator. **Personal:** Born in Chillicothe, OH; married Rosie Cheatham; children: Miguel Eugene & Madganna Mae. **Educ:** Ind Univ, Bloomington, BS, 1962, MS, 1966, EdD, 1971; Cleveland State Univ, post doctoral work; Univ Akron, psychol sch courses. **Career:** Indianapolis Pub Sch, teacher/coach, 1962-65; Ind Univ Div Univ Sch, instr, coach, 1966-69; New Castle Gunning Bedford Sch Dist, prin, 1971-73; St Dept Pub Instr, DE, state supt, 1973-76; Ment Retardation Prog, Lorain Co, OH, admin, consult, 1976-77; Akron Pub Sch, Akron, OH, unit prin, 1977-80; Stow City Sch, Stow, OH, cent off spec educ supvr, 1981-89, consult & special educ instr, 1990-. **Orgs:** Methodist Men's Orgn, 1980-91; Second Baptist Church, 1980-82; scholar comn Beautillion Militaire, 1980, 1981, 1983, 1985; founder, coordr, Minority Youth Recognition Prog, 1982-84; vpres, Akron Frontiers Club, 1982-84; chap consult, Jack & Jill Am Inc, 1986; exec bd, Neal-Marshall Alumni Club, 1986; ASCD; NABSE; Phi Delta Kappa; Alpha Phi Alpha; Coun Exceptional C. **Honors/Awds:** Presidential National Award, Frontiers Int, 1981; Commendation, Stow City Sch, 1985; President's Award, Akron Frontiers Club, 1986; Kentucky Colonel Award, IU Neal Marshall Alumni Club, 1987; Chillicothe High Sch Hall of Fame Inductee, 1993. **Home Addr:** PO Box 33592, Indianapolis, IN 46203-0592. **Business Addr:** Supervisor, Stow City Schools, 3227 Graham Rd, Stow, OH 44224, **Business Phone:** (330)678-0700.

MICKINS, ANDEL WATKINS
Educator. **Personal:** Born Oct 28, 1924, Central, SC; daughter of Ernest and Estelle Jamison; married Rev Isaac C, Jul 11, 1952; children: Isaac Clarence II. **Educ:** Tuskegee Inst, BS; Columbia Univ, MA. **Career:** Educator (retired); Head Home Econ Dept, sr, 1946-52; Holmes Elem Sch, teacher, 1953-62; Liberty City Elem, asst prin, 1962-67; Univ Miami, summer super teacher, 1965; RR Moton Elem, prin, 1967-72; Rainbow Park Elem, prin, 1972-81. **Orgs:** Pres, Friendship Garden Club; vpres, Baptist Women's Coun; supt, Sunday Sch; Temple Baptist Church; adv, Bus & profs Women's Club; pres, Ministers Wives Coun Greater Miami; spon Y-Teen; Alpha Kappa Alpha Sorority; Phi Lambda Theta Honor Soc; Kappa Delta Pi Honor Soc; Am Asn Univ Women; bd dir, Black Archives Found Res S Fla; chmn exec bd, Womens Conv Auxiliary,Fla Gen Baptist State Conv Inc; pres, Fla State Asn Ministers Wives; pres, Woman's Auxiliary, Fla E Coast Missionary Baptist Asn; chmn, Protocol, Woman's Auxiliary; Nat Baptist Conv USA Inc; Fac Int Asn Ministers' Wives& Ministers Widows; Gamma Zata Omega Chap, Alpha Kappa Alpha Sorority; Alpha Kappa Alpha; Phi Delta Kappa; Kappa Delta Pi; Pi Delta Kappa; life mem, Nat Educ Asn; Dade Co Adminr Asn; Nat Asn Elem Sch Prin; dir, Mem Temple Baptist Church, Early Childhood Educ Ctr. **Honors/Awds:** Sarah Blocker Award, Fla Mem Col; plaque Rainbow Park Elem Sch &Friendship Garden & Civic Club; plaque Alpha Kappa Alpha Sorority;Citation, City Miami; Nat Conf Christians & Jews.

MICKLE, ANDREA DENISE
School administrator. **Personal:** Born Jul 26, 1952, Kershaw, SC; daughter of John T and Mable Harris. **Educ:** Hampton Univ, BA, 1974; Adelphi Univ, cert, 1974; Howard Univ, MPA, 1985. **Career:** Howard Univ, financial aid officer; Minority Access Inc, pres & chief exec officer, currently. **Orgs:** Nat Asn Equal Opportunity Higher Educ, 1975-; Am Paralegal Asn, 1975-77;charter mem, Lawyer's Assts Inc, 1975; pres, Howard Univ Pi Alpha Alpha Honor Soc, 1984-85; DE-DC-MD Asn Stud Financial Aid Adminis; Am Soc Personnel Admin; Am Soc Pub Admin; Nat Asn Advan Colored People. **Honors/Awds:** Outstanding Service Award, Howard Univ Liberal Arts Stud Coun, 1979;Certificate of Service, Howard Univ Chap, ASPA, 1982; Certificate of Appreciation, Howard Univ Financial Aid Crisis Comn, 1989. **Home Addr:** 7201 Lena Way, Bowie, MD 20715. **Business Addr:** President,

Chief Executive Officer, Minority Access Inc, 5214 Baltimore Ave Suite 200, Hyattsville, MD 20781, **Business Phone:** (301)779-7100.

MICKS, DEITRA HANDY
Lawyer. **Personal:** Born May 26, 1945, Bronx, NY; daughter of John and Mabel; divorced. **Educ:** Howard Univ, BA, 1967; Howard Univ, JD, 1971. **Career:** Lawyer (retired); Jacksonville, legal aid, 1971-73; pvt prac, atty; Jackson & Micks; Univ N Fla, teacher; Duval Co, Fla, city council woman. **Orgs:** Bd dir, Legal Aid; life mem, Nat Advan Asn Colored People; Jacksonville chap; stud articles Ed Howard Law J, 1970-71; Gamma Sigma Sigma Sorority; Bethel Bapt Inst Church. **Home Addr:** 6650 Kinlock Dr W, Jacksonville, FL 32219, **Home Phone:** (904)764-9949. *

MIDDLEBROOKS, FELICIA
Television journalist, government official. **Personal:** Born May 29, 1957, Gary, IN; daughter of Raymond Middlebrooks Jr and Geraldine Rembert. **Educ:** Purdue Univ, Hammond, IN, BA, mass commun, 1982. **Career:** WBAA, anchor, 1976-77; WGVE Radio for Handicapped, anchor, 1978-81; Jones & Laughlin Steel, laborer, 1978-82; WJOB Radio, reporter & anchor, 1979-82; WLTH Radio, reporter & anchor, 1982-84; Total Living Network's Chicago Newsmakers, panelist; WBBM Radio, morning drive anchor & reporter, 1984-; Saltshake Productions, chief exec officer, currently; Purdue Univ Calumet. **Orgs:** Honorary chairperson, March of Dimes WalkAmerica, 1985-88; Chicago Asn Black Journalists, 1987-; bd mem, Cris Radio (Chicago land Reading Info Serv for the Handicapped), 1987-; Sigma Delta Chi Prof Journalists, 1987-; Women Commun, 1989; bd dirs, Chicagoland Radio Info Serv Blind; Ill News Broadcasters Asn; bd dirs, New Regal Theater Found; Women Film; trustee, C's Home; trustee, Aid Soc; bd dirs, WINGS; Hands of Hope; C's Home & Aid Soc. **Honors/Awds:** Benjamin Hooks Distinguished Achievement Recognition, Nat Asn Advan Colored People, 1987; Salute to Chicago's Up & Coming Black Bus & Prof Women, Dollars & Sense Mag, 1988; Tribute to Chicago Women, Midwest Women's Ctr, 1988; Sky Award of Merit, Outstanding Excellence Award, Outstanding Communicator, Women Commun, 1989; Best Reporter Award, Ill Assoc Press, 1989; Salute to Women in the Industry, Midwest Radio & Music Asn, 1992; Best Radio Reporter, Asn Black Journalists, 1987; Outstanding Young Citizens Award, Chicago Jaycees, 1991; Best Reporter Award, Assoc Press; Distinctive Imprint Award, Nat Asn Univ Women, 1993; Edward R. Murrow Award for Excellence in News; Outstanding Alumnus, Purdue Univ, 2003; Inductee, International Press Club's Chicago Journalism Hall of Fame. **Special Achievements:** First woman & first African American to co-anchor Morning Dr; first woman in Chicago to have survived the highly competitive timeslot for a record 22-years; her written work appears in a prestigious literary anthology, Souls of My Sisters; featured in Wash Jour Rev, 1987; been included in the Who's Who Among International Women in Cambridge England. **Business Addr:** Morning Drive Anchor, WBBM Newsradio 78, 630 N McClurg Ct, Chicago, IL 60611-4536, **Business Phone:** (312)202-3299.*

MIDDLETON, ERNEST J.
Educator. **Personal:** Born Dec 25, 1937, Franklin, LA; married Rosa Metz; children: Lance & Owen. **Educ:** Southern Univ, BA, 1962; Univ Colorodo, EdS, 1973; Univ Colo, EdD, 1974. **Career:** Univ KY, asso prof; St Mary Par Pub Sch, prof, 1962-63, 1965-70; St Mary Human Rel Coun, vpres, 1966; Southern Univ, EPDA fel, 1971; Univ Colo, EPDA fel, 1972; Race & Sex Desegregation, Training Inst, dir, 1974-; Clark Univ, Sch Educ, dean, 2001-07, prof curric, currently. **Orgs:** Pres, St Mary Educ Asn, 1967-70; chmn, St Mary Comm Action Agency, 1969;La Educ Asn; Southern Univ, 1958-62; Kappa Alpha Psi Fraternity; Nat Asn Advan Colored People; Phi Delta Kappa Fraternity; Nat Alliance Black Sch Educ; mem rep, Georgia Asn Independent Col of Teacher Education(GAICTE), 2006. **Honors/Awds:** ASCD Award, Bowling Green Univ, 1968; TDIS 1970-71; Outstanding Service Award, St Mary Par, 1970-71; Outstanding Achievement, La Educ Asn, 1974. **Military Serv:** AUS, 1963-65.

MIDDLETON, FRANK, JR.
Football player, football coach. **Personal:** Born Oct 25, 1974, Beaumont, TX; married Kristina; children: Kayla & Katlyn. **Educ:** Fort Scott Community Col, attended 1994; Ariz State Univ, criminal justice. **Career:** Football player (retired), Football coach; Tampa Bay Buccaneers, guard, 1997-2000; Oakland Raiders, guard, 2001-04; Monsignor Kelly High Sch, coach, currently. **Honors/Awds:** Rookie of the year, 1997.

MIDDLETON, HERBERT, JR. See **BLACQUE, TAUREAN.**

MIDDLETON, JOHN ALLEN
Educator. **Personal:** Born Nov 19, 1945, Hawthorne, FL; son of Theodore Agustus and Marguerite Ivey; children: Alicia, John II & LaTonya. **Educ:** Fla A&M Univ, BS, 1970; Univ Fla, MEd, 1974, EdD, 1984. **Career:** PCR Inc, chemist, 1970-72; Alachua County Sch Bd, teacher, 1972-78; Univ Fla, dir, 1978-79; Alachua County Sch Bd, prin, 1979-85; Volusia County Sch Bd, asst supt, 1985-90; Columbus City Sch, supt, 1990-92; Ohio State Univ, assoc prof, dir sch rel, 1992-94; Univ Cent Fla, assoc dean, 1994-97, assoc prof, 1997-. **Orgs:** Am Asn Sch Admr; SPP Fraternity; life mem, APA Fraternity. **Honors/Awds:** Science Hall Distinction, Fla A&M Univ, 1988. **Special Achievements:** A model preparation program for first year substitute teachers without a bachlors degree, 1984; first African supt in Columbus, Ohio. **Military Serv:** USAF, e-4, 1963-67. **Home Addr:** 10960 Dearden Circle, Orlando, FL 32817. **Business Phone:** (407)823-2835.

MIDDLETON, PHILLIP
Educator. **Personal:** Born Aug 10, 1947, Rocks, MD; married Theresa, Jun 20, 1987; children: Zoe Ross. **Educ:** Morris Brown Col, BA, 1969; Tenn State Univ, MA, 1974; Southern Ill Univ, PhD, 1979. **Career:** Al-Fetch Univ (Tripoli, Libya), asst prof Eng, 1978-80; Univ Niamey (Niger, W Afr), asst prof, 1980-83; Univ Khartoum (Sudan), Fulbright prof, 1984-87; Morris Brown Col, asst prof, 1987-89; Univ Cluj (Romania) Fulbright prof, 1995-97; Ferris State Univ, Col Arts & Sci, prof lang & lit, 1989-. **Orgs:** Nat Fulbright Asn; Sudan Studies Asn. **Honors/Awds:** Ford Found, fel PhD study, 1976-78; Coun Int Exchange Scholars, Fulbright-Hays Fel, Sudan, 1984-87, Romania, 1995-97. **Special Achievements:** Publ journs: Succrnochee Review, New Growth Arts Review, Catalyst, Old Mill Pond Anthology, other journals & books. **Military Serv:** AUS, E-4, 1969-71. **Business Phone:** (231)591-5878.

MIDDLETON, REV. DR. RICHARD TEMPLE
Educator. **Personal:** Born Jan 17, 1942, Jackson, MS; son of Richard T II and Johnnie Beadle; married Brenda Marie Wolfe; children: Jeanna E & Richard T IV. **Educ:** Lincoln Univ, BS, 1963, MEd, 1965; Univ Southern Mo, EdD, 1972. **Career:** Tougaloo Col, instr educ, 1967-70; Jackson State Univ, asst & assoc prof, 1970-76, dir student teaching, 1976-97; St Mark's Episcopal Church, priest, 1995-. **Orgs:** Security Life Ins Co, 1985; pres, Beta Gamma Boule Sigma Pi Phi Fraternity, 1985-87; bd mem, Opera S Co, 1986-90; Cath Charities, 1986-90; Nat Exec Coun, Episcopal Church, 1987-88; vpres, Miss Relig Leadership Conf, 1988-89; vice chmn, Jackson, MS Planning Bd, 1990-94; bd examiners, NCATE. **Honors/Awds:** Woodrow-Wilson King Fel, Doctoral Study, 1969. **Military Serv:** AUS, first lt, 2 yrs. **Home Addr:** 944 Royal Oak Dr, Jackson, MS 39209, **Home Phone:** (601)922-8047. **Business Addr:** Priest, St Mark's Episcopal Church, 903 Metro Pkwy, Jackson, MS 39203, **Business Phone:** (601)353-0246.

MIDDLETON, ROSE NIXON
Consultant, school administrator. **Personal:** Born Jun 3, 1932, Gum Tree, PA; daughter of Havard Downing Nixon and Margaret Black Nixon; married C T, Mar 12, 1951; children: Karen Ann Nixon Middleton & Tanya Hope Nixon Middleton. **Educ:** Univ Pa, Philadelphia, Pa, AB, 1954; Bryn Mawr Col, Bryn Mawr, Pa, MSS, 1958. **Career:** Child Care Serv Chester County, West Chester, Pa, child welfare worker, 1960-62; Child Study Ctr Philadelphia, Philadelphia, Pa, psychiat social worker, 1962-66; Ment Health Ctr, West Chester, Pa, sr psychiat social worker, 1966-68; Chester County Intermediate Unit, Coatesville, Pa, admin asst dir spec educ preSch prog, 1968-89; Expertise & Assistance, Coatesville, Pa, pres, 1990-. **Orgs:** Commun Task Force mem, Downingtown Area Sch Dist, 1991-; treas, bd dir, United Cerebral Palsy Asn, 1989-; pres, bd dir, 1985-86, mem, 1980-86, Chester County Head Start, Inc; bd dir, pres, Handi-Crafters Inc, 1971-73; secy, bd dir, Brandywine Red Cross, 1983-84; founder, Chester County Local C's Team, 1979; handicapped serv comt chmn, Rotary Int, 1988-. **Honors/Awds:** Scholar, Senate Pa, 1950-54; Scholar, Nat Inst Ment Health, 1956-58; Chester County Woman of Achievement for Public Service, 1996. **Home Addr:** Sky Vue Box 242A Rd Suite 1, Coatesville, PA 19320. **Business Addr:** President, Expertise and Assistance, 1263 Lone Eagle Rd, Coatesville, PA 19320, **Business Phone:** (215)383-4387.

MIKELL, CHARLES DONALD
Health services administrator. **Personal:** Born Jan 12, 1934, McKeesport, PA; son of Sadie Bell Qualls and Eugene Mikell; married Jacqueline Henry, Oct 20, 1961; children: Michelene Wofford & Charles D II. **Educ:** Lincoln Univ, AB, 1960; Univ Pittsburgh, Pittsburgh, PA, MPA, 1968, MPH, 1972. **Career:** Allegheny Co Health Dept, pub health san, 1960-64; Neighborhood develop worker, 1964-65; Hill Dist Community Action Prog, asst coord, 1965-66; Hill Emergency Lift Prog, supr, 1966-67; Hill Rehab Ctr, asst dir, 1967-68; acad & prof consult, 1968-69; Hill Rehab Ctr, dir, 1968-70; Alcoholic Couns & Recovery Prog CAP Inc, dir, 1970-; Univ Pittsburgh, field supr grad studs, 1971-; McKeesport Area Health Syst, asst adminr, 1978-89; Family Health Coun Inc, proj coordr, 1989-91; Primary Care Health Serv, consult, 1998-. **Orgs:** Pa HIV State Planning Com, Harrisburg, 1994-; Pa HIV Planning Coun, Harrisburg, 1997-; former pres, City Coun, McKeesport; former chair, McKeesport Redevelop Authority; former chair, McKeesport Housing Authority; bd mem, Allegheny County Ment Health; Ment Retardation, Drug & Alcohol Bd, Pittsburgh; former vpres, bd, McKeesport YMCA; Booker T. Wash Lodge 218. **Honors/Awds:** Bronze Key Award, Nat Coun Alcoholism Inc, 1975; Community Service Awards, Pittsburgh; Outstanding Achievements in the field of Alcoholism, Col Consults Inc. **Special Achievements:** Author: "The Delivery of HTH Services to Low Income People," dissertation; co-author: "Peer Networkers: One Key to HIV Prevention for Women in High Risk Communities," HIV Infection in Women Conference, 1995; "Teen Peers: HIV Prevention Through Teenage Peer Networkers," PA Pub Health Asn, 1996; "Peers in Public Housing: Case Studies in the Develop & Maintenance of Peer Networks for HIV & Unintended Pregnancy Prevention," Am Pub Health Asn meeting & exhibition, 1996. **Military Serv:** USNR, 1950-52; USMC, Cpl, 1952-55; US Presidential Unit Citation. **Home Addr:** 1726 Eagle Ridge Dr, Monroeville, PA 15146-1769.

MIKELL, JOHNNY
Executive director. **Career:** Novartis Pharmaceut Corp, dir quality, vpres qual assurance, currently. **Business Addr:** Vice President of Quality Assurance, Novartis Pharmaceuticals Corporation, 1 Health Plz, East Hanover, NJ 07936, **Business Phone:** (862)778-8300.*

MILBOURNE, LAWRENCE WILLIAM
Baseball player, baseball executive. **Personal:** Born Feb 14, 1951, Port Norris, NJ. **Career:** Baseball player (retired), Baseball executive; Houston Astros, infielder, 1974-76; Seattle Mariners, infielder, 1977-80, 1984-85; NY Yankees,infielder, 1981-83; Minn Twins, infielder, 1982; Cleveland Indians, infielder, 1982; Philadelphia Phillies, infielder, 1983; New York Mets, instructor.

MILBURN, DR. CORINNE M.
Educator. **Personal:** Born Sep 20, 1930, Alexandria, LA; daughter of Corinne Neal Martin Brown and Ramsey Martin (deceased); married Dr Sidney E, Jun 14, 1952 (deceased); children: Sidney E II & Deborah Anne. **Educ:** Marian Col Indpls, BS, 1950; Univ SD, MA, 1970, EdD, 1976. **Career:** Ind Univ Med Ctr, lab tech (clin biochem) 1950-53; Carver Found-Tuskegee Inst, tissue culture tech, 1954-57; Elk Point Pub Sch, high sch teacher, 1969-73, teacher corps team leader, 1973-75; grad intern sci consult, AEA12-Sioux City, 1975-76; proj writer-HEW grant, Univ SDak, 1976-77; Univ SDak, asst prof & dir outreach, assoc prof, assoc dean sch edu, 1990, profemer. **Orgs:** St pres, Epsilon Sigma Alpha Int, 1977-78; chap pres, Phi Delta Kappa(USD chpt), 1979-80; st pres, Asn Teacher Educators, 1979-80; exec dir, SDak Asn Middle Level Educ; int pres, Epsilon Sigma Alpha Int, 1986-87. **Special Achievements:** Published articles "Leaders of Amer Sec Educators" 1972; voc educ "AChallenging Alternative for the Gifted/Talented Student" 1976; voc educ "A New Dimension for the Gifted/Talented Student" 1976; "Education-A Life long Process" ESA Jour 1980; Helping to make the transition from high school to College, 1988. *

MILBURN, GLYN CURT
Football player. **Personal:** Born Feb 19, 1971, Los Angeles, CA. **Educ:** Univ Stanford, BA. public policy. **Career:** Football player (retired); Denver Broncos, wide receiver, 1993-95; Detroit Lions, 1996-97; Chicago Bears, 1998-01; San Diego Chargers, 2001; Austin Wranglers, gen mgr & dir player personnel, 2004-. **Business Addr:** General Manager, Director of player personnel, Austin Wranglers, 2209 w barker Lane, Austin, TX 78758, **Business Phone:** (512)491-6600.

MILES, ALBERT BENJAMIN
Executive. **Personal:** Born Jan 7, 1956, Brooklyn, NY; son of Albert Miles Sr and Marguerite; married Susan J Burns, Aug 23, 1981; children: A Benjamin III & Claire. **Educ:** Wesleyan Univ, BA, 1978, MLS, 1990; Northwestern Univ, Kellogg Exec Prog, Cert, 1987; RPI, MBA, 1992. **Career:** SNET, mgr, cre data ctr, 1988-94, dir, cre data network, 1994-95; Citizens Utilities, dir, pinnacle proj, 1995-96, dir, cre strategic archit, 1997-; Starcast Inc, chief technol officer. **Orgs:** Bd mem, Dixwell Community Ctr, 1988-93; Guide, 1988-90; Share, 1988-90; bd mem, New Haven Boys Club, 1989-90; Meriden CT SNET Bus Partnership, founding mem, 1990-93; bd mem, Community Health Ctr, 1990-95; bd mem, Lenua S Williams, MD, 1991-; commun dir, Spec Olympics World Games, 1995. **Honors/Awds:** Service Award, Dixwell Community Ctr, 1993. **Business Addr:** Director, Citizens Utilities, High Ridge Office Pk, Stamford, CT 06905, **Business Phone:** (203)595-6657.

MILES, CARLOTTA G.
Physician. **Personal:** Born Sep 19, 1937, St Augustine, FL; married Theodore A; children: Wendell Gordon, Cecily Allison, Lydia Carlotta. **Educ:** Wheaton Col, AB, 1959; Howard Univ Med Sch, MD, 1964. **Career:** Howard Univ Col Med, asst prof psychiat; Wash Sch Psychiat, fac; Pvt Pract, physician, 1968-; Area B Children's Prog, co-dir, 1969-71. **Orgs:** Am Psychiat Asn; Am Acad Child Psychiat; affil mem, Am Psychoanalytic Inst; trustee Wheaton Col; Black Stud Fund Wash; adv bd mem, Nat Urban Technol Ctr. **Honors/Awds:** Clerkship Prize, Howard Univ Med Sch, 1964. **Business Addr:** Psychiatrist, 3000 Conn Ave NW, Washington, DC 20008.

MILES, DR. E. W.
Educator. **Personal:** Born May 4, 1934, Hearne, TX; married Frances Winfield; children: Tony W & Christopher W. **Educ:** Prairie View Univ, BA, 1955; Ind Univ, AM, 1960, PhD, 1962. **Career:** Prairie View Univ, assoc prof, 1962-65; Univ NC, visiting fac scholar, 1965-66; IN Univ, visiting summer prof, 1966; San

Diego State Univ, prof polit sci, 1966; So Univ, 1967; Univ Tex, 1971. **Orgs:** San Diego Blue Ribbon Comn Charter Review, 1968; assoc ed, West Pol Sci Quarterly; exec, Comn CA State Assembly Fel Prog; State-Wide Anti-Discrimination Comn; Unit Prof CA; chmn, Comn Status Blacks Am Polit Sci Asn; past mem, exec coun, Western Polit Sci Asn; adv panel CA Bd Educ,1969-70; bd dirs, Law Am Soc Found; chmn bd, San Diego Urban League,1983-; pres, delegate-at-large, Nat Bd, ACL, 1989-; San Diego & Imperial Counties, 1990; trustee, Ctr Res & Develop Law Related Educ, 1991. **Honors/Awds:** Distinguished Teaching Award, San Diego State Univ, 1968. **Special Achievements:** Co-author of Vital Issues of the Constitution, 1975, author of various scholarly articles. **Military Serv:** USY, 1st lt, 1955-57.

MILES, DR. EDWARD LANCELOT
Educator. **Personal:** Born Dec 21, 1939; son of Louise Dufont Miles and Cecil B Miles; married Wanda Elaine Merrick (divorced); children: Anthony Roger & Leila Yvonne. **Educ:** Howard Univ, BA, 1962; Univ Denver Grad Sch Int Studies, PhD, 1965. **Career:** Univ Denver, instr, 1965-66, from asst prof to assoc prof, 1966-74; Univ Denver Grad Sch Int Studies, assoc prof, 1970-74; Univ Wash, prof, Marine Studies & Pub Affairs, 1974-, Virginia & Prentice Bloedel prof, 1994-, dir, Sch Marine Affairs, 1982-93, chmn Univ Comt Interdisciplinary Res & Grad Educ, 1991-92, chmn, Pres Task force Environ Educ, 1995-96, Va & Prentice Bloedel Prof, Marine Stud & Pub Affairs, 1994-; Joint Inst Study Atmosphere & Oceans, sr fel, 1995; CSES Dir, Climate Impacts Group (CIG), Univ Washington. **Orgs:** Bd ed, int org, 1969-77; Ocean Policy Comn; chmn, Nat Res Coun, 1970-79; exec bd, Univ Hawaii-Law Sea Inst, 1971-; assoc ed, Ocean Develop & Int Law J, 1973-; joint appointee, Micronesian Maritime Auth Fed States Micr, 1977-83; chief negotiator, Micronesian Maritime Authority, 1983-92; chmn,adv comn int prog, Nat Sci Found, 1990-93; US Nat Acad Sci, 2003; AAAS, 2005. **Honors/Awds:** Received numerous awards including Honors in history, Phi Beta Kappa, 1962; Int Affairs Fel, Coun Foreign Rel Inc, 1972-73; James P Warburg Fel, Harvard Univ, 1973-74; Coun Foreign Rel, 1990; Distinguished Research Award, Col Ocean & Fisheries Sci, Univ Wash, 1999; Sabbatical award, Univ Wash, 1986-87, 1993-94, 2001-02. **Business Addr:** Virginia & Prentice Bloedel professor, University of Washington, School of Marine Affairs, 3707 Brooklyn Ave NE, Seattle, WA 98105-6715, **Business Phone:** (206)543-7004.

MILES, FRANK J W
Executive. **Personal:** Born Dec 18, 1944, Orange, NJ; married Brenda. **Educ:** Hampton Univ, BA; Columbia Univ, MBA. **Career:** State NJ, maj acct relationships; Citibank NA, vpres. **Orgs:** Vol Urban Consult Minority Bus; former Mayor's Appointee Co Econ Develop Corp; Omego Psi Phi Fraternity; Urban Bankers Asn; NJ Real Estate Asn; Nat Black MBA Asn. **Military Serv:** AUS, capt.

MILES, FREDERICK AUGUSTUS
Psychiatrist. **Personal:** Born May 25, 1928, Boston, MA; married Cora Edythe; children: Frederick, Felix & Andre. **Educ:** Va State Col, BS, 1949; Columbia Univ, 1951; Hunter Col, 1955; Univ Basel, Switzerland, 1958; Univ Freiburg, W Germany, MD, 1964. **Career:** Kingsboro Psych Ctr, resident; Brooklyn-Cumberland Med Ctr, intern & resident pathol, 1966-68; Brooklyn State Hosp, residency psychiat, 1969-72; Pvt Pract, psychiatrist, currently; Brooklyn State Hosp, staff psychiatrist; Willia Hardgrow Mental Health Clinic, consult psychiatrist. **Orgs:** Am Med Asn; Am Psychol Asn; NY & Kings Co Med Soc; Am Asn Geriat Psychiat; Asn Comprehensive Energy Psychol; Am Col Physicians; Provident Med Soc Brooklyn; United Demo Club; Kappa Alpha Psi; Redeemer Baptist Church. **Military Serv:** AUS, German interrogator 1952-55. **Business Addr:** Psychiatrist, 808 New York Ave, Brooklyn, NY 11226.*

MILES, GEORGE L
Executive. **Personal:** Born Nov 13, 1941, Orange, NJ; son of George L Sr and Eula Miles; married Janet, Jun 25, 1966; children: Tammy Brown. **Educ:** Seton Hall Univ, BA, 1963; Fairleigh Dickinson Univ, MBA, 1970. **Career:** Touche & Ross, mgr, 1969-78; KDKA-TV, Pittsburgh, bus mgr, controller, 1978-80; WPCQ-TV, Charlotte, NC, sta mgr, controller, 1980-81; Westinghouse TV Group, vpres, controller, 1981; WBZ-TV, Boston, sta mgr, 1981-84; WNET-TV, NY, exec vpres/chief operating officer, 1984-94; WQED Multimedia, Pittsburgh, pres & chief exec officer, 1994-. **Orgs:** Bd mem, Sigma Pi Phi Frat; bd mem, Allegheny Conf Community Develop; bd mem, Black Broadcasters Asn; bd mem, Mentoring Partnership Southwestern Pa; bd mem, Pub Broadcasting Serv; bd mem, Urban League Pittsburgh; bd dirs, Harley-Davidson; bd dirs, Westwood One; bd dirs, WESCO Int Inc; bd dirs, Equitable Resources Inc; bd dirs, Citizens Financial Group Inc; bd dirs, Applied Technol Systs Inc; African Am Chamber Com Western Pa; Carnegie Mus Pittsburgh; WESCO Int Inc; chair, Urban League Pittsburgh; co-chair, Mentoring Partnership Southwestern Pa; bd dirs, Am Int Group. **Honors/Awds:** Hon Doctorate Law, St Joseph Col, 1989; Pinnacle Award, Fairleigh Dickinson Univ, 1989; Hon Doctorate, Robert Morris Univ. **Military Serv:** AUS, sp/4, 1964-66; Vietnam Service Medal. **Business Addr:** President, Chief Executive Officer, WQED Multimedia, 4802 5th Ave, Pittsburgh, PA 15213, **Business Phone:** (412)622-1370.

MILES, DR. NORMAN KENNETH
Clergy, educator. **Personal:** Born Dec 5, 1946, Toledo, OH; son of Mervin and Sadie; married Doris Calandra Goree; children: Erica Lynette, Norman Jr, Candace Renee, Kira Danette & Neal Mervyn. **Educ:** Oakwood Col, BA, theol, 1964-68; Andrews Univ, MDiv, 1972-73; Univ Mich, MA, 1974, PhD 1978. **Career:** Econ Opportunity Planning Asn, work counr, 1968-69; S Cent Conf & Seventh Day Adventists, pastor, 1969-72; Lake Regional Conf Seventh Day Adventists, pastor 1974-77; Seventh Day Adventists, prof 1977-; Univ Mich, adj prof relig, 1977-; Andrews Univ, Christian Ministry Dept, chmn, 1988-; Hyde Pk Seventh-Day Adventist Church, pastor, 1989-; Andrews Univ, Urban Ministry, assoc prof, adj prof, prof, currently. **Orgs:** Mp Ministerial Alliance, Hattiesburg, MS, 1969-72; bd dir, Southern Miss Chap, Am Red Cross; mem, Nat Black Pastors Conf, 1980-; dir, Inst Human Rels Seventh Day Adventist Church, 1983; bd trustees, Andrews Univ. **Honors/Awds:** John Pierce Award, Hist Scholar Univ Mich, 1975. **Business Addr:** Pastor, Minister, Hyde Pk Seventh-day Adventist Church, 4608 S Drexel Blvd, Chicago, IL 60653, **Business Phone:** (773)373-2909.

MILES, RACHEL JEAN
Educator. **Personal:** Born Sep 3, 1945, Memphis, TN; married Willie T; children: Lisa & Jason. **Educ:** Lemoyne-Owen Col, BS, 1967; Memphis State Univ, EdM, guid & coun, 1970; Memphis State Univ, post grad, 1971. **Career:** Memphis City Sch Syst, elem teacher, 1967-68; Memphis State Univ, counsr, 1969-70; Moorestown Township Col Prep, guid counr, 1971; Fairview Jr High Sch, counr eng teacher, 1971-72; Shelby State Community Col, prof counr, 1972-75, coord coun adv, 1975; Tenn Indust Develop Coun, econ develop rep, currently. **Orgs:** JUGS Charitable Orgn, 1967-; Cherokee Community Civic Club, 1969-; Kappa Delta Pi Honor Soc, Memphis State Univ, 1970; Phi Delta Kappa, Memphis State Univ, 1971; secy, Westlawn-Galveston Block Club, 1972-; pres & bd dirs, Human Employment Resources Inc, 1979-80; bd dirs, Miss Black Memphis Pageant, 1979-80; workshop presenter, Am Personnel & Guidance Asn, 1980. **Honors/Awds:** Col Aide De Camp, Gov Ray Blanton, 1977-78; Honorary Staff Member, Tenn House Rep, 1977-78. **Business Addr:** Economic Development Representative, Tennessee Industrial Development Council, 22 N Front St Suite 200, Memphis, TN 38103, **Business Phone:** (901)543-3561.

MILES, RUBY A BRANCH
Librarian. **Personal:** Born Sep 6, 1941, Houston, TX; daughter of Richard Andrew and Ernestine Phelps; married Emerson Edward, Apr 18, 1970 (died 1971). **Educ:** Prairie View A&M Univ, BS, educ, 1963; Atlanta Univ, MLS, 1969. **Career:** Atlanta Fulton Pub Libr, child/young adult librn, 1969-71, br head, 1971-77; Houston Independent Sch Dist, Houston Tech Inst, librn, 1977-79, Gregory-Lincoln Educ Ctr, librn, 1979-85, Bellaire High Sch, librn, 1986-90, DeBakey High Sch Health Prof, librn, 1990-; Houston Community Col Syst, part-time campus librn, 1985-; Houston Acad Med, Tex Med Ctr Libr, part-time librn, 1997-. **Orgs:** Am Asn Univ Women, 1971-; Am Libr Asn, 1984-, Young Adult Serv Asn Community, 1984-88, 1992-96; Tex Libr Asn, 1991-92. **Honors/Awds:** Houston Ind Sch Dist, Librarian of the Year, 1993-94. **Home Addr:** 4514 Connies Ct Lane, Missouri City, TX 77459. **Business Addr:** Librarian, Michael E DeBakey High School for Health Professions, Houston Independent School District, 3100 Shenandoah St, Houston, TX 77021, **Business Phone:** (713)746-5215.

MILES, STEEN
Television journalist, senator (u.s. federal government). **Personal:** Born Aug 20, 1946, South Bend, IN; daughter of Rev Austin A Davis (deceased) and Rose E Wheeler Davis (deceased); divorced; children: Kellie J King Middleton & Heather Lynne King. **Educ:** Ball State Univ, bus educ, eng; Ind Univ, commun; Daniel Sch Mgt. **Career:** Journalist (retired), media relations consultant (retired), senator; WNDU-TV, reporter, anchor & talk show hostess, 1969-73; WMAQ, NBC Radio, reporter & anchor, 1973-78; WGCI, news dir, 1978-80; United Press Int, broadcast ed, 1981-84; WXIA-TV, assignment ed, 1984-86, managing ed, 1986-89, reporter & anchor, 1989-99; MARTA, chief media rels officer & spokesperson; SMCI, pres & ceo, currently; Senate Dist 43, senator, 2004-. **Orgs:** Ga Asn Broadcasters, 1982-84; bd mem, Salvation Army Adv Bd, 1988-92; Atlanta Asn Black Journalists, 1989-; Nat Asn Media Women, 1989-; mentor, SCLC, 1995-; pres, Jack & Jill Am Stone Mountain, 1988-92; bd mem, Dekalb Co Chamber Com, 1988-91; bd mem, Nat Acad TV Arts & Sci, 1988-91; bd mem, Victims Witness Assistance Adv Bd, 1992-; charter mem, Decatur-Dekalb Coalition 100 Black Women; Dekalb Acad Leaders; bd mem, Proj Impact, 1994-. **Honors/Awds:** Numerous honors and awards including Pioneer Award, Nat Asn Media Women, 1976; Best Spot News, United Press Int, 1976; Woman of Achievement, 11 alive, YWCA, 1988; One Emmy; Three Emmy Nominations, Two Best Newscast, Best Feature, 1989-91; Four Best TV Feature, Nat Asn Black Journalists Award, 1989, 1992; Best Feature, Ga Associated Press, 1991; Community Service Award, Toney Gardens Civic Asn, 1992; AABJ, Pioneer Journalist of the Year, 1996; Ordinary Women Doing Extraordinary Things, Metro Atlanta. **Special Achievements:** Carter Administration White House Briefing, 1979, 100 Best and Brightest Women, Dollars and Sense Magazine, 1989, Bush Administration White House Luncheon, 1989. **Business Addr:** Senator, Georgia State Senate, District 43, 325 B Coverdell Office, Atlanta, GA 30334, **Business Phone:** (404)463-2598.

MILES-LAGRANGE, VICKI
Judge. **Educ:** Vassar Col, attended 1974; Howard Univ, Sch Law; Univ Ghana. **Career:** TV news reporter; Speaker US House Reps, Carl Albert, cong aide; US Dept Justice, criminal trial atty; Fed Ct, Dist Judge Woodrow Seals, SD Tex, law clerk; Oklahoma County, asst dist atty; Oklahoma Senate Judiciary Comt, chmn; Legislative Black Caucus; pvt pratice, 1986-93; US Dist Fed, Western Dist Okla, judge, currently. **Orgs:** Bd trustees, Vassar Col; bd dirs, Kirkpatrick Mus & Planetarium; Alpha Kappa Alpha Sorority; Links Inc; Urban League; Nat Asn Advan Colored People; Oklahoma Heritage Asn; Am Bar Asn; Okla Bar Asn; Oklahoma Black Lawyers Asn; US Judicial Conf's Int Judicial Rels Comm, 1999-05; chair, Comn Africa Working Group, 1999-05; regional dir, Midwestern Region; Judicial Coun US Ct Appeals 10th Circuit & Am Bar Asn; Africa Law Initiative Adv Coun; Int Judicial Rels Comt Judicial Conf United States. **Honors/Awds:** Honarary Doctor of Laws, Oklahoma City Univ. **Special Achievements:** first African Am woman to be sworn in as US atty Western Dist Oklahoma; the first African Am female elected to the Oklahoma Senate. **Business Addr:** US District Judge, US District Court Western District of Oklahoma, 200 NW 4th St Rm 5011, Ct Rm 501 5th Fl, Oklahoma City, OK 73102, **Business Phone:** (405)609-5400.*

MILLARD, DR. THOMAS LEWIS
Educator, editor. **Personal:** Born Mar 8, 1927, Newark, NJ; son of James and Elizabeth; married P Anne Kelsic; children: Elizabeth Millard Reaves, Thomas Lewis Jr & James Edward. **Educ:** Rutgers Univ, AB, 1952; Columbia Univ, The New York Sch Social Work, MS, 1956; New York Univ, MA, 1960; Columbia Univ, Third Yr Cert, 1969; The Drug Dependence Inst, Yale Univ Sch Med, attended 1971; Fairleigh Dickerson Univ, EdD, 1976; Acad Behav Med & Prof Coun, Prof Psychother Inst, dipl, 1983. **Career:** New York Youth Serv Bur, youth parole officer, 1956-59; United Parent Asn, New York City Bd Educ, consult commun sch rel, 1959-60; Irvington House, social worker, 1960-61; Public Schs, Newark Bd Educ, sch social worker, 1961-65; Montclair State Univ, prof educ, social work & coord sch social work; Clearing House J, consult ed, 1981-95; Marital & Family Therapist, NJ,1983; J Educators & Scholars, consult ed, 1985-90; Int J Adolescence & Youth, consult ed, 1990-; Monuclair State Univ, prof emer, currently. **Orgs:** Pres, Bd Educ Orange, NJ, 1968-71; del, White House Conf C, 1970; Ment Health Asn New Jersey; vice chmn bd trustees, New Jersey Neuro Psychiatric Inst, 1977-79; bd dir, New Jersey State Prison Complex, 1979-81; bd dir, Alcoholic Trmnt Fac Inc, 1981-84; fel, Am Orthopsychiatric Asn, 1982; bd dirs, Ment Health Asn Morris County, 1983-; app mem, Governor New Jersey State Bd Marriage & Family Therapist Examiners, 1988-95; vice chair, New Jersey State Bd Marriage & Family Therapist Examiners, currently. **Honors/Awds:** Honor, New Jersey State Assembly Resolution Citing Outstanding Teaching. **Special Achievements:** Presented scholarly papers at conferences in US, Canada, Puerto Rico, Africa, Europe, Australia, Japan and Mexico. **Military Serv:** AUS lt col USAR-RET ACTIVE & reserve; WW II Ribbon, Occupation Ribbon (Japan), Victory Medal, 1946. **Business Addr:** Professor Emeritus, Montclair State University, 1 Normal Ave, Montclair, NJ 07043, **Business Phone:** (973)655-7971.

MILLEDGE, DR. LUETTA UPSHUR
School administrator, educator. **Personal:** Born in Savannah, GA; children: Marshall L Upshur. **Educ:** Ft Valley State Col, BA, Eng, 1948; Atlanta Univ, MA, Eng, 1949; Univ Georgia, PhD Eng, 1971. **Career:** Ford Found fel, 1969-71; Savannah State Col, asst instr, assoc prof, prof, chr div human, 1973-80, head, Dept Eng, 1972-80, head, Dept Humanities/Fine Arts, 1980-84, head, Dept Humanities, 1984-91, prof emer, 1991-. **Orgs:** Bd mem, GA Endowment Humanities, 1980-83; Elder Butler Presbytery Church; pres, Community Future Savannah State Col; Phi Kappa Phi, Phi Beta Kappa; Ga Humanities Coun. **Honors/Awds:** George Washington Honor Medal; Freedoms Found Valley Forge Speech Vital Speech, 1973; Phi Kappa Phi, Phi Beta Kappa, Univ GA; Co-Teacher of the Year, Sch Humanities, 1989. **Home Addr:** 918 Carver St, Savannah, GA 31415. **Business Addr:** Professor Emeritus, Savannah State University, Department of Humanities/Fine Arts, PO Box 20029, Savannah, GA 31404, **Business Phone:** (912)356-2368.

MILLENDER, B PENNIE
Judge. **Educ:** Olivet Col, Southern Univ, BA, psychol, 1974; Wayne State Univ, MA, voc rehab coun, 1976; Detroit Col Law, PhD, 1987. **Career:** Nat Labor Rels Bd, Region 7, atty, 1987-90; 36th Dist Ct, magistrate, 1997-2004; 36th Dist Ct, judge, 2004-. **Orgs:** Vpres, Wolverine Stud Bar Asn; chairperson, Civil Liberties Comt, State Bar Mich, 1995-97; Asn Black Judges Mich; Robert L Millender Sr Mem Fund; life mem, Nat Asn Advan Colored People. **Honors/Awds:** Harold E Bledsoe Award for Academic Excellence; American Jurisprudence Book Award. **Business Addr:** Judge, Michigan's 36th District Court, Rm 2028 421 Madison Ave, Detroit, MI 48226, **Business Phone:** (313)965-8729.*

MILLENDER, DHARATHULA H.
School administrator. **Personal:** Born Feb 4, 1920, Terre Haute, IN; daughter of Orestes Hood and Daisy Ernestine Eslick Hood; married Justyn L, 1944 (deceased); children: Naomi Estelle, Justine Faye & Preston (Isaac). **Educ:** Ind State Univ, BS, 1941; Purdue Univ, MS, 1967. **Career:** School administrator (retired), Bettis Jr Col, librn, 1941-42; Pmoney HS, librn teacher, 1942-43; Netherlands Studies Unit Libr Cong, ref asst, 1943-44; Serv Club No 2 Ind Town & Gap Mil Reser, army librn, 1944; Lincoln Jr High Montgomery County, teacher 1952-53; Houston Jr High Sch Baltimore, librn, 1953-60; Dunbar-Pulaski Sch Gary, librn media specialist, 1960-78; Black Exper Film News Mag, ed, 1973-82; Gary Sch Syst, librn/media specialist, 1960-78, sch radio stn, 1978-83, reading lab coordr, 1979-82; Gary Hist & Cultural Soc Inc, chief exec officer. **Orgs:** Former state chmn; Hist & Cul 1966-72; libr, Multi-Media Coun Model Cities Dayton 1969-70; Gary Precinct Comt woman, 1972-80; prog coordr, Cable TV Gary channel 3a, 1973-; State Hist IN Black Pol Caucus 1973; hist, Gary Chap Ind State Black Caucus, 1973; mat from Black Exper State dir, Asn Study Afro-Am Life & Hist, 1973; chairperson & founder, Gary Hist & Cultural Soc, 1977; former organist, St Philip Luth Church; pres, NIMM Educ Media Serv Inc; Louis Armstrong-Rev Simon & Schuster, 1997; libr, Media Consul Model Cities Gary dev media ctr, Community Res Ctr Gary;radio prog, Lift Every Voice & Sing sta, WWCA; chrmn, Gary NAACP Black Hist Com, 1962-72; libr trustee, Gary Pub Libr, 1971-75, 1982-86; Gary Hist & Cultural Soc Inc, 1971-; historian, Nat Black Caucus - Nat League of Cities, 1984-92; consult, Follow Through Cultural Linguistic Approach1989-; Gary City Coun, 1980-92; historian, City Gary; vpres, Gary Sch Bd Trustees, 1992-; organizer & secy, Peace Lutheran Church Gary, 1989-. **Honors/Awds:** Commendable Book by an Indiana Author Awd for Crispus Attucks, Indiana Writers Conf, 1966; outstanding serv Rendered to Comm Award, Gary NAACP, 1966; Media Women's Award, Natl Assn of Media Women, 1974; Outstanding Women of Lake County, IN, 1984; author: Brief Note on the Early Development of Lake County & Gary, IN, published by Gary Historical & Cultural Society, Inc, 1988; History of Gary City Council, 1992, revised,1995. **Special Achievements:** Author, 4 Books & num articles in journ & educ mags. **Home Addr:** 2409 W 5th Ave, Gary, IN 46404. *

MILLENDER, MALLORY KIMERLING
Publisher, editor, educator. **Personal:** Born Jul 11, 1942, Birmingham, AL; married Jacqueline Stripling; children: Mallory Jr & Marlon. **Educ:** Paine Col, BA, eng lit, 1964; Univ Toulouse, 1966; Kans State Teachers Col, MS, foreign lang, 1969; Columbia Univ, MSJ, 1977; Clark Atlanta Univ, DA, 1996. **Career:** TW Josey High Sch, teacher, 1964-67; Paine Col, asst prof, 1967, coord foreign lang, 1977, dean admis, 1971, assoc prof, 2005; prof fr & jour, currently, assoc prof mass communications, currently; Augusta News Review, ed & publ, 1974-; Lucy Craft Laney Mus, exec dir, currently. **Orgs:** Pres, New Grow Inc, 1971-; vpres, Bd Trustees Antioch Baptist Church, 1971-; bd trustees, Paine Col, 1980-82; bd dirs, Paine Col Nat Alumni Asn; co-chmn, Blue Ribbon Comt. **Honors/Awds:** Fulbright US & Fr Govt, 1968-69; United Negro Col Fund, 1976-77; Merit Award, Nat Newspaper Publ Asn, 1983. **Business Addr:** Professor, Paine College, 1235 15th St, Augusta, GA 30901, **Business Phone:** 800-476-7703.

MILLER, DR. ANDREA LEWIS
Vice president (organization), dean (education), chancellor (education). **Personal:** Born Sep 10, 1954, Memphis, TN; married Robert A; children: Meredith Mechelle. **Educ:** Le Moyne Owen Col, BS, 1976; Atlanta Univ, MS, 1978, PhD, 1980. **Career:** NIH, Predoctoral fel, 1977-80; Univ Cincinnati Col Med, postdoctoral fel, 1980-82; LeMoyne Owen Col, prof biol assoc investr, 1982-83, prof biolprin investr, 1983, dept chair, asst dean curric & instr, assoc prof biol, vpres acad affairs, dean fac; NIH, res grant, 1983-86; United Negro Col Fund, premed educ grant, 1984-; Doe res grant; Univ Nev, Col Human &Community Sci, asst dean; Shelby State Community Col, interim vpresacad &stud affairs; Southwest Tenn Community Col, exec vpres acad stud affairs,exec vpres acad affairs admin & planning; SOWELA Tech Community Col,chancellor, 2007-. **Orgs:** Memphis Vol Placement Prog, 1973; Alpha Kappa, 1973; Am Soc Cell Biologist, 1981; pres, LeMoyne Owen Col Fac Orgn, 1984-86; Southeast Electron Micros Soc, 1985, Electron Micros Soc Am, 1985. **Honors/Awds:** Research Award, Lederle Labs, 1980. **Business Addr:** Chancellor, SOWELA Technical Community College, 3820 J Bennett Johnston Ave, PO Box 16950, Lake Charles, LA 70616-6950.

MILLER, ANNA M.
Association executive. **Personal:** Born May 15, 1923, New Orleans, LA; married Martin W; children: Walter P, Loretta E, Fatima M. **Educ:** Xavier Univ New Orleans, BS, 1943; Cath Sch Soc Serv Wash, DC, 1944; Howard Univ, 1945. **Career:** Chester Cit Info Cntr, chmn steering comt, 1969-; NAACP, chmn voter reg, 1963-; League Women Voters, chmn, 1964-70; Centennial Com IHMC, co-chairperson, 1971-74; Human Concerns Comn YWCA, chmn, 1971-. **Orgs:** Chester Rep Theatre, 1969. **Honors/Awds:** Community Service award, 5th United Presb Ch, 1967; Human Service award, Chester Br NAACP, 1973.

MILLER, ANTHONY
Basketball player. **Personal:** Born Oct 22, 1971, Benton Harbor, MI. **Educ:** Mich State Univ, criminal justice, 1994. **Career:** Los Angeles Lakers, forward, 1994-96; Continental Basketball Asn, Fla Beachdogs, 1996-97; Atlanta Hawks, 1997-98, 2000, 2004-05; Houston Rockets, 1999-2000, 2001; Philadelphia 76ers, 2000-01; Houston Rockets, guard, 2003; Continental Basketball Asn, Yakama Sun Kings, 2006. **Orgs:** Continental Basketball Asn.

MILLER, REV. ANTHONY GLENN
Clergy. **Personal:** Born Sep 24, 1959, Los Angeles, CA; son of Isaac Nimrod and Lillian Lois Gray. **Educ:** Univ Southern Calif, BA, 1984; Gen Theol Sem, MDiv, 1988; Grad Inst Religion & Health, certified pastoral counr, 1993; Yale Univ, STM, 1994. **Career:** Parish Trinity Church, seminarian, 1985-86; St Philip's Episcopal Church, seminarian intern, 1986-87; Church Heavenly Rest, seminarian, 1987; Church Transfiguration, assoc rector, 1989-91; Diocese Long Island, exec off bishop, 1988-92; St Andrew's Episcopal Church, vicar, 1993; St. Barnabas' Church, rector, currently. **Orgs:** Long Island rep Guatemala prog, Presiding Bishop's Fund World Relief, 1992; dean's search comt, 1992, jr tutorial prog, tutor, 1991, Gen Theol Sem; Diocese Long Island Comn Ministry, 1993; Diocesan Epsicopal AIDS Comt, 1993; GOE reader, Gen Bd Examining Chaplains, 1993. **Special Achievements:** I Am Somebody, essay contest, 1973. **Business Addr:** Rector, St. Barnabas Church, 1062 N Fair Oaks Ave, PO Box 93096, Pasadena, CA 91103, **Business Phone:** (626)798-2996.

MILLER, ARTHUR J
Management consultant. **Personal:** Born Oct 7, 1934, New York, NY; son of Theodore Roosevelt and Rosalie White; married Mary Lee, Feb 19, 1966 (deceased). **Career:** Chase Manhattan Bank, dividend clerk, 1952, supvr, 1961, sys planning off, 1968, vpres, 1970, vpres banking 1974-87; AJM Assoc Inc, pres, 1988-; Bus Syst Mgt Inc, prin, 1989, pres, 1992-. **Orgs:** Chair bd, Reality House Inc. **Honors/Awds:** Man of the Year, Angel Guardian Family Service, 1997. **Military Serv:** AUS, corp, 1955-58. **Business Addr:** President, Business Systems Management Inc, 150 Broadway Suite 812, New York, NY 10038, **Business Phone:** (212)385-4084.

MILLER, DR. BERNICE JOHNSON
School administrator, educational consultant. **Personal:** Born in Chicago, IL; married George Benjamin; children: Benita & Michael. **Educ:** Roosevelt Univ Chicago, IL, BA; Chicago Teachers Col, MA, 1965; CAS Harvard Univ Grad Sch Educ, attended 1969, EdD, 1972. **Career:** Chicago Bd Ed, teacher elem & hs, 1950-66; New Sch C Inc, headmistress, 1966-68; Jackson Col, assoc dean, 1968-70; Radcliffe, instr, 1970-73; Harvard Grad Sch Educ, assoc dir, 1971-75, High Tech Res Proj, dir, 1983-84; Boston Pub Sch Lucy Stone Sch, prin, 1977-78; Boston Pub Sch, sr officer, 1978-84; City Col Chicago, pres, pres emer, currently. **Orgs:** Bd mem, Children's World Day Care Ctr Boston, 1972-84, Blue Cross & Blue Shield Boston, United Way; trustee, Brigham's & Women's Hosp Med Found; pres, United Commun Planning Corp, 1983-85; bd mem, Chicago Metro Hist Fair Bd; Mayor's Comn Women. **Honors/Awds:** Educator's Award, Boston 350th Anniversary, Boston MA, 1980; Educator of the Year, Urban Bankers Ed Award, Boston, 1982; Woman of the Year Award, Asn Mannequins, 1984; Woman in Education, Bus & Prof Women Boston & Vicinity, 1984; Freedom Award, Roosevelt Univ, 1985; Distinguished Alumni, Chicago State Univ, NABSE, 1985; Outstanding Achievement Award, Educ YWCA, 1986; Minority Networking Org Focus & Seana Mag Service Award, 1986. **Special Achievements:** Written journals like: Inner City Women in White Schools, The Journal of Negro Education. **Business Addr:** President Emeritus, Harold Washington College, 30 E Lake St, Chicago, IL 60601.

MILLER, BUBBA (STEPHEN DEJUAN MILLER)
Football player, television talk show host. **Personal:** Born Jan 24, 1973, Nashville, TN; married Gina; children: Stephen III. **Educ:** Tenn State Univ. **Career:** Philadelphia Eagles, corner, 1996-01; New Orleans Saints, corner, 2002(retired); TV & Radio appearnces: Philadelphia Eagles, TV analyst; "Mathews' show", guest host; co-host with Chris Low; "Trade winds", host; ESPN 1180, "The Bubba Miller Show", host, currently. **Business Addr:** Host, ESPN 1180, Knoxville, TN 37902.

MILLER, C CONRAD, JR.
Advertising executive. **Personal:** Born Jul 16, 1950, Little Rock, AR; son of Clarence Conrad Miller Sr and Bernice Beatrice Jaudon Miller; married Sherrin Ellen Johnson, May 24, 1980; children: Andrew & Lauren. **Educ:** Fort Hays Kansas State Univ, BS, 1973; Univ Mich, MM, 1974, doctoral studies, 1976. **Career:** Ortho pharmaceut Corp, sales rep, 1977-78, sales training mgr, 1979-81, dist sales mgr, 1981-83, prod mgr, 1983-86, product dir, 1986-88, sr prod dir, 1988-90; Dudnyk Co, acct group dir, 1990-91; vpres, 1992; Adis Int, dir acct servs & bus develop; MTI Info Technologies, sr vpre bus develop, currently. **Orgs:** Bus Coun Arts, vol, 1983-84; Branchburg (NJ) Environ Comn, 1985-86; Healthcare Mkt & Communs Coun, 1991-. **Business Addr:** Sr Vice President Business Development, MTI Information Technologies, One Oxford Valley Suite 500, Langhorne, PA 19047, **Business Phone:** (267)569-2400.

MILLER, CHARLES D, JR.
Executive. **Personal:** Born Apr 13, 1952, Lexington, NC; son of Charles Sr; married Loretta W, Mar 30; children: Charles D III & Kellen A. **Educ:** NC A&T State Univ, BSME, 1974; Univ Ill, MBA, 1984. **Career:** John Deere, engr, 1974-77; Ford, sr engr, 1977; GE, dir eng, 1984-86, vpres mkt, 1986-91; Whirlpool Corp, vpres mkt kitchenaid, 1991-92, pres, Kitchenaid, 1992-93, vpres mkt, 1993-. **Orgs:** Dir, Whirlpool Found, 1992-; Am Mgt Asn, 1992-; trustee, Mkt Sci Inst, 1994-. **Honors/Awds:** Nat YMCA, Achievers, 1993; Am Marketing Asn, Organization of the Year, 1993; Baldridge, Gold Award, 1994. **Business Addr:** Vice President Marketing-North America, Whirlpool Corporation, 2000 M-63 N, Benton Harbor, MI 49022, **Business Phone:** (269)923-5000.

MILLER, CHERYL DE ANN
Athletic coach, television broadcaster, basketball player. **Personal:** Born Jan 3, 1964, Riverside, CA. **Educ:** Univ Southern Calif, BA, broadcast journalism. **Career:** Outstanding Col and amateur basketball player; teams include: Junior National Team, 1981; US National Team, 1982; JC Penney All-American FiveTeam; World Championship Team, 1983; Univ SC, Women's Basketball Team, player; US Olympics, Women's Basketball Team, player,1984; ABC Sports, commentator; Univ SC, head coach, women's basketball, 1993-95; Phoenix Mercury, head coach, 1997-2000; Turner Sports, TNT, TBS, NBA analyst; Sideline reporter, NBA games, TNT, currently. **Orgs:** U.S. Olympic gold medal women's basketball team. **Honors/Awds:** Sports Illustrated Player of the Week, 1983; member of US Olympic Gold Medal Basketball Team, 1984; ABA & USA Female Athlete of the Year, 1986; Naismith Player of the Year, three consecutive yrs; Kodak All-Am, four consecutive yrs. **Special Achievements:** Recipient of more than 1,140 trophies and 125 plaques; offered 250 scholarships to various college & univ teams; participant inchampionship games including: CIF state championship, Nat Sports Festival, 1981, Pan Am Games, 1983; FIBA World Championships, Goodwill Games; player for US Olympic team winning first Gold Medal for women'sbasketball, 1984; first female analyst to call a nationally televised NBAgame; U.S. Olympic gold medal women's basketball team. **Business Phone:** (404)827-1500.*

MILLER, CONSTANCE JOAN
Manager. **Personal:** Born Sep 8, 1945, Frederick, OK; daughter of Arthur Lee and Esther Bell Herd; married Norman Engelsberg (divorced 1982); children: Braswell, Michelle. **Educ:** Temple Univ, attended 1971; Univ Wash, attended 1974; Goddard-Cambridge Grad Sch, MA, attended 1976. **Career:** City of Seattle, 1979-81; The Phoenix Proj, 1982, managing dir, 1982-89; Med Legal Consult Wash, legal asst; Dalkon Shield, proj mgr, 1988-91; IUD Claim Info Serv, ICIS, managing dir, 1991-. **Orgs:** Founding bd mem, Int Dalkon Shield Victims Educ Asn, 1986-. **Special Achievements:** Co-author, From The Ashes, A Head Injury Self-Advocate Guide, The Phoenix Project Books, 1987-; author, Dalkon Shield Claims Information Guide, ICIS Books, 1989-; Dalkon Shield Claims Legal Guide, ICIS Books, 1990-; author, Dalkon Shield Claims Up-Date Service, ICIS Books; "Clap Your Hands el3," Essence, May 1990, p 112; "Day of Reckoning," Ms. Magazine, June 1989, p 50; "Are You a Victim of this Nasty-Looking Thing?" Woman's World Magazine, April 25, 1989, p 6. **Business Addr:** Founder, International Dalkon Shield Victims Education Association, PO Box 84151, Seattle, WA 98104.

MILLER, CYLENTHIA LATOYE
Lawyer, judge. **Personal:** Born Dec 13, 1962, Pine Bluff, AR; daughter of George Boyer Miller Jr and Sharon Elaine Bernard. **Educ:** Wayne State Univ, BA, 1988; Detroit Col Law MI State Univ, JD Cum Laude, 1996. **Career:** Wayne Co Neighborhood Legal Servs, mediator, 1988-89; MI Credit Union League, regulatory specialist, 1989-93; Neighborhood Servs Orgn, emergency phone counr, 1993-96; Dykema Gosset PLLC, assoc, 1996-98; Lewis & Munday PC, assoc; City Detroit, Employ & Training Dept, dir admin; Michigan's 36th Judicial Dist Ct, judge, 2006-. **Orgs:** Nat Asn Advan Colored People; Alpha Kappa Alpha Sorority Inc, 1984-; Am Bar Asn, 1993-; Nat Bar Asn, 1996-; State Bar MI, 1996-; Wolverine Bar Asn, 1996-; Women Lawyers Asn MI, 1996-; Arkansas Bar Asn, 1997-; Nat Asn Female Exec, 1993-; dir, City Detroit Employ & Training Dept; dir, Detroit Workforce Develop Dept. **Honors/Awds:** Book Award, Detroit Col Law, Probate Procedure; Book Award, RWA II; Honors, RWA I & II, 1992-93; Scholarship, Wolverine Bar Asn, 1994; Scholarship, Wolverine Stud Bar Asn, 1993-94. **Special Achievements:** First African Am female president of a graduating class, Detroit Col of Law at Mich State Univ, 1996. **Home Addr:** 620 Chrysler Dr Apt 202, Detroit, MI 48207-3054, **Home Phone:** (313)393-8736. **Business Addr:** Judge, Michigan's 36th Judicial District Court, 421 Madison Ave, Detroit, MI 48226, **Business Phone:** (313)965-2200.

MILLER, DR. DENNIS WELDON
Physician. **Personal:** Born Mar 12, 1949, Roanoke, VA; son of Henry and Rosa; married Carol; children: Damon & Jared. **Educ:** Fisk Univ, 1971; Meharry Med Col, 1975; KC Gen Hosp & Med Ctr, residency in Obstet & Gynec, 1975-76; Truman Med Ctr, 1976-79. **Career:** Pvt pract, physician, currently; Univ Kans, Med Ctr, Family Practice Dept, clinical prof, 1983-. **Orgs:** Gynecological Soc, Southwest Clinical Soc, Nat Med Asn, 1971-77; AMA, 1971-77; NAACP; secy, treas, Kan Valley Med Soc, 1988-90; Am

Asn Gynecological Laparoscopists, Wyandotte Co Med Soc, KS Med Soc, KS Found Med Care; Gyn Laser Soc; chmn, Dept Obstet & Gynec Providence; chmn, St Margarets Health Ctr, 1987-89. **Home Addr:** 21 N 12th St Suite 350, Kansas City, KS 66102. **Business Addr:** Physician, 21 N 12th St Suite 350, Kansas City, KS 66102, **Business Phone:** (913)371-1667.

MILLER, DONALD LESESSNE
Executive. **Personal:** Born Jan 10, 1932, New York, NY; son of John H and Mamie Johnson; married Gail Aileen Wallace, Jun 27, 1981; children: Lynn Ann, Mark L. **Educ:** Univ Md, BA, 1967; Harvard Bus Sch, 1969. **Career:** Inmont Corp, New York, NY, asst pres, 1968-70; Seatrain Shipbuilding, New York, NY, vpres indust rels, 1970-71; US Dept Defense, Wash, DC, asst secy defense, 1971-73; Columbia Univ, New York, NY, vpres personnel, 1973-78; Int Paper, New York, NY, dir personnel, 1978-79; Con Edison, New York, NY, vpres employee rels, 1979-86; Dow Jones & Co, New York, NY, vpres, employee rels, 1986-95; founder, Our World News; Bank of New York Inc, mem bd dir, currently; Shering-Plough Corp, mem bd dir, currently; HealthDataInsights Inc, adv bd mem, currently. **Orgs:** Trustee, Pace Univ, 1979-; dir, United Way, Tri State, 1981-; dir, Jackie Robinson Found, 1981-; chmn bd, Assoc Black Charities, 1982-. **Honors/Awds:** Distinguished Civilian Medal, US Defense Dept, 1973; Distinguished Alumnus Award, Univ Md, 1977. **Military Serv:** AUS, maj, 1948-68; Legion of Merit, 1968, Commendation Medal, 1961. **Business Addr:** Director, HealthDataInsights Inc, 2450 Fire Mesa St Suite 160, Las Vegas, NV 89128.*

MILLER, DORIS JEAN
School administrator, president (organization). **Personal:** Born Oct 13, 1933, River Rouge, MI; married Olie; children: Carla A, Darryl S & Felicia C. **Educ:** Wayne State Univ, BA, 1957; Mich State Univ, Cert, 1963; Wayne State Univ, MA, 1968. **Career:** School administrator (retired), president; River Rouge Pub Schs, teacher, 1959-73, prin, 1973-74, teacher, 1974-79; Mich Fed Teachers & Sch Related Personnel, field rep, 1979-96, asst to pres, 1996-98; Wayne County Community Col, trustee, 1978-88; Doris Miller Educ Consulting Servs, pres, 1998-. **Orgs:** Alpha Kappa Alpha Sor, 1952-; mem bd dir, Down river Guidance Clinic, 1970-88; chmn, Black Women's Task Force, 1982-85; Greater Metro Det Guidance Assoc, 1982-88; Women's Conf Concerns, 1982-89; mem bd dir, Wayne County Private Indus Coun, 1983-89; pres, Wayne County Community Col Found, 1982-84, treas, 1985. **Honors/Awds:** Scholar, Ford Motor Co Fund, 1951-55; Golden Apple Award, Wayne County Regional & Educ Serv Agency, 1998. **Home Addr:** 431 Palmerston Dr, River Rouge, MI 48218.

MILLER, DR. DORSEY COLUMBUS, JR.
Educator. **Personal:** Born Jan 7, 1943, Ocala, FL; son of Dorsey C Miller Sr and Eudora J; married Betty J Samuel, Dec 16, 1967; children: Kim Y, Eric T & Dorsey C III. **Educ:** Morehoues Col, BA, 1965; Univ Fla, Masters, 1971; Fla Atlantic Univ, EdD, 1980. **Career:** The Sch Bd Marion County, teacher, guidance counr, 1965-68; The Sch Bd Broward County, guidance counr, 1972-73; Fla dept Educ, counsult, 1973-75, regional counr, 1975-79; Southern Bell Telephone Co, mgr, 1979-80; The Sch Bd Broward County, migrant educ, 1980-91, special prog, dir, 1991-; DC Miller & Assoc, pres & chief exec officer, currently. **Orgs:** Grand basileus, OPP Fraternity Inc; bd trustees chr, Broward County Col; bd trustees, Mt Olive Baptist Church; bd gov, Greater Fort Lauderdale; Nat CNF Christians &d Jews, bd. **Honors/Awds:** Outstanding Young Man of Am, US Jaycees, 1977; OPP Fraternity 7th District, 'Citizen of the Year', 1983; Presidential appointee, US Motor Carrier Ratemaking Study Co, 1983; 'county Service Award', City Lauderdale, 1984; NCP, Act-So Award, 1991. **Special Achievements:** Dissertation: The Impact of Race on a Desegregated School District as Perceived by Selected School Administrators, 1980; author, "Migrant Student Record Transfer System," 1974. **Military Serv:** USY, spec-4, 1968-70; Good Conduct Medal, 1969. **Home Addr:** 6008 NW 62nd Ter, Parkland, FL 33064, **Home Phone:** (305)984-9777. **Business Addr:** President, DC Miller & Associates Inc, 545 N Andrews Ave, Fort Lauderdale, FL 33301.

MILLER, E. ETHELBERT
School administrator, writer, college teacher. **Personal:** Born Nov 20, 1950, New York, NY; son of Enid Marshall and Egberto; married Denise King, Sep 25, 1982; children: Jasmine Simone & Nyere-Gibran. **Educ:** Howard Univ, BA, Afro-Am Studies, 1972. **Career:** Howard Univ, African-American Resource Ctr, dir, 1974-; Univ Nevada, vis prof, 1993; African Am Rev, adv ed, currently; Art & Letters, contributing, currently; Bennington Col, fac, 2002; Inst Policy Studies, bd chairperson, currently; Am Univ, adj prof; Poet Lore mag, ed. **Orgs:** Bd mem, The Writer's Center and editor of Poet Lore magazine; former chair, Humanities Coun of Washington. **Honors/Awds:** Tony Taylor Award, Cult Alliance Wash, DC, 1986; Mayor's Art Award for Literature, 1982; Hon Doctorate Lit, Emory & Henry Col, 1996; Josephine Miles Award, Pen Oakland, 1994; Public Humanities Award, DC Humanities Coun, 1988; Columbia Merit Award, 1994; O. B. Hardison Jr. Poetry Prize, 1995; Honorary Doctorate of literature, Emory & Henry Col, 1996; Stephen Henderson Poetry Award, African-Am Lit & Cult Soc, 1997; Jessie Ball Du Pont Scholar, Emory & Henry Col, 1996; Stephen Henderson Poetry Award, African Am Lit and Cult Soc, 1997. **Special Achievements:** Published: Andromeda, 1974; The Land of Smiles & The Land of No Smiles, 1974; Migrant Worker, 1978; Season of Hunger/Cry of Rain, 1982; Where Are the Love Poems for Dictators", 1986; First Light, New & Selected Poems, Black Classic Press, 1994; Whispers, Secrets & Promises, Black Classic Pess, 1998; Beyond the Frontier, 2002; How we Sleep on the Nights We Dont Make Love, 2004; Synergy: An Anthology of Washington Do Co Poetry, 1975; Women Surviving Massacres & Men, 1997; In Search of Color Everywhere, 1994; Fathering Words, 2000; Buddha Weeping in Winter, 2001; poem: Trouble the Water, 250 Years of African-American Poetry; The New Cavalcade; Erotique Noire/Black Erotica; 360 A Revolution of Black Poets; Beyond Lament, Poets of the World Bearing Witness to the Holocaust; New Bones; Tales from the Couch; Sept 28, 1979 proclaimed as E Ethelbert Miller Day; made an honorary Citizen of Baltimore, MD, July 17, 1994; hosted MaidenVoyage, WDCU-FM; Vertigo on the Air, WPFW-FM; Humanities Profiled, WDC-TV;Honored by Laura Bush & the White House, Nat Book Festival, 2001, 2003. **Home Addr:** 1411 Underwood St NW, Washington, DC 20012. **Business Phone:** (202)806-7242.

MILLER, ERENEST EUGENE
High school principal, educator. **Personal:** Born Jun 13, 1948, Farmville, VA; son of William C and Maria G; married Alice Robinson, Jun 8, 1985. **Educ:** Va State Univ, BA, 1970, Ed.M, 1978. **Career:** Trophy & Plaque Luther P Jackson, fac, 1966; Gold Hill Elem Sch, teacher,1970-71; Cumberland High Sch, educr, 1971-92; Cumberland Co Sch, adult educ teacher, 1973-; Longwood Col Summer Inst Talented & Gifted Students,facilitator, 1979; Prince Edward Co Middle Sch, teacher, 1992-, asst prin, 1993-. **Orgs:** Scout master, Robert E Lee Scout Troop 6280, 1971-74; dir proj, Va Found Humanities & Pub Policy, 1979; pres, Cumberland Co Br, Nat Asn Advan Colored People 1976-80, bd mem, Va State Conf, 1978-, vpres, Va State,1988, pres, 1992-; sponsor, SCA Cumberland High Sch; dir, Summer Youth Employ & Training Prog; coach, Battle Brains, 1988; coach, Social Studies AC Team, 1988; vpres, Iota Tau Lambda Chap, Alpha Phi Alpha, 1988, pres,1991; Tearwallet & Sharon Baptist Church; vpres, Inspirational Choir; dir,Vocational Bible Sch; bd dir, Southside YMCA. **Honors/Awds:** Engraved Plaque Robt E Lee Scout Troop 6280, 1974; Certificate, Va State Conf, Nat Asn Advan Colored People, 1976; Plaque Plaque Cent Piedmont Action Coun, 1989; Man of the Year, Alpha Phi Alpha, 1991; Leon Monton Leadership Award, Southside & Cent Chap Alpha Phi Alpha, 1995; Assistant Principal of the Year, 2001. **Home Addr:** 1135 Plank Rd, Farmville, VA 23901, **Home Phone:** (804)392-9929. **Business Addr:** Assistant Principal, Prince Edward County High School, 35 Eagle DR, Farmville, VA 23901.

MILLER, EVELYN B
Association executive, writer. **Personal:** Born in Atlanta, GA; daughter of Thomas F Bailey (deceased) and Willie Groves Bailey (deceased); married Charles R, Aug 28, 1955 (deceased). **Educ:** Southeastern Univ, BA; Spelman Col; Hunter Col; Columbia Univ; New Sch Soc Res. **Career:** Association executive, Writer (retired); YMCA Greater New York, Harlem Branch, adult prog & pub rel. **Orgs:** Asn Black Soc Workers; life mem, Nat Asn Advan Colored People; Metro Comn 100 Inc; Asn Prof Dirs; pres, Knickerbocker Int Bus & Prof Women Inc; past mem, Comn Personnel & Security Matters YMCA; past reg co-commr on white racism YMCA; past chair, Comun Cabinet YMCA Greater New York; League Women Voters; deacon, Presbu Church; charter mem, Childsville Inc; trustee, Alexander Robertson Elem Sch, New York. **Honors/Awds:** Sr dir, Cert, YMCA; second place, Women of Year, Grehound Bus Co, 1967; & Devotion Award, Metro Comn 100 Inc, 1972; third place, Ten Leading Harlemites, NY Daily Challenge Paper, 1977; Auth: Footsteps on the Stair, pen name, Leslie Groves, 1977; Youth Service Award, YMCA Harlem Branch, 1984. **Home Addr:** 129 Parsons Pl SW, Atlanta, GA 30314.

MILLER, FRANK LEE, JR.
Military leader, vice president (organization). **Personal:** Born Jan 27, 1944, Atchinson, KS; son of Frank L and Evelyn A Wilson; married Paulette Duncan Miller, Sep 28, 1968; children: Frank L III, Michael W, Toni K. **Educ:** Univ Wash, BA, 1973; AUS Command & Gen Staff Col, Ft Leavenworth, KS, attended 1977; Troy State Univ, attended 1979; Naval War Col, Newport, RI, attended 1984. **Career:** Major general (retired), vice president; AUS, pvt, 1965-97, Commanding Gen III Corps Artil, major gen, currently; 101st Airborne Div, Rifle Co Comdr, rifle platoon leader, 1980-85; Spec Forces, spec forces officer, col, 1985; 1st Battalion; 1st Spec Forces Group; AUS War Col, Strategic Studies Inst, external researcher; Pub Opers Dell Comput Corp, vpres, currently. **Orgs:** Asn AUS, 1966-; Field Artil Asn, 1988-; Foreign Area Officer Prog. **Honors/Awds:** Meritorious Serv Medal; Distinguished Flying Cross; Joint Serv Commendation Medal. **Special Achievements:** First black chief of staff of the free world's ctr for fire support at Fort Sill, OK; First black commanding general of the Army's largest and most diverse Corps Artillery. **Military Serv:** AUS, 1965-; Legion of Merit with 3 OLC; Bronze Star Medal with "V" & 2 Oak Leaf Clusters; Air Medal with "V" and 19 Oak Leaf Clusters; Vietnamese Cross Gallantry with Silver Star. **Home Addr:** 7 Scenic Ter, Round Rock, TX 78664-9635. **Business Addr:** Vice President, Dell Computer Corporation, 1 Dell Way, Round Rock, TX 78758-4053.*

MILLER, FRED JUNIOR, JR.
Football player. **Personal:** Born Feb 6, 1973, Aldine, TX; married Kim; children: Grant & Evan. **Educ:** Baylor Univ, BA, sociol. **Career:** St Louis Rams, tackle, 1996-99; Tenn Titans, 2000-04; Chicago Bears, tackle, 2005-07; free agent, currently. **Honors/Awds:** Super Bowl XXXIV win, St louis. **Special Achievements:** Only Titans O-lineman to start all 80 regular-season games from 2000-04.

MILLER, FREDERICK A.
Management consultant. **Personal:** Born Nov 2, 1946, Philadelphia, PA; son of Frederick and Clarice Gaines; married Pauline Kamen Miller; children: Kamen Kaleel, Shay Clarice. **Educ:** Lincoln Univ, PA, BA, 1968. **Career:** Conn Gen Life Ins Co, admin, 1968-72, human develop consult, 1972-76, asst dir training, 1976-79; Kaleel Jamison Mgt Consult Group, partner, vpres, 1979-85, pres & chief exec officer, 1985-; Day & Zimmerman, dir; Seton Health Systs, dir; Sage Cols, dir; The Promise Diversity, managing ed. **Orgs:** Bd dir, The Living Sch, 1973-; mem, Orgn Develop Network, 1974-; mem, Am Soc Training & Develop, 1974-; mem, Nat Training Labs, 1976-; bd dir, Nat Training Labs Inst, 1980-85; bd dirs, Orgn Develop Network, 1986-94; bd, Ben & Jerry's Homemade; mem, Social Venture Network. **Special Achievements:** Co-author with Judith Katz, of "The Inclusion Breakthrough: Unleashing the Real Power of Diversity". **Military Serv:** AUS, sergeant, 1968-70. **Business Addr:** Chief Executive Officer, Kaleel Jamison Consulting Group Inc, 279 River St Suite 401, Troy, NY 12180-3270.*

MILLER, GEORGE CARROLL, JR.
Management consultant. **Personal:** Born Mar 3, 1949, Atlanta, GA; son of George and Beatrice; married Nawanna Lewis; children: George III, John Elliott, Mikah Alexis & Victoria Melissa. **Educ:** Am Inst Banking, attended 1971 & 1975; Ga State Univ, BBA, 1971, MBA, 1974; Univ Okla, 1975. **Career:** Trust Co Ga, com officer, 1971-76; US Treas Dept, exec asst, 1977-79; Cooper & Lybrand, dir state & local govt pract, 1980-89; Spectrum Consulting Assocs Inc, pres, currently. **Orgs:** Fundraiser YMCA, 1972-74, United Negro Col Fund, 1973-74, United Way, 1973-74; vchmn, treas, Atlanta Bus League, 1974-75; bd dir, Joint Action Community Serv, 1982-; pres, Ga State Univ Nat Capital Alumni Club, 1985-; bd dir, DC Lung Assoc, 1986-; Nat Asbestos Coun; bd dirs, Metrop Towers Inc; bd trustees, Metrop Baptist Church; bd dirs, Jobs Homeless People; bd dirs, Capitol City Bank & Trust Co; chmn, Messiah's Temple Church. **Honors/Awds:** WSB Beaver Award, 1968; Herbert Leman Educ Grant, 1968-71; Alumni Appreciation Award, Ga State Univ, 1976. **Military Serv:** USA ROTC 2 yrs. **Home Addr:** 1920 Sharpshooters Ct NW, Marietta, GA 30064, **Home Phone:** (770)499-9519. **Business Addr:** President, Spectrum Consulting Associates Inc, 1050 Connecticut Ave NW Suite 1000, Washington, DC 20036, **Business Phone:** (202)772-3177.

MILLER, GWENDOLYN MARTIN
Government official. **Personal:** Born Aug 2, 1934, Tampa, FL; daughter of Nathaniel Martin (deceased) and Wilma Rivers; married Lesley J Miller Jr, Nov 27, 1982; children: James Jones, Arthur Jones & Le. **Educ:** Fla A&M Univ, BS, educ, 1957, MS, educ, 1966. **Career:** Hillsborough County Sch District, human relations specialist, 1951-94; Miller Miller & Assocs Inc, chair, pres & ceo, 1994-; Tampa City Coun, councilwoman, 1995-2003, chairperson, 2004-08, chair pro-tem, 2008-. **Orgs:** Nat pres, The Charmettes Inc, 1971-; 1st nat vpres, Kappa Alpha Psi Fraternity Silhouettes, Inc, 1982-; pres, Nat Coalition 100 Black Women Inc, Tampa Bay Chap, 1982-; bd dir,Tampa Hillsborough, 1990-; Alpha Kappa Alpha Sorority, 1998-. **Honors/Awds:** Outstanding Service Award, Kappa Alpha Psi Fraternity Inc, 1993; Whitney Young Memorial Award, Tampa-Hillsborough Urban League, 1997; Eunice Thompson Merit Award, Nat Charmettes Inc, 1997; Florence Griffith Joyner Trailblazer Award, US Am Track & Field, 1998; Finer Womanhood Award, Zeta Phi Beta Sorority Inc, 1999; Distinguished Alumni Award, Fla A&M Univ, . **Business Addr:** Councilwoman, City of Tampa City Council, 315 E Kennedy Blvd, Tampa, FL 33602, **Business Phone:** (813)274-7072.

MILLER, HELEN S.
Nurse, college teacher. **Personal:** Born Mar 29, 1917, Atlanta, GA; daughter of Ola Sullivan and Floyd Sullivan; widowed; children: Ronald. **Educ:** Univ Hosp, Augusta, GA; Med Col Va; Tuskeegee Inst Sch Midwifery, BSNEd; Yale Univ Sch Nursing CNM, MSN. **Career:** Nurse, college teacher (retired); Ga Dept Pub Health, staff nurse,1947-49; US Pub Health Serv, area supvr, 1949-51; Army Nurse Corps, admin nurse, 1951-53; City Philadelphia Dept Health, dist suprv, 1953-54; Fla Agr & Mech Univ, pub health coord sch nursing, 1954-56; NC Cent Univ, Dept Nursing, chmn, 1956-82, assoc prof nursing res, 1977-82. **Orgs:** Secy, Undergrad Coun, NC Cent Univ; fac exec comn, NC Cent Univ; Long Range Planning Comt, NC Cent Univ; NC State Nurses Asn; Am Nurses Asn; comt mem,Write Hist Nursing, NC; bd dir, vpres, NC League Nursing, 1971-75; Yale Univ Alumnae Asn; Am Asn Univ Women; Adv Com on Cont Educ Sch Nursing Univ NC, Chapel Hill; YWCA; former bd mem, Local Chap ARC; exec comt, NC Lung & Resp Asn; Health Careers Comt, NC Cent Univ; Gubernatorial appt, NC Bd Nursing, 1966-70; nat pres, Chi Eta Phi Sor, 1969-73; life mem, Nat Coun Negro Women; life

mem, Chi Eta Phi Sor Inc. **Honors/Awds:** Mary Mahoney Award, Am Nurses Asn, 1968; Historical Preservations America, 1975-76; listed inMinority Groups in Nursing, Am Nurses Asn, 1976; Distinguished Alumni Award, Yale Univ, 1978; Miller Morgan Health Sci Building, named in honor. **Special Achievements:** Author, two abstracts in Abstracts of Nursing Research in the South, Vol1, 1979; author, The History of Chi Eta Phi Sorority Inc, Associationn forthe Study of Afro-American Life & History, 1968; co-author, ContemporaryMinority Leaders in Nursing, American Nurses Association, 1983; auth: MaryEliza Mahoney 1845-1926: America's First Black Professional Nurse - AHistorical Prospective. **Military Serv:** AUS, Nurse Corps, lt, 1951-53. **Home Addr:** 6000 Fayetteville Rd, PO Box 810, Durham, NC 27713. *

MILLER, HORATIO C.
Educator, pianist. **Personal:** Born Jan 8, 1949, Birmingham, AL; children: Allison. **Educ:** Univ Pa, BA, 1970; Temple Univ, MA, 1973. **Career:** Cheyney State Col, instr, 1973-74; Community Col Philadelphia, asst prof, 1974-. **Orgs:** Found Study Cycles. **Honors/Awds:** Acad Music Philadelphia, Inaugural Concert President Carter Washington, DC, 1976; Timer Digest, rated top 10 market timers in the gold market, 1988; Timer Digest, Rated No 3 gold market timer, 1990; Article, EliottWave & Gold, Stocks & Commodities Magazine, 1991. **Business Addr:** Assistant Professor, Community College of Philadelphia, Music Department, 1700 Spring Garden St, Philadelphia, PA 19130, **Business Phone:** (215)751-8295.

MILLER, INGER
Athlete. **Personal:** Born Jun 12, 1972, Los Angeles, CA; daughter of Lennox. **Educ:** Southern Calif, attended 1994. **Career:** Brad Tomasini, Track & field athlete. **Honors/Awds:** Gold medal, 1996; gold medal, 1997; World 200m champion, 1999; silvermedal, World Champs 100m, 1999; World Champs, 2001; silver medal, 2003; Olympian, 2004; gold medal, World Track & Field Champ, Seville, Spain. **Special Achievements:** Miller was a Tournament of Roses Princess in the 1990 court. *

MILLER, INGRID FRAN WATSON
Educator. **Personal:** Born Jul 4, 1949, Washington, DC; daughter of Dempsey and Matilda; married George E Miller III, May 3, 1980; children: Sean Gregory & Simon Geoffry. **Educ:** NC Cent Univ, BA, Span, 1971; Howard Univ, MEd, curric develop, 1983; Catholic Univ Am, MA, Span, 1993; Univ Md, College Park, 1994-96. **Career:** T Roosevelt SHS, Washington, DC, Span teacher, 1973-88; Jackson State Univ, lectr, 1983-85; Hampton Univ, asst prof Span, 1988-96; Norfolk State Univ, asst pro Span, 1996-99; Johnson C Smith Univ, 1999-2000; Bowie State Univ, Dir, off-campus Advisement, 2001-. **Orgs:** Alpha Kappa Alpha Sorority, Inc, pres, vp, parl, reporter, grand advisor, 1968-; Jack & Jill Am Inc, rec sec, pres, regional dir, nat ed, nat pres, 1998-00; Col Lang Asn, 1985-, constitution comm, 1994-95; Am Asn Teachers Span & Port, 1980-, workshop chair, 1991; Am Coun Teachers Fa, 1975-; PhiDelta Kappa Educ Frat, 1987-; Nat Coun Negro Women. **Honors/Awds:** Distinguished Florida Educator the Year, Greater DC Area Teachers Fa, 1987; Distinguished Mother of the Year, Jack & Jill Am, Chesapeake, 1991; Leadership in Afro-Hispanic Studies Award, Howard Univ, 1998; Distinguished AFA Woman Award, Phi Beta Sigma, 1999; 100 Most Influential African Americans, Ebony, 1999, 2000. **Special Achievements:** Publ, "Afro-Hispanic Literature: An anthology of Hispanic Writers of African Ancestry," 1989; language proficiency, Spanish. **Home Addr:** 3315 Dunwood Crossing Dr, Bowie, MD 20721. **Business Addr:** Director, Bowie State University, School of Continuing Education, 14000 Jericho Pk Rd, Bowie, MD 20715, **Business Phone:** (301)736-7667.

MILLER, DR. ISAAC H., JR.
Administrator. **Personal:** Born Sep 26, 1920, Jacksonville, FL; married Effie; children: Isaac, III, Kevin, Eric, Keith & Kay. **Educ:** Livingston Col, BS, 1938; Univ WI, MS, PhD, 1948, 1951. **Career:** Adminr (retired); Meharry Med Col Nashville, former prof bio chemistry; Bennett Col, Greensboro NC, past pres. **Orgs:** Am Chem Soc; Botanical Soc Am; Am Asn for Advan Sci; Asn S eastern Biologists; former vis sci Oak Ridge Inst Nuclear Studies; panelist Nat Sci Found Prgm. **Honors/Awds:** Recipient Lederle Medical Faculty Award, Meharry Col.

MILLER, JACQUELINE ELIZABETH
Library administrator, educator. **Personal:** Born Apr 15, 1935, New York, NY; daughter of Lynward and Sarah Ellen Grevious Winslow (deceased); children: Percy Scott. **Educ:** Morgan State Col, BA, 1957; Pratt Inst, MLS, 1960. **Career:** Educator, Library Administrator (retired); Brooklyn Pub Libr, 1957-68; New Rochelle Pub Libr, head exten serv, 1969-70; Yonkers Pub Libr, br admin, 1970-75, dir, 1975-96; Queens Col, Ny, adj prof, 1989-90. **Orgs:** Comnr Comn State-wide Libr Develop, 1980; NYS Govs CMS Libr, 1990-91; Rotary of Yonkers; Numerous other national, state, county professional library org. **Honors/Awds:** Honored Citizen of Yonkers, Church of Our Saviour, 1980; Annual Award West County Club, Nat Asn Negro Bus & Prof Womens Clubs, 1981; Mae Morgan Robinson Award, 1992; Womens Equality Day Award, 1992.

MILLER, DR. JAKE C
Educator. **Personal:** Born Dec 28, 1929, Hobe Sound, FL; son of Jake and Augustine White Paige; married Nellie Carrol; children: Charles, Wayne & Warren. **Educ:** Bethune-Cookman Col, BS, 1951; Univ Ill, MA, 1957; Univ NC, Chapel Hill, PhD, 1967. **Career:** Educator (retired); Martin Co Sch Syst, FL, instr, 1954-59; Bethune-Cookman Col, asst prof, 1959-64, prof, 1976-96; Fisk Univ, assoc prof, 1967-76; Nat Endowment Humanities, 1981-82; US Inst Peace, fel, 1989-90; Univ Ill, fac; Univ NC, Chapel Hill, fac. **Orgs:** Am Polit Sci Asn; Int Studies Asn; Caribbean Studies Asn; Trans Africa Nat Conf Black Polit Scientists; Alpha Phi Alpha Fraternity. **Honors/Awds:** Excellence in Research Award, 1979, 1985, 1989; Ja Flo Davis Faculty Member of the Year, Bethune-Cookman Col, 1980, 1985, 1988; Professor of the Year Finalist, Coun Adv & Support Educ, 1984; Distinguished Scholar, United Negro Col Fund, 1986-87; Distinguished Alumni Citation, Nat Asn Equal Opportunity Higher Educ, 1988; Dr Jake C Miller Political Science Scholarship, named in honor. **Special Achievements:** Published books, Black Presence in American Foreign Affairs, Univeristy Press of America, 1978, Plight of Haitian Refugees, Praeger 1984, Building A Better World, 1996, A Century of Hope, 2001, Prophets of A Just Society, 2002. **Military Serv:** USMC, corporal. **Home Addr:** 1103 Lakewood Pk Dr, Daytona Beach, FL 32117.

MILLER, JAMES
Banker. **Educ:** E Tenn State Univ, BS, attended; Univ Tenn, MBA, attended. **Career:** First Tenn Bank, vice chmn, vpres com banking, currently. **Orgs:** Pres, 100 Black Men Chattanooga; Chattanooga African Am Chamber; chmn, Greater Chattanooga Sports & Events Comn; vchmn, Sports Comt, chmn. **Honors/Awds:** Eagle Scout Award, 1968; Highest District Award, Boy Scouts Am Scout Reach Comt. **Business Addr:** Vice President, First Tennessee Bank, 701 Mkt St Suite 1128, Chattanooga, TN 37402, **Business Phone:** (423)757-4011.

MILLER, JAMES ARTHUR
Educator. **Personal:** Born Aug 27, 1944, Providence, RI; son of John and Elease; children: Ayisha & John. **Educ:** Brown Univ, Providence, RI, AB, 1966; State Univ NY, Buffalo, PhD, 1976. **Career:** State Univ New York, dir black studies, 1969-71; City Univ NY, Medgar Evers Col, asst prof humanities, 1971-72; WGBH Radio Found Boston,consult, 1978-80; Trinity Col, Hartford, CT, assoc prof eng to asst profeng, 1979-90; CT Pub Radio, humanities consult, 1979-80; Lafayette Col, Easton, PA, distinguished vis prof, 1982-83; Wesleyan Univ, Middletown, CT, vis assoc prof Afro-Am studies, 1985-86; Wesleyan Univ, Middletown,CT, vis assoc prof eng & Afro-Am studies, 1988-89; Trinity Col, Hartford,CT, prof eng & Am studies; Univ SC, prof eng & dir African- Am studies prog; George Washington Univ, prof Am Studies & eng, 1998-, chair Am Studies, 2006-. **Orgs:** Pres, Blue Hills Civic Assoc, Hartford, 1976-78; bd dir, Big Bro Greater Hartford, 1978-80; pres & bd dir, Artists Collective Inc, Hartford,1984-86; Conn Humanities Coun, 1985-91; trustee, Mark Twain Memorial, Hartford 1987-94. **Honors/Awds:** Outstanding Young Man of Am, 1978; fel, African Humanities Inst, Nat Endowment Humanities, 1979; fel, WEB DuBois Inst, Harvard Univ, 1993;Scholar In Residence, Schomburg Ctr, 1994; Conarroe Vis Scholar, Lafayette Col, 2000; Teacher of the Year, Carnegie Found Advan Teaching, DC, 2002. **Business Addr:** Professor of American Studies & English, George Washington University, 801 22nd St NW Room 761, Washington, DC 20052, **Business Phone:** (202)994-6743.

MILLER, JAMES S.
Educator. **Personal:** Born Feb 20, 1923, Gastonia, NC; married Anne E Grier. **Educ:** Howard Univ, BS, 1949; A&T State Univ, MS, 1956; Appalachian State Univ; UNC Exten Prog. **Career:** Educator (retired); CF Gingles Elem Sch, prin, 1952-70; Arlington Elem Sch, prin, 1970-88. **Orgs:** Nat Educ Asn; NC Asn Educrs; Gaston Co Educ Asn; Elder Loves Chapel Press; Omega Psi Phi Frat; Local Chap treas; treas Gaston Co Prin Asn; Excelsior Credit Union; Gastopn Boys Club; Gaston Co Red Cross; Gaston Co Bicentennial; Catherine's House; Community Share Food Prog; Mayors Task Force Against Crime; Presbytery Western NC Committee Ministry; comnr, Gen Assembly Witicka Kansas, 1994. **Honors/Awds:** Recip Omega Man of the Year, 1965-93; Outstanding service, 1974; Alliance Children, Caring Hands Children & Youth Award, 1992; Community Service Award, Guston County, Nat Asn Advan Colored People, 1992; Community Service Award, Guston County, 1994. **Military Serv:** USMC, first sgt, 1943-46.

MILLER, JAMIR MALIK
Football player, social worker. **Personal:** Born Nov 19, 1973, Philadelphia, PA; son of John Miller and Rhonda Hardy; married Racquel; children: Ashlynn & Amara. **Educ:** Univ Calif, Los Angeles. **Career:** Football player (retired); Ariz Cardinals, linebacker, 1994-98; Cleveland Browns, 1999-2003. **Orgs:** Founder, Jamir Miller Foundn.

MILLER, DR. JEANNE-MARIE ANDERSON
Educator, writer. **Personal:** Born Feb 18, 1937, Washington, DC; daughter of William (deceased) and Agnes C Johns Anderson (deceased); married Nathan J. **Educ:** Howard Univ, BA, 1959, MA, 1963, PhD, 1976. **Career:** Howard Univ, instr, Eng, 1963-76, grad asst prof, Eng, 1977-79; Inst Arts & the Humanities Howard Univ, asst dir, 1973-75, grad assoc prof, Eng, 1979-92; Acad planning office vpres acad affairs, asst, 1976-90, grad prof, Eng, 1992-97, prof emer, Eng, 1997-. **Orgs:** Ed Black Theatre Bulletin Am Theatre Assoc, 1977-86; exec coun, Black Theatre Prog, Am Theatre Assoc, 1977-86; proposal reviewer Nat Endowment Humanities, 1979-; adv bd, WETA-TV Ed prog, Black Folklore, 1976-77; Friends JF Kennedy Ctr Performing Arts, Am Theatre & Drama Soc, Asn Theatre Higher Edu; Am Assoc Univ Women, Am Civil Liberites Union, Am Film Inst; assoc mem, Arena Stage, Wash Performing Arts Soc, Langston Hughes Soc, Zora Neale Hurston Soc, Eugene O'Neill Mem Theatre Ctr, Am Soc Bus & Exec Women; assoc, Art Inst Chicago, Boston Mus Fine Arts, Studio Mus Harlem, Nat Mus Women Arts; Metropolitan Mus Art, Corcoran Gallery Art, Smithsonian Inst, Wash Performings Arts Soc, The Wash Opera Guild, World Affairs Coun Wash DC, Drama League New York, Modern Lang Assoc, Am Studies Assoc, Col Lang Assoc, Nat Coun Teachers Eng, Am Assoc Higher Educ; Nat Women's Studies Assoc; Hist Soc Wash, DC, DC Preserv League, Ibsen, SocAm, Nat Trust Hist Preserv, Folger Shakespeare Libr; Shakespeare Theatre; Metropolitan Opera Guild; Winterthur Guild. **Honors/Awds:** Adv Study Fel Ford Found, 1970-72; Fel So Fel Fund, 1972-74; Grantee, Am Coun Learned Societies; 1978-79; Grantee Nat Endowment for the Humanities, 1981-84; Grantee, Howard Univ Fac Res Fund, 1975-76, 1994-95, 1996-97; PiLambda Theta Nat Honor & Prof Asn Educ, 1987. **Special Achievements:** Edited book From Realism to Ritual: Form & Style in Black Theatre, 1983; The Journal of Negro History, Vol. 57, No. 4, 429-431, Oct., 1972; Published over 80 articles in various books, journals & magazines. **Business Addr:** Professor Emerita, Howard University, Deparment English, 2400 6th St NW, Washington, DC 20059, **Business Phone:** (202)806-6730.

MILLER, JOSEPH HERMAN
Insurance executive. **Personal:** Born Mar 5, 1930, Port Gibson, MS; married Cleo L Baines; children: Darryl, Stephen, Carrington, Vicki & Scott. **Educ:** Talladega Col, AB, 1950; Howard Univ, JD, 1957. **Career:** Miller Funeral Homes Inc, pres, 1972-; Freedom Nat Ins Co, pres, 1976-; Nat Inst Assoc, pres, 1976-; Reliable Life Ins Co, pres & chief exec officer, currently. **Orgs:** Bd dir, Monroe LA C C, 1976. **Special Achievements:** Black Enterprise's list of Top Insurance Companies, ranked no 10, 1999. **Military Serv:** AUS, corp, 1951-53. **Business Addr:** President, Reliable Life Insurance Company, 2932 Renwick St, PO Box 1157, Monroe, LA 71210, **Business Phone:** (318)387-1000.*

MILLER, JUANITA JACKSON
Lawyer. **Orgs:** NAACP. **Honors/Awds:** Juanita Jackson Mitchell Award for Legal Activism is awarded annually on her behalf to a NAACP unit that shows outstanding legal redress committee activities. **Special Achievements:** First African American woman admitted to the Maryland bar. Fought for school desegregation in Baltimore after the Brown vs. Board of Ed ruling. As a result, Maryland was the first southern state to integrate school system. *

MILLER, KEVIN
Media executive. **Personal:** Born Dec 17, 1957, St Louis, MO; son of Leroy A and Martha E; married Alyson, Oct 6, 1995; children: Chase T & Kathryn. **Educ:** Mil Acad-Westpoint, BS, 1979. **Career:** Leo Burnett USA, acct exec; Coca Cola USA, mkt mgr; Hal Riney & Partners, vpres mgt supvr; Pizza Hut Inc, vpres mkt, 1994-98; ABC Radio Networks, sr vpres bus develop & chief mkt officer, 1998-. **Orgs:** USMA Asn Grad, 1979-; Exec Leadership Coun, 2001; Advertising Awards Comt judge, Asn Nat Advertisers; bd mkt & commun comt mem, Nat Urban League. **Honors/Awds:** Corporate Executive of the Year, Am Diabetes Asn, 2003. **Military Serv:** AUS, capt, 1979-85. **Business Addr:** Senior Vice President, Chief Marketing Officer, ABC Radio Networks, 13725 Montfort Dr, Dallas, TX 75240-4455, **Business Phone:** (972)448-3180.

MILLER, REV. KEVIN D
Manager, clergy. **Personal:** Born Apr 9, 1966, New York, NY; son of Lawrence and Viera McAfee; married Myra Y. **Educ:** Syracuse Univ, Syracuse, NY, tv prod, 1988; Fordham Univ, Grad Sch Arts & Sci, MA, Liberal Studies, 1994; Drew Theol Sch, Madison, NJ, divinity degree. **Career:** Wash Arms, Syracuse, NY, work study, 1984-87; Roberto Clemente Pk, Bronx, NY, filter room, summer, 1987; Campus Convenience, Syracuse, NY, work study, 1987-88; Salt City Productions, Syracuse, NY, producer, 985-89; Expressive People Prod, New York, NY, producer, 1988-; Paragon Cable Manhattan, New York, NY, assoc producer & producer, 1988-89, access mgr, 1989-92, com use mgr, 1992-93; ABC Sports, assoc, 1994; Time Warner Cable; pdir admissions, Drew Theol Sch, Madison, NJ; pastor, Bethel African Methodist Episcopal Church, 2005-. **Orgs:** Bd mem, Am Cancer Soc, NYC, 1991-; comt chairperson, Phi Beta Sigma Fraternity Inc, 1985-; liason, mem, Harlem Week Inc, Uptown Chamber Com, 1990-; Nat Acad Cable Programming, 1990-; Black Filmmakers Found, 1989-; Prince Hall FM & AM, 1990-; bd mem, Morristown Community Develop Corp. **Honors/Awds:** Service Award, Beta Psi Sigma Chap, 1989; Brotherhood Award, Theta Xi Chap, 1988; President's Award, Nat Pan-Hellenic Coun, 1988; Sigma Man of the Year, Phi Beta Sigma-Theta Xi, 1985. **Business Addr:** Pastor, Bethel African Methodist Episcopal Church, 140 Plane St, Boonton, NJ 07005.

MILLER, DR. LAMAR PERRY
Educator. **Personal:** Born Sep 1, 1925, Ypsilanti, MI; married Deborah F Fox; children: LaMar Jr & Arianne E. **Educ:** Eastern

Mich Univ, BA, 1954; Univ Mich, MA, 1958, EdS, 1965, PhD, 1968. **Career:** NY Univ, sec ed & prof of metro studies present; Inst of Afro-Am Affairs,educ rsrch dir; Inst for Tchrs of Disad Youth, dir; Educ Ypsilani MI, asso prof; English Dept Willow Run, chmn; dir forensic activ; NY Univ, prof educ & exec dir metro Ctr, currently. **Orgs:** Chief consult, Nat Inst Educ Dept HEW; dir, Teachers Corps; ons Union Carbide Corp; NY Urban League; secy, Div G Am Educ Res Asn, 1972-74; edbd, NY Univ Quarterly, 1972-75; Nat Alliance of Black Sch Educ 1975-; publ comn Asn for Super & Curric Devel, 1975-77; asso ed, Am Educ Res JourAERA. 1975-78. **Honors/Awds:** Publs "equality of educ opport a handbook for rsrch" 1974; "the testing of black students a symposium" 1974; "edn for an open soc" 1974. **Military Serv:** AUS, 1944-46. **Business Addr:** New York University, Press Building, Room 72, 32 Washington Place, New York, NY 10003.

MILLER, LAUREL MILTON
Police chief. **Personal:** Born Apr 29, 1935, Richmond, VA; son of Dahlia and Alma; married Betty Loggins; children: Yasmin & Nicole. **Educ:** VA Union Univ, BS, 1972; NW Univ, attended 1974; Univ Louisville, grad study, 1975; Nova Univ, MS, 1980. **Career:** Police Chief (retired); Richmond Bur Police, patrolman, 1961-68, detective, 1968-69, sergeant, 1969-73, lt personnel officer, 1973-76, capt, 1976-77, major, 1978, dep chief police. **Orgs:** Police Benevolence Asn; bd mem, Nat Orgn Black Law Enforcement Execs; Alumni S Police Inst. **Honors/Awds:** Police Cit Certificate, 36 Public Serv Commendations; 1963; Police Medal 1972; Merit Police Duty, 1975. **Special Achievements:** First Black Traffic Sergeant Richmond; First Black Head Div Bur Police; First Black Capt Bureau; First Black Major and Deputy Chief of Police. **Military Serv:** USAF a/1c 1953-57. **Home Addr:** 9307 N Run Rd, Glen Allen, VA 23060.

MILLER, LAWRENCE A., JR.
Government official, manager. **Personal:** Born Aug 17, 1951, Bronx, NY; son of Lawrence A and Adella B Williams King; married Shirley; children: Keisha Yvette & Dahra Ayanna. **Educ:** York Col, BA, pub admin, 1974; Brooklyn Col, MPA, 1989. **Career:** Dept Juv Justice, juv counr, 1973-76; New York City Youth Brd, evaluation consult, 1976-79; New York State Div Youth, prog mgt specialist, spec projs coord, 1980-89; New York City Health Hosp Corp, dir equal employ opportunity & affirmative action, 1989-94; Suffolk County Human Rights Comn, exec dir, 1994; City Sarasota, interim asst city mgr. **Orgs:** Bd mem, Community Sch Brd 28, 1983-86; Comm Planning Brd 12, 1983-; Rochdale Village Inc 1985-; vpres, Fred Wilson Regular Dem Club, 1987; chmn brd, Youth Advocates Edn & Sports, 1987; exec dir, Community Advocates Better Living Environ, 1989; Nat Assn Advan Colored People. **Honors/Awds:** Certificate of Apppreciation, New York City Off Serv Cord, 1975;Outstanding Young Men Am, US Jaycees, 1980; Outstanding Serv Award, New York State Div Youth, 1981; Community Serv Award, Elmcor Youth & Adult Activites, 1984; Certificate of Apppreciation, Brd Edn New York City, 1986; Chancellor's Award Outstanding Alumni, 1986; Outstanding Community Serv Award, York Col, 1986; Community Serv Award, Nat Assn Negro Bus & Prof Women's Club, 1987; Honor Serv Award, Assn Black Educators New York, 1988; Columnist, New York Voice Newspaper, 1988; Central Islip Branch, Comm Serv Award, Nat Assn Advan Colored People, 1997. **Special Achievements:** Producer/Host, Community Affairs Talk Show, Radio 91.5 FM & Cable TV, 1986& 1989; Producer and host of radio program WNYE Comm Trustees Report for the Borough of Manhattan.

MILLER, LAWRENCE ANTHONY
Football player. **Personal:** Born Apr 15, 1965, Los Angeles, CA. **Educ:** San Diego State Univ, Pasadena City Col; Univ Tenn. **Career:** San Diego Chargers, wide receiver, 1988-93; Denver Broncos, 1994-96; Dallas Cowboys, wide receiver, 1997.

MILLER, LOREN, JR.
Judge. **Personal:** Born Mar 7, 1937, Los Angeles, CA; married Gwen Allain; children: Pamela Allain, Michael, Stephanie Allain, Robin, Nina, Gregory Allain. **Educ:** Univ Ore, BS, 1960; Loyola Law Sch Los Angeles, LLB, 1962. **Career:** Judje (retired); State Calif, Dept Justice, dep atty gen, 1962-69; McLaren, Miller & Monet, partner, 1969-73; Western Ctr Law & Poverty, dir litigation, 1969-70; Model Neighbor Legal Prog, exec dir, 1972-73; Pacific Lighting Corp, asst gen coun, 1973-75; Los Angeles Munic Ct, judge, 1975-77; Super Ct LA County, super ct judge, 1977-96. **Orgs:** Calif State Senate, 1973-75; exe comt, Los Angeles County Super Ct, 1993-94.

MILLER, LORRAINE
Government official. **Educ:** Georgetown Sch Bus, MA. **Career:** The White House, dep asst pres legis affairs, White House Community Empowerment Bd, 1994-96; Am Fed Teachers, lobbyist; Speaker Jim Wright, D-Texas, aide; Speaker Tom Foley, D-Wash, aide; John Lewis, D-Ga, aide; US House Minority Leader Pelosi's Off, sr advisor; U.S. House Reps, clerk, 2007-. **Orgs:** Pres, NAACP, Wash, 2004; Shiloh Baptist Church Wash; found bd dir, Shiloh's Henry C Gregory Family Life Ctr; Fed Communication Comn; Fed Trade Comn. **Special Achievements:** As Clerk of the House, Lorraine Miller is the first African American to serve as an official of the U.S. House of Representatives. **Business Phone:** (202)225-7000.*

MILLER, LOUISE T.
Educator. **Personal:** Born Mar 2, 1919. **Educ:** Univ Mich, BS, 1949; Syracuse Univ, MS, 1951; Yale Univ, MPH, 1961; Univ RI, PhD, 1970. **Career:** Syracuse Univ, res asst, 1951-60; Univ RI, res asst, 1962-63, res assoc Animal Pathol, 1963-72; Spelman Col, assoc prof biol, 1973-. **Orgs:** Instr educ, 900 Bio Workshop Elem Sch Teachers, 1965-66, 1968, 1972; Ad Hoc Comn Disabled Stud, 1968-69; Coun Spec Prog Talent, 1970. **Honors/Awds:** USPHS Trainee Grant Yale Univ, 1960-61.

MILLER, DR. M SAMMYE
Educator, administrator. **Personal:** Born Feb 23, 1947, Philadelphia, PA; son of Herman S and Sammye Elizabeth Adams-Miller; married Gloria J. **Educ:** DE State Univ, BA, 1968; Trinity Col, Wash, MAT, 1970; The Catholic Univ Am, PhD, 1977. **Career:** Nat Endowment Humanities, humanist admin & policy analyst, 1978-80; Stanford Univ, post doc fel, 1983; Asn Study Afro-Am Life & Hist Inc, exec dir, 1983-84; Bowie State Univ, dept chmn & prof hist, dean sch arts & sci & spec asst to the provost, currently. Walter J Leonard fel, Wolfson Col, currently. **Orgs:** Southern Hist Asn; Org Am Historian; The Am Historical Asn; life mem, Kappa Alpha Psi Fraternity Phi Alpha Theta Intl; Hon Soc Hist; ASALH; fel Knights Columbus; Catholic Univ, Penfield fel; Nat Asn Equal Opportunity Higher Educ. **Honors/Awds:** NAFEO Research Achievement Award, Nat Asn Equal Opportunity Higher Educ, 1984; fel, Knights of Columbus, 1970; Penfield fel; Bd Trustees Scholar, Catholic Univ. **Home Addr:** 7709 Wingate Dr, Glenn Dale, MD 20769. **Business Addr:** Professor of History, Special Assistant to Provost, Bowie State University, Department of History & Government, 14000 Jericho Pk Rd, Bowie, MD 20715, **Business Phone:** (301)860-3664.

MILLER, DR. MAPOSURE T
Dentist. **Personal:** Born Jul 17, 1934, Wadesboro, NC; son of Wade H Miller and Mary R Miller; married Bobbie J Grubbs; children: Teresa, Vickie & Gail. **Educ:** Bluefield State Col, BS, 1956; WV Univ Sch Dent, DDS, 1965. **Career:** Dr MT Miller Inc, pres, currently; pvt pract, currently. **Orgs:** Beta Kappa Chi hon soc, 1955-56; Nat Dent Asn; Am Dent Asn; Buckeye State Dent Asn; OH State Dent Asn; Cleveland Dent Soc; pres-elect, Forest City Dent Study Club, 1975-76; sec-treas, Lee road Dent Centres Inc; bd trustees, Olivet Inst Bapt Ch; chmn, health & welfare E Cleveland Bus Men Asn; Urban League; NAACP. **Honors/Awds:** Provincial Man of the Year, Kappa Alpha Psi, 1956. **Military Serv:** AUS, Sp4, 1957-59; USN, Lt, 1965-68. **Business Addr:** Physician, 13944 Euclid Ave Suite 206, Cleveland, OH 44112-3832, **Business Phone:** (216)761-0500.

MILLER, DR. MARGARET ELIZABETH BATTLE
Executive. **Personal:** Born Nov 19, 1934, Chapel Hill, NC; daughter of Johnnie M Battle and Ivy Battle; divorced; children: Lisa, Monica & William II. **Educ:** NC Cent Univ, AB, 1955, JD, 1982; Univ NC, MSLS, 1961. **Career:** Highland Jr & Sr HS, librn, 1955-59; Swannee River Jr Col, librn, 1959-66; Borgess Med Ctr, librn, 1968-79; Whitaker Sch, DHR adminr II, 1981-90; MLM Serv, pres, 1986-89; Miller's ARTrium, owner, 1989-. **Orgs:** Asst ed, Commnty Courier Newspaper, 1971-73; columnist, Kalamazoo Gazette Newspaper, 1973-75; comnr, Kalamazoo Co Bd Commns, 1975-78; chmn, Orange Co Rainbow Coalition Educ Comn, 1984-85; NAACP; Am Re-Educ Asn. **Honors/Awds:** Newspaper Fund Fellowship, 1965; US HEW Fellowship, 1967; recep Mary MBethune Award, Delta Sigma Theta Sor, 1978; Liberty Bell Award, 1978. **Business Addr:** Owner, Millers ARTrium, PO Box 413, Chapel Hill, NC 27514.

MILLER, DR. MARGARET GREER
School administrator. **Personal:** Born Jan 25, 1934, Indianapolis, IN; married Charles E; children: Gregory Charles & Jennifer Charmaine. **Educ:** Ind State Univ, BS, 1955, MS, 1965; Univ Fla, Doctorate Educ, 1978. **Career:** School administrator (retired). Orange County Pub Schs, speech clinician, 1957-70, asst supt planning, res & testing, 1981-83, assoc supt for personnel & off serv, 1983; Univ Cent Fla, asst prof, 1971-81, assoc prof exceptional educ, 1987, dir teacher educ ctr & extended studies, 1989-91, dir off multicultural issues, 1991-93, asst dean undergrad progs & cline xperiences, 1993-01. **Orgs:** Alpha Kappa Alpha Sorority; Am Speech & Hearing Asn; Am Soc Training & Develop; Fla Asn Sch Admin, Coun Exceptional C; Nat Sorority Phi Delta Kappa; Asn C Learing Disabilities; Ment Health Asn; Asn Supervised Curriculum & Develop; Phi Delta Kappa; Am Educ Res Asn, Am Asn Sch Personnel Admin; Fla Asn Sch Personnel Admin; comn secy, Orange County Adv Comn Bd Educ; comt mem, Walt Disney Community Awards, 1990; Howard Phillips Fund Eval Comt, 1986-90, bd mem, 1991-; pres, Fla Asn Staff Develop, 1994-95. **Honors/Awds:** Dr Emory O Jackson Memorial Journalism Award, S Atlantic Regional Conf, Alpha Kappa Alpha Sorority, 1983; Univ Cent Fla, Pioneer Award, First Minority Full Time Instr & Outstanding Leadership, 1985, Distinguished Black Educator, 1991-94; State Health, Rehabilitation Service Award for Outstanding Work in Child Abuse, 1987; Certificate of Appreciation for Outstanding Work and Contributions to the Community and State, Gov Robert Graham, 1987; Summit Award, Pioneering Work in Community Services & Volunteerism, Women's Resource Ctr, 1991; I Dream a World Community Award, Outstanding Pioneer in Education & the Arts, County Commission & Orlando Hist Soc, 1992; Outstanding Black Achiever, 1996. **Special Achievements:** Publ, "Multicultural teaching modules: A source of multicultural experiences for pre-school through high school curriculum", Col Educ, Univ Cent Fla, 1992. *

MILLER, MARQUIS DAVID
School administrator, executive director. **Personal:** Born Jan 22, 1959, Charleston, WV; son of Fredericka Inez Sherrill and Manuel Thurston; married Jennifer Jean Kee Miller, Jul 10, 1982; children: Janae Latise. **Educ:** Ohio State Univ, BA, social behavioral sci, 1981. **Career:** Buckeye Fed Savings & Loan, proj specialist, 1981-83; Continental Off, acct exec, 1983-90; Karlsberger Co, bus develop rep, 1990-91; Ohio State Univ, assoc dir, Corp Found, 1991-95; UNCF, nat dir corp gifts, 1995-98, vpres, field opers; Corp Scholars Prog United Negro Col Fund, vpres; External Affairs Chicago Urban League, vpres; Chicago State Univ Found, exec dir, currently; Inst Adv, interim vpres, currently. **Orgs:** Ohio State Univ Alumni Asn, 1981-; OH State Univ Black Alumni Soc, 1987-; Varsity "O", 1981-; Omega Psi Phi Fraternity, 1990-; Columbus Focus Comt, 1990-; bd dirs, Asn Fundraising Profs (AFP) Chicago Chapter; co-chair, Diversity & Fels Comt; Philanthropy Day Luncheon Comt. **Honors/Awds:** Ten Outstanding Young Citizens Award, Columbus Jaycees, 1987. **Home Addr:** 1200 N Veith St Suite 819, Arlington, VA 22201. **Business Addr:** Executive Director, Interim Vice President, Chicago State University Foundation, Cook Administration Bldg Suite 322, Chicago, IL 60628, **Business Phone:** (773)995-3839.

MILLER, MATTIE SHERRYL
School administrator. **Personal:** Born Jun 19, 1933, Adams, TN; daughter of Luetta Carney Washington and George Washington; married William Edward, Sep 19, 1953; children: Kori Edwin. **Educ:** Tuskegee Inst, Ala, BS, 1955; Ind Univ, MS, 1965, reading specialist, 1970; Univ Evansville, coun & admin cert, 1975. **Career:** School Administrator (Retired); Evansville-Vanderburgh Sch Corp, teacher, 1959-71, reading clinician, 1971-72, proj dir right read, 1972-75, guid counr, 1975-85, Harper Sch, prin, 1985; Univ Evansville, adj instr, 1967; Ind Univ, practicum supvr, 1970-73; Vincennes Univ, field couns-upward bound, 1975-77; Ball State Univ, Muncie, Ind, instr; Ind State Teachers Asn, pres; Ivy Tech Community Col, adj instr eng. **Orgs:** Bd dirs, Channel 9 WNIN, 1975-; sec bd dirs Leadership, Evansville, 1976-; bd dirs, Ind State Teachers Asn & Evansville Teachers Asn; Rotary Club Am, 1988; Nat Educ Asn; bd mem, Univ Southern Ind; pres, Vanderburgh Co Retired Educators chap; bd chair, US Selective Serv Draft Appeals Bd Dist 43. **Honors/Awds:** Woman of Year in education, Evansville YWCA Leadership Award, 1975; staff rep 8th dist Congressional Appointment, 1975-78; Black woman of the Year in education, Evansville Comn Action Award, 1978; Rep W African Countries, 1984; Rep France Sec Ed Schs, 1985; LLD, University Southern Ind, 2006; Sagamore of the Wabash award. **Home Addr:** 517 S Boeke Rd, Evansville, IN 47714. **Business Addr:** President, Indiana State Teachers Association, 150 W Market St Suite 900, Indianapolis, IN 46204, **Business Phone:** (317)263-3400.

MILLER, MELVIN ALLEN
Public relations executive. **Personal:** Born Nov 24, 1950, Hattiesburg, MS; married Alfredia Dampier. **Educ:** Univ So Miss, BS, 1972; Jackson State Univ, MS, 1978. **Career:** Jackson Plant DeSoto Inc, commun asst, 1975-76; Jackson State Univ, staff writer, 1976-77, asst to dir of pub info, 1977, acting dir pub info, 1977-78, dir pub info, 1978-86, dir of develop, 1987; W Jackson Community Develop Corp, exec dir, 2004. **Orgs:** Trustee, New Hope Baptist Church, Jackson, 1978-; 1st vice pres, Cystic Fibrosis Found, Miss Chap, 1980; unit commr, Boy Scouts Am, 1980; dean's list scholar, Univ of So Mississippi, 1970-72; Delta Omicron Hon Soc, Univ Miss, 1972; Phi Kappa Phi Natl Hon Soc, Jackson State Univ, 1978; pres, Coll Pub Relations Asn Miss, 1979-80; bd mem, Jackson Chap March Dimes. **Military Serv:** AUS, 1st lt, 1972-75. **Business Addr:** Executive Director, West Jackson Community Development Corporation, 1060 Jorhn R Lynch St, Jackson, MS 39217, **Business Phone:** (601)352-6993.*

MILLER, MELVIN B.
Television journalist, executive. **Personal:** Born Jul 22, 1934, Boston, MA; divorced. **Educ:** Harvard Col, AB, 1956; Columbia Law Sch, JD, 1964. **Career:** US Justice Dept, asst US atty, 1965-66; Bay State Banner, publ & ed, 1965-; Boston Bank Com, dir; Unity Bank & Trust Co, conservator, 1973-77; WNEV-TV Inc, vpres & gen coun, 1982-93; Fitch Miller & Tourse, partner, 1981-91; OneUnited Bank, bd dir, currently. **Orgs:** Trustee, Boston Univ, Milton Acad; past trustee, The Wang Ctr; New Eng Conserv Music; James Jackson Putnam Children's Ctr; Family Serv Asn Greater Boston; Family Couns & Guid Ctr; past dir, Greater Boston C C; past dir, Mass Counc Crime & Correction; past chmn, Boston Comn Media Com; Overseers Harvard Univ; Mass Small Bus Adv Coun; NE Reg Area One Exec Com BSA; exec bd, Minority Bus Opportunity Comn; trustee, Huntington Theatre Co; dir, US SAfrica Leadership Exchange Prog. **Honors/Awds:** Boston Ten Outstanding Young Men, Boston Jr C C 1967; Award of Excellece, Art Dir Club Boston 1970; First prize, Gen Excell New Eng Press Asn, 1970; Second prize Make-up & Typography, New Eng Press Asn, 1970; Second prize Spec Sect Award, New

Eng Press Asn, 1971; Annual Achievement Award, Nat Asn Advan Colored People, 1971; hon ment Gen Excell New England Press Assn 1975; DHL, Suffolk Univ, 1984. **Business Addr:** Board of Director, OneUnited Bank, 133 Federal St, Boston, MA 02110.

MILLER, NATE (NATHAN UDELL MILLER)
Football player. **Personal:** Born Oct 8, 1971, Tuscaloosa, AL. **Educ:** La State Univ, Baton Rouge, La, gen bus. **Career:** Atlanta Falcons, tackle, 1997. **Special Achievements:** Poetry: ''Heart of a Man'' & ''love''.

MILLER, NATHAN UDELL. See MILLER, NATE.

MILLER, NORMA ADELE
Dancer, writer. **Personal:** Born Dec 2, 1919, New York, NY; daughter of Alma and Norman. **Career:** Dancer, writer, currently. **Orgs:** Society of Singers. **Honors/Awds:** Stompin at the Savoy, nomination for choregraphy. **Special Achievements:** Redd Foxx Encylopedia of Black Humor, 1977; Savoy Home of Happy Feet, Temple University, 1996. *

MILLER, OLIVER J
Basketball player. **Personal:** Born Apr 6, 1970, Ft Worth, TX; children: Xavier. **Educ:** Univ Ark. **Career:** Basketball player (retired); Phoenix Suns, ctr, 1992-94, 1999-2000; Detroit Pistons, 1994-95; Dallas Mavericks, 1996-97; Toronto Raptors, 1997-98; Iraklion, Greece, 1998-99; Sacramento Kings, 1999; Harlem Globetrotters, 2000-01; Pruszkow, Poland, 2000-01; Roseto, Italy, 2002; Gary Steelheads, CBA, 2002-03;Southern Calif Surf, ABA, 2002; Dodge City Legend, USBL, 2002; Dakota Wizards, CBA, 2003, 2004; Minn Timberwolves, 2003-04; Indios de Mayaguez, Puerto Rico, 2004; Tex Tycoons, ABA, 2004-05; Ark Rimrockers, ABA, 2005.

MILLER, OLIVER O.
Executive. **Personal:** Born Jul 23, 1944, Battle Creek, MI; son of Oliver and Edith; married Jeannette Claire Walker. **Educ:** Dartmouth Col, BA, 1966; Stanford Univ, MBA, 1968. **Career:** Mckinsey & Co, mgt consult, 1973-75; McGraw-Hill Broadcasting Co, vpres planning, 1974-84, dir acquisitions, 1977-79; MECCO, vpres, 1975-77; Bus Week, ad sales, 1984-. **Home Addr:** 50 E 89th St, New York, NY 10028. **Business Addr:** Sales Staff, Business Week, 1221 Avenue of the Americas, New York, NY 10020.

MILLER, PERCY ROBERT
Rap musician, entrepreneur, actor. **Personal:** Born Apr 29, 1967, New Orleans, LA; married Lisa; married Sonya; children: 4. **Career:** No Limit Film, founder; No Limit Sports Mgt, founder; Wayne Fury, player, 1998; No Limit Rec, owner & chief exec officer, currently; Albums: Get Away Clean, 1991; The Ghetto's Tryin' to Kill Me, 1994; 99 Ways to Die, 1995, Ice Cream Man, 1996; Ghetto D, 1997; MP the Last Don, 1998; Only God Can Judge Me, 1999; Ghetto Postage, 2000; Game Face, 2001; Good Side, Bad Side, 2004; America's Most Luved Bad Guy, 2006; Films: I Got the Hookup, 1998; No Tomorrow, 1998; Foolish, 1999; Hot Boyz, 1999; Take down, 2000; Gone in 60 Seconds, 2000; Lock down, 2000; Popcorn Shrimp, 2001; Undisputed, 2002; Dark Blue, 2002; Hollywood Homicide, 2003; Uncle P, 2007; Paroled, 2007; Down and Distance, 2009; Toxic, 2008; TV series, Romeo!, Nickelodeon, 2003; "Robot Chicken", 2008; Las Vegas Rattlers, Amn Basketball Asn, Guard & Forward, 2003. **Honors/Awds:** American Music Awards, Award for Favorite Artist, R & B/Hip-Hop, 1998; Black Star Award, 2000. **Special Achievements:** Forbes list of top 10 most highly paid entertainer for 1998; five gold and platinum albums; Black Enterprise Top 100 Industrial/Service companies, No Limit Enterprises ranked #25, 2000. **Business Phone:** (225)291-8282.*

MILLER, PERCY ROMEO, JR. (LIL ROMEO)
Rap musician, baseball player, actor. **Personal:** Born Aug 19, 1989, New Orleans, LA; son of Master P. **Career:** Albums: We can make it right; Take my pain away, 1999; My Baby; Lil'Romeo, 2001; Game Time, 2002; Romeoland, 2004; Romeo!, 2005; Young Ballers: The Hood Been Good To Us, 2005; Lottery, 2006; God's Gift, 2006; Hip Hop History, 2007; Get Low LP, 2009; The College Boy, 2010; Films: Max Keeble's Big Move, 2001; Honey, 2003; Crashing with Master P, 2003; Decisions, 2004; Still 'Bout It, 2004; Don't Be Scared, 2006; Uncle P, 2007; Crush on U, 2007; Black Supaman, producer, 2007; Sweetwater, 2008; The Pig People, 2009; The Mailman, 2009; Down & Distance, 2009; TV Series: "The Brothers Garcia", 2001; "Oh Drama!", 2001; "Raising Dad", 2002; "Romeo!", Nickelodeon", 2003; "One onOne", 2003; "All Grown Up", 2004; "The Team", 2005; "Out of Jimmy's Head" 2009. **Special Achievements:** Beat Michael Jackson record of the youngest person to get a number 1; My Baby rose to the top of the Billboard Hot 100 before the album even hit the streets.

MILLER, PETE. See MILLER, WARREN F, JR.

MILLER, RAY
Executive, senator (u.s. federal government). **Personal:** Born Apr 6, 1949, Hampton, VA; son of Inus Ray and Inez Smith; married Marlene Rose; children: Inus Ray III. **Educ:** Ohio State Univ, BA, polit sci, 1972, MA, pub admin, 1974. **Career:** Ohio Legis Serv Comm, res assoc; former State Rep Richard F Celeste, legis asst; Rep CJ McLin Jr, admin asst; Correctional Inst Inspect Comm, exec dir; Am Fedn State, County, Municipal Employees, lobbyist; White House Staff Pres Jimmy Carter, dep spec asst; Columbus State Community Col, vpres minority affairs; Columbus Area Chamber Com, vpres community develop; Ohio House Rep, state rep, 29th dist, 1981-93, 1998-2002; Nat Urban Policy Inst, pres, 1993-; Ohio State Senate, senator, 2003-; Prof Employ Servs Am, pres & chief exec officer, currently. **Orgs:** Second Baptist Church; NAACP; Alpha Phi Alpha Fraternity; Ohio Comn African-Am Males; pres, AfriCare, Columbus Chap; bd dirs, King Cultural Arts Complex; bd dirs, Health Coalition Cent Ohio; bd dirs, Int Health Comn African, African-Am Summit; founder & chmn, Ohio Comn Minority Health; chair, Intl Inst Democracy. **Honors/Awds:** Inter-Nat Pathfinder Award, World Congress on the Family; Dr Martin Luther King Jr Humanitarian Award, Columbus Educ Asn; Chairman's Award, Ohio Comn Minority Health; Hubert H Humphrey Humanitarian Award, Akron Summit Community Action Asn; President's Award, Alpha Phi Alpha Fraternity; Award of Excellence, Columbus Urban League; Distinguished Service Award, Black Elected Democrats of Ohio; Distinguished Legislator of the Year Award, Am Pub Health Asn, 2004; Community Leader of the Year Award, Columbus Works Inc, 2004; District Legislative Award, Am Asn Counseling Develop; Trailblazer Award, Ohio Legislative Black Caucus; CJ Mclin, Jr Award, Drug Abuse Outreach Programs of Ohio. **Special Achievements:** Chief sponsor of legislation which established first time state funding for the Head Start program in Ohio; chief sponsor of some of the most significant health care legislation ever enacted in the state of Ohio, including the Indigent Health Care Act, Health Data Act, and the Mental Health Act of 1988. **Business Phone:** (614)466-5131.

MILLER, REGINALD WAYNE
Basketball player, entrepreneur. **Personal:** Born Aug 24, 1965, Riverside, CA; son of Saul Miller and Carrie; married Marita Stavrou, Aug 29, 1992 (divorced 2001). **Educ:** Univ Calif, Los Angeles, attended 1987. **Career:** Basketball player (retired), entrepreneur; Ind Pacers, guard, 1987-2005; Turner Sports, basketball analyst, 2005-; Boom Baby Productions, owner, currently. **Honors/Awds:** NBA All-Star, 1990, 1995-96, 1998; All-NBA Third Team, 1995, 1996;World Championship gold medalist, 1994; US Olympic Basketball Team, gold medal, 1996; J.Walter Kennedy Citizenship Award, 2004. **Special Achievements:** Became the first Pacer ever to start in an NBA All-Star Game, 1995; the first player in NBA history to hit 100 three-pointers in eight consecutive seasons, 1989-97; first player in Pacers' franchise hit to top 15,000 career points; co-auth: I Love Being the Enemy: A Season On Court With the NBA's Best Shooter & Sharpest Tongue, 1995; hoisted the first 3-ball of his post-playing career out in Hollywood last week as Boom Baby Productions premiered Beautiful Ohio at the American Film Institutes Film Festival.

MILLER, RICHARD CHARLES
School administrator, educator. **Personal:** Born Jul 26, 1947, Ithaca, NY; son of Richard (deceased) and Marjory; married Doris Jean Boyd, Jul 14, 1973; children: Carin Lea & Courtney Alison. **Educ:** Ithaca Col, BS, 1969, MS, 1971; Springfield Col, DPE, 1976. **Career:** Educator(retired), school administrator(retired); Tompkins Co Trust Co, bank teller, 1965-70; San Francisco Giants Baseball Club, prof baseball player, 1969-70; Springfield Col, instr, 1975-77; Bowie State Univ, from asst prof to prof, 1975-90, dir phys educ, 1976-90; Ithaca Col, Ithaca, NY, Sch Health Sci & Human Performance, dean, 1990-2001. **Orgs:** Am Alliance Health, Phys Educ, Recreation & Dance; Nat Asn Sport & Physl Educ; Asn Res, Admin, Prof Couns & Socs; Asn Schs Allied Health Professions; Bd dirs, Ithacare Sr Ctr; bd dirs, Tompkins County Pub Libr; bd dirs, Cayuga Med Ctr; bd trustees, Nat Sr Games Asn. **Honors/Awds:** Sports Hall of Fame Ithaca Col, 1979; Hall of Fame, NY State Pub High Sch Athletic Asn, 1998. **Special Achievements:** First dean of the Ithaca College's School of Health Sciences and Human Performance in 1990. **Home Addr:** 2326 Laurel St, Columbia, SC 29204-7823. *

MILLER, ROBERT, JR.
Librarian. **Personal:** Born Feb 27, 1947, New York, NY; son of Robert and Edythe Kitchens Miller; divorced; children: Nova Jean, Jennifer Ann & Robynn Marie. **Educ:** Wagner Col, BA, 1972; Columbia Univ, MLS, 1974. **Career:** NY Pub Lib, community liaison asst, 1972-74, librn I, 1974-75; Nat Col Educ, ref librn, 1975-79; Memphis & Shelby County Pub Libr & info Ctr, first asst, 1979-81; Memphis old & new, Tenn librn, 1980; Atlanta-Fulton Pub Libr, communs officer, 1981-86; Chicago Pub Libr, cur, 1986-. **Orgs:** Am Libr Asn, 1972; Black Caucus Am Libr Asn, 1987-91. **Honors/Awds:** Stephen A Douglas Award, Stephen A Douglas Asn, 1992. **Special Achievements:** Book: Harold Washington, 1982-87; A Select Bibliography, 1987; Ben Burns and Horace Cayton Papers, Illinois libraries, 1988; Genealogy Sources in the Vivian G Harsh Collection, Illinois libraries, 1989. **Business Addr:** Curator, Chicago Public Library, 400 S State St, Chicago, IL 60605, **Business Phone:** (312)747-4999.

MILLER, ROBERT LAVERNE
Football player. **Personal:** Born Jan 9, 1953, Houston, TX; married Lennie; children: Robert II, Samuel & Tiffanie. **Educ:** Univ Kans, Lawrence, bus admin, 1978. **Career:** James D Ryan Jr High, 1967; Jack Yates Sr High, 1968-70; Minn Vikings, right-back, 1975-80; CDC, admin 1981. **Orgs:** Nineth St Missionary Baptist Church; deacon Church Org; asst teacher Sunday Sch; Campus Crusade Christ; Fel Christian Athletes; bd ref, Hospitality House. **Honors/Awds:** Most Valuable Player, 1969-70; most determined & inspirational player, 1973; Jayhawk 1974.

MILLER, DR. RONALD BAXTER
Educator. **Personal:** Born Oct 11, 1948, Rocky Mount, NC; son of Elsie Bryant and Marcellus C; married Jessica Garris, Jun 1971 (divorced 1978); children: Akin Dasan; married Diana L Ransom, 2000. **Educ:** NC Ctrl Univ, BA (Magna Cum Laude), 1970; Brown Univ, AM, 1972, PhD, 1974. **Career:** State Univ Col NY, lectr, 1974; Haverford Col, asst prof eng, 1974-76; Univ Tenn, assoc prof, 1977-81, prof eng, 1982-92, dir & prof, Black Lit Prog, Lindsay Young Chair, 1986-87; LeMoyne Col, Black Scholar Prof, 1985; Univ Ga, prof eng & African Am studies, 1992-; Inst African Am Studies, dir, currently; TV Series: "The South", 1977-78; "WATU: A Cornell Journal in Black Writing", adv & contributing ed, 1978-79; "Obsidian: Black Literature in Review", 1979-; "Callaloo", 1981-; "Black American Literature Forum", African Am Review, 1982-, "Middle Atlantic Writers Asn Review", 1982-; "Langston Hughes Review", 1982-. **Orgs:** Consult, Nat Endowment Humanities; sponsor, participant & consult, Black Writers S, Ga Coun Arts & Humanities, 1980; exec, Comn Afro-Am Lit Discuss Group MLA, 1980-83; vpres, Black Hist Month Lecture Series, 1980; reader, Univ Tenn Press, 1980-; chmn, Black Studies CLA, 1982-83; chmn & founder, Div Black Am Lit & Culture, 1982-84; deleg, Modern Lang Asn Assembly, 1984-86, 1994-99; pres, Langston Hughes Soc, 1984-88; Zora Neale Hurston Review, 1986-; sr fel, Nat Res Coun, Ford Found, 1986-87; vis scholar, Irvine Found, Univ San Francisco, 1991; evaluator, Div Pub Progs Harlem Renaissance, Nat Endowment Humanities; chmn, Comm Lang & Lit Am, 1997. **Honors/Awds:** ACLS Conf Grant, Black Am Lit & Humanism Res, 1978; NEH Summer Res, 1975; Haverford Col Res, 1975; Natioal Fellowships Fund Dissertation Grant, 1973-74; Univ of Tennessee Committee Awards for Excellence in Teaching of English, 1978-79; Nat Res Coun sr Fellowship, Univ NC, 1986-87; Distinguished Scholar, United Negro Col Fund, Xavier Univ, 1988; Honored teacher, Alpha Delta Pi, 1988; Golden Key Award for Excellence, Univ Tenn, 1990; American Book Award, 1991; Irvine Foundation Visiting Scholar, Univ San Francisco, 1991; Regional Designation Humanities Award, ACOG, 1994; Regional Designation Humanities Award, Am Col Obstetricians & Gynecologists Cultural Olympiad & Southern States Humanities Coun Black & White Perspectives Am S, 1994; Golden Key Award for Excellence, Univ Ga, 1995; Sr Lilly Teaching Fellowship, 1994-95; Who's Who in America, Who's Who in Education, Who's Who in the World, 1996; Davis Fel Lect, Univ San Francisco, 1999; Langston Hughes Prize, 2000; Langston Hughes Prize, 2001; Love of Learning Award, Phi Kappa Phi, 2003; Who's Who Among America's Teachers, 2004; Student Government Asn Teacher Award, 2005-06. **Special Achievements:** Author of Reference Guide to Langston Hughes and Gwendolyn Brooks, 1978, Editor and Contributor of Black American Literature and Humanism, 1981, author of Black American Poets Between Worlds, 1986, Art and Imagination of Langston Hughes, 1989, Southern Trace of Black Critical Theory, 1991, co-author of Call and Response: Riverside Anthology in African American Literary Tradition, 1998, editor of "The Short Stories," The Collected Works of Langston Hughes, 2002, has given Black Scholar Lectures in Le Moyne College in 1985, has written scores of chapters, articles, and reviews for professional journals. **Business Addr:** Professor of English & African American Studies, University of Georgia, Institute for African American Studies, Hunter Acad Bldg 312 Holmes, University of Georgia, Athens, GA 30602.

MILLER, RUSSELL L., JR.
Physician, educator, administrator. **Personal:** Born Jun 30, 1939, Harvey, WV; son of Russel and Corinne; married Daryl Lawson; children: Steven & Laura. **Educ:** Howard Univ Col Liberal Arts, BS, 1961; Howard Univ Col Med, MD, 1965; Nat Bd Med Examrs, dipl, 1966. **Career:** NIH, Bethesda, Md, summer fel, 1961-63; Univ Mich Med Ctr, Ann Arbor, MI, summer fel, internal med res, 1965-68; Univ Calif, Cardiovascular Res Inst, Dept Internal Med, San Francisco Div Clin Pharm, res fel, 1968-69, 1971-73; Roche Inst Molecular Biol, Dept Cellular Biol Div Pharm & Immuno pharmacology, Nutley, NJ, visiting scientist, 1973-74; Howard Univ, Internal Med & Pharm, assoc prof, dir, sect clin pharm, 1974-79, dean colmed, 1979-88, prof internal med & pharm, 1979-93, vpres health affairs, 1988-90, sr vpres & vpres health affairs, 1990-93; NIH, visiting scientist, 1984; St Univ New York Health Sci Ctr, Brooklyn, NY, pres, 1994-97. **Orgs:** AAAS; Am Fed Clin Res; Am Soc Internal Med; Am Soc Clin Pharm & Therapeutics; DC Med Soc; DC Nat Med Asn; Med Chirurgical Soc; DC Gen Hosp Community, 1984-88; Mayor's Adv Comn Post-Sec Educ, 1987-89; Nat Adv Coun Aging, 1988-91; bd dir, Nat Res Matching Prog, 1988-91; Educ Community Foreign Med Grad, bd trustees, 1991-92; chmn, Coun Southern Deans, 1987-88; mem-at-large, Nat Bd Med Examr, 1988-91, exec bd mem, 1991-, chmn, 1995-99. **Honors/Awds:** Certified, Am Bd Internal Med, 1971; scholar, Clin Pharm Burroughs Welcome Fund, 1977-82; awarded grants, Dept Health Educ & Welfare Res Grant 1977-80; certificate of honor, National Med Fel, 1988. **Military Serv:** USAR, Major, 1969-71; Bronze Star. *

MILLER, SAUNDRA C
Consultant. **Personal:** Born Jul 4, 1943, New York, NY; daughter of Vivian Hedgepeth; widowed; children: Rodney, Anthony & Yvette. **Educ:** John Jay Col Criminal Justice, social sci, criminal law cert; Col New Rochelle, lib arts, 1982. **Career:** NYPD, invest counr, 1973-97; travel consult, currently. **Orgs:** Better Chance, NY-NJ Chap, 1980-; deleg, Nat Orgn Black Law Enforcement Exec, 1988-; trustee, Nat Black Police Asn, 1989-; 100 Black Women, 1992-; rec secy, New York NOBLE Chap. **Home Addr:** 353 Beach 57th St Suite 5A, Arverne, NY 11692.

MILLER, SHEILA
Judge, lawyer. **Personal:** Divorced. **Educ:** Mich State Univ, BA, 1984; Thomas Cooley Law Sch, JD, 1980. **Career:** Mich House Rep, legis asst, 1986-88; Mich Senate, admin asst, 1988-92; Cooley Law Sch, sr instr trial workshop, 2003 & 2004; 41B Dis Ct, judge, currently; asst co prosecutor. **Orgs:** State Bar Mich. **Special Achievements:** First African American to serve on any bench in Macomb County. **Business Addr:** Judge, 41B District Court, 22380 Starks Dr, Clinton Township, MI 48036, **Business Phone:** (586)469-9300.*

MILLER, SHERRE. See BISHOP, SHERRE WHITNEY.

MILLER, STEPHEN DEJUAN. See MILLER, BUBBA.

MILLER, TANGI
Actor, entertainer. **Personal:** Born Feb 28, 1974, Miami, FL. **Educ:** Ala State Univ; Univ Calif, Irvine, MA; Royal Nat Theater, London, Ala Shakespeare Festival. **Career:** Films: Rhinos, 1998; Actress, 1999; The Other Brother, 2000; The Other Brother, 2002; Leprechaun: Back 2 the Hood (voice), 2003; Hurricane in the Rose Garden, 2006; Madea's Family Re union, 2006; Love. & Other 4 Letter Words, writer, 2007; After School, 2008; TV series: "Felicity", 1998-02; "Playing with Fire", 2000; "The Enforcers", 2001; "Too Legit: The MC Hammer Story", 2001; "All the News" (voice), 2002; "The Twilight Zone", 2002; "Time Will Tell", 2002; "The Shield", 2002; "Throw away", 2002; "The Power of the Ex", 2002; "Spin the Bottle", 2002; "Felicity Interrupted", 2002; "Back to the Future", 2002; "Girls Own Juice", 2002; "Fast lane", 2002; "Harsh Mistress", 2002; "Kim Possible", ed, 2002; "The District", 2003; "Blind Eye", 2003; "In God We Trust", 2003; "Cold Case", 2004; "The Division", 2004; "Hail, Hail, the Gang's All Here", 2004; "Class Actions", 2004; "The Badlands", 2004; "Half & Half", 2005; "The Big Sexism in the City Episode", 2005; "Living with Fran", 2005; "The Reunion", 2005; "Half & Half", 2005; TV movies: "The Enforcers", 2001; "Too Legit: The MC Hammer Story", 2001, "Phantom Force", 2004; Producer: Hurricane in the Rose Garden, 2006; After School, 2007; Love. & Other 4 Letter Words, 2007; Los Angeles based African dance troupe, mem, currently. **Honors/Awds:** Nat Asn Advan Colored People Image Award, 2002; One of the Most Beautiful People of the Millennium, Ebony Mag. **Business Addr:** Actress, c/o Warner Bro TV, 15303 Ventura Blvd Suite 1200, Sherman Oaks, CA 91403.*

MILLER, TEDD
Educator, college administrator. **Personal:** Born Jan 4, 1946, Washington, DC; son of Theodore and Ruby; married Gail D Johnson, Feb 1, 1976; children: Tony, Tammy, Tyesha & Atiba. **Educ:** Bethune Cookman Col, BA, 1968; Rutgers Sch Law, JD, 1972. **Career:** Rutgers Univ, adj fac, 1972-75; Essex County Legal Serv, staff atty, 1972-75; Coun Legal Educ Opportunity, asst dir, 1975-80; Georgetown Univ Law Ctr, assoc dir admis, 1980-92; Howard Univ Sch Law, asst dean & dir admis; Phoenix Sch Law, dean stud, currently. **Orgs:** Asn Am Law Sch, chair sec pre legal educ & admis law sch, 1994-96; bd trustees, Law Sch Admis Coun, 1994-97. **Business Addr:** Dean of Students, Phoenix School of Law, 4041 N Central Ave Suite 100, Phoenix, AZ 85012, **Business Phone:** (602)682-6800.

MILLER, DR. TELLY HUGH
Educator, clergy. **Personal:** Born Jun 18, 1939, Henderson, TX; married Glory D Bennett; children: Alanna Camille. **Educ:** Wiley Col, BA, 1962; Interdenom Theol Ctr, MDiv, 1965; Vanderbilt Univ, DMin, 1973; Prairie View A&M Univ, EdM, 1980. **Career:** St Paul Baptist Church, St Albans, WV, pastor, 1965; WV State Col, relig counr, 1967; Wiley Col Marshall, TX, col minister 1968, financial aid dir, 1970, assoc prof & chmn, dept relig, 1973, vpres stud affairs, 1974, prof & chmn, dept relig & philos, 1976-. **Orgs:** YMCA St Albans, 1966-67; Mt Olivet Asn, 1966-67; relig consult, Bapt WV St Col Inst, 1967; Am Asn Univ Profs; chmn, Christmas Baskets Needy St Albans, 1967; Nat Asn Advan Colored People, 1967; Kanawha Co chap, 1967; George Washington Carver Elem Sch PTA, 1977; Gamma Upsilon Lambda Chap Alpha Phi Alpha Frat Inc, 1977; Christian Athletes; Harrison County United Way Fund Dr, 1983; Harrison Co Red Cross. **Honors/Awds:** East Texas Educational Opportunities Center Award, 1980; Kappa Alpha Psi Achievement Award, 1980; Omega Psi Phi Man of the Year Award, 1983; Gov of TX, East TX Regional Review Comm for the State's Comm Develop Block Grant Prog. **Special Achievements:** First Black Commissioner for Harrison County 1983. **Business Addr:** Professor & Chairman, Wiley College, Department of Religion & Philosophy, 711 Rosborough Springs Rd, Marshall, TX 75670.

MILLER, THOMASENE
Administrator. **Personal:** Born Dec 6, 1942, Newcastle, PA; married David Lamar; children: David. **Educ:** DePaul Univ. **Career:** City of Chicago, commndg adminstr; Model Cities, asst comndg adminstr, 1970-76; Chicago Com on Urban Oppty, asst chief clk, 1968-70, sec, 1965-68. **Orgs:** Rua Consult Firm; Metro Home Hlth Adv Com; Chicago Boys Club Martin Luther King Unit, 1977; NAACP; mem Nat Asn for Comm Devel; Am Soc Pub Admin. **Honors/Awds:** Recog of merit, Chicago Com on Urban Oppty; Englewood Childrens Club Award, 1970; recog of merit, Chicago State Univ 1970; recog of achvmt Model Cities/CCUO 1975.

MILLER, WADE THOMAS
Baseball player. **Personal:** Born Sep 13, 1976, Reading, PA. **Educ:** Alvernia, PA. **Career:** Houston Astros, 1999-04; Boston Red Sox, pitcher, 2005; Chicago Cubs, pitcher, 2006-07; Toronto Blue Jays,currently. **Business Addr:** 1 Blue Jays Way Suite 3200, Toronto, ON, Canada M5V1J1.*

MILLER, WARD BEECHER
Banker. **Personal:** Born Jun 22, 1954, Kingstree, SC; son of Clifton and Bertha McCray; married Vicki Smith. **Educ:** Col Charleston, BA, 1976. **Career:** Wachovia Bank, personal banker, 1977-79, br mgr, 1979-81, field analyst, 1981-83, br mgr, 1983-85, exec banker, 1985-88, Main Office br mgr, 1988-92, E & S Office mgr, 1992-. **Orgs:** Steward St James AME Church, 1979-; bd mem, Big Brothers/Big Sisters, 1982-; March Dimes, 1983-; fin partner, Forsyth Investment Partners, 1985-; Juv Justice Coun, 1986-; Lift Inc 1986-; Inner City Coun, Boy Scouts Am; Forsyth County Zoning Bd. **Honors/Awds:** Campaign Award, March of Dimes, 1984-86; YMCA Century Club Award, Big Brothers/Big Sisters Appreciation Award; Forsyth Investment Partners Appreciation Award; Outstanding Lay Leader Award. **Home Addr:** 2520 Treetop Lane, Winston-Salem, NC 27101. **Business Addr:** Vice President, Wachovia Bank & Trust Co, 701 Martin Luther King Jr Dr, Winston-Salem, NC 27101, **Business Phone:** (910)777-1898.

MILLER, WARREN F, JR. (PETE MILLER)
Educator. **Personal:** Born Mar 17, 1943, Chicago, IL; son of Warren F Miller and Helen R Miller; married Judith Hunter, Feb 21, 1969; children: David & Jonathan. **Educ:** US Military Acad, West Point, NY, BS, eng sci, 1964; Northwestern Univ, Evanston, Ill, MS, eng sci, 1970, PhD, eng sci, 1973. **Career:** Northwestern Univ, Evanston, Ill, asst prof, 1972-74; Los Alamos Nat Lab, Los Alamos, NM, staff mem, 1974-76, group leader, 1976-79, assoc dir, 1979-86, dep dir, 1986-90; Univ Calif, Berkeley, Calif, Pardee prof, 1990-92; Sci & Technol Base Progs, Los Alama Nat Lab, dir, 1992-2001; mem, Nuclear Energy Res Adv Coun, US Dept Energy, 1997-; mem, Nuclear Technol Adv Group, Los Alamos Nat Lab, 2001-; mem, Nuclear & Radiation Studies Bd, Nat Res Coun, 2005-; Tex A&M Univ, Texas Eng Exp Sta, res prof, 2005-, Nuclear Security Sci & Policy Inst, assoc dir, 2006-. **Orgs:** US Mil Acad, 1964; Nuclear Eng Educ Disadvantaged Comt, 1972-90, chmn, 1979-80; fel Am Nuclear Soc, 1982; Prof Devel & Accreditation Comt, 1988-93; adv ed, Nuclear Sci & Eng, 1989-; gen chmn, Math & Comput Div, Topical Meeting, 1989; Math & Comput Div Exec Comt, 1990-93, chmn, 1979-80; Nat Acad Eng, 1996; Nat Soc Black Engrs, 2004. **Honors/Awds:** Pullman scholar, Univ Ill, 1964; Walter P Murphy fel, Northwestern Univ, 1969-72; Martin Luther King Jr fel, Woodrow Wilson Nat Fel Found, 1969; NMex Eminent Scholar, 1988-; State of New Mexico Eminent Scholar, 1989; Alumni Merit Award, Northwestern Univ, 1993; Distinguished Performance Award, Los Alamos Nat Lab, 2004; Distinguished Engineer, Nat Soc Black Engrs, 2004. **Military Serv:** AUS, capt, 1964-69; Bronze Star, 1968; Army Commendation Medal, 1969. **Business Addr:** Associate Director, Research Professor, Texas A&M University, Department of Nuclear Engineering, 122E Zachry Eng Ctr 3133 TAMU, College Station, TX 77843-3133, **Business Phone:** (979)845-6093.

MILLER, WILLIAM
Association executive. **Personal:** Born Apr 14, 1934, Philadelphia, PA; son of Joseph M (deceased) and Ethel Reed; married N Terri Fisher; children: William C. **Educ:** Temple Univ, BS, 1957; Antioch Univ, ME, 1974. **Career:** Opportunity Indus Ctrs Inc, instr, 1965-73; Pa Urban Coalition, instr, 1968-80; Fitzsimons Jr HS, dir publicity, 1968-70; Fel Comn Pa, dir educ, 1975-76; OIC/A Pa, asst dir funds devel, 1976-83, dir, nat org & specevents, 1983-; Lincoln/Eagleville Prog, 1980-81. **Orgs:** Temple Univ Downtown Club; Grad Coun Antioch Univ; Pa Tribune Charities; Voters Crusade; Delaware Valley Chap Nat Soc Fund Raisers; bd dir, PaCivic Ballet; Prince Hall Masons King David No 52 F and A Penna PHA; AlphaPhi Alpha Fraternity; Deacon Bd Zion Baptist Church; Am League Lobbyist, Archival Comm OIC/Temple Univ. **Honors/Awds:** Legion Honor Award Chapel Four Chaplins, 1967-75; Second Mile Award Prince Hall Masons Pa, 1972; Distinguished Serv Award, Pa Chap NAACP, 1965. **Home Addr:** 520 A Glen Echo Rd, Philadelphia, PA 19119, **Home Phone:** (215)248-9793.

MILLER, WILLIAM NATHANIEL
Association executive. **Personal:** Born Mar 15, 1947, Perry, GA; married Shirley Jones; children: Corbett Burgess & William Franklin. **Educ:** Ft Valley State Col, BA, Econ, 1969; American Inst Banking, attended 1971. **Career:** Nat Bank Ga, banking officer, 1972-77; US Small Bus admin, disaster loan specialist, 1977-78; Atlanta Regional Minority Purchasing Coun, exec dir, 1978-. **Orgs:** Phi Beta Sigma Fraternity; life mem, Atlanta Chamber Com; chmn bd, John Harland Boys Club, 1976; Ft Valley State Col Alumni Asn; Atlanta & Nat Bus League; NAACP; chmn, bus com United Negro Col Fund, 1982; Nat Asn Exhibition Mgrs, 1985; graduate, Leadership Atlanta, 1985. **Honors/Awds:** Nat Top Achiever Atlanta Chamber Com, 1976; Bus Develop Honors Collections Life & Heritage, 1984. **Business Addr:** Executive Director, Atlanta Reg Minority Purch Company, 235 International Blvd, Atlanta, GA 30303, **Business Phone:** (404)586-8516.

MILLER, YVONNE BOND
Senator (U.S. federal government), educator. **Personal:** Born Jul 4, 1934, Edenton, NC; daughter of John Thomas Bond Sr and Pency Cola Bond; married Wilbert Roy Jr (divorced). **Educ:** VA St Coll, BS, 1956; Columbia Univ Tchrs Coll, MA, 1962; Univ Pittsburgh, PhD, 1973. **Career:** Young Pk Sch, teacher, 1956-66, headstart teacher, 1965-66; Norfolk City Sch, teacher asst, 1966-68; Norfolk State Univ, from asst prof educ to assoc prof educ to prof educ, 1968-2000, prof emer, former, head, Dept Early Childhood/Elem Educ, 1980-87; Norfolk/Chesapeake Tchr Corps Proj, from assoc dir to dir, 1972-74; Mid-Atlantic Teacher Corps Network Bd Dir, secy, 1974-75, dir, 1974-76; Old Dominion Univ, adj assoc prof, 1975-76; Norfolk Teacher Corps Proj, dir, 1975; Mid-Sch Teacher Corps Network, dir exec comn, 1976; Teacher Corps Corpsmen Train Inst, fac mem, 1976; Va House Delegates, delegate 89th dist, 1984-88; Va Senate, 5th sen dist, senator, 1988-. **Orgs:** Zeta Phi Beta Kappa Delta Phi, 1962; ed, Viewpoint Newsletter VAECE 1979-80; life mem, NEA; Am Asn Elem Kinder Nursery Edn; Asn Supv & Curric Develop; Nat Asn Educ Young Child; Asn Child Educ Internat; Va Asn Early Child Educ; Tidewater Pre-Sch Asn; Southern Asn Child Under 6; life mem, Nat Alliance Black Sch Educ; Am Asn Univ Prof; Va Educ Asn; CH Mason Memorial Church God Christ; Am Asn Univ Women; Chrysler Mus, Norfolk; Va Mus; Beta Theta Zeta Chap Zeta Phi Beta; adv bd, Southern Women Polit. **Honors/Awds:** Academic Excellence Award, Zeta Phi Beta, 1974; SERWA Award, Va Commonwealth Chap, Nat Coalition 100 Black Women, 1989; Hall of Fame Induction, Va Comn Women, 1991. **Special Achievements:** First African-American woman elected to the Senate. **Home Addr:** 2816 Gate House Rd, Norfolk, VA 23504. **Business Addr:** Senator, Virginia Senate, PO Box 396, Richmond, VA 23218, **Business Phone:** (804)698-7505.

MILLER-HOLMES, CHERYL
Manager, media executive. **Personal:** Born Sep 15, 1958, Detroit, MI; daughter of Hubert and Elzenia. **Educ:** Specs Howard Sch Broadcast Arts, Southfield, MI; Oakland Community Col, Farmington Hill, MI, AA; Spring Arbor Col, Spring Arbor, MI, BA, 1988; Wayne State Univ, Detroit, MI, MLS, 1990. **Career:** Wayne County Dept Soc Servs, caseworker, 1981; Mich Dept Corrections, libr dir, 1993; Wayne County Community Col, libr dir; Univ Park Creative Arts, media specialist; South Fulton, mgr, 2004. **Orgs:** Bd dirs, African Am Reparations Comt; Wayne County Dept Soc Serv, Affirmative Action Adv Comt. **Honors/Awds:** Paul Laurence Dunbar Award, Detroit Black Writers Guild, First Prize, Poetry Contest. **Home Addr:** 144 E Red Fox Ct, Midway, GA 31320. **Business Addr:** Midway Middle School, 425 Edgewater Dr, Midway, GA 31320.

MILLER-JONES, DR. DALTON
Psychologist, educator. **Personal:** Born Jul 6, 1940, St Louis, MO; married Cynthia L Miller; children: Dalton A Jones, Julie K Jones, M Luke Jones & Marcus N. **Educ:** Rutgers Univ, BA & BS, 1962; Tufts Univ, MS, exp psychol, 1965; Cornell Univ, PhD, devel psychol, 1973. **Career:** Cornell Univ Africana Studies, lectr & res assoc, 1969-73; Univ Mass, Amherst, asst prof, 1973-82; Rockefeller Univ, NY, Inst Comparative Human Cognition, adj prof & fel, 1974-76; Williams Col, Henry Luce assoc prof, 1982-84; City Univ NY Grad Sch, assoc prof & dep exec officer PhD prog psychol, 1984; Portland State Univ, vice provost acad affairs, 1991-96, prof psychol, chair, Black Studies Dept, 2004-; Ore State Bd Higher Educ, bd mem, 2006-. **Orgs:** Soc for Res in Child Devel, 1978-; empirical res consult in Black psychol; NY Bd Educ; Am Can Co & Black community orgns, 1980; Jean Piaget Soc, 1981-; Am Educ Res Asn, 1981-; Am Psychol Asn, 1982-. **Honors/Awds:** NSF & Off Educ Fel, 1966-69; NSF, 1972; Carnegie Corp NY Grant, 1972-73. **Special Achievements:** Articles & book chapt on Black C language & thought in J of Black Studies & Acad Press, 1979-84; Publications: Jour Higher Educ; Informal Reasoning in Educ; Am Psychologist; Contemporary Educ Psychol; New Directions in Child Develop; Develop curric guide: A prekindergarten & kindergarten curric guide; Speech & lang: Advan in Basic Res & Pract.

MILLER-LEWIS, S JILL
Art patron, machinist. **Personal:** Born in Detroit, MI; daughter of Margie K and Ruben H; married James A, Dec 29, 1984; children: Davida, Alake, Bakari & Mekeda. **Educ:** Tuskegee Inst; Howard Univ, BS; Mich State Univ, post-grad studies; Wayne State Univ. **Career:** Nat Day Care Asn, Wash, DC, educ consult, 1978-80; Detroit Bd Educ, Detroit, MI, teacher, 1980-82; Rosa Parks Ctr Museum, Detroit, MI, prog dir & designer, 1983-84; Charming

Shoppes Inc; Fashion Bug, Royal Oak, MI, asst mgr, 1985-86; Detroit Bd Educ, Detroit, Mich, teacher; Jill Perette Gallery, Detroit, Mich, owner; Aida-Akante Designs & Mfg, owner; Dabl's/Perette's African Bead Gallery, owner, currently. **Orgs:** Fashion designer, Celebrity Fashion Extravaganza, Rosa Parks Ctr, 1983; prog dir, Rosa Parks Ctr Mus, 1983-84; chairperson, Walk-a-thon 84, 1984; Convention Bureau Detroit, 1990-91; Mich Retailers Asn, 1992; network dir, Nat Asn Female Execs, 1992. **Honors/Awds:** Spirit of Detroit, City Coun Detroit, 1988; Certificate of Apppreciation, Childrens Ctr Wayne Co, 1982-83. **Special Achievements:** Author of Dressing Successfully, 1984-85, AFR Pattern Design, 1993, Scrapbook Styles, 2004. **Business Phone:** (313)898-3007.

MILLER-POPE, CONSUELO ROBERTA
Association executive, president (organization), chief executive officer. **Personal:** Born in Ayer, MA; daughter of Harold G and Consuelo D; divorced; children: Alexis Michelle-Dale Williams. **Educ:** Pa State Univ, BA, 1965; Univ Chicago, MA, 1969; Chicago-Kent Col Law. **Career:** Chicago Econ Develop Corp, vpres, 1969-81; Cosmopolitan Chamber Com, pres & chief exec officer, 1982-. **Orgs:** Vpres, Inst Urban Econ Develop; bd mem, Univ Ill Ctr Urban Bus; Nat Asn Advan Colored People. **Honors/Awds:** Service Award, Chicago Econ Dev Coun, 1987; Service Award, League Black Women, Econ Develop, 1988; Bridge-Builder Award, Southern Austin-Madison Develop Corp, 1988; Appreciation Certificate, Nat Sales Network, 1995. **Special Achievements:** Numerous articles published including in Crain's Chicago Business; Dollars & Sense Magazine; Talking to the Boss Newspaper; Organizer for minority bus participation in White House Conference on Small Business, 1995. **Business Phone:** (312)786-0212.

MILLER-REID, DORA ALMA
Educator. **Personal:** Born in Montgomery, AL; daughter of George Miller (deceased) and Mary-Frances Ingersoll Miller (deceased); married Willie J Reid, Sep 28, 1949. **Educ:** Fla Agr & Mech Univ, Tallahassee, FL, BS, 1954; Wayne State Univ, Detroit, MI, EdM, 1959. **Career:** Educator (retired); Escambia Co Bd Pub, Pensacola, FL, instr, teacher, 1955-71; Detroit Bd Educ, Detroit, MI, teacher, 1971-81. **Orgs:** Detroit Fedn Teachers, AFL-CIO, 1971-; Am Fedn Teachers, 1971-; bd dir, Co-Ette Club Inc, Detroit Chap, 1971-; Wayne State Univ Alumni Asn, 1975-; Nat Retired Teachers Asn, 1981-; Retirement Coord Coun, 1981-; mem, United Found Heart Gold Awards Coun, 1982-; Metro Detroit Teen Conf Coalition, 1983-; Women's Comn, Nat Asn Advan Colored People, 1983-. **Honors/Awds:** Outstanding Service to Community & State Award, Ed Bd Am Bio Inst, 1976-77; Certificat of Merit, Detroit Bd Educ, 1981; John F Kennedy Membership Award, Co-Ette Club Inc, Detroit Chap, 1987; Certificate of Appreciation, Detroit Bd Educ, 1988; Governor's Voluntary Honarary Roll, State Mich, Spec Tribute, 1989; Certificate of Appreciation, Ronald McDonald House, 1989; Heart of Gold Award, United Way, 1991. **Home Addr:** 9000 E Jefferson Ave, Detroit, MI 48214, **Home Phone:** (313)821-2679.

MILLER-RYCRAW, EUGENIA. See RYCRAW, EUGENIA.

MILLETT, KNOLLY E.
Physician. **Personal:** Born Aug 15, 1922; married Mavis DeBurg; children: Eileen, Mercedes, Denise, Maria, Jacques. **Educ:** Long Island Univ Brooklyn, BS, 1947; Univ Paris Faculty Med, MD, 1959. **Career:** Brooklyn Physicians, pvt practice. **Orgs:** Nat Med Asn; AMA; Kings Col Med Soc; Provident Clinic Soc Brooklyn; Phi Beta Sigma; Gamma Rho Sigma; Brooklyn-Cumberland Med Ctr Jewish Hosp Brooklyn; Urban League; NY Civil Liberties Union; Manhasset C C; dipl Am Bd Family Practice. **Business Addr:** 453 Franklin Ave, Brooklyn, NY 11238, **Business Phone:** (718)622-3113.

MILLETT, RICARDO A.
Association executive, consultant. **Personal:** Born May 10, 1945, Panama City, Panama; son of William G and Ometa Trowers; married Jan Stepto; children: Sundiata Madoda, Miguel Stepto, Maya Alegre. **Educ:** Brandeis Univ, BS, econ, 1968; Florence Heller Sch Brandeis Univ, MA, 1971, PhD, 1973. **Career:** Atlanta Univ, assoc prof, 1973-77; ABT Assocs, sr analyst, proj mgr, 1977-80; Dept Social Servs, dep asst comn mgr, 1980-81; Boston Univ, dir, adj prof, 1981-83; Roxbury Milti-Serv Ctr, exec dir, 1983-85; Neighborhood Housing Develop, asst dir, 1985-; W.K. Kellogg Found, dir prog evaluation; Woods Fund Chicago, pres; United Way Mass Bay, Boston, sr vpres planning & resource mgt; Philanthropies & Nonprofits, independent consult, currently. **Orgs:** Asst dir, Boston Redevel Auth, 1985-; bd mem, chmn, Hillside Pre-Release Prog; pres, Black Political Task Force; Mus Afro-Am History, African Meeting House Comt, 1987; bd overseers, Florence Heller Sch, Brandeis Univ; bd dir, Thomas Jefferson Forum; bd dir, Social Policy Res Group. **Special Achievements:** "St Corner Alcoholics", Alton Childs Publ, 1976; "Widespread Citizen Participation in Model Cities and the Demands of Ethnic Minorities for a Greater Decision Making Role in Amer Cities", 1977; "Simmering on the Calm Presence and Profound Wisdom of Howard Thurman", 1981-82; "Racism and Racial Relations in Boston", 1982-83; "Monuments for Social Justice: A Commentary from the Black Perspective", Toward Social & Econ Justice, 1985; "Faces to Watch in 1986", Boston Mag, 1986; "Urban Renewal and Residential Displacement in the South End", Boston Univ Afro-Am Studies Dept, 1987; "Enterprise Zones and Parcel to Parcel Linkage, The Boston Case", Univ Mass Sch Pub & Community Serv, 1987; "New Players in Urban Development", Boston Redevelop Authority, 1989; "elopment & Displacement in the Black Community," J Health & Social Policy, Vol I, No 4, 1990. *

MILLIARD, RALPH GREGORY
Baseball player. **Personal:** Born Dec 30, 1973, Curacao, Venezuela. **Career:** Fla Marlins, infielder, 1996-97; New York Mets, infielder, 1998; Summer Olympics, Netherlands, 2000, 2004. **Honors/Awds:** World Series Champion, 1997. *

MILLICAN, ARTHENIA J. BATES
Educator, writer. **Personal:** Born Jun 1, 1920, Sumter, SC; daughter of Calvin Shepherd Jackson and Susan Emma David Jackson; married Noah Bates (deceased); children: Willie Louis Lee; married Wilbert Millican. **Educ:** Morris Col, Sumter, SC, BA (Magna Cum Laude) 1941; Atlanta Univ, MA, 1948; La State Univ, Baton Rouge, PhD, 1972. **Career:** Educator (retired), Writer; Westside High Sch, Kershaw, SC, Eng teacher, 1942-45; Butler High Sch, Hartsville, SC, civics & eng teacher, 1945-46; Morris Col, head eng dept, 1947-49; Mary Bethune High Sch, Halifax, VA, eng teacher, 1949-55; MS Valley State Univ, eng instr, 1955-56; Southern Univ, eng instr, 1956-59, asst prof, 1959-63, assoc prof, 1963-72, prof eng, 1972-74; Norfolk State Univ, prof eng, 1974-77; fel, Nat Endowment Arts, 1976; Southern Univ, Baton Rouge, LA, prof eng & creative writing, 1977-80; Books: The Deity Nodded, 1973; Seeds Beneath the Snow; Vignettes of the South, 1975; Where You Belong, 1977; Such Things From the Valley, 1977; Journey to Somewhere, 1986; Trek to Polaris, 1989. **Orgs:** Baton Rouge Alumnae Chap, Delta Sigma Theta; comt mem, Arts & Letters Baton Rouge Sigma Alumnae Chap; Les Gayettes Civic & Social Club; life mem, Col Language Asn, 1948-; comt mem, La Folklore Soc, 1973-; Soc Study Southern Lit, 1986-; exec comt mem, Societas Docta Inc, 1988-90; Modern Language Asn Am; Nat Coun Teachers Eng; Asn Study Afro-Am Life & Hist; Phillis Wheatley Club. **Honors/Awds:** National Endowment for the Arts Award, 1976; Delta Pearl Award in Literature, Baton Rouge Sigma Alumnae Chap, 1989; Silver Anniversary Award, DST Sorority Inc, 1991. **Special Achievements:** Cover picture and interview "Nuance" with Adimu Owusu in March 1982; contributing editor of Heath Anthology of American Literature; Prepared Black Culture Registry, Louisiana, a first, 1985; author, Hand on the Throttle, 1993; works have been included in several anthologies including Revolutionary Tales, 1995; contributing author of A Critical Evaluation; Sturdy Black Bridges; Visions of Black Women in Literature. **Home Addr:** 325 W Oakland Ave, PO Box 723, Sumter, SC 29150. *

MILLIGAN, RANDALL ANDRE
Baseball player, baseball executive. **Personal:** Born Nov 27, 1961, San Diego, CA. **Career:** Baseball player (retired), baseball executive; NY Mets, 1987, Pittsburgh Pirates, 1988, Baltimore Orioles, 1989-92, scout, currently; Cincinnati Reds, 1993-94; Montreal Expos, 1994. **Honors/Awds:** The Sporting News Minor League Player of the Year, Tidewater Tides, Int League, 1987.

MILLINER, DAVID M
Editor, publisher. **Career:** Mkt exec; Chicago Defender, ed & publ, 2003-04, PublicMediaWorks, vpres, Real Times Inc, co-owner & bd mem, currently. **Orgs:** The Daily Gazette; African Am Chamber Com. **Business Addr:** Publisher, Editor, Chicago Defender, 2400 S Michigan Ave, Chicago, IL 60616-2329, **Business Phone:** (312)225-2400.

MILLINES DZIKO, TRISH
Association executive. **Personal:** Born Jan 1, 1957, New Jersey; daughter of Patricia Millines. **Educ:** Monmouth Col, BS, Comput Sci, 1979; Seattle Univ, Hon Doctorate Humane Letters, 2001. **Career:** Computer Sci Corp, programmer; Microsoft Corp: software tester, software developer, mgr, consult, database designer & sr Diversity adminr. **Orgs:** Co-founder & executive dir, Technology Access Found, 1996-; trustee, Monmouth col. **Honors/Awds:** Arthur Ashe Award for community service, 1998. **Special Achievements:** Full basketball scholarship to Monmouth Col. **Business Phone:** (206)725-9095.

MILLNER, DIANNE MAXINE
Executive director, lawyer. **Personal:** Born Mar 21, 1949, Columbus, OH; daughter of Charles and Barbara Johnson; married Herb Anderson, Aug 15, 1986; children: Ashley Anderson & Tori Anderson. **Educ:** Pasadena City Col, AA, 1969; Univ Calif, Berkeley, AB, 1972; Stanford Univ, JD, 1975. **Career:** Pillsbury Madison & Sutro Law Firm, atty, 1975-80; Hastings Col Law, instr, 1977-78; Alexander, Millner & McGee, atty, 1980-91; Steefel, Levitt & Weiss, atty, 1991-94; Calif Continuing Educ Bar, atty; Protection & Advocacy Inc, bd dir, chair, currently. **Orgs:** Phi Beta Kappa, Univ Calif, Berkeley, 1975; dir, Youth for Serv, 1978-80, bd mem; Community Redevel Agency Asn, 1983-94; Nat Bar Asn; comt chmn, Parents Div, Nat Fedn Blind, 1988-; Black Woman Lawyers Asn; Charles Houston Bar Asn; Am Asn Univ Women, 1990-92; Am Bar Asn; Calif State Bar; pres, Calif Sch Blind, Parents & Friends Asn; Nat Fed Blind; Better Chance Inc. **Honors/Awds:** President Award Womens Division, Nat Bar Asn, 1980. **Home Addr:** 32 Sequoyah View Ct, Oakland, CA 94605. **Business Addr:** Board Director, Chair, Protection Advocacy Inc, 100 Howe Ave Suite 185N, Sacramento, CA 95825, **Business Phone:** (916)488-9955.*

MILLOY, LAWYER
Football player. **Personal:** Born Nov 14, 1973, St Louis, MO; son of Larry Milloy and Mae; married Claudine; children: Amirah & Kiara. **Educ:** Univ Wash,Sociol. **Career:** New England Patriots, defensive back, 1996-02; Buffalo Bills, safety, 2003-05; Atlanta Falcons, 2006-08. **Orgs:** Founder, Lawyer Milloy foundation. **Honors/Awds:** Pro Bowl, 1998, 1999,2001,2002; Pardade All Am Honors,Assoc Press, Walter Camp,1995; AFC Def Player of the Week,1998. **Business Addr:** Professional Football Player, Atlanta Falcons, 4400 Falcon Pkwy, Flowery Branch, GA 30542, **Business Phone:** (770)965-3115.

MILLS, ALAN BERNARD
Baseball player. **Personal:** Born Oct 18, 1966, Lakeland, FL; married Shareese; children: Tyson. **Educ:** Polk Community Col, assoc degree. **Career:** NY Yankees, pitcher, 1990-91, Baltimore Orioles, 1992-98, 2000-01; Los Angeles Dodgers, pitcher, 1999-2000; Minor League Baseball, Erie SeaWolves, pitcher, 2007-.

MILLS, ALAN KEITH
Lawyer. **Personal:** Born Sep 5, 1957, Savannah, GA; son of Warne and Shirley; married Sally Mills, Aug 11, 1979; children: Alexis K & Adam K. **Educ:** Carthage Col, BA, 1979; Ind Univ Sch Law, JD, 1982. **Career:** Barnes & Thornbury, staff, 1982, partner, 1990-; Govt Mexico, official financial institutions counsel. **Orgs:** Pres, Marion County Bar Asn, 1988-89; chairperson, State Election Bd, 1988-92; bd mem, Madame C J Walker Urban Life Ctr, 1988-2000; co-chairperson, Marion County Judicial Study Comn, 1990; bd visitors, Ind Univ Sch Law, 1990-; bd mem, Ind Black Expo, 1993-96; bd mem, Indpolis Opera, 1993-96; bd mem, St Mary Woods Col, 1998-2002; Ind Univ, Pres's Coun. **Honors/Awds:** Harry S Truman Scholar, Truman Found, 1977; Facult Prize, Ind Univ Sch Law, 1982; Minority Achiever of the Year, Ctr Leadership Develop, 1990; Distinguished Alumni Award, Carthage Col, 1996. **Home Phone:** (317)293-4222. **Business Addr:** Partner, Barnes & Thornburg LLP, 11 S Meridian St, Indianapolis, IN 46204-3535, **Business Phone:** (317)231-7239.

MILLS, BILLY G.
Judge. **Personal:** Born Apr 5, 1929, Waco, TX; married Rubye; children: Karol, Karen, William Karl, John, James. **Educ:** Compton Col, AA, 1949; Univ Calif Los Angeles, BA, 1951; Univ Calif Los Angles Law Sch, LLB, 1954, JD, 1958. **Career:** Judge (retired); Los Angeles County, dep probation officer, 1957-60; pvt prac, atty, 1957-74; Los Angeles City Coun, city councilman, 1963-74; Sup Ct, State Calif, judge, 1974; Los Angeles Super Ct, Fam Law Dept, supv judge, 1979-87, judge Super Ct. **Orgs:** Chmn, Los Angeles County Dem Control Comt; Dept Justice Adv Com; exec bd, Los Angeles County Bar Asn; Calif State Bar Asn; Am Bar Asn; Am Judicature Soc; bd trustees, United Church Rel Sci; League of Calif Cities; United Negro Col Fund; Sickle Cell Found; Calif Black Correction Coalition; Calif Fed Black Leadership; Crippled Child Soc; Kiwanis Club. **Honors/Awds:** Outstanding Graduate, Compton Community Col; Outstanding Achievement S Cent Area Planning Coun United Way; Certificate of Merit, United Supreme Coun Prince Hall Affil; Hon DHL, United Church Rel Sci Sch of Ministry; Boss of the year, Civic Ctr Women's Coun. **Special Achievements:** Billy G Mills Manor Apartments in Los Angeles are named after him. **Military Serv:** AUS, 1955-57.

MILLS, CHERYL
Government official. **Educ:** Univ Va , BA, 1987; Stanford Law Sch, JD, 1990. **Career:** Pres Clinton, dep coun; Gore Transition Planning Found, assoc coun pres; Wash DC law firm, Hogan & Hartson, assoc; Oxygen Media, sr vpres corp policy & pub programming, 1999-01; The White House, assoc coun pres; New York Univ, Off Pub Affairs, sr vpres, gen coun, secy univ, acting sr vpres opers & admin, currently. **Orgs:** Secy, New York Univ; prin liaison, Univ Bd Trustees; co-owner, DC Works, 1990-99; bd, See Forever Found; Nat Partnership Women & Families; Leadership Conf Civil Rights Educ Fund; Jackie Robinson Found; Cent Am Progress & the William J Clinton Presidential Libr Found; bd dir, Cendant Corp. **Honors/Awds:** Susan B Anthony Achievement Award. **Business Phone:** (212)998-6840.*

MILLS, CHRISTOPHER LEMONTE
Basketball player. **Personal:** Born Jan 25, 1970, Los Angeles, CA; son of Claude. **Educ:** Univ KY, attended; Univ Ariz, BA, commun & sociol, 1993. **Career:** Basketball player (retired); Cleveland Cavaliers, forward, 1993-97; NY Knicks, 1997-98; Golden State Warriors, 1998-2003; 310 Auto, owner, currently. **Orgs:** Founder, Chris Mills Found; Alpha Phi Alpha. **Special Achievements:** Cameo appearance: Blue Chips.

MILLS, DOREEN C
Executive. **Personal:** Born Jan 5, 1959, New Haven, CT; daughter of Marcus Mills and Dolores Tyson. **Educ:** Hampton Univ, BS,

Psychol. **Career:** Ramada Renaissance Hotel, sales mgr, 1985-88; Philadelphia Conv & Visitors Bur, conv sales mgr, 1988-90; Los Angeles Conv & Visitors Bur, dir, conv sales, 1990-97; Continental Plaza Hotel, dir sales & mkt, 1997-. **Orgs:** Delta Sigma Theta, 1982-; LA Chap Urban League, 1990-; pres, Nat Asn Black Hospitality Profs, 1995-; Am Soc Asn Exec, 1996-; Meeting Profs Inst, 1997-; Religion Conf Mgt Asn, 1998-; exec chair, Southern CA Soc Asn. **Business Addr:** Director Sales, Marketing, Continental Plaza Hotel, 9750 Airport Blvd, Los Angeles, CA 90071, **Business Phone:** (310)649-7071.

MILLS, ERNIE
Football player, football coach. **Personal:** Born Oct 28, 1968, Dunnellon, FL. **Educ:** Univ Fla, BS, sports admin, exercise & sport sci, 1990. **Career:** Pittsburgh Steelers, wide receiver, 1991-96; Carolina Panthers, 1997-98; Dallas Cowboys, wide receiver, 1998-99; Miami Dolphins, intern wide receivers coach; Johnson C Smith Univ, wide receivers coach; Phillip O'Berry Acad, asst head coach, defense & special teams cord; Jacksonville Dolphins, wide receivers coach, currently. **Orgs:** Nat Alliance African Am Athletes. **Business Addr:** Wide Receivers Coach, Jacksonville Dolphins, 2800 Univ Blvd N, Jacksonville, FL 32277, **Business Phone:** (904)256-7771.

MILLS, JOEY RICHARD
Beautician. **Personal:** Born Apr 2, 1950, Philadelphia, PA. **Educ:** Temple Univ, BA, 1970. **Career:** Vogue, Make-up artist: Harper's Bazaar; Glamour; Red Book; Mccalls; Ladies Home Journal; Family Circle; Essence; Town & Country; The Next Man; "Eyes of Laura Mars", 1978; record album covers: Valerie Harper. **Honors/Awds:** Guest appear WNBC Not For Women Only; For You Black Woman; appeared "Kenneth" Beauty Talk Show; appeared "AM New York"; appeared "PM New York"; appeared "The Morning Show" w/Regis Philbin; appeared "Today in New York"; appeared "The Barbara Walters Special" with Brooke Shields; 3 beauty books; cosmetic line 1978; author of best seller, "New Classic Beauty"; introduced & created, The Joey Mills Makeup System, beauty compacts and sets in skin palettes of Ivory, Suntan, Bronze & Mahogany, 1994; appearances on BET. **Home Addr:** 1 Lincoln Plz Apt 37M, New York, NY 10023.

MILLS, JOHN. See Obituaries section.

MILLS, JOHN HENRY
Football player, football coach. **Personal:** Born Oct 31, 1969, Jacksonville, FL. **Educ:** Wake Forest Univ. **Career:** Football player (retired), coach; Houston Oilers, 1993-96; Oakland Raiders, 1997-98; SKILLS Enterprise Inc, Golf Classic Coordr, 1998-; Minn Vikings, 1999; Pin Oak Youth Football Camp Coordr, 2002; Bellaire Cardinals, coach defensive coordr, 2003. **Orgs:** Skills Inc. **Honors/Awds:** Hall of Fame Youth Football, 2004-06; Pro Bowl Selection for Special Teams, 1994-95.

MILLS, REV. DR. LARRY GLENN
Executive, clergy. **Personal:** Born Oct 6, 1951, Monroe, LA; son of Catherine; married Bernice Perry, Sep 17, 1982; children: Erma, Larry, Larita, Larnell, Yolando, Larone, Lantz, Tracie & Milania. **Educ:** Wayne State Univ, 1974; Bethany Col, BRE, 1990; Bethany Theol Sem, MA, 1992; Bethany Bible Col, 1994, THD, 1999; Univ Phoenix, BSBM, 2000, MA, organ donor, 2002. **Career:** Executive (retired), Clergy; OXY Metal Ind, mgr, pc, 1971-77; Portec Rail Car, supvr, pc, 1977-82; Gen Dynamics, mgr, pc, 1982-84; Lockheed Martin, vpres, human resources, 1984-2007; Mt Sinai Baptist Church, pastor, 1988-. **Orgs:** Vpres, SCLC; past chmn, Pvt Indus Coun; TASTD; moderator, past pres, W Coast Baptist Asn; YMCA Black Achievers; Citizen's Review Bd; APICS, 1973-90; Phi Beta Sigma Fraternity, 1974-; exec bd dir, Boy Scouts; exec bd dir, Inroads, currently. **Honors/Awds:** Certified Practitioner, Am Production & Inventory Soc, 1980; Top 100 Meritorious Achievement Award, Martin Marietta, 1988; Masonic, Meritorious Youth Community Work, 1989; Black Achievers Award, YMCA, 1991; Crime Prevention Award, State of Florida, Attorney General, 1992; Community Support Award, Urban League of Orlando,1992; Management Excellence Award, 1995. **Special Achievements:** Published chapter in book: Human Factors in Advanced Manufacturing, 1992; "Training Needs in CIM," Society of Manufacturing Engineers, 1989; Annual Conference Presenter, Society of Manufacturing Engineers, 1988; published first book, Recovery of God's Purpose, 2000. **Home Addr:** 6632 Crenshaw Dr, Orlando, FL 32835. **Business Phone:** (407)299-8820.

MILLS, LOIS TERRELL
Industrial engineer. **Personal:** Born Sep 24, 1958, San Francisco, CA; daughter of Warren C and Lois M Terrell Clark; married Roderick L, Jul 21, 1990. **Educ:** Univ Valencia, Valencia, Spain, 1978; Stanford Univ, Stanford, CA, BS, ind engineering, 1980. **Career:** Procter & Gamble, Albany, GA, line & staff mgmt, 1980-82, ind engr dept mgr, 1983-85; Procter & Gamble, Cincinnati, OH, corp planning mgr, 1985-88, corp distribution planning mgr, 1989-90; Ethicon Inc, div Johnson & Johnson, Albuquerque, NM, ind engr, 1991-92; Total Assoc Involvement, coordr, 1992; Forte, hr dir, currently. **Orgs:** Univ Black Alumni, 1982-; Toastmasters Int, 1987-90; Nat pres, Am Bus Women's Asn, 1990-91; Albuquerque Chamber Com Bd Dirs, 1991-92; Stanford New Mexico Network Women Sci & Engineering, 1991-. **Honors/Awds:** Top Ten Business Woman, Am Bus Women's Asn, 1985; Highest Fund Raiser, Boys Club Am, Albany, GA, 1985; YMCA Black Achiever, YMCA, 1987. **Home Phone:** (505)897-9136. **Business Addr:** Human Resources Director, Forte, PO Box 131477, Carlsbad, CA 92013, **Business Phone:** (919)942-7068.

MILLS, MARY ELIZABETH
Educator, government official. **Personal:** Born Jul 4, 1926, Franklin, TN; daughter of Daisy Johnson Knowles; married Latham L, May 31, 1951; children: Latham L & Joycelin M Blackman. **Educ:** Tenn State Univ, Nashville, Tenn, BS, 1946, MS, 1965, cert admin & supv. **Career:** Williamson Co Sch Syst, Franklin Tenn, teacher, 1953-55; Franklin Spec Sch Dist, Franklin Tenn, teacher, 1955-77, asst prin, 1977-80, prin, 1980-; Williamson Co, Dist 11, bd comnr, currently. **Orgs:** Pres, Franklin City Teachers Asn, 1977; bd trustees, William Med Ctr, 1983-; chmn, Community Child Care Ctr, 1983-; secy, Williamson County Tourism, 1983-; Nat Educ Asn; Tenn Educ Asn; Asn Elem Sch Prin; Asn Prin & Supvr; Franklin Spec Sch Dist Educ Asn; Phi Delta Kappa; regional dir, Nat Sorority Phi Delta Kappa Inc. **Honors/Awds:** Henry L. Hardison Humanitarian Award, Franklin Spec Sch Dist Educ Asn; Whitney M Young Jr Award, Boy Scouts Am; Helping Hand Award, Williamson County Chamber Com; Black History Month Achievement Award; Outstanding Achievement in the Field of Education, Black Perspective Newspaper; Member of the Year, Outstanding Chamber Com; Soror of the Year, Nat Sorority Phi Delta Kappa Inc; Educator of the Year. **Home Addr:** 1776 W Main St, PO Box 486, Franklin, TN 37065, **Home Phone:** (615)794-2270. **Business Addr:** Member of Board of Commissioners, Williamson County, 1777 W Main St, Franklin, TN 37064, **Business Phone:** (615)794-2270.

MILLS, CAPT. MARY LEE
Nurse. **Personal:** Born Aug 23, 1912, Wallace, NC; children: Lt Cmdr Robert S & David G. **Educ:** Lincoln Sch Nursing, dipl, 1934; Med Col VA, cert pub health nursing, 1937; Lobenstine Sch Midwifery, cert midwifery, 1941; NY Univ, BS, MA 1946; George Wash Univ, cert, 1973. **Career:** Nurse (retired); US Pub Health Serv, Off Int Health, Agency Int Develop, nurse, 1946-76. **Orgs:** Reg Adv Comt; Shiloh Columbia Volunteer Fire Dept; Black History County Comt; Nat Acad Sci; Am Col Nurse Midwives; Nat Orgn Pub Health Nursing; Nat Col Midwives; Asn Study Afro Am Life & Hist; Nat Asn Uniformed Serv; Nat Asn Advan Colored People. **Honors/Awds:** NC State Volunteer Award; James Rufus Herring Award; Lakes Chapel Baptist Church Award; Shiloh Columbia Volunteer Fire Dept Disting Service Award; Pleasant Hill Baptist Church Centennial Award; Seton Hall University, Honorary DL; Tuskegee Institute, Honorary Dsc; US Pub Health Serv Distinguished Service Award; Woodrow Wilson Sch Pub & Int Affairs, Rockefeller Pub Serv Award; NY Univ Citation, 1996. **Special Achievements:** First woman to receive the Rockefeller Award; Portrait included in exhibit of 33 Outstanding Americans of Afro-American Origin, Smithsonian Institution. *

MILLS, STEPHANIE
Actor, singer. **Personal:** Born Mar 22, 1957, New York, NY; married Michael Saunders; married Jeffrey Daniels, 1993 (divorced). **Educ:** Juilliard Sch Music. **Career:** Appeared in: The Wiz, 1975, 1984; Maggie Flynn; To Sir With Love; Singles: "What Cha Gonna Do with My Lovin", 1979; "You Can Get Over", 1979; "Sweet Sensation", 1980; "Never Knew Love Like This Before", 1980; "Two Hearts", 1981; "Night Games", 1981; "Last Night", 1982; "Keep Away Girls", 1982; "You Cant Run From My Love", 1983; "Pilot Error", 1983; "How Come U Don't Call Me Anymore?", 1983; "The Medicine Song", 1984; "Edge of the Razor", 1984; "Bit by Bit", 1985; "Stand Back", 1985; "I Have Learned to Respect the Power of Love", 1986; "Rising Desire", 1986; "I Feel Good All Over", 1987; "A Rush on Me", 1987; "Secret Lady", 1987; "If I Were Your Woman", 1988; "Where Is The Love", 1988; "Something in the Way", 1989; "Home", 1989; "Comfort of a Man", 1990; "Heart to Heart", 1991; "All Day, All Night", 1992; "Never Do You Wrong", 1993; Films: The Wiz, 1978; TV Series: "Miss Black America Page ant", 1985; "My Dad the Rock Star", Nick Toons, voice, 2004-06; Albums: Movin' in the Right Direction, 1974; For the First Time, 1976; Whatcha Gonna Do With My Lovin', 1979; Sweet Sensation, 1980; Stephanie, 1981; Tantalizingly Hot, 1982; Merciless, 1983; Stephanie Mills, 1985; If I Were Your Woman, 1987; Home, 1989; Something Real, 1992; Personal Inspirations, 1995; The Best of Stephanie Mills, 2000; Born For This, 2004; Gold, 2006. **Honors/Awds:** Drama Desk Award, 1974; American Music Award, 1979, 1980, 1981; 2 Gold Albums; Grammy Award for Best Female R&B Vocal, 1980; American Music Award for Best Female R&B Vocal, 1981; Nat Asn Advan Colored People Image Awards. **Business Addr:** Singer, Actor, Wenig-La Monica Associates Agency, 580 White Plains Rd Suite 130, Tarrytown, NY 10591, **Business Phone:** (914)631-6500.

MILLS, STEVE
Executive. **Personal:** Born Jan 1, 1960?; married Beverly; children: Kristen, Danielle. **Educ:** Princeton Univ, sociology, 1981. **Career:** Ecuador, prof basketball, 1981-82; Chemical Bank NY, mgr, 1982-83; NBA Properties, acc exec, 1983-86, nat prog mgr, 1986; NBA special events dept, 1987-93, vpres, 1989; NBA comnrs off, vpres corporate develop, 1993-95; NBA, vpres basketball & player develop, 1995-99; NY Knickerbockers, exec vpres, 1999-2001; Madison Square Garden sports team opers, pres, 2001-03; Salvation Army Greater NY, bd bir; Madison Square Garden Sports, pres & CEO, 2003-. **Orgs:** co chmn, Madison Square Garden Cheering C Found; Arthur Ashe Inst Urban Health & Econ Comn Nassau Co; bd trustees, Basketball Hall Fame; Bd Dirs, USA Basketball. **Honors/Awds:** Business Executive of the Year, Black Enterprise Mag; Sports Executive of the Year, Rainbow Coalition, 1999; TrailBlazer Award, Metrop Black Bar Asn, 2002.

MILLS, TERRY RICHARD
Basketball player, basketball coach. **Personal:** Born Dec 21, 1967, Romulus, MI; son of Emma. **Educ:** Univ Mich, attended 1990. **Career:** Basketball player (retired), basketball coach; Denver Nuggets, forward, 1990-91; NJ Nets, 1991-92; Detroit Pistons, 1992-97, 1999; Miami Heat, 1997-99; Ind Pacers, forward, 2001; Intl Basketball League, Macomb County Mustangs, head coach, 2005-06. **Honors/Awds:** Michigan Mr. Basketball Award, 1986; Co-Nat player of the Year, 1986.

MILNER, MICHAEL EDWIN
Banker. **Personal:** Born Mar 16, 1952, Atlanta, GA; son of Edwin R and Ethel M Minor; married Ocie Stiggers; children: Kimberly, Michaelyn, Therron & Tasha. **Educ:** Morehouse Col, BA, 1974. **Career:** Gen Finance Corp, mgr, 1974-78; Fed Res Bank Atlanta, fed bank examr, 1978-90; S Trust Corp, corp vpres, dir, community reinvestment, 1990-99; Fed Res Bank Atlanta, Regional Community develop dir, sr community develop mgr, currently. **Orgs:** Brotherhood St Andrews; Birmingham Asn Urban Bankers; bd dir, Ala Non-profit Resource Ctr. **Honors/Awds:** Competent Toastmaster Toastmaster Int, 1985. **Business Addr:** Regional Community Development Director, Federal Reserve Bank of Atlanta, 524 Liberty Pkwy, Birmingham, AL 35242, **Business Phone:** (205)968-6760.

MILNER, THIRMAN L.
Executive. **Personal:** Born Oct 29, 1933, Hartford, CT; son of Henry Marshall and Grace Allen; divorced; children: Theresa, Gary, Thirman Jr. **Career:** Retired: All State Ins Co, acct rep; Gen Electric Bus Div, acct rep; New York City Council Against Poverty CAA, exec asst; Comn Develop NYC, dep asst admin; Comn Renewal Team Community Action Agency, pub rels dir; State of CT, rep; House of Reps, asst maj leader 1978-81; City Hartford, mayor 1981-87; First Nat Supermarkets, Inc, dir, govt affairs, 1987; State senator, asst majority leader, 1993-94; Food Marketing Inst, chmn of govt rel. **Orgs:** Sub-comm chmn, Finance Revenue and Bonding legislative Comm, 1979-80; sub-comn chmn, Planning and Devel legislative Comm 1979-80; northeast region liaison, Minority Energy Tech Asst Prog, 1979-81; bd dir, Hartford Branch NAACP, 1979-81, pres, 2001-; regional coordr, Nat Caucus Black State Legislators, 1979-81; Nat Conf Black Mayors, first vice pres 1985-86, assoc mem 1987-; bd dir, Massachusetts Food Assoc, 1989-; bd mem, Connecticut Food Assoc, 1989-; life mem, NAACP; bd dirs, New York State Food Merchants Asn; Sons of the Am Revolution. **Honors/Awds:** Community Service Award, Omega Phi Epsilon Frat, 1980; Community Service Award, Guardians Af-Am Police, 1980; Community Service Award, NAACP 1980; Community Service Award, Gr Hartford Black Soc Workers, 1980; Jewish Tree of Life Award, 1986; Univ of Hartford Chair-Establishing Thirman L Milner Scholar, 1987; dedication of Thirman L Milner Public Elementary School, 1989; first African Amer mayor, New England popularly elected, 1981. *

MILSTEAD, RODERICK LEON, JR.
Football player. **Personal:** Born Nov 10, 1969, Washington, DC; son of Roderick L Sr and Veronica E. **Educ:** Delaware State Col, BA, sociol, criminal justice, 1992. **Career:** Football player (retired); Cleveland Browns, guard, 1993-94; San Francisco 49ers, 1994-97; Wash Redskins, guard, 1998-99. **Honors/Awds:** San Francisco's Super Bowl Championship Team, 1994; Hall of Fame, 2003.

MILTON, ISRAEL HENRY
Government official. **Personal:** Born Aug 30, 1929, Marianna, FL; son of Rogene and Lucille Barkley McRae; married Regina Wooden Milton, Apr 24, 1969; children: Addie, Otha, Charles, Israel I. **Educ:** Bethune Cookman Col, Daytona Beach, FL, BS, 1951; Atlanta Univ, Atlanta, GA, MSW, 1958. **Career:** Government official (retired); Dade County Model City Prog, Miami, FL, dir, 1974-77; Dade County Neighborhood Serv Ctr Div, Miami, FL, dir, 1977-80; Dade County Dept Human Resources, Miami, FL, deputy dir, 1980-82; Dade County Dept Human Resouces, Miami, FL. **Orgs:** bd nominee, Nat Forum Black Pub Adminrs, 1982-; policy bd mem, Florida Asn Social Serv Execus, 1982-; chmn & mem, YMCA & Family Christian Asn Am, 1974-; Bethune Cookman Col Alumni Asn, 1951-; Alcohol, Drug Abuse & Mental Health Coun, 1987-90. **Honors/Awds:** Citizen of the Year, Miami Chamber Com, 1978; Volunteer of the Decade, YMCA, 1984; JFK School of Government Program for Senior Executives, Harvard Univ, 1989. **Military Serv:** USAF, Airman 1st Class, 1951-55. *

MILTON, LEROY
Research scientist. **Personal:** Born Apr 7, 1924, Los Angeles, CA; married Alma M Melonson; children: James E & Angela H. **Educ:** Pepperdine Univ, BS, 1949. **Career:** Real estate investor, 1950-96; Secured Div LA Co, chief, 1961-63; LA Co, head col invest, 1963-68; exec asst, bldg serv, 1968-69; LA Co, admin dep coroner, 1969-70; Mental Health Dept, LA County, chief admin serv, 1976-96; Avacaclo Grower, 1985-; Potomac View Prop, financial consult, currently. **Orgs:** Pres, Milton Enterprise, 1960-; pres & dir, Pub Ser Credit Union, 1960-73; dir, Eye Dog Found, 1966-73; dir, Beverly Hills Hollywood NAACP, 1969-77; pres & mem, Cosmos Club, 1946-; Alpha Phi Alpha. **Military Serv:** USN, 1942-46. **Home Addr:** 17437 Tarzana St, Encino, CA 91316.

MIMMS, DR. MAXINE BUIE
Educator, social worker. **Personal:** Born Mar 4, 1929, Newport News, VA; married Jacques; children: Theodore, Tonie & Kenneth. **Educ:** Va Union Univ, BA, 1950; Union Graduate Sch, PhD, 1977. **Career:** Seattle Public Schs, teacher, 1953-61; adminr, 1964-69; Kirkland Pub Schs, teacher, 1961-64; Women's Bur Dept Labor, 1969-72; Evergreen State Col, prof, 1972-91; prof emer; Antioch Univ, Seattle, fac; Maxine Mimms Academies, founder. **Orgs:** Nat Consultances Educ; New Approaches Higher Educ; Nat Asn Advan Colored People; Urban League; Nat Educ Asn. **Honors/Awds:** Women of the year, Seattle St Louis Tacoma.

MIMS, BEVERLY CAROL
Educator. **Personal:** Born Jan 29, 1955, Washington, DC; daughter of Oscar L Sr and Barbara Crockett; divorced; children: Michael Armwood-Phillips Jackson. **Educ:** Howard UNV, BS, pharm, 1977, doctorate, pharm, 1987. **Career:** Prof Pharm, pharmacist, mgr, 1978-80; DC Gen Hosp, staff pharmacist, pharmacist-in-charge, 1980-85; Howard Univ, asst prof, pharm practice, 1987-, assoc prof, Clinic & Admin Pharm Scis, currently. **Orgs:** Am Soc Hosp Pharmacists, 1980-; Wash Metropolitan Soc Hosp Pharmacists, 1980-; Rho Chi Soc Nat Pharm Hon Soc, 1986-; Nat Pharmac Asn, 1990-; Antibiotics and Adverse Drug Events Sub-Comms; Am Soc Health-System Pharmacists; Am Soc Consult Pharmacists. **Special Achievements:** Medicating the Elderly in Minority Aging, 1990. Quality Assessment and Improvement: Clinical Impact on Distribution, 1992. **Business Addr:** Associate Professor, Clinical & Administrative Pharmacy Sciences, Howard University, College of Pharmacy and Pharmaceutical Sciences, 2300 4th St NW, Washington, DC 20059, **Business Phone:** (202)806-6452.

MIMS, CHRISTOPHER EDDIE. See Obituaries section.

MIMS, DR. GEORGE L.
School administrator. **Personal:** Born Feb 27, 1934, Batesburg, SC; son of George W Mims and Mary Aletha Corley; married Clara Ann Twigg; children: Cheryl Ann & Carla Aletha. **Educ:** Fla A&M Univ, BS, 1955; Teachers Col, Columbia Univ, MA, 1957, Prof Dip, 1967; Rutgers Univ, EdD, 1976. **Career:** School administrator(retired); Fisk Univ, head res counr, 1959-61; Volusia Co Community Col, Fla, dean of students, 1961-63; Hunter Col, New York, asst placement dir, 1963-67; Pace Univ, New York, dir spec progs, 1968, sch law. **Orgs:** Proposal reader, US Off Educ, New York, 1974-; pres, Eta Theta Lambda Chap, Alpha Phi Alpha, 1980-87, 1996-97; res, New York State Div AACD, 1982-83; pres AERA, Spec Int Group Black Educ, 1982-86; ed bd Jour, Educ &Psych Res, 1983-86; adv comt, Merck Sharp & Dohme, 1983-; chmn AERA, CommSpec Int Groups, 1984-87. **Honors/Awds:** Cert Merit, Big Bro New York, 1969; Leadership Award HEOP, 1975; HEOP Award, 1980; Minority Alumni Award, Pace Univ, NY, 1983; Brothers Award, Eta Theta Lambda Chap, 1987; Community Serv Award, Cent Nassau Club 1989; Humanitarian Award, Howard Univ LI Alumni, 1990; Youth Community Educ Award, Ministerial Alliance N Amityville & Vicinity (LI), 1991; African Am Youth Award, African Am Heritage Asn Long Island, 1993; Distinguished Community Serv Award, Nat Hampton Univ Alumni Asn, 1993; Distinguished Serv Award, Lakeview Branch, Nat Asn Advan Colored People, 1994; Jr League LI, 1994; Community Serv Award, Eta Theta Lambda Chap, Alpha Phi Alpha Frat Inc, 1995; Humanitarian Award, Lakeside Family & C Serv, Spring Valley, New York, 1996; Gentleman of Distinction Award, Holy Trinity Baptist Church, Amityville, New York, 1996; Appreciation Award, Hempstead Sch Dist, Hempstead, New York, 1996; Jewel Founders Award, Chapter NYACOA, Alpha Phi Alpha Frat, 1996; Founder's Award, Coalition Diversity, Pace Univ, 1998; Outstanding Senior Vol, Sch Bd Sarasota County, Fla, 1999-2000; Dr. George L. Mims Oratorical Contest; The African Hall of Fame, Mt Pleasant Bapt Church; Outstanding Serv Award, Dedication Higher Educ. **Military Serv:** AUS, sgt, E5; Good Conduct, 1957-59. **Home Addr:** 113 Shady Pkwy, Sarasota, FL 34232-2370.

MIMS, MARJORIE JOYCE
Association executive. **Personal:** Born Sep 14, 1926, Chicago, IL; married Thomas S Mims; children: John, Raleigh. **Educ:** Univ IL, BS, LAS, 1949, MS, Admin, 1974; Univ Chicago, advan study, 1976; DePaul Univ, advan study, 1981. **Career:** Jack & Jill Am Chicago Chapt, pres, 1974-78; The Moles, nat vpres, 1978-82; The Links Inc, central area dir, 1983. **Orgs:** Am & Guidance Asn, 1970-; bd mem, Ada S McKinley Asn, 1972-82, Asn Family Living, 1973-81; chmn, Nat Nominating Comt Jack & Jill Am, 1978. **Honors/Awds:** Woman of the Year, Radio Station WAIT, 1974; Anti-Basielus Theta Omega Chap Alpha Kappa Alpha Sor. *

MIMS, RAYMOND EVERETT, SR.
Manager, clergy. **Personal:** Born Apr 10, 1938, Bogalusa, LA; son of Edward A and Hattie L; married Shirley Humbles, Jun 26, 1971; children: Raymond E Jr. **Educ:** Southern Univ, BS, 1961; United Theol Sem, BTh, 1984, MTh, 1987. **Career:** Crown Zellerbach Corp, asst safety & supvr, 1969-74, schedule coordr prod, 1974, logging foreman, 1974-79, supvr employee rels, 1979-82, employee rels mgr, 1982-86; Gaylord Container Corp, personnel supvr, 1986-; Greater Ebenezer Baptist Church, pastor, currently. **Orgs:** Am Pu lpwood Asn, 1974-86; bd mem, Zellco Fed Credit Union, 1980-91; bd mem, Habitat Humanity, 1986-; Am Paper Inst, 1986-; bd chair, Good Samaritans Nursing Home, 1987-92; Bogalusa City Sch Bd, 1992-; chmn, Finance Comt & Transp Comt; La Home & Foreign Mission Baptist State Conv Inc. **Honors/Awds:** HH Jefferson Memorial Safety Award, Am Pulpwood Asn, 1981. **Military Serv:** USY, sergent, 1962-64; Soldier of the Month. **Home Addr:** 1714 St Louis St, Bogalusa, LA 70427, **Home Phone:** (504)732-8407. **Business Addr:** Pastor, Greater Ebenezer Baptist Church, 2301 Medora St, Lake Charles, LA 70601, **Business Phone:** (337)436-3999.*

MIMS, RHONDA
Executive. *

MIMS, ROBERT BRADFORD
Physician, educator, scientist. **Personal:** Born Mar 24, 1934, Durant, MS; son of Dawson and Laura; married Eleanor Veronica Meeseburgh; children: Sharon Beverly, Valerie Tracy, Robin Eleanor & Bari Allen. **Educ:** Shorter Col, attended 1954; Philander Smith Col, BS, 1956; Univ Ark, Sch Med, MD, 1960; Univ SC Med Sch, attended 1964. **Career:** Univ SC Sch Med, acad prof, 1964-77, assoc clin prof, 1978-86; John Wesley County Hosp, assoc med dir, 1970-74; Univ SC LAC Med Ctr, Home Health Servs, dir, 1974-78; Found Med Ctr, pres & bd dir, 1978-82; Endocrine Metab Clinic Santa Rosa, dir, 1984-; Mims Enterprise Diversified, chief exec officer; co-founder ACE-00; Peoples Network, independent sr exec; Thyroid Educ Inst, fac, 2001. **Orgs:** Pasadena Unified Sch Dist; Calif Med Asn; Endocrinol Soc; AAAS; Am Fedn Clin Res; Am Col Phys; Am Geriatric Asn; founder & pres, Endocrine Soc Redwoods, 1987-; Nat Asn Home Health; vpres & bd dir, Health Plan Redwoods, 1978-80; bd dir, Sonoma Co Diabetic Asn, 1978-88; bd dir, Tri-Co Found Med Care; dir, Dept Internal Med Family Pract Sonoma County Hosp, 1984-86; dir, Dept Internal Med Santa Rosa Memorial Hosp, 1984-86; bd dir, VNA Sonoma Co; Calif Asn Health Care Home; Am Diabetes Asn; Calif Polit Action Asn, 1984; dir, BSA, 1979-81; bd dir, Vis Nurses Asn, 1978-83;pres, N Calif Am Diabetic Asn, 1985-86; Altadena Family Serv; Altadena Neighbors; Pasadena Integration Plan; med admin advr, Southwest La Comity Med Corp; med lectr, various pub educ meeting 1977-; served numerous community & hosp comts; bd dir, exec comt, Calif Affiliate Am Diabetes Asn, 1986-89; vpres, bd dirs, Laura & Dawson Mims Educ Found & Mims Res Inst, 1985-; AACE, 1992; Col Endocrinol, 1986; Felon Col Endocrinol, 1986; N Am Menopause Soc, 2001. **Honors/Awds:** Nat Honor Soc Philander Smith Col, 1952-56, Summa Cum Laude, 1956; Hon Life Membership Calif & Nat Congress PTA, 1973; Nat Sci Soc; numerous Collegiate Awards & Honors; Award & Scholarship Pasadena Unified School Dist, Calif Congress Parents & Teachers Inc, 1971; Award for dedicated service to Med-Cor Affairs, Univ SC, Sch Med, 1972-74; numerous scientific presentations & publications. **Military Serv:** USN, lt comdr, 1966-68. **Business Addr:** Director, Endocrine Metabolic Clinic, 5202 Old Redwood Hwy, Santa Rosa, CA 95403.*

MIMS, TERRENCE
Executive. **Educ:** USC; Benedict Col. **Career:** New World Group, co-pres, currently. **Business Addr:** Co-President, New World Group, 1117 Peachtree Walk Suite 123, Atlanta, GA 30305, **Business Phone:** (404)876-6366.

MINCEY, W. JAMES, JR.
Association executive. **Personal:** Born Feb 27, 1947, Statesboro, GA. **Career:** NC Mut Life Ins, emp; Kroney - Mincey Inc, ins designer, currently. **Orgs:** Pres Bulloch Co Chapt; SCLC 1970-; co-chmn, Mcgovern campaign Bulloch Co, 1972-72; pub dir, NAACP, 1969-70; youth coun pres, NAACP, 1967-68; mem Wesley Lodge 161; Mason; Ins Underwriters Asn Thomas Grove Bapt Ch. **Honors/Awds:** Semi-finalist, Ford Found Leadership Develop Prog. **Business Addr:** Insurance Designer, Kroney Mincey Inc, 12221 Merit Drv Suite 1210, Dallas, TX 75251, **Business Phone:** (214)386-8500.

MINCY, CHARLES ANTHONY (CHUCK MINCY)
Football player. **Personal:** Born Dec 16, 1969, Los Angeles, CA. **Educ:** Pasadena City Col; Univ Wash. **Career:** Football player (retired); Kansas City Chiefs, defensive back, 1991-94; Minnesota Vikings, 1995; Tampa Bay Buccaneers, 1996-98; Oakland Raiders, 1999.

MINCY, CHUCK. See MINCY, CHARLES ANTHONY.

MINDOLOVICH, MONICA HARRIS
Book editor. **Personal:** Born Aug 2, 1968, Washington, DC; daughter of Benjamin L and Blanche R; married Paul D, Oct 5, 1996. **Educ:** Carnegie-Mellon Univ, Lit & Cult Studies, 1990, Proffessional Writing, 1990. **Career:** Dell Publ, ed asst, 1990-93; Kensington Publ, asst ed, ed, sr ed, 1993-96; Carol Publ Group, sr ed, 1996-99; Doubleday Direct, Black Expressions Book Club, ed, 1999-2001, ed consult, currently. **Orgs:** Black Women In Publ, 1990-93. **Honors/Awds:** NY Chap NAACP, Lifetime Achievement Award, 1996; 'Special Achievement Award', Waldenbooks Inc, 1995; 2003 Emma Trailblazers' Award. **Special Achievements:** Established, "Arabesque," the first African-Am Romance line from a major publ, 1994. **Home Addr:** 522 E 20th St Suite 6D, New York, NY 10009. **Business Addr:** Editorial Consultant, Doubleday Direct, Black Expressions Book Club (Dorchester African American Romances), 522 E 20th St, New York, NY 10009, **Business Phone:** (917)584-6915.

MINER, HAROLD
Basketball player, real estate executive. **Personal:** Born May 5, 1971, Inglewood, CA; married; children: 1. **Educ:** Univ Southern Calif. **Career:** Basketball player (retired), real estate executive; Miami Heat, guard, 1993-95; Cleveland Cavaliers, guard, 1996; real estate investor, currently. **Honors/Awds:** Col Basketball Player of the Year.

MINER, WILLIAM GERARD
Architect. **Personal:** Born May 12, 1950, Washington, DC; son of George and Charlotte. **Educ:** Princeton Univ, AB, 1972; Mass Inst Tech, 1974. **Career:** US Dept State, Foreign Bldgs Opers, chief, engineering support br, 1990-, prog mgr, 1985-90; CRS Sirrine Int Group, training & res coordr, 1983-85; Am Inst Architects, dir practice pubs, 1978-83; Univ Md Sch Archit, asst prof archit, 1977-81; Keyes Lethbridge & Condon, proj archit, 1974-77; MIT Sch Archit & Urban Planning, teaching asst, 1973-74; Keyes Lethbridge & Condon, intern archit, 1973; MIT Sch Archit, rehab consult, 1973; Keene Interior & Systems, designer draftsman, 1972; Peoples' Workshop, co-founder, designer, 1972-72; Irving Wasserman Gulf Reston Inc, asst head planner, 1971; Princeton Univ Sch Archit & Planning, res asst, 1970-71; Princeton Alumni Coun, travelling res, 1970; Joseph Minor Nat Capital Housing Authority, asst sr archit, 1970. **Orgs:** Stud Planning Team Metro Dist Comn, 1972; instr, Trenton Design Ctr, 1970-71; stud rep, bd dir, AIA, 1972. **Honors/Awds:** Design competition finalist, Nat Granite Quarry Asn, 1974. **Business Addr:** Chief, BDE/ESB, US Department of State, Foreign Buildings Operations, SA-6 Rm 326, Washington, DC 20520.

MINES, RAYMOND C
Executive. **Personal:** Born in Somerville, NJ; son of Raymond C Sr and Helen M Miller; married Joyce; children: Sean M & Kimara L. **Educ:** Acad Advanced Traffic & Transportation, traffic transportation mgmt. **Career:** McDonald's Corp, dir opers & training, 1982-84, regional mgr, 1984-85, sr regional mgr, 1985-86, regional vpres, 1986-91, zone vpres, 1991-93, sr vpres/zone mgr, 1993-98, exec vpres, system rels, 1998-. **Orgs:** Children's Mem Hosp, bd; DMSF, bd; Chicago Urban League, bd; Chipotle Mexican Grill, bd; United Negro Col Fund, adv bd; Northern Trust Bank, Naperville, adv bd; Nat Coun LaRaza, adv bd; Hispanic Asn on Corp Responsibility, adv bd; Nat Puerto-Rican Coalition, adv bd. **Special Achievements:** 50 Top BE Blacks in Corp America. **Business Addr:** Executive Vice President, McDonald, 2915 Jorie Blvd, Oak Brook, IL 60523, **Business Phone:** (630)623-6230.

MINGO, PAULINE HYLTON
Restaurateur, manager, real estate agent. **Personal:** Born Aug 8, 1945; daughter of Cecil and Martha Correoso; divorced; children: Martha Senetta, Elizabeth Joy & Nelson III. **Educ:** Univ Hartford, attended 1967; Nursing sch. **Career:** State Conn, private secy to chancellor higher educ, 1969-71; real estate agent, 1966-; National Black Bus & Prof Womens Org, chaplain, 1971-74; Pan Am World Airways Eleuthera Bahamas, asst to base oper mgr, 1967-74; Mingos World Travel Serv, Hartford, owner, mgr, 1974-94; Brass Key Bar-B-Que/Soul Food Restaurant, owner, 1998-; Century 21 Reale Realtors, real estate agent, currently. **Orgs:** Treas, NW Family Day Care Ctr, Hartford, 1972-; vpres, Greater Hartford Bus Devel Corp Hartford, 1975-78; Union Baptist Church, Hartford, Connecticut; Elks. **Honors/Awds:** Published pictoral article "The Watchman", Philadelphia Spring, 1977; A Woman Worth Knowing Award, Ujima Inc, 1978; appointed mem Gov's Vacation Council, 1978-80; publ "Making It", Black Enterprise Mag, 1980; featured CT Bus Times, 1980; writer Bi-Weekly Travel Article No Agents Newspaper 1980.

MINION, MIA
Computer scientist. **Personal:** Born Nov 5, 1960, Washington, DC; daughter of Jackson and Katherine; children: Daryn. **Educ:** Coppin State Col, BS, 1985. **Career:** Coppin State Col, clerk-typist, 1981-85; Social Security Admin, comput syst analyst, 1985-. **Orgs:** Alpha Kappa Mu Nat Honor Soc, 1983; vpres, Zeta Phi Beta Sor Inc, 1984-85; Nat Deans List, 1983, 1984, 1985. **Honors/Awds:** 'Outstanding Young Women of America', 1983,

1984, 1985; John S Sheppard Scholar, Baltimore Mkt Asn; 1983. **Home Addr:** 5801 Bland Ave, Baltimore, MD 21215, **Home Phone:** (410)578-8473. **Business Addr:** Computer Systems Analyst, Social Security Admin, 6401 Security Blvd, Baltimore, MD 21235, **Business Phone:** (410)594-6991.

MINOR, BILLY JOE
Educator. **Personal:** Born Nov 10, 1938, Pine Bluff, AR; married Mary McMillian; children: Billy, Devron & Darius. **Educ:** Calif State Col, Hayward, BA, 1968, MS, 1969; Ind Univ, PhD, 1974. **Career:** San Francisco Sch, sch psychologist, 1969-71; Oakland Univ, assoc prof, 1974-, Human Resource Develop Dept, chair, currently. **Business Addr:** Chairperson, Associate Professor, Oakland University, 435B Pawley Hall, Rochester, MI 48309, **Business Phone:** (248)370-4186.

MINOR, DALE MICHAEL
Counselor, educator. **Personal:** Born Jul 31, 1949, Cleveland, OH; son of James H and Emma Lucille; married Elizabeth, Jul 29, 1972; children: Ethan. **Educ:** Ohio Univ, BS, 1973, MED, 1999. **Career:** Hocking Col, Minority Affairs, Alcohol & Drug Educ Prog, judiciary sanction officer, coordr, currently; D M C & Assoc, counr, currently. **Orgs:** Chief instr, Am Bando Asn, 1973-2002; Ohio Asn Multicultural Counr Develop, 1998-99; Chi Sigma Iota Honors Soc, 1998-2000; Am Coun Asn, 1998-2001 . **Honors/Awds:** Spec Serv & Achievement, King Hussein of Jordan, 1988; 6th Degree Black Belt, Am Bando Asn, 1997. **Business Addr:** Counselor, D M C & Associates, 8699 Terrell Rd, Athens, OH 45701, **Business Phone:** (740)592-5195.

MINOR, DEWAYNE
Racehorse trainer, horseman or horsewoman. **Personal:** Born Nov 4, 1956, Detroit, MI; son of Thomas and Arleathier; married Annemette Christiansen, 1991. **Career:** Harness racing trainer & driver, 1976-. **Honors/Awds:** Dan Rathka Memorial Award, Mich Harness Horsemans Asn, 1996. **Special Achievements:** First African American driver and trainer duo to compete in the 75-year history of the Hambletonian. **Business Addr:** Horse Race Driver, cø Odds On Racing, 1550 E Bemes Rd, Crete, IL 60417, **Business Phone:** (708)672-3438.*

MINOR, EMMA LUCILLE
Educator. **Personal:** Born Mar 16, 1925, Pollard, AL; daughter of Berry Walton and Estella Dowell Walton; married James H, May 24, 1946; children: Dale Michael, Gail Christopher & Valerie E Alloy. **Educ:** Kent State Univ, Kent, OH, BS, 1971; Cleveland State Univ, Cleveland, OH, MA, educ admin, 1974. **Career:** Cleveland Pub Schs, Cleveland OH, cadet teacher, 1968-72, consult teacher, admin intern, asst prin, 1972-75, prin, 1975-85. **Orgs:** Nat Asn Reading & Lang Educ, 1975-85; Phi Delta Kappa Educ Frat, 1976-89; Nat Alliance Black Sch Educ, 1977-89; supreme basileus, nat officer, Nat Sorority Phi Delta Kappa Inc, 1977-89; Nat Asn Advan Colored People, 1977-89; local officer, Ohio Asn Sch Admin, 1980-85; Delta Sigma Theta Sorority, 1982-89; affil rep, Nat Urban League, 1985-89, Legal Coun Civil Rights, 1986-89, United Negro Col Fund, 1986-89; affil pres, Nat Coun Negro Women, 1986-89; co-chairperson, Assault Illiteracy, Prof Educ Comt, 1986-89; pres, Nat Sorority Phi Delta Kappa Perpetual Scholar Found Inc, 1997-2001. **Honors/Awds:** Distinguished Service Award, City Cleveland, 1982; Teaching Reading Competency, 1984; Distinguished Service, Cleveland Pub Schs, 1985; Orgn Growth & Change, 1986; Mission Make Difference, 1987; Distinguished Service, Nat Sorority Phi Delta Kappa Inc, 1987. **Special Achievements:** 100 Most Influential Black Am, Ebony Mag, 1989. **Home Addr:** 310 Autumn Glenn Cir, Fayetteville, GA 30215, **Home Phone:** (770)460-9960.

MINOR, GREG MAGADO
Basketball player. **Personal:** Born Sep 8, 1971, Sandersville, GA; son of Twiggs and Charley R Brown; married Stephanie; children: Kira, Greg Jr, Khalid & Chloe. **Educ:** Univ Phoenix, BA, criminal justice admin, 2006. **Career:** Basketball player (retired), basketball coach; Los Angeles Clippers, 1994; Boston Celtics, guard, 1994-99; Ind Pacers, 2004; Okla Cavalry, asst coach, currently. **Special Achievements:** First round pick, No 25, NBA Draft, 1994.

MINOR, JESSICA
Psychotherapist, consultant, president (organization). **Personal:** Born in Chicago, IL. **Educ:** Wittenberg Univ, BA, 1962; Univ Chicago, MA, 1964; Univ Calif, JD, 1988. **Career:** Mgt consult, corp exec & psychotherapist, 1970-; Minor & Co, pres, currently. **Orgs:** Phi Alpha Delta Law Frat United Nations Asn; Commonwealth Club Calif; Am Women Int Understanding; Planning Forum, Int Visitors Ctr; San Francisco Opera Guild; Founders Comt, United Nations World Ctr San Francisco; charter mem, San Francisco Symphony League. **Honors/Awds:** Semifinalist, White House Fellows Prog, 1973-74; Outstanding Professional in Human Services, 1974; Hon Consult, Republic of Liberia, 1979-84. **Business Addr:** President, Minor & Co, PO Box 15505, San Francisco, CA 94115, **Business Phone:** (415)563-5767.

MINOR, TRACEY L (TRACEY DE MORSELLA)
Publisher. **Personal:** Born Nov 9, 1963, Philadelphia, PA; daughter of C Wes and Evie R. **Educ:** Temple Univ, BA, communn, 1988. **Career:** Expression Modeling Agency, model, 1982-87; Ctr Social Policy, newsletter ed, intern, 1985-86; Click Modeling Agency, model, 1985-87; Horizon House, newsletter ed, intern, 1986-87; Atlantic Tech, newspaper assoc ed, 1987-88; Saint Benedict's Day Care Ctr, asst dir, 1988-89; EMSCO Scientific Enterprises, sales rep, 1989-91; Del Valley Network, publ; The Multicultural Advantage, pres, 2003, Managing Producer, currently. **Orgs:** Harriet Tubman Hist Preserv Soc, 1980-81; Screen Actor's Guild, 1983-87; Pub Rels Soc Am, 1987-89; Nat Asn Black MBA's, 1992-; Poor Richard Club, 1992-; New Penn Del Many Bus Coun, 1992-; Women Communs, 1992-. **Honors/Awds:** Entrepreneur of the Yr, Nat Black MBA Asn, 1992; Urban Profiles Mag, Honored in 30 Under 30, Thirty Top Bus Owners, 1992; Woman of the Yr, ZPB, 1992. **Business Phone:** 888-750-6132.

MINOR, WILLIE
School administrator. **Personal:** Born Jan 31, 1951, Navasota, TX; son of Carl Minor Jr and Marjorie Williams. **Educ:** Prairie View A&M Univ, BS (magna cum laude), 1973, MS, 1974; Univ Phoenix, MA, 1980; Ariz State Univ, EdD, 1976. **Career:** Fac Asn, secy, 1984-85; Admin Mgmt Soc, pres, 1984-85; Phoenix Col, prof bus; Phoenix Col, admin intern, 1989-97, assoc dean instruction, fac exec coun, pres, 2003-04; Rio Salado Col, fac chair bus & appl progs; Rio Salado Col, emer fac, currently. **Orgs:** Mem & sec, Delta Mu Delta, 1972; grad co-op, NASA Space Ctr, 1974; sponsor Afro Am Club, 1977; mem & sponsor, Phi Beta Lambda, 1972-; Bus Comm Asn, 1976-85; mem & officer Delta Pi Epsilon, 1976-; pres, Admin Mgt Soc, 1977-; Phi Delta Kappa, 1980-; arbitrator, Better Bus Bureau, 1984-. **Honors/Awds:** Academic Recognition, Prairie View Fac, 1976. **Home Addr:** 6442 W Fremont Rd, Laveen, AZ 85281-8519. **Business Addr:** Emeritus Faculty, Rio Salado College, 2323 W 14th St, Tempe, AZ 85339.

MINTER, BARRY ANTOINE
Football player. **Personal:** Born Jan 28, 1970, Mt Pleasant, TX; married Shawyna; children: Gia & Bari. **Educ:** Tulsa Univ. **Career:** Football player (retired); Dallas Cowboys, 1993; Chicago Bears, linebacker, 1993-2000; Cleveland Browns, 2001.

MINTER, ELOISE DEVADA
School administrator. **Personal:** Born Oct 24, 1928, Monroe County, AL; children: Clifford B & Brenda Y. **Educ:** Tuskegee Inst AL, BS, 1949; Tuskegee Inst, AL, MA, 1961; Wayne State & Merril Palmer Inst, Detroit, attended 1970 & 1974. **Career:** Southside Jr High Sch Mobile, asst prin, 1965-68; Jefferson Mid Sch, dept head, 1968-78; Telegram Newspaper, writer, 1970-80; City Detroit, real estate salesman & appraiser 1975-80; Long fellow Middle Sch Detroit, unit head 1978-79; Pershing High Sch Detroit, asst prin, 1979-. **Orgs:** Pub speaker, religious occasions civic groups & youth progs, 1960-80; dir Bd, Christian Educ Dexter Ave Baptist Church, 1968-80; Nat Orgn Sch Adminr Suprs, 1968-80; Sunday Sch & BTU Cong, 1970-80; Alpha Kappa Alpha, 1949; NAACP, 1965-80; PUSH, 1965-80; Marie Clair Block Club, 1970-80. **Honors/Awds:** Pub audio presentation Israel "In the footsteps of Jesus"; pub "A Dramafor Your Ch", 1980. *

MINTER, MICHAEL CHRISTOPHER
Football player. **Personal:** Born Jan 15, 1974, Lawton, OK; married Kim; children: 4. **Educ:** Nebr Univ, BE, 1996. **Career:** Football player (retired); Carolina Panthers, safety, 1997-2006. **Orgs:** Spokesperson, Salvation Army Boys & Girls Club.

MINTER, STEVEN ALAN
Foundation executive. **Personal:** Born Oct 23, 1938, Akron, OH; son of Lawrence L and Dorothy K Knox; married Dolores K; children: Michele, Caroline & Robyn. **Educ:** Baldwin Wallace Col, BA, educ, 1960; Case Western Reserve Univ, MA, Soc Admin, 1963. **Career:** Cuyahoga Co Welfare Dept, from caseworker to dir, 1960-70; Commonwealth MA, comnr public welfare, 1970-75; US Dept Educ Wash DC, 1980-81; US dept educ, under secy, 1970-75; Cleveland found, prof officer & assoc dir, 1975-84, pres & exec dir, 1984-2003; Cleveland State Univ, exec-in-residence, 2003-. **Orgs:** Dir, Goodyear Tire & Rubber co; trustee Col, Wooster; dir, Key Corp; life mem, NAACP; dir, Soc Corp; dir, Consolidated Natural Gas; dir, Rubbermaid Inc; bd overseers, Florence Heller Grad Sch Advan Studies Social Welfare, Brandeis Univ; bd trustees, Found Ctr; bd trustees, Leadership Cleveland; N Coast Harbor Inc; fel Ctr Nonprofit Policy & Practice. **Honors/Awds:** Distinguished Service Award, The Sch Applied Social Sci, Case Western Reserve Univ, 1979; Social Worker of Year, OH Chap Nat Asn Soc Workers, 1984; Black Prof Year, Black Professional Asn Cleveland, 1985; Hon PhD Humane Letters, Kent State Univ, 1988; Hon PhD Humane Letters, Case Western Reserve Univ, 1989; Ohio Governor's Award, 1991. **Business Addr:** Executive in Residence, Cleveland State University, Maxine Goodman Levin College of Urban Affairs, 2121 Euclid Ave, Cleveland, OH 44115-2214, **Business Phone:** (216)687-2135.

MINTER, THOMAS KENDALL
School administrator. **Personal:** Born Jun 28, 1924, Bronx, NY; married Rae Alexander; children: Thomas K Jr. **Educ:** NY Univ, BS, MA, 1950; Union Theol Sem NY, SMM; Harvard Univ, EdD. **Career:** MD State Teachers Col, instr, 1949-53; James Otis Jr High Sch, teacher, 1955-59; Music Dept Benjamin Franklin High Sch, teacher actg chmn, 1959-66; Human Resources Adminr NY, consult, 1967; PA Advan Sch, dir, 1970-72; Dist 7 Sch Dist Philadelphia, supt, 1972-75; NOVA Univ, Philadelphia Cluster Nat EdD Prog Educ Leaders, coord, 1973-76; Wilmington Pub Schs, supt, 1975-77; USOE, asst sec elem & sec educ, 1980; NYC Public Schs, dep chancellor instr, 1981-83; Lehman Col, City Univ NY, dean prof studies, 1983-95; York Col, City Univ NY, actg pres, 1996; Lehman Col, prof emer & dean emer, currently. **Orgs:** Phi Mu Alpha Hon Music Educ, 1949; Phi Mu Alpha Hon Music Educ, 1949; fel, NAACP John Hay Summer Inst Humanities Williams Col, 1965; Phi Delta Kappa Hon Educ Frat, 1966; consult, Nat Alliance Black Sch Educr; consult, Res Better Schs, PA; consult supt schs, Portland Learing Res & Develop Ctr, Rider Col; Carter Mondale Transition Planning Group, 1976; Asn Study Afro-Am Life & Hist. **Honors/Awds:** Villanova Univ (PA), ScD, 1978. **Special Achievements:** A study of NY city, bd ed demonstration proj IS 201 2 bridges ocean hill Brownsville, 1967; The Role of Conflict in Devel Operation of two New York City Decentralized Sch Proj, 1968; Covering the Desegregation Story current Experiences & Issues, 1976; Sch Desegregation Making It Work. **Business Phone:** (718)960-8000.

MINTER, WILBERT DOUGLAS, SR.
Administrator. **Personal:** Born Nov 17, 1946, Knoxville, TN; children: Wilbert Douglas, Jr. **Educ:** Knoxville Col, 1967; Univ Tenn, 1970. **Career:** Asn Records Managers & Adminirs, pres, 1974; Admin Mgt Soc, pres, 1982; Martin Marietta Corp, suprvr eng records. **Orgs:** Pres, Oak Ridge Comn Rels Coun, 1972-73; Atomic City Sportsmen Club Oak Ridge, 1975; Human Resources Bd Oak Ridge, 1980-82; Oak Ridge Sch Bd, 1983; State Advert Comn US Civil Rights Comn, 1983-85; Dept Energy Contractors & Micrographics Asn, 1985; Nat conf speaker Asn Records Mgrs & Admin. **Honors/Awds:** Distinguished service award, Shriners Knoxville, 1973; outstanding chap mem Records Mgrs & Adminrs, 1975; outstanding cert records mgr, 1982.

MINUS, HOMER WELLINGTON
Dentist, clergy. **Personal:** Born Mar 21, 1931, Wyoming, DE; son of George Greenfield and Luvenia Roberts; married Barbara; children: Carla Michele Minus Lewis, Felicia Yvette Minus Lewis. **Educ:** Univ Delaware, BS, 1953; Temple Univ Sch Dentistry, DDS, 1959; Howard Univ Sch Div, MDiv, 1987. **Career:** Dentist; United Methodist Church, clergyman. **Orgs:** Vestryman Dioc Coun Conv DE Protestant Episcopal Church; sch bd mem Dover DE, 1967-70; life mem, NAACP; life mem, Alpha Phi Alpha Fraternity Inc. **Military Serv:** USY, s & sgt, 1953-55; USY Reserve Dental Corp, capt, 1959-66. *

MINYARD, HANDSEL B.
Business owner, executive. **Personal:** Born Mar 11, 1943, Phoenix, AZ; son of Vivian and Richard (deceased); married Karen Flavell; children: Stacey B & H Blair. **Educ:** Stanford Univ, AB, 1964; Yale Law Sch, LLB, 1967. **Career:** NLRB San Francisco, law clerk, 1967-68; Fordham Univ NY, asst exec,1968-69; Sullivan & Cromwell NY, assoc coun, 1969-72; Temple Univ Sch Law Philadelphia, prof law, 1972-89; City Philadelphia, dep city solicitor, 1984-86, city solicitor, 1986-88; Graimark Realty Adv Inc, Philadelphia, Pa, exec vpres, 1989-2006, co-owner, currently; MIG Realty Advisors Inc,sr vpres. **Orgs:** Calif Bar Asn, 1968; NY Bar Asn, 1970; bd mem, N PA Sch Dist Authority,1975-79; dir, N PA Chap ARC, 1975-79; Philadelphia Bar Asn, 1979; bd mem, Friends Hosp, 1981-; bd overseers, Widener Law Sch, 1986-93; bd mem,Franklin Inst, 1988-98; dir, Penns Landing Corp, 1989-92; bd mem, PaInter governmental Coop Authority, 1992-94; bd, Crime Prevention Asn,1993-98; trustee, Philadelphia Univ, 1996-; bd mem, Young Scholars Charter Sch,1999-; dir, Health Ins Processors Inc, 2000-; asst secy, Temple's Bd Trustees. **Home Addr:** 3400 Warden Dr, Philadelphia, PA 19129-1418, **Home Phone:** (215)790-1660. **Business Addr:** Co-Owner, Graimark Realty Advisors, 500 River Place Dr Suite 5105, Detroit, MI 48207-4225, **Business Phone:** (313)259-9479.

MISSHORE, JOSEPH O, JR.
Insurance executive. **Career:** Gertrude Geddes-Willis Life Ins Co, New Orleans, LA, chief exec officer, 1941-. **Special Achievements:** Black Enterprise's list of Top Insurance Companies, ranked 10, 2000. **Business Addr:** Chief Executive Officer, Gertrude Geddes-Willis Life Insurance Co, 2120 Jackson Ave, New Orleans, LA 70113, **Business Phone:** (504)522-2525.*

MISTER, MELVIN ANTHONY
Executive, president (organization), consultant. **Personal:** Born Jun 18, 1938, Memphis, TN; son of Mack A Mister Sr and Mattie A Cunningham; married Joan Devereux; children: 4. **Educ:** Carnegie Inst Tech, BS, 1958; Princeton Univ, MPA, 1964. **Career:** US Conf Mayors, assoc dir comm rel serv, 1964-66; NW No 1 Urban Renewal Area DC, proj dir, 1966-68; Ford Found NY, prog officer, 1968-69; DC Redevelop Land Agency, exec dir, 1969-75; US Conf Mayors, dir off prog develop, 1975-80, dep exec dir, 1980-82; Citibank NA, vpres, 1982-84; Security Pac Bank NA, vpres, 1984-86; Chase Municipal Securities, vpres, 1986-91; Clayton Brown & Assoc, vpres, 1991-94; Twentieth Century Fund, fel,

1991-; WR Laidlawy & Mead, supvr, 1994-95; Melvin A Mister & Assocs, consult, pres, currently. **Orgs:** Nat Asn Housing & Redevelop Officials; bd Hispanic Develop Proj; bd, Seedco; Taconic Found; bd, Inst Pub Admin; exec dir, DC Redevelop Land Agency, 1969-74; act dep dir, DC Dept Housing & Comm Dev, 1974-75; dir, Urban Econ Policy League Cities Conf Mayors, 1975-77; asst exec dir, US Conf Mayors, 1977-. **Military Serv:** AUS, corp engrs 1st lt, 1958-62. **Business Addr:** President, Consultant, Melvin A Mister & Associates, 146 Maple St, Brooklyn, NY 11225, **Business Phone:** (718)941-3848.

MITCHAL, SAUNDRA MARIE
Marketing executive. **Personal:** Born Jun 3, 1949, Massillon, OH; daughter of Betty Jones Brown and Clyde; married John Higginbotham (divorced 1988). **Educ:** Kent State Univ, Kent, Ohio, BBA, 1967-71; Ind Univ, Bloomington, Ind, MBA, 1971-73. **Career:** Bristol Myers Co, New York, NY, prod mgr, 1973-81; Hunt Wesson Foods, Fullerton, Calif, mkt mgr, 1981-84; Neutrogena Corp, Los Angeles, Calif, vpres mkt, 1984-; Consortium Grad Studies fel, Ind Univ. **Orgs:** Corp Women's Network, currently; Delta Sigma Theta Sorority, 1968-; Motor Bd Hon Soc, Kent State Univ, 1971. **Honors/Awds:** Women of Achievement, Essence Mag, 1990. **Home Phone:** (213)293-9858. **Business Addr:** Vice President of Marketing, Neutrogena Corporation, 5760 W 96th St, Los Angeles, CA 90045, **Business Phone:** 800-582-4040.

MITCHELL, ARTHUR
Artistic director, dancer. **Personal:** Born Mar 27, 1934, New York, NY. **Career:** Premier Danseur New York Ballet, prin dancer, 1955-72; Dance Theatre Harlem, Everett Ctr Performing Arts, exec pres, artistic dir, choreographer & founder, currently; MacArthur fel, 1994. **Orgs:** Nat Conf Soc Welfare, 1973; adv panel, US Dept State Dance, 1973; Nat Soc Lit & Arts, 1975; council mem, NY Coun Arts. **Honors/Awds:** Certificate of Recognition, Harold Jackman Mem Comt, 1969; Special Tribute to Arthur Mitchell & Dance Theatre of Harlem, Northside Ctr Child Develop Inc, 1969; The Changers Award, Mademoiselle Mag, 1970; North Shore Commercial Arts Center Award, 1971; 20th annual Capezio Dance Award, 1971; Lifetime Achievement Award, Sch Am Ballet, 1995; John W. Gardner Leadership Award, 1996; Americans for the Arts Education Award, 1997; Dance Hall of Fame, 1999; Governor's Martin Luther King Award, 2000; Heinz Award, 2001. **Special Achievements:** First black dancer to become a principal artist in the New York City Ballet; first male recipient Dance Award High School of Performing Arts, 1951; ambassador at large, National Endowment for the Arts, 1994; inducted into the Cornelius Vanderbilt Whitney Hall of Fame at the National Museum of Dance in 2000. **Business Addr:** Artistic Director, Founder, Dance Theatre of Harlem, Everett Center of Performing Arts, 466 W 152nd St, New York, NY 10031.*

MITCHELL, BASIL MUCKTAR
Football player. **Personal:** Born Sep 7, 1975, Pittsburgh, TX; married Sharay Traylor; children: 5. **Educ:** Tex Christian Univ, BS, psychol. **Career:** Green Bay Packers, running back, 1999-2000; Memphis Maniax, Xtreme Football League, running back, 2001.

MITCHELL, BENNIE ROBERT, JR.
Clergy. **Personal:** Born Apr 24, 1948, Edgefield, SC; son of Bernie R; married Betty Tompkins, 1974; children: Benita Roshaunda, Bendette Renee & Bennie III. **Educ:** Benedict Col, BA, 1970; Morehouse Sch Religion, MDiv, 1974. **Career:** New York City & Housing Authority, housing officer, 1969; Mims Elementary, teacher, 1969-70; South Side Elem Sch, teacher, 1970-71; Rock Hill Baptist Church, minister, 1971-73; Connors Temple Baptist Church, minister, 1974-. **Orgs:** Exec Bd, Gen Missionary Baptist Conv Ga; Nat Baptist Conv; Nat Sunday Sch & Baptist Training Union; Savannah Baptist Ministerial Union; political action chmn, Interdenominational Ministerial Alliance; Spokesman, IMA Pilgrim Asn; Savannah Landmark Rehab Proj Inc; Savannah Emanicipation Asn; chmn, MKL Jr Observance; bd mem, Savannah Chap PUSH; life Mem, Omega Psi Phi Frat; Prince Hall Masonic Lodge; vol chaplain, Savannah Police Dept; bd dirs, Nat Baptist Conv; bd trustees, Morehouse Sch Religion; bd trustees, Savannah Voc & Tech Sch. **Honors/Awds:** Man of the Year, Savannah Tribune Newspaper; Ivan Allen Humantarian Award, Nat Chapter, Morris Brown Col Alumni; Chaplain of the Day, Georgia State Senate; Preacher of the Year, Gospel Music Workshop of Savannah; Citizen of the Year, Omega Psi Phi Fraternity; Person of the Week, WJCL-TV; Guest Evangelist for the FL Baptist Convention & Outstanding Community Service Award, Gamma Sigma Omega Chapter, AKA Sorority; Community Service Award, West Broad SDA Church. **Special Achievements:** Chaired the Jesse Jackson Campaign for Savannah, 1988. **Business Addr:** Pastor, Connors Temple Baptist Church, 509 W Gwinnette St, Savannah, GA 31401, **Business Phone:** (912)232-8291.

MITCHELL, BERT NORMAN
Consultant, administrator. **Personal:** Born Apr 12, 1938; son of Joseph and Edith; married Carole Harleston; children: Tracey, Robbin & Ronald. **Educ:** City Col New York, BBA, 1963, MBA, 1968; Harvard Grad Sch Bus, attended 1985. **Career:** JK Lasser & Co, CPA'S, sr auditor, 1963-66; Interam Ins Co, controller, 1966-67; Ford Found, asst controller, 1967-69; Lucas Tucker & Co CPA'S, partner, 1969-73; Mitchell/Titus & Co, chief exec officer; Mitchell & Titus LLP, founder, chief exec officer & chmn, currently. **Orgs:** Numerous memberships & affiliated positions organizations including dir, Greater New York Fund; treas, 100 Black Men Inc; trustee, Baruch Col Fund; Asn Better NY; pres elect, NY Soc CPA'S; pres, NY State Soc CPA's, dir/chmn; State bd pub acct, dir/chmn; dir, AICPA; dir, NYSSCPA; pres, Accountants Club Am, 1991-93; bd dirs, Harvard Bus Sch; comn mem, Consolidated CRE Fund Lincoln Ctr; Asn BlacK CPA Firms; bd dirs, BJ's Wholesale Club Inc, 1998. **Honors/Awds:** Numerous honors and awards including Outstanding Achievement Award, Nat Asn Black Accountants, 1977; Outstanding Alumnus Award, City Col New York, 1982; Hon Dr Laws, Baruch Col, 1988; CPA New York, NJ & DC; Townsand Harris Medal, City Col, New York, 1991; Hon Dr Letters Degree, Western New England Col, 1991; Human Relations Award, Anti-Defamation League B'Nai B'Rith, 1991; hon doctor humane letters, State Univ New York, 1993; Alumni Achievement Award, Harvard Univ Bus Sch, 1995; Gold Medal for Distinguished Service, AICPA, 1996; Marcus Garvey Lifetime Achievement Award, Inst Caribbean Studies, 1996. **Special Achievements:** Published over 50 articles in professional journals. **Business Addr:** Chairman & Chief Executive officer, Founder, Mitchell & Titus LLP, 1 Battery Pk Plz 27th Fl, New York, NY 10004.

MITCHELL, BRANDON (BRANDON PETE MITCHELL)
Football player. **Personal:** Born Jun 19, 1975, Abbeville, TX. **Educ:** Tex A&M Univ. **Career:** Football player (Retired); New England Patriots, defensive tackle, 1997-2001; Seattle Seahawks, 2002-04. **Honors/Awds:** Super Bowler XXXVI.

MITCHELL, BRANDON PETE. See MITCHELL, BRANDON.

MITCHELL, BRENDA K.
Government official. **Personal:** Born Jan 9, 1943, New York, NY; daughter of William Franklin and Ola Mae; married William Nelson (divorced 1974); children: Corrie Nelson. **Educ:** Fordham Univ, New York, NY, BA, liberal arts, 1975; Hunter Col, New York, NY, master's, urban affairs, 1976; Nova Univ, Fort Lauderdale, FL,doctorate, pub admin, 1981. **Career:** Control Data Corp, Minneapolis, MN, dir control data bus & technol ctr,1983-87; Commonwealth Pennsylvania, Dept Com, Harrisburg, PA, dep secy com, Governor's Office, spec asst, 1990-91; Dept State, secy commonwealth; Mgm & Environ Technologies Inc, pres, chief exec officer, currently. **Orgs:** Vpres, Philadelphia Regional Port Authority; co-founder, former vpres,Capitol Chap, Nat Forum Black Pub Adminrs; bd trustees, United Way Southeastern Pennsylvania; bd dirs, West Philadelphia Chamber Com; vpres,West Parkside Philadelphia Bus Asn; bd dirs, Ben Franklin Partnership Advan Technol Ctr Southeastern Pennsylvania; Greater Philadelphia First Neighborhood Econ Develop Task Force; bd dirs, Philadelphia Fund CommunityDevelop; bd trustees, Lincoln Univ; bd fin & revenue, PA Municipal Retirement System; PSU Econ Develop Coun; PA Econ Educ Coun. **Business Phone:** (215)546-7991.

MITCHELL, BRIAN KEITH
Football player, television game show host. **Personal:** Born Aug 18, 1968, Fort Polk, LA; married Monica; children: Bria. **Educ:** Southwestern La Univ. **Career:** Football player (retired), Talk show host; Wash Redskins, running back, 1990-99; Philadelphia Eagles, 2000-02; New York Giants, 2003; Brian Mitchell show, WTEM 980, Rockville, Md, host; John Thompson Show, co-host; Brian Keith Mitchell Comcast Sports Net, Washington, DC, co-host; WUSA-TV, Nat Football League analyst, co-host, currently. **Orgs:** Founder, Brian Mitchell Found. **Honors/Awds:** Special Teams Player of the Year, Nat Football League Alumni, 1996; USL Hall of Fame; Hall of Fame, Louisiana Sports, 2007. **Special Achievements:** First player in NCAA history to rush for 3,000 yards and pass for 5,000 yards in a career in leading USL to four straight winning seasons; one of the 70 Greatest Redskins, 2002. **Business Addr:** Co-host, WUSA-TV, 4100 Wis Ave NW, Washington, DC 20016, **Business Phone:** (202)895-5999.

MITCHELL, BRIAN STOKES
Actor, singer. **Personal:** Born Oct 31, 1957, Seattle, WA; married Allyson Tucker, Sep 3, 1994; children: Ellington. **Career:** Films include: Ghost Dad, 1990; Edward II, 1991; One Last Thing, 2005; TV series: "Roots: The Next Generations", 1979; "The Next Generations", 1979; "Trapper John MD", 1979; "Houston Knights", 1987; "Roots: "The Fresh Prince of Bel-Air", 1990; "Captain Planet & the Planeteers", 1990; "James Bond Jr.", 1991; Defenders of Dynatron City, 1992; "Capitol Critters", 1992; "The Fresh Prince of Bel-Air", 1992-93; "The Ernest Green Story", 1993; "Double Platinum", 1999; "Too Rich: The Secret Life of Doris Duke", 1999; "Call Me Claus", 2001; "Ruby's Bucket of Blood", 2001; "Crossing Jordan", 2002; "Frasier", 2002; "Great Performances", 2006; A Capitol Fourth, 2008; Singer: "Kiss Of The Spider Woman", 1994; "Lunch: A Modern Musical Myth", 1994; "Ragtime", 1998; "Kiss Me Kate", 1999; Brian Stokes Mitchell, 2006. **Honors/Awds:** Tony Award as Best Actor, 2000; Nominated Three times, Best Actor(musical), 1998, Portarying Colemen, Walker, 2003. **Business Addr:** Actor, c/o Roland Scahill, William Morris Agency, 1325 Avenue of the Americas, New York, NY 10019, **Business Phone:** (212)903-1327.*

MITCHELL, DR. BYRON LYNWOOD
Dentist. **Personal:** Born Mar 2, 1936, Miami, FL; divorced; children: Vanessa, Lynita, Patricia & Michael. **Educ:** Savannah State Col, BS, 1959; Howard Univ, DDS, 1966; Howard Univ, Orthod, 1969. **Career:** Pvt pract, gen dent, 1966-69; Family Health Ctr, chf family dentist 1969-70, dental dir, 1971-72; pvt pract, orthodontist, 1970-. **Orgs:** Alpha Phi Alpha Frat; Kiwanis Club, Elks; Dade Co Dent Soc; Dade Co Acad Med; Grtr Miami Acad Orthodon; mem, Miami, E Coast, FL Dent Socs; mem; Southern Soc Orthodon; mem, Amer Asn Orthodon. **Special Achievements:** First black specialist in dentistry to practice in state of Florida; first black orthodontist to practice in Forida; 2nd black orthodontist to practice in entire South. **Military Serv:** AUS, 1959-61. **Home Addr:** 17301 NW 27th Ave, Opa Locka, FL 33056, **Home Phone:** (305)751-4889. **Business Addr:** Dentist, 4885 NW 7th Ave, Miami, FL 33127, **Business Phone:** (305)751-4889.

MITCHELL, CARLTON S
Banker. **Personal:** Born Sep 7, 1950, New York, NY. **Educ:** Howard Univ, BA, 1972; Columbia Univ, MS, 1984. **Career:** Marine Midland Bank, vpres; Community Develop, Dept Youth & Community Develop, City Of NY, dep commnr. **Orgs:** Nat Asn Urban Bankers; Nat Bankers Asn; Long Island Asn; vpres, Union Black Episcopalians.

MITCHELL, CAROL GREENE
Marketing executive. **Personal:** Born Jul 22, 1960, Baltimore, MD; daughter of Thelma Stewart Greene Clardy; married A Stanley, Sep 5, 1987. **Educ:** Fisk Univ, Nashville, TN, BA, Econs & Mgt, 1982; Univ Wis, Madison, WI, MBA, Mkt, 1983. **Career:** Gen Mills, Minneapolis, MN, mkt res asst, 1983; RJ Reynolds Tobacco Co, Winston-Salem, NC, mkt res analyst, 1984-86, sr mkt res analyst, 1986-87, asst mkt res mgr, 1987-88, mkt res mgr, 1988-91, sr mkt res mgr, 1991-, dir, innovations res, currently. **Orgs:** Alpha Kappa Alpha sorority, 1979-; Nat Asn Advan Colored People, 1984-; Nat Black MBA Asn, 1984-; Barrister's Wives, 1987-. **Honors/Awds:** Outstanding Business and Professional Award, Dollars & Sense Magazine, 1992. **Special Achievements:** Who's Who in the Beverage and Tobacco Industries, Dollars and Sense Magazine, 1990-92. **Home Addr:** 4440 Gatlin Knoll Lane, Clemmons, NC 27012. **Business Addr:** Director of Innovations Research, R J Reynolds Tobacco Company, PO Box 2959, **Business Phone:** (336)741-5000.

MITCHELL, CHARLES, JR.
School administrator. **Personal:** Born Apr 21, 1938, Detroit, MI. **Educ:** Western Mich Univ, BS, 1959; Wayne State Univ, MEd, 1965, EdS, 1968; MassInst Tech, MS, 1970; Wayne State Univ, EdD, 1972. **Career:** Fed & St Prog, div dir, 1976-; Phys Edn, consult, 1959-60; Detroit, teacher, 1960-65; Highland Pk, coordr, 1965-67; Highland Pk, dir spec proj, 1967-69, asst supt personnel, 1970-72; supt sch, 1972-. **Orgs:** Asn Sch Col Univ Staffing; Am Asn Sch Adminrs; Am Asn Sch PersonnelAdminrs; Asn Supv Curric Devel; Acad Mgt; Booker T Wash Bus Asn; MI AsnSch Adminrs; MI Asn Sch Bds; MI Asn Supv Curric Devel; Nat Community SchEduc Asn; Nat Alliance Black Sch Adminrs; Black Causes Asn Inc; Nat AsnAdvan Colored People; YMCA; Rotary Internat; Civic League; Human RelationsCom; Civic & Indust Com; Jaycees; Caucus Club; Alumni Asn; MI Inst TechWestern MI Univ Wayne State; Varsity Club Inc; adv Mothers Club. **Honors/Awds:** Outstanding young man of yr, 1968; sloan fellow, MA Inst Tech 1969-70;Danforth NAES fellow, 1975; Ford Found fellow, 1973. **Business Addr:** School Administrator, Oakland Unified School District, 1025 2nd Ave, Oakland, CA 94606-2212.

MITCHELL, CHARLES E
Lawyer. **Personal:** Born Jul 7, 1925, Seymour, IN; married Julia Sarjeant; children: Charles L & Albert B. **Educ:** Temple Univ Sch Law, JD, 1954; Brooklyn Law Sch, attended; NY Univ, BA, 1949; Morehouse Col, attended. **Career:** Philadelphia Sch Dist, teacher, 1954-55; Financial Dept Philadelphia, mgt trainee, 1955-56; Atty Philadelphia, legal asst, 1956-60; Off Dist Atty Philadelphia, legal asst, 1956-60; NY US Soc Sec Admin, claim rep, 1960-64; Labor Mgt Rel Exam Nat Labor Rel Bd Phila, E I DuPont DeNemours & Co Inc, att labor mgt; Heritage Capital Credit Corp, bd dirs, Human Resources Comt, chair, currently. **Orgs:** Am Bar Asn; Nat Labor Rel Act; Corp Banking & Bus Law; Legal Educ & Admin Bar; Philadelphia Bar Asn; PA Bar Asn; pres, Fed Bar Asn, DE Chap; Am Judge Soc; Barristers Club Philadelphia; Lawyers Club Philadelphia; DE St Bar Asn; Com Promote Equal Opportunity Entry Legal Prof DE; Philadelphia Inter-alumni Coun; United Negro Col Fund; Indust Rel Res Asn; Philadelphia Chap; W Mt Airy Neighbors Asn; sub chmn, Zoning; Morehouse Col Club Phila; YMCA fund raiser; United Way DE solicitor; Interested Negroes Inc; Nat Asn Advan Colored People; Rotary Club Wilmington. **Military Serv:** USN, 1944-46. **Home Addr:** 5500 Wissahickon Ave Suite M907A, Philadelphia, PA 19144-5653, **Home Phone:** (215)844-0164. **Business Addr:** Directors,

Heritage Capital Credit Corp, 218 W Ninth St Suite 302, Wilmington, DE 19801, **Business Phone:** (302)778-4222.

MITCHELL, CHILL. See MITCHELL, DARYL.

MITCHELL, CLARENCE MARQUIS. See MITCHELL, KEITH.

MITCHELL, CONNIE R COHN
Educator. **Personal:** Born Jun 30, 1947, Memphis, TN; daughter of Joseph R Sr and Cleopatra Evans; married George, Jun 5, 1971; children: George C Jr & Carlotta. **Educ:** Central State Univ, bachelor's degree, 1969; Dartmouth Col, master's degree, 1993. **Career:** Detroit Pub Schs, teacher, 1969-95, teacher advocate/ human resources, 1995-, dir, Off Teacher Develop, currently. **Orgs:** Top Ladies Distinction Inc, status women chair, 1983-; Alpha Kappa alpha, 1995-; bd dir, Nat Bd Prof Teaching Standards, 1995-; bd dir, Inkster Community Partnership, 1998-; exec bd, Young Educrs Soc Mich, 1999-; bd dir, Methodist Children's Home Society, 1999-; bd advrs, Inkster Human Develop Agency, 2000-; Univ Mich, LUCY Initiative, bd advrs, 2001-. **Honors/Awds:** Christian Mother of the Year, Inkster Christians Action, 1993; Teacher of the Year, Post-Newsweek WDIV, 1994; Teacher of the Year, Detroit Pub Schs, 1994; Wayne County RESA, Golden Apple Teacher, 1994, 1995; State Mich Legis, Resolution #105, 1994. **Special Achievements:** Author: Using Technology to Fight Violence Among Youth: Sending Kids into ORBIT, 1993; Natl Bd Certification: Professional Development and Much More, 2000. **Business Addr:** Director, Detroit Public Schools, Division of Human Resources, 5057 Woodward Ave Rm 708, Detroit, MI 48202-4050, **Business Phone:** (313)494-7860.

MITCHELL, CRANSTON J
Law enforcement officer, city commissioner. **Personal:** Born Aug 25, 1946, St Louis, MO; son of Monroe M and Elizabeth; married Aleta Grimes, Jul 8, 1983; children: Leslie Barnes, Catherine J & Christie J. **Educ:** Univ Mo, St Louis, MO, BS, polit sci, 1973; Harvard Univ, Boston, MA, prog sr exec state & local govt, 1988. **Career:** City St Louis, MO, police officer, 1967-74; Mitchum-Thayer Inc, St Louis, MO, mkt rep, 1974-75; State Mo, St Louis & Kans City, MO, voc rehab counr & supvr, 1975-83; Jobs Mo Grads, St Louis, MO, regional supvr, 1983-84; State Mo, Mo Bd Probation & Parole, Jefferson City, MO, dir bd govt & chmn, 1984; Nat Inst Corrections, Dept Justice, correctional prog specialist; US Parole Comn, comnr, 2003-; Dept Elem & Sec Educ, Div Voc Rehab, counr & supvr. **Orgs:** Am Probation & Parole Asn, 1984-; Am Corrections Asn, 1984-; charter vpres, Nat Asn Blacks Criminal Justice, 1984-; regional vpres, Asn Paroling Authorities Int, 1988-90; comnr, Jefferson City Housing Authority, 1990-. **Honors/Awds:** Vincent O'Leary Award, Asn Paroling Authorities; Jonathan Jasper Wright Community Leadership Award, Nat Asn Blacks Criminal Justice. **Business Addr:** Commissioner, United States Parole Commission, 5550 Friendship Blvd Suite 420, Chevy Chase, MD 20815-7286, **Business Phone:** (301)492-5990.

MITCHELL, DANA S.
Architect. **Career:** URS Corp, vpres archit. **Orgs:** Res assoc, Nat Coun Archit Registration Bds.

MITCHELL, DARYL (CHILL MITCHELL)
Actor, executive. **Personal:** Born Jul 16, 1969, Bronx, NY; children: Kamari, Desmin & Justin. **Career:** Films: The PoFilms: The Pooch & the Pauper, voice, 1999; Lucky Numbers, 2000; Black Knight, 2001; 13 Moons, 2002; The Country Bears, 2002; Inside Man, 2006; TV series: "Ed", 2000; "Law & Order: Criminal Intent", 2004; "Eve", 2005; "I Love The 80's," 2005; "The Suite Life of Zack and Cody", 2007; The Game, 2007; Brothers, 2009; Daryl Mitchell Found, prin, currently. och & the Pauper, voice, 1999; Lucky Numbers, 2000; Black Knight, 2001; 13 Moons, 2002; The Country Bears, 2002; Inside Man, 2006; TV series: "Ed", 2000; "Law & Order: Criminal Intent", 2004; "Eve", 2005; "I Love The 80's," 2005; "The Suite Life of Zack and Cody", 2007; The Game, 2007; Brothers, 2009; Daryl Mitchell Found, prin, currently. **Business Addr:** Actor, William Morris Agency, 151 El Camino Dr, Beverly Hills, CA 90212.*

MITCHELL, DEAN LAMONT
Artist. **Personal:** Born Jan 20, 1957, Pittsburgh, PA; son of Hazel. **Educ:** Columbus Col Arts Design, BFA, 1980, hon masters degree. **Career:** Hallmark Cards, illusr, 1980-83; artist, currently. **Orgs:** Am Watercolor Soc; Nat Watercolor Soc; Allied Artist Am; Nat Soc Painters Casein, Acrylic; Knickerbocker Artist. **Honors/ Awds:** Top Prize, TH Saunders Int Artist in Watercolor, London, 1980; Allied Artist of America, Gold Medal, Oil, 1992, Gold Medal, Watercolor, 1990; Hardie Gramatky Award, Am Watercolor Soc, 1990; Honorary Masters Degree, Columbus Col Art Design, 1994; Gold Medal, Am Watercolor Soc, 1998; Grand Prize, Arts for the Park, 1999; Virtual Modern-Day Vermeer, New York Times, 2002; Newington Award for Best Painting, Am Artist Prof League. **Business Addr:** Artist, c/o Gadsen Arts Center, 13 N Madison St, Quincy, FL 32351, **Business Phone:** (850)875-4866.

MITCHELL, DENNIS ALLEN
Athlete, executive. **Personal:** Born Feb 20, 1966, Havelock, NC; son of Edward and Lenora; married Kristin, Nov 14, 1992. **Educ:** Univ Fla. **Career:** US Olympic Team, Barcelona, track & field athlete, 1992; Mind, Body & Soul Inc, pres, currently; Nat Training Ctr, sports performance coordr, currently. **Honors/Awds:** Gold Medalist, Barcelona Olympics 4 x 100 relay, 1992; Gold Medalist, Tokyo Olympics 4x100 m relay, 1991; Gold Medalist, Stuttgart Olympics 4x100 m relay, 1993; Bronze Medalist, Barcelona Olympics 100 m, 1992; Bronze Medalist, Tokyo Olympics 100 m, 1991; Bronze Medalist, Stuttgart Olympics 100 m, 1993; Am Champion 100 m, 1992; Second in the World 100 m, 1992; Silver Medalist, Atlanta Olympics 4 x100 Relay, Olympic Games, 1996. **Business Addr:** Sports Performance Coordinator, National Training Center, 1099 Citrus Tower Blvd, Clermont, FL 34711, **Business Phone:** (352)241-7144.

MITCHELL, DONALD MICHAEL
Actor. **Personal:** Born Mar 17, 1943, Houston, TX; married Judy Pace, Feb 19, 1972 (divorced 1986); children: Dawn Marie, Shawn Michelle & Julia Anette; married Emilie Blake, May 1, 1969 (divorced 1970); children: Dawn. **Educ:** Los Angeles City Col, drama directing; Lee Strasberg Actors Studio; Los Angeles Reportory Co, theatrical mgt; Beverly Hills Dirs Lab, directing; Univ Calif Los Angeles, ceramics sculpture; Tony Hill Ceramics, ceramics sculpture. **Career:** The Watts Training Ctr, co-founder, 1967; Los Angeles Opera Co, producer, 1979; Don Mitchell Productions, actor; TV Series: "I Dream of Jeannie", 1965-66; "The Fugitive", 1966-67; "The Virginian", 1967; "Insight", 1967-74; "Ironside", 1967-75; The Priest Killer, 1971; Short Walk to Daylight, 1972; "Wonder Woman", 1978; "CHiPs", 1979; "Capitol", 1982; "Matlock", 1986; The Return of Ironside, 1993; Films: Warning Shot, 1967; Scream Blacula Scream, 1973; Perfume, 1991; The Return of Ironside, 1993. **Orgs:** Numerous organizations including US Jaycees; Nat Asn Negro Bus & Prof-Women; Boy Scouts; Am Cancer Soc; New Sch Soc Res; Mot Pic Asn; MediaWomen; Calif Spec Olympics; Charles Drew Med Soc; Am Black Vet Admin; AmPolit Sci Asn; Handicapped Asn; Boys Club; Univ Calif Dept Theater Arts;Nat Park Serv US Dept Int; Nat Coun Negro Women; Involvement YoungAchievers Inc; LAPD Drug Abuse Prog; Los Angeles Urgan League; Int YearChild; Screen Actors Guild; El Monte City Counc; Ward Meth EpiscopalChurch; L A Thespians; Inner City Cult Ctr; New Fed Theater; NegroEmsemble Co; Mouehouse; Rockefeler Found; United Negro Col Fund; LosAngeles Unified Sch Dist; NAA AFTRA; Actors Equity Asn. **Honors/Awds:** Black Filmmakers Hall of Fame.

MITCHELL, DOUGLAS
Technician, government official. **Personal:** Born Apr 10, 1948, Leslie, GA; son of Albert Joe and Lula Mae Jenkins Winbush; married Velma Jean Floyd, Jun 27, 1971; children: Rodney Purcell. **Career:** Procter & Gamble, Albany, Ga, line technician, 1975-82, team leader, 1982-84, elec technician, 1984-; City Smithville, Smithville, Ga, mayor, currently. **Orgs:** Albany Area Primary Health Bd Dirs, 1985-86; Lee County Chamber Com Task Force, 1989; Hwy 19 Improv Task Force, 1989. **Military Serv:** AUS, E-4, 1968-70. **Home Addr:** Henry St, PO Box 72, Smithville, GA 31787, **Home Phone:** (912)846-2905. **Business Addr:** Mayor, City of Smithville, Main St, PO Box 180, Smithville, GA 31787, **Business Phone:** (912)846-2101.

MITCHELL, DR. EARL DOUGLASS, JR.
Educator. **Personal:** Born May 16, 1938, New Orleans, LA; married Bernice Compton, Jan 31, 2009; children: Karen, Doug & Mike. **Educ:** Xavier Univ Louisiana, BS, 1960; Mich State Univ, MS, 1963, PhD, 1966. **Career:** Mich State Univ, Dept Chem, grad teaching asst, 1960-63, Dept Hort, Plant Anal Lab, lab technician, 1962-63, Dept Biochem, grad res asst, 1963-66, res assoc, 1966; Okla State Univ, res assoc, 1967-69, from asst prof to assoc prof, 1969-78, Grad Col, prof & asst dean, 1978-82, Dept Biochem, prof, 1982-94, Dept Biochem & Molecular Biol, from interim assoc vpres to assoc vpres multicultural affairs, 1994-2004, prof biochem & molecular biol, 1994-2004, interim head & prof, 2004-07, prof emer, 2007-; Nat Heart & Lung Inst, NIH, res chemist, 1978-79; NSF Louis-Stokes Okla Alliance Minority Participation, proj dir, 1994-2007; OSU Talent search, proj dir, 2001-04. **Orgs:** Am Chem Soc, 1961; Okla State Adv Comt, US Comn Civil Rights, 1969-2007; res proposal reviewer, NSF, 1978-; mem comt, Am Soc Bio chem & Molecular Biol, 1979-81, Minority Affairs Comt, 1983-87; chmn, Okla State Personnel Bd, 1980-82; chmn, Okla Ethics & Merit Comn, 1982-84; mem consult, Biochem Study Sect, NIH, 1984-87; chair, Okla Merit Protection Comn, 1985-91; chmn, Merit Protection Comn, 1986-88; mem bd trustees, Okla High Sch Sci & Math, 1986-; Minority Biomed Res Support Prog, NIH, 1988-92; chair, Okla State Adv Comt, US Comn Civil Rights, 1989-; Minority Biomed Res Support Prog, NIH, chair, 1991-92; vpres, Soc Sigma Xi, 1991-93; Am Asn Univ Prof, Okla State Univ, 1991-95; Okla Acad Sci; AAAS. **Honors/Awds:** Oklahoma Human Rights Award, Okla Human Rights Comn, 2004; Oklahoma Higher Education Hall of Fame Inductee, 2005. **Special Achievements:** Published 40 research journal publications & 41 research abstracts; the first tenure-track Afro-American appointed to the OSU faculty. **Business Addr:** Professor Emeritus, Oklahoma State University, Department of Biochemistry & Molecular Biology, 246 NRC 408 Whitehurst, Stillwater, OK 74078-0117, **Business Phone:** (405)744-2009.

MITCHELL, REV. DR. ELLA PEARSON
Theologian, clergy. **Personal:** Born Oct 18, 1917, Charleston, SC; daughter of Rev Dr Joseph R Pearson (deceased) and Jessie Wright Pearson (deceased); married Henry H; children: Muriel, Elizabeth M Clement & Kenneth. **Educ:** Talladega Col, AL, BA, 1939; Union Theol Sem & Columbia Univ, MA, 1943; The Sch Theol, Claremont, DMin, 1974. **Career:** Berkeley Baptist Div Sch, instr christian educ, 1951-59; Sunset Unified Sch Dist Calif, kindergarten instr, 1961-66; Compton Col, CA, instr early child educ, 1967-69; Am Baptist Sem W & LaVernue Univ, adj prof, 1974-82; Claremont Unified Sch Dist CA, kindergarten teacher, 1973-80; Second Baptist Church, Los Angeles, CA, minister church educ, 1980-82; Sch Theol, VA Union Univ, assoc prof Christian educ, dir continuing educ, 1982-86; Spelman Col, Atlanta, dean sisters chapel, 1986-88; Interdenominational Theol Ctr, Atlanta, vis prof homiletics, 1988-2000; United Theol Sem, vis prof homiletics, 1988-2001. **Orgs:** Gov Bd Nat Coun Churches, 1971-75; Claremont City Human Resources Comn 1975-79; pres, 1969-73, Bd Educ Ministries Am Baptist Churches; Gen Bd Am Baptist Churches, 1984-87; regional chaplain, Delta Sigma Theta Sorority, 1993-; co-pres, Acad Homoletics. **Honors/ Awds:** Author/Editor Those Preachin' Women, vol 1 1985, vol 2 1988, vol 3 1996; Women: To Preach Or Not To Preach, 1991; Deputy Dir Martin Luther King Fellows Program 1972-75; Talladega College, LHD, Granted 1989. **Special Achievements:** Author: Together for Good, Ella P and Henry H Mitchell; Five in the Well, Sermons by Ella P and Henry H Mitchell, 2003; First woman Dean of the Sister's Chapel at Spelman College. **Home Addr:** 411 Angier Ct NE, Atlanta, GA 30312. *

MITCHELL, EMMITT W.
Executive. **Career:** Mitchell Lincoln Mercury, Kansas City, MO, chief exec, 1982; Urban Ministries, counsel, div election; M S Howell & Co, exec vpres, currently. **Orgs:** Bd mem, Urban Youth Leadership; bd dir, Sermant Christian Community Found.

MITCHELL, GEORGE L
Executive. **Personal:** Born in Greenwood, MS; married Carolyn; children: Cicely & Cydni. **Educ:** Morehouse Col, bus admin. **Career:** Ford Motor Co, mkt analyst; Dyersburg Ford Inc, Dyersburg, TN, chief exec, 1985-. **Orgs:** Ford Lincoln Mercury Minority Dealers Asn, pres, 2000-. **Business Addr:** President, Dyersburg Ford-Lincoln-Mercury, 920 US Hwy 51 By-Pass W, Dyersburg, TN 38024, **Business Phone:** (731)285-2500.

MITCHELL, REV. DR. HENRY HEYWOOD
Clergy, theologian. **Personal:** Born Sep 10, 1919, Columbus, OH; son of Orlando W (deceased) and Bertha Estis (deceased); married Ella Muriel Pearson; children: Muriel M Lawrence, Elizabeth M Clement & Kenneth. **Educ:** Lincoln Univ, AB, cum laude, 1941; Union Theol Sem, MDiv, 1944; Calif State Univ, MA, 1966; Claremont Sch Theol, ThD, 1973. **Career:** NC Central Univ, dean chapel & instr, 1944-45; Am Bapt Northern Calif, area staffer & ed, 1945-59; Second Bapt Church Fresno, pastor, 1959-66; Calvary Bapt Church Santa Monica, pastor, 1966-69; Colgate Rochester & Bexley Hall & Crozer, black church studies 1969-74; Fuller Theol Sem Pasadena & Am Bapt Sem W Berkeley & LaVerne Col, adj prof sch theol; Ecumenical Ctr Black Church Studies, LA, prog dir, 1974-82; Calif State Univ Northridge, prof rel & pan-African studies, 1981-82; Va Union Univ, Samuel Proctor Sch Theol, dean, 1982-86, prof hist & homiletics 1986-87; Interdenominational Theological Ctr, Atlanta, vis prof homiletics, 1988-90; United Theolo Sem, Dayton OH, vis prof homiletics, 1989-99. **Orgs:** Dir, ML King Prog Black Church Studies, 1972-75; Soc Study Black Relig, 1972; pres, N Calif Bapt Conv, 1963, chmn bd, Fresno Co Econ Oppor Community, 1964-65, pres, 1966; Nat Comn Black Churchmen, 1968-75; pastor, Calvary Bapt Church Santa Monica, CA, 1966-69; Second Baptist Church Fresno, CA, 1959-66; lit ed, Martin Luther King Fels Press, 1975-; Lyman Beecher lectr Divinity Sch Yale Univ, 1974; founding dir, Ecumenical Ctr Black Church Studies. **Special Achievements:** Co-author: Together For Good, 1999; Fire in the Well, 2003; Author: Black Preaching 1970, Black Belief 1975, The Recovery of Preaching 1977, Soul Theology with Nicholas Cooper Lewter, 1986, Celebration and Experience in Preaching, Abingdon Press, 1990, Black Preaching: The Recovery of a Powerful Art, Abingdon Press, 1990; Preaching for Black Self-Esteem, with Emil M Thomas, 1994; numerous articles in books magazines & journals. **Home Addr:** 411 Angier Ct NE, Atlanta, GA 30312.

MITCHELL, HORACE
Educator. **Personal:** Born Oct 4, 1944, Lambert, MS; married Barbara J; children: Angela & Kimberly. **Educ:** Wash Univ, AB, 1968; Wash Univ, MEd, 1969; Wash Univ, PhD, 1974. **Career:** Wash Univ, St Louis, asst dean, col arts & scis, 1968-73, asst prof educ & black studies, 1973-78, chair black studies prog, 1976-78; Univ Calif, Irvine, spec asst vice chancellor-stud affairs, 1978-80, lectr educ, 1978-79; lectr social scis, 1979-80; asst clinical prof, 1980-83; assoc clinical prof Psychiat & Human Behav, 1983-95; vice chancellor, Stud Affairs & Campus Life, 1984-95; Univ Calif, Berkeley, vice chancellor, Bus& Admin Servs, 1995-04; affil prof,

African Am Studies, 1996-04; Calif State Univ, Bakersfield, pres, 2004-. **Orgs:** Am Asn Higher Educ; Am Coun Asn, 1973-78; Consult, Midwest Ctr Equal Educ Opport, Kans State Univ, 1974-80; AAAS; Am Col Personnel Asn; Am Psychol Asn; exec bd, Asn Multicultural Coun & Develop, 1981-84; nat pres,1982-83; Asn Am Med Col; life mem, Asn Black Psychologists; Nat Forum Black Pub Adminrs, 1995-; APGA Com Standardized Testing Poten Disad; Kappa Delta Ph; Phi Delta Kappa; Phi Beta Sigma; Am Person & Guid Asn; Asn Black Psychol Asn; Non-White Concerns Person & Guid. **Honors/Awds:** Recieved numerous awards including 'Distinguished Psychologist Award', Asn Black Psychologists, 2002. **Special Achievements:** Published numerous articles which include, "The Testing Game", in Jones,R.L. (ed), Black Psychology, 3rd edition, Berkeley, CA: Cobb and Henry, 1991. **Business Addr:** President, California State University, 401 Golden Shore 6th Fl, Long Beach, CA 90802.

MITCHELL, HUEY P
Lawyer. **Personal:** Born Dec 10, 1935, Bivins, TX; married Nelvia G; children: Huey Jr & Janet H. **Educ:** Tex Southern Univ Sch Law, LLB, 1960. **Career:** Off Judge Advocate Gen; AUS Ft Hood, 1960-62; City Houston, asst city atty, 1964-67; Law Firm Mitchell & Bonner, atty; Reg Coun US Dept HUD, asst, 1967-73; Tex Christian Univ, teacher, Bus Law, 1968-73; Munic Ct Ft Worth, sub judge, 1973; Pvt Pract, atty, currently. **Orgs:** Mem chmn bd, Tarrant Co Legal Aid Found, 1972; mem & vpres, Ft Worth Chap Fed Bar Asn; Nat Bar Asn; Ft Worth Tarrant Co Sr Bar Asn; partner, Hex Learning Ctr; owner & org, HPM Mgt Develop & Co; Nat Bd Dir Planned Parenthood Fedn Am; Tarrant Co Health Planning Coun; organizing comt, Ft Worth Tarrant Community Develop Fund. **Honors/Awds:** First Black Asst City Attorney In History Of Houston, 1964; First Black Municipal Judge in Ft Worth, 1973. **Military Serv:** AUS, splst e-5 62. **Business Addr:** Attorney, 400 Weathford St, Fort Worth, TX 76106-9416.

MITCHELL, IVERSON O., III
Lawyer. **Personal:** Born Dec 20, 1943, Washington, DC. **Educ:** Georgetown Univ, BSFS, 1965; Wash Col Law, Am Univ, JD, 1968. **Career:** DC Corp Coun, asst, 1971-76; Wilkes & Artis, atty, 1976-85; pvt pract, atty, 1985; Speights & Mitchell, partner, 1986-. **Orgs:** DC Bar Asn; Wash Bar Asn, pres, 1982-84; Nat Bar Asn; DC Bd Labor Rels, 1977-79, chair, 1978-79; DC Bd Equalization & Review, 1987-93, chair, 1991-93. **Honors/Awds:** Certificate of Appreciation, Young Men's Christian Asn, 1973. **Military Serv:** USY, capt, 1969-70. *

MITCHELL, JACOB BILL
Executive. **Personal:** Born Jun 19, 1932, Boswell, OK; married Erma Jean Davis; children: Waymon, Victor, Erik, Mark & Kayla. **Educ:** Armed Forces Inst, AE, 1953; Univ Calif, Los Angeles, BSEE, 1958, MSEE, 1963; City Univ, Los Angeles, Wichita State, PhD, 1979. **Career:** Librascope Inc, sr engr analyst, 1956-60; N Am Aviation, syst design engr, 1960-62; Hughes Aircraft Co, sr electronic engr, 1962-64; NASA, sr res engr, 1964-68; Beech Aircraft, design engr, 1968-73; Cessna Aircraft, design engr, 1973-75; Jacob B Mitchell Assoc, eng consult, 1975-79; NCR, sys engr, 1979-81; Mitchell Enterprises, owner, 1981-89; Learjet Inc, systems engr, 1989-, aviation consult, currently. **Orgs:** Inst Elec & Electronics Engrs, 1963-. **Honors/Awds:** NASA consult; Learjet Mgt. **Special Achievements:** First group of black engineers ever hired by NASA. **Military Serv:** AUS, communs chief, 1951-54; European Occupation Medal, Good Conduct Medal. **Home Addr:** 1456 N Madison Ave, Wichita, KS 67214. **Business Addr:** Aviation Consultant, Learjet Inc, 1 Learjet Way, Wichita, KS 67209, **Business Phone:** (316)946-2000.

MITCHELL, JAMES H.
Automotive executive. **Personal:** Born Sep 15, 1948, Danville, VA; married Linda T. **Educ:** Va State Univ, BS, 1972. **Career:** Mel Farr Ford, used car mgr; Park Motor Sales, asst used car mgr; Crest Lincoln-Mercury, asst used car mgr; Ford Motor Dealer Training Prog; Detroit Lions Inc, pro football, 1970-78; Lynchburg Ford Inc, chief executive, pres, currently. **Orgs:** Children's Miracle Network. **Business Addr:** President, Lynchburg Ford Inc, 2113 Lakeside Dr, Lynchburg, VA 24501.*

MITCHELL, DR. JAMES WINFIELD
Scientist. **Personal:** Born Nov 16, 1943, Durham, NC; son of Willie and Eunice Hester; married Alice J Kea; children: Veronica, Duane & Tonya. **Educ:** NC A&T State Univ, Greensboro, BS, chem, 1965; Iowa State Univ, PhD, Anal Chem, 1970. **Career:** AT&T Bell Labs, mem tech staff, 1970-72, supvr, Inorg Anal Chem Res Group, 1972-75, head, analyst chem res dept, 1975-85, fel, 1985, Nat Acad Engineering, Mat Engineering sect, 1989, head, Process Chem Engineering Res Dept, 1994, dir, Materials Reliability & Ecol Res Lab, 1995, dir, Materials Processing Res Lab, 1997, VPres, Communs Materials Technol Res Lab, 2001-. **Orgs:** Omega Psi Phi Frat, 1963-; Adv bd, Anal Chem, 1977-80; adv bd, Mikro Chim Acta, 1978-82; bd, NRC, Chem Sci & Math, 1992-95; bd dir, Essex County Community Col, NJ, 1972-74; bd dir, Plainfield Sci Ctr, NJ, 1972-; ed bd, Talanta, 1978. **Honors/Awds:** Pharmacia Award in Analytical Chemistry; Percey Julian Industrial Research Award, 1980; IR100 Award, 1982; Nat Acad Engineering, 1989; Industrial Research Award, 1989. **Special Achievements:** Author, "Contamination Control in Trace Element Analysis" Wiley-Intersci Published, 1975; 56 jour articles; 3 patents. **Home Addr:** 17 Kingsbridge Rd, Somerset, NJ 08873. **Business Addr:** Vice President, Communications Materials Technology Research Laborator, Bell Laboratories, 700 Mountain Ave MH 1D239, Murray Hill, NJ 07974, **Business Phone:** (908)582-4436.

MITCHELL, JOANN
College administrator, vice president (organization). **Personal:** Born Sep 2, 1956, Augusta, GA; daughter of Earl and Alice King. **Educ:** Davidson Col NC, AB, psychol, 1978; Vanderbilt Univ Sch Law, JD, 1981. **Career:** Manson Jackson & Asn, assoc attorney, 1981-86; Tenn Human Rights Comn, law clerk, 1983-84; Vanderbilt Univ Opportunity Dev Ctr, asst dir, 1983-86; Univ Pa, dir affirmative action, 1986-93, vpres & chief staff, 2004; Princeton Univ, assoc provost & affirmative action officer, 1993-2001, vice provost admin, 2001-; Univ Pa, vpres & chief of staff, 2004-. **Orgs:** Am Bar Asn, 1981-; treas, bd dirs, Napier-Lobby Bar Asn, 1985-86; adv bd mem, Vanderbilt Women's Ctr, 1985-86; bd dirs, Asn Vanderbilt Black Alumni, 1985-86; financial secy, Usher Bd Mt, Oliver Miss Baptist Church, 1985-86; deacon, Mt Oliver Miss Baptist Church, 1986-; pres, Bd McCarter Theatre Ctr; bd mem, Int Schs Serv Inc; Asn Black Women Higher Educ; Women's Law Proj; Comn Minority Concerns, NJ Supreme Ct. **Honors/Awds:** Outstanding Young Women of America, 1983-; Affirmative Action Award, Vanderbilt Univ, 1986; Tribute Women Award, Princeton YWCA, 2002. **Business Phone:** (215)898-6630.

MITCHELL, JOANNE
Social worker. **Personal:** Born May 30, 1938, Evansville, IN; married Robert Bright; children: Howard Polk & Karen Polk. **Educ:** Roosevelt Univ Chicago, Sociol, 1971; Univ Chicago, Sch Social Serv Admin, AM SSA, 1973. **Career:** Ill Dept Corrections, community worker, 1969-73; Brunswick Chicago Job Corps Ctr, admin asst, 1966-69; Ill Dept Educ & Registration, social worker, 1973; Ill Dept Fin Inst, asst dir; Ill Comn on Deliquency Prevention, exec dir; Ill Law Enforcement Comn, assoc dir, juvenile justice, 1973-78. **Orgs:** Acad Cert Social Workers; Nat Asn Social Workers, 1973; panelist Assembly Behav & Social Sci Nat Acad Sci, 1979; League Black Women, 1976; NAACP; Nat Urban League. **Honors/Awds:** Appointment Gov Adv Coun Criminal Justice Legis, 1978; Outstanding Leadership & Dedicated Serv Ill Health & Human Serv Asn, 1978.

MITCHELL, JUDSON, JR.
Auditor. **Personal:** Born Oct 26, 1941, Jersey City, NJ; son of Judson (deceased) and Lucy Barnes; married Patricia Roberts (deceased); children: Mark A, Judson (deceased), Steven C, Guy (deceased). **Educ:** Rutgers Univ Col, BS, acct, 1975; Rutgers GSBA, MBA, 1979. **Career:** Pub Serv Elec & Gas Co, sr plant analyst, 1980-81, assoc acct, 1981-82, internal auditor 1982-, sr staff auditor, 1994. **Orgs:** pres, Northern NJ Chap Nat Asn Black Accountants, 1987-88; Nat Black MBA Asn; Am Inst CPA's, NJ Soc CPA's; Inst Internal Auditors, Minority Interchange; Nat Asn Cert Fraud Examr; Nat Asn Black Accountants. **Honors/Awds:** Cert Pub Accountant NJ, 1982; Cert Internal Auditor, Inst Internal Auditors, 1986; Black Achiever Bus & Educ, YMWCA Newark & Vicinity, 1988; Cert Fraud Examr, Nat Asn Cert Fraud Examr, 1989; Outstanding Mem of the Year, 1992. **Military Serv:** USMC, lance corp, 4 yrs. **Home Addr:** 15 Holly St, Jersey City, NJ 07305, **Home Phone:** (201)332-4839. *

MITCHELL, DR. JUDY LYNN
School administrator. **Personal:** Born Aug 19, 1951, Salisbury, MD; married Fred; children: Cortni Lee-Lynn. **Educ:** Bowie State Col, BS, 1972; Bowling Green State Univ, MEd, 1974; Nova Univ, EdD, 1985. **Career:** Salisbury State Col, academic counr, 1974-79, project dir, 1980-82, progs pecialist, 1982-83; Wicomico Co Pub Schs, supvr elem elem multi cultural educ & media serv. **Orgs:** Asn Study Afro Life & Hist; bd trustees, Wicomico Co Lib; bd dir, Eastern Seals Soc; Wicomico Co Hist Soc; Ctr Human Serv, educ specialist, 1983-84, residential admin. **Honors/Awds:** Outstanding Young Women of the Year, 1982-83. **Special Achievements:** Black Heritage Articles, "Salisbury Sunday & Daily Times" Salisbury, Md, 1979; religious black hist play, "Yester-Days Women, Gone But Not Forgotten", 1983. **Business Addr:** Elementary Supervisor of English, Wicomico County Public Schools, 101 Long Ave, Salisbury, MD 21802, **Business Phone:** (410)677-4400.

MITCHELL, DR. JULIUS P
Army officer, educator, school administrator. **Personal:** Born Nov 5, 1941, Rome, GA; son of Carrie and Pryor; married Gwendolyn McLeod; children: Toni L & Shaune. **Educ:** Clarkson Univ, Potsdam NY, Bachelor 1984; St Lawrence Univ, Canton NY, MED 1987. **Career:** AUS, spec forces, 1959-81; St Lawrence Univ, dir HEOP & pres, HEOP-PO; Clarkston Univ, Potsdam NY, dir, minority affairs, 1988-, assoc vpres. **Orgs:** Pres, Higher Educ Opportunity Prog Prof Orgn New York, 1984. **Military Serv:** AUS, First sgt 22 yrs; Bronze Star; Meritorious Service Award. **Home Addr:** PO Box 146, Potsdam, NY 13676. **Business Addr:** Director, Clarkson University, Department Pipeline for Education Programs, 101 Camp, PO Box 5512, Potsdam, NY 13676, **Business Phone:** (315)268-3785.

MITCHELL, KATHERINE PHILLIPS
Educator, administrator. **Personal:** Born Apr 16, 1943, Hope, AR; daughter of Parthenia Phillips and Clem Phillips; divorced; children: Jeffrey Allen. **Educ:** Philander Smith Col, BA, eng educ; Univ Wis, 1966; Cleveland State Univ, MEd, reading educ; Univ Ark, EdD, higher educ. **Career:** Cleveland Pub Sch, teacher, 1967-73; Univ Cent Arks, asst prof, 1977-78; City Little Rock, grant mgr, 1978-79, proj dir, 1979-81; Storer Cable, coord Channel 14, 1981-89; Independent Community Consult, 1982-; Philander Smith Col, div chair, educ, 1986-89, dean develop studies; Shorter Col, pres, 1990-97; Little Rock Sch Bd, pres, currently. **Orgs:** Immediate past pres, Little Rock Sch Bd, 1988-; Prof Coun Assoc, 1986-, past secy; Cent Ark Libr Syst, 1988-; past chap pres, Delta Sigma Theta, 1962-; Ouachita Coun Girl Scouts, 1987-; Minority AIDS Task Force, 1987-; AAUW; Ark Acad Advising Network, 2005-. **Honors/Awds:** Outstanding Contribution to Higher Education, Philander Smith Col Alumni Asn; Delta of the Year, Delta Sigma Theta; Black Achiever's Award, Mt Pleasant Baptist Church; Woman of the Year, Ward Chapel AME Church. **Home Addr:** 1605 Welch, Little Rock, AR 72202. **Business Addr:** President, Little Rock School Board, 810 W Markham, Little Rock, AR 72201, **Business Phone:** (501)447-1000.

MITCHELL, KEITH (CLARENCE MARQUIS MITCHELL)
Football player. **Personal:** Born Jul 24, 1974, Garland, TX. **Educ:** Tex A&M Univ. **Career:** New Orleans Saints, linebacker, 1997-2001; Houston Texans, 2002; Jacksonville Jaguars, 2003; free agent, 2003. **Honors/Awds:** Pro Bowl Selection, 2000. *

MITCHELL, LEMONTE FELTON
Labor relations manager, teacher. **Personal:** Born Feb 19, 1939, Wake Forest, NC; married Emma Jean Hartsfield (deceased); children: LaMarsha, Muriel, Andrea. **Educ:** Johnson C Smith Univ, BA, 1960; Loyola Univ Chicago, graduate study, 1964; Govt Exec Inst, Univ NC, Sch Bus Admin, 1979. **Career:** Retired: Classification Spec NC Dept Human Res NC Dept Transportation, 1980-92; NC Dept Correction, personnel dir, 1977; NC Dept of Admin, personnel analyst, 1969-77; jr & sr high sch tchr, 1960-69. **Orgs:** NC Chap IPMA; pres, Wayne & Co Tchr Asn; Omega Psi Phi Frat; minister music, Davie St Presbyterian Church, The Comt Ministries New Hope Presbytery. **Honors/Awds:** Outstanding Young Man of America, 1971-72. *

MITCHELL, LEONA PEARL
Opera singer. **Personal:** Born Oct 13, 1948, Enid, OK; daughter of Hulon and Pearl Olive; married 1971 (widowed 1973); married Elmer Bush III, 1980; children: Elmer IV. **Educ:** Okla City Univ, BA, music, 1971; Juilliard Sch Music, New York. **Career:** San Francisco Opera, soprano 1973-74, 1977; European debut, BarcelonaSpain 1974; Met Opera debut 1974; Edinburgh Scotland Festival 1977; SacriaUmbria Festival, Australia, 1978. **Orgs:** Am Guild Musicians Asn; Sigma Alpha Iota; Alpha Kappa Alpha; Church God Christ; honorary chair, Black Heritage Month. **Honors/Awds:** James H Schwabacher Award, San Francisco Opera Auditions, 1971; named Ambassadress of Enid, 1978; honorary doctorate, Okla City Univ, 1979; Okla Hall of Fame, 1983; honorary doctorate, Univ Okla. **Special Achievements:** Performed for Pres Ford, 1976, Pres Carter, 1978, 1979, Pres Clinton,1998. **Business Addr:** Singer, c/o Columbia Artists Management LLC, 1790 Broadway Suite 16, New York, NY 10019, **Business Phone:** (212)841-9527.*

MITCHELL, MARTHA MALLARD
Executive, executive director. **Personal:** Born Jan 1, 1940, Gary, IN; daughter of Louis B and Elizabeth Allen; divorced. **Educ:** Mich State Univ, E Lansing, MI, BA, 1963, MA, 1968. **Career:** Univ DC, Wash DC, dir continuing educ women, 1970-74; Drug Abuse Coun, dir info servs, 1974-77; US Govt Exec Office Pres, spec asst to pres, 1977-79, Dept Com, assoc dir, 1979-81; self-employed bus consult, 1981-84; Fleishman-Hillard Inc, St Louis, MO, vpres, 1985-87, sr vpres, 1987-93, partner, 1993-98; sr partner, 1998-2005; CBRL Group Inc, independent dir, 2005-. **Orgs:** Bd trustees, Nat Urban League; MO Women's Forum; bd dirs, vpres, Fair Found; bd dirs, Eugene Field House & Toy Mus; exec comt, St Louis Br, Nat Asn Advan Colored People; Links Inc. **Honors/Awds:** Public Service Award, Capital Press Club, 1978; Distinguished Achievement Award, Nat Asn Advan Colored People, Gary IN Br, 1985. **Special Achievements:** Hundred Top Black Business & Professional Women, Dollar & Sense Magazine, 1988. **Business Addr:** Independent Director, CBRL Group Inc, 305 Hartmann Dr, PO Box 787, Lebanon, TN 37088-0787, **Business Phone:** (615)444-5533.

MITCHELL, MELVIN LESTER
Architect, educator. **Personal:** Born Aug 11, 1939, New Orleans, LA; married Geraldine Vaughan; children: Marcus Quintana & Michelle Violet. **Educ:** Howard Univ, B Archit, 1967; Harvard Grad Sch Design, M Archit, 1970. **Career:** Howard Univ, asst prof archit, 1970-75; Univ DC, prof, 1972-92; Howard Univ, prof, 1972-92; Melvin Mitchell Architects, Wash DC, prin & owner, 1979; Grad Archit Prog Morgan, Baltimore, dir, 1997-2002; Am Inst Architects, fel, currently; Bryant Mitchell, PLLC, pres & chief exec officer, currently; Morgan State Univ, Sch Archit & Planning,

dir. **Orgs:** Past chmn, DC Bd Architects; past mem, DC Hist Preserv Rev Bd; Am Inst Architects; Nat Orgn Minority Architects. **Honors/Awds:** Awarded total expenses stipend to Harvard Grad Sch Design, 1968-70. **Special Achievements:** Author "The Case for Environmental Studies at Black U", AIP J, 1968, "Urban Homesteading", Wash Post, 1974, "The Crisis of the African-American Architect: Conflicting Cultures of Architecture and (Black) Power". **Military Serv:** AUS, spec 4 cl construct, 1960-62, Thule Greenland & Fort Belvoir VA. **Business Addr:** President, Chief Executive Officer, Bryant Mitchell, PLLC, 7826 Eastern Ave NW Suite 409, Washington, DC 20012.

MITCHELL, MICHELLE BURTON
Law enforcement officer. **Personal:** Born Jun 30, 1963, Richmond, VA; daughter of Arthur Burton and Claudette Moore; married William Thomas, Jun 30, 1984; children: Michael. **Educ:** Va Commonwealth Univ, BS, 1984. **Career:** Va Dept Corrections, 1983-86; Richmond City Sheriff's Off, 1986-, sheriff, currently. **Orgs:** Va Sheriff's Asn; Willing Workers Ministry; Bd Corrections Liaison Comn; Nat Sheriff's Asn; Nat Orgn Black Law Enforcement Exec. **Honors/Awds:** Charlotte J Harris Washington Service Award, Urban League Guild Greater Richmond, 1994; National Service Award, Nat Epicureans, 1994; Outstanding Alumni Award, Psychol Dept, Va Commonwealth Univ, 1994; Humanities & Sciences, Alumni Star for 1994, Va Commonwealth Univ. **Special Achievements:** Virginia's first female sheriff; Only one of fourteen female Sheriffs out of 3,095 in the United States. **Home Addr:** PO Box 8145, Richmond, VA 23223, **Home Phone:** (804)780-8630. **Business Addr:** Sherriff, Richmond City Sheriff, Office of the Sheriff, 1701 Fairfield Way, Richmond, VA 23223, **Business Phone:** (804)646-0930.

MITCHELL, MIKE ANTHONY
Basketball player. **Personal:** Born Jan 1, 1956, Atlanta, GA; married Diane; children: Kiah & Michael Jr. **Educ:** Auburn Univ, attended 1978. **Career:** Basketball player (retired); Cleveland Cavaliers, 1979-82; San AntonioSpurs, 1982-88; Filodoro Brescia, 1988-90; Filodoro Napoli, 1990-91;Maccabi Tel Aviv, 1991-92; Pallacanestro Reggiana, 1992-99. **Honors/Awds:** All-SEC. **Home Addr:** 2178 Wingate St SW, Atlanta, GA 30310, **Home Phone:** (404)691-2407.

MITCHELL, DR. NELLI LOUISE
Psychiatrist. **Personal:** Born Feb 11, 1926, Jersey City, NJ; daughter of Eloise Casey Mitchell and Cullie Mitchell; married Edward Henry Chappelle, Sep 11, 1953; children: Edward H Chappelle Jr. **Educ:** NY Univ, BA, 1945; Columbia Univ, MA, 1949; Howard Univ, MD, 1950; Am Bd Psychiat & Neurol, Psychiat, dipl, 1961. **Career:** St Elizabeth's Hosp, staff psychiat, 1956-57; Ment Health Ctr, med dir, youth consult serv, 1963-65; Rochester Ment Health Ctr, training dir/child psychiat, 1965-89, supv psychiatrist, 1983-89; Hillside Children's Ctr, psychiat consult, 1970-; pvt pract, Rochester, NY, psychiatrist, 1989-; Anthony Health Ctr, Rochester, NY, consult, 1989-90. **Orgs:** Fel Am Psychiat Asn, 1956; Nat Med Asn, 1956; Am Orthopsychiatric Asn, 1960; Hudson City Med Asn, 1960; bd mem, Camp Fire Girls Inc, 1967-73; Am Acad Child Psychiat, 1970; YWCA 1974-75; Synod Nebr; UPC US, 1975-79; Monroe Co Bd Ment Health, 1976-80; NY State Bd Visitors Monroe Develop Ctr, 1977-; Am Bd Psychiat & Neurol, Child Psychiat; Am Coun Psychiatrists, 1999. **Honors/Awds:** Psi Chi Hon Soc Psychol. **Business Addr:** Psychiatrist, 345 Highland Ave, Rochester, NY 14620-3027, **Business Phone:** (585)244-9068.

MITCHELL, ORRIN DWIGHT
Dentist, president (organization). **Personal:** Born Oct 1, 1946, Jacksonville, FL; son of Arthur O Mitchell (deceased) and Ella Mae; married Patricia Hill; children: Derrick, Kia. **Educ:** Howard Univ, BS, 1969, DDS, 1973, cert orthod, 1975. **Career:** Orrin D Mitchell DDS, PA, orthodontist, 1975-. **Orgs:** Am Asn Orthodontists; Am Dent Asn; Nat Dent Asn; Acad Gen Dent; Continental Orthod Study Club; Jacksonville Dent Soc; NE Dist Dent Asn; Fla Med, Dent & Pharmaceut Asn; Southern Soc Orthodontists; Jacksonville Med Dent & Pharmaceut Assn; Jacksonville Urban League; life mem, Alpha Phi Alpha Fraternity; Chi Delta Mu Fraternity; Howard Univ Alumni Asn; Sigma Pi Phi Fraternity; life mem, Nat Asn Advan Colored People; adv bd dirs, First Union Nat Bank Fla; Fla Asn Orthodontists; trustee, bd New Bethel AME Church; Fla Bd Dent; bd govs, Jacksonville Chamber Com, 1989; Stewart Bd New Bethel AME Church; secy, Howard Univ Orthod Alumni Asn; Pvt Indus Coun Jacksonville; pres, NW Coun, Jacksonville Chamber Com; bd dirs, Jacksonville Urban League, 1988-90; bd dir, Midas Touch Day Care Ctr; pres, Continental Orthod Study Club; fel Am Col Dentists; fel World Fedn Orthodontists. **Honors/Awds:** dipl, Am Bd Orthods, 1986; Alumni Achievement Award, Howard Univ Col Dent, 1986; Small Bus Leader, Jacksonville Chamber Com NW Coun, 1986; Alpha Phi Alpha Fraternity Alumni Bro of the Yr Fla, 1986, 1988; Achiever's Award, NW Coun Chamber of Com, 1992. **Business Addr:** Orthodontist, Orrin D Mitchell DDS, 1190 W Edgewood Ave Suite A, Jacksonville, FL 32208.*

MITCHELL, QUITMAN J.
Mayor. **Career:** Twentieth Century Barbershop, staff, 1964-98; City Bessemer, AL, mayor,1998-2002. **Orgs:** Bessemer Area Chamber Com. **Honors/Awds:** First Black mayor of Bessemer.

MITCHELL, RHONDA ALMA
Artist, writer, illustrator. **Personal:** Born Feb 22, 1954, Cleveland, OH; daughter of Melvin and Beatrice. **Educ:** Kent State Univ, BA, 1992. **Career:** Orchard Books, illusr & writer, 1992-97; Writer, illusr & artist, currently; Books: Joshua by the Sea, illusr, 1994; Rain Feet, illusr, 1994; Joshua's Night Whispers, illusr, 1994; Sleep Song, pictures, 1995; Talking Cloth, story & pictures, 1997; Mama Bird, Baby Birds, illusr, 1994; Little Red Ronnika, illusr, 1998. **Orgs:** Hudson Soc Artist, 1980-99; Cuyahoga Art Ctr, 1998-99. **Business Phone:** (330)296-0401.

MITCHELL, ROBERT C.
Football executive. **Personal:** Born Jun 6, 1935, Hot Springs, AR; son of Albert James Mitchell Jr and Avis Mitchell; married Gwendolyn E Morrow; children: Terri Sue & Robert Jr. **Educ:** Univ Ill, BS, 1958. **Career:** Football executive (retired); Pepsi Cola, mkt rep, 1963-69; Bobby Mitchell Ins Agency, owner, 1967-72; pro football scout, 1969-72; Wash Redskins, dir pro scouting, 1972-78, exec asst to pres, 1978, asst gen mgr, 1981-2003. **Orgs:** Univ Ill Presidents Coun; Univ Ill Found; chmn, Metrop Wash DC Area Leadership Coun; past bd mem, Am Lung Asn; Martin Luther King Fed Holiday Comn; NFL Alumni Exec Comt; Boys Club Wash; bd mem, Bike Found; adv coun, Variety Club Greater Wash; adv bd, UNCF; adv bd, Univ Ill Libr; adv bd, Provident Bank Va; bd trustees, Plymouth Church Unified Church Christ. **Honors/Awds:** Numerous honors & awards including Rookie of the Year 1958; Arkansas Hall of Fame 1977; NFL Pro Football Hall of Fame 1983; DC Stars Hall of Fame1979; Washington Touchdown Hall of Fame 1983; Hot Springs School District Hall of Fame, 1989; Outstanding Leadership Award, Univ Ill Found, National Network; Illini of the Year, Ill Varsity, 1995; Lifetime Achievement, Pigskin Club of DC; Bobby Mitchell Hall of Fame Golf Classic for Leukemia Foundation Charity. **Special Achievements:** First Black to play for Washington Redskins 1962. **Military Serv:** AUS, 1958-59 & 1961-62.

MITCHELL, DR. ROBERT L.
School administrator. **Career:** Edward Waters Col, Jacksonville, Fla, pres.

MITCHELL, ROBERT LEE, SR.
Executive. **Personal:** Born Nov 18, 1932, West Palm Beach, FL; son of Hezekiah and Grace; divorced; children: Verdette L, Marc A, Robert Jr. **Career:** Retired: Pratt & Whitney Aircraft, utility. **Orgs:** Founder, Afro-Amer Civ Action Unit Inc, 1960-69; bd of dir Palm Beach Co Comm Mental Health Center, 1979-81; state chmn, FL Minority Conf of Repub Clubs, 1980-82; pres, Frederick Douglass Repub Club, 1979-81; mem, Black Citizen's Coalition PB Co, 1979-84; NAACP; past gen bd mem, Urban League; Black Professional Caucus; bd mem ,Concerned Alliance Progressive Action Inc; Palm Beach co Repub Exec Comm, 1970-80; Policy Comm & Platform Com Rep Party of FL, 1975-77; organz & chmn, FL black Repub Councl, 1975; del GOP Conv, 1976; bd mem, Tri-Cnty Chapter Nat Business League, 1984-; Palm Beach Cnty Reagan-Bush Campaign - co-chmn Blacks for Reagan, 1984; Nat coordr, Commun Network of Negro League Players, 1996-; Crime Prevention Task Force; Tampa-Hillsborough Urban League Inc; Brotherhood of St. Andrews, St. James Episcopal House of Prayer; volunteer, YWCA, 2000; Yesterday Negro League Baseball. **Honors/Awds:** Community Serv Award, Tri-Cnty Nat Business League, 1984; Accomp Pres Ford on historic riverboat trip down the MS river, 1975; Man of the Year, Professional Men's Bus League, 1966; Official Particip, FL Human Rel Conf, 1977; Player KC Monarchs Baseball Team, 1954-57; Man of the Year, Omega Si Phi, 1967. **Special Achievements:** Successfully lobbied for some 155 Negro League legends who had been excluded from receiving a supplemental pension from Major League Baseball. **Home Addr:** 2009 Elmwood Ave, Tampa, FL 33605, **Home Phone:** (813)247-3357. *

MITCHELL, RODERICK BERNARD
Executive, president (organization). **Personal:** Born Aug 14, 1955, Reidsville, NC; son of Hunter Lee and Christine Odessa Dixon; married Monica Boswell, Aug 12, 1979; children: Marcus Galen Mitchell & Akia Lee Mitchell. **Educ:** Univ Calif, Los Angels, Calif, BA, econs, 1977; Columbia Univ, New York, NY, MBA, 1980. **Career:** Executive, president (retired); Collins & Aikman Corp, Charlotte, NC, indust engr, 1977-79; Celanese Corp, New York, NY, sr financial analyst, 1981-83; Bedford Stuyvesant Restoration Corp, Brooklyn, NY, 1984-85, dir operations, 1985-86, vpres phys develop, 1987-88, pres, 1988-2001. **Orgs:** Treas, Men 'N' Ministries, 1986-; bd dir, Brooklyn Acad Cult Affairs, 1988-; bd dir, Brooklyn Chamber Com, 1988-; bd dir, Brooklyn Bur Community Serv, 1989; 100 Black Men on Manhattan, 1989; Adult Sunday Sch Teacher, Bethel Gospel Assembly, 1989. **Honors/Awds:** NOMMO Outstanding Grad, Univ Calif, Los Angeles, 1983; Outstanding Businessman Award, Cent Baptist Church, 1988; Achievement Award, Brooklyn Urban League, 1988; RF Kennedy Minority Business Award, Brooklyn Chamber Com, 1988; Merit Award, Nat Asn Negro Bus & Prof Women's Club Inc, 1989.

MITCHELL, SADIE STRIDIRON
Clergy. **Personal:** Born Jan 4, 1922, Philadelphia, PA; daughter of Joseph Alfonso Stridiron and Lucinda Clifton; married Charles Mitchell Jr, Aug 19, 1946 (deceased); children: Sadye Mitchell Lawson, Chas T III & Charlene Mitchell Wiltshire. **Educ:** Temple Univ, BS, Educ, 1942; Univ Penn, MS, 1968; Nova Univ, EdD, 1978; Lutheran Theol Sem, MDiv, 1990. **Career:** Clergy (retired); Philadelphia Bd Edu, teacher, 1945-68, prin, 1968-81; sem, 1981-83; St Luke's, deacon & deacon training, 1983-89; Christ Church, priest in charge, 1989-90; St Luke's, asst rector, 1984-91; African Episcopal Church, St Thomas, asst rector. **Orgs:** Nat Asn Advan Colored People, 1944-; Union Black Episcopalians, 1961-; secy, Philadelphia Asn Sch Adv, 1968-81; founder, vpres, Black Women's Ed Alliance, 1975-; Diocesan Christian Ed Comn, 1981-92; Diocesan Phia Theol Inst; bd coun, Episcopal Comm Serv, 1990-. **Honors/Awds:** Highest Achievement Award, Administrative, PASA, 1981; Community Service, Mill Creek Comm Center, 1978; Achievement Award Women Clergy, 1994.

MITCHELL, SALLY RUTH
Executive. **Personal:** Born Oct 5, 1960, Dallas, TX; daughter of David Mitchell and Cerenia. **Educ:** Southern Methodist Univ, BBA, 1982. **Career:** Mitchell's Floor Covering Co, off asst, 1978-83; Internal Revenue Serv, taxpayer serv rep, 1983-85; EDS, employee rels specialist, 1985-91, 1994-; EGG Inc, hr adminr, eeo coord, 1991-94. **Orgs:** AKA Sorority Inc; Dallas Human Resource Mgt Asn. **Special Achievements:** Accreditation, Professional in Human Resources (PHR), Human Resources Cert Inst (HRCI), 1994-; Performed on TV: commercial, lead vocalist; shows, Insight, Good Day Dallas. **Business Addr:** Employee Relations Specialist, Electronic Data Systems Corp (EDS), 5400 Legacy Dr, Plano, TX 75024, **Business Phone:** (972)604-6000.

MITCHELL, SAMUEL E
Basketball player, basketball coach. **Personal:** Born Sep 2, 1963, Columbus, GA; married Anita; children: Morgann, Maya, Rhagan & Rhana. **Educ:** Mercer Univ, attended 1993. **Career:** Basketball player (retired), basketball coach; Wisc Flyers, CBA, forward, 1985-86; Rapid City Thrillers, CBA, 1986-87; Minn Timberwolves, 1989-92, 1995-2002; Ind Pacers, 1992-95; ilwaukee Bucks, asst coach, 2002-04; Charlotte Bobcats, asst coach, 2004; Toronto Raptors, head coach, 2004-. **Orgs:** Spec Olympics. **Honors/Awds:** Coach of the month, 2007; NBA Coach of the Year, 2007. **Business Addr:** Head Coach, Toronto Raptors, Air Canada Ctr, 40 Bay St, Toronto, ON, Canada M5J 2X2, **Business Phone:** (416)815-5600.

MITCHELL, SHANNON LAMONT
Football player. **Personal:** Born Mar 28, 1972, Alcoa, TN. **Educ:** Ga Univ. **Career:** Football player (retired); San Diego Chargers, tight end, 1994-97.

MITCHELL, SHARON L
Writer, psychologist, educator. **Personal:** Born Oct 27, 1962, Fort Deposit, AL; daughter of Curtis and Bertha. **Educ:** Carleton Col, BA, 1984; Ohio State Univ, MA, 1987, PhD, 1990. **Career:** Boston Univ, psychologist, 1989-94; Univ Del, psychologist & asst prof, 1994-; State Univ New York, Buffalo, NY, dir coun serv, currently; Books: Nothing But the Rent, 1998; Sheer Necessity, 1999; Near Perfect, 2001. **Orgs:** Am Psychologist Asn, 1988-; Am Coun Asn, 1997-; pres, Examiners Psychologists, 2001-; Nat Asn Advan Colored People. **Business Addr:** Director of Counseling Services, State University of New York, 120 Richmond Quad, Buffalo, NY 12246, **Business Phone:** (716)645-2720.

MITCHELL, STANLEY HENRYK
Lawyer. **Personal:** Born Sep 28, 1949, St Louis, MO; children: Stanley J P. **Educ:** Univ Mo, St Louis, BS, 1974; Wash Univ, MSW, 1976; Temple Univ Sch Law, JD, 1979. **Career:** Solo Practicioner, atty, 1980-; PA House Reps, exec dir, 1981-83; Elizabethtown Col Soc Welfare, adj prof, 1982-84; City Harrisburg, solicitor, 1984-; PA House Reps, chief coun; Shippensburg Univ, adj prof criminal law, 1991-96. **Orgs:** Chmn, Pro Bono Legal Redress City Harrisburg, Nat Asn Advan Colored People, 1981-; Omega Psi Phi Fraternity, 1984-; Democratic Nominee City Harrisburg City Coun, 1985; committee man, 11th Ward City Harrisburg; City Coun Harrisburg PA, 1986-90; pvt pract, atty, currently. **Honors/Awds:** American Jurisprudence Award Conract Remedies, 1976-77. **Business Addr:** Attorney, PO Box 425, Harrisburg, PR 17108-0425, **Business Phone:** (717)787-5379.

MITCHELL, TEX DWAYNE
Manager. **Personal:** Born Nov 19, 1949, Houston, TX; married Deborah Ann Earvin; children: Tonya DiBonne & Tess Dionne. **Educ:** Lee Jr Col, attended 1970; Tex Southern Univ, BA, 1977. **Career:** Courtesy Ford, parts delivery, 1968-69; Petro-Tex Chem Corp, plant oper, 1969; TX Petrochem, pumping suprv; Crosby ISD Trustee Bd, vpres. **Orgs:** Pres, Barrett-Crosby Civic League, 1976; Tenneco vols, 1979-83.

MITCHELL, THEO W
State government official, lawyer. **Personal:** Born Jul 2, 1938, Greenville, SC; son of Clyde D and Dothenia E Lomax; married Greta JoAnne Knight; children: Emily Kaye, Tamara JoAnne & Megan Dawn. **Educ:** Fisk Univ, AB, 1960; Howard Univ Law Sch, JD, 1969. **Career:** Clemson Univ, Greenville Tech Col, adj prof; SC Gen Assembly, sen & atty, 1975-95; Theo W Mitchell &

Assocs, atty, currently; Schiller Inst, bd dirs, currenlty. **Orgs:** Pres, Greenville Urban League Inc, 1971-73; chmn, SC Legislative Black Caucus; chmn, SC House Reps Task Force on Struct & Authority State Agencies; vice chmn, House Judiciary Comt; Health Care Planning & Oversight Comt; chmn, Region 5 Nat Black Caucus State Legislators; Omega Psi Phi Fraternity Inc. **Honors/Awds:** Senator of the Year, SC Probation Parole & Pardon Serv, 1989; Senator of the Year, SC Educ Asn, 1989; Gen Assembly Member of the Year, Transp Asn SC, 1988. **Home Addr:** 522 Woodland Way, Greenville, SC 29607. **Business Addr:** Attorney, Theo W Mitchell & Assocs, 9 Bradshaw St, Greenville, SC 29601, **Business Phone:** (864)235-6361.

MITCHELL, WILLIAM GRAYSON
Editor. **Personal:** Born Mar 8, 1950, Mobile, AL; married Renee Grant. **Educ:** Univ Ill, BS, econs, 1971. **Career:** Chicago Sun Times, polit reporter, 1970-72; Wash Post, gen assignment reporter, 1972-73; Ebony Jet Mag, 1973-74; Nat Endowment Humanities Journ, fel, 1975-76; Corp Commun Johnson Prod, dir, 1980; Chicago's first African American Mayor, press secy, 1983-85; Summit Consult Inc, founder, chmn & chief exec officer, currently; Johnson Pub Co, assoc ed. **Orgs:** bd dir, Lakefront Supportive Housing; bd dir, Ill Humanities Coun; bd dir, Fedn State Humanities Coun; Econ Club Chicago. **Business Addr:** Chairman & Chief Executive Officer, Founder, 50 N Mich Ave Suite 1000, Chicago, IL 60601.*

MITCHELL, WINDELL T
Government official. **Personal:** Born Feb 28, 1941; son of Thomas T and Eveline V; married Myrtle J Mitchell, Nov 22, 1964; children: Jonathan & Audrey. **Educ:** Univ Wash, bachelor's degree, architecture & urban planning, 1971, MBA, 1973. **Career:** King Co, Seattle, WA, spec asst pub works dir, fleet mgr, 1980-, div dir, currently. **Orgs:** Nat mem chmn, Nat Asn Fleet Adminr, 1990-, chap chmn, 1988-89; chap chmn, Am Pub Works Asn Equipment Serv; Forum Black Pub Adminr, 1984-. **Honors/Awds:** Larry Goill, 2001; Nat Achievement Award, Nat Asn Counties, 2005; Environmental Award, Am Lung Asn; Highest EnviroStar Award; Wastewise Award, US Environ Protection Agency; Nat Asn of Counties Award. **Special Achievements:** One of the top two finalists, Government Fleet Magazine, 2007. **Business Addr:** Fleet Manager, Division Director, King County Public Works, Department of Transportation, 201 S Jackson St Suite 822, Seattle, WA 98104-3856, **Business Phone:** (206)296-6521.

MITCHELL-BATEMAN, MILDRED
Psychiatrist. **Personal:** Born Jan 1, 1922?, Cordele, GA; married. **Educ:** Barber-19Scotia Col, attended 1939; Johnson C Smith Univ, BS, 1941; Women's Med Col PA, MD, 1946; Menning Sch Psychiatry, psychiatric residency cert, 1957. **Career:** Philadelphia, pvt practice; Lakin State Hosp WV, staff physician, Clinical dir & supt; WV State Dept Mental Health, Supvr, 1960-62, actg dir, 1962, dir, 1962-77; Am Psychiat Asn, vpres, 1973; chairperson, Psychiat Dept Marshall Univ Med Sch, 1977; Mildred Mitchell-Bateman Hosp, 1999-. **Orgs:** Am Psychiat Asn. **Special Achievements:** First African-American woman to be named to a high-ranking office in WV State Govt; First Woman to head such a dept in the US; First black in WV history to direct an exec dept; First black woman to serve as vice president of the American Psychiatric Association; One of four psychiatrists on the President's Commission on Mental Health, which resulted in the Mental Health Systems Act, passed in 1980. **Business Addr:** Mildred Mitchell Bateman Hospital, Charleston, WV 25305.

MITCHELL-KERNAN, DR. CLAUDIA IRENE
School administrator, educator. **Personal:** Born Aug 29, 1941, Gary, IN; daughter of Joseph Henry Mitchell and Claudia; married Keith, Dec 14, 1968; children: Claudia L & Ryan J. **Educ:** Ind Univ, BA, anthrop, 1963, MA, anthrop, 1964; Univ Calif, Berkeley, PhD, anthrop, 1969. **Career:** Harvard Univ, asst prof anthrop, 1969-73; Univ Calif, Los Angeles, fromasst prof anthrop to assoc prof anthrop, 1973-89, dir Ctr Afro-Am Studies, 1977, vice chancellor & dean, grad studies, 1994, prof, currently; dean residence, Coun Grad Schs/Nat Sci Found, 2005. **Orgs:** Researcher, Nat Inst Ment Health, 1971-75; consult, Nat Urban League,1973; fel rev commn, Nat Sci Found, 1974; bd trustees, Ctr Appl Ling,Wash, DC, 1979-81; bd mem, Crystal Stairs Inc, 1980-; vice chancellor, Acad Affairs & Dean Grad Div, Univ Calif, Los angeles, 1994-; Nat Sci Bd, (presidential appointment), 1994; Grad Rec Exam Bd, 1994-00, chair, 1999-00; Nat Sci Bd, 1994-00; chair, Sci & Engineering Indicators Sub comt, 1996-00. **Honors/Awds:** Fel, Nat Inst Ment Health, 1965-66; fel, Social Sci Res Coun, 1966-68;fel, Ford Found, 1968-69. **Business Addr:** Professor, University of California, Department of Anthropology, 1237 Murphy Hall, Los Angeles, CA 90095-1553, **Business Phone:** (310)825-4383.

MITCHELL-RANKIN, ZINORA M
Judge. **Personal:** Born 1956, Washington, DC; married Michael L Rankin; children: Lee, John Michael, Everett & Michael Joseph. **Educ:** Spelman Col, BA, polit sci, 1976; George Wash Univ Nat Law Ctr, JD, 1979. **Career:** Civil Div, Commercial Litigation Br, US Dept Justice, trial atty; US Atty's Off, Wash, DC, asst US atty; DC Super Ct, Wash, assoc judge, 1991-. **Orgs:** Nat Asn Women Judges; Nat Bar Asn; Am Bar Asn. **Business Addr:** Associate Judge, Superior Court of the District of Columbia, 500 Ind Ave NW Rm 2500, Washington, DC 20001, **Business Phone:** (202)879-7846.

MITCHEM, DR. ARNOLD LEVY
President (organization), school administrator. **Personal:** Born Sep 17, 1938, Chicago, IL; son of DeV Levy and Archie; married Freda Kellams, Apr 1, 1969; children: Nichelle, Adrienne, Michael & Thea. **Educ:** Pueblo Jr Col, AA, 1959; Univ Southern Colo, BA, 1965; Haverford Col, post bac study, 1966; Univ Wis, grad study, 1968; Marquette Univ, PhD, found educ, 1981. **Career:** Marquette Univ, hist dept instr, 1968-69, educ opportunity prog, dir, 1969-86; Coun Opportunity Educ, pres, 1986-. **Orgs:** Fel, hon Woodrow Wilson, 1965-66; fel, spec Woodrow Wilson fel, 1966-67, 1967-68; pres, Mid-Am Asn Educ Opportunity Prog Personnel, 1974-76; Inroads Nat Bd, 1975-77; chairperson, Nat Coord Coun Educ Opportunity Asn, 1977-81; bd dirs & trustee, Col Bd. **Honors/Awds:** Citation for outstanding service to higher education Region V Off Educ, 1974; Doctor of Humane Letters, Marycrest Col, 1990; Doctor of Laws, Univ Massachussets, 1990; Arturo Schomburg Distinguished Service Award, Asn Equality & Excellence Educ, Inc, 1996; Arnold L Mitchem Dissertation Fellowship Prog, named in honor, 2002. **Business Addr:** President, Council Opportunity Education, 1025 Vermont Ave NW Suite 900, Washington, DC 20005, **Business Phone:** (202)347-7430.

MITCHEM, DR. JOHN CLIFFORD
School administrator, dean (education). **Personal:** Born in Terre Haute, IN; son of Clifford and Clara; married Anna Maria; children: Terence & Melanie. **Educ:** Ball State Teachers Col, BS, chem, biol, educ; State Univ Iowa City, MA, Phys Educ, PhD, Phys Ed. **Career:** School administrator, Dean (retired); Northern Ill Univ, spec asst pres, 1969-72; Baruch Col, asst dean fac,1972-73, asst dean acad affairs, 1972-77; Bronx Community Col, prof, dean,1977-81; Univ Wis, LaCrosse, Col Health, PE & Rec, dean 1981-88, dean emer, 1988-. **Orgs:** Life mem, Am Alliance Health, PE & Rec 1966-; ed, Res Quarterly, 1969-74;policy adv bd, City Univ New York, Freshman Skills Assessment Prof, 1977-;personnel & budget community, Dept Compensatory Prog, Col Liberal Arts &Sci; univ coun instr, open admis coordr, City Univ New York; mid state eval accred team; N Cent Assoc Accred Team; Southern dist accred team;life mem, Phi Epsilon Kappa; Phi Delta Kappa; Am Assoc Univ Profs. **Honors/Awds:** PE & Rec Quarter Century Club Award, Ill Assoc Health, 1972; fel, Am Acad PE, 1973. **Special Achievements:** Numerous publications including, "Athletics: The Lab Setting for Character", 1967; "The Child that Bears Resentment", 1968; "Resolved that the Amer Acad of PE Support the Position that the Requirement of PE in Coll & Univ Should be Abolished", 1974. **Business Addr:** Dean Emeritus, University of Wisconsin-La Crosse, 1725 State St, La Crosse, WI 54601, **Business Phone:** (608)785-8000.

MITCHEM-DAVIS, ANNE
Educator. **Personal:** Born in Boston, MA; daughter of Marian Franklin and Robert T; married 1954; children: Leah Anne Davis-Hemphill. **Educ:** Lincoln Univ, BS, 1950; IN Univ Sch Nursing, Dipl, 1953; Simmons Col, MS, 1960; Boston Univ, CAGS, 1966. **Career:** Educator (retired); Vis Nurse Asn Boston, staff nurse, 1954-59, asst supvr, 1960-62; Hampton Inst, asst prof, 1962-65; Boston Univ, asst prof,1966-70; Mental Health/Retardation Ctr, pub health nurse consult, 1970-71; Boston City Hosp, nursing dir out patient dept 1971-73; Howard Univ, asst dean col nursing, 1973-75; assoc prof, 1980-89; Col Nursing Chicago State Univ, actg dean, 1982-83; chairperson, 1983-84; Howard Univ Col Nursing, chmn sr studies, 1989-96. **Orgs:** North Atlantic Regional dir, 1970-74; exec dir, Alpha Kappa Alpha Sorority, 1974-80; Am Nurses Asn; Nat League Nursing; Am Public Health Asn; Beta Kappa Chi; Sigma Theta Tau. **Honors/Awds:** Special Service Award, Alumni Asn IN Univ Sch Nursing, 1979. **Special Achievements:** Advisor of the Year, 1983; Outstanding Faculty of the Year, Chicago State University, 1984, 1985. Supreme Grammateus First to hold the title of Executive Director. First African-American to graduate from the school of nursing. **Home Addr:** 11104 Oak Leaf Dr, Silver Spring, MD 20901-1310.

MITCHUM, DOROTHY M
Media executive. **Personal:** Born Oct 7, 1951, Moncks Corner, SC; daughter of Frank Simmons and Laura Simmons; married Ronnie, Oct 21, 1973; children: Ronnie L & Melody. **Educ:** Denmark Technical Col, attended 1969; Charleston Southern Univ, BS, 1990; Univ SC, MA, 1995. **Career:** Dotty Sims Graphic Designs, owner, currently; WMCJ Radio, vpres, gen mgr, currently. **Orgs:** Kids Who Care. **Home Addr:** PO Box 1483, Moncks Corner, SC 29461. **Business Phone:** (803)761-9625.

MIX, BRYANT LEE
Football player. **Personal:** Born Jul 28, 1972, Water Valley, MS; married Tonette, Feb 8, 1997. **Educ:** NW Ms Comm Col; Alcorn State Univ. **Career:** Football player (retired); Houston Oilers, defensive end, 1996; Tenn Oilers, 1997.

MIXON, KENNY
Football player. **Personal:** Born May 31, 1975, Sun Valley, CA. **Educ:** La State Univ. **Career:** Football player (retired), Miami Dolphins, defensive end, 1998-2001; Minn Vikings, defensive end,2002-04. **Honors/Awds:** Rookie of the year, 1998.

MIXON, VERONICA
Writer, editor. **Personal:** Born Jul 11, 1948, Philadelphia, PA; daughter of William and Bertha Goodwine. **Educ:** Long Island Univ, BA, 1974. **Career:** Food Fair, bookkeeper, 1966-68; Social Sec Admin, admin asst, 1968-70; Doubleday & Co Inc, Starlight romance ed, 1974-88; Film Gazette, ed; E! Online, feature writer; NY Trends, film critic; Carib News, film ed, currently. **Orgs:** VM Media Serv, 1985-; film reviewer, Carib News, 1983-; mem, NY Online Film Critics. **Honors/Awds:** co-ed, Freshstones, Women's Anthology, 1979; author," The World of Octavia Butler," Essence Mag, 1979;" black agents," Emerge Mag, 1993; "Nick Gomez," The Independent Film & Video Mag, 1995. **Home Addr:** PO Box 694 Grand Cent Sta, New York, NY 10163-0694, **Home Phone:** (212)862-8487. **Business Addr:** Film Editor, The New York Carib News, 7 W 36th St, New York, NY 10018, **Business Phone:** (212)944-1991.

M- MIDDLETON, VERTELLE D
School administrator, counselor. **Personal:** Born Aug 10, 1942, Charleston, SC; daughter of Nazarene Baldwin Graham and Michael Graham; married James Middleton Jr, Dec 21, 1963; children: Jamela V, Gloria Holmes & Kylon Taylor Middleton. **Educ:** Johnson C Smith Univ, BS Psych/Soc, 1964; NYU, Adult Educ Cert, 1975; Bank Col, Adult Educ Cert, 1975; Temple Univ, Admin Training Cert, 1981; Webster Univ, Charleston SC, MA, 1989. **Career:** Immaculate Conception High Sch, teacher, 1964-67; Charleston County OIC Inc, exec dir, 1968-82; Trident Tech, Col Fair Break Ctr, ctr dir, 1982-84, Col Manpower Skill Ctr, dir, 1984-86, Berkeley Campus, Moncks Corner SC, JTPA dir, 1987-90, minority affairs dir, 1991-97, counr, 1997-; Beaufort Tech Col, Walterboro SC, dir Career Success, 1987. **Orgs:** Secy, Greater Bd Chapel Am Church, 1980-90; vchmn, Steward Bd Greater Bd Chapel, 1980-90; Alpha Kappa Alpha Sorority, 1982-86; secy, Burke High Sch Adv Bd, 1983-; Past Pres, SC Prof Asn Access & Equity; SC Chap SETA, 1984-; SC Tech Educ Asn, 1984-; coordr, S Atlantic Region-Cluster, 1988-90; chmn, Burke High Sch Improv Coun, 1988-90; adv coun, Trident Tech Col Employee Assistance Prog, 1989; S Atlantic regional dir, Alpha Kappa Alpha Sorority Inc, 1990-94; Am Jr Col Women Asn, 1990-; Charleston Speech & Hearing Adv Bd, 1993; Nat Mem Comn S Atlantic region; pres, South Carolina Prof Asn Access & Equity; pres, Charleston Intercolgiate Consortium; bd mem, CIty Charleston, SC, Site & Design; bd dir, City Charleston Smoking Ban Community; Nat Asn Advan Colored People; Young Women Chrisitian Asn Greater Charleston. **Honors/Awds:** Tribute to Women Young Women Christian Asn, 1980; Outstanding Community Service, WPAL Radio Sta, 1984; Outstanding Award S Atlantic Region, Alpha Kappa Alpha Sorority, 1986; Scholar-Key Leadership Award, Alpha Kappa Alpha, 1991; Frederica Wilson Sisterly Relations Award, Alpha Kappa Alpha, 1991; Alliance of Achievement Commendation Award, Women in SC Making a Difference; Black History Recognition Award, St Luke AME Church; Distinguished Service Award, Access and Equity South Carolina State Award, 1997; Martin Luther King Jr Outstanding & Distinguished Service Award, Black History Intercollegiate Consortium. **Home Addr:** 1861 Taborwood Circle, Charleston, SC 29407. **Business Addr:** Counselor, Trident Technical College, PO Box 118067, Charleston, SC 29423-8067.

MOANEY, ERIC R.
Educator. **Personal:** Born May 16, 1934, Easton, MD; children: Sara Elizabeth & Lucinda Jennifer. **Educ:** RI Sch Design, BFA, 1956; Syracuse Univ, MFA, 1965; San Diego State Univ, MS. **Career:** Rustcraft Greeting Cards, designer, 1956-57; Darrel Prutzman Assoc,asst art dir, 1957-62; freelance artist, 1962-63; Syracuse Univ, designer asst dir graphic arts 1963-65; Benton & Bowles Advert Agency, asst art dir,1965-66; New Frontiers Corp, 1965; NJ area libr, 1966-70; Calif State Univ, San Diego, Dept Art, asst prof, 1968-; Motown Record Corp, design consult, 1968; Terry Phillips Enterprises, 1968-69; Four Guys Stores, 1969; Thomas Corp, 1970; Core Fac Calif, Sch Prof Psychol, series co-ordr humanities, 1973-76. **Honors/Awds:** Commission sculpture bust of Beethoven to be completed for BeethovenBi-centennial NJ, 1970; Certificate of merit, CA Governor's comt, 1971.

MOBLEY, CHARLES LAMAR
Educator, consultant. **Personal:** Born Oct 9, 1932, Winter Garden, FL; son of Benjamin James and Mary Jayne Davis. **Educ:** Morehouse Col, attended 1955; Univ Miami, BMus, 1964, MMus, 1971; Fla Int Univ, attended 1983; Barry Univ, attended 1984. **Career:** Mt Zion Baptist Church, organist & choir dir, 1948-60; Beulah Baptist Church, organist & choir dir, 1953-55; Fine Arts Conservatory, teacher, 1963-64; Miami-Dade Community Col, teacher, 1971-79, dir choir, 1971-80; Dade County Pub Sch, teacher, consult. **Orgs:** Nat Asn Music Educ, 1964-; FEA, 1964-; treas, Del Music Educrs Asn, 1983-; UTD, 1964-; FEA, 1964-; AFT; 1964-; pub rel chmn, Dade Co Music Educ Asn, 1974-75; founder & dir, Liberty City Elem String Ensemble, 1976-; chmn, Tract II Model City Prog, 1974-75; bd dir, Greater Miami Youth Symphony, 1982-; vpres, Oakland Park Homeowners Asn, 1989-. **Honors/Awds:** Teacher of the Year, North Central Area, Dade Co, FL, 1977; Community Service Award, Nat Asn

Negro Bus & Prof Women's Clubs Inc, Miami Club, 1985; Achievement Award in Music Education, Nat Sor Phi Delta Kappa Inc; Gamma Omicron Chap, 1987; Achievement Award, Miami Alumni Chap, Kappa Alpha Psi Fraternity, 1989; Top Teens Award, Top Ladies of Distinction, 1990; Martin Luther King's Vision Award, Bayside Mkt Pl, 1991; Teacher of the Year, Liberty City Elem Sch, Dade County, FL, 1991; Outstanding Community Leader in Education, Zeta Phi Beta Sorority Inc, 1991; Black Music Festival Vanguard Award, African Heritage Cult Arts Ctr, Dade City, FL, 1992; Guest Conductor, Dade County, FL Pub Schs Superintendent's Honors Music Festival, Elem Orchestra, 1993; Unsung Hero Award, The Links Inc, 1993; Conductor, Liberty City Tri-String Ensemble, 1994.

MOBLEY, EMILY RUTH
Librarian, educator. **Personal:** Born Oct 1, 1942, Valdosta, GA; daughter of Ruth Johnson and Emmett. **Educ:** Univ Mich, AB Ed, 1964; Univ Mich, AM Libr Sci, 1967. **Career:** Chrysler Corp, engr librn, 1965-69; Wayne State Univ, librn, 1969-75; Libr Sci Comm Inst Coop, CIC Doctoral fel, 1973-76; Gen Motors Res Labs, 1976-81; Univ Mich, adj lectr, 1974-75 & 1983-85; GMI Engr & Mgt Inst, libr dir, 1982-86; Purdue Univ, assoc dir libr, 1986-89; Purdue Univ, dean libr, 1989-2004, Esther Ellis Norton Distinguished prof libr sci, prof, currently; Am Libr Assn, ACRL prof educ comm, 1990-92. **Orgs:** Resolutions Comt, 1969-71; Comn Positive Action, 1972-74; Mich Chap Bulletin ed, 1972-73; Ed Comt, 1974-76; Prog Comt, 1976-80; Res Comt, 1977-80; pres elect, 1979-8l; pres, 1980-81; Career Adv, 1980-83; Prog Comt, 1981-82; chmn, Long Range Planning Comt, 1981-82; chmn, Nominating Comt, 1982-83; Libr Mgt Div Sec, 1983-85; chap cabinet chmn elect,1984-85; chap cabinet chmn, 1985-86; pres-elect, 1986-87; pres, 1987-88;past pres, 1988-89; chmn, Awards Comt, 1989-90; rep, Int Fed Libr Assn,1989-93; Spec Libr Assn; brd trustees, Libr Mich, 1983-86; Alpha Kappa Alpha Sorority; brd dir, Asn Res Libr, 1990-93; fel, Spec Libraries Assn, 1991. **Honors/Awds:** Distinguished Alumnus, Univ Mich Sch Info & Libr Studies, 1989. **Special Achievements:** Various publications including "Spec Libraries at Work", Shoe String Press, 1984; "Libr Operations within a Decentralized Corp Orgn", Issues &Involvement, 1983; First African-American dean at Purdue. **Home Addr:** 1115 Trace Eleven, West Lafayette, IN 47906, **Home Phone:** (317)497-2945. **Business Addr:** Director, Purdue University, Library Science, G938, West Lafayette, IN 47907, **Business Phone:** (765)494-7190.

MOBLEY, EUGENIA L.
Educator, dentist. **Personal:** Born Dec 21, 1921, Birmingham, AL; married Charles W Mcginnis. **Educ:** Tenn State Univ, BS, 1943; Meharry Med Col, DDS, 1946; Univ Mich, MPH, 1948. **Career:** Sch Dent, Meharry Med Col, interim dean, 1976-; Dept Prev Dent & Community Health & Community Health Sch Dent, Meharry Med Col, assoc dean prof & chmn, 1974-76; Div Dent Hygiene, Meharry Med Col, dir, 1952-56; Meharry, pvt pract & part-time instr, 1950-57; Jefferson Co Bd Health, staff dentist, 1946-49. **Orgs:** Dent Health Res & Educ Adv Comn; Nat Inst Health PHS; Tenn State Dent Asn; Capital City Dent Soc; Pan-Tenn State Dent Asn; Nat Dent Asn; Nashville Dent Soc; Coun Community Agencies; Fed Int Dentaire, member of various other prof orgns; Delta Sigma Theta; Nat Asn Advan Colored People; Urban League; secy, Wash Bass Jr High PTA; St Vincent's Depaul Alter Soc & Ardent Gardners. **Honors/Awds:** Recipient of several research grants Omicron Kappa, Upsilon Hon Dental Soc, 1952; Kappa Sigma Pi Hon Dental Soc, 1954; outstanding educator Of America, 1972. **Business Addr:** Dean, School of Dentistry Meharry Medical College, 1005 18 Ave N, Nashville, TN 37208.

MOBLEY, DR. JOAN THOMPSON
Physician, health services administrator. **Personal:** Born Jun 2, 1944, New York, NY; daughter of Alfonso and Gertrude Porcher; married Stacey J; children: Michele T. **Educ:** Fisk Univ, BA, 1966; Howard Univ Col Med, MD, 1970. **Career:** Thomas Jefferson Univ Hosp, resident, 1971-75, staff pathologist, 1975-77; Howard Univ Hosp, asst prof, 1977-79; HHS Indian Health Serv, dir labs, 1979-83; St Francis Hosp, dir labs, 1983-; PNC Bank, bd mem; pvt pract, currently. **Orgs:** Fel, Col Am Pathologists; dir, Girls Clubs DE; dir, Blood Bank Delaware, 1991; State Arts Coun, 1989-; dir, Neumann Col, 1991; Bd Prof Responsibility Supreme Court Delaware; Univ Delaware, secy, treas, Acad Affairs & Exec Comns, mem, currently. **Honors/Awds:** Fel, Col Am Pathologists, Am Soc Clinical Pathologists. **Home Addr:** 10 Stone Tower Lane, Wilmington, DE 19803, **Home Phone:** (302)656-1973. **Business Addr:** Physician, 212 Cherry St, Wilmington, DE 19805, **Business Phone:** (302)655-5227.

MOBLEY, JOHN ULYSSES
Football player. **Personal:** Born Oct 10, 1973, Chester, PA; children: Jasmine, Kameron Yvonne & Tyson Lee. **Educ:** Kutztown State Univ. **Career:** Football player (retired); Denver Broncos, linebacker, 1996-2003. **Special Achievements:** First round pick, No 15, NFL Draft, 1996.

MOBLEY, SINGOR A.
Football player. **Personal:** Born Oct 12, 1972, Tacoma, WA. **Educ:** Wash State Univ. **Career:** Football player (retired); Canadian Football League, Edmonton Eskimos, linebacker, 1995-96, 2001-07; Dallas Cowboys, defensive back, 1997-99. **Orgs:** Hon chair, Kid Sport. **Honors/Awds:** Defensive Player of the Week, Canadian Football League, 2003; Grey Cup champion, 2003, 2005.

MOBLEY, STACEY J
Lawyer. **Personal:** Born Nov 19, 1945, Chester, PA; married Dr Joan C Thompson; children: Michele. **Educ:** Howard Univ Col Pharm, BPharm, 1968; Howard Univ Sch Law, JD, 1971. **Career:** Del Co Legal Asst Asn, atty, 1971-72; EI DuPont DeNemours & Co, atty, 1972-76, Wash coun, 1977-82, dir fed affairs, 1983-86, vpres, fed affairs, 1986-92, vpres commun external affairs, 1992, sr vpres, 1992-, chief admin officer, 1999-, gen coun, 1999-. **Orgs:** DC Bar, 1977; bd dir, Wilmington Trust Co; Wilmington Club; chmn, Delaware Strategic Econ Coun, 2001; bd trustees, Howard Univ; Pa, DC & US Supreme Ct bars; Nat Asn Corp Dir. **Honors/Awds:** Distinguished Alumni Award, Nat Asn Equal Opportunity Higher Educ, 1987; Trail Blazer Awd, MC Calif, 2000; Distinguished Service Awd, United Way Delaware, 2001; Howard Univ Distinguished Alumni Awd, Law, 2002; Gerald Kandler Award, Am Civil Liberties Union DE, 2006; Asn of Corporate Counsel Award, 2006. **Home Addr:** 141 Deer Valley Lane, Wilmington, DE 19807. **Business Addr:** Senior Vice President, General Counsel & Chief Administrative Officer, EI DuPont DeNemours & Company, Dupont Bldg, 1007 Market St, Wilmington, DE 19898-0001, **Business Phone:** (302)774-1000.

MOBLEY, DR. SYBIL COLLINS
School administrator, educator. **Personal:** Born Oct 14, 1925, Shreveport, LA; daughter of Melvin Collins and Cora Collins; married James Otis (deceased); children: James Jr, Janet Yolanda Sermon & Melvin. **Educ:** Bishop Col, BA, 1945; Wharton Sch Univ, Pa, MBA, 1961; Univ Ill, PhD, 1964; Fla State Univ, CPA. **Career:** Educator, School administrator (retired); Fla A&M Univ, Sch Bus & Indust, prof 1963-2003, dept head, 1971-74, dean, 1974-2003, prof & dean emer, currently. **Orgs:** Alpha Kappa Alpha; Int Assoc Black Bus Educr; bd dirs, Anheuser-Busch Co-Inc, Champion Int Corp, Hershey Foods Corp, Sears Roebuck & Co, Southwestern Bell Corp, Dean Witter, Discover Inc. **Honors/Awds:** Hon doctorate, Wharton Sch, Univ Pa, Babson Col, Bishop Col, Hamilton Col, Washington Univ, Princeton Univ, Univ Ill. **Home Addr:** 520 Hampton Ave, Tallahassee, FL 32310. **Business Addr:** Professor, Dean Emeritus, Florida A&M University, School of Business & Industry, 1 SBI Plz, Tallahassee, FL 32307-5200, **Business Phone:** (850)599-3565.

MOCK, JAMES E
Educator. **Personal:** Born Oct 26, 1940, Tuscaloosa, AL; son of Christopher Mock and Elizabeth Jemison Jackson; married Lorna Thorpe, Dec 1980; children: Che & Tekalie. **Educ:** Marquette Univ, Milwaukee, Wis, civil engr, 1958-60; Univ Memphis, Memphis, Tenn, BBA, economics, 1972; Univ Tenn, Nashville, Tenn, MPA, 1977; Univ Tenn, Knoxville, Tenn, PhD, 1981. **Career:** Austin Peay State Univ, Clarksville, Tenn, former chairperson, chair & prof pub mgt, prof emer, currently; Cuttington Univ, former vpres. **Orgs:** Former chairperson, Dept Pub Mgt, 1994-97; dir, Public Mgt Progs, 1981-91; chair, Polit Sci, 1991-94. **Honors/Awds:** Direct study abroad in Africa. **Home Addr:** 138 Queens Ct, Clarksville, TN 37043. **Business Addr:** Professor Emeritus, Austin Peay State University, Department of Public Management, PO Box 4454, Clarksville, TN 37044, **Business Phone:** (931)221-1480.

MOHAMED, GERALD R, JR.
Accountant, manager. **Personal:** Born Oct 3, 1948, New York, NY; son of Gerald R and Helen Brown; children: Gerald R III. **Educ:** Duquesne Univ, BS, 1970; Univ Pittsburgh, MBA, 1979. **Career:** Westinghouse Electric Corp, mgr gen acct, 1971-84, staff asst corp, financial planning & procedures, 1984-88, mgr financial planning, 1989-92; Ad Value Network, comptroller, 1992-95; UAAI, staff acct, 1996-99; Signal Apparel Comp, acct mgr, 1999-. **Orgs:** Black MBA Asn, 1983-86; mem, 1968-, basilius, 1969-70, treas, 1985-87, Omega Psi Phi Frat; Masonry PHA, 1985-. **Honors/Awds:** Omega Man of the Year, 1987. **Home Addr:** 4 Suttie Ave, Piscataway, NJ 08854. **Business Addr:** Accounting manager, Signal Apparel Co, 34 Englehard Ave, Avenel, NJ 07001, **Business Phone:** (732)382-2882.

MOHAMMAD, SANDRA B
Librarian. **Personal:** Born Nov 10, 1947, Chicago, IL; daughter of Mattie McGuire Matthews and Aubrey D Matthews; married Ali S; children: Nena & Christopher. **Educ:** Chicago State Col, Chicago, IL, BA, 1971; Univ Ill Urbana-Champaign, Urbana, IL, MS, 1973. **Career:** The Chicago Pub Libr, Chicago, IL, librn I, first asst, 1976-77, librn I, br head, 1977-80, librn I, unit head, 1980-82, librn II, ref asst, 1982-93, librn II, ref asst, 1993-2002, librn III, ref asst, 2002-04, librn IV, br mgr, 2004-. **Orgs:** Black Caucus Ala, Chicago chap, 1979, chair-elect, 1981-82, chair 1983, scholar chair, 1994. **Business Addr:** Branch Manager, The Chicago Public Library, 400 S State St, Chicago, IL 60605, **Business Phone:** (312)747-5281.

MOHAMMED, AL-IMAM WARITH DEEN. See MOHAMMED, W DEEN.

MOHAMMED, NAZR TAHIRU
Basketball player. **Personal:** Born Sep 5, 1977, Chicago, IL. **Educ:** Univ Ky, 1998. **Career:** Utah Jazz, 1998; Philadelphia 76ers, center, 1998-2000; Atlanta Hawks, 2000-03; New York Knicks, 2003-04; San Antonio Spurs, 2005-06; Detroit Pistons, 2006-07; Charlotte Bobcats, 2007-. **Business Addr:** Professional Basketball Player, Charlotte Bobcats, 333 ETrade St, Charlotte, NC 28202, **Business Phone:** (704)688-8600.

MOHAMMED, W DEEN (AL-IMAM WARITH DEEN MOHAMMED)
Clergy. **Personal:** Born Oct 30, 1933, Detroit, MI; son of Elijah and Clara. **Career:** Nation Islam, supreme minister, 1975-76; Ministry W Deen Mohommed (aka Am Soc of Muslims), founder, currently. **Honors/Awds:** Outstanding Leadership Award, Coun Am-Islamic Rels, 2005.

MOHR, DIANE LOUISE
Library administrator. **Personal:** Born Nov 24, 1951, Fairbanks, AK; daughter of Dean Burgette and Mary Louise Leonard. **Educ:** Alliance Francais Brussels Belg, Deuxieme deg, 1971; Calif State Univ, Long Beach, BA, Black Studies, 1977; Univ S Calif, Los Angeles, CA, MLS, 1978; George Washington Univ, Wash, DC, Cert Pub Admin, 1999. **Career:** Getty Oil Co, indexer reviewer, 1978-79; Woodcrest Pub Libr, librn incharge, 1979-82; View Pk Pub Libr, librn incharge, 1982-83; Compton Pub Libr, sr librn incharge, 1983-87; DC Pub Libr, Martin Luther King Jr Br, sociol librn, 1987-89, West End Br, br librn, 1990, asst coordr, adult servs, 1991-2000, adult collection coordr, 2001-. **Orgs:** Univ S Calif, Alumni Asn, 1978-; Am Libr Asn, 1980-; Calif Libr Asn, 1980-87; bd, Vesta Bruner Scholar, 1980-83; Calif Black Librn, Caucus, 1981-87; Alpha Kappa Alpha Sor Inc, 1981-; The Links Inc, 1985-87; DC Libr Asn, 1989-. **Honors/Awds:** Presidents Honor List, Calif State Univ, 1975-77; Phi Kappa Phi Honor Soc, Calif State Univ, 1977-. **Business Addr:** Adult Collection Coordinator, District of Columbia Public Library, 901 G St NW Rm 417, Washington, DC 20001, **Business Phone:** (202)727-1117.

MOHR, DR. PAUL B., SR.
Educator. **Personal:** Born Aug 19, 1931, Waco, TX; married Rebecca Dixon; children: Paul & Michelle. **Educ:** Fla A&M Univ, BS, 1954; Univ NMex, MS, 1969; Okla State Univ, EdD, 1969. **Career:** St Petersburg Jr Col, FL, instr, 1954-55; Fla A&M Univ, Tallahassee, acad dean, 1969; Norfolk State Univ, VA, acad affairs vpres; Talladega Col, AL, pres, 1983-. **Orgs:** Consult, S Asn Cols & Schs, 1971-; evalr proposals, Nat Inst Educ & DeptHEW, 1975-; S Regional Educ Bd, 1975-, Fla Coun Teacher Educ, 1976-; Am Asn Univ Profs. **Honors/Awds:** Phi Delta Kappa Award, 1974; Recipient Liberty Bell Award, Fla A&M Univ,Nat Alumni Asn, 1976. **Military Serv:** AUS, 1955-57.

MOLAIRE, MICHEL FRANTZ
Chemist. **Personal:** Born Jul 8, 1950, St Marc, Haiti; son of Marcel Molaire and Marie Therese; married Tulienne, Mar 11, 1977; children: Alexandra & Melissa. **Educ:** NY Tech Col, AAS; chem technol; Univ Rochester, BS, chem, MS, chem Engineering, MBA, exec develop. **Career:** Eastman Kodak, proj mgr, res assoc, 1974-99, Imaging Res Develop Group, res assoc, currently, NexPress Solutions LLC, res assoc, 1999-. **Orgs:** Chair, Am Chem Soc, Minority Affairs Comt; Greater Rochester United Way, Kids Track Comn; Hillside Children Ctr, Pub Rels Comn; past pres, African Am Leadership Develop, Rochester, NY; past pres, Rochester Nat Orgn Black Chem Engrs; Leadership Rochester. **Honors/Awds:** Eastman Kodak Company Distinguished Inventor's Award, Inventor's Hall of Fame; Kodak, Mees Award for Scientific Research Excellence; Modern Black Inventor, Ebony Mag. **Special Achievements:** 34 US patents and over 75 foreign patents; numerous scientific publications; author, African-American Who's Who, Past & Present-Greater Rochester Area, first and second editions; Shadow of Dreams, poems; publisher, Blackfirsts.com, Blackshoppersclub.com. **Business Addr:** Research Associate, Imaging Research and Development Group, Eastman Kodak Company, 1999 Lake Ave, Rochester, NY 14650-2110, **Business Phone:** (585)722-9104.

MOLAND, WILLIE C.
School administrator. **Personal:** Born Jan 19, 1931, Shamrock, OK; married Marianne; children: Charlotte, Debbie, Gary, Brent & Bryan. **Educ:** Denver Art Acad Denver Colo, cert, 1958. **Career:** Martin Luther King Young Adults Ctr, dir, 1955-68; Metrop State Col, coordr resources & support, 1968-69, affirmative action staff officer, 1971; Denver Community Comn relations, consult, 1970; Air Force Acct & Finance ctr, data devel technician. **Orgs:** Chmn, Black Faculty Staff Caucus Metro State Col; state dir, youth Prince Hall Grand Lodge Co; co-pres, Phillips Elem PTSA; secy, Syrian Temple 49 Chanters Group; pres, Syrian Temple 49 Arabic Patrol; exec bd mem, dir, youth prog, Greater Park Hill Community Inc. **Honors/Awds:** Citizens soldier of year 1959; man of year GPHC Tutorial Program, 1972; superior perf award USAF, 1965; Golden Rule Award accounting & finance center. **Military Serv:** USAF, AUS, 1951-54. **Business Addr:** Metropolitan State Coll, 250 W 14 Ave Room 208, Denver, CO 80204.

MOLDEN, ALEX M.
Football player. **Personal:** Born Aug 4, 1973, Detroit, MI; married Christin; children: Isaiah & Elijah. **Educ:** Univ Ore, BS,

psychol. **Career:** New Orleans Saints, corner back, 1996-2000; San Diego Chargers, 2001-02; Detroit Lions, 2003; Wash Redskins, corner back, 2003; Sports performance specialist, Nike world HQ; Dir, All-star performance athletics, currently. **Honors/Awds:** Univ oregon athletic Hall of fame, 2008.

MOLETTE, BARBARA J.
Educator. **Personal:** Born Jan 31, 1940, Los Angeles, CA; daughter of Baxter R Roseburr and Nora L Johnson; married Carlton W Molette, Jun 15, 1960; children: Carla E Molette, Andrea R Molette. **Educ:** Fla A&M Univ, BA, 1966; Florida State Univ, Tallahassee, FL, MFA, 1969; Univ Mo, Columbia, MO, PhD, 1989. **Career:** Fla State Univ, grad fel, 1967-69; Spelman Col, Atlanta GA, instr, 1969-75; Tex Southern Univ, Houston TX, asst prof, 1975-85; Univ Mo, grad fel, 1986-87; Mayor's Adv Comt Arts & Cult, Baltimore, MD, dir arts educ prog, 1988-90; Baltimore City Col, prof, 1990-93; Eastern Conn State Univ, assoc ed, prof, 1993-02, prof emer, 2002-; consult, workshops, theatre & mass commun. **Orgs:** Dramatist Guild Am, 1971-; pres, Nat Asn African-American Theatre, 1989-91. **Honors/Awds:** Distinguished Alumna Award, Univ Mo, 2000. **Special Achievements:** Author of Black Theatre, Wyndham Hall Publishers, 1986; Noahs Ark, published in Center Stage, 1981; Upstage/Downstage, column in Houston Informer, 1977-78; Rosalee Pritchett, performed at Negro Ensemble Company, 1971, published in Black Writers of America; collaborated on plays, scholarly papers, workshops. **Home Addr:** 3 Nutmeg Ct, Mansfield, CT 06250. *

MOLETTE, DR. CARLTON WOODARD
College teacher, playwright. **Personal:** Born Aug 23, 1939, Pine Bluff, AR; son of Carlton William Sr and Evelyn Richardson; married Barbara Roseburr, Jun 15, 1960; children: Carla & Andrea. **Educ:** Morehouse Col, BA, 1959; Univ KC, grad study, 1960; Univ Iowa, MA, 1962;Fla State Univ, PhD, 1968. **Career:** Educator,producer, playwright, director, designer/stage manager; Univ KC, grad fel theatre; Little Theatre Div Humanities, Tuskegee Inst, asst dir, 1960-61; Des Moines Comm Playhouse, designer tech dir, 1962-63; Howard Univ Dept Drama, asst prof tech prod & design, 1963-64; Fla A & M Univ, asst prof & tech dir, 1964-67, assoc prof, 1967-69; Spelman Col, assoc prof drama, 1969-75, Div Fine Arts, chmn, 1974-75; Atlanta Univ Summer Theatre, Director, 1972-75; Univ Mich, guest dir, 1974; Sch Commun Tex Southern Univ, dean, 1975-84; Lincoln Univ, ColArts & Sci, dean, 1985-87; Coppin State Col, Acad Affairs, vpres, 1987-91; Univ Conn, Dept Dramatic Arts, prof, sr fel, Inst African Am Studies, 1992-2008; Univ Conn, prof emer 2009-; **Plays:** Dr B S Black (musical), Booji, Noah's Ark; Fortunes of the Moor, The Frank Silvera Writers' Workshop, 1995; Presidential Timber, 2001; Our Short Stay, M Ensemble Theatre Co, 2005; Prudence, Conn Repertory Theatre, Univ Conn,2006; Fortunes Of The Moor, dir. **Orgs:** Dramatists Guild; pres, Natl Conf African Am Theatre; Natl Assn Dramatic & Speech Arts; ed, Encore; mem brd dir, Atlanta Arts Festival; vpres, Greater Atlanta Arts Coun; chmn brd trustees, Neighborhood Arts Ctr, Miller Theatre Adv Coun; mem & brd dir, Young Audiences Md, 1990-93. **Honors/Awds:** Ford Foundation Scholarship to Morehouse Col, 1955-59; Carnegie Foundation Doctoral Fellowship to Florida State Univ, Faculty Research Grant, Atlanta Univ Ctr, 1970-71. Playwright Grant, Conn Commission Culture and Tourism, 2005. **Special Achievements:** Co author of Premise & Presentation Wyndham Hall Press, second ed, 1986. **Military Serv:** AUS, sp5, 1963. **Business Addr:** Professor Emeritus, The University of Connecticut, Department of Dramatic Arts, 802 Bolton Rd Suite 1127, Storrs, CT 06269-1127, **Business Phone:** (860)486-4025.

MOLETTE-OGDEN, CARLA
Educator, administrator. **Personal:** Born Jan 1, 1970?, Atlanta, GA; daughter of Carlton W and Barbara J; married Christopher A, Dec 30, 1993. **Educ:** Spelman Col, BA, 1991; Wash Univ, St Louis, PhD, 1998. **Career:** State Univ NY, Stony Brook, asst prof, 1997-2000; J Walter Thompson, partner, sr strategic planner & bus develop mgr, 2000; vpres, sr brand planner, FitzgeraldCO, currently. **Business Addr:** Vice President, Senior Brand Planner, FitzgeraldCO, One Buckhead Plaza, 3060 Peachtree Rd Suite 500, Atlanta, GA 30305, **Business Phone:** (404)504-6900.

MOLOCK, GUIZELOUS O
Lawyer. **Personal:** Born Apr 10, 1958, Wilmington, DE; son of Inez and Guy; married Sherry Davis Molock PhD, Jun 7, 1986; children: Amber N, Jelani L & Diarra M I. **Educ:** Bethune-Cookman Col, BA, 1980; Howard Univ, Sch Law, JD, 1983. **Career:** US Air Force, asst judge advocate gen, 1985-89; US Atty Off, asst US atty, 1989-92; US Senate, Comt Judiciary Chief Nominations, coun, 1992-94; Admin Off US Ct, Article III Judges Div, sr atty, 1994-98, Bankruptcy Judges Div, special coun, 1998-2003, br chief, safetly, security & emergency preparedness, 2003-; **Orgs:** Am Bar Asn; Dist Columbia Bar Asn; Nat Bar Asn; J Franklyn Bourne Bar Asn; Am Bankruptcy Inst; Apa Fraternity Inc; Bethune-Cookman Col Nat Alumni Asn; Fort Foote Baptist Church. **Honors/Awds:** Outstanding Young Man America, 1982; InterNat Science Award, Optimist Club, 1987; Administrative Office Special Act Awards, 1994-99, certificates of appreciation, 1994-; Distinguished Alumni Award, Nat Asn Equal Opportunity Higher Educ, 1994. **Military Serv:** USAF, capt, 1985-89; Commendation Medal, 1989. **Business Addr:** Special Council,

Administrative Office of U S Courts, 1 Columbus Circle NE Suite 4-250, Washington, DC 20544, **Business Phone:** (202)502-1900.

MOMMA J. See HARRIS, JEANETTE.

MONAGAN, DR. ALFRIETA PARKS
Educator. **Personal:** Born Nov 27, 1945, Washington, DC; daughter of Frances Gordon Parks and Claude E; married; children: Venice Frances & Agra Charlotte. **Educ:** George Washington Univ, BA, 1969; Princeton Univ, MA, 1971, PhD, 1981. **Career:** Princeton Univ, fel, 1969-70, 1973-74; Hamilton Col, vis asst prof,1974-75; Univ Erlangen-Nuremberg, Am Studies, Fulbright Jr lectr, 1975-76;Univ Iowa, from instr to asst prof, 1976-86, from adj asst prof to adj assoc prof, 1986-90; Cornell Col, Dept Social & Anthrop, lectr, 1990-98, vis fac, 1999-2000, assoc prof, 2000-; Belin & Blank Ctr, instr, 1998; Cornell Col, Dept Social & Anthrop, prof, currently. **Orgs:** Am Anthrop Asn; Asn Black Anthropologists; Cult Survival Asn; Asn Princeton Grad Alumni; Long fel Neighborhood Asn; Citizens Police Acad Alumni; fel Soc Women Geogr. **Honors/Awds:** Gillen Scholarship, Fulbright Alumni Asn, 1968; Award Nat Asn Foreign Stud Affairs, 1982, 1987. **Business Addr:** Professor, Cornell College, Department Sociology & Anthropology, 600 1st St W, Mt Vernon, IA 52314, **Business Phone:** (319)895-4482.

MONCRIEF, SIDNEY A.
Executive, basketball player, basketball coach. **Personal:** Born Sep 21, 1957, Little Rock, AR; married Debra; children: Brett. **Educ:** Univ Ark, BS, phys educ. **Career:** Basketball player (retired), coach; Welch One One Competition, spokesman; Milwaukee Bucks, 1979-89; Atlanta Hawks, 1990-91; Sidney Moncrief Pontiac-Buick-GMC Truck Inc, pres, 1987-; Fort Worth Flyers, coach, 2006; Golden State Warriors, shooting coach, 2007; Glendale Mitsubishi, pres, currently. **Orgs:** Partner with Ark basketball coach Eddie Sutton to conduct clinics for the Special Olympics; bd dir, Arkla Corp. **Honors/Awds:** NBA Defensive Player of the Year, 1983, 1984; NBA All-Defensive First Team, 1983, 1984, 1985, 1986; SW CNF Player of the Year; All-Am & SW CNF Player of the Year, Univ Ark; 36th NBA All-Star Team. **Special Achievements:** Broke the record of 504 FTM by Kareem Abdul-Jabbar in 1971-72 season; Sporting News All-Am Second Team, 1979. **Business Addr:** President, Sidney Moncrief Pontiac-Buick-GMC Truck Inc, PO Box 4357, Troy, MI 48099-4357, **Business Phone:** (501)945-1601.*

MONCRIEFFE, PETER
Executive. **Career:** Citywide Broadcasting, KQXL-FM, pres; Citadel Broadcasting Corp, staff, currently. **Business Phone:** (702)804-5200.*

MONDAY, SABRINA GOODWIN
Sales manager. **Personal:** Born Aug 7, 1961, Tulsa, OK; daughter of Alquita and Ed Goodwin; married Kenny Monday, Sep 4, 1993 (divorced); children: Sydnee Kennedy, Quincy. **Educ:** Tenn State Univ, BS, 1983; Boston Univ, MA, 1985. **Career:** Boston Globe Newspaper, ed asst, 1989-92; Mary Kay Cosmetics, sr sales dir, 1989-00. **Orgs:** Beta Sigma Theta, 1982-; Nat Asn Advan Colored People, 1985-; The Moteis Group, 1996-; Community Service Coun, 1997-99; Black Women's Adv Comt, 1998-.

MONET, JERZEE (TANISHA MONET CAREY)
Singer. **Career:** Album: Love & War, 2002. **Business Addr:** Recording Artist, c/o Universal Music Group, 1755 Broadway, New York, NY 10019-3743, **Business Phone:** (212)841-8000.*

MONK, ART (JAMES ARTHUR MONK)
Football player, businessperson. **Personal:** Born Dec 5, 1957, White Plains, NY; son of Arthur and Lela Monk; married Desiree; children: James Arthur Jr, Danielle & Monica. **Educ:** Syracuse Univ, attended 1980. **Career:** Football Player (retired), Businessperson; Wash Redskins, wide receiver, 1980-93; New York Jets, 1994; Philadelphia Eagles, wide receiver, 1995; Record Den Inc, dir outside sales; Rich Walker's Scoreboard Restaurant, Herndon, VA, co-owner; WRC-TV, broadcaster; Cactus Advert Assoc, principal owner; Alliant Merchant Services, co-founder. **Orgs:** Bd dirs, Nat Capital Bank Wash; founder, Good Samaritan Found, 1992-. **Honors/Awds:** Player of the Year, Wash Touchdown Club & Quarterback Club; Offensive Player of the Game; Elected to Syracuse University Board of Trustees; Redskins Most Valuable Player, 1984; UPI: 1st team all-conf, 1985; Associated Press: 2nd team all-NFL, 1985; UPI: 2nd team all-conf, 1986; Pro Bowl, 1984-86; Pro Football Hall of Fame Inductee, 2008; Redskins' Ring of Fame. **Special Achievements:** First and only player to record over 100 receptions. **Business Phone:** (703)448-2510.*

MONK, JAMES ARTHUR. See MONK, ART.

MONROE, ANNIE LUCKY
Educator. **Personal:** Born Dec 6, 1933, Milledgeville, GA; married Semon V; children: Angela V & Michael V. **Educ:** Paine Col, BA, 1953; GA Col, MEd, 1977. **Career:** Boddie High Sch, teacher, 1953-68; Baldwin High Sch, teacher, 1968-76, asst prin, 1976-77; GA Col, instr eng, 1977-80. **Orgs:** Ga Libr Asn, 1976-

80; GA Col Alumni Asn, 1977-80; GA Col Women's Club, 1978-79; trustee, Mary Vinson Libr, 1976-80; asst pianist, Trinity CME Church. **Honors/Awds:** Teacher of the Year, Boddie High Sch, 1967; Most Effective Teacher in Classroom Study, Baldwin High Sch, 1977. **Special Achievements:** First Black Instr of Eng, Baldwin High Sch, 1968; First Black Woman chosen Bd of Trustees, Mary Vinson Libr, 1976; First Black Instr of Eng, GA Col,1977; First Black Woman asst prin, Baldwin High Sch, 1976-77. **Business Addr:** Instructor, Georgia College, Milledgeville, GA 31061.

MONROE, ANTHONY E
President (Organization). **Career:** St John Riverview Hosp, pres, currently. **Business Addr:** President, St John Detroit Riverview, c/o Administrative Office, 7733 E Jefferson Ave, Detroit, MI 48214, **Business Phone:** (313)499-4100.*

MONROE, BRYAN K
Newspaper executive. **Personal:** Born Aug 22, 1965, Munich, Germany; son of James W and Charlyne W. **Educ:** Univ Wash, BA, commun, 1987. **Career:** The Seattle Times; The Roanoke Times & World News; United Press Int; Univ Wash Daily, editor; The Poynter Inst Media Studies, visiting lectr; The Sun News, graphics ed, dir photog, 1988; Knight-Ridder Inc's 25/43 Proj, asst proj dir; San Jose Mercury News, asst managing ed, design dir; Ebony & Jet mag, vpres, ed dir, currently. **Orgs:** Co chair, Bay Area Black Journalists Asn; bd dir, Hillcrest Homeowners Asn; 100 Black Men Silicon Valley, Inc; pres, Nat Asn Black Journalists; bd dir, Unity: Journalists Color. **Honors/Awds:** Numerous journalism awards: The Society of Newspaper Design; Nat Press Photographers Asn; The South Carolina Press Asn; The Florida Press Asn; The Washington Press Asn. **Special Achievements:** Guest speaker on topics including newspaper design, graphics, photjournalism, technology, innovation and the future of American newspapers. **Business Addr:** Board of Director, Unity: Journalists of Color, 7950 Jones Br Dr, McLean, VA 22107, **Business Phone:** (703)854-3585.

MONROE, CHARLES EDWARD
School administrator. **Personal:** Born Dec 9, 1950, Laurel Hill, NC; married Edwina Williams; children: Jarrod, Keisha & Charles Jr. **Educ:** Johnson C Smith Univ, BA, summa cum laude, 1978, Univ NC, MEd, 1980, EdS, 1989. **Career:** Greensboro City Schs, teacher, 1980-84, asst prin, 1984-86, prin, 1986-. **Orgs:** NC Asn Educr, 1981-, Nat Asn Elem Sch Principals, 1986-, NC Asn Adminrs, 1986-; Cedar Grove Baptist Church, 1985-; pres, Alpha Kappa Mu Nat Honor Soc; vpres, Alpha Chi Nat Honor Soc; Pi Delta Tau Educ Honor Soc, Hon Prog. **Honors/Awds:** Teacher of the Year, Reidsville City Schs; Outstanding Young Educator, Reidsville City Schools, Reidsville Jaycees. **Military Serv:** AUS, E-4, 2 yrs; Purple Heart, Air Commendation Medal, Bronze Star, Soldier of the Month, Distinguished Grad Ranger Sch Vietnam, 1970-71. **Home Addr:** 2204 Cheltenham Blvd, Greensboro, NC 27407. **Business Addr:** Principal, Hugh M. Cummings High School, 2200 N Mebane St, Burlington, NC 27217, **Business Phone:** (336)570-6100.

MONROE, EARL (VERNON EARL MONROE)
Executive, basketball player, television show host. **Personal:** Born Nov 21, 1944, Philadelphia, PA; married Marita Green; children: Maya. **Educ:** Winston Salem State Univ, attended 1967. **Career:** Basketball player (retired), executive; Baltimore Bullets, 1967-71, NY Knicks, 1971-80; US Basketball League, comnr, 1985; ABC Radio, commentator; Pretty Pearl Recs, founder; Pretty Pearl Entertainment Co, pres; Madison Sq Garden, tv commentator, currently; NJ Urban Develop Corp, comnr, currently; Earl Monroe's Restaurant & Pearl Club, owner; The River Room Restaurant, owner, 2005-; Reverse Spin Records, pres, currently. **Orgs:** Groove Phi Groove Fraternity; spokesman, Am Heart Asn; President's Coun Physical Fitness & Health; Crown Heights Youth Collective; Lit Assistance Fund; Harlem Jr Tennis Prog. **Honors/Awds:** Rookie of the Year, 1967-68; All star team, 1969, 1971, 1975, 1977; NBA champion, 1973; Naismith Memorial Basketball Hall of Fame, 1990; Harlem Professionals Inspirational Award; Most Outstanding Model for American Youth; YMCA Citizenship Award; Big Apple Sportsman of the Year Award; Baltimore Pearls, named in honor, Am Basketball Asn, 2005. **Special Achievements:** One of the 50 Greatest Players in NBA History, 1996. **Business Addr:** TV Commentator, Madison Square Garden, 4 Pennsylvania Plz, New York, NY 10001, **Business Phone:** (212)465-6000.

MONROE, KEVIN
School administrator. **Personal:** Born Oct 29, 1951, Canton, OH; son of Joseph and Bettye Monroe; married Francine Monroe, May 25, 1974; children: Kevin, Patrice & Candice. **Educ:** Mount Union Col, BA, 1974; Univ Akron, MPA, 1994. **Career:** City Canton, income tax auditor III, 1974-77, dep personnel dir, 1987-88, supt pub works, 1988-; Brown & Williamson Tolo, sales rep, 1977-88; Consolidated Frtways, dock supvr, 1978-87. **Orgs:** Steering comt, Am Soc Pub Admin, 1993-; Am Pub Works Asn, 1996-; Int City/County Mgt Asn, 1998-; Water Environ Fedn, 1998-. **Honors/Awds:** Collection System Award, Ohio Water Environment Asn, 2000; Excellence in Public Service Award, Street Maintenance & Sanitation officials Ohio, 2000. **Special Achievements:** Publica-

tions: "Tomorrow's Cities Are Global Cities" in American Cities & Counties, 1992. **Home Addr:** 5971 Drenta Circle SW, Navarre, OH 44662, **Home Phone:** (330)484-6443. **Business Addr:** Superintendent of Public Works, City of Canton, 2436 30th St NE, Canton, OH 44705, **Business Phone:** (330)489-3033.

MONROE, MARY
Writer. **Personal:** Born Dec 12, 1951, Toxey, AL; daughter of Otis Sr and Ocie Mae; married Joseph, Jan 19, 1969 (divorced); children: Michelle & Jacquelyn. **Career:** Novels: The Upper Room, 1985; God Don't Like Ugly, 2000; Red Light Wives, 2002; Gonna lay down my burdens, 2004; Borrow trouble, 2006; God don't play, 2006; Borrow Trouble, 2006; Deliver me from evil, 2007; Spirit in the dark, 2008. **Honors/Awds:** Oakland Pen Award for Best Fiction of the Year, 2001; Best Southern Author Award. **Special Achievements:** Nomination for the Black Writers Alliance's Golden Pen Award. **Business Addr:** Author, Kensington Publ Corp, 850 3rd Ave, New York, NY 10022.

MONROE, ROBERT ALEX
Executive. **Personal:** Born in Somerville, NJ. **Educ:** Westchester Community Col, Hofstra Univ, 1964. **Career:** Calvert Distillers Co, asst eastern div sales mgr, eastern div mgr, vpres/dir mkt; Gen Wine, mgr, NY mgr, nat brand mgr, sales mgr, eastern div sales rep; Summit Sales Co/Perennial Sales Co, pres. **Orgs:** Bd dir, Joseph E Seagram & Sons Inc; Polit Action Comt. **Honors/Awds:** Outstanding Business & Professional Award, Blackbook Mag, 1983; Man of the Year Award, Anti-Defamation League, 1985; George M Estabrook Award, Hofstra Univ Alumni Asn, 1987. **Special Achievements:** First black to lead a major firm in the liquor industry. **Military Serv:** USMC, cpl, 1954-57. **Home Addr:** 1206 Parrilla De Avila, Tampa, FL 33613.

MONROE, VERNON EARL. See MONROE, EARL.

MONSON, ANGELA ZOE
Government official. **Educ:** Oklahoma City Univ, BS; Univ Oklahoma, MPA. **Career:** Exec dir, Oklahoma Health Proj; Probation & Parole Off, Oklahoma Dept Corrections; asst senate majority leader, Oklahama State Senate. **Orgs:** Pres, Nat Conference State Legislatures; bd mem, Families USA Found; exec comt mem, Nat Black Caucus State Legislatures. **Honors/Awds:** Kate Barnard Award, Okla Comn Status Women. **Special Achievements:** First woman to win a statewide elected office in the United States.

MONTAGUE, CHRISTINA P
County commissioner, educator, government official. **Personal:** Born Dec 25, 1952, Inkster, MI; daughter of Romo Watson and Mattie Lee Watson; married Larry Montague, Jun 1976 (divorced); children: Teesha Fanessa. **Educ:** Washtenaw Community Col, criminal justice, 1974; Eastern Mich Univ, BSW, 1984; Univ Mich, MSW, 1988. **Career:** Joint Ctr Polit & Econ Studies, exec dir, 1984-85; Ann Arbor Pub Sch, community agent, 1974-87, res asst, 1987-88; Franklin Wright Settlement, case mgr, 1989-90; Ann Arbor Pub Sch, social worker, 1988-90, child & family therapist, 1990-91, family serv supt, 1991-; Michiganders for Obama, state coordr, currently. **Orgs:** Judge, State Mich Licensed Prof & Amateur Boxing, 1984-88; vpres, Ann Arbor NCP, 1987-89; cent comt mem, Mich Dem Party, 1988-; founding pres, Nat Polit Congress Black Women, Washtenaw Co Chap, 1989; Nat Taxation & Finance Steering Comt Co Officials; nat pres, Terry Scholar Found; Sheriff's Community Rels Adv Bd; Drug Forfeiture Comt; Property Tax Foreclosure Prev Task Force; Workforce Develop Bd; Community Action Bd; Drainage Bd; Emergency Telephone Dist Bd. **Honors/Awds:** Political & Educational Award, Nat NCP, 1985; Outstanding Achievement, Nat Polit Congress Black Women, 1989; Certificate of Appreciation, African Am Youth Acad, 1991; Service to Washtenaw County Award, Washtenaw Co Dem Party. **Special Achievements:** First black to chair Ann Arbor Democratic Party, 1988-90; First African American woman ever elected Washtenaw County Commissioner, 1990. **Home Addr:** 1245 Island Dr Apt 201, Ann Arbor, MI 48105-2065. **Business Addr:** State Coordinator, Michiganders for Obama, 2734 Maitland, Ann Arbor, MI 48105, **Business Phone:** (734)662-9908.

MONTAGUE, NELSON C.
Scientist, clergy. **Personal:** Born Jul 12, 1929, Washington, DC; son of Nelson R and Rosmond P; married Nancy L; children: Lennis Lee. **Educ:** BS, Elec Engr, 1952. **Career:** Elec Engr (retired); Nat Bur Standards, elec engr, 1951-68; Defence Documentation Ctr, Defence Logistics Agency, physical scientist, elec engr, 1984; VIR, marriage celebrant. **Orgs:** Inst Elec & Electronics Engrs Inc, 1950's; Fairfax NCP; treas, N VA Baptist Asn, 1968-; exec bd, NVB Asn; vpres Comn Human Rights & Community Rels, Vienna VA; Mayor's Adv Comt, 1966-70; coach Little League VA, 1972-73; final sec Northern VA Baptist Ministers & Laymen's Union, 1985-94; life mem, NAACP, 1994. **Honors/Awds:** Recipient Group Award, Nat Bur Standards, 1964; Outstanding Performance Rating QSI, Def Documentation Ctr, 1974; finished 4 7 man race for 3 seats Vienna Town Coun, 1968; Achievement Award, Arlington Branch, NAACP, 1986; Faithful Service Award, Fairfax NAACP Branch, 1988. **Military Serv:** AUS, pfc, 1952-54. *

MONTAIGNE, ORTIZ. See WALTON, DR. ORTIZ MONTAIGNE.

MONTEIRO, DR. THOMAS
College teacher. **Personal:** Born Oct 6, 1939, New York, NY; son of John and Lovely Peters; married Joy Williams (divorced 1980); children: Thomas & Tod. **Educ:** Winston-Salem State Univ, NC, BS, 1961; City Univ New York, Queens Col, NY, MA, 1966; Fordham Univ, NY, profl dipl, 1969, EdD, 1971, PhD, 1974. **Career:** Bd Educ, New York, NY, teacher, 1961-68, dist curric dir, 1969-70; Brooklyn Col, City Univ New York, New York, prof, 1970-85, City Univ New York, Brooklyn Col, Dept Educ Admin & Supervision, chairperson & dir prin's ctr, 1985-95, prof emer, currently. **Orgs:** Educ co-chairperson, New York State, Nat Asn Advan Colored People, 1976-80; pres, New York Jamaica Br, Nat Asn Advan Colored People, 1977 & 1978. **Honors/Awds:** Educator of the Year Award, New York Asn Black Educators, 1988; Award of Excellence, New York, Alliance Black Sch Educators, 1988; Congressional Achievement Award, Congressman Floyd Flake, 1990; Educational Leadership Award, Coun Supervisors & Adminrs New York, 1991; Outstanding Educator Award, Success Guide George Fraser Ed, 1991. **Business Addr:** Professor Emeritus, Brooklyn College, Department of Education Administration and Supervision, 2900 Bedford Ave, Brooklyn, NY 11210, **Business Phone:** (718)951-5209.

MONTEITH, DR. HENRY C.
Nuclear engineer, educator. **Personal:** Born May 10, 1937, Columbia, SC; son of Frank Hull and Susie Elizabeth; divorced. **Educ:** Milwaukee Sch Engineering, BS, elec engineering, 1965; Univ Pa; Purdue Univ; Univ N Mex, MS, elec engineering, 1970, PhD, 1975. **Career:** Educator (retired), Nuclear Engineer; RCA Indianapolis, elec engr, 1965-67; Sandia Natl Labs, Albuquerque, N mex, math, comp programmer, elec engr, tech staff mem, 1967-80, nuclear engr, 1976-88; ITT Tech Inst,instr, 1990-92; Albuquerque Acad, math instr, 1992-93; Eastern N Mex Univ, instr, 1993-2003. **Orgs:** Writer & lectr on sci, philos subjects; priv res Parapsychology; Am Asn Advancement Sci, Soc Physics, Studs, Int Asn Math Physicists. **Honors/Awds:** Sigma Pi Sigma Physics Honor Soc. **Special Achievements:** Computer Determination of Decoder Parameters for Color Television, 1967; "The Time Theory of Nikolai A. Kozyrev", 1971; "Stimulated Emissions from Living Forms May Provide Clues to Novel Medical Techniques of the Future"; Dynamic Gravity and Electromagnetic Processes, 1987; Psychotronics: Yesterday, Today and Tomorrow, 1988; Preliminary design of the cooling system for a gas-cooled, high-fluence fas pulsed reactor; "Applications of Scalar Technology: The Liatronics Microscope", 1991. **Military Serv:** USN, Electron Tech second Class, 1958-62.

MONTEVERDI, MARK VICTOR
Executive, executive director. **Personal:** Born Jun 19, 1963, New York, NY; son of Monahan and Marcella F. **Educ:** Hiram Col, Hiram OH, BA, 1985. **Career:** Small Bus Admin, NY, NY, pub affairs specialist, 1985-87; Black Enterprise Magazine & Earl G Graves, Ltd, New York NY, nat networking forum coord, 1987-88; Mayors Office, NY, NY, mgr pub communs & outreach, 1988-89; Westchester Minority Com Asn, exec dir, 1989-90; Phillip Morris Co Inc, pub affairs coord, 1990-91, mgr pub prog, 1991-96; AT&T, dir corp affairs, 1996-. **Orgs:** Alpha Lamda Delta, 1981-; jr fel, US Small Bus Admin, 1981-85; Omicron Delta Kappa, 1983-; Asn Minority Enterprises NY, 1985-; Caribbean-Am Chamber Com, 1985-; Nat Minority Bus Coun, 1985-; adv bd mem, Self-Help Group, 1988-; Prog develop vip, Bus Policy Review Coun; Adv bd secy, Latin Am Mgt Asn; bd mem, Manhattanville Col Ential Coun; Vis prof, Nat Urban League's Black Exchange Prog; Nat Asn Market Developers; Proj prize mentor, Queensborough Community Col; NAT Coalition Black Meeting Planners. **Honors/Awds:** James A Garfield Memorial Award, Hiram Col, 1981; Outstanding Political Science Major, Hiram Col, 1985; Martin Luther King Junior Scholarship, Hiram Col, 1985; Presidents Award, Asn Money Enterprises NY, 1991;Award of Distinction, Communications Excellence to Black Audiences, 1992. **Special Achievements:** Received White House recognition for role as downstate coordinator for the 1985 White House Conference on Small Business, 1986; "Best & Brightest" Dollars & Sense Magazine; "40 under 40" African American influentials by The Network Journal, 1998. **Home Addr:** 23 S Elliot Pl, Brooklyn, NY 11217. **Business Phone:** (210)821-4105.

MONTGOMERY, ANNETTE
Archivist, educator. **Personal:** Born Jan 9, 1961, Suffolk, VA; daughter of Raymond Jones Jr and Edna M Montgomery. **Educ:** Norfolk State Univ, BA, Sociol, 1984, MA, Urban Affairs, 1992. **Career:** Norfolk State Univ Urban Affairs Grad Prog grad fel, 1990-91, asst archivist, 1996-, instr, 1999-. **Orgs:** Norfolk State Univ Asn Educ Off Profs (NSUAEOP), 1993-; Va Asn Govt Archivists & Records Adminstrators, 1998-; Mid-Atlantic Regional Archives Conf (MARAC), 1999-; MillionaireMommie. **Honors/Awds:** Employee of the Quarter, Norfolk State Univ Cluster, 1993, 1994; participant, res conf, Nat Endowment Humanities, 1995; Carter G. Woodson Inst Afro-Am Studies, UVA, Scholars Summer Seminar in African Am Studies, 1999. **Special Achievements:** Co-author: Policy and Guidelines for Records Management at Norfolk State Univ, revised 2008; A Guide to the Manuscript Collection in the Harrison B Wilson Archives at Norfolk State Univ, 1997; Black America Series, Suffolk, Arcadia Publishing 2005. **Business Addr:** Assistant Archivist, Norfolk State University, 700 Pk Ave Suite 2851, Archives Lyman B Brooks Library East Wing, Norfolk, VA 23504, **Business Phone:** (757)823-2003.

MONTGOMERY, CATHERINE LEWIS
Executive. **Personal:** Born in Washington, DC; daughter of Lloyd Lewis (deceased) and Catherine Branch Lewis Laster (deceased); married Alpha LeVon Montgomery Sr (divorced); children: Alpha LeVon Jr. **Educ:** Howard Univ, attended 1946; Univ Calif, attended 1949; Nat Inst Pub Affairs, attended 1968. **Career:** USN elect Lab San Diego, admin asst to tech dir, 1950-62; Republican State Cent Comn, admin asst field dir, 1966; Econ Opportunity Comn, San Diego County, personal dir admin serv, 1966-69; State Calif Fair Employ Prac Comn, comnr, 1969-75; USN Dept, consult, Urban Affairs, 1972-, mgt consult equal opportunity spec, 1978-90. **Orgs:** San Diego Planning Comnr, 1966-73; adv bd, Mental Health Serv, 1968-72; President's Adv Coun Minority Bus Enterprise, 1972-75; founder, bd mem, Women's Bank, 1974-78; Western Gov Res Asn; Nat Asn Planners; Am Soc Planning Officials; Commonwealth Club Calif; pres, Soroptimist Int San Diego, 1979-80; Nat Girls Clubs Am Inc; Urban League San Diego Inc; Univ Hosp Adv Bd; life mem Nat Asn Advan Colored People; life mem, Nat Coun Negro Women; League of Women Voters; San Diego Girls Club Inc; San Diego Links, Inc; bd mem, SE Economic Devlop Corp, 1987-94; govt & community relations comn, San Diego Convention Tourist Bureau, 1989-90; life mem, Friends VP Pub Libr, 1990. **Honors/Awds:** Essence Women of the Month, 1974; National Recognition Award, Lambda Kappa Mu, 1978; Woman of Dedication, Salvation Army Door of Hope, 1994; Humantarian Service Award, Catfish Club, 1994; Unsung Hero Award, San Diego Nat Asn Adavn Colored People, 1994; San Diegan of the Year, San Diego Home-Garden Mag, 1994; Making a Difference Award of Excellence, San Diego City Mayor Susan Golding, 1995; Appreciation Award, SE San Diego Develop Comn, 1996. **Home Addr:** 5171 Roswell St, San Diego, CA 92114. **Business Addr:** Urban Consultant, Montgomery, 5171 Rosewell St, PO Box 740041, San Diego, CA 92174, **Business Phone:** (619)263-3387.

MONTGOMERY, DR. CLYDE, JR.
Educator. **Career:** Langston Univ, Sch Arts & Scis, dean & prof music, currently, assoc vpres acad affairs, actg vpres acad affairs, vpres acad affairs, currently, chief acad officer, currently. **Orgs:** Okla Asn Col Teacher Educ; N Cent Asn Col & Sch. **Business Addr:** Vice President Academic Affairs, Dean, Langston University, School of Arts & Sciences, 219 Sanford Hall, PO Box 1500, Langston, OK 73050, **Business Phone:** (405)466-3419.

MONTGOMERY, DEBBIE
City council member. **Career:** State Dept Pub Safety, asst comnr; Saint Paul Police Dept, comdr; St Paul City Coun, councilwoman, currently. **Business Addr:** Councilwoman, St Paul City Council, Ward 1 Rm 310-A City Hall, Saint Paul, MN 55102, **Business Phone:** (651)266-8610.*

MONTGOMERY, DELMONICO LAMONT. See MONTGOMERY, MONTY.

MONTGOMERY, DWIGHT RAY
Clergy. **Personal:** Born Apr 8, 1950, Memphis, TN. **Educ:** Lane Col, BA, 1972. **Career:** Reg Sickle Cell Coun, dep dir, 1973-76; Goodwill Indust, counr, 1977; Annesdale Cherokee Baptist Church, minister, 1985-. **Orgs:** Kappa Alpha Psi Alumni Chap, 1969; Masonic Lodge; 32 deg Scotish Rite; Elks; Shriners 1969-71; found, dir Coalition of Benevolent Youth, 1974; pres, Southern Christian Leadership Conf. **Honors/Awds:** Memphis Hall of Fame, Alpha Kappa Alpha Sor, 1973-75; Outstanding Young Men Am, 1975; Outstanding Citizen Memphis, Tri-St Def Newspaper, 1976; 50 Future Black Leaders, Ebony Mag Chicago, 1978. **Business Addr:** Pastor, Annesdale Cherokee Baptist Church, 2960 Kimball Ave, Memphis, TN 38114, **Business Phone:** (901)743-2057.

MONTGOMERY, DR. EDWARD B.
Dean (education), educator. **Personal:** Born in New York; married Kari; children: Lindsay, Elizabeth & Edward. **Educ:** Pa State Univ, grad, 1976; Harvard Univ, PhD, econs, 1982. **Career:** Carnegie Mellon Univ, fac, 1981-86; Mich State Univ, fac, 1986-90; NJ Gov's Study Comn Discrimination Pub Works, consult; State Court Child Support Admin Office Mich, consult; Bd Govs Fed Res, consult; Fed Res Bank Cleveland, consult; Urban League Pa, consult; US Dept Labor, chief economist, dep secy, asst secy for policy, 2001;Univ Md, Col Behav & Social Scis, prof, 1990-, dean, 2003-;Center for the Study of Poverty and Inequality, Univ Stanford, fel, 2006-. **Orgs:** Vis Scholar, Bd Govs Fed Res & Fed Res Bank Cleveland; Res Assoc, Nat Bur Econ Res; US Dept Labor's Adv Coun Employee Welfare & Benefits; trustee,Coun Excellence Govt, 2004-; bd Visitors, Soc & Econs Scis Directorate; bd Visitors, Adv Panel Econs Nat Sci Found; Urban Inst; Upjohn Inst Employ; Joint Ctr Polit & Econ Studies; Mem, Economic Domain Design Group, Key Nat Indicators Initiative, 2005; affli-

ate, Center for Integrate Environmental Research, 2007-. **Special Achievements:** First African American chief economist at the US Dept of Labor;Publications: "Pensions and Wage Premia" (with Kathryn Shaw), Economic Inquiry, 1997, "Do Workplace Smoking Bans Reduce Smoking," (with WilliamEvans and Matthew Farrelly), American Economic Review, September 1999, Affirmative Action and Reservations in the American and Indian Labor Markets: Are They Really That Bad? in A Not So Dismal Science, edited by Mancur Olson, 2000, "Cross State Variation in Medical Programs and Female Labor Supply (with John Navin), Economic Inquiry, July 2000. **Business Addr:** Dean, Professor, University of Maryland, College of Behavioral and Social Sciences, 2141 Tydings Hall, College Park, MD 20742, **Business Phone:** (301)405-1691.

MONTGOMERY, ETHEL CONSTANCE
Executive. **Personal:** Born Jul 10, 1931, Morristown, NJ; daughter of Arnold and Aletha; widowed; children: Byron, Lisa. **Educ:** Fairleigh Dickinson Univ. **Career:** Executive (retired); Morristown Neighborhood House, prog dir, coordr, vol, group worker, secy, 1951-64; Warner Lambert Inc, coder, 1965; Silver Burdette, Morristown Ship, 1967; Bell Tel Co, typist, 1968; Western Elec Co, salaried personnal rels, personnal results investr, tech clerk, sec, steno secy, 1968-75; AT&T Bell Labs, affirm act coordr, 1975, group supvr, 1978, supvr, 1985-87, employment rep, 1987-90. **Orgs:** Leader Girl Scout, 1952; pres, PTA, 1957; Carettes Inc, 1959; sec, treas, vp, corrs sec Carettes Inc, 1959-76; mem, vp, pres Morristown Bd Ed, 1966-70; corrs sec Morris Co Sch Bd Asn, 1969; Morristown Civil Rights Comn, 1969; Morristown Community Act Comn, 1969; Urban Leag & Family Serv, 1970; Youth Empl Serv 1970; United Fund Adv Bd, 1970; vpres, Morris Sch Dist Bd Ed, 1972-74; St Bd Ed, 1975; Juv Conf, 1977; adv com, Memorial Hosp, 1977; Gov Byrn's Govt Cost & Tax Policy Com, 1977; 1982-, pres 1984, 1986, 1987; Morristown Council; newsletter chairperson, Concerned Citizens second Ward, 1989-90; Morris Count Democratic Comn , 1986-90; bd mem, Morristown Neighborhood Watch, 1987-90. **Honors/Awds:** Morris Co Urban League Award 1953, 1963; Outstanding Women New Jersey, Fairleigh Dickinson Univ, 1964; Morris Co NAACP Award, 1970; Lambda Kappa Mu Sor Award, 1970; Transcendental Meditation Award, 1977; Nat Black Achiever, 1979. **Home Addr:** 17 Liberty St, Morristown, NJ 07960, **Home Phone:** (201)539-2897.

MONTGOMERY, EVANGELINE JULIET
Artist, executive. **Personal:** Born May 2, 1933, New York, NY. **Educ:** Los Angeles City Col, AA, 1958; Calif State Univ, Los Angeles, attended 1962; Calif Col Arts & Crafts, BFA, 1969; Univ Calif, Berkeley, attended 1970. **Career:** Freelance artist, 1960-62; EJ Assocs, art consult to museums, comm orgns & cols, 1967-; Montgomery & Co, exhibits specialist, freelance art consult, 1969-73; Rainbow Sign Gallery, cur, 1971-76; ARK Urban Systs Inc, vpres & dir, 1973-78; Am Asn State & Local Hist, exhibit workshop coordr, 1979; WHMM TV Wash DC Community Affairs, dir, 1980; African Am Museums Asn, exhibit workshops coordr, 1982; Art Consults & Gallery, freelance artist represented by Unity Works, Los Angeles, CA; UFA Gallery, New York; Dist W Fine Art Gallery, Leesburg, VA, Mich Chap NCA Gallery, Detroit, Stella Jones Gallery, New Orleans, LA, Parish Gallery, Wash DC USIA, Arts Am, prog officer, 1983-99, US Dept State, Cult Prog, prog officer, 1999-. **Orgs:** Pres, Art W Asn N Inc, 1967-78; Am Museums Asn, 1970-; pres, Metal Arts Guild, CA, 1972-74; nat coordr regions, Nat Conf Artists, 1973-81; bd mem, Museum Nat Ctr Afro-Am Artists, 1974-85; art comnr, San Francisco Art Comn, 1976-79; nat fine arts & cult dir, Nat Asn Negro Bus & Prof Women Clubs Inc, 1976-78; adv bd, Parting Ways Ethnohistory Museums, Plymouth, MA, 1977-85; DC chap co-chairperson, Fine Arts & Cult Comm; Col Art Asn, 1983-; Coalition 100 Black Women, 1984-91; Womens Art Caucus, 1988-; bd dirs, DC Arts Ctr, 1989-99; Brandywine Workshop, 1990-; Mich Chap Nat Conf Artists, 1990-; bd mem, Year Craft Celebration, Am Craft Coun, 1993; Am Asn State & Local Hist, Nashville. **Honors/Awds:** Nat Program Award, NANB & P W Clubs Inc, 1977; Service Awards, Nat Conf Artists, 1970, 1974, 1976; Museum Grant, Nat Endowment Arts, 1973; Grant, Third World Fund San Francisco, 1974; Special Achievement Award, USIA Arts Am, 1989; Outstanding Woman Artist of the Year Award, Nat Womens Art Caucus, 1999; Outstanding Women on the Move in the Arts Award, IAM, 2001. **Special Achievements:** Work and exhibits appeared in The Oakland Museum, Oakland, CA, The Museum of the Natl Ctr for African American Artists, Boston, MA, The Brandywine Print Workshop Archives Philadelphia, PA, Nation Black Caucus Foundation, Washington, DC, James E. Lewis Museum of Art, Morgan State Univ, Baltimore, MD and many private collections. **Business Addr:** Artist, 1054 31st St NW off M St Canal Sq, Georgetown, DC 20007, **Business Phone:** (202)944-2310.

MONTGOMERY, GEORGE LOUIS, JR.
Banker, real estate agent. **Personal:** Born Jul 13, 1934, St Louis, MO; children: Gay & Kelly. **Educ:** St Louis Univ, BS, 1956; Wash Univ, AD, 1968. **Career:** St Louis Redevelop Authority, real estate spec, 1974; Kraft Foods Inc, salesman, 1963-68; Conrad Liquor, salesman, 1962-63; Universal Life Ins Co, salesman, 1961-62; Montgomery Real Estate, broker, 1968-. **Orgs:** St Louis Jr C C, 1961-63; Nat Asn Mkt Develop, 1961-63; Frontiers Int Inc, 1970-; Pres Coun St Louis Univ, 1973-; past chmn, Sel Ser Bd, 1974; Independent Fee Appraisers Asn, 1974-; Realtist Asn St Louis, 1974-; Wayman Temple AME Ch; bd mem, 1976-, pres, 1980-84, vice-chmn, Gateway Nat Bank St Louis, 1977; Annie Malone C Home. **Honors/Awds:** Citizen of the Wk, KATZ Radio, 1961; Most Eligible Bachelor, Ebony Mag, 1964; Man of the Yr, Frontiers Int, 1964; Alumni Merit Award, St Louis Univ, 1980; Distinguished Service Award, Top Ladies Distinction, 1981. **Military Serv:** USNR, seaman, 1956-58. **Home Addr:** 4615 Redfield Ct, Saint Louis, MO 63121. **Business Phone:** (314)381-0440.

MONTGOMERY, GREGORY B
Lawyer. **Personal:** Born Mar 23, 1946, McKeesport, PA; married Patricia A Felton. **Educ:** Rutgers Col, AB, 1968; Rutgers Law Sch, Newark, NJ, JD, 1975. **Career:** Matah Network, exec vpres; Pvt Pract, atty, 1985-; Forrestal Village Inc, corp sec, 1978-79; S & E Const Corp, corp sec, 1977-79; Fidelity First Corp, vpres, 1975-79. **Orgs:** Mem Nat Bar Asn; Kappa Alpha Psi Fraternity. **Military Serv:** USAF, capt, 1968-72, Commendtion Medal, 1972. **Business Addr:** Attorney, 361 Independence Blvd, Lawnside, NJ 08045-1033, **Business Phone:** (609)546-1446.

MONTGOMERY, JAMES C.
Clergy. **Personal:** Born Feb 8, 1918, Lake, MS; married Mary I Roberts. **Educ:** Rust Col, Holly Springs, MS, 1952. **Career:** Mt Sinai Missionary Bapt Ch, pastor; Radio Shop, owner. **Orgs:** Nat Asn Advan Colored People. **Honors/Awds:** Recipient Award Comm Sch Improvement Prog, 1961; Award of Appreciation, Metro Bapt Church, 1954; Award Dept of Christine Ed Nat Coun Chs; Hon State of MI 68 Dist Ct Flint. **Military Serv:** AUS, pvt first class, 1940. **Business Addr:** Sinai Missionary Baptist Church, 1215 Downey Ave, Flint, MI 48505.

MONTGOMERY, JOE ELLIOTT
Government official. **Personal:** Born Jul 10, 1942, Hemingway, SC; son of Elliott and Emma Jane; married Phyoncia, Apr 30, 1969; children: Charles Montgomery. **Educ:** Allen Univ, Columbia, SC, BA, l965; Univ SC. **Career:** City NY, counr, l965-66; Horry County Dept Educ, teacher, l966; Govt Neighbourhood Renewal Unit, head, 2002, dir gen, currently; Town Atlantic Beach, Atlantic Beach, SC, mayor. **Orgs:** SC Educ Asn; Nat Educ Asn; Horry County Educ Asn; Nat Coun Black Mayors; SC Coun Black Mayors. **Honors/Awds:** Costa Carolina Col, Cert, l979; Joint Ctr Polit Action, Cert, l979; Kappa Alpha Psi Fraternity, Cert, l982; Horry County Cult Asn, l982; Nat Conf Black, Cert, l984. **Home Addr:** 807 31st Ave S, PO Box l374, Atlantic Beach, SC 29582. **Business Addr:** Director General, Neighbourhood Renewal Unit.*

MONTGOMERY, JOSEPH
Football player, broadcaster. **Personal:** Born Jun 8, 1976, Robbins, IL; son of Joe and Renee. **Educ:** Ohio State Univ. **Career:** Football player (retired), analyst; New York Giants, running back, 1999-2000; Carolina Panthers, 2002; WBNS-AM & NBC Channel 4, broadcaster, col football analyst, currently. **Business Phone:** (202)885-4000.

MONTGOMERY, MONTY (DELMONICO LAMONT MONTGOMERY)
Football player. **Personal:** Born Dec 8, 1973, Dallas, TX. **Educ:** Univ Houston. **Career:** Indianapolis Colts, defensive back, 1997-99; San Francisco 49ers, 1999-2000; Philadelphia Eagles, 2001; New Orleans Saints, 2004.

MONTGOMERY, OLIVER R.
Administrator. **Personal:** Born May 31, 1929, Youngstown, OH; married Thelma Howard; children: Darlene, Howard, Brenda, Oliver, Jr, Edwin. **Educ:** BS, 1956. **Career:** United Steelworkers Am, assoc res asst. **Orgs:** chmn labor, Nat Asn Advan Colored People, 1960-63; Nat bd mem, Sec Nat Afro-Am Labor Coun, 1970-75; vpres, Unitedd Steelworkers Local 3657; nat bd & exec coun mem, Coalition Black Trade Unionists; bd mem, Gr Pittsburgh Am Civil Liberties Union, 1972-75; Kappa Alpha Phi Frat. **Honors/Awds:** A Philip Randolph Award; Award certification Merit, Nat Asn Advan Colored People Urban League; Testimonial Dinner, 1970; Award from Mayor, City Counc CAP officer, Off Equal Opportunities Progs. **Military Serv:** AUS, military sci instr. **Business Addr:** Research Dept United Steelwork, Pittsburgh, PA 15222.

MONTGOMERY, DR. OSCAR LEE
Educator. **Personal:** Born Jul 19, 1949, Chapman, AL; married Alfredia Marshall; children: Paula Onese, Renita Falana, Christa Ivana & Oscar Lee Jr. **Educ:** Ala A&M Univ, BS, 1972; Purdue Univ, MS, 1974, PhD, 1976; Trinity Theol Seminary, D.Min, 1997. **Career:** Ala A&M Univ, asst prof, 1976-81, assoc prof, 1981, vpres, prof; UHPBC, sr pastor, 1977-. **Orgs:** Ala Ctr Applications Remote Sensing, 1980-; GHIMF-Ministerial Fel, 1980-; Nat Asn Advan Colored People local chap, 1982-84. **Home Addr:** 3800 Milbrae Dr, Huntsville, AL 35810. **Business Addr:** Senior Pastor, Union Hill Primitive Baptist Church (UHPBC), 2115 Winchester Rd NW, Huntsville, AL 35810, **Business Phone:** (256)852-0170.

MONTGOMERY, DR. PATRICIA ANN FELTON
Educator, school administrator. **Personal:** Born Sep 11, 1946, Greenville, SC; daughter of Clifton Howard Felton and Ruth Elizabeth Beal; married Gregory Byron, Feb 7, 1970; children: Gregory Hassan & Clifton Amir. **Educ:** Douglas Col, Rutgers The State Univ, BA, 1968; Syracuse Univ, MEd, educ, 1971; Teachers Col-Columbia Univ, EdD, 1994. **Career:** Lawnside Pub Sch, stud-personnel Serv, 1975-79; Big Brothers/Big Sisters Am, asst vpres, 1979-82; Acad Advan, Teaching, mgt, educ prog specialist, 1984-89; Winslow Twp Sch, prin, 1989-93; Camden City Pub Sch, dir regional schs, 1993-97; West Deptford Twp Sch, asst supt, 1997-99; Willingboro Pub Sch, asst supt, 1999-2001; Temple Univ, lab stud success, dir, 2001-; Bridgeton Pub Schs, Bridgeton, NJ, asst supt, currently; US Dept Educ, Mid-Atlantic Regional Educ Lab, dir educ leadership lab stud success. **Orgs:** Am Asn Univ Women; Asn Curric & Supv; NJ Asn Curric & Supv; exec bd, NE Coalition Edu, Southern NJ Chap; NJ Chap, Black Sch Educrs; NJ Chap, Phi Delta Kappa; Rowan Univ Leadership NJ, Zeta Nu Chap; Coalition 100 Black Women, S Jersey Chap; Jack & Jill Am, S Jersey Chap; Camden Co Girl Scout Coun Bd; Continental Socs Inc; Delta Sigma Theta, S Jersey. **Honors/Awds:** Education Award, Coalition of 100 Black Women; Outstanding Young Women of America. **Special Achievements:** Published: "Leadership Is More Than Intuition", Academy Newsletter, Spr 1987; "School Districts Join Staff Leader Program", NJ School Boards Notes, Mar 3 1988; "Time on Task: A Key to Student Achievement", Instructional Insight, Sept 1995; "New Teacher Induction", 1999. **Home Addr:** 183 Echelon Rd, Voorhees, NJ 08043. **Business Addr:** Assistant Superintendent, Bridgeton Public Schools, 41 Bank St, Bridgeton, NJ 08302, **Business Phone:** (856)455-8030.

MONTGOMERY, PAYNE
Educator, government official. **Personal:** Born Nov 24, 1933, Bernice, LA; married Rosemary Prescott; children: Janice, Eric & Joyce. **Educ:** Grambling Col, BS, 1956; Tuskegee Inst, MS, 1969; NE La Univ, 1969. **Career:** Morehouse Par Sch Bd, hum rel cnsl; City of Bastrop, city cnclmn; Morehouse HS, basketball coach, 1959-69; Delta HS, soc stud teacher, 1969-72. **Orgs:** City Coun, 1973; La Ed Asn; Nat Educ Asn; Parish Rec Bd; C C; Am Leg; bd dir, Headstart; pres, Morehouse Community Orgn. **Honors/Awds:** Special recognition Coaching Record; Coach of Year, 1961. **Military Serv:** AUS, 1956-58. **Business Addr:** Government Officer, Human Relations Office, Bastrop HS, Bastrop, LA 71220.

MONTGOMERY, ROBERT E
Automotive executive, consultant, president (organization). **Personal:** Born Feb 1, 1948, Lake Wales, FL; son of Annie L Gadson; married Valorie A; children: Ryan & Raven. **Educ:** John B Stetson Univ, BBA, 1970; Columbia Univ, Grad Sch Bus, MBA, 1972. **Career:** Ford Motor Co, analyst, 1972-73; Chevrolet Motor Co, analyst & supvr, 1973-80; Gulf & Western, dir, bus planning, 1980-85; GM Dealer Sch, trainee, 1985-86; Self-Employed, consult, 1986-88; Mountain Home Ford, pres, chief exec, 1988-. **Orgs:** Alpha Phi Alpha; bd dir, Ford-Lincoln Mercury Minority Dealers Asn. **Military Serv:** USY, 1st lt, 1970-74. **Business Addr:** Chief Executive, MOUNTAIN HOME FORD-LINCOLN-MERCURY, INC, 491 W 6TH S, Mountain Home, ID 83647-3483, **Business Phone:** (208)587-3326.

MONTGOMERY, TIM
Track and field athlete. **Personal:** Born Jan 25, 1975, Gaffney, SC; children: 2. **Educ:** Norfolk State Univ, degree, 1996. **Career:** Athlete (retired); Nike, endorsement contract; track & field athlete. **Honors/Awds:** Silver Medal, Olymics, 1996; Bronze Medal, IAAF World Championship, 1997; Bronze Medal, Olympics, 1997; Gold Medal, IAAF World Championship, 1999, 2001; Gold Medal, Olympics, 2000; Silver Medal, World Championships, 2001; USA Outdoor champion, 2001; Gold Medal, World Championships, 2002; Jesse Owens Award, USA Track &Field, 2002. **Special Achievements:** The men's 100m world record, IAAF Grand Prix Final, 2002. *

MONTGOMERY, TONI-MARIE
School administrator, educator. **Personal:** Born Jun 25, 1956, Philadelphia, PA; daughter of Milton and Mattie Drayton. **Educ:** Philadelphia Col Performing Arts, Philadelphia, PA, BM, piano, 1980; Univ Mich, Ann Arbor, MI, MM, piano chamber music, 1981, DMA, piano chamber music, 1984. **Career:** Western Mich Univ, Sch Music, Kalamazoo, MI, asst dir & artistic dir, 1985-87; Univ Conn, Storrs, CT, Sch Fine Arts, asst dean, 1987-89; Ariz State Univ, Tempe, AZ, assoc dean, asst prof, 1990-96; Ariz State Univ, Sch Music, dir, 1996-2000; Univ Kansas, Sch Fine Arts, dean, 2000-03; Northwestern Univ Sch Music, dean, 2003-, prof piano, currently. **Orgs:** Pres, Sister Friends, African-Am Women, 1990-; bd dirs, pres, Fac Women's asn, 1990-; Tempe Arts Comn, 1991-93; Phoenix Symphony Bd, 1998-. **Honors/Awds:** Outstanding Keyboard Performer, Am Keyboard Artists, 1988; Black Women's Task Force Arts Award, 1998. **Business Addr:** Dean, Professor, Northwestern University, School of Music, Music Admin Bldg 711 Elgin Rd, Evanston, IL 60208-1200.

MONTGOMERY, DR. TRENT
Educator, college administrator. **Educ:** Southern Univ, BSEE, 1969; Univ Ill, MSEE, 1971; Univ Tex, PhD, 1976. **Career:** Univ Ill, fac; Univ Tex, fac; Southern Univ, Baton Rouge, LA, dean col eng & prof elec eng & comput sci; Ala A&M Univ, fac, 1996; Ala

A&M Univ, Dept Elec Eng, prof & Sch Eng & Technol, interim dean, currently; staff, AT&T Bell Labs; staff, Int Bus Mach. **Orgs:** Inst Elec & Electronics Engrs; Eta Kappa Nu; Am Soc Eng Educ; Nat Soc Prof Engrs; La Eng Soc; HKN Honor Soc; Asn Comput Mach. **Honors/Awds:** Outstanding Fac Award, Southern Univ, 1982, 1983, 1985; Inst Elec & Electronics Engrs Outstanding Educator Award, 2000. **Business Addr:** Professor, Interim Dean, Alabama A&M University, School of Engineering and Technology Department of Electrical Engineering, 222 Carver Complex N Rm 226, PO Box 1148, Normal, AL 35762, **Business Phone:** (256)372-5560.

MONTGOMERY, VELMANETTE
State government official. **Personal:** Married William Walker; children: William. **Educ:** NY Univ, MEd; Univ Accra, Ghana; St Josephs Col, LLD, 1991. **Career:** NY City Dist 13 Sch Bd, mem, 1977-80, pres, 1977-84; Child Care Inc, Advocacy Group, former co-dir; Day Care Forum, NY, teacher, adj prof, founder & dir; NY Senate, 18th Sen Dist, sen, 1984-. **Orgs:** Serves on many senate comns including: Finance; Crime Victims, Crime & Correction, Consumer Protection, Housing & Community Develop, Mental Health & Develop Disabilities, Educ, Health; chief dem, C & Families; chair, Dem Task Force on Primary Health Care; co-chair, Dem Task Force on Criminal Justice Reform; Robert Wood Johnson Found, Nat Adv Comm. **Honors/Awds:** fel, Inst Educ Leadership, 1981; fel, Revson Found, 1984; one of "America's Top 100 Black Bus & Prof Women", Parade Mag, 1992; Nat Teen Leadership Award, Advocates Youth,1994; Legislative Leadership Award, The Vis Nurse Asn Brooklyn; legislative Leadership Award, NY Therapeut Communities Inc; Revson Fel, Columbia Univ. **Business Addr:** State Senator, State of NewYork, 18th Senate District, 306 Legislative Office Bldg, Albany, NY 12247, **Business Phone:** (518)455-3451.

MOODY, ANNE
Writer. **Personal:** Born Sep 15, 1940, Wilkerson County, MS; daughter of Elmire Williams and Fred; married Austin Straus, Mar 9, 1967 (divorced); children: Sascha. **Educ:** Natchez Junior Col, attended 1961; Tougaloo Col, BS, 1964. **Career:** Cong Racial Equality, Washington, DC, organizer, 1961-63, fundaraiser, 1964; Cornell Univ, Ithaca, NY, civil rights proj coord, 1964-65; Coming of Age in Mississippi, auth, 1968; Mr.Death, auth, 1975; New York City Poverty Prog, coun, currently. **Orgs:** NAACP; Cong Racial Equality; Int PEN. **Honors/Awds:** Brotherhood Award, Nat Coun Christians & Jews, 1969; Best Book of the Year Award, Nat Libr Asn, 1969; Coming of Age in Mississippi, 1969; Silver Medal, Mademoiselle, 1970. **Business Addr:** c o Harper and Row, 10 E 53rd St, New York, NY 10022.*

MOODY, C DAVID
Executive. **Career:** CD Moody Construction Inc, pres & ceo, currently. **Special Achievements:** Black Enterprise's list of Top 100 Industrial & Service Companies, ranked 86, 2000. **Business Addr:** Chief Executive Officer, president, CD Moody Construction Company Inc., 6017 Redan Rd, Lithonia, GA 30058, **Business Phone:** (770)482-7778.*

MOODY, CAMERON DENNIS
Engineer, executive. **Personal:** Born Jun 17, 1962, Chicago, IL; son of Charles and Christella. **Educ:** BS, indust eng. **Career:** Ford Motor Co, engr, 1986-93; CD Moody Const, engr, 1991-92; Atlanta Olympic Comt, regional logistics mgr, 1994-96; Dem Nat Convention, dep dir transp; olumpics, 1996, 2000 & 2002; Denver Summit Eight, dir transp, 1997; Sinbad Soul Music Festival, Aruba, transp coordr, 1997; DJ Miller & Assocs, chief info officer, 1997-; CD Moody Const Co, chief information officer, 1998-99; Dem Nat Convention, dep dir opers, 2000, dir opers, dep chief exec officer opers comt, 2004-; Am Cancer Soc, dir strategic planning & opers. **Orgs:** Omega Psi Phi; Nat Alliance Black Sch Educators. **Business Addr:** Deputy Chief Executive Officer of Operations, Democratic National Convention Committee, 53 State 4th Fl, Boston, MA 02109, **Business Phone:** (617)342-2004.*

MOODY, CHARLES DAVID, SR.
Association executive, educator. **Personal:** Born Aug 30, 1932, Baton Rouge, LA; son of James Nathaniel and Rosetta Ella Hall; married Christella Delois Parks; children: Charles David Jr, Corey Derrick & Cameron Dennis. **Educ:** Cent State Univ, BS, biol, 1954; Chicago Teachers Col, MA, sci educ, 1961; Univ Chicago, cert adv study, 1969; Northwestern Univ, PhD, educ admin, 1971. **Career:** Mentally Handicapped Chicago Schs, educ teacher, 1959-62; Posen-Robbins Jr High Sch, asst teacher, 1963-67, asst prin, 1967-68; Schs Harvey, Il, supt, 1968-70; Northwestern Univ, TTT fel, 1969-70; Nat Alliance Black Sch Educr, founder, 1970-; Univ Mich, Sch Educ, dir prog educ opportunity, 1970-73, Div Educ Specialist, chmn, 1973-77, Proj Fair Admn Stud Disc, dir, 1975-80, prof educ, dir prog educ oppor, 1970-87, vice provost minority affairs, 1987-96, vice provost emer minority affairs & prof emer, 1996-; Ctr Sex Equity Schs, dir, 1981-87; South Africa Initiative Off, exec dir, 1993-. **Orgs:** Ex bd, Nat Alliance Black Sch Educr, 1970-; bd dir, Nat Asn Advan Colored People, Ann Arbor, 1983-85; bd dirs, Network Instrnl TV Inc; Phi Delta Kappa; Sigma Pi Phi; Omega Psi Phi Fraternity. **Honors/Awds:** Community Leader Award, Ann Arbor Veterans Admn Med Ctr, 1980; Doctorate of Laws Degree, Cent State Univ, 1981; Award of Respect, Washtenaw Comn Col, Ann Arbor, MI, 1984; Professional of the Year Award, Ann Arbor; Charter Inductee, Cent State Univ, Wilberforce, OH, 1989; Alumni Merit Award, Northwestern Univ; Living Legend Designation Award, Nat Alliance Black Sch Educr; received various awards and honors. **Military Serv:** AUS, second lt, 1954-56. **Home Addr:** Ann Arbor, MI 48105, **Home Phone:** (313)663-7508. **Business Phone:** (202)608-6310.

MOODY, DOMINIQUE FAYE
Artist. **Personal:** Born Dec 14, 1956, Augsburg, Germany; daughter of Theodore Robert and Barbara Spurlock Bundage; married Phillip Bannister III (divorced). **Educ:** Philadelphia Col Art, Philadelphia, PA, attended 1972; Pratt Univ, Brooklyn, NY, attended 1975; Univ Calif, Berkely, BFA, 1991. **Career:** Art ed, 1991-95; artist. **Orgs:** Nat Conf Artists, 1993-95; La County Museum Art, 1999; Friends Watts Towers, 1998-99; Pro Arts, Oakland, CA, 1994; Southern Exposure, San Francisco, 1994; Museum Children's Art, Oakland CA, 1993-95; Calif African Am Museum, 1997-. **Honors/Awds:** Univ Calif Berkely Hons, 1987-91; Fine Arts Award, Gordon Heinz, 1990; Fine Arts Award, Maybelle Toombs, 1990, 1991; Fine Arts Honor, Phi Beta Kappa, 1991; Seagram's Gin, Perspectives in African American Art, 1997. **Special Achievements:** Commissioned work through Seagram's Perspectives in African American was donated to the CA African American Museum, 1997. Publ: Ramsey Bell Breslin, The Figured identified (unpublished review from Bay Guardian Weekly), Oakland, CA James Brzezinski, Reassurance: The Figure Identified, Review Art Week, Richmond, CA November 17, 1991; G. Shontell, Multimedia Show, The Figure Identified, West County Times, Richmond, CA October 5, 1991; Jocelyn Stewart"Walkin on Water," Ramsess Publications, Los Angeles, CA 1994; David Pagel Reviews Into the Dream Box Exhibit at Watts Towers Arts Center, Calendar Section, Los Angeles Times, May 12, 1996; Angela Johnson Interview, Los Angeles Watts Times, June 20, 1996; Adrienne Johnson, feature article, "A Matter of Perception" Life & Style Section, Los Angeles Times, March 25, 1997; Donald James"Artist Weaves a Different Kind of Vision", first column, Los Angeles Watts Times, Feb. 27, 1997; Jocelyn Stewart self-published book of poetry"Walkin on Water" in collaboration with D. Moody in stallation"Walking on Water" March 12, 1998; Sharon Banister Arts Viewing Points: Art takes many forms Review for the Hanford Sentinel Carousel Weekly Mag a zine, Hanford, CA (February); American Visions Magazine"Perspectives in African American Art (Team sheet) Spring 1998; Emerge Magazine"Perspectives in African American Art", February 1998.

MOODY, ERIC ORLANDO
Lawyer. **Personal:** Born Jul 16, 1951, Petersburg, VA; married Sherrie Y Brown. **Educ:** Lafayette Col, AB, Philos, 1973; Univ Va Sch Law, JD, 1976. **Career:** Va Beach Police Dept, uniformed police officer, 1974; WINA/WOMC Radio, reporter & announcer, 1974-75; Neighborhood Youth Corps, client counr, 1975-76; Eric O Moody & Assoc, sr partner, 1976-; Norfolk State Col, instr, 1977-78. **Orgs:** Va State Bar; Portsmouth Bar Asn; Old Dominion Bar Asn; Am Bar Asn; Chesapeake Bar Asn; Twin City Bar Asn; bd dir, Chesapeake YMCA; Nat Asn Advan Colored People; Chesapeake Men Progress; Chesapeake Forward; Boy Scouts Am; fel United Church Christ. **Honors/Awds:** Dean's List; George F Baker Scholar; Substitute Judge City Chesapeake; Indust Develop Authority. **Business Addr:** Senior Partner, Eric O Moody & Assoc, 355 Crawford St, Ste 810, Portsmouth, VA 23704-2825.*

MOODY, HAROLD L.
Educator, businessperson. **Personal:** Born Sep 6, 1932, Chicago, IL; married Shirley Mc Donald; children: Michele Marcia. **Educ:** Chicago Teacher Col, BE, 1954, ME, 1961. **Career:** Educator, Businessperson (retired); Williams Elem Sch, teacher; Ray Elem Sch, teacher; S Shore HS, audio visual consult; Deneen Elem Sch, princ, 1970-90. **Orgs:** Elementary Press Assoc, Phi Delta Kappa, Chicago Princ Assoc, Chicago Area Reading Assoc, Intl Reading Assoc, Block Club, Steering Comm Police Comm Workshops 3rd dist; Salem House Luth Soc Serv Agency; First Unitarian Church. **Honors/Awds:** Chicago Bd Ed, Best Teacher Award; Scholarship Harvard Univ, 1963; Park Manor Neighbors Comm Org, Service Award, 1979. **Military Serv:** USNG, 2 yrs.

MOODY, WILLIAM DENNIS
Dentist. **Personal:** Born Jun 6, 1948, White Plains, NY; son of William Jr and Ellen Rebecca. **Educ:** North Cent Col, BA, 1970; State Univ NY, Buffalo, DDS, 1974. **Career:** Pvt prac, dentist. **Orgs:** Prog chmn, Greater Metrop Dent Soc, 1977-78; bd dirs, Greenburgh Neighborhood Health Ctr, 1979-81, Greenburgh Community Ctr, 1982-83, Thomas H Slater Ctr, 1984-91; White Plains Dent Forum, Scarsdale Dent Soc; bd dir, Union Child Day Care Ctr; Am Dent Asn; Alpha Omega Frat; Nat Dent Asn; Greater Metro NY Dent Soc; pres, Greater Metrop Dent Soc, 1987-89; corresp secy, Greater Metrop NY Dent Soc, 1990-91. **Business Addr:** Dentist, Private Practice, 48 Mamaroneck Ave Suite 42, White Plains, NY 10601.*

MOON, HAROLD. **See MOON, WARREN.**

MOON, WALTER D
Government official. **Personal:** Born Aug 10, 1940, Marietta, GA; married Winford G Strong; children: Sonja & Sonita. **Educ:** Kennesaw Jr Col; Savannah State Col; Inst Comput Technol, 1967. **Career:** Mails US Postal Serv, Marietta, GA, foreman; part-time bldg contractor. **Orgs:** Treas, Future Develop Asn Inc; pres, Concerned Citizens Marietta; Nat Asn Advan Colored People; Marietta Cobb Bridges Prog; vice chmn, Marietta Bd Educ; Marietta Civil Serv Comn; USN Manpower Speakers Team Freshman Scholastic Savannah State Coll, USN, 1960-64; Atlanta E Dist, African Methodist Episcopal Church, 2005-. **Military Serv:** USNR, chief petty officer, 1966-. **Business Addr:** Part Time Building Contractor, Private Business, 331 Hermitage Ct SW, Marietta, GA 30064, **Business Phone:** (770)428-6744.

MOON, WARREN (HAROLD MOON)
Football player, television broadcaster. **Personal:** Born Nov 18, 1956, Los Angeles, CA; son of Harold (deceased) and Pat; married Felicia Hendricks (divorced); children: Joshua, Chelsea, Blair & Jeffrey. **Educ:** Univ Wash. **Career:** Player (retired), owner; Edmonton Eskimos, CFL, quarterback, 1978-83; Houston Oilers, quarterback, 1984-93; Minn Vikings, 1994-96; Seattle Seahawks, 1997-98, Seahawks radio team, broadcast analyst, currently; KansCity Chiefs, quarterback, 1999-2000; Warren Moon's Chocolate Chippery, Edmonton, owner. **Orgs:** Founder, Crescent Moon Found. **Honors/Awds:** MVP, Rose Bowl; All NFL Rookie Team, Pro Football Writers, UPI & Pro Football Weekly; Football Digest's Rookie All-Star Team; NFL Man of the Year, 1989; Travelers NFL Man of the Year, 1989; AFC Passing Leader, 1992; Canadian Football Hall of Fame, 2002; Pro Football Hall of Fame, 2006. **Special Achievements:** One of nine African-American quarterbacks, largest number in NFL history, 1997.

MOONE, WANDA RENEE
Consultant. **Personal:** Born Oct 12, 1956, Greensboro, NC; daughter of Connell and Beulah; divorced; children: Dedrick L. **Educ:** NC A&T State Univ, BS, (cum laude), 1982; Univ NC Chapel Hill, MSW, 1983. **Career:** Bowman Group Sch Med, Amos Cotlage Rehab Hosp, social worker I, 1983-85; St James Nursing Ctr Inc, dir social serv, 1985-87; Rockingham Coun on Aging, case mgr, 1987-89; Piedmont Triad Coun Govts, reg long term care ombudsman, 1989-90; Youth Focus Psychiat Hosp, dir social work, 1990-94; Guilford Co Dept Soc Serv, child protection servs supvr, currently. **Orgs:** NASW, 1982-; Alpha Delta Mu, 1982-; field instr, Bennett Col, 1985-86; NC A&T State Univ & Univ NC, Greensboro, 1986-; NC Asn Black Social Workers, 1987-90; Nat Asn Advan Colored People, 1987-; NC Asn Health Care Facil, 1987-88; Acad Cert Social Workers, 1988; Alzheimer's Asn, 1989; adv comt mem, United Servs Older Adults, 1989-90. **Honors/Awds:** NC Dean's List, 1979-80; Certificate, Alpha Delta Mu; Nat Social Work Hon, Soc Rho Chap, 1982-. **Business Addr:** Supervisor, Guilford Co DSS, 1203 Maple St, Greensboro, NC 27405, **Business Phone:** (336)641-3813.

MOORE, ACEL
Editor. **Personal:** Born Oct 5, 1940, Philadelphia, PA; divorced; children: Acel Jr. **Educ:** Settlement Music Sch 1958; Charles Morris Price Sch 1964. **Career:** Philadelphia Inquirer, ed clerk, 1964-68, copy boy, 1965, staff writer, 1968-81, assoc ed & dir recruiting, columnist & mem ed bd, 1981-05, assoc ed emer, 2005-. **Orgs:** Pres, Philadelphia Asn Black Journalists; founding mem, Nat Asn Black Journalists Sigma Delta Chi; Am Soc Newspaper Eds; Pulitzer Prize Juror. **Honors/Awds:** Scales Of Justice Award, Philadelphia Bar Asn, 1970; Managing Editors Award, Philadelphia Asn Press, 1975-76; Philadelphia Prison Society Award; Humanitarian Award, House Umoja; Community Service Award, Youth Develop Ctr; Journalism Award, Philadelphia Party, 1976; Philadelphia Bar Association Award; Paul Robeson Award, Afro-Am Hist Mus, 1976; National Headliners Award; Nat clarion Award for Women in Communication; National Business League of Philadelphia Award; North Philadelphia Mothers Concern Award; Achievement Award, White Rock Baptist Church; Pulitzer Prize, 1976; Robert F Kennedy Journalism Award, 1976; Heywood Broun Award, 1976; Yvonne Motley McCabe Award, Swarthmore Col Annual Upward Bound, 1977; Nieman fellowship, Harvard Univ, 1979-80. **Military Serv:** AUS 1959-62. **Business Addr:** Associate Editor Emeritus, The Philadelphia Inquirer, 400 N Broad St, PO Box 8263, Philadelphia, PA 19101.*

MOORE, ALBERT
Public relations executive, school administrator. **Personal:** Born Feb 17, 1952, Johnsonville, SC; married Marie Durant; children: Porchia Atiya, Chelsey Maria. **Educ:** Friendship Jr Col, 1971; Benedict Col, BA, Pol Sci, 1974; Univ SC, Pub Admin, 1979; SC Criminal Justice Acad, Cert Correction Officer, 1981. **Career:** Crayton Middle Sch, sub teacher, 1974-75; Square D Co, prod coordr, 1975-76; US Auto Assoc, vpres mktg & pub rels, 1976-77; Al's Drive In Restaurant, owner, 1976-77; Benedict Col, equip mgr, 1977-79, tech asst, dean acad affairs, 1979-82; Nat Conf Black Mayors Prog, asst dir, 1979-82; Central Correctional Inst, correction officer II, 1981-83; Benedict Col, coordr spec servs, pub rels, 1982-84; St Augustines Col, dir pub rels, 1984; Florence County, treas, 1999-00. **Orgs:** Seminar, Robert R Morton Mem Inst, 1980; panalist, Am Census Bur Workshop, 1980; participant Assoc Rec Mgrs, 1981; Benedict Col Jr Alumni Club, Drexel Lake Residents Civic Org, NAACP, SCARMA, SC Correction Officers Asn; charter mem Benedict Col Tiger Club. **Honors/Awds:** Alternate delegate Richland Cty Dem Convention, 1984.

MOORE, ALFRED
Chief executive officer, executive director. **Personal:** Born Feb 24, 1956, Detroit, MI; divorced. **Educ:** Adrian Col, Adrian, MI, BA, acct, 1978; State Mich, certified pub acct. **Career:** Central City Health Serv Inc, Detroit, MI, exec dir, 1984; New Ctr Hosp, Detroit, MI, adminr, 1986-90, ceo, 1990; New Ctr Clin E, Detroit, MI, exec dir, 1986. **Orgs:** Life mem, Nat Asn Advan Colored People; pres, Block Club.

MOORE, ALICE EVELYN
Educator, secretary (organization). **Personal:** Born Feb 16, 1933, Washington, NC. **Educ:** Tuskegee Inst, Social Studies, 1955; NMex Highlands Univ, Hist Educ, 1962; Johns Hopkins Univ, Cert, Negro & Sou Hist, 1970; N Tex State Univ, Cert Aging Specialist, 1979,82; Southern Univ & UNO prof. **Career:** Young Women's Christian Asn, teen-age dir, 1955-56; Emerson Settlement House, group work, 1957-58; Friendship Jr Col, instr social sci, 1962-71; Elizabeth City State Univ, instr social sci, 1971-73; Claflin Col, asst prof social sci, 1974-80; Allen Univ, assoc prof social sci, 1981-, coordr geront prog, 1981-; interim dir acad affairs, 1985-86. **Orgs:** Counsr, Epworth C's Home, 1981; secy, Resource Mobilization Adv Coun Dept Social Serv Richland Co, 1981-84; founder, secy & treas, Orangeburg Br Asn Study Life & Hist. **Honors/Awds:** Volunteer of the Year, Epworth C's Home, 1986. **Special Achievements:** One of the first African-Americans to attend Tulane University.

MOORE, ALLYN D
Automotive executive. **Personal:** Born Aug 9, 1960, Chicago, IL; son of Buck and Elizabeth; married Cheryl, Oct 17, 1992; children: Cydney, Zackery & Camryn. **Educ:** Bradley Univ, Peoria, Ill. **Career:** Ford Motor Co, Ford Division Chicago, St Louis; Quality Ford-Mercury, owner, currently. **Orgs:** Bus comn, long range planning comt, Southside Bapt Church; Ford Lincolnmercury Minority Dealers Asn; secy, NADA; bd mem, Princeton Chamber Com; Optimist Club; past bd mem, United Way; bd mem, St Charles Community Col; St Charles Chamber Com; St Peter's Optimist Club. **Honors/Awds:** Contest Dealer of the Year, KY-TN Lease, 1993; Minority Business of the Year, Minority Bus Asn, 1997; Dealer Development, Alumni Award; Allyn Moore Automotive Group ranked #62, BE Top 100 Auto Dealers, 2001. **Business Addr:** Owner, Quality Ford Mercury, 311 US Hwy 62 W, Princeton, KY 42445, **Business Phone:** (270)365-3673.

MOORE, ANNIE JEWELL
Fashion designer. **Personal:** Born Sep 20, 1919, Daytona Beach, FL; daughter of James (deceased) and Ora Lee Hall (deceased). **Educ:** Spelman Col, BA, 1943; Fashion Acad, golden pen cert, 1952; Ecole Guerre-Lavigne, Paris France, cert, 1954; Marygrove Col, cert, 1976. **Career:** Ann Moore Couturiere Inc, fashion designer & pres, 1952-70; Detroit Pub Sch Syst, teacher, 1972-82; Atlanta Pub Sch Syst, teacher, 1985-86; Rich's Acad, couturiere teacher, 1986-91; Military Justice Clin Inc, receptionist, 1991; Dekalb & Futton Housing Coun, off asst, 2000-03; Social Security, clerical asst, 2003-. **Orgs:** Pres, Michigan Women's Civic Coun; vpres, Detroit Chap, Nat Alumnae Asn Spelman Col, 1980-82; chairperson, comm Atlanta Chap, Nat Alumnae Asn Spelman Col, 1986-87; Ad Hoc Comm Clothing & Textile; founder, Benefactors Educ, 1990. **Honors/Awds:** Michigan Women Civic Council Award, 1982; Honoree, Military Justice Annual Banquet, 1999.; Certificates of recognition, Detroit Chap Nat Alumnae Asn Spelman Col; Honoree, Nat Black Arts Festival Event, 2006. **Special Achievements:** Donated fashion designs created over a 40 year period to the Atlanta Historical Society, taught a practicum on costume design, Drama Department of Spelman College, 1983-84, produced Cent Fash Focus Spelman's 100th Anniversary 1981. **Home Addr:** 988 Palmetto Ave SW, Atlanta, GA 30314-3128.

MOORE, ANTHONY LOUIS
Executive. **Personal:** Born Jan 10, 1946, Chicago, IL; married Joyce M Watson; children: Jason A. **Educ:** Southern Ill Univ, BS, 1971; DePaul Univ, attended 1976; Univ Ill Chicago, attended 1978. **Career:** Vince Cullers Advert, media buyer, 1971-73, media planner, 1973-74; Proctor & Gardner Advert, assoc media dir, 1974-76, media dir, 1976-78, vip advert serv, sr vip advert serv, 1990. **Orgs:** Bd mem, Faulkner Sch, 1984-; Am Advert Fed, 1971-; Am Mgt Asn, 1976-; Nat Asn Mkt Develop, 1975-; adv bd, Chicago YMCA, 1976-; Alpha Delta Sigma, 1970-; Stepp Sch; Chicago Media Dirs Coun, 1986; Target Adv Pros. **Honors/Awds:** Creative Advertising Certificate, Asn Nat Advertisers; Black Media Merit, Black Media Inc; Employee of the Year, Proctor & Gardner; Achievement Award, YMCA. **Military Serv:** USMC, E-4, 1967-69, Combat Corres Asn, 1968-. **Business Addr:** Senior Vice President, Proctor Communications Network, 980 N Michigan Ave, Chicago, IL 60611.

MOORE, DR. ARCHIE BRADFORD, JR.
Educator. **Personal:** Born Jan 8, 1933, Montgomery, AL; son of Archie B Sr and Annie Ruth Jeter; married Dorothy Ann Flowers; children: Angelo Juan & Kimberly D. **Educ:** Ala State Univ, BS, 1959, MEd, 1961; Kans State Univ, PhD, 1974. **Career:** Educator (retired); Russell Co Pub Sch Syst, teacher, 1959-61; Montgomery Co Pub Sch Syst, teacher, 1961-69; Clarke Col, asst prof social sci, 1970-75; Ala St Univ, dir TCCP, 1975-77, coordr continuing educ, 1977-78, dean evening & weekend col & pub serv, 1978-83, prof educ & spec asst dean grad studies & cont educ, 1983-91. **Orgs:** Nat Educ Asn; Ala Asn Social Sci & Hist Teachers; Am Fedn Musicians Affil AFL-CIO; Phi Beta Sigma Frat; Phi Delta Kappa Prof Educ Frat; Asn Continuing Higher Educ; Nat Community Educ Asn; chmn, Catholic Charity Dr; Holy Name Soc; Ala Ctr Higher Educ Comm Serv Comm; Col Educ Curric Comm Ala St Univ; Ala St Univ Coun Acad Deans; chmn, Resurrection Catholic Sch Syst Bd Educ. **Honors/Awds:** State Award, Ala Social Studies Fair Teacher Recognition, 1968. **Military Serv:** USN, petty officer 3rd class, 1952-56. **Home Addr:** 2966 Vandy Dr, Montgomery, AL 36110.

MOORE, BARBARA CROCKETT
Association executive. **Educ:** Benedict Col, BS, biol; Univ Chicago, MS. **Career:** Benedict Col, Columbia, SC, vpres inst advan, 1975-; Zeta Phi Beta Sorority Inc, intl pres, 2002-. **Orgs:** Midlands YWCA; Nat Asn Female; chmn, Nat Capital Campaign; Richland County Nat March Dimes Found; Nat Asn Female Executives; Coun Advan Support Edu. **Honors/Awds:** Zeta's SC Hall of Fame; Zeta's Southeastern Regional Hall of Fame; Living the Legacy Award, Nat Coun Negro Women, 1983. **Business Addr:** International President, Zeta Phi Beta Sorority Inc, 1734 New Hampshire Ave NW, Washington, DC 20009, **Business Phone:** (202)387-3103.

MOORE, BEVERLY
School administrator, mayor. **Personal:** Married Larry; children: Bryan & Craig. **Educ:** Ohio State Univ, BS, social welfare, 1966; Western Mich Univ, MS, social welfare, 1984. **Career:** City Kalamazoo, vice mayor, 1989?93, mayor, currently; Western Mich Univ, Sch Social Work, dir admis, currently; Kalamazoo Pub Sch, Bd Educ, pres; Western Mich Univ, adminr; Health Connect, exec dir. **Orgs:** Greater Kalamazoo United Way Bd, pres; Kalamazoo Pub Educ Found; trustee, Bronson Hosp; found mem, WMU; Community Access Ctr Bd; Vol Ctr Bd; Planned Parenthood Southwest Mich Bd; Rotary Club Kalamazoo; Forum Kalamazoo; Irving S Gilmore Keyboard Festival Bd; League Women Voters; Nat Asn Advan Colored People; Alpha Kappa Alpha Sorority; Saturday Eves' Book Club. **Special Achievements:** First African American woman Mayor. **Business Addr:** Mayor, City of Kalamazoo, 241 W S St, Kalamazoo, MI 49007-4796, **Business Phone:** (616)337-8047.*

MOORE, CARMAN LEROY
Music critic, composer, educator. **Personal:** Born Oct 8, 1936, Lorain, OH; son of Claude Leroy and Jessie Lee; married Susan Stern (divorced); children: Martin & Justin. **Educ:** Ohio State Univ, BA, music, 1958; Juilliard Sch Music, MS, 1966. **Career:** The Village Voice, music critic, 1965-; NY Times, staff, 1969; Manhattanville Col, asst prof music & composer; New Sch Soc Res, Queens Col, NY, staff; Univ Yale Grad Sch Music; The Saturday Rev; The Am Dance Festival, rock lyricist; Sky music Inc, founder & conductor, currently; Compositions: Mass for the 21st Century, Lincoln Ctr Performing Arts; African Tears; Drum Major; Wildfires & Field Songs; Gospel Fuse; Hit, A Concerto for Percussion & Orchestra Wild Gardens of the Loup Garou music theatre work Paradise-Lost The Musical & Journey to Benares; Opera, The Last Chance Planet & Gethsemane Park (libretto by Ishmael Reed); Songs: Wellness for All; Zen Garden; In Gratitude; Garden of Time; Healing Music; The Home Galaxy; Star music; Spirit of Kamakura; Dream Time; At Peace; With Thee Conversing; Lots in Love; Oakland Blues; You Promised; BLUE.RED.GREEN, 2007. **Orgs:** Am Soc Composers, Authors & Publ. **Honors/Awds:** Meet-the-Composer Readers Digest Composer / Choreographer Award. **Home Addr:** 152 Columbus Ave, New York, NY 10023. **Business Addr:** Composer, Conductor, Skymusic Inc, 148 Columbus Ave, New York, NY 10023, **Business Phone:** (212)633-1456.

MOORE, CHANTE
Singer. **Personal:** Born Feb 17, 1967, San Francisco, CA; married Kadeem Hardison, Jan 1, 2002 (divorced); children: Sophia Milan; married Kenny Lattimore, Jan 1, 2002; children: Kenny. **Career:** Albums: Precious, 1992; A Love Supreme, 1995; This Moment Is Mine, 1999; Exposed, 2000; The Millennium Collection: The Best of Chante Moore; play Things That Lovers Do, 2003; Uncovered/Covered; "The Tom Joyner Show", 2005; Love The Woman, 2008. **Honors/Awds:** NAACP Image Award, 1996; nominee, Grammy Award, 1996; American Music Award, 1997; nominee, Soul Train Award. **Business Phone:** (310)865-4500.

MOORE, DR. CHARLES W
School administrator, executive. **Personal:** Born Nov 2, 1923, Macon, GA; son of Rose Bud Cornelius Moore and Henry Moore; married Mary Agnes DuBose; children: Tallulah Ragsdale. **Educ:** Morris Brown Col, AB, 1950; NY Univ, MBA, 1952; Daniel Payne Col, DHL, 1971; Univ UT, MS, 1975; Morris Brown Col, LLD, 1980. **Career:** Morris Brown Col, bus mgr, 1951-66; US Dept HEW, educ prog officer, 1966-78; US Dept HHS, financial mgr, 1978-85; Morris Brown Col, vpres finance, 1985-91; Brown & Moore Financial Serv LLC, vpres, currently, tournament co-chair, currently. **Orgs:** Bd stewards Big Bethel AME Church, 1955; treas, Atlanta Invest Asn Inc, 1956-; treas, Am Asn Col & Univ Bus Off, 1960-66; nat treas, Phi Beta Sigma Fraternity Inc, 1970-93; chmn, bd dir, Butler St YMCA, 1979-81; Asn Govt Acct, 1983-; pres, Nat Alumni Asn, Morris Brown Col, 1984-85. **Honors/Awds:** Alumnus of the Year, Morris Brown Col, Nat Alumni Asn, 1968 & 1975; Distinguished Service Award, Rust Col, 1971; Distinguished Service Award, Phi Beta Sigma Fraternity Inc, 1978; Special Achievement Award, US Dept Health & Human Serv, 1984; Distinguished Leadership Award, United Negro Col Fund, 1985. **Military Serv:** AUS, staff sgt; Good Conduct Medal. **Home Addr:** 734 Flamingo Dr SW, Atlanta, GA 30311. **Business Addr:** Vice President, Tournament Co-Chair, Brown and Moore Financial Services LLC, 34 Peachtree St NW Suite 2480, Atlanta, GA 30361, **Business Phone:** (404)522-7431.

MOORE, CHARLIE W. See Obituaries section.

MOORE, CHRISTINE JAMES
School administrator, consultant, social worker. **Personal:** Born in Windsor, NC; daughter of Henry and Maude Boxley; married Marcellus (died 1998); children: Lisa M Barkley. **Educ:** Morgan State Univ, Baltimore, BA, eng & hist, 1952; Columbia Univ, Teachers Col, New York, MA, guid & stud personnel admin, 1962; Johns Hopkins Univ, advan grad study; Syracuse Univ, advan grad study. **Career:** Social Worker, Consultant, Educational Administrator (retired); Booker T Washington Jr High Sch, teacher 1952-59; counr, 1959-64; Balt Sec Schs, specialist guid, 1965-69; Workshop Employment Opportunities Disadvantaged Youth, Johns Hopkins Univ, asst dir, 1966, instr, 1969-70; Community Col Baltimore, Md, dir develop Studies, 1969-74, Stud Serv, Harbor Campus-,dean, 1974-79, dean staff develop & urban resources, 1980-81, exec asst pres, 1981-83; House Delegates Gen Assembly State Md, reader, 1986-87; Morgan State Univ, acad adv, 1988-92. **Orgs:** Regional dir, Delta Sigma Theta, 1968-70; Mayor's Steering Com Baltimore Best Promotional Com, 1976-87; Middle States Asn Col & Sec Schs, 1977-83; Am Personnel & Guid Asn; Am Col Personnel Asn; bd dir, Mun Employees Credit Union Baltimore, 1975-83; bd dir, Arena Players Community Theater; bd dir, 4th Dist Dem Org, 1980-82; Am Fed Television & Radio Artists, 1983-; Nat Asn Advan Colored People; Nat Coun Negro Women; Coun&human rels, Urban League Consult; bd dir, Baltimore Md Metro YWCA, 1983-86; bd dirs, Baltimore Maryland Metrop, YWCA, 1983-86; bd examiners Speech Pathol, 1983-85; comnr, Comn Med Discipline Md, 1984-88; Comn Med Discipline State Md, 1985-88; bd, Physicians Quality Assurance State Md, 1988-98; bd trust, City Temple Baltimore Baptist Church, 1986-87; Md Stat eBd Physicians Quality Assurance, 1988-98; Screen Actors Guild, 1991-; Nat Coalition 100 Black Women; Links Inc; steering comt, Rev Characteristics Excellence Higher Educ: Stand Accreditation Mid States Asn Cols & Schs Comn Higher Educ, 1992-93. **Honors/Awds:** Outstanding Educators of America, 1973; Outstanding Delta of the Year,1974; 100 Outstanding Women in Baltimore, Delta Sigma Theta Sorority,1975; Arean Players Artistic Award, Community Theater Group, 1979; One Hundred Outstanding Black Women of Baltimore, Emmanuel Chirstian Community Church, 1988. **Home Addr:** 853 Woodward St, Baltimore, MD 21230.

MOORE, CHRISTOPHER PAUL
Writer, playwright, actor. **Personal:** Son of Willard and Norma K D; married Kim Yancey; children: 2. **Educ:** Northeastern Univ, attended 1974. **Career:** Author, playwright, actor, historian, journalist; ABC Radio News, ed; Nat Black Network News, ed; NY Pub Libr, Schomburg Ctr Res Black Cult, cur & res historian, currently; writer, currently; Books: Santa & Pete: A Novel of Christmas Present & Past, 1998; The Black New Yorkers: 400 Years of African-American History, 1999; Jubilee: The Emergence of African-American Culture, 2003; Standing in the Need of Prayer: A Celebration of Black Prayer; 2003; Fighting for America: Black Soldiers, The Unsung Heroes of World War II, 2005; Plays: The Last Season, 2004; TV: "The African Burial Ground: An American Discovery"; "Santa & Pete". "Black Soldiers Blue", 2005. **Orgs:** Northeastern Univ Alumni Asn; New York Landmarks Preserv Comt. **Special Achievements:** Interviewed every American president from Jimmy Carter to Bill Clinton. **Business Addr:** Writer, c/o Random House Inc, 1745 Broadway, New York, NY 10019, **Business Phone:** (212)782-9000.*

MOORE, CLEOTHA FRANKLIN
Association executive. **Personal:** Born Sep 16, 1942, Canton, MS; son of Sam A and Luevenia Lee McGee; married Normajo Ramsey Moore, Jun 26, 1965; children: Faith Veleen, Sterling Kent. **Educ:** IN Central Univ, BS, 1964; Ball State Univ, Ed, 1965; IN Univ Purdue Univ Indpls, Bus Studies, 1975. **Career:** Wood HS Indianapolis Pub Sch Syst, tchr, coach, 1964-69; IN Nat Bank, personnel admin, 1969-74; RCA & Consumer Electronics, emp rels mgr, 1974-90; United Way Cent Ind, dir human res, 1990-. **Orgs:** 1st vp, newsletter ed IN State Missionary Bapt Convention, 1968-79; mem NAACP, 1969-; trustee, asst treas S Calvary Bapt Church, 1977-; pres Audubon Terr Neighborhood Assoc, 1978-85; mem Mayor's Ridesharing Work Rescheduling Task Force 1979; bd mem Metro School Dist of Warren Twp; bd of dir, Near East Side Multi Serv Ctr, 1983-89; bd of dir, Indianapolis Day Nursery Assn, 1988-90; mentor, Business Encouraging Success for Tomorrow, 1990-; mentor, Indianapolis Pub Sch Syst, 1990-. **Honors/Awds:** Work study Grant IN Central Col, 1960-64; IN State HS Wrestling Champion IN HS Athletic Assoc, 1960; Col Wrestling

Championship Awds, IN Little State Col Conf, 1962, 1964; Spoke Aws Indianapolis Jaycees, 1971; Spark Awd Indianapolis Jaycees, 1972; Serv Awd Indianapolis Headstart Prog, 1974. **Business Addr:** Director, United Way Cent Ind, 1828 N Meridian St, Indianapolis, IN 46202, **Business Phone:** (317)923-1466.*

MOORE, COLIN A.

Lawyer. **Personal:** Born Apr 24, 1944, Manchester Village, Berbice, Guyana; son of Victor Emmanuel and Olive Muriel; married Ela Babb, May 18, 1985; children: Simone Moore. **Educ:** Univ WI, Kingston, Jamaica, BSc, 1963; Univ London, MA, 1968; Brooklyn Law Sch, attended 1978; Princeton Univ. **Career:** Douglas Col, Rutgers Univ, New Brunswick, NJ, lectr, 1971-75; Wachtell Lipton Rosen Katz, NY, paralegal, 1975-76; Atty Gen, State NY, law clerk, 1976-78; Bronx County, NY, asst dist atty, 1978-79; Brooklyn, NY, self-employed atty, 1979-. **Orgs:** Chmn, Legal Redress Comt, Nat Asn Advan Colored People, Jamaica Chap, 1978-81; St Albans Local Develop Corp, 1979-82; pres, Macon B Allen Bar Asn, 1980-83; pres, Carribean Action Lobby, 1981-82; bd mem, Nat Bar Asn, 1981-83; Nat Conf Black Lawyers, 1982-84; bd mem, Medgar Evers Ctr Law & Social Justice, 1986-. **Honors/Awds:** Am Jurisp Award, Lawyers Coop Publ House, 1976; Leadership Award, Sesame Flyers Int, 1987; Achievement & Community Serv Award, Medgar Evers Col, 1987; Distinguished Serv Award, Jamaica Nat Movement, 1988; Humanitarian Award, Vidcap Inc, 1989. **Special Achievements:** Author of The Simpson-Mazzoli Bill: Two Steps Forward, One Step Backward, 1984; author of The History of African Liberation Movements from Os Palmares to Montgomery, 1989; author of collection of articles, 1989. **Business Addr:** Attorney, Private Practice, 15 Ct St Suite 1212, Brooklyn, NY 11241.*

MOORE, CORNELL LEVERETTE

Lawyer, president (organization). **Personal:** Born Sep 18, 1939, Tignall, GA; son of Luetta T and Jesse L; married Wenda Weekes; children: Lynne M, Jonathon C & Meredith L. **Educ:** Va Union Univ, AB, 1961; Howard Univ Law Sch, JD, 1964. **Career:** US Treas, staff atty, 1962-64; Crocker Bank, trust admin, 1964-66; Comptroller Currency, US Treas, regional coun, 1966-68; NW Nat Bank Minneapolis, asst vpres & legal officer, 1968-70; Shelter Mortgage Co Inc, exec vpres & dir, 1970-73; Shelard Nat Bank, dir, 1973-78; Hennepin Co Bar Found, pres, 1975-78; Marquette, Golden Valley Bank, dir, 1978-2002; Lease More Equipment Inc, pres & chief exec officer, 1977-86; Miller & Schroeder Financial Inc, sr vpres & gen coun, 1987-95; Dorsey & Whitney, partner, 1995-. **Orgs:** Trustee, Dunwoody Inst; dir, Greater Minneapolis Housing Corp; trustee, Va Union Univ; trustee, Howard Univ; dir, Greater Minneapolis Visitors & Conv Assoc; trustee, Johnson C Smith Univ; chmn, Minneapolis Pub Housing Authority; Minneapolis Aquatennial Commodore, 1998; Sigma Pi Phi; Grand Sire Archon-elect, 2004. **Honors/Awds:** Whitney Young Award, Boy Scouts Am, Minneapolis, MN. **Business Addr:** Partner, Dorsey and Whitney LLP, 50 S 6th St Suite 1500, Minneapolis, MN 55402-1498, **Business Phone:** (612)340-6331.

MOORE, CYNTHIA M

Journalist. **Personal:** Born Nov 11, 1963, Columbus, OH; daughter of Jackie and Barbara Price Hughes. **Educ:** Ohio State Univ, Columbus, OH, BA, 1990. **Career:** WSYX, TV 6, ABC, Good Morning Columbus, producer, currently. **Orgs:** Nat Asn Black Journalists. **Honors/Awds:** American Heart Association Media Award, 1992. **Home Addr:** 3751 Rosewell Dr, Columbus, OH 43227. **Business Addr:** Producer, WSYX-TV 6 ABC, 1261 Dublin Rd, Columbus, OH 43215, **Business Phone:** (614)481-6659.

MOORE, DAMON E.

Football player. **Personal:** Born Sep 15, 1976, Fostoria, OH; son of Cleo (deceased) and Addie. **Educ:** Ohio State Univ. **Career:** Football player (retired); Philadelphia Eagles, defensive back, 1999-2001; Chicago Bears, 2002.

MOORE, DAVID BERNARD, II

Educator. **Personal:** Born Jul 13, 1940, Uniontown, AL. **Educ:** Ala State Univ, BS, 1960; Fordham Univ, Spec educ, 1962; Univ AL, MA, 1972. **Career:** Eductor (retired); Superior Graphics, dir, 1973-79; RC Hatch HS, teacher, 1981-90. **Orgs:** Pres, Uniontown Civic League, 1970-; city Counman, 1972-. **Honors/Awds:** Versality Award, 1975. *

MOORE, DAVID M

Executive. **Personal:** Born May 2, 1955, Chattanooga, TN; son of Clara S and David. **Educ:** Univ Wis, Eau Claire, Wis, BA, bus admin, 1986. **Career:** Miller Brewing Co, Milwaukee, Wis, group mgr, 1977-82; Miller Brewing Co, San Francisco, Calif, area mgr, 1982-85; Miller Brewing Co, Los Angeles, Calif, mkt develop mgr, 1986; Quali Croutons Inc, Chicago, Ill, founder, 1986-. **Business Addr:** Founder, Quality Croutons Inc, 825-29 W 37th Place, Chicago, IL 60609, **Business Phone:** (312)927-8200.

MOORE, DERRICK C.

Writer, football player, football coach. **Personal:** Born Oct 13, 1967, Albany, GA; married Stephanie; children: 2. **Educ:** Northeastern Okla State Univ. **Career:** Football player (retired),

author, motivational speaker; Atlanta Falcons, running back, 1992; Detroit Lions, running back, 1993-94; Carolina Panthers, running back, 1995; Ariz Cardinals, running back, 1996-2001; Ga Tech, Athletic Dept, adv & counr, campus dir, develop coach & chaplain; Books: The Great Adventure.Tv: The Big 4-0, Tv land. **Orgs:** Fel Christian Athletes; Best Friends Found. **Honors/Awds:** AIA All-American; Most Valuable Player, 1992; Hula Bowl. **Business Addr:** Member, Fellowship of Christian Athletes, 8701 Leeds Rd, Kansas City, MO 64129, **Business Phone:** (770)316-5273.

MOORE, EDDIE N., JR.

School administrator. **Educ:** Pa State Univ, BS, acct, 1968; Katz Bus Sch, Univ Pittsburgh, MBA. **Career:** Gulf Oil Corp, var positions, 1971-85; Commonwealth Va, asst controller, 1985-88, : Controller, Col William & Mary, 1988-90; Dept Treas, state treas, 1990-93; Va State Univ, pres, 1993-. **Orgs:** Omega Psi Phi Fraternity Inc; Forum Club; Virginia Heroes Inc; chmn, Finance Comn Cent Intercollegiate Athletic Asn; Va Bd Agr, Va Ctr Innovative Technol, Va Hist Soc & Am Asn Col Teacher Educ; chair, Vantagepoint Funds Bd; bd, Universal Corp; St James Baptist Church; Joint Comn Reporting Req; United Way Servs; The Greater Richmond Chamber Com. **Honors/Awds:** Dr Martin Luther King Jr Legacy Award, 1995; Distinguished Alumnus Award, Penn State Univ, 1999; Distinguished Educational Leadership Award, Thurgood Marshall Scholar Found, 2000; Distinguished Alumnus Award, KatzBus Sch, 2001. **Military Serv:** AUS, First Lt; Bronze Star, Army Commendation Medal. **Business Addr:** President, Virginia State University, 1 Hayden Dr, PO Box 9001, Petersburg, VA 23806.

MOORE, ELIZABETH D

Lawyer. **Personal:** Born Jul 29, 1954, Queens, NY; daughter of William A and M Doreen; married Jimmy L Miller, Dec 21, 1984. **Educ:** NY State Sch Indust & Labor Rels Cornell Univ, BS, 1975; St John's Univ Sch Law, JD, 1978. **Career:** Consol Edison Co New York, atty, 1978-79; Am Express Co, atty, 1979-80; Equitable Life Assurance Soc, mgr, equal opportunity, 1981; Off Coun Gov, asst coun, 1981-83, first asst coun, 1983-87; Gov Off Employee Rels, dir, 1987-90; NY State Ethics Comn, chairperson, 1988-90; NY State Gov, Off Coun Gov, coun gov, 1991-94; GovOff, dir; Nixon Peabody LLP, partner, currently. **Orgs:** Bd dirs, Ctr Women GOV; co-chair, Task Force NYS Pub Workforce 21st Century; chchair, NYS/CSEA COM Work Environ & Productivity; bd trustees, Cath Interracial Coun; Govs Exec Comn Affirmative Action; Int Personnel Mgt Asn; Nat Asn State DRRs Employee Rels; Nat Forum Black Pub ADRs; Nat Pub Employer Labor Rels Asn; NY Joint Labor/Mgt Coms; State Acad Pub Admin; Women Exec State Gov; Gov Task Force Work & Family; Governor's Spec Prosecutor Screening Com; Govs Task Force Bias-Related Violence; bd trustees, Rochester Inst Technol; gov, NY State Second Dept Judicial Screening Comt. **Honors/Awds:** Governor Mario M Cuomo, nominated for the 9th Annual Salute to Young Women Achievers Award, 1985; Legislative Mobilization Appreciation Award, Nat Asn Advan Colored People, 1986; Toll fel, Nat Coun State Govs, 1987; Westchester County Black Women's Political Caucus Leadership Award, 1989; John E Burton Award, State Univ NY, 1990; Honorary Doctor of Civil Law, St John's Univ; Diversity Champion Award, New York City Bar Asn, 2006; Groat Award, Cornell Univ Sch Indust Rels; Leaders for a New Century Legal Community Award, Asn Black Women Atty. **Business Phone:** (212)940-3052.

MOORE, EMANUEL A

Lawyer. **Personal:** Born Nov 22, 1941, Brooklyn, NY; son of Hubert and Hilda Waterman; married Hilda Rosa Garcia, Nov 24, 1999. **Educ:** New York Univ, BS, Willard J Martin Scholar, James Talcott Scholar 1963; NY Law Sch, JD Thurgood Marshall Scholar, 1966. **Career:** Justice Dept, Wash, Civil Rights Div, atty, 1966-68; Queens Co NY, asst dist atty, 1968; Off Gen Coun AID Wash, legal adv, 1968-70; Eastern Dist NY, US atty, 1970-72; US Atty Off Eastern Dist NY, chief consumer protect secy, 1972-74; US Fed Energy Admin, dir compliance & enforcement, 1974-77; Pvt Pract, atty 1977-; Sunshine Quest Realty Inc, atty law, currently. **Orgs:** Ed, NY Law Forum, 1965-66; Chinese Am Lions Club, NY, Knighted Order St George & Constantine, 1986; pres, Atlantic Palace Condo Asn, 1989-; app US magistrate, Selection Com, Eastern Dist, NY, 1992-; dir, Nat Macon B Allen Black Bar Asn; dir, NY Law Sch Alumni Asn. **Honors/Awds:** American Jurisprudence Award Academic Excellence in Law of Evidence, 1965; Vice President Award Academic Excellence, 1966. **Home Addr:** 125-10 Queens Blvd, Kew Gardens, NY 11415, **Home Phone:** (718)793-5535. **Business Addr:** Attorney at Law, Real Estate Broker, Sunshine Quest Realty Inc, 1330 N John Young Pkwy, Kissimmee, FL 34741, **Business Phone:** (407)931-0003.

MOORE, ETTA R

Manager, executive. **Personal:** Born Jan 9, 1957, Oklahoma City, OK; daughter of Myrtle Holloway; divorced; children: DeAngelo. **Educ:** Okla State Univ, BS, mkt, 1979. **Career:** Woolco Dept Store, asst div mgr, 1979-81; Pan Okla Commun, sales admin, 1981-83; Red Lands Girl Scout Coun, field dir, 1984-89; Girl Scouts-Lone Star Coun, dir mem & prog, 1989-92, asst exec dir, 1992-93, exec dir, 1993, chief exec officer, currently. **Orgs:** Grad adv, AKA Sorority Inc, 1981-83; treas, High Sch Alumni Class, 1985-; bd mem, exec staff, Asn Girl Scout; Am Bus Women's Asn,

1987-89; Urban League, 1987; YWCA Leader Luncheon Comt, 1989-93; Austin Independent Sch Dist Vol Adv Comt, 1989-92, chair 1991-92; Regist Prof Camp Planner, 1990; Capital Area Chamber Com, 1990-; St Stephen's Missionary Baptist Church: Sunday Sch Teacher, Vacation Bible Sch Worker, 1990-; vol, Dessau Elem Sch, 1991-93; vol, Hyde Park Baptist Elem Sch, 1993-95; bd dirs, Adopt-A-Sch, 1992-, comt chair, 1993, treas; E Austin Rotary Club Charter; Women's Chamber Com; exec coun chair, United Way/Capital Area; bd dirs, comt co-chair, Leadership Austin, 1995-; bd dirs, agency rep, UW/CA; County Invest Comt. **Honors/Awds:** Appreciation Pin, Girl Scouts-Lone Star Coun, 1992; Honor Pin, Girl Scouts-Lone Star Coun 1993; Thanks Badge, Girl Scouts-Lone Star Coun, 1994. **Business Addr:** Chief Executive Officer, Girl Scouts-Lone Star Council, 12012 Pk 35 Cir, Austin, TX 78753, **Business Phone:** (512)453-7391 Ext 108.

MOORE, EVELYN K.

Executive. **Personal:** Born Jul 29, 1937, Detroit, MI. **Educ:** Eastern MI Univ, BS, 1960; Univ MI, MA, 1960. **Career:** Nat Black Child Develop Inst Wash, DC, dir, 1973, pres & chief exec officer, currently. **Orgs:** bd dir, Children's Lobby; N Am Adoption Bd; adv, comt DC Citizens Pub Educ; consult, US Office Educ; Nat Asn Educ Young Children. **Honors/Awds:** Outstanding Young Woman of State of MI, 1970. **Business Phone:** (202)387-1281.

MOORE, EVIA BRIGGS

Educator. **Personal:** Born Jan 18, 1943, Ripley, MS; daughter of Vance and Ruby Simelton; divorced; children: Robert Vance Moore. **Educ:** Tougaloo Coll, BA, 1965; Syracuse Univ, MSLS, 1970; Univ Wis Madison, cert libr admin; Univ Pac, doctoral, candidate. **Career:** Tougaloo Col, acquisitions librn, 1966-74; Jackson State Univ, asst prof libr sci, 1974-75; San Joaquin Delta Col, periodicals & reference librn, 1977-90; librn & coordr pub serv, 1990-91, interim dir affirmative action, 1991-92, librarian & coordr pub serv, 1992-95, interim dir affirmative action, 1995-96, dir libr serv, Goleman Libr, div dean, currently. **Orgs:** Am Library asn; California Library asn; Phi Delta Kappa (Univ the Pacific Chapter); Amer Asn Univ Women, 1975-2003; Stockton Symphony League, 1980-93; The Links Inc, Stockton Chapter, 1977-2003; Jack & Jill America, 1988-94; Delta Sigma Theta Sorority, 1976-88; Stockton Seaport Rotary, 2001-03. **Honors/Awds:** Jackson/Tougaloo Coll, Alumin Club Awd, 1968; San Joaquin County Commission on the Status of Women, Susan B Anthony Awd, 1997; City of Stockton, certificate of recognition, July 2001. **Special Achievements:** Selected for Leadership Skills Seminar for Women, California Community Colleges, 1987, 1993; elected Academic Senate President Delta College, 1990-91.

MOORE, FLOREESE NAOMI

Educator, school administrator. **Personal:** Born Mar 15, 1940, Wilson, NC; daughter of Naomi Jones Lucas and Wiley Floyd Lucas; divorced; children: Lemuel Wiley, Lyndon Benjamin. **Educ:** W Chester State Univ, BS, 1974; Univ Delaware, MI, 1979; Nova Univ, EdD, 1984; OH State Univ. **Career:** Red Cross, Japan, gen off worker, 1961-63; Vita Foods Inc, bookkeeper, 1963-64; Chesapeake Potomac Telephone Co, operator, 1964-66; Doctors Bookkeeping, secy, 1966-68; New Castle Co, Del Pub Sch, human rels sp, teacher, 1968-79; Sch Bd Alachua, teacher, adminr, prin, asst supt, 1979-90; Fla Asn Exceptional Sch Adminrs, founder, 1984; Columbus Pub Sch, asst supt, 1990, elem prin, currently. **Orgs:** Exec bd, Coun Except C, 1980-84; Delta Sigma Theta Sorority int comn, 1982; secy, Phi Delta Kappa, 1983; Altrussa Club Gainesville; Fla Orgn Instrnl Leaders, 1984-90; arts comn, teens comn, Links Inc, 1985-; Am Asn Sch Adminrs, 1985-; Buckeye Asn Sch Adminrs, 1990-; Delta Sigma Theta. **Honors/Awds:** Sch Bd Merit Award, Sch Bd Alachua, 1981; Founder's Award, Fla Asn Exceptional Sch Adminrs, 1986; The Ebony Appreciation Award, City Gainesville, 1988; Mayor's Proclamation Award, 1988. **Special Achievements:** Author: "Operant Treatment of Asthmatic Responding with the Parent as Therapist," Behavior Journal, 1973; "Implementation of Residential School Age Children into the Public Schools," presented at the International Conference for the Council for Exceptional Children; "Applying Business Mgt and Organization Develop Practice to a Public School Organization," presented at the Fourteenth Annual Conference of the Nat Council of States on Inservice Education, 1989; Peer Assistance and Review: Helping Entry Year & Veteran Teachers, Third Annual National Evaluation Inst, 1994; Is Your Organization Ready, Fifth Annual National Conference of the National Association for Multicultural Education. **Business Addr:** Elementary Principal, Columbus Public Schools, 270 E State St, Columbus, OH 43215, **Business Phone:** (614)365-5715.*

MOORE, FRED HENDERSON

Lawyer. **Personal:** Born Jul 25, 1934, Charleston County, SC; married Louise Smalls; children: Fredena, Melissa, Fred, Louis, Rembert. **Educ:** SC State Col, 1956; Roosevelt Univ, Chicago, 1956; Allen Univ, BS, 1957; Howard Episcopal, JD, 1960; Teamers Sch Religion, DD, 1976; Stephens Christian Inst, 1976; Reform Episcapal Seminary. **Career:** self-employed atty, 1977. **Orgs:** Corp coun, Nat Advan Asn Colored People, 1960; Black Rep Party; Silver Elephant Club; 1st Dist Coun SC Conf Nat Advan Asn Colored People; assoc pastor, Payne RMUE Church; assoc coun, NC Mutual Ins Co; Omega Psi Phy Frat. **Honors/Awds:** Youth award, Nat Advan Asn Colored People, 1957; Memorial

Award, Charles Drew, 1957. **Special Achievements:** Book: Angry Black South, co-author, 1960. **Business Addr:** Attorney, 115 St Margaret St, Charleston, SC 29403.*

MOORE, GARY
Chief executive officer. **Career:** Texoma Ford, chief exec officer, pres, currently. **Orgs:** Sherman Chamber Com; Ford Motor Minority Dealers Asn; Pottsboro Area Chamber Com; Dension Chamber Com. **Business Addr:** Chief Executive Officer, Texoma Ford, 215 Hwy 75 N, PO Box 693, Denison, TX 75020, **Business Phone:** (903)465-5671.*

MOORE, GARY E
School administrator, manager. **Personal:** Born Dec 8, 1962, Rochester, NY; son of Frank Lewis and Christine Enge; married Marva Elaine, Jul 1, 1989. **Educ:** Clarion Univ Pa, BS, Acct, 1985, MS, Commun, 1988. **Career:** Clarion Univ, grad asst; 1985, admissions recruiter, 1987, project dir; Univ Pa, asst dir admissiona; 332nd Eng Co (DT), Kittanning Pa, Co comdr; GEM Presentation Graphics, pres, owner, currently. **Orgs:** Grad adv, Black Stud Union, 1985-87; chair, editor, Am Mktg Asn Newsletter, 1986-87; chmn, editor, Black Stud Union Newsletter, 1987; human relations subcomm, Clarion Univ; Acct Club, Am Mkt Asn; Soc Mil Engrs, 1987; Reserve Officers Asn, 1989. **Honors/Awds:** Black Stud Union Acad Achievement Award; Grad Assistantship, Clarion Univ Pa, 1985-87. **Military Serv:** USAR, second lt, platoon leader, training & evaluation, equipment accountability, 1984-86; AUS, second lt, 4 yrs; Merit of Achievement, 1986. **Business Addr:** Project Director, Clarion University of Pennsylvania, Department of Communication, PO Box 250, Clarion, PA 16214, **Business Phone:** (814)226-2306.

MOORE, GEORGE THOMAS
Scientist. **Personal:** Born Jun 2, 1945, Owensboro, KY; married Peggy Frances Jouett. **Educ:** KY State Univ, BS, chem & math, 1967; Univ Dayton, MS inorg chem., 1971; Environ Health Univ Cincinnati Med Ctr, PhD, 1978. **Career:** Monsanto Res Corp Mound Lab, res chemist, 1967-72; US DOE Pittsburgh Energy Tech Ctr, res indust hygienist, 1978-79, chief occup health br, 1979-; US Environ Protection Agency, industrial hygenist, currently. **Orgs:** Unity Lodge 115 Price Hall affil, 1963-; Omega Psi Phi Fraternity, 1964-; Am Chem Soc, 1975-; Air Pollution Control Asn, 1977-; Am Indust Hygiene Asn, 1978-; supt, Ebenezer Baptist Church Sunday Sch, 1980-. **Honors/Awds:** Hon French Award, Alpha Mu Gamma French Soc. **Business Addr:** Project Manager, U.S. Environmental Protection Agency, 26 W Martin Luther King Dr, Pittsburgh, PA 15236, **Business Phone:** (513)569-7991.

MOORE, GREGORY B
Electronics engineer, manager. **Personal:** Born Mar 27, 1962, New York, NY; son of Vera. **Educ:** Norfolk State Univ, BS, ind educ, 1987. **Career:** Norfolk State Univ, head resident asst, 1982-86, electrical lab asst, 1986-87; Cox Cable Hampton Roads, repair dispatch oper, 1987-88, radio dispatcher, 1988-89; signal leakage auditor, 1989-91; telecommunicator I, 1992-97, help desk tech, 1997-99, network monitoring coordr, 1999-2000, systs opers specialist II (residential), 2000-02; Sr Systs Support Opers Specialist II (commercial), 2002-03, Sr Technical Support Specialist (telephony), 2003-. **Orgs:** Nat Technical Asn, bd dirs, 1984-85, stud dir, 1984-85, 1987-89; Stud Nat Asn, pres, 1984-85, 1987-89, stud adv, 1985-86; Norfolk State Univ, SNTA; Stud Asn Norfolk State Univ, cofounder, 1982-86; Concerned Citizens for Polit Educ Norfolk, treas, 1988-; 3rd Dist Delegate, Norfolk City Democratic Comt Va, 1996-97; 89th Precinct Chairmen, Norfolk City Democratic Comt Va, 1996-99; 89th House Dist Norfolk City Democratic Comt, vchair, 1998-2001; 5th Senate Dist Norfolk City Democratic Comt Va, vchair, 2001-. **Honors/Awds:** Black Engineer of the Year Award, nominee, 1989; Outstanding Young Men of America, 1989; Outstanding Person of the 20th Century, 1998-01. **Home Addr:** 3017 Somme Ave, Norfolk, VA 23509-1859. **Business Addr:** Senior Technical Suppport Specialist, Commercial Test Desk Telephony Services, Cox Communications, Cox Business Services, System Operations Center, 4585 Village Ave, Norfolk, VA 23502-2034, **Business Phone:** (757)369-4584.

MOORE, GWEN
Executive, government official. **Personal:** Born in Michigan; married Ronald Dobson; children: Ronald Dobson II. **Educ:** Calif State Univ, LA, BA, teaching,1963; Univ Southern Calif, MPA. **Career:** Government Official (retired); LA County, dep probation officer, 1963-69; Gr LA Comm Action Agency, dir pub affairs & dir personnel, 1969-76; Social Action Res Ctr, LA, consult, 1970-72; LA Community Col, bd trustees, 1975; Compton Community Col, instr, 1975; Inner City Info Syst LA, consult, 1976-77; Calif State Assembly, 1978-94, chairperson assembly subcomm cable TV, 1982, chair assembly utilities & com comm, 1983-94; G & M Commun, pres, currently. **Orgs:** Western regional chairperson, Nat Black Caucus State Legislators; regional vice chairperson, Nat Conf Legis; Calif Pub Broadcasting Task Force; Common State Govt Orgn & Econ; platform comm, Dem Nat Comm; Calif Elected Women's Asn Educ & Res; Dem Women's Forum; LA Coalition 100 Black Women; Nat Women's Polit Caucus; YWCA; United Negro Col Fund; Calif Legis Black Caucus; regional dir, Women's Network Nat Caucus State Legis; secy, Nat Orgn Black Elected Legis Women (Nobel/Women). **Honors/Awds:** Newsmaker of the Year Award, Nat Asn Media Women, 1983; Legislator of the Year, Nat Alliance of Supermarket Shoppers Golden Shopping Cart Award, 1983; Nat Caucus of Black State Legislators Award, 1984; Calif State Package Store & Tavern Owner's Asn Award, 1984; Meritorious Award, Outstanding Service, Women Good Govt; Nat Asn Minorities Cable's. **Business Addr:** President, GEM Communications Group Public Relations Firm, 4201 Wilshire Blvd Suite 301, Los Angeles, CA 90010, **Business Phone:** (323)954-3777.

MOORE, DR. HAROLD EARL, JR.
Physician, educator. **Personal:** Born Sep 5, 1954, San Antonio, TX; son of Harold Earl Moore Sr and Barbara Stewart. **Educ:** Fla A&M Univ, 1972-76; Morehouse Col, BS, 1978; Morehouse Sch Med,1981-83; Howard Univ, Col Med, MD, 1985; Morehouse Sch Med, Dept Family Med, Fac Develop Fel, 1994-95. **Career:** Fla State Univ, Dept Psychol & Neuro-Histology, lab technician, res, Dr.Karen Berkley, 1974-75; Cornell Univ Col Pharmacol, lab technician,1979-80; Harlem Hosp, Gen Surg Internship, 1985-86; Morehouse Sch Med,family practice residency, 1986-88; Ga Regional Hosp, Atlanta, ER physician, 1988-89; Fulton County Teen Clinics, physician, 1988-89;Sterling Group, ER physician, 1989-95; Stewart-Webster Rural Health Inc, physician, 1989-91; Southeastern Health Servs Inc, physician, beginning1991; Emory Clinic Inc, physician, 1993-, asst prof, currently; pvt pract, currently. **Orgs:** Am Acad Family Physicians, 1987-; Ga State Med Asn, 1988-; Am Med Asn,1989-; Ga Acad Family Physicians, 1983-; Nat Med Asn, 1987-; Morehouse Sch Med Nat Alumni Asn, 1983, pres, 1993; Howard Univ Col Med Alumni Asn, 1985-; Kappa Alpha Psi Fraternity Inc, 1989-. **Honors/Awds:** Morehouse Sch Med, Dean's Leadership Award, 1982; 'Fellow of American Academy of Family Physicians', 1994; Outstanding Young Doctor Award,Dollar & Sense Mag, 1991; 'honorary doctor of medicine', Morehouse Sch Med, 2000. **Home Addr:** 11 Dunwoody Pk Suite 150, Atlanta, GA 30338, **Home Phone:** (404)778-6920. **Business Addr:** Physician, Emory Clinic Inc, 2764 Candler Rd, Decatur, GA 30034, **Business Phone:** (404)778-8600.

MOORE, HAZEL STAMPS
Librarian. **Personal:** Born Jan 10, 1924, Learned, MS; daughter of Andrew Stamps and Seretha Hicks Stamps; married Wilbur D, May 30, 1948 (died 1984); children: Wibur Dexter & Debra M Carter. **Educ:** Southern Christian Inst Jr Col, cert, 1945; Tougaloo Col, BA (cum laude), 1947; Atlanta Univ, MS, libr sci, 1955; Wash Univ, St Louis, Mo; Xavier Univ; La State Univ; Univ New Orleans; Tulane Univ. **Career:** Librarian (retired); Tougaloo Col, librn, 1947; Oakley Training Sch, teacher, librn, 1947-49; Tougaloo Col, Prep Sch, teacher, from asst librn to librn, 1949-57; Booker T Wash High Sch, head librn, 1957-61, 1962-66 & 1967-72; St Louis Pub Libr, sr ref librn, 1961-62; New Orleans Pub Schs, Proj 1089-B, 1095-A & 1200-G, asst supvr, 1966-67; Marion Abramson High Sch, head librn, 1972-91; New Orleans Pub Schs, Adult Educ Ctr, intern; One Church One School, Cent Congregational United Church Christ, dir, 1990-93. **Orgs:** Numrous memberships in various organizations including Am Libr Asn; Am Asn Sch Librarians; La Libr Asn; La Asn Sch Librarians; Catholic Libr Asn, Greater New Orleans Unit, 1958-91; La Asn Educ Commun & Technol; La Asn Comput Users Educr; United Teachers New Orleans Retired Chap; Southern Asn Cols & Schs Teams; Nat Coun Negro Women; Tougoloo Alumnae Club; Snacirema Club. **Honors/Awds:** PTA Outstanding Service Award, Abramson; Guidance Department Award, Landry; Modisette Award, La Libr Asn; Spec Citation, US Dept Educ. **Special Achievements:** Author, How to Conduct a Dial-an-Author Program, LLA Bulletin, 1989. **Home Addr:** 5931 Congress Dr, New Orleans, LA 70126, **Home Phone:** (504)282-0184.

MOORE, HELEN D S
Educator, founder (originator). **Personal:** Born Jan 21, 1932, Baldwyn, MS; married Elijah; children: Michelle, Pamela & Elijah. **Educ:** Miss Indust Col, BA, 1951; Tenn State Univ, MS, 1957; Delta State Univ, educ specialist, 1977. **Career:** Teacher (retired), clergy; Jr, Sr, HS, teacher, four yrs; Primary Grades, teacher, 1953-75; Greenville Municipal Sch Dist, elem prin, 1975-90; AME Church, ordained minister, 1994; Day spring Ministries Inc, founder & pres, currently. **Orgs:** Voter Reg; Polit Camp; Ad Hoc Comm; lectr, Wash County Polit Action Comm; pres, YWCA, 1950-51; pres, Greenville Teacher Asn; pres, Miss Asn Educ, 1978-79; youth adv, St Matthew AME Church, 1977; adv, Teenette Art & Civic Club; Modern Art & Civic Club, Nat Asn Advan Colored People, Nat Fed Colored Women's Club; bd dirs, NEA, 1984-88; pastor, Disney Chapel AME Church; Greenville Area Chamber Com. **Honors/Awds:** NSF Grant, Eastern Mich Univ, 1963; Citizen Award, NAACP, 1975; Citizenship Award, WB Derrick Masonic Lodge, 1976; Educ Award CivilLiberties Elks, 1976; Comm Seventh Day Adventist Church Award. **Home Phone:** (662)334-9914. **Business Addr:** Founder, President, Dayspring Ministries Inc, 3583 Forest Dr, Greenville, MS 38703.

MOORE, HERMAN JOSEPH
Football player, president (organization). **Personal:** Born Oct 20, 1969, Danville, VA; married Angela; children: Aaron & Ashton. **Educ:** Univ Va, BA, rhetoric & communs studies, 1991. **Career:** Football player (retired), executive; Detroit Lions, wide receiver,1991-2001; NY Giants, wide receiver, 2002; HJM Enterprises, pres & chief exec officer, 2001-; AH!MOORE Int Caf, owner, 2002-. **Orgs:** Founder, Catch 84 Found. **Honors/Awds:** Offensive Most Valuable Player, Detroit Lions, 1995; True Value & NFL Man of the Year, Detroit Lions, 1995, 1996; Pro Bowl selection, 1994-97; team All-Pro Selection, 1995-97. **Business Addr:** President, Chief Executive Officer, HJM Enterprises, 2600 Auburn Rd, Auburn Hills, MI 48326, **Business Phone:** (248)853-4013.

MOORE, HOWARD, JR.
Lawyer. **Personal:** Born Feb 28, 1932, Atlanta, GA; married Jane Bond; children: Grace, Constance, Kojo. **Educ:** Morehouse Col, AB, 1954; Boston Univ, LLB, 1960. **Career:** Moore & Lawrence, atty. **Orgs:** Nat Conf Black Lawyers; Charles Houston Law Club; Nat Lawyers Guild; Nat Emergency Civil Liberties Com; Am Civil Liberties Union; Fedn Southern Coop; gen counr, Stud Nonviolent Coord Comt. **Honors/Awds:** Martin Luther King Jr Award, Howard Univ, 1972; Distinguished Son Morehouse Col, 1973; Centennial Award, Boston Univ, 1973; Distinguished Service, Nat Col Advocacy, Asn Am Trial Lawyers, 1975. **Military Serv:** AUS pfc 1954-56. **Business Addr:** Attorney, Moore & Moore, 445 Bellevue Ave 3rd Fl, Oakland, CA 94610.*

MOORE, JANE BOND
Lawyer. **Personal:** Born Sep 1, 1938, Nashville, TN; daughter of Horace Mann and Julia Washington; married Howard; children: Grace, Constance & Kojo. **Educ:** Spelman Col Atlanta, AB, 1959; Boalt Hall Univ Calif, JS, 1975. **Career:** So Regional Coun, res asst, 1961-63; So Christian Leadership Conf, res asst, 1963-64; Moore & Bell, assoc atty, 1975-76; Open Rd, admin 1976-77; Bank Calif, asst coun, 1977-80; Fed Trade Comn, San Francisco, CA, atty, 1980-83; Moore & Moore Attorneys Law, Oakland, CA, partner, 1983-90; Oakland Unified Sch Dist, Oakland, CA, assoc coun, 1990-, dep gen coun, 1995-2001; pvt pract, 2001-; John F Kennedy Sch Law, fac, currently. **Orgs:** Charles Houston Bar Asn. **Home Addr:** 1880 San Pedro, Berkeley, CA 94707. **Business Addr:** Faculty, John F Kennedy School of Law, 100 Ellinwood Way Pleasant Hill, Oakland, CA 94523, **Business Phone:** (925)969-3300.

MOORE, DR. JEAN E.
Television producer, educator, radio host. **Personal:** Born in New York, NY; daughter of Hugh Campbell and Theodora Campbell; married Robert M Moore Jr; children: Robert III & Doreen Moore-Closson. **Educ:** Hunter Col, BA; Bryn Mawr Col, MSS; Temple Univ, EdD, 1978. **Career:** Vet Admin, Pa, Clin Social Work Serv, asst chief; Redevelop Auth City Philadelphia, social work specialist; Model Cities US Dept Housing & Urban Develop, human serv adv; Temple Univ, Sch Soc Admin, assoc prof, 1969-89, assoc prof emer, currently; Cheyney Univ, Pa, exec asst to pres, 1985-91; Univ Md Eastern Shore, Princess Anne, MD, vpres inst advan, 1991-97; WESM-FM, radio host, 1994-97; WRTI-Temple Univ, Univ Forum, creator, host & exec producer, currently. **Orgs:** Nat Assn Social Workers; Acad Cert Soc Workers; Coun Soc Work Educ; Pa Black Conf Higher Educ; team chairperson & team mem, Comn Higher Educ, Middle States Assn Col & Schs; Act 101 reviewer & eval Commonwealth Pa; US Dept Educ; reviewer & pres, Spectrum Health Serv; brd dirs comm, Y Eastern Del County; chairperson, Fair Housing Coun Suburban Philadelphia; elder,Lansdowne Presbyterian Church; Delta Sigma Theta Sorority; Phi DeltaKappa; Phi Beta Kappa; bd trustees, Community Col Philadelphia; LackawannaJr Col; brd, C's Serv Inc; int brd adv, Radio Peace Int; Alpha Chi Alpha. **Honors/Awds:** Bronze/Silver Medals for Writings; Outstanding Educator, 1977; Alumni Award, Col Educ, 1978; Educator Achievement Award, 1979; Award Chapel Four Chaplains; Community Service Award, Cheyney Univ, 1990, President's Dedication Award, 1991; Appreciation Award, Spectrum Health Serv, 1992; Community Award, 1999-2001; Crystal Award Excellence; Crystal Award Distinction; 6 CINDY Regional Awards; 5 CINDY Intl Awards, Achievement in Radio Crystal Award, 2000; Broadcast Education Assn Award, 2000. **Business Phone:** (215)204-8405.

MOORE, JERALD CHRISTOPHER
Football player. **Personal:** Born Nov 20, 1974, Houston, TX. **Educ:** Univ Okla. **Career:** St Louis Rams, running back, 1996-98; New Orleans Saints, 2000.

MOORE, JERRY A, JR.
Clergy. **Personal:** Born Jun 12, 1918, Minden, LA; son of Jerry A, Sr and Mae Dee; married Ettyce Hill, Jan 14, 1946; children: Jerry III & Juran D. **Educ:** Morehouse Col, BA, 1940; Howard Univ, BD, 1943, MA, 1957. **Career:** Clergy (retired); Nineteenth Street Baptist Church, pastor, 1946-96; Howard Univ, Baptist chaplain, 1958; Wash Baptist Sem, 1964; DC, councilman, 1969-84. **Orgs:** Mem-at-large, DC City Council, 1970-84; past pres Baptist Conv Wash DC & Vincinity; past pres, Int Soc Christian Endwavor; past pres, Wash Metro Area Coun Govts; past chair, public works Com DC Council; Rock Creek East Civic Asn; Nat Asn Advan Colored People; Pigskin Club; Urban League; Capitol City Rep Club; past exec secy, Home Mission Bd, NBC, 1985-97. **Honors/Awds:**

Washington Area Contractors Award, 1971; NAACP Service Award, 1972; Capitol City Rep Club Lincoln Award, 1974; Minority Transportation Officials Award, 1986. **Home Addr:** 1612 Buchanan St NW, Washington, DC 20011. **Business Addr:** Pastor Emeritus, Nineteenth St Baptist Church, 4606 16th St NW, Washington, DC 20011, **Business Phone:** (202)882-3127.

MOORE, JESSE A
Automotive executive, business owner, chief executive officer. **Career:** Warner Robins Olds-Cadillac-Pontiac-GMC, ceo, owner, currently; full service auto body shops, owner. **Orgs:** Metropolitan Bus League; Gen Motors Minority Dealer Develop prog. **Business Phone:** (912)929-0222.

MOORE, JOHN BRIAN
Basketball player. **Personal:** Born Mar 3, 1958, Altoona, PA; married Natalie. **Educ:** Univ Tex, Austin, phys educ, 1979. **Career:** Basketball player (retired); San Antonio Spurs, 1980-88; New Jersey Nets, 1988; San Antonio Spurs, 1990; Tulsa Fast Breakers, 1990; AAU basketball team, coach, currently. **Honors/Awds:** All-Southwest Conf, TX.

MOORE, JOHN WESLEY, JR.
Executive, vice president (organization). **Personal:** Born Mar 10, 1948, Martins Ferry, OH; married Brenda Scott; children: Kelly Shannon, Ryan Wesley, Johnathan Morgan & Nicholas Patrick. **Educ:** W Liberty State Col, BA, 1970; WV Univ Morgantown, MA, 1972. **Career:** Bridgeport HS, teacher, 1970-71; W Liberty State Col, dir coun ctr & asst dir financial aids, adj instr, 1971-76; WesBanco Inc, dir personnel, 1976-80, vpres personnel-human resources, 1980-86; vpres personnel, 1986-93;sr vpres personnel & human resources, 1993-2002; exec vpres human resources, currently. **Orgs:** Bd trustees, OH Valley Med Ctr, 1979; consult, Ctr Creative Comm, 1974-75; consult, No Panhandle Ment Health Ctr Wheeling, 1977-79; bd dir, Big Bros Big Sisters Wheeling, 1976-77; adv bd, OH Co Bd Vocational Educ, 1977-; bd dir, Am Inst Banking Wheeling Chap, 1979-; Ambassadors Club Wheeling Area C C, 1979-; adv comn, Upper OH Valley Employer Wheeling, 1979-80; pres & bd mem, Salvation Army, 1980; bd mem, Ohio Valley Bus Indust CMS. **Home Addr:** 7 Forest Hills, Wheeling, WV 26003. **Business Addr:** Executive Vice President-Human Resources, WesBanco Inc, 1 Bank Plz, Wheeling, WV 26003, **Business Phone:** (304)234-9000.

MOORE, JOHNNIE ADOLPH
Government official. **Personal:** Born Sep 28, 1929, Cuero, TX; son of Nelson and Eva Jones; married Tommye Dalphine Jordan, Jul 9, 1961; children: Carmalie Budgewater. **Educ:** Tuskegee Inst, AL, BS, 1950; George Williams Col, MS, 1957. **Career:** Int Personnel Mgt Asn, Chicago, IL, ed, 1963-66; US Dept Labor Chicago, IL, pub affil officer, 1966-67; US Civil Serv Comn, Wash, DC, pub affil officer, 1967-79; Bowie State Col, Bowie, MD, asst pres, 1980-82; US Off Personnel Mgt Wash, DC, pub affil officer, 1979-83; Am Nurses Asn, dir mkt & pub affil div, 1984-85; US Nuclear Regulatory Comn, pub affairs officer, 1985-90; US Dept Treas, Bureau Engraving & Printing, Wash, DC, pub affairs mgr, 1990-93, pub rels consult. **Orgs:** Bur ed, Norfolk J & Guide, 1958-59; night ed, Chicago Daily Defender, 1959-61; info specialist, Pres Comn Gov't Contracts, 1960-61; exec dir, Nat Ins Asn, 1961-62; pres, Capital Press Club, Wash, DC, 1972-74; Pub Rel Soc Am, 1977-; vis prof, NUL Black Exec Exchange Prog, 1978-; state coordr, AARP, 1997-; Kappa Alpha Psi Fraternity. **Honors/Awds:** Pearlie Cox Harrison Award, Capital Press Club, 1974; Image Maker Award, Nat Asn Media Women, 1976; Albert Gallatin Award, Treasury Dept, 1993. **Military Serv:** USAF, lt, 1953-55. **Home Addr:** 2212 Westview Ct, Silver Spring, MD 20910. *

MOORE, JOHNNY B
Guitarist, singer. **Personal:** Born Jan 24, 1950, Clarksdale, MS; son of Floyd. **Career:** Singer & guitarist; Albums: Hard Times, 1987; Lonesome Blues, 1993; Johnny B Moore, 1996; Live at Blue Chicago, 1996; Troubled World, 1997; 911 Blues, 1997; Born in Clarksdale, 2001. **Business Addr:** Singer, Guitarist, Delmark Records, 4121 N Rockwell St, Chicago, IL 60618, **Business Phone:** (773)539-5798.*

MOORE, DR. JOSSIE A.
Educator. **Personal:** Born Aug 20, 1947, Jackson, TN; married Jimmy L; children: Juan & Jerry. **Educ:** Lane Col, BA, 1971; Memphis State Univ, ME, 1975, EdD, 1986. **Career:** Lane Col, secy & dir AV, 1970-74; Memphis State Univ, Memphis City Sch, teacher corps intern, 1974-75; Lauderdale Co Sch, resource teacher, 1975-76; Covington City Sch, spec educ teacher, 1976-77; State Tech Inst, chmn, develop reading & writing, prof reading, 1999-2002; SW Tenn Community Col, fac, currently. **Orgs:** Secy, PTA Lincoln Sch, 1973-74; Sigma Gamma Rho; AUA; TEA, SCETC; CRLA; NEA, 1977-83; secy, adminr, vpres, Stimulus Toastmasters, 1978-84; consult, Fed Corrections Inst, 1978-79; rep, Parent Adv Comn, 1979-82; consult, Expert Secretarial Serv, 1981-84. **Honors/Awds:** Hon Mention, Third World Writer's Contest, 1979; Best Regional Bullet, Toastmasters Regional, 1981-82. **Special Achievements:** Book: "Practical Reading", 2002. **Business Addr:** Professor Developmental Studies & Reading, Southwest Tennessee Community College, 5983 Macon Cove, Memphis, TN 38134, **Business Phone:** (901)333-4277.

MOORE, JUANITA
Actor. **Personal:** Born Oct 19, 1922, Los Angeles, CA; married Charles Burris. **Educ:** Los Angeles City Col, drama, grad. **Career:** Dancer, singer, night clubs, New York City, London, England (Palladium), Paris, France (Moulin Rouge); actress, stage credits include: No Exit, Ebony Showcase production; Raisin Sun, London co; The Amen Corner, 1965; Films: Pinky, 1949; No Questions Asked, 1951; Skirts Ahoy!, 1952; Lydia Bailey, 1952; Affair in Trinidad, 1952; Witness to Murder, 1954; The Gambler from Natchez, 1954; Women's Prison, 1955; Lord of the Jungle, 1955; Not as a Stranger, 1955; Queen Bee, 1955; Ransom!, 1956; The Opposite Sex, 1956; The Girl Can't Help It, 1956; Something of Value, 1957; Band of Angels, 1957; The Helen Morgan Story, 1957; Bombers B-52, 1957; The Green-Eyed Blonde, 1957; Imitation of Life, 1959; Tammy Tell Me True, 1961; Walk on the Wild Side, 1962; Papa's Delicate Condition, 1963;The Singing Nun, 1966; Rosie!, 1967; Up Tight!, 1969; Angelitos negroes, 1970; Skin Game, 1971; The Mack, 1973; Fox Style, 1973; Abby, 1974; The Zebra Killer, 1974; Thomasine & Bushrod, 1974; Fox Style, 1974; Fugitive Lovers, 1975; Joey, 1977; Paternity, 1981; O'Hara's Wife, 1982; Two Moon Junction, 1988; The Kid, 2000; TV appearances: "Wagon Train"; "Breaking Point"; "Going My Way"; "77 Sunset Strip", 1958; "Ben Casey", 1961; "The Alfred Hitchcock Hour", 1962; "The Gentleman Caller", 1964; "Slattery's People", 1964; "Dragnet", 1967; "Mannix", 1967; "Adam-12", 1968; "MarcusWelby, MD", 1969; "Ellery Queen", 1975; "ER", 2000; "Judging Army", 2001. **Honors/Awds:** Second Place, Golden Laurel Award, 1959; Best Supporting Actress Oscar, 1959; Gloden Globe Nominee for Best Supporting Actress, 1959. **Special Achievements:** Fourth African American to be nominated for an Academy Award. **Business Phone:** (310)550-8606.*

MOORE, JULIETTE R
School administrator. **Personal:** Born Sep 30, 1953, New Orleans, LA; daughter of Frank. **Educ:** Xavier Univ, New Orleans, BS, 1975; Univ W Fla, MS, 1976. **Career:** Univ W Fla, grad teaching asst, 1975-76, sports club coordr, 1975-76, asst dir recreation & sports, 1976-84; Ariz State Univ, asst dir recreation, intramural sports & sports clubs, 1985-89; James Madison Univ, assoc dir stud activities prog & recreation, 1989-91; Northern Ill Univ, dir campus recreation, 1991; Ariz Univ, dir, Campus Recreation, currently. **Orgs:** Ariz Coll Personnel Asn, 1988-89; Nat Asn Campus Activities, 1989-91; Nat Asn Stud Personnel Admin, 1989; fac adv, Zeta Phi Beta Sorority Inc, 1991-. **Honors/Awds:** Outstanding Leadership & Service Award, Nat Intramural Recrational Sports Asn, 1989; Women of Color of the Year, James Madison Univ, 1991; Stacy Dolby Award, Northern Ill Univ, 1994; Outstanding Alumni Award, Univ W Fla, 1995; Ruth Haddock Award, Northern Ill Univ, 1996; Outstanding Leadership & Service Award, Nat Intramural-Recreational Sports Asn, 1996. **Special Achievements:** Melonball, Natl Intramural Recreational Sports Assn J, 1985; Diversity: Be a Part of the Solution, Natl Intramural Recreational Sports Assn J's, 1991. **Business Addr:** Director, The University of Arizona, Department of Campus Recreation, 1400 E 6th St, PO Box 210117, Tucson, AZ 85721, **Business Phone:** (520)621-8707.

MOORE, KATHERINE BELL
Executive, government official. **Personal:** Born Nov 30, 1941, Norfolk, VA; daughter of William Grant Bell and Katherine Scott Bell-Weller; divorced; children: Ira Braswell IV & Katherine Larilee. **Educ:** Univ NC-Wilmington, BA, 1972. **Career:** Mecklenberg & Cent Piedmont Community Col, teacher, 1972-73; Cape Fear Community Col, teacher, 1973-74; Fairfax County Schs, teacher, 1974-77; Eastern Transp Serv Inc, pres, 1977-; City Wilmington, mayor pro-tem, 1992-2002. **Orgs:** Numerous memberships including chair, New Hanover County Human Rels Comt, 1980-83; vice chair, New Hanover Dept Social Serv, 1980-82; adv bd, Duke Univ LEAD Prog, 1980-82; bd mem, Governor's Comn Econ Develop, 1982-84; bd mem, Lt Governor's Comn Jobs, 1984-86; trustee, Univ NC Ctr Pub Tv, 1990-; bd dirs, Carolina Savings Bank, 1986-; Wilmington City Coun. **Honors/Awds:** Numerous hhonors & awards including Achievement Award, Links, 1985; Women of Achievement in Business Award, YWCA, 1985; Minority Bus, second runner-up, Small Bus Admin, 1986; Avon, Women Enterprise, 1990; Blue Chip Enterprise Award, Conn Mutual, 1991. **Special Achievements:** Author, Under Oath: Memoirs of An Honest Politician. **Home Addr:** 4311 Appleton Way, Wilmington, NC 28412, **Home Phone:** (919)395-1510.

MOORE, KENYA
Actor, fashion model. **Personal:** Born Jan 24, 1971, Detroit, MI. **Educ:** Wayne State Univ, Detroit, Mich, child psychol. **Career:** Miss USA, 1993; Films: Senseless; Brothers in Arms, 2005; Cloud 9, 2006, I Know Who Killed Me, 2007; TV episodes: Girlfriends, 2004; The Parkers, 2002; Men, Women & Dogs, 2001; Nubian Goddess, 1999; The Parent Hood, 1999; The Jamie Foxx Show, 1999; In the House, 1999. **Orgs:** Founder, Kenya Moore found. **Special Achievements:** Second African-Am to gain both Miss Mich & Miss USA titles, 1993.

MOORE, KERMIT
Composer, cellist, educator. **Personal:** Born Mar 11, 1929, Akron, OH; married Dorothy Rudd. **Educ:** Cleveland Inst Music, 1951; NY Univ, MA; Paris Conservatory, 1956; Juilliard Sch Music. **Career:** Brooklyn Philharmonic Lincoln Ctr NY, conductor, 1984-87, 1992; Detroit Symphony, guest conductor, 1985, 1992; Berkeley CA Symphony, guest conductor, 1986-88, 1990, 1992; Summer Chamber Music Conf Bennington Col, mem fac, 1988-; NY Philharmonic, lectr, 1992-93; Rud/Mor Publ Co, pres; Class Heritage Ensemble, founder & conductor; Hartt Sch Univ Hartford, mem fac; Univ Hartford, prof; Nat Opera Ebony, guest conductor. **Orgs:** Founder & proj dir, Symphony New World, 1964-; founder, Soc Black Composers, 1968; founder, Riverside Symphony, 1975. **Honors/Awds:** Lili Boulanger Award, Paris, 1953; Special Medal, Queen Elizabeth Belgium, 1958; Edgar Stillman Kelly Award, State Ohio. **Special Achievements:** Conducted concerts in UN General Assembly Hall in 1976, composed "Many Thousand Gone", played Premiere of his composition, "Music for Cello and Piano", numerous concerts throughout US, Europe, Africa & Far East, toured NY Philharmonic to Argentina & Dominican Repub, 1978, commissioned to compose several works "Viola Sonata", classical Radio WQXR, premiered 1979, commissioned by St Louis Arts Festival to compose work for cello and piano, premiered work in Sheldon Hall, 1986, composed film score with Gordon Parks about Ida B Wells on American Experience Series, 1989, Recital at Kennedy center, 1992.

MOORE, KERWIN LAMAR
Baseball player. **Personal:** Born Oct 29, 1970, Detroit, MI. **Career:** Baseball player (retired); Kans City Royals, outfielder, 1988-92; Fla Marlins, 1993; Oakland Athletics, outfielder, 1996; free agent, 1996. **Honors/Awds:** Rookie of the Year, 1996.

MOORE, KEVIN
Writer, singer, guitarist. **Personal:** Born Oct 3, 1951, Compton, CA; children: one son. **Career:** Albums: Keb'Mo', 1994; Just Like You, 1996; Slow Down, 1998; The Door, 2000; Big Wide Grin, 2001; contributor, When Love Speaks: Sonnets of Shakespeare, 2002; Keep It Simple, 2004; Peace. Back by Popular Demand; Suitcase, 2006. **Honors/Awds:** Blues Artist of the Year, 1996; Grammy Award, Best Contemporary Blues Album, 1996, 1998, 2004. **Business Addr:** Singer & Songwriter, Guitarist, Keb' Mo' Music Merchandise, PO Box 210023, San Francisco, CA 94121.*

MOORE, LARRY LOUIS
Educator. **Personal:** Born Jul 21, 1954, Kings Mountain, NC. **Educ:** Western Carolina Univ, BA, 1978; Univ NC-Charlotte, Grad Sch, 1980-. **Career:** Cleveland Tech Col, instr black hist & world civilization, 1979-81; Southwest Junior High Sch, teacher chmn & foreign language dept. **Orgs:** NEA & NCEA 1982-84; NC Teachers Math, 1983-84; chmn, Student Activities Comn, 1984-85; sec Parents & Teachers Org, 1985-87; NAACP, 1987. **Honors/Awds:** Published articles black topics various newspapers.

MOORE, LARRY MACEO
Football player. **Personal:** Born Jun 1, 1975, San Diego, CA. **Educ:** Brigham Young Univ, bus mgt. **Career:** Indianapolis Colts, guard, 1998-2001; Wash Redskins, 2002-03; Cincinnati Bengals, 2004-05. **Honors/Awds:** Rookie of the year, 1998.

MOORE, LENARD DUANE
Consultant, educator, poet. **Personal:** Born Feb 13, 1958, Jacksonville, NC; son of Rogers Edward and Mary Louise Pearson; married Marcille Lynn, Oct 15, 1985; children: Maiisha. **Educ:** Coastal Carolina Community Col, attended 1976-78; Univ Md, attended 1980-81, NC State Univ, 1985; Shaw Univ, BA (magna cum laude), 1995; NC A & T State Univ, MA, eng, 1997. **Career:** Freelance Lectr/Workshop Conductor, 1981-; The Black Writer Chicago, mag consult, 1982-83; Pac Quarterly Moana Hamilton New Zealand, acting adv, 1982-83; Int Black Writers Conf Inc, Chicago, regional dir, 1982-83; Mira Mesa Br Libr, San Diego, Calif, poet-in-residence, 1983; NC Dept Pub Instr, educ media technician, 1984-95; United Arts Coun, Raleigh, NC, writer-in-residence, 1987-93; Enloe High Sch, Raleigh, NC, eng teacher, 1995-96; NC State Univ, Eng Dept, vis lectr, 1997, prof eng, currently. **Orgs:** Numerous memberships including Kuumba Festival Community, Nat Asn Advan Colored People Onslow Co Br, 1982; bd dirs, Int Black Writers Conf Inc, 1982; Toastmasters Int, 1982-84; exec comt, NC Haiku Soc 1983-; usher bd Marshall Chapel Missionary Baptist Church, 1984-85; Poetry Soc Am; Acad Am Poets; World Poetry Soc; NC Poetry Soc; Poets Study Club Terra Haute, NC Writers Network; Int Platform Assoc; Poetry Coun NC Inc; Haiku Soc Am; WV Poetry Soc; The Raleigh Writing Alliance; NC Writers Conf, 1989-; Nat Book Critics Cir, 1989-; Carolina African-Am Writers Collective, 1992-; chmn, NC Haiku Soc, 1995-96; bd dirs, La Jan Productions, 1995-. **Honors/Awds:** Numerous honors & awards including Haiku Museum of Tokyo Award, Haiku Soc Am, 1983 & 1994; CTM Award, Toastmasters Int, 1983; Dr Antonio J Waring Jr Memorial Prize, The Poetry Soc Ga, 1984; publishing grant, NC Haiku Soc, 1985; Emerging Artist Grant, City Raleigh Arts Comn, 1989;listed in Poets & Writers Inc; Alpha Chi Nat Col Hon Scholar Soc, 1995; Gold Medal for Creative Writing Contest in West Germany; The Sallie Paschall Award; Role Model Experiences Award, St. Louis Pub Schs, 1996-97; 1996 Indies Award; Margaret Alexander Walker Creative Writing Award, College Lang Asn, 1997; Tar Heel of the Week, News & Observer, 1998. **Special Achievements:** Author, The Open Eye, 1985, Forever Home, 1992; Desert Storm: A Brief History, 1993; Published in I Hear A Symphony: African Americans Celebrate Love, Anchor Books, 1994; In Search of

Color Everywhere, Stewart, Tabori & Chang Inc, 1994; The Garden Thrives; Twentieth-Century African American Poetry (Harper Collins), 1996; numerous works published including "The Open Eye," NC Haiku Soc Press 1985; "North Carolina's 400 Years, Signs Along the Way," The Acorn Press; "The Haiku Anthology", Simon & Schuster; The first African American to be elected as President of the Haiku Society of America. **Military Serv:** AUS, specialist 4/E-4; Honorable Discharge, Good Conduct Medal. **Home Addr:** 5625 Continental Way, Raleigh, NC 27610. **Business Addr:** Professor, Shaw University, English Department, 118 E S St, PO Box 8105, Raleigh, NC 27601, **Business Phone:** (919)546-8200.

MOORE, LENNY EDWARD
State government official. **Personal:** Born Nov 25, 1933, Reading, PA; son of George and Virginia; married Erma (deceased); married Edith; married Francis (divorced); children: Lenny, Leslie, Carol, Toni & Terri. **Educ:** Pa State Univ 1956; LA. **Career:** Football (Retired), WSID-RADIO, disc jockey sports dir, 1956-58; Baltimore Colts, prof football, 1956-67; pub rels nat brewery, 1958-63; WWIN Radio,sports dir, 1962-64; NW Ayer & Sons, field rep, 1970-74; Baltimore Colts Football Inc, prom dir, 1975-84; resource consult, 1984-; Juvenile Serv Admin State Md, staff, 1984-; prog specialist, 1989; crisis intervention counr, 1991. **Orgs:** Chmn, Heart Asn; Camp Concern; CBS Pro-Football, analyst, 1968; assoc Leukemia, Kidney Found, Multiple Sclerosis, Muscular Dystrophy, Spec Olympics 1975-; adv coun Juvenile Justice 1985; bd dir, The Door, 1991; Gov's Adv Comt "Violence in Schools", 1994. **Honors/Awds:** NFL Rookie of The Year, 1956; Pro Football Hall of Fame, 1975; PEN, Hall of Fame, 1976; East-West Shrine Game Hall of Fame, 2009; mem, The Pigskin Club of Washington. **Special Achievements:** Moore was ranked number 71 on The Sporting News' list of the 100 Greatest Football Players, 1999; The only player to have at least 40 receiving touchdowns and 40 rushing touchdowns. **Home Addr:** 8815 Stonehaven Rd, Randallstown, MD 21133. **Business Addr:** Worker, Maryland Department Juvenile Justice, Liberty and Fayette St, Baltimore, MD 21203.*

MOORE, LEWIS CALVIN
Labor activist, president (organization). **Personal:** Born Jun 22, 1935, Canton, MS; son of Sam A and Louvenia McGee; married Delores Thurman, Sep 29, 1956; children: Kelly, Thurman, Anderson. **Educ:** Manual HS Indianapolis, IN, 1954. **Career:** OCAW Local 7-706, pres, 1970-75; OCAW Dist Coun 7, pres, 1970-75; OCAW Dist 4 Houston, intl rep, 1975-77; OCAW Wash Off, citizenship-legis dir, 1977-79; Oil Chem & Atomic Workers Intl Union, vpres. **Orgs:** Labor instr Univ Ind; charter mem, Nat bd mem A Philip Randolph Inst; Nat Asn Advan Colored People; bd mem, Big Brothers Am; leader Boy Scouts Am; Tex Black Alcoholism Coun; instr, Health & Safety Seminars Kenya, 1984, 1988; Drugs in Contemporary Soc. **Honors/Awds:** Recognition for serv in field of alcoholism & drug abuse. **Business Addr:** Vice President, OCAW International Union, PO Box 2812, Denver, CO 80201.*

MOORE, LOIS JEAN
Executive. **Personal:** Born Oct 12, 1935, Bastrop, TX; daughter of Coronza and Cecelia; married Harold, Nov 13, 1958; children: Yolanda E. **Educ:** Prairie View A&M Univ, Prairie View, TX, nursing dipl, 1957; Tex Woman's Univ, Houston, TX, BA, sci nursing, 1970; Tex Southern Univ, Houston, TX, MA, educ, 1974. **Career:** Harris County Hosp Dist-Ben Taub Gen Hosp, Houston, TX, shift supvr, 1962-68, asst dir nursing serv, 1968-77, adminr, 1977-87, exec vpres, 1987-89, chief exec officer, 1987-99, pres, 1989-99; Jefferson Davis Hosp, chief exec officer, 1988-2001; Univ Tex, Harris County Psychiat Hosp, chief adminr, 2000-; Prairie View A&M Univ, Prairie View, interim dean. **Orgs:** Advan fel, Am Col Healthcare Exec, 1987-; bd mem, Nat Asn Pub & Non Profit Hosps; bd mem, Tex Asn Pub Hosp; bd mem, March Dimes Gulf Coast; chairperson, Houston Crackdown Treatment & Res Comt; Am Red Cross; March Dimes. **Honors/Awds:** Women on the Move, Medicine, The Houston Post, 1989; Outstanding Women of the Year, YWCA, 1989; Houston Women Leaders, Economic Summit, 1990; Distinguished Professional Woman's Award, Univ Tex Health Sci Ctr, 1990; Houston Nurse of the Year, Eta Delta Chap, Sigma Theta Fraternity Int, 1990; Tree of Life Award, Jewish Nat Fund, 1994; DHL, Our Lady of the Lake Univ, 1966. **Business Addr:** Chief Administrator.

MOORE, M ELIZABETH GIBBS
Librarian. **Personal:** Born in Boston, MA; daughter of Warmoth T and Marece A Jones (deceased); divorced. **Educ:** NC A&T State Univ, 1940; Univ Chicago, BLS, 1945, grad study, 1948-49. **Career:** Librarian (retired); NC A&T State Univ, instr, 1940-43; NC A&T State Univ, asst librn, 1943-44; Fisk Univ, cataloger, 1945-48, Libr Sci, instr, 1945-46; Detroit Pub Libr, cataloger, 1945-53; Detroit Pub Libr, ref librn, 1953-54; cataloging supvr, 1955-67; Burroughs Corp, Detroit area librn, 1967-71; Corp Libr Burroughs Corp, 1971-79; Libr MI Bell, human resources supvr, 1979-82, libr consult, 1982-85. **Orgs:** Women's Econ Club, Spec Libr Asn; Am Libr Asn, YWCA, Womens Nat Book Asn; bd dir, Delta Home for Girls, 1974-76; Friends Detroit Pub Libr, 1970-76, 1980-82, Your Heritage House, 1969-; bd dir, Spec libr Asn, 1981-84; Ctrl Adv Comn on Re-Accreditation Wayne State Univ, div Libr Sci, 1975-76; Adv Group Selection Head Sci Libr, Wayne State Univ, 1976-77; Delta Sigma Theta, NAACP; Guilford County, Bd Soc Serv, 1984-87, 1988-90; bd dir, Charlotte Hawkins Brown Historical Found, 1985-; Women's Econ Club Detroit, 1967-82; bd dir, Guilford Women's Network, 1989-90; Libr Serv & Construction Act Adv Coun NC State Libr, 1988-89; adv coun, NC Central Univ, Sch Libr & Info Serv, 1981-88, mem, 1988-, recording secy, 1990-, Friends Sch Educ, NC A&T State Univ. **Honors/Awds:** Saslow Medal for Scholarship in Soc Sci; Award for Meritorious Serv on Col Newspaper; Alumni Award for Outstanding Serv, 1969; Outstanding Grad in Field of Soc Sci Alumni Award, 1973; Hall of Fame, Spec Librs Asn, 1986; Sr Citizen, Greensboro, NC, 1990.

MOORE, DR. MARIAN J.
Historian, executive director. **Personal:** Born in Saginaw, MI; daughter of Eugene and Ann. **Career:** Nat Afro-Am Mus & Cult Ctr, dir; Mus African Am Hist, Detroit, MI, dir, 1988-93; Birmingham Civil Rights Inst, exec dir, 1993.

MOORE, MELBA (MELBA HILL)
Singer, actor. **Personal:** Born Oct 29, 1945, New York, NY; daughter of Melba Smith Hill and Bonnie Davis; married George Brewingston; married Charles Huggins (divorced 1991); children: 1. **Educ:** Montclair State Col, BA, music educ. **Career:** Films: The Sidelong Glances of a Pigeon Kicker, 1970; Cotton Comes to Harlem, 1970; Lost in the Stars, 1974; Hair, 1979; Def by Temptation, 1990; The Fighting Temptations, 2003; TV series: "The Melba Moore-Clifton Davis Show", 1972; Opryland, 1973; "NBC Special Treat", 1975; The American Woman: Portraits of Courage, 1976; "The Love Boat", 1979-84; "The Tim Conway Show", 1980; Flamingo Road, 1980; Purlie?, 1981; "Ellis Island",1984; Charlotte Forten's Mission: Experiment in Freedom, 1985; "ABC Weekend Specials", 1985; "Hotel", 1985; "Melba", 1986; "Falcon Crest",1987; "ABC After school Specials", 1987; "The Cosby Show", 1988; Mother's Day, 1989; "Monsters", 1989; "Mathnet", 1992; "Square One TV", 1992; "Loving", 1983; Albums: I got Love, 1970; Look What You're Doing to the Man, 1971; Live, 1972; Peach Melba, 1975; This is it, 1976; Melba, 1976; A Portrait of Melba, 1977; Burn, 1979; The Other Side of the Rainbow, 1982;A Lot of Love, 1986; I'm in Love, 1988; Soul Exposed, 1990; Singles: "This Is It"; "You Stepped Into My Life"; "Lift Every Voice & Sing"; Legends Ball, 2006; Melba Moore": Live in Concert, 2007; Hair, Let the Sun Shine In; 2007; Unsung; 2009. **Honors/Awds:** Tony Award, Best Supporting Actress, Purlie, 1970; Drama Desk Award, Purlie, 1970; Antoinette Perry Award, Purlie, 1970; New York Drama Critics Award, Purlie, 1970; Grammy Award, nomination, Read My Lips, 1985. **Special Achievements:** First black to perform solo, Metro Opera House, 1977. *

MOORE, DR. MILTON DONALD, JR.
Dermatologist. **Personal:** Born Aug 16, 1953, Aberdeen, MD; son of Dora Lee; divorced; children: Rahmon & Justin. **Educ:** Xavier Col Pharm, RPh, 1976; Meharry Medl Col, MD, 1980. **Career:** Hubbard Hosp, pharmacist, 1976-80; Baylor Col Med, derm dept, asst prof, 1985-; pvt pract, physician, 1985-. **Orgs:** Bd mem Ensemble Theatre, 1986. **Honors/Awds:** Outstanding Young Men of America, Am Acad Dermat. **Home Addr:** 9350 Kirby Dr Suite 100A, Houston, TX 77054. **Business Addr:** Physician, 9350 Kirby Dr Suite 100, Houston, TX 77054, **Business Phone:** (713)741-3376.

MOORE, MINYON
Association executive. **Personal:** Born May 16, 1958, Chicago, IL. **Educ:** Univ Ill, BS, 1982. **Career:** Enclopedia Britannica Educ Corp, promotional serv dir, 1982-85; Oper PUSH Inc, exec asst, 1985-87; Jackson '88 Campaign, nat dept field dir, 1988; Dukakis-Bentsen Gen Election Campaign, nat dept field dir, 1988; Nat Rainbow Coalition, sr adv, nat dep polit dir, 1988-93, DNC Voter Proj, proj dir, 1992; Dem Nat comt, dep chief staff, asst chair, dir Pub Liaison, Training, Voter Contact, Constituency Outreach, 1993-95, nat polit dir, 1995-97; The White House, dep asst to Pres, dep pol dir, 1997-98, asst to Pres, dir of Pub Liaison, 1998-99, asst Pres, pol dir, 1999-2001; Dewey Square Group's, principal, 2001-; Am Coming Together, founder; senior political consultant to Senator Hillary Clinton's, sr political consult, currently. **Orgs:** Nat Coun Negro Women; Push/Rainbow Coalition; Nat Polit Caucus Black Women. **Honors/Awds:** Mothers in Action Lifetime Award; Rainbow Push, Women on the Rise Award; ACE Award, 1998. **Special Achievements:** First African American political director of the Democratic Natl Committee; first African American political director in White House. **Business Addr:** Prinicipal, Dewey Square Group, 1001 G St NW Suite 400E, Washington, DC 20001, **Business Phone:** (202)638-5616.

MOORE, NAT. See MOORE, NATHANIEL.

MOORE, DR. NATHAN
Educator. **Personal:** Born Jun 26, 1931, Mayaro, Trinidad and Tobago; son of William B and Eugenie Samuel; married Mary Lisbeth Simmons, Jul 3, 1967; children: Christina & Serena. **Educ:** Caribbean Union Col, Trinidad, BA, 1958; Rockford Col, Ill, BA, 1963; Carleton Univ, Ottawa, Mass, 1965; Univ BC, PhD, 1972. **Career:** Educator (retired); Barbados Sec Sch, high sch teacher, 1958-61; Carleton Univ, teaching fel, 1963-65; sessional lectr, 1964-65; Barrier Sch Dist British Col, high sch teacher, 1966-67; Walla Walla Col, Wash, col teacher, 1967-79; Ala State Univ, prof eng, 1979-2001, chmn eng, 1980-2001. **Orgs:** Modern Lang Asn, 1965-; Am Soc 18th Century Studies, 1971-; S Atlantic MLA, 1980-. **Honors/Awds:** Scholar, Rockford Col, 1961; Scholar, Readers Digest, 1962; Carleton Fel,Carleton Univ, 1963-65. **Home Addr:** 2928 Moorcroft Dr, Montgomery, AL 36116, **Home Phone:** (334)281-2883. *

MOORE, NATHANIEL (NAT MOORE)
Executive, football player. **Personal:** Born Sep 19, 1951, Tallahassee, FL; son of Julia Mae Gilliam; married Patricia; children: Trellanee, Natalie, Melanie, Tiffanie & Maurice. **Educ:** Univ Fla. **Career:** Football player (retired), executive; Miami Dolphins, wide receiver, 1974-87; Superstar Rollertheque, owner; Inferno Lounge, owner; L&S Builders, past partner; Nat Moore & Assocs Inc, pres, currently; Sunshine Network, football broadcaster, currently; NFL Super Bowl Football Clin, exec dir, currently. **Orgs:** Bd dir, Orange Bowl Comt; bd dir, Genuity Championship; bd dir, Sun Trust Bank; bd dir, Doral Golf Resort & Spa; bd mem, Univ Fla Found; founder, Nat Moore Found, 1998. **Honors/Awds:** All NFL Honors AP Pro-Football Writers, 1977; All AFC Recognition; Tommy Fitzgerald Award Outstanding Rookie, 1974; Man of the Year, NFL, 1984; Byron "Whizzer" White Humanitarian Award, NFL Players Asn, 1986; Florida Hall Fame, Sports Hall Champions; Miami Dolphins Ring Honor, 1999. **Home Phone:** (305)770-0995. **Business Phone:** (407)648-1150.

MOORE, DR. OSCAR JAMES, JR.
Physician, educator. **Personal:** Son of Oscar Sr and Minnie B; children: Frederick & Elna. **Educ:** Morehouse Col, BS, 1955; Atlanta Univ, 1956; Howard Univ, MD, 1962, intern, 1963. **Career:** Harvard Univ, Thorndike Mem Lab, Boston City Hosp, resident, 1963-66; US Navy Submarine Base Hosp, dir med, 1966-68; St Francis Hosp, Hartford, Conn, physician, 1968-69; Mt Sinai Hosp, physician, 1968-69; Mile Square Ctr, Chicago, Ill, physician, 1969-72; Michael Reese Hosp, Chicago, Ill, physician, 1969-80; Presby St Lukes Hosp, Chicago, Ill, physician, 1969-80; Rush Med Col, asst prof, 1969-79; Cedar Sinai Hosp, LA, Calif, physician, 1970-99; Univ Calif Sch Med, asst clin prof, 1970, clinical prof; Ko Med Ctr, med dir, 1972-80; Univ Chicago Pritzker Sch Med, assoc prof; Calif Hosp, Loa Angeles, physician, 1990; Pvt pract, physician, currently. **Orgs:** Bd dirs, Hoover Inst, Stanford Univ, 1990-; bd dirs, Chicago Urban League; bd dirs, Olive Harvey Col; Chicago Junior Col Bd; bd dirs, Mid S Health Planning Orgn; consult, HEW Regional Planning; bd dirs, Abraham Lincoln Ctr, Chicago, Ill; Omega Psi Phi; Beta Kappa Chi; 33 Scotish Rite Mason. **Honors/Awds:** Citizen of the Year Award, Olive Harvey Col, Junior Col Bd, 1976. **Military Serv:** USN, Lt Comdr, 1966-70; chief Med, USN Hosp, New London, CT US Submarine Base. **Business Addr:** Physician, 8306 Wilshire Blvd Suite 21B, Beverly Hills, CA 90211, **Business Phone:** (213)386-9970.

MOORE, OSCAR WILLIAM
Clergy, educator. **Personal:** Born Mar 31, 1938, White Plains, NY; son of Oscar Sr and Helen; married Vicki Renee Bransford, Feb 14, 1990; children: Derrick, John, Sean, Mahla & William. **Educ:** Southern Ill Univ, BS, 1969, MS, 1970; Philadelphia Col Bible; Trinity Col Bible; Trinity Theol Sem. **Career:** Southern Ill Univ, asst dir, 1969-71; Glassboro State Col, asst prof, head track & field coach, currently; Mt Olive Baptist Church, Glassboro, NJ, assoc minister, currently. **Orgs:** Secy, treas, NJ Track Coaches Asn, 1975-; fac sponsor, Alpha Phi Alpha, Sigma Sor; dir, Glassboro Summer Martin Luther King; dir, Manna Bible Inst, Glassboro campus. **Special Achievements:** Olympian, track & field, 1964. **Military Serv:** USMC, sgt, 1956-60; Good Conduct Award, 1957. **Home Addr:** 6 Harrell Ave, Williamstown, NJ 08094. **Business Addr:** Assistant Professor, Rowan College New Jersy, Health & Exercise Science Department, 201 Mullica Hill Rd, Glassboro, NJ 08028, **Business Phone:** (856)256-4500.

MOORE, PENNY
Basketball player. **Personal:** Born Jan 25, 1969. **Educ:** Long Beach State Univ, attended 1991. **Career:** Charlotte Sting, forward, 1997; Wash Mystics, forward, 1998-99, 2002. *

MOORE, DR. QUINCY L
School administrator. **Personal:** Born Dec 31, 1949, Chicago, IL; son of N L and Hannah; widowed. **Educ:** Culver-Stockton Col, BA, 1972; Univ Nev, Las Vegas, MS, 1975; Univ Iowa, PhD, 1983; Harvard Grad Sch Educ, MDP dipl, 1992. **Career:** Univ Nev, Upward Bound Prog, dir, 1973-76; Clark County Community Col, CETA consult, 1976-77; Univ Nev, Spec Servs Prog, dir, 1977-78; Va Commonwealth Univ, Educ Support Prog, dir, 1985-89, pres's off admin asst, 1991, Off Acad Support, dir, 1989-98, exec dir acad success ctr, 1998-2001; W Chester Univ, dean undergrad studies & stud support serv, 2001-06; Palm Beach Community Col, vpres student serv, 2006-. **Orgs:** Concerned Black Men Richmond, 1990-94; chmn, Am Coun Asn, Task Force Black Males, 1991-92; Leadership Metro Richmond, 1991-92; adv bd mem, Richmond Jazz Soc; adv Bd mem, Richmond Community

High Sch, 1991-94; pres, Asn Multicult Coun & Develop, 1992-93; vice chmn, Coalition Access, Affordability & Diversity Higher Educ, 1992-93; adv bd, Richmond Javeline & Domestic Courts, 1993-. **Honors/Awds:** Distinguished Leadership Awards, United Negro Col Fund, 1985-88; ACA Legislative Award, Am Coun Asn, 1992; John L Lennon Professional Success Award, Asn Multicult Coun & Develop, 1992; Faculty of the Year Award, Delta Sigma Theta, Va Commonwealth Univ, 1992. **Special Achievements:** Co-author, Transcultural Counseling from an African-American Perspective, 1993. **Business Addr:** Vice President of Student Services, Palm Beach Community College, 4200 Congress Ave, Lake Worth, FL 33461-4796, **Business Phone:** (561)868-3142.

MOORE, RALPH G
Businessperson. **Personal:** Born Apr 7, 1949, Evanston, IL; son of William and Alberta. **Educ:** Southern Ill Univ, BD, acct, 1971. **Career:** Arthur Andersen & Co, acct staff; Minority Enterprise Small Bus Investment Co, vpres; Parker House Sausage Co, controller; Ralph G Moore & Assocs, founder & pres, 1979-. **Orgs:** Co founder & pres, Alliance Bus Leaders & Entrepreneurs; trustee, Univ Chicago Hosps & Health Syst, 1994-; trustee, City Col Chicago; Jr Achievement Chicago; Chicago Minority Bus Develop Coun. **Honors/Awds:** Governor's Minority Small Bus Advocate of the Year Award, former Ill Gov George Ryan; Entrepreneur of the Year, Inc. Magazine & Ernst & Young; Minority Bus Advocate Award, Minority Bus Comt of the Chicago Minority Bus Develop Coun; Minority Advocate Award, Ill Minority Enterprise Develop Week (MED-Week) Comt; Ill Minority Small Bus Advocate Award, US Small Bus Admin. **Special Achievements:** Appearances on the "Minority Business Report" television program; has held various positions including lecturer, writer and seminar presenter for strategic alliances between corporate America and minority businesses and the role of minority entrepreneurship and community economic development. **Business Phone:** (312)419-1911.*

MOORE, REV. RICHARD
Clergy, educator. **Personal:** Born Oct 19, 1956, Chicago, IL. **Educ:** Union Theol Sem, MDiv. **Career:** Holy Unity Day Care, dir; Holy Unity Baptist Church, pastor, currently. **Orgs:** NAACP; pres, Youth Unlimited Inc. **Business Addr:** Pastor, Holy Unity, 167-10 137th Ave, Jamaica, NY 11434, **Business Phone:** (718)723-7353.

MOORE, RICHARD BAXTER
Lawyer. **Personal:** Born May 26, 1943, Erie, PA; son of Jean and Lewis Tanner; divorced; children: Leonard, Richard Jr & Tiffiny. **Educ:** Central State Col, BS, 1965; Howard Univ Sch Law, JD 1969. **Career:** City Philadelphia, asst jury comnr, 1979-91; Philadelphia, Pa, asst dist atty, 1971-77; Pvt Pract, atty, currently. **Orgs:** IBPOEW; Phi Alpha Delta Law Fraternity; Omega Psi Phi Fraternity Inc; Nat Asn Advan Colored People; chmn, Veterans Comn; vice chmn, United Negro Col Fund, City Philadelphia; vice chmn, Juvenile Serv Sub Comn Pub Serv, 1973-74; Compensation Victims Crimes Comn, 1974-75; vpres, bd dirs, Nat Bar Found, 1975-78; Philadelphia Bar Asn; Sigma Pi Phi Fraternity. **Honors/Awds:** Service Award Chapel of Four Chaplains; Citation, United Negro Col Fund; Service Award, Boys & Girls Clubs Am. **Military Serv:** AUS, capt, 1969-71. **Home Addr:** 406 S 16th St, Philadelphia, PA 19146-1501, **Home Phone:** (215)545-2781. **Business Addr:** Attorney, 406 S 16th St, Philadelphia, PA 19146, **Business Phone:** (215)545-2781.

MOORE, RICK
Executive. **Personal:** Born Jun 16, 1951, Dayton, OH; son of Jessie and Dorothy; married Judi Moore, Apr 17, 1998; children: Troy & Brian. **Educ:** Wright State Univ; Sinclair Col; Wilberforce Univ, BS, 2002. **Career:** Griffin/ Blosser Color Labs, 1969-72; Wolpent Engineering, 1972-76; Price Brother's Co, 1976-83; Dayton Metropolitan Housing Authority, mgr, 1983-. **Orgs:** Bd mem, Buckeye Trails Girl Scouts, 1995-2001; City Dayton Citizens Awareness Comt, 1996-; Nat forum Black Pub Admin, 1998-; bd mem, Big Brother Big Sisters, 1998-. **Honors/Awds:** President's Award, Progessive Daytonview Neighborhood, 1994; Image Award, City Dayton, OH, 1998; Community Service Hope Ministry Award, 1999. **Business Addr:** Manager, Dayton Metropolitan Housing Authority, 400 Wayne Ave, Dayton, OH 45410, **Business Phone:** (937)910-7500.

MOORE, ROB
Football player. **Personal:** Born Sep 27, 1968, Hempstead, NY; married Drucilla; children: Dakota & Savoy. **Educ:** Syracuse Univ, BS, psy chol, 1990. **Career:** Football player (retired); New York Jets, wide receiver, 1990-94; Ariz Cardinals, wide receiver, 1995-2001; Denver Broncos, wide receiver, 2002. **Honors/Awds:** Role Model of the Year, New York City Coun, 1991; Marty Lyons Award, 1992; Edge Man of the Year, 1992.

MOORE, ROBERT EARL. See RASHAD, DR. AHMAD.

MOORE, ROBERT F
Socialist, educator. **Personal:** Born Jan 30, 1944, Tuskegee, AL. **Educ:** Fisk Univ, BS, 1965; Ind Univ, MS, 1966, EdD, 1969. **Career:** Coppin State Col, asst prof, 1968-70; Fisk Univ Nashville, from asst prof to assoc prof educ, 1970-75; Tenn State Univ, assoc prof, 1975; Univ Miami, assoc prof, 1975-2000, assoc dean, 1981-93, Dept Teaching & Learning, assoc prof, 1994-, Undergrad Spec Educ Prog, coord, currently; Milwaukee Pub Schs, Div Exceptional Student Educ, Early Childhood Audit, consult, 1985; Silny & Assocs, Coral Gables, FL, consult, 1988-; Dade Co Pub Schs, FL, consult, 1994-; Mahoney Residential Col, master, currently; Bel-Aire Elem Sch, prof residence, currently. **Orgs:** Bd dirs, Tenn Asn Retarded Citizens; Davidson Co Asn Retarded Citizens; Tenn Foster Grandparents Asn; Grace Eaton Day Home; Phi Delta Kappa; Am Asn Ment Retardation; Asn Supervision & Curric Develop; Golden Key Nat Honor Soc; Iron Arrow; Coun Except C. **Honors/Awds:** Professor of the Year & Golden Apple Award, Panhellenic Coun, Univ Miami, 1999. **Business Addr:** Associate Professor, University of Miami, School of Education, Merrick Bldg 319-B, PO Box 248221, Coral Gables, FL 33124, **Business Phone:** (305)284-4185.

MOORE, RODNEY GREGORY
Lawyer. **Personal:** Born Sep 1, 1960, Birmingham, AL; son of Tommie and Jethroe (deceased); married Yaslyn, Nov 20, 1994; children: Nyosha, Rodney G II & Imari. **Educ:** Univ Wash, BA, polit sci, 1982; Santa Clara Univ Sch Law, JD, 1985. **Career:** Wash State Atty General's Off, consumer protection claims rep, 1980-82; Bancroft Whitney Legal Publ, Am Law Review Series, assoc ed, 1984-85; Law Offices Williams, Robinson & Moore, partner/atty, 1987-89; Moore Law Firm, pres & chief exec officer, 1989-97; Lincoln Law Sch, pro, 1991-93; Santa Clara Co Black Chamber Com, gen coun, 1992-98; E Side Union High Sch Dist, sch bd mem, 1994-97; Eastside Union High Dist, gen coun, 1997-2000; Atlanta Pub Schs, gen coun, 2000-05; Greenberg Traurig LLP, gen coun, currently. **Orgs:** Pres, Univ Wash, Black Student Union, 1980-82; assoc ed, Santa Clara Comp & High TEC Law J, 1984-85; Stud Bar Asn treas, 1984-85; Nat Black Law Students Asn, western regional dir, 1984-85; Calif State Bar Asn, 1987-; pres, Santa Clara Co Black Lawyers Asn, 1989-91; bd trustees, Santa Clara Co Bar Asn, 1989-91; chief coun, Santa Clara Co Black Chamber Com, 1991-97; bd visitors, Univ Santa Clara Law Sch, 1993-2001; pres, Calif Asn Black Lawyers, 1993-94; alumni bd mem, Santa Clara Univ Law Sch, 1993-95; dir region IX, Nat Bar Asn, 1993-94, gen coun, 1997-99; bd mem, Hampton-Phillips Track & Field Classic, 1993-99; mem, San Jose Library Vision Comt, 1994-96; bd mem, 100 Black Men Am, Atlanta Chap; bd mem, Metrop Edu Dist, 1994-97, pres, 1996-97; chair, ed bd, Nat Bar Asn J, 1997-99, vpres, 2002-04, pres elect, 2007-08; bd dirs, Nat Sch Bd Asn, Coun Sch Atty, 2002-06; chair, Urban Law Comn, 2003-06; Atlanta Bar Asn; Gate City Bar Asn; State Bar Calif; State Bar Ga. **Honors/Awds:** Order of the Golden Hand, Santa Clara Co Black COC, 1991; Proclamation, City San Jose, 1994; Certificate of Recognition, Entreprenurial Spirit, Calif Legis, 1994; Loren Miller Award-Attorney of the Year, CA Asn Black Lawyers, 1997; Special Award of Merit, Nat Bar Asn, 1998; Best Lawyers in America, 2007-08. **Special Achievements:** Int Monitor, Independent Elections CMS, Republic of South Africa, 1994; chair, Nat Bar Asn, Int Delegation to United Nations Int Criminal Tribunal for Rwanda. **Business Addr:** General Counsel, Greenberg Traurig LLP, The Forum, 3290 Northside Pkwy Suite 400, Atlanta, GA 30327, **Business Phone:** (678)553-2100.

MOORE, RONALD
Football player, public utility executive. **Personal:** Born Jan 26, 1970, Spencer, OK; married Tammy; children: Ashlynn & Allison. **Educ:** Pittsburg State Univ. **Career:** Football player (retired); Ariz Cardinals, running back, 1993-94, 1997; New York Jets, 1995-96; St Louis Rams, 1997; Miami Dolphins, 1998; police officer & minister, currently. **Orgs:** Pres, PSU's Fellowship Christian Athletes; mem, Alpha Phi Alpha Fraternity, Inc. **Honors/Awds:** Harlon Hill Trophy winner, 1992; National Player of the Year, 1992.

MOORE, DR. ROSCOE MICHAEL
Veterinarian, chief executive officer. **Personal:** Born Dec 2, 1944, Richmond, VA; son of Roscoe Michael Moore Sr and Robnette Johnson; married Patricia Ann Haywood, Aug 2, 1969; children: Roscoe III & John H. **Educ:** Tuskegee Univ, BS, 1968, DVM, 1969; Univ Mich, MPH, 1970; Johns Hopkins Univ, MHS, 1982, PhD, 1985. **Career:** Nat Insts Health, veterinarian, 1970-71; Ctrs for Disease Control, epidemic intelligence serv officer, 1971-73; Ctr for Veterinary Med, sr veterinarian, 1973-74; Nat Inst Occup Safety & Health, sr epidemiologist, 974-81; Ctr for Devices & ad Health, sr epidemiologist, 1981-92; Univ Wash, Seattle, assoc prof, 1989-; Pub Health Serv, chief veterinary med officer, 1989-93; US Pub Health Serv, assoc dir, Office Int & Refugee Health, 1992, surgeon gen & rear admiral; Potomac Inst Policy Studies, sr fel & staff, 2003-; Global Flu Consortium, chief exec officer & vice chmn, currently. **Orgs:** Am Veterinary Med Asn, 1969-; bd dirs, FONZ, 1979-; pres, bd dirs, Friends Nat Zoo, 1984-87; fel, Am Col Epidemiology, 1984-; adv comn, Howard Univ Col Med, 1985-; consult, Sch Veterinary Med, Tuskegee Univ, 1988-; bd govrs, Univ Mich Pub Health Alumni, 1987-93; Omega Psi Phi Fraternity, 1995-; bd dirs, Montgomery Gen Hosp, 1992-. **Honors/Awds:** Commendation Medal, US Public Health Service, 1976,83; USPHS Career Develop Award to attend, Johns Hopkins Univ, 1977-79; Delta Omega Nat Honorary Public Health Soc, 1985; 'Honorary Doctor of Science', Tuskegee Univ, 1990; Surgeon Gen's Exemplary Service Medal, 1990. **Home Addr:** 14315 Arctic Ave, Rockville, MD 20853. **Business Addr:** Senior Fellow, Staff, Potomac Institute for Policy Studies, 901 N Stuart St, Arlington, VA 22203, **Business Phone:** (703)525-0770.

MOORE, SAMUEL D.
Actor, singer. **Personal:** Born Oct 12, 1935, Miami, FL; son of Louise White and John Richard Hicks; married Joyce McRae, Mar 26, 1982; children: Deborah, Nicole, Tangela, Lawanda Denise, Michelle Gayle, Vicky & JoAnn. **Career:** Singer, entertainer, actor; Singles: "You Don't Know Like I Know," 1966; "Hold On, I'm Comin", 1966; "Soul Man", 1967; "I Thank You", 1968; Albums: Sam & Dave, 1966; Best of Sam & Dave, 1969; One Trick Pony, 1980; Soul Men, 1986; Films: Tapeheads, 1988; Blues Brothers 2000, 1998; Night at the Golden Eagle, 2002; Only the Strong Survive, 2002; TV series: "Saturday Night Live", 1980; "Golden Age of Rock'n'Roll", 1991; "Tales of the City", 1993; The Roots of Country: Nashville Celebrates the Ryman, 1994; Elvis:The Tribute, 1994; The Life & Times of Conway Twitty, 1995; Rhythm & Blues 40: A Soul Spectacular, 2001; Sounds of Memphis, 2002; Soulsville, 2003; Soul Man: Isaac Hayes, 2003; "Late Night with Conan O'Brien", 2004-06; "Tavis Smiley", 2007; Respect Yourself: The Stax Records Story, 2007; "Ovenight Sensational"; "Plenty Good Lovin"; Worldwide Symphony Concert Tour, 2008-09. **Orgs:** Nat Acad Recording Arts & Sci; Soc Singers; Rhythm & Blues Foun Artist Bd. **Honors/Awds:** Grammy Award, Nat Acad Recording Arts & Sci, 1967; Rhythm & Blues Found, Pioneer, 1991; Rock & Roll Hall of Fame, inductee, 1992; two Country Music Association Awards nominations; NARAS Heroes Award; Grammy Song Hall of Fame for Soul Man, inductee; ETAM Living Legend Award; MOBO Lifetime Achievement Living Legend Award, 2006. **Special Achievements:** Command performance for Queen of England, 1967; command performance for Jimmy Carter, White House, 1975; Presidential Inauguration of George Bush, 1989. **Business Addr:** Singer, Buddy Lee Attractions, 38 Music Square East 300, Nashville, TN 37203, **Business Phone:** (615)244-4336.

MOORE, SHEMAR F.
Fashion model, actor. **Personal:** Born Apr 20, 1970, Oakland, CA. **Educ:** Santa Clara Univ. **Career:** Films: Hav Plenty, 1997; Butter, 1998; How to Marry a Billionaire: A Christmas Tale, 2000; The Brothers, 2001; Motives, 2004; Reversible Errors, 2004; The Seat Filler, 2004; Greener, 2004; Diary of a Mad Black Woman, 2005; TV Series: "The Young & the Restless", 1994-2002; "Mama Flora's Family", 1998; "Soul Train", host, 1999-2003; "Birds of Prey",2002-03; "Criminal Minds", 2005-09; "Living Single"; "The Jamie Foxx Show";"The Nanny", 2006; True Night, 2008; A Shade of Gray, 2009; The Big Wheel, 2009; Roadkill, 2009; Amplification, 2009; To Hell.. And Back, 2009. **Honors/Awds:** NAACP Image Awards, nominated, 1996; Emmy Award nomination, 1997;Oust standing Actor in a Daytime Drama Series, 1998, 2002. **Business Addr:** Actor, Craig Agency, 8485 E Melrose Pl Suite E, Los Angeles, CA 90069, **Business Phone:** (213)655-0236.

MOORE, THELMA WYATT CUMMINGS
Judge. **Personal:** Married Luke (deceased); children: Charles M. **Educ:** UCLA, BS; Emory Univ, JD. **Career:** Morris Brown Col; Univ Warwick, Coventry, England; Munic Ct, Atlanta, judge, 1977-80; City Ct, Atlanta, 1980-85; State Ct, Fulton County, judge, 1985-90; Fulton County, Superior Ct, GA, judge, 1990-. **Orgs:** Joint Ctr Polit & Econ Studies, bd govs, currently. **Honors/Awds:** John Hay Whitney Fel; Nat Urban League Fel; First Annual Distinguished Alumni Award, 1986, Emory Medal, 1992, Emory Black Law Studs Asn; School of Law's Distinguished Alumna Award, 1996; Generous Heart 2003 Award; Thurgood Marshall Award, 2006. **Special Achievements:** The first black woman appointed to the Superior Courts of Georgia; first black woman to serve on the State Court Bench of Georgia; first woman to serve full-time on the benches of the Atlanta Municipal Court and the Atlanta City Court. **Business Addr:** Judge, Fulton County Superior Court, 136 Pryor St SW Suite C-640, Atlanta, GA 30303, **Business Phone:** (404)730-4305.

MOORE, THOMAS L.
Executive. **Personal:** Born Jun 26, 1926, Burke Co, GA; married Alma Brown; children: Tommy, Yvonne, Dionne & Michael. **Educ:** Swift Meml Col; Knoxville Col. **Career:** TAM Inc Constrn Co, pres; Tommy Moore Enter, staff; Moore's Package Store, staff. **Orgs:** City & Co Bank of Knox Co; charter comnr, Knox Co Bd Comnr; pres Knoxville, Nat Bus League; Bus Develop Ctr C of C; BSA; pres, Coun Youth Oppt YMCA. **Honors/Awds:** Cert award Commonwealth of KY, YMCA.

MOORE, TRUDY S
Journalist. **Personal:** Born Jan 6, 1957, Paterson, NJ; daughter of Queen E; children: Taylor S Moore. **Educ:** Howard Univ, Wash, DC, BS, 1979; Northwestern Univ, Evanston, IL, MS, 1980. **Career:** Chicago Sun-Times, Chicago, IL, gen assignment reporter, 1980; Jet Mag, Chicago, IL, asst ed, 1980-83, assoc ed, 1983-89, feature ed, 1989; Ebony Man, Chicago, IL, contrib ed, 1988-90; Jet Mag, Johnson Publ Co, feature ed. **Orgs:** Vol, Big Brothers/Big Sisters, Chicago, IL, 1982-85; Chicago Urban

League, 1986-; NAACP, Women's Auxiliary, 1989; mem bd dir, NAACP, Chicago, S Side Br, 1989; Chicago Asn Black Journalists. **Home Phone:** (312)363-7887. **Business Addr:** Feature Editor, Jet Magazine/Johnson Publishing Co, 820 S Michigan Ave, Chicago, IL 60605, **Business Phone:** (312)322-9307.

MOORE, WALTER LOUIS
Government official. **Personal:** Born Mar 14, 1946, Pontiac, MI; married Daisy Barber. **Educ:** Ferris State Col, attended 1968, Oakland Univ. **Career:** Pontiac City, MI, firefighter; Oakland County, MI, comnr, 1978; Pontiac City, MI, mayor, currently. **Orgs:** Campaign mgr, Coalition Modern Charter, Pontiac City; I-75 Mayor's Conf; mem, US Conf Mayors; Nat Conf Black Mayors; dir, Pontiac Youth Assistance; charter mem, Pontiac Optimist Club; mason, Gibraltor Lodge #19 Prince Hall; bd mem, Offender Aid & Restoration. **Honors/Awds:** America's Outstanding Young Men, Jaycees of Am, 1984; Man & Boy Award, Boys & Girls Club of Pontiac, 1986; Community Serv Award, Oakland County Nat Asn Advan Colored People; Community Serv Award, Nat Org Negro Bus & Prof Women's Clubs. **Home Addr:** 37 Ottawa Dr, Pontiac, MI 48341.

MOORE, HON. WARFIELD, JR.
Judge. **Personal:** Born Mar 5, 1934, Chicago, IL; son of Warfield Sr and Sally Curry; married Jeane Virginia; children: Warfield III, Sharon, Sally Anne & Janet. **Educ:** Univ Mich, AB, 1957; Wayne State Univ, LLB, 1960. **Career:** Pvt Pract, atty, 1961-78; Recs Ct, judge, 1978; Circuit Ct, judge, currently. **Orgs:** Mich Bar Asn; Wolverine Bar Asn; Black Judges Asn. **Special Achievements:** Did Law Review in Wayne State University, editor, 1958-60. **Home Addr:** 1561 Lincolnshire Dr, Detroit, MI 48203. **Business Addr:** Judge, Circuit Court, 3rd Circuit, Civil Division, Rm 921 711 Coleman A Young Munic Ctr 2 Woodward Ave, Detroit, MI 48226, **Business Phone:** (313)224-5261.

MOORE, WENDA WEEKES
Research scientist. **Personal:** Born Dec 24, 1941, Boston, MA; daughter of Leroy R Weekes; married Cornell L; children: Lynne, Jonathon & Meredith. **Educ:** Howard Univ, BA, 1963; USC, grad work. **Career:** Gov Wendell R Anderson, staff asst; Wash, DC Libr, resr; Westminster Town Hall Forum, dir, currently. **Orgs:** League Women Voters, 1964, 1974; bd regents, Univ Minn, 1973; vice chairperson bd regents, 1975; chmn bd regents, 1977-83; Univ Minn Found; bd Minn Bd Continuing Leg Educ; dir, Gamble-Skogm Inc, 1978-82; leader, First Educ Exchange Deleg Univ Minn People's Repub China, 1979; Bd Adv US Dept Educ, 1980; Adv Coun, 1980-83; Nat Comn Foreign Lang, 1980; Alpha Kappa Alpha; pres, St Paul Chap Links, 1987-; Jacks & Jill; pres bd & chmn, Chart & Wedco 1989-90; trustee, Kellog Found, 1988-; bd, Am Judicature Soc, 1990. **Honors/Awds:** Torch & Shield Award, 1982; Outstanding Woman in Education, YWCA, 1983; Outstanding Alumni Achievement, Howard Univ, 1989. **Home Addr:** 2727 Dean Pkwy, Minneapolis, MN 55416. **Business Addr:** Director, Westminster Town Hall Forum, 83 S 12th St, Minneapolis, MN 55403, **Business Phone:** (612)332-3421.

MOORE, WILL H., III
Football player. **Personal:** Born Feb 21, 1970, Dallas, TX; married Phyllis. **Educ:** Tex Southern Univ, BA, bus, 1992. **Career:** Football player (retired); New England Patriots, wide receiver, 1995-96; Jacksonville Jaguars, 1997-98.

MOORE, YOLANDA
Basketball player, television sportscaster. **Personal:** Born Jul 1, 1974; children: Courtney & Ashley. **Educ:** Univ Miss, BA, eng & radio & tv, 2002. **Career:** Basketball player (retired), basketball analyst; Houston Comets, forward, 1997-98; Orlando Miracle, 1999; Miami Sol, 2000; Women's Korean Basketball League, Seoul, Korea, 2001-02; Dallas Mavericks, broadcast intern, 2004-05; Fox Sports Net, basketball analyst, 2006-; Memphis Grizzles game show, analyst, 2007;Mississippi Sports Magazine, writer. **Orgs:** Owner, Yolanda Moore Basketball Enterprises; owner, Yolanda Moore Motivational Training Systems. **Honors/Awds:** All-Am, 1996; WNBA Championship, 1997; All-Southeastern Conf, 1995, 1996. **Business Phone:** (310)369-1000.

MOOREHEAD, BOBBIE WOOTEN
Educator, meeting planner. **Personal:** Born May 26, 1937, Kelly, LA; daughter of Verdie C Wooten and Ora Lee Edwards Jones; married Erskine L; children: Eric Lyn & Jennifer Lynne. **Educ:** Atlanta Univ, attended 1958-59; Tex Southern Univ, BS, 1958, MEd, 1977; cert, admin supv, 1977. **Career:** Goose Creek Consolidated Sch Dist, teacher, 1959-62; Houston Independent Sch Dist, teacher, 1963-; Capt Campaign, meeting planner & consult, currently. **Orgs:** Comn Admin, YWCA, 1977-84; regional dir, Zeta Phi Beta Sorority, 1978-80, nat conv chmn, 1978, nat first vpres, 1980-84; Comn Accreditation Schs Tex, 1978-83; nat pres, Top Ladies Distinction Inc, 1983-87; hon bd mem, TSU Maroon & Grey Ex-Students Asn, 1983-84; nat bd conv chmn, Nat Coun Negro Women, 1985, 1987 & 1989; speakers bur, Houston Planned Parenthood Fedn, Houston Urban League Guild; nat exec Bd, Nat Coun Negro Women; nat chmn, Social & Legis Action Top Ladies Distinction Inc; nat vpres, Nat Coun Negro Women Inc, 1991-95. **Honors/Awds:** Service to the State Award, Govt Dolph E Briscoe, 1977; Woman of Achievement in Leadership, Sigma Gamma Rho Sorority, 1986; Leadership Award, Zeta Phi Beta Sorority, 1986; Jack Yates High School Hall of Fame, 1986; Distinguished Woman Award, South Cent Dist Women Achievement Inc, 1986; History Makers Award, Educ Riverside Hosp, 1987; Gem, Blue Triangle Br, YMCA, 1990; National Achiever's Award, Nat Women Achievement Inc, 1993; Community Leadership Award, S Cent Br, YMCA, 1993; Community Leadership Award-Education, Kappa Alpha Psi, 1994. **Business Addr:** Meeting Planner, Consultant, Captain Campaign, 3207 Parkwood Dr, PO Box 131894, Houston, TX 77021, **Business Phone:** (713)748-3119.

MOOREHEAD, ERIC K
Research administrator. **Personal:** Born Jun 21, 1958, Baltimore, MD; son of Archie Clarence and Rose Marie Lewis; married Gemma Arlene Arrieta, Dec 21, 1986; children: Bradford & Brookelyn. **Educ:** Univ Cent Arks, BA, 1980; Univ Southern Calif, Grad Sch, jour, 1984. **Career:** Western Electric, NY, intern pub Rels, 1980; City Los Angeles, Los Angeles, intern, press Off Mayor Tom Bradley, 1982; Los Angeles Bus Jour, Los Angeles, CA, edial intern, 1984; Arks Democrat, Little Rock, copy ed & reporter, 1986-90; Ark State Press, Little Rock, AR, reporter, 1990-91; Little Rock In View Magazine, Little Rock, ed, 1991; Univ Ariz Med Sci, Little Rock, res admin, 2002-, inst rev bd admnir, currently. **Orgs:** Nat Asn Black Journalists; Univ Cent Ark Alumni Asn; Univ Cent Ariz, African-Am Alumni Asn. **Honors/Awds:** AEJ/NYU Summer Internship, Asn Educ Journalism, New York Univ, 1980; Dean's List, Univ Cent Arks, 1979; Whos Who Among African Am; Grants Mgt Cert, 2005. **Home Addr:** 3512 Wynne St, Little Rock, AR 72204.

MOOREHEAD, JUSTIN LESLIE
Banker. **Personal:** Born Oct 31, 1947, St Thomas, Virgin Islands of the United States; married. **Educ:** Occidental Col Los Angeles CA, BA, hist, 1969; Woodrow Wilson Sch Princeton Univ, MPA, concentration, econ devel, 1971; NY Univ Grad Sch Bus Admin, transp econ, 1974; Univ Mich Exec Acad, 1977; Bank Am, Municipal Credit & Money Mkt Instr, 1978. **Career:** Govt Kenya, rural devel planner, 1970; Govt US Virgin Islands, economist off budget dir, 1971-72; Virgin Island Dept PubWorks, admin, 1972-73; Amerada Hess Corp, 1973-75; Virgin Island Off budget Dir, budget dir, 1975-79; Lehman Brothers Kuhn Loeb Inc, vpres publ fin, 1979-83; Dean Witter Reynolds Inc, managing dir pub finance. **Business Addr:** Managing Dir, Dean Witter Reynolds Inc, 2 World Trade Center, New York, NY 10048.

MOORE-POOLE, JESSICA CARE
Poet, chief executive officer, publisher. **Personal:** Born Oct 28, 1971, Detroit, MI; daughter of Thomas and Irene; married Sharrif Simmons; children: Omari. **Educ:** Mich State Univ; Wayne State Univ. **Career:** Moore Black Press Inc, founder & chief exec officer, 1997-; Detroit Read, singer, currently; Poet, currently; Poetry collections: The Alphabet Verses The Ghetto, 2002; The Words Don't Fit in My Mouth; God is Not an American; Plays: There Are No Asylums for the Real Crazy Women; Alphaphobia!, Moore Black Press. **Honors/Awds:** Small Press Award, African-Am Helping Auth Orgn NYC. **Special Achievements:** Apollo Legend, It's Showtime at the Apollo, won five consecutive weeks, poetry has appeared in numerous publications, including Rap Pages, Essence, African Voices, and Black Elegence, Black Issues Book Review's Publisher Power List, published Saul Williams, Ras Baraka, asha bandele, NBA basketball player, Etan Thomas, and Danny Simmons, 2006, honored by African Voices Mag for literary work, host, producer, Black Family Channel, in conjunction with Robert Townsend, Star of Bricktop! A musical cabaret, Atlanta, 2006. **Business Addr:** Founder, Chief Executive Officer, Moore Black Press, PO Box 10545, Atlanta, GA 30310, **Business Phone:** (404)752-0450.

MOORER, LANA MICHELE. **See MC LYTE.**

MOORER, MICHAEL (MICHAEL LEE MOORER)
Boxer. **Personal:** Born Nov 12, 1967, New York, NY; married Bobbie Moorer; children: Michael Jr. **Career:** Professional Boxer (retired), coach, bodyguard; prof boxer, 1988-2004; boxing trainer, currently; bodyguard, currently. **Honors/Awds:** United States Amateur Light Middleweight (156 pound) champion, 1986; World Heavyweight Boxing Champion, 1994-95.

MOORER, MICHAEL LEE. **See MOORER, MICHAEL.**

MOORE-STOVALL, DR. JOYCE
Physician. **Personal:** Born Nov 5, 1948, Washington, DC; daughter of Joseph Samuel and Ida Barnes; married Arthur J; children: Artis Jomar, Aaron Joseph, Arthur Jr & Kelly Ann. **Educ:** Fisk Univ, BA, 1970; Meharry Medical Col, MD, 1974. **Career:** Veteran's Admin, diagnostic radiologist; Mallinckrodt Inst Radiol, St Louis, MO, visiting fel, 1983; Va Med Ctr, Kans City, MO, visiting fel, 1984; Wash Sch Med, Mallinckrodt Inst Radiol, St Louis, MO, visiting fel, 1987; Wis Sch Med, Milwaukee, WI, visiting fel, 1990; Eisenhower Veteran's Affair Med Ctr, diagnostic radiologist, currently, pvt pract, currently. **Orgs:** NMA; Greater Kans City Radiological Soc. **Honors/Awds:** Bd Certified Radiol, 1989; A Consortium of Doctors Honoree, 1993. **Special Achievements:** Author: "Parosteal Osteosarcoma," 1982; "Anorectal Abscesses," 1983, Journal of the Kansas Medical Soc; "Pneumatosis Coli," Journal of the NMA, 1983; "CT, Detecting Intraabdominal Abscesses," Journal of the NMA, 1985; "AIDS: The Role of Imaging Modalities and Infection Control Policies," Journal of the NMA, 1988; "Magnetic Resonance Imaging of an Adult with Dandy Walker Syndrome," Journal of the NMA, 1988; "Serial Nonenhancing Magnetic Resonance Imaging Scans of High Grade Glioblastoma Multiforme," Journal of the NMA, 1993; "Ruptured Pancreaticoduodenal Arterial Aneurysms: Diagnosis and Treatment by Angiographic Interventional," Journal of NMA, 1995; "Multiple Glioblastomas," Journal of Applied Radiology, 2002. **Home Addr:** 1617 Ridge Rd, Leavenworth, KS 66048-6504. **Business Addr:** Diagnostic Radiologist, Eisenhower Veteran, 4101 S 4th Trafficway, Leavenworth, KS 66048-5055, **Business Phone:** (913)682-2000.

MOORING, DR. KITTYE D.
Educator. **Personal:** Born Mar 18, 1932, San Antonio, TX; married Leon. **Educ:** Prairie View A&M Univ, BA, 1953, MS, 1960; Univ Houston, EdD, 1969. **Career:** Carver HS, dept head, 1953-62; Prairie View A & M Univ, assoc prof, 1962-68; Bus Educ & Off Admin Tex Southern Univ, dept head; Sch Bus, assoc dean, 1990-93. **Orgs:** Nat & Tex Bus Asn; chmn, Tex Bus Teacher Educ Coun, 1973-75; Tex Asn Col Teachers; Am Asn Univ Prof; YWCA; chmn, Univ Curriculum Comn, 1980-; chmn, Fac Awards & Recognition Comt, 1985-; Chadwick Manor Civic Club; Community Stand, 1989-92. **Honors/Awds:** Many hon soc; State Service Youth Award; Leaders Black Am, 1974; Teacher of the Year, TBEA Col Bus, 1983; Teacher of the Year, McCleary, 1993. **Home Addr:** 2615 Hodges Bend Circle, Sugar Land, TX 77479.

MOORMAN, CLINTON R
Scout. **Personal:** Born Mar 10, 1924, Cincinnati, OH; son of Clinton and Thelma; married Tamiko Sanbe; children: Bobby & Kathy. **Educ:** Univ Md, BS, 1965. **Career:** Wiley Col, head football coach, 1966-68; San Diego Chargers, talent scout 1969-75; CEPO, area scouts, 1975-76; Cent Intercollegiate Athletic Asn, comnr, 1976-89; Old Dominion Univ, spec asst athletic dir, 1989-91; Nat Football League, Officials' Scouting Prog, scout. **Orgs:** Fellowship Christian Ath, 1969; Peninsula Sports Club, 1973; Big Bros Inc, 1973; Alpha Phi Alpha Res Officers Asn. **Military Serv:** AUS, corporal, 1943-46, major, 1949-66; Bronze Star, Purple Heart, AUS Commendation Medals. **Home Phone:** (757)851-2909.

MOORMAN, HOLSEY ALEXANDER
Military leader. **Personal:** Born May 18, 1938, Roanoke, VA; son of Holsey James and Grace O Walker; married Carrie Boyd, Aug 3, 1963; children: Gary Wayne. **Educ:** Thomas A Edison Col, AA; Hampton Univ, attended 1958; Park Col, BS, bus admin, 1986; Command & Gen Staff Col; US Army War Col, sr reserve component officer course; mediation & conflict mgt skills, 2000. **Career:** Military leader (retired); US Civil Serv, training officer, 1965-68, admin officer, 1968-80, EEO officer, 1980-86; Office Dept Chief Staff Personnel US Army, personnel policy integrator; Asst Secy Army, military asst, 1987-90; Asst Secy Army, Wa, DC, asst deputy, 1990-92; Army Reserve Forces Policy Comt, military exec, 1992-94; deputy adjunct gen, 1994. **Orgs:** Life mem, Nat Guard Asn NJ, 1964-, life mem, Nat Guard Asn US, 1964-; PHA, F&AM, 1978-; EEO investigator Nat Guard Bur, 1982-86. **Honors/Awds:** Service Award, NAACP, Roy Wilkens Renown Service, 1993. **Military Serv:** USY, col, 1961-; Meritorious Serv Medal, Army Commendation Medal, Army Serv Ribbon, Armed Forces Reserve Achievement Medal, Armed Forces Reserve Medal, NJ Medal Honor; Army Distinguished Service Medal; Legion Merit; National Defense Service Medal; Army Superior Unit Award; NJ Good Conduct Award; Desert Storm Ribbon; New Mexico Medal Merit; Governor's Unit Award; Unit Strength Award; National Guard Bureau Eagle Award, 1994, 2000. *

MOOSE, GEORGE EDWARD
Educator, government official. **Personal:** Born Jun 23, 1944, New York, NY; son of Robert and Ellen Amanda Lane Jones; married Judith Roberta Kaufmann, Jan 3, 1981. **Educ:** Grinnell Coll, BA, 1966, Hon Doctorate Law, 1990; Syracuse Univ, postgraduate, 1967. **Career:** Dept State Wash DC, spec asst under secy polit affairs, 1977-78, dep dir SAfrica 1978-79; Coun Foreign Rels New York, int affairs fel, 1979-80; US Mission UN New York City, dep polit counr, 1980-83; Dept State Wash DC, US ambassador Benin, 1983-86, dep dir off mgt operations, 1986-87, dir off mgt operations, 1987-88; US ambassador Senegal, 1988-91; US Alternate Rep UN Security Coun, 1991-92; Dept State, asst secy African affairs, 1993-97; Europ Off UN, Geneva, US Ambassador & permanent rep, 1998-2001; Ralph J Bunche Int Affairs Ctr, Howard Univ, 2001-02; US Inst Peace, bd mem, 2007-; Elliott Sch Int Affairs, George Wash Univ, adj prof, currently; int health diplomacy, consult, currently. **Orgs:** Am Foreign Serv Asn, 1967-; foreign affairs fel, Coun Foreign Rels New York, 1979-80; Asn Black Am Ambassadors, 1985-; Policy Coun Una Chapman Cox Found, 1986-89; Coun Foreign Rels, 1991-; bd dirs, African Develop Found, 1993-97; ambassador & permanent rep, UN Off Geneva, 1998-2001; sr fel, Ralph J Bunche Int Affairs Ctr, Howard Univ, 2001-02; sr inspector, Off Inspector Gen, US Dept State,

2002-. **Honors/Awds:** Superior Honor Award, Dept State, 1974 & 1979; Meritorious Honor Award, Dept State, 1975; Sr Performance Pay, 1985; Presidential Meritorious Service Award, 1989 & 1994; Doctorate Law, Grinnell Col, 1990. **Business Addr:** Adjunct Professor, The George Washington University, The Elliott School of International Affairs, 1957 E St NW, Washington, DC 20052, **Business Phone:** (202)994-6240.

MOO-YOUNG, LOUISE L.
Educator, nurse. **Personal:** Born Dec 29, 1942, Lexington, MS; married Ervin; children: Troy, Tiffany & Tricia. **Educ:** St Mary Nazareth attended 1963; Roosevelt Univ, attended 1974, MPA, 1975; Governors Univ, BA. **Career:** Mich Ave Hosp Chicago, staff nurse head nurse, 1963-64; Chicago Bd Health, pub health field nurse, 1964-70, pub health nurse supvr, 1970-72; Ryerson Stell, part-time indust nurse; Woodlawn Hosp, staff nurse; State Univ, instr; Marion Adult Educ Ctr, prof; Oak Forest Hosp, dir. **Orgs:** Chicago Bd Health Claude WB Holman Neighborhood Health Ctr, 1972-; chmn, Health Task Force Chicago Urban League, 1973-74; Pub Health Section Ill Nurses Asn, 1975; off mgr, Chicago Campaign Off, 1975; St Margaret Epis Church Vestery, 1976-77; Gov Adv Coun Develop Disabilites, 1976-77; Pres, Faulkner Sch Asn, 1977-78; Bd Trustees Faulkner Sch, 1977-78; beat rep, 21st Dist Police; Comprehensive Sickle Cell Anemia Community Adv Coun; Univ Chicago Neighborhood Health Ctr; past mem, Am Nurses Asn; Econ & Gen Welfare Com; Ill Nurses Asn; ARC Nurse Active Church & Comm Affairs; peer group educ comt, Loop Jr Col; adv bd, Claude WB Holman Neighborhood Health Ctr; Am Soc Pub Adminr; St Mary's Alumni Asn; Roosevelt Univ Alumni Asn. **Honors/Awds:** One of Chicago's Ten Outstanding Young Citizens, Jr Assn of Commerce Indus, 1973-74; Outstanding Achievement Award, fourth Ward Dom Orgn; recipient certificate The Emerging Women in Management Workshop.

MORAGNE, LENORA
Editor, publisher. **Personal:** Born Sep 29, 1931, Evanston, IL; daughter of Joseph Sr (deceased) and Linnie Lee (deceased). **Educ:** Iowa State Univ, BS; Cornell Univ, MS, PhD, 1969. **Career:** Community Hosp, Evanston, Ill, chief dietitian, 1955-57; Cornell Univ, asst prof, 1961-63; NC Col, asst prof, 1965-67; Gen Foods Corp, nutrit publicist, 1968-71; Columbia Univ, lectr, 1971-72; Hunter Col, prof, 1971-72; Food & Nutrit Serv USDA, head nutrit, ed & training, 1972-77; Agr Nutrit & Forestry Comn, US Senate, prof staff mem, first female, 1977-79; DHHS nutrit policy coordr, 1979-84; Nutrit Legis Serv, founder, pres, 1985-; Nat Acad Sci, sr proj officer, Inst Med, 1988-89; Nat Rainbow Coalition, consult, 1990; Environ Protection Agency, environ officer, 1994-. **Orgs:** Bd dir, Am Dietetic Asn, 1981-84; APHA Prog Develop Bd, 1984-87; nominee bd trustees, Cornell Univ, 1984; chmn, Cornell Univ Fed Govt Rels Comt, 1985-88; adv coun, Meharry Med Col Nutrit Ctr, 1986-90; founding ed, publ, Nutrit Legis & Regulatory News, Nutrit Funding Report, 1986-; founding ed, publ, Black Cong Monitor, 1987-; pres, Soc Nutrit Educ, 1987-88; founding mem, Joseph & Linnie Lee Monagne Memorial Scholar Fund, 1992-; Am Dietetic Asn; Soc Nutrit Ed; Am Pub Health Asn; Cornell Club DC; Nat Coun Women; adv Coun, Cornell Univ; adv coun, Iowa State Univ; adv coun, Univ Del; adv coun, Univ Md. **Honors/Awds:** Special Appreciation Award, Nat Asn Bus & Prof Women, 1971; Certificate of Apppreciation, USDA, 1973; Distinguished Alumni Award, Iowa State Univ, 1983; President's Coun Cornell Women, Cornell Univ, 2002. **Special Achievements:** Co-author Jr HS nutrition text, "Focus on Food"; co-authored baby record book for new parents "Our Baby's Early Years"; author of numerous food-nutrition related articles in professional publication. **Business Addr:** Founding Editor/ Publisher, Black Congressional Monitor, PO Box 75035, Washington, DC 20013, **Business Phone:** (202)488-8879.

MORAGNE, MAURICE S.
Executive, businessperson. **Personal:** Born Jan 22, 1964, Washington, DC; son of Jacquelyn D.; married Dana M Moragne, Mar 24, 1989; children: Mitchell M, Jordan A. **Educ:** Edinboro Univ Pa, BA, 1986. **Career:** Brown & Williamson, sales rep, Orlando, 1987-89, div mgr, Orlando, 1989-91, brand mkt assoc, Louisville KY, 1991-94, dist sales mgr, Champaign IL, 1994, dist sales mgr, Milwaukee WI, 1994-95, sect sales mgr, Baltimore, 1995-96, dir human resources, 1996-02, dir, Trade Mkt, 2000-02; Moragne & Assoc, prin, 2003-04; L'Oreal, AVP sales admin & oper, 2004-05; Chiquita Brands Int, dir sales & mkt, 2004-05, US Food Serv Div, dir, 2007-; Chiquita Fresh Exp, global dir sales, 2006-07. **Honors/Awds:** Black Achievers Award, Louisville, 1993. **Special Achievements:** Fluent in Spanish, 1977-80. **Business Phone:** (513)784-8000.

MORAGNE, RUDOLPH
Physician. **Personal:** Born Feb 5, 1933, Evanston, IL; married Kathlyn Elaine; children: Donna, Diana, Lisa. **Educ:** Univ Ill, BS, 1955; Meharry Med Col, MD, 1959. **Career:** Cook Co Hosp, intern & resident 1961-65; Hedd Surgi Ctr, abortionist, 1986. **Orgs:** Am Col Obstet & Gynec Surgeons; Am Med Asn; Nat Med Asn; Ill & Chicago Med Soc; Cook Co Physicians Asn; Univ Chicago Lying In Hosp staff; dir, S Side Bank; Urban League; Oper PUSH. **Honors/Awds:** Beautiful People Award, Chicago Urban League 1973. **Special Achievements:** Co-author Our Baby's Early Years 1974. **Military Serv:** USAF, capt, 1961-63. **Business Addr:** 8044 S Cottage Grove, Chicago, IL 60619.

MORAN, GEORGE H
Human services worker. **Personal:** Born Jun 30, 1941, Chicago, IL; son of George H and Wedell Johnson; divorced. **Educ:** Ind Univ-Purdue Univ, Indianapolis; Baker Col, AAS; Detroit Col, BS, comput info syst. **Career:** Instr, data processing; comput programming, instr; Employ Servc, Durable Veteran Outreach; Mich Employ Security Comn, employ analyst, chair emer, currently; Mich Employ Security Agency, veterans coordr, cuerrently. **Orgs:** Chair, Vietnam Veterans Monument Comn; VFW 3791; Southern Cross 39, free mason; Int Asn State Employ; Black Asn State Employers; Black Data Processing Asn, VVA, Vietnam, Vietnam Veterans Am. **Honors/Awds:** VVA Retraining Award, Veterans VVA, 1993; VFW Henry Wolfe Award, Henry Wolf Dept Mich, 1994; African Veterans Banquet, State of MI, 1994. **Military Serv:** AUS, ssgt, 1960-70; Vietnam, 1963-64, 1968-69. **Business Addr:** Chair Emeritus, Michigan Employment Security Commission, 7310 Woodward Ave, Detroit, MI 48202, **Business Phone:** (313)876-5901.

MORAN, JOYCE E
Lawyer. **Personal:** Born May 21, 1948, Chicago, IL; daughter of Theodore E and Irma Rhyne. **Educ:** Smith Col Northampton MA, AB, 1969; Yale Law Sch New Haven, JD, 1972; Univ Chicago, MBA, 1981. **Career:** Sidley & Austin, assoc atty, 1972-78; Sears Roebuck & Co, vpres, law, 1978-2002; Welfare Work Partnership, exec loan, 2000-02; Morityne Develop Co LLC, pres, 2002-. **Orgs:** Vpres, Smith Col Class, 1969, 1974-79; vpres, Chicago League Smith Col Clubs, 1972-; Jr Gov Bd Chicago Symphony Orchestra, 1973-85; bd dirs, vpres, pres, Legal Asst Found Chicago, 1974-88; Chicago Symphony Chorus & Chorale Omega, 1974-78; vpres, treas, Yale Law Sch Assoc, 1975-78; chmn, Lawyers Comt Chicago Urban League, 1980-82; coordr, Coppin AME Church Enrichment Prog, 1981-84; bd dir, Chicago Area Found Legal Serv, 1982-95; ed rev team leader, Mayor Wash Transition Comt Chicago, 1983; bd dir, vpres, Am Civil Liberties Union, 1983-92; bd dirs, Alumnae Asn Smith Col, 1984-87; bd dir, Chicago Found Women, vice chmn, 1985-88, adv coun, 1989-92; bd dir, vpres, treas, Chicago Sch Finance Authority, 1985-93; Kennedy-King COT Chorus, 1986-99; Ill Judicial Inquiry Bd, 1987-91; dir, Am Civil Liberties Union, 1987-89; bd trustees, Smith Col, vice chmn, chmn, pres, search comnr, AD Hoc chapel comt,1988-98; bd dir, Women's Asn Chicago Symphony Orchestra, secy, 1991-97, dir, exec leadership coun, 1997-. **Honors/Awds:** Distinguished Service Award, Coppin Am Church Chicago, 1972; Player of the Year Jr Master, Am Bridge Asn, 1977; Beautiful People Award, Chicago Urban League, 1979; YMCA of Metro Chicago Black & Hispanic Achievers of Industrial Recognition Award 1981; Ten Outstanding Young Citizen Award, Chicago Jr Asn Com & Indust, 1985.

MORANCIE, HORACE L.
Government official, management consultant. **Personal:** Born in San Fernando, Trinidad and Tobago. **Educ:** Polytech Inst Brooklyn, BS, civil eng, 1958; Cornell Univ, MS, civil eng, 1960; Brooklyn Law Sch, Harvard Univ, John F Kennedy Sch Govt, cert, 1982. **Career:** Cornell Univ, teaching fel, 1958-60; Port Authority NY & NJ, res & civil engr, 1960-68; Off Mayor, City NY, asst admin, 1968-74; Addiction Res Treat Corp (ARTC), founder, 1969-; Rockland Community Action Coun Inc, mgt consult, 1974-80, exec dir, 1976-80; State NY, Div Econs Opportunity, dir, 1980-82; City Harrisburg, Dept Community & Econs Develop, dir; Horace L Morancie & Assocs, develop housing & mgt consult. **Orgs:** Bd chmn, Urban Resources Inst, Addiction Res & Treatment Corp; vice chmn,Harrisburg Redevelop Authority; bd mem, Nat Community Develop Asn; chmn, Harrisburg Property Reinvestment Bd. **Honors/Awds:** Anheuser Busch Community Service Award; Exemplary Lifetime Award, 2006;Founders Award, ARTC/ URI Employees Recognition Comt, 2006. **Business Addr:** Consultant, Horace L Morancie & Associates, 469 Rockaway Pkwy, Brooklyn, NY 11212.

MORANT, MACK BERNARD
Publisher, educator, writer. **Personal:** Born Oct 15, 1946, Holly Hill, SC; son of Mack and Jannie Gilmore. **Educ:** Voorhees Col, Denmark, SC, BS, bus admin, 1968; Univ Mass, Amherst, MA, MEd Urban Educ, 1972, CAGS, educ admin, 1973, EdD, 1976. **Career:** SC Pub Sch Syst, hist, Eng, bus teacher, 1968-71; Univ Mass, grad stud, res asst, 1971-74; Belcher Town State Sch, ment health asst, 1974-76; Dillion-Marion Human Resources Com, dep dir, 1977-81; SC State Col, Orangeburg, SC, dir small bus develop, 1982-85; Va State Univ, Petersburg, VA, placement dir, 1985-92; Augusta Col, asst prog, teacher geog, 1992-96; Voorhees Col, stud support serv prog, dir, 1997-; Blackville Hilda High Sch, bus educ teacher, currently; Books: Teacher/student Work Manual: A Model for Evaluating Traditional U.S. History Textbooks, 1982; Face of African Americans on US & International Stamps: A Guide to Collecting & Investing, 1998; African Americans on Stamps, 2003; Articles: "Identifying & Evaluation of Black History in Textbooks"; "The Gigantic Asylumn" 1977; "Blues, Jazz, & American Blacks", 1978. **Orgs:** Alpha Kappa Psi Fraternity, 1985-; vice-chmn, VA State Univ Assessment Comt, 1986-87; Prince Hall Mason, 1986-; Am Philatelic Soc, 1988-. **Business Addr:** Teacher, Blackville-Hilda High School, Department Business Education, 76 Atkins Circle, PO Box 245, Blackville, SC 29817, **Business Phone:** (803)284-2280.

MORCOM, CLAUDIA HOUSE
Judge. **Personal:** Born in Detroit, MI; daughter of Walter House and Glady Stuart. **Educ:** Wayne State Univ, BA, 1953, LLB-JD, 1956. **Career:** Judge (retired); City Detroit Housing Comn, pub housing aid, 1956-60; Law Firm Goodman Crockett et al, atty, assoc mem, 1960-66; Nat Lawyers Guild So Legal Com, regional dir, 1964-65; City Detroit, dir neighborhood legal serv, 1966-68; State Mich Dept Labor, admin law judge, 1972-83; Wayne County Circuit Ct, judge, 1983. **Orgs:** Instr, Afro-Amer Studies Univ Mich, 1971-73; bd mgt, YMCA & YWCA 1971-; instr, Inst Labor Indust Rel, 1972-73; adv, Wayne State Univ Coun World Affairs Ctr Peace & Conflict Studies, 1974-; exec bd nat, Alliance Against Racist & Polit Repression, 1974-; State Bar MI; deleg, Asn Am Jurists, conf Nicaragua, 1981, Granada 1983, Argentina, 1985; Human Rights Workshop Nat Conf Nicaragua Const NY, 1986; bd mem, Merrill Palmer Inst; chmn adv bd, Renaissance Dist Boy Scouts Am; Detroit Police Dept, Jr Cadet Adv Comm, Detroit Strategic Plan Comm; bd dir, Renaissance Club, Harmony Park Playhouse; vpres, Millender Fund; Wilmington 10 Defense Comt; Alternatives Girls; KIND; Mich Democratic Black Caucus; Nat Asn Advan Colored People; Plymouth United Church Christ; Mich Black Judges Asn; Nat Bar Asn; adv bd, Detroit Int Jazz Festival. **Honors/Awds:** National Shrine Scholarship Award, Denver, 1953; Civil Rights Award, Nat Negro Women, 1965; Civil Rights Award, Cook County Bar Asn, 1966; Human Rights Award, Detroit Chap Am Civil Liberties, 1967; Human Rights Award, Detroit Com Human Rights, 1969; Mich State Legislative Certificate of Merit, 1977; Spirit of Detroit Award, 1977; Certificate of Recognition, YWCA Met Detroit, 1979; Damon J Keith Civic and Humanitarian Award, 1984; Commercial Leadership Award Coalition of 100 Black Women; Women of Wayne Headliner Award; Boy Scouts Appreciation Award; John F Kennedy Award of Co-Ettes Club; Heart of Gold Award Boy Scouts of America; National Honor Soc Award Cass Tech HS; HDL, Shaw Col; Liberty Bell Award, Wayne County Neighborhood Legal Serv; National Honor Society Award, Cass Tech High Sch; The Woman of Wayne Award, Wayne State Univ; Dauris Jackson Award, Wayne State Univ; Outstanding Alumni Award, Wayne State Univ; Service to the Handicapped Award, Eastern Mkt Bus Asn; The Center for Constitutional Rights Award, 1990; Silver Beaver Award, Boy Scouts Am, 1994; Certificate of Special Congressional Recognition, 1996; Service Award, Evergreen C Serv, 1996; Champion of Justice, State Bar Mich, 1996; Life Achievement Award, Mich Women's Hall Fame, 1996. **Home Phone:** (313)331-0692.

MORDECAI, DAVID K A
Economist. **Personal:** Born Sep 27, 1961, New York, NY; son of Kenneth and Vinette; married Samantha Kappagoda, Jul 18, 1996. **Educ:** King's Col, BA, 1983; NYU Stern Sch Bus MBA, 1987; Univ Chicago, PhD, financial econs, 2004. **Career:** NYU Stern Sch/Chase Manhattan fel, 1985-86; Bankers Trust, assoc, corp finance, 1987-88; West Deutsche Landesbank, asst vp, leveraged capital group, 1990; Bank Montreal, consult, foreign exchange trading, 1992-93; Univ Chicago, Grad Sch Bus fel, 1993-; Credit Suisse First Boston, consult, 1995; FITCHIBCA, dir, commercial ABS group, 1997-98; AIG Global Investments, vpres, financial eng, 1998-2001; AIG Structured Products, vpres, financial eng/ prin finance, 1998-2001; Clinton Group, managing dir, structured products, 2001-03; Columbia Univ, guest lectr; Risk Econs Ltd Inc, found, currently. **Orgs:** Int Investment Mgt Steering Comt, NY Mercantile Exchange, 1998-; Ins Indust Working Group, Nat Bur Econ Res, 1999-; adv bd & IRC Steering Comt, Int Asn Financial Engrs, 2000-; adv bd, Jour Alternative Investments, Euromoney/Insts Investor Jour, 2004-; co-chair, Liquidity Risk Comt 2005-; Financial Insts Risks Working Group, 2005-; adv/ edial bd, Int Encycl Derivatives; sr adv, Swiss Financial Serv. **Honors/Awds:** Stern School Dean's Service Awardd, NY Univ, 1986-87. **Special Achievements:** Ed in Chief, Journal of Risk Finance, Euromoney/Institutional Investor Journals, 1998-2004; Author: Emerging Market Credit Derivatives & Default Estimation, in Credit Derivatives: Applications for Investment, Portfolio Optimization & Risk Mgmt, 1998; The Use of Credit Derivatives In Credit-Enhanced & Credit-Linked Structuren Notes, The Handbook of Credit Derivatives, 1999; Alternative Risk Transfer, The Handbook of Alternate Investment Strategies, 1999. **Business Addr:** President/Partner, Founder, Risk Economics Limited Inc, S3 Asset Funding, c/o S3 Partners, 590 Madison Ave 32nd Fl, New York, NY 10022, **Business Phone:** (212)759-5222.

MORELAND, DR. LOIS BALDWIN
Educator, school administrator. **Personal:** Born in Washington, DC; daughter of Genis G and Fannie; married Charlie J, Dec 28, 1958; children: Lisa Carol. **Educ:** Sarah Lawrence Col, BA, 1955; Howard Univ, MA, 1957; Am Univ, WA, PhD, 1968. **Career:** Howard Univ, asst & instr social sci, 1956-57; SE reg youth field sec 1957-58; US Senator R Vance Hartke, legis asst, 1958-59; Spelman Col, instr, 1959-65, Political Sci Dept, asst prof & founding chmn, 1965-70, prof & chmn, 1970-90, 1991-92, acting dean instr, 1970-72, chmn soc sci div, 1980-90, prof polit sci, Int Affairs Ctr, founding dir, 1989-98, prof emer, 1999-. **Orgs:** Charter

mem & first treas, Nat Conf Black Polit Sci; former mem, Am Asn Univ Women; Nat Asn Advan Colored People; League Women Voters; former mem, Fulton Co Bd Elections; Fulton Co Jury Comn; Gov's Coun Human Rel; Am Southern & Ga Polit Sci Assoc; Assoc Polit & Life Sci; Alpha Kappa Alpha;former mem, advisory Coun, Nat Inst Neurological, Communicable Disease & Stroke; former mem, Adv Coun Deafness & Commun Dis; NIH; Prof Adv Bd, Nat Epilepsy Found, 1984-9; Am Political Sci Asn; Am Asn Univ Prof; Am Asn Univ Women; Nat Conf Black Political Scientists; Southern Political Sci Asn; Ga Political Sci Asn. **Honors/Awds:** American Legion Award; Ford Found Fel; American Univ Govt Intern Fel; Merit Achievement, Outstanding Educator, 1973; American Political Science Society Conference Award; United Negro Col Fund Fel; Sarah Lawrence Col Scholar; honorary life mem, Nat Assoc Bus Women; Presidential Award, Spelman Col, 1988-89; Professional Excellence Award, 1993; Distinguished Service Award, Spelman Col, 1998; hon mem, Alpha Lambda Delta Honor Soc, Spelman Col, 1999. **Special Achievements:** First professor Emerita, Spelman college, 1999; Books: "White Racism and the Law", 1970. **Home Addr:** 849 Woodmere Dr NW, Atlanta, GA 30318. **Business Addr:** Professor Emeritus, Spelman College, Department of Political Science, 350 Spelman Lane SW, Atlanta, GA 30314-4399, **Business Phone:** (404)681-3643.

MORELAND-YOUNG, DR. CURTINA

Educator. **Personal:** Born Mar 5, 1949, Columbia, SC; daughter of Gladys Evelyn Glover Moreland and Curtis Weldon Moreland; married James Young, Jun 20, 1983 (divorced); children: Curtis Jamel Turner. **Educ:** Fisk Univ, Nashville, Tenn, BA, 1969; Univ Ill, Urbana, MA, 1975, PhD,1976; Harvard Univ, Cambridge, MA, PhD, 1982. **Career:** Ohio State Univ, Dept Black Studies, Columbus, Ohio, instr asst prof, 1971-78; Jackson State Univ, Miss Col & Univ Consortium Int Study, Dept Polit Sci, coordr MA prog, assoc prof, 1978-84, prof & chair, pub policy & admin dept, 1984-2006. **Orgs:** Chair, pres, Conf Minority Pub Adminr, 1989-90; exec bd, Nat Conf Black Polit Scientist, 1989; Nat Coun Am Soc Pub Adminr, 1989-90; chair, Comt Orgn Rev & Eval, ASPA, 1990-91; exec bd, Jackson Int Visitors Ctr. **Honors/Awds:** John Oliver Killen Writing Award, Fisk Univ, 1969; Lilly Fel, Lilly Found,1979-80; Rockefeller Foundation Fel, Rockefeller Found, 1983; DuBois Scholar, DuBois Inst, Harvard Univ, 1983; Kellogg Nat Fel, Kellogg Found, 1989-92. **Business Addr:** Professor, Jackson State University, 3825 Ridgewood Rd, Jackson, MS 39211.

MORGAN, ALICE JOHNSON PARHAM

Health services administrator. **Personal:** Born Jul 17, 1943, Richmond, VA; daughter of Elmore W Johnson Jr and Fannye Mae Quarles Johnson; married Wilson M; children: Weldon Leo & Arvette Patrice. **Educ:** VA Union Univ, BA, 1965; VA Commonwealth Univ, MSW, 1967; Univ Southern Calif (WA Public Affairs Ctr), MPA, 1982. **Career:** Health services administrator (retired); Area D CMHC, supvr, soc worker, 1981; St Elizabeth's Hosp, soc work prog, 1981-82; Area D CMHC, soc worker, 1982-83, dir, spec apt prog, 1983-88, dir, Region IV Psychosocial Day Prog, 1988-91, Region 4 Housing, resource specialist, 1991-2002. **Orgs:** Bd dir, Nat Conf Christians & Jews, Alexandria Mental Health Asn; First Black/First Female Alex, VA, Planning Comm, 1971-79; chairperson (city of Alex, VA) Martin Luther King Planning Comm, 1973-; dir, comm placement office, Area D, CMHC, 1972-79; First Black Female City Coun Candidate, Alex, VA, 1979; ed & standards specialist, St Elizabeth's Hosp, 1979-80; prog analyst, Public Health Serv, 1980-81; dir, comm placement off, Area D, CMHC, 1980. **Honors/Awds:** Outstanding Commission Service Award, Alex Dept Pro Club, 1979; Intergovt Mgt Appointee, Dept Health & Human Serv 1980-81; Human Rights Award, Alex Comm Status Women, 1984; Dorothea Lynde Dix Award, St Elizabeth's Hosp, 1984; Community Service Award, Alex Commn Status Women, 1986; Community Service Award, Nat Asn Advan Colored People, 1988; Community Service Award, Lorraine B Funn Atkins, 1996. **Home Addr:** 1513 Dogwood Dr, Alexandria, VA 22302.

MORGAN, ALISHA THOMAS

Congressional representative (u.s. federal government). **Personal:** Born in Miami, FL; married David. **Educ:** Spelman Col, BA, Sociol & Drama. **Career:** Ga House, rep, currently, educ comn, C & youth comn, info comn & audits comn, currently; 1380 WAOK, comn talk, host, currently; Morganics, princ & ceo, currently. **Orgs:** Pres, NAACP, Miami Dade Youth Coun; pres, Spelman Col Chap; state pres, Spelman Col Chap, Youth & Col Div; Destiny World Church in Austell; Alpha Kappa Alpha Sorority Inc; Rho Zeta Omega Chap; NAACP; brd, Joseph E LoweryInst; Steering Comn, Ga Coalition for People Agenda; Austell CommunityT ask-force; Nat Coalition 100 Black Women, NW Ga Chap. **Honors/Awds:** Leadership Awards, NAACP; Outstanding Young Woman Award, Concerned Black Clergy; Unsung Heroine Award, Anti-Defamation League; Freshman Legislator of the Yr, Ga Legis Black Caucus, 2008; Flemming Fel, Ctr Policy Alternatives,2006. **Special Achievements:** First African-Am to serve in Ga House Representatives, Cobb Co, 2002; Youngest service mem entire Ga Gen Assembly; Featured in: Atlanta Tribune,Women Looking Ahead; Ga brightest 40 under 40, Ga Trend Mag; Nations 30Leaders who are under 30, Ebony mag; one ten Am Young Civil Rights

Heroes, AOL Black Voices; one six women in country featured in article "I Made in By 30 & You Can Too", Marie Claire Mag; selected as a deleg to travel to S Africa with Am Coun Young Polit Leaders; Flemming Fel, Ctr for Policy Alternatives, 2006; Launched "Closing the Achievement Gap", 2009; Author of "No Apologies: Powerful Lessons in Life, Love and Politics", 2009. **Business Addr:** Representative, GA House of Representatives, 6570 Brandemere Way, Austell, GA 30168, **Business Phone:** (404)656-0109.*

MORGAN, CLYDE ALAFIJU

Educator, dance teacher. **Personal:** Born Jan 30, 1940, Cincinnati, OH; son of Lee and Harriette Young; married Marie Lais Goes; children: Clyde G, Dyuna G & Lee Young G. **Educ:** Cleveland State Univ, Cleveland, OH, BA, 1963; Bennington Col, Bennington, VT, prof cert, 1965. **Career:** Bennington Col, VT, dance fel, 1963-64; Fed Univ Bahia, Salvador Bahia Brazil, choreographer & artistic dir, Fulbright prof, 1985-86; Univ Wis, Madison, WI, vis artist, 1979-80; Univ Wis, Milwaukee, WI, asst prof, 1980-87; State Univ NY Brockport, Sankofa African Dance & Drum Ensemble, artistic dir, 1985-; assoc prof African dance, currently; Fulbright Prof, Brazil, 1986-87. **Orgs:** Cong Res Dance, 1985-; United Univ Prof, 1987-; Dance Hist Scholars, 1991-. **Honors/Awds:** Academic Scholarship, Cleveland Found, 1961-62. **Business Addr:** Associate Professor of African Dance, Artistic Director of Sankofa, State University of New York, Department of Dance, Hartwell Hall 350 New Campus Dr, Brockport, NY 14420, **Business Phone:** (585)395-5789.

MORGAN, DARIAN. See TIGGER, BIG.

MORGAN, DEBBI

Actor. **Personal:** Born Sep 20, 1956, Dunn, NC; daughter of George Morgan and Lora Morgan; married Donn Thompson. **Career:** Soap operas: All My C, 1982-90; Generations, 1990-91; Loving, 1993-95; The City, 1995-97; Port Charles, 1997-98; tv movies: Roots, 1977; The Jesse Owens Story, 1984; The Runaway, 2000; tv series: "All my Children", 1982-2008; "Loving", 1983-95; "The city", 1995; "Soul Food", 2000; "Boston Pub", recurring role, 2000; "For the People", 2002; "Charmed", 2002-03; "Woman Thou Art Loosed", 2006; "Touching Evil", 2004; "Back in the Day", 2005; "Color of the Cross", 2006; "Prodigal Son", 2006; "Close to Home", 2006; films: Mandingo, 1975; Eve's Bayou, 1997; Asunder, 1998; She's All That, 1999; The Hurricane, 1999; Love & Basketball, 2000; "Charmed", 2003; Woman Thou Art Loosed, 2004; Back in the Day, 2005; Relative Strangers, 2005; Coach Career, 2005; Rel Strangers, 2006; "The Bold & the Beautiful", 2006-07. **Honors/Awds:** Emmy Award for Best Supporting Actress, All My Children (first black actress to win the award); Daytime Emmy Award for Outstanding Supporting Actress in a Drama Series, 1989; CFCA Award for Best Supporting Actress, 1998; Independent Spirit Award for Best Supporting Female, 1998; Image Award for Outstanding Supporting Actress in a Drama Series, 2002. **Business Addr:** Actress, Stone Manners, 8436 W Third St Suite 740, Los Angeles, CA 90048-4100, **Business Phone:** (213)654-7575.

MORGAN, DOLORES PARKER

Entertainer, musician. **Personal:** Born in New Orleans, LA; daughter of Joseph and Mabel Moton; married Vernon Smith, Jan 1, 1945; married E Gates; children: Melodie Morgan-Minott. **Educ:** Chicago Musical Col, 1941; Wilson Col. **Career:** Earl "Fatha" Hines, singer, 1945-47; Duke Ellington, singer, 1947-49; solo performer & singer, 1949-56; Local Charity Events, singer, 1960-; Traditions, soloist, 1999. **Orgs:** Bd mem, corres secn Ohio Ballet, 1983-87; exec bd trust, Visiting Nurses Serv, 1984-; develop coun, Akron Art Museum, Beacon Jour, 1986-; bd mem, Akron Symphony, 1986-; bd dir, Kent State Found, 1987-; hon mem, Alpha Kappa Alpha Sorority, 1990. **Honors/Awds:** Hall of Fame Best Dressed Akron, Beacon Jour, 1971; Ebony Best Dressed List, Ebony Mag, 1972; Dolores Parker Morgan Endowed Scholarship, Music Kent State Univ, named in honor, 1986; EL Novotny Award, Kent State Sch Art, 1989; Dolores Parker Morgan Day, City Akron, Ohio, named in honor, 1990. **Special Achievements:** Honored by Smithsonian Museum of American History as one of the five surviving female vocalists of the Duke Ellington Orchestra. **Home Addr:** 3461 S Smith Rd, Akron, OH 44333.

MORGAN, FLETCHER

Government official. **Personal:** Born Oct 6, 1920, Bay City, TX; son of Fletcher and Ella; married Alice Mae Riggins; children: Nadine, Rita & Dennis L. **Educ:** Prairie View A&M Univ, BS, 1943, MS, 1947; Lasalle Inst & Wharton Co Jr Col, addl study. **Career:** Government official (Retired); USDA Farmers Home Adm Bay City, TX, retired co supr, 1970-86, asst co supr, 1965-70; USDA FMHA Richmond TX Co, supr, 1949-51; Vets in Agri, instr & supr, 1946-49. **Orgs:** Bd dir, Ft Bend Co Taxpayers Asn; Centennial Coun Prairie View A&M Univ, 1968-70; Nu Phi; Omega Psi Phi; Tex Soc Farm & Ranch Mgrs & Appraisers; NAACP; AME Ch; 32 deg Mason; Shriner; Prairie View A&M Univ alumni asn; bd dir, Coastal Plain; Plains Soil & Water Conservation Dist; bd dirs, #1772 AARP; bd dirs & secy, treas, Sam Houston conservation Dist; bd dirs, Fort Bend County FSA Comt MNY Advr;

volunteer, Brazos Bend State Park; pres, Gulf Coast Asn Soil & Water Conservation Dist; advis comt, Cty Agr Extension Prog. **Honors/Awds:** Alumni citation Prairie View A&M Univ, 1969; distinguished Omega Man of Year, 1969; Omega Man of Year Nu Phi Chap Houston, 1973; Certificate of Appreciation, Tepos Agr Extension Serv, Years of Service, dir, Sun Houston Conservation & Develop, Aneas Inc, 2001; First Burton Award, 2002. **Military Serv:** MIL serv, 1943-45. **Home Addr:** PO Box 90, Thompsons, TX 77481-0090.

MORGAN, DR. GORDON D.

Educator. **Personal:** Born Oct 31, 1931, Mayflower, AR; son of Roosevelt and Georgianna Madlock; married Izola Preston, Jun 15, 1957; children: Marsha, Brian, Marian & Bryce (deceased). **Educ:** Ark AM & N Col, BA cum laude, soc, 1953; Univ Ark, MA, sociol, 1956; WashState Univ, PhD, sociol, 1961. **Career:** Pine State Sch, teacher, 1956-59; Wash State Univ, TA/RA, 1960-63;Teachers E Africa Proj, res asst, 1963-65; Lincoln Univ, asst prof sociol, 1965-69; Ark AM & N Col, instr, 1969-60; Univ Ark, assoc prof & prof, 1973-91, univ prof, currently; Wash State Univ, visiting distinguishedprof sociol, 1991-. **Orgs:** Consult, S Regional Educ Bd; consult, SW Minn State Col; consult,Philander Smith Col; consult, Ark Prog Basic Adult Educ; consult, Ark Tech Assistance Prog; consult, Quachita Baptist Col; consult, Nat Inst Ment Health; fly-in prof, St Ambrose Col, 1973; expert witness before Rockefeller Comm, Pop & Future, 1971; expert witness on fed judge panel onat-large voting AR, 1973; Wash Co Grand Jury, 1974; Rotary/Downtown, AR,1980-; fel Southern Studio Miss, 1987-88. **Honors/Awds:** Ford Foundation Postdoc, Lincoln Univ, 1969; Am Col Testing Postdoc,Lincoln Univ, 1969; The Ghetto Col Stut, ACT, 1970; Russell Sage Post doc,Univ Ark, 1972; Law Enforcement Assistant Administration Award, SUNY, 1975; NEH, Univ Wis, 1980; NEH, Queens Col, SUNY, 1983; Lawrence A Davis,Ark Educator, Asn Fac Press, 1985. **Special Achievements:** First black faculty members at the Univ Ark, 1956; Author: A Short Social History of the E Fayetteville Community with Izola Preston Morgan, 1978,The Training of Black Sociologists, Tolbert H Kennedy and Washington State University, Teaching Sociology, 1980, America Without Ethnicity, Kennikat,1981, The Little Book of Humanistic Poems, 1981, co-author of The Edge of Campus, A Jour of the Black Experience at the Univ Ark, 1990, The History of the Southeast Fayetteville Community Action Committee, The Fayetteville Action Group, 1990, Ida Rowland Bellegorde: Master Teacher, Scholar,McGraw-Hill, 1992, Toward an American Sociology; Questioning the European Construct, Westport, CT, Greenwood, 1997, he Firing of Nolan Richardson, 2004, Winners Never Quit: Marguerite Rogers Howie: Early Black Woman Sociologist, New Academia Press, Washington, DC 2006. **Military Serv:** AUS, 1953; AUS Reserves, comm, 1959. **Business Addr:** Professor of Sociology, University of Arkansas, 224 Old Main, Fayetteville, AR 72701, **Business Phone:** (479)575-3810.

MORGAN, DR. HARRY

Educator, publisher, writer. **Personal:** Born Jun 6, 1926, Charlottesville, VA; son of John and Cheyney Lewis; married Edwina, Jan 1, 1949 (divorced 1982); children: Parris & Lawrence. **Educ:** NY Univ, BS, 1949; Univ Wis, MSW, 1967; Univ Mass, EdD, 1970. **Career:** Bank State Col, prog coordr, 1966-69; Univ NH, prof, 1969-70; Ohio Univ, prof, 1970-72; Syracuse Univ, prof, 1972-84; Univ West Ga, prof early childhood & elem educ, 1984-, chmn early childhood educ; Author: The Learning Community, 1973; Historical Perspectives on the Education of Black Children, 1995; Cognitive Styles & Classroom Learning, 1997; The Imagination of Early Childhood Education, 1999; Real Learning: A Bridge to Cognitive Neuroscience, 2004; Early Childhood Education : History, Theory, and Practice, 2007. **Orgs:** US Govt Dir Project Head Start North East Region, 1964-66; fel Ford Found, 1967-69; consult, US Govt, Black Aged, 1970-74; Am Educ Res Asn, 1975-; Nat Asn Educ Young C, 1972-; Am Asn Univ Prof, 1980-; Am Asn Col Teacher Educ, 1984; Phi Delta Kappa, 1985. **Honors/Awds:** Research Award, Phi Delta Kappa, 1999. **Home Addr:** 2284 Lakeview Pkwy, Villa Rica, GA 30180. **Business Addr:** Professor, University of West Georgia, Department of Curriculum and Instruction, 1601 Maple St, 221 Education Annex, Carrollton, GA 30118, **Business Phone:** (678)839-6072.

MORGAN, HAZEL C BROWN

Educator. **Personal:** Born Oct 25, 1930, Rocky Mount, NC; daughter of Beulah McGee Brown (deceased) and Rollon Brown (deceased); married Charlie (deceased); children: Savoynne Ewell. **Educ:** A&T State Univ, BS, Nursing, 1960; East Carolina Univ, MS, Rehab Coun, 1977, MS, Nursing, 1980. **Career:** Educator (retired); Wilson Mem Hosp, charge nurse, 1964-66; Northern Nash High Sch, health occup teacher, 1966-73; Nash General Hosp, team leader, pt care, 1971-; East Carolina Univ Sch Nursing, asst prof nursing, 1973-93; Veteran's Admin Hosp, Richmond Va & E Orange NJ, staff nurse, 1960-62; Landis State Hosp Philadelphia Pa, asst head nurse & instr, 1963; Resurrection Ministries Christian Ctr, secy, currently. **Orgs:** Past mem, Am Nurses Asn; Asn Black Educr, NC; Nurse's Asn Dist 20; past mem, ECU Orgn Black Fac & Staff; Sigma Theta Tau 1988-; Asn Black Nursing Fac, 1987-; past health consult, Wright Geriatric Day Care Ctr, 1988-; pres, Carrie Broadfoot Nurses Club; secy, 1995, pres, Seasons Plus Srs,; prof retirees, 1997-98, treas, 1997,

Leisurettes Club; East Carolina Retired Fac Asn; comn mem, East Carolina Univ, Sch Nursing Emeriti; secy, Diabetic comn; Nash Cty Democratic Comn. **Honors/Awds:** Ten years Service Award, East Carolina Univ Sch Nursing, 1983; Service Award for Achievement, Black Fac Mem Greatest Numbers Yrs Serv, Omega Psi Phi Frat, 1984; Soc & Civic Award, Chat-a-While Civic Orgn La State Univ, Eunice, 1984; Creativity Documenting Nursing Interventions, Develop Slide-Tape Prog, 1989. **Home Addr:** 913 Beal St, Rocky Mount, NC 27804, **Home Phone:** (252)446-1554.

MORGAN, JANE HALE
Librarian. **Personal:** Born May 11, 1925, Dines, WY; daughter of Arthur Hale and Billie Wood; married Joseph C, Aug 12, 1955; children: Joseph Hale, Jane Frances & Ann Michele. **Educ:** Howard Univ, BA, 1947; Univ Denver, MA, 1954. **Career:** Librarian (retired). Detroit Pub Library, staff, 1954, exec asst dir 1973-75, dep dir, 1975-78, dir, 1978-87; Wayne State Univ, visiting prof, 1989-91. **Orgs:** Am Libr Asn; Mich Libr Asn; exec bd, Southeastern Mich Reg Film Libr; LSCA adv coun Lib; bd trustees, Womens Nat Book Asn; New Detroit Inc; bd dir, Rehab Inst; vpres United Way Southeastern Mich; bd dir, YWCA; Asn Municipal & Pressional Women; Alpha Kappa Alpha; bd dir, Univ Cult Ctr Asn; Urban League; NAACP; bd dir, Women's Econ Club; bd dir, United Community Serv; bd dirs, Delta Dental Plan; bd dirs, Metropolitan Affairs Corp; bd, New Detroit Inc; Mich Coun Humanities; Mich Women's CMS; Detroit Women's Community; Delta Dental Plan Ohio; pres, Delta Dental Fund; Detroit Exec Serv Corps; pres, Sorosis Art & Lit Club; bd mem, Mich Ctr Book; Detroit Women's Forum. **Honors/Awds:** Recipient, "The Anthony Wayne Award," Wayne St Univ, Col Ed, 1981; Detroit "Howardite of the Year," 1983; Summit Award, Greater Detroit Chamber Com, 1989. **Home Phone:** (248)539-9383.

MORGAN, JOE
Baseball player, broadcaster. **Personal:** Born Sep 19, 1943, Bonham, TX; married Gloria Stewart; children: Lisa & Angela. **Educ:** Calif State Univ, Hayward, BA, phys educ, 1990. **Career:** Baseball Player (retired), broadcaster; Houston Colt .45's (later Houston Astros), 1963-71, 1980; Cincinnati Reds, 1972-79, announcer, 1985; San Francisco Giants, 1981-82, announcer, 1986-95; Philadelphia Phillies, 1983; Oakland Athletics, 1984; KTVU, broadcaster; Joe Morgan Beverage Co, chief exec officer, 1988-95; ABC, announcer, 1988-89; ESPN, NBC, color analyst, baseball analyst, color commentator, 1994-2000, Emmy-winning commentator, currently. **Orgs:** Pres, Joe Morgan Youth Found; vice chmn, Nat Baseball Hall Fame, 2000; contribr, Young Am baseball prog; contribr, Oakland Unified Sch Dist Sports Prog. **Honors/Awds:** Nat League Rookie of the Year, 1965; Most Valuable Player, All-Star Game, 1972; Gold Glove, 1973, 1974, 1975, 1976; Nat League Most Valuable Player, Baseball Writers Asn Am, 1975, 1976; Most Valuable Player, San Francisco Giants, 1982; Willie Mac Award, 1982; Comeback Player of the Year, Sporting News, 1982; Cincinnati Reds Hall of Fame, 1987; Nat Baseball Hall of Fame, 1990; Sports Emmy, 1998, 2005. **Special Achievements:** Author: Joe Morgan: A Life in Baseball; Baseball for Dummies. **Business Addr:** Major League Baseball Analyst, ESPN, ESPN Plz, Bristol, CT 06010, **Business Phone:** (203)585-2000.

MORGAN, DR. JOHN PAUL
Dentist. **Personal:** Born Oct 23, 1929, Kokomo, IN; widowed 2004; children: Angela Marie. **Educ:** Ind Univ, pre-dental studies; Meharry Med Col, DDS, 1960. **Career:** Dentist (retired); 6510 USAF Hosp Edwards AFB Calif, officer-in-charge hosp dental, 1960-64; 439th USAF Hosp Misawa, AB, Japan, oic security serv dental asst base dent surgery, 1964-67; Lockbourne AFB, OH, chief prosthodontics, 1967-71; 377th USAF Disp Tan Son Nhut AB Vietnam, chief oral surgery, 1971-72; USAF Hosp Kirtland AFB NM, asst base dent surgeon, 1972-78; USAF Hosp Hahn AB Germany, base dental surgeon, 1978-81; USAF Med Ctr SGD Scott AFB IL, dep dir dental serv, 1981. **Orgs:** Nat Dent Assoc, Acad Gen Dent, Assoc Mil Surgeons, Prince Hall Lodge; life mem, NAACP, Alpha Phi Alpha. **Military Serv:** USAF, col, 28 yrs; Meritorious Serv Medal w/One Oak Leaf Cluster, Air Force Commendation Medal, Presidential Unit Citation AF Outstanding Unit Award; Republic of Vietnam Gallantry Cross w/Palm; Republic of Vietnam Campaign Medal, 1960-; The Legion of Merit, 1988.

MORGAN, JOSEPH C.
Manager. **Personal:** Born Jan 10, 1921, Douglas, GA; married Jane Hale; children: Joseph, Jane & Michele. **Career:** Pub Serv Employ Detroit, dir, 1974; Detroit Zoo Park, dep dir, 1974-. **Orgs:** Pres, Frame Div, UAW, 1955-67; pres, Detroit Chap Nat Negro Labor Coun, 1957-59; Int Rep Recruiter Coun, 1967-74. **Honors/Awds:** Meritorious Service Award, 1974. **Military Serv:** AUS, corp eng, 1946.

MORGAN, REV. MARY H ETHEL
Educator. **Personal:** Born Mar 11, 1912, Summerton, SC; married C M; children: Carolyn Marie Brown-Geli Revelle. **Educ:** SC State Col, BA, 1951; Ball State Uni, IN, MA, educ, 1975; Anderson Col Theological Sem, MA, religion, 1979; Anderson Univ, honorary doctor divinity degree. **Career:** Educator (retired); Bd Educ, SC, teacher, 1935-40; Nursery Sch, FL, teacher, 1941-44; IN Church Sch, teacher, 1960-70; Comm Sch, Anderson, IN, teacher & substitute teacher, 1970-82; Teacher Minister; Sherman St Church, minister. **Orgs:** Ordained Christian ministry, Indiana Ministry Assembly, 1984; NAACP Local & Nat, 1985; Ladies Republican Club Local & Nat, 1985; State Teachers Retirmnt Club, IN, 1985; Madison County retired Teachers org; Women United; bd dirs, CCCV; bd dirs, YWCA, 1987-; assoc minister, Church God, 1990-. **Honors/Awds:** Outstanding Teacher (Elem) of America, 1974; "Love Award", 1987; Women Ministers Organization Award for faithful service; Outstanding Alumnus Award, Ball State Univ, 1989; Distinguished Alumnus Award, Anderson Univ Seminary, 1990; Anderson-area elementary school, named in honor. **Special Achievements:** Missionary service in India for ten years. **Business Addr:** PO Box 2041, Anderson, IN 46018.

MORGAN, MELI'SA
Singer, songwriter, music producer. **Personal:** Born Jan 1, 1964, Queens, NY; married Shelly Garrett, Aug 28, 1993. **Educ:** Juilliard Sch, New York, NY. **Career:** Albums: Do Me Baby, 1986; Good Love, 1988; The Lady in Me, 1990; Still in Love With You, 1992; Tell Me How It Feels, 1995; Do You Still Love Me, 1996; Believe in Yourself, 1998; Fools Paradise, 2001; Don't Say Love, 2003; Back Together Again, 2005 I Remember, 2005. Singles: High Maintenance, 2007. **Business Addr:** Singer, c/o Capitol Records, 1750 Vine St Suite 6252, Los Angeles, CA 90028.*

MORGAN, MICHAEL
Conductor (music). **Personal:** Born Jan 1, 1957, Washington, DC. **Educ:** Oberlin Col Conservatory Music; Berkshire Music Ctr, Tanglewood, CA. **Career:** St Louis Symphony Orchestra, asst conductor; Buffalo Philharmonic, apprentice conductor; Chicago Symphony Orchestra, asst conductor, 1986-92; Civic Orchestra Chicago, conductor; Oakland Youth Orchestra, artistic dir; Sacramento Philharmonic, music dir; Festival Opera, Walnut Creek, artistic dir; San Francisco Conservatory Music, music teacher; Oakland E Bay Symphony, music dir & conductor, currently. **Orgs:** Bd mem, ASOL; Recording Acad; Am Soc Composers. **Honors/Awds:** First Prize, Hans Swarowsky Inter Nat Conductors Competition, Vienna, Austria, 1980; Two Nat Awards, 2005; Governors Award for Community Service, San Francisco Chapter, Recording Acad, 2005; Concert Music Awards, Am Soc Composers, Authors & Publ, 2005. **Business Addr:** Music Director, Conductor, Oakland East Bay Symphony, 400 29th St Suite 501, Oakland, CA 94609, **Business Phone:** (510)444-0801.

MORGAN, MONICA ALISE
Photojournalist. **Personal:** Born May 27, 1963, Detroit, MI; daughter of Barbara Jean Pace. **Educ:** Wayne State Univ, Detroit MI, BA, 1985. **Career:** Domino's Pizza, Ann Arbor, MI, promotional coordr; Detroit Pub Schs, Detroit, MI, pub rels coordr; WDIV-TV, Detroit, MI, prod asst; Palmer St Productions, Detroit, MI, host & pub rels dir; WQBH-radio, talk show host; Mich Chronicle, Detroit, MI, columnist & photojournalist, 1987-; US Dept Census, Detroit, MI, Community Awareness Specialist, 1988-90; Monica Morgan Photography, owner & photojournalist, currently. **Orgs:** Secy, Nat Asn Black Journalists, 1981-; Optimist Club, 1987-; be mem, Manhood Inc, 1988-; Elliottorian Bus Women Inc, 1988-; Nat Asn Broadcasters; Nat Asn Female Execs; Nat Press Photographers; Kindred Souls. **Honors/Awds:** Numerous awards & honors including Outstanding Young Woman of America, 1986 & 1987; Civic & Community Award, Wall Street Inc, 1989; Certificate of Appreciation, Rosa & Raymond Parks Inst Self Develop; SBC Ameritech African American Excellence Award, 2003; Detroit's Most Influential Woman; Leader of the 21st Century. **Business Addr:** Owner, Photojournalist, Monica Morgan Photography, 500 River Pl Suite 5109, Detroit, MI 48207, **Business Phone:** (313)259-7005.

MORGAN, RICHARD H., JR.
Lawyer. **Personal:** Born Feb 12, 1944, Memphis, TN; married Olga Jackson; children: Darrin Allan, Heather Nicole, Nia Abena, Amish Adzua & Erica. **Educ:** Western Mich Univ, BA, MA; Univ Detroit Law Sch, attended 1973. **Career:** Western Mich Univ, counr; Oakland Univ Proj Pontiac, dir; Stud Ctr, asst dir, asso dir, dean Stud asst; Community Serv Prog Urban Affairs Ctr, dir; Hatchett Mitchell Morgan & Hall, atty; Morgan & Hall, sr partner. **Orgs:** Am Pub Gardens Asn, Maine Prof Guides Asn; Mich State Bar; Oakland Co Bar; Wolverine Bar; Am Bar & Wayne Co Bar; Kappa Alpha Psi Frat; Big Bro Kalamazoo; Pontiac Area Urban Force dropouts; treasure & vpres, Black Law Stud Alliance Univ Detroit Law Sch; bd mem, Heritage Culture Ctr; Akan Priest; pres, Walton Acad Bd. **Business Addr:** Attorney, Morgan & Hall, 47 N Saginaw St, Pontiac, MI 48342-2153.

MORGAN, ROBERT
Transportation consultant, military leader. **Personal:** Born May 17, 1954, Donaldsonville, LA; son of Robert Sr and Ruby Fields; married Rowena Guanlao; children: Robyn Talana, Ryan Guanlao & Rubi Guanlas. **Educ:** Southern Univ, BS, 1972; Old Dominion Univ, attended 1976; Nat Univ, MBA, 1982; Armed Forces Staff Col, Cert, 1986; Fort Gordon Signal Sch, Augusta, GA, Cert, 1987; Univ Md, Foreign Lang Studies, 1989; Panama Canal Col, AS, comput sci, 1993; Tex Southern Univ, MS, Transp technol, 1995. **Career:** USS Am CV 66, Norfolk, VA, deck/ASW officer, 1977-79; USS Cleveland LPD 7, San Diego CA, navigator/weapons officer, 1979-80; Surface Warfare Officer Sch, Coronado, CA, instr, 1981-83; USNS Ponchatoula FAO 108, Philippines Island, officer in charge, 1983-84; USN, human resource mgr instr, 1983; Naval Station Guam, Guam MI, opers officer, 1984-85; Cent Tex Col, Guam MI, instr, 1984-85; Cent Tex Col, mgt prof, 1985; HQ Cent Command, Macdill AFB FL, comm staff officer, 1986-88; MSCO Korea, Pusan Korea, commanding officer, 1988-90; HQ US Southern Command, Quarry Heights, Panama, logistics staff officer, 1990-92; MSCO Panama, commanding officer, 1992-94; Tex Southern Univ, instr; Univ Houston, instr; Houston Port Authority, opers mgr, trade develop mgr cust serv, 1994-. **Orgs:** Life mem, Alpha Phi Omega Frat, 1973-; life mem, Omega Psi Phi Frat, 1980-; mem, Asn MBA Execs, 1981, Acct Soc, 1982; St Joseph Masonic Lodge, 1982; master scuba diver Micronesian Diver Asn, 1985; Certified PADL & NAUL diver; Nat Naval Officers Asn; NAACP; Armed Forces Commun & Electronics Asn, 1988-; Am Chamber Com, Korea, 1988-; Nat Defense Transp Asn, 1987. **Honors/Awds:** Outstanding Black American Award, Comnav Marianas, 1985; Outstanding Citizens of the Year, 1992, Omega Man of the Year, 1993. **Military Serv:** USN, lt cmdr, 1976-; Surface Warfare Officer, Humanitarian Service Medal, Navy Achievement Award; Expert Rifle & Pistol Marksmanship, 1976-; Joint Serv Commendation Medal, 1988; Commanding Officer, 1988-89; Defense Meritorious Service Medal, 1988; Navy Commendation Medal, 1990; Nat Defense Medal, 1991; Joint Specialty Officer, 1989; Joint Meritorious Unit Award, 1991; Meritorious Unit Commendation, 1988; Defense Meritorious Serv Medal, 1992, Meritorious Serv Medal, 1994. **Home Addr:** PO Box 890263, Houston, TX 77289-0263.

MORGAN, ROBERT LEE
Architect. **Personal:** Born Mar 6, 1934, Yazoo City, MS; married Janet Rogers; children: Allyson, Whitney, Peter. **Educ:** Lincoln Univ, Jefferson City, MO; Kans State Univ, BArch, 1964. **Career:** Architect (retired). Opus Architects & Engrs, 1984-99; Adkins-Jackels Asn Architects, exec vip partner, stockholder, architect, 1968-84; Hammel, Green & Abrahamson, architect, 1966-68; Cavin & Page Architects, architect, 1964-66. **Orgs:** Soc Architects Am Inst Architects; Nat Orgn Minority Architects; bd, secy, 1993-95, Minn Comt Urban Environ, 1968-76; Minn Schs Long-Range Facilities Planning Comn; pres, Minn CDC, 1971; Comt Archit Arts & Recreation, Am Inst Architects, 1974-77; Minn Bd Architect, Engrs, Land Surveying & Landscape Architect, 1983-91; Nat Coun Architect Regist Bds, 1991-95. **Honors/Awds:** Invested Col Fels, Am Inst Architects, 1995. **Home Addr:** 220 Oakshore Dr, Port Townsend, WA 98368. *

MORGAN, ROSE (ROSE META MORGAN)
Executive. **Personal:** Born Jan 1, 1912?, Shelby, MS; daughter of Winnie and Chappel; divorced. **Educ:** Morris Beauty Acad Chicago. **Career:** Executive (retired); Trim-Away Figure Contouring Ltd, franchiser; Mail Order Bus Nat & Int; Rose Morgan Enterprise, founder & pres; Rose Meta House Beauty, owner. **Orgs:** Charter mem, Cosmetic Career Women; NY State Beauty Culturists Asn; Nat Asn Negro & Prof Women; Nat Asn Bank Women Inc; incorporator, Bethune Fed & Savings Loan Bank; dir, Freedom Nat Bank NY; dir, Interracial Coun Bus Opportunity; vpres, Nat Coun Negro Women; Asn Asst Negro Bus; life mem, Nat Asn Advan Colored Peopel; Task Force Econ Adv Comm Mayor NYC; dir, Uptown COC NYC, Mt Morris Park Hosp; pres, Continental Soc NY; bd dir, Kilamanjaro African Coffee; bd trustee, Arthur C Logan Mem Hosp; bd trustee, Shaw Univ Raleigh NC; Convent Ave Bapt Church; bd mem, Asn Black Charities; treas, Nat Coalition 100 Black Women; New York City Partnership Inc. **Honors/Awds:** Outstanding Achievement Award, NY State Beauty Culturists Asn.

MORGAN, ROSE META. **See MORGAN, ROSE.**

MORGAN, STACEY EVANS (STACEY LYN EVANS)
Television producer, television writer. **Career:** Warner Bros, comedy writer training prog; BET, producer spec proj; TV series: "The Parkers", producer & writer, exec story ed & writer, 1999-2004; "After All", writer, 1999; "One on One", writer; Jamie Foxx Show, writer. **Business Addr:** Television Producer, United Paramount Network, 11800 Wilshire Blvd, Los Angeles, CA 90025, **Business Phone:** (310)575-7000.

MORGAN, STANLEY DOUGLAS
Football player, executive, president (organization). **Personal:** Born Feb 17, 1955, Easley, SC; married Rholedia; children: Sanitra Nikole & Monique. **Educ:** Univ Tenn, BS, educ, 1979. **Career:** Football player (retired), president; Industrial Nat Bank; New England Patriots, wide receiver, 1977-89; Indianapolis Colts, wide receiver, 1990; Denver Broncos, wide receiver, 1992; Mid-S Sports Mgt, pres, currently. **Honors/Awds:** Rookie of the Year, Patroits' 1776 Fan Club. **Business Phone:** (901)523-2535.

MORGAN, TRACY
Actor. **Personal:** Born Nov 10, 1968, Bronx, NY; son of Jimmy and Sabina; married Sabina, Jan 1, 1985 (divorced 2008);

children: Gitrid, Malcomb & Tracy. **Career:** Films: A Thin Line Btwn Love & Hate, 1996; Half Baked, 1998; Bamboozled, 2000; 30 Years to Life, 2001; WaSan Go, 2001; Jay & Silent Bob Stike Back, 2001; How High, 2001; Frank McKlusky, C.I., 2002; Head of State, 2003; The Longest Yard, 2005; Little Man, 2006; First Sunday, 2008; Superhero Movie, 2008; Deep in the Valley, 2009; G-Force, 2009; TV series: "Martin", 1994-96; "Saturday Night Live", 1996-2006; "Crank Yankers", 2002; "Comic Groove", 2002; "The Tracy Morgan Show", 2003-04; Saturday Night Live Weekend Update Halftime Special, 2003; "Where My Dogs At?", 2006; "Mind of Mencia", 2006; "Totally Awesome", 2006; Human Giant, 2008; "30 Rock", 2006-09. **Honors/Awds:** Nominee, Image Award, 2008 & 2009 and nominee, Emmy Award, 2009 for Outstanding Supporting Actor in a Comedy Series for: "30 Rock" (2006). **Business Addr:** Actor, c/o NBC, 30 Rockefeller Plz Suite 2, New York, NY 10112, **Business Phone:** (212)315-9016.*

MORGAN, WAYNE
Basketball player, basketball coach. **Personal:** Born Oct 7, 1950, Brooklyn, NY; married Maribeth; children: Jerusha, Shayne & Ciara. **Educ:** St Lawrence, phys educ, 1973; Ithaca Col, MA, phys educ, 1974. **Career:** Westchester Community Col, basketball player; St Lawrence, asst coach, 1972-73; Ithaca Col, assisted the basketball team, 1973-74; Dutchess Community Col, head coach, 1974-75; Dartmouth Col, asst coach, 1975-79; Xavier, asst coach, 1979-84; Syracuse Orange men, asst coach, 1984-96; Long Beach State Univ, head coach, 1996-02; Iowa State Univ, asst coach, 2002-03, head coach, 2003-06; Mid-Iowa Satellite, owner, currently. **Honors/Awds:** Dist 15 coach of the yr, Nat Assn Basketball Coaches, 2000. **Special Achievements:** Iowa State University first African American head basketball coach.

MORGAN-CATO, CHARLOTTE THERESA
Educator, college teacher. **Personal:** Born Jun 28, 1938, Chicago, IL; daughter of Eleazar Jack and Helen Juanita Brewer; married John David Cato; children: One. **Educ:** Univ Chicago, BA, 1960; Haile Selassie I Univ Addis Ababa, Cert Attendance, 1965; Columbia Univ, Sch Int Affairs, Master Int Affairs, 1967, Teachers Col, MEd, 1976, EdD, 1979. **Career:** Chicago Bd Educ, high sch social studies teacher, 1961-65; African-Am Inst, teacher Kurasini Sch, 1967-70; Phelps-Stokes Fund, asst for African progs, 1970-71; Lehman Col CUNY, assoc prof, 1972-02, dir, Women's Studies Prog, 1996-02, prof emer, currently. **Orgs:** adv comt adult learning, Follett Publishing Co, 1982-83; nat treas, African Heritage Studies Asn, 1984-88; alternate rep, United Nations NGO, Alpha Kappa Alpha Sor Inc, 1985-86; Am Asn Adult & Cont Educ; Asn Study African-Am Life & Hist; Nat Coun Black Studies; Alpha Kappa Alpha Sor; Links, Inc; bd mem, Free Rein Therapeut Riding & Educ Ctr. **Honors/Awds:** Fulbright Award, 1965; CUNY Faculty Fel Award, 1978-79; Award Nat Fel Fund Emory Univ, 1978-79; Kappa Delta Pi Honor Soc, 1979; Research Grant, Women's Res & Devel Fund CUNY, 1986-87; Prism Award, Lehman Col, 1998; Am Asn Univ Women, Community Devel Grant, 1998-99; Teacher of the Year, Lehman Col, 2000; published articles in Afro-Americans in NY Life & History, Grad Studies Jour (Univ DC); Hist Found of Adult Educ. **Home Addr:** 2385 Rosemont Ct, Hendersonville, NC 27891. **Business Addr:** Professor Emeritus, Lehman College, 250 Bedford Pk Blvd W, Bronx, NY 10468.*

MORGAN-PRICE, VERONICA ELIZABETH
Judge. **Personal:** Born Nov 30, 1945, Chas, SC; daughter of Robert and Mary Cross; married Jerome Henry; children: Jerome Marcus. **Educ:** Tenn State Univ, BS, eng, 1969; Univ Cincinnati Summer Law Scholar, cert; Tex S Univ, JD, 1972; Univ NV Nat Col Juv Judges, cert, 1980. **Career:** Judge (retired); Wade Rasmus & Wash, law clerk & atty, 1970-72; Baylor Col Med Alcoholism Prog, chief counr coord, 1972-75; Houston Community Col, law prof, 1972-78; Harris Co Dist Atty Off, asst dist atty, 1975-80; TX Paralegal Sch, prof law; Harris Co Juvenile Ct, assoc judge. **Orgs:** Tex State Bar, 1973-; Houston Lawyers Asn, 1973-; Nat Bar Asn, 1975-; adv bd, Safety Coun Great Houston, 1979-; chairperson, Med Legal Child Advocacy Comn, 1980; adv bd, Criminal & Juvenile Justice Educ Prog, 1980; Children's Defense Fund/Black Community Crusade Children, 1997; Ford Found Coun Legal Educ; bd dir, Asn Community TV Channel 8; Nat Coun Juvenile & Family Ct Judges; Metro Ct Judges; comt mem, Learning Disabilities & Juv Delinquincy; Nat Coun Juvenile & Family Ct Judges; chair, Judicial Leadership Coun; Black Women Lawyers Asn; Thurgood Marshall Sch Law Alumni Asn. **Honors/Awds:** Law School Scholarship, 1969-72; Hidden Heroine Award, Girls Scouts USA, 1996. **Special Achievements:** First black woman prosecutor TX Harris County District. **Home Addr:** PO Box 35323, Houston, TX 77489, **Home Phone:** (713)562-2951.

MORGAN-SMITH, SYLVIA
Executive. **Personal:** Born in Alabama; married William F II; children: Shiva, Andre, Melody & Ramon Morgan. **Educ:** Technol Community Col, nursing, 1959; Univ Colo-Denver, jour, 1970; Signal Broadcasting, dipl, 1971; Real Estate Col, dipl, 1976. **Career:** KBPI-FM Radio, radio producer & announcer, 1970-72; KWGN-TV 2, anchorwoman, 1972-77; Champion Realty, realtor, 1975-; Rockwell Int Rocky Flats, mgr pub affairs, 1977-81; Nat Solar Energy Res Inst, mgr communs, 1981-91; KOA-TV, announcer, 1981-92; Nat Renewable Energy Lab, Midwest Res Inst, dir creative communs, 1991-, Colo Govt Rels, mgr, currently; Colo Gospel Music Acad & Hall Fame, founder & pres, currently. **Orgs:** Comnr, Denver Comn Community Rels, 1973-79; dir, First Interstate Bank Golden, 1979-95; exec comt, Jefferson Co Priv Indstry Coun, 1980-97; dir, Childrens Hosp, 1981-85; pres, Police Retirement Comn & Citizens Appreciate Police 1981-; vice chairperson, Nat Small Bus Admin Adv Coun, 1990-92; Asn Blacks Energy. **Honors/Awds:** Trailblazer Award, Colo Martin Luther King Comn, 2001; Shaka Franklin Foundation for Youth Award; Award, Colo Asn Black Journalists; President's Special Award, Denver Ministerial Alliance; Chairman's Cup, Am Asn Blacks Energy, 2005; Outstanding Community Service Award, Urban League Metrop Denver, 2006. **Home Phone:** (303)233-3321. **Business Addr:** Director, Corporate Communications-Midwest Research, Colorado Governmental Relations Manager, National Renewable Energy Laboratory, 1617 Cole Blvd, Golden, CO 80401-3393, **Business Phone:** (303)275-3001.

MORGAN-WASHINGTON, DR. BARBARA
Dentist. **Personal:** Born Nov 9, 1953, Richmond, VA; daughter of Calvin T Sr and Florence Brown; married Fred S Washington Jr; children: Bria Renee & Fredrica Samone. **Educ:** Virginia State Univ, BS, 1976; Med Col Va Sch Dent, DDS, 1980. **Career:** USPHS, sr asst dent surgeon, 1980-82; pvt pract, assoc, 1983-86; Beaufort Jasper Community Health Servs, staff dentist, 1982-97; pvt pract, 1997-. **Orgs:** Acad Gen Dent, 1980-; Tabernacle Baptist Church, 1981-; Amer Dental asn, 1982-, SC Dental Asn, 1982-; Nat Asn Advan Colored People, 1986-; Alpha Pi Alpha Sorority; Beaufort Regional Chamber Com; Tings fa Tek. **Home Addr:** PO Box 325, Beaufort, SC 29901. **Business Addr:** Dentist, 102 Sea Island Pkwy Suite J, Beaufort, SC 29907, **Business Phone:** (843)986-0157.

MORGAN-WELCH, BEVERLY ANN
Executive, executive director, president (organization). **Personal:** Born Sep 15, 1952, Norwich, CT; married Rev Mark RP Welch Jr; children: Michael, Dominique & Alexandra. **Educ:** Smith Col, BA, 1970-74. **Career:** Creative Arts Comn, admin asst, 1975-76; Amherst Col, asst dean, 1976-77, asst dean admis, 1977-78; Conn Mutual Life, consult corp responsibility, 1979-83; Avery Theater, gen mgr; Wadsworth Atheneum, corp & mus serv officer, 1983-86; Wads Worth Atheneum, develop officer, 1986-87; Greater Hartford Arts Coun, exec dir, 1987-; Mus Afro-Am Hist, exec dir, currently. **Orgs:** Chair, Urban Affairs Coun, 1981-82; secy, Conn Mutual Life Found, 1981-83; charter bd mem, Conn Coalition 100 Black Women, 1982-85; United Way Allocations Com Capitol Area, 1982-86; bd dir, Newington C Hosp, 1983-86; bd dir, sec Jazz Inc, 1983-86; bus assoc, Greater Hartford C C, 1983-86; bd dir, Am Red Cross, Greater Hartford Chap, 1985-86; pres, Goodwin Track Conservancy, 1986-88; vpres, Horace Bushnell Mgt Resources Inc, 1985; exec comt, Hartford Downtown Coun, 1988-; vpres, Amistad Found, 1987-; corporator & dir, Inst Living, 1988-; Diaconate, First Church Christ, Hartford, 1989-; regional advisory coun, Capitol Community Tech Col Found, 1991-; corporator, Hartford Sem, 1991-. **Honors/Awds:** Gerald Penny Memorial Award, 1979; producer & co-founder, PUSH Performing Ensemble, 1980-82; Big Brothers/Big Sisters Award, 1982; participant, Leadership Greater Hartford Chair Poverty Task Force, 1984; coord producer, CPTV Video Documentary Paint by Mr Amos Ferguson, 1985; Greater Hartford Community College Recognition Award, 1990. **Business Addr:** Executive Director, Museum of Afro-American History, 14 Beacon St Suite 719, Boston, MA 02108, **Business Phone:** (617)725-0022.

MORIAL, DR. MARC (MARC H MORIAL)
President (Organization), mayor, chief executive officer. **Personal:** Born Jan 3, 1958, New Orleans, LA; son of Ernest Dutc and Sybil Haydel; married Michelle Miller. **Educ:** Univ Pa, BA, econs, 1980; Georgetown Univ, JD, 1983. **Career:** Barham & Churchill Law Firm, assoc, 1983-85; Harare Inc, chmn, 1983-86; Marc H Morial Prof Law Corp, managing partner, 1985-; Off Civil Sheriff, Orleans Parish, LA, legal coun auctioneer; Xavier Univ, adj prof polit sci, 1988; State La, sen; City New Orleans, mayor, 1994-2002; Nat Urban League, pres & chief exec officer, 2003-. **Orgs:** Dem campaign coord, Morial for Mayor New Orleans, 1977; dep campaign mgr, Russell Long for Senator, 1980; Jesse Jackson for Pres, 1984; deleg, Dem Nat Conv, 1988; La Voter Registration Educ Crusade Inc, 1986-; bd dir, La Spec Olympics, 1991-; Milne Boys Home, 1991-; US Conf Mayors, pres, 2001-02; pres, US Conf Mayors, 2001-02; Am Bar Asn; Nat Bar Asn; La Trial Lawyers Asn; Nat Conf Black Lawyers; La State Bar Asn; Gen counsel, La Asn Minority & Women Owned Bus Inc; New Orleans Asn Independent Cab Drivers Inc. **Honors/Awds:** Pro Bono Award, 1988. **Business Addr:** President, Chief Executive Officer, National Urban League Inc, 120 Wall St, New York, NY 10005, **Business Phone:** (212)558-5300.

MORIAL, MARC H. See MORIAL, DR. MARC.

MORIAL, SYBIL HAYDEL
College teacher, educator. **Personal:** Born Nov 26, 1932, New Orleans, LA; daughter of Eudora Arnaud and Clarence C; married Ernest Nathan, Feb 17, 1955 (deceased); children: Julie, Marc, Jacques, Cheri & Monique. **Educ:** Boston Univ, BS Ed, 1952, M.Ed, 1955. **Career:** Educator, college teacher (retired); Newton Pub Sch, teacher 1952-55; Baltimore Pub Sch, teacher, 1955-56; New Orleans Pub Sch, teacher, 1959-71; Xavier Univ, dir spec serv, 1977-85, Drexel Ctr Extended Learning, assoc dean, 1985-93, assoc vpres, pub & commun affairs, 1993-2005. **Orgs:** Founder, La League Good Govt, pres, pres emer, 1963-; pres, New Orleans Chap Links Inc, 1976-78; dir, Liberty Bank & Trust Co, 1979-; bd trustees, Amistad Res Ctr, 1980-; bd dir, WLAE-TV, 1979-81, adv bd, 1984-; founder, I've Known Rivers Afro-Amer Pavilion La World Exposition, pres, chmn, 1982-85; Nat Conf C Having C, Black Women Respond, 1983; co-chair, Year Healthy Birth, 1983; trustee, Nat Jewish Hosp, Nat Asthma Ctr, 1983-; pres, Women's Forum of La, 1985-; vpres, Int Women's Forum, 1987-; Tulane Univ President's Fund, 1988-; adv bd, Tulane Med Ctr, 1990-; bd dirs, Greater New Orleans Found, 1993-; bd dirs, Leadership Found, 1993; chair, Ernest N Morial Asthma & Respiratory Dis Ctr, La State Univ Med Ctr, 1994; Nat Hon Soc; Ed Pi Lambda Theta. **Honors/Awds:** Torch of Liberty Award, Anti-Defamation League of B'nai B'rith 1978; Whitney M Young Brotherhood Award, Urban League Greater New Orleans, 1978; Zeta Phi Beta Finer Women hood Award, 1978; Arts Council Medal, La Coun Music & Performing Arts Co, 1979; Weiss Award, Nat Conf Christians & Jews,1979; Woman of the Year, Links Inc, 1981; Citizen of the Year, Spectator News J, 1984; Lifetime Achievement Award, Martin Luther King Jr, 1995.

MORISEY, PATRICIA GARLAND
Educator. **Personal:** Born Aug 1, 1921, New York, NY; daughter of Arthur L Williams and Dagmar Cheatum; widowed; children: Paul Garland, Jean, Carroway Muriel Spence & Alex. **Educ:** Hunter Col, BA, 1941; Columbia Univ Sch Social Work, MSS, 1947, DSW, 1970. **Career:** Comm Serv Soc & NYANA, caseworker, 1944-51; Louise Wise Adoption Serv, caseworker consult, 1951-59; Bur Child Welfare NY Dept Social Serv, proj dir, dir training, 1959-63; Youth & Corrections, Community Serv Soc, staff consult, 1963-64; Family & Child Welfare Fedn Protestant Welfare Agency, dir, div family & child welfare, 1966-68; Catholic Univ Am, Wash, DC, assoc prof, 1968-69; Lincoln Ctr Fordham Univ, Grad Sch Social Sci, asst dean, 1975-86, prof emer, 1970-. **Orgs:** Pres, Comm Men Health, 1977-78; Greater NY Comn, Nat Coun Negro Women, 1984-; vpres, Leake & Wahs Children's Serv 1985-91; secy, Fedn Protestant Welfare Agencies, 1988-91; Mayor's Task Force on Child Abuse & Mayor's Task Force on Foster Care, 1980; New York Dept Ment & Retardation-Task Force Youth & The Law, Coun Social Work Educ, Nat Asn Social Workers; vpres, Leake & Watts C Svc; mem bd, Citizens Comm Children; bd dir, Fedn Protestant Welfare Agencies; Subpanel on Spec Pops. **Honors/Awds:** Hall of Fame, Hunter Col, 1975; Honoree, Nat Asn Women's Bus & Prof Club,1975; Bene Merente, Fordham Univ, 1989; Ninth Annual Award, Coun Adoptable Children, 1992; Keystone Award, Fedn Protestant Welfare Agencies, 1993; Josephine Shaw Lowell Award, Community Serv Soc, 1996; Louise Wise Services Award, 1996; Outstanding Mentor Award, Highbridge Advising Coun, 1997. **Home Addr:** 10 W 135th St Apt 16F, New York, NY 10037. **Business Addr:** Professor Emeritus, Fordham University, Rose Hill Campus, Bronx, NY 10458, **Business Phone:** (718)817-1000.

MORMAN, ALVIN
Baseball player. **Personal:** Born Jan 6, 1969, Rockingham, NC; son of Hettie F; married Pamela; children: Latydra Janae. **Educ:** Wingate Univ, BS, bus admin, 1991. **Career:** Player (retired): Counselor; Houston Astros, pitcher, 1996; Cleveland Indians, 1997-98; San Francisco Giants, 1998; Kans City Royals, 1999; Fuquay Varina Middle Sch; guidance counselor, currently. *

MORNING, JOHN
Financial manager. **Personal:** Born Jan 8, 1932, Cleveland, OH; son of John Frew Sr and Juanita Kathryn Brannan; divorced; children: Ann Juanita & John Floyd. **Educ:** Wayne State Univ, 1950-51; Pratt Inst, BFA 1955. **Career:** Mc Cann Erickson Inc, art dir, 1958-60; Dime Savings Bank, dir; John Morning Design Inc, pres, 1960-99. **Orgs:** Dir, Henry St Stlmnt, 1973-, chmn, 1979-86; dir, NY Landmarks Conservancy,1985-; trustee, Wilberforce Univ, 1987-; chmn, Pratt Inst Brd Trustees, 1989-92; trustee, Mus African Art, 1990-98; dir, Charles E Culpeper Found, 1991-99; trustee, Brooklyn Acad Music, 1993-; dir, Lincoln Ctr Theater,1995-; trustee, City Univ NY, 1997-02; chair, Assn Governing Brds Univs & Cols, 1998-2000; trustee, Rockefeller Bros Fund, 1999-; trustee, C S Mott Found, 2000-; trustee, Pratt Inst; found trustee, InterNatPrint Center New York; dir, New York Landmarks Conservancy. **Honors/Awds:** Alumni Medal, Pratt Inst 1972; Presidential Recognition Award, White House, 1984; Lillian D. Wald Humanitarian award of Henry Street Settlement in 1992. **Military Serv:** AUS, sp/3c, 1956-58. **Home Addr:** 333 E 45th St, New York, NY 10017. **Business Addr:** President, John Morning Design, 333 E 45th St, New York, NY 10017, **Business Phone:** (212)687-1914.

MORRIS, ARCHIE, III
Educator, manager. **Personal:** Born Mar 24, 1938, Washington, DC; married Irene Beatrice Poindexter; children: Giovanni & Ottiviani. **Educ:** Howard Univ, BA, 1968, MUS, 1973; Nova Univ, DPA, 1976. **Career:** US Dept Com, dep asst dir admin, 1972-73; US Dept Com, OMBE, R& D spec, 1973-74; DC Govt,

rent admin, 1974-76; The MATCH Inst, proj dir, cons, 1976-79; US Dept Agr, chief facilities mgt, 1979-82; US Dept Agr, chief mail & reproduc mgt, 1982-. **Orgs:** Bd dirs, HUD Fed Credit Union, 1971-76; instr, WA Ctr Learning Alternatives, 1976; instr, Howard Univ Dept Publ Admin, 1976-77; pres, Nat Capital Area Chap Nova Univ Alumni, 1980-81; Am Soc Publ Admin; Nat Urban League; dir social servs, Alexandria Redevel & Housing Authority, currently. **Honors/Awds:** Honors & Plaque HUD Task Force Against Racism WA, 1972; Spec Achievement Award, OMBE Dept Com WA, 1973; Outstanding Serv Award, HUD Fed Credit Union WA, 1976; Cert Appreciation, Mayor WA, 1976. **Military Serv:** USAF, a/1c, 1955-59. **Business Addr:** US Department of Agriculture, 12th and Independence Ave SW, Washington, DC 20250.

MORRIS, BERNARD ALEXANDER
Consultant, executive, college teacher. **Personal:** Born Jun 25, 1937, New York, NY; son of Herbert Anthony and Beryl Bernice Berry; married Margaret Mary Taylor, Jul 16, 1988; children: Myron, Michael, Loree V Smith & Quincy. **Educ:** Boston State Col, BS, 1975; Harvard Univ, EdM, 1978. **Career:** Mass Inst Technol, acad admin, 1971-77; NY City Bd Educ, sr policy analyst, 1979-80; Nolan Norton & Co, MIS consult, 1980-85; Morris Assocs, pres & consult, 1985-. **Orgs:** Transafrica; Pi Sigma Alpha; Phi Delta Kappa. **Military Serv:** USAF, electronics/radar, 4 yrs. **Business Addr:** President, Morris Associates, **Business Phone:** (617)354-2293.

MORRIS, DR. CAROLE V.
Educator. **Personal:** Born May 1, 1945, Conway, NC; daughter of Roland C Lassiter Sr; children: Diallo Kobie. **Educ:** Elizabeth City State Univ, BS, 1967; Antioch Col, MPh, 1973; Univ Miami, EdD, 1988. **Career:** City Univ NY, instr, 1968-69; Rutgers State Univ, instr, 1969-72; Univ Miami, grad teaching, 1986-88; Eastern VA Med, consult, 1980; Leadership in Education, VA Educational Policy, fel, 1990-92; Norfolk State Univ, assoc prof, dept chair, spec educ, prof spec educ, currently. **Orgs:** Bd chair, Speer Trust Fund, 1996-2000; bd mem, Nat Asn Investment Clubs, Hampton Roads Chap, 1997-; co-dir, Rehabil Servs Projects, 1998-2004; bd mem, 1998-2003, vpres, 2004-, Ecumenical Family Shelter Inc. **Honors/Awds:** IBM Leadership Award, 1971-73; Leadership Award, Phi Delta Kappa, 1986-87. **Special Achievements:** Coauthored Fundamental Reading Skills, 5th edition, Kendall-Hunt; Advanced Communication Skills, 4rd edition, Kendall-Hunt; co-editor, Enfranchising Urban Learners, Morris Publishing. **Business Addr:** Professor, Norfolk State University, Department of Special Education, 700 Pk Ave, 107 Bozeman Educ Bldg, Norfolk, VA 23504, **Business Phone:** (757)823-9109.

MORRIS, CAROLYN G
President (Organization), executive. **Educ:** NC Cent Univ, BS, math; Harvard Univ, MS, math. **Career:** Fed Bur Invest, Systs Develop Sect, chief, dep asst dir info technol, 1984-95, asst dir info resources div, 1995-2000; Innovative Mgt & Technol Approaches Inc, pres, 2000-. **Special Achievements:** Highest ranking African American female in FBI hist. **Military Serv:** AUS, Dept of Defense; Army PACE Award. **Business Phone:** (202)962-0000.

MORRIS, CELESTE
Publisher, political consultant. **Personal:** Born Oct 7, 1949, Brooklyn, NY; daughter of Edith Harding and Cuthbert Allsop; divorced; children: Oji, Kimya. **Educ:** Howard Univ, attended 1968; Brooklyn Col, BS, 1980. **Career:** BHRAGS Home Care Progs, prog dir, 1980-85; NY City Transit Authority, govt rels specialist, 1986-87; Congressman Major Owens, community specialist, 1987; Unlimited Creative Enterprises Inc, pres & founder, 1987-; State Senator Malcolm Smith, chief staff. **Orgs:** Nat Minority Bus Coun; Caribbean Am Chamber Com; vpres & bd dir, Nat Asn Market Developers; pres, Black Pages Pub Asn; bd mem, Workshop Bus Opportunities. **Honors/Awds:** Comm Serv Award, Mosaic Coun, 1990; Women of Color Entrepreneurs Award, Medgar Evers Col, 1991; NAMDer Award, Nat Asn Market Developers, 1992; Outstanding Minority Bus, Nat Minority Bus Coun, 1992; Communicators Award, Councilwoman Annette Robinson, 1992; Charles H Revson fel, Columbia Univ, 1993-94; Commendation, NY City, Controller, 1996. **Special Achievements:** The Big Black Book, 1987-95; NYs Black Pages, 1987-. **Business Addr:** Founder, President, Unlimited Creative Enterprises Inc, 576 Pacific St, Brooklyn, NY 11217, **Business Phone:** (718)638-9223.*

MORRIS, DR. CHARLES EDWARD, JR.
School administrator, president (organization). **Personal:** Born Sep 30, 1931, Big Stone Gap, VA; son of Charles E and Verta Edith Warner; married Jeanne A Brown; children: David & Lyn Elizabeth. **Educ:** Johnson C Smith Univ, BS, 1952; Univ Ill, MS, 1959, PhD, 1966. **Career:** William Penn High Sch, teacher, 1954-58; Univ Ill-Urbana, teaching & res assoc, 1959-66; Ill State Univ, fac, assoc prof math, sec univ, 1973-80, vpres admin, 1980-90, emer assoc prof math & emer vpres admin serv, 1995-; Ill Bd Regents, Springfield, Ill, from interim vchancellor acad affairs to vchancellor, 1990-95; CEM Assoc Inc, pres, currently. **Orgs:** Bd dirs, Presbyterian Found, 1974-83, Presbyterian Econ Develop Corp,1975-85, Western Ave Comm Ctr, 1978-86; chairperson, Ill Community Black Concerns Higher Educ, 1982-88, chmn emer, 1988-; adv bd, Col Potential Prog Coun Advan Experiential Learning, 1984-; chairperson, Ill Consortium Educ Oppor Bd, 1986-90; trustee emer, Monmouth Col, currently. **Honors/Awds:** Distinguished Alumnus Johnson C Smith Univ, 1976; Citizen's Awd for Human Rel Town Normal, 1979; Distinguished Alum of the Year Citation Nat Asn for Equal Oppor in Higher Educ, 1979; numerous speeches and articles on topics including mathematics educ, univ governance, blacks in higher educ; Doctor of Humane Letters, Monmouth Col, 1991. **Business Addr:** President, CEM Associates Inc, 1023 Barton Dr, Normal, IL 61761, **Business Phone:** (309)454-5459.

MORRIS, CHRISTOPHER VERNARD
Basketball player. **Personal:** Born Jan 20, 1966, Atlanta, GA; son of John and Patricia Ann Pittman Walton; married Felicia Michelle Hammonds, May 10, 1986; children: Micheal Christopher & Brenden Re. **Educ:** Auburn Univ, attended 1988. **Career:** Basketball player (retired); NJ Nets, forward, 1988-95; Utah Jazz, 1995-98; Orlando Magic, 1997; Phoenix Suns, 1998-99. **Honors/Awds:** All Rookie Second Team, Nat Basketball Asn, 1989; Number retired, Auburn Univ Tigers. **Special Achievements:** First round pick, No 4, NBA Draft, 1988.

MORRIS, PROF. CLIFTON
Educator, lecturer. **Personal:** Born Jun 21, 1937, Fredericktown, PA. **Educ:** Waynesburg Col, BS (summa cum laude), 1959; WVa Univ, MS, 1961; OH State Univ, PhD, 1968. **Career:** WV Univ, res fel, 1959-61; Ohio State Univ Columbus, teaching asst,1965-68; Ohio State Univ Lima, asst prof biol, 1969; Whittier Col, asso prof biol, 1972; Nat Dent Aptitude Test Rev Course, consult & instr,1977-; Nat Med Col Aptitude Test Rev Course, consult instr, 1977-; Educ Testing Serv Advan Placement, consult, 1978; City Hope Med Tech Training Prog, lectr, 1978; Whittier Col, chmn biol dept, 1979; James Irvine Foundation prof biol, 1980. **Orgs:** Xi Psi Epsilon Hon Scholastic Soc Waynesburg, PA, 1959; treas, Gamma Alpha Grad Sci Frat Columbus, OH, 1963-65; appointed James Irvine Chair Biol Sci, Whittier Col, 1980. **Honors/Awds:** Rockefeller Found Grant, WVa Univ Physiol Fung I, 1959-61; NSF Cooperative Grad Fellowship, OH State Univ, 1961; NSF summer fellowships, OH StateUniv, 1962-64; Muellhaupt Found fellowship, OH State Univ, 1964; Distinguished Teacher Award, OH State Univ Lima, 1971; Distinguished Teacher Award, Whittier Col, 1977-78; highest honors WVa Univ; highest honors, OH State Univ. **Special Achievements:** Joint authorship "Hormone-like substances which increase carotenogenesisin plus & minus sexes of Choanephora cucurbitarum" Mycologia, 1967. **Business Addr:** 13406 Philadelphia St, Whittier, CA 90608.

MORRIS, DR. DOLORES ORINSKIA
Clinical psychologist. **Personal:** Born in New York, NY; daughter of Joseph Morris and Gertude Elliott; divorced. **Educ:** City Univ NY, MS 1960; Yeshiva Univ, PhD, 1974; NY Univ, cert psychoanalysis, psychotherapy post doctoral prog, 1980. **Career:** Children's Ctr, Dept Child Welfare, psychologist, 1959-62; Urban League Greater NY, staff psychologist 1962-65; Bur Child Guid NYC, sch psychologist, 1965-74, supvr sch psychologists, 1974-78; Urban Res Planning Conf Ctr, tech asst, 1976; Bedford Stuyvesant St Acad, consult, 1977; Fordham Univ, asst prof, 1978-87; Pvt pract, 1980-; New York Pub Schs Div Spec Educ, Clin Prof Develop, educ admin, 1987-92, supvr sch psychologists, clin adminr, 1992-95; NYU Postdoctoral Prog, supvr, sychoanalysis, psychotherapy, supvr, currently; New Hope Guild Ment Health Servs, supvr, 1994-2001. **Orgs:** Treas, NY Asn Black Psychologists, 1967-75; co-chair, prof develop NY Asn Black Psychologists, 1975-77; chair Schs & Ment Health Am Orthopsychiat Asn, 1978-81, 1986-87; Nat Asn Sch Psychol; NY State Psychol Asn pres Div Sch Psychol, 1985-86; vice chairperson, Psychol NYS Educ Dept, 1988-2000; Diplte Psychoanalysis Psychol, 1996-; Division 39, 1998-; bd mem, Am Psychol Asn. **Honors/Awds:** Yeshiva Fellowship, NIMH, 1970-72; fellowship, Black Analysis Inc, 1972-74. **Business Addr:** Supervisor, Postdoctoral Program in Psychotherapy & Psychoanalysis, New York University, 240 Greene St 3rd Fl, New York, NY 10003, **Business Phone:** (212)998-7890.

MORRIS, EARL SCOTT
Fashion designer. **Personal:** Born May 24, 1966, Waukegan, IL; son of Velma D and Earle. **Educ:** Mich State Univ, BA, indust design, 1989. **Career:** Hasbro Inc, toy designer, 1990; Reebok Int, sr designer, 1990-. **Orgs:** Mich State Alumni Group, 1990; WIMA, Cult Diversity Group Reebok Int, 1992; Asn Black Sporting Goods Prof, 1992. **Honors/Awds:** Hasbro Inc, GI Joe action figure, codenamed Bulletproof, named after self, 1992. **Special Achievements:** Spoke as rep for Reebok at Association of Black Sporting Goods Professional's Career Awareness Program, 1992. **Military Serv:** US Marine Corps Reserves, sgt, 1985-93; Desert Storm veteran; Southwest Asia Campaign Medal; National Defense Medal; Naval Achievement Medal. **Business Phone:** (617)341-5000.

MORRIS, EFFIE LEE
Lecturer, librarian, consultant. **Personal:** Born Apr 20, 1921, Richmond, VA; daughter of Erma Lee Caskia (deceased) and William Hamilton (deceased); married Leonard V Jones, Aug 25, 1971 (deceased). **Educ:** Univ Chicago, 1941; Case Western Res Univ, BA, 1945, BLS, 1946, MLS, 1956. **Career:** Cleveland Pub Libr, br children's librn, 1946-55; Atlanta Univ, instr,1954; NY Pub Library, br children's librn, 1955-58; Libr Blind, children's spec, 1958-63; Univ San Francisco, lectr, 1974-76; San Francisco Pub Libr, coordr children's serv, 1963-78; Harcourt Brace Jovanovich, ed, 1978-79; Mills Col, lectr, 1979-89. **Orgs:** Consult reading proj, San Francisco Chap Nat Coun Chris & Jews 1967-70;Ohio, New York & Calif Libr Asns; Am Libr Asn; Newbery-Caldecott Award Comm, 1950-56, 1966-67, 1967-71, 1975-79, 1984-85; Laura Ingalls Wilder Award Comm, 1953-54, 1958-60; bd dir, Nat Aid Visually Handicapped; libradv bd, New Book Knowledge, 1966; con children's serv, Chicago Pub Libr Study, 1968-69, Oakland Pub Libr Study, 1974; adv comm, Title II ESEA State Calif, 1965-75; deleg, White House Conf Children, 1970; bd dirs,YWCA San Francisco, 1968-73; ALA dir, children's serv div, 1963-66, coun,1967-71, 1975-79, 1984-88; pres, Pub Libr Asn, 1971-72; chap pres,1968-70, Women's Nat Book Asn; pres, Nat Braille Club, 1961-63; Calif Libr Serv Bd, 1982-94, vpres, 1984-86; mem adv bd, Ctr Book Libr Cong, 1978-86;chairperson, Coretta Scott King Book Awd, 1984-88; Commonwealth ClubCalif, 1972-; Mayor's Adv Coun Child Care, 1978-96; chairperson, High Sch Essay contest, bd mem, Eng-Speaking Union, 1985-89; bd, Phoebe Hearst Nursery Sch, 1992-98; Golden Soror, 1996, Alpha Kappa Alpha Sorority; life mem, NAACP; Univ Calif, Berkeley Chancellor's, incentive scholar awd selection comm, 1993-00; chairperson, San Francisco Hist & Cult Soc Res Libr & Archives, 1998-99; adv bd & round table, Children's Defense Fund Langston Hughes Libr, 1999; co-chairperson adv bd, Langston Hughes Libr, Haley Farm Children's Defense Fund. **Honors/Awds:** Lola M Parker Award, Iota Phi Lambda Sor, 1978; Apprec Award, Jewish Bur of Ed, San Francisco, 1978; Distinguished Service to Librarianship, Black Caucus, AL, 1978; Distinguished Serv Award, Calif Librns Black Caucus,1978, 1997; Distinguished Alumni Award, Sch Libr Serv, Case Western Reserve Univ, 1979; Outstanding Negro Woman, Iota Phi Lambda Sor, 1964; EPDutton-John Macrae Award, Advan Libr Serv Children & Young People, 1958; Women's Nat Book Asn Award, 1984; San Francisco Pub Library, Effie Lee Morris Hist & Res Collection Children's Lit, 1982; Effie Lee Morris Day by Mayor Diane Feinstein, named in honor, June 12, 1984; Grolier Foundation Award of AL, 1992; Professional Award for Continuing Service and leadership in the Professional Black Caucus of ALA, 1992; Community Service Award, San Francisco Chapter Links, Inc, 1994; Effie Lee Morris Annual Lecture Children's Literature to San Fran Public Library funded by Women's Nat Book Asn, 1996; Reading the World Award, Univ San FranciscoCtr Multicult Lit, 1999; Ageless Hero, Blue Shield CA, 1999; African American Community Entrepeneur, Courageous Person Community Award, 2000;Silver SPUR honoree, San Francisco Planning & Urban Res Asn, 2000; Unites States Senate Certificate of Commendation from Senator Diane Feinstein,2000; Resolution of Commendation, Assembly Calif State Legis, 2000; First Community Service Award, celebration of 60 Yrs of Jones Methodist Episcopalian Church, 2003; Hon mem, American Library Association, 2008-. **Special Achievements:** First African American president of the Public Library Association. **Home Addr:** 66 Cleary Ct Suite 1009, San Francisco, CA 94109, **Home Phone:** (415)931-2733.

MORRIS, ELISE L.
Educator. **Personal:** Born Oct 25, 1916, Deridder, LA; widowed; children: Monica Wilson, John T, Gabriella Coleman. **Educ:** Xavier Univ, BA, 1937; Prairie View A&M Univ, MEd, 1965; TX S Univ, Univ Houston, Southwestern Univ, post grad study; Univ St Thomas, relig educ. **Career:** Archditoches Parish Training Sch, teacher, 1973; Our Mother Mercy Sch, 1942; Our Lady Star Sea Day Sch, dir, 1956; Galena Park Ind Sch Dist, teacher, 1962-. **Orgs:** Nat Educ Assn; Nat PTA & TX PTA; Delta Sigma Theta Sorority; TX State Teacher Asn; Nat Asn Univ Women; Nat Asn Univ Women Houston, 1965; Harris Co Grand Jury Adv Com, 1974-75; Supreme Lady Knights Peter Claver, 1970-75; steering com black participation 41st Int Eucharistic Congress, 1975; pres emer, The Drexel Soc, 1978. **Honors/Awds:** TSU listed Black Leader of Houston, 1970, KOCH & TSU Newman; Dict Intl Biog, 1975; Silver Medal Award outstanding serv Knights PC; Outstanding citizenship & serv commendation Mayor Houston; Woman Breaking New Ground Delta Sigma Theta, 1974; Outstanding Xavier Alumnae Houston; Papal Medal Honor, Congressional listing, 1996.

MORRIS, ELIZABETH LOUISE
Nurse. **Personal:** Born Dec 3, 1924, Cincinnati, OH; daughter of Malcolm and Ethel Ruth Brown; married Laurence Morris, Sep 28, 1962 (deceased); children: Donna Louise Higgins. **Educ:** Practical Sch Nursing, licensed practical nurse, 1954; pharmacol course completed, 1968. **Career:** Nurse (retired); Jewish Hosp Cincinnati, staff develop, 1978-89. **Orgs:** Am Bridge Asn; Gaines United Methodist church. *

MORRIS, ERNEST ROLAND
School administrator. **Personal:** Born Dec 15, 1942, Memphis, TN; son of Benjamin C Morris and Ernestine Edwards Morris; married Freddie Linda Wilson, Sep 3, 1966; children: Ernest Jr & Daniel. **Educ:** Rocky Mountain Col, BS (cum laude), 1967;

Eastern Ill Univ, MS, educ,1968; Univ Ill Urbana-Champaign, PhD 1976. **Career:** School administrator (retired); Minneapolis Pub Sch, hist teacher, 1968-69; Eastern Ill Univ, admissions officer, 1969-71; Univ Ill Urbana-Champaign, asst dean, assoc dean, 1971-78, exec asst chancellor, 1978-80; Univ Wash, Seattle, spec asst pres, 1980-82, vpres stud affairs, 1982. **Orgs:** Chmn, educ div, 1983 & 1984; admis & rev community, 1984-85, vice chmn bd dirs, 1985-88, chmn elect, 1990, chmn, 1991, Residential Care & Family Serv Conf Panel, 1984-85; vice chmn, planning & distribution comt, 1986, chmn, planning & distribution comt, 1987-89, first vice chair, 1989, finance comt, 1993-, United Way Seattle/King Co; class, 1983-84, bd dirs, 1985-96,exec comt, 1986-96, chmn, selection comt, 1987, vpres, 1992, pres, 1993, exec comt, 1992-94, chair bd dirs, 1994-95, United Way/Chamber of Commerce Leadership Tomorrow Prog; chmn, Fed Emergency Mgt Agency Local Bd Seattle/King Co 1984-86; founding trustee, Seattle/King Co Emergency Shelter Found, 1984-86; mem, bd trustees, First Funds of Am, 1990-93; bd dirs, Cent Puget Sound Coun Campfire, various bd committees, 1993-98; YWCA Isabel Colman Pierce Award Comt, 1992-98; King County Redistricting Comt, Chair (nonpartisan), 1996; bd dirs, Consumer Credit Coun Serv Seattle, 1997-2000; President's Cir, United Way of King County, 1998-; Endowment Bd, United Way King County, 1999-2000. **Honors/Awds:** Cark Mem Scholar, 1966; Outstanding History Student Award, 1966; Alumni Distinguished Achievement Award, Rocky MT Col, 1982; Nat Assoc Stud Personnel Adminr; Nat Assoc State Univ & Land Grant Cols; Outstanding Alumnus Award, Leadership Tomorrow, 1988; Ernest Thompson Seton Award, Cent Puget Sound Coun Camp Fire Boys & Girls, 1998.

MORRIS, EUGENE
Advertising executive, president (organization), chief executive officer. **Personal:** Born Jul 25, 1939, Chicago, IL; son of Willie Mae Mitchell and Eugene Sr. **Educ:** Roosevelt Univ, Chicago, BSBA, 1969, MBA, 1971. **Career:** Foote, Cone & Belding, Chicago, IL, acct exec, 1968-74; Burrell Advert, Chicago, IL, sr vpres, 1974-86; Morris & Co, Chicago, IL, pres, 1986-87; Morris & Randall Advert, Chicago, IL, pres, 1987-88; E Morris Commun Inc, Chicago, IL, chmn, pres & chief exec officer, 1988-. **Orgs:** Bd mem, Bethune Mus, 1989-; vice chmn, Sickle Cell Dis Asn Ill; dir, Cosmopolitan Chamber Com; bd dir, Jr Achievement, Chicago; ABLE, Alliance Bus Leaders & Entrepreneurs. **Honors/Awds:** Blackbook Business & Professional Award, Nat Pub, 1984; Citizen Professional Award, Citizen Newspapers, 1985; Entrepreneur of the Year Award, State Ill, 2000; Asn Fundraising Professionals Outstanding Volunteer Award, 2001. **Special Achievements:** Black Enterprise's List of Top Advertising Agencies, ranked 10th, 1999, ranked 8th, 2000, ranked 8th, 2001. **Military Serv:** AUS, E4, 1962-65. **Business Addr:** President, Chief Executive Officer, E Morris Communications Inc, 820 N Orleans St Suite 402, Chicago, IL 60610, **Business Phone:** (312)943-2900.

MORRIS, DR. FRANK LORENZO, SR.
School administrator. **Personal:** Born Jul 21, 1939, Cairo, IL; son of Frankie Mae Taylor (Honesty) and Lorenzo Richard Jr; married M Winston Baker, Jan 2, 1959; children: Frank Jr, Scott, Rebecca & Kristina. **Educ:** Colgate Univ, BA, 1961; Syracuse Univ, MPA, 1962; MIT, PhD, MS, 1976. **Career:** US Dept Housing & Urban Devel, Seattle WA, urban renewal rep, 1962-66; US Agency for Intl Develop, reg coord, 1966-72; Northwestern Univ, assoc prof, 1972-77; US Community Serv Admin, chief planning & policy, 1978; US AID, dep dir chief opers, 1979-83; Cong Black Caucus Found, exec dir, 1983-85; Colgate Univ, O'Connor prof, 1986; Univ MD Sch Pub Affairs, assoc dean, 1986-88; Morgan State Univ, Baltimore MD, dean grad studies & res,1988; Univ Md, prof; West Valley View, staff writer, currently; Diversity Alliance for a Sustainable Am, exec dir, chmn, currently. **Orgs:** Pres, NAACP Tacoma, 1963-66; vpres, NAACP Montgomery County, 1977-79; trustee, Lincoln Temple UCC, 1984; moderator Potomac Asn, United Church Christ, 1987-; treas, bd dir, Global Tomorrow Coalition, 1987-; Alpha Phi Alpha; bd dir, Ctr Immigration Studies, 1988-; bd homeland ministries, United Church Christ, 1988-; Coun Historically Black Grad Schs, pres, 1992-94; Grad Rec Exam, minority adv com, 1992-94; exec dir, chmn & dir, Congressional Black Caucus Found. **Honors/Awds:** NDEA Fel MIT, 1971; Dissertation Fel Russel Sage Found, 1972; Father of the Year, Chicago Defender, 1975; Education Policy Fel Inst Educ Leadership, 1977; three awards NAACP Evanston IN, Mont Cty MD; Superior Honor Award, Dept State 1982. **Military Serv:** US AID, sr foreign serv officer, 18 yrs. **Business Addr:** Chairman, Diversity Alliance for a Sustainable America, 1904 Franklin St Suite 517, Oakland, CA 94612, **Business Phone:** (510)835-5017.

MORRIS, FRED H., JR.
Executive. **Personal:** Born Oct 15, 1925, Bristol, VA; son of Fred H Sr (deceased) and Estella Ruth Charles; married Wilma J Booker Morris, Feb 4, 1957; children: Marvin L, Fred III, Karen, Kevin, Deborah. **Educ:** Univ State NY, acct, 1952; Blackstone Sch Law, LLB, 1969. **Career:** State Univ NY, educ dept, pub acct & taxation, 1960; Town of Babylon, comptroller, 1962; Sufflolk County, comnr, human rights adv bd, 1985-; Morris Mgt Consult Co, chmn & chief exec officer. **Orgs:** Masonic Lodge, King Tyre Affiliation, A F & AM; State New York, Northern Hemisphere; grandmaster, Fed Masons World, 1960-80; Am Legion Post 1218; Cpl Anthony Casamento Memorial Post 46; Italian Am War Veterans; founder, Vet Mem Park; founder, Suffolk County Black History Asn Inc Mus; founder, chmn, St Andrew Gen Masonic Congress. **Honors/Awds:** Newsday Editorial Award, 1979; honorary degrees, 33 Degree Mason. **Military Serv:** AUS, 2Yrs.

MORRIS, GARRETT GONZALEZ
Actor. **Personal:** Born Feb 1, 1937, New Orleans, LA; married Freda. **Educ:** Dillard Univ, BA; Juilliard Sch Music, Manhattan Sch Music. **Career:** Plays: Bible Salesman, 1960; Porgy and Bess, 1964; Show Boat, 1966; Hallelujah, Baby!, 1967; I'm Solomon, 1968; Slave Ship, 1969-70; Transfers, 1970; Operation Sidewinder, 1970; In New England Winter, 1971; The Basic Training of Pavlo Hummel, 1971; What the Wine-Sellers Buy, Don't Bother Me, I Can't Cope, Sweet Talk, 1974; The World of Ben Caldwell, 1982; The Unvarnished Truth, 1985; Films: Where's Poppa (also known as Going Ape), 1970; The Anderson Tapes, 1971; Cooley High, 1975; Car Wash, 1976; How to Beat the High Cost of Living, 1980; The Census Taker, 1984; The Stuff, 1985; Critical Condition, 1987; The Underachievers, Critical Condition, 1987; Dance to Win; Husbands, Wives, Money, and Murder, 1989; Blackbird Fly, Children of the Night, Motorama,1991; Severed Ties, Almost Blue, 1992; Coneheads, 1993; Black Rose of Harlem, Santa with Muscles, 1996; Black Scorpion II: Aftershock, 1997; Graham's Diner, Palmer's PickUp, Twin Falls Idaho, 1999; Little Richard, 2000; Jackpot, How High, 2001; Connecting Dots, 2003; The Salon, 2005; TV series: "General Hospital", 1963; "Roll Out", 1973-74; "Change at 125th Street", 1974; "Saturday NightLive", regular, 1975-80; "ABC Weekend Specials", 1978; "Diff'rent Strokes", 1982; "The Invisible Woman", 1983, 1984; "True Confessions", 1983, 1984; "The Jeffersons", 1983, 1984; "It's Your Move", 1984-85; "Murder, She Wrote", 1985; "Hill Street Blues", 1985; "The Twilight Zone",1985; "Scarecrow and Mrs. King", 1985; "Hunter", 1986-89; "227", 1987; "Married With Children", 1987, 1989; "Who's the Boss?", 1988; "Earth Angel", 1991; "Roc", 1991-92; "Maid for Each Other", 1992; "Martin", 1992-95; "ER", 1994; "The Wayans Bros.", "Black Scorpion", 1995; "Minor Adjustments", 1995; "Cleghorne!", 1995-96; "The Jamie Foxx Show", 1996; "Boston Common", 1997; "G vs E", 1999; "City of Angels", 2000; "Little Richard", 2000; "Static Shock", 2000; "Justice League", 2001; "The Hughleys", 2001; "Maniac Magee", 2003; "Noah's Arc", 2005; "All of Us", 2005; Amenic, Implanted, Fank, Who's Your Caddy?, 2007; Dog gone, The Longshots, 2008; Bed Ridden, Sonny Dreamweaver, 2009; Harry Belafonte Folk Singers, singer & musical arranger; Books: The Secret Place, 1972; Saturday Night Live, 1975; Daddy Picou and Marie LeVeau, 1981. **Orgs:** Am Soc Composers, Authors & Publishers, 1963-; Am Fedn TV & Radio Artists. **Honors/Awds:** Tanglewood Conductors Award, 1956; National Singing Contest Winner, Omega Psi Phi; Garrett Morris Day, Los Angeles mayor Antonio Villaraigosa, named in honor, 2007. **Special Achievements:** Nominated, Independent Spirit Award, 2001; Nominated, Emmy Award, 1979. *

MORRIS, GERTRUDE ELAINE
Clergy. **Personal:** Born Dec 20, 1924, Brooklyn, NY; daughter of Clifford Alphonso Morris and Estelle Justina Taylor Morris. **Educ:** Grailville Community Col, Loveland, OH, attended 1961; DeSales Sch Theol, Wash, DC, cert pastoral leadership, 1991. **Career:** Clergy (retired); Mobilization for Youth, New York, NY, off mgr, 1963-67; HR Admmn, New York, NY, dir cler training, 1967-73; Nat Off Black Catholics, Wash, DC, dir publ & evangelization, 1973-85; Catholic Archdiocese San Francisco, CA, dir African Am Ministry, 1985-94. **Orgs:** Grail, 1957; Nat Conf Catholic Bishops Commun Comt, 1980-84; bd dir, Nat Coun Catholic Evangelization, 1981-85; allocations panel, United Way Nat Capitol Area, 1981-85; comt mem, Campaign Human Dev-San Jose, 1988-90, San Francisco, 1990; vol, Laguna Honda Convalescent Hosp. **Honors/Awds:** The Fr Norman Dukette Award, Off Black Ministry, Brooklyn, NY, 1984; Outstanding Community Service, Pres Brooklyn, City NY, 1984; Imani Distinguished Service Award, Nat Off Black Catholics, 1985; Evangelist of the Year Award, Paulist Fathers, 1986. **Special Achievements:** Named one of People To Watch in the 90's, San Francisco Chronicle, 1990. **Home Addr:** 56 Navajo Ave, San Francisco, CA 94112.

MORRIS, HERMAN
Lawyer, president (organization). **Personal:** Born Jan 16, 1951, Memphis, TN; son of Herman and Reba Garrett; married Brenda Partee, Oct 4, 1980; children: Amanda Elizabeth, Patrick Herman & Geoffrey Alexander. **Educ:** Rhodes Col, Memphis, Tenn, BA, 1973; Vanderbilt Univ Sch Law, Nashville, Tenn, JD, 1977. **Career:** Dixie Homes Boys Club Inc, Memphis, TN, counr, 1969; Porter Leath Children Ctr, Memphis, TN, counr, 1970-73; RLS Assoc, Charleston, SC, dir minority recruiting, 1973-74; Sears, Nashville, TN, retail salesman, 1975; Tenn Commission Human Develop, Nashville, Tenn, law clerk, 1976; Ratner, Sugarmon & Lucas, Memphis, TN, law clerk, 1976; Ratner & Sugarmon, Memphis, TN, assoc atty, 1977-82, partner, 1982; Sugarmon, Salky & Morris, Memphis, TN, managing partner, 1982-86; Herman Morris & Associates, Memphis, Tenn, 1986-88; Morris & Noel Attorneys Law, Memphis, TN, partner, 1988-89; Memphis Light, Gas & Water Div, Memphis, Tenn, gen coun, 1989-96, pres/chief exec officer, 1997-2003; Baker, Donelson, Bearman, Caldwell & Berkowitz PC, partner, 2004-06; Univ Tenn Med Group, dir, currently; Tenn Valley Pub Power Asn, dir, currently; pvt pract atty, currently. **Orgs:** Chmn, Shelby County Homerule Charter Comn; chmn bd, Memphis Health Ctr Inc; chmn, Dixie Home Boys Club; exec bd, Southwestern Memphis Alumni Asn; Primary Health Care Adv Bd; pres, Ben Jones Chap, Nat Bar Asn; Memphis Pub Educ Fund; Nat Conf Christians & Jews; pres, Memphis Br, Nat Asn Advan Colored People; mem, Am Bar Asn; mem, Tenn Bar Asn; bd mem, Memphis Bar Asn; mem, Am Trial Lawyers' Asn; bd dir, Tenn Trial Lawyer's Asn; bd dir, Judicial Criminal Justice Ctr Adv Comt; vice chmn, Tenn Bd Professional Responsibility; Tenn Judicial Selection Comt, 1997; adv bd, Bank Am, 1998-; dir, Perrigo Co, 1998-; dir, Am Gas Asn, 1998-; dir, Tenn Valley Auth Reg Resource Adv Coun, 2000-; Am Asn Blacks Energy Energy, 2000-; dir, Tenn Quality Award, 2000-; Nat Petroleum Coun, 2000-01; treas, Am Pub Power Asn, 2000-. **Honors/Awds:** Best Lawyer, 1994-96; Executive of the Year, PSI Inc, 1996; Boss of the Year, Legal Secy Asn, 1992-93; Leadership Award, Mny Business League, 1999; Community Leadership Award, Memphis Urban League, 1999; Communicator of the Year, Pub Rels Soc Am, 2000; LEO Vol Leadership Award, Volunteer Ctr Memphis, 2000. **Special Achievements:** First African American president/CEO at Memphis Light, Gas and Water Division; first African American to lead the nation's largest three-service municipally owned utility company. **Business Addr:** Attorney at Law, 217 Exchange, Memphis, TN 38103.

MORRIS, HORACE W
Association executive. **Personal:** Born May 29, 1928, Elizabeth, NJ; son of Pringle and Evelyn Turner; divorced; children: Bradley, JoAnne, Horace Jr & Bryan. **Educ:** Syracuse Univ Sch Educ, BA, 1949; Rutgers State Univ, Grad Sch Educ, MEduc, 1962. **Career:** Labor relations manager (retired); Burlington Pub Sch, teacher, admin, 1956-64; Garmco Inc, pres ceo, 1968-70; Dade County Community Relations Bd, dep dir, 1970; Dade County Model Cities Prog, dir, 1971; New York Urban League, exec dir, 1974-83; Greater NY Fund United Way, exec dir, 1983-88; United Way New York City, exec vpres, 1988-91, consult. **Orgs:** Nat Conf Soc Welfare; Nat Asn Advan Colored People; Alumni Asn Syracuse Univ; Alpha Phi Alpha Frat; Frontiers Int; Charter mem, Civitan Int Springfield, OH Chap; AME Zion Ch; bd dir, New York City Partnership; chair, Black Agency Execs of New York City; trustee, Wesley A.M.E. Zion Church. **Honors/Awds:** Four Year Scholar, 1945-49; Pop Warner Service to Youth Award, S Jersey area, 1962; Outstanding Young Man of Year, Gr Burlington Area Jr C of C, 1962; Father of Year, Burlington Jr HS PTA, 1960; Letterman of Distinction, 1985, Syracuse Univ; Frederick Douglass Awardee, New York Urban League, 1992. **Home Addr:** 15 Ridgeview Pl, Willingboro, NJ 08046.

MORRIS, JAMIE WALTER
Football player, football executive. **Personal:** Born Jun 6, 1965, Southern Pines, NC. **Educ:** Univ Mich, attended 1987. **Career:** Football player (retired), football administrator; Wash Redskins, 1988-90; New England Patriots, running back, 1990; Univ Mich, Athletic Dept, develop mgr, currently.

MORRIS, JOE
Football player, real estate executive, insurance executive. **Personal:** Born Sep 15, 1960, Fort Bragg, NC; married Linda; children: Samantha Ashley. **Educ:** Syracuse Univ, BS, 1982. **Career:** Football player (retired), Business owner; New York Giants, running back,1982-88; Cleveland Browns, running back, 1991; AFL, New Jersey Red Dogs, co-owner, 1997-2000; real estate & ins bus, owner, currently. **Honors/Awds:** Independence Bowl Outstanding Offensive Player, 1979; Mark Hoffman Outstanding Back Award, 1981.

MORRIS, JOHN P, III
Shipping executive, business owner. **Personal:** Son of John P Sr (deceased). **Career:** Red River Shipping, owner, 1993-. **Special Achievements:** Red River Shipping is the first African-American controlled company to own and operate an oceangoing motor vessel under the US flag. **Business Addr:** Owner, Red River Shipping Corporation, 6110 Executive Blvd Suite 620, Rockville, MD 20852, **Business Phone:** (301)230-0854.

MORRIS, KELSO B. See Obituaries section.

MORRIS, LATICIA
Basketball player. **Personal:** Born May 26, 1974. **Educ:** Auburn Univ, attended. **Career:** Auburn Tigers, 1995-97; Portland Power, forward, 1997-98.

MORRIS, LEIBERT WAYNE
School administrator. **Personal:** Born Nov 20, 1950, Cleveland, OH; married Cathy L. **Educ:** OH Univ, BGS, 1973, MEd, 1980. **Career:** OH State Univ Office Minority Affairs, coord recruitment, 1974-75; Oberlin Col, asst dir admin, 1975-77; Col Osteopathic Med, OH Univ, assoc dir admis, 1977-79, asst regional dean, 1979-85; OH State Univ Col Med, assoc dean, 1985-90, dir admin, 1990-96; Columbus State Community Col, dir admin, 1996-, coord admin enrollment serv, 1998; Mayo Sch Med, asst dean stud affairs, 1998; Stricth Sch Med, asst dean stud af-

fairs, currently. **Orgs:** Adv bd, Staff Builders Home Health Care Agency, 1983-85; keeper records & seal, Omega Psi Phi Frat Inc 1984-85; bd trustees, Triedstone Missionary Baptist Church, 1985-88; nat nominations chair, Nat Asn Med Minority Educr, 1989-91; Ohio Comn Minority Health, 1989-92; New Salem Missionary Baptist Church. **Business Addr:** Assistant Dean, Stricth School of Medicine, 2160 S First Ave, Maywood, IL 60153, **Business Phone:** (708)216-3227.

MORRIS, MAJOR
Educator, photographer. **Personal:** Born May 12, 1921, Cincinnati, OH; son of Ellen Morris; married Anne-Grethe Jakobsen; children: Lia Jacqueline. **Educ:** Boston Univ, attended, 1951; Harvard Univ, Grad Sch Educ, EdM, 1976. **Career:** Educator (retired), Photographer; Mass Inst Technol, res technician, 1953-66; Tufts Univ, prog dir officer 1969-76; Southeastern Mass Univ, affirmative action officer, 1977-79; Portland State Univ, dir equity programs, 1979-87; photogr, currently. **Orgs:** Photographer/adminr, Educ Develop Ctr, 1966-68; dir, Deseg Training Inst, Univ Del, 1976-77; state coordr, Mass Region I AAAA, 1977-79; vice chair, Tri-County AA Assoc, Portland, 1981-83; state coordr, Oregon Region X AAAA, 1983-; Willamette Valley Racial Minority Consortium; dir/photographer, Foto MaJac, 1987-; bd mem, Beaverton Ore Arts Comn, 1989-91; Retirement Asn Portland State Univ. **Honors/Awds:** Monographs EEO/AA In Postsecondary Institutions, Concepts Multicultural & Intergroup Rels ed, Click & Tell, Our Street; contributor Intergroup Rels Curric. **Military Serv:** AUS, staff sgt, 1942-46; European Theatre; Po Valley; No Appenines; Good Conduct Medal; Victory Medal. **Business Addr:** Photographer, 9521 High Pk Lane, San Diego, CA 92129.

MORRIS, MARGARET LINDSAY
Educator. **Personal:** Born Dec 23, 1950, Princess Anne Co, VA; daughter of George Alfred and Lillie Mae Phelps; married Richard Donald, Aug 24, 1984; children: Kristin Richelle & Tyler Donald. **Educ:** Norfolk State Univ, BA, 1973; Iberian Am Univ Mexico City, 1975; Univ Ill Urbana-Champaign, MA, 1974; PhD, 1979; Univ Madrid, 1982; Mich State Univ, 1991. **Career:** Univ Ill, fel, 1973-74; Grad Col Univ Ill, fel, 1975; Lincoln Univ, asst prof span, 1980; Central State Univ Wilberforce Ohio, lang lab dir, 1980; Livingstone Col Salisbury NC, asst prof, 1981-85; Portsmouth City Schs, teacher, 1986; Ford Found, fel, 1992; Hampton Univ, asst prof span; Smith Univ, educr, currently. **Orgs:** Alpha Gamma Mu Spanish Hon Soc, 1972-; Alpha Kappa Mu Honor Soc, 1972-; Sigma Delta Pi Spanish Hon Soc, 1974-; Am Asn Teacher Span & Port,1976-80; Am Asn Univ Prof, 1976-80; Col Lang Asn, 1980; Alpha Kappa Alpha Soc, 1983-. **Special Achievements:** First Black received PhD Span from Univ of Ill, 1979. **Home Phone:** (804)543-3908. **Business Addr:** Educator, Smith College, Paradise Rd, Northampton, MA 01060, **Business Phone:** (413)584-2700.

MORRIS, MARLENE C.
Chemist. **Personal:** Born Dec 20, 1933, Washington, DC; daughter of Richard Cook and Ruby Cook; married Kelso B; children: Gregory A, Karen D, Lisa F. **Educ:** Howard Univ, BS, 1955; Polytechnic Inst NY, postgrad. **Career:** Chemist (retired); AUS, res assoc, High Temp Res Proj, 1953-55; NBS JCPDS Associateship, research assoc, 1955, dir & res assoc, 1975; Int Ctr Diffraction Data, res chemist, 1986-90. **Orgs:** Am Chemist Soc; Am Crystallographic Soc; AAAS; Joint Comn Powder Diff Stand; Int Union Crystallography; NBSSR Lunch Club; fel, Wash Acad Sci Sigma Xi; Beta Kappa Chi Hon Sci Soc; Unitarian Church. **Special Achievements:** Published 69 articles in professional periodicals; author of 4 books. **Home Addr:** 1448 Leegate Rd NW, Washington, DC 20012. *

MORRIS, MELVIN
Lawyer. **Personal:** Born May 7, 1937, Chicago, IL. **Educ:** Univ Wis, BS, 1959; John Marshall Law Sch, JD, 1965. **Career:** Pvt Pract, atty, currently. **Orgs:** Illinois State Bar. **Business Addr:** Attorney, 602 E 150th St, East Chicago, IN 46312, **Business Phone:** (219)398-6711.

MORRIS, NATHAN BARTHOLOMEW (ALEX VANDERPOOL)
Singer. **Personal:** Born Jun 18, 1971, Philadelphia, PA; son of Gail Harris and Alphonso Morris Sr. **Career:** Albums: Cooleyhighharmony, 1991; II, 1994; Evolution, 1997; Full Circle,2002; Boys II Men, founding mem; Int Stylings, owner, 1997-; Tv Appearances: The Jacksons: An American Dream (1992); Boyz II Men Motown: A Journey Through Hitsville USA Live,2008. **Business Addr:** Recording Artist, Arista Records, 6 W 57th St, New York, NY 10019.*

MORRIS, ROBERT V
Executive, consultant. **Personal:** Born May 13, 1958, Des Moines, IA; son of James B Jr and Arlene J; married Vivian E, Jun 3, 1989; children: Jessica, Robert Jr & Brandon. **Educ:** Univ Iowa, attended 1982. **Career:** Iowa Bystander, ed & writer, 1968-83; Des Moines Register, editorialist, 1990-; Morris Communs Int Inc, chief exec officer & pres, 1983-96; Future Electronic Mgt Inc, chief exec officer & pres, 1997-; Fort Des Monies Mem Pk & Educ Ctr, founder, chief exec officer; Morris Contracting Serv Inc, consult, currently. **Orgs:** Kappa Alpha Psi Fraternity, 1984; pres, Iowa City Chap, Nat Asn Advan Colored People, 1979-81; Iowa Tuskegee Airmen; founder, Iowa Air Nat Guard 132rd Fighter Wing. **Honors/Awds:** Black Hall of Fame, Univ Iowa, 1980; Chairs Award, Nat Asn Advan Colored People Iowa City Chap, 1980; TSB Entrepreneur of the Year, State Iowa, 1989; Meritorious Service Award, Nat Asn Advan Colored People, Iowa/NEB Conf, 1990. **Special Achievements:** Fifty Most Influential Iowans of the New Twenty Century; Author: Tradition and Valor, Sunflower Press, 1999. **Business Addr:** Consult, Morris Contracting Services Inc, 1223 Ctr St Suite 24, PO Box 35953, Des Moines, IA 50315-0308, **Business Phone:** (515)243-0400.

MORRIS, STANLEY E., JR.
School administrator. **Personal:** Born Nov 15, 1944, Brooklyn, NY; son of E Sr and Bernice Lambert; married Sandra Brito; children: Brooke Brito. **Educ:** Howard Univ, BA, 1968; Cornell Univ, pub rels bd, cert, neutral training, 1990. **Career:** Educator (retired); NY City Bd Educ, teacher, 1968-69; St Univ NY, asso dean, 1970-95, asst dir, 1969-70; Stan Morris, Conceptual Engineering, owner. **Orgs:** Pres & chmn bd, Elephant Ent Ltd; pres, SE Morris Mgt Asn; NY St Personnel & Guidance Asn; Afro Am Teacher Asn; rep, Univ Negro Col Fund, 1970; rep, ASG; mem, DC Sociol Soc; Nat Asn Stud Personnel Adminr, 1990-91; Am Asn Higher Educ, 1991; trainer, Nat Coalition Bldg Inst Prejudice Reduction, 1990-91. **Honors/Awds:** Claude McKay Award, 1960; Chancellor's Service Award, State Univ NY, 1990; Distinguished Service Award, Pres Comt Minority & Traditionally Under represented Stud, State Univ NY Oneonta, 1990; University Faculty Senate Award, State Univ NY Fac Senate, 1991. **Home Addr:** 632 W St, Oneonta, NY 13820, **Home Phone:** (607)432-4656. *

MORRIS, STEVLAND HARDAWAY. See WONDER, STEVIE.

MORRIS, VALERIE COLEMAN
Television news anchorperson. **Personal:** Born Nov 25, 1946, Philadelphia, PA; daughter of William O Dickerson and Vivien A Dickerson; married Robert L Morris Jr, Dec 31, 1993; children: Michon Coleman & Ciara Coleman Harris. **Educ:** San Jose State Univ, BS, 1968; Columbia Univ Grad Sch Jour, MS. **Career:** KRON-TV, researcher; KGO-TV, general assignment reporter, news anchor; KRON-TV, anchor; KCBS Newsradio, morning drive anchor; KCBS-TV, anchor, 1986-88; KCBS Radio, morning drive anchor, 1988-, "With the Family in Mind" radio commentary series, writer & narrator, 1986-; WPIX-TV Channel 11, anchor; CNN Financial Network, anchor & corresp; CNN Bus Anchor, currently. **Orgs:** Dd dir, Hearing Soc Bay Area. **Honors/Awds:** Three Emmy awards. **Special Achievements:** American Sign Language. **Business Addr:** Anchor/Correspondent, CNN, 1 Time Warner Ctr, New York, NY 10019, **Business Phone:** (212)275-7980.

MORRIS, VIVIAN LOUISE
Educator. **Personal:** Born Nov 8, 1925, Greenwood, LA; daughter of Bienville Greggs; married Rev George L, Apr 13, 1968 (deceased). **Educ:** Prairie View Univ, BA, 1949, ME, 1964. **Career:** Educator (retired); Thornton's Bus Sch, teacher typing, 1949-50; Grandview Independent Sch Dist, teacher, 1950-52 & 1961-86; City Houston Water Dept, billing clerk, 1952-59; Prairie View, money order clerk, 1959; Prairie View Univ & E Tex, regular & spec educ counr, 1980. **Orgs:** Pres, 1982-84, Classroom Teachers Grand Prairie; deleg, Nat Educ Asn 1876, 1977, 1982; Extended Sick Leave Bank, 1977-82; grade level chmn, 1979-80; life mem, PTA/Plaque, 1979; pres, Ethel Ranson Cult Club, 1986-95; Disabled Serv Comn. **Home Addr:** 706 Tusegee St, Grand Prairie, TX 75051.

MORRIS, WANYA
Singer, business owner. **Personal:** Born Jul 29, 1973, Philadelphia, PA. **Career:** Boys II Men, singer; Albums with Boys II Men: Cooleyhighharmony, 1991; II, 1994; Evolution, 1997; Full Circle, 2002; Film: An Invited Guest, 1999; The Co Entertainment Inc, owner, 2005-. **Business Addr:** Recording Artist, Arista Records, 888 7th Ave, New York, NY 10019, **Business Phone:** (212)489-7400.*

MORRIS, WAYNE LEE
Rancher, contractor, football player. **Personal:** Born May 3, 1954, Dallas, TX. **Educ:** Southern Methodist Univ, BA, 1976. **Career:** Rancher, Contractor, Football player (retired); St Louis Cardinals, 1976-83; San Diego Chargers, 1984; Wayne Morris Enterprises Inc, chmn bd; Landmark Northwest Plz Bank, loan officer, 1978; Wayne Morris Quarter Horse Ranch, owner, 1979. **Orgs:** Co-chmn, YMCA. **Honors/Awds:** Player of Year, Golden Knights, 1975-76; Most Valuable Player, Shriners C's Hosp, 1976; Most Improved Player, St Louis Quarterback Club, 1977. **Home Addr:** 5715 Old Ox Rd, Dallas, TX 75241.

MORRIS, WILLIAM HOWARD
Executive, educator. **Personal:** Born Sep 7, 1960, Detroit, MI. **Educ:** Northwood Inst, BBA, 1982; The Wharton Sch Univ Pa, MBA, 1988. **Career:** Peat Marwick, supvr, 1982-86; Chrysler Corp, senior treasury analyst, 1988-90; Wilmoco Capital Mgt, pres & chief invest officer, 1990-; Hillsdale col, pro finance & acct, 1991-. **Orgs:** Nat Black MBA Asn, 1987-; Mic Asn Cpa's, 1988; Fin Analysts Soc Detroit, Acct Comt, 1989-; secy & treas, State MIC Accountancy Bd, 1991-; Am Inst CPAs, invest comt, 1992-93; Nat Asn St Bd Accts, finance & admin comt, 1992-93. **Honors/Awds:** Outstanding Alumni Award, Northwood Inst, 1992. **Special Achievements:** Top 40 Business People Under 40 Years Age, Crain's Detroit Bus, 1991. *

MORRISON, CHARLES EDWARD (CHUCK MORRISON)
Executive, manager. **Personal:** Born Jul 18, 1943, Longview, TX; married Geri Brooks; children: Constance, Rani, Kristi & Jennifer. **Educ:** Bishop Col, BS, 1964; Wichita State Univ; Rust Col, Hon Doctorate, 1988; Grambling State Univ, Honorary Doctorate, 1989. **Career:** Gen Motors, acct, 1965-70; Procter & Gamble, sales, mkt, 1970-72; Schlitz Brewing Co, sales, mkt, 1972-77, 1979-81; Burrell Advert, advert acct sup, 1977-79; Coca-Cola USA, dir black consumer mkt, 1981; Don Coleman Advert, exec vpres, 2000; Uniworld Group Inc, exec vpres & gen mgr, currently. **Orgs:** Consult, WCLK Adv Bd, 1985-86; consult, Southern Arts Fedn, 1985; trustee, Bishop Col, 1985-86; bd mem, S DeKalb YMCA, 1986; life mem, NAACP, Urban League; bd mem, Atlanta Boys Club; Grambling State Univ Indust Cluster; chmn, Nat Asn Mkt Develop, 1991-92; trustee, Rust Col; bd mem, Jackie Robinson Found. **Honors/Awds:** Top 10 Black Businessperson Dollar & Sense Magazine, 1985; Beverage Executive of Year, Cal-PAC Org, 1986; several ad awards; CEBA's, CLIO's, Addy's. **Business Addr:** Executive Vice President, General Manager, Uniworld Group Inc, 100 Ave Of The Americas Fl 16, New York, NY 10013-1689, **Business Phone:** (212)219-1600.

MORRISON, CHUCK. See MORRISON, CHARLES EDWARD.

MORRISON, CLARENCE CHRISTOPHER
Judge. **Personal:** Born Feb 17, 1930, Charleston, SC; son of Clarence and Ida; married Grace Fulton; children: Derricott M & Mark E. **Educ:** Howard Univ Col Lib Arts, BS, Psych, 1954; Howard Univ Sch Law, LLB, 1959. **Career:** Judge (retired); Judge Carl B Shelly, law clerk, 1960-61; State PA Auditor Gen, legal asst, 1961-62; Commonwealth PA Dept Rev, asst atty gen, 1962-65; Dauphin Cty Prosecutors Off, asst dist atty, 1965-69; PA State Ed Assoc, staff coun, 1969-76; Marrison & Atkins, law partner, 1972-80; Ct Common Pleas, Dauphin Co Ct Common Pleas, judge, 1980; Am pres judge, 1993-2000. **Orgs:** Bd dir, pres, Harrisburg Housing Authority; Mayors Comn Human Rels; vpres, Yoke Crest Inc; vice chmn, bd trustees, legal adv, Sunday Sch teacher Tabernacle Baptist Church, Harrisburg, PA; co-chmn, S Cent PA Chap Heart Fund; legal adv, chmn bd dir, Opportunity Indust Ctrs Inc; pres, Harrisburg Club Frontiers Int; bd dir, Dauphin City, Nat Asn Advan Colored People; charter Optimist Club Harrisburg; Omega Psi Phi Fraternity; Dauphin County Bar Asn; Pa Bar Asn. **Honors/Awds:** Morrison Towers home for the elderly named after Clarence Morrison. **Special Achievements:** First African American president judge, 1993. **Military Serv:** AUS, comn officer, 1964-56.

MORRISON, GARFIELD E
Law enforcement officer. **Personal:** Born Apr 13, 1939, Boston, MA; son of Iona Blackman and Garfield E Sr; married Pearl P Johnson, Jul 27, 1963; children: Garfield E Morrison III & Melissa E Morrison. **Educ:** Mass Bay Community Col, Wellesley, MA, AS, 1978; Boston State Col, Boston, MA, BS, 1981; Anna Maria Col, Paxton, MA, attended 1982. **Career:** Law Enforcement Officer (retired); US Post Off, Boston, MA, letter carrier, 1966-74; Cambridge Police Dept, Cambridge, MA, police officer, 1974-84, sgt, 1984-94, lt, 1994-2001, dep supt, 2001-04. **Orgs:** Chmn, usher bd, Mass Ave Baptist Church, 1966-70; secy, Men's Club, Mass Ave Baptist Church, 1965-68; trustee, Mass Ave Baptist Church, 1968-72; treas, Cambridge Afro-Am Police Asn, 1977-86, pres, 1990 & 1992. **Honors/Awds:** WEB DuBois Academy Award, Recognition Serv, 1992; Outstanding Contribution in Aiding Police Service to the Citizens of Boston, Boston Police Dept, 1992. **Military Serv:** USAF, A/3C, 1957-59; Unit Citation, 485th Commun Squadron.

MORRISON, DR. GWENDOLYN CHRISTINE CALDWELL (WENDY MORRISON)
Educator. **Personal:** Born Dec 11, 1949, Cuney, TX; daughter of John and Josephine Pierce Ellis; married Ben Arnold, 1973; children: Paul, Brandon, Jonathan & Betsey. **Educ:** Stephen F Austin State Univ, Nacogdoches, TX, BS, home econ, 1970; Stephen F Austin State Univ, Med, 1971; Tex Womans Univ, Denton, TX, Phd, 1981;Univ North Tex, Denton, TX, educ leadership post doc studies, 1988; Tex Woman's Univ, Denton, TX, Ed.D, adult educ, 1988. **Career:** Palestine ISD,TX, homemaking teacher, 1971-73; Property Management Co,admin asst, 1973-77; Radio Shack, employee relations counr, 1977-81; City of Grand Prairie, TX, dir personnel, 1982-84; Fort Worth ISD, Fort Worth,TX, classroom teacher, 1986-87, dir employee staffing, 1988-90, dir of alternative cert, 1990-; E-Systems Inc, Garland, TX, EEO specialist, 1987-88; Ind Univ- Purdue Univ Indianapolis,

asst prof econs, currently; Regenstrief Inst Inc, prin investr, currently. **Orgs:** Trustee elected county wide, Trrant Co Jr Col Dist, 1976-; bd dirs, St Citizens Center Inc, 1976-82; gov, S Cent Dist Nat Asn Negro Bus Prof Women, 1978-83; mem appointed by gov, Coordinating Bd TX Col Univ Syst,1979-83; bd dirs, Ft Worth Girls Club, 1979-82; pres, Tex Alliance Black Sch Educr; chair, NABSE Coun Affil Presidents. **Honors/Awds:** Trailblazer of the Year Award, Ft Worth NB & PW Club, 1976. **Special Achievements:** Author: "Characteristics of Black Executive Females" 1981. **Home Phone:** (817)871-2206. **Business Addr:** Assistant Professor of Economics, Indiana University-Purdue University Indianapolis, Cavanaugh Hall 425 Univ Blvd, Indianapolis, IN 46202-5140, **Business Phone:** (317)274-1577.

MORRISON, JACQUELINE
Association executive. **Personal:** Born Aug 9, 1951, Plainfield, NJ; daughter of Wisteria Ingram McKnight and Caldwell; married Curtis Sr, Jul 1971 (divorced 1988); children: Curtis Morrison Jr (deceased). **Educ:** San Diego State Univ, BA, 1978; Univ Mich Sch Pub Health, MPH, 1983. **Career:** Public health consult, 1984-86; Wayne State Univ, pub health consult, 1986-88; Detroit Urban League, sr vpres progs, 1988-98; Planned Parenthood SE Mich, pres & chief exec oficer; AARP, MI, assoc state dir, currently. **Orgs:** Adv bd mem, Literacy Vols Am; bd mem, Life Directions, 1990-91; New Detroit Inc; bd mem, Sickle Cell Dis Asn; Brush park Develop Corp; Workforce Develop Bd; Am Pub Health Asn. **Honors/Awds:** Community Service Award, Nat Coun Negro Women, 1994. **Business Addr:** Associate State Director, AARP, 309 N Wash Sq Suite 110, Lansing, MI 48933-1222, **Business Phone:** (866)227-7448.

MORRISON, JAMES W.
Lobbyist, president (organization), consultant. **Personal:** Born Jan 14, 1936, Bluefield, WV; son of James W Sr and Winnie E Hendricks; married Jean M, May 15, 2001; children: Traquita Renee, James W III & Susannah Myerson. **Educ:** WVa State Col, BA, 1957; Univ Dayton, MPA, 1970. **Career:** Dayton AF Dept Def Electronics Supply Ctr, OH, inventory mgr, 1959-63; AF Logistics Command, Dayton, OH, mgt spec, 1963-72; NASA, Wash, DC, execasst dir mgt systs, 1972-74; Exec Off Pres OMB, Wash, DC, sr mgt assoc, 1974-79; Exec Proj State Univ NY, Albany, vis lectr publ, 1974-76; US Off Personnel Mgt, Wash, DC, asst dir econ & govt, 1979, dir congional rel, 1979-81, assoc dir compensation, 1981-87; CNA Ins Co, Rockville, MD, sr mgr prog support, 1987-88; pres, Morrison Assocs, Wash, DC/Scottsdale, AZ,1988-. **Orgs:** Adv comt mem, Dayton Bd Educ, 1971; Alpha Phi Alpha; Pi Delta Phi; Pi Alpha Alpha. **Honors/Awds:** Exceptional Service Award, Exec Off Pres OMB Wash, DC, 1977; President Certificate, Pres USA, Wash, DC, 1979; Meritorious Service Award, US Off Personnel Mgt, Wash, DC, 1980; President Meritorious Executive, Pres USA, Wash, DC 1983; Distinguished Executive, Pres USA, Wash, DC 1985. **Military Serv:** AUS, first lt, 1957-59. **Business Addr:** President, Morrison Associates, 35056 N 80th Way, Scottsdale, AZ 85266-1026, **Business Phone:** (480)515-2859.

MORRISON, JOHNNY EDWARD
Lawyer, judge. **Personal:** Born Jun 24, 1952, Portsmouth, VA; son of Mary Bernard; married Cynthia L Payton, Aug 21, 1976; children: Melanie Yvette & Camille Yvonne. **Educ:** Wash & Lee Univ, grad, 1974; Wash & Lee Univ Sch Law, grad, 1977. **Career:** Legal Aid Soc Roanoke Valley, staff atty, 1977-78; Washington & Lee Sch Law, Reginald Heber Smith fel, 1977; Norfolk Commonwealth Attys Off, prosecutor, 1978-79; Portsmouth Commonwealth Atty's Off, prosecutor, 1979-82; Overton, Sallee & Morrison, partner, 1982; Portsmouth Commonwealth Atty's Off, atty, 1982-91; Portsmouth Circuit Ct, judge, 1991-, chief judge, 1992-94, 1996-98. **Orgs:** Va State Bar Asn; VA Asn Commonwealths Attys; Kiwanis Int; bd mem, Tidewater Legal Aid Soc, United Way, Effingham St Branch YMCA; pres, Tidewater Legal Aid Soc; bd dirs Wash & Lee, Tidewater Alumni; Va Black Caucus; Cent Civic Forum; Old Dominion Bar Asn; Twin City Bar Asn; Nat Criminal Justice Asn; Nat Black Prosecutors Asn. **Honors/Awds:** Young Man of the Year, Eureka Club, 1982; Man of the Year, Disabled Am Vets Portsmouth, 1982; Outstanding Young Men of America, 1983; Martin Luther King Jr Leadership Award, Old Dominion Univ, 1987; Man of Year, Eureka Club, 1988. **Business Addr:** Chief Judge, Portsmouth Circuit Court, 601 Crawford St, Portsmouth, VA 23704, **Business Phone:** (804)393-8581.

MORRISON, DR. JUAN LARUE, SR.
Educator, clergy. **Personal:** Born Mar 22, 1943, Springfield, IL; son of Farries Sr and Margaret; married Clementine Lorraine; children: Juan L Jr, Daryl G & Cheryl L. **Educ:** IL State Univ, BS, educ, 1969, PhD, higher educ admin, 1980; IL State Univ, MA, Ed admin, 1972; Sangamon State Univ, MA, human dev & coun, 1975. **Career:** Springfield Sch Dist No 186, elem teacher, 1969-70, sec teacher, 1970-72; Prayer Wheel Church God Christ, copastor, 1980-84; Emmanuel Temple Church God Christ, pastor, 1984-; Lincoln Land Comm Col, counr & coordr, prof phsycol; Charles Harris Mason Bible Col, instr; Ill South Cent Fel Church of God in Christ, supt & 1st admin asst, founding overseer, currently. **Orgs:** Test admin Am College Test, 1979-; test admin, Am Registry Radiologic Technologists, 1982-; test admin, Nat Bd for Respiratory Care Mgmt Servs Inc, 1982-; publicity chmn, Springfield Ministerial Alliance, 1983-; test admin, Educ Testing Serv, 1984-; pres music Dept Cent IL Jurisdiction Church God Christ, 1984-. **Honors/Awds:** IL Guidance and Personnel Asn, 1982; Community Service Award, Nat Asn Advan Colored People, 1996. **Home Addr:** 260 Maple Grove, Springfield, IL 62707. **Business Addr:** Pastor, Emmanuel Temple Church Of God In Christ, 212 W Foote St, Po Box 481, Hamburg, AR 71646, **Business Phone:** (870)853-8820.

MORRISON, DR. K C (MINION KENNETH CHAUNCEY)
Educator. **Personal:** Born Sep 24, 1946, Edwards, MS; son of Elvestra Jackson and Minion; married Johnetta Bernadette Wade; children: Iyabo Abena. **Educ:** Tougaloo Col, BA, 1968; Univ WI, Madison, MA, 1969, cert African Studies, 1974, PhD, 1977; Univ Ghana, cert African Studies, 1972. **Career:** Tougaloo Col, instr, 1969-71, asst prof, 1975-77; Hobart Col, asst prof coordr, 1977-78; Syracuse Univ, assoc prof, 1978, chair afro am studies, 1982-89; Univ Mo, Columbia, vice provost, 1989-97, prof polit sci, currently. **Orgs:** African Studies Asn; Nat Conf Black Polit Scientists; Am Pol Sci Asn; consult, fel Ford Found, Danforth Frost & Sullivan Huber Found, 1968-84; NAACP; bd dirs United Way. **Special Achievements:** Author: Housing Urban Poor Africa, 1982; Ethnicity & Political Integration, 1982; Black Political Mobilization, 1987. **Business Addr:** Professor Political Science, University of Missouri, 202 Prof Bldg, Columbia, MO 65211, **Business Phone:** (573)882-0125.

MORRISON, PROF. KEITH ANTHONY
Artist, school administrator, educator. **Personal:** Born May 20, 1942, Linstead, Jamaica; son of Noel and Beatrice McPherson; married Alexandra, Apr 12, 1989. **Educ:** Sch Art Inst Chicago, BFA, 1963, MFA, 1965. **Career:** Fisk Univ, asst prof art, 1967-68; DePaul Univ, Dept Art, chmn, 1969-71; Univ Ill, Chicago, assoc prof art, 1971-79, Col Art, assoc dean, 1974-78; Univ Md, Dept Art, chmn, 1987, prof art, 1979-93; San Francisco Art Inst, dean, 1992-94; San Francisco State Univ, Col Creative Arts, dean, 1994; Temple Univ, Tyler Sch Art, dean, currently, prof painting, drawing & sculpture, currently. **Orgs:** Danforth Found Teaching Asn, 1970-71; chmn bd, Wash Proj Arts, 1984-85; adv bd, New Art Examiner, 1983-. **Honors/Awds:** Bicentennial Award for Painting, City Chicago, 1976; InterNat Award for Painting, OAU Monrovia, Liberia, 1978; Award for Painting, Nat Asn Equal Opportunity Educ, 1984. **Special Achievements:** Has had many solo exhibitions, has exhibited numerous paintings and prints, his work has been featured in many publications, has contributed articles to numerous publications and organizations, including The New Art Examiner, American Visions, The Washington Post, the USIA, the University of Chicago, and the Smithsonian Institution, has written catalog essays for museums such as the Baltimore Museum of Art, the Corcoran Gallery of Art, the MH de Young Memorial Museum, the Getty Museum and the Alternative Museum, has also written one book-length catalogue, Art in Washington and Its Afro-American Presence: 1940-1970. **Business Phone:** (215)782-2715.

MORRISON, PAUL-DAVID
Executive. **Personal:** Born Apr 28, 1965, Boston, MA; son of Paul E and Carole Vitale-Chase; married Nancy Morrison, May 28, 1994. **Career:** Digital Equip Corp, mech engr tech, 1983-88; Raytheon, supvr, 1988-91; Motorola, sr packaging engineering tech, 1991-94; P D Morrison Enterprises Inc, pres & chief exec officer, 1995-. **Orgs:** Bd mem, Central & S Tex Minority Bus Coun; bd dir, Capital City African-Am Chamber Com. **Honors/Awds:** United States Patent Office, Patent # 5,381,039, 1994. **Business Addr:** President, Chief Executive Officer, P.D. Morrison Enterprises, Inc., 1120 Toro Grande Dr Bldg 2 Suite 208, Cedar Park, TX 78613, **Business Phone:** (512)335-7173.

MORRISON, PEARL PATTY
School administrator, educator. **Personal:** Born Oct 11, 1938, Boston, MA; daughter of Annie Lenox and Harry Samuel Johnson; married Garfield E Morrison Jr, Jul 27, 1963; children: Garfield E III & Melissa E. **Educ:** State Teachers Col at Boston, BSED, 1960; State Col Boston, ME, 1967. **Career:** Educator, Sch Principal (retired); City of Somerville, teacher, 1960-87, vice prin, 1987-95, prin. **Orgs:** Mass Ave Baptist Church, treas, 1970-; African-Am Soc Arlington, pres; Arlington Civil Right Comt Arlington, pres; Somerville Racial Understanding Comm, sec, 1970-80; Somerville YMCA, bd mem, 1990-; Elizabeth Peabody House, bd mem, 1990-; Delta Kappa Gamma, MA Chap. **Honors/Awds:** Nat Conference of Christians & Jews, Humanitarian Award; MLK Jr Community Service Award; MLK Jr Educators Award, Somerville Coalition, City of Arlington; Somerville PTA, CNL Scholarship Given in her name, 1995; Millennium Education Award, Tuskegee Alumni Club, 1999.

MORRISON, RICHARD DAVID
Educator. **Personal:** Born Jan 18, 1910, Utica, MS; married Ethel. **Educ:** Tuskegee Inst, BS 1931; Cornell Univ, MS 1941; State Univ, PhD 1954. **Career:** Ala A&M Univ, dir agr, 1937-62; pres, 1962-84, pres emer. **Orgs:** Joint Coun Food & Agr Sci; adv comt Marshall Space Flight Ctr, AL A&M Univ, 1937-62; affiliated with numerous professional & civic groups. **Special Achievements:** Authored two books, a History of Alabama A&M University, 1875-1992, and Walking in the Wilderness. **Business Addr:** President Emeritus, Alabama Agricultural and Mechanical University, Normal, AL 35762.

MORRISON, ROBERT B., JR.
Government official. **Personal:** Born Jul 9, 1954, Orlando, FL. **Educ:** Loyola Univ, BA, Political Sci, Bus Admin, 1975; Univ Fla, JD, 1978. **Career:** Law Off Warren H Dawson, atty, 1978-79; Morrison Gilmore & Clark, Pa, partner, 1986-; City Tampa, exec asst mayor. **Orgs:** Am Bar Asn; Nat Bar Asn; Fla Bar Asn; Fla Chap Nat Bar Asn, 1979-; chmn, Bi-Racial Adv Comn Hillsborough City Sch Bd, 1978-81; chmn, Mayor's Cable TV Adv Comn, 1979-83; pres, St Peter Claver Parish Coun, 1979-83; Franklin St Mall Adv Comn, 1979-; Tampa Orgn Black Affairs, 1979-; mediator Citizen Dispute Settlement Prog, 1979-80; bd dir, Tampa Urban League, 1980-; March Dimes Hillsborough City, 1980-; Nat Advan Asn Colored People, 1981; bd dir, Boy Scouts Am, 1982-; State Job Training Coordr Coun, 1983-; Rotary Club Tampa, 1983-; pres, Fla Chap Nat Bar Asn, 1986-87; Bi-Racial Comn, 1987. **Honors/Awds:** Citizen of the Year, Omega Psi Phi, 1980; George Edgecomb Member Award for Outstanding Community Serv, 1981.

MORRISON, SAMUEL F.
Librarian, executive. **Personal:** Born Dec 19, 1936, Flagstaff, AZ; son of Travis B and Ruth Morrison Genes; divorced. **Educ:** Compton Junior Col, AA, 1955; Calif State Univ, Los Angeles, BA, Eng, 1971; Univ Ill, Champaign, MS, libr sci, 1972; Harvard Univ, Kennedy Sch Govt, attended 1989. **Career:** Frostproof Living Learning Libr, Frostproof, FL, dir, 1972-74; Broward County Libr Syst Fort Lauderdale, FL, asst to dir & dep dir, 1974-87; Chicago Pub Libr, Chicago, IL, dep comnr & chief librn, 1987-90; Broward County Libr Syst, Fort Lauderdale, dir, 1990-2003; Southeastern Consulting Group, Boca Raton, FL, assoc, 2003-. **Orgs:** Am Libr Asn, 1971-; Nat Urban League, 1972-; Nat Asn Advan Colored People, 1972-; bd mem, Broward County Libr Found, 1990; bd mem, Urban League Broward County; bd mem, Nat Forum Black Pub Adminr, South Fla Chapter, 1990; steering comt, Ctr Book; planning comn, Fla Libr Asn; Fontaneda Soc, Fort Lauderdale, FL; bd mem, United Way, 1995-97; bd mem, National Conf; bd mem, Gold Coast Jazz Soc; bd mem, Fla Humanities Coun; bd mem, Urban Libr Coun. **Honors/Awds:** Faculty Award, Univ Ill Libr Sch, 1972; Employee of the Year, Broward Co Libr Adv Bd, 1977-78; Freeman Bradley Award, Nat Asn Adavn Colored People, 1993; Broward Service Award, Urban League, 1993; Leader of the Year Award, Leadership Broward Found, 1996; Sun Sentinel Publisher's Award, 1997; hon doctorate St Thomas Univ, Ft Lauderdale, FL, 1998; Diversity Champion Award, Urban League, 1998; Nat Asn Advan Colored People President's Award, 1998; Distinguished Alumnus Award, Univ Ill Grad Sch Libr & Info Sci, 1999; Cato & Margaret Roach Award Exemplary Human Rels, 2003; Citizen Recognition Award, City Fort Lauderdale, 2003. **Special Achievements:** First recipient of the Dr. Mack King Carter Community Revitalization Summit Humanitarian Award. **Military Serv:** USAF, Airman 1st Class, 1955-59; Good Conduct Medal, 1958; Air Force Longevity Award, 1959. *

MORRISON, TONI (CHLOE ANTHONY WOFFORD)
Writer, educator, editor. **Personal:** Born Feb 18, 1931, Lorain, OH; daughter of George Wofford and Ramah Willis Wofford; married Harold, 1958 (divorced 1964); children: Harold Ford & Slade Kevin. **Educ:** Howard Univ, BA, 1953; Cornell Univ, MA, 1955; Oxford Univ, DLitt, 2005. **Career:** Tex Southern Univ, instr, 1955-57; Howard Univ, instr, 1957-64; Random House Publ Co, sr ed, 1965-; author, 1969-; State Univ NY, Purchase, assoc prof, 1971-72; Yale Univ, vis prof, 1976-77; State Univ NY, Albany, Schweitzer prof humanities, 1984-89; Bard Col, vis prof, 1986-88; Princeton Univ, Robert F Goheen prof humanities, 1989-93, prof emer, currently; Novels: The Bluest Eye, 1970; Sula, 1974; Song of Solomon, 1977; Tar Baby, 1981; Beloved, 1987; Jazz, 1992; Paradise, 1998; The Big Box, 2002; The Book of Mean People, 2002; Love, 2003; Playwright: Dreaming Emmett, 1986; ed: The Black book, 1974. **Orgs:** Am Acad & Inst Arts & Letters; Nat Coun Arts; Authors Guild; Authors League Am. **Honors/Awds:** Ohoana Book Award for Sula, 1975; Nat Book Critics Circle Award; Award for Song of Solomon, Am Acad & Inst Arts & Letters, 1977; New York State Governor's Art Award, 1986; Pulitzer Prize for Fiction, 1988; Robert F Kennedy Award, 1988; Nobel Prize, lit, 1993; Elizabeth Cady Stanton Award, Nat Orgn Women; Nat Book Foundation Medal, 1996; Nat Arts & Humanites Medal, presented by President Clinton, 2000. **Special Achievements:** First African-American to win a Nobel Prize in literature, 1993; nominee, National Book Award; 30 Most Powerful Women in America. **Business Addr:** Robert F. Goheen Professor Emeritus, Princeton University, Department of Creative Writing, 58 Prospect Ave, Princeton, NJ 08544-1099.

MORRISON, TRUDI MICHELLE
Presidential aide, lawyer. **Personal:** Born Jul 25, 1950, Denver, CO; daughter of George and Marjorie; married Dale Saunders, Jan 1, 1981. **Educ:** Colo State Univ, BS, 1971; Nat Law Ctr, George Wash Univ, JD, 1975; Univ Colo Denver, DPA, 1986. **Career:** States Atty Off, Rockville, MD, asst states atty, 1975-76; Gorsuch Kirgis Campbell Walker & Grover, atty, 1977; Denver Dist Atty

Off, atty, 1977-78; Colo Div Criminal Justice, criminal justice admin, 1978-81; US Dept HUD, actg dep asst secy, policy & budget, 1981-82; US Dept Health & Human Serv, reg dep dir, 1982-83; White House, assoc dir off pub liaison; US Sen, dep sgt arms; US Courts, chief fair employment pract, currently. **Orgs:** Exec secy stud body, Colo State Univ, 1969-71; bd dir, Nat Stroke Asn, 1983-87; Nat Coun Negro Women; founder, Colo Black Repub Coun; Nat Urban League; Nat Asn Advan Colored People. **Honors/Awds:** Outstanding Young Women of America, 1978, 1979, 1982; Young Careerist, Nat Org Bus & Prof Women, 1978; Highest Ranking Black Woman White House, 1983-; Black Republican of the Year, 1984; William E Morgan CSU Alumni Achievement Award, 1984. **Special Achievements:** First Black Homecoming Queen Colo State Univ, 1970-71; First woman & First Black Dep Sgt Arms, US Senate. **Business Phone:** (202)502-1380.

MORRISON, WENDY. See MORRISON, DR. GWENDOLYN CHRISTINE CALDWELL.

MORROW, CHARLES G, III
Manager, congressional representative (u.s. federal government). **Personal:** Born Jul 21, 1956, Chicago, IL; son of Lillian; married Sherri; children: 3. **Educ:** De LaSalle Inst; Ill Inst Technol. **Career:** Sch Dist, drivers educ instr, 1971-74; Metro Sanitary Dist, bookkeeper, 1975-76; Peoples Gas, customer serv rep, 1977; Ill Gen Assembly, 32nd Dist, rep, 1987-2005. **Orgs:** Boy Scouts Am; Nat Asn Advan Colored People; Urban League. **Business Phone:** (217)782-1702.

MORROW, DION GRIFFITH
Judge. **Personal:** Born Jul 9, 1932, Los Angeles, CA; son of Anna Griffith and Virgil; married Glynis Ann Dejan; children: Jan Bell, Kim Wade, Cydney, Carla Cavalier, Melvin Cavalier, Dion Jr. **Educ:** Loyola Univ Law Sch, LLB, 1957; Pepperdine Col. **Career:** Judge (retired); La City Atty, asst city atty, 1973-75; La, atty law, 1957-73; Munic Ct Compton, CA, judge, 1975-78; Super Ct, judge, 1978-95. **Orgs:** Vpres, Gen Counsel dir, Enterprise Savings & Loan, 1962-72; pres, John M Langston Bar Asn, 1969-71; life mem, Nat Asn Advan Colored People; Nat Bar Asn, 1969-; dir, Mercantile Nat Bank; Los Angeles County Bar Asn. **Honors/Awds:** Langston Bar Asn, Judge of the Year, 1992; Hall of Fame inductee, 1998. **Home Addr:** 5101 Bedford Ave, Los Angeles, CA 90056. *

MORROW, HAROLD, JR.
Football player. **Personal:** Born Feb 24, 1973, Maplesville, AL. **Educ:** Auburn Univ. **Career:** Minn Vikings, running back, 1996-2002; Baltimore Ravens, 2003-04; Ariz Cardinals, running back, 2005; free agent, currently.

MORROW, JESSE
Executive. **Career:** Leader Lincoln-Mercury-Merkur, Inc, St Louis, MO, chief executive, President, currently. **Business Addr:** President, Leader Lincoln-Mercury-Merkur Inc, 6160 S Lindbergh Blvd, St Louis, MO 63123.

MORROW, DR. JOHN HOWARD, JR.
Educator. **Personal:** Born May 27, 1944, Trenton, NJ; son of Dr John H Morrow Sr and Ann Rowena; married Diane Batts, Jun 14, 1969; children: Kieran & Evan. **Educ:** Swarthmore Col, BA (with honors), 1966; Univ Pa, Philadelphia, PhD, hist,1971. **Career:** Univ Tenn, Knoxville, from asst prof to prof & dept head, 1971-; Nat Aerospace Museum Wash, DC, Lindbergh prof hist, 1989-90; Univ Ga, Athens,GA, Franklin prof hist, 1989-, dpt chmn, 1991-93, assoc dean arts & sci, 1993-95. **Orgs:** Am Hist Asn, 1971-; consult, Col Bd & Ed Testing Serv, 1980-84, 1990-; AHAComn Comm, 1982-85, AHA Prog Comm 1984 Meeting, 1983-84; mem edit adv bds,Aerospace Historian, 1984-87, Military Affairs 1987-90; Smithsonian InstPr, 1987-93; chmn, Hist Adv Comm Secy Air Force, 1988-92; chmn, Col Bd NatAcad Asn, 1993-95, mem col bd, bd trustees, 1993-; Dept Army Hist AdvComm, 1999-01. **Honors/Awds:** Hon Soc Phi Kappa Phi, 1980; Lindsay Young Professorship, 1982-83;Outstanding Teacher UT, Nat Alumni Asn, 1983; UT Macebearer, 1983-84; Univ Distinguished Service Professorship, 1985-88. **Special Achievements:** Author of Building German Airpower 1909-14, 1976, German Airpower in World War I, 1982, The Great War in the Air, 1993, co-editor of A Yankee Ace inthe RAF, 1996; The Great War: An Imperial History, 2005. **Home Addr:** 130 Pine Tops Dr, Athens, GA 30606. **Business Addr:** Franklin Professor of History, University of Georgia, Department of History, 316 Leconte Hall, Athens, GA 30602, **Business Phone:** (706)542-2536.

MORROW, LAVERNE
Business owner. **Personal:** Born Mar 2, 1954, Kankakee, IL; daughter of George and Shirley Jackson Watson. **Educ:** Ill State Univ, Normal, IL, BS, 1976; Wash Univ, St Louis, MA, 1978. **Career:** Urban League, St Louis, MO, specialist, 1978-79; Mid town Pre Apprenticeship Ctr, St Louis, MO, dir, 1979-82; Coro Found, St Louis,MO, trainer, 1983-85; Emprise Designs Inc, St Louis, MO, pres founder, 1985-. **Orgs:** First vpres, Coalition 100 Black Women Prog, St Louis, MO, 1981-84; White House Conf Small Bus Minority Caucus, natl chap, 1986, 1995, rules comt,1995; comm chmn, Jr League St Louis, 1986. **Honors/Awds:** Appointed to the US Senate, Small Bus Nat Adv Coun. **Special Achievements:** Featured and profiled as an Outstanding Business Woman in the September1988 St Louis Business Journal. **Business Phone:** (314)972-9933.*

MORROW, PHILLIP HENRY
Administrator. **Personal:** Born Sep 30, 1943, New Haven, CT; son of Benjamin and Viola English; married Ann Jordan Morrow, Feb 6, 1985; children: Nicole, Haleema, Germaine. **Educ:** Univ Conn, Storrs, BA, 1965, MA, 1967; Mass Inst Technol, min developers prog, 1992. **Career:** Poor Peoples Fed, Hartford, CT, exec dir, 1968-71; Greater Hartford Process, dir social dev, 1971-75; Upper Albany Community Orgn, Hartford, CT, exec dir, 1975-79; US Dept Housing & Urban Develop, Wash, DC, dir office pub pri, 1979-81; Harlem Urban Develop Corp, New York, NY, dir dev, 1982, S Bronx Overall Econ Develop Corp, exec dir, 1994, pres & chief exec officer, 1996-. **Orgs:** Bd mem, Int Downtown Asn, 1987-94; bd mem, N Gen Attendant Project, 1986-; vice chair, 125st LDC, 1986-; pres, 260-262 Corp, 1985-; treas, PACC Housing Asn, 1988-; vice chair, Pratt Area Community Coun. **Honors/Awds:** All Am City Juror, 1990. **Business Phone:** (718)292-3113.*

MORROW, TRACY. See ICE-T.

MORROW, W DERRICK
Executive. **Personal:** Born May 26, 1964, Philadelphia, PA; son of Tammy and Ward. **Educ:** Howard Univ, attended 1983-87. **Career:** Wash Hilton & Towers, sales mgr, 1987-92; Hyatt Regency Atlanta, assoc dir sales, 1992-94; Hyatt Regency Bethesda, dir sales, 1994-95; Hyatt Regency Baltimore, dir sales & mkt, 1995-; Hyatt Regency O'Hare, Rosemont, Ill, dir mkt; Hyatt Regency Tampa, gen mgr, currently. **Orgs:** Black Prof Men Inc; Prof Conv Managers Asn. **Honors/Awds:** Nominee for Director of Sales of the Year, Hyatt Hotels, 1994 & 1995; Director of Sales of the Year, Hyatt Hotels, 1997. **Business Addr:** General Manager, Hyatt Regency Tampa, 211 N Tampa St, Tampa, FL 33602-5187, **Business Phone:** (813)225-1234.

MORSE, ANNIE RUTH W.
Educator. **Personal:** Born in Pendleton, SC; daughter of Walter Webb and Hester Lee Webb; married Wilford Morse, Dec 27, 1947 (deceased); children: Harry B, Rejetta Ruth. **Educ:** SC State A&M Col, Orangeburg, SC, BS Ed, 1937; Columbia Univ Teachers Col, MA, 1958; Clemson Univ Grad Prog, Dept Ed, 1974. **Career:** Educator (retired); Easley Elem, Easley, teacher, 1937-40; Whitmore High Sch, Conway, teacher, 1940-42; E End Elem, Seneca, teacher, 1942-43; Lancaster Tr Sch, Lancaster, teacher, 1943-44; Pickens County, Jeanes Sup-Elem. Sup, 1945, supvr, reading & spl serv, 1974. **Orgs:** SC & Nat ASCD; SC State Adoption Textbooks; SC & NEA Retired Educ Asn; AACP, & Person chap; founder/mem, & person chap, Delta Sorority; adv bd mem, SC Blacks & Native Am, 1977; pres/dir, Pendleton Found Black Hist & Cult, 1976-91; Educ Asn, County, Nat, State, 1990; resr, Historical Found, Humanities Coun State SCA; SCA Dept Archives & Hist, 1992; Curriculum Coun, Dist 4, 1992; SC African Am Heritage Coun, Pub Rels Comt, 1992-95; County comn Adv Bd, & person County Mus, 1997. **Special Achievements:** With the Found, SCA Dept Parks, Tours and Recreation CMS, involved in the production of brochures on Africa and the Afro AMR Arts and Crafts Festival, and a legacy of Pendleton, SC. **Home Addr:** 305 Morse St, PO Box 305 Morse, Pendleton, SC 29670. *

MORSE, BARBARA LYN
Television journalist. **Personal:** Born Nov 15, 1958, Zanesville, OH; daughter of Stanley LaVerne and Sylvia Barbara Yancich; married; children: Maryssa Ann, David Marko & Sydney Elaine. **Educ:** Ind Univ Indianapolis, Indianapolis, IN, BA, 1983. **Career:** Indy Today Newspaper, Indianapolis, IN, columnist, 1984-86; Visions Mag, Indianapolis, IN, staff writer, 1985-86; WNDE-AM, Indianapolis, IN, news anchor & reporter, 1986; WAND-TV, Decatur, IL, news reporter, 1987-88; WLNE-TV 6, Providence, RI, news reporter, 1988-89; WLVI-TV 56, Boston, MA, news reporter, 1989-94; WISH TV 8, Indianapolis, IN, reporter, 1994-95; WJAR TV 10, Providence RI, anchor & health reporter, news reporter, currently. **Orgs:** Nat Asn Black Journalists, 1987-. **Honors/Awds:** Emmy Nominations, 1993, 1998, 2001; American Heart Asn's First Annual Media Awards. **Business Addr:** News Reporter, WJAR-TV, 23 Kenney Dr, Cranston, RI 02920.

MORSE, JOHN E
Judge. **Educ:** Ga State Univ, Mercer Law Sch. **Career:** Chatham Co State Ct, state ct judge, 1992-, elected, 1994, super ct judge, 1995, elected, 1996. **Orgs:** State Bar Ga. **Business Addr:** Judge, Chatham County Court, Rm 213 133 Montgomery St, Savannah, GA 31401, **Business Phone:** (912)652-7236.

MORSE, DR. LAURENCE C
Executive. **Educ:** Howard Univ, BA, econ; Princeton Univ, MA, econ, PhD, econ. **Career:** Harvard Univ, fel; UNC Ventures, mgr, 1983-87; Equico Capital Corp, vpres, 1988-91; TSG Ventures, founding prin, 1992; Coopers & Lybrand Int, sr venture capital adv, 1993; Fairview Capital Partners Inc, co-founder, 1994-. **Orgs:** Syndicated Commun Venture Partners; Opportunity Capital Partners; MedVenture Assocs; Ascend Venture Group; chmn & bd dir, Nat Asn Investment Co; dir, Webster Financial Corp; Phi Beta Kappa. **Special Achievements:** Named one of "The Top Ten Minds in Small Business" by Fortune Small Business Magazine, 2003. **Business Addr:** Co-Founder, Fairview Capital Partners Inc, 10 Stanford Dr, Farmington, CT 06032, **Business Phone:** (860)674-8066.*

MORSE, MILDRED S
Executive, founder (originator), executive director. **Personal:** Born Oct 20, 1942, Dermott, AR; daughter of John Sharpe and Helen Wilson Sharpe; married Oliver "Reds" Morse; children: Stacey & Kasey. **Educ:** Bowling Green State Univ, attended 1962; Univ Ark, BA, 1964; Howard Univ, JD, 1968. **Career:** Civil Rights, specialist, 1968-71; HEW, staff asst dir, 1971-73; HUD, dir 1973-77 & 1979-80; Phase II White House Task Force Civil Rights Presidents Reorganization Proj, dep dir, 1977-79; Corp Pub Broadcasting, Wash, DC, asst pres, 1980-89; Morse Enterprises Inc, Silver Spring, MD, pres & chief exec officer, 1989-. **Orgs:** Nat Bar Asn; Nat Civil Rights Asn; steering comt, Dept Justice Title VI Proj; Blacks Pub Radio, 1980-90; Arcousa Sigma Phi Pi Frat, 1980-; Am Women in Radio & TV, 1980-90; Capital City Links Inc, 1981-; Nat Black Media Coalition, 1982-; bd dirs, Am Indians Media Asn, 1982-91; Delta Sigma Theta Sorority, 1983-; Americans Indian Opportunity, 1989-91; Adv Comn Minority Student Educ, Montg County Sch Bd, 1990-92, vice chair, 1991-92; adv bd, Channel 32, 1990-95; life mem, NAACP; Nat Tobacco Independence Campaign. **Honors/Awds:** Special Achievement Award, HUD 1980; Certificate of Service Award, Fed Serv, 1980; Award of Appreciation, Native Am Pub Broadcasting Consortium, 1984; Nat Black Programming Consortium, 1984; Extraordinary Record of Success, Nat Black Media Coalition, 1985; Presidential Award, Maryland Br, NAACP, 1987; Certificates of Merit, Inside Pub Rels, 1992 & 1993; Proclamation, City New Orleans; Certificate of Recognition, City New Orleans, 1996; Proclamation, City Detroit, 1997; Nat Tobacco Independent Campaign Founder's Award, 1998; Long Term Care Vested Agent's Award, GE, 2001. **Home Addr:** 98 Delford Ave, Silver Spring, MD 20904. **Business Addr:** President, Chief Executive Officer, Morse Enterprises Inc, 510 Wolf Dr 1st Fl, Silver Spring, MD 20904, **Business Phone:** (301)879-7933.

MORSE, DR. OLIVER
Educator. **Personal:** Born May 17, 1922, New York, NY; son of Hugh and Ethel Leftage Morse-Jackson; married Mildred; children: Stacey & Kasey. **Educ:** St Augustine's Col, BS, 1947; Brooklyn Law Sch, LLB, 1950; NY Univ, LLM, 1951; Brooklyn Law Sch, JSD, 1952. **Career:** Educator (retired); Howard Univ, Sch Law, acting dean, 1986, assoc dean, prof; Hunter Col, instr, 1959; S Univ, Sch Law, prof, 1956-59; BrooklynLaw Sch, prof, 1968-69; Morse Enterprises Inc, chmn, bd dirs, 1989-97. **Orgs:** Vice chmn, HEW Reviewing Authority; Beta Lamba Sigma; Phi Alpha Delta; Omega Psi Phi; Am Asn Law Schs; Nat Bar Asn; NY Bar Asn; first chmn sect legal educ, NBA, 1971-72; sire archon, 1986-87; Sigma Pi Phi Fraternity, Md Boule, 1981-; bd trustees, St Augustine's Col, 1991-. **Honors/Awds:** Most Outstanding Law Professor, Howard Law Sch, 1967, 70-72; written serveral publs including over 40 legal decisions of cases heard on appealto HEW Reviewing Authority. **Military Serv:** AUS, sgt, 1943-46. **Home Addr:** 98 Delford Ave, Silver Spring, MD 20904. *

MORSELL, FREDERICK ALBERT
Educator, entertainer. **Personal:** Born Aug 3, 1940, New York, NY; son of John Albert Morsell and Marjorie Ellen Poole Morsell. **Educ:** Dickinson Col, BA, 1962; Wayne State Univ, MA, 1974. **Career:** Educator, actor: Terry Schreiber Studio, New York, actor, dir, teacher, 1970-; Fremarjo Enterprises Inc, pres, currently; Plays; Hill St. Blues; LA law; Scarecrow & Mrs.King; Presenting Mr. Frederick Douglass. **Orgs:** Actor's Equity Assn; Screen Actor's Guild; Am Soc Composers, Auth & Publ;Am Fedn TV & Radio Artists; Dramatists Guild. **Special Achievements:** Performing nationally in a one-man show: "Presenting Mr Frederick Douglass". **Military Serv:** USY, 1st lt, 1962-65. **Home Addr:** PO Box 394, Emigrant, MT 59027, **Home Phone:** (406)333-4970. **Business Addr:** President, Fremarjo Enterprises Inc, PO Box 382, Emigrant, MT 59027, **Business Phone:** (406)333-4970.

MORSTON, GARY SCOTT
Educator. **Personal:** Born Oct 20, 1960, Queens, NY; son of Thelima Morston; children: 2. **Educ:** City Univ NY, AAS, child care, 1983, BS, spec educ, 1985, MS, spec educ, 1990; Bank St Col, educ leadership, 1992. **Career:** United Cerebral Palsy, health aide, 1983-91; NY Bd Educ, Cent Park E II, kindergarten teacher, 1985-. **Orgs:** Educ adv, Scholastic Inc, 1992-; City Univ Track Team; Mustang Track Club; NY Tech Col Theatre Works Performing Arts Group. **Honors/Awds:** Minnie Tib land Award, City Univ NY, 1985; Child Care Service Award, NY Tech Col; Theatre Works Skilled Craft Award; NYCTC Track; Field Team Award. **Special Achievements:** O0ne of the few African-American males teaching at the kindergarten level; Colaborator: "Recruiting New Teachers," nat advert campaign TV commercial, 1991. **Home Addr:** 468 W 141st St, New York, NY 10031, **Home Phone:** (212)281-7815. **Business Addr:** Kindergarten Teacher, Central Park East, 19 E 103rd St, New York, NY 10029, **Business Phone:** (212)860-5992.

MORTEL, DR. RODRIGUE
Physician, educator. **Personal:** Born Dec 3, 1933, St Marc, Haiti; married Cecilia; children: Ronald, Michelle, Denise & Renee. **Educ:** Lycee Stenio Vincent, BS, 1954; Med Sch Port Au Prince Haiti, MD, 1960. **Career:** Educator (retired), Physician; Pvt Practice, physician; Pa State Univ, consul; Lancaster Gen Hosp, prof; Pa State Univ, chmn, dept Ob-gyn, Pa State Geisinger Cancer Ctr, dir, Pa State Univ Cancer Ctr, assoc dean & dir, prof dept obstetrics & gynec, former chmn dept. **Orgs:** AMA; PA Med Soc; James Ewing Soc; Soc Synecologic & Oncologist; Amer Col Ob-Gyn; Amer Coll Surgeons; Amer Radium Soc; NY Acad Sci OB Soc Phila; Missions Off Archdiocese Baltimore. **Honors/Awds:** USPHS Award, 1968; Horatio Alger Award, 1985; Pennsylvania State Univ Faculty Scholar Award for Outstanding Achievement in the Area of Life and Health Sciences, 1986; Health Policy Fellow, Robert Wood Johnson Found, 1988. **Home Addr:** PO Box 532, Hershey, PA 17033.

MORTIMER, DELORES M.
College administrator. **Educ:** Howard Univ, Macalester Col, BA, 1971; Cornell Univ, masters, prof studies, 1973; Univ Mich, Int Educ, doctoral studies, 1993-94. **Career:** Cornell Univ, grad asst, 1971-72; African Bibliog Ctr, res coordr & projsupvr, 1972-75, tech resource person & broadcaster, 1973-76; freelanceconsult, 1973-89; Phelps-Stokes Fund Wash, adminr, 1974-75; SmithsonianInst, Res Inst Immigration & Ethnic Studies, social sci analyst, 1975-79;US Comn Civil Rights, social sci analyst, 1979-81; US Info Agency, sr intacad exchange specialist, 1981-89; Univ Mich Ctr Afro-Am & AfricanStudies, asst dir, 1988-90; Univ Mich Rackham Sch Grad Studies, srfinancial aid officer, 1990-94; US Dept State, Am Embassy Pretoria,foreign serv officer, currently. **Orgs:** Nat Asn Female Exec, 1981-; vpres, Thursday Luncheon Group, 1985-89; Int Studies Asn, 1987; Black Prof Int Affairs, 1988-. **Honors/Awds:** Recipient Grant, Howard Univ, Sponsors Educ Opportunity Scholar, 1967; Solarship Award, Lambda Kappa Mu, Black Prof Womens Sorority, 1969; Scholarship Award, Macalester Col, 1969; Scholarship Award, Sponsors Educ Opportunity, 1970; Fellowship Award, Cornell Univ, 1971; TravelstudyGrant, Cornell Univ, 1972. **Special Achievements:** Elected Member of Cornell University Senate 1971, 1972, elected member Smithsonian Institute Women's Council, 1976-79, published various essays &book reviews in "A Current Bibliography on African Affairs," 1970-74, published "Income & Employment Generation".

MORTON, BENJAMIN
Lawyer. **Personal:** Born Jan 2, 1966, Detroit, MI; son of McClenton and Ella Lee; married Brigette Monique, Apr 13, 1990. **Educ:** Eastern Ariz Col, AA, 1986; Univ Central Fla, BA, 1989; Touro Col, Jacob D Frischberg Law Ctr, JD, 1997. **Career:** US Atty's off, Dayton, OH, spec asst US Atty, 1999-2001; USAF, asst staff judge advocate, 1999-2001, trial atty, Air Force litigation team, 2001-; Legal Info-Graphics LLC, founder, pres & chief exec officer, currently. **Orgs:** Am Bar Asn; Nat Inst Trial Advocacy; Nat Bar Asn; Kappa Alpha Psi. **Special Achievements:** Author: The Federal Rules of Evidence-Simplified, 2003; Criminal Procedure-Simplified, 2004. **Military Serv:** AUS, 1990-92; USAF, capt, 1999-; Nat Defense Ribbon; Primary Leadership Dev Course; AF, Commendation Medal. **Business Addr:** Founder, President, Chief Executive Officer, Legal Info-Graphics LLC, 620 Opperman Dr, Eagan, MN 55123, **Business Phone:** (651)687-7000.

MORTON, REV. CHARLES E
Clergy, educator. **Personal:** Born Jan 31, 1926, Bessemer, AL; married Jean; children: Joan & Carla. **Educ:** Morehouse Col, Atlanta, GA, BA, 1946; Union Theol Sem, New York, NY, 1949; Heidelberg Univ, Heidelberg, Germany, 1955; Garrett Biblical Inst Northwestern Univ, 1956; Columbia Univ, New York, NY, PhD, 1958; Shaw Col, Detroit, LHD, 1970. **Career:** Mich Bd Educ, 1946-54; Morehouse Col, instr philos, 1949-51; Knoxville Col, assoc prof religion & philos, 1953-57; Div Humanities & Philos Dillard Univ, chmn; Albion Col, assoc prof philos; Ebeneze Baptist Church Poughkeepsie, NY, minister; Fayetteville State Univ, acad dean, 1962-63; Oakland Univ, Rochester, prof philos, 1972-93, adj prof philos, 1974-76; Metropolitan Baptist Church, Detroit, pastor, 1963-94, emer pastor, 1994-. **Orgs:** Pres, bd dirs, Metropolitan Baptist Church Non-Profit Housing Corp, 1969-; bd dirs, First Independence Nat Bank, Detroit, 1970-; chairperson emer, Inner-City Bus Improv Forum Detroit, 1972-; bd dirs, Brazeal Dennard Chorale, 1988-; pres, Mich Progressive Baptist State Convention, 1990-92; bd mem, Gleaners Community Food Bank, 1990-; pres, Mich Progressive Baptist Conv Inc; chairperson, bd trustees, Wayne Co Community Col, 1990-93; vice chair, bd dirs, First Independence Nat Bank, 1999-. **Special Achievements:** Author of : The African-Am Church at Work, "Modeling Church Outreach Projects as Strategy of Evangelism in Black Urban community" Hodale Press: St Louis, 1994; The Indeological Character of Moral Judgement, Hodal Press: St Louis, MO, 1996. **Business Addr:** Emeritus Pastor, Metropolitan Baptist Church, 13110 14th St, Detroit, MI 48238, **Business Phone:** (313)869-6676.

MORTON, JAMES A.
Executive. **Personal:** Born Dec 20, 1929, Ontario, VA; married Juanita; children: James A, David L. **Educ:** Am Acad Mortuary Sci, 1950; Lincoln Univ; Howard Univ. **Career:** Morton & Dyett Funeral Homes Inc, pres. **Orgs:** Past pres, Funeral Dir & Morticians Asn MD; past pres, Opportunities Industrial Ctr; bd mem, Nat Funeral Dir Mforticians Asn; chmn, Tri-state Conv Comn; mem Adv, com Bus bd; bd mem, Am Red Cross; committee man BSA; chmn, House Hope Financial Com; trustee, Wayland Bapt Ch; adv bd, Advance Fed Sav; bd mem, YMCA; life mem, NAACP; A Phillip Randolph Prince Hall Masons.

MORTON, JOE
Actor. **Personal:** Born Oct 18, 1947, New York, NY; divorced; children (previous marriage): Hopi; married Nora Chavooshian; children: Ara & Seta. **Educ:** Hofstra Univ, drama. **Career:** Stage: A Month of Sundays, off broad way, 1968; Hair, broad way; Salvation, 1969; Pretty belle, 1971; Charlie Was Here & Now He's Gone, 1971; Two if By Sea, 1972; Tricks, 1973; Raisin, 1973-75; Oh, Brother!, 1981; Honky Tonk Nights, 1986; Art, 1998-99; Films: And Justice for All, 1970; The Brother From Another Planet, 1984; Crossroads, 1985; Zelly & Me, 1988; There's City of Hope, 1991; Terminator 2, 1992; Blues Brothers 2000, 1997; The Astronaut's Wife, 1999; What Lies Beneath, 2000; Bounce, 2000; Ali, 2001; Dragonfly, 2002; Crossing, 2002; Paycheck, 2003; Lenny the Wonder Dog, 2004; Stealth, 2005; The Night Listener, 2006; Badland, 2007; American Gangster, 2007; La Linea, 2008; TV series: "Another World"; "MASH", 1976; Jack Reed: Death& Vengeance, 1996; "Y2K", 1999; "Law & Order", 1992-2005; "Touched by anAngel", 1996-2002; "Smallville", 2001-02; "All My Children", 2002; "Texas Jasper", 2003; "The Jury", 2004; E-Ring, 2005-06; "CSI: NY", 2005;Numb3rs, 2007; "Eureka", 2006-08. **Honors/Awds:** Theatre World Award, Best Actor Musical Raisin, 1974; nomination, Antoinette Perry Award, Best Actor Musical Raisin, 1974; Caixa de Catalunya award for Best Actor, Catalonian Int Film Festival, 1984; NAACP Awards, 1990 & 1993. **Business Addr:** Actor, Judy Schoen & Associates, 606 N Larchmont Suite 309, Los Angeles, CA 90004-1309, **Business Phone:** (213)962-1950.*

MORTON, JOHNNIE JAMES, JR.
Football player. **Personal:** Born Oct 7, 1971, Inglewood, CA. **Educ:** Univ Southern Calif. **Career:** Football player (retired); Detroit Lions, wide receiver, 1994-2001; KansasCity Chiefs, wide receiver, 2002-04; San Francisco 49ers, wide receiver, 2005; free agent, currently. **Orgs:** Screen Actors Guild; Am Fed Radio & TV Asn; DARE; Athletes & Entertainers Kids; Big Bros Am. **Special Achievements:** Appeared in several episodes of "The Young and the Restless," 1996; Appeared in the film "Jerry Maguire," 1996.

MORTON, KAREN VICTORIA (KAREN V MORTON-GROOMS)
Lawyer. **Personal:** Born Jun 16, 1956, Plainfield, NJ; daughter of Edward N and Eva S; married Kenneth B Grooms, Oct 10, 1981; children: Kya Nicole & Keenen Edward. **Educ:** Tufts Univ, Medford, MA, BA, polit sci, 1977; Northeastern Univ Law Sch, Boston, MA, JD, 1980. **Career:** City Boston, asst corp coun, 1980-81; Mass Comn against Discrimination, sr staff atty, 1981-83; US Equal Employment Opportunity Comn, spec asst atty adv, 1984-86; Delaney, Siegel, Zorn & Assocs Inc, sr staff coun & dir training, 1986-87; Dukakis for pres, admin coordr, 1987-88; John Hancock Mutual Life Ins Co, asst coun, 1988-89, from assoc coun to coun, 1990-97, sr coun, 1997, Employment & Labor Relations Law, 2nd vpres & coun, 1998-. **Orgs:** Mass Black Women Atty, 1987-89; bd mem, Ecumenical Soc Action Coun, 1988-91; bd mem, Int Inst Boston, 1991-93; bd mem, Am Corp Coun Asn, Northeast Chap, 1993-97. **Honors/Awds:** Hundred of the Most Promising Black Women in Corporate America, Ebony Mag, 1991. **Home Addr:** 41 Janet Rd, Newton, MA 02459, **Home Phone:** (617)965-0201. **Business Addr:** Vice President, Counsel, John Hancock Life Insurance Company, Employment & Labor Relations Law, John Hancock Pl, PO Box 111, Boston, MA 02117, **Business Phone:** (617)572-9201.

MORTON, LORRAINE H
Government official, mayor. **Personal:** Born in Winston-Salem, NC; married James T (died 1974); children: Elizabeth Morton Brown. **Educ:** Winston-Salem State Univ, BS; Northwestern Univ, MA; Kendall Col, Hon Doctorate, pub serv. **Career:** Foster Sch, various other schs, teacher, 1953-77; Haven Middle Sch, prin, 1977-89; Fifth Ward, alderman, 1991; US Conf Mayors, Chair Humanities Comn; Northwestern Munic Conf, legis comm; Workforce Develop Coun Northern Cook Co; Exec Bd Inventure; City Evanston, mayor, 1993, 1997, 2001, 2005-. **Orgs:** Deacon, Second Baptist Church; adv comn, Kellogg Grad Sch Mgt; Nat Asn Univ Women; life mem, Nat Asn Advan Colored People; N Shore Ill Chap; Alpha Kappa Alpha Sorority; Delta Chi Omega Grad Chap; Evanston Hist Soc; bd mem, Sr Action Serv; bd mem, Foster Reading Ctr; bd mem, Family Coun Serv; bd mem, Leadership Evanston Steering Comn; Evanston Township High Sch Comn Serv Comm; deleg, White House Conf on Libr & Info Serv. **Business Addr:** Mayor, City of Evanston, 2100 Ridge Ave Rm 2500, Evanston, IL 60201, **Business Phone:** (847)866-2979.

MORTON, MARGARET E.
State government official, executive. **Personal:** Born Jun 23, 1924, Pocahontas, VA; married James F Morton; children: James III, Robert Louis, Gerald Woods, Dawn Margaret. **Career:** State government official, executive (retired); Funeral dir; Conn Gen Assembly, 1972-79; Conn State Senate, sen, 1980-92, asst majority leader, senate co-chmn Exec & Legis Nominations Comm, dep pres pro tempore, 1990-92. **Orgs:** Vpres, 1970, exec bd, 1971-76, Nat Asn Advan Colored People; bd dir, Greater Bridgeport YWCA, 1970-72; Greater Bridgeport Chamber Com, 1973-79; bd dirs, Hall Neighborhood, 1973-76; St Marks Day Care Ctr, 1974-76; United Dem Club Bridgeport; State Fed Black Dem Clubs; Fed Dem Women; Org Women Legislators; Greater Bridgeport Chap Coalition 100 Black Women. **Honors/Awds:** AMORE Chapter Achievement Award, 1972; Sojourner Truth Award, Nat Coun Negro Women, 1973; Achievement Award, Barnum Festival, 1973; Achievement Award, Bridgeport Chap Bus & Prof Women, 1973; Margaret E Morton Lane, named in honor. **Home Addr:** 25 Margaret E Morton Lane, Bridgeport, CT 06607. *

MORTON, MARILYN M
Executive, manager. **Personal:** Born Jan 20, 1946, New York, NY; daughter of Wilma Hayes Pegg (deceased) and William Gaitha Pegg (deceased); divorced; children: Louis-Hale, Khaim & Micah. **Educ:** Howard Univ, Wash, DC, BA, 1967; UCLA Ext, Los Angeles, CA, 1974-77; CSU, Dominquez Hills, MBS, negotiation & conflict mgt, 1999. **Career:** Los Angeles 200 Bicentennial Comt, Los Angeles, CA, dir, pub rels, 1979-81; Mixner, Scott & Assocs, Los Angeles, CA, assoc, pub affairs, 1981-83; Times-Mirror Cable TV, Irvine, mgr pub affairs, 1983-84; Parsons Corp, Los Angeles, mgr community affairs, 1984-96, reg mgr, gov't rels, 1987-96; Metro Transp Authority, mgr external rels, Pub Affairs, ADA compliance officer, currently. Los Angeles County C, dir mgt serv, currently. **Orgs:** Co-founder, Women Color Inc, 1985-98; pres, Environment Affairs Comn, appointed by Mayor Tom Bradley, 1987-93; bd, co-chair, Ethnic Coalition, 1989-; bd dirs, Southern Calif Econ Partnership, 1994-. **Honors/Awds:** Environment Affairs CMS, Appointed by Mayor Bradley, 1987; NAACP, Black Women Achievement Award, 1992. **Business Addr:** Manager, Public Affairs/ADA Compliance Office, Metro Transportation Authority, 1 Gateway Plz, Los Angeles, CA 90012, **Business Phone:** (213)922-2218.

MORTON, NORMAN
Computer scientist. **Personal:** Born Jul 27, 1938, Washington, DC; son of Matthew and Bertha; married Robbie Clark Morton, May 26, 1967; children: Norman Jr, Mark. **Educ:** Grantham COL ENG, ASET, 1989; UNIV MAR, BS, mathematics; George Mason UNIV, MA, mathematics. **Career:** Self-employed, prof tutor, 1965-; USY, Finance & Acctg Off, comput programmer, 1966-68; Small BUS ADMIN, comput programmer, 1968-74; Minority BUS Develop ADMIN, comput systs analyst, 1974-75; Econ Develop ADMIN, comput systs analyst, 1975-88; Dept Com, Census Bureau, comput programmer, systs analyst. **Orgs:** MENSA, 98th percentile, IQ, 1992-; INTERTEL, 99th percentile, IQ, 1993; Boy Scouts AME, den leader, 1977-81, 1984-88; Good Shepherd Church, homeless shelter volunteer helper, 1986-87; Intl Soc Philosophical Enquiry, 99.9th percentile IQ, 1994-; Prometheus Soc, 99.9th percentile IQ, 1994-. **Honors/Awds:** DC TCRs COL, BKX SCI Honor Fraternity, 1963, PRES of the Math Club, 1963; Small BUS ADMIN, PRES of the SBA Statistical Club, 1972. **Special Achievements:** Volunteer tutor: Census Bureau, 1992-93; Crossland High School, 1991; inr: COBOL programming class, SBA, 1973; copywrights: "CLOAK," cryptographic software, TX 1675827, 1985; "Large Scale Number Manipulations on the PC," TX 1705169, 1985; "Hide It Find It," TX 4-332-687; author: "Why Does Light Disappear in a Closed Room after the Switch is Turned Off", Capital M, MENSA Publishing, 1993; scored at 99th percentile, IQ test, INTERTEL, 1993; scored at 98th percentile, IQ test, MENSA, 1993; IQ percentile of 99.997 ranks at 1 in 33,000 of the general population. *

MORTON, PATSY JENNINGS
Advertising executive. **Personal:** Born Oct 2, 1951, Fauquier County, VA; daughter of Thomas Scott and Louise Dickson; married Allen James Morton Jr, May 28, 1978; children: Valerie, Allen Christopher & Douglas. **Educ:** Jersey Acad, Jersey City, 1965-69; Oberlin Col, Oberlin, BA, 1969-73; Columbia Univ, New York, 1973-75. **Career:** Earl G Graves Publishing, New York, NY, mkt mgr, 1973-75; The New York Times Co, New York, sales rep, 1975-81, assoc group mgr, 1981-83, group mgr, 1983-87, advert mgr, 1987-, classified advert dir, 1989-92, advert managing dir, 1992-96; Educ Allicances, dir, 1997-. **Orgs:** Bus Comm, Admis Comn, Oberlin Col, 1986; task force, Five Star Newspaper Network, 1988; bd dir, New York State Food Merchants, 1989; Asn Newspaper Classified Advert Mgrs; exec coun, NYU Metro Ctr, 1993-. **Honors/Awds:** Rookie of the Year, Jersey Acad, 1965; Black Achievers Award, YMCA, 1989; Publisher's Award, 1994. **Business Addr:** Education Programs, The New York Times, 229 W 43rd St, New York, NY 10036, **Business Phone:** (212)556-8843.

MORTON, WILLIAM STANLEY
Lawyer. **Personal:** Born Jul 18, 1947, White Plains, NY; son of Clara E and William; married Mary; children: William Stanley Jr & Sydney Elaine. **Educ:** Col Arts & Sci, BS, 1969; Col Law Ohio State Univ, JD, cum laude, 1974. **Career:** Procter & Gamble Co, sr coun, 1974-88, div coun, 1988-, assoc gen coun, currently. **Orgs:** Cincinnati Bar Asn; Am Bar Asn; Ohio Bar Asn, 1974-;

Omega Psi Phi Fraternity; bd dir, ProKids, 1985-87; bd mem, Housing Opportunities Made Equal, 1990-94; vpres & bd mem, Cincinnati Opera, 1991-01; bd dir, Cincinnati Better Bus Bur, 2000-; bd dir, Nat Coun Better Bus Bur Exec Comn, 2000-. **Military Serv:** AUS, sp4, 1970-72. **Home Addr:** 8429 Preakness Lane, Cincinnati, OH 45249-1319. **Business Addr:** Associate General Counsel, Procter & Gamble Company, 7250 Poe Ave, Dayton, OH 45415, **Business Phone:** (937)898-7387.

MORTON-GROOMS, KAREN V. See MORTON, KAREN VICTORIA.

MOSBY, CARLA MANE (CARLA MOSBY WARD)
Immunologist. **Personal:** Born Apr 16, 1974, Heidelberg, Germany; daughter of Charles and Bennell; married Lance Ward, Apr 17, 2004. **Educ:** Univ Md, BS, 1996; MD, 2000. **Career:** Beth Israel Deaconess Med Ctr, resident, 2000-03; Kaiser Permanente, physician, internal med, 2003-04; Allergy & Immunol, Univ Med & Dent, fel, NJ; Univ Community Hosp, consult, currently. **Orgs:** Alpha Kappa Alpha Sorority; Nat Med Asn; Med Alumni Asn, 2000. **Home Addr:** 100 Dudley St 2340, PO Box 99, Jersey City, NJ 07302, **Home Phone:** (201)209-0088. **Business Addr:** Consultant, University Community Hospital Medical Center, 3645 Madaca Lane, Tampa, FL 33618, **Business Phone:** (813)969-0116.

MOSBY, CAROLYN ELIZABETH
Manager. **Personal:** Born Nov 27, 1967, Gary, IN; daughter of John O (deceased) and Carolyn Mosby (deceased). **Educ:** Indiana State Univ, BS, 1990. **Career:** Nicor Gas; Indiana State Dept Admin, Minority Bus Develop Div, 1990-94, mgr, 1994-95; Ind Black Expo, pub rels mgr, 1995-96; Ameritech Advert Serv, market rels mgr, 1996-97; USX Corp, mgr community affairs, 1997-2000; govt affairs rep, 2000-2002; Ind Black Expo, chair bd; USFilter Indianapolis Water LLC, dir commun & community affairs, 2002-2003, vpres commun & community affairs, 2003-2004; Veolia Water. **Orgs:** Mem exec comt, Circle City Classic, 1995-96; mem pub rel comt, NCAA Final Four, 1996-; Nat Asn Female Exec, 1994; pres, Soc Govt Meeting Planners, 1994; mem bd, Salvation Army, 1997-; mem bd, Hoosier Boystown, 1997-; vpres, Gary Police Found, 1997-. *

MOSBY, DR. CAROLYN LEWIS
Educator. **Personal:** Born Mar 6, 1937, Lynchburg, VA; daughter of William and Nannie Jackson; married Alexander, Aug 17, 1963. **Educ:** Va Union Univ, Richmond, Va, BS, math, 1958; Morgan State Univ, Baltimore,MD, MA, math, 1970; The Col William & Mary, Williamsburg, Va, Ed.D, higher educ, 1983. **Career:** East High Sch, Buffalo, NY, teacher, math, 1959-61; Blackwell Jr High Sch,Richmond, Va, teacher, math, 1961-65; John Marshall High Sch, Richmond,Va, teacher/asst prin, 1965-74; Va Union Univ, Richmond, Va, dir learning skills/genl educ, 1974-76; John Tyler Community Col, Chester, Va, dean,math, natural sci allied health, 1978-91; Richmond Public Schs, staff dev & officer, part-time; Va State Univ, adjunct prof, math, currently. **Orgs:** Charter mem, James River Chapter, The Links Inc, 1983-; mem, The Girl Friends Inc, Richmond, Va, 1984-; mem, Delta Sigma Theta Sorority, 1955-;nat pres, Nat Epicureans Inc, Richmond, Va, 1984-86; charter mem,Coalition 100 Black Women, Richmond, Va, 1984-; chair, Comn, pupil reassignment, Richmond Public Schools, 1985; bd mem, State Health Regulatory bd, Commonwealth Va, 1978-82; bd mem, United Giver's Fund,1970; bd dir, Girl Scout Commonwealth Coun Va, Inc 1995; chair, Strategic Planning; bd mem, Va League Planned Parent Hood, 1998; Bd mem, J. Sargeant Reynolds Commun Col, 2005. **Honors/Awds:** Outstanding Teacher of the Year, Richmond Jaycees, 1971. **Business Addr:** Adjunct Professor, Virginia State University, Mathematics Department, PO Box 9027, Petersburg, VA 23806.

MOS DEF (DANTE TERRELL SMITH)
Rap musician, actor. **Personal:** Born Dec 11, 1973, Brooklyn, NY. **Career:** Albums: Black Star, 1998; Black on Both Sides, 1999; Jam on It, 2001; Urban Renewal Program, 2002; The New Danger, 2004; True Magic, 2006; Mos Definite, 2007; The Ecstatic, 2008; Films: Monster's Ball, 2001; Showtime, 2002; Brown Sugar, 2002; The Italian Job, 2003; The Sky Is Green, 2003; From the Outside Looking In, 2003; 16 Blocks, 2006; Talladega Nights: The Ballad of Ricky Bobby, 2006; Prince Among Slaves, 2007; Be Kind Rewind, 2008; Next Day Air, 2008; Stringbean & Marcus, 2008; Toussaint, 2008; theater: Topdog/Underdog, Broadway prod, 2002; TV: "Chappelle's Show", 2003-06; "The Boondocks", 2005. **Honors/Awds:** Best Actor, 2003; Image Awards, 2003, 2005; Best Supporting Actor, 2004; Emmy Award, 2004; Best Actor TV Movie/Mini-Series, 2005; Grammy Award, 2005-08; Best Actor Independent, 2005; Best Supporting Actor, 2006. **Special Achievements:** 2004 Emmy Nomination for Outstanding Lead Actor In A Miniseries Or A Movie; 2005 Grammy nomination for Best Alternative/Urban Performance. **Business Addr:** Recording Artist, Rawkus Records, 676 Broadway Fl 4, New York, NY 10012, **Business Phone:** (212)358-7890.

MOSEBY, LLOYD ANTHONY
Baseball player, athletic coach. **Personal:** Born Nov 5, 1959, Portland, AR. **Career:** Baseball player (retired), coach; Toronto Blue Jays, outfielder, 1978-89; Pioneer League, outfielder, 1978, Fla State League, outfielder, 1979, Intl League, outfielder, 1980; Detroit Tigers, outfielder, 1990-91; Tokyo Giants, outfielder; Blue Jays, first base coach, 1998-99; Duane Ward Baseball Clinic, fielding instr, currently. **Honors/Awds:** Pioneer League All-Star, 1978; Fla State League All-Star Team, 1979; Tops Class A All-Star Team, 1979; co-winner, Labatt's Blue MVP, 1983; Am League All-Star Team, The Sporting News & UPI, 1983; Silver Slugging Team, 1983; Player of the Week, Am League,1983; Labatt's Blue Player of Month, 1983, 1986; Am League Player of Month, 1983; Am League All-Star Team, 1986.

MOSEKA, AMINATA (ABBEY LINCOLN)
Actor, artistic director, educator. **Personal:** Born Aug 6, 1930, Chicago, IL; married Max Roach, Jan 1, 1962 (divorced 1970). **Career:** Calif State Univ, African Am Theatre & Pan African Stud, asst prof,1974-; Films: The Girl Can't Help It, 1956; Nothing But a Man, 1964; For the Love of Ivy, 1968; A Short Walk to Daylight, 1972; Mo' Better Blues, 1990; TV shows: "Flip Wilson"; "Marcus Welby" "M.D."; "Mission Impossible"; "All in the Family"; Play: A Pig in a Poke, dir & producer; Albums: "Affair: A Story of a Girl in Love", 1956; "That's Him!", "Riverside",1957; "It's Magic", 1958; "Abbey Is Blue", 1959; "We Insist!: Freedom Now Suite", 1960; "Straight Ahead", 1961; "It's Time", 1962; "People in Me", 1979; "Golden Lady", 1981; "Talking to the Sun", 1984; 'Abbey Sings Billie", 1987; "The World Is Falling Down", 1990; "You Gotta Pay the Band", 1991; "Devil's Got Your Tongue", 1992; When There is Love, 1992; A Turtle's Dream, 1994; Painted Lady,1994; 'Who Used to Dance", "Wholly Earth", 1999: "Over the Years", 2000; "It's Me" 2003; "Abbey Sings Abbey", 2007. **Orgs:** Chairwoman, producers comt Tribute Black Woman, 1977. **Honors/Awds:** Best Actress, 1st World Festival Negro Arts, 1966; Best Actress, Fedn Italian Film Makers, 1965; Most Promising Screen Person, All Am Press Assn,1969; Natl Endowment For the Arts', NEA Jazz Masters Award, 2003. **Special Achievements:** Inductee, Black Filmmakers Hall of Fame, 1975; Author of A Pig in a Poke, 1975 & In a Circle, Everything Is Up.

MOSELEY, FRANCES KENNEY
Association executive. **Personal:** Born Mar 20, 1949, Cleveland, OH; married Monroe Avant Moseley; children: Gavin. **Educ:** Univ Denver, BA Psychol, 1971. **Career:** State St Bank & Trust, security analyst, 1974-77; Bank of Boston, trust officer, 1977-79; WGBH-TV, dir of promo, 1979-80; Boston Edison Co, sr pub info rep; John Hancock Financial Services Inc, sr mgr retail mkt and consumer affairs, until, 1993; Boys & Girls Clubs Boston, pres & ceo, 1992; Boston Partners, pres & ceo; One Family Inc, Chief Develop Officer, currently. **Orgs:** former officer, Boston Branch NAACP, 1976; Am Assoc Blacks in Energy, 1980-88; chmn, bd Big Sister Assoc Greater Boston, 1984; pres, bd Big Sisters Asn Greater Boston, 1982; bd mem, since, 1979; trustee, The Huntington Theatre; New England Aquarium; dir, PNC Bank, New England, 1996; dir, Tufts ASOed HTH Plans Inc, 1996; Beth Israel Deaconess Medical Ctr; Wang Ctr Performing Arts; The Children's Hosp Bd Overseers; founding mem, Boston Chapter of the Coalition 100 Black Women; chair Bell Atlanta Consumer Advisory Panel; bd mem, Massachusetts Sports Partnership. **Honors/Awds:** The Urban League, 75th Anniversary President's Award; The College Club 1993 Career Award, Soc Serv; Honorary Doctorate of Public Service, Bridgewater State Col, 1998; Named 1 of Boston's Most Powerful 100 People by Boston Magazine, 1997. **Business Addr:** Chief Development Officer, One Family Inc, 186 South St 4th Fl, Boston, MA 02111, **Business Phone:** (617)423-0504.*

MOSELEY BRAUN, CAROL ELIZABETH
Ambassador, president (organization). **Personal:** Born Aug 16, 1947, Chicago, IL; daughter of Joseph Moseley and Edna; married Michael (divorced); children: Matthew. **Educ:** Univ IL, Chicago, BA, 1969, JD, 1972. **Career:** Mayer Brown & Platt, law clerk 1970; Rose Hardies O'Keefe Babcock & Parsons, law clerk, 1971; Davis Miner & Barnhill, assoc 1972; US Dept of Justice, asst atty, 1973-77; Jones, Ware & Grenard, coun; 26th Legislative Dist, Chicago, state rep, 1978-88; Cook County, recorder deeds/ registrar of titles, 1988-92; US Senate, sen State Ill, 1993-99; US Dept of Education, consult, 1998-99; US ambassador to New Zealand, 1999-2001; Morris Brown Col, vis distung prof & scholar residence, 2001-02; DePaul Univ, Col Com, bus law prof, 2002-03; Moseley Braun LLC, owner; Ambassador Organics, founder & pres, 2005-. **Orgs:** Bar US Ct Appeals 7th Circuit, Bar US Dist Ct Northern Dist IL, Bar State Ill, Ill State Bar Asn, Nat Order Women Legislators, Dem Policy Comns Dem Nat Conv, Cook County Bar Asn, Chicago Coun Lawyers, Am Judicature Soc, Nat Conf State Leg; comn Cts & Justice; del Dem Nat Conv, 1984; League Black Women, Jane Addams Ctr Social Policy & Res, Alpha Gamma Phi, Chicago Forum, DuSable Museum, Chicago Public Schs Alumni Asn, IL women's Political Caucus, Coaltion to Save South Shore Country Club Pk, Urban League, NAACP, South Shore Comn. **Honors/Awds:** Awardee Atty Gen's Commendation; Woman Year Award, Lu Palmer Found, 1980; Best Legislator Award, Independent Voters Ill, 1980; Recog & Appreciation Cert IL Sheriffs Asn, 1981; Award Distinction Networking Together, 1981; Outstanding Woman Struggle Award, Chicago Alliance Against Racist & Political Repression, 1981; Dist Serv Award, Concerned Black Execs Social Serv Org, 1983; Outstanding Legislator Award, IL Public Action Coun, 1983; Leadership Award Asn Human Serv Providers, 1984; Legislative Leadership Award, Chicago Public Schs & Coaltion to Save Our Schs 1985; Beautiful People Award, Urban League 1985; Legislator of the Year Award, IL Nurses Asn, 1986; Cert of Appreciation, Chicago Bar Asn, 1986; Serv Award, IL Pro-Choice Alliance, 1986; Best Legislator Award, Independent Voters of IL Indepent Precinct Org, 1986; Friends Educ Award, IL State Bd Educ 1988; "Day Breaker" Award, Mayor Harold Washington, 1988; Chicago Black United Communities "Secrets" Award, St Mark's United Methodist Ch, 1989; Karunya Educational Award for Legislative Excellence; Certificate of Appreciation, PTA; Woman of the Year, Minority Economic Resources Corp, 1997; Martin Luther King Jr Excellence Award, InterdenomiNat Ministerial Alliance of Chicago, 1997; Magnificant 7 Award, Bus & Professional Women, 1996; and numerous honorary degrees and other awards. **Special Achievements:** First female African American US senator, 1992; presidential candidate, 2003-04. **Business Phone:** (773)288-3700.

MOSELEY-DAVIS, BARBARA M.
Executive. **Personal:** Born Feb 12, 1938, New York, NY; divorced. **Educ:** BS, math, 1960. **Career:** M-Cubed Info Systs Inc, strategic planning mgr; Delta Res & Educ Found, Sci & Everyday Experiences, nat proj mgr, currently. **Orgs:** Regional corresponding secy, Eastern Region, Delta Sigma Theta Sorority; First Combined Community Fed Credit Union; Morgan State Alumni Asn. **Honors/Awds:** Eliza P. Shippen Award, Delta Sigma Theta Sorority, 1993. **Business Phone:** (202)347-1404.*

MOSELY, KEN. See MOSELY, DR. KENNETH.

MOSELY, DR. KENNETH (KEN MOSELY)
Educator. **Educ:** Morgan State Univ, BS; Kans State Univ, MS; Ind Univ, PED. **Career:** Educator (retired); SC State Univ, Dept Health & Phys Educ, prof, chmn. **Honors/Awds:** Special Achievement Award, Morgan State Univ, 2007. *

MOSES, CHARLES T
Government official, executive director. **Personal:** Born Oct 2, 1952, New York, NY; son of Grace and Charles T; divorced. **Educ:** Howard Univ, BS, 1975; Baruch Col, MBA, 1985. **Career:** Newsday, reporter, asst bus ed, strategic planning dir, 1978-88; Bristol Myers-Squibb, commun exec, 1988-89; City New York, Comptroller's Off, dep press secy, 1991; State New York, Governor's Off, exec dir, 1991-95. **Orgs:** Nat Asn Black Journalists, 1976-88. **Honors/Awds:** Frank Tripp Award, Gannett Co, 1978; Outstanding News Feature Award, Nat Asn Black Journalists; Media Award, Odyssey Inst, 1980 & 1988; fel strategic planning, Am Newspaper Publ Asn, 1987; fel, Leadership New York, 1991.

MOSES, EDWIN
Athlete. **Personal:** Born Aug 31, 1955, Dayton, OH; son of Irving S and Gladys H; married Myrella Bordt (divorced 1992); children: Edwin Julian. **Educ:** Morehouse Col, BS, physics, 1978; Pepperdine Univ, MBA, 1994. **Career:** Olympic hurdler; The Platinum Group, partner; Robinson-Humphrey Co, financial consult; Laureus World Sports Academy, chmn, 2000-. **Orgs:** USOC, Substance Abuse Comt, chmn, exec comn, 1994-96, bd dirs, 1986-96; Intl Olympic Comt, Athletes Comn, 1982-96, Med Comn, 1994-96; pres, Intl Amateur Athletic Asn, 1982-; Comn White Fellowships, 1992-; vice chair, US Olympic Found, 1996-; 100 Black Men Atlanta, 1997-. **Honors/Awds:** Worlds Top Ranked Intermediate Hurdler; two times Olympic Gold Medalist, 1976, 1984, Bronze Medalist, 1988; Sportsman of the Year, US Olympic Comn; Sullivan Award, 1983; Sports Illustrated, Athlete of the Year, 1984; Track & Field, Hall of Fame, 1994; Georgia Sports Hall of Fame, 1998; ScD, Univ Mass, 2009. **Special Achievements:** First US athlete to be voted as delegate to Intl Amateur Athletic Federation; 122 consecutive victories in 400 hurdles, 1977-87; launched The Magic Bus Sports Program for street children in Bombay, India, 2003. **Business Addr:** Chairman, Laureus World Sports Academy, 460 Fulham Rd, London SW6 1BZ, United Kingdom, **Business Phone:** (442)07514-2797.

MOSES, HAROLD WEBSTER
Educator. **Personal:** Born Jun 6, 1949, Little Rock, AR; son of Tracie and Bishop; children: Harold & Corye. **Educ:** Univof Ark, Little Rock, AR, BA, 1973, MPA, 1984; Southern Ill Univ, Carbondale, IL, PhD, 1995. **Career:** Ark Int Lang Prog, Russellville, AR, Fr tutor, 1985-88; Ill Legis Res Unit, Springfield, IL, res asst, 1985-86; Southern Ill Univ, Carbondale, IL, grad admin asst to Ill Minority Fels, 1990, instr, 1991-92, Bethune Cookman Col, Daytona Beach FL, asst prof, Politl Sci; Cent Fla Legal Services, Daytona Beach, Fla, accounting asst, 1997-98; Little Rock Pub Sch Dist, Little Rock, Ark, teacher, 1998-. **Orgs:** Chair, Awards Comt, Southern Ill Univ Polit Sci Dept, 1985-91; Secy, Grad Assistantship Prog, Nat Conf Black Polit Scientists, 1989-91; African Studies Asn, 1991; Grad Politl Sci Comt; Nat Conf Black Polit Scientists. **Honors/Awds:** Gradate Deans Fellowship, Southern Ill Univ, 1986, 1988; Sammy Younge Award for Best Paper Nat Conf Black Polit Scientists, 1986; Rodney Higgins Award for Best Paper, Nat Conf Black Polit Scientists, 1987; Illinois Consortium of Educational Opportunity Award, Ill Bd Higher Educ, 1988-92;

Merit Scholarship for the Study of Chinese Beloit College, 1991. **Home Addr:** PO Box 17702, North Little Rock, AR 72117.

MOSES, DR. HENRY A.
Educator, school administrator. **Personal:** Born Sep 8, 1939, Gaston County, NC; son of Roy and Mary. **Educ:** Livingstone Col, BS, 1959; Purdue Univ, MS biochem, 1962, PhD, biochem, 1964. **Career:** TN State Univ, vis lectr biochem, 1966-70; GW Hubbard Hosp, Meharry Med Col, asst prof, Biochem, 1964-69, consult clin chem, 1968-74, assoc prof biochem nutrition, 1969-81, provost internal affairs, 1976-83, dir continuing educ 1981-, prof biochem, 1981-, asst vpres acad support, 1983-95, dir continuing educ area health educ ctrs, 1984-99, Mehary Med Col, prof emer biochem; Col Rels, & Lifelong Learning, assoc vpres, 1995-99, consult, Alumni Rels, currently; Fisk Univ, distinguished prof,chem & biol, currently; Mehary Med Col, interim exec dir, currently. **Orgs:** AAAS; ACS; Alpha Chi Sigma Frat for Chemists; Am Asn Univ Profs; Beta Kappa Chi Scientific Honor Soc, 1972-; chmn, Honors & Awards Comm; The Sch Med, 1976-99; Alpha Omega Alpha Honor Med Soc, 1980; adv, The Meharrian Stud Yr book, 1980-99; chmn, Acad Policy Comm, Th e Sch Med, 1985-97; McKendree United Methodist Ch. **Honors/Awds:** Service Award Meharry Med Col, 1971; Harold D West Award, Meharry Med Col, 1972; Kaiser-Permanente Award for Excellence in Teaching Meharry Medical Col, 1976; Alpha Omega Alpha Honor Med Soc, 1981; Meritorious Service Award Los Angeles Chap Meharry Medical Col Nat Alumni Asn, 1985, Los Angeles, Memphis and Orlando Chapters, 1998. Beta Kappa Chi Scientific Honor Soc Special Recognition Award, 1986; Presidential Citation as Outstanding Alumnus NAFEO, 1986; also 29 publications; Distinguished by Alumni Purdue Univ, 1995; Building dedicated, 1996; Henry A Moses Chair in Molecular Genetics, Mehary Medical Col, est, 2000; Presidential Distinguished Serv Medal, Meharry Med Col. **Business Addr:** Professor Emeritus, Off Alumni Affairs, Meharry Med Coll, 1005 DB Todd Jr Blvd, Nashville, TN 37208.

MOSES, MACDONALD
School administrator, bishop. **Personal:** Born May 20, 1936, Bailey, NC; married Marie Biggs; children: Alvin, Jacqueline, Reginald, Kenneth. **Educ:** Westchester Community Col; Alexander Hamilton Brooklyn Tech; IBM Educ Ctr; Am Mgt Asn. **Career:** Church of Christ, Disciples of Christ, gen bishop. **Orgs:** Mgr, MIS Botway Media Assocs; pastor, Mt Hebron Church of Christ. **Honors/Awds:** Honorary Doctor of Divinity, Goldsboro Disciple Inst, 1978. **Home Addr:** 14 Granada Cres, White Plains, NY 10603-1230.

MOSES, MILTON E.
Chief executive officer. **Personal:** Born Aug 5, 1939, Chicago, IL; son of Jeffery and Mary; married Shirley C; children: Timothy E, Melody L & Milton E Jr. **Educ:** DePaul Univ, attended 1965. **Career:** Supreme Life Ins Co of Am, agt, 1963; The Robbins Ins Agency Inc, underwriter, 1965; Prof Independent Ins Agts of Ill, regional dir, 2002; Community Ins Agency Inc, pres & ceo, currently. **Orgs:** Pres, Men Provident Hosp, 1971; mem, Ind Ins Agts Am, 1980; Chicago Bd Underwriters, 1980; Ins Inst of Am, 1980; chmn bd, Human Resources Develop Inst, 1980; pres, We Can Found Inc, 1980. **Honors/Awds:** Outstanding Support Award, South town YMCA, 1974; Dedicated Serv Award,Third Ward Dem Party, 1976; Black Businessman of the Year, Black book Bus &Ref Guide, 1980. **Business Addr:** President, Chief Executive Officer, Community Insurance Center Inc, 526 E 87th St, Chicago, IL 60619, **Business Phone:** (773)651-6200.

MOSES, YOLANDA T.
School administrator, president (organization). **Educ:** Perris High Sch, Valley Col, attended 1966; Calif State Univ, San Bernardino, attended; Univ Calif, Riverside, PhD, anthropol, 1976. **Career:** Calif State Polytech Univ, fac, 1985-88, Ethnic & Women's Studies Dept, chair, Sch Liberal Arts, dean; Calif State Univ, Dominguez Hills, anthropol prof & vpres acad affairs, 1988-93; City Univ NY, City Col, pres, 1993-99; Am Coun Educ, sr scholar; City Col NY, pres, 1993-99; Anthropologist; Ctr Adv Studies, Behavioral Sci, Andrew Mellon postdoctoral fel. **Orgs:** Women's Forum; Ford Found Bd Trustees, 1996-; bd chair, Am Cols & Univs, 2000-; Free Angela Davis Comt, 1970; pres, Am Anthropol Asn. **Honors/Awds:** Alumni Hall of Fame, San Bernardino Valley Col, 1994; Distinguished Alumni, Univ Calif, Riverside, 1997. *

MOSLEY, BENITA FITZGERALD
Athletic director, president (organization). **Personal:** Born Jul 6, 1961, Warrenton, VA; daughter of Roger and Fannie; married Ron, May 11, 1996; children: Isaiah & Maya. **Educ:** Univ Tenn, UT, BS, industrial ngineering, 1984. **Career:** PRO, athlete, 1980-88; med spokesperson, 1988; Tracor inc & MHP Fu-Techinc, indust systs & software engr, 1991-95; Special Olympics Int Inc, regdir, 1991-92, sports mktg mgr, 1992-93; Atlanta Comt Olympic Games, prog dir mkt div, 1993-95; Atlanta Centennial Olympic Properties, prog dir,1993-95; ARCO Olympic training ctr, San Diego, dir, 1995-97, dir pub rels prog, 2000-01; US Olympic Comt, Olympic Training Centers, dir, 1997-2000; Women Cable Telecommunications, pres & chief exec officer, 2001-09; USA Track & Field, chief sport performance, currently. **Orgs:** Pres & bd trustees, Womens Sports Fed; US Olympics comt, 1995; chair,diversity comt, 2000-01; athletes advisory coun; bd mem, USA track &field; Delta Sigma Theta Sorority Inc; women sports & events; trustee &past pres, Bd Trustees, Womens Sports found, currently. **Honors/Awds:** Olympic Gold Medalist, 100 Meter Hurdles, 1984; Distinguished Serv Award, US Sports Acad, 1996; Hall of Fame, Univ Tenn, 1994; Hall of Fame, VIR Sports, 1998; Hall of Fame, Penn Relays; Hall of Fame, UT Lady Vols, 2001; Cable TV Executive of the Year, Television Week Mag; Hall of Fame, Va Sports; Hall of Fame, Va High Sch. **Special Achievements:** Named "Hurdler of the Decade" for the 1980s by Track and Field News, she was honored with a street named Benita Fitzgerald Drive in her hometown of Dale City, VA in 1987. **Business Addr:** President, Chief Executive Officer, Women in Cable Telecommunications, 14555 Avion Pkwy Suite 250, Chantilly, VA 20151, **Business Phone:** (703)817-9801.

MOSLEY, CAROLYN W
Educator. **Personal:** Born Nov 2, 1952, New Orleans, LA; daughter of Johnny Washington Sr and Lillie Lee Washington; married Shantell Nicole (divorced 1984); children: Shantell Nicole. **Educ:** La State Univ, Med Ctr, Sch Nursing, BSN, 1974, MN, 1980; Texas Woman's Univ, Houston, PhD, 1994. **Career:** Charity Hosp New Orleans, staff nurse, 1974-75 & 1987-91; Vet ADM New Orleans, head nurse, 1975-81; La State Univ, Med Ctr, Sch Nursing, bd regents fel, 1987-90, asst prof, 1981-87 & 1989, assoc prof, currently, prof, assoc dean acad admin, currently; Tex Woman's Univ, Mary Gibbs fel, 1988. **Orgs:** Chi Eta Phi Sorority Blacks, 1976-; pres-elect, Sigma Theta Tau, Epsilon NU, 1982-; Am Nurses Asn, 1990-; New Orleans Dist Nurses Asn, 1990-; Nat League Nurses, 1990-; pres-elect, La League Nurses, 1990-; Asn Black Nursing Fac, 1990-; vol, Cope-line, 1992-; ANA Coun Nursing, Res Exec Comt; Am Acad Nursing. **Honors/Awds:** Doctoral fel, Am Nurses Asn, 1988-91; Soror of the Year, Chi Eta Phi Sorority Inc, 1992; Vigor Volunteer of the Year, City New Orleans; Lederle Award; Rosalyn Carter Caregiving Award; Vol Distinction. **Special Achievements:** A Call to Action: Health Care Reforms as a Priority, 1992; plenary session speaker, NAT CTR for Advancement Blacks in Health Professions; speaker at nat confs by Contemporary Forum. **Home Phone:** (504)822-5886. **Business Addr:** Professor, Associate Dean of Administration, Louisiana State University Health Sciences Center, School of Nursing, 1900 Gravier St, New Orleans, LA 70112, **Business Phone:** (504)568-4200.

MOSLEY, CHRIS. See MOSLEY, CHRISTOPHER D.

MOSLEY, CHRISTOPHER D (CHRIS MOSLEY)
Financial manager, association executive. **Personal:** Born Jul 12, 1960, Atlanta, GA; son of Lamar T and Annie B. **Educ:** W Geo Col, BS, 1983. **Career:** NationsBanc Securities Inc, investment specialist, 1986, margin specialist, 1986-89, retirement plan dir, 1989-. **Orgs:** Toastmasters Int; bd mem & treas, Rehab Exposure; vol, Income Tax Assistance; pres, Mays Manor Neighborhood Asn, currently. **Honors/Awds:** Outstanding Young Men of America, US Jaycees, 1983; External Client Services Award, NationsBanc Securities Inc, 1992. **Special Achievements:** Americas Best & Brightest Professional Men, Dollars & Sense Mag, 1992. **Home Addr:** 3796 Benjamin Ct, Atlanta, GA 30331. **Business Addr:** President, mays Manor Neighborhood Association, 3796 Benjamin Court SW, Atlanta, GA 30331, **Business Phone:** (404)505-8687.

MOSLEY, EDNA WILSON
Administrator, government official, president (organization). **Personal:** Born May 31, 1925, Helena, AR; married John W; children: Edna L. **Educ:** Univ Northern Colo, 1943; Adams State Col, 1969; Met State Col, BA, 1969; Univ Colo, 1976. **Career:** Univ Denver, affirmative action dir, 1978-; Colo State & Dept Personnel, asst state affirmative action coordr, 1974-78; Colo Civil Rights Comn, community rels coordr, 1970-74; Co Civil Rights Comn, civil rights specialist, 1969-70; Women's Bank NA Denver, founder, 1975; Aurora Colo, councilwoman; Colo Bus Bank, pres & chairwoman, currently. **Orgs:** Women's Forum Colo Inc Best Sustaining Pub Affairs Prog Colo Broadcasting Asn, 1972; cochmn, Denver/Nairobi Sister-/City Comm, 1976-80; bd dir, Women's Bank NA Denver, 1978-80; comnr, Nat Social Action Comn Delta Sigma Theta Sorority, 1979-81; dir, Higher Educ Affirmative Action; Nat Asn Affirmative Action Officers; Colo Black Women Polit Action; Delta Sigma Theta Denver Alumnae Chap. **Honors/Awds:** Lola M Parker Achievement Award, Iota Phi Lambda Far Western Region, 1977; Headliner Award Women, Commun Inc, 1978; Appreciation Award, Nat Asn Black Accts, 1978; Distinguished Service Award, Int Stud Orgn Univ Denver, 1979; honorary doctoral degrees, CSU, 2004. **Special Achievements:** The first person of color to be elected to the Aurora City Council. **Business Addr:** President, Chairwoman, Colorado Business Bank, 821 17th St, Denver, CO 80202, **Business Phone:** (303)293-2265.

MOSLEY, EDWARD R.
Physician. **Personal:** Born in Chicago, IL; married Marian Kummerfeld; children: Cary, Laura, Kia, Rennie, Christopher, Caroline. **Educ:** Meharry Med Col, MD, 1948. **Career:** Pvt Prac, Physician, 1956-; Psychiatric Serv Va Hosp, Tuskegee, AL, med coordr, 1954-56; Va Hosp, Tuskegee, AL, residency, 1949-52; Harlem Hosp, internship, 1948-49; Reg Med Consult State Dept Rehab. **Orgs:** Pres & bd dir, Westview Convalescent Hosp; John Hale Med Ctr; Nat Med Asn; Am Med Asn; Golden State Med Asn; Calif Med Asn; Daniel Hale William Med Forum; Fresno Co Med Soc; Am Soc Internal Med; Fresno Co Soc Internal Med; Alpha Phi Alpha; F & AM Prince Hall Shrine; 20th Century Elks; chmn, Citizen's Resource Com State Ctr Community Col, 1969; bd trustees, State Ctr Community Col, 1971-, pres, 1975-; bd dir, Sequoia Boy Scout Coun; Co Parks & Recreation Comn, 1958-68; Mayor's Biracial Comn on Human Rel, 1966-68; bd dir, Easter Seal Soc TB Asn; bd chmn, Sequoia Community Health Ctrs, Fresno, CA, currently. **Honors/Awds:** AUS, med corp capt, 1952-54.

MOSLEY, ELWOOD A
Government official. **Personal:** Born May 12, 1943, Philadelphia, PA; son of John and Ethel Glenn; married Eileen Carson, Jan 14, 1967; children: Danielle Mosley. **Educ:** St Joseph's Univ, Philadelphia Pa, Bus Admin, 1972; Harvard Univ, Cambridge Mass, MA, 1989. **Career:** Chase Manhattan Bank, New York NY, asst treas, 1972-76; CIGNA Ins, Philadelphia Pa, vpres, 1976-82; USF&G Ins, Baltimore Md, vpres, 1982-85; Huggins Financial, Philadelphia Pa, vpres, 1985-87; US Postal Serv, Wash DC, asst postmaster gen, training & devel, 1987, S Jersey Dist, dist mgr; MBNA America Bank, exec vpres, currently. **Honors/Awds:** National Diversity Award. **Military Serv:** USMC, corporal, 1964-70. **Home Addr:** 1684 Kingsbridge Court, Annapolis, MD 21401-6408, **Home Phone:** (410)849-2261. **Business Addr:** Executive Vice President, MBNA America Bank NA, 100 King St, Wilmington, DE 19801.

MOSLEY, GERALDINE B.
Educator, nurse. **Personal:** Born Oct 22, 1920, Petersburg, VA; married Kelly (died 1996). **Educ:** Hunter Col, NY, BS, 1945; Col Columbia Univ NY, MA, psychol, 1950; NY Univ, PhD, 1970. **Career:** Educator, nurse (retired); Dept Health NY, pub health nurse, 1947-52; instr/supvr, 1952-56; Queens Col NY, lectr, nursing, 1956-58, 1961-68; Columbia Univ, asst prof dept nursing, 1968-71; Mayor's Org Task For Comprehensive Health Planning, health planner, 1970-71; Dept Psychiat, Harlem Hospital Ctr, asso dir nursing, 1971-73; Div Nursing Dominican Col Blauvelt, dir, 1973-91. **Orgs:** Asn Univ Profs, 1973-80; Bd dirs, Nat League for Nursing, 1974-76; secy, NY State Nurses Asn; Am Nurses Asn; vpres, Metro Regional Task Force Nursing, 1975-. **Honors/Awds:** Outstanding Professional Leadership Award, Dept Psychiat, Harlem Hosp Ctr, 1973; Distinguished Service, Rockland County, 1976; Professional Award, Westchester County Club; Nat Asn Negro Bus & Prof Women's Clubs Inc, 1977; The Estelle Osborn Certificate of Achievement, Div Nursing, NY Univ, 1996. **Home Addr:** 635 S 8th Ave, Mount Vernon, NY 10550. *

MOSLEY, JAMES EARL
Law enforcement officer. **Personal:** Born Jan 19, 1939, Hackensack, NJ; son of Charles and Hattie Mae; married JoAnn, Jan 9, 1960; children: Paulette, Beverly Allen & James Jr. **Educ:** Bergen Community Col, AAS, 1975. **Career:** Law Enforcement Officer (retired); City Englewood, chief police, 2003. **Orgs:** MT Zion Baptist Church, 1953-; dean instrn, Shiloh Masonic Lodge No 53-F&AM, 1983-; Nat Orgn Black Law Enforcement Execs, 1990-; NJ State Police Chief's Asn, 1994-; Holy Royal Arch Masons, Joshua Chap No 15, 1994-. **Honors/Awds:** Honorable Mention Award, City Englewood, 1968; Dedicated Service Award, 1983, Outstanding Service Award, 1985; Exec Certificate Commendation, Bergen County, 1993; 30 Year Service Award, 1994; Pastor's Award, Comunity Serv, First Baptist Church Englewood. **Special Achievements:** Presented a resolution from the New Jersey State Gen, 1993. **Military Serv:** USM, sgt, 1958-61; Good Conduct Medal, 1961.

MOSLEY, MARIE OLEATHA
Educator, nurse. **Personal:** Born Jul 14, 1941, Miami, FL; daughter of Jimmie Pitts and Bertha Lee Pitts; divorced; children: DaShawn Lynette Young. **Educ:** Hunter Col Bellevue Sch Nursing, BSN, 1976, MSN, cum laude, 1983; Columbia Univ Teachers Col, EdM, 1986, EdD, 1992. **Career:** Educator (retired), Nurse; Jackson Memorial Hosp; Boone Municipal Hosp Ctr, head nurse, 1971-80; staff relief, Staff Builders, 1980-82; Hunter Col Bellevue Sch Nursing, asst prof, 1983, assoc prof; LaGuardia Community Col, asst prof, 1985-86; AUSR, Army Nurse Corp, asst medical officer, 1989-. **Orgs:** Rep, Nurses Polit Action; chairperson, nominating comt, Sigma Theta Tau, Inc, Alpha Phi Chap, 1984-; prog comnr, Asn Black Nursing Fac Higher Educ, 1987-; New York State Nurses Asn, educ comt, 1988-; Civil Affairs Officers Asn, New York/ NJS Chap, 1989-; Nat Black Nurses Asn, 1991-; Am Asn Hist Nursing, 1992-; educ comt, NYSNA Dist 13. **Honors/Awds:** Certificate of Service, 1970, Merit Award, 1970, Commencement Award, 1971, Student Governance Service Award, 1971, Bronx Community Col; Professional Nurse Traineeship, Hunter Col, Bellevue Sch Nursing, 1982-83; Professional Nurse Traineeship, 1985-91, NY Scholarship, 1990-91, Columbia Univ Teachers Col; Nurse Educ Fund, M Elizabeth Carnegie Scholarship, Nurses Scholarship & Fellowship Award, Mead Johnson & Corp Scholarship, 1989.Dissertation Award, Asn Black

Nursing Faculty in Higher Educ, 1990. **Special Achievements:** A History of Black Leaders in Nursing: The Influences of Four Black Community Health Nurses on the Establishment Growth & Practice of Public Health Nursing in NewYork City 1900-30, National Association Colored Graduate Nurses, Dr Mary Elizabeth Osborne, Estelle Riddl Carnegie, 1992. **Military Serv:** USY Reserve, Nurse Corp, major, 1978-. **Home Phone:** (212)926-1647.

MOSLEY, MAURICE B.
Lawyer. **Personal:** Born Jun 4, 1946, Waterbury, CT. **Educ:** SC St Col, BS, 1968; Cent Conn St Col, MS, 1972; Univ Conn, Sch Law, JD, 1975. **Career:** Teacher, 1968-72; Urban Leag, legis consult, 1974; Conn St Treas, exec asst, 1975-77; Conn, legislature, 1976-; State Conn, Rep, Atty; Mosley & Sinclair LLP, pvt pract, currently. **Orgs:** Adv bd, Colonial Bank & Trust Co; chmn, Legis Black Caucus; bd trustees, Waterbury Hosp; exec bd, Nat Asn Advan Colored People, 1974-77. **Honors/Awds:** Business Award, SC St Dist, 1968. **Business Addr:** Attorney, Mosley & Sinclair LLP, 32 Linden St, Waterbury, CT 06702-1301.

MOSLEY, ROOSEVELT CHARLES
Insurance executive. **Personal:** Born Jul 29, 1972, Saginaw, MI; son of Roosevelt and Evelyn; married Yashica Mosley, Aug 13, 1994; children: Tanisha & Bria. **Educ:** Univ Mich, BS, actuarial sci, 1993, BS, statistics, 1993. **Career:** State Farm, sr asst actuary, 1994-98; Vesta Insurance, actuarial mgr, 1998-99; Miller, Herbers, Lehmann & Associates Inc, 1999-2002; Pinnacle Actuarial Resources Inc, sr consult, 2003-, prin, 2006-. **Orgs:** Kappa Alpha Psi Fraternity Inc, 1991-; Am Acad Actuaries, 1996-; assoc mem, Casualty Actuarial Soc, 1996-, fel, 1999-; Midwestern Actuarial Forum, 1996-; Joint CAS/SOA Comt on Minority Recruiting, 1999-2003; CAS Comt Profism Educ, 1999-2005; vpres, InterNat Asn Black Actuaries Found, 2003-04, bd dirs, 2004-; CAS Exam Comt, 2003-05; CAS Ratemaking Seminar Comt, 2004-05; CAS Bd Dirs, 2005-; CAS Long Range Planning Comt, 2005-. **Special Achievements:** Estimating Claim Settlement Values Using GLM, 2004 CAS Discussion Paper Program? Applying and Evaluating Generalized Linear Models; Detecting a Pattern, Best's Review, May, 2005, pp. 68-70. **Business Phone:** (309)665-5010.

MOSLEY, SHANE
Boxer. **Personal:** Born Sep 7, 1971, Lynwood, CA; son of Jack and Clemmie; married Jin; children: Najee Jamarr, Taiseki Justin & Mee-Yon Jinae. **Career:** Boxer; Sugar Shane Inc, owner, currently. **Honors/Awds:** US Championship winner, 1989; Jr Worlds champion, 1989; US Amateur Champion, 1992; US Olympic Team, 1992; Int Boxing Fedn Champion, 1997; Fighter of the Year, Boxing Writers Asn, 1998; World Boxing Coun Champion, 2000; Champion, World Boxing Asn; Champion, World Boxing Coun, 2003. **Business Addr:** Boxer, Sugar Shane Inc, PO Box 8318, La Verne, CA 91750.

MOSLEY, TIMOTHY Z. See TIMBALAND.

MOSLEY, WALTER
Writer, educator. **Personal:** Born Jan 1, 1952?, Los Angeles, CA; son of LeRoy and Ella; married Joy Kellman. **Educ:** Goddard Col; Johnson State Col, polit theory; City Col NY, grad writing prog. **Career:** Publ: The New Yorker; GQ; Esquire; USA Weekend; Los Angeles Times Mag; Savoy; Black Betty; A Little Yellow Dog Cinnamon Kiss; NY Times bestsellers; Books: Devil in a Blue Dress, 1990; A Red Death, 1991; White Butterfly, 1992; Black Betty; Norton, 1994; Always Outgunned, Gone Fishin', 1997; Blue Light, 1999; Walkin' The Dog, 1999; RL's Dream; A Yellow Dog; Always Outnumbered; Workin' on the Chain Gang: Shaking off the Dead Hand of History, 2000; Fearless Jones; What next, 2003; The Man in My Basement, 2004; Little Scarlet, 2004; The Wave, 2006; Fortunate Son, 2006; Black Genius, ed & contribr; NY Univ, prof Eng, currently; auth, currently. **Orgs:** Bd dir, Nat Book Awards; bd, Full Frame Doc Film Festival; Poetry Soc Am; TransAfrica; past pres, Mystery Writers Am. **Honors/Awds:** Shamus Award, 1990; Lit Award, Black Caucus Am Libr Asn, 1996; O'Henry Award, 1996; Am Soc Mag Ed honored a story he published in GQ: The Black Woman in the Chinese Hat, 2000; Anisfield Wolf Award; Grammy award, 2002; Risktaker Award, Robert Redford's Sundance Inst; hon doctorate, City Col. **Special Achievements:** Devil in a Blue Dress was nominated for Edgar Award; finalist for the NAACP Award in fiction. **Business Phone:** (212)522-7200.*

MOSS, ALFRED A
Educator, clergy. **Personal:** Born Mar 2, 1943, Chicago, IL; son of Alfred Alfonso Sr and Ruth Watson; married Alice E Foster (divorced 1985); children: Daniel Clement. **Educ:** Lake Forest Col, Lake Forest, IL, BA, hon, 1965; Episcopal Divinity Sch, Cambridge, MA, MA, divinity, 1968; Univ Chicago, Chicago, IL, MA, 1972, PhD, hist, 1977. **Career:** Episcopal Church Holy Spirit, Lake Forest, IL, asst minister urban ministry, 1968-70; Univ Chicago, Episcopal Chaplaincy, Chicago, IL, assoc chaplain, 1970-75; Univ Md, Dept Hist, Col Park, MD, lectr, 1975-77, asst prof hist, 1977-83, assoc prof hist, 1983-, affil assoc prof hist, currently. **Orgs:** Phi Beta Kappa; mem ed bd, Wash Hist & Studies Anglican & Episcopal Hist; trustee & first vpres, Hist Soc Episcopal Church. **Honors/Awds:** Award for Excellence in Teaching, Col Arts & Humanities. **Special Achievements:** Publications: The American Negro Academy, Louisiana State Univ Press, 1981; Looking at History, People for the American Way, 1986; From Slavery to Freedom, Alfred A Knopf, 1994, 1997, 1999, 2000; The Facts of Reconstruction, Louisiana State Univ Press, 1991; Dangerous Donations, UNV of MO Press, 1999; Ordained Episcopal Priest. **Business Addr:** Associate Professor, University of Maryland College Park, Department of History, 2101H Francis Scott Key Hall, College Park, MD 20742-7315.

MOSS, ANNI R.
Actor, writer, fashion model. **Personal:** Born in Alabama; daughter of Samuel D and Rebecca C. **Educ:** WVA State Col, BS, educ, math, french, 1966; Boston Univ, Theatre Inst,1988; State Univ NY, 1984, 1991. **Career:** NASA Lewis Res, math asst, 1965; IBM CRP, syst engr, 1966-74, instr,1974-75, IBM Germany, consult, writer, 1976, prod planner, 1976-81, systrequirements specialist, 1981-82; IBM Worldwide, IS auditor, 1983-84, systeng mgr, 1984-89, hq market planner, admnr, 1989-92; ARM Int, pres, 1992-;actress, Films: Bed of Roses, The Last Good Time; Movin' Up, Boston Cable;Mountain Don't Move for Me; Television Series: Law & Order; The CosbyMysteries; NY Undercover; Nat & Reg TV commercials; Press Coun PhysFitness PSA, corporate videos; Community Scene, WICZ-TV; Black HistVignettes, WBNG-TV; Black Women's Spec, WSKG-TV; host producer: dreamUpwith Anni, cable TV show; radio show dream Sounds, WRTN/WVOX; GospelRenaissance Music, WENE/WMRV; theatrical appearances include: Joe Turner'sCome & Gone, Huntington Theatre, Boston; Antigone, Boston Univ; Over theDamn, Playwright's Platform; concert soloist of gospel, jazz, & pop; SabbyLewis Band, Charlie Bateman Band, jazz singer, 1991-92; concert producer. **Orgs:** AFTRA, 1988-; Screen Actors Guild, 1992-. **Honors/Awds:** Black Achievers Award, 1985; IBM Hundred Percent Club & Golden Circle,1985-88. **Special Achievements:** Unex corporate video, spokesperson, 1992; Nat Fire Protection Asn Int MagPubl, first female & first AFA to appear on the cover, 1992; IBM's System,390: originator, planner, producer, & executor of worldwide photography &videos for the system, 1990; Author of Marketing publications for thesystem, 1990-92; Published writer: Women's News, Mentor Magazine, numerousothers. **Business Addr:** President, ARM International, PO Box 1272, White Plains, NY 10602, **Business Phone:** (212)724-2800.

MOSS, ERIC
Football player. **Personal:** Born Sep 25, 1975. **Educ:** Ohio State Univ. **Career:** Minn Vikings, guard, 1997-98; Columbia Lions, quater back, 1999; Scottish Claymores, guard, 1999; Jacksonville Jaguars, 2000. **Military Serv:** AUS, 1992.

MOSS, ESTELLA MAE
Government official. **Personal:** Born Sep 15, 1928, Providence, KY; daughter of Eugene Jones and Odessa; married Charles E Moss Sr; children: Phyllis Johnson, Ardell, Sheila Spencer, Deborah L Ray & Charles E Jr,Angie V. **Educ:** Ind State Univ, Evansville, IN, Sch Pub & Environ Affairs, attended 1975. **Career:** Government official (retired); Super Ct, clerk probate; Pigeon Twp Assessor; chief dep appointed, 1974-76; Vanderburgh Co, recorder, comnr, 1976-84. **Orgs:** Vpres, Comm Action Prog, 1969-77; brd dir, Carver Comm Day Care, 1970-76; Natl Assn Advan Colored People Coalition 100 Black Women Polit Black Caucus, 1978-85; brd dir, Liberty Baptist Housing Authority; appointed supt, City Cemeteries, 1987-91. **Honors/Awds:** Community Leadership Award, Young Women's Christian Assn, 1976; Black Woman of the Yr, Politics Black Women Task Force, 1977; State of Ind Black Expo, 1978; Selected & Honored as one of 105 Outstanding Black Women of Ind, Natl Coun of Negro Women, 1983; Spec Recognition Community Serv Award, Black Women Task Force, 1990; Jefferson Award, 2004. **Home Addr:** 804 E Mulberry St, Evansville, IN 47713, **Home Phone:** (812)425-8789. *

MOSS, JAMES EDWARD
Police officer. **Personal:** Born Jan 8, 1949, Columbus, OH; son of Frank P and Ernestine Coggins; married Andria Felder, Jan 23, 1970; children: Shondrika, Marquai & Jamarran; married Jun 27, 1992; children: Jamelah. **Educ:** Columbus Bus Univ, AA, bus admin, 1973; OH Dominican Coll, BA, bus admin, 1975; Capital Univ, attended 1978; OH State Univ, MA, black studies, 1989, MA, US hist, 1993, PhD, cand hist, 1994. **Career:** Police officer (retired); Columbus Police Dept, Columbus, OH, sgt, 1970-94. **Orgs:** Pres, Police Officers Equal Rights, 1988-; Am Historical Asn, 1990-; Orgn Am Historians, 1990-; bd mem, Columbus Police Athletic League; OH Guardians, 1988-; pres, Nat Black Police Asn, 1993-; columbus chap, Nat Asn Advan Colored People, 1994-; Nat Coun Black Studies; Asn Study Afro Am Life & Hist. **Honors/Awds:** Jefferson Award, 1985; Coach of the Year, Police Athletic League, 1983; Service Award, Police Athletic League, 1986, 1987, 1990; Police Officer of the Year, Nat Black Police Asn, 1993. **Military Serv:** AUS, sgt, E-5, 1967-70; Vietnam War Veteran; Good Conduct Medal; Combat Infantry Badge; Vietnam Service Medal; Tet Offensive Medal; Two Unit Citation; Vietnam Campaign Medal; Parachute Medal-Jump Wings.

MOSS, NIKKI
Labor relations manager. **Educ:** Oakland Univ, BS & MBA, human resource. **Career:** Detroit Edison, col recruiter; Ford Motor Co, panelist; DTE Energy, supvr orgn learning, currently. **Orgs:** Leader, Youth Fel; Chairperson, Black Hist Month Celebration, Women's Retreat Comt; DTE Energy's Diversity Leadership Coun; Hope United Methodist Church, Southfield, Mich. **Honors/Awds:** Sarah Sheridan Award, 1997; Recipient Walter J McCarthy Award, DTE Energy. **Business Addr:** Supervisor, Organizational Learning, DTE Energy, 2000 2nd Ave, PO Box 2859, Detroit, MI 48226-1279, **Business Phone:** (313)235-4000.

MOSS, REV. OTIS, JR.
Clergy. **Personal:** Born Feb 26, 1935, LaGrange, GA; son of Otis and Magnolia; married Edwina Hudson; children: Kevin, Daphne (deceased) & Otis III. **Educ:** Morehouse Col, BA, 1956, DD, 1977; Morehouse Sch Religion, BD, 1959; Interdenominational Theol Ctr, spec studies, 1961; United Theol Seminary, PhD, 1990; Temple Bible Col, DD. **Career:** Raymond Walters Col, instr; Old Mt Olive Baptist Church, La Grange, pastor, 1954-59; Providence Baptist Church, Atlanta, pastor, 1956-61; Mt Zion Baptist Church, minister, 1961-74; Mt Olivet Instnl Church, Cleveland, pastorn 1975-. **Orgs:** Bd dirs, Morehouse Sch Religion & Morehouse Col; bd dir, ML King Jr Ctr; bd dir, vice chmn, Oper PUSH; Alpha Phi Alpha; past vpres, NAACP, Atlanta; past pres & founder Cincinnati Chap SCLC; bd trustees, Leadership Cleveland Civil Right Activist; former columnist, Atlanta Inquirer, Atlanta, GA, 1970-75; mem rev comn, Harvard Divinity Sch Harvard Univ, 1975-82; mem bd trustees, Morehouse Col, 1979-; delivered speeches, sermons & addresses, Atlanta Univ, Colgate Rochester Divinity Sch, Col Mt St Joseph, Dillard Univ, Eden Theol Ctr, Howard Univ, Kalamazoo Coll, Miami Univ, Fisk Univ, Univ Cincinnati, Vanderbilt Univ, Wilberforce Univ, Wright State Univ, Morehouse Col. **Honors/Awds:** Keynote speaker March, Cincinnati, 1963; served as part of clergy mission to the Far East Hong Kong, Taiwan & Japan 1970; invited to act as delegate to World Bapt Conf in Beirut; twice honored by Ohio House of Reps, Resolutions, 1971,75; Human Relations Award, Bethune Cookman Col, 1976; consult with govt officials as part of clergy mission to Israel, 1977-78; Consult with Pres Carter Camp David, 1979; Ranked as one of Clevelands 10 Most Influential Ministers, Cleveland Press, 1981; Govs Award in Civil Rights Gov Richard F Celeste; Special Award in Leadership, Central State Univ, 1982; Black Professional of the Year, Black Professional Asn, Cleveland, OH, 1983; Greatest Black Preachers, EbonyMag, 1984; invited as part of clergy mission to Republic of China Taiwan 1984; sermon "Gg from Disgrace to Dignity" Best Black Sermons 1972; essays "Black Church Distinctives", "Black Church Revolution" The Black Christian Experience; listed in Ebony Success Library. **Business Addr:** Pastor, Olivet Institute Baptist Church, 8712 Quincy Ave, Cleveland, OH 44106, **Business Phone:** (216)721-3585.

MOSS, RANDY
Football player. **Personal:** Born Feb 13, 1977, Rand, WV; son of Randy Pratt and Maxine; children: Sydney. **Educ:** Marshall Univ, bus admin. **Career:** Minn Vikings, wide receiver, 1998-2004; Oakland Raiders, 2005-06; New England Patriots, wide receiver, 2007-. **Honors/Awds:** NFL Best at Each Position Award, 1998; Offensive Rookie of the Year, Associated Press, 1998; AFC Player of the Month, 2007. Pro Bowl selection, Pro Bowl AFC Starters, 2008. **Business Addr:** Wide Receiver, New England Patriots, Gillette Stadium One Patriot Pl, Foxboro, MA 02035, **Business Phone:** (508)543-8200.

MOSS, ROBERT C., JR.
Consultant, baseball umpire. **Personal:** Born May 30, 1939, San Diego, CA; son of Robert C Sr and La Verne; married Edna Jean, Mar 17, 1962; children: Anita Louise & Parry Donald. **Educ:** San Diego State Univ, BA, 1961, MS, 1975; US Int Univ, teaching cred, 1965. **Career:** Lincoln High Sch, biol teacher, 1965-66; Mission Bay High Sch, biol instr, football, baseball coach, 1966-69; prof baseball umpire, 1969-71; San Diego High Sch, black studies teacher, black stud motivation counr, 1969-71; Phys Educ Dept Univ Calif San Diego, supvr, 1971-92; Moss-Cess Unlimited, founder & dir, 1973. **Orgs:** Kappa Alpha Psi Fraternity; Am Alliance Health, Phys Educ Recreation &Dance; Am Coun Asn; Calif Asn Health, Phys Educ Recreation & Dance; Calif Asn Couns & Develop; Calif & Am Asn Multicultural Coun & Develop; vpres, San Diego County Baseball Umpires Asn. **Honors/Awds:** Ted Williams Award, 1960; Byron Chase Memorial Award, 1960; Most Outstanding San Diego State University Senior Athlete, 1961; Associated Students Man of the Month, San Diego State Univ, 1961; Blue Key Honorary Soc, 1961; Ashanti Weusi Award, Southeast San Diego community; Unit Meritorious Service Award, Calif Asn Health Phys Educ Recreation & Dance,San Diego, 1975; Calif Asn Health Phys Educ Recreation & Dance President's Citation, 1981; Oustanding Teacher Award, Univ Calif, San Diego African Am graduates, 1985; Calif Asn Health Phys Educ Recreation & Dance Emmett Ashford Community Spirit Award, 1986; Am Asn Cosmetic Dentist President's Citation, 1986; CACD Black Caucus Service Award, 1986; Calif Asn Health Phys Educ Recreation & Dance Honor Award, 1987; Special Recognition Award,Univ Calif San Diego Athletics Prog; Special Recognition Award, US Int Univ basketball team, 1988; CACD Black Caucus Dedicated

Service Award,1989; CACD-CAMC President's Outstanding Professional Service Award, 1989; Outstanding Service Award, Camperd Multicultural Dynamics Section, 1991; CACD Human Rights Award, 1993; ACA-AMCD Professional Development Award,1994. **Special Achievements:** Author: booklet on positive uses of laughter. **Military Serv:** Served USMC 1961-65. *

MOSS, SHAD GREGORY. See BOW WOW, LIL.

MOSS, TANYA JILL
Government official, association executive, lawyer. **Personal:** Born Dec 20, 1958, Chicago, IL; daughter of Hiawatha and Arzelia. **Educ:** Univ Chicago, BS, 1983. **Career:** Carson Pirie Scott & Co, personnel asst, 1980-83; Quaker Oats, acct rep, 1983-84; City Chicago, proj coordr, 1985-; atty. **Orgs:** Alpha Kappa Alpha Sorority Inc, 1979-; Order Eastern Star, 1982-; Nat Asn Female Execs, 1984-; Nat Forum Black Pub Admins, 1985-; bd mem, ETA Creative Arts Found; exec bd mem, Polit Action League. **Honors/Awds:** Appraising Real Property, Soc Real Estate Appraisers, 1990. **Special Achievements:** Developed the City of Chicago's Indebtedness Program, Scofflaw Program, 1989; assisted in the development of the False Burglar Program, 1994. **Home Addr:** 8910 S E End Ave, Chicago, IL 60617-2807, **Home Phone:** (312)747-1127. *

MOSS, THYLIAS
Poet, educator. **Personal:** Born Jan 1, 1954, Cleveland, OH; daughter of Calvin Brasier and Florida. **Educ:** Oberlin Col, grad, 1981; Univ New Hampshire, MFA. **Career:** MacArthur "Genius" fel; Guggenheim fel; Nat Endowment Arts fel; Mass Arts Coun, artist's fel; Univ Mich, Ann Arbor, MI, prof eng & poet, currently; Poetry: Hosiery Seams on a Bowlegged Woman, 1983; Pyramid of Bone, 1989; At Redbones, 1990; Rainbow Remnants in Rock Bottom Ghetto Sky, 1991; Small Congregations: New and Selected Poems, 1993; Last Chance for the Tarzan Holler, 1998; Slave Moth: A Narrative in Verse, 2004; Tokyo Butter: Poems, 2006; Prose: Talking to Myself, 1984; The Dolls in the Basement, 1984; I Want to Be, 1995; Someone Else Right Now, 1997; Tale of a Sky-Blue Dress, 1998. **Honors/Awds:** Whiting Award; Witter Bynner Award; Dewar's Profiles Performance Award.

MOSS, WAYNE B
Manager, executive director. **Personal:** Born Jul 28, 1960, Cleveland, OH; son of Ceasar and Earlene Hill. **Educ:** Howard Univ, Wash, DC, broadcast jour, 1982; Ohio Univ, Athens, OH, sports admin, 1988. **Career:** Ohio Bur Employ Serv, Maple Heights, OH, acct exec, 1984-87; Cleveland Browns, Cleveland, OH, pub rels asst, 1988; Baltimore Orioles, Baltimore, MD, asst dir community rels, 1989; Detroit Lions, Pontiac, MI, asst dir pub rels, 1989-91; City Cleveland, Cleveland, OH, comnr recreation, 1991-95; Dekalb County, dep dir recreation; Boys & Girls Clubs Am, dir prog planning, sr dir sports, fitness & recreation, currently. **Orgs:** Career Beginnings, 1988; United Negro Col Fund, 1989. **Business Addr:** Senior Director of Sports, Fitness and Recreation, Boys & Girls Clubs of America, 1230 W Peachtree St NW, Atlanta, GA 30309, **Business Phone:** (404)487-5761.

MOSS, WILMAR BURNETT, JR.
Educator, commissioner. **Personal:** Born Jul 13, 1928, Homer, LA; married Orean Sanders; children: Dwight, Victor, Gary, LaDonna. **Educ:** Ark Baptist Col, attended 1949; Southern State Col, attended 1957; AM&N Col Pine Bluff, BS, bus admin, 1960; Univ Ark, Fayetteville, MEd, educ admin, 1970. **Career:** McNeil Cleaners, cleaner spotter presser; McNeil Lumber Co, tractor truck driver lumber grader; Partee Lumber Co, tractor driver; Navel Ordnance Plant Camden, light mach oper; Stuttgard, teacher, 1960; E Side Lincoln Elem Schs Stuttgart, head teacher, 1961-63; E Side Lincoln Holman, prin, 1964-69; Holman Northside Elem Schs, prin, 1969-72; Walker School Dist No 33, supt schs, 1972-; Ark Fair Housing Comn, comnr, currently. **Orgs:** Ark Sch Admin Asn; Ark Educ Asn; S Ark Admins Asn; Columbia County Educ Asn; Nat Educ Asn; Nat Asn Advan Colored People; Nat Alliance Black Sch Supts; Phi Delta Kappa; Bethany Baptist Church McNeil; Golden Diadem Lodge No 41; McNeil Jaycees; bd mem Pres Johnson's Concentrated Employ Prog, 1971-72; Stuttgart Civic League; Walker Alumni Asn, 1974. **Honors/Awds:** Outstanding Service Award, Stuttgart Faculty Club, 1970; Community Service Award, Stuttgart Civic League, 1972. **Military Serv:** AUS, 1951-53. **Business Addr:** Commissioner, Arkansas Fair Housing Commission, 101 E Capitol Ave Suite 114, Little Rock, AR 72201.

MOSS, WINSTON
Writer. **Personal:** Born in Selma, AL. **Educ:** Bellarmine Col, KY, 1964; Western Ky Univ, attended 1968. **Career:** The Flip Wilson Show, staff writer, 1970; Laugh In, staff writer, 1972; That's My Mama, story ed, 1975-76; The Jackson-5 Show, staff writer, 1977; Writers Guild Am/WST, freelance writer; Staff writer: Love, American Style, 1969; Clifton Davis Spec, 1977; All in the Family, 1977-79; Archie Bunkers Place, 1979-80; Sanford, 1980; Cissy and the Nephew, 1980. **Orgs:** Vice chmn, Black Writers Comt, 1979-81; Hollywood Br mem, Nat Asn Advan Colored People. **Honors/Awds:** Golden Globe Award, 1977. **Special Achievements:** First Black story editor for Network TV, 1975. **Military Serv:** AUS, specialist 4, 1965-67. **Home Addr:** 4714 Rodeo Lane Suite 3, Los Angeles, CA 90016.

MOSS, WINSTON (WINSTON N MOSS)
Football player, football coach. **Personal:** Born Dec 24, 1965, Miami, FL; married Zoila; children: Winston Jr, Robert, Marcus & Victoria. **Educ:** Univ Miami, FL. **Career:** Football player (retired), Football coach; Tampa Bay Buccaneers, linebacker, 1987-90; Los Angeles Raiders, linebacker, 1991-94; Seattle Seahawks, linebacker, 1995-97, defensive quality control coach, 1998; New Orleans Saints, defensive asst & quality control, 2000, linebackers coach, 2000-05; Green Bay Packers, linebackers coach, 2006-07, asst head coach & defense, 2007-. **Honors/Awds:** Ed Block Courage Award, 1993; Unsung Hero Award, Nat Football LeaguePlayers Asn, 1996. **Business Phone:** (920)569-7500.

MOSS, WINSTON N. See MOSS, WINSTON.

MOSS, YOLANDA M
School principal. **Personal:** Married Kerry. **Career:** Pierre Laclede Elem Sch, prin, currently. **Business Phone:** (314)385-0546.*

MOSS, ZEFROSS
Football player. **Personal:** Born Aug 17, 1966, Tuscaloosa, AL. **Educ:** Ala State Univ. **Career:** Football player (retired); Indianapolis Colts, tackle, 1989-94; Detroit Lions, 1995-96; New England Patriots, 1997-99.

MOTEN, EMMETT S, JR.
Executive. **Personal:** Born Feb 6, 1944, Birmingham, AL; son of Emmett S Sr and Marie Creighton; married Loran Williams, May 29, 1965; children: Eric & Alicia. **Educ:** Grambling Univ, Grambling, LA, BS; La State Univ, New Orleans, LA, Masters Degree. **Career:** St Augustine High Sch, New Orleans, LA, athletic dir, football coach, 1966-70; City of New Orleans, New Orleans, LA, rec dept-deputy dir, 1970-73, dir policy planning & analysis, 1973-75, asst chief admin officer, 1975-78; Detroit Econ Growth Corp, Detroit, MI, exec vpres, downtown develop authority, 1978-79; City of Detroit, Detroit, MI, dir, community & econ develop, 1979-88; Little Caesar Enterprises Inc, vpres, 1989-96; Twinpines Paper Corp, chmn; United Am Healthcare Corp, secy subsidary opers, currently. **Orgs:** Chmn, Boys Hope; bd mem, Orchard Childrens Serv; bd mem, Inst Bus; bd mem, Detroit Downtown Develop Authority; bd mem, Detroit Econ Develop Authority; pres, Joint Fraternal Devt Corp; Kappa Alpha Psi, Detroit chap. **Honors/Awds:** Hall of Fame, Grambling State Univ, 1983; Honorary Alumnus, Univ Detroit, 1988; Martin L King Award, 1991. **Business Phone:** (313)393-4571.

MOTHERSHED, SPAESIO W
Librarian. **Personal:** Born Jun 30, 1925, Bloomburg, TX; married Juliene Craven; children: Spaesio jr & Willa Renee. **Educ:** Jarvis Christian Col, BA, 1952; Syracuse Univ, MS, 1956; N TX State Univ, attended 1963. **Career:** Syracuse Univ Libr, grad asst, 1954-56; State Libr Mich, cataloger, 1956-60; Jarvis Christian Col, head librn, 1960-66; Tex Southern Univ, dir librn. **Orgs:** Tex Libr Asn; SW Libr Asn; Houston Met Archives; ed, News Notes, 1968-72; COSATI Sub-com Negro Res Libr, 1970-73. **Honors/Awds:** English award; Journalism award. **Military Serv:** USN, 1943-46; 2 gold stars, USN, 1945. *

MOTLEY, DAVID LYNN
Manager. **Personal:** Born Sep 11, 1958, Pittsburgh, PA; son of Thomas A and Lillie M. Law; married Darlene Gambill, Aug 18, 1990; children: Renee, Carrington. **Educ:** Univ Pittsburgh, Pittsburgh, PA, BSME, 1980; Harvard Bus Sch, Boston, MA, MBA, 1988. **Career:** PPG Indust Inc, Pittsburgh, PA, analyst, 1980-82, St Louis, MO, sales rep, 1982-84, New York, NY, res sales rep, 1984-86; MBA Develop, Wash, DC, consult, 1988-89; PPG Industs Inc, Pittsburgh, PA, dir corp invest, 1989; Alcoa Inc, dir mkt & vpres. **Orgs:** chair, Langley High Sch Future Jobs, 1989-; bd dirs, E Liberty Develop Corp, 1989-; alumni steering comn, NEED, 1990-; Bd dirs, Urban League Pittsburgh, 1990-; treas, Harvard Sch Club, Pittsburgh, 1990-; Pittsburgh C's Mus; Sewickley Acad Bd Trustees; Bd Pittsburgh Zoo; exec dir, Inner City Jr Tennis Prog; founder, Univ Pittsburgh Eng Endowed Scholar Fund. *

MOTLEY, J. KEITH
Chancellor (education). **Personal:** Children: Keith Jr, Kayla & Jordan. **Educ:** Northeastern Univ, BS, MS; Boston Col, PhD. **Career:** Univ Mass, Boston, vice chancellor stud affairs, vpres bus mkt & pub affairs, interim chancellor, chancellor, 2007-; Newbury Col, Bd Trustees, chair; Concerned Black Men Mass Inc, founder & educ chair; Paul Robeson Inst, founder & educ chair. **Orgs:** Iota Phi Theta Fraternity; Sigma Pi Phi Fraternity; Beta Beta Boule; Am Red Cross; Freedom House; United Way Mass Ba; Boston Pvt Indust Coun; Dimock Community Health Ctr. **Business Addr:** Chancellor, University of Massachusettes, Rm 0054A Quinn Admin Bldg 3 100 Morrissey Blvd, Boston, MA 02125-3393, **Business Phone:** (617)287-6800.*

MOTLEY, DR. RONALD CLARK
Physician, educator. **Personal:** Born Jan 25, 1954, Dayton, OH; son of Claude L Dunson (stepfather) and Birdella M Rhodes Dunson; married Charlyn Coleman, May 6, 1983; children: Melissa Charon. **Educ:** Northwestern Univ, BA, 1976; Howard Univ, Col Med, MD, 1983. **Career:** Northwestern Univ, lab tech, 1972-74; Ind Biotest Labs, toxicologist & group leader skin sensitization, 1976-77; Avon Products Inc, process control chemist, 1977-78; Southern Ill Univ, Sch Med, visiting asst instr, 1978-79; Howard Univ, Col Med, instr & tutor, 1980-81; Howard Univ, Col Med, Health Scis Acad, gen coordr, 1981-83; Mayo Clinic, gen surg internship, 1983-84, urol residency, 1984-88; pvt pract, currently. **Orgs:** Equal opportunity comm, Mayo Clinci, 1985-; assoc mem, Minority Fellows Mayo Clinic, 1985-; Nat Med Asn, 1985-; educ comn, Dept Urol Mayo Clinic, 1987-88; bd dirs, Family Serv Agency San Bernardino, CA, 1989-. **Honors/Awds:** Who's Who Among Students in Am Univs & Cols, 1983; Lang Book Award, Health Scis Acad Award, Outstanding Geriatrics Award, Excellence in Psychiatry Award, CV Mosby Surgery Award Howard Univ Col Med, all rec'd in 1983; also numerous presentations and articles. **Business Addr:** Physician, 200 Veterans Ave, Beckley, WV 25801.

MOTT, STOKES E, JR.
Lawyer. **Personal:** Born Mar 11, 1947, Tifton, GA; son of Stokes E Sr and Kathleen M; married Neilda E Jackman; children: Ako K & Khari S. **Educ:** Long Island Univ, BS, 1968; New York Univ, MS, urban planning, 1971; Seton Hall Law Sch, JD, 1979. **Career:** Essex Co Community Col, instr; Stokes E Mott Jr PC, atty, currently. **Orgs:** Alpha Phi Alpha; Pa Bar Asn; Philadelphia Bar Asn. **Business Addr:** Attorney, Stokes E Mott Jr PC, Architects Bldg 117 S 17th St Suite 909, Philadelphia, PA 19103, **Business Phone:** (215)587-0440.

MOULDS, ERIC SHANNON
Football player. **Personal:** Born Jul 17, 1973, Lucedale, MS. **Educ:** Miss State Univ, psychol. **Career:** Buffalo Bills, wide receiver, 1996-2005; Houston Texans, wide receiver, 2006; Tennessee Titans, 2007; free agent, currently. **Orgs:** Nat Asn Advan Colored People. **Honors/Awds:** Rookie of the Year, Buffalo Bills, 1996.

MOURNING, ALONZO
Basketball player. **Personal:** Born Feb 8, 1970, Chesapeake, VA; married Tracy; children: Alonzo Mouring III & Myka Sydney. **Educ:** Georgetown Univ, BA, sociol. **Career:** Charlotte Hornets, ctr, 1992-95; Miami Heat, 1995-2001, 2004-06, 2006-; NJ Nets, ctr, 2003-04. **Orgs:** The Children's Home Soc; founder, Zo's Summer Groove; founder, Alonzo Mourning Charities. **Honors/Awds:** NBA All-Rookie First Team, 1993; All-NBA First Team, 1999; NBA Defensive Player of the Year, 1999, 2000; All-NBA Second Team, 2000; J Walter Kennedy Citizenship Award; NBAOCOs J Walter Kennedy Sportsmanship Award, 2002; Hometown Hero, Fla Sports Awards, 2002; Good Guy, The Sporting News, 2002; Silver Medallion Community Serv Award, Nat Conf Community & Justice, 2003; Outstanding Community Serv Award, Nat Urban League, 2003; NBA Champion, 2006. **Special Achievements:** First round pick, No 2, NBA Draft, 1992; Book: Resilience, 2008. **Business Addr:** Professional Basketball Player, Miami Heat, AmericanAirlines Arena, 601 Biscayne Blvd, Miami, FL 33132, **Business Phone:** (786)777-4667.

MOUSE, MIGHTY. See MCMILLIAN, MARK.

MOUTON, JAMES RALEIGH
Baseball player. **Personal:** Born Dec 19, 1968, Denver, CO. **Educ:** St Mary's Col Calif. **Career:** Baseball player (retired); Baseball coach; Houston Astros, outfielder, 1994-97; San Diego Padres, 1998; Montreal Expos, 1999; Milwaukee Brewers, 2000-01; Fort Bend Texans, hitting & fielding coach, 2006-. **Honors/Awds:** National League Stolen Bases Award, 1994. **Business Phone:** (832)444-2307.

MOUTON, LYLE JOSEPH
Baseball player. **Personal:** Born May 13, 1969, Lafayette, LA; married Aimee Churchill; children: Alexis Leigh & Kayla Lynn. **Educ:** La State Univ. **Career:** Chicago White Sox, outfielder, 1995-97; Yakult Swallows, 1998; Baltimore Orioles, 1998; Milwaukee Brewers, 1999-2000; Fla Marlins, 2001; Montreal Expos, 2002; Philadelphia Phillies, 2003; Cleveland Indians, 2003. **Honors/Awds:** NY-Penn League All-Star Team, 1991. *

MOUTOUSSAMY-ASHE, JEANNE
Photographer. **Personal:** Born Jul 9, 1951, Chicago, IL; married Arthur Ashe, 1977 (died 1993); children: Camera. **Educ:** Cooper Union, NT, BFA, photog, 1975. **Career:** Prof photogr; Arthur Ashe Found Defeat AIDS, chairwoman, currently. **Honors/Awds:** CEBA Award for IBM Advertisement, 1979; City of Chicago, Mayoral Citation for Viewfinders, 1986; Distinguished Alumni Citation, The Cooper Union, 1990; LISC Award for Art, 1999; Hon Dr of Fine Arts, Long Island University, C.W. Post Campus, 2001; Hon Dr of Fine Arts, Queens Cil, 2002; Essence Photography Literary Award, 2007. **Special Achievements:** Books: "Daddy and Me," Knopf, 1993; "Viewfinders: Black Women Photographers, 1839-1985," New York: Dodd, Mead and Company, 1986; "Daufuskie Island: A Photography Essay," Columbia, SC: University of South Carolina Press, 1982. Exhibitions: "America: Another Perspective," New York University, 1986; "Three Photographers," Black Gallery, Los Angeles, CA, 1985; "Art Against Apartheid: 3 Perspectives," Schomburg Center

for Research in Black Culture, New York Public Library, 1984; "Image and Imagination," Jazzonia Gallery, Detroit, MI, 1982; one woman shows, NY, Chicago, Florence, Paris; one woman exhibition, Leica Gallery, 1996-97; work appears in Columbia Museum of Art & Sci, Natl Portrait Gallery, Studio Museum of Harlem; "Reflections In Black, A History of Black Photographers, Debroah Willis", WW Norton & Co, 2000; Committed to Image Contemporary Black Photographers, Merril Publ, LTD, 2001. **Business Addr:** Photographer, The Leica Gallery, 670 Broadway 5th Fl, New York, NY 10012.

MOWATT, OSWALD VICTOR
Surgeon. **Personal:** Born in Spanishtown, Jamaica; married Glenda; children: Cecilia, Oswald Jr, Cyril, Raoul, Enrico, Mario. **Educ:** Roosevelt Univ, BS, 1959; Loyola Univ Med Sch, MD, 1963; Am Bd Surg, dipl, 1976. **Career:** Cook Co Hosp, intern, 1963-64; Michale Reese Hosp, resident surg, 1964-65; gen pract, 1965-67; Univ Ill, 1967-60, chief, resident surg; Westside VA Hosp, 1969-76; instr surg, 1969-76; Westside VA, resident surg, 1969-70; St Bernard Hosp, attend surg, 1970-73; Provident Hosp, sr attend surg, 1971-; Proficent Hosp, chief emer serv, dir med affairs, 1972-74; St Bernard Hosp, Dept Surg, chmn, 1976-, consult surg 1973-; Self-employed, Surgeon, currently. **Orgs:** Am Med Asn, 1965-; Ill State Med Soc, 1965-; Chicago Med Soc, 1965-; Nat Med Asn; Judicial Coun Nat Med Asn, 1975-; nominating comt, Nat Med Asn, 1977-; Asn Hosp Med Educ, 1973-74; chmn bd dir, Martin L King Boys Club 1977; chmn, Bylaws com Cook Co Physicians Asn, 1974-76; pres, Cook Co Physicians Asn, 1977; fel, Am Col Surgeons, 1977. **Business Addr:** Surgeon, 2011 E 75th St, Chicago, IL 60620.

MOWATT, ZEKE
Football player. **Personal:** Born Mar 5, 1961, Wauchula, FL. **Educ:** Fla State Univ. **Career:** Football player (retired); NY Giants, tight end, 1983-89, 1991; New Eng Patriots, tight end, 1990. **Honors/Awds:** Post-season play, 1986: NFC Championship Game; NFL Championship Game.

MOYO, YVETTE JACKSON
Publishing executive. **Personal:** Born Dec 8, 1953, Chicago, IL; daughter of Rudolph and Pauline; married Karega Kofi Moyo, 1985; children: Angela Saunders, Kweli, Ki-Afi, Kilolo Shalomeet, Rael, Yosheyah Gavriel, Kush & Kevani Zelpha (deceased). **Educ:** Eastern Ill Univ, BS, 1974. **Career:** Black United Fund, local conv coordr, 1976-77; Nat Pub Sales Agency, acct exec, 1977-79, sales mgr, 1979-81, vpres dir sales, 1984-84, sr vpres, dir sales, 1984-88; Dollars & Sense Mag, sr vpres sales & promotion, 1977-88; Resource Assocs Int, pres & co-founder, 1988-; Real Men Cook, pres, 1988-; US Postal Serv, pr & mktg consult, 1994-2000; Time Warner Inc, consult, 1992-2000. **Orgs:** Life mem, Nat Asn Advan Colored People, 1985; Oper PUSH, 1987; League Black Women, 1987. **Honors/Awds:** Black Achievers Award, YMCA, 1983; Kizzy Award Black Women's Hall of Fame, 1985. **Business Phone:** (312)324-5200.*

MSHONAJI, BIBI TALIBA. See BELLINGER, REV. MARY ANNE ALLEN.

MUCKELROY, WILLIAM LAWRENCE
Lawyer. **Personal:** Born Dec 4, 1945, Los Angeles, CA; son of John and Josie; married; children: William Jr, William II, William III & Heather. **Educ:** Univ Texas, BA, math, 1967; Am Univ, MS 1970, JD 1974. **Career:** Prothon Cyber Ltd, dir & pres; Riggs Liquor, dir & pres; Iram Am Invests Ltd, dir, pres, chmn bd; Am Univ, teaching asst; Harry Diamond Labs, WA, patent adv; RCA Corp, David Sarnoff Res Ctr, patent coun; Muckelroy & Assoc, patent atty; Litton Indust, div patent & licensing coun, 1977-78; US Patent Soc Inc, patent coun; William Lawrence Muckelroy PC, atty, currently. **Orgs:** Pres, Int Soc Hybrid Microelectronics Capital Chap; pres elect, Nat Patent Law Asn, dir; NJ, Am Bar Asn; trustee, Montclair State Col; dir, Trenton Bus Asst Corp; trustee, Montclair State Col, NJ, 1982-88; fel Wash Col Law Am Univ; Teaching fel, Am Univ; chmn, NJ Patent Law Asn Ethics Comt; dir, Trenton Bus Assistance Corp; dir, US Patent Soc Inc; Int Intellectual Property Law Soc; Am Intellectual Property Law Asn; NJ Intellectual Property Law Asn; Tex Acad Sci; Mercer County Bar Asn; US Ct Appeals DC; Third, & Tenth Circuits; US Ct Customs & Patent Appeals; Fed Circuit Ct; DC Ct Appeals; NJ Supreme Ct. **Honors/Awds:** Honors Univ, TX, 1963-64; Apa Scholar; NSSFNS Scholar; Lawrence D Bell Scholar; 70 patents granted. **Home Phone:** (215)321-0818. **Business Addr:** Attorney, William Lawrence Muckelroy PC, 1901 N Olden Ave Ewing Prof Pk Suite 3, Ewing Township, NJ 08618-2101, **Business Phone:** (609)882-2111.

MUDD, LOUIS L.
Marketing executive. **Personal:** Born Jul 29, 1943, Louisville, KY; married Marcella; children: Latonya, Darron, Bryan. **Educ:** Tenn State Univ, BS. **Career:** KY Commerce Cabinet, sr bus develop off; Brown & Williamson Tobacco Corp, Louisville, KY, asst prof planning mgr; Kool Cigarettes, asst brand mgr; KY Procurement, br mgr. *

MUDIKU, MAESGARA. See MUDIKU, MARY ESTHER.

MUDIKU, MARY ESTHER (MAESGARA MUDIKU)
Educator. **Personal:** Born Jan 1, 1943, Greenville, MS; daughter of Cornelius Members and Rose Esthers Jones; children: Mark K Greer & Masavia N Greer. **Educ:** Memphis State Univ, BFA, 1968; Memphis Acad Art, attended 1971; Howard Univ, MFA, prog. **Career:** DC Pub Schs, art teacher, 1986-89; Carter Global, art therapy consult, 1990-92; DC Dept Corrections, art therapist, 1992-97; CCA Corrections Corp Am, art therapist, 1997-; Season of Rebirth, founder. **Orgs:** Nat Conf Artists, 1990-97; GABA, 1990-2000; co-founder, New Age African Elders, 1995-2001; founder, Sacred Sisterhood, 1997-2001; ADACI. **Honors/Awds:** Tulani & Fana, Sisterlove Award, 1988; African American Achievement Award, Morgan State Univ, 1989; Emerging Artist Award, Fed City Alumni, Delta Sigma Theta, 1994-95. **Business Addr:** Art Therapist, Corrections Corporation of America, DC Lifeline Addiction Treatment Program, 1901 E St SE, Art Studio Rm B1-181 Leisure Skills, Washington, DC 20003, **Business Phone:** (202)698-3139.

MUHAMMAD, AKBAR A
Association executive, business owner, foreign correspondent. **Personal:** Born Jun 9, 1942, Hampton, VA; son of Celeste Brown-Prescott; married Maryam Aziz, Nov 21, 1960; children: 7. **Educ:** Hunter Col. **Career:** Former NY Minister Louis Farrakhan, asst, 1965-75; Imam Muhammad, spec asst, 1976; own bus, 1977-82; Nation Islam, int rep, Louis Farrakhan, 1982-; Adventure in Africa Tours, founder/owner, currently. **Orgs:** Nation Islam. **Special Achievements:** One of the most historical trips of any Black leader in the history of the United States; coordinated the publishing of Minister Farrakhan's book, "7 Speeches", published in 1973; responsible for producing four albums by Minister Farrakhan titled "Black Family Day", "Our Time Has Come", "Let Us Unite" with Rev. Jesse Jackson and "Heed the Call."; featured in weekly in more than 100 African-American newspapers nationally and also in several newspapers internationally; currently working on Minister Farrakhan's biography and a book on the history of the Nation of Islam from 1930-1985. **Business Addr:** Speaker, Ghana Mission - Nation of Islam, 8816 Manchester Rd, Saint Louis, MO 63144, **Business Phone:** (314)963-0913.

MUHAMMAD, ALI SHAHEED
Rap musician. **Personal:** Born Aug 11, 1970, Brooklyn, NY. **Career:** A Tribe Called Quest, mem; The Ummah, mem; Lucy Pearl, mem; Albums: "People's Instinctive Travels & the Paths of Rhythm", 1990; "The Low End Theory", 1991; "Midnight Marauders", 1993; "Kids, writer", 1995; Beats, "Rhymes & Life", 1996; "The Love Movement", 1998; "Lucy Pearl", 2000; "Shaheedullah & Stereotypes", 2004; Singles: "Bonita Applebum", "I Left My Wallet in El Segundo", "Can I Kick It?", "Check the Rhime", "Jazz (We've Got)", "Scenario", "Hot Sex", "Award Tour", "Electric Relaxation", "Oh My God", "1nce Again", "Stressed Out", "Find a Way" & "Like It like That". **Honors/Awds:** ASCAP Song writer Award. **Business Addr:** Musician, c/o BMG Entertainment Inc, 1540 Broadway Suite 9W, New York, NY 10036, **Business Phone:** (212)930-4000.*

MUHAMMAD, ASKIA
Journalist. **Personal:** Born Mar 28, 1945, Yazoo City, MS; married Alverda Ann Muhammad; children: Nadirah I, Raafi. **Educ:** Los Angeles State Univ, attended 1963; Los Angeles City Col, attended 1965; San Jose State Univ, attended 1970. **Career:** Newsweek Mag, corresp, 1968; Multi-Cult Prog Foothill Col, dir, 1970-72; Muhammad Speaks News, ed chief, 1972-75; Chicago Daily Defender, Wash, corresp, 1977-78; Black Journ Rev, founder, Pac Radio Nat News Bur, diplomatic corresp, 1978-79, reporter, 1979-80; Nat Sci Mag, ed, 1978-80; Nat Pub Radio, commentator, 1980-93; The WPFW Paper, ed; WPFW, news dir, 1991-93, prog dir, 1994, photojournalist, currently; Christian Sci Monitor Radio, 1993-; The Final Call Newspaper, White House corresp & Wash bur chief, 1996-; Book Written : "Behind Enemy Lines". **Orgs:** Nat Press Club; Sigma Delta Chi; Wash Automotive Press Asn; Capital Press Club; Nat Asn Black Journalists; Soc Profl Journ. **Honors/Awds:** Fred Douglass Award, Howard Univ Sch Comt, 1973; Annual Award; Fred Hampton Community Service Award, 1975; Outstanding Journalism Achievement Award, Nat Conf Black Lawyers, 1977, Univ DC, 1979; DuPont-Columbia Journalism Award, 1990; President's Award, Wash Asn Black Journalists, 1993; DC Mayor's Award for Excellence in Service to the Arts, 1994. **Special Achievements:** Man-of-words-and-images; Written Many Books. **Military Serv:** USNR, e-4 (ocs), 1963-70. **Business Addr:** White House Correspondance Reporter, Final Call Newspaper, 236 Mass Ave NE Suite 610, Washington, DC 20002, **Business Phone:** (202)543-7796.*

MUHAMMAD, AVA
Clergy. **Personal:** Born Jan 1, 1951, Columbus, OH; married Darius, 1988. **Educ:** Georgetown Univ Law Ctr, 1975. **Career:** Head, Muhammad Mosque No 15, 1998; Nat Islam, southern region rep, 1998; Real Love, auth; Queens of the Planet Earth: The Birth & Rise of the Original Woman, auth; Nation Islam, minister & nat spokesperson, currently; Minister Louis Farrakhan, nat spokesperson, currently. **Orgs:** New York Bar Asn. **Special Achievements:** Featured in Essence Magazine; The Islamic publication New Trends named her one of the 5 most important Muslim women of the 20th Century; Appointed as first woman to head a Mosque; Lecturer and writer who had authored five books. **Business Addr:** Minister, National Spokesperson, Nation of Islam, 734 W 79th St, Chicago, IL 60620, **Business Phone:** (866)602-1230.

MUHAMMAD, BENJAMIN CHAVIS (BENJAMIN FRANKLIN CHAVIS, JR.)
Association executive, talk show host. **Personal:** Born Jan 22, 1948, Oxford, NC; married Martha; children: 8. **Educ:** Univ NC, BA, chem, 1969; Duke Univ Divinity Sch, MA, divinity, 1980; Howard Univ, PhD, theol, 1982. **Career:** United Church Christ, Comn Racial Justice, dir, 1972, minister, 1972-, dep dir, exec dir; polit prisoner, NC, 1976-80; Nat Asn Advan Colored People, exec dir, 1993-94; WOL-AM, Wash, DC, talk show host, 1995-97; Hip-Hop Summit Action Network, pres & chief exec officer, 2001; Nation of Islam, E coast regional minister, Million Family March, nat dir, currently. **Orgs:** Civil rights organizer, Southern Christian Leadership Conf, 1967-69; labor organizer, AFSCME, 1969; co-chmn, Nat Alliance Against Racism & Polit Repression, 1977-; co-chmn, Southern Organizing Comn Econ & SocialJustice, 1977; chmn, Nat Coun Churches, Prophetic Justice Unit; chairperson, Southern Organizing Comt Economic & Social Justice; pres, Angola Found; pres bd, Wash Off Africa; Phi Beta Sigma Fraternity; chief exec officer & founder, Nat African Am Leadership Summit; co-founder, Nat Black Independent Polit Party. **Honors/Awds:** George Colins Community Service Award, Congressional Black Caucus, 1977; William L Patterson Award, Patterson Found, 1977; Shalom Award, Eden TheolSem, 1977; Gertrude E Rush Distinguished Service Award, Nat Bar Asn; J E Walker Humanitarian Award, Nat Bus League; Martin Luther King Jr Freedom Award, Progressive Nat Baptist Conv. **Special Achievements:** Author, An American Political Prisoner; Appeals for Human Rights; Psalms From Prison, Pilgrim Press, 1983; United Church of Christ Commission on Racial Justice, 1979. **Business Addr:** East Coast Regional Minister, National Director of the Million Family March, Nation of Islam, 106-108 W 127th St Muhammad Mosque Suite 7, New York, NY 10027, **Business Phone:** (212)865-1200.

MUHAMMAD, JAMES A
Executive. **Personal:** Born Sep 11, 1970, Columbia, SC; son of James Arthur Williams; married Shelia Culpepper; children: Salih Rafiq. **Educ:** Stillman Col, BA, 1992. **Career:** Bradley Univ, WCBU-FM, prog dir, 1998-2001; WVa Pub Broadcasting, dir radio programming, 2001-. **Orgs:** Alpha Phi Alpha Fraternity; Sigma Pi Phi Fraternity; Pub Radio Prog Dirs; Eastern Pub Radio. **Honors/Awds:** Gabriel Award; The Communicator Crystal Award of Excellence; The Communicator Award of Distinction. **Special Achievements:** Black History in Live Performance, national radio show for PRI; Her Vision, Her Voice, Her Song, national radio show for PRI. **Business Addr:** Director of Radio Programming, West Virginia Public Broadcasting, 600 Capitol St, Charleston, WV 25301, **Business Phone:** (304)556-4900.

MUHAMMAD, MARION
President (Organization). **Personal:** Born in Wilson, NC; son of Marvin Wilkins Sr and Helen. **Career:** Intl Boxing Fedn, exec secy, 1983-2001, treas, 1999-2001, pres, 2001-. **Orgs:** Am Cancer Soc; Schomburg Ctr Res Black Cult; Abandoned Babies Ctr; Essex County Educ Servs Comn; Nat HIV-AIDS Found; Peoples Org Progress; Nat Asn Advan Colored People; Nat Campaign Tolerance; Nat Asn Female Execs; Juvenile Diabetes Found. **Business Addr:** President, International Boxing Federation, United States Boxing Association, 516 Main St 2nd Fl, East Orange, NJ 07018, **Business Phone:** (973)414-0300.

MUHAMMAD, MUHSIN, II
Football player. **Personal:** Born May 5, 1973, Lansing, MI; married Christa; children: Jordan Taylor & Chase Soen. **Educ:** Mich State Univ. **Career:** Carolina Panthers, wide receiver, 1996-2004, 2008-; Chicago Bears, wide receiver, 2005-07. **Orgs:** Founder, M2 Found Kids; spokesperson, Muscular Dystrophy Asn. **Honors/Awds:** Panthers Man of the Year. **Business Addr:** Founder, M2 Foundation For Kids, 6420 A1 Rea Rd Suite 367, Charlotte, NC 28277.

MUHAMMAD, SHIRLEY M.
Executive. **Personal:** Born Apr 28, 1938, Chicago, IL; married Warith Deen Muhammad; children: Laila, Ngina, Warithdeen, Sadrud-Din. **Educ:** Cortez Peters Business Col, attended 1957, Wilson Jr Col, attended 1958. **Career:** Clara Muhammad Memorial Fund, pres, 1976-. **Orgs:** Pres, CMMEF, 1976-; bd dirs, Pkwy Comm House, 1982; Provident Hosp, 1983. **Honors/Awds:** Outstanding Woman of the Year, Provident Womens Aux, 1982-; Outstanding Business Woman, Pkwy Community House, 1982-83; Appreciation Award, Masjid Saahin Jr Youth 1984; Key to the City Newark, NJ, 1987. **Home Addr:** 8752 So Cornell, Chicago, IL 60617. **Business Addr:** President, Clara Muhammad Memorial Education Foundation Inc, 634 E 79th St, Chicago, IL 60619.

MUHAMMAD, DR. TIY-E
Physiologist. **Career:** Man II Man Develop, Inc., founder; 1-Step Above, founder;Men Against Molestation, founder; Hot 107.9 FM, host; Morris Brown Col; Clark Atlanta Univ, prof psychol; life coach; sex therapist; playwright; radio/television personality; dancer & athlete. **Honors/Awds:** Phi Beta Sigma Fraternity; Prince Hall affiliated Masons. **Special Achievements:** First black professor on the TBS reality series; named one of Ebony's "Most Eligible Bachelors; Book: Secrets Men Keep; My Mind, My Body, My Spirit.

MUHAMMAD, WALLACE D. (WARITH DEEN MUHAMMAD)
Clergy, clergy. **Personal:** Born Oct 30, 1933, Hamtramck, MI; son of Elijah and Clara; married Shirley; children: Laila, N'Gina, Wallace II, Sadrud-Din. **Educ:** Muhammad Univ Islam, vocational training in welding; Wilson Junior Col, microbiol; Loop Jr Col, Eng, hist & social sci. **Career:** Son of Elijah Muhammad; Philadelphia Temple, minister; Arabic & Islamic studies; leader of the American Muslim Mission (formerly World Community of Al-Islam in the West, formerly Nation of Islam and the Black Muslims). **Orgs:** Made pilgrimage to Mecca 3 times; adv Panel for Religious Freedom Abroad, Secy State Madeline Albright; World Supreme Coun Mosques. **Honors/Awds:** Recipient four Freedom Awards; Pioneer Award, Black Press; Humanitarian Awards from many cities & groups. **Business Addr:** MACA Fund, PO Box 1061, Calumet City, IL 60409.

MUHAMMAD, WARITH DEEN. See MUHAMMAD, WALLACE D.

MULDROW, JAMES CHRISTOPHER. See Obituaries section.

MULLEN, HARRYETTE
Poet. **Personal:** Born Jul 1, 1953, Florence, AL. **Educ:** Univ Tex, Austin, BA, 1975; Univ Calif, Santa Cruz, MA, 1989, PhD, 1990. **Career:** Austin Community Col, TX, Instructional Asst, instr, 1975-77; Manpower, Austin, TX, temp office worker, 1977-79; Tex Comn Arts, Beaumont & Galveston, artist schs, 1978-81; Dobie-Paisano writer's fel, Tex Inst Letters & Univ Tex, 1981-82; Univ Calif, Santa Cruz, teaching asst, 1985-89, vis lectr/dissertation fel, 1988-89; Cornell Univ, Ithaca, NY, asst prof, 1989-95; Univ Calif, Los Angeles, assoc prof, 1995-2002, prof 2002-. **Honors/Awds:** Artist grant, Helene Wurlitzer Found NM, 1981-82; Literature Award, Black Arts Acad, Dallas, 1986; Rockefeller Fel, Susan B Anthony Ctr for Women's Studies, Univ Rochester, NY, 1994-95; Katherine Newman Award for Best Essay, MELUS, 1996; artist residency, Va for the Arts, 1999; Nat Book Award, poetry finalist, 2002; Los Angeles Times Book Prize, poetry finalist, 2003; Nat Book Critics Circle Award, poetry finalist, 2003; award in poetry, Found for Contemporary Arts, 2004; fel award, John Simon Guggenheim Mem Found, 2005; PEN Beyond Margins Award, 2007. **Special Achievements:** Poetry collection: Sleeping with the Dictionary (2002), was a finalist for a National Book Award, National Book Critics Circle Award, and Los Angeles Times Book Prize; Blues Baby, 2002; Dim Lady, 2003; Recyclopedia: Trimmings, S*PeRM**K*T, and Muse and Drudge, 2006. **Business Phone:** (310)825-7553.

MULLEN, RODERICK
Football player. **Personal:** Born Dec 5, 1972, Baton Rouge, LA; married Deneca; children: Roderick MJ Mullen II, Meagan & Layla. **Educ:** Grambling State Univ, BS, criminal justice. **Career:** Green Bay Packers, defensive back, 1995-97; Carolina Panthers, corner back, 1999; Minn Vikings, safety, 2000; Las Vega prop, Investor, 2001-02; Bally Total Fitness, gen mngr, 2002-. **Honors/Awds:** Rookie of the Year, 1995.

MULLENS, DELBERT W
Executive. **Personal:** Born Nov 14, 1944, New York, NY; son of Edythe J; married Lula Sweat; children: Dorian & Mandy. **Educ:** Tenn State Univ, Nashville, TN, BS, 1968; Univ New York, Buffalo, NY, MS, 1974. **Career:** Flint Coatings Inc, Flint, MI, pres, dir, chief exec officer, 1983-98; Wesley Financial Corp, pres & chief exec officer, 1990-; Margate Industries Inc, dir, 1990-; NHF, pres, 1992-; Prod-SDL Chem Inc, chmn, currently. **Orgs:** Omega Psi Phi Fraternity, 1965-; pres, Nat Asn Black Automotive Suppliers, 1990-; sr mem, Soc Mfg Engrs, 1984-; trustee, Univ Buffalo. **Honors/Awds:** Business of the Year, Black Enterprise Mag, 1991; Business of the Year, Nat Minority Bus Devt Coun, 1990; Business of the Year, Mich Minority Bus Devt Coun, 1990. **Military Serv:** USAF, lt, 1968. **Business Addr:** Chief Executive Officer, President, Wesley Financial Corp, 100 N Woodward Ave Suite 395, Bloomfield Hills, MI 48302-5005, **Business Phone:** (248)203-9906.*

MULLETT, DR. DONALD L.
School administrator, chief executive officer. **Personal:** Born Apr 10, 1929, New York, NY; son of Josephine Reid; married Mildred James; children: Barbara L, Donna M King, David R James & Lisa J James. **Educ:** Lincoln Univ, AB, 1951; NY Univ, MBA, 1952; Univ Del, PhD, 1981. **Career:** United Mutual Life Ins Co, vpres & secy, 1954-62; Equitable Life Assurance Soc, cost analyst, 1962-63; Lincoln Univ, comptroller, 1963-69, vpres fin, 1969-89, interim pres, 1985-87; Tex Southern Univ, Houston, vpres fin, 1989-90; Jarvis Christian Col, Hawkins, TX, vpres fiscal affairs, 1990-93; Cheyney Univ PA, vpres bus affairs, 1993, chief exec officer, 1995-96. **Orgs:** Omega Psi Phi Frat Inc, 1948; mem & trustee, Rotary Int, 1969-; NY Univ Club, 1981-; dir, Pan African Devel Corp, DC, 1981-89; dir, Urban Educ Found Philadelphia, 1983-89; dir & treas, Lincoln Univ Found, 1986-89; trustee, Lincoln univ; trustee, Oakwood Col; dir, Unity Natl Bank, 1990; dir, Community Music Ctr, Houston, 1989-90. **Honors/Awds:** Achievement Award, Omega Psi Phi Frat, 1969; Distinguished Alumnus Award, Lincoln Univ, Pa, 1991. **Military Serv:** AUS, Finance Corps, sgt, 1952-54. **Home Addr:** 722 Laurel Grove Ln, Pearland, TX 77584. *

MULLINGS, PAUL
Executive. **Educ:** Inst Acct Staff, London, Eng. **Career:** Glendale Fed Bank; First Interstate Mortgage Co, pres & chief exec officer; Mortgage Electronic Registration Systems Inc, pres & ceo; JP Morgan Chase, Home Finance, sr vpres; Freddie Mac, sr vpres single family mortgage sourcing, 2005-. **Business Phone:** (703)903-2000.

MULLINS, JARRETT R
Executive. **Personal:** Born Nov 16, 1957, South Bend, IN; son of Ralph and Mary; married Kathy; children: Kevin & John. **Educ:** Auburn Univ, BS, 1980. **Career:** Fed Express Corp, sr mgr, cust serv, 1984-88; US Sprint, group mgr sales, 1988-91; Purator Courier, managing dir, customer serv & sales, 1991-93; TLI, dir, customer serv, 1993-94; Zenith Electronics, vpres sales, 1994-. **Orgs:** Kappa Alpha Psi; Nat Asn Minorities in Cable; CTAM.

MUMFORD, ESTHER HALL
Writer, editor, publisher. **Personal:** Born Jan 20, 1941, Ruston, LA; daughter of Nona Mae Hall and Shellie O Hall; married Donald Emerson Mumford; children: Donald Toussaint & Zola Marie. **Educ:** Southern Univ, 1959; Univ Wash, BA, 1963. **Career:** Washington State Archives, oral history interviewer; Ananse Press, co-publisher, writer/researcher, 1980-, managing ed; Off Archaeol & Hist Preserv, researcher; King Co Hist Preserv Off, oral hist interviewer; Wash Comn Humanities, lectr; Yesler Terrace Comn Coun, outreach worker; assoc curator, Mus Hist & Indust; Douglass-Truth Libr, African Am Mus, Tacoma; proj consult, State Centennial Exhibitions; lectr, African Americans Northwest; Ananse Press, founder, ed, currently; Publ: Seattle's Black Victorians: 1852-1901; Seven Stars & Orion: Reflections of the Past, editor; The Man Who Founded A Town; Calabash: A Guide to the History, Culture & Art of African-Am in Seattle & King Co. **Orgs:** Founding mem, Black Heritage Soc Wash State,; Nat Trust Hist Preserv; Asn King County Hist Orgns; Episcopal Women's History Proj; bd dir, Raven Chronicles; Festvial Sundiata Prog Comm. **Honors/Awds:** Aspasia Pulakis Award, Ethnic Heritage Council NW; Washington Living Treasure, Wash State Centennial Comn; Peace & Friendship Medal, Wash State Capital Museum; Award for Outstanding Scholarly Achievement in Black Studies, Natl Coun For Black Studies, Pacific NW Region; Voices of Kuumba Award, NW African Am Writers Workshop; Seattle Heritage Award, Museum of History & Industry; Cert of Recognition for Preservation of King Co, WA, History. **Business Addr:** Editor, Ananse Press, 1504 32nd Ave S, Seattle, WA 98144-3918, **Business Phone:** (206)325-8205.

MUMFORD, JEFFREY CARLTON
Educator, composer. **Personal:** Born Jun 22, 1955, Washington, DC; son of Thaddeus Q and Sylvia J; married Donna Coleman, Nov 16, 1985; children: Blythe Coleman. **Educ:** Univ Calif, Irvine, BA, 1977; Univ Calif, San Diego, MA, 1981. **Career:** Settlement Music Sch, theory, comp inst, 1985-89; Westchester Conserv Music, theory instr, 1986-89; Wash Bach Consort, asst dir, 1989-90; Wash Conserv Music, theory, comp instr, 1989-; Concert Soc, MD, sem coordr, prod supvr, 1990-95; Bowling Green State Univ, artist-in-residence,1999-2000; Oberlin Col, asst prof composition music, composer-in-residence, 2003-06; Lorain County Community College, Distinguished vis prof, 2008-; Recordings: Fragments From The Surrounding Evening; The Focus Of Blue Light; A Window Of Resonant Light; the promise of the far horizon; wending; A landscape of interior resonances; The Milliner's Fancy, barbaglio dal manca. **Orgs:** Bd dirs, League Composers, Int Soc Contemporary Music, US Chap, 1990-; bd dir, Nat Acad Recording Arts & Sci, 1997-99; adv bd, Bascom Little Fund, 2005-. **Honors/Awds:** Grants, ASCAP Found, 1979; Martha Baird Rockefeller Fund Music Inc, 1979, 1981; DC Comn Arts & Humanities, Technical Assistance Prog, The Minn Composers Forum, 1985-86; DC Comn Arts & Humanities, 1992-94; Guggenheim Found, 1995-96; Aaron Copland Scholar, Am Soc Composers, Authors & Publishers; ACCAP Standard Panel Awards, 1981; winner, Atlanta Symphony Orchestra Composition Competition, Nat Black Art Festival, 1994; Guggenheim Foundation Fellowship, 1995; Alpert Award U Cross Residency Prize, 2003; Academy Award in Music, Am Acad Arts & Letters, 2003; Individual Excellence Award, OH Arts Coun, 2006; Residency with the Milwaukee Youth Symphony, 2006. **Special Achievements:** Comns include: Cincinnati Symphony Orchestra, 2008, Cleveland Orchestra, 2006, Chicago Symphony, 2004, Cleveland radio station, WCLV, 2002, Corigliano Quartet, Cleveland Chamber Symphony, 2002; Nat Symphony Orhestra, 2001; violist Wendy Richman, 2001; saxophonists Rhonda Taylor & David Reminick, 2001;Nancy Ruyle Dodge Charitable Trust, 2000; pianist Margaret Kampmeier,1999; Reston Prelude Festival, 1997; Meet the Composer & Arts Endowment Commissioning, 1996; Nat Symphony Orchestra, 1995; Cincinnati radiostation, WGUC, 1994; cellist, Joshua Gordon, 1994; Walter W Naumburg Found, 1991;; From Music Found, 1990;Amphion Found Da Capo Chamber Players, 1989; McKim Fund in the Libr Cong,1986; Works performed both in the US & abroad including: US Libr Cong; London's Purcell Rm; Vienna's Musikverein; Aspen Music Festival; Bang on aCan; Finland's Helsinki Festival; Festival Musica nel Nostro Tempo Festival; Minn Orchestra; Atlanta Symphony Orchestra; St Paul Chamber Orchestra; Am Composer's Orchestra; Group for Contemporary Music; Amelia Piano Trio; pianist, Amy Briggs; Krannert Ctr for Performing Arts, Univ Ill, Urbana-Champaign Pacifica Quartet; Chicago Symphony Orchestra,2004; violinist, Ole Bohn, Norway, 2005; Haydn Trio Eisensatdt, Vienna, Network New Music, 2005; Cleveland Orchestra, 2005; Milwaukee Youth Symphony Orchestra, 2006,Alba Muisc Festival (Italy) 2008, Chamber Music Conference and Composers Forum of the East 2008, Fortnightly Musical Club Cleveland, 2006;Empyrean Ensemble, recordings included on Bang On A Can Live, Vol 2, the focus of blue light, Dark Fires, Telling Tales, the promise of the far horizon & Bachmann to Music. **Business Addr:** Composer, Carlson & Carlson Arts Contarctors, Lorain County Community College, 10208 Lake Gardens Dr, Dallas, TX 75218.

MUMFORD, THADDEUS QUENTIN
Television producer, writer. **Personal:** Born Feb 8, 1951, Washington, DC. **Educ:** Hampton Univ, attended 1969; Fordham Univ, attended 1971. **Career:** Twentieth Century Fox, Los Angeles CA, "MASH", writer & producer, 1979-83; Alien Prod, Los Angeles, CA, "ALF", writer & supv producer, 1986-87; "The Cosby Show", writer, 1986; Carsey-Werner, Studio City CA, "A Different World," writer & supv producer, 1987-88, head writer & co-exec producer, 1988-90; CBS Entertainment, "Bagdad Cafe," head writer & co-exec producer,1990; "Home Improv", 1991; Time Out: The Truth About HIV, AIDS & You, 1992; "Judging Amy", 2001. **Orgs:** Writers Guild Am, 1971-; Am Soc Composers, Artists & Performers, 1973-; Humanitas Comt, 1984; NAACP, 1984; Save the C, 1986-; Friends Friendless,1986-; Los Angeles Partnership Homeless, 1986-. **Honors/Awds:** Emmy Award, "The Electric Co", 1973; Writers Guild Award, "The Alan KingShow", 1974; Writers Guild Award, "MASH", 1979.

MUMPHREY, JERRY WAYNE
Baseball player. **Personal:** Born Sep 9, 1952, Tyler, TX; married Gloria; children: Tamara & Jerron. **Career:** Baseball player (retired); St Louis Cardinals, outfielder, 1974-79; San Diego Padres, outfielder, 1980; San Diego Padres, 1980; NY Yankees, outfielder, 1981-83; Houston Astros, outfielder, 1983-85; Chicago Cubs, outfielder, 1986-88. **Honors/Awds:** Nat League All-Star Team, 1984. **Special Achievements:** First professional baseball player to practice yoga.

MUNDAY, DR. CHERYL CASSELBERRY
Clinical psychologist, educator. **Personal:** Born Jan 20, 1950, Osaka, Japan; married Reuben Alexander Munday; children: Reuben Ahmed. **Educ:** Cornell Univ, BA, 1972; Univ Mich, MA, 1978, PhD, 1985. **Career:** Detroit Psychol Inst, dir psychol, pvt practice, Birmingham, MI; Sinai Hosp, consult/fac; Univ Detroit Mercy, asst prof, assoc prof psychol, currently. **Orgs:** Am Psychological Asn; Mich Psychological Asn. **Honors/Awds:** Represented UDM in March at the 14th Annual Equity in the Classroom Conference sponsored by the Michigan Dept of Labor with a presentation entitled "Cultural Competency in Psychology Professional and Graduate Education". **Special Achievements:** Co-author, "Differences in Patterns of Symptom Attribution in Diagnosing Schizophrenia Between African American and Non-African American Clinicians in the Journal of Orthopsychiatry, and "Clinician Race, Situational Attributions and Diagnoses of Mood Versus Schizophrenia Disorders" in the Cultural Diversity and Ethnic Minority Psychology. **Home Addr:** 18994 Birchcrest St, Detroit, MI 48221. **Business Addr:** Associate Professor in Psychology, University of Detroit Mercy, 725 S Adams Rd Suite 218, Birmingham, MI 48009-6947, **Business Phone:** (313)578-0518.

MUNDAY, REUBEN A
Lawyer. **Personal:** Born Mar 2, 1947, Orange, NJ. **Educ:** Cornell Univ, BA, 1971, MPS, 1974; Univ Mich, JD, 1976. **Career:** Cornell Univ, staff writer, 1972-74; Lewis & Munday Law Firm, atty, partner & shareholder, 1977-. **Orgs:** Detroit Bar Asn; Wolverine Bar Asn; life mem Nat Bar Asn; Am Bar Asn; bd dirs, Fund Detroits Future; bd dirs, City Detroit Bd Ethics, 2001-; bd dirs, St John Detroit Macomb Hosp Corp, Big Brothers Big Sisters Am, Leadership Detroit Prog Detroit Regional Chamber Com; bd dirs, Wyoming Sem Col Prep Sch. **Business Addr:** Partner, Attorney, Lewis & Munday Law Firm, 2490 First Nat Bldg, Detroit, MI 48226, **Business Phone:** (313)961-2550 Ext 103.

MUNOZ, ANTHONY
Football player, social worker. **Personal:** Born Aug 19, 1958, Ontario, CA; married DeDe; children: Michael & Michelle. **Educ:** Univ SC, BS, pub admin, 1980. **Career:** Football player (retired), social worker; Cincinnati Bengals, offensive tackle, 1980-93; Tampa Bay Buccaneers, 1993; Fox Sports, NFL Telecasts, color commentator, 1994-95; Anthony Munoz Found, founder, 2002-. **Orgs:** Crusade life; United Appeal; chmn, Billy Graham Mission, 2002. **Honors/Awds:** Man of the Year, Cincinnati Bengals, 1981; Lineman of the Year, Nat Football League, 1981; NFL Man of the Year in 1991; Pro Football Hall of Fame, 1998; Walter Payton Award, 2004. **Special Achievements:** Only Pro Football Hall of

Fame inductee in Cincinnati Bengals history. **Business Addr:** Founder, Anthony Munoz Foundation, Longworth Hall 700 W Pete Rose Way Suite 54, Cincinnati, OH 45203, **Business Phone:** (513)772-4900.

MUNROE, ANTHONY E
Chief executive officer. **Educ:** Excelsior Col, Albany, NY, Lib Arts; Columbia Univ, New York City, MA, pub health; Northwestern Univ, Evanston, IL busin admin. **Career:** Brookdale Hosp Med Ctr, Brooklyn, NY, adminr; pres & chief exec officer, Econ Opportunity Family Health Ctr, Miami, FL; St John Detroit Riverview Hosp, pres, 2003-05; St John Detroit Riverview Hosp, St John Health Syst, Warren, Mi, pres; Advocate Trinity Hosp, pres, 2005-; The Munroe Mgt Group, LLC, chmn & chief exec officer, currently. **Orgs:** Fel, ACHE; Memorial Sloan-Kettering Cancer Ctr; NY City Health & Hosps Corp; New York City Dept Health; dir Community Health Promotion, DeKalb County Bd Health, Decatur, GA. **Honors/Awds:** Robert S Hudgens Memorial Award, 2003; Upcomer of the Year, Am Col Healthcare Execs. **Special Achievements:** Recognition by Modern Healthcare magazine as one of the Top 25 Minority Executives in Healthcare in the United States, 2006. **Business Addr:** President, Advocate Trinity Hospital, 2320 E 93rd St, Chicago, IL 60617, **Business Phone:** (773)967-5017.*

MUNSON, CHERYL DENISE
Executive. **Personal:** Born Aug 3, 1954, Milwaukee, WI; daughter of John and Mattie Waldon. **Educ:** Univ Wis, Madison, WI, BA, jour, 1975. **Career:** Leo Burnett Advert, Chicago, IL, intern, 1975; Kloppenberg, Switzer & Teich Advert, Milwaukee, WI, writer/producer, 1976-80; Foote, Cone & Belding Advert, San Francisco, CA, copywriter, 1980-84; Love Auntie Cheryl Greetings Inc, San Francisco, CA, chief exec officer & founder, 1984; advert creative dir & insight & shopper mkt expert, currently. **Orgs:** Greeting Card Asn Am, 1985; Third Baptist Church, 1980-. **Honors/Awds:** Outstanding Business Woman, Governor, State Calif, 1989; Outstanding Alumnus, Univ Wis, 1984. **Business Phone:** (404)806-9211.

MUNSON, EDDIE RAY
Certified public accountant. **Personal:** Born Aug 4, 1950, Columbus, MS; son of Ray and Rosetta Moore; married Delores Butler, Jun 9, 1973; children: Eddie III & Derek. **Educ:** Jackson State Univ, BS, 1972. **Career:** Peat Marwick Main & Co, partner, 1972, audit partner, 1983; Bearingpoint Inc, chief financial officer, 2008-. **Orgs:** MS Soc CPAs, 1977-, Am Inst CPAs, 1980-, Mich Asn CPAs, 1980-; bd dir, Acct Aid Soc, 1984-, Black Family Develop Inc, 1984-, Boys & Girls Clubs, 1989-; bd dir, YMCA, Detroit, MI; bd dir, Urban League, Detroit, MI; Nat Asn Black Acct; dir, United Am Healthcare Corp. **Home Addr:** 5879 Murfield Dr, Rochester Hills, MI 48306, **Home Phone:** (313)357-4116. **Business Phone:** (248)430-3030.

MUNSON, ROBERT H
Engineer. **Personal:** Born Jan 15, 1931, Detroit, MI; married Shirley C Segars; children: Renee Angelique & Rochelle Alicia. **Educ:** Detroit Inst Technol, BS, 1966; Mich State Univ, MBA, 1977. **Career:** Ford Scientific Lab, metall engr, 1956; Ford Motor Co, mats design engr, sect supvr front end sect, bumper sect, body engineering office, dept mgr elec components lighting dept body & elec engineering office, exec engr paint corrosion & mats engineering body & elec engineering office, exec engr lighting bumpers & grills, exec engr advanced & pre-prog engineering, exec engr instrument panels & elec systs, chief engr N Am design, chief plastics engr plastics prods div, dir automotive safety office environ & safety engineering staff; Automotive Safety & Engineering Standards Office, exec dir, currently. **Orgs:** Am Soc Body Engineering; Am Metals Soc; Ford Col Recruiting Prog; Adv Bd Col Engineering, Univ Detroit; engineering sch sponsor, NC A&T State Univ; Engineering Soc Detroit, Soc Automotive Engrs; Motor Vehicle Safety Res, adv comt; life mem, NAACP. **Honors/Awds:** Blue Ribbon Award, Am Soc Metals, 1963; Congress & Exposition Detroit. **Special Achievements:** Co-author, [b5]A Modified Carbide Extraction Replica Technique in Transactions', Quart, 1963; [b5]Metallographis Examination of the Corrosion Mechanism of Plated Plastics', 1969; [b5]SAE Int Automotive Engr'; Air Bag Supplemental Restraint Systems: Progress to Date and Future Challenges. **Business Addr:** Executive Director, Automotive Safety Engineering Standards Office, 330 Town Ctr Dr Suite 400, Dearborn, MI 48126, **Business Phone:** (313)845-4320.

MURDOCK, ERIC LLOYD
Basketball player. **Personal:** Born Jun 14, 1968, Somerville, NJ. **Educ:** Providence Col. **Career:** Basketball player (retired); Utah Jazz, 1991-92; Milwaukee Bucks, guard, 1992-96; Vancouver Grizzlies, 1996; Fortitudo Bologna, Italy, 1996-97; Denver Nuggets, 1997; Miami Heat, 1997-98; NJ Nets, 1999; Los Angeles Clippers, guard, 2000; Virtus Bologna, 2002-03. **Orgs:** March Dimes, Blue Jeans For Babies; Bucks/YMCA Basketball Clin, Athletes For Youth Prog.

MURDOCK, DR. NATHANIEL H
Physician, college teacher, gynecologist. **Personal:** Born in Texas, TX. **Educ:** Howard Univ, Wash DC, BS, chem, 1958; Meharry Medical Col, Nashville, TN, MD. **Career:** Homer G. Phillips Hosp, St. Louis; Wash Univ, fac, 1969-; Barnes-Jewish Hosp, asst prof, currently. **Orgs:** Cent Eastern Missouri Prof Rev Org Comt; Missouri State Med Asn; Mound City Med Forum; St. Louis Gynec Soc; St. Louis Metrop Med Soc; past pres, Nat Med Asn. **Business Addr:** Assistant Professor, Obstetrics & Gynecology, Barnes-Jewish Hospital, One Barnes-Jewish Hosp Plaza Suite 16310 W Pavilion, St Louis, MT 63110, **Business Phone:** (314)361-0313.*

MURDOCK, PATRICIA GREEN
Educator, school administrator. **Personal:** Born Dec 12, 1949, Richmond, VA; daughter of William and Josephine Evelyn; married Hugh Murdock Jr; children: Elwin Michael, Patrice Michelle Cotman. **Educ:** Va Union Univ, BA, 1972; Va Commonwealth Univ, MSW, 1974; Am Univ, WA, DC, MSPR, 1980. **Career:** Va Union Univ, Richmond Va, dir practicum, dir urban studies, 1974-76; Nat Coun Negro Women-Opn Sisters United, Nat resource developer, nat dir, nat prog vol coordr, 1977-81; Women's Ctr & Shelter Greater Pittsburgh, community outreach cordr, 1983-87; Community Col Allegheny County, Pittsburgh, adj prof sociol, 1988-89; Partnerships in Educ, cordr, open doors, 1991; La Roche col, dir pub relations, adj prof, 1992-; Duquesne Univ, adj prof, 1995-. **Orgs:** Nat Coun Negro Women, pres, Pittsburgh secy, 1989-92; YWCA Nominating Comt, 1992; bd di, Am Wind Symphony Orchestra, 1992; bd dir, Myasthenia Gravis Asn Western Pa, 1991-; Pub Relations Soc Am, 1996; Pa Black Conf Higher Educ, 1993; bd dir, Beginning with Books, 1996. **Honors/Awds:** Pa Coun Arts, FAME Fellowship in Arts Mgt, 1989; Women in Communications, First Place Matrix Award, Annual Report category, 1987. **Special Achievements:** Co-authored a domestic violence training manual for nurses, 1986; co-authored National Council of Negro Women juvenile prevention article for "Vital Issues," 1978; Western Regional Committee Chair, Dr Martin Luther King Jr Youth Assembly, 1993. **Business Phone:** (412)536-1272.*

MURFREE, DR. JOSHUA, JR.
Civil rights activist. **Career:** Chairman of the Dept. of Psychology , Sociology, and Social Work, Albany State University; Center for the African-American Male, Director; Albany State University, Executive Assistant to the President, Administrative Chief of Staff, and Director of Athletics. **Orgs:** Vice Chairman of Programs, 100 Black Men of America; Advisory Group Member, RIF (Reading is Fundamental) Multicultural Literacy Campaign. **Home Addr:** 008830. *

MURPHY, CALVIN JEROME
Basketball player, radio host. **Personal:** Born May 9, 1948, Norwalk, CT; married Vernetta; children: 3. **Educ:** Niagara Univ, NY, attended 1970. **Career:** Basketball player (retired), radio host; Purple Eagles, 1967-68; San Diego Rockets, guard, 1970-71; Houston Rockets, guard, 1971-83, 1976-77, television broadcaster, currently;; ESPN, The Calvin Murphy Show, host, currently. **Orgs:** Conn Coaches Assn. **Honors/Awds:** NBA All-Rookie Team, 1971; NBA All-Star Game, 1979; Connecticut Coaches Association Hall of Fame; Connecticut Sportswriters Gold Key Award; Naismith Memorial Basketball Hall of Fame, 1993; NBA All-Rookie Team 1971, NBA All-Star 1979. **Special Achievements:** Used his voice as a color commentator for Play Station NBA Live, 2003. **Business Phone:** (713)266-1000.

MURPHY, DR. CHARLES A
Surgeon. **Personal:** Born Dec 29, 1932, Detroit, MI; son of Charles L and Hazel C Robinson; married Sandra Marie Scott, Jul 17, 1971; children: Charles A III. **Educ:** Wayne State Univ, attended 1953; Col Osteopathic Med & Surg, DO, 1957; Flint Osteopathic Hosp, internship, 1958. **Career:** Martin Place Hosp, chief staff, 1964-65; Art Ctr Hosp, chief staff, 1971-73; Detroit Police Dept, sr police surgeon, 1977-79; Calif Murphy DO PC, physician surgeon, 1958; Mich State Univ Col Osteop Med, clin prof, 1973. **Orgs:** Psi Sigma Alpha, 1955; Mich Osteop Med Ctr, 1972-87; House Delelgate Am Osteop Asn, 1975-89; Mich Osteop Asn, 1977; pres, Wayne Co Osteop Asn, 1977-79; Omnicare Health Plan Org, 1978-98; Mich Osteop Asn, 1981-89; Mich Peer Rev Org, 1985; Osteop Rep Central Peer Rev Comn Mich Dept Health; pres, Mich Asn Osteop Physicians & Surgeons, 1987.

MURPHY, CHARLES WILLIAM
Insurance executive. **Personal:** Born Dec 6, 1929, Kinston, NC; son of Edgar D Sr and Blanche Burden; married Geneva McCoy, Aug 9, 1954; children: Charles Jr, Donald Seth, Deanna Faye, Bryan Keith. **Educ:** NC Agr & Tech State Univ, Greensboro, NC, BS, bioscience & chem, 1954; Butler Univ, Indianapolis, IN, 1969. **Career:** City-County Govt, Indianapolis, IN, mgt analyst, 1974-75; Indianapolis Life Ins Co, Indianapolis, IN, vpres off admin, 1975-89. **Orgs:** Personnel dir, Indianapolis Chap Admin Mgt Soc, 1975-80; life mem, Indianapolis Chap Nat Asn Advan Colored People, 1979-; Zeta Phi Chapter, Omega Psi Phi Fraternity, 1979-81; exec comt, Admin Serv Comm Life Off Mgt Asn, 1979-90; Indianapolis Education Adv Coun, 1983-85; Econ Develop Comm, Indianapolis Chap Urban League, 1984-87; bd trustees, N United Methodist Church, 1985-89; Ind Minority Supplier Develop Coun, 1985-90; vol action ctr, United Way Bd, 1988-; exec comt, Interfaith Housing Bd, 1988-92; chair, Nat Urban League Conf, Minority Vendors Showcase, 1994. **Honors/Awds:** Achievement in Military, NC A&T State Univ, 1974; Advan Minority Enterprises, Minority Supplier Develop Coun, 1987, Achievement in Business, Ctr Leadership Develop, 1988; Citizen of the Year, Indianapolis Chap, Omega Psi Phi Fraternity, 1994. **Military Serv:** AUS, lt col, 1954-74. **Home Addr:** 412 Shallow Brook Dr, Columbia, SC 29223-8114. *

MURPHY, CLYDE EVERETT
Lawyer. **Personal:** Born Jun 26, 1948, Topeka, KS; son of Everett E; married G Monica Jacobs; children: Jamal Everett, Akua Edith & Naima Lorraine. **Educ:** Yale Col New Haven, BA, 1970; Columbia Univ, Sch Law, NY, JD, 1975. **Career:** Kings Co Addictive Disease Hosp, asst dir, 1970-72; Columbia Univ, Sch Law, Charles Evans Hughes fel, 1973-75; Vassar Col, lectr, 1981-84; Nat Asn Advan Colored People Legal Defense & Educ Fund Inc, asst coun, 1975-90, dep-dir coun, 1990-95; Chicago Lawyers' Comt Civil Rights Under Law Inc, exec dir, 1995-. **Business Addr:** Executive Director, Chicago Lawyers Committee for Civil Rights Under Law Inc, 100 N LaSalle St Suite 600, Chicago, IL 60602, **Business Phone:** (312)630-9744 Ext 232.

MURPHY, DANIEL HOWARD
Marketing executive. **Personal:** Born Aug 13, 1944, Washington, DC; son of John Henry and Alice Adeline Quivers; married Bernadette Francine Brown, Feb 15, 1969; children: Brett Nicole & Lynn Teresa. **Educ:** Wharton Sch, Univ Pa, Philadelphia, Pa, BS, econs, 1962-66. **Career:** McCormick Spice Co, Baltimore, Md, proj supvr mkt res, 1966-70; Gen Foods, White Plains, New York, brand research supvr, 1970-73; Hunt Wesson Foods, Fullerton, Calif, prod res mgr, 1973-76; RJ Reynolds Tobacco Co, Winston-Salem, NC, bd res mgr, 1976-80, brand mgr, 1980-85, sr group mkt res mgr, 1985-. **Orgs:** Bd dirs, Winston-Salem Tennis Inc, 1986-; grammateus, Sigma Pi Phi Fraternity, 1986-; bd mem, YMCA, Winston Lake, 1988-; Alpha Phi Alpha Fraternity, 1990-. **Home Addr:** 321 Stanaford Rd, Winston-Salem, NC 27104, **Home Phone:** (336)765-8407. **Business Addr:** Senior Manager of Communications Research, RJ Reynolds Tobacco Co, Business Information Department, 401 N Main St, Winston-Salem, NC 27102, **Business Phone:** (336)741-5000.

MURPHY, DR. DONALD RICHARD
Lawyer. **Personal:** Born Aug 1, 1938, Johnstown, PA; married Carol Handy; children: Steven, Michael & Richard. **Educ:** Wilberforce Univ, BA, econ, 1960; New York Law Sch, JD, 1969. **Career:** IBM Corp, acct supvr, 1963-66; Chem Bank NY, oper mgr, 1966-69; Soc Nat Bank, vpres, 1969-73; Sherwin Williams Co, staff atty & asst dir labor rel, 1973-83; Forest City Enterprises Inc, atty, currently. **Orgs:** EEO Sub Comt, Am Bar Asn, 1974-; bd dir, Health Hill Hosp, 1970-78; bd trustees, United Way Serv, 1980-; Cleveland Comn OH Fund Independent Col, 1970-; Cuyahoga City Bar Asn, 1972-; adv mem, United Negro Col Fund, 1974-82. **Honors/Awds:** Distinguished Service Award, Wilberforce Univ, 1972; Outstanding Alumnus of Year, Wilberforce Univ, 1972. **Special Achievements:** First Black recruited for IBM Management and Training Course in 1963. **Military Serv:** AUS, 1st lt, 1959-62; Grad Army, Adj Gen Sch, 1960. **Business Addr:** Attorney, Forest City Enterprises Inc, 10800 Brookpark Rd, Cleveland, OH 44130-1199, **Business Phone:** (216)267-1200.

MURPHY, EDDIE (EDWARD REGAN MURPHY)
Singer, comedian, actor. **Personal:** Born Apr 3, 1961, Brooklyn, NY; son of Charles and Lillian Murphy Lynch; married Tracey Edmonds, Jan 1, 2008; married Nicole Mitchell, Mar 18, 1993 (divorced 2006); children: Bria, Myles Mitchell, Shayne Audra, Zola Ivey & Bella Zahra. **Educ:** Nassau Community Coll. **Career:** Stand-up comedian, 1978-; Panda Merchandising, owner, currently; TV:Saturday Night Live, cast mem, 1980-84; The PJs, 1999; The Jeffersons, voice, 2000; Robbin' HUD, voice, 2000; The Last Affirmative Action Hero, voice, 2000; Shrek the Halls, voice, 2007; Clip Show, voice, 2008; films: 48 Hours, 1982; Trading Places, 1983; Best Defense, 1984; Beverly Hills Cop, 1985; The Golden Child, 1986; Beverly Hills Cop II, 1987; Eddie Murphy Raw, 1987; Coming to Am, 1988; Another 48 Hours, 1990; Harlem Nights, 1990; Boomerang, 1992; Beverly Hills Cop III, 1994; Vampire in Brooklyn, 1995; The Nutty Prof, 1996; Metro, 1997; Dr Doolittle, 1998; Holy Man, 1998; Mulan, 1998; Bowfinger, 1999; Life, 1999; Nutty Prof II:The Klumps, 2000; Shrek, 2001; Dr Doolittle 2, 2001; Showtime, 2002; The Adventures of Pluto Nash, 2002; I Spy, 2002; Daddy Daycare, 2003; Haunted Mansion, 2003; Shrek 2, 2004; The Incredible Shrinking Man, 2005;Dreamgirls, 2006; Norbit, 2007; Shrek the Third, 2007; Shrek the Halls, 2007; Meet Dave, 2008; Imagine That, 2009; film actor & dir: Harlem Nights, 1990; comedy albums: Eddie Murphy, 1982; Eddie Murphy: Comedian, 1983; music album: How Could It Be, 1984; So Happy, 1989; Love's Alright, 1993; appeared in Michael Jackson's video, Remember the Times, 1992; Writer:Saturday Night Live, 1982-84; Eddie Murphy Delirious, 1983; Beverly Hills Cop II, 1987; Eddie Murphy Raw, 1987; Another 48 Hrs, 1990; Boomerang, 1992; Vampire in Brooklyn, 1995; The PJs, 1999; Norbit, 2007; Producer:Eddie Murphy Delirious, 1983; Eddie Murphy Raw, 1987; What's Alan Watching", 1989; The Royal Family, 1991; Vampire in Brooklyn, 1995; Life, 1999; Nutty Professor II: The Klumps, 2000; Norbit, 2007; Dir: Harlem Nights, 1989. **Honors/Awds:** Emmy Award nomina-

tion for outstanding comedy performance and outstanding comedy writing, for Saturday Night Live; Grammy Award nomination for best comedy album, 1982; Image Award, NAACP, 1983; Golden Globe Foreign Press Award, 1983; Grammy Award for best comedy album, 1984; Golden Globe Award nomination for best actor, 1985; Star of the Year Award, 1985; People's Choice Award, 1985; Saturn Award, Acad Sci Fiction, Fantasy & Horror Films, 1997; Natl Soc of Film Critics, Best Actor, The Nutty Prof, 1996; Blockbuster Entertainment Award, 1997; NSFC Award, Nat Soc Film Critics Awards, USA, 1997; Annie Awards, 2001; People's Choice Award, Best Motion Picture Star in a Comedy, 2002; Critics Choice Award, Broadcast Film Critics Asn, 2007; COFCA Award, Cent Ohio Film Critics Asn, 2007; Golden Globe Award, 2007; Blimp Award, Kids Choice Awards USA, 2008.

MURPHY, HARRIET LOUISE M.
Judge, educator, lawyer. **Personal:** Born in Atlanta, GA; married Patrick H; children: Charles Wray. **Educ:** Spelman Col, AB, 1949; Atlanta Univ, attended 1952; Johns Hopkins Sch, attended 1954; Univ Tex Law Sch, JD, 1969; Univ Gratz, Austria, 1971. **Career:** Educator, judge (retired), lawyer; Fulton Co, GA, high sch teacher, 1949-54; Southern Univ, teacher, 1954-56; Prairie View A&M Univ, teacher, 1956-60; Womack Sr High, high sch teacher, 1960-66; Houston- Tillotson Col, prof gov, 1967-78; US State Dept Adv Coun African Affairs, 1970-72; State Tex, goodwill ambassador, 1976; City Austin, assoc judge, 1978-88, presiding judge, 1988-94; pvt pract lawyer, currently. **Orgs:** Delta Sigma Theta Sorority, 1964-; bd mem, Greater Austin Coun Alcoholism, 1970-93; Links Inc, 1982; bd mem, Judicial Coun Nat Bar Asn; bd mem, Tex Munic Ct Found; Nat Bar Asn; Tex Bar Asn; Austin Black Lawyers Asn; J Travis Co Women Lawyers Asn; Travis County Bar Asn; financial secy, Judicial Coun; financial secy bd, Habitat Humanity; Int Hosp Coun Austin; Gender Bias Implementation Task Force; Munic Ct Found; Austin Black Lawyers Asn; Travis Co Women Lawyers Asn. **Honors/Awds:** Outstanding Sorority Woman, Delta Sigma Theta Sorority, 1974; U T Award, Thurgood Marshall Legal Soc, 1986; Distinguished Service Chairman's Award, Greater Austin Coun Alcoholism, 1990; Judicial Coun, 1987; De Witty Award Civil Rights, Austin Nat Asn Advan Colored People, 1989; Hall of Fame, Spelman Col, 1993; Hall of Fame, Nat Women Achievement, Austin Chap, 1996; National Meril Award, Spelman Col, 1999; Gertrude E. Rush Award, Nat BarAsn, 2003; Raymond Pace Alexander Award, Judicial Coun Nat Bar Asn, 2005. **Special Achievements:** First black woman to be appointed a permanent judge in Tex, 1974; First black woman democratic presidential elector for Tex, 1976; most outstanding class member, Spelman Col, 1984; selected as one of the 10 Legal Legends of Austin, TX, Travis County Bar Asn, 2001. **Home Addr:** 3638 Quictte Dr, Austin, TX 78754. **Business Addr:** Attorney, 6635 Greensboro Dr, Austin, TX 78723-3919.*

MURPHY, IRA H.
Lawyer. **Personal:** Born Sep 8, 1928, Memphis, TN; married Rubye L Meekins. **Educ:** Tenn State Univ, BS; City Col, NY; NY Univ, grad sch bus; NY Univ Sch Law, LLB, LLM. **Career:** Gen law prac, 1956-; Riverside San & Hosp Nashville, acct; Geeter HS, com teacher. **Orgs:** State Rep, 1986, 1987, 1988, 1989, 1990, & 1991st Gen Assembly; chmn, Labor Com House Rep 87th Gen Assembly; chmn, Jud Com House Rep, 1988, 1989, 1990 & 1991st Gen Assemby del Limited Constis Conv, 1971; Slpha Phi Alpha; Kappa Delta Pi; Elks; Masons; Shriners; past pres, 26 Ward Civic Club; former legal adv, Bluff City Coun Civic Clubs; legal adv, IBPOE W Tenn. **Military Serv:** AUS.

MURPHY, JOHN H, III
Executive. **Personal:** Born Mar 2, 1916, Baltimore, MD; son of Daniel H (deceased) and Sarah M Clements; married Alice Quivers, 1940 (died 1979); children: Sharon & Daniel; married Camay Calloway, 1980. **Educ:** Temple Univ, BS, 1937; Columbia Univ, Am Press Inst, 1952, 1971; Towson State Univ, DHL, 1984. **Career:** Wash Afro-Am, mgr, 1937-48, dir, 1946-67, asst bus mgr, 1948-61, pres, 1967-74, bd chmn & publ, 1974-86; Baltimore Times, photogr, 1987. **Orgs:** Churchman's Club; vestryman, St James Episcopal Church; adv bd, Morgan State Univ; Sch Bus, Morgan State Univ Cluster Prog, Sigma Pi Phi, Omega Psi Phi; bd mem,Amalgamated Publs Inc, Nat Newspaper Publ Asn, Counc Equal Bus Opportunity, Nat Aquarium Baltimore, Provident Hosp, Baltimore Sch Arts, Baltimore City Literacy Comn; Governor's Comn Crime Prev. **Honors/Awds:** City of Baltimore Citizen Award, 1977; Publisher of the Year Award, Univ DC, 1979; Father of the Year Award, Redeemer's Palace Baltimore MD, 1980; Certified MD Communication on Sickle Cell Anemia,1980; US Dept Commerce Award, 1980; Appreciation Award Race Relations Institution, Fisk Univ, 1981; Distinguished Citizens Public Service Award, Coppin State Col, 1983.

MURPHY, DR. JOHN MATTHEW, JR.
Dentist, executive. **Personal:** Born Mar 12, 1935, Charlotte, NC; son of John Matthew Sr and Elizabeth Benton; married Claudette Owens, Jan 3, 1983; children: Alicia Williams, Snowden Williams, John Matthew III & Brian Keith. **Educ:** Morgan State Col, BS, 1959; MeHarry Med Col Sch Dent, DDS, 1965; Va Hosp, cert, 1966. **Career:** Meharry Med Col Sch Dent, res assoc dept orthod, 1966; VA Ctr Dayton OH, staff dentist, 1967-70; Charles Drew Health Ctr Dayton, OH, clin dir dentistry, 1971-73; pvt pract, gen dentist, 1973-; Metrolina Urban Health Initiative, Charlotte NC, originator & co-founder, 1979. **Orgs:** Pres elect, Dayton Hosp Mgt Asn, 1970-73; fel Royal Soc Health, 1974-; bd trustees, Little Rock AME Zion Church, 1975-; Charlotte C C, 1975-; treas, Martin Luther King Mem Comn, 1976-; life mem, Nat Asn Advan Colored People, 1977-; life mem, Omega Psi Phi Fraternity, 1978-; coun comm chmn, Boy Scouts Am, 1978; Charlotte Bus League, 1979-; Sigma Pi Phi, 1980; fel Acad Gen Dentistry, 1980; NC Chap Guardsmen, 1983-; pres & founder, A J Williams Dent Study Club, 1985-. **Honors/Awds:** Scroll of Honor, Omega Psi Phi, 1970; Certificate of Appreciation, Boy Scouts Am, 1972. **Military Serv:** AUS, spec 4, 1959-61. **Business Addr:** Dentist, 1075 Gauguin Lane, Fort Mill, SC 29708, **Business Phone:** (803)333-2104.

MURPHY, LAURA W.
Association executive. **Personal:** Born Oct 3, 1955, Baltimore, MD; daughter of Judge William H and Madeline; divorced; children: Bertram M Lee Jr. **Educ:** Wellesley Col, AB, 1976. **Career:** Off Congressman, Parren Mitchell, legis asst, 1976-77; Off Congresswoman, Shirley Chisholm, legis asst, 1977-79; ACLU, legis rep, 1979-82, ACLU Found Southern Calif, dir develop & planning giving, 1983-84; Mixner Scott Inc, proj mgr, 1984-87; Assembly Speaker, Willie L Brown Jr, chief staff, 1986-87; Jesse Jackson Pres Campaign, nat finance dir, 1987-88; Fund-raising consult, 1988-90; Exec Off Mayor Sharon Pratt Kelly, mayor's tourism consult, 1990-92; DC Govt, Off Tourism, dir, 1992-93; Am Civil Liberties Union, Wash Legis Off, dir, 1993-. **Orgs:** DC Comt Promote Wash, acting chair, 1993-95; Leadership Conf Civil Rights, exec comt, 1993-; Pub Defenders Serv Wash, bd mem, 1993-95; numerous past memships. **Honors/Awds:** Congressional Black Caucus, William L Dawson Award, 1997; Mayor Sharon Pratt Kelly, Distinguished Public Service Award, 1994; Capital Entertainment Servs, Honorary Tour Guide DC, 1992; NAACP Legal Defense & Educ Fund Inc, Black Women Achievement Award, 1987; ACLU, Wash Off, Human Rights Award, 1982; State Md, Citation Public Service, 1980; numerous others. **Special Achievements:** First African American and first female director of ACLU. **Business Phone:** (202)546-0738.*

MURPHY, MARGARET HUMPHRIES
Government official, administrator. **Personal:** Born in Baltimore, MD; married Arthur G (deceased); children: Terry M Bailey, Arthur G Jr & Lynn M Press. **Educ:** Coppin State Col, BS, 1952, ME; Morgan State Col. **Career:** Baltimore City Pub Sch, teacher, 1952-78, educ asn, 1978-; Md State, deleg, 1978-95. **Orgs:** Pub Sch Teachers Asn, 1952-; Md St Teachers Asn, 1952-; Nat Educ Asn; Nat Asn Advan Colored People; Lambda Kappa Mu; Red Cross; secy, Leg Black Caucus; treas, Orgn Women Legislators; Delta Sigma Theta; Forest Park Neighborhood Asn; chmn, Baltimore City Health Sub-Comm; bd mem, Threshold Inc.

MURPHY, MICHAEL MCKAY
Executive. **Personal:** Born Aug 13, 1946, Fayetteville, NC; son of Charles L Murphy (deceased) and Eleanor McKay Murphy (deceased); married Gwendolyn Ferguson; children: L Mark. **Educ:** St Louis Univ, BS, commerce, 1968. **Career:** John Hancock Insurance Co, life underwriter, 1968-71; Ford Motor Co, bus mgt specialist, 1971-75; Dunkin Donuts, purchasing mgr, 1975-79, dir quality control beginning, 1979-, dir consumer affairs; Renewal Inc, pres. **Orgs:** Zeta Kappa Sigma Chapter, 1988-89; clerk, Canton, MA Bd Health, 1996; pres, Phi Beta Sigma Fraternity, Inc; past pres, Blue Hill Civic Asn; Nat Restaurant Asn. **Honors/Awds:** Governor's Coun, Republican, elected, 1990; Congressional Candidata, MA Dist 9, 1994. **Business Addr:** President, Renewal Inc, 100 Boylston St No 300, Boston, MA 02116, **Business Phone:** (617)338-1904.

MURPHY, PAULA CHRISTINE
Librarian. **Personal:** Born Dec 15, 1950, Oberlin, OH; daughter of Paul Onieal and Vivian Chiquita Lane. **Educ:** Rosary Col Dominican Univ, River Forest, IL, BA, 1973; Dominican Univ, Sch Libr Sci, MALS, 1975; Northern Ill Univ, Dekalb, IL, MA, 1982. **Career:** Chicago Pub Libr, Chicago, IL, libr I, 1974-76; Gov's Libr State Univ, Univ Park, IL, circulation/media librarian, 1976-80; Columbia Col Libr, Chicago, IL, head audiovisual servs, 1980-89; Loyola Univ Libraries, Chicago, IL, head audiovisual servs, 1989-96; Dominican Univ, head access servs, 1996-98; Univ Pittsburgh Semester At Sea, 1998; Chicago Hist Soc, Research Serv, libr, 1998-03; Paula Murphy Consult, 2003-. **Orgs:** Am Libr Asn Divs & Roundtables, 1974-; Ill Libr Asn, 1975-80; Black Caucus Am Libr Asn, 1987-;treasurer, Jr Members Roundtable Am Libr Asn, 1980-82; chair, arts sect, Asn Col & Res Libraries Am Libr Asn, 1989-90; exec bd mem, Am Film & Video Asn, 1992-95; chair, ACRL New Publs Adv Bd, 1993-95; chair, ACRL Arts Dance Subcommittee Inter libr Loan Video, 1994-96; Ala Elections Comt, 1994-96; chair, Video Roundtable, Am Lib Asn, 1997-98; chair, ACRL Arts Dance Comt, 1999-02; chair, ACRL Arts Standards Comt, 2001-04. **Honors/Awds:** Elected to Membership in Beta Phi Mu, 1973; 3M/JMRT Professional Development, 3M Company and JMRT; Grant, American Library Association, 1977; African-American Women's Achievement Award, African-Am Alliance, 1989; Speaker, Art Libraries Soc NA & Consortium Col & Univ Media Ctrs, 1986, 1989; Judge, Am Film Festival, 1989-92; Speaker, Charleston Conference on Book & Serial Acquisitions, 1991; Nat Conf African Am Librns, 1994; Speaker 6th Biennial Symposium of Arts and Technology, 1997. **Special Achievements:** Author "Visual Literacy, Libraries & Community Development in Collection Building," March 1981; Films for the Black Music Researcher in Black Music Research Journal, Center for Black Music Research, 1987; "Documentation of Performance Art," Coll and Research Libraries News, Apr 1992; "Audio Visual Services for the Performing Arts Programs at Columbia Coll, Chicago," in Performing Arts Resources, Vol 15, 1990; Senior Advisory Viewing Race Project, 1997-; contributor, Int Dictionary of Modern Dance, 1998; "What Classroom Teachers Should Know About Using Interactive Multi Media Materials," Media Horizons, vol 13, Spring 1997; grant panelist, Nat Initiative to Preserve America's Dance, 1998-02; speaker, Am Libr Asn Conf, 2000; speaker, Dancing in the Millenium Conf, 2000; contributor, Amer Women Writers; advisor, Nat Video Resources Viewing Races project; speaker, 5th Nat African Am Librarians Conf, 2002. *

MURPHY, RAYMOND M.
State government official. **Personal:** Born Dec 13, 1927, St Louis, MO; married Lynette; children: Clinton, Krystal, Leslie, Raymond, Anita, James, Brandon & Alicia. **Educ:** Detroit Inst Tech, Wayne State Univ, attended. **Career:** Michigan State House of Representatives, state rep, 1983-98. **Orgs:** Mem Nat Black Caucus State Legislators; lifetime mem NAACP; imperial grandcncl Ancient Arabic Orders; Nobles the Mystic Shrine; mem MI Legislative Black Caucus; exec bd mem Detroit Transit Alternative; mem Metro Elks Lodge; mem Eureka Temple No 1; Lions Club; Optimist Club. **Honors/Awds:** Legislator of the Year Minority Women Network, 1987. **Home Addr:** 610 Chicago Blvd, Detroit, MI 48202.

MURPHY, ROMALLUS O.
Lawyer, educator. **Personal:** Born Dec 18, 1928, Oakdale, LA; son of Jimmy and Mary Celeste Collins; married Gale L Bostic; children: Natalie, Kim, Romallus Jr, Lisa, Verna & Christian. **Educ:** Howard Univ, BA, 1951; Univ NC, JD, 1956. **Career:** Pvt law pract, 1956-62; Erie Human Rel Comn, exec dir, 1962-65; Mitchell & Murphy, 1965-70; Mayor's Comm Rel Comt, exec secr, 1968; Shaw Univ, spec asst pres, 1968-70; Shaw Col Detroit, pres, 1970-82; NC State Conf Branches NAACP, gen coun; Gen pract emphasis civil rights; pvt pract, atty, 1983-. **Orgs:** Intermittent consult conciliator, 1966-69; Am Arbit Asn, Arbitrators & Community Dispute Settlement Panel; ACE; Am Asn Health Educ; NBL; NEA; Task Force Detroit Urban League Inc; Nat Asn Advan Colored People; bdmem, Metro Fund Inc; Cent Gov Bd & Educ Comn Model Neighborhood Agency; charter mem, Regional Citizens Inc; Greensboro Task Force One; bd mem; Good News Jail & Prison Ministry; trustee, sec trust bd, Shiloh Baptist Church; pres, Laymen's League Shiloh Baptist Church; Omega Psi Phi; bd mem, Greensboro Br Nat Asn Advan Colored People; Foreign Travel Int Community Agency; NC Asn Am Bar Asn; NC Black Lawyers Asn. **Honors/Awds:** Omega Man of the Year, 1968; Detroit Howardite for Year, Howard Univ Alumni, 1974; Educator of the Year, Gamma Phi Delta Sorority, 1975; Citizen of the Year Award, Omega Psi Phi, 1977; Tar Heel of the Week, NC; Community Service Award, Greensboro Br, Nat Asn Advan Colored People, 1985, William Robert Ming Advocacy Award, 1990. **Military Serv:** USAF, First Lt, 1951-53. **Business Addr:** Attorney, 1106 E Market St, PO Box 20383, Greensboro, NC 27405, **Business Phone:** (336)274-3785.

MURPHY, VANESSA
Fashion model. **Career:** Model. **Honors/Awds:** Ms Plus USA, 1997. **Business Addr:** Ms Plus USA 1997, Ms Plus USA Beauty Pageant, c/o Dimensions Plus, 551 36th St NW, Canton, OH 44709, **Business Phone:** (330)649-9809.

MURRAIN, GODFREY H
Lawyer. **Personal:** Born Mar 14, 1927, New York, NY; son of Walter Herbert and Ellouise Pearl Jones; married Peggy Gray; children: Michelle Pearl. **Educ:** Howard Univ, attended, 1948-49; New York Univ, BS, 1951; Brooklyn Law Sch, LLB, JD, 1955. **Career:** Treas Dept, IRS agt, 1953-58; Godfrey H Murrain Esq, atty coun, law tax consult advising & coun individual corp estates, 1958-. **Orgs:** Am Arbitration Asn; NY Co Lawyers Asn; Metrop Black Bar Asn; Nat Bar Asn; Am Civil Liberties Union; elder, Hollis Presbyterian Church; Task Force Justice Presbytery City NY; adv bd, Borough Manhattan Community Col, 1970; secy gen, coun, One Hundred Black Men Inc; bd trustees, Great Neck Libr; bd mem, Nat Asn Advan Colored People, Great Neck Manhasset Port Wash Br; Dept Disciplinary Comn, First Judicial Dept Supreme Ct, State NY; NY Surrogate's Ct Adv Comt; grand gammateus & exec sec, Grand Boule Sigma Pi Phi. **Honors/Awds:** One Hundred Black Men of New York Inc, hon mem, Bd Dirs. **Military Serv:** AUS, 1945-46. **Home Addr:** 240 Shoreward Dr, Great Neck, NY 11021. **Business Addr:** Attorney at Law, Godfrey H Murrain Esq, 225 Broadway Suite 3504, New York, NY 10007, **Business Phone:** (212)619-1250.

MURRAY, ALBERT L.
Educator, writer. **Personal:** Born May 12, 1916, Nokomis, AL; son of Hugh and Mattie; married Mozelle Menefee; children:

Michele. **Educ:** Tuskegee Inst, BS, 1939; NY Univ, MA, 1948; Tuskegee Univ, doctor letters, 1999; State Univ NY, 2000. **Career:** Tuskegee Inst, instr Engr, 1940-43, 1946-51; Colgate Univ, O'Connor, prof Eng, 1970; Emory Univ, writer res, 1978; Colgate, prof humanities, 1982; Barnard, adj prof writing 1981-83; Drew Univ, Woodrow Wilson Fellow 1983; Washington and Lee, Dupont visiting prof, 1993; lectr & partic, Symposia. Author:"Omni Americans," "South to A Very Old Place," "The Hero and the Blues," "Train Whistle Guitar," "Stomping the Blues," "The Spyglass Tree," 1991, "The Seven League Boots," "The Blue Devils of Nada," 1996; Lillian Smith Award for "Train Whistle Guitar," ASCAP Deems Taylor Award for "Stomping the Blues" 1977; "Good Morning Blues", The Autobiography of Count Basie as told by Albert Murray 1986; Spring Hill College, doctor of humane letters, 1996; Natl Book Critics Circle, Literature Achievement Award, 1997; AL Writer's Forum, Harper Lee Award for Literary Excellence, 1998; poetry: "From the Briarspatch File," "Conjugations and Reiterations," 2001. **Orgs:** Amer Academy of Arts and Letters, 1997; Amer Academy of Arts and Science, 1998. **Honors/Awds:** Alumni Merit Award, 1972; Lillian Smith Award, 1974; Deems Taylor Award ASCAP, 1976; Lincoln Ctr Dir Emeriti Award, 1991; Lit Achievement Award, Nat Book Critics Circle, 1997; Harper Lee Award, for Literary Excellence, Ala Writer's Forum, 1998; Litt.D, Colgate Univ, 1975; DHL, Spring Hill Col, 1996. **Military Serv:** USAF major, 1943-1962. **Home Addr:** 45 W 132nd St, New York, NY 10037. *

MURRAY, ALBERT R
Law enforcement officer. **Personal:** Born Jan 25, 1946, Ripley, TN; son of Rossie G and Pearl L; married Connie Graffread, Aug 31, 1969; children: Andrea & Camille. **Educ:** Tenn State Univ, Nashville, TN, BS, eng, 1969; Middle Tenn State Univ, Murfreesboro, TN, MA, educ, 1973; Tenn Govt Exec Inst, grad, 1988. **Career:** Spencer Youth Ctr, Nashville, TN, counr, 1970-76; Tenn Youth Ctr, Nashville, TN, asst supt, 1976-81, supt, 1981-; Tenn Dept C Servs, Nashville, TN, asst comnr; Kans Juvenile Justice Authority, comnr, 1997-2003; Ala Dept Corrections, dep comnr prog, 2003-; Ga Dept Juvenile Justice, comnr, 2004-. **Orgs:** Phi Beta Sigma Fraternity, 1968-; Govs Adv Coun Voc Ed, 1984; bd Mgrs, YMCA, 1987-; auditor, Am Correctional Asn, 1988-; bd Govs, Tenn Correctional Asn, 1990. **Home Addr:** 109 Bella Ct, Nashville, TN 37207, **Home Phone:** (615)865-6054. **Business Addr:** Commissioner, Georgia Department of Juvenile Justice, 3408 Covington Hwy, Decatur, GA 30032, **Business Phone:** (404)508-6500.

MURRAY, ANNA MARTIN
Educator. **Personal:** Born Oct 31, 1910, Birmingham, AL; married Willie Alca (deceased). **Educ:** AL State Col, BS, 1952; Samford Univ, Cert Early Childhood Educ, 1975; The CA Inst Metaphysics, 1952; George Peabody Col; A&M Univ, attended 1964. **Career:** Educator (retired); St Clair Bd Educ, teacher, 1944-46; Birmingham City Bd Educ, teacher, 1947-72; Helping Hand Day Care, teacher, 1976-77; Birmingham City Bd Educ, substitute teacher, 1977-87. **Orgs:** Ultra Modern Club, 1930-87; Gamma Phi Delta Alpha Mu Chap, 1968-; vpres, Deaconess Bd Macedonia Baptist Church, 1970-85; sec, Alert Professional Club, 1980-85; sec, Tyree Chap 77 OES, 1981-85; AL Retired Teachers Assoc Montgomery AL; Am Assoc Retired Persons Long Beach CA; Nat Ed Assoc WA DC; Fraternal OES, Alert Twelve Profl, Alpha Mu Gamma Phi Delta Sor; Macedonia Missionary Baptist Church, Ensley, AL. **Honors/Awds:** Meritorious Service Award, Birmingham Educ Assn, 1973; New verses in American Poetry, Vantage Press NY, 1976; Inspiration from a Save in Action Vantage Press NY, 1977; Award Nat Black Women's Polit Leadership Caucus, 1978; Meritorious Service Award Field Jour, 1980; Dipl The Inst Mentalphysics; Outstanding Service Award, Supreme Chap Zeta Phi Lambda Sor, 1983. **Special Achievements:** "From A Soul In Action", author.

MURRAY, CALVIN D.
Baseball player. **Personal:** Born Jul 30, 1971, Dallas, TX; married Kelli Nichols, Nov 30, 1996. **Educ:** Univ Tex, Austin. **Career:** Baseball player (retired); San Francisco Giants, outfielder, 1999-02; TexRangers, 2002; Chicago Cubs, outfielder, 2004. *

MURRAY, CECIL LEONARD
Clergy. **Personal:** Born Sep 26, 1929, Lakeland, FL; son of Edward W and Minnie Lee; married Bernadine Cousin, Jun 25, 1958; children: Drew David. **Educ:** Fla A & M Univ, BA, 1951; Sch Theology, Claremont, Doctor Religion, 1964. **Career:** Clergy (retired); USF, captain, Jet Radar interceptor & Navigator; First African Methodist Episcopal Church, sr minister. **Orgs:** gen bd, African Methodist Episcopal Church, 1972-92; gen bd, Nat Coun Churches, 1972-92; Alpha Phi Alpha Fraternity, 1948-; NCP; Southern Christian Leadership Conf; CORE; Urban League; United Nations Asn, USA; gen bd, Nat Coun Aging, 1988-93. **Honors/Awds:** Ralph Bunche Peace Prize Award, United Nations Asn, 1992; Alpha Man of the Year, Alpha Phi Alpha, 1951; Daniel Alexander Payne Award, African Methodist Epicopal Church, 1992; Community Achievement Award, NCP, Los Angeles, 1986; Outstanding Role Model, Nat Asn Univ Women, 1992. **Special Achievements:** Sermon in "Dreams of Fire," compendium of sermons after Los Angeles riots; named by PRS George Bush: 177th Point of Light, First AME Church; Excerpts in Time Mag, Wall St J, BBC, CNN. **Military Serv:** USAFR, maj, 1951-61; Soliders Medal Heroism, 1958. *

MURRAY, DESMOND. See ADEYEMI, BAKARI.

MURRAY, EDDIE CLARENCE
Baseball player, athletic coach. **Personal:** Born Feb 24, 1956, Los Angeles, CA; son of Charles and Carrie. **Educ:** California State Univ, Los Angeles, attended. **Career:** Baseball player (retired), athletic coach; Baltimore Orioles, infielder, 1977-88, 1996; Los Angeles Dodgers, infielder, 1989-91, 1997, bench coach, hitting coach, 2006-07; NY Mets, infielder, 1992-93; Cleveland Indians, 1994-96; Anaheim Angels, 1997. **Orgs:** United Cerebral Palsy; Sickle Cell Anemia; Am Red Cross; United Way; Johns Hopkins C's Ctr; New Holiness Refuge Church & Pk Heights Acad; Proj 33. **Honors/Awds:** American League Rookie of the Year, Baseball Writers' Asn Am, 1977; Am League All-Star Team, 1978, 1981-86, 1991; New Holiness Refuge Church & Pk Heights Acad which dedicated a classroom in his honor; Golden Glove Award, 1982, 1983, 1984; Baseball Hall of Fame, 2003. **Special Achievements:** Named first baseman on The Sporting News Am League All-Star fielding teams, 1982-84; named first baseman on The Sporting News Am League Silver Slugger teams, 1983, 1984.

MURRAY, EDNA MCCLAIN
Educator, association executive, businessperson. **Personal:** Born Jan 2, 1918, Idabel, OK; daughter of Swingley Lee Moore and Ruberda Lenox Moore; married Mar 31, 1938 (widowed); children: Ruby J McClain Ford, Jacquelyn McClain Crawford (deceased). **Educ:** Roosevelt Univ, BA; Chicago State Univ, MEd; admin & coun & human rels. **Career:** Ru-Jac Charm Center & Beauty Shop, Chicago Ill, owned & operated, 1948-59; Chicago Bd educ, sch teacher, 1959-, Learning Disabilities, resource teacher, 1974-95, Teacher Corp unit leader, 1970-71; Chicago State Univ, guest lecturer; Short Stop Restaurant, co-owner. **Orgs:** Nat Sorority Phi Delta Kappa; nat supreme grammateus sorority, 1979-83; basileus, Local Chap, 1968-72, bd, exec coun, nat exec secy; organizer, Chicago Chap; Top Ladies Distinction; nat officer, local pres, TLOD; Chicago Psychological Club; Nat Advan Asn Colored People; United Negro Col Fund; Nat Coun Negro Women; Urban League; bd, exec coun, Chicago Africa TCR Asn; Phidelka Found; MIC Ave Block Club; Mich Ave Condo Bd; voting del, Chicago Teachers Union; Phi Delta Kappa Nat Sorority, exec secy, 1982-92. **Honors/Awds:** Woman of the Year, Chicago Daily Defender, 1966; Outstanding 100 Black Women, Copin Church, 1986; Woman of the Year, Top Ladies Distinction, 1981; Senior Citizens Hall of Fame, Mayor Wash, 1987; Special Honor & Recognition, Women's History Month, 1988; Outstanding Achievements, Chicago Asst Prin Asn, 1990; Educator of the Year Award, Phi Delta Kappa, Chicago State Univ, Chap Ed-320, 1991. **Special Achievements:** Pioneer, African women as own & operator, Ru-Jac Charm Ctr & Beauty Shop, 1948-59.

MURRAY, GARY S., SR.
Computer executive, manager, business owner. **Educ:** Howard Univ, B.B.A. **Career:** Falcon Microsystems, Chief Operating Officer; Sylvest Mgt Syst Corp, vpres; Integrated Spatial Inform Solutions, chmn & bd dir, 2003; Greater Washington Board of Trade, Bd mem; Maryland Science Center, Bd mem; Hi-Tech Council of Prince George's County, founder; Greater Prince George's Business Round table, founding chr; Bio Tech Institute, Univ Md, Bd mem; Greater Washington Board of Trade Mem. Pappas Commission; Human Vision LLC, founder & managing dir, currently. **Honors/Awds:** Executive of the Year, Bus Gazette, 2003; Business Gazette Newspaper Executive of the Year, 2004; Economic Development Association Volunteer of the Year, 2005. **Business Phone:** (301)577-3300.*

MURRAY, J RALPH
Insurance executive. **Personal:** Born Oct 4, 1931, Manatee, FL; married Alaine; children: James, Janmarie & Jodi. **Educ:** BS, 1960. **Career:** Am Cyanamid Co Res Labs; Travelers Ins Co, 1967; Ins & Financial Serv Inc, owner, currently. **Orgs:** Bd finance, dir, Liberty Nat Bank, City Stamford, 1970; SW CT Life Underwriters Asn; bd dirs, St Lukes Infant Child Care; former ch, bd trustees, Congregational Ch; Secy, Stamford Ctr Arts, currently. **Honors/Awds:** Travelers Inner Circle Award, 1970; Outstanding Political Service Award, Afro-Am Club, 1972; Civic Award, Planning Bd City Stamford, 1970. **Military Serv:** AUS, 1952-54. **Business Addr:** Owner, Insurance & Financial Services Inc, 832 Bedford St, Stamford, CT 06901, **Business Phone:** (203)359-1326.

MURRAY, JAMES HAMILTON
Educator, dentist. **Personal:** Born Nov 22, 1933, Washington, DC; married Joan; children: Christina, Michelle. **Educ:** Howard Univ, BS, 1956; Meharry Med Col, DDS, 1960; Jersey City Med Ctr, rotating dental internship, 1961; Johns Hopkins Sch Hygiene & Pub Health, MPH, 1969. **Career:** Educator, dentist (retired); VIR Pub Health Dept, clin dentist, 1964-68; Howard Univ Col Dent, Dept Prosthodontics, asst prof, 1964-68; Howard Univ Col Dentistry, Dept Community Dent, asst prof, 1968-69; Shaw Community Health Proj, Nat Med Asn Found, dent dir, 1969-70; Matthew Walker Health Ctr, Meharry Med Col, proj dir; Dept Family & Community Health, prof, 1970-71; Dept Health Educ & Welfare Family Health Serv, Rockville MD, health adminr, 1972-74; Dept Human Resource Comt Health & Hosp Admin, Washington, DC, 1974-75; Howard Univ Col Dent, Dept Clin Dent, assoc prof, 1975-92. **Orgs:** Nat Dent Asn; Am Soc Dent C; Am Acad Gen Dent; Am Pub Health Asn; Am Dent Asn; Urban League; secy, Am Pub Health Asn, 1974-75; fel Am Col Dentists; fel Acad Gen Dent; fel Acad Dent Int. **Honors/Awds:** Award, Am Soc Dent C, 1960; Award for Clinical Dentistry, Nashville Dent Supply Co, 1960; US Public Health Traineeship Grant, 1968-69; DC Dental Soc Award, 1969; Dental Alumnus of the Year, Meharry Med Col, 1970-71; Honorary Dental Society Award, Omicron Kappa Upsilon, 1960. **Special Achievements:** Published articles for dental journals. **Military Serv:** USAF, capt, 1961-63. **Home Addr:** 1433 Locust Rd NW, Washington, DC 20012.

MURRAY, JAMES P
Executive, manager. **Personal:** Born Oct 16, 1946, Bronx, NY; son of Eddie and Helena; married Mary; children: Sean Edward, Sherron Anita & Angela Dawn. **Educ:** Syracuse Univ, BA, 1968. **Career:** White Plains Reporter Dispatch, copy ed, 1968; ABC-TV News, news trainee, 1968-71; Western Electric Co, pub relations assoc, 1971-72; freelance writer, 1972-73; NY Amsterdam News, arts & entertainment ed, 1973-75; Nat Broadcasting Co, press rep, 1975-83; Black Creation Mag, ed in chief, 1972-74; free lance-writer, 1983-85; USA Network, mgr public relations, 1985-90, dir corporate relations, 1990-91, freelance publicist, 1991-93; The Terrie Williams Agency, acct supvr, 1993, publicity consult, 1993-94; The Valley Youth Agency, dep dir, fund dev & public relations, 1994-. **Orgs:** Volunteer Fire Co, 1968; judge, Newspaper Guild Page One Award, 1976-86; cont ed, The Afro-Am Almanac, 1976, 1989; pres, Fairview Engine Co #1, 1980. **Honors/Awds:** Man of the Year, Fairview Engine Co #1 1971; Humanitarian Achievement Award MLK Players 1975; ordained elder Christs Temple White Plains NY, 1978; judge Gabriel Awards, 1986. **Special Achievements:** First Black Member in Fairview Engine Co #1 Greenburgh NY; first Black elected to Nwe York Film Critics Circle, 1972; Author, "To Find An Image", 1974. **Military Serv:** AUS, first lt, 1968-70. **Business Addr:** Deputy Director, Fund Development and Public Relations, The Valley Inc, 1047 Amsterdam Ave, New York, NY 10025, **Business Phone:** (212)222-2115.

MURRAY, REV. J-GLENN
Educator, clergy. **Personal:** Born Apr 22, 1950, Philadelphia, PA; son of Lillian Marie Hilton Murray and James Albert Murray. **Educ:** St Louis Univ, BA, 1974; Jesuit Sch Theol Berkeley, MDiv, 1979; Aquinas Inst, MA, 1996; Catholic Theol Union Chicago, DMin, 1996; Cath Theol Union Chicago, Dr Ministry, 2006. **Career:** St Frances Acad, asst prin, 1981-88; Off Pastoral Liturgy, asst dir, 1989-95, dir, 1995-2007; St Mary Sem, homiletics prof, 1992-; parochial vicar, St Aloysius Gonzaga Church, currently. **Orgs:** Nat Black Cath Clergy Caucus, 1979-; Cath Asn Teachers Homiletics, 1992-; Acad Homiletics, 1992-; N Am Acad Liturgy, 1993-; Black Cath Theol Symp, 1994-.; Cath Asn Liturgy; Jungmann Soc. **Honors/Awds:** Youth Ministry Medal of Honor, Archdiocese of Baltimore, 1988.; coordr, Nat Black Cath Cong, wash DC, Baltimore, liturgical consult, New Orleans. **Special Achievements:** Editor: Plenty Good Room: the Spirit and Truth of African American Worship. **Business Addr:** Parochial Vicar, St Aloysius Gonzaga Church, 4366 Bridgetown Rd, Cincinnati, OH 45211, **Business Phone:** (513)574-4840.

MURRAY, KAY L.
Government official. **Personal:** Born Sep 8, 1938, Greenville, MS; daughter of Preston Mike Lance and Ann De Jackson Lance; children: Gary Michael. **Educ:** Roosevelt Univ, Chicago, Ill, BA, pub admin, 1976; Northeastern Ill Univ, Chicago, Ill, MA, 1993. **Career:** City Coun, Chicago, IL, secy pres pro-tempore, 1960-74; City Dept Pub Works, Chicago, IL, equal employ officer, 1974; Dept St & Sanitation Comnr's Off, Chicago, IL, staff asst, 1974-82; Bureau Rodent Control, Chicago IL, asst comnr, 1983-84; Dept St & Sanitation Rodent Control, Chicago, IL, dep comnr; Ill Dept Prof Regulation, Chief Staff, 1991-. **Orgs:** Nat Asn Women Exec; Hyde Pk Community Orgn; assoc, Howard Univ Sch Bus Mgt Minority Women; Am Pub Works Asn; community developer, John Marshall Law Sch; Nat Advan Asn Colored People, 1977; 21st Dist Steering Comn; Chicago Police Dept, 1979; Int Toastmistress Am & Sirrah Br, 1980; Chicago Urban League, 1986; vpres, Jackson Pk Hosp, 1989-98; vpres, Bus & Prof Women, 1988-89; co-founder, Women Govt, 1984-89; pres, Genesis House Exec Bd; treas, N Wash Park Community Corp. **Honors/Awds:** Outstanding Community Efforts Award, 1986; WGRT Great Guy Award; Dedication & Loyalty to Fel Man Award; Outstanding Contributions to Dept of Health, Police, Fire & Citizens of Chicago; Cert of Achievement, Mid-Southside Health Planning Orgn. **Business Phone:** (312)814-4500.*

MURRAY, LAMOND MAURICE
Basketball player. **Personal:** Born Apr 20, 1973, Pasadena, CA; married Carmen; children: Lamond Jr & Ashley. **Educ:** Univ Calif, attended. **Career:** Los Angeles Clippers, forward, 1994-99; Cleveland Cavaliers, 2000-02; Toronto Raptors, forward, 2004-05; NJ Nets, forward; Los Angeles Clippers, 2006-07; Santa Barbara Breakers, 2007; Long Beach Breakers, 2007-08; Guang-

dong Southern Tigers, currently. **Business Addr:** Professional Basketball Player, Guangdong Southern Tigers, **Business Phone:** (861)06711-1476.

MURRAY, DR. MABEL LAKE
Educator. **Personal:** Born Feb 24, 1935, Baltimore, MD; daughter of Moses Oliver Lake and Iantha Alexander Lake; married Elmer R, Dec 16, 1968; children: Mark Alfonso Butler & Sarita Murray. **Educ:** Coppin State Teachers Col, Baltimore, MD, BS, 1956; Loyola Col, Balitmore, MD, MED, 1969; Va Polytech Inst, Blacksburg, VA, Case, 1981, EdD, 1982. **Career:** Baltimore City Pub Schs, teacher, 1956-68; Prince Georges County Pub Schs, reading specialist, 1968-70; Proj KAPS, Baltimore, Md, reading coordr, 1970-72; Univ Md, reading coordr, 1972-76; Johns Hopkins Univ, adj prof, 1972-76; Carroll County Pub Schs, supvr, 1976-87; Baltimore City Schs Special Educ, guest lect, 1979; Sojourner Douglass Col, Baltimore, Md, prof, 1987, supvr, Stud Teaching, currently; NAACP Educ Dept, nat coordr NTE; Sojourner-Douglass Col, Human Growth Dev, coordr. **Orgs:** Delta Sigma Theta Sorority, 1972-; Baltimore County Alumnae Chap, Delta Sigma Theta; adv, Lambda Kappa & Mu Psi Chapters, Delta Sigma Theta; consult, Piney Woods Sch, 1984-89; comn chair-instruction, 1987-96, exec bd, 1987-, Nat Alliance Black Sch Educators; consult, AIDS Proj MSDE, 1988; consult, Dunbar Middle Sch, 1989; consult, Des Moines Iowa Schs; Nat Coun Educating Black C; pres, Md Coun Deltas; nat pres, Pinochle Bugs Social & Civic Club; nat treas, The Societas Doctas; Baho Chap, The Soc; Coalition 100 Black Women; Nat Coalition Black Women; The Soc Inc Pinochle Bugs. **Honors/Awds:** Service Award, Baltimore City Chapter, Delta Sigma Theta, 1983. **Special Achievements:** Designed curriculum material for two school systems, 1968-72; Conducted numerous workshops, 1969-89; Guest speaker at variety of educ/human relations activities, 1969-89; Outstanding Educator, State Md Int Reading Asn, 1979; Developed reading program for state mental hospital, 1981; Mayor's Citation, 1982; Mem Congressman Louis Stokes Committee Black Health Issues, 1989; Miss Maryland Senior America, 2005. **Home Addr:** 3 Kittridge Ct, Randallstown, MD 21133.

MURRAY, SYLVESTER
School administrator, educator. **Personal:** Born Aug 15, 1941, Miami, FL; son of Tommy Lee and Annie Anderson; children: Kimberly & Joshua. **Educ:** Lincoln Univ Pa, BA, hist, 1963, LLD, 1984; Univ Pa, MGA, govt admin, 1967; Eastern Mich Univ, MA, Econ, 1976. **Career:** City Inkster Mich, city mgr, 1970-73; City Ann Arbor Mich, city admin, 1973-79; City Cincinnati Ohio, city mgr, 1979-85; City San Diego Calif, city mgr, 1985-87; Coopers & Lybrand, mgr; Am Soc Pub Admin & Int City mgt Asn Cleveland State Univ, educ adminr, currently; Maxine Goodman Levin Col Urban Affairs, prof, currently. **Orgs:** Pres, Int City mgt Asn, 1984; pres, Am Soc Pub Admin, 1987; fel, Nat Acad Pub Admin; bd mem, Nat Civic League. **Honors/Awds:** Public Service Award, Am Soc Pub Admin, 1984. **Military Serv:** AUS, sp5, 1965-67. **Business Addr:** Professor, Cleveland State University, Maxine Goodman Levin College of Urban Affairs, 1717 Euclid Ave, Cleveland, OH 44115, **Business Phone:** (216)687-2135.

MURRAY, DR. THOMAS AZEL, SR.
Educator, consultant, government official. **Personal:** Born Jan 15, 1929, Chicago, IL. **Educ:** Ohio State Univ, BA, bus, 1974; Univ Ill, MA, coun, 1976, MA, interpersonal commun, 1977; Southern Ill Univ, PhD, 1982. **Career:** Military official (retired); government official (retired), consult; Univ Ill, Chicago, proj coordr, 1959-72; Chicago Baptist Asn, dir, 1971-72; Fed Civil Serv, US Dept Housing & Urban Develop, supvry equal oppportunity specialist, 1973-75; Fed Hwy Admin, civil rights officer, 1975-78; Ill State Bd Educ, officer & parliamentarian, 1978-84 & 1994-96; Sangamon State Univ Alumni Asn, dir, 1979-85; US Dept HUD Region V, dir compliance; Off Civil Rights, dep dir, 1984-85, prog opers div, dir, 1985-87; US Off Personnel Mgt; Prof Serv Corps, Ill State Bd Educ, 1989; US Dept Transp, supvr & complaint investigators; Ill State Bd Educ, affirmative action officer; State Ill & Chicago Bd Educ, consult; NMex State Univ-Grants, instr; consult, currently. **Orgs:** Dir, Springfield Sangamon Co Youth Serv Bur, 1974-75; adv comt mem, Land Lincoln Legal Act Found, 1978-80; adv coun mem, Region IV Career Guid Ctr, Springfield, Ill, 1982-83; Prof Serv Corps, Ill State Bd Educ, 1989-96; Chicago Bd Educ, Admin Acad, 1989-96; presenter, Educ Serv Ctr VI, 1989-96. **Honors/Awds:** Black Affiliate Council Award of Merit, Southern Ill Univ, 1981; HE Honor, Phi Kappa Phi Soc, Southern Ill Univ. **Military Serv:** USAF; USAFR; USAR, first sgt; AUS; USANG. **Home Addr:** PO Box 430, Ramah, NM 87321. **Business Addr:** Consultant, PO Box 430, Ramah, NM 87020-0000, **Business Phone:** (505)775-3634.

MURRAY, THOMAS W., JR.
Clergy. **Personal:** Born Mar 11, 1935, Wilmington, NC; married Mable; children: Thomas R, Dean W & Darrell L. **Educ:** BS, Ed, 1966; ThM, 1969; MEd, 1973; DD, 1973. **Career:** Shawtown HS, educr, 1968-69; Community Col, educr, 1969-70; Bolivia HS, educr, 1969-70; Philadelphia Sch Sys, educr, 1970-74; Union Baptist Church, pastor. **Orgs:** Black Econ Develop Self Help Prog; Founder & Dir Oper Shout; Positive Self Image & Metaphys Inst Cited Chapel 4 Chaplains, 1974. **Military Serv:** USAF, E5, 1955-64. **Business Addr:** Clergy, Union Baptist Church, 1910 Fitzwater St, Philadelphia, PA 19146.

MURRAY, TRACY LAMONT
Basketball player, basketball executive. **Personal:** Born Jul 25, 1971, Los Angeles, CA. **Educ:** Univ Calif, Los Angeles, hist, 1993. **Career:** Portland Trail Blazers, forward, 1992-95, 2003-04; Houston Rockets, 1995; Toronto Raptors, 1995-96, 2000-02; Wash Wizards, 1996-2000; Denver Nuggets, 2000; Los Angeles Lakers, 2002-03; NY Knicks, forward, 2004-05; PAOK BC, 2005-06; Chalon, 2006?07; Bakersfield Jam, mentor, 2007-. **Orgs:** Co-chmn, Toshiba Celebrity Golf Classic; founder, Tracy Murray Summer Basketball Camp; Nat Basketball Asn. **Honors/Awds:** Most Improved Player, 1995-96.

MURRAY, VIRGIE W.
Editor. **Personal:** Born Sep 4, 1931, Birmingham, AL; daughter of Virgus Williams and Martha Miller Reese (deceased); married McKinley C Murray, Jun 1, 1949 (divorced); children: Charles Murray. **Educ:** Miles Col; Booker T Wash Bus Col. **Career:** Editor (retired); Dr John W Nixon, bookkeeper, 1954-58; Thomas Floorwaxing Serv, bookkeeper, 1954-64; Birmingham World, clerk/reporter, 1958-64; First Baptist Church Graymont, secy, 1960-64; Los Angeles Sentinel Newspaper, relig ed, 1964-2006. **Orgs:** Pres, Nat Baptist Conv USA INC; Secy, Relig Newswriters Asn, 1971; West Coast PR Dr Frederick Eikerenkoetter, 1974-; bd mem, Inst Sacred Music, 1979-; bd mem, Ecumenical Black Campus Ministry Univ Calif Los Angeles, 1982-; Trinity Baptist Church; Nat Asn Advan Colored People; Urban League; Angeles Mesa; Young Men's Christian Asn; Boy Scouts Am; Los Angeles Chap Bus & Prof Women's Club Inc; spec task force, UN Asn USA's Ralph Bunche Awards; mem, Los Angeles chapter Lane Col & Mileans & Parker High Sch Alumni; Relig Heritage Am, 1989-90; bd dirs, Los Angeles Sentinel Inc. **Honors/Awds:** Award of Merit, Crenshaw Christian Ctr, 1980; Christian Example First Church of God, 1982; Tribute Award, Good Shepherd Baptist Church, 1983; City Colo State Councilman Supvr & Assemblymen, 1983; spec award & honors, Southern Conf Christian Methodist Episcopal Church, 1988; Nat Newspapers Publs Asn. **Special Achievements:** Journalist: participated & covered the Friendship Tour of Seoul, Korea, 1992; covered the Church of God in Christ 85th Holy Convocation, 1992; covered the dedication of the Civil Rights Inst & the dedication of Rev Fred Shuttlesworth's statue, Birmingham, AL, 1992; Covered the African Am tour of the Holy Land, 1993, the CME Gen Conf in Memphis, TN, 1994; covered W Angeles COGIC retreat, 1995, Mexican Riviera Cruise retreat, 1996; covered AME Gen Conf, 1996; covered CME Gen Conf, 1998; World Pentecostal Conf, Seoul, Korea, 1998. *

MURRELL, ADRIAN BRYAN
Football player, president (organization), chief executive officer. **Personal:** Born Oct 16, 1970, Lafayette, LA; son of Angelo and Patricia; married Tanya; children: Tylan. **Educ:** West Virginia Univ. **Career:** Football player (retired), President, Chief Executive Ofiicer; NY Jets, running back, 1993-97; Ariz Cardinals, 1998-99; Wash Redskins, 2000; Dallas Cowboys, running back, 2003-04; Water Eng Serv Inc, pres & chief exec officer, 2003-. **Orgs:** Alpha Phi Alpha. **Honors/Awds:** Marty Lyons Award, 1995. **Business Addr:** President, Chief Executive Officer, Water Eng Serv Inc, 4008 S 23rd St, Phoenix, AZ 85040-1477, **Business Phone:** (602)252-5198.

MURRELL, BARBARA CURRY
Founder (Originator), school administrator. **Personal:** Born Jan 12, 1938, Starksville, MS; married Robert N Murrell. **Educ:** Tenn State Univ, BS, 1960, MS, 1963; Univ Ill, Post Grad Cert, 1970. **Career:** Tenn State Univ, dir, stud activities, 1965-75, asst vpres, stud affairs, 1975-81, vpres, stud affairs, 1981; Fisk Univ, adj prof social sci, currently, RealSports Leadership Acad, founder & exec dir, currently, vpres Student Life, 2007-. **Orgs:** Task Force Human Resources Asn Col Unions Int, 1968-79; state coordr, Nat Asn Stud Personnel Admins, 1973; Harvard Univ Inst Educ Mgrs Prog, 1984; consult, Prof Develop Workshop Asn Col Unions Int; bd dirs, Bordeaux YMCA; Asn Col Unions Int; Nat Entertainment & Campus Activities Asn; Beta Kappa Chi Nat Hon Soc; Delta Sigma Theta Sorority Inc. **Honors/Awds:** Omega Psi Phi Frat Sweetheart, 1958-59; Miss Tenn State Univ, 1960; Kappa Alpha Psi Frat Perpetual Sweetheart, 1960. **Business Addr:** Founder & Executive Director, Vice President for Student Life, Fisk University, RealSports Leadership Academy, 1000 17th Ave N, Nashville, TN 37208-3051.

MURRELL, DR. PETER C
Dentist. **Personal:** Born May 14, 1920, Glasgow, KY; son of Samuel Murrell and Nellie Murrell; married Eva Ruth Greenlee; children: Peggy, Peter Jr, Linda & James. **Educ:** Ky State Col, BS (Cum Laude), 1943; Marquette Univ, DDS, 1947. **Career:** private practisioner (retired); Howard Univ Col Dentistry, instr, 1947-48; pvt pract, 1948-51, 1953-92. **Orgs:** Am Wisc & Gr Milwaukee Dent Asn; pres, Greater Milwaukee Dent Asn; Am Soc Prev Dent; Am Acad Gen Pract; treas, bd mem, Childrens Serv Soc, 1962-77; Garfield Found; former mem, Frontiers Int; past pres, Delta Chi Lambda, Alpha Phi Alpha; fel, Int Col Dentists, 1978; Acad Gen Dent, 1981; trustee, Wis Dent Asn, 7th Dist, 1983-84; adv coun, Marquette Univ Sch Dent, 1988; Wis State Med Asst Adv Comt; Pierre Fauchard Acad, 1989; fel, Am Col Dentists, 1989. **Honors/Awds:** Distinguished Serv Award, Opportunity Industrialization Ctr, 1971; Service to Dent, Greater Milwaukee Dent Asn, 1987; Lifetime Achievement Award, Wisc Dent Asn, 1993; Founders Plaque, Frontiers Int, 1995. **Military Serv:** AUS, 1942-44; USAF Dent Corps, capt, 1951-53. **Home Addr:** 1302 W Capitol Dr, Milwaukee, WI 53206.

MURRELL, HON. SYLVIA MARILYN
Administrator. **Personal:** Born Sep 7, 1947, Arcadia, OK; daughter of Inez Traylor Parks and Ebbie Parks Jr; divorced; children: Monica A, Alfred H & Cypreanna V. **Educ:** Cent State Univ, Edmond, Okla, 1964-66; Rose State Col, Midwest City, Okla, 1981-82; Langston Univ, Oklahoma, Okla, 1986-87. **Career:** Okla Bus Develop Ctr, Okla City, Okla, variety of positions, 1975-94, exec dir, 1985-94; Town Arcadia, mayor, 1988-; M & M Bus Consult, pres & ceo, 1988-; Okla City Northeast, Inc, independent consult, 1991-93; Okla Consortium for Minority Bus Develop Inc, chmn, 1991?; Team One Consult Inc, owner, currently. **Orgs:** Okla City Chamber Com, 1977-; secy & chmn, Econ Develop Comt, Conf Black Mayors, 1986-; bd mem, Youth Serv Okla County, 1986-; bd mem, Okla City Chap Assault Illiteracy, 1986-; steering comt, Okla City Crime Prev Task Force, 1988-; Cent Okla econ Develop Task Force, 1988-; Teamwork Okla, 1988-; vice chair, Okla Consortium Minority Bus Develop, 1988-89; Okla Conf Black Mayors; pres, 2002-03, Nat Conf Black Mayors; chmn, Nat Small Town Alliance, currently; adv bd, NEW Leadership. **Honors/Awds:** Creative Christian Award, Forrest Hill AME Church, 1987. **Business Addr:** Owner, Team One Consulting Inc, 1301 N Martin Luther King Ave, Oklahoma City, OK 73117, **Business Phone:** (405)606-7460.

MUSE, J MELVIN (JO MUSE)
Advertising executive. **Career:** Reid Advert, new bus acct exec; Olin Corp, pub rels mgr; Mcc, Creative Develop Advert, mgr; Muse Cordero Chen & Partners, chmn, exec creative dir, chief exec officer; Muse Commun Inc, exec creative dir, chmn & chief exec officer, currently. **Orgs:** Am Asn Advert Agencies. **Business Addr:** Chief Executive Officer, Chairman, Muse Communications Inc, 6100 Wilshire Blvd, Los Angeles, CA 90048, **Business Phone:** (323)954-1655.*

MUSE, JO. See MUSE, J MELVIN.

MUSE, DR. WILLIE L
School administrator. **Educ:** Selma Univ, ThB; Ala State Univ, educ; Interdenominational Theol Ctr. **Career:** Selma Univ, prof relig pres, interim pres; Selma Univ, pres, 1994-. **Honors/Awds:** Hon Doctorate, Selma Univ.

MUSGROVE, MARGARET WYNKOOP
Writer, teacher. **Personal:** Born Nov 19, 1943, New Britain, CT; daughter of John T and Margaret Holden; married George Gilbert, Aug 28, 1971; children: Taura Johnene & George Derek. **Educ:** Univ Conn, BA, 1966; Cent Conn State Univ, MS, 1970; Univ Mass, EdD, 1979. **Career:** Hartford, Conn, high sch eng teacher, 1967-69, 1970; W Bershireshire Community Col, Pittsfield, MA, teacher; Community Col Baltimore, MD, eng teacher, dir develop studies, coordr ctr educ develop & coordr early childhood educ, 1981-91; Loyola Col, writing media dept & writing teacher, 1991-, Women's Ctr, dir, currently. **Orgs:** Soc Children's Book Writers, Md Writer's Proj & Int Women's Writers Guild. **Honors/Awds:** Fulbright Scholar, 1997-98. **Special Achievements:** Author of Ashanti to Zulu: African Traditions, Dial, 1976 (on Horn Book honor list and a Caldecott Award Winner, 1977), The Spider Weaver: A Legend of Kente Cloth (2001). **Business Addr:** Director, Loyola College, Women's Center, 4501 N Charles St, Baltimore, MD 21210-2699.

MUTCHERSON, JAMES ALBERTUS
Physician. **Personal:** Born Mar 22, 1941, Tampa, FL; married Katherine; children: Rovenia & Kimberly. **Educ:** Fla Agr & Mech Univ, 1962; Am Intl Col, BA, 1965; Howard Univ Col Med, 1971. **Career:** Howard Univ Hosp, clinical instr 1975; Howard Univ Hosp, pediatric allergy fel, 1973-75; Childrens Hosp, DC, pediatric resident, 1971-73; pvt pract, currently. **Orgs:** DC Med Soc; DC Social Asthma & Allergy, Amr Acadamy Asthma Allergy & Immunol; Pediatric Allergy Fel, 1973-75. **Home Addr:** 1140 Varnum St NE Suite 030, Washington, DC 20017-2151, **Home Phone:** (202)269-4223. **Business Addr:** Physician, 1140 Varnum St NE Suite 030, Washington, DC 20017-2151, **Business Phone:** (202)269-4223.

MUTOMBO, DIKEMBE
Basketball player. **Personal:** Born Jun 25, 1966, Kinshasa, Republic of the Congo; married Rose; children: Carrie Biamba, Jean Jr, Ryan, Reagan, Harouna, Pearla & Nancy. **Educ:** Georgetown Univ, BA, lings & diplomacy. **Career:** Denver Nuggets, ctr, 1991-96; Atlanta Hawks, 1996-2001; Philadelphia 76ers, 2001-02; New Jersey Nets, 2002-03; New York Knicks, 2003-04; Chicago Bulls, 2004; Houston Rockets, reserve ctr, 2004-; The Africa Channel, owner, currently. **Orgs:** Founder, Dikembe Mutombo Found, 1997-. **Honors/Awds:** NBA All-Rookie first team, 1992; NBA Defensive Player of the Year Award, 1995, 1997, 1998, 2001; seven time NBA All-Star; Nat Civil Rights Museums Sports Legacy Award, 2007. **Special Achievements:** NBA Draft, First round pick, No 4, 1991, passed Kareem Abdul-Jabbar as the

second highest shotblocker of all time, behind only Hakeem Olajuwon. **Business Addr:** Professional Basketball Player, Houston Rockets, 2 Greenway Plz Suite 400, Houston, TX 77046, **Business Phone:** (713)627-3865.

MUWAKKIL, SALIM (ALONZO JAMES CANNADY)
Writer, editor. **Personal:** Born Jan 20, 1947, New York, NY; son of Alonzo and Bertha; married Karimah; children: Salimah & Rasheeda. **Educ:** Rutgers Univ, attended; Newark Col Arts & Sci, attended 1973. **Career:** Bilalian News, managing ed, 1975-77; Muhammad Speaks, news ed, 1974-75; copy ed, 1974; AP, bur newsman, 1972-74; Addiction Planning & Coordr Agency Newark, res specialist, 1972; Livingston Neighborhood Educ Ctr, co-founder educ, 1971; Black Journalism Rev, consult ed bd; Columbia Col, Chicago, IL, journalism lectr, 1986-90; Assoc Col Midwest, Chicago, IL, part-time fac, 1990-; In These Times Mag, Chicago, IL, sr ed, 1990-; contributing columnist, CHI Suntimes, 1993-97; contributing columnist, CHI Tribune, 1998-. **Orgs:** Pres, Black Students Union, 1970-72; consult, Livingston Col Neighborhood Educ Ctr, 1972-74; bd, Gov S Shore Community Ctr Several Publ; Spl Observer Orgn African Unity, 1975; Crime & Communities Media Fel, Open Soc Inst. **Honors/Awds:** International Reggae Music Awards, Outstanding Music Criticism, 1983-84; Article of the Year, Int Black Writers Conference, 1984; Outstanding Service Award, African-Am Alliance Columbia Col, Chicago, 1990; Top Ten Media Heroes, IST Alternative Journalism, 1994; Black Rose Achievement Award, League Black Women, 1997; Studs Terkel Award for Journalistic Excellence, COT Media Workshop, 2001. **Military Serv:** USAF, 1964-69. **Business Addr:** Senior Editor, In These Times Magazine, 2040 N Milwaukee Ave, Chicago, IL 60647, **Business Phone:** (773)772-0100.

MUYUMBA, FRANCOIS N. See Obituaries section.

MWAMBA, ZUBERI I
Educator. **Personal:** Born Jan 3, 1937, United Republic of Tanzania. **Educ:** Univ Wis, BS, 1968; Univ Pitts, MA, 1968; Howard Univ, PhD, 1972. **Career:** Govt Tanzania, radio announcer, court clerk, interpreter, info asst, 1957-62; Fulbright fel, 1965-68; Howard Univ, instr, 1968-72; US State Dept, staff, 1969-70; Tex Southern Univ, African Studies, prof pub admin & dir, 1982-; Gen Elections, S Africa, int election observer, 1994. **Orgs:** Pres, Pan African Stud Orgn, 1965-67; Tanzania Stud Union, 1968-70, 1971-72; exec comt, East African Stud Orgn, 1968-70; Howard Univ Trust, 1969-70; Am Polit Sci Asn, 1971-; Nat Coun Black Polit Scientists, 1971-; Educr Africa Asn, 1972-; adv, Tex Southern Univ, Stud Govt Asn, 1974-75; fac, TSU Young Demo, 1974-75. **Honors/Awds:** Distinguished Service of the Year Award, Tex Southern Univ, 1997. **Business Addr:** Professor of Public Administration, Texas Southern University, 3100 Cleburne Ave, Houston, TX 77004, **Business Phone:** (713)313-7332.

MYATT, HON. GORDON J
Judge. **Personal:** Born Jan 2, 1928, Brooklyn, NY; son of Frances Simons and Carlton O Sr; married Evelyne E Hutchings; children: Gordon jr, Kevin & Craig. **Educ:** New York Univ, BS, 1950, Sch Law, LLB, 1956. **Career:** Pvt Pract, atty, 1956-60; US Dept Justice, Nat Labor Rels Bd Chicago, trial atty, 1960-62, supv atty, 1962-64, legal adv, admin law judge, 1989. **Orgs:** Nat Bar Asn; Nat Bar Judicial Coun; Am Bar Asn; Alpha Phi Alpha Fraternity, 1945-; Alpha Gamma Boule Sigma Pi Phi, 1989-.

MYERS, ANDRE
Insurance executive, consultant. **Personal:** Born Aug 2, 1959, Philadelphia, PA; son of George and Pauline; divorced. **Educ:** Community Col, retail mkt mgt, 1984; Eastern Col, orgn mgt, 1996. **Career:** Independence Blue Cross, enrollment specialist, 1998, electronic data interchange specialist, currently; Church Mentoring Network, coordr & comnr. **Orgs:** Enon Tabernacle Baptist Church; vpres, Young Democrats Pa, 1992-94; subscripting life mem, NAACP; coordr, 1996, comnr, Church Mentoring Network; Philadelphia Prison Ministry. **Honors/Awds:** Bulldog Award & MUP Award, Independence Blue Cross; Regional Outreach Award, 2002. **Home Addr:** 23 E Slocum St, Philadelphia, PA 19119. **Business Addr:** Electronic Data Interchange Specialist, Independence Blue Cross, 1901 Market St 38th Fl, Philadelphia, PA 19103-1480, **Business Phone:** (215)241-2400.

MYERS, BERNARD SAMUEL
Veterinarian. **Personal:** Born Jun 2, 1949, Moultrie, GA. **Educ:** Rollins Col, BA, 1970; Cornell Univ, DVM, 1974. **Career:** Harvard Sch Pub Health, res asst, 1973; Bruce Animal Hosp, asso vet, 1974-75; Stoneham Animal Hosp, asso vet, 1975-77; Needham Animal Hosp, asso vet, 1977-80; Lynn Animal Hosp, vet, 1985; Williamsburg Vet Clin, physician, currently. **Orgs:** Am Vet Med Asn, 1974-80; Mass Vet Med Asn, 1974-80; asst moderator, Shiloh Bapt Church, 1980; Vet Emergency Clin Cent Fla. **Honors/Awds:** Acad Scholar, Rollins Col, 1966-70; Algernon Sidney Sullivan Award, Rollins Col, 1969; Health Professions Scholarship, Cornell Univ, 1970-74. **Business Addr:** Physician, Williamsburg Veterinary Clinic, 5518 Central Florida Pkwy, Orlando, FL 32821.

MYERS, DWIGHT. See HEAVY D.

MYERS, EMMA MCGRAW
Educator, chief executive officer. **Personal:** Born Nov 15, 1953, Hartsville, SC; married Kenneth E Myers. **Educ:** FL State Univ, BA, 1974, MSW, Social Work Admin, 1975. **Career:** United Way Am, united way intern, 1976-77, consul planning & allocations div, 1979-80; United Way Tarrant Co, mgr vol training, 1977-78, campaign div dir, 1978-79; UWA, assoc dir nat relations, 1980-83; United Way Midlands, dir planning & allocations div; United Way Aiken County Aiken SC, Pres & chief exec officer, 1988-92; United Way Richland County Aiken SC, Pres & chief exec officer, 1992-94; USC Inst Families soc, Res Assoc, 1999-2003; EM Consultants, Pres & chief exec officer, 1994-; DeSaussure Col Social Work, Adjunct Faculty, 2001-; Communities Schs Midlands, Dir Develop, 2003-05. **Orgs:** Parlimentarian Episcopal Ch Women, 1985; treas, FSU Black Alumin Asn; bd mem, Nat Asn Black Social Workers; pres, Dutch Fork Citivans; pres, Alpha Kappa Alpha; corresp sec, Columbia Chap NABSW; Alpha Kappa Alpha Sorority, 1972; Leadership Aiken, 1995; NAACP; chmn, Woman Yr Pageant Aiken Br, 1995, 1997; pres, Watkins Elementary Sch PTA, 1996-2000; Paul Harris, 1997; Rotary Club Aiken, 1996-97; Richland Sch Dist One Blue Ribbon Comt, 1999-; pres, The RichLand Found, 2001-; pres, Columbia Luncheon Club, 2000-01; Richland Sch Dist One Calendar Comt, 2001, 2004; pres, WA Perry Middle Sch PTA, 2001-04; Ctr Religion S, 2002-05; vpres, CA Johnson Preparatory Academy PSTA, 2002-; pres, Asn Fundraising Prof, Central SC Chap; Committee on 100 Black Women, 2005-; Past Pres, Parliamentarian, 2005-; pres, Jones McDonald Community Club, 2005; City Columbia Community Promotions Comt, 2005-. **Honors/Awds:** Nominee Outstanding young Women of America, 1983; Living the Legacy Award, NCNW, 1986; Civitan of the Year, 1986; Certified Fundraising Exec, CFRE Intl Bd, 2005. **Special Achievements:** First African-American in SC to receive designation as Certified Fundraising Executive by CFRE International Board, 2005. **Business Addr:** Adjunct Faculty, DeSaussure College of social Work, University of South Carolina, Columbia, SC 29208, **Business Phone:** (803)779-4241.

MYERS, DR. ERNEST RAY
Writer, educator, vice president (organization). **Personal:** Born in Middletown, OH; son of David Sr and Alma Harper; married Carole E Ferguson. **Educ:** Howard Univ, BA, 1962, MSW, 1964; Am Univ, PhD, 1974; Union Inst Univ, PhD, 1976. **Career:** US Pres Task Force War Against Poverty, consult, 1964; VISTA, Proj Develop Div, prog officer, 1964-66, sr eval officer, 1964-66, proj develop officer, 1966-67, prog plans & policy develop officer, 1967; Dept Housing & Urban Develop, neighborhood serv prog officer & coordr, 1967-68; Nat Urban League, asst dir, 1968; Westing house Learning Corp, mgr prog develop, 1968-69; Fed City Col, dir col community eval off, 1969-71; Bur Higher Educ US Off Educ, dir servicemen's early educ coun prog, 1971; Fed City Col, asst prof, 1972-77; Univ DC, assoc prof, 1977-86, chmn depthuman resource dev, 1986-94, Dept Psychol & Counseling, prof, 1994; TRI-Austin Inc, vpres, defense bus level, currently. **Orgs:** Nat Asn Social Workers, 1969-; Asn Black Psychologists, 1972-; Acad Certified Soc Workers, Nat Asn Social Workers, 1974-; Am Psychol Asn, 1975-; pres, ERM Consult Corp, 1980-; trustee, Woodley House Rehab, 1982-88; grievance comt, Nat Asn Social Workers, 1984-86; chmn, DC Ment Health Asn Prof Adv Comn, 1984-86; chmn, DC Govt Mental Health Admin Adv Bd, 1984-86; chmn, Howard Univ Alumni Sch Social Work Fund Raising Comn, 1984-86; Kiwanis Club, Ga Br, 1985-86; mem adv, Zest Inc, 1990-; fel APA, 1995-. **Honors/Awds:** Outstanding Leadership, Univ DC Col Educ & Human Ecology, 1981; Outstanding Scholar, Asn Black Psychologists, 1981; Outstanding Alumni Howard Univ Sch Soc Work, 1982; Outstanding Service, Mental Health Asn, 1982; Outstanding Leadership Award, Univ DC, 1985; Outstanding Scholar Award, Univ DC 1986; Service Recognition Plaque, Nat Asn Advan Colored People, 1993; Outstanding Services Plaque, Grad, SGA Univ DC, 1994; Outstanding Alumni, Union Inst, 1996; Image Award & Faculty Award, Univ DC, 1996. **Special Achievements:** Author: Race & Culture in the Mental Health Service Delivery System, 1981; Challenges of a Changing America, 1994. **Military Serv:** USAF Tech Sch Flight comdr, Personnel Specialist, 1956-60; 2 Good Conduct Medals. **Home Addr:** 5315 Colorado Ave NW, Washington, DC 20011, **Home Phone:** (202)882-8124.

MYERS, DR. JACQUALINE DESMONA
Educator, college teacher. **Personal:** Born Jan 5, 1951, Charleston, SC; daughter of William Nicholas Myers and Daisy Elouise Brown Myers. **Educ:** Benedict Col, Columbia, SC, BS, 1971; Ind Univ, Bloomington, MS, 1972; Univ Wis, Madison, PhD, 1980. **Career:** Benedict Col, work study secy, 1968-71; Med Univ SC, clin acct, 1971; Ind Univ, asst instr, 1971-72; Ala State Univ, asst prof, 1973-86, assoc prof, bus educ, co dir, 1986-. **Orgs:** Nat Bus Educ Asn, 1971-; Am Educ Res Asn, 1980-; asst corresp secy, Delta Sigma Theta Montgomery Alumnae, 1983-84; fac staff alliance, Am Fed Teachers; Phi Delta Kappa, AL; Southern Bus Educ Asn, 1989-91; fac senate, Ala State Univ. **Honors/Awds:** Cum Laude, Benedict Col, 1971; Outstanding Young Women of America, 1977,1980, 1984; Consortium of Doctors, 1991-97. **Special Achievements:** Published article in SBEA Bulletin, 1980. **Home Addr:** 501 Deerfield Dr, Montgomery, AL 36109-3312. **Business Addr:** Associate Professor of Business Education, Alabama State University, 206 McGehee Hall, PO Box 80, Montgomery, AL 36101-0271, **Business Phone:** (334)229-4447.

MYERS, L LEONARD
Executive. **Personal:** Born Jan 25, 1933, Aliquippa, PA; son of Joseph and Eddie Mae Ham; married R Elizabeth; children: Linda Ann & Larry Leonard. **Educ:** Univ Pittsburgh, BA; Life Underwriter Training Coun LUTC; Chartered Life Underwriters, Calif Lutheran Univ; Am Col Am Inst Property & Liability Underwriter, Casualty & Property Ins Underwriters. **Career:** First Summit Agency Inc, chief exec officer, pres, currently. **Orgs:** Pres, Long Island Chap, Casualty & Property Ins Underwriters; Long Island Chap, Calif Lutheran Univ; Hempstead Chamber Com; pres, Nat Inst Ind Asn; Lakeview Lions Club. **Military Serv:** AUS, spec, 4 2 yrs. **Home Addr:** 19 Surrey Lane, Hempstead, NY 11550, **Home Phone:** (516)485-7067. **Business Addr:** President, First Summit Agency Inc, 100 Main St Unit D, Hempstead, NY 11550-2427, **Business Phone:** (516)483-3300.

MYERS, DR. LENA WRIGHT
Educator. **Personal:** Married Julius Jr (deceased); children: Stanley. **Educ:** Tougaloo Col, BA, sociol; Mich State Univ, MA, sociol & anthropol, 1964, PhD, sociol & social psychol, 1973. **Career:** Utica Jr Col, instr, sociol & psychol, 1962-68; Washtenaw Comm Col, asst prof psychol, 1968; Center for Urban Affairs Mich State Univ, urban res, 1970-73; Jackson State Univ, prof social, 1973-; Ohio Univ, prof sociol, research agenda, currently. **Orgs:** Community Status Women Sociol Am Sociol Assoc, 1974-77; res consult, TIDE, 1975-78; pres, Asn Social Behav Scientists Inc, 1976-77; res consult, KOBA, 1979-80; bd dirs, Soc Study Social Problems, 1980-83; res consult, Nat Sci Found, 1983; pres, Asn Black Sociologists, 1983-84. **Honors/Awds:** State of MS House of Rep Concurrent Resolution No 70 Commendation, 1981; Distinguished American Award, 1981; Marguerite Rogers Howie Distinguished Service Award, Asn Social & Behavioral Scientists; James Blackwell Founder's Award, Asn Black Sociologist. **Special Achievements:** Author of numerous essays like:"Black Male Socialization: A Broken Silence with Empirical Evidence," published in CHALLENGE, 1996; "Systemic Oppression or Family Structure: Voices in Retrospect," published in Nat Journal of Soc, 1997; "Black Male Socialization: A Symbolic Interactionist Perspective," pub in National Soc Sci Persp Jnl, 2000; "Realities of Academe for Afr Amer Women," pub in Women in Higher Ed, 2000; "The Academic Pendulum & Self Esteem of Afr Amer Males," pub in Perspectives, Fall 2000; Author of books, including, Black Male Socialization Revisited in the Minds of Respondents, JAI Press, 1998. **Home Addr:** 2320 Queensroad Ave, Jackson, MS 39213. **Business Addr:** Research Agenda, Ohio University, Department of Sociology & Anthropology, Bentley Annex 103, Athens, OH 45701-2979, **Business Phone:** (740)593-1375.

MYERS, LEWIS HORACE
Executive. **Personal:** Born Apr 28, 1946, Carlisle, PA; married Cheryl; children: Donnell L, Marrielle & Lewis H III. **Educ:** Franklin & Marshall Col, BA, 1968; Univ NC, MBA, 1974; Univ NC, Cert Basic Ind Dev Course, 1979; Govt Exec Inst, attended 1981. **Career:** Off Spec Progs Franklin & Marshall Col, assoc dir, 1968-69; Upward Bound Prog Harvard Univ, exec dir, 1969-71; Soul City Found Inc, assoc dir, 1971-75; Soul City Co, vpres, 1976-79; NC Minority Bus Dev Agency, dir, 1980-82; NC Dept Com Small Bus Develop Div, asst sec, 1982-88; Construct Control Serv Corp, vpres mkt, 1988-91; LHM Assocs, pres, 1991-; Freelon Group, dir bus develop, currently. **Orgs:** NC Econ Develop Asn, 1979-; founder, mem, NC Asn Minority Bus; life mem, NAACP; NC Citizens Bus & Indus; chair, Econ Comn; 100 Black Men, Triangle East Chap; NCM/WBE Coordinators Network. **Honors/Awds:** Minority Business Advocate of the Year, Med Week Atlanta Reg Off, 1995. **Business Addr:** President, LHM Associates, 5119 Shady Bluff St, Durham, NC 27704, **Business Phone:** (919)477-1662.

MYERS, MICHAEL
Football player. **Personal:** Born Jan 20, 1976, Vicksburg, MS; married Brandy; children: Mykayla. **Educ:** Ala Univ. **Career:** Dallas Cowboys, defensive tackle, 1998-2002; Cleveland Browns, 2003-04; Denver Broncos, 2005-06; Cincinnati Bengals, defensive tackle, 2007. Free agent, currently.

MYERS, PETER E.
Basketball player, basketball coach. **Personal:** Born Sep 15, 1963, Mobile, AL. **Educ:** Univ Ark, little rock. **Career:** NBA career: Chicago Bulls, 1986-87, 1993-97; San Antonio Spurs, 1988; Philadelphia 76ers, 1988; New York Knicks, 1988-90, 1997-98; New Jersey Nets, 1990; San Antonio Spurs, 1990-91; Washington Bullets, 1992; Chicago Bulls, asst coach, 2001-; CBA career: Rockford Lightning, 1987-88; Italian League career: Mang Bologna, 1991-92; Scavolini Pesaro, 1992-93. **Business Addr:** Assistant Coach, Chicago Bulls, United Ctr, 1901 W Madison St, Chicago, IL 60612-2459, **Business Phone:** (312)455-4000.*

MYERS, SAMUEL L, SR.
Educator, association executive. **Personal:** Born Apr 18, 1919, Baltimore, MD; son of David and Edith; married Marion R Ri-

eras; children: Yvette M, Tama M Clark & Samuel L Jr. **Educ:** Morgan State Col, AB, 1940, LLD, 1968; Boston Univ, MA, 1942; Harvard Univ, MA, 1948, PhD 1949; Univ Md, LLD, 1983; Sojourner & Douglass Col, DH, literature, 1992; Univ DC, LLD, 1997. **Career:** Harvard Univ, res assoc, 1949; Bureau Statistics US Dept Labor, economist, 1950; Morgan State Col, prof & div chmn soc sci, 1950-63; Inter-Am Affairs US Dept State, adv, 1963-67; Bowie State Col, pres, 1967-77, pres emer, 1977-; Nat Asn Equal Opportunity Higher Educ; pres, Nat Asn Equal Opportunity, 1977-95, pres emer, 1995-; Minority Access Inc, chair & sr educ advr, 1998-. **Orgs:** Md Tax Study Comn, 1958; Gov Comn Prevailing Wage Law Md, 1962; vice chmn, Md Community Humanities & Publ Policy; Alpha Kappa Mu, State Scholarship Bd, 1968-77; vice chmn, Gov Community Aide Educ, 1969-70; pres, MD Asn Higher Educ, 1971-72; chmn, Comn Int Prog, Am Asn State Col & Univ; rep, Nat Adv Coun Int Teacher Exchange; steering comt, Comn Future Int Studies; vpres & bd dir, Nat Asn Equal Opportunity Higher Educ; pres comn, Foreign Lang & Int Studies, 1978-80; mem bd dir, Rassias Found, 1980; Baltimore Urban League; res fel, Rosenwald Fellow Harvard Univ. **Honors/Awds:** DHL, Shaw Univ, 1994; Samuel Z Westerfield Award, Nat Econ Asn, 1995; Hall of Fame, Morgan State Univ Alumni, 1998. **Military Serv:** AUS, capt, 1942-46. **Business Addr:** Chairman, Senior Educator Advisor, Minority Access, 5214 Baltimore Ave Suite 200, Hyattsville, MD 20781, **Business Phone:** (301)779-7100.

MYERS, DR. SAMUEL L
Economist. **Personal:** Born Mar 9, 1949, Boston, MA. **Educ:** Morgan State Univ, BA, econ (Magna Cum Laude), 1971; Mass Inst Technol, PhD, 1976. **Career:** Bowie State Col, visiting instr, 1972; Boston Col, instr, 1973; Cuttington Univ Col, Liberia, West Africa, Fulbright Lectr, 1975-76; Univ Tex, Dept Econ, vis fac fel, 1976-80; Univ Wis-Madison, vis res fel; 1979-80; Nat Inst Justice, US Dept Justice, vis fac fel, 1979-80; Federal Trade Comn, sr economist, 1980-82; Dubois Inst, Harvard Univ, assoc, 1984; Cornell Univ, vis assoc prof, 1985; Grad Sch Public & Intl Affairs, Univ Pittsburgh, assoc prof, 1982-86; Afro-Am Studies Prog, Univ Md, dir, 1986-82; Univ Md, Dept Econ, prof, 1986-92; Univ Minn, Human Relations & Social Justice, Hubert H Humphrey Inst Public Affairs, Roy Wilkins Prof, 1992-; Univ NC, Dept Econ, Hanes-Willis Lectr 1994; Fac Aboriginal & Islander Studies, Univ South Aus, Fulbright Scholar, 1997; Ctr Urban & Regional Studies, Univ NC, Floyd McKissick Scholar, 1998; Benedict Col, Distinguished Vis Scholar, 1998-99. **Orgs:** Am Econ Asn; Nat Econ Asn; Am Acad Political & Social Sci; Am Asn Advancement Sci; Alpha Phi Alpha; co-coordr, Black Grad Econ Asn, 1973; Asn Pub Policy Analysis & Mgmt, vp, 1997-99. **Honors/Awds:** Alpha Kappa Mu Merit Award, 1970; Inst Fel, MIT, 1971-73; Nat Fel Fund Fel, 1973-75; Fulbright Lectr Econ, Cuttington Col, Liberia, 1975-76; Fulbright Scholar, Univ S Australia, Fac Aboriginal & Islander Studies, 1997. **Special Achievements:** Co-author: Bittersweet Success: Faculty of Color in Academe; Persistent Disparity: Race & Economic Inequality in the US 1998; The Black Underclass: Critical Essays on Race and Unwantedness, 1994; Editor: Civil Rights and Race Relations in the Post Reagan-Bush Era 1997; Co-editor: Economics of Race and Crime, Transaction Press, 1988; author, editor, and contributor of articles, chapters, and reviews to newspaper, periodicals, books, and journals. **Home Addr:** 9 Island View Lane, North Oaks, MN 55127, **Home Phone:** (651)482-8749. **Business Addr:** Roy Wilkins Chair Professor, University of Minnesota, H H Humphrey Institute of Public Affairs, 257 Humphrey Ctr, Minneapolis, MN 55455, **Business Phone:** (612)625-9821.

MYERS, SERE SPAULDING
Dentist. **Personal:** Born Feb 8, 1930, Oklahoma City, OK; married MaryJane Barbara Stewart; children: Dr Serese Si C'Annon, Dr Sere S Jr, Robin Lynn, Stewart, Sheryll. **Educ:** Morehouse Col, BS, 1950; Univ Mo, Kansas City, MS, 1951; Howard Univ, DDS, 1958; Queens Hosp, cert oral surgery, 1959. **Career:** Forbes AFB, chief oral surg, 1959-61; Meyers Dent Clin, owner, currently. **Orgs:** Pres, Kansas City, Howard Univ Alumni, 1972-73; Nat Howard Univ Dent Asn, 1983-85; Kansas City, Dist Dent Soc; Mo Dent Asn; Am Dent Asn. **Honors/Awds:** Legacy Award, Black Chamber of Com, 1994. **Special Achievements:** One of the 100 Most Influential Blacks of Kansas City, 1993. **Military Serv:** USAF, capt, 1959-61. **Business Addr:** Dentist, Owner, Meyers Dental Clinic, 5240 Prospect Ave, Kansas City, MO 64130.*

MYERS, VICTORIA CHRISTINA
Parole officer, executive. **Personal:** Born Nov 23, 1943, Indianapolis, IN; daughter of Stanley Louis Porter and Victoria Knox Porter; married Albert Louis, Sep 4, 1965; children: David, John & Matthew. **Educ:** Ind Univ, Bloomington, IN, AB, sociol, 1966; Webster Univ, Webster Groves, MO, MA, corrections, 1975. **Career:** Marion County Juv Ct, Indianapolis, IN, juvenile probation officer, 1967-69; Mo Bd Probation & Parole, St Louis, MO, probation & parole officer, 1970-73; Mo Bd Probation & Parole, St Louis, MO, supvr, 1973-84; Mo Bd Probation & Parole, Jefferson City, MO, bd mem, 1984-96, probation & parole adminr, 1996-2000, dir parole serv, 2000-01; Mo Dept Corrections, dir human serv, 2001-. **Orgs:** Pres, Mo Corrections Asn, 1978-79; bd mem, Am Probation & Parole Asn, 1982-88; bd mem, 1982-88, nat secy, 1983-88, nat prog chair, 1989-; Nat Asn Blacks Criminal Justice; chmn, Ethics Comt, 1990-92, prog chair, 1994-96, vpres, 1996-98, bd governors, delegate assembly, Am Correctional Asn; comnr, 1982-94, exec comt, 1988-92, Comn Accreditation Corrections; vestry, Grace Episcopal Church, 1992-95 & 2000-03, sr warden, 1993-95; Episcopal Diocese Mo, diocesan coun, 1995-2000 & 2003-06; bd dirs, United Way Cent Mo, 1994-99, secy, 1999-2000; pres, AKA Sorority, 1996-99, financial secy, 2000-04; Gamma Epsilon Omega. **Honors/Awds:** Outstanding Employee, Mo Bd Probation & Parole, 1975; Dedicated Service Award, Nat Asn Blacks Criminal Justice, St Louis Chap, 1985; Chairman's Award, Nat Asn Blacks Criminal Justice, 1987; ER Cass Correctional Achievement Award, Am Correctional Asn, 1994; Ben Baer Award, Asn Paroling Authorities Int, 2001. **Home Addr:** 2408 Parkcrest Dr, Jefferson City, MO 65101. **Business Addr:** Director of Human Services, Missouri Department of Corrections, Division of Human Services, 2729 Plaza Dr, PO Box 236, Jefferson City, MO 65109, **Business Phone:** (573)751-2389.

MYERS, WALTER DEAN
Executive, writer. **Personal:** Born Aug 12, 1937, Martinsburg, WV; son of George Ambrose Myers and Mary Green Myers (Deceased); married Constance Brendel, Jun 19, 1973; children: Karen, Michael Dean & Christopher; married Constance Brendel, Jun 19, 1973. **Educ:** Columbia Univ; State Univ NY, Empire State Col, BA, 1984. **Career:** NY State Dept Labor, Brooklyn, employ supvr, 1966-69; Bobbs-Merrill CoInc, New York City, sr trade book ed, 1970-77; writer, 1977-; Books: Where Does the Day Go?, 1969; The Dragon Takes a Wife, 1972; The Dancers, 1972; Fly, Jimmy, Fly!, 1974; The World of Work: A Guide to Choosing a Career, 1975; Fast Sam, Cool Clyde & Stuff, 1975; Social Welfare, 1976; Brainstorm, 1977; Mojo & the Russians, 1977; Victory for Jamie, 1977; It Ain't All For Nothing, 1978; Young Landlords, 1979; The Black Pearl & the Ghost; 1980; The Golden Serpent, 1980; Hoops, 1981; The Legend of Tarik, 1981; Won't Know Till I Get There, 1982; The Nicholas Factor, 1983; Tales of a Dead King, 1983; Mr. Monkey & the Gotcha Bird, 1984; Motown & Didi, 1984; The Outside Shot, 1984; Adventure in Granada, 1985; The Hidden Shrine, 1985; Fallen Angels, 1988; Scorpions, 1988; Now Is Your Time, The African American Struggle for Freedom, 1992; Sort of Sisters, 1993; Brown Angels, Harper Collins, 1993; The Party, 1993; The Prince, 1993; The Glory Field, 1994; Malcolm X: A Fire Burning Brightly, 2000; The Blues of Flats Brown, 2000; 145th Street: Short Stories, 2000; The Greatest: The Life of Muhammad Ali, 2000; Bad Boy: A Memoir, 2001; The Journal of Biddy Owens:The Negro Leagues, 1948, 2001; Patrol: An American Soldierin Vietnam,2002; Three Swords for Granada, 2002; Handbook for Boys: A Novel, 2002; A Time to Love: Stories from the Old Testament, 2003; Blues Journey, 2003;The Dream Bearer, 2003; The Beast, 2003; Shooter, 2004; I've Seen the Promised Land; Martin Luther King, 2004; Constellation, 2004; Antarctica,2004; Here In Harlem: Poems in Many Voices, 2004; Autobiography of My Dead Brother, 2005; The Hell fighters: When Pride Met Courage, 2006; Jazz, 2006;Street Love, 2006; What They Found: Love on 145th Street, 2007; Harlem Summer, 2007; Game, 2008. **Orgs:** PEN, Harlem Writers Guild; fel NJ State Coun Arts, 1981. **Honors/Awds:** Nat Endowment Arts Grant, 1982; Newbery Honor Book Award, two-time winner;Coretta Scott King Award, five-time winner; Margaret A Edwards Award,1994; Nat Book Award; Michael L Printz Award, Am Libr Asn. **Military Serv:** AUS, 1954-57. **Home Addr:** 2543 Kennedy Blvd, Jersey City, NJ 07304. **Business Addr:** Writer, c/o The Book Report Network, 250 W 57th St Suite 1228, New York, NY 10107, **Business Phone:** (212)246-3100.

MYERS, DR. WOODROW AUGUSTUS, JR.
Health services administrator. **Personal:** Born Feb 14, 1954, Indianapolis, IN; son of Woodrow and Charlotte; married Debra Jackson; children: Kimberly Leilani & Zachary Augustus. **Educ:** Stanford Univ, BS, BS, 1973; Harvard Med Sch, MD, 1977; Stanford Univ Grad Sch Bus, MBA, primary sector & health care mgt, 1982. **Career:** US Senate Comt Labor & HR, physician health adv, 1984; Univ Calif, asst prof, 1982-84; San Francisco Gen Hosp Med Ctr, qual assurance prog chmn, 1982-84, cost containment task force chmn, qual assurance dept med-comput syst mgr, dept med gen internal med div-attending physician, med surg intensive care unit-assoc dir; Univ Calif Inst Health Policy Studies, affiliated fac; Ind Univ Med Ctr, asst prof med; Stanford Univ Med Ctr, physician specialist surgery, attending physician; St IN, st health comnr; City New York, health comnr; The Assoc Group, sr vpres, corp med dir; Ford Motor Co, dir; WellPoint, exec vpres & chief med officer, 2000-05; Estes Pk Inst, fac, 2005; Genomic Health Inc, dir, 2006-. **Orgs:** Am Col Physicians; AMA; Nat Med Asn; Soc Critical Care Med; IN State MedAsn; Marion County Med Soc; dipl, Am Bd Internal Med, 1980; bd trustees,Stanford Univ, 1987-92; Harvard Univ Bd Overseers; chmn Vis Comt Harvard Sch Public Health. **Honors/Awds:** Dr Charles F Whitten Award, The Sickle Cell Found NW Ind, 1985; Sagamore of the Wabash, Gov Robert D Orr, 1986; Hoosier Freedom Award, Ind Trial Lawyers Asn, 1986; US Public Health Service Award, US Surgeon Gen CEverett Koop, 1989; Distinguished Mentor Award, Stud Nat Med Asn, RegionV, 1990; Sagamore of the Wabash, Gov Evan Bayh, 1990; Above & Beyond Award, Indiana Black Expo, Ind St Sen Carolyn B Mosby, 1990; Key to the City of Indianapolis, Indiana, Mayor William Hudnut, 1990; Spirit of the Heartland Award, Gov Evan Bayh, IN, 1990; Living Legend Award, Hoosier Minority Chamber Com, 1992. **Special Achievements:** Author: Problems of Minorities at Majority Institutions: A Student's Perspective; 23 articles; medical licenses in states of Indiana, California and DC; appointed by President Reagan to 13 member committee to find a strategy for battling AIDS, 1987. **Business Phone:** (650)556-9300.

MYLES, DESHONE J.
Football player. **Personal:** Born Oct 31, 1974, Las Vegas, NV. **Educ:** Univ Nev, Reno. **Career:** Football player (retired); Seattle Seahawks, linebacker, 1998-99; New Orleans Saints, 2001.

MYLES, STAN, JR.
Television show host, television producer. **Personal:** Born May 2, 1943, Los Angeles, CA; divorced. **Educ:** Calif State Univ, BA, 1966. **Career:** KABC-TV, LA, host-producer; manpower develop specialist, 1969-71; Mich Mining Mfg Co, sales rep, 1968-69; La Hair Co, pub rels rep, 1968-69; Ala Locke HS, LA, teacher, 1968; TV movie: "Louis Armstrong-Chicago Style", producer, 1976. **Orgs:** Dir pub info, Westminister Neighborhood Asn, LA, 1965-68; Nat Asn Mkg Developers; Am Fedn TV & Radio Artists; Kappa Alpha Psi; YMCA; life-time mem, Nat Asn Advan Colored People; Urban League. **Honors/Awds:** John Sweat Award, Calif Teachers Asn; Urban Affairs Community Relations Award, La City Schs; Man of the Year Award, Bahai Faith.

MYLES, TOBY (TOBIATH MYLES)
Football player. **Personal:** Born Jul 23, 1975, Jackson, MS. **Educ:** Miss State Univ; Jackson State Univ, 1999-2001. **Career:** Football player (retired); New York Giants, tackle, 1998-99; Oakland Raiders, 2001; Cleveland Browns, 2002.

MYLES, WILBERT
Executive, vice president (organization). **Personal:** Born Aug 28, 1935, Winnsboro, LA; son of John Myles and Armeather Myles; married Geraldine C Pinkney; children: Wilbert Anthony Jr & Nicole Denise. **Educ:** Am Inst Banking, attended; Pace Univ. **Career:** Baltman & Co, nyc porter, 1961; Mail Clerk Home Ins Co, 1961-62; clerk typist, 1962-64, asst cashier, 1968-73; Corp Trust Dept Nat Bank North Am, asst vpres, 1973-. **Orgs:** Stock Transfer Asn, 1968; BANWY's Black & Non-white YMCA's Black Comn; Black Achiever's Comt, Harlem YMCA, Greater New York, 1974-; Reorganization Group, Securities Industries Asn, 1975; bd mgrs, Harlem Br YMCA, 1975; Nat Task Force Steering Comt, YMCA Black Comt, 1975. **Honors/Awds:** Plaque Harlem Br YMCA Greater New York, 1974; A Salute to Black Achievers in Industry; Plaque Honor of Bank, Harlem Br, YMCA, Greater New York in Appreciation Banks Support of 1975 Black Achievers Proj. **Military Serv:** US Air Force, a/2c, 1956-61.

MYLES, WILLIAM
Athletic director. **Personal:** Born Nov 21, 1936, Kansas City, MO; son of Vera L Phillips Myles and William Myles Sr; married Lorita Thompson, Jun 30, 1957; children: Debbie & Billy. **Educ:** Drake Univ, Des Moines, IA, BS, 1962; Central MO State, MS, 1967. **Career:** Manual High Sch, Kansas City, MO, asst football & basketball coach, 1962-63; Lincoln High Sch, Kansas City, MO, asst football & basket ball coach & head football coach, 1963-69; SE High Sch, Kansas City, MO, head football coach, 1969-72; Univ NE, Lincoln, NE, asst football coach, 1972-77; OH State Univ, Columbus, OH, asst football coach, 1977-85, assoc dir athletics, 1985-2007. **Orgs:** Christian Science Church, Fel Christian Athletes, 1964-, Am Football Coaches Asn, 1972-; dir Athletics, Nat asn col, 1985-; Boy Scouts Am. **Honors/Awds:** Kansas City Area Man of Year; Greater Kansas City Coach of Year, 1971; Double D Award, Drake Univ, 1981; Drake National Distinguished Alumni Award, Drake Univ, 1988.

MYRICK, BISMARCK
Diplomat. **Personal:** Born Dec 23, 1940, Portsmouth, VA; children: Bismarck Jr, Wesley Todd & Allison Elizabeth. **Educ:** Univ Tampa, BA, 1972; Syracuse Univ, MA, 1973; postgrad, 1980. **Career:** US Dept State, Somalia, 1980-82; Monrovia, 1982-84; action officer, Office Strategic Nuclear Policy, 1985-87; dep dir, Policy Plans & Coord Bur, 1987-89; Una Chapman Cox Fel, US-African Policy, 1988-90; consult gen, Durban, South Africa, 1990-93; Capetown, SAfrica, 1993-95; ambassador Kingdom Lesotho, Maseru, 1995-98; Spelman Col, dipl residence, 1998-99; Ambassador to Liberia, 1999-2002; Old Dominion Univ, ambassador-in-residence, adj fac, currently; Goodwill Ambassador for Goree Island to Senegal, 2008-. **Honors/Awds:** Most Meritorious Order of Mohlomi, Gov Lesotho; Department of State's Superior Honor Award; four Meritorious Honor Awards. **Special Achievements:** Author: Three Aspects of Crisis in Colonial Kenya, 1975. **Military Serv:** AUS, 1959; Decorated Silver Star, Purple Heart, 4 Bronze stars, inducted in the US Army Hall of Fame, 1996. **Business Phone:** (757)683-3000.

MYRICK, DR. HOWARD A.
Educator, television broadcaster. **Personal:** Born Jun 22, 1934, Dawson, GA; son of Howard Myrick and Lenora Pratt Myrick; married Roberta Bowens, Oct 8, 1955; children: Kyl V & Keris J. **Educ:** Fla A&M Univ, Tallahassee, FL, BS, 1955; Univ Southern Calif, Los Angeles,MA, 1966, PhD, 1967. **Career:** Corp Pub Broadcasting, Washington, DC, dir res, 1977-82; Am Forces

Radio-TV Network, Repub Korea, dir & gen mgr; Howard Univ, Sch Commun,prof; Educ TV Div, AUS Command & Gen Staff Col, Fort Leavenworth, dir &gen mgr; Off Asst Secy Defense Pub Affairs, audio visual officer; Clark Col, Atlanta Univ Ctr, Atlanta, GA, prof, 1982-83; Temple Univ, chmn radio, tv & film dept, 1983-89; Temple Univ, Sch Commun & Theater, Philadelphia, prof commun, currently. **Orgs:** Edn brd, J Natl Acad Television Arts & Sci, 1989-91; chmn, comn minorities, Broadcast Educ Assn, 1988-90; bd dirs, Int Assn Knowledge Engrs, 1988-91; consult, Nat Telecom & Info Agency, 1986-90; brd experts, Natl Endowment Arts, 1988-91. **Honors/Awds:** Soldier's Medal, Republic China, 1969; Distinguished Graduate, Florida A & M Univ, 1989. **Military Serv:** AUS, Lt.col, 1955-77; Vietnam Combat Service Medal, 1969; Joint Service Commendation Medal, 1973; Legion Merit, 1977. **Business Addr:** Professor, Temple University, School of Communication & Theater of Philadelphia, Rm 212 Tomlinson Hall Main Campus, Philadelphia, PA 19122-6080, **Business Phone:** (215)204-8431.

MYRICKS, DR. NOEL
Lawyer, educator. **Personal:** Born Dec 22, 1935, Chicago, IL; son of Wyman and Mollie Palmer; widowed; children (previous marriage): Toussaint L & Mollie; married Sherralyn L Faine. **Educ:** San Francisco State Univ, BA, 1965, MS, 1967; Howard Univ, JD, 1970; Am Univ, EdD, coun psychol & higher educ, 1974. **Career:** Howard Univ, prof, 1967-69; Univ DC, educ adminr, 1969-72; Pvt Pract, atty, 1973-; Univ Md, prof, assoc prof, assoc prof emer, currently. **Orgs:** NFL Players Asn, 1984-; assoc ed, Family Rels J, 1978-82; Kappa Upsilon Lambda; Alpha Phi Alpha, 1984-; Am Bar Asn; Groves Asn; educr, atty coach, Nat Intercollegiate Mock Trial Champions, UMCP, 1992; Omicron Delta Kappa Hon Soc, 1992. **Honors/Awds:** Outstanding Citizen of the Year, Omega Psi Phi Fraternity, 1979; Outstanding & Dedicated Service Youth & Community Easton, PA, Nat Asn Advan Colored People, 1984; Faculty Minority Achievement Award, Pres Comn Ethnic Minority Issues, Univ Md, 1990; Outstanding Advisor for a Student Organisation, Campus Activities Off Md, 1990; Super Teaching Award, Univ Md, 1990; Outstanding Mentor, UMCP, 1992; Outstanding Teacher of the Yearr, UMCP, 1992; Outstanding Teacher, Col Health & Human Performance, 1998; Outstanding Mentor, Omicron Delta Kappa, 1998; Kirwan Undergraduate Education Award, 2003; Board Regents Faculty Award for Excellence in Mentoring, Univ Syst Md, 2003. **Special Achievements:** published numerous articles. **Military Serv:** USN, Musician 3rd Class, served 4 yrs. **Home Addr:** 2000 Golf Course Dr, Reston, VA 20191-3802. **Business Phone:** (301)405-3672.

N

NABORS, JESSE LEE
Educator. **Personal:** Born May 17, 1940, Columbus, MS; married Rebecca Gibson; children: Sherri, Tejia, Jesse Jr & Marcellus III. **Educ:** Tuskegee Inst, BS, 1965, MEd, 1968. **Career:** Stockton Unified Sch Dist, child welfare attendance, 1971, asst prin, 1993; Tuskegee Inst, coordr, 1966; Sanders Unified Sch Dist, teacher,1968; Tuskegee Inst, residence hall counr, 1967-68; City Stockton, vice-mayor, 1975; Amos Alonzo Stagg High Sch, head security team, currently. **Orgs:** Pres, Stockton Br Nat Asn Advan Colored People, 1971-73; pres, BTA, 1972-73; Stockton Alumni Chap, 1975-77; polemarch, Kappa Alpha Psi Frat. **Honors/Awds:** Outstanding service, Nat Asn Advan Colored People, 1973; Outstanding Service, BTA, 1973; Outstanding Service, City Stockton, 1976. **Business Addr:** Head of Security Team, Amos Alonzo Stagg High School, 1621 Brookside Rd, Stockton, CA 95207.

NABORS, MICHAEL C.R.
Clergy, president (organization). **Personal:** Born Nov 12, 1959, Kalamazoo, MI; children: Simone Charice, LaNez Domimic, JaRell Desmond, Spencer Alexandria. **Educ:** Western MI Univ, BS, 1982; Princeton Theol Sem, MDiv, 1985, ThM, 1986; United Theol Sem, DMin, 1992. **Career:** Galilee Missionary Baptist Church, youth minister, 1980-82; First Baptist Church, interim pastor & pastor, 1983-92; Joint Action in Community Service, Inc, regional dir, 1993; C's Home Soc, prog dir, 1994-96; Shiloh Baptist Church, asst pastor, 1994-98; Borough & Township of Princeton, civil rights dir, 1996-98; New Calvary Baptist Church, sr pastor, 1998-; Ashland Theol Sem, adjunct prof; Marygrove Col & Ecumenical Theol Seminary, adj prof, currently. **Orgs:** Nat Asn Advan Colored People, Cent NJ br, pres, 1986-89, Trenton br, pres, 1995-97, Detroit br, bd mem, 2000-; Princeton Clergy Asn, pres, 1987-88; co chair, NJ Religious Task Force; bd mem, NJ Health Dept's Cardiac Surg Adv Comt; chair, Urban Agenda Comt Black Ministers Coun NJ;dir, Cong Christian Educ Eastern Region PNBC Inc; Mich Progressive Baptist Convention Inc, first vpres, 2000-; United Way, Oakland County, bd mem, 2001-. **Honors/Awds:** Kalamazoo Rotary Club, Outstanding Youth of the Year, 1977; Princeton, NJ, Oct 12, 1991 declared Michael CR Nabors Day; Samuel DeWitt Proctor Fellow, United Theol Sem Dayton. **Business Addr:** Pastor, New Calvary Baptist Church, 3975 Concord, Detroit, MI 48207.*

NABORS, ROB
Government Official. **Personal:** Fort Dix, NJ; son of Robert L. Nabors. **Educ:** Univ of Notre Dame, BA, 1993; Univ of North Carolina-Chapel Hill, MA, 1996. **Career:** Office of Management and Budget (OMB) program examiner, 1996-98; Special assistant to the director, 1998; assistant director and executive secretary, 2000; minority staff director, 2004; majority staff director; Deputy Dir of the Office of Management and Budget, 2009-. **Special Achievements:** Recognized as a "budding wunderkind" by OMB Director Jacob Lew; as a graduate, co-authored a paper political scientist Thomas Oatley, published in journal Intl Organization, 1996. **Business Addr:** The Office of Management and Budget, 725 17th St, NW, Washington, DC 20503, **Business Phone:** (202)395-3080.*

NABRIT, JAMES M
Lawyer. **Personal:** Born Jun 11, 1932, Houston, TX; son of James M Nabrit Jr and Norma W; married Roberta Jacquelynn Harlan. **Educ:** Bates Col, AB, 1952; Yale Law Sch, JD, 1955. **Career:** Lawyer (retired); Reeves, Robinson & Duncan; NAACP Legal Def & Educ Fund Inc, assoc dir, coun, atty, 1959-89. **Orgs:** Dir, Lawyers Comn Civil Rights; secy, Nat Asn Advan Colored People Legal Defense & Educ Fund Inc. **Honors/Awds:** Hon Doctorate, Univ DC, Sch Law, 1998; Hon Doctorate, Univ DC, 2000; William J Brennan Award, DC Bar Asn, 2000. **Military Serv:** AUS, corporal, 1956-58.

NAEOLE, CHRIS (CHRISTOPHER KEALOHA NAEOLE)
Football player. **Personal:** Born Dec 25, 1974, Kailua, HI; married Tara; children: Azure Ke'alohilani & Christian Kaiwikani. **Educ:** Univ Colo, BA, sociol. **Career:** New Orleans Saints, guard, 1997-01; Jacksonville Jaguars, guard, 2002-09; free agent, currently. **Honors/Awds:** All-Am first-team, Assoc Press, Am Football Coaches Assn; Walter Camp & Football News; second-team hons, The Sporting News; John Mack Award. *

NAEOLE, CHRISTOPHER KEALOHA. See NAEOLE, CHRIS.

NAGAN, WINSTON PERCIVAL
Educator. **Personal:** Born Jun 23, 1940, Port Elizabeth, Republic of South Africa; married Judith Mattox; children: Jean, Catherine & Arthur. **Educ:** Univ Ft Hare, BA, 1965; Oxford Univ, BA, 1966, MA, 1970; Kuke Univ, LLM, 1970, MCL, 1970; Yale Univ, JSD 1977. **Career:** Duke Sch Law, Rule Law Res Ctr, res asst, 1967-68; African-Am Inst fel, 1967-68; Va Polytechnic Inst & State Univ, asst prof political sci, 1968-71; Valparaiso Univ Sch Law, asst prof law, 1971-72; De Paul Univ Col Law, from assoc prof to asst prof, 1972-75; Univ Fla Col Law, prof, 1975-; Monash Univ Sch Law Australia, vis prof, 1979; Yale Univ, lectr, 1974-75; CLEO Inst, assoc prof, 1974; Expedited Arbitration Proc, arbitrator, 1972-74; Valparaiso Univ Sch Law, asst prof, 1971-72; Va Polytech Inst State Univ, asst prof, 1968-71; AALS Law Teachers Clin, 1971; Duke Law Sch, res asst, 1968; Ross Arnold atty-at-law, law clerk, 1967; Valparaiso Univ Sch Law, asst prof, 1971-72; DePaul Univ, asst prof law, 1972-73; Univ Fla Law Sch, assoc prof, 1975-77, prof, 1978-, affiliate prof anthrop, 1989-, Inst Human Rights & Peace Develop, founder & dir, 1994-, Samuel T Dell Res Scholar prof law, currently; British PEN, mem, 1993-; High Ct Republic S Africa, Western Cape Div, acting justice, 2006-07. **Orgs:** Am Soc Int Law; test UN, 1968-73; African Stud Asn; Asn Am Law Sch; Ctr Study Dem Inst; Am Soc Social Philos & Philos Law; Arts & Civil Sem Univ Fla; Am Civil Sem Univ Fla; ed, Soviet Pub Int Law 1970; trustee, Int Def Aid Fund, 1971-74; secy, Int Campaign vs Racism Sports, 1972-74; Minority Comt; Prom Tenure Comt; Curr Comt; Libr Comt; fac, Recruit Comt; chmn, Admin Foreign Lawyers Comt, Univ Senate; Int Def & Aid Fund S Africa, 1972-74; fel James B Warburg, 1974-75; consult, Am Bar Asn, 1976; S Africa Constitution Watch Comn, 1989-90; fel World Acad Art & Sci, 1998-; trustee res fel, Univ Fla, 1998; vis fel, Brasenose College, 2002-03; fel Royal Soc Arts, 2003-; Am Soc Social Philosophy & Philosophy Law; Am Bar Asn; Nat Democratic Lawyers Asn. **Honors/Awds:** English Dept Prize, Univ S Africa, 1962; Faculty of Law prize, Ft Hare, 1963; Princess Beatrix InterNat Scholarship Award, 1964; Brasenose Oxford Overseas Scholar, 1964-67; African-American Inst Fellowship, 1967-68; James B. Warburg Fel, Consortium for World Order Studies, 1974-75; Senior Fulbright Scholar, Monash Univ, 1979; Bahai Human Rights Award, 1990; Rosa Parks Award, Accepted on behalf of AIUSA, 1990; Senior Fulbright Law Scholar Award, 1993; Professorial Excellence Award, 1997, Unviersity Step Award, 2001; Honorary Professor, Univ Cape Town, State Fla, 2002-; Distinguished Int Educr, Univ Fla, 2005. **Special Achievements:** Numerous appearances on radio & television, numerous publications of papers & speeches. **Business Addr:** Professor, Founding Director, University of Florida, College of Law, 312L Holland Hall, PO Box 117625, Gainesville, FL 32611, **Business Phone:** (352)273-0935.

NAGIN, C. RAY (CLARENCE RAY NAGIN, JR)
Mayor. **Personal:** Born Jun 11, 1956, New Orleans, LA; married Seletha Smith, 1982; children: Jeremy, Jarin, Tianna. **Educ:** Tuskegee Univ, BS, 1978; Tulane Univ, MBA, 1994. **Career:** General Motors, Detroit, 1978-81; Assoc Corp, Dallas, 1981-85; Cox Communications, New Orleans, LA, controller, 1985-89, vpres & gen mgr, 1989-02; City New Orleans, mayor, 2002-. **Orgs:** Pres, 100 Black Men of Metro New Orleans; pres, LA Cable TV Asn; chmn, UNCF Walkathon; bd mem, Greater New Orleans Educ Found; Orleans & Jefferson Parish Bus Coun; bd mem, United Way; bd mem, Covenant House; Nat Conf Democratic Mayors; Nat Black MBA Asn. **Honors/Awds:** Excellent Customer Service Award, Better Business Bureau, 1993; Distinguished Business Partner Award, LA State Bd Educ, 1994; Diversity & Role Model, Young Leadership Coun, 1995; Spirit of Greatness Award, 1997; New Orleanian of the Yr, Gambit Weekly, 1998; Natl Telly Award, 2001. **Special Achievements:** First New Orleans mayor to rise to the post in nearly 60 years without holding a previous elected office. **Business Addr:** Mayor, City of New Orleans Mayor's Office, 1300 Perdido Rm 2E04, New Orleans, LA 70112.*

NAGIN, CLARENCE RAY, JR. See NAGIN, C. RAY.

NAILS, JAMIE MARCELLUS
Football player, football coach. **Personal:** Born Jun 3, 1977, Baxley, GA. **Educ:** Fla A&M, 1997. **Career:** Football player (retired), football coach: Buffalo Bills, tackle, 1997-00; Miami Dolphins, 2001-04; Miami Morays, NIFL, offensive line coach. **Business Addr:** Offensive Line Coach, Miami Morays, Miami Arena, 701 Arena Blvd, Miami, FL 33136, **Business Phone:** (305)530-4400.*

NAILS, JOHN WALKER
Lawyer. **Personal:** Born Sep 5, 1947, Florence, AL; son of Rudolph Jr and Mary Ester; married Phyllis Johnson, Mar 9, 1974; children: Tanique Yvette, Rudolph IV. **Educ:** Howard Univ, BA, 1969; Villanova Law Sch, JD, 1972. **Career:** Community Assistance Proj, legal rep, 1972-75; pvt pract atty, 1975-; City of Chester, asst city solicitor, 1978-87, city solicitor, 1988-91. **Orgs:** PA Bar Asn, 1972-; Delaware County Bar Asn, 1975-; Nat Bar Asn, 1985-; trustee, Calvary Baptist Church, 1987-. **Honors/Awds:** Outstanding Community Service, Chester Scholar Fund, 1983; co-winner Riemel Moot Court Competition, Villanova Law Sch, 1972. **Special Achievements:** City of Chester, first black city solicitor, 1988. **Business Addr:** Attorney-at-Law, 19 W Fifth St, Chester, PA 19013, **Business Phone:** (610)876-0306.*

NAJEE, J. (JEROME NAJEE RASHEED)
Musician. **Personal:** Born Nov 4, 1957, New York; children: Noah & Jamal. **Educ:** Bronx Community Col, 1978; New England Conserv Music, 1982. **Career:** Recordings include: Najee's Theme, 1987; Day By Day, 1988; Tokyo Blue,1990; Just An Illusion, 1992; Share My World, 1995; The Best of Najee, 1998; Morning Tenderness, 1998; Embrace, 2003; My Point of View, 2005; Songs from the Key of Life; Love Songs; Rising Sun, 2007; Mind Over Matter, 2009. **Honors/Awds:** Soul Train Music Award, 1993, 1995; NAACP Image Award, 2006; Trumpet Award, 2008. **Special Achievements:** Plays soprano, alto & tenor sax & flute; performed as a spec guest artiston Hit & Run tour with Prince; nominated for Grammy music award, 1987; performed for Nelson Mandela for the S African leaders birthday celebration, 1998; guest of Bill Clinton in a spec performance, 1999.

NALL, ALVIN JAMES, JR.
Photojournalist, accountant. **Personal:** Born Nov 27, 1960, New York, NY; son of Alvin J and Emma. **Educ:** Cayuga Community Col, AAS, 1995; Ithaca Col, Roy H Park Sch Communs, BS, TV & radio studies, 1997, MS, communs, 1998. **Career:** NY Air Nat Guard, media specialist, master sgt, 1998-, human resources advr, 1998-; Portrait Photogr, 1981-82; WTVH-TV, Syracuse, NY, photojournalist/ed, 1982-93, prod tech, 1993, 1995; USF, tech sgt, 1990-91; Eric Mower & Assocs, Pub Rels Servs Group, sr acct exec, currently. **Orgs:** Nat Press Photogr's Asn, 1988-94; Nat Asn Broadcasters, 1989-; Syracuse Asn Black Journalists, 1991-; NCP, ACT-So Prog, mentor/coach, 1989-; bd mem, Nat Asn Advan Colored People's Afro-Cultural Technol Sci Olympics prog. **Honors/Awds:** NY Emmy Award, Nat Acad TV, Arts & Scis, 1988-89; Spot News Award, Assoc Press, 1985; Clips Awards, Nat Press Photographer's Asn, 1989, 1992; Five Professional Recognition Awards, Syracuse Press Club,1985-90; Park Fellowship, Ithaca Col, 1998. **Military Serv:** USF, tech sgt, 1990-91; SW Asia Service Medal w/3 Devices, Kuwait Liberation Medal, AF Commendation Medal; Air Force Achievement Medal. *

NALLS, PATRICIA
Founder (Originator), chief executive officer. **Career:** The Women's Collective, founder & exec dir, currently. **Orgs:** Consult, Health Resources & Servs Admin. **Honors/Awds:** Courage Award, Whitman-Walker Clin, 1999; Award of Merit, Solutions 1999, 2000; Caribbean People's International Award, 2003; Washington Free Clinic Community Leadership Award, 2003; Tribute to Working Women Award, WJLA Channel 7, 2003; Outstanding Leadership Award, Nat Asn Advan Colored People Youth Coun, 2004; Linowes Leadership Award, Community Found Nat Capital Region; Thurlow Evans Tibbs Jr. Award. **Business Addr:** Founder, Executive Director, The Womens Collective, 1436 U St NW Suite 200, Washington, DC 20009, **Business Phone:** (202)483-7003.*

NAMPHY, ANDRE
Lawyer. **Educ:** Yale Law School, JD 2001; University of Oxford, D.Phil 1998; Harvard Univ, AB 1994. **Business Addr:** Sullivan and Cromwell LLP, 125 Broad St., New York, NY 10004.

NANCE, BOOKER JOE, SR.
Government official. **Personal:** Born Apr 10, 1933, Crockett County, TN; married Everlena Lucas; children: Alice Eison,

Booker J Jr, Mary, Phyllis, Gladys, Marvin. **Career:** Town of Gates, town board, alderman, 1973; Nance's Construction & Contracting, pres, 1984-; city mayor, currently. **Orgs:** Chmn, Parents Adv Comt Halls Elem. **Military Serv:** AUS, pfc, 1953-55; Nat Defense Serv Medal. **Home Addr:** 1191 7th St, Gates, TN 38037. **Business Addr:** Mayor, City Hall 10085 2nd St, Gates, TN 38037.*

NANCE, FREDERICK R
Executive. **Personal:** Born in Ohio; married Jacquelyn Jones Nance, Apr 24, 1999; children: Melanie & Ricky. **Educ:** Harvard Col, AB, 1975; Univ Mich, Law Sch, JD, 1978. **Career:** City Cleveland, primary outside counsel; fed & state courts, jury trial litigator; RPM Int Inc, bd dir; BioEnterprise Inc, bd dir; McDonald & Co Investments Inc, audit & compensation comt; Squire Sanders & Dempsey, Cleveland, OH, managing partner, currently. **Orgs:** Vchmn, advocacy, Exec Comt Greater Cleveland Partnership; Cleveland's 16,000 plus; Exec Comt 50 Club Cleveland; chmn, Cleveland Defense Ind Alliance; Bds Cleveland Found; United Way Greater Cleveland; Catholic Charities Found; US Court Appeals Sixth Circuit Judicial Conf. **Honors/Awds:** Cardinal Robert J Bellarmine Award, St Ignatius High Sch, 1999; Best Lawyers in America; Ohio Super Lawyer; Inside Business Leading Lawyer in Northeast Ohio; Service to Mankind Award, Leukemia & Lymphoma Soc, 2004; Norman S Minor Trailblazer's Award, 2004; America's Best Corporate Lawyers Award, Corporate Board Member's Mag, 2004; American ORT Jurisprudence Award, 2005; Community Leaders of the Year, NE Ohio Chapter of the Arthritis Found, 2005; Regional Vision Award, NE Ohio Regional Leadership Task Force, 2007; Tribute to the Public Service Award, Cleveland State Univ, 2007. **Business Phone:** (216)479-8623.

NANCE, HERBERT CHARLES, SR.
Lawyer, auditor, consultant. **Personal:** Born Dec 30, 1946, Taylor, TX; son of Henry Jr and Alice Lavern Sanford; married Linda Lee Brown; children: Charlinda Audlice, Herbert Jr. **Educ:** Huston Tillotson Col, BA, 1969; Univ Tex, San Antonio, MA, 1979. **Career:** Ross Jr High Sch, teacher & coach, 1974-76; Kitty Hawk Jr High Sch, teacher & coach, 1976-80; Vietnam Era Veterans Outreach Prog, counr, 1980-81; Kelly AFB, Base Educ Serv Off, guidance counr; Base Educ Serv SA-ALC & DPE, Tex, Educ Serv Specialist; Sam Houston High Sch, San Antonio, Tex, Col counr, 2003; San Antonio Indep Sch Dist, sch attendance auditor, nontraditional prog, currently. **Orgs:** Am Asn Coun; bd trustees, Lackland Indep Sch Dist; adv counsel, Comn Col Air Force, 1986; asst keeper records, Omega Psi Phi Frat, San Antonio Chap, 1986; bd mem, Bexar County Sickle Cell Anemia; vBasileus, Psi Alpha Chap; Omega Psi Phi Fraternity. **Military Serv:** USY, sp-5, 3 1/2 yrs; Army Commendation & Expert M-14. **Business Addr:** Attendance Auditor, San Antonio Independent School District, Student Attendance Office, 141 Lavaca St, San Antonio, TX 78210.*

NANCE, JESSE J., JR.
Educator. **Personal:** Born Aug 2, 1939, Alamo, TN; son of Jesse J and Lillie L Nunn. **Educ:** Tenn State Univ, Nashville, BS, 1961; Univ Wis Madison, MS, 1971; Univ Tenn, additional graduate studies. **Career:** Tenn High Sch, teacher, 1961-67; Oak Ridge Assoc Univ, special training in atomic energy, 1967, instr nuclear sci, 1967-69; Atlantic Comm Col, asst prof biol, 1971-76; Univ Tenn Med Units Memphis, special training, 1972; Jackson St Comm Col, instr biol, 1976-78; Vol Comm Col, assoc prof biol, 1978. **Orgs:** Phi Beta Sigma, 1959; Intl Wildlife Fed, 1972; church choir mem, dir malechorus, minister of educ, church sch teacher. **Honors/Awds:** Serv Key Award, Baptist Student Union, 1961; Danforth Fellowship Award, Danforth Found, 1969; Acad Grant, NSF & Atomic Energy Commn, 1972; Teacher of the Year, 1984-85; Martin Luther King Brotherhood Award, 1988. *

NANCE, LARRY DONELL
Basketball player, race car driver. **Personal:** Born Feb 12, 1959, Anderson, SC; married Jaynee; children: Casey, Larry Jr & Pete. **Educ:** Clemson Univ, attended 1981. **Career:** Basketball player (retired); Phoenix Suns, 1981-87, 1988; Cleveland Cavaliers, 1988-94; Catch-22Racing, NHRA, prof stock car racer, owner, 1986-. **Honors/Awds:** NBA slam dunk champ; NBA Player of Week; hon mention, Assoc Press All-Am team, 1980-81; NBA All-Star Player; winner, IHRA, Pro Stock mountain stock class, 1996. **Business Addr:** Stock Car Racer, NHRA, Catch-22 Racing, 2035 Financial Way, Glendora, CA 91741, **Business Phone:** (626)914-4761.*

NANULA, RICHARD D
Executive, vice president (organization), chief financial officer. **Personal:** Born May 9, 1960, Los Angeles, CA; married Tracey; children: Anthony & Samantha. **Educ:** Univ Calif, Santa Barbara, BS, econ; Harvard Sch Bus, MBA. **Career:** Deloitte, Haskins & Sells, Atlanta, staff, 1980; Walt Disney & Co, sr planning analyst, 1986-87, strategic planning mgr, 1987, dir strategic planning, 1988-89, vpres & treas, 1989-91, sr vpres & chief financial officer, 1991-95; Disney Stores, pres, 1994-96, sr exec vpres & chief financial officer, 1996-98; Starwood Hotels & Resorts Worldwide Inc, pres & chief executive officer, 1998-99; Broadband Sports Inc, chmn & chief executive officer, 1999-2001; Amgen Inc, exec vpres & chief financial officer, 2001-. **Orgs:** Bd dir, Boeing Co; bd mem, Amateur Athletic Found, LA; bd trustee, UCSB Found. **Business Phone:** (805)447-1000.

NAPHTALI, ASHIRAH SHOLOMIS
Lawyer, consultant. **Personal:** Born Apr 6, 1950, Kingston, Jamaica. **Educ:** NY Med & Dent Sch, physician asst cert, 1974; NY Univ, BA, 1979; Hofstra Univ, JD-MBA, 1984. **Career:** Urban Develop, consult/res asst, 1978-80; MAKKA Prod, mgt consult, 1980-82; Nassau County Off Employ, legal asst, 1982-83; Colin A Moore Esq, legal asst, 1983; S Brooklyn Legal Servs, law asst, 1983-84; Michael M Laufer Esq, assoc, 1984; Helen Gregory Law Off, assoc, 1987-; NACA Inc, pres, 1984-; Law Off Barbara Emmanuel, Queens, NY, assoc, 1989-; Law Off Alarid, Alexander Al, law asst & assoc, 1989-90; Ashirah Naphtali Laurelton, NY, atty & finance counsult, 1990-. **Orgs:** WIBO; Nat Bar Asn; Int Soc Financiers, 1986-; Am Consult League, 1986-; Kiwanis Club Cambria Heights, 1990-97; Queens Bar Asn, 1990-95; NY State Bar Asn, 1990-91; Macon B Allen Bar Asn, 1991-92; BESLA, 1991-92. **Honors/Awds:** Certificate of Recognition, Cambria Heights Kiwanis Club Inc, 1996; Certificate of Recognition, NYC Off Vet Affairs, 1995; Editors Choice Award, Nat Libr Poetry, 1996; Merit Award, Beth Elohim Ethiopian Hebrew Congregation Inc, 1996. **Military Serv:** USAF, sgt, 1969-74; USAR, sgt, 1980-83. **Business Addr:** Attorney, Law Office of Ashirah Sholomis Naphtali, 130 33 217 St Suite B, Laurelton, NY 11413-1230.*

NAPOLEON, BENNY NELSON
Police chief, lawyer. **Personal:** Born Sep 10, 1955, Detroit, MI; son of Harry N and Betty Lee Currie; children: Tiffani Chanel. **Educ:** Mercy Col Detroit, Detroit, MI, AA, cum laude, 1980, BA, cum laude, 1982; Detroit Col Law, Detroit, MI, JD, 1986; FBI Nat Acad, US Secret Serv Dignitary Protection Sch, Northwestern Univ Sch Police Staff & Command, Aresty Inst Exec Develop Wharton Sch Univ PA. **Career:** Police chief (retired), atty: Sibley's Shoes; Detroit Police Dept, sergeant, 1983, lt, 1985, inspector, 1987, comdr, 1993, dep police chief, 1994, asst chief, 1995, chief police, 1998-01; self-employed, atty, 1987-; Capri Capital, exec vpres, 2001; Dozier Turner & Braceful P C, atty, currently. **Orgs:** bd dirs, GDIRT, NCCJ, 1990-; secy, Coalition DEMH, 1990-91; NOBLE, 1985-; FBI NAA, 1987-; IAATI, 1990-; State Bar Mich, 1987-; Am Bar Asn, 1986-; chair, Mich Civil Rights Comn, currently; Nat Asn Advan Colored People, currently; Cass Tech Hall Fame, currently. **Honors/Awds:** Trustee Scholar, DCL, 1982; Dean's Award for Outstanding Scholar, DCL, 1983; Distinguished Alumni Award, MCD, 1988; Police Community Service Award, Greater Detroit Chamber Com, 1990; Distinguished Alumni Award, Wolverine Stud Bar Asn, Detroit Col Law, 1991. **Business Phone:** (313)226-0260.

NAPOLEON, HARRY NELSON
Clergy. **Personal:** Born Nov 12, 1922, Brownsville, TN; son of Harry and Geneva Estes; married Betty Lee Currie Napoleon, Apr 17, 1951; children: Geneva Smitherman, Bobbie Napoleon Rearton, Anita Napoleon Taylor, Hilton, Benny N, Kathryn Napoleon Brogdon, Sharon Napoleon Seaton. **Career:** Tenn Missionary Baptist Church, pastor, currently. **Orgs:** Coun Baptist Pastors, Detroit, MI. **Business Addr:** Pastor, Tenn Missionary Baptist Church, 2100 Fischer St, Detroit, MI 48214, **Business Phone:** (313)823-4850.*

NAPPER, BERENICE NORWOOD
Musician. **Personal:** Born Dec 10, 1916, S Norwalk, CT; divorced; children: Patricia Knudsen, Alver Woodward Jr. **Educ:** Howard Univ, Washington, DC, MusB, 1940; Westport Famous Writer's Sch, Westport, CT, dipl, 1950. **Career:** Concert artist, 1940-; Conn Welfare Dept, social worker, 1945-; Conn Labor Dept, unemployment comp supvr, 1946-53; Napwood Assocs, owner & dir, 1953-; Am Cyanamid Co, librarian foreign div, 1964. **Orgs:** Bd mem, Sigma Gamma Rho Sorority, 1940; bd mem, State & Nat LWV/PPLI Social Serv, 1940-; exec dir, Urban League, White Plains, 1942-; field sec & troubleshooter, Nat Asn Advan Colored People, NY, 1951; Dist 12 RTM Greenwich Conn Town Gov, 1960-68; comnr, Conn State Bd Parole, 1971-75; bd mem, Norwalk Comm Col, 1973-; founding mem, Conn Br Nat Coun Negro Women. **Honors/Awds:** Distinguished Alumni Award, Howard Univ Alumni NY Chap, 1970; Humanitarian Award, Nigeria, 1975; Outstanding Negro Woman, Conn Bicentennial Comn, 1976; Distinguished Black Women, YWCA, Greenwich, 1977. **Special Achievements:** First Negro vol nurse's aide Greenwich Chap ARC, 1942-; first Negro woman candidate Reb Nomination CT US Senate, 1970; first Negro woman candidate GOP Greenwich Nom 2nd Selectman, 1979.

NAPPER, HYACINTHE T.
Government official. **Personal:** Born Feb 26, 1928, New York, NY; daughter of Georgiana Bergen Tatem and Charles A Tatem; divorced; children: Cynthia, Guy & Geoffrey. **Educ:** Fisk Univ, 1947; Howard Univ, AB, 1951. **Career:** Government Official (retired); US Dept Labor, Sec Thomasina Norford Minority Groups, consult, 1951-53; Hon John Conyers Jr, admin asst; self employed financial mgr; Wash Figure Skating Club, The Blade newsletter, ed, 1990-97. **Orgs:** Alpha Kappa Alpha Sor; interest in bringing greater polit awareness to African Am comm improve voter turnout; US Figure Skating Asn; Ft Dupont Skating Club; Cong Staff Club, 1965-95; Wash Figure Skating Club; bd gov, 1992-96; DC Specl Olympics, ice skating coach; DC Police Boys & Girls Club. **Honors/Awds:** DC Spec Olympics Figure Skating Coach Award; Miscellaneous figure skating Awards.

NAPPER, JAMES WILBUR
Educator. **Personal:** Born Feb 25, 1917, Institute, WV; son of Walter J and Zanphra D Robinson; married Cassie McKenzie, Dec 23, 1950; children: Gregory S, David M. **Educ:** W Va State Col, BS, 1937, MS, 1949; Univ Calif, Berkeley, attended 1964. **Career:** Educator (retired); Boyd Sch, Charleston, WV, teacher, coach, 1950; Alameda City Oakland, CA, dep probation officer, 1954; DeAnza High Sch Richmond, teacher, 1958; Richmond Unified Sch Dist, guidance consult, 1965; Santa Rose Jr Col, counr, 1969-82. **Orgs:** Calif Teacher Asn, 1958-; Nat Educ Asn, 1969, Phi Delta Kappa Educ Group, 1976-; ed adv, Alpha Phi Alpha; exec bd, Nat Asn Advan Colored People; pres, Kiwanis Club; bd dirs, AGAPE. **Honors/Awds:** Letters of Commendation, Santa Rose City School, 1969-70; Certificate of Appreciation Dept Calif Youth Auth, 1974. **Military Serv:** AUS, staff sgt, 1944-46; ETO 5 Battle Stars. **Home Addr:** 1010 Bristol Lakes Rd, Mount Dora, FL 32757. *

NASH, BOB J.
Government official. **Personal:** Born in Texarkana, AR; married J anis F Kearney; children: 3. **Educ:** Univ Ark, Pine Bluff, BA, sociol, 1969; US Dept Ag, grad prog, Cert Mgmt, 1971; Howard Univ, MA, urban studies, 1972. **Career:** City Wash, DC, asst dep mayor; City Fairfax Va, asst city mgr; Nat Training & Develop Serv, admin officer; Ark State Dept Planning, dir, community & regional aff; Winthrop Rockefeller Found, vp; Office Former Ark, Gov Bill Clinton, sr exec asst, econ develop; Ark State Develop Fin Authority, pres; White House Personnel, assoc dir, personnel chief, 1995; US Dept Agr, under secy agr, 1993-95; Shore Bank Corp, vice chmn, currently. **Orgs:** Chmn bd dirs, Shore Bank Enterprise Group, Cleveland; chmn bd dirs, Shore Bank Enterprise, Detroit; Chmn bd dirs, Winthrop Rockefeller Found, Little Rock; Mercy Housing bd, Denver; Chicago Children's Advocacy Ctr; S Side YMCA, Chicago; The Mercy Housing Bd Denver. **Special Achievements:** First black male VIP in Clinton White House. **Business Addr:** Vice-Chairman, ShoreBank Corporation, 7054 S Jeffery Blvd, Chicago, IL 60649, **Business Phone:** (773)420-4776.

NASH, CURTIS
Lawyer. **Personal:** Born Jul 11, 1946, Tallulah, LA; married Betty Jean Gordon. **Educ:** Southern Univ, Baton Rouge, La, BA, 1969; Univ Col Law, JD, 1972. **Career:** Firm Kidd & McLeod Monroe, LA, law clerk, 1971; Vermillion Co Legal Aid Soc Danville, Ill, law clerk, 1972; Corp Tax Br IRS Nat Off, tax law spec, 1972-75; Tax Div Criminal Enforcement Section Northern Region, Justice Dept, DC, trial atty, 1975-. **Orgs:** Vpres, Fairfax Co Wide Black Citizens Asn, 1980; Pi Gamma Mu; Omega Psi Phi Frat. **Business Addr:** Trial Attorney, Tax Division Criminal Enforcement Section Northern Region, Justice Department, 950 Pa NW, Washington, DC 20530-0001.

NASH, DR. DANIEL ALPHONZA, JR.
Physician. **Personal:** Born Jul 15, 1942, Washington, DC; son of Ruby I and Daniel A Sr; married Bettie Louise Taylor; children: Cheryl L & Daniel E. **Educ:** Syracuse Univ, BS, 1964; Howard Univ, MD, 1968. **Career:** Georgetown Med Serv DC Gen Hosp, internship first Yr res, 1968-70; Brooke Army Med Ctr, resd nephrol fel, 1970-73, asst chief, 1973-76; Walter Reed Army Med Ctr, asst chief, 1976-77, chief nephrol serv, 1977-83; Pvt Pract, physician 1983-. **Orgs:** Am Col Physicians, 1974, fel, 1976; Nat Med Asn, 1974; AMA 1975; Am Soc Nephrol, 1975; Int Soc Nephrol, 1975; med licensure Wash, DC, 1969; MD, 1977; assoc prof, med Howard Univ Col Med, 1978; diplomat Am Bd of Int Med, 1973; subspecialty Bd Nephrol, 1974. **Honors/Awds:** 10 major medical pubs; 12 publ abstracts; 4 sci presentations. **Military Serv:** USY col MC, 1970-83; USAR, 1983-92. **Business Addr:** Physician, 6196 Oxon Hill Rd Suite 300, Oxon Hill, MD 20745, **Business Phone:** (301)567-8000.

NASH, EVA L.
Executive. **Personal:** Born Jul 25, 1925, Atlantic City, NJ; widowed; children: Michele, Sharon. **Educ:** Howard Univ, AB, 1945; Univ Chicago, Sch Soc Serv Admin, 1946; Univ Pgh Sch Soc Work, MSW, 1959. **Career:** Hubbard Hosp, med soc worker, 1947-49; Atlantic City NJ, sub teacher, 1954-55; City Pgh, mkt surveyor, 1956-57; Travelers Aid, 1957; Freedman's Hosp, 1961-64; Child Guid Clinic, clinical soc worker, 1964-67; DC Developmental Serv, chief soc worker, 1967-69; DC Model Cities Prog, health planner, 1969; HUD, comm serv officer, 1969-72, asst dir, admin on aging. **Orgs:** Comn Chest Area Capt Nashville, 1951; World & Polit Disc Grp Pgh, 1955-57; Bunker Hill Sch PTA, 1959-64, chmn, nominating comn, 1960; chmn, Sch Fair, 1961; Marriage Prep Inst Bd, 1963-64; V St Proj Com, 1963-64; Mental Health Sub-Comn Urban League, 1963-64; Howard Univ & Interdisciplinary Faculty Seminar, 1963-64; Western HS PTA, 1965-66; Am Orthopsychiatric Assn, 1965; NAACP; Nat Coun

Negro Women; workshop ldr Howard Univ Sch Soc Work Sch Agency Inst, 1967; Nat Comn Support Pub Sch; consult, Group Counseling Prog Model Sch Div Sec Sch, 1967-68; bd dir, DC Planned Parenthood, 1968; NASW Regional Conf Buffal, 1968; conslting seminar ldr, Wash Sch Psychiatry 1968-69; staff, DC Public Sch Model Sch Div sum, 1968; Educ Working Party Mental Retardation Planning Comn DC, 1968; co-chmn spec serv comm, DC Citizens Better Pub Sch Educ, 1968-70; Nat Assn Soc Workers; Academy Certified Soc Workers; pres, NW settlement House Aux, 1972-73; Budget Comn Wash Coun Planned Parenthood. **Honors/Awds:** Urban League Voluntary Service Award, 1967.

NASH, HENRY GARY
Executive, president (organization). **Personal:** Born May 3, 1952, Macon, GA; son of Henry and Elizabeth Cason; children: David & Gary Alton. **Educ:** Univ Southern Cali, Los Angeles, MS, 1979; Savannah State Col, Savannah, GA, BSEE, 1974. **Career:** Automation Industs, Silver Spring, MD, systs engr, 1974-77; Raytheon Co, Burlington, MA, sr proj engr, 1977-81; Gen Elec Co, Arlington, VA, sr systs engr, 1981-85; Tracor Applied Sci Inc, Arlington, VA, prog mgr, 1985-87; Gen Scientific Corp, Arlington, VA, pres, chief exec officer, 1987-. **Orgs:** Kappa Alpha Psi Fraternity, 1972; Arlington County Chamber Com, 1987. **Business Addr:** President, Chief Executive Officer, General Scientific Corporation, Maritime Plaza I 1201 M St SE Suite 120, Washington, DC 20003-3711, **Business Phone:** (202)547-4299.*

NASH, JOHN LESTER, JR
Singer, business owner. **Personal:** Born Aug 19, 1940, Houston, TX; son of John Nash; married Carlie; children: two. **Career:** Songs: "A Teenager Sings The Blues", 1957; "A Very Special Love", 1958, "Stir It Up"; Albums: Johnny Nash, 1958; I Got Rhythm, 1959; Quiet Hour, 1959; Let's Get Lost, 1960; Starring Johnny Nash, 1961; Composer's Choice, 1964; Hold Me Tight, 1968; Prince of Peace, 1969; Let's Go Dancing, 1969; I Can See Clearly Now, 1972; Celebrate Life, 1974; What a Wonderful World, 1977; The Johnny Nash Album, 1980; Here Again, 1986; Tears on My Pillow, 1987; The Reggae Collection, 1993; Movie: Take A Giant Step, 1958; Key Witnes, 1960; Johnny Nash Indoor Arena, owner & operator, 1980-. **Honors/Awds:** Grammy Award, 2000; Silver Sail Award. **Special Achievements:** First regular African-American performer on Houston television. **Business Addr:** Owner, Johnny Nash Indoor Arena, 6200 Willardsville Rd, Houston, TX 77048.*

NASH, MARCUS DELANDO
Football player. **Personal:** Born Feb 1, 1976, Tulsa, OK; married Lorie. **Educ:** Univ Tenn. **Career:** Denver Broncos, wide receiver, 1998-99; Miami Dolphins, 1999; Baltimore Ravens, 1999-2000; Detroit Fury, 2003; Las Vegas Gladiators, 2004-06; Dallas Desperados, 2007-. **Honors/Awds:** All-American, 1997; Two times Super Bowl champion (XXXIII, XXXV); AFL Offensive Player of the Year, 2004. **Business Phone:** (972)785-4900.

NASH, NIECY (ENSLEY CAROL DENISE)
Actor. **Personal:** Born Feb 23, 1970, Palmdale, CA; married Don, May 14, 1991; children: 3. **Educ:** Calif State, BA. **Career:** Films: Boys on the Side, 1995; Cookie's Fortune, 1999; The Bachelor, 1999; Malibu's Most Wanted, 2003; Spider Man 2, Voice, 2004; Hair Show, 2004; Japardee, 2005; Guess Who, 2005; Here Comes Peter CottonTail: The Movie, Voice, 2005; Cook Off, 2006; Code Name: The Cleaner, 2007; Reno 911: Miami, 2007; G-Force, 2009; TV Episodes: "Spring Breaks: Part 1", 1996; "Fifeteen Candels", 2001; "He's having a baby", 2002; "Psychics Wanted", 2003; "Illegal Aliens", 2006; "Satisfaction", 2008; "Deputy Dance", 2009. **Orgs:** Spokesperson, Mothers Against Violence In Schools. **Honors/Awds:** Nominee, Day Time Emmy, 2009. *

NASH, TROY
Government official, executive. **Personal:** Born Apr 10, 1969, Kansas City, MO. **Career:** Lathrop & Gage; Univ Mo Bd Curators, curator; City Coun, Kans City, admin asst; Mayor Emanuel Cleaver, spec asst; Kans City, Mo City Coun, mem, 1999, 2003-07; Zimmer Real Estate Serv LC, vpres Pub Sector Consult & Develop, currently. **Orgs:** Vice chair, Planning, Zoning & Econ Develop Comt, 1993-03; chmn bd trustees, People to People Int, 1998-; Mid-America Regional Coun, 1999-03; Jazz Dist Redevelop Corp, 1999-; Greater Downtown Develop Authority, 2003-07; vice chair, Budget & Audit Comt, 2003-05; chair, Int Comt, 2006-07; Neighborhood Develop & Housing Comt; Legis, Rules, & Ethics Comt; Pub Interest & Int Law Asn; Am Royal Bd Gov; Downtown Minority Develop Corp; Econ Develop Corp Kansas City. **Military Serv:** USAF, chief honor flight 048; Air Force Training Medal; Nat Defense Serv Medal; Air Force Achievement Medal; Good Conduct Medal. **Business Addr:** Vice President of Public Sector Consulting & Development, Zimmer Real Estate Services LC, 1220 Wash St Suite 200, PO Box 411299, Kansas City, MO 64141-1299.

NATHAN, REV. TIMOTHY ERIC
Clergy. **Personal:** Born Oct 12, 1970, Columbus, GA; son of Thomas L and Hattie F. **Educ:** BS, art educ, 1994; MDiv, christian edu, 1998. **Career:** Oak Grove AME Church, Newell, AL, pastor, 1993-98; St Paul AME Church, Lanett, AL, pastor, 1996-98; Greater St Paul AME Church, pastor. **Orgs:** Nat Art Educrs Asn; United Asn Visual Arts; exec bd, Univ N Ala, Campus Ministry; Coop Task Force City Florence; Alpha Phi Alpha; asst dir, Christian Educ, Ninth Episcopal Dist-AMEC; exec bd, N Ala Habitat Humanity. **Honors/Awds:** The Interdenominational theol Ctr, The Bishop WD Fountain Award-AME, The Issac Clark Preaching Award, 1998. *

NATHAN, TONY CURTIS
Football coach. **Personal:** Born Dec 14, 1956, Birmingham, AL; son of William Nathan and Louise Nathan; married Johnnie F Wilson; children: Nichole, Natalie & Nadia. **Educ:** Univ Ala. **Career:** Player (retired), Coach: Miami Dolphins, running back, 1979-87, asst coach, 1988-95; Tampa Bay Buccaneers, asst coach, 1996-01; Dade Christian Sch, 2002; Fla Int Univ, coach running backs, 2003-05; Baltimore Ravens, running backs coach, 2006-08; San Francisco 49ers, running backs coach, 2008. **Orgs:** FCA; Am Football Coaches Assn. **Honors/Awds:** Inducted into the Senior Bowl Hall of Fame, 2006. **Home Addr:** 15110 Dunbarton Pl, Hialeah, FL 33016, **Home Phone:** (305)820-1490. *

NATT, KENNY
Basketball player, basketball coach. **Personal:** Married Jolene; children: Ki & Yazmine. **Educ:** Northeast La Univ, BA, bus admin, 1980. **Career:** Basketball player (retired), basketball coach; Ind Pacers, 1980-81; Kans City Kings; Utah Jazz; Minor League Basketball, Albuquerque, Leth bridge, Can, Las Vegas, Lancaster, PA, Casper, WY; CBA, Rockford; World Basketball League, Fresno, Youngstown, pro player, player personnel dir, scout, 1989; CBA, Columbus Horizon, OH, asst coach, 1992; Natl Basketball League,Canada, Cape Breton, Nova Scotia, head coach, 1992-93; Youngstown State Univ, asst coach, 1994-95; Utah Jazz, scout, asst coach, 1995-2004; Cleveland Cavaliers, asst coach, 2004-07; Sacramento Kings, asst coach, 2007-08; Head coach, 2008-09. **Honors/Awds:** All-Trans Am Conf, NBA Draft, 1980.

NATTA, CLAYTON LYLE
Educator, physician. **Personal:** Born Nov 17, 1932, San Fernando, Trinidad and Tobago; son of Samuel and Leonora; married Stephenie Lukowich, Jul 4, 1964; children: Laura & Andrea. **Educ:** McMaster Univ, BA, 1957; Univ Toronto, MD, 1961; Royal Col Physicians,Can, FRCP, 1972; Royal Col Pathologists, FRC, pathol, 1990. **Career:** Ottawa Civic Hosp, 1965-66; NY Univ Med Ctr, fel clin hematol, 1966-68; Columbia Univ, instr, assoc, 1970-73, asst prof med & pathol, 1973-81, assoc prof clin med, 1981, spec lectr med, currently. **Orgs:** AAAS, 1969-; Am Soc Hematol, 1969-; fel Royal Col Physicians Can, 1972; NY Acad Sci, 1973-; NY State Soc Internal Med, 1974-; chair, Soc Study Blood, 1977; fel Am Col Nutrit, 1980; Int Soc Hematol, 1983-; Biochem Soc London, 1983-; Nutrit Soc London, 1985-; Am Soc Clin Nutrit, 1987-; Fel Royal Col Pathologists London, 1992. **Honors/Awds:** Second Annual George M Howard Jr Memorial Lecture, Meharry Med Col, 1987; consult, Nat Heart, Lung, & Blood Inst, 1992. **Special Achievements:** Co-author, Erythrocyte Poly amines Normal Individuals & Patients with Sickle Cell Anemia, 1988; Co-author, Alteration in IgG Subclass Distribution in AIDS, 1989; Co-author, Anti sickling Properties Pyridoxine Derivatives: Cellular & Clinal Studies, 1990; Co-author, Selenium & Glutathione Peroxidase Levels in Sickle Cell Anemia, 1990; Co-author, Antioxidant status & free radical-induced oxidative damage Sickle Erythrocytes, 1992. **Home Addr:** 300 W 55th St Apt 14B, New York, NY 10019, **Home Phone:** (212)305-3595. **Business Addr:** Special Lecturer in Medicine, Columbia University, College of Physicians and Surgeons, 630 W 168th St, New York, NY 10032, **Business Phone:** (212)305-2645.

NATTIEL, RICKY. See NATTIEL, RICKY RENNARD.

NATTIEL, RICKY RENNARD (RICKY NATTIEL)
Football player. **Personal:** Born Jan 25, 1966, Gainesville, FL. **Educ:** Univ Fla, rehab coun, 1987. **Career:** Denver Broncos, wide receiver, 1987-92. **Honors/Awds:** Post-season play, 1987, 1989: AFC Championship Game, NFL Championship Game.

NAVES, LARRY J
Judge. **Personal:** Born in Birmingham, AL; married; children: 3. **Educ:** Univ Denver, attended 1968; Univ Colo Sch Law, JD, 1974. **Career:** Pvt pract, atty; Colo Pub Defender, dep state pub defender, 1974-79; US Pub Defender, asst fed pub defender, 1979-84; Denver Dist Ct, judge, 1987; Denver Dist Ct, Second Judicial Dist, judge, chief judge, 2006-. **Orgs:** Bd trustee, Denver Bar Asn, 1992-94; bd trustee, Colo C Chorale, 1999-2005; Childrens Chorale; Colo Bar Asn; Sam Carey Bar Asn; Colo Supreme Courts Civil Jury Instr Comt; Colo Comn Judicial Discipline. **Business Addr:** Chief Judge, Denver District Court, Second Judicial District, Rm 256 City & County Bldg 1437 Bannock St, Denver, CO 80202, **Business Phone:** (720)865-9063.

NAYLOR, GLORIA
Movie producer, novelist, business owner. **Personal:** Born Jan 25, 1950, New York, NY; daughter of Roosevelt Naylor and Alberta McAlpin. **Educ:** Brooklyn Col, BA, eng, 1981; Yale Univ, MA, Afro-Am Studies, 1983. **Career:** George Washington Univ, vis lect, 1983-84; New York Univ, vis prof, 1986; Princeton Univ, vis lectr, 1986; Boston Univ, vis prof, 1987; Soc Humanities, sr fel, 1988; US Info Agency, cultural exchange lectr; One Way Productions, New York, NY, founder & pres, 1990-, Univ Kent, Eng, vis prof; Novels: The Women of Brewster Place, 1982; Linden Hills, 1985; Mama Day, 1988; Bailey's Cafe,1992; The Best Short Stories by Black Writers, volume II, editor, Sept 1995; The Men of Brewster Place, 1998. **Orgs:** Exec bd mem, Book the Month Club, 1989-94. **Honors/Awds:** Nat Book Award, 1983; American Book Award 1983; Lillian Smith Award, 1989. **Business Addr:** Founder, President, One Way Productions, 638 2nd St, Brooklyn, NY 11215, **Business Phone:** (718)965-1031.

NAYMAN, ROBBIE L.
Psychologist. **Personal:** Born Nov 1937, Dallas, TX; married Dr Oguz B. **Educ:** BS, 1960; MS, 1962; PhD, 1973. **Career:** So IL U, cnslr, 1960-62; St Univ Col, asst dean studs, 1962-64; Univ Wis, teaching asst, 1964-69; Wis St Dept Health & Soc Servs, affirm acct coord, 1969-70; Calif State Univ Fullerton, sr counr Univ Counselling Ctr, dir Univ Learning Lab, vpres stud affairs. **Orgs:** Am Personnel & Guidance Asn; Am Psychol Asn; Pi Lambda Theta; Urban Leag Nat Advan Asn Colored People.

NDIAYE, MAKHTAR VINCENT
Basketball player. **Personal:** Born Dec 12, 1973, Dakar, Senegal. **Educ:** NC State Univ. **Career:** Vancouver Grizzlies, forward, 1999-2001; Levallois, 2006. **Honors/Awds:** African Championship, Senegal National Team, 1997.

NDIAYE-DIATTA, ASTOU
Basketball player, basketball coach. **Personal:** Born Nov 5, 1973, Kaolack, Senegal; married Ousman; children: Boubacar, Bineta & Ndiaysse. **Educ:** Southern Nazarene, BA, bus, 1997. **Career:** Basketball player (retired), basketball coach; Detroit Shock, 1999-2003; Indiana Fever, 2004; Houston Comets, 2006; Seattle Storm, 2007; Utah State Univ, asst coach, currently. **Honors/Awds:** Sooner Athletic Conference Player of the Year. **Business Addr:** Assistant Coach, Utah State University, 1400 Old Main Hill, Logan, UT 84322-1400, **Business Phone:** (435)797-1850.

NEAL, BRANDON
Executive. **Educ:** Howard Univ, BA, african-am studies, 2000. **Career:** Nat Asn Advan Colored People, nat youth coun coordr, 2000, Nat Off, mid-atlantic youth field dir, Youth & Col Div, nat dir, 2003-, asst dir, currently. **Special Achievements:** Featured in EBONY magazine as a "top thirty leader in America under thirty". **Business Addr:** National Director, Assistant Director, National Association for the Advancement of Colored People, Youth and College Division, 4805 Mt Hope Dr, Baltimore, MD 21215, **Business Phone:** (410)580-5658.*

NEAL, BRENDA JEAN
Manager. **Personal:** Born Jan 3, 1952, Greenville, SC; children: Damon Yusef. **Educ:** NMex State Univ; Onondaga Community Col, AA, social work, 1976; Le Moyne Col, BA, sociol, 1978. **Career:** Lincoln First Bank, teller, 1974; Syracuse City Sch Dist, sch social worker, 1982-83; Xerox Corp, internal control mgr, customer serv mgr, 1983. **Orgs:** YWCA. **Honors/Awds:** Black Achievers Award, 1490 Enterprise Buffalo, 1983; Special Merit Award, Xerox Corp, 1984. **Military Serv:** AUS, Specialist 4; Outstanding Trainee Award, ranked 1st out of 34 men, 1971. **Home Addr:** 114 - Kay St, Buffalo, NY 14215. *

NEAL, CHARLIE
Broadcaster. **Personal:** Born Oct 28, 1944, Philadelphia, PA; son of Robert Parrish and Elizabeth. **Educ:** Villanova Univ, 1966. **Career:** CBS TV, sports broadcaster, 1982-85; TBS TV, sports broadcaster, 1986-88; Greyhound Lines Inc, safety instr, 1971-; BET TV, sports broadcaster, 1980; Premier Basketball League, supvr officials, 2007-; ESPN, play-by-play announcer, currently; ABL, off; IBL, off; USBL, off; ABA, off; NCAA Div I Games, off. **Orgs:** Am Fedn TV & Radio Artists, 1982-; Blue Knights Safety Comt, 1985-; spec oper sect, Arlington Co Police, 1986-. **Honors/Awds:** Numerous broadcasting awards including Sportcaster of the Year, 100% Wrong Club, 1989; Outstanding Volunteer, Arlington Co, Va, 1991. **Business Addr:** Supervisor of Officials, Premier Basketball League, 4958 W Irving Pk Rd, Chicago, IL 60641, **Business Phone:** (773)844-7251.

NEAL, CURTIS EMERSON, JR.
Consulting engineer. **Personal:** Born Feb 20, 1931, Yoakum, TX; son of Ellie Neal and Curtis Emerson Neal Sr; married Evelyn V Spears, Sep 21, 1963. **Educ:** Prairie View A&M Univ, BS, archit eng, 1958; Dept Defense Fallout Shelter Anal Cert; Dwyer Sch Real Estate. **Career:** St Philip's Col, instr, 1958-63; WA Moore Eng Co, vpres, 1963-71, vpres, 1973-75; GW Adams mfg Co, pres, 1971-73; Curtis Neal Assoc, prin, 1975-; St Philips Col, Drafting Dept, San Antonio, Tex, instr. **Orgs:** Tex Soc Prof Engrs; Nat Soc Prof Engrs; Prof Engrs Pvt Pract; Nat Asn Black Consult Engrs; bd mem, Alamo City Chamber Com; bd mem, San Antonio Water Serv Bd; San Antonio Energy Study Technical Adv Panel; Waste water Adv Comt, City San Antonio; trustee & secy, San Antonio Water Syst; bd mem, San Antonio Coun Eng Educ; vice chmn, Alamo Conserv & Reuse Dist; asst Dist Comnr, Polaris District Boy Scouts of Am; Prof Engr State Tex; Nat Asn Black

Consulting Engrs. **Honors/Awds:** The United Negro Col Fund, Leadership in the Minority Community, 1980; Legislative Black Caucas, State of Texas, Outstanding Contribution to the Business Field, 1983; Community Award Prof Bus, Alamo City Chamber Com; Outstanding Serv Community, City of San Antonio; Outstanding Serv Community, Legis Black Caucus State Tex; Rotary Club Merit Award, Northwest San Antonio; Scouter's Training Award, Alamo Area Coun Boy Scouts of Am. **Military Serv:** USY, staff sgt, 1952-54. **Business Phone:** (210)579-0913.*

NEAL, ELISE
Actor. **Personal:** Born Mar 14, 1966, Memphis, TN. **Educ:** Univ Arts, PA; Am Acad Dramatic Arts. **Career:** Stage: Oh, Kay!, 1991; TV series: "Loving," 1994; 'SeaQuest," 1995-96; 'The Hughley's," 1998; "All of Us," 2003; TV movies: "Brian's Song," 2001; "Law & Order; Family Matters"; "Chicago Hope"; "The Steve Harvey Show"; "Fantasy Island"; AUSA, 2003; "Something About Brenda," 2004; "Bodies in Motion," 2005; "CSI: Crime Scene Investigation," 2005; "K-Ville", 2007; Films: Malcolm X, 1992; Rosewood, 1997; How to Be a Player, 1997; Money Talks, 1997; Scream 2, 1997; Restaurant, 1998; Mission to Mars, 2000; Sacred Is the Flesh, 2001; Paid in Full, 2002; The Rising Place, 2002; Playas Ball, 2003; Hustle & Flow, 2005. **Honors/Awds:** Best Ensemble Cast, SAG Awards, 2006; Best Supporting Actress in Film, Nat Asn Advan Colored People, 2006; Hottest Ensemble Cast, 2006; Trailblazer Award, 2006. **Business Addr:** Actress, Star File Photo Agency Ltd, 11 W 20th St Fl 7, New York, NY 10011, **Business Phone:** (212)929-2525.

NEAL, FREDERIC DOUGLAS
Basketball player, public relations executive, basketball coach. **Personal:** Born May 19, 1941, Greensboro, NC; son of Katie C Carter and Alfonza Lowdermilk; married Rose Allen, Sep 8, 1976; children: Lavern, Frederic Jr, Pamela, Toi & RoCurl. **Educ:** Johnson C Smith Univ, attended 1963, BS, 1975. **Career:** Basketball player, basketball executive, public relations executive(retired); Harlem Globetrotters, Los Angeles, CA, basketball player, coach & pub rels exec, 1963-85; Cernitin Am, Yellow Springs, Ohio, pub rels exec, 1985; Orlando Magic, Orlando, Fla, ticket chmn & dir spec proj, 1986-; Celebrity Golf Asn, PGA, prof golfer, 1990. **Orgs:** Screen Actors Guild; Am Fedn Television & Radio Artists. **Honors/Awds:** Numerous honors & award including Outstanding Athlete, All State Basketball, NC, 1958-59; Best Athlete, CIAA, 1960-63; Best Five Award, GIT, 1961; Hall of Fame, CIAA, 1985 & 1986; J C Smith 100 Club Sports Hall of Fame, 1989; Outstanding Contribution to Youth, Spec Olymipics, 1988-89; Contribution to Youth, Youth Basketball Am, 1988; Outstanding Contributor to the Youths of Greensboro, Greensboro Recreation Dept, 1970; Superior Performance as a Dribbler, Harlem Globetrotters, 1970; Dedication toYouth, United Way, United Youths Sports League, 1988. **Special Achievements:** Appeared in numerous TV shows, including Harlem Globetrotters Popcorn Machine, Wide World of Sports, Donnie and Marie Osmond Show, The Mandrell Sisters, The Love Boat, BBC TV Special, MTV, Don't Just Sit There, Comedyhour, Johnny Carson, Dick Cavett, David Frost, Good Morning America; spokesperson for Boeing, McDonalds, Coca Cola, Sherwin Williams Paint, and others.

NEAL, DR. GREEN BELTON
Physician. **Personal:** Born Sep 4, 1946, Hopkins, SC; married Linda Mattison; children: Green II, Tiffany & Marcus. **Educ:** Benedict Col, BS, 1966; Meharry Medical Col, MD, 1971; GW Hubbard Hosp, resident, 1973. **Career:** Providence Hosp, med staff; Columbia; SC Richland Mem Hosp; Meharry Med Col, asst prof med; GW Hubbard Hosp, dir cardiac catherization lab, 1975-76; pvt pract, currently. **Orgs:** Fel, Vanderbilt Univ Med Sch, 1973; GA St Med Asn, 1975; LA St Med Asn, 1975; consult Physician, Tuskeegee Inst; Nat Med Asn; AMA; bd mem, Boys Club Grtr Columbia; Columbia Med Asn; Am Heart Asn; Congaree Med Dental & Pharm Asn. **Honors/Awds:** Fel Grant Cardiol, NIH. **Home Phone:** (803)256-7985. **Business Addr:** Physician, 3010 Farrow Rd Suite 230, Columbia, SC 29201, **Business Phone:** (803)256-7985.

NEAL, DR. HOMER ALFRED
Educator, scientist. **Personal:** Born Jun 13, 1942, Franklin, KY; married Donna Daniels; children: Sharon & Homer Jr. **Educ:** Indiana Univ, BS, Physics, 1961, DSc Hon Degree, 1984; Univ Mich, MS, 1963, PhD, 1966. **Career:** Ind Univ, asst prof, 1967-70, from asso prof to prof, 1970-81, dean, res &grad develop, 1976-81; State Univ New York, Stony Brook, provost, 1981-86,Univ Mich, prof, 1987-97, dept physics, chair, 1987-93, emer vpres, res,1993-97, interim emer pres, UM-ATLAS Project, dir, 1997-, Samuel AGoudsmit prof, 2000-; European Lab Particle Physics, res. **Orgs:** Am Phys Soc, 1972-; US Dept Energy, High Energy Physics Advisory Panel,1977-81; Nat Sci Bd, 1980-86; New York Seagrant Inst, 1982-86; AAAS 1983;Univ Res Asn Bd, trustee, 1983; Covanta Corp, 1985; Nat Sci Found PhysicsAdv Panel, 1986; Smithsonian Inst, 1989-2001; Ind Univ, Inst Adv Study,1992; Ford Motor Co, 1997-; External Adv coun Nat Computational Sci Alliance, 1997-; Appln Stategy Coun, Univ Corp Advan Internet Develop, 2000-; mem, Smithsonian Coun of the NatMuseum for African Am History and Culture; mem, Oak Ridge NatLaboratory Advisory Board. **Honors/Awds:** Sloan Found, 1968; Argonne Zero Gradient Synchrotron Users Group, 1970-72; JS Guggenheim Found, 1980-81; The Stony Brook Medal, 1986; Ind Univ Distinguished Alumni Award, 1994; Edward A Bouchet Award, Am Phys Soc, 2003. **Business Addr:** Samuel A Goudsmit Professor, Director UM-ATLAS Collaboratory Project, University of Michigan, Department of Physics, 375 W Hall 2477 Randall Laboratory, Ann Arbor, MI 48109-1120, **Business Phone:** (734)764-4375.

NEAL, DR. IRA TINSLEY
School administrator. **Personal:** Born Nov 14, 1931, Memphis, TN; son of James and Ogie; married Jacqueline Elaine Wiley. **Educ:** Evansville Col, Ind, BA, 1960; Ind Univ, Bloomington, MS 1964. **Career:** Evansville-Vanderburgh Sch Corp, teacher, 1960-65, exec dir, 1966-70; supr, 1970-77, dir fed projs, 1977-; Neighborhood Youth Corps, dir, 1965-66. **Orgs:** Kappa Alpha Psi Frat, 1966-80; pres, Pride Inc, 1968-78; bd mem, Vanderburgh Co Judiciary Nominating Com, 1971-80; bd mem, Inner City Cult Ctr, 1977-80; sec-treas, New Hope Housing Inc, 1979-80; ctr assoc, Ill /Ind Race Desegregation Assistance Ctr, 1979-80. **Special Achievements:** Nominated NEA's Carter G Woodson Award, Local Black Teachers, 1978; Black Community Award, Black Community Evansville, 1978; Plaque Service Rendered Head Start Evansville, Ind, 1979. **Military Serv:** AUS SFC, 1947-56. **Home Phone:** (812)437-9944. **Business Addr:** Director of Field Projects, Evansville-Vanderburgh School Corporation, 1 SE 9th St, Evansville, IN 47708, **Business Phone:** (812)435-8159.

NEAL, JOSEPH C., JR.
Insurance agent, financial manager. **Personal:** Born Mar 23, 1941, Memphis, TN; son of Joseph C Sr and Hattie Counts Owens; children: Lisa M & Thomas Joseph. **Educ:** Trade Tech Col LA, AA, 1960; Calif State Col LA, BA, 1973. **Career:** Phoenix Life Ins Co & WS Griffith, 1969-; Christian Method Episcopal Church, gen secy finance, currently, chief financial officer, currently. **Orgs:** Nat Asn Advan Colored People, 1965-; 32nd degree mason, Prince Hall Grand Lodge, 1966-; Los Angeles Life Underwriters Asn, 1969-; La Kiwanis Club, 1972-; lic rep, Nat Asn Securities Dealers, 1974-. **Honors/Awds:** Honorary Doctor of Laws, Lane Col, 1989; Outstanding Sales, Phoenix Life Ins Co; Blue Vase Winner, Pres Club. **Business Addr:** General Secretary of Finance, Chief Financial Officer, Christian Methodist Episcopal Church, 4466 Elvis Presley Blvd, Memphis, TN 38116-7100, **Business Phone:** (901)345-0580.

NEAL, LANGDON D
Lawyer. **Personal:** Born in Chicago, IL. **Educ:** Cornell Univ, BA, 1978; Univ Ill Law Sch, JD, 1981. **Career:** Am Inst Real Estate Appraisers, lectr; Col Taylor Bank, bd dir; Support Group; Cook Co Bar Asn, lectr; Earl L Neal & Assocs, managing partner, 1968-; Chicago Gary Regional Airport Authority, chmn, 1995-; Ill State Bd Elections, chmn, 1991-93; Chicago Bd Election Comners, chmn, 1997-; Neal & Leroy LLC, atty, currently, High Jump Orgn, co-chair, 2008-; Cole Taylor Bank, bd dir; Am Inst Real Estate Appraisers, lectr; Cook County Bar Assoc, Judicial Candidates Symp, lectr. **Orgs:** Cook County Bar Asn; Chicago Bar Asn; Am Bar Asn; Ill State Bar Asn; Chicago Hist Soc; W DePaul Neighbors; Cs Place Asn; Chicago Pub Educ Fund; Jane Addams Juvenile Ct Found; Bar Admiss Supreme Ct Ill; US Dist Ct; Northern Dist Ill; Trial Bar; Children's Pl Asn. **Special Achievements:** Only the second African Am to be elected to the Chicago Bd of Election Commissioners. **Business Addr:** Attorney, Co-chair, Neal & Leroy LLC, High Jump Organization, 203 N LaSalle St Suite 2300, Chicago, IL 60601, **Business Phone:** (312)641-7144.

NEAL, LAVELLE E, III
Writer. **Personal:** Born Sep 28, 1965, Chicago, IL; son of Lillian E Neal and La Velle E Neal Jr. **Educ:** Univ Ill, Champaign, 1983-86; Univ Ill, Chicago, BA, commun, 1989. **Career:** Chicago Illini, sports ed, 1986-89; Southtown Economist, Chicago, Ill, sports writer, 1988-89; Kans City Star, Kans City, Mo, sports writer, 1989; Star Tribune, baseball writer & reporter, currently. **Orgs:** Kansas City Asn Black Journalists, secy, 1989-; Nab, 1987-. **Honors/Awds:** Chancellor's Student Service Award, Univ Il, 1989; Kans City Assn Black Journalists, PRS's Award, 1992. **Home Addr:** 8013 N Hickory Suite 737, Kansas City, MO 64118-8338, **Home Phone:** (816)468-8748. **Business Addr:** Sports Writer, Kansas City Star, 425 Portland Ave S, Minneapolis, MN 55488, **Business Phone:** (612)673-4000.

NEAL, LORENZO LAVON
Football player, business owner. **Personal:** Born Dec 27, 1970, Hanford, CA; married Denisha; children: Lorenzo, Nylya & Mia. **Educ:** Fresno State Univ. **Career:** New Orleans Saints, running back, 1993-96; New York Jets, 1997; Tampa Bay Buccaneers, 1998; Tennessee Titans, 1999-2000; Cincinnati Bengals, 2001-02; San Diego Chargers, 2003-07; M & N Service Inc, owner. **Business Addr:** Onwer, M & N Service Inc, Fresno, CA.

NEAL, MARIO LANZA
Banker, vice president (organization), president (organization). **Personal:** Born Aug 3, 1951, Haines City, FL; son of Warren Neal Jr and Mary E Wolfe; married Emma L Woodward Neal, Dec 23, 1973; children: Warren Keith & Jennifer Woodard. **Educ:** Fla State Univ, BS, finan & mgt, 1973; Univ Delaware, Stonier Grad Sch Banking, 1989. **Career:** First Union Corp, area prest/Fla panhandle, 1973; Ed, Charlotte Citizen, publ Charlotte Jaycees, 1975-76; First Union Nat Bank, sr vpres & consumer bank dir, area pres, currently. **Orgs:** Pres, Family Housing Services, Inc, 1974-76; treas, Energy Committed to Ex-Offenders, Inc, 1978-83; Mecklenburg County Personnel Comn, 1980-85; chair-elect, United Way of the Big Bend Tallahassee, FL; chair-elect, Econ Develop Coun; bd dirs, Tallahassee Area Chamber of Com; bd dirs, March Dimes; bd dirs, Regional 5 Workforce Develop Bd; bd dirs, Fla State Univ Alumni; Fla State Univ Col Bus Adv Bd; comt mem, Davis Productivity Awards, Florida Tax Watch; bd dirs, Capital Cultural Ctr, Tallahassee; bd mem, INROADS of Tampa Bay, Inc, 1989-; YMCA Black Achievers Inc, 1992; Bd mem, Ctr drug-Free Living Inc, 1992-; bd mem, Hi-Tech Learning Center, Inc, 1992. **Honors/Awds:** Central Florida YMCA Black Achievers Inc, 1992. **Special Achievements:** Recognized as One of Two areas within First Union Corp for top performance, 1995. **Business Addr:** Senior Vice President, Consumer Bank Director, First Union National Bank, 11510 E Colonial Dr, Orlando, FL 32817, **Business Phone:** (407)273-2300.

NEAL, RICHARD
Law enforcement officer. **Career:** Philadelphia Police Dept, patrolman, 12th dist, community rels, Internal Affairs Div, head, Housing Police, interim chief, Patrol Bureau, chief inspector, comnr, 1992-98.

NEAL, SYLVESTER
Firefighter, lieutenant governor, president (organization). **Personal:** Born Sep 21, 1943, Austin, TX; son of Willis and Ima L Jenkins; married Doris Marie (Mims) Neal; children: Sylvia, Sylvester L, Keith, Todd, Angela Williams. **Educ:** Univ Alaska, Fairbanks, degree in criminal justice (magna cum laude), 1983. **Career:** Firefighter (retired); City of Austin, Austin TX, firefighter, 1965-68; AUS, Fort Wainwright AK, firefighter, crew chief, 1968-70; State Alaska, Dept Transp, Fairbanks AK, firefighter, security police, 1970-79, fire/security chief, 1979-83; Dept Pub Safety, Anchorage, AK, state fire marshal, 1983; Anchorage Daily News, safety dir, 1994. **Orgs:** bd mem, Alaska Fire Chiefs Asn, 1976-; Alaska Peace Officers Asn, 1979-; secy, Fairbanks Kiwanis Club, 1982-83; Int Fire Chiefs Asn, 1983-; Fire Marshals Asn N Am, 1984-; consult, Alaska Asn Pub Fire Educ, 1985-; pres, Anchorage Kiwanis Club, 1987-88; bd dir, Community Action Drug Free Youth, 1988-; Kiwanis/Alaska-Yukon Div, lt gov elect, 1989-90, gov-elect, 2001-02, gov, 1989-90, 2002-03; hon chair, Pacific Northwest Dist Kiwanis/SIGN proj. **Honors/Awds:** Student of the Year Justice Dept, Univ of Alaska Fairbanks, 1982; Kiwanian of the Year, Fairbanks Kiwanis Club, 1983; Outstanding President, Kiwanis/Pacific Northwest Dist, 1989. **Military Serv:** AUS, sergeant, 1968-70. **Home Addr:** 1720 64th St SE, Auburn, WA 98092-8022. *

NEAL-BARNETT, ANGELA M.
Educator, business owner. **Personal:** Born Feb 13, 1960, Youngstown, OH; daughter of Andrew and Doris L; married Edgar J Barnett Jr, Jun 17, 1995; children: Reece L Barnett. **Educ:** Mt Union Col, BA, 1982; De Paul Univ, MA, 1985, PhD, 1988. **Career:** Englewood Community Health Orgn, clin therapist, 1985-87; Western Psychiatric Inst & Clin, intern, 1987-88, fel, 1988-89; Kent State Univ, asst prof, 1989-95, res fel, 1991-, assoc prof, 1995-, scientific med staff, 1996-; Rise Sally Rise Inc, chief exec officer, 2000-. **Orgs:** Am Psychol Asn, 1989-; Anxiety Disorder Asn Am; Trichotillamania Learning Ctr; Asn Black Psychologist; Arlington Church God; adv comm, Am Psychol Asn Minority Fel Prog, 2003-06; Asn Advan Behavior Therapy; Soc Res Child Develop. **Honors/Awds:** Kenneth and Mamie Clark Award, Am Psychol Asn, 2000; University Teaching Council Graduate Applause Award, Kent State Univ, 2000; Ohio Senate Spec Resolution, 2000; Kent State Univ Creative Contribution Award, 2000; Status of Women Award, Greater Cleveland Chap Top Ladies Distinction, Inc, 2005; named her one of the 500 most influential women in Northeastern Ohio, Northern Ohio Live Magazine. **Special Achievements:** Author of Soothe Your Nerves: The Black Woman's Guide to Understanding and Overcoming Anxiety, Panic, and Fear, Forging Links: African American Children Clinical Developmental Perspectives, numerous articles and book chapter son anxiety disorder among African Americans, video, Strand by Strand: A Black Trichotillomnic Story; Believe And Succeed: Applying & Getting Into Graduate School for Students of Color an Interactive CD, was featured in the November 2006 Womens Network newsletter, was interviewed & featured in the Beacon Journal. **Home Addr:** 361 Starr Lane, Tallmadge, OH 44278, **Home Phone:** (330)633-5990.

NEALS, FELIX
Judge. **Personal:** Born Jan 5, 1929, Jacksonville, FL; married Betty Harris; children: Felice, Felix, Julien. **Educ:** Idaho State Univ, BS; Washburn Univ, LLB, JD, 1958. **Career:** Appellate Law NY, pvt pract, 1960-64; ITT & RCA, mgt positions, 1965-69; NY Dept State, supervising admin law judge; pvt pract, corp law. **Orgs:** Arbitrator Community Dispute Serv, Am Arbit Asn, NY; founder, "Psycho-Systematics"; authority & collector mats Black Magic; bd mem, State Coun Soc Prevention Cruelty C Inc, 1988-; exec vpres, NY State Admin Law Judges Asn; Nat Asn Admin Law Judges. **Honors/Awds:** US Nat Intercoll Oratorical

Champion, 1954-55. **Military Serv:** AUS, corpl, 1946-49. **Business Addr:** Supervising Administrative Law Judge, NY State Department of State, 123 William St 19th Fl, New York, NY 10038.

NEARN, ARNOLD DORSEY, JR.
Executive. **Personal:** Born Jun 7, 1949, Philadelphia, PA; son of Arnold Dorsey Sr and Isabelle Lawrence; married Sharon Anderson, Oct 22, 1983. **Educ:** Del State col, BS, bus admin, 1971; Temple Univ Law Sch, 1971-72; Rutgers Univ, Grad Bus Sch, 1976; Fairleigh Dickinson Univ, 1981. **Career:** Allstate Insurance Co, casualty claims adjuster, 1971-82; Ethicon Inc, head prod supvr, 1972-76; Monsanto Co, mfg foreperson, 1976-77; Calgon Corp, prime prod foreperson, 1977-78, asst mgr, 1978-81; Schering-Plough Corp, Warehouse Opers, mgr, 1981-82, mgr, 1983; Belle-Sue Assocs, pres, 1983-87; Millennium Fire & Safety Equip, secy, currently. **Orgs:** Dania coun, exec comt, 1988-; Coun Black Economic Develop, 1985-; Broward County Boys & Girls Clubs, 1989-; Fla Reg Purchasing coun; bd dirs, Fla Fire Equip Dealers Asn; alumni leadership coun, DE State Univ. **Honors/Awds:** Coun Black Econ Develop Top 50 Bus Awards, 1988-91; Price Waterhouse Up & Comers Award Outstanding Entrepreneur, 1989; Small Bus Year Award, Dania Coun, 1989; Distinguished Alumni Award, Del State Univ, 1990; Nat Distributor Spotlight, Brooks Equip Co, Charlotte NC. **Special Achievements:** Publications: Plant Environmental Protection Program; Operational Training Guide; Preventive Maintenance Program; Warehouse Operations Employee Safety Manual; Warehouse Operations Policy Manual; spotlighted on television on 3 separate occasions by the Visual Communications Groups and Channel 17 (Miami, FL) on a program entitled The Black Entrepreneur on Location; received numerous council service awards from the Broward County Boys & Girls Clubs. **Home Addr:** 425 SE 6th St, Dania, FL 33004. **Business Addr:** Secretary, Millennium Fire & Safety Equipment, 1496-1502 Dixie Hwy, Dania, FL 33004, **Business Phone:** (954)922-9136.

NEAVON, JOSEPH ROY
Clergy. **Personal:** Born Dec 4, 1928, New York, NY. **Educ:** Manhattan Col, NY, BA, 1950; Gregorian Univ, Rome, Italy, STD, 1973. **Career:** Blessed Sacrament Fathers, rev, dr, prof, 1985. **Orgs:** Parliamentarian Cath Theol Soc Am, 1970-; Black Catholic Clergy Caucus, 1978-; Faculty Fellowship, John Carroll Univ Cleveland OH, 1980-81.

NEDD, CATHY
Business owner. **Career:** Nedd/Detroit Pub Rels, owner & pres, 1994-; Hass Assocs-Nedd; The Hair Network, founder & owner, currently. **Business Addr:** Founder/Principal, Owner, The Hair Network, 703 Livernois, Ferndale, MI 48220, **Business Phone:** (313)350-4241.

NEDD, JOHNNIE COLEMON. See COLEMON, REV. DR. JOHNNIE.

NEELY, DAVID E.
School administrator, educator, lawyer. **Personal:** Born in Chicago, IL. **Educ:** Fayetteville State Univ, BA, sociol, 1975; Univ ID, MA, sociol, 1978; Univ IA, Sch Law, JD, 1981; Univ Ill, Chicago, PhD, educ, 1997. **Career:** Univ IA, Univ Ombudsman, 1979-81; Ill State Univ, assoc prof, Polit Sci,1981-83, dir affirm action, 1981-83; Nat Bar Asn, reg dir; John Marshall Law Sch, practicing atty, prof law, consult, K-12, col & univ, asst dean. **Orgs:** Legal coun, Ill Affirm Action Officer Asn; Ill Human Rels Asn,; Ill Comn Black Concern Higher Ed; Chicago Southside Branch NAACP. **Special Achievements:** Works: Capital punishment discrimination An Indicator of Inst Western Jrnl ofBlack Studies, 1979; innovative approach to recruiting minority employeesin higher ed EEO Today, 1982; Blacks in IL Higher Ed A Status Report Jrnlfor the Soc of Soc & Ethnic Studies, 1983; The Social Reality of BlacksUnderrepresentation in Legal Ed Approach Toward Racial Parity, 1985. Author of articles, "Pedagogy of Culturally Biased Curriculm in PublicEducation," 1994; "Social Reality of African American Street Gangs," 1997. **Business Addr:** Assistant Dean, The John Marshall Law School, 315 S Plymouth Ct, Chicago, IL 60604, **Business Phone:** (312)427-2737.

NEELY, HENRY MASON
Lawyer. **Personal:** Born Jan 13, 1942, Washington, DC; married Elsie T; children: Allen, Frank. **Educ:** Morgan St Col, BA, 1963; Howard Univ Sch Law, LLB, 1966. **Career:** DC, spec US dep marshal, 1964; Met Police Dept, DC, mem, 1965; Armstrong Adult Educ Ctr, bus law & polit sci instr, 1966-70; Clinton W Chapman Firm, assoc atty, 1967-71; pvt prac law; Pub Serv Comn, DC, vice chmn, 1971-. **Orgs:** Wash Bar Asn; Jud Br DC Bar Asn; Great Lakes Conf Utility Comnr; Nat Asn Regulatory Untility Comnr; Gamma Theta Upsilon Fraternity; Nat Soc Pershing Rifles; Int Moot Ct Team; Sigma Delta Tau Legal Fraternity; active, Howard Univ Child Develop Ctr; past mem, Wash Bar Asn Legal Comt; former vol, supr, atty, Howard Univ Legal Interns; trustee, DC Inst Ment Hygiene. **Honors/Awds:** Recipient of Association of AUS Medal, 1962; American Jurisprudence Prize; Outstanding Academic Achievement in Commercial Law, 1985. **Special Achievements:** "Design and development of a reversible plastic blade fan", 1963. **Military Serv:** AUS. **Business Addr:** 1625 I St NW, Washington, DC 20006.

NEIGHBORS, DOLORES MARIA
Clergy. **Personal:** Born Aug 29, 1929, Chicago, IL; daughter of Roscoe Cokiegee and Ruth Smith; divorced; children: Deborah Ann, Eric Chanlyn & Lori Dee. **Educ:** Seabury Western Theol Sem, MDiv, 1988; advan seminar, psychiat & pastoral coun, 1992; Claret Ctr, internship, spiritual direction, 1997. **Career:** Clergy (Retired); Univ Chicago, Nat Opinion Res Ctr, area supvr, 1967-78; Ill Human Rights Dept, human rights investr, 1978-86; Seabury Western Theol Sem, seminarian, 1985-88; St George & Matthias Episcopal Church, seminarian asst, 1988; Church Epiphany, assoc priest, 1988-90; St Edmund Episcopal Church, asst priest, 1990-96, spiritual dir, 1996; St James Episcopal Cathedral, canon, 1997-2000; St Chrysastoms Episcopal Church, assoc priest, 2000-01. **Orgs:** Nat Alliance Mentally Ill, 1981-89; Alliance Mentally Ill, 1981-90; Black Union Episcopalians, 1985-; Chicago Episcopal Diocese, 1990-97; Clergy Family Proj Comt, 1993-96; Standing Comn, Diocese Chicago, 1999-2001; Network Biblical Storytellers, 2000-01; pres, Standing Comn, 2001; Pastoral Asn St Paul & The Redeemer Episcopal Church, 2001. **Special Achievements:** Ordained to the Diaconate, Deacon, June 1988; Ordained to the Sacred Order of Priests, Dec 1988. **Home Addr:** 5555 S Everett Ave C4, Chicago, IL 60637-1968, **Home Phone:** (773)493-3429.

NEIL, EARL ALBERT
Clergy. **Personal:** Born Dec 17, 1935, St Paul, MN; son of Earl Willus Neil and Katherine Louise Martin; married Angela, Aug 31, 1991; children: Latoya. **Educ:** Carleton Col, Northfield, MN, BA, 1957; Seabury-Western Theol Sem, MDiv, 1960, DDiv, 1989; Univ Calif-Berkeley, MSW, 1973. **Career:** Clergy (Retired); St Augustine's Wichita, KS, vicar, 1960-63; Christ Church, Chicago, IL, vicar, 1964-67; St Augustine's, Oakland CA, rector, 1967-74; Episcopal Church Ctr, New York, NY, exec, 1974-90; Church Province Southern Africa, SAfrica, 1990-93; Wash Nat Cathedral, WDC, canon missioner, 1994-97; Calvary Episcopal Church, WDC, interim rector, 1997-2000. **Honors/Awds:** Alumni Award, Carleton Col, 1971. **Home Addr:** 4545 Connecticut Ave NW Suite 929, Washington, DC 20008.

NEIZER, MEREDITH ANN
Vice president (government), president (organization). **Personal:** Born Jul 24, 1956, Chateauroux, France; daughter of Donald Neizer and Roberta Marie Faulcon Neizer. **Educ:** US Merchant Marine Acad, Kings Point, NY, BS, (honors), 1978, USCG Third Mate License, 1978; Stanford Grad Sch Bus, Stanford, Calif, MBA, 1982. **Career:** Arco Marine, Long Beach, Calif, third mate, 1978-80; Exxon Int, Florham Park, NJ, sr analyst, 1982-86; US Dept Defense, Wash, DC, spec asst, 1986-87; New York/New Jersey Port Authority, New York, NY, bus mgr, 1987-; Martin-Brower, Canada, vpres; Mbx Logistics, pres, currently. **Orgs:** Kings Point info rep, Kings Point Alumni Assn, 1979-91; minority rep, Stanford Grad Sch Bus Admissions, 1982-89; corp liason comm, New Jersey Black MBA Assn, 1983-89; consult, Morris Co Bus Vol Arts, 1986; chair sub comt no 1; Defense Adv Comm on Women in the Serv, 1987-90; mem, Navy League, 1988-89; young exec fel, Fund For Corp Initiatives, 1989; mem, Transp Res Forum, 1989-; mem, Leadership NJ, 1991-. **Honors/Awds:** Partner, Creative Renovations Assoc, 1984-85; White House Fel, Pres's Commn on White House Fel, 1986, 1987; Leadership Award, New Jersey Black MBA Assn, 1986; Woman Pioneer, Kings Point Assn, 1988; Secy Defense Medal for Outstanding Pub Serv, 1990. **Business Addr:** President, Mbx Logistics LLC, 7699 Commerce Center Dr, Orlando, FL 32819.

NELLUM, ALBERT L
Executive, management consultant. **Personal:** Born Apr 1, 1932, Greenville, MS; son of Daniel F and Thurma B Moore; married Velma Love, May 26, 1984; children: Brian, Judith Rebecca & Daniel. **Educ:** Loyola Univ, Chicago, IL, BS, 1955. **Career:** Cath Interracial Coun, Chicago, IL, asst dir, 1957-60; Chicago Comn Youth Welfare, Chicago, IL, dir, 1960-62; Nat Asn Intergroup Rels, Spec & Emergency Serv, Chicago IL, asst dir, 1962-63; Bur Labor Statist, Chicago, IL, regional youth consult, 1963-65; A L Nellum & Assoc, Wash, DC, pres & chief exec officer, 1964-. **Orgs:** Vpres, Cong Black Caucus Found, 1973-; trustee, bd mem, Martin Luther King Jr Ctr Nonviolent Social Change, 1978-90; Martin Luther King, Jr Fed Holiday Comn, 1985-90; Dem Nat Comt Site Selection, 1986. **Military Serv:** AUS, specialist 3rd Class, 1955-57. **Business Phone:** (202)466-4920.

NELLUMS, MICHAEL WAYNE
School administrator, businessperson. **Personal:** Born Aug 6, 1962, England, AR; son of Shirley Nellums and Silas Nellums; married Brenda Kay Clipper, Sep 5, 1987; children: Michael Brandon. **Educ:** Univ Cent Ark, BSE, 1985, MSE, 1991. **Career:** Little Rock City, pool mgr, 1983-; Pulaski Co Spec Sch Dist, teacher, adr, 1985, Mills Univ Studies High Sch, asst prin, Jacksonville Jr High Sch, prin, currently; Sigma One Productions, owner, 1985-; Power 92-Radio, on-air announcer, 1990-. **Orgs:** Educ comt, Phi Beta Fraternity, Mu Beta Sigma, 1983-; Ark Educ Asn, 1985-; Nat Educ Asn, 1985-; curric develop, ASSCD, 1989-; dir, Teachers Tomorrow Academy, 1992-. **Honors/Awds:** Phi Beta Sigma Leadership Award, local chapter, 1989; Distinguished Service Award, North Hills Jaycee, 1992. **Business Addr:** Principal, Jacksonville Jr High School, Pulaski County Special School District, 1320 School Dr, Jacksonville, AR 72204, **Business Phone:** (501)982-1587.

NELLY (CORNELL HAYNES, JR.)
Rap musician. **Personal:** Born Nov 2, 1974, Austin, TX; son of Cornall Haynes Sr. **Career:** Albums: Country Grammar, 2000; Free City, 2001; Nellyville, 2002; Da Derrty Versions: The Reinvention, 2003; Iz U, 2004; Sweat, 2004; Suit, 2004; Tilt Ya Head Back, 2005; Sweatsuit, 2005; Who's The Boss, 2006; Brass Knuckles, 2008; TV: "Saturday Night Live," 2002-04; "Cedric the Entertainer Presents," 2003; Films: The Longest Yard, 2005; Singles: "Country Grammar", 2000; "E.I.", 2000; "Ride wit Me", 2001; "Batter Up", 2001; "#1", 2001; "Hot in Herre", 2002; "Dilemma", 2002; "Air Force Ones", 2002; "Work It", 2003; "Pimp Juice", 2003; "Iz U", 2003; "Na-Nana-Na", 2004; "My Place", 2004; "Flap Your Wings", 2004; "Tilt Ya Head Back", 2004; "Over & Over", 2004; "N Dey Say", 2005; "Errtime", 2005; "Fly Away", 2005; "Grillz", 2005; "Wadsyaname", 2007; "Party People", 2008; "Kill Ya Self", 2008. **Honors/Awds:** Source Awards, Best New Artist of the Year, Best Album of the Year, 2001; American Music Award, Favorite Rap & Hip-Hop Artist, 2002; Grammy Awards, 2003. **Special Achievements:** Ranked 39 on Entertainment Weekly's 2002 "101 Most Powerful" List. **Business Addr:** Recording Artist, Universal Records, 1755 Broadway, New York, NY 10019, **Business Phone:** (212)373-0600.

NELMS, OMMIE LEE
Association executive. **Personal:** Born Jul 4, 1942, Houston, TX; son of Wiley H and Thelma O; married Donna Marie Ashley. **Educ:** Dillard Univ; Univ MO KC, BA, 1965; St Paul Sch Theology, Kansas City, MO, Master Divinity, 1980. **Career:** exec (retired); MO Dept Ins, Western Div, asst mgr; Allstate Ins Co, KC Reg Off, underwriting div mgr, 1969-75; Jr HS, teacher; United Methodist Ch, W Conf, MO, minister. **Orgs:** Nat Underwriters Soc, 1970-75; youth coord, KC Br NAACP; dist lay, ldr MO W Conf United Methodist Ch, 1974; S Central Jurisdictional Conf United Methodist Ch, 1972; lay ldr, Centennial United Methodist Ch KC, 1967-75; Delegate World Methodist Conf, 1985, 1991. **Honors/Awds:** Paragon Award, 1971; Arch Bow Award, 1973. *

NELOMS, HENRY
Executive. **Career:** Premium Distribr Inc, chief exec officer, currently. **Business Phone:** (202)526-3900.*

NELSON, CHARLES J
Government official. **Personal:** Born Mar 5, 1920, Battle Creek, MI; son of Schuyler A and Dayse; married Maureen Tinsley. **Educ:** Lincoln Univ, BA, 1942; NY Univ, MPA, 1948. **Career:** Res assoc state govt, 1949-52, prog asst MSA Manila, 1942-53, pub admin analyst FOA 1953-54, pub admin spec, 1954-55, dep spec asst for cot develop ICA, 1955-57, chief commun develop adv Tehran, 1958, commun develop adv dept state, 1960, chief Africa-Latin Am br, 1960-61, detailed African br, 1961; Off Prog Develop & Coordr PC Wash, assoc dir, 1961-63; Off Develop Resources AID, dir, 1963-64; No African Affairs, dir, 1964-66, dep dir, Addis Ababa, 1966-68, dir, Dar es Salaam, 1968-71; Botswana, Lesotho, Swaziland, Garborone, ambassador 1971-74, dir aid Nairobi, 1974-78; Howard Univ Sch Human Ecol, admin, 1978-81, int consult, 1981-. **Orgs:** Nat Bd Dir Sister Cities Int, 1986-, vpres, bd dirs, 1990; chmn, mayors Int Adv Coun; bd dir, Girl Scouts; Coun Nation's Capital; Georgetown Citizens Asn; Voice Informed Community Expression; Smithsonian Inst; Am Polit Sci Asn; Soc Int Develop Clubs; Fed City Club WA; co chair, Africa Round Table SID; Beijing Friendship Coun, DC Dakar Friendship Coun Bangkok; Coun Overseas Development Coun; Univ Club, Wash, DC. **Honors/Awds:** Lincoln Univ Hall of Fame. **Special Achievements:** Council of American Ambassadors; Assoc of Black American Ambassadors. **Military Serv:** AUS, capt, 1942-47. **Business Addr:** Honarary Member, Sister Cities International, 2853 Ontario Rd NW Apt 115, Washington, DC 20009, **Business Phone:** (202)248-0892.

NELSON, CURTIS. See NELSON, OTHA CURTIS.

NELSON, DARRIN MILO
Football player, executive director. **Personal:** Born Jan 2, 1959, Sacramento, CA; married Camilla; children: Jordan. **Educ:** Stanford Univ, BS, urban & environ planning, 1981. **Career:** Football player (retired), Executive director; Minn Vikings, running back, 1982-89 & 1991-92; San Diego Chargers, 1989-90; Piper Capital Mgt; Stanford Univ Cardinal, asst athletic dir community relations, 1997-99, assoc athletic dir external rels, sr assoc athletic dir external relations, 2005-. **Orgs:** Acad All-Am; Nat Football Found Scholar Athlete. **Honors/Awds:** Miller NFL Man of Year Award, 1984; NFC Championship Game, 1987. **Business Phone:** (650)723-4591.

NELSON, DEBRA J
Manager, vice president (organization). **Personal:** Born in Birmingham, AL; daughter of James Nelson. **Educ:** Univ Ala,

Tuscaloosa, BA, commun, 1980. **Career:** WSGN Radio, Birmingham, dir pub affairs, 1980-84; WBRC-TV, Birmingham, dir community affairs, 1984-88, news anchor, noon show, 1987-88; Univ Ala, Birmingham, spec studies instr, 1988-; Univ Ala Syst, Tuscoosa, dir media rels, 1994; Mercedes-Benz, mgr corporate diversity, Daimler Chrysler, sr mgr, human resources, diversity & extern commun; Mercedes-Benz, adminr Extern Affairs, 1998; Daimler Chrysler sr mgr, Group Mkt & Diversity Commun, sr mgr, human resources, labor, mfg Gov Affairs Commun, 2001; MGM Mirage, vpres corporate diversity & community affairs, currently. **Orgs:** Convener, Birmingham Literacy Task Force, 1987-88; US Libr Literacy Rev Panel, 1988-91; dir, Am Heart Asn, Ala Affiliate, 1986-; commun chmn, Am Heart Asn, 1986-; Ala Japan Leadership Prog, 1988-89; Military Acad Rev Comt, 6th Cong Dist, 1999; Ed Davis Edu Found Bd; William Paterson Univ Found Bd; chair, Edward Davis Edu Found, 2002; chair, Edward Davis Edu Found bd, 2003. **Honors/Awds:** Distinguished Leadership Award, United Negro Col Fund, 1985, 1987, 1988; Award of Distinction, Int Asn Bus Communicators, 1985; Nominee, Career Woman of the Year, Birmingham Bus & Prof Women's Club, 1987; Honorary Lieutenant Colonel, Ala Militia Governor's Office, 1987; Woman of Distinction, Iota Phi Lambda Service Sorority, 1985; Outstanding Leadership Award, Am Heart Asn, 1987-89; Outstanding Volunteer Service Award, American Red Cross, 1985; Human Rights Award, Southern Christian Leadership Conf; Outstanding Corp & Comm Relations Award, Human Resources Develop IST; Woman of the Yr, African Am Wheels Mag, 2001; Prism Award, 2002. **Business Addr:** Vice President of Corporate Diversity & Community Affairs, MGM Mirage, 3600 Las Vegas Blvd S, Las Vegas, NV 89109, **Business Phone:** (702)891-1111.

NELSON, EDWARD O.
Engineer. **Personal:** Born Feb 2, 1925, Johnsonville, TN; son of Edgar and Lucille; married Pauline; children: Stanley, Michael, Michelle, Cozetta, Richard, Viola. **Educ:** St Louis Univ; Rankin Tech Inst; Wash Univ, St Louis, MO, BS, eng, 1975. **Career:** Engineer (retired); Rockwell Int Environ Monitoring Serv Ctr, tech staff; US Environ Protection Agency St Louis, engr technician. **Orgs:** Am Radio Relay Leag; Am Asn Retired Persons; IBEW-LU Suite 4; Am Legion; Disabled Am Vet. **Special Achievements:** First black admitted to the International Brotherhood of Electrical Workers. **Military Serv:** AUS, WWII, tech 5th grade, 1943-45; Phillipine Island Liberation Medal, Asiatic Pacific Theater. **Home Addr:** 4614 Elmbank Ave, Saint Louis, MO 63115, **Home Phone:** (314)383-0107. *

NELSON, EILEEN F
Artist. **Personal:** Born in Chicago, IL; daughter of Frances Irons Anderson and Summers Anderson; married Alphonzo George, Dec 7, 1975; children: Maisha Eileen Nelson. **Educ:** Art Inst Chicago, attended 1964; Ill Inst Tech, attended 1969; Los Angeles City Col, attended 1974; Indian Valley Col, attended 1979. **Career:** Studio F, artist & designer; self employed artist & designer, currently. **Home Addr:** 7 Regent Ct, Novato, CA 94947. **Business Addr:** Designer, Artist, Studio F, 7 Regent Ct, Novato, CA 94947, **Business Phone:** (415)892-4471.

NELSON, FLORA SUE
Administrator. **Personal:** Born Dec 14, 1930, Chicago, IL; daughter of William Jarrett Martin (deceased) and Clara Payne Martin (deceased); married Herman Nelson, Jul 6, 1962 (died 1981); children: Lisa, Tracey. **Educ:** Univ Wis-Madison, WI, attended 1949; Roosevelt Univ, Chicago, BA, 1951; Univ Chicago, Chicago, IL, MA, 1957. **Career:** Administrator (retired); Cook County Juv Ct, Chicago, IL, 1951-58; Dept Housing, Chicago, IL, specialist, 1958-67; asst relocation, 1967-76; dir relocation, 1976-80, dep comnr, 1980-92. **Orgs:** Delta Sigma Theta Sorority, 1951-. **Home Addr:** 6707 S Bennett Ave, Chicago, IL 60649. *

NELSON, GILBERT L.
Consultant. **Personal:** Born Oct 5, 1942, Princeton, NJ; son of Gilbert and Lillian; married J Mary Jacobs; children: Christine E Cave & Jessica L. **Educ:** Trinity Col Ct, BA 1964; Georgetown Law Sch, JD 1967. **Career:** State NJ, dep pub defender, 1968-70; self employed atty at law, 1968-87; Middlesex Co, NJ, asst prosecuter, 1970-72; New Brunswick, NJ, city atty, 1975-86; Mayor New Brunswick, NJ, 1978; consult, currently. **Orgs:** Dir, Urban League Greater New Burnswick, 1968-70; Nat Bar Asn, 1968-87; NJ Bar Asn, 1968-87; dir, Damon House, 1975-81. **Military Serv:** USAR, sgt, 1968-74. **Home Addr:** 29 Goodale Cir, New Brunswick, NJ 08901. *

NELSON, DR. H. VISCOUNT
Educator. **Personal:** Born Jul 10, 1939, Oxford, PA; son of H Viscount Sr and Leanna; married Joan K Ricks; children: Christer V & Berk William. **Educ:** West Chester State Col, BS, 1961; Univ Pa, MA, 1962, PhD 1969. **Career:** Oxford High Sch, teacher, 1962-64; Abington High Sch, teacher, 1964-66; Univ Pa, teaching fel, head teaching asst, 1966-69; Dartmouth Col, assoc prof, 1975; asst prof, 1972-75; Univ Calif, Los Angeles, asst prof,1969-72; Ctr Stud Programming, dir, currently. **Orgs:** Am Hist Asn; Orgn Am Historians; former mem, Examining Comt Adv Placement US Hist Educ Testing Serv; Danforth Asn Unofficial Part-Time Track &

Field Coach; Simon Wiesenthal Mus Tolerance; Golden Key Int Honour Soc, Univ Calif, Los Angeles. **Honors/Awds:** Books: "The Philadelphia NAACP Race vs Class Consciousness During the Thirties", "Journal of Black Studies", 1975; "Black Philadelphia & the Great Depression". **Business Addr:** Director Center for Student Programming, University of California at Los Angeles, 105 Kerckhoff Hall, Los Angeles, CA 90095-1376.

NELSON, HAROLD E
Police chief. **Career:** Ill State Police; Cairo outpost, dist comdr, 1979-87; Cairo Police dept, asst chief, 1992, chief, 1992-94. **Special Achievements:** First African Police Chief, Cairo, IL, 1992. **Business Addr:** Police Chief, Cairo Police Department, 1501 Washington, Cairo, IL 62914, **Business Phone:** (618)734-2131.

NELSON, DR. IVORY V.
College administrator, educator. **Personal:** Born Jun 11, 1934, Curtis, LA; son of Elijah and Mattie Nelson; married Patricia Ann, Dec 27, 1985; children: Cherlyn, Karyn, Eric Beatty & Kim Beatty. **Educ:** Grambling State Univ, BS, chem, 1959; Univ Kans, PhD, chem, 1963. **Career:** Southern Univ Baton Rouge, chair, natural sci div, 1966-68; Prairie View A & M, asst acadc dean, prof chem, 1968-72, vpres res, prof chem, 1972-82,acting pres, prof chem, 1982-83; Tex A&M Univ System, exec asst chancellor, 1983-86; Alamo Community Col Dist, chancellor, 1986-92; Centl Wash Univ, pres, 1992-99; Lincoln Univ, pres, 1999-. **Orgs:** AAAS, 1963-; Am Chem Soc, 1963-; Tex Acad Sci, 1968-; Africult Res Inst;Am Asn Col Teachers; Nat Asn Federal Rel Officers, 1975-83; Nat Asn State Univ & Land Grant Col, exec comm; Nat Coun Univ Res Admin, 1976-83; NY Acad Sci, 1976-83; Western Interstate Regional Policy Comm on Higher Ed, 1986-88; Phi Delta Kappa, Southeast Consortium Int Develop; exec comm, Tex-Pub Community, Jr Col Asn, 1989-91; exec comm, Nat Jr Col Athletic Asn,1991; Nat Asn Intercollegiate Athletics, 1993-98; Am Coun Ed Comm Int Ed,1995-98; Pres Coun Division III, NCAA, 2001-; Sigma Xi; Phi Kappa Phi; Phi Lamda Upsilon. **Honors/Awds:** Am Men Sci, 1966; Outstanding Young Men America, 1967; Leaders of Ed,1970; Personalities of the South, 1971; Buildings of Mathematics, Computer Science, Biology, Chemistry and Physics, Lincoln Univ, named in honor, 2009. **Special Achievements:** DuPont Teaching Fellowship, Univ of Kansas, 1962; Fulbright Lectureship,1966; Distinguised Alumni, University of Kansas, Grambling State Univ;National Urban League, Fellowship, 1969. **Military Serv:** USAF, staff sgt, 1951-55. **Business Addr:** President, Lincoln University, 1570 Baltimore Pke, PO Box 179, Lincoln University, PA 19352, **Business Phone:** (484)365-7400.

NELSON, JILL
Writer, journalist. **Personal:** Born in Harlem, NY. **Educ:** City Col NY; Columbia Univ's Sch Jour. **Career:** Wash Post Mag, journalist, 1986-; City Col New York, prof jour, 1998-2003; USA Weekend, contrib ed; MSNBC.com, columnist; Books: Volunteer Slavery: My Authentic Negro Experience, 1993; Straight, No Chaser: How I Became A Grown-Up Black Woman, 1997; Police Brutality: An Anthology, 2000; Finding Martha's Vineyard: African Americans at Home on an Island, 2005. **Honors/Awds:** Washington DC Journalist of the Year Award; American Book Award. **Special Achievements:** Writings have appeared in numerous publications including The New York Times, Essence, The Nation, Ms, The Chicago Tribune and The Village Voice.

NELSON, JONATHAN P.
Executive. **Personal:** Born Jun 5, 1939, New York, NY; married Dorothy Higgins. **Educ:** Howard Univ, BSEE, 1963; St John's Univ, MBA, 1974. **Career:** Pfizer Inc, mgr oral prod pkg dept, 1968-94; EG & G Inc, electronics engr, 1967-68; ACF Ind Inc, electronics design engr, 1963-67; Nat Bur Standards, stand trainee, 1961-63; The Haagen Dazs Co, eng mgr, 1994-; Strategic Mfg Initiatives Inc, proj dir, 1995-. **Orgs:** Inst Elec & Electronics Engrs; Nat Mgt Asn; exec bd, Brooklyn BSA; Omega Psi Phi; Nat Black MBA Asn; Am Fin Asn. **Honors/Awds:** Recipient Achievement Award, Nat Asn Negro Bus & Prof Women, 1969; Black Achiever Ind Harlem YMCA, 1972, 1974. **Business Addr:** Project Director, Strategic Manufacturing Initiatives Inc, 242 Old New Burnswick Rd Suite 100, Piscataway, NJ 08854.

NELSON, KIM
President (Organization). **Educ:** Georgetown Univ, BA, Intl Relations, 1984; Columbia Univ, MBA, 1988. **Career:** General Mills, VP; General Mills Snacks Unlimited Division, Pres. **Orgs:** Member, Congressional Black Caucus Foundation Board; Member, Executive Leadership Council; Member, National Executive Women Network; Chairperson, Minneapolis YWCA Board; Founding Member, Black Champions Network; Founding Member, Women in Marketing Network. *

NELSON, LARRY
Association executive, vice president (organization). **Educ:** Rutgers Univ, BS; Univ Pittsburgh Sch Law, JD. **Career:** Wendy's Int Inc, officer, 1991, vpres & asst gen couns, sr vpres & assoc gen coun develop, currently. **Orgs:** Bd dirs, Big Brother/Big Sister Asn Greater Columbus; bd, King Arts Complex Columbus. **Special**

Achievements: The first Black senior vice president and associate general counsel of development for Wendy's International Inc. **Business Addr:** Sr Vice President, Associate General Councel of Development, Wendy, 4288 W-Dublin-Granville Rd, Dublin, OH 43017, **Business Phone:** (614)764-3100.*

NELSON, MARIO
Marketing executive. **Personal:** Born Jan 19, 1955, Los Angeles, CA; son of George and Martha; married Cheryl, Nov 20, 1971; children: Mario Umjamo & Ahree Kashawn. **Educ:** Riverside City Col, Assoc Art, 1981; Calif State Col, San Bernardino, BA, 1983; Calif State Univ, San Bernardino, MBA, 1986. **Career:** Brown-Forman Beverages Worldwide: merchandiser, sales rep, reg mgr, chain channel mgr, convenient store mgr, reg sales mgr, div mkt mgr. **Orgs:** Nat Black MBA Asn. **Honors/Awds:** Top Sales Team, 1991; Fleet Owner Graphics Award, 1997. **Military Serv:** AUS, E-5, 1974-77. **Business Addr:** Division Marketing Manager, Brown-Forman Beverages Worldwide, North American Group, PO Box 74338, Richmond, VA 23236, **Business Phone:** (804)674-6432.

NELSON, MARY ELIZABETH
Lawyer, president (government), government official. **Personal:** Born Feb 6, 1955, St Louis, MO; daughter of Clyde H and Kathryn E; divorced. **Educ:** Princeton Univ, BA, polit philos, 1977; Univ Miss-Columbia Sch Law, JD, 1981. **Career:** Wilson Smith & McCullin, assoc 1981-82; Mary E Nelson LLC, pvt pract; Off Bus Develop, minority bus develop dir, 1982-86; St Louis Develop Corp, gen coun, atty; Vickers Moore & Wiest, PC, assoc, 1986-88; Lashley & Baer, PC, assoc, 1988-92, partner, 1992; House Redistricting & Reapportionment Comn, 2001; St Louis Police Bd Comnrs, vpres, pres, 2002; Speaker Miss House Reps, gen coun. **Orgs:** Vpres, Mound City Bar Asn, 1988, corresponding secy, 1985-87; Bar Asn Metrop St Louis, long-range planning comn, 1989-; bd dirs, Bar Found St Louis, 1990-; bd dirs, People's Health Ctr, 1991-; bd comnrs, Regional Arts Comn, 1991-; bd dirs, Opera Theatre of St Louis, 1992-; Nat Bar Asn, entertainment law comn, 1992; Black Entertainment & Sports Lawyers Asn, 1992; bd mem, Doorways, 2002-. **Honors/Awds:** Best Pract Award, 2001. **Home Addr:** 4100 Laclede Ave 202, St Louis, MO 63108.

NELSON, NATHANIEL W.
Podiatrist. **Personal:** Born Nov 28, 1921, Birmingham, AL; married Lee E; children: Altamease, Beth, Nolita, Stanley, Pierre & Milford. **Educ:** Wayne Univ Detroit; Detroit Inst Technol. **Career:** Podiatrist, foot & ankle surg; podiatrist admitted hosp surgical staff; Old Kirwood Hosp, chief podiatry serv. **Orgs:** Mich Podiatry Asn; Am Podiatry Asn; Nat Podiatry Asn; Ohio Col Podiatric Med Alumni Asn; Bethal AME Ch BTA. **Special Achievements:** First black podiatrist to be appointed as examiner & consult in Detroit area of Aetna Life & Casalty Ins Co for foot & ankle disabilities Quarter Master Serv & Corp, 1943-46. **Home Addr:** 18000 Indiana Ave, Detroit, MI 48221. **Business Addr:** 16451 Schoolcraft Rd, Detroit, MI 48227.

NELSON, NOVELLA C.
Actor, singer, administrator. **Personal:** Born Dec 17, 1939, Brooklyn, NY; daughter of James and Evelyn Hines; children: Alesa Novella Blanchard. **Educ:** Brooklyn Col. **Career:** J Papp, consult; Sundance Theatre Prog, dir; Lincoln Ctr Dirs prog, dir; Hartford Stage, dir; KY Humana Fest, dir; Eugene O'Neill Ctr, dir; MTC, dir; Pub Theatre, dir; Negro Ensemble Co, dir; New Fed Theatre, dir; Films: Seattle Rep; ACT; Alliance; Mark Taper Forum; Long Wharf Theatre; Caucasian Chalk Circle; He Doctor's Story; One Life to Live; You Are There; All My Children; As The World Turns; The Equalizer; Orphans; The Cotton Club; The Flamingo Kid; An Unmarried Woman, The Seduction of Joe Tynan; Green Card; The Devil's Advocate; A Perfect Murder; Clockers; Girl Six; Performed in: Purlie; Hello Dolly; The Little Foxes; Caesar & Cleopatra; Having Our Say; Passing Game; Division Street; A Piece of My Heart; Trio; The Skin of Our Teeth; In New England Winter; South Pacific; Widows; Mecuba; Judy Berlin, 2000; Antwone Fisher, 2002, Taboo; Death 2002, Head of State, 2003; Birth, 2004; Dear Wendy, 2005; Preaching to the Choir, 2005; Stephanie Daley, 2006; Premium, 2006; Griffin & Phoenix, 2006; King, 2007; The Ten, 2007; The Toe Tactic, 2008; Sweet Kandy, 2009; My Place in the Horror, 2009; Night Catches Us, 2009; TV series: "100 Centre Street," 2001; "Things Change," 2001; "Third Watch", 2003; "Whoopi", 2003; "The West Wing", 2004; "The Starter Wife", 2007; "Law & Order: Special Victims Unit", 1999-2008. **Orgs:** ACT; Alliance Theatre; Nat Counc Negro Women; Delta Sigma Theta; mem bd, DST Community Arts & Letters; Harlem C Theatre; New Heritage Theatre; bd mem, Studio WIS; NY State Coun Arts Theatre panelist, Young Playwrights Festival Selection Comt. **Honors/Awds:** Mary M Bethune Lifetime Achievement Award, Nat Coun Negro Women; Image Award, Nat Asn Advan Colored People. **Special Achievements:** DRR, Hunana Festival, ATL; Appeared in Hawk; Law & Order; The Littlest Victim; He's Hired She's Fired; Chiefs; album, Novella Nelson; numerous singing engagements. **Home Addr:** 43 Midwood St, Brooklyn, NY 11225, **Home Phone:** (718)941-8415. **Business Addr:** Producer, DBA, 10 E 44th St, New York, NY 10012.

NELSON, OTHA CURTIS (CURTIS NELSON)
Lawyer. **Personal:** Born Feb 28, 1947, Marion, LA; son of Jeremiah and Wilma Pearson; married Vernita Moore, Sep 1, 1968;

children: Nelson & Otha Curtis Jr. **Educ:** Southern Univ, Agr & Mech Col, BA, 1969; Southern Univ, Sch Law, JD, 1972. **Career:** Capital Area Legal Serv Corp, law clerk, 1971-72, staff atty, 1973-74; Southwest La Legal Serv Corp, staff atty; Off Gen Coun, staff atty, state La, 1974-82; Simmons & Nelson Law Firm, founding partner, 1974-80; Otha Curtis Nelson Sr, atty-at-Law, notary pub, 1980-. **Orgs:** Chaplain, Louis A Martinet Soc, 1972-92; co-pastor, Pentecostal Assembly Christ, 1975-78; pres, Pentecostal Assemblies World La State Choir, 1975-76; Sunday Sch superintendent, Holy Ghost Temple Church God Christ, 1979-91, asst pastor, 1985-; founder, Christians Basketball Teams, sponsor, coach, 1982-87; chmn bd dirs, Martinet Fin Serv Inc, 1991-; co-chaplain, Southern Univ Law Sch Alumni, 1992-; Nat Asn Coun C. **Honors/Awds:** Valuable Services Rendered, Louis A Martinet Soc, 1991; Honorary Secretary of the State of Louisiana Award, 1980. **Special Achievements:** Coach, basketball champion teams, 1st place, 1985-86. **Business Addr:** Attorney, 1606 Scenic Hwy, Baton Rouge, LA 70802, **Business Phone:** (225)334-7665.

NELSON, PRINCE ROGERS (PRINCE)
Television producer, actor, singer. **Personal:** Born Jun 7, 1958, Minneapolis, MN; son of John L (deceased) and Mattie D Shaw; married Manuela Testolini, Dec 31, 2001 (divorced 2006); married Mayte Garcia, Jan 1, 1996 (divorced 2000). **Career:** Singer, songwriter, actor, producer, dir, currently; Albums: Summer Lovers, 1982; Still Smokin, 1983; Risky Business, 1983; Purple Rain, 1984; The Slugger's Wife, 1985; Krush Groove, 1985; Band of the Hand, 1986; Fire with Fire, 1986; Under the Cherry Moon, 1986; Sign o the Times, 1987; Bright Lights, Big City, 1988; My Stepmother Is an Alien, 1988; Batman, 1989; Pretty Woman, 1990; Without You Im Nothing, 1990; Graffiti Bridge, 1990; Gett Off, 1991; The Last Boy Scout, 1991; Innocent Blood, 1992; Poetic Justice, 1993; Prince Interactive, 1994; 3 Chains o Gold, 1994; Frauen sind was Wunderbares, 1994; PCU, 1994; Blankman, 1994; Vampire in Brooklyn, 1995; Showgirls, 1995; Waiting to Exhale, 1995; Girl 6, 1996; Striptease, 1996; Romeo Juliet, 1996; Eine unmogliche Hochzeit, 1996; Scream 2, 1997; Down in the Delta, 1998; An Audience with Tom Jones, 1999; Bamboozled, 2000; Jay and Silent Bob Strike Back, 2001; Stella Shorts 1998-2002, 2002; Head of State, 2003; Are We There Yet?, 2005; Filthy Gorgeous: The Trannyshack Story, 2005; Get Rich or Die Tryin, 2005; Happy Feet, 2006; Her Best Move, 2007; License to Wed, 2007; Rush Hour 3, 2007; Young at Heart, 2007; Dan in Real Life, 2007; P S I Love You, 2007; Forgetting Sarah Marshall, 2008; Nel nome del male, 2009; Songs: "Saturday Night Live", 1981-2006; "Knight Rider", 1984; "Fame", 1984-85; "Lo Kolel Sherut", 1990; "Tiny Toon Adventures", 1992; "Beavis and Butt-Head", 1993-95; "Muppets Tonight", 1997; "Quelli che il calcio", 2001; "Fergus's Wedding", 2002; "Operacion triunfo", 2001; "Ha-Shminiya", 2006; "Verbotene Liebe", 2006; "20 to 1", 2006; "American Idol: The Search for a Superstar", 2007; "Las Vegas", 2007; "La tele de tu vida", 2007; "60/90", 2008; "Sputnik", 2008; "Banda sonora", 2009; "Late Night with Jimmy Fallon", 2009. **Honors/Awds:** Academy Award Best Original Song Score for Purple Rain, 1985; three American Music Awards; three Grammy Awards; 3 gold albums; 2 platinum albums; No 1 album of the year Purple Rain; Rhythm & Blues Musician of Year, down beat Readers Poll, 1984; Best Soul/Rhythm & Blues Group of Year, downbeat Readers Poll, Prince & Revolution, 1985; Grammy Award, 1995; Oscar Award, 1985; Razzie Award, 1987; ASCAP Award, 1990, 1991; Special Award, 2004; Golden Globe Award, 2007. **Business Addr:** The Artist, EMI, 304 Pk Ave S, New York, NY 10010.

NELSON, RAMONA M
Broker, executive. **Personal:** Born Mar 23, 1950, Pittsburgh, PA; daughter of Ramona L Collie and Pronty L Ford; divorced; children: Tawana R Cook & John Nelson. **Educ:** Knoxville Col, psychol, 1972; Univ Penn, MGA, govt admin, 1984. **Career:** PEN Housing Finance Agency, housing mgt rep, 1979-84; Remanco Inc, regional mgr, 1985-87; Nelson & Assoc Inc, pres & chief exec officer, 1987-; Lic Real Estate Broker; Cert Property Mgr, 1984. **Orgs:** Greater Cincinnati Chap IREM, past pres, 1991; Nat Asn Realtors; Nat Asn Real Estates Brokers; Greater Cincinnati Chamber Com; Delta Sigma Theta Sorority. **Honors/Awds:** Black Achiever, YMCA, 1992. **Home Phone:** (513)489-2707. **Business Addr:** President, Chief Executive Officer, Nelson & Associates Inc, 2516 Pk Ave, Cincinnati, OH 45206, **Business Phone:** (561)504-2110.

NELSON, REX
Sports manager. **Career:** Detroit Pistons, vpres, community develop & player progs; Skill man Found, prog off, 2006-. **Orgs:** Exec dir, Pistons Palace Found; ABFE, 2003-04; Asn Black Found Exec; Mich Col Found; pres, Rosa Parks Found. **Business Addr:** Program Officer, The Skillman Found, 600 Renaissance Ctr Suite 1700, Detroit, MI 48243, **Business Phone:** (313)393-1185.

NELSON, RICHARD Y., JR.
Executive director, government official. **Personal:** Born Aug 27, 1939, Atlantic City, NJ; married Nancy Allen; children: Michael, Michele, Cherie, Gregg, Nancy. **Educ:** San Fran State Univ, BA 1961; Temple Univ Law Sch, JD 1969. **Career:** Def Support Agency, Philadelphia, purchasing agt, 1961-65; Philadelphia Regional off, Dept Housing & Urban Develop, area coord, 1965-70; Nat Asn Housing & Redevelop officials, dep exec dir, 1970-01; NJ Bar, admitted, 1969; Housing Opportunities Comn Montgomery County, comnr, 1991, chair, 2003-; Univ Md, Sch Pub Policy, sr fel; Dept Housing & Community Affairs, Montgomery County, dir, currently. **Orgs:** Am Soc Asn Exec; Alpha Phi Alpha Frat; NAACP; officer, Local PTA; bd mem & vice chair, Camp Hill Square Housing Develop Corp; emer mem, Housing & Develop Law Inst; bd mem, Housing & Develop Reporter; life dir, Nat Housing Conf; bd mem, Town Ctr Housing Corp; life mem, Nat Asn Housing & Redevelop officials; hon mem, Chartered Inst Housing UK; mem adv bd, Maryland Dept Housing & Community Develop; US China Residential Bldg Coun. **Honors/Awds:** M. Justin Herman Award, Nat Asn Housing & Redevelop officials. **Business Addr:** Director, Department of Housing and Community Affairs, 100 Maryland Ave 4th floor, Rockville, MD 20850.

NELSON, RICKY LEE
Police officer. **Personal:** Born May 8, 1959, Eloy, AZ; son of Ebb Corelius and Willie Pearl Whitehead; married Deanna Christina Perez, Sep 25, 1982; children: Alexis, Ashley & Austin. **Educ:** Ariz State Univ, Tempe, BA, 1991. **Career:** Police Officer (retired); Seattle Mariners, outfielder, 1983-86; NY Mets, outfielder, 1986; Cleveland Indians, outfielder, 1987; A L Williams Financial Serv, Phoenix, regional mgr, 1985-91; Durango Juvenile Ct, youth supvr, probations officer. **Orgs:** Calif All-Star Team, 1982. **Special Achievements:** Attended Arizona state univ winning All-Pac 10 honors while playing for the 1981 College World Series champions. **Home Phone:** (602)438-2733.

NELSON, ROBERT WALES, SR.
Physician. **Personal:** Born Mar 26, 1925, Red Bank, NJ; married Pamela Diana Fields; children: Debra C, Renae V, Desiree M, Jason D, Roxanne W, Robert W. **Educ:** Howard Univ, attended 1951; Howard Med Sch, attended 1956; Univ SC Med Ctr, attended 1957. **Career:** Pvt Pract, 1957-65; LA Co, bd educ, 1959-60, health dept, 1965-66; Gardena Med Ctr, physician; W Adams Emergency Med & Group, emergency physician 1967-80. **Orgs:** Am Col Emergency Physicians; Am Arabian Horse Asn, 1974-77; Int Arabian Horse Asn, 1974-77; breeder of Arabian Horses, 1974-; breeder of Black Angus, 1975-. **Military Serv:** USMCR, corp, 1943-46.

NELSON, RONALD DUNCAN
Police chief, executive. **Personal:** Born Jun 17, 1931, Pasadena, CA; son of Harold O and Zenobia D; married Barbara Dorsey, Jul 3, 1954; children: Rhonda & Harold. **Educ:** Drake Univ, Des Moines, Iowa, BA, 1956; Calif State Col, attended, 1961-66; Pepperdine Univ, Malibu, Calif, MA, 1977. **Career:** Police chief (retired), Corporate Executive; Los Angeles Police Dept, Los Angeles, Calif, police lt, 1956-77; Compton Police Dept, Compton, Calif, police comdr, 1977-79; China Lake Police Dept, China Lake, Calif, police chief, 1979-80; City Compton, Compton, Calif, city mgr, 1980-82; Berkeley Police Dept, Berkeley, Calif, police chief, 1982-90; Univ Calif, San Francisco, Police Dept, police chief, 1990-2002; Satellite Housing Inc, secy, currently. **Orgs:** Kappa Alpha Psi Fraternity, 1955-; Pasadena Planning Comn, 1976-79; Kiwanis Int, 1978-88; Berkeley Boosters Asn, 1983-; Berkeley Breakfast Club, 1984-; Nat Forum Black Pub Admin, 1987-; nat pres, Nat Orgn Black Law Enforcement Exec, 1988-89; pres, Alameda Co Chief Police & Sheriffs Asn, 1989; Berkeley Booster Asn; Nat League Cities; Comn Accreditation Law Enforcement Agencies; Black Men United Change; United Black Clergy Berkeley. **Honors/Awds:** Community Service Award, City Berkeley; Community Service Award, Nat League Cities; Community Service Award, Nat Orgn Black Law Enforcement Agencies; Community Service Award, Nat Forum Black Pub Admin, 1988. **Military Serv:** AUS, sgt, 1951-53; Good Conduct Award, 1953. **Home Addr:** 1460 Lincoln St, Berkeley, CA 94702, **Home Phone:** (510)644-1237. **Business Addr:** Secretary, Satellite Housing Inc, 1521 Univ Ave, Berkeley, CA 94703-1422, **Business Phone:** (510)647-0700.

NELSON, RONALD J
Automotive executive. **Career:** Genl Motors, dealer; Bill Nelson Chevrolet Inc, pres & chief exec officer, currently. **Business Addr:** Chief Executive Oficer, President, Bill Nelson Chevrolet Inc, 3233 Auto Plz, Richmond, CA 94806-1994, **Business Phone:** (510)222-2070.*

NELSON, TANYKA SHINELL
Psychologist. **Educ:** Ala State Univ & Calif State Univ, Northridge, Calif. **Career:** Los Angeles Unified Sch Dist, sch psychologist, currently. **Business Addr:** School Psychologist, Los Angeles Unified Sch Dist, 333 S Bleaudry Ave, Los Angeles, CA 90001, **Business Phone:** (213)241-1000.*

NELSON, DR. WANDA JEAN
Association executive. **Personal:** Born Jul 5, 1938, Kingfisher, OK; married Earl Lee Sr; children: Marie, Stephen A & Earl Lee Jr. **Educ:** Madam CJ Walker's Beauty Col, attended 1958; Nat Inst Cosmetology, Wash DC, BA, 1966, MA, 1968, PhD, 1973; Penn Valley Community Col Sci, attended 1973; Univ Ottawa, Ottawa, KS, BS, 1979. **Career:** Le Cont'e Cosmetics, tech hairstylist & instr; Air Cargo TWA, supvr; USDA, keypunch & verifier; US Postal Servs, guard, 1979-80; Ms Marie Cosmetics, owner; Associated Hairdresser Cosmetologist, MO, pres. **Orgs:** Founder & first pres, Young Progressors Beauty & Barbers; MO State Asn Cosmetology; pres, Nat Beauty Culturist League Inc, vpres; Women's Polit Caucus; parliamentarian, Black Chamber Com, 1987-. **Honors/Awds:** Certificate, Jackson Co State Sch Retarded C; Top 100 Influential Black Americas in Greater Kansas City, 1985; Woman of the Year, Theta Nu Sigma Nat Sorority, 1986; Woman of the Year, Alpha Beta Local Chap, 1986. **Home Phone:** (913)469-4389.

NELSON, DR. WANDA LEE
School administrator. **Personal:** Born Nov 16, 1952, Franklin, LA; daughter of James Green and Geraldine Minor Green; married Elridge Nelson; children: Michael & James. **Educ:** Grambling State Univ, BA, 1973; Ball State Univ, MA, 1975; Nat Cert Counr, 1984; La State Univ, EdS, 1985; Northern Ill, Univ DeKalb, Ill, EdD, 1989. **Career:** Bicester Am Elem Sch, Eng, learning specialist, 1974-76; Summer Enrichment Prog LSUE, music teacher, 1984; La State Univ Eunice, counr; Northern Ill Univ, counr & minority prog coordr, 1985-89; assoc dean students, Univ Tex, Austin, Tex, 1989-92, assoc dean students, 1992-95, exec dir, Univ Outreach Centers, 1995-, asst vpres, assoc vpres, currently. **Orgs:** Adv, Awareness Cult, Educ & Soc Student Club, 1978-85; Anti-Grammateus Epsilon Alpha Sigma Chap, 1979-80; adv, Zeta Nu Chap, 1984-89; organized Mu Upsilon Chap, 1992; Basileus Alpha Kappa Sigma, Chap, 1994-98; adv, Innervisions Gospel Choir, Univ Texas, 1993-95; life mem, Sigma Gamma Rho Sorority Inc; Jack & Jill AME Inc, 1996-99; life mem, Grambling State Univ Alumni asn; Am Asn Coun & Develop; Am Asn Higher Educ; Am Col Personnel Asn. **Honors/Awds:** Magna Cum Laude, Grambling State Univ, 1973; President's Award, Little Zion BC Matrons, Opelousas, La, 1985; Alpha Kappa Mu Honor Soc, Grambling State Univ; Kappa Delta Pi Hon Soc, Northern Ill Univ, 1988; Best Advisor of the Year, 1989; Alpha Golden Image Award, Northern Ill Univ; Outstanding Educr, Tex Employees Retirement System, 1991; African Fac/Staff of the Year, 1995; Pan-Hellenic Image Award, Univ Tex; Leadership Austin Class, 1997-98; Governor's Exec Develop Prog, 1998. **Home Addr:** 10206 Cripple Creek Cove, Austin, TX 78758. **Business Addr:** Associate Vice President, Executive Director, The University of Texas at Austin, 1301 E 7th St, Austin, TX 78702, **Business Phone:** (512)232-4630.

NELSON, DR. WILLIAM EDWARD
Educator. **Personal:** Born Mar 19, 1941, Memphis, TN; married Della Jackson; children: Nicholas. **Educ:** AM & N Col Pine Bluff, Ark, BA, 1962; Atlanta Univ, MA, 1964; Univ Ill, PhD, 1971. **Career:** Southern Univ, instr, 1963-65; Univ Ill, res assoc, 1966-69; OH State Univ, prof, 1969-, res prof, currently, chmn, Dept Black Studies. **Orgs:** Regl dir, Alpha Phi Alpha Frat, 1976-82; proclamation Ohio Senate, 1977; proclamation Columbus City Coun, 1977; pres, Nat Conf Black Polit Scientists, 1978-79; pres, Black Polit Assembly, 1979-81; exec bd, African Heritage Studies Asn, 1980-; chmn, Nat Coun Black Studies, 1980-82; pres, African Heritage Studies Asn, 1991-96; NAACP; Urban League. **Honors/Awds:** Outstanding adminstr Black Stdnt Caucus, 1976; vip, Am Polit Sci Asn, 1996-97; Best Book Award, Am Polit Sci Asn, 2001. **Special Achievements:** Coed, "Black and Latino/a Politics: Issues in Political Development in the United States". **Business Addr:** Professor, The Ohio State University, Department of African-American and African Studies, 486F Univ Hall 230 North Oval Mall, Columbus, OH 43210, **Business Phone:** (614)292-0453.

NELSON-HOLGATE, GAIL EVANGELYN
Singer, educator, actor. **Personal:** Born Mar 29, 1944, Durham, NC; daughter of William Tycer (deceased) and Jane Avant (deceased); married Daniel A, Sep 27, 1987. **Educ:** Mozarteum Conserv, Salzburg Austria, 1963-64; Oberlin Col, MusM, 1965; New Eng Conserv Music, Boston MA, MusM, 1967; Metropolitan Opera Studio, attended 1970-72; Am Inst Musical Studies, Graz Austria, 1972. **Career:** Henry Street Music Settlement, priv vocal teacher, 1986-87; NYC Col, adj prof contemporary pop-vocal music, 1986-89; D & G Productions Inc, vpres, prof vocalist, currently. **Orgs:** AEA, 1968; AGMA, 1967; Am Fed Television & Radio Artists, 1968; SAG 1968; Oberlin Alumnae; New England Conserv Alumnae; Am Cancer Soc, 1975-; Mu Phi Epsilon, 1967-; Black Women Theatre, 1985-87. **Honors/Awds:** Lucretia Bori Award, NY Metro Opera Studio Performance Scholar, 1970-72; Humanitarian Plaque, Oakwood Col, 1977; Stone Soul Festival "97", Springfield, MA, 1995; In Recog of Your Valuable Contrib to Human Life & Dignity and to Black Cultural Enrichment in Particular United Student Movement, 1977. **Special Achievements:** Films: The Way We Live Now, I Never Sang for My Father, Cotton Comes to Harlem; Recordings: Gail Nelson Sings! (on cassette), That Healin' Feelin & Phase III from the US of Mind w/Horace Silver, Blue Note Label, the original broadway cast album of Tap Dance Kid; Lady Day at Emerson's Bar &Grill (Cast Recording Starring Gail Nelson as Billie Holiday); many television & radio commercials, voice overs, indust films & shows; numerous operas; orchs: The Maggio Musicale Orch Florence Italy, The Ball of the Silver Rose Deutsches Theatre, Munich, Germ, The Madame Mag Ball Baden Baden, Detroit Symph Gala,

Buffalo Philharm, Philadelphia Pops, St Louis, Hartford, Tulsa, Chicago Ravinia Fest, Wmsburg Fest; Omaha, Oklahoma City Philharmonic, Edmonton, Calgary Philh, Indianapolis; One Life to Live (ABC); Another World (CBS), Guiding Light (NBC); Maya Angelou's "King", as Coretta Scott King, Jan, 1997; Broadway theatre, Hello Dolly, Applause, On The Town, Music Music, Eubie; Tap Dance Kid;Porgy and Bess (as Bess) with Houston Grand Opera, tour 1977; Bubbling Brown Sugar; (as Irene Page) 1986; Lady Day at Emerson's Bar & Grill, on tour 1994-03; AMR Symphony at Carnegie Hall, debut, London Philharmonic, debut, guest artist Queen Elizabeth II Cruise Ship, Holland America CruiseLines; New Jersey Symphony, debut, Buffalo Philharmonic New York, soloist; Indianapolis Symphony, debut, 1992; "Lady Day at Emerson's Bar & Grill, "An Evening of the Life and Music of Billie Holiday (as Billie Holliday), Seabourn Spirit Cruise Ship thru Asia, guest artist, Soloist: Connecticut Symphony; New Jersey Symphony; Portland Maine Symphony; Indianapolis Symphony; "Funny, You Don't Look Like A Grandma", "By Strouse", Talking Books, Inc, narrator for the American Foundation for the Blind, NY; Boston "Pops" Orchestra, Brevard Music Festival; Carnegie Hall Soloist for Nicholas Brothers tribute, 1998; the Palm Beach Pops, soloist; "Gershwin and Friends," "this Joint is Jumpin!" and "Puttin' on the Ritz "; television commercials; teaches voice privately in New York City. **Home Addr:** 160 West 73rd St Suite 9B, New York, NY 10023-3058, **Home Phone:** (212)580-8116. **Business Addr:** Vice President, D & G Productions Inc, 160 W 73rd St Studio 9B, New York, NY 10023, **Business Phone:** (212)580-8116.

NENGUDI, SENGA (SENGA NENGUDI FITTZ)
Artist. **Personal:** Born Sep 18, 1943, Chicago, IL; daughter of Samuel Irons and Elois Jackson Irons; married Ellioutt, Dec 29, 1976; children: Sanza & Oji. **Educ:** Calif State Univ, Los Angeles, BA, art, 1966, MA, sculpture, 1971; Waseda Univ Tokyo, Japan, foreign studies prog, 1967. **Career:** Watts Tower Art Ctr, Watts, CA, art instr, 1965-66; Pasadena Art Museum, art instr, 1969-71; C's Art Carnival, NYC, art instr, 1971-74; Watts Towers Art Ctr, LA, art instr, 1965, 1978; Calif State Univ, substitute instr, 1980; Comm Artists Prog, LA, prog coordr, 1982-88, arts prog developer, 1990-, dance instr comm & pvt classes, 1992-98; Fairburn Elem Sch, Coordr, 1985-86; Univ Southern Calif, asst slide curator, 1986-88; "Mouth to Mouth Conversations on Being", creator & independent radio producer, 1988-; African Dance & Diaspora, Colo Col & Pikes Peak Comm Col, Colo Springs, guest dance instr, 1993-98; Univ Colo, Colorado Springs, Afro Am Art Studies, art history lectr, 1998-; Sante Fe Art Inst, vis artist, 2005; Chicago Art Inst, guest artist, 2006; Univ, guest artist, 2007. **Orgs:** Curatorial comm perf art, Womans Bldg, LA, 1984-85; bd dirs, 1990-, co-pres, Performing Arts Youth, 1991-92; Bus Arts Ctr, 1990-92; Nat Black Women's Health Proj; Black Life Support Sisterhood, 1990-94; community liaison, Kennedy Ctr Imagination Celebration, 1992-95; Bd trustees, Tutmose Acad Sch, 1996-; Col Art Asn; Toni Morrison Soc. **Honors/Awds:** Dance scholarship, Orchesis Calif State Univ, LA, 1964; CAPS Grant Sculpture, Creative Artists Pub Serv Prog, 1972; Distinguished Service Award, Bd Regents Univ Colo, 1994; Anonymous Was A Woman Award, 2005; Louis Comfort Tiffany Foundation Award, 2005;Penny McCall Foundation Ordway Prize, 2005. **Special Achievements:** "Art as a Verb" Group Travelling Exhibit, 1988-89; "Coast to Coast," Group Travelling Exhibit, A Women of Color Artists Box and Books Exhibit 1988-92; Shaping the Spirit, Exhibit CAP St Project/AVT-Experimental Projects Gallery, San Francisco, CA, 1990; artist-in-residence, Mitchell High School, Artists Space-20th Anniversary Show, New York City, 1993, Homecoming Watts Tower Art Center, 25th Anniversary Show, 1995, curator for "Whisper! Stomp! Shout! A Salute to African-American Performance Art," Colorado Springs Fine Art Center, Co, a festival of video documentation of performing art, 1996, lecture/performance "Making a Scene of Ourselves The Black Arts: Happy Ruminations on Life in America," University of Colorado, 1996, At Banff Arts Center in Canada, 1996, Solo Exhibit "Wet Night Early Dawn Seat Chant Pilgrims Song," Thomas Erben Gallery, NYC, 1996, participated in as an artist, "Incandescent" part of "Now Here," Intl Art Exhibit, Louisiana Museum of Modern Art, 1996, represented by Thomas Erben Gallery, New York, NY, 1995; solo exhibit "Populated Air" Thomas Erben Gallery, 1997, Univ of Illinois at Chicago School of Art and Design, visiting artist, 1997, participated as artist, "Out of Action: Between Performance and the Object, 1949-1979," "Resonances," Galerie Art'O Paris, France, 1997, Guest artist, Maryland Inst, College of Art, 1997-00, Museum of Contemporary Art Los Angeles, 1998, participated in 16 pieces: "The Influence of Yoruba on Cont Artists," the Brickhouse, London; "A Love Supreme," La Criere Centre d'Arta; Solo exhibit, Colorado Springs Fine Arts Center, 2001, guest artist, Kerry Marshall's exhibit "One True Thing: Meditations on Black Aesthetics," Museum of Contemp Art, Chicago, 2003, "Widefield", Wildfield, Colo, 2001, "Watch!", Wooten Studio Gallery, 2002, "RSVP Retrospective", Thomas Erben Gallery, 2003, solo exhibit, Thomas Erben Gallery, NYC, 2003, "Prospect Lake", Photo Exhibit under the pseudonym Propecia, Leigh, 2004, "Asp-Rx", Thomas Erben Gallery, 2005, Fabric Workshop and Museum - Artist in Residence, 2006. **Home Addr:** 4160 Brigadoon Lane, Colorado Springs, CO 80909, **Home Phone:** (719)596-3551. **Business Addr:** Artist, University of Colorado, Visual Arts & Performing Arts Department, PO Box 10255, Colorado Springs, CO 80909-1255, **Business Phone:** (719)262-4360.

NESBITT, PREXY-ROZELL WILLIAM
Educator, government official, consultant. **Personal:** Born Feb 23, 1944, Chicago, IL; son of Rozell Rufus and Sadie Alberta Crain; divorced 2002; children: Samora Nesbitt. **Educ:** Antioch Col, BA, 1967; Univ Chicago, PhD, 1971; Columbia Univ, Cert in African Studies 1968; Northwestern Univ, MA 1974, PhD, 1975. **Career:** Educator, Speaker, Consult: Amilcar Cabral Comm Organizers Training Inst, dir, 1970-72; World Coun Churches, dir 1979-83; Dist 65 United Auto Workers Union, adminr 1983-86; Sch Art Inst Chicago, lectr african Lit, 1983-90; City Chicago Mayor's Off, asst dir comm rels 1986-88; Govt Mozambique, sr consult, 1987-92; Assoc Col Midwest, Multiculturalism coord & hist lectr, 1990-93; John D & Catherine T MacArthur Fndn, Prog on Peace & Int Cooper, sr prog Officer, 1993-96; ed bd Chicago Reporter, 1995-2000, 2002-04; Francis W Parker Sch, dean, 1996-2001; Am Ctr for Int Labor Solidarity, Southern African rep, 2001-03; Am Friends Serv Comt, interim dir, 2001-03; Chicago Teachers Ctr, Northern Ill Univ, sr multiculturalism & diversity specialist, 2003-; Columbia Col, instr African hist; Francis W Parker Sch, consult, 2003-; Univ Chicago Lab Sch, consult, 2003-; speaker & educator pvt pract, currently. **Orgs:** NAACP, 1970-; Asn Concerned African Scholars, 1980-; bd dirs, CA Newsreel 1980-; consult, Am Comn Africa, 1980-; bd dirs, TransAfrica, 1981-86, Inst for Food & Devel Policy, 1994-; Anti-Racism Inst, Chicago, consult, 1994-; bd dirs, Shared Interest, 1996-2000, 2002-06; Nat Asn Independent Sch. **Honors/Awds:** Swords into Plowshares Peace Award, Clergy and Laity Concerned, Chicago, 1986; Steve Biko Award, Chicago TransAfrica, 1987; Drylongso Award, Boston, 1994-, Order Friendship & Peace, Mozambique Govt, 1989; Peacemaker of the Year, Peace Mus, Chicago, 1996; Harold Wash Studs Terkel Award, IL Peace Action, 1998; Horace Mann Award for Serv to SOC, Antioch Col, 1998. **Special Achievements:** Author: Apartheid in Our Living Room, 1986; 15 pubations including "Beyond Divestment Movement," Black Scholar 1986; "Apartheid in Our Living Rooms, US Foreign Policy on SAfrica," Midwest Res 1987; "Desbin Straight: A Reflection on Basil Davidson" Race & Class, 1994. **Business Addr:** Speaker, Educator, 502 Jackson Blvd, Oak Park, IL 60304-1402, **Business Phone:** (708)445-7359.

NESBITT, ROBIN ANTHONY
Lawyer. **Personal:** Born May 17, 1956, New York, NY; son of Robert and Vivian Nimmo; married Michelle Ponds, Dec 19, 1987; children: Robin Anthony Jr, Christine Michelle. **Educ:** Morehouse Col, BA, econ, 1977; Atlanta Univ Sch Bus, MBA, 1980; Southern Univ Sch Law, JD, 1984. **Career:** First Fed Savings & Loan, managing atty, 1984-87; Southern Univ, asst prof, 1984-89; Nesbitt & Simmons, atty, partner, 1984-. **Orgs:** Kappa Alpha Psi, 1974; Toastmasters, 1977; Phi Alta Delta, 1982; Community Asn Welfare Sch Age C, 1989; O'Brien House, 1990. **Honors/Awds:** Licensed registered rep, series No 6, Nat Asn Securities Dealers. **Home Addr:** 7928 Wimbledon Ave, Baton Rouge, LA 70810, **Home Phone:** (225)767-3107. **Business Addr:** Attorney, Nesbitt & Simmons, 118 S 19th St, Baton Rouge, LA 70806-3636, **Business Phone:** (225)344-9555.*

NESBY, ANN (ANN BENNETT)
Singer. **Personal:** Born Jan 1, 1955?, Joliet, IL; married Timothy Lee; children: 3. **Career:** Sounds Blackness, vocalist; solo, 1996; Albums: I'm Here for You, 1996; Love Is What We Need: The Essentials, 2001; Put It on Paper, 2002; Make Me Better, 2003; In the Spirit, 2006; This Is Love, 2007; The Lula Lee Project, 2009; Singles: Keep Ya Head Up, 2001; Best Friends, 2007; Film: Gigli, 2003; The Fighting Temptations, 2003. **Honors/Awds:** Two Grammy awards as part of Sounds of Blackness; Has been nominated for three solo Grammys. *

NESBY, DONALD RAY, SR.
Law enforcement officer. **Personal:** Born Feb 16, 1937, Austin, TX; married Ruby J Thomas; children: Donald R Jr & Alex L. **Educ:** San Diego City Col, 1964; Austin Community Col, 1975. **Career:** Travis City Sheriff Dept, dep sheriff, 1973-76; Co Travis, Constable Pct 1, constable 1976-. **Orgs:** Tex Peace Officers Asn, 1978-; pres, WH Passon Hist Soc, 1983-85. **Honors/Awds:** Outstanding Community Service, Alpha Kappa Zeta Chap, 1977; Outstanding Service Award, St Mary's Community, 1978; Recognition Award, MW Mt Carmel Grand Lodge, 1982. **Special Achievements:** First elected black law enforcement officer in the county. His first book is "try the impossible and achieve the impossible". **Home Addr:** 5505 Ameswood Dr, Austin, TX 78723. **Business Addr:** Constable, County of Travis, 1811 Springdale Rd Suite 120, Austin, TX 78721-1354, **Business Phone:** (512)854-7510.

NESMITH, KIMBLIN E
Educator. **Educ:** Morehouse Col; Univ Miami Sch Law, JD. **Career:** Edward Waters Col, Dept Criminal Justice & Study Law, asst prof & chair, currently. **Business Addr:** Assistant Professor, Chair, Edward Waters College, Department of Criminal Justice, 1658 Kings Rd, Jacksonville, FL 32209, **Business Phone:** (904)470-8000.

NETTERS, TYRONE HOMER
Secretary (office). **Personal:** Born Oct 11, 1954, Clarksdale, MS; married Beverly Bracy; children: Malik & Toure. **Educ:** Calif State Univ, Sacramento, BS, 1976. **Career:** Off Majority Consultants, campaign specialist, 1979-82; Assembly Ways & Means, consult, 1982-83; Off Assembly woman Moore, legis asst; Sacramento Valley Organizing Community, organizer, currently. **Orgs:** Bd dirs, Magalink Corp, 1984-; Philip Randolph Inst, 1985; founding mem, Fannie Lou Hamer Demo Club, 1985. **Honors/Awds:** SABC Community Service Award, 1980; National Black Child Development Merit Award 1981. **Home Addr:** 8767 Carissa Way, Elk Grove, CA 95624-3887. **Business Addr:** Organizer, Sacramento Valley Organizing Community, 455 Univ Ave Suite 370, Sacramento, CA 95825.

NETTLEFORD, HON. REX MILTON
Dancer, choreographer, educator. **Personal:** Born Feb 3, 1933, Falmouth, Jamaica; son of Charles and Lebertha Palmer. **Educ:** Univ Col West Indies, London, BA, 1956; Oxon, MPhil, 1959. **Career:** Jamaica, Trinidad & Tobago, resident tutor, 1956-57, 1959-61, staff tutor polit educ, 1961-63; Trade Union Educ Inst, dir studies, 1963-98; Univ West Indies, Kingston, Jamaica, Dept Govt, tutor, lectr & polit thought; Extra-Mural Studies, deputy dir, 1969-71, dir, 1971, prof, 1975-98, pro-vice chancellor, 1990-96, prof & dep vice chancellor, 1996-98; prof & dir sch continuing studies, 1990-96, vice chancellor, prof extra mural studies, currently; Comn Nat Symbols & Nat Observances, chmn, 1996. **Orgs:** Founder & artistic dir, Jamaica Nat Dance Theatre Co, 1962-; gov, Int Develop Res Ctr, 1970-; chmn, Tourism Prod Develop Co, Jamaica, 1976-78; cult adv to Prime Minister Jamaica, 1972-80; chmn, Inst Jamaica, 1978-80; trustee, AFS Int, New York; chmn, Commonwealth Arts Orgn, 1980; int trustee, AFS Int, 1980-89; Comn Experts Open Learning & Distance Educ, Commonwealth Secretariat, London, UK, 1986-87; bd dirs, Nat Com Bank Jamaica, 1987-; bd dirs, Jamaica Mutual Life Assurance Soc, 1989-; Group experts Monitoring Sanctions Against Apartheid, ILO, 1989-; cult adv, Prime Minister Jamaica, 1989-; bd dirs, Panos Inst, 1990-; West Indian Comn, 1990-92; exec bd, UNESCO, 1991-92; chmn, Comm Adv Govt Structure, Jamaica, 1992; chmn, Nat Coun Educ, Jamaica, 1992; UNESCO Steering Comm Cult & Develop, 1993-; rapporteur, UNESCO, Int Sci Comm "Slave Route" Proj, 1994; chmn, Comn Nat Symbols & Nat Observances, 1996; Caricom Comn Cult, 1997; Assoc fel, Ctr African & African-Am Studies, Atlanta Univ; acad counr, Latin Am Studies, Int Soc Hist Ideas, Wilson Ctr, Wash DC; CIDEC, Orgn Am States. **Honors/Awds:** Order of Merit Award, Govt Jamaica, 1975; Gold Musgrave Medal, Inst Jamaica, 1981; UCWI Exhibition Scholar, 1953: Issa Scholar, 1956; Rhodes Scholar, 1957; Patton lect, Ind Univ, 1989; Pelican Award, Univ WI Alumni, 1990; Living Legend Award, Nat Black Arts Festival, USA, 1990; 1991; Zora Neale Hurston-Paul Robeson Award, 1994; Hon Doctor of Letters, St Johns Univ Hartford, 1995; Presidential Medal, Brooklyn Col, City Univ NY, 1995; Man of the Year Award, Am Biog Inst, 1995; Honorary Doctorate, City Univ NY, 1996; Honorary Doctorate, St Johns Univ, 1996; Honorary Doctorate, Univ Conn, 1997; Honorary Doctorate, Ill Weslyn Univ, 1997; Honorary Doctorate, Univ Hartford, 1998; Honorary Doctorate, Emory Univ, 1999; Honorary Doctorate, Grand Valley State Univ, 2000; Honorary Doctorate, Queens Univ, CA, 2000; Honorary Doctorate, Univ Sheffield, UK, 2000; Honorary Doctorate, Col Oxford, UK, 2001; Honorary Doctorate, Toronto Univ, Canada, 2002; Honorary Doctorate, Oxford Univ, UK, 2003. **Special Achievements:** Choreographer, over 50 major works for the National Dance Theatre Co of Jamaica, 1962-, author of many books and articles on Caribbean cultural development, editor, principal dancer, author, choreographer: leader of Cultural Missions to the USA, Canada, Latin American, Australia, and the USSR, is the author of Manley and the New Jamaica, The African Connexion, and In Our Heritage, and his latest published book is Caribbean Cultural Identity, the Case of Jamaica. **Business Addr:** Professor of Extra Mural Studies, University of the West Indies, Extra Mural Studies, Mona Campus, PO Box 42, Kingston, Jamaica, **Business Phone:** (876)977-0237.

NETTLES, WILLARD, JR.
Educator, executive. **Personal:** Born Jan 17, 1944, Hooks, TX; son of Willard and Gladys Hammick; married Rosemary. **Educ:** Lewis & Clark Col, BA, 1967 & MAT, 1973. **Career:** Vancouver, WA, city councilman; Portland Sch Dist, teacher; Crown Zellerbach Corp, prod planner, 1967-70; Vancouver Pub Sch, Vancouver, WA, teacher math & spanish, 1978-91; Trailblazer Fence Co, Vancouver, WA, owner, 1982-91. **Orgs:** Nat Asn Advan Colored People. **Honors/Awds:** Washington State Athletic Association of Community Colleges Championship. **Special Achievements:** First Black & Youngest Councilman of Vancouver, WA. **Home Phone:** (360)254-0441.

NEUFVILLE, DR. MORTIMER H
School administrator, educator. **Personal:** Born Dec 10, 1939, Portland, Jamaica; married Masie Brown; children: Sonetta, Nadine & Tisha. **Educ:** Jamaica Sch Ag, Dipl, 1961; Tuskegee Inst, BSc, 1970; Univ Fla, MSc, 1971, PhD, 1974. **Career:** Univ Fla, grad asst, 1971-74; Prairie View A&M, head dept animal sci, 1974-78; Lincoln Univ Sch Appl Sci MO, assoc dean, 1978-83; Univ MD Eastern Shore, dean agr, res dir, 1983-91, assoc vpres,

1991-93, Acad Affairs, vpres, 1994-96; Nat Asn State Univ & Land-Grant Cols, exec, vpres, 1997-. **Orgs:** Agr rsch asst, Ministry Agri-Jamaica, 1961-68; Gamma Sigma Delta Hon Soc, 1970, Alpha Zeta Hon Soc, 1971, bd dir, N Cent R&D Ctr, 1982-83; Sigma Pi Phi, 1984; Nat Higher Ed Comm, 1985; N E Regional Coun, 1986; Govs Comn Educ Agr, 1987; Int Sci & Educ Coun, 1987; Asn Res Dirs, vice chmn, chmn, 1989-90; JCARD-CSRP Rev Comt, chair, 1990; ACOP, 1993, Budget Comt, chair, 1992; Northeast Regional Ctr Rural Develop, 1990. **Honors/Awds:** Most Outstanding Junior, Agr Tuskegee Inst, 1969; Most Outstanding Grad Senior, Tuskegee Inst, 1970; Review of Animal Science Research, 1890 Univ Develop Res Hist Black Land Grant Inst 1-75. **Business Phone:** (202)478-6040.

NEVERDON-MORTON, DR. CYNTHIA
Educator. **Personal:** Born Jan 23, 1944, Baltimore, MD; daughter of James Neverdon and Hattie Neverdon; married Lonnie George. **Educ:** Morgan State Univ, BA, 1965, MS, 1967; Howard Univ, PhD, 1974. **Career:** Baltimore Pub Sch Syst, teacher hist, 1965-68; Peale Mus, researcher & jr archivist, 1965; Univ Minn, admis assoc, 1968-69, coordr spec progr, 1969-71; Inst Afro-Am Studies, instr curric develop, 1968; MN Lutheran Synod Priority Prog, consult, 1969; Coppin St Col, asst dean stud & prof hist, 1971-72, assoc prof hist, 1972-81, chmn, dept hist & geog, int studies, 1978-81, prof hist, 1981-; Historically Black Col & Univ Fel, Dept Defense, EEO & Spec Emphasis Prog, 1989-93, Fiftieth Anniversary WWII Commemoration Comt, 1993-95; Mich St Univ, Res CD-ROM Immigration & Migration US 1900-2000, consult, 1996; Md Mus African Am Hist & Cult, head acad team, 1998-. **Orgs:** Study grant to selected W African Nations, 1974; partic, Caribbean-Am Scholars Exchange Prog, 1974; adv bd, Md Comn Afro-Am Life, 1977-; Asn Black Female Historians, 1979-; adv bd, Multicultural Educ Coalition Comt, 1980-; Asn Study Afro-Am Life & Hist; reader & panelist, Nat Endowment Humanities Smithsonian Inst Fel, 1986; Nonstandard Eng & Sch Environ TaskForce, Baltimore County Pub Sch, 1990; Md St Dept Educ Task Force Teacher Social Studies, 1991; Accreditation Team; Nat Forum Hist Stand, 1992-94; reviewer, hist dept, Howard Univ, 1995; bd ed, Twentieth Century Black Am Officials & Leaders; bd mem, Great Blacks In Wax. **Special Achievements:** Publ "The Impact of Christianity Upon Traditional Family Values" 1978;"The Black Woman's Struggle for Equality in the South" 1978; publ"Self-Help Programs as Educative Activities of Black Women in the South, 1895-1925, Focus on Four Key Areas" 1982; "Blacks in Baltimore 1950-80,An Overview" with Bettye Gardner 1982; "Black Housing Patterns inBaltimore 1895-1925" publ MD Historian 1985; recent publications book,"Afro-American Women of the South and the Advancement of the Race1895-1925" Univ of TN Press 1989; essay, "Through the Looking Glass:Reviewing Bo about the African American Female Exerience" in Feminist-Studies 1988; wrote eight chapters, African American History in the Press,1851-1899, Gale Press, 1996; "Securing the Double V: African-American andJapanese-American Women in the Military During World War II" in A Woman'sWar Too: "In Search of Equality: Maryland and the Civil Rights Movement,1940-70," Black Classic Press, 1997; "Interracial Cooperation Movement,"The Readers Companion to US Women's History, Houghton Mifflin, 1998;"Fanny Jackson Coppin," Encyclopedia of Africa-American Educ", GreenwoodPress, 1996; "Advancement of the Race Through AFA Women's Organization inthe South, 1895-1925," AFA Women End the Vote, 1837-1965, Univ of MAPress, 1997; "Atlanta Neighborhood Union" and "Baltimore Civic, Literacy,and Mutal Aid ASC," Organizing BLK AME: "An Encyclopedia of AFA Assns",Garland Publ, Inc, 2001. **Business Addr:** Professor, Coppin State University, 2500 W North Ave, Baltimore, MD 21216-3698, **Business Phone:** (410)951-3433.

NEVILLE, AARON
Singer. **Personal:** Born Jan 24, 1941, New Orleans, LA; son of Arthur (deceased) and Amelia (deceased); married Joel Roux (deceased); children: Ivan, Aaron Jr, Ernestine & Jason. **Career:** Albums: Aaron Neville Greatest Hits, 1967; Orchid in the Storm, 1985; The Classic Aaron Neville - My Greatest Gift, 1990; Tell It Like It Is, 1991; Warm Your Heart, 1991; Aaron Neville's Soulful Christmas, 1993; The Grand Tour, 1993; The Tatoo ed Heart, 1995; Can't Stop My Heart, 1995; Doing It Their Own Way, 1996; To make Me Who I Am, 1997; The Very Best of Aaron Neville, 2000; Devotion, 2000; Aaron Neville - The Ultimate Collection, 2001; The Best of Aaron Neville - The Millennium Collection, 2002; Humdinger, 2002; Gospel Roots, 2003; Love Songs, 2003; Believe, 2003; Orchid in the Storm Bonus Tracks, 2003; Nature Boy: The Standards Album, 2003; Christmas Prayer, 2005; Bring It On Home, 2006; Mojo Soul, 2006. **Honors/Awds:** Numerous honors & awards including 14 Grammy Awards, 3 Big Easy Awards &Rolling Stone Critics' Poll. **Business Phone:** (310)859-4000.*

NEWBERRY, CEDRIC CHARLES
Executive. **Personal:** Born Aug 10, 1953, Perry, GA; son of Charlie C and Rubye L Allen; married Lillie Ruth Brown; children: Carnice, Candice & Clayton. **Educ:** Fort Valley State Col, BS, 1975; Univ Wis-Madison, MS, 1977; Southern Ill Univ, Edwardsville, MBA, 1982. **Career:** Monsanto Co, sr res biologist, 1977-83; Meineke Discount Mufflers, CC Newberry Automotive Corp, pres, gen mgr, 1983-. **Orgs:** Am Soc Agron, 1977-83; Comm Support Black Bus & Prof, 1983-; chmn educ comn, Nat Black MBA Assoc, 1986-87. **Honors/Awds:** Honors Convocation Fort Valley State Col; Shion Univ Wis fel, 1975-77. **Business Addr:** President, General Manager, CC Newberry Automotive Corp, 7760 Reading Rd, Cincinnati, OH 45237, **Business Phone:** (513)761-9900.

NEWBERRY, TRUDELL MCCLELLAND
School administrator. **Personal:** Born Jan 30, 1939, Junction City, AR; daughter of Roosevelt and Margaret Knighten; divorced; children: Fe Lesia Michelle & Thomas Walter III. **Educ:** Univ Ariz, Pine Bluff, BA, 1962; Roosevelt Univ, Chicago, MA, 1980; Gov State, post grad Work, 1984; Northern Ill Univ, post grad work, 1989. **Career:** Almyra Pub Sch System, teacher, 1962-65; Franklin-Wright Settlement, social worker, 1965-69; N Chicago Grade Sch, teacher, 1970-90; Foss Park Dist N Chicago, recreational supvr, 1982-83; City Coun N Chicago IL, alderwoman fifth ward, 1983-87; N Chicago Unit Sch District, N Chicago, IL, dean students, 1990-92; Neal Elementary Sch, teacher, 1992-93. **Orgs:** Eureka Temple no 1172, 1972-; UAPB Alumni Asn, 1982-; N Chicago Teachers Asn, 1982-87; N Chicago High Sch PTO, 1984-88; N Chicago Booster Club,1984-88; bldg rep, NCTA, 1985-87; N Chicago Libr Bd, 1986-87; exec bd, Coun Rep Lake County Fed Teachers, 1987-89; Comt Ten Unification N Chicago Sch Sys, 1988-89; pres, N Chicago Elemen Coun Federated Teachers, 1989-90; N Chicago Unit Dist Coun, 1992-. **Honors/Awds:** Ark Travelers Award, Ambassador of Goodwill, signed by Governor BillClinton, 1992. **Home Addr:** 2111 S Lewis Ave, North Chicago, IL 60064-2544.

NEWBILLE, CYNTHIA
Manager, association executive. **Career:** Charles Drew Univ Med & Sci, head start, prog dir; Nat Black Women's Health Proj, exec dir; City Richmond, VA, dist mgr & chief staff, currently. **Orgs:** Founder, Parent Policy Coun. **Business Phone:** (804)646-7970.

NEWBOLD, SIMEON EUGENE, SR.
Clergy. **Personal:** Born Sep 4, 1954, Miami, FL; son of David Jerome Sr and Catherine Melvina Armbrister; married Audrea Stitt, Aug 21, 1982; children: Simon Eugene Jr & Krishna Alanna. **Educ:** Tuskegee Inst, BS, social work, 1977, MEd, personnel admin, 1979; Seabury-Western Theol Sem, MDiv, 1989. **Career:** Barnett Bank, credit analyst; Oper PUSH Nat, financial analyst; Messiah-St Bartholomew Episcopal Church, asst; St Simon's Episcopal Church, rector; St Peter's Episcopal Church, vicar, currently. **Orgs:** Union Black Episcopalians; Opp Fraternity Inc; Nat Asn Black Suba Divers, Inc. **Business Addr:** Vicar, St Peter Episcopal Church, 1719 N 23rd St, Richmond, VA 23223, **Business Phone:** (804)643-2686.

NEWBORN, DR. ODIE VERNON, JR.
Physician. **Personal:** Born Nov 5, 1947, Nashville, TN; married Trina. **Educ:** Tenn State Univ, BS; Meharry Med Col, MD, 1973; Flint Mich, Intern, Residency. **Career:** Physician, family practitioner, currently. **Orgs:** NMA; Ga State Med Soc; Colquitt Co Med Soc; NCP. **Home Addr:** 116 Southlake Ct, Columbia, SC 29223, **Home Phone:** (912)985-9660. **Business Phone:** (615)254-9345.

NEWELL, DARYL
Banker, executive. **Personal:** Born Oct 5, 1963, Chicago, IL; son of Hallie and Eli; married Verlena Mooney Newell, Feb 17, 2001; children: Daryl Isaac & Grant Eli George. **Educ:** Northwestern Univ, BA, sociol, 1986; Keller Grad Sch Mgt, MBA, 1991. **Career:** Green Bay Packer Football Club, free agt profl athlete, 1986; Dean Foods, mgt trainee, 1986-89; Harris Bank, unit mgr & operations officer, 1989-92, sect mgr & asst vpres, 1992-95; br mgr & vpres, 1995-97; financial consult & vpres, 1997; ShoreBank Corp, sr vpres retail banking, currently. **Orgs:** Bd mem & vpres develop, 100 Black Men Chicago Inc, 1995-; treas, Northwestern Black Alumni Asn, 1995-; NFL Retired Players Asn, 1996-; dir, South East Chicago Comn, 1996-; Big Ten Av Comn, 1998. **Honors/Awds:** 1st Team Defense Freshman All-America, Football News, 1982; Best Conditioned Athlete, Northwestern Athletic Dept, 1984; 1st Tean All State Defensive Tackle, Bloomington Herald, 1981; Illuminati Honoree, Inst Positive Learning Open Book Prog, 2002. **Special Achievements:** Author: International Banks Initiate Strategic, 1998; co-author, Partnerships with Small and Medium Size Enterprises in the Emerging Global Market Place. **Business Addr:** Senior Vice President Retail Banking, ShoreBank Corporation, 7054 S Jeffery Blvd, Chicago, IL 60649, **Business Phone:** 800-669-7725.

NEWELL, KATHLEEN W
Judge, lawyer. **Personal:** Born Aug 30, 1943, Alexandria, LA; daughter of Leroy and Juanita Mandebourgh; widowed; children: Oliver Joseph. **Educ:** Univ Calif Los Angeles, attended; Wayne State Univ Sch Law, JD, 1972. **Career:** Mich Dept Treas, admin law judge, 1979-97; Ernst & Young LLP, sr tax mgr, 1997-99; pvt pract, atty, currently. **Orgs:** Probate & Estate Planning & Taxation Sect, 1985-88, chair, elder law & advocate secy, State Bar Mich, 1996-97; pres, New Home Community Develop & Non-Profit Housing, 1995-96; adv coun, Denby Home/Salvation Army, 1995-, pres, 1998-2001. **Business Addr:** Attroney, 22433 Chippewa St, Detroit, MI 48219-0301, **Business Phone:** (313)592-1187.

NEWELL, VIRGINIA K.
Educator. **Personal:** Born in Advance, NC; daughter of William S Kimbrough (deceased) and Dinah; married George (deceased); children: Virginia D Newell Banks & Glenda Newell-Harris. **Educ:** Talladega Col, AB, 1940; NY Univ, 1956; Univ Sarasota, EdD, 1976; Winston-Salem State Univ, LHD, 1989. **Career:** Educator (retired); Winston-Salem State Univ, assoc prof, math & comput sci, chairperson. **Orgs:** ASF fel Univ Chicago, 1959; Winston-Salem Chap Links Inc; pres, NC Coun Teachers Math; life mem, Nat Educ Asn; ed, newsletter Nat Asn Math; Am Math Sci; Math Asn Am; NCTM; life mem, Nat Asn Advan Colored People; State Comnr Nat Coun Negro Women; Alpa Kappa Alpha Sorority; Phi Omega Chap; bd dirs, Chamber Commerce; bd dirs, Arts Coun; bd dirs, Winston-Salem Symphony. **Honors/Awds:** Outstanding Teacher Award, 1960; Woman of Yr, Zeta Phi Beta's, 1964; Eastward, elected to alderman, 1977; Woman of the Yr, Winston-Salem Chronicle, 1983, Citizen of the Yr, 1987; The Math & Sci Acad Excellence, Winston-Salem State Univ, 1988; WW Rankin Excellent in Teaching Award, NC Coun Teachers Math, 1999. *

NEWFIELD, MARC ALEXANDER
Baseball player. **Personal:** Born Oct 19, 1972, Sacramento, CA. **Career:** Ariz League, Ariz Mariners, player, 1990; Calif League, San Bernardino, player, 1991; Southern League, Jacksonville Suns, player, 1992-93; Seattle Mariners, outfielder, 1993-95; Pac Coast League, Calgary, player, 1994; Pac Coast League, Tacoma Rainers, player, 1995; Pac Coast League, Las Vegas 51s, player, 1995; San Diego Padres, player, 1995-96; Milwaukee Brewers, player, 1996-98; Eastern League, Trenton Thunder, player, 1999; Vancouver, 1999; Oakland Athletics, player, 1999.

NEWHOUSE, MILLICENT DELAINE
Lawyer, educator. **Personal:** Born May 28, 1964, Detroit, MI; daughter of Benjamin and Janette. **Educ:** Univ Mich, BA, 1986; Howard Univ, JD, 1989. **Career:** State Atty Gen Off, asst atty gen, 1989-98; legal asstistance, 1998-; Nat Acad Paralegal Studies, teacher, 1992; Univ Wash Sch Law, Career Planning & Pub Serv Ctr, dir, 2001-04. **Orgs:** Secy, Loren Miller Bar Asn, 1992-93; volunteer, atty coordr, Neighborhood Legal Clinic, 1992-; Equality Practice Comn; mentor, Boys & Girls Club, 1990-91; tutor, Maddona Presbyterian Church, 1990-92; Municipal League Candidate Comn, 1992; Howard Univ Alumni Asn; Wash Women Lawyers Orgn Pres, 1997-98. **Honors/Awds:** Diversity Award's Outstanding Recruitment Coordinator, Atty Gen Off; Outstanding Young Lawyers of the Year, King County Bar Asn; Outstanding Young Lawyers of the Year, Wash State Bar Asn; Outstanding Young Lawyers of the Year, Loren Miller Bar Asn. **Business Addr:** Gender Study Committee, University of Washington School, Law Gender Study, 1325 4th Ave Suite 600, Seattle, WA 98101-2539, **Business Phone:** (206)443-9722.*

NEWHOUSE, QUENTIN
Psychologist, research scientist, educator. **Personal:** Born Oct 20, 1949, Washington, DC; son of Quentin Newhouse Sr and Berlene Byrd; married Debra Carter, Jul 7, 1984; children: Alyse Elizabeth Belinda. **Educ:** Marietta Col, BA, psychol, 1971; Howard Univ, MS, gen exp psychol, 1974, PhD, exp social psychol, 1980. **Career:** Antioch Univ, asst prof social scis, 1976-79; Quentin Newhouse Jr & Assocs, pres, 1981-84; Howard Univ, asst prof social scis, 1982-88; United Synagogue Youth, comput syst analyst, 1984-85; Univ DIS, adj prof psychol, 1984, 1991-; US Census Bureau, 21th Century staff, comput supt, 1988-91, Ctr Survey Methods Res, statistician, 1991-93; Bureautots Inc, adv bd, vpres, 1990-91; Prepare Our Youth Inc, adv bd, 1990-94; Market Res Analyst, 1994; PG Private Ind Coun, job developer, 1994; Bowie State Univ, Bowie Md, Dept Behav Scis & Human Servs, asst prof, 1995-, interim chair, 1996-; Strayer Univ, Nasville Campus, dean, currently. **Orgs:** Life mem, Tau Epsilon Phi, 1980-; Am Psychol Asn, 1981, 1993-; affil, Social Sci Comput Asn, 1990-94; PG County CMS C & Youth, 1991-92; PG County Children's Comn C & Families, 1992-95; P G County rep, State Adv CMS C, Youth, & Families, 1992-95; co-chair, CENSUG, Census SAS User's Group, 1992-; Am Statist Asn, 1993; Asn Black Psychols, 1994-; bd dirs, Mental Health Asn PG County, 1994-95; Regional Adv Bd, United Way PG County, 1994-; bd dirs, Metropolitan Police Boys & Girls Clubs, 1994-. **Honors/Awds:** Service Award, Univ DIS, 1982, 1984; Letter of Commendation for Outstanding Performance, United Synagogue Youth, 1988; Certificate Appreciation, PG County, 1995, 1996; Governor's Certificate of Achievement, State Md, 1995. **Business Addr:** Dean, Strayer University, Nashville Campus, 30 Rachel Dr Suite 200, Nashville, TN 37214, **Business Phone:** (615)871-2260.

NEWHOUSE, ROBERT F
Executive, football player. **Personal:** Born Jan 9, 1950, Gregg County, TX; married Nancy; children: Roddrick, Dawnyel, Shauntel & Reginald. **Educ:** Univ Houston, MTH, 1973; Univ Dallas, MBA, 1984. **Career:** Dallas Cowboys, player, 1972-83, dir community affairs, currently; Tymeshare, computer oper; Tex Bank & Trust, loan officer; Trans Global Airlines, pres, 1984; Dallas Tex, real estate broker; Lone Star Delivery, pres; R Newhouse Enterprises Inc, pres. **Orgs:** Young Men Chrisitan Asn; United Way; Boys Club; panel trustee, Northern Dist Dallas Div. **Honors/Awds:** Sport Hall of Fame, Univ Houston. **Home Addr:** 1412

Main St Suite 2450, Dallas, TX 75202, **Home Phone:** (214)752-0999. **Business Addr:** President, R Newhouse Enterprises Inc, 6847 Truxton Dr, Dallas, TX 75231, **Business Phone:** (214)343-9064.

NEWKIRK, DR. GWENDOLYN
School administrator, educator. **Personal:** Born in Washington, DC; daughter of Rachel Cornelia Polk and William Henry. **Educ:** Tillotson Col, Austin, TX, BS, 1945; Columbia Univ, Teachers Col, New York, NY, MA, 1946; Cornell Univ, Ithaca, NY, EdD, 1961. **Career:** Cornell Univ, Ithaca, NY, grad teaching & res asst, 1960-61; Bennet Col, Greensboro, NC, instr, 1946-50; Lincoln Univ, Jefferson City, MO, prof, 1950-62; NC Col, Durham, NC, prof, 1962-69; Univ Minnesota, assoc prof, 1969-71; Univ Nebr, Lincoln, NE, dept chmn & prof, prof emer, currently; Univ Okla, Home Econs Women's Scholars Prog, visiting scholar, 1976; Ind Univ, PA, visiting scholar, 1982. **Orgs:** Life mem, Am Home Econs Asn; Nebr Home Econs Asn; life mem, Am Voc Asn; Nebr Voc Asn, 1971-; Nebr Educ Asn; bd dir, Child Guidance Ctr, currently. **Honors/Awds:** Women Helping Women Recognition, Soroptimist Int Lincoln Chap, 1975; Doctor of Humane Letters, Tillotson Col, 1990. **Special Achievements:** Recognized by Optimists Club Lincoln in 1986. **Business Addr:** Professor Emeritus, University of Nebraska-Lincoln, Consumer Science & Education, 128 501 Bldg, Lincoln, NE 68588-0244, **Business Phone:** (402)472-2600.

NEWKIRK, PAMELA
Educator, journalist, writer. **Personal:** Born Nov 13, 1957, New York City, NY; daughter of Louis and Gloria; married Michael Nairne, Nov 5, 1983; children: Marjani & Mykel. **Educ:** New York Univ, BA, 1983; Columbia Univ, MS, 2001. **Career:** Knickerbocker News, reporter, 1984-89; Gannett News Serv, Capitol Hill correspondent, 1988-89; New York Post, reporter, 1989-90; NY Newsday, reporter, 1991-93; NY Univ, adj prof, 1991-93, Undergrad Studies, dir, 1994-96, asst prof, 1993-2000, assoc prof, 2000-; Books: "Kerner Project: Dream for Their Kids Fulfilled," Gannett News Service, Jan 5, 1989; foreword, "Thinking Black: Some of the Nation's Best Black Columnists Speak Their Mind," Crown Publishers, Inc, 1996; "Courting Rap Stars With Clothes," The New York Times, June 16, 1996; "A Rich Caste of Characters: Benilde Little Punctures Airs With Her Pen," The Washington Post, Style section, Dec 1, 1998; "Whitewash in the Newsroom," The Nation, Mar 16, 1998; guest on "Radio Nation," Mar 1998; "Controversial Silhouette: A Kara Walker piece is removed," ARTnews, Sept 1999; "A Look at Black Journalists, White Media," Washington Post, Sept 24, 2000; "Shaping the Story of Black Art," Artnews, May 2000; "Ida B Wells-Barnet: Journalism as a Weapon Against Racial Bigotry," Media Studies Jnl, Spring/Summer 2000; "Within the Veil: Black Journalists, White Media", 2000; "Searching for An Afr Amer Audience," Artnews, May, 2001; A Love No Less: Two Centuries of African American Love Letters, 2003. **Orgs:** Exec bd mem, Support Network, 1993-; adv bd mem, Annenberg Found Comn Press, 2003; adv bd mem, Press Am (documentary), PBS; co-dir, NYU Urban Jour Workshop, 2003-. **Honors/Awds:** NY Asn Black Journalist, Int Reporting Prize, 1990; Columbia Univ, Pulitzer Prize, Spot News (Team Coverage), 1992; Golden Dozen Award for Excellence in Teaching, NYU, 1994; Scholar-in-Residence, Spelman Col, 1996; Nat Press Club Award for Media Criticism, 2000. **Business Addr:** Associate Professor, Journalism, New York University, Department of Journalism & Mass Communication, 10 Wash Pl, PO Box 1286 Cooper Sta, New York, NY 10003, **Business Phone:** (212)998-7966.

NEWKIRK, THOMAS H.
School administrator, executive. **Personal:** Born in New York City, NY; son of Climith J Sr and Esther; divorced; children: Kori, Kisan, Kamila, Tori. **Educ:** Univ Mas, Amherst, MEd, 1974, EdD, 1985. **Career:** Pres, consult Newkirk Assoc Tax & Bus, 1958-; educ consult, 1958-; ins broker, 1959-63; Haryou-Act NYC, coord training testing youth div, dir mgt training; State Univ NY, Cortland, dir emer spec ed prog. **Orgs:** Founding mem, Holcombe Rucker Scholar Fund, 1967; consult, State Ed Dept, 1967-72; vpres, United Black Ed, 1969; founding mem, NYS Spec Prog Personnel Assoc, 1973; chmn, Spec Prog Inst on Teaching & Coun, 1979; Mayors Adv Comt Cortland; swimming instr, Cortland; lectr, Social Found Ed; past vpres, Spec Progs Pers Assoc State NY. **Honors/Awds:** Superlative Community Service Award, Int Key Women, 1974; Chancellors Award for Excellence in Professional Service, State Univ NY, 1979; Arthur Eve Award, Outstanding Public Service, 1991. **Special Achievements:** Publisher of books and articles. **Military Serv:** NY Nat Guard, 1946-48. **Business Addr:** Prseident, Newkirk Associates, 2628 7th Ave, New York, NY 10039-2601, **Business Phone:** (212)926-4103.

NEWLAND, DR. ZACHARY JONAS
Podiatrist. **Personal:** Born Dec 15, 1954, Ft Lee, VA; son of Archie J and Adeline M; married Camillia Sutton; children: Yolanda. **Educ:** SC State Col, BS, Chem, 1975; Med Univ SC, BS, Pharm, 1978; Pa Col Podiatric Med, DPM, 1984. **Career:** Thrift Drugs, asst mgr pharmacist, 1978-80; SC Army Nal Guard, med platoon leader, 1978-80; Laurel Pharm, pharmacist, 1982-84; Lindell Hosp, resident podiatric surg, 1984-85; Lindell Hosp, chief resident podiatric surg, 1985-86, resident teaching staff & lectr, 1986-; Metro Community Health Ctr, dir podiatric med & surg, 1986-88; People's Health Ctr, staff podiatrist, 1988-; pvt med practice, 1990-. **Orgs:** SC Pharmaceut Asn, 1978-, Nat Health Serv Corps, 1980-, Am Podiatric Med Asn, Omega Psi Phi Frat. **Honors/Awds:** Article published in Journal of Foot Surgery, 1984. **Military Serv:** AMSC Reserves, capt, 1978-. **Home Addr:** 4106 Sheridan Meadows Dr, Florissant, MO 63034-3484. **Business Addr:** Podiatrist, 4585 Washington St, Florissant, MO 63033, **Business Phone:** (314)972-1040.

NEWLIN, DR. RUFUS K
College administrator. **Career:** Morristown Col, Morristown, TN, pres, currently.

NEWMAN, ANTHONY
Personal: Born Nov 21, 1965, Bellingham, WA; married Teri; children: Baylee & Anthony Jr. **Educ:** Univ Ore. **Career:** Football player (retired), TV host; Los Angeles Rams, defensive back, 1988-94; New Orleans Saints, 1995-97; Oakland Raiders, 1998-99; Oregon Sports Network, show host,currently. **Orgs:** Founder, Anthony Q Newman Foundn. **Honors/Awds:** Rookie of the Year, 1988.

NEWMAN, CONSTANCE BERRY
Government official. **Personal:** Born Jul 8, 1935, Chicago, IL; daughter of Joseph Alonzo and Ernestine Siggers; married Theodore (divorced 1980). **Educ:** Bates Col, Lewiston, ME, AB, 1956; Univ Minn, Sch Law, Minneapolis, MN, BSL, 1959. **Career:** Vol Serv Am, Wash, DC, dir, 1971-73; Consumer Prod Safety Comn, Wash, DC, comnr, 1973-76; US Dept Housing & Urban Develop, Wash, DC, asst secy, 1976-77; Newman & Hermanson Co, Wash, DC, pres, 1977-82; Govt Lesotho, Ministry Interior, consult, 1987-88; Bush-Quayle 1988 Campaign, Wash, DC, dep dir, Nat voter coalitions, 1988; Presial Transition Team, Wash, DC, co-dir outreach, 1988-89; US Off Personnel Mgt, Wash, DC, dir, 1989-92; Smithsonian Inst, Wash, DC, under secy; US Dept State, Bur African Affairs, asst secy, 2004-05; Carmen Group, Special Counsel African Affairs, currently. **Orgs:** Bd trustees, Brookings Inst; bd trustees, Bates Col; vice chair, DC Financial Responsibility & Mgt Asst Authority; Intl Republican Inst.; pres, Inst Am Bus; vchmn, Consumer Product Safety Comn. **Honors/Awds:** Hon Doctors Laws, Amherst Col, 1980; Hon Doctors Laws, Bates Col, 1972; Secy Defense Medal for Outstanding Pub Serv, 1985; Secy's Award for Excellence, US Dept Housing & Urban Develop, 1977; Washingtonian of the Year, 1998; Smithsonian Institution Joseph Henry Medal, 2000. **Home Addr:** 114 Duddington Pl SE, Washington, DC 20003, **Home Phone:** (202)546-7013.

NEWMAN, DAVID, JR. See Obituaries section.

NEWMAN, DR. GEOFFREY W
Educator. **Personal:** Born Aug 29, 1946, Oberlin, OH; son of Arthur Eugene and Bertha Battle. **Educ:** Howard Univ, Wash, DC, BFA, 1968, PhD, 1978; Wayne State Univ, MI, MA, 1970. **Career:** Howard Univ, Wabash Col, Drama Dept, chmn; Montclair State Col, Sch Arts, dean, 1988-; World Premiere Owen Dodson's Sound Soul & European Premiere Robert Nemiroff's Raisin, dir; Park Place Productions, DC, artistic dir; Young Audiences Dist Columbia, artistic dir; Ira Aldridge Theatre, Howard Univ, Wash DC, artistic dir; Takoma Players, Takoma Theatre, Wash DC, artistic dir, cofounder. **Orgs:** Grant screening panels, Dist Columbia Comn Arts & Humanities, Penn State Coun Arts & Ill State Arts Coun; nominator, Wash Awards Soc Helen Hayes Awards. **Honors/Awds:** Received Amoco Award, Theatrical Excellence, John F Kennedy Ctr Permorming Arts Conjunction Am Theatre Asn; Special commendations, Mayor Marion Barry Jr, Washington DC, Mayor Pat Screen, Baton Rouge La, & Gov Harry Hughes, State Md. **Special Achievements:** Actor, educator, consultant, theorist and director in theatre; Published articles in professional journals. **Business Addr:** Dean, Montclair State University, School of the Arts, LI-130E 1 Normal Ave, Montclair, NJ 07043-1624.

NEWMAN, JOHN SYLVESTER
Basketball player. **Personal:** Born Nov 28, 1963, Danville, VA; married Tina; married Dawn Lewis (divorced). **Educ:** Univ Richmond, attended 1986. **Career:** Basketball Player (retired); Cleveland Cavaliers, forward, 1986-87; NY Knicks, 1987-90; Charlotte Hornets, 1990-94; NJ Nets, 1994, 2000-01; Milwaukee Bucks, 1995-97; Denver Nuggets, 1997-98; Cleveland Cavaliers, 1998-99; Dallas Mavericks, forward-guard, 2002. **Orgs:** Kappa Alpha Psi Fraternity; Sickle Cell Anemia Found. **Honors/Awds:** Citation, Sickle Cell Anemia Found. **Special Achievements:** Established a permanent athletic scholarship in his name at the University of Richmond in 1989.

NEWMAN, KENNETH J.
Accountant, auditor, executive director. **Personal:** Born Nov 7, 1944; married Barbara B; children: Kenneth J Jr, Eric J. **Educ:** Gramblin Col, BS, 1967; Vet Admin Data Processing, Austin, TX, prog instr courses, 1968; SACUBO & NACUBO, continued educ workshops, 1969; Univ Nebr, course bus mgr, 1977. **Career:** Grambling Col, asst dir comput ctr, 1967; Veteran Admin Data Processing Ctr, acct trainee, 1967-68, data processor, 1968-69, asst auditor, 1969-70; Grambling State Univ, bus mgr, 1970-73; Mary Holmes Col, bus mgr, 1974-79; City Monroe, prog auditor, 1979-81, dir planning & urban develop. **Orgs:** Visiting comt, S Asn Col & Schs Atlanta, 1976; Alpha Phi Alpha Fraternity, 1979; bd trustees, Zion Travelor Baptist Church, 1979-; bd mem, Tri Dist Boys Club; United Way, 1981-; PIC mem, JTPA, 1984-90; Indust Develop Bd, 1986-92; pres, Carroll HS PTA, 1986; Monroe Chamber Com; Adv bd mem, Spec Serv Mary Holmes Col; adv bd, Gourmet Serv. **Honors/Awds:** Outstanding Young Man of Am, 1978-79.

NEWMAN, MILLER MAURICE
Salesperson. **Personal:** Born Oct 31, 1941, Terrell, TX; son of Miller and Lillie Vee Coleman Whestone; married Alice Faye Keith, Feb 10, 1963; children: Keith, Donald & Mark. **Educ:** Eastern Okla State Col, attended 1971. **Career:** Hunt's Dept Store, Shipping & Receiving, staff, 1960-66; Rockwell Int, mach oper, 1966-83, stock clerk, 1983-; B&B Skelly Sta, staff, 1968-76; Eastside Exxon, owner, 1970-75; Eastside Supperette, owner, 1976-81; Teen's Vill USA, co-owner. **Orgs:** Model Cities, 1971-76; scoutmaster, Boy Scouts Am, 1971-73; Keddo, 1972-; pres, Pitts Co Nat Asn Advan Colored People, 1972-; pres, UAW Local Suite 1558, 1985-91; Pitts County Holiday Comn, 1985-; chmn, McAlster Housing Auth, 1989-92; recording secy & chair trustees, Okla State UAW CAP/PAC, 1992-. **Honors/Awds:** Martin Luther King Jr Award, Nat Alliance Against Racism, 1984. **Military Serv:** Okla Nat Guard, Msg, ARCOM, Award for Valor, 1959-82; USAR School, 1982-91.

NEWMAN, NATHANIEL
Government official, clergy. **Personal:** Born Aug 6, 1942, Altheimer, AR; son of Abraham Henry and Marguerite Ruth Gordon; children: Mia Ruth Newman Williams & Angelique Marie. **Educ:** Merritt Col, Oakland, CA, AA, 1971; San Jose State Univ, BS, 1974, MS, 1976; Spring Valley Bible Col, Alameda, CA, BA, 1983; Fuller Theol Sem, Pasadena, CA, cert relig studies, 1985; FBI Nat Acad, US Dept Justice, grad; Pacific Western Univ, PhD, criminol, 2001. **Career:** Oakland City, Oakland, CA, patrolman, 1968-74; Santa Clara County, San Jose, CA, inspector, 1974-; Antioch Baptist, San Jose, CA, assoc minister, 1981-86; Concord Missionary Baptist, San Francisco, CA, youth minister, 1986-90; Santa Clara County Dist Atty's Off, 1990-, asst chief bur invest, currently; Good News Missionary Baptist Church, pastor, 1991-. **Orgs:** Chaplain, Alpha Phi Alpha, 1973-; life mem, Alpha Phi Alpha Fraternity, 1975-; pres, Black Peace Officers Asn, 1980-88; vchmn, Minority Citizens Adv Coun, Metro Transportation Comn, 1980-; pres, Dist Attorney's Investigators Asn, 1982-84; pres & ceo, Frank Sypert Afro-Am Community Serv Agency, 1982-88; chaplain, Nat Black Police Asn, 1982-; chmn, Pack Comy, Boy Scouts Am, 1986-; bd mem, Santa Clara County Dist Atty's Investigators Asn, 1990-; pres, 1991-92, exec comt mem, Nat Asn Advan Colored People, San Jose Branch, 1993-; vchmn, San Jose Traffic Appeals Comnr, 1991-; Mayor's Citizens Adv Group, 1992-. **Honors/Awds:** Doctor of Divinity, School of Gospel Ministry, 1982; Peace Officer of the Year, Santa Clara County Black Peace Officers, 1983, 1985, 1988; community recognition, Omega Psi Phi, 1985; Community Service Award, San Jose Black Chamber Commerce, 1986; Humanitarian Award, Ministers Alliance of San Jose, 1986; Brother of the Year, Alpha Phi Alpha Fraternity, Western Region, 1990; Certificate of Appreciation, Calif Dist Atty Investrs Asn, 1992; Good Neighbor Award, Martin Luther King Jr Asn Santa Clara County, 1993; Outstanding Service Award, San Jose State Univ, 1996; Certificate of Appreciation, San Jose African Am Parents Group, 1997; Certificate of Appreciation, San Jose Traffic Appeals Commission, 1998. **Home Addr:** 2047 Quail Creek Rd, Hot Springs, AR 71901-7307.

NEWMAN, PAUL DEAN
Automotive executive. **Personal:** Born Dec 15, 1938, Zanesville, OH; son of Sarah Margaret and Delbert F; married Norma Jean Guy; children: Vicki, Paula, Valerie, Paul II, Scott & Sharri. **Educ:** Tri State Univ, BS, 1966; Univ Va, Exec Develop Prog, Dipl, 1985; Univ Mich, Exec Develop Prog, Dipl, 1986. **Career:** Executive (retired): General Motors Corp, dir urban affairs. **Orgs:** Exec leadership coun, Mich League Human Serv; Insight bd mem, Bus Policy Rev Coun; vpres, pres, Genesee Intermediate Sch Dist Bd Educ, currently. **Honors/Awds:** Distinguished Service Award, Tri State Univ, 1986. **Home Addr:** 3020 Westwood Pkwy, Flint, MI 48503.

NEWMAN, TERENCE
Football player. **Personal:** Born Sep 4, 1978, Salina, KS. **Educ:** Kans State Univ. **Career:** Dallas Cowboys, corner back, 2003-. **Orgs:** Breakfast Buddy prog; Cowboys Rookie Club, 2003. **Honors/Awds:** Jim Thorpe Award, 2002; Nagurski Award; Co-All Iron Award, 2007; Pro Bowl, 2007. **Business Addr:** Corner Back, Dallas Cowboys, Cowboys Ctr 1 Cowboys Pkwy, Irving, TX 75063, **Business Phone:** (972)556-9900.

NEWMAN, DR. THEODORE ROOSEVELT, JR.
Judge. **Personal:** Born Jul 5, 1934, Birmingham, AL; son of Theodore R Newman Sr and Ruth O. **Educ:** Brown Univ, AB, philos,

1955, LLD, 1980; Harvard Law Sch, JD, 1958. **Career:** Judge (retired); Civil Rights Div, Dept Justice; pvt pract, Wash, DC,1962; Houston, Bryant & Gardner, 1962-68; Pratt, Bowers & Newman, partner,1968-70; DC Superior Ct, assoc judge, 1970-76; Brown Univ, trustee, 1979-83; DC Ct Appeals, chief judge, 1976-84, assoc judge, 1984-91, sr judge, 1991-. **Orgs:** Fel Am Bar Found; Am Bar Asn; pres, Nat Ctr State Cts, 1981-82; Nat Bar Asn; chmn, Judicial Coun Nat Bar Asn; Ala Bar Asn; DC Bar Asn; Kappa Alpha Psi. **Honors/Awds:** C Francis Stradford Award, Nat Bar Asn, 1984; William H Hastie Award, Judicial Coun, Nat Bar Asn, 1988. **Military Serv:** USAF, judge advocate, France, 1959-61.

NEWMAN, WILLIAM THOMAS, JR.
Lawyer, government official. **Personal:** Born Sep 11, 1950, Richmond, VA; son of William T and Geraldine Nunn. **Educ:** Ohio Univ, Athens OH, BA, 1972; Catholic Univ Sch Law, Wash DC, JD, 1977. **Career:** US Dept Com, Wash DC, atty, 1977-80; Self-Employed, Arlington VA, atty, 1980-; Arlington County Bd, 1988-, chr, 1991-, judge, 1993-; Arlington County Circuit Ct, chief judge, currently. **Orgs:** Va State Bar Asn, 1977-; DC Bar Asn, 1978-; bd dir, Northern Va Black Atty's Asn, 1984-88; chmn, Arlington County Fire Trial Bd, 1985-87; trustees coun, Nat Capital Area YMCA, 1985-; bd dir, Arlington County United Way, 1985-86; Arlington Com PO, 1985-; Northern Va Urban League Adv Com, 1985-; vpres, Old Dominion Bar Asn, 1986; Va Med Malpract Review Panel, 1986-; comn chancery, Arlington County Circuit Ct, 1986-; vice chmn, Arlington Civic Coalition Minority Affairs, 1986-88. **Honors/Awds:** Corpus Juris Secundum, Catholic Univ Sch Law, 1977; SAA, US Dept Com, 1979; Community Serv, Alpha Kappa Alpha, Zeta Chi Omega, 1988; Community Serv, Alpha Phi Alpha, Theta Rho Lambda, 1990. **Business Addr:** Chief Judge, Arlington County Circuit Court, 1425 N Courthouse Rd Suite 6700, Arlington, VA 22201, **Business Phone:** (703)228-4370.

NEWSOME, REV. BURNELL
Manager, clergy, accountant. **Personal:** Born Apr 13, 1938, Wesson, MS; son of James; married Gloria J Wilson; children: Burnell Jr & Kenneth. **Educ:** Marion Col, Cert Bus Admin, 1962; Copiah Lincoln Jr Col Wesson MS, Cert Carpentry, 1977; MS Baptist Sem Jackson MS, BTh. **Career:** Towne Shoes, store mgr, 1965; Com Credit Corp, dist rep, 1968; St Regis Paper Co, acct, 1973; BF Goodrich, budget control mgr; St Mary's United Methodist Church, pastor, currently; Mt Salem United Methodist, pastor, currently. **Orgs:** Trustee, Hazlehurst MS Separate Sch Dist, 1982; adv comt, SW MS Elec Power Asn, 1983; bd mem, MS Dept Educ Comn Accreditation, 1984; chmn steering comt, Copiah County Crusade for Christ, 1985; secy, Copiah County InterdenomiNat Ministerial Alliance. **Honors/Awds:** FHA Farm Family of the Year, USDA Farmers Home Admin, 1977. **Business Phone:** (601)892-4483.

NEWSOME, DR. CLARENCE GENO
Educator. **Personal:** Born Mar 22, 1950, Ahoskie, NC; son of Annie Butler Lewis and Clarence Shaw; married Lynne DaNean Platt, Jul 29, 1972; children: Gina Lynn & Brittany Ann Byuarm. **Educ:** Duke Univ, BA, 1971, PhD, 1982; Duke Divinity Sch, attended 1975. **Career:** Duke Univ, Dept Minority Affairs, asst prof, dean, 1973-74, Am religious thought, asst prof; Mt Level Baptist Church, Durham, NC Dem Nat Comn, asst staff, dir, demo charter comn, 1974-75; Duke Divinity Sch, instr, 1978-82, asst prof, 1982; Howard Univ, DC, Divinity Sch, from asst dean to assoc dean, 1986-91, from acting dean to dean, 1991-2003; Shaw Univ, pres, 2003-. **Orgs:** Am Soc Church Hist, 1980-; Finance Comt Creative Ministries Assoc, 1981; chmn bd, NC Gen Baptist Found Inc, 1982; Comt Educ Durham Comm Affairs Black People 1983; co-chmn, Comt Educ Durham InterdenomiNatMinisterial Alliance, 1983-84; planning coord, Euro-Am Theol Consult Group; Am Acad Religion, 1987-; pres, Soc Study Black Religion, 1989-. **Honors/Awds:** Athletic Grant-in-Aid Scholar, Duke Univ, 1968-72; United States Senate, 1998; Distinguished Service in Education Award, Progressive Nat Baptis Conv Inc, 2000; Distinguished Alumnus Award, Duke Divinity Sch, 2001. **Special Achievements:** First Black to be named to the All Atlantic Coast Conf Acad Team Duke Univ, 1970-71; First Black stud Comm Speaker, Walter Cronkite Keynote, Duke Univ, 1972; Published number of articles & completed book length manuscript on Mary McLeod Bethund, A Religious Biography. Author of several scholarly articles. **Home Addr:** 6761 Sewells Orchard Dr, Columbia, MD 21045. **Business Addr:** President, Shaw University, 118 E South St, Raleigh, NC 27601, **Business Phone:** (919)546-8200.

NEWSOME, ELISA C
Journalist. **Personal:** Born Jul 6, 1964, Detroit, MI; daughter of William York and Gwendolyn; children: Andrew I Lee. **Educ:** Miami Dade Community Col, Miami, Fla, AA & AS, 1986; Univ Miami, Coral Glades, Fla, BS, 1988. **Career:** Palm Beach Post, West Palm Beach, FL, reporter, 1989. **Orgs:** Nat Asn Black Journalists, 1987-. **Home Phone:** (305)628-1402.

NEWSOME, DR. EMANUEL T.
Educator. **Personal:** Born Mar 21, 1942, Gary, IN; married Nellie Smith; children: Kim, Eric & Erika. **Educ:** Western Mich Univ, BS, 1964; MA, 1965; Indiana State Univ, PhD counseling guidance & Psychol Serv, 1976. **Career:** Grad asst physical educ, 1964-65; head scout & asst basketball coach, 1964-65; IN St Univ, asst dean student life stud activities; financial aid couns & field rep, 1965-66; dir coordr st educ talent search search prog, 1966-68; Univ Toledo, 1976-; dir student activities, 1976-, VPres Student Affairs, currently; Palm Beach Atlantic Col, Adjunct Prof, 1990. **Orgs:** Midwest Stud Financial Aid Asn, 1965-68; bd dir Big Brother Orgn Kalamazoo, MI, 1965-66; NAACP, 1960-; Urban League, 1967-; Nat Asn Student Personnel Asn, 1969-; bd dir Hyte Comn Ctr, 1973-; basketball coach Terre Haute BoysClub, 1973-; Gov Steering Comt Volunteerism, 1975; adv bd, Toledo March Dimes; Western MI Univ Athletic Hall Fame, 1974. **Honors/Awds:** IN All-star Basketball Team, 1960; All Mid-am Conf basketball 3 yrs, 1961-64; All American in basketball, 1964; 2nd leading scorer nation majorcol, 1964; participant Olympic Trials basketball; Athletic Hall of Fame, 1980. **Business Addr:** Vice President Student Affairs, University of Toledo, 2801 W Bancroft St, Toledo, OH 43606, **Business Phone:** (419)530-1470.

NEWSOME, DR. MOSES, JR.
School administrator. **Personal:** Born Sep 6, 1944, Charleston, WV; son of Rev Moses and Ruth G Bass; married Barbara, Jun 8, 1968; children: Ayanna & Mariana. **Educ:** Univ Toledo, BA, 1966; Univ Mich, MSW, 1970; Univ Wis, PhD, 1976. **Career:** Howard Univ Human Serv Eval Design Div, asst dir, 1977-78; Howard Univ Sch Social Work, asst dean, 1979-80, assoc dean, 1980-84; Norfolk State Univ, Ethelyn R. Strong Sch Social Work, dean, prof, 1984-; Jackson State Univ, vis prof, 2000-01; Rutgers Univ, vis prof, currently; Miss Valley State Univ, vpres res, planning, community & econ develop, currrently. **Orgs:** Nat Steering Comt; Nat Assoc Black Soc Workers, 1979; Delegate Assembly Nat Assoc Soc Workers, 1983-84; chmn, Va Social Work Educ Consortium; distchmn, Va Chap Nat Asn Social Workers, 1989-90; chmn, Norfolk City Counl Task Force on Children in Need of Services, 1988-89; vchmn, Norfolk Area Health Study, Advisory Bd, 1987-88; Bd Accreditation Coun on Social Work Educ, 1988-90; State Bd Va Coun on Social Welfare, 1989-91; Planning Coun, Norfolk, Va, bd, 1987-90. **Honors/Awds:** Outstanding Young Man in Am US Jaycees, 1977; Outstanding Macro Faculty Member, Howard Univ Sch Soc Work 1978; "Frequency and Distribution of Disabilities Among Blacks," in Equal to the Challenge, Bureau Educ Res, Washington, DC, 1986; "Job Satisfaction and Work Relationships of Social Service Workers," Dept Human Resources, Norfolk, Va, 1987. **Military Serv:** USAF. **Business Addr:** Vice President, Research, Planning, Community & Economic Development, Mississippi Valley State University, 14000 Hwy 82 W, Itta Bena, MS 38941, **Business Phone:** (662)254-9041.

NEWSOME, OZZIE, JR.
Football player, football executive. **Personal:** Born Mar 16, 1956, Muscle Shoals, AL; son of Ozzie Sr and Ethel; married Gloria Jenkins; children: Michael. **Educ:** Univ Ala, BS, recreation & park mgt, 1978. **Career:** Football player (retired), manager; Cleveland Browns, tight end, 1978-90;Baltimore Ravens, vp player personnel, 1996-2002, sr vp football opers,gen mgr, 2002-, exec vp, 2003-; Active Fellowship Christian Athletes, Big Brothers, Athletes Action. **Orgs:** Bd dirs, Police Athletic League. **Honors/Awds:** Alabama Amateur Athlete of Year, Ala Sportswriters Asn, 1977; Teams Outstanding Player, 1981; Ed Block Courage Award, 1986; Whizzer White Award, 1990; Col Football Hall Fame, 1994; NFL Hall Fame, 1999. **Special Achievements:** First African Am gen mgr in NFL history. **Business Addr:** General Manager, Executive Vice President, Baltimore Ravens, 1 Winning Dr, Owings Mills, MD 21117, **Business Phone:** (410)701-4000.

NEWSOME, DR. PAULA RENEE
Optometrist, president (organization). **Personal:** Born Jul 3, 1955, Wilmington, NC; daughter of Mercedes and Carter; divorced; children: Ayana Renee. **Educ:** Univ NC-Chapel Hill, BA, 1977; Univ Ala, Birmingham Med Ctr, OD, 1981, MS, 1981. **Career:** Eye Inst Philadelphia, residency, 1982; Univ MO, St Louis Sch Optom, asst prof, 1982-84; VA Hosp St Louis, optom consult, 1983-84; pvt pract, optom, 1984-; Advantage Vision Ctr, pres, currently, optometrist, currently. **Orgs:** Delta Sigma Theta Sorority Inc, 1974-; Am Optom Asn, 1981-; Nat Optom Asn, 1981-; NC State Optom Soc, 1982-; Mecklenburg Co Optom Soc, 1984-; Charlotte Med Soc, 1984-; state legis affairs adv comm Scope Prac AOA, 1984-; free visual screening area churches, 1984-; speaker Role Model Series Charlotte-Mecklenburg Sch Syst, 1985-; urban optom, Am Optom Assoc, 1986-; bd mem, Charlotte Women Bus Owners, 1986-87; charter mem, Doctors Heart, 1986-90; free visual screenings Mecklenburg Co Parks & Recreation, 1986; Leadership Charlotte, 1986-; pres, bd dirs, Focus Leadership, 1986-90; Mecklenburg Co, YWCA, 1988-90; Coalition Lit, 1988-90; bd dirs, Charlotte Chamber Comn, 1990-96; bd dirs, Cent Piedmont Community Col, 1991-95; chmn, Discovery Pl, 2000-01; bd dirs, Univ NC-Chapel Hill, Gen Alumni Asn; Crown Jewel Chap; Delta Sigma Theta Sorority Inc; treas, Charlotte Chap. **Honors/Awds:** Irv Borish Award for Outstanding Clinical Research, 1981; The Las Amigas Outstanding Service in Business Award, 1985; Crystal Award, Nan BPW, 1998; Harvey Beech Outstanding Alumni Award, Univ NC, 2000; Alumnus of the Year, Univ Ala Birmingham Sch Optom, 2001. **Special Achievements:** First African American to chair the Board of Discovery Place; First African American to serve on the Executive Committee of Discovery Place. **Business Addr:** President, Optometrist, Advantage Vision Center, 1016 S Church St, Charlotte, NC 28203, **Business Phone:** (704)375-3935.

NEWSOME, RONALD WRIGHT
Banker, vice president (organization). **Personal:** Born Jan 21, 1949, Charleston, WV; son of Moses and Ruth; married Toni, Jun 21, 1973; children: Nicole & Kristine. **Educ:** Philander Smith Col, BA, 1971; Clark/Atlanta Univ, MBA, 1973. **Career:** Nat Bank Detroit, asst br mgr, credit officer, commerical loan officer, 1973-81; Bank One, Columbus, NA, commercial loan officer, sr loan officer, asst vpres res, 1981-86, asst vpres res, unit mgr, vpres, 1988-; Huntington Nat Bank, asst vpres/com lender, 1986-88, asst vpres & unit mgr, vpres & group mgr, 1988-98; Franklin Univ, adj prof, 1986-96; Bank One COT Develop Corp, vpres & mgr small bus group, sr vpres & mgr small bus group, 1998-; Wilberforce Univ, adj prof, 1999; Small Bus Investment Alliance Inc, dir & mgr, Banc One CDC, sr vpres, currently. **Orgs:** Univ Club Columbus, 1983-; bd dirs, exec comt mem & secy, Columbus Urban League, 1989-; bd mem & vchmn, Pvt Indust Coun Columbus & Franklin County Inc, 1991-; bd mem & second vpres, Columbus Metropolitan Area Community Action Org, 1990-; pres, Mark D Philmore Urban Bankers Forum Cent Ohio Inc, 1994-; Univ Club; Columbus Regional MNY Supplier Develop Coun; OH Found Entrepeneurship Ed; chair, Pvt Indus CNL Columbus & Franklin County; APA. **Honors/Awds:** Philander Smith Col Distinguished Alumni Award; UNCF Inter-Alumni C James E Stamp Alumni Recognition Award. **Home Addr:** 1020 Zodiac Ave, Gahanna, OH 43230, **Home Phone:** (614)855-0120. **Business Addr:** Senior Vice President One CDC, Manager, Small Business Investment Group, 127 Pub Sq 7th Fl, Cleveland, OH 44114-1306, **Business Phone:** (614)248-2975.

NEWSOME, RUTHIE
Educator. **Personal:** Born Mar 16, 1940, Marvell, AR; daughter of Sam and Josephine. **Educ:** Ark Baptist Col, BA, 1962; Webster Univ, attneded 1976; Northeast State Univ, attended 1986. **Career:** St Louis Public Sch, teacher. **Orgs:** Antioch Bapt Church; Stevens Middle Sch Community Coun; secy, Ark Baptist Col Alumni, St Louis Chap; nat pres, Ark Bapt Col Alumni; St Louis Teacher Union; YWCA, Phyllis Wheatley Br; group leader, ABC Alumni Club, currently. **Home Addr:** 7720 Nacomis Dr, Saint Louis, MO 63121. **Business Addr:** Group Leader, ABC Alumni Club, 7720 Nacomis Dr, St Louis, MO 63121, **Business Phone:** (314)382-7681.

NEWSOME, STEVEN CAMERON
Museum director. **Personal:** Born Sep 11, 1952, Norfolk, VA; divorced; children: Sanya. **Educ:** Trinity Col, BA, 1974; Emory Univ, MLS, 1975. **Career:** Northwestern Univ Libr, Afro-Am studies librn, 1975-78; Univ Ill Chicago Univ Libr, asst ref librn 1980-82, head ref, 1982-83; Vivian Harsh Collection Afro-Amer Hist & Lit Chicago Pub Libr, curator, 1983-86; MD Comn Afro-Am Hist & Cult, exec dir; State of MD Dept Housing & Community Develop, Off Cult & Educ Serv, chief, 1991; Anacostia Mus, dir, 1991-. **Orgs:** Bd dirs, MD Humanities Coun, 1991-; bd gov, 1991-94, vpres, 1994-; Mid Atlantic Asn Mus; bd dirs, Cult Alliance Greater Wash, 1992-; John F Kennedy Ctr for the Performing Arts, comm & firends bd, 1993-. **Business Addr:** Director, Anacostia Museum, 1901 Fort Pl SE, Washington, DC 20020, **Business Phone:** (202)633-4820.*

NEWSOME, VINCENT KARL
Football executive, football player. **Personal:** Born Jan 22, 1961, Braintree, England; married Tasha; children: Candace & Emerald. **Educ:** Univ Wash, psychol. **Career:** Football player (retired), football executive; Los Angeles Rams, safety, 1983-90; Cleveland Browns, safety, 1991-92, spec assignment scout, 1993-95; Baltimore Ravens, W area scout, 1996-99, Western Col supvr, 2000-02, asst dir pro personnel, 2003-. **Orgs:** Alpha Phi Alpha, Alpha Xi Chap. **Honors/Awds:** Ed Block Courage Award, 1988. **Business Addr:** Assistant Director of Pro Personnel, Baltimore Ravens, Player Personnel Department, 1 Winning Dr, Owings Mills, MD 21117, **Business Phone:** (410)701-4000.

NEWTON, ANDREW E., JR.
Lawyer, photographer. **Personal:** Born Mar 9, 1943, Boston, MA; married Joan Ambrose. **Educ:** Dartmouth Col, AB, 1965; Columbia Univ, JD, 1969. **Career:** Winston A Burnett Construct Co, asst gen coun, 1969-70; Amos Tuch Sch Bus Admin, Dartmouth Col, 1970-71; Burnett Int Develop Corp, gen coun, 1971-72; Honeywell Info Systs Inc, opers coun, 1972-74, staff coun, 1974-75, regional coun, Western Region, 1975-77; Amdahl Corp, dir mkt oper coun, 1977; Digital Res Inc, gen coun; Frame Technol Corp, vpres, gen coun & secy; Infoseek Corp, vpres, gen coun & secy; Propel Software Corp, co-founder, vpres, gen coun & secy, currently. **Orgs:** Am Bar Asn; Boston Bar Asn; Fed Bar Asn; Mass Bar Asn; Nat Bar Asn; NY Bar; Mass Bar; Peninsula Asn Gen Coun; Comput Lawyers Asn; Nat Contract Mgt Asn.

NEWTON, DEMETRIUS C
Lawyer. **Personal:** Born Mar 15, 1928, Fairfield, AL; son of Caiphus and Eola Williams; married Beatryce Thomas, Jun 19, 1954;

children: Deirdre Cheryl & Demetrius C Jr. **Educ:** Wilberforce Univ, BA, 1949; Boston Univ, JD, 1952. **Career:** Law firm Newton & May; City Brightond city, atty, 1973-; City Brownsville, city judge, 1975-; Ala House Rep, Alab State House, atty, 1986-. **Orgs:** Pres, Tittisville & Powderly Br, Nat Asn Advan Colored People; former nat pres, Wilberforce Univ Alumni Asn, 1958-60; former pres, Fairfield Voters League, UMDCA; nat pres, Phi Beta Sigma, 1981-85; Ala Bankers Asn; Ala Educ Asn; Am Bar Asn; Am Judicature Soc; 101 Black Men; Vulcan Gold Club; Nat Asn Advan Colored People. **Honors/Awds:** Hon DHL, Wilberforce Univ, 1984; Outstanding Lawyer Award, Ala Lawyer Asn; Outstanding Legislator Award, Ala Poultry & Egg Asn. **Special Achievements:** Man of the Year; Man of the Year, S Beauty Cong; Man of the Year, Phi Beta Sigma; counr, 82nd Airborne Div, 1952-54; Outstanding Alabama Lawyer's Asn, 1982. **Business Addr:** Representative/Attorney, Alabama House of Representatives, Alabama State House, 11 S Union St Rm 516 B, Montgomery, AL 36130.

NEWTON, ERIC CHRISTOPHER
Consultant, software developer, chief executive officer. **Personal:** Born Apr 5, 1965, Detroit, MI; son of John Henry Newton and Willie Bell Duncan; married Kimberly, Nov 28, 1992; children: Brittany Delamere, Haley Christine, Naomi Annabelle & Gabrielle Leigh. **Educ:** Mich State Univ, BS, 1988. **Career:** Gen Motors, claims processor, 1983-84; Unisys Corp, programmer, analyst, 1984-85; Stroh Brewery Corp, Programmer, analyst, 1987; Alpha II, syst, dir, 1988-93; Info Services, Inc, pres, owner, div mgr, 1993-96, vpres opers, 1998, pres & ceo, 2001-05; Gilbar Engineering, info systs mgr,1996-98; SDE Business Partnering LLC, dir sales, currently. **Orgs:** Mentor prog, Detroit Pub Schs, 1983-; Phi Beta Sigma Fraternity Inc,1985-; Apple Programmers & Developers Assn, 1988-; Mich Assn for Computer Users in Learning, 1989-; IBM Developer Assistance Prog, 1991-. **Home Addr:** 6566 Horncliffe Dr, Clarkston, MI 48346, **Home Phone:** (248)625-5498. **Business Addr:** Director of Sales, SDE Business Partnering, 400 Renaissance Center Suite 1010, Detriot, MI 48243, **Business Phone:** (313)656-2200.

NEWTON, ERNEST E., II
Government official, executive, association executive. **Personal:** Born Feb 21, 1956, Fort Belvoir, VA; married Pamela A; children: Ernest E III, Chad J Newton. **Educ:** Winston-Salem State Univ, BA, 1978; Univ Bridgeport, grad prog, 1980. **Career:** Bridgeport Bd Educ, music teacher, 1980-84; Bridgeport City Coun, pres, 1981; Conn Nat Bank, personal banking rep, 1984; Peoples Bank, admin supv, 1986; State House Reps, mem, 1989; chmn, legis Black & Puerto Rican Caucus, Conn, 1991-92; House Reps, asst majority leader, 1995-96; 23rd Dist Spec Election, state senator, 2003, dep pres pro tempore. **Orgs:** Pres, alderman, mem Bd, Aldermen 139th Dist; Alpha Phi Alpha Frat; bd mgrs, YMCA; policy coun Head Start; adv bd, Greater Bridgeport Regional Narcotics Prog; comn Sikorsky Mem Airport; coun pres Red Cross; vice chmn, 150th Anniversary Bridgeport; Alpha Phi Alpha; Mount Airy Baptist Church; NAACP; Prince Hall Masons; chmn exec, Legis Nominations Comt. **Honors/Awds:** Outstanding Merit Award, Nat Bulk Teachers Asn, 1974; Scholarship Award, Alpha Phi Alpha Grad Chap, 1976; Outstanding Young Men of Am Award, Nat Jaycees, 1983; Comn Serv Award, Bus & Prof Women Youth Dept; Heritage Award, Alpha Kappa Alpha Sor, 1983; City Govt Award, Omega Psi Phi Frat Inc, 1983; Outstanding Achievement Award, Nat Asn Negro Bus & Prof Women, 1983; TGBOIC Proj Saga Sponsorship Award; has received a number of awards. **Special Achievements:** Becoming the youngest age 25 and first black person to ever hold the position as council president.

NEWTON, JACQUELINE L.
Counselor, accountant. **Personal:** Born in Oklahoma City, OK; daughter of Jack Jefferson and Josephine Jefferson; divorced; children: Jeffrey, Richard. **Educ:** So Univ Lab Sch, Grad; Univ Okla, BBA, MEd, 1974. **Career:** Univ Okla, Norman, OK, acad adv, 1972-78; Okla Univ, finan aids couns; Apco Oil Corp, Okla City, OK, from clerk to acct; Okla City Law Firm, bookkeeper; Okla Univ, Mobil Oil Co, admin phys res coun, equal employee opp Com; Univ Nev, Las Vegas, NV, athletic acad counselor, 1978-. **Orgs:** Chrd empl orgn representing all non-teaching employees at univ, 1972-73; active Okla Univ Prof Employee Group; pres, Okla Univ Asn Black Personnel, 1975-76; Nat Asn Advan Colored People; supr training sem in Jan 1974; Alpha Kappa Alpha Sor; chmn, Comt Okla Black Coalition Educ; chair, Student Athlete Recognition Comn; Nat Asn Acad Adv Athletics, 1988-93; secy, Univ Nev Las Vegas Alliance Black Prof, 1984-. **Honors/Awds:** Voted outstanding achievement Award, fel prof emplyee Okla Univ, 1973.

NEWTON, JAMES DOUGLAS, JR.
Government official, nurse. **Personal:** Born Sep 3, 1929, Malakoff, TX; daughter of Hillary Cook and Mary Glenn Cook; widowed; children: Carolyn Andrenia Barron & Audry Laverne. **Educ:** Henderson City Jr Col, LVN, 1962-63; Navarro Col, attended 1975; El Centro Col, attended 1975. **Career:** Nurse, Government official (retired); Lakeland Med Ctr, lic voc nurse, 1979-93. **Orgs:** Youth counr, Cedar Forks Baptist Church, 1970; counr, Galilee Griggs Mem Dist Youth Conf, 1975-; nursing fac, Lakeland Med Ctr, 1979-87; E Tex Coun Governments, 1980-; Trinidad Chamber Com, 1980; appointed mem, State Task Force Indigent Health Care, 1984. **Honors/Awds:** Outstanding Black Henderson Countian Award; Black History Committee, 1989; attended & participated in the inauguration of President George Bush, 1989.

NEWTON, JAMES DOUGLAS, JR.
Government official. **Personal:** Born Jun 11, 1949, New Haven, CT; children: Bonita, Melissa, Tomeka, James D Newton III & Allen W Newton II. **Educ:** NH Col, BS, Human Serv Admin, 1979; Yale Univ, Sch Pub Health & Hosp Admin, 1980; Southern Conn State Univ, MS, 1991. **Career:** New Haven City Personnel Dept, records syst consult, 1979-82; New Haven Bd Aldermen, chmn, 1983-87; Conn Nat Bank, mgt trainee, 1984-85, temple St Br, mgr, 1984-85, Church St Br, mgr, 1986-87; Greater New Haven Chamber Com, Jobs Compact Prog, assoc dir, 1987-88; N & N Construct Co, chmn, 1987-; New Haven City, Bd Educ, assoc dir, 1988-90; YMCA Youth & Fitness Ctr, gen mgr, 1990-91; New Haven Job Ctr, mgr, 1991-. **Orgs:** Chmn, Yale Univ; New Haven City, Sci Park Dev Corp, 1992-. **Honors/Awds:** Community Services Award, Rotary Club Int, 1990.

NEWTON, DR. JAMES ELWOOD
College teacher, school administrator. **Personal:** Born Jul 3, 1941, Bridgeton, NJ; son of Charles C Newton Sr and Hilda H Newton; married LaWanda Williams, Dec 1967; children: Regina, Walidah & KaWansi. **Educ:** NC Cent Univ, BA, 1966; Univ NC, MFA, 1968; Ill State Univ, PhD, 1972. **Career:** Univ NC, art instr, 1967-68; W Chester State Col, Pa, asst prof art, 1968-69; Ill State Univ, asst prof art, 1969-71; Western Ill Univ, asst prof art 1971-72; Univ Del, Newark, asst prof educ, 1972-73; prof, Black Am Studies, 1973-2005; prof emer, Black Am Studies, 2005-. **Orgs:** Ed bd, Nat Art Ed Assoc; ed bd educ 1974-; exec counr, Assoc Study Afro-Am Life & Hist, 1976-77; bd mem, Western J Black Studies 1983-; bd mem, past chmn, Walnut St YMCA, Del, 1983-; state dir, Asn Study Afro-Am Life &Hist 1988-; sr fel, Ctr Community Res & Serv. **Honors/Awds:** First prize, Sculpture & Graphics 19th Annual Exhib Afro-Am Artists, 1972; 23rd Annual Mid-States Art Exhibit, 1972; Nat Print & Drawing Show, 11th Midwest Bienniel Exhib, 1972; Purchase Award, 13th Reg Art Exhibit, Univ Del, 1974; A Curric Eval Black Am Studies Rel Stud Knowledge Afro-Am Hist& Cult, R&E Assoc Inc, 1976; Roots Black Am; Audio-Tapes Slave Artisans &Craftsmen, Contemporary Afro-Amer Art Miami-Dade Comm Col, 1976; Del Afro-Am Art Exhib, 1980; Excellence Teaching Award, Univ Del, 1988; Eastern Region Citation Award, Phi Delt appa National Sorority, 1989; Hometown Hero Award, Wilmington News Jour, 1990; Jefferson Award, Am Inst Pub Serv; Joseph Del Tufo Award Distinguished Service Humanities, 1998; Louis L. Redding Diversity Award, Univ Del, 2004. **Special Achievements:** Document verifier, Little Known Facts of Black History; published numerous articles in various journals; Author, The Principles of Diversity, A Curriculum Evaluation on Student Knowledge of Afro-American Life and History; Co-editor, The Other Slaves: Mechanics, Artisans and Craftsmen. **Military Serv:** AUS, spec 4th class 1959-62. **Home Addr:** 217 Harris Circle, Newark, DE 19711. **Business Addr:** Professor Emeritus, University of Delaware, 401 Acad St, Newark, DE 19716, **Business Phone:** (302)831-2392.

NEWTON, GEN. LLOYD W
Military leader. **Personal:** Born in Ridgeland, SC; married Elousie M Morning. **Educ:** Tenn State Univ, BS, 1966; Armed Forces Staff Col, 1978; Indust Col Armed Forces, 1985; George Wash Univ, MS, 1985; Harvard Univ, nat security sr exec course, MA, 1987. **Career:** Williams AFB, AZ, 1966-67; US House Representatives, cong liaison officer, 1978-82; Twelfth Flying Training Wing, Randolph AFB, TX, comdr, 1990-91; 833rd Air Div, Holloman AFB, NMex, 1991; 49th Figher Wing, Holloman AFB, NMex, 1991-93; US Sepec Opers Command, MacDill AFB, FL, 1993-95; HQ USAF, Wash, DC, asst vice chief staff, 1995-97; HQ Air Educ & Training Command, Randolph AFB, comdr, 1997-2000; Pratt & Whitney, exec vpres, 2000-05; TSU Air Force Reserve Officer Training Corp, group wing comdr. **Orgs:** Goodrich Corp, bd dir; Torchmark Corp, bd dir, currently. **Honors/Awds:** Distinguished Service Medal; Legion of Merit with oak leaf cluster; Distinguished Flying Cross with oak leaf cluster; Meritorious Service Medal with oak leaf cluster; Air Medal with 16 oak leaf clusters; Air Force Commendation Medal; Air Force Outstanding Unit Award with "V" device and two oak leaf clusters; Vietnam Service Medal; Philippine Presidential Union Citation; Republic Vietnam Campaign Medal. **Special Achievements:** First African American to fly with US Air Force Aerial Demonstration Squadron, the Thunderbirds; 1 of 12 Four Star Generals in the US Air Force. **Military Serv:** Defense Distinguished Service Medal. **Business Addr:** Board of Director, Torchmark Corporation, 3700 S Stonebridge Dr, PO Box 8080, McKinney, TX 75070-8080, **Business Phone:** (972)569-4000.

NEWTON, NATE (NATHANIEL NEWTON)
Football player, television broadcaster. **Personal:** Born Dec 20, 1961, Orlando, FL; married Dorothy, Jan 30, 1992 (divorced 2000); children: Nathaniel III & Nate King. **Educ:** Fla A&M Univ. **Career:** Football player (retired); Tampa Bay Bandits, USFL, 1984-85; Dallas Cowboys, guard, 1986-98; Carolina Panthers, 1999-2000; ESPN radio, commentator; BET television, analyst. **Orgs:** N Dallas Community God. **Honors/Awds:** NFL Offensive Lineman of the Year, Nat Football League Alumni Asn, 1994; six time Pro Bowler, 1992, 1994-97.

NEWTON, NATHANIEL. See NEWTON, NATE.

NEWTON, OLIVER A., JR.
Educator. **Personal:** Born Jan 31, 1925, Long Branch, NJ; married Eleanor M Simmons; children: Martha Louise. **Educ:** Howard Univ, BS, 1949, MS, 1950. **Career:** Educator (retired); Inter-Am Inst Agr Sci Turrialba Costa Rica, res, 1950-52; Univ So CA, lab assoc, 1952-56; Howard Univ, instr botany, 1956-58; William Paterson Col NJ, assoc prof, 1958-90. **Orgs:** AAAS, AAUP, AIBS, Botanical Soc Am, Alpha Phi Alpha, Ridgewood Glen Rock Coun Boy Scouts Am, Soc Econ Botany, Glen Rock Adult Sch Coun, Glen Rock Civic Asn; dir, Glen Rock Human Rels Coun, Cits Comn Sch Plant & Classroom Eval; local asst bd Glen Rock, 1966-74; Glen Rock Bd Ed, 1969-75; State Comn Study Student Activism & Involvement Ed Progs, 1970; Community Rels Bd Ridgewood & Glen Rock, 1991. **Honors/Awds:** Pan Am Union Fellowship, 1950-52; Nat Sci Found Col Faculty Fellowship Rutgers Univ, 1964. **Military Serv:** USAF, sgt, 1943-46; USAFR, maj, retired. *

NEWTON, PYNKERTON DION
Physician. **Personal:** Born Nov 9, 1960, Marion, IN; son of John W and Olivia McNair. **Educ:** Ball State Univ, BA, 1983, MA, 1986; Logan Col Chiropractic, DC, 1992. **Career:** Operation Crossroads Africa, group leader, 1986; Ball State Univ, asst dir, 1986; Marine Midland Bank, corp analyst, 1986-87, mgr, 1987-89; Logan Col Chiropractic, coordr, admissions dept, 1989-92, consult, 1992-; Pynkerton Chiropractic Group, PC, dir, 1992-. **Orgs:** Am Black Chiropractic Asn, exec dir, 1995-96; Am Chiropractic Asn, 1989-; Nat Asn Med Minority Educrs, 1990-91; Indiana State Chiropractic Asn, 1989-; Nat Asn Advan Colored People. **Honors/Awds:** Meritorious award, Logan Col Chiropractic, 1992. **Special Achievements:** Proficient in Spanish. **Business Addr:** Chiropractor, Pynkerton Chiropractic Group, 2102 E 52nd St Suite E, Indianapolis, IN 46205, **Business Phone:** (317)257-7463.

NEWTON, ROBERT
Lawyer. **Personal:** Born Nov 13, 1944, Fairfield, AL; married Ruth Ann Boles; children: Robert Wade & Reginald Alan. **Educ:** Harvard-Yale-Columbia, intensive summer studis cert summer, 1966; Lincoln Univ, Jeff City MO, BS, 1968; Howard Univ Sch Law, JD, 1971. **Career:** Mo Comn Human Rights, spec field rep, 1968; Econ & Opportunity Wash, legal asst ofc, 1969; US Atomic Energy Comn, staff atty, 1971-74; Newton Coar Newton & Tucker Law Firm, atty. **Orgs:** Am Bar Asn; Ala Bar Asn; Nat Asn Advan Colored People; Legal Defense Fund Earl Warren fel; Jeff City Mo Comn Fiar Housing, 1966-67; Omega Psi Phi Fraternity Inc; pres, Lincoln Univ Stud Govt Asn, 1966-67; Law J Howard Univ Law Sch, 1969-70; Earl Warren Legal fel, Nat Asn Advan Colored People, 1974-75. **Honors/Awds:** Man of the Year, Lincoln Univ, 1966-67; Cobb-trustee Scholar, Howard Univ Law Sch, 1969-71. **Military Serv:** AUSR, first lt. **Home Addr:** 3524 Squire Lane, Birmingham, AL 35211, **Home Phone:** (205)969-7494.

NEYLAND, LEEDELL WALLACE
School administrator. **Personal:** Born Aug 4, 1921, Gloster, MS; son of Sam Matthew and Estella McGehee; married Della Louise Adams; children: Beverly Ann, Keith Wallace & Katrina Denise. **Educ:** Va State Col, AB, 1949; NY Univ, MA, 1950, PhD, 1959. **Career:** School administrator (retired); Leland Col Baker LA, prof social sci, dean Col, 1950-52; Grambling Col, assoc prof social sci, 1952-58; Elizabeth City Col, dean, 1958-59; Fla A&M Univ, prof hist, dean humanities/social sci, 1959-84, Col Arts & Sci, dean, 1968-82, vpres, acad affairs, 1982-85; consult, lectr Black hist & educ. **Orgs:** Co-chmn, Gov Dr Martin Luther King Jr Com memorative Celebration Comn, 1985-87; bd dirs, Leon County/Tallahassee Chamber Com, 1984-86; vchmn, Tallahassee Preservation Bd, 1984-88; Presbyterian Nat Comt Self-Devel People, currently; Fla Hist Records Adv Bd, currently; Phi Beta Sigma; Sigma Pi Phi; 32 Degree Mason, Modern Free & Accepted Masons of the World. **Honors/Awds:** Co-auth: Hist Fla A&M Univ, 1963; Twelve Black Floridians, 1970; Hist Fla State Teachers Asn, 1977; Hist Fla Interscholastic Asn, 1982; Fla A&M Univ: A Centennial History, 1987; Historical Black Land-GrantInsts & Devel Agr & Home Econ, 1890-90, 1990; author of numerous articles appearing in prof publs; Carnegie Grant, 1965. **Special Achievements:** Author, Unquenchable Black Fires, Leney Educational and Publishing Inc, 1994. **Military Serv:** USNR, 1941-46. *

N'GAI JONES, COBI. See JONES, COBI N'GAI.

NIBBS, ALPHONSE, SR.
Executive, government official. **Personal:** Born Nov 10, 1947, Charlotte Amalie, Virgin Islands of the United States; son of Elenora Charles and Ernest Albert; married Paulette E Shelford, Oct 30, 1967; children: Berecia Nibbs-Cartwright, Alphonse Jr, Antoninette Nibbs, Annette Garces, Anthony & Alyssa. **Educ:** Col

VI, attended 1980; Cert Labor Rels, Pub Admin, Personnel Mgt, 1980; Inst Prof & Econ Develop, attended 1981; Ga Inst Technol, Atlanta, Ga, Contract Admin, 1986. **Career:** Water & Power Authority, distribution engr, 1967-76; Nibbs Brothers Inc, secy, treas, 1974-; Dept Housing, asst comnr, 1977-84; Lt Governors Off, temp housing off hd-gar team, terr coord off, 1979-86; VI Housing Authority, exec dir, 1985-87; Legisl VI, exec dir 1991-93; VI Cong Off, dist chair staff, 1995-97. **Orgs:** Comn Aging, 1977-87; Bd Elections, elected 1978-87; VI Soc Pub Admin, 1980-87. **Honors/Awds:** Lt Col/AIDE DeCamp, State Ga Nat Guard, Civilian Appointment. **Business Addr:** Secretary & Treasurer, Nibbs Bros Inc, 4A Estate Thomas, PO Box 7245, St Thomas, Virgin Islands of the United States 00801, **Business Phone:** (809)774-2108.

NICCO-ANNAN, LIONEL
Executive. **Career:** Clipper Int Corp, Detroit, chief exec, 1963-. **Business Phone:** (313)366-6210.

NICHOLAS, BOB
Executive. **Personal:** Married Arita. **Career:** Channel 2 News, Houston, TX, anchorperson; BNE Fine Printing, founder & chair, 1999-; Nicholas Earth Printing LLC, pres, currently. **Orgs:** Bd, Mental Health Asn; bd, Houston Citizens Chamber Com; Super Bowl Host Comt; bd mem, Greater Houston Partnership. **Honors/Awds:** Best printing among medium-sized facilities, Printing & Imaging Asn, 2001; Emerging E-10 Award, 2002. **Special Achievements:** First African American TV news reporter in the south in Charlotte, NC; first African American TV news anchor in Houston at KHOU-TV, 1971. **Business Addr:** Owner, Nicholas Earth Printing, 7021 Portwest Dr Suite 100, Houston, TX 77024.

NICHOLAS, BRENDA L.
Gospel singer. **Personal:** Born Dec 16, 1953, Salem, NJ; daughter of John H Watson and Janette Coleman; married Philip, Feb 18, 1978; children: Jennifer & Philip Jr. **Educ:** Career Educ Inst, AS, 1974. **Career:** Command Recs, gospel singer; Nicholas Ministries Int, gospel vocalist, currently; Song: "God's Woman"; "A Love Like This"; "The Closer I Get To You"; "Dedicated"; "I Do"; "The Love CD". **Honors/Awds:** Excellence Awards, Gospel Music Workshops Am, 1983; Dove Award, 1987; Grammy Award, ARAS, 1986; Golden Eagle Award, Southern Cal Motion Picture, 1986; Halo Award, Best Foreign Rec, 1988. **Home Addr:** PO Box 1869, Van Nuys, CA 91401, **Home Phone:** (818)995-6363. **Business Addr:** Gospel Singer, Nicholas Ministries International, PO Box 10151, Palm Desert, CA 92255, **Business Phone:** (760)836-0776.

NICHOLAS, DENISE (DONNA HILL)
Socialist, actor, writer. **Personal:** Born Jul 12, 1944, Detroit, DE; daughter of Otto Nicholas and Louise Carolyn Burgen; married Bill Withers, Jan 1, 1973 (divorced 1974); married Gilbert Moses, Jan 1, 1964 (divorced 1965); married Jim Hill, Jan 1, 1981 (divorced). **Educ:** Univ Mich, 1965; Univ Southern Calif, Professional Writer's Prog 1985. **Career:** Negro Ensemble Co, actress, 1967-69; TV series: "Room 222", actress, 1969-74; "Baby I'm Back", actress, 1978; "In the Heat of the Night", actress, 1988; "My Wife & Kids", actress, 2002; Films: The Soul of Nigger Charley, actress, 1973; Blacula, actress; Let's Do It Again, actress, 1975; Mr Ricco, actress, 1975; A Piece of the Action, actress, 1977; Ghost Dad, actress, 1990; Ritual, actress, 2000; Proud, actress, 2004; Author:Freshwater Road, 2005; producer; Media Forum Inc, producer 1980-. **Orgs:** Neighbors Watts Inc 1976-; bd dir, Communs Bridge Video Sch, 1983-; mem & fund raiser, Artists & Athletes Against Apartheid; Mus African Am Art, LA; Mus Afro-Am Hist & Cult. **Honors/Awds:** Two LA Emmy Awards producer/actress Voices of our People in Celebration of Black Poetry, 1981; 2 CEBA Awards Excellence for Advertising & Communications to Black Comn, 1981, 1982; 3 Emmy nominations Room 222; author, The Denise Nicholas Beauty Book, 1971; Black Filmmakers Hall of Fame, 1992; Zora Neal Hurston/ Richard Wright Award, 2006; American Library Asns Black Caucus Award, 2006. **Business Addr:** 9300 Wilshire Blvd Suite 555, Beverly Hills, CA 90212.

NICHOLAS, GWENDOLYN SMITH
Government official. **Personal:** Born Jan 27, 1951, San Francisco, CA; married. **Educ:** Univ San Francisco, BA, 1972; Atlanta Univ, MSW, 1974. **Career:** Fireman's Fund Ins Co, bus syst analyst, 1976-77; W Oak Ment Health Dept, psychiat social worker, 1977-78; State Calif Dept Ment Health, psychiat social worker, 1978-81, ment health prog specialist, 1981-83; State Calif,Dept Social Serv, lic prog analyst II, 1984-91; Calif Pub Utilities Comn, 1991-95, Dept Alcohol Drug Progs, analyst, 1995-. **Orgs:** Alpha Kappa Alpha, 1972; area pub info officer, chap rec sec, Nat Nominating Comn SF Chap Links Inc, 1975-; Bay Area Asn Black Social Workers, 1977-; contributor, United Negro Col Fund, 1978-; contributor, Bay Area Black United Fund, 1980-; Soroptimist Int Oak Founder Club, 1986-91; Black Advocates State Serv, Bay Area Heath Consortium. **Honors/Awds:** Outstanding Young Women of America, 1983. **Home Addr:** PO Box 1175, Sacramento, CA 95812-1175.

NICHOLAS, PHILIP
Gospel singer, executive. **Personal:** Born Feb 18, 1954, Chester, PA; son of Julia B Shade and Ross B Nicholas; married Brenda L Watson, Feb 18, 1978; children: Jennifer & Phil Jr. **Educ:** Drexel Univ, BS, 1977. **Career:** Command Rec, Nicholas Ministries, pres, gospel vocalist, currently. **Honors/Awds:** Excellence Awards, Gospel Music Workshops Am, 1983; Grammy Award, nomination, ARAS, 1986; Golden Eagle Award, Southern CAL Motion Picture, 1986; Dove Award, nomination, 1987; Halo Award, Best Foreign Recording, Can, 1988. **Special Achievements:** Songs: God's Woman; A Love Like This; The Closer I Get To You'; Dedicated; I Do; Fired Up-God Will See you Through; The Nicholas Love Cruise; Nicholas' Classic Wedding & Love Songs. **Business Addr:** President, Nicholas Ministries Int, PO Box 10151, Palm Desert, CA 92255, **Business Phone:** (760)836-0776.

NICHOLLS, FRANCIS. See KNUCKLES, FRANKIE.

NICHOLS, ALFRED GLEN
Printer. **Personal:** Born Mar 20, 1952, Jackson, MS; married Sylvia Lauree Robinson; children: Derek Allen, Shaunte Latrice. **Educ:** Purdue Univ, BS, 1975; Univ Chicago, MBA, 1985. **Career:** RR Donnelley & Sons Co, price admin estimator, 1975-78, indust engr, 1978-80, project engr, 1980-86, supvr planning & facil engr, 1986-. **Orgs:** Dir, Hazel Crest Jaycees, 1982-85. **Honors/Awds:** Outstanding Young Men in America, 1985; Black Achiever of Industry, Young Men's Christian Asn, Chicago, 1986. **Home Addr:** 2918 Greenwood Rd, PO Box 315, Hazel Crest, IL 60429. **Business Addr:** Supervisor Planning, Facility Engineer, RR Donnelley and Sons Company, 3075 highland Pkwy, Downers Grove, IL 60515.

NICHOLS, CHARLES HAROLD
Educator. **Personal:** Born Jul 6, 1919, Brooklyn, NY; son of Charles F and Julia King; married Mildred Thompson, Aug 19, 1950; children: David G, Keith F & Brian A. **Educ:** Brooklyn Col, BA, 1942; Brown Univ, PhD, 1948. **Career:** Educator (retired); Morgan State Col, assoc prof, Eng, 1948-49; Hampton Inst, prof Eng, 1949-59; Free Univ, Berlin, GE, prof, Am lit, 1959-69; Brown Univ, Providence RI, prof Eng, 1969-89. **Orgs:** Modern Lang Asn; Am Studies Asn; Soc Multi-Ethnic Lit US. **Honors/Awds:** Fulbright Prof Denmark, 1954-55; Sr fellow, Nat Endowment Humanities 1973-74; O'Connor Distinguished Vis Prof, Colgate Univ, 1977. **Special Achievements:** First chairman of the Afro-American Studies program at Brown Univ; Author, "Many Thousand Gone," "The Ex-Slaves Account of their Bondage & Freedom" Brill, Leiden 1963, IN Univ Press, 1969, "Black Men in Chains" 1971, Instr Manual for Cavalcade, Houghton, Mifflin, 1971, "African Nights, Black Erotic Folk Tales" 1971, "Arna Bontemps - Langston Hughes Letters 1925-67," Dodd Mead, 1980. **Home Addr:** 56 Fosdyke St, Providence, RI 02906.

NICHOLS, CRYSTAL FAYE
Manager. **Personal:** Born Apr 11, 1969, Lansing, MI; daughter of Charles and Dorthy. **Educ:** Brook Col, AA, 1982; Lee Strasburg Acting Sch. **Career:** Ashford Properties, apt mgr, 1987-; bartender; Prof Int Basketball League, basketball official, 1989-; LA Unit, football official, line judge, 1994-. **Special Achievements:** First woman to officiate high school football playoff games in Los Angeles, 1999. **Home Addr:** 3865 Nicolet Suite 19, Los Angeles, CA 90008, **Home Phone:** (323)293-4198. **Business Addr:** Apartment manager, Ashford Properties, Inc., 5126 Clareton Dr Suite 206, Agoura Hills, CA 91301, **Business Phone:** (818)865-1088.

NICHOLS, DAVID G
Physician, educator. **Educ:** Yale Univ, BA, 1973; NY Mt Sinai Sch Med, MD, 1977; Johns Hopkins Univ Sch Prof Studies Bus & Educ, MBA, 2000. **Career:** C?s Hosp Philadelphia, resident, 1977-80, chief resident, 1980-81, Pediat Anesthesia & Critical fel, 1983; Univ Pa Sch Med, instr, 1980-81; Hosp Univ Pa, residency anesthesiol, 1981-83; Johns Hopkins Sch Med, from asst prof to assoc prof anesthesiol/critical Care Med & Pediat, 1984-98, Residency Educ Prog, assoc dir, 1984-87, Pediatric Intensive Care, from assoc dir to dir, 1987-97, Div Pediat Anesthesia & Critical Care Med, 1997-2001, prof anesthesiol/critical Care Med & Pediat, 1998-, vice dean educ, 2000-, Mary Wallace Stanton Prof Educ, 2005-. **Orgs:** Fel Am Acad Pediat; fel Am Col Critical Care Med; Am Soc Anesthesiol; Int Anesthesia Res Soc; Soc Pediatric Anesthesia; Am Thoracic Soc; Soc Critical Care Med; Soc Pediat Res; Asn Univ Anesthesiologists; Am Bd Pediat; Alpha Omega Alpha Honor Med Soc. **Honors/Awds:** Medical Attendings Award, Mt Sinai Sch Med, 1977; Benjamin Ritter Award, Dept Pediat, C's Hosp Philadelphia, 1981; Medical Student Teaching Award, Dept Anesthesiol, Univ Pa, 1982; Outstanding Teacher Award, Dept Anesthesiol, Johns Hopkins Univ, 1986; Teacher of the Year Award, Johns Hopkins Emergency Med Residency Prog, Johns Hopkins Univ, 1997-98; Distinguished Career Award, Am Acad Pediat, Sect Critical Care, 2006. **Special Achievements:** Best Doctors in Baltimore, Baltimore Magazine, 2002; Best Doctors, Black Enterprise Magazine, 2002. **Business Addr:** Professor & Vice Dean for Education, Johns Hopkins University School of Medicine, Department of Pediatrics, 33 N Broadway Suite 115 Blalock 904, Baltimore, MD 21205, **Business Phone:** (410)955-8401.

NICHOLS, DIMAGGIO
Executive. **Personal:** Born May 8, 1951, Byhalia, MS; son of Emmitt Nichols Jr and Lucille Bougard; married Lizzie Emma Shelton Nichols, Mar 16, 1974; children: Dimeka W, Dondra O. **Educ:** Rust Col, Holly Spring, BS, 1973; Gen Motor Inst, Flint, Dealer Develop, 1983. **Career:** Buick Motor Div, Flint Mich, dist sales mgr, 1974-83; Gen Motor Inst, Flint Mich, trainee, 1983-84; Sentry Buick, Omaha, salesperson, 1984-85; Noble Ford-Mercury Inc, Indianola, pres, 1985-. **Orgs:** Bd mem, Chamber Com, Indianola, 1987-; bd mem, Black Ford Lincoln Mercury Asn, 1988-. **Honors/Awds:** Iowa Up & Comers Des Moines Regist, 1986; Quality Care Prog Award Excellence, Ford Motor Co, 1987. **Special Achievements:** Top Return on Invest, Ford Motor Co, 1988. Noble Ford-Mercury Inc ranked 1993. BE Top 100 Auto Dealers, 2001. **Business Addr:** President, Noble Ford-Mercury Inc, 947 Hwy 65 69 N, PO Box 579, Indianola, IA 50125.

NICHOLS, EDWIN J.
Psychologist, industrialist, clinical psychologist. **Personal:** Born Jun 23, 1931, Detroit, MI; married Sandra; children: Lisa, Edwin. **Educ:** Assumption Col, CAN, attended 1955; Windsor Can; Eberhardt Karls Univ, Tubingen, Ger, 1957; Leopoline-franciscea Univ, Innsbruck, Austria, Phd, psychol & psychiatry; Fel Austrian Ministry Educ, PhD, 1961. **Career:** Nat Inst Mental Health, Rockville, MD, chief Applied & Social Proj Rev Br, 1969-89; Kans Neurol Inst Cleveland Job Corps Ctr Women Meharry Med Col & Fisk Univ, psychologist; Univ Ibadan Nigeria, dir Childs Clin, 1974-77; Ctr Mgt Develop Lagos Nigeria, mgt consult, 1974-77; Ctr Excellence Pub Leadership, George Wash Univ, fac, currently; Nichols & Assocs Inc, dir, currently. **Orgs:** Veteran, Korean War. **Business Addr:** Director, Nichols & Associates Inc, 1650 Arch St Suite 2703, Philadelphia, PA 19103, **Business Phone:** (215)587-1200.

NICHOLS, ELAINE
Archaeologist. **Personal:** Born Oct 5, 1952, Charlotte, NC. **Educ:** Univ NC, Charlotte, BA, 1974; Case Western Reserve Univ, MSSA, 1980; Univ SC, MA, pub serv archaeol, 1988. **Career:** Planned Parenthood Charlotte, crisis intervention counr, 1974-75; Big Brothers Big Sisters, social caseworker, 1975-78; City Cleveland, neighborhood planner, 1980-81, asst mgr planners, 1981-82; Univ NC, Charlotte, lectr, 1982-85; Univ SC, grad stud, dept anthrop, 1985-88; SC State Museum, curator hist, 1987-. **Orgs:** Charter mem, Afro-Am Serv Ctr, 1974; Delta Sigma Theta Sor, 1977-; Co-chairperson, Afro-Am Hist Soc, Charlotte, 1982-83; bd mem, Metrolina Asn Blind, 1983-85; researcher, Am Heart Asn, Charlotte, 1985. **Honors/Awds:** "Pulse of Black Charlotte" Urban Inst Grant UNCC 1984; Research Assistantship, Dept of Anthrop, USC, 1985-; Service Award, Alpha Kappa Alpha Sor, 1986; Sigma Xi Science Award, 1987. **Home Addr:** PO Box 3536, Columbia, SC 29230. **Business Addr:** Curator of History, South Carolina State Museum, 301 Gervais St, PO Box 100107, Columbia, SC 29202-3107, **Business Phone:** (803)898-4953.

NICHOLS, GEORGE
Insurance executive. **Personal:** Born May 25, 1960, Bowling Green, KY; son of George Jr and Vera; married Cynthia J, Jul 14, 1984; children: Courtney, Jessica & George IV. **Educ:** Alice Lloyd Col, AA, 1980; Western KY Univ, BA, 1983; Univ Louisville, MA, 1985. **Career:** KY Dept Ment Health, Ment Retardation Serv, exec asst, 1984-89; Cent State Hosp, chief exec officer, 1989-92; Southeastern Group Inc, BCBS KY, exec dir, 1993; Athena N Am Inc, vpres mkt, 1993-95; KY Health Policy Bd, exec dir, 1995-96; KY Dept Insurance, comnr, 1996-2000; NY Life Ins Co, sr vpres, AARP Tampa Oper, exec charge, 2003-07, Office of Govt Affairs, head, 2007-. **Orgs:** Bd dir, Repub Bank & Trust Co, 1993-96; youth mentor, chair youth prog, 100 Black Men Louisville, 1992-94; bd dirs, vice chair, United Way KY, 1993-96; bd dirs, Actors Theatre Louisville, 1993-95; bd dirs, Louisville Zoo Soc, 1993-95; bd dirs, Lincoln Found, 1993-95; bd dirs, Big Brothers & Big Sisters, 1992-94; exec comt, NAIC, 1996-; vice chair, SE Zone, 1997; chair, secy, treas, Banking & Ins, 1997-2000, 1998-; vpres, pres, Nat Asn Ins Comnrs, 1998-99, 2000-. **Honors/Awds:** Social Science Student of the Year, Alice Lloyd Col, 1980; Top 200 Basketball Players in Jr Col, Sporting News Nat, 1980; Adult Black Achiever, Louisville YMCA, 1993; Hall of Fame, Bowling Green Sr High, 1994; First 40 Under 40 Foremost Young Business Leader, Metro Louisville Bus, 1996; Wm E Summers Award, Outstanding Bus Person, Shelby Ministerial Coalition, 1994. **Special Achievements:** Cent State Hosp, first African-Am State Hosp Dir, Youngest, 1989; NAIC, first African-Am Ins Comnr, in KY, 1996, first African-Am Pres Nat Asn Ins Comnrs in 137 yrs history, 1998. **Home Addr:** 6449 Renwick Circle, Tampa, FL 33647, **Home Phone:** (813)558-0539. **Business Addr:** Head, Office of Governmental Affairs, New York Life Insurance Co, 51 Madison Ave Suite 3200, New York, FL 10010, **Business Phone:** (212)576-7000.

NICHOLS, GRACE. See NICHOLS, NICHELLE.

NICHOLS, NICHELLE (GRACE NICHOLS)
Actor, singer. **Personal:** Born Dec 28, 1932, Robbins, IL; daughter of Samuel Earl and Lishia Parks; married Foster Johnson, Jan 1, 1951 (divorced); children: 1; married Foster Johnson (divorced 1951); children: Kyle Johnson; married Duke Mondy, Jan 1, 1967 (divorced 1972). **Educ:** Chicago Ballet Acad, Chicago, attended 1950-56; Columbia Law Sch. **Career:** Actress, singer, dancer;

Duke Ellington; Women In Motion, pres; NASA,minority recruitment officer; Films: Star Trek; A-R Way Productions, pres,1979-; Films: Porgy & Bess, 1959; Made in Paris, 1966; Mister Buddwing, 1966; Doctor, You've Got to Be Kidding!, 1967; Truck Turner, 1974; StarTrek: The Motion Picture, 1979; Star Trek: The Wrath of Khan, 1982; StarTrek III: The Search for Spock, 1984; The Supernaturals, 1986; Star Trek IV: The Voyage Home, 1986; Star Trek V: The Final Frontier, 1989; StarTrek VI: The Undiscovered Country, 1991; The Adventures of Surge of Power,2004; Captain Zoom in Outer Space, 1995; Trekkies, 1997; Snow Dogs, 2002;Are We There Yet?, 2005; Mirror Universe: Part 1, 2008; Lady Magdalene's, 2008; Tru Loved, 2008; The Torturer, 2008; TVSeries: Great Gettin' Up Mornin', 1964; "Tarzan", 1966; "Star Trek",1966-69; "Star Trek", 1973-74; Antony & Cleopatra, 1983; "Inside Space", 1992; "Gargoyles", 1994-96; "Renunciation", 2000; "Buzz Light year of Star Command", 2000; "Heroes", 2007; Albums: Uhura Sings & Hauntingly. **Orgs:** Kwanza Found, 1973-; bd gov, Nat Space Soc; Nat bd adv, SEDS-MIT; Hon mem, Alpha Kappa Alpha Sorority. **Honors/Awds:** Women of the Year, Nat Educ Asn, 1978; Distinguished Pub Serv Award Agency, 1989; ACTSO Award Performing Arts, Acad Olympics, 1991; Hollywood Walk of Fame, 1992. **Special Achievements:** First African-American to place her handprints in front of Hollywood's Chinese Theatre. Books: Beyond Uhura: Star Trek & Other Memories, 1994; (With Margaret Wander Bonanno) Saturn's Child, 1995; Played prominent role in the recruitment of minorities and women by NASA. **Business Addr:** President, AR-Way Productions, 22647 Ventura Blvd Suite 121, Woodland Hills, CA 91364, **Business Phone:** (818)340-7929.

NICHOLS, DR. OWEN D.
Educator. **Personal:** Born Apr 8, 1929, Raleigh, NC; son of William and Pearl; married Delores Tucker; children: Bryan K & Diane Maria. **Educ:** Shaw Univ, BS, 1955; Howard Univ, MS, phy chem, 1958; HIghland Univ, EdD, 1975. **Career:** Educator (retired); SC State Col, assoc prof, 1958-59; US Naval Res Lab Washington DC, res chemist, 1959-62; Dept Defense Alexandria VA, physical sci analyst, 1962-66; Air Pollution Tech Info Ctr, Nat Air Pollution Control Admin Washington DC, deputy dir, 1966-68; Off Tech Info & Pub Nat Air Polllution Control Admin Washington DC, dir, 1968-69; Howard Univ Washington DC, exec asst to pres, 1969-71; Howard Univ, vpres admins & secy, 1971-88. **Orgs:** Alpha Kappa Mu Soc; Beta Kappa Chi Sci Soc; Am Chem Soc; Air Pollution Control Asn; Soc Sigma XI; Intl Platform Asn; Am Mgt Asn; Am Asn High Educ; Am Asn Univ Admin; Comn Educ Statis & Admin Affairs, Am Coun Educ MD Congress; PTA; Adv Con Hosp Construct MD; town Counman, Seat Pleasant MD; Prince Georges County Housing Authority; legislative chmn, 2nd vpres Prince Georges Co Coun, PTA; Lay Speaker United Methodist Church; montgomery col, bd trustee, 2001-03, bd mem, currently. **Honors/Awds:** Comn Campus Ministry & Higher Educ; Baltimore Washington Conf United Methodist Church. **Military Serv:** AUS, Corps Engrs, 1st lt, 1950-53. *

NICHOLS, DR. RONALD AUGUSTUS
Hospital administrator. **Personal:** Born Jun 4, 1956, Louvain, Belgium; son of Rufus and Janet Watson; married Sati Harris, Jun 21, 1986; children: Aaron. **Educ:** Boston Univ, Boston, Mass, BA, 1974-78; Brown Univ, Providence, RI, MD, 1978-82; Harvard Univ, Boston, Mass, MPH, 1981-82. **Career:** Mt Sinai Hosp, New York, residency in Obstet & Gynec, 1982-86; Univ Cincinnati, Cincinnati, Ohio, dir, univ obstet practice, 1987-88; Mich State Univ, Sparrow Hosp, Lansing, Mich, dir, perinatal ctr, 1988-. **Orgs:** Bd mem, Mich Bd Med, 1990-94; bd mem, Mich Hosp Asn, 1989-91; bd mem, Perinatal Asn Mich, 1989-92; bd mem, Boy Scouts Am, Mich, 1989-; bd mem, Lansing Urban League, 1989-. **Honors/Awds:** Fel maternal-fetal med, Univ Cincinnati, Cincinnati, Ohio; Sigma Xi Honor Society for Res, 1980-81. **Business Addr:** Chief Doctor in Obstetrics and Gynecology, Abortion Clinic of Grand Rapids, 3212 Eastern Ave SE, Grand Rapids, MI 49508, **Business Phone:** (616)361-8800.

NICHOLS, SYLVIA A.
Manager. **Personal:** Born Nov 15, 1925, Washington, DC; daughter of Charles Perry and Nellie Perry; married Herb Nichols (died 07/21/1999); children: Cynthia, Louie, Albert Blalock-Bruce, Carl, Donna. **Educ:** Univ DC, Wash, MA. **Career:** Retired: Dept of Labor, Occupational Safety & Health Admin, public affairs specialist, 1971-87; US Dept of Labor, pub affairs specialist, 1987. **Orgs:** Delegate Central Labor Coun, DC 1972-85; founding mem, Wash Womens Forum 1977-; exec bd Nat Assoc DOL Chapter Blacks In Govt DC, 1979-; pres, Local 12, AFGE, Dept Labor 1982; dir Fed Credit Union, Dept Labor 1982-87; delegate Nat AFGE Convention 1984; delegate Nat AFGE Convention 1986; second vice pres, 12 AFGE 1986-87; Black Democratic Council Inc PG MD 1986-87; supervisory comt, Federal Credit Union Dept, 1988; social activities comt, Greater Southeast Healthcare Sys, Iverson Mall Walkers, 1990-; Nat Political Conf black Women, delegate, 1993; Nat Political Conf of Black Women, 1992-95; Prince George's County Chapter, Iverson Mall Walker's Choral Group, PG County, MD, 1990-95, Activities Comt, 1990-95; Election Judge, 26th District, PG County, Maryland, 1994, 1999-00; Global Ages Club, St Paul United Methodist Church. **Honors/Awds:** Special service Commission Award, The PG County Chapter of the Nat Hook Up of Black Women, Dept of Labor, 1982; Fed Serv Award, thirty years of honorable serv to the Dept of Labor. **Special Achievements:** Seabrook Elementary School, Career Day Speaker, Maryland, 1995. *

NICHOLS, WALTER LAPLORA
Educator. **Personal:** Born Aug 31, 1938, Bolton, MS; married Louise Faye Harris; children: Anthony & Kala Faye. **Educ:** Miss Valley State Univ, BS, 1964; Northern Ill Univ, MS, 1978; Independence Univ, DEd, 1979. **Career:** Sheridan Ind Boys, teacher, 1965-67; Fairmont Jr High Sch, teacher, coach, 1967-71; Argo Comm High Sch, teacher, coach, 1971-. **Orgs:** Vpres, Dist 86 Sch Bd, 1981-; Nat Sch Bd Asn, 1981-; Ill Sch Bd Asn, 1981-; consult, Joliet Job Corp, 1982-83; bd mem, PUSH, 1983-; Marquette Joliet Consistory, 1983; Shriner, 1984. **Special Achievements:** Article "You Either Move Up or Move Out" Chicago Tribune, 1967, "Title Triumph by Charger Something Special, Walt", 1967, "Remember Walter Nichols Offensive Tackle", Joliet Herald newspaper, 1964-67, "Stand by Valley State Alumni Urge Official" Clarion Ledger Paper, 1983. **Home Addr:** 406 Church St, Clinton, MS 39056-5308.

NICHOLSON, ALEATHIA DOLORES
Educator, clergy. **Personal:** Born Apr 10, 1937, Salisbury, NC; daughter of John Wadsworth and Leathia Williams. **Educ:** Hampton Univ, BS, 1959; Univ Conn, MA, 1965; George Peabody Col/Verbilt Univ, EdS, 1968; Episcopal Theol Sem Ky, Licentiate Servant Ministry, 1989. **Career:** Educator, (retired): Pub Pvt Schs, music specialist, 1959-78; Meharry Med Col, stud affairs dir & nursing educ, 1978-81; Tenn State Univ, stud affairs dir & sch nursing, 1981-85; Fisk Univ, dir teacher educ progs, 1985-92; Episcopal Diocese Tenn, voc deacon, 1989; Teach Am, curric consult, 1990-92; Metro Bd Educ, music specialist, 1992-2002; Christ Church Cathedral, deacon, 2007-. **Orgs:** Zeta Phi Beta Sorority Inc, 1960-; N Am Asn Diaconate, 1989-2001; bd mem, Neighborhood Educ Proj, 1989-91; bd trustees, Dubose Scholarship Fund, 1998; Nat Educ Asn Affiliates. **Honors/Awds:** Award for JTPA Exceptional Youth Sub-Contracting, Gov Tenn, 1989; Outstanding Teacher, Fisk Univ, Social Sci Div, 1992. **Special Achievements:** Co-author: 1980; An Afro-Anglican Mass Setting, St Anselm's Episcopal Church, composer, 1980; Epic Lives, Visible Ink, contributor, two profiles, 1992; Notable Black American Woman, Gale, contributor, five biographies, 1992; Instructional Approaches to Classroom Management, TFA, editor/author, 1992; Contributed 19 biographies to Notable Black American Women; contributed 25 biographies to Notable Black American Men. **Home Addr:** 3729 Creekland Ct, Nashville, TN 37218-1803, **Home Phone:** (615)876-7914.

NICHOLSON, ALFRED
Educator. **Personal:** Born Jun 3, 1936, Edgefield, SC; children: Sharon Michell & Althea Gail. **Educ:** Community Col, Philadelphia, AAS, 1968; LaSalle Univ, BS, 1974. **Career:** AAA Refinishing Co, tanner & inspector, 1956-59; Strick Corp, elec wireman, 1961-68, personnel asst, 1968-69; Community Col Philadelphia, personnel officer & aa dir, 1974-. **Orgs:** Treas, Col & Univ Personnel Asn, 1972-74; bd trustees, United Way Southeastern, PA. **Military Serv:** AUS, corpl, 2 yrs; Good Conduct Medal; Honorable Discharge. **Business Addr:** Personnel Officer, AA Dir, Community College of Philadelphia, 1700 Spring Garden St, Philadelphia, PA 19130.

NICHOLSON, GEMMA
Executive, educator. **Personal:** Born Jul 28, 1959, Port-Au-Prince, Haiti; daughter of Jean and Rachel Gaetjens; children: Felicia & Carlos. **Educ:** Univ Virgin Islands, 1994; Univ Md, BS, 1996; Harvard, ABS, 2000. **Career:** Davenport Univ, instr; Horizons Conf Ctr, food & beverage dir. **Orgs:** Horizon's Conference Ctr. **Special Achievements:** Publ articles, Virgin Island Daily News, 1995-96. **Military Serv:** AUS, 1979-86; Army Achievement Medal; Army Commendation Medal. **Business Addr:** Hospitality Director, Horizons Conference Center, 6200 State St, Saginaw, MI 48603, **Business Phone:** (517)799-4122.

NICHOLSON, JESSIE R
Lawyer. **Personal:** Born in Waterloo, IA; married Charles E, Jul 22, 1972; children: Ephraim Nicholson. **Educ:** Univ Northern Iowa, BA, 1974, MA, 1975; William Mitchell Col Law, JD, 1985. **Career:** Ramsey County, Sr Leadership Atty; Southern Minn Regional Legal Servs Inc, dep exec dir, 2001-07, exec dir & chief exec officer, 2007-. **Orgs:** Am Bar Asn, 1985-90; conciliator, Due Process Bd, Conciliator Minneapolis-St Paul Archidocese, 1988-; bd mem, Housing Trust Adv Comn, 1989-91; Ramsey & Wash Co Bar Asn, 1989-; Minn Asn Black Lawyers, 1996; bd gov, Minn State Bar Asn, 1998-; legal asst, Disadvantage Comn, Minn State Bar Asn, 1998-. **Honors/Awds:** Service Recognition Award, Minn State Housing Finance Agency, 1991; Distinguished Service Award, William Mitchell Col Law, 2000; 15 yr Recognition Award for distinguished service, Southern Minn Regional Legal Serv, 2000; Anderson Trailblazer Award, William Mitchell Col Law. **Military Serv:** USN Reserve, 3rd class, 1975-77. **Business Addr:** Executive Director, Chief Executive Officer, Southern Minnesota Regional Legal Services Inc, 166 E 4th St Suite 201, St Paul, MN 55102, **Business Phone:** (651)228-9823.

NICHOLSON, LAWRENCE E
Educator. **Personal:** Born Jul 10, 1915, St Louis, MO. **Educ:** Lincoln Univ, MO, BA, 1938; Chicago Univ, MA, 1942; Columbia Univ, MA. **Career:** Educator (retired); Soc Caseworker, 1939-41; Va Coun Ctr, chief, 1946-47; High Sch, teacher, 1948-49; Harris Teachers Col, prof. **Orgs:** Chmn, Nat Scholarship Comn Omega Psi Phi Frat, 1950-60; Nat Bd ADA, 1968-70; pres, St Louis Dist, MO St Teachers Asn, 1970-72; chmn bd, Adult Welfare Serv, St Louis, 1968-; comnr chmn, St Louis House Auth, 1972-; bd, St Louis Coun Human Rel, 1972-; F St Louis Sch Bd, 1977; Bond Issue Super Comn, St Louis, 1968-; bd, St Louis Urban League, 1972-; bd, Chrctr Rea Asn, 1965-69; bd, NAACP, 1963-65; bd, Dept Chmn Relat Episcopal, 1953-55; bd, St Louis Voc Couns Serv, 1960-64; W End Comn Conf, 1958-63; St Louis Opera Theatre, 1963-65; C Welfare Comn, MO, 1968-70. **Honors/Awds:** Distinguished Service to Community Medal, Univ Chicago, 1971; Dirstingushed Service Award, Nat Fraternity Omega Psi Phi 1972; Man of the Year, St Louis ADA, 1972; The Nicholson Prize, named in honor, Harris Teachers Col. **Military Serv:** USN, 1942-45.

NICHOLSON, TINA
Basketball player. **Personal:** Born Sep 27, 1973. **Educ:** Pa State Univ, BS, exercise & sports mgt, 1996. **Career:** Basketball player (retired), coach; Cleveland Rockers, guard, 1997; asst coach, Lady Lions. **Honors/Awds:** Records of Big Ten, NCCA.

NICKERSON, DON CARLOS
Lawyer. **Personal:** Born Aug 24, 1951, Wilmington, DE; son of David B and Floretta W; married Aug 24, 1989 (divorced); children: Christen, Jordan & Dariann. **Educ:** Iowa State Univ, BS, sociol, jour, 1974; Drake Univ Law Sch, JD, 1977. **Career:** WHO Radio & TV, news reporter, 1972-74; Parrish & Del Gallo, assoc atty, 1977-78; Des Moines, Iowa, asst US atty, 1978-80; Babich & Nickerson, partner, atty; Wellmark Blue Cross & Blue Shield Iowa, assoc gen coun; Southern Dist Iowa, US atty, 1993-2001; Polk Co Dist Ct, Dist Ct 5C, judge, 2003-. **Orgs:** Iowa Comn the Aging, 1983-85; United Way Cent Iowa, 1985-88; Drake Univ Law Sch Bd Counrs, 1989-92; Iowa State Bar Asn; Nat Bar Asn, 1991-; Iowa Nat Bar Asn, 1991-92; Nat Asn Criminal Defense Lawyers, 1991-; Atty General's Health Care Fraud Adv Comm, 1994. **Honors/Awds:** Iowa Governor's Volunteer Award, 1984, 1985, 1992; Des Moines Register, Up & Comer, 1989; Certificate Recognition, Amnesty Int, 1991; Top lawyer rating, Martindale-Hubbell, AV, 1992; Medal of Honor, Drake Univ; SBA Community Service Award. **Special Achievements:** Conference presenter, first annual state conference on the Black Male, Criminal Justice, 1992. **Home Addr:** 3416 SW Rose, Des Moines, IA 50321, **Home Phone:** (515)222-9617. **Business Addr:** Judge, Polk County District Court, District 5C, 500 Mulberry St Suite 212, Des Moines, IA 50309, **Business Phone:** (515)286-3198.

NICKERSON, HARDY OTTO
Football player, executive, football coach. **Personal:** Born Sep 1, 1965, Compton, CA; married Amy; children: Ashleigh, Hardy & Haleigh. **Educ:** Univ Calif, Berkeley, BA, sociol, 1989. **Career:** Football player, Football coach (retired), Executive; Pittsburgh Steelers, linebacker, 1987-92; Tampa Bay Buccaneers, 1993-99; Jacksonville Jaguars, 2000-01; Green Bay Packers, 2002; Chicago Bears, coach, 2007; Buccaneer Radio Network, color analyst, currently; Nickerson Realty Group, founder & chief exec officer, currently. **Business Addr:** Founder, Chief Executive Officer, Nickerson Realty Group, 14120 Ballantyne Corp Pl Suite 160, Charlotte, NC 28277, **Business Phone:** (704)295-0093.*

NICKSON, SHEILA JOAN
College administrator. **Personal:** Born May 20, 1936, Buffalo, NY; daughter of William Harris and Genevieve Martha Briggs; children: Stephen Dwight & Roderick Matthew. **Educ:** Buffalo State Col, 1953; Erie County Col, 1966. **Career:** College administrator (retired); Buffalo State Col, asst to chair dept chem, 1966-74, asst to pres dir affirmative action, 1974; State Univ NY, asst chancellor coordr compus prog, 1980-83. **Orgs:** Exec bd, State Univ NY Black Faculty & Staff Asn, 1980; educ adv comt, Nat Urban League, 1983; bd dirs, YWCA, Buffalo, 1983; vice chair, NY State Human Rights Adv Coun, 1984-; pres, Nat Org Am Asn Affirmative Action; bd mem, vpres, Girl Scouts Am; Nat Asn Advan Colored People, 1987; bd mem, Sheehan Mem Hosp, 1988. **Honors/Awds:** Citation for Service to State Governor Carey NY State, 1982; Citation of Appreciation, Nat Alliance Black Sch Educrs, 1984; Citation for Service to Nation Commonwealth Va, 1986; Alpha Kappa Alpha Award, Women Involved in Gloval Issues, 1987; Truth Meritorious Service Award, 1989. **Home Addr:** 151 Sanders Rd, Buffalo, NY 14216, **Home Phone:** (716)871-1810. *

NICOLE NOLOAN, DEANNA TWEETY. See NOLAN, DEANNA.

NIGHTINGALE-HAWKINS, MONICA R
Marketing executive, president (organization), vice president (organization). **Personal:** Born Feb 6, 1960, Topeka, KS; daughter of Floyd Nightingale and Carol Lawton; married Thomas, Apr 9, 1989. **Career:** Office of the Mayor, on-the-job training prog mgr,

1982-83; KSNT-TV 27, opers engr, 1984-85; KSNW-TV 3, news producer, 1985-87; KPRS/KPRT Radio FM, music dir, 1987-89; AA Productions, vpres mkt & promotions, 1989-; Church of The Ascension, youth minister, 1989-; The Wyandotte City Proj, exec dir, 1989-. **Orgs:** Bd mem, Turner House Episcopal Social Services, 1987-90; State Kans, Comn AIDS in the Black, 1988-89; artist in educ, Governors Artist in Residence, 1988-; pres, Episcopal Church Women, 1989-91. **Honors/Awds:** Mayor Richard Berkey, Key to The City, 1989; Salute to Women, Am Bus Women 1988; Outstanding Female Broadcaster, A & M Records, 1989; $32k grant to train inner-city youth, State Kans. **Special Achievements:** Appeared in local, state, and national A A music trades magazines for involvement & work in the inner-city, 1989-92; Appeared on "Mass Communications Project for Youth Intervention and Training," NBC television, Aug 1992; "President's Glass Ceiling" Witness, Dec 1992.

NILES, ALBAN I
Judge. **Personal:** Born Jun 10, 1933, St Vincent, West Indies; son of Isaac and Elsie; children: Maria, Gloria & Angela. **Educ:** UCLA, BS, 1959, JD, 1963. **Career:** Judge (retired); Ernst & Ernst, auditor, 1963-64; Pvt pract, atty, 1964-82; Kedren Comm Health Ctr Inc, pres, 1968-79; LA Cty Civil Serv Comm, pres comn, 1980; LA Munic Court, judge, 1982; LA Super Ct, judge, 2002; Parliamentarian 100 Black Men Inc, Los Angeles; Urban Exec Leadership, Carnegie Found fel; Los Angeles Munic Ct, judge; Munic Ct, asst presiding judge, 1992-93; presiding judge, 1994-95. **Orgs:** Langston Bar Asn; chmn bd, Bus Devel Ctr S CA, 1978-91; Nat Asn Advan Colored People, Urban League; Commander Post 116 Am Legion; chair, Munic Court Judges Asn, 1992-93; treas, Judicial Div, Nat Bar Asn, 1991-93; 33 degree Mason & Hon Past Potentate Shriners rank Ambassador Large; pres, Los Angeles County Civil Serv Comn. **Honors/Awds:** Passed the CPA examination, 1960; Selected as person of Caribbean birth to make signif contrib, 1976; Univ Calif Los Angeles Law Reviewappointed to the bench Feb 3, 1982; Honored by the State Legislature, The County Bd of Supervisors, The Los Angeles City Council, 1996. **Military Serv:** USAF, a/2c, 1951-55.

NILES, PROF. LYNDREY ARNAUD
Chairperson, educator. **Personal:** Born May 9, 1936; married Patricia Aqui; children: Kathryn Arlene & Ian Arnaud. **Educ:** Columbia Union Col, BA, 1963; Univ Md, MA, 1965; Temple Univ, PhD, 1973. **Career:** Columbia Union Col, lectr, 1964-65; Univ DC, instr, 1965-68, asst prof, 1968-74; Univ Md, lectr, 1971-75; Leadership Resources Inc, mgt consult, 1974-75; Howard Univ, prof & assoc dean, 1975-79, Sch Commun, Commun Arts & Sci Dept, chmn, 1979-, Human Commun Studies, prof emer, currently. **Orgs:** Pres, Met Wash Commun Asn, 1974-75; Speech Commun Asn; Int Commun Asn; Am Soc Training & Develop; Nat Asn Adv Colored People. **Special Achievements:** Publ article: "Listening & Note TakingMethods", 1965; publ dissertation: "The Defel of Speech Educ Problems at Predominately Black Colls", 1973; "black rhetoric five yrs of growth, Encoder", 1974; "Communication ind Dental Office", article in Encoder 1979. **Business Addr:** Professor Emeritus, Howard University, School Communication, 2400 6th St, Washington, DC 20059, **Business Phone:** (202)806-7692.

NIMMONS, DR. JULIUS F., JR.
School administrator. **Career:** Jarvis Christian Col, Hawkins, TX, pres; Harford Community Col, Bel Air MD, dean arts & scis, 1990-93; Univ DC, provost & vpres acad affairs, 1993-96, actg pres, 1996-98; pres, 1998-2001, prof urban affairs. **Orgs:** Nat Asn Equal Opportunity, Wash, DC; trustee, Fed City Coun, DC; Wash Econ Coun, DC; Leadership Wash, DC; DC Pvt Indust Coun; DC Sch Careers Gov Coun; bd dirs, DC Workforce Investment Coun. **Honors/Awds:** Outstanding Leadership & Service Award, Alpha Phi Alpha Fraternity; Camp All America Certificate Achievement, Fort Bragg, NC, Dept Army. **Business Addr:** President, Professor of Urban Affairs, University of the District of Columbia, 4200 Connecticut Ave NW, Washington, DC 20008, **Business Phone:** (202)274-5100.

NIPSON, HERBERT
Journalist, association executive. **Personal:** Born Jul 26, 1916, Asheville, NC; married E Velin Campbell; children: Herbert, Maria. **Educ:** Penn State Univ, Jour, 1940; Univ IA, Writers Workshop, MFA, 1948. **Career:** Journalist (retired) assoc exec; Cedar Rapids Gazette, corres; Ebony Mag, assoc ed, 1949-51, co-managing ed, 1951-64, managing ed, 1964-67, exec ed, 1972-87; S Side Community Art Ctr, pres emer, currently. **Orgs:** IL Arts Coun, Joseph Jefferson Community; bd govs Urban Gateways; Chicago community; life mem, UI Alumni Asn; Nat Asn Advan Colored People. **Honors/Awds:** IA Press Photographers Asn Awards; Outstanding Journalist, Capital Press Clubs Award, 1965; Distinguished Alumnus, Penn State Univ, 1973; Phi Eta Sigma & Sigma Delta Chi Fraternities; Distinguished Alumni Award, Univ IA. **Special Achievements:** Became the first African-American elected to Sigma Delta Chi, the national journalism honor society. **Military Serv:** Armed Serv, m & sgt, 1941-45. **Business Addr:** President Emeritus, South Side Community Art Center, 3831 S Michigan Ave, Chicago, IL 60653, **Business Phone:** (773)373-1026.

NISSEL, ANGELA
Writer. **Personal:** Born Dec 5, 1978, Philadelphia, PA; daughter of Jack and Gwen. **Educ:** Univ Penn, BA, med anthrop, 1998. **Career:** Okayplayer.com, co-founder, site mgr, 1999; Scrubs tv series, staff writer, 2002; Books: The Broke Diaries: The Completely True & Hilarious Misadventures of a Good Girl Gone Broke, 2001; Mixed: My Life in Black & White, 2006. **Honors/Awds:** Online Hip-Hop Award, Best New Website, 2001. **Business Addr:** c/o Author Mail, Random House, 299 Pk Ave, New York, NY 10171.*

NIVENS, BEATRYCE THOMASINIA
Writer, lecturer, executive. **Personal:** Born Apr 1, 1948, New York, NY; daughter of Thomas J (deceased) and Surluta Bell (deceased). **Educ:** Fisk Univ, Nashville TN, BA, 1969; Univ Ghana Legon, Ghana W Africa, Summer Sch Cert, 1970; Hofstra Univ, Hempstead NY, MS, 1971. **Career:** Denison Univ, Granville OH, asst dean women, 1969-71; Hosftra Univ, Hemptead NY, pre-law counr, 1971-73; Queens Col, Flushing NY, counr 1974-79; Dist Coun 37, New York NY, part-time counr, 1979-87; Essence Mag, columnist, 1977-90; US Dept of Health & Human Serv, Bronx NY, expert, 1980-83; Career Mktg Int, New York NY, pres, lectr, writer, 1985-; IBM, consult; Verizon, NY, consult; NJ Port Authority, consult; Am Express, consult; Smart Biz Coaching Co, chief coach & pres, 2005-; JP Morgan Chase, career mgt consult; Beatryce Nivens.com, owner, currently; Books: The Black Woman's Career Guide, 1982, 1987; How to Change Careers, 1990; How to Choose a Career, 1992; How to Re-Enter the Work Force, 1992; Success Strategies for African Americans, 1998. **Orgs:** Delta Sigma Theta Sorority, 1987-. **Honors/Awds:** Nal Madame C.J. Walker Award; Pub Serv Award, US Dept of Labor 1982; author: Fel, Virginia Ctr for the Creative Arts, 1985; Winthrop Rockefeller Distinguished Lectr, Univ of AK, 1986; Careers for Women Without Coll Degrees, 1988. **Special Achievements:** numerous workshops and sem for coll and univ, corps, libr, women's professional assn, Black civic and professional assn, educ conf, and govt agencies; author of six career books and has written more than 170 career articles for major publ.

NIX, RICK (JAIME RICARDO)
Administrator. **Personal:** Born Jan 6, 1950, Toledo, OH; son of Ulysesses S and Viola Crain; children: Noel. **Educ:** St Joseph's Col, Rensselaer, IN, BS, philos, 1972. **Career:** Ohio Civil Rights Comn, Toledo, OH, field rep, 1973; City Flint, MI, mgt intern, 1974, community develop, 1975; Genesee Co, Flint, MI, community coordinating specialist, 1974-75; Gen Motors Corp, Flint, MI, inspector, 1976-82; Catholic Diocese Saginaw, MI, Off Black Concerns, dir, Mission Off, assoc dir, 1982-. **Orgs:** Vice chmn, City-Wide Adv Comt Community Develop, 1974-; Nat Asn Black Catholic Adminrs, Communs Comt, 1982-; Knights St Peter Claver, 1989-; founder & chmn, Black Fathers Day March Against Drugs & Crime, 1989-; co-chair & co-founder, First Annual Bridge Walk (Bridging the Gap); United Saginaw Against Crime, 1993; pres & founder, Ministry Black Catholic Men, 1995-; US Conf Catholic Bishops. **Honors/Awds:** Human Rights Award, City Flint, MI, Human Rels Comt, 1990; Voluntary Action Award, Pres George Bush, 1990; Community Service Award, Phi Delta Kappa Sorority, Saginaw Chap, 1991; Community Service Award, Frontiers Int Saginaw Chap, 1993; Community Service Award, The Diocese of Saginaw, St Joseph's Parish, Black History Month Award, 1993; Dr Martin Luther King Jr Unity Award, Iota Chi Lambda Chap, Alpha Phi Alpha Fraternity Inc, 1994. **Special Achievements:** Manual: "How to Drive Drug Dealers Out of Your Neighborhood", 1989. **Business Addr:** Director, Office for Black Concerns, Associate Director, Mission Office, Catholic Diocese of Saginaw, 5800 Weiss St, Saginaw, MI 48603, **Business Phone:** (989)799-7910.

NIX, ROSCOE RUSSA
Government official. **Personal:** Born Jun 22, 1921, Greenville, AL; son of Comer Payton and Jimmie Mae; married Emma Coble; children: Veretta Tranice & Susan Lynette. **Educ:** Howard Univ, AB; Am Univ, grad work, 1952. **Career:** Government official (retired); Labor Lodge No 12, Civil Rights Comn, US Dept Labor, chmn, 1964-66; US Dept Justice Community Rels Serv, field rep, 1966-68; MD Community Hum Rels, exec dir, 1968-69; US Dept Justice, Community Rels Serv, chief state & local agencies secy, 1969-73, chief technol support, 1973; Off Tech Assistance, Community Rels Serv, US Dept Justice, assoc dir, 1980-86; Weekly polit analyst, "Twenty-One This Week"; columnist, Montgomery Times; Pres, Roscoe R nix elem sch, currently. **Orgs:** Bd trustees, Stillman Col, Nat Asn Advan Colored People, Urban League, 1964, Am Civil Liberties Union, 1969; Community Church, Union Presbyterian Church; vpres, Montgomery County Nat Asn Advan Colored People, 1979, pres, 1980-90; Community Assembly Oper Presbyterian Church, 1979-; exec bd, Montgomery County Chap, Nat Conf Christians & Jews, 1979; Alpha Phi Alpha, United Way Montgomery County; Montgomery County Sch Bd, 1974-78; co-founder, African Am Family Festival Acad Excellence, 1990. **Honors/Awds:** Martin Luther King Jr Award, Montgomery County Gov, 1990; Wiley Branton Award, Wash Lawyer's Comn Civil Rights Under Law, 1991; honorary PhD, Montgomery Col, 2001; Community Service Award, African Am COC, Montgomery County, 2002; APA Award, 2002. **Special Achievements:** Second African-American to win election; Publ, "When the Sword is Upon the Land," "What Color Are Good Neighbors?", "If We Must Die", "The Ghost of Exec Order 9066", "Wanted Missionaries to the Suburbs", "God Is White", "Wanted, A Radical Black Church". **Military Serv:** AUS, T/4, 1943-46. **Home Addr:** 1100 Corliss St, Silver Spring, MD 20903. *

NIX, THEOPHILUS RICHARD
Lawyer. **Personal:** Born Jul 21, 1925, Chicago, IL; married Lulu Mae Hill; children: Theophilus R. **Educ:** Lincoln Univ, PA, BA, 1950; Howard Univ Law Sch Wash, DC, LLD, 1954. **Career:** Pvt practice, atty, 1954-; City Wilmington, asst city solicitor, 1955-56; EEOC Phila, supr trial atty, 1974-75; E I Du Pont De Nemours & Co, atty. **Orgs:** Del Bar Asn 1956-; Bar State Mich, 1957-; Nat Bar Asn, 1970-; Bar Mass, 1975-; Nat Advan Asn Colored People, 1946-; legal coun, Del Adolescent Prog, 1966-79; Correct Comn Del Bar Asn, 1973-76; bd mem, Martin Luther King Ctr, 1976-76; ETO & EUROPEAN Bandsmen & Drummajor, AUS, 1943-46; Meritorious Serv, DE PTA, 1959; Meritorious Community Serv Del Martin Luther Comn, 1978. **Honors/Awds:** District Service Award, Del Adolescent Prog, 1979. **Special Achievements:** Book: How To Operate a School of Business, 1959; St Tutorial & Job Training Program, 1962; Statistical Analysis NCC Sup Court Drug Sentencing, 1972. **Military Serv:** AUS, t/5 Bandsmen, 1943-46. **Business Addr:** Attorney, 2807 W 4th St, Wilmington, DE 19805.

NIX, THEOPHILUS RICHARD, JR.
Lawyer. **Personal:** Born Oct 12, 1953, Washington, DC; son of Theophilus R and Lulu Mae; married Myrtice Servance. **Educ:** Cincinnati Col Mortuary Sci, 1975; Ithaca Col, BFA 1979; Howard Univ Sch Law, JD 1982. **Career:** Funeral dir & embalmer; Bechtel Corp, sr contract formation specialist procurement; Boston Housing Authority, construct & contract atty; Pvt Pract, currently; EI Du Pont De Nemours & Co, corp, coun, currently; Red Orange USA, gen coun & vpres develop, currently. **Orgs:** Philadelphia Contractors Asn, 1984-87; bd dirs, Bd DE Contractors Asn, 1985-86; Philadelphia Barristers Asn, 1986-87; Nobles Mystic Mason Shrine; Am Arbit Asn; Nonprofit Develop Inst. **Home Addr:** 26 Bayes Hill Rd, PO Box 2298, Oak Bluffs, MA 02557, **Home Phone:** (508)693-8658. **Business Addr:** General Counsel, Vice President of Developmen, Red Orange USA, 2900 W 5th St, Wilmington, DE 19805, **Business Phone:** (302)654-8818.

NIXON, REV. FELIX NATHANIEL
Clergy. **Personal:** Born May 27, 1918, York, AL; son of Nathan Nixon and Savannah Carlisle Nixon; married Callie Cotton Nixon, 1944; children: Felix Jr, Donald Roland, Charles, Samuel, Joe Rome, Josiah, John K, Jewel, Katie, Jeanette, Mildred, Joyce, Savannah, Zeala, John. **Educ:** Meridian Baptist Sem, Meridian, MS, BTH, 1959; Union Baptist Sem, Birmingham, AL, BD, 1972; Selma Univ, AL, DD, 1988. **Career:** Mt Hermon Baptist Church, pastor, 1948-64; Morningstar Baptist Church, pastor, 1963-65; Sumter Co Day Care Ctr, owner, 1974-75; Nixon Ready to Wear Shop, owner, 1974-75; Elim Baptist Church, pastor, 1976-. **Orgs:** Sumter County Movement for Human Rights, 1960-67; Sumter Co Br Nat Asn Advan Colored People, 1964-75; dir, Sumter Econ Devel Corp Inc, 1970-75; Ensley Pratt City Br Nat Asn Advan Colored People, 1968-75; chmn, Sumter Co Dem Conf, 1967-75; chmn, Sumter Co Bd Educ, 1978-80; pres, Nat Asn Advan Colored People, 1964-91; bd mem, Sumter County Bd Educ, 1976-91; bd mem, Nat Baptist Conv; pres, Ala Baptist Conv. **Honors/Awds:** Recepient The Most Dedicated Leader, W AL, 1971; city of York, AL, Felix Nixon Day, Sept 1990. **Home Addr:** 510 Lincoln St, York, AL 36925. *

NIXON, GEORGE W.
Airplane pilot. **Personal:** Born Mar 13, 1935, Pittsburgh, PA; son of James and Annie; married Heather Mary White; children: Lynnora, Rhonda, Nannette, George II & Vanessa. **Educ:** Univ Pittsburgh Sch Eng, 1954; USAF Aviation Cadet Sch, attended 1956; USAF Navigator Eng Sch, attended 1957; USAF Aerial Bombardment Sch, attended 1959; USAF Pilot Sch, attended 1962. **Career:** Pilot (retired); United Airlines, pilot, 1966-87, capt, 1987-95. **Orgs:** United Airlines Pilot Speakers Panel, Arline Pilots Asn; United Airlines Black Prof Org; Orgn Black Airline Pilots; Alpha Phi Alpha. **Honors/Awds:** Won recognition & acclaim, filmed interview, Emmy Award winning Realities Black, 1974; Nominee Cty Grand Jury. **Special Achievements:** Featured on United Airlines Safety Video, 1989-95. **Military Serv:** USAF, mil combat Korea Loas & Vietnam, comdr, Boeing 707, B-47 Bombardier, B-36 engr; USAF capt 1954-66; National Defense Service Medal; AF Expeditionary Medal; AF Reserve Medal; AF Outstanding Unit Award; Vietnam Serv Medal; AF Longevity Serv Award.

NIXON, HAROLD L
Educator, administrator. **Personal:** Born May 31, 1939, Smithfield, NC; son of Mark A and Lizzie O; married Brenda Flint, Jun 8, 1962; children: Eric F & Leah. **Educ:** Fisk Univ, BA, 1962; NC Cent Univ, MA, 1976; Univ NCA, Chapel Hill, PhD, 1988. **Career:** Food & Drug ADM, res biologist, 1963-64; Nat Inst Health, res biologist, 1966-69; Fayetteville State Univ, dir financial aid, 1969-80, assoc dean spec progs & stud life, 1980-83, vice chancellor stud develop, 1983-88; Wright State Univ, vpres stud affairs, pro edu, 1988; Urban Develop partner, partner, currently; Univ S Fla, vpres Student Affairs. **Orgs:** Chr, legis comt, NCA Asn Fin Aid ADRs, 1975, pres, 1976; exe bd, Southern Asn

Fin Aid ADRs, 1976; nat mem-at-large, Nat Asn Fin Aid ADRs, 1977; Nat Asn Stud Personnel ADRs, 1983-; Ohio Asn Stud Personnel ADRs, 1988-; Ohio Col Personnel Asn, 1988-; Mid-Western Res Asn, 1990-. **Honors/Awds:** Outstanding Leadership Award, NCA Asn Financial Aid ADRs, 1976; Fayetteville State Univ, Outstanding Service Award, 1983-88; Rookie Administrator of the Year, Wright State Univ, Student Gov Asn, 1989; Alpha Phi Alpha Fraternity Inc, 1989. **Special Achievements:** Factors ASOd with Enrollment Decisions of Black Students and White Students in Colleges Where They Are in the Minority, Thoughts for ADRs, 1990; White Students at the Black Univ, A Report on Their Experiences Regarding Acts of Intolerance, 1992; The Adult Learner, A Comparison of Counseling Needs Between AFA and Caucasusian Univ Students, 1992; AFAs in the 21st Century, The Agony and Promise of Higher Edu, 1993. **Home Phone:** (813)278-5054. **Business Addr:** Partner, Urban Development Partners, 8630 M Guilford Rd Suite 409, Columbia, MD 21046.

NIXON, JAMES I, JR. (JIM NIXON)
Executive, business owner, automotive executive. **Personal:** Born Jun 21, 1933, Pittsburgh, PA; son of James I Nixon Sr and Annie Forest Nixon; married LaRue Saunders Howard, Apr 5, 1961; children: GiAnna Watkins & Edward T IV. **Educ:** Carnegie-Mellon Univ, BSME, 1956; Univ Cincinnati, 1958-59; Union Col, Schenectady, NY, 1963-64. **Career:** General Electric Corp, dist sales mgr, 1956-74; ITT Corp, vpres Equal Opportunity Opers, dir, 1974-87; N Am Venture Develop Group, founder, 1987-; Metropolitan Transp Authority, dir-AA, 1989-91; Inline Brake Mfg Corp, pres & chief exec officer, 1991-97; Beacon Partners Inc, managing dir, 1997-. **Orgs:** Bd mem, Nat Urban Affairs Coun, 1980-81; bd mem, Equal Employ Adv Coun, 1981-82; bd mem & chair policy comt, Asn Black Charities Inc, 1984-96; small bus adv coun, Fed Res Bank NY, 1995-97; regional adv bd, Bank Boston & Conn, 1997-. **Honors/Awds:** Outstanding Public Service Award, Jr Chamber Com,1965, 1966, 1968; Gerald L Phillipps Service Award, General Electric Co, 1970; Black Achievers in Industry Award, Harlem YMCA, 1972, 1982; NAACP of NY, 1983. **Military Serv:** Army CEngr, sgt first class, 1950-52; achieved rank sgt at age 17 yrs old; sgt first class at age 18 yrs old. **Home Addr:** 337 Mayapple Rd, Stamford, CT 06903-1310, **Home Phone:** (203)329-3515. **Business Addr:** Managing Director, Nixon Beacon Partners Inc, 97 Libbey Pkwy Suite 310, Weymouth, MA 02189, **Business Phone:** (781)982-8400.

NIXON, JAMES I, JR. (JIM NIXON)
Executive. **Personal:** Born Jun 21, 1933, Pittsburgh, PA; son of James I Nixon Sr and Annie Forest Nixon; married Lea Young Nixon, Aug 5, 1988; children: James I Nixon III, Danita H Brown, James E Hair Jr, Janette S Dent; married Joan B Nixon (divorced 1976). **Educ:** Carnegie-Mellon Univ, BSME, 1956; Univ Cincinnati, 1958-59; Union Col, Schenectady, NY, 1963-64. **Career:** General Electric Corp, dist sales mgr, 1956-74; ITT Corp, vpres Equal Opportunity Opers, dir, 1974-87; N Am Venture Develop Group, founder, 1987-; Metropolitan Transp Authority, dir-AA, 1989-91; Inline Brake Mfg Corp, pres & chief exec officer, 1991-97; Beacon Partners Inc, managing dir, 1997-. **Orgs:** Bd mem, Nat Urban Affairs Coun, 1980-81; bd mem, Equal Employ Adv Coun, 1981-82; bd mem & chair policy comt, Asn Black Charities Inc, 1984-96; small bus adv coun, Fed Res Bank NY, 1995-97; regional adv bd, Bank Boston & Conn, 1997-. **Honors/Awds:** Outstanding Public Service Award, Jr Chamber Com,1965, 1966, 1968; Gerald L Phillipps Service Award, General Electric Co, 1970; Black Achievers in Industry Award, Harlem YMCA, 1972, 1982; NAACP of NY, 1983. **Military Serv:** Army CEngr, sgt first class, 1950-52; achieved rank sgt at age 17 yrs old; sgt first class at age 18 yrs old. **Home Addr:** 337 Mayapple Rd, Stamford, CT 06903-1310, **Home Phone:** (203)329-3515. **Business Addr:** Managing Director, Nixon Beacon Partners Inc, 97 Libbey Pkwy Suite 310, Weymouth, MA 02189, **Business Phone:** (781)982-8400.

NIXON, JAMES MELVIN
Association executive. **Career:** C of C, assoc exec prof dir. **Orgs:** Nat Ctr Youth Outreach Workers; Omega Psi Phi.

NIXON, JIM. See NIXON, JAMES I, JR.

NIXON, JIM. See NIXON, JAMES I, JR.

NIXON, NORM ELLARD
Executive, basketball player. **Personal:** Born Oct 11, 1955, Macon, GA; son of Elmer Nixon and Mary Jo; married Debbie Allen; children: Vivian & Norm Jr. **Educ:** Duquesne Univ, attended 1977. **Career:** Basketball player (retired), Executive, Analyst; Los Angeles Lakers, 1978-83, San Diego Clippers, 1984, Los Angeles Clippers, 1985-86, 1989; Nixon-Katz Assocs, personal mgr/sports agents; Ga Restaurant, owner; KABC-TV, analyst, 2005-07; FSN West, studio color analyst, currently; Debbie Allen Dance Acad, Culver City, Calif, founder. **Orgs:** Bd dirs, MM VII Operation Hope, 1995-97. **Honors/Awds:** NBA All-Rookie Team, 1978. **Business Phone:** (310)286-3800.

NIXON, OTIS JUNIOR
Baseball player, minister (clergy). **Personal:** Born Jan 9, 1959, Columbus County, NC; married Pebbles, Jan 1, 2001 (divorced 2004); married Juanita Leonard, Dec 24, 1992 (divorced). **Educ:** MDiv. **Career:** Baseball player (retired), minister; NY Yankees, 1983; Cleveland Indians, 1984-87; Montreal Expos, 1988-90; Atlanta Braves, 1991-93, 1999; Boston Red Sox, 1994; Tex Rangers, 1995; Toronto Blue Jays, 1996-97; Los Angeles Dodgers, 1997; Minn Twins, 1998; Atlanta Braves, prof baseball player, 1999; On-Track Ministries, minister, currently.

NKONGOLA, MUYUMBA WA. See MUYUMBA, FRANCOIS N. in the Obituaries section.

NKONYANSA, OSAFUHIN KWAKU. See PRESTON, GEORGE NELSON.

NNAJI, BARTHOLOMEW O
College teacher. **Personal:** Born Jul 13, 1956, Oruku Enugu, Nigeria; son of Emmanuel and Nev; married Patricia, Aug 16, 1980; children: Chik & Nev. **Educ:** St John's Univ, NY, BS, 1980; Va Polytech Inst & State Univ, MS, 1982, PhD, 1983. **Career:** Univ Mass, asst prof, 1983-91, prof, 1991; Fed Repub Nigeria, hon minister, 1993; Univ Pittsburgh, Mfg Eng, ALCOA found chair, 1996, William Kepler Whiteford prof eng & dir, ALCOA Found prof mfg eng, currently. **Orgs:** Fel Int Soc Productivity Enhancement, 1994; sr mem, Inst Indust Eng; sr mem, Soc Mfg Engrs; bd mem, Robotics Int; Am Inst Physics; dir, US Nat Sci Found Ctr. **Honors/Awds:** Outstanding Teaching Award, United Technol Corp, 1992; M Eugene Merchant Best Textbook Award, 1994; St John's Univ Sports Hall of Fame, 1994; Award of Commander of the Order of the Niger, 1999; ARCO Excellence in Science & Technology Award, 2001; Baker Distinguished Research Award, 2001. **Special Achievements:** Numerous editorials and articles including editor, SME Transactions on Robotics Research, Society of Manufacturing Engineers Publications, 1992; International Journal of Design & Manufacturing, Chapman-Hall Publishers, editor in chief, 1990-; Design & Manufacturing book series, Chapman-Hall Publishers, series editor, 1990-; co-author, Modern Manufacturing Planning & Control, Prentice Hall, 1995; co-author, Design by Product Modelling, Chapman and Hall. **Business Addr:** ALCOA Foundation Professor in Manufacturing Engineering, University of Pittsburgh, School of Engineering, Indust Eng Dept, 1048 Benedum Hall, Pittsburgh, PA 15261, **Business Phone:** (412)624-9857.

N'NAMDI, CARMEN ANN
Educator, school principal. **Personal:** Born May 13, 1949, Cincinnati, OH; daughter of Carl and Dorothy Jenkins; married George N, Aug 14, 1971; children: Kemba, Nataki (deceased), Jumaane & Izegbe. **Educ:** Ohio State Univ, Columbus, Ohio, BS, educ, 1971; Wayne State Univ, Detroit, Mich, MA, educ, 1978. **Career:** Nataki Talibah Schhouse, Detroit, MI, founder & headmistress, 1978-95, principal, 1995-. **Orgs:** Bd mem, Detroit Children's Museum Friends; exec bd, Detroit Chap Jack & Jill, 1987-; Greater Wayne County Links, 1990-, pres, 1997-99; chair Bd, Nat Charter Sch Inst; mem bd, Mich Asn Pub Sch Academies. **Honors/Awds:** Maharishi Award, World Govt Age Enlightenment, 1983; Black Women of Michigan Exhibition, Detroit Historical Museum, 1985; Headliners Award, Women Wayne State Alumni Asn, 1985; Spirit of Detroit Award, Detroit City Coun, 1985; 'Salute to Black Women Who Make It Happen', National Council Negro Women, 1989; Michigan State Resolution, Mich Senate, 1989; Professional Best Award, Learning Mag, Mich State Univ, Col Educ, 1990; "Michigan House of Representatives Resolution", Mich House Reps, 1990; Award for Education, Black Women's Expo Detroit, 2000. **Home Phone:** (734)697-5474. **Business Addr:** Principal, Nataki Talibah Schoolhouse, 19176 Northrop St, Detroit, MI 48219-1857, **Business Phone:** (313)531-3720.

N'NAMDI, GEORGE RICHARD
Art museum director. **Personal:** Born Sep 12, 1946, Columbus, OH; son of George Richard Johnson and Ima Jo Winson Watson; married Carmen Ann Kiner N'Namdi, Aug 14, 1971; children: Kemba, Nataki (deceased), Jumaane, Izegbe. **Educ:** Ohio State Univ, Columbus, BS, 1970, MS, 1972; Univ Mich, Ann Arbor, 1974, PhD, psychol, 1978. **Career:** Univ Cincinnati, OH, dir head start training, 1970-72; Univ Mich, Ann Arbor, instr, 1973-76; Wayne State Univ, Detroit, MI, asst prof, 1976-86; Wayne Co Health Dept, Detroit, MI, psychologist, 1978-82; Jazzonia Gallery, Detroit, MI, dir, 1981-84; G R N'Namdi Gallery, Birmingham, MI, owner & dir, 1984-. **Orgs:** Chmn bd, Cass Food Co-op, 1983-86; Paradigm Dance Co, 1986-88; treas, Nataki Talibah Schoolhouse, 1989-; Birmingham Bloomfield Cultural Coun, 1990-; bd, Friends African & African Am Detroit Inst Art; Detroit Artist Mkt. **Honors/Awds:** Spirit of Detroit Award, City Detroit, 1981, 1985; Art Achievement Award, Delta Sigma Theta Sorority, 1982. **Business Phone:** (313)831-8700.*

NNOLIM, CHARLES E.
Educator. **Personal:** Born May 10, 1939, Umuchu, Nigeria; son of Lolo Ezelibe and Obidegwu; married Virginia Onwugigbo, Oct 26, 1966; children: Emeka, Chinyere, Amaeze & Azuka. **Educ:** Benedictine Col, Atchison, KS, BA, 1966; Bemidji State Univ, Bemidji, MN, MA, eng, 1968; Catholic Univ Am, Wash, DC, PhD, 1975. **Career:** Ferris St Col, Big Rapids, MI, asst prof eng, 1969-70; Babson Col, Wellesley, MA, asst prof eng, 1970-76; Univ Port Harcourt, Port Harcourt, Nigeria, prof eng, 1980-, fac humanities, dean. **Orgs:** African Lit Asn, 1974-; African Studies Asn; Modern Lang Asn Am; Nat Soc Lit & Arts; pres, Literary Soc Nigeria, 1986-; West African Asn Common wealth Lit & Lang Studies, 1988-. **Honors/Awds:** Doctoral Fellowship, Catholic Univ Am, 1968-72; Nigerian National Order of Merit Award, 2006. **Special Achievements:** Author of Melville's Benito Cereno: A Study in Mng of Name-Symbolism, 1974, author of Pessimism in Conrad's Heart of Darkness, 1980, author of critical essays on African literature published in US and British journals, author of the book-Justice of the Jungle. **Business Addr:** Professor of English, Dean, University of Port Harcourt, Department of English Studies, East/West Road, PO Box 5323, Rivers State, Rivers, Nigeria, **Business Phone:** (000)23408423-0890.

NOAH, LEROY EDWARD
Government official. **Personal:** Born Jul 25, 1934, Clarksdale, MS; son of Jesse and Lilliam Mae White; married Grace Fulghum, Dec 7, 1952; children: Sharon Davis, Carolyn Mann & Brenda. **Educ:** Forest Park Community Col, AAS, 1975; Nat Inst Cosmetology, PhD, 1987. **Career:** Government official (retired); City Kinloch, pres, bd aldermen. **Orgs:** Pres, Sch Bd, 1963-75; financial secy, Assoc Hairdresser, CosmetologistMo, 1980-94; United Beautician, 1991-; first vpres, Sigma Nu ThetaFraternity; pres, United Beauticians, St Louis, MO, 1992-00; pres, AssocHairdressers & Cosmetologist of MO, 2001-; Nat Beauty Culturist League,2003-. **Honors/Awds:** Citizen of the Year, Ward Chapel AME Church, 1981; Man of the year, AssocHairdresser, Cosmetologist Mo, 1988-; Nat King, Nat Beauty CulturistLeague, 1987-88; Dr John Bryant Memorial Award, 1988. **Military Serv:** USAF, sgt; Korean Defense; Presidential Unit; Good Conduct; Korean Medal. **Home Addr:** 11849 Northport Dr, Florissant, MO 63033-6736. *

NOBLE, JOHN CHARLES
School administrator, school superintendent. **Personal:** Born Sep 21, 1941, Port Gibson, MS; married Colleen L; children: Michaelle, Leketha, Carlos, Tracy & Stephanie. **Educ:** Claiborne Co Training Sch, attended 1959; Alcorn State Univ, BS, 1962; Tenn A&I State Univ, MA, 1971; Jackson State Univ, attended. **Career:** MS Chicago, teacher; Chicago, juvenile probation officer; Medgar Evers Comprehensive Health Ctr, dir res & eval; Opportunity Industrialization Ctr, instr; Claiborne Co Sch, supt educ. **Orgs:** Omega Psi Phi; Am Asn Sch Admins; fel Inst Politics; Rising Sun MB; chmn, Bd trustees Hinds Jr Col; bd trustee, Utica Jr Col; advan ind instr, Dr Thomas Gordons Parent Effectiveness Training & Teacher EFfective Training; Claiborn Co Chap, Nat Asn Advan Colored People; Port Gibson Masonic Lodge 21; bd dir, MS Action Prog; bd dir, Urban League LEAP Prog. **Business Addr:** Superintendent, Claiborne County Public School, PO Box 337, Port Gibson, MS 39150.

NOBLE, JOHN PRITCHARD
Administrator. **Personal:** Born May 31, 1931, West Palm Beach, FL; son of Floyd Grafton and Aurelia; married Barbara Norwood, Aug 30, 1958; children: John Jr, Michael. **Educ:** FL A&M Univ, BS, 1959; Columbia Univ NYC, MA Hosp Admin, 1963; Cornell Univ, Ithaca, attended 1969. **Career:** Retired: Arabian Amer Oil Co Dhahran Saudi Arabia, hosp admin, 1962-69; Winston-Salem NC Hosp Authority, pres & chief exec officer, 1969-71; Forsyth Hosp Authority Winston-Salem, vice pres planning & develop, 1971-73; Homer G Phillips Hosp St Louis, admin, 1973-78; Acute Care Hosp City of St Louis, dir, 1978-79; Dept of Health & Hosp City of St Louis, hosp com; Lambert-St Louis Intl Airport, asst dir. **Orgs:** Amer Col of Hosp Admins, 1965-; Amer Pub Health Asn, 1976-; chmn, Nat Asn of Health Serv Exec, 1978-80; bd mem, Family & Children Serv, 1977-; bd mem, King Fanon Mental Health, 1978-; life mem, Alpha Phi Alpha Frat; bd mem, Tower Village Nursing Home, 1978-; Nat Assoc of Guardsmen, 1994-; Sigma Pi Phi Frat, 1994-. **Honors/Awds:** Meritom Citation. **Military Serv:** USAF, A & 2C, 1951-53. **Home Phone:** (314)367-6324. **Business Addr:** Saint Louis, MO 63145, **Business Phone:** (314)426-8034.*

NOBLE, RONALD K
Educator. **Personal:** Born in Fort Dix, NJ; married; children: 1. **Educ:** Univ NH, BA, econ & bus admin, 1979; Stanford Univ, Law Sch, JD, 1982. **Career:** US Court Appeals Third Circuit, law clerk for judge, 1982-84; US Dept Justice, asst US atty & dep asst atty gen, 1984-89; 26-nation Financial Action Task Force, pres; US Dept Treas, asst secy enforcement, undersecretary enforcement, 1993-96; Int Crim Police Orgn, chief; Interpol, 69th Gen Assembly, secy gen, 2000; Interpol, 70th Gen Assembly, secy gen, 2005-; NY Univ Law Sch, from asst prof to assoc prof, 1990-99, prof, 1999-, fac dir Root-Tilden-Kern scholarship prog, currently. **Orgs:** Int Crim Police Orgn Exec Comm; pres, 33-mem Financial Action Task Force. **Honors/Awds:** US Dept of the Treasury, Alexander Hamilton Award, 1996. **Special Achievements:** President Clinton named Noble as the lead investigator of the disastrous BATF raid in Waco, Texas, 1993; Highest ranking African Am in the hist of fed law enforcement, 1994; first Am to lead Interpol; first elected to the position of Secy Gen of Interpol, 69th Gen Assembly in Rhodes, Greece, 2000; second five-yr term, 74th Gen Assembly, Berlin, Germany, 2005. **Business Addr:** Professor, New York University School of Law, 40 Wash Sq S 302B, New York, NY 10012, **Business Phone:** (212)998-6702.

NOBLES, PATRICIA JOYCE
Lawyer. **Personal:** Born Jun 3, 1955, St Louis, MO; daughter of Henry Stovall and Gwendolyn Bell Stovall. **Educ:** Southwest Baptist Col, BA, 1976; Univ Alaska, JD, 1981. **Career:** US District Judge, law clerk, 1981-83; Southwestern Bell Telephone Co, attorney, 1983-99; SBC Commun Inc, sr coun, 2000-. **Orgs:** Exec bd, Urban League, 1981-84; Am Asn Trial Attys, 1983-87; Alaska Bar Asn, 1983-87; pres, Alaska Asn Women Lawyers, 1985-86; mem bd, KLRE Pub Radio Station, 1986-87; Nat Advan Asn Colored People; Mo Bar Asn; Tex Bar Asn; mem bd, Literacy Instr Tex. **Business Addr:** Senior Counsel, SBC Communication Inc, 1 SBC Plz, 208 S Arkard Rm 3021, Dallas, TX 75202.*

NOEL, GERALD T, SR. (GERALD THOMAS NOEL)
Physicist. **Personal:** Born Oct 10, 1934, Westchester, PA; son of Charles F and Helen Madelyn Thomas; married R Gail Walker, Mar 28, 1992; children: Gerald T Jr, Charles F, Owen R & Brandan J Walker. **Educ:** Drexel Univ, BS, physics, 1962; Temple Univ, MS, physics, 1965, PhD, course work solid state physics, 1966-68. **Career:** David Sarnoff Res Ctr, technical staff mem, 1962-70; RCA Astro Electronics Div, engr staff mem, 1970-72; Univ Pa, res staff mem, 1972-77; Battelle Mem Inst, sr res scientist, 1977-85, res leader, 1985-, adv bd mem, 1997; Cent State Univ, prog dir lean transition emerging com technologies, currently. **Orgs:** Am Inst Physics; Materials Res Soc, 1985-; Am Vacuum Soc, 1984-; Nat Technical Asn, bd, chair, 1978-; Inst Environ Scis, sr mem, 1980-88; Nat Asn Blacks in Energy, 1989-; Int Soc for Hybrid Microelectronics, 1991-; IEEE Photovoltaic SPTs Comt, 1976-89. **Honors/Awds:** Nat CNF Chair Award, Nat Tech Asn, 1990; Technology Commercialization Award, Battelle Mem Inst, 1989. **Special Achievements:** Numerous publications in the fields of solar energy, microelectronic circuits, thin film materials and devices. **Military Serv:** USN, electronic tech 3, 1952-55. **Home Phone:** (614)844-6944. **Business Addr:** Program Director, Central State University, PO Box 1004, Wilberforce, OH 45384, **Business Phone:** (937)376-6216.*

NOEL, GERALD THOMAS. See NOEL, GERALD T, SR.

NOEL, PATRICK ADOLPHUS
Physician, consultant. **Personal:** Born Nov 9, 1940; married Evelyn Sebro; children: Carlita, Patrick Jr & John. **Educ:** Howard Univ, BS, 1964; Howard Univ, MD, 1968. **Career:** Howard Univ, residence, 1969-73; fel John Hopkins Univ, 1972; Pvt Pract, physician, 1973-; Bowie St Col, physician, 1973-; Howard Univ, instr ortho surg, 1973-; Univ Md, consult, 1973-76; Bowie St Col, Football Team, orth consult, 1973-76; Howard Univ Hosp, attend surg; Leland Hosp; SSE Comm Hosp; Laurel Hosp. **Orgs:** Fel Int Col Surgeons, 1974; Am Bd Orthop Surg, 1974; fel Am Acad Ortho Surg, 1976; treas, Soc Health Prof, 1977. **Honors/Awds:** Meritorious Serv, Bowie State Col, 1976.

NOGUERA, DR. PEDRO ANTONIO
Sociologist, educator. **Personal:** Born Aug 7, 1959, New York, NY; son of Felipe Carl and Millicent Yvonne Brooks; married Patricia Vattuone, Jul 6, 1982; children: Joaquin, Amaya, Antonio & Naima. **Educ:** Brown Univ, BA, sociol, 1981, MA, sociol, 1982; Univ Calif, Berkeley, PhD, sociol, 1989. **Career:** Univ Calif, Berkeley, Dept Ethnic Studies, course instr, 1983-84, Dept Sociol, course instr, 1984-85, res specialist, 1985-86, asst to vice chancellor, 1988-89, coordr multicultural action team, 1989-90, asst prof, 1990-94, assoc prof, 1994-2000; Goldberg & Assocs, Oakland, CA, consult, 1985; S Berkeley Youth Proj, dir, 1985-86; City Berkeley, exec asst & mayor, 1986-88; Fulbright fel, 1987-88; Harvard Univ, prof; NY Univ, Steinhardt Sch Educ, prof teaching & learning, currently. **Orgs:** Vpres, Berkeley Black Caucus, 1985-; bd mem, Daily Calif Newpaper, 1985-88; mem congressman, Dellums Exec Comt, 1986-; pres, Black Men United Change, 1987-90; bd mem, YMCA, Berkeley, 1988-; bd dirs, Berkeley Unified Sch Dist, 1990-94; pres, Caribbean Studies Asn, 2006; Am Sociol Asn; bd dirs, S African Educ Fund; bd dirs, S Berkeley Neighborhood Develop Corp; Caribbean Studies Asn; bd dir, Berkeley Community Found; pres, Berkeley Sch Bd Orgn; bd dir, S African Educ Fund. **Honors/Awds:** Teaching Assistant Prize, Brown Univ, 1981; Samuel P Lambert Prize, 1981; Rhodes School Finalist, RI, 1981; San Francisco Foundation School Improvement Research Award, 1992; Engineering & Science Award, Eisenhower Mathematics, 1993; Wellness Foundation Award, 1995; Distinguished Teaching Award, Univ Calif, Berkeley, 1995; Centennial Medal, Philadelphia Univ, 2002; Whitney Young Award of Leadership in Education, 2006; Honorary Doctorate, Univ San Francisco. **Special Achievements:** Tracking as a Form of Second Generation Discrimination and Its Impact on the Education of Latino Students, La Raza Law Jour, 1995; Taking Chances, Taking Charge: A Report on a Drug Abuse Intervention Strategy Conceived, Created and Controlled by a Community, International Quarterly Community Health Educ, 1995; Education and Popular Culture in the Caribbean: Youth Resistance in a Period of Economic Uncertainty, Cult Transition: Latin America the Caribbean and Canada, Carleton Univ Press, 1995; Ties That Bind, Forces That Divide: Confronting the Challenge of Integration Forty Years After Brown, Univ San Francisco Law Rev, 1995; Preventing Violence in Schools, Harvard Educ Rev, 1995; author, The Imperatives of Power: Regime Survival and the Sound Basis of Political Support in Grenada, 1951-1991; Pettier Lang Publ, 1997. **Business Addr:** Professor of Teaching and Learning, New York University, Steinhardt School of Education, 82 Wash Sq E, New York, NY 10003, **Business Phone:** (212)998-5787.

NOISETTE, RUFFIN N
Clergy. **Personal:** Born Mar 20, 1923, Summerville, SC; son of Joseph and Louise; married Thelma Anderson; children: Shelley, Karin, Robin & Louis. **Educ:** Howard Univ, AB, 1946; Howard Univ, BD, 1949. **Career:** Fisk Univ Nashville, asst dean chapel, 1949-50; Ebenezer African Meth Episcopal Church, Rahway, NJ, pastor, 1950-51; Bethel African Meth Episcopal Church, Wilmington, Del, pastor, 1951-65; Delaware OEO, dep dir, 1965; EI Dupont De Nemours & Co, prof staffing consult, 1965-85; Emily P Bissell Hosp, Wilmington, Del, chaplain, 1986-92; United Metrop Missionary Baptist Church, minister, currently. **Orgs:** Eastern Col Personnel Officers; Del Personnel & Guidance Asn, 1968; mem bd dir, YMCA, Wilmington, Del; Boys Club Wilmington; Opportunity Ctr Inc; Golden Beacon Col; Del Coun Crime & Justice Inc; New Castle Co Bd Elections; mem bd trustees; Del State Col. **Honors/Awds:** Citizenship Award, Alpha Phi Alpha, 1959; Meritorious Service Award, YMCA, 1964; Recruiter of Year Award, LaSalle Col, 1973; Black Heritage Disting Service Award, 1981; Outstanding Service Award, Del State Univ Div Stud Affairs, 1984; Meritorious Service Award, Del State Univ Trustee, 1997. **Business Addr:** Minister, United Metropolitan Missionary Baptist Church, 450 Metrop Dr NE, Winston-Salem, NC 27101, **Business Phone:** (336)761-1358.*

NOLAN, DANIEL KAYE
School administrator. **Personal:** Born May 20, 1949, Newbern, TN; married Margaret M; children: Richard A Owens, Kyra D & Daniel M. **Educ:** Ball State Univ Admin, attended; Butler Univ, BSEd, attended; St Frances Univ, MS Counseling, attended. **Career:** South side High, guidance counr, 1973-79; YMCA, br exec, 1979-89; Magnavox Corp, eng coordr, 1989-93; NBS-Imaging, purchasing mgr, 1993-93; FWCS,vice prin, 1993-95; Northrup High Sch, counr, 1996-, asst prin, currently. **Orgs:** Omega Psi Phi. **Honors/Awds:** Omega Man of the Year, 1999. **Business Addr:** Assistant Principal, Northrop Highschool, 7001 Coldwater Rd, Fort Wayne, IN 46825, **Business Phone:** (260)467-2329.

NOLAN, DEANNA (DEANNA TWEETY NICOLE NOLOAN)
Basketball player. **Personal:** Born Aug 25, 1979, Flint, MI; daughter of Philip Murray and Virginia Nolan. **Educ:** Ga Univ, BA, 2001. **Career:** Detroit Shock, guard & forward, 2001-. **Honors/Awds:** Mich Miss Basketball, 1995; WNBA All-Star, 2003-07; WNBA Community Assist Award, 2007. WNBA Player of the Week twice in 2008; Detroit Sports Broadcasters Association Player of the Year, 2007. **Business Addr:** Basketball Player, Detroit Shock, 3 Championship Dr, Auburn Hills, MI 48326, **Business Phone:** (248)377-0100.*

NOLES, EVA M.
Nurse. **Personal:** Born Apr 5, 1919, Cleveland, OH; daughter of Charles Bateman (deceased) and Ola Neal (deceased); married Douglas Noles; children: Tyrone M. **Educ:** EJ Meyer Mem Hosp Sch Nursing, RN, 1940; Nursing Univ Buffalo, BS, 1962; State Univ NY Buffalo, MEd, 1967. **Career:** Nurse (retired); Roswell Park Mem Inst, staff nurse & head nurse, 1945-63, instr nursing & asst dir nursing, 1963-68; State Univ NY, Buffalo, clin assoc prof nursing, 1970-77; Roswell Park Mem Inst, chief nursing serv & training, 1971-74; EJ Meyer Mem Hosp, Nurses Practitioner Prog, coordr family planning, 1974-77; Med Personnel Pool Inc, home care supervisor & staff develop, 1977-84. **Orgs:** NY State Nurses Asn; Am Nurses Asn, 1941-; bd dirs, Am Cancer Soc, 1965-; NY State Bd Nursing, 1972-92; comt adv coun, State Univ NY, Buffalo, 1975-; chmn, Nursing & Health Serv ARC Greater Buffalo Chap, 1978-84; bd govs & chairwoman, Community Mental Health Ctr, Buffalo, NY, 1979-; bd dirs, ARC; bd trustees, Buffalo Gen Hosp; bd dirs, Boys & Girls Clubs Buffalo & Erie Co, 1985; bd dir, Greater Buffalo Chap Am Red Cross. **Honors/Awds:** Distinguished Serv Award, 1972; Distinguished Award, AAUW, 1972; Community Award, 1986; Culture Keepers Award, Uncrowned Queens Inst, 2002; Cert Merit, ARC Greater Buffalo Chap; Nat Award. **Special Achievements:** First AFA nurse educated in Buffalo NY EJ Meyer Mem Hosp, 1936-40; published "Six Decades of Nursing 1914-74", 1975; published Buffalo's Blacks "Talking Proud", 1987; author: Black History "A Different Approach - A Compilation", 1988; The Church Builder: The Life of Bishop Charles N McCoy, 1990; ; published Black History-A Different Approach. **Home Addr:** 780 Maryvale Dr, Buffalo, NY 14225. *

NOONAN, DR. ALLAN S.
Dean (education), physician. **Personal:** Born Dec 10, 1942, Providence, RI; son of Herbert Noonan and Agnes Noonan; married Martha Prescod. **Career:** New York State Health Dept, assoc comnr; Commonwealth Univ, Pa, secy health; Morgan State Univ, Sch Pub Health & Policy, prof & dean, currently; Dept Health DC, dir. **Military Serv:** US Public Health Service. **Business Addr:** Professor, Dean School Public Health & Policy, Morgan State University, School of Public Health and Policy, 1700 E Cold Spring Lane, Baltimore, MD 21251, **Business Phone:** (443)885-3238.

NORFLEET, JANET
Postmaster general. **Personal:** Born Aug 14, 1933, Chicago, IL; daughter of Willis Richards and Blanche Gilbert Richards; married Junious; children: Cedric Williams. **Educ:** Olive Harvey Col, AA, 1977; Duke Univ, The FUQA Sch Bus, exec develop prog, 1998; Univ Va Grad Sch Bus Admin, The Prog Postal Exec, 1988; Chicago State Univ, BA, 1997. **Career:** Postmaster general (retired); US Postal Serv, supt customer serv reps, pub affairs officer, mgr retail sales & serv, mgr delivery & collection, mgr N Suburban Ill mgt sect ctr, field div mgr, postmaster S Suburban Ill div,1986-87; field div gen mgr; postmaster Chicago Ill Div, 1987-90. **Orgs:** Bd dir, Carson Pirie Scott & Co, 1988-; bd mem, Red Cross; bd mem, Federal Executive; Chairman's Leadership Group, Nat Asn Advan Colored People. **Honors/Awds:** First Woman Postmaster of the US Postal Service Chicago Div; Partnership For Progress Award Postmaster General TISCH, 1986; Appointment Congressional Records by Congressman Savage 1987; Proclamation by Mayor Washington Janet Norfleet Day in Chicago 1987; American Black Achievement Award, Bus & Prof, Johnson Publ, 1987; African-American Award, Bus & Prof Women, Dollars & Sense Mag, 1989; Women's Hall of Fame, City of Chicago, 1990. **Home Addr:** 8217 S Evans Ave, Chicago, IL 60619-5305.

NORMAN, BOBBY DON
Artist, geologist. **Personal:** Born Jun 5, 1933, Dallas, TX; son of Bessie Taylor Gregory and Ruben; divorced; children: Parette Michelle Barnes. **Educ:** San Francisco City Col, 1951; USAF, Radio Electronics Tech, 1955; SW Sch Bus Admin, cert, 1959; Biblical Geol, 1 Corinthians 12=8, 1998. **Career:** Artist, writer & scientist, 1955-; Mile High Club Restaurant & Cabins, gen mgr, 1955-57; D H Byrd Properties, property mgr, 1957-65; US Post Serv, city distro clerk, 1959-66; Univ Chicago-Dallas, Nat Opinion Res Ctr, field eval researcher, 1969-70; AAAW, Inc Cult Gallery, dir, 1972; SCLC Dallas, TX, co-founder, off mgr & co-dir, 1970-72; Planned Parenthood NE Tex, community liaison, 1974-76; Davis Norman Zanders Inc, vpres & gen mgr, 1976-77, exec vpres, 1977-78; Davis,Norman, Zanders Inc, exec vpres, 1977-78; Halfway House Tex Dept Corrections, supvr, 1983-84; free-lance artist & inventor anti-collision car; biblical geologist, 1987-; self-employed tectonic analyst, 1988-; Books: 500 Shaft Tbl-Sports, 1973; Time of Babel: Biblical Geology & Tectonics, 1998; Biblical Geology & Tectonics, 1998; Tectonic Analyses & Notes of Modern Biblical Geology & Earth Science, 1998; Tectonic Fundamentals of Biblical Geology, 1998; Tectonic Verbal Posturing & Various Advanced Studies of Earth Science, 1998; Religious Art & Artistic Evangelism, 1998; Glossary & Cross Reference of Biblical Geology & Tectonics, 1999; Biblical Geology: Events, Writings & Geo-Morality, 2003. **Orgs:** Vpres, Forest Lakes Sportsmans Club; hunter safety instr, NRA, 1963; pres & founder, Asn Advancing Artists & Writers, 1969-74; Citizenship training, SCLC, 1969; founder & off mgr, Southern Christian Leadership Conf Dallas Br, 1969-73; comnr, Greater Dallas Comm Rels Comn, 1970-73; organizer & tech consult, Greater DFW Coalition FFI, 1971-74; alumnus Chi Rho Int Bus Fraternity; committeeman, Block Partnership Comm Greater Dallas Coun Churches, 1971-72; serv, GDCRC, 1973; fine arts, Dallas Black Chamber Com, 1973; Int Platform Asn Pub Speakers, 1977-78. **Honors/Awds:** Citizenship Training Award, SCLC, 1969; Art Award, Dallas Black Chamber Commerce, 1973. **Military Serv:** USAF, cpl, 1951-55; Korean Service Medal; UN Serv Medal; Good Conduct Medal; Nat Defense Medal. **Business Addr:** Artist, Art Religious, PO Box 191904, Dallas, TX 75219-8509.

NORMAN, CLIFFORD P
Executive. **Personal:** Born Mar 22, 1943, Detroit, MI; son of Leavi and Claudia Cloud; married Pauline C Johnson; children: Jays S & Rebecca L. **Educ:** Wayne State Univ, BA, 1974, MA, 1980. **Career:** Fisher Body Div GM, engr test, 1967-71, sr analyst qc, 1971-72, sr serv & tool spec, 1972-74, div process engr, 1974-76; Ford Motor Co, div staff engr, 1976-80; Glasurit Amer Inc, acct exec; BASF Corp, acct exec, mkt coordr, currently. **Orgs:** ESD, 1975-; Soc Engr & Applied Scis, 1975-82; Budget & Allocation Comn, UCS, Detroit, 1981-84, 1995-; u-f Speakers Bureau, 1985-; Big Bros Big Sisters, Metro Detroit, exec comt, 2000-; Big Bros Big Sisters Am, Region IV, pres, 2000-. **Honors/Awds:** One In A Million WDME Radio Detroit, 1976. **Military Serv:** USAF, a/2c, 1963. **Business Addr:** Marketing Coordinator, BASF Corporation, 26701 Telegraph Rd, Southfield, MI 48034-2442, **Business Phone:** (248)304-5771.

NORMAN, GEORGETTE M.
Educator. **Personal:** Born Jan 27, 1946, Montgomery, AL; daughter of George J Norman Jr and Thelma Juliette Graham. **Educ:** Fisk Univ, Nashville, TN, BA, hist, 1967; Hampton Inst, Hampton, VA, MA, educ, 1970; Univ Miami, cert humanistic Educ. **Career:** Leadership Montgomery Alumni Asn, 1987-; bd dir, chair, Homeowner Asn Montgomery Habitat Humanity, 1987-; panel mem, Lit & Rural Initiative Ala State Coun Arts, 1988-; bd dir, secy, Springtree/Snowhill Inst for Performing Arts, 1991; adv bd, multicultural chair, Armory Learning Ctrfor performing Arts, 1991; Am Arts Alliance, 1992-99; Troy Univ Rosa Parks Museum, dir, currently; Auburn Univ, Dept Communication & Dramatic Arts Montgomery, adj instr, currently. **Orgs:** Leadership Montgomery Alumni Asn, 1987-; bd dir, chair, Homeowner Asn

Montgomery Habitat Humanity, 1987-; panel mem, Lit & Rural Initiative Ala State Coun Arts, 1988-; bd dir, secy, Springtree/Snowhill Inst for Performing Arts, 1991; adv bd, multicultural chair, Armory Learning Ctr for performing Arts, 1991; founder, Am Arts Alliance, 1992-99. **Honors/Awds:** Teacher of Year, Claude O Markoe Jr High, 1974; Regional Grant for Theater Productions Womanrise: Her Story/Her Self, American Asn Univ Women, 1981; Teacher of the Year, St Joseph the Worker Catholic High, 1982; Citizen of Year, St Croix, Rotary Club West, 1984. **Business Addr:** Director, Troy University Rosa Parks Museum, 252 Montgomery St, PO Box 4419, Montgomery, AL 36103-4419, **Business Phone:** (334)241-8608.

NORMAN, JAMES H
Administrator. **Personal:** Born Aug 14, 1948, Augusta, GA; son of Silas Sr (deceased) and Janie M King (deceased); children: James H Jr. **Educ:** Mercer Univ, Macon, Ga, BA, psychol, 1970; Western Mich Univ, Kalamazoo, MSW 1972. **Career:** Western Mich Univ, Full Univ Grad fel, 1970-72; Douglass Community Asn, Kalamazoo, Mich, coordr job develop & placement, 1972-74; Kalamazoo Mich Pub Schs, parent consult, 1974-75; Oakland Livingston Human Serv, Pontiac, Mich, div mgr community develop, 1975-78; Mich Dept Labor, dir bur community serv, 1978-87; Mich Dept Labor, dep dir, 1987-92; Action For Better Community Inc, exec dir, pres & chief exec officer, currently. **Orgs:** Chmn & legis comn chair, Nat Asn State Community Serv Prog, 1981-82 & 1985-87; exec secy, Mich Econ & Social Opp Comn, 1983-87; Am Soc Pub Admin, 1984-; Assoc State Govt Execs, 1986-92; Nat Coun State Building Code Officials, 1988-90; Int Asn Personnel Employ Security, 1988-90; bd mem, Mich Asn Black Orgn, 1988-92; Greater Lansing Urgan League, 1989-92; adv coun mem, EOC, State Univ New York, 1993-; adv coun, Leadership Rochester, 1993-; life mem, Nat Asn Advan Colored People; Asn Black Social Workers; Phi Mu Alpha Nat Music Frat; Omega Psi Phi Frat Inc; life mem, Western Mich Univ Alumni Assoc. **Honors/Awds:** Community Serv Award, Nat Alliance Businessmen, 1973 & 1974; Outstanding Young Man of America, US Jaycees Publ, 1978 & 1979; Hall of Distinction, Western Mich Univ, 1980; Service Award, Nat Asn State Community Serv Prog, 1983. **Business Addr:** President, Chief Executive Officer, Action For a Better Community Inc, 550 E Main St, Rochester, NY 14604, **Business Phone:** (585)325-5116.

NORMAN, JESSYE
Opera singer. **Personal:** Born Sep 15, 1945, Augusta, GA; daughter of Silas Norman Sr and Janie King Norman. **Educ:** Howard Univ, BM (Cum Laude), 1967; Peabody Conserv Music, 1967; Univ MI, M Mus, 1968. **Career:** Deutsch Opera, Berlin, debut, 1969; Deutsch Opera, Italy, 1970; Opera: Die Walkure, Idomeneo, L'Africaine, Marriage of Figaro, Aida, Don Giovanni, Tannhauser, Gotterdammerung, Ariadne auf Naxos, Les Troyens, Dido & Aeneas, Oedipus Rex; La Scala Milan, Italy, 1972; Salzburg Festival, 1977; Hollywood Bowl, US debut, 1972; appeared with Tanglewood Festival MA, Edinburgh, Scotland Festival; Covent Garden, 1972; appeared in first Great Performers Recital Lincoln Ctr, New York, 1973; guest performances: LosAngeles Philharmonic Orch, Boston Symphony Orch, Am Symphony Orch, Chicago Symphony Orch, San Fran Symphony Orch, Cleve Orch, Detroit Symphony, NY Philharmonic Orch, London Symphony Orch, London Philharmonic Orch, BBC Orch, Israel Philharmonic Orch, Orchestre de Paris, National Symphony Orch Australia; albums: Brava, Jessye!; Sacred Song: "With a Song in My Heart";"Christmastide", 1990; "Amazing Grace", 1991; "Jessye Norman at Notre Dame", 1991; "Lucky to Be Me", 1992; "In the Spirit", 1996; "Jessye Norman", 1999; "I Was Born in Love With You", 2000; Soundtrack: Revolution francaise, La, 1989; Wild at Heart, 1990; The Hours, 2002. **Orgs:** Gamma Sigma Sigma; Sigma Alpha Iota Pi Kappa Lambda. **Honors/Awds:** Numerous recordings Columbia, EMI, Philips Records; recip first Prize Bavarian Radio Corp Intl Music Competitor; Grand Prix du Disque Deutsch Schallplatten; Preis Alumniat MI 1982; Outstanding Musician of the Year Award, Musical Am, 1982; 5 Grand Prix du Disque, Acad du Disque Francais; Grand Prix du Disque, Academie Charles Cros, 1983; thirty hon doctorates from col & universities, decorations and distinctions from governments around the world including Hon Doctor Music, Howard Univ, 1982; hon Doctor Humane Letters, Am Univ Paris, 1989; hon Doctor Music, Cambridge Univ, 1989; Hon fel, Newnham Col, Cambridge, 1989; hon fel, Jesus Col, Cambridge, 1989; Musician of the Year, High Fidelity Musical/America, 1982; Grammy Awards for Best Opera Recording for Wagner: Lohengrin, 1984; Grammy Award for Best Classical Vocal Soloist Performance for Ravel: Songs of Maurice Ravel, 1988; appointment in 1990 as an hon UN ambassador; Women of the Arts Award, Coun Fashion Designers Am, 1992; Youngest Recipient of the US Kennedy Ctr Honor, 1997; Awarded hon doctorate for services to music from the Univ PA, Philadelphia, PA, 1998; Grammy Award for Best Opera Recording for "Bartok: Bluebeard's Castle, 1998; Georgia Music Hall of Fame, 1999; Outstanding Alumnae by Howard Univ, 2000; Eleanor Roosevelt Val-Kill Medal, 2000; Hammond Award, 2002; Grammy Lifetime Achievement Award, 2006; Named in honor, The Amphitheatre & Plz, Augusta, GA; Ace Award, Nat Acad Cable Programming; Amsterdam's Edison Prize. **Special Achievements:** The youngest recipient of the US Kennedy Ctr Honor, 1997; In Augusta, Georgia, the Amphitheatre and Plaza overlooking the tranquil Savannah River have been named for Jessye Norman. **Business Addr:** Opera Singer, Grabow Entertainment, 4219 Creekmeadow Dr, Dallas, TX 75287-6806, **Business Phone:** (972)250-1162.

NORMAN, KENNETH DARNEL
Basketball player. **Personal:** Born Sep 5, 1964, Chicago, IL. **Educ:** Wabash Valley Col, attended 1983; Univ Ill-Urbana Champaign, attended 1987. **Career:** Basketball player (retired); Los Angeles Clippers, forward, 1987-93; Milwaukee Bucks, 1993-94; Atlanta Hawks, 1995-97.

NORMAN, MOSES C
Educator. **Educ:** Clark Col, BA, 1957; Univ Mich, MA; Ga State Univ, PhD. **Career:** Luther Judson Price High Sch, eng dept chair, humanities proj leader, area supt & asst supt sec educ; Clark Atlanta Univ, dir alumni rels, Sch Educ, assoc prof & chmn educ leadership, currently; MASTER Inst, assoc dir, currently. **Orgs:** Grand basileus, Omega Psi Phi, Wash, DC, 1984-88. **Honors/Awds:** DHL, Clark Col. **Business Phone:** (404)880-8495.

NORMAN, P. ROOSEVELT
Dentist, air force officer. **Personal:** Born Sep 8, 1933, Mound Bayou, MS; married DeLois Williams; children: Philippa J, David W. **Educ:** Tougaloo Col, BS, 1955; Meharry Med Col, DDS, 1959. **Career:** Pvt Pract, dentist; Babe Ruth League Baseball Coach; Mound Bayou Community Hosp, dent consult; Frances Nelson Health Ctr, adv consult; Union Med Ctr Dental Serv, co-dir; Gen Dent Malcom Grow Reg Med Ctr USAF, officer in charge; Sheppard AFB TX, preventive dent officer; Misawa AFB Japan, air base oral surg; VA Hosp Tuskeegee, rotating dent internship. **Orgs:** Nat Dent Asn; Am Dent Asn; Acad Gen Dent; Am Soc Preventive Dent; Am Endodontic Soc; Military Surgeons Asn; LicensedPrac in IL, TX, DC, MD, NH, PA, MS; Omega Psi Phi Frat; Champaign Co C of C; Neighborhood Comdr Boy Scouts of Am; Career Counseling HS; bd dir, Boys Club Am Champaign Co; Univ Dent Res Team. **Honors/Awds:** Recipient music scholrship; Athletic Scholrship; mosby scholrship award for Scholastic Excellance. **Military Serv:** USAF; presently serving USAFR maj.

NORMAN, WALLACE
Controller, executive. **Personal:** Born 1961, Atlanta, GA. **Educ:** Univ Ga, polit sci degree, MBA (finance); Ga State Univ, master's prog, acct. **Career:** Fed Express, assoc financial analyst; Atlanta Falcons, controller, payroll & benefits mgr, 1989-. **Honors/Awds:** First minority controller, NFL. **Business Phone:** (770)965-3115.

NORMAN, DR. WILLIAM H
Psychologist. **Personal:** Born Dec 14, 1946, Sharon, PA; married Belinda Ann Johnson; children: Monica & Michael. **Educ:** Youngstown State Univ, BA, 1968; Howard Univ, MS, 1971; Duke Univ Med Ctr, psychol internship, 1974-75; Penn State Univ, PhD, 1975. **Career:** Butler Hosp, dir psychol consult prog, 1976-93, dir psychol, 1982-91, coordr, eating dis prog, 1987-; Brown Univ Internship Consortium, coordr adult clin psychol track comn 1983-92; Brown Univ Med Sch, assoc prof psychiat & human behav, 1986-. **Orgs:** Am Psychol Asn, 1975-; Asn Advan Behav Therapy, 1975-; Soc Psychotherapy Res, 1986-. **Honors/Awds:** Reviewer for several journals; J Abnormal Psychol & J Consulting & Clin Psychol; Master Arts ad eundem, Brown Univ, 1987; recipient/co-recipient, NIH grants, 1979, 1981, 1983, 1990, 1992. **Home Phone:** (401)294-6170. **Business Phone:** (401)455-6352.

NORMAN, WILLIAM STANLEY (BILL NORMAN)
Executive, president (organization), chief executive officer. **Personal:** Born Apr 27, 1938, Roper, NC; son of James Colbitt and Josephine Cleo Woods; married Elizabeth Patricia Patterson, May 31, 1969; children: Lisa Renee & William Stanley II. **Educ:** WVa Wesleyan Univ, BS, chem, 1960; Am Univ, MA, int rel, 1967; Stanford Univ Grad Sch Bus, exec prog, 1976. **Career:** Executive (retired); Wash High Sch, Norfolk, VA, teacher, 1961; Cummins Engine Co Inc, Columbus, IN, dir corp action, 1973-74, exec dir corp responsibility, 1974-76, exec mkt mgr, 1976-77, exec dir distrib & mkt, 1977-78, vpres eastern div, 1978-79; Amtrak, Nat RR Passenger Corp, Wash DC, vpres sales & mkt, 1979-81, group vpres, 1981-84, exec vpres, 1984-94; Travel Indust Asn Am-,Wash, DC, pres & chief exec officer, 1994-2005. **Orgs:** Bd dir, USN Mem Found, 1980; bd gov, UN Asn US, 1983; bd adv, Am Univ Kogod Col Bus Admin, 1990; bd dir, Best Foods Inc, 1993; bd trustees, Logistics Mgt Inst, 1993; bd dir, An-Bryce Found, 1994; bd trustees, W VA Wesleyan Col, 1996; bd dir, Corn Prod Int Inc, 1997. **Military Serv:** USN, naval flight officer, Airborne Early Warning Squadron Eleven, 1962-65, staff officer air weapons systs anal, Off Chief Naval Opers, Pentagon, Washington, 1965-66, social aide, The White House, 1967-69, history & foreign affairs instr, US Naval Acad, 1967-69, carrier div staff officer SE Asia, 1969-70; spl asst to Chief Naval Opers for Minority Affairs, 1970-72, asst to Chief Naval Opers for Spl Proj, 1972-73, capt, 1973.

NORMENT, LYNN A
Editor. **Educ:** Univ Memphis, attended 1973. **Career:** Johnson Publ Co, managing ed; Ebony Mag, managing ed, 1977-; Publicity Club Chicago, panelist, currently. **Orgs:** Vpres print, Nat Asn Black Journalists. **Special Achievements:** Published numerous articles. **Business Addr:** Managing Editor, Ebony Magazine, 820 S Mich Ave, Chicago, IL 60605, **Business Phone:** (312)322-9200.

NORRELL-NANCE, ROSALIND ELIZABETH
Government official. **Personal:** Born May 17, 1950, Atlantic City, NJ; daughter of Vivian M Rhoades-Norrell and Albert V Norrell Jr; married Nelson W; children: Kimberly, Alisha, Nelson Jr, Antonio, Noel & Patrick. **Educ:** Hampton Inst 1967-69; Atlantic Comm Coll, AS, 1974-76; Glassboro State Coll, BA, 1976-78. **Career:** Pleasantville Sch Dist, educr, 1976-84; City Atlantic City, mayoral aide, 1984-90; Atlantic City, councilwoman, 1992-, pres, 1994-2000; Atlantic City Pub Sch, Drug & Weapon Free Schs Prog, 1991-96; Atlanticare Family Ctr, dir, 1997; State NJ, Dept Educ, Atlanticare Behav Health, proj dir, currently. **Orgs:** Exec bd/youth adv, Atlantic City Nat Asn Advan Colored People, 1969-95; bd dirs, Atlantic Human Resources Inc, 1981-97; Nat Sorority Phi Delta Kappa Delta Lambda Chap, 1982-; govt affairs chairperson, 101 Women Plus, 1982-85; bd dirs, Minority Entrepreneur Develop Co, 1984-85; bd dirs, United Way S Jersey, 1984-85; bd dirs, Black United Fund, NJ, 1987; vpres, bd dir, Inst Human Develop; bd dirs, Atlantic City Coastal Mus, 1985-89; NJ State Bus & Prof Women; bd dir, Atlantic Human Resources; chairperson, Atlantic County Comprehensive Network Task Force Homeless Serv; Atlantic City Pub Rel Adv Bd; Nat Coun Colored Women's Clubs; bd dir, Atlantic Community Concerts, 1984-87; Ruth Newman Shapiro Cancer Fund; bd dir, Atlantic City Local Assistance; Healthy Mothers/Healthy Babies Coalition Atlantic City Hampton Alumni Asn; pres, mayor's youth adv bd, chair educ task force Cong Black Caucus; NJ State Div Youth & Family Services Adv bd, 1985-; bd dirs, Coalition 100 Black Women, 1987-; Atlantic County Red Cross, 1988-92; founder, Atlantic County Welfare Mothers Support Group, 1992-; Atlantic County Human Serv Adv Bd; Atlantic City Drug Alliance, 1990-; bd dirs, Atlantic County Transp Authority, 1986-92; Atlantic City Inc, 1994-; Links Inc, 1995-. **Honors/Awds:** Community Service Award, W Side Parent Adv Coun, 1976; Outstanding Leadership Award, Black Atlantic City Mag, 1983; Phi Delta Kappa-Leadership, NJ Div Youth & Family Serv, 1995. **Home Addr:** 101 Cherry Dr, Egg Harbor Township, NJ 08234. **Business Addr:** Project Director, Atlanticare Behavioral Health, Uptown School Complex 323 Madison Ave, Atlantic City, NJ 08401, **Business Phone:** (609)345-1994.

NORRELL-THOMAS, SONDRA
Athletic director, teacher. **Personal:** Born May 31, 1941, Richmond, VA; daughter of Faith Morris Norrell and Edinboro A Norrell; married Chauncey S Thomas, Jun 1, 1978 (died 1999). **Educ:** Hampton Inst, BS, phys educ & biol, 1961; Howard Univ, MS 1973. **Career:** Charlottesville Schs, teacher 1961-63; Richmond Pub Schs, teacher,1963-64; Howard Univ, teacher 1964-77, womens athletics coordr, 1972;assoc dir athletics, 1974-86, exec asst to vpres student affairs, 1986-2000, dir athletics, 2000, interim athletics dir, exec asst to vpres Stud Affairs, sr womens adminr athletics, dir athletics, 2001-04. **Orgs:** Spec Comn Womens Interest Nat Col Athletic Asn, 1983-85; coun, Nat Collegiate Athletic Asn, 1983-87; Div I Steering Comt, Nat Col Athletic Asn, 1983-87; spec liaison, Mid-Eastern Athletic Conf, 1983-; pres, Capital City Chap, Links Inc, 1987-89; Nat Col Athletic Asn Coun, 1995-99;Alpha Kappa Alpha Sor; Just Good Friends Inc; HUAA; Nat Coun Negro Women; Nat Asn Advan Colored People; United Way Dist Columbia Bd; consult, counpres & chancellors, Mid Eastern Athletic Conf; Acad-Eligibility &Compliance Cabinet & Nat Col Athletic Asn; Championships & Competition Cabinet, Nat Col Athletic Asn; chair SWAs Mid-Eastern Athletic Conf; nominating comt, Nat Asn Collegiate Women Athletic Adrs. **Honors/Awds:** Woman in Male-Dominated field, DC City Coun, 1983; IAA Administrator of the year, Nat Col Athletic Asn, 2004. **Special Achievements:** First female inducted into the Mid-Eastern Athletic Conference (MEAC) Hallof Fame, 1993; first female director of athletics in the history of Howard Univ; first female member of the committee that selected the conference's first full-time commissioner; first to serve as a consultant to the MEAC Council of Presidents & Chancellors. **Home Addr:** 1611 Webster St NW, Washington, DC 20011.

NORRIS, CHARLES L, SR.
Clergy. **Personal:** Born Aug 14, 1926, Williston, SC; married Ruby Dent; children: Keith & Charles Jr. **Educ:** National Theol Sem, BS, 1979, MDiv, 1984; Blanton Peale Inst, cert coun. **Career:** Kitchen Modernization, prod mgr, 1950-69; Bethesda Missionary Baptist Church, pastor, 1973, sr pastor, currently. **Orgs:** New York City Mission Soc Urban Ministries, 1981-; United Negro Col Fund Clergy Consortium, Queens County, 1985-; co-chair, Concerned Citizens South Queens, 1986-; The City New York Comn Human Rights, 1993-; vice moderator, Eastern Baptist Asn, Long Island Inc. **Honors/Awds:** Leadership & Dedication Award, Inwood-Nassau Community Health Comt, 1981; Outstanding Clergy Award, Nat Asn Negro Bus & Prof Women Queens Borough Club, 1983; Meritorious Service Award, 1985; Outstanding Leadership & Dedicated Service, 1986; United Negro College Fund. **Business Addr:** Senior Pastor, Bethesda

Missionary Baptist Church, 179-09 Jamaica Ave, Jamaica, NY 11432, **Business Phone:** (718)297-5908.

NORRIS, DR. DONNA M
Psychiatrist. **Personal:** Born May 28, 1943, Columbus, OH; married Lonnie H; children: Marlaina & Michael. **Educ:** Fisk Univ, Nashville, TN, BA, 1964; OH State Univ, Col Med, MD, 1969; Mt Carmel Med Ctr, Columbus, OH, intern, 1970; Boston Univ Med Ctr, residency, 1972; Childrens Hosp, Judge Baker Guidance Ctr, 1974. **Career:** Mass Rehab Community Roxbury & Quincy MA, psychol consult, 1974-79; Boston Juvenile Court Clinic, sr psychol, 1974-88; Harvard Med Schl, instr psychol, 1974-; asst psychol, 1974-83; Family Serv Assoc Greater Boston, med dir, 1981-89; C Hosp Med Ctr & Judge Baker Guidance Ctr, assoc psychol, 1983-; pvt pract, currently. **Orgs:** Am Acad Child Psychol, 1974-; Am Psychol Asn, fel, speaker assembly; Black Psychol Am; Soroptomist Asn, 1985-89; Links Inc, Middle Clearwater Chap, 1988-; Jack & Jill Am, 1978-; staff consult, Levison Inst, 1981-; Falk Fel, 1973-75; Exec Comt & Steering Comt to plan Conf on Psychol Educ, 1974-75; Task Force of Films, 1975-77; ed bd, Psychol Educ, Prologue to the 1980s, 1976-; Comn on Women, 1976-79; ed newsletter, Comn on Women, 1977-79; Spouses Sub-comn, 1977-78; Dep Rep to Leg Assembly Am Psychol Asn, 1981-83; Rep to Leg Assembly Am Psychol Asn, 1983-; Task Force on mem, Non-participation, 1983-85; Comn Black Psychol, Am Psychol Asn, 1984-; Site Visitor Ach Awards Bd, 1984; Mass Psychol Soc Boston, 1973-; Ethic Comn, 1978-88; Am Acad Child Psychol, 1974-; Rep to Mass CoMrthopsychiatric Asn Inc, 1983-; sr Mass rep, leg Assembly for Am Psychiatric Asn, 1986-; chp, membership comt, Am Psychiatric Asn, 1990-91; Mass Bd Regn Med, 1988-91; Bd Trustees, Univ Lowell, 1987-88; Secy-Treas, APA, currently. **Honors/Awds:** Falk Found, Am Psychol Asn, 1973-75; Am Bds Psychol & Neurol, 1978. **Special Achievements:** First woman and first African American to be named speaker of the American Psychiatric Asn. **Home Addr:** 54 Cartwright Rd, Wellesley, MA 02482. **Business Addr:** Secretary-Treasurer, American Psychological Association, Boston, MA 02133-2002.

NORRIS, FRED ARTHUR, JR.
Administrator. **Personal:** Born Nov 25, 1945, Ecorse, MI; son of Fred Arthur and Annie B Davis; married Betty Sue Graves, Nov 26, 1982; children: Tracy M Graves & Shawna L Norris. **Educ:** Wayne City Community Col; Wayne State Univ; Ind Univ; Univ Wis; Mich State Univ; George Meany Sch Labor. **Career:** City of Ecorse, council member 1974-87; Local 616 Allied Ind Workers, pres, beginning 1977; Detroit AFL-CIO, pres, currently. **Orgs:** United Black Trade Unionist, 1976; SPIDER, 1979; bd mem, Mich Downriver Comn Conf, 1979-; bd mem, Metro Detroit Chap A Philip Randolph Inst, 1984; Allied Indust Workers Human Rights; pres, Independence Alliance; Nat Black Elected Officials; secy, treas, New Ctr Med CLin; personal ministry dir, Ecorse Seventh Day Adventist Church; Elder Ecorse Seventh Day Adventist Church, 1989. **Honors/Awds:** Community Serv Award, Ecorse, 1981; Community Serv Award, Wayne County 1982; Little League Award, Ecorse Little League, 1982. **Business Addr:** President, Metropolitan Detroit AFL-CIO, 600 W Lafayette Suite 200, Detroit, MI 48226, **Business Phone:** (313)389-7038.

NORRIS, DR. JAMES ELLSWORTH CHILES
Surgeon. **Personal:** Born May 12, 1932, Kilmarnock, VA; son of Theresita Chiles Norris and Morgan E Norris, Sr; married Motoko Endo, Jun 21, 1967; children: Ernest Takashi. **Educ:** Hampton Inst VA, BS, 1953; Case Western Res Cleveland OH, MD 1957; Grasslands Hosp, internship, 1958; Queens Hosp Ctr Jamaica, gen surg res, 1966; Univ Mich Med Ctr, plastic surg res, 1974. **Career:** Kilmarnock Va & Melbourne, Fl, gen practr, 1958-62; Va Hosp, Tuskegee, chief Surg serv & dir surg res prog, 1969-72; Burn Unit Div Plastic Surg Harlem Hosp Ctr, chief, 1974-77; Hosp Joint Diseases & Med Ctr, assoc attend plastic surg, 1975-88; Jamaica Hosp, Jamaica, attend & chief plastic surg, 1975-88, consult plastic surg, 1988-90; Col Physicians & Surgeons, Columbia Univ, asst prof, clin surg, 1976-87; Div Plastic Surg Harlem Hosp Ctr, attend, 1977-87; St Lukes-Roosevelt Hosp Ctr, Manhattan, assoc attend plastic surg, 1981-97; Pvt pract, physician; Jamtak Int, consult & founder, currently. **Orgs:** Reed O Dingman Soc, 1974; Am Burn Asn, 1975-94; NY County Med Soc, 1975; NY State Med Soc, 1975; Am Soc Plastic & Reconst Surgeons, 1975, NY Regional Soc ASPRS, 1976, Lipoplasty Soc N Am, 1987-97, Am Cleft Palate Asn, 1988-94, Am Soc Laser & Med & Surg Inc, 1987-97; NY Acad Med, 1992-; vol surgeon, Juazerio do Norte, Brazil, 1999, Phillipines, Vietnam, 2001; Vietnam, 2002, 2003; Nat Asn Advan Colored People. **Honors/Awds:** Certified Nat Board of Medical Examiners, 1958; Certified American Board of Surgery, 1967; Certified American Board of Plastic Surgery, 1975. **Special Achievements:** Numerous med articles in various med journals. **Military Serv:** USNR, comdr, 1967-69. **Business Addr:** President, Jamtak International Inc, 144 E 90th St, New York, NY 10128-1139, **Business Phone:** (212)831-9313.

NORRIS, LAVENA M.
Real estate agent. **Personal:** Born in Chicago, IL; daughter of Robert W Collins and Annie M Collins; married Alvin Norris, Sep 6, 1970. **Educ:** De Paul Univ, BS, 1981. **Career:** LaVena Norris Real Estate, pres, 1986-; US Bur Census, Minority Bus Opportunity Comt, exec dir, 1991-. **Orgs:** Rho Epsilon, Prof Real Estate Fraternity, 1980-; C & Adolescents Forum, 1984-; pres, Dearborn Real Estate Bd, 1991-; Physicians Nat Healthcare Prog, 1991-; Nat Asn Real Estate Brokers, Invest Div, 1991-; bd dirs, Chicago Gray Panthers, 1992-; adv bd mem, Health & Med Res Group, 1992-. **Honors/Awds:** Kellogg Nat fel, WK Kellogg Found, 1991; Fair Housing Advocate Award, Nat Asn Real Estate Brokers Region IX, 1988; Presidential Serv Award, Nat Asn Real Estate Brokers, 1989; Dedicated Serv Award, Dearborn Real Estate Bd, 1985; Unsung Herione Award, Nat Asn Advan Colored People, 1983. **Special Achievements:** Author, "House Hunting", Black Family Magazine, 1982. **Home Addr:** 2772 E 75th St, Chicago, IL 60649, **Home Phone:** (773)978-0550. **Business Addr:** President, LaVena Norris Real Estate, 27 E Monroe St 11th fl, Chicago, IL 60603, **Business Phone:** (312)641-0084.*

NORRIS, LONNIE H
School administrator. **Personal:** Born in Houston, TX; married Dr Donna M Norris. **Educ:** Fisk Univ, BA; Harvard, MA, public health, MPH, dent med, DMD. **Career:** Tufts Univ Dent Sch, tenured prof oral & maxillofacial surg, currently, interim dean, 1995-96, dean, 1996-, resident. **Orgs:** Am Bd Oral & Maxillofacial Surg; Phi Beta Kappa; Am Dent Asn; consult, CMS Dent Accreditation; Am Acad Dent Sci; Am Col Dentists; Int Col Dentists; Pierre Fauchard Acad; rep, Am Dental Educ Asn. **Honors/Awds:** Distinguished Practitioner, Nat Acad Practice. **Special Achievements:** First African American dean of Tufts' dental school. **Business Addr:** Dean, Tenured Professor, Tufts University Dental School, 1 Kneeland St Ballou Hall, Medford, MA 02155, **Business Phone:** (617)627-3310.

NORRIS, WALTER
Government official. **Personal:** Born Jan 9, 1945, Jackson, MI; son of Walter Sr and Willie Mae Glaspie-Neely; married Rosie Hill, Aug 7, 1963; children: Gloria J, Anthony W, Vernon D & Shannon D. **Educ:** Spring Arbor Col, Spring Arbor, MI, BS, 1970; Mich State Univ, E Lansing, MI, Grad Study Educ Admin, 1979. **Career:** Jackson Community Col, Jackson, MI, fin aid dir, 1968-70; Norris Real Estate, Jackson, MI, owner & broker, 1970-76; Jackson Pub Sch, Jackson,MI, dir, minority affairs, 1970-76; Jackson Housing Comn, Jackson, MI, exec dir, 1976-79; Lansing Housing Comn, Lansing, MI, exec dir, 1978-88; Ypsilanti Housing Comn, exec dir, 1988-. **Orgs:** Nat Asn Housing & Redevelopment Officials; Mich Chap NAHRO; chmn, bd dir, Legis Comn; cert trainer, HAHRO Pub Housing Mgmt; Pub Housing Authority Dirs Asn; Tex Housing Asn; assoc mem, Galveston Historical Found, 1988-, Galveston Chap, Nat Asn Advan Colored People, 1988-; bd mem, Galveston Boys Club, 1988-, Galveston Chamber Com, 1988-, Rotary Club Galveston,1988-; bd dir, SOS community serv. **Honors/Awds:** Mens Union Award, Most Outstanding Young Man of the Year, Jackson Community Col, 1965; Sophomore Class Pres, Jackson Jr Col, 1965; Outstanding Young Man of the Year, Jackson Jaycees, 1968; Service Award,Outstanding Service & Contribution, HUD Prog, 1982; NAHRO Pub Housing Mgmt Cert. **Business Addr:** Executive Director, Ypsilanti Housing Commission, 601 Armstrong Dr, Ypsilanti, MI 48197, **Business Phone:** (734)482-4300.

NORRIS, WILLIAM E.
Automotive executive. **Career:** Utica Chrysler Plymouth Inc, chief exec officer, currently. **Business Addr:** Chief Executive Officer, Utica Chrysler Plymouth Inc, PO Box 214, Yorkville, NY 13495.*

NORTHCROSS, DR. DAVID C. **See Obituaries section.**

NORTHCROSS, DEBORAH AMETRA
School administrator. **Personal:** Born Jun 27, 1951, Nashville, TN; daughter of Theron and Nell. **Educ:** Mt Holyoke Col, BA, french, 1973; Memphis State Univ, MEd, spec educ, 1975. **Career:** School administrator (retired); Shelby St Comm Col, counr, 1973-76, dir spec serv prog, 1976-79, coordr fed affairs, 1979-81, asst dir, stud develop, 1981-83, dir stud retention, 1982-83, grants officer 1983-84, dir develop 1984; Univ Tenn Health Sci Ctr, Ronald E McNair Post bacca laureate Achievement Prog, dir, 2004-. **Orgs:** Field reader, US Dept Educ; pres, Tenn Asn Spec Prog, 1977-79; bd mem, Southeastern Asn Educ Opportunity Prog Personnel, 1978-79, currently; tutor, Memphis Literacy Coun, 1983-87; chairperson, Christian Educ Comn MS Blvd Christian Church, 1984-; chair nominating comt, YWCA, 1985, bd dir, 1986-, vpres, 1987, chair, Fin Develop Comt, 1988-; eval consult, US Dept Educ Spec Prog Training Grant, 1986-; vpres alumni asn, Leadership Memphis, 1987-88, bd mem, 1987-89, vice chair bd trustees, 1989-; bd trustee, Campaign Steering Comt, Mt Holyhoke Col, currently; Pres Comn, Diverse Community. **Honors/Awds:** Kate Gooch Leadership Award, leadership Memphis, 1989; Alumnae Medal of Honor, 2003. **Business Phone:** (413)538-2000.

NORTHCROSS, WILSON HILL, JR.
Lawyer. **Personal:** Born Dec 8, 1946, Detroit, MI; son of Wilson H Sr and Gwendolyn Pinkney; married Winifred C Wheelock, Apr 9, 1977; children: Jill Inez & Christopher Wilson. **Educ:** Wayne State Univ, BS, 1969; Harvard Univ, Law Sch, JSD, 1972. **Career:** Vice chmn, First Dist Young Dem, Detroit, 1967; Canfield, Paddock & Stone, atty, 1975-77, assoc, 1973-75; pvt law pract, 1975-77, 1981-83, 1987-; Mich Supreme Ct, assoc comnr, 1977-78; UAW Legal Serv Plan, Detroit, sr atty, 1978-81; Sr Citizens Law Prog, Legal Serv Southeastern Mich, Ann Arbor, dir, 1983-87. **Orgs:** Am Bar Asn; Mich State Bar Asn; bd dirs, Wolverine Bar Asn, 1973-74; Mem Church Christ. **Special Achievements:** Publication of "The Limits on Employment Testing," University of Detroit Journal of Urban Law, Vol 50, Issue 3, 1973. **Military Serv:** USAF, 1st lt, 1969-73. **Business Addr:** Attorney, 801 Sunrise Ct, Ann Arbor, MI 48103-3544, **Business Phone:** (734)668-6036.

NORTHERN, CHRISTINA ANN
Lawyer. **Personal:** Born May 21, 1956, Kansas City, KS; daughter of Emanuel and Christine. **Educ:** Wash Univ, BA, 1978; Antioch Sch Law, JD, 1981. **Career:** Self-employed, atty, 1987-. **Orgs:** Bd mem, chair fund raising & asst treas, New Columbia COT Land Trust, 1990-; Nat Bar Asn, 1981-; Am Friends London Econs, 1989-. **Business Addr:** 9039 Sligo Creek Pkwy Suite 707, Silver Spring, MD 20901, **Business Phone:** (301)562-9212.

NORTHERN, DAVID A
Executive. **Personal:** Born Sep 4, 1973, Lake County, Western Samoa. **Educ:** Ball State Univ, BS, acct, 1997; Ind Univ Northwest, MPA, pub mgt, 2003. **Career:** City E Chicago Housing & Community Develop, dir capital improv; Lake Co Housing Authority, dep dir, 2002-. **Orgs:** Lake Co Affordable Housing Team; adv bd, NICASA Women Servs; adv bd, Youth Build Lake Co; Allocations Comt, Lake Area United Way; life mem, Irish Universities Athletics Asn; Neal-Marshall Alumni Club NWI; Hoosiers Higher Educ; Ind Univ Alumni Club Chicago; Inst Innovative Leadership; Pi Alpha Alpha; Nat Honor Soc; Omega Psi Phi Fraternity. **Business Addr:** Deputy Director, Lake County Housing Authority, 33928 N Rte 45, Grayslake, IL 60030, **Business Phone:** (847)223-1170 Ext 203.*

NORTHERN, GABE. **See NORTHERN, GABRIEL O.**

NORTHERN, GABRIEL O. (GABE NORTHERN)
Football player, business owner. **Personal:** Born Jun 8, 1974, Baton Rouge, LA. **Educ:** La State Univ. **Career:** Football; Co owner: Buffalo Bills, linebacker, 1996-99; Minnesota Vikings, linebacker, 2000; Anytime Fitness,2002-. **Honors/Awds:** Most Valuable Player, 1995.

NORTHERN, ROBERT A.
Educator, musician, lecturer. **Personal:** Born May 21, 1934, Kinston, NC; son of Ralph and Madie. **Educ:** Manhattan Sch Music, attended 1953; Vienna State Acad Music Vienna, Austria, attended 1958; Howard Univ, grad. **Career:** Sym Air Orchestra, NYC, stage band, 1958-70; Metro Opera, NYC, 1958-59; Radio City Music Hall, Orchestra, 1963-66; Brass Instruments Pub Sch Syst, NYC, instr, 1964-67; Broadway Theatre Orchestra, NYC, staff, 1969-71; Jazz Composer Orchestra, NYC, staff, 1969-71; Dartmouth Col, Music Dept, artist-in-residence, lectr, 1970-73; Brown Univ Afro Am Studies Prog, lectr, 1973-82; Umoja Music Publ Co, owner & founder, 1973-; Divine Recs,owner, 1975-; World Music Ensemble, founder & dir, 1986; World Community Sch Music, founder & exec dir, 1986-; WPFW-FM, Wash, DC, founder &producer, 1993; CD "Celebration", World Music Ensemble Maple shade Recs, producer, 1993; composer & dir: Ode to Creation Dartmouth Col, 1970; Ti-Jean Dartmouth Col, 1971; Confrontation & Commun Dartmouth Col, 1971; Magical Mode Dartmouth Col, 1971; Forces Nature Brown Univ, 1974; Symbols Dartmouth Col, 1972; Child Woman Brown Univ, 1973; recordings: Meditation; Light from Womb; Open Sky. Smithsonian Inst, lectr, currently. **Orgs:** Charter mem, Soc Black Composers, 1965; founder, NY Wind Octet, 1966; founder, Sound Awareness Ensemble, 1968; founder, Radio Series Dimensions Black Sounds WBAI-FM, New York, 1970; Sound Awareness Vol Move Ever Onward III, 1975; New World Vol III, 1980; founder, World Community Sch Music; music dir, Black Fire Performing Arts Co, Birmingham. **Honors/Awds:** Mayor's Arts Award for Artistic Excellence, Wash, DC. **Military Serv:** USAF, a/1c, 1953-57. **Business Addr:** Founder, Chief Executive Officer, World Community School of Music, PO Box 56481, Washington, DC 20011, **Business Phone:** (202)829-5345.

NORTON, DR. AURELIA EVANGELINE
Clinical psychologist, educator. **Personal:** Born Feb 14, 1932, Dayton, OH; daughter of Joseph Turner and Aurelia DeMar; divorced. **Educ:** Wayne State, BA, 1961, MA, PhD; Central State Univ, Dayton. **Career:** Wayne State, res psychologist; Children & Emergency Psychiat Clin Detroit Gen Hosp, staff psychologist; Oak Park Sch Syst, psychologist; Chrysler Corp, psychologist; Children Hosp Consult Psychologist, res psychologist; Univ Cincinnati Multi Ethnic Br Psychol Serv, assoc prof psychol; Univ Cincinnati, Psychol Serv Ctr, dir training, emer fac, currently. **Orgs:** Numerous organizations including Am Psychol Asn; Asn Black Psychologists; Nat Asn Advan Colored People; Mt Zion Baptist Church. **Business Addr:** Emeritus Faculty, University of Cincinnati, Department of Psychology, 316 Dyer Hall, Cincinnati, OH 45221-0037, **Business Phone:** (513)556-0648.*

NORTON, CHERYL WEEK
Singer, songwriter. **Personal:** Born Oct 13, 1958, Los Angeles, CA. **Career:** Tabu Rec, rec artist, 1984-88; CBS Rec Inc, singer,

currently; Albums:Fragile, 1984; High Priority, 1986; Affair, 1988; The Woman I Am, 1991;The Best Of Cherrelle, 1995; The Right Time, 1999; Greatest Hits, 2005; Songs: "Artificial Heart", 1986; "Never In My Life", 1991; "Tears Of Joy", 1991; "Still In Love With You", 1991; "The Right Time"; "Just Tell Me", 1999; "I Wanna Get Next To You", 1999. **Business Phone:** (212)975-4321.*

NORTON, EDWARD WORTHINGTON
Government official. **Personal:** Born Apr 10, 1938, New York, NY; married Eleanor K Holmes; children: Katherine Felicia & John Holmes. **Educ:** Yale Univ, BA, 1959; Columbia Univ, LIB, 1966. **Career:** Lawyers const Def Com, 1966; Paul, Weiss, Rif kind, Wharton & Garrison, assoc, 1966-68; Legal Serv Prog NE Region OEO, dep dir, 1968-70; NY Health Serv Admin, spec asst to adminr, 1970-73; NY Univ Law Sch; adj asst proj, 1971-73; NY Housing Authority, gen coun, 1973-77; Dept Housing & Urban Develop, dep gen coun; Bus Humanitarian Forum USA Bd, chair, currently. **Orgs:** Equality comt, Am Civil Liberties Union, 1967-73; treas, Columbia Law Sch Alumni Asn, 1970-74; bd dir, NY Civil Liberties Union, 1971-74; vpres,Scholar Ed & Def Fund for Racial Equality, 1972-; 100 Black Men Inc,1974-; bd dir, Save The C Fedn, 1975-; Harlem Lawyers Asn, 1976-. **Military Serv:** USN, lt, 1959-63.

NORTON, ELEANOR HOLMES
Congressional representative (u.s. federal government), educator. **Personal:** Born Jun 13, 1937, Washington, DC; daughter of Coleman Holmes and Vela Holmes; married Edward, Jan 1, 1965 (divorced 1993); children: Katherine & John. **Educ:** Antioch Col; Yale Univ, MA, 1963; Yale Law Sch, JD, 1964. **Career:** Am Civil Liberties Union, asst legal dir, 1965-70; NY Univ Law Sch, adj asst prof law, 1970-71; NY Comn Human Rights, chair, 1970-77; US Equal Employ Opportunity Comn, chair, 1977-81; The Urban Inst, sr fel, 1981-82; Georgetown Univ Law Ctr, prof law, 1982; US House Rep, WA, DC, congresswoman, 1991-. **Orgs:** Rockefeller Found; Bd Gov, DC Bar Asn. **Honors/Awds:** Outstanding Alumna, Yale Law Sch; Yale Wilbur Cross Medal, Yale Grad Sch; Distinguished Public Service Award, Ctr Nat Policy, 1985; 60 honorary doctorates; Louise Waterman Wise Award. **Special Achievements:** First woman to chair the Equal Employment Opportunity Commission; publ articles: "Public Assistance, Post New-Deal Bureaucracy and the Law: Learning from Negative Models," Yale Law Jour, 1983; "The Private Bar and Public Confusion: A New Civil Rights Challenge," Howard Law Jour, 1984; "Equal Employment Law: Crisis in Interpretation, Survival against the Odds," Tulane Law Rev, 1988; author, Sex Discrimination and the Law: Causes and Remedies; listed in "100 Most Important Women", Ladies Home Jour, 1988; listed in "100 Most Powerful Women in Washington", The Wash Mag, 1989; featured on "Better Know A District" segment of Comedy Central's "The Colbert Report", 2006. **Business Addr:** Congresswoman, US House of Representatives, National Press Bldg, 529 14th St NW Suite 900, Washington, DC 20045, **Business Phone:** (202)783-5065.

NORTON, KENNETH HOWARD
Football player, football coach. **Personal:** Born Sep 29, 1966, Jacksonville, FL; son of Ken Norton Sr; married Angela; children: Brittney, Sabrina Brooke & Ken III. **Educ:** Univ Calif, Los Angeles, Bachelor's Degree, sociol, 1999. **Career:** Football Player (retired), Football Coach; Dallas Cowboys, linebacker, 1988-93; San Francisco 49ers, linebacker, 1994-2000; radio & TV commentator & analyst; Hamilton High Los Angeles, defensive coordr, 2003; Univ Southern Calif Trojans, defensive asst/ linebackers coach, 2004, linebackers coach, 2005-. **Honors/ Awds:** Linebacker, Sporting News Col, All-Am Team, 1987; Super Bowls XXVII-XXIX, 1992-94; Pro Bowl appearances, 1993, 1995 & 1997. **Special Achievements:** Autobiography: Going The Distance: The Ken Norton Story; Only player in NFL history to win three consecutive Super Bowl rings, 1992-94. **Business Phone:** (213)740-2530.

NORVEL, WILLIAM LEONARD
Clergy. **Personal:** Born Oct 1, 1935, Pascagoula, MS; son of William L Sr and Velma H. **Educ:** Epiphany Apostolic Col, 1956; St Joseph's Sem, BA, 1959; St Michael's Col, 1961; St Bonaventure Col, 1963; Marquette Univ, attended 1967. **Career:** Holy Family, asst pastor, 1965; St Augustine HS, teacher, 1965; Josephite Training Ctr, dir, 1968; St Joseph's Sem, staff asst, 1970; St Benedict Moor, pastor, 1971; St Brigid, pastor, 1979-83; consult Black Catholic Parishes USA, 1983-; Josephite Soc, consultor gen, 1983; Most Pure Heart Mary Church, pastor, 1987-91; St Peter The Apostle Parish, Pascagoula, pastor, currently. **Orgs:** Bd mem, Lithurgical Conf, 1978-82; bd mem, SCLC & LA, 1979, 1983; NAACP, 1983-85; pres, Black Catholic Clergy Caucus, 1985-87; trustee, bd Nat Black Catholic Congress, 1987. **Honors/Awds:** Community Action Award, Secretariat Black Catholics, 1978; Ecumenical Fellowship Award, Baptists, Muslims, AME, CME, 1981; Church God Christ & Holiness Churches LA Achievement Award, SCLC & LA, 1983; Service Award, Loyola Marymount Univ, 1983. **Business Addr:** Pastor, St Peter The Apostle Parish, 1715 Telephone Rd, Pascagoula, MS 39567, **Business Phone:** (228)762-1759.*

NORVELL, DR. MERRITT J.
Executive, athletic director, dean (education). **Personal:** Married; children: 2. **Educ:** Univ Wis, Madison, BS, MS & PhD. **Career:** IBM Corp, nat mgr mkt support servs & collegiate merchandising progs mgr; Mich State Univ, athletic dir, 1995; asst dean grad sch admin; asst vice chancellor; head football coach; TV & radio; officer & psychiat social worker; educ pract group, leader; Norvell group mkt firm, founder; DHR Int, exec vpres & managing dir & leader educ pract group, currently; NCAA Minority Male Leadership Inst, lectr, currently; Black Coaches Asn's Prof Develop Prog, lectr, currently; Div 1A Athletic Dirs & Minority Opportunities Athletic Asn Inc, consult, currently; Pres Principal, TNG and Associates, currently. **Orgs:** Bd mem, United Negro College Fund; NCAA Budget & Finance Cabinet; Big Ten Conference Budget Comt; chair, Madison Urban League; bd mem, Wis Special Olympics & Madison Wis Community Found Boar; mem, Kappa Alpha Psi Fraternity, mem, 100 Black Men, Inc. **Business Addr:** Executive Vice President, Managing Director, DHR International, 6639 Centurion Dr Suite 140, Lansing, MI 48917, **Business Phone:** (517)886-9010.

NORVILLE, ERLEIGH
Judge. **Educ:** Tex Tech Univ; Univ Tex Law Sch, JD, 1988. **Career:** Kaufman Co, Co Ct law judge, currently. **Orgs:** Tex State Bar Asn, 1989-. **Business Addr:** County Court at Law Judge, Kaufman County, Co Courthouse, 100 W Mulberry St, Kaufman, TX 75142, **Business Phone:** (972)932-4331.*

NORWOOD, BRANDY (BRANDY RAYANA NORWOOD)
Actor, singer. **Personal:** Born Feb 11, 1979, McComb, MS; daughter of Willie Sr and Sonja Bates; married Robert Smith, 2002; children: Sy. **Educ:** Pepperdine Univ. **Career:** Singer, actor, currently; Albums: Brandy, 1994; Never Say Never, 1998; Full Moon, 2002; Afrodisiac, 2004; The Best of Brandy, 2005; TV: "Thea", 1993-94; "Moesha", 1996-2001; "The Parkers", 2001; "Sabrina, the Teenage Witch", 2002; "Reba", 2002; "American Dreams", 2004; "House", 2005; "One on One", 2006; "I Love LA", 2006; TV movies: Cinderella, 1997; Double Platinum, 1999; Films: Arachnophobia, 1990; I Still Know What You Did Last Summer, 1998; Osmosis Jones, 2001. **Honors/Awds:** Grammy Award; Am Music Award, favorite new artist, 1996. **Special Achievements:** Song "Baby" climbed to no 5 on Billboard's pop charts. **Business Addr:** Vocalist, c/o Atlantic Recordings, 1290 Ave of the Americas, New York, NY 10104, **Business Phone:** (212)275-2000.

NORWOOD, BRANDY RAYANA. **See NORWOOD, BRANDY.**

NORWOOD, CALVIN COOLIDGE
State government official. **Personal:** Born Apr 1, 1927, Tunica, MS; son of Hester and Willie; married Ida Williams, Feb 14, 1946; children: Doris Norwood Jernigan, Deloris Norwood Sanders, Demetrice NorwoodBurnette & Regina. **Educ:** Coahoma Jr Col, GED, 1979. **Career:** Co Rd Dept Co Turstee Bd Rosa Fort Sch, foreman; Miss St Highway Dept,Tunica County, black jury comn supvr; Miss Dept Transp, road supvr. **Orgs:** Pres, Nat Asn Advan Colored People, 1966-97; EDA Bd; Co Dem Party; Legal Aide Bd Joint Commun Activ & Job Care; mem st bd, Nat Asn Advan ColoredPeople; VFW. **Honors/Awds:** Job Core Cert Job Core, 1979; Politician Action Award, Nat Asn Advan Colored People, 1980; Ed Award, Nat Asn Advan Colored People, 1980; Programmatic Award, Nat Asn Advan Colored People, 1985-86, 1990; Recognition Appreciation, Miss State Highway Dept, 1989. **Military Serv:** USN, std third class, 1944-46; served overseas Island of Guam 18 mo's.

NORWOOD, KIMBERLY JADE
Educator. **Personal:** Born Aug 18, 1960, New York, NY; daughter of Ahmad Akbar and Marietta Holt; married Ronald Alan, Jul 2, 1988; children: Candice Jade, Ellis Grant & Donnell Bussey. **Educ:** Fordham Univ, BA, 1982; Univ Mo, JD, 1985. **Career:** Hon.Clifford Scott Green, law clerk, 1985-86; Bryan Cave et al, litigation assoc, 1986-90; Univ MO-Columbia, vis lectr, Cleo Prog, 1990; Wash Univ Sch Law, prof law, 1990-, prof African & African Am Studies, currently. **Orgs:** Am Bar Asn, 1986-; Mound City Bar Asn, 1986-; Bar Asn Metro St Louis, 1986-; Ill Bar Asn, 1987-; bd mem, St Louis Women Lawyers Asn, 1993-94; bd mem, Greeley Comn Asn, 1993-94; Am Asn Law Sch, 1993-; Jack & Jill Am, 1994-96; bd mem, Girls Inc, 1994. **Honors/Awds:** American Jurisprudence Award, 1983; Judge Shepard Barclay Prize, 1984-85; Bernard T Hurwitz Prize, 1984. **Special Achievements:** Articles include: "The Virulence of Blackthink & How Its Threat of Ostracism Shackles Those Deemed Not Black Enough," 93 Kentucky Law Journal 144 (2005), "Shopping for a Venue: The Need for More Limits on Choice," Miami Law Review (1996), & "Double Forum Shopping & the Extension of Ferens to Federal Claims that Borrow State Limitations Periods," Emory Law Journal (1995). **Business Addr:** Professor of Law, Professor of African and African American Studies, Washington University School of Law, 1 Brookings Dr Anheuser-Busch Hall Rm 561, PO Box 1120, Saint Louis, MO 63130, **Business Phone:** (314)935-6416.

NORWOOD, DR. TOM
School administrator, lecturer. **Personal:** Born Jul 19, 1943, Baton Rouge, LA; son of Edward A Norwood Sr and Corinne Burrell; married Marjorie Marshall; children: Teri Lynn & Tony. **Educ:** Southern Univ A&M Col, BS, art & eng, 1964, MEd, educ admin, 1969; Univ NE Lincoln, PhD, educ admin, 1975. **Career:** Dean (retired); Omaha Pub Sch, traveling art teacher, 1964-65, jr high art teacher, 1965-68, jr high coun, 1968-70; Col Educ Univ NE Omaha, asst dean, 1970-83, assoc prof, 1983-88; Univ Wisc-River falls, asst dean & prof. **Orgs:** Pres, 1981-83, vpres, NE Coun Teacher Educ; workshop dir, Joslyn Art Mus"Forever Free Exhibit" 1981; workshop dir, Sioux Falls SD City Dept Heads,"Racism & Sexism" 1979; vpres Greater Omaha Comm Action, 1975; Appointedby US Dist Court Judge Albert Schatz, 1976; Urban League NE, 1983-84;consult Omaha Pub Sch re Implementing Discipline Based Art Educ Prog,1987-87. **Honors/ Awds:** Phi Delta Kappa Southern Univ & A&M Col, 1964; hon mention Water color Coun Bluffs IA Art Fair, 1972; book "Contemporary Nebr Art & Artists" Univ NE Omaha, 1978; article "Facilitating Multicultural Educ Via the Visual Arts" NE Humanist 1980; 1st pl award NE Art Educ Competition, 1982; paintings selected nat & int juried competitions, Nat Miniature Competition, 1983, Nat Exhibit Contemporary Realism, 1983, Mo Int Miniature Competition, 1983, Int Small Fine Art Exhibit, 1984, Int Miniature Competition, 1984, Biennial Juried Competition, Nat 1984, Tenth Int Miniature Competition, 1985; commissioned St NE create poster design for first state observance of Martin Luther King, Jr holiday, 1986; First Annual Nat NC Miniature Painting Show Cert of Merit, 1985; Second Annual NC Nat Miniature Painting Show Second Place Watercolor, 1986; Arts W juried Competition, Eau Claire, WI, 1993-94; participated in 17 exhibition, 1985-87; commissioned by Chancellor of UW-RF to produce painting "Celebration of Diversity," 1990; Achiever of the Year, Greater St Paul YMCA Black Achievers Prog, 1991. **Home Addr:** 11 Morningview Pl, Pueblo, CO 81008. *

NORWOOD, WILLIAM R.
Pilot. **Personal:** Born Feb 14, 1936, Centralia, IL; son of Sam and Allingal; married Molly F Cross; children: William R, George A. **Educ:** Southern Ill Univ, BA, 1959; Univ Chicago, MBA, 1974. **Career:** Pilot (retired); Airline pilot first officer, 1968-83; second officer, 1965-68; United Airlines, capt, 1983-96. **Orgs:** Bd trust, Southern Ill Univ, 1974-01; commencement speaker, Shawnee Community Col, 1975; NAACP, 1985-; Airline Pilots Asn; United Air Lines Speakers Panel; charter mem, Org Black Air Line Pilots; bd dirs, Suburban Chap, SCLC; pres, bd trustees, State Univ Retirement Syst; Ill Comt Black Concerns Higher Educ; Southern Ill Univ Alumini Asn. **Honors/Awds:** United Airlines Corp Community Rels Award, 1991; O'Hare Capt of the Year, United Airlines, 1995; Chicagoan of the Year, 1995; Southern Ill Reunion Coun Founders Award, 1996; United Airlines Black Prof Orgn Outstanding Achievement & Leadership Award, 1996; Alpha Kappa Alpha Monary Award Winner, 1997; Destiny Church Community Serv Award, 1997; Southern Ill Univ Distinguished Alumni Award; Ill Educ Asn Friend of Educ Award; Flight Opers Div Spec Achievement Award; Carbondale ROTC Hall of Fame, Southern Ill Univ; Carbondale Athletic Hall of Fame, Southern Ill Univ; Boeing 727 Aircraft Named in Honor of Capt William R Norwood; Black Wings, Smithsonian Inst Nat Air & Space Mus, Washington. **Special Achievements:** First African-Am Pilot with United Air Lines;Ffirst African-Am Quarterback SIU. **Military Serv:** AUS, pilot B-52 & capt, 1959-65. *

NOTICE, REV. GUY SYMOUR
Clergy, educator. **Personal:** Born Dec 6, 1929; son of Eugena Amanda Young and Daniel Ezekiel; married Azelma Matilda, Nov 9, 1955; children: Donald Hylton & Sandra Simone. **Educ:** Bethel Bible Col, cert, 1954; Amer Divinity Sch, BTh, 1972; Fordham Univ & Goddard Col, BA, 1974; Luther Rice Sem, MA, 1991; European Theol Sem, PhD, 1998; Logos Grad Sch, PhD, religious philos, 1999. **Career:** Tutorial Col, vice chmn, 1965-69; conv speaker, England, Canada, Dallas TX, Mexico, Eastern Caribbean, US Virgin Islands, 1968-81; Bethel Bible Col, dir educ 1973-77; Jamaica Theol Sem, bd mem; New Testament Church God, supt, 1982; justice of the peace, 1985. **Orgs:** Chmn, Nat Chest Clinic, 1982; guest speaker, Conf PR, 1985; chmn, Hope Inst; chmn bd, Bethel Bible Col. **Honors/Awds:** Certificate of merit, Opa Locka City, 1982. **Special Achievements:** Authored - Prison Life: The Jamaican Experience, 1991. **Business Addr:** PO Box 680205, Orlando, FL 32818.

NOWLIN, BETTYE J ISOM
Educator, publicist. **Personal:** Born in Knoxville, TN; daughter of Jettie Isom and Elizabeth; married Thomas A Nowlin III, Mar 12, 1957; children: Thomas IV, Mark & Brett. **Educ:** Tenn A&I State Univ, BS, 1956; St Lukes Hosp & Med Ctr, Dietetic Internship, RD, 1957; Univ Calif, Los Angeles, MPH, 1971. **Career:** Cook County Hosp, therapeutic dietitian, 1957-59; Michael Reese Hosp, admin dietitian, 1959-61; Chicago Bd Educ, teacher, 1961-63; Chicago Bd Health, pub health nutritionist, 1962-68; Delta Sigma Theta, Head Start, nutritionist, 1968-70; Dairy Coun CA, mgr, adult nutrition prog, 1970-90, pub affairs mgr, 1990-. **Orgs:** Alpha Kappa Alpha Sorority, 1952-56; deleg, Am Dietetic Asn, 1957-, media spokesperson, 1982-; deleg, Calif Dietetic Asn, 1968-; Calif Nutrit Coun, 1970-; Soc Nutrit Educ, 1971-; Am Pub Health Asn, 1972-; Nutrit Educ Pub, 1980-; Nat Asn Female Exec, 1995-; Am Sch Food Serv Asn, 1993-; dietitians bus & comm, pub health, Am Dietetic Asn, Practice Groups. **Honors/Awds:** Distinguished Serv

Award, Excellence Community Nutrit, 1990; Medallion Award, Am Dietetic Asn, 1994. **Special Achievements:** Publications: Development of a Nutrition Educ Program for Homemakers; Society for Nutrition Educ Journal; Leader-Led and Self Instruction Work Site Programs; Keep It Short & Simple, Journal of American Dietetic Assn; Marketing Social Programs, The Competetive Edge, ADA Mkting Manuel, 2nd Editon. **Business Addr:** Public Affairs Manager, Dairy Council of California, 1101 Nat Dr Suite B, Sacramento, CA 95834-1901, **Business Phone:** (916)263-3560.

NOWLIN, FRANKIE L
Foundation executive, executive. **Personal:** Born in Huntington Beach, CA. **Educ:** Marshall Univ, grad; W Va Univ, grad sch; Ohio State Univ, grad sch. **Career:** Tri-State Opportunities Industrialization Ctr Inc, exec dir, 1973-84; Pvt Indust Coun Columbus & Franklin Co, Prog Oper Dept, dir, 1984-89; Borden Found, prog adminr, 1987-89, adminr, 1989-91, exec dir, 1991, pres, 1996-2001; Borden Inc, dir social responsibility, 1996-2001; YWCA, Columbus, dir anti-racism & race rels, vpres racial justice. **Orgs:** Marshall Univ Found; United Way, Safety Vision Coun; adv, The Col Fund/UNCF; trustee, Keystone Col; trustee, secy, Mt Carmel Col Nursing; trustee, pres, Ctr New Directions; trustee, vpres, Martin Luther King Arts Complex; trustee, The Conf Bd, Contribs Coun II.

NUNERY, LEE. See NUNERY, DR. LEROY DAVID, II.

NUNERY, DR. LEROY DAVID, II (LEE NUNERY)
Administrator. **Personal:** Born Dec 22, 1955, Jersey City, NJ; son of Leroy C and Thelma Jones; married Carolyn Thomas, Apr 24, 1982; children: Leroy David Nunery III. **Educ:** Lafayette Col, BA, hist, 1977; Wash Univ, MBA, finance, 1979; Univ Pa, EdD, 2003. **Career:** Leroy Nunery & Sons Inc, vpres, 1973; Edward D Jones & Co, res analyst, 1978-79; Northern Trust Co, community banking officer, 1979-83; First Nat Bank Chicago, vpres, 1983-87; Swiss Bank Corp, dir, 1987-93; Nat Basketball Asn, vpres, human & info resources, 1993-97; Univ Pa, vpres bus serv, 1999-2005; Edison Schs, Charter Sch Div, pres, 2005-. **Orgs:** Bd dir, Chicago Community Ventures, 1980-83; nat pres, Nat Black MBA Asn, 1986-89; dir, Family Resource Coalition Inc, 1988-90; trustee, Lafayette Col, 1988-; nat conf chairperson, Nat Black MBA Asn, 1991; bd dir, Pitney Bowes Inc, 1991-94; Nu Beta Beta Chap, Omega Psi Phi Fraternity Inc; dir, 1997-99; Fin Performance & Stand Comt Blue Cross Blue Shield Asn Inc; dir, WXPN-FM; dir, Enterprise Ctr W Philadelphia; dir, Enterprise Ctr Capital Corp; dir, W Philadelphia Partnership; dir, Univ City Dist; Philadelphia Conv & Visitors Bur; dir, Philadelphia Sports Cong. **Honors/Awds:** Black & Hispanic Achievers, YMCA, 1983, 1986; Outstanding MBA of the Year, Nat Black MBA Asn, 1984; Am Best & Brightest, Dollars & Sense Mag, 1987; Alumni Recognition Award, Wash Univ Bus Minority Coun 1987. **Home Addr:** 56 Hawthorne Pl, Montclair, NJ 07042-2604. **Business Addr:** President, Edison Schools Inc, Charter School Division, 521 Fifth Ave Fl 11, New York, NY 10175, **Business Phone:** (212)419-1600.

NUNES KIRBY, MIZAN ROBERTA PATRICIA (MIZAN ROBERTA PATRICIA KIRBY)
Actor. **Personal:** Daughter of Joe and Bertina. **Educ:** Colby Col, Waterville, ME, 1970; Univ Chicago Divinity Sch, attended 1974; Franklin & Marshall Col, AB, 1973; Am Conserv Theatre, San Francisco, attended 1978. **Career:** Ctr Theatre Tech Educ, actor & teacher, 1983-85; NY Univ Creative Arts Team, Crisis Resolution Through Drama, co-creator, 1985-87, Schomburg Ctr Res Black Cult Tribute Langston Huges I've Known Rivers Ceremonial Actor, 1991; Frank Silver as Writers Workshop, am reporter, 1992; Almas Rainbow, actor & contrib feature film, 1994; Angel Child Prods, LLC, founder & chief exec officer, 1997-2002; NY Univ & Actors Equity Asn, CAGE Afro Centric, writer & performer, 1998-2000; Lock Down, 2000-01; campaign rep, 2001; Taking Back New York, reading series, 2001; INN Report, anchor, 2002-; Film: The voice of "Midnight Ravers; Ethnic Bacchanal; The Occultist; Crooklyn, The Mind, 2009; dir; Married To The Mob, dir; Sounds that waft through his film heighten the visual impression of pure, free wheeling vitality; Fortunes of the Moor; Shakin' The Mess Outta Misery. **Orgs:** Nat Asn Advan Colored People, 1970-; Screen Actors Guild, 1988-2000; dist coordr, Nichiren Shoshu Temple, 1998-2002; judge, Nat Acad Arts & Sci, 1996-2000. **Honors/Awds:** Award in the Arts, Lincoln Ctr, 1969; Actress Extra ordinaire, State NY, 1981; Nominee, Recognition Award, Audience Develop Comt Inc, 1990; Clifford A Ridley Citation for Notable Achievement in Theater, Philadelphia Inquirer, 1992-93; Golden Reel Award, 2003. **Special Achievements:** Awarded one year course of study in African political studies at Univ of Lagos, Nigeria, 1971, History of Religions, co-presenter, Univ of Chicago, 1974, Theatre for the Forgotten, 1981, United Nations, "I, Marcus Garvey", benefit performer, 1990, Abysinnian Baptist Church, "The Glory of the African Diaspora", commentator, 1991, WBAI, Pacifica Public Radio, "Tribute to the Martyrs", presenter, 1991, "Tribute to Nestor Robert Marley", guest speaker, 2000, wrote and acted in "Incidents" at Playwrights Horizons Voice & Vision Production: 1,000 years of women playwrights, 1997. **Business Addr:** Actor, Andreadis Talent Agency, 119 W 57th St Suite 711, New York, NY 10019, **Business Phone:** (212)315-0303.

NUNEZ, MIGUEL A
Actor, movie producer, movie director. **Personal:** Born Aug 11, 1964, New York City, NY. **Career:** TV Series: "Rhythm & Blues', 1992; "My Wildest Dreams", 1995; "Sparks", 1996; "The Faculty", 1996; "Homeboys in Outer Space", producer, 1996; "Tour of Duty", 1987; "Tarzan", 2003; "Joey", 2005-06; "Joey & the Critic", 2006; "Joey & the Wedding", 2006; TV Films: Secrets, 1992; WEIRD World, 1995; films: For Richer or Poorer, 1997; Why Do Fools Fall in Love, 1998; Life, 1999; If You Only Knew, 2000; Nutty Professor II, 2000; MacArthur Park, 2001; Flossin, 2001; ZigZag, 2002; Scooby Doo, 2002; Juwanna Man, 2002; Pluto Nash, 2002; Up Against the 8 Ball, dir, 2004; Bathsheba, 2005; Flip the Script, producer, 2005; Clean Up Men, 2005; Kickin It Old Skool, 2007; All Lies on Me, co-producer, 2007. **Business Addr:** Actor, Abrams Artists Agency, 9200 Sunset Blvd Suite 1130, West Hollywood, CA 90069, **Business Phone:** (310)859-0625.

NUNN, JOHN
Executive. **Personal:** Born Sep 19, 1953, Berkeley, CA; son of John and Yvonne Hunter; married Valmere Fischer, Jul 3, 1977; children: Arianna M, Julian G & Micheala Y. **Educ:** St Mary's Col, Moraga CA, BS, Biol, 1971-76; Univ Calif, Berkeley 1975. **Career:** World Savings, Alamo CA, asst vpres br mgr, 1976-78; Am Savings, Oakland CA, asst vpres br mgr, 1979-80, El Cerrito CA, vpres regional mgr, 1980-85, Stockton CA, sr vpres office chief admin officer, 1985-87, Stockton CA, sr vpres, NC Aea Mgr, 1987-89; Community Outreach & Urban Develop, sr vpres dir, 1989; Washington Mutual Bank, sr vpres, currently. **Orgs:** Alumni Bd, Bishop O'Dowd HS Prep, 1980-85, pres, 1985-87; Stockton Chamber Com, 1987-; Stockton Black Chamber Com, 1987-; Sacramento Chamber Com, 1987-; Calif League Savings Inst, 1988-; Bus Sch Adv Bd, Calif State Univ, 1988-. **Business Phone:** (206)461-2000.

NUNN, ROBINSON S.
Judge, legal consultant. **Personal:** Born Sep 29, 1944, Blytheville, AR; married Glanetta Miller. **Educ:** Mich State Univ, E Lansing, MI, BA, social sci, 1966; Am Univ, Wash Col Law, Wash, DC, JD, 1969. **Career:** US Tax Ct, Wash, DC, legal asst, 1969; Little Rock, AR, gen prac law, 1976; Small Bus Admin, Gen Coun Off, chief coun ethics, 1977-; US Tax Ct Bar, 1978; US Supreme Ct Bar, 1978. **Orgs:** Am Bar Asn; Nat Bar Asn, 1973-; Ark Bar Asn, 1973-; US Dist Ct, Eastern Dist Ark, 1973; US Dist Ct, Western Dist Ark, 1973; Nat Asn Advan Colored People; Kappa Alpha Psi Fraternity; pres, Mich State Black Alumni Asn, 1982-. **Military Serv:** USMC, capt, 1974-77. **Business Addr:** Chief Counsel for Ethics, Small Business Administration, General Counsel Office, 409 3rd St SW 7th Fl, Washington, DC 20416-0005.

NUNN, RONNIE
Basketball player, basketball coach, basketball executive. **Personal:** Born in Brooklyn, NY. **Educ:** George Washington Univ, phys educ; Brooklyn Tech, educ, sixth yr cert in admin & supv. **Career:** Basketball player (retired), basketball coach; Nat Basketball Circuit, basketball player; NY Knicks, basketball player; Houston Rockets, basketball player; NJ Nets, basketball player; Brooklyn Tech, asst coach; Pace Univ, asst coach; Nat Basketball Asn, prof staff; Nat Pro-Am, mem; Western CT State Univ, coaching staff; Nat Basketball Asn, referee, 1984-03; Nat Basketball Asn, dir of officials, currently. **Orgs:** Concerned Black Men for Youth; Hord Found; Officiating Develop Alliance.; mem, Nat Pro-Am. **Honors/Awds:** Inducted, George Wash Univ Hall of Fame; Basketball Player Decade, Leon Mexico, 1970. **Special Achievements:** Created Nunn-Better referee camp. **Business Addr:** Director of Officials, National Basketball Association, 645 5th Ave Fl 10, New York, NY 10022-5986, **Business Phone:** (212)407-8000.*

NUNNALLY, DAVID H.
Educator, executive. **Personal:** Born Oct 16, 1929, Athens, GA; married Ileane I Nesbit; children: 1. **Educ:** Union Bapt Inst; Tuskegee Inst; Atlanta Univ; Univ Ga; Gov State Univ, MS; Loyal Univ Chicago, PhD. **Career:** Educator (retired), executive; Kennedy-Ing Col, counr, teacher, Jr HS counr, HS counr, residential counr, Stud Personnel Serv, dir; Comm Adult HS, asst dir, athletic coach employ counr, camp counr; Ga Dome, personnel asst; Clarke County Sch Dist, brd dir, currently. **Orgs:** Parent Teacher Assn; Am Fedn Teachers; Nat Educ Assn; Phi Delta Kappa; Vet Foreign Wars; APGA; IGPA; Int Chiropractic Pediat Assn; Ga Assn Educr; past dir, Dist IX Assn Educ; past mem, Assn Educ Brd Dir; Chicago Heights Leadership Forum; founder, Athens Chap Ita Iota Lambda; Lions Int Club;Alpha Phi Alpha; Masonic Lodge; sponsor, Comm Serv Club; troop scoutmaster; Sch Brd, Clarke County Sch Dist, 1992-; mem, Exec Comt, North east Ga Boy Scouts Coun. **Honors/Awds:** BSA Outstanding Male Teacher, Am Teacher Assn, 1964; Martin Luther King Hum Rel Award, Eta Iota Lambda Chap, 1970; Man of Yr, Eta Iota Lambda Chap & Ga Alpha Phi Alpha, 1970; Athens Rotary Club; Four Way Test Award, 2001; GFuneral Svc Practitioners Asn Inc COT Award, 2001; South Atlantic RegionAKA Sorority Inc Trailblazer Award, 2001; Outstanding Community ServiceAward, Creative Vision Found Inc, 2001. **Military Serv:** AUS, sp 2, 1951-53. **Business Addr:** Board of Directors, Clarke County School District, Clarke County Board of Education, 185 N Rocksprings St, Athens, GA 30606.

NUNNALLY, JONATHON KEITH
Baseball player. **Personal:** Born Nov 9, 1971, Pelham, NC. **Educ:** Miami-Dade Community Col. **Career:** Baseball player (retired); Baseball coach; Kansas City Royals, 1995-97; Cincinnati Reds, 1997-98; Boston Red Sox, 1999; New York Mets, 2000; Orix BlueWave; 2000. Milwaukee Brewers, left fielder; Pittsburgh Pirates, outfielder, 2005; Kinston Indians, hitting coach, 2006-. *

NUNNERY, WILLIE JAMES
Lawyer, government official. **Personal:** Born Jul 28, 1948, Chicago, IL. **Educ:** Univ Kans, Lawrence, BS, 1971; Univ Wis Sch Law, JD, 1975. **Career:** Atlantic Richfield, jr anal engr, 1971; Energy Res Ctr, Univ Wis, Col Eng, asso dir; Atlantic Richfield, legal intern, 1972; Univ Wis, Col Eng, asst dean, 1972-75; State WI, dep sec energy, 1975-; Midwestern Gov Energy Task Force; Four Lakes Area Boy Scout Coun, WI, scout master & exec dir; Univ Wis, Sch Eng, adj assoc prof, 1984-85; pvt prac atty; Nunnery Law Firm, atty, currently. **Orgs:** WI State Bar, 1976-; Downtown Kiwanis Club Madison & Greenfield; Baptist Church; Pres Comt, Nat Medal Sci, 1989; bd dir, Young Men Christian Asn. **Business Addr:** Attorney, Nunnery Law Firm, Bank 1 Bldg 802 W Broadway, Madison, WI 53713-1866, **Business Phone:** (608)224-1900.

NURSE, RICHARD A
School administrator. **Personal:** Born Sep 1, 1939, New York, NY; son of Reginald and Bernice Lawless; divorced; children: Allison & Richard C. **Educ:** Brown Univ, Providence, RI, BA, 1961; NY Univ, New York, NY, 1968; Univ Rhode Island, Kingston, RI, MPA, 1973. **Career:** Vpres (retired), exec dir; AUS, France & Ger, counter intelligence, 1962-64; Prudential Ins Co, Newark, NY, actuarial correspondent, 1964-66; AUS Electronics Command, Fort Monmouth, NJ, contract specialist, 1966-68; Brown Univ, Providence, RI, assoc dir admis, 1968-73; Stockbridge Sch, Stockbridge, MA, headmaster, 1973-76; Rutgers Univ, New Brunswick, NJ, asst vpres, undergrad educ, 1976; Crossroads Theatre Co, exec dir, 2004-. **Orgs:** Bd trustees, Princeton Friends Sch, 1986-94; coun mem, New Jersey Basic Skills Coun, 1978-90; state chmn, New Jersey Alumni Brown Univ, 1986-90; bd dirs, Planned Parenthood League Middlesex County, 1989-94; co-chmn, Dance Power, 1988-; bd trustees, Princeton Ballet; treas, Ctr Health & Social Policy; bd trustees, Arbor Glen Quaker Continuing Care Retirement COT; Grad Sch Bd, New School Univ. **Honors/Awds:** Pres, Brown Univ, 1961 class; Alumni Service Award, Brown Univ, 1990; Alumni Trustee Nominee, Brown Univ, 1976, 1978, 1988, Admin Service Award, NJ Asn Veterans Prog Adminrs, 1985. **Military Serv:** AUS, Spec 4th Class, 1962-64, 513th Intelligence Group Award, 1964. **Home Addr:** 27 Lilac Way, Piscataway, NJ 08854-3596, **Home Phone:** (732)627-9229. **Business Addr:** Executive Director, Crossroads Theatre Company, 7 Livingston Ave, New Brunswick, NJ 08903, **Business Phone:** (732)545-8100.

NUTT, REV. MAURICE JOSEPH
Clergy. **Personal:** Born Dec 20, 1962, St Louis, MO; son of Haller Levi and Beatrice Lucille Duvall. **Educ:** Holy Redeemer Col, BA, philos, 1985; Cath Theol Union, MDiv, 1989; Xavier Univ, LA, ThM, 1989; Aquinas Inst Theol, DMin, 1997-. **Career:** St Alphonsus Rock Church, St Louis, Mo, from assoc pastor to pastor, 1989-93; St. Louis Univ, adj prof theol, 1990-91; Redemptorist priest; Bd Police Comnr, pres, St. Louis, MO; Holy Names, pastor, currently. **Orgs:** Pres, Nat Black Cath Seminarians Asn, 1986-87; mem bd dir, Nat Black Cath Clergy Caucus, 1986-89; Seminarians Asn, 1988; organizer & speaker, Redemptorist Conf Black Ministry, 1989; pres, bd dirs, Better Family Life Inc, 1990-98; bd dirs, St Charles Lwanga Ctr, 1990; Portfolio Art Gallery, 1993; St Louis Civil Rights Comn, 1994; exec comt, Nat Asn Advan Colored People, St Louis Br, 1994; Young Democrats St Louis, 1994; vpres, bd dir, Nat Coun Drug & Alcohol Abuse, St Louis Chap, 1995. **Honors/Awds:** Man of the Year Award, St Joseph Preparatory Col, 1980; The Fr Clarence Williams Award, Nat Black Cath Seminarians Asn, 1988; Rodel Model Award, St. Louis Pub Sch, 1990; Forty Under Forty Award, St. Louis Mag, 1990; Trumpet of Justice Award, Institute for Peace & Justice, 1994; Young Democrats St Louis, 1994; Finalist, Greater Preacher Award, Aquinas Inst Theol, 1995; Steller Performer Award, St Louis American Newspaper, 1996; The John Simon Civic Service Award, Maryville Univ, 1997. **Special Achievements:** The first Black pastor of the hist St Louis Parish; publ: Black Vocations: The Responsibility and Challenge 1987. **Business Addr:** Pastor, Holy Names, 3141 Sandwich St, Windsor, ON, Canada N9C 1A7.

NWA, WILLIA L DEADWYLER
Educator, pianist. **Personal:** Born in Cleveland, OH; daughter of Thurman and Josephine; married Umoh Nwa, Sep 4, 1971; children: Idara, Jakitoro, Ayama, Ifiok & Uko. **Educ:** Cleveland Inst Music, 1965-66; Ohio State Univ, BS, 1971; Wittenberg Univ, 1973-74; Univ Akron, MS, 1975, PhD, 1992. **Career:** Seventh Avenue COT Baptist Church, pianist, organist, 1970-71; Northeastern Local Schs, educr, 1971-74; Canton City Schs, educr, 1975-; Univ Akron, supvr, 1989; Malone Col, adj prof, 1997-. **Orgs:** Exe comt, Coun Exceptional C, Chap 464; Nat Educ Asn; Ohio Educ Asn; Canton Prof Educr's Asn; Ohio Teachers Exceptional C; Asn Supv & Curric Develop; Am Educ Res Asn; Kappa Delta Pi, Alpha Theta Chap; Pi Lambda Theta, Beta

Lambda Chap, exec com; Nat Alliance Black Sch Educrs; Leila Green Alliance Black Sch Educrs; Nat Congress Parents & Teachers Asn; Sunday Sch; Deaconess Bd, former asst soc; Missionary Soc; E Cent Ohio Educ Asn. **Honors/Awds:** Forest City Foundaries, Charles F Seelback Scholar, 1966; Ohio State Univ, Alice A White Scholar, 1970; Canton City Schs, grant; Univ Akron, Univ Scholar, 1989; Recognition by Coun for Exceptional Children, 1993; Kurdziel Ed Grant, 1995; Educ Partnership Grant, 1995; Outstanding Educr, 1996; YWCA Hall of Fame, Stark County, 1998. **Special Achievements:** Co-author, "Reading for Survival," 1988; Presentation at the 38th Biennial Convocation, Memphis, Tenn, Kappa Delta Pi, theme: Excellence in Educ, 1992; dissertation, "The Extent of Participation in Extracurricular Activities at the Secondary Level of Students with Different Exceptionalities in an Urban School District," 1992; Lecturer 13th-17th Annual Intl Conference of Critical Thinking and Educational Reform, Sonoma State Univ, 1993-96. **Business Addr:** Educator, Canton City Schools, 521 W Tuscarawas St, Canton, OH 44702, **Business Phone:** (216)456-8779.

NWAGBARAOCHA, JOEL O
School administrator, dean (education), college president. **Personal:** Born Nov 21, 1942; son of John Oluigbo and Christiana; married Patsy Coleman; children: Eric, Jason, John & Jonathan. **Educ:** Norfolk State Univ, BS, 1969; Harvard Univ, MEd, 1970, EdD, 1972. **Career:** Inst Serv, Div Acad Planning & Fac Develop, dir, 1972-74; Morgan State Univ, vpres plan & opers anal, 1978-84; Tech Systs, pres, 1982-86; Voorhees Col, vpres, acad affairs, 1985-90; Barber-Scotia Col, pres, 1990-94; Strayer Univ, dean grad studies, campus dean of fac, 1994-, interim univ pres, 2006, provost, currently. **Orgs:** Bd dirs, Harvard Univ Coop Soc; bd dir, Harvard Univ Phi Delta Kappa Chap; bd dir, C Inst; bd dir, Higher Educ Support Serv; bd dir, African Relief Fund Inc; Higher Educ Group Wash, DC; Am Coun Educ; Nat Coun Social Studies; Am Humanist Asn. **Honors/Awds:** Training Teachers of Teachers; Beta Kappa Chi; Phi Delta Kappa. **Business Addr:** Provost, Dean of Faculty, Strayer University, 8335 IBM Dr Suite 150, Charlotte, NC 28262-4329, **Business Phone:** (704)717-2380.

NWANNA, DR. GLADSON I N
Educator. **Personal:** Born May 12, 1954, Mbonge, Cameroon. **Educ:** Essex County Col, AS, acct, 1977, AA, 1978; Rutgers State Univ, BA, acct, 1979; St Johns Univ, MBA, fin, 1980; Fordham Univ, PhD econ, 1984; Am Inst Banking, cert, 1985. **Career:** NJ Blood Ctr, distrib clerk, 1978-79; St Benedict High Sch, math teacher, 1979-80; Essex County Col, adj prof math & bus, 1981-84; Kean Col, NJ, asst prof fin & econ, 1983-85; Rutgers State Univ, adj prof math, 1984; Morgan State Univ, prof fin, 1985-. **Orgs:** Who's Who in Am, Jr Col Essex County Col, 1978; Rutgers State Univ, Int Stud Org, 1978-79, Am Econ Asn, 1983-, Eastern Fin Asn, 1985; Alpha Epsilon Beta, Essex County Col, 1979; Omicron Delta Epsilon, 1980; Beta Gamma Sigma, St Johns Univ, 1981; World Acad Devel & Coop, 1986-; Nat Asn Advan Colored People, 1986; Nat Urban League, 1986; World Acad Devel &Coop, 1986; Soc Int Devel, 1986. **Honors/Awds:** Student of the Month, Essex County Col, 1978. **Special Achievements:** Co-Author: Savings Mobilization in the Rural Sector: Strategic Options for Developing Economies: Proceedings of the Annual Meeting of the International Academy of African Business and Development, 2001; "Stock Dividend Announcement & Information Signaling theory", "Savings Mobilization in the Rural Sector: Strategic Options for Developing Economies", 2003; "Debt Burden and Corruption Impacts: African Market Dynamism", 2003; "Market Liberalization & Exchange Rate Exposure: The Case of Taiwanese Exporting Firms", 2003; Author and publ for several articles and books. **Business Addr:** Professor of Finance, Morgan State University, Department of Accounting and Finance, 608 McMechen Hall 1700 E Cold Spring Lane, Baltimore, MD 21251, **Business Phone:** (443)885-3254.

O

O, FREDRICK WILLIAM, JR.
Engineer, consultant, government official. **Personal:** Born Dec 8, 1948, Chicago, IL; son of Fredrick W and Essie M Reed. **Educ:** Roosevelt Univ, Chicago, IL, BS, 1985; Keller Grad Sch Mgmt, Chicago, IL, MBA, 1987. **Career:** Commonwealth Edison Co, Chicago, IL, efficiency technician, 1966-71; Western Union Telegraph Co, Chicago, IL, computer technician, 1972-88; City Chicago, Dept Fleet Mgmt, prin systs eng, 1988-96, dir, data processing, 1996-. **Orgs:** Telecommunications Profs; City Chicago, Dept Fleet Mgmt, Dir Info Systs, 2002-. **Business Addr:** Director of Data Processing, City of Chicago, Department of Fleet Management, 1685 N Throop St, Chicago, IL 60622, **Business Phone:** (312)744-7587.

OAKLEY, CHARLES
Basketball player. **Personal:** Born Dec 18, 1963, Cleveland, OH. **Educ:** Va Union Univ, Richmond, 1985. **Career:** Basketball player (Retired); Chicago Bulls, forward, 1985-88, New York Knicks, 1988-98; Co-Founder, Oaktree Entertainment; Toronto Raptors, 1998-2001; Chicago Bulls, 2001-02; Washington Wizards, 2002-03; Houston Rockets, forward, 2003-04. **Honors/Awds:** Led NCAA Division II in rebounding 1985; NBA All-Rookie Team, 1986; NBA All-Defensive Team, 1994; NBA All-Star, 1994; NBA All Star, 1994; NBA All Defensive Team Selection, 1998. *

OATES, CALEB E.
Clergy. **Personal:** Born Apr 5, 1917, Shelby, NC; married Authella Walker; children: Bernard D, David C. **Educ:** Union Sem; Jewish Theol Sem. **Career:** Baptist Church, ordained minister, 1947; Bethany Baptist Church, pastor, 1947-. **Orgs:** Fed Baptist Church Orgn; pres, chmn, Howell-Farmingdale Juv Bd, 1965-; pres, Howell-Farmingdale Coun Churches, 1968-72; bd dir, Howell Rotary Club, 1973-; pres, Farmingdale Howell Rotary Club, 1974; pres, Gen Baptist State Conv, NJ, 1980-88; vpres, Nat Baptist Conv, 1980-88; pres, Black Ministers Conf, NJ, 1990-; Elem Sch C Howell, mentor. **Honors/Awds:** Pastor of the Yr, NJ, 1953; Cert of Merit, Community Act Jewish War Veterans, 1961; Honoree, Nat Baptist Conv, 2005; Outstanding Citizen, Howell Township. **Special Achievements:** Celebrated his 53 year as pastor, Bethany Bapt Ch, Farmingdale, NJ. **Military Serv:** AUS, ETO, chaplain, 1943-45; Bronze Star; 5 Battle Stars, NJ Distinguished Serv Medal, 1998. **Business Addr:** Pastor, Bethany Baptist Church, W Farms Rd, Farmingdale, NJ 07727.*

OATES, GISELE CASANOVA. **See CASANOVA, DR. GISELE M.**

OATES, WANDA ANITA
Athletic director. **Personal:** Born Sep 11, 1942, Washington, DC; daughter of Robert L Oates Sr and Ruth Dorothy. **Educ:** Howard Univ, Wash DC, BS, 1965; George Wash Univ, Wash DC, MA, 1967. **Career:** Athletic dir (retired); F W Ballou High Sch, athletic coach, athletic dir, 1988-94. **Orgs:** Delta Sigma Theta Sorority. **Honors/Awds:** Coach of the Yr, Eastern Bd of Athletic Officials; Outstanding Achievement Award, Howard Univ Alumni Club; Coach of the Yr, Inter high East, 1991; DCPS & DCIAA Service Award, 1997; Sports Pioneer Award, Nat Assn of Black Journalists, 1998; Distinguished Service Award, DC Coaches Asn, 1999; inductee, DC Coaches Hall of Fame, 2000, Athletic Coaches Association's Hall of Fame, 2009. **Home Addr:** 5700 4th St NW, Washington, DC 20011. *

OBAMA, BARACK
President (U.S. federal government). **Personal:** Born Aug 4, 1961, Honolulu, HI; son of Barack Obama Sr and Ann Dunham; married Michelle, Jan 1, 1992; children: Malia & Sasha. **Educ:** Occidental Col; Columbia Univ, BS, polit sci, 1983; Harvard Law Sch, JD, 1991. **Career:** Baskin-Robbins, staff; Chicago, community organizer, 1983-87; Church-based Group, staff, 1985; Univ Chicago Law Sch, sr lectr const law, 1991-2004; Miner, Barnhill & Galland Law Firm, lawyer; Ill State Senate, 13th Cong Dist, rep, 1997-2004, US sen, 2005-2008, President of the United States, 2009-. **Orgs:** Pres, Harvard Law Rev; Senate Health & Human Serv Comt, 2003; chair, Chicago Annenberg Challenge. **Honors/Awds:** Hon Doctorates of Law, Knox Col; Hon Doctorates of Law, Univ Mass; Hon Doctorates of Law, Northwestern Univ; Hon Doctorates of Law, Xavier Univ; Newsmaker of the Year Award, Nat Newspaper Publ Asn, 2004; Chairman's Award, NAACP, 2005; Grammy Award, 2006. **Special Achievements:** first African American president of the Harvard Law Review; author, autobiography, Dreams From My Father, 1992; named among "Forty under Forty," Crain's Chicago Bus, 1993; named among "Fifty Most Intriguing Blacks of 2004," Ebony; listed as one of "10 people who could change the world" by New Statesman, 2005; appeared on various TV shows; auth, The Audacity of Hope Crown, 2006; first African American Democratic presidential nominee, 2008; first African American U.S. President, 2009. **Business Addr:** President, The White House, 1600 Pennsylvania Avenue NW, Washington, DC 20500, **Business Phone:** (202)456-1414.

OBAMA, MICHELLE
First Lady (U.S. federal government).**Personal:** Born Jan 17, 1964, Chicago, IL; daughter of Fraser Robinson and Marian Robinson; married Barack Obama; children: Malia, Sasha. **Educ:** BA, Princeton Univ, 1985; JD, Harvard Law School, 1988. **Career:** Univ of Chicago, VP Comm Affairs, 2005-; First Lady of the United States, 2009-.**Business Addr:** First Lady, The White House, 1600 Pennsylvania Avenue NW, Washington, DC 20500, **Business Phone:** (202)456-1414.*

O'BANNER-OWENS, JEANETTE
Judge. **Personal:** Born in Detroit, MI. **Educ:** Wayne State Univ, Monteith Col, BA, Wayne State Law Sch, JD. **Career:** Thirty Sixth Dist Ct, Detroit, MI, judge, 1988-, pres, currently. **Orgs:** Pres, Mich Dist Judges Asn; Asn Black Judges, 1997; Fed Bar Asn; Am Bar Asn; State Bar Mich; Am Judges Asn; Detroit Bar Asn; treas, bd mem, Wolverine Bar Asn; Judicial Conf; Nat Bar Asn; Nat & Int Asn Women Judges; fac adv, Nat Judicial Col; Supreme Ct Update; Harvard Law Sch; Wayne State Univ Law Sch; Friends Wayne Med Sch; 36th Dist Ct, Law Day, organizer; Wayne County Criminal Advocacy Prog; Phi Alpha Delta Fraternity; founders soc, Detroit Inst Arts; Downtown Detroit Lion's Club; Nat Judicial Col; Founder's Soc, Detroit Inst Arts; Mich Cancer Found; Feed C; Citizen Ambassadors, Zinta Int; Nat Assocs Women Judges; Int Assocs Women Judges. **Special Achievements:** Guest speaker, Continuing Legal Advocy Lawyers, Criminal Div. **Business Addr:** Judge, 36th District Court, 421 Madison Ave Suite 3068, Detroit, MI 48226, **Business Phone:** (313)965-8724.

O'BANNO, DONNA EDWARDS (DONNA MARIA)
Lawyer. **Personal:** Born Jun 26, 1957, New York, NY; daughter of Theodore U (deceased) and Ione Dunkley; divorced; children: Danielle Salone & Dionne Teddie. **Educ:** Wellesley Col, BA, 1979; Univ Va Law Sch, JD, 1982. **Career:** Exxon Co USA, tax atty, 1982-85; Harris County DA, asst, DA, 1985-87; US Equal Employment Opportunity Comn, atty, 1987-88; sr atty, 1988-89, admin judge, 1994-; FDIC, Consolidated Off, staff atty, 1989-90, Litigation Dept, head, 1990-92, sr regional atty, 1992-94. **Orgs:** Hundred Black Women, 1989-94; int trends chair, Links Inc, 1992-94, historian, 1994-96, corresp secy, 1996-; adv coun, Thurgood Marshall Recreation Ctr, 1996-, vpres, 1994-96, pres, 1996-; Jack & Jill Am Inc. **Honors/Awds:** Pinkston Camp Award, Mooreland YMCA, 1991. **Special Achievements:** Tax article, UVA Tax Rev, 1982. **Home Addr:** 2122 Elderoaks Lane, Dallas, TX 75232-3309, **Home Phone:** (214)339-0309. **Business Addr:** Administrative Judge, US Equal Employment Opportunity Commission, 207 S Houston St, Dallas, TX 75202, **Business Phone:** (214)253-2700.

O'BANNON, CHARLES EDWARD
Basketball player. **Personal:** Born Feb 22, 1975, Lakewood, CA. **Educ:** Univ Calif, Los Angeles, 1997. **Career:** Detroit Pistons, guard & forward, 1997-99; Polonia, Polish Basketball League, Warsaw, Poland, player, 2002; Italian League, Suns. **Honors/Awds:** CBS & Chevrolet Most Valuable Player of the Game. *

O'BANNON, EDWARD CHARLES, JR.
Basketball player, car dealer. **Personal:** Born Aug 14, 1972, Los Angeles, CA. **Educ:** Univ Nev, Las Vegas, attended. **Career:** Basketball player (retired), car salesman; New Jersey Nets, 1995-96; Dallas Mavericks, 1997; car salesman, Las Vegas auto dealership, currently. **Honors/Awds:** NCAA Champion, 1995; NCAA Basketball Tournament Most Outstanding Player, 1995. *

OBAYUWANA, ALPHONSUS OSAROBO
Physician. **Personal:** Born Jul 26, 1948, Benin City, Nigeria; son of William and Irene Osemwegie; married Ann Louise Carter, Jun 11, 1977; children: Alphonsus, Anson. **Educ:** High Point Univ, BS, 1973; Howard Univ, MS, 1977, Col Medicine, MD, 1981. **Career:** South Baltimore Gen Hosp, intern, 1981-82; Harbor Hosp Ctr, resident, 1982-85; Johns Hopkins Univ, Sch Med, instr, 1985-86; Group Health Assoc, obstetrician/gynecologist, 1986-93; Univ Md, Col Med, dept obstet & gynec, clinical fac position; Mitchell-Trotman Med Group, 1993-97; Kaiser-Permanente Med Group, 1997; Eastern Va Med Sch, asst prof, currently; EVMS Ghent Family Prac, Div Family Obstet & Gynec, physician, currently. **Orgs:** Prin investr, Inst Hope, 1982-; Am Med Asn; Nat Med Asn; Am Soc Psychosomatic Obst & Gynec; consult, Female Care Ctr, Silver Spring, MD, 1985-; pres, Asn Nigerian Physicians Americas, 2000. **Honors/Awds:** fel, Am Col Obstet & Gynec; Dipl, Nat Bd Med Examiners; Dipl, Am Bd Obstet & Gynec; National Resident Research Paper Award. **Special Achievements:** Co-author "The Hope Index Scale," 1982; "Psychosocial Distress and Pregnancy Outcome", 1984. **Business Addr:** Obstetrician, Gynecologist, Private Practice, 2700 London Blvd, Portsmouth, VA 23707.*

OBEN, ROMAN DISSAKE
Football player, founder (originator). **Personal:** Born Oct 9, 1972, Cameroon; son of Marie; married Linda; children: Roman Jr & Andre. **Educ:** Louisville, BA, econ, 1995; Fairleigh Dickinson Univ, MPA, 2001; ForkUnion Mil Acad. **Career:** Football player (retired); NY Giants, tackle, 1996-99; Cleveland Browns, 2000-01; Tampa Bay Buccaneers, 2002-03; San Diego Chargers, tackle, 2004-08; internship with US Congressmen Dennis Kucinich, OH & Bill Pascrell, NJ. **Orgs:** Vpres, Alpha Phi Alpha Fraternity; founder, Roman Oben Found, 2002; charter mem, NFLPA Benefits Com; vpres, Corporate Playbook, 2009. **Honors/Awds:** Louisville Community Serv Award, 1994; four-time Athletic dir Hon Roll;offensive game ball, 1999; Vince Lombardi Champion, Vincent T Lombardi Found, 2003; Alumni Player of Week, 2004-05; Super Bowl XXXVII, Man of the Yr, Big Brothers Big Sisters San Diego, 2007. **Business Phone:** (727)786-2223.*

OBI, JAMES E.
Manager, chairperson. **Personal:** Born Sep 2, 1942, Lagos, Nigeria; married Olubosede Cecilia; children: Funke, Femi, Siji, Uche. **Educ:** St Peter's Col, Oxford Eng, BA, 1963; Am Col, Life Underwriters, CLU, 1973. **Career:** Equit Life Assurance Soc of the US, agent, 1967-68, dist mgr, 1968-72, agency mgr, 1972, dir of mgt dev, 1991; The Obi Group, chmn, 1992-. **Orgs:** bd mem, Nigerian-Am Friendship Soc, 1979-; past mem, Bus Adv Comn of the Bus Coun for the United Nations; past mem, Corp Coun on Africa; Million Dollar Round Table; Crescent Investment Group Inc; TLC Beatrice Int Foods Inc; Glaucoma Trust Found; Forum

for World Affairs; Nigerian-Am Alliance. **Honors/Awds:** National Management Award; Master Agency Award. **Business Phone:** (203)329-7500.*

OBINNA, DR. ELEAZU S.
Educator. **Personal:** Born Jun 4, 1934, Ogbeke-Obibi, Imo, Nigeria; married Carol Jean Miles; children: Iheanyi, Obageri & Marvin. **Educ:** Bishop Col, BA, 1969; Inst Bookkeepers London, FCBI, 1972; Loyola Univ, Los Angeles, MEd, 1973; Univ Calif, Los Angeles, EdD, 1978; Univ Hull England, post doc. **Career:** Redman Indust Inc, acct controller, 1968-69; Security Pac Nat Bank, Los Angeles, financial planning specialist, 1970-71; Calif St Univ, Dept Pan-African Studies, chmn & assoc prof, 1971-75, assoc prof bus & consumer educ, 1975-83, prof, 1983-; Consult & Serv Los Angeles Unified Sch Dist, black educ comnr, 1974-81; US Govt Small Bus Admin, Los Angeles, minority enterprise rep, 1974-76. **Orgs:** Phelp Stokes fel, 1966-69; life mem, NAACP, 1972; Bd Dir, NAACP San Fernando Valley, 1973-74; Univ Calif Los Angeles, Phi Delta Kappa, 1975-; vpres, African-Am Educ Comn, Los Angeles Unified Sch Dist; chmn, Nat Bus Alliance Youth Motivation, Washington, D.C. 1982-; pres, United Crusade Found, 1982-; Calif St Univ Northridge, Stud Affirmative Action Comt, Outreach, 1984; Calif State Univ Northridge Affirmative Action Comt, Retention, 1984; Univ Calif Los Angeles, Consumer Educators Asn; Am Inst Consumer Affairs, 1984-; Asn Int Educ Bus, Houston, 1984-. **Business Addr:** Professor, California State University, Northridge, Department of Pan-African Studies, Rm SN 214 18111 Nordhoff St, Northridge, CA 91330, **Business Phone:** (818)677-3265.

O'BRIEN, MARY NELL
Labor activist, business owner. **Personal:** Born Mar 23, 1945, Bolton, MS; married Hank; children: Edgar Whipps Jr. **Educ:** Utica Jr Col, attended 1964; Campbell Jr Col, attended 1965. **Career:** Business owner, Labor activist (retired); IBEW Local Union 2262, negotiating comn, 1970, fin sec, 1971-78, int rep, retired, 2000; Hammond Jr High Sch PTA, first vpres; A Philips Randolph Conf, resource person & workshop instr; catering bus, co-owner, 2000-. **Orgs:** Corresp sec, MS A Philip Randolph Inst, 1973-76; sec, treas, Jackson Central Labor Union, AFL CIO COPE Dir, 1974-78; labor sect chairperson, United Way Kick Off Fund Dr; secy, Ind Employee Credit Union, Brd Dirs; Labors' Panel on Easter Seal Telethon; vpres, pres, Ramsey Rec Ctr Alexandria, 1980-82; natl exec brd, Coalition Labor Union Women, 1984-86; steering committee, Natl A Philip Randolph Inst, 1984; IBEW Minority Caucus, 1974-78. **Honors/Awds:** Among first Black females at Presto Mfg Co; delegate to many Union activities including MS AFL CIO Convention, Jackson Central Labor Union, MS Electrical Workers Assn, Natl Conference A Philip Randolph; crowned Miss Mississippi A Philip Randolph; 2 Outstanding Service Awards, MS A Philip Randolph Inst; Service Awards IBEW Local 2262, IBEW Syst Council EM 6. **Special Achievements:** First black female Intl Rep of Intl Brotherhood of Elect Workers AFL CIO (IBEW); Labor's Ad Hoc Committee Natl Coun Negro Women. **Home Addr:** 10722 Castleton Turn, Upper Marlboro, MD 20774, **Home Phone:** (301)350-1295.

O'BRYANT, BEVERLY J.
Educator. **Personal:** Born Aug 21, 1947, Washington, DC; daughter of James C and Gertrude Robb; married Michael T O, Jun 7; children: Kimberly Michelle & Michael Tilmon II. **Educ:** Dunbarton Col, BA (cum laude), 1969; Univ Maryland, MA, 1972; Bowie State Univ, PhD, Counselor Educ, attended. **Career:** James C. Jones Builders Inc, asst estimator, 1965-80; Mazima CRP, tech writer, ed, res analyst, 1979-80; Dis Pub Schs, counr, 1978-88, 1990-92, reg counr, 1986-88, Elem Div, pupil personnel team coordr, 1988-90, exec asst to supt, 1992-94, dir community serv/serv learning progs, 1994-; Bowie State Univ, prof, Minority Male Health Proj, dir, asst prof & coordr res; Coppin State Univ, dean, currently. **Orgs:** Pres, Am CounAsn, 1993-94, Governing CNL, 1989-94, Ethics Comt, chap, 1988-90, Counr/CounImage Task Force, 1985-86, N Atlantic Region, vpres, 1985-87; Am Sch Counr Asn, pres, 1990-91, Leadership Develop CNF, chap, 1986, Inter prof Rels, chap, 1983-85; AKA Sorority Inc; Barrister's Wives Dis; Jack Jill Inc Am; Kiwanis Wives Dis; Am Asn Teachers Col Edu; Nat Bd Certified Counselors; Am Public Health asn; Asn Multicultural Coun& Develop; Nat Organization Fetal Alcohol Syndrome; Asn Supervision & Curriculum Develop. **Honors/Awds:** Arkansas Traveler Award, Ark Sch Counr Asn, Governor Bill Clinton, 1990; J Harold McCully Recognition Award, DC Counseling Asn, 1991; City-Wide Parent CNF Appreciation Award, Parents Dis, 1992; Exemplary Nat Leadership Award, Supt DC Pub Schs, 1992; Carl D Perkins Governor Rels Award, Am Counseling Asn, 1992. **Special Achievements:** Author: Marketing Your Sch Counseling Prog, A Monograph, ERIC/CAPS, 1992; presentations: Face lift 90's: Enhancing Counselor Image through Creative Partnerships, NEB Sch Counselor ASN; Empowering Positive Human Potentialin Ourselves, IDA Sch Counselors; A New Vision Guidance, PBS EDU Series. **Business Phone:** (410)951-3000.

O'BRYANT, CONSTANCE TAYLOR
Judge. **Personal:** Born Apr 12, 1946, Meherrin, VA; daughter of Joseph E Taylor and Mattie Naomi Taylor; divorced; children: Taylora Laurece & Kristal Cherrie. **Educ:** Howard Univ, Col Liberal Arts, BA, 1968, Sch Law, JD, 1971. **Career:** DC Pub Defender Serv, sr staff atty, 1971-81; Dept Health & Human Serv, Social Security Admin, admin law judge, 1981-83, admin appeals judge, 1983-90, Dept Appeals Bd, admin law judge, 1991, Social Security Adm, dep chief admin law judge, 1991-94; Harvard Law Trial Advocacy Workshop, vis fac, 1985-86, 1996-97; Dept Housing & Urban Develop, admin law judge, 1994-; Sch Law, John Marshall Univ, vis fac, 1997-98. **Orgs:** Secy, Friends DC Youth Orchestra, 1987-89; secy, Banneker Sch Coun, 1989-91; exec bd, Nat Asn Advan Colored People, Nat Urban League Off Hearings & Appeals, SSA Law J, 1991-94; SSA Strategic Planning Comn, 1991-94; chair, bd trustees, DC Pub Defender Serv, 1992-98; exec bd, Fed Admin Law Judge Conf, 1995-97; tutor, DC Pub Sch-Reading & Math, 1995-96; vol, Proj Champ, 1996-97; tutor & mentor, Nat Coun Negro Women, 1998; Nat Bar Asn; Judicial Coun NBA; Nat Asn Women Judges; adv bd, Joint Educal Facilities. **Honors/Awds:** Outstanding Leadership & Service as Jurist & Lawyer, Women Lawyer's Div NBA, Greater Wash Area Chap, 1982; Asniate Commissioner Citations, 1984, 1985, 1986; Deputy Commissioner Citation, Social Security Admin, 1992. **Special Achievements:** First Woman and First African American Deputy Chief Admin Law Judge, Social Security Admin; First Woman & First African American, Admin Law Judge, Dept of Housing & Urban Development; Annual Panelist, Natl Bar Assn, Convention on Social Security Law & Procedures, "How to Become an Admin Law Judge," 1990-95; Moderator, National Judicial Council's seminar on administrative law issues, 1992. **Business Addr:** Administrative Law Judge, Office of Administrative Law Judges, Department Housing & Urban Develop, 451 7th St SW, Washington, DC 20024, **Business Phone:** (202)708-1112.

O'CONNOR, DR. RODNEY EARL
Dentist. **Personal:** Born Jun 25, 1950, Sharon, PA; son of Helena B McBride and Dr Lauriston E; divorced; children: Elena Moi & Candance Nicole. **Educ:** Ky State Univ, Frankfort, KY, 1971; Univ Ky, Lexington, KY, Col Dent, DMD, 1975; Eastman Dental Ctr, Rochester, NY, 1976; Rochester Inst Technol, 1983. **Career:** Rushville Clinic, dent, consult, 1976-77; Rochester Health Network, dent consult, 1978-87; RE O'Connor DDS, vpres, 1978-; Anthony L Jordan Health Ctr, consult, 1981-85; Westgate Nursing Home, consult; Dr. Rodney O'Connor Family Dent, dent, curently. **Orgs:** Fel, Strong Hosp Dent Res, 1972; Treas, Operation Big Vote, 1983; Acad Gen Dent, 1984-, Am Dent Asn, Nat Dent Asn, Northeast Regional Dent Bd; mentor, Urban League Mentorship Prog, 1990-91; The Dent Soc State NY; 7th District Dent Soc. **Honors/Awds:** Abstr & patent search, Method Ultrasonic Pyrogenic Root Canal Ther, 1976; Distinguished Service, 1991; Distinguished Chefs, 1991, 1992; Community Service Award, Ward Asn, 1999; American Top Dentists, 2000. **Special Achievements:** Recorded CD of original music, Time Traveled, 1998. **Home Addr:** 311 Aberdeen St, Rochester, NY 14619, **Home Phone:** (716)436-9518. **Business Addr:** Vice President, Dr. Rodney O'Connor Family Dent, 521 Beahan Rd Gates, Rochester, NY 14624, **Business Phone:** (716)436-1640.

O'CONNOR, THOMAS F, JR.
Lawyer. **Personal:** Born Mar 16, 1947, New Bedford, MA; married Donna L Dias; children: Jolon Thomas, Justin Kahil & Quinton Kolby. **Educ:** Roger Williams Col, Bristol, RI, AA, BA, 1975; New England Sch Law, Boston, MA, JD, 1993. **Career:** War II Providence, city councilman, sch comt man, 1973-79; City Coun, 1979-89; Dept Planning, 1989-90; Port Comn, assoc dir proj mgt & construct, 1990-94; Dept Planning & Develop, spec assoc dir, dep dir. **Orgs:** ILA Local 1329; bd dir, Afro Arts Ctr; bd dir, S Providence Tutorial; pres, Omni Dev Corp; treas, RI Black Lawyers Asn. **Military Serv:** USMC, 1966-70. **Home Addr:** 202 Cong Ave, Providence, RI 02907.

ODEN, DR. GLORIA (CATHERINE)
Educator, poet. **Personal:** Born Oct 30, 1923, Yonkers, NY; married John Price Bell. **Educ:** Howard Univ, BA, 1944, JD, 1948; NY Univ, grad study, 1971. **Career:** John Hay Whitney Found, Creative Writing Fel, 1955-57; Middlebury Col, Bread loaf Writers Sch, 1960; Am J Physics, ed, 1961-66; New Sch Social Res, lectr, 1966; Inst Elec & Electronic Engr, sr ed, 1966-67; Appleton-Century-Crofts, supvr sci & math books, 1967-68; Holt Rinehart & Winston, sr ed in-chg math & sci books, proj dir sci & lang arts books, 1968-71; State Univ New York, vis lectr eng, 1969-70; Univ MD, Baltimore County, asst prof, 1971-75, assoc prof, 1975-83, full prof Eng, 1983-86. **Orgs:** The Poetry Soc Am; The Soc Study Multi-Ethnic Lit US. **Honors/Awds:** Living Black Am Auth, 1973; Black Writers Past & Present 1975; Distinguished Black Women's Award, Towson Univ, 1984; William H Hastie Symp Award, 1981; Numerous others. **Special Achievements:** Author: The Naked Frame: A Love Poem and Sonnets, Exposition Press, 1952; Resurrections, Olivant Press, 1978; The Tie That Binds, Olivant Press, 1980; Appearances, 2003; Chair or panelist at numerous meetings and conferences, 1964-; Interviewed for Black Oral History Prog Fisk Univ Library in 1973; Guest on television and radio programs. **Home Addr:** 707 Maiden Choice Lane Apt 8119, Catonsville, MD 21228-5915. *

ODEN, WALTER EUGENE
Educator. **Personal:** Born Feb 26, 1935, Stuart, FL; married Edith; children: Walter II & Darin. **Educ:** Bethune-Cook man Col, BS, 1956; Fla Atlantic Univ, MEd, 1966; Fla Atlantic, EdD, 1975. **Career:** Brownsville Jr High Sch, prin, 1955-68; Radio Sta W STU, anchor, dj; Univ Miami, teacher, 1956-63, dir, 1963-66; prin, 1966-67; consult, 1967; guid consult, 1968-69; asst prin, 1969; Fla Atlantic Univ, asst prof, 1971; adj prof, 1971-76; Jan Mann Opportunity Sch N, prin, 1982. **Orgs:** Phi Delta Kappa; Second Baptist Church; Omega Psi Phi; Bethune-Cook man Col Alumni Asn; Dade City Sec Sch Prin Asn. **Honors/Awds:** Distinguished Service Award, Recruiting Students Bethune-Cook man Col, 1968; Outstanding Leadership Award, Col Entrance Exam Bd Club Martin Co,1969; Outstanding Service Plaque, 1973; Outstanding Service Award, Young Mens Prog Orgn, 1975. **Special Achievements:** Book: A study of selected single grade junior high schools in the State of Florida, 1975. **Home Phone:** (305)235-9561. *

ODOM, CLIFTON LEWIS
Football player, executive. **Personal:** Born Sep 15, 1958, Beaumont, TX. **Educ:** Univ Tex, Arlington, BA, bus admin. **Career:** Football player (retired), Owner; Cleveland Browns, linebacker, 1980-81; Baltimore Colts, linebacker, 1982-83; Indianapolis Colts, linebacker, 1984-90; Miami Dolphins, linebacker, 1990-94; Blockbuster Video Franchisee, owner, currently. **Orgs:** Athlete Action; Optimist Club Arlington; Nat Football Leaue Alumni; Univ Tex Alumni Asn; Fellowship Christian Athletes. **Business Addr:** Owner, Blockbuster Video, 1521 Marlandwood Rd, Temple, TX 76502, **Business Phone:** (254)774-8480.

ODOM, DARRYL EUGENE
Manager, administrator. **Personal:** Born Mar 14, 1955, Houston, TX; son of Cleveland and Elizia Amboree; married Rene; children: Matthew, Crystal, Russell & Brittany. **Educ:** Morgan State Univ, Baltimore, MD, BA, 1977; Tex Southern Univ, Houston, TX, MPA, 1985; Rice Univ, Houston, TX, 1986. **Career:** City Houston, Houston, TX, ctr adminr, Multi-Serv Ctr, asst, prog mgr, adminr, currently. **Orgs:** Am Red Cross, 1986-91; bd mem, Boy Scouts, 1989-91; literacy advan, Literacy Advan, 1989-91; Family to Family, 1990-91. **Honors/Awds:** Outstanding Young Man of America, US Jaycees, 1979; Mayor's Appreciation Award, City Houston, 1980; Community Service Award, YWCA, 1989; Mayors Award, Young Black Achievers, 1999. **Home Phone:** (936)857-5745. **Business Addr:** Administrator, Sunnyside Multi-Service Center, City of Houston, 4605 Wilmington St, PO Box 1562, Houston, TX 77051, **Business Phone:** (713)732-5030.

ODOM, JOHN YANCY
Consultant, writer. **Personal:** Born Sep 22, 1948, Jackson, MS; son of Rev Corey Franklin Sr and Rosa B; married Annie S, Aug 15, 1970; children: Nikki Annette. **Educ:** Lane Col, BA, 1969; Univ Wis, Madison, MS, 1973, PhD, 1978. **Career:** Sch Dist Beloit, eng teacher, 1969-72; Madison Schs, asst dir human rels, 1973-76, dir/human rels, 1976-80, middle sch prin, 1980-85; Univ Wis, Madison, acad specialist, 1986-86; Odom & Associates LLC, pres, 1985-; Dissertion: Educational Admin & Human Relations, 1978; actor: Oscar Mayer Theatre, The Wiz; Joseph & The Amazing Tech Dreamcoat; The Fantasticks; The Wiz; John Odom in Concert, 1981-97; book: Saving Black America: An Econ Plan for Civil Rights, 2001. **Orgs:** Bd mem, Big Bros/Sister Dane County, 1973-82; founder, Mu Eta Lambda Chap, Alpha Phi Alpha, 1978-; bd mem, Children's Theatre Madison, 1981-95; Nat Res Ctr Eng Learning & Achievement, 1996-; vpres, chair, ed comt, 1998-, pres, 1990-93, NAACP-Madison, WI; NAACP, Nat Educ Task Force, 2000-01; pres, Charles Hamilton Houston Inst, 2001-. **Honors/Awds:** Outstanding Alumni, Lane Col, 1979; Leadership Forum, Southwestern Bell Corp, 1991; Martin Luther King Humanitarian of Year, Madison City, WI, 1992; Madison Opera, Frank Lloyd Wright Shining Brow, 1993; Educational Leadership, Prairie View A&M Univ, 1999; Human Rights Award-,Madison City, 2002; One of 50 Most Influential Citizens, Madison Mag, 2002-; Community Service Award, 2002, President's Service Award, 2002, NAACP. **Business Addr:** President, Odom & Associates, LLC, PO Box 56155, Madison, WI 53705, **Business Phone:** (608)836-5555.

ODOM, MELANIE
Association executive. **Career:** Comerica Bank, vpres civic affairs, currently. **Business Addr:** Vice President of Civic Affairs, Comerica Bank, Comerica Tower at Detroit Ctr, 500 Woodward Ave MC 3391, Detroit, MI 48226, **Business Phone:** (313)222-9668.

ODOM, STONEWALL
Executive, government official. **Personal:** Born Nov 1, 1940, Petersburg, VA; son of Stonewall Faison and Flossie Odom; married Marlena Hines, Jan 29, 1989; children: Terrance, Jacqueline, Latisha, Nicole, Stonewall III, Marlena, Marcus, Malcolm, Mandela, Muhammad, Malik & Myles. **Educ:** John Jay Col Criminal Law. **Career:** Metropolitan Life, sales rep; City NY, police officer, 1965-73; CORE, chief coordr & interim chmn, 1989-; Black Men Opposed to Drugs & Violence, Yonkers NY, past chmn; Odom & Sons Vending Co, principal owner. **Orgs:** Samuel H Dow Am Legion Post 017; master mason, James H Farrell Lodge; Vietnam Veterans Am; coord mem, Yonkers Crack Task Force; founder &

chmn, Tower Soc Citizens Responsible Govt, 1985-89; legis chmn, Sammuel H Dow Post 1017 Am Legion; Nat Asn Advan Colored People, 1986; vice chair, Petersburg Repuban Comn, 2000-; bd comnrs, Petersburg Dinwiddie Airport, 2002; bd comnrs, Petersburg Redevelop & Housing Authority, 2002. **Honors/Awds:** Two Meritorious Awards, New York Police Dept, 1969-72; Chairman of Veterans; Ethiopian Orthodox Church Public Award, 1988; ran for The New York State Assembly on the Conservative Line and Right to Life (received 7,000) votes, 1988; African American Asn Community Service Award, 1996. **Military Serv:** AUS, Sp4, Airborne, 1961-64. **Business Addr:** Owner, Stonewall Odom Vending Co, 1844 Fort Rice St, Petersburg, VA 23805.

ODOMES, NATHANIEL BERNARD
Football player. **Personal:** Born Aug 25, 1965, Columbus, GA. **Educ:** Univ Wis. **Career:** Football player (retired), football coach; Buffalo Bills, cornerback, 1987-93; Atlanta Falcons, cornerback 1996; Columbus Wardogs, defensive back coach. **Honors/Awds:** AFC Championship Game, post-1988 season.

OFFICER, CARL EDWARD
Mayor, vice president (organization), funeral director. **Personal:** Born Apr 3, 1952, St Louis, MO. **Educ:** Western Col, Miami, BA, polit sci & philos, 1974; John F Kennedy Sch Govt, Harvard Univ; Southern Ill Univ, Carbondale, mortuary sci, 1975. **Career:** Officer Funeral Homes PC, E St Louis IL, v pres, 1970-; St Clair County, IL, dep coroner, 1975-77; State Ill, Drivers Servs, dep dir, 1977-79; City E St Louis, IL, mayor, 1979-91, 2003-07; AME Church, ordained elder, 2001-. **Orgs:** US Conf Mayors; Nat Conf Black Mayors; Urban League; Jaycees; Nat Asn Advan Colored People; Sigma Phi Sigma; life mem Kappa Alpha Psi; bd mem, E W Gateway Coun Govts; Ill Funeral Dir Asn; St Clair County Funeral Dir Asn; Nat Funeral Dir Asn; Int Order Golden Rule. **Honors/Awds:** Certificate of Commendation, Top Ladies Distinction, 1980; Humanitarian Award, Campbell Chapel AME Church, 1980. **Special Achievements:** First African American Cadet to graduate from the Mormion Military Academy in Aurora, IL. **Military Serv:** Ill Nat Guard, second lt, 2 yrs. **Business Addr:** Vice President, Officer Funeral Homes PC, 2114 Mo Ave, East St Louis, IL 62205, **Business Phone:** (618)271-6055.

O'FLYNN-PATTILLO, PATRICIA
Executive. **Personal:** Born Jul 28, 1940, E St Louis, IL; daughter of James E and Margarette Matthews; married Roland A Pattillo, Jul 1995; children: Terence (deceased) & Todd. **Educ:** Southern IL Univ, BS, 1963; Univ Wis-Milwaukee, MA, 1973; St Martins Acad, Hon Doctoral, 1983. **Career:** Nat Newspaper Publ Asn, pres, 1987-90, vpres secy, 1983-86; Milwaukee Minority C of C, dir, 1986; Milwaukee NAACP, dir, 1983; Milwaukee Community Jour Inc, newspaper publ, pres; PPP Inc, pres; Speech of the singing group, Arrested Develop, agent, currently. **Orgs:** Founder, Eta Phi Beta Milwaukee Chap, 1976; founder, Milwaukee Comm Pride Expo 1976; mayoral, appt Lakefront Design Comm, 1979; founder, Milwaukee Chap Squaws, 1980; gov appt, Comm Small Bus, 1980; dir, Milwaukee Chap PUSH, 1980; deleg, White House Comm, 1980. **Honors/Awds:** Publisher of the Year, NNPA, 1986. **Business Addr:** Publisher, Chief Executive Officer, Milwaukee Community Journal Inc, 3612 N Martin L King Dr, Milwaukee, WI 53212, **Business Phone:** (414)265-5300.

OFODILE, FERDINAND AZIKIWE
Surgeon. **Personal:** Born Oct 20, 1941, Nnobi, Anambra State, Nigeria; son of Julius and Regina Eruchalu; married Caroline Okafor Ofodile, Jul 5, 1969; children: Uchenna, Ikechukwu, Nnaemeka, Nnamdi. **Educ:** Northwestern Univ, Evanston, IL, BS, 1964; Northwestern Med Sch, Chicago, IL, MD, 1968. **Career:** St Lukes & Roosevelt Hosp, New York, NY, assoc attending surg, 1982-; Harlem Hosp Ctr, New York, NY, dir plastic surg, 1982-; Columbia Univ, New York, NY, clin prof surg, 1996-. **Orgs:** Am Soc Plastic & Recon Surgeon, 1986; fel, Am Col Surgs, 1986; Intl progs Comt ASPRS, 1992; New York County Med Soc, 1988-; chmn plastic surg, Am Asn Acad. **Honors/Awds:** Author of many scientific articles; lect many intl symposiums; Fellow, Am Asn Plastic & Reconstructive Surgs. **Special Achievements:** Designed the "Ofodibe Nasal Implant" for augmentation Rhinoplasty AFA & Hispanic noses. **Business Addr:** Director plastic surgery, Harlem Hospital Center, 506 Lenox Ave Rm 11 101, New York, NY 10037, **Business Phone:** (212)939-3538.*

OGBOGU, ERIC O.
Football player. **Personal:** Born Jul 18, 1975, Irvington, NY; son of Louis (deceased). **Educ:** Univ Md. **Career:** Football player (retired); New York Jets, defensive end, 1998-2001; Cincinnati Bengals, 2002; Dallas Cowboys, linebacker, 2003-05. **Honors/Awds:** Hula Bowl; Rookie of the Year, 1998. **Special Achievements:** Official star & spokesperson of the famous Under Armour brand, and is named Big E in the Under Armour commercials; Actor, The Game Plan, 2007.

OGDEN, CHRISTOPHER A.
Financial manager. **Educ:** BS, bus mgt; MBA, int bus studies. **Career:** Protein Technologies Int, bus develop mgr, regional sales, mgr; Merrill Lynch, NY, financial adv; Ogden Capital Group LLC, pres, currently. **Honors/Awds:** Won numerous performance rewards. **Business Addr:** President, Ogden Capital Group LLC, 980 Oriole Dr SW, Atlanta, GA 30311, **Business Phone:** (404)755-2257.

OGDEN, JONATHAN PHILLIP
Football player, football coach, social worker. **Personal:** Born Jul 31, 1974, Washington, DC; son of Shirrel and Cassandra; married Kema; children: Jayden. **Educ:** Univ Calif. **Career:** Football player(retired), Patterson High Sch, acad tutor; Baltimore Ravens, offensive tackle, 1996-2007. **Orgs:** Bd trustees, Nat Urban League; founder, Jonathan Ogden Found; founder, The Ogden Club; chmn, Beacon Inst; participated in various social prog. **Honors/Awds:** Outland Trophy winner, 1995; All-America first team, The Sporting News, 1995; All-Rookie Team, USA Today, 1996; UCLA Athletics Hall Of Fame in 2006; Pro Bowl AFC Starters, 2001-05, 2007.

OGDEN, STEVEN
Real estate executive. **Personal:** Son of Sharon. **Educ:** Mich State Univ, BA, pub policy, 1985. **Career:** Sterling Group, vpres & dir real estate. **Orgs:** Bd mem, Habitat Detroit; Habitat for Humanity; Music Hall for Performing Arts; Detroit Discovery Mus; Eastside Emergency Ctr Inc. *

OGILVIE, LANA
Fashion model, television show host. **Personal:** Born in Ontario;married; children: 1. **Career:** Ford & Elite Modeling Agencies, model; paraded catwalks Dior, Prada, Calvin Klein & Gucci; print campaigns include: CoverGirl, Banana Repub, Gap & Tia Maria; model: Sports Illustrated, Elle, Vogue, Glamour, Flare, Mademoiselle, Essence & Harpers Bazaar; advertisements for clients including: Gap, Guess Jeans, Victoria's Secret, John Galliano & Katherine Hamnett; Fashion TV Channel, "The Review", co-host, "This Week in Fashion", segment contribr, 2002-; fashion model, currently. **Orgs:** Christian Children's Fund. **Special Achievements:** First black model to sign an exclusive deal with CoverGirl cosmetics, 1992. **Business Addr:** Fashion Model, c/o Ford Models, 111 Fifth Ave, New York, NY 10003, **Business Phone:** (212)219-6500.

OGLESBY, BORIS
Executive. **Educ:** Grambling State Univ, Grambling, La. **Career:** Jim Beam Brands Co, vpres super premium & cordials, 2002-; Miller Brewing Co, gen mgr, Capital Market Area; Kraft Foods Inc, Ethnic Mkt & External Rels, dir. **Business Addr:** Vice President, Jim Beam Brands Co, 510 Lake Cook Rd, Deerfield, IL 60015, **Business Phone:** (847)948-8888.*

OGLESBY, JOE
Newspaper editor. **Personal:** Born Aug 1, 1947, Tampa, FL; son of Northern and Terrie Del Benniefield Yarde; married Linda Blash, Feb 14, 1988; children: Lee Erin; married Bloneva McKenzie (divorced 1984); children: Joy Denise. **Educ:** Fla Agr & Mech Univ, BA, eng, 1970. **Career:** The Miami Herald, day city ed, ed writer, reporter, 1972-87, asst managing ed, 1990-, ed Page ed, currently; The Philadelphia Inquirer, suburban ed, 1987-90. **Orgs:** Nat Asn Black Journalists, 1977-. **Honors/Awds:** Pulitzer Prize, Columbia Univ, 1983. **Business Addr:** Editorial Page Editor, The Miami Herald, 1 Herald Plz, Miami, FL 33101.

OGLETREE, CHARLES J
Lawyer, educator. **Personal:** Born Dec 31, 1952, Merced, CA; son of Charles J Ogletree Sr and WillieMae Reed Ogletree; married Pamela Barnes, Aug 9, 1974; children: Charles J III & Rashida Jamila. **Educ:** Stanford Univ, Stanford, Calif, BA, 1974, MA, 1975; Harvard Law Sch, Cambridge, MA, JD, 1978. **Career:** DC Pub Defender Serv, Wash, DC, staff atty, 1978-82, dir staff training, 1982-83, dep dir, 1984-85;; Am Univ, Wash Col Law, Wash, DC, adj prof, 1982-84; Antioch Law Sch, Wash, DC, adj prof, 1983-84; Jessamy, Fort & Ogletree, Wash, DC, partner, 1985-89; Harvard Law Sch, Cambridge, Mass, vis prof, 1985-89, dir, introd trial advocacy workshop, 1986-, asst prof, 1989-93, prof law, 1993-; Jessamy, Fort & Botts, Wash, DC, legal coun, 1989-; Harvard Law Sch, Criminal Justice Inst, Cambridge, Mass, dir, Jesse Climenko Prof Law, currently; Charles Hamilton Houston Inst Race & Justice, exec dir, currently. **Orgs:** Am Bar Asn; Nat Conf Black Lawyers; Nat Bar Asn; Am Civil Liberties Union; Bar Asn DC; Wash Bar Asn; defender comt mem, Nat Legal Aid & Defender Asn; Asn Am Law Sch; DC Bar; chmn, Southern Ctr Human Rights Comt. **Honors/Awds:** Hall of Fame, Calif Sch Bd Found, 1990; Nelson Mandela Service Award, Nat Black Law Stud Asn, 1991; Richard S Jacobsen Certificate of Excellence in Teaching Trial Advocacy, 1990; Honoree, Charles Hamilton Houston Inst, 1990; Award of Merit, Pub Defender Serv Asn, 1990; Personal Achievement Award, NAACP & Black Network, 1990; "Supreme Court Jury Discrimination Cases and State Court Compliance, Resistance and Innovation," Toward a Usable Past, 1990; Boston Mus Afro-Am Hist, Man of Vision Award, 1992; honoree, Award for Outstanding Contribution in Criminal Law Education, NY State Bar Asn-Criminal Justice Sect, 1992; Outstanding Service Award, Transafrica-Boston Chap, 1992; Albert M Sacks-Paul A Freund Award for Excellence in Teaching, Harvard Law Sch, 1993; A Champion of Liberty Award, Criminal Practice Inst, 1994; co-auth: Beyond the Rodney King Story; "Just Say No! A Proposal to Eliminate Racially Discriminatory Uses of Peremptory Challenges," 31 American Criminal Law Rev1099, 1994; "The Quiet Storm: The Rebellious Influence of Cesar Chavez," Harvard Latino Rev, vol 1, 1995; Peoples Lawyer of the year, Nat Conf Black Lawyers; A Leon Higginbotham Lawyer of the Year Award, Nat Bar Asn Young Lawyers Division; Carter G Woodson History Maker Living Legend Award, Clio Exchange, 2004; Dr Martin Luther King, Jr Legacy Award, 2005; City University of New York Public Interest Law Asn Lifetime Achievement Award, City University of New York. **Special Achievements:** Moderator of television programs including: "Surviving the Odds: To Be a Young Black Male in America," Public Broadcasting System, 1994; "Political Correctness and the Media," C-Span, 1994; "Don't Say What You Think!; Limits to Free Speech," C-Span, 1994. **Home Addr:** 54 Pemberton St, Cambridge, MA 02140, **Home Phone:** (617)868-3330. **Business Addr:** Jesse Climenko Professor of Law, Harvard Law School, Hauser 516, 1563 Mass Ave, Cambridge, MA 02138, **Business Phone:** (617)495-5097.

OGLETREE, JOHN D, JR.
Clergy, lawyer. **Personal:** Born Mar 1, 1952, Dallas, TX; son of John D Sr and Marion Deckard; married Evelyn Horn, Apr 14, 1973; children: Johnny, Lambrini, Joseph & Jordan. **Educ:** Univ Tex, Arlington, BA, 1973; South Col Law, JD, 1979. **Career:** Fulbright & Jaworski Law Firm, messenger, 1976-77; Harris County Sheriff dept, baliff, 1977-79; Caggins, Hartsfield & Ogletree Law Firm, partner, 1979-93; Antioch Missionary Baptist Church, minister Christian develop, 1985-86; First Metropolitan Baptist Church, pastor, founder, sr pastor, currently. **Orgs:** Nat Bar Asn, 1979-; State Bar Tex, 1979-; Nat Baptist Conv USA, 1986-; Urban Alternative, 1987-; instr, Eastern Progressive Baptist Missonary Dist Asn, 1987-; Baptist Missionary & Educ State Conv, 1987-; Evangelist Gulf Coast Asn, 1989; NE Baptist Church; bd trustee, Cypress-Fairbanks ISD. **Special Achievements:** Keynote speaker Gulf Coast Keswick, 1990; ctr, Workshop Cooperative Baptist Fel, 1992. **Home Addr:** 7863 Maple Brook Lane, Houston, TX 77095, **Home Phone:** (713)550-0566. **Business Addr:** Senior Pastor, First Metropolitan Baptist Church, 5249 Dow Rd, Houston, TX 77040, **Business Phone:** (713)460-8000.

OGLIVIE, BENJAMIN A.
Baseball player, athletic coach. **Personal:** Born Feb 11, 1949, Colon, Panama; married Tami; children: Trianni & Benjamin. **Educ:** Bronx Community Col, Northeastern Univ, Wayne State Univ. **Career:** Baseball player (retired); Athletic coach; Boston Red Sox, Outfielder, 1971-73; Detroit Tigers,outfielder, 1974-77; Milwaukee Brewers, outfielder, 1978-86; Kintetsu Buffaloes, 1987-88;Montgomery Biscuits, coach, currently. **Honors/Awds:** Harvey Kuenn Award, 1978; All-Star Teams, 1980; Silver Slugger Award, Sporting News 1980; An League Home Run Champion, 1983. **Business Addr:** Coach, Montgomery Biscuits Baseball, 200 Coosa St, Montgomery, AL 36104, **Business Phone:** (334)323-2255.

OGUNDE, ADEYEMI
Clergy. **Personal:** Born Oct 10, 1950, West Africa, Nigeria; son of Ogunde Adejoke; children: Aderonke, Adeyemi, Adeola, Adewale. **Educ:** Yoba Col Technology, Nigeria, OND, 1972, HND, printing, 1974; Univ Logos, Nigeria, BA, cosmology, 1978; Univ Nortttingham, attended 1983. **Career:** Inst African Wisdom, chief priest, founder, 1988-. **Orgs:** Nat African Religion Congress; The Ijebu Descendant Asn; Nat Black United Front; Nat Asn Advan Colored People. **Honors/Awds:** African Letter Excellence, National Black United Front, 1985; Certificate of Special Congressional Recognition, 1996; Proclamation from the City of Houston, Mayor Lee Brown, 1998, 1999, 2001; Certificate of Appreciation, Members of African Wisdom, 2001. **Special Achievements:** Presented Meditation for Unity Church Convention in Portland, Oregon, 1999; Special Presentation to Maya Angelo/Ku Lamanjaro, 2001. *

OGUNLESI, ADEBAYO O
Lawyer, investment banker. **Personal:** Born Jan 1, 1953?, Nigeria; children: 1. **Educ:** Oxford Univ, Oxford, Eng; Harvard Law Sch, magna cum laude; Harvard Bus Sch, JD, MBA. **Career:** Harvard Law Rev, ed; Dist Columbia, US Ct Appeals, staff; Supreme Ct Justice Thur Marshall, staff; Cravath, Swaine & Moore, atty; Yale Sch Org, lectr; Credit Suisse First Boston Inc, 1983, managing dir, 1993, headed global energy group, 1993-2002, exec vice chmn & chief client officer, head global invest banking, 2002-, bd dirs, 2002-. **Honors/Awds:** Lamond Godwin Bridge Builders Award, 2003. **Special Achievements:** One of the top 25 "Hottest Blacks on Wall Street" listed in Black Enterprise, October, 1992. **Business Addr:** Executive Vice Chairman & Chief Client Officer, Head of Global Investment Banking, Credit Suisse First Boston Inc, 11 Madison Ave, New York, NY 10010-3629, **Business Phone:** (212)325-2000.*

O'HARA, LEON P
Clergy, oral surgeon. **Personal:** Born May 13, 1920, Atlanta, GA; married Geraldine Gore; children: Scarlett, Leon, Michael, Jeri, Mark & Miriam. **Educ:** Talladega Col, AL, BA & BS, 1942; Meharry Med Col, DDS, 1945; Wash Univ, attended 1952;

Providential Theol Sem, DD. **Career:** Oral surgeon, St Louis; Holy Metro Bapt Chap, fdr, pastor, 1955; City St Louis, pub health oral surg. **Orgs:** Vpres, pres Mound City Dental Soc, 1952-56; pres, Midwestern States Dental Soc; staff, St Mary's Hosp; Peoples Hosp; Faith Hosp; Christian Hosp; commr St Louis Mayor's Coun Human Rels; chmn, Way Out Drug Abuse Prog; parole adv, Penal Adoption Prog; bd dirs, Urban League, St Louis; bishop Indep Peng Assemblies Chap; Omega Psi Phi; W Urban Renewal Dirs, 1968-70; life mem, Nat Asn Advan Colored People; mem CORE; Ecumenical Coun Chap. **Honors/Awds:** Pub Serv Award, Pres Johnson; ETO Tennis Champ 1947; Ft Monmouth Tennis Champ, singles & doubles, 1945; shotgun skeet shooting champ, 1966. **Military Serv:** AUS, maj Dental Corps, 1943-48.

OHENE-FREMPRONG, KWAKU
Physician, association executive, executive director. **Educ:** Yale Unive Sch Med, pediat, 1980; Sub-Bd Hemat & Oncol, cert pediat, 1980. **Career:** Nat Assn for Sickle Cell Dis Inc, nat pres; Children's Hosp, Comprehensive Sickle Cell Ctr, Philadelphia, dir, currently; Univ Pa, Children's Hosp Philadelphia, pediat hemat fel. **Business Phone:** (215)590-3423.

OHUCHE, EMEKA
Entrepreneur, chief financial officer, president (organization). **Educ:** Univ Iowa, bachelors, engineering & bus; Univ Mich, MBA. **Career:** Deloitte Group, int bus consult; IKobo Inc, co-founder, pres & chief financial officer, 2001-. **Business Addr:** Co-Founder, President, Chief Financial Officer, Ikobo Inc, 2030 Powers Ferry Rd Bldg 200 Suite 222, Atlanta, GA 30339, **Business Phone:** (678)483-4562.

OJUMU, AYODELE
Librarian. **Personal:** Born Mar 15, 1972, Buffalo, NY; daughter of Ochun and Vivian. **Educ:** Univ Rochester, BA, 1994; Univ Buffalo, MLS, 1997, advan studies cert, Info & Libr Studies, 2006; NYU, dipl paralegal studies, 2001. **Career:** New York Pub Libr, 1997-2000; NYC Bd Educ, sch librn, 1999-2000; SUNY Col, Fredonia, sr asst librn, 2001-04; Rochester City Sch Dist, librn, currently. **Orgs:** Black Caucus Am libr Asn, 1996-; Am Libr Asn, 2001-; SUNY Libr Asn, 2001-04; Asn Col 2nd Res Libr, WNY/Ontario Chap, 2001-04. **Special Achievements:** Publications: "5th Natl Conf of African American Librarians: Source of Professional Rejuvenation 2nd Affirmation," Newsletter of the Black Caucus of the American Library Assn, Oct/Dec 2002. **Business Addr:** Librarian, Rochester City School District, 131 W Broad St, Rochester, NY 14614, **Business Phone:** (585)262-8100.

OKANTAH, MWATABU S
Writer, educator. **Personal:** Born Aug 18, 1952, Orange, NJ; son of Wilbur and Gladys Smith; married Aminah M, May 18, 1991; children: Janeia, Ta-Seti, Jamila, Afrikiti, Ile-Ife, Sowande & Berhane. **Educ:** Kent State Univ, BA, Eng & African studies, 1976; City Col NY, MA, creative writing, 1982. **Career:** Cleveland State Univ, Black Studies Prog, asst to dir, 1981-89; Kent State Univ, Pan-African Studies, adj fac, 1991-96, instr, 1996-99, lectr, Ctr Pan-Africa Cult, dir, 1999-, asst prof, dir, currently; Author: Cheikh Anta Diop: Afreeka Brass, 1983; Collage, 1984; Legacy: for Martin & Malcolm, 1987; Poem For The Living, 1997; Reconnecting Memories: Dreams No Longer Deferred, 2004. **Orgs:** Leader, Muntu Kuntu Energy Ensemble, 1989-; Cavani String Quartet, 1990-; bd mem, Poets & Writers Inc, 1991-; bd mem, Poet's League Greater Cleveland, 1996-; Iroko African Drum & Dance Soc. **Honors/Awds:** Outstanding Teaching Award, Kent State Univ Alumni Asn, Univ Teaching Coun, 1999; Outstanding Writers of the 20th Century, 2000. **Home Addr:** 2180 Thurmont Rd Suite 1, Akron, OH 44313. **Business Addr:** Director, Kent State University, Department Pan-African Studies, PO Box 5190, Kent, OH 44242-0001, **Business Phone:** (330)672-2300.

OKHAMAFE, IMAFEDIA
Educator. **Personal:** Son of Obokhe and Olayemi. **Educ:** Purdue Univ, PhD, Philosophy & English, 1984. **Career:** Univ Nebr, Omaha, prof philos & Eng, 1993-, Goodrich Scholar Prog & DeptEng, prof, currently. **Orgs:** Am Mod Lang Asn; Am Philos Asn. **Honors/Awds:** Omaha's Excellence in Teaching Award, Univ Nebr. **Special Achievements:** Articles have appeared in periodicals such as Black Scholar, J of the British Soc for Phenomenology, UMOJA, Intl Journal of Social Educ, Auslegung, Rsch in African Literatures, Soundings, Philosophy Today & Africa Today; Publ: Husserliana Analecta: The Yearbook of Phenomenological Research, Vol. IC. **Business Addr:** Professor Philosophy and English, University Nebraska-Omaha, Ash Suite 205, Omaha, NE 68182-0265, **Business Phone:** (402)554-2628.

OKINO, BETTY. See OKINO, ELIZABETH ANNA.

OKINO, ELIZABETH ANNA (BETTY OKINO)
Gymnast, actor. **Personal:** Born Jun 4, 1975, Entebbe, Uganda; daughter of Francis C and Aurelia. **Career:** Gymnast (retired), actress; Olympic Team, gymnast, 1992; "Undressed", MTV, 1999; Films: The District, 2000; Creature Unknown, 2004. **Honors/Awds:** Silver Team Medal, Bronze on Bean, World Championships, Indianapolis, 1991; Spec Sports Award, Chicago State Univ, 1992.

OKORE, CYNTHIA ANN
Social worker. **Personal:** Born Nov 15, 1945, Philadelphia, PA; daughter of William (deceased) and Jessie M; married Caleb J; children: Elizabeth A. **Educ:** Cheyney Univ, BA, 1974; Rutgers Univ, MSW, 1981. **Career:** Presbyterian Univ Pa Hosp, Philadelphia, PA, social worker, 1977-79; John F Kennedy Community Ment Health & Ment Retardation Ctr, Philadelphia, PA, social worker, 1981-84; Philadelphia Veterans Affairs Med Ctr, social worker, 1984-. **Orgs:** Nat Asn Social Workers, 1980-; Pa Chapter Social Workers, 1980-; Philadelphia Chap Social Workers, 1980-; Nat Coun Negro Women, 1989-; Nat Black Alcoholism Coun, 1989-; Nat Black Women's Health Proj, 1990-. **Honors/Awds:** Technical Art & Publishers Competition Award of Excellence, Soc Tech Commun, Puget Sound Chapter, 1990-91. **Special Achievements:** Author: The Nurse Practitioner, The Jour of Primary Health Care, July 1990; The Cocaine Epidemic: A Comprehensive Review of Use, Abuse, & Dependence. **Home Addr:** 5543 Windsor Ave, Philadelphia, PA 19143. **Business Addr:** Social Worker/Family Therapist, Philadelphia Veterans Affairs Med Ctr, 39th & Woodland Ave, Philadelphia, PA 19104, **Business Phone:** (215)823-5814.

OKOYE, CHRISTIAN E
Football player, executive. **Personal:** Born Aug 16, 1961, Enugu, Nigeria. **Educ:** Azusa Pac Univ, phys educ degree, 1987. **Career:** Kans City Chiefs, running back, 1987-92; Golden Baseball League, investor, currently; Okoye Fitness & Nutrition, owner, currently; Calif Sports Hall Fame, pres, currently; Montclair High Sch, head football coach, currently. **Orgs:** Sporting News All-Star Team, 1989. **Business Addr:** Owner, Okoye Fitness & Nutrition, PO Box 1323, Alta Loma, CA 91737, **Business Phone:** (909)481-3541.

OKPARA, MZEE LASANA. See HORD, DR. FREDERICK LEE.

OKUNOR, DR. SHIAME
School administrator, chairperson, educator. **Personal:** Born Jun 2, 1937, Accra, Ghana; son of Benjamin and Dorothea; divorced; children (previous marriage): Dorothy Ometse; married Ivy Okunor. **Educ:** New York Univ, Cert, 1968; Grahm Jr Col, AAS, 1971; The Univ NMex, BA, Speech Communs, 1973, MPA, 1975, PhD, 1981; Yale Divinity Sch, MDiv, 1995. **Career:** The Univ NMex, African-Am studies, 1981-82, dir, acad affairs Afro-Am studies, 1982-, acting dean univ col, 1985-86, dean gen col, 1986-87, asst prof educ found, assoc dean, Grad Studies, 1988-89, prof, currently, Summer Inst African-Am Studies, dir, currently; Charlie Morrisey Res Hall, dir; Cult & Edu Proj, dir; Team Excellence Mentoring Prog; AME Church, Grant Chapel, assoc pastor, Howard Chapel, sr pastor. **Orgs:** Exec bd, NAACP, 1975-86; Affirmative Action Policy Comm; bd dirs, pres, NM Sickle Cell, 1981-91; secy, treas, NMex Endowment Humanities, 1987-92; NMex Jazz Workshop, 1991-92; chair, The Ghana Free Community Libr, currently. **Honors/Awds:** Outstanding Senior Award, 1971; Outstanding InterNat Award, 1971; President Recognition Award Univ, New Mexico, 1981-85; AP Appreciation Award, Albuquerque Pub Sch, 1981; Community Service Award, NAACP, 1982; WM Civitan Merit Awd, 1984; Black Community Service Award, 1984; Presidency Award, Schomburg Ctr, New York City, 1985-86; NM Sec State Certificate of Appreciation, 1985; NM Asn Bilingual Teachers Award, 1986; US Military Airlift Command Certificate Recognition, 1987; Certificate Appreciation, US Corps Engrs, 1987; Yvonne Ochillo, Southern Conference on African Am Studies, 1990; Award Outstanding Achievement, Intercultural Initiatives, Univ NMex, Commun & Jour Dept, 2000; Outstanding Alumni, Univ NMex; Outstanding Teacher Awd, Univ NMex, 2004. **Home Addr:** 1432 Summerfield Pl SW, Albuquerque, NM 87121. **Business Addr:** Professor, Director African American Studies, University of New Mexico, College of Education, Mesa Vista Hall Rm 4023, Albuquerque, NM 87131, **Business Phone:** (505)277-5644.

OLAJUWON, HAKEEM ABDUL
Basketball executive, basketball player. **Personal:** Born Jan 21, 1963, Lagos, Nigeria; son of Salim and Abike; married Abisola, Jan 1, 1900 (divorced); children: 1; married Abisola Dalia Asafi, Aug 8, 1996; children: Rahmah & Aisha. **Educ:** Univ Houston, attended 1984. **Career:** Basketball player (retired), basketball executive; Nigerian Nat Team, 1980; Houston Rockets, ctr, 1984-2001; Toronto Raptors, 2001-02; Barakaat Holdings Ltd, mgr; Big Man Camp, founder, 2006-. **Honors/Awds:** Most Valuable Player Award, 1994; NBA World Champion Houston Rockets Basketball Team, 1994; Gold medal, Olympics Dream Team, 1996; Texas Sports Hall of Fame, 1999. **Special Achievements:** Film appearance: Heaven Is a Playground, 1991; one of 50 Greatest Players in NBA History, 1996; author, autobiography, Living the Dream, 1996; life-sized Olajuwon statue, Rockets new downtown arena, 2004.

OLAPO, OLAITAN
President (Organization), consulting engineer. **Personal:** Born Apr 2, 1956, Lagos, Nigeria; son of F A Osidele and J O Osidele; married Oluwayimika Aduloju, Dec 23, 1989; children: Olabamigbe & Ayoola. **Educ:** Va Community Col, AAS, 1980; Milwaukee Sch Engineering, BSc, 1982; Marquette Univ, MSc, 1986. **Career:** Wisc Dept Transp, 1983-90; Toki & Assoc Inc, founder & pres, 1987-. **Orgs:** Int Inst Wisc, bd dir, 1991-; Am Soc Civil Engr; Concrete Reinforcing Steel Inst. **Honors/Awds:** Secretary's Award, Wisc Dept Transp, 1992. **Home Addr:** W147N6945 Woodland Dr, Menomonee Falls, WI 53051, **Home Phone:** (414)250-9868. **Business Addr:** President, Toki & Associates Inc, 7100 W Fond du lac Ave Suite 201, Milwaukee, WI 53218, **Business Phone:** (414)463-2700.

OLAWUMI, BERTHA ANN
Counselor, executive. **Personal:** Born Dec 19, 1945, Chicago, IL; married Aina M; children: Tracy, Tanya. **Educ:** Thronton Comm Col, AAS, 1979; John Marshall Law Sch, Cert, 1980; Governors State Univ, BA, Human Justice, 1981. **Career:** Tinley Park Mental Health Ctr, mental health tech, 1979; Robbins Juvenile Advocacy, juvenile advocate, 1979-83; John Howard Assoc Prison Watch Group, intern student, 1984; Minority Econ Resources Corp, employment spec & instr. **Orgs:** chairperson, Thornton Community Col Mental Health Club, 1978-79; bd dir Worth Twp Youth Serv, 1981, mem, 1981-83, pres, 1982; Am Criminal Justice Assoc; Blue Island Recreation Comn, 1982-84; bd mem, Sch Dist 143 1 & 2. **Honors/Awds:** Student Found Scholarship Award, Thornton Community Col, 1979; Certificate, Cook Cty Sheriffs Youth Serv, 1980; Certificate, Citizens Info Serv, 1980; Certificate, Morraine Valley Community Col, 1980; Certificate, St Xavier Col, 1981. *

OLDHAM, ALGIE SIDNEY, JR.
Educator. **Personal:** Born May 18, 1927, Dyersburg, TN; married Sarah Mae Graham; children: Roslynn Denise, Bryan Sidney. **Educ:** TN State Univ Nashville, BA, 1949; Univ Notre Dame, MA, 1954. **Career:** Educator (retired); S Bend Comm Sch, elem prin, 1966-75, asst high sch prin, 1975-83, Riley High Sch, prin, 1983-89. **Orgs:** Phi Delta Kappa Educ Frat, Nat Assoc Secondary Sch & IN Prin's Asn; adv bd Voc/Spec Educ Handicapped S Bend Community Schs; Nat Asn Advan Colored People; bd mem S Bend Police Merit Bd; Kappa Alpha Psi Frat; Most Worshipful Grand Master Prince Hall Grand Lodge Jurisdiction Ind, 1981-83; Dep Orient Ind, Ancient Accepted Scottish Rite Prince Hall Grand Lodge IN, 1986-92; grand minister state, United Supreme Coun, Ancient Accepted Scottish Rite Freemasonry, Prince Hall Affil, northern jursidiction, 1992, 1998-; Lt Grand Comdr, USC, AASR; fel Paul Harris Rotary. **Honors/Awds:** Invited to the White House during President Carter's administration for conference on Energy 1980; Sovereign Grand Inspector Gen Ancient Accepted Scottish Rite Prince Hall Northern Jurisdiction, 1980; elevated to 33 degree United Supreme Council AASR, PHA, NJ, 1971. **Special Achievements:** First Black High School Principal in South Bend Indiana, 1983. **Military Serv:** AUS, supply sgt, 1950-52. **Home Addr:** 6521 Waterstone Dr, Indianapolis, IN 46268. *

OLDHAM, CHRIS. See OLDHAM, CHRISTOPHER MARTIN.

OLDHAM, CHRISTOPHER MARTIN (CHRIS OLDHAM)
Football player. **Personal:** Born Oct 26, 1968, Sacramento, CA. **Educ:** Univ Ore. **Career:** Football player (Retired); Detroit Lions, defensive back, 1990; Phoenix Cardinals, Buffalo Bills, 1991; Phoenix Cardinals, 1992-93; Ariz Cardinals, 1994; Pittsburgh Steelers, 1995-99; New Orleans Saints, 2000-01. *

OLDHAM, JAWANN
Basketball player. **Personal:** Born Jul 4, 1957, Seattle, WA. **Educ:** Seattle Univ. **Career:** Basketball player (retired); Denver Nuggets, ctr, 1980-81; Houston Rockets, ctr, 1981-82; Chicago Bulls, ctr, 1982-86; New York Nets, 1986-87; Sacramento Kings, 1987-88; Orlando Magic, 1989; Los Angeles Lakers, 1990; Ind Pacers, 1991; Jawann's Basketball Acad, Dubai, dir, currently. **Honors/Awds:** Olympic Gold Medalist with USA team. **Special Achievements:** First NBA superstar to open up a basketball training academy in Dubai. **Business Addr:** Director, Jawann's Basketball Academy, Canadian University of Dubai, Sheikh Zayed Rd PO 117781, Dubai 31961, Saudi Arabia, **Business Phone:** (971)50140-2271.*

OLDS, LYDIA MICHELLE
Administrator. **Personal:** Born Aug 25, 1961, Sanford, FL; daughter of Oliver Glover Sr (deceased) and Ruth Y; married; children: Rashonda Jamil. **Educ:** Roberts Wesleyan Col, BS, orgn mgt, 1996. **Career:** Xerox Corp, sr commodity mgr; Am Airlines, purchasing mgr, currently. **Orgs:** Nat Asn Purchasing Mgr, 1997. **Business Addr:** Purchasing Manager, American Airlines, PO Box 582809, Tulsa, OK 74158, **Business Phone:** (918)292-2724.

O'LEARY, HAZEL R. See O'LEARY, HAZEL R.

O'LEARY, HAZEL R (HAZEL R O'LEARY)
Government official, consultant, college president. **Personal:** Born May 17, 1937, Newport News, VA. **Educ:** Fisk Univ, attended; Rutgers Univ, law. **Career:** State NJ, state & co prosecutor; Coopers & Lybrand, partner; US Community Serv Admin, gen coun; Ford Admin, fed energy post; Carter Admin, fed energy post; Northern States Power Co, Minneapolis, MN, exec vpres; Clinton Admin, US Dept Energy, secy, 1993-97; O'Leary & Assocs Inc, pres, 1997-; Blaylock & Partners, LP, pres & chief oper officer, 2001-02; Fisk Univ, pres, currently. **Orgs:** Bd trustee,

Morehouse Col, 1998-; bd trustee, Africare; bd trustee, AES Corp; bd trustee, Ctr Democracy; bd trustee, Keystone Ctr; bd trustee, ICF Kaiser Inc; bd trustee, World Wildlife Fund. **Honors/Awds:** Trumpet Award, 1997. **Business Addr:** President, Fisk University, 1000 17th Ave N, Nashville, TN 37208-3051, **Business Phone:** (615)329-8500.

O LEARY, TROY FRANKLIN
Baseball player. **Personal:** Born Aug 4, 1969, Compton, CA. **Educ:** Chaffey Col. **Career:** Baseball player (retired); Milwaukee Brewers, outfielder, 1993-94; Boston Red Sox, 1995-2001; Montreal Expos, 2002; Chicago Cubs, 2003; baseball leagues, South Korea. **Special Achievements:** Currently writing a book about his career in Major League Baseball.

OLINGER, DAVID Y, JR.
Lawyer. **Personal:** Born Jan 8, 1948, Hazard, KY; son of David Y Sr and Zetta M; married Betty Hyatt, Jun 2, 1969; children: Joslyn Hyatt. **Educ:** Berea Col, BA, 1969; Univ Ky, JD, 1976. **Career:** Ky Dept Transp, staff atty; US Dept Justice, Eastern Dist Ky, asst US atty, currently. **Orgs:** Pres, Kiwanis Club Berea, 1987; Ky-Tenn Div Nine, lt gov, Kiwanis Club, 1992-93; master, Ashler Lodge 49 F & AM; gov elect, Kiwanis Club Berea, 2006-07. **Military Serv:** USN, sm3, 1969-73; Ameriman Spirit, 1970. **Home Addr:** 307 Brown St, Berea, KY 40403, **Home Phone:** (859)986-8716. **Business Addr:** Assistant US Attorney, United States Department of Justice, Eastern District of Kentucky, 110 W Vine St Suite 400, Lexington, KY 40507, **Business Phone:** (606)233-2661.

OLIVER, AL
Baseball player, executive. **Personal:** Born Oct 14, 1946, Portsmouth, OH; married Donna; children: Felisa & Aaron. **Educ:** Ky State Univ. **Career:** Baseball player (retired); Pittsburgh Pirates, outfielder & infielder, 1968-77; Tex Rangers, outfielder & infielder, 1978-81; Montreal Expos, outfielder & infielder, 1982-83; San Francisco Giants, outfielder & infielder, 1984; Philadelphia Phillies, outfielder & infielder, 1984; Los Angeles Dodgers, outfielder, 1985; Toronto Blue Jays, infielder, 1985; Al Oliver Enterprises Inc, pres, currently. **Honors/Awds:** Nat League batting title winner, 1982; first player in history to have 200hits & 100 RBI in same season in both leagues (1980, Tex, 1982, Montreal);named to The Sporting News Natl League All-Star team, 1975, 1982; NatLeague All-Star Team, 1972, 1975, 1976, 1982, 1983; Am League All-StarTeam, 1980, 1981; collected the 2500 hit of his career, 1983; played 2000 major league game, 1983; Seven Times All-Star selection, 1972, 1975, 1976, 1980, 1981, 1982, 1983; World Series champion, 1971; 3 Times Silver Slugger Award winner, 1980, 1981, 1982.

OLIVER, BILAL SAYEED (JAZZ BILAL)
Singer. **Personal:** Born Aug 21, 1979, Philadelphia, PA. **Educ:** Mannes Music Conserv, NY. **Career:** Soul Sista; "The 6th Sense"; appearances: Common's Like Water for Chocolate, Guru's Jazzmatazz Street Soul; UNI/Motown, mama's gun album,2000; Soul Aquarians collective; Albums: 1st Born Second, 2001; Love for Sale, 2006; "Air Tight's Revenge", 2009; Singles: "Fast Lane"; "Love It"; "Soul Sista". **Special Achievements:** Hit single "Soul Sista" on Love and Basketball soundtrack. **Business Addr:** Recording artist, Interscope Records Inc, 2220 Colorado Ave, Santa Monica, CA 90404, **Business Phone:** (310)865-1000.*

OLIVER, BRIAN DARNELL
Basketball player. **Personal:** Born Jun 1, 1968, Chicago, IL. **Educ:** Ga Inst Technol, attended 1990. **Career:** Basketball player (retired); Philadelphia 76ers, guard, 1991-92; Wash Bullets, 1995; Viola Reggio Calabria, 1996-97, 1998-2000; Polti Cantu, 1997-98; Atlanta Hawks, guard, 1998; Pallacanestro Messina, 2001-03; Coop Nordest Trieste, 2003-04; Upea Capo d'Orlando, 2004-05; Carifabriano, 2005-06; Cimberio Novara, 2006-07.

OLIVER, CECELIA. See BLANKS, CECELIA.

OLIVER, DARREN CHRISTOPHER
Baseball player. **Personal:** Born Oct 6, 1970, Kansas City, MO; son of Robert. **Career:** Texas Rangers, pitcher, 1993-98 & 2000-01; St. Louis Cardinals, pitcher, 1998-99; Boston Red Sox, pitcher, 2002; Colorado Rockies, pitcher, 2003; Florida Marlins, pitcher,2004; Houston Astros, pitcher, 2004; New York Mets, pitcher, 2006; LosAngeles Angels Anaheim, pitcher, 2007-. **Business Addr:** Pitcher, Los Angeles Angels Anaheim, 2000 E Gene Autry Way, Anaheim, CA 92806, **Business Phone:** (714)940-2000.

OLIVER, DONALD BYRD
Clergy. **Personal:** Born Nov 13, 1948, New York, NY; son of Byrd and Deforest; married Marionette, Jul 15, 1974; children: Marlo, Donald Jr & David. **Educ:** Point Loma Pasadena Nazarene Univ, BA, 1971; Princeton Theol Sem, MDiv, 1975; Fort Valley State Univ, MS, 1984; Oxford Grad Sch, PhD, 1989. **Career:** Bethel Presby Church, pastor, 1976-79; Wash Ave Presby, pastor, 1979-84; Coliseum Psychiatric Hosp, psychotherapist, 1984-85; Med Ctr Cent Ga, assoc dir pastoral care, 1985-92; Mercer Univ, adj asst prof-psychol, 1990-92; Hoag Memorial Hosp Presby, dir pastoral care, 1992-; San Francisco Theol Sem, adj prof ministry, 1996-. **Orgs:** Clin mem, Asn Clin Pastoral Education, 1985-; prof mem, InterNat Enneagram Asn, 1997-; pres, Presby Chapter Black Caucus, 1998-2000; chairperson, Presby Black Adv Comt, 1998-2000; pres, Newport Mesa Irvine Interfaith Coun, 1999-; trustee, San Francisco Theol Sem, 1999-; moderator, Synod Southern CA/ Hawaii, 2000-01. **Business Addr:** Director, Hoag Memorial Hospital Presbyterian, Rm 204 Fishback Bldg One Hoag Dr, PO Box 6100, Newport Beach, CA 92658-6100, **Business Phone:** (949)764-8358.

OLIVER, EVERETT AHMAD
Executive. **Personal:** Born Nov 22, 1961, Memphis, TN; son of George Oliver Sr and Evelyn Minor; married Kim Manning, Aug 17, 1985; children: Trevor & Shane. **Educ:** Univ Northern Colo, BA, criminal justice, 1985. **Career:** Coors, security rep, 1985-, mgr invest recovery, currently. **Orgs:** Bd mem, Colo State Juv & Delinq Prevention Adv Coun, 1989-92; Bd mem, Coors African-Am Asn; Chairperson, Systems Monitoring; Colo Uplift. **Honors/Awds:** Americas Best and Brightest Business and Professional Men, Dollars & Sense Mag, 1992. **Special Achievements:** Developed, implemented, and managed the Coors Office Watch Program, 1992-; featured in Professional Security Training Network video on corporate security, 1992; featured in Security Management magazine, 1992. **Business Addr:** Manager Investment Recovery, Coors Brewing Co, 311 10th St, Golden, CO 80401, **Business Phone:** (303)279-6565.

OLIVER, GARY DEWAYNE
School administrator. **Personal:** Born Sep 30, 1968, Montgomery, AL; son of George Oliver and Minnie. **Educ:** Savannah State Col, BA, 1992. **Career:** Savannah State Univ, dir stud progs & orgn, asst adv, currently. **Orgs:** Alpha Phi Alpha; Nat Asn Stud Affairs Profs; Ga Col Personnel Asn; Nat Orientation Dir Asn; Nat Asn Advan Colored People; Delta Eta Chap, Alpha Phi Alpha. **Honors/Awds:** Outstanding Young Men in America, 1992; Student Leadership Award, Nat Operatic & Dramatic Asn, 1992; Outstanding Young America, 1997. **Home Addr:** 12409 Largo Dr Suite 73, Savannah, GA 31419, **Home Phone:** (912)927-1703. **Business Addr:** Director of Student Programs and Organizations, Assistant Advisor, Savannah State University, Rm 208 King Frazier Stud Ctr, PO Box 20316, Savannah, GA 31404, **Business Phone:** (912)353-3149.

OLIVER, JERRY ALTON
Law enforcement officer. **Personal:** Born Mar 2, 1947, Phoenix, AZ; son of Florine Goodman and Fred A; married Felicia; children: Jerry II, Hope, Jacob, Joshua & Jordan. **Educ:** Phoenix Col, Phoenix, AZ, AA, 1972; Az State Univ, BA, 1976, MPA, 1988; Fed Bur Invest, Nat Exec Ins, grad. **Career:** Phoenix Police Dept, asst police chief, 1970-90; City Memphis, TN, dir, off drug policy, 1990-91; City Pasadena, chief police, 1991-95; City Richmond, chief police, 1995-2002; City Detroit, chief police, 2002-03; Oliver-Sage & Associates, Proprietor, currently. **Orgs:** Nat Orgn Black Law Enforcement, 1985-; past bd pres, Valley Leadership, 1985-86; Kappa Alpha Psi Fraternity; Nat 100 Black Men Inc, 1990; nat steering comt, Urban Youth Educ, Off Substance Abuse Prev, 1991. **Honors/Awds:** Veterans of Foreign Wars J, 1989; Hoover Award Hall of Fame Inductee, Az State Univ Pub Progs, 1988; Distinguished Alumni, Alumni Asn Phoenix Col, 1985; Distinguished Leadership Award, Nat Comt Leadership Orgn, 1990; Image Award, Nat Asn Advan Colored People, Phoenix Chapter, 1990. **Military Serv:** USN, E-4, 1966-68. **Business Addr:** Proprietor, Oliver-Sage & Associates, PO Box 93696, Phoenix, AZ 85070.

OLIVER, JESSE DEAN
Government official, lawyer, school administrator. **Personal:** Born Oct 11, 1944, Gladewater, TX; married Gwendolyn Lee. **Educ:** Dallas Baptist Univ, BCA, 1976; Univ Tex Sch Law, JD, 1981. **Career:** Sanger Harris Dept Stores, asst dept mgr, 1971-72, dept mgr, 1972-73; Int Bus Mach Corp, admin specialist, 1973-78; Univ Tex Sch Law, stud asst assoc dean; Byron Fullerton, 1979-80; Mahomes Biscoe & Haywood, assoc atty, 1981-83; Tex House Rep, mem 68th & 69th Tex Legis; Attorney Law,pract atty, 1983-; Lannen & Oliver PC, atty; Univ Tex Southwestern Med Ctr, assoc dir, currently. **Orgs:** Adv Comt, Licensed Voc Nurses Asn; partic, Info Sem Am Opinion LeadersHamburg & Berlin Germany, 1983; Nat Forum Excellence Educ, 1983; PlanningComt, Secretarial Initiative Teenage Alcohol Abuse Youth Treatment Regional Conf, 1983; Exec Comt Mayor's Task Force Housing & Econ Develop S Dallas, 1983-84; partic, 19th Annual Women's Symposium, Polit Power &Conscience, 1984; Nat Ctr Health Serv Res User Liaison Prog, 1984; speaker, Tex Pub Health Asn Conf, 1984; speaker, Nat Conf State Legislators Conf Indigent Health Care, 1984; speaker, Tex Pub Health Asn Conf; chmn, DART Bd. **Honors/Awds:** Honor, Univ Tex; Perigrinus Award for Outstanding Leadership, Tex Sch Student Bar Asn Bd Govs; Board of Governors Award, Student Bar Asn, Tex Sch Law; Consultant Award for Outstanding Service, Tex Sch Law; Gene Woodfin Award, Univ Tex Sch Law; J L Ward Distinguished Alumnus Award, Dallas Baptist Col, 1984; Certificates of Appreciation, E Garland Neighborhood Serv Ctr, 1974 & 1975; Distinguished Signal Service Award, Prairie View A&M Univ; Civics Award, Elite News; Legislative Achievement Award, Tex Pediat Soc, Tex Perinatal Asn. **Business Addr:** Associate Director, University of Texas, Southwestern Medical Center, 5323 Harry Hines Blvd, Dallas, TX 75390-9023, **Business Phone:** (214)648-9811.

OLIVER, JOHN J., JR.
Publishing executive, publisher, chief executive officer. **Personal:** Born Jul 20, 1945, Baltimore, MD. **Educ:** Fisk Univ, BA, 1969; Columbia Univ Sch Law, JD, 1972. **Career:** GE Information Serv Co, counr asst sec, 1980; Assigned Components GE Co,counr, 1978-80; Davis Polk & Wardwell, corp atty, 1972-78; Afro American Newspapers, vice chmn, 1982, publisher, 1982-, chmn bd of Dir, 1983-. **Orgs:** Kappa Alpha Psi; assoc mem, Mus Nat Hist; Columbia Law Sch Alum Asn; pres, Nat Newspaper Publishers Asn. **Business Addr:** Chairman of the Board, Publisher, Afro American Newspapers, 2519 N Charles St, Baltimore, MD 21218, **Business Phone:** (410)554-8200.

OLIVER, KENNETH NATHANIEL
Executive. **Personal:** Born Mar 6, 1945, Montgomery, AL; married Thelma G Hawkins; children: Tracey, Karen & Kellie. **Educ:** Univ Baltimore, BS, 1973; Morgan State Univ, MBA, 1980. **Career:** Equitable Bank NA, sr banking officer, 1973-83; Coppin State Col, asst prof; Harbor Bank, MD, vpres, currently; Baltimore Coun County, councilman, currently. **Orgs:** Pres, Baltimore Mkt Asn; Baltimore Cty Pvt Ind Coun; State Md Adv Bd; Walter P Carter Ctr; Baltimore Co Planning Bd; treas, Investing Baltimore; adv coun, John Hopkins Univ; Dem State Cent Community; bd mem, Hannah More Sch. **Special Achievements:** First African-American elected to Baltimore County Council, 2002. **Military Serv:** AUS, E-5, 4 yrs. **Home Addr:** 8818 Greens Lane, Randallstown, MD 21133, **Home Phone:** (410)655-5891. **Business Addr:** Councilman, Baltimore Council County, Ct House 2nd Fl 400 Washington Ave, Towson, MD 21204, **Business Phone:** (410)887-3389.

OLIVER, LOUIS
Real estate executive, football player. **Personal:** Born Mar 9, 1966, Belle Glade, FL. **Educ:** Univ Fla, BS, criminology, law, 1989. **Career:** Football player (retired), co-founder; Miami Dolphins, safety, 1989-93; Cincinnati Bengals, 1994; Miami Dolphins 1995-96; Sports & Entertainment Realty Advisors, co-founder, currently. **Business Phone:** (305)535-9686.

OLIVER, DR. MELVIN L
Educator, dean (education). **Personal:** Born Aug 17, 1950, Pittsburgh, PA; son of Rev Loman and Ruby. **Educ:** William Penn Col, BA, 1972; Wash Univ, MA, 1974, PhD, 1977; Univ MI, attended 1979. **Career:** Ford Found, Asset Bldg & Comm Develop, vpres; Univ MO, vis asst prof, 1977-78; Univ Calif, LA, from asst prof to assoc prof, 1978-2003; Rockefeller Found, res fel, 1984-85; Univ Calif, Santa Barbara, dean social sci & prof sociol, 2004-. **Orgs:** Fac assoc, Univ Calif, LA, Ctr Afro-Am Studies, 1978-; mem, Resource Allocation Comt, 1981-86, chair 1986-; mem bd, Urban Inst, Wash; mem adv bd, Div Behavioral & Social Sci & Educ, Nat Res Coun; mem adv bd, Gerald R Ford Sch Pub Policy, Univ Mich. **Honors/Awds:** Distinguished Alumni Award, Wash Univ; California Professor of the Year, 1994; Harriet and Charles Luckman Distinguished Teaching award, Univ Calif, LA Alumni Asn, 1994; Distinguished Scholarly Publication Award, Am Sociol Asn; C Wright Mills Award, Soc Study Social Problems; Award for the outstanding book on the subject of human rights from the Gustavus Myers Ctr. **Special Achievements:** Co-authored Black Wealth/White Wealth: A New Perspective on Racial Inequality. **Business Addr:** Dean of Social Sciences, Professor of Sociology, University of California, 552 Univ Rd, Santa Barbara, CA 93106, **Business Phone:** (805)893-4327.

OLIVER, PAM (PAMELA DONIELLE OLIVER)
Broadcaster. **Personal:** Born Mar 10, 1961, Dallas, TX. **Educ:** Fla A&M Univ, BS, broadcast jour, 1984. **Career:** WFSU-TV, reporter/producer, 1984-85; WALB-TV, Albany, Ga, polit/news reporter, 1985-86; WAAY-TV, Huntsville, Ala, sci/mil reporter, 1986-88; WIVB-TV, Buffalo, NY, news reporter/anchor, 1988-90; WTVT-TV, Tampa, Fla, news reporter/anchor, 1990-91, sports reporter/anchor, 1991-92; KHOU-TV, Houston, Tex, sports anchor/reporter, 1992-93; ESPN, sportscaster, 1993-95; Fox Sports, NFL Games, sideline reporter, 1995-; TNT, NBA Playoffs, sideline reporter, 2005-. **Honors/Awds:** Outstanding Woman in Journalism, Ebony Mag, 2004. **Business Addr:** Reporter, Fox Sports, 10201 W Pico Blvd, Los Angeles, CA 90064, **Business Phone:** (310)369-1000.

OLIVER, PAMELA DONIELLE. See OLIVER, PAM.

OLIVER, WINSLOW PAUL
Football player. **Personal:** Born Mar 3, 1973, Houston, TX; married Julie; children: Christopher, Steven & Lauren. **Educ:** Univ NMex. **Career:** Football player (retired); Carolina Panthers, running back, 1996-98; Atlanta Falcons, 1999-00. **Honors/Awds:** Hula Bowl MVP, 1996. *

OLIVER-SIMON, GLORIA CRAIG
Government official. **Personal:** Born Sep 19, 1947, Chester, PA; daughter of Lavinia C Staton and Jesse Harper; married Joseph M;

children: James R Norwood. **Educ:** Prince George Community Col, AAS, 1983; Bowie State Univ, attended 1986; Univ Md, BS, 1987; Wash Col Law, JD, 1990; Am Univ, MS, 1992. **Career:** Government offical (retired); PMC Col, Widener Univ, admin asst, 1966-68; Veterans Admin, Med Ctr, personnel specialist, 1975-80, sr personnel specialist, 1980-90; Dept Vet Affairs, Recruitment & Examining Div, chief, 1990-96; sr human resources consult, 1996, adv human resource mgt. **Orgs:** Am Bar Asn, 1987-; Nat Bar Asn, 1987-; Am Univ, Stud & Fac Comt, 1987-88; vice chair, Black Law Stud Asn, AU Chap, 1988-89; Phi Delta Phi Legal Frat, 1988-; Nat Black Law Stud Asn; coordr, Mid-Eastern Region, Frederick Douglass Moot Ct Annual Competition, 1989; Pa Bar Asn, 1991-; Fed Bar Asn, 1992; Pub Employees Round table, VA, coordr, PSRW, 1991-92; Leadership Va Alumni Asn, 1992; Am Soc Law, Med & Ethics, 1992-94; Fed Circuit Bar Asn, 1993; DC Bar, 1997; DAV Auxiliary, 1993-; AKA Sorority Inc, 1995; bd chair, Promotions Comt, 1996-2000; Asn Trial Lawyers Am, 2000-; Asn Conflict Resolution, 2000-; DC Bar Asn, 2000-; Dept HAS Sharing Neutrals Prog, 2000-; fel Soc Fed Labor & Employee Rels Prof, 2001-, bd secy,2001-; Md Asn Nonprofit Orgn, 2001-03; VFW Auxiliary, 2003-. **Honors/Awds:** Word Master Award, Veterans Admin, 1981; Prince George Community Col, Phi Theta Kappa Hon Frat, 1983; Director's Commendation, Med Ctr,Philadelphia, 1980; Appreciation Plaque, Black Law Students Asn, 1989;Special Contribution Award, 1996, 1997, 2000 & 2003; Recognition Award,2001.

OLLEE, MILDRED W.
School administrator, college president. **Personal:** Born Jun 24, 1936, Alexandria, LA; daughter of Robert L Wilkerson and Pearl Herbert Wilkerson; married Henry P Ollee Jr, Dec 21, 1957; children: David Michael & Darrell Jacques. **Educ:** Xavier Univ LA, BA, 1956; Univ SW LA, Grad Courses 1960; Walla Walla Col.Masters, 1967; Univ Wash Grad Work, 1977-78; Seattle Univ, Seattle, WA, EdD, 1988. **Career:** High Sch teacher, 1956-62; George Wash Carver High Sch, LA, soc sci lead teacher, 1960-61; WA Asn Retarded Children Walla Walla Lillie Rice Activ Ctr Youths & Adults, dir, 1964-66; Walla Walla County Sup Ct, marriage counr, therapist, 1967; Walla Walla Community Col, instr fac, 1968-70; Birdseye Frozen Foods Div of Gen Foods Walla Walla WA, consult, 1968; Seattle Cent Community Col, dist VI, couns fac, 1970-73, dir spec serv to disadv stud, 1973-; AIDP SSDE FIPSE Dept HEW Office Ed, consult, 1977-80; Seattle Community Col Dist VI, assoc dean stud, 1976-, dean stud develop serv, 1988-, Stud Serv, vpres, 1992-; Seattle Central Community Col, pres, Currently. **Orgs:** Bd mem, Am Red Cross Walla Walla, 1962-64, Puget Sound Black Educ Asn, Seattle 1970-72; chmn pres search comm, Seattle Cent Community Col, 1979; pres, NASP, NW Asn Spec Prog Regional X, 1979-81; Delta Sigma Theta, Citizens Transit Adv Comm, METRO Coun, 1979-80; area rep, Fed WayCommunity Coun, 1979-80; fin secy, Links, Inc, 1983-90; exec bd, Leadership Synthesis, 1989-91. **Honors/Awds:** Most Outstanding Young College Woman Award, Xavier Univ, 1956; Workshop Leader Compensatory Ed for the New Learner, Univ of WA 1975; Co-author, SSDS-TRIO Project Dir Manual Dept of HEW Office of Ed 1978; Presented paper "3 R's for Black Students, Recruitment Requirements & Retention" 4thAnnual Conf of Council on Black Affairs. **Business Phone:** (206)587-6946.

OLLISON, RUTH ALLEN
Journalist. **Personal:** Born Apr 1, 1954, Mount Pleasant, TX; daughter of Vera Lewis; married Quincy L, Dec 28, 1980; children: Jacob Waelder Allen. **Educ:** Univ Tex, Arlington, bus courses; Am Univ, bus courses; Univ N Tex, BA, radio-tv-film, 1975; Wesley Theol Sem, pursuing masters theol studies. **Career:** KKDA-FM, news dir, 1975-78; KRLD Radio, reporter, 1978-80; KXAS TV, news mgr, 1980-84; KDAF TV, news dir & asst news dir, 1984-86; KETK TV, news dir & anchor, 1986-87; Fox TV, asst news dir, 1987-; KEGG Radio Sta, co-owner & mgr, 1990-; Houston's Beulah Land Community Church, pastor, currently; Houston Baptist Univ, adj prof applied theol, currently. **Orgs:** Nat Asn Black Journalists; Shiloh Baptist Church. **Honors/Awds:** Best Newscast, United Press Int, 1987; Outstanding News Operation, Assoc Press, 1988; Regional Overall Excellence Award, Radio TV News Dirs Asn, 1989. **Home Phone:** (713)522-2344. **Business Addr:** Adjunct Instructor, Houston Baptist University, Department of Christianity and Philosophy, 7502 Fondren Rd, Houston, TX 77074, **Business Phone:** (281)649-3000.

OLOWOKANDI, MICHAEL
Basketball player. **Personal:** Born Apr 3, 1975, Lagos, Nigeria; son of Ezekiel. **Educ:** Univ Pac, econ, 1998. **Career:** Los Angeles Clippers, ctr, 1998-2003; Minn Timberwolves, ctr, 2003-06; Boston Celtics, ctr, 2006-07; free agent, currently. **Honors/Awds:** Big W Player of the Week. **Business Addr:** Free Agent.

OLUGEBEFOLA, DR. ADEMOLA
Arts administrator, educator, artist. **Personal:** Born Oct 2, 1941, Charlotte Amalie, St Thomas, Virgin Islands of the United States; son of Harold Thomas II and Golda Matthias Thomas; children: Mona, Monica, Rahim, Alejandro, Tanyeni, Solar, Khari & Denise. **Educ:** Fashion Inst Tech, 1961; Yoruba Acad West African Cult, attended; Weusi Acad African Arts & studies, New York, attended; Printmaking Workshop, New York, attended. **Career:** Artist; designer; educr, businessman; Pomusicart's Jazz Art Develop & Res Pro, dir; Harlem Cult Coun, consult; Metrop Mus Art, New York, spec consult; Ori-Gem, founder; Caribbean Media Assoc Inc, pres; Tetrahedron, founder, 1978; Robert Gumbs, consult & partner, currently. **Orgs:** Vpres, Int Commun Asn; chmn, Educ Dept Weusi Acad Arts & Studies. **Honors/Awds:** Hon Doc, Weusi, 1969; Commendation, City of New York, 2000. **Business Addr:** Artist, Grinnell Fine Art Collection, 800 Riverside Dr Suite 5E, New York, NY 10032.

OMOLADE, BARBARA
Educator. **Personal:** Born Oct 29, 1942, Brooklyn, NY; daughter of Hugh Jones (deceased) and Mamie Taylor Jones (deceased); children: Kipchamba, Ngina, Eskimo & Krishna. **Educ:** Queens Col, BA, 1964; Goddard Col, MA, 1980; City Univ NY, New York, NY, PhD, sociol, 1997. **Career:** Feminist-run domestic violence Ctr; Ctr Elimination Violence Family, co-dir, 1977-78; Women's Action Alliance, 1979-81; Empire State Col, Ctr Labor Studies, instr, 1980-81; WBAI Radio, producer & commentator, 1981-83; CCNY-CWE, higher educ officer & adjunct fac, 1981, assoc prof; freelance writer, 1979-; City Univ NY, New York, NY, coordr curric change fac develop sems, 1988-; Calvin Col, dean multicultural affairs, dean emer, currently. **Orgs:** Bd mem, Sisterhood Black Single Mothers, 1983-; co-founder, CUNY Friends Women Studies, 1984-; career fac mem, CCNY-CWE; NAACP; staff mem, Student Non-Violent Coord Comt. **Honors/Awds:** Unit Awards in Media, Lincoln Univ, MO, 1981; Malcolm X Award, The East, 1982; Susan B Anthony Award, New York City Nat Org Women, 1987. **Special Achievements:** Author of The Rising Song of African Am Women; first dean of multicultural affairs of a major Christian college. **Home Addr:** 231 Ocean Ave Suite 4B, Brooklyn, NY 11225, **Home Phone:** (718)462-9428. **Business Addr:** Dean Emeritus, Calvin College, 3201 Burton St SE, Grand Rapids, MI 49546, **Business Phone:** (616)526-6000.

ONASSIS, ERICK. See SERMON, ERICK.

O'NEAL, REV. EDDIE S
Clergy. **Personal:** Born Mar 28, 1935, Meridian, MS; son of Eddie S and Sara Lenora. **Educ:** Tougaloo So Christian Col, BA, 1963; Andover Newton Theol Sch, BD, 1967, STM, cum laude, 1969, DMin, 1972. **Career:** Clergy (Retired); Rockefeller Protestant fel, 1962-66; Woodrow Wilson fel, 1963; Peoples Baptist Church, assoc minister; Clinton Ave Baptist Church, copastor; Myrtle Bapt, pastor; St Mark Congregational, assoc pastor; Mt Olive Baptist Church, pastor; Pine Grove Baptist Church, pastor; Andover Newton Theol Sch, prof. **Orgs:** Chmn, Black Studies Comn Boston Theol Inst, 1970-76; Ministries Black Higher Educ; Interfaith Coun Ministry & Aging; Rockefeller Protestant Fel Prg; trustee, Andover Newton Theol Sch; auditor & parl, United Baptist Conv Mass & RI; Nat Comn Black Chmen; Soc Study Black Religion; City Missionary Soc Boston; Am Bapt Conv; Nat Asn Advan Colored People; Omega Psi Phi Frat; consult, Women's Serv Club. **Honors/Awds:** Key to the City of Newton, MA, 1969; Andover Newton Quar, 1970. **Special Achievements:** Articles Christian Century, 1971.

O'NEAL, JERMAINE
Basketball player. **Personal:** Born Oct 13, 1978, Columbia, SC; son of Angela Ocean. **Career:** Portland TrailBlazers, forward, 1996-2000; Ind Pacers, ctr-forward, 2000-; Bogota Entertainment, owner, currently. **Honors/Awds:** NBA All-Star, 2002, 2003, 2004, 2005, 2006, 2007; NBA Most Improved Player Award, 2002; Magic Johnson Award, Pro Basketball Writers Asn, 2004. **Business Addr:** Professional Basketball Player, Indiana Pacers, 125 S Penn St, Indianapolis, IN 46204, **Business Phone:** (317)917-2500.

O'NEAL, LESLIE CORNELIUS
Football player. **Personal:** Born May 7, 1964, Pulaski County, AR. **Educ:** Okla State Univ. **Career:** Football player (retired); San Diego Chargers, defensive back, 1986-95; St.Louis Rams, 1996-97; Kansas City Chiefs, 1998-99. **Honors/Awds:** NFL Defensive Rookie of the Year, Associated Press, 1986.

O'NEAL, MALINDA KING
Executive. **Personal:** Born Jan 1, 1929, Cartersville, GA; daughter of Dan; married Sheppard Dickerson Sr; children: Sheppard D Jr & Sherod Lynn. **Educ:** Morris Brown Col, BA (cum laude), 1965; Atlanta Univ, MA, 1970; Alumni Admin Am Alumni Coun, Wash, DC, cert; Skillings Bus Col, Kilmarnock, Scotland, prof cert. **Career:** Radio Station WERD, rec librn, disc jockey & continuity writer, 1949-50; Mammy's Shanty Restaurant Atlanta, sec bookkeeper, 1951-53; MKO Graphics & Printers, Atlanta, GA, owner & pres, 1987-; Nat Cong Colored Parents & Teachers Atlanta, off dir; Emory Univ Ctr Res Soc Change, field supvr spec proj; Morris Brown Col, dir alumni affairs, gov rels, dir admiss & dean stud. **Orgs:** Better Bus Bureau, 1988; Atlanta Bus League, 1988; United Negro Col Fund; Nat Asn Advan Colored People; YWCA; Kappa Omega chap, Alpha Kappa Alpha; vol, Atlanta Coun Int Visitors; trustee bd, Ebenezer Baptist Church. **Honors/Awds:** Outstanding Dedicated Serv Dir Alumni Affairs, 1974; Business of the Year Award, 1992; WA Fountain & JH Lewis Status Achievement Award Recipient. **Special Achievements:** Editor of "The Alumni Mag" Morris Brown College 8 years, editor of "The Ebenezer Newsletter", writings include "How to Rear a Blind Child" 1959; Hon by Nat Cong Colored Parents & Teachers on 2 occasions outstanding & dedicated serv; cited on 2 occasions for outstanding service as Advisor to the Undergrad Chapter of Alpha Kappa Alpha; Distinguished Alumni, NAFEO 1991. **Home Addr:** 215 Piedmony Ave NE Apt 306, Atlanta, GA 30308-3319, **Home Phone:** (404)523-0845. **Business Addr:** President, Owner, MKO Graphics & Printers, 846 M L King Jr Dr SW, Atlanta, GA 30314, **Business Phone:** (404)523-1560.

O'NEAL, RAYMOND W, SR.
Lawyer. **Personal:** Born Sep 22, 1940, Dayton, OH; son of Carrie B and Henry L; married Brenda, Jun 22, 1963; children: Raymond Jr & Terisa. **Educ:** Ohio Univ, BA, 1968; Howard Univ, MA, 1968, JD, 1973. **Career:** US Dept Trea, financial analyst, 1971-74; Wilberforce Univ, polit sci asn prog, 1977-79; Miami Univ, econs instr, 1978-84; Atty Law, sole practitioner, 1981-; Advance Eldercare Law Firm, lawyer, currently. **Orgs:** Founder, Dayton-Miami Valley Minority Chamber Com; APA Fraternity Inc, 1970-; Ohio Bar Asn, 1981-; Cent Steering Comt, second vpres, Montgomery County Republican Party, 1981-; Am Bar Asn, 1982-; bd mem, Dayton Educ & Legal Comn, Nat Asn Advan Colored People, 1987-92; bd mem, Montgomery County Arthritis Found, 1990-92; O'Neal Fund, 2000. **Honors/Awds:** Economics Honorary, Omicron Delta Epsilon, 1968; Business Leadership Award, Middletown Ohio, 1984; Citizens Volunteer Award, City Dayton, 1992; Assistance To Indigent Clients Award, Dayton Bar Asn, 1992. **Special Achievements:** The Black Labor Force in the USA: Critical Analysis (master's thesis), 1968; 39th House District candidate to Ohio Legislative, 1992. **Home Phone:** (937)222-7773. **Business Addr:** Lawyer, Advance Eldercare Law Firm, 211 S M St Suite 1130, Dayton, OH 45402-2419, **Business Phone:** (937)222-7773.

O'NEAL, RODNEY
Automotive executive, president (organization). **Personal:** Born Aug 27, 1953, Dayton, OH; son of James H and Ida B; married Pamela Estell O, Aug 20, 1983; children: Heather Marie & Damien Cain. **Educ:** Gen Motors Inst, BA, indust admin, 1976; Stanford Univ, MBA, 1991. **Career:** Gen Motors, stud co-op prog, 1971, Inland Div, staff, 1976-91, dir indust eng, 1991; Gen motors, Delhi Interior Syst, dir manufacturing, 1992-94, gen mgr, 1997-98, pres, 1998-00; Gen Motors, Delphi Automotive Systs Corp, ad dir, exec vpres, Dynamics Propulsion & Thermal sector, 2000-03, pres, 2003-05, pres & chief operating officer, 2005-07, pres & chief exec officer, 2007-. **Orgs:** Kappa Alpha Psi Fraternity, 1977-; adv, Gen Motors Inst, Black Unity Cong, 1987-88; Windsor, Ontario, Can Chamber Com, 1987-90; Indust Mutual Asn Flint, MI, 1995-96; One Hundred Club Flint, MI, 1995-; Mich Manufacturers Asn. **Honors/Awds:** Am Best & Brightest Young Businessmen, Dollars & Sense Mag, 1990; Distinguished Serv Award, Consortium for Grad Study in MGT, 1993. **Special Achievements:** Presenter at the Annual Trumpet Awards, Aired on TBS, 1995-. **Business Addr:** President, Chief Executive Officer, Delphi Automotive Systs Corp, 5725 Delphi Dr, Troy, MI 48098-2815, **Business Phone:** (248)813-2000.

O'NEAL, SHAQUILLE RASHAUN
Actor, basketball player, business owner. **Personal:** Born Mar 6, 1972, Newark, NJ; son of Joseph Toney and Lucille O'Neal Harrison; children (previous marriage): Taahirah; children: Shareef Rashaun, Amirah Sanaa & Shaquir Rashaun. **Educ:** La State Univ, BA, 2000; Univ Phoenix, MBA, 2005. **Career:** Orlando Magic, ctr, 1992-96; Los Angeles Lakers, 1996-2004; TWISM Rec Label, founder, 1997-; Miami Heat, ctr, 2004-08; TWISM Clothing Co, founder & owner; Phoenix Suns, ctr, 2008-. **Honors/Awds:** Eddie Gottlieb Award, 1993; NBA Rookie of the Year, 1993; NBA All-Rookie First Team, 1993; NBA All-Star, 1993-98; Gold Medal, US Olympic Basketball Team, 1996; NBA Most Valuable Player, 1999-00; NBA Champions, 2000; NBA Most Valuable Player 2000-01. **Special Achievements:** First pick, overall, NBA draft, first round, 1992, Selected as one of the 50 Greatest Players in NBA Hist, 1996, was ranked No 9 on SLAM Magazine's Top 75 NBA Players of all time in 2003; Films: CB4, 1993; Blue Chips, 1994; Kazaam, 1996; Good Burger, 1997; Stell, 1997; He Got Game, 1998; Freddy Got Fingered, 2001; The Wash, 2001; The Year of the Yao, 2004; After the Sunset, 2004; The Kid & I, 2005; Scary Movie 4, 2006; Albums: Shaq Diesel; Shaq Fu: Da Return; You Can't Stop the Reign; Respect. **Business Phone:** (602)379-7900.

O'NEAL, STANLEY
Executive. **Personal:** Born Oct 7, 1951, Roanoke, AL; married Nancy Garvey; children: 2. **Educ:** General Motors Inst, BS, indust admin, 1974; Harvard Bus Sch, MBA, finance, 1978. **Career:** Gen Motors Corp, analyst, 1978-80, dir, 1980-82, Spanish subsid, treas, 1982-84, asst treas, NY, 1984-87; Merrill Lynch & Co Inc, investment banker, dir investment banking, managing dir financial servs group, head client strategies group, 1987-96, exec vpres, coheadglobal mkt & investment banking, 1997-98, chief financial officer 1998-2000, pres, & chief exec officer, 2000-02, chmn, 2003-07; Alcoa Inc, dir, 2008-. **Orgs:** Exec Leadership Coun & Fedn; bd mem GM Corp; bd mem, Lower Manhattan Develop Corp; bd mem, NASDAQ Stock Exchange; bd mem, Nat Urban League; bd

mem, Ronald McDonald House; bd mem, Bronx Preparatory Sch; trustee, Buckley Sch; trustee, Ctr Strategic & Int Studies. **Honors/Awds:** Corporate Executive of the Year, Black Enterprise, 2000; Achievement Award, Exec Leadership Coun, 2000. **Business Addr:** Chief Executive Officer, Director, Alcoa Inc, 201 Isabella St, Pittsburgh, PA 15212-5858, **Business Phone:** (412)553-4545.*

O'NEALE, SONDRA
School administrator, dean (education). **Educ:** Asbury Col, BA, eng lit; Univ Ky, MA, Am lit, doctorate degree, Am lit. **Career:** Univ Ky; Emory Univ; Univ Calif, San Diego; Univ Wisc-La Crosse, chairperson, Dept Women's Studies; Wayne State Univ, Col Liberal Arts, dean, 1994-98, prof eng, 1999-. **Orgs:** Phi Beta Kappa. **Special Achievements:** Has published twenty articles, author of Jupiter Hammon & the Biblical Beginnings of African-Am Lit, editor of Call & Response: An Anthology of African-American Literature. **Business Phone:** (313)577-2545.

O'NEILL, ANTHONY B., SR.
Lawyer. **Educ:** St. Augustine's College, BA, 1969; University of Iowa College of Law, JD, 1975. **Career:** O'Neill & Fair Attorneys at Law, Attorney. **Orgs:** National Secretary, 100 Black Men of America; Board of Directors, Neighborhood Legal Assistance Program; South Carolina Black Lawyers Association; Thurgood Marshall Law Society; NAACP; National Bar Association. **Business Addr:** 1847 Ashley River Rd., Ste. 200, Charleston, SC 29407, **Business Phone:** (843)763-3900.*

ONLI, TURTEL
Artist, educator, publisher. **Personal:** Born Jan 25, 1952, Chicago, IL. **Educ:** Olive-Harvey Col, AA, 1972; L'Academie De Port-Royal, attneded 1977; Sch Art Inst, Chicago, BFA, 1978; Art Inst Chicago, MAAT, 1989. **Career:** Columbia Col, Chicago, instr, 1978-81; Dysfunctioning Child Ctr, art therapist, 1978-82; Ada S McKinley Develop Sch, art therapist; Onli-Wear Studio, master artist, 1978-85, dir, currently; Black Black Love, Fine Arts Ctr, actg dir, 1984-85. **Orgs:** Founder, Black Arts Guild, 1971-76; USA rep, FESTAC, Second World Festival African Art & Cult, 1976; founder, Rhythmistic Sch Art, 1976. **Honors/Awds:** Certificate of Award, Nat Conf Artists, 1972,1974; premiere prix aux foyer, Internatl D'Accueil De Paris, 1978; Award Of Excellence, Artist Guild Chicago, 1979. **Special Achievements:** Publisher of NOG Protector of the Pyramides and Future Funk News, the only black-owned & published comic characters, curator, Bag Retrospective Exhibition, 1991, publisher, Malcolm-10 Spawning The Black Age of Comics, 1992, Organizer & promoter of the Black Age of Comics National Convention, Chicago. **Business Addr:** Director, Onli Studios, 1448 E 52nd St, PO Box 468, Chicago, IL 60615, **Business Phone:** (773)536-0755.

ONO, MUSASHI
Chief executive officer. **Personal:** Married LaKeyshia Graves. **Career:** Black Child Films, chief exec officer, currently. **Business Addr:** Chief Executive Officer, Black Child Films, 100 Oceangate Blvd Suite 100, Long Beach, CA 90802, **Business Phone:** (562)628-5537.*

ONWUDIWE, EBERE C
School administrator, editor. **Personal:** Born Oct 10, 1952, Isu-Njaba, Imo, Nigeria; son of Nwamgbede Onyegbule Achigaonye and Onwudiwe Simon Achigaonye; married Mamle, Jul 11, 1992; children: Chinwe & Mbamemme. **Educ:** Am Col Switzerland, AA; Univ Sci & Arts Okla, BA; Fla State Univ, Tallahassee, Fla, MA, int rel, 1981, MSc, econ, 1983, PhD, polit sci, 1986. **Career:** Cent State Univ, Wilberforce, OH, assoc prof, 1986-; Antioch Col, Yellow Spring, OH, adj prof; Centr State Univ, dir Nat Res Ctr African Studies & prof polit sci, currently; Int J African Studies, ed. **Orgs:** African Studies Asn; Acad Int Bus; Nat Asn Black Pol Scientists; World Acad Develop & Coop; vpres, Asn Nigerian Scholars Dialogue. **Honors/Awds:** Cong Citation, Publ Ed, US Senate, Cong Record, 1990. **Home Addr:** 1026 Trianon Dr, Xenia, OH 45385, **Home Phone:** (513)372-4596. **Business Addr:** Professor, Director, Central State University, Center for African Studies, PO Box 1004, Wilberforce, OH 45384-1004, **Business Phone:** (937)376-6264.

ONYEJEKWE, DR. CHIKE ONYEKACHI
Physician. **Personal:** Born Jun 8, 1960, Okigwe, Nigeria; son of Engr E Onyejekwe. **Educ:** Western Ky Univ, BS, Biol, BS, Chem, 1981; Howard Univ, MD, 1986. **Career:** DC Gen Hosp, med officer, currently; pvt pract, currently. **Orgs:** Secy, Int Red Cross, 1976-78; Int Forum WKU, 1978-81; capt, WKU Soccer Club, 1980-81. **Honors/Awds:** Alpha Epsilon Delta Premed Hon Soc; Chief Resident, Howard Med Serv, DC Gen Hosp. **Home Addr:** 1930 E Orman Ave, Pueblo, CO 81004. **Business Phone:** (719)565-3320.

OPOKU, EVELYN
Physician. **Personal:** Born Jun 14, 1946, Accra, Ghana; daughter of Ebenezer and Barbara; divorced; children: James Boye-Doe. **Educ:** Univ Ghana Med Sch, W Africa, MD, 1971; Columbia Univ, MPH, 1990. **Career:** Korle Bu Teaching Hosp, house officer, 1971-72, med officer, 1972-75; Health & Hosp Corp, Harlem Hosp, pediat res, 1976-79; Southern Med Group, pediatrician, 1979-82; Hunts Pt Multiservice, pediatrician, 1982-85; City NY Dept Health, sr med specialist, 1986-91; Graham Windham, dir, health servs, beginning 1991; NYHHC/Cumberland Diagnostic & Treat Ctr, Med Dir, 2001-02; Woodhull Med & Ment Health Ctr, pediatrician; pvt pract, currently. **Orgs:** Fel, Am Acad Pediat, 1990-; Am Pub Health Asn, 1987-; NY Task Force Immigrant Health, 1991-. **Home Addr:** 408 Pondside Dr, White Plains, NY 10607. **Business Addr:** Pediatrician, Woodhull Medical & Mental Health Center, 760 Broadway, Brooklyn, NY 11206, **Business Phone:** (718)963-8124.

ORDUNA, DR. KENNETH MAURICE
Educator. **Personal:** Born Dec 27, 1939, Omaha, NE; son of Alonzo and Florence; married Nancy Baker, Aug 12, 1989; children: Alon, Damian, Terry Lynn, Alisa & Kela. **Educ:** City Univ, MBA, 1998; Pac Theol Univ, PhD, 2000, ThD, 2001. **Career:** US Congress, chief staff, 1980-92; Customer Service Inc, vpres, 1992-; Pac Theoll Univ, dean, prof, 2001-. **Orgs:** Life mem, Nat Asn Advan Colored People, 1959-; pres, Coalition Better Govt, 1969-76; pres, Comt Peace & Democracy Middle East, 1971-80; field dir, A Philip Randolph Inst, 1972-76; deacon, St Paul Bapt Church, 1989-; dir educ, Western Bapt Conf USA, 1999-. **Special Achievements:** Author: History of the African American Church - by African Slaves: Study of the Ethnicity of the Biblical Patriarchs and their Linage to Jesus Christ. **Military Serv:** USN, Petty Officer 1st class, 1956-60. **Home Addr:** 4436 W 58th Pl, Los Angeles, CA 90043. **Business Addr:** Dean/ Professor, Pacific Theological University, 11555 La Cienega, Los Angeles, CA 90043, **Business Phone:** (323)338-6900.

OREE, WILLIAM. **See OREE, WILLIE.**

OREE, WILLIE (WILLIAM OREE)
Hockey player, hockey executive. **Personal:** Born Oct 15, 1935, New Brunswick;son of Rosebud; married Deljeet; children: Chandra. **Career:** Prof hockey player (retired), exec; Boston Bruins, 1957-58, 1960-61; Nat Hockey League, dir youth develop, currently. **Orgs:** NHL, Diversity Task Force. **Honors/Awds:** Los Angeles Blades Western Hockey League, goal scoring 1964; three all star teams; San Diego Gulls, Western Hockey League, goal scoring 1969; New Brunswick Sports Hall of Fame, 1984. **Special Achievements:** First Black player in the National Hockey League; Referred to as the Jackie Robinson of ice hockey due to breaking the colour barrier in the sport; played professional hockey for 21 years with only one eye; Author: The Willie O'Ree Story: Hockey's Black Pioneer. **Business Addr:** Director of Youth Development, National Hockey League, 1251 Ave of the Americas Fl 47, New York, NY 10020, **Business Phone:** (212)789-2000.

ORLANDERSMITH, DAEL (DONNA DAEL THERESA ORLANDER SMITH BROWN)
Playwright, poet. **Personal:** Born 1959, New York, NY. **Educ:** Hunter Col; HB Studios, acting; Actors Studio, acting. **Career:** Plays: Beauty's Daughter, 1995; Monster, 1996; The Gimmick, 1998; Yellowman, 2002; Books: Beauty's Daughter, Monster, The Gimmick: Three Plays, 2000; Yellowman, My Red Hand, My Black Hand: Two Plays, 2002; Film: Get Well Soon, 2001; New Dramatists, playwright-in-residence, 2002-. **Honors/Awds:** Obie Award, Beauty's Daughter, Village Voice, 1995; Hellen Merrill Emerging Playwrights Award, 2003; Roger Stevens Playwrighting Award, 2003, Susan Smith Blackburn Award, 2003; PEN/Laura Pels Foundation Award for Drama, 2005. **Business Addr:** Playwright, c/o Judy Boals, 208 W 30th St Suite 401, New York, NY 10001, **Business Phone:** (212)868-1068.*

ORMSBY, WILLIAM M
Judge. **Career:** Los Angeles Munic Ct, judge; State Calif Munic Ct, Inglewood Dist, judge, 1981-. **Business Addr:** Judge, State of California Municipal Court Inglewood District, 1 Regent St Rm 205, Inglewood, CA 90301-1261, **Business Phone:** (213)419-5121.

ORR, CLYDE HUGH
Executive. **Personal:** Born Mar 25, 1931, Whitewright, TX; son of Hugh and Melissa; married Maizie Helen Stell; children: 3. **Educ:** Army Command Gen Staff Col, Grad, 1965; Prairie View Agri & Mech Col, BA, Polit Sci, 1953; Univ Oklahoma, Masters Public Admin, 1974. **Career:** Fort Ord, CA, mgr, 1968-70, mil adv / Ethiopia-Haile Salassie Body Guard div, 1970-72; Lincoln Univ, adminr, ROTC, 1973-75; Metrop St Louis Sewer Dist, dir human resources. **Orgs:** St Louis Bi-state Red Cross; mem of corp, YMCA Bd; Bd of City Unit, Am Cancer Soc; Pkwy Sch Dist Affirmative Action Comt; vice chair, Hopewell Ctr. **Honors/Awds:** Lay Participant Award, St Louis Sch Syst; Boy Scouts of America Award, St Louis Chap, 1984; Lay Participant Award, Vounteer of the Year Award, Am Cancer Soc, 1992. **Military Serv:** AUS, Lt, col 22 yrs; Legion of Merit; Bronze Star & Air Medal, 1975. **Home Addr:** 12866 Topping Manor Dr, Saint Louis, MO 63131.

ORR, DR. DOROTHY J
President (Organization), insurance executive. **Educ:** Atlanta Univ, attended; Columbia Univ, accelerated grad study. **Career:** Fordham Univ Sch of Social Work, assoc prof; Equitable Life Assurance Soc, vpres; Orr DaCosta Balthazar & Orr, pre & sr partner; NY State, Dept of Human Rights, comnr; Equitable Life Financial Co, vpres corp social responsibility; Dorothy J Orr Assoc Consult, founder & pres, currently. **Orgs:** Former comnr NY State Comn Human Rights. **Honors/Awds:** Carter G Woodson Award, Mercy Col, 2003. **Special Achievements:** Organized the first course on "Culture and Social Work" in response to student requests for courses on cultural diversity.

ORR, LOUIS M.
Basketball player, basketball coach. **Personal:** Born May 7, 1958, Cincinnati, OH; married Amerine Lowry; married Yvette; children: Monica & Chauncey. **Educ:** Syracuse Univ, attended 1980. **Career:** Basketball player (retired), basketball coach; Ind Pacers, 1980-82; NewYork Knicks, 1982-88; Xavier, asst coach, 1991-94; Providence, asst coach, 1994-96; Syracuse, asst coach, 1996-2000; Siena, 2000-01; Seton Hall Univ, head coach, 2001-06; Bowling Green, head coach, currently. **Honors/Awds:** All-East, Baketball Writers & Basketball Weekly; Big East Coach of the Year, 2003. **Business Addr:** Head Coach, Bowling Green Falcons, Perry Stadium E, Bowling Green, OH 43403, **Business Phone:** (419)372-2255.*

ORR, MARLETT JENNIFER
Educator. **Personal:** Born Sep 30, 1970, Detroit, MI; daughter of Remal. **Educ:** Mich State Univ, BA, 1992; Univ Mich-Dearborn, MA, 1994. **Career:** Detroit Bd Educ, educr, 1993-. **Orgs:** Coun, Except Stud, 1990-. **Honors/Awds:** Young Educrs Soc, Detroit Bd Ed, 1993. **Home Addr:** 14730 Quincy St, Detroit, MI 48238-2162. **Business Addr:** Educator, Detroit Public Schools, 28545 Thorn Apple Dr, Southfield, MI 48034, **Business Phone:** (313)873-0379.

ORR, RAY
Executive. **Personal:** Born Feb 13, 1953, Marks, MS; son of Ella Kuykendall; married Patrice Ann Clayton; children: Jacqueline Denise, Ray Jr & Reuben Patrick. **Educ:** Memphis State Univ, BS, bus admin, 1978. **Career:** US Post Off Memphis, clerk, loader & sorter, 1975-77; Methodist Hosp, distrib agt, 1977-78; Fed Express Corp, cargo handler, sales trainee, sales rep sr sales rep, 1978-82; Big D Mailing Serv Inc, chmn, pres & ceo, 1983-. **Honors/Awds:** Outstanding Sales Performance, Fed Express Corp, 1980; Quest for Success Award, Dallas Black Chamber, 1987. **Special Achievements:** Businessman of the Day KKDA Radio Dallas, 1985; Entrepreneur of the Week Dallas Morning News, 1986. **Business Addr:** President, Chief Executive Officer, Big D Mailing Services Inc, 1007 E Levee St, PO Box 565841, Dallas, TX 75207, **Business Phone:** (214)747-9400.

ORTICKE, LESLIE ANN
Consultant. **Personal:** Born Dec 28, 1960, Los Angeles, CA; daughter of Lester Lionel and Gertrude Kathryn. **Educ:** Univ Calif, Los Angeles, BA, 1983. **Career:** United Negro Col Fund, asst to the area dir; HIV Educr, Job Trainer, YWCA Los Angeles, adolescent pregnancy childwatch, consult, fund develop assoc; Ariz State Univ, Southern Calif, Develop & Alumni Asn, coord, 1991-. **Orgs:** United Negro Col Fund, Delta Sigma Theta; Congregational Church Christian Fel, United Church Christ; YWCA; Junior League Los Angeles; Nat Comt Mem, chapter pres, Delta Sigma Theta Sorority; Congregational Church Christian Fel, UCC; Jr League Los Angeles; Lullaby Guild of the Child's Home Soc; Nat Asn Female Execs; LA Bruin Club. **Honors/Awds:** Recipient of several awards and certs for volunteer services; Outstanding Young Woman, Delta Sigma Theta Sorority; Women's Hist Month Honoree, Los Angeles Black Employees Asn; numerous awards & cert for volunteer serv. **Business Addr:** Fund Development Associate, YWCA of Greater Los Angeles, 3345 Wilshire Blvd Suite 300, Los Angeles, CA 90010, **Business Phone:** (213)365-2991.

ORTIQUE, REVIUS OLIVER, JR.
Judge. **Personal:** Born Jun 14, 1924, New Orleans, LA; son of Revius Oliver Ortique (deceased) and Lillie Long (deceased); married Miriam Marie Victorianne; children: Rhesa Marie McDonald. **Educ:** Dillard Univ, BA, sociol, 1947; Ind Univ, MA, 1949; Southern Univ, JD, 1956; Campbell Col, LLD; Ithaca Col, LHD; Univ Ind, LLD; Morris Brown Col, LLD; Loyola Univ, LLD; Dillard Univ, LLD. **Career:** Judge (retired); Full-time practicing atty, New Orleans, LA, 1956-78; Orleans Parish Civil Dist Ct, 1978; Civil Dist Ct, judge, 1979-92; Urban League, Greater New Orleans, pres; La Supreme Ct, justice, 1992-94. **Orgs:** US Dist Ct Eastern Dist LA; US 5th Circuit Ct Appeals; former pres, Nat Legal Aid & Defender Asn; Am Lung Asn; Nat bd dir; bd dir, Antioch Col Law; exec bd, Nat Bar Asn; exec bd, Nat Bar Found; Former mem bd, Nat Sr Citizens Law Ctr, LA; exec comn, Am Bar Asn; Am Bar Asn Comn Legal Aid & Indigent Defenders; Am Bar Asn House Dels; La State Bar Asn House Dels; sr vpres, Metro Area Comn MAC Affiliate Urban Coalition; bd trustees, Dillard Univ; exec comn, Criminal Just Coord Comt; former bd mem, Law Enforcement Alliance Am; former bd mgt, Flint Goodridge Hosp; former bd, City Trusts City New Orleans; former exec comn, Indust Develop New Orleans Metro Area; adv bd, League Women Voters Greater New Orleans; bd, New Orleans Legal Asst Corp; former bd dir, United Fed Savings & Loan Asn; former bd

dir, Community Rels Coun; men's bd, YWCA; La State Bar Asn; Ad Hoc Comn Develop Cent Bus Dist New Orleans; gen coun eight dist African Methodist Episcopal Church, La & Miss; former mem Pres, Comn Campus Unrest & Scranton Comn; past pres Am Lung Asn, La; chart mem, World Peace Through Law; chmn, New Orleans Aviation Bd. **Honors/Awds:** Alpha Kappa Delta Honor Soc; Blue Key Honor Soc; Arthur von Briesen Medal, Distinguished Serv Disadvantaged Am, 1971; Brotherhood Award, Nat Conf Christians & Jews; Lifetime Achievement Award, La State Bar Asn, 1976; Outstanding Person La, 1976; Gertrude Rush Award, Nat Basketball Asn; Lifetime Achievement Award, La State Bar Asn; Award for Excellence, United Negro Col Fund; President's Award, Int Honors, World Trade Ctr; Martin Luther King Lifetime Achievement Award, Consortium Loyola, Tulane & Xavier Univ; Honorary Doctor Laws, Campbell Col; Honorary Doctor Humane Letters, Univ Ind; Honorary Doctor Laws, Loyola Univ; many other citations, awards and plaques. **Special Achievements:** First African-American lawyer elected to the House of Delegates of the Louisiana State Bar Association; first African American elected to La Supreme Court, 1992-94. **Military Serv:** USY, 1st Lt, Co Commander. *

ORTIZ, DELIA
School administrator. **Personal:** Born Nov 25, 1924; married Steve Oritz; children: Rosie, Vickie, Steven Jr, Clara, Sandra & Beinaldo. **Educ:** Columbia, 2 yrs. **Career:** PS 43-PS125, pres; Fama Film Prod, pres; Knickerbocker Hosp Ambulatory Care, pres; Drug Referral, pres; Community Sch Bd, pres, 1973-75, secy, 1982-. **Honors/Awds:** Tenant of the year Grant, Housing Project, 1966; Community Award, Salinas Socia Club, 1970; School Service Award, Pres' coun Dist 5, 1972. **Business Addr:** Secretary School Board, Community School District 5, 333 7th Ave, New York, NY 10001-5004.*

ORTIZ, VICTOR
Judge. **Personal:** Born Dec 12, 1946, New York, NY; son of Wendell and Manda Mays. **Educ:** BBA, mkt, 1970; JD, 1973. **Career:** Pvt pract civil & criminal law, 1977-78, 1981-85; Off Dist Atty, Dallas County, TX, asst dist atty, 1978-81; Dallas County Ment Health Ctr, hearing officer, 1984-85; City Dallas, TX, asst city atty, 1974-77, assoc munic judge, 1977-78, 1984-85, munic judge, 1985-. **Orgs:** J L Turner Legal Asn, 1974-; Progressive Voters League, 1975-86; bd dir, Dallas Minority Repertory Theatre, 1976-81; vpres & mem dir, Comt 100, 1976-82; bd dir, Pk S YMCA, 1978-81; stewards bd, St Paul AME Church, 1978-; bd dir, Dallas Black Chamber Com, 1979-81; Nat Bar Asn, 1982-; coun pres, Charles Rice Learning Ctr, 1999-. **Honors/Awds:** American Jurisprudence Award, Bancroft Witney Co, 1972; Community Service Award, United Negro Col Fund, 1975; Extra Mile Award, St Paul AME Church, Usher Board No 2, 1985; Man of the Year, Nat Coun Negro Women, 1986; Man of the Year, St Paul AME Church, 1997; Hall of Fame, Charles Rice Learning Ctr, 1999. **Business Addr:** Municipal Judge, City of Dallas Municipal Court, 2014 Main St Suite 210, Dallas, TX 75201, **Business Phone:** (214)670-5573.

OSAKWE, PROF. CHRISTOPHER
Educator. **Personal:** Born May 8, 1942, Lagos, Nigeria; married Maria Elena Amador; children: Rebecca Eugenia. **Educ:** Moscow State Univ Sch Law, LLB, first class hons, 1966, LLM, 1967, PhD, law, 1970; Univ IL Col Law, JSD, 1974. **Career:** Univ Notre Dame Law Sch, prof law, 1971-72; Russian Res Ctr Harvard Univ, res fellow, 1972; Univ PA law Sch, vis prof, 1978; Tulane Univ Sch Law, prof law, 1972-81; Univ PA sch law, vis prof law, 1978; St Anthony's Col, Oxford Univ, vis fel, 1978; Univ Mich Sch Law, vis prof law, 1981; Tulane Univ Sch Law, prof comparative law, 1981-; Wash & Lee Univ Sch Law, visit proflaw, 1986; World Bank & USAID, resident legal adv, 1994-97; Kazak State Law Acad, vis prof & dir, 1997-99; Moscow State Univ, prog dir, vis prof, 1999-2007; Am Russian Law Inst, consult, currently. **Orgs:** Carnegie doctoral fel Hague Acad Int'l Law, 1969; ABA, 1970; Am Soc Int IL, 1970; Am Law Inst, 1982-; res Fel Russian Res Ctr, Harvard Univ, 1972; dir, Eason-Weinmann Ctr Comparative Law, 1978-86; dir, bd dir, Am Asn Comparative Study Law, 1978; vis fel, Ctr Russian & East Europ Studies Univ MI, 1981; scholar, Sr US-Soviet Exchange Moscow State Univ Law Sch, 1982; dir, bd of review & devel, Am Soc Int Law, 1982-87. **Special Achievements:** Auth, The Participation of the Soviet Union in Universal Intl Orgs, 1972; co-auth, Comparative Legal Traditions in a Nutshell, 1982; co-auth, Comparative Legal Traditions-Text, Materials, Cases, 1985. **Business Phone:** (212)656-1810.

OSBORNE, DR. ALFRED E., JR.
Educator, school administrator. **Personal:** Born Dec 7, 1944; son of Alfred and Ditta. **Educ:** Stanford Univ, BSEE, 1968, MA, econs, 1971, MBA, finance, 1971, PhD, bus econs, 1974. **Career:** Western Develop Labs, elec engr, 1968; Sec & Exchange CMS, econ fel, 1977-80; UCLA Grad Sch Mgt, asst prof, 1972-78; assoc prof, 1979-; asst dean, MBA Prog, dir, 1979-83; assoc dean, 1984-87; Entrepreneurial Studies Ctr, dir, 1987-. **Orgs:** Dir, The Times Mirror Co, 1980-; past pres, Nat Econ Asn, 1980-81; dir, chair, Municipal Financial Adv Comt City Los Angeles, 1981-; bd economists, Black Enterprise Magazine, 1982-85; dir, Nordstrom Inc, 1987-; dir, Indust Bank, 1983-93; co-chair, Nat Conf Christians & Jews, 1985-94; dir, First Interstate bank CA, 1993-; dir, US Filter Corp, 1990-; dir, Greyhound Lines, Inc, 1994-; governor, Nat Asn Securities Dealers Inc,1994-; Coun Econ Advs CA, 1993-; dir, Equity Mkt Inc; dir, K2 Inc; dir, Kaiser Aluminum. **Honors/Awds:** Outstanding Faculty Award, UCLA Grad Sch Mgt, 1975-76; Fellow, Brookings Inst Econ Policy, 1977-78. **Special Achievements:** Author: Several scholarly articles in economics and finance. **Business Addr:** Co-Director, University California Los Angeles Graduate School of Management, Entrepreneurial Studies Center, 405 Hilgard Ave, PO Box 951521, Los Angeles, CA 90024-1481, **Business Phone:** (310)825-2985.*

OSBORNE, CLAYTON HENRIQUEZ
Executive. **Personal:** Born Aug 16, 1945, Canal Zone, Panama; son of Clayton F and Hilda Rogers; married Dorelis Agnes, Jul 1975; children: Clayton C & Sheldon R. **Educ:** Ohio Northern Univ, Ada, OH, 1965; State Univ New York Albany, Albany, NY, BA, 1968, Sch Soc Welfare, MSW, 1972; Univ Massachusetts Amherst, ABD. **Career:** Rochester Inst Technol, Rochester, NY, asst prof, 1974-75; NYS Div Youth, Rochester, NY, dist supvr, 1976-79, regional dir, 1979-88; Monroe County, Rochester, NY, dir opers, 1988-92; Bausch & Lomb, corporatwe dir employee rel, workforce diversity, 1992-94, dir strategic staffing & diversity, 1994-99, vpres, staffing & diversity, 1999-2000, vpres, human resources, 2000, vpres, Global Diversity Orgn Effectiveness, chief privacy officer, currently. **Orgs:** Chmn, drug abuse, NYS Asn Counties, 1988-92; Monroe County Bd thics, Monroe County, 1988-92; bd mem, Monroe Co Employer Credit Union, 1988-92; bd mem, Urban League Rochester, 1986-; bd mem, NYS Disabilities Counc, 1989-93; bd mem, Asn Battered Women, 1992-; bd mem, Rochester bus Opportunities Inc, 1992-93; chmn, Mayor Comn Against Violence, 1992-93; bd trustees, St Marys Hosp; Career Develop Serv Bd; United Way Rochester; Black Bus Asn; chair, Career Develop Servs, Nat Multi-cultural inst; bd trustees, Equity Inc; founder, Greater Rochester Diversity Coun. **Honors/Awds:** Distinguished Service, City of Rochester, 1979; Distinguished Service, Urban League of Rochester, 1985; Distinguished Alumni, Gov Rockefeller Sch Pub Affairs, 1987; Father of the Year, Bethel AME Church, 1988. **Home Addr:** 30 Stonebury Crossing, Pittsford, NY 14534-4211. **Business Addr:** Vice President, Chief Privacy Officer, Bausch & Lomb Inc, 1 Bausch & Lomb Pl, Rochester, NY 14604, **Business Phone:** (716)338-5358.

OSBORNE, ERNEST L.
Government official. **Personal:** Born Nov 15, 1932, New York, NY; married Elizabeth; children: Mrs. **Educ:** Long Island, Du, 1953. **Career:** Travelers Corp, dir nat & community affairs; Dept Health & Human Serv, depunder sec inter govt affairs; Dept Health Educ & Welfare Wash, DC, comnrAPS/OHDS, 1978-80, dir OSCA/OHDS, 1977-80; Sachem Fund New Haven, CT, exec dir, 1972-77; Yale County Community Affairs Yale Univ, exec dir, 1968-71. **Orgs:** Bd mem, Coop Asst Fund Wash, 1972-75, 1980; bd mem, Howard Univ Press Wash, DC 1979-80; bd mem, Coun Found Wash, DC 1980-81; Nat Asn Advan Colored People. **Honors/Awds:** Distinguished Service Award, Dept Health Educ & Welfare Wash, DC, 1980.

OSBORNE, GWENDOLYN EUNICE
Activist, manager. **Personal:** Born May 19, 1949, Detroit, MI; daughter of George William and Ida Juanita Jackson; married Harry Kaye Rye, Feb 12, 1977; children: Kenneth Anthony Osborne Rye. **Educ:** Detroit Conserv Music, AA, 1966; Mich State Univ, BA, eng educ, 1971; Medill Sch Jour, NW Univ, MSJ, 1976; Roosevelt Univ, litigation cert, 1986. **Career:** Penguin, Inc Ed Serv, 1968-; Crisis Nat Asn Advan Colored People, contrib ed, 1973-78; Players Mag, bk ed, 1974-78; Unique Mag, arts bk & entertainment writer, 1976-78; Scott-Foresman & Co, asst ed permissions asst, 1978-79; Pioneer Press Newspapers Inc, lively arts ed, 1978-80; Rand McNally, prod ed, 1979; News Election Serv, Chicago regnl personnel mgr, 1980; Am Bar Asn, publ specialist, 1980-82; Southeastern Mich Transp Authority, publ specialist, 1982-84; Debbie's Sch Beauty Cult Debbie Howell Cosmetics, spec asst pres, 1985-86; Twenty first Century Woman, assoc ed, 1986; ABA Comn Opportunities Minorities Legal Prof, commun consult, 1988-89; Am Civil Liberties Union Ill, pub info dir, 1989-91; Univ Ill Chicago, arts & cult ed, 1991-95; Ill Inst Technol, Downtown Campus, pub affairs dir, 1995-; Romance Reader, contribr, 1997-; Mystery Reader, contribr, 1998-; Black Issues Bk Rev, regional ed, 1999, assoc ed, currently; Bk Mag, contribr, 2000. **Orgs:** Mich State Univ Black Alumni Asn; Second Baptist Church; Delta Sigma Theta; Nat Asn Black Journalists; Nat Black Publ Rel Soc; Nat Endowment Arts Off Partnership; Am Bar Asn; Am Civil Liberties Union; Nat Asn Advan Colored People. **Honors/Awds:** Editorial Award, Arts Category, Pioneer Press Newspaper, 1980; Certificate of Merit, Family Law Sect, Am Bar Asn, 1981-82; Proclamation, Off Mayor, City Detroit, 1983; Certificate of Appreciation, Off Gov, State Ill, 1983; Editorial Award, Arts Category, Pioneer Press Newspapers, 1980. **Home Addr:** 635-5 Chicago Ave Suite 218, Evanston, IL 60202-2372. **Business Addr:** Associate Editor, Black Issues Book Review, 350 Fifth Ave Suite 1522, New York, NY 10118, **Business Phone:** (212)947-8515.

OSBORNE, JEFFREY LINTON
Singer, drummer. **Personal:** Born Mar 9, 1948, Providence, RI; son of Clarence and Wanita; married Sheri; children: Tiffany, Dawn & Jeanine. **Career:** Love Men Ltd, singer, 1969; L.T.D., producer & singer; solo performer, currently; Singles: "On the Wings of Love", 1982; "I Really Don't Need No Light", 1982; "She's On the Left"; Albums: Jeffrey Osborne, 1982; Stay With Me Tonight, 1983; Don't Stop, 1984; Emotional, 1986; Space balls, 1987; One Love, One Dream, 1988; Only Human, 1991; Something Warm for Christmas, 1997; That's for Sure, 2000; Undercover Brother, 2002;Space balls Music Is Life, 2003; From the Soul, 2005; Film: The Young Messiah - Messiah XXI, 2006; The Office, 2006; TV Series: "A Celebration of Life: A Tribute to Martin Luther King, Jr", 1984; "The Beach Boys: 25Years Together", 1987; "We Are the World", 1985; "The Parent 'Hood", 1995; "Christmas with the Stars", 2001; "Celebrity Duets", 2006. **Business Phone:** (516)484-1000.

OSBORNE, OLIVER HILTON
Educator. **Personal:** Born Feb 17, 1931, Brooklyn, NY; son of Mildred Branch and Deighton Hamilton; married Mary P; children: Zarth Gazvoda; married Julianne Nason, Aug 25, 1985; children: Martin, Mary Ann, Michael, Michelle & Mathew. **Educ:** Hunter Coll NY, BS, Nursing, 1958; NY Univ, MA, Psychiatric/Mental Health Nursing, 1960; MI State Univ, PhD, 1968. **Career:** Wayne State Univ, assoc prof nursing/adj prof anthrop, 1960; McGill Univ Montreal, mental health consult, 1969; Univ WA, Dept Psychosocial Nursing, assoc prof & chmn 1969-74; Univ Botswana S Africa, assoc res fel, 1976-78; Sch Nursing, Yale Univ, vis prof, 1979; Dept Afro-Am Studies, Sch Nursing Univ, vis prof, 1979; Sch Nursing, E Carolina Univ, distinguished lectr, 1979; Am Acad Practice, fel, 1985; Univ WA, Dept Anthrop, adj prof; Univ WA, Dept Psychosocial Nursing, prof, prof emer. **Orgs:** Am Anthrop asn; Am Nurses' asn; Soc Applied Anthrop; sec & treas, Soc Med Anthrop,1970-73; Coun Nursing & Anthrop; numerous consultations including, East Model Cities Health Task Force, Seattle, WA, 1971; Rockefeller Found Univ del Valle Cali, Columbia, 1973; Mental Health Clinic Group, Hlth Coop, Seattle, WA 1974; ANA Fellowship Prog; Doctoral Training Racial/Ethnic Minorities, Clin Mental Hlth Serv, 1977-82; Interdiv Cncl, Cert Am Nurses Asn, 1976-80; Nat Adv Center for Health Care & Res Sch Nursing Univ TX, Austin, 1979-80; Psychiatric Nursing Educ Review Comn, NIMH, 1980-83; Nat Comn Develop Minority Curric Psychiat & Mental Health Disciplines, Howard Univ, NIMH, 1980-; lay mem Judicial Screening Comn, Seattle-King County Bar Asn; 1982-; Ogboni Soc Ibara Abeokuta Nigeria; Northwest Asn Clinical Specialists Psychosocial Nursing; Am Acad Practice. **Honors/Awds:** Chief Adila of Ibara, Ibara Abeokuta Nigeria, 1972; Frederick Douglass Scholar's Award, Natl Conf Black Scholars, 1988. **Special Achievements:** Numerous papers including, "Violence and the Human Condition, A Mental Health Perspective" Univ of WI Milwaukee, WI 1979; "Psychosocial Nursing Research, The State of the Art" presented at the Conference, "Perspectives in Psychiatric Care," 1980 Phila, PA; Research Approaches to the Social Ecology of Health Sch of Nursing Columbia Univ New York, NY 1982; Occasioning Factors of Urban Violence, African-American Studies Ctr Madison, WI; "Point Prevalence Study of Alcoholism and Mental Illness among Downtown Migrants" (with Whitley, Marilyn P and Godfrey, M) Social Science & Medicine, an Intl Journal in 1985. **Business Addr:** Professor Emeritus, University of Washington, Health Sci Bldg Rm T-310 1959 NE Pacific St, PO Box 357260, Seattle, WA 98195.

OSBORNE, DR. WILLIAM REGINALD, JR.
Health services administrator, educator. **Personal:** Born May 10, 1957, Worcester, MA; son of William Reginald Sr and Dolores Everett; married Cheryl Lowery, Jun 1980; children: Justin, Blake & Maya. **Educ:** Morehouse Col, BS, 1979; Howard Univ Col Med, MD, 1983; Emory Univ Sch Med, Dept Internal Med. **Career:** Morehouse Col, asst instr, anat & physiol, 1979-80, summer careers prog instr physics, 1980, Medicine Dept Internal Med, clin instr, 1986-; Health South, internist 1986-89; Southside Healthcare Inc, med dir, 1989-91; Henry Med Ctr, chief staff, 1999-2001. **Orgs:** Omega Psi Phi Fratenity, 1976-; Southern Christian Leadership Conf, 1978-; Am Col Physicians, 1986; Nat Med Asn; Ga State Med Asn, 1989-. **Honors/Awds:** Scholastic Award, Omega Psi Phi Frat, 1978,79; Atlanta Univ Ctr Biol Honor Soc; Fraternity 7th District Scholar Award Omega Psi Phi Frat, 1978; Beta Kappa Chi Scientific Honor Soc; Bd Cert Internal Medicine. **Business Addr:** Physician, Harsch Osborne MD PC, 105 Carnegie Pl-103, Fayetteville, GA 30214-3905, **Business Phone:** (770)716-7999.

OSBY, GREGORY THOMAS
Saxophonist, composer. **Personal:** Born Aug 3, 1960, St Louis, MO; son of Georgina; married Kay Vaughn. **Educ:** Howard Univ, attended 1978-80; Berklee Col Music, MA, 1980-83. **Career:** Saxophonist, composer, producer & educator; Oztone Productions, ceo, currently; Albums: Greg Osby & Sound Theater, 1987; Mind Games, 1989; Season of Renewal, 1990; Man-Talk for the Moderns V.X., 1991; 3-D Lifestyles, 1993; Black Book, 1995; Art Forum, 1996; Further Ado, 1997;Zero, 1998; Banned in New York, 1999; Invisible Hand, 2000; Symbols of Light (A Solution), 2001; Inner Circle, 2002; St. Louis Shoes, 2003; Public (Live), 2004; Channel Three, 2005. **Honors/Awds:** Recieved numerous awards. **Home Addr:** Jug Hollow Rd, Phoenixville, PA 19460, **Home Phone:** (610)935-0108. **Business Phone:** (610)935-0108.

OSBY, PARICO GREEN
Nutritionist, educator. **Personal:** Born Feb 7, 1945, Selma, AL; daughter of Marion L Sr and Rosetta Wilson; married Porter Jr, Sep 12, 1965; children: Patrick, Phyllis & Portia. **Educ:** Tuskegee Univ, BS, 1968; Baptist Hosp, ADA dipl, 1973; Cent Mich Univ, MA, 1977. **Career:** Univ Nev, Las Vegas, Nev, stud foodservice mgr, 1968-70; Baptist Hosp, dietetic trainee, 1970-73; St Francis Xavier Hosp, clin & adm dietician, 1973-75; St Elizabeth Hos, Dept of Nutrit, dir, 1976-87; Tuskegee Univ, instr, 1989-92, hospity Mgt Prog, actg cordr, instr, 1992-93; Ala Coop Exten Syst, regional exten agent III, currently. **Orgs:** Am Dietetic Asn, 1973-; NCP, 1975-; Ala Dietetic Asn, Scholarship Comn, 1988-; Am Hotel/Motel Asn, 1991-. **Honors/Awds:** Graduate of Leadership, Dayton Prog Promising Community Leaders, 1985; Faculty Service Award, Tuskegee Univ, 1990; Teacher of the Year, Sch Agr & Home Econs, 1991. **Business Addr:** Regional Extension Agent III, Alabama Cooperative Extension System, South East Alabama F&CP Region 3, 306 S 3 Notch St, Troy, AL 36081, **Business Phone:** (334)566-0985.

OSBY, PATRICIA ROBERTA
Social worker. **Personal:** Born Jul 6, 1958, Toledo, OH; daughter of Katherine L Osby; children: Imari, Isaiah & Ileah. **Educ:** Univ Toledo, Assoc, 1983, BASW, 1994. **Career:** Ohio Youth Advocate Program, treatment coord, 1996-. **Orgs:** Miss Junior Toledo, pres, founder, chief exec officer, 1995-; Gamma Phi Delta, 1999. **Home Addr:** 2124 Calumet Ave, Toledo, OH 43607, **Home Phone:** (419)536-0250.

OSEYE, EBELE. See SOUTHERLAND, ELLEASE.

OSHIYOYE, DR. EMMANUEL ADEKUNLE, SR.
Physician, lawyer. **Personal:** Born Jan 1, 1951, Lagos, Nigeria; son of Alfred (deceased) and Grace; married Irene, Dec 28, 1991; children: Emmanuel Adekunle Jr & Justice. **Educ:** Univ State NY, BS, 1974; Columbia Univ, Sch Med, med, 1974-78; Am Univ Sch Med, MD, 1979; Thomas Cooley Law Sch, JD, 1997. **Career:** Chicago Bd Health, gynecologist, 1989-93; St Joseph Hosp, Obstet-Gynec, 1993-95; Wayne County Health Dept, family planning consult, 1995-96; Residential Home Care, dir care mgmt, staff physician, 1995-; Law Office Dr Oshiyoye, CEO/atty-at-law, 1998-. **Orgs:** State Bar, MI, Health Comm, 1998-; Oakland County Bar Asn, Young Lawyers Comn, 1998-; MI Trial Lawyers Asn, 1998-; Mich State Med Soc, delegate, 1998-; Wayne County Med Soc, Med-Legal Comn, 1998-; Detroit Med Soc, Legislative Comn, 1998-; Am Immigration Lawyers Asn, 1998. **Honors/Awds:** Howard Univ, scholar, 1972-74; Fed Govt Nigeria, scholar, 1972-79; Cerebral Palsy Medical Award, 1974; Beta Kappa Chi, Honor Society, 1974; Alpha Phi Alpha, Recognition Award, 1992. **Home Phone:** (248)357-7821. **Business Addr:** CEO/Attorney-at-Law, Emmanuel Oshiyoye Law Offices, 23300 Greenfield Rd Suite 127, Oak Park, MI 48237-8408, **Business Phone:** (248)968-1006.

OSSE, MCGHEE WILLIAMS. See WILLIAMS, MCGHEE.

OTHOW, HELEN CHAVIS
Educator. **Personal:** Born Apr 21, 1932, Oxford, NC; daughter of Benjamin F Sr; widowed; children: Ajulonyodier Elisabeth. **Educ:** St Augustine's Col, BA, 1952; NC Cent Univ, MA, 1958; Univ Wis-Madison,PhD, 1971. **Career:** NCA Secondary Sch, Eng, Fr teacher, 1952-63; St Augustine's Col, Enginstr, 1963-66; St Augustine's Col, eng assoc prof, 1971-74; Johnson CSmith Univ, assoc prof, Chair Div, 1974-79; Howard Univ, eng asst prof, 1980-81; Univ Juba, Juba, Sudan, eng assoc prof, 1981-82; NCA Cent Univ, eng assoc prof, 1982; Univ NCA, Chapel Hill, assoc prof, 1983; St Augustine's Col, prof eng, 1984-2001; NC Cent Univ, prof eng, 2001-; Louisberg Col, part-time fac, 2007-. **Orgs:** Col Lang Asn, 1989-; Modern Lang Asn, 1984-; Nat Coun Teachers Eng, 1989-98; Am Asn Univ Women, 1984-; Asn Study Africa Am Life & Hist, 1990-; pres, John Chavis Hist Soc, 1986-; Nat Presenters Asn, 1990-; Zora Neale Hurston Soc, 1993-. **Honors/Awds:** Outstanding Faculty Plague Trophy, St Augustine's Col 1995; President Prezell R Robinson Award, 1985; UNCF Faculty Research Grant, 1987-88; NEH fel, Princeton Univ, 1988. **Special Achievements:** Author: Biography of John Chavis, 2000; Anthology of African Literature, 2000; "African Continuity in Toni Morrison's Beloved;" Zora Neale Hurston Forum, Vol VII, No 1, Fall, 1992; "Roots and the Heroic Search for Identity," CLA Journal, 1983; "The New Decorum: Moral Perspectives of Black Literature," PhD Dissertation, 1971; author, John Chavis: Afr Amer Patriot, Preacher, Teacher & Mentor (1763-1838), McFarland & Co, 2001. **Business Addr:** Part time Faculty, Louisburg College, 501 N Main St, Louisburg, NC 27549, **Business Phone:** (919)496-2521.

OTIENO-AYIM, LARBAN ALLAN
Dentist. **Personal:** Born Sep 15, 1940; son of Jonathan and Dorcas; married Agness Auko; children: Peter, Paul, James, Anna. **Educ:** Univ Wis, attended 1969; Meharry Med Col Nashville, TN, DDS, 1973; Univ Minn Sch Pub Health, MPH, 1975. **Career:** Dentist, pvt pract, 1977-; State Minn Dept Pub Welfare, staff dent, 1975-77; Pilot City Health Ctr Minneapolis, clin dent, 1974-75. **Orgs:** Am Dent Asn; Minneapolis Dist Dent Soc; Minn Dent Asn; Am Pub Health Asn; Minn Pub Health Asn; Masons. **Business Addr:** Broadway Penn Dent Bldg, 2126 W Broadway, Minneapolis, MN 55411-180.

OTIS-LEWIS, ALEXIS D
Judge. **Educ:** Wash Univ Sch Law, JD. **Career:** St Clair Co, Ill, asst state's atty; pvt pract, E St Louis, Ill, 1989-92; St Clair County 20th Judicial Circuit, judge, 1992-. **Orgs:** Alpha Kappa Alpha Sorority; Jack & Jill Inc. **Special Achievements:** First African-American woman judge elected to serve in the 20th judicial circuit which includes St Clair, Monroe, Perry, Wash & Randolph Counties; First African Am fed law clerk, Southern Dist of Ill. **Business Addr:** Judge, St Clair County Circuit Court, St Clair County Courthouse, 10 Pub Sq, Belleville, IL 62220, **Business Phone:** (618)277-7325.

OTTLEY, AUSTIN H.
Association executive. **Personal:** Born Jun 17, 1918, New York, NY; married Willie Lee; children: Federic Wayne, Dennis. **Educ:** Empire State Col, BS. **Career:** Mayors Comn Exploitation Workers NY, sr rep, 1965-67; IBEW Local 3, shop steward, 1959-65; NY City Ctr Labor Coun ALF-CIO, asso dir; BTULC, secy. **Orgs:** F Div Adv Bd, Local 3 IBEW; Lewis Howard Latimer Progressor Asn; Chap 80 St Geo Asn, 1972; Labor Comn Jamaica; NAACP, 1962-66; Negro Am Labor Coun, 1962. **Military Serv:** USAF, sgt, 1942-46; USAFR, s & sgt, 1948-52, active duty, 1951-52.

OURLICHT, DAVID E.
Investment banker, vice president (organization). **Personal:** Born Oct 22, 1957, Detroit, MI; son of Borus and Myrtle; married Marybeth, Aug 21, 1983; children: David E II, Christine F. **Educ:** State Univ NY, Col Buffalo, BS, bus, 1979. **Career:** Nat Asn Securities Dealers, sr examr, 1981-84; Daniels & Bell, vpres, 1984-87; Marine Midland Bank, vpres, 1987-88; Drexel Burnham Lambert, vpres, 1988-90; Chase Manhattan, consult, 1990-91; State NY, exec dir, Coun Fiscal & Econ Priorities, 1991-93; Dillon Read & Co Inc, vpres, 1993-; Swarthmore Group, sr vpres, 2003-. **Orgs:** Trustee, S St Seaport Mus, 1992-; bd mem, Univ Settlement Soc, 1992-. **Honors/Awds:** Black Achiever Indust, YMCA Harlem, 1989. **Business Phone:** (215)557-9300.*

OUSLEY, HAROLD LOMAX
Music publisher, music producer. **Personal:** Born Jan 23, 1929, Chicago, IL; son of Nellie Ousley Farabee; married Alice Inman; children: Sheronda Jordan, Saundra Hepburn & Renee Watson. **Career:** Broadcast Music Inc, composer, music publ, 1967-; Jazz Interactions, music cord, 1980-85; Jamaica Art Ctr, music dir & cord, 1982-; Queens Coun Arts, jazz mus cord, 1982-85; Jazz Circle Friends, OPTV, 1990; Manhattan Neighborhood Network, jazz cable show producer, 1992; Time, NY, 1998; Time Flushing, NY, "Harold Ousley Presents," cable jazz producer; Leader Muse Records, Bethlehem Records, J's Why Records, rec artist; Albums: The Kid!, 1972; The People's Groove, 1977; Sweet Double Hipness, 1980; Singles: The Grass Roots, 1972; Backlash That's Jazz 26, 1977; It's Uptown / The George Benson Cookbook, 1985; So Blue, So Funky - Heroes Of The Hammond, 1994; Funky Good Time The Freedom Jazz Dance Series, 1995; Full Cooperation, 1998; Giblet Gravy, 2000; Living In The Streets 2, 2001; The Grass Is Greener, 2005; Hot Grits Volume 1, 2006; Hammond's Delight, 2008; Return Of The Prodigal Son, 2008; Organist . **Orgs:** Therapeutic music cord, Key Sch York Manor, Branch Key Women Am, 1970-85; Nat Jazz Orgn, 1991-; Jazz Bur, 1991-. **Honors/Awds:** Jazz achievement, Jazz Home Club, 1972; wrote movie theme, "Not Just Another Woman", 1974; Key Women of America, Comn Serv, 1981; Jazz Pioneer Award, Broadcast Music Inc, 1984; Award, Greater Jamaica Develop Corp, 1997.

OUTLAW, BO. See OUTLAW, CHARLES.

OUTLAW, CHARLES (BO OUTLAW)
Basketball player. **Personal:** Born Apr 13, 1971, San Antonio, TX. **Educ:** S Paines Col; Houston Univ, attended 1993. **Career:** Basketball Player (Retired); Los Angeles Clippers, forward-center, 1993-97; Orlando Magic, forward, 1997-02, 2006-08; Phoenix Suns, forward, 2001-03; Memphis Grizzlies, 2004-04; Phoenix Suns, forward, 2004-05. *

OUTLAW, JOHN
Basketball coach, basketball player, football player. **Personal:** Married Linda; children: John Jerome. **Educ:** Jackson State Univ, BS, industrial eng; Coppin State, MS, criminal justice. **Career:** Basketball player (retired), football player(retired) basketball coach;New England Patriots, corner back, 1968-73; Philadelphia Eagles, 1974-79;NC Central Univ, asst football coach, 1979-90; Denver Nuggets, scout/asst coach, 1990-97; Washington Wizards, asst coach, 1997-99; St Louis Swarm,asst coach & dir player personnel; Nat Youth Sports Prog, dir; Consult US Dept Educ, off safe & drug free schs, consult; Charlotte Bobcats, asst coach, 2003-. **Business Phone:** (704)688-8600.

OUTLAW, DR. PATRICIA ANNE
Psychologist, educator. **Educ:** Mt Providence Jr Col, AA, 1966; Towson State Univ, BA, 1968, MA, 1971; Univ MD Col Park; PhD, 1977; St Mary's Seminary & Univ, MA, Th, 1985. **Career:** Baltimore City Sch, sch psychologist, 1970-71; Towson State Univ, dir study skills ctr, 1971-77, assoc dean students, 1977-79; Cheltenham Ctr, staff psychologist, 1979-83; Walter P Carter Ctr, sr psychologist, 1985-94; Spring Grove Hosp, staff psychologist, 1994-97; Outlaw & Assocs, pres, 1993-; Accessible Health Assocs Inc, vp, 1995; Samford Univ, Beeson Divinity Sch, assoc prof divinity, currently. **Orgs:** St John AME Church, assoc minister, 1984-87; Hemingway Temple AME Church, assoc minister, 1987-88; Mt Joy AME Church, pastor, 1988-92; Payne Memorial AME Church, assoc minister, 1992-. **Honors/Awds:** Strong Blacks in Health, 1995. **Special Achievements:** First woman to graduate from Beeson Divinity School's Doctor of Ministry Program, 2002; auth, Soul Food For Hungry Hearts. **Business Addr:** Associate Professor of Divinity, Beeson Divinity School, Samford University, 800 Lakeshore Dr, Birmingham, AL 35229-2252.

OUTLAW, WARREN GREGORY
Counselor. **Personal:** Born Mar 25, 1951, South Bend, IN; married Iris L Hardiman; children: Lauren & Gregory. **Educ:** Lincoln Univ, BS, 1974; Ind Univ-South Bend, MS, educ, 1980. **Career:** South Bend Sch Corp, substitute teacher, 1974-75; YMCA Community Serv Br, asst dir, 1975-80; Univ Notre Dame, Educ Talent Search, assoc dir, 1980-83, dir, 1983-, assoc prof specialist TRIO Prog, currently; Ind Univ, exec coun mem, currently. **Orgs:** Chmn scholar comn, NAACP, 1984-; chmn, financial develop comn, Ind Mid-Am Asn Educ Opportunity Prog, 1985-; chmn, Black Comm Sch Comn, 1986-; Martin Luther King Jr Found St Joseph County, 1986-; Alpha Phi Alpha, Theta XI Lambda Chap, 1996-; Community Found St Joseph County, 1997-2002; bd dtrustees, Stanley Clark Sch, 1997-2001. **Honors/Awds:** Service Citation, YMCA, 1980; Ind Black Achievers Ind Black Expo, 1984; Youth Leadership & Service, John Adams High Sch, 1985; Groups Program Services Award, Ind Univ, 1994; Distinguished Consultant Award, Southern Asn Educ Opportunity Prog Personnel, 1995; Michiana Neal-Marshall Distinguished Alumnus Award, Ind Univ, 1998. **Home Addr:** 2902 Bonds Ave, South Bend, IN 46628. **Business Addr:** Director, University of Notre Dame, Educational Talent Search program, PO Box 139, Notre Dame, IN 46556, **Business Phone:** (574)631-5670.

OVERBEA, LUIX VIRGIL
Journalist, writer. **Personal:** Born Feb 15, 1923, Chicago, IL; married Elexie Culp. **Educ:** Northwest Univ, PhB, 1948; MS, 1951. **Career:** Asn Negro Press, chief copy desk, 1948-54; Okla Eagle Tulsa, city ed, 1954-55; The Winston-Salem Jour, staff writer, 1955-68; The St Louis Sentinel, managing ed, 1968-70; Winston-Salem State Col, teacher, 1965-68; The St Louis Globe-Dem, asst ed, staff & reporter, 1970-71; Christian Sci Monitor, staff writer, 1971-. **Orgs:** Sigma Delta Cig; managing ed, The Black Chap Mag, 1974; commentator, Black News TV Show, 1973-; Nat Asn Advan Colored People; Kappa Alpha Psi; Parents Coun; Metco; 2nd Church Christ; co-founder, Nat Asn Black Journalists. **Honors/Awds:** Special Honor Lifetime Achievement, Nat Asn Black Journalists, 1993. **Military Serv:** AUS, Army Specialized Training Prog, corporal, 1943-46. **Business Addr:** 1 Norway St, Boston, MA 02115.

OVERSTREET, DR. EVERETT LOUIS
Civil engineer. **Personal:** Born Oct 9, 1941, Dekalb, MS; son of Pervis and Myrtha Crawford; married JoAnn Gregory, Jun 28, 1970; children: Lorie Danielle & Piper Sabrina. **Educ:** Ohio Univ, Athens, OH, BSCE, 1967; Carnegie Mellon Univ, Pittsburgh, PA, MSCE, 1973; Calif Coast Univ, Santa Ana, CA, PhD, 1988. **Career:** Alyeska Pipeline Service Co, staff engr; Contra Tech Inc, Anchorage, AK, partner, 1978-85; Anchorage Times, editorial columnist, 1980-86; Tundra Times, editorial columnist, 1986-88; Anchorage Sch Dist, Anchorage, AK, exec dir, 1986-92; Trigen-Peoples Dist Energy Co, gen mgr, currently. **Orgs:** Bd Trustees, Alaska Pacific Univ, 1985-92; bd dirs, Alaska Black Caucus, 1980-92; life mem, Golden Heritage; life mem, NAACP, 1994-. **Honors/Awds:** Author, Black on a Background of White, 1988; Cited for Volunteer Serv, Alaska Legislature, 1988. **Home Addr:** 3120 Blue Monanco St, Las Vegas, NV 89117-2510.

OVERSTREET, HARRY L
Architect. **Personal:** Born Jun 30, 1938, Conehatta, MS; son of Cleo Huddleston; divorced; children: Anthony, Harry II & Nile. **Educ:** Contra Costa Col, San Pablo, CA, 1956; Calif Col Arts, Oakland, CA, 1957. **Career:** Gerson/Overstreet, San Francisco, CA, vpres & prin, 1968-85, pres, 1985-; CA Poltechnic Univ, San Luis Obispo, adj fac mem. **Orgs:** Past pres & mem, Berkeley Planning Comt, 1967-73; bd mem, Hunter Point Boys Club, 1975-; pres, Nat Org Minority Archits, 1988-90; co-founder, Northern CA Chap Nat Org Minority Architects, 1972; San Francisco Chap; bd mem, Calif Coun Am Inst Architects, 1992-93; co-chair, San Francisco Ho Chi Minh City Sister City comt, 1997-98. **Honors/Awds:** Award of Merit, Palace Fine Arts, 1975; Service for Engineering Career Day, U C Davis, 1979; Career Workshop, City Berkeley, 1979. **Military Serv:** AUS, 1957-60. **Business Phone:** (415)989-3830.

OVERSTREET, MORRIS L
Educator, judge. **Educ:** Angelo State Univ, San Angelo, Tx, BA, sociol; Tex Southern Univ-Thurgood Marshall Sch Law, Houston,

Tx, JD, 1975. **Career:** Dist Atty Off, Amarillo, first asst dist atty; Tex Ct Criminal Appeals, judge, 1990-98; Tex Southern Univ, Thurgood Marshall Sch Law, distinguished vis prof law, 1999-2000, prof law & dir clin legal studies prog, Pvt Pract, atty, currently. **Orgs:** Life mem & nat legal coun, Phi Beta Sigma Fraternity Inc; life mem, NAACP; gen coun, Tex State Baptist Conv; Mount Zion Baptist Church; Sigma Pi Phi Fraternity; Nat Bar Asn; cert contract adv, Nat Football League Players Asn; Am Bar Asn; auxillary, Nat Med Asn 1999-2000. **Special Achievements:** First African-American to be elected to Statewide Off, TX. **Business Addr:** Attorney, 200 Williams, Prairie View, TX 77446.

OVERTON, DOUGLAS M.
Basketball player, basketball coach. **Personal:** Born Aug 3, 1969, Philadelphia, PA; married Chanel; children: Miles Randall & Maya. **Educ:** LaSalle Univ, attended. **Career:** Basketball player (retired), basketball coach; Rockford Lighting, 1991-92;Washington Bullets, guard, 1992-95; Denver Nuggets, 1995-96; Philadelphia76ers, 1996, dir players, 2005-06; Chicago Bulls 2002-03; Los AngelesClippers, 2003-04; St Joseph's Hawks, asst coach, 2006-08; New JerseyNets, asst coach, currently. **Honors/Awds:** Big 5 Hall of Fame, 1997; La Salle's Hall of Athletes. **Business Addr:** Assistant Coach, New Jersey Nets, 390 Murray Hill Pkwy, E Rutherford, NJ 07073, **Business Phone:** (201)935-8888.

OVERTON, SPENCER
College teacher. **Personal:** Married Leslie; children: Sterling & Langston. **Educ:** Hampton Univ, Hampton, VA, BA, mass media/journ, 1990; Harvard Law Sch, Cambridge, MA, JD, cum laude, 1993. **Career:** Harvard Law Sch, Cambridge, MA, Charles Hamilton Houston fel, 1999-2000; Univ Calif, Davis, CA, actg prof law, 2000- 2002; The George Wash Univ, Wash, DC, assoc prof law, prof, currently. **Orgs:** Md Bar; Mich Bar; Wash Bar; bd mem, Nat Voting Rights Inst, 1999-; bd mem, Fannie Lou Hamer Proj, 2000-; sr fel, Jamestown Project at Yale. **Special Achievements:** Book: Stealing Democracy: The New Politics of Voter Suppression, 2006. **Business Addr:** Associate Professor, George Washington Univ Law School, 2000 H St NW, Washington, DC 20052, **Business Phone:** (202)994-9794.

OVERTON-ADKINS, DR. BETTY JEAN
School administrator. **Personal:** Born Oct 10, 1949, Jacksonville, FL; daughter of Miriam Crawford and Henry Crawford; married Eugene; children: Joseph A, Jermaine L & Kevin. **Educ:** Tenn State Univ, BS, eng, 1970, MA, eng, 1973; George Peabody Vanderbilt Univ, PhD, educ leadership, 1980. **Career:** Metrop Nashville Sch Bd, teacher, 1970-72; Tenn State Univ, teacher, prog dir, 1972-76; Univ Tenn, Nashville, instr, 1973-78; Nashville State Tech Inst, asst prof, 1976-78; Fisk Univ, asst prof, asst dean, 1978-83; Univ Ark, assoc dean, dean 1983-91; W K Kellogg Found, coordr, higher educ, prog dir, asst dir, 1991-; Spring Arbor Univ, vpres acad affairs, currently. **Orgs:** Race Rels Info Ctr, reporter, 1970-71; Nashville Panel Am Women, bd mem, 1973-83; Nat Coun Teachers Eng, 1979-; ACE, admin fel, 1980; bd mem, Ark Women's Hist Inst, 1983-; bd mem, Teak Reportory Theatre, 1983-; bd mem, Women Color United Against Domestic Violence, founding mem, 1985; W K Kellogg Nat Leadership Develop fel, W K Kellogg Found, 1988-91; consult, Scarritt Col; consult, YMCA; Comn Higher Learning, N Cent Asn Col & Univ; Am Asn Higher Educ; ed bd, Lib Educ, Asn Am Col & Univ; bd mem, Coun Grad Schs. **Honors/Awds:** Outstanding Leadership Award, Alpha Kappa Alpha, 1981; articles publ in: Southern Quarterly, 1985; Award for Meritorious Achievement, Off Res & Sponsored Progs, Univ Ark, Little Rock, 1989. **Home Addr:** 223 Berkley Ave, Battle Creek, MI 49017. **Business Addr:** Vice President for Academic Affairs, Spring Arbor University, 106 E Main St, Spring Arbor, MI 49283, **Business Phone:** (517)750-6357.

OWAN, DR. RANSOME E
Executive. **Personal:** Born Aug 23, 1957, Cross River, Nigeria; son of Louis and Anna Etok; divorced; children: Lemmy Owan & Lauren. **Educ:** City Univ, NYC Barach Col, BBA, 1980; Hofstra Univ, MBA, 1982; Univ Pa, MSC, 1998, PhD, 1998. **Career:** Pace Global Energy Serv, sr analyst, 1999-2002; Wash Gas Energy Serv, dir, regulatory & external affairs; Nigerian Elec Regulatory Comn, chmn & chief exec officer, currently. **Orgs:** Pres & found, ETung Heritage Found, 2002. **Honors/Awds:** Energy Manager of the Year, Asn Energy Engrs, 1997. **Business Addr:** Director, Regulatory & External Affairs, Nigerian Electricity Regulatory Commission, Plot 1099 First Ave Cent Area, PO Box 136, Abuja, Nigeria, **Business Phone:** (234)9672-3206.

OWENS, BISHOP ALFRED A, JR.
Clergy. **Personal:** Born Mar 18, 1946, Washington, DC; son of Alfred A Owens, Sr and Susie E; married Susie C, Apr 22, 1972; children: Alfred T & Kristel Moneek. **Educ:** Miner Teachers Col, BS, eng; Howard Univ, MA, 1985, MDIV, 1993, Doctrate Ministry, 1997. **Career:** Cardoza High Sch, eng instr; Howard Univ, eng instr; Greater Mt Calvary Holy Church, pastor, currently. **Orgs:** Mt Calvary Holy Church Am Inc, vice bishop, 1976-. **Honors/Awds:** Hon doctorate, 1980. **Special Achievements:** Office of Sr Bishop, conferred upon by Carribean Ministries Intl, 2002. **Business Addr:** Pastor, Greater Mount Calvary Holy Church, 610 Rhode Island Ave NE, Washington, DC 20002, **Business Phone:** (202)529-4547.

OWENS, ANDI
Educator, army officer. **Personal:** Born Jul 21, 1934, Minneapolis, MN. **Educ:** Columbia Univ, BA, 1962; NY Sch Social Work, grad work, 1963. **Career:** Church of St Edward the Martyr, dir recreation, 1962-65; Indus Home Blind, asst dir recreation, 1965-72; Genesis II Gallery African Art, co-fdr, 1972; The Met Mus Art, Rockefel fel, 1973-74Black Hist Mus Nassau Co, mus curator, 1974-75; Afro-Am Cultural Found Westchester Co, coordr, 1976-77; Brooklyn Mus, mus prep 6 curatorial depts work proj, 1978-80; Genesis II Mus Int Black Culture, dir, 1980-. **Orgs:** Fed experimental drama group, The Queens Revels Columbia Univ, 1958-62; Workshop Document & Exhib Mus Educrs, 1974; Fedn Prot Welfare Agys "Creative Comm Involvement" 1974; Met Mus of Art "Art Discovery Workshop for Comm Grps" 1974; Met Mus rep designer for YM-YWHA 1974; chmn, Visual Arts Discipline for Mid-West Regn; 2nd World Festival of Black & African Arts & Culture, 1975; panelist, Blacks & Mus; Am Asn Mus, 1974; bd adv, Bronx Comm Bd 7 Cultural Arts Ctr, 1974; NY State chmn exhib Nat Conf of Artists, 1974; part NY State Coun Arts, 1975; Smithsonian Inst Mus Prog, 1975; panel chmn Mus & Visual Art Inst Regional, Nat Conf of Artists, 1976. **Honors/Awds:** Grant recipient NY State Coun on Arts for Genesis II Traveling Exhib Prog, 1973. **Military Serv:** USAF, sergeant, 1953-57. **Business Addr:** 509 Cathedral Pkwy, New York, NY 10025.

OWENS, ARLEY E., JR.
State government official, administrator. **Personal:** Born Oct 14, 1948, Lima, OH; son of Arley E Sr and Loretta J; married Audrey M Bankston, Nov 9, 1968; children: Scott, Kevin. **Educ:** Ohio State Univ, BA, commun, 1977. **Career:** CONSOC, housing consult, 1976-78; Ball Realty, property mgr, 1978-79; Lane Realty, sales mgr, 1979-80; Ohio Dept Natural Resources, proj supvr, 1980-81, employee rels coordr, 1981-85, commun admin, 1985-. **Orgs:** Commun comt chair person, vpres, Nat Orgn Minorities Recycling & Waste Mgt, 1991-; bd dirs, Nat Recycling Coalition, 1991-; chair person, NRC Commun & Educ Comn, 1993-; chair person, NRC Minority Coun, 1993-; comt mem, Pub Rels Soc Am, 1994. **Honors/Awds:** Employee of the Month, 1985; Outstanding Prof Employee Award, Ohio Dept Natural Resources, 1988; Nat Recycling Award, Keep Am Beautiful Inc, 1989; Citizen of the Week Award, Black Communicator, 1990; Nat Winner, US Dept Interior, Take Pride Am, 1991, 1992. **Special Achievements:** Creator: Nation's first Pride in Public Housing Campaign, Ohio's Pub Housing Authorities, 1990, state-wide Recycling Awareness Campaign involving Ohio's five major zoos, 1989. **Military Serv:** USAF, sergent, 1967-70; Vietnam Serv Campaign Medal; Distinguished Unit Citation. **Home Addr:** 7954 Slate Ridge Blvd, Reynoldsburg, OH 43068. **Business Addr:** Administrator, Ohio Department of Natural Resources, Div Litter Recycling Prev, 1889 Fountain Sq Bldg F 2 Suite 203, Columbus, OH 43224, **Business Phone:** (614)265-6363.

OWENS, BILLY EUGENE
Basketball player. **Personal:** Born May 1, 1969, Carlisle, PA; married Nicole; children: 5. **Educ:** Syracuse Univ, attended 1992. **Career:** Basketball player (retired), basketball coach; Golden State Warriors, forward-guard, 1992-94, 2000; Miami Heat, forward-guard, 1995-96; Sacramento Kings, forward-guard, 1996-98; Seattle Supersonics, forward-guard, 1998; Philadelphia 76ers, forward-guard, 2000; Detroit Pistons, forward-guard, 2001; Dallas Mavericks, asst coach, player develop coach, currently. **Honors/Awds:** NBA All-Rookie first team, 1992. **Special Achievements:** NBA Draft, First round pick, No 3, 1991.

OWENS, BRIGMAN
Executive, football player, president (organization). **Personal:** Born Feb 16, 1943, Linden, TX; son of Alfred L and Roxie Love; married Patricia Ann, Jun 26, 1965; children: Robin & Tracey Lynn. **Educ:** Univ Cincinnati, BA, 1965; Potomac Sch Law, JD, 1980. **Career:** Dallas Cowboys, prof athlete, 1965-66; Wash Redskins, prof athlete, 1966-78; NFL Players Asn, asst exec dir, 1978-84; Brig Owens & Assocs, pres, currently. **Orgs:** Exec bd, Boy Scouts Am, 1974; vpres, Mondale's Task Force on Youth Employ, 1978; Comn on Caribbean Gov Fla, 1978; bd dirs, USA Telecomm Inc 1985; bd dirs Nat Bank Com, 1985; bd dirs, Big Bros Am, 1985; vpres, Leukemia Soc 1985; president's bd, Univ Cincinnati, 1990. **Honors/Awds:** All American Univ of Cincinnati 1965; author "Over the Hill to the Superbowl" 1971; Distinguished Alumni Fullerton Jr Coll 1974; Washingtonian of the Year Washington magazine 1978; Washingtonian of the Year Maryland Jaycees 1978; Hall of Stars Washington Redskins; Hall of Fame Univ of Cint; Hall of Fame Orange Co CA, NCAA Silver Anniversary Award Winner, 1990. **Military Serv:** ANG, 1965-70. **Business Addr:** Board Director, Venture Philanthropy Partners, 1201 15th St NW Suite 420, Washington, DC 20005, **Business Phone:** (202)955-8085.

OWENS, CHANDLER D.
Clergy, bishop. **Career:** Church God Christ Inc, gen bd mem, presiding bishop, jurisdictional prelate bishop, currently. **Business Addr:** Jurisdictional Prelate Bishop, Church of God In Christ Inc, World hq 938 Mason St, PO Box 38, Memphis, TN 38101, **Business Phone:** (901)578-3838.*

OWENS, DR. CHARLES CLINTON
Dentist. **Personal:** Born Sep 3, 1942, Smithville, TX; son of Dr E A Owens; married Dianne Burdel Banks; children: Euau Cha & Chelsi Dion. **Educ:** A&M Univ, Prairie View, BS, 1965; Howard Univ Sch Dent, DDS, 1970. **Career:** Model Cities Lawton, dentist, 1971-72; Okla State Health Dept, dentist, 1972-79; pvt pract, dentist, currently. **Orgs:** Consult, Okla State Health Dept, 1972-79; vice pres, PIC Invest Corp, 1978-; treas, Northside C C, 1979; treas, PIC Invest Corp; mem, OK Health Planning Com, 1973; mem, Alpha Phi Alpha Fraternity; mem, Selective Services; mem, United Way; mem, Lawton Chapter Red Cross. **Honors/Awds:** Outstanding Young Man of the Year, Lawton Jaycees, 1972; Appreciation Award Great Plains, Vo Tech, 1979; Appreciation Award, Eisenhower Sr High Sch, 1979. **Home Addr:** 402 NW Sheridan Rd, Lawton, OK 73505, **Home Phone:** (580)357-6519. **Business Addr:** Physician, 1316 NW Ferris Ave, Lawton, OK 73507, **Business Phone:** (580)248-6062.

OWENS, CHARLES EDWARD
Educator. **Personal:** Born Mar 7, 1938, Bogue Chitto, MS; married Otis Beatrice Holloway; children: Chris Edward, Charles Douglas & Bryant Holloway. **Educ:** WVa State Col, BA, 1961; WVa Univ, MA, 1965; Univ NM, EdD, 1971. **Career:** Wheeling, WVa, teacher, 1965-66; Charleston Job Corps Ctr Women, WVa, coordr testing & referals, 1966-67; Albuquerque Job Corps Ctr Women, NMex, counr, 1967-68; Univ Wis Madison, counr, 1969-71; Va Commonwealth Univ Richmond, counr, 1971-73; Univ Ala, Psychol Dept, assoc prof, 1973, Dept Sociol, Anthrop & Criminal Justice, prof; Univ N Fla, Dept Sociol, Criminal Justice & Anthrop, adj fac, currently. **Orgs:** Plemarch Kappa Alpha Psi, WVa St Col, 1960-61; Phi Delta Kappa, WVa Univ, 1965; fel US Off Educ, Univ NMex, 1968-69; Am Psychol Asn; Nat Asn Black Psychol; Nat Asn Blacks Criminal Justice; Nat Asn Adv Colored People; Tuscaloosa Ment Health Asn. **Honors/Awds:** Books: Blacks & Criminal Justice, 1977; Mental Health & Black Offenders,1980. **Military Serv:** AUS, 1st lt, 1961-64. **Business Addr:** Adjunct Faculty, University of North Florida, Department of Sociology, Criminal Justice & Anthropology, 4567 St Johns Bluff Rd S, Jacksonville, FL 32224, **Business Phone:** (904)620-2850.

OWENS, CURTIS
Executive. **Personal:** Born Oct 18, 1938, Philadelphia, PA; children: Curtis Derek. **Educ:** Cent State Univ Wilberforce, OH, BS, 1962; Temple Univ, MPA, 1970; Calif Coast Univ Santa Ana, Calif, PhD. **Career:** Mercy Douglass Hosp, Pa, asst adminr; Gen Elect Pa, oper & res analyst; Philco Ford Corp, sr instr; Neighborhood Health Svc, ctr admin; Temple Univ, Comprehensive Health Serv, prog adminr, dir; African Am Unity Ctr, pres; Rainbow PUSH Coalition, trade bur dir, chmn; Watts Health Found Inc, pres & ceo; Owens Development Co, advisor, 2004-. **Orgs:** Polit Sci Soc; Nat Health Consumer's Orgn; pres, Nat Asn Neighborhood Health Ctr Inc; Health Task Force Philadelphia Urban League; bd dir, Regional Comprehensive Health Planning Coun. **Honors/Awds:** Congressman's Medal of Merit, 1975; Key to City of San Francisco, 1975; MLK Jr Social Justice Award, Calif State Univ, Dominguez Hills. **Military Serv:** AUS, 1st Lt Med Serv Corp. **Home Addr:** 1525 N Cahuenga Blvd Suite 14, Los Angeles, CA 90028. **Business Addr:** Advisor, Owens Development Company, 1425 K St NW Suite 350, Washington, DC 20005, **Business Phone:** (443)324-1030.

OWENS, CYNTHIA DEAN
Physician. **Personal:** Born Mar 14, 1952, Detroit, MI; daughter of Jimmie and Annie; divorced; children: Luke Stewart. **Educ:** Hughland Park Jr Col, 1971; Wayne State Univ, BA, 1975; Mich Osteopathic Med Ctr, DO, 1979. **Career:** Gen med physician, 1981-82; Priv Pract, internist, 1984-86; Gulf Coast Primary Care, internist, 1986-95; Biloxi VA Med Ctr, ER physician, 1995-97; Gulf Coast Primary Care, internist, 1997-; pvt pract, currently. **Orgs:** Bd mem, Slavation Army Soc Battered Women, 1991-94; prof ed chairperson & bd mem, Jackson County Am Cancer Soc, 1992-94; bd mem, Jackson County Sickle Cell Soc, 1996-. **Honors/Awds:** Citizen of the Year, Moss Point MS, 1998. **Business Addr:** Physician, Gulf Coast Primary Care, 2900 Melton Ave, Pascagoula, MS 39581, **Business Phone:** (228)549-2000.*

OWENS, DANA ELAINE. See LATIFAH, QUEEN.

OWENS, DAVID KENNETH
Engineer, executive. **Personal:** Born Jun 14, 1948, Philadelphia, PA; son of Erwin D and Grace; married Karen P, Nov 20, 1971; children: Pharis, Phyllis & Kenneth. **Educ:** BS, elec engr, 1969; Howard Univ, MSEE, 1977; George Wash Univ, MSEA, 1977. **Career:** Securities & Exchange Comn, chief engr, 1974-80; Fed Power Comn, 1970-74; Gen Elec Co, 1969-70; Pa Elec Co, 1968; Edison Electric Inst, sr vpres, exec vpres, currently. **Orgs:** Inst Elec & Electronics Engrs; Kappa Alpha Psi Frat; Nativity BVM Ch; Blacks in Energy; Nat Black Engr's Asn. **Honors/Awds:** Frat Schroller of Year Award, Kappa Alpha Psi, 1969; Superior Perf Award, 1972; Outstanding Award, 1974; Outstanding Employee of the Year Award, EEI, 1987; Most Distinguished Professional, EEI, 1988; Special Rec Award, EEI, 1990. **Business Addr:** Executive Vice President, Edison Electric Institute, Fl 4 701 Pennsylvania Ave NW, Washington, DC 20004-2696, **Business Phone:** (202)508-5527.

OWENS, DR. DEBBIE A.
Journalist, college teacher. **Personal:** Born Jan 23, 1956, Brooklyn, NY. **Educ:** Brooklyn Col City Univ NY, BA, 1977; Univ Ill, Urbana-Champaign, MS, 1982; Univ Fla, PhD, 1994; Univ Fla, cert geront, 1994. **Career:** Chicago Tribune Newspaper, reporter intern, 1976; NY Amsterdam Newspaper, reporter intern, 1977; NY City Bd Educ, Eng teacher, 1978-79; JC Penney Co, NY, catalog copywriter, 1979-81; Freedom ways Mag, NY, book reviewer, 1980; WPGU-FM, Black Notes, pub affairs reporter, 1981-82; Univ Ill, Urbana-Champaign, grad fel, 1981-82; Univ Ill, grad newsletter writer, 1981-82; WCIA-TV, news reporter/minority affairs prog prod, 1982-85; Edward Waters Col, radio/tv broadcast instr, 1985-86; East Carolina Univ, commun lect/instr, 1986-88; Bethune Cookman Col, pub speaking adj, 1991; Washington & Lee Univ, jour vis scholar, 1993-94; Fel Voice Am, reporter/writer, 1994; Bowling Green St Univ, jour asst prof, 1994-98; Fayetteville St Univ, commun assist prof, 1998-2002; ASNE fellow The Charlotte Observer, reporter/ed, 2000; RTNDF Fel WRAL-TV5, Capitol Broadcasting Co, 2002; Univ Nebr-Lincoln, jour visiting sum scholar, 2002; Murray State Univ, Dept Journ & Mass Commun, assoc prof, currently. **Orgs:** Mayor's Vol Action Ctr NY, 1980; NY Vol Urban Consult Group, 1980;Radio-TV News Dir Asn, 1982-; Ill News Broadcasters Asn, 1983-85; Nat Broadcasting Soc-Alpa Epsilon Rho; JMC Nat Honor Soc-Kappa Tau Alpha; Broadcast Educ Asn; Asn Am Univ; Collegiate Press Ed Adv Bd; Cumberland-Fayett Arts Coun; WTVD-TV Durham Adv Comn, 2001-02; Black College Radio Adv Bd, 2002-03; Broadcast Educ Asn Publications Bd, 2003-;Women; chair, Gender Issues Div, 2006-07; vpres, Black Fac Staff Asn, 2007. **Honors/Awds:** Florida Governor's Award, 1986; Outstanding Young Women of America, 1988; Teacher of the Year Award, Fayett St Univ Perf/Fine Arts, 2001-02; FayettSt Univ, Col of Arts & Sci Conf, Res, & Pub Award, 2000-02; Key to theCity, Murray, KY, 2004; Murray-Calloway NAACP Appreciation, 2004. **Business Addr:** Associate Professor, Murray State University, Department of Journalism & Mass Communications, 114 Wilson Hall, Murray, KY 42071-3311, **Business Phone:** (270)762-6318.

OWENS, EDWARD GLENN
Government official. **Personal:** Born Apr 23, 1958, Huntsville, TX; son of Edward and Hattie; married Rissie, Aug 20, 1983; children: Edward (Trey). **Educ:** Sam Houston State Univ, BS, crimino & corrections, 1980. **Career:** Government Official (retired); Tex Dept Criminal Justice, correctional officer, 1977-81; Tex bd Pardons & Parole, parole caseworker, 1981-83; Tex Dept Criminal Justice, line supvr, 1983-90, warden, 1990-95, regional dir, 1995-97, dep dir, 1997-2001, opers div dir, 2001-02, dep exec dir, 2002-07. **Orgs:** Alpha Phi Alpha fraternity, 1979. **Honors/Awds:** Service Award, TX Dept of Criminal Justice, 2003.

OWENS, GEOFFREY
Actor, special education teacher. **Personal:** Born Mar 18, 1961, Brooklyn, NY; son of Major Owens. **Educ:** Yale Univ. **Career:** TV series: "ABC Afterschool Specials", 1990; "The Cosby Show", 1985-92; "Built To Last", 1997; "Law & Order", 1999; "Law & Order: Special Victims Unit", 2002; "That's So Raven", 2007; "The Wedding Bells", 2007; "It's Always Sunny in Philadelphia", 2007; "Boston Legal", 2007; "Las Vegas", 2007; "Journeyman", 2007; "Medium", 2008; Films: The Paper, 1994; Stonebrook, 1999; Forgiven, 1999; The Cross, 2001; Brooklyn Shakespeare Co, founder & artistic dir, currently; Gene Frankel Studio, teacher; HB Studio, teacher. **Orgs:** New York Church Christ. **Honors/Awds:** Danny Kaye Award; BACA Brooklyn Bridge Award; Young Artist Award for Best Young Actor/Actress Ensemble in a TV Comedy, Drama Series or Spec, 1989. **Home Addr:** 6231 Medici Ct Apt 205, Sarasota, FL 34243-5603.

OWENS, DR. HUGO ARMSTRONG
Dentist. **Personal:** Born Jan 21, 1916, Chesapeake, VA; son of James E Owens and Grace M Owens; married Helen West Owens, Sep 2, 1941; children: Paula C Parker, D Patrice & Hugo A Jr. **Educ:** Va State Univ, BS, Gen Sci & Sci educ, 1939, hon doctorate; Howard Univ Col Dent (cum laude), DDS, 1947. **Career:** Dentist (retired); Crisfield MD Pub Schs, sci & math teacher, asst prin; pvt pract, dent; Chesapeake City Coun, vice mayor, 1970-80; Norfolk State Univ, bd visitors; Va State Univ, rector, bd visitors, 1982-86; Howard Univ, prof; Med Col Va, prof; Old Dominion Univ, rector, 1993-97. **Orgs:** Founder, John L McGriff Dent Soc; founding mem, Am Soc Preventive Dent, 1969; Comt Concerned Citizens; NCP; African Am Cult Ctr, Old Dommion Univ, 1991, bd visitors, 1990-94, rector bd, 1992-93. **Honors/Awds:** Citizen of the Decade, Norfolk-Virginian-Pilot, 1980; Citizen of the Decade, Norfolk Ledger Dispatch, 1980; First Citizen, City Chesapeake, 1988; Distinguished Alumni, Howard Univ; Distinguished Alumni, honorary doctorate degree, Virginia State Univ; Most Influential African Americans, Ebony. **Special Achievements:** First African Am elected to Chesapeake, VA, city council, 1970; Auth, articles in Jour Am Soc Preventive Dent; Nat Dent Assoc; Am Dent Asn; Nat Med Asn; Va Teacher Asn; Jour Prosthetic Dent. **Military Serv:** AUS, personnel officer. **Home Addr:** 4405 Airline Blvd, Chesapeake, VA 23321.

OWENS, IKE. See OWENS, ISAIAH HUDSON.

OWENS, ISAIAH HUDSON (IKE OWENS)
Educator, executive, football player. **Personal:** Born Jan 8, 1921, Columbus, GA; son of Isaiah H and Mary D; married Nell Craig; children: Whitlynn, Isaiah Jr, Bert & Barrington. **Educ:** Univ Ill, B FA, 1948; Ind Univ, BS, 1959. **Career:** Roosevelt High Sch, Gary, teacher; Owens & Craig's Inc, pres; Stand Oil, indust distribr, 1950-58; Owens' Gift & Toy Shoppe, owner, 1949-65; Chicago Rockets, pro football, 1948. **Orgs:** Vpres, Midtown Businessmen Asn, 1970-73; Residence Com Model Cities; chmn, Econ Task Force; Gary Alumni Chap, Kappa Alpha Psi; Nat Asn Advan Colored People; Roosevelt High Sch Alumni Asn. **Honors/Awds:** Big Ten Football, 1941, 1945, 1947; All American, 1947; Most Valuable to Team, 1947; All Big Ten, 1947; All Midwest, 1947. **Military Serv:** AUS, sgt, 1941-45. **Business Addr:** 1638 Broadway, Gary, IN 46404.

OWENS, JAMES E, JR.
Executive, insurance executive. **Personal:** Born Sep 7, 1937, Stonewall, MS; married Evelyn Robinson; children: James III. **Career:** Chicago Metrop Mutual Ins Co, mgr, 1959-71; Supreme Life Ins Co, sr vpres, 1971-82, bd dir, 1976-82; Am Investors Life Ins Co, reg dir, 1983-; JEO Ins & Financial Serv Inc, pres, currently. **Orgs:** Bd dir, Chicago Inst Asn; asst dean, Cosmopolitan CC Free Sch Bus; sect Nat Inst Asn; instr, Chicago Inst Asn; Southend Jaycees; NAACP; Boy Scouts Am; Am Asn Comm & Indust; Chicago Ins Asn, 1975-76; Nat Asn Life Underwriters. **Honors/Awds:** Chicago Merit Chicago Asn Life Underwriters, 1968-69; Outstanding Man of the Year, Chicago Southend Jaycees, 1973; Golden Scepter Award, 1974. **Military Serv:** AUS, E4, 1960-62. **Business Addr:** President, JEO Insurance & Financial Services Inc, 523 E 67th St, Chicago, IL 60637, **Business Phone:** (773)752-5500.

OWENS, JAMES ROBERT
Trumpet player, composer, educator. **Personal:** Born Dec 9, 1943, New York, NY; children: Milan & Ayan. **Educ:** Univ Mass, Amherst, MEd, 1975. **Career:** BMI, writer & publisher, 1966-; MUSE, jazz workshop staff, 1968-73; Am Guild Authors & Composers, publisher & composer, 1968-85; State Univ New York, Stony brook, lectr demonstration & concert, 1975; McLennan Community Col, Waco, TX, concerts & workshops, 1978; Queens borough Community Col, adj prof, 1984-85; State Univ New York, Col Old West bury, adj prof,1981-86; Jazz mobile Inc, workshop prog dir, 1984-90; New Sch Social Res,Jazz Prog, part-time fac, 1990-; Oberlin Conserv Music, vis prof, 1992-93; Univ Pittsburgh, clin & trumpet master class, 1992, 1997; Youngstown State Univ, Col Fine Arts, workshop & master class, 1997; Greenwich High Sch,CT, workshop & adjudication, 1997; City Univ New York, vis prof, 1998. Compositions: Complicity; Dreaming My Life Away; Look Softly; Milan is Love; Never Subject to Change; Jazz Fusions; Against Great Odds; TV documentary sound tracks: "Conversations with Roy DeCarava"; "Hookers atthe Point 1 & 2", "Pimps up, Ho's Down". **Orgs:** Mech Copyright Protection Soc, 1967-76; bd govs, Nat Acad Rec Arts & Sci, New York, 1971-; jazz panelist, Nat Endowment Arts, 1972-76, 1990, 1998; Int Asn Jazz Educrs, 1974-; Int Trumpet Guild, 1975-; exec comt & bd dirs, Am Arts Alliance Inc, 1977-83; panelist, Mass Arts & Humanities Found, 1977; presenting Orgn panel, NY Coun Arts, 1978-81; bd dirs, Jazz Found AmInc, 1991-. **Honors/Awds:** America Achievement Award, Jazz Home Club Am, 1972; New Leaders for the'80s Award, Black Enterprise Mag, 1979; Survival of the Black Artist Award, Howard Univ, Washington, DC, 1980; International Success Award, Marabu Club, Italy, 1983; Manhattan Borough President's Award for Excellence in the Arts, 1986. **Special Achievements:** Presidential Citation, Clark Col, Atlanta, GA, 1972; live performances of original orchestral works with Jimmy Owens Plus; Rochester Philharmonic Orchestra; Brooklyn Philharmonic Orchestra; Hannover Philharmonic; Metro pole Orchestra. **Business Addr:** Musician, Jay-Oh Productions Inc, 236 Park Ave S, New York, NY 10003, **Business Phone:** (212)475-0358.*

OWENS, JAY R.
Dentist. **Personal:** Born Feb 17, 1944, Pine Bluff, AR; married Staggie Darnelle Gordon; children: Kevin, Jay II, Latitia. **Educ:** Howard Univ, BS, 1967; Meharry Med Col, DDS, 1971. **Career:** Pvt Pract, dentist, currently. **Orgs:** Pres, Ark Med Dent Pharmaceut Asn, 1982-83; vice speaker house, Nat Dent Asn, 1984-85; bd dirs, Urban League Ark, 1984. **Military Serv:** AUS, capt, 2 yrs. **Home Addr:** 1117 So Arthur Dr, Little Rock, AR 72204. **Business Addr:** Dentist, 1123 S Univ Ave Suite 714, Little Rock, AR 72204.

OWENS, DR. JERRY SUE
School administrator. **Personal:** Born Jan 16, 1947, Kentucky; married Ronald L. **Educ:** Murray State Univ, BA, 1969, MA, 1970; Univ Tex, PhD, 1983. **Career:** Earlington Elem Sch, 6th grade educ, 1970; Murray High Sch, Jr/Sr eng, 1970-71; Triton Col, instr, 1971-77, asst, assoc & dean of arts & scis, 1978-85; Lakewood Community Col, pres, 1985-. **Orgs:** Nat Coun Teachers Eng; Am Asn Comm & Jr Cols; Am Asn Higher Educ; Women Higher Educ; vice pres bd, YWCA, St Paul, Minn; bd mem, United Way St Paul; Urban League, Nat Asn Advan Colored People. **Honors/Awds:** Chief Executive Officer Award, Asn Community Col Trustees, 1991. **Business Phone:** (612)779-3200.

OWENS, DR. JOAN MURRELL
Educator. **Personal:** Born Jun 30, 1933, Miami, FL; daughter of William Henry and Leola Peterson; married Frank A; children: Adrienne Johnson-Lewis & Angela. **Educ:** Fisk Univ, BA, 1954; Univ MI, MA, 1956; George Wash Univ, BS, 1973, M Phil, 1976, PhD, 1984. **Career:** Educator (retired); Children's Psychol Hosp Univ MI, reading the rapist, 1955-57; Howard Univ Dept Eng, reading specialist, 1957-64; Inst Servs Educ DC & MA, curriculum Spec, 1964-71; Smithsonian Inst DC, mus technician, 1972-73; Ford Fellowship NatFellowships Fund, Atlanta 1973-76; Howard Univ Wash DC, 1976-95, assoc prof Geol, 1976-91; assoc prof Biol, 1991-95. **Orgs:** Speaker, 4th Intl Symposium Fossil Cnidaria, 1983; Minority Affairs Comt,Nat Asn Geol Teacher, 1988-90; geol counr, Coun Undergrad Res, 1990-91. **Honors/Awds:** College Reading Skills, Alfred J Knopf, 1966; "Microstructural Changes in the Micrabaciidae and their Taxonomic & Ecologic Implications, "Palaeontographica Americana", 1984; Delta Sigma Theta; "Evolutionary Trends in the Micrabaciidae, An Argument in Favor of Pre-Adaptation", 1984, Geologos Vol II No 1; "Rhombopsammia: New Genus Family Micrabaciidae," 1986, Proceedings Biological Soc Washington Vol 99 No 2; "On the Elevation of the Stephanophyllia Subgenus Letepsammia to Generic Rank," Proceedings the Biological Soc Wash Vol 99 No 3; Scientist, Black Achievers Sci, Exhibit Chicago's Mus Sci & Indus, 1988; Distinguished African American Scientists of the 20th Century, 1993; "Letepsammia Franki, A New Species Deep-Sea Coral," 1994; Proceedings Biol Soc Washington, Vol 107, No 4. **Special Achievements:** First Black American Woman to earn a doctorate in Geology. *

OWENS, DR. JUDITH MYOLI
Educator. **Personal:** Born Jun 18, 1940, Carlisle, PA; daughter of Benjamin Myoli and Estella Pickens. **Educ:** Shippensburg Univ, BS, educ, 1962; Monmouth Univ, MS, educ, 1975; Nova Univ, Ed.D, 1990. **Career:** Educator (retired); NJ Educ Asn, pres, 1975-77; Asbury Park Bd Educ, Bradley Sch, prin, 1987-91, elem teacher, math resource room teacher, chair person spec educ, affirmative action officer, supvr, vice prin; Col NJ, asst prof, 1991-95; Educ Testing Serv, consult. **Orgs:** Mensa Int, 1990-; Nat Educ Asn; NJ Educ Asn; Order Ky Colonels; Ctr Jersey Club NANB PWC Inc. **Honors/Awds:** Woman of Year, Camden Area Club NANBPW Inc, 1976; The Status of Women, Monmouth County Adv Comt, 1986; Nat Achiever Award, Nat Asn Negro Bus & Prof Women's Clubs; Educ Achiever Award, Ctr Jersey Club NANBPW Inc; Education Achiever Award, Asbury Park Study NJ Org Teacher; Educ Achiever Award, Psi Upsilon Chap, Omega Psi Phi Frat; Education Achiever Award, Monmouth City Bus & Prof Women's Coun; Gold Award, United Way; Woman of the Year. **Home Addr:** 64 Kathy Ct, Brick, NJ 08724.

OWENS, KEITH ALAN
Journalist. **Personal:** Born May 1, 1958, Denver, CO; son of Sebastian C and Geneva M. **Educ:** COl Col, BA, 1980. **Career:** Littleton Independent, intern, 1984; Denver Post, intern, 1984-85; Los Angeles Times, Jour trainee, 1985-86; Ann Arbor News, reporter, 1986-89; Fort Lauderdale Sun-Sentinel, ed writer, reporter, 1989-93; Detroit Free Press, ed writer, columnist; Detroit Metro Times, ed & freelance writer, currently. **Orgs:** Nat Asn Broadcasters, 1984-; pres, Mid-Mich Asn Black Journalists, 1988-89; chmn, Phillips Exeter Acad Com Excellence thru Diversity, 1988-89; secy, 1991, parlimentarian, 1992, Palm Beach Asn Black Journalists, 1991. **Honors/Awds:** Presidents Award, Phillips-Exeter Acad, 1990; Service to PEA Award, Class 1976, 1991. **Home Addr:** 3430 E Jefferson Ave Suite 535, Detroit, MI 48207-4200.

OWENS, KELLY D
Association executive. **Personal:** Born Jan 1, 1966. **Career:** Cong Black Caucus Found Inc, dir educ prog, currently. **Orgs:** Leadership Inst Pub Serv. **Business Addr:** Director of Educational Programs, Congressional Black Caucus Foundation Inc, 1004 Pennsylvania Ave SE, Washington, DC 20003, **Business Phone:** (202)675-6739.

OWENS, KENNETH, JR. See Obituaries section.

OWENS, LYNDA GAYLE
Consultant, educator. **Personal:** Born Jun 16, 1956, Elizabethtown, NC; daughter of Eunice Bryant Owens Houston and David P Owens; children: LaTisha, Larry, Solomon, Aljawanna. **Educ:** Rutledge Col, Richmond, Va, 1981; ICC Career Ctr, Richmond, Va, nurses aide, cert; Richmond Va Seminary, J Sargeant Reynolds Col. **Career:** Richmond Pub Lib, Richmond, Va, pager, libr asst, 1979-81; Henrico Co Jail, Richmond, Va, supvr, 1982-85; City Richmond Recreation & Parks, Richmond, Va, vol, 1985-; Richmond Pub Sch, Richmond, Va, instrnl asst, 1985-; HEAL, Richmond, Va, AIDS health educr, 1991-; self-employed parental & family consult, Richmond, VA, 1989-; The Carver Promise, exec dir, 1992-96; Va Dept Juvenile Justice, coordr youth serv, currently. **Orgs:** Exec Secy, RAAC, 1991; vpres, Mosby PTA, 1989-; shared Decision Making Comt, 1990-91; Richmond Educ Asn, 1985-; Speaker's Bur, 1989-; Greater Mt Moriah Baptist Church, assoc minister; NAACP; Eastern Star; Crusade Voters; Sistercare; N-Pac. **Honors/Awds:** Lynda G Owen Day, Dec 10, 1990, named in honor; America's Award, Positive Thinking Found, 1990; Proclamation, Mayor, City of Richmond, 1990; Resolution, Richmond City Coun, 1990; Outstanding Employee

& Parent, Richmond Pub Sch Bd, 1990; Outstanding Citizen & Role Model, Bd Commissioners Richmond Redevelopment & Housing Authority; Community Service Award, Richmond Times Dispatch, 1992; Ascended Woman Award, 1992;Governor's Comn Citizen Empowerment Commonwealth Va, 1994; Person of the Week, ABC Nightly News; ABC-Family Values Special; ABC Special-Real Kids, Real Solution. **Special Achievements:** First woman ever recognized nationally as a National Unsung Hero who personified the American Dream for sacrificing and devoting her life to children in oppressed communities; numerous speeches, articles, and documentaries.

OWENS, MAJOR R

Congressperson (U.S. federal government). **Personal:** Born Jun 28, 1936, Memphis, TN; son of Ezekiel Owens and Edna Davis Owens; married Ethel, 1956 (divorced 1985); children: Christopher, Geoffrey & Millard. **Educ:** Morehouse Col, BA, 1956; Atlanta Univ, MLS, 1957. **Career:** Congressman (retired), politician; Brooklyn Pub Libr, comm coord, 1964-66; Brownsville Comm Coun, exec dir, 1966-68; NYC, commr, 1968-73; Columbia Univ, prof; Communovation Assoc, pres cons; State of New York, sen, 1974-82; NY State Senate Albany NY, sen, 1975-82; NY City Dep Adminr Community Develop Agency; US House Rep, 11th Cong Dist, congressman, 1982-2007. **Orgs:** Comn on XVI Intl Conf Hague Netherlands 1972; 100 Black Men; NY State Black & Puerto Rican Caucus; Beta Phi Mu; Central Brooklyn Mobilization Polit Action; chmn, Congressional Black Caucus; Am Library Asn, 1986-; Brooklyn Nat Asn Advan Colored People, 1987-; founder, Nat Comn African Am Educ, 1991-2001; NY chmn Brooklyn Congress Racial Equality; Lifetime mem, NAACP; Progressive Caucus; SECME Inc, 2000-; Morehouse Col Alumni Asn. **Honors/Awds:** Awards in Black Found for Rsch & Educ in Sickle Cell Disease, 1973; Honoree Award, Fed Negro Civil Serv Org, 1973; Achievement Award, Widow Sons' Lodge #11 Prince Hall Masons, 1973; Major R Owens Day, Pres of Borough of Brooklyn, Sept 10 1971; pub author & lecturer on library sci; keynote speaker White House Conf on Libraries 1979; Honorary Doctorate of Law Degree Atlanta Univ 1986; Appointed Chairman House Subcommittee on Select Education 1987-95; President's Award, Nat Alliance Black Sch Educators, 1996.

OWENS, MERCY P

Banker. **Personal:** Born Sep 30, 1947, Jenkinsville, SC; daughter of Fred Pearson Sr (deceased) and Unita; divorced; children: Tia & Trey. **Educ:** St Augustines Col; Cannon Trust Sch. **Career:** Citizens Bancshares Corp, dir, 2004-; FNB/SCN, floater, customer serv opers officer; SCN/Wachovia Bank SC, C/D IRA coordr, trust officer, asset mgt acct officer; Wachovia Bank SC, corporate compliance officer, CRA adminr, sr vpres. **Orgs:** Trumpeter gala, Richland Mem Hosp Ctr Cancer Treatment; bd mem, Eboni Dance Theatre; compliance comm, SC Bankers Asn; adv bd, SC Low Income Housing Coalition; proj blueprint, United Way Midlands; Nat Asn Advan Colored People; exec comm, James R Clark Sickle Cell Found; SC Asn Urban Bankers. **Honors/Awds:** Eboni Keys Award, United Black Fund/Eboni Keys, Women Opening Doors, 1991; Minority Bankers of the Year, Minority Bus Develop Ctr, 1994; Positive Image Award, Pee Dee Times & Carolina Tribune, 1995. **Business Addr:** Director, Citizens Bancshares Corporation, 175 John Wesley Dobbs Ave NE, Atlanta, GA 30303, **Business Phone:** (404)659-5959.

OWENS, NATHANIEL DAVIS

Judge. **Personal:** Born Feb 17, 1948, Hartsville, TN; married Barbara Catlin; children: Marsha. **Educ:** Univ S Sewanee, TN, BA (with honors), 1970; Emory Univ, Law Sch, JD, 1973; Northwestern Univ, Sch Law, grad prosecutors course, 1976; Univ NV, Reno, Grad Nat Judicial Col, 1979. **Career:** Atlanta, GA, res, 1971-72; USMC Ast Defense Coun, spec prog, 1972; Atlanta Legal Aid Soc, 1972; Thelma Wyatt Atty, 1972-73; Kennedy Bussey Sampson Attys, 1973-74; Huie Brown & Ide Attys, 1974-; AUS AGO Basic Course AGOBC, 1974, Ft McClellan 1974-76; Jacksonville State Univ, adj prof, 1975-; 7th Judicial Circuit, asst dist atty, 1976-79; Dist Ct Cleburne & Calhoun Counties, dist ct judge, 1979-. **Orgs:** Mt Olive Baptist Church, 1975-; 32nd Degree Master Mason, 1976-; Royal Arch Mason Chap 47; Hartsville Commandry No 5 TN, 1976-; first vpres, Asn AUS, 1978-; bd dir, Anniston Area Chamber Com, 1978-79; pres, Club Ala State Demo Party, 1978-; Omega Psi Phi Theta Tau Chap, 1978-; chmn, State & Local Govt Com Chamber Com, 1978-80; co-chmn, Citizens Orgn Better Ed, 1979-82; Beta Kappa Boule Sigma Pi Phi, 1981-. **Honors/Awds:** Omega Man of the Year Award, Theta Tau Chap, 1979; Outstanding Service Award, Alpha Kappa Alpha Sorority Inc, 1980; Case Club Award, Appellate Arguments; Moot Court Competition Award, Emory Univ, Sch Law. **Military Serv:** AG/FA/CML, capt, 1974-; comdr 496, chem detachment. **Home Addr:** 111 S Quintard Ave, PO Box 2641, Anniston, AL 36202. **Business Addr:** Judge, Calhoun County, District Court, 161 E Michigan Ave, Battle Creek, MI 49014, **Business Phone:** (616)969-6504.

OWENS, RICH DARRYL

Football player. **Personal:** Born May 22, 1972, Philadelphia, PA. **Educ:** Lehigh Univ. **Career:** Wash Redskins, defensive end, 1995-97; Miami Dolphins, defensive end, 1999-2000; Kansas City Chiefs, defensive end, 2001-02; Seattle Seahawks, defensive end, 2002. **Honors/Awds:** Rookie of the Year, 1995. *

OWENS, RISSIE LOUISE

Government official. **Personal:** Born Jun 9, 1959, Texas; daughter of Oliver and Louise Anderson; married Edward G Owens Jr, Aug 20, 1987; children: Edward G Owens III. **Educ:** Sam Houston State Univ, BS, criminal justice, 1980; Univ Houston, MA, psychol, 1994. **Career:** Brajos County 272nd Dist Ct, ct coordr, 1981-82; Ment Health/Ment Health Retardom Brojos Valley, case mgr, 1982-84; Tex Dept Criminal Justice, coordr, 1984-90; Galveston County Adult Probation, probation officer, 1991-93; Amarillo ISD, drug prev coordr, 1993-95; Huntsville ISD, assoc sch psychol, 1995-97; Tex Bd Pardons & Paroles, chmn, 2004-, presiding officer, currently. **Orgs:** Leadership Tex, 1995-; Asn Paroling Authorities Int, 1997-; Tex Corrections Asn, 2000. **Honors/Awds:** Outstanding Community Leader, Nat Coun Negro Women, 2003. **Business Addr:** Chairman, Presiding Officer, Texas Board of Pardons & Paroles, 209 West 14th St Suite 500, PO Box 13401, Austin, TX 78701, **Business Phone:** (936)291-2161.

OWENS, ROBERT LEON, III

Educator. **Personal:** Born Nov 3, 1925, Arcadia, FL; married Nancy Gray; children: Raymond, Ronald & Nancy. **Educ:** Tuskegee Inst, BS, summa cum laude, class valedictorian, 1949; State Univ Iowa, MA, 1950, PhD, 1953. **Career:** State Univ La, instr psychol reading, 1953; Southern Univ, asst prof psychol, 1953-55, assoc prof psychol, 1956; prof psychol & educ, 1957, dean grad sch, prof psychol & educ, 1958-62, prof psychol & educ, 1962-66; Knoxville Col, pres, prof psychol, 1966-71; Univ Tenn, vis prof educ psychol, 1969-71; Howard Univ, Col Lib Arts, dean, 1971, prof emer, currently. **Orgs:** Exec comt, Land Grant Asn Deans Grad Schs, 1959-71; Exec Comt Deans Arts & Sci Land Grant Univs, 1963-65; LHD, N Park Col, 1968; mem exec comt, Am Soc Curric Develop, 1970; symposium leader, Ann Conf Inst Int Educ1971-76; discussant, Am Conf Acad Deans, 1973; exec Comt, Coun Religion & Higher Educ Res Asn, 1974-77; group leader, Am Conf Acad Deans, 1977; chmn nominating comt, Am Conf Acad Deans, 1976; bd dir, Am Conf Acad Deans, 1977-80; life mem, Phi Delta Kappa. **Home Addr:** 822 52nd St NE, Washington, WA 20019, **Home Phone:** (202)399-8498. **Business Addr:** Professor Emeritus, Howard University, 2400 Sixth St NW, Washington, DC 20059, **Business Phone:** (202)806-6100.

OWENS, RONALD C

Lawyer. **Personal:** Born May 1, 1936, Conway, AR; married Lois Adamson; children: Ronald, Alan & Veronica. **Educ:** Morehouse Col, 1954; Univ Ark, Pine Bluff, BS, 1957; Univ Baltimore Law Sch, JD, 1973. **Career:** Johns Hopkins Univ, asst dir admis, 1969-73, pre-law adv, 1975-; pvt prac, atty, 1974-; Ft Howard Am Bar Asn, corrective therapist; Baltimore City, asst states atty; asst city solicitor. **Orgs:** Monumental City Bar Asn; Phi Beta Gamma Legal Frat; Steward Douglas Memorial Church. **Honors/Awds:** Outstanding Advocate, 1972-73. **Military Serv:** AUS. **Business Addr:** Lawyer, 3705 Dorchester Rd, Baltimore, MD 21215, **Business Phone:** (410)542-6791.

OWENS, TERRELL ELDORADO

Football player. **Personal:** Born Dec 7, 1973, Alexander City, AL; son of Tit Russell and Marilyn Heard. **Educ:** Univ Tenn, Chattanooga. **Career:** San Francisco 49ers, wide receiver, 1996-2003; Philadelphia Eagles, wide receiver, 2004-05; Dallas Cowboys, wide receiver, 2006-09; Buffalo bills, wide receiver, 2009-. **Orgs:** Founder, Terrell Owens Found. **Honors/Awds:** Won the celebrity slam dunk competition NBA All-Star Game, 2000; ESPY Award, 2003. **Special Achievements:** TV skit, Desperate Housewives. **Business Addr:** Wide Receiver, Dallas Cowboys, Cowboys Ctr 1 Cowboys Pkwy, Irving, TX 75063, **Business Phone:** (972)556-9900.

OWENS, TREKA ELAINE

Accountant, vice president (organization), chief financial officer. **Personal:** Born Dec 6, 1953, Chicago, IL; daughter of Alfred Berry and Pauline Berry; married Johnny C; children: Kellie. **Educ:** DePaul Univ, BSC, acct, 1975; DePaul Univ, Col Law, Chicago, IL, JD, 1990. **Career:** Arthur Young & Co, auditor, 1975-77; Avon Products, staff acct, 1977-78; Borg-Warner Corp, corp acct, 1978-80; Johnson Pub Co, chief acct, 1980-86, vpres & cfo, 1986-. **Orgs:** Am Inst CPA's, 1982-, Il Soc CPA's 1982-; Am Bar Asn, 1991; Ill Bar Asn, 1991; Chicago Bar Asn, 1991. **Business Addr:** Vice President, Chief Financial Officer, Johnson Publishing Company, 820 So Mich Ave, Chicago, IL 60605, **Business Phone:** (312)322-9200.

OWENS, VICTOR ALLEN

Executive. **Personal:** Born Sep 30, 1945, Bronx, NY; married Ruth Morrison; children: Malcolm. **Educ:** Wilberforce Univ, BA, 1967; Univ Dayton, MA, 1971. **Career:** Ohio Bell Telephone, mgr, 1967-71; YWCA, bus mgr, 1971-76; Colonial Penn Group, mgr, 1976-79; Equitable, vpres, 1979-. **Orgs:** Chmn, Minority Interchange; assoc mem, Big Brothers; Int Commun Asn. **Home Addr:** 169 Rutland Rd, Brooklyn, NY 11225. **Business Addr:** Vice President, The Equitable, 787 7th Ave The Equitable, New York, NY 10019, **Business Phone:** (212)554-2909.

OWENS, WALLACE, JR.

Educator, painter (artist), executive. **Personal:** Born Dec 28, 1932, Muskogee, OK; son of Wallace Owens and Sarah. **Educ:** Lang-ston Univ, BA, art educ, 1959; Univ Cent OK, MA, art educ, 1965; Inst Allende-Mexico, MFA Painting, 1966; Univ Rome, Italy, Fulbright Scholar, 1970; Northern Tex State Univ, Doctoral Studies, 1970-71. **Career:** Educator (retired), Executive; Sterling HS Greenville SC, art instr, 1969-71; Lockheed Missile Co Sunnyvale, Ca, electronics tech, 1971-74; Langston Univ, prof art, 1966-80; Cent State Univ, prof art, 1980-2005; Owens Arts Place Mus Found Inc, owner & dir, currently. **Orgs:** Lions Int, 1976; Nat Conf Artists. **Honors/Awds:** Educators to Africans, African Am Inst Study Tour W Africa, 1973. **Special Achievements:** Executed Centennial Sculpture for Langston Univ, 1997. **Military Serv:** AUS cpt. **Home Addr:** 3374 Sunny Acres Lane, Guthrie, OK 73044. **Business Addr:** Owner, Director, Owens Arts Place Museum Foundation Inc, 1202 E Harrison Ave, Guthrie, OK 73044, **Business Phone:** (405)260-0204.

OWENS, WILLIAM

State government official, senator (u.s. federal government). **Personal:** Born Jul 6, 1937, Demopolis, AL; son of Jonathan and Mary A Clemons; married Cindy Edwards; children: Laurel, Curtis, William Jr, Adam, Sharra & Brenda. **Educ:** Harvard Univ, MEd 1971; Boston Univ, 1970; Univ MA, doc cand. **Career:** Sunrise Dry Cleaners, owner & mgr, 1960-68; Urban League Geater Boston, proj coord, 1968-70; St Dept Educ, dir career oppt prog, 1970; Proj Jesi-Jobs Univ Mass, local proj dir, 1971-72; Mass St, st rep, 1973-75, state sen, 1975-90. **Orgs:** Mass Leg Black Caucus; Mass Black Polit Assembly; Nat Black Polit Assembly; Dept Corrections Adv Task Force Voc Educ; bd dir, Roxbury Defenders; Resthaven Corp; Boston Black Repertory Co; S End Neighborhood Action Prog; Harvard Club Boston; Caribbean Am Carnival Day Asn; New Hope Baptist Church; Urban League Greater Boston; Boston Black United Front; Nat Asn Sch Administrators; Nat Asn Advan Colored People; Nat Educrs Asn. **Honors/Awds:** Man of Year Award; Black Big Bros Award of Excellence; Houston Urban League Plaque; Big Black Brother Alliance Award. **Home Addr:** 115 Hazelton St, Boston, MA 02126, **Home Phone:** (617)296-8568.

OWENS, REV. ZELBA RENE

Clergy. **Personal:** Born Feb 25, 1950, Rochester, NY; daughter of Robert Lee Carson and Shadie; children: Barbara Ann Spencer. **Educ:** Mich State Univ, BS, MA, 1971; Univ Mich Sch Med, attended 1973; Ashland Sem, cert, 1997. **Career:** Octagon House Inc, clin dir, 1973-79; Univ Mich Grad Sch Bus, res, 1980-81; Univ Mich Hosp, Allied Health Hosp, Mgt Assessment Ctr, role player res, 1980-81; Ann Arbor Community Ctr, substance abuse counr, 1986-87; Shelter Asn Ann Arbor, prog dir, 1987-91; Detroit Health Care Homeless, ment health prog dir, 1990-91; Harambee Inc, ceo, 1992-; Univ Mich Sch Pub Health, res assoc, 1995-96; African Methodist Episcopal Zion Church, itinerate elder, 1997-; Huron Residential Servs Youth, asst treatment supvr. **Orgs:** Delta Sigma Theta, 1969-; bd mem, Martin Chapel House Corp, 1980-; chair, Beyer Mem Hosp, Ethics Comm, 1994-99; bd dir, Metro Jail Ministries, 1995-; African Methodist Episcopal Zion Church, 1996-; Nat Coun Negro Women, 1996-; bd mem, Christine Therry Ministries, 1998-. **Honors/Awds:** Public Service Award, Community Develop Black Grant Agency, 1977-79; Outstanding Staff Commendation, Huron Residential Serv Youth, 1986; Coordinating Proj Women, 1989;Community Award, Brown Chapel AME Church, 1996; Community Award, Huron Valley Asn Black Social Workers. **Business Addr:** Chief Executive Officer, Harambee Inc, 1508 Hanover St, Chicago Heights, IL 60411, **Business Phone:** (708)870-9333.

OWENS-HICKS, SHIRLEY

State government official. **Personal:** Born Apr 22, 1942, Demopolis, AL; daughter of Johnathan and Mary; married; children: Dawn Deirdre & Stephanie Alicia. **Educ:** Chandler Sch Women, cert, 1961; Boston Univ Sch Educ, attended 1971; Harvard Univ Grad Sch Educ, EdM, 1972. **Career:** State government official (retired); Mass Sen, chief aide to sen, 1975-80; Urban League Eastern Mass Inc, dep dir, 1980-81, pres, exec dir, 1981-83; Boston Sch Comt, vpres, 1984-88; Univ Mass Boston, advocacy counr, 1984-86; Commonwealth Mass, 1987. **Orgs:** Delta Sigma Theta Sorority; Harvard Univ Alumni Asn; Urban League; Mass Black Legis Caucus; Nat Asn Advant Colored People; chair Joint (House & Senate) Comn Educ, 1995-97; Nat Black Caucus State Legislators; bd member, Brookview House Honary; Safe Futures, Mattapan goverance bd; Boston State Citizens Adv Comt; Phi Delta Kappa. **Honors/Awds:** Cert Appreciation Simmons Col 1978; Achievement Plaque Urban League Guild Eastern Mass 1983; Woman Year Zeta Phi Beta Sorority 1984; Cert Appreciation Boston Studs Adv Coun 1985, 1987; Promoting Excellence in Educ Award Freedom House Inst on Schs & Educ 1986; Educ Award Black Educrs Alliance MA 1986; Bilingual Master Parents Adv Coun Award 1986; Woman Year Univ MA at Boston Black Studs Org 1987; Cent Boston Elder Servs Distinguished Service to Older Bostonians, 1989; Womans Ministry Outstanding Leadership Award, Berea 7th Day Adventist, 1993; City Boston, African American Achievement Award in Pub Service, 1995; Network for Women in Polit & Govt, 1996; Woman Year Award; Distinguished Service to Education Award, Black Educrs Alliance MA, 1997. **Home Addr:** 15 Outlook Rd, Mattapan, MA 02126.

OWSLEY, BETTY JOAN

Educator, librarian. **Personal:** Born in Chicago, IL; daughter of Holsey C and Willa H. **Educ:** Fisk Univ, Nashville, TN, BA;

Howard Univ, Wash, DC, MA; Ind Univ, Bloomington, IN, MLS. **Career:** Indianapolis Pub Sch, Indianapolis, IN, teacher; Howard Univ, Allen M Daniel Law Lib, Wash, DC. **Orgs:** Bd mem, Indianapolis Coun Int Visitors, 1984-90; Am Library Asn; ALA Int Rels Round Table; Black Caucus Am Libr Asn; Delta Sigma Theta Sorority, Indianapolis Alumnae Chap; librn, founder, Willa H Owsley Inst; adv comt & Host Family Comt; Coun Int Prog; Ind Univ; Int Ctr Indianapolis; Nat Asn Advan Colored People; Nat Coun Negro Women; Ind Int Coun Inc; Corinthian Baptist Church. **Home Addr:** 505 W 40th St, Indianapolis, IN 46208, **Home Phone:** (317)283-7883.

OXENDINE, KEN QWARIOUS. See OXENDINE, KENNETH.

OXENDINE, KENNETH (KEN QWARIOUS OXENDINE)
Football player, football coach. **Personal:** Born Oct 4, 1975, Richmond, VA; son of Carl Waller and Viola. **Educ:** Va Tech Univ. **Career:** Football player (retired), Football coach; Atlanta Falcons, running back, 1998-99; Los Angeles Xtreme, XFL, 2001; Va Tech Univ, asst strength & conditioning coach, 2002-03; Duluth High Sch, running backs coach, 2003; Ga Southern Univ, wide receivers coach, 2004; Nat Football League, Europe, Cologne Centurions, offensive asst & running backs coach; Notre Dame Academy, phys educ, 2006-. **Business Phone:** (678)387-9385.

OXLEY, DR. LEO LIONEL
Psychiatrist. **Personal:** Born Jul 9, 1934, Raleigh, NC; children: Keith Charles & Claire Elaine. **Educ:** St Augustine Col, Raleigh NC, BS, 1955; Meharry Med Col, MD, 1959. **Career:** William Beaumont Gen Hosp, internship; Walter Reed Gen Hosp, chief resident, 1960-63; Brooklyn-Staten Island Mental Health Serv Health Ins Plan, Greater NY, dir, 1971-73; Natchaug Hosp, staff psychiatrist, 1973-74; Newington Veterans Admin Hosp, chief psychiatry serv, 1974-78; Ga Mental Health Inst, supt, 1978-80; The Inst Living, sr staff psychiatrist, 1980-82; Va Med Ctr, Chillicothe, OH, chief psychiatry serv, 1982-83; Va Med Ctr, Leavenworth, KS, chief psychiatry serv, 1983-84; Brecksville, Va Med Ctr, Nat Ctr for Stress Recovery, assoc clinic dir, 1984-85; Va Med Ctr, chief mental hygiene clinic, 1985-86; Va Med Ctr, Cleveland, staff psychiatrist; Va Outpatient Clinic, chief med officer, 1991-; Morehouse Sch Med, Adjunct Clinic Prof, psychiatry, 1996-. **Orgs:** Alpha Phi Alpha Frat; Alpha Omega Alpha Honor Med Soc; Am Psychiatric Asn, DAV, ROA, licensed to practice med in MO, GA. **Honors/Awds:** Publication, "Issues and Attitudes Concerning Combat Experienced Black Vietnam Veterans," Journal, Nat Med Asn, Vol 79, No 1, 1987, pp 25-32. **Military Serv:** USY, col, 1958-67; USAR, 1977-. **Business Addr:** Adjunct Clinical Professor, Psychiatry, Morehouse School of Medicine, Department of Psychiatry & Behavioral Sciences, 720 Wview Dr SW, Atlanta, GA 30310-1495, **Business Phone:** (404)756-1500.

OYEKAN, DR. SONI OLUFEMI
Engineer. **Personal:** Born Jun 1, 1946, Aba, Nigeria; son of Emilia Ikpe Inyang and Theophilous Oyekan; married Priscilla Ann Parker, Jun 2, 1970; children: Ranti Valdez, Ima, Femi & Arit. **Educ:** Yale Univ, BS, 1970; Carnegie Mellon Univ, MS, 1972, PhD, chem eng, 1977. **Career:** Univ Pittsburgh, lectr, coordr, 1972-77; Exxon, sr engr, 1977-80; Engelhard, section head, mgr, res assoc, 1980-90; Dupont, eng assoc, 1991-93; Sun Oil Co, process coordr, 1993-97; BP Amoco, sr process consult, 1997-99; Marathon Oil Co, Marathon Ashland Petrol LLC, sr refining technologist, 1999-. **Orgs:** Am Inst Chem Engrs, 2000-02, CWRT/CCPS, 2000-02, chair, Minority Affairs, 1998-99, Fuels & Petroleum Div, chair, 1995; prog chair, Spring Mtg, 1994, fel; chair, Pet Programming Comm, 1989-91; Sigma Xi; Phi Kappa Phi Soc. **Honors/Awds:** AICHE, fel, 1999; New Jersey YMCA, Black Achiever in Bus & Educ, 1984; Sigma Xi, Phi Kappa Phi, 1977; Yale, Manuscript, 1969; Distinguished Senior Award, Am Inst Chem Engrs, 2000; Distinguished Service Award, Fuels & Petrochemicals Div, Am Inst Chem Engrs, 2002. **Special Achievements:** US patent 4,539,307, Novel Activation Procedure, 1985; US patent, Novel Catalyst System. **Business Addr:** Senior Refining Technologist, Marathon Oil Company, Marathon Ashland Petrol LLC, PO Box 1, Findlay, OH 45839, **Business Phone:** (985)535-7415.

OYESHIKU, DR. PATRICIA DELORES WORTHY
Educator. **Personal:** Born Nov 3, 1944, Miami, FL; daughter of Inez Brantley; married Anthony A, May 25, 1968; children: Kama Charmange Titilola & Chaundrissa Morenike. **Educ:** Knoxville Col, Knoxville, Tenn, BS, eng, 1964; San Diego State Univ, San Diego Calif, MA, curric, 1971; US Int, San Diego Calif, PhD, educ leadership, 1980. **Career:** Peace Corp, Brazil, vol, 1964-66, San Francisco, Calif, recruiter, 1966-67, Boston, Mass, dep dir, recruiter, 1967-68; San Diego City Sch, San Diego Calif, eng teacher, 1970-. **Orgs:** Vol, Homeless Shelter, San Diego Calif. **Honors/Awds:** Outstanding Peace Corps Volunteer, Hubert Humphrey, 1966; California Teacher of the Year, 1980-81; National Teacher of the Year Finalist, 1980-81; Press Club Award, San Diego Calif; Outstanding Alumni in Education, San Diego State Univ; doctoral dissertation "The Effect of the Race of the Teacher on the Student". **Home Addr:** 7985 Hillandale Dr, San Diego, CA 92120, **Home Phone:** (619)286-3922. **Business Addr:** English Teacher, Morse High School, 6905 Skyline Dr, San Diego, CA 92124, **Business Phone:** (619)262-0763 Ext 4032.

OYEWOLE, DR. SAUNDRA HERNDON
Educator. **Personal:** Born Apr 26, 1943, Washington, DC; daughter of Laurence Homer and Helen Kirkland; married Godwin G, Mar 21, 1970; children: Ayodeji Babatunde, Monisola Aramide & Kolade Olufayo. **Educ:** Howard Univ, BS, zoo (Magna Cum Laude, Phi Beta Kappa, Beta Kappa Chi), 1965; Univ Chicago, MS, microbiol, 1967; Univ Massachusetts, Amherst, PhD, microbiol, 1973. **Career:** Electron microscopist; Hampshire Col, asst prof microbiol, 1973-79, assoc prof microbiol, 1979-81; Trinity Col, Wash, DC, assoc prof bio, 1981-87, chair, health professions adv Comm, 1982-, prof bio, 1988-, chair, bio dept, 1990-98, dean fac, 1998, Col Arts & Sci, dean; prog dir, Div Undergraduate Educ, Nat Sci Found, 1994-96. **Orgs:** Pres, Epsilon Chap Phi Beta Kappa, 1983-85; Am Soc Microbiol; mem, Comm Status Minority Microbiologists Am Soc Microbiol, 1984-, treas, 1989-; exec comm, Northeast Asn Advs Health Professions, 1984-87; chairperson, Health Professions Adv Comm Trinity Col; coordr, Pre-Nursing Prog Trinity Col; adv coun, Northeast Asn Advs Health Professions, 1987-; founder & dir, Post-Baccalaureate Premed Prog Trinity Col, 1993-; Nat Asn Advs Health Professions, bd dirs, 1993-95, secy bd, 1994-96; pres-elect, 1996-98, pres, 1998-00; vice chairperson, governing coun, Wye Fac Seminar, 1997-; chairperson, MNY Educ Comm, Am Soc microbiol, 1997-. **Honors/Awds:** Danforth Associate, 1979; Clare Boothe Luce Professor of Biology, 1990-93. **Business Addr:** Professor of Biology, Trinity College, 125 Michigan Ave NE, Washington, DC 20017, **Business Phone:** (202)939-5000.

OZANNE, DOMINIC L.
President (organization). **Personal:** Born Apr 10, 1953, Cleveland, OH; son of Leroy and Betty Peyton; married Gaile Cooper, Jun 30, 1984; children: Dominic & Monique. **Educ:** Boston Univ, Boston, MA, BS, BA, 1975; Harvard Law Sch, Cambridge, MA, JD, 1978. **Career:** Thompson, Hine, Flory, Cleveland, OH, assoc, 1978-80; Ozanne Construction Co, Cleveland, OH, pres, 1980-. **Orgs:** Pres, Nat Asn Minority Contractors, 1989-90; bd dirs, Notre Dame Col, 2005-; mem exec comt, Ohio Found Independent Col . **Honors/Awds:** Top Black Stud, Black Enterprise Mag, 1975; 1990 Marksman, Engineering News Mag, 1990. **Special Achievements:** Co listed at no. 61 on Black Enterprise's list of the top 100industrial/service companies, 1998. **Business Addr:** President, Chief Executive Officer, Ozanne Construction Co Inc., 1635 E 25th St, Cleveland, OH 44114-4214, **Business Phone:** (216)696-2876.

OZANNE, LEROY
Executive. **Career:** Cleveland building inspector;n Ozanne Construct Co Inc, founder & chief exec officer, 1956-. **Honors/Awds:** Listed No 88 of 100 top indust serv companies, Black Enterprise, 1992. **Business Addr:** founder, Chief Executive Officer, Ozanne Construction Company, 1635 E 25th St, Cleveland, OH 44114-4214, **Business Phone:** (216)696-2876.

OZIM, DR. FRANCIS TAINO
Surgeon. **Personal:** Born Oct 1, 1946, Lagos, Nigeria; married Margaret Fay Taylor; children: Brion Olufemi, Frances Adetola & Melissa Funmilayo. **Educ:** St Finbarr's Col, Lagos, Nigeria, WASC, 1965; St Gregory's Col, Lagos, Nigeria, HSC, 1967; Howard Univ Med Sch, MD, 1976; Univ Albuquerque, NM, 1969-72. **Career:** Georgetown Univ Med Ctr, intern, 1976-77; Howard Univ Hosp, resident surg, 1977-81; Dist Columbia Gen Hosp, attend surg, 1981-82; Charlotte Mem Hosp & Med Ctr, active staff, 1982-86; Norfolk Community Hosp, active staff, 1987-; Louise Obici Mem Hosp, Suffolk, 1987-; Norfolk Gen Hosp, 1987; Sufnor Surg Group, gen surgeon; pvt prac, currently. **Honors/Awds:** fel, Southeastern Surg Cong, 1982-; Am Col Surgeons, 1986-. **Home Phone:** (757)382-9191. **Business Addr:** Physician, 113 Gainsborough Sq Suite 400, Chesapeake, VA 23320, **Business Phone:** (757)549-2492.

P

PACE, ORLANDO LAMAR
Football player. **Personal:** Born Nov 4, 1975, Sandusky, OH; married Carla; children: Justin & Jalen. **Educ:** Ohio State univ, BMT. **Career:** Saint Louis Rams, offensive tackle, 1997-2008; Chicago Bears, offensive tackle, 2009-. **Orgs:** Sokesman, Diversity Awareness Partnership, 2000; spokesperson, Our Little Haven "Safe & Warm" expansion project, 1998. **Honors/Awds:** Lombardi Award, 1995-96; Outland Trophy, 1996; National Offensive Player of the Year, Football News, 1996; UPI Lineman of the Year, 1996; Jim Parker Award, 1996; Big Ten Football MVP, 1996; Super Bowl champion. **Special Achievements:** First Overall Pick in NFL Draft, 1997; First-team All-Pro, 1999-2001 & 2003; Pro Bowl selection, 1999-2005. **Business Addr:** Professional Football Player, Chicago Bears, Halas Hall at Conway Pk, 1000 Football Dr, Lake Forest, IL 60045.*

PACK, ROBERT JOHN
Basketball player. **Personal:** Born Feb 3, 1969, New Orleans, LA; children: Robert III. **Educ:** Tyler Jr Col; Univ Southern Calif, BS, sociol, 1991. **Career:** Basketball player (retired); Portland Trail Blazers, guard, 1991-92; Denver Nuggets, 1992-95; Wash Bullets, 1995-96; Dallas Mavericks, 1996-2000; Denver Nuggets, 2001; Minn Timberwolves, 2001-02; New Orleans Hornets, 2002-03; NJ Nets, 2003; Pamesa Valencia, 2004; Zalgiris Kaunas, Euroleague, 2004-05; Toronto Raptors, point guard, 2005. **Orgs:** Founder, Robert Pack Found, 1997.

PACKER, DANIEL FREDRIC, JR.
Manager, president (organization), chief executive officer. **Personal:** Born Dec 8, 1947, Mobile, AL; son of Daniel F and Algie V Ervin; married Carlene (deceased); children: Timothy & Vanice; married Catherine August, Jul 7, 1983; children: Randall Ross, Reginald Ross & Maria Ross. **Educ:** Tuskegee Univ, Tuskegee, Ala, 1965-68; Middlesex Community Col, Middletown, Conn, AS, 1978; Charter Oak Col, Hartford, Conn, BS, 1980. **Career:** Conn Yankee Atomic Power, Haddam, Conn, sr reactor operator, 1975-81; Gen Physics Corp, Columbia, Md, sr engr, 1981-82; La Power & light, Tact, La, training mgr, 1982-90; Entergy Opers Inc, training mgr, plant mgr o&m,1990, dir, 1996-, pres, 1997-2007, ceo, 1998-2007. **Orgs:** Chmn, Am Asn Blacks Energy; Am Nuclear Soc, 1982-; chmn, NFL Stadium Advisory Comn, 2001; chmn, New Orleans Regional Chamber Com, 2001; chmn, New Orleans Aviation Bd, 2002; Bring New Orleans Back Comn, 2005-, mem, Fore kids foundation, currently. **Honors/Awds:** Black Achievement Award, YMCA, 1988; Sr Nuclear Plant Mgr Course, Inst Nuclear Power Opers, 1990; Weiss Award, Tulane Univ, 2001; Whitney Young Service Award, Boy Scouts Am, S E La Coun, 2004; Most Powerful African-American Executives, Black Enterprise's, 2005. **Special Achievements:** First African American to manage a nuclear power plant. **Military Serv:** USN, e-6, 1969-75.

PACKER, ZZ
Educator, writer. **Personal:** Born Jan 12, 1973, Chicago, IL. **Educ:** Yale Univ, BA, 1994; Johns Hopkins Univ, MA, 1995; Univ Iowa, MFA, 1999. **Career:** Wallace Stegner & Truman Capote fellowships, Stanford Univ; Calif Col of the Arts, sr vis prof creative writing, writers in residence, currently; Working on a first novel, about the adventures of the Buffalo Soldiers, currently; Books: Drinking Coffee Elsewhere, 2003. **Honors/Awds:** Whiting Writers' Award; Rona Jaffe Found Writers' Award; Rona Jaffe Writers Foundation Grant, 1997; Ms. Giles Whiting Award, 1999; Bellingham Review Award, 1999; Guggenheim Fellowship for fiction, 2005. **Business Addr:** Writers in Residence, California College of the Arts, 1111 Eighth St, San Francisco, CA 94107, **Business Phone:** (415)703-9523.*

PADDIO, GERALD (GERALD JAMES PADDIO)
Basketball player, basketball coach. **Personal:** Born Apr 21, 1965, Lafayette, LA. **Educ:** Univ Nevada, Las Vegas. **Career:** Basketball player (retired), basketball coach; Cleveland Cavaliers, 1990-91; Seattle Supersonics, 1992-93; Ind Pacers, forward & guard, 1993-94; NY Knickerbockers, forward & guard, 1994; Wash Bullets, forward & guard, 1994; Petroleros, Mexico, asst coach, 2004.

PADDIO, GERALD JAMES. See PADDIO, GERALD.

PADDIO-JOHNSON, DR. EUNICE ALICE
Clergy, school administrator. **Personal:** Born Jun 25, 1928, Crowley, LA; daughter of Henry Paddio and Ce; married John David Johnson Sr (died 1992); children: Deidre Reed Dyson (deceased), Clarence III, Henry P, Bertrand J & Ce. **Educ:** Leland Col Baker, LA; Grambling State Univ, Grambling LA, BS, 1949; UCLA, MA, 1960; La State Univ, Baton Rouge, attended 1966; Univ Minn, St Paul, 1975; State Univ New York, Albany, 1980; Cornell Univ, Ithaca, MS, 1988; Progressive Univ, PhD, 1993. **Career:** St Helena Parish Sch, LA, teacher, counr, 1949-72; St Helena Summer Hd Start, LA, assoc dir, 1965-69; St Helena Assis Resource Est, LA, pres & dir, 1972-73; Cornell Univ, NY, admin, 1973-85; St Helena Head Start, dir, 1986-87; Paddio-Johnson Enterprises Inc, pres, 1987-; Greater Rising Star AME Church, pastor, 1995-98; Gaines Chapel AME Church, pastor, 1998-99; Crystal Springs AME Chruch, pastor, 1999-2000. **Orgs:** Ed jour, exec comt mem La Educ Asn, 1964-69; sch bd mem, St Helena Parish Sch, LA, 1972-74; Ithaca City Sch, NY, 1975-82; Ithaca Neighborhood Housing Servs; P-R Found; Atlanta Child, 1975-; pres, Paddio-Johnson Human Rels Consult, 1980-; Am Asn Univ Women, 1980-; bd dir, Family & Childs Serv, Planned Parenthood, Tompkins Co; pres emer, Martin Luther King Jr Scholar Fund Ithaca Inc, 1982-86; Delta Sigma Theta Sorority; Nat Asn Advan Colored People; exec bd, African Methodist Episcopal Women Ministry, 1996-2000. **Honors/Awds:** Graduate Asniate, Matron La Esther Grand Chapter OES, 1963-74; Outstanding Citizen, New Orleans, 1973; Black Gold Award, Grambling State Univ, 1973; Citizen of the Year, 1974; Creat Career Express Program, 1975; Outstanding Humanitarian & Trailblazer Award, 1992. **Special Achievements:** Co-author: Wng Behavior Skills, 1976-77. **Home Addr:** PO Box 245, Greensburg, LA 70441, **Home Phone:** (225)222-4388. **Business Addr:** President, Paddio-Johnson Enterprises, 731 Hall Rd, PO Box 245, Greensburg, LA 70441, **Business Phone:** (225)222-4388.

PADGETT, JAMES A
Artist, educator. **Personal:** Born Nov 24, 1948, Washington, DC; son of James Padgett and Pauline C Flournoy; married Joan M

Jemison; children: Anthony A. **Educ:** Corcoran Sch Art, WW; Howard Univ, BFA, 1972; Howard Univ Grad Sch, MFA, 1974. **Career:** Wilberforce Univ, Dept Art & Scis, prof, currently. **Orgs:** Howard Univ Mural Proj Comn, 1968-; DC Comn on the Arts Mural Proj Comn, 1968-72; murals erected & various sites, Howard Univ, Anacostia Museum, Smithsonian Inst, Sch Soc Work, Howard Univ; Shaw Com Comp Health Ctr Nat Med Asn, Found Howard Univ Hosp Col Med; co-dir, Martin Luther King Jr Arts Festival. **Honors/Awds:** Selected to participate in touring art exhib "Paintings from Am U"; Cert of Appreciation Univ Neighborhood Coun, 1964; Cert of Accom Summer Enrich Prog Art Dir, 1965; Wash Rel Arts Exhib Am Savings & Loan Assn DC; first prize Collage & Painting, 1966; Cert of Commen Upward Bound Col Prog Howard Univ, 1966; Corcoran Scholarship Award, W W Corcoran Sch Art, 1967; Cert Art DC Rec Dept Art & Splst Instr, 1967-68; second prize The Town Square Art Show Inc Collage & Painting, 1969; third prize Outdoor Art Exhib Painting, 1969; third prize Artists Unlmtd Painting, 1969; first & second prize Artists Unlmtd Painting, 1970; Monitor Asst Grant Howard Univ Col of Fine Arts 1970; first prize Hon Mention Ch of the Brethren Arts Exhib Painting, 1971; Scholarship Award, Howard Univ Col of Fine Arts, 1-72; Scholarship Award, Howard Univ Grad Sch of Fine Arts, 1972-73; Scholarship Award, Skowhegan Sch of Painting & Sculp summer, 1971; Afro-Am Artist a bio-bibliog directory; Images of Change-1 Art Society in Transition; Chrmn 4th InterNat Conference on Art, in honor of her majesty Queen Elizabeth II, 1977; K Miller Galleries LTD, the Old Bank Gallery, 1979; Galerie Des Deux Mondes Gallery of Art, 1980. **Business Addr:** Professor of Arts, Wilberforce University, PO Box 370, Wilberforce, OH 45384, **Business Phone:** (937)708-5676.

PADULO, DR. LOUIS
Educator. **Personal:** Born Dec 14, 1936, Athens, AL; son of Helen Margaret Yarbrough Padulo and Louis Padulo; married Katharine Seamans; children: Robert & Joseph. **Educ:** Fairleigh Dickinson Univ, BS, 1959; Stanford Univ, MS, 1962; Ga Inst Tech, PhD, 1966. **Career:** RCA, systs analyst, 1959-60; San Jose State Col, asst prof, 1962-63; Ga State Col, asst prof, 1966-67; Ga Tech Eng Experiment Sta, consult, 1966-69; Morehouse Col, assoc prof & chmn math dept, 1967-69; Stanford Univ, assoc prof, 1969-75; Columbia Univ, 1969; Harvard Univ, vis prof, 1970; Atlanta Univ & Ga Tech, founder & dir dual degree prog; Boston Univ, dean col engineering prof math & engineering, 1975-88, assoc vpres, 1986-87; Mass Inst Techno, Cambridge, MA, vis prof, 1987-88, vis scientist, 1991-92; Univ Ala Huntsville, Huntsville, Ala, pres, 1988-90; Univ City Sci Ctr, pres & chief exec officer, 1991-97, pres emer, 1997-; Invictus, chmn, 1997-; GLOSAS & USA, vchmn; Congress Higher Educ, pres. **Orgs:** Chmn planning comn, Expanding Minority Opportunities Engineering, 1973-; Nat Acad Engineering Com Minorities Engineering; fel Am Soc Engineering Educ, 1988; fel Inst Elec & Electronic Engineers, 1991; pres, Congress Higher Educ, 1992-; trustee, Fairleigh Dickinson Univ, 1992-. **Honors/Awds:** Walter J Gores Award, Stanford Univ, 1971; W Elec Fund Award, 1973; Award for Excellence in Science & Engineering, Educ Nat Consortium Black Professional Develop, 1977; Reginald H Jones Award, Nat Action Coun Minorities Engineering, 1983; Vincent Bendix Award, 1984; Pinnacle Award, Fairleigh Dickinson Univ, 1989. **Business Addr:** President Emeritus, University City Science Center, 2020 Walnut St Suite 32A, Philadelphia, PA 19104, **Business Phone:** (215)564-6405.

PAGE, HON. ALAN CEDRIC
Judge. **Personal:** Born Aug 7, 1945, Canton, OH; son of Howard Felix and Georgianna Umbles; married Diane Sims, Jun 5, 1973; children: Nina, Georgianna, Justin & Khamsin. **Educ:** Univ Notre Dame, BA, 1967; Univ Minn Law Sch, JD, 1978. **Career:** Football player (retired), judge; Minn Vikings, prof football player, 1967-78; Chicago Bears, 1978-81; Nat Football League Players Asn, rep, 1970-74, 1976-77, execcomt, 1972-75; Lindquist & Vennum, assoc, 1979-84; Turner Broadcasting Syst, "Col Football Game of the Week", color commentator, 1982; Nat Pub Radio, commentator, 1982-83; St Minn, spec asst atty gen, 1985-87, asst atty gen, 1987-93; MinnSupreme Ct, assoc justice, 1993-. **Orgs:** Rep, Nat Football League Players Asn, 1970-74, 1976-77; Nat Football League Players Asn Exec Comt, 1972-75; Am Bar Asn, 1979-; Nat Bar Asn,1979-; Minn St Bar Asn, 1979-85, 1990; Minn Asn Black Lawyers, 1980-; Adv Bd, Mixed Blood Theater, 1984-; Bd Dir, Minneapolis Urban League, 1987-90; Page Educ Found, 1988; Bd Regents, Univ Minn, 1989-92; Inst BillRights Law Task Force Drug Testing Workplace, 1990-91; Am Law Inst, 1993-. **Honors/Awds:** Most Valuable Player Award, 1971; Pro Football Hall of Fame, 1988; Alan Page Drive, named in honor, 1989; Nike Walk of Fame, 1990; Friend of Education Award, Nat Educ Asn, 1991; Chicago's Inner City Sports Hall of Fame, 1991; Babe Hollingbery Award, E-W Game, 1992; Silver Anniversary Award, NCAA, 1992; Reverend Edward Frederick Sorin CSC Award, Univ NotreDame, 1992; Theodore Roosevelt Meritorious Service Award, US Sports Acad, 1992; Distinguished Good Neighbor Award, WCCO Radio, 1993; Col Football Hall of Fame, 1993; LLD, Univ Notredame, 1993, 2004; LLD, St John's Univ, 1994; Aetna Voice of Conscience Arthur Ashe Jr Achiever Award, 1994; hondegree, Westfield State Col, 1994; hon degree, Luther Col, 1995; The 50 Greatest Sports Figures from Ohio, Sports Illustrated, 1999; 100 Influential Minnesotans of the Century, Star Tribune, 1999; hon degree, Univ New Haven, 1999; 100 Most Important Sports Figures of the Century, Star Tribune, 1999; DHL, Winston-Salem State Univ, 2000; Academic All-American Hall of Fame, 2001; Dick Engberg Award, 2001; InterNat Scholar-Athlete Hall of Fame, 2002; hon degree, Gustavus Adolphus Col, 2003; Theodore Roosevelt Award, NCAA, 2004; Distinguished American Award &Col Hall of Fame, Nat Football Found, 2005; Equal Justice Award, Coun Crime & Justice, 2007; 9 Times Pro Bowl Selection, 1969-77; 6 Times All Pro Selection, 1969-75; Thrice Second Team All Pro Selection, 1968, 1972, 1976. **Special Achievements:** First defensive player in NFL history to receive "Most Valuable Player" Award in 1971; First active NFL player to complete a marathon (26.2 miles) in 1979; Selected by U.S. Jaycees as one of America's Ten Outstanding Young Men in 1981. **Business Addr:** Associate Justice, Minnesota Judicial Center, 25 Rev Dr Martin Luther King Jr Blvd, St Paul, MN 55155, **Business Phone:** (651)297-7650.

PAGE, CLARENCE
Journalist. **Personal:** Born Jun 2, 1947, Dayton, OH; married Lisa Johnson, Aug 26, 1987; children: Grady Page. **Educ:** Ohio Univ, BS, jour, 1969. **Career:** The NewsHour, essayist; WBBM-TV, community affairs dir, reporter & planning ed; Chicago Mag, writer; The Chicago Reader, writer; Wash Monthly, writer; The New Repub, writer; The Wall St J, writer; New York Newsday, writer; Emerge, writer; Chicago Tribune, reporter, asst city ed & columnist, 1984-, mem ed bd, currently. **Honors/Awds:** Pulitzer Prize, 1972; Edward Scott Beck Award, 1976; Ill UPI Award, 1980; Am Civil Liberties Union James P McGuire Award, 1987; Pulitzer Prize, 1989. **Special Achievements:** Author of The Jaws of Success and Showing My Color: Impolite Essays on Race & Identity. **Business Addr:** Columnist, Chicago Tribune, Tribune Co, 1325 G St NW Suite 200, Washington, DC 20005.

PAGE, DR. GREGORY OLIVER
Dentist. **Personal:** Born Feb 26, 1950, Philadelphia, PA; son of William and Bernice; children: Dylan Mikkel, Erin Leah. **Educ:** Howard Univ, BS, 1972; Univ Pennsylvania, DMD, 1976. **Career:** Hostos Community Col, CCNY, assoc adjunct prof; Harlem community; N Cent Bronx Hosp, attending dentist, 1978-80; Health Ins Prog NY, Bronx, dir dent, 1978-82; Am Dent Foreign Serv Inc; pvt practice, dentist, 1982-. **Orgs:** Howard Univ Alumni Club NY City; Acad Gen Dent; Am Dent Assn; Am Dent Foreign Serv; Acad Gen Dent; St Phillip's Ch NY City; Am Cancer Soc, 1991. **Special Achievements:** Some Wisdom About Teeth, Ebony mag, author, 1987. **Business Addr:** Dentistry, 10 W 135th St, New York, NY 10037, **Business Phone:** (212)281-5775.

PAGE, HARRISON EUGENE (HARRY PAGE)
Television producer, writer, actor. **Personal:** Born Aug 27, 1941, Atlanta, GA; son of Roberta Fambro Hunter and Harry; married Christina Giles, Dec 30, 1989; children: Delisa Hutcheson & Terry Lynn. **Career:** NBC Television, Los Angeles, CA, actor, 1975-83; ABC television, Los Angeles, CA, actor, 1984-85; New World Television, Los Angeles, CA, actor, 1985-87, actor, 1989; Universal Pictures & Imperials Pictures, Los Angeles, CA; actor, 1989; Orion Pictures, Los Angeles, CA, actor, 1991; Universal Pictures, Off Balance Producer, Los Angeles, CA, 1991; TV Episodes: "Boy Next Door", "Turning Thirty", 2000; "Queen Bee", "Raptor", "I'll Be Home for Christmas", "Dog Robber: Part 2", "Mixed Messages", 2001; "Chaos Theory", "Lockdown", "By gones", "Family Business", "First Casualty", 2002; "Back in the Saddle" "Blast from the Past", 2003; "Cold Case", 2005; "The Kids in the Hall", 2007; "Standoff", 2007; Deadland, 2008. **Orgs:** Buddhist, NSA, 1985-91; lifetime mem, Lee Strasberg. **Honors/ Awds:** Bronze Wrangler Award, 1970; Emmy Award, 1992. **Military Serv:** Military service. **Business Phone:** (818)980-8092.

PAGE, JOHN SHERIDAN
Dean (Education), librarian, administrator. **Personal:** Born Dec 29, 1942, Pace, MS; son of John Sheridan Page Sr and Mary Lee. **Educ:** Tougaloo Col, Tougaloo, MS, BA, 1964; Long Island Univ, Greenvale, NY, MS, 1967. **Career:** Oceanside Free Libr, Oceanside, NY, young adult librn, 1966-68; Stone-Brandel Ctr, Chicago, IL, librn, 1968-69; Fed City Col, Wash, DC, sr media specialist, 1969-76; Univ DC, Wash, DC, assoc dir, tech servs, 1976-84, asst dir, learning resources, 1984-99, Learning Resources Div, assoc dean, 2000-. **Orgs:** Am Libr Asn; DC Libr Asn; Asn Col Res Libr, 1988-90, chair, 1990-92, stand & accreditation comt; Black Caucus Am Libr Asn, Literary Award Comn, Choice Ed Bd, 1999-2003. **Honors/Awds:** Mellon ACRL Internship, Univ Calif, Berkeley, 1974-75. **Home Addr:** 3003 Van Ness St NW W522, Washington, DC 20008, **Home Phone:** (202)363-4990. **Business Addr:** Associate Dean, University of the District of Columbia, Learning Resources Division, 4200 Conn Ave, Washington, DC 20008, **Business Phone:** (202)274-6030.

PAGE, MURRIEL
Basketball player. **Personal:** Born Sep 18, 1975, Louin, MS. **Educ:** Fla Univ, sports mgt, 1998. **Career:** Wash Mystics, forward, 1998-05; Hondarrabia, Spanish Pro League, 2003-04, 2005-06, 2006-07; Valencia, Spanish Pro League, 2004-05; Los Angeles Sparks, forward, 2006-. **Honors/Awds:** Most Valuable Player, State Farm Classic; Most Valuable Player, Dial Classic; silver medal, US Jones Cup Team, 1997; All-America Team, Kodak, 1997-98. **Business Addr:** Basketball Player, Los Angeles Sparks, 888 S Figueroa St Suite 2010, Los Angeles, CA 90017, **Business Phone:** (213)929-1300.*

PAGE, ROSEMARY SAXTON
Lawyer. **Personal:** Born Jan 29, 1927, New York, NY; daughter of Oliver W (deceased) and Earle Day (deceased); divorced; children: Marjorie & Christopher. **Educ:** Fisk Univ, BS, 1948; Howard Univ, Sch Law, 1959. **Career:** Lawyer (retired); Legal Aid Soc New York City, assoc coun, 1967-70; Nassau Co Law Servs, atty, 1970-72; Am Arbitration Asn, assoc gen coun, 1973-95; Fordham Univ, Sch Law, adj prof, 1983-95; Touro Law Sch, adj, 1986. **Orgs:** NY State Bd, 1961-; US Dist Ct, Southern Dist NY, 1969; US Dist Ct, Eastern Dist NY, 1969; Ed Digest Ct Decisions, 1973-76; Arbitration Com Bar Asn NY, 1974-77; Labor & Employment Comn Bar Asn NY, 1981-85; Nat Bar Asn, 1977-; NBA Bd Govs & chmn, NBA Arbitration Sect, 1981-95; USDC, NDNY, 1984; US Ct Appeals, 1969; bd dir, Huntington Youth Bd, 1972-77, vice chmn bd, 1976-77; US Supreme Ct, 1973; Bahai Missionary S Africa, 1996-02. **Special Achievements:** Published "Arbitration Proceedings and the Automatic Stay in Bankruptcy", "Recent International Cases", "Employment-Related Women's Issues", "Enforceability of Oral-Contract Award", 1991-92. **Home Addr:** 528 E Broadway, Bel Air, MD 21014.

PAGE, SOLOMON
Football player. **Personal:** Born Feb 27, 1976, Pittsburgh, PA. **Educ:** Univ WVa. **Career:** Football player (retired), Football coach; Dallas Cowboys, tackle, 1999-2002; San Diego Chargers, 2003; New York Giants, 2004; Detroit Lions, 2004; offensive line coach; Carrollton Christian Acad, 2008.

PAGE, WILLIE F
Educator. **Personal:** Born Jan 2, 1929, Dothan, AL; married Gracie Tucker. **Educ:** Wayne State Univ, BSME, 1961; Adelphi Univ, MBA, 1970; NY Univ, PhD, 1975. **Career:** Educator (retired); Boeing Co, engr, 1961-63; Grumman Aerospace, asst dir, prod, 1967-70; Glen Cove Coop Col Ctr, SUNY, dir, lectr, 1971-72; Nassau-Suffolk CHES, exec dir, 1972-74; Brooklyn Col, Dept Africana Studies, chmn, assoc prof, 1974-79, CUNY, assoc prof, 1979, prof emer, currently; New York City Head Start Regional Training Off, consult, 1975-79; Nat Endowment Humanities, consult, 1977-78; NY Educ Dept, consult, 1977-79. **Orgs:** African Heritage Studies Asn, 1974-80; Am Educ Res Asn, 1974-80; bd mem, Weeksville Soc Brooklyn, 1979-80. **Honors/Awds:** EPDA Fel, USOE, NYU, 1973; Dissertation Yr Fel, Nat Fel Fund Atlanta, 1975; Henry Meissner Res Award, Phi Delta Kappa, NYU, 1975; NEH, Fel Sem Slavery, Harvard Univ, 1978. **Special Achievements:** Author "The Dutch Triangle: The Netherlands and the Atlantic Slave Trade, 1621-1664 ", "Encyclopedia of African History and Culture 5-Volume Set", "The Encyclopedia of African History and Culture Set", " Encyclopedia of African Kingdoms". **Military Serv:** AUS, 1st lt, 1950-53. **Business Addr:** professor Emeritus, C U N Y, Brooklyn College, Afro-American Studies, 2901 Bedford Ave, Brooklyn, NY 11210-2813, **Business Phone:** (718)951-5000.*

PAIGE, ALVIN
Artist, school administrator, educator. **Personal:** Born Jul 13, 1934, LaGrange, GA; son of Edward and Dora Jane McGee; married Susan Lee, Feb 29, 1988; children: Monica L, Paige, Gaila R Paige, Alvin Jr & Shaneane Paige Foster. **Educ:** Am Int Col, BA, Polit Sci, 1980; Antioc Col, MA, Admin, 1981; Harvard Univ, advan graduate studies. **Career:** The Beeches Resort Rome, NY, art dir, 1965-67; Display workshop Hartford, CT, chief designer, 1967-68, dir art, 1968-69; Paige Innovations Enterprise, managing dir, 1970-75; Am Int Col, Springfield, MA, resident artist/designer & dir cult arts ctr, 1978-. **Orgs:** Bd dirs, Nat Col Conf Asn, 1979; bd dirs, Berkshire Ballet, l987-89; bd dirs, Springfield Mayors Office Cult Affairs, 1988-89; bd dirs, Springfield Neighborhood Housing Serv, l988-89; cooperator, Stage West Theatre Co, l988-89; chmn, Symphony Hall Prom Community; Inst Urban Design Archit League NY; Nat Sculptors Soc; British Sculptors Soc; Free Painters & Sculptors London, Eng; Shanghai Sculptors Soc; Sculpture Soc Can. **Honors/Awds:** Nat One man sculptors exhibit tour, 1984-85; Acad Polit Sci Achievement, Am Int Col, 1980; US Steel Cost Incentive Award, 1982; Alvin Paige Day LaGrange, GA, 1983; Coun Advan Support Educ "Except Achievement" Award, 1982; Outstanding American Spirits of Honor Medal, 1957; Governor TX Citizenship Award, 1958. **Special Achievements:** 3 Int Art ExhibitsPeople's Republic of China 1989; Invitational Intlxhibit Royal Hibernian Academy Dublin Ireland l988; Ebony Mag, 1969. **Military Serv:** USAF 8 years; Maj; Non-Commissioned Officers Award (4-times). **Business Addr:** Director, American International College, Department Cultural Arts 1000 State St, Springfield, MA 01109, **Business Phone:** (413)737-7000.

PAIGE, EMMETT, JR.
Military leader, president (organization). **Personal:** Born Feb 20, 1931, Jacksonville, FL; son of Elizabeth Core Paige and Emmet Paige; married Gloria Mc Clary, Mar 1, 1953; children: Michael, Sandra, Anthony. **Educ:** Univ Md, BA, 1972; Penn State, MA, 1974; Army War Col, 1974. **Career:** military officer (retired),

president; AUS, 1947; 361st Signal Brigade AUS Vietnam, comdr, 1969; 11th Signal Brigade AUS, Ft Huachuca, AZ, comdr, 1975; AUS Commun Electronics Eng Installation Agency's, comdr, 1976-79; AUS Info Syst Eng Command, commanding gen; AUS Commun Res & Develop Command, comdr, 1979-81; Armed Forces Commun & Electronics Asn, bd dir, 1980; AUS Electronics Res & Develop Command, 1981-84; AUS Info Systs Command, lt gen, 1984-88; OAO Corp, pres & chief oper officer, 1988-93 & 1997-; asst secy defense command, control, commun & intelligence, 1993-97; bd visitors, Univ Md Univ Col, currently; bd dir, Gtech Holdings, currently. **Orgs:** Am Leg Post 224, 1976-; Am Radio Relay League. **Honors/Awds:** Alumni Award, Univ Md Univ Col, 1988. **Military Serv:** AUS, gen, 1947-1988, 1993-97; Distinguished Service Medal, Legion of Merit, Bronze Star for Meritorious Service, Meritorious Service Medal, Army Commendation Medal. **Business Phone:** (301)220-7193.

PAIGE, DR. RODERICK RAYNOR
School administrator, secretary of education (u.s. federal government). **Personal:** Born Jun 17, 1933, Monticello, MS; son of Raynor C and Sophie; married Gloria Crawford (divorced 1982); children: Rod Paige Jr. **Educ:** Jackson State Univ, BS, 1955; Ind Univ, MS, 1964, DPEd, 1969. **Career:** Utica Jr Col, head football coach, 1957-67; Jackson State Univ, head football coach, 1966-68; Tex Southern Univ, asst football coach, asst prof, dean & athletic dir, 1971, head football coach, 1971-75; Houston Independent Sch Dist, Bd Educ, trustee, 1989-94; Houston Independent Sch Dist, Bd Educ, officer, 1990-94; Houston Independent Sch Dist, supt, 1994-2000; US secy educ, 2001-05; Chart well Education Group LLC, chmn,2005-. **Orgs:** Pres, Hirma Clarke Civic Club; secy, Houston Job Training Partnership Coun; adv bd mem, Prof United Leadership League; mem dirs, Tri-Civic Assoc; comnr, Nat Comn Employ Policy; coordr, Harris Co Explorer Olympics Boy Scouts Am; Nat Ctr Educ & Econ. **Honors/Awds:** Richard R Green Award as Outstanding Urban Educator, 1999; Hon doctorate, Univ Houston, Tex, 2000; Brent wood Dolphins Community Service Award; Nat Superintendent of the Year, Am AsnSch Administrators, 2001; Harold W McGraw Jr Prize in Education; Nat Alliance of Black School Educators' Superintendent of the Year award. **Special Achievements:** Named one of top two educrs in Am Coun of Great City Schs, 1999; First African American to serve as the US education chief. **Military Serv:** USN, hosp corpsman, 2 yrs. **Business Addr:** Chairman, Chartwell Education Group LLC, 350 5th Ave Suite 7506, New York, NY 10118, **Business Phone:** (212)488-1596.

PAIGE, STEPHONE
Football player. **Personal:** Born Oct 15, 1961, Long Beach, CA. **Educ:** Fresno State Univ, Saddleback Col. **Career:** Football player (retired); Kans City Chiefs, wide receiver, 1983-91.

PAILEN, DONALD
Lawyer. **Personal:** Born Mar 25, 1941, Washington, DC; son of William and Cora Johnson; married Wendy Boody, Jun 10, 1967; children: Donald Jr & William. **Educ:** Howard Univ, Wash, DC, BA, 1968, JD, 1971. **Career:** US Dept Justice, Civil Rights Div, Wash, DC, atty, 1971-82; City Detroit, Detroit, MI, corp coun, 1982-88; Trinity Lutheran Seminary, bd dirs, 2006-. **Orgs:** Nat Bar Asn, 1971-; Nebr State Bar Asn, 1972-; Mich State Bar Asn, 1982-. **Honors/Awds:** Exceptional Performance Awards, US Justice Dept, 1975-82; Award Appreciation, Guardians Police Orgn, Chicago, 1977; Spec Commendation, US Justice Dept, 1981. **Military Serv:** AUS, E-5, 1960-63. **Home Phone:** (313)345-2032. **Business Addr:** Board of Director, Trinity Lutheran Seminary, 2199 E Main St, Columbus, OH 43209-2334, **Business Phone:** (614)235-4136.

PAINTER, DR. NELL IRVIN
Educator. **Personal:** Born Aug 2, 1942, Houston, TX; daughter of Frank Edward and Dona Donato McGruder; married Glenn R Shafer, Oct 14, 1989. **Educ:** Univ Calif, Berkeley, BA, 1964; Univ Calif, Los Angeles, MA, 1967; Harvard Univ, PhD, 1974. **Career:** Ghana Inst Lang, lectr Fr, 1964-65; Harvard Univ, teaching fel, 1969-70, 1972-74; Ford Foundation fel, 1971-72; Univ Pa, asst prof, 1974-77, assoc prof, 1977-80; Am Coun Learned Soc fel, 1976-77; Charles Warren Ctr Studies Am Hist fel, Harvard Univ, 1976-77; Radcliffe Inst fel, 1976-77; Nat Humanities Ctr fel Am Hist, 1978-79; Univ NC, Chapel Hill, prof hist, 1980-88; Princeton Univ, prof hist, 1988-91, Edwards prof, 1991, dir, Prog African Am Studies Studies, 1997-2000, Edwards prof Am Hist emer, currently; Kate B & Hall J Peterson fel, Am Antiquarian Soc, 1991. **Orgs:** Dir, Nat Asn Black Women Historians, 1982-84; Am Coun Learned Socs, 1982-; Orgn Am Historians, 1984-87, pres, 2007; Harvard & Radcliffe Alumnie Against Apartheid; Ctr Adv Study Behav Sci fel, 1988-89; Am Studies Asn, 1989-92; Am Hist Asn, 1990-94; mem exec bd, Am Acad Polit & Social Sci, 2003-; Inst Southern Studies; pres, Southern Hist Asn, 2007; Asn Study Afro-Am Life & Hist; Berkshire Conf Women Historians; Asn Black Women Historians; Nat Book Found; Schomburg Ctr Res Black Cult; Social Sci Res Coun; Southern Regional Coun; Phi Beta Kappa; counr, Soc Am Historians; Am Antiquarian Soc. **Honors/Awds:** Coretta Scott King Award, Am Asn Univ Women, 1969; John Simon Guggenheim Found, 1982-83; Graduate Society Medal, Radcliffe Col Alumnae, 1984; Candace Award, Nat Coalition 100 Black Women, 1986; Alumnus of the Year, Black Alumni Club, Univ Calif, Berkeley, 1989; Nat Endowment Humanities fel, 1992-93; DHL, Wesleyan Univ, 1996; DHL, Dartmouth Col, 1997; DHL, State Univ NY-New Paltz, 1998; Service Award, Asn Black Princeton Univ Alumni, 1998; Roelker Mentorship Award, Am Hist Asn, 2000; DHL, Yale Univ, 2003. **Special Achievements:** Published numerous books, articles, reviews and other essays. **Business Addr:** Edwards Professor of American History Emerita, Princeton University, History Department, 129 Dickinson Hall, Princeton, NJ 08544-1017, **Business Phone:** (609)258-4159.

PAJAUD, WILLIAM E, JR.
Executive, watercolorist. **Personal:** Born Aug 3, 1925, New Orleans, LA; married Donlaply. **Educ:** Xavier Univ, BFA, 1946; Chouinard Art Inst, MFA. **Career:** Golden St Mutual Life Ins Co, pub rels. **Orgs:** Life Ins Advertisers Asn; Pub Rel Soc Am; Graphic Designers Asn; Nat Watercolor Soc; pres, Art Ed Found. **Honors/Awds:** Second Annual Samella Award, CAAD Inc, 2004.

PALCY, EUZHAN
Television director, movie director. **Personal:** Born Jan 13, 1958, Martinique, Martinique; daughter of Leon and Romauld. **Educ:** Sorbonne, Paris, France, BA, French lit; Vaugirard, Paris, France, filmmaking. **Career:** Film dir; TV Series dir; Writer; TV: "The Messenger", 1975; "Sugar Cane Alley", 1984; "A Dry White Season", 1989; "The Ruby Bridges Story, Disney", 1998;" Winds Against the Wind", 1998; "The Killing Yard", 2001; "Parcours de dissidents", 2006; Mariees de l'isle Bourbon, Les, 2007; films: Rue cases negres, 1983; A Dry White Season, 1989; Comment vont lesenfants, 1993. **Honors/Awds:** Candace Award, Nat Coalition of 100 Black Women, 1990; Best Lead Actress Award, Venice Film Festival; Sojourner Truth Award, Cannes Film Festival, 2001. **Special Achievements:** First black woman to ever direct a hollywood studio movie with filmography, biography, photos, articles; first woman of African descentto ever direct a Hollywood Studio movie MGMs A Dry White Season.

PALMER, DR. ANNETTE
College teacher. **Personal:** Born in Trinidad, West Indies. **Educ:** Carleton Univ, Ottawa, Can, BA; Fordham Univ, MA, PhD. **Career:** Howard Univ, Wash, DC; Nat Endowment Humanities, prog officer; Morgan State Univ, hist dept, chairperson, currently. **Orgs:** Am Hist Assn; treas, Assn Study African Am Life Hist. **Special Achievements:** Author: 'World War II in the Caribbean: a Study of Anglo-American Partnership and Rivalry".

PALMER, DARLENE TOLBERT
Administrator. **Personal:** Born Jul 4, 1946, Chicago, IL; married Mickey A; children: Terri, Jonathan, Tobi. **Educ:** St Univ NY Albany, BA, 1973, MA, 1974; Harvard Grad Sch Bus Admin, Cert Broadcasting Mgt, 1979. **Career:** Minority Telecomm Dev Nat Telecomm & Info Admin, prog mgr, 1979-; Nat Asn Broadcasters Wash DC, asst dir broadcast mgt, 1977-79; Little Enterprises Wash DC div, pres, 1975-77; WTEN-TV Albany, prod, 1973-75; Palmer Media Assoc Schenectady, partner, 1970-75. **Orgs:** Media rels dir Nat Hookup Black Women, 1976-78; rec sec Am Women Radio & TV, 1980; chmn, Affirm Act Am Women Radio & TV, 1980; co-chmn, MinorityOwnership Cong Black Caucus Commun Brain Trust DC, 1977-78; Comt Media & Natural Disaster Nat Acad Sci DC, 1979; bd dirs, Am Nat Metric Coun Wash DC, 1979. **Honors/ Awds:** Prod "Black English" WTEN-TV Albany; Nat Med Asn.

PALMER, DAVID LEE
Football player. **Personal:** Born Nov 19, 1972, Birmingham, AL; married Carmelita; children: David, Davin, Davida & Davia. **Educ:** Univ Ala. **Career:** Football player (retired); Minn Vikings, running back, 1994-2000.

PALMER, DR. DOREEN P
Physician. **Personal:** Born Jun 1, 1949, Kingston, Jamaica; daughter of Granville and Icilola. **Educ:** Herbert H Lehman Col, Bronx, NY, BA, 1972; Downstate Med Sch, Brooklyn, NY, MD, 1976; Johns Hopkins Univ, Baltimore City Hosp, fel gastroenterologist, 1981. **Career:** NY Med Col, Valhalla, NY, asst prof, 1981-86; Metropolitan Hosp, NY City, asst chief, GI, 1981-88, chief GI, 1983-86; Lenox Hill Hosp, NY City, adjunct physician, 1986-; Cabrini Hosp, NY City, attending physician, 1986-; Doctors Hosp, NY City, attending physician, 1986-; pvt pract, currently. **Business Phone:** (212)860-7477.

PALMER, DOUGLAS HAROLD
Mayor. **Personal:** Born Oct 19, 1951, Trenton, NJ; son of George H and Dorothy P; married Christiana Foglio; children: Laila Rose. **Educ:** Hampton Inst, BS, bus mgt, 1973. **Career:** Trenton Bd Educ, sr acct, 1976-78, coordr of comm educ, 1981-82, asst sec purchasing, 1982; Mercer Co Legislator, freeholder; City Trenton, NJ, mayor, 1990-. **Orgs:** Pres & mgr, W End Little League; treas, Trenton Branch the Nat Asn Advan Colored People; bd dirs, Am Red Cross; Forum Project, Boy Scouts, WE Inc, Carver Ctr, Urban League Guild Metro Trenton, Project Help; pres, Freeholder Bd; mem comn, Comn on the Status Women, TRADE Adv Bd, Disabled Adv Bd, Mercer Co Bd Social Serv, Cult & Heritage Comn; past pres, NJ Conf Mayors; past pres, Nat Conf Democratic Mayors; Mayors Against Illegal Guns coalition; pres, US Conf Mayors. **Honors/Awds:** Comn Serv Awards: Fai-Ho-Cha Club, Twig Mothers, Hub City Distributors, Voice Publ, NJ Asn of Black Social Workers; Outstanding Chmn, DE Valley United Way, 1977; Man of the Year, Omega Psi Phi Frat, 1984; Community Serv Awd, Lifeline Energy Shelter; Twenty Year Alumnus Award, Hampton Univ; Spirit of St. Francis Award, St Francis Hosp, Trenton; Peace Medal Award. **Special Achievements:** First African American mayor of the Trenton, NJ. **Business Addr:** Mayor, City of Trenton, 319 E State St, Trenton, NJ 08608, **Business Phone:** (609)989-3030.

PALMER, EDGAR BERNARD
Counselor, educator. **Personal:** Born Aug 12, 1953, Hartford, CT; son of Clitus Vitelius and Emma Frances Ragins; married Carie Lyn Treske, May 25, 1985; children: Rachel Erin, Jordan Michael, Andrew & David. **Educ:** Gallaudet Univ, BA, hist, 1977, MS, 2003; Western Maryland Col, MEd, 1980. **Career:** Md Sch Deaf, Columbia Campus, instructional counr, 1980-81, Frederick Campus, instructional counr, 1981-82; Md State Dept Educ, voc rehab counr, 1982-88; Model Sec Sch Deaf, guidance counr, 1988-; Gallaudet Univ, adj prof hist, progs coordr, 1993, Eng Lang Inst, SUS, assoc dean, 2007-, dir, currently. **Orgs:** Co-chair, Nat Asn Deaf, 1983-85; adv bd mem, Tele Communs Exchange Deaf, Inc, 1985-87; bd mem & vpres, Am Deafness & Rehab Asn, Metro-Wash Chap, 1988-90; bd mem, Black Deaf Advocates, Inc, 1989-92; Black Deaf Advocates, Inc, 10th Anniversary Celebration, 1991; bd mem, People Encouraging People, Inc, 1992-94; microcosm planning comt, Model Secondary Sch Deaf; bd dirs, Penn Visions, 1994-; Asn Late-Deafened Adults; reg dir, Md Sch Deaf. **Honors/Awds:** Certificate of Achievement, Md State Dept Educ, 1985; Counselor of the Year, Md State Dept Educ, 1986; Model Secondary School for the Deaf Coaching Award, Cross Country Girls Potomac Valley Athletic Conf Champions, 1990; Outstanding Achievement Award, Am Deafness & Rehab Asn, Metro Wash Chapter, 1991. **Special Achievements:** Preview Magazine, Pre-College Programs, Gallaudet University, Special Edition: Communication and Cultural Issues, fall 1990; Montgomery County Journal, write-up related to multi-cultural program sponsored by A G Bell, Associate & Gallaudet University, 1992. **Home Addr:** 4412 Stockbridge Ct, Bowie, MD 20720, **Home Phone:** (301)464-4184. **Business Addr:** Director, Associate Dean, Gallaudet University, 800 Fla Ave NE, Washington, DC 20002, **Business Phone:** (202)651-5755.

PALMER, DR. EDWARD
Physician. **Personal:** Born Jul 25, 1937, New York, NY; son of Edward Palmer Sr and Thelma Lester; married Maria; children: Neeco. **Educ:** Adelphi Univ, attended 1960; Meharry Med Col, MD, 1964; Kings Co Hosp Cen, attended 1965. **Career:** Elmhurst Hosp Ctr, staff attending; Mt Sinai Sch Med, lectr; Hosp Albert Einstein Col Med, staff attending; Montefiore Hosp & Med Ctr, staff attending; State Univ NY, assoc prof; Univ Hosp & Kings County Hosp Ctr, dir eye serv; Palmer Eye Care & Laser Ctr, admin, currently. **Orgs:** Mem Cen NY State Ophthalmogic Soc; Amer Acad of Ophthalmology & Otolaryngology; fellow Amer Col of Surgeons; NY Clinical Soc; Intl Eye Found The Soc of Surgeons; Amer Asn of Ophthalmology; rsch to prevent blindness; diplomate, associate examiner, Am Bd of Ophthalmology. **Honors/Awds:** Founding editor Journal of Cataract; numerous publs; listed as one of best black physicians in America, Black Enterprise Magazine, 1988. **Military Serv:** USN, lt, 1965-67. **Business Addr:** Founder, Palmer Eye Care & Laser Center, 100 Casals Pl, Bronx, NY 10475-3002, **Business Phone:** (718)671-8888.

PALMER, ELLIOTT B., SR.
Executive. **Personal:** Born Mar 7, 1933, Durham, NC; son of Ada Brown Palmer (deceased) and Clarence Palmer (deceased); married Juanita Brooks; children: Elliot, Douglas, Ruth, Tonya. **Educ:** NC Central Univ, AB, 1955, MA, 1961; Duke Univ; Bemidji State Univ, MN; UNC, Chapel Hill, NC. **Career:** Executive (retired); Little River HS Durham Co, teacher, 1956-60; Lakeview Elem Sch Durham Co, prin, 1960-64; NC Teachers Asn Raleigh, exec sec, 1964-70; NC Asn Educr, asso exec dir, 1970-82; African Am Cult Complex Museum, founder, chief exec officer & curator, 1984. **Orgs:** Nat Ed Asn; pres, Standard Gov, 1954; pres, Comn Urban Redev Durham, 1958; found Diversified Invest Spec Org, 1960; chmn, Nat Coun Off State Teachers Asn, 1969-71; Pi Gamma Mu Nat Soc Sci Honor Soc; NAACP; Hunter Lodge FM & AM; gov comm Study NC Pub Schls 1972; co-chmn, NEA Joint Comn Publ & Textbook Comn, 1972-73; Boy Scouts Raleigh, 1974; Mayor's Comn Plan & Dev, Raleigh, 1974; nat pres, Official Black Caucus Nat Ed Asn, 1985; 1st Black chairperson Nat Comn Ed Hum Rights; exec dir, Hammocks Beach Corp. **Honors/ Awds:** Invited to White House Conf Educ, 1964; Rec H Coun & Trenholm Award, NEA protection educ rights; cited by two Govs for Outstanding Contrbution to Fld of Educ, 1972-73; Outstanding Alumni Award, Hillside High Sch, Durham, 1974; Outstanding Contributions Towards The Advancement of Human Rights & Fundlemental Freedoms, United Nations & NEA Educ Comt, 1978; consult minority artifacts, NC State Museum Hist, 1990; Distinguished Community Service Award, City Raleigh, 1996; Omega Comm Service Award, 1998. **Special Achievements:** featured in the Ebony Magazine as one of the most influential Blacks in Educ, May 1978. **Home Addr:** 119 Sunnybrook Rd, Raleigh, NC 27610, **Home Phone:** (919)231-0625. *

PALMER, DR. JAMES DIBBLE. See Obituaries section.

PALMER, JAMES E.
Educator, clergy, teacher. **Personal:** Born Jul 6, 1938, Butler, AL; married; children: two. **Educ:** Selma Univ, BTech; State Univ, Montgomery, BS; Appalachian State Boone, NC, addn study; NC State Univ; Birmingham Baptist Col, DD. **Career:** Iredell County Pub Schs, Statesville, NC, teacher; Jones Chapel Baptist Church, Mooresville, NC; Catawba Col & Catawba County Pub Sch, teacher & counr; NDEA grant; Teachers grant; Univ Park Baptist Church, Charlotte, pastor, 1972, sr pastor. **Orgs:** Moderator, Mt Catawba Asn; Jaycees; Mayor's Coun; bd mem, Gen State Bd Conv NC Inc; Nat Educ Asn; BSA; exec bd mem, YMCA; Black Pol Caucus; Nat Asn Adv Colored People.

PALMER, NOEL D.
School administrator. **Personal:** Born Nov 14, 1926, Jamaica, WI; son of Ruth and Septimus; married Daisy Mae; children: Janet, John & Jules. **Educ:** Union Theological Col, attended 1954; William Pa Col, BA, 1956; Columbia Univ Teachers Col, BSc, 1977, MA, 1959. **Career:** SUNY Farmingdale, asst pres, 1968-70, vpres Urban Ctr, 1970-73, vpres, Educ Opportunity Ctr, 1973-80, vpres stud affairs, 1980-05. **Orgs:** Supt, Swift Purscell Boys Home, 1964-66; dir, on-the-job training Five Towns Community House, 1966-68; part-time teacher, Lawrence Pub Sch, 1967-69; pres, Adv Coun-BOCES, 1978-82; pres, Half Hollow Hills Rotary, 1980-81; vchmn, WLIW Educ TV, 1982-84; Religious Soc Friends; pres, Westbury Friends Sch Bd. **Honors/Awds:** Outstanding Educrs Am, 1972-74. *

PALMER, ROBERT L., II
School administrator. **Personal:** Born Mar 1, 1943, Tuscaloosa, AL; son of Robert L and Arnetta Greene; married Beverly Spencer Palmer, Feb 10, 1990; children: Anthony, Tracie, Monifa, Reginald, Robert. **Educ:** Ind Univ, Bloomington, IN, BS, Educ, 1969, MS, Col Personnel Admin, 1973; State Univ NY, Buffalo, NY, PhD, 1979. **Career:** State Univ Col Buffalo, Buffalo, NY, counr educ opportunity prog, 1972-74, asst dir educ opportunity prog, 1973-74; State Univ NY Buffalo, Buffalo, NY, asst vpres stud affairs, 1974-82, assoc provost, 1982-87, provost stud affairs, 1987-; CA State Univ, Fullerton, vpres, stud affairs, currently. **Orgs:** Bd dirs, Buffalo Area Engineering Awareness, 1982-; Chmn, bd dirs, Buffalo Urban League, 1987-90; The Western New York Health Sci Consortium Minority Manpower Task Force Minorities, 1989-; Co chair, United Negro Col Fund, Buffalo & Western New York Campaign, 1989-; bd dirs, Coordinated Care, 1989-. **Honors/Awds:** Outstanding Leadership Award, Univ Buffalo Campus Ministry, 1985; Buffalo Black Achievers Award, Buffalo 1840 Enterprise Inc, 1985; Human Relations Award, Buffalo Nat Asn Advan Colored People, 1988; Outstanding Service Award, Buffalo Urban League, 1989; Award of Excellence, United Way Buffalo & Erie County, 1989. **Military Serv:** USAF. **Business Addr:** Vice President Student Affairs, California State University Fullerton, Langsdorf Hall 805, Fullerton, CA 92834, **Business Phone:** (714)278-3221.*

PALMER, RONALD DEWAYNE (RONALD DEWAYNE FAISAL PALMER)
Consultant, educator, ambassador. **Personal:** Born May 22, 1932, Uniontown, PA; son of Wilbur Fortune and Ethel Roberts; married Evna Johnson, Jul 25, 1987 (deceased); children: Derek R & Alyson C; married Tengku Intan Badariah Abubakar; children: Natasha Elina & Nadiah Raha. **Educ:** Howard Univ, BA, 1954; Inst de'Etudes Politiques, Univ Bordeaux, France, 1954-55; Sch Advan Int Studies, Johns Hopkins Univ, MA, 1957. **Career:** US State Dept, foreign service officer, 1957-89, fac mem, US Mil Acad, West Point, 1967-69; US ambassador extraordinary & plenipotentiary Togo, 1976-78; US Govt, foreign service dep dir gen, 1979-81; US ambassador extraordinary & plenipotentiary Malaysia, 1981-83, foreign service officer CSIS/Georgetown, 1983-86, US ambassador extraordinary & plenipotentiary Mauritius, 1986-89; George Washington Univ, prof, 1990-2001; George Washington Univ, prof emer prac int affairs, 2001-. **Orgs:** Kappa Alpha Psi, 1952-; Am Foreign Service Asn, 1957-; Coun Foreign Rels, 1979-; Africare; Wash Inst Foreign Affairs; Malaysian-Am Soc; Royal Asia Soc; Inst Int Studies, United Nations Asn, DC Coun Humanities; Friends of the Chapel, Howard Univ; Am Acad Diplomacy. **Honors/Awds:** Knight Commander, Order Mono, Republic Togo, 1978; Commander, Setia Mahkota Johor, Malaysia, 1984; Award, Nat Asn Equal Opportunity, 1988; Award, Nat Asn Advan Colored People, 1988. **Special Achievements:** Publication: Building ASEAN: 20 Years of Southeast Asian Cooperation, Praeger, 1987; Nominated for Teacher of the Year, 1997; Writes on local history and genealogy for Journal of the Afrian-American Historical and Geneological Society and other National journals. **Business Addr:** Professor Emeritus Practice of International Affairs, Elliott School of International Affairs, The George Washington University, 1957 E St NW, Washington, DC 20052, **Business Phone:** (202)994-0563.

PALMER, RONALD DEWAYNE FAISAL. See PALMER, RONALD DEWAYNE.

PALMER, STEPHANIE
Association executive. **Personal:** Born Sep 23, 1952, Philadelphia, PA; daughter of Luther and Mae; divorced; children: Matthew Palmer Bowman. **Educ:** Middleburg Col, BA, am studies, hist, 1974; Temple Univ, MA, educ, 1978. **Career:** NYC Private Industry Coun, dir oper, 1985-93; Human Services Coun NYC, admin, 1993-96; NYC Mission Soc, exed dir, 1996-. **Orgs:** Harlem Little League; vpres, Black Agency Executives, 1994-; Non Profit Coordinating Comt NY, 1998-; Human Services Coun, 1996-. **Honors/Awds:** Jack & Jill, Metropolitan Chap, Mother of The Year, 1999; Charls A Wolberg Multi Service Org Certificate of Honor, 2002; Leadership Insititute for African American Female Executives 1st Annual Isis Award for Leadership by Example, 2004; Baruch Col School of Public Affairs Alumni Asn Recognition Award for Outstanding Work in the Nonprofit Community, 2004; Charter Revision Commissioner, 2004. **Special Achievements:** Honored for being First African American woman to lead City's oldest social services organization. **Business Addr:** Executive Director, New York City Mission Society, 105 E 22nd St 6th Fl, New York, NY 10010, **Business Phone:** (212)674-3500.

PALMER, VIOLET
Manager, basketball coach. **Personal:** Born Jan 1, 1964?, Compton, CA. **Educ:** Calif Poly Pomona Univ, BS, admin. **Career:** Cal Poly Pomona Col, point guard, 1985; City Placentia Off High Sch-Basketball, recruting leader; City Los Angeles Nat Collegiate Athletic AsnDiv I Col, recruiting supr & point guard, 1986; Violet Palmer's Off Camp,founder, 2001-; Women Nat Basketball Asn & Nat Basketball Asn, referee,currently; coord women's basketball officials, W Coast Conference, 2009-. **Orgs:** Nat Collegiate Athletic Asn; Women Nat Basketball Asn; Nat Basketball Asn. **Special Achievements:** First African Am female to officiate games in the Nat Basketball Asn; first black female referee in the Nat Basketball Asn; first woman to referee an all-male professional sports league regular-season game from Ebony; one of two women officials to referee in any men's pro sports league; guest speaker & clinician, Nat Basketball Asn Training - Pro Summer Leagues; featured in mag including: Ebony & Sports Illustrated; the frequent target of sports critics, including ESPN . **Business Addr:** Referee, National Basketball Association, 645 5th Ave Fl 10, New York, NY 10022.*

PALMER, WENDY. See DANIEL, WENDY PALMER.

PALMER-HILDRETH, BARBARA JEAN
Educator, social worker. **Personal:** Born Jan 10, 1941, Jackson, MS; daughter of John and Thelma; married Truman A, Aug 15, 1970. **Educ:** Jackson State Univ, BS, 1964; Nat Louis Univ, MS, 1986. **Career:** Social Worker, Teacher (retired); Canton Pub Sch, teacher, 1964-67; Rockford Bd Educ, from teacher to headteacher 1967-92. **Orgs:** Big Sisters Inc, 1975-89; Second vpres & life mem, Nat Council Negro Women, 1984; Legis Community, IEA 1986-87; Nat Asn Advan Colored People; Nat Alliance Black Sch Educr; Provident Baptist Church; Beta Pi Sigma; Delta Sigma Theta; Am Asn Univ Women; vol, Rockford Memorial Hosp; Winnebago County Health Bd; Little People Place Day Care Bd. **Honors/Awds:** Mary McLeod Bethune Service Award, Nat Coun Negro Women, 1976; Service Award, Rockford Memorial Hosp, 1989; Red Apple Teacher Award, Rockford Sch Dist #205; Golden Apple Nominee, Winnebago County. **Home Addr:** 2228 Pierce Ave, Rockford, IL 61103.

PALMORE, LYNNE A. JANIFER
Advertising executive, public relations executive. **Personal:** Born Oct 3, 1952, Newark, NJ; married Roderick Palmore; children: Jordan, Adam. **Educ:** Yale Univ, BA, 1974. **Career:** J Walter Thompson, media trainee, 1975-76, media planner, 1976-78; Creamer Inc, media supvr, 1978-80; Needham Harper Worldwide Inc, v pres assoc media dir. **Orgs:** Northshore Chap Jack & Jill.

PALMORE, RODERICK A
Executive. **Personal:** Born Feb 14, 1952, Pittsburgh, PA; son of Jefferson and Sophie; married Lynne Palmore, Jun 3, 1978; children: Jordan & Adam. **Educ:** Yale Unic, BA, 1974; Univ Chicago Law Sch, JD, 1977. **Career:** Berkman Ruslander, assoc, 1977-79; US Atty, asst US atty, 1979-82; Wildman Harrold Allen & Dixon, partner, 1982-93; Sonnenschein Nath & Rosenthal, partner, 1993-96; Nuveen Investments, dir; Sara Lee Corp, vpres & deputy gen coun, 1996-99; Sara Lee Corp, sr vpres, gen coun & secy, exec vpres, gen coun & secy, currently. **Orgs:** Bd mgrs, Chicago Bar Asn, 1992-94; bd dirs, Chicago Bar Found, 1993-94; Ill Judicial Ethics Comn, 1996-; bd dirs, Legal Assistance found Chicago, 1994-97; bd dirs, Pub Interest Law Initiative, 1993-96; bd dirs, Boys & Girls Clubs Chicago, 1997-; bd dir, Ctr New Horizons, 1997-; bd dir, The Village Found, 1997-; bd dir, Chicago Bd Options Exchange, 1999-. United Way Metrop Chicago; dir, Asn Corp Coun; trustees, Chicago Symphony Orchestra. former chmn, Publ Arts Adv Comn. **Honors/Awds:** Best & Brightest African American Bus People, Dollars & Sense Mag, 1991. **Business Addr:** Executive Vice President, General Counsel, SCY, Sara Lee Corp, 3 First National Plz, 70 W Madison St, Chicago, IL 60602, **Business Phone:** (312)726-2600.

PALMS, SYLVIA J
Executive, president (organization), chief executive officer. **Personal:** Born Jun 23, 1962, Honolulu, HI; daughter of Goldie Royal; divorced; children: Royal Christine Jones. **Educ:** Evergreen State Col, Tacoma, WA, BA, lib studies, 1991; City Univ, Leadership Inst Seattle, MA, appl behavioral scis, 1993. **Career:** US West, strategic acct mgr, 1988, Fed Servs, dir & lobbyist; Supplier Diversity, dir, 1998-99, vpres, 1999; The Greater Phoenix Black Chamber Com, pres & ceo, 2001. **Orgs:** Nat chairs, Nat Minority Supplier Develop Coun, 2000; chair, Rocky Mountain Minority Supplier Develop Coun, 1999; bd mem, Urban League Metropolitan Denver, 1998-. **Honors/Awds:** Woman of the Year, Colo Fedn Bus & Prof Women, 2000; Denver Women of Distinction Award, 2000; Advocate of the Year, Rocky Mountain Minority Supplier Develop Coun, 1999; Young Careerist, Bus & Prof Women, Seattle, 1989; US West, President's Club, 1998, 1999; Woman of The Year, Colo Bus & Prof Women orgn. **Business Phone:** (602)307-5200.

PANDYA, HARISH C. (H CHRISTIAN POST)
Executive. **Personal:** Born Oct 22, 1945, Zanzibar, United Republic of Tanzania. **Educ:** Univ London, 1964; Univ Cambridge, 1966; NE MO State Univ, BS, 1968; Univ Ind, MA, 1971. **Career:** Westinghouse Corp, 1969-70; Clopton HS, counr, teacher, 1969; Johnson Pub Co, mkt-ed res, 1970-71; Tuesday Publs, dir mkt, 1971-76; Essence Mag, mid-west dir advert, 1977. **Orgs:** MO Hist Soc; Writers & Educators Guild; Nat Asn Mkt Developers; Chicago Advert Club; Chicago Press Club; Am Mkt Asn; bd mem, Pullen Sch Exceptional C, 1973; Pro & Con Screening Bd, 1975; bd dirs, Coalition Concerned Women War Crime, 1977. **Honors/Awds:** 10 Outstanding Young Citizens Jr C & Off C, 1976; Spec Achievement US Citizen, 1976.

PANNELL, WILLIAM E
Administrator, college teacher. **Personal:** Born Jun 24, 1929, Sturgis, MI; son of William and Olive Pannell; married Hazel Lee Scott; children: 2. **Educ:** Wayne State Univ, BA, black hist, attended; Univ South Calif, MA, social ethics; Malone Coll, hon doctorate, attended. **Career:** Itinerant evangelist, 1951-78; Brethren Assemblies, asst pastor, youth dir, 1955-65; Christian Assemblies, pastor; Sch Theol, Fuller Theol Sem, dir black ministries, assoc prof evangelism; Fuller Theol Sem, spec asst pres & sr prof preaching, currently. **Orgs:** Tom Skinner Asn, vpres; Staley Found, lectr George Fox Col, Newburg, OR; speaker at many conferences including consultation on the Gospel & Culture Lausanne Comm, 1978; US Consultation Simple Lifestyle, Ventnor, NJ, 1979; Church & Peacemaking in a Nuclear Age Conf, speaker, Pasadena, CA, 1983; chmn, Youth for Christ USA, 1980; pres, Acad Evangelism, 1983-84; Obsidian Soc. **Special Achievements:** Author, "My Friend My Enemy", 1968; Div Malone Coll, 1975; Delta Epsilon Chi Honor Soc of the Accrediting Asn of Bible Colls; numerous articles in: Eternity, The Other Side, Sojourners, The Amer Scientific Affiliation, The Herald, The Gospel Herald, Theology, News & Notes, Christianity Today, Leadership Magazine, etc. **Business Addr:** Special Assistant President, Senior Professor Preaching, Fuller Theologival Seminary, 135 N Oakland Ave, Pasadena, CA 91101, **Business Phone:** (626)584-5592.

PAPPILLION, GLENDA M
Government official. **Personal:** Born Nov 28, 1951, Lake Charles, LA; daughter of John and Viola; divorced. **Educ:** McNeese State Univ, BS, acct, 1973. **Career:** Internal Revenue Serv, criminal investr, Houston, 1976-81, CI coord, 1981-82, criminal investr, Chicago, 1982-84, group supv, CI div, Chicago, 1984-86, br chief, CI div, Chicago, 1986-88, chief, criminal invest, Houston, 1988-91, asst dist dir, 1991-93, asst regional comnr criminal invest, 1993-, actg spec agent-in-charge, dir, dir cent area field opers. **Orgs:** AKA, 1971-; Big Sister/Big Brother, 1978-90; Nat Orgn Black Law Enforcement Execs, 1988-. **Honors/Awds:** Distinguished Performance Award, Internal Revenue Serv, 1986, 1987, 1988, 1989. **Special Achievements:** First female chief in hist IRS, Criminal Investigation Div, 1988. **Business Addr:** Assistant Regional Commissioner, Director, Internal Revenue Service, 915 2nd Ave Rm 2498 M/S 600, Seattle, WA 98174, **Business Phone:** (206)220-6011.

PARHAM, BRENDA JOYCE
Nurse, educator. **Personal:** Born Jun 3, 1944, Ft Lauderdale, FL; daughter of Clarence Ray Sr; divorced; children: Grant III, Valorie, Stephanie & Deidra. **Educ:** Fla A&M Univ, BS, 1966; Memphis State Univ, MEd, 1972; Univ Tenn, Ctr Health Sci, MSN, 1981. **Career:** Holy Cross Hosp, staff nurse, 1966-67; Methodist Hosp, charge nurse, 1966-69, instr 1969-71; Plantation Gen Hosp, staff nurse, 1967; USAF, staff nurse, 1967-68; Shelby State Community Col, dept head nursing; Baptist Memorial Hosp, liaison nurse & supvr, 1971-72; Memphis State Univ, asst prof, 1972-80; Regioanl Med Ctr, staff nurse, supvr, asst dir, 1973-81; Methodist Hosp, staff develop coordr, 1982; Shelby State Community Col, assoc prof, instr, 1982-83, dept head nursing, 1984-87; asst prof nursing. **Orgs:** Tenn Nurses Asn, 1984-; Nat League Nurses, 1985. **Honors/Awds:** Pastor - Temple of Joy Deliverance Ctr Church, 1983; Advisory Bd Mem Am Home Health Agency 1984. **Military Serv:** USAF, First Lt. **Home Addr:** 946 Roland St, Memphis, TN 38114.

PARHAM, DASHTON DANIEL
Arts administrator. **Personal:** Born Jan 22, 1956, Brunswick Co, VA; son of John and Sarah; divorced; children: Erin & Sarah.

Educ: Va Commonwealth Univ, BFA, commun art & design, 1978. **Career:** Finnegan & Agee Advert, asst art dir, 1978; Cent Fidelity Bank, designer & pub rels dept, 1979; Kell & Assoc, art dir, 1980; Designer's Folio, art dir, illusr, 1980-83; USA Today, illusr, 1983-85; USA Weekend, art dir, 1985-86; USA Today, art dir, 1986-96, dir graphics, 1996-99, design ed, 1999-; Howard Univ Sch Jour, adj prof, publ design. **Orgs:** Art Dirs Club Metrop Wash, 1980-86; Soc Newspaper Design, 1983-86; Nat Asn Black Journalist, 1994. **Honors/Awds:** 3 awards of excellence, Soc Newspaper Design, 1984-86; 8 awards of excellence, Art Dirs Club Metro Wash, 1980-85; Olympic Media Award, Seoul, Korea, 1998-; Washington Illustrators Club Award, art direction, 1999. **Special Achievements:** Designer of publication entitled Information Illustration, Dale Glasgow in 4 languages, 1994. **Business Phone:** (703)276-5588.

PARHAM, FREDERICK RUSSELL
Electrical engineer. **Personal:** Born Aug 13, 1953, Columbus, OH; son of E A Parham and Madeline Inez Holland; married Barbara Ann Kimble, Dec 31, 1979; children: Jonathan. **Educ:** Northwestern Univ, Evanston, IL, BA, biomed engineering, 1976, MA, biomed engineering, 1977. **Career:** Batelle Mem Inst, Columbus, OH, sr lab technican, 1972; G D Searle, Skokie, IL, res assoc, 1973-76; 3M, Maplewood, MN, sr elec engr, 1977-. **Orgs:** Dir, Region 1, Nat Tech Asn, 1979-80; dir, Music Dept, Jubilee Christian Church, 1982-; dir, IBM Spec Interest Group, 3M, 1982-. **Honors/Awds:** Genesis Grant Recipient, 3M, 1987; Golden Step Award, 3M, 1989. **Home Addr:** 8185 Ivywood, Cottage Grove, MN 55016. **Business Addr:** Senior Electrical Engineer, The NTA Electronic Bulletin Board System (EBBS), PO Box 4544, St Paul, MN 55104, **Business Phone:** (612)733-6001.

PARHAM, JAMES B. (JIM PARHAM)
School administrator. **Personal:** Born Dec 6, 1942, Chattanooga, TN; son of James W and Pearl Parham; married Loretta O'Brien Parham, Apr 9, 1997; children: Francia Greer, Scott, Trace, Quantrell, Perry O'Brien, Leah O'Brien, Aaron Walton. **Educ:** Central State Univ, BS, mathematics, 1964; Eastern Kentucky Univ, MS, criminal justice, 1973; Nat Univ, MBA, 1983; Univ Mich, Ann Arbor, PhD, bus admin, 1992. **Career:** Univ Pittsburgh, asst prof, 1972-96; Dept Army, proj mgr, comput assisted traning, 1977-80; Readiness group, dir, sr consult, 1980-83; Dept Army Traning Prog, depy dir, 1983-85; Central State Univ, dept chair, mil sci, 1985-88; Hampton Univ, dean, sch bus, 1996; Norfolk State Univ Bus Sch, dean. **Orgs:** Acad Mgt; Am Mgt Asn; Strategic Mgt Soc; Int Soc Strategic Mgt & Planning. **Honors/Awds:** Rackman Merit Award, Acad Excellence, Acad Fel Univ Mich, Rackman Grad Sch; res fel, Inst Social Res, 1990-91; Excellence in Teaching, Teaching Award, Thomas W Leabow Fel, Univ Mich, 1991; Teaching Award, Col Gen Studies, Univ Pittsburgh, 1993; Instrnl Develop Grant, Int Bus Ctr, 1995. **Special Achievements:** Czechoslovak Management Ctr, Celakovice, Czech Republic, contracted by US AID to provide instruction and evaluate the instruction being provided to Czech citizens attending a US sponsored school of management, provided consultations with the center's dean and selected faculty members, summer 1994; Consulting experience, executive trng prog, Hurgdga, Egypt, contracted by Dallah-Albarka Group to provide instructor to senior executives going through leadership trng program, summer 1996. **Military Serv:** AUS, lt colonel, 1964-99; BS 3, AM 4, MSM 3. *

PARHAM, JIM. See PARHAM, JAMES B.

PARHAM, JOHNNY EUGENE, JR.
Association executive, executive director. **Personal:** Born Jan 22, 1937, Atlanta, GA; son of Johnny and Carolyn Anderson; married Ann Cox Parham, Jun 24, 1961; children: Johnny Eugene III. **Educ:** Morehouse Col, Atlanta, GA, BA, 1958; Atlanta Univ, Atlanta, GA, MSW, 1960; Woodrow Wilson Col Law, Atlanta, GA, JD, 1978. **Career:** Association executive, executive director (retired); NY Urban League, Brooklyn, NY, br dir, 1962-65; Training Resources Youth, Brooklyn, NY, dep dir, 1965-66; Opportunities Industrialization Ctr, Brooklyn, NY, exec dir, 1966-67; Curber Assocs, New York, NY, exec vpres, 1967-70; Social Dimensional Assocs, New York, NY, pres, 1970-75; United Negro Col Fund, New York, NY, vpres, 1979-94; Thurgood Marshall Scholarship Fund, exec dir, 1994-99. **Orgs:** Bd mem, Community League Retarded C, 1991; bd mem, Big Brothers New York, 1970-75; bd mem, Nat Soc Fund Raising Execs, New York Chap, 1995-. **Home Addr:** 689 Columbus Ave, New York, NY 10025. *

PARHAM, MARJORIE B.
Publisher, editor. **Personal:** Born in Batavia, OH; married Hartwell (deceased); children: William M Spillers Jr. **Educ:** Wilberforce Univ; Univ Cincinnati; Chase Sch Bus. **Career:** Federal Gov Cincinnati, staff, 1946-61; Cincinnati Herald, pres, owner, 1963-66, publ emer, currently. **Orgs:** Bd mem, Comn Chest & Coun United Appeal; chairwoman, Nat Afro-Am Mus & Cult Ctr; Hamilton County YMCA; Nat Newspaper Publ Asn; trustee, Univ Cincinnati; bd mem, Cincinnati OIC; Hamilton County Am Red Cross; Greater Cincinnati Urban League; chmn bd, Cincinnati Tech Col; Women Commun Inc; Iota Phi Lambda Bus Women's Sor; St Andrew's Episcopal Church; Metropolitan YMCA; Dan Beard Coun, Boy Scouts of Am; Great Rivers Coun Girl Scouts; Better Bus Bur; bd chair ,Cincinnati Technical Col, Univ Cincinnati. **Honors/Awds:** Iota Phi Lambda Bus Woman of the Yr, 1970; Outstanding Woman Commun, 1973; named 1 of 12 most influential to the Queen City, 1974; Outstanding Citizen Award, Omega Psi Phi 1975; Community Serv Media Award, Nat Conf Christians & Jews, 1977; Hon DTL, Cincinnati Tech Col, 1977; Black Arts Festival Award, Univ Cincinnati, 1980; Cincinnati Jour Hall of Fame, 1980; Top 100 Black Business Prof Am, Dollars & Sense Mag, 1988; Trailblazer Award, Nat Asn Black Journalists, 1993; Lifetime Achiever Award, Applause Mag, 1994; Ohio Women's Hall of Fame & YWCA Career Women of Achievement Award, 1994; Govs Outstanding Journalism Award, Glorifying the Lion Award, Urban League, 1994; Publisher, Pioneer & Mentor Awarded, 2007. **Special Achievements:** One of 12 Women Who Have Influenced The Queen City by The Cincinnati Post in 1974; Named one of Cincinnati's Most Influential Blacks over the past 50 years by WCIN in 2003. **Business Addr:** President, Publisher Emeritus, Cincinnati Herald, 354 Hearne Ave, Cincinnati, OH 45229, **Business Phone:** (513)961-3331.*

PARHAM, RICHELLE
Manager. **Educ:** Drexel Univ, BS, mkt, design & merchandising. **Career:** Citibank, acct exec; Digitas LLC, gen mgr & vpres, 2004-. **Orgs:** Steering comt, United Way Young Leaders Soc. **Business Addr:** General Manager, Digitas LLC, 33 Arch St, Boston, MA 02110, **Business Phone:** (617)867-1000.*

PARHAM HOPSON, REAR ADM. DEBORAH L. (REAR ADM. DEBORAH PARHAM HOPSON)
Nurse, government official. **Personal:** Born Apr 20, 1955, Glouster, OH; daughter of William M Parham Jr and Rose L Parham; married Kevin M, Feb 14, 1998; children: William. **Educ:** Univ Cincinnati, BSN, 1977; Univ NC, Chapel Hill, MSPH, 1979, PhD, 1990. **Career:** Dept Health & Human Servs, presidential mgt intern, 1979-81; Inst Med, res assoc, 1981-83; Nat Health Serv Corps, pub health analyst & chief nurse, 1983-86; Bur Health Care Delivery & asst, perinatal coordr, 1988-89, off surgeon gen, dep staff dir & spec asst, 1989-91, public health analyst, 1990-91, br chief, 1991-97; HIV/AIDS Bur, DHHS, div dir, 1997-2000, dep bur dir, 2000-01, bur dir, 2002, assoc adminr, currently; US Pub Health Serv, rear admiral & asst surgeon gen, 2003-. **Orgs:** Am Pub Health Asn, 1977-; Asn Nurses AIDS Care, 1997-; Nat Minority Health Asn, 1992-94; Acad Mgt, 1988-95; Am Nurses Asn, 1984-95, 1999-; Nat Black Nurses Asn, 1985-95; Coalition 100 Black Women, 1992-98; Urban League, 1992-94; life mem, NCNW; prin adv, assoc admin; Nat Acad Scis; Inst Med. **Honors/Awds:** Delta Omega Serv Award, Univ NC, 1979; Administrator's Citation, HRSA, 1984; Director's Award, 1986; Chief Nurse Officer Award, 1991; Hildrus A Poindexter Award, Black Commissioned Officers Adv Group, 2003. **Special Achievements:** Elected as a Fellow in the American Academy of Nursing. **Military Serv:** USPHS: Citation, 1986, 1990, 1991; Emergency Preparedness Ribbon, 1989; Commendation Medal, 1986; Unit Commendation, 1984, 1988, 1992, 1994, 1995; Achievement Medal, 1985; Outstanding Unit Citation, 1996; Outstanding Serv Medal, 1997; Meritorious Service Medal, 2002. **Home Addr:** 16119 Llewellyn Manor Way, Silver Spring, MD 20905, **Home Phone:** (240)342-2254. **Business Addr:** Associate Administrator for HIV/AIDS, Health Resources and Services Administration, Department of Health and Human Services, 5600 Fishers Lane Suite 705 Parklawn Bldg, Rockville, MD 20857, **Business Phone:** (301)443-1993.

PARIS, CALVIN RUDOLPH
Marketing executive, entrepreneur. **Personal:** Born Sep 5, 1932, New Haven, CT; son of Samuel Felix and Nellie Belle Baker; divorced 1990; children (previous marriage): Calvin Jr (adopted), Priscilla Naomi, Theodore Thurgood, April Nell; married Claudette, 1992; children: Samuel Joshua. **Educ:** Howard Univ, BS, 1956; Meharry Medical Col Dental Sch, 1958. **Career:** Marketing executive (retired); Fla Enterprises Educ Corp, asst vp, gen mgr sales, 1958-81; Paris Health Systs Mgmt Inc dba Nutri & Systs Weight Loss Centers, pres & treas, 1981-90; Baskin Robbins 31 Flavors, Chicago IL, franchisee, 1980-90; Estates Mango de Paris, developer, 1993; Fed Auto Plz & Shopping Ctr owner, 1999; RPS, co-owner. **Orgs:** Life mem, Nat Asn Advan Colored People. **Honors/Awds:** Thirty plus Honors & Awards, Field Enterprises Edl Corp, 1957-81; William H Douglass Citizen of the Yr Award, Dixwell Community House Alumni Asn, 1984; Pres & major stockholder in largest black owned chain of weight loss centers in world. **Home Addr:** 601 NW 12th St, Delray Beach, FL 33444, **Home Phone:** (561)243-0153. *

PARIS, WILLIAM H.
Football player, public speaker. **Personal:** Born Oct 6, 1960, Louisville, KY; married Lynne; children: Wayne, David, Austin, Brandon, Courtney & Ashley. **Educ:** Univ Mich, attended 1982. **Career:** Football player (retired), Public speaker; Paris Enterprises, founder, 1982-, pub speaker & head, currently; San Francisco 49ers, offensive tackle, 1983-90; Indianapolis Colts, 1991; Detroit Lions, 1991-92; Bubba Paris Friends Homeless, founder; Champions Christ Crusade Ministries, pres & founder, currently. **Special Achievements:** Sports analyst for Channel 7 TV San Francisco; CO-hosted a weekly live talk show on KNBR radio; produced a special segment called "Behind the Face Mask."; special segment reporter and a producer of sports features entitle "Heart of a Champion."; sideline reporter for CBS covering 49erspre-season football and CO-hosted the 49er preview show for KPIX Channel 5; poet & ordained minister serving as an evangelist. **Business Phone:** 888-600-4937.*

PARISH, ROBERT
Basketball coach, consultant, basketball player. **Personal:** Born Aug 30, 1953, Shreveport, LA; married Nancy Saad (divorced); children: 1. **Educ:** Centenary Col. **Career:** Basket player (retired), coach, consult; Golden State Warriors, ctr,1976-80; Boston Celtics, ctr, 1980-94, consult, 2005-; Charlotte Hornets, 1994-96; Chicago Bulls, 1996-97; USBL's Maryland Mustangs, coach, 2000-01. **Honors/Awds:** All-Am First Team, The Sporting News, 1976; Gold Medalist, World Univ Games, 1975; NBA, Championship, 1981, 1984, 1986; NBA, All-Star game,1981-87, 1990-91; All-NBA Second team, 1982; Naismith Memorial Basketball Hall of Fame, 2003. **Business Addr:** Consultant, Boston Celtics, 226 Causeway St 4th Fl, Boston, MA 02114, **Business Phone:** (617)854-8000.

PARKER, ANTHONY
Football player. **Personal:** Born Feb 11, 1966, Sylacauga, AL; children: Colin. **Educ:** Ariz State. **Career:** Football player(retired; Indianapolis Colts, defensive back, 1989; Kansas City Chiefs, 1991; Minn Vikings, 1992-94; St Louis Rams, 1995-96; Tampa Bay Buccaneers, 1997-98.

PARKER, ANTHONY
Football player. **Personal:** Born Dec 4, 1975, Denver, CO. **Educ:** Weber State Univ. **Career:** Football Player (Retired); San Francisco 49ers, defensive back, 2001-01. *

PARKER, ANTHONY L
Association executive. **Educ:** Howard Univ Sch Archit & Urban Planning, Wash, DC, BA, archit. **Career:** Wayne County Sheriff's Dept, Dept Pub Serv, properties mgr, 1993-99; Farbman Group NAI, vpres develop, 1999-2001; Parkstone Develop LLC, pres & chief exec officer, currently. **Orgs:** Residential Builders & Maintenance & Alteration Contractors Bd, 2003-06. **Business Addr:** President, Chief Executive Officer, Parkstone Develop LLC, 649 Van Dyke St, Detroit, MI 48214, **Business Phone:** (313)926-4200.

PARKER, ANTHONY MICHAEL
Basketball player. **Personal:** Born Jun 19, 1975, Naperville, IL; son of Larry and Sara; married Tamy; children: Alonso. **Educ:** Bradley Univ, attended. **Career:** Philadelphia 76ers, guard, 1997-99; Orlando Magic, 1999; Quad City Thunder, 2000; Maccabi Tel Aviv, 2001-02; Lottomatica Roma, 2002-03; Maccabi Tel Aviv, guard, 2003-06; Toronto Raptors, 2006-09; Cleveland Cavaliers, currently. **Honors/Awds:** Missouri Valley Conference MVP, 1995; Most Valuable Player, MVC Conf, 1995-96; Euroleague Champion, 2001-05; Most Valuable Player, Israeli League, 2003-04; Most Valuable Player, Euroleague Final Four, 2004; All-Euroleague first team, 2004-05; Israeli League MVP, 2004; Most Valuable Player, Euroleague, 2005-06. **Business Addr:** Professional Basketball Player, Cleveland Cavaliers, One Center Ct, Cleveland, OH 44115-4001, **Business Phone:** (216)420-2000.

PARKER, AVERETTE MHOON
Physician, psychiatrist. **Personal:** Born Jan 27, 1939, Memphis, TN; divorced; children: Rosalind. **Educ:** Hillsdale Col, BS, 1960; Howard Univ, MD, 1964. **Career:** C & Family Ment Health & Ment Retardation Unit, N Cent Philadelphia Comm, Ment Health & Ment Retardation Ctr, dir; Hillcrest Children's Ctr to DC Headstart Prog, consult, 1968; Area B to DC Pub Sch, consult, 1969-70; Com Ment Health Ctr, dir adult outpatient dept, 1970-71; N County Ctr Fairfax Falls C Ment Health Ctr, dir 1972-73; Corinthian Guidance Ctr for Srvs to C, assoc dir 1973-74; Woodburn Ctr Comm Ment Health, dir, 1973; WNVT TV Nat Instrumental TV, consult, 1973-74; ARCH Inst Inc, pres & CEO, currently. **Orgs:** Selected for externship Obstet & Gynecol, 1963; Am Psychiatric Asn, 1969-; prof adv com, Soc Ctr, 1973-75; adv coun N VA Hot Line, 1973; PA Psychiatric Soc, 1974-; appearance in WKBSTV DE Vly Today Ment Health Srvcs 1975; SPVI TV Woman's Perspective & Perspective on Yth "The Black Family", 1975; panel mem, Blk Health Consumer Conf N Cent Philadelphia Comm Ment Health & Ment Retardation Ctr 1975; panel mem, PA Asn Ment Health Providers-Annual Meeting, 1975; panel mem Orthopsychiatry Annual Meeting Primary Prevention & Early Intervention Progs, 1976; panel mem, lectr "Hostility in the Blk Male-Fact or Fiction", N Cent Philadelphia Comm Ment Health& Ment Retardation Ctr,1976; lects Blk Family Roles Swarthmore Col Upward Bound Parents, 1976; "Hostility in the Black Male", 1976; "Aggression in Children & Adolescents", 1976; "Crisis Intervention-effects on Women & their Family", 1976. **Honors/Awds:** Award for Achievement, Rec Neuro-Psychiatry Dept, 1964. **Business Addr:** President, Chief Executive Officer, ARCH Institute Inc, 3645 Veazey St NW, Washington, DC 20008, **Business Phone:** (202)362-4550.

PARKER, BARRINGTON D, JR.
Judge. **Personal:** Born Aug 21, 1944; son of Barrington D Sr (deceased). **Educ:** Yale Univ, BA, 1965, Law Sch, LLB, 1969.

Career: Hon Aubrey E Robinson Jr, law clerk, 1969-70; Sullivan & Cromwell, atty, 1970-77; Parker Auspitz Neesemann & Delehanty, partner, 1977-87; Morrison & Foerster, partner, 1987-94; US Dist Ct, Southern Dist NY, judge, 1994-2001; US Ct Appeals Second Circuit, chair, States Circuit Judge, 2001-. **Orgs:** Trustee, Yale Corp; bd trustees, Gov Inst. **Business Addr:** States Circuit Judge, US Court of Appeals for the Second Circuit, 300 Quarropas St, White Plains, NY 10601, **Business Phone:** (914)390-4177.

PARKER, BERNARD F., JR.
Government official, county commissioner. **Personal:** Born Dec 16, 1949, Detroit, MI; married Sandra Bomar; children: Bernard III, Bukika, Bunia, Damon Bomar, Deric Bomar. **Educ:** Univ Mich, BA, 1973. **Career:** Oper Get Down, exec dir, 1973-, cofounder & chief exec officer, currently; Wayne Co, Detroit, comnr, 1991-. **Orgs:** Vpres, Universal Variable Staffing, 1979; bd mem, Southeast Mich Food Coalition, 1979; vpres, Midwest Group Mgt, 1980; bd mem, Govrs Task Force Infant Mortality, 1985, Mich Bell Citizen Adv Group, 1986; comn mem, Detroit Strategic Planning Comn, 1987; pres, CAD Cable 1987-. **Honors/Awds:** Nat Community Serv Award, United Community Serv, 1979; Detroit City Coun Community Award, 1984; Michelob Comn Serv Award, 1985. **Business Addr:** Co-founder, Chief Executive Officer, Operation Get Down, 10100 Harper Ave, Detroit, MI 48213.*

PARKER, CHARLES MCCRAE
Scientist. **Personal:** Born Aug 13, 1930, Farmville, NC. **Educ:** NC A&T State Univ, BS, 1951, BS, 1958; Nat Inst Health. **Career:** Scientist (retired); Nat Inst Health, messenger clerk, 1961-65; USDA, biol sci tech, 1965-67, biol sci tech path, 1967-80, sr biol sci tech, 1980-87, FSIS, 1990; Armed Forces Inst Pathology, histotechnologist, 1990; Fed Am Socs Experimental Biol. **Orgs:** Phi Beta Sigma. **Honors/Awds:** Quality Increase APHIS USDA, 1975; Letter Achievement FSIS USDA, 1983; Special Achievement FSIS USDA, 1985. **Military Serv:** AUS, sp3, 1954-57; Honor Graduate NCO Sch, 1956.

PARKER, CHARLIE
Basketball coach. **Educ:** Univ Findlay, health & phys educ & sociol, 1972. **Career:** Univ Findlay, asst coach & head track; Bowling Green, asst coach; Wayne State, head coach, 1983-88; George Raveling, asst, 1989-94; USC, head coach, 1995-96; Dallas Mavericks, asst coach, 1996-04; New Orleans Hornets, asst coach, 2006-07. **Honors/Awds:** GLIAC Coach of the Yr, 1984, 1987; Michigan Coach of the Yr, 1984. *

PARKER, CLARENCE E
Automotive executive. **Career:** Gresham Chrysler Plymouth Jeep Eagle, chief exec officer. **Business Addr:** Chief Executive Officer, Gresham Chrysler Plymouth Jeep Eagle, 1975 E Powell Blvd, Gresham, OR 97080, **Business Phone:** (503)665-7121.

PARKER, CLAUDE A.
Quality control inspector. **Personal:** Born Oct 24, 1938, Branchville, VA; son of Claude A Parker Sr and Alma Virginia Wyche; married Constance Yvonne; children: Ryan. **Educ:** Community Col Baltimore, AA 1960; Morgan State Univ, BS, 1964. **Career:** Joseph E Seagram & Sons Inc, chemist, 1965-66, supvr quality control 1966, distiller, 1967-70, quality control mgr, 1970. **Orgs:** Am Mgt Asn, 1971, Appl Mgt Sci Inc, 1972, Wine Adv Bd Ca, 1972; Meritocrats Inc, YMCA. **Honors/Awds:** Ebony Success Libr, 1975.

PARKER, DAVID GENE
Baseball player, athletic coach, executive. **Personal:** Born Jun 9, 1951, Calhoun, MS; son of Richard and Dannie M; married Kellye Crockett; children: Danielle, David II & Dorian. **Career:** Baseball player (retired), baseball coach, executive; Pittsburgh Pirates, outfielder, 1973-83, spec hitting instr; Cincinnati Reds, outfielder, 1984-87; Oakland Athletics, hitter, 1988-89; Milwaukee Brewers, outfielder, 1990-91; Calif Angels, outfielder, 1991; Toronto Blue Jays, 1991; Anaheim Angels, first base coach; St. Louis Cardinals, batting coach, 1998; Popeye's Chicken & Biscuits, owner, currently. **Honors/Awds:** Nat League All-Star Team, 1977-81, 1985, 1986 & 1990; Gold Glove Award1977, 1978 & 1979; Nat League Most Valuable Player, Baseball Writers AsnAm, 1978; All-Star game MVP, 1979; Cincinnati Reds MVP, 1984, 1985 &,1986; MVP, Milwaukee Brewers, 1990; Designated Hitters Award, 1989-90. **Special Achievements:** First black player to command one million dollars in 1979. **Business Addr:** Owner, Popeye's Chicken & Biscuits, 7131 Reading Rd, Cincinnati, OH 45237, **Business Phone:** (513)731-1997.

PARKER, DE (DEMOND KEITH PARKER)
Football player. **Personal:** Born Dec 24, 1976, Tulsa, OK. **Educ:** Okla State Univ. **Career:** Green Bay Packers, running back, 1999-2000; Detroit Lions, 2001; Buffalo Bills, 2003. *

PARKER, DORIS S
Association executive. **Personal:** Born Aug 23, 1931, Marvel, AR; daughter of Earlie Mae Sims (deceased) and Percy L (deceased); divorced; children: Karen Parker Stewart & Terri L. **Educ:** Ind Cent Col, BA, 1959. **Career:** AUS, Finance Ctr, military pay clerk, 1952-66; Veterans Admin Reg Off, adjudicator veteran claims examr, 1966-73; Ind Voc Tech Col, asst dir, stud serv, 1973-75, reg relations coord, 1975-82; YWCA, exec dir, 1982-85; independent consult, 1985; Alpha Kappa Alpha Educ advan Found, Chicago, exec secy, 1987-. **Orgs:** Pres, Hoosier Capital Girl Scout Coun, 1978-82; Nat Comt Campaign Human Develop, US Catholic Conf, 1973-77, chmn, 1976-77; St Felicitas Roman Catholic Church; Fund for Hoosier Excellence, 1983-; St Mary Woods Col, bd trustees, 1985-94, trustee emer, 1994-; Blacks in Develop, 1990-; Asn Black Found Exec, 1993-; US CMS Civil Rights, Ind adv cms, currently; Asn Forum of Chicago; Alpha Kappa Alpha Sorority. **Honors/Awds:** Brotherhood Award, Ind Chapter, Nat Conf Christians & Jews, 1975; Human Relations Award, Indianapolis Educ Asn, 1976; Harriet Tubman Award, Community Action Against Poverty, 1982; Thanks Badge, Hoosier Capital Girl Scouts Coun, 1982. Achievement Plus Pub Serv, Ctr Leadership Develop, 1985. **Business Phone:** (312)684-1282.

PARKER, E CHARMAINE ROBERTS
Editor, journalist. **Personal:** Born May 30, 1956, Salisbury, NC; daughter of James Deotis and Elizabeth Caldwell; married Ricardo, Sep 10, 1988; children: Jazmin Monet & Tangela. **Educ:** Howard Univ, BFA, 1977; Am Univ, graduate studies, jour, 1978; Univ Southern Cal, MA, print jour, 1983. **Career:** The Wash Times, ed, copy ed, reporter, 1984; Strebor Books Int, publ dir, currently. **Orgs:** Nat Asn of Black Journalists, 1991. **Honors/Awds:** Soc Newspaper Design, Feature Section/Lifestyle, 1991-92; Design & Layout Awards, 1995-96. **Home Addr:** 9511 Gwynndale Dr, Clinton, MD 20735, **Home Phone:** (301)856-1423. **Business Addr:** Publishing Director, Strebor Books International, PO Box 6505, Largo, MD 20792, **Business Phone:** (301)583-0616.

PARKER, G JOHN, SR.
Firefighter. **Personal:** Born Dec 29, 1941, Drew, MS; son of Loys and Anna Mae Tyler (deceased); married Eva M Semien, Sep 1, 1990; children: Jannie Lynn, G John Jr, Dannette Shaton, Toni Michelle & Stephanie A. **Educ:** Ill Cent Col, East Peoria, IL, AA, 1975, AAS, 1979. **Career:** Caterpillar, Peoria, IL, mach operator, 1964-65; Peoria Fire Dept, Peoria, IL, 1965-91, fire chief, 1988; City Pomona, Pomona, CA, fire chief, 1991. **Orgs:** Int Asn Black Prof Firefighters, 1975-; Am Soc Pub Adminr, 1988-; Int Asn Fire Chiefs, 1988-; bd mem, Peoria Urban League, 1989-; bd mem, Aro Hall Fame, 1989-; bd mem, Pomona Valley Red Cross, 1991; Nat Forum Black Pub Adminr, 1991; Greater Pomona Kiwanis, 1992. **Honors/Awds:** Outstanding Service Arson Investr, Gov Ill, 1982; Outstanding Alumni Award, Ill Cent Col, Am Coun Educ, 1989; Dr Martin Luther King Leadership Award, South Side Pastors Asn, 1990; Sigma Image Award, Sigma Gamma Rho, 1990; Applaud Peoria-Outstanding Serv, Peoria Chamber Achievers, 1990. **Military Serv:** USMC, master sgt, 1960-64; Outstanding Commissioned Officer, 1989; 182nd Ill Air Nat Guard, 1976-, Dep Fire Chief.

PARKER, GEORGE ANTHONY
Executive. **Personal:** Born Jan 29, 1952, Norfolk, VA; son of Milton A and Lillian B Carr; married Michele Annette Fleuranges; children: Jenifer Ann. **Educ:** Wake Forest Univ, BS, math, 1974; Univ NC, Chapel Hill, MBA, 1976. **Career:** Continental Ill Nat Bank, banking assoc, 1976-78, banking officer, 1979-80, vpres, 1980-82; DPF Comp Leasing Corp, vpres & treas, 1982-84; Atlantic Comp Funding Corp, chmn bd & pres, 1984; Conn Bancorp Inc, dir, 1986-88; Norwalk Bank, dir, 1986-88; Leasing Tech Int Inc, dir, vpres & chief financial officer, 1984-95, exec vpres, chief financial officer & chief mkt officer, 1996-. **Orgs:** Vpres, Urban Bankers Forum Chicago, 1981-82; Glenwood Lake Comm Asn, 1983-, Nat Black MBA Asn, 1986-; YMCA, 1986; Wake Forest Univ Alumni Letterman Club, 1986-; dir, treas, St Bernard's Ctr Learning; bd dir, Eastern Asn Equipment Lessors; Equipment Leasing Asn. **Honors/Awds:** Western Electric Scholarship Award, 1971-73; Consortium for Grad Studies in Mamangement Fellowship Award, 1974-76. **Business Addr:** Founder & Executive Vice President, Chief Financial Officer, Leasing Technologies International, 221 Danbury Rd, Wilton, CT 06897.

PARKER, H WALLACE
Lawyer. **Personal:** Born Dec 8, 1941, North Carolina; married Patricia W; children: Meriel S. **Educ:** Winston-Salem State Univ, BS, 1967; NCC Univ, JD, 1970. **Career:** Reg Herb Smith Lawyer fel Prog, 1970-72; Legal Dept, City Pontiac, Dep City atty, 1971-75; Bloomfield Law Ctr, pres, 1975-; Check Mate Transp Syst, pres, owner, 1974-; V-Tech Corp, vpres, atty, 1976-; Nat Asn Advan Colored People, gen coun, atty, chief coun. **Orgs:** Wolverine Bar Asn; chief legal counr, Nat Asn Advan Colored People, 1984-; atty, bd dir, OAR Prog, 1987-; Am Judicature Soc; chair, Criminal Law Div, Am Trial Lawyers Asn, Oakland County Corrections Adv Bd; Criminal Defense Attorneys Mich; Am Bar Asn; Nat Bar Asn; Oakland County Criminal Adv Bd; bd mem, N Oakland County Girl Scouts Inc; Pontiac Area Urban League; bd trustees, St John United Methodist Church; State Mich Econ Develop Comn. **Honors/Awds:** First black Deputy City Attorney, City Pontiac, 1971; Norcroff Award, Nat Asn Advan Colored People, 1986; Outstanding Service Award, 0AR, 1987; Theophilus Jefferson Northcross Award, Nat Asn Advan Colored People; Lifetime Achievement Award, Dept Justice, Fed Bur Investn, Detroit Chap; Diversity Award, Waterford Sch Dist, 2004. **Military Serv:** USMC, sgt, 1960-63; Outstanding Soldier Award, 1962. **Home Addr:** 3332 Barlyn Lane, PO Box 99, Bloomfield Township, MI 48302, **Home Phone:** (248)332-8472.

PARKER, HARRY
Vice president (Organization). **Personal:** Born Oct 20, 1954, Richlands, NC. **Educ:** NC State Univ, BS, mech engineering, 1976. **Career:** Dupont Spruance site, engr; Dupont Nylon Supplex, brand mgr, 1991; Dupont Dacron filament, global mkt mgr, 1992, global bus dir, 1996; Dacron staple, dir, 1994; DuPont Dacron, vpres & gen mgr, 1998-00; DuPont Surfaces, vpres & gen mgr, 2000-03; DuPont Sales Effectiveness, vpres, 2003-. **Orgs:** Int Rotary; Alpha Phi Alpha; Nat Asn Advan Colored People.

PARKER, HENRY ELLSWORTH
Government official, health services administrator. **Personal:** Born Feb 14, 1928, Baltimore, MD; married Janette; children: Curtis & Janet. **Educ:** Hampton Inst, BS, 1956; Southern CT State Univ, MS, 1965; Sacred HeartUniv, JD, Hon, 1983. **Career:** State CT Hartford, treas, 1975-86; Atlanta Sosnoff, sr vpres, pub fundsector, 1986-; Connecticut Health Found, treas, 1975-86, bd mem, currently. **Orgs:** Pres, Nat Assoc State Treas, 1985; pres, Kappa Alpha Psi Found, 1981-86; mem, Fed Nat Mortgages Assoc Adv Comm, 1982-84; Past Grant Exalted Rulerthe Elks; 33 Degree Mason; trustee, Instnl Responsibility Res Corp; bddirs, Inst Living. **Honors/Awds:** Prince Hall Masons Bicentennial Award, 1975; Civil Rights Award, CT, NAACP, 1976; One of Ebony Mag 100 most influential Black Am, 1976-86; Lovejoy Award Elks, 1984. **Military Serv:** AUS, 1951-53. **Business Addr:** Board Member, Connecticut Health Foundation, 74B Vine St, New Britain, CT 06052, **Business Phone:** (860)224-2200.

PARKER, DR. HENRY H.
Educator. **Personal:** Born Sep 11, 1933, Memphis, TN; son of Ben Parker. **Educ:** St Thomas Univ, BA, 1956; Univ Minn, MA, eng, 1959; Univ Ill, PhD, latin & greek, 1975. **Career:** Univ Minn, asst prof, 1961-65; NDEA Rhetoric, lectr, 1965; Univ Northern Iowa, from asst prof to prof, 1965-84; Univ Ill, asst prof, 1968-71; Ford Found fel, 1969; Univ Tenn, Martin, Dept Psychol, prof psychol, 1990-; producer & star "the Hank Parker Show" Channel 7. **Orgs:** Pres, Off-Campus Univ consulting firm; founder & principal, Waterloo-Pre-Sch Acad; pres, Parker Reading Co; pub, Parker Reader Elem Sch Newspaper; co-dir, Marilyn Crist CP Collegians Gifted Children's Prog; Nat Dir Curric, Jesse Jackson's PUSH-Excel. **Honors/Awds:** Danforth Asn, Danforth Found; Iowa's Most Outstanding Professor Award, 1972; Geo Wash Carver Distinguished Lecturer Award, 1975. **Special Achievements:** Dr Henry participated in "Oprah Winfrey Show" for his work with medical hypnotherapy, with which he helps alleviate pain in incurable pain sufferers. **Business Addr:** Professor of Philosophy, University Tenn Martin, Department of History and Philosophy, 322 Humanities Bldg, Martin, TN 38238.

PARKER, DR. HERBERT GERALD
School administrator, consultant. **Personal:** Born May 13, 1929, Fayetteville, AR; son of Otis James and Anna Fisher; married Florida Fisher; children: Christie Lynne. **Educ:** Univ Nebr, BS, 1962; NC A&T State Univ, MS, 1970; Fla State Univ, PhD, 1982. **Career:** School administrator, (retired), consultant (retired); Rep China, Taipei,Taiwan, adv ministry nat defense, 1962-65; NC A&T State Univ, prof milt sci, 1965-68; AUS Spec Forces The Delta Vietnam, comdr, 1968-69; US Army Civil Affairs Sch Fort Bragg, dir, 1969-73; Fla A&M Univ, prof milt sci, 1973-77; State Fla Bur Crimes Compensation, 1979-87; Fla Dept Educ, Tallahassee, FL, chief internal auditor, 1987-91, dir admin serv, 1991-94; consultant, 1994. **Orgs:** Kappa Alpha Psi; Sigma Pi Phi Fraternity; Rocks Inc; bd dir, Civil Affairs Asn, 1970-73; Nat Asn Soc Scientist, 1973; bd dir, Three C's Corp, 1974-79; Tallahassee Area C of C, 1974-82; bd dirs, Opportunity Indust Ctrs, 1975-78; bd dirs, United Way Leon Co 1978-82; bd dirs, Tallahassee Urban League, 1981; pres, Nat Asn Crime Victim Compensation Bd, 1984-87; bd dirs FL Victim & Witness Network 1984; bd chmn, 1986-88, 2002-04; Tallahassee Nat Asn Advan Colored People, capital chordsmen; pres- elect, Capital City Rotary, 1998-99, pres, 2000-01; Retired Officers Asn; Military Order of the World Wars; bd dirs, Salvation Army, 2002; pres, one of Tallahassee s Rotary Clubs. **Honors/Awds:** Distinguished Serv Award, Boy Scouts of Am, 1968; Distinguished Serv Award, Civil Affairs Asn, 1974; Outstanding Serv Award, Col Humanities &Soc Sci, Fla A&M Univ, 1977; Phi Kappa Phi Hon Soc, 1979; Distinguished Serv Award, Nat Asn Crime Victim Compensation Bds, 1986; Fla Network Victim Witness Serv; James Fogarty Distingushed Serv Award, 1988;Distinguished Black Achiever Award, Tallahassee Nat Asn Advan Colored People, 1991; James Hudson Citizenship Award, 1998; Silver Star Award, 2001. **Special Achievements:** Youngest African promoted to Col, United Synagogue Youth, 1969; first African-American to serve as president of one of Tallahassee Rotary Clubs. **Military Serv:** USY, col, 1947-77; 2 Legion of Merit; Silver Star; 3 Bronze Stars; Purple Heart; Meritorious Serv Award; 12 other awards Airborne Ranger & Spec Forces Qualified; Joint Service Commendation Medal; 3 Air Medals; 2 Army Commendation Medals; United Nations Ribbon; Korean Campaign Award; Vietnamese Cross of Gallantry with Palm; Reserve Forces Award with 10 year device, Good Conduct Medal. **Home Addr:** 3510 Tullamore Lane, Tallahassee, FL 32309, **Home Phone:** (850)893-2671. *

PARKER, JACQUELYN HEATH
Association executive. **Personal:** Born in Memphis, TN; daughter of Fred Heath and Nezzie Heath; married William A Parker; children: Kimberly & Shane. **Educ:** Southern Ill Univ, BS, 1963, MS, 1967; Univ Ill. **Career:** Olive-Harvey COT Col, asst dean, 1996-; Top Ladies Distinction Inc, nat pres, 1987-91, prog crd, 1996-, dean, 1999-. **Orgs:** Scholar chmn, Build Inc, 1983-90; sponsor, NIA Club, 1985-95; pres, Theta Rho Omega Chap Alpha Kappa Alpha Sor, 1987-89; Jack & Jill, Inc; Links, Inc; exec bd, 1991-95, Ill State Convener, Nat Coun Negro Women. **Honors/Awds:** Soror of the Year, Theta Rho Omega Chap Ark Sorority; Lady of the Year, Top Ladies Distinction Chicago, 1985; Top 40 Finest Women COT, Women Together South Suburban Chicago, 1988; nominee, Top Women Chicago Midwest Ctr Chicago, 1989; Orchid Award, Top Ladies Distinction, Inc, 1989; Ten Community Builders Award, South Suburban Chicago Ark, 1990; Jacquelyn Parker's Day, 1990; Mayor Cincinnati, OH, 1990; A Woman of Distinction Award Chicago, Top Ladies Distinction, 1991; winner, "Those Who Excel", Ill State Bd Educ, 1991; Outstanding Teacher Award, Univ Chicago, 1994. **Home Addr:** 254 E Denell Dr, Crete, IL 60417, **Home Phone:** (708)672-9217. **Business Addr:** Illinois State Convener, National Council of Negro Women Inc, 254 E Denell Dr, Crete, IL 60617, **Business Phone:** (708)672-9217.

PARKER, JAMES L.
Administrator. **Personal:** Born Oct 29, 1923, Salina, KS; son of John Henry and Classie (Meadows); married Berma Jeane (Wells) Parker, Jan 16, 1946 (deceased); children: Cheri D Ware, Jami L, Kathleen L Sullivan, Beryl J, Rosalind A Crutcher, Donna J, Janice E, Gloria J Shelton. **Educ:** Kansas Wesleyan Univ, attended 1949; Brown-Makie Sch Bus, BA, 1950. **Career:** Adminr (retired); Salina Recreation Dept, Carver Rec Ctr, Salina, KS, asst rec dir, 1946-50; E Side Rec Ctr Freeport IL, exec dir, 1951-66; Sundstrand Advanced Tech Div, contract adminstr, 1967-87; tax acct. **Orgs:** Gov Comn Minority Entrepreneurship; Gov Comn Emancipation Centennial; Freeport Hum Rels Comn; IL Law Enforcement Comn; Freeport Adult Educ Coun Freeport Northwestern IL Comt Act Prog Bd; Int Toastmasters Club; adv bd, Freeport Jr Col; ML King Jr Comm Ctr Bd N IL Constr Affirm Act Prog; steward, St James CME Church; Stephenson County Jury Comnr. **Honors/Awds:** Youth Award Freeport Children of Children, 1956. **Military Serv:** AUS, Sgt maj, 1943-45; NATO & ETO Battle Clusters. *

PARKER, DR. JEFF, SR.
Physician. **Personal:** Born Aug 19, 1927, Big Cane, LA; son of Edmond Parker and Stella Parker; married Patricia O; children: Jeff Jr, Jacqueline, James & Janice. **Educ:** Howard Univ, BS, 1962, MD, 1966; Union Mem Hosp, Baltimore, MD, rotating internship 1966-67; Sinai Hosp Baltimore, MD, asst resid internal med, 1967-69; Univ MD Hosp, fel cardiol, 1969-70. **Career:** Pvt Pract, internist/cardiol. **Orgs:** Black Cardiologists Asn, 1974-; active staff Md Gen Hosp, Union Memorial Hosp; pres, Med Found Baltimore Inc; pres, Reliable Med rental & Serv Inc. **Honors/Awds:** Phi Beta Kappa, Howard Univ, 1962; Presidential Medallion/Recognition of Medical Arts by Church of God in Christ Bishop JO Patterson 1984; Alan Locke Memorial Plaque, Howard Univ,1958; Dean's Honor Roll Under-Grad Howard Univ, 1962; Nat Honor Soc, Psychol Psi Chi, Howard Univ, 1962; Magna Cum Laude Col Liberal Arts, Howard Univ; Honors Col Med Ped & Psych, Howard Univ, 1966. **Special Achievements:** Author: A christian Guide to the War on Drugs. **Military Serv:** AUS, sgt 1st class, 1947-58; Good Conduct Medal. **Home Addr:** 1012 Argonne Dr, Baltimore, MD 21218, **Home Phone:** (410)366-7604. **Business Addr:** Physician, 1012 Argonne Dr, Baltimore, MD 21218, **Business Phone:** (410)366-7604.

PARKER, JERRY P.
Lawyer. **Personal:** Born Mar 1, 1943, West Blocton, AL; married Patricia Wall; children: Jerry & Jennifer. **Educ:** Bowling Green State Univ, BS, BA, 1965; Cleveland Marshall Sch Law, JD, 1970. **Career:** E Ohio Gas Co, syst analyst, 1965-68; c, tax supr, 1968-73; Sears Roebuck & Co, tax atty, 1973-. **Orgs:** Am Bar Asn; Nat Bar Asn; Cook Co Bar Asn; Chicago Bar Asn; Ill Bar Asn; Ill & Ohio St Bar Bd Trust Consult Prot Asn; bd trustee, Exec Comt Child Serv; bd trustee, Friendly Inn Settle House. **Business Addr:** Tax Attorney, Sears Roebuck & Co, Suite 568 Sears Twr, Chicago, IL 60684.

PARKER, JOSEPH CAIAPHAS, JR.
Educator, lawyer. **Personal:** Born Sep 25, 1952, Anniston, AL; son of Joseph C Sr (deceased) and Addie Ruth Fox; married J LaVerne Morris, Aug 14, 1976; children: Jessica & Jennifer. **Educ:** Morehouse Col, BA, 1974; Univ Ga, M Public Admin, 1976; Univ Tex, Austin, JD, 1982. **Career:** City Dallas, admin asst mgt serv, 1976-77, admin asst office city mgr, 1977-79, mgr summer youth employ prog, 1979; Travis Co Atty Office, trl atty, 1983-84, chief trl div, 1985-86; David Chapel Missionary Baptist Church, assoc pastor 1984-92, pastor, 1992-; Long, Burner, Parks & Sealy PC, atty, dir, vpres; Univ Tex, Austin, instr trl advocacy, 1991. **Orgs:** Nat Conf Minority Pub Adminrs, 1974-80; Am Soc Pub Admin; bd dirs, Morehouse Col Nat Alumni Asn; bd dir, Austin Child Guidance Eval Ctr; Conf Christians & Jews; Black Austin Democrats; Urban League, NAACP, Austin Jaycees; Travis County Pub Defender Task Force; State Bar Tex, Austin Young Lawyers Asn, Nat Bar Asn; Austin Black Lawyers Asn & Fed Bar Asn; Asn Tr Lawyers Am. **Honors/Awds:** Man of the Year, Spelman Col Stud Govt Asn, 1973-74; Univ GA fel, 1974-76; Pi Sigma Alpha Honor Soc, 1976; Dallas Jaycees Rookie of the Yr, 1978-79, Presidential Award, 1978-79; Outstanding Achievement Award, Nat Conf Minority Pub Adminrs, 1979; Gene Woodfin Award, Univ Tex, 1982; Leadership Austin 1984-85; Distinguished Morehouse Col Alumni Citation of the Year, 1986; Baptist Gen Conv Tex Theol Scholar, 1986-87; Benjamin E Mays fel Ministry, Fund Theol Studies; Distinguished Alumnus of the Year, George W. Truett Theoll Seminary, 2004. **Special Achievements:** First African American president of the Travis County Bar Association.

PARKER, KAI J
Executive, government official. **Personal:** Children: Darren & Darnel. **Educ:** Compton Col, AA, social welfare, 1965; Loyola Marymount Univ, grad studies psychol & guid coun, 1979, Human Construct Sexuality, 1980, Alcohol & Drug Studies, 1982; Univ Redlands, BA, mgt, 1981. **Career:** Am Telegraph & Tele, customer serv rep, 1966-68; Los Angeles County Dept Social Serv, eligibilty worker, 1968-70, eligibility supvr, 1970-79; Aide Sanitary & Supply Co, mgt consult, 1979-80; Los Angeles County Assessment Appeals Bd, comnr, 1980-82; Group W Cable, pub affairs & govt rels coordr, 1982-91; Los Angeles County, Dept C Serv, spec progs coordr, 1991-. **Orgs:** Nat Asn Advan Colored People; Asian-Pac legal Defense & Educ Bd Dirs; United Negro Col Fund; Gardena Local Manpower Adv Bd; Gardena Interagency Health Comn; Gardena Martin Luther King Cultural Comn; Asian Am Drug Abuse Prog; Calif Afro-Am Mus Art Coun; Mus African Am Art; vpres, S Bay Coalition Alcoholism; adv bd, Los Angeles County Child Health Disease Prev; vpres, Gardenia Valley Lions. **Honors/Awds:** Outstanding Leadership Award, City Gardena; Recognition Award, Gardena Elks Leadership; Outstanding Service Award, AFL-CIO; Community Involvement Award, Soroptimist Int; Community Involvement Award, Gardena Sorptomist; Community Service Award, Calif Black Comn Alcoholism; Commendations, Los Angeles County; Outstanding Service Award, Bd Supervisors, Dept Pub Social Serv, 1982; Political Award, Zeta Phi Beta; Founder, Gardenia African Centered Saturday Sch; Nat Asn Counties Award, 1992-96; Women of the Year, US Cong House Representatives, 35th Dist, 1996. **Business Addr:** Coordinator of Special Programs, Los Angeles County Department of Children Services, 425 Shato Pl Rm 604, Los Angeles, CA 90020.

PARKER, KAREN LYNN
Journalist. **Personal:** Born Dec 21, 1943, Salisbury, NC; daughter of Fred and Clarice; married Barry Lambert (divorced 2000); married Christopher L Roe (divorced 1995); married Peter A Kuttner (divorced 1978); children: Jonah Evan Kuttner. **Educ:** Univ NC, BA, jour & mass comn, 1965. **Career:** Winston-Salem J, 1962-65, copy ed, 1997-; Grand Rapids, MI, Press, 1965-67; Rochester Democrat & Chronicle, 1967; Los Angeles Times, sunday news ed, 1978-93; Salt Lake Tribune, asst nat ed, 1994-96. **Orgs:** Nat Asn Black Journalists, 1997-; Am Copy Eds Soc, 1997-; UNC Bd Visitors, 2005-; bd dirs, UNC Gen Alumni Asn, 2005-08. **Honors/Awds:** Harvey E Beech Outstanding Alumni Award, Univ NC, 2004. **Special Achievements:** First African American woman to graduate from University of NC, Chapel Hill, 1965; Journal of 1963-64 placed in Southern Historical Collection, UNC Library, 2007. **Home Addr:** 2 Laurel Brook Ct, Greensboro, NC 27407, **Home Phone:** (336)855-6936. **Business Addr:** Copy Editor, Winston-Salem Journal, 416 N Marshall St, Winston-Salem, NC 27101, **Business Phone:** (336)727-7211.

PARKER, DR. KEITH DWIGHT
Educator. **Personal:** Born Oct 15, 1954, Philadelphia, MS; married Emery D Woodruff, Jun 20, 1981; children: Narroyl & Malcolm. **Educ:** Delta State Univ, BA, 1978; Miss State Univ, MA, 1981, PhD, 1986. **Career:** Delta State Univ, asst dean, 1979-82; Miss State Univ, resident asst, 1982-85, teaching asst, 1982-86; Auburn Univ, asst prof, 1986-89; Univ Nebr-Lincoln, from asst prof to assoc prof, 1994-2003, African Am & African Studies Prog, dir, 1993-98, from asst dean grad studies to assoc dean grad studies, 1999-2002; coordr undergrad res, 2002-03; Univ Ga, assoc provost inst diversity, 2003-05, prof sociol, 2003-. **Orgs:** Adv, Black Student Orgn, 1982; Minority Fels, Miss State, 1982; pres, Grad Black Stud Orgn, 1983; Alpha Kappa Delta, Miss State, 1983; adv, African People's Union, Univ Nebr, 1990-94; Inst Res Adv Bd, 2004-05; Am Soc Criminology; Am Sociol Asn; Mid-South Sociol Asn; Southern Sociol Soc. **Honors/Awds:** Ladies of Elegance Organization Citizenship Award, November 2006; Outstanding Student, 1986; Outstanding Minority Faculty, Auburn Univ, 1989; Barbara Jordan Award, Big 8 Conference Black Student Government, 1991-94. **Special Achievements:** Numerous publications including, "The Extended Family as a Source of Support Among African Americans.", 1999; "Achieving Diversity in Graduate Education: Impact of the Ronald E. McNair Postbaccalaureate Achievement Program.", 2003. **Business Addr:** Professor, University of Georgia, Department of Sociology, 213C Baldwin Hall, Athens, GA 30602, **Business Phone:** (706)542-3220.

PARKER, LAWRENCE KRISNA
Rap musician. **Personal:** Born Aug 20, 1965, Brooklyn, NY; son of Sheffield Brown and Jacqueline Jones; married Ramona Scott, 1987 (divorced 1992); married Simone; children: Randy Hubbard (deceased). **Career:** Boogie Down Productions, DJ Scott LaRock, 1985; Edutainer Records & Human Educ Against Lies, founder, 1990; lectr; producer; A&R, Reprise, vpres, 1998-2000; Temple Hip-Hop, founder; Albums: Criminal Minded, 1987; By All Means Necessary, 1988; Ghetto Music: The Blueprint of Hip Hop, 1989; Edutainment, 1990; Live Hardcore Worldwide, 1991; Sex & Violence, 1992; Return of the Boom Bap, 1993; KRS-One, 1995; I Got Next, 1997; A Retrospective, 2000; The Sneak Attack, 2001; Best of B-Boy Records, 2001; Strictly for the Breakdancers & Emceez, 2001; Spiritual Minded, 2002; The Mix Tape, 2002; Kristyles, 2003; D.I.G.I.T.A.L., 2003; Keep Right, 2004; Life, 2006; Hip-Hop Lives (withMarley Marl), 2007; Adventures In Emceeing (with Duck Down Records), 2008; Singles: "The Bridge Is Over", 1987; "Sound of da Police", 1993; "I Can't Wake Up", 1993; "MC's Act Like They Don't Know", 1995; "Rappaz R. N.Dainja", 1995; "East Coast West Coast Killas", 1997; "Men of Steel", 1997; Step Into A World, 1997; "Clear 'Em Out", 2002; "Classic (Better Than I'veEver Been)", 2007. **Honors/Awds:** Four gold records. **Special Achievements:** Receipient, Lifetime Acheivement Award, 2008. **Business Addr:** Singer, c/o Jive Records, 137 W 25th St Suite 139, New York, NY 10001, **Business Phone:** (212)727-0016.*

PARKER, LEE
Educator, consultant. **Personal:** Born May 31, 1949; married; children: 2. **Educ:** LeMoyne Owen Col, BS, BBA, 1979; Trevecca Nazarene Col, MEd, 1990. **Career:** US Treas, assoc nat bank examr, 1979-83; Nat Bank Com, Memphis, vpres, 1983-84; Gospel TV Network Inc, bus consult, 1984-; Memphis City Sch, teacher, BASIC prog & math, 1985-. **Orgs:** Co-chmn, Memphis Housing Comn; Securities & Exchange Comn; LeMoyne Owen Col Relig Life Comn; naval adv, NAUSUPPACT forces. **Honors/Awds:** National Science Award, Eastman Kodak Co; Distinguished Alumnus, Nat Asn Equal Opportunity Higher Educ; UNCF Award. **Military Serv:** USN, petty officer, 1966-76; Naval Commendation Medal. **Home Addr:** 301 Walker Ave, Memphis, TN 38126.

PARKER, MARYLAND MIKE
Journalist. **Personal:** Born Feb 5, 1926, Oklahoma City, OK; married John Harrison (deceased); children: Norma Jean Brown, Janice Kay Shelby, Joyce Lynn, John H Jr, Cherie D Hite,Patrick Scott, Charles Roger & John H III. **Educ:** Univ Ariz, Pine Bluff, 1970-71; Mary mount Col, Salina, KS, 1974-77. **Career:** Md House Beauty, Salina, KS, beautician, 1964-69; NAACP, Salina, youth adv, 1970-72; BACOS Newsletter, newspaper reporter, 1971-77; KINA BACOS, Reporter, radio announcer, 1973-84; Kans State Globe, reporter & photographer, currently. **Orgs:** YWCA, 1958-, Saline County Democratic Women, 1960-, VFW Aus, 1971-, Am Leg Aux, 1973-, Nat Fed Press Women, 1973-, Kans Press Women, 1973-; bd dir,Salina Child Care Asn, 1973; part time volunteer, Salvation Army, 1979-; Int Platform Asn, 1983-; bd dir, Gospel Mission, 1984; Am Bus Women Asn, 1991-. **Honors/Awds:** NAACP, 1980; Good Citizenship Award, VFW 1432, Salina, KS, 1982; Award of Merit, Salina Human Rels, 1986; Woman of the Year, Am Bus Asn, 1997. **Home Addr:** 920 Birch Dr, Salina, KS 67402. **Business Addr:** Reporter, Photographer, Kansas State Globe, PO Box 1309, Kansas City, KS 66104, **Business Phone:** (913)825-0468.

PARKER, MATTHEW
Executive. **Personal:** Born Nov 14, 1945, Cincinnati, OH; son of Matt (deceased) and Ruth Spann (deceased); married Karon Lanier, Aug 8, 1981; children: Matthew Lloyd Jr, Tiffany Barbara, Michael Jones & Kelly Betsy. **Educ:** Grand Rapids Sch Bible & Music, dipl Bible, 1970; Wheaton Col, BA, Sociol 1976; Univ Detroit, MA, Educ Admin, 1981. **Career:** Campus Crusade Christ, black campus staff, 1971-72; Wheaton Col, minority student adv, 1973-77; Great Comn Community Church, founder, pastor, 1978-83; Detroit Afro-Am Mission Inc, consult, 1979-80; J Allen Caldwell Schs, admin, 1979-81; William Tyndale Col, fac mem, 1982-87, assoc vpres urban acad affairs; Inst Black Family Develop, pres, currently. **Orgs:** Nat Religious Broadcasters; Christian Mgt Asn. **Honors/Awds:** Achievement Award & Minority Student Award, Wheaton Col, 1974; Outstanding Young Men of America, 1980-81; Missions Leadership Award from Destiny, 1987; Leadership Development National Black Evangelical Asn, 1988.amily: A Christian Legacy, film. **Business Phone:** (313)493-9962.

PARKER, PAUL E
School administrator. **Personal:** Born Oct 23, 1935, Jenkins Bridge, VA; son of Edward L and E Alma Logan; married Ann Withers; children: Paul Jr & Kenneth. **Educ:** NC A&T State Univ, BSME, 1961; State Univ New York Buffalo, MSME, 1969. **Career:** Sch Administrator (retired); Bell Aerosystems, stress analyst, 1961-67; NC A&T State Univ, asst prof mech engineering, 1967-73, asst dean engineering, 1971-73; Univ Ill, asst dean & dir morrill engineering prog. **Orgs:** Engineering dir, NC A&T State Univ, 1970-73; pres, Nat Asn Minority Engineering Prog Adminr, 1985; consult, Battelle Lab, 1984; bd dirs, Urban League Champaign Co, 1983-90; bd trustees, Mt Olive Baptist Church, 1980-; chmn adv comn, Unit 4 Sch, 1975-78; bd dir, GEM, 1986-; ed, ASEE CIP newsletter, 1989-; Pi Tau Sigma Hon Soc; Tau Beta Pi Hon Soc. **Honors/Awds:** Vincent Bendix Minorities Engineering, Am Soc Engineering Educ, 1990; Black Engineer of the Year,

US Black Engineer, 1991, Promotion Higher Educ; 2007 STAR Award for Educator of the Year, Univ Ill. **Military Serv:** AUS, sp3 instr engrs sch, 1955-57.

PARKER, PAULA JAI
Actor. **Personal:** Born Aug 19, 1969, Cleveland, OH; married Forrest Martin. **Educ:** Howard Univ, BA. **Career:** TV series: "The Apollo Comedy Hour", 1992; "Townsend Television", 1993; Cosmic Slop, 1994; "Roc", 1994; "Pointman", 1995; "The Wayans Bros", 1995-96; "The Weird Al Show", 1997; "The Parent 'Hood", 1997; Riot, 1997; "Cosby", 1997; Always Outnumbered?, 1998; "NYPD Blue", 1998; "Snoops", 1999-2000; "Touched by an Angel", 2000; "The Proud Family", 2001-05; "Express Yourself", 2001; "I Love the '80s Strikes Back", 2003; "My Coolest Years", 2004; "The Shield", 2004; "Lilo & Stitch: The Series",2005; "CSI: Miami", 2005; "CSI: Crime Scene Investigation", 2006; "Side Order of Life", 2007; "Baisden After Dark", 2007; Something with Bite, 2009; "Fear Itself", 2009; Films: Friday, 1995; Tales from the Hood, 1995; Don't Be a Menace to South Central While Drinking Your Juice in the Hood, 1996; Get on the Bus, 1996; Riot, 1997; Sprung, 1997; Always Outnumbered, 1998; Woo, 1998; Why Do Fools Fall In Love, 1998; The Breaks, 1999; 30Years to Life, 2001; High Crimes, 2002; Phone Booth, 2002; Love Chronicles, 2003; My Baby's Daddy, 2004; She Hate Me, 2004; Hustle & Flow,2005; The Proud Family Movie, 2005; Animal, 2005; Idle wild, 2006; The Genius Club, 2006; Cover, 2007; Angels Can't Help But Laugh, 2007; So You Want Michael Madsen?, 2008. **Business Addr:** Actress, c/o William Morris Agency, 1 William Morris Pl, Beverly Hills, CA 90212, **Business Phone:** (310)859-4000.*

PARKER, RAY, JR.
Singer, television producer, songwriter. **Personal:** Born May 1, 1954, Detroit, MI; children: 4. **Career:** Singer, music producer, actor; Raydio, mem, 1977-; Albums: Ray dio, 1978; Rock On, 1979; Two Places at the Same Time, 1980; A Woman Needs Love,1981; Greatest Hits, 1982; The Other Woman, 1982; Woman Out of Control, 1983; Chart busters, 1984; Sex & the Single Man, 1985; After Dark, 1987; The Best of Ray Parker Jr. & Raydio, 1990; I Love You Like You Are, 1991; Two Places at the Same Time, 1993; Greatest Hits, 1993; The Best of Ray Parker Jr., 1999; Ghost busters: The Encore Collection, 1999; The Heritage Collection, 2000; Featuring Ghost busters, 2004; The Best of Ray Parker Jr, 2004; I'm Free!, 2006; Singles: "Jack & Jill", 1978; "Is This A Love Thing", 1978; "You Can't Change That", 1979; "More Than One Way To Love A Woman", 1979; "Two Places At The Same Time", 1980; "For Those Who Like To Groove", 1980; "A Woman Needs Love (Just Like You Do)", 1981; "That Old Song", 1981; "It's Your Night", 1981; "The Other Woman", 1982; "Let Me Go", 1982; "It's Our Own Affair", 1982; "Bad Boy", 1983; The People Next Door", 1983; "I Still Can't Get Over Loving You", 1983; "Woman Out Of Control", 1984; "Ghost busters", 1984; "Jamie", 1984; Girls Are More Fun", 1985; "One Sunny Day/Dueling Bikes From Quicksilver", 1986; I Don't Think That Man Should Sleep Alone", 1987; "Over You", 1988; "Than It", 1989; "The Past", 1990; "All I'm Missing Is You", 1990; Films: Up town Saturday Night, 1974; Enemy Territory, 1987; Disorderlies, 1987; TV series:"Berrenger's", 1985; The Kid Who Loved Christmas, 1990; Ray dio Music Corp,owner, currently. **Honors/Awds:** BAFTA Film Award, 1985. **Business Phone:** (818)225-2412.*

PARKER, RIDDICK
Football player. **Personal:** Born Nov 20, 1972, Emporia, VA. **Educ:** Univ NC, hist. **Career:** San Diego Chargers, 1995; Seattle Sea hawks, defensive tackle, 1997-2000; New England Patriots, 2001; Baltimore Ravens, 2002-03; San Francisco49ers, defensive tackle, 2004.

PARKER, STAFFORD W
Government official. **Personal:** Born Sep 12, 1935, Kansas City, MO; son of Cato and Erma Thurston Freeman; married Anita McBride, Aug 17, 1963; children: Monique V Parker & Dana V Parker. **Educ:** Univ Kans, Lawrence, KS, BA, 1958, LLB, 1963. **Career:** Government official (retired); City Lawrence, KS, probation Offr, 1962; Travelers Insurance Co Agency, Cleveland, OH & Oakland, CA, claims examiner, adjuster, 1963-66; San Francisco Redevelop Agency, San Francisco, CA, admin asst to proj dir, 1966-67, asst bus relocation supvr, 1967-68, salvage section coordr, 1967-68, community servs supvr, 1968; Fresno Redevelop Agency, Fresno, CA, proj Mgr gen neighborhood renewal area, 1968-70, asst dir, 1970-77; City Fresno, asst dir Housing & Community Develop Dept, 1977-82, asst dir Develop Dept, 1982-88, dir Housing & Community Develop Dept, 1988-91; Econ Develop Agency, City San Bernardino, dep dir, 1991-94; City Lancaster, redevelop dir & housing authority dir, 1995-2002. **Orgs:** Nat Asn Advan Colored People, 1968-; Nat Asn Housing & Redevelop Offs, 1975-; pres, Black Lawyers Asn Fresno,1986-89; pres, Boys Club, West Fresno Chap, 1979-81. **Honors/Awds:** Hon Year, Govt Category, NAACP, 1988; Recognition Award for Work With Youth, Boys Club Am, 1981. **Military Serv:** AUS, Spc 4, 1958-60; received Good Conduct Medal.

PARKER, DR. STEPHEN A.
Educator, consultant. **Personal:** Born Jan 1, 1945, Chicago, IL; son of Ilena Parker; married Diana Louise; children: Stephen A II & Daniel Edmond. **Educ:** Ill Teacher Col S, BS, 1965; Chicago State Col, MS, 1970; North western Univ Evanston, PhD, 1974; Ill State Brd Cert Coun; Nat Brd Cert (NCC); Clin Cert Forensic Counr, Am Col Cert Counr, 2000. **Career:** Educator (retired), consultant; Chicago Brd Educ, teacher, 1965-70, recreational instr, 1966-70; Chicago State Univ, instr psychol, 1970-74, from asst to dir financial aid, 1970-74, from asst to assoc prof psychol, 1978-83, prof psychol, 1983, dean admis & records, 1983-86, full prof psychol, 1983-2003; consult, currently. **Orgs:** Affiliate Henry Horner Chicago Boys Club, 1957-; Am Psychol Assn, 1974-; Phi Delta Kappa, 1975-; Natl Res Coun, Ford Found; panel mem, doctoral fel, 1987; Int Coun Educ Teachers, 1987-; Ill Coun Asn. **Honors/Awds:** Black Studs Psychol Assn, 1975; Chicago Urban League Achievement Award,1976; Spec Teaching Recognition Award, Chicago State Univ, 1977; Natl Assn Bahamian Cosmetologists, 1979; Appreciation Award, Bus Educ Stud Assn CSU, 1982; Distinguished Alumni Award Crane HS Hall Fame, 1985; Special Guest Speaker Award, 1986; Distinguished Service Award, Henry Horner Boys & Girls Club, 1987; Distinguished West sider Award, West side Org, 1988; Appreciation Award, Crane High Sch, 1990; Volunteer Award, Tougaloo Alumni Assn, Chicago Chapter, 1990; Alumni of the Yr, Boys & Girls Clubs Am, 1991; Faculty Excellence Award, Chicago State Univ, 1992; Certificate of Apppreciation, Black Stud Psychol Assn, 1996; Recognition Award, Natl Coun Negro Women, 1997; Special Award, Sunshine Chapter 116, OESPHA, 2000.

PARKER, THOMAS EDWIN, III
Manager. **Personal:** Born Dec 11, 1944. **Educ:** Princeton Univ, MPA, 1971; Howard Univ, BA, 1967; Woodrow Wilson Sch Pub & Int Affairs. **Career:** Wash Concentrated Employ Prog, prog coordr, 1967-69; City Coun DC, legis asst, 1971-74; Am Soc Pub Admin Wash, dir progs, 1974-76; Stand Oil Co, prog coordr, pub & govt affairs, 1985. **Orgs:** NAACP; Int City Mgt Asn; Urban League; Opportunities Industrialization Ctr, NJ; admin prog develop consult, Ghana W Africa. **Honors/Awds:** Woodrow Wilson Fel; Pub Affairs Internship; Outstanding Young Men of America, 1972.

PARKER, VAUGHN ANTOINE
Football player. **Personal:** Born Jun 5, 1971, Buffalo, NY. **Educ:** Univ Calif, sociol. **Career:** Football player (retired); San Diego Chargers, tackle, 1994-2003; Wash Redskins, 2004.

PARKER, VERNON B
Lawyer, consultant. **Personal:** Born Nov 16, 1959, Houston, TX; son of Lillie Mae Parker; married Lisa Farringer, Apr 27, 1991; children: Sonya Zepeda & Ian Bernard. **Educ:** Bilingual & Cult Inst, Cuernavaca, Mexico, 1980; Calif State Univ, Long Beach, BS, 1983; Georgetown Univ, JD, 1988. **Career:** Rockwell Int, financial analyst, 1983-85; US Off Personnel Mgt, counr dir policy, 1989-91, gen coun, 1992; White House, spec asst pres, 1992-93; Kenny Rogers Roasters Chicago, vpres, 1993-94; Multinational Legal Serv, partner, 1994-; Parian Int, pres & chief exec officer; Parker, Farringer, Parker, atty, currently; Belsante Int LLC, pres & chief exec officer; Calvary Church, interim sr pastor; USDA, asst secy civil rights, 2003; VBP Group LLC, pres & chief exec officer, currently. **Orgs:** Nat Bar Asn, 1991-; DC Bar, 1989-; Va Bar Asn, 1995; Stud Bar Asn; vpres, Georgetown Univ Law Ctr, 1986-87. **Honors/Awds:** Foreign Language Scholar recipient, 1980; Outstanding Leader, Georgetown Univ Law Ctr, 1988, Outstanding Tutor, 1988. **Special Achievements:** Editor-in-chief, Georgetown American Criminal Law Review; Author, "Annual Survey of White-Collar Crime Attorney Client Privilege," American Criminal Law Review, Winter 1986-1987; Selected by President to represent US at swearing in of President of Ghana, 1993; First ever Assistant Secretary for Civil Rights at the United States Department of Agriculture. **Business Addr:** President, Chief Executive Officer, VBP Group LLC, 740 15th St NW Third Fl, Washington, DC 20250, **Business Phone:** (202)399-7921.

PARKER, DR. WALTER GEE
Physician. **Personal:** Born Feb 11, 1933, Branchville, VA; son of Roosevelt and Theresa; married Henri Mae Smith; children: Jennifer L, Walter G Jr & Brian K. **Educ:** Hampton Inst, BS, 1955; Meharry Medical Col, MD, 1962; Univ Mich, MPH, 1967. **Career:** Physician (retired); Univ Mich, Ann Arbor, MI, instr pediatrics, 1966-69; Univ Mich, Sch Pub Health, res assoc, 1967-69; Wayne County Health Dept, pub health physician, 1969-75; Univ Mich, Ann Arbor, MI, clinical instr pediatrics, 1969-; Southwest Detroit Hosp, vpres med affairs, 1975-86; W Wayne Correctional Facility, State Mich Dept Corr, med dir, 1986-2000. **Orgs:** Am Public Health Asn, 1967-, Am Acad Pediatrics, 1973-, Detroit Med Soc, 1975-, Wayne Co Med Soc, 1975-. **Honors/Awds:** Delta Omega Pub Health Honorary Soc, 1967-; Bd Certified Am Bd Pediatrics, 1971. **Special Achievements:** Article "Michigan Rheumatic Fever Study," in Michigan Med, 1969. **Military Serv:** AUS, sp-3, 1956-58; Good Conduct Medal. **Home Addr:** 3626 Deerfield Pl, Ann Arbor, MI 48103.

PARKER, DR. WILLIAM C, JR.
President (Organization), chief executive officer. **Personal:** Born Apr 16, 1939, Mt Gilead, NC; son of William Carter Sr and Vallie Simon; married Markethia Baldwin; children: Kamala O & Keisha D. **Educ:** NC A&T State Univ, BS, 1961, MS, 1965; Univ NC, Chapel Hill, med, 1967; Ind Univ, 1971. **Career:** Piedmont Develop Corp, founder, pres & chief exec officer, 1974; Shepargib Foods Inc, Burger King Franchise Greensboro & Winston-Salem, founder, pres & chief exec officer, 1976-84; Wilpar Develop Corp, founder, pres & chief exec officer, 1977; Wilpar Construct Co, founder, pres & chief exec officer, 1977; Parker Brothers Restaurant, founder, pres & chief exec officer, 1980; Wilpar Corp, founder, pres & chief exec officer, 1983; Southeastern Develop Group, founder, 1985; Joint Ctr Econ Develop, founder, 1985. **Orgs:** Omega Psi Phi Frat, 1963; Phylaxis Soc, 1975; Nat Restaurant Asn, 1976; Univ NC Chapel Hill Alumni Asn, 1977; Nat Bd Realtors, 1979-; adv bd, Carolina Peacemaker Newspaper, 1980; Greensboro Bd Realtors, 1979; dep grand master, Prince Hall Grand Lodge NC Jurisdictions, 1980-; secy, A&T Univ Found Inc, 1982; bd dirs, Found Greater Greensboro, 1983; The Greensboro Conversation Club, 1985-, Greensboro Mens Club, 1985; chmn, NC A&T State Univ Bd Trustees, 1985; Beta Epsilon Boule Sigma Pi Phi Fraternity, 1986; Greensboro Nat Bank Adv Bd, 1986; vpres, NC Black Leadership Caucus, 1986; bd trustees, chmn long range planning comt, Shiloh Baptist Church, 1986; Nat Asn Advan Colored People; Greensboro Merchants Asn; Grand Master, Prince Hall Grand Lodge, 1987-94. **Honors/Awds:** James T Isler Community Service Award, Family C Serv Greater Greensboro, 1982; Order of the Long Leaf Pine, Gov James B Hunt, 1985; Economic Development Award, Nat Asn Advan Colored people, 1985; Outstanding Alumnus Award, Nat Assoc Higher Educ, 1985; Levi Coffin Award, Greensboro Area Chamber Com, 1986. **Military Serv:** USY.

PARKER, WILLIAM HAYES, JR.
Movie director. **Personal:** Born May 2, 1947, Mt Vernon, NY; married Yvonne Kelly; children: Eric Hayes, Steven Lee & Stella Cailan. **Educ:** Univ Cincinnati, 1965-66; Macomb Co Col, 1967-69; Los Angeles City Col, 1973-75. **Career:** EUE Screen Gems, prod mgr, 1977-78; New Genesis Prods, producer, 1978-79; BAV Inc, producer & ld, 1980-82; BPP, dir & producer, 1982; Renge Films Inc, dir & producer, currently. **Orgs:** C's Fund Defense. **Military Serv:** USAF, sgt, 1966-70. **Business Addr:** Director, Producer, Renge Films Inc, 8400 DeLongpre Ave Suite 212 W, Los Angeles, CA 90069, **Business Phone:** (213)656-5941.

PARKER KODJOE, NICOLE ARI (NIKKI KODJOE)
Actor. **Personal:** Born Oct 7, 1970, Baltimore, MD; daughter of Donald and Susan; married Boris Kodjoe, May 21, 2005; children: Sophie Tei Naaki Lee & Nicolas Neruda Kodjoe; married Joseph Falasca, Jan 1, 2001 (divorced 2001). **Educ:** NY Univ, Tisch Sch Arts, drama, 1993. **Career:** Paramount Hotel, phone operator; Baltimore Actors Theatre, Washington Ballet Co, Signature Theatre Co, Metropolitan Playhouse, and the New Group, stage actor, 1990-; film actor, 1995-; television actor, 2000-; Films: The Incredibly True Adventure of Two Girls in Love, 1995; Stonewall, 1995; Boogie Nights, 1997; The End of Violence, 1997; Spark, 1998; The Adventures of Sebastian Cole, 1998; 200 Cigarettes, 1999; Mute Love, 1999; Mirar Mirror, 1999; Loving Jezebel,1999; Blue Streak, 1999; A Map of the World, 1999; Harlem Aria, 1999; A Map of the World, 1999; Blue Streak, 1999; Dancing in September, 2000; Remember the Titans, 2000; Brown Sugar, 2002; King's Ransom, 2005; Welcome Home, Roscoe Jenkins, 2008; TV series: "Divas", 1995; "Rebound: The Legendof Earl The Goat Manigault", 1996; "SUBWAY Stories: Cosby", 1996-2000; "SUBWAYStories: Tales from the Underground", 1997; "Exiled", 1998; "MindPrey", 1999; Cosby, 1999-2000; "The Loretta Claiborne Story", 2000; "Soul Food", 2000; "CSI-:Crime Scene Investigation", 2000; "All of Us", 2003;"Second Time Around", 2004-05. **Honors/Awds:** Special Award for outstanding work as an actress, Urban World Film Festival, 1999. **Special Achievements:** Appeared in shows with Naked Angels, Metropolitan Playhouse & Circle Rep Lab. **Business Addr:** Actress, Showtime Networks Inc, 1633 E Broadway, New York, NY 10019, **Business Phone:** (212)708-1600.*

PARKER-ROBINSON, D LAVERNE
Executive. **Personal:** Born Jan 14, 1949, New York, NY; daughter of Tommie B (deceased) and Emma Smith; married Guy, Aug 28, 1990. **Educ:** Bernard M Baruch Col, City Univ New York, BA, 1974; Fordham Univ, MSW, 1978. **Career:** Harlem Dowling Children's Servs, caseworker, 1974-77; Greater New York Fund Tri-State United Way, tech asst internal, 1977-78; Abraham & Straus Dept Stores, coordr pub affairs, 1978-79, asst mgr, comput operator, 1979-81, internal consult, spec proj mgrs, 1981-82, data processing financial controller, 1982-85; Strategic Intelligence Inc, vpres, chief financial officer, prod res, 1985-; New York City Admin Children's Servs, Agency Child Develop, dir social servs & info referral. **Orgs:** Dinner Comt, Randolph Evans Scholar Awards, 1979-; bd mem, Strategic Intelligence Inc, 1985-; Mgt Assist Comt Greater New York Fund United Way, 1985-87; sch vol, New York City Sch Vol Prog, 1986-87; pres, Brooklyn Mgt Club, 1986-87; bd mem, New York Ubran League, Manhattan Br, 1991-94; Nat Asn Social Workers; bd dir, Citizens' Comt C New York, currently. **Honors/Awds:** Distinguish Service Award, Salvation Army Brownsville Corps, 1979. **Business Phone:** (212)673-1800.

PARKER-SAWYERS, PAULA
Government official, administrator. **Personal:** Born in Indianapolis, IN; daughter of Thomas and Dorthea Shelton; mar-

ried James Sawyers, Oct 9, 1982 (deceased); children: Elizabeth, Parker & Patrick. **Educ:** Ball State Univ, Muncie, IN, attended 1971; George Wash Univ, Wash, DC, attended 1972; Purdue Univ, Indianapolis, IN, BA, Polit Sci, 1980. **Career:** LS Ayres & Co, Indianapolis, IN, 1974-78; AT&T, Ind Bell, Indpolis, IN, 1978-85; Browning Investments, Indianapolis, IN, 1985-86; Blue Cross/ Blue Shield, 1986-89; City Indianapolis, Indianapolis, IN, dep mayor; Governor's Off Faith Based & Community Initiatives, exec dir, 2005-08; Nat Campaign Prevent Teen & Unplanned Pregnancy, Wash, DC, dir outreach & partnership, 2008-. **Orgs:** Indianapolis Mus Art; Coalition 100 Black Women; Nat Coun Negro Women; Indianapolis Campaign Healthy Babies; bd dir, Boys & Girls Clubs Indianapolis; bd dir, Christian Theol Sem; bd dir, Pacer's Foundation. **Honors/Awds:** Madame CJ Walker Women of the Year, Ctr Leadership Develop, 1989. **Business Addr:** Director of Outreach & Partnership, National Campaign to Prevent Teen & Unplanned Pregnancy, 1776 Mass Ave NW Suite 200, Washington, DC 20036.

PARKINSON, NIGEL MORGAN
Executive, contractor. **Personal:** Born Aug 26, 1953, Freetown, Sierra Leone; married; children: Nigel Jr & Malcolm. **Educ:** Florida A & M, BS, 1974; Fla State Univ, MSPA, 1975; Leadership Wash, 1992; MIT, Ctr Real Estate, 1993. **Career:** Davis Found, jr exec, 1975-78; Mgt Support Serv, 1978-83; Parkinson Construct, pres, 1983-. **Orgs:** Adv bd, US Gen Serv Adminr, 1991; bd mem & treas, DC Contractors Asn, 1988-93; treas, 1992-94, pres, 1994-, Nat Asn Minority Contractors; US Chamber Com; Masonry Inst. **Honors/Awds:** Excellence Award, DC Contractors Asn, 1991; Contractor of the Year Award, Nat Asn Minority Contractors, 1992; Public Service Award, US Gen Serv, 1993. **Business Addr:** President, Parkinson Construct Co, 3905 Perry St, Brentwood, MD 20722, **Business Phone:** (301)985-6080.

PARKS, DR. ARNOLD GRANT
School administrator. **Personal:** Born Nov 19, 1939, St Louis, MO; son of Noble Grant Parks and Estella Victoria Smith Parks; married Lennette Bogee; children: LaShawn M Hampton, Anna L Holt & Alicia V. **Educ:** Harris Teachers Col, AA, 1959; Wash Univ, BS, 1962; St Louis Univ, MA, 1964, PhD, 1970. **Career:** St Louis Univ, instr, 1964-66; Delta Educ Corp, dep dir, 1966-69; Malone & Hyde Inc, training dir, 1969-71; Memphis State Univ, assoc prof, 1971-76; NSF, fac fel, 1976-79; Ethel Percy Andrus Geront Ctr, fel, 1979; Lincoln Univ, prof sociol; Parks Consult LLC, pres, currently, consult, currently. **Orgs:** Life mem Alpha Phi Alpha; United Methodist Church; Mo E Conf Congregational Develop Team; Am Diabetes Asn; bd trustees, Mo River Regional Libr; bd dir, treas, Mo Sch Religion/Ctr Rural Ministry; bd govs, Capital Region Med Ctr; deleg, Nat White House Conf Aging, 1995; mem, St. Paul UMC. **Honors/Awds:** Numerous other federal and state grants; fel SW Soc Aging, 2002; Sumner High School Hall of Fame. **Special Achievements:** Author: Urban Education: An Annotated Bibliography, Century 21 Publishing Co, 1981; Black Elderly in Rural America: A Comprehensive Study, Wyndham Hall Press, 1988; Aging and Mental Health: Aging in the Heartland, Kendall-Hunt Publishing Co, 1996; published numerous articles in journals. **Home Addr:** 1817 Chelle Ct, Jefferson City, MO 65101, **Home Phone:** (573)635-0725. **Business Addr:** President, Consultant, Parks Consulting LLC, 1817 Chelle Ct, Jefferson City, MO 65101, **Business Phone:** (573)635-0725.

PARKS, BERNARD
Lawyer. **Personal:** Born Jun 10, 1944, Atlanta, GA; married Joyce Williams; children: Bernard Jr. **Educ:** Morehouse Col, BA, 1966; Emory Univ, Sch Law, JD, 1969. **Career:** Patterson Parks Jackson & Howell, ptr, 1973-; Jackson Patterson Parks & Franklin, ptr, 1970-73; Jackson & Handler Assoc, 1970; Jud Elbert Parr Tuttle United Cir Ct Appeals, law clerk, 1969-70; Atlanta Legal Aid Soc Inc, law asst, 1968-69; Sen Horace Ward Atlanta, leg intern, 1968; Aldmn QV Williamson Atlanta City, gov intern, 1967; Ga Supreme Ct; Ga Ct Appeals; US Dist Ct; US Ct Appeals; US Supreme Ct. **Orgs:** Co-chmn, Men Health Comn Young Law Sect; Am Bar Asn; Atlanta Bar Asn; bd dir, Atlanta County Young Law; co-chmn, Ment Health Comn, Ga Bar Asn; vpres, Ga Legal Serv Prog Inc; Gate County Bar Asn; Nat Bar Asn; Law Com Civ Rights under Law; chmn, bd dir, Opp Ind Cent Atlanta; bd dir, Opp Ind Cent Am; chmn, bd mgrs, E Cent Br Butler St Young Men's Christian Asn; bddir, Butler St Young Men's Christian Asn; Gov Ment Health Community Task Force; Met Atlana County Crime & Juv Del; chmn Pri Alloc Com Uni Way Allo Com Comm Sec; Local Govt Task Force Com Atla C C; Atlanta Crim Just Coord Com; bd dir, Big Bros Asn; Atla Bus League; Atla Urban League; Nat Asn Advan Colored People; Am Civ Lib Un; SE Region Bd Young Men's Christian Asn; Atlanta Coal Curr Comm Aff; Omega Psi Phi Fraternity; Phi Alpha Delta Fraternity; Y Men Int. **Honors/Awds:** Outstanding Young Man of Year, Omega Chap; Mr Psi of 1967, Omega Psi Phi Fraternity, Psi Chap, Morehouse Col; WSB Nesmaker Award, 1972; five Outstanding Young Men In 1974. **Business Addr:** 101 Marietta Towers, Atlanta, GA 30303.

PARKS, BERNARD C.
Police chief, city council member. **Personal:** Born Dec 7, 1943, Beaumont, TX; married Bobbie; children: Felicia, Michelle, Trudy, Bernard Jr. **Educ:** Los Angeles City Col, Pepperdine Univ, BS, 1976; Univ Southern Calif, MA, pub admin, 1976; Loyola Univ, Interpersonal & Interracial Relationships, attended 1974; Fed Bureau Invest Nat Acad, attended 1976; Univ Southern Calif, Mgt Policy Inst, cert grad, 1983; Peace Officers Stands & Training Exec Develop Course, cert grad, 1984; Nat Exec Inst, Fed Bureau Invest, cert grad, 1993; New York Police Dept, Comp Stat Conf, cert completion, 1997. **Career:** Los Angeles Police Dept, from police officer to sergeant, 1965-70, lt, 1973, capt, 1977, comdr, 1980, dep chief, 1988, asst chief, 1992, dep chief, 1994, chief police, 1997-02; Bureau Spec Invest, dep chief & comndg officer; Calif State Bar Asn, Judicial Eval Comn, Former Comnr; Los Angeles City Coun, councilman, chmn budget & finance comt, vpres coliseum comn ,2003-. **Orgs:** Int Asn Chiefs Police; Nat Asn Black Law Enforcement Exec; Fed Bureau Invest Nat Acad Asn; founding mem, Oscar Joel Bryant Asn; pres, Drug Abuse Resistance Educ; bd mem, Challenger Boys & Girls Club; Police Exec Res Forum; Metrop Transportation Bd Comnrs, 2005; Nat Asn Advan Colored People. **Business Addr:** Councilman, City of Los Angeles Council District 8, 200 N Spring St room 460, Los Angeles, CA 90012, **Business Phone:** (213)473-7008.

PARKS, DR. DONALD B
Physician. **Personal:** Born Nov 2, 1950, Philadelphia, PA; son of Dewitt and Bertha; married Sharon, Jun 20, 1976; children: Laurie, Drew & Sharon-Candace. **Educ:** Temple Univ, 1968; Jefferson Med Col, Thomas Jefferson Univ, 1973; Mercy Catholic Med Center-Philadelphia, PA, residency, 1978. **Career:** SmithKline-French, group dir clinic invest, 1981-85; Parkstone Med Asn, physician, med dir, 1985-; Temple Univ, assoc prof community med, currently, asst dean, currently, med dir, currently. **Orgs:** Dept Health Educ & Welfare, consult, 1979-82; Health Policy & Manpower Comn, consult, 1980; Philadelphia Police & Fire Dept, consult, 1983; Exec Excellence Prog/National Urban League, bd mem, 1989-92; Am Found for Negro Affairs, bd mem, 1988-; Chmn, Development Comn/Morehouse School of Medicine, 1994-; PA Blue Shield, bd mem, 1994-97. **Honors/Awds:** President James F Carter, Education & Community Involvement, 1980; Alpha Beta Alpha Sorority, Commun Involvement and Services to the Afro-American Historical & Cultural Museum, 1980. **Business Addr:** President, Parkston Medical Associates, 2305 N Broad St, Philadelphia, PA 19132, **Business Phone:** (215)229-2022.

PARKS, EDWARD Y
Lawyer. **Personal:** Born Feb 5, 1951, Thomson, GA; son of Roy L Sr; married Sequoyah, May 25, 1975; children: Akil-Dabe T & Alkebu S. **Educ:** Otterbein Coll, BA, 1973; Howard Univ, JD, 1979. **Career:** Ohio Pub Interest campaign, assoc dir, 1979-81; Legal Aid Soc, atty, 1981-83; Pub Utilities Comn, atty examr, 1983-86; Ohio Dept Health, legal coun, 1986-89; Edward Y Parks Law Off, atty, pres & chief exec officer, 1989-; Pvt Pract, lawyer, currently. **Orgs:** Nat Asn Advan Colored People, 1979-; Columbus Bar Asn, 1980-; Nat Conf Black Lawyers, 1980-; presiding officer, Asn Juvenile Atty, 1989-; Legal Aid Soc Lawyer Referral, 1989-; Urban League, 1991-; trustee, Shiloh Baptist Church, 1993; Nat Bar Asn, 1993-. **Honors/Awds:** Outstanding Legal Advocate, Welfare Rights, 1983; Community Service Award, Nat Asn Advan Colored People, 1985; Outstanding Service, Softball Prog, Shiloh Baptist Church, 1987 & 1988. **Special Achievements:** Shiloh Baptist Church Plan, 1990; Book of Poems-In Progress. **Business Phone:** (614)252-8111.

PARKS, GEORGE BROOKS. **See Obituaries section.**

PARKS, GILBERT R.
Psychiatrist. **Personal:** Born May 14, 1944, Arcadia, OK; married Jenice L; children: Garmez, Melanese, Ronee. **Educ:** Central State Univ, BS, 1967; Thomas Jefferson Med Col, MD, 1973. **Career:** Topeka St Hosp, psychiatrist; Menninger Found, Topeka; Pvt Prac; psychiatry asst, Univ Okla hosp 1965-67; HEW, psychiatry complete, 1976. **Orgs:** Rancher, 1960-69; Okla State Dept Pub Health, Environ Health Div Water Quality Control, 1967-69; dir, Health Career Progs, Philadelphia, 1970-72; chmn bd, Stud Nat Med Asn, 1972-73; admin consult, adv Student Nat Med Asn; Kans Dist Br, Am Psychiatric Asn; consult Off Health Resources Opp, Health Resources Admin Dept HEW; secy, Nat Asn Post Grad Physicians; bd dirs Boys Club Topeka. **Honors/Awds:** Outstanding Leadership Award, Nat Med Asn; Solomon Fuller Fel, 1975.

PARKS, JAMES CLINTON
Marketing executive. **Personal:** Born May 12, 1944, Kannapolis, NC; married Corine Musgrave; children: Crystal Westray, James III & Shawnda M. **Educ:** Livingstone Col, BS, 1965. **Career:** EI Du Pont, employ supvr, 1965-77; Miller Brewing Co, mgr spec mkt prog, 1977-. **Orgs:** Mem Phi Beta Sigma, 1963-; bd dir, Milwaukee Min Chamber Com, 1983-86, Waukesha County WI Nat Asn Advan Colored People, 1984-86; Frontiers Int, 1987-; bd mem, Fayetteville State Univ Found; bd mem, Cal-Pac Corp Adv Bd. **Honors/Awds:** Order of Long Leaf Pine St NC, 1984; Distinguished Alumnus, Livingstone Col, 1989. **Military Serv:** AUS, 1st lt, 1966-69. **Business Addr:** Manager-Special Marketing Programs, Miller Brewing Co, 3939 W Highland Blvd, Milwaukee, WI 53208, **Business Phone:** (414)931-2000.

PARKS, JAMES EDWARD
Lawyer. **Personal:** Born Mar 22, 1946, Pine Bluff, AR; son of James and Cora; married Gwendolyn Jean Fane, Sep 4, 1965; children: James Jr, Latina, Lisa. **Educ:** Calif State Univ, Fresno, BS, 1972; Harvard Law Sch, JD, 1975. **Career:** Dawson & Ninnis Fresno, CA, atty, 1977-82; San Fernando Val Neighborhood Legal Serv Van Nuys CA, atty, 1975-77; Parks & Smith, Fresno, CA, 1982-89; pvt practice, atty, 1989-. **Orgs:** Fresno Co Bar Asn; Calif State Bar & Asn; Asn Defense Coun; bd dirs, Fresno Co Legal Servs Legan Adv, Black Polit Coun, Fresno, 1980; Fresno City Bar Asn; Fresno Trial Lawyer's Asn; United Black Men; Black Lawyers Asn Fresno; Nat Advan Asn Colroed People; bd mem, Fresno Tomorrow. **Business Addr:** Attorney, 7750 N Fresno St Suite 101, Fresno, CA 93720, **Business Phone:** (559)436-6575.*

PARKS, KENNETH
Executive. **Career:** United Parcel Serv, vpres hr, proj mgr, currently. **Orgs:** Bd mem, ACT-SO; BC Chamber Com. **Business Addr:** Project Manager, United Parcel Service, 55 Glenlake Pkwy NE, Atlanta, GA 30328, **Business Phone:** (770)698-9703.

PARKS, PAUL
Executive. **Personal:** Born May 7, 1923, Indianapolis, IN; son of Cleab and Hazel; married Virginia Loftman; children: Paul, Pamela & Stacey. **Educ:** Purdue Univ, BS, 1949; Mass Inst Technol, post grad, 1958; Univ Mass, Amherst, MA, DEd (ABD), 1985; Northeastern Univ, Doctor of Engineering, 1994. **Career:** Ind St Highway Comn Indianapolis, 1949-51; Fays Spofford & Thorndike, Boston; Stone & Webster Eng, designer, 1951; Chance Vought Aircraft; missile designer, 1952-53; Pratt & Whitney Aircraft, nuclear engr, 1953-57; Archit & Eng Firm, Boston, partner, 1957-67; Boston Model City Admin, admin, 1968-75; Commonwealth Mass, secy educ affairs, 1975-; Tufts Univ, Sch Eng, Medford, Mass, prof, 1976-90; Paul Parks & Assocs Inc, pres, 1979-; Mayors Comn Admin Justice, consult gen acct off. **Orgs:** Chmn, Urban Affairs Com, Mass Fed Fair Housing & Equal Rights, 1961-67; Comn Educ & Coun, 1961-73; pres, Comn Educ Develop Inc, 1968-74; adult leader, Youth Progs Roxbury UMCA; trustee, Peter Bent Brigham Hosp; bd dir, Mass Planned Parenthood Asn; Mass Mental Health Asn; Mass Soc Prev Blindness; Boston Col, Upward Bound Prog; Am Soc Civil Engrs; Nat Soc Prof Engrs; Nat Acad Pub Admin; Nat Asn Advan Colored People; Nat Bd Am Dem Action, 1970-74; St Bd Am Dem Action, 1970-74; Steering Comt, Educ Comn States; pres, Bd Libraries, City Boston, Mass; educr, Commonwealth States, 1976-80; Zoning Bd Appeals, City Boston, 1983-; pres, Boston Pub Lib, 1987-93; chmn, Boston Sch Comt, 1992-95. **Honors/Awds:** Outstanding Service Award, Goodwill Indust; Honorary Doctorate, Northeastern Univ, 1997; Honarary Degree, Franconia Col; Wallanberg Award, 2000; Raoul Wallenberg Award, 2000; Distinguished Engineer Alumnus, Purdue Univ Sch Eng, 2001. **Special Achievements:** Author: "Racism", "Elitism", "Professionalism Barriers to Community Mental Health", 1976; Appointed by Pres Carter to Pres Comn on Educ Progs for Women; represented Pres Clinton at 50th anniversary liberation Belgium in WW II; guest & prinipal speaker, Haitian Liberation Day, Reggio Amoli, Italy, 2002. **Military Serv:** AUS, first sgt, 1942-46. **Home Addr:** 78 Woodhaven St, Mattapan, MA 02126. **Business Addr:** President, Paul Parks and Associates, 100 Boylston St, Boston, MA 02116.

PARKS, SONIA A.
Executive director. **Career:** Urban health Initiative, fel, 1999-02; Blue Cross Blue Shield Mich, assoc med dir, Provider Rels Admin, sr assoc med dir.

PARKS, SUZAN-LORI
Playwright, educator. **Personal:** Born Jan 1, 1964?, Kentucky; married Paul Oscher. **Educ:** Mt Holyoke Col, MA, BA, eng & ger lit (Phi Beta Kappa), 1985. **Career:** Playwright & educator; Drama studio, London, mem, 1986; Pratt Inst, NY, guest lectr, 1988; Univ Mich, Ann Arbor, guest lectr, 1990; Yale Univ, New Haven, Conn, guest lectr, 1990-91; NY Univ, guest lectr, 1990-91; Eugene Lang Col, NY, playwriting prof, 1990; New Sch Social Res, NY, writer-in-residence, 1991-92; Guggenheim fel, 2000; Calif Inst Arts, Valencia, dir, 2000; Yale Sch Drama, New Haven, assoc artist; Wilma Theater, Philadelphia, Pa, playwriting residency; Plays: The Sinner's Place, 1984; Imperceptible Mutabilities in the Third Kingdom, 1989; Betting on the Dust Commander, 1990; The Death of the Last Black Man in the Whole Entire World, 1990; Pickling, 1990; Third Kingdom, 1990; Locomotive, 1991; Girl 6, 1996; Devotees in the Garden of Love, 1992; The America Play, 1994; Venus, 1996; In The Blood, 1999; Fucking A, 2000; Topdog/Underdog, 2001; Their Eyes Were Watching God, 2005; 365 Days/365 Plays, 2006; RAY CHARLES LIVE! - A New Musical, 2007; The Great Debaters, 2007. **Honors/Awds:** Numerous honors & awards including Obie, 1990; Playwriting Fellow, Nat Endowment Arts, 1990, 1991; Whiting Writers' Award, 1992; W Alton Jones Grant Kennedy Center Fund for New Am Plays, 1994; Lila-Wallace Reader's Digest Award, 1995; Obie, 1996; John D & Catherine T MacArthur genius grant, 2001; Pulitzer Prize for Drama, 2002; Eugene McDermott Award, Coun Arts, Mass Inst Technol, 2006; hon doctorates, Brown Univ. **Special Achievements:** Novel: Getting Mother's Body, 2003; TIME magazine's One of 100 Innovators for the Next New Wave. **Business Addr:** Playwright, Steven Barclay Agency, 12 Wern Ave, Petaluma, CA 94952, **Business Phone:** (707)773-0654.

PARKS, THELMA REECE
Government official, educator. **Personal:** Born in Muskogee, OK; daughter of Thomas and Estella Reece; married; children: Dia Denise Parks Carter. **Educ:** Langston Univ, BS, 1945; Univ Okla, MS, 1955; Cent State Univ, prof cert, 1963, additional study, 1980-81. **Career:** Educator (retired), Board member; Dunbar & Truman Elem Schs, teacher, 1951-61; Douglass High Sch, english teacher & dept head, 1961-70, counsr, 1970-71; US Grant High Sch, counsr & dept head, 1973; Okla City Housing Authority, comnr, 1977-84; Okla City Bd Educ, pres; Okla City Pub Schs, teacher; Okla City Pub Schs Bd Educ, bd mem, currently. **Orgs:** Pres, Okla City Guidance Asn, 1976-77; life mem, Nat Educ Asn; OEA COA; McFarland Br, YWCA, 1973-; adv, Capitol Improvement Plan, Okla City, 1975-; Adv Com Black Family; NE YMCA; Alpha Kappa Alpha Sorority; NAACP; Urban League; bd dirs, Urban League Guild; Womens Day speaker, Tabernacle Baptist Church, 1992, Wildwood Christian Ch, 1978; chmn, Blue Ribbon Comn Fund Raising, 1982-86; bd dir, YWCA, 1983-86; secy, Okla City Langston Alumni, 1986-88; panelist, Okla State Dept of Ed Conf on Educ, 1987; bd mem, Langston Univ Alumni Assoc, 1987-90; task force comn, OEA improving schs Okla, 1987-; Nat Sorority of Phi Delta Kappa; Okla Sch Bd Asn, bd dirs, 1992; bd dirs, Black Caucus, 1992; panelist, Urban League Equal Opportunity Day, 1991; Okla City Educ Round Table, 1991-; pres, Nat Sorority Phi Delta Kappa, gamma Epsilon Chap, Ok, 1997; bd dirs, Black Caucus, Nat Sch Bds Asn. **Honors/Awds:** Nat Black Col Alumni, Hall of Fame, inductee, Atlanta, GA, 1991; Lady of Distinction, Nu Vista Club, 1991; Okla Achiever's Award, 1989; Soror of the Yr, Alpha Kappa Alpha Sorority, 1990; Soror of the Yr, Phi Delta Kappa, 1990; Volunteer of the Yr Award, Urban League of Okla City, 1990; Distinguished Alumni, Langston Univ, 1990; Men of Distinction, Outstanding Citizen, 1991; Okla Black Pub Adminr Award, 1992; Top Ladies of Distinction, Outstanding Achievement Award, 1997. **Special Achievements:** Elementary Sch named in her honor, Okla City, 1997; First African-Am female trustee, Faith Mem Bapt Ch, 1975; first African-Am female mem, Kappa Delta Pi, Gamma Chap, Univ Okla, 1955; Langston University Distinguished Alumnus Award; Whos Who Among Black Americans; Whos Who Among Women in the World; Whos in America and Urban League Volunteer of the Year Award; Outstanding Public Service Award. **Home Phone:** (405)427-2053. **Business Addr:** Board Member, Oklahoma City Public Schools, 900 N Klein St, Oklahoma City, OK 73119.

PARMALEE, BERNARD A. (BERNIE PARMALEE)
Football coach, football player. **Personal:** Born Sep 16, 1967, Jersey City, NJ; married Angela; children: Nakia Marie, Torian & Tre Bernard. **Educ:** Ball State Univ, bus admin, 1991. **Career:** Football player (retired), Football coach; Ball State Univ, running back, 1987-90; Miami Dolphins, running back, 1992-98, asst spec teams coach, 2002, asst spec teams coach & offensive asst coach, 2003, tight end coach, 2004; New York Jets, running back1999-2000; Univ Notre Dame, tight ends coach & spec teams coach, 2005-. **Honors/Awds:** MAC Freshman of the Year. **Business Addr:** Tight Ends Coach, Special Teams Coach, University of Notre Dame, 100 Univ Village Apt, Notre Dame, IN 46556-5664, **Business Phone:** (574)631-5000.

PARMALEE, BERNIE. See PARMALEE, BERNARD A.

PARMS, EDWIN L.
Lawyer. **Personal:** Born Jun 18, 1937; son of Ophelia Parms and Johnson Parms; married Margaret; children: Stephanie, Deborah. **Educ:** Univ Akron, BA, 1960, JD, 1965. **Career:** Parms, Purnell & Gilbert, atty, 1965; Akron Pub Schs, teacher, 1960-65; St Univ Akron, co-coun; pvt prac atty, currently. **Special Achievements:** First black chosen Young Man of Year, Akron Jr C C. **Military Serv:** AUS, lt. **Business Addr:** Attorney, 209 S Main St, Akron, OH 44308-1136, **Business Phone:** (330)376-6136.*

PARNELL, ARNOLD W
Executive. **Personal:** Born Jan 21, 1936, Philadelphia, PA; son of Jesie Parnell and Eva; married Thelma; children: Steven, Paula & Michael. **Educ:** Villanova Univ, BSCE, 1957; USC, MSCE, 1962; USC & UCLA. **Career:** N Am Aviation, sr res engr, 1957-62; Nellson Candies, owner & founder, 1962-68; TRW Syst Group, div staff mgr, 1962-82, dir indust res ctr, 1982-86; P&L Mgt Syst, corp dir, 1972-; ELI Mgt Corp, gen mgr, 1986; ADP & Assoc, pres; Forte Comput Easy Inc, dir, currently. **Orgs:** Am Inst Aeronaut & Astronaut, 1967-; assoc fel, AIAA, 1970; Prof Lic Mech Engineering; Small Bus Develop Adv Bd. **Home Addr:** 2506 13 Ave, Los Angeles, CA 90018. **Business Addr:** Director, Forte Computer Easy Inc.

PARNELL, JOHN V, III
Executive, president (organization), manager. **Personal:** Born Oct 4, 1944, Boston, MA; married Patricia Meehan; children: Elizabeth, Monica & Andrea. **Educ:** Univ Mass, BS, 1966. **Career:** General Foods Corp, sr food tech, 1966-72; Latouraine Bickford's, new prod develop mgr, 1972; Miralin Co, prod develop mgr, 1972-74; Gen Foods Corp, lab mgr, sr lab mgr, 1974-90; Kraft Gen Foods, group dir, 1990-95; Kraft Foods, group dir, 1995-99, res & develop, consult. **Orgs:** Pres, AEPI Frat, 1965, vpres, Class 66; Inst Food Technologist; bd dir, 1970-80pres, 1975-77, vpres, 1973-75, Univ Mass Alumni Asn; Univ Mass Found Inc, 1977-80; past mem Sportsmens Club Greater Boston. **Honors/Awds:** Outstanding Senior Award, 1966; Distinguished Service to University Award, Univ Mass, 1977; Black Achievers in Industry Award, YMCA Greater New York, Harlem Br, 1979. **Business Addr:** 5 Libra Lane, Mashpee, MA 02649, **Business Phone:** (508)477-7120.

PARNELL, WILLIAM CORNELLUS, JR.
Accountant. **Personal:** Born Feb 10, 1940, Burton, SC; married Carolyn E Howard; children: Wanda, Debra & Monique. **Educ:** Howard Univ, BA, 1962; Mil Comptrollership; honor cert, 1969; Univ Detroit, MBA 1974; Wash Col Bus. **Career:** Defense Contract Audit Agency, Alexandria VA, auditor, 1965-66; Citizens Crusade Against Poverty, Wash, comptroller, 1966-68; Ford Mtr Co Birmingham MI, fin anal, 1968-74; Vickers Inc, bus anal, 1974-86; practicing acct & tax practr; Independent Fin Serv Inc, pres, chief finance dir, currently. **Orgs:** Nat Asn Advan Colored People, 1980; treasurer, Hope United Methodist Church, 1990-93; vice chmn, fin, Hope UM Church, 1994-95; MI Ind Accts Asn; Nat Asn Accts; Inst Mgt Accts; Nat Black MBA Asn; Asn MBA Exec; Nat Asn Black Accts; Nat Soc Enrolled Fed Tax Agents; treas, vpres, Howard Univ; Alumni Club Detroit; Omega Psi Phi Frat; Luth Int Mens League; panelist Detroit Ind Adv Group. **Honors/Awds:** Community Award Bus Leadership, City Detroit, 1990; Alumni Award Outstanding Commitment, Howard Univ, 1992; Outstanding Leadership, Hope United Methodist Church, 1993. **Military Serv:** AUS, lt, 1962-64; USAR, capt, 1964-75; Mil Hon Ribbon, 1961; Army QM Theater Operations, Ft Lee, VA, 1967; Lett Commendation Command Post Exercise; Fin & Acct Officer, AUS Reserve, Detroit, Mich. **Home Addr:** 17225 Sherfield Pl, Southfield, MI 48075-1968, **Home Phone:** (248)557-4672. **Business Addr:** President, Chief Financial Director, Independent Financial Services Inc, 19750 James Couzens Dr, Detroit, MI 48235, **Business Phone:** (313)342-1880.

PARRIS, REV. ALVIN, III
Clergy. **Personal:** Born Sep 23, 1951, Washington, DC; son of Alvin Jr and L Edith Simmons; married Debra Bryant, Jul 16, 1976; children: Benjamin James, Christopher Alvin, Jonathan Gregory & Cherise Danielle. **Educ:** Eastman Sch Music, Rochester, NY, BMusEd, 1973. **Career:** Rochester City Sch Dist, John Marshall High Sch, Rochester, NY, orchestra dir, 1973-79; Parris Community Sch Performing Arts, Rochester, NY, dir, 1975; Univ Rochester, Rochester, NY, gospel choir dir, music instr, 1976-; Golden Heights Christian Ctr, Brockport, NY, music pastor, 1987-90; Syracuse Symphony Orchestra, Syracuse, NY, dir, Project 2000 prog, composer, conductor, 1990-; New Life Fel, Rochester, NY, assoc pastor, music minister, 1990-. **Orgs:** Music dir, Greater-Rochester Martin Luther King Festival Comn, 1986-; Rochester Rotary Club, 1987-89; New Life Ministries Inc. **Honors/Awds:** Community Service Award, Saint Monica School, 1986; Artistic Achievement Award, Colgate-Rochester Divinity School, 1987. **Business Addr:** Music Director, New Life Ministries, Inc., 330 Wellington Ave, Rochester, NY 14619-1210, **Business Phone:** (585)436-0085.

PARRISH, ALEX L.
Lawyer, college teacher. **Personal:** Born Jan 1, 1955. **Educ:** Howard Univ, BA, 1977; Harvard Univ Law Sch, JD, 1980. **Career:** US Ct Appeals, Sixth Circuit, law clerk, 1980-81; Honingman Miller Schwartz & Cohn LLP, Wash, DC, atty, 1981-85, Mich, partner, 1985-; MichInst Continuing Legal Educ, fac, 1990-. **Orgs:** Pi Sigma Alpha; trustee, Music Hall Ctr Performing Arts; Am Bar Asn; State Bar Mich. **Honors/Awds:** Martindale-Hubbell Award; Listed in The Best Lawyers in America 2008. **Special Achievements:** Listed in the Best Lawyers in America 2007; Michigan's Outstanding Young Business Leaders, Crain's Detroit Business. **Military Serv:** AUS, asst to gen coun, 1981-85. **Business Phone:** (313)465-7000.

PARRISH, ANTHONY W. See PARRISH, TONY.

PARRISH, JAMES NATHANIEL
Insurance executive. **Personal:** Born Feb 3, 1939, Winter Park, FL; son of Amos L and Celeste Colston. **Educ:** Fisk Univ, BA, 1958; Univ Wis, MS, 1960. **Career:** Western & Southern Life Ins Co, asst actuary, 1960-67; Inter-Ocean Insurance Co, vip, actuary, 1967-74; Sun Life Ins Co AME, second vpres, New Bus, 1974-75; Towers, Perrin, Foster & Crosby, consult, 1975-79; Fidelity Mutual Life Ins Co, vpres, actuary, 1979-86; NC Mutual Life Ins Co, sr vpres, actuary, 1986-90; NC Mutual Life Ins Co, exe vpres, 1990-. **Orgs:** Am Acad Actuaries, 1969-; Soc Actuaries, 1971-; Asn NC Life Co. **Business Addr:** Executive Vice President, North Carolina Mutual Life Insurance Company, 411 W Chapel Hill St, Durham, NC 27701, **Business Phone:** (919)682-9201.

PARRISH, JOHN HENRY
Clergy. **Personal:** Born Dec 14, 1924, Clarkdale, AR; married Marie Jones; children: John Jr & Roland. **Educ:** Manassas High Sch, dipl, 1942. **Career:** Hammond Br, Nat Asn Advan Colored People, pres, 1959 & 1972; Third Dist Hammond, councilman 1972-91; First Tabernacle Baptist Church, pastor 1977-. **Special Achievements:** John Henry Parrish was the first Black to serve as a city councilman of Hammond, IN. **Military Serv:** USN seaman first class, 3 yrs. **Home Addr:** 1108 Cleveland St, Hammond, IN 46320. **Business Addr:** Pastor, First Tabernacle Baptist Church, 643 W 41st St, Gary, IN 46408, **Business Phone:** (219)884-6170.

PARRISH, MAURICE DRUE
Museum director, vice president (organization). **Personal:** Born Mar 5, 1950, Chicago, IL; son of Maurice and Ione Yvonne Culumns; married Gail Marie Sims, Sep 2, 1978; children: Theodore, Andrew, Brandon & Cara. **Educ:** Univ Pa, Philadelphia, PA, BA, 1972; Yale Univ, New Haven, CT, masters, archit, 1975. **Career:** Museum Director (retired); H I Feldman fel, 1974-75; City Chicago, city planner, 1975-81; John D Hilts cher & Assoc Architects, Chicago, IL, vpres, 1981-83; Barnett, Jones, Smith Architects, Chicago, IL, prin, 1983-84; City Chicago, zoning adminr, 1984-87, bldg comnr, 1987-89; Detroit Inst Arts, Detroit, MI, dep dir, 1989-97, interim dir, 1997-99; exec vpres, 1999-2006; Compass Group Associates, vpres, 2007-. **Orgs:** Chmn, St Philip Neri Sch Bd, 1982-85; pres, S Shore Comn, 1983-85; Lambda Alpha Land Use Soc, 1985; Chicago Econ Develop Comn, 1987-89. **Honors/Awds:** Nat Achievement Scholar, NMSC, 1968-72; Franklin W Gregory Scholar, Yale Univ, 1973-74.

PARRISH, TONY (ANTHONY W PARRISH)
Football player. **Personal:** Born Nov 23, 1975, Los Angeles, CA. **Educ:** Univ Wash, BS, psychol. **Career:** Football player (retired); Chicago Bears, defensive back, 1998-2001; San Francisco 49ers, strong safety, 2002-06; Dallas Cowboys, 2006. **Orgs:** Spokesperson, Ill State Liquor Control Comn; 49ers Reading Team. **Honors/Awds:** Brian Piccolo Award; NFC Defensive Player of the Week, 2003; Ed Block Courage Award; Len Eshmont Award. **Special Achievements:** First 49ers player to win the Len Eshmont Award.

PARROTT-FONSECA, JOAN
Government official. **Educ:** Howard Univ, BA, 1973; George Washington Univ, MA, educ & human resource mgt, 1974; EEP Appeal Officer Training, cert, 1980; Georgetown Univ LawSch, doctorate jurisprudence, 1981; Harvard Univ, John F Kennedy Sch Govt,master, pub admin, 1998; Tufts Univ, Fletcher Sch Law & Diplomacy, Int Leadership & Mgt, cert, 1998; Univ Pa, Wharton Sch Bus, cert, fundamentals money mgt, 2002. **Career:** AM Herman & Assocs, sr assoc, 1986; US Gen Servs Admin, Off Enterprise Develop, assoc adminr, 1995; Minority Bus Develop Agency, Dept Com, dir, 1995-; Jpf & Assoc, founder & pres, currently; Harvest Capitol Investments LLC, sr vpres bus develop; Dist Columbia's, Dept Consumer & Regulatory Affairs, actg dir & dep dir; Governor's Off Minority & Women, dir bus serv; Off Econ Develop Opportunity & Compliance, NY State Dept Transp, dir; Annual Spring Meeting Moderator. **Orgs:** Moderator, African Am Chamber Com Westchester & Rockland Counties, 2002. **Special Achievements:** First woman named director of Minority Business Development Agency. **Business Addr:** Director, Minority Business Development Agency, US Department of Commerce, 1401 Const Ave NW, Washington, DC 20230, **Business Phone:** (202)482-2000.

PARSON, RICHARD DEAN
Executive. **Personal:** Born Apr 4, 1948, Brooklyn, NY; son of Lorenzo Locklair and Isabelle; married Laura Ann Bush, Aug 30, 1968; children: Gregory, Leslie & Rebecca. **Educ:** Univ Hawaii, 1968; Univ Ala Law Sch, JD, 1971. **Career:** Asst coun to NY Gov Nelson Rockefeller, 1971-74; dep coun to US vpres, 1975; White House Domestic Coun, gen coun & assoc dir, 1975-77; Patterson, Belknap, Webb & Tyler, atty, 1977-78, partner, 1979-88; Dime Savings Bank, NY, coo, 1988-90, chmn & ceo, 1990-95; Mayor-Elect Transition Coun, head, 1993; NY Econ Develop Corp, chmn; Time Warner Inc, pres, 1995-99; AOL Time Warner, co-chief operating officer, 1999-2002, ceo, 2002-07, chmn & coo, 2003-. **Orgs:** Presidential Drug Task Force; chair, Wildcat Service Orgn; bd dir, Fed Nat Mortgage Asn; bd dir, Philip Morris Co; bd dir, New York Zool Soc; bd dir, Am TV & Commun Inc; trustee, Rockefeller Bros Fund; trustee, Howard Univ; trustee, Metrop Mus Art; bd mem, Estee Lauder; bd mem, Citigroup; Co-chmn, Mayor's Comn Econ Opportunity, NY; chmn, Apollo Theatre Found; Mus Modern Art; Am Mus Natural Hist. **Honors/Awds:** Americas Best CEO, Instnl Investor Mag, 2005. **Business Addr:** Chairman, Chief Executive Officer, Time Warner Inc, 1271 Ave of the Americas, New York, NY 10019-8016, **Business Phone:** (212)484-8000.

PARSON, WILLIE L.
Educator. **Personal:** Born Apr 25, 1942, Newellton, LA; married Sylvia Sanders. **Educ:** Southern Univ Baton Rouge, BS, Bacteriology, 1963; Wash State Univ, MS, Bacteriology & Pub Health, 1968, PhD, Microbiol, 1973. **Career:** Educator (retired); So Univ Baton Rouge, instr biol dept, 1963-65; WA St Univ, teaching asst, 1965-67, res asst, 1965-67; The Evergreen St Col, mem faculty, 1971-74, sr acad dean, 1974-78, mem faculty microbiol. **Orgs:** Panelist grants review Nat Sci Found, 1977-80; Am Soc Microbiol; Am Asn Advan Scis; Phi Delta Kappa Educ Soc; Alpha Phi Alpha Frat. **Honors/Awds:** Outstanding Young Man of America, Outstanding Young Men Am Inc, 1977.

PARSONS, KARYN (KARYN ROCKWELL)
Actor. **Personal:** Born Aug 10, 1966, Hollywood, CA; married Alexandre Rockwell, Feb 8, 2003; children: Lana & Nico; married

Randy Brooks (divorced). **Career:** Films: Class Act, 1992; Major Payne, 1995; Death Spa, 1998; Mixing Nia, 1998; The Ladies Man, 2000; 13 Moons, 2002; 13 Moons, 2002; TV series:"The Bronx Zoo", 1987; "Hunter", 1988; "The Fresh Prince of Bel Air", 1990-96; "Lush Life", 1996; "Melrose Place", 1999; "The Job", 2001; "Gulliver's Travels", 1996; "Static Shock", 2002; Nobody Wants Your Film, 2005; "Tavis Smiley", 2006; "E! True Hollywood Story", 2007. **Business Phone:** (818)840-4444.*

PARSONS, PHILIP I
Executive. **Personal:** Born Nov 18, 1941, Cherry Hill, NJ; son of Nathaniel I Banks and Kathyrn M Beverly-Brooks; children: Andrea LaVerne. **Educ:** Gettysburg Col, BA, 1964; Harvard Bus Sch, MBA, 1972; Ill Inst Technol, MPA, 1988. **Career:** Scott Paper Co, sales mgr, 1964-70; Quaker Oats Co, mkt mgr, 1973-78; AT&T, staff mgr, 1979-82; Perfect Pinch Inc, Soft Sheen Prod, gen mgr, 1982-90; Equitable Financial Servs, mgr, 1991; Ubia Financial Servs, pres & chief exec officer, currently. **Orgs:** Bd mem, Hyde Park Neighborhood Club, 1978; pres, Condo Asn, 1984-87; trustee, Gettysburg Col, 1986-91; E Bank Club, 1987; bd mem, Chicago Youth Ctr, Robbins, IL, 1992. **Honors/Awds:** Trainee of the Cycle, Fort Dix, NJ, 1964; Outstanding Salesman, Scott Paper Co, 1968; Regional Representative, Tau Kappa Epsilon, 1975; Calvary Youth Council Award, Calvary Baptist Church, 1982; Chicago Boys Club Award, 1989. **Special Achievements:** Article on Minority Business Grocery Marketing, 1986. **Military Serv:** USY, lt.

PASCHAL, ELOISE RICHARDSON
Educator. **Personal:** Born Feb 7, 1936, Hartsville, SC; married Willie Lee; children: William. **Educ:** Benedict Col, AB, 1954-58; Atlanta Univ, MSLS, 1967. **Career:** Tooms County Ga Pub Schs, teacher, 1958-60; Am Pub Sch, teacher, 1960-65; Staley Mid Sch, career media spec, 1965. **Orgs:** Sumter County Ment Health Assoc, 1971-, Flint River Girl Scout Coun, 1982-; chmn, bd dir, Sumter County Ment Health Ment Retardation, 1982-84; Am LibrAssoc, Am Asn Sch Librns, Nat Ed Assoc, Ga Assoc Educ, GA Libr Assoc, Third Dist Dept; pres, GA Libr Media; GEO Southwestern State Univ Fund; adv coun, Rosalynn Carter Carenet; elected, Am City Coun; Delta Sigma Theta Sorority. **Honors/Awds:** Woman of the Year, Boy Scout Units No 226, 1980; Distinguished Service Award, Sumter County Ment Health Asn, 1982. **Home Addr:** 310 Vista Dr, Americus, GA 31709. **Business Addr:** Career Media Specialist, Staley Middle School, 915 N Lee St, Americus, GA 31709.

PASCHAL, TIA
Basketball player, manager. **Personal:** Born Mar 22, 1969. **Educ:** Fla State Univ, criminal justice, 1993. **Career:** Basketball player (retired), proj mgr; AB Contern, Luxembourg, 1993-95; Visby Ladies, Sweden, 1997-98; Charlotte Sting, 1997; IBM Security, Atlanta, Ga, proj mgr, currently. **Honors/Awds:** Metro Conference, Player of the Year, 1990; Player of the Year, 1992, 1993; Hall of Fame, 1999; ACC's 50th Anniversary Team for women's basketball, 2002. **Business Phone:** (404)814-1806.

PASCHAL, TRISA LONG
School administrator. **Personal:** Born May 13, 1958, Akron, OH; daughter of Pauline Long and George W Long Jr. **Educ:** Univ Akron, BS, 1981, MS, 1987. **Career:** Spelman Col, inst advancement, asn vpres Instn advancement, 1996-97; vpres, currently; Mjr Gifts, campaign dir, 1993-96; Univ Akron, assoc dir develop & dir annual giving, 1988, asst dir, asst dir alumni relations, 1983-85, assoc dir, 1985-88. **Orgs:** Bd trustees, Hammonds House Gallery; Leadership Atlanta; Antioch Baptist Church North; Jr League Atlanta, 1995; Delta Sigma Theta Sorority; CASF. **Honors/Awds:** Outstanding Employee, Univ Akron Bd Trustees, 1985; Woman of the Year, Akron Women's History Proj, 1988; Delta Sigma Theta Service Award, 1988; Delta Sigma Theta Sisterhood Award, 1990; Buchtel Grad Scholar, 2007. **Business Addr:** Vice President, Spelman College, 350 Spelman Lane SW, PO Box 1551, Atlanta, GA 30314-4399, **Business Phone:** (404)681-3643.

PASCHAL, TRISA LONG
School administrator. **Personal:** Born May 13, 1958, Akron, OH; daughter of George W Long Jr and Pauline Long; married Nelson, May 11, 1996. **Educ:** Univ Akron, BS, 1981, MS, 1987. **Career:** Univ Akron, assoc dir develop & dir annual giving, 1988, asst dir asst dir alumni relations, 1983-85, assoc dir, 1985-88; Spelman Col, Mjr Gifts, campaign dir, 1993-96, Inst Advancement, asn vpres inst advan, 1996-97, vpres, 1997-. **Orgs:** Leadership Atlanta; Hammonds House Gallery, bd trustee; Delta Sigma Theta; CASE; Antioch Baptist Ch N; Jr League Atlanta, 1995. **Honors/Awds:** Outstanding Employee, Univ Akron Bd Trustees, 1985; Woman of the Year, Akron Women's History Proj, 1988; Delta Sigma Theta Service Award, 1988; Delta Sigma Theta Sisterhood Award, 1990. **Business Addr:** Vice President for Institutional Advancement, Spelman College, 350 Spelman Lane SW, PO Box 1551, Atlanta, GA 30314, **Business Phone:** (404)223-1485.

PASCHAL, WILLIE L.
School administrator. **Personal:** Born May 9, 1926, Americus, GA; married Eloise Richardson; children: William Stanley. **Educ:** Morehouse Col, BA Bus Admin 1949; Atlanta Univ, MA Educ & Admin 1957; GA State Univ Atlanta GA, EdS EAS 1978. **Career:** Webster City Bd Educ Preston, Ga, prin & teacher, 1949-52; Twiggs City Bd Educ, teacher, 1952-53; Sumter City Bd Educ, prin & teacher, 1953-72; Am Bd Pub Educ, prin; Eastview Elem Sch, prin. **Orgs:** Life mem, Alpha Phi Alpha Frat; asst secy, Am & Sumter City Payroll Develop; sr vice comn, Am Legion Dept Ga, 1984-85; Nat Asn Elem Sch Prin; Ga Asn Elem Sch, Prin 3rd Dist, 1984-85; Phi Delta Kappa, 1984-85; Ga Asn Educ Leaders, 1984-85; mem team chmn, Chamber Com, 1985. **Honors/Awds:** Distinguished Citizen, Ment Health Asn Sumter City, 1982; Distinguish Service Ment Health Asn Sumter City, 1982. **Military Serv:** AUS, corpl, 1 yr 4 mo's. *

PASCHALL, EVITA ARNEDA
Lawyer, publisher, judge. **Personal:** Born May 18, 1951, Augusta, GA; daughter of Marion R and Lucille T; married Felix Bryan Andrews, May 5, 1990; children: Iman Andrews, Felix Bryan Andrews Jr & Evita Lucille Young. **Educ:** Howard Univ, BA, 1973; Univ Ga, JD, 1976. **Career:** Augusta Judicial Circuit, asst dist atty, 1976-79; Brown & Paschall Attys Law, atty, 1979-81; Evita A Paschall PC, atty, 1981-; State Ct Ga, Augusta, asst solicitor, 1982-84; Magistrate Ct, Augusta, asst solicitor, 1984-86, solicitor, 1986-94; Augusta Today Mag, ed, publ, currently; Municipal Ct, judge, 1994-97. **Orgs:** Augusta Jaycees; Leadership Augusta; NBA, 1983-; bd dirs, Bethlehem Community Ctr, 1984-95; pres, Augusta CNF AFA Atty, 1992-93; Augusta Bar Asn. **Honors/Awds:** Woman of the Year, WHAM, 1973; Outstanding Young Women of America, 1979. **Business Addr:** Attorney, Evita A Paschall PC, 137 Broad St, PO Box 2201, Augusta, GA 30901-1551, **Business Phone:** (706)722-0173.

PASCHALL, JIMMIE WALTON
Association executive, vice president (organization). **Personal:** Married Matthew. **Educ:** Howard Univ, grad. **Career:** XO Commun, vpres & chief human resources officer; Vols Am Nat Bd Dir; Sodexho, staff; HMSHost Corp, staff; Vols Am, exec vpres external affairs, currently; Marriott Int Inc, sr vpres external affairs, currently, global diversity officer, currently. **Orgs:** Bd dir, Generations United, currently. **Business Addr:** Senior Vice President External Affairs, Global Diversity Officer, Marriott International Inc, Marriott Dr, Washington, DC 20058, **Business Phone:** (301)380-3000.*

PASSMORE, JUANITA CARTER
Marketing executive. **Personal:** Born Mar 4, 1926, Chicago, IL; married Maymon. **Educ:** Long Beach City Col; Columbia Col. **Career:** Marketing executive (retired); Johnson Prod Co, dir, spec promotions, exec nat coord, 1990. **Orgs:** Founder, 69 Choppi Block Club; chmn, Nat Media Women; parliamentarian, Chicago Chapter, Women's Bd, Operation PUSH; chmn, Fashion Therapy Ment & Health; Operation Snowball. **Honors/Awds:** Media Woman of Yr Award, Chicago Chap, 1974; Outstanding Woman of Yr, Chicago S End Jaycees Women Asn, 1977; Comm Worker Debutante Master AME Ch, 1977.

PATE, ALEXS D
Writer, college teacher. **Personal:** Born Jan 1, 1950?, Philadelphia, PA; son of Alexander and Lois; children: Gyanni, Alexs & Chekesha. **Career:** Macalester, lectr, 1992-98; Univ Minn, lectr, African-Am & African Studies, asst prof, assoc prof, 1993-; Poems: Losing Absalom, 1994, Finding Makeba, 1996, Contemporary African American Literature: Anywhere The Wind Blows, 1996, Amistad, 1997, Innocent, 1998, West of Rehoboth, 2001. **Honors/Awds:** Minn Book Award; Best First Novel, Black Caucus, Am Lib Asn; Minn Book Award for Finding Makeba & The Multicultiboho Sideshow, 2000; Award West of Rehoboth for Finding Makeba & The Multicultiboho Sideshow. **Military Serv:** USN, E-5, 1968-72. **Home Addr:** 1425 W 35th St, Minneapolis, MN 55408, **Home Phone:** (612)824-3208. **Business Addr:** Associate Professor, University of Minnsota, Department of African Am & African Studies, 808 Social Sci Bldg 267 19th Ave S, Minnepolis, MN 55455, **Business Phone:** (612)626-7587.

PATE, JOHN W., SR.
Conductor (music), musician, composer. **Personal:** Born Dec 5, 1923, Chicago Heights, IL; son of Charles H Pate Sr and Nora R; married Carolyn; children: John Jr, Yvonne, Donald & Brett. **Educ:** Midwestern Conservatory Music, Chicago, 1950-53; Univ Calif, Los Angeles, Elec Music, Script Writ, Act-Dir workshop. **Career:** Musician (retired); professional bass player, composer, producer, arranger, 1946-; Johnny Pate Trio, Chicago, founder & musician, 1957-62; ABC Rec, Chicago, midwest dir A&R, 1963-65; MGM-Verve Rec, NY, east coastdir artists & repetoire, 1966-68; UNLV, teacher film scoring. currently; Composer: Shaft in Africa, 1973; Satan's Triangle, 1975; Bucktown, 1975; Dr Black & Mr. Hyde, 1976; Sudden Death, 1976; Every Girl Must Have One, 1978; musical dir TV productions: "The Lou Rawls Special," 1979; "Future Stars," 1979; "The Richard Pryor Show," 1977. **Orgs:** Pres, Yvonne Publ & Nod-Jon Mus pub cons; BMI. **Honors/Awds:** Unsung Hero of Popular Music, 2003. **Special Achievements:** First African-American to become president of Local NARAS Recording Academy, Chicago Chapter. **Military Serv:** AUS, 1943-46. **Home Addr:** 7463 Trudy Lane, Las Vegas, NV 89123.

PATERSON, BASIL ALEXANDER
Lawyer. **Personal:** Born Apr 27, 1926, New York, NY; son of Leonard J and Evangeline Rondon; married Portia Hairston; children: David & Daniel. **Educ:** St John's Col, BS, 1948; St John's Univ Sch Law, JD, 1951. **Career:** Paterson Michael Jones & Cherot Esqs, partner, 1956-77; Inst Mediation & Conflict Resolution, pres & chief exec officer, 1972-77; City New York, dep mayor labor rels, 1978; State New York, secy state, 1979-82; Meyer, Suozzi, English & Klein, PC, partner, mem & co-chair, currently; Hunter Col, vis prof; Fordham Uni Sch Educ, adj prof; State Univ New Paltz, vis prof. **Orgs:** NY Senate, 1965-70; NY Temp Comn Revision NY Charter; vice chmn, Dem Nat Comm, 1972-78; chair, Judicial Screening Comn Second Dept, 1985-95; NY Judicial Nominations Comn, 1986-; comnr, Port Authority New York & NJ, 1989-95; chmn, Mayor's Comm Judiciary, 1990-93; Comn Promote Confidence Judical Elections, 2003-; chmn, Keyspan Fund, 2003-. **Honors/Awds:** Eagleton Institute of Politics Award, Excellence in Politics, 1967; Black Expo Award, 1973; Interracial Justice Cath Interracial Coun, 1978; Humanitarian Award, Coalition Black Trade Unionists, 1980; Medal of Excellence, St John's Univ; Kibbee Award for Outstanding Public Service & Achievement, City Univ NY, 1987; PSC Friend of CUNY Award, 1989; Pierre Toussaint Award, Catholic Archdiocese New York; President's Award, St. John's Univ Law Sch, 2003. **Special Achievements:** Is rated "AV" by Martindale-Hubbell, the highest level in professional excellence and ethics. **Home Addr:** 40 W 135th St, New York, NY 10037. **Business Addr:** Member, Co-Chair, Meyer, Suozzi, English & Klein, PC, 1350 Broadway Suite 501, PO Box 822, Garden City, NY 10018.

PATERSON, DAVID A (DAVID ALEXANDER PATERSON)
Government official. **Personal:** Born May 20, 1954, Brooklyn, NY; married Michelle; children: Ashley & Alexander Basil. **Educ:** Columbia Univ, BA, 1977; Hofstra Law Sch, JD, 1982. **Career:** Queens Dist Attys Off; State NY, state sen, 1985-, dep minority leader, 1995-2002; Minority Leader, 2003, Lt gov, 2006-08; State New York, governor, 2008-. **Orgs:** Am Found Blind; Achilles Track Club; Am Found Blind; Jewish Guild Blind; bd mem, Nat Asn Advan Colored People. **Special Achievements:** First African American to become Lieutenant Governor of New York. **Business Addr:** Senator, NY State Senate, Current Dist 30, 250 Broadway Suite 1930, New York, NY 10007, **Business Phone:** (212)298-5585.

PATERSON, DAVID ALEXANDER. **See PATERSON, DAVID A.**

PATES, HAROLD
School administrator. **Educ:** PhD. **Career:** School administrator (retired); Kennedy-King Col, Chicago Ill, pres. **Orgs:** Bd mem, Black United Fund Ill, currently. **Business Phone:** (773)324-0494.

PATHON, JEROME
Football player. **Personal:** Born Dec 16, 1975. **Educ:** Univ Wash, Psychol. **Career:** Indianapolis Colts, wide receiver, 1998-01; New Orleans Saints, widereceiver, 2002-04; Atlanta Falcons, wide receiver, 2005. **Honors/Awds:** CIAU Football Rookie of the year, 1994.

PATIN, JOSEPH PATRICK
Physician. **Personal:** Born Jan 10, 1937, Baton Rouge, LA; son of Henry W Patin and Harriet D; married Rose; children: Joseph & Karla. **Educ:** Univ Mich, BS, attended; Meharry Med Col, MD, 1964. **Career:** Pvt Prac, physician; 85th Evac Hosp, chief surg, 1970-71; Raymond W Bliss Army Hosp, 1969; St Elizabeth Hosp, res, 1964-69; LA State Univ, assoc prof. **Orgs:** Baton Rouge Parish Bd Health; Kappa Alpha Psi; Cancer Soc Greater Baton Rouge; Oper Upgrade Baton Rouge; Baton Rouge Med Soc; Soc Med Asn; Nat Med Asn Dipl Bd Surgeons, 1970; dir, Burn Unit; asst dir, Trauma Unit; Dipl, bd surg critical care, 1992. **Honors/Awds:** Fel, Am Col Surgeons. **Military Serv:** AUS, maj; Bronze Star, Dist Med.

PATIN, JUDE W. P.
Military leader. **Personal:** Born Jan 25, 1940, Baton Rouge, LA; son of Henry Wilmot and Mary Harriett Domingue; married Rose Marie Darensbourg Patin, Aug 22, 1964; children: Michelle, Steve. **Educ:** Southern Univ, Baton Rouge, LA, BS, architectural eng, 1962; Arizona State Univ, Tempe, AZ, MA, indus eng, 1971; Harvard Univ, Cambridge, MA, John F Kennedy Sch Govt & Pub Mgt Sr Exec Course, 1990; US Army Engineer Officer Advanced Course; US Army Cmd & Gen Staff Col; Nat Security Mgt Course, Industrial Col Armed Forces; US Army War Col. **Career:** Military leader (retired); US Army; brigadier gen; Secy, Transportation & Develop La; US Army Corps Engrs North Central Div, Commanding Gen, currently; consult, currently. **Orgs:** Alpha Phi Mu Industrial Engineering Honor Soc; US co-chair Four intl joint comns dealing w & elem water resource mgt Great Lakes; vpres, Soc Am Military Engrs, 1991; Am Pub Works Asn; Asn US Army. **Honors/Awds:** Alpha Phi Mu Industrial Engineering Honor Society; Black Engineer of the Year, 1991; numerous public presentations involving engineering & military defense concerns, including speeches, briefings, articles & pub letters; registered prof engr Wisconsin. **Military Serv:** Legion Merit w & Oak Leaf Cluster; Bronze Star Medal w & Oak Leaf Cluster;

Meritorious Service Medal, w & Oak Leaf Cluster; Air Medal; Army Commendation Medal; Nat Defense Service Medal; Army Service Ribbon w & Oak Leaf Cluster; Overseas Service Ribbon w & Oak Leaf Cluster; Republic Vietnam Campaign Medal; Republic Vietnam Cross Gallantry w & Palm; Meritorious Unit Citation; Republic Vietnam Civil Actions Meritorious Unit Citation; AUS Parachutist Badge. **Business Addr:** Commanding General, US Army Corps Engineers North Central Division, 111 N Canal St 12th Fl, HQ NCD Command Suite, Chicago, IL 60604, **Business Phone:** (312)353-6310.*

PATNETT, JOHN HENRY
Executive, president (organization). **Personal:** Born Nov 21, 1948, New Orleans, LA; son of Melvin and Mary; married Lynn J. **Educ:** Southern Univ New Orleans, BA, 1971; Southern Univ, Baton Rouge, La, Cert Furniture Upholstery, 1980. **Career:** La Black Republican Coun, dir pub rels, 1983-85; Mel & Son Upholstery Inc, pres. **Orgs:** Bd mem, US Selective Serv, 1980. **Honors/Awds:** Certificate of Merit, Outstanding Community Service, 1974; Appointed Orleans Parish Republican Exec Comn, 1985. **Home Addr:** 7009 Queensway Dr, New Orleans, LA 70128. **Business Addr:** President, Mel & Son Upholstery Inc, 2001 Touro St, New Orleans, LA 70116, **Business Phone:** (504)945-5187.

PATRICK, CHARLES NAMON, JR.
Executive. **Personal:** Born Feb 5, 1949, Birmingham, AL; son of Charles and Rutha Mae Robbins; married Gwendolyn Stephanie Batiste, Apr 13, 1975; children: Gentry Namon Patrick, Jessica Sherrie Patrick, Charles Stephan Patrick III, Hope Naomi Patrick & John Paul Patrick. **Educ:** Col Data Processing, Los Angeles, CA; Life Underwriters Training Coun, certif completion, 1979. **Career:** VIP Mfg, North Hollywood, CA, sales dist, 1970-76; Prudential Insurance Co, Los Angeles, CA, sales agent/mgr, 1976-82; Pioneer Capital & Assoc, Dallas, TX, western reg vpres, 1982-83, owner, 1982-84; Patrick, Patrick & Associates, Lawndale, CA, pres, 1984; Austin Diversified Products, Ingelwood, CA, corp sales mgr, 1985-88; PPA Industries, Compton, CA, owner, 1988-; fdr, Fragment House Mission Intl Inc, 1994, Est Hish Sch, 2001. **Orgs:** Admin/asst, Way Church Ingelwood, 1981; block club pres, Action Block Club, 1982-85; Greater LA Visitors & Convention Bur, 1984, prog coord, Black Am Response African Community (BARAC), 1987-88; counr, Fel West Youth Ministries, 1987-88; NABSE (Nat Alliance Black Sch Educr), 2001. **Honors/Awds:** Business Man of the Year, ACC News, 1985. **Business Addr:** Owner, PPA Industries/Pioneer Patrick & Associates Industries, PO Box 5365, Compton, CA 90224-5365, **Business Phone:** (213)774-5984.

PATRICK, DEVAL L
Government official. **Personal:** Born Jul 31, 1956, Chicago, IL; son of Laurdine Kenneth and Emily Mae Wintersmith; married Diane Louise Bemus Patrick; children: Sarah Baker & Katherine Wintersmith. **Educ:** Milton Acad, Eng & Am lit; Harvard Col, BA, 1978; Harvard Law Sch, JD, 1982. **Career:** US Ct Appeals, law clerk; NAACP Legal Defense & Educ Fund, litigator; Hill & Barlow, partner, 1986; Dept Justice, asst atty gen civil rights, 1994-; Nat Church Arson Task Force, 1996-97; Day, Berry & Howard, pvt pract, 1997; Texaco, chair, 1997-99, vpres & gen coun, 1999-2001; Coca-Cola Co, exec vpres & gen coun, 2001-06, corp secy, 2002-06; Mass Gov, 2006-. **Orgs:** Mass Bar Asn; Black Lawyers Asn; Boston Bar Asn; Harvard Club Boston; dir, Harvard Alumni Asn, 1993-96; Fed Election Reform Comn; Mass Judicial Nominating Coun. **Honors/Awds:** George Leisure Award, Harvard Law Sch, 1981; Rockefeller Fel, United Nations Sudan & Nigeria, 1978. **Special Achievements:** First African American to be elected governor in Massachusetts. **Business Addr:** Governor, Massachusetts State House, Office of the Governor, Rm 360, Boston, MA 02133, **Business Phone:** (617)725-4005.

PATRICK, ISADORE W
Judge. **Personal:** Born Mar 27, 1951, Jackson, MS; son of Isadore W Sr and Esterline; married Deborah Williams, Dec 18, 1971. **Educ:** Jackson State Univ, Jackson, MS, BS, 1973; Univ MS, Oxford, MS, JD; Nat Judicial Col, Reno, NV, judicial cert. **Career:** IBM, Manassas, VA, comput programmer, 1973-78; Hinds Co Pub Defender Off, Jackson, MS, pub defense atty; State Miss, Nineth Dist Circuit Ct, Vicksburg, MS, asst dist atty, 1981-89, Warren County Circuit Ct, ruling judge, 1989-. **Orgs:** Nat Judges Asn; MS Conf Judges; MS State Bar; Magnolia State Bar; Warren Co Bar; bd dir, Salvation Army; Jackson State Alumni Asn; Am Bar Asn; Am Trial Lawyers Asn; Nat Bar Asn. **Honors/Awds:** Legal Award, Nat Asn Advan Colored People, 1989. **Home Addr:** 112 Moonmist Dr, Vicksburg, MS 39180, **Home Phone:** (601)636-7378. **Business Addr:** Circuit Court Judge, State of Mississippi, Ninth Circuit Court District, 1009 Cherry St, PO Box 351, Vicksburg, MS 39181-0351, **Business Phone:** (601)634-8042.

PATRICK, DR. JENNIE R
Engineer. **Personal:** Born Jan 1, 1949, Gadsden, AL; daughter of James (deceased) and Elizabeth (deceased); married. **Educ:** Tuskegee Inst, 1967-70; Univ Calif, Berkeley, BS, 1973; MIT, ScD, 1979, PhD, chem eng. **Career:** Dow Chem Co, asst engr, 1972; Stauffer Chem Co, asst engr, 1973; MIT, res assoc, 1973-79; Chevron Res, engr, 1974; Arthur D Little Inc, engr, 1975; Gen Elect Co, res engr, 1979-83; Phillip Morris Inc, sr engr, 1983-85; Rohm & Haas Co, res sect mgr, 1985-90; Southern Co Servs Inc, asst to exec vpres, 1990-92; Tuskegee Univ, Cheml Engineering Dept, 1993-97; Raytheon Engrs & Constructors, sr consult, 1997-99; Bus & Home Environ Review, consult, 1999-. **Orgs:** Sigma Xi, AIChE, NOBCChE. **Honors/Awds:** 'Outstanding Women in Science & Engineering Award', NOBCChE, 1980; a subject in Exceptional Black Scientists Poster Prog, CIBA-GEIGY, 1983; Tuskegee Inst, Hon PhD, 1984. **Special Achievements:** First African Am female in the US to earn doctorate in chem engrg 1979. **Business Addr:** Consultant, Business and Home Environmental Review, PO Box 51678, Amarillo, TX 79101, **Business Phone:** (806)353-1401.

PATRICK, JULIUS, JR. See Obituaries section.

PATRICK, LAWRENCE CLARENCE, JR.
Lawyer. **Personal:** Born Feb 8, 1945, Detroit, MI; son of Ada D and Bishop Lawrence C; married Raynona P Fuller, Jun 23, 1973; children: Lawrence C III, Joseph E, Ayana B & Goldie E Patrick. **Educ:** Wayne State Univ, Detroit, Mish, BA, 1972; Harvard Univ, JD, 1975. **Career:** Honigman Miller Schwartz & Cohn, Detroit, Mich, assoc, 1975-77; Patrick, Fields & Preston-Cooper, Detroit, Mich, partner, 1977-93; Detroit Bd Educ, pres, 1989-92, chair, Detroit 2000, vis fel, Hudson Inst, 1992-; Jaffe Raitt Heuer & Weiss PC, partner & atty, currently. **Orgs:** Mich Bar As, 1975-; Wolverine Bar Asn, 1977-, bd dir, 1978-81; corp dir & bd chmn, Black United Fund, 1978-88; Mich Transp Commn, 1979-84, vice chmn, 1981-84; chmn bd, Black United Fund, 1985-88; chmn bd, Wayne County Social Serv Bd, 1986-88; Detroit Bd Educ, 1989-95; pres, Cass Tech Alumni Asn, 1997-; chmn, N End Community Develop Corp; State Bar Mich; bd gov, Cranbrook Inst Sci; Nat Coun Sch Atty; Mich Coun Sch Atty; Asn Educr Pvt Pract; bd dir, Mich Future Inc. **Honors/Awds:** Michingan Senate, Mich Senate Resolution, 1981; Trio, Wayne State Univ, 1988; Founder's Award, Stud Motivational Prog, 1989, Outstanding Service, Church God Christ, 1989. **Home Addr:** 237 King St, Detroit, MI 48202, **Home Phone:** (313)873-0165. **Business Addr:** Attorney, Partner, Jaffe Raitt Heuer & Weiss PC, 500 Griswold Suite 2400, Detroit, MI 48226, **Business Phone:** (313)961-1200.

PATRICK, ODESSA R.
Personal: Born Oct 22, 1933, Mt Gilead, NC; married Joe L; children: Krystal, Joseph & Jasmine. **Educ:** NC A&T State Univ, BS, 1956; Univ NC, Greensboro, MA, 1969. **Career:** Univ NC, Greensboro, lab technician, 1958-69, Biol Dept, instr hist, 1968, prof emer, 1996-. **Orgs:** Am Asn Univ Women; Delta Sigma Theta; Elisha Mitchell Sci Soc. **Special Achievements:** Scientific paper published in Journal of Elisha Mitchell Scientific Soc, 1969; Leader, Girl Scout. **Business Addr:** Professor Emeritus, University of North Carolina, 1000 Spring Garden St, Greensboro, NC 27403, **Business Phone:** (336)334-5000.

PATRICK, DR. OPAL LEE YOUNG
Educator. **Personal:** Born Jul 16, 1929, Tatums, OK; daughter of L P Young Jr and Connie V Mitchell; married Charles; children: Jacqueline R. **Educ:** Langston Univ, BA, 1951; Univ NM, MA, 1963; Univ UT, PhD, 1974. **Career:** Educator (retired); Pub Sch, Okla, teacher, 1951-56; Bur Ind Affairs, inst counr, 1956-63; Univ Md, Educ Ctr Independent Sch, 1963-66; USAFE W Ger,instr, lectr & teacher; Clear field Job Corp, inst counr & adminr, 1966-70;Univ Utah, instr educ, 1971-74, asst prof educ, 1974-77; guest lectr, coordr, consult & tutor, 1979-91, 1994. **Orgs:** Presenter, various conf; partic & presenter, Nat Org; guest lectr & coord, various projects & res activ; State Mental Health Asn, 1973-; Utah Acad Sci, 1974-; Nat Col Soc Studies, 1976-; Asn Teach Educ, 1974-; Nat Coun Teachers Eng, 1973-; vpres, Nat Coun Teachers Eng, 1973; Asn Sch & Curric Develop, 1975-; pres, Davis Co, Nat Asn Advan Colored People, 1978.

PATRICK, VINCENT JEROME
Marketing executive. **Personal:** Born Oct 21, 1959, Delray Beach, FL; son of Freddie W and Mattie Hough. **Educ:** Univ Fla, Gainesville, FL, BS, jour, 1981. **Career:** Jordan Marsh, Miami, FL, assoc buyer, 1981-85; Rouse Co, Miami, FL, asst mkt mgr, 1985-88; Rouse Co, Atlanta, GA, mgr, sales & mkt, 1988-; VJP Mkt & Commun Inc, Hapeville, Ga, owner, currently. **Orgs:** Bd dirs, Atlanta Downtown Partnership; bd dirs, Travel Ga; Downtown Pub Rels Coun; Fernbank Mus Natural Hist Commun Adv Comt. **Honors/Awds:** Underground Atlanta Grand Opening, MAXI/Mkt, 1990, Bayside Marketplace Grand Opening, MAXI/Mkt, 1989, Int Coun Shopping Ctrs; Paper Clip Award/Advertising, Underground Atlanta Advert Campaign, Atlanta Jour Const, 1990; Silver Anvil/Pub Relations, 1989, Phoenix Award, Pub Rels, 1989, Underground Atlanta. **Home Addr:** 4955 Wynhurst Way, Stone Mountain, GA 30088, **Home Phone:** (770)987-8407. **Business Addr:** Owner, Vincent J Patrick Marketing & Communications Inc, 631 N Cent Ave, Hapeville, GA 30354, **Business Phone:** (404)762-0048.

PATTEN, DAVID
Football player. **Personal:** Born Aug 19, 1974, Columbia, SC; son of David Patten and Betty; married Galiena; children: Daquan, Quintin & David. **Educ:** Western Carolina Univ. **Career:** Albany Firebirds, defensive back & wide receiver, 1996; New York Giants, wide receiver, 1997-99; Cleveland Browns, wide receiver, 2000; New England Patriots, wide receiver, 2001-04; Wash Redskins, wide receiver, 2005-06; New Orleans Saints, wide receiver, 2007-08; Clevand Browns, 2009-. **Honors/Awds:** Super Bowl Champion Thrice, XXXVI, XXXVII, XXXIX. **Business Phone:** (504)733-0255.

PATTERSON, ALONZO B., JR.
Clergy, administrator. **Personal:** Born Nov 5, 1937, New Orleans, LA; married Shirley May Smith; children: Edna, Mitchell, Norris, Janet, Kim. **Educ:** Am Bible Inst, ThD, 1977; Univ Alaska, AA 1973, BA, 1974; AA, 1974. **Career:** Shiloh Missionary Baptist Church, pastor, 1970-; Anchorage Sch Dist, person specialist, 1976; Shiloh Baptist Church, relig admin, 1970-75; MHE, supv, 1966-70; Alaska Ministries Am Baptist Nat Ministries, coordr; Corinthian Baptist Church, Fairbanks. **Orgs:** chair, Alaska State Bd Parole, 1984-; Nat Asn Adv Colored People; Community Action; Human Rels Comn; Anchorage OIC; Ministerial Alliance; Civilian & Mil Coun; Anchorage Community Health Ctr; Minority Cult Asn; vpres, March Dimes; chmn, Martin Luther King Jr Found, Alaska; Alaska Black Leadership Conf; Greatland State Baptist Conv. **Military Serv:** AUS, food serv supv, 1956-66. **Business Addr:** Pastor, Shiloh Missionary Baptist Church, 855 E 20th Ave, Anchorage, AK 99501.*

PATTERSON, ANDRAE MALONE
Basketball player. **Personal:** Born Nov 12, 1975, Riverside, CA. **Educ:** Ind Univ, attended 1998. **Career:** Panellinios; Zadar; Ricoh Man; Estudiant; Minn Timberwolves, forward,1998-2000; Adecco Estudiantes, 2001-02; Ricoh Manresa, 2002-02; Adecco Estudiantes, 2003-05; Ricoh Manresa, 2005-06; KK Zadar, 2006; Ironi Ashkelon, Power Forward, 2006; Panellinios, 2006-07; Egaleo AO, 2007-09. **Special Achievements:** US Jr World Championship Team, 1997; named Texas Mr.Basketball & First-team Parade All-American. *

PATTERSON, BARBARA ANN
President (Organization), association executive. **Personal:** Born in Pennsylvania; married Billy W Patterson; children: Gwendolyn Patterson-Cobbs, Kimberly & Damali. **Educ:** Trinity Col, Wash, DC, BA, educ, 1984, MA, counseling, 1993. **Career:** Independent & Pub Schs, teacher; pvt pract; Cross-Racial Communs & Personal Growth Counseling prof; Black Stud Fund, IST Equity, Race & Educ, pres, currently. **Orgs:** Bd gov, Trinity Col; adv bd, Wash Nat Cathedral Scholars; Friends for COT Future. **Honors/Awds:** Washingtonians of the Year, 1999. **Special Achievements:** Publisher: Chapter contributor "Promoting Independent School Enrollment," Visible Now Blacks in Private School by Slaughter & Johnson 1989; "Respecting the Strength of Black Youth," Black Issues in Higher Educ; researcher & resource for a History Deferred, A Guide for Teachers; "Pioneering Multiracial Education," Independent School, vol 53, 1993. **Business Addr:** President, Black Student Fund, 3636 16th St NW 4th fl, Washington, DC 20010, **Business Phone:** (202)387-1414.

PATTERSON, CECIL BOOKER, JR.
Judge. **Personal:** Born May 15, 1941, Newport News, VA; son of Cecil B Sr and Marie E; married Wilma M Hall; children: Angela D & Cecil M. **Educ:** Hampton Univ, Va, BA 1963; Ariz State Univ, JD, 1971. **Career:** Judge (retired); Maricopa Co Legal Aid Soc, staff atty, 1971-72; Law fel, Reginald Heber Smith Prog, 1971; Bursh & Patterson, pvt law pract, 1972-73; Phoenix Urban League, house coun, 1973-75; Maricopa Co Pub Defend Off, trial atty, 1975-80; Maricopa Co Superior Ct, judge, 1980-91; Atty General's Off, Human Serv Div, Ariz, chief coun, 1991-95; Ariz Ct Appeals, 1995-2003; Ariz Ct Appeals, Div One, judge. **Orgs:** Nat Asn Atty Gen Civil Rights Comn; bd dir, Maricopa Co Br, Nat Asn Advan Colored People; Southminster Community Serv Forum; Minority Adv Comt, Ariz State Univ; bd dir, YMCA; Valley Sun United Way; Legal Aid Soc, 1971-75; Grant Martin L King Jr Woodrow Wilson Found, 1969; Ariz Acad, 1975 & 1978; bd gov, Ariz State Bar, 1977-79; rep, Am Bar Asn House Del, 1978-80; bd mem, Maricopa Co Red Cross, 1978; pres, Ariz Black Lawyers Asn, 1979-80; Nat Conf Christians & Jews, 1981-; bd mem, Valley Sun, Ariz United Way, 1984-; chair, Nat Bar Asn Judicial Coun, 2001-02. **Honors/Awds:** Law Scholarship Scholarship, Educ & Defense Fund, 1970; Marvin Award, Nat Asn Atty Gen, 1994-95; Martin Luther King Living the Dream Award, City Phoenix Ariz, 1998. **Military Serv:** AUS, cpt, 1963-68; Marksmanship Ribbon, 1967; Outstanding Weapons Controller Officer 27th Air Div Luke AFB, 1968; Good Conduct Ribbon. **Home Addr:** 1955 E Bendix Dr, Tempe, AZ 85283, **Home Phone:** (480)730-8864.

PATTERSON, CECIL LLOYD
School administrator, college teacher. **Personal:** Born Jun 10, 1917, Edna, TX; married Vivian Rogers. **Educ:** Samuel Huston Col, AB, engineering, 1941; Univ Pa, MA, eng, 1947, PhD, eng, 1961. **Career:** School administrator (retired); Ft Valley State Col, GA, instr, 1947-48; NC Cent Univ, instr & prof, 1950-68, Undergrad Sch, dean, 1968-78, vice chancellor acad affairs, 1978-86; NC Cent Univ, prof emer eng, 1986-. **Orgs:** Conf Deans & Acad

Vpres, 1970-96; chmn, NC Comn Col Transfer Stud, 1974-78; chaplain, Gen Bd Exam Chaplains Epis Church, 1976-90; pres, Durham Coun Sr Citizens, 1996-01. **Military Serv:** USY, engrs col, 1941-74; Southwest Pac Theater; Misc Battle Stars; Campaign Medals. **Home Addr:** 409 E Lawson St, Durham, NC 27707. *

PATTERSON, CHERYL ANN
Accountant. **Personal:** Born Jul 5, 1957, Columbus, OH; daughter of John B and Geraldine; married Dale, May 31, 1981. **Educ:** Columbus State Community Col, AS, optom technol, 1979; Franklin Univ, BS, acct, 1984, MBA, 1998. **Career:** Ohio State Univ, Col Optom, optom technican; Ohio Dept Taxation, tax agent; Columbus Conv Ctr, jr acct, sr acct, vp treas, dir finance, currently. **Business Addr:** Director of Finance, Greater Columbus Convention Center, 400 N High St, Columbus, OH 43224, **Business Phone:** (614)825-2532.

PATTERSON, CHRISTINE ANN
School administrator. **Personal:** Born Sep 9, 1949, Wilkes-Barre, PA; daughter of James Samuel and Stella Bienwski; married Walter DeFrantz, Feb 15, 1968 (divorced 1983); children: Waltrina, Felicia & Amanda. **Educ:** Wilkes Univ, Wilkes-Barre, BA, commun, 1983-86, MS, educ, 1987-89; Penn State Univ, Univ Park, PhD, currently. **Career:** Penn State Univ, Media, coord minority advan placement prog, 1986, minority stud counsr, coordr, 1986-88, exten agent/4-H urban youth, 1988-89, dir, minority stud serv, 1989-; Nat Multiple Sclerosis Soc, br coordr, 1987-88. **Orgs:** Martin Luther King Comt Social Justice, 1983-; coordr, Wilkes-Barre chap, Nat Asn Advan Colored People, 1986-88; President's Coun Undergrad Recruitment & Retention, Pa State Univ, 1989-; chair women, Color Winter Ball, 1990; chair, Forum Black Affairs, 1990. **Honors/Awds:** Scholarship Award, Col & Univ Pub Rels Asn Penn Minorities Commun, 1986; Special Friend Award, Luzerne County Head Start, 1987; Publicity Award, Nat Asn Advan Colored People Press, 1987; Recognition Award, Forum Black Affairs, 1990. **Special Achievements:** Author of "The Black Experience in Wyoming Valley". **Home Addr:** 1652 Oxford Circle, State College, PA 16803. **Business Addr:** Director, Pennsylvania State University, School of Communications, 205 Carnegie Bldg 416 Old Main, University Park, PA 16802, **Business Phone:** (814)863-6081.

PATTERSON, CLARENCE J. See Obituaries section.

PATTERSON, REV CLINTON DAVID
Clergy, manager. **Personal:** Born Nov 11, 1936, Uniontown, AL; son of David and Mattie Mason; married Lillie Young, Dec 24, 1961; children: Michael, Florencia, Donnetta, Clintonia, Edshena, Bernita. **Educ:** Birmingham Bapt Col, 1963; Liamia, 1969; Elba Sys, 1970; Liamia, 1973. **Career:** Beulah Baptist Church, pastor; Booker T Wash Inc Co, mgr; New Morning Star Baptist Church, pastor, 1965-72; Demopolis Fed Credit Union, former vpres; Fed Credit Union, loan off teller; asst trea mgr; BBM Fed Credit Union; Beulah Baptist Church, pastor, currently. **Orgs:** Pres, Demopolis Ministerial Fellow, 1966-72; bd dirs, Together Demopolis, AL; bd dirs, BBM Fed Credit Union; Prof Bus Men's Asn, 1964-75; bd dirs, BBM Birmingham, AL; Demopolis Fed Credit Union; Ala Cent Credit Union; Ala Bapt State Conv & Congress; Nat Bapt Sunday Sch & Training Union Congress; Nat Bapt Conv; Birmingham Bapt Min Conf; Jeff Co Dist Asn; NW Dist Conv; lecturer, Jeff Co Dist Sun Sch & BTU Congress; hon mem, Ala Sheriff Asn, 1974; Ala Motorist Asn, 1974; past pres, S Pratt City Civic Leag, 1967; Ala Fed Civic Leag; trustee bd, Peace Bapt Ch, 1957; Geometry Lodge 410; Nat Advan Asn Colored People; Ala Chris Movement Human Rights; Tuxedo Height Civic Leag; moderator, Jefferson County Asn; pres, NW Dist Convention. **Honors/Awds:** C J McNear Award, 1963; Community Service Award, Pratt City, 1971; Community Service Award, Demopolis, AL, 1972; Outstanding Salesmanhip Award, NIA, 1974. **Business Addr:** Pastor, Beulah Baptist Church, 1022 2nd Ave N, Bessemer, AL 35020, **Business Phone:** (205)424-0861.*

PATTERSON, CURTIS RAY
Educator, college teacher. **Personal:** Born Nov 11, 1944, Shreveport, LA; married Gloria M Morris; children: Curtis R. **Educ:** Grambling State Univ, BS, educ, 1967; Ga State Univ, MVA, 1975. **Career:** Atlanta Pub Sch, art instr, chairperson, 1970-76; Caddo Parish Sch Bd, Shreveport, LA, art instr, 1968-70; Muscogee Co Sch, Columbus, GA, art instr, 1967-68; Gov Hon Prog, instr, 1973; Atlanta Col Art, GA, art instr, 1976-; Atlanta Life Ins Co, Adv Comt Art, 1979-80; Piedmont Arts Festival, juror, 1980; Atlanta Col Art, prof, currently. **Orgs:** Black Artist Atlanta, 1974-80; 13 Minus One Sculpture Group, 1975-80; adv bd mem, Atlanta Bur Cult Affairs, 1975-80; Sculpture Park Comn, Atlanta Bur Cult Affairs, 1977; Sculpture Comn Metrop Atlanta Rapid Transit Authority, 1978; Atlanta Int Airport Sculpture Comn, Atlanta Bur Cult Affairs, 1980. **Honors/Awds:** Rep, Visual Arts Festival Arts & Cult, Lagos, Nigeria, 1977; Bronze Jubilee Award, WETV Network Channel 30, 1979. **Business Addr:** Professor, Atlanta College of Art, 1280 Peachtree St NE, Atlanta, GA 30309, **Business Phone:** (404)733-5000.

PATTERSON, DESSIE LEE
Government official, mayor. **Personal:** Born Jul 6, 1919, Grand Cane, LA; daughter of Clinton Jackson Sr and CarLee Guice Jackson (deceased); widowed; children: Willie Leroy, Betty Marie P Smith, Corrie Jean P Reed. **Educ:** Attained 9th grade. **Career:** Mansfield Desoto, LA, Nat Asn Advan Colored People, secy, 1971-; City S Mansfield, mayor, 1971-. **Orgs:** Desoto Parish Chamber Com, 1979-; libr bd controls; Desoto Parish Sch Bd Adv Coun; Desoto Parish Lib Bd. **Special Achievements:** First Black female Mayor of the State of Louisiana; first Black female Mayor in the US. **Business Addr:** Mayor, City of South Mansfield, PO Box 166, Mansfield, LA 71052.*

PATTERSON, DR. ELIZABETH ANN
Radiologist. **Personal:** Born Feb 2, 1936, Wilkes-Barre, PA; daughter of Benjamin A and Edythe E; divorced; children: Tonya L Henry. **Educ:** Univ MI, BS, 1957; Howard Univ Col Med, MD, 1961. **Career:** Radiologist (retired): Mercy Hosp, radiol, 1972-80; Univ Pgh/Magee Women's Hosp, asst prof radiol, 1981-85; Central Med Ctr & Hosp, diagnostic radiologist, 1985-88; Breast Imaging, Dept radiol, Hosp Univ Pa, 1988-98. **Orgs:** Pres, Pittsburgh Roentgen Soc, 1982-83; pres, Gateway Med Soc, 1983-88; Counor, Am Col Radiol, 1985-91; Radiol Sect Nat Med Assoc, secy/program chair, 1985-87, vice chmn, 1987-89, chair, 89-91; bd dirs, Am Cancer Soc, Pittsburgh Div, 1986-88, Philadelphia Div, 1992-; mem, Am Asn Women Rad, Alpha Kappa Alpha; Intercultural Cancer Coun, 2004-; pres, Philadelphia Roentgen Ray Soc, 1994-95; Soc Breast Imaging; chmn, Nat Mammography Quality Assurance Adv Comm, 1994-97; pres, Pa Radiological Soc, 1996-97; adv coun, Susan G Komen Found; vpres, FSNW Ski Club Officers, 2001-02; Am Col Radiol, fel.

PATTERSON, ELIZABETH HAYES
Lawyer, school administrator. **Personal:** Born Jun 25, 1945, Boston, MA; daughter of Alan L Young and Lucille Young; married Jerome Alexander Patterson; children: Sala Elise, Malcolm Atiim. **Educ:** Sorbonne Univ Paris, dipl, 1966; Emmanuel Col, AB, French, 1967; Stanford Univ, 1968; Columbus Sch Law Cath, Univ Am, JD, 1973. **Career:** Hon Ruggero Aldisert US Ct Appeals, law clerk, 1973-74; Hogan & Hartson Law Firm, assoc, 1974-77; Columbus Sch Law Cath Univ, adj prof, 1976; DC Pub Sev Comn, comnr, 1977-80, chmn, 1978-80; Georgetown Univ Law Ctr, assoc dean JD & grad prog, 1993-97, asso prof, 1980-. **Orgs:** Trustee, secy, Nat Florence Crittenton Mission Found Bd; bd dirs, Child Welfare League Am, 1997; Am Law Inst; Trst Family & Child Sevr, Wash, DC, 1977-; bd dirs, Frederick B Abramson Found, 1992-; trustee, Emmanuel Col, 1994-; Am Civil Liberties Union Litigation Screening Comn, 1977-80; DC Bar Div I Steering Comn, 1980-82, DC Bar Screening Comn, 1985-86; bd ed, Wash Lawyer, 1986-91; Secy State's Adv Comn, pvt Int Law; adv comn, Procedures Judicial Coun DC Circuit, 1981-84; DC Law Revision Comn, 1990-93; treasurer, Dist Columbia Bar, 1987-88. **Honors/Awds:** Center's Frank F. Flegal Teaching Award, 2001. **Business Addr:** Associate Professor of Law, Georgetown University Law Center, 600 New Jersey Ave NW, Washington, DC 20001, **Business Phone:** (202)662-9000.*

PATTERSON, EVELYNNE
School administrator. **Personal:** Born Feb 28, 1930, Meadville, PA; married Herman; children: Alice & Patricia. **Educ:** NY Univ, BS, 1962; NY Univ, post grad. **Career:** NY Univ, exec asst to pres, dir off affirmative action, assoc dir, 1968-72, dir off community rel, assoc prof, 1972-, asst dep chancellor. **Orgs:** Adv bd, Harvard Univ, 1974-77; Comt Bd 2 Borough Manhattan, 1977-; bd dir, WA Sq Asn, 1977-. *

PATTERSON, GERALD WILLIAM
Executive. **Personal:** Born May 9, 1953, Cleveland, OH; son of William Robert Johnson and Willa Mae; married Diana Crump; children: Monique Camille. **Educ:** Michigan State Univ, BA, 1975; Wayne State Univ, specialist, 1977; Cent Mich Univ, MA, 1978; Univ Wis, transp cert, l987. **Career:** Ford Motor Co, sr transportation agent, 1978-80; Amway Corp, traffic coordinator, 1980-82, traffic supvr, 1982-83; Kellogg Co, truck pricing mgr, 1984-87, mgr logistics services, 1988, mgr outside warehouses & dist centers, 1988-91, logistics mgr, 1992; Walker Int Trans LLC, vpres, currently. **Orgs:** Phi Beta Sigma, 1975-; Delta Nu Alpha, 1982-89; Southwest Mich Traffic Club, 1984-; Battle Creek Area Urban League, 1985-; adv, Jr Achievement, 1986-88; 60NR Comt, 1987-88; Nat Asn Advan Colored People, 1988-; adv, Upward Bound, 1989-; Coun Logistics Mgt, 1989. **Honors/Awds:** Transportation Negotiation Strategies, 1987; Service Award, Gov Tenn, 1989. **Business Addr:** Vice President, Walker International Transportation LLC, 70 E Sunrise Hwy Suite 604, Valley Stream, NY 11581-1260, **Business Phone:** (516)568-2080.

PATTERSON, BISHOP GILBERT EARL
Clergy. **Personal:** Born Sep 22, 1939, Humboldt, TN; son of Bishop WA Sr and Mary Louise; married Louise. **Educ:** Detroit Bible Col, attended; LeMoyne Owen Col, attended. **Career:** COGIC, minister, 1958-61, Holy Temple, Memphis, co-pastor, 1961-75, jurisdictional bishop, 1988-92, general bd mem, 1992-2000, presiding bishop, 2000-; Deliverance Temple, Cathedral Bountiful Blessings, founder & pastor, 1975-88; Charles H. Mason Bible Col, pres. **Honors/Awds:** Hon Doctorate, Oral Roberts Univ. **Special Achievements:** Bishop Patterson is the publisher of Bountiful Blessings Magazine and a contributing writer in the Spirit Filled life Bible (King James Version) published by Thomas Nelson Publishers and edited by Dr. Jack W. Hayford. In July 2002, Whitaker House Publishers released Bishop Patterson's first book entitled "Here Comes The Judge". **Business Addr:** Bishop, Temple of Deliverance COGIC, 369 G E Patterson Ave, Memphis, TN 38126, **Business Phone:** (901)521-9160.*

PATTERSON, GRACE LIMERICK
Librarian. **Personal:** Born Nov 21, 1938, New York, NY; daughter of Robert and Frieda Sajac; married Joseph Nathaniel Patterson, Oct 30, 1956; children: Lorrayne & Joseph Jr. **Educ:** City Col NY, New York, NY, BA, 1971; Columbia Univ, New York, NY, MLS, 1975; Col New Rochelle, New Rochelle, NY, MS, 1989. **Career:** Paterson Pub Libr, Paterson, NJ, outreach coordr, 1975-79; Passaic County Col, Paterson, NJ, media specialist, 1979-81; Irvington Pub Libr, Irvington, NJ, br coordr, 1981-84; Rockland Community Col, Suffern, NY, assoc prof, 1984-89; Hudson County Col, libr dir, 1989-. **Orgs:** Am Libr Asn, 1978-; chair, Outreach Servs Comt, New Jersey Libr Asn, 1981-85; deleg, State Univ NY Libr Asn, 1984-89; chair, ALA Louise Giles Scholar Comt, 1985-87; Arts Coun Rockland County, 1987-89; chair, Pub Rels Comt, Black Caucus Am Libr Asn, 1988-90; chair, Instrnl Resources Comt, HCCC, 1995-98; secy & treas, INT FED Libr Asn, Kipert, 1996-97; Asn Col & Res Librs; rep, Am Libr Asn, Freedom Read Found. **Honors/Awds:** Title IIB Fel, Dept Educ, 1974-75; Pubic Relations Award, NJ Libr Asn, 1979, 1996; basic tutor, Literacy Vols Am, 1978; Professional Librarian Certification, Educ Dept, NJ, 1981; Community Development Asniate, Mott Found, Flint, MI, 1983. **Business Addr:** Library Director, Hudson County Community College, 25 Journal Sq, Jersey City, NJ 07306, **Business Phone:** (201)714-2229.

PATTERSON, JAMES
Executive. **Personal:** Born May 10, 1935, Augusta, GA; married Phyllis Black; children: Katy, Jacqueline & Jennifer. **Educ:** St Col, MD, 1957. **Career:** Mutual of NY, field underwriter, 1966-; Supreme Life Phila, debit & staff mgr, 1960-66 business unlimited inc, pres, 1975-. **Orgs:** Million Dollar Round Table; Mutual of New York Hall of Fame; mutual of NY Pres's Coun; Nat Assoc of Life Underwriters; past mem Philadelphia Jaycees; Philadelphia chap Nat Bus League, vpres, 1972. **Honors/Awds:** Rec'd Mutual of New York's highest honor Hall of Fame, 1974; agcy Man of The Year, 1967. **Military Serv:** Mil srv, 1958-60. **Business Addr:** 146 Montgomery Ave, Bala Cynwyd, PA 19004.

PATTERSON, JOAN DELORES
Military leader. **Personal:** Born Mar 17, 1944, Columbia, SC; daughter of David Creech; married; children: Torrey. **Educ:** City Col Chicago, AA, 1976; Chicago State Univ, BA, 1979; Univ N Fla, MEd, 1982. **Career:** USN, dir personal serv, 1982-83, educ tech, 1983-84, personnel clerk, 1984; USAF, guidance counr, 1984-88, educ specialist, 1988-96, educ servs flight, chief, 1996-. **Orgs:** Am Soc Training & Develop, 1982-85; chief counr, Equal Employment Opportunity, 1984-85; mgr, Fed Women's Prog, 1984; Am Coun Asn, 1985-; Military Educators & Counselors Asn, 1985-; Asn Multicultural Coun & Develop, 1985-; bd dir, Military Educators Coun Asn, 1989-94; secy, Tuskegee Airman Inst, 1990-; Am Counselors & Educators Gout, ACEG, 1994-. **Honors/Awds:** Outstanding Performance Award, USF, 1992,US Navy, 1983; Letters of Commendation, USAF, 1986. **Military Serv:** USAR, staff sargent, 1977-85. **Business Addr:** Chief, Education Services & Human Resources Flight, US Air Force, US Air Force, 1271 White Oak Circle, Melbourne, FL 32934.

PATTERSON, KAY
State government official. **Personal:** Born Jan 11, 1931, Darlington County, SC; son of James Hildred and Lelia (Prince); married Jean Millicent James; children: Eric Horace (deceased) & Pamela Maria. **Educ:** Allen Univ, AB, 1956; SC State Col, MEd, 1971. **Career:** Educator (retired); Wash Perry Middle Sch, teacher, 1956-70; Benedict Col, teacher, 1968; SC Educ Asn, uniserv rep 1970-86; SC House Rep, rep, 1975-85; SC Legis, sen, 1985-2006; SC Sen, Richland County, Dist 19, mem, currently. **Orgs:** Nat Educ Asn; Nat Asn Advan Colored People; Educ Comm States 1978-84; Southern Regional Educ Bd, 1985; trustee, Univ SC, 1985; Omega Psi Phi Fraternity. **Military Serv:** USMC, sgt, 1951-53.

PATTERSON, KEVIN L.
Technologist. **Personal:** Married Charlene Price Patterson; children: Charise and Craig. **Career:** IBM, Worldwide Director of Sales for the POWER System Unit. **Orgs:** Founder, Focus On Leadership; President, 100 Black Men of America (Greater Charlotte Chapter); Conventions and Meetings Chairperson, 100 Black Men of America; President of the Board of Directors, United Way for North Carolina. **Honors/Awds:** Charlotte Observer and Charlotte Post voted him one of the Top 10 Leaders in Charlotte. **Home Addr:** 001850. *

PATTERSON, LLOYD
Consultant, executive. **Personal:** Born Feb 2, 1931, Cleveland, OH; son of Willa Byrd and Ambrose; married Lena Burgan, Dec 31, 1975. **Educ:** Cuyahoga Community Col, attended 1966; FBI

Nat Acad, grad 1975; Nat Training Ctr Polygraph Sci New York, grad; Dignitary Protection Sch, US Treasury Dept; OPOTA Hypnosis Sch. **Career:** Cleveland PD, police officer patrolman lt, 1957-82, dep chief police, 1982-83; CWRU Law Med Ctr, staff instr, 1978-83; L & L Patterson Consults, Las Vegas, exec dir, currently. **Orgs:** Life mem, Nat Rifle Asn, 1951-; potentate, El Hasa Temple #28 Shriners, 1961-; Thirty Second Degree Bezaleel Consistory AASR, 1961-; Eureka Lodge 52 Prince Hall Masons 1961-; distinguished fel, Acad Cert Polygraphists, 1976; pres, Black Shield Police Asn, 1980-; trustee, Cleveland Police Hist Soc, 1982-; co-owner, Bar 2 L Ranch 1983-; Ohio Police & Fire Retirees, 1983-; chmn, Project PRIMES, Cleveland Urban League, 1982-83; parliamentarian, Las Vegas Appaloosa Club, 1985; pub info officer, Las Vegas Valley Water Dist, 1989-96; imp dir, Nat Asn Advan Colored People; charter mem, Nat Orgn Black Law Enforcement Execs; NBPA; FOP; Int Asn Chiefs Police; Black Shield Police Asn; NV Black Police Officers Asn; FBI-NAA; bd mem, Clark Co Coun Ctr; Nat Organization Black Law Enforcement Exec. **Special Achievements:** Appeared in Disney Movie: "You Ruined My Life," 1987; HBO Special: "VIVA-SHAF", 1987; movie: Crime Story, 1988; movie: Midnight Run, 1988; Author of Chicken Every Sunday, Chicken Every Sunday & Profiles of Blacks in Blue (history). **Military Serv:** AUS, sgt, 1952-53; Good Conduct Medal, 1952-53, National Service Defense Medal, Presidential Unit Citation, Solider of the Month 2 times. **Home Addr:** 5654 Smithsonian Way, Las Vegas, NV 89130, **Home Phone:** (702)645-8893. **Business Addr:** President, L & L Patterson Consultants, 5654 Smithsonian Way, Las Vegas, NV 89130, **Business Phone:** (702)645-8893.

PATTERSON, LYDIA R
Consultant, educator. **Personal:** Born Sep 3, 1936, Carrabelle, FL; daughter of Richard D Ross and Johnnie Mae Thomas Ross; married Berman W Patterson; children: Derek Kelley Corley. **Educ:** Hunter Col, BA, 1958. **Career:** US Energy Dept, indus res specialist, 1966-68; NY State Div Human Rights, reg dir/mgr 1962-66, 1969-76; Extend Consult Serv, pres & chief exec officer, 1982-94; Lydia Patterson Communications, founder, 1995-; Bankers Trust Co, vpres, 1976-87; Merrill Lynch & Co, vpres, mgr corp, chief exec officer, serv dept 1987-90; Borough Manhattan Community Col, NY, adj lectr, 1991; DBA, Practical Resources, 2001-. **Orgs:** Govt affairs comn, Fin Women Asn/Nat Asn Bank, Women, 1978-87; prof develop comn, Urban Bankers Coalition, 1978-86; Soc Human Resources Mgt, 1979-87, Nat Urban League, 1979-93; exec bd, NY Women Employment Ctr, 1985-87; exec bd, mem EDGES, 1985-87; Women's um (Nat & Int), 1988-89; City Univ NY Vocational & Tech Educ Adv Coun, 1990-91; bd dir, VP mktg, Wellington Edu Comm found, 1993, 1994; Leadership Palm Beach Co, 1997-, bd, 1999-2001; Palm West Chamber Com, chair, Edu Comm, 1996-2000, bd, 2000-01; bd, Gulf Stream Goodwill Industries, 1997-; bd, Am Heart Asn. **Honors/Awds:** Women in Industry, Nat Coun Negro Women, 1978; Women Who Make A Difference, Minorities and Women in Business Magazine, 1989; Corporate/Community Partnership Award, Greater New York Chapter Links, 1989; Economic Justice Award, Judicial Council, Nat Bar Asn; Giraffe Award, Women's Chamber Com PBCO, 2000. **Special Achievements:** Seminar speaker: Columbia Univ; Wharton Sch Harvard Univ; Duke Univ; Cornell Sch IDL Rels, 1976-89; article, Columbia Sch IDL Social Welfare J, 1981. **Business Phone:** (560)790-5514.

PATTERSON, MICHAEL DUANE
Manager, lawyer. **Personal:** Born Jul 27, 1949, Detroit, MI; son of Harry B and Myra Howard; children: Lisa Marie. **Educ:** Ferris State Col, Big Rapids MI, attended, 1968; Western Mich Univ, Kalamazoo MI, BS, 1970; Nat Law Ctr, George Washington Univ, Wash DC, JD, 1974. **Career:** Mayor Robert B Blackwell, Highland Park MI, spec asst to mayor, 1971; US Sen Birch Bayh, Wash DC, legal intern, 1971-72; US Sen Philip A Hart, Wash DC, staff asst, 1972-74; Herman J Anderson PC, Detroit MI, law clerk, 1974; Wayne Co Community Col, Detroit MI, instr, 1974-81; Community Youth Serv Prog, Detroit MI, legal coord, 1975; Mich & US Dist Ct, Eastern Dist Mich, 1976; US Ct Appeals, Sixth Circuit, 1977; Stone, Richardson, Grier & Allen PC, Detroit MI, assoc, 1975-80, partner, 1978-80; Dist Columbia, 1980; US Supreme Ct, 1982; Phifer, Phillips & White PC, partner, currently. **Orgs:** NY Bar Asn, Joint Ctr Polit Studies, 1971-72; chmn bd trustees, Renaissance Baptist Church Detroit, 1984-86, 1987-89; vice chmn, Comt Property Ins Law, Tort & Ins Pract Sect, 1986-88, vice chmn, Comt Mem Involvement, 1987-88, chair elect, Mem Comt, 1988-, NY Bar Asn; State Bar Mich; DC Columbia Bar Asn; Wolverine Bar Asn; Nat Bar Asn; Nat Asn Advan Colored People; Am Bar Asn. **Honors/Awds:** Spirit of Detroit Award; Mayor's Certificate of Merit Award. **Business Addr:** Partner, Phifer, Phillips & White PC, 1274 Libr St Suite 500, Detroit, MI 48226, **Business Phone:** (313)964-2360.

PATTERSON, DR. ORLANDO HORACE
Educator. **Personal:** Born Jun 5, 1940, Jamaica, West Indies; married Nerys (divorced 1994); children: Rhiannon & Barbara; married Anita, 1995. **Educ:** London Univ, BS, econs, 1962; London Sch Econs, PhD, 1965; Harvard Univ, MA, 1971; Trinity Col, DHL, 1992; The New Sch, NY, DHL, 2000; Northeastern Univ, DHL, 2001; Univ Chicago, DHL, 2002; La Trobe Univ, DHL, 2006. **Career:** London Sch Econs, asst lectr, 1965-67; Univ West Indies, lectr, 1968-70; Harvard Univ, prof, dept Sociol, 1971-93, actg chmn, 1989-90, John Cowles prof sociol, 1993-; Allston Burr Sr, tutor, 1971-73; Univ Chicago, vis prof, 1994-95. **Orgs:** AAAS; Am Acad Polit & Social Sci; Am Sociol Asn. **Honors/Awds:** Distinguished Contribution Scholarship Award, 1983; Ralph Bunche Award, Am Polit Sci Asn, 1983; Walter Channing Cabot Faculty Prize, Harvard Univ, 1983 & 1997; National Book Award, 1991; Medal Merit, Univ Calif, LosAngeles, 1992; Order Distinction Commander Class, 1999; Best Paper onCulture Award, Am Sociol Asn, 2006. **Special Achievements:** Author: The Sociology Slavery, 1967; The Children Sisyphys, 1964; An Absence Ruins, 1967; Die the Long Day, 1972; Freedom, Vol 1, Basic Books, 1991; Ethnic Chauvinism: The Reactionary Impulse, Stein & Day, 1977; Slavery & Social Death, Harvard UNV Press, 1982; The Ordeal Integration: Progress & Resentment in AME's "Racial" Crisis, Civita sCounterpointBooks, 1997; Rituals Blood: Consequences of Slavery in Two AmericanCenturies, Civitas-Counterpoint, 1998. **Business Addr:** Professor, Harvard University, Department of Sociology, 520 William James Hall 33 Kirkland St, Cambridge, MA 02138, **Business Phone:** (617)495-3707.

PATTERSON, PAUL
Manager, administrator. **Personal:** Born Aug 6, 1926, Aurora, IL; married Shirley Glenn; children: Charles & Carrie. **Educ:** Univ Ill, attended 1950. **Career:** Capitol Dairy, 1950; Anheuser-Busch, sales rep, 1965; owned & oper food & liquor store, 1965; Chicago Bears, scout dir player rel, 1967, traveling sec, 1973; Anheuser-Busch Inc, sales supr. **Orgs:** Rose Bowl, 1947; bd dir, IL Athletic Asn, Univ IL, 1974; St IL Athletic Bd, 1974; bd chmn, Athletic Bd St IL, 1975; Jr Mens Hon Soc SACHEH; Mawanda Sr Men Hon Soc; Kappa Alpha Psi. **Military Serv:** USN, 1945-46.

PATTERSON, PAUL A
Executive. **Personal:** Born Mar 5, 1929, Richmond, IN; divorced; children: 3. **Educ:** Earlham Col, BS, 1951; Ind Mortuary Col, 1964. **Career:** Wayne Co, coroner, 1984-93, 1997-2000; Patterson's Funeral Home, mortician, owner, currently. **Orgs:** Past pres, Richmond Community Sch Bd, 1966-77; Mayor's Select Group, 1972-73; Lions Club; Townsend Community Ctr; pres, Wayne Co Fed Welfare Adv Bd; bd, Am Red Cross; bd, Boys Club; bd, Jr Achievement; past pres, Ind Voc Tech Col; bd, Salvation Army; Richmond Funeral Dirs Asn; IFDA & NFDA; Buckeye State Funeral Dir Asn Ohio; past exalted ruler, IBPOEW 479; Nat Disaster Team, REG V FEMA. **Honors/Awds:** Gov Evan Bayh, Sagamore of the Wabash, 1992. **Business Addr:** Owner, Patterson's Funeral Home, 110 S 8th St, Richmond, IN 47374, **Business Phone:** (765)962-0335.

PATTERSON, PICKENS ANDREW
Lawyer. **Personal:** Born Aug 1, 1944, Cotton Plant, AR; son of Rev Pickens A and Willie Mae; married Gloria P, Nov 25, 1967; children: Pickens A III & Staci E. **Educ:** Fisk Univ, BA, 1965; Harvard Law Sch, JD, 1968. **Career:** Atlanta Legal Aid, managing atty, 1969-70; Jackson, Patterson & Parks, partner, 1970-77; N Cental Legal Asst, exec dir, 1977-78; Dept HUD, atty advisor, 1978-81; City Atlanta, asst city atty, 1981-82; Arrington Patterson Thomas, partner, 1982-85; Thomas, Kennedy, Sampson, Patterson, partner, sr partner, currently. **Orgs:** Alpha Phi Alpha Fraternity, 1962-; Comt Specialization & Recertification, State Bar Ga, 1976; pres, Atlanta Guardsmen, 1993-; vpres, Sadie G Mays Nursing Home, 1994-; State Bd Bar Examrs, 1997-; State Bar GA, Adv Opinion Comt, 1998-; Sigma Pi Phi Fraternity, 1998-; Formal Legal Adv Opinion Com, 1998-; Nat Asn Bond Lawyers, 1999; Nat Conf Bar Examrs, Comt Technol, 1999; Atlanta Charter Study Comn; chmn, Atlanta Judicial Comn; pres, Gate City Bar Asn; trustee, Louisville Presbyterian Theol Sem, Louisville, Ky. **Honors/Awds:** Alumni Award for Scholarship, Fisk Univ Alumni, 1962; Valedictorian, AE Beach High Sch, 1961; Departmental Honors, Fisk Univ, 1965; Man of the Year, Cascade United Methodist Church, 1988; Man of the Year, Black Pages, 1995. **Special Achievements:** "Got Land Problems" pamphlet designed for landowners, 1972. **Business Addr:** Senior Partner, Thomas, Kennedy, Sampson & Patterson, 3355 Main St, College Park, GA 30337, **Business Phone:** (404)688-4503.

PATTERSON, ROBERT. See ALI, RASHIED.

PATTERSON, ROBERT L.
Judge. **Personal:** Born Aug 2, 1945, Detroit, MI; son of Clarence (deceased) and Florence; married Joyce Hurst; children: Kevin, Robert II. **Educ:** Colo State Univ, Ft Colins, BS, sociol, 1968; Univ Colo, Boulder, JD, 1974. **Career:** Univ Colo, dir black educ prog, 1969; Colo State Univ, asst dir proj go, 1970-71; Legal Aid Soc, staff atty, 1974-76; Colo State Pub Defender, Dep Pub Defender, 1976-80; Western Dist Wash, asst fed defender, Fed Pub Defender, 1980-81; Colo Atty Gen, asst atty gen, 1981-85; Denver County Ct, judge, 1985, presiding judge, 1998-00; Colo Supreme Ct; US Dist Ct, CO; US Dist Ct, Western Dist Wash; US Ct Appeals, Ninth Circuit; Best Best & Krieger LLP, atty, currently. **Orgs:** Nat Bar Asn, 1980-; pres, Delta Eta Boule, 1991-; Judicial Coun Nat Bar Asn; Colo Bar Asn; Denver Bar Asn; Sam Cary Bar Asn; Am Judges Asn; Am Judicature Soc; Colo Supreme Ct Comn Delay Reduction; Nat Asn Ct Mgt, 1998-01; Western Regional Officer, Sigma Pi Phi Fraternity, 1997-01; chair, Justice Ctr Planning Comn Denver Co Ct, currently. **Honors/Awds:** Man of Distinction, Lane Col Alumni Asn, 1990; Who's Who in American Law; Dynamic Duo Award, Am Asn Univ Women, 1999; Distinguished Service Award, Judicial Coun Nat Bar Asn, 2001; Living Sr Hall of Fame Award 4th Ann, Clyburn Sr Village, 2001; Living Legend Award, 2003; Outstanding Toastmaster, Toastmasters Int Downtown Speakeasy Club, 2002-03. **Special Achievements:** First African-American Presiding Judge in the history of the Denver Colorado Court , 1998-01.

PATTERSON, RONALD E
Banker. **Career:** Commonwealth Nat Bank, Mobile, AL, chief exec. **Business Phone:** (205)476-5938.

PATTERSON, RUBEN NATHANIEL
Basketball player. **Personal:** Born Jul 31, 1975, cleveland, OH; son of Charlene; divorced; children: 3. **Educ:** Univ Cincinnati, attended 1998. **Career:** Los Angeles Lakers, forward, 1998-99; Seattle Supersonics, 1999-01; Portland Trailblazers, 2001-06; Denver Nuggets, 2006; Milwaukee Bucks,small forward, 2006-07; LA Clippers, 2007; Denver Nuggets, 2008; free agent, currently. **Honors/Awds:** Silver medal, US Olympic Festival, 1995; Most Outstanding Player, US Olympic Festival, 1995; AP, All-Am Hon Mention, 1997-98. *

PATTERSON, SALADIN K
Writer, movie producer. **Career:** Producer & witer; Films: One Flight Stand, producer & writer, 2003; The Fighting Temptations, screenplay, 2003; TV series: Teen Angel, 1998; "The PJs", writer, 2000; "Frasier", writer, 2000-03; "The Bernie Mac Show", co-exec producer, 2003-05; "Stacked", consult producer, 2005; Psych, co-exec producer, 2007-08. **Business Addr:** Writer, Producer, c/o The 20th Century Fox, 10201 Pico Blvd, Century City, CA 90035, **Business Phone:** (310)369-1000.*

PATTERSON, WILLIAM BENJAMIN
Administrator, vice president (government). **Personal:** Born May 19, 1931, Little Rock, AR; son of William Benjamin Sr and Perrish Childress; married Euradell Logan; children: William & David. **Educ:** Calif State Univ, San Francisco, BS, 1956, MS, 1963. **Career:** City Oakland, Off Parks & Recreation, recreation dir, 1952-56, head recreation dir, 1956-62, dist suprvr, 1962-74, admin supvr, 1964-74, visitor serv mgr, 1974-87, recreation serv mgr, 1987-89; City Oakland, Off Mayor Lionel J Wilson, spec consult, 1989; Growth Opportunities Inc, pres & chief exec officer; E Bay Munic Utility Dist Bd, bd dir, 1997, pres, 2004-06, vpres retirement bd, currently. **Orgs:** Foreman Alameda County Grand Jury 1982-83; mem Oakland Baseball Athletics Adv Bd 1982-; NAACP, 1982-87; treas, bd dirs Joe Morgan Youth Found, 1983-; vpres & dir, Mitre Bus Org, 1983-88, pres & chief exec officer, 1988-; past pres 1984, chair bd, New Oakland Comn, 1985-; pres & bd chair, Greater Acorn Community Improvement Asn, 1985-87; mem Calif Parks & Recreation Soc, East Bay Recreation Exec Asn; Am Asn Zool Parks & Aquariums; life mem, Kappa Alpha Psi Frat, 1982-; mem Sigma Pi Phi Frat, 1984-. **Honors/Awds:** Outstanding Contributions Award, Calif Youth Authority, 1977; Outstanding Serv Award, Alameda County Bd Supvrs, 1977; Comn Testimonial, McClymonds Alumni Asn, 1982; Commendation Community Serv, Oakland City Coun, 1983; Christian Leadership Award, Downs mem Methodist Church, Oakland, 1990; Outstanding Community Serv, Cong US, 1988; Senate Resolution Recognition of Public Serv, Calif Assembly, 1988; Resolution, Commendation for Outstanding Public Serv, Alameda County, bd supvrs, 1988; mgt, Oakland City Coun, 1986; Outstanding Contributors Award, Nat Parks Serv, 1988. **Military Serv:** AUS, pfc EII, 1951. **Business Addr:** Director, Vice President of Retirement Board, East Bay Municipality Utility District Board, Oakland Administration Center and Business Office, 375 11th St, PO Box 24055, Oakland, CA 94607.

PATTERSON, WILLIS CHARLES
Entertainer, educator. **Personal:** Born Nov 27, 1930, Ann Arbor, MI; married Frankie Bouyer; children: Sharon, Kevin, Shelia & Jamal. **Educ:** Univ Mich, BMusEd, M Mus, PhD. **Career:** Southern Univ, Baton Rouge, LA, 1959-61; Va State Col, assoc prof, 1962-68; Our Own Thing Inc, performer; Univ Mich, prof, prof emer & assoc dean, currently. **Orgs:** Nat Opera Asn; Nat Asn Teachers Singing; Alpha Phi Alpha; NAACP; pres, Nat Asn Negro Musicians; exec secy, Nat Black Music Caucus. **Honors/Awds:** Marian Anderson Award. **Military Serv:** USAF, staff sgt, 1949-52. **Business Addr:** Associate Dean, Professor Emeritus, University of Michigan, School of Music, Theatre & Dance, EV Moore Bldg 1100 Baits Dr., Ann Arbor, MI 48109-2085, **Business Phone:** (734)764-0583.

PATTERSON-TOWNSEND, MARGARET M.
Administrator, technologist. **Personal:** Born Jul 4, 1951, Flint, MI; daughter of Albert Patterson and Zelma V Stewart; divorced; children: Marc A Patterson, Sommer C Green. **Educ:** Bakers Bus Col, bus admin, 1987; Univ MI, health care admin, 1992; Univ MI Med Ctr, polysomnography, 1992. **Career:** Flint Gen Hosp, admin asst, 1978-86; HealthPlus of MI, asst to dir spec accts, 1986-89; Manpower Inc, admin troubleshooter, 1990-91; Sleep

Disorders Inst MI, asst coordr, 1991-92; Genesee Co Substance Abuse, asst to dir develop, 1991-92; Mich Sleep Diagnostics & Res Ctr, dir, 1992-, chief exec officer, currently. **Orgs:** Flint Chamber Com, ambassador; dir, National Asn Female Execs; Am Bus Women's Asn; Flint Women's Forum, bus; dir, Mid Michigan's Coordr Nat Narcoleptic Found. **Honors/Awds:** Nomination for Athena Award, Flint Area Chambers Com. **Special Achievements:** First minority female successfully own & operate a sleep disorders treatment center in the US. **Business Addr:** Chief Executive Officer, Mich Sleep Diagnostics & Research Center, 3237 Beecher Rd Suite M, Flint, MI 48503-3695, **Business Phone:** (810)733-8338.*

PATTILLO, JOYCE M
Executive, consultant. **Personal:** Born Apr 28, 1951, Little Rock, AR; daughter of Johnnie C and Mable Stubblefield; married Conrad S, Dec 24, 1977; children: Conrad Peyton. **Educ:** Univ Ark Pine Bluff, BA, social & hist, 1972; Webster Univ, MA, pursing human resources. **Career:** Social Security Admin, claims rep, 1973-80; US Dept Labor, investr, 1980-82; US Dept Army, chief tech serv, 1982-87; EEOC, investr, 1987-90; Alltel Info Serv, mgr affirmative action, diversity, 1990-. **Orgs:** Alpha Kappa Alpha Sorority, 1970-; adv coun Lions World Services Blind, 1990-; bd mem, Ark ABIE, 1992-; Toastmasters, CTM, 1992-; Urban League, 1992; educ comm, Greater Little Rock Chamber Com, 1992-; Ark Human Resources Asn; Soc Human Resources Mgt; bd mem, Leadership Greater Little Rock, Class IX; Help Individuals Receive Employ Inc; Lions World Serv adv coun Ourtown 1; bd mem, Ark C Mus; bd mem, United Way, allocations comn, 1993-. **Honors/Awds:** Univ Ark, Cum Laude Grad, 1972, Means McClellan Award, hist dept, 1972; Prof Achievement award, Alpha Kappa Alpha Sorority, 1986; SBA Region IV Nat Award, Systematics Info Serv Inc, 1991; Black Corp Exec Nat Asn Advan Colored People, 1994; Agency Leader for Partners in Educ, Supt Award, 1994. **Special Achievements:** Author: Diversity, 1994. Grad Leadership Greater Little Rock Class IX, 1994. **Military Serv:** AUS, Spec Act Award, 1986. **Business Addr:** Human Resources Executive, Rank Video Services America Inc, 9201 Faulkner Lake Rd, North Little Rock, AR 72117.

PATTILLO, ROLAND A
Physician, educator. **Personal:** Born Jun 12, 1933, DeQuincy, LA; son of James Pattillo and Rhena Pattillo; married Patricia; children: Catherine, Michael, Patrick, Sheri & Mary. **Educ:** Xavier Univ, BS, 1955; St Louis Univ, MD; Johns Hopkins Univ, fels, 1967. **Career:** Med Col Wis, prof; Harvard Univ, fel, resident, 1960-64; Obstet & Gynecol J NIH, fel, 1965-67; World Health Orgn, consult, 1977, prof, dir, cancer res & res sci; Med Col Wis, physician, 1968-; Marquette Univ; Morehouse Sch Med, interim chmn, 1996, dir residency prog, Dept Obstet & Gynecol, prof, currently. **Orgs:** Bd dir, Am Cancer Soc; Milwaukee Div Sci Jour Reviewer; J Nat Cancer Inst Sci; Cancer Res; Am J Obstetricians & Gynecologists. **Honors/Awds:** Research Award, Am Col Obstetricians & Gynecologists, 1963, Found Thesis Award, 1975; Physician of the Year, Cream City Med Soc, 1990; Distinguished Service Award, Med Col Wis, 1994; Medallion, Trophoblast Soc, 2003. **Special Achievements:** Atlanta Top Doctors, Atlanta Mag, 2002; Health Heroes, Atlanta Bus Chronicle, 2005. **Business Addr:** Director, Professor of clinical obstetrics and gynecology, Morehouse School of Medicine, Department of Obstetrics and Gynecology, 720 Westview Dr SW, Atlanta, GA 30310-1495.

PATTMAN, VIRGIL THOMAS, SR.
Engineer. **Personal:** Born Nov 29, 1940, Detroit, MI; children: Virgil Thomas Jr, Randall H, Tiffaney Lynn. **Educ:** Lawrence Inst Tech, BS, 1969; Detroit Inst Tech, BS, 1981; Central MI Univ, MA, 1983. **Career:** Gen Elec Co, electronic tech, 1964-67; GM Corp Proving Ground, elec engr, 1967-78; GM Corp Tech Ctr Mfg Div, safety engr, 1978-82; GM Corp Tech Ctr Adv Eng Staff, sr safety engr, 1983-. **Orgs:** Bd trustees, 1968-84, church treas & finance sec asst, 1972-84, audio engr, 1984-, church sch teacher, 1985-, bd christian educ, 1986- Peace Bapt Church Detroit; Am Soc Safety Engrsk 1980-. **Honors/Awds:** Appeared in Ebony Magazine Who's Who, 1982. **Special Achievements:** First black senior safety engr at the GM Tech Ctr responsible for staff of 1500 persons. **Military Serv:** AUS, Reserves, sgt, 1963-69; instr, chem biol & radiol warfare.

PATTON, ANTWAN ANDRE (BIG BOI)
Singer, actor, business owner. **Personal:** Born Feb 1, 1975, Savannah, GA; children (previous marriage): Bamboo; children: Jordan & Cross. **Career:** Hip-hop duo Out Kast, currently; Pitfall Kennels, owner, currently; Albums: Southern playalist icadillacmuzik, 1994; ATLiens, 1996; Aquemini, 1998; Stankonia, 2000; Speaker boxxx/The Love Below, 2003; Ghetto Musick; Got Purp? Vol 2, xXx: State of the Union, 2005; Idle wild, 2006; Films/TV: "Benz or Beamer", 1995; "In Due Time", 1997; "High Schoolin'", 1999; "Speed ballin'", 2001; "B.O.B (Bombs Over Baghdad)", 2001; "B.O.B. (Bombs Over Baghdad)", 2002; "So Fresh, So Clean", 2002; "Land of a Million Drums", 2002; "Players Ball", 2002; "On & On & On", 2003; Films: Idle wild, co-producer, 2006; ATL, 2006; Who's Your Caddy, 2007; How 2 Build a Rapper, 2008; "Law & Order: Special Victims Unit", 2008; "BET News", 2008; Kiss and Tail: The Hollywood Jump off, 2009. **Honors/Awds:** Player's Ball went gold, 1993; Southern playalist icadillacmuzik went platinum, 1993; Aquemini went double platinum, 1998; Two Grammy Awards for Stankonia, 2001; three Grammy Awds for Speaker boxxx/The Love Below, 2004. **Business Addr:** Recording Artist, Singer, c/o Outkast, PO Box 161652, Atlanta, GA 30321.*

PATTON, DR. CURTIS LEVERNE
Scientist, educator. **Personal:** Born Jun 13, 1935, Birmingham, AL; married Barbara Beth Battle, 1963; children: Lynne Martine. **Educ:** Fisk Univ, BA, 1956; Mich State Univ, MS, 1961, PhD, microbiol, 1966. **Career:** Mich State Univ, asst microbiologist, 1960-63, from asst instr to instr, 1963-67; Rockefeller Univ, guest investr, 1967-70; Yale Univ, Sch Med, asst prof microbiol, 1970-74, dir grad studies, 1972-74, asst prof epidemiol, pub health & microbiol, 1974-76, assoc prof epidemiol, pub health & microbiol, 1976-2006, researcher, prof emer, 2006-. **Orgs:** Dir, Interdisciplinary Parasitol Training Prog; Minority Access Res Careers & Nat Ins Gen Med Sci, 1978-82; Nat Res Coun Community Human Res Eval Panel, 1979-81; consult, US Army Med Res & Develop Command, 1979-82; Am Asn Advan Sci; Am Soc Parasitologists; Soc Protozoologists. **Honors/Awds:** Biomedical Science Support Grant, 1966-67; Parasitology Fellowship, Rockefeller Univ, 1967-70; Training Grant, USPHS, 1967-69, Research Grants, 1972-77, 1978-86; Edward A. Bouchet Leadership Award, 2004; Award for Excellence in Leadership Promoting Public Health, Social Justice & Human Rights, 2006. **Special Achievements:** First African-American graduate of Yale College. **Military Serv:** AUS, spec sixth class, 1956-59. **Business Addr:** Professor Emeritus, Yale School of Public Health, 60 College St, PO Box 208034, New Haven, CT 06520-8034, **Business Phone:** (203)785-2869.*

PATTON, JEAN E
Executive, educator, consultant. **Personal:** Born Mar 14, 1947, Bronx, NY; daughter of John Henry and Estelle Witherspoon. **Educ:** City Univ NY, BA, psychol, 1971; Columbia Univ, advanced cert, orgn develop & human resources mgt, 1999; Univ Mich, advanced cert, orgn develop & human resources mgt, 1999. **Career:** Training Living Inst, group facilitator, 1971-73; Harlem Confrontation Drug Rehab Ctr, dir educ, 1973-75; Nat Westminster Bank, asst vpres, corp training & develop mgr, 1975-83; Second Skin Cosmetics, founder, pres, 1983-87; Color Educ Resources, founder, pres, 1986-; Securities Indust Automation Corp, dir training, 1992. **Orgs:** Local & int bd, var community; Asn Image Consults Int. **Honors/Awds:** Black Achievers in Industry Award, Harlem YMCA, 1983; Image Makers Merit & Industry Excellence Award, Asn Image Consults Int, 1992. **Special Achievements:** Created the first skin tone analysis system that makes it easy to accurately select complexion flattering colors for ethnic skin tones; Author, Color to Color, 'The Black Woman's Guide to a Rainbow of Fashion and Beauty', Simon & Schuster, 1991; introduced the first personal color analysis course at Parsons Sch of Design, Sch of Continuing Educ, 1986; auth of numerous articles on color analysis, image & color psychology. **Home Addr:** 321 W 29th St, New York, NY 10001, **Home Phone:** (212)564-3082. **Business Addr:** Director of Training, Securities Industry Automation Corporation, 2 Metrotech Ctr, Brooklyn, NY 11201, **Business Phone:** (212)383-7673.

PATTON, JOE. See PATTON, JOSEPH.

PATTON, JOSEPH (JOE PATTON)
Football player. **Personal:** Born Jan 5, 1972, Birmingham, AL. **Educ:** Ala A&M. **Career:** Wash Redskins, guard, 1994-98; Jacksonville Jaguars, 1999.

PATTON, JOYCE BRADFORD
School administrator, educator. **Personal:** Born May 31, 1947, Shreveport, LA; married Jerry A Patton (deceased); children: Blythe. **Educ:** Grambling State Univ, BA, 1969; SUNY Teacher Col Buffalo, MS, 1972; LA State Univ Shreveport, 1983. **Career:** Caddo Mid Magnet, teacher earth sci, asst prin, curric & instr, currently. **Orgs:** Prog Scholarship Comn Alpha Kappa Alpha Inc, 1966-; Nat Educ Asn, 1972-, YWCA 1983-, Nat Sci Teachers Asn, 1984-; local sch chmn, Substance Abuse Prevention Educ, 1984-; local bd 1st vpres, Parent Teacher Student Asn, 1984-85; Nat Earth Sci Teachers Asn, 1986-; youth Sunday sch supt Mt Canaan Baptist Church, 1986-; Phi Delta Kappa, 1987-; pres, Northwest Louisiana Sci Teachers Asn, 1991-92; exec bd mem, Louisiana Sci Teacher Asn, 1990-93; AKA Sorority Inc, Ebony Fashion Fair, chair, 1993-94. **Honors/Awds:** Presidential Awards for Excellence Science & Math Teaching, LA State winner, 1986, national winner, 1986; Teacher Enhancement Program Evaluator, Nat Sci Foundation, 1987; Educator Distinction Louisiana PTA, 1987; Middle School Teacher of the Year, Caddo Parish Sch Bd, 1988; Selected for the National Science Foundation, Sposored "Operation Physics," 1988; Teacher Enhancement Program Evaluator, Nat Sci Foundation, 1988-94; educator of the Year, LOU Middle Sch asn, 1992-93. **Special Achievements:** LOU's tcr representative to the first Japan & AME Grassroot Summit Tokyo & Kyoto, Nov 1991. **Business Addr:** Assistant Principal of Curriculum and Instruction, Caddo Middle Magnet, 7635 Cornelious Lane, Shreveport, LA 71106, **Business Phone:** (318)868-6588.*

PATTON, LEROI. See PATTON, LEROY.

PATTON, LEROY (LEROI PATTON)
Cinematographer. **Personal:** Born Apr 14, 1944, Alabama; son of Charles H and Neuria; married Jessie Maple; children: Mark A, Edward L & Audrey Maple. **Educ:** Ind Cent Col; Ind Univ, 1967; Calif Film Inst Filmmakers, 1971. **Career:** Cinematographer, camera operator; Films: Fame, asst camera, 1980; Fort Apache the Bronx, second camera operator, 1981; Brewster's Millions, collab dir photog, 1985; School Daze, second camera operator, 1988; Drop Squad, dir photog, 1994; The Walking Dead, camera operator, 1995; Rosewood, camera operator, 1997; Up Against the Wall, cinematographer, 1991; Women Behind the Camera, cinematographer, 2007; TV series: The Simple Life of Noah Dearborn, camera operator, 1999; The Last Brickmaker in America, camera operator, 2001; LJ Film Productions Inc, founder & owner, 1974. **Orgs:** Pres, Concerned Black Filmmakers NYC; 100 Black Men Inc mem found independent video & film; Cameraman Union Iatse Local 644. **Honors/Awds:** First & Second prize, NY Black Film Festival, 1977; Freedoms Found Award, WCBS-TV spec "My Seeds Are Gone", 1979. **Special Achievements:** Published "How to Become a Union Camerawoman Film-Videotape", 1977. **Business Addr:** Cinematographer, 20 W 120th St, New York, NY 10027.

PATTON, MARVCUS RAYMOND
Football player, business owner. **Personal:** Born May 1, 1967, Los Angeles, CA; son of Raymond (deceased) and Barbara; married Ina. **Educ:** Univ Calif, Los Angeles, BS, polit sci, 1990. **Career:** Football player (retired); Buffalo Bills, linebacker, 1990-94; Wash Redskins, 1995-98; Kans City Chiefs, 1999-2002. **Business Addr:** Owner, Girls Like Math LLC, 14001-C St Germain Dr Suite 820, Centreville, VA 20121, **Business Phone:** 800-425-0119.

PATTON, PRINCESS E
Journalist, editor. **Personal:** Born Jan 1, 1954, Nashville, TN; daughter of Gill H Gordon Sr and Mary Frances Corder (deceased); married Alexander Patton Jr, Aug 25, 1990; children: Keisha RaNese Simmons Clopton & Ayesha Patrice Patton, H Eric Simmons. **Educ:** Fisk Univ, BA, 1978. **Career:** United Methodist Publ House, Abington Press, copy ed; Vanderbilt Univ, staff reporter, calendar ed, 1984-86; The Tennessean, forum ed, columnist, ed writer, 1986-92; Meharry Medical Col, publ ed, 1994-. **Orgs:** Nat Asn Black Journalists, 1986-; Nashville Asn Minority Communicators, 1986-; Minority Journ Workshop, exe comt mem, 1991-92; Parents for Pub Edu, steering comt mem, 1990-91; Parents Against Paddling, adv comt mem, 1989-. **Honors/Awds:** 'Peace and Justice Award', Domestic Violence Prog, 1990. **Home Addr:** PO Box 22698, Nashville, TN 37202. **Business Addr:** Publications Editor, Meharry Medical College, 1005 D B Todd Blvd, Nashville, TN 37208, **Business Phone:** (615)327-6273.

PATTON, RICARDO MAURICE
Basketball coach. **Personal:** Born Oct 23, 1958, Nashville, TN; son of Leroy Reed and Juanita Patton; married Jennifer; children: Ricardo Jr & Michael. **Educ:** Belmont Col, BA, phys educ, 1980; Trevecca Nazarene Col, MA, admin & supv,1989. **Career:** Basketball Coach (retired); WTVF-TV, cameraman; Two Rivers Mid Sch, head coach, 1985-86; Hillwood High Sch, head coach, 1986-87; Mid Tenn State Univ, Murfrees boro, asst coach, 1988-90; Ark-Little Rock Univ, asst coach, 1990-91; Tenn State Univ, asst coach, 1991-93; Univ Colo, Boulder, from asst coach to head coach, 1993-2007; Northern Illinois univ, head coach, 2007-. **Orgs:** Nat Asn Basketball Coaches. **Honors/Awds:** Belmont's Sports Hall of Fame. **Business Addr:** head men's basketball coach, Northern Illinois University, Intercollegiate Athletics, Convocation Center, Dekalb, IL 60115.

PATTON, ROBERT
Government official, educator. **Personal:** Born Jun 29, 1947, Clarksdale, MS; married Dorothy J Johnson; children: Kamela, Darrell & Karen. **Educ:** Jackson State Univ, atnd, 1968; Delta State Univ, MA, 1976. **Career:** Shelby, Miss, vice mayor, 2001-05, mayor, currently; Bolivar County Sch Dist 3, teacher; Bolivar County, city alderman. **Orgs:** Jackson State Alumni Asn; St Andrews Baptist Church; vpres, PTA Broad St Sch; trustee, St Andrews Baptist Church; Bolivar County Develop Bd. **Honors/Awds:** Outstanding Comm Leader, 1974-75.

PATTON, ROSEZELIA L.
Consultant. **Personal:** Born Sep 25, 1934, Cincinnati, OH; daughter of Robert L Leahr and Rosezelia Bradshaw Leahr (deceased); married Walter B, Sep 6, 1958 (deceased); children: Councill M Harris III & Rebecca Leah Harris-Ragland. **Educ:** Western Col, attended 1972; Miami Univ, attended 1984;. **Career:** DuBois Bookstore Oxford, Ohio, trade buyer 1962-69; Western Col, Oxford,Ohio, registr, 1969-74; Miami Univ Sch Educ & Allied Prof, prog consult,1974-82; Miami Univ Roudebush Hall Oxford, asst dir aff act, 1982-84; Sears Roebuck & Co, sales rep, 1987-88; Acme Wrecking, Cincinnati, Ohio, consultant, 1990-. **Orgs:** Housemother, Alpha Phi Alpha, Miami Univ, 1959-62; treas, Church Women United Oxford, 1962-63; Minister, Music Bethel AME Oxford, 1962-72, 1977-;vol, Planned Parenthood, 1965-70; bd dirs, Butler Co MentHealth/Retardation, 1966-69; vpres, 1973-74, treas, 1974-75, Oxford Bus &Prof Women; pres, Women's Missionary Soc, 1977-84; chair budget & fin estimates Conf, Br Women's Missionary Soc, 1978-86; bd dir, Oxford Crisis& Referral Ctr, 1984-91; citizens adv comt, Butler

County C Serv Bd, 1990-92, 1993-. **Home Addr:** 520 S Main St, Oxford, OH 45056-2363. **Business Addr:** Consultant, Acme Wrecking Company Inc, 3111 Syracuse St, Cincinnati, OH 45206, **Business Phone:** (513)281-5151.

PAUL, DR. ALVIN
Educator, school administrator. **Personal:** Born Feb 17, 1941, New Roads, LA; son of Alvin Paul Jr and Pearl H; married Vera; children: Alvin Jerome, Calvin James & Douglas Fairbanks. **Educ:** Southern Univ, Baton Rouge, LA, BS, 1961; Northeastern Ill Univ, MEd,1970; Nova Southeast Univ, Ft Lauderdale, EdD, 1979. **Career:** Sch Administrator (retired); Pointe Coupee Parish Schs, New Roads, LA,math & sci teacher, 1961-62; Gary Pub Schs, math teacher, 1962-71, team leader & asst prin, 1967-69; Prairie State Col, math & educ teacher, 1971-90; Marcy Newberry Ctr, Chicago, acting exec dir & dir, 1971; Our Lady of Solace Catholic Sch Chicago, prin, 1974-75; Triton Col, River Grove Ill, math teacher, 1979-93; Prairie State Col, prof, math dept, 1990-2005. **Orgs:** St Dorothy Parish Coun, 1976-79; pres, St Dorothy Sch Bd, 1976-79; Personalized Learning Prog Adv Bd, Prairie State Col, 1976-87; Human Serv Adv Bd, Prairie State Col, 1977-90; Archdiocese Chicago, Bd Educ, 1979-84; chmn, Human Serv, Dept Prairie State Col, 1980-83; metric adv bd, Prairie State Col, 1980-82; Keeper Records, Chicago Height Alumni, 1982; Kappa Alpha Psi Chap Guide Right Comn, 1982, 1985, 1987; chmn, Acad Prog Review Comn, PSC, 1983-85; vpolemarch, Chicago Heights Alumni Kappa Alpha PsiFrat, 1985-87; dep grand knight, Knights Peter Claver Coun #158, 1987-89; former chmn, Financial Comn, St Dorothy Sch Bd; treasurer, PSC Fed Teacher Union, 1995-98; Curric Comt & Fac Senate (PSC); chmn, Teacher Aide Adv Bd, Prairie State Col; former bus mgr, Our Lady Peace Home Sch Asn; formermem, Our Lady Peace Parish Coun; polemarch, Chicago Hts Alumni, Kappa Alpha Psi Frat, 1987-88; keeper records, Chicago Alumni, Kappa Alpha Psi, 1993-; bd mem, Chicago Heights, BRCEDA, 1983-; pres, Asn Black Personnel, PSC; chair, Spiritual Life CMS; prayer group, promise keepers at St Dorothy Catholic Church, 1996-2000; chair, NCAAAE COM, PSC; St Dorothy Parish, pastoral coun, chair, 1998-2003. **Honors/Awds:** Faculty of the Year, Prairie State Col; Polemarch Award, 1981, 1996; Distinguished Alumni Award, N Central Province, KAY, 1996; Father Augustus Tolton Award, Archdiocese Chicago, 1998. **Special Achievements:** Dissertation, 'Perceived Satisfaction of Traditional Students with Traditional College Programs', Nova Southeast Univ, 1979.

PAUL, JOHN F.
Executive. **Personal:** Born Sep 13, 1934, Miami, FL; married Betty; children: Dana, Derek, Darryl & Darin. **Educ:** Cert Mgt Develop Inst, 1970; Cert Inst Ct Mgt, 1971; Cert Inst Labor & Indust Rels, 1972; Cert Nat Inst Corrections, 1974. **Career:** Calif Youth & Corrections Agency, Norwalk CA, sr group supvr, 1960-64; CA Youth & Corrections Agency, parole officer, 1964-67; State Serv Ctr, Los Angeles, supvr, counr, 1967, asst mgr, 1968-69; CEA Dept Human Resources Develop, Los Angeles, CA, mgr, 1969-71; Circuit Ct Probation Dept, dir. **Orgs:** Consult, US Dept Justice Comn Rels Officer, 1974; consult, Univ S Calif Ctr Admin Justice, 1974; Am Soc Pub Admin; Nat Coun Crime & Delinquency; MI Correctional Assoc; Acad Ct Admin; NAACP; fel, Univ Denver Inst Ct Mgt; Trade Unionist Leadership Conf; MI Black Caucus. **Honors/Awds:** China Serv Award. **Military Serv:** USN petty officer 3rd class, 1952-56; Good Conduct Award.

PAUL, TITO (TITO JERMAINE PAUL)
Football player. **Personal:** Born May 24, 1972, Kissimmee, FL. **Educ:** Ohio State Univ, econ. **Career:** Football player(retired); Ariz Cardinals, defensive back, 1995-97; Cincinnati Bengals, 1997; Denver Broncos, 1998; Wash Redskins, 1999.

PAUL, TITO JERMAINE. See PAUL, TITO.

PAUL, VERA MAXINE
Educator. **Personal:** Born Dec 14, 1940, Mansfield, LA; daughter of Virginia Elzania Smith Hall and Clifton Hall; married Alvin James Paul III, Jun 14, 1964; children: Alvin Jerome, Calvin James & Douglas Fairbanks. **Educ:** Southern Univ, Baton Rouge, BS, 1962; Chicago State Univ, Chicago, 1968-69; Roosevelt Univ, Chicago, MA, 1975. **Career:** Educator (retired) Union State High Sch, Shreveport, La, teacher, 1962-64; S Bend Community Sch Syst, S Bend, Ind, 1967-68; Chicago Bd Educ, Chicago, Ill, teacher, 1964-67; Chicago Bd Educ, Chicago, Ill, asst prin, 1968. **Orgs:** Chicago Teacher Union, 1964; Nat Asn Advan Colored People, 1965; Ill Teacher Union, 1968; Nat Math Asn, 1969-88; Ill Math Asn, 1975-88; Oper Push, 1975-88; Am Fedn Teachers, 1978; Urban League, 1980-88; Chicago Area Alliance Black Sch Educrs, 1982-87; life mem & Great Lakes regional dir, Zeta Phi Beta Sorority Inc, 1986-90; bd dir, Retired Teachers Asn Chicago, 2002-04. **Honors/Awds:** Distinguished Vol Leadership, March of Dimes, 1982; Mayoral Tribute from City of Pontiac, MI, 1987; Zeta of the Year, Zeta Phi Beta Sorority Inc, 1988; Distinguished Service Award, City Coun Detroit, 1988; Award Excellence in Education, New Sch Adminr, 1988; Distinguished Service Award, Prog Dir, Zeta Phi Beta Sorority Inc, 1992; Outstanding Leadership Award, Zeta Phi Beta Sorority Inc, 1996; Outstanding Leadership & Direction, Chicago Women Connecting UIC Ctr Res Women & Gender, 1997. **Home Addr:** 8505 S Phillips Ave, Chicago, IL 60617.

PAUL, WANDA D
Executive, vice president (organization). **Personal:** Born May 3, 1957, Philadelphia, PA; daughter of Henry and Maude Daniels; married Patrick. **Educ:** Temple Univ, BBA, 1979. **Career:** Deloitte Haskins & Sells, auditor, 1980-82; Goode Mayor Campaign, dir commun fundraising, 1983-84; Philadelphia Convention Bur, vpres finance & admin, 1985, sr vpres finance & admin, currently. **Orgs:** Nat Asn Black Accountants, 1980-; chairperson-bd dir, 1980, chair, 1993-95, 1998-2000, Urban League Philadelphia; Am Inst CPA's, 1990-; Int Asn Convention & Visitors Bur, 1989-; Int Asn Hospitality Accountants, 1990-; Pa Inst CPA's, 1990-; treas, bd dirs, Steppingstone Scholars Inc, currently; bd dir, Nat Adoption Ctr, currently. **Honors/Awds:** Whitney Young Community Service Award, Urban League of Philadelphia, 1989; Certified Public Accountant, Commonwealth Pa, 1990; Professional Achievement Award, NABA's Pro, 1990; Communication Award, Toastmasters Int, 1992; Service Award, Alumni Coun Conf, United Negro College Fund, 1993; Service Award, Urban League Guild, 1993; Volunteer of the Year, Urban League Philadelphia, 2003; Teenshop Woman of Distinction Award, 2004; Movers & Shakers Award, 2005. **Business Addr:** Senoir Vice President of Finance, Administration, Philadelphia Convention & Visitors Bureau, 1515 Market St Suite 3000, Philadelphia, PA 19102, **Business Phone:** (215)636-3300.

PAWLEY, THOMAS D., III
College teacher. **Personal:** Born Aug 5, 1917, Jackson, MS; son of Thomas D and Ethel John Woolfolk; married Ethel Louise Mc Peters; children: Thomas IV, Lawrence. **Educ:** Va State Col, AB, 1937; Univ Iowa, AM, 1939, PhD, 1949. **Career:** College teacher (retired); Prairie View A&M State Col, instr, 1939-40; Lincoln Univ MO, fac, 1940, div chmn, 1967-77, dean arts & scis, 1977-83, instr, from asst prof to prof, writer in residence, head dept commun, 1983-85, curators, disting prof of speech & theatre, head dept communs, 1985-88, curators, distinguished prof emer, speech & theatre, 1988; ; vis prof, Univ Calif, Santa Barbara, 1968; vis prof, Northern IL Univ, 1971; vis prof, Univ IA 1976. **Orgs:** Pres, Nat Asn Dramat & Speech Arts, 1953-55; adv comt, Am Educ Theatre Asn, 1953-55; delegate, Episcopal Diocesan Conv, St Louis, 1963; pres, J C Library bd, 1970-72; ; treas, Jefferson Reg Libr Bd 1974; vpres, Alpha Phi Alpha Frat, 1975-79; Theatre Educ Am Theatre Asn, 1977-79; pres, Speech & Theatre Asn, Mo, 1977-78; delegate Governor's Conf on Libr Services 1978, 1990; Theatre Adv Comm Mo Arts Coun, 1979-87; vis prof, Univ Mo, 1980, 1988, 1990; exec Com Black Theatre Prog, Am Theatre Asn, 1980-83; bd dirs, Mid Am Arts Alliance, 1981; Mo Arts Coun, 1981-87; Nat Endowment Arts Theatre Panel, 1986-88; pres, Nat Conf African, 1987-90; Mo Humanities Coun, 1989-95; delegate, White House Conf on Libr & Info Serv, 1991; Historian Alpha Phi Alpha Fraternity Inc, 1993-96; Vestry, Grace Episcopal Church, 1994-97; vice chmn, Mayor's Comm Res Stand; Org comn Jefferson City Coun Race & Religion. **Honors/Awds:** Shields-Howard Creative Writing Award, Va State Col, 1934; Nat Theatre Conf Fel,1947-48; First Prize Jamestown, Va Corp Playwriting Contest, 1954;"FFV" Full-length drama, 1963; First production by Stagecrafters Lincoln Univ, 1963; The Tumult and the Shouting Drama Two Acts, 1969; First prod by Inst in Dramatic Arts Lincoln Univ 1969; Publ Hatch & Shine 1974; Nat Asn Dramatic & Speech s Outstanding Serv Award, 1984; Nat Conf African Am Theatre Mister Brown Award, 1986; Distinguished Alumnus NAFEO, Va State Univ, 1988; Am Theatre Fel, 1989; Distinguished Alumnus Achievement Award, Univ Iowa Alumni Asn, 1990; Award of Merit, Alpha Phi Alpha Fraternity Inc, 1996; Mo Arts Coun Award, 1999; Winona Lee Fletcher Award, Black Theatre Network, 2000. **Home Addr:** 1014 Lafayette St, Jefferson City, MO 65101, **Home Phone:** (573)635-2719. *

PAXTON, GERTRUDE GARNES. See Obituaries section.

PAYDEN, REV. HENRY J, SR.
Clergy. **Personal:** Born Apr 3, 1923, Columbus, OH; married Phyllis M Smith; children: Garnet, William B, Linda, Henry J, Wendy M & Paula Y. **Educ:** Cert Clin Psychol & Pastoral Coun, Ashland Theol Sem, 1971; Capital Univ; Cleveland Bible Col, Westminster; Western Res Univ. **Career:** Holy Trinity Baptist Church, organizer & pastor, 1961-; St Paul Baptist Church, New Castle PA, former pastor; Macedonia Baptist Church, Toledo; Gr Abyssinia Baptist Church, Cleveland; Black Shield Cleveland Police Unit, chaplain. **Orgs:** Cleveland Women's Sym Orch; Chaplain Amvets; Mt Pleasant Community Ctr; Pub Bd & Teacher Prog Nat Baptist Conv Inc. **Honors/Awds:** Awarded automobile as Soloist in Burts Hour Cleveland, 1947; Pastor of Year, 1956. **Military Serv:** AUS, 9 Cav sargent. **Business Addr:** Pastor, Holy Trinity Baptist Church, 3808 14 E 131 St, Cleveland, OH 44120, **Business Phone:** (216)561-4121.

PAYNE, ALLEN
Actor. **Personal:** Born Jul 7, 1968, Harlem, NY. **Educ:** Studied dance. **Career:** Films: Rooftops, 1989; Cookie, 1989; New Jack City, 1991; CB4, 1993;Jason's Lyric, 1994; Vampire in Brooklyn, 1995; The Walking Dead, 1995; A Price Above Rubies, 1998; The Perfect Storm, 2000; 30 Years to Life, 2001; Blue Hill Ave, 2001; From the Outside Looking In, 2003; Playas Ball, 2003;Crossover, 2006; TV series: "The Jeffersons", 1983; "The Cosby Show", 1990-92; "The Fresh Prince of Bel-Air", 1992; "A Different World", 1992; Roc, 1993; "The Tuskegee Airmen", 1995; "Malcolm & Eddie", 1996; Double Platinum, 1999; "Commitments", 2001; "All of Us", 2004; "CSI: NY", 2004; "Cross Over", 2006; "House of Payne",2006-09. **Honors/Awds:** Black Reel, 2002. **Business Phone:** (212)997-1818.*

PAYNE, ALLISON GRIFFIN
Television journalist. **Personal:** Born Feb 12, 1964, Richmond, VA; daughter of Dana and Kathryn. **Educ:** Univ Detroit, BA, liberal arts, 1985; Bowling Green State, MA, radio, tv & film, 1992. **Career:** WNWO-TV, Toledo, Ohio, intern, reporter, anchor, 1987-88; WNEM-TV, Saginaw, MI, anchor, 1988-90; WGN-TV, Chicago, IL, reporter, 1990-, "People to People", co-anchor, currently; WVAZ-FM 102.7, "The Real Show", co-host, 2005-. **Orgs:** Delta Sigma Theta. **Honors/Awds:** Numerous awards including 9 Emmy awards, Regional Award, Radio TV News Dirs, 1991; Mark of Excellence Award, Chicago Asn Black Journalists, 1992; Peter Lisage Award, Soc Prof Journalists, 1991; Silver Dome Award, Ill Broadcasters Asn, 1991-92. **Business Addr:** Reporter, Co-Anchor, WGN-TV, 2501 W Bradley Pl, Chicago, IL 60618-4718, **Business Phone:** (773)528-2311.

PAYNE, CECILIA
Manager, executive director. **Personal:** Born Dec 5, 1962, Bronx, NY; daughter of Noah Blount and Patricia McKinney; married George T Payne, Jul 24, 1988; children: George M. **Educ:** Sch Visual Arts, BFA, 1984; Rensselaer Polytech Inst, MS, mgt & mkt. **Career:** Juvenile Diabetes Mag, assoc art dir & prod, 1987-88; Philip Morris Mag, assoc art dir & prod, 1987-88; Signs & Unique Designs, dir, co founder & cheif exec officer, 1991-99; St Joseph Col, creative design dir, 1999-. **Orgs:** Literacy Vols, CT; Dept Social Servs, Hartford, CT; Family Life Educ, Hartford, CT; The Nat Conf Community & Justice, Windsor, CT. **Special Achievements:** Art Gallery Exhibitions : West Hartford Art League, Juried Art Show, West Hartford, CT, 1997; Art Space Gallery, Colors and Textures, Hartford, CT, 1998; Art Space Gallery, Women in Art, Hartford, CT, 2001; State Treasures' Office: Art in Public Spaces, Hartford, CT, 2001; The Pump House Gallery, CP2, Hartford, CT, 2003. **Business Addr:** Creative Design Director, St Joseph College, 41 Clarendon Ave, W Hartford, CT 06110-1208.*

PAYNE, DEBRA K
Administrator, state government official. **Personal:** Born Aug 18, 1964, Memphis, TN; daughter of Robert and Dorothy. **Educ:** Capital Univ, BA, eng, prof writing. **Career:** Ohio Civil Rights Comn, civil rights rep, 1989-93; Ohio Dept Health, labor rels officer, 1993-98, acting EEO chief, 1998-99, EEO chief, 1999-. **Orgs:** Secy, exec comt, Columbus Asn Black Journalists, 1992-95; King Arts Complex, 1999-; YWCA, 2000-; Human Resources Asn Cent Ohio, 2000-; Nat Asn African Am Human Resources; Nat Asn Female Execs; OH Investigator's asn; United Way Key Club; Junior League Columbus. **Honors/Awds:** Mary Margaret Doonan Scholar for Excellence in Creative Writing, Capital Univ, 1987; Employee of the Month, Ohio Dept Health, 1999; Director's Award for Citizenship, 2002. **Special Achievements:** United Way Campaign, agency coordinator, record breaking campaigns, 1999, 2000 & 2001; Operation Feed, agency coordinator, record breaking campaign, 1999. **Business Addr:** EEO Chief, Ohio Department of Health, 246 N High St 1st Fl, Columbus, OH 43215, **Business Phone:** (614)466-6258.

PAYNE, DONALD M.
Congressperson (u.s. federal government). **Personal:** Born Jul 16, 1934, Newark, NJ; son of William Evander and Norma Garrett; married Hazel Johnson, Jun 18, 1958 (died 1963); children: Donald Milford & Wanda. **Educ:** Seton Hall Univ, BA, social studies, 1957, 1963. **Career:** S Side High Sch, Newark, NJ, teacher, 1957; Robert Treat Jr High Sch, Newark, NJ, teacher, 1957-59; Pulaski Ele Sch, Passaic, NJ, teacher, 1959-64; Prudential Ins Co, Newark, NJ, affiliated with, 1964-69, mgr,1969; Urban Data Syst, Newark, NJ; Atlantic Western Ins Co, Hamilton, Bermuda, dir & pres; Essex Co Bd Chosen Freeholders, Newark, NJ, mem, 1972-77, dir, 1977-82; Newark Muni Coun, council mem, 1982-88; Dem Steering Comt, mem; US House of Rep, mem, 1988, 10th Congressional Dist NJ, congressman, 1988-, House Comt Educ & Labor, mem. **Orgs:** Pres, Nat Coun YMCA's; chmn, World Refugee & Rehab Comn; bd dirs, Congional Award Found; Trans Africa; Nat Endowment for Dem; Boys & Girls Clubs Newark; Newark Day Ctr; Fighting Back Initiative; Democratic Whip Orgn; chmn, Congressional Black Caucus; Congressional rep, UN. **Honors/Awds:** Hon doctorates: Chicago State Univ, Drew Univ, Essex County Col & William Paterson Univ. **Special Achievements:** First Black pres of the YMCA; First African Am Congressman, 10th Congressional Dist NJ. **Business Addr:** Congressman, 10th Congressional District New Jersey, US House of Representatives, 2310 Rayburn House Off Bldg, Washington, DC 20515-3010, **Business Phone:** (202)225-3436.

PAYNE, FREDA CHARCELIA
Singer, actor, television actor. **Personal:** Born Sep 19, 1942, Detroit, MI; married Gregory Abbott (divorced); children: Gregory Jr. **Career:** Singer & actress; Albums: Band of Gold, 1970; Payne & Pleasure, 1974; Come See About Me, 2001; Films: Book of Numbers, 1973; Private Obsession, 1995; Sprung, vocal-

ist, 1997; Rag doll, 1999; Nutty Professor II: The Klumps, 2000; Deadly Rhapsody, 2001; Cordially Invited, 2007; TV Series: "The Tonight Show Starring Johnny Carson", 1973; "Love & Payne", 2003; "Today's Black Woman", 1981; "Living Single", 1993; "Fire & Ice", 2001; "Saurian", 2006. **Honors/Awds:** Appeared on American Idol, 2009. **Business Addr:** Actress, Fleischer Studios, 10160 Cielo Dr, Beverly Hills, CA 90210-2037, **Business Phone:** (310)276-7503.*

PAYNE, JACQUELINE LAVERNE
Lawyer. **Personal:** Born Dec 15, 1957, Atlanta, GA; daughter of Doris Hanson and Amos Jr; married Timothy Beckum, May 21, 1994; children: Alexis Payne-Scott, Brooke Payne-Scott & Jordan T Beckum. **Educ:** Spelman Col, BA, 1977; Univ Ga, JD, 1980. **Career:** Atlanta Legal Aid Soc Inc, staff atty, 1980-85, managing atty, 1985-86, managing atty, supervising atty, currently; Reginald Heber Smith Community Lawyer, fel, 1980-82; Hyatt Legal Servs, managing atty, 1986-88. **Orgs:** State Bar Ga, 1982-; troop leader, Northwest Ga Girl Scout Coun, 1991-99; exec comt, Atlanta Fulton Co Comn C & Youth, 1992-2000; Ga Asn Black Women Attys; bd dirs, Atlanta Bar Asn. **Honors/Awds:** Families First Award, Atlanta Bar Asn, Family Law Sect, 2001; Don Bradley Award, State Bar Ga, 2002. **Home Addr:** 1582 Arden Dr SW, Marietta, GA 30008. **Business Addr:** Supervising Attorney, Atlanta Legal Aid Society Inc, 151 Spring St NW, Atlanta, GA 30303-2097, **Business Phone:** (404)524-5811.

PAYNE, JAMES EDWARD
Lawyer. **Personal:** Born Jul 7, 1944, Cleveland, OH; son of Booker T and Vito; married Margaret Ralston Payne, Dec 5, 1976; children: Maya Renee. **Educ:** Cleveland State Univ, BBA, 1973; Univ Akron Sch Law, JD, 1977. **Career:** Lawyer (retired); Cleveland Trust Co, staff asst, 1975-77; Ford Motor Co, labor rels rep & ind rels analyst, 1977-83; Western Reserve Legal Serv, staff atty, 1983-84; Parms, Purnell & Gilbert, assoc atty, 1984-87; City Akron, asst prosecutor, asst law dir, 1984-87, dep dir law. **Orgs:** Past coun deleg mem, Ohio State Bar Asn, 1979-; past pres, Sigma Pi Phi Fraternity, Beta Rho Boule, Past Sire Archon, 1983-; past pres, Akron Bar Asn, 1983; Alpha Phi Alpha Fraternity Inc, 1986; life mem, Akron Br, Nat Asn Advan Colored People, 1988; Leadership Akron Alumni Asn, 1990; Salvation Army Adv Bd, 1993; Akron Barristers Asn. **Honors/Awds:** Service Award, Akron Urban League, 1988; Service Award, Univ Akron Black Law Students Asn, 1992; Harold K Stubbs Humanitarian Award, St Paul AME Church, 1994; Meritorious Service Award, Akron Bar Asn, 1998. **Military Serv:** AUS, first lt, 1965-68.

PAYNE, JERRY OSCAR
School administrator. **Personal:** Born Jul 31, 1953, Madera, CA; son of Oscar (deceased) and Sallie Ophelia Smiley; children: Deidre Avery, Jonathan & Keri. **Educ:** San Jose State Univ, San Jose Ca, BA, 1975; Ariz State Univ, Tempe, MA, 1978; Lewis & Clark Col, Portland, educ admin cert, 1984; Calif Sch Leadership Acad, 1987-90; Univ Mich, Ann Arbor, Horace Rackham doctorate fellow, 1990; Harvard Prin Ctr, 1992; UC Davis, CSU Fresno Joint Doctoral Prog, EdD, 2002. **Career:** Fremont Unified Sch Dist, Sunnyvale, CA, Title VII, instr, 1974-76; Phoenix Union High Sch, Phoenix, spec educ, Ariz hist instr, 1976-78; El Dorado High Sch, Las Vegas NV, spec educ instr, 1978-80; Clark County Classroom Teachers Asn, Las Vegas, negotiations chmn, 1978-80; Grant High Sch, Portland, spec educ instr, 1980-82; Benson Polytechnic High Sch, Portland, integration counsr, 1982-84, from admin asst to prin, 1984-87; Lincoln Summer High Sch Portland, prin, 1985-87; Martin Luther King, Jr, Junior High Sch, Sacramento Ca, prin,1987-90; Parker Elem Sch(K-6), Oakland, prin, 1990-96; Hayward Unified Dist, Hayward, dir stud serv, 1996-2002; St Helen Parish Sch, supt schs, 2002-. **Orgs:** Asn Calif Adminrs; Asn Supv & Curric Develop; Am Asn Sch Adminrs; Comn Dist Adminrs; bd dir, treas, found Bd mem, & life mem, Nat Alliance Black Sch Educs; Am Voc Asn; Nat Coun Local Admin Voc, Tech & Practical Arts Educ; Hugh O'Brian Alumni Asn; Calif League Middle Sch; Nat Asn Elem Sch Prin; Ariz State Univ Alumni Asn; Kiwanis Int; Toastmasters Int; Harvard Principal's Ctr Alumni; NAACP, life mem; NAACP Legal Redress Comt; La Asn Sch Supts; La Asn Sch Bds; IEL Alumnus. **Honors/Awds:** Distinguished Leadership & Service, Nat Alliance Black Educrs, Outstanding Contribution C; Partnership in Educ Award, Xerox Corp; Appreciation Award, US Navy; Outstanding Volunteer Service, Marcus Foster Found; Dedicated Volunteer Service, Castlemont High Sch. **Special Achievements:** Author: Turning Around an Urban School: The Vision Versus the Reality, Far West Regional Lab, San Francisco, CA, 1989; author, Effects of Low Expectations on Minority and Low Socio-Economic Students, Educational Research Project, 1985; author, Do Children Whose Parents Have Less Than a High School Diploma Impact Their Child's Academic Achievements?, Arizona State University Graduate School, 1978; co-author, Administrators and Choice, UC Davis CSU, Fresno, 1992; State of California Commission on Teacher Credentialing, admin advisory panel, 1990-96. **Business Addr:** Superintendent of Schools, St Helena Parish Schools, PO Box 912, Greensburg, LA 70441, **Business Phone:** (225)222-6016.

PAYNE, DR. JUNE P
Psychologist. **Personal:** Born Jun 11, 1948, Charlottesville, VA; daughter of Walter A and Theola Reaves; married Charles R; children: Lauren R & Gregory A. **Educ:** Va State Univ, BA, 1970; Ball State Univ, MA, 1974, PhD, 1980. **Career:** Charlottesville Dept Pub Welfare, social worker, 1970-72; Cambridge House Inc, counr, 1974-75, dir treat, 1976-78; Comprehensive Ment Health Serv East Cent Ind, psych, 1980-83; Ball State Univ, Coun & Psychol Serv Ctr, coun psychol, 1983-, dir coun & health servs, currently. **Orgs:** Pres, secy, Ind Asn Black Psych, 1984-85; bd dir, Hospitality House; Nat Asn Advan Colored People; Delta Sigma Theta Sor; Coalition 100 Women; bd dirs, Altrusa Club Muncie; vpres, Altrusa Internation, 2007-08, pres elect, 2008-09. **Honors/Awds:** Jack Beyerl Outstanding Professional, 2002; Indiana Women of Achievement, 2007. **Home Addr:** 7405 N Landings Trail, Muncie, IN 47303. **Business Addr:** Director, Counseling and Health Services, Ball State University, Counseling Center, 2000 W Univ Ave, Muncie, IN 47306, **Business Phone:** (765)289-1264.

PAYNE, KENNETH VICTOR
Basketball player, basketball coach. **Personal:** Born Nov 25, 1966, Laurel, MS; son of Cleveland Payne; married Michelle; children: Alexander & Alexis. **Educ:** Univ Louisville, BS, sports admin, 2000. **Career:** Basketball player (retired), basketball coach; Philadelphia 76ers, forward-guard, 1989-93; Continental Basketball Asn; Taipans Cairns; Univ Ore, asst coach, 2004-. **Business Phone:** (503)725-3055.

PAYNE, LES. See PAYNE, LESLIE.

PAYNE, LESLIE (LES PAYNE)
Journalist. **Personal:** Born Jul 12, 1941, Tuscaloosa, AL; married Violet S Cameron; children: Tamara Olympia, Jamal Kenyatta & Haile Kipchoge. **Educ:** Univ Conn, BA, eng, 1964. **Career:** Newsday, babylon town, beat reporter, 1969, asst ed, 1970, ed, writer 1971, investigative reporter, 1972-80, minor affairs specialist, 1973-78, nat corresp & columnist, 1980-85, asst managing ed, assoc managing ed emer, currently; United Muslim Asn, Toledo, dep managing ed, currently; Columbia Univ, Grad Sch Jour, David Laventhol Chair. **Orgs:** NY Asn Black Journalists, 1977-80; Int Press Inst; Nat Asn Black Journalists, 1978. **Honors/Awds:** Headliner Award, 1974; Sigma Delta Chi Award, 1974; United Nations Hunger Award, 1983; Tobenkin Award, Columbia Univ, 1978; Man of the Yr Award, Nat Asn Black Bus & Prof Women, 1978; Frederick Douglass Prize, Nat Asn Black Journalists, 1978; Pulitzer Prize, 1974; Pulitzer Prize nominee Foreign Reporting, 1978; Pulitzer Prize Cable TV Ace Award, 1990; AP & UPI Commentary Awards, 1983-84; Jour Prize, 100 Black Men; Unity Awards, Lincoln Univ; Hon Doctorate, Medgar Evers Col; Hon Doctorate, Long Island Univ. **Special Achievements:** Author: The Heroin Trail; Life and Death of the Symbionese Liberation Army. **Military Serv:** AUS, capt, 6 yrs; Bronze Star, 2 Commendation Medals. **Business Addr:** Assistant Managing Editor Emeritus, Newsday, 235 Pinelawn Rd, Melville, NY 11747-4250, **Business Phone:** (631)843-2805.

PAYNE, MARGARET RALSTON
School administrator, educator. **Personal:** Born Jan 31, 1946, Louisville, KY; daughter of Henry Morris and Rena Owens; married James Edward, Dec 5, 1976; children: Maya Renee. **Educ:** Kalamazoo Col, BA, 1968; Fourah Bay Col, Univ Sierra Leone, attended 1967; Kent State Univ, MA, 1972. **Career:** Kent State Univ, asst prof psychol, 1972-78, adj asst prof psychol, 1978, asst dean, prof develop serv, 1973-89, spec asst vice provost stud affairs, 1989-92, Corp & Found Rel, dir, 1992-96, Bd Trustees, exec asst pres & secy, 1996-; Ralston Payne Enterprises, vpres, currently. **Orgs:** Ohio & Nat Asn Women Educ, 1979-2000; bd mem, Portage Co Comn Action Coun, 1979-85; pres, Kent Area Chap Links Inc, 1984-88; dist adv, Nat Alpha Lambda Delta, 1985-87; Nat Adv Comt, SAGE: bd mem, Akron Urban League, 1988-91; dir, Links Found Inc, 1992-94; pres, Kathryn Sisson Phillips Trust, 1994-96; dir, Summa Health Syst Found, 1995-; bd mem, Women's Endowment Fund, Akron Community Found, 1995-2000; chair, Grant, Awards & Scholar, Links Inc, 1998-2002; dir, Summa Health Syst, 1998-; bd mem, Western Res Girl Scout Coun; Nat Asn Black Journalists. **Honors/Awds:** Award, Fed Dept Health Educ & Welfare Dept Educ, 1974, 1978-89; Nat Finalist, White House Fel Prog, 1979; Service Certificate, Asn Handicapped Stud Serv Prog Post Sec Educ, 1987; Leadership Award, Kent State Univ Upward Bound, 1989; Hilda A Davis Award for Educational Leadership, NAWE, 1992; Josseph D Lewis Trailblazer Award, Ohio Asn Educ Opportunity Prog Personnel, 2003; Akron YWCA Woman of Professional Excellence Award, 2003. **Home Addr:** 797 Cliffside Dr, Akron, OH 44313-5609. **Business Addr:** Executive Assistant to President, Secretary, Kent State University, PO Box 5190, Kent, OH 44242-0001, **Business Phone:** (330)672-2210.

PAYNE, MITCHELL HOWARD
School administrator. **Personal:** Born Feb 2, 1950, Shelbyville, KY; son of Llewellyn and Hattie Cohrell; married Karen W Bearden, Jul 11, 1987; children: Janell Mitchet, William Mitchell. **Educ:** Western Kentucky Univ, BA, 1972, MPA, 1973; Univ Louisville, JD, 1978. **Career:** Univ Louisville, dir minority affairs; Commonwealth Kentucky, Frankfort KY, exec asst to sec of finance comm admin; Univ Louisville, assoc vpres admin, 1990-. **Orgs:** Nat Bar Asn; Am Soc Pub Admin; Nat Asn State Dir Admin & Gen Serv, 1987-; Kappa Alpha Psi Frat; bd mem, Prichard Comm Acad Excellence, 1987-; adv coun, Kentucky State Univ Sch Pub Affairs, 1987-; Nat Forum Black Pub Admin, 1988-; steering comt, YMCA Black Achievers Prog, 1989-; Sigma Pi Phi Frat, 1989-; NACUBO, 1990; Ky Coc, Mny Bus, bus adv bd, 1992; Ky Heritage Coun, Afa heritage task force, 1992; 100 Black Men of Louisville, founding mem. **Honors/Awds:** Kappa Alpha Psi Frat Alumni Achievement Award, 1985; Dr Martin Luther King Appreciation Award, Western Kentucky Univ, 1986; Alpha Kappa Alpha Sorority, "Men Who Cook," 1988; Volunteer of the Year, Louisville YMCA Black Achievers, 1989; Shelbyville KY, Black Achiever of the Year Award, Nat Asn Advan Colored People, 1989; Sigma Pi Phi, Man of the Year Award, 1991. **Business Addr:** Associate Vice President for Business Affairs, University Louisville, Off VPres Admin, Louisville, KY 40292, **Business Phone:** (502)852-5155.*

PAYNE, DR. N JOYCE
School administrator. **Personal:** Born Jan 29, 1941, Washington, DC; daughter of Eunice Brown Johnson Tyson and Jesse Maryland Tyson; married Charles Harrington (divorced 1984); children: April A & Wynton K. **Educ:** DC Teachers Col, Wash, DC, BS, 1971; Atlanta Univ, Atlanta, GA, MS, 1976, EdD, 1976. **Career:** Ford Fellowship, Ford Found, 1971; Presidential Coun Women's Educ Progs, DC specialist, 1977-79; President's Adv Coun Women, DC, educ specialist, 1979-81; Global Systs Inc, pres; Nat Asn State Univs & Land-Grant Cols, DC dir; Off Advan Pub Black Cols, dir, 1979-; Thurgood Marshall Scholar Fund, founder, 1984-. **Orgs:** Foreign Serv Performance Eval bd, US State Dept; Zeta Phi Beta Sorority; founder, Coalition 100 Black Women, Inc, Wash DC Chap; bd trustee, univ DC. **Special Achievements:** Dr. Payne has published and presented a number of papers on "Women in Administration in Higher Education"; "Women in Urban School Systems, New Women, & The Consequences of Power"; "Maintaining the Competitive Tradition" in Minorities in Higher Education; "Hidden Messages in the Pursuit of Equality" in Academe; and "Black Colleges in an Expanding Economy" in the American Council on Education's Educational Record. **Business Addr:** Founder, Thurgood Marshall College Fund, 80 Maiden Lane Suite 2204, New York, NY 10038.

PAYNE, OSBORNE ALLEN
Consultant. **Personal:** Born May 26, 1925, Bedford, VA; married Famebridge Cunningham; children: Andrea Kyles, Famebridge S & Sarita S. **Educ:** Va Union Univ, BS, 1950, MS, 1955; Univ Va, attended 1961; Univ MD,attended 1974. **Career:** Consultant (retired), Director; Richmond, VA, teacher, 1950-57, prin, 1957-62; Cuttington Col Liberia, W Africa, act dean instr, 1963-65; TAPRoanoke, Va, field dir, 1965-66, educ dir, 1966-68; NEA Search, dir, 1968-70; NEA Spec Serv, field coordr, 1970-73; Baltimore-Specialty Tours, pres; Broadway-Payne Inc, pres, owner, operator, 1973-97; Nat Educ Asn, consumer adv, 1974-75; Columbia Bancorp, dir emer. **Orgs:** Bd trustees, Va Union Univ, 1978; pres, Presidents Roundtable; Greater Baltimore Comn, 1984-86; founder, Asn Black Charities Baltimore; founder, Baltimore Black McDonald's Owner Operator Asn, 1986-. **Honors/Awds:** Golden Arch Elite McDonald's Award, 1976-77; Governor's Citation for Outstanding Service MD, 1982; Presidential Citation, Nat Asn Equal Opportunity Higher Educ, 1983; President's Citation, Baltimore City Coun, 1985; Congressional Merit, Citations Md House Deleg, 41st Dist Baltimore, US Sen, 1985; Businessman of the Year, Int Asn Negro & Prof Women; Ronald McDonald Award Community Involvement, 1985; Small Business Award, Mayor Baltimore, 1985; Honorary Degree Doctor International Law, 1985; Man of the Year, Baltimore Mkt Asn, 1985. **Military Serv:** USN, 3rd Class Petty Officer, 1943-46.

PAYNE, RONNIE E
Consultant, executive, founder (originator). **Personal:** Born Jun 12, 1940, Palmersville, TN; son of Noel and Thelma Williams; married Jerry, 1959 (died 1983); children: Angela, Sherri Williams, Anita & Antoinette Benford; married Norris, Feb 9, 1985. **Educ:** Tenn State Univ, BS, 1961; Geo State Univ, 1968. **Career:** Lockheed, Missiles & Space, subcontract crd, 1961-64, GA, div purchasing supr, 1965-67; IBM, sr buyer, 1968-70, central purchasing procurement mgr, 1971-76; Digital Equip corp, Springfield plant mgr, 1978-83, corp purchasing mgr, 1983-88, corp purchasing vpres, strategic resources group staff mgr & vpres, 1988-93; Excel Partners Inc, gen partner, managing dir, 1993-95; Purchasing Services Inc, founder & managing dir, 1995-. **Orgs:** Nat Minority Supplier Develop, 1987-; Shawmut Middlesex Bank, 1986-; Boston Univ, SchTheol, 1990-; adv, Digital's african Heritage Alliance, 1990-; steering comt co-chair, Digitals Nat Asn Advan Colored People & ACT-SO, 1987-92. **Honors/Awds:** "A Blueprint for Success" Leadership Ctr StudyBlack exec, subject of study. **Special Achievements:** First african ceo of the Greater Springfield Co, 1981-82. **Business Addr:** Founder, Managing director, Purchasing Services Inc, 4950 Parkside Ave Suite 550, Philadelphia, PA 19131-4746, **Business Phone:** (215)477-4799.

PAYNE, ULICE, JR.
Baseball executive, executive director, lawyer. **Personal:** Born Jan 1, 1955?, Donora, PA; son of Ulice Sr and Mary; married Car-

mella; children: Amber & Ulice III. **Educ:** Marquette Univ, BA, business admin, 1978, JD, 1982; Univ London, England, master's law prog, 1988. **Career:** US Dist Co, E Dist WI, law clerk, 1982-83; WI comnr securities, 1985-87;pvt pract attny, 1988-98; Foley & Lardner Law Firm, attny, 1998-02; Milwaukee Brewers, ceo, 2002-03; Addison-Clifton LLC, pres, 2002; WisEnergy Corp, dir, 2003; Addison-Clifton, Managing Member. **Orgs:** Bd of dirs, Milwaukee Brewers Baseball Club; WI chp, Nat MS Society; YMCAof Metro Milwaukee; bd of dirs, WI Energy Corp; bd of dirs-Badger MeterInc; bd of dirs, Midwest Express Holdings; bd of dirs, State FinancialServices Corp; bd of dirs, Bradley Ctr Sports & Entertainment Corp; bd ofdirs, Children's Hosp of WI; Trustee, Northwestern Mutual Life InsuranceCompany. **Honors/Awds:** Ranked 14, 101 Most Influential Minorities in Sports, Sports Illustrated, 2003. **Special Achievements:** First Afr Am to head a major baseball franchise, 2002. **Business Addr:** Director, Addison-Clifton, 13555 Bishops Court Suite 245, Brookfield, WI 53005.*

PAYNE, VERNON
School administrator, basketball coach. **Personal:** Born Apr 20, 1945, Michigan City, IN; married Dorphine; children: Linda, David & Arthur. **Educ:** Ind State Univ, BS, speech pathol & audiol, 1968, MS, guid & coun, 1972. **Career:** Int Bus Mach Corp, res intern, 1967; City Mich, Off Econ Opportunity, asst exec dir, 1968-70; Indiana Univ, basketball coach; Univ Denver, basketball coach; Wayne State Univ, head basketball coach, 1977-82; Western Mich Univ, head basketball coach, 1982-89, off admis & orientation, asst dir, 1989-92, Univ recreation prog & facility, dir,1992-98; asst vpres stud affairs, 1998-2001, assoc vpres stud affairs, 2002-. **Orgs:** Chair, Detroit Edison Sch County, Personnel Comn, 1977-79; mem scholar comn, Western Mich Univ, Fund Advan Minorities Educ, 1989-, diversity comn, 1989-; brd dirs, Am Cancer Soc Kalamazoo County, 1990-91; brd dirs, Lakeside Home, 1990-; adv bd, Kalamazoo County Walk Warmth, 1990-; chair, Resource Develop Comn, 1991; Mich Higher Educ Facilities Authority, 1993-2001; Info Tech Strategic Plan Comn, WMU, 1999-; Restricted Weapons Policy Comn, WMU, 1999-; Emergency Plan Comn, WMU, 1999-; Vertical Portal Develop Comn, 1999-; USAG, 2001-; SIS, 2001-. **Honors/Awds:** Man of the Year, 1987; Merit Award for Distinguished Coaching, Nat Assn Basketball Coaches US, 1988; Indiana Basketball Hall of Fame, Silver Anniversary Team, Inductee, 1989; Michigan Volunteer of the Year; Outstanding Service Award, Detroit Pub Sch System, 1990; Faculty Member ofthe Year, 1992; Western Mich Univ, Nat Pan-Hellenic Conf, 1992; Vernon Payne Day, named in honor, Mayor Austin, Tex, Aug 1, 1997. **Home Addr:** 1412 W Kilgore Rd, Kalamazoo, MI 49008. **Business Addr:** Associate Vice President for Student Affairs, Western Mich University, 2120 Faunce Stud Serv Bldg, Kalamazoo, MI 49008.

PAYNE, WILFORD ALEXANDER
Executive director. **Personal:** Born Jan 4, 1945, Youngstown, OH. **Educ:** Blufton Col, Blufton OH, attended 1965; Youngstown State Univ, OH, BA, 1973; Ohio State Univ, MHA, 1975. **Career:** Health & Welfare Asn, scholar, 1973-75; St Joseph's Riverside Hosp, Warren OH, admin resident, 1974; OH State Univ Hosp, Columbus, admin asst, 1975; Monongahela Valley Asn Health Centers Inc, Fairmont, WV, admin asst, 1976-77; Monongahela Valley Asn Health Centers Inc, health main coordr, 1976-77; Alma Illery Med Ctr, Primary Care Health Serv Inc, proj dir, 1977-. **Orgs:** Bd dir, Eastern Allegheny Co Health Corp, 1977-; bd dir, Family Planning Coun Southwestern, PA, 1977-; Nat Asn Comt Health Centers Inc, 1977-; instr, Tri Reg Cluster Training Ctr, NY, 1979-; comt mem, United Way Rev Comt Planning & Allocations. **Military Serv:** USAF, sgt, 1966-70. **Business Addr:** Project Director, Alma Illery Medical Center, Primary Care and Health Services, 7227 Hamilton Ave, Pittsburgh, PA 15208, **Business Phone:** (412)687-1250.

PAYNE, WILLIAM D
Government official. **Educ:** Rutgers Univ, BA, polit sci. **Career:** Bus consult; NJ Gen Assembly, assemblyman, 1998-2008, dep majority conf leader, 2002-08. **Orgs:** Essex County Improv Authority, vice chair, 1980-86; chair, Newark Housing Authority, 1986-89; NJ Coun Adult Literacy, 1992; NJ Cong Award Coun, 1995; NJ Tourism Adv Coun, 1998; NJ Joint Comt Mentoring, 1999-; Essex County, dep chief staff, 2003-; pres, Bd Trustees, Chad Independent Sch, 2003-; NJ Criminal Disposition Comn, 2004-. **Honors/Awds:** Man of the Year Award, Nat Asn Negro Bus & Prof Women's Club, N NJ Unit, 2000.

PAYNE-NABORS, COLLEEN J
Executive. **Personal:** Born in Oklahoma City, OK. **Career:** Frontier City Amusement Pk, staff; MCI Diag Ctr, founder & chief exec officer, 1998-; CP Enterprises LLC, founder & chief exec officer, currently. **Orgs:** Am Col Radiol; Am Healthcare Radiol Adminrs; Am Registry Regist Technologists; Am Soc Regist Technologists; Internal Soc Accreditation Echocardiography; Internal Soc Accreditation Nuclear Med; Northeastern Okla Soc Nuclear Med; Soc Nuclear Med; Okla State Univ Women's Found; Planned Parenthood; Mothers Group. **Honors/Awds:** Business Innovator of the Year, Black Enterprises Mag, 2003; Community Serv Award, Omega Psi Phi Fraternity Inc, 2003; Pinnacle Award, Tulsa Comn Status Women, 2004; Female Entrepreneur of the Year Award, AXA Advisors, 2004; Business Person of the Year, 2004; Business Innovator & Entrepreneur of the Year, 2004; Business Excellence Award, Tulsa People Mag, 2004; Woman of the Year, Jour Rec, 2006; Oklahoma Small Business Person of the Year, 2006, 2007. **Special Achievements:** Oklahoma Venture of the Year finalist, Grace Franklin Bernsen Found, 2004; featured in several magazines & news publications & has received numerous media releases in the Tulsa World, Oklahoma Eagle, Tulsa People, Oklahoma Herald, Oklahoma Magazine, Tulsa Beacon & Ebony Tribune; featured in the Black Enterprise Report & has made many media appearances. **Business Addr:** Founder, Chief Executive Officer, CP Enterprises LLC, 7018 S Utica Ave, Tulsa, OK 74136, **Business Phone:** (918)744-1001.

PAYTON, ALBERT LEVERN
Organic chemist. **Personal:** Born Feb 8, 1944, Hattiesburg, MS; married Maggie Belle Smith, 1965; children: Al Michaelis, Andriae Monique. **Educ:** Alcorn State Univ, BS, 1965; Southern Univ Syst, Baton Rouge, LA, MS, 1969; Univ Southern Miss, PhD, chem, 1976. **Career:** Hattiesburg Public High Sch, teacher chem, physics, & math, 1965-67; Southern Univ, asst teacher chem, 1967-69; Dillard Univ, instr chem & math, 1969-71; Univ Southern Miss, teaching asst, chem, 1971-74; Miss Valley State Univ, assoc prof, chem, 1974-; Broward Community Col, prof, currently. **Orgs:** Am Chem Soc; Nat Inst Sci. **Honors/Awds:** Southern Fel Fund, Atlanta, 1972-73; res grant, Acetylenic Acid Syntheses, Nat Sci Found, 1978-81; Outstanding Young Men Am, 1979; res article, Lithium-Amine Reduction, J Org Chem Asn, 1979. **Business Addr:** Professor, Broward Community College, 111 E Las Olas Blvd, Fort Lauderdale, FL 33301, **Business Phone:** (954)201-7400.*

PAYTON, DR. BENJAMIN FRANKLIN
Educator. **Personal:** Born Dec 27, 1932, Orangeburg, SC; son of Rev Leroy R and Sarah M; married Thelma Plane; children: Mark Steven & Deborah Elizabeth. **Educ:** SC State Univ, BA, social studies, 1955; Harvard Univ, BD, philos theol, 1958; Columbia Univ, MA, philos relig, 1960; Yale Univ, PhD, social ethics, 1963. **Career:** Danforth grad fel, 1955-63; Howard Univ, Washington, DC, asst prof, Community Serv Project, dir, 1963-65; Off Church & Race, Protestant Coun City NY, dir, 1965-66; Comn Relig & Race & Dept Social Justice Nat Coun Churches USA, exec dir, 1966-67; Benedict Col, pres, 1967-72; Ford Found Higher Educ & Res, prog officer, 1972-81; Tuskegee Univ, pres, 1981-; Seven Nation Tour Africa, educ adv to vpres George Bush, 1982; Presidential Task Force Agr Develop, Zaire, team leader, 1984. **Orgs:** Bd mem, ITT Corp, 1987-98; Am S Bancorp; Bus-Higher Educ Forum; Am Soc Scholars; Nat Consortium Educ Access; Leadership Ala; Ala Shakespeare Festival Royal Coun; Am S Bank; bd mem, Liberty Corp; bd mem, PRAXAIR Inc; bd mem, Ruby Tuesday Inc; bd mem, Morrison Mgt Specialists Inc; Phi Beta Kappa; Alpha Kappa Mu Honor Soc, SC State Univ. **Honors/Awds:** First Place, Harvard Billings Prize, 1957; Gold Medal Award, Napoleon Hill Found, 1987; Benjamin E Mays Award, SC State Univ, 1988; George Washington Carver Lect, Nat Asn State Univs & Land-Grant Col, San Francisco, 1999; Honorary Degree, Eastern Mich Univ; Honorary Degree, Morris Brown Col; Honorary Degree, Benedict Col; Honorary Degree, Morgan State Univ; Honorary Degree, Lehigh Univ; Honorary Degree, Univ Md; Honorary Degree, SC State Univ; Preston Williams Alumni Award, Harvard Univ Divinity Schs, 2008. **Home Addr:** 399 Montgomery Rd, Tuskegee, AL 36083. **Business Addr:** President, Tuskegee University, Fl 3 308 Kresge Ctr, Tuskegee, AL 36088, **Business Phone:** (334)727-8501.

PAYTON, GARY DWAYNE
Basketball player. **Personal:** Born Jul 23, 1968, Oakland, CA; son of Al and Annie; married Monique James, Jul 26, 1997; children: Gary Jr, Julian & Raquel. **Educ:** Oregon State Univ, attended 1990. **Career:** Basketball player (retired); Seattle Supersonics, guard, 1990-2003; Milwaukee Bucks, guard, 2003; Los Angeles Lakers, guard, 2003-04; Boston Celtics, guard, 2004-05; Miami Heat, guard, 2005-07; NBA, free agent, currently. **Orgs:** Founder, Gary Payton Found, 1996. **Honors/Awds:** NBA All-Star, 1995, 1996, 1997, 1998; NBA Defensive Player of the Year Award, 1995-96; Gary Payton Day, named in hon, 2000, NBA Champion, 2006. **Special Achievements:** Appeared on "The Jamie Foxx Show". **Business Addr:** Free Agent, NBA, 477 Madison Ave, New York, NY 10022.

PAYTON, JARRETT
Football player. **Personal:** Born Dec 26, 1980, Arlington, IL; son of Walter payton. **Educ:** Miami Univ, Fla, lib arts. **Career:** Tenn Titans, running back, 2004; Nat Football League, Europe, Amsterdam Admirals, running back, 2005; Tennessee Titans, 2005; Montreal Alouettes, 2007-08; Toronto Argonauts, currently. **Orgs:** The walter & connie payton Foundn. **Honors/Awds:** Hall of Fame, Nat Football League; MVP of the Orange Bowl, 2004. *

PAYTON, JEFF
Lawyer. **Personal:** Born Sep 11, 1946, Canton, MS; married Carol E Rooks. **Educ:** Ashland Col, BS, 1969; John Carroll U, attended; John Marshall Col Law-Cleveland State Univ, JD, 1975. **Career:** Cleveland HS OH, biol instr, 1969-71; US Dept Just, legal intern, 1972-73; Cleveland Legal Aid Soc, atty staff, 1975-77; Richland Co Legal Serv, dir, 1977-; Mansfield Munic Ct, judge, 1987-. **Orgs:** OH State Bar Asn; Richland Co Bar Asn; bd trustees, Ashland Alumni Asn; bd trustees, Planned Parenthood Asn 1979-; bd trustees, Heritage Trials Girl Scouts Coun, 1979-; bd trustees, Richland Co Juvenile Just Comn, 1980; exec comt, Mansfield Chap, Nat Asn Advan Colored People, chmn, Legal Redress Comn; pres, Ohio Munic/Co Judges Asn, 2001; bd mem, Ohio Criminal Sentencing Comn; Ohio Jury Task Force; Ohio Futures Comn. **Home Addr:** 743 Courtwright Blvd, Mansfield, OH 44907-2217, **Home Phone:** (419)756-7783. **Business Addr:** Judge, Mansfield Municipal Court, Munic Bldg 30 N Diamond St, Mansfield, OH 44902, **Business Phone:** (419)755-9616.

PAYTON, NICHOLAS
Musician. **Personal:** Born Sep 26, 1973, New Orleans, LA; son of Walter and Maria. **Educ:** Univ New Orleans. **Career:** Trumpeteer, currently; Albums: From This Moment, 1994; Gumbo Nouveau,1995; Peyton's Place, 1997; Toured with Marcus Roberts, 1992, Jazz FuturesII, 1994; Elvin Jones, 1994; Fingerpainting: The Music Of Herbie Hancock,1997; Doc Cheatham & Nicholas Payton, 1997; Payton's Place, 1998;Nick****ht, 1999; Trumpet Legacy, 1999; Dear Louis, 2001; Sonic Trance,2003; Mysterious Shorter, 2006; Into The Blue, 2008. **Honors/Awds:** Grammy Award, Best Solo Jazz Performance, Nat Acad Recording Arts & Sci, 1997. **Business Phone:** (215)248-5296.

PAYTON, NOLAN H
Lawyer. **Personal:** Born Dec 23, 1919; married; children: 1. **Educ:** Ariz St, BA; USC, MA, 1940; Am Col Life Underwriters, CLU, 1954, LLB, 1962; Certificates for attending legal seminars in London, England; Oxford, England; Moscow, Russia; Bombay, Delhi, India; Madrid, Spain; The Holyland. **Career:** Golden St Mut Life Ins, agent, 1938-42, mgt 1942-49; Pvt Pract, atty, 1969-; Payton Law Ctr, atty, currently. **Orgs:** Am Bar Asn; Beverly Hills Bar Asn; Langston Law Asn; Los Angeles County Bar Asn; Lawyers Club Los Angeles; SW Bar Asn; Am Arbitration Asn; Nat Asn Advan Colored People; Sigma Lambda Sigma; Alpha Phi Alphi; Alpha Mu Gamma; Desert Bar Asn; life mem, Sigma Pi Phi Fraternity; USC Alumni Asn; Legion Lex; Ariz State Alumni Asn. **Business Addr:** Attorney, Payton Law Center, 4232 W Martin Luther King Jr Blvd, Los Angeles, CA 90043, **Business Phone:** (323)296-4971.

PAYTON-NOBLE, JOMARIE (JO MARIE PAYTON-NOBLE FRANCE)
Actor. **Personal:** Born Aug 3, 1950, Albany, GA; married Marc France (divorced); children: Chanele; married Landrus Clark; married Rodney Noble (divorced). **Career:** Southern Shadows, 1999; Films: The Hollywood Knights, 1980; Deal of the Century, 1983; Crossroads, 1986; Disorderlies, 1987; Colors, 1988; Troop Beverly Hills, 1989; Echoes of Enlightenment, 2001; In the Eyes of Kyana, 2002; Gas, 2004; The Rev, 2005; "The Proud Family Movie", 2005. TV series: "The New Odd Couple", 1982-83; "Silver Spoons", 1986; "Perfect Strangers", 1987-89; "Family Matters", 1989-98; "ABC TGIF", 1990; "Moesha", 1996-99; "Will & Grace", 1999-2000; "The Proud Family", 2001-05; "In the Eyes of Kyana", 2002; "Reba", 2005; "Desperate Housewives", 2006; "Meet the Browns", currently. **Orgs:** Alpha Kappa Alpha Sorority. **Honors/Awds:** Nominee for Image Award, 2003, 2005 & 2006. **Business Phone:** (310)276-5677.

PEACE, EULA H
Educator. **Personal:** Born Jul 22, 1920, Norfolk, VA; children: Wesley H III. **Educ:** Va Union Univ; Va St Col & NJ State Teacher Col. **Career:** City Playground, teacher; World Book, mgr. **Orgs:** Norfolk Chap Asn Col Women; pres, former bd mem, League Women Voters & Demo Women's Club; pres, Norfolk Club Asn Negro Bus & Prof Women; Phi Delta Kappa; city-wide Girls' Week, 1948-68; Demo Comt woman, 1968-77; City Dem Comn, 1972-74; build rep, Educ Asn Norfolk, 1973-80; del, Va Educ Asn, 1974-80; bd mem, Hunterville Heighborhood Ctr, 1974; adv bd mem, Area III Model City Prog, 1974; Va Educ Asn Women Educ, 1977-78; del, Nat Educ Asn, 1978-80; secy & treas, Dist 19 Year Child, 1978-80; part Gov Conf Educ; bd mem, Educ Asn Norfolk; chmn, Women Educ Asn Norfolk; Legislator & Polit Action Comn & Women Abuse Comn & Ment Retard Asn & C Need Comn & Les Gemmes Civic & Soc Club; City coordr Gov's campaign.

PEACE, DR. G. EARL
Educator, scientist. **Personal:** Born Feb 4, 1945, Norfolk, VA; son of George Earl and Margaret Douthit; married Renee Marlene Filas; children: Trevor D & Nicole K. **Educ:** Lafayette Col, BS, chem, 1966; Univ Ill, Urbana-Champaign, MS, chem, 1968,PhD, analyt chem, 1971. **Career:** Lafayette Col, from asst prof chem to assoc prof chem, 1971-79; Colo State Univ, vis assoc prof chem, 1985-86; Col Holy Cross, assoc prof chem,1979-92, USAF, summer fac fel, 1980, AAAS/EPA Environ Sci & Eng, fel,1981, Am Coun Educ, fel, 1990-91, asst dean, dean of the class of 2005,dean of the class of 2009, currently; Univ Wis Syst, Off Acad Affairs,acad planner; Univ Wis-Madison, fac assoc & lectr chem. **Orgs:** Am Chem Soc, 1967-92, 1995-; mem exec comt, NE Asn Advisors Health Prof,1974-79; Citizen Adv Coun Pa Dept Environ Resources, 1976-79; AAAS,1979-92; Shrews bury Conserv

Comn, 1989-92; Am Asn Higher Educ, 1993-. **Honors/Awds:** Student Government Superior Teaching Award, Lafayette Col Stud Govt, 1974;Superior Teaching Award, Lafayette Col, Col Holy Cross. **Business Addr:** Director of the Natural World Cluster, College of the Holy Cross, 1 Col St, Worcester, MA 01610-2395, **Business Phone:** (508)793-2532.

PEACOCK, NICKI. See PEACOCK, NICOLE.

PEACOCK, NICOLE (NICKI PEACOCK)
Government official. **Career:** US Dept State, Bur African Affairs, pub affairs specialist, currently. **Special Achievements:** Led the effort to have the main library at the US State Department named in honor of Ralph Bunche; mobilized the American Foreign Service Association & Thursday Luncheon Group. **Business Addr:** Public Affairs Specialist, US Department of State, Bureau of African Affairs, 2201 C St NW, Washington, DC 20520, **Business Phone:** (202)663-0519.

PEAGLER, OWEN FAIR
Educator. **Personal:** Born Nov 28, 1931, New Milford, CT; son of Myrtle E Gary and Robert J; married Joyce Hancock, 1983 (divorced); children: Catherine Ann & Robert G; married Teresa Balough, Mar 20, 1985; children: Kirin. **Educ:** Western Conn State Univ, BS, 1954; New York Univ, MA, 1958, Prof Dipl, 1962; PhD. **Career:** New York State Office Econs, dep dir; Sci fel, Weslyan Univ, 1956; New York City Metro Area, dir, 1966-69; Pace Univ, Sch Continuing Educ, dean, 1969-78; Eastern Conn State Univ, Sch Continuing Educ, dean, 1978-99; Dept Commun Affairs Del, secy, 1982-83; acad adv, Mitchell Col; educ adv, Mohegan Tribe, 2004-. **Orgs:** Pres, 70001 Development Found, 1976-88; bd dirs, 70001 Training &Employment Inst, 1975-; chmn, Presidents Adv Coun Disadvantaged C,1973-80; pres, Conn Asn Continuing Educ, 1985-86; chmn bd dir, WAVE Inc, 1988-96. **Honors/Awds:** Centennial Award, Western Conn State Univ; Young Man of the Year, New York State Jr Chamber Com, 1964; Distinguished Service Award, New York State Jr Chamber Com, White Plains, 1964; Outstanding Educator, Conn Nat Guard,1988; Association for Continuing Higher Education Emeritus Award, 1998. **Home Addr:** 57 Boughton Rd, Old Lyme, CT 06371. **Business Addr:** Dean, Eastern Connecticut State University, School of Continuing Education, 83 Windham St Shafer Hall 100, Willimantic, CT 06226, **Business Phone:** (860)465-5125.

PEAGLER, DR. RICHARD C
Colonial administrator. **Personal:** Born Feb 14, 1946, Oak Grove, LA; son of Charles and Orel; married Vashti Peagler, Dec 23, 1975; children: Richard C Peagler II. **Educ:** Central State Univ, Ohio BS, 1968; Univ Conn, MA, 1971; Syracuse Univ, EdD, 1993. **Career:** Wooster Prep Sch, dir, upward bound prog, 1968-70; Western Conn State Col, admis off, 1972; State Univ New York, Cortland, sr counr, 1972-96, sr counr & dir stud support serv, 1996-98, dir coun & stud devel, 1998-, interim vpres stud affairs, currently. **Orgs:** Asn Counseling Ctr Dirs; Int Asn Coun Serv, 1980-2004; vpres, Seven Valleys Coun Alcoholism, 1993-95; vol, Red Cross, 1996-2004; Cortland High Sch Shared Decision Making Team, 1996-97; Cortland City Sch Bd, 1998-2004; Am Col Personnel Asn, 1998-2004; Phi Kappa Phi. **Honors/Awds:** Excellence in Professional Service Award, United Univ Professionals, 1990; Chancellor's Award for Excellence in Professional Service, 1999; Excellence in Professional Service, SUNY Cortland, 2003; Dedicated Service Award, SUNY Cortland, 2003. **Special Achievements:** Author: Proactive Steps Taken to Prevent Racial Confrontation, Innovative Counseling Services, International Assn of Counseling Services, 1986; Co-author: Counseling in a Litigious Society, New York Assn of Counseling Development, 1998. **Military Serv:** Army Reserves, SPEC 5, 1971-77. **Business Addr:** Interim Vice President for Student Affairs, State University of New York College Cortland, Corey Union Rm 407A, Cortland, NY 13045, **Business Phone:** (607)753-4721.

PEAKE, EDWARD JAMES, JR. See Obituaries section.

PEAL, DARRYL ALAN
Association executive, educator. **Personal:** Born Jun 15, 1963, Springfield, OH; son of Clinton Edward and Joann Marie; married Regina Randall Peal. **Educ:** OH Weslyn Univ, BA, print & broadcast jour, 1986; OH Univ, master's, social sci, 1991. **Career:** OH Univ, Health Edu & Wellness, asst dir, 1991-92; Wilberforce Univ, Counseling Services, dir, 1992-92; Otterbein Col, asst dean stud, coordr or ethnic diversity, 1993-2000, adj prof black studies, 1996-2000; Wilberforce Univ, adj prof orgn mgt, 2000-; United Way Cent OH, dir diversity, 2000-. **Orgs:** Life mem, OH dist dir, Alpha Phi Alpha; OH Univ Alumni Asn, Columbus Black chap; Nat Asn Advan Colored People; Alliance of Ethnic Dirs & Prof. **Honors/Awds:** Alumni Brother of the Year-OH, Alpha Phi Alpha, 1997; Ten Oustanding Young Citizens Award, Columbus Jaycees, 1998; Martin Luther King Jr Award for Peace & Justice, Otterbein Col, 1999. **Business Addr:** Director, United Way of Central Ohio, 360 S Third St, Columbus, OH 43215, **Business Phone:** (614)227-2714.

PEAL, DR. REGINA RANDALL
School administrator. **Personal:** Born Dec 26, 1964, Washington, DC; daughter of James Roland Randall and Marian Laverne Randall; married Darryl Alan Peal, Aug 29, 1992. **Educ:** Ohio Univ, BSHEC, food serv mgt, 1988, MHSA, health admin, 1990, PhD, higher educ admin, 1998. **Career:** Columbus State Community Col, Coun & Adv Serv, counr, 1993-98, Off Stud Activities, coordr, 1998-99, Dept Stud Activities & Athletics, dir, 1999-2002, registr, 2002-. **Orgs:** Regional coordr, Alpha Kappa Alpha Sorority Inc, Educ Advan Found; exec asst great lakes regional dir, 1998-2002, pres, 2001-02, Alpha Sigma Omega chap; Top Ladies Distinction Inc; pres, Columbus Moles, 2002-04; NAACP; membership campaign co-chair, Urban League, 2001-02; co-chair, United Way Young Leadership Group, 2002-03; Trinity Baptist Church; life mem, Ohio Col Personnel Asn; exec bd, Nat Asn Stud Personnel Admin, 2001-02; Am Col Personnel Asn; Am Asn Collegiate Registrars & Admis Officers. **Honors/Awds:** Outstanding Young Women of America, 1997; Award of Excellence, Alpha Phi Alpha, Phi chap; Presidential Leadership Award, Alpha Kappa Alpha, Alpha Sigma Omega Chap, 1998, 1999 & 2000; Oh Bd Regents; NASPA IV E Regional Conf, 2001; Forty Under 40 Award, Business First Magazine. **Special Achievements:** Publications: "Sister Friends: CSCC Creates Innovative Support Group for African-American Women," OCPA News, spring 1995; "Student Orientation for Success at Columbus State Comm Coll," OCPA News, summer 1998. **Home Addr:** 660 Culpepper Dr, Reynoldsburg, OH 43068. **Business Addr:** Registrar, Columbus State Community College, Department of Student Activities & Athletics, 550 E Spring St, Columbus, OH 43215, **Business Phone:** (614)287-5343.

PEARCE, OVETA W
Educator. **Personal:** Married. **Career:** Harrand Creek Elem Sch, Enterprise, AL, teacher & prog specialist, prin; Enterprise City Schs, dir fed prog, currently. **Orgs:** Delta Sigma Theta; pres, Ala State Dept Educ Fed Prog Div Bd Practr; secy, Enterprise City Chamber Com. **Honors/Awds:** Educator Award, Milken Family Found, 1998. **Business Addr:** Director of Federal Programs, Enterprise City School System, 502 E Watts Ave, PO Box 311790, Enterprise, AL 36331, **Business Phone:** (334)347-9531.*

PEARCE, RICHARD ALLEN
Executive. **Personal:** Born Oct 4, 1951, New York, NY; son of Marvin and Edith Burwell; married Lois A Mayo; children: Alysia Daphine, Ryki Desiree & Zuri Damita. **Educ:** Hampton Inst, BS, 1973; Univ Bridgeport, MBA; Williams Col, Williams Sch Banking, 1978; Rutgers Univ, Stonier Grad Sch Banking, 1986. **Career:** Union Trust Co, Ct, staff; State Nat Bank, Ct, staff; Colonial Bank Ct, staff; Conn Savings Bank, govt serv; City West Haven, dir finance & comptroller, 1989-91; Fleet Bank, vpres; Rampart Financial Group, prin, 1994-2001; Evolution Enterprises LLC, founder, founder, 2002-. **Orgs:** Carver Fed Savings & Loan Asn, New York, NY; Carteret Savings & Loan Asn, Newark, NJ; bd dir, Hampton Alumni Fed Credit Union, 1973-74; Alpha Phi Alpha; bd dirs, New Haven Community Investment Corp; bd dirs, W Haven Community House; bd dirs, Childrens Ctr Hamden CT; bd dirs, Conn Afro-Am Hist Soc; bd dirs, Greater New Haven Bus & Prof Asn; chair, Regional Workforce Develop Bd Greater New Haven; comnr, Econ Devlop Comn, Hamden, CT. **Home Addr:** 151 Promenade Dr, Hamden, CT 06514. **Business Addr:** Founder, Evolution Enterprises LLC, PO Box 185636, Hamden, CT 06518, **Business Phone:** (203)248-3677.

PEARMAN, RAVEN-SYMONE CHRISTINA. See SYMONE, RAVEN.

PEARSON, BISHOP CARLTON DEMETRIUS
Writer, public speaker, clergy. **Personal:** Born Mar 19, 1953, San Diego, CA; son of Adam and Lillie Ruth; married Gina Marie Gauthier, 1993; children: Julian & Majeste. **Educ:** Oral Roberts Univ, BA, 1975. **Career:** Oral Roberts Evangelistic Asn, traveling evangelist, 1975-77; Higher Dimensions Evangelistic Ctr, founder, pastor, 1981; AZUSA Fellowship Int, Inc, 1991; Higher Dimensions Ministries, founder, pastor, 1977-2005; New Dimensions Worship Ctr founder, pastor 2006-; Warner Brothers Records, recording artist, 1992-99; Atlantic Records, 1999-; TV host. **Orgs:** AZUSA Fellowship Int; Higher Dimensions Family Church; New Dimensions Worship Center; Dimensions Life. **Honors/Awds:** NARAS, Grammy nomination, "Live at Azusa 3", 2000; GMA, Dove & Stellar Award nomination, "Live at Azusa 3", 2000. **Special Achievements:** Is There A Man in the House, Treasure House Books, 1999; Everything Gonna Be All Right, Harrison House, 1992; Crisis At the Crossroads, Dmetrius Publishing, 1990. **Business Addr:** Pastor, New Dimensions Worship Center, 15 E 5th St Suite 2950, Tulsa, OK 74103, **Business Phone:** (918)392-9982.

PEARSON, CLIFTON
School administrator, educator, consultant. **Personal:** Born Jun 24, 1948, Birmingham, AL; married Clementene Hodge; children: Monica Denise & Clifton Anderson. **Educ:** Ala A&M Univ Normal, AL, BS, art, 1970; Ill State Univ, MS, 1971, EdD, art, 1974. **Career:** Ill State Univ, grad teaching asst, 1971-73; Ala A&M Univ, acting chmn, 1973-74, art educ consult, 1973-, chmn & assoc prof, 1974; Univ Montevallo, Dept Art Glass & Art Educ, coordr art dept, prof art & visual art dept chair, currently; Ford Found fel, NY; Ill State Univ, acad fel; Ala A&M Univ, acad scholar; For Arts Sake, creator. **Orgs:** Southern Fel Fund. **Business Addr:** Professor of Art, Chair, University of Montevallo, Department of Art Glass & Art Education, Sta 6001, Montevallo, AL 35115, **Business Phone:** (205)665-6000.

PEARSON, DREW
Executive, football player, broadcaster. **Personal:** Born Jan 12, 1951, South River, NJ; children: Tori & Britni. **Educ:** Univ Tulsa, grad, 1972. **Career:** Football Player (retired), exec; Dallas Cowboys, wide receiver, 1973-83; CBS Sports, color commentator; Smokey's Express Barbecue Restaurant, partner; Drew Pearson Mkt, founder, currently. **Orgs:** Past chmn, March Dimes Crusade; Nat spokesman, Distilled Spirits Coun. **Honors/Awds:** President's Award, Univ Tulsa; NFL Alumni Career Achievement Award, 2005. **Business Addr:** Founder, Drew Pearson Marketing Inc, 15006 Beltway Dr, Addison, TX 75001, **Business Phone:** (972)702-8055.

PEARSON, HERMAN B.
Government official. **Personal:** Born Mar 2, 1947, Omaha, NE; divorced; children: Nicole, Carmen, Selina & Quatica. **Educ:** Univ Nebr, BS, 1972. **Career:** Minister, 1973-; Mayor's Off, City Omaha, contract coordr. **Orgs:** Evaluator Ment Retardation Prog; Community Leader Among Young Adults; Prof football Player, Wash Redskins, 1972; prof dj co-founder, First Black Owned Radio Sta Omaha Area, 1969; asst pastor, Tabernacle Bapt Ch Coun Bluff, IA; Recreational Activities Leader; NATRA. **Business Addr:** 723 N 18 St, Omaha, NE 68111.

PEARSON, JESSE S.
Executive. **Personal:** Born Apr 24, 1923, Gasden, AL; son of Donia and Jesse; married Mary Lee; children: Milbrun, Eric Hart, Peter Hart, Kelli Hart. **Educ:** Wayne State Univ, BS bus admin 1969. **Career:** Executive (retired); Bon Secours Hosp, asst controller, 1967-71, controller, 1971-86; Highland Park Gen Hosp, dep dir, 1971; Hartford Baptist Church, adminr, 1986. **Orgs:** Pres, Eastern MI Chap HFMA, 1976-77; nat bd mem, Health Care Financial Mgt Asn, 1978-80; dir, Homemaker's Agency MI, 1982-83; dir, Agape House Hartford Chap, 1985; pres, Detroit Set, 1985-94; dir, Le Chateau Condominium, 1991. **Honors/Awds:** William G Follmer Award, HFMA Eastern MI, 1974; Robert Reeves Award, HFMA Eastern MI, 1978; Ernest C Laetz Award HFMA 5 MI Chapts, 1978; Frederick C Muncie Award, HFFMA Eastern MI, 1981. **Military Serv:** AUS sgt, 2 yrs; South Pacific Combat Ribbon. *

PEARSON, MARILYN RUTH
Consultant. **Personal:** Born Nov 12, 1955, Saginaw, MI; daughter of Hollis Townsend and Bernice Richard; married Tommie L Pearson Sr, Aug 9, 1975; children: Tamara Bernice & Tommie L Jr. **Educ:** Saginaw Valley State Univ, Univ Ctr Mich, BA, 1978. **Career:** Ford Motor Credit Co, Saginaw MI, credit investigator, 1977-80; Merrill Lynch, financial consult, 1980-84, sr training consult, 1984-87, AVP mgr sel & devel, 1987, vpres & retirement plan consult, currently; Salomon Smith Barney, vpres. **Orgs:** First vpres, Zeta Phi Beta Sorority Epsilon XI Zeta, 1980-; Exec Club Merrill Lynch, 1981-82; President's Club, Merrill Lynch, 1983; Nat Asn Securities Prof, 1987-; bd mem, Jr Achievement Mercer County, 1987-; bd mem, Literacy Volunteers Am State NJ, 1988-; bd mem, YWCA, Trenton, 1989-; Nat Asn Advan Colored People; Shiloh Baptist Church. **Honors/Awds:** Achievement Award, Nat Asn Negro Bus & Prof Women, 1982; CEBA Award, 1988; Zeta of the Year, Epsilon Xi Zeta Zeta Phi Beta Sorority, 1988; Faith, Hope & Charity Award, FAI HO CHA, Trenton NJ, 1988; Black Achievers in the Industry Award, Harlem Branch YMCA, 1989. **Special Achievements:** Designed, developed & implemented Auditors Training Prog, 1984; creative director Black FC ads; featured in Merrill Lynch ad in Black Enterprise, Essence, Ebony, 1988-89; Int Bus & Prof Women Dolars & Sense, 1989. **Military Serv:** Special tributes from State of Michigan and Mercer County NJ. **Business Addr:** AVP Financial Consultant Training, Merrill Lynch, PO Box 9032, Princeton, NJ 08543-9032, **Business Phone:** (609)282-1814.

PEARSON, MICHAEL NOVEL
Banker, president (organization). **Personal:** Born Feb 12, 1956, Memphis, TN. **Educ:** Fisk Univ, BS, 1978; Pepperdine Univ, MBA, 1980; Col Financial Planning, CFP, 1984. **Career:** Ford Motor Credit Co, cust acct rep, 1978-79; M-Bank Houston NA, energy loan officer, 1981-83; Pearson Assoc, financial planner, 1982-; First City Bank Corp, sr loan rev officer, 1984-89, Healthcare Group Wholesake Banking Div, vpres, 1989-92; Tex Com Bank, sr loan officer, 1992-99; JP Morgan Chase Bank, sr loan preview officer, 1999-2001; Southwest Bank Tex, sr credit process officer, 2001-05; Amegy Bank Tex, vpres, pres. **Orgs:** Life Health Disability Ins license State TX, 1986; Enrolled Agt-IRS; Alpha Phi Alpha Frat; Inst Cert Financial Planners, Int Asn Financial Planners; Series 7 Registered Rep, HD Vest, 2001. **Home Addr:** PO Box 55708, Houston, TX 77255.

PEARSON, PRESTON JAMES
President (organization), football player. **Personal:** Born Jan 17, 1945, Freeport, IL; married Linda; children: Gregory & Matthew. **Educ:** Univ Ill. **Career:** Football player (retired), President; Baltimore Colts, 1967-69; Pittsburgh Steelers, 1970-74; Dallas

Cowboys, 1975-80; Time Inc & Am Tel Comun, mktexec; Pro-Style Assos, pres, currently. **Orgs:** Founder, treas, Consult Mgt Enterprises. **Special Achievements:** Broke his own record 47 Catches 1978; only player to appear in Super Bowl with three different teams Colts, Steelers, Cowboys; led NFL in kickoff returns and kickoff returns for touchdowns; set Cowboy record for running back with 46 receptions, 1977; author of "Hearing the Noise".

PEARSON, RAMONA HENDERSON (RAMONA ESTELLE HENDERSON)
Government official, president (organization). **Personal:** Born Oct 3, 1952, Baltimore, MD; daughter of Robert and Doris Green; married Edward, Nov 20, 1989; children: Leora. **Educ:** Morgan State Univ, BS, 1975, MBA, 1982. **Career:** Arthur Young & Co, sr auditor; Linwood Jennings Pa CPA's, assoc, 1977-79;Constant Care Comm Health Ctr Inc, controller, 1976-77; Ernst & Ernst,auditor, 1975-76; Wayne State Univ, dir internal audit, 1985-87; Wayne County Govt, auditor gen; Highland Park, financial mgr, 2001-. **Orgs:** Am Inst CPA's, 1976-; pres, Nat Asn Black Accountants; Nat Asn Advan Colored People; Big Brothers & Sisters Am; Mich Asn CPA's, 1981-; Inst Internal Auditors, 1985-; Govt Accountants Asn, 1988-; Govt Finance Officers Asn, 1988-; Local Govt Auditors Asn, 1988-. **Honors/Awds:** Outstanding Member award, Nat Asn Black Accts, 1983. **Special Achievements:** Article "How to Start a Small Business" Afro-American Newspaper, 1977. **Business Addr:** Auditor General, Wayne County Michigan, 600 Randolph Suite 208, Detroit, MI 48226, **Business Phone:** (313)224-0924.*

PEARSON, DR. STANLEY E
Physician. **Personal:** Born Oct 21, 1949, Quitman, GA; son of Rev Oliver Pearson and Jr Mattie A Bowles. **Educ:** Univ FL Gainesville, attended 1971; Meharry Med Col, MD, 1975; Am Bd Internal Med, dipl, 1978. **Career:** Providence Hosp, residency, 1975-78; Fitzsimons Army Med Ctr, fellowship, 1978-80; Landstahl Army Regional Med Ctr W Ger, chief cardiolo serv, 1981-83; US Army Europe 7th Med Command, cardiolo consult, 1982-83; Madigan Army Med Ctr, staff cardiologist 1983-84; CIGNA Health Plan Ariz; dir, cardiac rehab, 1984-, chief staff, 1986-88; chmn, dept internal med, 1988, chief med off & sr med dir, currently. **Orgs:** Mem Alpha Omega Alpha Honor Med Soc; fel Am Col Cardiolo; Colo Med Soc; Tau Epsilon Phi Frat; Asn Black Cardiologists; Am Col Physician Execs; chmn, Specialty Care CIGNA Health Care Ariz, 1998. **Honors/Awds:** Am Bd Internal Med Cardiovasc Dis, 1981. **Military Serv:** AUS, retired Col; Army Commendation Medal 2nd Oak Leaf Cluster. **Home Addr:** 5530 N Camelback Canyon Dr, Phoenix, AZ 85018-1239. **Business Addr:** Chief Marketing Officer, Chief Medical Officer, CIGNA HealthCare of Arizona, 755 E McDowell Rd, Phoenix, AZ 85006, **Business Phone:** (602)271-5426.

PEASE, DENISE LOUISE
State government official, banker. **Personal:** Born Mar 15, 1953, Bronx, NY; daughter of William Henry Pease Jr and Louise Marion Caswell. **Educ:** Columbia Univ, NY, BA, 1980; Columbia Univ Grad Sch Bus, Spl Cert, 1982; Bernard Barauch Grad Sch Pub Admin, attended 1982-83. **Career:** Elmcor Youth & Adult Activities, dir community servs, 1980-82; Essex County, Newark NJ, spl asst to co exec, 1982-83; NY State Dept Banks, urban anal III, 1983-86, exec asst to supt, 1986-87; deputy supt, 1987, Com Banking Off NY Comptroller, found bd mem, asst controller & dir, currently. **Orgs:** bd mem, Handier, 1974-; Govr's Econ Develop Sub-Cabinet, 1985-; bd mem, Cornell Univ Coop Ext Adv Comn, 1986-; bd mem, Elcor Youth & Adult Activities, 1986-87; Coalition of 100 Black Women, 1988-; life mem, Nat Coun Negro Women, 1988-; rep, Govr's, Housing Policy Cabinet, 1989; Financial Women's Asn, 1989; Soc Consumer Affairs Profs Bus; life mem, Nat Coun Negro Women; life mem, Nat Asn Advan Colored People; Coalition of 100 Black Women; bd dirs, Financial Womens Asn NY; Epilepsy Found. **Honors/Awds:** Prof Achievement Award, Nat Asn Negro Bus & Prof Women, 1980; Charles H Revson Fel on the Future of NY, Columbia Univ, 1981; Nat Urban Fel, Nat Urban Fellows Org, 1982; Cit Merit, NY State Assembly, 1989; Salute to Outstanding African Am Bus & Prof Women, Dollar & Sense Mag, 1990; Cit Merit, NY State Assembly, 1988; Gov Cit, 1993; Community Service Award, NY State Black & Puerto Rican Legislators Asn, 1993. **Business Addr:** Director, Assistant Controller, Commercial Banking, Off NYC Comptroller, 103 21 35th Ave, Corona, NY 11368.*

PEAVY, JOHN W., JR.
Judge. **Personal:** Born Apr 28, 1943, Houston, TX; married Diane Massey; children: 4. **Educ:** Howard Univ, BA, 1964; Howard Univ School Law, attended 1967. **Career:** Judge (retired); Nat Aero & Space Coun, The White House, Washington DC, acct, 1961-64, admin asst, 1964-67; Berry Lott Peavy & Williams, practice law, 1967-72; Harris Cty Comn Action Assoc, assoc field coord, 1967-68; County Judge Bill Elliott, exec asst, 1968-70; Home Pilot Prog, Am Bar Asn, Houston Bar Asn, assoc counr proj, 1970-71; Harris County Court Precinct 7, judge, justice peace position, 1973-77; 246th Dist Judicial Dist Ct Harris County Houston, judge. **Orgs:** Chmn, WL Davis Div Sam Houston Boy Scouts, 1976; Alpha Phi Alpha; Harris Cty Coun Orgs; life mem, NAACP; comn Houston Bus & Professional Men's Club, YMCA Century Club; former dem precinct chmn, Precinct 292 Houston TX; mem adv bd, KYOK Radio Sta; legal adv, Riverside Lion's Club; bd dir, Mercy Hosp; steering comt, Phillip Randolph Inst; bd dir, Houston Citizens Chamber Com Proj Pull; Eliza Johnson Ctr Aged; Southern Ctr Br YMCA; United Negro Col Fund; Julia C Hester House, St Elizabeth Hosp; Houston Coun Human Rel; Vol Am; app mem, Housing Asst Tech Adv Group, 1974; hon cochmn, Citizens Better Transit, 1978; Downtown Rotary Club Houston, Urban Policy Task Force City Houston, 1978; Pol Acting Comt Houston Lawyers Asn; bd dir, Nat Bar Found, Houston Bar Asn; Nat Bar Asn; Am Bar Asn; State Bar TX; Jr Bar Asn Houston; St Jr Bar Small Claims Court Handbook Comn, 1977; State Bar TX Ctr Reorg Comt, Judicial Coun. **Honors/Awds:** Outstanding Military Student Chicago Tribune Award; Eagle Scout & mem Order of the Arrow of Boy Scouts of Am, 1960; Distinguished Achievers Award, YMCA, 1973, 1977; YMCA Award for Outstanding Serv to the Community, 1974; Nat Judicial Int Achievement Award; Houston Lawyers Asn Achievement Award, 1980; Outstanding Young Bus & Prof Man, Houston Young Adult Club, 1979; Appreciation Award, Exploring Div, Sam Houston Area BSA, 1979. **Special Achievements:** Certificate of Citation by the State of TX House of Reps, 1975. *

PEAY, FRANCIS
Football coach. **Personal:** Born May 23, 1944, Pittsburgh, PA; married Patricia; children: Aryca & Aisha. **Educ:** Univ Mo. **Career:** Football coach (retired); New York Giants, 1966-67; Green Bay Packers, 1968-72; Kansas City Chiefs, 1973-75; Univ Sr HS in St Louis, defensive coord; Notre Dame, jr varsity & offensive line coach; Univ CA, outside linebacker coach; Northwestern Univ, defensive coordr, head coach; Indianapolis Colts, defensive line coach. *

PEAY, SAMUEL
Judge, lawyer. **Personal:** Born Jun 2, 1939, Ridgeway, SC; son of Geneva Peay and English Peay; married Lillian Bernice Chavis; children: Clifton Delmineo & Ira Aloysius. **Educ:** Basic Law Enforcement Training, cert; Univ Nev Nat Judicial Acad, 1985, 1986. **Career:** Richland County Sheriff's Dept Columbia, SC, dep sheriff, 1964, sergeant law enforcement, 1969, juv, arson, criminal invest, 1971-78; Richland County, judge, currently. **Orgs:** Nat Sheriff's Asn; SC Law Enforcement Asn; SC Summary Ct Judges Asn; pres, Richland County Summary Ct Judges Asn, 1986-88; Nat Judges Asn; Zion Canaan Baptist Church, Columbia, SC. **Honors/Awds:** Outstanding South Carolinian, Nat Coun Negro Women, 1980; Honored, Capital City Lodge No 47, Columbia, SC 1985; "Respect for Law" Award, Optimist Club Columbia, 1986; Benedict Col Service Award, 1986; Honor, Columbia, SC Br Nat Asn Advan Colored People, 1991; Honor, Columbia Lawyers Asn, 1996; Honor, SC Black Lawyers Asn, 1996. **Home Addr:** 954 Campanella Circle, Columbia, SC 29203. **Business Addr:** Judge, Richland County, 4919 Rhett St, Columbia, SC 29203-4522.

PECK, CAROLYN
Basketball coach, basketball player. **Personal:** Born Jan 22, 1966, Jefferson City, TN. **Educ:** Vanderbilt Univ, BA, commun, 1988. **Career:** Basketball player (retired) basketball coach; Nashville TV station, mkt consult; pharmaceut sales person; Nippondenso Corp, professional basketball player, 1991-93; Tenn Univ, asst coach, 1993-95; Univ Ky, asst coach, 1995-96; Purdue Univ, asst coach, recruiting coordr, head basketball coach, 1996-98; Orlando Miracle, head coach, 2000-01; Florida Gator, head basketball coach, 2002-07; ESPN, basketball analyst, currently. **Honors/Awds:** Tennessee's Miss Basketball, 1984; Winged Foot Award, New York Athletic Club; Purdue's women's basketball coach, 1999; Associated Press National Coach of the Year; WBCA National Coach of the Year, 1999; Big Ten Coach of the Year, 1999. **Special Achievements:** First African American female to coach a team to the women's NCAA national championship; First African American to win the Winged Foot Award. **Business Addr:** Basketball Analyst, ESPN, ESPN Plaza 935 Middle St, Bristol, CT 32611, **Business Phone:** (860)766-2000.

PECK, LEONTYNE CLAY
Educator. **Personal:** Born Nov 14, 1958, Keyser, WV; daughter of Suellen Gaiter Clay and Russell Clay Sr; married Lyle, Jun 2, 1990; children: Whitney & Alexis. **Educ:** Am Univ, Wash, DC, BA, polit sci; WV Univ, Morgantown, WV, Higher educ admin; Am Univ Rome, Rome, Italy, cert Italian studies. **Career:** US Dept Housing & Urban Dev, Wash, DC, consumer affairs specialist, 1978-81; Congressman Cleve Benedict, LB Johnson legis intern, 1981-82; US Conf Mayors, Wash, DC, pub affairs officer, 1984-88; Ctr Black Culture, Morgantown, WV, prog mgr, 1989-91; WV Univ, prog mgr, Potomac State Col WV; Gaye Clay Pottery, owner; Afritique. founder & chief exec officer, currently. **Honors/Awds:** Ford Foundation Grant, Nat Coun Black Studies, 1990; Outstanding West Virginian for Public Service, Common Cause, 1989; Comnr African Am History & Culture MD, 1997. **Business Addr:** Founder, Chief Executive Officer, Afritique, 1069 Somer Chase Ct, Charlottesville, VA 22911, **Business Phone:** (434)975-3943.

PEEBLES, ALLIE MUSE
Educator. **Personal:** Born Apr 12, 1926, Danville, VA; daughter of Maude B Smith Muse and William Brown Muse Sr; married Millard R Peebles Sr, Aug 16, 1947 (deceased); children: Martha Elaine Peebles Brown, Brenda LaVerne & Millard R Jr. **Educ:** Hampton Univ, Va, BS, 1943-47; St Augustine's Col, NC, cert renewal; NC Cent Univ, attended 1965-69. **Career:** Prince Edward Co Sch Syst, Va, eng teacher, 1947-48; Raleigh-Wake Co Sch Syst, NC, eng teacher, 1963-78; M R Peebles & Son Masonry Contractors, owner, pres, 1978-82; Telamon Corp, Smithfield NC, job counsr, 1983-86; The Carolinian (newspaper), columnist, 1984-; St Augustine's Col, Raleigh, eng instr, 1987-. **Orgs:** Martin St Baptist Church, 1955-; pres, Raleigh Hampton Univ Alumni Asn, 1962-64, 1984-86, vpres, 1979-84, recruitment chmn; treas, Jack Jill Am, 1966-68; sec, Delta Sigma Theta-Raleigh Alumnae Chap, 1972-74, chmn publicity & pub rels, 1985-89, historian; chmn nat recruitment, Nat Hampton Alumni Asn, 1978-82, 2nd vpres NC reg, 1983-89, pres, currently; life mem, chmn, Raleigh-Apex Nat Asn Advan Colored People, 1978-; Wake Co Private Indust Coun, 1980-82; Raleigh Civil Serv Comn, 1980-82; bd mem, YWCA Wake Co, 1980-86; consult, Women Commun Workshop, 1987; Delta's Nat Comm Heritage & Archives; sec, Finance Comt, Martin Baptist Church, Raleigh, NC, 1989-93; chmn, Publicity Com, 1990-; pub rels dir, Delta Sigma Theta, Raleigh Chap, 1990-93, journalist, 2000-02; chmn publicity, Capital City Sertoma Club; Nat Coun Negro Women, Capital Area Sect; publicity chmn & adv, James P West, Raleigh Dist C City Councr, 1999-01. **Honors/Awds:** NC Hamptonian of the Year Award, Hampton Univ, 1974; Million Dollar Club, Nat Asn Advan Colored People, 1981-89; Recognition of Service, Nat Asn Advan Colored People; National Million Dollar Award, NCP, 1990-01; Merit Award, Hampton Univ, 2000; Cot Service Award, Achievement Area Media, Nat Pan-Hellenic Coun, 2001. **Home Addr:** 721 Calloway Dr, Raleigh, NC 27610. **Business Addr:** Instructor, St Augustine College, 1315 Oakwood Ave, Raleigh, NC 27610, **Business Phone:** (919)516-4640.

PEEBLES, DANIEL PERCY
Football player, president (organization). **Personal:** Born May 30, 1966, Raleigh, NC; children: Damiya, Danny, Dylan & Jada. **Educ:** NC State Univ, acct & bus mgt, 1988. **Career:** Tampa Bay Buccaneers, wide receiver, 1989-90; Cleveland Browns, 1991; Rise & Walk Min, owner, currently. **Orgs:** Bd mem & pres, Rise and Walk Ministries; Nat Honor Soc.

PEEBLES-WILKINS, DR. WILMA CECELIA
Educator. **Personal:** Born Apr 21, 1945, Raleigh, NC; daughter of Mary Myatt Peebles and Millard Peebles. **Educ:** NC State Univ, BA, 1967; Case Western Res Univ, MSSA, 1971; Univ NC Chapel Hill, PhD, 1984. **Career:** Cuyahoga Co Div Child Welfare, social worker, 1967-72; Ment Develop Ctr, dir intake, 1972-76; Eastern KY Univ, asst prof, 1976-77; NC Memorial Hosp, chief pediat social worker, 1977-78; NC State Univ, assoc prof & dir social work, 1978-91; Boston Univ, assoc dean, 1991-93, acting dean, 1993-94, dean, dean emer & prof emer, currently. **Orgs:** Nat Asn Black Social Workers, 1976-; consult, Wake Co Coun Aging, 1979; Raleigh Housing Authority, 1979; vice chmn, NC Cert Bd Social Work, 1984-; competence cert bd, Nat Asn Social Workers, 1984-; comn minority group concerns, Coun Social Work Educ, 1985-87; serves on several ed bd; past chmnn, New Eng Asn Deans & Dir Sch Social Work. **Honors/Awds:** Irene Sogg Gross Service Award, 1971; Swedish Int Fel Youth Leaders & Social Workers, 1980; articles Encycl Social Work, J Social Work; Black Caucus J, C & Youth Serv Rev, J Educ Social Work; Outstanding Practitioner, Nat Acad Pract, 2000; Hall of Fame, Cardinal Gibbons High Sch, 2001; Greatest Contribution to Social Work Education, Nat Asn Social Workers, Massachusetts Chap, 2002; Social Work Pioneer, Nat Asn Social Workers, 2006. **Special Achievements:** Published several articles and has been on many editorial boards. **Home Addr:** 4801 Newham Ct, Raleigh, NC 27612, **Home Phone:** (919)571-4685. **Business Addr:** Dean Emerita, Professor Emerita, Boston University, School of Social Work, 264 Bay State Rd, Boston, MA 02215.

PEEK, BOOKER C.
Educator. **Personal:** Born May 22, 1940, Jacksonville, FL; son of Oscar Peek and Estella Peek; married Annette Jones, Jun 29, 1958; children: Cheryl, Joseph & Angela. **Educ:** Fla Agr & Mech Univ, BA, 1964; Oberlin Col, MAT, 1966; Univ Fla, attended. **Career:** Hampton Jr Col, teacher; Matthew W Gilbert High Sch, teacher; Ribault Sr High Sch, teacher; Albany St Col, fac; Oberlin Col, assoc prof African Am studies, currently. **Orgs:** Pres, Toward Am Togetherness Common Orgn, 1968; Fla Star Teacher, 1968; coordr, Words Are Very Empowering; Am Asn Univ & Prof; Nat Asn Advan Colored People; Int Longshoremen's Asn. **Honors/Awds:** Scholar, Jacksonville Univ, 1969; Civic-Engagement Advocate Award. **Business Addr:** Associate Professor of African American Studies, Oberlin College, African American Studies Department, 323 Rice Hall 10 N Prof St, Oberlin, OH 44074, **Business Phone:** (440)775-8479.

PEEK, GAIL LENORE
College teacher, vice president (organization), lawyer. **Personal:** Born Jan 18, 1950, Brooklyn, NY; married. **Educ:** City Col Univ NY, BA, polit sci, 1972; Princeton Univ, MA, 1974, PhD, 1978; Univ Chicago, Law Sch, JD, 1984. **Career:** Williams Col, asst prof, 1976-80; Kirkland & Ellis, assoc, 1984-87; Premark Int Inc, sr atty, 1987-90, corp coun, 1990-91, gen coun, 1991-93; Ralph

Wilson Plastics Co, vpres & gen coun, 1993-95; Wilsonart Int Inc, in-house coun, vpres & gen coun, 1993-2005; Beard Kultgen Brophy Bostwick & Dickson LLP, atty, currently. **Orgs:** State Bar Tex; Am Bar Asn; Bell County Bar Asn; bd dirs, Scott & White Health Plan; bd dirs, United Way Cent Tex; pres, Ralph Wilson Youth Clubs Temple; comnr, Bd Cent Tex Housing Consortium; vis comt mem, Univ Mary Hardin Baylor; vis comt mem, Scott & White Hosps & Clins; Rotary Club Temple. **Business Addr:** Attorney, Beard Kultgen Brophy Bostwick & Dickson LLP, 5400 Bosque Blvd, Central Tower Suite 301, Waco, TX 76710, **Business Phone:** (254)776-5500.

PEELER, ANTHONY EUGENE
Basketball player. **Personal:** Born Nov 25, 1969, Kansas City, MO; children: Marcus Anthony & Chynna. **Educ:** Univ Miss, attended 1992. **Career:** Basketball player (retired); Los Angeles Lakers, guard, 1992-96; Vancouver Grizzlies, 1997-98; Minn Timberwolves, 1998-2003; Sacramento Kings, guard, 2004; Wash Wizards, guard, 2005; Akasvayu Girona, guard, 2005. **Honors/Awds:** Big Eight Conf Player of the Year; Male Athlete of the Year. **Special Achievements:** First round pick, No 15, NBA Draft, 1992.

PEELER, DIANE FAUSTINA
Educator. **Personal:** Born Mar 14, 1959, Greeneville, TN; daughter of Segeet and Marilyn. **Educ:** Univ Tenn, Knoxville, BS, 1982; Southern Univ New Orleans; Xavier Univ. **Career:** Orleans Parish Sch Bd, instr, 1982-; Orleans Parish Comn Schs, modern dance teacher, 1983-85; Off Employment & Develop, summer youth counr, 1986. **Orgs:** Vpres, Delta Sigma Theta Sor Inc, 1980-81; phys therapy volunteer, Meadowcreast Hosp, 1985-86.

PEEPLES, AUDREY RONE
Association executive. **Personal:** Born May 22, 1939, Chicago, IL; daughter of John Drayton Rone and Thelma Shepherd Rone; married Anthony Peeples (deceased) (deceased); children: Jennifer Lynn & Michael Anthony. **Educ:** Univ Ill, BA, 1961; Northwestern Univ, MBA, attended. **Career:** Association executive (retired); Continental Bank, trust admin, 1961-72; Girls Scouts USA, asst reg dir, 1973-76; GS Chicago, from assoc exec dir to exec dir, 1976-87; YWCA Metrop Chicago, chief exec officer, 1987-2001. **Orgs:** Nat bd GS USA, 1971-73; Jack & Jill Chicago, 1973-; Chicago Network, 1988-; Econ Club Chicago, 1988; bd mem, United Way Chicago, 1988-92; bd mem, Chicago Network, 1991-95; trustee, First Non Profit Trust, 1992-97; bd mem, treas, Chicago Found Women, 1992-97; comnr, Gov Comn Women, 1997-; vpres & bd mem, Am Civil Liberties Union, 1999-; chair, YWCA USA Nat Coordinating Bd, 2002-; bd mem, Exec Serv Corp, 2002-; chief exec officer, Young Women's Christian Asn. **Honors/Awds:** Kizzy Award; Outstanding Achievement Award, Girl Scouts Chicago; Merit Award, Nat Coun Negro Women, Cosmopolitan Sect; Thomas & Eleanor Wright Award, City Chicago Comn.

PEER, WILBUR TYRONE
Educator, government official, administrator. **Personal:** Born Apr 28, 1951, Lee County, AR; married Patricia Nelson; children: Andre B, Yolanda & Wilbur T II. **Educ:** Univ Ark, Pine Bluff, BA, hist; Univ Ark, Fayetteville, MA, voc educ. **Career:** Phillips Col, vet counselor, 1974-76; Lee County Coop clinic, community develop specialist, 1976-82; Phillips County Community Col, dean continuing educ, 1982-88, dir econ develop, 1992-93; Southern Develop Bank Corp, Arkadelphia, Ak, consult; Delta Improvement Corp, Marianna, exec dir; Int Filter Mfg Corp, vpres of sales, 1988-91; Ark Land & Farm Develop Corp, Fargo, mgt consult, 1991-92; Rural Develop Admin, 1992-93; Rural Bus-Coop Serv, 1994. **Orgs:** Phi Beta Sigma 1972; owner & oper, Wilbur Peer Farm, 1977-; justice of the peace Lee County quorum Court, 1980-; owner & broker, Wilbur T Peer Realty Co, 1982-; exec dir, Delta Improvement, 1982-; PIC East AR Pvt Indust Coun, 1983-. **Military Serv:** USAR, 1lt transport, 8 yrs.

PEERMAN-PLEDGER, VERNESE DIANNE
Foundation executive, president (organization), chief executive officer. **Personal:** Born Jan 1, 1958, Pinehurst, NC; daughter of William Donald and Otelia Cooke; married Vincent Lewis, Oct 4, 1988. **Educ:** NC Cent Univ, BA, jour, 1979. **Career:** Eunice Advert, sr acct exec, bus mgr; Carrington & Carrington Advert, partner, bus mgr; Dudley Products Co Inc, nat advert mgr; Western Career Col, PR dir, high sch crd; Chapel Hill Carrboro Downtown CMS, dir spec projs; St Joseph's Historic Found Inc, coo, exec dir, pres & ceo, currently; Hayti Heritage Ctr, pres & ceo, currently. **Orgs:** NC Cultural Network, pres, 1992-; bd dirs, Scrap Exchange; Delta Sigma Theta Sorority Inc, Chapel Hill Carrboro Alumnae Chap; South Orange Black Caucus; vol, Am Cancer Soc; choir mem, St Paul Am Church, Steward Bd; bd, Chapel Hill Women's Ctr; Arts Advocates bd. **Business Phone:** (919)683-1709.

PEERY, BENJAMIN FRANKLIN, JR.
Astronomer, educator. **Personal:** Born Mar 4, 1922, St Joseph, MO; married Darnelle; children: Yvany. **Educ:** Univ Minn, BS, physics, 1949; Fisk Univ, MA, 1955; Univ Mich, PhD, astrophys, 1962. **Career:** Agricultural & Techical Col NC, instr, 1951-53; Univ Mich, instr, 1958; Ind Univ, prof, 1959-76; Calif Inst Tech, vis assoc, 1969-70; Harvard Univ, vis assoc prof, 1971; Kitt Peak Nat Observer, vis res astronomist, 1975-76; Howard Univ, prof, 1977, prof emer, currently. **Orgs:** US Nat Comt Int Astron Union, 1972-77; mem Am Astron Soc; chmn Comn Manpower & Employment, 1977; Astron Adv Panel Nat Sci Found, 1974-78; consult, NSF NASA Ind Syst Sci Instr Fla State Univ; writ Elem Sch Sci Prog, 1961-66; participant Vis Prof, AAS 1964-; trustee, Adler Planetarium; Astron Soc The Pac; fel AAAS; NSF Res. **Honors/Awds:** Grants; published numerous articles in Astrophys Jour Astron Soc and in Japan Astron & Astrophysics Jour. **Special Achievements:** Second Black to be awarded the PhD in astronomy from University of Michigan in 1962; Has the distinction of being the first Black astronomer to be seen and heard by a mass audience thanks to a televised documentary on PBS stations in 1991 called "The Astronomers". **Military Serv:** AUS 1942-45. **Business Addr:** Professor Emeritus, Howard University, Department Physics & Astronomy, 2355 6th St NW, Washington, DC 20059.*

PEETE, CALVIN
Golfer, educator, president (organization). **Personal:** Born Jul 18, 1943, Detroit, MI; son of Dennis and Irenia Bridgeford; married Pepper; children: Aisha & Aleya; married Christine (divorced 1987); children: Calvin, Rickie, Dennis, Kalvanetta & Nicole. **Educ:** Wayne State Univ, degree, 1983. **Career:** Golfer (retired), instructor; farm laborer, FL, 1957-60; itinerant peddler, 1961-71; prof golfer, 1971-2001; PGA Tour Golf Acad, instr; Calvin Peete Enterprises, pres, currently. **Orgs:** Prof Golfers Asn. **Honors/Awds:** Ben Hogan Award, 1983; Jackie Robinson Award, 1983; African American Ethnic Sports Hall of Fame, 2002. **Special Achievements:** Mem, US Ryder Cup team. **Business Addr:** President, Calvin Peete Enterprises, 2050 Collier Ave, Fort Myers, FL 33901.

PEETE, RODNEY
Talk show host, football player. **Personal:** Born Mar 16, 1966, Mesa, AZ; son of Willie; married Holly Robinson, 1995; children: Rodney Jackson, Ryan Elizabeth & Robinson James. **Educ:** Univ Southern Calif, BS, commun, 1989. **Career:** Football player (retired), talk show host; Detroit Lions, quarterback, 1989-93; Dallas Cowboys, 1994; Philadelphia Eagles, 1995-98; Wash Redskins, 1999; Oakland Raiders, 2000-01; Carolina Panthers, quarterback, 2002-04; Fox Sports Net, "The Best Damn Sports Show Period", co-host, currently. **Orgs:** Founder, HollyRod Found. **Special Achievements:** Appearance on ABCs Hangin With Mr. Cooper. **Business Addr:** Host, Fox Sports Interactive Media LLC, Fox Sports Net, 407 N Maple Dr, Beverly Hills, CA 90210, **Business Phone:** (310)969-7192.

PEGRAM, ERRIC DEMONT
Football player, athletic trainer. **Personal:** Born Jan 7, 1969, Dallas, TX; children: Talor Marie. **Educ:** Univ N Tex. **Career:** Football player (retired), athletic trainer; Atlanta Falcons, running back, 1991-94; Pittsburgh Steelers, 1995-96; San Diego Chargers, 1997; NY Giants, 1997; personal trainer; web engr; Match.com, configuration mgr, currently. **Honors/Awds:** Super bowl XXX.

PEGUES, FRANCINE
Insurance executive. **Personal:** Born Jun 18, 1947, Youngstown, OH; daughter of Charles and Edwina; children: Dwaylon, Jake, E'lida, Edwina & Tailor. **Educ:** Miami Univ, Ohio, BA, 1969; Ohio State Univ, attended 1977. **Career:** State Ohio, various mgmt positions, 1971-78; City Detroit, census coordr, 1979-80; Mich Republican State Comn, urban dir, 1981-82; Health Care Network, regional dir, 1983-87; Blue Cross Blue Shield Mich, Mkt & Regional Sales Dept, dir, 1987-. **Orgs:** Blue Cross Blue Shield Mgt Asn, 1987-; chair, Mich Metro Girl Scout Coun, develop comn, 1991-; bd mem, BluesPac, 1991-; Leadership Detroit XVI Grad, 1995; African Develop Found Adv Coun, 1992-94; chairperson, Civic Ctr Comn, City Detroit, 1997-; bd dir, Oakland Com Bank, 1997-; trustee, Parade Co, 1997-. **Honors/Awds:** Pioneer Award, Frederick Douglass Soc, 1966; Certificate of Honor, Sojourner Found, 1997; Crain's Detroit Business, Black Business Leadership 100, 1998. **Special Achievements:** Author: Wages Incentives: Good News or Bad, Hospital Topics, June 1976; LEAA Compliance Procedures, Cities and Villages, 1976; selected by the American Asn of Health Plans, Exec Leadership Prog, 1998-99. **Business Addr:** Regional Sales Director, Blue Cross Blue Shield of Michigan, 600 E Lafayette, PO Box 341 Blvd Suite 2022, Detroit, MI 48226-2998, **Business Phone:** (313)225-9000.

PEGUES, ROBERT L., JR.
School administrator, army officer. **Personal:** Born Mar 6, 1936, Youngstown, OH; children: Tamara Pegues Brooks, Robert L III. **Educ:** Youngstown State Univ, BS, 1958; Westminster Col PA, MS, 1963; Kent State Univ OH, Doctoral Prog. **Career:** Youngstown City Schs, teacher & admin, 1959-72; Educ Res Coun Am, Cleveland, OH, dir urban educ, 1969-70; Youngstown City Schs, superintendent, 1972-78; Youngstown State Univ, dir & instr, 1978-79; Warren City School Dist, supt of schools. **Orgs:** Bd of trustees, St Elizabeth's Med Ctr Youngstown, OH; bd dir, Warren Redevel & Planning Corp Warren, OH; bd dir, Warren-Trumbull Urban League. **Honors/Awds:** Humanitarian Award, Trumbull Co Br Nat Asn Advan Colored People, 1984; Outstanding Educator, Warren-Trumbull Urban League, 1981; Finis E Engleman Scholarship, Am Asn Sch Admin, 1981; Bowman Fellowship, Kent State Univ, 1979. **Military Serv:** AUS, capt (active & reserves), 1954-68. **Business Addr:** Superintendent of Schools, Warren City School District, 261 Monroe NW, Warren, OH 44483.

PEGUES, WENNETTE WEST
Educator. **Personal:** Born Nov 25, 1936, Pittsburgh, PA; married Julius; children: Mary Pamela, Michael David & Angela Suzette. **Educ:** Carlow Col Pittsburgh, BSN, 1958; Univ Tulsa, MS, 1975, EdD, 1978. **Career:** RN adminr, teacher & staff position, 1958-74; Univ Tulsa, grad asst, 1974-75, grad res fellow, 1975-76, asst dean, 1976-78; Langston Univ Urban Center, assoc acad dean, 1979-80; Okla State Univ, Psychiat & Behav Sci, adj asst prof, asst dean students, registrar & fin aid, emer, currently. **Orgs:** Osage Co Dept, Dist #55 Acad Cent Sch, 1979-80; comnr, Okla State, Dept Human Serv, 1979; Delta Sigm Theta, 1980; sch bd pres, Osage Co Dept, Dist#55 Acad Cent Sch, 1980-81; mem bd dir, Tulsa Sr Citizens, 1980; Am Asn Univ Women; Am Personnel & Guidance Asn; Nat Conf Acad Advising; Pub Welfare Asn Sch Bd; Tulsa Alumni Asn; Okla State Univ Emer Asn. **Honors/Awds:** Educ Honor, Soc Kappa Delta; Outstanding Women, Community N Tulsa B&P Women; Distinguish Alumni Service Award, Educ Calow Col, 1979. **Military Serv:** ANC, 2 lt, 1956-59. **Home Addr:** 1741 W Virgin St, Tulsa, OK 74127. **Business Phone:** (405)744-5000.

PEGUESE, CHARLES R.
Librarian, school administrator. **Personal:** Born Aug 3, 1938, Philadelphia, PA. **Educ:** LaSalle Col, Philadelphia, PA, BS, 1960; Drexel Univ, Philadelphia, PA, MLS, 1965. **Career:** Librarian (retired); NE Area Young Adult Free Libr, Philadelphia, PA, coordr, 1960-69; Action Libr Learning Ctr, Philadelphia Sch Dist, dir, 1970-74; State Libr PA, coordr networking & acad libr, 1974-88; Harrisburg Area Community Col, dir, McCormick Libr, dean, instrnl resources, 1988. **Orgs:** OPP, 1957; pres, bd, N City Cong Philadelphia, PA, 1966-74; comt mem, Penn Libr Asn, 1970; comt chmn, Am Libr Asn, 1971; adv bd, Philadelphia United Way, 1972-74; chair, Harrisburg Hist Archit Rev Bd, 1980-90; Hist Harrisburg Asn, 1980; City Harrisburg, Redevelopment Authority Bd, 1989; Leadership Harrisburg Area, Class of 1993. **Honors/Awds:** Nat Leadership Award, Am Libr Asn & Asn Col & Res Libr, 1990. **Special Achievements:** Writer, articles in PA Library Asn Bulletin, Libr Jour. **Military Serv:** USY, sgt, 1961-66. **Home Addr:** 1108 Green St, Harrisburg, PA 17102, **Home Phone:** (717)232-7926. *

PEGUESE, HERMAN A
Executive. **Personal:** Born Nov 9, 1940, Philadelphia, PA; son of Herman R and Edmonia F; married Diana Lynn, Feb 14, 1994; children: Angela M, Kimberly Vicchiollo, Benjamin Myer, Christopher C, Nathaniel Myer & Cameron Myer. **Educ:** Howard Univ, BS, psychol, 1970; Univ Mo, MBA, mgt, 1974. **Career:** USAF, radar technician, 1959-62, col, 1970-93; Atlantic Mgt Ctr Inc, prog mgr, 1994-99, sr prog dir, 1999-. **Orgs:** Vpres, Psi Chi, 1970; life mem Air Force Asn, 1970-; comdr, Quuantico Yacht Club, 1990; recorder, Knights Columbus, 1991; Refined Officers Asn, 1992-; prog chair, Nat Contract Mgt Asn, 1995; sr warden, St Clement Church, Vestry, 1999-2000; Phi Beta Kappa. **Special Achievements:** Written several course text books, 1995-; written articles for various newsletters, periodicals, 1990-. **Military Serv:** USAF, col, 1959-62, 1970-93; AUS, 1963-66; Legion Merit, 1993; Meritorious Service Medal, 1991. **Home Addr:** 1806 Tarpon Bay Dr S, Naples, FL 34119-8713, **Home Phone:** (239)591-3931. **Business Addr:** Senior Program Director, Atlantic Management Center Inc, 6066 Leesburg Pke Suite 700, Falls Church, VA 22041, **Business Phone:** (703)256-0509.*

PEGUS, CHERYL
Association executive. **Educ:** Cornell Univ Med Col, MD; Columbia Univ Sch Pub Health, MPH. **Career:** New York Hosp Cornell Med Ctr, Mem Sloan Kettering Hosp, fel; Pfizer Pharmaceut, Cardiovasc Risk Factors Group, med dir, 1996-2001; Lipo-Science, Prod Develop & Sci Alliances, vpres; Health Power Inc, vice chair; Aetna Inc, Blue Bell, PA, nat med dir women health, Clin Prog Develop, nat med dir, 2004-. **Orgs:** Bd dir, Heritage Affil of the Am Heart Asn; Dean Circle Cornell Univ Med Col; ed adv bd, Disease Mgt Advr; mem corp adv coun, Soc Women Health Res; Nat Med Asn Coun Concerns Women Physicians; Am Col Cardiology Inst. **Business Addr:** National Medical Director Member Avantage Programs, Aetna Inc, 1425 Union Meeting Rd, Blue Bell, PA 19422, **Business Phone:** (215)628-4800.

PELOTE, DOROTHY B
Government official. **Personal:** Born Dec 30, 1929, Lancaster, SC; daughter of Abraham Barnes and Ethel Green; married Maceo R (deceased); children: Deborah Pelote Allen & Miriam Pelote Heyward. **Educ:** Allen Univ, BS, 1953; Savannah State Col. **Career:** Government official (retired); Chatham Co Bd Educ, teacher, 1956-85; Chatham Co GA, co comnr. **Orgs:** Phi Delta Kappa Educ Frat, 1978; pres, Savannah Fedn Teachers, 1982-83; Legis Study Comm Memorial Med Ctr; pres, Carver Height Organ; Adv Comm Local Govt; Water & Sewer Auth Chatham Co;

Chatham Asn Educ; Coastal Comm Food Bank; mem, bd dir, YMCA; bd mem, United Way; Bus & Prof Women's Club; bd mem, Phoenix Proj; Nat Coun Negro Women Inc; Chatham Co Employees Retirement Bd; Coastal Area Planning & Devel Commn for Seminar Agendas; Nat Asn Advan Colored People. **Honors/Awds:** Carver Heights Community Serv Award, 1981-82; Rep Roy Allen Award, 1982; Minority Women of the Year, Zeta Phi Beta, 1984; Dorothy Pelote Day City Savannah & Chatham Co, 1985. **Special Achievements:** First Female elected Co Comn Chmn Pro Tem; one of the first Black females to be elected to the Chatham Co Comn; State Bd Postsecondary Voc Educ by appointment of the Gov Ga elected vpres Black Caucus Asn Co Comnr Ga; Testimonial Banquet by Constituents of Eighth Comn Dist.

PELSHAK, TROY (ZENRET TROY PELSHAK)
Football player. **Personal:** Born Mar 6, 1977, Charlotte, NC. **Educ:** NC A&T Univ, mkt. **Career:** St Louis Rams, linebacker, 1999 & 2000; Jacksonville Jaguars, linebacker, 2000; NFL Europe, Barcelona Dragons, 2001-02; Arena Football League, Columbus Destroyers, 2005; New York Dragons, offensive line & defensive line, 2006. **Honors/Awds:** All-Conf hon; Defensive Most Valuable Player, NC A&T Univ; first-team All-Mid-Eastern Athletic Conf hons; Super Bowl XXXIV, 2000; Rookie of the Year, 1999.

PELSHAK, ZENRET TROY. See PELSHAK, TROY.

PEMBERTON, DAVID MELBERT
Insurance executive. **Personal:** Born Apr 24, 1926, Chicago, IL; son of David M Jr and Cleo Davis Ward; married Masseline Gibson, Jun 26, 1949; children: Dianna, Debra, Denise & Kim. **Career:** Midwest Nat Life Ins Co, reg mgr, 1965; Insurance Agent, currently. **Orgs:** Life Underwriters Asn Miami; elder Bethany SDA Church; Nat Asn Advan Colored People; treas, Locka Br; chmn, Commun Act Neighbourhood Coun; exec bd chair, OPA Locka Comm Develop Corp. **Honors/Awds:** Civic award, 1969; National Quality Award; Nat & Sales Achievement Award, 1974; 51st All-Star Hon Roll, 1973; Father of the Yr, Urban League, 1993. **Home Addr:** 2520 NW 156th St, Opa Locka, FL 33054.

PEMBERTON, DR. GAYLE R.
Educator, writer. **Personal:** Born Jun 29, 1948, St Paul, MN; daughter of Lounneer and Muriel E Wigington. **Educ:** Lake Forest Col, attended 1968; Univ Mich, BA, 1969; Harvard Univ, MA, 1971, PhD, 1981; Wesleyan Univ, MAA. **Career:** Columbia Univ, lectr, 1974-77; Middlebury Col, instr, 1977-80; Northwestern Univ, asst prof, 1980-83; Reed Col, vis assoc prof, 1983-84; Bowdoin Col, African-Am Studies, vis assoc prof, acting dir, 1986-88, Minority Affairs, dir, 1988-90; Princeton Univ, African-Am Studies, assocdir, 1990-93; John Simon Guggenheim Fel, 1993; Wesleyan Univ, African-AmStudies, chair, William R. Kenan Prof Humanities, 1994; WW Norton,writer. Author: "It's The Thing That Counts," State of Black America,1991; "A Sentimental Journey," Race-ing Justice En-Gendering Power, 1992;The Hottest Water in Chicago, 1992; The Colored Girls Go; Black Women &American Cinema; prof emeritles, currently. **Orgs:** Modern Lang Asn. **Honors/Awds:** WEB DuBois Found, 1975; Ford Found, Doctoral Fel, 1969-74; SW Review,Margaret Hartley Mem Award, 1992; Book of the Year Award for Hottest Water, NJ Comt Humanities; Binswanger Teaching Award. **Business Addr:** Professor Emeritus, Wesleyan University, Department of African-American Studies, 215 Long Lane, Middletown, CT 06457, **Business Phone:** (860)685-2420.

PEMBERTON, HILDA RAMONA
Government official. **Personal:** Born Jun 29, 1940, Norman, NC; daughter of Archie C (deceased) and Judy Pearl; divorced; children: Eugenia & Charles. **Educ:** NCA Central Univ, BS, 1961; Southeastern Univ, masters, 1981. **Career:** Government official (retired); Prince Georges County govt: psychiatric social worker, chief, employee rels div, office personnel, dep dir personnel, coun mem, chiar. **Orgs:** Bd, Nat Asn Counties; past pres, Nat Asn Black County Officials; bd mem, Prince George's County Econ Develop Corp; chair bd, Coun Govts; bd, Wash Sanitary Transit Authority; Nat Coun Negro Women; Alpha Kappa Alpha; First Baptist, Highland Park. **Honors/Awds:** One of 100 Most Influential Women, WASian Mag, 1989; County Leader of the Year, Am City & County Mag, 1991; Presidential Citation for outstanding dedication to the career development of our nation's youth; Governor's Award for dedicated service to the homeless.

PEMBERTON-HEARD, DANIELLE MARIE
Lawyer. **Personal:** Born Nov 29, 1964, New York, NY; daughter of Dennis and Andrea; married Gregory McQuade, Aug 26, 1995. **Educ:** Tufts Univ, BA, 1986; Case Western Reserve Univ, Sch Law, JD, 1989. **Career:** Time Life Inc, vip bus affairs; Cowan Luiebowitz & Latman, atty assoc, 1991-93; Wiggin & Dana, atty assoc, 1989-91; Discovery Commun, dir, sr coun legal & bus affairs, 1993-96; Walker Mem Dinner Gala,Wash, DC, co-chair; Pub Broadcasting Syst, Arlington, Va, group coun prog bus affairs, currently. **Orgs:** Delta Sigma Theta Sorority Inc, 1984-; vip prog, Prof Alliance, 1994-; Habitat Humanity, N Va, 1996-; Toy Indust Asn. **Special Achievements:** Contributing Author, Journal of The Copyright Soc, 1992; 1991 Letter Updates, Trademark & Unfair Conpetion Law, Cases & Materials, The Michie Corp, 1990. **Home Phone:** (301)208-8916. **Business Addr:** Group Counsel Program Business Affairs, Public Broadcasting System, 2100 Crystal Dr, Arlington, VA 22202, **Business Phone:** (703)739-5000.

PENA, ROBERT BUBBA
Actor, executive, football player. **Personal:** Born Aug 8, 1949, Falmouth, MA. **Educ:** Dean Jr Col, AA; Univ Mass, attended 1972. **Career:** Offensive guard (retired), president; Cleveland Browns, offensive guard, 1972; Film: Love of Life; Dogs of War; Ft Apache; The Four Seasons; TV pilot; business ventures, Domingo's Chowder House Restaurant; W Falmouth Fish Market; Health Club Enterprises; Robert Pena & Assocs, pres; Mortgage Security Inc, pres & chief exec officer, currently. **Orgs:** Founder & co-chmn, Roche Pires Scholarship Fund; Cape Verdean Club, Falmouth; Lambda Chi Alpha Frat; volunteer work, Northampton Jail. **Honors/Awds:** Award from Falmouth MA Local Real Estate Beautification Comt for restoringa piece of historically zoned real estate. **Business Addr:** President, Chief Executive Officer, Mortgage Security Inc, 31 Teaticket Hwy Suite 2-7, Teaticket, MA 02536-5644, **Business Phone:** (508)548-6618.

PENA, TONY (ANTONIO FRANCESCO PENA)
Baseball player. **Personal:** Born Jun 4, 1957, Montecristi, Dominican Republic; married Amaris; children: Tony Jr & Jennifer Amaris. **Career:** Pittsburgh Pirates, infielder, 1980-86; St Louis Cardinals, infielder,1987-89; Boston Red Sox, infielder, 1990-93; Cleveland Indians, 1994-96;Chicago White Sox, 1997; Houston Astros, 1997; Kansas City Royals, mgr, 2002-05; New York Yankees, Base Coach, 2006-08; New York Yankees, Bench coach, 2009-. **Honors/Awds:** Gold Glove Awd; TOPPS Rookie All-Star; Nat League All-Star Team, 1982,1984, 1985, 1986, 1989; Gold Glove Award, Nat League, 1983-85; Gold Glove Award, 1991; 2003 AL Manager of the Year, 2003. **Special Achievements:** First base coach of the New York Yankees, 2005. *

PENCEAL, DR. BERNADETTE WHITLEY
Educator. **Personal:** Born Dec 16, 1944, Lenoir, NC; daughter of Walter Andrew Whitley and Thelma Simmons Whitley; married Sam, Apr 29, 1967. **Educ:** Syracuse Univ, NY, BS, 1966; City Col, NY, MA, 1973; Fordham Univ, NY, PhD, urban educ, 1989. **Career:** Fashion Inst Technol, NY, instr eng, 1973-74; Green Haven Maximum Security Prison, Stormville NY, instr eng, 1974-76; Malcolm-King Col, NY, instr eng, 1974-78; Hunter Col, NY, instr reading, 1974-79; Col New Rochelle, NY, instr eng, 1977-89; New York Univ, NY, mentor eng, 1980-, instr, currently. **Orgs:** Asn Black Fac & Admin; Phi Delta Kappa, 1981-; pres, Asn Black Women Higher Educ Inc, 1985-87, J & B Whitley's Inc, 1985-; bd mem, Urban Women's Shelter, 1985-87; New York Urban League, 1987-, Am Asn Univ Women, 1989-. **Honors/Awds:** Bernadette Penceal Day, Off Pres Borough Manhattan, City New York, 1987. **Home Addr:** 129 W 147th St, New York, NY 10039, **Home Phone:** (212)368-7046. **Business Addr:** Instructor, New York University, 239 Greene St Suite 811, New York, NY 10039, **Business Phone:** (212)998-5677.

PENDER, MEL
Executive. **Educ:** Adelphi Col, BS, social sci. **Career:** U.S. Military Academy, head track coach; Nat Asn Homebuilders, southeast regional coordr; Atlanta Hawks, dir community affairs, currently. **Orgs:** pres, Atlanta Hawks Found; Intl Track Asn; Georgia spec Olympics; 100 Black men Dekalb County. **Honors/Awds:** Olympic Games, gold medal, 4x100-meter relay, 1968; hall fame, bob hayes. **Special Achievements:** Olympic Games, 1964. **Military Serv:** retired: USA, capt; Vietnam War, Bronze Star. *

PENDERGRAFT, MICHELE M
Banker. **Personal:** Born Sep 6, 1954, Trenton, NJ; daughter of Leon Edward Meekins Sr and Lena Mae Kelly; married James William Pendergraft Sr, May 17, 1980; children: James William Jr. **Educ:** Mercer County Community Col, Trenton, NJ, 1977; Am Inst Banking, Anchorage, AK, 1983. **Career:** Mercer St Friends Ctr, Trenton, NJ, dance instr, 1970-78; Ginger Bread House, Anchorage, AK, asst mgr, 1978-79; First Nat Bank Anchorage, Anchorage, AK, customer serv rep, 1979-80, asst vpres, br mgr; First Nat Bank Alaska, br mgr, currently. **Orgs:** Bus Prof Women Club, 1990. **Home Addr:** 7041 Scalero Circle, Anchorage, AK 99507. **Business Addr:** Manager, First National Bank Alaska, 5305 E Northern Lights Blvd, PO Box 200788, Anchorage, AK 99520-0788, **Business Phone:** (907)777-4362.

PENDERGRASS, EMMA H
Lawyer. **Personal:** Born in Orangeburg, SC; daughter of W W Humphrey and Catherine; children: Bailey III & Gary W. **Educ:** Howard Univ, Wash, DC, BS; Westfield State Col, MEd, 1964; Armstrong Law Sch, JD, 1976; Calif Western Univ, Santa Ana, CA, PhD, 1977. **Career:** US Govt, chemist, 1955-56; Chicopee High Sch, sci teacher, 1960-67; Hayward Unified Sch Dist, sci teacher, 1967-71; Hayward Unified Sch Dist, career educ coun, 1971-76; Law Off Emma H Pendergrass, atty of law, 1976-. **Orgs:** Past pres, Charles Houston Bar; bd dirs, Young Men Chrisitan Asn Oakland; Nat Bar Asn; Delta Sigma Theta Sorority Inc; Alameda Co Bar Asn, 1977-; Pro Bono Serv Judicare Prog Charles Houston Bar Asn, 1977-80; past pres, Calif Asn Black Lawyers Links Inc. **Home Addr:** 7677 Oakport St Suite 1050, Oakland, CA 94621-1929, **Home Phone:** (510)567-6100. **Business Addr:** Attornet at Law, Emma H Pendergrass Law Office, 7677 Oakport St Suite 1050, Oakland, CA 94621, **Business Phone:** (510)567-6100.

PENDERGRASS, THEODORE DEREESE
Singer. **Personal:** Born Mar 26, 1950, Philadelphia, PA. **Career:** Singer (retired); Mc Intyre Elem Sch Choir, singer; All-City Stetson Jr High Sch Choir, singer; The Cadillacs b &, drummer; Harold Melvin & the Blue Notes, drummer & backup vocalist, 1968, lead singer, 1970-77; solo performer, 1977-2006; Solo LPs include: Life is a Song Worth Singing, 1978; Teddy, 1979; TP, 1980; Live Coast to Coast, 1980; It's Time for Teddy, 1981; Teddy Pender grass, 1982; This One's For You, 1982; Heaven Only Knows, 1983; Greatest Hits, 1984; Love Language, 1984; Workin' It Back, 1985; Joy, 1988; Truly Blessed, 1991; Teddy Live Coast to Coast,1993; You & I, 1997; A Touch of Class, 1998; This Christmas I'd Rather Have Love, 1998; Auth, Truly Blessed, 1998; From Teddy With Love, 2002; Pure Love, 2002; From the Front Row Live, 2003; Anthology, 2003; Turn Off the Lights, 2004; Greatest Hits: Love TKO, 2004; Timeless Classics, 2004; Golden Legends (St Clair), 2004; Live! Coast to Coast & TP, 2005; Believing Love: The Very Best of Teddy Pender grass, 2005; Golden Legends (Madacy), 2006; Teddy Pendergrass/Live Is a Song Worth Living, 2006. **Honors/Awds:** Recipient of numerous civic & pub service awards; Image Award, Nat Asn Advan Colored People, 1973, 1980; Black Achievement Award, Ebony Mag,1979; Keys to Cities: Detroit, Savannah, Lakeland, FL, Memphis; Nominee for 5 grammy Awards. **Special Achievements:** Twelve gold & seven platinum albums; Co-author, Biography, Truly Blessed.

PENDLETON, BERTHA MAE OUSLEY
School administrator, school superintendent. **Personal:** Born Oct 15, 1933, Troy, AL; married Oscar Pendleton; children: Gregory. **Educ:** Knoxville Col; US Int Univ; Univ San Diego, educ leadership. **Career:** Sch Administrator, Sch Suprintendent (retired); Tenn Valley Authority, cartographic eng aide, 1954-55; Chattanooga Pub Sch, 1956-57; Mem Jr High Sch, teacher & counr, 1957-68; Morse High Sch, parent counr, 1968-70; Compensatory Educ Unit, coordr, 1970-72; Crawford High Sch, vice prin, 1972-74; Lincoln High Sch, prin, 1974-76; Prog Div, dir compensatory educ, 1976-83; Sch Opers Div, asst supt, 1983-85; Supt's Off, spec asst supt, 1985-86; Dep Supt's Off, dep supt, 1986-93; San Diego Unified Sch Dist, supt, 1993-98; Pt Loma Nazarene Col, adj prof. **Orgs:** United Way San Diego County; Natural Hist Mus; Nat Ctr Educ & Economy; Danforth Found Adv Comt; Asn Calif Sch Adminrs; Alpha Kappa Mu Hon Soc; Elementary Inst Sci; YMCA; adv coun, US Dept Defense; Alpha Kappa Alpha Sorority; Inst Educa Inquiry; bd dirs, I Have Dream Found. **Honors/Awds:** George Edmund Haynes Award, San Diego Urban League; Legislative Woman of the Year, Senator David Kelley; Educator of the Decade, Phi Delta Kappa, 1993; Woman of Change, Pt Loma Col, 1994; Woman of Distinction, Salvation Army; Chairman's Award, San Diego Chamber Com; Woman of Distinction, Nat Coun Negro Women; Frederick D Patterson Award, United Negro Col Fund, 1996; Author E Hughes Career Achievement Award, Univ San Diego, 1996. **Special Achievements:** First female & first African Am supt, San Diego Unified School Dist; selected as one of 100 role models in the "Songs of My People" exhibit at the San Diego Museum of Art. **Business Phone:** (702)734-2220.

PENDLETON, FLORENCE HOWARD
School administrator, senator (u.s. federal government). **Personal:** Born in Columbus, GA; daughter of John Milton and Elease Brooks; married Oscar Henry Sr, 1943; children: Oscar Henry Jr & Howard Thompson. **Educ:** Howard Univ, BS, 1949, MS, 1957; Am Univ, SScD, 1976; Cath Univ, SScD, 1970. **Career:** DC Pub Sch, teacher, 1958-70, asst prin, 1970-80, prin, 1980-; Ward Five Dem Comt, chairperson, 1979-82, mem, 1979-; Ward Five CO7, Adv Neighborhood Comt, comnr, currently; DC, shadow senator. **Orgs:** Secy, Alpha Kappa Alpha; DC Asn Sec Sch Prin, 1980-; Nat Asn Sec Sch Prin. **Honors/Awds:** Outstanding Principal, Hine Jr High Sch, Stud Govt Asn, 1981; Outstanding Community Leader, Ward Five, Berean Baptist Church, 1981.

PENDLETON, TERRY LEE
Athletic coach, baseball player. **Personal:** Born Jul 16, 1960, Los Angeles, CA; son of Alfred and Ella; married Catherine; children: Stephanie, Terry & Trinity. **Career:** Baseball player (retired), baseball coach; St Louis Cardinals, third baseman, 1984-90; Atlanta Braves, 1991-94, 1996, hitting coach, 2001-; Fla Marlins, 1995-96; Cincinnati Reds, 1997; Kansas City Royals, 1998. **Honors/Awds:** Gold Glove Award, 1987, 1989, 1992; MLB Most Valuable Player Award, 1991; All-Star, 1992. **Special Achievements:** Fifth player to Steal 20 Bases, 1984. **Business Phone:** (404)522-7630.

PENELTON, BARBARA SPENCER
Educator. **Personal:** Born Apr 8, 1937, Chicago, IL; married Richard; children: Kim & Lisa. **Educ:** Univ Ill, BS Elem Educ, 1958; Univ IL, MS Guidance & Counseling, 1961; Univ IN, ed.D

Higher Educ, 1977. **Career:** McCosh Elementary Sch Chicago, teacher, 1958-66; Tri-County Urban League Peoria, dir educ progs, 1966-69; Bradley Univ Peoria IL, assoc prof educ,1969-, dir student teaching, 1978-; Ten-year Review Team IL State Bd Educ, eval team Consult, 1979; IL Coun Right Read, adv & consult, 1980; Rockefeller-Kellogg Found Leadership Training Proj, consult, 1980; Assoc Prof Educ, emer; Bradley Univ, Teacher Educ Chair. **Orgs:** Bd trustees, Nat Urban League, 1980; bd trustees, Proctor Hosp Peoria,1980; pres, bd dirs Tri County Urban League, 1980. **Honors/Awds:** Outstanding Educator, Young Women's Christian Asn, 1973; Outstanding Graduate Advisor, Central Region Alpha Kappa Alpha Sorority, 1975. **Business Addr:** Teacher Education Chair, Bradley University, 1501 W Bradley Ave, Peoria, IL 61625, **Business Phone:** (309)676-7611.

PENHA, GAIL A.
Chief executive officer. **Career:** Gap Enterprises Natural Solutions, chief exec officer, currently. **Business Addr:** Chief Executive Officer, Gap Enterprises Natural Solutions, 6030 Marshalee Dr, PO BOX 103, Elkridge, MD 21705, **Business Phone:** 877-917-5170.

PENISTON, CECE (CECELIA PENISTON)
Singer. **Personal:** Born Sep 6, 1969, Dayton, OH. **Career:** A & M Rec, singer; Albums: Overweight Pooch's Female Preacher; I Like It, 1991; Finally, 1992; We Got A Love Thang, 1992; Keep On Walkin, 1992;Inside That I Cried, 1992; Crazy Love, 1992; Thought Ya Knew, 1994; Finally, 1992; I'm In The Mood, 1994; Remix Collection, 1994; I'm Not Over You, 1994; Hit By Love, 1994; Keep Givin' Me Your Love, 1995; Thought 'Ya Knew; Good News in HardTimes, 1995; Movin' On, 1996; Before I Lay, 1996; I'm Movin' On, 1996; Somebody Else's Guy, 1998; Nobody Else, 1998; My Boo (The Things You Do), 1998; The Best of, 1998; The Best Of CeCe Peniston, 1998; He Loves Me 2, 1999; Lifetime To Love, 2001; Reminiscin', 2001; 20th Century Masters: The Millennium Collection, 2001; For My Baby, 2003; Eternal Lover, 2004; Deeper Love, 2005; Shame Shame Shame, 2007; Other Appearences: The Wendy Williams Show, 2009. **Honors/Awds:** Miss Black Arizona, 1989; Miss Galaxy; Hall of Fame, Phoenix Col. **Special Achievements:** Album "Finally", topped Billboard magazine's dance chart, following the abolition of apartheid, she was the first female entertainer to visit and perform in South Africa. **Business Phone:** (213)856-2755.

PENISTON, CECELIA. See PENISTON, CECE.

PENN, ALGERNON H
Executive. **Personal:** Born Oct 18, 1956, Chicago Hts, IL; son of Edward H and Vernell; married Suzanne Y, Aug 28, 1999; children: Jamula M McClinton, Drake E & Alexandra K. **Educ:** Thorton Community Col, AA, 1978; Governors State Univ, BA, 1987. **Career:** Nehemiaa Prog, regional dir, 2000-01; Nareb Housing Am Fund, nat prog dir, 2002-03; Residential Loan Centers Am, sr vpres, corp & indust rels, 2003-; Home Gift USA Inc, vpres strategic partnerships; E4E Financial Serv, dir enterprise sales, currently. **Orgs:** Life mem, President's coun, Univ Ill, Chicago, 2002-; nat chair, down payment assistance progs, Nat Asn Real Estate Brokers, 2002-; trustee, Village Univ Park, IL, 2003-; Dearborn Realist Bd, 2003-; Rainbow-PUSH Coalition's Real Estate & Mortgage Trade Bur; chmn, Friends Abraham Lincoln Nat Airport Comn; vpres, Dearborn REALTIST. **Honors/Awds:** Spirit of Greatness Award, New Orleans Ctr Successful Living's, 2002; Proclamation, New Orleans City Council, 2002; Certificate of Merit, City New Orleans, 2002; Meritorius Serv, US Senator Mary L Landrien, 2003; Image Award, NAACP; President's Club Award, CenTrust Mortgage's; Platinum Club Award, Commonwealth-United Mortgage's; Roundtable Award, N Am Mortgages Producer's Asn. **Business Addr:** Director, E4E Financial Services, 109 Koramangala Industrial Layout, 4th Cross 5th Block, Bangalore 560095, India, **Business Phone:** (918)02552-6061.

PENN, AUDREY
Physician; Administrator. **Educ:** Swarthmore College, BA, 1956; Columbia University College of Physicians and Surgeons, MD 1960. **Career:** Special Advisor, Dir NINDS/NIH, 2007-present; Deputy Dir, NINDS 1995-2007. **Business Addr:** Special Advisor to the Director, NIH/NINDS, Neuroscience Center, Rm.2101, 601 Executive Blvd, MSC9531, Bathesda, MD 20892.*

PENN, CHRISTOPHER ANTHONY
Football player. **Personal:** Born Apr 20, 1971, Nowata, OK; son of James. **Educ:** Northeastern Okla A&M col; Univ Tulsa. **Career:** Football player (retired); Kans City Chiefs, wide receiver, 1994-96; Chicago Bears, wide receiver, 1997-98; San Diego Chargers, wide receiver, 1999.

PENN, JAMES T, JR.
Funeral director. **Career:** Penn Funeral Home, owner & funeral dir, currently. **Business Addr:** Owner, Funeral Director, Penn Funeral Home, 3015 S Inkster Rd, Inkster, MI 48141, **Business Phone:** (313)278-6300.*

PENN, MINDELL LEWIS
Manager. **Personal:** Born Mar 27, 1944, Detroit, MI; daughter of Artis Underwood and Mamie Underwood; married Leon Penn, Feb 3, 1974; children: Michael Artis, Courtney Leon. **Educ:** Wayne State Univ, Detroit, MI BS, bus admin, 1964. **Career:** Michigan Consolidated Gas Co, Detroit, MI, tele type operator, 1961-64; San Diego Gas & Elec Co, San Diego, CA, credit rep, 1964-67; Pacific Gas & Elec Co, Sacramento, CA, small bus affairs adminr, 1967-02, City Richmond, coun mem, 1999-05. **Orgs:** Chair, Sacramento Girl Scout Adv Bd; chair, bd dirs, Sacramento Urban League; bd mem, St Hope Acad; Sacramento Metropolitan Arts Comn's County Cultural Awards Comt. *

PENN, DR. NOLAN E
Educator. **Personal:** Born Dec 1, 1928, Shreveport, LA; son of Bessie Penn and Henry Penn; married Barbara Pigford; children: Joyce & Carol. **Educ:** Calif State Univ, AB, 1949; Univ So Calif, MS, 1952; Metro State Hosp, psychol intern, 1955; Univ Denver, PhD, 1958; Harvard Med Sch, Cert Comm Ment Health, 1969. **Career:** Larue Carter mem Hosp Indianpolis, staff psychologist, 1958-59; Univ Wis, Sch Med, postdoctoral fel, 1959-61, from asst prof to prof, 1963-70; Mendota State Hosp, staff psychologist, 1961-63; Univ Calif, Sch Med, La Jolla, prof psychiat, 1970-97, reg dir, area health ed ctr off dean, 1982, prof emer psychiat, 1997-; Univ Calif-San Diego, assoc chancellor, 1988-; Cross-Cultural Personality Res Studies Team, Sch Psychol, Fielding Grad Univ, Santa Barbara, CA, dir, 1999-, fac, currently; San Diego County Mental health Servs, San Diego, sr forensic psychologist, 2000-04. **Orgs:** Pres, Wis State Psychol Assoc, 1967-68; Wis Leg Comt recodify Ment Health & Ment Retardation Codes, 1967-70; founder & chmn, Afro-Am Studies Dept, Univ Wis, Madison, 1969-70, Urban & Rural Studies, Univ Calif, San Diego, 1970-73; examiner, Am Bd Prof Psychol, Am Psychol Asn, 1970-;dir, Comt & Forensic Psychol Trg UCSD, 1974-88; Am Psychol Assoc, Inter-Am Soc Psychol, Sigma Xi; ed bd, J Consult & Clin Psychol, Am J Pub Health; fel, Am Group Psychotherapy Asn; Nat Registry Certified Group Psychotherapists, 1994-; Acad Psychotherapists, 1997; Acad Experts Traumatic Stress, 1998; ethics comt, Calif Psychol Asn, 2002-05; fel, Am Acad Experts Trauma; fel, Am Asn Advan Sci; fel, Am Forensics Soc; fel, Am Orthopsychiatry Asn; fel, Am Psychotherapy Asn; Am Psychol Asn; fel, Am Psychol Soc; Am Pub Health Asn; Asn Acad Minority Physicians; Asn Black Psychologists; Gerontological Soc Am; InterAm Soc Psychologists; Int Congress Social Psychol; Int Coun Psychologists; Int Soc Study Hypertension Blacks; fel, Soc Personality & Assessment; fel, Western Psychol Asn. **Honors/Awds:** Helen Margulies Mehr PhD Award, Div Pub Interest, Calif Psychol Assoc. **Military Serv:** AUS, corpl, 1952-54. **Business Addr:** Faculty, Director, Fielding Graduate University, School of Psychology, 2112 Santa Barbara St, Santa Barbara, CA 93105, **Business Phone:** 800-340-1099.

PENN, SHELTON C.
Judge, lawyer. **Personal:** Born Dec 9, 1925, Winston Salem, NC; married Sadie W. **Educ:** Morehouse Col, BA, 1948; Univ Mich Law Sch, JD 1951. **Career:** Atty pvt pract, 1951-75; asst pros atty Calhoun County, MI, 1957-66; chief asst pros atty, 1963-66; practicing atty & civil rights hearing referee, 1973-75; appointed judge Tenth Dist Ct Calhoun County; pvt pract, currently. **Orgs:** Calhoun Co Bar Asn; Mich Bar Asn; Am Bar Asn; Nat Bar Asn; Nat Conf Black Lawyers; bd dir, Cripple Childrens' Soc; YMCA; Urban League; Humane Soc; Battle Creek Human Rel Comn; past pres, Battle Creek Nat Asn Advan Colored People; Legal Aid Soc; bd dir, S Cent Mich Planning Coun; Mich Crime Comn; bd dir, Big Brothers & Big Sisters S Cent Mich. **Honors/Awds:** NBA Hall of Fame; Whitney Young Award; Distinguished Citizen Boy Scout Award; Frederick Douglass Award. **Military Serv:** AUS, WWII. **Home Addr:** 225 W Columbia Ave Apt 16, Battle Creek, MI 49015. **Business Addr:** Attorney, 225 Columbia Ave W Suite 16, Battle Creek, MI 49015-3361.*

PENN, DR. SUZANNE Y.
Business owner. **Personal:** Born in Chicago, IL; daughter of Willie B McDonald and Essie McDonald; married Algernon H; children: Jamila McClinton, & Alex. **Educ:** Univ Ill-Chicago, BA, 1976; Univ Chicago, MBA, 1978; Kennedy-Western Univ, PhD, 2006. **Career:** First Nat Bank Chicago, portfolio mgr, 1977, security analyst, 1978-79; CEDCO Commercial Credit, co-mgr, 1979-81, mgr, 1981-82; McClinton Mgt Serv Inc and McClinton Financial Services, Inc., founder & chief exec officer, 1981; Christian Financial Ministries, pres. **Orgs:** Probe Inc, 1982; Chicago Reg Purchasing Coun, 1984-86; Cosmopolitan Chamber Com, treas, 1984-89; YWCA, dir, 1987; Christian Financial Ministries, pres, 2004-. **Honors/Awds:** Kizzy Award Prof Achievement, Images-Leadership Award; Black Women's Hall Fame, 1985; Dollar & Sense, Chicago's Up & Coming Black Bus & Prof Women, 1985; Outstanding Prof Award, CCUP, 1986; Nat Asn Negro Bus & Prof Women's Club Inc, 1986; Black Rose Award, League Black Women, 1988; Chicago Defender Women of Excellence Award, 2009. **Special Achievements:** Author, "How to Finance Your Salon," 1984; co-author, "Family Networking Makes Good Business Sense," 1990; interviewed, "Are You Living Beyond Your Means?" 1991; "The Pink Corner Office - Women Achieving Power In The Workplace," 2006; featured in Newsweek, Today's Chicago Woman and Crain's Chicago Business Magazines. **Business Phone:** 800-374-5616.

PENN, TENESIA SHARONE
Consultant. **Educ:** La State Univ. **Career:** Towers Perrin, benefits consult assoc, currently. **Business Addr:** Benefits Consulting Associate, Towers Perrin, 2107 Wilson Blvd Suite 500, Arlington, VA 22201-3062, **Business Phone:** (703)351-4700.

PENN-ATKINS, BARBARA A.
Executive. **Personal:** Born Nov 11, 1935, Gary, VA; married Will E Atkins; children: Lawrence Nichols, Cheryl Nichols Smith, Brian L Nichols. **Educ:** Mich State Univ, 1955; Wayne State Univ, 1964; Oakland Community Col, 1979; Wayne Co Community Col, 1979. **Career:** Univ Detroit, admin asst; Wayne Co Community Col, accts rec supvr, 1968-72; BPA Enterprises Inc, vpres, 1972; Pica Systems Inc, pres, 1980. **Orgs:** Pres, Am Bus Women's Asn & MCCC 1981; gen co-chair & MI United Negro College Fund 1983-85; Allocations rev United Found, 1983-85; vpres & bd dirs, Minority Tech Coun Mich, 1985; bd dir, Detroit C of C. **Honors/Awds:** Woman of the Year, Motor City Charter Chap, Am Bus Women's Asn, 1979; Spirit Detroit Detroit Conv Bur, 1980; Founders Award, United Negro Col Fund, 1984; Minority Bus Award Mich Dept Com, 1984; Pioneering Bus Award, Nat Asn Women Bus Owners, Mich Chap, 1985.

PENNICK, JANET
Law enforcement officer. **Personal:** Born Feb 6, 1946, Philadelphia, PA; daughter of Roosevelt and Ella; married Frank Nelson, Jan 27, 1966 (divorced); children: Kelly Lynn. **Career:** Philadelphia Dep Sheriff's Off, lt, 1996-. **Orgs:** Philadelphia Guardians Peace, pres, 1997-. **Military Serv:** USAR, master sgt, 1977-; Bronze Star Metal, Desert Storm, 1991. **Home Addr:** 1315 N 57th St, Philadelphia, PA 19131, **Home Phone:** (215)877-7462. **Business Phone:** (215)686-3530.

PENNIMAN, RICHARD WAYNE. See LITTLE RICHARD.

PENNINGSFELD, GLORIA DAVY. See DAVY, GLORIA.

PENNINGTON, JESSE C
Lawyer. **Personal:** Born Jul 1, 1938, Percy, MS; married Roberta; children: Bradford & Johnny. **Educ:** Howard Univ, BA, 1964, JD, 1969; Wright Jr Col, AA, 1969; Cent YMCA Real Estate Inst, cert; Nat Col Criminal Lawyers & Pub Defenders, attended 1974. **Career:** US Postal Serv, clerk, 1957-60; Seyfarth, Shaw, Fairweather & Geraldson Law Firm, off boy, 1957-60; Travis Realty Co, real estate broker, 1960-61; Sen Paul H Douglas, legis asst, 1964-67; Nat Labor Rels Bd, legal asst, 1967-68; Reginald Heber Smith fel, 1969-71; Northern Miss Rural Legal Serv, managing staff atty, 1969-72; Fed Home Loan Bank Bd, staff, 1968-69; Mary Holmes Col, instr, 1970-71; Pennington Walker & Turner, sr partner, 1973-; Micronesian Legal Serv Corp, directing atty; pvt pract atty, currently. **Orgs:** Bd dirs, Northern Miss Rural Legal Serv, 1973-; mem, Trust Terr Pac Bar, 1976-; Miss Bar Asn; IA Bar Asn; Nat Bar Asn; Nat Conf Black Lawyers; pres, Miss Asn Attys; Nat Defense Lawyers Asn; Black Appalachian Comn; Clay County Community Develop Prog Inc. **Business Addr:** Attorney, Rm 315 Moore Bldg 1400 Lynch St, Jackson, MS 39217-0001, **Business Phone:** (601)373-0902.

PENNINGTON, LEENETTE MORSE
Educator. **Personal:** Born May 10, 1936, Webster, FL; married Bernard; children: Bernadette & Brigette. **Educ:** Morgan State Col, BS, 1956; Univ Miami, EdM, 1970; Univ Fla, attended 1974. **Career:** Fla State Welfare, case worker, 1958-63; educr, 1963-69; curriculum writer, 1969-70; Dade Co, admin asst, 1970-72; Inst Dade Co Div Staff Dev, coordr, 1971; Elem Basic Skills Project Dade Co Pub Schs, Miami, proj mgr, 1973; Edward Waters Col, interim pres. **Orgs:** Adv Coun, Elem Educ Fla Int Union; Asn Supervision & Curriculum Develop; Int Reading Asn; pres, Nat Coun Negro Women; Sigma Gamma Rho; consult, Desegration Ctr, Univ Miami; Dade Co Comn Status Women; African Meth Epis Chap. **Honors/Awds:** Outstanding Religious Service AME Chap, 1970; Outstanding Education Achievement Award, Sigma Gamma Rh, 1972; Outstanding Young AME Church woman 11 Epis Dist.

PENNINGTON, RICHARD
Law enforcement officer. **Personal:** Born in Little Rock, AR. **Educ:** Am Univ, BA, criminal justice; Univ DC, MA, coun; FBI Nat Acad George Wash Univ, Exec Develop Prog; FBI Nat Exec Inst; Harvard Univ John F Kennedy, Sch Govt, sr Exec Prog. **Career:** Wash Metrop Police Dept, law enforcement, police officer, asst chief, 1968; New Orleans Police Dept, police chief, supt, 1994-02; Atlanta police Dept, polic chief, 2002-. **Orgs:** Nat Pres, Nat Orgn Black Law Enforcement Exec; Int Asn Chiefs Police; Major Cities Chiefs Police Asn; Ga Asn Chiefs Police; 100 Black Men Atlanta; Kappa Alpha Psi Fraternity; Cascade United Methodist Church. **Honors/Awds:** Public Official of the Year. **Business Addr:** Chief Of Police, Atlanta Police Department, 675 Ponce de Leon Ave, Atlanta, GA 30308, **Business Phone:** (404)817-6900.*

PENNIX, JAMES A
College administrator. **Personal:** Born Apr 10, 1966, Lynchburg, VA; son of Anna R; married Lisa B, Jul 7, 2001; children: Damian

East, James II & Jordan. **Educ:** Roanoke Col, BS, 1988; Radford Univ, MSW, 2001. **Career:** Herr Foods Inc, salesperson, 1988-93; UTZ Qual Foods, sales supvr, 1993-98; Roanoke Col, asst basketball coach, 1998-2001, asst dir admis, 2001-03, dir admis, currently, Multicultural Recruitment coordr, currently. **Orgs:** NABC, 1998-; NASW, 1999-; NACAC, 2001-. **Honors/Awds:** Salesperson of the Year, Herr Foods, 1990, 1991; Salesman of the Year, UTZ Qual Foods, 1993. **Military Serv:** USNR, second class petty officer, 1985-93; National Service Medal, 1991. **Business Addr:** Director of Admissions, Multicultural Recruitment Coordinator, Roanoke College, 221 Col Lane Roselawn, Salem, VA 24153, **Business Phone:** (540)375-2270.

PENNY, DR. ROBERT
Physician. **Personal:** Born Jun 6, 1935, Cincinnati, OH; son of Ralph and Marie; married Joselyn E, May 21, 1971; children: Angeline E. **Educ:** Univ Cincinnati, BS, 1959; OH State Univ, MD, 1963. **Career:** Children's Hosp, Columbus, internship pediatrics, 1963-64; Children's Hosp, Cincinnati, residency pediatrics, 1964-66; Loma Linda Univ, instr pediat, 1967-68; Johns Hopkins Hosp, Baltimore, fellow ped endocrinol, 1968-71; Univ Southern Calif, from asst prof to assoc prof pediat, 1971-81, prof pediat; Univ Southern Calif Med Ctr, dir, div pediat endocrinol, 1985-91, pro, res med, 1991, dir, Core Molecular Biol Lab, GenClin Res Ctr; Univ Southern Calif, prof emer, currently. **Orgs:** The Endocrine Soc; The Lawson Wilkins Ped Endocrine Soc; Soc for Pediat Res; Am Pediat Soc; ed bd, AJDC, 1988; Am Bd Pediat, assoc mem, 1989-91; Am Pediat Asn, adolescent med sect, chair. **Honors/Awds:** Published 53 articles in peer review journals; 9 chapters; 48 abstracts; chairperson, Endocrinology Sect Western Soc for Ped Res, 1983; question writer, Pediat Endocrinol Examination, 1984, 1989, 1991; Rho Chi Soc Beta Nu Chap, Cincinnati, 1959; reviewer, J Endo & Metabolism, AJDC & pediatres. **Military Serv:** USAF, Med Corps capt, 1966-68. **Business Phone:** (803)255-3400.*

PENNYWELL, PHILLIP, JR.
School administrator. **Personal:** Born Aug 1, 1941, Shreveport, LA; son of Phillip Pennywell Sr and Rosa; married Janet E M; children: Phyllis, Twanda, Pamela & Phillip Wayne. **Educ:** Southern Univ, BS, 1972, MEd, 1974; N Tex State Univ, PhD, 1980. **Career:** Caddo Parish Sch Bd, teacher, 1972-74; Parish Govt, police juror, 1984-85; Southern Univ, chmn, Div Behav/Sci Educ, ful bright prog adv, currently. **Orgs:** Phi Delta Kappa, 1976; Kappa Alpha Psi Frat, 1983; bd dirs, Shreveport Leadership, Shreveport Chamber Comn; chmn bd dirs, Socialization Serv Inc; exec dir, SSI Drug Alcohol Abuse Educ Prog; Dem State Cent Comt; City Shreveport River Front Develop; Citizens Adv Comt; Shreve Square; bd dirs, Caddo-Bossier Port CMS Adv Bd; bd dirs, La Asn Blind. **Home Addr:** 7412 McArthur Dr, Shreveport, LA 71106. **Business Addr:** Fulbright Program Adviser, Southern University, Department of Behavioral Sciences/Education, 3050 Dr Martin Luther King Jr Dr, Shreveport, LA 71107, **Business Phone:** (318)674-3300.

PEOPLES, ALICE LEIGH
President (organization). **Career:** Jack & Jill Am Found Inc, nat pres, currently. **Home Addr:** 5445 Scott Ct, Ypsilanti, MI 48197, **Home Phone:** (734)487-7725. **Business Addr:** National President, Jack & Jill of Am Foundation Inc, 1930 17th St NW, Washington, DC 20009.*

PEOPLES, DANITA L
Dermatologist. **Educ:** Wayne State Univ, Detroit, MI, med training, dermat residency, 1986. **Career:** William Beaumont Hosp, Royal Oak, internal med internship, dermat residency, 1986; Henry Ford Health Syst, W Bloomfield, div head dermat; pvt pract, dermatalogist, 1986-; MidMichigan Dermatol, Midland, MI, pvt pract, 1994-; pvt pract, Bloomfield Hills, 1999-; Peroxsys Corp, founder, 2006-. **Business Addr:** Dermatologist, Founder, Peroxsys LLC, PO Box 1764, Midland, MI 48641-1764, **Business Phone:** 877-832-2292.

PEOPLES, DOTTIE
Singer, artistic director. **Personal:** Born in Dayton, OH. **Career:** Gospel singer, currently; Albums: Live at Salem, 1993; On Time God, 1994; Christmas With Dottie, 1995; Count On God, 1996; Testify, 1997; Collection-songs of Faith and Love, 1998; God Can & God Will, 1999; Show Up & Show Out, 2000; Greatest Hits, 2001; Churchin' With Dottie, 2003; The Water I Give, 2003; Live in Memphis, 2005. **Honors/Awds:** Stellar Awards; Female Vocalist, Choir of the Year (Traditional), 1995; Vision Award, Bobby Jones Gospel Show, 1995; Atlanta Gospel Choice Award, Song of the Year. **Special Achievements:** Best Gospel Album nominee, Soul Train Music Awards; Traditional Gospel Album nominee, Dove Awards. **Business Addr:** Gospel Singer, Atlanta International Record Company, 881 Memorial Dr, Atlanta, GA 30316, **Business Phone:** (404)524-6835.*

PEOPLES, ERSKINE L.
Salesperson. **Personal:** Born Oct 16, 1931, Gadsden, AL; married Dorothy Thompson; children: E Ladell Jr, Tamatha M. **Educ:** Mus Educ TN A&I State Univ, BS, 1953; TN A&I State Univ, Addl Studies; Chattanooga Asn Life Underwriters. **Career:** ins agent (retired); Mutual Benefit Life Ins Co, salesman; BT Wash HS Chattanooga, band dir; Security Fed Savings & Loan Asn Chattanooga, vpres, dir. **Orgs:** Chmn, Hamilton Co Sch Bd Chattanooga, 1973-75; mem bd, Greater Chattanooga C C; Goodwill Industries Inc; Meth Neighbrohood Ctrs; deacon Mt Calvery Bapt Ch; Alpha Phi Alpha; Chattanooga Underwriters; pres, Club Mutual Benefit Life. **Honors/Awds:** Man of Year, Psi Lambda, 1968. **Military Serv:** AUS, spl, 1956-58. *

PEOPLES, FLORENCE W
Health services administrator. **Personal:** Born Jul 21, 1940, Charleston, SC; married Earl Calvin; children: Patricia Peoples Lowe, Jonelle Elaine Washington, Deborah Simmons Jones, Sheyla Simmons, Pamela & Calvin. **Educ:** Roper Hosp Sch Practical Nursing, dipl, 1963; Northeastern Univ, BSN, 1977. **Career:** New Eng Reg Black Nurses, bd dir, 1982-85; H McCall Nurses Unit Grant Am Methodist Episcopal Church, pres, 1986-87; Am Cancer Soc, William Price Unit, bd dir, co-chairperson, 1987; Mass Ment Health Ctr, Boston, hosp supvr, currently. **Orgs:** Nat Black Nurses, 1978-; New Eng Regional Black Nurses Asn, 1978-; Am Nurses Asn, 1978-; Mass Nurses Asn, 1978-; Nat Asn Advan Colored People, 1982-; Eastern Mass Urban League, 1983-. **Honors/Awds:** Public Serv Award, New Eng Regional Black Nurses Asn, 1982; Committee of the Year, New Eng Regional Black Nurses Asn, 1987. **Home Addr:** 70 Nelson St, Dorchester Center, MA 02124. **Business Addr:** Supervisor, Massachusetts Mental Health Center, 74 Fenwood Rd, Boston, MA 02115, **Business Phone:** (617)734-1300.*

PEOPLES, DR. GERALD C
Chancellor (Education). **Career:** Chancellor (retired); City Grambling, city councilman; Southern Univ, Baton Rouge, vice chancellor for stud affairs; Southern Univ New Orleans, chancellor, 1997-2000.

PEOPLES, GREGORY ALLAN
School administrator. **Personal:** Born May 17, 1951, Ravenna, OH; married Alice Leigh; children: Allaina Terice, Ashleigh Gail & Angela Marie. **Educ:** Allegheny Col, BA, 1973; Kent State Univ, MEd, 1977. **Career:** Allegheny Col, asst dir admis, 1973-75; Kent State Univ, resident hall dir, 1975-77; Ctr-Eastern MI Univ, coordr campus info, 1978-80; Eastern MI Univ, asst dir admis, 1980-82, assoc dir admiss, 1982-83; GMI Engineering & Mgt Inst, admis, corp spec, 1983-84, dir admis; Washtenaw Community Col, dir enrollment mgt, 1985-91; Eastern Mich Univ, assoc dean stud, 1991-, ombudsman, currently. **Orgs:** Delta Tau Delta, 1973-; treas, Black Faculty & Staff Asn, 1978-82, 1991-95; Delta Sigma Pi, 1980; bd dir, Nat Orientation Dir Asn, 1981-; adv, Delta Sigma Pi, 1981-83, Delta Tau Delta, 1984-. **Honors/Awds:** Outstanding Young Men America, 1984. **Business Addr:** Ombudsman, Eastern Michigan University, 112 Welch Hall, Ypsilanti, MI 48197, **Business Phone:** (734)487-0074.*

PEOPLES, HARRISON PROMIS, JR.
Executive, consultant, business owner. **Educ:** Chapman Col, Orange, Calif, BA, 1976; Pepperdine Univ, Malibu, Calif, MS, 1986. **Career:** Motorola, Cupertino, Caluf, mgr, 1980-85; Transition Strategies, Los Altos, Calif, vpres, 1985-88; Nat Traffic Safety Ins, San Jose, Calif,instr, 1988-89, regional dir, 1989-96; US Census Bur, San Jose, Calif, mgr, 1989-; Lighthouse Worldwide Solutions Inc, vpres, 1996-97; Peoples & Assocs, owner, consult, 1997-; Valerie Frederickson & Co, Exec coach, Sr HR, OD & Outplacement consult. **Orgs:** Penninsula Assoc Black Personnel Admin, 1981-88; recorder, Human Resources Planning Soc, 1983; Orgn Develop Network, 1984-86; Nat Asn Advan Colored People, pres state, 1987-89, vpres, 1989. **Honors/Awds:** Recognition, Salinas Nat Asn Advan Colored People, 1983; Service Award, Palo Alto NAACP, 1988; DEA Appreciation, Drug Enforcement Admin, 1988; Omega Man of the Year, Omega Psi Phi. **Military Serv:** AUS, maj, 1959-80. **Business Phone:** (408)279-3134.

PEOPLES, DR. JOHN ARTHUR, JR.
School administrator. **Personal:** Born Aug 26, 1926, Starkville, MS; son of John A Peoples Sr and Maggie Rose; married Mary E Galloway, Jul 13, 1951; children: Kathleen Peoples-Sedlak & Mark. **Educ:** Jackson State Univ, BS, 1950; Univ Chicago, MA, 1951, PhD, 1961. **Career:** Gary IN Pub Sch Syst, prin, 1951-64; Jackson State Univ, asst to pres, 1964-65; Am Coun Educ, fel, 1965-66; State Univ NY, Binghamton, asst to pres, 1965-66; Jackson State Univ, vpres, 1966-67, pres, 1967-84, pres emer, currently. **Orgs:** Bd trustees, Am Col Test Corp, 1973-79; bd control, Southern Regional Educ Bd, 1974-86; chair, Am Coun Educ; consult, Kellogg Found, 1981-84; consult, Killy Endowment Fund, 1976-77; Noon Optimist Club Jackson, 1981-; life mem, NAACP; bd dirs, MS Ballet Intl Inc, 1980-; bd dirs, Piney Woods City Life Sch; bd dirs, Jackson Hinds Comprehensive Health Ctr; bd dirs, Smith Robertson Mus & Cult Ctr; bd dirs, Jackson State Nat Alumni Asn; Jackson Civil Serv Comn; deacon, Farish St Bapt Church; Omega Psi Phi; Sigma Pi Phi; 33rd degree Mason. **Honors/Awds:** Man of Year, Alpha Chi Chap, 1962; Education Specialist, US State Dept, 1977; Sports Hall of Fame, Jackson State Univ; S western Athletic Conference Hall of Fame; Hall of Fame Lifetime Achievement Award, Nat Black Col, 1993; Distinguished Alumni Award, NAFEO, 1993; Walter Wash Humanitarian Award; John A Peoples Jr Science Building, named in honor, Jackson State Univ; Mississippi Medal of Service, Miss Governor, 2009. **Special Achievements:** First African American to chair ACE; wrote book "To Survive and Thrive". **Military Serv:** USMC, sgt, 1944-47. **Home Addr:** 386 Heritage Pl, Jackson, MS 39212. **Business Addr:** President Emeritus, Jackson State University, 1400 Lynch St, Jackson, MS 39217, **Business Phone:** 800-848-6817.

PEOPLES, JOHN DERRICK, JR.
Journalist. **Personal:** Born Jul 23, 1951, Seattle, WA; son of J D Peoples Sr and Gertrude Johnson; married Julie Selman, Jun 1989. **Educ:** Univ Montana, Missoula, MT, 1969-71; Tex Southern Univ, Houston, TX, 1978-79; Univ Wash, Seattle, WA, BA, commun, 1984. **Career:** The Times Seattle, Seattle, WA, sports reporter, currently. **Orgs:** NABJ, 1984. **Home Addr:** 4731 S Hudson St, Seattle, WA 98118, **Home Phone:** (206)723-5036. **Business Phone:** (206)464-8283.

PEOPLES, JOYCE P.
Educator. **Personal:** Born Aug 27, 1937, Huntsville, AL; divorced; children: Alycia Peoples-Behling. **Educ:** Ala A&M Univ, BS (Cum Laude), 1957, MS, 1965; The Am Univ, PhD (with Distinction), 1977. **Career:** Ala A&M Univ, asst prof, 1967-76; Voorhees Col, dir, interdisciplinary studies, 1976-77; Univ MD-ES, asst vice chancellor, 1977-78; Inst for Serv to Educ, special asst to pres, 1978-83; Southern Univ, vice chancellor acad affairs, 1983; Atlanta Metropoliton Col, prof Eng. **Orgs:** Regional dir, Black Women Academicians, 1982-83; consult, Am Coun Educ, 1982-86; parliamentarian, NAUW, 1985-87; pres, Top Ladies Distinction Inc, 1985-87; bd mem, Nat Asn Univ Women, 1986-87. **Honors/Awds:** Listed in Int Dictionary of Biography London, England, 1973; Nat Citation for Assault on Illiteracy, AOIP, 1985-86; selected Woman of the Year, Nat Asn Univ Women, 1986-87; Nat Top Lady of the Year, TLOD Inc, 1986-87; listed in Who's Who of Am Women, 1986-87.

PEOPLES, DR. L KIMBERLY
School administrator. **Career:** Golightly Career & Tech Ctr, prin, 1985-92, dir, currently. **Orgs:** Asn Sec Sch Prin; Asn Supv & Curric Develop; Am Voc Asn; Alpha Kappa Alpha. **Honors/Awds:** MetLife NASSP Michigan Principal of the Year, Michigan Asn Sec Sch Prin, 1997; Michiganian of the Year, Detroit News, 1997; Cent Mich Univ Commencement Speaker & Hon Deg, Doctor Educ. **Business Addr:** Director, Golightly Career And Technical Center, 900 Dickerson Ave, Detroit, MI 48215-2900, **Business Phone:** (313)822-8820.

PEOPLES, SESSER R.
Educator. **Personal:** Born Dec 7, 1934, Newark, NJ; married Irma; children: 4. **Educ:** Jersey City State Col, BA 1963; Kean Col, MA. **Career:** Jersey City State Col, Black Studies dir, 1969-73, affirmative action officer, 1973, presidential assts; Mentally Retarded Plainfield Pub Sch, teacher; Urban Processes Coordinated, coor, 1971. **Orgs:** Third World Enterprises, 1968; African-Am Studies Asn, 1970-73; Urban Processes Coordinated Consult Firm, 1971; Nat Asn Black & Urban Ethnic Dirs, 1971-72; African Heritage Studies Asn; Phi Delta Kappa, 1972; mem bd dirs Leaguers Inc. **Military Serv:** AUS, 1957-59.

PEOPLES, VEO
Lawyer. **Personal:** Born Sep 13, 1947, St Louis, MO; married Linda Sing; children: Nicole & Nissa. **Educ:** Univ Mo Rolla, BS Chem Engr 1970; St Louis Univ Sch Law, JD, 1975. **Career:** Ralston Purina Co, patent agt 1973-75; Ralston Purina Co, patent atty 1975-78; Monsanto's Patent Dept, patent trainee; Monsanto Co's Control Eng Dept, process design engr; Monsanto Co, eng intern; Anheuser-Busch, assoc gen coun 1978-84; pvt pract, patent atty; Haverstock, Garrett & Rogers, partner, currently. **Orgs:** Spec task force Mo Bar Assoc 1976-77; entertainment chmn Mound City Bar Assoc 1976-77; secy exec comn, bd dir, Legal Serv Eastern Mo Inc; dist comn Western Dist St Louis for Boy Scouts Am; bd dir, W Co Am Cancer Soc; dist exec Mark Twain BSA 1976-; Ralston Purina Corp Devel Bd 1977; Optimist Club St Louis; circuite comn 22nd Judicial Bar, 1984-92; chmn, patent sect, BAMSL; pres, founder CADRE 19 Inc; bd dirs, Fed Reserve Bank St Louis, 1994-99; Bar Asn Metrop St Louis; Nat Bar Asn. **Honors/Awds:** Rosalie Tilles Scholar 1966-70; Curators Scholar, Univ Mo 1966; Stud Chap Award Excellence AIChE 1970; Univ Scholar Award Univ Mo 1967; Undergrad Research Fel 1970; Achievement Award Urban League 1975; Acad Chem Engrs Univ Mo Rella, 1998; Theodore McMillian Award, St Louis Univ, 1998. **Home Addr:** 342 Jamboree Dr, Manchester, MO 63011. **Business Phone:** (314)231-9775.

PEOPLES, VERJANIS ANDREWS
Educator, college administrator. **Personal:** Born Aug 8, 1955, Monroe, LA; daughter of Willie and Vernita; married Gerald C Peoples, Aug 9, 1975; children: Takiyah & Nicholas. **Educ:** Grambling State Univ, BS, 1976, MS, 1978; Kansas State Univ, PhD, 1990. **Career:** Bienville Parish Sch Syst, teacher, 1976-79; Grambling State Univ, lab sch, teacher, 1979-88, Col Educ, prof, 1989-90; Southern Univ, Col Educ, prof, 1991-92; Southern Univ & A&M Col, asst dean acad & stud affairs & Dept Curric & Instr,

assoc prof, currently. **Orgs:** La Asn Teacher Educr, 1996; Asn Teacher Ed, 1996; Asn Supv & Curric Develop, 1996; La Alliance Educ Reform, 1996; La Coun Teacher Educ, 1996; Am Asn Col Teacher Educ, 1996. **Honors/Awds:** Teacher of the Year, Grambling Lab Sch, 1989. **Special Achievements:** Created proposal for teachers Alumni As-Partners Program (TAAP), instituted "First Class teachers Program," developed Partnership prog surrounding parishes, Publ article, "Restoring Human Dignity: A Model for Prevention & Intervention," Publ chapter, "Teacher Preparation Prog Hist Black Col". **Business Addr:** Assistant Dean of Academic & Student Affairs, Associate Professor, Southern University & A&M College, College of Education, W W Stewart Hall Rm 242, PO Box 9983, Baton Rouge, LA 70813, **Business Phone:** (225)771-3762.

PERARA, MITCHELL MEBANE
Physician. **Personal:** Born Feb 11, 1924, Tulsa, OK; married Jean Wolfe; children: Susan, Mark, Georgianna. **Educ:** Va Union Univ, BS, 1944; Howard Univ, MD, 1948. **Career:** Am Col Surgeons, dipl, 1955-85; Pvt Prac, physician, 1955-85. **Honors/Awds:** Fel Am Cancer Soc, 1955.

PERDREAU, CONNIE. See PERDREAU, CORNELIA WHITENER.

PERDREAU, CORNELIA WHITENER (CONNIE PERDREAU)
Educator, college administrator. **Personal:** Born in Beacon, NY; daughter of Henry Whitener and Mazie Martin; married Michael, Jun 14, 1969; children: Maurice. **Educ:** Potsdam Col, Potsdam, New York, BA, 1969; Ohio Univ, Athens, Ohio, MA, 1971, MA, 1972. **Career:** Ohio Univ, Athens, Ohio, lectr & study abroad coordr, 1976-98, dir off Educ Abroad, dir emer educ abroad, currently. **Orgs:** Pres, Ohio Teachers Eng Speakers Other Lang, 1987-88; trustee, Ohioana Libr Asn, 1988-96; team mem, NAFSA: Asn Int Educr, 1988-90, 1991-93; Black Professionals Int Affairs, 1989-; Ohio Univ African-Am Fac, Adminr & Staff Caucus, 1990-91; Coop Grants Community, 1990-95; pres, Fulbright Enrichment Ctr Community, 1991-96; founder & chair, Black Prof Teachers Eng Speakers other Lang, 1992-; adv bd, USIA Eng Lang Prog, 1995-98; pres elect, 1995-96, pres, 1996-97, Educ Testing Serv Policy Coun Test Eng Second Lang, 1998-01; Chair, Adminr & Teachers Eng as a Second Lang. **Home Addr:** 92 Grosvenor St, Athens, OH 45701. **Business Addr:** Director Emeritus, Ohio University, Office of Education Abroad, 107 Gordy Hall, Athens, OH 45701, **Business Phone:** (740)593-2200.

PERDUE, REP. GEORGE, JR.
State government official. **Personal:** Born Mar 15, 1943; married Delores; children: Cindy & Joy. **Educ:** Morehouse Col, BS; Atlanta Univ, MS. **Career:** Univ Ala, Human Resources Syst, proj coordr, vpres fin affairs & admin, currently; Ala House Reps, Dist 54, state rep, 1983-. **Orgs:** NAACP; YMCA; bd dirs, Birmingham Girl's Club; Alpha Phi Alpha; SCLC; Fourth Ave YMCA Century Club; bd dirs, Univ Credit Union Supvry Comn. **Honors/Awds:** Minority Advocate of the Year, US Dept Com. **Business Addr:** State Representative, Alabama Legislative of Black Caucus, 11 S Union St Room 626, PO Box 2473, Montgomery, AL 36130, **Business Phone:** (205)934-2693.

PERDUE, WILEY A
School administrator. **Educ:** Morehouse Col, grad 1957; Atlanta Univ, MBA; Ind Univ-Bloomington, advan studies. **Career:** Sch Administrator (retired); Savannah State Col, registr; Morehouse Col, bursar, bus mgr, vpres fiscal affairs; Morehouse Col, acting pres, 1994-95.

PEREZ, ALTAGRACIA
Clergy. **Personal:** Born Sep 19, 1961, New York, NY; daughter of Ramon Eduardo and Esther Zoraida Maceira-Ortiz. **Educ:** New York Univ, SEHNAP, BS, 1982; Union Theol Sem, MDiv, 1985, STM, 1986. **Career:** Astor Ment Health Ctr, special educ teacher, 1982; Church Living Hope, day camp dir, 1984; Union Theol Sem, co-coordr, Women's Ctr, 1984-85; Mission San Juan Bautista, youth leader/minister, 1985-86; Pilsen Cath Youth Ctr, assoc dir, 1986-89; Diocese Chicago, coordr youth ministries, 1990; Episcopal Church Ctr, Nat provincial youth coordr, 1991; Episcopal Church St Phillip, rector, currently. **Orgs:** Founding bd mem, Hispanic AIDS Network, 1986-, bd dir, 1992-; educ leadership coun, Hispanic Designers Inc, 1990-; Comn End Racism, Episcopal Diocese Chicago, 1990-92; staff liaison, AIDS Task Force, Episcopal Diocese Chicago, 1990-; adv coun, Chicago Women's AIDS Proj, 1991-; co-chair, Chicago Area AIDS Care Givers Retreat, 1991-92; secy, Gen Conv Joint Comn AIDS, Episcopal, 1992-; bd dir, Urban Environ Policy Inst. **Honors/Awds:** Bertha Dixon Memorial Award, New York Higher Educ Opportunity Program, 1982. **Special Achievements:** A Faith of One's Own, "Este Es Mi Cuerpo," Crossing Press article in anthology, 1987; "The Spiritual Cost of Abuse," Prevention Resource Services: Journal on Abuse, 1992. **Business Addr:** Rector, Episcopal Church St Phillip, 2800 Stanford Ave, Los Angeles, CA 90011, **Business Phone:** (213)232-3494.*

PEREZ, ANNA
Executive. **Personal:** Born Jan 1, 1951?, New York, NY; married Ted Sims; children: 3. **Educ:** Hunter Col. **Career:** Tacoma Facts, Tacoma, WA, publ; Sen Slade Gordon, press secy; Rep John Miller, press secy; Barbara Bush, Wash, DC, press secy, 1989-93; Chevron Corp, 1998-2001; vpres Calif; Creative Artists Agency Inc, head media rels & external affairs; dep asst pres; Nat Security Coun, dir commun; Walt Disney Co, vpres Calif govt rels; Chevron Corp, gen mgr corp commun & progs, 1998-2001; Nat Sec Adv Condoleezza Rice, dep asst to pres & counr, 2001-04; NBC, exec vpres commun, 2004; Universal Studios, head; NBC Universal, exec vpres commun, currently. **Orgs:** Calif Int Rels Found; Greek Theatre Los Angeles Found; Black Filmmakers Found; Int Womens Media Found Adv Comt; Ariel Capital Mgt; Gulf Found; felInst Politics John F Kennedy Sch Govt, Harvard Univ; California Film Comn; Joint Ctr Polit & Econ Studies. **Special Achievements:** First Black press secretary to First Lady Barbara Bush.

PERINE, JAMES L.
Educator. **Personal:** Born Jun 23, 1943, St Louis, MO; married B Rosalie Hicks; children: Lori, Keith & Kelly. **Educ:** NE Mo State Univ, BA, 1964; Univ Md, MA, 1967; Pa State Univ, PhD, 1979. **Career:** Wash, res psychol, 1964-68; Univ Md, oeo grad & teaching asst, 1965-67; Pa State Univ, Col Human Develop, asst to dean, currently. **Orgs:** Phi Delta Kappa; Nat Educ Hon Fraternity; Am Voc Asn; Am Personnel & Guid Asn; Am Psychol Asn; St Paul's United Methodist Church State Col; Nat Asn Adv Colored People; adv bd, Lewisburg Prison; bd dirs, State Col Comn Theatre; Comn Vol Mountain view Unit Ctr Community Hosp; State Col Kiwanis Club. **Honors/Awds:** Spec Citation, Optimists Club, 1970; Blue Key.

PERINE, MARTHA LEVINGSTON
Executive. **Personal:** Born Jun 27, 1948, Mobile, AL; married David Andrew; children: David Jr, Alissa, Alison. **Educ:** Bus Adminstr Clark Col, Atlanta GA, BA 1969; Wash Univ St Louis, MA, econ, 1971. **Career:** Fed Res Bank of St Louis, sr br exec, asst vpres, 1971-. **Orgs:** Nat Asn Bank Women, 1985; mem, Am Inst Banking, 1985; financial sec Gamma Omega Chap Alpha Kappa Alpha Sor Inc, 1985; fin sec Holy Metro Missionary Bapt Chap, 1985. **Honors/Awds:** Outstanding Young Woman, Am Outstanding Young Am's, 1970, 1979; Achievement Nominee St Louis Jaycee Wives, 1978. **Business Addr:** Senior Branch Executive, Federal Reserve Bank of St Louis, 1 Fed Res Bank Plz Broadway and Locust St, PO Box 442, Saint Louis, MO 63166-0442, **Business Phone:** (314)444-8444.

PERKINS, BERNICE PERRY
Government official. **Personal:** Born Apr 5, 1931, West Point, MS; daughter of Willie B and Statie M. **Educ:** Univ Ill, Champaign-Urbana, IL, BS, 1954. **Career:** Government official (Retired); Dept Veterans Affairs, Chicago, clinic dietician, 1964-66, dietetic servs asst chief, 1966-72, Salem, VA, dietetic servs chief, 1972-74, Cincinnati, dietetic servs chief, 1974-76, Boston, dietetic servs chief, 1976-82, Wash Dist, dietetic servs chief, 1982-87; Dept Veterans Affairs, dietetic servs dir, 1987-96. **Orgs:** Food admin sect co-chair, Ill Dietetic Asn, 1968-69; career guidance chap, Dist Dietetic Asn, 1985-86; Am Soc Hosp Food Serv Admin, 1986-96; Qual mgmt, Am Dietetic Asn, dietetics educ task force, 1992-94; Dist Dietetic Asn, mgmt practices chair, 1992-93; treas, Nat Soc Healthcare Food Serv Mgmt,1994. **Honors/Awds:** Certificate of Apppreciation, Dist Pub Sch, 1986; Cert Pride in Public Serv, Veterans Admin, 1989, Honor Award, 1989; Presidential Rank Award, Dept Veterans Affairs, 1992; Am Heart Asn, Cert of A; Am Asn Retired Persons. **Special Achievements:** Speaker: Dietetic Interns, 1987, 1997; speaker: Nat Educ CNF, NV, 1991; Dietetic Interns, MD, 1992; Speaker, Am Dietetic Asn, 1993. **Home Addr:** 10200 Rock Oak Terr, Cheltenham, MD 20623.

PERKINS, CHARLES WINDELL
Executive. **Personal:** Born Mar 12, 1946, New Orleans, LA; children: Evany Joy. **Educ:** Univ Calif, Berkeley, BA, 1968; Southwestern Grad Sch Banking SMU Dallas, grad degree banking, 1978. **Career:** Security Pac Nat Bank, vpres; San Leandro, vpres & mgr, 1978. **Orgs:** Asst vpres, San Mateo & SF; mgr, Foster City, 1974; asst mgr, Hayward Fremont; asst cashier, SF; supvr, SF & Berkeley; mgt trainee Security Pac Bank, 1968; bd mem, Hunters Point Boys' Club SF, 1972; treas Foster City CC, 1974; co-founder, Black Officers Group Sec Pac Bank, 1980; Univ CA Alumni Asn. **Honors/Awds:** All-conference basketball, Univ CA Berkeley, 1967; $1,000,000 trust award, Security Pac Bank, 1979.

PERKINS, DANIEL T
Chief executive officer, foundation executive. **Personal:** Born in Washington, DC. **Educ:** Univ Pittsburgh, Johnstown, Pa, attended, 1974; Pepperdine Univ, Masters Degree. **Career:** Booz Allen & Hamilton Inc, mgr staffing; Dual & Assocs, mem bd dirs, vpres admin; MTS Technols Inc, owner, ceo, 1991-. **Orgs:** Founder, The Challenge Prog, 2003-. **Military Serv:** USMC, comn officer, commun officer, dir the performance coun ctr. **Business Addr:** Owner, Chief Executive Officer, MTS Technologies Inc., 2800 Shirlington Rd Suite 1000, Arlington, VA 22206, **Business Phone:** (703)575-2900.*

PERKINS, EDWARD JOSEPH
College teacher, government official. **Personal:** Born Aug 19, 1928, Sterlington, LA; son of Edward Joseph Sr and Tiny Estella Noble Holmes; married Lucy Cheng-mei Liu, Sep 9, 1962; children: Katherine Karla Shih-Tzu & Sarah Elizabeth Shih-Yin. **Educ:** Univ Md, BA 1968; Univ Southern CA, MPA 1972, DPA 1978; St Augustine Col, DHL, Honis Causa, 1993. **Career:** AID Far E Bur Wash, asst gen serv officer; US Opers Mission to Thailand, Bangkok, asst gen serv Officer 1967-69, mgt analyst 1969-70, dep asst dir mgt 1970-72; Off Dir Gen Foreign Serv Wash, staff asst, 1972, personnel officer, 1972-74; Bur Near Eastern & South Asian Affairs, admin officer, 1974-75; Off Mgt & Opers, mgt anal Officer, 1975-78; Accra, counr polit affairs 1978-81; Monrovia, dep chief mission, 1981-83; Bur African Affairs Off West African Affairs, dir 1983-85; Dept State, ambassador to Liberia, 1985-86, ambassador to S Africa 1986-89, dir gen Foreign Serv 1989-92; United Nations & UN Security Coun, ambassador, 1992-93; US ambassador, Australia, 1993-96; Univ Okla, Int Progs Ctr, William J Crowe chair & exec dir, 1996-. **Orgs:** Epsilon Boule Sigma Pi Phi Fraternity; Kappa Alpha Psi Fraternity; Navy League; Hon Soc Phi Kappa Phi; Am Soc Pub Admin, 1971-; Veterans Foreign Wars, Chevy Chase Chap; Am Acad Diplomacy; Am Foreign Serv Asn; Am Polit Sci Asn; World Affairs Coun, Cent Okla & Wash, DC; Cranlana Prog, bd; Am Legion; Chester A Arthur Soc; Coun Foreign Rels; Foreign Policy Asn; Int Studies Asn; Pac Coun Int Policy; Pub Serv Comn; Am Consortium Int Pub Admin; bd dirs, Ctr Study Presidency; Asn Diplomatic Studies & Training; adv bd, Inst Int Pub Policy; bd trustees, Lewis & Clark Col; adv coun, Univ Off Int Progs, Pa State Univ; bd trustees, Woodrow Wilson Nat Fel Found; bd visitors, Nat Defense Univ; bd dirs, Nat Acad Pub Admin. **Honors/Awds:** Dept State, Dir Gen's Cup, 2001; Honee Beta Gamma Sigma Chap Univ Okla, 1998; Distinguished Alumni Award, Univ Southern Calif, 1991; Achievement Award, Southern Univ, 1991; C Rodger Wilson Leadership Conf Award, Kappa Alpha Psi, 1990; Living Legend Award, Links, Inc, 1989; Award for Distinguished Service as US Ambassador to SAfrica, Eastern Province, Kappa Alpha Psi, 1989; Presidential Distinguished Service Award, 1989; Una Chapman Cox Found Award, 1989; Presidential Meritorious Service Award, 1987; Kappa Alpha Psi Fraternity Award for Outstanding Achievement in Foreign Service, 1986; Dept State, Superior Hon Award, 1983; Agency for Int Develop, Meritorious Hon Award, 1967; Nat Acad Pub Admin, fellow; Statesman Year, George Wash Univ, 1992; Distinguished Honorary Award, Dept State, 1992; Beloit Col, Doctor Humanities, 1990; & numerous other Honary degrees. **Special Achievements:** Author: "New Dimensions in Foreign Affairs: Pub Admin Theory in Pract,"Pub Admin Review, July-August 1990; "Diversity in US Diplcy," Burcrat, Vol 20, No 4, 1991-92; "The United States & UN", Yale Univ Law Journal, 1993; "Global Institutions (Action for Future)," U.S. Cath Conf, 1995;"Resolution Conflict, Attainment Peace", Univ Sydney, Centre for Peace & Conflict Studies, 1996; "An International Agenda for Change," Am Behavorial Scientist, Vol 40, Number 3, Sage Publishers, 1997; "ThePsychology Diplcy: Conflict Resolution in a Time Minimal or Unusual Small-Scale Conflicts, "Chap 4, Psychology Peace keeping, edited by Harvey J. Langholtz, Westport, CT: Praeger, 1998; Preparing Am's Foreign Policy for 21st Century, co-ed, Univ OK Press, 1999; Palestinian Refugees: Traditional Positions & New Solutions, co-ed, 2001; Democracy, Morality & Search for Peace in Am's Foreign Policy, co-ed, 2002; Middle East Peace Process: Vision versus Reality, co-ed, Univ Okla Press, 2002; Distinguished Jerry Colins Lectr in Pub Admin, Fla State Univ; presial appointment to Presial/Congional Comn on Pub Serv, 1992-93; Presial appointment to White House Adv Comt on Trade Policy & Negotiation, 2003; Mr Ambassador: Warrior for Peace, Univ Okla Press, 2006. **Military Serv:** USMC, 1954-58; AUS, 1951-54. **Business Addr:** Executive Director, University of Oklahoma, Political Science Department, 400 Whitehand Hall, Norman, OK 73019-5144.

PERKINS, FRANCES J
Educator, counselor. **Personal:** Born Dec 14, 1919, Boston, MA; married W Wentworth; children: Joseph W. **Educ:** Boston State, BSE, 1941; Tufts Univ, EdM, 1957; Boston Univ, EdM, counseling, 1981. **Career:** St Mark Nursery Sch, Boston, MA, founder & dir, 1941-53; Parent COOP, NS Belmont, MA, dir, 1953-57; Red Barn Nursery Sch, dir, 1957-61; Tufts Univ, summer fac Eliot-Pearson Dept Child Study, 1960-65, lectr; Garland Jr Col, instr, 1965-66; Lemberg Lab Pre Sch, Brandeis Univ, dir, 1961-73; Head Start Training Prog Wheelock Col Sum, dir, 1966-67; Peace Corps, Tunisia, proj dir, 1966-67; EPDA Inst Garland Jr Col, asst dir 1969; Wheelock Col, instr psychol, 1970-73, assoc prof psychol, 1973-85, prof emer, Boston, MA, 2000-; Head Start Progs, evaluator, 1970-85; Jackson-Mann Early Childhood Prog, Horace Mann Sch Deaf, consult, 1974-75; Ctr Individual & Family Servs, consult; Family Mediation Prog, consult; Head Start progs, consult. **Orgs:** Nat Asn Educ Young C; Am Asn Univ Women; past pres & bd dir, Freedom House Inc; Parents & C's Serv; MA Comn C & Youth; Prof Adv Comn Ft Hill Mental Health Asn; bd mem, Urban League Eastern MA; bd mem, NAUSET Workshop; past pres, Ctr Individual & Family Servs, Cape Cod, MA; First Parish Unitarian Universal Church; bd mem, Eastham Coun Aging, Mass Appeal; Anti-Racism, First Parish Unitarian Universal Church. **Special Achievements:** One of the team of 3 to create Boston Head Start Program for Action for Boston Community Develop-

ment, 1965. **Business Addr:** Professor Emeriti, Wheelock College, 200 Riverway, Boston, MA 02215.

PERKINS, HUEL DAVIS
Educator. **Personal:** Born Dec 27, 1924, Baton Rouge, LA; married Thelma O Smith; children: Huel Alfred. **Educ:** Southern Univ, BS, highest hons, 1947; Northwestern Univ, MusM, 1951, PhD, 1958. **Career:** Lincoln Univ, instr music, 1948-50; Southern Univ, assoc prof music, 1951-60; Southern Univ, dean col arts & humanities, 1968-78; La St Univ, vis prof, 1972, 1974; Nat Endowment Humanities, dep dir educ prog, 1978-79; Acad Affairs, La St Univ, asst vice chancellor, 1979-90, exec asst chancellor, 1990-98, spec asst chancellor, 1998-2005, prof emer,currently; Huel D Perkins & Assocs, pres, currently. **Orgs:** Vis fac prog, Harvard Univ, 1968; Mayor's Comn Youth Activ, 1969; bd dirs, Blundon Orphanage, 1970-71; Baton Rouge Symphony Orchestra, 1971-; So Assembly, 1973; Caribbean-Am Scholars Exchange Prog, 1974; Nat Bd ConsultNat Endowment Humanities; bd dir, La Arts & Sci Ctr; Alpha Phi Alpha; Pi Kappa Lambda; Phi Mu Alpha; Pi Gamma Mu; Alpha Kappa Mu; Sigma Pi Phi; Omicron Delta Kappa; Phi Kappa Phi; Golden Key Honor Soc; Rotary Club Baton Rouge; Sunburst Bank, bd dir, Fedn State Humanities Coun; bd dir, AmSoc Composers Authors Publ; pres bd dir, Capital Area United Way, 1986; bdmem, Baton Rouge Opera, New Orleans Museum Art, Salvation Army; Rotary Club Baton Rouge; Baton Rouge Chamber Com; Omicron Delta Kappa Leadership; Baton Rouge Area Found; La Pub Broadcasting Corp; Com Bank Community Develop Corp; dir, Union Planters Bank; trustee, Mt Zion First Baptist Church. **Honors/Awds:** Outstanding Prof, Student Govt Asn, 1970, 1974; Brotherhood Award, National Conf Christians & Jews, 1987; Humanist of the Year, 1988; Educator of the Year, 1988; Volunteer Activist, 1990; Service Award, 1990; Humanitarian Award, 1990; Distinguished Citizen Award, 1991; LHD, La St Univ, 2005. **Special Achievements:** The first African American to achieve professional tenure at La St University. **Military Serv:** USN, musician first class, 1943-46. **Business Addr:** President, Huel D Perkins & Associates Inc, Consult Firm & Speakers, 1923 79th Ave, Baton Rouge, LA 70807-5528, **Business Phone:** (504)357-3751.

PERKINS, DR. JAMES CONNELLE
Clergy. **Personal:** Born Mar 14, 1951, Williamson, WV; son of Cecil (deceased) and Chaddy B (deceased); married Linda Carol Adkins, Mar 2, 1979; children: Tamaria Yvette, Lindsey Camille. **Educ:** Wiley Col, BA, 1972; Andover-Newton Theol Sch, MDiv, 1974; United Theol Sem, DMin, 1990. **Career:** St Paul Baptist Church, St Albans, WV, pastor, 1974-80; Greater Christ Baptist Church, pastor, 1981-. **Orgs:** bd dir, Detroit Empowerment Zone; bd dir, Detroit One-Stop Capital Shop; bd dir, Detroit Design Collab; cot advisory coun, St John Health System; bd dir, Detroit East COT Health Ctr; past pres, Mich Progressive Bapt Convention; Detroit Pastors Coun; Nat Advan Asn Colored People, Detroit chap; Kappa Alpha Psi; founder, Fellowship Nonprofit Housing Corp, 1992; founder, Benjamin E Mays Male Acad, 1993; founder, Detroit Eastside Coalition Churches, 1993. **Honors/Awds:** Charles A Hill Award, 1997; Samuel Dewitt Proctor fellow, United Theological Seminary, 1990; Caroll E Whittemore Award, Andover Newton Theological Sch, 1974. **Home Addr:** 19575 Renfrew Rd, Detroit, MI 48221. **Business Addr:** Pastor, Greater Christ Baptist Church, 3544 Iroquois St, Detroit, MI 48214, **Business Phone:** (313)924-6900.*

PERKINS, JOHN M.
Executive. **Personal:** Born Jan 1, 1930?, New Hebron, MS; son of Maggie; married Vera Mae; children: Spencer, Phillip, Joan, Derek, Debbie, DeWayne, Priscilla, Betty. **Career:** Voice Calvary Ministries, pres, 1960-81; Fed S Cooper, co-fed, 1967; S Cooper Devel Fund, co-fed; Voice Calvary Cooper Health Clinic; People Develop Inc; Gen Session spkr Urbana, 1976; MS Billy Graham Crusade, steering com, 1975; Tom Skinner MS Mgt Sem, sponsor, 1975; Voice Calvary Bible Ins; Berean Bible Church; child care ctr; Pres Reagan Task Force, 1983-84. **Orgs:** bd mem, Bread world; Nat Black Evangelical Asn; Convenant Col; S Devel Found; Koinonio Partners; num lecuring posts travelled over US Ford Found, 1972-73; Harambee Christian Family Ctr & John Perkins Found, 1982. **Special Achievements:** Author, Let Justice Roll Down; A Quiet Revolution; contrib editor Sojourners mag; The Other Side mag, Radix mag; Decision mag. **Military Serv:** AUS, 1951-53.

PERKINS, LOUVENIA BLACK (KITTY BLACK-PERKINS)
Fashion designer. **Personal:** Born Feb 13, 1948, Spartanburg, SC; daughter of Luther Black and Helen Goode Black; married Gary Perkins, May 1, 1981 (divorced); children: Erika Nicole. **Educ:** Los Angeles Trade Tech Col, AA, fashion design, 1971. **Career:** fashion designer: Miss Melinda of Calif, Debbie Ross, A & O Couture; Mattel Toys, El Segundo, CA, prin designer, 1976-. **Honors/Awds:** Chairmans Award, 1985; Employee of the Month, 1986; Chairmans Award, 1987; The Doty Award; Woman of the Year honoree at the annual 'Woman Keeping the Dream Alive' banquet, Nat Coun Negro Women, 1994. **Special Achievements:** A special doll, designed & donated to the SC State Mus, 2001; recognized and pursued by some of the industry's top mag and newspapers: Ebony; Essence; LA Mag; Woman's Day; Sister to Sister; Los Angeles Mag; Fox TV's Personalities; The Tim & Daphne Show; I've Got a Secret, SC, 2002; African-Am Hist Calendar; guest speaker, Career Day events; Black Hall of Fame, 2001-. **Business Addr:** Principal Designer, Mattel Inc, 333 Continental Blvd, El Segundo, CA 90245-5012.*

PERKINS, MYLA LEVY
Educator, business owner. **Personal:** Born Feb 25, 1939, Pueblo, CO; daughter of Naomi and Addison; married Edgar L; children: Julie, Steven, Todd & Susan. **Educ:** Wayne State Univ, BS, 1960. **Career:** Detroit Pub Sch, teacher, 1960-66; Sugar N Spice Nursery Sch, co-owner, 1966-; Pyramid Elem Sch, co-owner, 1976-92. **Orgs:** Alpha Kappa Alpha Sor, 1957-; Tots & Teens Am, 1967. **Special Achievements:** Author, Black Dolls, 1820-1991, An Identification & Value Guide, Collector Books; NAACP, Black Dolls Book II, 1994. **Business Addr:** Co-Owner, Sugar N Spice Nursery School, 16555 Wyoming Ave, Detroit, MI 48221, **Business Phone:** (313)368-2899.

PERKINS, ROBERT E. L.
Oral surgeon. **Personal:** Born May 17, 1925, Carthage, TX. **Educ:** Wiley Col, BS, 1945; Howard Univ, DDS, 1948; Tufts Univ, MSD, 1956. **Career:** Childrens Hosp Mich, courtesy staff, 1960-87; Metro Hosp Detroit, 1965-87; Hutzel Hosp, jr staff mem, 1983-87; oral & maxillofacial surgeon, currently. **Orgs:** Am Dent Asn, 1949-87; Nat Dent Asn, 1963-87; pres & founder, DSACE, 1964-87; Mich & Am Asn Oral & Maxillofacial Surgeons, 1970-87; bd dir, treas, Your Heritage House, 1977-87; bd dirs, Detroit Symphony Orchestra, 1980-87; life mem, Nat Asn Advan Colored People; Nat Urban League; United Negro Col Fund; Alpha Kappa Alpha; bd mem, Detroit Inst Arts; pres, Howard Univ Alumni Asn. **Honors/Awds:** Key to the City of Detroit; Patron of the Arts Award, Detroit Musicians Assn; Alumni Awards, College of Dentistry; Howard University Alumni Award 1983. **Military Serv:** US Air Force, major, 1949-54. **Business Addr:** Oral Maxillofacial Surgeon, 2673 W Grand Blvd, Detroit, MI 48208.

PERKINS, SAM BRUCE
Basketball player, businessperson, vice president (organization). **Personal:** Born Jun 14, 1961, Brooklyn, NY. **Educ:** NC State Univ, BA, commun, 1984. **Career:** Basketball player (retired), businessperson, vice president; Dallas Mavericks, forward-ctr, 1984-90; Los Angeles Lakers, 1990-93; Seattle SuperSonics, 1992-98; Indiana Pacers, 1998-2001, vpres player relations, 2008-; Neo Soul Cafe LLC, owner, currently. **Orgs:** United Negro Col Fund; The Lupus Found; Big Brothers & Big Sisters; founder, 848 prod. **Honors/Awds:** Won a gold medal with the US Olympic Basketball team, 1984; NBA All-RookieTeam, 1984-85; NCAA Champion, NC Tar Heels, 1982; NCAA Mens Basketball Champion, 1982. **Special Achievements:** Co-captain of the gold medal winning 1984 Olympic team; Hosts "BigSmooth's Coolout" for Pediatric AIDS Prog, Children Hosp; hosts own local radio show. **Business Addr:** Owner, Neo Soul Cafe LLC, PO Box 2233, Addison, TX 75001, **Business Phone:** (972)923-1585.*

PERKINS, TONY
Meteorologist. **Personal:** Born Jan 1, 1960?. **Educ:** Am Univ, Wash, DC, BA. **Career:** WKYS-FM, "The Donnie Simpson Show", on-air contribr & producer, 1985-92; WDCA-TV, "DC20 Breakaway", producer & host, 1986-88; WTTG-TV, "Fox Morning News", co-anchor, 1998-99, weather forcaster, 2005-; ABC News, "Good Morning America", weather forecaster, 1999-2205, "Less Than Perfect", cameo appearance, 2004, "Jimmy Kimmel Live," guest appearance, "American Music Awards", presenter, VH1, "I Love the '90s Part Deux", comic commentator, "Stealing Scenes". **Orgs:** Dean's Adv Coun, Am Univ Sch Commun. **Honors/Awds:** Emmy Award, 1988. **Business Addr:** Weather Forecaster, Fox Television Stations, Inc, 5151 Wis Ave NW, Washington, DC 20016, **Business Phone:** (202)895-3000.

PERKINS, WILLIAM O., JR.
Government official. **Personal:** Born Jun 5, 1926, Gregory, NC; married Arthur; children: 4. **Educ:** Elizabeth City State Univ, BS, 1949; Atlanta Univ; Univ Ga. **Career:** Morgan Co Schs, teacher, 1949-51, 53-56; Turner Co Schs, teacher, 1952-53; Atlanta Pub Schs, teacher, 1957-76; New Jersy St Bar Found, atty. **Orgs:** YWCA, 1957-77; NEA, 1957-77; Gate City Teachers Asn, 1957-70; mem bd dir, Metro Atlanta Girls Club, 1972-75; bd dir, Atlanta Asn Educ, 1973-75; Ga Asn Educ, 1976-77; Nat Asn Advan Colored People; Secy, Atlanta Dist Baptist Missionary Soc, 1976-77; Beulah Baptist Church; Alpha Kappa Mu Nat Hon Soc; mem bd dirs, Ga Asn Classroom Teachers; Metro Atlanta Coun Int Reading Asn. **Honors/Awds:** Nom Bronze Woman, 1976; Atlanta Classroom Teacher of the Year, 1976-77; GA Classroom Teacher of the Year, 1976-77.

PERRIMON, VIVIAN SPENCE
Educator, association executive. **Personal:** Born Jun 5, 1926, Gregory, NC; daughter of Hallard Dozier Spence (deceased) and Edmund Clay (deceased); married Arthur Perrimon (deceased); children: Petronia P Martin, Geraldine P Thomas. **Educ:** Elizabeth City State Univ, NC, BS, 1949; Atlanta Univ, GA, attended 1957; Univ GA, attended 1960. **Career:** Teacher (retired), association executive; Morgan Co Schs, Madison, GA, teacher, 1949-51, 1953-56; Turner Co Schs, Ashburn, Ga, teacher, 1952-53; Atlanta Pub Schs, Atlanta, GA, teacher, 1957-76; DeKalb County Community Coun Aging, meals wheels vol, 1978-86; Atlanta Metro Alumni Chap, charter pres, 1978-91, vpres, 1986-90; Metro Atlanta YWCA, bd dir, 1979-85; DeKalb Co EOA, bd dir, 1979-85; Metro Atlanta Girls Club, bd dir, 1980-83; Atlanta Chamber Com, Sch Partnership Prog, vol tutor; Fifth Dist, Gen Missionary Baptist Conv GA Inc, prog coord, 1991, hosting comm secy, 1997; Lambda Epsilon Omega Chap, Alpha Kappa Alpha Sorority, mem, 1991-. **Orgs:** Life mem, Elizabeth City State Univ Gen Alumni Asn, 1978-91. **Honors/Awds:** Georgia Classroom Teacher of the Year, 1976, 1977; Alumni Community Service Award, ECSU Gen Alumni Asn, 1979; Nat Asn Equal Opportunity Higher Educ Pres Citation, Wash, DC, 1981; Atlanta Metro Alumni Service Award, 1982; Outstanding Alumni Service Award, Atlanta Metro Chapter, Elizabeth City State Univ, 1992; Vip Memorial Award, Mem Campaign, 1992. **Home Addr:** 2930 Edna Lane, Decatur, GA 30032. **Business Addr:** Member, Lambda Epsilon Omega Chapter, Alpha Kappa Alpha Sorority Inc, PO Box 370337, Decatur, GA 30037.

PERRIN, DAVID THOMAS PERRY
Clergy, bishop. **Personal:** Born May 16, 1951, Cleveland, OH; married Allethia Yvonne Campbell, Oct 24, 1998; children: Caleb Karamo, Quianne Shapearl & Mileah Niambi; married Elizabeth Ann Jackson (deceased). **Educ:** Carnegie Mellon Univ, BFA, 1975; Gordon-Conwell Theol Sem, MTS, 1978; Howard Univ, ABD; Andersonville Baptist Sem, PhD. **Career:** Corning Comm Col, instr, 1981-83; Friendship Baptist Church, pastor, 1981-83; Elmira Correctional Inst, visiting lectr, 1982-83; TDX Systems Inc, sales analyst, 1984-85; Parkway Baptist Church, pastor; Church Great Comn, sr pastor, 1986-99, bishop, currently. **Orgs:** Prince George's County Baptist Asn; Collective Banking Group Inc; Prince George's County Am Christian TV Inc. **Special Achievements:** Bishop's Epistle is quarterly publication from the office of Bishop David T P Perrin, Bishop Perrin is co-host of several TV ministries aired on PG Acts Network. **Home Addr:** 13216 Glenmore Dr, West Palm Beach, FL 33349. **Business Addr:** Bishop, Church of the Great Commission, 5032 Forsyth Commerce Rd, PO Box 780609, Orlando, FL 32878-0609, **Business Phone:** (321)206-4946.

PERRINEAU, HAROLD, JR. (HAROLD WILLIAMS, JR.)
Actor. **Personal:** Born Aug 7, 1963, Brooklyn, NY; son of Harold Sr and Perrineau; married Brittany, Aug 27, 2002; children: Aurora Robinson & Wynter Aria. **Educ:** Shenandoah Conserv, music & theater. **Career:** Films: Flirt, 1995; Smoke, 1995; Romeo Juliet, 1996; The Edge, 1997; Come To, 1998; Shakedown, 1998; King of New York, 1990; Lulu on the Bridge, 1998; The Best Man, 1999; Macbeth in Manhattan, 1999; A Day in Black & White, 1999; Woman on Top, 2000; Overnight Sensation, 2000; Someone Like You, 2001; Prison Song, 2001; On_Line, 2002; The Matrix Reloaded, 2003; Enter the Matrix, 2003; The Matrix Revolutions, 2003; The Matrix Online, 2005; Random Acts of Kindness, 2005; 28 Weeks Later, 2007; Gardens of the Night, 2007; Ball Don't Lie, 2008; Felon, 2008; Your Name Here, 2008; The Killing Jar, 2009; TV series: "Law & Order", 1990-93; I'll Fly Away", 1991-93; "Oz," 1997-2003; The Tempest, 1998; "Dead Like Me," 2003; "HBO First Look," 2003; "Players," 2003; "The Matrix Recalibrated", 2004; "The Burly Man Chronicles," 2004; "Lost," 2004, 2005, 2006; "The View", 2005; "Jimmy Kimmel Live", 2005; "Entertainment Tonight", 2005; "Lost", 2004-08; Demons, 2007; "Lost: Missing Pieces", 2007-08; "The Unusuals", 2009. **Orgs:** Screen Actors Guild. **Honors/Awds:** Independent Spirit Award, 1995; Image Award Nominee Outstanding Supporting Actor in a Motion Picture for: The Best Man (1999/I), 2000; Won Screen Actors Guild Award for Outstanding Performance by an Ensemble in a Drama Series for: "Lost" (2004), 2006. **Business Addr:** Actor, c/o The Gersh Agency, 232 N Canon Dr, Beverly Hills, CA 90210, **Business Phone:** (310)274-6611.

PERRY, DR. AUBREY M.
Psychologist, educator. **Personal:** Born Jan 14, 1937, Petersburg, VA; married Clarie; children: Vanessa, Aubrey Jr & Kenneth. **Educ:** Va State Col, AB, 1958, MS, 1960; Ind Univ Med Ctr, Diploma, 1972; Fla State Univ, PhD, 1972. **Career:** Crowns ville Hosp, psychologist intern, 1959; Cent State Hosp, staff psychologist, 1960; Fla Agr & Mech Univ, asst prof psychol, 1961-68, assoc prof psychol, 1969; Col Arts & Sci, dean, 1972, prof psychol, 1997-2003, prof emer, 2003-, dir, currently; NSF, summer fel, 1964; fel, Carnegie,1968; Ind Med Ctr, psychologist intern, 1971; Apalachee Comm Mental Health Serv, clin psychologist, 1972-. **Orgs:** Asn Black Psychologists; Psi Chi, Seastern Psychol Asn; Fla Psychol Asn; Asn Social & Behavioral Scientists; Phi Delta Kappa; Pi Gamma Mu; Leon Co Mental Health Asn; Omega Psi Phi. **Honors/Awds:** Teacher of the Year, Fla A&M Univ, 1961-62; Psychology Teacher of theYear, Fla A&M Univ, 1974-75; Famuan of the Century, 2000. **Business Addr:** Professor Emeritus, Florida Agricultural And Mechanical University, Department of Psychology, 501 Orr Dr GEC-C Suite 302, PO Box 1123, Tallahassee, FL 32307, **Business Phone:** (850)599-3014.

PERRY, BETTY HANCOCK
Government official. **Career:** Cook County, Bur Finance, Off Contract Compliance, head, dir, adminr, currently. **Orgs:** Cook

County Rep Cent Comn. **Business Addr:** Contract Compliance Administrator, Cook County Bureau of Finance, Office of Contract Compliance, 118 N Clark St Rm 1020, Chicago, IL 60602, **Business Phone:** (312)603-5502.

PERRY, CLIFFORD, III
Banker. **Personal:** Born Feb 8, 1945, Chicago, IL; son of Clifford Jr and Gloria Dixon; married Mattie Pointer; children: Michele Walton, Renee Scott, Clifford R & Michael S. **Educ:** Gov State Univ, BA, mkt, 1991. **Career:** Harris Bank, dept vpres, 1971; Northwest Bank, pres; Wells Fargo Bank, mgr; Fifth Third Bank, community rels mgr, sr vpres community develop, 2005-, currently. **Orgs:** Nat Bankers Asn, 1975-; investment comt bd,YMCA, 1992; bd mem, Boys Club, 1992; bd mem, Boy Scouts, 1992; bd mem, Omaha Small Bus Network, 1992; bd mem, N Omaha Bus Develop Corp, 1992; chmn, Greater Omaha Pvt Indust Coun, 1992-; adv chmn, SBA Region VII, Omaha Adv Coun, 1992-; Greater Omaha Chamber Com; Chicago Community Ventures. **Business Addr:** Senior Vice President Community Development, Manager of Community Relations, Fifth Third Bank, Bldg 4 810 Crescent Ctr Dr Suite 160, Franklin, TN 37067, **Business Phone:** (615)771-5814.

PERRY, DARREN
Football player, football coach. **Personal:** Born Dec 29, 1968, Chesapeake, VA; married Errika; children: Danielle, Dominique, Dedriana & Devan. **Educ:** Pa State Univ, BA, bus admin & mgt, 1992. **Career:** Football player (retired), football coach: Pittsburgh Steelers, defensive back, 1992-98; San Diego Chargers, 1999; New Orleans Saints, safety, 2000; Cincinnati Bengals, safeties coach, 2002; Pittsburgh Steelers, asst Defensive backs coach, 2003, defensive backs coach, 2004-06; Oakland Raiders, defensive back coach, 2007-08; Green Bay Packers, secondary safeties coach, 2009-. **Orgs:** Bd, Chesapeake Care Free Clinic. **Business Phone:** (510)864-5000.

PERRY, EDWARDCCC
Football player. **Personal:** Born Sep 1, 1974, Richmond, VA; married Sonja (divorced); children: Kamaya & T J. **Educ:** James Madison Univ. **Career:** Miami Dolphins, tight end, 1997-2004; Kans City Chiefs, 2005; free agent,currently.

PERRY, ELLIOTT
Basketball player. **Personal:** Born Mar 28, 1969, Memphis, TN. **Educ:** Univ Memphis, attended 1991. **Career:** Basketball player-(retired); Los Angeles Clippers, guard, 1991; Charlotte Hornets, 1991-92; Portland Trail Blazers, 1992, 1993; Phoenix Suns, 1994-96; Milwaukee Bucks, 1996-99; NJ Nets, 1999-00; Phoenix Suns, guard, 2001; Orlando Magic, 2001; Memphis Grizzlies, guard, 2002. **Honors/Awds:** Most Improved Player Award, Nat Basketball Asn, 1995; Outstanding Young Alumnus, 2002. *

PERRY, EMMA BRADFORD
Librarian. **Personal:** Born in Hodge, LA; daughter of Ibe and Mattie Stringfellow; married Huey L Perry, Aug 26, 1972; children: David Omari & Jeffrey Donovan (deceased). **Educ:** Grambling State Univ, Grambling, LA, BS; Atlanta Univ, Atlanta, GA, MLS; Western Mich Univ, Kalamazoo, MI, EdS. **Career:** Battle Creek Pub Sch, Battle Creek, MI, librn, 1971-72; Evanston Pub Libr, Evanston, br head, 1972-76; Tex A&M Univ, Col Sta, Tex, asst prof, 1977-83; State Libr La, Baton Rouge, LA, libr consult, 1985-87; Harvard Univ Bus Sch, Cambridge, MA, assoc lib dir, 1987-89; Dillard Univ, New Orleans, LA, dir, univ libr, 1989-92; Southern Univ, John B Cade Libr, dean libr, 1992-. **Orgs:** Am Libr Asn, 1973-, ed bd, Col & Res Libr, accreditation team; Tex Libr Asn, 1977-87; La Libr Asn, 1985-; Asn Col & Res Libr, 1988-; bd dirs, chair, Solinet, 1995-96; vpres, LLA; Southern Asn Cols & Schs. **Business Addr:** Dean of Libraries, Southern University, John B Cade Library, 167 Roosevelt Steptoe Ave, Baton Rouge, LA 70813, **Business Phone:** (225)771-4991.

PERRY, EMMITT, JR. **See PERRY, TYLER.**

PERRY, EUGENE CALVIN, JR.
Executive. **Personal:** Born Feb 8, 1953, Charlottesville, VA; son of Eugene C Sr and Elizabeth Blair; married Shelia Herndon, Sep 1, 1978; children: Shannon Janine Xavier & Eugene Calvin III. **Educ:** Wash Univ, BA, hist, 1975; Lee Univ, JD, 1978. **Career:** Justice Dept Fed Bur Invest, spec agt, 1978-86; Pop Warner Football, coach, currently; Wilkinson & Perry Ltd, pres, 1986-; Perry Group Int Inc, pres, 1987-89; Visions Video Ltd Inc, partner, currently. **Orgs:** Phi Alpha Delta Legal Fraternity, 1977-; parliamentarian, Jr Chamber Com, 1979-; Am Mgt Asn, 1983-; Wash & Lee Alumni Coun, 1985-; Wash & Lee Univ Alumni Bd Dirs, 1987-; Spec Olympics, Philadelphia Adopt-A-Sch Prog, Omega Psi Phi Inc; Nat Asn Advan Colored People, 1991-; First Baptist Church Lincoln Gardens; bd dirs, First Baptist Community Develop Corp, 1994-; life mem, Omega Psi Phi Fraternity Inc. **Honors/Awds:** Honor Award, Norfolk Jaycees, 1980; Omega Man of the Year, Ma Gamma Gamma Chap, 1993.

PERRY, FELTON
Actor, playwright. **Personal:** Born Sep 11, 1945, Chicago, IL. **Educ:** Roosevelt Univ, BA, Spanish/French; Univ Chicago, grad study; Univ Calif, Santa Barbara, MA, Spanish, 2003. **Career:** Films: Medium Cool, 1969; Night Call Nurses, 1972; Brute Corps, 1972; Trouble Man, 1972; Walking Tall, 1973; The Fuzz Brothers, 1973; Magnum Force, 1973; The Towering Inferno, 1974; Sudden Death, 1977; Mean Dog Blues, 1978; Down & Out in Beverly Hills, 1986; RoboCop, 1987; Weeds, 1987; Checking Out, 1989; RoboCop 2, 1990; Talent for the Game, 1991; Perfume, 1991; Let's Kill All the Lawyers, 1992; Relentless 3, 1993; RoboCop 3, 1993; Puppet Master 4, 1993; Dumb & Dumber, 1994; Dark Breed,1996; The Sweeper, 1996; At Face Value, 1999; Buck & the Magic Bracelet, 1999; Hollywood Vampyr, 2002; TV series: Room 222, 1969; "Here Come the Brides", 1969-70; "Ironside", 1969-73; "Dragnet 1967", 1970; "Bracken's World", 1970; Dial Hot Line, 1970; "Nanny & the Professor", 1970; "Matt Lincoln", 1970; "The Partridge Family", 1970; "The Name of the Game", 1970; "Owen Marshall: Counselor at Law", 1971; "O'Hara, U.S. Treasury", 1971-72; "Adam-12", 1971-72; "Marcus Welby, M.D.", 1972; Jigsaw, 1972; Here Comes the Judge, 1972; "Mannix", 1972; "Cool Million", 1972; "The New Perry Mason", 1973; "Medical Center", 1974; "McMillan & Wife", 1974; "Police Story", 1975; The City, 1977; "Barnaby Jones, 1978; The Critical List, 1978; Hunters of the Reef, 1978; The Ordeal of Patty Hearst, 1979; Hill Street Blues, 1982-85; "Automan", 1984; "Legmen", 1984; "The Atlanta Child Murders", 1985; Seduced, 1985; Cagney & Lacey, 1985; "What's Happening Now!", 1986; "Stingray", 1987; "Harry", 1987; "Hooperman", 1987; "227", 1989; "Amen", 1989; "L.A. Law", 1986-90; Daughter of the Streets, 1990; "Murphy Brown", 1991; "The Fresh Prince of Bel-Air", 1991-92; Civil Wars, 1992; "Human Target", 1992; "Hangin' with Mr. Cooper", 1993; "The Adventures of Brisco County Jr.", 1993; Percy & Thunder, 1993; The American Clock, 1993; Menendez: A Killing in Beverly Hills, 1994; NYPD Blue", 1994; Derby, 1995; "Living Single", 1995; "The Pretender", 1996; "Sports Night", 1998; "Strong Medicine", 2001; "The West Wing", 2000-02; "Judging Amy", 2002; The Members, 2007; Theater appearances: Mac Bird, 1968; Chemin de Fer, 1969; The Meeting, 1987; Ritual, 1989-90; Killing Time, 1990; Hamlet, 1995; YAY Prod Co, founder; La Unified Sch Dist, teacher; TV: The Last Payment, writer, 1973. **Orgs:** Am Fedn TV & Radio Artists; Actors' Equity Asn; Screen Actors Guild. **Honors/Awds:** Image Award for Playwrighting, Nat Asn Advan Colored People. **Military Serv:** US Marine Corps, sgt, 4 yrs. **Business Addr:** Actor, William Morris Agency, 1 William Morris Pl, Beverly Hills, CA 90212, **Business Phone:** (310)859-4000.

PERRY, GARY W
Automotive executive. **Personal:** Born Jun 3, 1952, Roanoke, VA; son of Leroy Sr and Rosetta; married Carlleena Herring, Oct 15, 1977. **Educ:** Winston-Salem State Univ, BA, 1975; Northwood Inst, Cert, 1978-79; Wharton Sch Bus, Cert, 1990; Univ Mich, bus, Cert, 1990; Univ Pittsburgh, Execs Sch Mgt, Katz Grad Sch Bus, grad, 1998. **Career:** Gen Motors, Oldsmobile Div, asst off mgr, 1976-77; Oldsmobile Div, Boston Zone, dist mgr sales, 1977-80; Oldsmobile Div, Wash Zone, dist mgr sales, 1980-83, car distributor, 1983-86; Oldsmobile Div, Detroit Zone, area fleet mgr, 1986-89, asst zone mgr sales, 1989, mkt area mgr, currently. **Orgs:** Tau Phi Tau Frat, pres, 1972; Appointed by Gen Sales Mgr to Bus Process Reengineering Team-Oldsmobile. **Honors/Awds:** Distinguished Manager of the Year, Gen Motors, Oldsmobile Div, 1978, 1982 & 1983; Robert Stempel, Highest Achievement, Gen Motors, 1991; Dale Carnegie, Highest Achievement Award, 1991, Highest Award, Human Rels, 1991, Highest Award, Reporting, 1991; John F Smith President's Coun Exceptional Performance Award, Gen Motors, 1992, 1993, 1994 & 1995; Appointed vpres Gen Motors-Oldsmobile to Exec Leadership Team. **Business Addr:** Area Manager of North Central Region, General Motors Corp, 387 Shuman Blvd, Naperville, IL 60560, **Business Phone:** (630)961-6350.

PERRY, GERALD
Baseball player, athletic coach. **Personal:** Born Oct 30, 1960, Savannah, GA. **Career:** Baseball player (retired), Athletic coach; Atlanta Braves, infielder & outfielder, 1983-89; Kansas City Royals, infielder, 1990; St Louis Cardinals, infielder, 1991-95; Seattle Mariners, hitting coach, 2000-02; Pittsburgh Pirates, hitting coach, 2003-05; Oakland Athletics, hitting coach, 2005; Chicago Cubs, hitting coach, 2006-09. **Honors/Awds:** Player of the Year Award, Bill Lucas Minor League, Atlanta Braves, 1982; All-Star Team, Nat League, 1988. **Special Achievements:** First baseman in Major League Baseball who played from 1983 to 1995 for the Atlanta Braves, Kansas City Royals and St. Louis Cardinals.

PERRY, JEAN B.
Educator, teacher. **Personal:** Born Aug 31, 1946, New York, NY. **Educ:** Fashion Inst Tech, AA, 1968; NY Univ, BS, 1970; NY city Tech Col, AA, 1980; Teacher Col Columbia Univ, MA, 1986. **Career:** NY Daily News "Good Living" section, feature writer; NY Daily News, reporter, 1970; Black Enterprise Mag, wrote "Black Bus in Profile" column on free lance basis, 1973-74; Daily News Conf for HS Editors, speaker, 1974 & 75; Essence Mag, health & fitness editor, 1982-84; Ethical Culture Sch, asst teacher, 1985-87; Los Angeles Unified Sch Dist, teacher, 1987-. **Orgs:** Kappa Tau Alpha 1970-, Kappa Delta Pi 1986-. **Honors/Awds:** Recipent Martin Luther King Alumni Asn Award, Print Jour NY Univ, 1978; Media Award, NY Heart Asn, 1979; William Harvey Award, Squibb Corp & Am Med Writers Asn, 1984; Media Award, Am Diabetes Asn, 1984. **Special Achievements:** Author:"Lights, Action, Camera, Women!", 1976. **Business Addr:** Educator, Los Angeles Unified School, 315 Holmby Ave, Los Angeles, CA 90024.

PERRY, JEFFERY STEWART
Consultant. **Personal:** Born Nov 15, 1965, Cleveland, OH; son of Elder and Rudolph Sr; married Dena Dodd, Apr 26, 1997; children: Jonathan Stewart & Donovan Rudolph. **Educ:** Babson Col, BS, 1987; Harvard Univ, MBA, 1991. **Career:** BP Chem Inc, com assoc, 1987-89; co-chair, Chicago Children's Museum; Booz-Allen Hamilton, assoc, 1991-94; CSC Index Inc, prin, 1994-97; AT Kearney Inc, vpres; Ernst & Young LLP,integration practice leader, currently. **Orgs:** Bd dir, Nat INROADS Alumni Asn, 1987-89; bd dirs, DuBois Group, 1991-93;Nat Black MBA Asn, 1991-; vpres, bd dirs, Martin Luther King Jr Boys &Girls Club Chicago, 1999-; Bd mem, Chicago Children's Museum; Chicago Coun Foreign Rel, Chicago comt, 2001-;vpres, Sigma Pi Phi Fraternity, 2002-. **Honors/Awds:** Roger W Babson Achievement Award, Babson Col, 1987; Meritorious Service Award, United Negro Col Fund, 1989; Chicago Alumni of the Year, INROADS,1998. **Special Achievements:** Completed advanced intermediate study of French language, Sorbonne, Paris,1991; Nominated/attended Harvard Exec Educ Prog, Leadership in Professional Service Firms, 1997; HBS Afr Amer Alumni Conf, Creating &Preserving Wealth, co-chair, 1999. **Business Addr:** Integration Practice Leader, Ernst & Young LLP, Times Sq, New York, NY 10036-6530, **Business Phone:** (312)879-5316.

PERRY, REV. JERALD ISAAC, SR.
Consultant, clergy. **Personal:** Born Jun 3, 1950, Edenton, NC; son of John Isaac and Evelyn Jones; married Deborah Mayo, Mar 19, 1989; children: Jerald I Jr, Davin E & Felicia Shantique Mayo. **Educ:** Automation Machine Training Ctr, Dipl, 1968; Roanoke Theol Sem, BA, Divinity; Shaw Divinity Sch, MA matriculating; Aviation Storekeeper "A" Sch Meridian MS. **Career:** Elizabeth City State Univ, comput oper, programmer; Whosoever Will Church God, pastor, currently. **Orgs:** NC Consortium Comn 1972; gospel disc jockey/acct mgr, WZBO-AM, 1975-; Edenton Housing Authority, bd mem, 1979-86; Am Heart Fund Asn, bd mem, 1980-86; bd mem, Edenton Chowan Bd Educ, 1982-86; NC State Sch Bd Asn, 1982-; Nat Sch Bd Asn, 1982-; NC Humanities Comn, 1982-; bd mem State Employees Asn NC, 1985; Black State Ministers Coalition; bd mem, EdentonChowan Civic League; disc jockey/acct mgr, WBXB-Love 100 FM Sta; Sunday sch supt Eastern NC Greater NC Diocese Church God in Christ Inc; Meridian Lodge 18; JW Hood Consistory 155 United Supreme Coun; 33 degree AASR Freemasonry Prince Hall Affil; bd mem, Church God in Christ Trustee Bd. **Honors/Awds:** Outstanding Young Man of America, 1979;1983; Kappa Delta Phi Honor Soc. Eliz City State Univ, 1982-83; Letter of Accomodation Commanding General for ExpeditingH1 Priority Documents; Letter of Accomodation for Serving as Wing NCO of Barracks when received Barracks of Quarter Selection; Bluejacket of the Month and Bluejacket of the Quarter MCAS Cherry Point, NC. **Military Serv:** USN. **Home Addr:** 201 Dillard Ave, Edenton, NC 27932. **Business Addr:** Pastor, Whosoever Will Church Of God, RR 3, Edenton, NC 27932, **Business Phone:** (252)482-0272.

PERRY, JOSEPH JAMES
Clergy. **Personal:** Born Oct 8, 1936, Sprott, AL; son of Calloway Alphonso and Ola Mae Ford; married Dorothy M Cutts, Sep 22, 1957; children: Sherron, Joseph Jr, Kenneth, Keith & Andrea Perry Davis. **Educ:** Union Baptist Sem, BTh, 1974; Southern Bible Sem, MTh, 1975; Univ Seattle, BA, 1976; New Era Baptist Sem, DTh, 1977. **Career:** Little Rock Missionary Baptist Church, pastor, 1957-62; Good Hope Missionary Baptist Church, pastor, 1960-62; Holly Grove Missionary Baptist Church, pastor, 1962-65; Exodus Missionary Baptist Church, pastor, 1971-; Wayne County Sheriff's Dept, chaplain, 1988-; PWR & W Inc, partner. **Orgs:** Nat Asn Advan Colored People, 1957-; vpres, Nat Baptist Conv USA Inc, vice pres, 1960-; treas, One Church One Child Mich, 1989-; exec dir, SCLC, Mich Chap, 1989-; pres, Baptist Missionary & Educ Conv Mich, 1991-96; Detroit Comn Fair Banking, 1992-; Plight Black Doctor, 1992-. **Honors/Awds:** Hon Citizen, Mobile Alabama, 1988; Distinguished Serv Award, State Mich, 1990; Outstanding Citizen, SCLC, 1991; Martin Luther King Jr Award, Detroit Rescue Mission, 1993. **Business Addr:** Pastor, Exodus Missionary Baptist Church, 8173 Kenney St, Detroit, MI 48234, **Business Phone:** (313)921-3690.

PERRY, REV. JOSEPH NATHANIEL
Clergy. **Personal:** Born Apr 18, 1948, Chicago, IL; son of Joseph N Sr and Mary Elizabeth Williams. **Educ:** St Joseph Col, Rensselaer, IN, BA, philos, 1971; St Francis Sem, MDiv, 1975; Catholic Univ Am, JCL, canon law, 1981; St Mary Sem, Crown Point, IN, BA, theol. **Career:** St. Nicholas Parish, Milwaukee, priest, 1975-90; Milwaukee Archdiocese Tribunal, chief judicial officer, 1983-95; All Saints Church, pastor, 1995-99; Titular Bishop Lead, 1998; Marquette Univ Law Sch, Milwaukee, instr, 1996-98; St. Mary Lake Sem, Mundelein, Illinois, instr, 1997-; Archdiocese Chicago, auxilary bishop, 1998-; Sacred Heart Sch Theol, canon law studies, prof. **Orgs:** Nat Chaplain Knights St Peter Claver & Ladies Auxiliary, 2004-; chmn, US Conf Catholic Bishops Comt African

Am Catholics; vpres, Nat Black Catholic Congress; nat chaplain, Knights St. Peter Claver & Ladies Auxiliary; Canon Law Soc Am; bd mem, Archbishop Quigley Preparatory Sem. **Business Addr:** Auxiliary Bishop, Archdiocese of Chicago, PO Box 733, South Holland, IL 60473, **Business Phone:** (708)339-2474.

PERRY, JUNE CARTER
Government official. **Personal:** Born Nov 13, 1943, Texarkana, AR; daughter of Bishop W and Louise E Pendleton; married Frederick M; children: Chad Douglass & Andre Frederick. **Educ:** Loyola Univ, BA (cum laude), 1965; Univ Chicago, Woodrow Wilson, fel, MA,1967; Hamline Col, St Paul, MN, Middle East Inst, fac fel, cert, 1968. **Career:** Col instr & high sch teacher, 1967-70; WGTS-FM & WTOP-AM, producer &commentator, 1973-74; WGMS-AM/FM, dir pub affairs, 1974-77; US Community Serv Admin, spec asst pub affairs, 1977-79; ACTION Peace Corps, dir pub affairs, 1979-83; Am Embassy, Lusaka, 1983-85, Harare, 1986-87; Dept State, polit officer, desk officer Botswana, 1987-89; Secy State, specasst, 1989-90; Am Embassy, Paris, first secy, polit affairs, 1990-93; Polit Mil Policy, state asst dir, 1993-95; Am Embassy Banguin, Cent Africa, dep chief mission, 1996-97, sr adv dep chief mission asst sec state, 1997-98, Antanarivo, dep chief missions; Int Orgn Bur, Off Social & Humanitarian Affairs, dir; Kingdom Lesotho, ambassador, 2007; Republic of Sierra Leone, ambassador, 2007-. **Orgs:** Am Asn Univ Women, 1973-76; AFTRA, 1974-78; vpres adv coun, Women's Inst,Wash, DC, 1975-; bd mem, Greater Wash Boys & Girls Club, 1975-79; Finance Comm Nat Capital YMCA, 1975-79; vpres, Friends Advan African Civilization,1979; Am Foreign Serv Asn, 1985-. **Honors/Awds:** Blacks in Industry Award, Harlem Y & Time Mag, 1975; Sup Achiever Award, RKO Genl Broadcasting, 1976; Human Rights Award, UN Nat Capital Chap,1977; Distinguished Alumna Award, Mundelein Col, 1980; Special Achievement Award, Action Agency, 1980; Outstanding Performance Award, Action Agency, 1982; Meritorious Service Award, 1985, 1987, Meritorious Honor Award, 1990; Superior Honor Award, Dept State, 1995, 1997; Diplomat-in-Residence of the Year Award, 2002. **Special Achievements:** Author of "Ancient African Heroines," Washington Post, 1983. **Business Addr:** Ambassador, US Department of State, Republic of Sierra Leone, 2201 C St NW, Washington, DC 20520, **Business Phone:** (202)647-4000.

PERRY, JUNE MARTIN
Association executive, consultant. **Personal:** Born Jun 10, 1947, Columbia, SC; daughter of Mark Anthony and Junie Alberta; divorced; children: Kevin & Krystle. **Educ:** NC Cent Univ, BS, Psychol, 1969; Univ Wis, MSW, Social Welfare, 1971; Univ Wis, PhD, cand. **Career:** Milwaukee Co DSS, social worker, 1971-73, purchase serv coord, 1973-75; New Concept Self Develop Ctr, Milwaukee WI, co-founder, chief exec officer & exec dir, 1975-2006; Access to Success, prin, currently. **Orgs:** Delta Sigma Theta Sorority, 1969; NASW, l971; Nat Black Child Develop Inst, 1986; bd dir, Girl Scouts Am, 1986-88; bd dir, Wis Coun Human Concerns, 1986; bd dir, Wis Advocacy Coalition, 1987; bd dir, Milwaukee Mgt Support Orgn, 1987; Nat Forum Black Pub Admin, 1988. **Honors/Awds:** Sojourner Truth Award, Eta Phi Beta, 1986; Trailblazer of the Year, Black Women's Network, 1986; Toast & Boast Award, Nat Women's Polit Caucus, 1986; Top Ladies of Distinction Community Service Award, 1987; Social Worker of the Year, Health Serv Profs Wis, 1988; Leadership America Alumnae, 1990; UWM School of Social Work, Alumni of the Year, 1993; Milwaukee NOW, Woman of the Year, 1994. **Special Achievements:** Author of Parents As Teachers of Human Sexuality, 1986; Wisconsin's Unsung Hero, Newsweek, 1988; Woman of the Year, Calvary Baptist Church, 1990. **Business Addr:** Principal, Access to Success, 204 E Reservoir Ave, Milwaukee, WI 53212, **Business Phone:** (414)313-9762.

PERRY, LAVAL
Automotive executive, president (organization). **Educ:** Univ Detroit, BE, mech eng mfg, MBA, finance, 1982. **Career:** All Am Lincoln Mercury Inc, pres & owner, currently; DTP Trans Inc, founder; All Am Ford, Saginaw, MI, pres, currently. **Orgs:** Chmn, Greater Mich Ford Dealer Advert Fund Asn, 1999; bd dir, Mich Ford Dealers Advertisers Fund; vpres & bd mem, Ford Lincoln-Mercury Minority Dealers Asn; bd mem, OIC Indust Coun; mem, Univs Presidents Club; pres, Mich Automobile Dealer Asn, 2002; Saginaw Chamber Com; bd dirs, Ferris Found. **Special Achievements:** Co is ranked 75 on Black Enterprise mag's list of top 100 auto dealers, 1998. **Business Addr:** President, All American Ford, 4201 Bay Rd, Saginaw, MI 48603-1298, **Business Phone:** (989)792-1700.*

PERRY, LEE CHARLES, JR.
Executive. **Personal:** Born Feb 22, 1955, St Louis, MO; married Rena Armstrong; children: Raimon & Jonathan. **Educ:** Forest Park Comm Col, AS, elec eng tech, 1974; Comm Col Air Force, Electronics Honor Grad, 1975; Eastern KY Univ, BS, 1980; Indust Tech. **Career:** IBM St Louis, customer engr, 1980-83, program support rep, 1983-85; IBM Reg Off Kansas City, sr nsd specialist, 1985-87; IBM availability, serv mgr, 1987-. **Orgs:** Minister United Pentecostal Church, 1984-. **Honors/Awds:** IBM Means Service Award. **Military Serv:** USAF, e-5 staff sgt equipt chief, 4 yrs; USAF, Good Conduct Medal, Certificate of Recognition Outstanding Performance, peer instr. **Business Addr:** Availability Services Manager, IBM Corporation, 860 Ridge Lake Blvd Suite 200, Memphis, TN 38120, **Business Phone:** (901)762-5238.

PERRY, LEONARD DOUGLAS, JR.
School administrator. **Personal:** Born Mar 14, 1952, Philadelphia, PA. **Educ:** Temple Univ, BS, MEd. **Career:** Temple Univ, resident coord, 1976-77, assoc dean stud, 1977-80; Purdue Univ, asst dean stud, 1980-85; Fla State Univ, assoc dean studs, 1985-92; Brown Univ, assoc dean stud life, 1992; Iowa State Univ, assoc dean & dir, 2007. **Orgs:** NAACP; Urban League; Am Soc Training & Develop; Nat Asn Stud Personnel Adminr; Southern Asn Col Stud Affairs; Nat Soc Performance & Instr; bd dirs, Black Families Am Inc; bd, CHOICES Inc; Rhode Island Inc; 21 Century Youth Leadership Movement. **Honors/Awds:** Martin Luther King Award, Florida State Univ, 1987; Advisor of the Year Award, Black Stud Union, Florida State Univ, 1987; Seminole Community Leadership Award, Fla State Univ, 1992; NAACP Chapter Award, 1992; Community Color Builders-Elders Award, Brown Univ. **Home Addr:** PO Box 1555, Ames, IA 50014-1555. *

PERRY, LOWELL WESLEY, JR.
Executive, actor, manager. **Personal:** Born May 10, 1956, Ypsilanti, MI; son of Lowell Wesley Perry Sr and Maxine Lewis Perry; married Kathleen Tucker, Mar 21, 1987; children: Lowell Wesley III, Tucker Nichol & Trenton Lewis. **Educ:** Yale Univ, BA, Admin Sci, 1978; graduate work marketing, Seattle Univ, 1987. **Career:** Nutone Div Scovill, sales rep, 1978-81; Seattle Seahawks, dir sales & mkt, 1981-88; Access Plus Commun, field sales mgr, 1988-89; Seattle Mariners, acct exec, 1989-90; Perry Mkt Group, Inc, pres, 1990-94; Hiram Walker & Sons Inc, integrated mkt mgr, 1994-; coms, indust training films, print ads, actor & model; Films : Deja Vu, 2006; Nothing But the Truth, 2008. **Orgs:** Equal Opportunity Comm, chmn, 1975; Corresp secy, Zeta Pi Lambda Chap of Alpha Phi Alpha, 1983-84; Pub relcomm, Eastside Ment Health Ctr, 1983-84; First vpres, Zeta Pi Lambda of Alpha Phi Alpha, 1984-; Bd mem, Kirkland C of C, 1984-; bd, Kidsplace-Action Agenda Taskforce, 1985; Bd, East Madison YMCA 1985-; Bd, Coop Charities; Bd, Washington Gens; Nat Asn Advan Colored People. **Honors/Awds:** Rookie of the Year, Nutone Div Scovill, 1978-79; Chmn, Sustaining Membership Drive East Madison YMCA, 1984-85; Project Developer & Coord of "Blow the Whistle on Drugs" a statewide family substance abuse prog; speaker of the house Seattle Marketing Executives. **Business Addr:** Integrated Marketing Manager, Hiram Walker & Sons Inc, 3000 Town Ctr Suite 3200, Southfield, MI 48075, **Business Phone:** (810)948-6500.*

PERRY, MARC AUBREY
Marketing executive, president (organization). **Personal:** Born in Michigan; son of Lawrence C and Carrie O; married Pamela E, Mar 23, 1995; children: Aubrey Mariah. **Educ:** Eastern Mich Univ, mkt, 1978. **Career:** Chevrolet, mkt spec 1978-90; Donald Coleman, acct supvn, 1990-94; Perry Mkt Group Inc, pres, ceo, 1994-2000; Infiniti Energy Inc, mkt mgr, 2001-. **Orgs:** Bd mem, Black United Fund; founder, Blacks In Advert, Radio & Television; comm chair, Eastern Mich Almuni. **Business Phone:** (248)443-0382.

PERRY, MARGARET
Librarian. **Personal:** Born Nov 15, 1933, Cincinnati, OH; daughter of Rufus Patterson and Elizabeth Munford Anthony. **Educ:** Western Mich Univ, BA, 1954; Univ de Paris, cert d'Etudes Sum, 1956; NY City Col, attended 1958; Cath Univ Am, MSLS, 1959. **Career:** NY Pub Libr, young adult & ref librn, 1954-55, 1957-58; AUS Europe, post librn, 1959-67; US Military Acad W Point, circulation librn, 1967-70; Univ Rochester, Libr Bulletin, assoc ed, 1970-73, head educ libr, 1970-75, assoc prof, 1975-82, joint appt asst prof eng dept, 1973-75, head reader serv div actg dir libr, asst dir libr reader serv, 1975-82; Valparaiso Univ, dir libraries & assoc prof, 1982-93, univ librn emer & assoc prof emer, currently. **Orgs:** Chair educ comt, 19th Ward Community Asn Rochester, 1972-73; second vpres, Urban League Rochester, 1978-80; pres, Northern Ind Area Libr, 1986-88; Am Libr Asn. **Honors/Awds:** Scholarship to Seminar of American Writing and Publishing, Schloss Leopoldskron Salzburg, Austria, 1956; First Prize, Armed Forces Writers League, Short Story Contest, Honorable Mention, 1965, 1966; Second Prize, Frances Steloff Armed Forces League Short Story Contest, 1968; First Prize, Arts Alive, Short Story Contest, 1990; Second Prize, Willow Review, Short Story Contest, 1990. **Special Achievements:** Author, works include: A Bio-Bibliography of Countee P Cullen, Greenwood Press 1971; Silence to the Drums: A Survey of the Literature of the Harlem Renaissance, Greenwood Press 1976; Harlem Renaissance: An Annotated Bibliography and Commentary, Garland 1982; Short Fiction of Rudolph Fisher, Greenwood Press 1987; An Interview Margaret Perry, Cobblestone Magazine, 1991; Gwendolyn Brooks, Notable Black American Women, ed by Jessie Carney Smith, Gale Publishing, 1992; Contributor to Michigan Land Use Insitute, 1994-2000; Carol Moseley Braun, Notable Black Am Women, ed by Jessie Carney Smith, Gale Pub, 1995. **Home Addr:** 15050 Roaring Brook Dr, Thompsonville, MI 49683. **Business Addr:** University Librarian Emerita, Associate Professor Emerita, Valparaiso University, Kretzmann Hall, Valparaiso, IN 46383-6493, **Business Phone:** (219)464-5000.

PERRY, MARLO
Football player. **Personal:** Born Aug 25, 1972, Forest, MS. **Educ:** Jackson State Univ. **Career:** Buffalo Bills, linebacker, 1994-99. **Honors/Awds:** SWAC Freshman of the Year, 1993; Dick Butkus Award, 1993.

PERRY, MICHAEL DEAN
Football player. **Personal:** Born Aug 27, 1965, Aiken, SC; married Trini; children: Taylor Denise, Amber & Tyrah. **Educ:** Clemson Univ. **Career:** Football player (retired); Cleveland Browns, defensive tackle, 1988-94; Denver Broncos, defensive tackle, 1995-97; Kans City Chiefs, defensive tackle, 1997. **Honors/Awds:** NFL All-Star Team, Sporting News, 1989; Defensive Player of the Year, United Press Int, 1989; Defensive Player of the Year, Cleveland Touchdown Club, 1991; Pro Bowl, 1989-94, 1996.

PERRY, PAM ELAINE
Publicist, writer. **Personal:** Born May 26, 1960, Detroit, MI; daughter of Ted and Connie Hunt; married Marc, Mar 23, 1995; children: Aubrey. **Educ:** Wayne State Univ, BA, Jour, 1983. **Career:** Detroit Free Press, acct exec & freelance writer, 1983-90; Joy Jesus, develop dir, 1990-92; The Salvation Army, dir pub rels, 1992-96; Ferry Marketing Group, vpres pub rels, 1996-2001; Detroit Pub Schs, jour teacher, 2001; Hermanoff & Assoc, publicist, 2001-03; Ministry Mkt Solution, co-founder & publicist currently. **Orgs:** Pub Rels Soc Am, 1983-85; founder & pres, Blacks Advert, Radio & TV, 1990-00; Am Christian Writers, pres, 2000-; Christian African Am Booksellers Asn, 2003-. **Honors/Awds:** One to Watch, Am Women in TV & Radio, 1993; Emmy Award, Detroit Academy of TV Arts, 2002. **Special Achievements:** Founder of non-profit group ACW/Det, 2000; columnist: Mich Chronicles, 2000-; author: Fruit Juice, 2002. **Business Addr:** Publicist, Ministry Marketing Solutions, 33011 Tall Oaks, Farmington, MI 48336, **Business Phone:** (248)426-2300.

PERRY, DR. PATSY BREWINGTON
Educator, administrator. **Personal:** Born Jul 17, 1933, Greensboro, NC; daughter of James C and Rosa Kirby; married Wade Wayne, Dec 23, 1955; children: Wade Wayne Jr. **Educ:** NC Col, Durham, BA, 1954, MA, 1955; Univ NC, PhD, 1972. **Career:** Educator, Administrator (retired); Georgetown High Sch, Jacksonville, NC, teacher, 1955-56; NC Cent Univ, Durham, NC, res librn, 1956-58, instr, 1959-63, asst prof, 1964-71, assoc prof, 1972-74, prof, 1974, Eng Dept, chmn, 1979-90, Univ Honors Prog, spec asst to chancellor & dir, 1993-95, Acad Affairs, provost & vice chancellor, 1995-98; Univ NC, career teaching fel, 1968-69; NC Cent Univ, fac fel, 1968-71; Duke Univ, vis prof, 1975; Ford Found, writing fel, 1989. **Orgs:** Alpha Kappa Mu Honary Soc, 1953; bd mem, Links Inc, 1976-; Sigma Tau Delta Int Eng Honor Soc, 1983-; reader, Col Bd Eng Composition Test, 1985-; sen, Philol Asn Carolinas, 1986-; bd mem, Women in Action Prev Violence, 1990-; bd gov & secy, Univ NC, 1999-2007; life mem, Col Lang Asn; S Atlantic Modern Lang Asn; Asn Dept Eng; Langston Hughes Soc. **Honors/Awds:** Notable Black Am Women, Jessie Smith, 1991; Silver Medallion Award for Excellence in Education, YWCA, Durham, 1991; Research Award, NC Cent Univ, 1991; Distinguished Alumni Award, Nat Asn Equal Opportunity Higher Educ, 1999; Women of Vision Award in Educational Leadership, Durham Alumnae Chap, Bennett Col, 2006. **Special Achievements:** Author: "The Lit Content of Frederick Douglass' Paper Through, 1860," CLA Jour, 1973; "Before The North Star: Frederick Douglass? Early Journalistic Career", Phylon 35, 1974; "One Day When I Was Lost: Baldwin's Unfulfilled Obligation," chapter in James Baldwin: A Critical Evaluation, edited by Therman B O'Daniel, Howard Univ Press, 1977; "Benjamin Griffith Brawley," "Leslie Pinckney Hill," Chester Bomar Himes," and Jay Saunders Redding." Southern Writers " BiographicalDictionary, Ed. Robert A. Bain, Joseph M. Flora, and Louis D. Rubin, Jr. Baton Rouge: Louisiana State UP, 1979; Le jour ou j'etais perdue une obligation que Baldwin n'a pas remplie"James Baldwin et son oeuvre, Trans Catherine Kieffer. Paris, Nouveaux Horizons, 1980; "James Alan McPherson." The Dictionary of Literary Biography, Ed, Thadious Davis and Trudier Harris, Columbia, S.C, BC Research, 1985; "A Tribute to W. Edward Farrison 1902-1985: Scholar, Educator, & Churchman," CLA Journal 28, 1985; "Leslie Pinckney Hill," "Willis Richardson." The Dictionary of Literary Biography, B. C. Research, 1986; "Alice Dunbar-Nelson," "Muriel Rahn," Notable Black American Women, Gale Research Books, 1991; "Nikki Giovanni," Southern Writers of the Second Renascence'Poets, Dramatists, Essayists, & Others, Greenwood Press Inc, 1994.

PERRY, RICHARD
Educator, novelist. **Personal:** Born Jan 13, 1944, New York, NY; son of Henry Perry and Bessie Draines Perry; married Jeanne Gallo, Sep 14, 1968; children: Malcolm David & Alison Wright. **Educ:** City Col, City Univ New York, BA, 1970; Columbia Univ, MFA, 1972. **Career:** Pratt Inst, Brooklyn NY, prof Eng, 1972, prof emer, currently, dean lib arts & sci, 1993-; Novels: Montgomery's Children, Harcourt, 1984; No Other Tale to Tell, William Morrow, 1994; The Broken Land, St. Martin's Press, 1996. **Orgs:** PEN, Teachers & Writers Collab, Nat Coun Teachers Eng. **Honors/Awds:** Arts Award, NJ State Coun, 1980; NJ Writers Conf Citation, 1985; auth: Changes, Bobbs-Merrill, 1974; New Jersey

Council on the Arts Award for Fiction, 1983, 1985, 1990; Black History Month Award, Asn Study Afro-Am Life & Hist, 1986; Fel Writing, Nati Endowment Arts, 1989. **Military Serv:** AUS, 1968-70. **Home Addr:** 182B Central Ave, Englewood, NJ 07631. **Business Addr:** Professor Emeritus, Pratt Institute, 200 Willoughby Ave, Brooklyn, NY 11205, **Business Phone:** (718)636-3600.

PERRY, RITA EGGLETON
Photographer, publisher, writer. **Personal:** Born Jul 24, 1943, Atlantic City, NJ; daughter of Christine Archer Luffborough and Jesse B Eggleton Jr; divorced; children: Sylvia Rosella Eggleton Carter-Perry. **Educ:** Univ detroit; Norfolk state Univ. **Career:** Muziki Publ Co, adminr, 1965-68. Macon Times Newspaper, managing ed, 1968-71; Fla Star Newspaper, from asst to publ, 1971-73; Mel-Lin, Pres-Jas Broadcasting Co, vpres sales, 1973-85; Jacksonville Free Press, publ, owner, 1985-. **Orgs:** Pub rel officer, Bold City Chapter the Links Inc, 1993-; A L Lewis YWCA Bd; One Church/One Child Bd; former pres, Jacksonville Negro Bus & Prof Women; former secy, Southeast Black Publs Asn; former pres, Jacksonville Coalition of Community Clubs; Nat Assault on Illiteracy Prog Bd (AOIP); bd visitors, Edward Waters Col. **Honors/Awds:** Jacksonville Urban League Award, 1988; Award for Dedication to Black History Educ, Florida Jr Col, 1990; Martin Luther King Found, Community Serv, 1990, 1996; Alpha Kappa Alpha Sorority, Community Serv, 1992, 1994, Academy Award, 1995; Sickle Cell Found, Partner for Caring, 1991; Numerous Awards. **Special Achievements:** Edward Waters Col, 1987; Visions of Jacksonville, 1990; One of 14 publishers called by Pres Bush for consultation, 1991; State of Florida Commendation for Voter Educ Projects, 1993. **Home Phone:** (904)384-7667. **Business Addr:** Publisher, Writer, Jacksonville Free Press, PO Box 43580, Jacksonville, FL 32203, **Business Phone:** (904)634-1993.

PERRY, DR. ROBERT LEE
School administrator. **Personal:** Born Dec 6, 1932, Toledo, OH; son of Rudolph R and Katherine Bogan; married Dorothy Larouth Smith; children: Baye. **Educ:** Bowling Green St Univ, BA, sociol & psychol, 1959, MA, sociol, 1965; Wayne St Univ, PhD, sociol, 1978. **Career:** Lucas Co Juv Ct Toledo, OH, probation counr, 1960-64, juvenile ct ref, 1964-67; Detroit Inst Techn, asst prof, 1967-70; Bowling Green State Univ, Dept Ethnic Studies, chmn, 1970, dir, chair, 1979-96; Univ Calif, Los Angles, Am Soci Soc Inst Soc Res, postdoctoral fel, 1980; licensed prof counr, 1988; Ohio cert prev consult, 1989-; Eastern Mich Univ, Dept African Am Studies, prof & dept head, 1997-2003, African Am Ctr Applied Res & Serv, coordr grad studies, prof African Am studies & dir, currently. **Orgs:** Sigma Delta PiNat Spanish Hon Soc, 1958; Alpha Kappa Delta Nat Soc Honor Soc, 1976; consult, Nat Inst Law Enf & Crimin Just, 1978-82; bd mem, Citizens Rev Bd Lucas County Juv Ct Toledo, OH, 1979-91; consult, Div Soc Law & Econ Sci, NSF, 1980; consult, C Def Fund Task Force Adoption Asst, 1980; bd mem, Inst Child Advocacy Cleveland, OH 1981-85; chair, Status Women & Minorities Comm N Cent Sociol Soc, 1983-85. **Honors/Awds:** Charles C Irby Distinguished Service Award, Nat Asn Ethnic Studies, 1994. **Special Achievements:** Published hundreds of publications, refereed journal articles, book chapters. **Military Serv:** USAF, A/IC air man first class, 1953-57. **Home Addr:** 1906 Potomac Dr, Toledo, OH 43607, **Home Phone:** (419)536-2503. **Business Addr:** Professor of African American Studies, Director, Eastern Michigan University, African American Center for Applied Research & Services, Off 201 Boone 620 Pray Harrold Bldg, Ypsilanti, MI 48197, **Business Phone:** (734)487-0185.

PERRY, TIMOTHY D
Basketball player. **Personal:** Born Jun 4, 1965, Freehold, NJ. **Educ:** Temple Univ, attended 1988. **Career:** Phoenix Suns, forward, 1988-92; Philadelphia 76ers, forward, 1992-95; NJ Nets, forward, 1995-96; NJ Bullets, Eastern Basketball Alliance, ctr, currently. **Business Phone:** (717)986-0720.

PERRY, TYLER (EMMITT PERRY, JR.)
Playwright, actor, theatrical producer. **Personal:** Born Sep 13, 1969, New Orleans, LA; son of Emmitt Perry Sr. **Career:** Plays: I Know I've Been Changed, 1998; Woman Thou Art Loosed, 1999; I Can Do Bad All By Myself, 2000; Diary of a Mad Black Woman, 2001; Madea's Family Reunion, 2002; Madea's Class Reunion, 2003; What's Done In the Dark; Film: Diary of a Mad Black Woman, 2005; Madea Goes to Jail, 2006; Why Did I Get Married?, 2007; Daddy's Little Girls, 2007; Meet the Browns, 2008; The Family That Preys, 2008; Madea Goes to Jail, 2009; I Can Do Bad All by Myself, 2009; Star Trek, 2009. **Honors/Awds:** Helen Hayes Award for Excellence in Theater, 2001; Black Business Professionals Entrepreneur of the Year, 2004; Quill Award: Best in Humor, 2006; Quill Award: Book of the Year, 2006; BET Tribute Award, 2007. **Special Achievements:** Ranked #7 on EW's The 50 Smartest People in Hollywood. **Business Addr:** Director, Actor, Atlanta, GA 30318.*

PERRY, VICTORIA
Counselor. **Educ:** Nova Southeastern Univ, EdD. **Career:** Bishop State Community Col, Div Stud Develop Serv, counselor, 1996-. **Business Addr:** Counselor, Bishop State Community College, 351 N Broad St, Mobile, AL 36603-5898.*

PERRY, WAYNE D
Educator. **Personal:** Born Oct 14, 1944, Denton, TX; married Linda Jackson; children: LaNitha, Chelese & Wayne. **Educ:** Tuskegee Inst, BS, 1967; Univ NMex, MS, 1969; Carnegie Mellon Univ, PhD, 1975. **Career:** Ford Motor Co, co-op student mfg eng, 1964-67; Tuskegee Inst, res & teaching asst, 1963-67; Sandia Lab, mech engr dir adv comput aided design proj, 1967-71; Manpower Studies Proj Carnegie Mellon Univ, instr mgr res coordr, 1971-75; Housing Studies Defense Manpower & Energy Pol Studies; The RAND Corp, econ pol proj dir; Rand Grad Sch Policy Studies, supvr; Fla Agr & Mech Univ, prof & dir, div mgr sci MBA prog; Texas Agr & Mech Univ Syst, dean & prof indust eng, col eng & architect; George Mason Univ, prof pub policy & opers res, currently. **Orgs:** Am Statis Asn; The Inst Mgt Sci; Economet Soc N Am; Am Soc Mech Engr; Omega Psi Phi; Nat Asn Advanc Colored People; co-founder, Concerned Black Employees Sandia Lab; Black Coalition, Albuquerque & Pitts; La Youth Motivat Task Force; dir, La Carnegie-Mellon Univ Alum Asn; dir, Ladera Heights Civic Asn; Asn Black Fac Adminr & Staff; Tau Beta Pi; Pi Tau Sigma. **Honors/Awds:** Res Grant, US Dept Labor, Dept Energy, Dept Defense; Sandia Lab & Serv Award, Nuclear Weapons Devel Atomic Energy Comm, 1969; Res Paper Winner, Am Soc Mech Engr, 1967; Fel Carnegie-Mellon Univ, 1971-75; edit reviewer "Policy Analysis" Univ of CA Berkeley 1978; White House Award, Pres Reagan; Distinguished Alumni Award, Carnegie-Mellon Univ; Nuclear Weapons Service Award, US Atomic Energy Comn. **Business Addr:** Professor, George Mason University, 4400 Univ Dr, MSN 3C6, Fairfax, VA 22030, **Business Phone:** (703)993-2273.

PERRY, WILMONT
Football player, football coach. **Personal:** Born Feb 24, 1975, Franklinton, NC. **Educ:** Livingstone Col. **Career:** Football player (retired), Football coach; Nat Football League, New Orleans Saints, running back, 1998-99; Carolina Panthers, running back, 2000; Arena Football League, Cape Fear Wildcats, running back & linebacker, 2002-03; Arena Football League, Columbus Destroyers, running back & linebacker, 2004-05; Louis burg Col, offensive line coach; Free agt.

PERRY-HOLSTON, WALTINA D
Economist. **Personal:** Born Jan 6, 1959, Augusta, GA; daughter of James W and Mabel Wingfield; married Kevin, Jun 22, 1991. **Educ:** Spelman Col, BA, 1980; Ga State Univ, attended, 1982. **Career:** Gen Servs Admin, technical support clerk, 1980-82; US Dept Edu, Litigation Unit, legal technician, 1982-83; US Dept Labor, economist, 1983-. **Orgs:** Spelman Col Alumni Asn, 1980-; Nat Asn for Female Execs Inc, 1980-; Am Econ Asn. **Honors/Awds:** 'Performance Management System Award', US Dept Labor, 1992, 91, Combined Fed Campaign CRD, 1991, Savings Bond Canvasser, 1990; Women's Executive Leadership Prog 1994-95. **Home Addr:** 3768 Ozmer Ct, Decatur, GA 30034, **Home Phone:** (404)243-7252. **Business Addr:** Economist, US Department of Labor, Bureau of Labor Statistics, 100 Alabama St SW Suite 6B-90, Atlanta, GA 30303-8750, **Business Phone:** (404)347-7575.

PERRYMAN, ANGELO R.
Business owner. **Personal:** Born Jan 1, 1960?; son of Jimmie L Sr. **Career:** Brown & Root; Perryman Bldg & Construct Serv, pres & chief exec officer,1998-. **Business Addr:** President, Chief Executive Officer, Perryman Building & Construction Service, 4548 Market St, Philadelphia, PA 19139, **Business Phone:** (215)243-4109.

PERRYMAN, BOB. **See PERRYMAN, ROBERT.**

PERRYMAN, LAVONIA LAUREN
Executive, vice president (organization). **Personal:** Born in Detroit, MI. **Educ:** Wayne State Univ, BA, 1971; Ferris Col, 1969; Howard Univ, MA, 1978. **Career:** Soc Res Applic Corp, comn dir; owner opr, first girls bsketball clinic; Pizazzz Corp, pres; Afbony Modeling & Talent Agency, prof model instr; Teai & Record, pub rel dir; WRadio, report, 1973-76; WTVS-56, black jour reprt; Smith, Sanders & Perryman, vpres, currently. **Orgs:** Vpres, Nat Asn Media Women; Nat Asn Advan Colored People; Negro Counc Women; Black Communicators; All Star Bsketball Player; Congressman John Conyers Women Org; Stud Non-violents Org; Congress Black Women; Nat Coalition 100 Black Women. **Honors/Awds:** Athletic award, Ferris State Col, 1969; Ms Soul Mich & Mass Autorama, 1972; speech award, VFW, 1973-74; Ms Black Mich; Ms Black Detroit; Ms Elks; Ms Swimsuit; Ms Congeniality; Ms Misty Mich, 1974-75; Media Woman of the Year; Spirit Detroit Award, City Detroit; Citizen Award, Booker T Wash Bus Asn; Most Unique Dresser Detroit News, 1976-77; Citizen Award, Detroit City Counc; Detroiter's Award, Detroit Experience; Disco Martin Citizen Award; Wash DC's 10 Most Admired Women Award. **Business Phone:** (202)682-4728.

PERRYMAN, ROBERT (BOB PERRYMAN)
Football player, football executive, football coach. **Personal:** Born Oct 16, 1964, Raleigh, NC; married Sonya; children: Krista, Robert & Jason. **Educ:** Univ Mich, BS, sports mgt & commun, 1987. **Career:** Football player (retired), football exec; New Eng Patriots, running back, 1987-90; Denver Broncos, 1991-92; United Way Merrimack Valley, Mkt & Labor Rels, vpres, regional coordr, currently; NFL, Jr Player Develop Prog, regional dir, 2005-; Merrimack Col, quaterback coach, currently. **Orgs:** NFL Alumni Asn; Pentuckey Bank Inc; Kiwanis club. **Business Addr:** Quarterback Coach, Merrimack College, 315 Turnpike St, North Andover, MA 01845, **Business Phone:** (978)837-5000.

PERRY-MASON, GAIL F
Banker. **Personal:** Born Dec 4, 1962, Detroit, MI; daughter of Clarence and Frankie; married Lance W, Aug 3, 1985; children: Brandon, Dexter & Scott. **Career:** Wayne County Commun Col, instr; Henry Ford Commun Col, instr; Marygrove Col, instr; Native Detroiter Mag, writer financial sect; Comcast Cablevision, host, "Detroit Bus Exchange," host, "Building Wealth," host & exec producer, "Women's Issues"; "Building Wealth", host radio show; Fahnestock & Co, Inc, vpres investments, currently; Oppenheimer & Co, vpres. **Orgs:** Bd dir, Salvation Army; bd adv, Women-Detroit Entrepreneurs Inst,; Nat Asn Securities Prof; finance comt, Women's Econ Club; Women's Exec Golf League; bd dir, That's What Friends Are For; Nat Asn Female Exec; Nat Asn Advan Colored People; founder's soc, Detroit Inst Arts; Bus Women's Alliances; Blue Monday Network; adv bd, YWCA; Hope United Methodist Church; Blacks Advert Radio & TV; bd dir, Mariners Inn; African Am Women Tour; Spaulding C; mentor; founder, First Money Camp, dir; Wall Street J Youth Investment Club; Nat Asn Securities Prof; Bus Women's Alliance; treas, Detroit Compact Bd Dir; Detroit 300 Adv Bd; Catherine Ferguson Acad Mentorship Prog, Pershing HS; founder, Money Matters Youth. **Honors/Awds:** Community Achievement Award, Gentlemen Wall St; Super Achiever's Award, WJLB Radio; Women of Excellence Oakland Cty Polit Action Comn; Who's Who Professional Bus Women's Award; Phenomenal Bus Woman of the Yr; Crain's 40 Under 40. **Special Achievements:** Author of articles published in Michigan Chronicle, Ebony, AAA, Black Enterprise, The Detroit News and Free Press, Research Magazine, Oakland Press and Tomorrow Magazine; author of Money Matters for Families, Pearson Publishing, 1999; author of "Girl Make Your Money Grow," Broadway Book, hosted the first Money Camp for Children in Detroit; hosted the first shareholders of Sara Lee Bus trip; Rosa and Raymond Parks Inst, Pathway to Freedom, 1996; Pershing High School, Catherine Ferguson Academy Mentorship Program; MFS Mutual Funds for Women and Investments, spokesperson; Keynote speaker for: Blacks in Govt Natl Conf, African Amer Women on Tour, Women of Excellence, Wall St Conf, County & Hosp Workers, Natl Assn of Securities Professionals, Natl Assn of Female Exec, Tavis Smiley Youth to Leaders Conf; Detroit's One of the Most Influential Women in the Financial Industry. **Home Addr:** 1176 Buckingham, Grosse Pointe Park, MI 48230, **Home Phone:** (313)885-5786. **Business Addr:** Vice President of Investments, First of Michigan Corp., 131 Kercheval Suite 131, Grosse Pointe Farms, MI 48236, **Business Phone:** (313)259-2600.

PERSAUD, INDER
Executive. **Personal:** Born Oct 23, 1926, Georgetown, Guyana; married Nalini Singh; children: 4. **Educ:** London Engl, hosp admin Inst, Hosp Admin, 1956. **Career:** Berbice Group Guyana, hosp admin, 1958-60; Georgetown Hosp, 1960-67; Morrisania Hosp Bronx, actg admin, 1967-68; Cumberland Hosp Brooklyn, assoc exec dir, 1968-73, exec dir, 1973. **Orgs:** Health Comn Nat Urban League; pres, NY City chap Nat Asn Health Serv Exec, 1972; founder, Consumers Accreditation Counc; fed vchmn, Ft Greene Coop.

PERSIP, CHARLES LAWRENCE
Educator, artist. **Personal:** Born Jul 26, 1929, Morristown, NJ; son of Francis and Doris; married Sophia Miller, Oct 30, 1955; children: Jean Michelle & Erma Evangeline. **Educ:** Julliard Conserv, attended, 1960. **Career:** New Sch Univ, jazz instructor, 1993-; Queensborough Community Col, adj lectr, assoc prof, currently; New Sch Jazz & Contemp Music, instr, currently. **Orgs:** Local 802 Am Fedn Musician, 1954-; Int Asn Jazz Educr, 1993-. **Honors/Awds:** Contribution Jazz, Greater Jamaica Develop Corp, 1995; Outstanding Service to Jazz Education Award, IAJE, 1998; Zildjian Hall of Fame, Zildjian Cymbal Co, 1999. **Special Achievements:** Published: How Not to Play Drums, 1987; Performed with Brooklyn Philharmonic Orchestra, May 1989. **Business Addr:** Instructor, The New School for Jazz and Contemporary Music, 55 W 13 St 5th Fl, New York, NY 10011, **Business Phone:** (212)229-5896.

PERSON, CHUCK CONNORS
Basketball player, basketball coach. **Personal:** Born Jun 27, 1964, Brantley, AL. **Educ:** Auburn Univ, Auburn, AL, attended 1986. **Career:** Basketball player (retired), coach; Ind Pacers, forward, 1986-92, Minn Timberwolves, 1992-94; San Antonio Spurs, 1994-98; Charlotte Hornets,1998-99; Seattle Supersonics, forward, 1999-2000; Ind Pacers, asst coach; Sacramento Kings, asst coach, 2007-. **Honors/Awds:** NBA Rookie of the Year, 1987; NBA All-Rookie Team, 1987. **Special Achievements:** Tv appearances: The Rifleman. **Business Phone:** (916)928-0000.

PERSON, DR. DAWN RENEE
College teacher. **Personal:** Born Dec 10, 1956, Sewickley, PA; daughter of Conrad Sr and Fannie Mae Thomas (deceased); married Harold Eugene Hampton, Aug 2, 1986; children: Bryson

Thomas Person-Hampton & Amara Renee Person-Hampton. **Educ:** Slippery Rock Univ, BS, educ, 1977, MEd, 1979; Teachers Col, Columbia Univ, EdD, 1990. **Career:** Slippery Rock Univ, human relations counsr, 1978-79, minority affairs coord, 1979-80, advr black & int stud, 1980-81; Colo St Univ, dir, black stud serv, 1981-85; Lafayette Col, asst dean acad serv, 1985-90; Teachers Col, Columbia Univ, asst prof higher educ, 1990-97; Stud Develop Higher Educ, assoc prof; Calif St Univ, prof, co-dir, 1997-. **Orgs:** Workshop facilitator Male/Female Relation, 1978-; ACPA; NAACP Easton PA Chap 1985-87; Black Conf-Higher Educ PA, 1986-87; NASPA; Leadership Lehigh Valley 1989-90. **Honors/Awds:** Outstanding Black Achiever, Pa, Black Opinions, 1989; Service Award, Lafayette Col Alumni Chapter Black Collegians, 1988; Excellence in Higher Education, Lafayette Col Minority Stud, 1990. **Special Achievements:** Publication & Research in Minority Student Retention, Student Cultures, & Multicultural Issues in Higher Education. **Home Phone:** (562)598-6283. **Business Addr:** Professor, California State University, Department of Educational Psychology, Administration, & Counseling, Rm AS - 216 1250 Bellflower Blvd, Long Beach, CA 90840, **Business Phone:** (562)985-8026.

PERSON, EARLE G.
Dentist. **Personal:** Born Apr 28, 1928, Mt Vernon, IL; married Estelle Mccraty. **Educ:** Univ Ill, BS, 1950; Creighton Univ, Omaha, DDS, 1958. **Career:** Pvt Pract dent, 1958-; Creighton Univ, fac, 1960-62; cert dent consult; Archbishop Bergan Mercy Hosp, surg staff; Doctor's Hosp Omaha, surg staff. **Orgs:** Pres, Urban League, 1965-68; Acad Gen Dent, 1972-; Nat Dem Conv, 1972; deleg, Nat Black Conv Gary, 1972; Creighton Univ Adv Coun, 1972-; assemblyman, Nat Black Polit Assembly, 1972-; pres bd dir, Comprehensive Health Asn Omaha, 1973-; pres, NE Soc Clin Hypnosis, 1973; state chmn, NDA Coun Dent Care Prog, 1974-; Int Platform Asn, 1974-75; Little Rock, 1974; Alpha Sigma Nu; Omicron Kappa Upsilon; IL Soc Microbiologists; Am & NE Dent Asn; Alpha Sigma Nu; Am Asn Dent Consult; bd dir, KOWH AM/FM Radio. **Honors/Awds:** Owler's Award, Dist serv dent & civic affairs, 1968; Black Hall of Fame; Dental Hall of Fame. **Military Serv:** AUS, second lt 1950-52, first lt 1952-53.

PERSON, LESLIE ROBIN
Executive. **Personal:** Born Nov 14, 1962, St Louis, MO; married Kyro Jonathan Carter. **Educ:** Nichols State Univ, attended 1980, Kent State Univ, attended 1981; Univ Cincinnati, BA, 1982. **Career:** US Air Force, 2012 commun squadron atc officer trainee, 1984-85, 1903 commun squadron dep atc opers officer, 1985-86, 2146 commun group dep atc operas officer 1986-. **Orgs:** Adv Coun 2012 CS Unit, 1984-85; assoc mem, Pima Country Special Olympics Group, 1985; secy, Davis-Monthan Co Grade Officer GP, 1985-86; founding mem, Davis-Monthan Special Olympics GP, 1985-86; Santas Blue, 1985-86; base chmn, Combined Fed Campaign, 1985. **Military Serv:** USAF, 1st lt, 3 1/2 yrs; Air Force Commendation Medal, 1985-86. **Business Addr:** Deputy ATC Operations Officer, United States Air Force, 2146 CG PSC, PO Box 2431, APO, CA 96366.

PERSON, ROBERT ALAN
Baseball player. **Personal:** Born Oct 6, 1969, St Louis, MO. **Career:** Cleveland Indians, 1989-90; Chicago White Sox, 1991; Florida Marlins, 1992; New York Mets, pitcher, 1994-96; Toronto Blue Jays, 1997-99; Philadelphia Phillies, 1999-2002; Boston Red Sox, 2003; Chicago White Sox, 2004-05.

PERSON, WAVERLY J.
Geophysicist, executive director. **Personal:** Born May 1, 1927, Blackridge, VA; son of Santee and Bessie Butts; married Sarah Walker Person, Nov 6, 1954. **Educ:** St Paul's Col, Lawrenceville, VA, BS, 1949; Am Univ, Wash, DC, 1960; George Wash Univ, Wash, DC, 1963. **Career:** Dept Com, Nat Oceanic & Atmospheric Admin, Boulder, CO, geophysicist, 1958-73; US Geol Survey, Denver & Golden, CO, geophysicist, 1973-94, US Geol Survey, Nat Earthquake Info Ctr, CO, staff, 1962, dir, 1977-. **Orgs:** Seismol Soc of Am, 1965-, eastern sect treasurer, 1968-; past pres, Flatirons Kiwanis, 1972-; Am Geophys Union, 1975-; bd of dir, Boulder Co Crimestoppers, 1986-; mem retention chmn, Rocky Mountain Dist. **Honors/Awds:** Honorary Doctorate, St Paul's Col, 1988; Outstanding Government Communicator, Nat Asn Govt Communicators, 1988; Distinguished Alumni: Citation of the Year Award, Nat Asn Equal Opport Higher Educ, 1989; Meritorious Service Award, US Geol Survey, 1989; Annual Minority Award, Community Servs Dept, Boulder, CO. **Special Achievements:** First African American to serve as the director of the US Geological Survey; many publications on earthquakes in scince journals & contributed a number of text books in the Earth Sciences. **Military Serv:** AUS, First Sergeant, 1944-46, 1951-52; Good Conduct Medals, Asian Pacific Medal. **Home Addr:** 5489 Seneca Pl, Boulder, CO 80303. **Business Addr:** Director, US Geological Survey National Earthquake Information Center, Denver Federal Centre, Mail Stop 967, PO Box 25046, Denver, CO 80225-0046, **Business Phone:** (303)273-8500.*

PERSON, WESLEY LAVON
Basketball player. **Personal:** Born Mar 28, 1971, Crenshaw, AL; married Lillian; children: Wesley Jr, Wesley II, Nykeia & Aleyah. **Educ:** Auburn Univ. **Career:** Basketball player (retired); Phoenix Suns, forward-guard, 1994-97; Cleveland Cavaliers, 1997-2002; Memphis Grizzlies, 2003-04; Portland Trail Blazers, 2004; Atlanta Hawks, 2004; Miami Heat, 2005; Denver Nuggets, forward-guard, 2005. **Honors/Awds:** NBA All-Rookie Second Team, 1995.

PERSON, DR. WILLIAM ALFRED
Educator. **Personal:** Born Aug 29, 1945, Henderson, NC; married Juanita Dunn; children: William Alfred II & Wilton Antoine. **Educ:** Johnson C Smith Univ, BA, 1967; Univ Ga, MEd, 1973, EdD, 1977. **Career:** Wilkes City Bd Educ, teacher, 1967-72; Univ Ga, grad asst & admin asst, 1973-77; Miss State Univ, asst prof, 1977-80, assoc prof, 1980, prof curric, instr & dir grad studies, currently; Univ Southern Miss, interim dir, assoc dean, 1991-99, Alliance Grad Educ Miss, prin investr. **Orgs:** Treas, Phi Delta Kappa, 1982-83; vpres, Phi Beta Sigma, 1982-83; pres, Phi Beta Sigma, 1983-; bd dir, Starkville Kiwanis Breakfast Club, 1984-. **Honors/Awds:** Two Acad Scholar, 1963-65; Sigma Man of the Year, Phi Beta Sigma, 1979. **Home Addr:** PO Box 424, Starkville, MS 39759. **Business Addr:** Director of Graduate Studies, Professor of Curriculum and Instruction, Mississippi State University, Office of Graduate Studies, PO Box G, Mississippi State, MS 39762-5507, **Business Phone:** (662)325-7400.

PERSONS, W RAY
State government official, educator, lawyer. **Personal:** Born Jul 22, 1953, Talbottan, GA; son of William and Frances Crowell; married Wendy-Joy Mottley, Sep 24, 1977; children: Conrad Ashley & April Maureen. **Educ:** OH State Univ, attended 1972; Armstrong State Univ, BS, 1975; OH State Univ, JD, 1978. **Career:** Armstrong State Col, col prof, 1979-80; Nat Lab Rel Bd, atty, 1980-82; Wells Braun Persons Law Firm, partner, 1982-; Cong Lindsay Thomas, legis coun; Arrington & Hollowell, PC, atty, 1986-95; Ga State Univ Col Law, adj prof litigation, 1989-98; State Ga, spec asst atty gen, 1989-99; Swift Currie McGhee & Hiers, partner, 1995-99; Hinton & Williams, partner, 1999-2001; King & Spalding, partner, 2001-. **Orgs:** Fel Am Col Trial Lawyers; fel Int Soc Barristers; Am Bd Trial Advocates; Fedn Defense & Corp Coun; Int Asn Defense & Corp Coun; chair-Evidence Study Comt, State Bar Ga; bd dir, Tommy Nobis Found; Nat Coun, Moritz Col Law, Ohio State Univ; bd dir, Ohio State Univ Found; pres, Atlanta Bar Asn, 2007-08. **Honors/Awds:** Regents Scholar, Armstrong State Col, 1973-75; Distinguished Alumnus Award, Armstrong Atlantic State Univ, 2001; Distinguished Alumnus Award, Ohio State Univ, Moritz Col of Law, 2005; Distinguished Service Award, Ohio State Univ, 2006. **Home Addr:** 6330 Riverside Dr NW, Atlanta, GA 30328. **Business Addr:** Partner, Attorney, King & Spalding, 11180 Peachtree St NE Suite 3600, Atlanta, GA 30309-3521, **Business Phone:** (404)572-2494.

PETERS, AULANA LOUISE
Lawyer, executive. **Personal:** Born Nov 30, 1941, Shreveport, LA; married Bruce Franklin. **Educ:** Notre Dame Sch Girls, dipl, 1959; Col New Rochelle, BA, philos, 1963; Univ S Calif, JD, 1973. **Career:** Publimondial Spa, secy/eng corresp, 1963; Fibramianto Spa, secy/eng corresp, 1963-64; Turkish Delegation Org Econ Coop & Develop, eng corresp, 1965; Cabinet Braconnier AAA Transl Agency, translator/interpreter, 1966; Org Econ Coop & Develop Sci Res Div, admin asst, 1966-67; Gibson Dunn & Crutcher, assoc & atty, 1973-84; US Securities & Exchange Comn, 1984-88; Gibson, Dunn & Crutcher, partner, 1988-2000, Minn Mining & Mfg Co, Northrop Grumman & Merrill Lynch & Co Inc, dir, currently; Deere & Co, bd dir, 2002-. **Orgs:** Los Angeles Co Bar Asn; State CA Bar Asn; Langston Hughes Asn; Black Women Lawyers Asn; Am Bar Asn; Univ S Calif Law Sch Law Alumni Asn; Coun Foreign Rels Inc NY; pub oversight bd panel, Am Inst Cert Pub Accts, 2001-02; Mayo Clinic Bd Trustees. **Honors/Awds:** Washington Achiever Award, Nat Asn Bank Women Inc, 1986; Director's Choice Award, Nat Women's Econ Alliance Found, 1994; Women in Business Award, Hollywood Coc, 1995; One of the 50 Most Influential Women Attorneys in USA, Nat Law Jour. **Special Achievements:** First African American ever to serve as a commissioner of the SEC, and only the third woman ever to do so. **Business Addr:** Board of Directors, Deere & Company, One John Deere Pl, Moline, IL 61265, **Business Phone:** (309)765-8000.

PETERS, CHARLES L, JR.
Executive, real estate developer, president (organization). **Personal:** Born Sep 20, 1935, New Orleans, LA; married Doris Jackson; children: Leslie Jean & Cheryl Lynne. **Educ:** So Univ, BS, cum laude, 1955; USC, MS, 1959, grad study. **Career:** Nat Housing Consult Inc, pres, chmn bd, 1973-; NHC Data Serv, pres & ceo; Trinity COT Develop Corp, ceo & exec dir. **Orgs:** Omega Psi Phi; La Urban League; YMCA; Nat Asn Housing & Redev Officials, Omega Life Mem Found. **Honors/Awds:** Nat Asn Homebuilders Man of Yr, Omega Psi Phi 1964, 1974, 1983; Outstanding Educator, La City Coun, 1970; service award, 2004. **Military Serv:** AUS, capt, 1955-67. **Home Addr:** 5323 Stillwater Dr, Los Angeles, CA 90008. **Business Addr:** President, National Housing Consult Inc, PO Box 8180, Universal City, CA 91618.

PETERS, DR. FENTON
School administrator, educator. **Personal:** Born Jul 10, 1935, Starkville, MS; son of Pellum and Cora Gandy; married Maggie Teresa Malone; children: Avis Campbell Wilcox, Pellum & Alton. **Educ:** Rust Col, AB, 1958; Miss State Univ, MEd, 1969, EdD, 1983. **Career:** Henderson High Sch, prin, 1968-70; Henderson Jr High Sch, prin, 1970-76; Starkville High Sch, prin, 1976-81; Starkville Pub Schs, chap 1 coordr, 1981-84, admin asst to supt; Holly Springs Pub Schs, supt, 1986-92; Christ Missionary & IDL Sch, prin; Miss St Univ, Meridian campus, adj lectr, currently. **Orgs:** Presenter Student Teaching Miss St Univ, 1978; presenter, Continuing Educ Miss St Univ, 1979; bd dirs, Starkville Chamber Com, 1983-84; bd trustees, Oktibbeha County Hosp, 1984-; st choir dir, Church Christ, 1983; bd dir, Holly Springs Chamber Com, 1988-89; St Supts Comm of 12, St Supt Educ, 1987-88; Arts Educ Task Force, Miss Arts Comn, 1991; PhiDelta Kappa. **Honors/Awds:** NSF Science Fellowship, 1962, 1962-63, 1967; Public Service Award, United Way 1985; Presidential Citation, Nat Asn Equal Opportunity Educ, 1987; Northeast MS Baptist Convention Hall of Fame, 1995; T E Veitch Community Service Award, 2006. **Home Addr:** 108 Old W Pt Rd, Starkville, MS 39759. *

PETERS, DR. JAMES SEDALIA, II. **See Obituaries section.**

PETERS, KENNETH DARRYL
Government official. **Personal:** Born Jan 27, 1949, Englewood, NJ; son of John C Jr and Lena Jones; married Katie M Coleman, Nov 27, 1976; children: Kenneth Jr & Kevin. **Educ:** Fisk Univ, BA, 1971; Univ Kans, MSW, 1973; Univ Calif, cert, 1973; Acad Health Sci Ft Sam Houston, cert, 1981. **Career:** Cath Social Serv, sch consult, 1973-78; State Calif Stockton, psychiat soc worker, 1978-80; Dept Develop Disabilities, Stockton, Calif, placement coordr, 1978-80; State Calif Sacramento, social serv consult, 1980-84, prog analyst, 1984, social serv admin; Calif Dept Transp, dist contracts officer, 1987-95; NIH, grant reviewer, 2002-; Calif Dept Health Serv, health trainer, currently; Ctr Disease Control, Atlanta, Ga, part time consult, currently. **Orgs:** Bd dir, Fisk Stud Enterprises, 1968; vpres, NAACP-Colegiate Chap Nashville, 1968-69; minority recruitment comr, Univ Kans, 1971-72; San Joaquin Ment Health Adv Bd, 1978-88; bd dir, Maternal & Child Health Disability Prev Bd, 1979-86; secy, Alpha Phi Alpha Fraternity Inc, 1980; Nat Conf Social Welfare, 1982-88; Calif Respiratory Exam Bd, 1983-92. **Honors/Awds:** Eligible Bachelor, Ebony Mag, 1975; Commendations: Calif Assemblyman Pat Johnston, 1983; Calif Senator John Garamendi, 1983. **Military Serv:** USAR, lt col, 1979-; Appt Asst Detach Cmdr, 1982; Commend for Combat Environ Transition Training, 1983; Appt Annual Training Module Officer in Charge, 1985; participated in Team Spirit '86 in Republic of Korea; Mobilization Officer for 6253d AUS Hosp, Santa Rosa, CA, 1994-; Equal Opportunity officer; Family Readiness officer for 921st Field Hosp, Sacramento, CA, 2000-. **Home Addr:** 2911 Sleepy Hollow Dr, Stockton, CA 95209, **Home Phone:** (209)475-0199. **Business Addr:** Health Consultant, Trainer, California Department of Health Services, MS 7700, PO Box 997413, Sacramento, CA 95899-7413, **Business Phone:** (916)445-4171.

PETERS, DR. REV. PAMELA JOAN
Business owner, president (organization), founder (originator). **Personal:** Born Feb 3, 1947, York, PA; daughter of Maurice E and Ruth V. **Educ:** Tenn State Univ, BA, 1969; Southern Ill Univ, MS, counselling educ, 1975; Walden Univ, PhD, 1992. **Career:** Pan Am World Airlines, airline stewardess, 1969-70; Delaware State Col, dir stud activ, 1970-74; Johnson & Johnson Corp, compensation admin, supvr traffic, 1974-76; Xerox Corp, personnel rep, 1976-78; ICI Americas, Inc, recruiter, eeo analyst, 1979-84; Univ Del, dir coop educ, 1984-86; Center for Stress, Pain & Wellness, Mgt Inc, pres, 1986-. **Orgs:** Wilmington Women Bus, 1980; Founding mem, chair, prog nomination comts, Brandywine Prof Assoc, 1981; chairperson, Forum Minority Engrs, 1981-83; bd dir, exec comt, chair personnel comm, YMCA, 1982-84; bd dir, Girl Scouts Am, 1984-86; Civil Rights Comn, 1985-86; Dela Guidance Assoc, 1986-87; bd mem, Mental Health Asn, 1988; life mem, Delta Sigma Theta. **Honors/Awds:** Outstanding athlete of the year, West York Area High Sch, 1965; Sigma Rho Sigma Honor Society, 1968-69; Outstanding service, Brandywine Professional Org, 1990; Outstanding Graduate, Walden Univ, 2001. **Special Achievements:** Dissertations, Lifestyle Changes of Selected Therapeutic Touch Practitioners, an Oral History; Papers, copyright, Prevention & Treatment Using Alternative Therapies for Injuries and Stress, Sports and Socialization of Youth into Health and Wellness; Published Article, Pregnancy/Childbirth, Therapeutic Insight; Author: My Hands: My Feet: standing out, My Heart: Loving Enough to Let Go, 1996; ordained interfaith minister, 2002. **Home Addr:** 315 W 36th St, Wilmington, DE 19802. **Business Addr:** Founder, President, The Center for Stress, Pain, and Wellness Management Inc., 315 W 36th St, Wilmington, DE 19802, **Business Phone:** (302)654-1840.

PETERS, ROBERT
Executive. **Career:** Nextgen Mgt Group Inc, prin, currently. **Business Addr:** Principle, Nextgen Management Group Inc, 1887 O Toole Ave Suite C207, San Jose, CA 95131.*

PETERS, SAMUEL A.
Lawyer. **Personal:** Born Oct 25, 1934, New York, NY; son of Clyde and Amy Matterson; married Ruby M Mitchell; children:

Robert, Samuel Jr, Bernard. **Educ:** New York Univ, BA, 1955; Fordham Univ Sch Law, LLB, 1961. **Career:** Federal Commun Community, law clerk, 1961; Lawyer's Community Civil Rights Under Law, staff atty, 1968-69; US Dept Justice, trial atty, 1961-68; Atlantic Richfield Co, employ rels coun, 1970-85, sr coun pub affairs; Rio Hondo Col, prof law; mediator, currently. **Orgs:** Nat Bar Asn; Am Bar Asn; Fordham Law Review Alumni Asn; Calif Musem Afro-Am Hist & Culture; Nat Advan Asn Colored People OC Chap; bd dirs, Weingart Ctr Assoc; Cent City E Task Force; Alpha Phi Alpha Fraternity, Nu Tau Lambda Chap; Toastmasters Int Club, 1391; bd dirs, Women's Transitional Living Ctr. **Military Serv:** AUS, sp-2, 3 yrs. **Home Addr:** 11471 Kensington Rd, Los Alamitos, CA 90720. **Business Addr:** B100j 3600 Workman Mill Rd, Whittier, CA 90601.*

PETERS, SHEILA RENEE
Psychologist. **Personal:** Born Jun 27, 1959, Columbus, MS; daughter of Dr James Calvin Sr and Anne Glover; divorced. **Educ:** Univ NC Chapel Hill, BA, psychol, 1981; Vanderbilt Univ, MS, 1985, PhD, 1989. **Career:** Luton Community Ment Health Ctr, dept psychol, human develop doctoral candidate clin psychol prog, clin therapist; coordr, community servs, Meharry Med Col, "I Have A Future" teenage pregnancy prev prog, partner; Greene, Peters & Assoc, clin & consult psychol prog, partner; Fisk Univ, asst prof psychol, sr prog mgr, Gender-specific Prog Training & Tech asst, Off Juv Justice & Delinq Prev, interim assoc provost, currently, Regist Reinvention Workgroup, chair, currently, Race Rel Inst, interim dir, currently. **Orgs:** Pres, Org Black Grad & Prof Studs, 1982-85; steering comn, 1983 Eco-Psychol Conf, 1982-83; dir, youth ministries Key-Stewart UM Church, 1983-87; treas, Asn Black Psychologists, 1984-85; Div Psychol Women, 1984-87, Div Comn Psychol, 1984-87, Southeastern Psychol Asn, 1986-87, Nashville Alum Chap Delta Sigma Theta, 1986-87; tres, Nashville Asn Black Psychologist, 1989-; nominations chairperson, Tenn Conf United Methodist Women, 1989; dir, Youth Ministries Ernest Newman UM Church, 1988-91; bd mem, Wesley Found, dist trustee, UM Church. **Honors/Awds:** Outstanding Young Woman of America, 1981; Peabody Minority Fel Vanderbilt, 1981-84; Crusade Scholar Bd Global Ministries, 1982-85; NIMH Traineeship, 1984-85. **Home Addr:** 4811 Fairmeade Ct, Nashville, TN 37218. **Business Addr:** Interim Director, Interim Associate Provost, Fisk University, Race Relations Institute, 1000 17th Ave N, Nashville, TN 37203, **Business Phone:** (615)329-8575.

PETERS, WILLIAM ALFRED
Manager. **Personal:** Born Mar 1, 1940, Atlantic City, NJ; married Warren Davidson. **Educ:** Temple Univ, BS, 1963; Pace Univ, MBA, 1978. **Career:** Time Inc, dir educ; Emerson Hall Pub, vpres mkt, 1970-72; Harper & Row Pub, ed, 1968-70, mkt & rep, 1976-80; Fortune Mag Time Inc, asst circulation dir, 1978-79; Ft Lauderdale's Gay & Lesbian Community Ctr, exec dir; Rainbow Endowment, co-chair bd dirs, currently; Equality Fla, bd dirs, currently; Lambda Legal Defense & Educ Fund, develop dir; Greater New York Campaign United Negro Col Fund, dir; Fortune Circulation Time Inc, nat sales dir; Gay Men African Descent, exec dir. **Honors/Awds:** Black Achievers in Industry Award, Harlem Br YMCA, 1978. **Home Phone:** (954)267-8973. **Business Addr:** Co-Chair, Rainbow Endowment, c/o Friends Ctr, 1501 Cherry St, Philadelphia, PA 19102, **Business Phone:** (215)241-7280.

PETERSEN, ALLAN ERNEST
Manager. **Personal:** Born Dec 13, 1918, New York, NY; married Florence Ridley; children: Robert. **Educ:** W Hervey Bus Col, AD, 1952; City Col NY, 1954. **Career:** Manager (Retired); NY State Div Unemployment Ins, supvr, 1946-52; Our World Mag, bus mgr, 1952-54; Distilled Brands, sales rep, sales mgr, 1954-78; Gotham Merchants Div Peerless Importers, gen sales mgr, 1987. **Orgs:** Nat Asn Advan Colored People; Urban League; Bottle & Cork Sales Club; Nat Negro Golf Asn. **Military Serv:** AUS, lt, 1941-45.

PETERSEN, ARTHUR EVERETT, JR.
Consultant. **Personal:** Born Feb 5, 1949, Baltimore, MD; son of Arthur E Sr and Marguerite. **Educ:** Comm Col Baltimore, AA,urban dev, 1971; Morgan State Univ, BS, urban stud, 1973; Atlanta Univ, MBA, transportation 1975. **Career:** Transp Inst NC A &T State Univ, res assoc, 1975-77; Exec Office Transp & Construct, sr planner, 1977-79; Simpson & Curtin Inc, consult, 1979-80; Lawrence Johnson & Assoc, res assoc, 1980-82; Ctr Transp Studies, Morgan St Univ, proj dir, 1982-83; Pub Tech proj mgr, 1983-88; Baltimore Minority Bus Develop Ctr, procurement specialist, 1986-86; Assoc Enterprises Inc, consult, 1988-89; Boone, Young & Assoc Inc, Baltimore Minority Bus Develop Ctr, Mgt Serv, dir, 1989-92, exec dir; John Milligan& Assoc, PC, Baltimore Minority Bus Develop Ctr, exec dir, 1992-93; David j Burgos & Assoc, Wash, DC, Minority Bus Develop Ctr, bus develop specialist, 1994-96; Coun Econ & Bus Opportunity Inc, dir, contract procurement serv, 1996-2001; AEP advisors, princ cons, 2001-06; Ezcertify.com LLC, vpres, 2006-07; Capital Region Small business Development Center, bus couns, 2007-08; AEP Adv, princ con, currently. **Orgs:** Conf Minority Transp Officials Transp Res Brd, Nat Forum Black Pub Admin, Baltimore Mkt Assn. **Business Addr:** Principal Consultant, AEP Advisors, Metro Area, WA 20001.

PETERSEN, EILEEN RAMONA
Judge, educator, government official. **Personal:** Born Apr 18, 1937, St Croix, Virgin Islands of the United States; daughter of Hugo R and Anna Leevy. **Educ:** Hampton Inst, BA, speech ther & eng, 1958, MA, 1959; Howard Univ, JD, 1966; George Wash Univ, MA, advan studies, 1970. **Career:** Judge (retired), educator; Christian sted High Sch, teacher Eng; Cath Univ PR, Extension Program, instr; US VI, asst atty gen, actg atty gen; Territorial Ct VI, judge. **Orgs:** Am Bar Asn, 1967-; Nat Asn Women Judges; Am Judges Asn; World Assoc Judges World Through Peace Law Ctr; League Womens Voters & Bus & Prof Women's Club; coun mem, VI Coun Boy Scouts Am; bd mem, VI Girl Scouts Am, 1982-85; chmn, VI Casino Control Comn; Int Gaming Regulators; VI Bar Asn; Nat Bar Asn; DC Bar Asn; Am Bar Asn; Nat Asn Women Lawyers; Am Judges Asn & Nat Coun Juvenile Ct Judges. **Honors/Awds:** Outstanding Woman of the Year, Howard Univ, 1970; Women of the Year, Bus & Prof Women's Club, 1976; William Hastie Award, Nat Bar Asn, 1982; Image Award, Nat Asn US VI Affairs; Thurgood Marshall Award, Nat Bar Asn. **Special Achievements:** First Woman to serve as a Judge in the United States Virgin Islands; First female to be selected to the Virgin Islands Council of Boy Scouts of America. **Business Addr:** Member, Virgin Islands Casino Control Commission, Five Orange Grove, St Croix, Virgin Islands of the United States 00820, **Business Phone:** (340)773-3616.

PETERSEN, FRANK EMMANUEL, JR.
Executive. **Personal:** Born Mar 2, 1932, Topeka, KS; son of Edith Sutthard and Frank Emmanuel; married Alicia Joyce Downs, 1975; children: Gayle, Dana, Frank III & Lindsey Monique. **Educ:** George Washington Univ, BS, 1967, MS, 1973. **Career:** Executive (retired); USN, 1950-52; USMC, 1952-88, lt gen, 1986-88, spec asst to chief staff, 1988; Du Pont, vpres. **Orgs:** Tuskegee Airmen, 1960-; Montford Pt Marines, 1960-; chmn, bd dir, Nat Bone Marrow Found, 1988-; bd dir, Higher Educ Assistance Found, 1989-; vpres, Opportunity Skyway, 1990-; IST Study Am Wars, bd dir, 1990-93; Nat Aviation Res & Educ Found, bd dir, 1990-92; Bus Exec Nat Security, 1991-;Nat Asn Advan Colored People. **Honors/Awds:** Man of the Year, Nat Asn Advan Colored People, 1979; Distinguished Graduate, George Washington Univ, 1986; Honarary Doctorate Law, Va Union Univ, 1987; Distinguished Service Medal; Defense Superior Service Medal; Legion of Merit; Distinguished Flying Cross; Purple Heart; Meritorious Service Medal; Air Medal; Navy Commendation Medal; Air Force Commendation Medal. **Special Achievements:** First African American pilot, USMC, 1952; first African American general, USMC, 1979.

PETERSON, ALAN HERBERT
Association executive, writer. **Personal:** Born Jul 9, 1948, East Orange, NJ; son of William Willis (deceased) and Evelyn Lucretia Hughes; married Michelle Monica Morrison Peterson, Sep 27, 1986. **Educ:** Cent Tex Col, Criminal Invest Cert, 1970; LaSalle Law Sch, Cert, 1971; Essex Co Police Acad, 1972; Bergen Co Police Acad, Cert, 1978; Law Enforcement Officers Training Sch, Cert, 1979; Doctor Divinity, 1985; Nat Inst Study Satanology, Las Vegas, NV, cert, 1990. **Career:** Rutgers Univ Police Dept, police officer, 1971-72; East Orange NJ Aux Police, patrolman, 1972-; Essex Co Sheriff's Dept NJ, spec dep, 1972-75; Mod Carpet Serv NJ, vpres, 1972-75; Conrail Police Dept, police officer/investr, 1975-85; Survival Asn, pres & chief exec officer, 1975-; Masters of Philanthropy, chief exec officer, 1982; Suicide Prevention Group PA, exec dir, suicidologist, 1985-; ordained minister, 1985; Law Enforcement Spec Agent, Law Enforcement Div, NJ Soc Prev Cruelty Animals, 1988; US Citizens' Comn Crime & Narcotics, founder, pres & chief exec officer, 1988; Montgomery Co Constable's Off, Precinct 2, ritual crime investr, 1990; US Citizens' Comn Crime & Narcotics, nat exec director, currently. **Orgs:** NJ Narcotic Enforcement Officers Asn NJ, 1976-; Am Criminal Justice Asn, 1979-, Police Benev Asn NJ 304, 1982-; Nat Disabled Law Officers Asn NJ, 1983-; Candlelighters Fnd DC, 1984-; first black sec, 1984, first black pres, 1985 NJ Law Enf Lions Club; Tex Narcotic Officers Asn, 1991-; Tex Ritualistic Crime Info Network, 1991-; Nat Asn Black Achievers, 1990-; nat pres, Nat Police Officers' Asn Am, 1991-; Int Narcotic Enforcement Officers Asn; Nat Org Black Law Enforcement Execs. **Honors/Awds:** Citation Bravery Nat Police Officers Asn Am, Louisville, KY, 1985; Veterans Admin, Leadership Award, 1985, Voluntary Serv Award, 1985; Jerseyan of the Week, Newark, NJ Star Ledger, result of receipt of Citation for Bravery; Cert Appreciation Southern NJ Region Hadassah; Outstanding Community Serv Award, Int Youth Org, 1988; auth: Am Focus on Satanic Crime - Volume 1, 1988, Volume 2, 1990, Volume 3, 1991; Satanic Crime & the SPCA, 1988; Cert Merit, Nat Police Officers' Asn Am, 1989; coproducer, Satanism in Prisons - Video Volume 1; coproducer, Exorcism - Video Volume 1; foreword contribr, The Christian Approach to Spiritual Warfare by Rev Frank M Brim. **Special Achievements:** First black Southern NJ Police Invest Conrail Police Ctr Div, 1978; first black bd mem, vpres, chmn, bd Make A Wish Found NJ, 1983-86; first black Heroism Commendation Recipient from Conrail Police Dept for heroic actions during Jan 7, 1983 Texaco Oil Co explosion, 1984. **Military Serv:** AUS, 1967-70; Vietnam Campaign Medal, Vietnam Serv Medal; Good Conduct Medal. **Home Addr:** 4535 W Sahara Ave Suite 105 126M, Las Vegas, NV 89102. **Business Addr:** National Executive Director, US Citizen's Commission on Crime and Narcotics, PO Box 1092, South Orange, NJ 07079.*

PETERSON, ALPHONSE
Dentist, educator. **Personal:** Born Sep 9, 1926, St Louis, MO; son of Alphonse H Peterson and Pearl Peterson; married Jessie Clark; children: Alphonse Jr, Alan & Alex. **Educ:** Howard Univ, Wash DC, BS, 1948; Meharry Med Col, Sch Dent, Nashville, TN, DDS, 1954; Royal Soc Health, Engl, DDS, 1954; Northwestern Univ Dent Sch, attended 1961; State Univ Iowa, attended 1963; St Louis Univ, attended 1965; Wash Univ Sch Dent, attended 1969; Univ Nebraska Med Ctr, attended 1971; Harvard Univ, attended 1971; Armed Forces Inst Path, attended 1972. **Career:** Gen practe dentist, 1957-; Wash Univ Sch Dent Med, St Louis MO, assoc prof oral diag & radiol, 1972-84; Homer G Phillips Hosp & Ambulatory Ctr, St Louis MO, asst chief, dept oral surg, dir, cardiopulmonary resuscitation educ, 1973-85; Meharry Med Col, Sch Dent, Nashville TN, assoc prof, adj prof, 1981-. **Orgs:** Sec-treas, Guam Dent Soc, 1956-57; pres, Am Acad Dent Electrosurgery, 1977; mem, Downtown St Louis Lions Club, pres, 1983; Kappa Alpha Psi Frat; Pleasant Green Missionary Baptist Church; Chi Delta Mu Med-Dent Fraternity; Thirty third Degree Prince Hall Free Masons; Medinah Temple; bd dir, Ferrier Harris Home Aged; bd dir, St Louis Br Opportunities Industrialization Ctr. **Honors/Awds:** Sixty sixth Ann World Dent Cong Fedn Dentaire Internationale, Madrid Spain, 1978; Hall of Fame, Charles Summer High Sch, 1995. **Special Achievements:** published "Diagnostic Electrosurgery, To Rule In or Out Malignacy of Oral Tissues," Quintessence Intl-Dental Digest, 1977, and "The Use of Electrosurgery in Reconstructive and Cosmetic Maxillofacial Surgery," Dent Clin North Am, 1982; author, "Electrosurgical Correction of Maxillary Double Lip", Dent Digest, 1972; Elected Fel, Am Acad Dent Electrosurgery, 1989; Elected Fel, Am CLG Dentists, 1991; Selected to represent the US at the Third Kenyan-Am Dent Seminar, Nairobi, Kenya, 1973; elected Fel, Royal Soc Health, Eng, 1972; mem Kappa Sigma Pi Scholastic Hon Frat; mem Gamma Chap, Omicron Kappa Upsilon Nat Dent Hon Soc; lect "The Use of Electrosurgery in Reconstructive Surgery of the Tongue, Lip, Ear and Nose. **Military Serv:** USF, oral surg resident, capt, 1955-57, chief oral surg, maj, 1970-72. **Business Addr:** 3737 N Kingshighway Blvd, Saint Louis, MO 63115, **Business Phone:** (314)261-5176.

PETERSON, ANTHONY WAYNE. See PETERSON, TONY.

PETERSON, COLEMAN HOLLIS
Executive, president (organization). **Personal:** Born Apr 6, 1948, Birmingham, AL; son of George and Doris; married Shirley, May 31, 1975; children: Rana & Collin. **Educ:** Loyola Univ, BA, 1972, MS, 1977. **Career:** Venture Stores, dist personnel mgr, 1978-79, regional personnel mgr, 1979-82, vpres, Organizational Devel, 1982-84, sr vice pres, Human Resources, 1984-94; Wal-Mart Stores Inc, exec vice pres, people div, 1994-2004; Hollis Enterprises, LLC, pres & chief exec officer, 2004-. **Orgs:** Life mem, Kappa Alpha Psi Fraternity; Sigma Pi Phi Fraternity; Nat Asn Advan Colored People; mem advisory Bds, Univ Fl, Florida A&M Univ; fel, Nat Acad Human Resources; bd mem, Northwest Ark Community Col. **Honors/Awds:** Award of Excellence, Soc Human Resource Mgt, 1998; Executive of the Year, Black Retail Action Group, 1998; Hon doctorate, Smith Col, 2003; Award for Professional Excellence, Soc Human Resource Mgt, 2004; Martin Luther Kind Lifetime Achievement Award, 2007. **Business Addr:** President, Chief Executive Officer, Hollis Enterprises LLC, 1204 SE 28th St Suite 14, Bentonville, AR 72712, **Business Phone:** (479)254-3642.

PETERSON, GERARD M.
Government official. **Personal:** Born Sep 10, 1932, Hartford, CT; son of Edythe and Rufus; divorced; children: Brian & Bradford. **Educ:** Univ Connecticut, BA, econ, 1957; Cert Data Processing, 1965. **Career:** Aetna Life & Casualty, admin roles, 1957-69, dir mkg, 1974-83; OUR Corp, pres, 1969-72; Nat Alliance Businessmen, exec vpres, 1969-70; Stanford Univ, asst dean grad sch bus, 1970-73; Star Lite Indust, dir, 1970-71; Hartford Civic Ctr, exec dir & CEO, 1983-93; Johnson Controls Inc, proj mgr, 1995-96; GMP Enterprises, gen mgr, currently. **Orgs:** Alpha Phi Alpha; Nat Asn Advan Colored People; Urban League; Int Asn Auditorium Mgrs; chmn, Greater Hartford Red Cross; dir & trustee, Hartford Club; Hartford Hosp; St Francis Hosp; Kaisen Permanente; St Joseph Col; Bay Bank Connecticut; comm, US Golf Asn. **Honors/Awds:** Arena & Manager of the Year, Performance Mag Readers Poll, 1986. **Military Serv:** AUS, corporal, 1953-55.

PETERSON, JAMES
Guitarist, singer. **Personal:** Born Nov 4, 1937, Russell County, AL; children: Judge Kenneth "Lucky" Peterson. **Career:** Musician, 1952-; club owner, 1965-80; recording artist, 1970-; Albums: The Father, The Son, & The Blues, 1970; Rough & Ready, 1990; Too Many Knots for the Kingsnake, 1991; Don't Let the Devil Ride, 1995; Preachin' the Blues, 1996; Wrong Bed!, 1999. **Business Addr:** Singer, HownDog Records & Artist Management, PO Box 1742, Palmetto, FL 34220, **Business Phone:** (941)729-0758.*

PETERSON, LLOYD
School administrator. **Personal:** Born Jul 20, 1958, San Antonio, TX; son of Lloyd Peterson, Sr and Dorothy Garrett Phifer; mar-

ried Debra Gay Culbertson; children: Jaela Culbertson Grayson. **Educ:** CO State Univ, BA, eng, 1980, MA, 1982. **Career:** Colo State Univ, admis counr, 1982-83; Colo Col, asst dir admis; Yale Univ, assoc dir admis; Vassar Col, dir admis; Col Coach, vpres educ, 2002-. **Orgs:** Bd dir, Jolly Jills Civic & Social Club, 1983-; bd dir, Urban League Colo Springs, 1984-. **Honors/Awds:** Mem Outstanding Young Men of America, 1983. **Special Achievements:** First vice president of El Paso County Black Caucus, 1984-86. **Home Addr:** 1224 N Weber Suite 8, Colorado Springs, CO 80903. **Business Addr:** Vice President of Education, College Coach, 233 Needham St Suite 200, Newton, MA 02464, **Business Phone:** (617)527-4441.

PETERSON, PROF. LORNA INGRID
Librarian. **Personal:** Born Jul 22, 1956, Buffalo, NY; daughter of Raymond George and Sybil Odette Lythcott. **Educ:** Dickinson Col, Carlisle, PA, BA, 1977; Case Western Res Univ, Cleveland, OH, MS libr sci, 1980; Iowa State Univ, PhD, 1992. **Career:** Wright State Univ, Dayton, OH, humanities ref libr & spec col cataloger, 1980-81; Ohio Univ, Athens, OH, spec col cataloger, 1982-82; Iowa State Univ, Ames, IA, cataloger, 1983-85, bibliog instr, 1985-91; State Univ NY Buffalo, Buffalo, NY, asst prof, assoc prof, Sch Libr & Information Studies, currently. **Orgs:** Black Caucus Am Libr Asn, 1980, 1988-; bd mem, Ames, ISU YWCA, 1984-89; chair communs comt, Iowa Libr Asn; Asn Col Res Librs, 1984-86; rep Am Libr Asn; RTSD Org & Bylaws, Am Libr Asn, 1984-86; chair mem comt, Iowa Libr Asn; Asn Col Res Librs, 1987-88; African Am Librn Asn Western NY, 1990-; Am Libr Asn; RASD & MOPSS, Catalog comt, 1992-96; Am Libr Asn-Lirt Res comt, 1994-96; Am Libr Asn; Asn Col Res Librs; BIS, Educ Biblio Instr, 1994-96; comt Accreditation, 1997-2001. **Home Addr:** 1088 Delaware Ave Apt 7C, Buffalo, NY 14209-1628, **Home Phone:** (716)886-1973. **Business Addr:** Associate Professor, The State University of New York, 534 Baldy Hall, Buffalo, NY 14260, **Business Phone:** (716)645-2412 Ext 1165.

PETERSON, ROCKY LEE
Lawyer. **Personal:** Born Apr 29, 1952, New York, NY; son of Natalia Lee; married Paulette Sapp, Dec 21, 1985; children: Malik, Danita & Corrie. **Educ:** Cornell Univ, BA, 1974, JD, 1977. **Career:** Admin Office Courts, clerk-civil pract, 1977-78; NJ Div Criminal Justice, deputy atty gen, 1978-83; Hill Wallack, partner, 1983-; City Trenton, city atty, 1990-98. **Orgs:** Bd trustees, Nat Asn Advan Colored People, 1988-89; YMCA, 1988-89; Granville Acad, 1988-89; NJ Bar Asn Minorities Profession, 1988-; Mercer Cty Bar Asn, 1989-; Disciplinary Review Bd NJ Supreme Ct, 1991-; Kappa Alpha Psi, 1993-. **Honors/Awds:** Service Award, NJ Bar Minorities iProfession, 1995; Service Award, Crossroads Theatre Co, 1994. **Business Addr:** Attorney, Partner, Hill Wallack, 202 Carnegie Ctr, Princeton, NJ 08540, **Business Phone:** (609)924-0808.

PETERSON, TONY (ANTHONY WAYNE PETERSON)
Football player. **Personal:** Born Jan 23, 1972, Cleveland, OH; married Anita; children: Anthony. **Educ:** Notre Dame Univ. **Career:** San Francisco 49ers, linebacker, 1994-96, 1998-2000; Chicago Bears, 1997;Wash Redskins, 2000; Univ Minn, passing game coordr, currently. **Business Addr:** Passing Game Coordinator, University of Minnesota, 321 Nineteenth Ave S Suite 4-201, Minneapolis, MN 55455, **Business Phone:** (612)624-0875.

PETETT, FREDDYE J WEBB
Association executive. **Personal:** Born Dec 27, 1943, Monroe, LA; daughter of Barbara Mansfield; divorced; children: Andre. **Educ:** Portland State Univ, BS, bus admin, 1973; Union Inst Cincinnati, OH, PhD, sociol. **Career:** Portland Community Col, programmer analyst, 1969-70; Portland Model Cities, syst coordr, 1970-71; Nero & Assocs, proj dir, 1971-73; Off Emergency Servs, coordr, 1973-74; Crime & Prevention Bur, dir, 1974-76; Mayors Off City Portland, asst to mayor, 1976-79; Portland Urban League, exec dir; 1979-86; State Ore, pub welfare admin, 1987-90; W K Kellogg Found, Battle Creek, MI, assoc prog dir, 1990-92, Kellogg Int Leadership Prog, dir, 1993-98, Found's Mid S Delta Initiative, coordr, 1998-2005; Univ Ark, Clinton Sch, asst prof leadership & philanthropy, Ctr Community Philanthropy, founding dir, emer asst prof, currently. **Orgs:** Bd dir, Housing Auth Portland; Delta Sigma Theta Sorority; World Affairs Coun; bd mem, Fed Home Loan Bank Seattle; Battle Creek Urban League. **Honors/Awds:** Woman of Excellence, Delta Sigma Theta Sorority, 1985. **Special Achievements:** Author: My Life's Journey in Voices of Women Moving Forward with Dignity & Wholeness, 1995. **Business Addr:** Emeritus Assistant Professor, University of Arkansas, Clinton School of Public Service, Sturgis Hall 1200 President Clinton Ave, Little Rock, AR 72201, **Business Phone:** (501)683-5200.

PETIONI, DR. MURIEL M
Educator, physician. **Personal:** Born Jan 1, 1914; children: Charles M Woolfolk. **Educ:** New York Univ, attended, 1930-32; Howard Univ, BS, 1934, MD, 1937; Harlem Hosp, Internship, 1937-39. **Career:** Educator, physician (Retired); New York City Dept Health, sch phys, 1950-80, pvt prac, 1950; NY Health & Hosp Corp Harlem Hosp, med staff, 1960-80; New York City Dept Health, supervisor, sch phys, 1980-84; Harlem Hosp Dept Peds, supervising phys & consult, 1982-; Dept Peds Columbia Univ, asst clin prof, 1982-85; Harlem Hosp Ctr, founder, chair, pres bd dirs, 1987. **Orgs:** Nat Med Asn; Doctors Coun City NY, 1950-80; Empire State Med Asn; tres, Manhattan Ctr Med Asn; Am Acad Family Phys; Howard Univ Med Alumni Asn; founder pres, Susan SmithMcKinney Steward Med Asn, 1974-84; founder, chairperson, Med Women NMA, 1977-83; tres, Doctors Coun City NY, 1980-84; Upper Manhattan Empowerment Zone, founding mem, bd mem, 1995-2000; pres, Trinidade & Tobago Gyap Orgn; Delta Sigma Theta Soc; Coalition of 100 Black Women; New York City Dept Health Child Health Forum; Nat Asn Advan Colored People; NY Urban League; pres, Howard Univ Med Alumni Asn, Trinidad & Tobago Gayap Org; Manhattan Cent Med Soc; adv coun, Breast Exam Clin Harlem; Empire State Med Asn; adv coun, Columbia Univ Coun Social Work; bd mem, Schomburg Ctr Res Black Cult; bd mem, Handmaids of Mary; bd mem, Harlem Coun Elders; bd mem, Sister to Sister; bd mem, Greater Harlem Nursing Home; community adv bd, Harlem Health Promotional Ctr; NYC & Harlem br, Am Cancer Soc. **Honors/Awds:** Woman of year, Morrisania Youth & Comm Serv Ctr Inc,1969; Awards Black Found, Res & Ed Sickle Cell Disease, 1973; First Harlem Humanitarian Award, NY Coun Churchs, 1975; Martin Luther King, Jr Democrates Salute, 1975; Harlem Br YMCA World Serv Award, Harlem YMCA 1978; Women of Year, Everybody's Mag, 1979; Practitioner of Year, Nat Med Asn, 1979; Distinguished Service Award, Lehman HS Bio-Med Inst, 1981; Professional ed Award Harlem Unit/Am Cancer Soc 1982; Black Acheivement Award Comm Church, NY 1983; Cert Pioneer Treatment Drug Abuse Edward I Koch Mayor, City of NY, 1983; Harlem Week 83 Health Serv Award, Harlem Week Inc, 1983; Harlem Hosp Meritorious Serv Award, Harlem Hosp Ctr & NY Heallth & Hosp Corp, 1983; Whitney M Young Jr Comm Relations Award, Annual African-Am Heroes & Heroines Day, 1984; Distinguished Service Award Doctors Coun, 1984; Distinguished Alumni Award, Howard Univ, 2000; Renaissance Award, Abyssinian Develop Corp, 2001; Generations Public Serv Award, City Col NY, 2002; Mary McLeod Bethune Award, Nat Coun Negro Women, 2003; Community Service Award, Thurgood Marshall Acad, 2003. **Special Achievements:** Ed, dept award City Tabernacle SDA,Chruch 1979; spec recognition Muriel Petioni MD Founder NMA Women Med Task Force, Conserns of Women Phys. **Home Addr:** 114 W 131st, New York, NY 10027, **Home Phone:** (212)926-2464.

PETRICK, PHD, JANE ALLEN
Psychologist, journalist. **Personal:** Born Apr 12, 1945, Bridgeport, CT; daughter of William A Allen and Jane Briscoe; married John Andrew Banyat; married Jonathan Schiesel; children: Seth Briscoe Schiesel. **Educ:** Barnard Col, BA, 1967; Teacher's Col, Columbia Univ, NY, MA, 1970; State Univ New York, Albany, NY, MS, 1980; Saybrook Inst, San Francisco, CA, PhD, 1985. **Career:** Univ Calif, Berkeley, fac; Herbert H Lehman Col, fac; State Univ NY, Albany, fac; Ulster County Community Col, fac; JEA Assocs, Woodstock, NY, pres, 1977-89; Knight-Ridder Inc, Miami, FL, internal consult, 1989-; Knight-Ridder News Serv, Wash, DC, columnist, 1989-; Miami Herald Publ Co, Miami, FL, columnist, 1989-; Capella Univ Grad Sch Bus, prof, currently; Good Catch Publishing, proj mgr/ed, currently; Informed Decisions Int, vpres, currently. **Orgs:** Am Psychol Asn, 1978-; Soc Indust Orgn Psychologists, 1980-. **Special Achievements:** Author: Beyond Time Management: Organizing the Organization, Addison-Wesley, 1985; Making the Connection: Getting Work to Work, Informed Decisions Publising, 1995. **Business Phone:** 800-632-7246.

PETROCELLI, HERNANDO. See HARRIS, PEP.

PETTAWAY, CHARLES
Educator, pianist. **Personal:** Born Jun 7, 1949, Philadelphia, PA; son of Charles Henry and Lorraine Thornton; divorced; children: Ashley. **Educ:** Philadelphia Mus Acad, BM, 1971; Fontainbleau Acad France, attended 1973; Ravel Acad France, cert, 1974; Temple Univ, MM, 1976. **Career:** Lincoln Univ, Lincoln, PA, tenured prof music, assoc prof music & interim dept chair, visual & performing arts, currently; Musical performances: Tour Switz summer, 1981; Great Hall Moscow Conserv, Russia; Carnegie Hall, NY; Acad Music Philadelphia; Philharmonic Hall, NY; Yacht Club Chicago; Boston Univ; Music Hall Ciboure; Palais de Fontainebleau France; Center Col, KY; Windsor Sch, NC; Tanglewood Music Fest Recanti Auditorium Tel Aviv, Israel; Kennedy Ctr, Wash, DC; Orchestra Hall, Chicago; Settlement Sch Music, concert pianist & teacher. **Orgs:** Bd mem, Manyunk Coun Arts, 1990-; bd mem, Philadelphia Gospel Sem, 1996; founding mem, Bonalis Piano Trio, 2001. **Honors/Awds:** First Place Winner, Robert Casadesus Int Int Piano Competition, France, 1974; De Bose Artist, Southern Univ, Baton Rouge, LA, 1997; First Prize, Bartok-Kabalevsky Int Piano Competition, Radford VA, 1998. **Special Achievements:** Article published in Society Newsletter (musical publication) "The American Audience" 1984, first commercial recording released "Charles Pettaway Performs Music by Russian Composers" 1985. **Home Phone:** (215)706-0617. **Business Addr:** Associate Professor of Music, Interim Department Chair, Visual and Performing Arts, Lincoln University, Department of Visual and Performing Arts, 144 Ware Ctr, Lincoln, PA 19352, **Business Phone:** (610)932-8300 Ext 7419.

PETTIES, CAROLYN D.
Manager. **Career:** MATA, Human Resource mgr. **Orgs:** Dir, Mid-South Transp Mgt.

PETTIGREW, GRADY L., JR.
Judge. **Personal:** Born Jun 21, 1943, Forrest City, AR; married Carolyn Landers; children: Dawn Karima, Grady Landers. **Educ:** Ohio State Univ, BA, 1965; Howard Univ Sch Law, attended 1969; Ohio State Univ, JD, 1971. **Career:** Columbus State Hosp, activities therapist, 1965; Huntington Nat Bank Columbus, mgr trainee, 1968; Legal Aid Agency DC, investr law clerk, 1969; Vorys Sater Seymour & Pease, assoc atty, 1971-77; US Bankruptcy Court, judge, 1977-86; Arter & Hadden, partner; Pettigrew And Associate, Partner, 2000-. **Orgs:** Columbus & Ohio State Bar Asn; Am Bar Asn; corr sec, Robert B Elliott Law Club, 1977-, Nat Conf Bankruptcy Judges; Law Capital Univ; Ohio State Univ; bd trustees chmn, Community Develop Comt Ctrl Community House, 1972-75; bd trustees, Ecco Manor, 1973; United Way Franklin City, 1974-75; solicitor, Village Urbancrest OH, 1975-76. **Honors/Awds:** Nat Moot Ct Championship Young Lawyers Comt, NY Bar Asn, 1971; Outstanding Young Men Am Chicago, 1972. **Military Serv:** AUS, 1st Lt, 2 yrs. **Business Addr:** Partner, Pettigrew And Associate LLC, 1 Columbus, 115 W Main St Ste 400, Columbus, OH 43215-5099.

PETTIGREW, DR. L EUDORA
School administrator, educator. **Personal:** Born Mar 1, 1928, Hopkinsville, KY; daughter of Warren C and Corrye L Newell; children: Peter W Woodard. **Educ:** WVa State Col, BMus, 1950; Southern Ill Univ, MA, counseling, 1964, PhD, educ psychol, 1966. **Career:** Southern Ill Univ, instr, 1964-66; Univ Bridgeport, assoc prof, 1966-70; Mich State Univ, prof, chair, 1970-80; Univ Del, assoc provost, 1981-86; SUNY Col, Old Westbury, pres, 1986-97. **Orgs:** Am Asn State Col & Univs, 1991-94; N Am Coun IAUP, exec bd, 1992-; Long Island Forum Technol, 1987-; Long Island Reg Adv Coun Higher Educ, 1986-, chair, 1988-91; adv com, Economists Allied Arms Reduction, 1996; Int Asn Univ Presidents (IAUP/UN), chair, Comm Disarmament Educ, Conflict Resolution & Peace, 1996-; Comm Univ Peace, Costa Rica, 1997; bd, Univ Pretoria Fund, SAfrica, 1997. **Honors/Awds:** BWA Achievement Award, Black Women's Agenda Inc, 1988; Woman of the Year, Nassau/Suffolk (NY) Coun Ade Women Edu, 1989; Distinguished Educ Leadership Award, Long Island Women's Coun Equal Edu, Training & Employ, 1989; Distinguished Alumna Award, Nat Asn Equal Opportunity Higher Educ, 1990; Long Island Distinguished Leadership Award, Long Island Bus News, 1990; Distinguished Black Woman Educ Award, NCW Inc, 1991; Distinguished Alumna, Southern Ill Univ, 1997. **Special Achievements:** Papers submitted on, "Old Westbury: Access and Excellence for All," Campus Commentary: SUNY Research '88, Albany, NY, Jan-Feb 1988; " Business, Industry and Universities: Partners for Multicultural Education," guest column, Economic Times of Long Island, Mineola, NY, Feb 1990; Int Conf on the New Role of Higher Educ in the Context of an Independent Palestinian State, An-Najah Natl Unit, Nablus, Palestine, guest speaker, Nov 1996; conducted workshop "Conflict Resolution the Woman's Role in Our World," UN Conference on Women, China, 1995; Numerous guest lectures. **Business Phone:** (516)876-3160.

PETTIS, BRIDGET
Basketball player. **Personal:** Born Jan 1, 1971. **Educ:** Univ Fla, attended 1993. **Career:** Fenerbache, guard, 1993-95; Anatalya Koleji, Turkey, 1995-96; Faenza, Italy, 1996-97; Phoenix Mercury, 1997-2001; Ind Fever, guard, 2002-03; Phoenix Mercury, asst coach, 2006-. **Business Addr:** Assistant Coach, Phoneix Mercury, 201 East Jefferson St, Phoenix, AZ 85004, **Business Phone:** (602)514-8331.*

PETTIS, GARY GEORGE
Baseball player, athletic coach. **Personal:** Born Apr 3, 1958, Oakland, CA; married Peggy; children: Paige, Shaye, Kyler & Dante. **Educ:** Laney Col, Oakland, CA. **Career:** Baseball player, (retired), Athletic coach; California Angels, 1982-87, Detroit Tigers, 1988-89, 1992; Tex Rangers, 1990-91; San Diego Padres, 1992; Oakland Athletics, 1993; Chicago White Sox, coach, 2001-02; New York Mets, coach, 2003-04; Nashville Sounds, hitting coach, 2005-06; Tex Rangers, coach, 2006-. **Honors/Awds:** A.L. Gold Glove Award, 1985-86, 1988-90. **Business Phone:** (817)273-5222.*

PETTIS, DR. JOYCE OWENS
Educator. **Personal:** Born Mar 14, 1946, Columbia, NC; daughter of Howard and Victoria Hill; married Bobby (deceased); children: Darryl; married Enoch Charles Temple. **Educ:** Winston Salem State Univ, BA, 1968; E Carolina Univ, MA, 1974; Univ NC Chapel Hill, PhD, 1983. **Career:** NC Pub Schs, teacher, 1968-71; Pitt Tech Inst, teacher, 1972-74; Carolina Univ, asst prof Eng, 1974-85; NC State Univ, asst prof eng, prof English, prof emer, 2006-. **Orgs:** Alpha Kappa Alpha; Popular Cult Asn; Col Lang Asn; NC History Summer Inst, 1984; Summer Inst Inc New Scholar Women, 1984. **Honors/Awds:** Minority Presence Fel, Univ NC, 1978-80; UNC Board of Gov Doctoral Award, Univ NC, 1981; National Humanities Faculty Member Award, 1984; Scholar Award, Col Lang Asn. **Home Addr:** 1108 Cedarhurst Dr, Raleigh, NC 27609. **Business Addr:** Professor Emeritus, North Carolina

State University, Department of English, Rm 221 246 Tompkins Hall, PO Box 8105, Raleigh, NC 27695-8105, **Business Phone:** (919)515-3866.

PETTWAY, JO CELESTE
Judge. **Personal:** Born Mar 18, 1952, Consul, AL; daughter of Joseph and Menda G. **Educ:** Auburn Univ, BA, 1973; The Univ Ala, BSW, 1976, MSW, 1978, JD, 1982. **Career:** Children's Aid Soc, social worker, 1975-77; Jefferson Co Dept Pensions & Security, social worker, 1977; Miles Col, instr social work, 1978-79; Legal Serv Corp Ala, clerk, 1980; England & Bivens PC, assoc, 1982-84; Jo Celeste Pettway Atty Law, solo practitioner, 1984; Wilcox County, district judge 1984-, chair currently. **Orgs:** Nat Bar Asn; Am Bar Asn; Nat Asn Women Judges; Nat Asn Juvenile & Family Ct Judges; Ala Lawyers Asn; pres, Zeta Eta Omega Chap Alpha Kappa Alpha Sor Inc; bd dirs, Health Improvement Project; Nat Coun Negro Women; Past Basileus - Zeta Eta Omega Chapter Alpha Kappa Alpha Sor Inc. **Honors/Awds:** Outstanding Achievement Award, BLSA Univ Ala; Outstanding Alumni, Black Law Students Asn, Univ Ala, 1987; Humanitarian Award Concordia Col, 1988; Soror of the Year, South Eastern Region, 1989. **Business Addr:** District Judge, State of Alabama District Court Wilcox County, PO Box 549, Camden, AL 36726-0549, **Business Phone:** (334)682-4619.

PETTY, BOB
Journalist, television news anchorperson. **Personal:** Born Nov 26, 1940, Memphis, TN; married Cora; children: Bobby & Cory. **Educ:** Ariz State Univ, BS, 1970; Gov State Univ, MS, commun, 1979. **Career:** KAET TV, Tempe, Ariz, news cameraman, soundman, film ed & lighting dir, 1968; KPHO TV News, 1969; KOOL TV News, writer, reporter & producer, 1969-71; Univ Chicago, urban jour fel prog, 1970, William Benton fel prog, 1986; ABC 7 Chicago, weekend anchor, reporter & host, 1971-2002, Action 7, reporter, 1975-77, "Weekend Ed", host, 1978-83. **Orgs:** Mem fundraising comn, Hyde Park YMCA; Provident St Mel Cath HS only black cath HS Chicago's Westside. **Honors/Awds:** William Benton Fellow in broadcast journalism, 1987. **Special Achievements:** One of several black broadcasters honores by Club Date Magazine of Chicago 1974.

PETTY, JERVIE SCOTT
Educator. **Personal:** Born Jan 28, 1947, Andrews, SC; daughter of Leroy Scott and Carrie Scott; married John Anthony, Nov 1, 1969; children: Donoval Anthony, William Scott & Lynnette Maria. **Educ:** Allen Univ, attended 1967; NC A&T State Univ, BS, 1970; Bowie State Univ, MEd, 1981. **Career:** Lackey High Sch, fac; Thomas Stone High Sch, Waldorf, Md, vice prin, 1987-94; Somers Middle Sch, LaPlata, Md, prin, 1994-98; Henry E Lackey High Sch, Charles County, Md, prin, currently. **Orgs:** Charter pres, Delta Sigma Theta Sorority, Ft Washington Alumnae Chap, 1990-94; pres, Metropolitan Prince George's Chap, Nat Polit Cong Black Women; Nat Asn Sec Sch Prin; Md Asn Sec Sch Prin. **Honors/Awds:** Outstanding & Dedicated Service, Ebenezer AME Church Usher Bd, 1990; Outstanding Principal Award, Washington Post, 2000; Outstanding Educator Award, Coalition Concerned Black Christian Men, 2001. **Home Addr:** 114 Cross Foxes Dr, Fort Washington, MD 20744. **Business Addr:** Principal, Henry E Lackey High Sch, 3000 Chicamuxen Rd, Indian Head, MD 20646, **Business Phone:** (301)743-5431.

PETTY, OSCAR
Educator, musician. **Personal:** Born Apr 5, 1960, Newark, NJ; son of Oscar Petty, Sr and Bessie. **Educ:** Montclair State Univ, BMusic, 1984; Rutgers Univ, MMusic, 1993. **Career:** Orange Public Schs, music educator, woodwinds, 1985-89; Orchestra of Saint Peter by the Sea, principal oboe, 1986-92; Roselle Public Schs, music educator, band, 1990-94; Arts High Sch, Newark, fac, 1994-. **Orgs:** Amer Fed Musicians, 1987-; Int Double Reed Soc, 1997-; Day Nursery Mountclair NJ Bd, 1999; Arts High Sch, Whole Sch Reform Committee, 1996-99. **Honors/Awds:** Aspen Music School Fel, oboe, 1983; Newark Municipal Coun, Jazz Education, Youth, 1999; Orchestra at William Paterson Univ, Outstanding Music Educator, 2002. **Special Achievements:** First African American solo oboist to record a classical CD with a symphony orchestra, 1994. **Business Addr:** Teacher of Woodwinds/Music Theory, Arts High School, Music Department, 550 Dr Martin Luther King Blvd, Newark, NJ 07102, **Business Phone:** (973)733-7102.

PETTY, DR. RACHEL MONTEITH
Psychologist, educator. **Personal:** Born Jun 21, 1943, Columbia, SC; daughter of Frank H Sr (deceased) and Susie E; married LaSalle Petty Jr, Sep 3, 1966; children: Adrienne & Erin. **Educ:** Howard Univ, BS, 1964, MS, 1968; Univ Md, PhD, 1980. **Career:** Howard Univ, lecturer 1968-71; Prince Geo Pub Sch, sch psychol, 1968-72; DC Pub Sch, sch psychol, 1967-68; Univ DC, chairperson & asst prof psychol, assoc prof psychol, dean currently. **Orgs:** Asn Black Psychol; AAAS; Md Asn Sch Psychol; res Black Child; consult, DC Dept Human Services, 1987-88; consult, psych St Ann's Infant Home Hyattsville, MD, 1974-; bd mem, Lutheran Soc Serv Nat Capital Area, 1989-. **Home Addr:** 2124 Sudbury Place NW, Washington, DC 20012, **Home Phone:** (202)829-4533. **Business Addr:** Dean, University of the District of Columbia, College Of Arts And Science, Rm 405 Bldg 41 4200 Connecticut Ave NW, Washington, DC 20008, **Business Phone:** (202)274-5707.

PETTY-EDWARDS, LULA EVELYN
School administrator. **Personal:** Born Mar 10, 1945, Cedar Bluff, MS; daughter of William Jr and Omy A Deans; married Ozzie L Edwards; children: Brett Tirrell Edwards, Daryl Westfield Edwards & Omy Lela Edwards. **Educ:** Mary Holmes Col, assoc deg, 1965; Knoxville Col, BD, 1968; Ill State Univ, MD, 1973. **Career:** Univ Mich, lectr, 1974-78; Mary Holmes Col, fac, Dir Reading Ctr, dir, Alumni, 1980-81; Univ Louisville, part-time fac, 1982-85; Imani Inst, pvt elem sch Roxbury, MA, co-found; N eastern Univ, coord, reading, writing, study skills, 1985-93, asst dir, acad & cult prog, 1989-93, assoc dean, dir, special asst to dean, currently. **Orgs:** Nat Coun Teachers Eng; Nat Asn Stud Personnel Adminrs; Black Educator's Alliance MA; Nat Polit Congress Black Women Inc. **Honors/Awds:** Positive Force Award, Northeastern Univ, Black Stud Asn, 1986-88; Black Women Achievers Award, African Methodist Episcopal Women, New Eng Area, 1991; Distinguished Alumni Award, Nat Asn Equal Opportunity Higher Educ, 1995. **Business Addr:** Special Assistant to Dean, Northeastern University, College of Arts & Sciences, 360 Huntington Ave, Boston, MA 02115, **Business Phone:** (617)373-3996.

PEYTON, JASPER E.
Administrator. **Personal:** Born Dec 30, 1926, Richmond, VA; widowed; children: Rose La Verne Abernathy. **Educ:** Univ Philippines, attended 1946; City Col NY, 1952. **Career:** Local 66 Int Ladies Garment Workers, trade unionists, shop steward, 1952-64; ILGWU, educ dept, 1963-82; Civil Rights Comm Dir Educ, exec bd mem dir, 1965-69, asst dir educ. **Orgs:** Council Chs Brooklyn Div; Assoc minister Bethany Bapt Ch; bd dir, CLICK-COMMERCE Labor Industry Corp of Kings for Brooklyn Navy Yard; bd mem, Fulton Art Fair. **Honors/Awds:** Award, Pub Rel Dir Bethany Bapt Ch. **Military Serv:** AUS, sgt. *

PHARRIS, CHRYSTEE
Actor, singer. **Personal:** Born Mar 7, 1976; married Tron Larkins, Aug 29, 2003. **Educ:** Emerson Col, BFA, theater. **Career:** Films: Understanding Me; Guilty or Not, 1999; Let's Be Real, 2000; Leprechaun in the Hood, 2000; Buds for Life, 2004; Paved with Good Intentions, 2006; Only in Your Dreams, 2006; Lord Help Us, 2007; My girl friend's back; TV Series: WB, "The Steve Harvey Show", 1998; WB, "Sister Sister", 1998; UPN,"Moesha", 1998; NPN, "Grown Ups", 2000; WB, "7th Heaven", 2000; ABC,"General Hosp", 2000; "Eve", 2004; "Scrubs", 2005; "Cuts", 2005;"Teachers", 2006; "Passions", 2006; "All of Us", 2006; "Lincoln Heights", 2007. **Orgs:** Faithful Cent Bible Church; Save Our Youth. **Business Addr:** Actress, Coast to Coast Talent Group, 3350 Barham Blvd, Los Angeles, CA 90068, **Business Phone:** (323)845-9200.

PHELPS, CONSTANCE KAY
School administrator, educator. **Personal:** Born Sep 16, 1940, Topeka, KS; daughter of Lucille Mallory Phelps and C Kermit Phelps. **Educ:** St Marys Col, BA, 1962; Wash Univ, St Louis, AM, 1970, PhD, 1977; Ctr Concern, Wash, DC, 1986; Bryn Mawr, 1991. **Career:** Denver Parochial Sch Syst, teacher, 1962-68; St Mary Col, prof sociol, 1970-; Long Range Planning proj, proj mgr, 1977-78, dean students, 1986-95, vpres stud life, 1995, interim pres, 1997; Harvard MIT, research asst 1970; Comn Crisis Intervention Ctr, res asst, 1974-75; HEW, grant reviewer, 1979; Carroll Col, bd trustees, currently; St Francis Health Ctr, bd mem, currently. **Orgs:** Sisters Charity Leavenworth, 1959-; Am Soc Assoc, 1969-; on campus coordr, small col consortium, Wash, DC, 1977-80; consult, Nat Consult Network,1977-; assoc mem, Danforth Asn, 1980; asst documents, Ghana Mission UN,1981; coordr, Social Justice Network Sisters Charity Leavenworth, 1985; bd dir, Leavenworth City-County Alcohol & Drug Abuse Coun, 1985; Civilian Based Defense, 1986; bd dirs, St Vincent Clin, 1988-94; Catholic Social Serv, 1988-93; consult & evaluator, N Cent Asn Cols & Schs, 1988-; Nat Asn Stud Personnel Admin; chair, Leavenworth County Human Rels Comn, 1990-; bd dirs, Providence & Saint John Hosp, 1997-; bd dirs, Leavenworth Catholic Schs, 1997-. **Honors/Awds:** Nat Delta Epsilon Sigma Acad Honor Soc, 1970-; fel, Hamline Univ, 1973; fel, Wash Univ, 1973-75; Fulbright Hays fel, Ghana, W Africa, 1975-76. **Business Addr:** Board of Trustees, Carroll College, 1601 N Benton Ave, Helena, MT 59625, **Business Phone:** (406)447-4300.

PHIFER, B JANELLE BUTLER
Lawyer. **Personal:** Born Jul 26, 1949, Springfield, MA. **Educ:** Howard Univ Sch Bus, BA, 1971; Howard Univ Sch Law, JD, 1975; Ohio State Bar, 1975. **Career:** State Ohio, asst atty gen, 1975-78; Toledo Legal Aid Soc, exec dir, 1978-; Toledo Legal Aid Soc, staff atty, 1990-; Munic Ct, chair, currently. **Orgs:** Toledo Bar Asn; pres, Thurgood Marshall Law Asn; Toledo Chap, The Links Inc; Delta Sigma Theta Sorority, Toledo Alumnae Chap; Jack & Jill Inc, Toledo Chap; co-leader, troop 1077, Maumee Valley Girl Scout Coun; St Paul Baptist Church. **Honors/Awds:** Outstanding Young Women of America; Delta Sigma Theta Sor Toledo Alumnal Chap; Outstanding Professional Develop, Toledo Legal Aid, 1982, 1992; Woman of the Year in Law, Model Neighborhood Develop Asn, 1983; Certificate of Appreciation, Supreme Court Ohio Continuing Legal Educ Comn, 1989, 1990; ProBono Pub-Toledo Bar Asn, 1990. **Business Addr:** Chairperson, Municipal Court, **Business Phone:** (419)724-0030.

PHIFER, MEKHI (MEKHI THIRA PHIFER)
Actor, rap musician, movie director. **Personal:** Born Dec 29, 1974, Harlem, NY; married Malinda Williams, Jan 1, 1999 (divorced 2003); children: Omikaye; children: Mekhi Thira Phifer Jr. **Career:** Films: Clockers, 1995; Sureshot, 1996; Girl 6, 1996; High School High, 1996; Hav Plenty, 1997; Soul Food, 1997; Hell's Kitchen, 1998; I Still Know What You Did Last Summer, 1998; Lover Man, 1998; An Invited Guest, 2000; Shaft, 2000; Head Games, 2001; O, 2001; The Other Brother, 2002; Imposter, 2001; Paid in Full, 2002; 8 Mile, 2002; Honey, 2003; Dawn of the Dead, 2004; Slow Burn, 2005; Easier, Softer Way, 2006; Puff, Puff, Pass, producer & dir, 2006; A day in the Life, 2007; This Christmas, exec producer, 2007; A Talent for Trouble, 2008; Nora's Hair Salon II, producer, 2008; TV series: "Homicide", 1993; "New York Undercover", 1995-96; "Models Inc", 1995; "The Tuskegee Airmen", 1995; "Homicide: Life on the Street", 1996-98; SUBWAY Stories: Tales from the Underground, 1997; "A Lesson Before Dying", 1999; "Carmen: A Hip Hopera", 2001; "Brian's Song", 2001; "ER", 2002-08; "Curb Your Enthusiasm", 2005; "Lie to Me", 2009; Album: New York Related: The HF Project, 1999. **Orgs:** Screen Actors Guild, 1995-. **Honors/Awds:** Black Reel Award, 2000; Rising Star Award, 2002; Image Award, 2004 & 2005; Icon Award, 2009. **Business Addr:** Actor, William Morris Agency, 1 William Morris Pl, Beverly Hills, CA 90212, **Business Phone:** (310)859-4000.*

PHIFER, MEKHI THIRA. **See PHIFER, MEKHI.**

PHIFER, ROMAN ZUBINSKY
Football player. **Personal:** Born Mar 5, 1968, Plattsburgh, NY; married Alexis Eggleston (divorced); children: Jordan; married Linda, Jan 1, 2003; children: Angelo & Milan. **Educ:** Univ Calif, Los Angeles. **Career:** Football player (retired); coach; Los Angeles Rams, linebacker, 1991-94; St Louis Rams, 1995-98; New York Jets, 1999-2000; New England Patriots, 2001-04; New York Giants, 2005; Denver Broncos, linebackers coach, currently. **Honors/Awds:** Ed Block Courage Award, 1994; Super Bowl champion; Pro Bowl Alternate, 1995-96. **Business Addr:** Assistant Linebackers Coach, Denver Broncos, 13655 Broncos Pkwy, Englewood, CO 80112, **Business Phone:** (303)649-9000.

PHILANDER, DR. S. GEORGE H.
Scientist, educator. **Personal:** Born Jul 25, 1942; son of Peter J and Alice E; married Hilda Storari; children: Rodrigo. **Educ:** Univ Cape Town, BS, 1963; Harvard Univ, PhD, 1970. **Career:** Mass Inst Tech, res assoc, 1970-71; NOAA, Dept Com, sr res oceanographer, 1978; Princeton Univ, res assoc, 1971-78; Princeton Univ, full prof, Dept Geol & Geophys Scis, 1990, Atmospheric & Oceanic Scis Prog, dir, 1990-, Dept Geol & Geophys Scis, chmn, 1994-; Knox Taylor prof geo sciences, currently. **Orgs:** Consult, World Meteorol Org, 1973-; Nat Acad Scis Gate Comn, 1977-79; chmn, EPOCS Steering Comn, 1978-85; SEQUAL Steering Comn, 1981-87; chmn, CCCO Atlantic Panel, 1981-; Mass Inst Tech Visiting Comt; Nat Acad Scis TOGA Panel, 1985-; Dynamics Atmospheres & Oceans; Geofisica Int;Oceanographie Tropicale; lectr with rank prof, geol & geophys scis, Princeton Univ, 1980-; Univ Consortium for Atmospheric Res, bd mem, 1991-; elected mem, Am Acad Arts & Scis, 2003. **Honors/Awds:** NOAA Environ Res Labs, 1979; Distinguished Authorship Award, 1979; NOAA Environ Res Labs, 1983; Distinguished Authorship Award, 1983; Awarded Sverdrup Gold Medal by Am Meteorol Soc, 1985; Dept Com, 'Gold Medal', 1985; Elected 'Fellow of the Am Meteorol Soc', 1985. **Special Achievements:** Numerous articles in oceanographic research journal; contributor, "The Sea", 1977; El Nino, La Nina & The Southern Oscillations, Acad Press, 1989; Author, Is The Temperature Rising? The Uncertain Science of Global Warming, Princeton Univ Press, 1998; Sextant to Satellite; the Education of a Land-based Oceanographer Chapter in History of Physical Oceanography Developments since 1960, Springer/New York, 2006. **Home Addr:** 81 Woodside Lane, Princeton, NJ 08540-5417. **Business Addr:** Knox Taylor Professor of Geosciences, Director, Atmospheric & Oceanic Science Program, Princeton University, Department of Geosciences, M47 Guyot Hall, Princeton, NJ 08544.

PHILLIP, DR. MICHAEL JOHN
Educator. **Personal:** Born May 27, 1929, Port-of-Spain, Trinidad and Tobago; married Germaine Victor; children: Roger & Brian. **Educ:** Univ Toronto, BS, 1960, MS 1962; Mich State Univ, PhD, 1964. **Career:** John Carroll Univ, Cleveland, assoc prof biol, 1969-72; Univ Detroit, prof microbiol, 1977-, dir genetics 1982; Univ Fla, dean grad minority prog; Univ Northern Colorado, minority affairs, vpres. **Orgs:** Vice chmn bd dirs, Alexandrine House Detroit, 1979-; bd trustees, St Mary's Hosp, 1983-. **Honors/Awds:** Outstanding Foreign Student, Mich State Univ, 1963; Distinguished Fac Award, Univ Detroit Black Alumni, 1983. **Home Addr:** 4401 NW 19th Ave, Gainesville, FL 32605.

PHILLIPS, REV. ACEN L.
Clergy, executive, chief executive officer. **Personal:** Born May 10, 1935, Hillhouse, MS; married E La Quilla Gaiter; children: Acen

Jr, Gregory, Delford, Vicky Lynn, Aaron La Bracc & Carole Knight. **Educ:** Denver Univ, BA, MA; Conservative Baptist Theol Seminary, BD; Iliff Sch Theol, MRC; Am Baptist Theol Seminary, DD. **Career:** Denver Public Schs, educr; Ace Enterprises, pres; Mt Gilead Baptist Church, minister; Am Church United, pres & ceo, currently. **Orgs:** Pres, WSBC; state vpres, NBC USA Inc; pres, E Denver Ministers Alliance; organizer, Denver OIC; organizer, founder, first chmn bd & pres, Productions Inc; organizer, founder, pres & bd chmn, Ace Enterprises Inc; pres, Nat Am Church Union Inc; chmn, Int InterdenomiNatMinisters Alliance; bd chmn, DTP Ministers Inc; 4th vpres, Nat Baptist Convention USA Inc; pres, Ala Phillips Ministry. **Honors/Awds:** Brought opening prayer for US Congress, 1976; listed in Congressional Record; Man of the Year; gave opening prayer for US Senate, 1981. **Business Addr:** Chief Executive Officer, American Church United, 195 S Monaco, Denver, CO 80224.

PHILLIPS, ANTHONY DWAYNE
Football player. **Personal:** Born Oct 5, 1970, Galveston, TX. **Educ:** Trinity Valley Community Col; Tex A&M-Kingsville. **Career:** Atlanta Falcons, defensive back, 1994-96; Minn Vikings, 1998.

PHILLIPS, BASIL OLIPHANT
Administrator. **Personal:** Born Feb 19, 1930, Kansas City, MO. **Educ:** Roosevelt Univ & Inst Design, IL Inst Tech. **Career:** Johnson Pub Co Inc, photo editor; JPC Book Div, dir spec mrkts, promo, former sales mgr, 1950-; Abraham Lincoln Bookstore, former employee.

PHILLIPS, CHARLES E, JR.
President (Organization). **Educ:** AUS Acad, BS, comput sci; Hampton Univ, MBA; New York Law Sch, JD. **Career:** Morgan Stanley & Co, prin, 1994-95, managing dir, 1995-2003; Oracle Corp, exec vpres, 2003-04, pres & bd dirs, currently. **Orgs:** Bd, Viacom Corp; bd, Jazz at Lincoln Ctr New York City; bd, New York Law Sch; bd, Viacom Inc; bd, Morgan Stanley. **Military Serv:** USMC, capt. **Business Addr:** President, Oracle Corp, 500 Oracle Pky, Redwood Shores, CA 94065, **Business Phone:** (650)506-7000.*

PHILLIPS, DANIEL P
Executive. **Personal:** Born Feb 20, 1917, Sharon, PA; married Dorothy Weston; children: Dana Jean Johnson & Robin Dale. **Educ:** Lincoln Univ, BA, 1939. **Career:** Chem Proc Fed Tool & Plastics Co, plant mgr div ethyl corp; Cyrus Realtors Inc, realtor; Coldwell Banker Realtor, sales assoc, currently. **Orgs:** Pres, Evnstn Pk & Rec Bd, 1953-73; vpres, Evanston YMCA Bd, 1959-76; pres, Evnstn HS Bd Educ 1969-73, 1987,88; dir, Evanston Rotary Club, 1969-; bd dirs Ill Asn Sch Bds, 1983-89; pres, Evanston Rotary Club, 1989-1990;bd mem, Youth Orgns Umbrella Inc. **Honors/Awds:** State Award Outstanding Rehab Employee, 1973; Recipient Outstanding School Bd Mem State Ill, 1974; Distinguished Comm Contrib Nat Asn Advan Colored People, 1974. **Business Addr:** Sales Associate, Coldwell Banker Realtors Inc, 2929 Cent St, Evanston, IL 60201.

PHILLIPS, DELORES
Writer. **Personal:** Born Jan 1, 1950?. **Educ:** Cleveland State Univ, BA, eng, attended. **Career:** State psychiat hosp, nurse, currently; freelance writer, currently; Author: The Darkest Child, Beloved or The Color Purple. **Home Addr:** 242 Armstead Circle, Griffin, GA 30223, **Home Phone:** (770)229-9612. *

PHILLIPS, EDWARD ALEXANDER
Manager. **Personal:** Born Jul 27, 1942, Cordele, GA; son of Sylvester and Eloise Moore; married Maxine Broussard, Feb 15, 1986; children: Kimberly L. **Educ:** Tuskegee Univ, Tuskegee, AL, BSME, 1965; Univ Idaho, Moscow, ID, 1981. **Career:** Pac Gas Transmission Co, Bend, OR, eng, 1966-73; Pac Gas & Elec Co, Oakland, CA, sr engr, 1973-74, dist gas supt, 1979-81, San Rafael, CA, supt opers/engr, 1974-79, San Francisco, CA, gas engr, 1981-82, Salinas, CA, div gas supt, 1982-85, Sacramento, CA, region gas mgr, 1982-90, region gen serv mgr, 1990-; M&M Power Prods, pres & gen mgr, currently; Phillips Enterprises Inc, prin, pres & owner, currently. **Orgs:** Awards comt, Pac Coast Gas Asn, 1970-; Pac Coast Elec Asn, 1970-; bd mem, Sacramento Black Employees Asn, 1986-; Sacramento Urban League, 1989-; pres, chmn, Sacramento Black Chamber Com, 1989-; bd mem, Nat Asn Advan Colored People, 1990-. **Honors/Awds:** Community Service Award, Pacific Gas & Elec Co, 1989 & 1990. **Business Addr:** President, Owner, Phillips Enterprises Inc, 3600 Sunset Ave, Ocean, NJ 07712, **Business Phone:** (732)493-3191.

PHILLIPS, EDWARD MARTIN
Chemical engineer, educator. **Personal:** Born Dec 23, 1935, Philadelphia, PA; son of Edward M Sr and Sylvia D; married Audrey Henrietta Longley. **Educ:** Lafayette Col, BS, chem, 1958; Northwestern Univ, MS, chem, 1959; Univ Pittsburgh, PhD, chem, 1969. **Career:** Univ Pittsburgh, NASA predoctoral fel, 1964-68; Arco Res & Engr, engr, 1959-64; Exxon Engr Co, proj engr, 1968-72; Tufts Univ, assoc prof, 1972-74; Air Prod & Chem Inc, eng assoc, 1974-86; Rutgers Univ, prof packaging sci & eng, 1987-. **Orgs:** Am Inst Chem Eng, 1958-; Am Chem Soc, 1969-; dir, Lehigh Valley Child Care, 1977-; Fel, Am Inst Chem Engrs, 1992-. **Business Addr:** Professor, Rutgers University, Bldg 3529 Busch Campus, Piscataway, NJ 08855.

PHILLIPS, ERIC MCLAREN
Manager. **Personal:** Born Oct 19, 1952, Mahaicony, Guyana; married Angela; children: Takeisha Sherrill, Eric McLaran & Ashley Nicole. **Educ:** McMaster Univ, BS, Engineering 1976; New York Univ, MBA, 1983; Stevens Inst Tech & Bell Labs, Cert Telecommunication Engineering, 1985. **Career:** Apollo Technologies, test engr, 1977-78, proj engr, 1978-79, sr proj engr, 1979-80, r&d prod develop leader, 1980-82; AT&T Commun, staff mgr local area networks, 1983-85, staff mgr network planning, 1985-86; AT&T Bell Labs, supvr mem tech staff, 1986-; AT&T Cent Europe Ltd (Belgium), managing dir, 1993; AT&T Africa & The Middle East, managing dir, 1994; AT&T Subsaharan Africa, sales vpres, 1994; African Continental Telecommunications Ltd, coo, dir, 1995; Matrix Cellular Inc, pres, 1995. **Orgs:** Pres, Phillips Smith & Assocs Inc, 1982; exec dir, The Caribbean Theatre Performing Arts New York City, 1983; pres, NY Univ Black Alumni Asn, 1985, prog dir, 1986. **Honors/Awds:** R&D Scientific Achievement of the Year Award, Apollo Technologies Inc, 1981; Merit Award, Grad Sch Bus Admin New York Univ, 1983; Outstanding Serv Award, AT & T Bell Labs. **Special Achievements:** Top Engineer 6 consecutive Quarters, Apollo Technologies Inc 1979, 1980. **Business Addr:** President, Matrix Cellular Inc, 544 Irvington Ave, Maplewood, NJ 07040, **Business Phone:** (201)761-7373.

PHILLIPS, REV. F ALLISON
Clergy. **Personal:** Born Jan 5, 1937, Brooklyn, NY; married Velma Carr; children: Denise Mitchell & Alyson. **Educ:** Va Union Univ, BA, 1958; Colgate Rochester Divinity Sch, BD, 1967; New York Theol Sem, STM, 1975, DMin, 1981. **Career:** YMCA, assoc dir, 1958-64; Garrison Blvd Community Ctr, dir, 1967-71; N Congregational Church, pastor, 1971-82; Mt Zion Congregational Church, pastor, 1982; Div Am Missionary Asn, gen secy, currently. **Orgs:** Alpha Phi Alpha. 1955-; bd mem. Am Red Cross. 1983-87; pres. Inner City Renewal Soc, 1984-; moderator, African Am Family Congress, 1986-; bd mem, Greater Cleveland Roundtable, 1986-; Leadership Cleveland 1986-; bd dir, Amistad Res Ctr, currently. **Honors/Awds:** Serv Awards, YMCA, 1966; Serv Awards, Coun Churches, 1971; Serv Awards, UCC Clergy Black Caucus, 1981; Leadership Award, ISTEM, 1982. **Special Achievements:** F. Allison Phillips is the first African American to serve as General Secretary of the American Missionary Association. **Business Addr:** Board of Director, Amistad Research Center, Tulane University, Tilton Memorial Hall 6823 St Charles Ave, New Orleans, LA 44115-1100, **Business Phone:** (504)862-3222.

PHILLIPS, FRANCES CALDWELL
Educator. **Personal:** Born Feb 13, 1923, Concord, NC; daughter of Robert and Cora Louise; married Jonas H Phillips, Nov 15, 1986; children: Deborah Waddell Williams. **Educ:** Winston Salem State Univ, BS, 1942; A & T State Univ, Greensboro, NC, MS, 1955. **Career:** Educator (retired); Martin County Sch System; Stanley County Sch System; Charlotte Mecklenburg Sch System; Barber Scotia Col upward Bound Prog. **Orgs:** Steering Comt, Albemarle City Sch Accredations; Phi Delta Kappa Basileus; YWCA, Charlotte, NC; golden life mem, Delta Sigma Theta Sorority; First United Presbyterian Church, Charlotte, NC; steering comt, NCP Legal Defence Fund; Urban League; Urban League Guild; bd trustees, Barber-Scotia Col; First Baptist Church W, deaconess. **Honors/Awds:** Woman of the Year, 1997-98. *

PHILLIPS, FRANK EDWARD
Government official. **Personal:** Born Mar 3, 1930, Pittsburgh, PA; son of Emanuel and Annie Evans; married Mary E Britt, Jun 19, 1953 (divorced); children: Nancy Phillips-Perry, Judith Lynne Phillips & Yvette Jacobs Davis; married Thelma Harrison, Jun 10, 1989 (divorced); children: Jay Clark; married Saundra Thompson-Kuy Kendall, Nov 29, 1997; children: Michael & Michelle. **Educ:** Shaw Univ, AB, 1952; Howard Univ, LLB, 1955. **Career:** Government official (retired); IRS, Wash DC, rev officer, 1955-62; IRS Los Angeles, CA, off chief coun tax atty, 1962-66, sr tax atty, 1966-69, staff asst to regional coun, gen litigation, 1969-72, asst dist coun, tax ct litigation, 1972-86. **Orgs:** Nat Bar Asn; Fed Bar Asn; VA St Bar; bd dir, Crenshaw YMCA; Christian Dcsn Dept Episcopal Church; bd dir, Crenshaw Neighbors; Alpha Kappa Mu Honor Society; Omega Psi Phi; bd dirs, African Am Unity Ctr; bd dirs, African Am Unity Ctr. **Honors/Awds:** First Chief Counsel, EEO Award, IRS, 1980; 3 Outstanding Award, IRS, 1980; Gallatin Award, 1986; Outstanding Award, Treasury Dept; Shaw Univ, Athletic Hall of Fame, 1996; Hall of Fame, Nat Bar Asn, 1997. **Home Addr:** 4194 S Cloverdale Ave, Los Angeles, CA 90008. *

PHILLIPS, DR. FREDERICK BRIAN
Psychologist. **Personal:** Born Sep 2, 1946, Philadelphia, PA; married Vicki Altemus, May 25, 1986; children: Jamali & Jasmine. **Educ:** Penn State Univ, BA, 1968; Univ Penn, MSW, 1970; The Fielding Inst, PsyD, 1978. **Career:** Dist Columbia Govt, psychologist, 1978-81; Inst Life Enrichment, assoc dir, 1981-83; Progressive Life Inst, dir, pres. **Orgs:** Kappa Alpha Psi, 1965-85; Asn Black Psychologists, 1978-85. **Military Serv:** AUS, capt, 3 yrs. **Business Addr:** Director, President, Progressive Life Center, 1704 17th St NE, Washington, DC 20002, **Business Phone:** (202)842-4570.

PHILLIPS, DR. GLENN OWEN
Educator, school administrator. **Personal:** Born Sep 26, 1946, Bridgetown, Barbados; son of Dorothy E and E Owen; married Ingrid Denise Tom, Aug 27, 1972; children: Mariette. **Educ:** Atlantic Union Col, BA, 1967; Andrews Univ, MA, 1969; Howard Univ, PhD, 1976. **Career:** Caribbean Union Col, lectr, 1969-71; Howard Univ, asst prof hist, 1981-82; Morgan State Univ, asst prof hist, asst dir Univ Hons Prog, 1981-82, res assoc, 1982-92, acting dir, Inst Urban Res, 1986-89, asst prof, 1989-90, acting chair, Dept History, 1989-90 & 1995-96, assoc prof, prof currently. **Orgs:** MSU Liaison Officer NAFEO, DC, 1985-94; pres, Barbados Nat Asn Wash Dist Columbia, 1985-89; Community Coun Caribbean Orgn, DC, 1985-89; Sch Bd Chair, 1991-94; G E Peters Elem Sch, 1987-92; bd trustees, Caribbean Union Col, 1989-94; Asn Am Univ Professors, 1995-97. **Honors/Awds:** HBCU Fac Fel, United Negro Col Fund/US Dept Lab, 1980; Morgan State Univ Hon Mem, Promethean Kappa Tau, 1982; Cited Nat Dir Latin Americans; Asn Ed Afro- Hispanic Rev, 1982-84; Fulbright Summer Scholar, Cairo, Egypt, 1994; African Diaspora Experience, 1998, 2000 & 2003. **Special Achievements:** Author, The Making of Christian College, 1988; co-editor, The Caribbean Basin Initiative, 1987; Over a Century of Adventism, 1991. **Business Addr:** Professor, Morgan State University, Department of History, Holmes Hall Rm G 04, Baltimore, MD 21239, **Business Phone:** (443)885-1793.

PHILLIPS, HELEN M.
Educator. **Personal:** Born May 29, 1926, Norfolk, VA; daughter of Thomas Battle and Rosa; children: Marcia Anita Baynes & Brian OD. **Educ:** Va State Univ, Petersburg, VA, BS, 1954; Suffolk Univ, Boston, MA, M.Ed,1983; Univ Md; Fairleigh Dickinson Univ; Salem State Col; Cath Univ Am; Boston Univ; Univ Mass, cert geront, 1994; advan cert geront, 1998. **Career:** Educator (retired); Norfolk State Col, fac, 1951; Carnegie Inst, dir progmed sect & asst; E Boston High Sch, Boston Sch Bus, fac; Malden Pub Sch Syst, Malden MA, teacher word processing, money & banking. **Orgs:** Nat bd dir & rep 17th Dist, Va State Univ Alumni Asn, 1982-85, 1986-87;task force comm, Restructuring Malden High Sch, 1988-89; Nat Bus Educ Asn; Nat Educ Asn; Mass Teachers Asn; Malden Teachers Asn; Eastern Bus Teachers Asn; Resolutions Comn Mass Teachers Asn; Va State Univ Alumni Asn; bd dirs& charter mem, Cynthia Sickle Cell Anemia Fund; Concord Baptist Church, Boston MA; proj dir, Women Community Serv Boston; founder, Black Stud Union MHS; Alpha Kappa Alpha Sorority; columnist, Boston Graphic & Boston Sun newspapers; Ad Hoc Comt. **Honors/Awds:** First Place Distinguished Representative Award, Va State Univ Alumni Asn, 1986. **Special Achievements:** One of Five Educators in Malden School System Selected as a Member of Needs Assessment Committee for Students at Risk, Dropout-Prevention Program, 1987, recognized by North Shore Black Women's Association for positive image and involvement in the Malden community at the 1997 Martin L King Luncheon, "Involvement Makes A Difference". **Home Addr:** 41 Acorn St, Malden, MA 02148.

PHILLIPS, DR. JAMES LAWRENCE
Physician, school administrator, educator. **Personal:** Born Mar 1, 1932, Sharon, PA; son of Daniel S and Roxie B; married Barbara A Eiserman; children: James Jr, Jeffrey & Steven. **Educ:** Washington & Jefferson Col, BA, 1954; Case Western Res Univ Sch Med, MD, 1958; Am Bd Pediat, cert, 1963; Harvard Univ, advan mgt prog, 1979. **Career:** W Ohio Permanente Med Group Inc, physician chief, 1968-86; Kaiser Found Hosp Parma, 1970-; Case Western Res Univ Sch Med, asst clin prof pediat, 1972-87, assoc dean stud affairs & minority prog; Cleveland Cavaliers Basketball Team, asst team physician, 1973-79; Rocky River Med Off, physician incharge, 1986-87; Baylor Col Med, Dept Pediat, Sect Acad Gen Pediat, sr assoc dean & prof, 1993-. **Orgs:** Bd trustees, Mt Pleasant Church God, 1976-82; pres, Case Western Res Univ Sch Med Alumni Asn, 1980-81; bd trustees, Wash & Jefferson Col, 1982-; chmn, United Way Serv New Progs Comt, 1985; pres, Northern Ohio Pediat Soc, 1988-89; bd trustees, Wash & Jefferson Col, 1988-94; Cleveland Med Asn, 1988-; Acad Med Cleveland; Ohio State Med Asn; N OH Pediat Soc; Am Acad Pediat; Ambulatory Pediat Asn. **Honors/Awds:** Birch Scholar Award, Wash & Jefferson Col, 1954; Jessie Smith Noyes Found Med Sch Scholar, 1954-55; Leadership Award, Cleveland, 1989-90; Honorary Doctorate of Science, Washington & Jefferson Col. **Military Serv:** USNR, lt comdr, 2 yrs; Commendation from Commanding Officer. **Business Addr:** Senior Associate Dean, Professor, Baylor College of Medicine, Department of Pediatrics, 1 Baylor Plaza 1709 Dryden Suite M108, Houston, TX 77030, **Business Phone:** (713)798-6598.

PHILLIPS, JERRY P
Executive. **Personal:** Born Jul 24, 1939, Lyons, GA; son of P T and Ase Lue; married Maxine Glass, Jun 20, 1964; children: Damon J & Dyelan J. **Educ:** Savannah State Col, 1959; Rollins Col, BS, 1985. **Career:** USF, supt, 1976-80; Harris Corp, receiving & shipping supvr, sr material adv, 1980-89; Alphatech Systems, Inc, pres, 1989-. **Orgs:** NCP, 1975-; Historical Underutilized Bus Coun; Palm Bay Chamber Com, 1990-; Nat Minority Supplier Develop Coun, 1990-; trustee, bd mem, building Comt, chair, Macedonia Baptist Church, 1991-; honorary chair, United Negro Col Fund, Men Who Cook, 1991-; Palm Bay FL, Citizen As-

sistance Comt, 1994-96; Palm Bay FL, Citizen Saturday Comt, 1994-; treas, Melbourne/Palm Bay Area, 1996-; mgr, Brevard County Workforce Develop Bd, 1996-. **Honors/Awds:** Minority Business Enterprise of the Year, Greater Fla Develop Coun, 1990; Governor's Award for Excellence in Manufacturing, Governor Fla, 1991; Minority Business Enterprise of the Year, Harris Corporation, 1991; Minority Business Enterprise of the Year, Sun Bank, 1990, 1991; One of the top 20 Small Disadvantaged Businesses in Florida, Fla High Tech & Indust Coun, 1991; Man of the Year, Macedonia Baptist Church, 1994; Business of the Year, Nat Minority Supplier Develop Coun Fla, 1995; Small Business Person of the Year Nominee, Melbourne, Palm Bay, 1996; Community Business Award Outstanding Services, 1996; Economic Development Commission Industry Appreciation, 1996. **Special Achievements:** Quality Work on Change Perception, Fla Today Paper, 1992; The US Air Force F-22/F119 Mentor-Protect Program, participation with Pratt & Whitney, 1995. **Military Serv:** USF, Master Sargent, 1960-80; Air Force Commendation Medals, 1966, 1970, 1973, 1977; Vietnam Service Medal with 2 Devices. **Business Phone:** (321)729-0419.

PHILLIPS, JULIAN MARTIN
Television journalist. **Personal:** Born Dec 5, 1955, New York, NY; son of Cecil and Enola; married Barbara King, Dec 3, 1983. **Educ:** Purdue Univ, BA, 1977. **Career:** ABC-TV, desk asst, 1977; Black Enterprise Mag, staff, 1980; WNEW-TV, Channel 5, prod asst, 1981; WNBC-TV, Channel 4, mgr community rels, 1984, anchor & journalist; WPIX-TV, on-air corresp; Fox News Channel, anchor & gen assignment reporter, 2002-. **Orgs:** Adv bd mem, Nat Puerto Rican Forum, 1984-90; sr employ adv bd, New York Dept Aging, 1985-89; region vpres, Nat Broadcast Asn Community Affairs, 1985-89; adv bd mem, Crohns & Colitis Found Am, 1989-92; bd dir, NY Coalition Adoptable Children, 1992-; Nat Asn Black Law Enforcement Execs, 1994-. **Honors/Awds:** Emmy Award, New York Acad TV Arts & Sci, 1986; Distinguished Alumni Award, Purdue Univ, 1988; Edward R Murrow Award, Best National Newscast, Best Spot News, Radio & TV News Dir Asn, 1994; New York Broadcasters Award, Outstanding Pub Affairs Series; Nominated for 4 Emmy Awards, 1994-96; First Place News Award, Assoc Press, 1996. **Business Addr:** General assignment reporter, Anchor, Fox News Channel, 1211 Ave of the Americas, New York, NY 10036, **Business Phone:** (212)301-3000.

PHILLIPS, JUNE M J
Educator, writer. **Personal:** Born May 31, 1941, Ashdown, AR; married A W; children: Roderick & Calandra Camille. **Educ:** Philander Smith Col, BA, English (Magna Cum Laude), 1963; La State Univ, MA, English, 1971; NW State Univ, doctoral candidate; Bakers Prof Real Estate Col, license, 1977. **Career:** Port Arthur Texas Schs, teacher, 1963-65; Caddo Parish Schs, Shreveport, teacher, 1965-68; Board La Cols & Univs, trustee, 1983-; const educ minorities; orator & poet; Southern Univ, Shreveport, asst prof, english, 1968-, Div Humanities, chair, currently. **Orgs:** Sales assoc, Century 21, 1977-79; Lester Realty, sales assoc, 1979-83; Ferdinand Realty, sales assoc, 1984-; Lynell's Cosmetics, consult, 1984-; United Way NW, La, 1979-; Caddo Parish Charter Study Com, 1981-82; Democratic Nat Conv, 1984; NAUW; OEO #175; Shreveport Chap of Links; Zeta Phi Beta Sor; La Philos Educ Soc; CODAC; La Cols & Univs, gubernatorial apptmt; chairs acad affairs comm for 9 La cols. **Honors/Awds:** Woman of the Yr, Zeta Phi Beta Sor Inc, 1975; Caddo Parish Sch Board, 1976-77; NDEA, Texas So & So Univ; editor & critic, Holbrook Press, NY & Roxbury Press, Calif; City Shreveport, "Woman Who Has Made a Difference". **Special Achievements:** First black woman to serve on state board. **Home Phone:** (318)221-5957. **Business Addr:** Assistant Professor of English, Chair, Southern University, 3050 Martin Luther King Dr, Shreveport, LA 71107-4795, **Business Phone:** (318)674-3365.*

PHILLIPS, LIONEL GARY
Media executive. **Personal:** Born May 1, 1950, New York, NY; son of Oscar and Johnetta; divorced. **Educ:** City Col New York, BA, eng/sociol, 1973. **Career:** WCBS TV News, desk asst, assignment ed & writer, 1972-80, segment producer, 1987-96, news mgr, 1987-96; CBS News, producer, 1980-86, field producer, 1985, CBS Morning News, producer, 1986-87; NJ Network News, exec prod, 1987-88; Phillips Media, owner, 1997-; NJ Network News, exec producer, 1986-87, news mgr, 1999-2001; NBC, freelance assignment ed, 1997-98; Mag Rack, 2001-03; MSNBC, segment producer, 2003-04; IDT, mgr media rels, 2005-06; CBS2 News, freelance writer, 2006; CNN, freelance writer, 2006-07; NJ Dept Labor Prof Serv Group, trainer, 2006; ABC News, freelance producer, 2007-. **Orgs:** Nat Asn Black Journalists; Writers Guild Am; instr, NABJ Jour Short Course, Temple Univ, 1995; Cathedral Int; Khalfani Big Brothers Ministry. **Honors/Awds:** New York State Regents Scholar, 1968; National Merit Scholar, 1968; Black Achievers in Industry, Harlem YMCA, 1976; Emmy Award, Nat Acad TV Arts & Sci, 1978, 1989; Writers Guild of America Award, 1987; Alfred I Dupont Gold Baton Award, 1987. **Business Addr:** Freelance producer, ABC News, 77 W 66th St, New York, NY 10023, **Business Phone:** (206)664-4000.*

PHILLIPS, MILDRED EVALYN
Physician. **Personal:** Born May 21, 1925, New York, NY; daughter of Fitzgerald and Kathleen; children: Tippi Brooke Phillips. **Educ:** Hunter Col, NY, BA; Howard Univ Col Med, MD. **Career:** Physician (retired); NY Univ Med Ctr, instr, assoc prof, 1957-73; State Univ NY, assoc prof, 1973-95. **Orgs:** Am Soc Exp Pathol, 1960-95; Int Acad Pathol, 1960-95; Am Asn Cancer Res, 1960-67; Am Soc Dermatopathology, 1982-; Int Acad Dermatopathology, 1982-; Asn Academic Minority Physicians, 1990-. **Honors/Awds:** Hall of Fame, Hunter Col, 1983; hon med soc, Alpha Omega Alpha, 2000. **Special Achievements:** Numerous publications. **Home Addr:** 511 E 20th St, New York, NY 10010, **Home Phone:** (212)228-1056. *

PHILLIPS, RALPH LEONARD
Manager. **Personal:** Born May 11, 1925, Sacramento, CA; son of Harry Wendall Jr and Bessie Wundus; married Alice Hall, Dec 1, 1990. **Educ:** Univ Calif Berkeley, AB (Cum Laude) 1949, MA; Inst African Studies Northwestern Univ, spec studies. **Career:** Manager (retired); Bur Int Rels Univ Calif Berkeley, res assoc, 1950, teaching fel polit sci, 1952-55; USIA, info officer, cult attache, 1956-68; Arabic lang training, Beirut, 1959-61; spec asst to dir, E & Southeast Asia, serving Middle E, Wash Hq, 1963-64; Mobil Oil corp, 1969-93; Community & Pub Affairs Tripoli Libya, 1969-71; sr planning analyst, Int Div, 1971-93. **Orgs:** Sir, Planning, Educ Task Force, Coun Econ Develop NY, 1971-72; bd dirs, DPF Inc (NYSE), 1972-74; Mayor's Adv Coun Housing, Princeton, 1973-75; bd dir, Coun Int Prog, 1975; Zoning Bd Princeton, 1977-79; vpres, Princeton Republican Asn, 1978-80; Princeton Regional Planning Bd, 1981-86; bd trustees, St Paul's Col Lawrence VA, 1983-84; Prince Hall F&A Masons Aaron No 9 Princeton NJ; 32nd Degree Ophir Consistory, Trenton NJ; Shriner Prince Hall Masons Kufu, Princeton NJ; Am Legion Post No 218 Princeton NJ. **Honors/Awds:** Merit Award, Hon Stud Soc, Univ Calif; Dept St, 1956; Pi Sigma Alpha Nat Polit Sci Hon Soc; Delta Sigma Rho, Nat Forensic Hon Soc. **Military Serv:** AUS, T/4 Med & Phil Islands, 1943-46; AUS Ready Reserve Presidio of San Francisco Mil Intelligence, 1957-61. **Home Addr:** 156 13th St SE, Washington, DC 20003.

PHILLIPS, DR. ROBERT HANSBURY
Labor relations manager. **Personal:** Born Nov 19, 1924, Detroit, MI; son of William and Bertha Hansbury; married Rose Mary Franklin, Sep 4, 1946 (died 1998); children: Hilanius Hansbury; married Consuelo Q, Oct 1, 1999; children: Eric Quintong. **Educ:** Wayne State Univ, Detroit, MI, BS, 1952, MPA, 1967, PhD, 1987. **Career:** Labor relations manager (retired); City Detroit Personnel Dept, Detroit, MI, personnel mgr, 1953-88. **Orgs:** Int Personnel Mgt Asn, 1953-; past dir, Personnel Mgt Asn, Mich Chap, 1953-; Pub Personnel Admin; Am Polit Sci Asn, 1983-88; Detroit Personnel Coun, 1953-88. **Honors/Awds:** Equal Employment Opportunity, Affirmative Action, Mayoral Initiatives & Bureaucratic Responses: The Case Detroit, Dissertation, 1987. **Special Achievements:** Author: A Peek Through the Curtain: A Trilogy; Men Are Like A Puff of Wind; Lives of Tears; Up Jumped the Canaille, 1991. **Military Serv:** AUS, sgt, 1943-46; Victory Medal, Am Theatre Ribbon, Asiatic Pacific Theatre Ribbon with 2 Bronze Battle Stars, Philippine Liberation Ribbon with 1 Bronze Star, 3 Overseas Serv Bars, Good Conduct Medal. **Home Addr:** 2900 Cove Cay Dr Apt 7G, Clearwater, FL 33760. *

PHILLIPS, DR. ROMEO ELDRIDGE
Educator. **Personal:** Born Mar 11, 1928, Chicago, IL; son of Sissieretta Lewis and James M Sr; married Deloris R Jordan; children: Pamela Marlene & Arthur JH. **Educ:** Roosevelt Univ, BB, 1949, MM, 1951; Eastern MI Univ, MA, 1963; Wayne State Univ, PhD, 1966. **Career:** Chicago IL Pub Schs, teacher, 1949-55; Detroit MI Pub Schs, teacher,1955-57; Inkster MI Pub Schs, teacher, 1957-66; Kalamazoo Col, tenured prof educ & music, 1968-93, chmn dept educ, 1974-86, prof emer, 1993-; Mich Col, Comt Scholars Accreditation, mem, 1982-84; Portage MI, city coun man, 1991-. **Orgs:** Am Asn Col Teacher Educ; Music Educrs Nat Conf; MI Sch Vocal Asn; Asn Supervison & Curriculum Develop; MI Asn Supervision & Curriculum Develop; MI Asn Improvement Sch Legislation; Nat Alliance Black Sch Educr; Nat Asn Negro Musicians; Phi Delta Kappa; Kappa Alpha Psi; conductor, African-Am Chorale; bd mem, SW Mich Black Heritage Soc; pres, Kalamazoo Chap NAACP. **Honors/Awds:** Omega Psi Phi Leadership Award, 1982; Kalamazoo Nat Asn Advan Colored People Appreciation Award, 1982; Fulbright Scholar Liberia West Africa, 1984-85. **Special Achievements:** First tenured African American professor at Kalamazoo College; 13 jour publs; 1 mag article; 2 book reviews; chapters contributed to or credit given in 6 books; Invited by the govt of the Republic of Nigeria West Africa to be a guest to the World Festival of Black & African Art, 1977. **Military Serv:** AUS, sgt, 1951-53. **Home Addr:** 6841 Welbury, Portage, MI 49024. **Business Addr:** Professor Emeritus, Kalamazoo College, 1200 Acad, Kalamazoo, MI 49006, **Business Phone:** (616)337-7033.

PHILLIPS, TARI LYNN
Basketball player. **Personal:** Born Mar 6, 1969, Winter Park, FL; daughter of John and Doris. **Educ:** Univ Cent Fla, BS, commun, 1991. **Career:** Seattle Reign, forward, 1996-97; Colorado Xplosion, forward, 1997-98;Orlando Miracle, 1998-99; NY Liberty, 2000-04; Houston Comets, 2005-06. **Honors/Awds:** Gold medal, USA World University Games, 1993; All-Star Team, 1997-98;All-Star Game, 1996-97. Gold Medal, Basketball World Championship, 2002.

PHILLIPS, THERESA LAWRENCE
Basketball coach, athletic director. **Personal:** Born Jun 15, 1958, Chatanooga, TN; married Michael; children: Micah & Kyle. **Educ:** Vanderbilt Univ, BA, 1980; TN State Univ, MA, 1999. **Career:** Vanderbilt Univ, asst basketball coach, 1981-84; Fisk Univ, head women's basketball coach, 1986-89; TN State Univ, assoc athletics dir, 1995-2001,interim athletics dir, 2001-02, head men's basketball coach, 2003; TN State Univ, athletics dir, 2002-. **Orgs:** Fel, Christian Athletes; chair, Ohio Valley Conf Athletic Dirs Comt. **Honors/Awds:** Sportsmanship Award, Nashville Citian, 1979, 1980; Natl Coach of the Year, USA Today, 1990; OH Valley Conf Co-coach of the Year, 1990; OH Valley Coach of the Year, 1993, 1994; 101 Most Influential Minorities in Sports, 2003; Lookout Mountain Hall of Fame, 2008. **Special Achievements:** First woman to ever coach an NCAA Division. **Business Addr:** Athletics Director, Tennessee State University, 3500 John A Merritt Blvd Keen Hall Room 131, Nashville, TN 37209, **Business Phone:** (615)963-5000.*

PHILLIPS, W THOMAS
Executive, vice president (organization). **Personal:** Born Aug 2, 1943, Charleston, MS; son of Jessie and Walter; married Carline Bradford; children: Craig, Lee & Ernest. **Educ:** Univ Northern Iowa, bus admin, 1966; Northeastern Univ, Boston, Mass, mgt develop, 1978; Harvard Univ, Grad Sch Bus, advan mgt prog, 1988. **Career:** Executive, Vice president (retired); Gen Foods, sales rep dist mgr, 1966-72; Quaker, sales planning zone mgr, 1973-77, mgr sales develop, 1978-79, mgr dir corp prog, 1980-84, vpres corp progs, 1984-94; Pioneer Hi-Bred International Inc, dir community investments, 1994-2007. **Orgs:** Loaned Exec Assoc, United Way Chicago, 1979-; bd mem, Chicago Hearing Soc, 1979-82, Donors Forum Chicago, Nat Charities Info Bur, 1984-; Asn Black Found Executives. **Honors/Awds:** East High Hall of Fame, 1987; Lifetime Achievement Award Philanthropy, Nat Ctr Black Philanthropy Inc, 2005; guest speaker, Annual Martin Luther King Jr. dinner, Waterloo; African American Hall of Fame, 2006. **Special Achievements:** First Black Vice President & Corporate Officer elected by Quaker. **Home Addr:** 2415 N Douglas Ave, Arlington Heights, IL 60004.

PHILLIPS, WILBURN R.
Banker. **Career:** Home Fed Savings Bank, Detroit, MI, pres/chief exec officer, dir emer & bd dirs; Cape Code Realty, St Clair Shores, broker/owner, currently. **Orgs:** Chmn Trustee Bd, Plymouth United Church Christ, 1949-, past secy Deacon Bd, 1957; Credit Union Nat Asn, Am's Community Bankers. **Business Addr:** Chairman Of Trustee Board, Plymouth United Church of Christ, 600 E Warren Ave, Detroit, MI 48201.

PHILPOTT, ETHEL
Vice president (Organization). **Career:** Retired Teachers Asn Chicago, vpres, currently. **Business Addr:** Vice President, Retired Teachers Association of Chicago, 220 S State St Suite 2100, Chicago, IL 60604, **Business Phone:** (312)939-3327.

PHILYAW, DINO (DELVIC DYVON PHILYAW)
Football player. **Personal:** Born Oct 30, 1970, Dudley, NC. **Educ:** Taft Col; Univ Oregon. **Career:** Football player(retired); Carolina Panthers, running back, 1995-96; New Orleans Saints, running back, 1999.

PICHON, RISE JONES
Judge. **Personal:** Born Oct 3, 1951, Tacoma, WA; daughter of LaVerta and Fairbanks; married Ulysses Pichon, Jul 7, 1974; children: Evann. **Educ:** Xavier Univ; Santa Clara Univ, BS, 1973; Santa Clara Univ Sch Law, JD, 1976. **Career:** County Santa Clara, dep pub defender, 1976-79, dep county coun, 1979-83, ct comnr, 1983-84County Santa Clara, dep pub defender, 1976-79, dep county coun, 1979-83, ct comnr, 1983-84, Munic ct judge, 1984-98; Calif Judicial Col, instr, 1989, 1990; Nat Judicial Col, instr, 1991, 1992; State Calif, superior ct judge, 1998-.Munic ct judge, 1984-98; Calif Judicial Col, instr, 1989, 1990; Nat Judicial Col, instr, 1991, 1992; State Calif, superior ct judge, 1998-. **Orgs:** Calif Judges Asn, 1984-; Nat Bar Asn, 1985-; bd dir, Santa Clara Univ Sch Law Alumni, 1988-93, pres, 1990-91; bd visitors, Santa Clara Univ Sch Law, 1989-97; Calif Judicial Coun, 1994-97; Joint Venture Silicon Valley, Vision Leadership Team, 1998; co-chair, Civic Action Network Planning Comn, 1998-99; Comn Judicial Performance, State Calif, 1999-2003; Trial Ct Budget Comn, Calif Judicial Coun, 1999-2003. **Honors/Awds:** Women of Distinction, Santa Clara Univ Women Studs, Challenges Conf, 1991; Thurgood Marshall Achievement Award, Santa Clara Univ Black Law Studs Asn, 1992; Owens Lawyer of the Year, Santa Clara Univ Sch Law, 1994. **Business Addr:** Superior Court Judge, Santa Clara County Superior Court, 191 North First St, San Jose, CA 95113, **Business Phone:** (408)808-7170.

PICKARD, VIVIAN
Executive. **Educ:** Ferris State Univ, BS; Cent Mich Univ, MS. **Career:** Gen Motors Corp, admin & mgt positions, 1978, vice chair, dir community rels, dir corp relations, currently. **Orgs:** Bd dir, Gleaners Community Food Bank Livingston; bd mem, Nat Coun Negro Women; pres, Renaissance Chap The Links Inc; nat chair corp rels, Corp Rels Comt, The Links Inc; life mem, Nat

Black MBA Asn; life mem, Nat Asn Advan Colored People; Inforum; NAACS; Detroit Inst Arts; FAAAA. **Honors/Awds:** Chairman's Award, 100 Black Men Am Inc, 2004. **Business Addr:** Director of Corporate Relations, General Motors Corporation, 300 Renaissance Ctr, Detroit, MI 48265-3000, **Business Phone:** (313)556-5000.

PICKARD, DR. WILLIAM FRANK
Executive, chief executive officer. **Personal:** Born Jan 28, 1941, La Grangee, GA; son of Willie H Pickard and Victoria Woodyard Pickard. **Educ:** Flint Mott Col, Flint, Mich, AS, 1962; Western Mich Univ, Kalamazoo, Mich,BS, 1964; Univ Mich, Ann Arbor, Mich, MSW, 1965; Ohio State Univ,Columbus, Ohio, PhD, 1971. **Career:** Ment Health NIMH fel, 1964; Cleveland Urban League, dir educ, 1965-67; Nat Urban League, Haynes fel, 1965; Nat Asn Advan Colored People, exec dir, 1967-69; Wayne State Univ, prof, 1971-74; Mc Donalds Res, owner, 1971-; Cleveland State Univ, Cleveland, Ohio, assoc dir urban studies, 1971-72; Wayne State Univ, Detroit, Mich, assoc prof, 1972-74; Global Automotive Alliance, chmn & ceo, 1985-; Regal Plastics Co, Roseville, Mich, chmn & ceo, 1985-. **Orgs:** Bd dir, Standard Fed Bank, 1989-; bd dir, Nat Asn Black Automotive Suppliers, 1986-; bd dir, Fed Home Loan Bank, Indianapolis, Ind, 1990-. **Honors/Awds:** Hon Doctorate Bus Admin, Cleary Col, 1980; Michiganian of the Yr Award,2002. **Special Achievements:** Black Enterprise's list of top 100 industrial & service companies, ranked42, 1998, 19, 2000. **Home Addr:** 335 Pine Ridge Dr, Bloomfield Hills, MI 48304, **Home Phone:** (313)258-6520. **Business Addr:** Chairman, Chief Executive Officer, Global Automotive Alliance, 211 W Fort St, Detroit, MI 48226, **Business Phone:** (313)297-6676.

PICKENS, CARL MCNALLY
Football player. **Personal:** Born Mar 23, 1970, Murphy, NC. **Educ:** Univ Tenn. **Career:** Football player (retired); Cincinnati Bengals, wide receiver, 1992-99; Tenn Titans, 2000. **Honors/Awds:** AFC Rookie of the Year, Assoc Press, 1992; Offensive Rookie of the Year, Nat Football League, 1992; Pro Bowl, 1995, 1996.

PICKENS, JAMES, JR.
Actor, television actor. **Personal:** Born Oct 26, 1954, Cleveland, OH; married Gina, May 27, 1984; children: Carl & Gavyn. **Career:** Films: F/X, 1986; Hotshot, 1987; Trespass, 1992; Boiling Point, 1993; Menace II Society, 1993; Hostile Intentions, 1994; Jimmy Hollywood, 1994; Dead Presidents, 1995; Nixon, 1995; Power 98, 1996; Sleepers, 1996; Ghosts of Mississippi, 1996; Gridlock'd, 1997; Rocket Man, 1997; Sphere, 1998; Bulworth, 1998; How Stella Got Her Groove Back, 1998; Liberty Heights, 1999; Traffic, 2000; Home Room, 2002; White Rush, 2003; Venom, 2005; Ball Don't Lie, 2008; TV series: "Another World", 1986-90; "Roseanne", 1990-96; Blossom, 1992; "Beverly Hills, 90210", 1991-92; Exclusive, 1992; "NYPD Blue", 1993-2000; Sodbusters, 1994; A Child's Cry for Help, 1994; Lily in Winter, 1994; Sharon's Secret, 1995; Trial by Fire, 1995; Bloodhounds, 1996; "Something So Right", 1996-97; The Uninvited, 1996; "The Practice", 1997-2000; "Brooklyn South", 1997-98; "Any Day Now", 1998-2000; "The X Files", 1998-2002; "A Slight Case of Murder", 1999; "Vengeance Unlimited", 1999; "City of Angels", 2000; "Family Law", 2000; Philly, 2001-02; "SemperFi", 2001; "Crossing Jordan", 2002; "Six Feet Under", 2002-03; Becker, 2002-03; "CSI: Miami", 2003; "The Lyon's Den", 2003; "Line of Fire", 2004; "Curb Your Enthusiasm", 2005; "Grey's Anatomy", 2005-08; "Private Practice", 2007. **Honors/Awds:** Nate Love Lifetime Achievement Award, Western States Black Res Educ Ctr, 2005; Outstanding Performance by an Ensemble in a Drama Series (shared), Screen Actors Guild, 2007. **Business Addr:** Actor, William Morris Agency, 1 William Morris Pl, Beverly Hills, CA 90212, **Business Phone:** (310)859-4000.*

PICKENS GLASS, ERNESTINE W. MCCOY
Educator. **Personal:** Born Dec 21, 1936, Braden, TN; daughter of Ernest W Williams and Rhobelia Alexander Williams; married William G Pickens, Sep 30, 1977; children: Marcus Christopher McCoy, Leslie, Reese, Todd. **Educ:** Tenn State Univ, BS, 1958; Atlanta Univ, MA, 1975; Emory Univ, PhD, 1986. **Career:** Educator (retired); Shelby County Bd Educ, Barret's Chapel High Sch, teacher, 1958-60; Cassopolis High Sch, teacher, 1961-62; Weaver High Sch, teacher, 1964-71; John Overton High Sch, teacher, 1971-73; Atlanta Univ, commun skills instr, 1973-78; Clark Col, asst prof Eng, assoc prof, 1975-86; Clark Atlanta Univ, prof Eng, chair, dept Eng. **Orgs:** Col Lang Asn Standing Comn, Eng Curriculum; Am Studies Asn; Nat Coun Teachers Eng; Toni Morrison Soc; Langston Hughes Soc; founding pres, Charles Waddell Chessnutt Asn. **Honors/Awds:** Outstanding Teacher Award, Clark Col, 1978; Dana Award, 1981; Appreciation Award, Nat Coun Teacher Eng, 1990; Appreciation Award, US Labor Dept, 1992. **Special Achievements:** Book: Charles W Chesnutt and the Progressive Movement, 1994; Charles W Chesnutt's The Conjure Woman, Masterpieces AFA Literature, Harper and Collins, 1992; Charles W Chesnutt's The House Behind the Cedars in Master Plots, Salem Press, 1993; Scholar in Residence, New York Univ, 1996.

PICKERING, ROBERT PERRY
Government official, educator, executive director. **Personal:** Born Oct 23, 1950, Charleston, SC; married Deborah DeLaine; children: Robert, Richard, Russell & Randall. **Educ:** Voorhees Col, BS, 1972. **Career:** Chas Co Health Dept, environ teacher, 1976; SC Swine Flu Prog Col, state coordr, 1979; DHEC SC State, epidemiologic asst, 1978-80; Health Dept Chas Co, SC, prog dir, 1980-81; Congressman T H Harnett, spec asst; Garrett Acad Community Educ Prog, dir, currently. **Orgs:** Treas, Mitchell Elem Sch PTA, 1978-85; pres, St Patrick Parish Coun, 1979-82; chmn, Mitchell Elem Sch Adv Coun, 1979-83; bd mem, Charleston OIC, 1980-83; bd mem, Morris Col Indus Bd, 1983-86; adv, SC Nat Black Republican Coun, 1984-. **Honors/Awds:** Community Service Award, Omega Psi Phi Frat, Mu Alpha Chas, SC, 1978; Outstanding Young Men of America, US Jaycees, 1981 & 1982. **Home Addr:** 179 Line St, Charleston, SC 29403. **Business Addr:** Director, Garrett Academy, Community Education Program, 2731 Gordon St, North Charleston, SC 29405, **Business Phone:** (843)529-3926.

PICKETT, CECIL BRUCE
Biologist. **Personal:** Born Oct 5, 1945, Canton, IL; married Shirley; children: 2. **Educ:** Calif State Univ, Hayward, CA, BS, biol, 1971; Univ Calif, Los Angeles, PhD, cell biol, 1976. **Career:** Univ Calif, Los Angles, fel cellular biol, 1976-78; Merck Res Labs, Montreal, Canada, sr res chemist, 1978-93, sr vpres, 1993; Howard Univ, Col Med, vis asst prof, 1978-83; NJ Sch Med & Dent, adjunct assoc prof, 1985-88; Univ Montreal, assoc prof, 1990; McGill Univ, adjunct prof, 1990; Schering-Plough Corp, exec vpres, 1993-2002, pres, 2002-06; Biogen Idec, pres, 2006-; Zimmer Holding Inc, dir, 2008-. **Orgs:** US Food & Drug Admin (FDA) Sci Bd; Am Soc Cellular Biol; Am Soc Biochem & Molecular Biol; Am Asn Cancer Res; Am Asn Advancement Sci; Adv Comt, Dir Nat Insts Health; Adv Comt, Nat Cancer Policy Bd Inst Med. **Honors/Awds:** Alumni Association Award for Scholarly Achievement and Academic Distinction, UCLA, 1976; Macy Scholar, Marine Biol Labs, Woods Hole, Mass, 1978; 'first Robert A. Scala Award and Lectureship in Toxicology', Rutgers Univ; Univ Med & Dent, New Jersey, 1993; Disting Lecturer, Jonsson Comprehensive Cancer Ctr, UCLA, 1995; Founders Award, Chem Ind Inst Technol Ctrs Health Res, 2001. **Special Achievements:** Published extensively in leading research journals and has been a frequent speaker at scientific symposia and conferences. **Business Addr:** President, Biogen Idec, 14 Cambridge Center, Cambridge, MA 02142, **Business Phone:** (617)679-2000.*

PICKETT, DONNA A
Executive. **Personal:** Born Jun 11, 1949, Lexington, VA; daughter of Mallory Wayne Harris and Gladys Jones Harris; married Edward E; children: Monica & Aaron. **Educ:** Va Commonwealth Univ, Richmond, VA, BA, eng. **Career:** Va Power, Richmond, VA, off supvr, supvr personnel servs, supvr rec mgt, Minority Affairs & Pub Affairs Dept, dir currently, 1969-. **Orgs:** Bd mem, Va Black Hist Mus & Cult Ctr, 1989-; chairperson, Va Coun Status Women, 1991-94; chairperson, bus adv coun, Orgn Chinese Am; vpres, external rels, Am Asn Blacks Energy. **Honors/Awds:** Suggestion Patent Award, 1984; Achievement Award, 1984, 1985; Performance Award, 1985; Mentorship Program Award, Va Power; Award, Bennett Col Bd Trustees, Black Exec Exchange Prog, 1989, 1991, 1992. **Home Addr:** 7805 Kahlua Dr, Richmond, VA 23227, **Home Phone:** (804)262-4670. **Business Addr:** Director, Virginia Power, Minority Affairs & Public Affairs Department, 120 Tredegar St Fl 20, PO Box 26666, Richmond, VA 23261, **Business Phone:** (804)771-4797.

PICKETT, REV. HENRY B, JR.
Educator, clergy. **Personal:** Born Mar 21, 1938, Morehead City, NC; married Mary Louise Hoffler; children: Marquis DeLafayette & Sherry Louise. **Educ:** Elizabeth City State Univ, BS, 1961; NC Central Univ, MA, 1973; Shaw Divinity Sch, Shaw Divinity Sch, MDiv, 1977. **Career:** Educator, clergy (Retired); Raleigh City, elem teacher, 1963-72; St Augustine's Col, counr foreign student adv, 1972-73; Fuguay Varina, counr, 1973-76; East Millbrook Middle Sch, coun, 1976-91; Oberlin Baptist Church, pastor, 1977-80; Wendell First Baptist Church, pastor, 1982-85; Wake County Pub Sch, staff. **Orgs:** Pres, Black Dem Caucus; chmn, Wake Co, 1974; bd trustees, Elizabeth City State Univ, 2001; Baptist Minister Wake Co Bd Edn; Am Personnel & Guidance Asn; Am Sch Counr Asn; NEA; NCPGA; NC Asn Educr; Phi Delta Kappa; Nat Asn Advan Colored People; Kingwood Forest Comn Asn Inc; Omega Psi Phi Frat Inc. **Honors/Awds:** Man of the Year, Oberlin Baptist Church, 1968; Boy Scout District Award Merit, 1971; Omega Achievement Award; Citizen of Year, 1974; Phi Delta Kappa, 1975; Outstanding Alumni Service Award, Elizabeth City State Univ, 1995; Downtown Housing Improvement Award, 1995; Sertoma Club Service to Mankind Award, 1997; NC Conference of Branches, NAACP; President Award, 1997; State of NC The Order of the long Leaf Pine, 2000; bd trustees, Elizabeth City State Univ, 2001; Presidential Citation recognition of exemplary experiences honor Elizabeth City State Univ, NAFEO, 2003. **Special Achievements:** State NC The Order of the long Leaf Pine, 2000; Presidential Citation recognition of exemplary experiences honor Elizabeth City State Univ, NAFEO, 2003. **Military Serv:** AUS, chaplin, 1961-63. **Home Addr:** 1604 E Davie St, Raleigh, NC 27610.

PICKETT, ROBERT E.
Educator. **Personal:** Born Sep 8, 1936, Brookhaven, MS; married Dorothy Owens; children: Deborah Denise & Ritchie Elyot. **Educ:** Alcorn State Univ, BS, 1957; Miss Jackson State Univ, MS, educ admin, 1969; Miss State Univ, Univ Miss & Atlanta Univ, attended. **Career:** Educator (retired); Randolph High Sch Pass Christian, MS, teacher & coach, 1957-59; Weathers High Sch Rolling Park, MS, teacher, 1959-60; Temple High Sch Vicksburg, MS, teacher, coach & admin asst, 1960-64; Mc Intyre Elem Jr High Sch Vicksburg, MS, prin, 1964-87; Jefferson Jr High Sch Vicksburg, MS, prin, 1966-73; Vicksburg High Sch, admin prin, 1973-77, prin, 1980-87; Vicksburg Jr High Sch, prin, 1977-80; Vicksburg Warren Sch Dist, deputy supt, 1987-94, supt, 1994-; Warren County Sch Dist, supt, 1994-99. **Orgs:** Bd mem, mgt, chmn, Jackson St YMCA, 1966-70; Vicksburg Teachers Asn; Nat Educ Asn; Am Asn Sch Admin; vice chmn, Elks Fidelity Lodge #507; ETA TAU Chap Omega Psi Phi Frat Basileus, 1969-71; pres, Warren Co United Fund, 1973; Vicksburg Park Comm, 1970-80; pres, Port City Kiwanis Club, 1975-76; bd dirs, Commun Improvement Inc WLBT-TV 3; bd dirs, Vicksburg Warren County; bd dirs, Merchant Bank; Miss Asn Sec Sch Prin; Nat Asn Sec Sch Prin; Phi Delta Kappa; Asn Supv & Curric Develop; Miss Asn Sch Adminr; Miss Asn Sch Bus Officials; Miss Asn Sch Supt & Southeastern Asn Sch Bus Officials; Three Rivers Dist Boy Scouts Am; Vicksburg Chapter Am Red Cross; bd dirs, Hinds Comm Col; Warren County Port Comn. **Honors/Awds:** YMCA Service Award, 1969; UGF Service Award, 1973; Golden Lamp Award, MSAsn, 1997. **Home Phone:** (601)636-0999.

PICKLES, PATRICIA L.
School administrator, executive. **Career:** Tex Educ Agency, sor dir; N Chicago Sch Dist 187, supt; Portland Pub Schs, chief acad officer. **Honors/Awds:** Crown Award; Distinguished Alumnus Award, Ill Community Col Trustees. **Special Achievements:** The Most Influential African American of Lake County for the Year, 2001. **Business Addr:** Chief Academic Officer, Portland Public Schools, 501 N Dixon St, Portland, OR 97227-1807.

PICKRUM, LISA M.
Businessperson. **Personal:** Born 1970?. **Educ:** Vassar College, BA; Univ of Pennsylvania, MBA, Stanford Law School, JD. **Career:** Exec VP and COO of the RLJ Companies, 2004-; Principal at Katalyst Venture Partners, 1999-03;Senior consultant for Accenture, 1998-99; attorney with the Federal Communications Commission (FCC), 1994-96;. **Orgs:** Board of directors for Rollover Systems and CW Wellspring Entertainment;. **Special Achievements:** Named one of the "50 Most Powerful Black Women in Business" by Black Enterprise, Feb, 2006. **Business Addr:** The RLJ Companies, 3 Bethesda Metro Center, Suite 1000, Bethesda, MD 20814, **Business Phone:** (301)280-7700.*

PICKRUM, MICHAEL
Executive, chief financial officer. **Educ:** Stanford Univ, BE, elec engr, ME, engineering-econ systs; Wharton Sch Bus, Univ Pa, MBA. **Career:** Mercer Mgt Consult, strategy consult; BET Interactive, vpres bus develop, exec vpres & chief operating officer, 2003-07, chief financial officer, 2007-. **Business Addr:** Chief Financial Officer, BET Interactive LLC, 2000 M St NW Suite 602, Washington, DC 20036, **Business Phone:** (202)533-1900.*

PIERCE, AARON
Football player. **Personal:** Born Sep 6, 1969, Seattle, WA; son of Samuel. **Educ:** Univ Wash. **Career:** Football player (retired); New York Giants, tight end, 1992-97; Baltimore Ravens, 1999; New York Gaints, free agt, currently.

PIERCE, AARONETTA HAMILTON
Association executive. **Personal:** Born Jan 8, 1943, Somerville, TN; daughter of David A and Clementine Lofties; married Joseph A Pierce Jr, M.D., Mar 1, 1964; children: Joseph Aaron, Michael Arthur. **Educ:** Tenn State Univ, Nashville, TN, 1961; State Univ Iowa, Iowa City, IA, BA, 1963. **Career:** San Antonio Independent Sch Dist, San Antonio, TX, teacher, 1964-67; Camino Real Bank, dir, 1994-01; Premier Artworks Inc, pres, currently. **Orgs:** Bd trustees, Fisk Univ, 1992-; Comnr, Tex Comn Arts, 1985-91; chairperson, Mayor's Blue Ribbon Comt Arts San Antonio, 1988-89; chairperson, first Martin Luther King Jr. Comn & Celebration San Antonio, Nat Arts dir, Links Inc, 1994-98, 1986-87; chairperson, Tex Arts Award, Texas Arts Alliance, 1988; reg arts comt chairperson, Alpha Kappa Alpha Sorority, 1991; exec comt, United Way San Antonio, 1988-94; founding mem, Southwest Ethnic Arts Soc. **Honors/Awds:** San Antonio Women's Hall of Fame, City of San Antonio, 1984; Texas Black Women's Hall of Fame, 1986; Nominee, Inductee into Texas Women's Hall of Fame, 1993; Headliner Award, Women in Communications, 1989; JC Penney Golden Rule Award, Cultural Category, 1984; barge named for her, carries tourists along San Antonio River; Texas Women's Hall of Fame, 1993; First African-American woman appointed to the Texas Commission on Arts. **Business Phone:** (210)490-4084.*

PIERCE, ABE, III
Mayor. **Personal:** Married Dorothy. **Career:** Mayor, Monroe (LA), 1996; Ouachita Parish sch syst, asst supt. **Orgs:** Ouachita Parish Police Jury. **Special Achievements:** First African American mayor of Monroe (LA) since Reconstruction. **Military Serv:** AUS, Second Lt.

PIERCE, DR. CHESTER MIDDLEBROOK
Educator. **Personal:** Born Mar 4, 1927, Glen Cove, NY; son of Samuel and Hettie; married Jocelyn Patricia Blanchet, Jun 15,

1949; children: Diane Blanchet Williams & Deirdre Anona. **Educ:** Harvard Col, AB, 1948; Harvard Med Sch, MD, 1952; Tufts Univ, ScD (hon), 1984; Westfield State, ScD (hon), 1977, DEng (hon), 1997. **Career:** Univ Cincinnati, instr, 1957-60; Univ Okla, from asst prof to prof, 1960-69; Harvard Grad Sch Educ, prof, prof emer, currently; Mass Gen Hosp, sr psychiatrist, currently. **Orgs:** Sr consult, Peace Corps, 1965-69; advisor, C's TV Workshop (Sesame St),1969-; founding nat chmn, Black Psychiatrists Am, 1969; nat consult, USAF,1976-82; pres, Am Bd Psychiat & Neurol, 1978; pres, Am OrthopsychiatricAsn, 1983; chair, NASA's Life Sci & Microgravity Sci Res Adv Comn, 1996;Am Acad Arts & Sci, 1997; chmn, Behavior & Performance Working Group,currently. **Honors/Awds:** Pierce Peak (in Antartica for biomedical res), 1968; Special Recognition Award, Nat Med Asn, 1974; hon fel, Royal Australian & New Zealand Col Psychiat, 1978; Solomon Carter Fuller Award, Am Psychiat Asn, 1986; Chester M Pierce Annual Res Sem, Nat Med Asn, 1988-; Masserman Award, World Psychiat Assoc, 1989; hon fel, Royal Col Psychiat, 1995; Division of Global Psychiatry, Mass gen Hosp, named in honor, 2009. **Military Serv:** USNR, comdr. **Home Addr:** 17 Prince St, Jamaica Plain, MA 02130. **Business Addr:** Professor Emeritus Psychiatry, Harvard Graduate School of Education, Nichols House Appian Way, Cambridge, MA 02138, **Business Phone:** (617)495-4929.

PIERCE, CYNTHIA STRAKER
Educator. **Personal:** Born Jan 1, 1929, Brooklyn, NY; daughter of Enid Bayley Straker and Milton; married Lawrence W. **Educ:** Hunter Col, AB, 1950; Brooklyn Law Sch, LLB, 1953, LLM, 1956. **Career:** Educator (retired); Pvt Pract, atty, 1954-56; Howard Univ, fac, 1956-62; FAA, atty adv, 1962-69; US Dept Transp, atty office sec, 1969-82; StJohn's Sch Law, assoc prof, 1983. **Orgs:** New York, Wash & DC Bar Asn; US Supreme Ct Nat Bar Asn; Fed Bar Asn; Nat Asn Advan Colored People; Nat Urban League. **Honors/Awds:** Fed Women's Award, Dept Transp, 1979; Hall of Fame, Hunter Col, 1983; Outstanding Service Award, St. John's Univ. **Special Achievements:** Author of "DC Lawyer's Handbook". **Home Addr:** 83 Hhempstead St, PO Box 2234, Sag Harbor, NY 11963-0111. *

PIERCE, DR. GREGORY W
Physician. **Personal:** Born Sep 25, 1957, Vallejo, CA; son of Raymond O Pierce Jr and Geraldine Brunridge Pierce; married Eurica Hill, Aug 4, 1990. **Educ:** Wabash Col, BA, 1979; Meharry Med Col, MD, 1983. **Career:** Univ Tenn Jackson-Madison Co Gen Hosp, intern & resident 1983-86; Family Health Assocs, staff physician 1986-; Bd Cert, Am Bd Family Pract, 1986-99; Patient First, med dir, Continuing Med Educ, dir & staff physician, currently; pvt pract, currently. **Orgs:** Chmn, J Comm Malcolm X Inst Black Studies Wabash Col; jr class pres, sr class pres Meharry Med Col; term trustee, Meharry Med Col Bd Trustees; cert instr, Advan Cardiac Life Support; Am & Tenn Med Asns; Am & Tenn Acad Family Physicians; Southern Med Asn; NMA; chmn, Dept Med, Middle Tenn Med Ctr, 1990-91; Alpha Omega Alpha Honor Med Soc. **Honors/Awds:** Honor Scholarship & Dean's List Wabash Col; Alvin P Hall Scholarship; Mosby Scholarship Book Award; Upjohn Award for Excellence, Clin &Academic Obstet & Gynecol; Pre-Alumni Asn Annual Senior Recognition Award. **Business Addr:** Director, Staff Physician, Patient First, 5000 Cox Rd, Glen Allen, VA 23060-9200, **Business Phone:** (804)968-5700.

PIERCE, JOSEPH
Lawyer. **Career:** Jacksonville Jaguars, assoc gen coun Ltd, currently. **Business Addr:** Associate General Counsel, Jacksonville Jaguars, 1 Alltel Stadium Pl, Jacksonville, FL 32202.*

PIERCE, KAMA B
Educator. **Career:** St Mark's Sch, dir mkt; Episcopal Acad, Lower Sch, Merion, assoc dir admis, currently. **Business Addr:** Associate Director of Admission, Episcopal Academy, Lower School, 376 N Latches Lane, Merion, PA 19066, **Business Phone:** (610)667-9612.*

PIERCE, HON. LAWRENCE WARREN
Judge. **Personal:** Born Dec 31, 1924, Philadelphia, PA; son of Leora Bellinger and Harold E; married Wilma Taylor, Sep 1948 (died 1978); children: Warren Wood, Michael Lawrence & Mark Taylor; married Cynthia Straker, Jul 8, 1979. **Educ:** St Joseph Univ, BS, 1948; Fordham Univ Sch Law, LLB, 1951. **Career:** Judge (retired); Gen law pract, New York City, 1951-61; Kings Co, NY, asst dist atty, 1954-61; New York City Police Dept, dep police comnr, 1961-63; NY State Div Youth, Albany, dir, 1963-66; NY State Narc Addiction Cont Comn, chmn, 1966-70; State Univ NY, Albany, Grad Sch Crim Justice, vis prof, 1970-71; S Dist New York, US dist judge, 1971-81; US Foreign Intelligence Surveillance Ct, judge, 1979-81; US Ct Appeals, Second Circuit, judge, 1981-90; sr judge, 1990-95; Cambodian Ct Training Proj Int Human Rights Law Group, 1995. **Orgs:** Pres, Cath Inter Coun, 1957-63; NBA; Am Bar Asn; bd mem, Lincoln Hall Boys, 1972-92; trustee, Fordham Univ, 1985-91; bd mgrs, Havens Relief Fund Soc; Am Law Inst, CARE USA; bd mem, St Joseph's Univ, Philadelphia, Pa; bd trustees, Practising Law Inst; Am Law Inst; deleg, Africa, Sweden, England, Japan, Vietnam, Korea, W Ger & People's Rep China study legal, judicial & correctional systems; Coun Foreign Rels. **Honors/Awds:** BALSA's Ruth Whitehead Whaley Award for Distinguished Legal Achievement, Fordham Univ Sch Law; Judicial Friends' Judge Jane Bolin Award; DHL, St Joseph Univ, 1967; LLD, Fairfield Univ, 1972; LLD, Fordham Univ, 1982; LLD, Hamilton Col, 1987; LLD, St John's Univ, 1990. **Military Serv:** AUS, sgt, 1943-46.

PIERCE, PAUL
Basketball player. **Personal:** Born Oct 13, 1977, Oakland, CA; son of Lorraine Hosey. **Educ:** Univ KS, crime & delinquency studies. **Career:** Boston Celtics, forward & capt, 1998-. **Honors/Awds:** Freshman of the Year, 1995-96; Most Valuable Player, Big 12 Conf Tournament, 1996-97; 1997-98; Rookie of the Month, 1999; Player of the Month Award, NBA, 2001; Player of the Week award, NBA. **Business Addr:** Professional Basketball Player, Boston Celtics, 151 Merrimac St Suite 400, Boston, MA 02114, **Business Phone:** (617)523-6050.

PIERCE, PONCHITTA A
Television show host, journalist, editor. **Personal:** Born Aug 5, 1942, Chicago, IL; daughter of Alfred and Nora. **Educ:** Cambridge Univ, Eng, attended 1962; Univ Southern Calif, BA (cum laude), jour, 1964. **Career:** Ebony Mag, asst ed, 1964-65, assoc ed, 1965-67; Johnson Publ Co, New York ed bur chief, 1967-68; CBS News, spec corresp, 1968-71; McCall's Mag, contrib ed, 1973-76; Reader's Digest, staff writer, 1975-77, roving ed, 1977-80; PBS, WNET Channel 13, host; WNBC-TV, mag writer & TV host; Parade Mag, contrib ed, 1994; Univ Southern Calif, Ctr Pub Diplomacy, adv bd mem, currently. **Orgs:** Bd dirs, Foreign Policy Asn; Thirteen/WNET; Inner-City Scholarship Fund Catholic Archdiocese NY; Housing Enterprise Less Privileged; Josephson Inst Ethics; Women's Foreign Policy Group; Cuban Artists Fund; External affairs comt mem, Hirshhorn Mus; external affairs comt mem, Sculpture Garden; Econ Club NY; Lotos Club; Columbia Presby Health Sci Adv Coun; exec comt mem, Coun Adv, Nat Ctr Children Poverty; Theta Sigma Phi NY Chap; Am Fedn TV & Radio Artists; Am Women Radio & TV; Nat Acad TV Arts & Sci, NY Chap; Women's Forum. **Honors/Awds:** Penney-Mo Mag Award, 1967; Headliner Award, Nat Theta Sigma Phi, 1970. **Business Addr:** Advisory Board Member, University of South California, Center on Public Diplomacy, 3502 Watt Way Suite 103, Los Angeles, CA 90089-0281, **Business Phone:** (213)821-2078.

PIERCE, DR. RAYMOND O., JR.
Educator, physician. **Personal:** Born May 17, 1931, Monroe, LA; married Geraldine Brundidge; children: Raymond III, Gregory, Leannette, Geralyn & Lori. **Educ:** Fisk Univ Nashville, TN, BA, 1951; Meharry Med Col Nashville, TN, MD, 1955. **Career:** Self-employed physician, 1963-69; Va Hosp Des Moines, resident; Univ Iowa, resident, 1963; Methodist Hosp, courtesy staff, 1969-; Winona Hosp, hon staff, 1969-; Ind Univ Med Ctr, from asst prof to prof, 1970-2000, dept chair, prof emer orthopedic surg, 2000-; AUS Hosp Ft Benjamin Harrison, consult staff, 1976-79; Martin Univ, med dir, currently; J Robert Gladden Orthopedic Soc, chief exec officer, 2002-; Wishard Hosp, chief orthopedic surg. **Orgs:** Bd dir, Martin Ctr, 1970-; bd dir, St Elizabeth's Home, 1980-83; bd dir, Flanner House, 1980-; pres, Aesculapian Med Soc, 1972-75; Am Acad Ortho Surg; AAAS; Am Asn Surg Trauma; examnr, cert Am Bd Ortho Surg, 1976-84; credentials comn, Am Col Surgeons, 1983-84; Am Fracture Asn; Am Soc Sports Med; chrtr mem, Am Trauma Soc; chmn bd, Group Pract Inc, 1973-79; secy & pres, Hoosier State Med Asn, 1968-75; pres, secy & treas, IN Bone & Joint Club, 1980-; chmn, IN Ortho Soc, 1970-80; Int Col Surgeons; bd trustee, MDDS, 1968-74; house delegates co-chmn, Nat Med Asn, 1963-76, Pan-Pacific Surg Soc; Sigma XI-Res Soc. **Honors/Awds:** Summer Furness Award, Outstanding Community Service, 1977; Physical Recogoniton Award, Am Med Asn, 1977-83; Physical Recogoniton Award, NMA,1981-83; Scientific Award, IN State Med Asn Meeting, 1980; Scientific Award, IN State Med Asn, 1982; Government Award, Coun Sagamore Wabash, 1984; Health Profession Public Health Award, 2003. **Special Achievements:** Publications: Alcohol, Underlying Cause of Many Skeletal Lesions, Ortho News, Vol 6 2 Mar/Apr 1984 p3; The Effect of Alcohol on Skeletal System, Ortho Review, Vol XIV 1 Jan 1985 pp45-49; Treatment of Subtrochanteric Fractures with a Flexible Intramedulla Rod Ortho Transactions, Vol 8 3Fall 1984 441. **Military Serv:** USAF, capt, 1956-58. **Business Addr:** Professor Emeritus of Orthopaedic Surgery, Indiana University Medical Center, 400 E Seventh St, Bloomington, IN 47405-3085, **Business Phone:** (812)855-1162.

PIERCE, RICKY CHARLES
Basketball player. **Personal:** Born Aug 19, 1959, Dallas, TX. **Educ:** Rice Univ, Houston, TX, BS, 1983. **Career:** Basketball player(retired); Detroit Pistons, 1982-83; San Diego Clippers, 1983-84; Milwaukee Bucks, 1984-91; Milwaukee Bucks, 1997-98; Seattle SuperSonics, 1991-94; Golden State Warriors, 1994-95; Indiana Pacers, 1995-96; Denver Nuggets, 1996-97; Charlotte Hornets, 1997; AEK Athens, 1997. **Honors/Awds:** Sixth Man of the Year Award, NBA, 1987, 1990; All-Star game, 1991. *

PIERCE, RUDOLPH F
Lawyer. **Personal:** Born Aug 12, 1942, Boston, MA; children: Kristen & Khari. **Educ:** Hampton Inst, BA 1967; Harvard Law Sch, JD, 1970. **Career:** Goulston & Storrs, atty, 1991-; Mass Superior Ct, judge; US Dist Ct Mass, Fed Magistrate; Keating Perretta & Pierce, partner, 1975-76; Crane Inker & Oteri, asso, 1972-74. **Orgs:** Pres, Boston Bar Asn, 1989-90; Am Col Trial Lawyers; Int Acad Trial Lawyers; New Eng Aquarium; trustee, Children's Hosp; chmn, Nat Inst Trial Advocacy; trustee, Inst Healthcare Improvement. **Honors/Awds:** "American Leading Business Lawyers", Chambers & Partners, 2003-07; Best Lawyers in Am, 2006 & 2008. **Special Achievements:** First African American president of the Boston Bar Association; co-author, The "Other" Costs of Securities Class Action Settlements, FindLaw, 2004. **Military Serv:** AUS, Sp-4, 1960-63. **Business Addr:** Attorney, Goulston & Storrs, 400 Atlantic Ave, Boston, MA 02110-3333, **Business Phone:** (617)574-4078.

PIERCE, WALTER J
Educator. **Personal:** Born Jan 16, 1941, Minden, LA; married Iopha Douglas; children: Gay, Gwenevera & Iopha Anita. **Educ:** BS, 1964. **Career:** Educator (retired); Atascadero State Hosp, recreation therapist, 1964-69; Kiwanis Club, counr, 1968-70; Tulare View, dir rehab, 1969-70; Northside Hosp, dir activities, 1970-71; Calif State Univ, affirmative action coordr, 1972-74, asst coord advising & testing serv, 1974, Advising Serv, asst dir. **Orgs:** Kiwanis Club, 1968-70; Nat Asn Advan Colored People; Black Educator, Fresno, CA; Fresno Housing Affirmative Comt; Baptist Sunday Sch Supt; Plan Variation; chmn, Man Power & Econ Area 6. **Honors/Awds:** Outstanding Young Men America, 1970; Certificate of Merit, Nat Acad Adv Asn, 1986.

PIERCE, WILLIAM DALLAS
Psychologist. **Personal:** Born Nov 16, 1940, Sunbury, NC. **Educ:** Univ of Pittsburg, BS, 1962; OH State Univ, MA, 1965; OH State Univ, PhD, 1967. **Career:** Pvt Pract San Francisco CA, clin psychologist 1969-; Dept Psychol Univ Calif Berkeley, lectr, 1970-; Westside Community Ment Health Ctr, dir clin serv, 1971-73; Westside Community Ment Health Ctr, San Francisco, exec dir, 1973-77; Dept Ment Health Comn Mass, regional serv admin, 1979-80. **Orgs:** Founding mem, Asn Black Psychologists, 1968; chmn comn ment health, Asn Black Psychologists 1971-73; pres, Bay Area Asn Black Psychologists, 1978-79. **Honors/Awds:** Appreciation Award, Asn Black Psychologists, 1970; Blacks in the West Hall of Fame, San Francisco African Hist Cult Soc 1976; Annual Award for leadership & Serv Asn Black Psychologisgts, 1980. **Business Addr:** President, William D Pierce PhD, 361 Upper Terr, San Francisco, CA 94117, **Business Phone:** (415)771-3938.

PIERRE, DR. DALLAS
Dentist. **Personal:** Born Jun 9, 1933, Charenton, LA; son of Russell Sr; married Carol Ann Yates; children: Dr James Pierre. **Educ:** Prairie View A&M Col, BS, 1955; Tex State Univ, MS, 1963; Univ Tex, Dental Br, DDS, 1968; Trinity Univ, adv study. **Career:** Pvt pract, dent, currently. **Orgs:** E Tex Area BSA; Nat Platform Asn; Phi Beta Sigma; Univ Tex Alumni Asn; Citizens C of C Angelina Co; Baptist Church; pres, Gulf State Dental Asn; secy, E Tex Med Dent Phar Asn; Golden Heritage mem, NAACP; E TX Minority Bus Develop Found Inc, 1974-; Lufkin Daily News Ed Roundtable; Am Dental Asn; Nat Dental Asn, house delegates, Acad Gen Dentistry; Tex Dental Asn; E Tex Dental Soc; Lufkin ISD Sch Bd; Int Platform Asn; Acad Gen Dentistry. **Honors/Awds:** Honoree, Colgate Dental Health Educ Adv Bd; Top Ladies of Distinction; Citizen of the Yr, Prof Activ Club Nacogdoches & Angelina Counties; NAACP, Golden Heritage Mem; honoree, Notable Am Bicentennial Era; honoree, Community Leaders & Noteworthy Americans. **Military Serv:** USAF, airman, 1st class, 1956-60. **Business Addr:** Dentist, Private Practice, 809 Kurth Dr, Lufkin, TX 75904-2037, **Business Phone:** (936)632-5255.*

PIERRE, JENNIFER CASEY
Executive. **Personal:** Born Aug 25, 1953, Baltimore, MD; daughter of Johnny Casey and Mary L Murreld; married Clifford Marston, May 9, 1987; children: Marianne Alicia Pierre & Marissa Janelle Pierre. **Educ:** Carnegie-Mellon Univ, Pittsburgh, Pa, BS, math, 1975; Columbia Bus Sch, New York, NY, MBA, 1977. **Career:** Gen Foods Corp, White Plains, New York, asst brand mgr, 1977-79; American Can Co, Greenwich, Conn, assoc brand mgr, 1979-81; RJ Reynolds Tobacco Co, Winston-Salem, NC, mgr fulfillment, 1981, mgr tracking/ eval, currently. **Orgs:** Vol, Forsyth Ct Vols, 1981-84; bd mem, Baldwin Sch, 1985; vis prof, Nat Urban League BEEP, 1986-. **Special Achievements:** Scholarship for Boarding School, A Better Chance, 1968-71; Graduate Fellowship/Internship, General Foods Corp, 1975-77. **Business Phone:** (336)741-5000.

PIERRE, DR. PERCY ANTHONY
Dean (Education), educator, executive. **Personal:** Born Jan 3, 1939, St James, LA; son of Percy Pierre and Rosa Villavaso Pierre; married Olga A Markham, Aug 7, 1965; children: Kristin Clare & Allison Celeste. **Educ:** Univ Notre Dame, BS, 1961, MS, 1963; Johns Hopkins Univ, PhD (elec eng), 1967; Univ MI, PhD, 1968. **Career:** Johns Hopkins Univ, instr elec eng, 1963-64; Morgan State Col, instr physics, 1964-66; Univ MI, instr info & control eng, 1967-68; Univ Calif, Los Angles, instr systems eng, 1968-69; RAND Corp, res engr commun, 1968-71; Off Pres, White House, fel spl asst, 1969-70; Howard Univ, dean sch eng, 1971-77; Alfred

P Sloan Found, prog officer eng educ, 1973-75; Percy A. Pierre & Assoc, eng mgt consult, 1981-83; Prairie View A&M Univ, pres 1983-89, Hitachi, bd dir, 1988-; Honeywell, prof elec eng, 1989-90; CMS Energy Corp, bd mem, 1990-; Mich State Univ, vpres, 1990-95, dir Sloan Scholar prog, prof elec & comput eng, 1995-2005, vpres & prof emer, 2005-; Aerospace Corp, bd mem, 1991-; Dual Inc, bd mem, 1992; Old Kent Financial Corp, dir, 1992-; IDL Technol IST, bd dir, 1992-94; Univ Notre Dame, Trustee, currently. **Orgs:** Ctr Naval Analysis, 1987-94; trustee, Univ Notre Dame, 1974-; Inst Elec & Electronis Eng; Sigma Xi; Tau Beta Pi; Sci Res Soc Am. **Honors/Awds:** Hon Doctoral Degree, The Univ Notre Dame, 1977; Award of Merit, Sen Proxmire, 1979; Reginald Jones Award, Nat Action Coun Minorities Engineering, 1984; Hon Doctoral Degree, Rensselaer Polytech Inst, 1984; Superior Public Service Award, US Navy, 1993; Frazier Thompson Pioneer Award, Black Alumni Univ Notre Dame, 1997; The Golden Torch Award, Nat Soc Black Eng, 2003; Frederick Scott Award, Soc Black Alumni Johns Hopkins Univ, 2003; Founder's Award, Nat Action Coun Minorities Engineering, 2004; Diversity Award, Mich State Univ, 2004. **Special Achievements:** Author of over thirty articles on engineering research, engineering education, systems analysis and military research and development; In 1967 Percy Pierre became the first African American to earn a doctorate in electrical engineering. **Military Serv:** AUS, asst secy res, Devel & acquisition, 1977-81; Distinguished Civilian Serv Award, Dept Army, 1981. **Business Addr:** Professor Emeritus, Michigan State University, Department of Electrical & Computer Engineering, 3224 Engineering Bldg, East Lansing, MI 48824, **Business Phone:** (517)432-5148.

PIERRE-LOUIS, DR. CONSTANT
Physician. **Personal:** Born Feb 11, 1939; married Jeany; children: Marilyn, Pascale & Carolyn. **Educ:** State Univ Port-au-Prince Med Sch, MD, 1963. **Career:** Physician (retired); Columbis Univ, 1971-75; Downstate Univ, clinic asst prof urol; Adelphi Med ARt Asn, fndg mem partner; Brookdale Hosp, St John's Epis Hosp, Unity Hosp, staff mem; Pvt Pract, urologist. **Orgs:** Am bd urol; fel, Am Col Surg; NY State Med Soc, Nat Med Ass; bd mem & pres, Asn Haitian Drs Abroad, 1975-76. **Honors/Awds:** Essay Contest 3rd prize, 1969. **Special Achievements:** Publisher: "Lymphoma of the Urethra Masquerading as a Caruncle" 1972; "Morphologic Appearance of Leydig Cells in Patients with Prostatic Cancer & Benign Prostatic Hypertrophy", NY Acad Med Urol Resd; "Delayed Subcapsular Renal Hematoma" Urol, 1977.

PIERSON, DERRON
Executive, vice president (organization). **Career:** Solo Construct Corp, vpres, currently. **Business Phone:** (305)944-3922.

PIERSON, KATHRYN A
Lawyer, chief executive officer. **Personal:** Born May 27, 1956, Chicago, IL; daughter of Edward and Myrtle; married Cedric Hendricks, Jul 17, 1982; children: Malcolm, Marcus & Nikki Henricks. **Educ:** George Wash Univ, BA, jour, polit sci, 1979; Howard Univ, JD, 1985. **Career:** Pierson & Archibald, lawyer & partner, 1987-93; Minority Asset Recovery Contractors Asn, exec dir, 1993-95; Tradewinds Int, dir bus develop, 1995, bus develop consult, 1996; Malnikus Real Estate Enterprises Inc, chief exec officer. **Orgs:** Chair, bd dirs, WPFW-FM, 1982-84; secy, chair, develop comt, Pacifica Found Corp, 1984-90; bd mem, Marshall Heights Community Develop Orgn, 1989-91; bd trustees, Rhythm & Blues Found, 1990-; chair, bd dirs, Dist Curators, 1991-.

PIERSON, RANDY
Executive, founder (originator), chief executive officer. **Career:** Solo Construct Corp, co-founder, 1978-, chief exec officer, currently. **Business Phone:** (305)944-3922.

PIGGEE, JAMES
School administrator. **Career:** Horace Mann High Sch, dean studs; Lew Wallace High Sch, high sch asst or vprin, 2005-06.

PILE, MICHAEL DAVID MCKENZIE
Administrator. **Personal:** Born Jan 28, 1954, New York, NY; son of Ernest S and Ulalie; married May 20, 1989. **Educ:** Colgate Univ, Hamilton, NY, BA, 1976; New York Univ, New York, NY, MPA, 1983. **Career:** Queens Hosp Ctr, Queens, NY, asst dir, 1978-86; Long Island Jewish Hillside Med Ctr, Queens, NY, 1984-86; Syracuse Univ, Syracuse, NY, health serv adminr, 1983-89; Calif State Univ, Sacramento, CA, dir univ health Ctr, 1989-. **Orgs:** Am Pub Health Asn, 1981; Am Col Health Asn, 1984-; chair, Constitution & Bylaws, Pacific Coast Col Health Asn, 1990-92. **Business Addr:** Director of Health, California State University Sacramento, Psychological Services, 6000 J St Health Center, Sacramento, CA 95819-6045, **Business Phone:** (916)278-6011.

PILGRIM, DAVID
Educator. **Personal:** Born Jan 3, 1959, Manhatten, NY; son of Eustace and Jean Shears; married Margaret Ryan, Dec 28, 1991; children: Haley Grace, Gabrielle Lynn & Eustace Jamison. **Educ:** Jarvis Christian Col, BA, 1980; Ohio State Univ, MA, 1982, PhD, 1984. **Career:** St Mary's Col, asst prof, 1984-89; Ferris State Univ, prof sociol, 1990-, chief diversity officer, currently; Jim Crow Mus, cur, 1998-. **Orgs:** Bd dirs, Mich Mus Asn, 2003; dir, Am Black Studies Libr. **Honors/Awds:** Distinguished Teaching, Mich Bd Govrs, 1998; VP Award for Academic Excellence, Ferris State Univ, 2000; Medal, Dept Defense, 2002. **Special Achievements:** Numerous scholarly and popular articles about racial and ethnic relations. Several books including, Above the Veil. **Business Addr:** Professor, Chief Diversity Officer, Ferris State University, Department of Social Science, 1201 S State St CSS 312, Big Rapids, MI 49307-2225, **Business Phone:** (231)591-3946.

PILLOW, VANITA J.
Salesperson. **Personal:** Born Dec 16, 1949, Nashville, TN. **Career:** Des Moines Main PO Supply & Procurement Asst; TN State Univ, part time instr, 1971; Exp Theatre sponsor; Electric Dance Workshop Sponser, 1972; Fayette Co Bd Educ, sec instr & Beta Honor Soc sponsor, 1973; speech dramatics arts grad asst; S Central Bell Bus Off, sales rep teller. **Orgs:** Theta Alpha Phi, 1969; USO Tour Ger, Holland, Belgium, 1970; Women's Bowling League, 1971; Univ Couns; pres, TN State Players Guild; NAACP; Minority Consumer Commun Theatre Nashville, 1974. **Honors/Awds:** Best female actress, 1971; C Theatre Chicago Grad top 10 percent class.

PILOT, ANN HOBSON
Musician. **Personal:** Born Nov 6, 1943, Philadelphia, PA; daughter of Harrison and Grace Stevens Smith; married R Prentice; children: Lynn & Prentice. **Educ:** Cleveland Inst, BM, 1966. **Career:** Pittsburgh Sym Orchestra, second harpist, 1965-66; Wash Nat Sym, prinharpist, 1966-69; Ambler Music Festival, fac, 1968-69; New Eng Conserv Music, Boston, MA, harp teacher, 1971-; Boston Sym Orchestra, asst prinharpist, prin harpist, 1980-09; Tanglewood Music Ctr, Lenox, MA, harp fac, 1989-; Pa Musical Acad, fac. **Orgs:** Partic, Marlboro Music Festival; fac, New Eng Conserv Music, Berkshire Music Ctr; soloist, Boston Sym Orchestra; founder mem, New Eng Harp Trio, 1971-; Contemp Music Ensemble, Col performances Europe, Japan, ChinaHaiti; bd dir, Holy Trinity Sch Haiti; bd trustees, Longy Sch Music, 1993-96; bd dirs, Boston Music Educ Collab. **Honors/Awds:** Hon Professional, Arts Soc Philadelphia, 1987; Honorary Doctorate of Fine Arts, Bridgewater State Col, 1988; Distinguished Woman of the Year, 1991;Sch Music Alumni Achievement Award, 1992; Distinguished Alumni Award,1993; Col Club Career Award, 1997. **Special Achievements:** Recordings for Boston Records, Ann Hobson Pilot, solo harp. Contrasts,music for flute and harp with Leone Buyse. for Koch Intl, Ginastera and Mathias Concerti with the English Chamber Orchestra. Dello-Joie harpconcerto with the New Zealand Symphony. Chamber Music of William Mathiasand Arnold Bax, performed the Mozart Concerto again at Tanglewood in 2005. **Business Phone:** (617)266-1492.

PINADO, ALAN E., SR.
Educator, real estate agent. **Personal:** Born Dec 15, 1931, New York, NY; son of Herman E and Agnes Steber; married Patricia LaCour; children: Alan E Jr, Jeanne M Pinado-Getter, Anthony M & Steven L. **Educ:** Fordham Univ, Col Bus Admin, BS Mktg, 1953; Univ Notre Dame, MBA, 1958. **Career:** Educator, Real estate agent (retired); Wm R Morris Agency S Bend IN, real estate sales, devel, 1960-61; Allied Fed Savings & Loan Jamaica NY, exec vpres, mortgage loan officer, 1961-67; IBM Corp NY, mktg rep, 1967-68; NY LIfe Ins Co NY, vpres re finance, 1968-84, vpres, mgt coordr & training,1984-85; Real Estate Inst of Clark Atlanta Univ Morehouse Col, dir, 1986-02. **Orgs:** Dir, Oppty Funding Corp, 1979-90, Urban Home Ownership Corp, 1980-92; NY Life Pac, 1983-85; Wilton CT United Way, 1983-85; dir emer, Minority Interchange, 1975-; United Mutual Ins Co, 1985-87; dir, Univ Comt Devel Corp, 1996; adv comt, The Prudential bank, 1995-97; dir, Nat Housing Coun, 1994-98; Archdiocesan Planning & Devel Coun. **Honors/Awds:** Dr of Literary Letters Mary Holmes Col, 1976; Horace Sudduth Award, Nat Bus League, 1978; James J & Jane Hoey Award, Catholic Interracial Coun NY, 1972. **Military Serv:** AUS, 1st lt, 1953-55; Commendation Medal, 1954. **Home Addr:** 4670 Guilford Forest Dr SW, Atlanta, GA 30331-7391. *

PINCHAM, R. EUGENE, SR.
Judge. **Personal:** Born Jun 28, 1925, Chicago, IL; married Alzata Cudalia Henry; children: 3. **Educ:** Tenn State Univ, BS, 1947; Northwestern Univ Sch Law, JD, 1951; admitted to the bar Illinois, 1951. **Career:** Judge (retired); Atty Joseph E Clayton Jr, assoc, 1951-55; Atty Charles B Evins, assoc, 1955-76; Attys T Lee Boyd Jr & Isaiah S Gant, assoc, 1974-76; criminal trial lawyer appellate litigation; Circuit Ct Cook Co, judge, 1976-84; lectr/instr, Notre Dame Univ Sch Law; Northwestern Univ Sch Law; Univ Ill Sch Law; Univ Houston Bates Col Law; Nat Col Criminal Defense Lawyers & Pub Defenders; Univ Colo-Boulder Col Law; Nat Inst Trial Advocacy, Univ Nev. **Orgs:** Chicago Bar; Cook County Bar; Ill Bar; Nat Bar; Am Bar Asn; Chicago Coun Lawyers; life mem, Nat Asn Advan Colored People; life mem, Am Civil Liberties Union; Kappa Alpha Psi Frat; Am Judicature Soc; former trustee Faith United Methodist Church. **Honors/Awds:** Richard E Westbrook Award, Outstanding Contrib Legal Prof, Cook County Bar Asn; cert serv, Lawyers Const Def Comm Am Civil Liberties Union, 1965; cert appreciation, Chicago Bar Asn, 1974; Award of Merit, Northwestern Univ Alumni Asn, 1975. *

PINCKNEY, ANDREW MORGAN, JR.
Administrator. **Personal:** Born Jul 2, 1933, Georgetown, SC; married Brenda Cox; children: Meika & Margo. **Educ:** Morris Brown Col, Atlanta, BS, 1960; Lasalle Col Phila, Bus Admin, 1968; Univ PA, Phila, Wharton Mgt, 1976. **Career:** Franklin Inst Lab Phila, res chemist, 1961-62; Skin & Cancer Hosp Phila, res assoc, 1962-63; Merck Sharp & Dohme W Pt PA, adminr; Merck Sharp & Dohme, res Biol, 1963-73. **Orgs:** Am Mgt Asn; Black Univ Liasion Comt Merck & Co; steering comt United Way; Campaign Merck Sharp & Co, 1976-79; pres, Philadelphia Alumni Chap Morris Brown; pres, Club Noble Gents; financial sec Black Polit Forum, 1975. **Honors/Awds:** Morris Brown Col Athletic Hall of Fame, TAY Club Atlanta, 1975; Purple & Black Service Award, Morris Brown Col Nat Alumni Atlanta, 1979. **Military Serv:** USAF, 1951-55.

PINCKNEY, CLEMENTA C.
Government official. **Personal:** Born Jul 30, 1973, Beaufort, SC; son of John and Theopia; married Jennifer Benjamin, Oct 23, 1999; children: Eliana Yvette. **Educ:** Allen Univ, BA, 1995; Univ SC, MPA, 1999; Lutheran Southern Seminary,grad, 1999. **Career:** Princeton Univ, res fel summer, 1994; Mt Horr AME Church Yonges Island,pastor; State Rep, SC, serv in house, 1997-2000, sen, 2001-. **Orgs:** Bd mem, STOP Tax. **Business Addr:** Senator, State South Carolina, 512 Gressette Bldg, Columbia, SC 29201.

PINCKNEY, EDWARD LEWIS
Basketball coach, basketball player. **Personal:** Born Mar 27, 1963, Bronx, NY; married Rose Marie; children: Shea, Spencer, Austin & Andrea. **Educ:** Villanova Univ, Villanova, PA, 1985. **Career:** Basketball Player (retired) & basketball coach: Phoenix Suns, 1985-87;Sacramento Kings, 1987-88; Boston Celtics, 1989-94; Milwaukee Bucks,1994-95; Toronto Raptors, 1995; Philadelphia 76ers, 1996; Miami Heat, 1996-97; Miami Heat orgn, radio & TV analyst, 1997-2003; Villanova Wildcats, asst coach, 2003-07; Minnesota Timberwolves, asst coach, 2007-. **Special Achievements:** NBA Draft, First round pick, 10, 1985. **Business Addr:** Assistant Coach, Minnesota Timberwolves, 600 1st Ave N, Minneapolis, MN 55403, **Business Phone:** (612)673-1600.

PINCKNEY, JAMES
Government official. **Personal:** Born Jun 24, 1942, Fairfax, SC; married Gladys M Simmons; children: Janet, Jerome, Zachary, Lorraine. **Educ:** Allen Univ, BS, phys educ, 1964. **Career:** Lower Saunnal Coun Govts, bd mem, 1984-; Allendale County, coun mem & legis deleg, 1985-, coun chmn, 2005-. **Orgs:** Bd mem, Allendale-Fairfax HS Advy Coun, 1982-84. **Business Addr:** Council Chairman, Allendale County, PO Box 677, Allendale, SC 29810.*

PINCKNEY, LEWIS, JR.
Hospital administrator. **Personal:** Born Dec 25, 1932, Columbia, SC; son of Louis Pinckney Sr and Channie Hopkins; married Johnnye Caver; children: Lewis III & Johnette V. **Educ:** Benedict Col, 1952-53; Cook Co Grad Sch Med, ARRT, 1956-57; DePaul Univ, 1975. **Career:** Cook County Hosp, staff tech, 1957-64, qual control supv, 1964-68, chief x-ray tech educ dir, 1968-69, from admin asst to chmn, 1969-73, admin; St Bernard Hosp, dir radiological serv. **Orgs:** John Jones Lodge No 7 F & AM Ill, 1963-; Ill State Soc Radiologic Tech, 1971-74; Lions Asn, 1971-73; Am Soc Radiologic Tech, 1973; Am Hosp Radiol Admin, 1973-76; WA Park YMCA, 1974; conf leader, Inst Graphic Commun, 1974; evaluating qual control, Cook Co Grad Schl Med, 1977. **Military Serv:** AUS, sgt, 1953-56. **Business Addr:** Director, St Bernard Hospital, 64th & Dan Ryan Expressway, Chicago, IL 60612, **Business Phone:** (773)962-3900.

PINCKNEY, STANLEY
Artist, educator. **Personal:** Born Sep 30, 1940, Boston, MA. **Educ:** Famous Artist Sch, Westport, CT, com art, 1960; Sch Boston Mus Fine Arts, Boston, MA, Dipl, 1967, Cert, Grad Prog, 1969. **Career:** Teacher (retired), artist; Boston Univ Prog In-Artisanry, guest artist, 1967; Sch Boston Mus Fine Arts, teacher, 1972-2006; Blanche E Colman fel, Blanche E Colman Found, Boston, MA, 1978; Albert H Whitin fel, Sch Boston Mus Fine Arts, 1978; Col Art, guest artist, 1979. **Orgs:** African-Am Artists-in-Residency Northeastern Univ, Boston, MA, 1978. **Honors/Awds:** Ford Found Grant, Music Sch Fine Arts, Boston, MA, 1978.

PINDELL, HOWARDENA D
Curator, artist, educator. **Personal:** Born Apr 14, 1943, Philadelphia, PA; daughter of Howard Douglas and Mildred Lewis. **Educ:** Boston Univ, Sch Fine & Appl Arts, BFA, painting, 1965; Yale Univ, Sch Art & Archit, MFA, 1967. **Career:** Pratt Inst, guest lectr, 1972; Hunter Col, fac, 1972; Morivian Col, fac, 1973; Queens Col, fac, 1973; Sch Visual Arts, fac, 1973, 1975; Montclair State Col, fac, 1974; Brooklyn Mus, staff, 1976; Guggeneheim Fel 1987-88; Joan Mitchell Fel, 1994; Yale Univ, vis prof, 1995-98; State Univ NY, Stony Brook, prof, currently. **Orgs:** Afro-Am Artists, 1973; Int Art Critics Asn; Int House Japan; Col Art Asn; ACASA. **Honors/Awds:** Alumni Award Distinguished Service to Professor, Boston Univ, 1983; Most Distinguished

Body of Work or Performance Award, Col Art Asn, 1990; Studio Museum Harlem Award, 1994; Women Caucus Art Distinguished Contribution to the Professor Award, 1996; Honorary Doctorate of Fine Arts, Mass Col Art, 1997; Community Service Award, NY State United Teachers, 1998. **Business Addr:** Professor, State University of New York at Stony Brook, Art Department, Rm 4211 2225 Staller Ctr, Stony Brook, NY 11794, **Business Phone:** (631)632-7250.

PINDER, NELSON W.
Clergy. **Personal:** Born Jul 27, 1932, Miami, FL; son of George and Coleen Saunders; married Marian Grant; children: Gail, Squire. **Educ:** Bethune Cookman Col, BA, 1956; Nashotah House Sem, BD, 1959; Inst IN Univ, Adult Educ, 1959; Urban Training Ctr, 1964; FL A&M, MEd, 1974; Bethune Cookman Col Daytona Beach FL, DD, 1979. **Career:** Clergy (retired); St John Baptist Episcopal Church, vicar, 1959-69; Awareness Ctr Orlando, dir, 1969-71; Diocese Ctr FL, staff mem, 1971; St John Baptist Episcopal Church Orlando, priest, 1974. **Orgs:** Joint Comn Church Small Comt, 1970-; Chmn Recruitment & Equal Employ Oppor Comn Province VI Episcopal Church, 1972-; mem bd dir, Union Black Episcopalians, 1973-74; assoc trustee, Bethune Cookman Col; bd trustees Bethune Cookman Col; Orlando C C; Dept Urban Affairs; Phi Delta Kappa; Walt Disney World Awards Comt, 1973; past Pres, Delta Ix Lambda; trustee, Univ South, Sewanee, TN, 1983-; Nat Comn Social & Specialized Ministry, 1989-. **Honors/Awds:** United Negro College Fund Award, 1971; 1st Annual Disney World Community Service Award, 1972; black community Award, 1972; Alpha Kappa Alpha Community Award, 1972; US Congress Chaplains Award, 1973; Knights Columbus Citizenship Award, 1974; Bethune Cookman medallion, 1975. **Military Serv:** AUS, 1953-55. *

PINKARD, BEDFORD L
Government official, commissioner. **Personal:** Born Oct 9, 1931, Jacksonville, TX; son of Adela Pinkard and Dee Pinkard; married Irene Stephens, Aug 1, 1987; children: Derek Louis & Keven D. **Educ:** La State Col, 1958, Calif Polytech Col, 1951; Ventural Col, AA, 1953; Calif State Univ., Northridge, BS, 1973. **Career:** Oxnard City, Community Youth Pro, dir, 1979-80, recreation supvr, 1959-91, councilman; Venutura County, Harbor Comn, comnr. **Orgs:** Oxnard Noontimers Lions Club 1964-; pres Bd of Educ Oxnard Union High School Dist, 1972-92. **Honors/Awds:** PTA Honrary Service Award; Esquire Social Club Citizen of the Year Award; Resolution of the Oxnard City Council for Dedicated Services; 22 Years Perfect Attendance Oxnard Noontimers Lions Club. **Military Serv:** USY, pfc, 2 yrs. **Home Addr:** 2047 Spyglass Tr E, Oxnard, CA 93030. **Business Addr:** Commissioner, Ventura County, Harbor Commission Hall of Justice, 800 S Victoria Ave 300 W 3rd St, Ventura, CA 93009.

PINKARD, DR. DELORIS ELAINE
Educator, college administrator. **Personal:** Born Oct 22, 1944, Kansas City, KS; daughter of Andrew D Jackson and Ella Mae Williams Jackson; widowed; children: Karisse Grigsby Whyte & Robert C Edwards. **Educ:** Emporia State Univ, BS (cum laude), elem educ, 1966, MS, educ admin, 1984; Univ Kansas, MS, educ psychol & res, 1980; Univ Kans, doctorate educ, 1995. **Career:** Educator, Col Administrator (retired); Wash Dist Schs, Kans City, KS, teacher, 1966-69; Kans City KS Cath Diocese, Kans City, KS, teacher, 1970-72; Kansas City KS Pub Schs, Kansas City KS, teacher, 1972-82, adminintern, 1982-83, prin, 1983-86, personnel dir, 1986-92; KS Kans Comm Col, dean human resources, 1992-94, vpres exec serv, 1994-2000. **Orgs:** Kappa Delta Pi, 1966; bd mem, Yates Br YWCA, 1969; bd dir, Wyandotte County Ment Health Comn, 1971; Phi Delta Kappa, Emporia State Univ; conf presenter, Networking Women Educ Admin, 1984; induction speaker, Lyons County Phi Delta Kappa, Fighting Teacher Burnout, 1985; keynote speaker, Sorority Founders Recognition, Equity With Excellence, 1986; Mo Valley Sch Personnel Admin Asn, 1986-; Asn Sch, Col & Univ Staffing, 1986-; Am Asn Sch Personnel Admin, 1986-; evangelism chairperson, Mason Mem UM Church; pres & bd dir, Kans City KS Womens Chamber Com, 1987-; conf presenter, Direction Educ Minority Stud & Legis Alternatives, Kans Black Legis Conf,1987; secy, Kans-Nat Alliance Black Sch Educ, 1988-; bd dir, Martin Luther King Urban Ctr, 1988-; interim secy, Nat Asn Advan Colored People, 1989; coordr, United Negro Col Fund Dr, 1989; community adv bd, Jr Gordens CsProj, 1995-; bd dirs, Univ Kans Alumni Asn, 1998-. **Honors/Awds:** Woman of Distinction for Community Service, Friends Yates, 1986; Hearts of Gold Education honoree, Greater KC YMCA, 2002. **Special Achievements:** Research thesis, Teacher Attitudes as Related to the Differences in Achievements of Reflective & Impulsive Children, 1980; Dissertation:School Reform Success: Critical Issues for Teachers/Determining Teachers' Concerns During the Process of Planned Change in Schools, 1995.

PINKETT, ALLEN JEROME
Salesperson, football player. **Personal:** Born Jan 25, 1964, Washington, DC. **Educ:** Univ Notre Dame, BBA, mkt, 1986. **Career:** Football player (retired), Salesperson; Houston Oilers, running back, 1986-92; New Orleans Saints; Notre Dame Football, Westwood One, color commentator, 2001-; ESPN 1000, host, currently; Hartford Financial Services Group Inc, sales rep, currently. **Business Phone:** (860)547-5000.*

PINKETT, JADA KOREN. See PINKETT SMITH, JADA.

PINKETT, DR. RANDAL D
Entrepreneur, executive. **Personal:** Born Apr 9, 1971, Philadelphia, PA; son of Leslie Pinkett and Elizabeth. **Educ:** Rutgers Univ, BS, 1994; Univ Oxford, England, MS, 1996; MA Inst Technol (MIT), MBA, 1998, MS, 1998, PhD, 2001. **Career:** MBS Enterprises, pres & chief exec oficer, 1993-2001; Gen Elec, analog & digital design engr, 1994; AT&T Bell Labs, technical staff, 1995; Lucent Technologies, tech staff, 1997-98; Partners Inc, Bus & Cot Technol, dir, 2000-; BCT Partners LLC, pres & chief exec officer, 2001-. **Orgs:** Nat exec bd, Nat Soc Black Engrs, 1993-94; Asn Am Rhodes Scholars, 1996-; Black Grad Stud Asn, 1996-; Nat Black MBA Asn, 2000-. **Honors/Awds:** Col All-Academic First Team, USA Today, 1993; Nat Soc Black Engineers, Nat Member of the Year, 1994; Rhodes Scholarship, The Rhodes Trust, 1994; NCAA, Acad All-Am, 1994; NSF Graduate Fellowship, Nat Sci Found, 1996; Rockefeller Next Generation Leadership Program Fellowship, 2002. **Special Achievements:** Mass Inst Technol (MIT) "Product Development Process Modeling and Analysis of Digital Wireless Telephones" masters thesis, 1998; Univ Oxford, England, "Hardware/Software Co-Design and Digital Speech Procssing" masters thesis, 1996; 30 Leaders for the Future, Black Enterprise Magazine, 2000; 30 Leaders for the Future, Ebony Magazine, 2001; MIT, "Creating Cot Connections; Soiocultural Constructionism & An Asset-Based Approach to Comm Tech & Comm Building In Low-Income Comm," doctoral disseration, 2001; Men's Track and Field Team as a high jumper, long jumper & sprinter winning NCAA Academic All-American honors. **Business Addr:** President, Chief Executive Officer, BCT Partners LLC, 105 Lock St Suite 207, Newark, NJ 07103, **Business Phone:** (973)622-0900.

PINKETT SMITH, JADA (JADA KOREN PINKETT)
Actor, singer. **Personal:** Born Sep 18, 1971, Baltimore, MD; daughter of Robsol Pinkett Jr and Adrienne Banfiled; married Sheree Zampino (divorced); children: Willard Christopher Smith III; married Will Smith, Dec 31, 1997; children: Jaden & Willow. **Career:** TV series: "A Different World", 1991-93; "If These Walls Could Talk", 1996; "Maniac Magee", 2003; Films: Menace II Society, actress, 1993; The Inkwell, actress, 1994; A Low Down Dirty Shame, actress, 1994; Jason's Lyric, actress, 1994; Demon Knight, actress, 1995; The Nutty Professor, actress, 1996; Set It Off, actress, 1996; Scream 2, actress, 1997; Woo, actress, 1998; Bamboozled, actress, 2000; Kingdom Come, actress, 2001; Ali, actress, 2001; The Matrix Reloaded, actress, 2003; The Matrix Revolutions, actress, 2003; Collateral, actress, 2004; Madagascar, actress, 2005; Reign Over Me, actress, 2007; Theater roles: August's Wilson's Joe Turner's Come & Gone; The Nutcracker; Carol's Daughter, co-owner; Planet Hollywood, owner, currently. **Orgs:** Alpha Kappa Alpha Sorority Inc. **Honors/Awds:** Outstanding Actress in a Mini-Series/Television Movie If These Walls Could Talk, 1997; Outstanding Actress in a Motion Picture: Set It Off (Nominated), 1997; Best Actress Bamboozled (Nominated), 2001; Outstanding Actress in a Motion Picture: Bamboozled (Nominated), 2001; Outstanding Supporting Actress in a Motion Picture: Ali (Nominated), 2001; Outstanding Supporting Actress in a Motion Picture: The Matrix: Revolutions (Nominated), 2004; Outstanding Supporting Actress in a Motion Picture: Collateral (Nominated), 2005; Best Supporting Actress, 2005. **Special Achievements:** Miss Md, 1988; one of the 10 sexiest women of the yr, Black Men Mag, 2000. **Business Addr:** Actress, United Talent Agency, 9560 Wilshire Blvd Fl 5, Beverly Hills, CA 90212, **Business Phone:** (310)273-6700.

PINKINS, TONYA
Singer, actor. **Personal:** Born May 30, 1962, Chicago, IL; daughter of Thomas Swoope and Anita Pinkins; children: Maxx Brawer & Myles Brawer. **Educ:** Columbia Col, BA, 1996; Carnegie Mellon Univ, music theatre prog, 1981. **Career:** Films: Beat Street, 1984; See No Evil, Hear No Evil, 1989; "Above the Rim", 1994; "Romance & Cigarettes," 2005; "Premium," 2006; "Enchanted", 2007; TV: "American Dream," 1981; "All My Children," 1991, 2004-; "Love Hurts," 2002; "The River", 2006; "Working in the Theatre", 2007; Theatre appearances: Death & the Kings Horseman, 1979-80; Merrily We Roll Along, 1981-82; Five Points, 1982; Just Say No, 1988; Joe Turner's Come & Gone, 1989-90; Jelly's Last Jam, Broadway, 1992-; TV appearances: "The Guardian," 2001-04; "In Loco Parentis," 2002. **Orgs:** Bd dir, Nontraditional Casting Proj; bd dir, Carousel Theatre; Actors Equity Asn; Am Fed TV & Radio Artists; Org Black Screen Writers. **Honors/Awds:** Tony Award, Am Theater Wing, 1992; Clarence Derwent Award, Social Coun Actors Equity, 1992; Drama Desk, NY Drama Critics, 1992; Monarch Award, NCAA, 1992; Best Actress, Daytime Drama, nominated, NAACP, 1992; Black Theatre Alliance Award; 1998; Los Angeles Drama Critics Circle Award, 2005. **Business Addr:** Actress, The Gersh Agency, 41 Madison Ave Fl 33, New York, NY 10010-2210.

PINKNEY, ARNOLD R.
Educator, insurance agent. **Personal:** Born Jan 6, 1931, Youngstown, OH; married Betty; children: Traci. **Educ:** Albion Col MI, BA, Political Sci & History & minor Econ; Case Western Res Univ Sch Law; Agency Mgt Training Course; Cent State Univ, Wilberforce, Ohio, Hon Doctorate Law Degree. **Career:** Cleveland Bd Educ, pres; Mutual Life Ins Co, Great lakes, Ins agent & mem mgt; Prudential Life Ins Co; Betpin & Assocs Inc, Sr Consult & Chief Opers Officer, 1996; Cuyahoga Community Col, consult, 1996; Williams Mayor City Warren, Ohio, 1999; Bryan Flannery Secy State Ohio, Campaign Mgr, 2002; Pinkey-Perry Ins Agency Cleveland, bd chmn, currently; betpin & assoc inc, sr consult & chief opers officer consult firm, currently. **Orgs:** Pres, Independent Men's Union; treas, Athletic Club; All Mich Intercollegiate Athletic Asn Team; Ohio Nat Life Underwriters Asn; exec comnr, Cleveland Growth Asn; Cleveland Bus League; City Cleveland Sch Bd, 1967; orgn dir, The First Nat Bank Asn; vpres & pres, Cleveland Bd Educ; bd, tst Albion Col; pres bd, tst Cent State Univ; chmn, Develop & Goals Comn; Comn, Black Phys; bd trustee, Coun Human Rel; Phyllis Wheatley Found; Urban League Greater Cleveland; bd mem, Metro Health Planning Corp; past treas, Black Econ Union; bd, tst The Citz League; life mem, Nat Advan Asn Colored People; cand Mayor, Cleveland, 1971, 1975; dir, Nat Dep Campaign Senator Humphrey's, 1972; exec comn, vchmn, Cuyahoga Co Dem Party, 1973; chmn, Dem Party's vpres, Selection Com, 1973; co-chmn, Dem Nat Cpgn Comn, 1974; bd elections, Cuyahoga Co, 1974; steering comt, Nat Caucus Black Dem, 1974; del, Dem & Mini-conv Kansas City, 1974; Dem Conv,1976; adv, Local State & Nat Dem Officials, 1976; state chmn, Ohio State Voter Registration Dr, 1976; headed crive Get Out The Vote, 1976; Olivet Int Baptist Ch; bd mem, Southern Christian Leadership Coun. **Special Achievements:** Thousand Successful Black in Ebony Mag; Apt Exec Order of the OH Commodore; numerous lects; first African Am to become a Million-Dollar Producer. **Military Serv:** AUS, 1952-54. **Business Addr:** Chairman, Pinkney-Perry Insurance Agency Inc, 2143 Stokes blvd, Cleveland, OH 44106-3066, **Business Phone:** (216)795-1995.

PINKNEY, DR. BETTY KATHRYN
Government official, lawyer, school administrator. **Personal:** Born in Cleveland, OH; daughter of Naomi Inez Yates Butts and Emmett Maceo; married Charles E; children: Jacqueline Pinkney Royster, Pamela & Merle. **Educ:** Cent State Univ, BA, 1956; Case Western Res Univ, MA, 1961; Cleveland State Univ Marshall Law Sch, JD, 1976; Levin Col Urban Affairs, doctoral degree, currently. **Career:** Cleveland Pub Sch, teacher, adminr, 1961-77; Carl J Character Law Firm,assoc, 1977-79; EEOC, Cleveland, trial atty, 1979-81; E Ohio Gas Co, sratty, 1981-96; Const Commun Sys, dist dir, currently; Stephanie Tubbs Jones, Shaker Heights Off, dist dir, currently. **Orgs:** Bd trustees, supt, Judge Lloyd O Brown Scholar Fund, 1984-; vol, Cleveland Bar Assn, 1984-; adv comt, supt, Cleveland Pub Sch Syst, 1987-; ABA; Ohio St Bar Assn; Nat Bar Assn; Delta Sigma Theta; chmn, Cent State Univ Brd Trustees, 1987; bd mem, Cleveland C's Mus; Ohio Bar; Levin col vistinh comm mem, currently. **Business Addr:** District Director, Stephanie Tubbs Jones, Shaker Heights Office, 3645 Warrensville Ctr Rd Suite 204, Shaker Heights, OH 44122, **Business Phone:** (216)522-4900.*

PINKNEY, DOVE SAVAGE
Government official. **Personal:** Born in Macon, GA; daughter of Edward Warren Savage Sr (deceased) and Mildred G; divorced; children: Rhonda Michelle Pinkney Washington & Roderick Stephen. **Educ:** Talladega Col, attended 1954; Inst Path Case-Western Res Univ, cert med tech, 1955; Univ Denver; Univ Calif Los Angeles. **Career:** Univ Hosp Cleveland, technologist & supvr, 1955-59; Children's Hosp Los Angeles, technologist in-charge out-patient clin lab, 1960-73, hematologyclin lab mgr, 1973-94, gov affairs coor dr, 1994-95; Los Angeles Chap,pres, currently. **Orgs:** Delta Sigma Theta Head Start Bd, 1970-76; Chairperson, Children's Hosp Los Angeles Employee Recog Comm, 1973-89; campaign chairperson Children's Hosp Los Angeles United Way Campaign, 1975; treas, 1978-80, 1981-, chair, 1988-90, bd mgrs, Crenshaw/28th St YMCA; del 20 nat conventions; chairperson ASMT Forum Concerns Minorities By-Laws Com, 1979-86; pres-,Calif Asn Med Lab Technol, Los Angeles Chap, 1982-83, treas, 1978-80; trustee & exec bd, 1978-95; treas, New Frontier Democratic Club, 1989-90, pres, 1992-93, bd 1989-; dir, CA Soc for Medical Technol, 1981 -83, 1983-85; coord CSMT Stud Bowl, 1983; del 15 state conventions; nat pres, Talladega Col Alumni, 1984-87; reg pres, 1997-01, bd, fund raiser, United Negro Col Fund, 1981-, life mem, Nat Coun Negro Women; life Delta Sigma Theta Sorority; Urban League, NOW, PUSH, NAACP; Comm Rels Coun Southern CA; Black Women's Forum, African-Am Mus, Mus Afro-Am Hist & Cult, Trinity Baptist Church; bd dir, Delta Sigma Theta Life Develop (senior citizens program), 1982-92; fin secy, 1989-93, 1998- Coalition of 100 Black Woman; LA County Comnr, 1994-; Los Angeles Delta Minerva Found, 1998-; Los Angeles Care Community Adv Bd; vice chair, Base Hosp Adv Comm. **Honors/Awds:** Awards received from Delta Sigma Theta Los Angeles Chap, Talladega Col Local Alumni Asn, Talladega Col Nat Alumni Asn, Crenshaw YMCA, UNCF, AmSoc Med Technol, New Frontier Democratic Club, Children's Hosp Los Angeles Employees, Fed Credit Union. **Special Achievements:** Co-author of two professional (scientific) papers; CA Assembly; CA State Senate; LA Care. **Home Addr:** 5601 Coliseum St, Los

Angeles, CA 90056-0337, **Home Phone:** (310)837-5495. **Business Addr:** President, Los Angeles Chapter, PO Box 56337, Los Angeles, CA 90056-0337.*

PINKNEY, ENID C.
Educator, social historian. **Personal:** Born Oct 15, 1931, Miami, FL; daughter of Henry Curtis and Lenora Curtis; married; married Frank; married Frank. **Educ:** Talladega Col, AB, 1953; Barry Univ, MS, 1967. **Career:** Educator (retired); Social Worker; YWCA, Miami, adult prog dir; Chicago,group worker; social worker, 1953-55; Dade County Pub Sch System, teacher,1955, counsr, 1967, asst prin, 1971, asst prin guid, 1985; S Miami Mid-Sch, asst prin, 991; African Am Comt, co founder; Brownsville & The N CentDade community, historian; The Hist Hampton House Community Trust, founder& pres. **Orgs:** NEA; FEA; Dade Co Adm Asn & Guid Asn; S Fla Guid Asn; Am & Sch Coun Asn; Am Guid & Personal Asn; AAUW; Hi Delta-Kappa; bd dir, Miami YWCA; bd dir, Fla Conf United Church Christ; charter mem, Chair Open Door; UCC Fruits States; Miami Inter Alumni Coun, UNCF; Sigma Gamma Rho Sor; pres, Dade Heritage Trust Hist Preserv Orgn, 1998. **Honors/Awds:** Cert of Appreciation, Sigma Gamma Rho Sorority; Enid C. Pinkney Humanitarian Award, The Miami Talladega Col Alumni Asn, named in honor. **Special Achievements:** First Black President of Dade Heritage Trust, 1998; Produced several videos on history. **Home Addr:** 4990 NW 31st Ave, Miami, FL 33142.

PINKNEY, JERRY
Educator, illustrator. **Personal:** Born Dec 22, 1939, Philadelphia, PA; son of James H and Willie Mae Landers; married Gloria Jean Maultsby, 1960; children: Troy Bernardette Pinkney Johnson, Jerry Brian, Scott Cannon & Myles Carter. **Educ:** Univ Arts, Philadelphia PA, 1957-59. **Career:** Rustcraft Publ Co, Dedham, MA, designer, 1960-62; Barker-Black Studio, Boston, MA, designer-illusr, 1962-64; Kaleiodoscope Studio, Boston, MA, designer-illusr, 1964-66; Jerry Pinkney Studio, Boston, MA, designer-illusr, 1966-70; Rhode Island Sch Design, visiting critic, 1969-70; Jerry Pinkney Inc, Croton-on-Hudson NY, pres, 1970-; Pratt Inst, Brooklyn NY, assoc prof, 1986-87; Univ Del, distinguished visiting prof, 1986-88, assoc prof art, 1988-92; US Military Acad, West Point, NY, lectr; Univ of Buffalo, Buffalo, NY, visiting prof art. **Orgs:** Soc Illusrs; US Postal Serv Citizens Stamp Adv Comn, 1982; Artist Team NASA, Space Shuttle Columbia, 1982; US Postal Serv Quality Assurance Comn, 1986-92. **Honors/Awds:** Annual Show, NY Soc Illusrs, 1965-83, 1986-95; Caldecott Honor Book, Am Libr Asn, 1989; CEBA Award, World Inst Black Communications, Inc, 1989; Am Visions Mag, 1989; The Years Best Illustrated Books for C, New York Times, 1989; First Place, New York Book Show, 1989; designer eleven commerative postage stamps, US Postal Serv; Randolph Caldecott Medal-Honor Book, Am Libr Asn, 1990; Retrospective, Schomburg Ctr Res, NY, 1990, Univ Buffalo, NY, 1991; Soc Childrenss Book Writers, 1990 Golden Kite Award, 1991; State CO, CO childrens Book Award, 1991; NY Book Show, NY Honor Book, 1991; 34th Soc Illusrs Annual Show, Gold Medal, 1992; Phila Sch Art & Design, Univ Arts, Alumni Award, 1992; Drexel Univ, Phil PA, Drexel Citation for C's Lit, 1992; Farmington State Coll, Framingham, MA, David McCord Award, 1992; Nebraska Lib Asn, Nebraska C's Book Award, 1992; Soc Illusrs Annual 35, Gold Medal, 1993, Silver Medal, 1993, Hamilton King Award, 1993; Am Inst Graphic Arts, NY, Fifty Best Books, 1993; Book Binders Annual, NY, Second Place, Book Jackets, 1993; M Dobbins Voc High Sch, PA, Alumni Award, 1993; One Man Show, The Art Inst Chicago, 1993; One Man Show, Univ Arts, Phila, PA, 1994; Orig Art Show, Soc Illusrs, Gold Medal, 1994; New York Times, Year's Best Illustrated Books for C, 1994; Parents Choice "John Henry," Parents Choice Award for Story Book, 1994; Parents Choice "The Sunday Outing," Parents Choice Award for Story Book, 1994; Honor Book "John Henry," Randolph Caldecott Medal, 1994.

PINKNEY, JOHN EDWARD
Manager, chief executive officer, business owner. **Personal:** Born May 6, 1948, Landover, MD; married Gloristine Wilkins; children: Nikole, John & April. **Educ:** Prince George Community Col, AA, 1973; Bowie State Col, BS, 1976. **Career:** Dept Agr, comput oper 1970-71; Shady side Barber & Beauty Salon, hairstylist & co-owner 1971-77; Philip Morris USA, sales rep, 1977-79, miliary mgr, 1979-80, div mgr, 1980-88; An Answer 4 U Telecommunications Co, owner & ceo, 1991-. **Orgs:** Youth task force partic Nat Alliance Bus 1981-83; Nat Bus League, southern Md, pres, 1981-83, bd dirs 1984-. **Honors/Awds:** Community Service Award, Dist of Columbia; Presidential Citation, Natl Asn Equal Opportunity Higher Educ. **Military Serv:** AUS, Sgt; Bronze Star; Vietnam Serv Medal; Vietnam Campaign Medal; Natl Defense Serv Medal. **Home Addr:** 6110 Joyce Dr, Camp Springs, MD 20748. **Business Addr:** Owner, Cheif Executive Officer, An Answer 4 U.

PINKNEY, ROSE CATHERINE
Executive, vice president (organization). **Educ:** Princeton Univ, BA, sociol; Anderson Sch mgt Univ Calif Los Angeles, MBA, entertainment mgt & mkt. **Career:** Twentieth Century Fox TV, dir programming; Uptown Entertainment, vpres & head tv; Paramount Network TV, vpres comedy develop, 1995-2002, sr vpres dept head; TV One, LLC, exec vpres programming & prod, currently. **Orgs:** Bd mem, Women in Film; treas, The New Leaders. **Business Addr:** Executive Vice President, Programming & Production, TV One, 1010 Wayne Ave 10th Fl, Silver Spring, MD 20910, **Business Phone:** (301)755-0400.

PINKNEY, WILLIAM D
Executive, vice president (organization). **Personal:** Born Sep 15, 1935, Chicago, IL; son of William Pinkney Sr and Marion Henderson; married Yvonne Glover, 1957 (divorced 1962); children: Angela Walton; married Ina, 1964 (divorced 2001); married Migdalia Vachier, 2003. **Educ:** New York City Community Col; Adelphi Univ. **Career:** Executive (retired); Astarte, nat sales mgr, 1971-72; Cleopatra Creations, vpres, 1972-73; Revlon, mkt mgr, 1973-77; Johnson Products Co, dir mkt, 1977-80; Dept Human Serv City Chicago, dir family serv, 1980-84; Combined Construction Co, vpres; The Dessert Kitchen Ltd, dir. **Orgs:** Nat Assoc Broadcast Engineering & Technol, 1970-, Lake Mich Yacht Racing Asn, 1974-; past commodore Belmont Yacht Club; life mem, Lake Mich Singlehanded Soc; Royal Yacht Club Tasmania, Australia; Chicago Yacht Club; Mystic Seaport Mus, Freedom Schooner Amistad Project, captain, 2000-03. **Honors/Awds:** Guest Lectr, Wharton Sch Bus, Univ Pa, 1978; Contrib Writer Great Lakes Boating Mag, 1982-83; LMYA, Chicago Yachting Asn; Yachtsman of the Year, 1992; Martin Luther King, Jr Legacy; Boy's and Girls Clubs Chicago; Monarch Award, Alpha Kappa Alpha Sorority; Founders Award; Cosmopolitan COC; Chicagoan of the Year, Chicago Mag, 1999; Ill Gov's Disting Achievement Award. **Special Achievements:** First African Am to Solo Circumavigate, The World Via Cape Horn, 1992. **Military Serv:** USN, hm2, 1953-60, USC, licensed capt, 1990-92; 2 Good Conduct Medals, 1953-57. *

PINN, DR. MELVIN T, JR.
Physician. **Personal:** Born Oct 6, 1947, Lynchburg, VA; son of Vera Ferguson and Melvin Pinn; married Evora, Jul 24, 1971; children: Tanika, Melva & Melvin III. **Educ:** Johnson C Smith Univ, BS, 1970; Univ Va, MD, 1976; Univ NC-Chapel Hill, MPH, 1986-91. **Career:** Neighborhood Health Ctr, med dir, 1979-96; The Wellness Plan of NC (Va Premier Health Plan Inc), med dir, 1996, sr med dir, 2003-. **Orgs:** AAFP; NCAFP; NMA; MCMS; Omega Psi Phi, 1967-. **Honors/Awds:** Am Acad Family Physicians, fel, 1980, Nat Family Physician of the Year, 1998; Omega Psi Phi, Omega Man of the Year, 1989, Citizen of the Year, 1998; Community Pride, Citizen of the Year, 1998. **Military Serv:** AUS, E-5, 1970-72, Medal Distinction. **Home Addr:** 5611 Ruth Dr, Charlotte, NC 28215. **Business Addr:** Senior Medical Director, Virginia Premier Health Plan Inc, 600 E Broad St Suite 400, PO Box 5307, Richmond, VA 23220-0307, **Business Phone:** (804)819-5151.

PINN, SAMUEL J
Educator. **Personal:** Born May 25, 1935, Brooklyn, NY; married Cynthia; children: Samuel III, Gregory & Charles. **Educ:** Morgan State Univ, BA, 1959; Rutgers Univ, MSW, 1970. **Career:** SJP Consult, pres, 1968-; Mayors Action Task Force, dir, 1968-71; Wiltwick Sch, dir, 1971-72; Ramapo Col, assoc prof social sci, currently. **Orgs:** Col Human Serv, 1973-75; Nat Conf Penal Reform, 1975-76; consult, Nassau & Co Equal Opptunity Comn, 1976; chmn, Comm Sch Bd Dist, 1996; pres, Bedford Study Inst Afro-Am Studies & Continuing Educ; chmn & founder, Ft Greene Sr Citzen Ctr; chmn, Brooklyn Core; sr citizen columnist, NY Amsterdam News; Human Resource Dist 11; Omega Psi Phi; Asn Black Social Workers; Youth Leadership Recreation Teacher Asn. **Honors/Awds:** Community Service Award, John Jay Col; Civic Leadership, Brooklyn Civic Asn. **Special Achievements:** Books: Committee Organizing for Small Groups, 1970. **Military Serv:** AUS, first lt, 1959. **Business Addr:** Associate Professor of Social Science, Ramapo College of New Jersey, Department of American Studies, Rm G226 505 Ramapo Valley Rd, Mahwah, NJ 07430-1623, **Business Phone:** (201)684-7500 Ext 7424.

PINSON, HERMINE DOLOREZ
College teacher, writer. **Personal:** Born Jul 20, 1953, Beaumont, TX; daughter of Robert B and Enid Davis Harris; married Donald E, Sep 10, 1976; children: Leah Courtney. **Educ:** Fisk Univ, BA, 1975; Southern Methodist Univ, MA, 1979; Rice Univ, PhD, 1991. **Career:** Community Col, Houston, 1977-79; Tex Southern Univ, asst prof, 1979-92; Col William & Mary, assoc prof eng, 1992-. **Orgs:** Acad Am Poets; ASCAP; Southern Conf African-Am Studies Inc; Am Lit Asn; Southern Modern Lang Asn; Collegium African Am Res; Arbor Asn; fel, Ford Postdoctoral, 1991; Macdowell Colony, 1996; Yaddo Colony, 1996; Vermont Studio Ctr, 1997; Nat Endowment Humanities, 1988; Va Found Humanities; Callaloo Fel. **Honors/Awds:** King Chavez-Parks Visiting Professor, Univ Mich, Ann Arbor. **Special Achievements:** Author, poetry collections: Mama Yetta and Other Poems 1988, Ashe 1992; work published in anthologies: Common Bonds, 1986; Loss of Ground Note, Callaloo, 1999; co-ed: Critical Voicings of Black Liberation in FORECAAST; fiction published in: Callaloo 2001; Sacred Bearings 2001; Sou'wester, 2003; CD, Changing the Changes: In Poetry & Song, 2006; Dolores is Blue / Dolorez is Blues, 2007. **Business Addr:** Associate Professor, College of William & Mary, Department of English, Tucker 307A, PO Box 8795, Williamsburg, VA 23187-8795, **Business Phone:** (757)221-2437.

PINSON, MARGO DEAN
Administrator. **Personal:** Born Oct 29, 1937, Washington, DC; daughter of Dr Millard R and Irene F C; married Dr Thomas J Pinson, Aug 21, 1969; children: Wendie F Barbee. **Educ:** Howard Univ, cert, dent hygiene, 1959, BS, 1977; Catholic Univ, summer session, 1973, 1974. **Career:** Administrator (retired); Michael Reece Hosp, clinic dent hygienist, 1959-61; Jewish Memorial Hosp, clinic dent hygienist, 1961-62; DC Gov, clinic dent hygienist, 1966-68, dent hygiene counr, 1968-77; Howard Univ, spec events officer, 1977; Southeastern Univ, exec asst pres. **Orgs:** Pres, Sigma Phi Alpha Dental Hygiene Hon Soc, 1963-64; Howard Univ Alumni Asn, 1977-; Howard Univ Dent Hygiene Alumni Asn, 1960-; Nat Asn Adv Colored People Montgomery Co Br, 1991-, fundraising dinner comt, 1992, 1993; bd gov, Westover Sch, 1986-92, bd govs, chair annual fund, 1990-92; pres, Northeasterners Inc, Wash Chap, 1988-90, nat vip, 1990-92, nat pres, 1992-; bd comnrs, town treasurer, Town Highland Beach, 1984-99, appointed comnr finance, 1992-99; Nat Coalition 100 Black Women, 1990-93; Southwest Neighborhood Assembly, currently. **Home Addr:** 3316 Brooklawn Terr, Chevy Chase, MD 20815, **Home Phone:** (301)656-3284. *

PINSON, VALERIE F.
Legislator. **Personal:** Born Apr 30, 1930, Newburgh, NY; divorced; children: Tracey. **Educ:** Howard Univ, atteded 1950; Bus Sch, 1951. **Career:** Legislator (retired); Sen Thomas J Dodd, asst, 1960-64; White House Hon Hobart Taylor, exec asst, 1965-66; Ofc Econ Opp, 1966-71; Comm Action Spec, 1971-72; Congress woman Yvonne B Burke Dem CA, admin asst; The White House, spl asst for cong liaison, 1977-81; Nat Asn Counties, leg repr. **Orgs:** Bd mem, Wash Urban League; bd Family & Child Serv; Com Minority Fel Prog Am Univ.

PIPER, ADRIAN MARGARET SMITH
Educator, artist. **Personal:** Born Sep 20, 1948, New York, NY; daughter of Daniel Robert and Olive Xavier Smith. **Educ:** Sch Visual Arts, NY, NY, AA, fine arts, 1969; City Col NY, NY, BA, philos, 1974; Harvard Univ, Cambridge, MA, philos, 1977, PhD, philos, 1981. **Career:** Harvard Univ, grad teaching asst, 1976-77; Visual Artists fel, Nat Educ Asn, 1979, 1982; Univ Mich, asst prof, 1979-86; Stanford Univ, mellon res fel, 1982-84; Georgetown Univ, assoc prof, 1986-88; Guggenheim fel, 1988-89; Univ Calif, San Diego, assoc prof, 1988-90; Woodrow Wilson Int Scholars fel, 1989-90; Wellesley Col, prof philos, 1990-; Nat Endowment Humanities Col Teacher's res fel, 1998; Internationales Forschungszentrum Kulturwissenschaften, fel, 2004. **Orgs:** N Am Kant Soc, 1979-; Am Philos Asn, 1979-; Am Asn Univ Prof, 1979-; Asn Polit & Legal Philos, 1979-; Col Art Asn, 1983-; Soc Philos & Pub Affairs; Phi Beta Kappa. **Honors/Awds:** First Prize in Drawing, Sch Visual Arts. Annual Stud Exhib, 1968; Sperling Prize for Excellence in Philosophy, City Col NY, 1974, Phi Beta Kappa Medal for the Best Honors Essay in the Social Sciences, 1974, Research Honors in Philosophy, 1974; Awards in the Visual Arts fellowship, 1990; DHL, Calif Inst Arts, 1992; DA, Mass Col Art, 1994; Skowhegan Medal for Sculptural Installation, 1995; Distinguished Scholar, Getty Res Inst, 1998-99. **Business Addr:** Professor of Philosophy, Wellesley College, Department of Philosophy, 106 Central St, Wellesley, MA 02481.

PIPER, ELWOOD A
Educator, business owner. **Personal:** Born Apr 13, 1934, Bastrop, TX; son of John H and Ruby; married Ora Lean Williams; children: Malcom, Karen, Adrian & Kenneth. **Educ:** Wiley Col, BA, 1956; Tex Southern Univ, MA, 1965. **Career:** Educator (retired), business owner; Houston Independent Sch Dist, teacher & coach, 1958-65, asst prin to prin, 1965-85; Piper's Automotive Serv Ctr, owner, currently. **Orgs:** Pleasantville Civil Club; Rotary Houston; Phi Delta Kappa; Nat Asn Sect Prin; Boy Scouts Am; Big Broth Am; Tex J Prin Asn. **Honors/Awds:** Man of the Year, Civic Club, 1965; Service Award, Negro Hist, 1968; Citation of the week, KNUZ-Radio, 1973; Silver Beaver Award, Boy Scouts Am, 1976; Outstanding Administrator, 1980; Certificate of Technical Competence Award, 1984. **Business Addr:** Owner, Piper's Automotive Service Center, 2004 N Main, Baytown, TX 77520, **Business Phone:** (281)420-2374.

PIPER, DR. PAUL J
Physician. **Personal:** Born Jun 19, 1935, Detroit, MI; married Mary K Harris; children: Paul & Michael. **Educ:** Univ Mich, BS 1962; MS 1967; Wayne State Univ, MD, 1973. **Career:** Mich Dept Corrections, physician; Pvt Pract, physician. **Orgs:** Detroit Med Soc; Sigma Phi Pi; Detroit Surg Soc; Nat Med Asn. **Military Serv:** USAF, 1955-58.

PIPER, DR. W ARCHIBALD
Physician, surgeon. **Personal:** Born Apr 13, 1935. **Educ:** Mt Allison Univ, BSc, 1961; Dalhousie Univ, MD, 1966; McGill Univ Can, MSc, 1969; FRCS 1972; FACS, 1976. **Career:** Physician, Surgeon (retired); W Archibald Piper PC, plastic surgeon; Mich St Univ, asst prof surg. **Orgs:** AMA; Mich State Med Soc; Am Col Surgeons; Am Soc Plastic Recons Surgeons; Flint Acad Surgeons; Mich Acad Plastics Surgeons; Rotary Club; pvt pilot; Int Col Surgeons. **Honors/Awds:** Bd cert Am Bd Plastic Surg; MSc thesis "The Fibroblast in Wound Healing"; Dr Clement A Alfred Humanitarian Award, 2008.

PIPKINS, ROBERT ERIK
Athlete. **Personal:** Born Feb 23, 1973, Buffalo, NY; son of Joan E Pipkins and Robert E Pipkins. **Educ:** Drexel Univ, BS,

architectural eng & civil eng, 1995. **Career:** Athlete (retired); luger Olympics, Mens Singles, US, junior development team, mem, 1987-88; jr candidate team, mem, 1988-89; jr nat team mem, 1989-92; Lake Placid Track Record Holder, 1992; Junior World Champion, 1992; sr nat team mem, 1992-94; luger Olympics team, US, mem, 1994. **Honors/Awds:** US National Champion, 1993-95. **Home Phone:** (718)720-1957.

PIPPEN, SCOTTIE
Basketball player, basketball coach. **Personal:** Born Sep 25, 1965, Hamburg, AR; married Karen McCollum, Jan 1, 1988 (divorced 1995); children: 1; married Larsa Younan, Jul 20, 1997; children: 2. **Educ:** Univ Cent Ark, attended 1987. **Career:** Basketball player (retired), Basketball coach; Chicago Bulls, forward-guard, 1987-98, 2003-04; Houston Rockets, 1999; Portland Trail Blazers, 1999-2003; Los Angeles Lakers, spec asst coach, 2005; ESPN, part-time analyst; ABC, studio analyst, 2005-06; Torpan Pojat, 2008; Sundsvall Dragons, 2008; speaker, currently. **Honors/Awds:** All-NBA First Team, 1994-96; All-NBA Second Team, 1992, 1997; NBA All-Defensive First Team, 1992-97; NBA All-Star, 1990, 1992-97; NBA All-Star Game Most Valuable Player, 1994; NBA Champions, Chicago Bulls, 1991-98; won gold medals with the US Olympic Basketball Team, 1992, 1996; Selected as one of the 50 Greatest Players in NBA Hist, 1996. **Special Achievements:** Personality behind the Scottie Candy Bar, 1993; Author: Reach Higher, 1997; Film: He Got Game, 1998. **Business Addr:** Speaker, Playing Field Promotions, 277 S Forest St, Denver, CO 80246-1148.

PITCHER, FREDDIE, JR.
Educator, judge. **Personal:** Born Apr 28, 1945, Baton Rouge, LA. **Educ:** Southern Univ, BA, polit sci, 1966, JD, 1973. **Career:** Judge (retired), Educator; Baton Rouge City Ct, judge; La Supreme Ct, assoc justice ad hoc; special counsel, Office of the Attorney General for the State of Louisiana; asst district attorney, East Baton Rouge Parish; Phelps Dunbar LLP, partner; Southern Univ Law Ctr, adj fac mem, chancellor & prof law, currently. **Orgs:** Am Bar Asn; Nat Bar Asn; La State Bar Asn; Baton Rouge Bar Asn. **Special Achievements:** First African American elected to a judgeship in Baton Rouge,1983; first African American elected to the 19th Judicial District, 1987; first with his election to the Louisiana First Circuit Court of Appeal, without opposition, 1992. **Business Addr:** Chancellor, Professor of Law, Southern University Law Center, 2 Roosevelt Steptoe Dr Suite 261, PO Box 9294, Baton Rouge, LA 70813, **Business Phone:** (225)771-2552.

PITCHER, CAPT. FREDERICK M A
Pilot, airplane pilot. **Personal:** Born Mar 9, 1932, Washington, DC; son of Hardy and Sylvia Saunders; divorced; children: Frederick II, Riccardo, Tia Pitcher Clarke, Mikela, Ericka & Elliott. **Educ:** DeVry Tech Inst, Dipl, 1953; Northrop Univ, Cert, Lic A&P, 1965; Fowler Aeronaut, Dipl, 1966; LA Trade Tech Col, AS Dean's List, 1969; UCLA, Teaching Credential, 1977; Nat Radio Inst, Dipl, 1977; KIIS Radio Broadcasting, Dipl, 1979. **Career:** US Naval Model Basin, engrg aide 1955; Burroughs Corp Computers, electronic tech 1955-59, electronics engr 1959-64; Tech Enterprises, owner, oper 1961-; Electronic Memories Inc, quality control 1964; Rose Aviation, flight instr 1975-85; Western Airlines, airline pilot, 1966-87; Delta Airlines, airline pilot, 1987-. **Orgs:** Pilot & instr, Civil Air Patrol, 1948-; cert flight instr Worldwide, 1961-85; station engr, KFAR-TV, 1962-63; builder, Experiment Aircraft Asn, 1965-; chief exec officer, Tech Enterprises 1966-; guestlectr LA Sch Dist 1968-85; Educare USC Alumni 1977; dir mem, Northrop Univ Alumni, 1979-; chief fin Officer, DW Ford Corp Inc, 1982-85; pres, Mkt Int Ltd, 1983-; dir, DW Ford Seminar Asn, 1983-85; exec vpres, Worldwide Tax & Bus Consult Inc, 1984-85; reading tutor CA Literacy Prog 1984-87; LA Urban Bankers Asn, 1984-85; west reg vpres, Orgn Black Airline Pilots, 1984-86; indust resource person, Los Angeles Sch Dist, 1986-; restorer, March Air Force Base Mus, Calif, 1988-89; founder, Socr Preserv Antique Tech Equip, 1989; comm rel Offr AirlinePilots Assoc 1983-85. **Honors/Awds:** Scholarship Sci Bosch & Lomb 1950; People & Choices Harcourt BraceJovonovich Publ Co, 1971; Community Service, LA Sch Dist, 1971; Distinguished Alumni, Northrop Univ, 1976; Good Samaritan Award, Church Jesus Christ of Latter Day Saints, 1976; Commendation CA State Senator Green Comm Asst 1980; Professional Recog Edges Group Inc of Fortune 500 1984; Certificate of Recognition, State Senator Bill Greene, California, 1989. **Military Serv:** USNR-R atr-2 10 yrs. **Home Addr:** PO Box 73CN Broadway-Manchester Station, Los Angeles, CA 90003, **Home Phone:** (213)750-7275. **Business Addr:** Airline Pilot, Delta Airlines, 6060 Avlon Dr Dept 030, Los Angeles, CA 90009, **Business Phone:** (323)309-9515.

PITCHFORD, GERARD SPENCER
Executive. **Personal:** Born Dec 8, 1953, Jersey City, NJ; son of Gordon and Gloria Oliver; married Janet F Hardy, Nov 25, 1987; children: Uonisha & Paris. **Educ:** Rutgers Univ, attended 1970. **Career:** Dynamic Serv Unlimited, sales mgr, 1976; Time to Order Corp, pres, 1984-86; Commun Equip Repair, pres, 1977; Corp Promotions Int, pres; GC Capital Inc, prin, currently. **Orgs:** Bd mem, treas, Chicago Regional Purchasing Coun, 1980-; bd mem, Chicago State Univ Found, 1982-; bd mem, Private Indust Coun, 1984-; deacon, Chicago United, 1987; bd mem, Push Int Trade Bur; comnr, City Chicago Dept Human Rights; chmn, Chicago Reg Purchasing Coun Comt. **Honors/Awds:** Vendor of the Month, State Ill, 1986. **Business Phone:** (773)810-9004.

PITRE, MERLINE
School administrator, educator. **Personal:** Born Apr 10, 1943, Opelousas, LA; daughter of Robert and Florence Pitre. **Educ:** Southern Univ, BS, 1966; Atlanta Univ, MA, 1967; Temple Univ, MA, 1972, PhD, 1976. **Career:** St Augustine's Col, prof, 1967-70; Tex Southern Univ, prof & dean, 1976-. **Orgs:** Southern Conf Afro-Am Studies; Southern Hist Asn; Black Women Historian; Tex State Hist Asn; Org Am Historian. **Special Achievements:** Through Many Dangers, Toils & Snares: The Black Leadership of Texas, 1868 to 1900; In Struggle against Jim Crow: Lulu B. White and the NAACP, 1900 to 57. **Business Addr:** Professor, Dean, Texas Southern University, 3100 Cleburn St, Houston, TX 77004, **Business Phone:** (713)313-7795.

PITT, DR. CLIFFORD SINCLAIR
School administrator. **Personal:** Born in Georgetown, GA; son of Alphonso and Carmen; divorced; children: Amanda & Carolyn. **Educ:** Newbold Col, BA, 1971; Andrews Univ, MA, 1972; Univ London, PhD, 1976. **Career:** British Union Seventh-Day Adventists, minister; Oakwood Col, assoc prof; Miles Col, dean acad affairs, currently. **Orgs:** Valedictorian & pres, Newbold Col Sor Class, 1971. **Special Achievements:** Author of Church, Ministry & Sacraments: A Critical Evaluation of the Thought of Peter Taylor Forsyth, Univ Press of America, 1983. **Business Addr:** Dean of Academic Affairs, Miles College, PO Box 3800, Birmingham, AL 35208, **Business Phone:** (205)929-1000.

PITTMAN, DR. AUDREY BULLOCK
Educator. **Personal:** Born Dec 16, 1916, Philadelphia, PA; daughter of Oscar Wyle and Annie Beaden; married James, Jan 17, 1942 (died 1989); children: Joyce Ann. **Educ:** Morgan State Univ, BA, 1948; Univ Penn, MSW; Waldon Univ, PhD, 1984. **Career:** Philadelphia Dept Welfare, supvr, 1951-57; Children's Aid Soc, adoption supvr & consult, 1957-64; Penn State Dept Welfare, day care dir, 1964-69; Temple Univ, assoc prof 1969-84, prof emer, currently. **Orgs:** Founding mem, Philadelphia Asn Black Social Workers, 1969-; bd pres, Christian Educ AME Church, 1971-; trustee, Cheyney Univ, 1977-; adv bd, Philadelphia Dept Welfare 1981-88; bd mem & vpres, Black Family Serv, 1984-; bd mem, Women's Christian Alliance, 1986-89; mem, Philadelphia County Bd Assistance, 1990-; trustee, Valentine Found, 1990; bd mem & vpres, Phila Child Guid Clin, 1994-. **Honors/Awds:** Linback Award of Excellence in Teaching, Temple Univ, 1981; Service Award, Nat Alliance Black Social Workers, 1984; Alumni of Year Award, William Penn High Sch, 1985; Meritorius Christian Serv, AME Womens Missionary Soc, 1992; Outstanding Christian Service, Dorothy M Jenkins, 1993; Distinguished Service Award, Morgan State Univ & Phil Alumnu Chapter, 1994; Achievement in the Field of Educ, 1995; African Am Community Award, Blacks Networking Progress Inc; The Alpha African Am Heritage Award, Rho Chapter Alpha Phi Alpha Fraternity; Christian Educ Award. **Business Addr:** Professor Emeritus, Temple University, 1801 N Broad St, Philadelphia, PA 19107, **Business Phone:** (215)204-7000.

PITTMAN, DARRYL E.
Government official. **Personal:** Born Jul 11, 1948, Pittsburgh, PA; son of J Ronald and Eunice W; married Deborah Durham, Aug 8, 1980; children: Darryl M, Sholah, Jordan, Cassi & Nolan. **Educ:** Columbia Col, New York, NY, BA, 1970; Columbia Univ Sch Law, New York, NY,JD, 1973. **Career:** Hahn Loeser, Freedheim, Dean & Wellman, Cleveland, OH, assoc; City East Cleveland OH, mayor; Pittman, Alexander, Cook & Assocs, Cleveland, OH, partner, currently. **Orgs:** Pres, Software Specialist; Norman Minor Bar Asn; former pres, Ohio Chapter Black Mayors; 21st Dist Cong Caucus, bd mem, Cleveland Br Nat Asn Advan Colored People. **Home Addr:** 16119 Oakhill Rd, East Cleveland, OH 44112. **Business Addr:** Partner, Pittman, Alexander, Cook & Associates, 2940 Noble Rd Suite 202, Cleveland, OH 44121, **Business Phone:** (216)291-1005.*

PITTMAN, KAVIKA CHARLES
Football player. **Personal:** Born Oct 9, 1974, Frankfurt, Germany. **Educ:** McNeese State Univ. **Career:** Dallas Cowboys, defensive end, 1996-99; Denver Broncos, defensive end, 2000-02; Carolina Panthers, defensive end, 2003; free agent, currently. **Honors/Awds:** Rookie of the Year, 1996.

PITTMAN, KEITH B.
Government official, vice president (government). **Personal:** Born Jan 1, 1971?. **Career:** New Orleans Metrop Conv & Visitors Bur, dir govt affairs, 1997, vpres govt affairs, currently. **Special Achievements:** First African American director at the Visitor's Bureau, as well as the youngest dir. **Business Addr:** Vice President governmental affairs, New Orleans Metropolitan Convention & Visitors Bureau, 1520 Sugar Bowl Dr, New Orleans, LA 70112, **Business Phone:** (504)566-5055.*

PITTMAN, MARVIN B.
Dentist. **Personal:** Born May 31, 1931, Blakely, GA; son of Johnnie Will and Lucile Brewster; married Amanda B Nelson; children: Marvin B Jr. **Educ:** Savannah State Col, BS, 1953; Univ Mich, MS, 1957; Howard Univ, DDS, 1966. **Career:** VA Ctr Los Angeles, res biochemist, 1957-62; Los Angeles, pvt pract dent, 1970-. **Orgs:** Am Dent Asn; CA Dent Asn; Angel City Cent Soc; Century Club Univ SC; Holman Meth Church; Urban League, NAACP; Alpha Phi Alpha; Young Men's Christian Asn; Res Officers Asn; bd dirs, pres, JW Ross Med Ctr; bd dirs, Omicron Kappa Upsilon; bd dirs, Beta Kappa Chi; bd dirs, Los Angeles Free Clinic. **Military Serv:** AUS, NCO, 1953-56; US Navy Res, 1964-66; AUS, dent officer, 1966-70; AUS Reserves Col, 1971; Bronze Star, Army Commendation, Good Conduct, Army Achievement. **Business Addr:** Dentist, 1828 SW Ave Suite 402, Los Angeles, CA 90006.*

PITTMAN, MICHAEL
Football player. **Personal:** Born Aug 14, 1975, New Orleans, LA; son of Henry and Mae; married Melissa; children: Jordanne, Michael Jr, Mycah & Mykava Kaelyn. **Educ:** Fresno State Univ. **Career:** Ariz Cardinals, running back, 1998-2001; Tampa Bay Buccaneers, runningback, 2002-07; Denver Broncos, 2008; Florida Tuskers, 2009-. **Honors/Awds:** Super Bowl XXXVII, 2002. **Special Achievements:** First team All-Eastern League League honoree. **Business Addr:** Professional Football Player, Florida Tuskers, 501 Riverside Ave Suite 904, Jacksonville, FL 32202.

PITTMAN, DR. SAMPLE NOEL
Educator. **Personal:** Born Apr 22, 1927, Texas; married Vivian Jo Byars; children: Sample Jr, Ava, Nicole & Nicholas. **Educ:** Samuel Huston Col, BA, 1949; Tex Southern Univ, MA, 1952; NY Univ, PhD, 1974. **Career:** Ill Youth Comn, juvenile parole officer, 1957; Mayors Comn New Residents, 1959; Chicago Comm Col, instr, 1962; Chicago Comn Race Relations, asst dir; St Charles St Training Sch; Dillard Univ, dean students, prof Sociol, 1964; New York City Housing & Redevel Bd Hudson Consev Project, asst dir, 1966; Inst Strategic Study United Presbyterian Church, New York City, res assoc, 1967; Poverty Prog, Training Resources Youth Educ Dept, dir, 1969; Borough Manhattan Comm Col City Univ NY, dean admin, 1970-, assoc dean stud, 1971; Corp Consortium-Harlem Inst Teachers NYC, dir teacher, 1970. **Orgs:** Alpha Phi Alpha, 1948; Chicago City Comm Col Fac Rep Intercollegiate Coun, 1961; mem bd dir, Chicago Halfway House, 1962; consult lectr, Nat Conf Christians & Jews Chicago, 1962; Chicago City Comm Col Fac Rep United Nat Inst, 1962; vpres, Parents Teachers Stud Asn, 1962; vpres, Greenview Comm Coun, Chicago, 1962; panelist, DePaul Univ & Nat Conf Christians & Jews, Chicago, 1962; Phi Delta Kappa, 1966; treas, Comm Bd 9 Manhattan NY. **Honors/Awds:** Administrator of the Year Award, Borough Manhattan Comm Col, 1974; Founders Day Award, NYU, 1974; Diploma de hon Borough, Manhattan Comm Col, 1975; Outstanding Educ Am Award, 1975; Bertha Lockett Achievement Award, Brownwood TX, 1975. **Military Serv:** AUS. **Business Addr:** Dean, Borough Manhattan Community College, 199 Chambers St, New York, NY 10031, **Business Phone:** (212)346-8000.

PITTMAN, WINSTON R., SR.
Automotive executive. **Career:** Cardinal Dodge Inc, owner, currently. **Orgs:** bd mem, Fifth Third bd. **Business Addr:** President, Cardinal Dodge Inc, 5311 Dixie Hwy, Louisville, KY 40216-1557, **Business Phone:** (502)449-1900.

PITTS, BRENDA S
Executive. **Personal:** Born Aug 29, 1950, Madison, IN; daughter of Kenneth W and Theola I; married Joseph David; children: Nichole & Christopher. **Educ:** Ind Univ, BS, educ, 1972. **Career:** Knox Co News, writer, 1972-73; Cummins Engine Co Inc, commun spec, 1974, couns 1975, personnel admin, 1975-78, mgr EEO, 1978-82, mgr personnel, 1982-83, dir personnel, 1983-88, exd personnel, 1988-92, vpres, human resources, 1992-97; vpres, diversity & corp responsibility, 1997-. **Orgs:** Alpha Kappa Alpha Sorority, 1970-72; scholar chmn, Laws Found, 1975-79; comnr, Columbus Human Rights Comn, 1978-79; vpres, Columbus NAACP. **Honors/Awds:** Freshman Hon Soc Ind Univ, 1968-69; Dean's List Ind Univ, 1968-72.

PITTS, CORNELIUS
Lawyer. **Personal:** Born Aug 3, 1933, Detroit, MI; son of Percy Jame and Zenolia O; married Mildred D Johnson, Aug 2, 1959; children: Byron Horace. **Educ:** Wayne State Univ, BA, 1959, LLB, 1964. **Career:** Pvt Pract, atty, 1965-. **Orgs:** Wolverine Bar Asn, 1965-; Nat Bar Asn, 1965-; Detroit Bar Asn, 1965-; Mich Bar Asn, 1965-. **Military Serv:** USY, cpl, 1953-55. **Business Addr:** Attorney, 645 Griswold St Suite 3650, Detroit, MI 48226, **Business Phone:** (313)964-0066.

PITTS, DONALD FRANKLIN
Judge. **Personal:** Born Aug 30, 1933, Pontiac, MI; married Patricia Florence Washington; children: Gregory Leroy, Gail Lynn, Kimberly Marie Thomas, Mark Robert Brown, Donald F Jr & Maureen Alyce. **Educ:** East Los Angeles Col, AA, 1952; Calif State Univ, BA, 1954; Southwestern Univ, JD, 1962. **Career:** Judge (retired); LA Calif, probation officer, 1955-63, atty law, 1963-71; Calif State Univ Long Beach, assoc prof, 1972-75; Super

Ct, ref, 1969-71, comnr 1971-84, judge, 1984. **Orgs:** State Bar Calif; Nat Bar Asn; John M Langston Bar Asn; LA Cty Bar Asn; Long Beach Bar Asn; YMCA; Nat Asn Advan Colored People; bd dir, Comm Develop Inc.

PITTS, GEORGE EDWARD
Writer, photojournalist. **Personal:** Born Sep 10, 1951, Pennsylvania; son of George Sr and Phyllis; married Janis Pitts, Dec 25, 1978. **Educ:** Howard Univ, 1970; Skowhegan Sch Painting & Sculpture, 1971; Bennington Col, BA, 1973. **Career:** Phillips Exeter Acad, art teacher, Summer, 1972; Time Inc Picture Collection, picture researcher, 1979-90; Sports Illusr Picture Collection, picture reseacher, 1982; Entertainment Weekly Mag, asst picture ed, 1990-93; Vibe Mag, dir photog, 1993-2004; Parsons New Sch Design, facult, 1998-, asst prof & assoc Chair, currently; Sch Visual Art, teacher, 2001; LIFE Magazine, dir Photography, 2004-07. **Orgs:** Soc Publ Design, 1994-. **Honors/Awds:** Winner, Skowhegan Sch Painting & Sculpture, 1971; Photography Award, Commun Arts, 1991-93; Best Photography, Vibe Magazine, 1994, 1995, 2000; Exhibition of Vibe Fashion Photography, Festival De La Mode, Louvre Museum, Paris, 1994; Certificate of Merit, Am Photog, 1995. **Special Achievements:** Group Art Exhibition: Social Studies: Truth, Justice, and the Afro-American Way, Illinois State University, 1989; Men, Myth, and Masculinities, Ledisflam Gallery, NYC, 1993; The Return of the Cadavre Exquis, The Drawing Center, NYC, 1993; Go Back and Fetch It, Gallery Annex I & II, 1994, 1995. **Business Addr:** Assistant Professor, Associate Chair, The New School For Design, 66 5th Ave, New York, NY 10011, **Business Phone:** (212)229-8900.

PITTS, LEE H.
Athletic coach, swimmer. **Personal:** Born Jul 7, 1960, Birmingham, AL; son of Johnnie Pitts. **Educ:** Talladega Col, BBA, 1982; Atlanta Univ, MA, economics, 1985. **Career:** A G Gaston Boys Club, swim instr, 1979; Colville Pool, head swim instr, 1981; Norwood Pool, head swim team, coach, 1982; Adams Park Pool, heads wim instr, 1984; Star Complex Ft Myers, FL, head swim instr; Dr Martin Luther King Pool, head swim team, coach, 1992; WEVU-TV Talk Show, Lee Pitts Live, exec producer & host, currently; Lee Pitts Swim Sch, Ft Myers, Fl, founder, 1999-. **Orgs:** Nat Assn Black Scuba Divers, 1992; Nat Assn Swim Instr, 1993; brd dirs, Am Red Cross, 1990; Nat Assn Urban Bankers, 1988; Phi Beta sigma fraternity;US swim; Quality Life Ctr. **Honors/Awds:** Outstanding Community Involvement Award, Nat Assn Advan Colored People,1984; Alumni Spotlight Award, Talladega Col, 1991; Outstanding Youth Devt Award, Edison Community Col, 1991; Outstanding Contribution to Swimming,Am Red Cross, 1991; Distinguished Service award, Nat Assn Advan Colored People, 1993; Crime Prevention Among Black Youths, Fl, 1994; Alumni Hallof Fame, Boys & Girls Clubs Am, 1998; Intl Swim Hall of Fame. **Special Achievements:** First and only African American swim instructor in the role; First African American to produce, direct, write, and star in a swim lesson video, 1993; First African American to be a spokesman on swim instruction commercials for NBC-TV, 1992; author of 25 published swimming-related articles; Keynote speaker at numerous elementary, high schools & colleges around the country; Inducted into the SW Florida Black History Museum, 1995; spokesman for WFLA, Channel 8, NBC, pool safety commercials in Tampa Bay; Author of article, "Black Splash: The History of African-American Swimmer". **Business Phone:** 877-830-0391.

PITTS, MEAGAN R
Executive. **Educ:** Univ Mich, BA, eng lang & lit, 2003. **Career:** City Detroit, Off Mayor, exec asst & team leader, currently. **Business Addr:** Executive Assistant, Team Leader, City of Detroit, Mayor?s Office of Community Affairs, 2 Woodward Ave Suite 1126, Detroit, MI 48226, **Business Phone:** (313)224-0869.

PITTS, RONALD JAMES, SR.
Lawyer. **Personal:** Born Nov 2, 1942, Wheeling, WV; married Nellie M Price; children: Ronnelle, Rhonda; Ronald J II. **Educ:** BS, 1966; LLB, 1969; JD, 1970. **Career:** Atty, pvt prac; IRS Estate & Gift Tax Reg Analyst Cincinnati, estate tax group mgr; IRS, atty; Greensboro Dist Greensboro NC, quality & productivity coord, currently; tech revr, 1997-. **Orgs:** Vpres, Nat Asn Advan Colored People Huntington WVa; Huntington URA Comnr; Legal Coun Bluefield St Alumni; secy, Nat Asn Advan Colored People, 1973-74; chmn, C-H Human Rights Coun, 1970-73; WVa Black Caucus; supv C/UNIDN chmn; pres, Chap 64 Nat Treas Employment Union; secy, Mtn St Bar Asn, 1972-73, histrn; WVa St Bar Asn; Am Bar Asn, 1969; pres Coun Wheeling Col; EEO Consult RJP Consult Fed Fed Basketball Leag, 1970; comnr, 1970-75; bd mem, Tri-St Tax Inst, 1975; St Legist Interim Com; quality instr Reg, 1987; nat exec bd, AIM-IRS, 1986-87, nat parliamentarian, 1986-; OD, consult. **Honors/Awds:** Distingushed Performer, 1986, 1987. *

PITTS, DR. VERA L.
Educator, school administrator. **Personal:** Born Jan 23, 1931, Wichita, KS; daughter of Wade and Maggie; married Leonard (deceased). **Educ:** Mills Col, AA, 1950; NC Berkeley, BA, 1953; Sacramento State Univ, MA, 1962; MI State Univ, PhD, 1969. **Career:** Stockton Unified Sch Dist, teacher, counselor & admin, 1954-65; City Col NY, asst prof, 1967-69; Palmer Handwriting Co, consult 1975-; Rockefeller Postdoctoral Fel, 1978-80; Calif St Univ, Hayward, prof, dept chair & ed admin, Dept Educ, prog mgr, 1986-87; Oakland Unified Sch Dist, assoc supt, 1987-88; Oakland Pub Schs, Oakland, CA, interim supt, 1989; Nat Hispanic Univ, San Jose, CA, provost, 1990-91. **Orgs:** League Women Voters, 1975-; Western Assoc Accrediting Teams 1975-; SanMateo Br Am Assoc Univ Women, 1976-77; Calif St Div Am Assoc Univ Women, 1978-80; Foster City Ed Facilities Comm, 1983; Univ Calif Alumni Assoc, 1979-83; Nat Urban League Ed Adv Community, 1979; Nat Coun Admin Women Educ, 1982; Phi Delta Kappa, 1982-85; bd trustees, Pacific Sch Religon, 1989; Rotary Int, 1988-; Family Serv Agency, 1999-; Sr FocusMills Peninsula Hosp, 1999; Am Social Health Asn, 1999-; Arthritis Found Advocacy Com, 1999-. **Honors/Awds:** National Award of Michigan, 1965-67. **Home Addr:** 1557 Beach Pk Blvd, Foster City, CA 94404-1437, **Home Phone:** (650)573-9459. **Business Addr:** Professor Emeritus, Department Chair, California State University, 25800 Carlos Bee Blvd, Hayward, CA 94542, **Business Phone:** (914)881-3106.

PLATT, RICHARD A
Executive. **Career:** Platt Construct Inc, Franklin, owner, currently. **Orgs:** Am Col Cardiol; Wis Underground Contractors Asn; MWCA; Turkish Cypriot Community Asn. **Honors/Awds:** SCY's Award, DPT Transportation, 1988; Regl V, 8A Graduate of the Year Award, 1992; National Graduate of the Year Award, SBA, Wash, DC, 1992. **Business Phone:** (414)761-3868.

PLEAS, JOHN ROLAND
Psychologist. **Personal:** Born Nov 11, 1938, East St Louis, IL; son of Henry and Daisy Walton; married Katherine, Dec 26, 1985; children: Chandra. **Educ:** McKendree Col, BA, 1960; Univ IL, Urbana, MEd, 1967; Vanderbilt Univ, Nashville,Tenn, PhD, 1980. **Career:** Univ Chicago, Billings Hosp, res tech, 1963-67; St Leonards House, dir com develop, 1967-71; Competence Inc, pres, 1975-; Vanderbilt Univ, weight Mgt prog, co-dir, 1977-84; Columbia Col, asst prof, 1984-85; Middle Tenn State Univ, assoc prof, 1985, prof, prof emer, currently. **Honors/Awds:** Danforth Fel, Vanderbilt Univ, 1971-73; Recognition Award, Natl Med Assn Northwest Indiana, Inc, 1988; Am Soc Engineering Educ, Certicate of Recognition Award, Naval Health Res Ctr, San Diego, CA, 1990. **Military Serv:** AUS, 1960-63; Good Conduct Medal. **Business Addr:** Professor Emeritus, Middle Tennessee State University, Department of Psychology, 1301 E Main St, Murfreesboro, TN 37132-0001, **Business Phone:** (615)898-2706.

PLEASANT, ALBERT E, III
Administrator, accountant. **Personal:** Born May 22, 1944, Cincinnati, OH; son of Albert E Jr and Margaret Nesbitt; married Barbara Greene, Apr 28, 1989; children: Dennis R Green Sr; married Byrdean (divorced 1987); children: Albert E IV. **Educ:** Univ Cincinnati, BS, 1973. **Career:** Univ Cincinnati, dean's off, Col Med, fiscal asst, 1969-74; C's Hosp Med Ctr, Div Neonatology, bus mgr, 1974-89; Univ Cincinnati, Dept Peds, bus affairs asst, 1974-79, sr bus admin, 1979-89; Howard Univ, dir off res adminr, 1989-90; Univ Cincinnati Med Ctr, Dept Environ Health, assoc dir admin & bus serv, exec dir, 1990-93; Pharm Sources Int Inc, bus mgt consult, 1995-96; Sears Indust Sales, acct mgr, 1996. **Orgs:** Nat Coun Univ Res Adminr, 1974-; Soc Res Adminr, 1974-; lay delegate fifty first Reg Conv Lutheran Church Mo Synod, 1975; Asn Am Med Cols Group Bus Affairs, 1982-; assoc mem, Nat Health Lawyers Asn, 1984-; Bus Mgt Consult, NICHHD, PHS, DHHS, 1985-; Ohio Dist Bd Parish Serv, 1985-87. **Honors/Awds:** Elected mem, Repub Cent Comm Hamilton Co, Cincinnati Ohio, 1982-86. **Military Serv:** AUS, specialist 5th class, 1967-69; Vietnam Serv Medal; Good Conduct Medal; Army Commendation Medal. **Home Addr:** 3401 York W, Cincinnati, OH 45215. **Business Phone:** 800-776-8666.

PLEASANT, ANTHONY DEVON
Football player. **Personal:** Born Jan 27, 1968, Century, FL; married Renita; children: Hannah Denette. **Educ:** Tenn State Univ, criminal justice. **Career:** Football player (retired); Cleveland Browns, defensive end, 1990-95; Baltimore Ravens, 1996; Atlanta Falcons, 1997; New York Jets, 1998-99; San Francisco 49ers, 2000; New Eng Patriots, 2001-03.

PLEASANT, MAE BARBEE BOONE
School administrator. **Personal:** Born Jul 8, 1919, Kentucky; daughter of Minnie Mae Burks and Zelma Clarence Barbee; married Noel J, 1966 (deceased); children: Eugene Jr; married Eugene Boone (divorced). **Educ:** Tennessee State Univ, BS, 1941; Hampton Inst, MA, 1962; George Washington Univ. **Career:** School administrator (retired); Va State Sch Deaf & Blind, past sec supt 1944; Clark Col, past exec sec pres, 1953-57; Hampton Inst, admin asst to pres, 1957-63, sec corp beginning 1973, faculty mem, 1968-71, business mgr, 1946-53; African Am Affairs, assoc dir, 1971-73; OEO, educ specialist 1966-68; Univ MD, dean women, 1963-66. **Orgs:** Alpha Kappa Mu; Girl Scout Leader; area chmn, UNCF; historian, Diocese Southern Va Daughters King; chmn, Human Rels Comm, League Women Voters; pres Peninsula Pan Hellenic Coun; state chmn, Asn Study Negro Life & History 1973-75; bd dir, YWCA, 1953-57; vice chmn, Prof Sec, 1955-57; Vestry & Register, St Cyprian's Episcopal Church, 1974, 1984, 1989, 1997; basileus, Alpha Kappa Alpha, Gamma Upsilon Omega, 1977-79; pres, Quarter Century Club Hampton Univ; bd dir, Children's Home Soc; former vice chmn, King St Community Ctr; trustee, Va Theol Seminary; first black lay person, 1979-89; tres, bd mem, Downtown Day Care Ctr; treasurer, St Anne Chap, Daughters King St Cyprian's Episcopal Church Peninsula Pastoral Counseling, bd finance community & retreat community, Nominating Community; secy, Exec & Prog Co, Miss Peninsula Chap, Nat Conf Community & Justice. **Honors/Awds:** Woman of Year, Hampton Inst, 1957, 1963; Outstanding Soror, 1978; Community Woman of the Year, Delta Sigma Theta Sorority, 1994; Outstanding Contributions to the Community, Peninsula Pan-Hellenic Coun, 1994; Eula Edmonds Glover Volunteer Community Service Award, Alpha Kappa Alpha Sorority Inc, 1994; Golden Soror, Alpha Kappa Alpha Inc, 1999. **Home Addr:** 11 Mimos Cres, Hampton, VA 23661.

PLEASANTS, CHARLES WRENN
School administrator. **Personal:** Born Feb 28, 1937, Newport News, VA; children: Charles W Jr, Michael L & Linda Y. **Educ:** Norfolk State Univ, BA, 1961, MA, 1973; The Col William & Mary, Harvard, advan study. **Career:** Carver HS, instr 1962-69; Va Sch Deaf & Blind, dir stud serv, 1969-73; Norfolk State Univ, dir intensive recruitment, 1978-81, alumni dir, 1973-81, asst dir admis, 1981-84, admis, assoc dir, 1984-95, athletics, assoc dir, 1995. **Orgs:** Past dist treas, Coun Advan & Support Educ, 1981-83; Nat Educ Asn; Nat Asn Col Admiss Couns; Va Asn Col Admis Officers; pres, Nat Alumni Asn Norfolk State Univ, 1973; Omega Psi Phi Frat; Norfolk State Athletic Found. **Honors/Awds:** Outstanding Leadership and Service Award, Norfolk State Univ Nat Alumni Asn, 1981; Cert Merit, Inter-Collegiate Press, 1983; Distinguished Alummus, Norfolk State Univ, 1988. *

PLEDGER, VERLINE S.
Educator. **Personal:** Born May 11, 1927, Macon, GA; married Charles L; children: Charles III & Bever Lyne. **Educ:** Morris Brown Col, BS, 1957. **Career:** Atlanta Girls Club, teacher, 1946-48; Pilgrim Health & Life Ins Co, bookkeeper, 1950-51; Atlanta Bd Educ, teacher except c (EMR), 1957-. **Orgs:** Exec bd, NAACP; chmn voter regist, Atlanta Br; AAE; NEA; CEC; pres-,Atlanta Chap, Las Amigas, 1969-71; Wheat St Baptist Church; secy, Deacon's Wives' Circle; treas, Adams ville Garden Club, 1972-74; parliamentarian & founding mem, Atlanta Chap Cont Socs Inc, 1972-; vpres, Loyal Friends Birthday Club 1972-; Altanta C Theatre Guild 1969-; Breast Cancer Screening Proj. **Honors/Awds:** Award Merit Civic Work, Gov GA, 1971; most dist exhib award, Conclave Las Amigas, 1970; merit outstation work, CF Harper, 1965; yearly cert, Voter Reg Fulton Co, 1968; asst chmn procedure book, CF Harper; chmn, Girl Scout Prog.

PLESS, WILLIE
Football player. **Personal:** Born Feb 21, 1964, Anniston, AL; children: 3. **Educ:** Univ Kans. **Career:** Football player (retired); Canadian Football League, Toronto Argonauts,linebacker, 1986-89; BC Lions, quarterback, 1990; Edmonton Eskimos,linebacker, 1991-98; Saskatchewan Roughriders, 1999. **Honors/Awds:** CFL All-Star, 1986, 1988, 1990-98; West Division All-Star, 1990, 1992, 1993, 1994, 1996-99; East Division All-Star, 1986, 1988; BC Lions outstanding player, 1990; Edmonton Eskimos outstanding defensive player: 1991-97; Outstanding Defensive Player, Canadian Football League, 1992, 1994 & 1995-97; TGrey Cup victories, 1993; oronto Argonauts Outstanding Defensive Player, 1986, 1988; Toronto Argonauts Outstanding Rookie, 1986; Norm Fieldgate Trophy, 1992, 1994-97; Edmonton Eskimo Wall of Honour, 1999; Grey Cup victories: 1993; Saskatchewan Rough riders outstanding defensive player, 1999; Univ Kansas Sports Hall of Fame, Canadian Football Hall of Fame, 2005.

PLUMMER, DR. DIANE LORETTA
Educator. **Personal:** Born Feb 11, 1956, Montgomery, AL; daughter of Edward and Grace Plummer; widowed; children: Jonathan Wise. **Educ:** Morris Brown Col, BA, 1978; Univ Ga, MS, 1982, PhD, 1985. **Career:** Univ Md, S Korea, prof, 1985-86; Morris Brown Col, Learning Res, dir, 1985-; Four County Comprehensive Ment Health Ctr, coordr res, 1986-87; Line berger Consult Serv, res assoc, 1998-; Clark Atlanta Univ, assoc prof, psychol, 1987-, fac adv, currently. **Orgs:** Am Psychol Asn; Southeastern Psychol Asn; Ga Psychol Asn, Acad Affairs Comn; exec bd, Continental Colony Elem Sch PTA; Univ Senate, bd trusteees, 1993-96, Clark Atlanta Univ; den leader, Boys Scout Am; adv bd, Ctr Acad Comput. **Honors/Awds:** Grad & Prof Opportunity Fel, DOE, 1980-84; Outstanding Research in Graduate School, SEPA, 1982; Martha Jo Walker Johnson Memorial Award for Superior Research, UGA, 1983; Fulbright Scholar, Brazil, DOE, 1993; Exemplary Leadership, Southeastern Asn Educ Opportunities Prog. **Special Achievements:** Academic & Social Consequences of Grade Retention, Current Topics in Early Childhood ****U, 1986; "The Effect of Suffering on Juror's Sentencing,"(JPSP), 1986; Applying to Graduate School: Minority Students, 1977; "Performance Management: Quality and Productivity Supporting," TQM, 1989; "An Assessment of Self-Destructive and Pro social Behavior as Predictors of Subsequent Behavioral Patterns," current research. **Home Addr:** 3936 Kenner

Dr SW, Atlanta, GA 30331-3728, **Home Phone:** (404)505-8814. **Business Addr:** Faculty Advisor, Clark-Atlanta University, Department of Psychology, Knowles Hall Room 210, 223 James P Brawley Dr SW, Atlanta, GA 30314-4381, **Business Phone:** (404)880-8238.

PLUMMER, GLENN
Actor. **Personal:** Born Aug 18, 1961, Richmond, CA; married DeMonica Santiago; children: 2. **Career:** Films: Who's That Girl, 1987; Hearts of Stone, 1988; Colors, 1988; Funny Farm, 1988; Downtown, 1990; Past time, 1991; Wedlock, 1991; Frankie & Johnny, 1991; South Central, 1992; Trespass, 1992; Menace II Society, 1993; Speed, 1994; Showgirls, 1995; Strange Days, 1995; Things to Do in Denver When You're Dead, 1995; Beyond the Edge, 1995; Small Time, 1996; The Destiny of Marty Fine, 1996; The Substitute, 1996; Psalms from the Underground, 1996; Up Close & Personal, 1996; Speed II, 1997; Tear It Down, 1997; One Night Stand, 1997; A House Divided, 1998; Thursday, 1998; Heist, 1998; Interceptors, 1999; History is Made at Night, 1999; Love Beatthe Hell Outa Me, 2000; Road Dogs, 2000; MacArthur Park, 2001; Knight Club, 2001; Deadly Rhapsody, 2001; The Salton Sea, 2002; Go For Broke, 2002; Pool hall Junkies, 2002; How to Get the Man's Foot Outta Your Ass, 2003; Road Dogs, 2003; Shade, 2003; Vegas Vampires, 2003; Gang of Roses, 2003; Last Night with Angel, 2003; The Day After Tomorrow, 2004; Lexie, 2004; Sugar Valentine, 2004; Constellation, 2005; Brothers in Arms, 2005; Saw II, 2005; VooDoo Curse: The Giddeh, 2006; El Cortez, 2006; The Long shots, 2008; The Joshua's Soul Film Short, 2009; Janky Promoters, 2009; TV series: Hands of a Stranger, 1987; The Father Clements Story, 1987; Terrorist on Trial: The United States vs. Salim Ajami, 1988; "Tour of Duty", 1988; "L.A. Law", 1988-89; The Women of Brewster Place, 1989; Heat Wave, 1990; "Murderous Vision", 1991; "Wedlock", 1991; "ER", 1994-2007; "Convict Cowboy", 1995; "Pronto", 1997; "Lawless", 1997; Bad Cop, 1998; "The Hunger", 1999; "The Corner", 2000; "Ruby's Bucket of Blood", 2001; "Three Blind Mice", 2001; "Reversible Errors", 2004; "Go for Broke 2", 2005; "Bones", 2006; Dexter, 2007; "Sons of Anarchy", 2008; "Raising the Bar", 2009. **Honors/Awds:** Black Reel Award for Network/Cable, Best Supporting Actor, 2001. **Business Phone:** (310)553-5200.*

PLUMMER, MATTHEW W, SR.
Lawyer. **Personal:** Born Apr 14, 1920, Bexar Co, TX; son of M William and Minnie; married Christine J; children: 4. **Educ:** Tuskegee Inst, Trade Dipl, 1939, BA, 1947; Tex S Univ, LLB, 1951. **Career:** Atty, pvt prac; former dist judge. **Orgs:** Pres, Tuskegee Civic Club, 1945-46; second pres, TCV; chmn, Tex Del Nat Black Polit Conv; pres, Harris Coun Orgs, 1962; fed, past pres, Bronze Eagles Flying Club; past pres, Houston Lawyers Asn; Dist Judge 133rd Court Harris County. **Honors/Awds:** Outstanding Student, 1947. **Military Serv:** USY, flight instr, 1941-45; US-AAF Res, WW II. **Home Addr:** 3438 Lydia St, Houston, TX 77021. **Business Phone:** (713)759-2020.

PLUMMER, MICHAEL JUSTIN
Sociologist, educator. **Personal:** Born Apr 15, 1947, Cambridge, MA; son of Justin and Kathleen. **Educ:** Trinity Col, BA, Religion 1970; Harvard Univ, Grad Sch Educ, MEd, 1972; Brandeis Univ, Florence Heller Sch, MMHS, 1986; Boston Col, MA, 1993, ABD, Sociol, 1994, PhD, Sociol, 2002. **Career:** Integrated Systems Info Serv Co, founder, prin, 1986-; Northeastern Univ, Boston, MA, vis lectr sociol, 1989-90; Boston Col, Chestnut Hill, MA, teaching fel, adjunct prof, Sociol, 1990-2001; Univ Mass, Boston & Lesley Col, Cambridge, MA, adj prof, sociol, 1994-; Bunsai Gakuen Intercultural Sch, Lincoln, MA, esl instr, 1994-95; Boston Univ, lectr, social. **Orgs:** Chmn, Proposal Review Comt, 1983 & bd mem, Cambridge, Somerville, MA, Coun Children, 1983-84; Human Servs Comn, 1995-96. **Honors/Awds:** Lifetime certification, Commonwealth Mass, 'Teacher of Secondary School Social Studies'; Certificate of Accomplishment, Mass Gov Dukakis, 1986; Winner, Boston Col, Men's Intermediate Tennis Intraminrals, 1996. **Special Achievements:** Publ, "Financial Services," in The World Trade Organization: Legal, Economic & Political Analysis, 2005. **Home Addr:** 156 Fayerweather St, Cambridge, MA 02138. **Business Addr:** Staff, Boston College, 140 Commonwealth Ave, Chestnut Hill, MA 02467-3407.

PLUMMER, MILTON
Banker. **Career:** City Nat Bank NJ, Newark NJ, chief exec. **Business Phone:** (201)624-0865.

PLUMMER, ORA BEATRICE
Educator, nurse. **Personal:** Born May 25, 1940, Mexia, TX; daughter of Macie I Echols; children: Kimberly, Kevin & Cheryl. **Educ:** Univ NMex Col Nursing, BS, 1961; Univ Calif, Los Angeles, MS, 1966; Fac Practr Nursing Course, 1973; Univ Colo, postgraduate; variety of continuing educ courses, 1973-92. **Career:** Nurse (retired); Staff Nurse, 1961-64, 1967-68; Staff Nurse & ReliefSuper, 1962-64; USPHS, nurse traineeship, 1964-66; NM Col Nursing, Albuquerque, instr, 1968-69; Univ CO Sch Nursing, sr instr, 1971-74, asst prof, 1974-76; West Interstate Comn Higher Educ, staff assoc III, 1976-78; Garden Manor, dir nursing serv, 1978-79; CO Dept Health, nursing consult, 1979-87, long term care process trainer, 1986, training coordr, 1987-96. **Orgs:** Black Educ Day Boulder, 1971; coordr, Comm Bacc Prog; Minority Affairs Comm, 1971-74; Navy Orientation trip for educrs & admins, 1971; Air Force Orientation Trip, 1971; fWICHE Project Fac Develop Meet Minority Group Needs, 1971-73; coordr & implementation pre-nursing prog, Univ Colo Sch Nursing, 1972; ac devel comn, Sch Nursing, 1974-; Inter disciplinary AMSA Proj, 1975-76; res, The Effects Nursing Reassurance Patients Vocal Stress Levels, 1976; Nat Black Nurses Asn, 1976-; adv bd, Sickle Cell Anemia, 1976-; St Institutional Child Abuse & Neglect, 1983-92; adv comm, Metrop St Col, 1989-94, bd trustees, Colorado Acad, 1990-96; Am Soc Training & Develop, 1990-; Nat Asn Female Execs, 1990-; bd dir, Domestic Violence Initiative, 2001; Am & Co Nurses Asn; Alpha Tau Delta; Phi Delta Kappa; Colo Black Nurses Coun. **Honors/Awds:** Certificate of Apppreciation, 1994; Certificate of Apppreciation, Dept of Pub Health & Environ, 1999; Nightingale Nominee, 2003. **Special Achievements:** Author: Long Term Care, Implications of Med Practice, 1988; co-auth: "A Demonstration Model for Patient Educ, A Final Report", Western Interstate Commission Higher Education, 1978; "Improvement of Rehabilitative Nursing Serv to the Elderly in Long Term Care Facilities in Colo, A Final Report," 1989; Co-auth, "Nursing Reassurance, Patient Denial & Vocal Distress, Nursing Res," 1976; Scholar, Am Bus Women's Asn, 1958-60; scholar, Confederated Art Club, 1958-59; scholar, NM Med Soc Women's Aux, 1960.

PLUMPP, STERLING DOMINIC
Educator. **Personal:** Born Jan 30, 1940, Clinton, MS; son of Cyrus Hampton and Mary Emmanuel; married Falvia Delgrazia Jackson, Dec 21, 1968; children: Harriet Nzinga. **Educ:** St Benedict's Col, Atchison, KS, 1962; Roosevelt Univ, Chicago, IL, BA, 1968, attended 1971. **Career:** US Postal Service, Chicago, IL, distribution clerk, 1962-69; N Park Col, Chicago, counr, 1969-71; Univ Ill, Chicago, African Am Studies & Eng Dept, assoc prof, 1971; Univ Ill, Chicago, African Am Studies & Eng Dept, prof, African Am Studies & Eng Dept, prof emer, 2001-; Chicago State Univ, vis prof. **Orgs:** Black Am Lit Forum, 1980-89. **Honors/Awds:** Illinois Arts Council Literary Awards, 1975, 1980 & 1986; Carl Sandburg Literary Award for Poetry, 1983. **Special Achievements:** The author of 14 books including "Black Rituals"(Third World Press, 1987); "Ornate with Smoke" (Third World Press, 1998); "Blues: The Story Always Untold"; and "Blues Narratives" (Tia Chucha Press, 1999). **Military Serv:** AUS, spec-4, 1964-65. **Business Phone:** (312)996-4694.

PLUNKETT, RAPHAEL HILDAN
Manager, editor. **Personal:** Born Feb 11, 1966, Chicago, IL; daughter of Ralph B Marrs Sr and Hettie Perry Mahan; children: Tabitha Talai Marrs. **Educ:** De Paul Col, lib arts. **Career:** Helene Curtis, Chicago, IL, customer support specialist, beginning 1987. **Orgs:** Ed, Helene Curtis Newsletter, 1989-92; United Way/Crusade of Mercy Vol, 1987-93. **Honors/Awds:** Crusade of Mercy Rep, 1992-93.

POCKNETT, LAWRENCE WENDELL
Insurance executive. **Personal:** Born Sep 23, 1934, Boston, MA; married Mary Seiter, May 6, 1977; children: Lawrence Jr, Lorraine. **Educ:** Boston Univ Sch Lib Arts, BA, 1962. **Career:** Insurance executive (retired); Liberty Mutual, chief underwriter, 1971-73; Aetna Ins, underwriting mgr, 1973-76; Hartford Ins Group. **Honors/Awds:** Black Achiever's Award, ITT, 1979. **Military Serv:** AUS, spc4, 1955-58. *

POE, ALFRED
Executive, executive director. **Personal:** Married Carol; children: 2. **Educ:** Polytech Inst Brooklyn, BS, 1971; Harvard Univ, MBA, 1975. **Career:** Mars Inc, vpres, brands dir, commercial dir, 1982-91; Campbell's Soup Co, corp vpres, 1991-96; Meal Enhancement Group, pres, 1993-96; State St Corp, bd dir, 1994; Super Nutrit Corp, chief exec officer, 1997-2002; AJA Restaurant Corp, chief exec officer, 1999-; B&G Foods, dir, 1997-; MenuDirect, pres, chief exec officer, 2001; Centerplace Inc, bd dir, 2004; Gen Foods, staff. **Business Phone:** (973)401-6500.

POE, DR. BOOKER
Physician. **Personal:** Born Jul 9, 1936, Eustis, FL; son of Rev William Poe (deceased) and Janie Jackson Poe (deceased); married Gloria Reeves Poe, Aug 15, 1959; children: Janita L & Brian D. **Educ:** Tenn State Univ, BS, (hons), 1957; McHarry Med Col, MD, 1963. **Career:** Pvt pract, pediatrician, currently. **Orgs:** Chmn, med legs GA State Med Asn, 1976; breakfast prog chmn, Atlanta Med Asn, 1970-76; chmn, GA State Med Asn, 1977; comm advisor, MinDent/Physicians, GA 1980; pub rels Atlanta Med Asn; chmn bd, dir GA Med Asn, 1973; bd dir prec, Morehouse Sch Med; exe bd, Atlanta Br NAACP; assoc clin prof pediat, GA Univ; leglt GA Am Acad Pediat; Chmn's Coun Scholarship Fund, Morehouse Sch Med; bd dir/treasr, Health 1st HMO, 1979-89. **Honors/Awds:** Young Physician of the Year, Atlanta Med Asn, 1974; Physician of the Year, Atlanta Med Asn, 1980; Doctor of the Year, GA House Rep, 1980; Pres Award GA Med Asn, 1982; President's Award, GA State Med Asn, 1982, 1986; 25 years of Service Award, Atlanta Med Asn, 1989; President's Award, 25 years of service McHarry Med Col, 1989; Distinguished Service Medallion, GA State Med Asn, 1990; Nash Carter Honoree, Atlanta Med Asn, 1992; Father of the Year Award, Concerned Black Clergy of Atlanta, 2000; Cot Service Award, Southwest Hosp & Med Ctr, 2001; honoree, field med, Eustis Afr-Am Heritage Comm, 2002; Distinguished Alumni Medallion, Tenn State Univ, 2002. **Special Achievements:** publisher: "EPSDT and the Black Medical Community in Georgia", Nat Med Assoc J, 1979, "Why Attend a Legislative Breakfast?", The Microscope Newsletter, 1980. **Military Serv:** USAF, capt, 1965-69. **Home Addr:** 3518 Lynfield Dr SW, Atlanta, GA 30311, **Home Phone:** (404)696-5970. **Business Addr:** Physician, 2600 Martin Luther King Jr Dr Suite 202, Atlanta, GA 30311, **Business Phone:** (404)691-4354.

POE, FRED J
Chief executive officer. **Career:** Southgate Automotive Group, chief exec officer, 1994-. **Business Addr:** Chief Executive Officer, Southgate Automotive Group, 15800 Eureka Rd, Southgate, MI 48195, **Business Phone:** (734)282-1010.*

POE, KIRSTEN NOELLE
Consultant, president (organization). **Personal:** Born Mar 30, 1965, New York, NY; daughter of Robert L Poe Jr and Dolores; married Lawrence Vincent Hill Jr. **Educ:** Syracuse Univ, BS, TV, Radio & Film Mgt; NY Univ, MA, Media Ecol. **Career:** Time Warner Cable, sales coordr, 1986; WNBC, sr sales admin, 1987-91; CNBC, media rel mgr, 1991-94; Noelle-Elaine Media, co-pres & chief exec officer, 1993-. **Orgs:** Syracuse Univ, Pub Rel Coun; Newhouse Prof Gallery Syracuse Univ; sch volunteer, Learning Leaders; former volunteer, Literacy Volunteers; lectr, Am Womens Economic Develop; lectr, Learning Annex; peer tutor, Syracuse Univ, Nat Asn Clack Female Exec, 2001; Nat Asn Black Journalists, Nat Asn Black Female Exec Music & Entertainment. **Honors/Awds:** Natl Academy of TV Arts & Science, finalist, 1987; CEBA Award, produc team, 1988; Walter Raitz Foundation, Fellow, 1991; Newhouse Professional Gallery, 2001; awarded the Chancellor Citation Award, Excellence in Public Relations. **Special Achievements:** Beginning Spanish; Basic Sign Language (ASL). **Business Addr:** Co-president, Noelle-Elaine Media Inc, 118 E 28th St Suite 207, New York, NY 10016, **Business Phone:** (646)424-9750.

POELLNITZ, FRED DOUGLAS
Administrator, educator. **Personal:** Born Aug 3, 1944, Philadelphia, PA; married Stephanie Snead; children: Andrew & Michelle. **Educ:** Univ Pittsburg, BSEE, 1966; NY Univ, MSEE, 1970; Harvard Univ, MBA, 1972; Wilmington Univ, EdD. **Career:** Bendix Corp, project engr, 1967-70; Touche Ross & Co, consult, 1972-76; Sor bus Inc, dir acct, 1976-80; Smith Kline Beckman, asst mgr, 1980-81; Meharry Med Col, vpres; Peirce Col, prof bus admin, 1999-; co-ACBSP facilitator, currently. **Orgs:** Bd dirs, Electronic Typesetting Corp, 1972-76; Alpha Phi Alpha Fraternity; Nat Asn Accountants; Fin Exec Inst; bd adv, Tenn State Univ Bus Sch. **Business Addr:** Professor, Peirce College, 1420 Pine St, Philadelphia, PA 19102, **Business Phone:** (215)545-6400.

POGUE, BRENT DARYL
Executive. **Personal:** Born Sep 3, 1954, Sumter, SC; son of Clarence W and Arnetta McCain Ellison. **Educ:** Cornell Univ, Ithaca, NY, BS, 1976, ME, 1977; Univ St Thomas, IT/IS, 2000. **Career:** Polaroid Corp, Cambridge, MA, technical supvr, 1977-80; Bechtel Power Corp, San Francisco, CA, sr engr, 1980-85; Impell Corp, Walnut Creek, CA, lead sr engr, 1985-88; Pacific Gas & Electric, San Francisco, CA, nuclear generation engr, 1988-95; individual consult, currently; Beckman & Assoc, sr engr. **Orgs:** Cornell Univ Soc Engrs, 1980-; Am Soc Mech Engrs, 1980-; Am Asn Blacks Energy, 1989-; Am Nuclear Soc, 1984; Urban Service Proj San Francisco, 1995; San Francisco Proj Inform, 1996-; Commonwealth Club Calif, 1997-. **Special Achievements:** Representative, Calif Comn Environ & Econ Balance, 1980-81; Col Recruiter, Polaroid Corp, 1977-79; various volunteer awards. **Home Addr:** 1958 Greenwich St, San Francisco, CA 94105, **Home Phone:** (415)775-2309.

POGUE, D ERIC
Labor relations manager, executive. **Personal:** Born Feb 12, 1949, Southampton, NY; son of Isaiah P (deceased) and Virginia Mines; married J Marie, Aug 21, 1982; children: Eric Spencer. **Educ:** Heidelberg Col, BS Psychol, 1970; Bowling Green State Univ, MA, 1971. **Career:** Case Western Reserve Univ, asst dir acad support, 1971-72; Cleveland State Univ, staff devel trainer, 1972-76; Diamond Shamrock Corp, mgr human resources, 1976-82; Cuyahoga Community Col, adj prof, 1978-79; Reichhold Chem Inc, White Plains NY, vpres human resources, 1982-87, sr vpres, 1987-88; Am Red Cross, sr vpres, human resources & chief diversity officer, 2003-; Philip Morris Co Inc, New York, NY, vpres employee relations. **Orgs:** Mem Soc Human Resource Mgt, 1980-; coordannual dir, United Way Greater Cleveland, 1982; Westchester/Ct Personnel Round Table, 1983-88; Human Resources Coun; Am Mgt Asn, 1987-; bd adv, Cornell Univ Sch Indust & Labor Rels, 1990-; bd dirs, Nat Alliance End Homelessness. **Business Phone:** (202)303-4498.

POGUE, FRANK G., JR.
Educator, school administrator. **Personal:** Born Nov 3, 1938, Mobile, AL; son of Annie B; married Dorothy Dexter; children:

Constance L. **Educ:** Bishop Jr Col, attended 1959; Ala State Univ, BA, sociol, 1961; Atlanta Univ, MA, sociol, 1966; Univ Pittsburgh, PhD, sociol, 1973. **Career:** Educator(retired), school administrator(retired); Philander Smith Col, Little Rock, asst prof, 1962-66; Chatham Col, Pittsburgh, instr, 1969-71; Meharry Med Col, Nashville, asst prof, 1971-73; State Univ NY, Albany, assoc prof, 1973-, chair, dept African & Afro-Am Studies, 1973-83, assoc vpres res educ develop, 1982-83, vpres stud affairs, 1983-86, vice chancellor stud affairs & spl progs, 1986-96; Edinboro Univ Pa, pres, 1996. **Orgs:** Nat Asn Stud Personnel Adminrs; Nat Asn Study Afro-Am Life History; Col Stud Personnel Asn NY State; Chief Stud Affairs Adminrs State Univ NY; Sigma Pi Phi Fraternity; Nat Coun Black Studies; Delta Sigma Pi Prof Bus Fraternity. **Honors/Awds:** Most Outstanding Young Men Am, Alpha Kappa Mu Hon Soc, 1968-69. **Business Addr:** President, Edinboro University Pennsylvania, 200 Meadville St, Edinboro, PA 16444.*

POGUE, RICHARD JAMES
Government official, baptist clergy. **Personal:** Born May 25, 1943, Cortelyou, AL; married Birdie Raine; children: Tiffany Denise & Karen Lanise. **Educ:** Ala State Univ, BS, high hon, 1971; Pepperdine Univ, 1977; Int Sem. **Career:** Robins AFB, personnel mgt specialist, 1971-73; Air Force Reserves, personnel mgt specialist, 1973-75; Keesler AFB, chief employ & staffing, 1975-76; Randolph AFB, personnel mgt specialist, 1976-79; HQ USAF Pentagon WA DC, dep eeo, 1979-80; Robins AFB, GA, equal oppor/affirmative action officer, 1980-86, chief employee devt & training sect, 1986-91, chief, Employ & Staffing, Classifications, 1992-; Friendship Memorial Baptist Church, pastor, currently. **Orgs:** Nat Asn Advan Colored People, 1980-; pres, K&R Shoes Inc, 1983-85; pres, Int Personnel Mgt Asn, 1984-85; Better Mgt Asn, 1985-; Blacks Govt, 1985-; bd career advs, Atlanta Univ, 1986; historian, Alpha Phi Alpha Frat Inc, 1986-87; bd dirs, Middle Ga Educ Talent Search, 1986-; bd dirs, Air Force Asn, 1986-; bd dirs, Combined Fed Campaign. **Honors/Awds:** Outstanding Young Men of America Award, 1971; Affirmative Action of the Yr Robins AFB, 1981. **Special Achievements:** Key to the City of New Orleans, 1975. **Military Serv:** USN, third class petty officer, 1963-67; Nat Defense. **Home Addr:** 110 River Valley Ct, Kathleen, GA 31047-2154. **Business Addr:** Pastor, Friendship Memorial Baptist Church, 2832 Ledo Road, Albany, GA 31707, **Business Phone:** (229)436-5700.

POINDEXTER, CHARLES L. L.
Clergy. **Personal:** Born Apr 11, 1932, Richmond, VA; son of Walter E and Pearl Maria Robinson; married Judith L Owens, Feb 24, 1962; children: Maria, Byroh, Evangeline. **Educ:** West VA State Col, BA, 1954; Philadelphia Divinity Sch, MDiv, 1958. **Career:** Clergy (retired); St Ausgustine's Church, vicar, 1958-65; St Monica's Church, rector, 1963-65; St Barnabas Church, rector, 1965-68; St Luke's Church, rector, 1968. **Orgs:** Nat jr vpres, Phi Beta Sigma, 1953-54; The Brahaman Soc, 1955-; bd, Springside Sch, 1974-80; bd, All Saints Hosp, 1975-81; Sigma Pi Phi Boule, 1980-; pres, Home Homeless Fund, 1985-nat vpres, Union Black Episcopalians, 1986-92, Aids Task Force, pres, 1987-92. **Honors/Awds:** Doctor of Humane Letters, St Augustine's Col, 1988; Achievement, Col Four Chaplins, 1988; Achievement Award, St Barnaba's Founders, 1989; Achievement Award, Union Black Episcopalians, 1991. **Special Achievements:** St Barnabas Episcopal Sch, headmaster, 1969-75, founder; Wissahickon Deanery, dean, 1975-81; Pamphlet, Aids in the Black Church, 1990; Book, History St Luke's Church, 1991. *

POINDEXTER, GAMMIEL GRAY
Lawyer. **Personal:** Born Sep 22, 1944, Baton Rouge, LA; daughter of Lee Ethel and James; married Geral G; children: John L R & Christopher R. **Educ:** Univ Ind, AB, 1965; La State Univ, JD, 1969. **Career:** Judge (retired); Off Solicitor, US Dept Labor, staff atty, 1968-70; Richmond Legal Aid Soc, dept dir, 1971-73; Poindexter & Poindexter, partner, 1973-; Surry Co, Va, commonwealth's atty, 1976-95, commonwealth judge, 1995-2001; Sussex Co Gen Dist Ct, chief judge, 1999-2002, Sixth Judicial Dist Gen Dist Ct, judge, 2002-07. **Orgs:** Pres, Old Dominion Bar Asn, 1980-82; bd vis, Old Dominion Univ, 1982-; chmn, Surry Co Democratic Party, 1983-95; bd dirs, Va Asn Black Elected Off; bd mem, Va State Ct Col Syst, 1990-95; Va State Bar Coun, 1991-95. **Home Addr:** PO Box 187, Prince George, VA 23875.

POINDEXTER, MALCOLM P
Television news anchorperson, manager. **Personal:** Born Apr 3, 1925, Philadelphia, PA; son of Malcolm Poindexter Sr and Alda F Palmer; children: David, Lynne E Poindexter & Malcolm III. **Educ:** Several pvt & mil schs, 1943-47; Temple Univ, 1953. **Career:** Television news anchorperson, manger (Retired); Philadelphia Bulletin; Jet; Ebony & KYW-Newsradio; The Philadelphia Tribune, reporter, columnist, bus mgr, controller, 1949-60; The Evening Bull, reporter, 1960-65; KYW-TV, ed spokesman, reporter, producer, prog host, 1965-89, host, producer, Eyewitness Newsmakers, host, producer, jour, 1990; CBS-TV 3. **Orgs:** Hon bd, Norris Sq Neighborhood Proj, 1990; bd mem, Mann Music Ctr; Philadelphia Asn Black Jour. **Honors/Awds:** Received more than 300 awards for prof & civic achievement; Lifetime Achievement Award. **Military Serv:** AUS, t-sgt.

POINDEXTER, DR. ZEB F
Dentist. **Personal:** Born Apr 5, 1929, Fort Worth, TX; son of Leonra Camilla Wilburn (deceased) and Zeb F Poindexter Sr (deceased); married Ruby Revis, Oct 30, 1953; children: Merlene, Patricia & Zeb III. **Educ:** Wiley Col, BS, 1945; Tex Sothern Univ, MS, 1952; Univ Tex, Dental Br, DS, 1956. **Career:** Zeb F Poindexter DDS Inc, founder, 1956; Gulf St Dental Assn, pres, 1966-67; Natl Dental Assn, local conv chmn, 1968; Univ Tex, asso prof Comm, dent, 1973. **Orgs:** NAACP; bd mem, Negro Coll; treas, Charles A George Dent Soc; bd mem, Baker-Jones Invest Co; Houston Dist Dent Soc; Nat Dent Asn; Alpha Phi Alpha Frat, 1947; YMCA Century Club; Eldorado Soc Club; Gulf St Dent Asn; Am Dent Asn; trustee NDA, 1973; del NDA, 1971 & 1973; del Tex, Dent Asn 1968; Minority Fac Asn, 1987-; chairperson, Multicultured Fac Commt, 1986-88; Acad Gen Dentistry; Am Asn Dent Sch; Nat Minority Recruiting Orgn. **Honors/Awds:** YMCA Century Man, 1972; Outstanding Alumnus, Univ Tex Dental Sch, 1990; Tex Acad Gen Dent, Outstanding Dentist of the Year, 1991; Intl col Dentists, Fel, 1992. **Special Achievements:** First african american to finish University of texas as Dentist, 1956. **Military Serv:** USA, capt. **Home Addr:** 2811 Blodgett St, Houston, TX 77004, **Home Phone:** (713)533-1522. **Business Addr:** Founder, Zeb F Poindexter DDS Inc, 7703 Cullen Blvd, Houston, TX 77051, **Business Phone:** (713)734-7611.

POINTER, DR. RICHARD H
Scientist, educator. **Personal:** Born Jun 4, 1944, Covington, GA; son of Hugh Brooks and Sarah Eunice Weaver; married Rosie Lee Davis, Apr 30, 1966; children: Richard Hamilton Jr, Rawlinson Lee & Robert Lewis. **Educ:** Morehouse Col, BS, 1968; Brown Univ, ScM, 1973, PhD, 1975. **Career:** Vanderbilt Univ, res assoc, 1975-77; Mass Gen Hosp, res biochemist, 1977-78; Harvard Univ, instr, 1977-80; Howard Hughes Med Inst, res fel, 1978-80; Howard Univ, Dept Biochem & Molecular Biol, asst prof, 1980-87, assoc prof, prof, currently; Membrane Regulatary Sect, Lab Cellular & Develop Biol, Nat Inst Diabetes & Digestive & Kidney Dis, NIH, vis scientist, 1992; African Sci Inst, fel, 2006. **Orgs:** AAAS, 1972-; Sigma Xi, 1973; secy exec bd, PACE, 1973-74; Am Physiol Soc, 1975-; Am Diabetes Asn, 1979-; Adult Leader Boy Scouts Am, 1979-; sci fair judge, Southern Md Sch Area, 1988-; bd dir, PG County Chap, Am Diabetes Asn, 1988-89; vpres, PG Co Chap, Am Diabetes Asn, 1989-90; pres, PG County Chap, Am Diabetes Asn, 1990-92; Am Soc Biochem & Molecular Biol, 1995-; Nat Acad Critical Thinking, 1999-; Omicron Kappa Upsilon, Pi Pi Chap, 2006. **Honors/Awds:** Commissioners Award, Boy Scouts Am, 1988; Meritorious Service Award, Am Diabetes Asn, 1992; Sharp Hands Award, NASA Goddard Space Flight Ctr, 1995, 1996; Johnetta Davis Mentorship Award, Grad Sch Arts & Scis, 1996; Outstanding Teacher Award, Col Dent, Howard Univ, 2002; Science Spectrum Trailblazer Award, 2006. **Special Achievements:** Publications in Biochemistry, Physiology & Pharmacology Journals. **Home Addr:** 7501 Epping Ave, Fort Washington, MD 20744. **Business Addr:** Professor, Howard University College of Medicine, Department of Biochemistry & Molecular Biology, 520 W St NW, Washington, DC 20059, **Business Phone:** (202)806-6367.

POITIER, SIDNEY
Administrator, television producer, actor. **Personal:** Born Feb 20, 1927, Miami, FL; son of Reginald and Evelyn Outten; married Juanita Hardy (divorced); children: Beverly, Pamela, Sherri & Gina; married Joanna Shimkus, 1969; children: Anika & Sydney. **Career:** Acted & starred in over 38 motion pictures; made film debut in No Way Out 1950; others include: Cry the Beloved Co, 1952; Go Man Go, 1954; Blackboard Jungle, 1956; Edge of the City, 1957; Something of Value, 1957; Porgy & Bess, 1959; Lillies of the Field, 1963; In the Heat of the Night, 1967; Guess Who's Coming to Dinner, 1968; They Call Me Mister Tibbs, 1971; Buck & the Preacher, 1972; The Wilby Conspiracy, 1975; Little Nikita, 1987; In the Hall of the Mountain King, 1987; Hard Knox, 1987; Deadly Pursuits, 1988; Sneakers, 1992; The Jackal, 1998; directed & starred in Buck & the Preacher, A Warm December, Uptown Saturday Night, Let's Do it Again, A Piece of the Action, 1977; starred in Broadway prod of Raisin in the Sun, 1959; directed Richard Pryor & Gene Wilder in Stir Crazy, 1980; directed Gene Wilder & Gilda Radner in Hanky Panky, 1982, directed youth musical Fast Forward, 1985; Ghost Dad, 1990; A Century of Cinema, 1994; Wild Bill: Hollywood Maverick, 1996; The Jackal, 1997; US Ambassador to the Bahamas; actor & exec producer in TV movie, Free of Eden; starred in the TV movie, The Simple Life of Noah Dearborn; TV: David & Lisa; 1998; Free of Eden, 1999; The Simple Life of Noah Dearborn, 1999; The Last Brickmaker in Am, 2001; Tell Them Who You Are, 2004; The Black Movie Awards, 2005; "The Oprah Winfrey Show", 2005; UNESCO, bahamas ambassador, 1997-; Verdon Cedric Productions, pres & chief exec officer, currently. **Orgs:** Walt Disney Co, bd dirs, 1994-. **Honors/Awds:** BAFTA Award, 1958; Academy Award, 1963, 2002; Golden Globe Award, 1964, 1982; AFI Life Achievement Award, 1992; SAG Life Achievement Award, 1995; Lifetime Achievement Award, Screen Actors Guild, 2000; NAACP Hall of Fame Award, 2001; Grammy, Best Spoken Word Album, 2001; honorary Oscar, 2001; Actor: Living Legend Award, Trumpet Awards, 2002. **Special Achievements:** Author: This Life, Alfred Knopf, 1980; publ Sidney Poitier-The Measure of a Man, Harper Collins, 2000; First black man to win the Academy Award for Best Actor; first Black actor to rec footprints in concrete of Grauman's Chinese Theater, 1967; first black actor to win an Oscar; named to the Am Film Inst's 50 Greatest Film Legends. **Military Serv:** AUS, WWII. **Business Addr:** Bahamas Ambassador, UNESCO, Ministry of Foreign Affairs, E Hill St, PO Box N-3746, Nassau, Bahamas, **Business Phone:** (809)322-7624.

POITIER, SYDNEY TAMIIA
Actor. **Personal:** Born Nov 15, 1973, Los Angeles, CA; daughter of Joanna Shimkus and Sidney. **Educ:** NY Univ. **Career:** Films: True Crime, 1999; Happy Birthday, 2000; MacArthur Park, 2001; The Devil Cats, producer, 2004; I'mPerfect, 2005; Nine Lives, 2005, Hood of Horror, 2006; Grey's Anatomy, 2006; The List, 2006; Death Proof, 2007; Grindhouse, 2007; TV movies: "East of Eden", 1999; "Noah's Ark", 1999; TV series: "First Years", 2001; "Abby", 2003; "Veronica Mars", 2004; Knight Rider, 2008. **Special Achievements:** 50 Most Beautiful People, People Mag's, 2001. **Business Addr:** Actress, International Creative Management Inc, 8942 Wilshire Blvd, Beverly Hills, CA 90211, **Business Phone:** (310)550-4000.

POLITE, DR. CRAIG K., II. See Obituaries section.

POLK, ANTHONY JOSEPH
Military leader. **Personal:** Born Mar 8, 1941, New Orleans, LA; son of Middleton Brooks Polk (deceased) and Edolia Stephens (deceased); married Maxine Polk (divorced 1986); children: Patricia, Michael, Stephen. **Educ:** McNeese State Univ, Lake Charles, BS, 1966; Bowling Green State Univ, MS, 1974. **Career:** Clin Lab Serv, Fort Hood Tex, dir, 1967; US European Command Tri-Serv Blood Prog, dir, 1974-78; Shape, dir, 1974-78; NATO Blood Prog, officer, 1982-84; Dept Defense Tri-Serv Blood Prog, dir, 1984-92; ANRC, chief staff, 1992-96; ARC Southeast Reg Blood Testing Ctr, chief exec officer, 1996-98, diversity officer, 2000-. **Orgs:** Clin lab mgr, Fort Rucker, 1967-68; joint blood prog officer, CP Zama, Japan, 1968-72; lab mgr blood bank manage, Fort Hood, 1974-78; comdr blood bank, Landstuhl, Ger, 1978-81; joint blood prog officer, Stuttgart, Ger, 1981-83; NATO blood prog officer, Shapie BE, 1983-84; dir DVD Armed Serv blood prog, Pentagon, 1984-91. **Honors/Awds:** Numerous military awards. **Special Achievements:** Publication in military journal. **Military Serv:** AUS, col, 1966-92; Defense Meritorous Medal, 1, Meritorious Sevice Medals, 3. **Home Addr:** 12047 Bridle Post Pl, Manassas, VA 20112-5515. *

POLK, DON
Chief executive officer, president (organization). **Career:** The Romar Group Inc, pres & chief exec officer, currently; Romar Studios Inc, chmn, currently. **Business Addr:** Chairman, Romar Studios Inc, 837 Traction Ave Suite 406, Los Angeles, CA 90013, **Business Phone:** (213)621-4403.*

POLK, EUGENE STEVEN S, SR.
Consultant. **Personal:** Born Oct 24, 1939, Detroit, MI; son of Wardell and Josephine; married Barbara Jean Edwards; children: Camille, Kent, Eugene Jr & Chris. **Educ:** Shaw Col, Detroit, BA, 1971. **Career:** Ford Motor Co, employment coord, 1966-69; Pontiac General Hosp, asst dir personnel, 1970-74; Comprehensive Health Serv, Detroit, personnel dir, 1975-79; Kelly Serv Inc, mgr hq personnel, 1980-87; Mazda Mfg, Prof,personnel adminr, 1987-93, employee relations, leader; Madison Madison Int Inc, HR dir, 1993-98; Edwards-Polk & Assoc Inc, sr hr consult, 1998-. **Orgs:** Bd mem, pres, Arc Detroit; bd mem, S.T.E.P.; bd mem Metro Detroit Youth Found,1983-87; polemarch Detroit Alumni Chap Kappa Alpha Psi Frat,1984-88; bd mem, North side Family YMCA, 1985-88; pres, Indust Rel Assoc Detroit, 1985-86; chmn bd dir, S Oakland Family YMCA, 1986-87; bd mem, DonBosco Hall, 1986-89; Nat Asn Advan Colored People, Detroit Urban League. **Honors/Awds:** Minority Achiever, Kelly Service Inc Metro, Detroit YMCA, 1987. **Business Addr:** Senior Consultant, Edwards-Polk & Associates Inc, 220 Bagley Ave Suite 408, Detroit, MI 48226-1412, **Business Phone:** (313)964-3106.

POLK, DR. GENE-ANN (GENE-ANN POLK HORNE)
Physician, educator. **Personal:** Born Oct 3, 1926, Roselle, NJ; daughter of Dr Charles C (deceased) and Olive Bond (deceased); married Dr Edwin C Horne, Aug 23, 1952; children: Carol Anne Horne Penn & Edwin Christian Horne. **Educ:** Oberlin Col, BA, 1948; Women's Med Col PA, MD, 1952; Columbia Univ, MPH, 1968. **Career:** Physician (retired); Dept Pediat, attending physician, 1955-93; Englewood NJ, pvt practr, 1959-68; Columbia Univ, Harlem Hosp Ctr, Pediat Clin, chief, 1968-75, prof clin pediat, 1969-93, acting dir pediat, 1975-77, prof emer clin pediat, 1995-; Ambulatory Care Servs, dir, 1977-88. **Orgs:** Fel Am Bd Med Examiners, 1952; fel Int Col Pediat, 1978; fel Am Acad Pediat, 1958; Sch phys City Englewood, NJ, 1960-67; Basileus Aka Sorority Iota Epsilon Omega Chap, 1971-73; bd mem, Greater Harlem Nursing Home, 1982-84; UNCF, 1970-92; bd mem, Bergen County Girl Scouts; bd mem, BergenYouth Orchestra; bd mem, Englewood Adult Sch; The Links Inc. **Honors/Awds:** Proclamation: Dr Gene-Ann Polk Day, by President of the Borough of Manhattan, 1987; Proclamation by Mayor of the City of New York, Dr GeneAnn Polk Day, 1993; Child Advocacy Award, Barristers' Wives of New York Inc, 1985; UNCF NJ Volunteer Recognition Award for Outstanding Serv, 1990; Leadership in Med, Susan Smith McKinney Steward Med Soc, 1980; Outstanding Prof Achievement, Englewood-Teaneck B&P, 1980; Second Century Serv Award, Harlem Hosp Cent Auxiliary, 1993;

Friends of Harlem Hosp Ctr, 1997. **Home Addr:** 374 Miller Ave, Englewood, NJ 07631, **Home Phone:** (201)567-4767. *

POLK, DR. LORNA MARIE
Federal government official. **Personal:** Born Aug 3, 1948, St Louis, MO; daughter of Louise and Ora. **Educ:** Fisk Univ, Nashville, Tenn, BA, psychol, 1968; George Wash Univ, DC, MA, Human Resource Develop, 1973; Catholic Univ Am, EdD, educ admin, 1982. **Career:** US Dept Educ, ed prog spec, Ed Personnel Develop, 1968-69; Career Opp Prog, 1969-73; Post-secondary Ed, 1973-75; Migrant Educ, 1975-83; White House Initiative Historically Black Col & Univ, educ admin, 1983-95; Fedl Trio Prog, prog office, 1994-97; US Dept Educ, Regional Rep, Chicago, IL, 1997-2006; US Dept Educ, Higher Educ Rep, Washington, DC, 2006-. **Orgs:** US Dept Educ Action Planning Team; Am Asn Public Admin; Am Soc Prof & Exec Women; Phi Delta Kappa; Nat Alliance Black Sch Edu; Blacks Govt; vpres personnel, Flair Promotions Inc, 1985-89; exec bd, E Coast Chapter, Tuskegee Airmen Inc; exec bd, Black Airline Pilots; Am Soc Training & Develop; Pres, Toastmasters Org, Chicago Chpt; Higher Educ Group, Washington, DC; Alfred Street Baptist Church, Va. **Honors/Awds:** Cert Excellence for Outstanding Work on an Action Team; Thurgood Marshall Scholarship Fund Leadership Inst Awards; Quality Service Award, Dept Educ, 1982, 1988; Special Service Act Award, 2003; Org Black Airline Pilots Leadership Award, 2002; Tuskegee Airmen Award for Achievement, 1998; Nat Honoree Women in Aviation Award, 1996; Tuskegee Airmen Outstanding Serv Award, 1994, Outstanding Young Women of Am, 1981-85. **Special Achievements:** Published "The Effects of Migrant Educ Ctr in the State of FL" 1981; presented article in the Nat Soc Black Engineers Jour Annual Commemorative Issues, 1986-87; presentations on "Multicultural Competence" at the International Conferences on the First-Year Col Experience - Univ Bath, England, 2002, Westin Kannapali, Maui, Hawaii, June 2004; and Waikola Village, Kona, Hawaii, July 2007. **Business Addr:** Higher Education Representative, US Department of Education, Institutional Development & Undergraduate Educational Service, 1990 K St NW Suite 6038, Washington, DC 20006, **Business Phone:** (202)502-7518.

POLK, RICHARD A.
Association executive. **Personal:** Born Jun 4, 1936, Moss Point, MS; married Mary Dennis; children: Clay, Phyllis, Beverly, Richard. **Educ:** Alcorn St Univ, Lorman, MS, BS, 1957; TN A&I Univ, Nashville, MS, 1965. **Career:** Fed Equal Empl Opport Comm, invstgtn supr; Newton & Carthage MS, tchr, athletic coach 1957-66; STAR Inc, 1966-70; Mound Bayou Community Hosp, dir, 1970; Hosp & Health Ctr, dir 1972. **Orgs:** NAACP; Jackson Urban League, 1968-70; STAR Inc, 1971-; Delta Ministry, 1975-; S Legal Rights Corp, 1975-; Leake Co Voters League, 1975-; Delta Found Greenville, MS, 1975-; MS Cncl Hum Rels, 1970; MS ACLU, 1974; MS Cath Found, 1975; pres, Parish Cnsl St Anne Cath Ch Carthage MS; Epilepsy Found, Mich, bd dir. **Honors/Awds:** Applicant, oper rights, Jackson MS TV sta OEO Award, 1969; MS Inst of Politics Fellow, 1971. **Business Addr:** 203 W Capitol St, 203 Bldg, Jackson, MS 39201.

POLK, REV. DR. ROBERT L
Clergy, school administrator. **Personal:** Born May 8, 1928, Chicago, IL; son of Tillman and Lillie Bell; divorced; children: George R. **Educ:** Doane Col, BA, 1952, DDiv (hon), 1971; Hartford Theol Sem, Mdiv, 1955; Huston-Tillotson, DDiv (hon), 1984. **Career:** Congregational Church Berthold ND, pastor, 1955-57; YMCA Minot ND, youth prog coord, 1957-60; Riverside Church, minister youth, 1960-66, minister urban affairs, 1969-76; Dillard Univ New Orleans, dean chapel & dean stud, 1966-68; Edwin Gould Serv C, exec dir, 1976-80; Coun Churches City NY, exec dir, 1980-88; City Col New York, City Univ New York, acting vpres, 1988-. **Orgs:** Chmn, CUNY Constr Fund; Mayor's Comm Religious Leaders, Assoc Black Charities, Hole-in-the-Wall-Gang Camp Inc; New York City Bd Educ, Capital Task Force Construct & Renovation Pub Sch; New York State Dept Educ Interfaith Educ Adv Coun Commr Educ; Governor's Comm Scholastic Achievement; Health Watch Adv Bd. **Honors/Awds:** Distinguished Service Award, Black Christian Caucus Riverside Church, 1983; Sam Levinson Memorial Award, Jewish Community Relations Council, New York City, 1984. **Business Phone:** (212)690-5361.

POLK, PROF. WILLIAM C.
Educator. **Personal:** Born Aug 2, 1935, Philadelphia, PA; son of Ruby and William Sr; married Aundria Willis; children: Catherine Collette & William David. **Educ:** W Chester State Col, BS, 1958; Columbia Univ, MA, 1961; Pa State Univ, D.Ed, 1970. **Career:** Neshaminy Sch Dist, teacher, 1958-68; PA St Univ, grad asst, 1968-70, asso prof; Slippery Rock, prof educ, prof educ emer, currently. **Orgs:** Bd dirs, EL Cunningham Comm Ctr, 1963-70; Phi Delta Kappa, 1968-; fac sponsor, Black Action Soc, Slippery Rock St Col, 1972, 1975-77; Nat CounSoc Studies; comnr, Teacher Cert & Rural Educ; secy, Md wstrn PA Coun Soc Studies 1973-; guest lectr, Int Studies Inst, Westminster Col, 1974-75; consult, Commodore Perry Sch, 1976; Nat Geographic Soc; Alpha Tau Chpt; Rho Chap Alpha Phi Alpha. **Honors/Awds:** Outstanding Educator, 1972. **Business Addr:** Professor Emeritus, Slippery Rock University, 1 Morrow Way, Slippery Rock, PA 16057, **Business Phone:** (724)738-2015.

POLLARD, ALFONSO MCINHAM
Musician, government official. **Personal:** Born Jun 13, 1952, Washington, DC; son of Alfonso and June Reynolds; married Lynda Lea Harrod, Sep 1, 1973; children: Prentice Odell & Lauren Jamille. **Educ:** Boston Univ, attended 1972; Juilliard Sch, BS, 1975; Cath Univ, MS, 1978. **Career:** Wash DC Youth Orchestra, 1970-92; USF Band, bandsman, tech sergeant, 1975-79; Howard Univ, assoc prof music, 1979-91; Metrop Cult Productions, pres, 1986-; Orchestra Found Metro Wash DC, chief exec officer, 1989-92; Am Fedn Musicians, Local 161-710 AFL-CIO, Local 40-543, dir; Am Univ, Residence Conductor, 1994-96; Am Fedn Musicians, nat legis dir, 1995-; Commun Workers Am, legislative rep, polit dir, currently. **Orgs:** Am Fedn Musicians, 1968-; prin timpanist, Annapolis Symphony Orchestra, 1976-87; prin timpanist, Filene Ctr Orchestra, Wolf Trap, 1986-; Am Symphony Orchestra League, 1988-; prin timpanist, Baltimore Opera Orchestra, 1989-99; Coalition Black Trade Unionists, 1999-. **Honors/Awds:** Performance Fellowship, Young Artist Prog, Tanglewood, 1968; Academic fellowships, Music Assistance Fund, 1972-75; Individual Fellowship Performance Award, DC Comm Arts & Humanities, 1986; Travel Award to Brazil, Am Partner, 1990; teaching & conducting grant, US Info Agency, 1990; Maestro Alfonso Pollard Day, Wash DC, City Coun, 1991; Outstanding Service to Education, Wash DC Bd Educ, 1992. **Military Serv:** USAF, tech sgt, 1975-79; BMT Distinguished Honor Graduate, 1975, Good Conduct Medal, 1978. **Home Addr:** 3013 Memory Lane, Silver Spring, MD 20904, **Home Phone:** (301)890-1941. **Business Addr:** Political Director, Legislative Representative, Communications Workers of America, 501 3rd St NW, Washington, DC 20001, **Business Phone:** (202)434-1334.

POLLARD, DR. ALTON BROOKS, III
Educator. **Personal:** Born May 5, 1956, St Paul, MN; son of Alton Brooks Pollard Jr and Lena Laverne Evans; married Jessica Bryant; children: Alton Brooks IV & Asha Elise. **Educ:** Fisk Univ, BA, 1978; Harvard Univ, Divinity Sch, MDiv, 1981; Duke Univ, PhD, 1987. **Career:** John St Baptist Church, pastor, 1979-82; Clark Univ, dir, 1981-82; New Red Mountain Baptist Church, pastor, 1984-86; St Olaf Col, asst prof, 1987-88; Wake Forest Univ, from asst prof to assoc prof, 1988-98; Emory Univ, Candler Sch Theol, Black Church Studies, dir & assoc prof religion & cult; Historic Howard Univ Sch Divinity, dean, currently. **Orgs:** Soc Sci Study Religion, 1984-, Assoc Sociol Religion, 1985-; Am Baptist Conv; Nat Asn Advan Colored People; Am Acad Religion, 1987; Religious Research Asn, l988-; Soc Study Black Religion, 1989-. **Honors/Awds:** Thomas J Watson Fel, Fisk Univ, 1978; Fund Theological Educ Fel, Princeton, NJ, 1978-81, 1983-86; Andrew Mellon Fel, Duke Univ, 1986-87. **Special Achievements:** Article "Religion, Rock, & Eroticism," The Journal of Black Sacred Music, 1987; "The Last Soul Singer in Am," Black Sacred Music, 1989; review "The Color of God" & "Black Theology in Dialogue," Perspectives in Religious Studies, l989; "Howard Thurman & the Experience of Encounter," Journal of Religious Thought, 1990; "Of Movements and Motivations," AME Zion Quarterly Review, 1991; "The Promise and Peril of Common Ground," BRIDGES, 1991; Mysticism & Social Change, Peter Lang, 1992. **Business Addr:** Dean, Howard University School of Divinity, 1400 Shepherd St, Washington, DC 20017, **Business Phone:** (202)806-0500.

POLLARD, DR. DIANE S.
Educator. **Personal:** Born Oct 31, 1944, Richmond, VA; daughter of Clara Bayton Stewart and Elric; married Scott; children: Amina & Almasi. **Educ:** Wellesley Col, BA, 1966; Univ Chicago, MA, 1967, PhD, 1972. **Career:** Roosevelt Univ, instr, 1969-72; Univ Wis, from asst prof to assoc prof, 1972-79, assoc prof, educ psychol & dir, ctr study minorities & disadvantaged, 1979-85, prof emer, 1993-. **Orgs:** Am Educ Res Asn, 1972-; Asn Black Psychologists, 1973-; Eta Phi Beta Inc, 1978-; Soc Psychol Study Social Issues; Alpha Kappa Alpha. **Honors/Awds:** Faculty Distinguished Public Service Award, 1993; Willystine Goodsell Award, AERA/SIG RES Women & Educ, 1996. **Special Achievements:** Author: "A Profile of Black Professional Women in Education, Psychology and Sociology"; "Perceptions of Black Parents Regarding the Socialization of their Children"; "Against the Odds: A Profile of Academic Achieversfrom the Urban Underclass," Journal of Negro Education, 1989; "Patterns of Coping in Black School Children;" Motivational Factors Underlying Achievement; book chapter, Black Women, Interpersonal Support and Institutional Change in Changing Education: Woman as Radicals and Conservators; "Reducing the Impact of Racism on Students," in Educational Leadership, 1990; He is author and co-author of many books. **Business Addr:** Professor Emeritus, University of Wisconsin-Milwaukee, PO Box 413, Milwaukee, WI 53201-0413, **Business Phone:** (414)229-1122.

POLLARD, MARCUS LAJUAN
Football coach. **Personal:** Born Feb 8, 1972, Lanett, AL; married Amani; children: Myles Ashton, Micah Jayden & Aja. **Educ:** Bradley Univ, criminal justice. **Career:** Football player (retired); football coach; Indianapolis Colts, tight end, 1995-2004; Detroit Loins, tight end,2005-06; Seattle Seahawks, 2007; New England Patriots, 2008; Atlanta Falcons, tight end, 2008; coach, Lanett High Sch; free agent, currently.

POLLARD, MURIEL RANSOM
Engineer. **Personal:** Born Nov 5, 1953, Isola, MS; daughter of Arthur Ransom; divorced; children: Kendra, Eyphra & Elverna. **Educ:** Meharry Med Col, attended biomed sc, summer prog, 1974; Dillard Univ, New Orleans, BA, Chem, 1975. **Career:** S Central Bell Telephone Co, engr supvr, 1977-. **Orgs:** Delta Sigma Theta Sorority, 1973-; Telephone Pioneers Am, 1981-; consult religious speech writing & delivery, 1984-; admin comn, S Political Action Community S Central Bell, 1986-. **Honors/Awds:** President's Award, Miss Head Start Parents Asn, 1989; Recognition Serv, Miss Delta Community Col, 1989; BellSouth Area Operations Counc Recognition Award, 1990; BellSouth Dept Head Award, 1996; BellSouth PRIDE Award, 1996; BellSouth, VIP's GALAXY Award, 1997. **Business Addr:** Engineering Supervisor, BellSouth, 268 N Raceway Rd, Greenville, MS 38701, **Business Phone:** (601)378-5000.

POLLARD, PERCY EDWARD, SR.
Manager. **Personal:** Born Jun 3, 1943, King and Queen, VA; son of George T (deceased) and Hattie Bell Taylor (deceased); married Annie Randolph, May 22, 1965; children: Tracie Anita & Percy Jr. **Educ:** Va State Univ, BS, 1966, MS, 1997; Emory Univ, Cert Mgt Develop Prog, 1985. **Career:** Manager (retired). IBM Corp, jr instr, 1966, sr educ specialist, 1969, equal oppor admin, 1970, mgr of equal opportunities, 1972, mgr equal opportunites & comm progs, Gaithersburg, 1973, dist personnel prog mgr Off Prods Div, 1976, regional personnel mgr Wash & Baltimore Metro area 1977, personnel planning mgr Off Prods Div Franklin Lakes, NJ, 1979, corp mgr equal opportunities prog, 1981, admin asst to the vpres of personnel 1982, personnel mgr Res Div Yorktown, NY, 1984, mgr staff servs White Plains, NY 1986-, Spec Asst for Employee Charitable Contrib 1988, IBM Corp HQ, personnel mgr, 1989, dir, Cultural & Human Servs Prog, 1991-93; IBM Fac Loan, 1993-95; Pollard Consult Serv, 1997. **Orgs:** Bergen Co Urban League; trustee, Franklin Lakes United Methodist Church; President's Exec Exchange Assoc; steering comt, Organizational Resource Counselors; Va State Univ Alumni Asn, NJ Chapt; Kappa Theta Lambda Chap Alpha Phi Alpha Frat; founder & chmn, Va State Univ Spec Action Team; deacon, First Mt Olive Baptist Church; chmn bdn Environ Careers Org; chm, adv coun, Richmond Technical Ctr; Southside Baptist Asn, 1999; Richmond Rotary Club, pres, 2001-; chair, First Mount Alive Baptist Church; Bay Consortium Workforce Investment Bd. **Honors/Awds:** Certificate of Merit, Broome Co New York, NAACP, 1972; Family & Children's Soc Special Recognition Certificate, 1973; Kiwanis Club President's Award, 1975; Alpha Phi Alpha Outstanding Tenure Award, 1976; Sustained Serv Award, 1977; President's Impact Award, 1978; IBM Office Products Div People Management Award, 1979; Division Excellence Award, IBM, 1988; Lead IBM's Charitable Contribution, 1988; Presidential Exec Exchange, 1980-81; Sr Management Citation Dept of Health & Human Serv, 1981; Outstanding National Achievement Award, 1981; Alpha Phi Alpha Iota Theta Lambda Chap Award, 1983; SES Candidates Certificates of Recognition Dept of Health & Human Service, 1983; Alpha Phi Alpha New York/New Jersey Archives Award, 1983; NAFEO Presidential Citation Award, 1986;Alumnus of the Year, Va State, 1989; President's Special Recognition Award, Alpha Phi Alpha, 1990; ed, Sphinx Magazine, Alpha Phi Alpha; Award of Merit, Am Vocational Asn, 1998. **Home Addr:** PO Box 280, St Stephens Church, VA 23148.

POLLARD, RAYMOND J.
School administrator. **Personal:** Born Mar 31, 1932, Lamar, SC; son of Gussie and Ethel; married Eloise Wilson. **Educ:** Fla State Univ, EdB, 1953; Univ Pa, M.Ed, 1957; Antioch Col, MS, 1977. **Career:** School administrator (retired); Internal Revenue, mail clerk, 1953-54; Kenderton Sch, spec educ teacher, 1957-58; McIntyre Sch, teacher, 1958-61; CPA, caseworker male clerk, 1961-62; LP Hill Sch, 1962-64 & 1967-71; Levering Sch, 1966-67; Turner Middle Sch, phys educ teacher, 1971-73; Penn Fed Teachers, staff rep, 1973, gen vpres. **Orgs:** Vpres, Negro Trade Union Leadership Coun, 1971; vice-chmn, Phillip Randolph Inst, 1972; finance sec mem, Usher Bd C Sch Scholar Comt; co-dir, Met Bapist Church; pres, Fayetteville State Univ Alumni, bus mgr, chmn, hospitality comt; exec bd, Progressive Philadelphia Fed Teachers, co-chmn;bldg rep, LP Hill Sch & JP Turner Sch; Nat Asn Advan Colored People; PUSH; CORE; SCLC; APHI; treas, BSA. **Military Serv:** AUS, commun coding clerk, 1954-56.

POLLARD, DR. WILLIAM LAWRENCE
Educator. **Personal:** Born Nov 27, 1944, Raleigh, NC; son of Bettie Pollard and Linwood Pollard; married Merriette Maude Chance; children: William Lawrence & Frederick Touissaint. **Educ:** Shaw Univ, AB, 1967; Univ NC Chapel Hill, MSW, 1969; Univ Chicago, PhD, 1976. **Career:** Livingstone Col, instr, 1969-71, asst prof & dir social welfare prog, 1973-76; Univ Pittsburgh, asso prof & chmn comn orgn skill set sch social work, 1976-82; Grambling State Univ, assoc prof & dir undergrad social work, 1984-; Syracuse Univ, Syracuse, NY, dean, 1989-; Univ DC, Wash, pres; Nat Asn State Univ & Land-Grant Col, vpres, 2007-. **Orgs:** House of dels Coun Social Work Educ, 1974-77, 1979-82; bd dir, Friendship House Salisbury, NC, 1974-76; sec bd dir, Dial Help Salisbury, 1974-76; bd dir, YMCA Salisbury, 1975-76; bd dirs, Coun Social Work Educ; adv comn Citizen Educ Action Group Criminal Justice; bd dir, Nat Asn Deans & Dirs Schs Social Work, 1991-; bd dirs, Salvation Army; bd dirs, Elmcrest C's Ctr. **Honors/Awds:** Fel Grant Met Applied Res Corp, 1974; A Study of Black Self Help R&E Res Assocs, 1978; "The Black Child" in

proceedings of New Concepts in Human Serv for the Developing Child, 1978; Distinguished Grad, Shaw Univ, 1991; Awardee, Frst Ann NY Gov's Award for African-Am of Distinction. **Special Achievements:** Co-Auth, "How Do We Get There: Strategic Planning for Schs of Social Work," J Social Work Educ, 1992. **Business Addr:** Vice President, National Association of State Universities and Land-Grant Colleges, 1307 NY Ave NW Suite 400, Washington, DC 20005-4722, **Business Phone:** (202)478-6040.

POLLARD-BUCKINGHAM, ALICE F
Police officer. **Career:** City St Louis, from exec asst to the dir pub safety, comnr corrections, supt corrections, currently. **Orgs:** MCA Legis Comt; Am Jail Asn; Am Correctional Asn; Sigma Gamma Rho Sorority; Lincoln Univ Alumni. **Special Achievements:** First female to hold the position of commissioner of corrections in St Louis. **Home Addr:** 4403 Arco Fl 2, St Louis, MO 63110, **Home Phone:** (314)531-0986. **Business Phone:** (314)621-5848 Ext 8312.

POLYNICE, OLDEN
Basketball player, basketball coach. **Personal:** Born Nov 21, 1964, Port-au-Prince, Haiti; son of Jean-Lester and Suzanne; married Raechel; children: Nikolas Justin, Chase, Tiara Alysha & Alexis. **Educ:** Univ Va, attended 1986. **Career:** Basketball player (retired), basketball coach; played in Italy, 1986-87; Seattle SuperSonics, ctr, 1987-91; Los Angeles Clippers, ctr, 1991-92; Detroit Pistons, ctr, 1992-94; Sacramento Kings, ctr, 1994-98; Seattle Supersonics, ctr, 1998-99; Utah Jazz, ctr, 1999-2001; Los Angeles Clippers, ctr, 2003-04; Los Angeles Aftershock, ctr, 2004-05; Long Beach Jam, Am Basketball Asn, play coach; Long Beach Breakers, head coach, currently. **Orgs:** Founder, Helping Out Our People Found. **Special Achievements:** Film: Eddie. **Business Phone:** (562)987-4487.

POMARE, ELEO. See Obituaries section.

PONDER, EUNICE WILSON
Educator. **Personal:** Born Sep 4, 1929, Kansas City, MO; daughter of Kate Wilson and Austin Wilson; married Henry; children: Cheryl & Anna. **Educ:** Langston Univ, BS, 1951; Okla State Univ, MS, 1958; Univ SC, EdD, 1977. **Career:** Educator (retired). Okla teacher pub schs, 1951-58; Planning Res & Mgt Benedict Col, inst researcher, 1977-84; Benedict Col, teacher, 1977-84; Millie Lewis Agency, Columbia, SC. **Orgs:** NatDelta Pi Epsilon Bus Frat, 1958-; Nat Asn Instnl vol worker Red Cross; NCATE Self-Study Team HEW, 1978-80; reader tite IV HEW 1979-80; life mem, Delta Sigma Theta Sor. **Honors/Awds:** Dissertation: A Study of Selected Characteristics Affecting the Survival Rate of Black & White Students at the Univ of SC", 1977.

PONDER, DR. HENRY
School administrator, consultant. **Personal:** Born Mar 28, 1928, Wewoka, OK; son of Frank and Lillie; married Eunice Wilson, Nov 22, 1952; children: Cheryl & Anna. **Educ:** Langston Univ, BS, 1951; Okla State Univ, MS, 1958; Ohio State Univ, PhD, 1963. **Career:** Okla State Univ, res asst, 1956-58; Va State Col, asst prof, 1958-61, Dept Agr & Bus, chmn, 1963-64; Ohio State Univ, res asst, 1961-63; Fort Valley State Col, chmn dept bus & econ, 1964-66; Irving Trust Co, econ consult, 1968; Fed Res Bank, consult; Philadelphia Nat Bank, consult; Chase Manhattan Bank, consult; Irving Trust Co, consult; Omaha Nat Bank, consult; Ala A&M Univ, dean, 1966-69, vpres acad affairs, 1969-73; Tennessee Univ, pres; Benedict Col, pres, 1973-84; Fisk Univ, pres, 1984-96; Fisk Univ, Nat Asn Equal Opportunity Higher Educ, ceo & pres, 1996-2001; Talladega Col, pres, 2002-. **Orgs:** Am Econ Asn; Am Farm Econ Asn; Mason 32nd Deg C C; gen pres, Alpha Phi Alpha, 1989-92; Nat Asn Equal Opportunity Higher Educ; chmn bd dirs, Fed Res Bank Richmond; bd dirs, JP Stevens & Co Inc; Bd ETV Endowment; bd dirs, Sun trust Bank Nashville; bd dirs, SCANA Corp SC; bd dirs, Comm Col Air Force. **Honors/Awds:** Distinguished Alumnus Award, Okla State Univ, 1986; Distinguished Alumnus Award, Ohio State Univ. **Special Achievements:** Hundred Most Effective College Presidents in US, 1986. **Military Serv:** AUS, chief comput fdc sgt, 1953-55. **Business Addr:** President, Talladega College, 627 W Battle St, Talladega, AL 35160, **Business Phone:** (256)761-0206.

PONDER-NELSON, DEBRA
Association executive, chief executive officer, president (organization). **Personal:** Born Jun 8, 1957, Midwest City, OK; daughter of Bishop Alonzo L Ponder and Beulah Jacobs Ponder; married; children: Kristen & Karmen. **Educ:** Okla State Univ, BS, 1979. **Career:** Okla City Limousine Serv, owner, 1979-81; B & P Maintenance, gen mgr, 1981-83; Gen Mills Inc, territory mgr, 1983-89; Okla Minority Supplier Develop Coun, exec dir, 1990, pres & chief exec officer, currently. **Orgs:** Okla State Alumni Asn; Soc Women Bus; vol, Delta Sigma Theta Sorority; Jack & Jill Am; Okla Consortium Minority Bus Develop. **Honors/Awds:** Resident Hall Academic Achievement Award, Okla State Univ, 1976-77; Dean's Honor Roll of Distinguished Students,Okla State Univ, 1979; Ralph Ellison Library Circulation Drive Community Appreciation Award, Nat Hon Soc, 1986; General Mills Salesperson of the Year, 1986-87, District 600, 1987; The Oklahoma Ebony Tribune Newspaper-Keepers of the Dream Award, Outstanding Achievement, 1993; selected as one of the 50 finalists, Journal Record Woman of the Year, 1999; Regional & Local Minority Advocate of the Year, Minority Bus Develop Agency; America's Women Who Mean Business, Minority Bus News USA. **Special Achievements:** US Senate, internship, 1978. **Home Addr:** PO Box 18228, Oklahoma City, OK 73154-0228. **Business Addr:** President, Chief Executive Officer, Oklahoma Minority Supplier Development Council, 6701 W Broadway Exten Suite 216, Oklahoma City, OK 73116, **Business Phone:** (405)767-9900.

POOL, VERA C
Police officer, president (organization). **Personal:** Born Jul 27, 1946, Greenwood, MS; daughter of Alberta Lofton Corbin and Rayfield Corbin; married John Pool, Jul 26, 1969; children: Sheina Karia. **Educ:** Portland Community Col, Portland, OR, AA, 1969; Univ Portland, Portland, OR, BA, Psychol, 1972, MA, Educ, 1974, MS, Criminal Justice, 1978. **Career:** Veterans Admin, Portland, OR, food services, 1965-70; Multnomah Co Sheriff's Dept, Portland, OR, Lt, 1970; NOBLE Northwest Chap, pres, currently. **Orgs:** App nat bd, NABCJ, 1979-86, 1989-; elected Nat assist secy, Bd on Police Standards & Training, 1981-89; Found & former chap pres, Nat Asn Black Correctional Justice, 1984-91; sgt-at-arms, Delta Sigma Theta Sorority, 1989; Gov Steering Comt on Sex Offenders, 1990. **Honors/Awds:** Woman of the Year, Am Bus Women's Asn Chap (Mt Hood), 1979; Service to the Community, 1987, The Chairman Emeritus Award, 1989, Nat Asn Black Correctional Justice; Professional Achievement, Delta Sigma Theta Sorority, 1988; Award for Dedicated Services in Corrections/Prison, Albina Ministrial Alliance, 1990. **Business Addr:** President, NOBLE Northwest Chapter, 1120 SW 3rd Ave, Portland, OR 97204, **Business Phone:** (503)988-3397.*

POOLE, DILLARD M.
Educator. **Personal:** Born Sep 15, 1939, Birmingham, AL. **Educ:** BA, 1971; MA, 1977. **Career:** State OH, clerk; Warner & Swasey Machine Tool Co, tool supply worker; Cleveland State Univ, asst to dean student life, 1971-72; Afro-Am Cultural Ctr, Cleveland State Univ, dir. **Orgs:** Nat Conf Artists, 1973-74; trustee, Parkwood CME Ch, 1974-. **Honors/Awds:** Dean's list Cleveland State Univ, 1970. **Military Serv:** USAF, airman 2nd class, 1959-63.

POOLE, JAMES F.
Financial manager. **Personal:** Born Apr 12, 1936, Laurens, SC; married Martha; children: Stephanie & Heather. **Educ:** Benedict Col, 1959; Univ Pa, Univ CO & CO Col, grad work. **Career:** Central High Sch, Pueblo, teacher math, 1962-67; Am Capital Financial Serv Inc, investment couns div mgr, 1967; Advantage Capital Corp, currently. **Orgs:** East Planning Coun Colo Springs; Sale & Mkt Exec Club; Alpha Phi Alpha Frat; Pueblo Country Club; Colo Centennial-Bicentennial Comn, 1975; bd trustee, Benedict Col, Columbia, SC; Millionaires Club Am Capital Financial Serv Inc; Southern Col Financial Planning Asn; Securities Investor Protection Corp; Financial Indust Regulatory Authority. **Military Serv:** AUS, e-5, 1959-62. **Business Addr:** Owner, James F Poole Associate Inc, 119 W 8th, Pueblo, CO 81003.

POOLE, DR. RACHEL IRENE
Nurse, consultant. **Personal:** Born Dec 2, 1924, Uniontown, PA; married Marion L; children: Andrea Lynell & Adriene Charisse Dilworth. **Educ:** Univ Pittsburgh PA, BSN 1947, M Litt, nursing educ, 1952, PhD, 1977. **Career:** Nurse, consultant (Retired); Dept Psychiatric Ment Health Nursing Sch Nursing Univ Pittsburgh, assoc prof & assoc chmn, 1967-72, assoc prof, 1972-73; health integrator, 1972; Inst Higher Educ Sch Educ Univ Pittsburgh, lectr, admin asst, 1974-77; Community Col Allegheny Co, adminsr intern, admin asst to pres, 1977-79; Allegheny Campus Community Col Allegheny Co Pittsburgh PA, asst dean life sci & dir nursing prog, 1979-84; Home wood-Brushton Br Allegheny Comm Col, part-time adv, counsr, 1984; Western Psychiatric Inst & Clin, dir nursing. **Orgs:** Bd dirs, Ille Elegba, 1968-74; org, treasurer, Black Women's Forum, 1969-71; Am Nurses Asn; Am Asn Higher Educ, 1975-76; adv bd mem, Visions: Women's Art Collective, 1989-; Univ Pittsburgh African Am Alumni Scholarship Comt, 1989-. **Honors/Awds:** Black Achiever of Year, NIP Magazine, 1986; Special Recognition Award, Community Col Alleg County, 1986; Outstanding Dedicated Services Award, Student Advisory Bd, Community Col Allegheny County Allegheny Campus, 1990; Distinguished Alumnus Award, Univ Pittsburgh Sch Nursing, 1990; Outstanding Black Nurse Citation, City Coun, Pittsburgh. **Special Achievements:** Author of many writings; Sigma Theta Tau, 1953; Selected PA Nurses Asn "Brain Trust", 1965-67; Interviewee "Racism" WIIC's TV Prog Face to Face, 1968; "Proposal for a Plan of Action" Com on Recruitment of Minorities into Nursing Dept of Health Common wealth, 1973; Penn Bar Asn, legal assistants, paralegals, single mothers, sec, nurses, ex-convicts, fed women employees, & women in military on the subject of "Assertiveness", 1979-88, 1988-90; Panelist Minorities and Nursing WQED's TV Prog Black Horizons, 1981; Panelist Nursing Programs WTAE's TV Prog Pgh Today 1982; first African American assoc prof of Department of Mental Health at Western Psychiatric Institute and Clinic.

POOLE, TYRONE
Football player. **Personal:** Born Feb 3, 1972, LaGrange, GA. **Educ:** Fort Valley State Univ, bus. **Career:** Carolina Panthers, defensive back, 1995-98; Indianapolis Colts, 1998-2000; Denver Broncos, 2001-02; New Eng Patriots, corner back, 2003-05; Oakland Raiders, defensive back, 2006; Houston Texans, 2007; Denver Broncos, corner back, 2008. Tennessee Titans, corner back, 2008-. **Special Achievements:** Selected in the first round/22nd overall pick in the 1995 NFL Draft. **Business Addr:** Cornerback, Tennessee Titans, 460 Great Circle Rd, Nashville, TN 37213, **Business Phone:** (615)565-4200.

POOL-ECKERT, MARQUITA JONES
Journalist. **Personal:** Born Feb 19, 1945, Aurora, IL; daughter of Mark E and Jeanne Boger; married Stephen C Pool, Sep 9, 1975 (divorced 1980); married Knut Eckert, May 11, 1988. **Educ:** Boston Univ, BS, 1966; Columbia Univ, MA, Jour, 1969. **Career:** WABC-TV NY, producer, 1970-74; WNET/13 Public TV, producer, 1974-75; CBS News, assoc producer, 1975-84, producer, 1984-90, sr producer, Sunday Morning, 1990-. **Orgs:** Pres, 1976-85, bd dirs, 1976-89, Nzingha Soc Inc; NY Assoc Black Journalists, 1985-; Womens Media Group, 1986-; bd dirs, NY Women in Film, 1994-; bd dirs, Frederick Douglas Creative Arts Ctr, 1994-98; Coun on Foreign Rels; Friends Mus Modern Art, NY, 1995-; Links Inc; Metro-Manhattan chap. **Honors/Awds:** Emmy Award foProducer, "The Bombing of Beirut", 1983, "The Black Family A Dream Deferred", 1983, "Racism", 1986, "Pan Am 103 Crash", 1988, "Diana, Princess of Wales", CBS Sunday Morning, 1998; Dollars & Sense Magazine Award,100 Top Professional Black Women, 1986; Nat Monitor Award, 1988; InterNat Monitor Award, "80's Remembered", 1990; Career Achievement Award, Norfolk State Univ, 1996; Black Career Women Lifetime Achievement Award, 1997; Muse Award, NY Women In Film & Television, 1999; Alumni of the Year Award, Columbia Univ, 2002. **Business Addr:** Senior Producer, CBS News, 524 W 57th St, New York, NY 10019, **Business Phone:** (212)975-6708.

POPE, REV. COURTNEY A
Clergy. **Personal:** Born Mar 29, 1964, Philadelphia, PA; son of Cromwell and Gloria J; married Audrey D Pope, Aug 1, 1987; children: Jazmine & Chaz. **Educ:** Temple Univ, BA, comun, 1988; Int Christian Univ, DDiv. **Career:** Eastern Atlantic Diocese Youth Congress, pres, 1984-97; Church Living God, Nat HYPBC, vpres, 1985-87; Holy Temple Church, pastor, 1995, bishop, currently; Eastern Atlantic Diocese, district elder, 1996-99. **Orgs:** Philadelphia Music Alliance, 1992; Pennsgrove Carney's Point Ministerium, 1995-; Salem County Men Christ, 1995; pres, Jhazzi Music Publ, 1997-; bd dirs, Bishop L Colene Williams Comm Ctr, 1998-; bd dirs, Fresh Harvest Ministries, 1998-; US Chaplains Asn, 1999-; adv bd, LIFELINES, 1999-. **Honors/Awds:** Youth of the Year, Holy Temple Church, 1990; 15 Years in the Gospel Ministry, 1991; Gift of Time, Am Family Inst, 1995; Mayor's Award, Borough Penns Grove, NJ, 1996; Outstanding Young Man of American Award, 1996; Volunteer of the Year for Salem County, State of New Jersey, 1999. **Special Achievements:** Performed and recorded "Make A Joyful Noise," 1984; wrote & performed musical score for drama, "Practical Spirits," 1985; performed & recorded, "All My Help," 1986; performed on "Spirit of Philadelphia," cruise, 1994; performed & recorded, "Living to Live Again," 1996. **Business Addr:** Bishop, Holy Temple Church of the Fresh Harvest, Willis & Cumberland Sts, PO Box 541, Penns Grove, NJ 08069, **Business Phone:** (856)299-2737.

POPE, DERRICK ALEXANDER
Educator, lawyer. **Personal:** Born Dec 7, 1964, Atlanta, GA; son of Howard and Sallie Pope. **Educ:** Morris Brown Col, BA, polit sci, 1987; Loyola Univ Sch Law, JD, 1992. **Career:** Morris Brown Col, adj prof law, beginning 1992; Spec Judiciary Comt, legal coun, 1992-93; Ga Gen Assembly, lawyer & asst legis coun, 1993-94; pvt pract, currently; Col Law, Ga State Univ, adj prof, currently; Med Asn Ga, lawyer, leg coun; spec proj dir, Asn Black Cardiologists. **Orgs:** Alpha Phi Alpha Fraternity Inc, 1984-; State Bar Ga, 1992-; Atlanta Inner Circle, 1993-; Am Bar Asn, 1993-; Phi Alpha Delta Law Fraternity; US Supreme Ct Hist Soc. **Honors/Awds:** Sterling Performance Award, Coun on Legal Educ Opportunity, 1987; Top Attorney Award, Nat Intercollegiate Mock-Trial, 1987; American Jurispudence Award, NCCU Sch Law, 1989; Foti Criminal Advocacy Award, Loyola Univ Sch Law, 1992. **Special Achievements:** A Const Gem of Interpretive Reason: Or in Other Words The Ninth Amendment, 37 Hon LJ, 201, 1994; Auth: Thy Will Be Done: An African-american Guide To Estate Planning,; And A Three-part Political Treatise Entitled, With Liberty And Justice For All, Volume 1 Of The Series; Is Entitled, A Declaration Of Independence For Colored Folks, Negroes, Black People, And African-americans. **Business Phone:** (404)588-1066.

POPE, HAROLD D
Lawyer. **Personal:** Born Aug 29, 1955, Newton, NJ; son of Harold Pope and Getrude Taylor Pope; married Renay, Aug 11, 1979; children: Daman & Ebony. **Educ:** Concordia Col, BA, 1976; Duke Univ Sch Law, JD, 1980. **Career:** Lamb, Chappell, Hartung, Gallipoli & Coughlin, law clerk, 1979, assoc, 1980-84; Lewis, White & Clay, PC, assoc, 1984-88, shareholder, 1989-94; Segue, Adams & Pope, PLC, partner, 1994-99; Jaffe, Raitt, Heuer & Weiss, PC, partner, 1999-. **Orgs:** Garden State Bar Asn, 1982-84; Wolverine Bar Asn; bd dir, Nat Bar Inst, 1992-94, exec comt, 1992-94, vpres, 1994-98, pres-elect, 1998-99, pres, 1999-2000, chair, 2002-06;

Renaissance Optimist Club, 1987-89; treas, Detroit Pub Schs Stud Motivational Prog, 1988-89; Pontiac Area Transitional Housing, bd dir; Alpha Phi Alpha; NAACP; NJ Bar Asn; Am Bar Asn. **Honors/Awds:** Michigan State Bar Champion of Justice, 2000; C.Stratford Francis Award, Nat Bar Asn, 2006. **Business Addr:** Partner, Jaffe, Raitt, Hever & Weiss, Professional Corp, 27777 Franklin Rd Suite 2500, Southfield, MI 48034, **Business Phone:** (248)351-3000.

POPE, HENRY
Psychiatrist, army officer. **Personal:** Born May 1, 1922, Athens, GA; married; children: 4. **Educ:** Howard Univ, BS, 1949; Meharry Med Col, MD, 1958. **Career:** Provident Hosp, intern 1958; St Elizabeth's Hosp, 1960; St Elizabeths Hosp, staff physician, 1960-65; Self-employed, 1960-; Crownsville Hosp Ctr, res psychiat & staff psychiat 1970-. **Orgs:** Nat Med Asn, 1960-; DC Med Soc, 1970. **Military Serv:** Sgt, 1943-45. **Business Addr:** Psychiatrist, 1509 Penn Ave Se, Washington, DC 20003.

POPE, DR. ISAAC S
Physician. **Personal:** Born Mar 6, 1939, S Pittsburgh, TN; married Joan Darby; children: David, Stephen & Theresa. **Educ:** Gonzaga Univ, Spokane, WA, BS, 1965; Univ WA Seattle, MPA, 1970; Univ WA, Seattle, MD, 1974. **Career:** Peace Corps, Sierra Leone, vol, 1965-67; Peace Corps Training Prog Gambia, dir, 1969; model cities prog Seattle, asst dir employee economic develop, 1969-70; US Army Ft Leonard Wood, MO, staff pediatrician, 1977-79; pvt pract, pediatrician, 1979-; Popes Kids Place, Vol Pediatrician, currently. **Orgs:** Regional dir Student Nat Med Asn, 1972-73; WA State Med Asn Lewis Co Med Soc; WA State Soc Pediat; Kiwanis, 1979-92, pres, 1985; bd mem, Lewis County Work Opportunity, 1981-86; bd mem, Lewis County Special Olympic, 1983-86; Twin Cities, pres, 1987; Chehalis City Coun. **Honors/Awds:** Conc patient care Ft Leonard Wood Army Hosp, 1978; Army Commendation Medal, AVS, 1979; Businessmen of the Year, Daily Chronicle, 1988; Service to Mankind Award, Sertoma Club, 1989; Distinguished Alumni Merit Award, Gonzaga Univ, 1990; Distinguished Citizenship Award, Elks, 1991; Service to Mankind Award, Sertoma Club, 1994; Duncan Award, 1994; Award for Excellence, Nat Asn Counties, 1995; Best of Lewis County Med Doctor, 1997, 1998, 1999, Real Heroes Award, AMR Red Cross, 1998; Citizen of the Year, WA State Elks, 1999; Jefferson Award Washington State, 2002; Physician Excellence Award, Providence Centralia Hosp, 2005. **Military Serv:** USAF, airman l/c 1956-59; USY, maj, 1974-79. **Home Addr:** 1631 SW Gails Ave, Chehalis, WA 98532.

POPE, MCCOY S
Police officer. **Personal:** Born Oct 5, 1937, New York, NY; son of Travis M and Rose Murphy Pope; married Geraldine Cooper, Jul 22, 1963; children: David C & Jason McCoy. **Educ:** Thomas Edison Col, AA, 1977; Southern Ill Univ, BS, 1980. **Career:** Police officer (retired); USAF, military police supvr, investr, 1959-80; US Defense Invest Serv, Croton, CT field off, spec agent in charge, 1981-94; New London Alternative Incarceration Ctr, counr & substance abuse specialist, 1994. **Orgs:** Air Force Asn, 1980-; bd mem, Kiwanis Club Int, 1994-; Nat Asn Advan Colored People New London, CT, 1995-; bd chmn, Alderhouse Inc, 1995-; vpres, New london, CT Hist Soc, 1996-. **Honors/Awds:** Hixson Medallion Award, Kiwanis Int, 1999. **Special Achievements:** USAF Certification for Fluency in Spanish, Italian & French Languages; initiated New London Amistad lead & began progs to promote then unknown event, 1996; First Afr Am field office chief a fed investigative agency in New England history. **Military Serv:** USAF, technical sgt, 1959-80; Meriterious Service Medal; Air Force Commendation Medal. **Home Addr:** 25 Starr St, New London, CT 06320.

POPE, MIRIAN ARTIS
Executive. **Personal:** Born Nov 3, 1952, Franklin, VA; married Johnnie Lee Pope Jr; children: Ebonee Johndrea, Courtney LaVerne. **Educ:** Norfolk State Univ, BS, 1975; Old Dominion Univ. **Career:** United Va Bank, br mgr, 1975-81; Community Fedl S/L Asn, managing officer, 1981-. **Orgs:** Adv bd, Jr Achievement Tidewater, 1976; Adv bd banking & fin comt, Norfolk State Univ, 1977-81; Nat Asn Bank Women, 1977-81; dir, Am Red Cross Tidewater Chap, 1979-81; Order Eastern Star Va, 1979-; dir, Norfolk C C, 1980; dir, United Way, 1981-82; Norfolk Conv & Visitors Bur. **Honors/Awds:** Scholar, Norfolk State Univ, 1971; appreciation Junior Achievement of Tidewater, 1976; appreciation, Norfolk Chamber Com, 1980; appreciation, Am Red Cross, 1981. **Home Addr:** 387 Brock Circle, Norfolk, VA 23502. **Business Addr:** Member, Norfolk Convention and Visitors Bureau, 232 E Main St, Norfolk, VA 23510.

POPE, RUBEN EDWARD, III
Labor relations manager, lawyer. **Personal:** Born Jun 28, 1948, Cleveland, OH; son of Ruben Jr and Marie Danzy (deceased); married Cheryl Ann Jones; children: Walter, Yolanda & Yvonne. **Educ:** Kenyon Col, BA, 1970; Boston Col Law Sch, JD, 1973. **Career:** Arthur Andersen & Co, auditor, 1973-75; Wyman-Gordon Co, develop benefits mgr. **Orgs:** Ohio Bar, 1978; Am Bar Asn 1978; bd dir, United Way Cent Mass; treas, Youth Guide Asn Inc; bd dir, Prospect House Inc, 1980; fin secy, Quinsigamond Lodge, IBPOE W Elks; sec, Belmont St AME Zion Church. **Home Addr:** 15 Westport Rd, Worcester, MA 01605, **Home Phone:** (508)852-3159.

PORCHE-BURKE, LISA
Educator. **Personal:** Born Nov 9, 1954, Los Angeles, CA; daughter of Ralph and June; married Peter Burke, Oct 27, 1984; children: Mallory, Dominique, Lauren. **Educ:** Univ Southern calif, BA, 1976; univ Nortre Dame, MA, 1981, PhD, 1983. **Career:** Calif Sch Prof Psychol, asst prof, prof training fac, 1985-87, asst prof, 1987-90, Ethnic MNY Mental HTH Proficiency, coordr, 1987-90, assoc prof, 1990-91, Multicultural COT Clinical Proficiency, coordr, 1990-92, acting provost, 1991-92, chancellor; Phillips Grad Inst, Pres, currently. **Orgs:** Asn Black Psychologists, 1980-; NAT Coun Schs Prof Psychol, exec comt, 1990-92, chair, 1992-; CAL Psychological Asn found, bd mem, 1992-; AMR Psychological Asn, DIV 45, SOC Study Ethnic MNY Issues, exec comt, 1985-, sr exec, 1991-, DIV Psychotherapy, exe bd, 1991-; AM Asn Higher EDUC, 1993-. **Honors/Awds:** Distinguished faculty Contribution Award, CAL Sch Prof Psychol; Jack B Krasner Award, DIV 29, AM Psychological ASN; Exemplary Prof Service Award, ASN Black Psychologists; Honorary Doctor of Letters, 1994; Distinguished Contributions to Service award, Am Psychological Asn. **Special Achievements:** Author: "Minority Student Recruitment and Retention: Is There a Secret to Success?" Towards Ethnic Diversification in Psychology Education and Training, Stricker, 1990; "The Particularly Insidious Effects of Stress on Women of Color," w/Funk, 1991; "Recommendations From the Working Group on Predoctoral Training," 1991, "Ethnic MNY Issues in Clinical Training at CSPP-LA," 1991, Ethnic Minority Perspectives on Clinical Training and Service in Psychology, Myers; "The Insidious Impact of Gang Violence: Strategies for Prevention and Intervention," Substance Abuse and Gang Violence, Cervantes, 1992. **Business Phone:** (818)386-5639.*

PORCHER, ROBERT, III
Football player, businessperson. **Personal:** Born Jul 30, 1969, Wando, SC; married Kimberly; children: Morgan Latreese. **Educ:** SC State Univ, BA, criminal justice. **Career:** Football player (retired); Detroit Lions, defensive tackle, 1992-2003. **Orgs:** Omega Psi Phi Fraternity; Chairperson,Metro Detroit Am Heart Asn Heart Walk, 1997. **Honors/Awds:** First-round draft pick, 1992; Pro Bowl, 1997; Extra Effort Awd, NFL, 2003. nominee, Sprint NFL Man of the Year, NFL, 1998. *

PORTEE, REV. DR. FRANK
Clergy. **Personal:** Born Jun 16, 1955, York, SC; son of Frank Jr and Alvon Pendergrass; married Yvonne Fersner, Sep 10, 1983; children: Alyssa Shanee. **Educ:** Carson-Newman Col, BA, 1977; Interdenominational Theol Sem, MDiv, 1980. **Career:** New Light United Methodist Church, pastor, 1980-83; United Methodist Church SC, coordr youth ministry, 1980-83; Charleston Col, campus minister, 1983-; Old Bethel United Methodist Church, pastor, 1983; Redeemer Church, pastor, 1991-; Interfaith Impact, dir empowerment & organizing; Union Inst, Fuller Theol Seminary, adj prof; Southern Calif Sch Ministry, adj fel; Emory Univ, Candler Sch Theol, res fel; Amandla Group, prin, currently; Pac Inst Word & Witness, conf dean. **Orgs:** Vpres, Nat Kidney Found, 1984-; bd mem, Action Coun Community Mental Health, 1984-; columnist, Charleston Chronicle, 1985-; bd mem, Community Rels Coun, 1985-; Florence Crittenton Homes, 1986; consult, Gen Bd Global Ministries, 1987; chmn, First Congressional Dist Rainbow Coalition, 1988; pres, Greater Charleston Community Develop Inc, 1988-; chmn, Avery Research Bd, 1988-; exec bd, Los Angeles Metrop Churches; exec secy, African Am Ministries; nat shalom coordr, Gen Bd Global Ministries, United Methodist Church; Lincoln Memorial United Church Christ. **Honors/Awds:** Research Fellow, Emory Sch Theol, 1982-83; Distinguish Service, Prince Hall Lodge #46 F&AM 1986; Distinguish Service, Chas Air Force Base, 1987; Delegate, Democratic Nat Conv, 1988. **Home Addr:** 513 Huger St, Charleston, SC 29403. **Business Addr:** Pastor, Church of the Redeemer, 900 E Rosecrans Ave, Los Angeles, CA 90059-3513, **Business Phone:** (310)537-1372.

PORTER, DR. ARTHUR T
Executive, physician. **Personal:** Born Jun 11, 1956, Freetown, Sierra Leone; married Pamela; children: 4. **Educ:** Cambridge Univ, BA, anat, 1978; Cambridge Univ Sch Med, MBB Chir, MD, 1980; Cambridge Univ, MA, natural sci, 1984; Royal Col Radiologists, DMRT, 1985; Royal Col Physicians & Surgeons, FRCPC, 1989; Univ TN, MBA, 1998. **Career:** Harper Hosp, Gershenson Radiation Oncol Ctr, chief, 1991-99; Radiation Oncol Res & Develop Ctr, pres & chief exec officer, 1991-99; Detroit Med Ctr, radiation oncologist-in-chief, 1991-99, exec vpres & chief oper officer, 1999, pres & chief exec officer, 1999-; Univ Radiation Oncol Physicians PC, pres, 1994-; Karmanos Cancer Inst, dir clin care, 1995-98; McGill Univ Health Ctr, dir gen & chief exec officer, 2004-. **Orgs:** Canadian Oncology Soc, 1987-; Am Radium Soc, 1989-; Am Soc Clinal Oncology, 1990-; Am Col Radiation Oncology, charter mem, 1991-; Detroit Med Soc, 1991-; Mich State Med Soc, 1991-; AMA, 1991-; Am Acad Med Admin, 1992-; chmn Oncol, Victoria Hosp Corp; fac med mem, Univ Western Ont. **Honors/Awds:** Physicians Recognition Award, Am Med Asn, 1986; Award for Excellence, Detroit Med Soc, 1993; Distinguished Service Award, Am Acad Med Admin, 1996; Tree of Life Award, Jewish Nat Fund, 1997; Healthcare Executive of the Year, Am Acad Med Admin, 1998; Pathfinders Award, Wayne State Univ Sch Med, 2000; named one of the Best Doctors in America for eight consecutive years from 1992-2000. **Special Achievements:** Numerous publications. **Business Addr:** Chief Executive Officer, Director General, McGill University Health Center, Montreal Children's Hospital, 2300 Tupper St, Montreal, QC, Canada H3H 1P3, **Business Phone:** (514)412-4400.

PORTER, BLANCHE TROULLIER
Educator, elementary school teacher. **Personal:** Born Nov 22, 1933, New Orleans, LA; divorced; children: Louis Porter II. **Educ:** Dillard Univ, BA, 1955; Univ S Calif; Xavier Univ. **Career:** Elem sch teacher, resource teacher. **Orgs:** Nat PTA Grammeteus Alpha Kappa Sorority, 1954; United Teacher New Orleans; Nat Educ Asn; Am Fedn Teachers; LA Educ Asn; Parent Teacher Asn, Andrew Jackson Ele Sch; McDonogh 35 High; admin bd, Grace United Methodist Church; secy, United Methodist Women; secy, Coun Ministries; Parents Aux Club BSA Troop 155. **Special Achievements:** Granted key to city of Louisville, KY, 1968.

PORTER, CHARLES WILLIAM
Publisher, educator, editor. **Personal:** Born Oct 6, 1939, Mobile, AL; son of Quillie Porter and Rosie Porter; married Joyce A Wallace; children: Nikki, Terri, Michael & Stanley. **Educ:** Bishop State Jr Col, AS, 1960; Ala State Univ, BS, 1962; Univ Ala, MA, 1970; Chicago City Col, 1973; Ala Interdenominational Sem, Mdiv, 1972. **Career:** Public sch teacher, 1962-68; Mobile Press Regist, news reporter, 1968-69; The Univ Ala, Tuscaloosa Inst, 1969-70; Tougaloo Col, Tougaloo, MS, dir public rels, 1970-71; Northwestern Univ, sr publ ed, 1971-74; Mobile Beacon, ed, 1974-76; Inner City News, ed & publ, 1976-; Inner City Printers, owner, 1977-; Bishop State Jr Col, dir public rels, 1982-86, instr Jour, 1984-87; Inner City Pub Rels, rels consul, 1986-; past exec dir, Human Rels Comn; exec dir, Minority Tech & Entrepreneural Ctr, Bishop State Community Col, currently. **Orgs:** Founder & pres, Media Coalition 1976-; chmn bd, OIC Mobile Area 1980-81; Sigma Delta Chi; Nat Asn Black Journalist; Am Col Pub Rels Asn; Educ Writers Asn; Nat Coun Col Pub Adv; NAACP; Sickle Cell Res Found; Omega Psi Phi Fraternity Inc; Concerned Citizens for Police Reform, Chicago; Southern Christian Leadership Conf: YWCA (Honary); YMCA; Urban League. **Honors/Awds:** Nat, regional & local honors for establishing the Southern Ala Task Force on Illiteracy; honorary doctorate, Ala InterdenomiNat Sem, 1991; Numerous honors for community serv. **Business Addr:** Executive Director, Bishop State Community College, Minority Technology & Entrepreneurship Center, 351 N Broad St, Mobile, AL 36603, **Business Phone:** (251)405-7118.

PORTER, DR. CLARENCE A.
Educator. **Personal:** Born Mar 19, 1939, McAlester, OK; son of Myrtle; children: Richard & Cory. **Educ:** Portland State Univ, BS, 1962; OR State Univ, MS, 1964, PhD, 1966. **Career:** Educator (retired); OR St Univ, grad asst, 1961-64, asst vet med, 1964-66; Portland St Univ, asst prof, 1966-70, exec asst to pres & assoc prof, 1970-72; Univ NH, asst vice provost acad affairs, 1972-76; St Univ MN, assoc vice chancellor acad affairs, 1976-78; Phyllis Wheatley Comm Ctr, exec dir, 1979-83; Cheyney Univ Penn, vpres acad affairs, 1983-84; Montgomery Col, Takoma Park, MD, instructional dean, 1985-04, coll vpres, provost. **Orgs:** Sigma Xi; Helminthological Soc Wash; Nat Coun Instructional Adminrs; NatCoun Black African Am Affairs; Col Mgt Prog, Carnegie Mellon, 1988; League Innovation Community Col, Exec Leadership Inst, 1997. **Honors/Awds:** Summer Fel, LA State Univ, 1968.

PORTER, EDWARD MELVIN
Businessperson, lawyer. **Personal:** Born May 22, 1930, Okmulgee, OK; son of Victor E and Mary Cole; married Jewel, Jan 1, 1955; children: E Melvin II & Joel Anthony. **Educ:** Tenn State Univ, BS, 1956; Vanderbilt Univ, LLB, 1959; Shorter Col, LLD. **Career:** Okla Nat Asn Advan Colored People, head, 1961-; Okla State Senate, sen,1964-86; Okla County Accessor, staff, 1992-94; Okla City atty, currently. **Orgs:** Okla County Bar Asn; Okla Bar Asn; Am Bar Asn; Am Judicature Soc; YMCA;Okla City Chamber Com; Sigma Rho Sigma; Kappa Alpha Psi; Okla Hist Soc. **Honors/Awds:** Kappa of the Month. **Special Achievements:** First Black Person to be admitted to Vanderbilt Law School; First Black State Senator elected in the State of Oklahoma. **Military Serv:** AUS, cpl, 1948-52.

PORTER, ELLIS NATHANIEL
Clergy. **Personal:** Born Apr 26, 1931, Sumter, SC; son of Frances Jenkins and Nathaniel. **Educ:** SC State Col, Orangeburg, BS, 1959; Philadelphia Divinity Sch, MDiv, 1963; Howard Univ Sch Divinity, DMin, 1985. **Career:** Clergy (retired); Episcopal Diocese NC, Durham, vicar/dir urban crisis prog, 1966-72; Episcopal Diocese Wash, Univ chaplain, 1972-87; Episcopal Church Ctr, coordr & ministry higher educ, 1988-92; St Edward Martyr Church, priest-in-residence, 1988-; Staff Officer Africa, 1992-94; Episcopal Church Ctr, 1994; Interim Rector Church St Mark, head master St Mark's Day Sch, 1994-95; Canon Trinity & St Philips Catheral, Newark, 1995-99; St Mary's Episcopal

Church, interim priest-in-charge, 1998-00. **Orgs:** Smithsonian Inst Copr, 1952-55; exec bd, Citz anti Poverty Comn, 1956-66; Citz Comm on Adoption, 1965-66; bd mem, Union Black & Epis; Angus Dun Fel Comn; exec bd, Better Health Found, 1968-72; Black Sol Comn, 1968-72; Diocesan Comn on Peace, 1975-87; convenor, Coun Ecumenical Stud Christian Ministry, 1990-94; Afro-Anglican Steering Comt, 1991-94. **Honors/Awds:** Appreciation Award, The Absalom Jones Stud Asn, Howard Univ, 1978; EFMM Unit Award, Chateau De Bossey, Celigny, Switzerland, 1988; Recognition Award, Union Black Episcopalians, 1996. **Military Serv:** AUS, specialist 2, 1953-55. *

PORTER, REV. DR. GLEN EUGENE
Minister (Clergy). **Educ:** Va Union Univ, Samuel D Proctor Sch Theol, MA, 1989, PhD, 2001; Rowan Univ, BA, mass comunications & jour, 2000. **Career:** Div Clergy Baptist Gen Convention Va, pres; pastor, Mount Zion Baptist Church; pastor, Gillfield Baptist Church, Petersburg, Va; Am Baptist Churches NJ, assoc regional pastor & area minister, currently. **Special Achievements:** Author of the book "Facing the Rising Sun". **Business Phone:** (609)587-8700.*

PORTER, GLORIA JEAN
Administrator. **Personal:** Born Apr 15, 1951, Baltimore, MD; daughter of Lillian and Percy. **Educ:** Adelphi Univ, BSW,Summa Cum Laude, 1973; Univ Ill, MSW, Summa Cum Laude, 1974. **Career:** Univ Mass Ment Health Serv, therapist, 1975-78; Univ Southern Calif Coun Serv, psychotherapist, asst dir, dir, 1978-84; Univ Southern Calif; Dataproducts Corp, employee asst mgr, 1984-90; Los Angeles County, Employee Assistance Prog, dir, 1991; Greene Co, CASA Coordr, currently. **Orgs:** Bd dir, Ebonics; Alcohol Info Ctr San Fernando Valley Coun Alcoholism; Nat Asn Advan Colored People; Black Women's Forum; Black Women's Network; Black Agenda; Women Mgmt, Am Personnel & Guidance Asn; NASW Reg Clin Soc Workers; Nat Asn Soc Workers; Asn Black Soc Workers; Nat Health Attitudes Res Proj; Am Personnel & Guidance Asn; NASW Regist Clin Social Workers. **Home Addr:** 5250 Village Green, Los Angeles, CA 90016. **Business Addr:** Coordinator, Greene Co, CASA, 2100 Greene Way Blvd, Xenia, OH 45385, **Business Phone:** (937)562-4000.

PORTER, GRADY J
Law enforcement officer. **Personal:** Born Sep 1, 1918, Carrollton, GA; son of James and Amandie; married Marcella M Larriere; children: Liliane, J Anthony, Sylviane & Patricia. **Career:** Dem Ward Chmn, 4 yrs; State Conv, delegate, 30 yrs; Oldsmobile Gen Motors Corp, employee; Ingham Co, comnr, 1967-; Law & Cts Comn, chmn pro-tem; Ingham County, bd comnr, chmn; City Lansing, police comnr, currently. **Orgs:** Chmn, Fair Prac Anti-Discrim Com Local 652 UAW; chmn, Local 652 UAW, 1952-54; transp officer, US Zone Germany UNRRA & ORT, 1945-48; Mich Asn Co; NACO; Capitol Lodge AF & AM Prince Hall; life mem, Nat Asn Advan Colored People; Union Baptist Ch; Boy Scouts; Urban League; Lansing Human Rel Community, 1952-53; spl comm Sch Needs & Sights, 1953; NABCO; chmn, Laymen League Union Baptist Church; mall adv bd Mayor comt; br treas, 4 yrs, Mich State Conf; bd mem, RSVP Lansing; Block Develop Comn, Capital Area, West Lansing; VAW; PTA; KDP. **Honors/Awds:** Nominated Outstanding Man of Year, 1966; Fredrick Douglass Award, 1986; Outstanding Community Service Award, Nat Asn Advan Colored People; Ingham County Bd Comnr Service Award, 1988; Distinguished Service Award, Nat Asn Black County Officials, 1990. **Special Achievements:** First person in State of MI to use civil rights legislations, 1948;Ingham County Bldg, Lansing, Mich, renamed in honor for outstanding contributions to cot by Ingham County Bd CMSers, 1992; first Black Unit CHP, Local 652 UAW Oldsmobile, Fair Practice Comm; Graduation Class Speaker, Sexton High School Breslin Center MSU, 1995. **Military Serv:** AUS, S/Sgt, four invasions, five battle stars, 1941-45. **Home Phone:** (517)487-9422.

PORTER, BISHOP HENRY LEE
Bishop. **Personal:** Born Jan 2, 1948, Sarasota, FL; son of Lee Ernest and Hazel Elkins; married Cynthia E Johnson; children: Henry, Etienne Jaberly, Zacchur Chalome & Tsadok Hazel. **Educ:** Fla Agr & Mech Univ, BS, 1969; Yale Univ, doctoral studies, PhD Math, 1971. **Career:** Westcoast Ctr Human Develop, founder, 1971; Westcoast Gospel Chorus Fla, founder, 1969; Fla Agr & Mech Univ, prof, math, 1973-75; Henry L Porter Evangelistic Asn, pres, founder, 1971-; Westcoast Sch Human Develop, prin, founder, 1981-; Trinity Col Ministerial Arts, vis prof, 1985-; Westcoast Magazine, Publisher, 2003-; Black Action Magazine, publisher, 1986-; Henry L. Porter Nursery Primary Sch, Takum, Nigeria, W Africa, 1990-; Westcoast Theol Sem, pres, 1989-; HL Porter Sch of music, pres, currently. **Orgs:** Ivy League Club Sarasota; life mem, Grand Chap Kappa Alpha Psi Fraternity, 1967-, pres, 1968-69; pres, Alpha Kappa Mu Nat Hon Soc, 1968-69; Am Asn Univ Profs, 1973-; Math Asn Am, 1973-; Yale Club Sun Coast, 1989-; bd mem, Bobby Jones Gospel, 1989; silver life mem, Nat Asn Advan Colored People; Nat Acad Recording Arts & Sci Grammy; Gospel Music Asn; bd mem, Adv Bd Educ Nigeria, 1993. **Honors/Awds:** Harvard Prize Book, Harvard Univ, 1964; Scholar of the Year, Alpha Kappa Mu, 1968; Doctoral Fellowship in Mathematics, Ford Found, 1969; one of The 100 Most Influential People in Sarasota, Sarasota Magazine, 1993, 2002; Men Give Back to the Community, Ebony Man Magazine, 1993; Nat Asn for Advancement of Colored People Freedom Award, 1999; Commendation from Governor Jeb Bush of Florida, 1999; White House performance, Wash, DC, 2000; Governor's Point of Light Award, 2002; Henry Porter & The Love Campaign; Florida Gospel Music Hall of Fame, 2003; The Gospel Awards; Henry L Porter Award 2003; Broadcasters Hall of Fame, Akron, OH, 2004; Sarasota Hall of Fame, 2004; The Golden Gavel Award, Sarasota Herald Tribune; Honorary Degrees, United Bible Col, 1986; Honarary Degreees, Trinity Col Ministerial Arts, 1989. **Special Achievements:** Cover Story, The Master's Touch, Charisma Magazine, May, 1981; Manuals: "How to Start a Prayer Group" 1991; "Africa Alive" video 1993, "Forgiveness Manual" 1990, "Duties of an Assistant" 1991; featured: Westcoast School for Human Development, "Street Stories with Ed Bradley," CBS-TV 1993; Poerty Books: Therapy 1990, Faces of Love 1990; Books: Child of the Thought 1989, Healing, A Gift from God1988, Seasons of the Rains 1999; Higher Thoughts and Peaceful Ways 1990; Composed over 2000 songs; Recorded 17 Albums/DVDs; Senate Advisory Board on Education, Federal Republic of Nigeria, 1992; Visiting Professor, Trinity College of Ministerial Arts 1992-; Television Broadcast, "Henry Porter and the Love Campaign"; Intl Lusanne Conference of Upcoming Christian Leaders, US Delegate to Singapore, 1988. **Business Addr:** Founder, President, Henry L Porter Evangelistic Assn, Westcoast Ctr, PO Box 49168, Sarasota, FL 34230 -616, **Business Phone:** (941)365-7543.

PORTER, JOHN T
Executive, vice president (organization). **Personal:** Born Feb 21, 1941, Brady, TX; children: John Jr & Christian (deceased). **Educ:** Ill Col, BA, 1968; Sangamon State Univ, MA, 1971. **Career:** Executive, vice president (retired); Ill Bell Telephone Co, dist mgr training, 1979-80, dist mgr, 1980-90, dir, human resources, 1990-91; Power Process Engineering, vpres, gen mgr. **Orgs:** Mem Disabled Am Veterans, 1963-; pres, Hope Sch, 1975-81; Chairperson, Ill Planning Coun on Developmental Disabilities, 1984-; bd mem, Ill State Asn Retd Citizens, 1984-; bd mem, Ill Self Sufficiency Trust, 1989-; bd mem, The Hope Sch Trust, 1989-; Nat Asn Developmental Disability Councils, 1994. **Military Serv:** USY, sargent, 3yrs. **Home Addr:** 190 S Wood Dale Rd Suite 905, Wood Dale, IL 60191.

PORTER, DR. JOHN W
Administrator. **Personal:** Born Aug 13, 1931, Ft Wayne, IN; son of James and Ola Mae; widowed. **Educ:** Albion Col, Albion, Mich, BA, 1953; Mich State Univ, E Lansing, Mich, MA, 1957, PhD, 1962. **Career:** Administrator (Retired). Lansing Pub Schs, Lansing Mich, counr 1953-58; Mich Dept Pub Instruction, consult, 1958-61; Mich Dept HE Asst Authority, dir, 1961-66; Mich Dept HE, assoc supt, 1966-69, state supt, 1969-79; Eastern Mich Univ, Ypsilanti Mich, pres, 1979-89; Detroit Pub Schs, gen supt, 1989-91; Urban Educ Alliance Inc, chief exec officer, 1989-2003. **Orgs:** Chmn, Nat Sel Comm for Outstanding HS Seniors sponsored by NASSP/Cent III 1981; chmn, AASCU Task Force on Excellence in Educ, 1983; chmn, Col Ent Exam Bd NY, 1984; app by Sec HEW Jos Califano Nat Adv Counc on Soc Svcs; chmn, Am Assoc State Cols & Univs Task Force on Excellence in Educ, 1984-86; Mich Counc for the Humanities; holiday commn, Mich Martin Luther King 1986; Nat Commn for Coop Educ, 1986, Governor's Blue Ribbon Commn on Welfare Reform, 1986-87; vice chmn, Nat Commn on the Future of State Cols & Univs 1986; life mem, NCP. **Honors/Awds:** 'Marcus Foster Distinguished Educator Award', Nat Alliance Black Sch Educrs' Conv, 1979; Cert Recog Alpha Kappa Alpha Sorority Eastern Mich Univ, 1979; State Admin Bd Ten-Year Serv Resolu State Cap Lansing, Mich 1979; Educator of the Decade Award Mich Asn State & Fed Prog Spec, 1979; 'Michigan Public School of Certificate Award', Pontiac Pub Sch, 1979; Res of Serv as Supt of Pub Instr Metro Detroit Alliance of Black Sch Educators 1979; Anthony Wayne Award, Co Educ, Wayne State Univ, 1979; Distinguished Alumni Award Mich State Univ, 1979; Recong Award for Contrib to Educ Wayne Cnty Comm Col, 1979; Momento for Serv as Supt Pub Inst Col Educ Alumni Asn Wayne St Univ, 1979; Cert Commendation Educ Serv Award Mich Cong Parents Teachers and Studs, 1979; President's Award as Distinguished Educr Nat Alliance Black Sch Educrs, 1977; Mich Edn Hall of Fame, inductee, 1992, Greater Detroit COC, Summit Awd, 1991; Mich State COC, Dist Svc & Lead Awd, 1991-; Tuskeegee Airmen, Dist Svc Awd, 1991; Albion CLG, Lifetime Achievement Award, 2003. **Special Achievements:** Numerous publications include: "Better Education Through Accountability, Research, Program Budgeting," Michigan Challenge, 1973; "Education, The Challenging Frontier," Colorado Jour Educ Res, 1976; "Why Minimum Competency Now?" JC Penney Forum, 1980; "The Counselor as Educationalist," The Personnel and Guidance Journal, 1982; John W. Porter Disting Chair endowed at East Mich Univ, 1999, Col Educ bldg named for him, 1999.

PORTER, KARL HAMPTON
Musician, conductor (music), educator. **Personal:** Born Apr 25, 1939, Pittsburgh, PA; son of Reginald and Naomi Arzetta; divorced; children: Marc, Turin, Nadia, Kenneth, Michael, Kelly, Kevin & Elizabeth. **Educ:** Carnegie-Mellon; Peabody Conserv; Juilliard Sch Music; Domaine Sch Conductors; Fordham Univ; State Univ New York, 1987. **Career:** Univ Denver, instr, 1963-64; Denver Symphony Orchestra, 1963-64; Gil EvansBand, 1967-69; Harlem Youth Symphony, 1968; Harlem Philharmonic Orchestra, 1969-; Newark Community Arts Ctr, teacher, 1969-71; Woodwind LI Inst Music, instr, 1969-75; New Breed Brass Ensemble, Harlem String Quartet, Harlem Woodwind Quintet, 1970; BMI Composers Competition, judge, 1970-74; New York Tech Col, instr, 1972-90; Finale Productions, pres; Baltimore Sym, conductor, 1971-72; Massapequa Sym, conductor, 1975-78; Park W Sym, conductor; Harlem Philharmonic, conductor; NYCTC/CUNY, instr; Josephine Baker, music dir & conductor, 1974; Harlem Music Soc, dir, 1980-91; ColNew Rochelle, instr, 1980; St Thomas Apostle, choir dir, 1988-99; NY Coun Arts, consult, 1990-99; freelance bassoonist & guest conductor, currently. **Orgs:** Dance Theatre Harlem, 1971-78; Sickle Cell, 1970-; Arts & Letters, 1974-; pres, Finale Prods, 1978-87; coach, NAACP, Act-So, 1988-2001. **Honors/Awds:** Martha Baird Rockefeller Grant, 1969; Nat Endowment Grant, 1970. **Special Achievements:** First Black bassoonist to perform with a major orchestra. **Home Addr:** 425 Cent Pk W, New York, NY 10025. **Business Addr:** Bassoonist, Conductor, 425 Cent Pk W, New York, NY 10025, **Business Phone:** (212)865-5280.

PORTER, REV. DR. KWAME JOHN R.
Clergy. **Personal:** Born Apr 2, 1932, Mineral Springs, AR; married June Carol McIntosh; children: John Thomas, Joseph Dubois, Julia Magdilene, Jessica Retha, Jorja Angela, Jerrianne Carol. **Educ:** IO Wesleyan Col, BA, 1959; Garrett Evan Theol Sem, MDiv, 1962; Union Grad Sch, PhD, 1975. **Career:** Christ United Meth Ch, pastor, 1962-71 & 1979-95; Urban Young Life, vpres, 1974-79; Chicago Ctr Black Religious Studies, dir, 1971-74; Sch Human Dignity, dir, 1967-70; Fel United Methodist Church, pastor, 1996-; Nat Urban Black Church Growth Inst, Chicago, dean. **Orgs:** Stud Asn Garrett Theol Sem, 1961; founding mem, Oper Breadbasket PUSH, 1966; Garrett Theol Sem, adj prof; Int Black Writers, 1980; pres, community trainer, JCPT/CAPS, Chicago Alliance Neighborhood Safety, 1995-96. **Honors/Awds:** Pub book "Dating Habits of Young Black Ams" 1979; pub articles best black sermons Vol II Judson Press, 1979; pub articles Metro Ministry David C Cook Pub, 1979; Three awards for work in 7th District's CAPS projects; Alumnus of the year, 1996 Iowa Wesleyan Col, 1994-95. **Special Achievements:** Author, "The Dating Habits of Young Black Americas," 1979; Res writer, proposal develr, chair, Englewood's New Village, EZEC proj, 1994-95; Pending publications "Black Male Violence," 1997; "How Blackfolk and Others Die," 1997; "Basic Training Manual for 21st Century Christians". **Military Serv:** AUS, sergeant, 1954-57. **Business Addr:** Pastor, Fel United Methodist Church, 447 W 120th St, Chicago, IL 60628.*

PORTER, LINSEY
Mayor. **Personal:** Born Jan 1, 1954?; married Patricia. **Career:** Colonial Life & Accident Ins Co, sales dir; City Highland Pk, councilman, 1983-87, coun pres, 1987-91, mayor, 1991-2002. *

PORTER, LIONEL
Executive. **Personal:** Born Jan 26, 1943, Canton, MS. **Educ:** IN State Univ, BA, 1966; Univ CT, MA, ABD, 1975, JD, 1985. **Career:** Arsenal Tech HS, eng teacher, 1966-68; Aetna Life & Casualty, mgt trainee, 1968-69; Hartford Pub HS; eng teacher, 1969-70; Univ Hartford, instr & am lit, 1975-78; Univ Conn Health Ctr, title XX cons, trng dir, 1978-. **Orgs:** Vp Blue Hills Civic Assoc, 1978-80; participant, Leadership Greater Hartford, 1980-81; bd mem, Community Coun Capitol Reg, 1981-82, Am Heart Assoc, 1984-. **Honors/Awds:** Outstanding Young Men in America Award; EPDA Fellowship, Univ CT, 1970-75.

PORTER, MIA LACHONE
Computer scientist. **Personal:** Born Jan 21, 1965, Birmingham, AL; daughter of John T and Dorothy Rogers. **Educ:** Univ Ala, Birmingham, attended 1985; Ala State Univ, BS, 1988; Samford Univ, attended 1991. **Career:** Southern Co Servs, client comput analyst I, currently. **Orgs:** Alpha Kappa Alpha Sorority Inc, 1987-; Alpha Kappa Psi Prof bus Fraternity, 1988; Nat Mgt Asn, 1989-; fin secy, Am Asn Blacks Energy, 1990-91. **Business Phone:** (404)668-4523.

PORTER, MICHAEL ANTHONY
Engineer. **Personal:** Born Sep 4, 1968, Bronx, NY; son of Ryland and Delrose; married Tanya, Jul 28, 1990. **Educ:** Howard Univ, BSME, 1993. **Career:** Ford Motor Co, production engr, 1987-91; Environ Protection Agency, envr engr, 1992-93; Martin Marietta Control Systems, product design engr, 1993-. **Orgs:** Prof advisor, Nat Soc Black Engrs, 1992-; chmn, Engineering Explorer Post, 1993-. **Home Addr:** 921 Lehigh Dr, Vestal, NY 13850. **Business Phone:** (607)770-2100.

PORTER, MICHAEL C
Vice president (Organization). **Educ:** Univ Mich, Dearborn, BBA, mkt; Univ Detroit, MBA, finance. **Career:** Am Motors Corp, mkt staff; Stroh Brewery Co, staff, 1983-94; vpres mkt, 1990-94; McCann-Erickson, Detroit, sr vpres, 1994-97; DTE Energy Co, vpres corp commun, 1997-. **Orgs:** DTE Energy Found; Children's Hosp Mich; Detroit Pub TV; dir, Univ Detroit, Jesuit High Sch;

Dean's Adv Coun, Univ Mich, Dearborn Sch Mgt; Citizen's Adv Coun, Univ Mich, Dearborn; Commun Adv Coun, Nuclear Energy Inst; bd dir, Metrop Affairs Coalition. **Business Addr:** Vice President of Corporate Communications, DTE Energy Company, 2000 2nd Ave, Detroit, MI 48226-1279, **Business Phone:** (313)235-4000.

PORTER, MICHAEL LEROY
Administrator. **Personal:** Born Nov 23, 1947, Newport News, VA; son of Doretha Bradley and Leroy. **Educ:** VA State Univ, BA, (hon) sociology 1969; Atlanta Univ, MA, hist 1972; Leonardo DaVinci Acad, Rome, Italy, MCP Contem 1984; Emory Univ, PhD hist/Amer studies 1974; Sorbonne Univ, postdoctorate, hist, Paris France, 1979; Harvard Univ, further study, 1980; Thomas Nelson Community Col, cert crim justice 1981; US Armed Forces Staff Col, Norfolk VA, US Pres Appt, 1987. **Career:** WA State Univ, asst prof of history, black studies prog 1974-75; Mohegan Comm Col, Dept History lectr 1975-76; Newport News VA, asst educ coordr, educ comp, target proj prog 1977; Hampton Univ, asst prof history 1977-80; NC Mutual Ins Co, life ins underwriter 1980-81; Mullins Prot Serv VA Bch, private investigator, 1981-83; Amer Biographical Inst Raleigh, media free-lancer 1984-85, publications dir/deputy governor 1985-; Old Dominion Univ, Norfolk VA, consultant 1985; Michael Porter Enterprises INT, prs, fdr, 1985-88; Int Biographical Ctr, Cambridge England, dep dir gen, 1986. **Orgs:** Life patron World Inst of Achievement 1985; curator "Michael L Porter Historical & Literary Collection"; World Literary Acad 1984-85; World Biographical Hall of Fame 1985; Republican Ntl Convention, 1988; FDL Braintrust, 1990; Intl Advisory CNL, 1989-99; African American Hall of Fame, 1994; Elite INT, 1992; bd of governors, Amer Biog Inst, 1986; Phi Beta Kappa; Intl Academy of Intellectuals, 1993; Famous Poet's Society, 1996; chr, US Selective Service Bd 32, 1986-92; chief delegate, Intl Congress on Arts & Commun, Nairobi, Kenya, 1990; Speaker's Circle, 2000; Schomburg SOC, 2000; Outstanding People of the 20th Century, 1999; Intl Honor SOC, 2002; Honors, Supria Omnia, 2002; Arte & Labore, 2002; World Peace & Diplomacy Forum, 2003; Colonial Williamsburg Burgesses, mem, 2003; Intl Biographical Ctr, vice-counsel, United Cultural Convention, secty general, 2002-05. **Honors/Awds:** 1st Black Concert Pianist to play Carnegie Hall, 1963; Lyon Dissertation Prize, 1974; Ebony Magazine, Eligible Bachelor, 1975; Jet Magazine Society World, 1978; US Presidential Inauguration, Guest of Honor, 1989; Outstanding Black, 1992; Hero, 1992; International Honors Cup, 1992; Abira Genius Grant, 1992; World Greetings, 1992; Pioneer Award, 1992; Great American, 1991; World Intellectual, 1993; Golden Academy Award, 1991; One of 500 Leaders of Influence in the 20th Century; Intl Hall of Leaders, Amer Biographical Inst, 1988; porter streets: Chicago, New York City, Richmond Virginia, Hong Kong China, SAO Paulo, Brazil; San Juan, Pureto Rico; participant (exhibit), DuSable Museum of Black History, 1988; honoree, Intl Exhibit, Singapore, Malaysia, 1988; Outstanding Man of the World, Ormiston Palace, Tasmania, Australia, 1989; Exhibit, Intl Music Museum, London, ENG, 1989; Poetry Reading, Royal Palace, Lisbon, Portugal, 1998; Michael Porter Poetry Exhibit, Internet Intl Poetry Hall of Fame, 1997-02; honoree, poetry recognition, Pope Paul VI, Krakow, Poland, 2002; Lecture, Oxford Univ, Oxford, ENG, 1997; Famous Quote, Leningrad, Russia, 1998; 20th Century Award for Achievement, 1990; 21st Century Gallery of Achievement, Black History Maker, 1992; International Man of the Year, 1992; Most Admired Person of the Decade, 1990-99; Recipient, Grant For Exceptionally Gifted Poets, 1998; NTL Science Foundation, Loner of Appreciation, 2003; US Congress, Certificate of Appreciation, 1991; Atlanta African American Festival, Honoree, 1992; Honorary US Congressman, 1993; Hampton History Center, Historical Marker, 1992; Appearances before US President's Council of Economic Advisors & Senate Finance Committee, 1992; Honorary Knighthood, 1997; US Presidential Medal of Freedom, 1993; Prize Winner, International Golf Classic, Bermuda UPA Masters, 1995; US Presidential Legion of Merit, 1996; Great Thinker, 1999; Living Legends Awd, 2003; Selected Works: Black Atlanta, 1974; Read Between the Lines, 1985; Outstanding Speaker/Golden Gavel, 2000; honoree, Millenium Celebration Giza, Egypt, 2000; honoree, VA General Assembly, 2000; Intl Ambassador of Goodwill, 2003; ABI World Laureate, 2003; Great honoree, 40th Anniversary March on Wash, DC, 2003; Intl Peace Prize, 2002; 100 Most Intriguing People of 2003; Minds of The 21st Century. **Special Achievements:** Television Programs: Cited On World News Tonight; Hard Copy; 60 Minutes; Current Affairs; Entertainment Tonight; 27th American Music Awards; CBS Evening News; The Remarkable Journey; Journey of African American Athelete, 1995; Eve's Bayou, 1997; 4 Little Girls; Kennedy Center Honors, 1998; NBC Nightly News; Miss World Pagent, 2002; People In The News, 2003; Soul Train, 2003; Film: The Making of Black Atlanta, 1974; 1st Black Elected to Intl Academy of Intellectuals, Paris, France, 1993; Radio: Empire State Bldg Broadcasting Ctr, WRIN, 1997; Radio FM 95.7, Black Man Legacy of Achievement, 2003; Publications: Ebony, Jet, Intl, Digest, Talent; Contemporary Authors; Directory of American Scholars. **Military Serv:** USY pfc, 1969-71; Nat Defense Medal, 1971; Cert of Appreciation, Vietnam Vets Nat Medal, 1986; Meritorious Commendation, Sec, of Navy, 1991; Good Conduct Medal, 1971; cert of Recognition, Sec of Defense, 2000. **Home Addr:** 3 Adrian Cir, Hampton, VA 23669-3814. **Business Phone:** (757)722-6815.*

PORTER, RUFUS
Football player. **Personal:** Born May 18, 1965, Amite, LA; married Anita; children: Atina & Rufus Jr. **Educ:** Southern Univ. **Career:** Football player (retired); Seattle Sea hawks, linebacker, 1988-94; New Orleans Saints, 1995-96; Tampa Bay Buccaneers, 1997. **Honors/Awds:** Pro Bowl, 1988 & 1989.

PORTER, DR. SHIKANA TEMILLE
Association executive. **Educ:** Calif Sch Prof Psychol, San Diego, PhD, MA; San Diego State Univ, bachelor degree; Conn Valley Hosp, Middletown, CT, APA. **Career:** Licensed Clin Psychologist; Saint John's Child & Family Develop Center's APA-Accredited Psychol Training Prog, CA, dir; Calif State Univ, Stanislaus, dir coun servs; Univ Southern Calif, dir disability servs & progs; USC Student Coun Ctr, sr staff psychologist; USC Student Coun Ctr, staff psychologist; San Diego State Univ, Depts Africana Studies, Women's Studies, lectr; Whittier Col Student Coun Servs, dir, currently; Positive Action Coun Serv, staff. **Business Addr:** Director, Whittier College Student Counseling Services, 13406 E Philadelphia, PO Box 634, Whittier, CA 90608-4413, **Business Phone:** (562)907-4239.

PORTER, TERRY
Basketball player, basketball coach. **Personal:** Born Apr 8, 1963, Milwaukee, WI. **Educ:** Univ Wis, Stevens Point, attended 1985. **Career:** Basketball player (retired), Basketball coach; Portland Trail Blazers, guard, 1985-95; Minn Timber wolves, 1995-98; Miami Heat, 1998-99; San Antonio Spurs, guard (retired), 1999-2002; Sacramento Kings, asst coach,2002-03; Milwaukee Bucks, head coach, 2003-05; Detroit Pistons, asst coach, head coach, 2006-07; Phoenix suns, head coach, 2008-09. **Orgs:** Proj Grad; Smart Moves; Sixth Man Found; Boys & Girls Club. **Honors/Awds:** J Walter Kennedy Citizenship Award, 1993. **Special Achievements:** First black head coach for Milwaukee Bucks.

PORTER-ESMAILPOUR, CAROL
Graphic artist. **Personal:** Born Mar 4, 1948, Washington, DC; daughter of Wiley Waverly and Alma Dodson; married Assad Esmailpour, Jan 2, 1998. **Educ:** Howard Univ, attended 1967; Independent Study Tour European Capitals, 1970; Moore Col Art, BFA, 1971; Sterling Inst, 1975; Hartford Grad Ctr, 1976; Poynter Inst Media Studies, 1986; Sch Visual Arts; Corcoran Sch Art; Torpedo Factory Art Ctr. **Career:** WJLA-TV7 Wash, graphic artist, 1971-73; WBBM-TV2 Chicago, graphic artist, 1973-75; WFSB-TV3 Hartford, art dir, 1975-77; WDVM-TV9, asst art dir, graphic designer, 1977-79; Needham Harper & Steers Advertising Falls Church, art dir, graphic designer, 1979-80; Ketchum Advertising, art dir, 1984-85; Wash Post, graphic designer, 1980-84, 1985-. **Orgs:** Alpha Kappa Alpha Sor; sec, Nat Acad TV Arts & Scis; Capital Press Club; volunteer Family Place; freelance design, art dir; Speakers Bureau Wash Post; Broadcast Designers Assoc; Soc Newspaper Design; second vpres, Capital Press Club, 1987-89; moderator, participant, Howard Univ Community Conference: workshop on careers in newspaper commun, 1988. **Honors/Awds:** Wash Art Dirs Club Awds Merit, 1973, 1979, 1981, 1983; Emmy Award Outstanding Individual Achievement in Scenic Design, 1972; Awards Excellence Chicago '75 Communs Collaborative Show for TV Spots, 1975; bd govs, Wash Chap Nat Acad TV Arts and Scis, 1979; Award Merit Soc Newspaper Design, 1986; Award Excellence "Page Design," Print Magazine, 1988; Award Excellence "Portfolio of 6 Page Designs," Soc of Newspaper Design, 1989; Award of Excellence "Page Design" Wash Art Dirs Club, 1989; Award of Excellence "Portfolio Page Design," Soc Newspaper Design, 1990; Award of Excellence "Page Design," Wash Metro Art Dirs Club, 1990; Soc Newspaper Design, 2 Awards Excellence: "Portfolio of 6 Bus News Pages" and "Page Front Show Section," Bronze Award: "One Page Front," ("Summer"), Print Magazine Award: Award of Excellence for "Food" page for locally brewed beer ("Brewed Near Here"); Society of Newspaper Design Competition, Nat Design Contest, judge, 1993; Moore Col Art & Design, bd mgrs (appointed alumna), 1990-93, 1993-96; distinguished Alumna of the Year, Moore Col Art & Design, 2002; John Albano Memorial Grand Prize for Design, 2003. **Business Addr:** Graphic Designer, The Washington Post, 1150 15th St NW, Washington, DC 20071, **Business Phone:** (202)334-4551.

PORTIS, KATTIE HARMON (JESSIE KATE HARMON)
Association executive. **Personal:** Born Oct 28, 1942, Kinterbish, AL; married Jesse; children: Dawn, Luther, Torris, James, Faye & Raymond. **Educ:** Franconia Col, BA, 1976; Antioch Col, MA, Human Serv Mgt. **Career:** Women Inc, Dorchester, Mass, founder & exec dir; Concilio Drug Prog, counr, 1974; Stamford Outreach Proj Turnabout, 1973; First Residental Drug-Free Prog Women & C Abusing Alcohol Drugs, founder, 1973; Women & Aids Risk Network Proj, community coordr & founder, 1987-; New Eng Med Ctr, community coordr, 1992-97; Mass Sober Housing Corp, dir, currently. **Orgs:** Third World Womens Caucus, 1974; consult, Women & Health, 1975; Res & Demonstratn Proj, 1975; Treatmnt Conf Women, 1976; chmn, Boston Univ Screening Bd; Mayor Coord Coun Drug Abuse; Mass Comn C & Youth Adv Bd. **Honors/Awds:** Certificate, Yale Univ, 1973; Hero Award, Boston Parents Paper; Abigal Adams Award; Metro Boston Alive Leadership Award; Leadership Award, Dept Pub Health; Outstanding Service for Children, Off C. **Home Addr:** 31 Radcliff Rd, Hyde Park, MA 02136. **Business Addr:** Director, Massachusetts Sober Housing Corporation, PO Box 2230, Worcester, MA 01602-0013, **Business Phone:** (508)987-3388.

PORTLOCK, DR. CARVER A.
School administrator, executive. **Personal:** Born Jun 8, 1934, Muskogee, OK. **Educ:** Bethune Cookman Col, BA, relig & philos, 1955; Syracuse Univ, attended1957. **Career:** Administrator, Executive (retired): Bethune Cookman Col, asst instr speech & drama, 1955-56; Dade Cty Jvnl Miami, counr boys, 1959-61; CME Church Paine Col, admin asst, 1960-62; Nat Alumni Assoc & Bethune Cookman Col, exec sec, 1962-66; Smith Kline Corp, info servs coord, 1966-68, mgr community rels, 1968-88; Bethune-Cookman Col, Northeast Regional Off, dir, 1988, Nat Celebrity Series Event, narrator; Smithkline Corp, mgr. **Orgs:** Pres, Nat Alumni Asn & Bethune Cookman Col, 1982-84; mem bd dirs, Big Brother & Big Sister Asn, 1981-; Catholic and Diocese of Philadelphia; Omega Psi Phi Fraternity; life mem, B-CC Nat Alumni Asn; Bd Philadelphia Tribute Charities. **Honors/Awds:** Fund Achievement Award, United Negro Col, 1984; Community Service Award, Berean Inst, 1983; Professional Service Award, Crisis Intervention Network,1981; LLD, Bethune-Cookman Col, 1986; LHD, Orthodox Catholic Archdiocese Philadelphia, 1985; Mary McLeod Bethune Award; Merit Award, City of Philadelphia; Shaft of Light Award. **Military Serv:** AUS, 1957-59.

POSEY, ADA LOUISE
Government official. **Educ:** Carleton Col, BA, attended. **Career:** Prudential Ins Co, expense mgt & pension oper staff, 1978-85, internal auditing staff, 1985-89; Minn Mut, corp budgeting staff, 1989-93; The White House, Wash, assoc dir gen svcs, off admin, 1993-96, dep dir off admin, 1996-97, dir off admin, 1997-99; Off Nat Drug Control Policy, Wash, spl adv, 1999; US Dept Energy, Wash, sr policy adv, 1999-01; Posey Cons Group, pres, 2001-03; Raytheon Tech Svcs, dir diversity & compliance, 2003-. **Orgs:** Trustee, Carleton Col; Capital City Links Chap.

POSEY, BRUCE KEITH
Lawyer. **Personal:** Born Mar 22, 1952, Baton Rouge, LA. **Educ:** Univ Ore, BS, 1974; Univ Mich, JD, 1977. **Career:** US W Commun; Pacific NW Bell; Stoel Rives Boley Fraser & Wyse, atty, 1977-; Urban League Portland, dir, 1979-; Martin Luther King Jr Scholar Fund Ore, pres; iPass Inc, gen coun, sr vpres, secy, 2002-. **Orgs:** Am Civil Liberties Union; secy, Ore State Bar Affirmative Action Steering Comn; Asn Ore Black Lawyers. **Business Phone:** (650)232-4100.

POSEY, DEBORAH
Executive. **Personal:** Born Dec 16, 1949, Detroit, MI; daughter of James and Kathleen Parker; divorced; children: Kelly M McGee & Raymond Posey Jr. **Educ:** Wayne State Univ, BA, 1975. **Career:** Bus Communications, sales mgr, 1982-83; Frontier Communications, supvr customer serv, 1984-90, supvr credit collection, 1990-94, sr mgr credit collections, 1994-96, vpres credit & collections, rev protection, 1996-. **Orgs:** NACM, 1990-; WTDE; Nat Asn Toll Fraud mgrs.

POSEY, DR. EDWARD W
Psychiatrist. **Personal:** Born May 29, 1927, Youngstown, OH; son of Alex and Margie King; married Fanny Berryman; children: Bruce, Ada & Michael. **Educ:** Ohio State Univ, attended 1944-48; Meharry Med Col, MD, 1952; Univ Minn, psychiat, 1965. **Career:** Minneapolis VA Med Ctr, dir day hosp, 1965-71, chief psychiat serv, 1971-79, chief outpatient psychiat, 1979-; Univ Minn, psychiatrist, asst prof, 1965, emer psychiatrist, currently; pvt pract, currently. **Orgs:** Const Pilot City Health Ctr, 1969-; chmn, minority studies prog comm Univ Minn Med Sch, 1971-; Sigma Pi Phi; Nat Med Asn. **Honors/Awds:** examr, dipl Am Bd Psychiat, Neurol, 1968; Am Psychiat Asn, 1972. **Military Serv:** USNR, lt, 1953-55. **Home Addr:** 2808 W Highland Dr, Burnsville, MN 55337. **Business Addr:** Physician, 1313 Penn Ave N, Minneapolis, MN 55411, **Business Phone:** (612)302-4600.

POSEY, JEFF
Football player. **Personal:** Born Aug 14, 1975, Bassfield, MS. **Educ:** Univ Southern Miss. **Career:** Football player (retired), San Francisco 49ers, defensive end, 1998-2000; Carolina Panthers, 2001; Jacksonville Jaguars, defensive end, 2001; Houston Texans, defensive end, 2002; Buffalo Bills, line back, 2003-05; Wash Redskins, line back, 2006.

POSEY, JOHN R
Entrepreneur, educator, chief executive officer. **Personal:** Born Nov 17, 1953, Evanston, IL; son of John R Sr and Lois; married Margo, Sep 8, 1979; children: Mercedes. **Educ:** Dartmouth, BA, hist, 1975. **Career:** Fort Worth Mayor's Off Spec Events, dir mkt, 1984-87; Events Mkt & Mgt, pres, 1987-89; North HTH Corp, dir mkt, 1989-90; Fort Worth Black Chamber, exec dir, 1990-92; writer, consult, 1991-; AALR, founder, 1992-94; BSPIN Media

Group, chief exec officer & founder, 1998-; Urban Sports News, publ & chief exec officer, 2004-. **Orgs:** Founding mem, Freelance Writer's Network; Nat Press Photographer's Asn; Am Mgt Asn; Nat Asn Black Journalists; Fuji Prof Servs; Rotary Int; Am Mkt Asn; Tex Black Sports Hall Fame; Tex Photographic Soc; Dallas & Fort Worth Asn Black Communicators; Austin Writer's League; TCU Creative Writing Workshop. **Honors/Awds:** Outstanding Business and Professional Award, Dollars & Sense Mag; Special Recognition Award, Talented 10th Club; Honorary Citizen of Shelby County; Fellowship, Mag Publ Am; Certificate of Excellence, Commun Collaborative. **Special Achievements:** Co-ed: anthology, Kente Cloth; Curator & the Band Played on Photo Exhibition; Auth: more than 1300 articles, essays, short stories, including, Portraits of Excellence, "A Closed Society", A World of Fiction, 1993, 411; sports photographer, more than 750 published photo credits; Ed: Business Report newsletter; Creator of People's Law, a cable access TV show. **Business Addr:** Chief Executive Officer, Publisher, Urban Sports News, 14902 Preston Rd, Dallas, TX 75254, **Business Phone:** (214)929-8573.

POST, H CHRISTIAN. See PANDYA, HARISH C.

POSTELL-BOYD, GLORIA
Social worker. **Personal:** Born May 1, 1954, Detroit, MI; daughter of Charles and Jeanette; divorced; children: Charlene Lynette Boyd. **Educ:** Western Mich Univ, BA, 1975; MSW, 1977. **Career:** State Mich, social worker, 1977-. **Orgs:** Delta Sigma Theta, 1972. **Home Addr:** 17534 Edinborough, Detroit, MI 48219. **Business Addr:** Social Worker, State of Michigan, 2929 Russell, Detroit, MI 48207, **Business Phone:** (313)396-0414.

POSTEN, WILLIAM S
Judge. **Personal:** Born Mar 10, 1931, E Moline, IL; son of Aquilla Teague and Vernie Teague; married Pauline Ann; children: Karen, Scott, David, Elaine & Melissa. **Educ:** Minneapolis Col Law, BSL, 1953; William Mitchell Col Law, JD, 1959. **Career:** US Govt SS Admin, 1960-61, asst city atty, 1961-73; Hennepin Co, munic ct judge, 1973-76; Minneapolis Dist Ct, judge; pvt atty, currently. **Orgs:** Adv Bd, Turning Point; adv bd, Genesis II; adv bd, Salvation Army; MN & Hennepin Co Bar Asn; Am Asn Black Lawyers; Am Legis, Nat Asn Advan Colored People; Health & Welfare City; Metrop Minneapolis March Dimes. **Military Serv:** Mil Serv, 1953-55. **Business Phone:** (612)338-1553.

POSTON, CARL
Sports agent, lawyer. **Personal:** Born in Detroit, MI. **Educ:** Fisk Univ, BS, math & bus, 1977; Wayne State Univ, JD, 1981; Saginaw Valley Univ, MBA, 1981; New York Univ, LLM, 1983. **Career:** O'Melveny & Myers, atty; Howeter Corp, exec dir, pres oshobori div; McKenzie & Poston, managing partner; Professional Sports Planning Inc, chmn, currently. **Orgs:** Sports Lawyer Asn; Nat Bar Asn; Am Bar Asn; Omega Psi Phi Fraternity Inc. **Honors/Awds:** All-America Tennis Player, NCAA; American Jurisprudence Record in Contracts; Z Alexander Looby Award. **Business Addr:** Chairman, Professional Sports Planning Inc, 909 Fannin St Suite 2090, Houston, TX 77010, **Business Phone:** (713)659-2255.

POSTON, CARL C, JR.
Lawyer. **Personal:** Born Oct 13, 1921, Memphis, TN; married Thelma Kirkland; children: Carl, Keith, Kevin & Craig. **Educ:** LeMoyne Col, BA, 1942; Univ Training Ctr Florence Italy, 1945; Wayne State Univ, 1950. **Career:** Lawyer (retired); Human Rels, 1961-68; Asst Co Prosecutor, 1966-68; Civil Rights Referee, 1967-70; Saginaw City Coun, 1970-73; Mayor Pro Tem, 1971-73. **Honors/Awds:** Frontiersman of Year, 1968; Outstanding Service Award, 25 Yrs Serv OIC, Metropolitan Saginaw Inc, 1968-95. **Special Achievements:** Alpha Phi Alpha Fraternity; city rep, Saginaw Co Bd Supvr, 1960-66, 1968-70; Workmens Comp Sec, 1960; Negligence Sec, 1960-; pres, Saginaw Co Youth Protection Coun, 1962-; pres, Frontiers, 1963; vpres, Big Brothers, 1966-67; treas, OIC Metropolitan Saginaw, 1968; State Bar Econ Comt, 1969; Fraternities; Press Club; MI State Bar Grievence Referee, 1972; State Bar Legis Comt, 1972-73; Nat Asn Advan Colored People. **Military Serv:** AUS, sgt tech, 1943-46. **Home Phone:** (989)754-8798.

POSTON, KEVIN D
Sports agent, sports manager. **Personal:** Born in Saginaw, MI; married; children: 3. **Educ:** Fisk Univ, BA, bus admin, 1981; Tex Southern Univ, Thurgood Marshall Sch Law, JD. **Career:** Miller Canfield, atty; Miro, Miro & Weiner, partner & shareholder; Prof Sports Planning Inc, owner, pres & chief exec officer, currently. **Special Achievements:** Negotiated an unprecedented thirteen-year, $68 million dollar contract for Orlando Magic star Anfernee Hardaway. **Business Addr:** President, Chief Executive Officer, Professional Sports Planning Inc, 909 Fannin St, Houston, TX 77010, **Business Phone:** (713)659-2255.

POTTER, JAMIE
President (Organization), association executive. **Career:** Cut Core Demolition Inc, founder, currently. **Business Addr:** Founder, President, Cut Core Demolition Inc, 515 Montebello Way, Montebello, CA 90640, **Business Phone:** (323)722-1249.*

POTTER, JUDITH DIGGS
Educator. **Personal:** Born Jul 23, 1941, Norwood, MA; divorced; children: Wende Beth & Kimberly Ann. **Educ:** Lesley Col, BS, educ, 1964; Wheelock Col, MS, educ, 1977. **Career:** Boston Pub Schs, teacher, 1964-65; Medway Pub Sch, teacher, 1965-66; Brookline Headstart, teacher, 1968; Boston Pub Schs, teacher, 1968-. **Orgs:** Found secy & treas, Black Caucus Boston Teachers Union, 1966, 1978-83; deleg, MA Fed Teachers, Am Fed Teachers, 1977-85; deleg, Boston Labor Coun, Bldg Rep-Boston T Union, 1977-87; coordr, Try Arts & Chap 188 Boston Pub Sch, 1978-86; grad adv, Delta Sigma Theta Inc Boston Alumnae, 1980-81. **Honors/Awds:** Teacher of the Year, Boston Pub Schs, 1983.

POTTER, MYRTLE STEPHENS
Executive. **Personal:** Born Sep 28, 1958, Las Cruces, NM; daughter of Albert and Allene Baker; married James; children: Jamison & Lauren Elizabeth. **Educ:** Univ Chicago, Chicago, Ill, AB, 1980. **Career:** Executive (retired); Int Bus Mach, mkt intern, 1979-80; Procter & Gamble, sales rep, 1980-81, dist sales training mgr, 1981-82; Merck Sharp & Dohme, sales rep, 1982-84, mkt analyst, 1984-85, training & planning mgr, 1985-86, field meeting serv mgr, 1986-87, dist sales mgr, 1987-89, prod mgr, 1989-90; Astra/Merck affairs, dir, 1990-92, sr dir sales planning, sr dir mkt planning, 1992-93, vpres NE region bus group, human health div, 1993-96; Bristol-Myers Squibb, vpres strategy & econs, 1996-97, group vpres worldwide mkt & sales force effectiveness, 1997, vpres worldwide meds group, 1997-98, US Cardiovascular Metabolics, sr vpres sales, 1998, pres, 1998-2000; Genentech, chief operating officer, exec vpres comm operations, exec comt mem, 2000, pres, 2005. **Orgs:** Philadelphia Urban League, 1988-96; bd trustees, Del Valley Boys & Girls Club, 1996-00; indust fac assoc, Univ Mich Bus Sch, 1996-2000; bd dirs, Calif Healthcare Inst, 2002-; adv bd, Healthcare Bus Women's Asn, 2003-; Citizens Fin Accountability Oversight Comt, currently. **Honors/Awds:** Chairman's Award, Merck; Leadership Development Award, Briston Myers Squibb; Woman of the Year, HBA, 2000; ranked 18 among Americas Most Powerful Black Executives, Fortune, 2003; Woman of the Year, Am Diabetes Asn, 2006. **Special Achievements:** First African American female president of a major pharmaceutical company. **Business Addr:** Member, Citizens Financial Accountability Oversight Committee, PO Box 942850, Sacramento, CA 94250-5872, **Business Phone:** (916)322-4224.*

POTTINGER, ALBERT A.
Lawyer. **Personal:** Born Apr 24, 1928, Topeka, KS; married Delores Johnson. **Educ:** Washburn Munic Univ, BBA, 1951; Cleveland St Law Sch, LLB, 1959. **Career:** City Cleveland, coun man, 1968-69, relocator, property mgr, 1968-69, 1st asst prosecutor, 1964-65, atty pvt pract, currently. **Orgs:** Bd trustee, C Serv; Cath Big Bros; Cath Charities; Harvard-Lee Comm Serv. **Business Addr:** Attorney, 16106 Delrey Ave, Cleveland, OH 44128.*

POTTS, ROOSEVELT BERNARD
Football player. **Personal:** Born Jan 8, 1971, Rayville, LA; married Tenisha; children: Taylor, Ragan & Roosevelt Jr. **Educ:** Northeast La Univ. **Career:** Football player (retired); Indianapolis Colts, running back, 1993-97; Miami Dolphins, 1997; Baltimore Ravens, 1998; Memphis Maniax, 2000-. **Honors/Awds:** Offensive Player of the Year, Thundering Herd Fan Club.

POTTS, SAMMIE
School administrator. **Career:** Mary Holmes Col, West Point MS, pres. **Business Addr:** President, Mary Holmes College, PO Drawer 1257, West Point, MS 28025.

POUNDER, C. C. H. (CAROL CHRISTINE HILARIA POUNDER)
Actor. **Personal:** Born Dec 25, 1952, Georgetown, Guyana; daughter of Ronald Urlington (deceased) and Betsy Enid Arnella James; married Boubacar Kone, Jan 1, 1991. **Educ:** Ithaca Col, BFA, 1975. **Career:** Films: All That Jazz, 1979; Union City, 1980; I'm Dancing as Fast as ICan, 1982; Prizzi's Honor, 1985; Out of Rosenheim, 1987; Postcards From the Edge, 1990; The Importance of Being Earnest, 1992; Benny & Joon, 1993;Sliver, 1993; Robocop 3, 1993; Tales from the Crypt: Demon Knight, 1995;Face/Off, 1997; Blossoms & Veils, 1998; Melting Pot, 1998; End of Days,1999; Things Behind the Sun, 2001; The Big Day, 2001; Tet Grenne, 2002;Baby of the Family, 2002; Rain, 2008; Orphan, 2009. TV series: "Hill Street Blues", 1981-86; Booker, 1984; Go Tell It on the Mountain, 1985; "The Atlanta Child Murders", 1985; "Cagney & Lacey", 1986; Valerie", 1986; As Summers Die, 1986; Resting Place, 1986; If Tomorrow Comes", 1986; "Women in Prison", 1987; Run Till You Fall, 1988; No Place Like Home, 1989; Third Degree Burn, 1989; Common Ground, 1990; Murder in Mississippi, 1990; "Cop Rock", 1990; Psycho IV: The Beginning, 1990; "Return to Lonesome Dove",1993; The Disappearance of Christina, 1993; For Their Own Good, 1993; The Ernest Green Story, 1993; "Biker Mice from Mars", 1993; "ER", 1994-97; Jack Reed: One of Our Own, 1995; "Living Single", 1995; White Dwarf, 1995; Zooman, 1995; "Millennium", 1996-98; If These Walls Could Talk, 1996; AllShe Ever Wanted, 1996; Things That Go Bump, 1997; House of Frankenstein,1997; Final Justice, 1998; Little Girl Fly Away, 1998; A Touch of Hope,1999; "Detention", 1999; Funny Valentines, 1999; To Serve & Protect, 1999;Net Force, 1999; "Batman Beyond", 1999; Disappearing Acts, 2000; CoraUnashamed, 2000; "The Outer Limits", 2000; "Rude Awakening", 2000; "The West Wing", 2000; "Static Shock", 2000-01; "Law & Order: Special Victims Unit", 2001-05; "Strong Medicine", 2001; Boycott, 2001; The Practice,2001; "The District", 2001; "For the People", 2002; "The Shield", 2002-08;"Girlfriends", 2004; Redemption: The Stan Tookie Williams Story, 2004;"Justice League", 2004-06; "Numb3rs", 2005; "W.I.T.C.H.", 2006; "American Masters", 2007; "The Tower", 2008; "Law & Order: Special Victims Unit" (4 episodes), 2001-08; "The No. 1 Ladies' Detective Agency", 2009; "The Boy with an African Heart", 2009; "Warehouse 13", 2009; "11-04-08: The Day of Change", 2009. **Orgs:** Artists for a New South Africa, 1989. **Honors/Awds:** Golden Satellite Award, 2003 & 2004; Black Reel Award, 2005. **Business Addr:** Actress, c/o Susan Smith & Associates, 121 N San Vicente Blvd, Beverly Hills, CA 90211, **Business Phone:** (213)852-4777.*

POUNDER, CAROL CHRISTINE HILARIA. See POUNDER, C. C. H.

POUNDS, DR. AUGUSTINE WRIGHT
College administrator. **Personal:** Born Jul 20, 1936, Wadley, AL; daughter of Cortelyou Busbee and Flossie Wilkes; married Russell G Pounds, Jul 4, 1981; children: Karen Williams & Georgina Young. **Educ:** Pontiac Bus Inst, attended 1960; Oakland Community Col, attended 1965; Oakland Univ, BA, 1973, MA, 1975; Iowa State Univ, PhD, 1980. **Career:** Oakland Univ, consult black cult ctr, 1966-68, admin asst to vpres urban affairs, 1968-71, asst dir community serv, 1971-73, asst dir stud ctr, 1973-75; Iowa State Univ, asst dir minority stud affairs, 1975-76, from asst dean stud life to dean stud life, 1976-84; Univ Zambia, vis prof, 1984; Murray State Univ, vpres stud develop, 1988-90; Anne Arundel Community Col, col develop & intercollegiate athletics, vpres stud servs, 1990-95, vpres emer, currently. **Orgs:** White House Conf Families, Des Moines, IA, 1980; consult evaluator, N Cent Asn Col & Schs, 1987; bd mem, Iowa Stud Personnel Jour, 1987-; chair exec comt, ACPA/CMA, 1988-89; vpres Asn rels, pres, Nat Asn Women Deans, Adminr & Counselors, 1993-94; vpres, Women's Action Coalition, 2000-02; chair, Am Asn Univ Women, Women Color Caucus, 2001-; Am Human Rels Comn; bd mem, United Way Ames, Am Col Personnel Asn; adv bd, Fine Arts Inst Region V US Off Educ; staff adv, Asn Black Studies; City Human Rel Comn; bd mem, Family Serv Oakland Co; vpres, Oakland Co Nat Asn Advan Colored People; bd mem, New Horizons Oakland Co; Am Coun Educ, Nat Identification Prog, IA; Stud Personnel Asn; Nat Asn Stud Personnel Adminr; admin bd, All Univ Community Coun; founding co-chair, Iowa State Univ birthday celebration comn, Martin Luther King Jr; Nat Asn Women Deans Admin & Counrs; Alumni Bd Govs, Iowa State Univ; pres, AAUW Legal Advocacy Comn. **Honors/Awds:** Certificate of Appreciation Citation, Finance Study Comn, City Pontiac Sch Dist, 1968; Citizen of Year, Oakland Co Ministerial Asn, 1970; Service Award, OU Credit Union Adv Coun, 1973; Matilda Wilson Award, 1974; Outstanding Contributor to Quality of Life, Studs Oakland Univ, 1977; Woman of the Year, Story Co Women's Polit Caucus, 1983; ISU Educ Leadership Award, Adv Fundraising Comn, 1994-; MLK Zeitgeist Award, 1996; Martin Luther King Service Award, MLK Inc, IA. **Home Addr:** 8210 Woburn Abbey Rd, Glenn Dale, MD 20769-2023. **Business Addr:** Vice President Emeritus, Anne Arundel Community College, 101 College Pkwy, Arnold, MD 21012-1895, **Business Phone:** (410)777-2222.

POUNDS, DARRYL LAMONT
Football player. **Personal:** Born Jul 21, 1972, Fort Worth, TX. **Educ:** Nicholls State Univ. **Career:** Football player (retired); Wash Redskins, defensive back, 1995-99; Denver Broncos, defensive back, 2000. **Honors/Awds:** Rookie of the Year, 1995.

POUNDS, ELAINE
Public relations executive. **Personal:** Born Dec 31, 1946, Detroit, MI; daughter of George and Ethel Loyd; divorced; children: Adrian Molett, Allen Parks. **Educ:** Los Angeles Southwest Col, attended 1971; Calif State Univ, Los Angeles, BA, 1978; Los Angeles City Col & Santa Monica City Col, attended 1980. **Career:** KNBC Television, former prod asst; KACE Radio, former producer, former corp mktg asst; Theta Cable Television, former programming asst; Group W Cable & Westinghouse Broadcasting Co, former promotions coordr & traffic mgr; KTTV & Metromedia Television, former asst traffic mgr; Los Angeles Black Media Coalition, exec dir, currently. **Orgs:** Nat Asn Media Women; Alliance Black Entertainment Technicians; Women Show Bus; Nat Asn Advan Colored People; REEL Black Women; Southern Christian Leadership Conf; comnr, Los Angeles City Cultural Affairs. *

POUNDS, DR. MOSES B
Health services administrator. **Personal:** Born Feb 18, 1947, Baltimore, MD; son of Moses B Pounds Sr and Katherine McCutcheon; married Ann P McCauley, Dec 28, 1981; children: M Andrew. **Educ:** Univ Calif, Santa Cruz, AB, Anthrop, 1974; Univ Calif, Berkeley, MA, Anthrop, 1975; Univ Calif, Berkeley & San Francisco, PhD, Med Anthrop, 1982. **Career:** The Johns Hopkins Univ, Sch Hyg & Pub Health, Dept Behav Scis & Health Educ, asst prof, 1982-88; Univ Md, Baltimore, asst to the pres, Mid-Atlantic AIDS Regional Educ & Training Ctr, project dir, princ investr, 1988-91; US Pub Health Serv, Health Resources Servs Admin, Bur Health Resources Develop, Office Sci & Epidemiol, sr

staff fel, 1991-94, med anthropologist, 1994-. **Orgs:** Am Anthrop Asn; Soc Med Anthrop; Kroeber Anthrop Soc; Am Pub Health Asn. **Honors/Awds:** Biol Sci Res Grant, NIH, The Johns Hopkins Univ, 1982-84, 1984-85; Fel, Grad Minority Fel, Univ Calif, Berkeley, 1979-81; Trainee Nat Inst Gen Med Serv, NIH Grant, 1977-79; Fel Nat Sci Found, Pre-doctoral Fel, 1974-77; Am Found for AIDS Res Grant, 1987-88; Nat Cancer Inst Grant, 1988; Health Resources & Servs Admin Grant, 1988-91. **Military Serv:** USY, admin asst, Sgt, 1966-70. **Home Addr:** 5224 Even Star Pl, Columbia, MD 21044. **Business Addr:** Medical Anthropologist, HAB Health Resources Services Administration, Office of Science and Epidemiology, 5600 Fishers Lane Rm 7C-07, Rockville, MD 20857, **Business Phone:** (301)443-2894.

POUSSAINT, DR. ALVIN FRANCIS
Educator. **Personal:** Born May 15, 1934, East Harlem, NY; son of Harriet and Christopher; married Tina Young, 1993; children: Alan & Alison. **Educ:** Columbia Col, BA, 1956; Cornell Univ Med Col, MD, 1960; Neuro psychiatric Inst Univ Calif, Los Angeles, MS, 1964. **Career:** Tufts Univ Med Sch, sr clin instr, 1965-66, asst prof, 1967-69; Med Comn Human Rights, Jackson, MS, southern field dir, 1965-66; Columbia Pt HealthCtr, dir psychiat, 1968-69; Mass Mental Health, assoc psychiatrist,1969-78; Harvard Med Sch, assoc dean students, 1969-, Judge Baker Children's Ctr, Boston,dir & sr assoc psychiat, 1978-, prof psychiat & fac assoc dean stud affairs, currently. **Orgs:** Mem bd trustees, Wesleyan Col, 1968-69; treas, Nat Med Comn Human Rights, 1968-69; mem bd trustees, Nat Afro Am Artists, 1968; mem bd dirs, Oper PUSH, 1971-85; fel, Am Psychiat Asn, 1972-; chmn bd, Solomon Fuller Inst,1975-81; Nat Med Asn, 1968-; fel AAAS, 1981-; Am Acad Child Psychiat,1985-; fel Am Ortho psychiatric Asn, 1987-; Med Alumni Asn, Univ Calif Los Angeles; Nat Asn Advan Colored People; Urban League. **Honors/Awds:** Dr, Wilberforce Univ, 1972; DHL, Govs State Univ, 1982; American Black Achievement Award in Business and the Professions, Johnson Publ, 1986;John Jay Award for Distinguished Professional Achievement, 1987; Medgar Evers Medal of Honor, Beverly Hills/ Hollywood, chap NCP, 1988; Award of Professional Achievement, Univ Calif Los Angeles, 1990; New England Emmy Award for Outstanding Children's Special, 1997. **Special Achievements:** Co-author of Raising Black Children, 1992; co-author of Lay My Burden Down, 2000, has written dozens of articles for lay and professional publications; Co- author of Come On People: On the Path from Victims to Victors, 2007. **Business Addr:** Professor of Psychiatry, Faculty Associate Dean for Student Affairs, Harvard Medical School, Judge Baker Children's Center, 53 Parker Hill Ave, Boston, MA 02120-3225, **Business Phone:** (617)278-4105.

POUSSAINT, RENEE FRANCINE
Journalist, educator, chief executive officer. **Personal:** Born Aug 12, 1944, New York, NY; married Henry J Richardson. **Educ:** Sorbonne Paris France & Yale Law Sch, attended 1967; Sarah Lawrence Col, Bronxville, NY, BA, 1966; Univ Calif, Los Angeles, MA, 1971; Ind Univ, PhD, 1972; Columbia Univ Sch Jour, attended 1973. **Career:** African Arts Mag Los Angeles, ed, 1969-73; Ind Univ Bloomington, lectr & doctoral candidate, 1972-73; WBBM-TV Chicago, reporter, anchor & show host, 1973-77; CBS Network News Chicago, WA DC, reporter, 1977-79; WJLA-TV, anchor & reporter, 1978-; Wisdom Works, Inc, pres & chief exec officer, currently. **Orgs:** Prog dir, AIESEC NY, 1967-69; dancer, Jean Leon Destine Haitian Daznce, 1967; translator UC Press, 1970; peaker, various pvt & govt orgn, 1977-; Sigma Delta Chi; lifetime mem, Nat Asn Advan Colored People; Women Communications Awards TV Reporting Nat Asn Media Women, 1975; Ill Ment Health Asn, 1975; Young Achiever YMCA Chicago, 1976; Am Fire fighters Asn,1977; Am Asn Univ Women, 1979; Sr Fel Univ Maryland's Acad Leadership. **Honors/Awds:** Outstanding serv US Dept of Labor Ed Women, 1979; emmy Nat Acad of TV Arts & Scis, 1980; religiton in Media, 1980; hon doctorate, George town Univ. **Business Phone:** (314)361-9473.*

POUSSAINT-HUDSON, DR. ANN ASHMORE
Psychologist. **Personal:** Born Jun 23, 1942, Atlanta, GA; married James L Hudson Esq; children: Alan Machel Poussaint. **Educ:** Spelman Col Atlanta, BA, 1963; Simmons Col Sch Soc Work, MS, 1965; Univ Calif, Berkeley, MA 1976, PhD, 1979; John Hopkins Univ, writing prog. **Career:** Pacific Psychother Assn, consult clinician, 1970-73; State Univ Calif, San Francisco, lectr, 1968-70; pvt pract, 1974-81; Urban Psychol Associates, founder & pres, 1980-95; State Dept, Sr Foreign Svc Selection Bd, 1996; United States Information Agency, Selection Bd, 1998; Howard Univ, Franklin Frazier Inst, vis scholar, 2000. **Orgs:** Mem pub rel com Am Psychol Asn; bd dir, Sasha Bruer Youth Works, 1994-; mem, Links Inc, Potomac Chapter Links, vpres programs, 1999-; bd dir, Wash Ballet, 1999-; Former bd dir, United Way Mass, 1992-94. **Honors/Awds:** Lectr & Contributor of articles in field to mags/ newspapers; Fellowship US Pub Health Scholar 1971-73; Precedent Setting in Jury Selection Assn of Black Psychologists 1974; Harvard Univ, DuBois Institute fellow, 1985-88; Cambridge YWCA, Volunteer of the Year. **Home Addr:** 2200 20th St NW, Washington, DC 20009.

POWE, JOSEPH S.
Engineer. **Personal:** Born Jul 26, 1946, Bremerton, WA. **Educ:** Univ WVa, BS, 1968; MS, Physics, 1971; MS, Aeronaut & Astronaut Engineering, 1972. **Career:** Hughes Aircraft Co, sr scientist. **Orgs:** Mensa. **Home Addr:** 5335 Village Green, Los Angeles, CA 90016.

POWELL, ADAM CLAYTON, III
Foundation executive. **Personal:** Born Jul 17, 1946, New York, NY; son of Hazel Dorothy Scott and Adam Clayton Jr; married; children: Adam Clayton IV & Sherman Scott. **Career:** CBS News, New York, mgr & producer, 1976-81; Gannett Ctr Media Studies, Columbia Univ, New York, fel lectr & consult, 1985-94, ctr fel, 1990 & 1993; Nat Pub Radio, Wash, DC, news vpres, 1987-90; Quincy Jones Entertainment, producer, 1990-91; The Freedom Forum Media Studies Ctr, dir technol studies & progs, 1994-96; The Freedom Forum, vpres technol & progs, currently. **Orgs:** Acad Polit Sci; Am Asn Polit & Social Sci; AAAS; Nat Asn Black Journalists; Soc Prof Journalists; Songwriters Guild Am; bd adv, Black Col Commun Asn; bd dirs, Int Webcasting Asn; bd dirs, Internet Policy Inst; Internet Soc Nominations Comt; ed bd, Jour Studies Quarterly; Mass Inst Technol, Tech Comt; Nat Soc Black Engineers; Tech Adv Comt, Nat Urban League; bd visitors, Syracuse Univ, Info Studies; bd counr, USC, Integrated Media Systems Ctr; adv fund, Web Development Fund. **Honors/Awds:** World Technology Award, 1999; Overseas Press Club Award. **Special Achievements:** Co-author of Lethargy '96: How the Media Covered a Listless Campaign; Online News; contributed to: Next Media; The Internet for the Broadcasters; Demystifying Media Technology; Death by Cheeseburger: High School Journalism in the 1990s and Beyond; written articles: Media Ethics Quarterly; Reason; RTNDA Communicator; Wired Magazine. **Home Addr:** 1350 Beverly Rd Suite 115, PO Box 251, McLean, VA 22101-3917. **Business Addr:** Vice President of Technology and Programs, The Freedom Forum, 1101 Wilson Blvd, Arlington, VA 22209, **Business Phone:** (703)528-0800.

POWELL, ADDIE SCOTT
Activist, writer. **Personal:** Born Nov 14, 1922, Augusta, GA; daughter of Tillie Lyons and Matthew Marion; divorced; children: Frances Powell Harris. **Educ:** Paine Col, BA, 1943; Univ Iowa, MA; Atlanta Univ, MA, 1949. **Career:** Brooklyn Pub Libr, dist supvr adult serv, 1970-74; Br Lib Augusta, GA, 1961-62; librn, 1949-74; freelance writer, researcher & lectr. **Orgs:** Fel, Carnegie, 1951-52; Am Libr Asn; Round Table Col Res Libr; So Coun Human Rels, 1960-62; YMCA; community serv, Seventh-day Adventist Church, 1982; bd dirs, Ga Housing Coalition, 1983-; bd dirs, Fund Southern Communities, 1984-87; Sickle Cell Anemia Asn; Leadership Augusta, 1986. **Honors/Awds:** Citizen's Participation, Study Black Residents Bethlehem, 1980-81; Citizen of the Year, Augusta Unit, Nat Asn Social Workers, 1983. **Special Achievements:** TV appearance "Voices of Bklyn" (intercultural series Brooklyn College), author of various works, tech publications, Economic Development Study: Marketable Skills Among Low Income Residents of Bethlehem, Land Use Study of Low Income Community of Bethlehem 1985-86. **Business Phone:** (706)722-3406.

POWELL, ALMA JOHNSON
Activist. **Personal:** Born Oct 27, 1937, Birmingham, AL; daughter of Robert Johnson and Mildred; married Colin L Powell, Aug 25, 1962; children: Michael Kevin, Linda Margaret, Annemarie. **Educ:** Fisk Univ, BA, 1957, Emerson Col, PhD. **Career:** Boston Guild Hard Hearing, audiologist, 1959-62; Kennedy Ctr, vice chairman, currently. **Orgs:** Chmn, 1989-00, bd dir, 1989-, Nat Coun Best Friends Found; Kennedy Ctr, Community & Friend Bd, 1991-; bd trustees, vice chair, John F Kennedy Ctr Performing Arts, 1993-; bd chmn, America's Promise Alliance; adv bd, Pew Ctr Civic Change; hon pres, Assoc Am Foreign Serv Worldwide; adv bd, Hospitality & Info Serv; hon mem, Dept State Fine Arts Comt; adv bd, Our Military Kids. **Honors/Awds:** DHL, Emerson Coll, 1996; Nat Pollit Congress Black Women, 1998; Washingtonian of the Year, 2000; Leadership Award, Women's Ctr, VA. **Special Achievements:** Author: My Little Wagon; America's Promise, 2003. *

POWELL, DR. ARCHIE JAMES
Educator. **Personal:** Born Jun 1, 1950, Lakeland, FL; children: Kevin J. **Educ:** Univ Nantes, France, cert, 1971; Morehouse Col, BA, 1972; Brown Univ, MA, 1974, PhD, 1984. **Career:** Morehouse Col grant, 1970-71; The Ford Found fel, 1972-75; RI Dept Educ, planning specialist, 1978-81; Brown Univ, minority affairs officer, 1981-85; Albany Medical Col, asst prof, 1985-, asst dean minority affairs, 1985-. **Orgs:** New Eng Asn Black Educators; Org Am Historians; Am Hist Soc; Asn Study Afro-Am Life & Hist; Rhode Island Black Heritage Soc; Nat Asn Med Minority Educators, NE regional coord, 1987, conference co-chair; Albany Symphony Orchestra, bd dir, 1986-; Albany Boys Club, bd dir, 1986-; Black Dimensions Art, bd dir, 1986-; Israel African Methodist Episcopal Church, trustee, 1986-. **Honors/Awds:** Distinguished service as as reg dir, Phi Beta Sigma, 1985; distinguished service as board pres, Mt Hope Day Care Center, 1985; Outstanding Young Men of America 1986. **Home Addr:** 285 Hudson Ave, Albany, NY 12210. **Business Addr:** Assistant Dean for Minority Affair, Albany Medical College, 47 New Scotland Ave, Albany, NY 12208.

POWELL, ARTHUR F
Executive, banker. **Personal:** Born in Atlanta, GA. **Educ:** Purdue Univ, BS, math. **Career:** AGH Financial Corp, pres & founder; Grigsby Brandford Powell Inc, prin; Powell Capital Markets Inc, founder, chief exec officer & pres, currently. **Orgs:** Bd trustees, St James Prep Sch; bd trustees, Newark Mus; bd trustees, NJ Inst Technol; Omega Psi Phi; Nat Asn Guardsmen; Sundowners Inc; bd trustees, Hosp Ctr Orange; NJ Develop Authority Small, Women, Minority Owned Bus; Newark Progressive Develop Corp; NJ Tennis & Sports Found; Seton Hall Leadership Coun; bd visitors, SC State Univ. **Special Achievements:** Black Enterprise's list of Top Investment Banks, co ranked No 10, 1998; ranked No 11, 1999-00. **Business Addr:** Chief Executive Officer & President, Founder, Powell Capital Markets Inc, 7 Becker Farm Rd, Roseland, NJ 07068, **Business Phone:** (973)740-1230.

POWELL, BETTYE BOONE
Banker. **Personal:** Born Apr 10, 1947, Garysburg, NC; daughter of James W Boone Jr; married Carlie W, Mar 28, 1970; children: Carlton G. **Educ:** NC Central Univ, BA, 1969. **Career:** Hibernia Nat Bank, employee rels coord, 1981-84; asst personnel off, benefits coord, 1984-88; AVP, sr compensation analyst, 1988-90; EEO/AA officer & vpres, 1990-. **Orgs:** Human Rels, adv comt, 1994-; bd dirs, Children's Bureau, 1992-; bd dirs, YMCA Greater New Orleans, 1992-; found bd, Southern Univ New Orleans, 1990-; New Orleans Chapter Links Inc, 1975-. **Honors/Awds:** Black Achiever In Business, Oryades YMCA, 1989; Business Coordinator of the Year, Inroads/New Orleans Inc, 1990-91. **Home Addr:** 7031 W Renaissance Ct, New Orleans, LA 70128. **Business Addr:** VP, EEO Affirmative Action Officer, Hibernia National Bank, PO Box 61540, New Orleans, LA 70161, **Business Phone:** (504)533-3262.

POWELL, BILL J. See POWELL, WILLIAM.

POWELL, C. CLAYTON
Optometrist. **Personal:** Born Apr 11, 1927, Dothan, AL; son of Willie and Evelyn; married Romae Turner, Mar 11, 1954 (deceased); children: C Clayton, Jr, Rometta E; married Deborah S Goodlett, Jul 30, 1994. **Educ:** Morehouse Col, AB; Ill Col Optometry, BSc; Col Optom, OD; Univ Mich, grad study MPH prog; Atlanta Univ, MEd; Ill Col Optom, Hon DOS, 1987. **Career:** Pvt Pract, 1953-; Metro-Atlanta Child Develop Ctr & Health & Vision Clin, develop vision specialist, exec dir; Atlanta Southside Comprehensive Health Ctr, exec dir, 1973-76, chief optom Dept, 1968-73; Jr high sch teacher, asst prin; Pa Col Optom; Sou Col Optom; Develop Authority Fulton Co, chmn, exec dir, currently. **Orgs:** Nat Eye Inst, NH; adv comt, State Univ, NY; Nat Asn Neighborhood Health Ctr; Am Pub Health Asn; legis comt, NANHC; Am Nat Optom Asn; Ga Vision Serv; organizer, chmn, Metro Atlanta OEP Study Group; Beta Kappa Chi; Nat Sci Hon Soc; Tomb & Key Nat Hon Optom Soc; Beta Sigma Kappa Int Hon Optom Soc; Mu Sigma Pi Prof Fraternity; Omega Psi Phi Fraternity. **Honors/Awds:** Outstanding Man of the Year, Clark Col; Outstanding Man of the Year, Morehouse Col; Outstanding Man of the Year, Morris Brown Col; Outstanding Achievement Award, Fulton Co Rep Club; Outstanding Achievement Award, Atlanta Postal Acad; Outstanding Achievement Award, Pine Acres Town & Country Club; Optometrist of the Year, Nat Optom Asn, 1984; Honorary Degree, Doctor of Ocular Science, Ill Col, 1987; Founders Award, Nat Optom Asn; The Kaufman Award, Nat Asn Advan Colored People; Outstanding Leadership Award, St Peter Missionary Baptist Church. **Home Addr:** 1347 Cascade Falls Dr SW, Atlanta, GA 30311-3637. **Business Addr:** Executive Director, Development Authority of Fulton County, 2039 Metropolitan Pkwy SW, Atlanta, GA 30315.*

POWELL, CARL
Football player. **Personal:** Born Jan 4, 1974, Detroit, MI. **Educ:** Univ Louisville. **Career:** Indianapolis Colts, defensive end, 1991-98; Rhein Fire, defensive end, 1999; Baltimore Ravens, defensive end, 2000; Chicago Bears, defensive end, 2001; Wash Redskins, defensive end, 2002; Cincinnati Bengals, defensive end, 2003-05. **Orgs:** Life Athletes mems.

POWELL, CHARLES ARTHUR
Publisher. **Personal:** Born May 22, 1933, Atlantic City, NJ; son of John and Colleen; divorced; children: Charles A II & Martin Kennedy. **Educ:** Lincoln Univ, BS, hist, 1962; Univ PA, MSW, 1966. **Career:** Child Guidance Clin, Media, PA, psych social worker; Headstart Progs, Deleware County, PA, dir; Chester, PA, Anti-Poverty Prog, dir; Bell Atlantic Corp, dir econ devel prog Philadelphia; Quantum Leap Publ, owner, 1990-; Author: Servants of Power, 1990. **Business Addr:** Publisher, Quantum Leap Publisher Inc, 2604 Christy St, Tracy, CA 95376, **Business Phone:** (209)839-1643.

POWELL, CLARENCE DEAN, JR.
Airplane pilot. **Personal:** Born Aug 26, 1939, Kansas City, MO; son of Clarence Powell Sr and Capitola; children: Pamela Diane. **Educ:** Univ Kansas City, 1957-60; Troy State Univ, Montgomery, AL, 1965-66. **Career:** TWA Inc, first officer, 1966, capt; Darben Clifton & Gordon Construction Co, proj engr, 1968-69; Hadden Invest & Develop Co, proj engr & cons, 1971-72; Afro Air Inc, pres & chief exec officer, 1974-77; Org Black Airline Pilots, eastern relig vpres, 1979; Prof Photogr. **Orgs:** Negro Airmen Int, 1967; NAACP, 1967-; consult, Nat Urban League 1967-77; Tuske-

gee Airman Inc, 1990-. **Honors/Awds:** Honor grad AUS Basic Training & Warrant Officer Training, 1962-63; Award of Excellence, TWA Airlines, 1979. **Military Serv:** AUS, WO, 1962-66; Vietnamese Cross Gallantry; Gold Leaf Air Medal w & 4 Silver Leaf Clusters & v Valor; Commendation Medal w & v Valor.

POWELL, GEN. COLIN LUTHER
Military leader, executive, businessperson. **Personal:** Born Apr 5, 1937, New York, NY; son of Luther Theophilus and Maud Ariel; married Alma Vivian Johnson, Aug 25, 1962; children: Michael, Linda & Anne Marie. **Educ:** City Col NY, BS, geol, 1958; George Wash Univ, MBA, 1971; Nat War Col, attended 1976. **Career:** AUS, second lt, 1957, career army infantry officer, 1958, first lt, 1959, capt, 1962, maj, 1966, lt col, 1970, 101st Airborne Div, brig comdr, 1976-77, brig gen, 1979, fourth Inf Div, Ft Carson, CO, asst div comdr, 1981-82, Dep Sec Def, mil asst, 1982-86; lt gen, 1986, nat security adv, 1987-89, maj gen, 1989, gen, 1989; Joint Chiefs Staff, chmn, 1989-93; US George W Bush Admin, secy state, 2001-05; Kleiner, Perkins, Caufield & Byers, strategic ltd partner, 2005-. **Orgs:** Founding chmn, Am Promise; Alliance Youth; bd trustee, Howard Univ; bd dir, United Negro Col Fund; bd gov, Boys & Girls Club Am; adv bd, C Health Fund. **Honors/Awds:** Inducted Horatio Alger, Asn of Distinguished Americans, 1991; Sylvanus Thayer Award, US Mil Acad, 1998; Living Legend Award; Liberty Medal, 2002; Bishop John T Walker Distinguished Humanitarian Service Award, 2005; Andrus Award, AARP, 2006; Presidential Medals of Freedom; President's Citizens Medal; Congressional Gold Medal; Secretary of State Distinguished Service Medal; Secretary of Energy Distinguished Service Medal; Silver Buffalo Award, Boy Scouts Am. **Special Achievements:** First African American Secretary of State; Author, biography, My American Journey. **Military Serv:** AUS, 1957-89; Purple Heart, 1963, Bronze Star, 1963, Legion of Merit awards, 1969 & 1971, District Service Medal. **Business Addr:** Strategic Limited Partner, Kleiner, Perkins, Caufield & Byers, 2750 Sand Hill Rd, Menlo Park, CA 94025, **Business Phone:** (650)233-2750.

POWELL, CRAIG
Football player, military leader. **Personal:** Born Nov 13, 1971, Youngstown, OH. **Educ:** Ohio State Univ, econ, 1994. **Career:** Football player (retired), Military leader; Cleveland Browns, linebacker, 1995; Baltimore Ravens, linebacker, 1996; New York Jets, linebacker, 1998; San Francisco Demons, linebacker, 2001. **Military Serv:** AUS, Supply officer.

POWELL, DANTE
Baseball player. **Personal:** Born Aug 25, 1973, Long Beach, CA. **Educ:** Calif State Univ. **Career:** San Francisco Giants, outfielder, 1997-98; Arizona Diamondbacks, 1999; San Francisco Giants, 2001; Anaheim Angels, centerfield, 2005-. *

POWELL, DARLENE WRIGHT
Lawyer. **Personal:** Born Dec 1, 1960, Brooklyn, NY; daughter of Franklin P Wright III and Elaine; married Clayton J Jr, Jul 28, 1984; children: Jessica Marie. **Educ:** Cornell Univ, Ithaca, NY, BS, 1981; Harvard Law Sch Cambridge, Mass, cert, 1987; Univ Md, Sch Law, Baltimore, MD, JD, 1985. **Career:** Frank, Berstein, Conaway & Goldman, law clerk, 1983-84; Daily Record, staff writer, 1983-84; Burke, Gerber, Wilen, Francomano, & Radding, law clerk, summer, 1984; Fidelity & Deposit Co Md, atty, 1986; Md-Nat Capital Park & Planning Comn, assoc gen coun, 1986-87; Kaiser Permanente, assoc regional coun, 1987-88; Md Off Pub Defender, part-time atty, 1989-90; Powell & Powell PC, prin atty, 1990-92; Law Off Darlene Wright Powell PA, prin atty, 1992-; Mission Love Inc, chairperson, 1997-98, advisor, dir, 1997-2002, exec bd mem. **Orgs:** Dist Bar Asn; bd trustees, State Md Pub Defender Syst, 1990-92; bd mem, Univ Md Prince George's County Alumni Club, 1990-91; Md Pub Defender Syst, 1990-92; Prince George's County Bar Asn Comt Comts, Continuing Legal Educ Comt; Bar Asn Baltimore City; Pub Serv Comt Md State Bar Asn's Young Lawyers' Sect; chairperson, Charles Co, Cornell Alumni Admis Ambassador Network Comt, 2002-, Prince George's County, 2002-; Prince George's County Mgt Oversight Panel, 2002; Am Asn Justice. **Honors/Awds:** Participant, Harvard Law School's Prog Instr Lawyers, June 1987; Young Careerist, Bus & Prof Women's Clubs, Bowie-Crofton Chap, 1987-88; Finalist Award, Young Career Woman Competition, Md Fed Bus & Prof Women's Clubs, 1987-88. **Home Addr:** 2116 Bermondsey Dr, Mitchellville, MD 20721, **Home Phone:** (301)249-3024. **Business Phone:** (301)464-6260.*

POWELL, DARRELL LEE
Television journalist. **Personal:** Born Mar 20, 1959, Cumberland, MD; son of Gloria Louise; married Jacqueline Lavern Barnes-Powell. **Educ:** Frostburg State Univ, Frostburg, MD, BS, sociol, 1983. **Career:** Frostburg State Univ, Frostburg, MD, librarian aid, 1978-83; Western Md Consortium, Cumberland, MD, counr, 1983; Allegany County Sch Bd, Cumberland, MD, teacher, 1985-87; TCI Cable Vision, Cumberland, MD, photographer & writer, 1984-87; WTBO/WKGO Radio, Cumberland, MD, disc jockey, 1987; WHAG-TV 25, Hagerstown, MD, rep, 1987-; City Cumberland, Dept Community Develop, fair housing specialist. **Orgs:** Treas, Nat Asn Advan Colored People, 1980-; Human Resource Develop Comn Bd, 1990-; Voc Educ Adv Coun, 1990-; Cumberland Theatre bd, 1993-. **Business Addr:** Fair Housing Specialist, City of Cumberland, 57 N Liberty St, PO Box 1702, Cumberland, MD 21501-1702.*

POWELL, DEBRA A
Mayor. **Personal:** Born Apr 30, 1964, East St Louis, IL; married Anthony Tarvin (divorced 1990); children: Anthony Tarvin Jr & Karmeen Powell-Childress. **Educ:** Univ Nebr, attended 1985. **Career:** City of East St. Louis, pub rel asst, 1986, city coun person, 1993-98, mayor, 1999-2003; munic pub rels prof, Pasadena, CA, 1986-90; Gateway East Metropolitan Ministries, news anchor & news dir, 1990-98. **Orgs:** Batari Inst Youth; Youth-A-Flame. **Honors/Awds:** Ambassador for Peace, Interreligions & Int Fedn World Peace; Distinguished Community Service Award, State Mo; Leadership Award, Nat Asn Blacks Criminal Justice 2002. **Special Achievements:** First female mayor in East St Louis.

POWELL, DOC (WILLIAM POWELL)
Guitarist. **Personal:** Born in New York. **Career:** Luther Vandross & Group, B B & Q Band, musical dir; The Five Heartbeats, musical dir; Down & Out In Beverly Hills, musical dir; songs: "Love Is Where It's At", 1987; "The Doctor", 1992; "Inner City Blues", 1996; "Laid Back", 1996; "I Claim The Victory", 1999; "Life Changes", 2001; "97th & Columbus", 2003; "cool like that", 2004; DPR Music Group Inc, owner, guitarist; Headsup Int; jazz label, owner. **Honors/Awds:** Grammy nominated. **Business Addr:** Recording Artist, c/o Headsup International, 23309 Commerce Park Rd, Cleveland, OH 44122, **Business Phone:** (216)765-7381.

POWELL, DOROTHY A.
Educator. **Personal:** Born in Temple, TX; daughter of Norman and Josephine Armstrong; married Allison B Powell (deceased). **Educ:** Prairie View A&M Univ, BS, 1954, MA, 1963. **Career:** Educator (retired); Temple Independent Sch Dist, teacher, 1959-71, prin, 1971-95. **Orgs:** Tex State Teachers Asn; Nat Educ Asn, 1959-95; Phi Beta Kappa Sorority; Zeta Phi Beta Sorority; Rotary Int; Campfire Boys & Girls; Top Ladies Distinction; vpres, Tex Retired Teachers Asn. **Honors/Awds:** Educator of the Month, Rotary Club, 1989. *

POWELL, DUDLEY VINCENT
Executive, pharmacist, physician. **Personal:** Born Jul 23, 1917; married Beryl Mae Prettigar Henry; children: Dudley Vincent Jr, Hubert Barrington & Tyrone Anthony. **Educ:** Syracuse Univ Hosp, internship; Met Hosp Cleveland, residency Obstet-Gynec, 3 yrs; Univ Rochester, Sch Med & Dent, New York, MD, 1950. **Career:** Western Reserve Univ, instr, 1yr; Ft Carson Co, chief ob-gyn, 2yrs; Dallas, pvt prac ob-gyn 1958-; Ob-Gyn Health Sci Ctr, Univ Tex, clinical prof; St Paul Presb Med Arts Hosp. **Orgs:** Dir Planned Parenthd NE Tex, 1960-76; Nat Planned Parenthood Bd, 1968-72; life mem, Nat Asn Advan Colored People. **Honors/Awds:** Margaret Sanger Award; Man of the Year, Omega Psi Phi. **Military Serv:** AUS, Reserve col 1958-77; Merit Award, AUS, Reserve; Legion Merit, AUS, Reserve. **Business Addr:** St Paul Professional Bldg 1906 Peabody Ave, Dallas, TX 75215.*

POWELL, ELAINE
Basketball player. **Personal:** Born Aug 9, 1975, Monroe, LA; daughter of James Powell and Merlene Powell. **Educ:** La State Univ, attended 1997. **Career:** Portland Power, guard, 1997; Orlando Miracle, 1999-02; Detroit Shock, guard, 2002-. **Honors/Awds:** Community Assist Award, WNBA off-season, 2002-03; All-SEC, Associated Press,1997; WNBA champion, 2003, 2006. **Special Achievements:** The 19.1 career scoring average is fourth-best in LSU history; Voted 1997District 6 Kodak All-American; WNBA Community Assist Award, 2003. **Business Addr:** Professional Basketball Player, Detroit Shock, Palace of Auburn Hills, 2 Championship Dr, Auburn Hills, MI 48326.*

POWELL, GAYLE LETT
Executive, consultant, fur trader. **Personal:** Born Dec 18, 1943, Manhattan, NY; daughter of Robert A and Claire G. **Educ:** Cent Univ, BSE, 1966. **Career:** Newark Bd Educ, teacher, 1966-72; She Creations Inc, corp pres, 1969-80; Essex Col Bus, teacher, 1980-81; The Fur Vault, fur sales, 1981-82; Antonovich Furs Inc, fur sales, 1982-84; Fur You Inc, Outside Fur Sales, corp off, 1984-; The Fur Mart Inc, retail furs & serv mfr, ceo, 1985-. **Orgs:** Alpha Kappa Alpha Sorority, Master Furriers Guild, Am Bridge Asn; Nat Asn Female Exec; Fur Info Coun Am. **Business Addr:** Chief Executive Officer, Fur Mart Inc, PO Box 43153, Upper Montclair, NJ 07043, **Business Phone:** (973)744-1844.

POWELL, GEORGETTE SEABROOKE
Educator, artist, founder (originator). **Personal:** Born Aug 2, 1916, Charleston, SC; married George W (deceased); children: George W III, Phyllis A Manson & Richard V. **Educ:** Cooper Union Art Sch; Fordham Univ; Turtle Bay Music Sch; Dept Agr Grad Sch Wash, DC; DC Teachers Col; WA Sch Psychiatry, Howard Univ, BFA. **Career:** DC Gen Hosp, art therapist, 1963-66; Art in Action, inceptor & consult, 1967-68; Comn Art Happening Annual Art Show, inceptor & dir, 1967; George Wash Univ Grad Sch Art & Sci, art therapy prog, 1972; Flagler County Bunnell, FL, minority arts coordr, 1982; Oper Heritage Art Ctr, founder, 1970-75; Tomorrow's World Art Ctr, dir & founder, 1975. **Orgs:** Des cover & illus, Black Arts Calendar Josephite Pastoral Ctr, 1976-80; Black Artists Nat Afro-Am Hist Kit, 1977; Int NCA Nat Conf Artists Dakar Senegal, 1984; guest, Comm Folk Art Gallery, 1986; Am Art Therapy Asn; Am Art League; DC Art Asn; bd mem, Howard Theatre Found; Nat Conf Artists; consult bd, Create a drama Educ Ctr IN; Women Arts WI, NY, DC; DC Mental Health Asn; DC Comn Arts & Humanities; Nat Endowment Arts; panelist, WPA & the Harlem Artists Guild NY; designer, Sidwell Friends Summ Prog. **Honors/Awds:** Outstanding Performer Award, DC Pub Health Art Therap Acute Psychiat, 1964; First Prize, Cooper Union Art Sch, Dillard Univ, Am Art League, 1967; Quality Performance Award, DC Dept Rec, 1974; Nat Achievement Award,Nat Conf Artists, 1975; DC Art Asn Award, 1977; Festac Ptcpt Award, 1977; Merit Award, Howard Univ Community Action Prog, DC, 1978; Community Service Award, Neighborhood Planning Coun, 1979; Jos Parks Special Award, Nat Conf Artists, 1979; Juris Art Citation, Plaque WA Bar Asn, 1980; Humanities Award, Black Hist Month Peos Congregational Church, 1985; Outstanding Community Service in the Arts Award, St Patrick's Episcopal Church Sr Ctr, 1986; Honoree Salute to Georgette Seabrooke Powell, 1986; Art Service Award, Plaque NCA Conf, Los Angeles, CA, 1987; Community Service Award, Plaque DC Art Asn. **Special Achievements:** Listed in, Ebony, Jet Mag & Wash Artists Dir, 1972, Artists USA, 1973, WA Post, Evening Star News, Afro-Am Newspapers, International Artist Dir, 1974-75. **Business Addr:** Founder, Tomorrow's World Art Center, Inc., PO Box 56197, Washington, DC 20011.

POWELL, REV. GRADY WILSON, SR.
Clergy. **Personal:** Born Aug 6, 1932, Brunswick Co, VA; son of Herbert V and Lillie T; married Bertie J; children: Sandra Z, Dorthula H, Grady W Jr, Herbert C & Eric C. **Educ:** St Paul's Col, BS, 1954; Va Union Univ Sch of Theol, MDiv 1959. **Career:** Clergy (Retired); Amity Baptist Church, S Hill, VA, pastor, 1953-58; Greensville Co Pub Schs, Emporia, VA, teacher, 1954-56; Quioccasin Baptist Church, Richmond, pastor, 1958-61; Richmond Pub Schs, teacher 1959-60; Gillfield Bapist Church, pastor, 1961-97. **Orgs:** Treas, bd mem, Children's Home Va Baptist Inc, 1959-70; secy, Va Coun Churches, gov bd, 1960-66; Petersburg Biracial Comn, Petersburg, VA, 1961-62; bd mem, secy, State Bd Corrections, VA, 1974-78; gov bd, Nat Coun Church Christ, 1979-; adv bd, Nations Bank, 1988-; adv bd, Energy Share, Va Power, 1989-; adv bd, United Way, Petersburg, VA, 1989-; corp bd, WCVE-TV, 1990-; Hosp Authority Southside Regional Med Ctr, 1991-. **Honors/Awds:** Distinguished Service, Nat Asn Advan Colored People, 1961; Man of the Year, Omega Psi Phi Frat, Petersburg, 1963; Hon Degree, St Paul's Col, 1976; Presidential Citation, Nat Asn Equal Opportunity Higher Educ, 1979.

POWELL, JOSEPH T
Clergy. **Personal:** Born Nov 11, 1923, Baltimore, MD; married Alice Pettiford; children: Cynthia R & Jo Anne M. **Educ:** Oakwood Col, Huntsville, AL, BA, 1946; Andrews Univ, Berring Springs, MI, MA, 1951. **Career:** Clergy (Retired); Acad Church, pastor, 1948-52; AUS, chaplain, 1952-57; Immanuel Temple Seventh Day Adventist Church, Durham, NC, chaplain, 1957-60; AUS Ft Ord CA, chaplain, 1960. **Orgs:** Durham Interden Ministries Asn, 1957-60; Durham Com Negro Affairs, 1957-60; Nat Asn Advan Colored People. **Honors/Awds:** Merit Service Award, Durham Com Negro Affairs, 1960; Achievement Award, Oakwood Col, 1974; Col AUS Res; numerous medals & commendatiosn Korea, Viet Nam, Armed Forces. **Special Achievements:** Joseph T. Powell was the first Black SDA chaplain who entered the U.S. Army as a chaplain on November 26, 1960.

POWELL, JUAN HERSCHEL
Manager, chief executive officer. **Personal:** Born Aug 11, 1960, Roanoke, VA; son of John Henry and Shirley Oliver; married Eugenia Toliver; children: Jamaal Khari. **Educ:** Howard Univ, BSCE, 1982; Univ Md, MBA, 1988. **Career:** The CECO Corp, construction engr, 1983-85; The George Hyman Construction Co, project engr 1985-89, project mgr, 1990-; Buildtech Construction Co, prin; Carr America Develop Inc, vpres & sr proj mgr; Neighborhood Develop Co, co-ceo, 2005-. **Orgs:** Am Soc of Civil Engrs, 1979-; Alpha Phi Alpha Frat Inc, 1980-; Tau Beta Pi Nat Engineering Honor Soc, 1982-; Nat Black MBA Asn, 1986-; pres, George Hyman Chap, Toastmasters Inc, 1988; DC Contractors Asn, 1989; pres, Howard Univ Engineering Alumni Asn, 1989-92. **Honors/Awds:** Leadership Award, ASCE Howard Univ, 1982; Certificate of Appreciation, Alpha Phi Alpha Beta Chap, 1983. **Business Addr:** Co-Chief Executive Officer, Neighborhood Development Company, 4110 Kansas Ave NW Washington, Bethesda, MD 20814, **Business Phone:** (202)722-6002.

POWELL, KEMPER O
Banker. **Personal:** Born in Chicago, IL. **Educ:** Univ Chicago, BS, econs, 1994. **Career:** Northern Trust Corp, securities custody adminr, internal vpres, 1993-. **Orgs:** Pres, Urban Financial Serv Coalition, Chicago Chap, 2000-; Alpha Phi Alpha Frat Inc. **Business Addr:** Internal Vice President, Northern Trust Corp, 50 So La Salle St, Chicago, IL 60675, **Business Phone:** (312)630-6000.

POWELL, KENNETH ALASANDRO
Management consultant. **Personal:** Born Nov 26, 1945, Mobile, AL; son of William O Sr and Myrtle E. **Educ:** Howard Univ, BS,

Math, 1967; Harvard Bus Sch, MBA, Fin, 1974. **Career:** McKinsey & Co, associate mgmt consulting, 1974-77; Chase Manhattan Bank, second vpres, strategic mgmt, 1977-83; Marine Midland Bank, vpres & mgr, mgt info sys, 1983-90; Powell Consulting Corp, pres, strategy, mkt, real estate, fin, 1990-; Key Exec Servs, Right Mgt Consults, sr vpres, 2002. **Orgs:** E 87 Tenants Corp, pres 1983-90; Harvard Bus Sch Club NY, pres, 1983-86, life bd mem, 1986-; Harvard Bus Sch Asn (all alumni), pres, 1986, bd, 1983-88; Found Dance Promotion bd mem, 1987-90; Safe Horizon (Victim Services/Travelers Aid), bd mem, 1989-2003; Am Soc Training & Develop (ASTD), 1988-90; New York Am Inst Banking, trustee, 1990; Found Leadership Quality & Ethics Practice, bd mem, 1991-94; Jobs for Youth, bd chmn, 1995-2004, vchmn, treas, 1991-95 & bd mem, 1991-2004; Inwood House, vpres, bd mem, chair investment comt, 1993-2004; Harvard Bus Sch African Am Stud Union, adv bd, 1995-97; 245 Harvard Bus Sch African Am Alumni Asn, pres, 1997-; Harvard Club NY, bd mem, 2005-; . **Honors/Awds:** COGME Fel (Honorarium) Coun Grad Mgmt Educ, Boston, 1972-74; Martin Luther King Fel, Woodrow Wilson Found, 1972-74; Howard Univ Distinguished Alumnus, Nat Asn Educ Oppor, 1984; Harvard Bus Sch, 'Bert King Service Award for Alumni Distinction', 1997. **Military Serv:** Nat Guard & Reserves, ltcol (retired) 5 yrs active (RA), 23 yrs reserves; Bronze Star; Vietnam Cross Gallantry, 1969; Ranger Qualified.

POWELL, MARVIN, JR.
Football player. **Personal:** Born Aug 30, 1955, Fort Bragg, NC; married Kristen; children: Amerique & Beronique. **Educ:** Univ Southern Calif, BA, speech & polit sci, 1977. **Career:** Football player (retired); New York Jets, offensive tackle, 1977-85; Tampa Bay Buccaneers, offensive tackle, 1986-87; New Orleans Saints, 1999. **Orgs:** Vpres, Nat Football League Players Asn; player rep, New York Jets, 1977-85, Tampa Bay Buccaneers, 1986-87. **Honors/Awds:** Most Valuable Player, 1979; Forrest Gregg Offensive Lineman of the Year, 1982.

POWELL, MICHAEL K
Government official. **Personal:** Born Mar 23, 1963; son of Colin and Alma; married Jane Knott; children: Jeffrey & Bryan. **Educ:** Col William & Mary, BA, 1985; Georgetown Univ Law Ctr, JD, 1993. **Career:** AUS, cav off, 1985-88; Dept Defense, asst to secy, 1988-90; US Ct Appeals, judicial clerk chief judge, 1993-94; O'Melveny & Myers LLP, assoc, 1994-96; Dept Justice, Antitrust Div, chief staff, 1996-97; Fed Communs Comn, comnr, 1997-, chair, 2001-05; Col William & Mary & Georgetown Univ Law Ctr, bd visitors, currently. **Orgs:** Henry crown fel, Aspen Inst, 2005. **Military Serv:** AUS, 3/2 Armored Calvary Regt, cavalry platoon leader, troop exec off, 1985-88. **Business Addr:** Rector, College of William & Mary, PO Box 8795, Williamsburg, VA 23187-8795, **Business Phone:** (757)221-4000.

POWELL, MIKE (MICHAEL ANTHONY POWELL)
Athlete, television sportscaster. **Personal:** Born Nov 10, 1963, Philadelphia, PA; son of Preston and Carolyn Carroll. **Educ:** Univ Calif, Irvine, UCLA, BA, sociol, 1986. **Career:** Athlete (retired), Television Sportscaster; US Olympics, long jumper,1988, 1992; Univ Calif, Los Angeles, coach; Yahoo Sports Olympic Track & Field coverage, analyst, currently. **Orgs:** Alpha Phi Alpha. **Honors/Awds:** Southern Califorina Athlete of the Year, Amateur Athletics Found, 1991; Overseas Personality of the Year, BBC TV Sports, 1991; James E. Sullivan Memorial Award; Outstanding Amateur Athlete, 1991; Jim Thorpe Pro Sports Award, 1992; silver medals, 1988 & 1992. **Special Achievements:** World record holder in the long jump since 1990; He came third at the 1995 World Championships in Athletics. *

POWELL, DR. MYRTIS H
Educator. **Personal:** Born Feb 6, 1939, Evergreen, AL; daughter of Arthur Lee and Lula B Jones; widowed; children: Kimberly, Robin, Judy & Lavatus III. **Educ:** Univ Cincinnati, AS, 1968, BS, 1969, MA, 1974, PhD, 1978; Harvard Univ, cert higher educ mgt, 1975; Salzburg Seminar Am Studies Salzburg Austria, cert, 1980. **Career:** Univ Cincinnati, teacher asst, 1969-71, asst to dean & lectr, 1971-73, assoc dean, adj & asst prof 1973-78, United Black fac; Edna McConnell Clark Found, prog dir, 1978-81; Miami Univ Oxford Campus, exec asst to pres, adj & asst prof, vpres stud affairs, 1989-2002; Public Welfare Found, dir, 2002-; Seven Hills Neighborhood Houses Inc; Nat Network Runaway & Youth Servs Inc, Wash, UNIFI Mutual Holding Co, dir, currently; Union Cent Mutual Holding Co, dir, currently; Greater Cincinnati Found, dir, currently; Union Cent Life Ins Co, dir, currently. **Orgs:** Leadership Cincinnati Alumni Asn; Mayerson Acad Human Resource Develop; Clin Ctr Women's Health Initiative; Nat Child Labor Comm, New York; Hamilton County Alcohol & Drug Addiction Serv; Univ Cincinnati, CLG Med, COT Gerontology Prog, bdm. **Honors/Awds:** Alumni Achievement Award by Class, Univ Cincinnati, 1966, African American Alumni Asn, Sankofa Award for Excellence in Higher Educ, 1997; Asn Black Excellence Award, 1973, 1978; Leadership Education & Service Award, 1976, 1978; Cincinnati Urban League Guild Leadership Award, 1977; Nat Coun Urban League Guilds Leadership Award, 1978; Salute Outstanding Volunteer, 1978; COT Service Award, 1978; Cincinnati COT Chest & CNL Outstanding Leadership Award Allocations Div, 1979; Carver COT Ctr Leadership Award, Peoria Ill, 1981; New Hope Baptist Church Outstanding Black American Recognition Award, 1983; Career Woman Achievement, YWCA, 1984, Black Achiever Award, 1991; Leadership Cincinnati Graduate Class VIII, 1984-85; Brotherhood Award, Nat CNF Christians & Jews, 1988; Woman Year Award, Cincinnati Enquirer, 1991; Beacon Light Award, Lighthouse Youth Services, 1996; Joseph A Hall Award, United Way & Community Chest, 1996; New Voices Award, Mallory Hist Asn, 1998; Woman Distinction Award, Great Rivers Girl Scout Coun, 1998. **Home Phone:** (513)793-9320. **Business Addr:** Director, Public Welfare Foundation, 1200 U St NW, Washington, DC 20009-4443, **Business Phone:** (202)965-1800.

POWELL, PATRICIA
Educator, writer. **Personal:** Born May 4, 1966, Spanish Town, Japan; daughter of Philip Powell and Winifred Powell. **Educ:** Wellesley Col, BA, 1988; Brown Univ, MFA, 1991. **Career:** South Boston High Sch, lectr, 1987-88; Univ Mass, Boston, lectr, 1990-91, creative writing asst prof, 1991-; Brown Univ, teaching asst, 1990-91; Mass Inst Technol, Martin Luther King Jr Vis Prof Writing, currently; Novel: Me dying trial, 1993; The Pagoda, 1998; A Small Gathering of Bones, 2003. **Orgs:** Acad adv, Wellesley Col Acad Adv, 1987-88; peer adv, 1987-88, Caribbean lit course consult, 1991, Boston Pub Sch,; ed, Elerestory, Brown RISD J Arts, 1990-91; African Writers Conf, 1991; Independent Black Filmmakers Series, 1991; chmn Black Studies, Search Comn, 1992. **Honors/Awds:** Grad Fel, Brown Univ, 1989; Poets, Essayists, Novelists, PEN, New England Award, 1991; MacDowell Fel, MacDowell Writers Colony, 1992; Lila-Wallace Readers Digest Writers Award; finalist, Granta Best of Young American Novelists Award, 1993; Bruce Rossley Literary Award; Ferro-Grumley Award for Fiction. **Business Addr:** Martin Luther King Jr Visiting Professor of Writing, Massachusetts Institute of Technology, 77 massachusetts ave, cambridge, MA 02139-4307, **Business Phone:** (617)253-1000.

POWELL, RENEE
Golfer. **Personal:** Born May 4, 1946; daughter of Dr William J and Marcella. **Educ:** Ohio Univ & Ohio State Univ. **Career:** Joined PGA, 1967; retired PGA Tour, 1980; Clearview Golf Club, East Canton, OH, head prof, currently. **Honors/Awds:** Hon mem, Exec Comn LPGA & Club Pro Div; Budget Serv Award, 1999; designated Pro Class A mem LPGA & PGA of Am; Hon mem, Exec Comn of the LPGA; First Lady of Golf Award, Prof Golfers' Asn, 2003. **Special Achievements:** One of only three African American women to ever play on the Ladies Professional Golf Association's (LPGA) Tour. *

POWELL, RICHARD MAURICE
Banker. **Personal:** Born Jan 8, 1951, Baltimore, MD; son of John J and Peggy A; married Debra S, Jun 28, 1990; children: Richard Jr, Hakim & Qiana. **Educ:** Temple Univ, Philadelphia, PA, BS, 1974. **Career:** First Pennsylvania Bank, Philadelphia, PA, com loan officer, 1974-79; Crocker Nat Bank, San Diego, CA, asst vpres, 1979-81; San Diego Trust & Savings Bank, San Diego, CA, vpres & mgr, 1981-89; First Interstate Bank, San Diego, CA, vpres, 1989-. **Orgs:** Healthcare Fin Mgmt Asn, 1982-85; treas, Southeast San Diego Rotary Club, 1981-87; Door of Hope Salvation Army, 1981-83; Lay Adv Comt, Mercy Hosp & Med Ctr, 1988-89. **Home Addr:** 6565 Farm Rd 1699, Avery, TX 75554. **Business Addr:** Vice President, Corporate Banking, First Interstate Bank of California, 401 B St Suite 2201, San Diego, CA 92101, **Business Phone:** (619)699-3127.*

POWELL, ROBERT JOHN
Vice president (Organization), executive. **Personal:** Born May 20, 1961, New York, NY; married Carlotta, Jun 1987; children: Selene, Jonathan & Courtney. **Educ:** Fla State Univ, attended 1981; Univ Cent Fla, BA, 1990. **Career:** Walt Disney World, prof musician, personnel rep, sr personnel rep, HRD rep, 1983-94; Carlson Companies, mgr employee rel, dir employee rel, vpres, human resources, 1994-98; Porex Corp, corp vpres, human resources, 1999-2000; AT&T Broadband, vpres, human resources, 2000-01; Archer Daniels Midland, vpres, HR Oper & Workforce Planning, 2001-. **Orgs:** Human resources adv bd, Am Heart Asn, 1997-; regional mem large, vpres, Kappa Kappa Psi; bd dirs, Cochran Mill Nature Ctr; Corpsvets Sr Drum & Bugle corps, 2000-01. **Honors/Awds:** Outstanding Young Man of America, 1984. **Home Addr:** 1401 Waterford Pl, Champaign, IL 61821. **Business Phone:** 800-637-5843.

POWELL, SIS PAULA LIVERS
Historian, educator, administrator. **Personal:** Born Jul 3, 1955, Indianapolis, IN; daughter of Bellwood Livers and Mary Evans; children: Carmin & Camira. **Educ:** FisK Univ, BS, 1977; Butler Univ, Indianapolis, IN, MS, 1987; Univ Calif-Santa Cruz, MA, 1989, Doctoral Studies, 1991. **Career:** Ind Christian Leadership Conf, planning dir, 1977-80; Martin Luther King Ctr Social Change, asst dir protocol, 1980-81; All state Ins Co, sales agt, 1981-83; Indianapolis Pub Schs, Grad Sch, teacher, 1983-87; UCSC-Graudate Div, GOP fel, 1987; Univ Calif, Santa Cruz, founding dean/dir African-Am Resource & Cult Ctr, 1991-; Black By the Bay, Inc, educ & cult Consults, founder & chief exec officer, 1997-; Cabrillo Col, adj prof African-Am hist, 2001-. **Orgs:** Pres, Nat Asn Advan Colored People-Santa Cruz County Br, 1994-; Grad advr, Alpha Kappa Alpha Sorority Inc, 1994; Links, Montery Bay Chap, Int Trends & Servs, 1995-; Jack & Jill Am Inc; Nat Forum Black Pub Admin, 1996-; Am Asn Univ Women, 1999-; Nat Alliance Black Sch Educrs, 1999-; SCLC Women, Inc, Nat Adv Bd, Asn Black Cult Ctrs. **Honors/Awds:** Student Affairs, Incentive Award, Thumbs Up Award, UCSC, 1995, 1996, 1997; Community Service award, Alpha Kappa Alpha Sorority Inc, 1996; Vision Award, Univ Calif Berkeley Black Leadership Conf, 1997; Appreciation, The Links Inc, Monterey Bay, 1998; Living Historymakers Award, Turning Point Mag; NAACP Outstanding Leadership Award. **Business Addr:** Director, University of California-Santa Cruz, African American Student Life Resource & Cultural Center, 1100 High St Suite 347 Baytree Bldg, Santa Cruz, CA 95064, **Business Phone:** (831)459-3651.

POWELL, WAYNE HUGH
Financial manager. **Personal:** Born Jul 29, 1946, Petersburg, VA; son of Willie and Lena; married Leslie J; children: Farrah, Brandi & Kristin. **Educ:** Lincoln Univ, BS Bus Admin, 1970; Rockhurst Col, MBA, Fin, 1979. **Career:** Gen Mills, reg office mgr, 1975-79, reg credit mgr 1980-81, mgr group anal, 1981-82, mgr admin, 1982-85.

POWELL, WILLIAM. See POWELL, DOC.

POWELL, WILLIAM (BILL J POWELL)
Executive. **Personal:** Born Jan 1, 1917?; married Marcella (deceased); children: Renee & Lawrence. **Career:** Timken Bearing & Steel Co, security guard; Clearview Golf Club, owner, currently. **Honors/Awds:** The Jack Nicklaus Golf Family of the Year Award; Cornerstone of Freedom Award; Diamond in the Rough Tribute, Nat Goulf Found. **Military Serv:** AUS, WWII. **Business Addr:** Owner, Clearview Golf Club, 8410 Lincoln Hwy, East Canton, OH 44730, **Business Phone:** (330)488-0404.

POWELL, WILLIAM
Dentist, air force officer. **Personal:** Born Mar 6, 1935, Greenville, MS; married Carolyn M. **Educ:** Xavier Univ New Orleans, 1957; Mehary Med Col Sch Dent, 1963. **Career:** DDS Inc Bakersfield CA, pvt prac dent, 1965-. **Orgs:** Am Dent Asn; CA Dent Asn; Kern Co Dent Soc; Am Endodontic Soc; Aca Gen Dent; Pierre Favehard Acad; Asn Military Surg; Nat Dent Asn; Kern Co Dent Soc, treas 1971, secy, 1972, pres, 1974; Kappa Alpha Psi Frat; Nat Asn Advan Colored People. **Military Serv:** USAF, capt, 1963-65.

POWELL, DR. WILLIAM O
Dentist, educator. **Personal:** Born Sep 19, 1934, Andalusia, AL; son of William O Powell Sr and Myrtle Estelle; married Anna D Thompson; children: Rosalyn F & Michelle R. **Educ:** Talladega Col, AB, 1955; Howard Univ, Col Dentistry, DDS, 1967. **Career:** Ft Detrick, Dept Defense, histopath tech, 1958-61; Mt Sinai Hosp, internship, 1968; Walter Reed Army, Med Ctr, res biologist, 1961-63; Howard Univ, Col Dentistry, asst prof, 1968-69, dir, dent therapist training, 1969-75; Pvt Practice, dentist, 1968-. **Orgs:** Omega Psi Phi Frat; Am Dent Asn; Nat Dent Asn; Md State Dent Asn; Southern Md Dent Soc; Robert T Freeman Dent Soc; Kiwanis Int; Montgomery County Md Drug Abuse Adv Coun; NNGA; Nomads Golf Asn; Pro Duffers Golf Club; Sigma Pi Phi Frat; Rotary Int; Guardsmen DC. **Honors/Awds:** Fel, Am Col Dentists, 1989. **Special Achievements:** Published paper on "Comparison of Dental Therapists Trainee and Dental Students" Journal of Dental Education. **Home Addr:** 14803 Waterway Dr, Rockville, MD 20853. **Business Addr:** Dentist, Private Practice, 809 Viers Mill Rd Suite 213, Rockville, MD 20851, **Business Phone:** (301)762-5575.

POWELL, WILMA D
Executive. **Personal:** Married LeVon. **Career:** Marine Exchange Los Angeles, pres; Port Long Beach, dir trade & maritime serv, 1999-. **Orgs:** City Long Beach Black Managers Asn; Leadership Long Beach; Long Beach YMCA. **Honors/Awds:** Secretary of Defense Award for Outstanding Public Service; Woman of the Year, Nat Woman's Political Caucus of Long Beach, 1993; Dollars for Scholars Humanitarian Award, 1995; US Coast Guard Distinguished Service Medal, 1998. **Special Achievements:** First female president of the Marine Exchange of Los Angeles. **Business Addr:** Trade and Maritime Services Director, Port of Long Beach, 925 Harbor Plz, PO Box 570, Long Beach, CA 90802, **Business Phone:** (562)590-4109.

POWELL, YVONNE MACON (YVONNE MACON COOK)
Administrator. **Personal:** Born Dec 8, 1936, Harlem, NY; daughter of James Macon and Eugenia Wright Jackson; married Alfred J Powell Jr, Sep 2, 1962; children: Richard L Cook III, Stacy D Powell, Alfred Edward Powell, Natasha N Powell, Ronald L Gardner, Towano Y Pittman, Terrence L Gardner, Sharon M Gardner. **Educ:** Tennessee State Univ, Nashville TN, 1957; Mercy Col, Dobbs Ferry NY, BS criminal justice, 1980; Nat Acad Corrections, Denver CO, 3 certificates, 1981, 1982; Long Island Univ, Dobbs Ferry NY, 1981. **Career:** Retired: Dept Public Safety, White Plains NY, parking enforcement, 1962-65; Westchester County Sheriff's Dept, White Plains NY, deputy sheriff, 1967; West County Dept Correction, Valhalla NY, correction officer, 1969-71,

sergeant, 1971-82, captain, 1982-84, asst warden, 1984-88; assoc warden, 1988-91. **Orgs:** NAACP; Urban League Westchester; Daughter Elks-Rosebud Temple; Alpha Kappa Alpha; Alpha Psi Epsilon. **Honors/Awds:** Commissioner's Award, Westchester County Dept Correction, 1981, 1983; Community Service, Central 7, Greenburgh NY, 1982; Member of the Year, Northeast Region Nat Black Police Asn, 1983; Guardian of the Year, Westchester Rockland Guardians Asn, 1984; Contribution to Law Enforcement, Tri-County Fed Police, 1984; Community Serv, Westchester Co-op, 1985; Coach of the Year, Kenisco Little League, 1986; Achievement Award, Nat Negro Bus & Prof Women, 1989; Honorary Doctrate Deg, Dr Humane Letters, Col New Rochelle, New Rochelle NY, 1994; Inductee, Wesichester Women's Hall Fame, 1994. *

POWELL-JACKSON, DR. REV. BERNICE
Administrator, president (organization). **Personal:** Born Mar 9, 1949, Washington, DC; daughter of Otis Fletcher and Bernice Fletcher; married Robert C S (deceased); married Franklin, 1991. **Educ:** Wilson Col, BA, 1971; Columbia Univ Grad Sch Jour, MS, 1975; Union Theol Sem, MDiv, 1991. **Career:** Administrator, president (retired); Wash DC Sch Syst, teacher, 1971-72; Nat Coun Ch, Africa dept asst, 1972-74; Renewal Mag, asst managing ed, 1974-75; Nat Urban League, commun specialist, 1975-77; Equitable Life Assur Soc, assoc mgr pub rel, 1977-79; Women's Div Gov Off NY, spec asst pub info, 1979-; United Church Christ, exec assoc pres, 1989-93, exec dir, CMS Racial Justice, 1993-2000, exec minister, Justice & Witness Ministries; World Coun Churches, pres, North Am, 2004-05. **Orgs:** Bd mem, Manhattan Br NY Urban League, 1978-80; chrmn, Riverside Ch Video Proj, 1979-80; vpres, Coalition 100 Black Women, 1980-81; pres, NY Coalition 100 Black Women, 1981-85. **Honors/Awds:** Hon Doctorate Humane Letters, Defiance Col, 1994. **Business Phone:** (212)870-3260.

POWERS, CLYDE J
Sports manager. **Personal:** Born Aug 19, 1951, Pascagoula, MS. **Educ:** Okla Univ. **Career:** Basket ball Player (retired), dir; NY Giants, defensive back, 1974-78; Kans City Chiefs, defensive back, 1978-79; Indianapolis Colts, asst coach, 1980-82, col scout, 1982-85, 1988-91, dir pro player personnel, 1985-87, 1992-. **Orgs:** Bd dir, Kids' Voice Indiana, 2006-08. **Special Achievements:** Earned All-Big Eight hons at cornerback as a sr at Okla Univ; Coaches All Am "Ernie Davis" Award Winner; played in Blue Gray Football Classic, 1973; Sr Bowl Classic, 1974; capt, Coaches All-Am Team, 1974. **Business Addr:** Director of Pro Player Personnel, Indianapolis Colts, 7001 W 56th St, Indianapolis, IN 46254, **Business Phone:** (317)297-2658.

POWERS, GEORGIA M.
Government official. **Personal:** Born Oct 19, 1923, Springfield, KY; daughter of Frances Walker Montgomery and Ben Montgomery; married James L (deceased); children: William F Davis (deceased), Cheryl Campbell & Deborah Rattle. **Educ:** Lou Munic Col, attended 1943. **Career:** Senator (retired); KY State Senate, sen. **Orgs:** Chmn, Senate Libr & Indust Com; Jeff Co Dem Exec Comm, 1964-66; Libr & Indust Comn; Cities Comm; YWCA; NAACP; Urban League; former Bd overseas Univ Louisville; bd dir, Fund Women Inc. **Honors/Awds:** Kennedy King Award, Young Dem Ky, 1968; Kentucky Congress of Barb & Beau Achievement Award, 1968; Merit award, Zion Bapt Church, 1969; AKA Recognition Award, 1970; Outstanding Service Award, Zeta Phi Beta Sorority, 1971; Isaac Murphy Award, 1981; Clarence Mitchell Award, 1983;Hon Doctor Laws, Univ Ky; DHL, Univ Louisville, 1988; DHL, Ky State Univ, 1990. **Special Achievements:** Author: "I Shared the Dream" (New Horizon Press), 1995; The Adventures of the Book of Revelation (Seng Powers Pub), 1998; First woman and the first Black to be elected to the Kentucky State Senate in 1967. **Home Addr:** 800 S 4th St Apt 2705, Louisville, KY 40203-2135.

POWERS, MAMON M
Executive. **Personal:** Born Mar 10, 1948, Gary, IN; son of Mamon and Leolean; married Cynthia R Berry, Jul 23, 1972; children: Kelly & Mamon. **Educ:** Purdue Univ, BS, civil eng, 1970. **Career:** Am Oil Co, Whiting, Ind, design engr, 1970-71; Powers & Sons Const Co, sec-treas, 1971-87, pres 1987-. **Orgs:** Former pres, Calumet Chap Ind, Soc Prof Engrs; bd dirs, Constr Advance Found; Asn Gen Contrs; former chmn, Const Advanc Found, 1983-85; former pres, Calumet Builders Asn, 1985-87; Nat Asn Minority Contractors; Black Contractors United; Young Press Org; bd trustees, Purdue Univ, 1996-; trustee, Operating Engineers #150 Health, Welfare & Apprenticeship Funds; World Presidents Organization; bd dir, Fifth Third Bank Northern Ind; bd mem, past pres, Boys & Girls Club NW Ind; bd mem, Methodist Hosp; Golden Heritage mem, Nat Asn Advan Colored People; past pres, Ind Soc Engrs-Calumet Chapter & Calumet Builders Asn. **Honors/Awds:** African Am owned business standing 60th largest (industrial & service) 1995; NCP, Benjamin Hooks Award for Achievement; Civil Engineering Alumni Achievement Award, Purdue Univ, 2002; Distinguished Engineering Alumnus Award, Purdue Col Eng, 2003. **Special Achievements:** Company ranked #97 on Black Enterprise's list of top 100 industrial service companies, 1998; featured on the cover of Northwest Indiana Business Quarterly. **Business Addr:** President, Powers & Sons Construction Company Inc, 2636 W 15th Ave, Gary, IN 46404, **Business Phone:** (219)949-3100.

POWERS, RAY
Executive. **Personal:** Born Mar 6, 1946, Topeka, KS; son of Margaret Clark; married Rheugena, Mar 16, 1968; children: Rachelle Spears & Brian. **Educ:** Johnson County Community Col, AA, bus admin, 1980; Cent Mont State, BS, graphic arts tech mgmt, 1982; Baker Univ, MS, mgmt, 1996. **Career:** Hallmark Cards, sect mgr, 1967-77, litho engr, 1977-79, dept mgr, GA technical develop, 1979-87, corp safety, environ dir, 1987-89, prod mgr, 1989-92, plant mgr, KC Mfg Prod Facility, 1992-95, Graphic Arts/N Am Prod, vpres, creative officer, 1995-2000, opers vpres mfg, currently; Commercial Arts Enterprise, Inc, owner, 1971-73. **Orgs:** Bd mem, Minority Supplier Coun; graphic arts adv bd, Central Mont State Univ; bd chair, Minority Suppiler Coun, 2001. **Military Serv:** AUS, 1965-67. **Business Addr:** Operations Vice Pres Graphics Arts/Directory Product Quality Execution, Hallmark Cards, 2501 McGee St, Kansas City, MO 64141-6580, **Business Phone:** (816)274-5111.

POWERS, DR. RUNAS, JR.
Physician. **Personal:** Born Dec 11, 1938, Jackson, AL; son of Runas Powers Sr and Geneva; married Mary Alice, Feb 4, 1969; children: Tiffany, Trina & Runas III. **Educ:** Tenn State Univ, BS 1961; Meharry Med Col, MD, 1966. **Career:** Pvt Pract, physician, currently. **Orgs:** Arthritis Found; Am Rheumatism Asn; Nat Med Asn; Am Fed Clin Res; Am Col Rheumat; AMA. **Honors/Awds:** Man of the Year, Alexander City, 1991. **Military Serv:** USN, Res lt cmdr, 1967-69. **Business Addr:** Physician, 3368 Hwy 280 Bypass Suite 108, Alexander City, AL 35010, **Business Phone:** (256)329-8417.

PRATER, DR. OSCAR L
School administrator, college president. **Personal:** Born in Sylacauga, AL; married Jacqueline P; children: Lamar & Marcus. **Educ:** Talladega Col, BA, 1961; Hampton Univ, MA, 1967; Col William & Mary, MS, 1968, EdD, 1977. **Career:** Educator, col administrator (retired); Middlesex Co Pub Schs, math teacher, 1961-62; Wmsbg-James City Pub Schs, math teacher, 1962-72; Rappahanock Community Col, chmn div math, 1972-79; Hampton Univ, vpres admin serv, 1979-90; Fort Valley State Col, pres, 1990; Talladega Col, pres, 2005-07. **Orgs:** Human Serv Bd, Hampton Roads Cult Action Comn; trustee & chmn, First Baptist Church, 1980-84; instnl rep, Am Coun Teacher Educ, 1980-; mgt consult, Human Admin Leadership Team, 1982-83-84; bd visitors, Va State Univ, 1982-. **Honors/Awds:** Citizen of the Year, Chamber Com, 1970; Outstanding Man of the Year, Omega Psi Phi Fraternity, 1982. **Special Achievements:** Published Fac Perceptions of Selected Stud Characteristics, 1978.

PRATHER, JEFFREY LYNN
Administrator. **Personal:** Born May 14, 1941, New York, NY; son of James Basil and Mary Jane Dickerson. **Educ:** Howard Univ Wash, DC, 1959-60; Queens Col CUNY Flushing NY, BA, 1965; CA State Univ Northridge, CA, MS Equiv, 1967; Rockdale Col, hon doctorate, 1971. **Career:** Operation Head Start, Brooklyn, NY, consult psychologist, 1967-71; MDTP Bd Educ, City NY, asst guid, 1968-72, coun suprvr, 1969-72, admin asst adult training ctr, 1969-72; Sacramento City Col, instr, 1978; Malcoln-King Harlem Col Ext NYC, instr, interim chmn psych, 1979-80; Dept State USA, escort & interpreter, 1979-2002; Sacramento CA, consult juristic psych, 1982-; Pratherian Enterprises, dir, 1972-. **Orgs:** Action Co-op Vol, Attica Correctional Facil, Literacy Vol Am, 1975-76; co proj dir, NY, CA Literacy Vol Am, 1976-77; consult, CA State Dept Educ, Migrant Ed, 1977-79; Int Assoc GP Psychotherapy, Int Coun Psychol, Assoc Black Psychol. **Special Achievements:** Author, "A Mere Reflection, The Psychodynamics of Black & Hispanic Psychology," Dorrance & Co, 1977; author, "400 Days at Attica," Dorrance & Co, 1983. **Home Addr:** 21031 Woodfield Rd, Gaithersburg, MD 20882, **Home Phone:** (301)963-4862. **Business Addr:** Director, Pratherian Enterprises, 21031 Woodfield Rd, Gaithersburg, MD 20882, **Business Phone:** (301)963-4862.

PRATHER, SUSAN LOUISE
Educator, hospital administrator. **Personal:** Born Nov 15, 1959, Norfolk, VA; daughter of William L and Rebecca J. **Educ:** Grambling State Univ, 1992; Hampton Univ, MS, Advan Adult Nursing & Educ, 1987; Hampton Inst, BS, 1984; Norfolk State Univ, AS, 1982. **Career:** Eighteenth Field Hosp, USAR, Norfolk, Va, coordr code blue team, 1985-92, asst weight control officer, 1985-92, security clearance officer, 1986-92, head nurse, ICU, 1986-92, CV Mosby Co, item writer, 1989-92; Norfolk State Univ, asst prof, 1987-89, 1995; Nursing Educ Servs, dir, 1990-; Grambling State Univ, asst prof, 1992-94; Univ Fla, vis asst prof, 1993; Univ Guam, instr, 1999; Publicity Club Chicago, co-pres, currently, Long Range Planning chair, currently. **Orgs:** Asn Black Nursing Fac Higher Educ, 1987; Sigma Theta Tau Soc, 1987; Am Med Detachment Regt, 1987; Tidewater Heart Asn, 1988; Va Cot Cols Asn, 1990; Nat Asn Female Execs; bd dirs, Chicago Athletic Asn; Delta Iota Chap, Sigma Theta Tau Hon Nursing Soc. **Honors/ Awds:** Achievement Award, AUS 1st Army, 1987; Honorary Army Recruiter Commander, AUS Recruiting, 1991; Outstanding Teacher, 1996. **Business Phone:** (312)861-0980.

PRATT, A MICHAEL
Lawyer. **Personal:** Born Apr 1, 1959, Grindstone, PA; son of Joan A Richardson and Brady; married Carla Denise; children: Jeanine, Payton & Christopher. **Educ:** Washington & Jefferson Col, BA, 1981; Univ Stockholm, Int Grad Sch, 1983-84; Harvard Law Sch, JD, 1985. **Career:** Hon Nathaniel R Jones, Sixth Circuit Ct Appeals, law clerk, 1985-86; City Philadelphia Law Dept, chief dep city solicitor, 1992-94; Pepper Hamilton LLP, atty & partner, 1986-92, 1994-. **Orgs:** Pres, Barrister Asn Phila Inc, 1991-92; Philadelphia Bar Asn, Young Lawyers Sect, 1991; bd govs, Nat Bar Asn, 1992-; house deleg, Pa Bar Asn, 1993-; Omega Psi Phi Fraternity; bd dir, City Philadelphia Activities Fund Inc, 1995; Found Educ Excellence Inc; Community Legal Serv Philadelphia Inc; Standing Comt Pro Bono & Pub Serv, Am Bar Asn, 1998-. **Honors/Awds:** Ten Fresh Faces for the 90's, Del Valley Counr, 1989; 40 Under 40 Business Award, Philadelphia Bus Jour, 1991; Nelson Mandela Service Award, Nat Black Law Students Asn, 1992; Equal Justice Award, Community Legal Serv Inc, 1993; Presidential Award, Nat Bar Asn, 1994. **Home Phone:** (215)879-9587. **Business Addr:** Attorney, Partner, Pepper Hamilton LLP, 3000 Two Logan Sq Eighteenth & Arch St, Philadelphia, PA 19103-2799, **Business Phone:** (215)981-4386.

PRATT, ALEXANDER THOMAS
School administrator. **Personal:** Born Sep 18, 1938, St Martinville, LA; son of Louise Thompson and Oliver Thompson; married Mable Agnes Lee; children: Thomas & Thaddeus. **Educ:** Prairie View A&M, BA, 1961, MA, 1963. **Career:** Prairie View A&M, asst circulation libr, 1962-63; La Marque Ind Sch, teacher & head hist dept, 1963-70; Col Mainland, instr, 1970-76, soc sci div, chmn, assoc acad dean, Dept Soc & Behavioral Sci, assoc prof, prof emer, currently. **Orgs:** Mayor, pro tem City La Marque, 1974-; Galveston Co Hist Comn, 1975-; Galveston Co Mayors Asn,1979-80; TX State Comt Urban Needs, 1980-; Phi Alpha Theta; Galveston Hist Found. **Honors/Awds:** HK "Griz" Eckert Award, Col Mainland, 1975; Jaycee of the Year, The La Marque Jaycee, 1975-76; Distinguished Service Award, La Marque Jaycee, 1978; Outstanding Community Service, Delta Sigma Theta, 1980. **Business Addr:** Professor Emeritus, College Mainland, Department Society & Behavioral Science, 1200 Amburn Rd, Texas City, TX 77591, **Business Phone:** (409)938-1211.*

PRATT, AWADAGIN
Pianist, educator. **Personal:** Born Mar 6, 1966, Pittsburgh, PA; son of Theodore and Mildred. **Educ:** Univ Ill, Urbana, violin scholar; Peabody Conserv Music, piano/violin,conducting; Banff Ctr Arts, Canada. **Career:** Albums include: A Long Way From Normal, 1994; Beethoven Piano Sonatas,1996; Live From South Africa, 1997; Transformations, 1999; The Caveman's Valentine, 2002; Univ Cincinnati, Col-Conservatory Music, asst prof piano & artist-in-residence, 2004-; Cramer/Marder Artists, pianist, currently; Next Generation Festival, artistic dir, currently. **Orgs:** Founder, Pratt Music Found; Am Symphony Orchestra League. **Honors/Awds:** Performer's Certificate, Peabody Conserv Music; first prize, Naumburg Competition, NY, 1992; Prestigious Avery Fisher Career Grant, 1994; numerous others. **Special Achievements:** Published numerous articles. **Business Addr:** Associate Professor of Piano, Artist-in-Residence, University of Cincinnati, College-Conservatory of Music, PO Box 210003, Cincinnati, OH 45221-0003, **Business Phone:** (513)556-2063.

PRATT, JOAN M
Government official. **Educ:** Hampton Univ, BS, acct, 1976; Univ Baltimore, MS, taxation, 1978. **Career:** City Baltimore, comptroller, 1995-, Bd Estimates, secy, currently; Coopers & Lybrand; Baltimore Legal Aid Bur, comptroller, 13 yrs; Joan M Pratt CPA & Assoc, pres, currently. **Orgs:** Trustee, Bethel AME Church; bd mem, Park Reist Corridor Coalition; Walters Art Gallery, African Am Steering Comt; Baltimore Mus Art; AKA, Rho Xi Omega Chap. **Special Achievements:** Second African American female city comptroller in the history of Baltimore; One of Maryland's Top 100 Women, Baltimore Mag, 1995. **Business Addr:** Comptroller, City of Baltimore, Office of Comptroller, Rm 204 City Hall 100 N Holliday, Baltimore, MD 21202, **Business Phone:** (410)396-4755.

PRATT, KYLA ALISSA
Actor. **Personal:** Born Sep 16, 1986, Los Angeles, CA; daughter of Johnny McCullar and Kecia Pratt Mccullar. **Educ:** Hamilton Acad Music. **Career:** Actor, 1995-; Films include: The Baby-Sitter's Club, 1995; Mad City, 1997; Riot, 1997; Barney's Great Adventure, 1998; Doctor Dolittle, 1998; Love & Basketball, 2000; One on One, 2000; Dr Dolittle 2, 2001; The Seat Filler, 2004; Fat Albert, 2004; The Proud Family Movie, 2005; Dr. Dolittle 3, 2006; Dr. Dolittle: Tail to the Chief, 2008; Hotel for Dogs, 2009; Dr Dolittle Million Dollar Mutts, 2009; I Can Do Bad All By Myself, 2009; TV series: "Barney & Friends", 1995; "The Parent' Hood", 1995-99; "In the House", 1996; "Sisters", 1996; "Smart Guy", 1997-98; "A Walton Easter", 1997; "Monday After the Miracle", 1998; Jackie's Back!, 1999; Moesha, 1999-2000; "Smart Guy", 1998; "Jackie's Back", 1999; "Strong Med", 2000; "The Proud Family", 2001-05; "Lizzie McGuire", 2001; "One on One", 2001-06; "Maniac Magee", 2003; The Picnic, 2005; The Beach, 2005; Hell on Earth, 2007; ER, 2009. **Honors/Awds:** Nickelodeon Kids Choice Award, Favorite Rising Star, 1999. **Special Achieve-**

ments: Best Nominee for NAACP Image Awards, Young Artist Award & Blockbuster Entertainment Awards. **Business Addr:** Actress, ACME Talent & Literary, 4727 Wilshire Blvd Suite 333, Los Angeles, CA 90010, **Business Phone:** (323)954-2263.*

PRATT, MABLE
Government official, educator. **Personal:** Born May 27, 1943, Houston, TX; married Alexander; children: Thomas & Thaddeus. **Educ:** Prairie View A&M, BS, home econ educ, 1967; Univ Houston, MS, educ mgt, 1978; doctoral prog, 1985. **Career:** Queen Peace Sch Lamarque, second teacher, 1969-70; Sacred Heart Sch Galveston, third grade teacher, 1970-71; Rosenberg Elem Galveston, fifth grade teacher, 1971-77; Rosenberg Elem Galveston, title I reading/math teacher, 1977-82; Alamo Elem Galveston, fifth grade teacher, 1982-; LaMarque Sch Dist, bd mem; McMasters Elem Sch, prin, currently. **Orgs:** Asn Childhood Educ; Tex Classroom Assoc; Tex Prof Educ; Alpha Kappa Alpha Sorority; Am Bus Women's Asn; Am Sch Bd Assoc; Gulf Coast Area Asn Sch Bds; Lamarque Gifted & Talented, Sch Home Adv Panel Educ; dir, LaMarque Youth Aid Proj, United Way Mainland; LaMarque School Bd; Queen Peace Instr, Interior Decorating COM; LaMarque Parent Teachers Asn; Helped to organize Non-Graded Reading Prog, GISD; Teacher Adv Coun; Policy Revision Comn, Pres & several other offs ACE, state vpres, Asn Childhood Educ; hospitality chmn, Rosenberg; served Admin, Designee, ARD Meetings. **Honors/Awds:** Jaycee-ette of the Year, 1974 & 1975; Tex Hon Life Mem, Jaycee-ettes, 1978; Texas Hon Life Mem, PTA, 1980; Service Above Self-Rotary International Award, 1978; Outstanding Young Woman of America, 1979. **Special Achievements:** Attended many seminars on HB 246, HB 72, Chap 75. **Home Addr:** 2616 Lake Park Dr, La Marque, TX 77568.

PRATT, MARVIN E.
Politician, mayor. **Personal:** Born May 26, 1944, Texas; son of Joyce; married Diane Sherrill; children: Michael Pratt. **Educ:** Marquette Univ, attended 1972. **Career:** Milwaukee Common Coun, mem, 1968-87; Milwaukee Common Coun, chmn, 1996-00, pres, 2000; Milwaukee Common Coun, actg mayor, 2004. **Military Serv:** AUS.

PRATT, DR. RUTH JONES (RUTH J KING)
Educator. **Personal:** Born Aug 2, 1923, Baltimore, MD; married James; children: Karl. **Educ:** Coppin State Teachers Col, BS, 1943; Howard Univ, MA, 1948; Johns Hopkins Univ, Univ Md, Towson State Univ & Morgan State Univ, attended. **Career:** Educator (retired); Baltimore City Pub Sch, sr educ officer supt pub instr present; elem prin, 1968-75; asst prin elem sch, 1963-68; curriculum specialist elem sch, 1961-63; sr teacher master teacher, 1959-61; supr teacher, 1952-55; demo teacher, 1945-49; teacher, 1943; Morgan State Univ, asst prof reading develop & educ psychol, 1969-73; Reading Workshops, consult, 1968-71; Human Rels Inst Towson State Univ, consult, 1968-70; Youth Summer Human Rels Workshop Nat Conf Christians & Jews, 1969-70; cosmetics consultant wig stylist, 1968-77. **Orgs:** Chmn, Miss United Negro Col Fund Contest, 1972-76; vpres, Provident Hosp Aux, 1974-75; exec, com dir search talent, 1969-76; chmn, 85th Anniv Sharon, 1970; Comn, Leaders Am, 1971; chmn, United Fund CICHA Campaign Baltimore City Pub Schs, 1975-77; allocation panel United Fund, 1976-77; bd dir, United Way, 1976-79; chmn, Baltimore Employ Adv Com, 1976-77; pres, Prof United Serv Cherry Hill Comn, 1970-75; long range planning comn, Girl Scouts Cent, Md, 1976-79; bd dir, YWCA Cent Md, 1977; comn, Preserv Orchard St Ch, 1977; pres, Baltimore Alumnae Chap Delta Sigma Theta Sor, 1974-76; Mayor's Bicent Ball Comn, 1976; Afro Am Expo Steering Com 1976-77; Sharon Bapt Ch; organ dir, Sunday Sch Choir; chmn, Annual Mus Scholarship Benefit. **Honors/Awds:** Serv Cert, SE Br Kiwanis Club, 1975; Certificagte Award, plaque Delta Sigma Theta Sor; sincere serv, plaque PUSH, 1975; outstanding woman, panelist St John's Bapt Ch, 1977; Community Service Award, United Fund-CICHA Campaign, 1975-76.

PRELOW, ARLEIGH
Movie director, writer, graphic artist. **Personal:** Born Feb 1, 1953, Los Angeles, CA; daughter of Leona Kern and Clifford Nathaniel; children: Alison Guillory & Kara Guillory. **Educ:** Univ Calif, Berkeley, BA, 1974; Laney Col, Oakland, CA, 1986; Univ Calif, Los Angeles, 1989. **Career:** Black Thoughts Newspaper, feature ed & writer, 1973-74; Portland Observer, writer, 1975; KQIV-Radio, Portland, OR, prog producer, host, writer, & spot announcer, 1975; KPIX-TV, San Francisco, CA, segment producer & writer, researcher, prod asst & secy, 1975-77; WTBS-TV, Atlanta, GA, producer, writer, researcher & on-air dir, 1977-78; WSB-TV, Atlanta, segment writer & researcher, 1977; Inspirit Commun, founder; WETA-TV, Wash, DC, assoc producer, 1978-80; Scott Hall Prod, San Anselmo, CA, adminr, 1980-81; Moti-Vision, Richmond, CA, exec dir & producer, 1981-84; Arleigh Prelow Design, Los Angeles, owner & graphic designer, 1984-90; ROJA Prod, Boston, MA, filmmaker & adminr, 1990-93; Inspirits Commun, founder, 1993-; freelance writer, Boston, MA; Double-Take Summer Documentary Inst, teaching fel. **Orgs:** Writer, Soul Newsmagazine, 1978; secy & mem, Nat Asn Negro Bus & Prof Women's Clubs, 1986-89; Worship 89 Conf Planning Comm, Synod Southern Calif & Hawaii Presbyterian Church USA, 1988-89; treas & mem, Presbyterian Women, Redeemer Presbyterian Church, Los Angeles, 1988-. **Honors/Awds:** Emmy Award, Acad TV Arts & Sci, Atlanta, 1978; Cappy Awards, Calif Pub Info Officers Asn, 1988; Mercury Awards, Gold Winner Mag Design Int, 1988; City Hall Digest Awards, Ggrand Prize, Best Publ, US & Canada, 1988. **Special Achievements:** We're Power Together, a video documentary exploring the Committee for Boston Public Housing's impact on the lives of Boston's public housing residents, Men of Vision for the Boston Museum of Afro American History, and two segments of Simon and Schuster's interactive videodisc on Harriet Tubman for eighth grade classrooms. **Business Addr:** Founder, Inspirit Communications, 2342 Shattuck Ave Suite 203, Berkeley, CA 94704, **Business Phone:** (510)666-0075.

PRESLEY, OSCAR GLEN
Veterinarian. **Personal:** Born Dec 19, 1942, Kosciusko, MS; married Ethel Rita Scott; children: Wanda, Glen Jr, Corey. **Educ:** Rust Col, BS, 1966; Tex Southern Univ, MS, 1971; Tuskegee Inst, DVM, 1974. **Career:** Meridian Pub Sch, teacher, 1967-69, dir independent study, 1968-69; Tuskegee Sch Vet Med Freshman Class, pres, 1969-70; Lexington Animal Clinic, pres; Hanging Moss vet Clin, veterinarian, currently. **Orgs:** Bd mem, Jackson Chap Nat Bus League 1977-; bd mem, K & S Chem,l 1979-; bd mem New Hope Church, 1980-84; vpres, Miss Vet Med Asn, 1983; Nat chmn Fund Raising Rust Col, 1983; Phi Beta Sigma, 1985; Lexington & hanging Moss Clinics, pres. **Honors/Awds:** Outstanding Young Man of America, 1972; Outstanding Service Award, Jackson State Univ Minority Student 1985, 86. **Military Serv:** AUS, capt, 2 yrs. **Home Addr:** 571 Woodson Dr, Jackson, MS 39206. **Business Addr:** Veterinarian, Hanging Moss vet Clin, 1250 Forest Ave, Jackson, MS 39206.*

PRESS, DR. HARRY CODY, JR.
Educator, physician. **Personal:** Born Aug 22, 1931, Chesapeake, VA; son of Harry Press and Vianna; married Francella Jane Teele; children: H Cody III & Lillian Jan. **Educ:** Va Union Univ, BS, 1952; Med Col Va, MD, 1957; Am Bd Radiol, Dipl, 1965; Am Col Radiol, attended 1980. **Career:** Educator(retired), Physician; Howard Univ, chmn, dept radiol, 1966-79, prof radiol, 1978-; pvt practice, currently. **Orgs:** Const radiol, Commty Group Found, 1969-; adv bd, Wash Inst Technol, 1970-78; comt grants James Picker Found, 1972-74; bd dir, Silver Spring Boys Club, 1971-74; sr warden Trinity Epis Church, 1972-74; phys Bethesda Chevy Chase Football Team, 1984. **Honors/Awds:** Special Service Award, Howard Univ Const, 1975; invested foreign bds, Am Jour Roentol, 1976; Med team Urban League Track Run, 1981-82. **Military Serv:** USN, lt med Officer, 2 yrs. **Home Addr:** 6745 Newbold Dr, Bethesda, MD 20817, **Home Phone:** (301)365-3435.

PRESSEY, JUNIUS BATTEN, JR.
Executive. **Personal:** Born Apr 6, 1947, Hampton, VA; married Elaine F Jenkins. **Educ:** Central State Univ, bus admin, 1972; Ind Univ, BS, 1975; Col Financial Planning, attending. **Career:** Magnavox Corp, acct, 1972-73; City Utility Ft Wayne, IN, acct trainee, 1974; Nat Life & Acct Ins Co, life ins agent, 1975-76; Metrop Life Ins Co, sales rep, 1976-79; Lincoln Nat Sales Corp, tax deferred prog mgr, 1979-; Lincoln Nat Life Employee Benefits Div, pensions mkt, 1984-86; Pressey Financial Planning Group Inc, pres, chmn, Communications consult, currently; BreadFromHeaven Int Ministries, Sch Trust, pres, currently. **Orgs:** Bd mem, Ft Wayne Opportunity Indust Ctr Inc, 1975-; Ft Wayne Nat Life Underwriters Asn, 1976-, Ind Life Ins Leaders Club; bus consult, Proj Bus Jr Achievement 1978; bd mem, Ft Wayne Sickle Cell Found, 1978-; pres, Nat Asn Advan Colored People, Ft Wayne, 1978-; chmn, Econ Task Force Ft Wayne Future Inc C of C, 1978-79; chmn, Ft Wayne Affirmative Action Adv Coun, 1980-86; Harvest Food Bank, 1983-87; chmn, Ft Wayne NBE/WBE Coun, 1984-86; Ft Wayne Anti-Apartheid Action Comn, 1985; pres, Ft Wayne/Allen City Martin Luther King Jr Mem Inc, 1985-87; bd mem, Ft Wayne Bus Coun, 1986; Int Fin Planners Asn, 1986. **Honors/Awds:** Metropolitans Leader Club Met Life Ins Co, 1976; National Sales Achievement Award, Nat Life Underwriters Asn, 1978-79; Agent of the Year Award, Gen Agent & Mgt Asn, 1978; The Cosmopolitan Outstanding Leadership Award, 1982; The Frederick Douglass Award, 1982; Indiana Grand Lodge Prince Hall Freedom Award, 1983; Marjorie D Wickliffe Award, Nat Asn Advan Colored People, 1983. **Military Serv:** USAF, a/1c, 1966-70; National Defense Award. **Home Phone:** (219)485-5133. **Business Addr:** President, BreadFromHeaven International Ministries, School of Truth, 6005 Sawmill Woods Dr Suite 7007, Fort Wayne, IN 46835, **Business Phone:** (260)486-3735.

PRESSEY, PAUL MATTHEW
Basketball coach, basketball player. **Personal:** Born Dec 24, 1958, Richmond, VA; married Elizabeth; children: Angela, Phillip, Ashley & Matthew. **Educ:** Univ Tulsa, BS, phys edn, 1982. **Career:** Basketball player (retired), basketball coach; Milwaukee Buck, 1983-90; San Antonio Spurs, 1990-92; Golden State Warriors, player & asst coach,1992-94; San Antonio Spurs, asst coach; Orlando Magics, asst coach, 2000-04; Boston Celtics, asst coach, 2004-07; New Orleans Hornets, asst coach, currently. **Honors/Awds:** MVC Player of the Year Award, 1982; All America honor. **Business Phone:** (504)593-4833.*

PRESSLEY, CONDACE L
Journalist. **Personal:** Born Jan 1, 1964?, Marietta, GA. **Educ:** Univ Ga, BA, 1986. **Career:** WSB Radio, anchor & reporter, 1986-88, news assignment ed, 1988-94, asst news dir, 1994-99, asst prog dir, 1999-. **Orgs:** Atlanta Asn Black Journalists, 1986-, pres, 1992-95; Nat Asn Black Journalists, 1987-, Region IV, regional dir, 1995-99, vpres broadcast, 1999-01, pres, currently; UNITY: Journalists Color, treasurer, 2003-; bd dirs & regional dir, RTNDA, 2003. **Honors/Awds:** One of Ten Outstanding People in Atlanta, Outstanding Atlanta, 1994; Murrow Award, RTNDA; Outstanding Young Alumnus, Univ Ga; Radio News Woman of the Year, Am Women Radio & Television. **Business Addr:** Assistant Program Director, WSB Radio, 1601 W Peachtree St, Atlanta, GA 30309, **Business Phone:** (404)897-6297.*

PRESSLEY, DELORES
Manager, consultant, founder (originator). **Educ:** Univ Akron, BA. **Career:** Motivational Speaker, trainer, consultant; BornSuccessful, pres, currently; Dimensions Plus, founder & dir, currently. **Orgs:** Nat Speakers Asn; vice-pres, Asn Better Community Develop, currently; founder, Plus USA Woman Beauty Pageant and Convention. **Honors/Awds:** Outstanding Community Service Award, Univ Akron; Successful Business Women & Leadership Award, Women's Leadership Caucus; Successful Entrepreneur, Madelyne Blunt Found. **Special Achievements:** Top Ten Ohio Women Business Owners by the National Association of Women Business Owners (NAWBO) & Key Bank Corporation; ATHENA Finalist sponsored by Inside Business Magazine; author, Clean Out the Closets of Your Life,Advanced Revelations to Modelingand Believe in the Power of You; host of the "DeLores Pressley Show", a success and inspirational show, heard on Joy 1520 am radio and a television host of The BornSuccessful Show. **Business Addr:** Director, Founder, Dimensions Plus, 551 36th St NW, PO Box 9049, Canton, OH 44711, **Business Phone:** (330)649-9809.

PRESSLEY, SYLVIA. See WOODS, SYLVIA.

PRESSON, RONALD TYSON. See TYSON, RON.

PRESTAGE, JAMES J.
Educator. **Personal:** Born Apr 29, 1926, Deweyville, TX; son of James and Mona Wilkins; married Jewel Limar Prestage, Aug 12, 1953; children: Terri, James Grady, Eric, Karen, Jay. **Educ:** Southern Univ, Baton Rouge, BS, biol, 1950; Univ Iowa, MS, zoology, 1955, PhD, zoology, 1959. **Career:** Educator (retired); Prairie View A&M Univ, Prairie View, instr, biol, 1955-56; Southern Univ, Baton Rouge, from asst prof to assoc prof, biol, 1959-68, dir comput ctr, chair, comput sci, 1968-73; La Coordinating Coun Higher Educ, asst dir, 1972-73; Southern Univ, Baton Rouge, LA, dean acad affairs, 1973, vpres, 1973-82, chancellor, 1982-86; Dillard Univ, distinguished prof biol, 1987-97, chair, div Nat Sci, 1991-97. **Orgs:** Vpres, Conf LA Cols & Univ, 1974-75; comn scholars, State Ill Bd Higher Educ; pres, Beta Iota Lambda Chap, Alpha Phi Alpha Fraternity, 1975; exec bd, Istrouma Coun, Boy Scouts Am; bd trustees, Am Col Testing, 1983-88. **Honors/Awds:** Jour Morphol; Jour Parasitol; Cum Laude, Southern Univ, 1950; Sigma Xi Scientific Honors Soc, 1958; Alpha Kappa Mu Honor Soc, Southern Univ, 1949; Fel Nat Med Fellowships Inc, 1956-59; Outstanding Faculty Mem, Southern Univ, 1966-67. **Military Serv:** USN, 1944-46, 1950-52. **Home Addr:** 2145 77th Ave, Baton Rouge, LA 70807. *

PRESTAGE, DR. JEWEL LIMAR
Educator, school administrator. **Personal:** Born Aug 12, 1931, Hutton, LA; daughter of Sallie Bell Johnson Limar and Brudis L Limar; married Dr James J; children: Terri, J Grady, Eric, Karen & Jay. **Educ:** Southern Univ & A&M Col, BA 1951; Univ Iowa, MA, 1952, PhD, 1954; Loyola Univ, Chicago, DHL, 1999. **Career:** Prairie View A&M Col, assoc prof Polit Sci, 1954-56; Southern Univ, assoc prof Polit Sci, 1956-62, prof Polit Sci, 1965, chairperson polit sci, 1965-83, dean sch Pub Policy & Urban Affairs, 1983-89, dean Sch PubPolicy & Urban Affairs, currently; Benjamin Banneker Honor Col, interim dean & honors prof polit sci, 1989, dean, 1990-98. **Orgs:** Pres, SW Soc Sci Asn Scientists, 1973-74; state chmn & mem, La St Adv Comt US Comn Civil Rights, 1974-81; vpres, Am Polit Sci Asn, 1974-75; chairperson, La State Adv Comt, US Comn Civil Rights, 1975-81; pres, Southern Polit Sci Asn, 1975-76; pres, Nat Conf Black Polit Scientist, 1976-77; mem bd, Voter Educ Project, Atlanta, Ga, 1978-; bd mem, La CommonCause, 1983-; bd mem, La Capital Area Chap Am Red Cross, 1985-; AlphaKappa Alpha Sor Inc; Jack & Jill Am Inc; Links Inc; pres, Nat Asn African Am Honors Progs, 1993-94; life mem, Alumni Asn; Ford Found Comt; Progs Assist Black Col; bd dirs, Voter Educ Proj, Atlanta, Ga; pres carter, Nat Adv Coun Women's Educ Progs, US Dept Educ; consultant to 26 organizations. **Honors/Awds:** Res fel Ford Found, 1969-70; Citizen of the Yr, Alpha Kappa Alpha Sorority S Central, 1971; co-author, A Port Marginality The Polit Behavior Am Women, 1977; Distinguished Alumni Award, Nat Asn Equal Opportunity Higher Educ, 1981; Baton Rouge Women of Achievement Award, 1983; Honor, Women's Pavillion, 1984; World's Fair, 1984; Honored Contributer, Prof Am Polit Sci Asn, 1984; Distinguished Alumni Achievement Award, Univ Iowa, 1986; Hancher-Finkbine Medallion, Univ of Iowa, 1989; Fannie Lou Hamer Award, Nat Conf Black Polit Scientists, 1989; Univ Dist Columbia, LHD, 1994; hondoc Law, Spelman Col, 1999; Frank Goodnow, Am Polit Sci Asn, 1998. **Business Addr:** Dean of the School of Public

Policy & Urban Affairs, Political Scientist, Southern University, PO Box 3677, Baton Rouge, LA 70813, **Business Phone:** (225)771-4500.*

PRESTON, EDWARD LEE. See Obituaries section.

PRESTON, EDWARD MICHAEL (MIKE PRESTON)
Columnist, journalist. **Personal:** Born Mar 7, 1959, Baltimore, MD; son of James Sr and Grace; married; children: Eboni & Marcellus. **Educ:** Towson Univ, BA, mass commun, 1981. **Career:** News Am, agate clerk, 1978-79; Baltimore Sun, agate clerk, 1982-87, soccer writer, 1987-88, Col football writer, 1988-93, feature writer, 1993-96, Ravens beat writer, 1996-2000, sports columnist, 2000-. **Orgs:** Asst dir, Sports Ministy, Westminster, MD, 2000-; Bd Selectors, Nat Football League Hall Fame, 2001-; Md Youth Lacrosse Asn. **Honors/Awds:** Best Enterprise Reporting, Asn press sports eds, 1994; first place in sports story, Md SPJ Soc, 1995. **Special Achievements:** All-State offensive tackle, 1980, 1981; Outstanding Student Athlete, Townson Univ, 1980 & 1981; Baltimore County Wrestling Hall of Fame, inductee, 1998. **Business Addr:** Sports Columnist, Baltimore Sun, 501 N Calvert St, Baltimore, MD 21278, **Business Phone:** (410)876-3055.

PRESTON, EUGENE ANTHONY
Executive. **Personal:** Born Jan 10, 1952, Zanesville, OH; married Karen Y Booker. **Educ:** Cent State Univ, Wilberforce, Oh, 1971; Franklin Univ, Columbus, OH, AS Bus Mgt, BS; Eastern Union Bible Col, Columbus; Ashland Theol Seminary, MA. **Career:** Perry Community Drug Abuse Coun, pres, 1973-80; Rendville, mayor, 1975-80; Rendville Housing Auth, vpres, 1976-80; Perry Community Planning Comn, chmn, 1976-80; Arvin Systems Inc, former asst serv mgr; Am Electric Power, contract dir, currently. **Orgs:** Committeeman, Dem Cent, 1971-79; Rendville Village Coun, 1973-75; exec dir, Perry Community Planning Comn, 1976-78; deacon, New Salem Bapt Ch; past pres, OH Bapt Gen Conf Laymens Aux, 1978-82; pres, Lancaster-Fairfield Co NAACP, 1980-84; former vpres, Providence Baptist Asn, BTU; former treas, Providence Baptist Asn Laymen's Aux; fel N Am Baptist Men; spec projects comn Nat Baptist Conv USA Laymens Aux; Omega Psi Phi Fraternity. **Special Achievements:** Listed in Nat Jaycee's Outstanding Young Men of America, 1983. **Home Addr:** 348 Kendall Pl, Columbus, OH 43205.

PRESTON, FRANKLIN DEJUANETTE
Automotive executive. **Personal:** Born Nov 28, 1947, Kansas City, KS; son of Vivian A Wilson and Beryl L Sr; married Alpha Theresa Johnson, Oct 8, 1972; children: Kameron DeJon, Ashley Terese, Christopher Franklin. **Educ:** Gen Motors Inst, BSME, 1970; Univ Mo, indust eng prog, 1977; Gen Motors Inst Engineering & Management Inst, MS, mfg mgt, 1991. **Career:** Executive (retired); Gen Motors, Assembly Div, Fairfax, engr, supvr, 1970-76, hq sr proj engr, 1977-79, Doraville, qual control supt, 1979, Fisher Body Div, div & plant engr, 1982-85, BOC, FAD, facil engr, dir, 1985-92, CLCD, mfg tech staff, mgr, 1992-94, N Am Opers Metal Fabricating Div, Pontiac Site Oper, mgr, 1994-. **Orgs:** choir & men's fel, Trinity Baptist Church, 1977-; Oakland County Chap, Jack & Jill Am, 1978-; sunday sch teacher, Trinity Baptist Church, 1983-; Bd Deacons, Trinity Baptist Church, secy, 1985-89; Adv Bd, ASPIRE, 1986-88; vice chmn, Trinity Baptist Church, 1989-; bd dir, Kettering Univ; bd dir, Metro Housing Partnership Flint & Genesse Co, 1992-95. **Home Addr:** 1647 Caliper Dr, Troy, MI 48084, **Home Phone:** (313)649-3129.

PRESTON, GEORGE NELSON (OSAFUHIN KWAKU NKONYANSA)
Educator. **Personal:** Born Dec 14, 1938, New York, NY; married Adele Regina; children: Matthew, Afua-Magdalena & John. **Educ:** City Col NY, BA, 1962; Columbia Univ, MA, 1967, PhD, 1973. **Career:** Rutgers Univ, asst prof art & art hist, 1970-73; Livingston Col, Dept Art, fac; City Univ, City Col, Dept Art & Hist, from asst prof art to assoc prof, 1973-80, prof emer, currently. **Orgs:** Special consult, New York State Community Arts, 1967-68; special consult,New World Cultures, Brooklyn Mus, 1968; foreign area fel, Joint Comt Am Coun Learned Soc & Soc Sci Res Coun, 1968-70, 1972; assoc, Columbia Univ Seminar Primitive & Precolumbian Art, 1973-80; bd dir, Bd Adult Educ, Mus African Art, Wash, DC, 1972-80; Roger Morris-Jumel Hist Soc, 1973-80; bd dir, Cinque Gallery, New York, NY, 1977-79. **Special Achievements:** Numerous publications. **Business Addr:** Professor Emeritus, City University of New York, City College, Art Department, CG M258 160 Convent Ave, New York, NY 10031-9101, **Business Phone:** (212)650-7431.*

PRESTON, JOSEPH
State government official. **Personal:** Born May 28, 1947, New Kensington, PA; son of Joseph and Therese Mae Buckner; married Odelfa Smith; children: Joseph III & Diana. **Educ:** Univ Pittsburgh, BA, 1979. **Career:** Pa House Rep, 24th Legis Dist, rep, 1983-. **Orgs:** Bd mem, Homewood Revit Develop Corp; bd mem, Allegheny Acad; Pittsburgh Water & Sewer Authority; Nat Orgn Women; Nat Conf Black State Legis; Nat Asn Advan Colored People; Pittsburgh River Life Task Force; trustee, Temple Baptist Church; E Liberty Chamber Com. **Business Addr:** Legislator, Pennsylvania House of Representatives, 330 K Leroy Irvis Office Bldg, PO Box 202024, Harrisburg, PA 17120-2024, **Business Phone:** (717)783-1017.

PRESTON, DR. MICHAEL B
School administrator, college teacher. **Personal:** Born Aug 20, 1933, Tyler, TX; son of Dwight M Preston and Marie B Preston Bicknell; married Mary E; children: Sherry, Sonja, Adrienne & Rymicha. **Educ:** Wiley Col, Marshall, Tex, BA, social sci, 1954; Univ Calif, Berkeley, Calif, MA, polit sci, 1971, PhD, polit sci, 1974. **Career:** Univ Calif, Berkeley, Calif, lectr, 1968-73, supvr social sci, prof, 1968-73; Univ Ill, Urbana, Ill, asst prof to prof, 1973-86; Univ Chicago, vis assoc prof, 1983-84; Univ SC, Los Angeles, Calif, prof & chair polit sci, 1986-95, Ctr Multiethnic & Transnational Studies, dir, currently; Western Polit Sci Asn, pres, 1995-96. **Orgs:** Pres, Nat Conf Black Polit Scientists, 1985-86; vpres, Midwest Polit Sci Asn, 1985-87; Nat Adv Comt, Inst Govt & Pub Affairs, Univ Ill, 1986-; Exec Coun, Western Political Sci Asn, 1988-90, pres; vpres, Am Polit Sci Asn, 1989-90; Task Force Los Angeles Urban League. **Honors/Awds:** Distinguished Scholar Award, Am Polit Sci Asn, 1990; Leadership Award, Champaign County Urban League, 1982. **Special Achievements:** Author, The New Black Politics, second ed, Longman Press, 1987, The Politics of Bureaucratic Reform: the Case of California State Employment Service, Univ Ill Press, 1984; Co-editor, Race, Sex, and Policy Problems, Lexington Books, 1979; Racial and Ethnic Politics in California, Vol second (ed with Bruce Cain and Sandra Bass), Inst Government Press, Univ Calif, Berkeley, 1998; "Coalition Politics in the twenty first Century: Problems and Opportunities," in African Americans in Los Angeles: Prospects for the twenty first Century, J Eugene Grisby III, ed The Planning Group, August, 2000; Revision of Racial and Ethnic Politics in California Vol III, 2004. **Military Serv:** AUS, 1955-57. **Business Addr:** Director, University of Southern California, Center for Multiethnic and Transnational Studies, 363 VKC Univ Park, PO Box 0044, Los Angeles, CA 90089-0044, **Business Phone:** (213)740-8501.

PRESTON, MIKE. See PRESTON, EDWARD MICHAEL.

PRESTON, ROELL
Football player. **Personal:** Born Jun 23, 1972, Miami, FL. **Educ:** Univ Miss. **Career:** Football player (retired); Atlanta Falcons, wide receiver, 1995-96; Wash Redskins, 1997; Green Bay Packers, 1997-98; Tenn Titans, 1999; Miami Dolphins, 1999; San Francisco 49ers, wide receiver, 1999; Chicago Enforcers, Xtreme Football League, wide receiver, 2001. **Honors/Awds:** Pro Bowl (x1), 1998; All-Pro, 1998.

PRESTON, SWANEE H. T., JR.
Physician. **Personal:** Born Mar 10, 1924, Dallas, TX; son of Swanee and Beulah M Williams; married Hazel Elizabeth Bjorge; children: Dorrlyn Jean, Tyrone Hudson, Wayne Raynard. **Educ:** Wiley Col Marshall, Tx, BS, 1943; Great Lakes Col, OH, MM, 1948, DM, 1952; Am T Univ Arcade MO, ND, 1953; Univ Cincinnati CT, Coun. **Career:** Physician (retired); pvt pract, 1952; Hair Weev Inc, adv, 1957-72; City Cleveland, EMT para medic, 1973-79; Operation Newstart, soc worker, drug counseling spt, 1976-80; Salvation Army, supvr stores, 1980-83; Dept Intimate Serv, actg unit dir soc serv, 1982-92. **Orgs:** vpres, NY Naturapathic Soc; founder, Phys Med Soc; Am Technol Asn; 1st aid & emergency care, Am Red Cross; CPR, Am Heart Asn; bd, YMCA; Nat Hole One Asn; USGA; PGA; ordained elder, Presbyteria USA; North Lake Presbyterian Church, leader, Extended Holy Communion Table Ministry, asst teacher, Bible group, choir mem, small group leader. **Honors/Awds:** Aus Man of the yr, Hair Inc, 1964; Busn Man Day Radio Sta WDOK; Myr Coun City Cleve Carl Stokes Mayor; LA soc Int Who's Who; Int Man of the Year, Twentieth Century Award for Achievement, IBC, 1999-00. **Military Serv:** USCG, lt 1/c, 3 yrs, 5 Battle Stars & Medals & Theater Ribbons, 1943-46. **Home Addr:** 9378 SE 174 Loop, Summerfield, FL 34491, **Home Phone:** (352)347-1370. *

PRESTONIA, ANU. See FRANKLIN, PRESTONIA D.

PRESTON-WILLIAMS, RODENA
Musician, business owner. **Personal:** Born Apr 7, 1938, Houston, TX; daughter of George and Robbie; divorced; children: Deborah Del Cambre, Henry Sloan jr, Renee Hence & Regina McDuel. **Career:** La Unified Sch Dist, admin asst, 1980-2000; Preston Music Group, owner & musician, currently. **Orgs:** Choir coordr, McDonald's Gospelfest, 1996-00; dir music/pianist, Brookins AME Ch, 1999-; bd mem, performance div chair, Gospel Music Workshop; chap rep, Los Angeles Chap, Gospel Music Workshop Am, currently. **Honors/Awds:** Musician of the Year, Gospel Music Workshop, 1985, 1986, 1995, Founders Award, 1990. **Home Addr:** PO Box 56167, Los Angeles, CA 90056, **Home Phone:** (323)937-7102. **Business Addr:** Owner, Musician, Preston Music Group, 6709 LaTijera, PO Box 305, Los Angeles, CA 90045-2017, **Business Phone:** (323)937-7102.

PRESTWIDGE-BELLINGER, BARBARA ELIZABETH
Banker, vice president (organization). **Personal:** Born Dec 5, 1945, Baltimore, MD; daughter of Algernon A and Gladys Thompson (deceased); married George M, Oct 7, 1989; children: Monique A Jackson & Melanie K Jackson. **Educ:** Howard Univ, BA, 1967; Southern CT State Univ, MS Ed, 1972; CT Sch Broadcasting, graduate, 1979. **Career:** Essex Co Coll, adj instructor, 1972-77; South End Community Day Care Ctr, exec dir, 1972-74; Kean Col, adj instructor, 1974-77; Farleigh Dickinson Univ, adjunct instructor, 1975-77; Messiah Luthern Day Care Ctr, dir, 1976-77; Child Care Gtr Bpt, exec dir 1977-78; Sacred Heart Univ, adjunct instructor, 1980; Peoples Bank Bridgeport, branch mgr, 1984, asst treasurer, 1984-86, asst vice pres, mgr, Boston Ave Office, 1986, vpres, 1987-94, vpres, mgr, Sales Serv & Tech Training, 1994-96, vpres, mgr, Recruiting, 1996-98, vpres, mgr, Employee Rel, 1998, vpres human resources, currently. **Orgs:** Vice chmn, 1982, chmn, 1982-87, Action for Bridgeport Comm Dev, Inc; allocation comm, 1980-, loaned exec, 1983, United Way of Fairfield Co 1983; mem, Coalition of 100 Black Women, 1986-; moderator "Today's Woman" radio talk show WICC Radio Bridgeport, 1979; advisory bd mem, Bridgeport Public Educ Fund, 1984-; bd mem, Greater Bridgeport Symphony, 1989-. **Honors/Awds:** Alpha Phi Alpha Sweetheart, 1965; Pi Sigma Alpha Pol Sci Honor Soc, 1967; Chairman's Award People's Bank, 1984; Hawley Award for Public Service, People's Bank Bridgeport, 1987; Woman of Distinction Award, Housatonic Girl Scout Council, 1996; Bus Award, Bridgeport Regional Bus Coun, 1995. **Home Addr:** 135 Brooklawn Ave, Bridgeport, CT 06604, **Home Phone:** (203)384-9228. **Business Addr:** Vice President, Human Resources, People, 850 Main St, Bridgeport, CT 06604, **Business Phone:** (203)338-2389.

PRETTYMAN, QUANDRA
Educator. **Personal:** Born Jan 19, 1933, Baltimore, MD. **Educ:** Antioch Col, BA, 1954; Univ Mich, grad study, 1957. **Career:** New Sch Social Res, lectr, 1959-62; Col Ins, instr, 1962-67; Scholastic Book Serv, NY, Open Boat & other short stories by Stephen Crane, ed, 1968; Barnard Col, Women's Studies Dept, sr assoc eng lectr, currently. **Special Achievements:** Out Of Our Lives: A Selection of Contemporary Black Fiction, Howard Univ Press, 1975, poems in many anthologies Most Notable Arnold Adoff, The Poetry of Black America, Black World Barnard Publication'; Her poem "When Mahalia Sings? was included in the landmark book I Am the Darker Brother published in 1968. **Business Addr:** Associate professor of English, Barnard College, English Department, 3009 Broadway, 415 Barnard Hall, New York, NY 10027-6598, **Business Phone:** (212)854-2110.

PREVOT, RAPHEAL M
Lawyer. **Personal:** Born Nov 22, 1958, Memphis, TN; son of Rapheal Sr and Flossie Prevot; married Roberta M Gumbel, Sep 14, 1991; children: Rapheal M III. **Educ:** Ind Univ, BS, 1981, JD, 1984. **Career:** Dade County FL, asst state atty, 1984-89; Adorno & Zeder, et al, assoc coun, 1989-91; Nat Football League, labor rels coun, 1991-. **Orgs:** Bd mem, Ind Univ Law Alumni, 1994-2001, pres, 1999-2000; chmn, Labor Law Sect, Nat Bar Asn, 1996-98, bd gov, 1996-2002, region II dir, 1998-2002, exec comt, 1998-2002; Ind Univ Law Bd Visitors, 1997-, chair 2007-08; Ind Univ, exec comt, 2000-03; bd mem, Nat Bar Inst, 2004-. **Honors/Awds:** Thomas J Hennessy Award, Ind Univ, 1999; President Award, 1999; Outstanding Region Award, 1999; Distinguished Service Award, Ind Univ Sch Law Bloomington, 2004; Person of the Year Award, BALSA Ind Univ, 2007. **Business Addr:** Labor Relation Counsel, National Football League, 280 Pk Ave Suite 12W, New York, NY 10017, **Business Phone:** (212)450-2000.

PREWITT, AL BERT
Educator, government official. **Personal:** Born Feb 17, 1907, Tuscaloosa, AL; married Audrey Monroe; children: Jean, AB, Jr, Juan, Maryann Davis, Gloria P Cooke, Jessee D. **Educ:** Langston Univ, BSA, 1935. **Career:** Langston Univ, instr, 1934-47; Langston High Sch, teacher, 1947-57; Boley High Sch, teacher, 1958-65; City Langston, chmn-trustee bd. **Honors/Awds:** Al Bert Prewitt Sr Scholar, Langston Develop, 1999. **Business Addr:** Chairman Board of Trustees, City of Langston, PO Box 116, Langston, OK 73050.

PREWITT, J EVERETT
Writer, real estate agent. **Personal:** Children: Eric & Lia. **Educ:** Lincoln Univ, Pa, BA, Bus Admin; Cleveland State Univ, MS, Urban Studies. **Career:** White Motors, int Div, mgr admin; AUS, United States & Vietnam, officer; Housing Info Serv, Cuyahoga Plan Ohio, Inc, Dir; Northland Res Corp, pres, 1982-; bk, nonfiction: Urban Residential Real Estate Market Analysis; bk, fiction: Snake Walkers. **Orgs:** Pres, Cleveland Asn Real Estate Brokers; pres, Cleveland Area Bd Realtors; chmn, bd East End Neighborhood House; vice-chmn, bd Greater Shaker Square Develop Corp. **Honors/Awds:** distinguished alumni, Lincoln Univ, Pa; distinguished alumni, Cleveland State Univ; Realtor of the Year award, Cleveland Area Bd Realtors; Award for Civic Service, Citizen's League Greater Cleveland; Bronze Award, 2005; Fiction Honor Award, Black Caucus Am Library Asn, 2006. **Business Addr:** President, Northland Publishing Company, 11811 Shaker Blvd Suite 414, Cleveland, OH 44120, **Business Phone:** (216)707-1300.*

PREWITT, DR. LENA VONCILLE BURRELL
Educator. **Personal:** Born Feb 17, 1932, Wilcox, AL; daughter of Cornelia Burrell and Leo Burrell; married Sep 5, 1959; children:

Kenneth Burrell Prewitt. **Educ:** Stillman Col, BS, bus educ, 1954; Ind Univ, MA, bus educ, 1955, EdD, bus educ, 1961, postdoctoral study, 1965; postdoctoral study France, Czechoslovakia & Germany, 1968-69; postdoctoral study, Tex Southern Univ, 1969, Univ Calif, Los Angeles, attended 1978; Ga Tech Univ, attended 1980; Harvard Univ, attended 1987; Univ Scand, attended 1987; Univ Bocconi, Milan Italy, attended 1988. **Career:** Stillman Col, from asst prof to prof, 1955-67; Marshall Space Flight Ctr, Huntsville, AL, employee develop officer, 1964; Tex Southern Univ, assoc prof, dept chmn, 1967-69; Pacific Tel & Tel, Los Angeles, Calif, spec mgt consult, 1968; Florence State Univ, assoc prof, 1969-70; Univ Alabama, assoc prof, 1970-74, prof, 1974-94; interim vpres fiscal affairs, 1998-99; distinguished prof mgt, 1999-2000, prof emerita, currently; IBM, consult; USAF, consult; US Fire Col, Charlespfizer, NY, consult; US Cong, adv; Union IST, core prof, currently. **Orgs:** Fel Presbyterian Church US, 1958-60; fel Ford Found, 1965; fel Urban League, 1966; Acad Mgt; Europ Found Mgt Develop, 1968-; Spec res consult, TTT Proj, Tex Southern Univ, 1969; Southern Mgt Asn; Am Asn Univ Women; Nat Bus Educ Asn; Delta Pi Epsilon; gen exec bd, Presbyterian Church US, 1973-; vpres, FOCUS Sr Citizens; Century Club YMCA; chmn, US Selective Serv Appeals Bd, 1980-; bd dir, AMI-West Alabama Hosp, 1986-. **Honors/Awds:** Outstanding Educator of the Year Award, Lucy Sheppard Art Federated Club, 1976; High Profile Professor of Year Award, Univ Ala Crimson White, 1991. **Special Achievements:** First female African American faculty member at the University of Alabama; named one of Top 5 Faculty Women, Univ Ala, 1978; published numerous articles. **Home Addr:** 412 Woodbridge Dr, Tuscaloosa, AL 35401. **Business Addr:** Professor Emeritus, University of Alabama, PO Box 870221, Tuscaloosa, AL 35487-0221, **Business Phone:** 800-486-3116.

PREZEAU, LOUIS E
Banker. **Personal:** Born Mar 4, 1943, Port-au-Prince, Haiti; son of Yia Roy and Emile; married Ramona A Prezeau, Apr 4, 1964; children: Jasmine, Louis Jr & Rodney. **Educ:** Bernard M Baruch, New York, NY, BBA, 1970; Baruch Col, public acct. **Career:** Freedom Nat Bank NY, chief operating officer, 1975-, act pres, 1987-88, controller; Fonkoze Financial Servs, inventor; City Nat Bank NJ, Newark, NJ, pres & chief exec officer, 1989-. **Orgs:** New York State Soc Cert Pub Acct, 1973-; treas, trustee, Community Serv Soc, 1985-; investment comn, Nat Coun Churches, 1988-; trustee, Newark Chamber Com, 1991; NJ Bankers Asn, exec comn. **Honors/Awds:** Golden Door Award, Intl Inst NJ. **Business Addr:** President, Chief Executive Officer, City National Bank of New Jersey, 900 Broad St, Newark, NJ 07102, **Business Phone:** (973)624-0865.

PREZEAU, DR. MARYSE
College teacher. **Personal:** Born Feb 20, 1942, Port-au-Prince, Haiti. **Educ:** City Univ NY, Hunter Col, BA, 1970, MA, 1971; City Univ NY, PhD, 1976. **Career:** Hunter Col, adj lectr, 1970-76; York Col, adj asst prof, 1973-77; Barnard Col, lectr, 1977-78; NY Inst Tech, asst provost, 1978-87; LaGuardia Community Col, CUNY, dean inst advan, 1987-90; New York Inst Technol, vpres stud affairs, 1990-, prof eng, currently, prof humanities, currently. **Orgs:** Bd mem, Nassau Community Med Ctr, 1978-88; NYIT Corp rep, Am Asn Univ Women, 1982-87; Coun Grad Sch, 1990. **Honors/Awds:** Educational Award, VIDCAPT Caribbean Cult Heritage Festival, 1991; Presidents Service Award, NYK Inst Technol, 1992. **Business Addr:** Professor of English, Vice President Student Affairs, New York Institute of Technology, Rm 208 Balding House NYIT Old Westbury Northern Blvd, Old Westbury, NY 11568-8000.

PRICE, PROF. ALFRED DOUGLAS
Educator. **Personal:** Born Jul 6, 1947, Buffalo, NY; son of Alfred D and Virginia M Allen; married; children: A Douglas V. **Educ:** Princeton Univ, AB, Sociol, 1969, M Arch & Urban Planning, 1975. **Career:** Harvard Univ, co dir, AAEO, 1969-71; Sch Arch-NJ, Inst Tech, asst dean,1975-77; Sch Archit & Planning, State Univ NY, Buffalo, assoc dean,1977-84; UB Sch Architecture & Planning, assoc prof planning, currently. **Orgs:** Bd dir, Seventy-Eight Restoration Corp, 1979-; chmn, City Buffalo Urban Design Task Group, 1980-; US Assn Club Rome, 1980-; chair, selection Buffalo City Arts Comn, 1980-97; chmn, archit comn Episcopal Diocese Western NY, 1980-; brd dir, Buffalo Conventional Ctr, 1981-84; exec coun,Episcopal Ch USA 1997-2003; chair, comm state church (Episcopal). **Honors/Awds:** Grants Exceeding 1/4 Million Dollars Harvard, 1969-71; Butler Travelling fel, Princeton Univ, 1973; Jamaican Ambassador to the US; Marcus Garvey Medal of Distinction, 1991; Chancellor's Award for Excellence in Teaching, St Univ NY, 2000. **Special Achievements:** Jury mem, 975 Honor Awards, Am Inst of Architects, 1975; Published : "Housing Affordability :An African American Perspective, 1997; "Buffalo's New Testament Leaves; Greenhouse Crops lead the Way", 1998; "Bethel Neighborhood Redevelopment Plan: A Proposal For action, 2001. **Home Addr:** 77 Huntington Ave, Buffalo, NY 14214. **Business Addr:** Associate Professor of Planning, UB School of architecture & planning, 3435 Main St, Buffalo, NY 14214, **Business Phone:** (716)829-3485.

PRICE, ANDREA R
Hospital administrator. **Personal:** Born Jun 16, 1959, Flint, MI; daughter of Jones and Clara; married Edward Johnson. **Educ:** Univ Mich, Ann Arbor, Mich, BA, psychol, 1981; Tulane Univ, Sch Pub Health, New Orleans, La, MHA, 1983. **Career:** DC hosp Asn, ambulatory resident, 1983-84; DataCom Systems Corp, mgr, ambulatory care servs, 1984-85; Children's Nat Medical Ctr, fel, 1985-86, asst vpres ambulatory servs, 1988-89, vpres prof servs, 1989-99; Howard Univ, Grad Sch Bus, adj asst Prof, 2000; Hurley Medical Ctr, Flint, Mich, exec vpres & chief operating officer, 2000-06, interim pres & chief executive officer, 2001-02; Sparrow Health Syst, Lansing, exec vpres & chief operating officer, 2006-. **Orgs:** Pres, Am Col Health Care Exec Women's Forum, 1988-89; pres, Asn Health Care Admins DC, 1991-92; nat bd member & membership chmn, Nat Asn Health Servs Execs, 1986-91; vpres, secy, DC chap, Nat Asn Health Servs Execs. **Honors/Awds:** Excellence in Health Care Industry, Int Bus Network, 1987; Young Health Services Excellence Award, NAHSE, 1992; Early Career Award, Am Col Health Care Execs, 1992; Senior Healthcare Executive of the Year Award, 2003. **Business Addr:** Executive Vice President, Chief Operating Officer, Sparrow Health System, 1215 E Mich Ave, Lansing, MI 48912, **Business Phone:** (517)364-1000.

PRICE, BRENDA G
Executive, administrator. **Educ:** Oakland Univ, BA, polit sci, 1979; Wayne State Univ, MEd, 1993. **Career:** DaimlerChrysler Corp, assembly line worker; Detroit pub sch, substitute teacher; Blue Cross & Blue Shield Mich, local govt liaison; Community Found Southeastern Mich, prog consult, sr prog officer, prog dir; John S James L knight Found, Community Liaison Prog Officer, 2004-, prog dir, currently. **Orgs:** Dir, African Am Legacy Prog; SW Detroit Bus Asn. **Special Achievements:** Selected as one of the most influential black women in metropolitan Detroit, by Women's Informal Network, 2001. **Business Addr:** Program Director, John S & James L Knight Found, Wachovia Financial Ctr Suite 3300, 200 S Biscayne Blvd, Miami, FL 33131-2349, **Business Phone:** (313)964-1114.

PRICE, CHARLES
Judge. **Personal:** Born May 9, 1940, Montgomery, AL; married Bernice B; children: Susan Y & Charles II. **Educ:** VA Union Univ, BS, 1969; Nat Law Ctr; George Wash Univ, JD, 1972. **Career:** US Dept Justice, Wash, DC, intern, 1972-73; St Ala, asst atty gen, 1973-75; Escambia County, AL, actg dist atty, 1974; Montgomery County AL, dep dist atty, 1975-78, asst munic judge, 1978-83; pvt law pract, 1978-83; St Ala, circuit judge, 1983-. **Orgs:** Nat Bar Asn; asst munic judge, Montgomery, 1978-83; pres, Montgomery City Trial Lawyers Asn, 1982-83. **Honors/Awds:** John F Kennedy Profile in Courage Award, 1998; Dr. Martin Luther King Humanitarian Award, Nat Educ Asn, 1998. **Military Serv:** USAR, Judge Advocate Corps, ltc, (retired); Active Duty-3 years 82nd Airborne; 3 years 8th Spl Forces, (Green Beret). **Home Addr:** 501 Wiltshire Dr, Montgomery, AL 36117. **Business Addr:** Judge Circuit Court, State of Alabama, 251 S Lawrence St, Montgomery, AL 36104.

PRICE, SR. FRED L
Executive. **Personal:** Born in Pittsburgh, PA. **Educ:** Reed Col, Portland, BA, 1971; Univ Calif, Berkeley, MS Amer Studies, Journ, 2008. **Career:** Medgar Evers Col, spokesperson, sr develop officer & spec projs, currently. **Orgs:** Life mem, NAACP; 100 Black Men, NY. **Honors/Awds:** Tom Boyland Award, Black & Puerto Rican Legislators; 100 Black Women Citation. **Special Achievements:** Produced and Directed "Home" a film documentary on Ghana; published article on "Samana" the African American Community in the Dominican Republic. **Military Serv:** USAAF. **Business Addr:** Senior Development Officer, Medgar Evers College, 1650 Bedford Ave, Brooklyn, NY 11225, **Business Phone:** (718)270-5190.*

PRICE, GEORGE BAKER
Manager, military leader. **Personal:** Born Aug 28, 1929, Laurel, MS; son of James A; married Georgianna Hunter; children: Katherine, James, William, Robert. **Educ:** SC State Col, BS, 1951; AUS Command & Gen Staff Col, cert, 1965; AUS War Col, cert, 1971; Shippensburg State Col, MS, 1971. **Career:** Military leader (retired), Manger; AUS, platoon leader 3rd Bn, 30 Inf Rgt, 1951, platoon leader L Co, 179 Inf Rgt, 1952, co comdr specialist training regiment, 1953-57, opers officer, 1957-61, personnel mgr, 1961-62, adv 1st Vietnamese infantry div, 1964-65, dept army staff, 1965-68, battalion comdr, 1968-70, brigade comdr, 1971-73, Am city, Nurnberg, Ger, city mgr, 1971-76, chief staff, 1973-74, asst div comdr, 1974-76, chief staff, 1976-78; Tech dyn Syst Corp, dir govt oper, 1978-81; Unified Indust, spl asst to pres, 1981-82; Southern Brand Snack Inc, exec vpres, 1978-81; Price Enterprises, personal mgr Leontyne Price, currently. **Orgs:** Kappa Alpha Psi Frat; Military & Veterans Adv Comm Nat Urban League; Vietnam Vet Mem Fund, 1980-85; bd visitors, US Military Acad, W Point; bd Advrs Womans Vietnam Vet Mem. **Honors/Awds:** Distinguished Patriot Award, Nat Womens Republican Club; Distinguished Serv Award, SC State Col, 1975; Distinguished Vietnam Vet Nat Asn Paramedics, 1989-. **Military Serv:** AUS, brigadier gen, 1951-78; Legion of Merit; Bronze Star; Meritorious Serv Medal; Commendation Medal; Air Medal; Purple Heart; Combat Infantryman Badge, airborne, ranger. *

PRICE, GLENDA DELORES
School administrator, educator. **Personal:** Born Oct 10, 1939, York, PA; daughter of William B Price and Zelma E McGeary. **Educ:** Temple Univ, BS, 1961, MEd, 1969, PhD, 1979. **Career:** Temple Univ, Clin Lab Sci, prof, 1969-79, Col Allied Health, asst dean, 1979-86; Univ Conn, Sch Allied Health Prof, dean, 1986-92; Spelman Col, provost, 1992-97; Temple Univ, Alumni fel, 1992; Marygrove Col, Detroit, pres, 1998-. **Orgs:** Pres, Am Soc Med Technol; Alpha Kappa Alpha Sorority Inc, 1959-; Am Asn Higher Educ; Asn Fel Sch Allied Health Professions, 1988. **Honors/Awds:** Member of the Year Award, Pa Soc Med Technol, 1979; Warren Perry Allied Health Leadership Award, State Univ NY, Buffalo, 1982; Medallion Award, Univ Conn, 1992. **Special Achievements:** Author: "Ethics in Research," Clinical Laboratory Science, July/Aug, 1979; "Consulting as a Professional Role," Textbook of Clinical Laboratory Science, 1988; "Health Care Technologies: Political & Ethical Considerations," Healing Technology: Female Perspectives, 1989; The Role of Professional Asn in the Educ Process in Allied Health Educ, 1989; "Reimbursement Mechanisms: Their Link with Professional Organizations," Interpersonal Skills and Health Professional Issues. **Business Addr:** President, Marygrove College, 8425 W McNichols, Detroit, MI 48221.

PRICE, HUBERT, JR.
State government official, president (organization). **Personal:** Born Sep 28, 1946, Pontiac, MI. **Educ:** Mich State Univ, BS. **Career:** Oakland County Bd Comnrs, comnr; Mich House Rep, state rep, currently; Synergistics Consult Bus, pres, currently. **Orgs:** Nat Asn Advan Colored People; Pontiac Area Urban League; OIC Oakland County; Coalition Black Trade Unionists; Nat Asn County Officials; Nat Asn Black County Officials; Trinity Missionary Baptist Church. **Honors/Awds:** Outstanding Legislator, Honorary Lay Membership MIch Asn, Osteopathic Physicians & Surgeons Inc, 1995; Pontiac Area Achievers Award, Boy Scouts Am, 1996. **Business Phone:** (517)373-0475.

PRICE, HUGH BERNARD
Educator, association executive. **Personal:** Born Nov 22, 1941, Washington, DC; son of Kline Armond Price Sr and Charlotte Schuster; married Marilyn Lloyd; children: Traer, Janeen & Lauren. **Educ:** Amherst Col, BA, 1963; Yale Law Sch, LLB, 1966. **Career:** New Haven Legal Assistance Asn, atty, 1966-68; The Black Coalition New Haven, exec dir, 1968-70; City New Haven HR, admin; Cogen Holt & Assoc, partner, 1970; New Haven, hr comnr, 1976; Urban Renewal Agency New Haven Redevel Agency, asst couns; New Haven Legal Asst Asn, neighborhood atty; City New Haven, Human Resources Admin, dir, 1977-78; NY Times, ed bd, 1978-82; WNET & Thirteen, NY, sr vpres, 1982-88; Rockefeller Found, NY, vpres, 1988-94; Nat Urban League, pres, 1994-2003; Metropolitan Life Inc,dir; Sears, Roebuck & Co, dir; Nynex Corp, Corp Gov Comt, mem; DLA Piper Rudnick Gray Cary US LLP, sr adv & co-chair, 2003-05; Brookings Inst, srfel, Econ Studies Prog, 2006-. **Orgs:** Bd dir, Ctr Comt Change Wash DC; bd dir exec comt & real estate comt, New Haven Water Co; Distrib Comt New Haven Found; bd dir & vpres, United Way Greater New Haven; Nat Bus League; NAACP; Alpha Phi Alpha Frat; Proj Planning Comt, Greater New Haven Black Soc Civic Orgn Higher Educ Fund; Metrop Life Insurance Co; Verizon; bd dir, New Haven Legal Asst Asn Day top Inc; Polly T McCabe Ctr; Greater New Haven UMCA; Lewis Latimer Found;trustee, Rochefeller Bros Fund, 1987-88; trustee, NAACP, Legal Defense & Educ Fund, 1988; trustee, Munic Art Soc, 1990-; trustee, Pub Develop Corp, 1991-; Am Philos Soc; Mayo Clinic Found; co-chair, Asn Supervision Curriculum Develop, 2006-07; Alpha Phi Alpha Frater. **Honors/Awds:** President's Medal, Hunter Col, 1995; Award of Merit, Yale Law Sch, 1996; William C. Dawson Award, Congressional Black Caucus Found, 2003; Excellence in Public Service Award, Committee Economic Develop, 2005; Dateline Award, 2006; Leadership Award, Nat Urban League, 2006. **Special Achievements:** First executive director of the Black Coalition of New Haven, 1960; Co-authored several articles; Author: Destination: The American Dream, 2001; Achievement Matters: Getting Your Child The Best Education Possible, 2002. **Business Addr:** Senior Fellow, Brookings Institution, 1775 Massachusetts Ave NW, Washington, DC 20036, **Business Phone:** (202)797-6058.

PRICE, JOANN H
President (Organization), executive. **Educ:** Howard Univ. **Career:** Nat Asn Investment Cos, pres; Fairview Capital Partners Inc, pres, founder, 1994-, meminvest comt, currently. **Orgs:** Black Enterprise/Greenwich St Corp Growth Partners; New Vista Capital; Pacesetter Growth Fund; The Initiative for a Competitive Inner City. **Business Addr:** President, Fairview Capital Partners Inc, 75 Isham Rd Suite 200, West Hartford, CT 06107, **Business Phone:** (860)674-8066.*

PRICE, JOHN ELWOOD
Educator, musician. **Personal:** Born Jun 21, 1935, Tulsa, OK; son of Carter Elwood and Irma Verila. **Educ:** Lincoln Univ, BMus, 1957; Univ Tulsa, MM, 1963; Wash Univ, attended 1968. **Career:** Karamu Theatre Cleveland, staff composer, pianist & vocal, 1957-59; Fla Mem Col, Miami, chmn music & fine arts, composer-in-residence, 1967-74; Eastern Ill Univ, mem music dept, 1970-71, 1974-80; Tuskegee Univ,composition hist, 1980, mem music dept, 1982; Portia, Wash-Pittman fel, 1981-82. **Orgs:** Life mem Alpha Phi Alpha, 1954-; Phi Mu Alpha Sinfonia, 1954-; ASCAP, 1970-;

Asn Study Afro-Am Life & Hist, 1970; Am Music Soc, 1970-; Soc Ethnomusicol, 1974; Medieval Acad Am, 1975; Spirituals Young Pianist BookI Belwin Mills NY, 1979; Menes, Uniter Unaccompanied C Bass, 1979; Nat Asn Composers USA, 1982; Slave Ship Press Tuskegee Inst AL, 1983; Moomery Symphony Bd, Ala Coun Arts; Nat Black Music Caucus; Lamp Fla Mem Col. **Honors/Awds:** Black Musician as Artist & Entrepreneur Award, Phelps-Stokes Fund Scholar Exchange, 1974; Distinguished Faculty Award, Eastern Ill Univ Charleston, 1979-80; Distinguished Faculty Award, Black Stud Union E Ill Univ, 1980; ASCAP Award, 1990-91; Most Outstanding Composition, Black Arts Festival,Atlanta, 1991; ASCAP Award, 1993-94; Links Arts Award, 1994. **Special Achievements:** Author: Invention I for Piano, 1952, Blues & Dance I Clarinet & Piano,1955, Scherzo I Clarinet & Orch, 1952 & 1955; Two Typed Lines, 1959; The Lamp FMC, 1969; Prayer, Martin Luther King Baritone Solo SSAATTBB acappella, 1971; Barely Time to Study Jesus third Version Solo Gospel Choir7 speakers percussion ensemble, 1971; pub A Ptah Hymn Unaccompanied Cello,1978; featured in Ala Adver Jour, 1987; Composers of the Ams Pan Am Un Vol 19, 1977 Wash DC; The Sphinx mag of Alpha Phi Alpha Frat, 1976; photographic posters of the Tuskegee City Dance Theatre in 8 rest areas for the St of AL; honored as one of the musical "gems" of Okla Musical History during Am music week, 1988; listed in: "Fifteen Black Am Composers," by Alice Tischler, 1981, Black Am Music Vol II, by Hildred Roach, 1985; Biographies of Black Composers & Songwriters, Ellistine Holly, 1990; Woodwind Music by Black Composers & Piano Music by Black Composers, Arron Horne. **Military Serv:** AUS, sp4, 1959-61.

PRICE, JOHN WILEY
County commissioner. **Personal:** Married; children: John Jr, John Nicholas & Angelina Monique. **Career:** Dallas County Comnr Ct, Dist 3, county comnr, 1984-. **Orgs:** Chmn, Dallas County Civil Serv Comn; vpres, Dallas County Juv Bd; chmn, Comnrs Ct Sheriff Liaison Comt; chmn, Delinquent Tax Collection Selection Comt; Loop 9 Policy Adv Group; vpres, Dallas County Housing Finance Corp; chmn, Pub Health Adv Comt; Adult & Juv Health Adv Comt; Tex Juv Crime Comn; Dallas Housing Acquisition & Develop Corp Bd; pres, Tex Orgn Black County Comnrs; founder & pres, KwanzaaFest Inc, 1991; St Luke Community United Methodist Church. **Honors/Awds:** Juanita Craft Award in Politics, NAACP; NAACP Medgar Evers Award; Lifetime Achievement Award, Dallas & Fort Worth Asn Black Communicators; Community Leadership Award, Malcolm X Day Organizing Comt; Newsome Award, Black United Fund Tex. **Special Achievements:** KKDA-AM, "Talk Back", talk show host. **Business Addr:** Dallas County Commissioner, Dallas County Commissioner, District 3, 1506 E Langdon Rd, Dallas, TX 75216, **Business Phone:** (214)653-6671.

PRICE, DR. JOSEPH L.
Clergy, business owner, real estate agent. **Personal:** Born Dec 25, 1931, Gary, IN; married Edria Faye; children: 6. **Educ:** East Los Angeles Jr Col; Moody Bible Inst; Chicago Baptist Bile Inst; Ind Christian Theol Sem, attended 1969. **Career:** Church God Christ, bishop dist supt & pastor, 1963-71; St Jude Deliverance Centers Am, pastor, Evangelist Minister organ & founder, 1971-; photo, welder, owner, furniture & appliance store; real estate & ins broker. **Honors/Awds:** Community Service & Leadership Award, Mayor Richard Lugar; DDiv, Nat Inst Relig Sci & Arts. **Military Serv:** AUS, airborne spl/4c, 1951-56.

PRICE, JUDITH
Executive. **Personal:** Born Feb 10, 1937, New York, NY; married; children: Toni & Marc. **Educ:** City Col NY; Bernard Baruch Sch, Bus Admin. **Career:** James B Beam Import Corp, vpres & dir, 1972-, admin dir & asst secy. **Orgs:** Traffic Asn, Liquor Industry. **Business Addr:** 5800 Arlington Ave, Riverdale, NY 10471.

PRICE, KELLY
Singer. **Personal:** Born Apr 4, 1973, New York, NY; daughter of Rev Joseph and Claudia; married Jeffrey Rolle; children: Jeffrey Jr & Jonia. **Career:** R&B vocalist, composer, arranger, producer, currently; Albums: Soul of A Woman, 1998; Mirror Mirror, 2000; One Family: A Christmas Album, 2001; Priceless, 2003; This Is Who I Am, 2006; Singles: "Friend of Mine", 1998; "Secret Love", 1999; "Love Sets You Free", 2000; "You Should Have Told Me", 2000; "Mirror or Mirror", 2001; "Take It To The Head", 2002; "In Love At Christmas", 2002; "Someday", 2002; "How Does It Feel?", 2002; "He Proposed", 2003; God's Gift", 2006; "Healing", 2006; EcclectiSounds Recs, owner, 2006-. **Orgs:** Sigma Gamma Rho Sorority Inc, 2006-. **Honors/Awds:** Soul Train Music Award, Best New R&B/Soul Artist, 1999. **Special Achievements:** nominee, Grammy Award. **Business Addr:** Singer, Universal Music Group, 825 Eigth Ave, New York, NY 10019, **Business Phone:** (212)333-8000.

PRICE, LEONTYNE (MARY VIOLET LEONTYNE PRICE)
Actor, activist, opera singer. **Personal:** Born Feb 10, 1927, Laurel, MS; daughter of James A and Kate Baker; married William C Warfield, Aug 31, 1952 (divorced 1973). **Educ:** Cent State Col, BA, 1948; Juilliard Sch Music, 1952; Florence Page Kimball, pvt study. **Career:** Opera singer (retired); Porgy & Bess, Europe, 1952-54; recitalist, soloist with symphonies in US, Canada, Australia, Europe, 1954; performed in Tosca, NBC Opera Theater, 1954; soloist, Hollywood Bowl, 1955-59, 1966; appeared in concert, India, 1956-64; San Francisco Opera, 1957-59, 1960-61, 1963, 1965, 1967, 1968, 1971; RCA recording artist, 1958; Vienna Staatsopera, 1958-59, 1960-61; Berlin Festival, 1960; opened new Metrop Opera House Lincoln Ctr, 1968; six performances at the White House; performed Live from Lincoln Ctr; performed at 2 presidential inaugrations & for the Pope; Films: Romeo Juliet, voice, 1996. **Orgs:** Bd mem, Campfire Girls; co-chair, Rust Col Upward Thrust Campaign; trustee, Int House; hon vice chmn, US Comt UNESCO; Am Fedn TV & Radio Artists; Am Guild Mus Artists; Actors Equity Asn; Sigma Alpha Iota; Delta Sigma Theta; Nat Inst Music Theater; Nat Asn Advan Colored People; Whitney Young Found; bd trustees, NY Univ. **Honors/Awds:** Twenty Grammy Awards; Spirit of Achievement Award, Albert Einstein Col Med, 1962; Silver Medal of San Francisco Oper Italy's Order of Merit; Presidential Medal of Freedom, 1964; Spingarn Medal, Nat Asn Advan Colored People, 1965; Schwann Catalog Award, 1968; Kennedy Center Honarary, 1985; Nat Medal of Arts, 1985; Handel Medallion New York; Grammy Life time Achievement Award, Asn Black Charities; 26 hon doctorates.

PRICE, MARCUS
Football player. **Personal:** Born Mar 3, 1972, Port Arthur, TX. **Educ:** La State Univ, finance, 1995. **Career:** Football player (retired), Jacksonville Jaguars, 1995-96; San Diego Chargers, tackle, 1997-99; New Orleans Saints, 2000-01; Buffalo Bills, 2002-04; Dallas Cowboys, guard,2005.

PRICE, MARY VIOLET LEONTYNE. See PRICE, LEONTYNE.

PRICE, PAMELA ANITA
Librarian. **Personal:** Born Nov 30, 1952, Washington, DC; daughter of John Robert and Gwendolyn Elizabeth Moses. **Educ:** NC Agr & Tech State Univ, Greensboro, BS, 1974; Univ Wis-Madison, MS, 1975. **Career:** Univ Md, Col Park, MD, serials cataloger, 1975-76; Del State Col, Dover, coordr eve reader serv, 1976-81; Mercer County Community Col, Trenton, NJ, libr supvr, 1981, dir, currently. **Orgs:** Am Libr Asn, 1974-; Kappa Delta Pi, 1974-; Delta Sigma Theta Sorority Inc, 1977-; YWCA, Trenton, NJ, 1987-; United Way Princeton Area Community, 1987-; Cent Jersey Regional Libr Coop. **Business Addr:** Director, Mercer County Community College, 1200 Old Trenton Rd, Trenton, NJ 08690.

PRICE, DR. PAUL SANFORD
Librarian. **Personal:** Born Mar 30, 1942, Coffeyville, KS; son of Ovie and Anna Belle. **Educ:** Univ Connecticut, Storrs, CT, BA, 1971, MA, 1974, PhD, 1982; Univ Denver, Denver, CO, MA, attended 1985. **Career:** Librarian (retired); Univ Conn Libr, Storrs, CT, dept mgr, 1972-84; The Quinoco Cos, Denver, CO, records adminr, 1985-87; Three Rivers Community Tech Col, dir, Learning Resources, 1987-2001. **Orgs:** Southeastern CT Libr Asn, 1987-; Conn Libr Asn, 1987-; New Eng Libr Asn, 1987-; Am libr Asn, 1987-; Mountain/Plains Libr Asn, 1984-87. **Honors/Awds:** Delegate to White House Conference on Library and Information Services, Governor's Conference on Libraries, Connecticut, 1991; Governor's Blue Ribbon Commission on the Future of Libraries in Connecticut. **Military Serv:** AUS, Sgt, E-5, 1964-70; Commendation Medal, Air Medal, Vietnam Medal, Bronze Star with OLC, Good Conduct Medal, Nat Defense Service Medal, 1964-66. **Home Addr:** 516 E 6th St, Coffeyville, KS 67337-6305.

PRICE, PHILLIP G
Automotive executive. **Career:** Red Bluff Ford-Lincoln-Mercury Inc, owner, currently. **Honors/Awds:** Ranked 55 of 100 auto dealers, Black Enterprise, 1992; ranked 64 on Black Enterprise's 2007 Top 100s Auto Dealers; Business Entrepreneur Award, Torrance Area Chamber Com & GLAAACC, 2008. **Business Addr:** Owner, Red Bluff Ford Lincoln Mercury, PO Box 1050, Red Bluff, CA 96080, **Business Phone:** (530)527-2816.*

PRICE, RAY ANTHONY
Television producer, educator. **Personal:** Born Jun 21, 1957, High Point, NC; son of Johnny and Carrie; married Gayle Lynnette Price, Sep 3, 1977; children: Samuel Ray, Rajeana Lynn & Michael Terrell. **Educ:** Yuba Col, AS, 1984; Calif State Univ, BA, 1986; Regent Univ, MA, 1993. **Career:** Continental Cablevision, Channel 5, producer, 1984-91; KVIE, Channel 6 PBS, prod asst, 1990-91; Yuba Community Col, TV instr, 1990-91; Portmouth Pub Sch, Channel 28, assoc producer, 1992-; Portmouth City Channel 29, video technician, 1992-; Newport News Pub Sch, educ supvr telecommunications, 1992-; Hampton Univ, adj prof, 1998. **Orgs:** Bd mem, Marysville Chamber Com, 1987-91; bd mem, Big Brother Big Sister, 1988-91; bd mem, Yuba-Sutter Regional Arts Coun, 1990-91; vpres, Marysville Kiwanis Club, 1990-91; Hampton Roads Black Media Professionals, 1994-; bd mem, Youth Entertainment Studios. **Honors/Awds:** Distinguish Honor, Grad Sch Aerospace Med, 1981; Outstanding Service, Yuba City & Marysville, CA, 1989; Communicator Award "Newport News Sports Highlights" prog, 1999. **Special Achievements:** Developer of "The Classified Channel," 1984; Music Video "Believe In Yourself," 1993. **Military Serv:** US Air Force, tech sargent, 1976-03, master sargent, 2003; Air Force Commendation, 1997. **Home Addr:** 245 Vicky St, Newport News, VA 23602-6352. **Business Addr:** Education Supervisor Telecommunications Education, Newport News Public Schools Telecommunications Center, 4 Minton Dr, Newport News, VA 23606.

PRICE, WILLIAM S., III
Judge. **Personal:** Born Sep 30, 1923, Hennessey, OK; married Dilys A. **Educ:** Washburn Univ, AB, JD, 1950. **Career:** Genesee County, atty, asst pros, 1951-72, asst pros, 1956-59; 68th Dist Ct Flint MI, presiding judge, currently. **Orgs:** Pres, Genesee County Bar Asn, 1970-71; Genesee County Legal Aid, 1956-57; pres, Flint Civil Serv Comn, 1969-72; jud counc, Nat Bar Asn. **Honors/Awds:** Achieve award, No Province Kappa Alpha Psi. **Military Serv:** Capt A&M Soc Corps ETO, 1944-45; ETO, 1942-46. **Business Addr:** Judge, 68th District Court, 630 S Saginaw St, Flint, MI 48502-1526.

PRIDE, CHARLEY FRANK
Singer, baseball player. **Personal:** Born Mar 18, 1938, Sledge, MS; son of Mack; married Rozene, Dec 28, 1956; children: Kraig, Dion & Angela. **Career:** Baseball player (retired), singer: Negro Baseball League, Detroit, Birmingham Black Barons, Memphis Red Sox, Los Angeles Angels, baseball player; Anaconda Mining; solo rec artist; Albums include: Very Best of Charley Pride, 1987-89, 2003; RCA Country Legends, 2000; A Tribute to Jim Reeves, 2001; Comfort of Her Wings, 2003; Country Legend, 2003; Anthology, 2003; 20 Classics, 2004; Greatest Songs, 2005; The Pride of Country Music American Legends, 2005; Country Music Superstars: Charley Pride & Conway Twitty, 2005; 16 Biggest Hits, 2005; Sings His Best, 2006; The Essential Charley Pride, 2006; Pride & Joy: A Gospel Music Collection, 2006. **Honors/Awds:** First Golden Opal Award, Australia; Grammy Award for Sacred/Inspirational/Relig, 1971; Grammy Award for Gospel, 1971; Grammy Award for Country Male Vocal, 1972; Best Gospel Performance "Let Me Live", 1971, Best Sacred Performance "Did You Think to Pray", 1971; Entertainer of the Year Award, 1971; Best Male Vocalists Award CMA; Am Music Award Favorite Male Vocalist in Co Music, 1976; received a star on the Hollywood Walk of Fame, 1999; Country Music Hall of Fame, 2000; Mississippi Arts Commission's lifetime achievement award, 2008. **Special Achievements:** Listed in Book of Lists as one of the top fifteen all-time world-wide recsellers; author, The Charley Pride Story, 1995. **Military Serv:** AUS, 1956-58. **Business Addr:** Singer, Cecca Productions, 3198 Royal Lane Suite 200, Dallas, TX 75229, **Business Phone:** (214)350-8477.

PRIDE, CURTIS JOHN
Baseball player. **Personal:** Born Dec 17, 1968, Washington, DC; married Lisa. **Educ:** Col William & Mary. **Career:** Baseball player (retired), coach; Montreal Expos, outfielder, 1993, 1995 & 2001; Detroit Tigers, outfielder, 1996-97; Boston Red Sox, outfielder, 1997 & 2000; Atlanta Braves, outfielder, 1998; NY Yankees, outfielder, 2003; Anaheim Angels, outfielder, 2004; Los Angeles Angels of Anaheim, outfielder, 2005-06; Atlantic League, Southern Maryland Blue Crabs, outfielder, 2008; Gallaudet Univ, coach, currently. **Orgs:** Together With Pride Found. **Honors/Awds:** Tony Conigliaro Award, 1996. **Special Achievements:** Excellent soccer player who played for the United States at the Under 17th World Championships in China, 1985.

PRIDE, HEMPHILL P, II
Lawyer. **Personal:** Born May 19, 1936, Columbia, SC; son of Maud Pendergrass and Hemphill P; divorced; children: Hemphill III & Elliott Caldwell. **Educ:** SC State Col; Johnson C Smith Univ; Fla A&M Univ. **Career:** Self Employed, atty; Nat Asn Advan Colored People, cola br, 1964-; Jenkins Perry & Pride, partner, 1965; SC Housing Authority, vice chmn, 1972-77; Nat Bar Asn, adv bd, 1972-76; SC Taxpayers Asn, atty, 1973; Co Columbia, asst pros, 1973; Gov's Bi-Centennial Comn, 1976; Pvt pract, atty, currently. **Orgs:** SC Bar, 1963; Nat Bar Asn, 1964; State Dem Comn 100, 1970; gen coun, Allen Univ, 1977; legal coun, Nat Asn Advan Colored People, 1977. **Special Achievements:** First Black to construct 55 unit high-rise 236 housing project in 1970. **Business Addr:** Attorney at Law, 1401 Gregg St, PO Box 4529, Columbia, SC 29201, **Business Phone:** (803)256-8015.

PRIDE, J. THOMAS
Executive. **Personal:** Born Jan 18, 1940, Highland Park, MI; married Vernester Green; children: Leslie, Thomas & Alesia. **Educ:** Highland Park Jr Col, 1958-59, 1962; Wayne State Univ, 1962-64. **Career:** J Walter Thompson Co Detroit, media buyer, 1964-69; Campbell Ewald Co, acct exec, 1969-72; Ross Roy Inc, vpres; Am Asn Advertising Agency, teacher; Health Alliance Plan, dir commun, assoc vpres, currently. **Orgs:** Blacks Against Racism, 1969; spkr Black Applied Res Ctr, 1972; trustee, Kirkwood Gen Hosp Club; Adcraft Club Detroit Nat Asn Market Devel; Black Applied Res Ctr; Detroit Boat Club. **Business Addr:** Associate Vice President, Health Alliance Plan, 2850 W Grand Blvd, Detroit, MI 48202, **Business Phone:** (313)872-8100.*

PRIDE, JOHN L.
Association executive. **Personal:** Born Nov 4, 1940, Youngstown, OH; married Sallie Curtis; children: Jacqueline, Curtis. **Educ:**

Capital Univ Columbus, BA, 1963; Howard Univ, Psy. **Career:** US Office Educ, chief SE oper Bran, 1970-72, deputy asst dir oper, 1972-74; US Dept HEW, spec asst dep asst sec human dev, dep exec dir, 1974-. **Orgs:** Consult, White House Conf Food Health & Nutrition 1969; US Senate Select Comn Human Needs, 1968; Nat Adv Comn Civil Disorders, 1968; Adv Comn Special Educ Montgomery Co, MD Pub Schls; Adv Comm Family Life & Human Dev Mont Co, MD Pub Schs; pres, Mont Co Asn Lang Handicapped C; Big Brothers Nat Capital Area. **Business Addr:** Deputy Executive Director, The US Department of Health and Human Services, 200 Independence Ave SW, Washington, DC 20201, **Business Phone:** (202)619-0257.

PRIDE, WALTER LAVON
Lawyer. **Personal:** Born Apr 4, 1922, Birmingham, AL; son of George Thomas and Althea; divorced; children: Karen & Pamela. **Educ:** Roosevelt Univ, BS; John Marshall Law Sch, JD; Univ Mich, Roosevelt Univ, grad study. **Career:** Chicago Asn Defense Lawyers, pres, 1967-69; Pride Leaner Stewart & Elston Chicago, atty-at-law. **Orgs:** Chicago Bar Asn; Ill State Bar Asn; Alpha Phi Alpha; bd dir, Stuart Town homes Corp; Chicago Conf Brotherhood; Cook Co Bar Asn; Nat Bar Asn; Nat Asn Defense Lawyers; Nat Asn Advan Colored People. **Honors/Awds:** Sr Counselor of the Year, Cook Co Bar Asn, 1995. **Military Serv:** AUS, sgt, WW II. **Home Addr:** 19801 NE 19th Ave, Miami, FL 33179-3102. **Business Addr:** Attorney, Pride Leaner Stewart & Elston, 180 N La Salle St, Chicago, IL 60602.

PRIDE, WILLIAM L., JR.
Automotive executive. **Personal:** Born Apr 25, 1948, Crenshaw, MS; son of William L and Savannah Pride; married Sarah B, Jan 2, 1971; children: Cynthia P, William L III. **Educ:** Northwest Community Col, BA, electronics, 1982; Ford Training, cert, 1996. **Career:** Pride Auto Sales Inc, owner & gen mgr, 1985-96; Pride Ford Lincoln Mercury Inc, gen mgr & chief exec officer, 1996-. **Orgs:** bd mem, Boy & Girl Club; bd mem, Chamber Com; bd mem, Coahoma Co Arts & Craft. **Honors/Awds:** Business Man of Year Award, 2000; Top 100, Black Enterprise Award, 2001-02; Black Entrepreneur Award, 2001. **Business Addr:** Chief Executive Officer, Prideford Lincoln Mercury Inc, 730 S State St, PO Box 1474, Clarksdale, MS 38614-4802, **Business Phone:** (662)627-2800.*

PRIEST, DR. MARLON L
Physician, educator, school administrator. **Personal:** Born in Moulton, AL; son of Charlie W Sr and Odra McKelvy. **Educ:** Univ N Ala, Florence, BS, 1974; Univ Ala, Birmingham Sch Med, Birmingham, 1977. **Career:** Baptist Med Ctr, Birmingham, dir outpatient Med, 1980-81; Univ Ala Birmingham, dep Med dir, Emerg Dept, 1982-85, Med dir, Univ Hosp emerg dept, 1985-89, asst prof surg, 1985-86, assoc prof surg, 1986-94, prof, 1994, asst vpres for health affairs, 1988-92, div dir/emergency servs, 1989-90, dir, emergency Med residency prog, 1989-90; Univ Ala, Sch Med, assoc dean, 1992-98, prof emergency med, currently; scholar, Lister Hill Ctr Health Policy, currently. **Orgs:** Nat counr, 1990-93, Ala Chap, pres, 1988-90, bd dirs, 1982-, Am Col Emergency Physicians; pres, Mineral Dist Med Soc, 1988-90; bd dirs, Am Heart Asn Jefferson/Shelby, 1984-; Ala Affiliate Am Heart, pres, 1994-95; underGrad curric comt, Soc Acad Emerg Med, 1984-86; pres, Beta Beta Beta, 1973; admiss comt, Univ Ala Sch Med, 1983-86; bd dirs, Univ Ala Birmingham Nat Alumni Asn, 1989-93; pres's adv coun, Univ Ala Birmingham, 1982-; Cath Health Asn, bd trustees, 2000-; bd dirs, Sisters Mercy Health Syst. **Honors/Awds:** Hon Grad, Univ North Ala, 1974, Alumus Year, 1989; Outstanding Contribution, Stud Nat Med Asn, 1986; Outstanding Contribution, Am Heart Asn, 1985; "The Trauma Cardiorespiratory Arrest," Basic Trauma Life Support, 2nd Ed, 1987-94; "Advan Systic Effect Ocular Drug Therapy," Clinal Ocular Pharmacol, 2nd Ed, 1988-94; Exec Mgt Fel, PEW Found, 1988; Leadership Develop, Birmingham Area Chamber Com, 1990; "Injury: A New Perspective on an Old Problem," Nat Med Asn, 1991; Stud Nat Med Asn Mentor Year Award, 1992; Asn Acad Med Ctrs, Scholar in Acad Admin & Health Policy, 1994; Nat Environment Policy Comn, 2000-; Adv Panel on Med Educ, Ctrs for Medicare, Dept HHS, 2002-; RWJF Health Policy Fel.

PRIESTER, JULIAN ANTHONY
Jazz musician, composer, educator. **Personal:** Born Jun 29, 1935, Chicago, IL; son of Lucius Harper and Colelia Smith; married Jaymi; children: Julia Antoinette, Claudette Ann Campbell, Adebayo & Atuanya. **Educ:** Sherwood Sch Music, Chicago, IL. **Career:** ECM Recs, Riverside Recs, trombonist & band leader, 1954-91; Sun Ra Arkestra, trombonist & soloist, 1954-56, 1990; Max Roach Quintette, trombonist & soloist, 1959-61, 1964-65; Art Blakey's Jazz Messingers, trombonist & soloist, 1968; Duke Ellington Orchestra, lead trombonist, 1970; Herbie Hancock Sextet, trombonist & soloist, 1971-73; Lone Mountain Col, fac, 1976-77; Dave Holland Quintet, trombonist & soloist, 1984-87; Cornish Col Arts, Music Dept, admin fac, 1979-; Albums: Keep Swinging, 1958; Spiritsville; Love Love & Polarization; Hints on Light & Shadow, 1997; In Deep End Dance, 2003. **Orgs:** Prog dir & fac, Cazadero Music Camp, 1978-80; Music Adv Coun, 1979-80; fac, Naropa Inst, 1981-83; fac, Banff Ctr Arts, 1984-87; bd dirs, Pac Jazz Inst, 1987; comnr, Seattle Arts Comn, 1988-91. **Honors/Awds:** Commemorative Plaque Msingi Workshop, 1972; Grant, NEA, 1975; Best Horn Player Award, Bay Area Music Mag, 1978; Commemorative Plaque San Francisco Jazz Comt, 1979; King County Arts Comn Grant, 1987; Seafirst Faculty Award, 1990; Record of the Year, In Deep End Dance, Earshot Jazz, 2002; Honor, Pac NW Chap Rec Acad, 2005. **Military Serv:** Fifth Army Reserves, corpl, 1955-63. **Business Addr:** Faculty, Cornish College of the Arts, Department of Music, 1000 Lenora St, Seattle, WA 98121, **Business Phone:** (206)726-5151.

PRIESTLEY, MARILYN
Association executive, vice president (organization). **Educ:** Rider Univ, BS, labor relations. **Career:** Novartis Pharaceuticals Corp, vpres human resources & vpres diversity & Inclusion, currently. **Honors/Awds:** The Top 100 Blacks in Corporate America. Black Prof Mag. **Special Achievements:** The first African-American Vice President at Novartis Pharmaceuticals Corporation. **Business Addr:** Vice President of Diversity & Inclusion, Vice President of Human Resources, Novartis Pharaceuticals Corp, 1 Health Plz, East Handover, NJ 07936-1080.

PRIGMORE, KATHRYN TYLER (KATHRYN BRADFORD TYLER)
Architect. **Personal:** Born Nov 21, 1956, St Albans, NY; daughter of Richard and Shirley Tyler; married James Craig, Jun 20, 1986 (divorced 1992); children: Crystal Andrea & Amber Sheriesse. **Educ:** Rensselaer Polytech Inst, BS, bldg Sci, 1977, BArch, 1978; Cath Univ, MS, Engineering, 1981. **Career:** VVKR Inc, architect, 1979-81; Robert A Hawthorne, architect, PC, architect, 1982; Robert Traynham Cols, architect, PC, proj mgr, 1982-84; Segreti Tepper Architects, assoc, 1984-92; Howard Univ, Sch Archit & Planning, assoc prof, 1991-, assoc dean, 1992-98; Col Engineering, Archit & Comp Sci, asst dir, 1997-98; Einhorn Yaffee Prescott Archit & Engineering, sr assoc, 1998-. **Orgs:** Northern Va Urban League, 1980-81; Am Inst Architects, 1981-; Nat Orgn Minority Architects, 1990-; archivist, Black Women in Archit, 1990-; et al, 1993-, chmn, 1996-97, 1999-2000, 2001-02, Va Bd for Architects, Prof Engrs, Land Surveryors; adv coun, exam comnr, 1993-2001, chmn, 2000, Nat Coun Archit Regist Bds. **Honors/Awds:** Oustanding Young Women in America, 1983. **Special Achievements:** One of the first African Am women licensed to pract archit in US. **Business Addr:** Senior Architect, Einhorn Yaffee Prescott, Architecture and Engineering PC, 1000 Potomac St NW, Washington, DC 20007, **Business Phone:** (202)471-5000.

PRIMM, DR. BENY JENE
Executive, physician. **Personal:** Born May 21, 1928, Williamson, WV; married Annie Delphine Evans (deceased); children: Annelle Benne, Martine Armande, Jeanine Bari, Eraka & Jene. **Educ:** WVa State Col, BS, 1950, postgrad work; Univ Heidelberg, 1954; Univ Geneva Switzerland, MD, 1959. **Career:** Interfaith Hosp, Medical Aff, dir, 1965-69; Harlem Hosp, Ctr, assoc anesthesiologist, 1963-69; Harlem Hosp Ctr, Narcotics Control Hosp Orientation Ctr, founder, dir, 1968-69; Control Hosp Orientation Ctr, Columbia Univ, founder, dir, 1968-69; Addiction Res & Treatment Corp, founder & exec dir, 1969-; Nat Ctr Substance Abuse Treatment, 1989-93; Consult. **Orgs:** Urban Resource Inst, pres, 1980-; US Info Agency, E & W Africa, US speaker, 1989; World Summit on Substance Abuse & AIDS, US rep; presidential appointee, Presidential Comn HIV, 1987-88; bd dirs, Meharry Medical Col, 1988-; bd dirs, Black Leadership Comn AIDS, 1989; bd dirs, WVa State Col Found, 1993-; bd dirs, Nat Med Asn, Minority AIDS Coun, 1994. **Honors/Awds:** HHS, Cert of Appreciation, 1988; J Michael Morrison Award for Sci Admin, 1993; WVa State Col, Hon Doctor Sci, 1994; Surgeon General Medal, 2001. **Military Serv:** AUS, first lt, 1950-53. **Business Addr:** Executive Director, Addiction Research & Treatment Corporation, 22 Chapel St, Brooklyn, NY 11201, **Business Phone:** (718)260-2950.

PRIMOUS, EMMA M.
Educator. **Personal:** Born Oct 5, 1942, Olive Branch, MS; married Commodore Cantrell; children: Commodore & Christopher. **Educ:** Memphis State Univ, BS, 1964, MEd, 1971. **Career:** Memphis Pub Schs, teacher, 27 years; MSU Reading Workshop Elem Sch Teachers, cons; WKNO-TV County Schs Prog, panel mem; Open-Space Schs Benoit, cons; MSU TN State Univ LeMoyne-Owen Col, supr teacher & stud teachers; Prog Problem-solving Skills Memphis City Bd Educ, staff teacher; night adminr, Adult High Sch; Memphis City Schs, instrnl facilitator; Delta fine arts, secy, currently. **Orgs:** Ant Educ Asn; TN Educ Asn; Memphis Educ Asn; vip Rubaiyats Inc; LesCasuale Bridge Club; Cherokee Civic Club; NAACP; Delta Sigma Theta Sorority; Kappa Delta Pi; Int Reading Asn. **Honors/Awds:** Outstanding Young Educator of the Year, Parkway Village Jaycees, 1974; Outstanding Teacher Award, Phi Delta Kappa, 1990. **Home Addr:** 1575 Galveston St, Memphis, TN 38114. **Business Addr:** Secretary, Delta Fine Arts, Memphis, TN 38117.

PRIMUS-COTTON, DR. BOBBIE J
Educator, research scientist. **Personal:** Born Jul 20, 1934, Daytona Beach, FL; daughter of William (deceased) and Lillie Rose (deceased); married Rev Jesse; children: Robyn & Jonathan R. **Educ:** Fla A&M Univ, Tallahassee, FL, BS, 1952; Univ NC, Chapel Hill, NC, MPH, 1972; Va Polytech Inst & State Univ, Blacksburg, VA, EdD, cert pub policy, 1984; Univ Calif Los Angeles, Berkeley, CA, post-doctorate, 1986. **Career:** Am Asn State Cols & Univs, Wash, DC, Allied Health Proj, assoc coordr, 1980-82; Howard Univ, Col Allied Health, Wash, DC, assoc coordr allied health proj, 1982-84; Cancer Prevention Awareness, assoc coordr, 1984-86; Nat Insts Health, Bethesda, Md, Am Red Cross, Wash, DC, Black Elderly Proj, assoc coordr, 1984-86; Nat Cancer Inst, Cancer Prevention Awareness Prog Black Am, Co-Authored with J Hatch, L Monroe, 1985; Morris Brown Col, Atlanta, GA, Dept Nursing, chair, 1986-88; Univ Cent Fla, Orlando, FL, assoc prof nursing, coordr spec proj, 1988-93; Bethune Cookman Col, Daytona Beach, FL, assoc prof, currently. **Orgs:** Dir, Proj SUCCEDS, 1987-; vpres & chmn, Nat Black Nurses Asn, 1990-; pres, Prof Images Int Inc, 1984-; minority grantsmanship chmn, Nat Insts Health, 1988-90; trustee, Daytona Beach Community Col, 1988-93. **Honors/Awds:** Merit Award, Univ Cent Fla. **Special Achievements:** Author, Mentor/ProtTgT Relationships Among Black Professionals in Allied Health: Professional Development (dissertation), 1984; co-author, Introduction to the Preceptor Role in the BS Program, 1989; The SEEED Report: A Cultural Diversity Workshop, 1990; Developing Intuition in Youth Through Empowerment: A Step Toward Professionalism Through Mentoring, 1990; author with M Lenaghan & W Primus, 'Making Cultural Diversity a Reality Within the College of Health and Professional Studies at the University of Central Florida', 1990. **Home Phone:** (904)672-7148. **Business Addr:** Associate Professor of Nursing, Bethune-Cookman College, 640 Dr Mary McLeod Bethune Blvd, Daytona Beach, FL 32114, **Business Phone:** (386)481-2000.

PRINCE. See NELSON, PRINCE ROGERS.

PRINCE, ANDREW LEE
Basketball coach, football executive, basketball player. **Personal:** Born Dec 14, 1952, Victoria, TX; son of Hazel Lewis Prince and Andrew Prince. **Educ:** Abilene Christian Univ, BS, 1975, MS, sch admin, 1980. **Career:** Basketball player (retired), basketball coach, football executive; Barcelona, Spain, pro basketball, 1975; Graz, Austria, pro basketball,1979; Gottingen, Germany, pro basketball, 1981; Abilene Christian Univ, asst coach, 1983; Stephen F Austin State Univ, asst coach; Abilene Christian Univ, Multi-Cult Ctr, dir; TX Tech, acad couns specialist; Univ Ill, Fighting Illin football squad, lead acad counr, 2001-. **Orgs:** Black Coaches Assn; Nat Assn Basketball Coaches. **Honors/Awds:** Inducted into the Abilene Christian University Sports Hall of Fame, 1994; NAIA All-America, All-Lone-Star. **Business Phone:** (217)333-1400.

PRINCE, EDGAR OLIVER
Government official. **Personal:** Born Sep 13, 1947, Brooklyn, NY. **Educ:** City Univ NY, NY, Christian Coun Ctr, AA, Lib Arts, 1968; State Univ NY, Stony Brook, BA, sociol, 1971, MA, sociol, 1974; CW Post Ctr Long Island Univ, MPA, pub admin, 1980; NY Univ, PhD, pub admin. **Career:** Mission Immaculate Va, 1968; St Agatha's Home C, 1969; St Vincent Hall, 1970-71; sr residential child care counr; State Univ NY, Stony Brook, sociol grad teaching asst ship, 1971-73; Suffolk Co Summer Intern Prog Youth Bd, res analyst, 1972; CW Post Ctr Long Island Univ, dept Criminal Justice, adj asst prof, 1974-79; Suffolk Co Criminal Just Coordr Coun, co exec off sr res analyst, 1974-75; Suffolk Co Dept Health Serv, sr res analyst, 1975-. **Orgs:** Am Public Health Asn, 1975-; Am Soc Pub Admin, 1976-; Int Soc Syst Sci Health Care, 1980-; Nat Forum Black Pub Admins, 1983-; charter mem, Statue Liberty Ellis Island Found Inc, 1984-; Cong Black Caucus Health Brain Trust, 1984-; charter mem & trustee, Repub Presidential Task Force, 1984-. **Honors/Awds:** Presidential Medal Merit, 1985; Presidential Honor Roll, 1985; Certificate of Merit, Presidential Comn Repub Presidential Task Force, 1986; Certificate of Recognition, Nat Repub Cong Comn. **Special Achievements:** numerous publ. **Military Serv:** USAR, Med Serv Corp Commissioned 2nd lt, 1981.

PRINCE, GINA MARIA. See PRINCE-BYTHEWOOD, GINA.

PRINCE, JOAN MARIE
Hematologist. **Personal:** Born Jan 14, 1954, Milwaukee, WI. **Educ:** Univ Wis-Milwaukee, BA, 1977, BS, 1981, MS, 1992, PhD, urban Educ, 1999. **Career:** St Joseph's Hosp, hematologist, 1981-; Med Sci Labs, supvr, hemat, 1988; Univ Wis Med Sch, mgr health professions partnership initiative, asst chancellor, vice chancellor, currently. **Orgs:** Assoc mem, Am Soc Clin Pathologists, 1981-; mem, Delta Sigma Theta Sor, 1974-; Black Women's Network, pres; mem Cancer & The Black Amer Comm, 1982-; task force mem, Black Women's Health Project, 1983-; speakers bureau Ronald McDonald House 1984-86; bd dirs, Am Cancer Soc, 1985-; assoc mem, Am Soc of Med Technologists; bd dir, UW Milwaukee Alumni Assoc, 1985-86; mem, Citizens Review Bd, 1987; mem, Future Milwaukee, 1988-; bd mem, Greater Milwaukee Found; vice chmn, Nat Kidney Found of Wis; bd, Wis Women's Coun. **Honors/Awds:** Published article "Black Women & Health," 1984; 1989 Black Role Model Milwaukee Public Library 1989; 12 articles in The Business Journal magazine, topic: "Instilling Entrepreneurial Spirit In Youth" 1989; Future Milwaukee Community Service Award, 1992; Women of Color Recognition Award, 1991; Future Milwaukee Community Svc Awd, 1993; WITI-TV 6 & The Milwaukee Times, Black Excel-

lence Awd for Community Svc, 1994; First Annual Executive Committee Awd for Volunteerism-Community Brain Storming Conference, 1996. **Special Achievements:** Ffirst African American graduate of the bachelor?s program in Medical Technology, as well as the Masters Program in Clinical Laboratory Sciences at University Wisconsin Milwaukee. **Home Addr:** 8712 W Spokane, Milwaukee, WI 53224. **Business Addr:** Vice Chancellor, University of Wisconsin-Milwaukee, Chapman Hall 118 2200 E Kenwood Blvd, PO Box 413, Milwaukee, WI 53201-0413, **Business Phone:** (414)229-3101.

PRINCE, RICHARD EVERETT
Journalist. **Personal:** Born Jul 26, 1947, New York, NY; son of Jonathan Joseph and Audrey Elaine. **Educ:** New York Univ, BS 1969. **Career:** Newark Star-Ledger, reporter, 1967-68; Wash Post, reporter 1968-77; Democrat & Chronicle, asst metro ed, 1979-81, asst news ed, 1981-85, ed writer/columnist, 1985-93, op-ed ed, 1993-94; Gannett News Serv, columnist, 1988-93; Communities In Sch Inc, publ ed, 1994-98; Nat Asn Black Journalists, interim dir communs, 1998-99; Wash Post, part-time foreign desk copy-editor, 1999-; Ctr for Public Integrity, ed, The Public i, online newsletter, 1999-. **Orgs:** Nat Assoc Black Journalists, 1984-; pres, Rochester Assoc Black Communicators, 1986-87; Writers & Books, 1988-94; Nat Conf Ed Writers, 1993-; Nat Soc Newspaper Columnists, 1989-; NABJ Jour, co-ed, 1990-93, assoc ed, 1994-97. **Honors/Awds:** Second place writing competition, Nat Soc Newspaper Columnists 1989; Third place writing competition, commentary, Nat Asn Black Journalists, 1987, 1988, 1989. **Military Serv:** USSAFR, sgt, 1968-73. **Home Addr:** 11 E Oxford Ave, Alexandria, VA 22301. **Business Addr:** Part-time Foreign Desk Copy Editor, The Wash Post, 1150 15th St NW, Washington, DC 20071, **Business Phone:** (202)334-6000.

PRINCE-BYTHEWOOD, GINA (GINA MARIA PRINCE)
Administrator, writer, movie producer. **Personal:** Born Jun 10, 1969; married Reggie Rock, May 24, 1998; children: Cassius & Toussaint. **Educ:** Univ Calif Los Angeles, Sch Theatre, attended 1991. **Career:** Producer: TV Series: "Courthouse", 1995; "Felicity", 1998; Biker Boyz, 2003; Film: Love & Basketball, dir, 2000; Biker Boyz, 2003; dir: TV Series: "Disappearing Acts", 2000, "The Bernie Mac Show", 200; "Everybody Hates Chris", 2005; "Everybody Hates the Laundromat", 2005; "Girlfriends", 2005; "Odds & Ends", 2005; "Fits & Starts", 2005; Reflections, co-producer, 2007. **Honors/Awds:** Gene Reynold's Scholarship, Univ Calif Los Angeles; Image Award, Nat Asn Advan Colored People; Black Reel, 2000; Humanitas Prize, 2000; Independent Spirit Award, 2000. **Business Addr:** Actor, International Creative Management, Jeanne Williams (agent), 8942 Wilshire Blvd, Beverly Hills, CA 90211, **Business Phone:** (310)550-4000.

PRINGLE, MIKE
Football player. **Personal:** Born Oct 1, 1967, Los Angeles, CA. **Educ:** Wash State Univ; Calif State Univ, Fullerton, Criminal Justice. **Career:** Football player (retired); Nat Football League, Atlanta Falcons, 1990-91; Canadian Football League, Edmonton Eskimos, running back, 1992, 2003-04; World League Am Football, Sacramento Surge, running back, 1992; Canadian Football League, Sacramento Gold Miners, running back, 1993; Canadian Football League, Baltimore Stallions, 1994-95; Nat football league, Denver Broncos, 1996; Canadian Football League, Montreal Alouettes, running back, 1996-2002, 2005. **Honors/Awds:** Most Outstanding Player, Canadian Football League, 1995; Canadian Football Hall of Fame, 2008. **Special Achievements:** One of the CFL's Top 50 players of the league's modern era by Canadian sports network, 2006.

PRINGLE, NELL RENE
Counselor, educator. **Personal:** Born Jun 21, 1952, Baytown, TX; daughter of Elsie M Fontenot and Earlest Fontenot Sr; married Danny C Sr, Aug 23, 1983; children: Danny Jr, Courtney Tenille & Jaime Reshaude. **Educ:** Lee Col, AA, 1971; Lamar Univ, BS, 1973; Tex Southern Univ, MEd, 1976, EdD, 1991. **Career:** Crosby Independent Sch Dist, educator, 1975-89; San Jacinto Col, dir couns, 1989; Kellogg fel, 1997; San Jacinto Col, assoc dean instr technol, currently. **Orgs:** Tex Jr Col Teachers Asn. **Honors/Awds:** Scholar, Ford Found, 1971; Most Representative Student Award, Lee Col, 1971; Fellows Award, Tex A&M Univ, 1990. **Home Phone:** (713)451-6233. **Business Addr:** Associate Dean of Instructional Technology, San Jacinto College North Campus, Brightwell Techl Bldg 5800 Uvalde, Houston, TX 77049, **Business Phone:** (281)458-4050 Ext 7122.

PRIOLEAU, OSCAR EUGENE
Lawyer. **Personal:** Born Oct 11, 1963, Columbia, SC; son of Oscar Sr and Lillian; married Edilinda, Oct 26, 1992; children: Monica, Oscar III & Antonio. **Educ:** Univ SC, BS, bus, 1985; Tex Southern Univ, JD, 1988; Georgetown Univ Law Ctr, LLM, labor law, 1989. **Career:** Prioleau & Assocs, owner, atty, currently. **Orgs:** Omega Psi Phi, 1982-; Phi Delta Phi, 1985; Fulfur County Off Workforce Develop Bd, 2001-. **Military Serv:** USN, 0-3 lt, 1988-93. **Business Addr:** Attorney, Owner, Prioleau & Associates, 41 Marietta St NW Suite 600-B, Atlanta, GA 30303, **Business Phone:** (404)526-9400.

PRIOLEAU, PETER SYLVESTER
Banker. **Personal:** Born Dec 10, 1949, Hopkins, SC; son of Jessie Prioleau and Ruth Byrd; married Brenda Mickens, Nov 24, 1984. **Educ:** Midland Tech Col, AA Retail Mgt, 1974; Benedict Col, BS, Bus, 1975. **Career:** Davision-Macy's Dept Store, assoc mgr, 1972-75; Bank Am, vpres, 1975-2001; NationsBank, vpres, currently. **Orgs:** SC Bankers Asn, 1975-2001; Greater Columbia Chamber Com, 1975-2001; NCP, 1978-; Comt, 100 Black Men. **Honors/Awds:** Award of Appreciation, United Negro Col Fund, 1983-85; Appreciation Award, United Way of the Midlands SC, 1983; Nat Asn Equal Opportunity in Higher Educ, 1986. **Military Serv:** AUS, sgt 2 yrs; SC Air Natl Guard; USAF Res CMSAF, 1975-. **Home Addr:** PO Box 1823, Columbia, SC 29202. **Business Addr:** Vice President, NationsBank, PO Box 727, Columbia, SC 29222, **Business Phone:** (803)343-7930.

PRIOLEAU, PIERSON
Football player. **Personal:** Born Aug 6, 1977, Alvin, SC; married Alicia; children: Pierson Jalen & Parker Jayden. **Educ:** Va Tech Univ, interdisciplinary studies. **Career:** San Francisco 49ers, defensive back, 1999-2000; Buffalo Bills, 2001-04; Wash Redskins, defensive back, 2005-07; Jacksonville Jaguars, 2008-09; New Orleans Saints, defensive back, 2009-. **Honors/Awds:** First-team All-Big East, 1997. **Business Addr:** Professional Football Player, New Orleans Saints, 5800 Airline Dr, Metairie, LA 70003, **Business Phone:** (504)733-0255.

PRIOLEAU, DR. SARA NELLIENE
Administrator, dentist. **Personal:** Born Apr 10, 1940, Hopkins, SC; daughter of Willie Oree and Wilhelmina; married William R Montgomery; children: Kara I & William P. **Educ:** SC State Col, BS, 1960, MS, 1965; Univ Pa, DMD, 1970. **Career:** Comph Group Health Serv, pub health dent, 1971-72; Hamilton Health Ctr, dir dent serv, 1972-97; Community Dent Assoc PC, pres, 1976-; Seltnsgrace Ctr, 1999-2001. **Orgs:** Nat Dent Asn, 1970-; Am Dent Asn, 1970-; Harrisburg Dent Soc, Links Inc, Hbg Chap, 1976-, pres, 2002; Exec Women Int Hbg Chap, 1984-90; vchmn, Status Women, 1986-87; chmn health, 1988-89, Soroptomist Int N Atlantic Region; pres, Soroptomist Int Hbg, 1989-90; bd dir, Ment Health Assoc Tri County Inc, 1986-88; pres, Soroptomist Int Harrisburg 1987-89; med assistance, Dent SubComt State Pa; bd trustees, Harrisburg Area Community Col. **Honors/Awds:** Working Woman of the Year, Health Service Pomoys, 1982; Woman of the Year, Black Women's Caucus; Cumberland Co Ment Retardation Award, 1987 & 1995; Koser Award, Athena Recepient, 1995; fel, Int Col Dent, 1996; Pa Best 50 Women Bus, 1997. **Home Addr:** 1094 Cardinal Dr, PO Box 5188, Harrisburg, PA 17111. **Business Addr:** President, Community Dental Associates PC, 2451 N 3rd St, Harrisburg, PA 17110, **Business Phone:** (717)238-8163.

PRIOR, ANTHONY
Football player, writer. **Personal:** Born Mar 27, 1970, Mira Loma, CA; children: Anthony Jordan. **Educ:** Wash State Univ. **Career:** Football player (retired), author, owner; NY Jets, defensive back,1993-95; Minn Vikings, 1996-97; Oakland Raiders, 1998; Calgary Stampeders, defensive back; BC Lions, defensive back; author & pub speaker, currently;Stone Hold Books Corp, owner, currently. **Business Addr:** Founder, Author, Stone Hold Books Corporation, 10504 Latour Lane, Mira Loma, CA 91752.

PRITCHARD, DARON
Government official. **Personal:** Born Aug 26, 1954, Vicksburg, MS; married Juanita Hill; children: LaTonzia, LaToya, LaKeita & Daron Jamaal. **Educ:** Utica Jr Col; Alcorn State Univ, Lormaums, BA, 1977. **Career:** Eastern Foods Inc, br mgr; Town Edwards, mayor, currently. **Orgs:** Deacon Friendship MB Church. **Business Addr:** Mayor, Town of Edwards, PO Box 215, Edwards, MS 39066.

PRITCHARD, MICHAEL ROBERT
Football player. **Personal:** Born Oct 26, 1969, Shaw AFB, SC. **Educ:** Univ Colo. **Career:** Football player (retired); Atlanta Falcons, wide receiver, 1991-93; Denver Broncos, wide receiver, 1994-95; Seattle Seahawks, wide receiver, 1996-99; ESPN 920 radio sta, caller, currently.

PRITCHARD, ROBERT STARLING, II
Composer, pianist, founder (originator). **Personal:** Born Jun 13, 1927, Winston-Salem, NC; son of Lucille Pickard Pritchard and R Starling Pritchard Sr. **Educ:** Syracuse Univ, Syracuse NY, BS, 1948, MM, 1950; private piano study with Edwin Fischer, Arturo Benedetti Michelangeli, Carl Fried berg, Hans Neumann, and Robert Golds band, 1948-59. **Career:** Touring concert pianist, 1951-; Conservatoire Nationale D'Haiti, Port-au-Prince, Haiti, artist-in-residence, 1958; Univ Liberia, Monrovia, artist-in-residence, 1959; New Sch Social Res, New York, NY, fac mem, 1962; Black Hist Month, founder, 1965; Panamerican & Panafrican Asn, Baldwinsville, NY, cofounder & chmn, 1968-; Kahre-Richardes Family Found, Baldwinsville, cofounder & chmn, 1972-; Impartial Citizen Newspaper, Syracuse, NY, publi, 1980-; Lincoln Univ Pa, artist-in-residence, 1988-. **Honors/Awds:** Doctorate honoris causa, Nat Univ Haiti, 1968; citation, Orgn Am States, 1969; founder & organizer, Louis Moreau Gotts chalk Int Pianists &Composers Competition, Dillard Univ, 1970; artistic dir, Gala Concert Peace & Reconsiliation DAR Constitution Hall, Wash DC, 1970; artistic dir, UN Gen Assembly Concert Gala US, Bicentennial & 13th Anniversary Orgn African Unity, 1976; artistic dir, Martin Luther King Concerts, Riverside Church & Cathedral St. John Divine, 1978; Black Hist Month Founder's Citation, Gov New York, 1987; Bayard Rustin Human Rights Award, A Philip Randolph Inst, 1988; President's Centennial Medal, Lincoln Univ, 1988;artistic dir, Black Hist Month Concert Gala, Lincoln Univ, 1989. **Special Achievements:** First African American concert pianist to tour Europe, the Middle East, and North Africa as a solo performer. **Business Phone:** (315)638-7379.

PRITCHETT, KELVIN BRATODD
Football player. **Personal:** Born Oct 24, 1969, Atlanta, GA. **Educ:** Univ Miss. **Career:** Football player (retired); Detroit Lions, defensive tackle, 1991-94, 1999-2004; Jacksonville Jaguars, 1995-98. **Special Achievements:** TV show: ''Super Bowl Fever''.

PRITCHETT, STANLEY JEROME
Football player, football coach. **Personal:** Born Dec 12, 1973, Atlanta, GA; married; children: 4. **Educ:** Univ SC, BA, hist. **Career:** Football player (retired), Football coach; Miami Dolphins, running back,1996-99; Philadelphia Eagles, 2000; Chicago Bears, 2001-03; Atlanta Falcons, 2004; Booker T. Wash High Sch, teacher & football coach, currently. **Orgs:** Kappa Alpha Psi Fraternity, Inc. **Business Addr:** Acting President, Morris Brown College, 643 Martin Luther King Jr Dr, Atlanta, GA 30314, **Business Phone:** (404)739-1010.

PROBASCO, JEANETTA
Counselor, educator. **Personal:** Born in Needville, TX; married James A (deceased); children: Wardell. **Educ:** Prairie View A&M Univ, BS 1941, MEd, 1950; Univ Tex, cert, 1965. **Career:** Educator, counselor (retired); Kilfore Jr High Sch, counr; CB Dansby High Sch, counr & teacher math, 1953-59; Fredonia Sch, teacher homemaking, 1953-59; Fredonia High Sch, teacher homemaking math, 1942-53. **Orgs:** Asst chmn, Texarkana Dist New Homemakers Am, 1958-59; Comn Kilgore Jr High Sch; secy, Parents Teachers Asn; Kilgore Br TSTA; NEA; Piney Woods Personnel & Guidance Asn; Tex Am Personnel & Guidance Asn; Control Steering Comt Kilgore Indepent Sch Dist, 1972-73; elected chmn, TEPS, 1974-75; Fedonia Baptist Church Kilgore; Heroines of Jerioch; Am Asn Univ Women; Gregg Co Home Econs Asn; Marquis Libr Soc. **Honors/Awds:** State 4-H Alumni Award, 1967; State 4-H Adult Leaders Award, 1969; WD McQueen 4-H Award, 1971; Nat 4-H Alumni Recognition Award, 1975.

PROCOPE, ERNESTA
Insurance executive. **Personal:** Married John L Procope, Jan 1, 1953; married Albin Bowman, 1954 (deceased). **Educ:** Brooklyn Col; Pohs Inst Ins. **Career:** EG Bowman, founder, pres, chief exec officer, 1953-; Bowman-Procope Assoc, 1970; Brinkerhoff Homes, Jamaica, NY, developer. **Orgs:** Chubb Corp; Columbia Gas Syst Inc; trustee, Cornell Univ; Avon Products; S St Seaport Mus; New York Zoological Soc; Boys & Girls Clubs Am; trustee, Adelphi Univ. **Honors/Awds:** Woman of the Year, Tuesday mag, 1972; Entrepreneurial Excellence, Dow Jones / Wall St Jour, 1992; Crain's New York Business All-Star Award, 1993; Small Business Person of the Year, US Small Bus Admin, 1993; Helen Garvin Outstanding Achiever Award, Nat Asn Ins Women, 1995; Woman of the Year, Police Athletic League, 1995; Minority Business Enterprise Legal Defense & Reeducation Fund, Parren J. Mitchell Award; Heritage Award, Exec Leadership Council & Foundation, 1997; honorary degrees from Howard Univ, Adelphi Univ, Marymount Manhattan Col, Morgan State Univ. **Special Achievements:** E.G. Bowne is now America's largest minority-owned and woman-owned insurance brokerage firm. **Business Addr:** President/Chief Executive Officer, EG Bowman Co., 97 Wall St, New York, NY 10005-3518.

PROCTER, HARVEY THORNTON, JR.
Automotive executive. **Personal:** Born Dec 29, 1945, Monongahela, PA; son of Harvey T Sr (deceased) and Charlene McPherson (deceased); divorced; children: Karyn Michele. **Educ:** Southern IL Univ, BA, 1967; Roosevelt Univ, MA, 1970; Wayne State Univ, JD, 1976. **Career:** Univ Ill Law, fel; Ill Gen Assembly, scholarship;Chicago Comn Youth Welfare, asst zone dir, 1966, dir spec events, 1967; Ford Motor Co, union rels mgr, 1968-; Univ Mich, Sch Bus, LEAD Prog, lectr, 1986-; Nat Urban League, Black Exec Exchange Prog, vis prof, 1988-. **Orgs:** Detroit Bar Asn, MI; Asn Trial Lawyers Am; Am Mgt Asn; Soc Human Resource Mgt; Midwest Co op Educ Asn; Employ Mgt Asn; life mem, Alpha Phi Alpha ; life mem, Nat Asn Advancements Colored People; parish coun, St Thomas Apostle Church; chmn, Midwest Col Placement Asn, 1983-; pres, bd dirs, Earhart Village Homes; Bus Adv Coun Mgt Inst, 1987-90; pres, exec bd, Midwest Col Placement Asn, 1988-; Bus Adv Coun Univ Mich Comprehensive Studies Prog, 1989-; Bus Adv Coun Clark Atlanta Univ Ctr, 1988-89; pres, Nat Asn Employ, 1997-; vpres, employ rels, bd governors, Col Placement Coun, 1991-; task force mem, Nat Governors Asn, 1990-; pres, Midwest Asn Col & Employ, 1990-91. **Honors/Awds:** Vice President's Award Youth Motivation, VPres US, 1970; Citation of Merit, City Detroit Police Dept, 1990, 1991; Award of Merit, Jarvis Christian Col, 1990, 1992. **Business Addr:** Union Relations Manager, Ford Motor Company, The Am Rd Suite 367, Dearborn, MI 48121.*

PROCTOR, BARBARA GARDNER
Executive, chief executive officer. **Personal:** Born Nov 30, 1932, Black Mountain, NC; divorced; children: Morgan. **Educ:** Talledega Col, BA, Psych Sociol, BA, Engl Ed. **Career:** Downbeat mag, contrib ed; Vee Jay Records Int, int dir, 1961-64; Post-Keyes-Gardner Advt, 1965-68; Gene Taylor Asn, 1968-69; N Advertising Agency, copy suprv, 1969-70; Proctor & Gardner Advertising Inc, pres. **Orgs:** Contg ed Down Beat Mag, 1958; Chicago Econ Devel Corp; Chicago Media Women; Nat Radio Arts & Sci; Chicago Advertising Club; Chicago Womens Advertising Club; Female Exec Assoc; Better Bus Bur, Cosmopolitan C of C; chmn, WTTW TV Auction; Chicago Econ Devel Corp, Chicago Urban League, NAACP; Seaway Nat Bank, Mt Sinai Hosp, IL State C of C, Coun of Univ of IL. **Honors/Awds:** Industry 20 Awds incl Clio-Amer TV Commercial Festival; 2 CFAC Awds; Frederick Douglass Humanitarian Awd 1975; Amer TV Commercial Awds, 1972; Black book Businesswoman of the Yr; Chicago Advertising Woman of the Yr, 1974-75; Small Bus of Yr, 1978; Headline Awd, 1978; Charles A Stevens Int Org of Women Exec Achievers Awd, 1978.

PROCTOR, EARL D.
Executive. **Personal:** Born May 20, 1941, Philadelphia, PA; son of Earl M and Louise Culbreath; married Jean E Matlock, Sep 27, 1978; children: Denise, Eric, Monica. **Educ:** Temple Univ, BS, 1963; Temple Univ, attended 1965; NY Univ, attended 1969; Harvard Bus Sch, MBA, 1975. **Career:** Ford Motor Co, 1968-73; Cummins Engine Co, mkt dir; Rockwell Int, mkt dir, 1977-79; Ferguson &Bryan Assoc, partner, 1979-80; DOT & MBRC, exec dir, 1980-81, Comn Bicentennial United States Const dep dir mkt; Hidden Creek Indust, vpres; TGP Inc, Va, pres, ceo. **Orgs:** Am Acad Polit & Soc Sci; PA Soc World Affairs Coun; life mem, Nat Asn Advan Colored People; PA Soc, Nat Urban League-Black Exec Exchange Prog vis prof. **Honors/Awds:** Honorary Citizen New Orleans; US Small Bus Nat Award of Excellence, 1983.

PROCTOR, SONYA T
Law enforcement officer. **Career:** DC Metrop Police Dept, police officer, lt, capt, Spec Events Br, comdr, inspector, asst chief police, interim chief, actg chief police, 1997-. **Special Achievements:** First female to head the Wash DC police force; first African American woman to head the 3,700-member department. **Business Phone:** (202)727-4383.

PROCTOR, WILLIAM H
Educator. **Personal:** Born Jan 15, 1945, Baltimore, MD. **Educ:** Pa State Univ, BS, 1967; NC Cent Univ Law Sch, JD, 1970; Univ PA, MBA, 1973. **Career:** Fed Trade Comn, examr mgt mkt, 1970-71; Pagan & Morgan, consult, 1973; Morgan St Univ, Earl G Graves Sch Bus & Mgt, Bus Admin Dept, asst prof bus & mgt, assoc prof, currently. **Orgs:** Kappa Alpha Psi Frat, 1963; pres, CBH Invest Corp, 1966-; Phi Alpha Delta Law Frat, 1971; Rapid Transit Coal Balt, 1973-; bd mem, Harris & Proctor, 1973-; bd mem, Proctor Enterprises, 1974-; US Supreme Ct, 1976; US Supreme Ct, 1976; Phi Alpha Delta; Kappa Alpha Psi; Am Bar Asn; Pa Bar Asn; York Co Bar. **Military Serv:** AUS, res capt. **Business Addr:** Associate Professor, Morgan State University, Earl G Graves School of Business and Management, Rm 213D McMechen Com Bldg 1700 E Cold Spring Lane, Baltimore, MD 21251, **Business Phone:** (443)885-1689.

PROFIT-MCLEAN, RENE. **See MCLEAN, RENE.**

PROTHRO, GERALD DENNIS
Executive director, computer executive. **Personal:** Born Sep 27, 1942, Atlanta, GA; son of Charles Emery and Esther Jones; married Brenda Jean Bell, Feb 14, 1976; children: Gerald Dennis. **Educ:** Howard Univ, BS, 1966, MS, 1969; Harvard Grad Sch Bus, postgraduate studies, 1975. **Career:** Goddard Space Flight Ctr, physicist, 1965-69; Int Bus Mach, Burlington, VT, assoc syst analyst, 1969, sr syst anaylst, 1969-71, mgr process line cent eng syst, 1971, mgr process line cent anaylsis syst, 1971-73, proj mgr syst facilities & support, 1973-74, Syst Prod Div, mgr info syst strategy, 1974-75, dir syst assurance & data processing prod group, 1975-78, Poughkeepsie Develop Lab, Data Syst Div, mgr processors syst, 1978-79, mgr site resources & bus planning, 1979-81, quality assurance mgr, 1981, vpres & site gen mgr, 1989, secy mgt bd, 1989-98; NDEA Fel, 1967-69; Nationwide Financial Serv Inc, dir, 1997-; IKT Inc, managing dir, 1998-99; BroadStream Commun Inc, sr vpres & chief technol officer, 1999-2000; IKT Investments Ltd, staff, 2000-; Nationwide Life Ins Co, dir, 2002-. **Orgs:** Nat Asn Advan Colored People; Urban League; Am Inst Phys; AAAS; Automatic Comput Mach Asn. **Honors/Awds:** Black Achievers Award, YMCA, 1976; received numerous award. **Special Achievements:** Author of numerous articles on computer science. **Business Phone:** (614)249-6918.

PROTHRO, DR. JOHNNIE WATTS
Educator. **Personal:** Born Feb 26, 1922, Atlanta, GA; son of Theresa Louise Young and John Devine Hines; married Charles E Prothro Jr; children: 1. **Educ:** Spel man Col, BS, 1941; Columbia Univ, MS, 1946; Univ Chicago, PhD, 1952. **Career:** Educator (retired); Tuskegee Inst, asst prof, 1952-63; Univ Conn, assoc prof, 1963-68; Emory Univ, prof, 1975-79; Ga State Univ, prof nutrit,1979-90. **Orgs:** Special fel NIH, 1958-59; OEEC fel, NSF, 1961; bd mem, Int Food & Agr Develop, 1978-81; Geo Washington Carver Res Found, 1979-85; Int Union Nutrit Scientists, 1982-85; fel March of Dimes, 1984. **Honors/Awds:** Borden Award, Am Home Ec Asn, 1950-51; Academic Excellence Award, Ga State Univ.

PROTHROW-STITH, DEBORAH BOUTIN
Physician, educator. **Personal:** Born Feb 6, 1954, Marshall, TX; daughter of Mildred Prothrow and PW Prothrow Jr; married Charles, Aug 30, 1975; children: Percy, Mary & Mildred. **Educ:** Spelman Col, BA, 1975; Harvard Univ, Med Sch, MD, 1979; Wheelok Col, EdD,1992. **Career:** Boston City Hosp, sr resident in charge Med & Surg unit, 1982, staff physician, 1982-87; coprin investr, 1984-87; City Boston, Dept Health & Hosps, Health Prog Ctr Urban Youth, co-dir, 1985-87; Harvard Street Neighborhood Health Ctr, clin chief, 1986-87; Commonwealth MAS, cms pub health, 1987-89; Community Care Systs Inc, vpres, Med dir, 1989-90; Harvard Univ, Sch Pub Health, asst dean gov & comunity progs, 1990-97,assoc dean fac develop, 1997-, prof pub health pract, 1994-97, dir, Division Pub Health Pract, 1997-, Henry Pickering Walcott prof pract pub Health, 1997-. **Orgs:** Trustee, Spelman Col, 1989-; trustee, Hyams Found, 1990; Am Pub Health Assn. **Honors/Awds:** PSD, N Adams State Col, 1988; Exceptional Achievement in Public Service, SCY Louis Sullivan, 1989; Rebecca Lee Award, Mass Dept Pub Health, 1990; Hildrus A Poindexter Distinguished Service Award, Black Caucus of Health Workers, 1992; Honorary Degrees; World Health Day Award, Am Assn World Health, 1993; inducted into IST of Medicine, 2003. **Special Achievements:** First woman Commissioner of Public Health for the Commonwealth of Massachusetts; Author, numerous works include: Violence Prevention Curriculum for Adolescents, 1987; Deadly Consequences: How Violence is Destroying Our Teenage Population, 1991; Health Skills for Wellness,Prentice Hall, 1994; Murder Is No Accident: Understanding and Preventing Youth Violence In America, 2003. **Business Addr:** Professor of Public Health Practice & Associate Dean Faculty Developme, Harvard School of Public Health, Department Health Policy & Management, 841 Parker St, Boston, MA 02120, **Business Phone:** (617)495-7777.

PROUT, PATRICK M
Banker. **Personal:** Born Jul 8, 1941, Port-of-Spain, Trinidad and Tobago; son of Iris Smith and Rupert; married Faye Whitfield, Apr 17, 1976; children: Nicole, Danielle & Dominique. **Educ:** US Naval Acad Annapolis, BS, eng, 1964; Harvard Univ, Grad Sch Bus, Cambridge, MBA, gen mgt, 1973. **Career:** IBM, Wash, mkt rep, 1968-71; Miller Brewing Co, Milwaukee, prod mgr, 1973-75; Chase Manhattan Bank, New York, vpres, 1975-82; Ranier Bank, Seattle, vpres, 1982-84; Seafirst Bank, Seattle, sr vpres, 1984-90; Bank Am, San Francisco, exec vpres, 1990; Bank One Cleveland, pres, chief operating officer, vice chmn; Bankers Trust New York, managing dir, head; Prout Group, pres & ceo, currently. **Orgs:** Exec Leadership Coun; HBS Alumni Asn, Cleveland Chapter; US Naval Acad Alumni Asn; NAUB. **Military Serv:** US Marine Corp, capt, 1964-68; Bronze Star with Combat "V", Vietnam Campaign, Vietnam Operations. **Business Phone:** (212)593-8240.

PROVOST, MARSHA PARKS
Counselor. **Personal:** Born Feb 6, 1947, Lynchburg, VA; married George H; children: Geoffrey. **Educ:** Hampton Inst, BA, 1969; Univ TN Chattanooga, MEd, 1976; Univ TN Knoxville, EdD, 1982; Univ Mich, C3 Experience, counr comput & creative change, 1984; Univ Tenn, Inst Leadership Effectiveness, 1984. **Career:** Guilford Co Dept Social Servs, counr-intern, 1968; City Hampton, juvenile probation officer, 1969-71; Guilford Co Dept Social Serv, social worker II, 1971-75; Counseling & Career Planning Ctr UTC, counr, 1977-81, asst dir. **Orgs:** Am Asn Coun & Develop; Am Col Personnel Assoc; Chattanooga Area Psychological Asn; vpres Women Higher Educ Tenn, 1981-82; pres mem, Chattanooga Alumnae Chap Delta Sigma Theta Inc; New Dimensions Club Toastmistress Inc; Chattanooga Bus & Prof Women's Club, 1982-83; Chattanooga Chap Am Soc Training & Develop, 1982-84; Leadership Chattanooga, 1984-85. **Honors/Awds:** Outstanding Young Woman Am, Outstanding Young Women Am Inc, 1981; Woman of the Year, Chattanooga Bus & Prof Women's Clubs, 1981-82; Nat Cert Counr, Nat Bd Cert Counrs, 1984. **Business Addr:** Assitant Director Counseling, University of TN at Chattanooga, 231 University Ctr, Chattanooga, TN 37403.

PRUDHOMME, NELLIE ROSE
Educator. **Personal:** Born Aug 28, 1948, Lafayette, LA; daughter of Richard and Mary; married Hilton James Prudhomme (divorced); children: Eunisha & Shannon. **Educ:** Univ Southwestern LA, BS, Nursing, 1970; Tulane Univ Sch Pub Health, M Publ Health, 1974; Univ Southern, MS, 1977; Univ Southwestern LA, 1984; LA State Univ Med Ctr, Doctorate Nursing Sci, 1997. **Career:** Lafayette Charity Hosp, staff nurse, 1970; Vermilion Parish Sch Bd, health nurse, 1971-72; Touro Infirmary City Health Dept, staff nurse, 1972-73; Univ Southern MS Nursing Sch, asst prof, 1973-78; Family Health Found, staff nurse summer, 1973; Univ Southwestern LA Nursing Sch, asst prof, 1978-81; Univ Med Ctr, staff nurse II, 1981-82; TH Harris Vo-Tech Sch, instr, 1983-84; Univ Med Ctr Lafayette, RN iv nurse consult, 1986-; LA State Univ, asst prof; Univ Southwestern LA, asst prof; Pennigton Biomed Res, fac scholar, 1997-98; Southern Univ & A&M Col, assoc prof & dir, nursing res, currently. **Orgs:** Sigma Theta Tau, 1978-, USL Nursing Hon Soc, 1981-; Zeta Phi Beta Sorority Inc, 1988; March Dimes Birth Defects Found, 1989-; Mayor's Human Servs Comn, 1989-; bd pres, SW LA Health Educ Coun, 1997; Phi Kappa Phi Honor Soc, 1999-; Southern Nursing Res Soc; Am Nurses Asn. **Honors/Awds:** Aaron Fellowship, Tulane Univ Sch Pub Health, 1972-73; USPHS Traineeship, Univ Sch Pub Health, 1972-73; Outstanding District RN, 1989; Career Achievement Award, 1994; Ethnic Minority Fellow, Am Nurses Asn, 1994-97. **Military Serv:** AUS Res, lt col, 20 yrs; 4 yrs Achievement, 1983; Army Commendation, Meritorious Service, 1990; Army Nurse Corps, Ltcol, 1989-; active duty Desert Storm, 1991. **Home Addr:** 157 S Richter Dr, Lafayette, LA 70501. **Business Addr:** Director, Southern University & A&M College, Office of Nursing Research, PO Box 11784, Baton Rouge, LA 70813.

PRUITT, FR. ALONZO CLEMONS
Clergy. **Personal:** Born Feb 20, 1951, Chicago, IL; son of Alonzo and Louise Clemons Hodges; married Doris Brown, Aug 28, 1983; children: Alexander & Nicholas. **Educ:** Roosevelt Univ, Chicago, IL, BA, pub admin, 1975; Univ Ill, Chicago, IL, MSW, 1978; Seabury-Western Theol Sem, Evanston, IL, MDiv, 1984. **Career:** Chicago Urban League, Chicago, IL, community organizer, 1971-73; Lake Bluff Homes C, Park Ridge, IL, 1973-79; Mary Bartelme Homes, Chicago, IL, dir, social worker, 1979-84; St George & St Matthias Church, Chicago, IL, pastor, 1984; Seabury-Western Theological Sem, Evanston, IL, adj prof, 1989-; The Episcopal Church Center, New York, NY, interim national staff officer black ministries, 1990; St. Philips Episcopal Church, rector, currently; Richmond Sheriff's Chaplains, exec dir, 2006-. **Orgs:** Past pres, Chicago Chap, Union Black Episcopalians, 1979-; Mayor Wash Ministers, 1982-87; former convenor, Soc St Francis, 1982-; bd vpres, Chicago Work Ethic Corp, 1987; diocesan coun mem, The Episcopal Diocese Chicago, 1987-; dean, Chicago South Episcopal Deanery, 1989-. **Honors/Awds:** Community Service Award, Oak Village, Community Rels Comn, 1974; Field Prize for Preaching, Cotton Award, Seabury-Western Theol Sem, 1984. **Military Serv:** AUSR, Chaplain, First Lt, 1990. **Business Addr:** Executive Director of Chaplains, Richmond City Sheriff's Office, Richmond City Jail, 1701 Fairfield Way, Richmond, VA 23223, **Business Phone:** (804)321-1266.

PRUITT, REV. EDDIE JAY DELANO
Clergy. **Personal:** Born Apr 17, 1946, Detroit, MI; son of Samuel and Norma; married Bonita Joyce Phillips, Oct 11, 1997; married AlAnne Izzard, 1965 (divorced 1968); children: Eddie J D Pruitt Jr. **Educ:** Lawrence Univ, attended 1984; Ashland Univ Sem, MDiv, 1994. **Career:** Christian Methodist Episcopal Church, pastor, currently. **Orgs:** Detroit Police Chaplan Corps. **Honors/ Awds:** Spirit Detroit Award, City Coun Detroit, MI; Certificate Honorable Community Service, Detroit Police Dept; Certificate of Completion, HIV & Substance Abuse prevention for African American Communities of Faith, 2002. **Business Addr:** Pastor, Christian Methodist Episcopal Church, 35757 Vinewood St, Romulus, MI 48174, **Business Phone:** (734)326-0210.

PRUITT, FRED RODERIC
Physician, president (organization). **Personal:** Born Dec 17, 1938, Birmingham, AL; married Joan Simmons; children: Christopher, Lisa. **Educ:** TN State Univ, BS 1961; Howard Univ, MS 1963; Meharry Med Col, MD 1967. **Career:** Phys specialist internal med, 1973-; St Elizabeth Hosp, resident, 1971-73; St Elizabeth Hosp, intern, 1967-68. **Orgs:** Med dir, Mahoning Co Drug Prog Inc; Lions Internat; pres & bdman, Lions Club; Nat Med Asn; Boh State Med Asn; Alpha Phi Alpha Frat; Mahoning Co Med Soc. **Military Serv:** USAF, mc maj, 1968-71. **Business Addr:** 333 Park Ave, Youngstown, OH 44504.

PRUITT, DR. GEORGE ALBERT
School administrator, educator. **Personal:** Born Jul 9, 1946, Canton, MS; married Pamela Young; children: Shayla Nicole. **Educ:** Ill State Univ, BS, 1968, MS, 1970; Union Grad Sch, PhD, 1974. **Career:** Ill State Univ, asst to vpres acad affairs, 1968-70; Towson State Univ, dean stud, 1970-72; Morgan State Univ, vpres, exec asst to pres, 1972-75; Tenn State Univ, vpres, 1975-81; Coun Advan Experiential Learning, exec vpres, 1981-82; Thomas Edison State Col, pres, 1982-. **Orgs:** Comn Higher Educ & Adult Learner, ACE, 1982-88; bd trustees, CAEL, 1983-87; chair, Comt Alternatives & Innovation Higher Educ, Am Asn State Col & Univ, 1985-87; bd trustees, Union Inst, 1988-; bd dir, Mercer Co Chamber C, 1988-; bd dir, Mercer Med Ctr, 1989-97; bd dir, NJ Asn Cols & Univs, 1989-93; US Educ Dept, Nat Advisory Comt Accreditation & Instnl Eligibility, 1989-92; adv, Kellogg Nat Fel Prog, Group XII, 1990-93; bd dir, SEEDCO, 1990-; bd mgrs, Trenton Savings Bank, 1991-99; bd dir, Am Cancer Soc, NJ, 1992-97; nat adv comt mem, Inst Qual & Integrity, 1993-; adv, Kellogg Nat Fel Prog, Group XV, 1994-97; bd dir, Sun Bancorp, 2001-; bd trustee, Rider Univ, 2001-; bd dir, SEEDCO. **Honors/Awds:** Governor's Citation for Outstanding Service Gov Alexander, Tenn, 1981; Outstanding Service to Education Award, Tenn State Univ, 1981; Outstanding Alumni Achievement Award, Illinois State Univ, 1984; Achievement in Education Award, Nat Asn Negro Bus & Prof Clubs Inc, NJ, 1987; Doctor of Public Service, Bridgewater State Col, MA, 1990; Good Guy Award, George

Washington Coun, Boy Scouts Am, 1991; Humanitarian Award, Nat Conf Christians & Jews, 1992; Elder of the Year, Black NJ Mag, 1993; Col of Education Hall of Fame, Ill State Univ, 1995; DHL, Empire State Col, 1996; DHL, Ill State Univ, 1994; Distinguished Alumni Award, Ill State Univ, 1996; Citizen of the Year, Mercer Co Chamber Com, 1997. **Special Achievements:** Named one of the most effective college presidents in the United States, EXXon Education Foundation Study, 1986. **Business Addr:** President, Thomas Edison State College, 101 W State St, Trenton, NJ 08608-1176, **Business Phone:** (609)984-1105.

PRUITT, GREGORY DONALD, JR.
Football player. **Personal:** Born Aug 18, 1951, Houston, TX. **Educ:** Univ Okla, BA, jour. **Career:** Football player (retired); Cleveland Browns, running back, 1973-81; Los Angeles Raiders, running back, 1982-84; Pruitt-Vaughn Inc, Sports Mgt, pres & chief exec officer. **Orgs:** OPP Fraternity. **Honors/Awds:** All-American, 1972-73; Heisman Trophy, 1973; Pro Bowl, 1973-77, 1983;Offensive Player of the Yr, Cleveland Browns, 1974; led Browns Rushing1974-79; Okla Football Hall of Fame, 1998. **Special Achievements:** One of only two Players that has 2,000 yards in four categories: rushing,receiving, punt and kickoff returns; Greater Cleveland Sports Hall ofFame, 2003; Cleveland Browns Legends, Class of 2000; 4th All Time Rushes,Cleveland Browns, 5,672 yards. **Home Addr:** 13851 Larchmere Blvd, Cleveland, OH 44120. *

PRUITT, JAMES BOUBIAS
Football player. **Personal:** Born Jan 29, 1964, Los Angeles, CA. **Educ:** Calif State Univ, Fullerton. **Career:** Miami Dolphins, wide receiver, 1986-88, 1990-91; Indianapolis Colts, wide receiver, 1988-89; Cleveland Browns, 1993.

PRUITT, MICHAEL
Business owner, football player. **Personal:** Born Apr 3, 1954, Chicago, IL; married Karen Boulware; children: Aaron. **Educ:** Purdue Univ, BA, bus admin. **Career:** Football player (retired), Business owner; Cleveland Browns, full back, 1976-84; Buffalo Bills, 1985; Kansas City Chiefs, 1985-86; Pruitt & Grace Develop Corp, pres; Mike Pruitt's Honda, owner, currently. **Honors/Awds:** Best Offensive Player, TD Club Cleveland, 1980; Miller Man of the Year, 1980; Cleveland's Player of the Year, Akron Booster Club, 1981; Pro Bowler, 1979 & 1980. **Business Addr:** Owner, Mike Pruitt Honda, 43 Pruitt Rde, Akron, OH 44310, **Business Phone:** 800-603-9461.

PRUITT-LOGAN, DR. ANNE SMITH
School administrator, consultant. **Personal:** Born in Bainbridge, GA; daughter of Loring Smith and Anne Ward Smith; married Harold G; children: Harold J, Minda & Andrew; married Ralph L (died 1985); children: Leslie, Diane, Sharon, Ralph Pruitt Jr & Pamela Pruitt-Green. **Educ:** Howard Univ, BS, 1949; Teachers Col, Columbia Univ, MA, 1950, EdD, 1964. **Career:** Howard Univ, counr, 1950-52; Hutto HS, dir guidance, 1952-55; Albany State Col, dean students, 1955-59; Fisk Univ, dean students, 1959-61; Case Western Res Univ, prof educ, 1963-79; Ohio State Univ, assoc dean grad sch, 1979-84, assoc provost, 1984-86, dir, Ctr Teaching Excellence, 1986-94, prof Educ Policy & Leadership, 1979-95, prof emeritus, 1995-; Coun Grad Sch, dean residence, 1994-96, scholar residence, 1996-2002; consult, currently. **Orgs:** Alpha Kappa Alpha Sorority; Links Inc; Cosmos Club; Deacon, Peoples Congregational United Chap Christ; consult, Women's Job Corps creation; pres, Lyndon Johnson's War on Poverty, 1964; bd trustees, Cleveland Urban League, 1965-71; consult, Southern Regional Educ Bd, 1968-81; bd trustees, Cent State Univ, 1973-82; moderator, Mt Zion Congregational Church, 1975-78; Research Task Force Southern Educ Found, 1978-87; consult, Southern Regional Education Bd; Adv Comm US Coast Guard Acad, 1980-83; Am Asn Counseling & Develop; secy, J bd mem, pres-elect, pres, Am Col Personnel Asn, 1976-77; Am Educ Res Asn; Am Asn Higher Educ; Am Asn Univ Prof; Columbus, OH, Mayor's Task Force Pvt Sect Initiatives, 1986-88, bd trustees, Case Western Res Univ, 1987-2002; bd dirs, Columbus Area Leadership Prog, 1988-92; Columbus Educ Comn, 1988-92; co-chairperson, Ohio State Univ United Way Campaign, 1990-91; Nat Sci Found, Comn Equal Opportunities Sci & Eng, 1989-95; coordr, CIC Alliance Success Planning Comn, 1989-90; ETS Vis Panel Res, 1996-2002; pres, Black Women's Agenda, 1998-2002; NSF GK-12 External Experts Panel mem, 2001-; BEST Expert Panel, 2002-; fel Am Coun Educ. **Honors/Awds:** Outstanding Alumnus Howard Univ, 1975; DHum, Cent State Univ, 1982; Named one of America's Top 100 Black Bus & Professional Women, Dollars & Sense Mag, 1986; Distinguished Affirmative Action Award, Ohio State Univ, 1988; Senior Scholar Award, Am Col Personnel Asn, 1989, William H Watson Jr Memorial Award, Ohio State Univ, 1994; Diplomate, 1996; Phi Beta Delta Honor Soc for Int Scholars, 1989; Hall of Fame, Ohio State Univ, Col Educ, 2004; Distinguished Service Award, Ohio State Univ, 2005. **Special Achievements:** First Black woman president; first African American woman full professor in Ohio State Univ. **Home Addr:** 8340 Greensboro Dr Suite 1023, McLean, VA 22102. **Business Addr:** Professor Emeritus, Ohio State University, 2120 Fyffe Rd, Columbus, OH 43210, **Business Phone:** (614)292-1868.

PRYCE, EDWARD L.
Sculptor, artist. **Personal:** Born May 26, 1914, Lake Charles, LA; son of George S and Dora C; married Woodia Smith; children: Marilyn Alim, Joellen G Elbashir. **Educ:** Tuskegee Inst, BS, agr, 1937; Ohio State Univ, BLA, 1948; Univ Calif, Berkeley, MS, 1953. **Career:** Ornamental Hort, Tuskegee Inst, head dept, 1948-55; pvt pract landscape architect, 1948-77; supt bldgs & grounds, 1955-69; Dept Archit, emer prof, 1969-77. **Orgs:** Tuskegee Model Cities Comt, 1968-72; Tuskegee City Planning Comt, 1970-76; fel Phelps-Stoke African Fac Exchange Prog, 1976; Ala State Outdoor Rec Planning Bd, 1978-; fel Am Soc Landscape Architects, 1979; chmn, Ala State Bd Examiners Landscape Architects, 1981-83. **Honors/Awds:** Alumni Merit Award, Tuskegee Inst, 1977; Distinguished Alumnus Award, Ohio State Univ, 1980; Distinguished Alumnus Award, Tuskegee Univ. **Special Achievements:** Exhibition held titled Edward L. Pryce: African Visions / American Spirit; first African-American to be elected a Fellow of the American Society of Landscape Architects; one of 10 artists for inclusion in the Smithsonian Artists' Curriculum Guide; inducted into the Tuskegee University George Washington Carver Society.

PRYCE, TREVOR
Football player. **Personal:** Born Aug 3, 1975, Brooklyn, NY; children: Khary & Kamryn. **Educ:** Clemson Univ, commun, attended. **Career:** Denver Broncos, defensive tackle, 1997-2005; Baltimore Ravens, defensive tackle, 2006-08. **Honors/Awds:** Pro-Bowl Player, 1999, 2000, 2001, 2002; First Team All Pro, 1999. **Special Achievements:** NFL Draft, First round pick, #28, 1997. **Business Addr:** Defensive Tackle, Baltimore Ravens, 1 Winning Dr, Owings Mills, MD 21117, **Business Phone:** (410)701-4000.

PRYDE, ARTHUR EDWARD
Engineer, business owner. **Personal:** Born Jul 8, 1946, Providence, RI; married Lydia. **Educ:** RI Sch Design, BA, 1972. **Career:** AVID Corp E Prov RI, designer, 1971-74; Gen Motors Corp, designer, 1974-85; LPA Design, Owner, 1983-85. **Orgs:** Design consult to Different Drummer; crew tech C Little Racing, 1983-85; racing 2 liter Can-Am Championship Car, 1984.

PRYOR, CALVIN CAFFEY
Lawyer. **Personal:** Born Oct 16, 1928, Montgomery, AL; divorced; children: Linda Pryor Elmore & Debra E. **Educ:** Ala State Univ, BS, 1950; Howard Univ, LLB, 1957. **Career:** Lawyer (retired); Sole pract, atty, 1958-70; US Dept Justice, asst atty, 1971-94. **Orgs:** Ala State Bar Asn. **Honors/Awds:** Special Achievement Award, Dept Justice, 1975; Special Alumni Award, Ala State Univ. **Home Phone:** (334)263-1389.

PRYOR, CHESTER CORNELIUS, II
Ophthalmologist. **Personal:** Born Jan 2, 1930, Cincinnati, OH; married Audrey; children: Marcus. **Educ:** Cent State Univ, BS, 1951; Howard Univ Col Med, MD, 1955. **Career:** Boston City Hosp, resident, 1957-58; MA Eye & Ear Infirmary, heed fel, 1959; Univ Cincinnati Col Med, asst prof; Deaconess & Christ Good Samaritan Hosp, assoc; Jewish Bethesda & Children's Clermont County Hosp, staff; pvt pract ophthal, 1961-. **Orgs:** Beta Kappa Chi, 1950; Alpha Kappa Mu, 1950; Am Chem Soc, 1951; diplomat, Am Bd Ophthal, 1960; Coun Aging, 1962-68; FA&M, 1962; King Solomon Consis 20, 1962; treas, Delta Gamma Lambda Chap, 1963-77; bd dir, Cincinnati Asn Blind, 1968-; treas, Cincinnati Acad Med, 1969; chmn sec ophtal, Nat Med Asn, 1970-71; dir, Unity State Bank, 1970-76; fel Am Col Surgeons, 1971-; Worshipful Master, 1972; comdr chief, King Solomon Consis 20, 1972-73; GIG, 1975; Pres, Cincinnati Ophthal Soc, 1976; Eye & Ear Infirmary; charter mem, Delta Xi; NAACP; Argus Club; True Am Lodge 2; Noble Sinai Temple 59; Alpha Phi Alpha Fraternity. **Military Serv:** AUS, capt, 1959-61. **Business Addr:** 2828 Highland Ave, Cincinnati, OH 45219.

PRYOR, LILLIAN W
Educator. **Personal:** Born Dec 13, 1917, New Orleans, LA; divorced; children: Mignon M Schooler. **Educ:** Univ Calif, Berkeley, BA, 1942; Roosevelt Univ, MA, 1966; Loyola Univ Sch Soc Work. **Career:** Dept Pub Asst, social worker, 1943-48; Chicago Bd Educ, elem teacher, 1948-53; Cook Co Hosp, med social worker, 1948-53; teacher physically handicapped children 1963. **Orgs:** Co-chmn, Ill State Educ; women's bd, Am Cancer Soc; Mus Contemp Art; Art Inst; bd mem, Chicago S Side Nat Asn Advan Colored People; bd mem, Coun Except Children; bd mem, S Side Comn Art Ctr; Women's Benefit Bd Oper PUSH; Bravo Chap, Lyric Opera; comt mem, Harris "Y"; Nat Asn Adv Colored People; Urban League Women's Coun Proj 75. **Honors/Awds:** Service Award, Women's Aux Nat Asn Adv Colored People; Top Tagger, Nat Asn Adv Colored People.

PRYOR, MALCOLM D.
Banker, chairperson. **Educ:** Howard Univ, BA, 1968; Wharton Sch Bus, MBA, 1980. **Career:** Goldman Sachs & Co, salesman; formed investment partnership, 1979; Pryor, Govan, Counts & Co, founder, 1981; Pryor, Mc Clendon, Counts & Co, chmn; Pryor, Counts & Co, chmn, currently; South African Econ Develop Fund, pres & chief exec officer, currently; bd dirs, CAL Bank Ltd, currently. **Special Achievements:** Co is largest African-Am-owned investment bank in the US; Black Co is ranked No 2 on Black Enterprise's list of top 12 Black-owned investment banks. **Business Addr:** Chairman, Pryor, Counts & Company Inc, 1515 Mkt St Suite 819, Philadelphia, PA 19102, **Business Phone:** (215)569-4544.

PUALANI, GLORIA
Executive director, manager. **Personal:** Born Nov 30, 1950, San Augustine, TX; daughter of Mary Lee Phelps and R C Phelps; married Jeffrey Ortiz, Apr 14, 1984; children: Ronald Bree. **Educ:** Calif State Univ, BA, 1976; Univ Calif, Los Angeles, purchasing cert, 1981; Nat Univ, MBA, 1989. **Career:** ABC TV, script supvr, prod asst, 1976-80; Pac Aircraft, buyer, 1980-81; Northrop Grumman Corp, adminr, 1981-, Socio-Econ Bus Prog, Integrated Syst, corp dir, currently. **Orgs:** Dept Com Minority Enterprise Develop, 1988; Black Bus Asn Adv Bd, 1988-; vpres, External Affairs, Southern Calif Regional Purchasing Coun, 1989-; Nat Asn Women Bus Owners, 1989-; Asn Black Women Entrepreneurs Adv Bd, 1990-; Orange Co Regional Purchasing Coun, 1991-; Nat Veteran Owned Bus Asn. **Honors/Awds:** 100 Most Promising Black Women in Corp Am, Ebony Mag, 1991; Am Best & Brightest, Dollars & Sense Mag, 1991; Service Award, Ga Asn Minority Entrepreneurs, 1992; Business Development Award, Mentor Network, 1992; Mayor Tom Bradley Recognition Award, 1992; 25 Influential Black Women in Business, Network J, 2006. **Special Achievements:** Mus African-Am Art, 1991. **Business Addr:** Corporate Director, Socio-Economic Business Program, Northrop Grumman Corporation, Integrated Systems, 1000 Wilson Blvd Suite 2300, Arlington, VA 22209, **Business Phone:** (703)875-8451.

PUGH, DR. CLEMENTINE A.
Educator. **Personal:** Born in Raleigh, NC; daughter of Alberta Harris High and Otho; married George Douglas; children: Douglas & Janet. **Educ:** Shaw Univ, BA, 1945; Columbia Univ, MSW, 1948; Univ Mass, Amherst, EdD, 1982. **Career:** Hunter Col, soc worker, res assoc educ clin; Comm Serv Soc Family, psych soc; Herbert H Lehman Col, prof educ, 1970-90, prof emer, 1991-. **Orgs:** Fel Am Orthopsychiatric Asn, 1975-, prog fac, 1980-; Nat Asn Black Social Workers, 1980-; bd dir, Homes Homeless; Assoc Black Women Higher Educ, Nat Women's Studies Assoc; life mem, Nat Asn Advan Colored People; bd trustees, Bank Street Col, 1990-94. **Special Achievements:** Book Published: "Those Children" Wadsworth Publishing, 1970; Articles:"Multi-Ethnic Collaboration to Combat Racism" Journal of Applied Behaviorial Sci 1977; Numerous articles & publishings, 1980-85. **Business Addr:** Professor Emeritus, Herbert H Lehman College, 250 Bedford Pk Blvd W, Bronx, NY 10468, **Business Phone:** (718)960-8000.

PUGH, G. DOUGLAS
Government official. **Personal:** Born Dec 14, 1923, New York, NY; married Clementine A; children: Douglas E & Janet A. **Educ:** Columbia Univ, BS, 1951, MBA, 1957. **Career:** Urban League Greater NY, ind rel dir, 1955-60; Trafalgar Hosp, personnel dir, 1960-62; Fed Mediation & Conciliation Serv, coms, 1962-67; Haryou Act Inc, assoc exec dir; Ford Found, prog adv urban affairs, 1966-69; Dormitory Auth NY, dir labor rel & urban affairs, 1970-75; Unemploy Inst Appeal Brd, comsr & mem brd, 1976-87; chmn, 1987-. **Orgs:** AFSCME AFL-CIO, officer, 1958-. **Special Achievements:** Published "Black Economic Development" in 1969. **Business Phone:** (518)457-9000.

PUGH, MARY E
Executive. **Educ:** Yale Univ, BA, econs. **Career:** Wash Mutual Bank, Portfolio Mgt Div, sr vpres; Fed Res Bank San Francisco, Seattle, dir; Pugh Capital Mgt Inc, founder & pres, 1991-, chief investment officer, currently; Wash Mutual Inc, dir, 1999-, Wash Mutual Corp, chmn Finance Comt, currently. **Orgs:** Trustee, Seattle Found; Investment Comt, YWCA Greater Seattle; Investment Comt, Univ Wash; Cascade Natural Gas Corp, 2001. **Business Phone:** (206)322-4985.

PUGH, ROBERT WILLIAM, SR.
Executive. **Personal:** Born May 10, 1926, New York, NY; son of William R and Vennette I; married Barbara Johnson; children: Robert Jr & Lori. **Educ:** Newark Sch Fine Indust Art, 1949; Mus Modern Art, 1946; New York Univ, 1948. **Career:** Wynson Inc, designer, 1945-46; Desagnet Housing Corp, 1946; Nowland & Schladermundt, designer, 1949-51; Asn Granite Craftsman's Guild Inc, pres, 1975; Keystone Monument Co Inc, founder, pres; Edward M Blesser Co, pres, currently. **Orgs:** Indust Designer's Inst; Design Guild NJ; bd mgrs, Harlem YMCA; bd trustees, Youth Consult Serv; pres, Asn Granite Craftmen's Guild Inc, 1976-77 & 1979-80; bd mem, NY State Monument Builders Asn Inc; Monument Builders N Am; bd dirs, NY State Monument Builders Asn Inc; Frank Silvera Workshop. **Honors/Awds:** Distinguish Service Award Asn, Granite Craftsman's Guild, 1976; Man of the Year, Harlem YMCA, 1977; Excellent Achievement Award, Nancy R Cherry Asn, 1989; Archie L Green Award for Excellence, Monument Builders North Am, 1990. **Special Achievements:** First Black man to serve as president of Association Granite Craftsman Guild of NY. **Military Serv:** AUS, pvt, 1944-45. **Business Addr:** President, Edward M Bleser Co, 37 Conway St, Brooklyn, NY 11207, **Business Phone:** (718)455-5153.

PUGH, DR. RODERICK WELLINGTON
Clinical psychologist, educator. **Personal:** Born Jun 1, 1919, Richmond, KY; son of George W Pugh and Lena B White; divorced. **Educ:** Fisk Univ Nashville, TN, BA, 1940; OH State

Univ, MA, 1941; Univ Chicago, PhD, clin psychol, 1949. **Career:** Clinical Psychologist, Educator (retired): Hines VA Med Ctr Chicago, staff psychol, 1950-54, asst chief, clin psychol psychotherapy, 1954-58, chief clin psychol secy, 1958-60, supvr psychol & coordr psychol internship training, 1960-66; Pvt pract, clin psychol, 1958-99; Loyola Univ Chicago, assoc prof psychol, 1966-73, prof psychol, 1973-89, prof emer, psychol, 1989. **Orgs:** Ill Div Voc Rehab, 1965-; Chicago Va Reg Psychol Training Prog, 1966-, Am Psychol Asn & Nat Inst Ment Health, Vis Psychol Prog, 1968-; Nat Inst Ment Health Juve Problems, res rev comt, 1970-74; prof adv comn, Div Ment Health City Chicago, 1979-; Nat Adv Panel, Civilian Health & Med Prog Uniformed Serv Am Psychol Asn, 1980-83; civilian adv comn, AUS Command & Genl Staff Col, 1981-83; Joint Coun Prof Educ Psychol, 1987-90; fel, Am Psychol Asn, Am Psychol Soc, Soc Psychol Study Soc Issues; Asn of Behavior Anal; IL Psychol Asn; Alpha Phi Alpha; vis scholar & prof psychol, Fisk Univ, 1966, 1994; mem, 1968-78, secy, 1970-77, Fisk Univ Bd Trustees; Psi Chi, Sigma Xi, Univ Chicago, 1948; dipl clin psychol, Amer Bd Prof Psychologists, 1975. **Honors/Awds:** Author, "Psychology & The Black Experience" 1972, "Psychological Aspects of the Black Revolution;" Distinguished Serv Awd, Am Bd Prof Psychol, 1986; Ill Psychol Asn, Distinguished Psychologist Award (top annual IL State Award), 1988; Asn Black Psychologists, Chicago Chapter, Award for Distinguished Service to Black Community, 1984 & 1988; Nat Asn Black Psychologists Guiding Light Award for Pioneering Service, 1979; hon doctorate Humane Letters, Chicago Sch Prof Psychol, 1998; Outstanding Contribution to the Profession of Psychology, 2001. **Military Serv:** AUS, 1943-46; Battlefield Commn, 2nd lt; Patton's 3rd AUS, Alsfeld Germany, 1945. **Home Addr:** 5201 S Cornell Ave Apt 25-C, Chicago, IL 60615.

PULLEN-BROWN, STEPHANIE D
Lawyer. **Personal:** Born Dec 11, 1949, Baltimore, MD; married Gerald O; children: Margot. **Educ:** Md Inst Art, BFA, 1970; Coppin State Col, Med, 1973; Loyola Col, Med, 1979; Univ Md, JD 1991. **Career:** Baltimore City Pub Sch, teacher, 1970-74, admin specialist, 1974-80; Univ Md, coop extn serv city dir, 1980-86, from asst to vpres, dean, 1986-91; atty, currently. **Orgs:** Comnr Baltimore City Comn Women, 1984-86; Johnson Found Bd Baltimore Mus Art, 1985-; bd mem, YMCA, 1985-. **Honors/Awds:** Search for Professional Excellence, Nat Asn Co Agr Agts, 1983; Woman Manager of the Year, Conf Women MD State Serv, 1984. **Home Phone:** (410)669-7263.

PULLEY, BRETT A.
Writer. **Personal:** Married Stacey; children: Zoe & Blake. **Educ:** Hampton Univ, BA; Northwestern Univ, MJ. **Career:** CEO, NewYork.com; Sr Ed, Forbes Magazine. *

PULLEY, PROF. CLYDE WILSON. See Obituaries section.

PULLIAM, BETTY E
Clergy, executive. **Personal:** Born Jun 4, 1941, Woodruff, SC; daughter of Shewerl Douglas Ferguson and Gertrude Greene Ferguson; married Herman; children: Trudy, Vanessa & Herman Jr. **Educ:** Wayne State Univ; Nat Judicial Col, Reno, NV, attended 1989. **Career:** St Mark's Community Church, secy, 1958-64; Mayor's Youth Employment Prog Comn Human Resources Develop, 1965-69; Robert Johnson Assoc Training Inst, off mgt, 1971-73; Payne-Pulliam Sch Trade & Com, pres, co-owner, 1973-; Mich State Liquor Control Comn, comnr, 1989-; ordained minister. **Orgs:** Assoc minister, Greater New Mt Moriah Baptist Church; pres & chair, Evangelistic comm, Inter Prayer Group; pres & chairwoman, Booker T Washington Bus Assoc. **Honors/Awds:** Business Woman of the Month; Pinch Cert Ach, 1978; Spirit of Detroit Award, 1983; Detroit City Council Community Award, 1983; Proclamation from the Mayor Detroit, 1983; Golden Heritage Award for Education Excellence, 1984; Black History Month Recognition Award, 1985; Achievement Award, Wayne County Exec Office, 1986; Certificate of Appreciation, Nat Business Week 1985; Certificate of Recognition, Highland Park city, 1987; Certificate of Recognition from the Mayor, 1987; Outstanding Achievement, Historical Accomplishment, 1987; Community Service Award, Councilwoman Barbara R Collins 1988. **Special Achievements:** First Woman licensed to preach at Gtr New Mt Moriah Bapt Church. First female pres & chairwoman of the board Booker T Washington Buisness Associates. **Home Addr:** 18945 Woodingham, Detroit, MI 48221. **Business Addr:** President, Payne-Pulliam School of Trade & Commerce, 2345 Cass Ave, Detroit, MI 48201-3305, **Business Phone:** (313)963-4710.

PULLIN, DENNIS
Hospital Administrator. **Educ:** Texas Lutheran Univ, BA; Texas A&M Univ, Masters. **Career:** COO, Washington Hospital Center; VP St. Luke's Health System. *

PURCE, DR. THOMAS LES
Engineer, dean (education). **Personal:** Born Nov 13, 1946, Pocatello, ID. **Educ:** BA, Psychol, 1969; MEd, 1970; Idaho State Univ, EdD, 1975; Harvard Univ, Inst Educ Mgmt, attended. **Career:** Wash State Univ, counr psychologist, 1970-72; Idaho State Univ, dir co op educ, 1974-75, asst prof counr educ, 1975-77; Pocatello, Idah, mayor, 1976-77; State Idaho, Dept Admin, adminstr, div gen serv, 1977-79, dir, 1979-81; State Idaho, Dept Health & Welfare, dir, 1981-83; Power Engineering Inc, chief operating officer, beginning 1983; Wash State Univ, VPres, Extended Univ Affairs, Dean, Extended Acad Progs, 1995; Evergreen State Col, vpres col advancement, 1989, interim pres, 1990-92, exec vpres, 1992-95, pres, 2000-. **Orgs:** Asn Univ Prof; Asn Counr Educ & Supr; Asn Idaho Cities; Asn Black Psychologists; vchmn, City Coun; Idaho Water & Sewage Cert Bd; NAACP; Pres, Counc Pub Liberal Arts Cols, 2001-02; Bd Dirs, Asn Am Cols & Univs; Urban League Task Force; SE Idaho Counc Govt; Idaho Housing Agency; Kappa Alpha Psi; City Coun man. **Honors/Awds:** Outstanding Young Men of Amer; mem State Exec Com Dem Party. **Special Achievements:** First black elected as official in the state of Idaho as councilman and then mayor of Pocatello. **Home Addr:** PO Box 2187, Hailey, ID 83333. **Business Addr:** President, The Evergreen State College, Office of the President, 2700 Evergreen Pkwy NW Libr Bldg Room 3109, Olympia, WA 98505, **Business Phone:** (360)867-6100.

PURDEE, NATHAN
Artist, actor, photographer. **Personal:** Born Aug 6, 1950, Tampa, FL; son of Emmanuel Purdee Johnson and Anna Beatrice Alston; married Roberta Morris, Nov 9, 1991; children: Taylor Armstrong. **Educ:** Metro State, AA, mental health; Linfield Col, theatre arts, criminol. **Career:** TV Series: Dynasty, 1983; St. Elsewhere, 1984; Knots Landing, 1985; Santa Barbara, 1984; The Young & the Restless, 1985-92; You Again??, 1986; Cheers, 1988; One Life to Live, 1995-2009; Karmic Release Ltd, pres; Wallowitch & Ross: This Moment, exec producer, 1999; Films: The Return of Superfly, 1990; Daytime's Greatest Weddings, 2004; Nathan Purdee Studios,owner & photogr, currently. **Orgs:** NATAS/ATAS, 1985-93; Installations Art Gallery, charter mem, 1988-93; Art Studios League, artist, 1993. **Honors/Awds:** NATAS, Emmy Honors, Best Drama, 1985, 1986; Hollywood Tribute to Soaps,Favorite Newcomer, 1985; Soap Opera Digest, Top Ten TVQ, 1990, 1991, 1992. **Special Achievements:** Featured artist, Am Dream Art Festival, 1988; "I Will Not Be Denied,"performance art, 1990; "The Other Side of Daytime", variety show, 1990,1991; "Stars Behind Bars," self-motivational seminar, 1987-88. **Home Addr:** c/o Karmic Release Ltd, 227 Riverside Dr Suite 7N, New York, NY 10025, **Home Phone:** (212)222-5840. **Business Addr:** Owner, Photographer, Nathan Purdee Studios, PO Box 3561, Easton, PA 18043, **Business Phone:** (212)222-5840.

PURNELL, CAROLYN J
Lawyer. **Personal:** Born Aug 16, 1939, Memphis, TN; married; children: Monica & Mardine. **Educ:** Univ WA, BA, 1961; Univ WA Sch Law, JD, 1971. **Career:** Pros Atty Off, sr legal intern, 1971, civil dep, 1972-74; City Seattle, legal couns to mayor; Weyerhaeuser Co Fed Way Wash, corp atty, dir corp matls; Wash Round Table, exec, Metro, chief coun, 1989-93, Metro dep dir, 1993; Metro exec dir, 1994-96, mgt consult, 1996-; pvt consult, currently. **Orgs:** Vpres, Housing Corp Devel Wash; panelist Human Rights Comn Tribunal; past exec bd secy, March Dimes; bd trustees, Epiphany Sch; Phi Alpha Delta Legal Frat; sec Delta Sigma Theta Sor; Providence Hosp Found; Wash State Bd Bar Examrs, City Seattle Bd Adjustments, Scholastic Hon Soc; Pacific Med Ctr Bd, Mayors Centennial Parks Comn, Mayors Zoo Comn. **Honors/Awds:** Outstanding Young Women Director US, 1976; 1 of 100 Lawyers in US to attend Amer Assembly on Law. **Business Addr:** Consultant, 16 W Harrison, Seattle, WA 98119.

PURNELL, LOVETT
Football player. **Personal:** Born Apr 7, 1972, Seaford, DE; son of Ronald Harmon and Betty Harmon. **Educ:** Univ WVa. **Career:** Football player (retired); New England Patriots, tight end, 1996-98; Baltimore Ravens, 1999; Tampa Bay Buccaneers, tight end, 2000. **Honors/Awds:** Delaware Sports Museum & Hall of Fame, 2007.

PURNELL, MARK W.
Consultant. **Personal:** Born Oct 23, 1957, Wilmington, DE; son of Ernest W Purnell Sr and Yolanda V; married Brenda Dillard Purnell, Jun 28, 1980; children: Devon, Faith, Brandon. **Educ:** Del State Col, BS (high honors), acct, 1979; Univ Wis Madison, MBA, finance/invest, 1982. **Career:** Peat Marwick Mitchell, sr acct; Arthur Andersen & Co, consult; Offerman & Co Inc, div mgr; Kemper Securities Inc, sr vpres, invest; Purnell Wealth Mgt Group, managing dir & portfolio mgr, currently; bd dirs, Univ Wis, Milwaukee, currently. **Orgs:** Nat Asn Black Acct, 1995; chair, Nat Conv; Univ Wis Alumni Asn; Milwaukee Athletic Club. **Honors/Awds:** Distinguished Serv Award, Consortium Grad Study Mgt, 1991; Invest Mgt Consult Asn, CIMA Designation. **Special Achievements:** "Managed Money: The Dynamics of Personalized Investing," Research Magazine, June 1992. **Home Addr:** 2877 N 117th St, Wauwatosa, WI 53222, **Home Phone:** (414)778-0916. **Business Addr:** Managing Director, Portfolio Manager, Purnell Wealth Manaement Group, 815 N Water St 2nd Fl, Milwaukee, WI 53202, **Business Phone:** (414)347-3357.*

PURNELL, MARSHALL E
Architect. **Personal:** Born Jun 8, 1950, Grand Rapids, MI; son of Curtis and Lelia Givens; married Tawana Cook; children: Justin, Tara & Austin. **Educ:** Univ Mich, Ann Arbor, MI, BS, archit, 1973, MA, archit, 1973. **Career:** Univ Md, Washington, DC, lectr teaching 2nd year studio, 1973-74; Fry & Welch Architects, Wash, DC, architect, 1973-74; The Am Inst Architects, Wash, DC, adminr, 1974-78, pres, 2007-; Devrouax & Purnell Architects, Wash, DC, principal, 1978-. **Orgs:** Pres, Nat Org Minority Architects, 1975; DC chmn, United Way, 1999. **Honors/Awds:** Univ Mich Alumni Scholar, Univ Mich. **Special Achievements:** First African-American President in AIA History. **Home Addr:** 98 Hodges Lane, Takoma Park, MD 20912, **Home Phone:** (301)587-6747. **Business Addr:** President, American Institute of Architects, 1735 NY Ave NW, Washington, DC 20006-5292, **Business Phone:** (202)626-7300.

PURVIS, ANDRE
Football player. **Personal:** Born Jul 14, 1973, Jacsonville, NC. **Educ:** Univ NC. **Career:** Cincinnati Bengals, defensivetackle, 1997-99, 2000; Arena Football League, Carolina Cobras, offensive line & defensive line, 2002; free agt, Cincinnati Bengals, currently.

PURVIS, ARCHIE C.
Consultant, executive. **Personal:** Born May 24, 1939, New York, NY; son of Archibald Sr and Millicent; married Candace H Caldwell; children: Christian. **Educ:** Univ Munich, attended 1960; City Col NY Sch Bus, BS, 1969. **Career:** Gen Foods Corp, acct mgr, 1963-66; Polaroid Corp, nat sales mgr, 1966-74; Lear Purvis Walker & Co, exec vpres, 1974-75; MCA Inc Univ Studios, vpres ind mkt, 1975-79; Am Broadcasting Co, vpres, gen mgr video sales div; ABC Distribution Co, pres; Capital ABC Inc, Ambroco Media Group, pres, 1980-95; Purvis Enterprises Inc, pres, 1995-; Orphalese Global Strategies Inc, media consult, currently. **Orgs:** Dir, San Fernand Fair Housing, 1979; dir, Corp Pub Broadcasting, 1987; bd dir, GTE Calif, 1988-; dir, GTE West; YMCA Metrop; secy, Keep Calif Beautiful; adv, Los Angeles Community Col; Yosemite Nat Inst; dir, Resn 8Technol & Communs; Am Mkt Asn; Am Mgt Asn; Sales Exec NY; dir, Int C Sch; Acad Motion Picture Arts & Sci, Hollywood Radio & TV Soc. **Honors/Awds:** Los Angeles County Outstanding Adopt-A-Highway Volunteer of the Year, 1997. **Military Serv:** AUS, sp-5; Advan Commendation Award. **Business Addr:** President, Purvis Enterprises Inc, 510 W 6th St Suite 400, Los Angeles, CA 90014-1305, **Business Phone:** (213)891-0677.

PURYEAR, DR. ALVIN NELSON
Educator. **Personal:** Born Apr 6, 1937, Fayetteville, NC; son of Byron and Gladys; married Catherine, Aug 30, 1962; children: Pamela, Susan & Karen. **Educ:** Yale Univ, BA, 1960; Columbia Univ, MBA, 1962, PhD, 1966. **Career:** Mobil Oil Corp, employee relations adv, 1965-66, financial analyst, 1966-67; Allied Chem Corp, comput systs specialist, 1967-68; Rutgers Univ, assoc prof, 1968-70; Baruch Col, assoc prof, 1970-72, dean, 1972-75, prof mgt, 1972-; Ford Found, vpres org & mgt, 1980-82; City NY, first deputy controller, 1983-85; North Fork Bank, dir; Baruch Col City Univ New York, Lawrence N. Field prof entrepreneurship & prof mgt, currently. **Orgs:** Smithsonian Nat Bd, 1989-95; trustee, Green Point Savings Bank, 1992-; trustee, Yale Univ, 1994-96; dir, Green Point Fin Corp, 1994-; dir, Bank Tokyo-Mitsubishi Trust Co, 1997-; trustee, Comm Serv Soc New York, 1997-; dir, Am Capital Strategies Ltd, 1998-; trustee, Union Theological Seminary & Presbyterian Sch Christian Educ. **Special Achievements:** Author of several articles and has spoken at numerous conferences and professional meetings. **Business Addr:** Lawrence N. Field Professor of Entrepreneurship, Professor of Management, Baruch College of the City University of New York, 17 Lexington, New York, NY 10010, **Business Phone:** (646)312-3636.

PURYEAR, MARTIN
Artist. **Personal:** Born May 23, 1941, Washington, DC; married Jean Gordon, 1986; children: one daughter. **Educ:** Catholic Univ Am, BA, 1963; Swedish Royal Academy Art, Stockholm, Sweden, attended 1968; Yale Univ, MFA, 1971. **Career:** MacArthur Found fel, 1989; Fisk Univ, asst prof art, 1971-73; sculptor, currently. **Orgs:** Vol, Peace Corps, 1964-66; Am Acad & Inst Arts & Lett, 1992. **Honors/Awds:** NEA, fellowship, 1978; grant, Guggenheim Memorial Found, 1984; Grand prize, Sao Paulo Bienal, 1989; John D. and Catherine T. MacArthur Found Award; Louis Comfort Tiffany grant; Skowhegan Medal for Sculpture; honorary doctorate, Yale Univ, 1994. **Business Addr:** Artist, c/o McKee Gallery, 745 5th Ave, New York, NY 10151.*

PUTNAM, GLENDORA M
Lawyer. **Personal:** Born Jul 25, 1923, Lugoff, SC; daughter of Simon P McIlwain (deceased) and Katherine Stewart McIlwain (deceased). **Educ:** Barber Scotia Jr Col, Cert, 1943; Bennett Col, AB, 1945; Boston Univ, JD, 1948. **Career:** Lawyer (retired); MA Off Atty Gen, asst atty gen, 1963-69; MA Comn Against Discrimination, chair, 1969-75; US Dept Housing & Urban

Develop, dep asst secy, 1975-77; MA Housing Finance Agency, equal opportunity officer, 1977-88; Exec Serv Corps New England, nat pres. **Orgs:** MA Bar Asn, 1949-; Fed Bar 1st Dist, 1956-; US Supreme Court Bar, 1964-; bd trustee, Boston Conserv, 1972-; pres, YWCA USA, 1985-91; bd mem, Nat Asn Advan Colored People Legal & Educational Defense Fund; Boston Bar Asn; Boston Lawyers Comt Civil Rights Under Law; life mem, Exec Comt Boston Univ Law Sch Alumni Asn; adv bd, Exec Serv Corps New England, currently. **Honors/Awds:** Women of the Year Greater Boston Bus & Prof Club, 1969; Humanitarian Award, Boston Br, Nat Asn Advan Colore People, 1973; Honarary Doctor of Laws, Southeastern Mass Univ, 1986; Woman of Achievement, Boston Big Sisters, 1985; Silver Shingle for Distinguished Public Service, Boston Univ Law Sch, 1988; Academy of Distinguished Bostonians, Greater Boston Chamber Com, 1988; LLD, Bennett Col, 1991; LLD, Leslie Col, 1999. **Home Addr:** 790 Boylston St, Boston, MA 02199.

PYLES, J. A.
School administrator. **Personal:** Born Feb 23, 1949, Sanford, FL. **Educ:** Bethune-Cookman Col, BA, 1971; Roosevelt Univ, MA, 1975. **Career:** United Negro Col Fund, asst area dir; Alpha Kappa Alpha Sorority Inc, prog specialist; Social Security Admin St Petersburg, 1970; Bethune Cookman Col, vpres develop, spec asst pres, 1990-. **Orgs:** Soc Fund-Raising Execs; Nat Soc Fund-Raising Execs; Bethune-Cookman Col Alumni Asn; Roosevelt Univ Alumni Asn; consult, AGAPE Ministries; MtCarmel Baptist Church. **Honors/Awds:** Alumni Achievement Award, United Negro Col Fund, 1980; Salute to Leadership Award, United Negro Col Fund Inc; Recognition Award, Black Col Fund; Intern Honors Program, Coun Advan & Support Educ, 1982, 1983. **Business Addr:** Special Assistant to the President, Bethune-Cookman College, 640 Dr Mary McLeod Bethune Blvd, Daytona Beach, FL 32114, **Business Phone:** (904)255-1401.

Q

QAMAR, NADI ABU
Composer, musician. **Personal:** Born Jul 6, 1917, Cincinnati, OH; son of William Givens and Alberta Bennett Givens; married Rose Ann Dolski; children: Fabian Billie & Alberta Edith. **Educ:** Int Univ Found Independence MO. **Career:** Jazz pianist, composer & arranger, 1934-65; Inaugural History Jazz series, composer & musician, 1965-77; Bedford Study Youth Action, oratorio composer & mus dir; Countee Cullen, concerts, 1965-68; New Lafayette Theatre, artist residence, 1970-72; Nina Simone World Tours, 1972-74; "Wy Mbony Sita," ballet, New York City, 1973; Mus Natural History NY, perf series, 1976; Bennington Col, prof voice, piano & orchestra, 1978-85; lectr, leader workshops various universities & study ctrs, 1977-89; Nuru Taa African Idiom & Nuru Taa Music, afromusicologist, dir & composer, currently. **Orgs:** Broadcast Music, 1958-; Am Fedn Musicians; Nat Music Publ's Asn Inc. **Honors/Awds:** Drummer & singer with Zulu Singers & Dancers at World's Fair African Pavillion, Flushing Meadows, NY, 1965; composer, scorer & dir, premiere perf Likembican Panorama, 1969; asst mus dir "Black Picture Show" Jos Papp Shakespeare Festival, 1974; Likembi/mbira Performance Workshop Series Dir Mus Natural History Dr Barbara Jackson Co-ord, 1976; Certificate of Recognition for Exemplary Representation of African Am Artistic & Cultural Expression, FESTAC, 1977; recs Nuru Taa African Idiom, The Mama Likembi Instruction Manual CRB 14, The Likembi Songbook Manual of Annotated Songs & Recorded Compositions CRB 15 Folkway Recs; citation concerts, FESTAC, 1977; performed Detroit Inst Art Inaugural Nok Igbo Sculpture Show, 1980; Folkways rec artist; Debut Fantasy rec strings & keys duo w/Charles Mingus, Max Roach original composition, Blue Tide Art, Music & Publs, 1989; Wis Pub TV, Prime Time Wis, 1990-91. **Home Addr:** Rte 1, Kewaunee, WI 54216, **Home Phone:** (920)388-2941. **Business Addr:** Composer, Nuru Taa Arts, Rte 1, PO Box 274, Kewaunee, WI 54216, **Business Phone:** (920)388-2941.

QUANDER, ESQ. ROHULAMIN
Administrative court judge. **Personal:** Born Dec 4, 1943, Washington, DC; son of James W and Joheora Rohualamin; married Carmen Torruella; children: Iliana Amparo, Rohulamin Darius & Fatima de los Santos. **Educ:** Howard Univ, BA 1966, JD, 1969. **Career:** Neighborhood Legal Serv, staff, 1969-71; Geo Wash Univ, fac, 1970-72; Int Investors Inc, mkt consult, atty, state dir, 1973-; pvt pract, 1975-; Off Adjudication DC Govt, staff, 1986-2002; Off Employee Appeals DC Govt, staff, 2002-; DC Dept Consumer & Regulatory Affairs, admin law judge, sr admin judge & Mayors agent Hist Preserv, currently. **Orgs:** Omega Psi Phi Frat, 1964-; Phi Alpha Delta Law Fraternity, 1967; founder, Howard Univ, Chap Black Am Law Studs Asn, 1968; pres, Stud Bar Asn, 1968-69, vpres, 1967-68; bd dir, Wash Urban League, 1969-70; pres, Howard Univ Alumni Club, Wash, DC, 1970-71; bd mem, Super Ct, DC, 1975; US Dist Ct, DC, 1976; bd dir, Wash DC Parent & Child Ctr, 1977-81; chief archivist, Quander Family Hist, 1977-; reg chmn, Howard Univ Alumni, 1979-87; chmn, Educ Inst Licensure Comn, DC, 1979-; Quanders United, Inc, 1983-; Columbia Hist Soc, Int Platform Speakers Asn, 1985-; pres, founder, Quanders Hist Soc Inc, 1985-; MLK Holiday Comn, DC, 1987-89; bd dir, Pigskin Club 1986-; dir & vpres, Torruella-Quander Gallery Ltd, 1988-; co-chair, founder, Benjamin Banneker Orial Community Inc, 1991; founder & pres, IliRoFa Int Inc, 1991-; Ct Appeals DC; Phi Alpha Theta His Soc; Am Bar Asn; Nat Bar Asn; DC Bar Asn; Bar Supreme Ct, PA; US Dist Ct Eastern PA. **Honors/Awds:** Man of Year Award, Omega Psi Phi Fraternity, 1965, 1968; Special Award, Howard Univ, 1969; Outstanding Service Award, Quanders United Inc, 1991. **Special Achievements:** Author: The History of the Quander Family, 1984; have published numerous articles for Howard Univ Alumni newspaper. **Business Addr:** Senior Administrative Judge, Mayors Agent for Historic Preservation, District of Columbia Government, Office of Employee Appeals, 717 14th St NW 3rd Fl, Washington, DC 20005, **Business Phone:** (202)727-0004.

QUANSAH-DANKWA, DR. JULIANA ABA
Dentist. **Personal:** Born Aug 11, 1955, Apam, Ghana; daughter of S T Quansah and Elizabeth Quansah; married Joseph Ofori. **Educ:** Univ Mich Dent Sch, zoology, 1974-76, DDS, 1980. **Career:** Lawrence D Crawford,DDS,PC, assoc dentist, 1980-83; Comm Action Comm, dental dir, 1981-85; Riverfront Dental Ctr, dentist, 1982-83; pvt pact,dentist,1984-. **Orgs:** NAACP,1984; chmn, Intl Trends & Serv Tri City Links Inc,1984-; African Greater Flint Inc, 1984-; Saginaw Chamber Com,1985; bd mem, Headstart Saginaw,1985-. **Honors/Awds:** Commendation Award, Ross Med Educ Ctr, 1986; Appreciation Award, Averill Career Opportunities, 1986. **Home Phone:** (989)753-1993. **Business Addr:** Physician, 1928 E Genesee Ave, Saginaw, MI 48601, **Business Phone:** (989)753-1993.

QUARLES, GEORGE R.
School administrator. **Personal:** Born Jul 14, 1927, Morgantown, WV; son of George and Mabel; married Barbara; children: Nia Caron Martin & Niama Burnley. **Educ:** Hampton Inst, BS, 1951; NY Univ, MA, 1956. **Career:** School administrator (retired); US Dept Educ, Wash, DC, Off Voc & Adult Educ, dep asst secy, 1980-81; Sewanhaka Cent High Sch Dist, Floral Park, NY, dir occup educ, 1985-90; Southern Westchester Bd Coop Educ Serv, Richard Lerer Ctr Tech & Occup Educ, asst dir, 1991-95; Ctr Career & Occup Educ, chief admin; NY City, bd educ; City Univ NY, dir regional opportunity ctr; Sam Harris Assoc Ltd, Wash, DC, exec vpres; NJ State Educ Dept, dir voc educ; Newark Skills Ctr, dir; New Rochelle High Sch, New Rochelle, NY, teacher. **Orgs:** US Aid African Bur, 1983-84; Acad Educ Devel, 1984-91; consult, Mitshita Educ Found, 1988-89; New Rochelle Civil Serv Comn, 1998; NY St Adv Coun Voc Educ; New Sch Soc Res; Voc Educ, Omega Psi Phi Fraternity; tech revpanel, Nat Inst Educ Study Voc Educ; Nat Fac Nat Ctr Res Voc Educ, Ohio St Univ; consult, US Dept Educ Regarding Grant Awards, Nat Projects; co-founder, chair, bd dir, Community Ctr Employ & Trainning; Am Voc Asn. **Honors/Awds:** Community Serv Award, Interreligious Coun New Rochelle, 2000; NY State Sidney Platt Award; Winged Trophy, Newark Anti-Poverty Agency; Omega Man of the Year, Omicron Iota Chap; Educ Secy Spec Achievement Pin. **Special Achievements:** Numerous radio & TV appearances articles for various newspapers on vocational education; major paper on Equity in Vocational Education, National Center for Research in Vocational Education; numerous articles & studies on vocational education & youth employment. **Military Serv:** First lt field artil; Bronz Star, Valor; Purple Heart Oak Leaf Cluster. **Home Addr:** 22 Vaughn Ave, New Rochelle, NY 10801. *

QUARLES, HERBERT DUBOIS
Educator, journalist, teacher. **Personal:** Born Feb 24, 1929, Charlottesville, VA; son of John Benjamin and Mattie Virginia Davis. **Educ:** James Millikin Univ, BA, music educ, 1952; Howard Univ, BA, music, 1962; Cath Univ Am, MA, music, 1965. **Career:** Educator (retired), Editor; Fed Govt, Wash, DC, clerk typist, 1955-61; Pub Schs, Wash, DC, music teacher, 1959-60, 1962-80, Pub Schs, Alexandria, VA, music teacher, 1961-62; Pub Schs, PT Eve, Wash, DC, teacher, 1967; Wash Afro Am Newspaper, Wash, DC, columnist & reporter, 1972, arts column ed, currently. **Orgs:** Vpres, Phi Mu Alpha Fraternity, 1950-52; pres, Wash Bridge Unit, 1977-83; vpres, Mid-Atlantic Sect, Am Bridge Asn, 1983-88, 1994-95; several church groups. **Honors/Awds:** Service Award, Francis Jr High Sch, 1980. **Military Serv:** Army Res, sgt major, E-9, 1952-79; several letters of commendation. **Home Addr:** 5616 13th St NW Suite 109, Washington, DC 20011-3529.

QUARLES, NANCY L
Legislator (U.S. state government). **Personal:** Born Jun 6, 1954; married Larry. **Educ:** Univ Detroit, BS, bus admin; Cent Mich Univ, MA, mgt; Western Mich Univ, PhD pub affairs & pub admin. **Career:** IBM, sr mkt consult, 1976-92; Mich House of Reps, house rep, 1996-2002; Cent Mich Univ, adj prof, 2002-; Advantage Consult Group, founder & pres, currently; Oakland County, comnr. **Orgs:** Pres, Southern Oakland County Nat Asn Advan Colored People; Mich Capitol Comt. **Honors/Awds:** Citizen of the Year Award, Omega Psi Phi Pub; Distinguish legislator of the Year, Independent Col & Univ Asn; Award of Recognition, Nat Polit Caucus Black Women. **Business Addr:** President, Advantage Consulting Group, 5000 Merrick Rd, Massapequa, NY 11759, **Business Phone:** (516)795-7300.

QUARLES, NORMA R.
Journalist. **Personal:** Born Nov 11, 1936, New York, NY; divorced; children: Lawrence & Susan. **Educ:** Hunter Col; City Col NY. **Career:** Katherine King Assocs, Chicago, IL, real estate broker, 1957-65; WSDM-FM,Chicago, IL, news reporter, 1965-66; NBC News Training Prog, 1966-67; WKYC-TV, Cleveland, OH, news reporter & anchorwoman, 1967-70; NBC-TV, news reporter, 1970; CNN, day time anchor, 1988-90, corresp, 1990-98; freelance journalist, 1998-. **Orgs:** Bd gov, Nat Acad TV Arts & Sci; Sigma Delta Chi; Nat Asn Black Journalists. **Honors/Awds:** Front Page Award, WNBC-TV, 1973; Deadline Club Award, Sigma Delta Chi, 1973; Inducted into NABJ Hall of Fame, 1990; CINE Golden Eagle, 1993. **Special Achievements:** Selected as a panelist, The League of Women Voters Vice Presidential Debate.

QUARLES, SHELTON EUGENE
Football player, scout. **Personal:** Born Sep 11, 1971, Nashville, TN; married Damaris; children: Gabriela Nicole, Shelton Jr & Carlos Antonio. **Educ:** Vanderbilt Univ, human & orgn develop. **Career:** Football player(retired); British Columbia Lions, 1995-96; Tampa Bay Buccaneers, linebacker, 1997-06, pro scout, currently. **Orgs:** Founder, Shelton Quarles IMPACT Found; mem, Nat Hon Soc. **Honors/Awds:** Pro Bowl selection, 2002; Super Bowl champion XXXVII; JB Award, NFLPA PLAYERS INC. **Special Achievements:** Hosted the All Pro Dad seminar. **Business Addr:** Pro Scout, Tampa Bay Buccaneers, One Buccaneer Pl, Tampa, FL 33607, **Business Phone:** (813)870-2700.

QUARLES SIMMONS, SYLVIA JEANNE. **See SIMMONS, DR. SYLVIA Q.**

QUEEN, EVELYN E CRAWFORD
Judge, educator. **Personal:** Born Apr 6, 1971, Albany, NY; daughter of Richard Carter and Iris Crawford; married Charles A Queen, Mar 6, 1971; children: Angelia Y & George Y. **Educ:** Howard Univ, BS, 1968, JD, 1975. **Career:** Judge, Educator (retired); NIH, support staff, 1968-75; Metrop Life Ins Co, atty, 1975-77; US Dept Com, Maritime Admin, atty-adv, 1977-79; US Atty Off, asst US atty, 1979-81; DC Super Ct, comnr, 1981-86, judge, 1986-2001; Howard Univ Law Sch, adj prof, 1990; Univ DC Sch Law, adj prof, 1991-92; Sigma Delta Tau. **Orgs:** ABA, 1975-; NBA, 1975-. **Honors/Awds:** Special Achievement Award, Dept HEW, 1975; Special Achievement Award, Dept Justice, 1981; Trefoil Award, Hudson Valley Girl Scout, 1988; Directory of Distinguished Americans, Achievement in Law, 1985; Personalities of America, Contributions Govt & Justice, 1986; Judicial Service Award, Sigma Delta Tau. **Home Addr:** 1727 Kalmia Rd NW, Washington, DC 20012, **Home Phone:** (202)291-4780.

QUICK, GEORGE KENNETH
Banker. **Personal:** Born Apr 14, 1947, Orangeburg, SC; son of Oscar and Geneva Shokes; married Gloria Grainger, Jun 10, 1972; children: Jeffrey George & Erica Camille. **Educ:** SC State Univ, Orangeburg, SC, BS, 1968; Atlanta Univ, Atlanta, GA, MBA, 1975; Sch Banking S La State Univ, Baton Rouge, LA, cert, 1984-86. **Career:** First Union Nat Bank, Charlotte, NC, asst vpres, 1975-86; Mutual Savings & Loan Asn, Durham, NC, exec vpres & COO, 1986-; Mutual Community Saving Bank Inc, pres, 1994-2001; Durham County Gov, finance dir, 2001-. **Orgs:** Chmn bd, UDI/CDC, 1987-; bd dirs, Chamber Com, 1991-; chmn, Pvt Ind Coun, 1989-; bd trustee & mem, St Joseph AME Church, 1990-; bd dirs, NC Mus Life & Sci, 1989-; bd trustees, Durham County Hosp Corp. **Honors/Awds:** Distinguished Alumnus of the Year, NAFEO, 1990; Distinguished Business Alumnus, SC State Univ, 1992. **Military Serv:** AUS, capt, 1968-74; Bronze Star, Air Metal, Vietnam Service Medal. **Home Addr:** 1326 Elmira Ave, Durham, NC 27707, **Home Phone:** (919)688-7497. **Business Addr:** Director, Durham County Government, 200 EMain St 4th Mezzanine Old Courthouse, Durham, NC 27701, **Business Phone:** (919)560-0035.

QUICK, MIKE
Football player, television broadcaster. **Personal:** Born May 14, 1959, Hamlet, NC; son of James Quick and Mary Quick. **Educ:** NC State col. **Career:** Football player (retired), Television broadcast; Philadelphia Eagles, wide receiver 1982-90; Philadelphia Eagles radio broadcasts on 94.1 WYSP, announcer, currently. **Orgs:** Active in community affairs especially Big Brothers/Big Sisters; made TV announcements for KYW-TV's Project Homeless Fund, WCAU-TV's School Vote Program, the Franklin Inst, 7-Eleven/Coca Cola Freedom Run for Sickle Cell; co-owner All Pro Fitness and Racquet Club in Maple Shade NJ. **Honors/Awds:** Played in the Blue-Gray Game; Olympia Gold Bowl; first team all-pro selections by AP; Newspaper Enterprises

Assoc, Col & Pro Football Newsweekly, The Sporting News, Sports Illustrated & NFL Films 1985; first team All-NFC, UPI; led NFC with 11 TD receptions 1985; honored with a special night The Pride of Hamlet-The Fantastic Four, 1985. **Special Achievements:** First Eagle in history to surpass 1,000 yards receiving in 3 straight seasons. **Business Addr:** Announcer, Philadelphia Eagles, 1 NovaCare Way, Philadelphia, PA 19145, **Business Phone:** (215)463-2500.

QUICK, R EDWARD
Manager, president (organization). **Personal:** Born Jan 22, 1927, Youngstown, OH; son of William and Loretta; married Constance D; children: Cheryl Pope & Renee C. **Educ:** Ohio State Univ, attended 1945, 1949; Howard Univ, LLB, 1952. **Career:** Rural Electrification Admin, USDA, spec asst adminr, 1968-69; Fed Hwy Admin US Dept Transp, contract compliance Div, chief, 1969-76, actg dept dir, 1976-77, office civil rights dir, 1977-86; El Dorado Travel Serv, Wash DC, pres, 1982-. **Orgs:** Nat Asn Human Rights Workers; bd dirs, El Dorado Travel Serv, 1982; MD Asn Affirmative Action Officers, 1984; vpres, Wash Sub Chapter Am Soc Travel Agents, 1988-89; Nat Asn Advan Colored People; Urban League; Pac Area Travel Asn; S Am Travel Asn; Africa Travel Asn; InterAm Travel Agts Soc; bd mem, Cent Atlantic Chap, Am Soc Travel Agents. **Honors/Awds:** Administrator's Special Achievement Award, Fed Hwy Admin, 1977; Senior Executive Service Bonus Award, Fed Hwy Admin, 1980. **Military Serv:** USAF, sgt, 1 1/2 yrs. **Business Addr:** President, El Dorado Travel Service, 2446 Reedie Dr, Wheaton, MD 20906.

QUIGLESS, DR. MILTON DOUGLAS, JR.
Surgeon, educator. **Personal:** Born Oct 15, 1945, Durham, NC; son of Milton Douglas Sr and Helen Gordon; divorced; children: Leslie, Matthew, Christine, Ashley & Maryanna. **Educ:** Morehouse Col, BS, 1970; Meharry Med Col, MD, 1971. **Career:** Meharry Medical Col, instr surg, 1976-77; Univ NC, Chapel Hill, clin assoc prof surg, 1986-; Wake County Med Ctr, pres/medical staff, 1986-87; pvt pract, currently. **Orgs:** St Augustine Col Bd, 1985-88. **Honors/Awds:** Doctor of the Year, Old N State Med Soc, 1984. **Home Addr:** 3410 Six Forks Rd, Raleigh, NC 27609. **Business Addr:** Surgeon, 3362 Six Forks Rd, PO Box 20127, Raleigh, NC 27609, **Business Phone:** (919)571-1170.

QUINCE, KEVIN
Government official, president (organization), business owner. **Personal:** Born Jul 4, 1950, Atlantic City, NJ; son of Remer and Doris Pratt Griffith; married Regina Gumby, Jan 8, 1972; children: Gyasi & Khary. **Educ:** Hampton Univ, BA, sociol, 1972; Rutgers Univ, city & regional planning, 1974; Univ Pa, Wharton Sch, attended 1980. **Career:** NJ Housing & Mortgage Finance Agency, sr develop officer, 1974-80, syndication officer, 1980-84, asst dir res & develop, 1984-86, dir res &develop, 1986-88, asst exec dir, 1988-90, exec dir, 1990-; Kevin Quince Assoc Inc, Real Estate Develop Consult, owner & pres, currently. **Orgs:** Vpres, E Windsor Planning Bd, 1982-83; chmn, Mercer County Housing Adv Bd, 1987-89; vpres & secy, Housing Assistance Corp, 1988-; bd dirs, Police Athletic League, 1989; bd mem, Coun Affordable Housing, 1990-; Harvard Univ, Prog Sr Execs, 1990. **Honors/Awds:** Achievements in Affordable Housing, NJ Chap Housing & Redevelop Off, 1989; Achievements in Affordable Housing, NJ Black Housing Adminr, 1990. *

QUINCE, PEGGY A.
Judge. **Personal:** Born in Norfolk, VA; daughter of Solomon; married Fred L Buckine, Apr 19, 1976; children: Peggy LaVerne Buckine, Laura LaVerne Buckine. **Educ:** Howard Univ, BS, zool, 1970; Catholic Univ Am, JD, 1975. **Career:** Rental Accommodations Off, Wash, DC, hearing officer; pvt pract, 1977-80; FL Atty Gen's Off, Criminal div, asst atty gen, Tampa bur chief, 1980-93; FL Second Dist Ct Appeals, judge, 1993-98; Fla State Supreme Ct, judge, 1998-. **Orgs:** FL Bar Asn; VA State Bar; Nat Bar Asn; Tallahassee Asn Women Lawyers; George Edgecomb Bar Asn; Alpha Kappa Alpha; Urban League; Jack & Jill Am; Nat Asn Advan Coloured People; Tampa Orgn Black Affairs; The Links Inc, currently; New Hope Missionary Baptist Church. **Honors/Awds:** Jurist Award, Nat Bar Asn, Women Lawyers Div; Virgil Hawkins Bar Asn Award; Virgil Hawkins Bar Asn certificate; Appreciation Award, Broward County Sch Bd; Appreciation Award, Hillsborough County Sheriff's Black Adv Coun; Honorary Doctor of Law, Stetson Univ Col Law, 1999; William H Hastie Award, Judicial Coun, Nat Bar Asn, 2002; Florida Girls State Award, 2002; Helping Hand Award, 2003; Southern Women in Public Service Pacesetter Award, 2003; Florida Girls State Award, 2003; Pioneering the Future in our Community Award, 2003; Outstanding Jurist & Howard University Alumna Award, 2003; honorary doctor of laws degree, St Thomas Univ Sch Law, 2004; Key to the City of Winter Haven, 2005; Richard W Ervin Equal Justice Award, 2005; Margaret Brent Women Lawyers of Achievement Award, 2006; Rickards High School Outstanding School Volunteer Award, 2006; Florida Women's Hall of Fame award, 2007. **Special Achievements:** First African American female appointed to a FL district court of appeal, 1993. **Business Addr:** Justice, Supreme Court Florida, 500 S Duval St, Tallahassee, FL 32399-1925, **Business Phone:** (850)922-5624.*

QUINN, DIANE C
Government official. **Personal:** Born May 9, 1942, Chicago, IL; children: Caren Clift. **Educ:** Am Univ. **Career:** Nat Alliance Business, lectr, 1972-74; Ill Bell Telephone Co, sales mgr, 1974-79; C&P Telephone Co, indust mgr, 1978-79; AT&T, mkt mgr, 1979-83, mgr mgt employ, 1983-84, mgr univ rels, 1984-87; Col Bd Conf Indust Partnerships, lectr, 1986; Dept Pub & Assisted Housing, regional mgr, 1989-94; DC Dept Recreation & Parks, exec asst dir, 1994, admin res, policy & planning, currently. **Orgs:** AT&T Rep Nat Urban League, 1972-; consult Wilberforce Univ, 1979; consult, R Burton & Co Inc, 1986. **Honors/Awds:** Black Achiever, YMCA, 1973, 74; AT&T Loaned Executive, Univ MD, 1987. **Home Addr:** 1708 15th St NW, Washington, DC 20009. **Business Addr:** Administrator of Research, Policy & Planning, DC Department of Recreation & Parks, 1800 Anacostia Dr SE, Washington, DC 20009, **Business Phone:** (202)645-3940.

QUINONES, LELA ROCHON. See ROCHON, LELA.

QUINTON, BARBARA ANN
Educator. **Personal:** Born Jul 1, 1941, Sharptown, MD; children: Keith F Nichols & Kyle B Nichols. **Educ:** Morgan State Univ, BS, 1963; Meharry Med Col, MD, 1967. **Career:** Hubbard Hosp, internship, 1967-68; St Louis Children's Hosp, resident, 1968-69; St Louis Children's Hosp, fel, 1969-71; Howard Univ, fel, 1971-74, asst prof, 1974-76, assoc prof, Col Med, Med Genetics Clin, dir; Howard Univ Hosp, practices Pediatrics, currently. **Orgs:** Hon mem, Intern/Resident Asn, Howard Univ, 1983; church rep, Nat Asn Advan Colored People, 1985-; Am Zion Methodist Church Lay Coun. **Honors/Awds:** Outstanding Teacher Award, Howard Univ, 1975 & 1978. **Business Addr:** Pediatrics Practioner, Howard University Hospital, 2041 Georgia Ave NW Suite 5100, Washington, DC 20060-0002, **Business Phone:** (202)865-6100.

QUIVERS, DR. ERIC STANLEY
Physician. **Personal:** Born Oct 27, 1955, Winston-Salem, NC; son of William Wyatt and Evelyn Cecelia; married Mara Williams, Feb 15, 1987; children: Micah Stanley & Lucas Sorrell. **Educ:** Morehouse Col, BS, magna cum laude, 1979; Howard Univ Col Med, MD, 1983; Pediat Cardiol, pediatrics, Bd Certified. **Career:** Howard Univ Hosp Dist Columbia, pediatric resident,1983-86; Park W Med Ctr, staff pediatrician, 1986; Sinai Hosp, provisional med staff, 1986-88; Mayo Clin, pediat cardiol fel, 1988-91; Children's Nat Med Ctr, Dept Cardiol, staff cardiologist, prevent cardiol & Exercise Labo, dir; Children's Hosp Pittsburgh, Prev Cardiol Clin, dir, currently; Univ Pittsburgh Sch Med, asst prof pediat, currently; pvt pract, currently. **Orgs:** Phi Beta Kappa, 1977; Beta Kappa Chi, 1977; AMA; Nat Med Asn, 1983-; Am Acad Pediat, jr fel; Dis Hunger Project, 1992; Mayor's CMS for Food, Health & Nutrit, 1993-; Asn Black Cardiologists, 1990-; Take AIM, chair, int adv comt; Int Soc Heart & Lung Transplantation. **Honors/Awds:** Certificate of Appreciation, Howard Univ Col Med SGA, 1983; Roland B Scott Departmental Award in Pediatrics, 1983; Healthcare Forum's Cardiovascular Health Fel, 1998-99; Co-Teacher of the Year Award, 2000; Outstanding Resident Faculty Teaching Award, 2000. **Special Achievements:** Co-author: "Hepatic Cyst Associated with Ventricular Peritoneal Shunt in a Child with Brain Tumor," Child's Nervous System, 1985; "Variability in Response to a Low-fat, Low-cholesterol Diet in Children with Elevated Low-density Lipoprotein Cholesterol Levels," Pediatrics, 1992; Echocardiographic Evidence for Ductal Tissue Sling Causing Discrete Coarctation of the Aorta in the Neonate: Case Report, 1997; "Pediatric Preventive Cardiology: Healthy Habits Now, Healthy Hearts Later.". **Home Addr:** 14 Foxlair Ct, Gaithersburg, MD 20882, **Home Phone:** (301)212-9748. **Business Addr:** Director, Children's Hospital of Pittsburgh, Division of Pediatric Cardiology, 3705 5th Ave, Pittsburgh, PA 15213, **Business Phone:** (412)692-5540.

QUIVERS, WILLIAM WYATT, SR.
Physician. **Personal:** Born Sep 14, 1919, Phoebus, VA; son of Robert McKinley and Irma Robinson Branch; married Evelyn C Seace; children: William Jr, Eric, Celia. **Educ:** Hampton Inst, BS 1942; Atlanta Univ, attended 1947; Meharry Medical Col, MD 1953; Pediatric Cardiology Fellowship USPH grant at Univ Los Angeles 1963, 1965. **Career:** Physician (retired); KB Reynolds Memorial Hosp, internship & pediat residency, 1953-55; Meharry Med Col Hubbard Hosp, pediat resident, 1959-63; Meharry Med Col, asst prof pediat, 1963-64, asst prfo pediat, 1965-68, med dir child & youth proj, 1967-68; Reynolds Memorial Hosp, dir pediat, 1968-72; Bowman-Gray Sch Med, assoc prof ped, 1968-72; Provident Hosp Inc, dir pediat, 1972-85; Univ Md Sch Med, assoc prof pediat, 1972-85; Liberty Med Ctr, actg chief pediat, 1986-91; Total Health Care, consult/provider; Author: "Rheumatic Heart Disease: A Review," Volunteer State Journal, 1962; co-author: "Use of Isoproterenol in the Evaluation of Aortic and Pulmonic Stenosis," Am J Cardiol, 1963, "The Electrocardiogram and Vectorcardiogram in Children with Severe Asthma," Am J Cardiol, 1964, "Congenital Duplication of the Stomach," J Abdominal Surg, 1982; "My Activities During WWII," Md Med J, 1995. **Orgs:** Fel Am Acad Pediat; Nat Med Asn; diplomate Am Bd Pediat; Royal Soc Health; Am Heart Asn; Chinese Am Sci Soc; East Coast Church Tuskegee Airmen; bd dirs Homewood Sch & Bear Sch; Asn Black Cardiologists; Cent Md Heart Asn. **Honors/Awds:** First Annual Physician Appreciation Award, 1990; Medical Staff Award for Outstanding Contributions in Ambulatory Services, Liberty Med Ctr, 1990; Hampton Univ Alumni Asn, 14th Annual Nat Conf Black Family, Honored Black Family, 1992. **Military Serv:** USAF 1st lt 1942-46. **Home Addr:** 6110 Benhurst Rd, Baltimore, MD 21209. *

R

RAAB, MADELINE MURPHY
Executive, executive director. **Personal:** Born Jan 27, 1945, Wilmington, DE; married Dr Maurice F Rabb Jr; children: Maurice F III & Christopher. **Educ:** Univ Md, attended 1963; Md Inst Col Art, BFA, 1966; Ill Inst Tech, MS, 1975. **Career:** Tuesday Publ, asst dir art & prod, 1966-68; Myra Everett Design, vpres bus mgr, 1977-78; Corp Concierge, acct exec, 1978-79; Rabb Studio & Gallery, artist, 1978-83; Chicago Off Fine Arts, exec dir, 1983-. **Orgs:** Univ Chicago Women's Bd, 1980-85; bd mem, Hyde Park Arts Ctr, 1981-83; Afro-Amer Newspaper Co, Baltimore, MD, 1981-84; adv, Folk Art Exhib Field Mus Nat Hist, 1984; treas, US Urban Arts Fed, 1984-86; adv, Black Creativity Celebration Mus Sci & Indust, 1985-86; Chicago World's Fair, 1985; bd mem, Channel 20 WYCC-TV, 1985-86, Ill Arts Alliance, 1986-88; co-chair, Special Interest Areas Nat Assembly Local Arts Agencies, 1986-88; panelist, Nat Assembly Local Arts Agencies Conv, WA DC, 1986; moderator, Ill Arts Alliance Annual Conf, 1986; panelist, Local Arts Agencies, Ill Arts Coun; panelist, Nat Assembly Local Arts Agencies Annual Conv, Portland, OR, 1987; panelist, Local Progs Nat Endowment Arts, 1987-88; Arts Culture & Entertainment Comn, 1992; bd Columbia Col, Chicago, currently; adv bd, Md Inst Col Art. **Business Addr:** President, Murphy Rabb Inc, 400 S Green St Suite G, Chicago, IL 60602, **Business Phone:** (312)243-5070.

RABOUIN, E MICHELLE
Lawyer, educator. **Personal:** Born Nov 7, 1956, Denver, CO; daughter of John V and Eva M Thomas; divorced; children: Dion Malik. **Educ:** Univ Colo, BS, 1977; Univ Denver, MBA, 1984, JD, 1984. **Career:** Coal Employ Proj, asst dir, 1983-85; Colo Off Atty Gen, asst atty gen, 1986-89; Colo Educ ASn, legal coun, 1989-90; Comm Colo Denver, mgt chairperson & fac, 1991-94; Tex Southern Univ, visiting prof law, 1994-95; Washburn Univ Sch Law, assoc prof law, 1994-; Tex Wesleyan Univ Sch Law, vis prof, 1999-2000. **Orgs:** Bd mem & ed, Colo Black Women Polit Action, 1979-; Bd mem, Northeast Women's Ctr, 1980-82; fel, Colo Energy Res, 1983; Colo Bar Asn, 1984-; founding mem, Colo Chapter, Nat Asn Black Women Atty, 1987-; Colo Women's Bar Asn, 1988-; Jr League Denver, 1988-91; Colo Coalition Mediators & Mediation Orgn, 1990-; bd mem, Am Civil Liberties Union, 1991-92. **Honors/Awds:** President's Academic Scholarship, Colo Black Women Polit Action, 1974-77; Community Service Award, Colo Black Women Polit Action, 1981. **Special Achievements:** Co-author of "1992 Tenth Circuit Court of Appeals Survey of Corporate and Commercial Law", Denver Univ Law Review, 1601, Valuing Diversity: Train the Trainer Manual, Mahogany Mountain Press, 1992, "The Legal Dimensions of Diversity: the Civil Rights Act of 1991, and the ADA," City of Boulder, Department of Social Services, 1992, lecturer, "Pro Bono: Enforceable Duty of Voluntary Obligation," "Intersection of Race and Poverty, Common Issues," Statewide Legal Services Conference, 1992. **Home Addr:** 4986 Worchester St, Denver, CO 80239.

RABY, CLYDE T
Government official. **Personal:** Born Sep 14, 1934, Baton Rouge, LA; married Elaine Miller; children: Dwight Tillman, Iris R Locure, Wayne A, Eric C & Trudi E. **Educ:** Southern Univ, BS, 1960; Tuskegee Inst, DVM, 1964; La State Univ, MS, 1992. **Career:** prof (retired), Veterinarian; Southern Univ, asst prof, 1964-70; Plank Road & Port Allen Animal Hosps, owner, 1970-; La Dept Agr, asst comnr, 1980-96; Plank Road Animal Hosp, vet, currently. **Orgs:** Beta Kappa Chi, 1962; AVMA 1963-; Beta Beta Beta Biol Soc, 1970-; chmn, La Vet Med Asn, 1982; bd dirs, Reddy Cult Ctr, 1985; bd dirs, Arts Coun Baton Rouge, 1988-98; African Sci Inst; Hon Biol Soc. **Honors/Awds:** Veterinarian of the Year, La Vet Med Asn, 1982; Bigger & Better Business Award, Phi Beta Sigma Frat, 1986. **Special Achievements:** Numeorus articles published in Journal of Dairy Science, Journal of Animal Science & American Journal of Veterinary Research. **Military Serv:** USAF, airman second class, 1954-57. **Business Addr:** Veterinarian, Plank Road Animal Hospital, 7660 Plank Rd, Baton Rouge, LA 70811, **Business Phone:** (225)355-5676.

RACINE, KARL A
Lawyer. **Educ:** Univ Pa, BA, 1985; Univ Va, JD, 1989. **Career:** Venable LLP, litigation assoc, 1989-92, deputy managing partner, managing partner, currently; DC Pub Defender Serv, staff atty;

White House, assoc coun; Cacheris & Treanor, atty, 1994-97. **Orgs:** DC Bar Asn; Md Bar Asn. **Honors/Awds:** Spoon Award, 1985. **Business Addr:** Attorney, Venable LLP, 575 7th St NW, Washington, DC 20004, **Business Phone:** (202)344-8322.

RACKLEY, LURMA M
Writer. **Personal:** Born Apr 24, 1949, Orangeburg, SC; daughter of Gloria Blackwell and L G Rackley (deceased); children: Rumal Blackwell Rackley. **Educ:** Clark Atlanta Univ, BA, 1970; Columbia Univ Sch Jour, Special Masters, 1970. **Career:** Wash Star, reporter & ed, 1970-79, freelance writer, 1970-; District Columbia Govt, 1979-90; Off Planning, Dep Press Secy, Dep Commun dir, press secy to the Mayor; Hill & Knowlton Public Affairs Worldwide, vpres, media rel, 1993-95; Amnesty Int USA, dep exec dir commun, 1995-98; Eddie Bauer, dir public affairs & social responsibility, 1998-; Sister 2 Sister Magazine, writer, currently; Care, pub relation officer, currently. **Orgs:** Alpha Kappa Alpha; DC Clark Atlanta Univ Club; bd, Seattle Urban Enterprise Ctr. Capital Press Club; Black Public Relations Soc; DC Hampton Univ Parents Club; bd mem, Unitarian Universalist Service Comt. **Honors/Awds:** Commitment to Excellence Award Dep Mayor for Economic Devel, 1985; Outstanding Women DC Govt, 1989-90; Corp Leadership Award, Ncp Youth, Col & Young Adult Div, 2001. **Home Addr:** 28519 Ne 151st St, Duvall, WA 98019. **Business Addr:** Writer, Sister 2 Sister Magazine, 6930 Carroll Ave Suite 200, Takoma Park, MD 20912, **Business Phone:** (301)270-5999.

RADCLIFFE, DR. AUBREY. See Obituaries section.

RAGLAND, SHERMAN LEON, II
Real estate developer, president (organization), chief executive officer. **Personal:** Born Jul 4, 1962, Stuttgart, Germany; son of Lt Col Sherman L and G Anita Atkinson. **Educ:** Towson Univ, Towson, MD, BS, mass commun, 1984; The Wharton Sch Univ Pa, MBA, fin & real estate, 1986; Univ Va, MA, 2000; Concord Univ Sch Law, JD. **Career:** Xerox Realty Corp, Stamford CT, 1986-87, Leesburg VA, assoc develop dir, 1987-88; The Oliver Carr Co, Wash DC, develop mgr, 1988-89; Tradewinds Realty Partners LLC, Managing dir, 1989-; fin adv, 1990-; Tradewinds Int Inc, founder, pres & ceo, currently. **Orgs:** Chmn, Bowie Economic Development Comn; The Net Am Found, bd dirs, Pres, Nat Asn Black Real Estate Prof, 1988; bd dir, Christmas April USA, 1988; Christmas April Alexandria, 1988; bd advs (alumni), Wharton Real Estate Ctr, 1988; bd dir, Towson State Univ Alumni Asn, 1989; comnr, Alexandria Human Rights Comn, 1989, Alexandria Equal Opportunities Comn, 1989; pres,The Wharton Alumni Club Wash, 1989-; Alexandria Bd Zoning Appeals, 1990-93; v chmnm, Alexandria bd Zoning Appeals, 1990-93; Alexandria Planning comn, 1993. **Honors/Awds:** Johnson & Johnson Leadership Award, Johnson & Johnson, 1984; Wharton Public Policy Fellowship, The Wharton Sch, 1985; Alumni of the Year Award, Towson State Univ, 1999; author of several pub, Motivation, 1985, Lease vs Purchase Real Estate, 1989; "50 Future Leaders", Ebony Mag, Nov, 1992; "Dead Men Walking" ASAE Mag; Blue Vase Award, 2002; Investor of the Year, National Real Estate Investors Conference in Atlanta, GA, 2002. **Business Addr:** Founder & President, Chief Executive Officer, Tradewinds International Inc, PO Box 1359, Conover, NC 28613, **Business Phone:** (828)465-2300.

RAGLAND, DR. WYLHEME HAROLD
Clergy. **Personal:** Born Dec 19, 1946, Anniston, AL; son of Howard Ragland and Viola Pearson; children: Seth H III & Frederick D. **Educ:** Jacksonville State Univ, BA, 1972; grad sch, 1973; Emory Univ, MDiv, Cum Laude, 1975; Vanderbilt Univ, DMin, 1978. **Career:** Ctr Grove United Methodist Church, pastor, 1975-77; King's Memorial United Methodist Church, sr pastor, 1977-; N Ala Regional Hosp, Decatur, AL, dir relig serv, coordr employee assistance prog, 1984-, patient rights implementer, 1989-; staff develop officer, chaplain, currently. **Orgs:** Charter mem, The Employee Assistance Soc N Am, 1985; chairperson, The Rights Protection Advocacy Comt, 1987-89; adv comt, The Albany Clin, 1989; The Ministerial Alliance Decatur, 1989; Quest Adv Bd, 1990-; N W Coun Ctr Bd, 1991; key vommunicator, Decatur Educ Bd; Phi Alpha Theta; Pi Gamma Mu; Sigma Tau Delta; The N Ala Study Club; The Morgan County Hist Soc; The Mental Health Asn Morgan County; The Needs Assessment Comt; The Decatur City Bd Educ. **Honors/Awds:** Pierce Pettis, Guitar Man Speaking Out Newspaper, Decatur, AL, 1984. **Special Achievements:** Editor, Patient Rights Handbook, North Alabama Regional Hospital, 1991. **Military Serv:** USNR communication yeoman, Third class 3 yrs; Highest Honor & First in Class CYN Sch. **Home Addr:** 511 Walnut St NE, Decatur, AL 35601. **Business Addr:** Chaplain, North Ala Regional Hosp, 4218 Hwy 31 S, PO Box 2221, Decatur, AL 35609, **Business Phone:** (256)353-9433.

RAGSDALE, PAUL B.
State government official. **Personal:** Born Jan 14, 1945, Jacksonville, TX. **Educ:** Univ Tex, Austin, BA, sociol, 1966. **Career:** State government official (retired); Tracor Inc, Austin, social scientist,1966-68; Dallas, chief planner, 1968-72; State rep, 1973-87. **Orgs:** Bd mem, Black C C; numerous others. **Honors/Awds:** Numerous awards. **Special Achievements:** One of the first African American legislators in Texas. *

RAHMAN, MAHDI ABDUL. See HAZZARD, WALTER R., JR.

RAIFORD, ROGER LEE
Orthopedic surgeon. **Personal:** Born Nov 1, 1942, Greensboro, NC; son of Ernest L Raiford and Blanche Reynolds Raiford; married Pamela Gladden; children: Gregory & Brian. **Educ:** Howard Univ, BS, 1964; Howard Med Sch, MD, 1968. **Career:** Bowie State Col, team physician, 1974-75; Leland Hosp, chief orthop surg, 1992-93; Howard Univ, asst prof orthop surg; Prince Georges Hosp Ctr, Cheverly, active staff, currently; Doctors Community Hosp, active staff; Pvt pract physician. **Orgs:** Am Bd Orthop Surg; Am Acad Orthop Surg; DC Med Soc. **Honors/Awds:** Oath & Honors Day, Howard Univ Med Sch, 1968; Diplomate, Nat Bd Med Examr, 1969. **Home Phone:** (301)345-0377. **Business Addr:** Active Staff, Prince George's Hospital Center, 3001 Hospital Dr, Cheverly, MD 20785, **Business Phone:** (301)618-2000.

RAINBOW-EARHART, DR. KATHRYN ADELINE
Psychiatrist. **Personal:** Born Mar 21, 1921, Wheeling, WV; daughter of John Henry Rainbow and Addaline Holly Rainbow; married William, Jul 29, 1966; children: Frederic B Jr & Holly R Bryant. **Educ:** Ft Valley State Col, BS, 1942; Meharry Med Col, MD, 1948; Menninger Sch Psychiat, 1965. **Career:** Psychiatrist (retired); Rocky Mount, pvt pediat pract, 1952-54; Lakin State Hosp, staff physician, 1954-59, clin dir, 1959-60, supt, 1960-62; Topeka State Hosp, staff psychiatrist, 1965-79; Shawnee Community Ment Health Ctr Inc, staff psychiatrist, 1979-81; Kans Reception & Diag Ctr, staff psychiatrist, 1981-83. **Orgs:** Bd dirs, Topeka Asn Retarded Citizens, 1972-78, 1983-87; bd dirs, Stormont-Vail Hosp Found, 1993-99; Shawnee County Med Soc; past pres, WV Med Soc; KS Med Soc; AMA; Am Med Women's Asn; Am Psychiat Asn; Black Psychiatrists Am; Nat Med Asn; emeritus courtesy staff, Stormont-Vail & St Francis Hosps; Alpha Kappa Alpha Sor; past pres, Topeka Chap Links Inc; past pres, Quota Int Topeka; Nat Am Advan Colored People; St John Am Church; Nat Coun Negro Women; hon mem, Delta Kappa Gamma Soc Int. **Honors/Awds:** 25-Year Service to Humanity, Meharry Med Col, Plaque; NIMH Fellowship, 1962-65; Honoree of the Consortium of Doctors, 1993; Certificate of Recognition; An Outstanding Woman of African Decent, 5th Episcopal District of the AM Church, 1994; Positive Image Award, The Links Inc, Topeka chp, 2001. **Home Addr:** 2916 Kentucky Ave, Topeka, KS 66605.

RAINES, COLDEN DOUGLAS
Dentist, president (organization). **Personal:** Born Oct 17, 1915, Apex, NC; married Frances Johnson; children: Tajuana Raines Turner, Colden Jr, Romley H. **Educ:** Shaw Univ, BS, 1940; Howard Univ, DDS, 1946. **Career:** Mary C Leonie Guggenheim Dental Clin, intern, 1948; pvt pract, currently. **Orgs:** Pres, Howard Univ Dent Alumni, 1977; fel Acad Med NJ fel Acad Gen Dent, 1979; fel Am Col Dentists, 1979; fel Am Soc Advan Anesthesia Dent, 1982; Bergen Co Dent Soc; Am Dent Asn; Nat Dent Asn; Essex Co Dent Soc; Commonwelath Dent Asn; pres, Dent Sect Acad Med; Acad Gen Dent; Soc Oral Physiol & Occlusion; trustee, Acad Med NJ; pres, Bergen Passaic Howard Univ Alumni Club; Alpha Phi Alpha Frat; Chi Delta Mu Frat. **Honors/Awds:** Alumni Award, Howard Univ Col Dent, 1975; Howard Univ Alumni Achievement Award, 1984. **Military Serv:** AUS, maj, 1957. **Business Addr:** Dentists, Private Practice, 603 Clinton Ave, Newark, NJ 07108.

RAINES, FRANKLIN D.
Government official. **Personal:** Married Wendy; children: Sarah. **Educ:** Harvard Law Sch, 1976; Rhodes Scholar. **Career:** Lazard Freres & Co, gen partner, 1979; Fed Nat Mortgage Asn (Fannie Mae), vice chmn, 1991-96; Off Mgt & Budget, dir, 1996-98; Fannie Mae, vice chmn, 1991, chmn, 1997, chief exec officer & chmn, 1999-. **Orgs:** Horatio Alger Asn Distinguished Ams. **Honors/Awds:** Equal Justice Award, Legal Defense & Educ Fund. **Special Achievements:** Instrumental in creating "Access," a program designed to increase minority participation in Fannie Mae's $380 billion-plus securities business; Created "Fannie Neighbors," a program that helps low-income homebuyers qualify for mortgages; First African American White budget chief. **Business Addr:** Chairman, Chief Executive Officer, Fannie Mae, 3900 Wis Ave NW, Washington, DC 20016-2892, **Business Phone:** (202)752-7000.*

RAINES, TIMOTHY
Athletic coach, baseball player. **Personal:** Born Sep 16, 1959, Sanford, FL; married Shannon Watson, Jan 1, 2007; married Virginia Hilton, Jan 1, 1979; children: Tim Jr & Andre. **Career:** Baseball outfielder (retired), coach; Montreal Expos, outfielder, 1979-90,2001; Chicago White Sox, outfielder, 1991-95, coach, 2004-06; New York Yankees, outfielder, 1996-98; Oakland Athletics, outfielder, 1999; Baltimore Orioles, outfielder, 2001; Fla Marlins, outfielder, 2002; Brevard County Manatees, mgr, 2003; World Series Championship, base coach, 2005, bench coach; Harrisburg Senators, hitting coach, currently. **Honors/Awds:** Rookie of the Year, Sporting News, 1981; Nat League MVP Award, 1983, 1986, 1987; The Sporting News Gold Shoe Award, 1984; Silver Slugger Award, 1986; Most Valuable Player Award, 1987. **Business Addr:** Hitting Coach, Harrisburg Senators, Commerce Bank Pk City Island, Harrisburg, PA 17101.

RAINEY, TIMOTHY MARK
Editor, clergy. **Personal:** Born Jul 27, 1956, Mobile, AL; son of Rev W D Rainey (deceased) and E S Rainey; married Gloria Johnson, Apr 7, 1979; children: Tiria & Mark. **Educ:** Troy State Univ, BS, 1977; Huntsville Bapt Inst, Theol, 1994. **Career:** Mobile Press Register, reporter, 1977-78; Ala A&M Univ, publ & news specialist, 1978-82; Huntsville Times, ed, 1982-; Mt Lebman Presbyterian Church, pastor, 1991-96; Indian Creek PB Church, pastor, 1996-. **Orgs:** Huntsville Ministerial Alliance; Sch Relig; asst dean relig, Tri-State PB Convention; bd trustees & sch registr, Huntsville Baptist Inst. **Honors/Awds:** Excellence in Journalism, Sigma Delta Chi, 1974; Associated Press Newswriting Award, Second Place, 1984; Alabama Press Asn Award, Honorable Mention, 1987; Douglas L Cannon, Med Jour Award, 1990; Journalism Alumnus of the Year, Troy State Univ, 1997. **Business Addr:** Pastor, Indian Creek PB Church, 884 Indian Creek Rd, Huntsville, AL 35810, **Business Phone:** (256)837-2890.

RAINSFORD, GRETA M.
Pediatrician. **Personal:** Born Dec 28, 1936, New York, NY; daughter of George Maurice and Gertrude Eleanor Edwards; married Samuel K Anderson. **Educ:** AB 1958; MD 1962; Internship 1963; Pediat Res 1965; Dipl Bd Ped 1967. **Career:** Mercy Hosp, assoc attending pediatrician, 1965-; NCMC, asst attending pediatrician, 1965-; Pvt Pract, physician & pediatrician, 1965-; Sickle Cell Clin, dir, 1971-85; Planned Parenthood of Nassau County, med adv bd, 1971-; Roosevelt Sch Dist, sch physician, 1975-; Hempstead Sch Dist, sch pediatrician, 1975-77; Old Westbury Campus State Univ, NY, clinic physician, 1976-; Hofstra Univ, Hempstead, NY, exec dir, community serv ctr, 1990-00; Ctr Developmentally Disabled, staff pediatrician, 1991-. **Orgs:** Community Health & Educ, 1971-; bd mem, Nassau Pediatrician Soc; bd dir, Roosevelt Ment Health Ctr, 1976-85; fel Am Acad Pediat, 1977; bd trustees, Hofstra Univ, 1978-90; pres bd dirs, Long Island Gate, 1979-81; SUNY Stony Brook Coun, 1981-95; Nassau Co Med Soc; NY Med Soc; bd mem, Planned Parenthood, Nassau County, 1986-91; bd, Nassau Health Care Corp, 1996-; Nassau Chap Am Red Cross, mem, 1991-96, chair, 1997-00; Comn to End Racial Disparity in Healthcare. **Honors/Awds:** Plaque Serv Sickle Cell Anemia, 1972; Plaque Serv Youth & Mankind, 1974; Commendation Serv Youth Hempstead C of C,1974; Distinguish Serv Award, HCTA, 1974; Community Serv Award, Nat Asn Norwood Bus & Prof Women's Club, 1974; Community Serv Award, Black Hist Mus, 1977; Med Serv Award, LI Sickle Cell Proj, 1977; MLK, JR Birth Celebration Award, 1988; Equal Award, Nass NOW, 1991; FSA Community Lead Award, 1991; Women of Dist, March of Dimes, 1992; Community Serv, AMWA, 1994. **Business Addr:** Pediatrician, 756 Front, Hempstead, NY 11550-4626, **Business Phone:** (516)485-6633.*

RAKESTRAW, KYLE DAMON
Engineer, executive. **Personal:** Born Apr 9, 1961, Dayton, OH; son of Delores Robinson. **Educ:** Univ Cin, BSIM, 1984; Xavier Univ Cincinnati, MBA, 1988. **Career:** Gen Motors Corp, prof practice, 1982-84, Delco Moraine Div, Dayton, purchasing agent, 1986-89, sr proj engr, 1990-92; Pepsi Cola Co, Indianapolis, warehouse operations mgr, 1989-90; ITT Automotive Elec Syst, N Am, bus planner & pricing adminr, 1994-96; Allied Signal Inc, pricing mgr, 1996-. **Orgs:** Nat Black MBA Asn, 1987. **Honors/Awds:** Voorheis Col Scholarship, Univ Cin, 1979, Dorothy Gradison Memorial Scholarship, 1983. **Business Addr:** Pricing Manager, Allied Signal Inc, 15001 Laguna N 36th St, Redmond, WA 98053, **Business Phone:** (425)376-2098.

RALPH, SHERYL LEE
Singer, entrepreneur, actor. **Personal:** Born Dec 30, 1956, Waterbury, CT; daughter of Stanley and Ivy; married Eric George Maurice; children: Etienne Maurice & Ivy Victoria. **Educ:** Rutgers Univ, BA, theater arts & eng lit. **Career:** TV Series: "It's a Living", 1986-89; "New Attitude"; "Designing Women"; "George"; "Moesha"; Films: A Piece of the Action, 1977; Oliver & Co, voice, 1988; The Mighty Quinn, 1989; Skin Deep, 1989; To Sleep With Anger, 1990; Distinguished Gentlemen, 1992; Sister Act 2, 1993; White Man's Burden, 1995; Bogus, 1996; Mistress; Personals, 1999; Deterrence, 1999; Unconditional Love, 1999; Lost in the Pershing Point Hotel, 2000; Baby of the Family, 2002; Whoopi, 2003; Kink in My Hair, 2004; Barbershop, 2005; c-wear designer; Broadway: Dreamgirls, 1992; Secrets; Island Girls Productions, owner; Annual Int Jamaican Film Festival, creator & dir; actress, singer, writer, dir & producer, currently. **Orgs:** Screen Actors Guild; Actor's Equity; Am Fed TV & Radio Artists; Diva, AIDS fundraiser. **Honors/Awds:** Miss Black Teen-Age NY, 1973; Best Col Actress, 1974; Nominated Image Award Outstanding Supporting Actress in a Comedy Series, 2002. Won numerous awards. **Special Achievements:** Tony Award nomination & Drama Desk nomination for Dreamgirls, 1982; Host of video and auth of book: Sheryl Lee Ralph's Beauty Basics, 1987; recorded album, In the Evening, 1984. **Business Addr:** Actress, MKS & Associates, 8695 W Washington Blvd Suite 204, Culver city, CA 90232.

RAMBISON, DR. AMAR B
Clergy. **Personal:** Born Nov 22, 1950, El Dorado, West Indies; son of Ram Bisoon and Chando; married Eutrice, May 30, 1971;

children: Candis. **Educ:** Luther Rice Sem, BDiv, 1979; Andersonville Baptist Sem, DTh, 1994, Phd, 1995; Lake Charles Bible Col, DMin, 1996; Southwest Bible Col, doctor, Phd, christian educ, 1997. **Career:** Deeper Life Assembly, sr pastor, 1990-; Metro Orlando District, supvr, 2002-; New York City Metro District, supvr, 2003-; Southwestern Bible Col, adj prof. **Orgs:** Pres, Independent Ministers Asn, 1997-; div supt, Church Foursquare Gospel, 2000-. **Special Achievements:** Written: The Unfinished Man; Jumping Jehoshaphat: The Ups and Downs of Leadership; Prospering Through Good Leadership; The Biblical Art of Personal Evangelism; 18 Missing Years of Christ Found. **Home Addr:** 13137 Plum Lake Circle, Clermont, FL 34711. **Business Addr:** supervisor, New York City Metro District, 8825 A D Mims Rd, Orlando, FL 32818-8604, **Business Phone:** (407)290-8510.

RAMBO, BETTYE R.
Educator. **Personal:** Born Sep 2, 1936, Jasper, CO; married Leon Taylor, Jan 1, 1980; children: Valencia A & Sherryle B. **Educ:** Stillman Col, BA, 1959; Ind Univ, MA, 1968; Univ Ill, post grad study; Laverne Col; Moray House Col, Edinburgh, Scotland, attended 1974; Ill State Univ. **Career:** Educator (retired); Springfield Bd Educ, educr, 1968-2000. **Orgs:** Jasper Co Teachers Asn, 1959-68; life mem, Nat Educ Asn, 1959-74; Miss Teachers Asn, 1959-68; Ill Educ Asn, 1968-74; human rels coordr Region 32, Human Rels Comn, Ill Educ Asn, 1974-75; secy, PDK, 1985-87; educ chair, ABWA, 1986; life mem, Springfield Civic Garden Club, 1988; Order Eastern Star, 1989; secy, St Patrick's Sch Bd, 1992-94; chair, Zion bapitst Trustee Bd, Springfield Educ Asn, vice chmn. Zion Missionary Baptist Church; bd dir, Stillman Col Alumni Asn; NDEA Inst Culturally Disadvantaged Youth; deleg, NEA Conv; Nat Asn Advan Colored People, Smithsonian Asn, NRTA; St Missions Bd; Airline Passengers Asn. **Honors/Awds:** Education Award, Nat Asn Advan Colored People, 1983; Teacher of Excellence, Iota Phi Lambda Sorority, 1986; Spotlight Feature, Springfield Pub Schs, 1986. **Home Addr:** 2025 Gregory Ct, Springfield, IL 62703.

RAMEY, ADELE MARIE
Lawyer, government official. **Personal:** Born Jun 30, 1954, New York, NY; daughter of Wilburn Taylor Sr and Delphenia A Taylor; married Martin G, Nov 2, 1991. **Educ:** Ohio Wesleyan Univ, BA, 1976; Ind Univ, paralegal cert, 1985, JD, 1989. **Career:** Sears, Roebuck & Co, mgr trainee, 1976-77; Churches Chicken, mgr, 1977-79; Red Lobster, asst mgr, 1979-81; Lucky Steer Restaurant, exec asst mgr, 1981-82; McDonalds, asst mgr, 1982-84; Marion Co Pub Defender's Off, paralegal, 1984-89; State Ind Pub Defenders Off, dep pub defender, 1989. **Orgs:** Am Bar Asn, 1989-; Ind Bar Asn, 1989-; Nat Bar Asn, 1989-.

RAMEY, FELICENNE H
School administrator, educator. **Personal:** Born in Philadelphia, PA; married Melvin R Ramey; children: 2. **Educ:** Pa State Univ, Pa, BS; Duquesne Univ, MS; Univ Calif, JD; Calif State Univ, MA. **Career:** Self-employed atty, Davis, Calif, 1975-84; City & County Sacramento, dir litigation, 1975-76; Calif State Univ, Sacramento Col Bus Admin, Calif, prof bus law, 1975-2003, asst pres, 1984-86, dept chair, 1986-88, assoc dean, 1988-94; Off Chancellor, Univ Calif, Davis, exec officer, 1994, interim dean, 1997-2000, dean, prof emer bus law, 2003-; Ebon Art, owner. **Orgs:** Bd dir, chair, Educ Comt, Sacramento Black Chamber Com, Sacramento, Calif, 1990-; bd dir, Cal Aggie Alumni Asn, 1989-; pres, Western Bus Law Asn, 1975-; Nat Asn Women Deans, Adminrs, & Counrs, 1990-; Calif Bar Asn, 1973-; Nat Asn Women Edu, 1989-; fel, Univ Calif, Am Coun Edu, 1992-93; bd trustee, Sutter Davis Hosp; Am Coun Educ Nat Identification Prog; Women Educ; Am Leadership Forum, Mountain Valley Chap; Comstock Club; Discovery Mus Hist; Greater Sacramento Urban League; Sacramento Entrepreneurship Acad; Sacramento Valley Forum. **Honors/Awds:** Citation for Excellence, 1994, Cal Aggie Alumni Asn; Woman of Color Achievement Award, 1994, Calif State Univ, Sacramento, Calif; Distinguished Faculty Award and order of the Hormet Award, CSU Sacramento Alumni Asn, 2002; Excellence in Education, Calif, 2003; Medellion Honoree, Bus, Observer Newspaper, 2003; Sacramento Business Journal's "Women Who Mean Business" Award. **Business Addr:** Professor Emeritus of Business Law, California State University, College of Business Administration, Sacramento, CA 95819-6088, **Business Phone:** (916)278-7030.

RAMEY, MELVIN R
Educator. **Personal:** Born Sep 13, 1938, Pittsburgh, PA; son of Ethrem and Eleanor; married Felicenne, Sep 5, 1964; children: David & Daina. **Educ:** Pa State Univ, BS, 1960; Carnegie Mellon Univ, MS, 1965, PhD, 1967. **Career:** Pa Dept Highways, bridge design engr, 1960-63; Univ Calif, Davis, prof, 1967-96, chairperson, 1991-96, prof emer, currently; Ga Inst Technol, vis prof, 1980; Mass Inst Technol, vis prof, 1988; Ctr Advan Health & Human Performance, 1997-99, Dept Exercise Sci, vice chairperson, 1998-99. **Orgs:** Hon mem, Golden Key Nat Hon Soc, 1992; Am Soc Biomechanics; Am Soc Civil Engrs; Am Concrete Inst; Am Asn Higher Educ. **Honors/Awds:** Outstanding Teacher, Stud Chap Am Soc Civil Engrs, 1974; Maynor Ronning Award for Teaching Excellence, Asn Stud Univ Calif, 1985; Black Engineer of the Year, Coun Engineering, Deans Historically Black Cols & Univs, 1993; Outstanding Faculty Advisor Award, Col Engineering, Univ Calif. **Special Achievements:** Published over 50 articles & reports, was slected by US Black Engineer & Information Technology magazine (www.blackengineer.com) as one of the "50 Most Important Blacks in Research Science" for 2004. **Business Addr:** Professor Emeritus, University of California, Department of Civil & Environment Engineering, 1 Shields Ave 2001 Engineering III, Davis, CA 95616, **Business Phone:** (530)752-0896.

RAMIREZ, RICHARD M
Executive. **Career:** Apex Securities Inc, pres, chief exec officer, 1987; AG Edwards & Sons Inc, staff; Chase Securities Tex Inc, staff, currently. **Business Addr:** Staff, Chase Securities of Texas Inc.

RAMISTELLA, JOHN HENRY. See RIVERS, JOHNNY.

RAMPERSAD, ARNOLD
Educator, college administrator. **Personal:** Born Nov 13, 1941, Port of Spain, Trinidad and Tobago; married Jan 1, 1985. **Educ:** Bowling Green State Univ, Bowling Green, OH, BA, 1967, MA, 1968; Harvard Univ, MA, 1969, PhD, 1973. **Career:** Univ VA, asst prof, 1973-74; Stanford Univ, assoc prof, 1974-83, Sara Hart Kimball prof humanities, currently, sr assoc dean humanities, 2003-06, Cognizant dean humanities, currently; Rutgers Univ, NB, NJ, prof, 1983-88; Columbia Univ, NY, prof, 1988-90; Princeton Univ, Woodrow Wilson prof Lit, 1990-98, Prog Am Studies, 1990-95. **Orgs:** AAAS; Am Philos Soc. **Special Achievements:** Collected Poems of Langston Hughes, editor, 1994; Jackie Robinson: A Biography, author, Knopf, 1998. **Business Phone:** (650)736-2133.

RAMSEUR, ANDRE WILLIAM
Poet, human services worker. **Personal:** Born Jan 15, 1949, Manhattan, NY; son of Otho William Ramseur Jr and Creola Howard. **Educ:** St Augustines Col Raleigh, BA Eng, 1971; Miami Univ, Oxford, OH, 1972; George Wash Univ DC, 1980; VA Polytechnic Inst & State Univ, MS, educ; Emphasis Adult educ, 1992. **Career:** Miami Univ Oxford OH, grad asst, 1971-72; St Augustines Col, instr eng, 1972-74; Equitable Life Assurance Soc US, agency sec; asst suprv; New Bus Indianapolis, Wash DC admin trainee, 1974-77; Eton Towers Tenants Assoc, legal coordr, 1975; Pres Comn White House Fel, staff asst, 1977-79; Office Personnel Mgt Washing DC, ed specialist, 1979-86; Defense Info Systs Agency, supervry employee develop specialist, 1986-92; Strayer Univ, adjunct prof, 1996-; Dept Com, Human Resources Specialist, 2002; Northern VA Interdenominational Mass Choir, bus mgr. **Orgs:** Co-founder, Sta to Sta Performance Poets & Writers Collective, 1980; Fed Educations & Technol Assoc (FETA). **Honors/Awds:** Outstanding Young Man Dees & Fuller Org, 1975; author, poetry: "You Never Tried" Clover Publ 1976, "After the Fact" Young Publ, 1978, "Greenhouse Poetry" Collection of Love Poems Triton Press, 1977-78, "Greenhouse Poetry" Vol 2, 1979-80; Vintage Poetry, 2002; The Journey, 2003; finalist Clover Int Poetry Contest Wash DC, 1975; Notable Am Award Notable Historian Soc Raleigh, 1976-77; Spec Achievement Award, Pres Comn White House Fel, 1979; group performances Sta 2 Sta, 1980-85; annual 1 man poetry performance, 1982; spec achievement OPM Director's Award, 1984; spec act serv Info Systs Agency, 1986; Spec Achievement, DISA, 1987-88; poetry collection progress Its About Time 1989; outstanding Act or service, Def Info Systems Agency 1990; Letter Appreciation, DISA Inspector Gen Participation & Performance, org Assessment Audit Team, 1996; DISA Award HRM Team Proj, 2000; DISA, Great Performer Award, 2002.

RAMSEUR, ISABELLE R
Government official. **Personal:** Born Feb 21, 1906, North Carolina; married Charles; children: Harold D & Albertine. **Career:** Philadelphia Gen Hosp, nursing vol work; Mercy Douglas Hosp; Nursery Sch Fernwood, teachers asst; Boro Darby, councilwoman. **Orgs:** Needlework Guild Am, 1933; Ladies Aux, WMCA, Philadelphia; Blessed Virgin Mary Church; Nat Asn Advan Colored People; matron, Order E Star; chartered mem, Rose Sharon Chap. **Honors/Awds:** First Prize, ARC Talent Rally Rose Sharon.

RAMSEY, DAVID P.
Actor. **Personal:** Born in Detroit, MI; son of Nathaniel and Jeraldine. **Educ:** Wayne State Univ, fine arts. **Career:** Films: The Line, 1980; Scared Stiff, 1987; The Nutty Professor, 1996; AVery Brady Sequel, 1996; Con Air, 1997; A Short Wait Between Trains, 1998; Three to Tango, 1999; Pay It Forward, 2000; Mr Bones, 2001; Big Fish, 2003; Runaway Jury, 2003; Hair Show, 2004; Central Booking, 2005; Resurrection: The J.R. Richard Story, 2005; Bathsheba, 2005; Jane Doe: The Wrong Face, 2005; Hello Sister, Goodbye Life, 2006; The Death & Life of Bobby Z, 2007; TV appearances: "Lovers & Friends/For Richer, For Poorer",1977; "Sanctuary of Fear", 1979; "Deutschland lied", 1996; Her Costly Affair, 1996; "The Good News", 1997; "Mama Flora's Family", 1998; CHiPs'99, 1998; "Mutiny", 1999; "For Your Love", 2000-01; "Ali: An American Hero", 2000; "Thieves", 2001; The Long Con, 2001; "Girl friends", 2001;"Romeo Fire", 2002; One on One, 2002-03; "It's a Miserable Life", 2003;"Navy NCIS: Naval Criminal Investigative Service", 2003; The Flannerys, 2003; "Wannabe", 2004; "Crossing Jordan", 2004; "Ghost Whisperer", 2005-08; All of Us, 2005; Huff, 2005; CSI: Crime Scene Investigation, 2006; Love Still Won't Die", 2006; "The West Wing", 2006; Fatal Contact:Bird Flu in America, 2006; "Criminal Minds", 2007; "Journeyman", 2007; Wildfire, 2008; Hollywood Residential, 2008. **Business Addr:** Actor, c/o Nils Larsen, Elements Entertainment, 1635 N Caheunga Blvd 5th Fl, Los Angeles, CA 90028, **Business Phone:** (323)461-2000.*

RAMSEY, DONNA ELAINE
Librarian. **Personal:** Born Oct 10, 1941, Charlotte, NC; daughter of William A Epps and Mabel Brown Tatum; married Reginald E, Apr 9, 1979 (died 1985); children: Gina M Clark (deceased), Ona B & Reginald E II. **Educ:** Johnson C Smith Univ, BA, 1969; Atlanta Univ, MSLS, 1971; Univ NC, attended 1973, 1977; Kent State Univ, attended 1976. **Career:** Barber-Scotia Col, Concord, NC, reference/circulation librn, 1971-73; Friendship Junior Col, Rock Hill, SC, chief librn, 1973-77; New Mexico State Univ, Las Cruces, NM, asst serials librn, 1977-81; Cochise Col, Fort Bliss, Tex, librn, 1984-85; US Army Air Defense Artillery Sch Libr, Fort Bliss, Tex, supervisory librn, 1985-89, librn, 1989-92; US Army Sergeants Major Acad, Fort Bliss, Tex, librn, 1992-97; US Army Air Def Art Sch, Mickelsen Libr, librn, 1997-2001; Van Noy Library, Ft Belvoir, Va, librn, 2001-. **Orgs:** Am Libr Asn, 1976-; Black Caucus Am Libr Asn, 1978-; NAACP, 1989-; golden life mem, Delta Sigma Theta Sorority Inc, 1989-; chair, prog planning, Fort Bliss Black Employment Prog Comt, 1989-90; Am Platform asn, 1995-; Am Biographical Inst, 1994-2000; Staff Organization Roundtable, ALA, 1979-; Constitution & Bylaws Chair, 1993; chair-elect, 1990-91; chair, 1991-93; Annual Prog Chair, 1991-93; Armed Forces Libraries Roundtable; Tex Libr Asn Leadership Develop Comt, 1998-2001; Tex Libr Asn Leadership Develop Comm, chair, 1999-2000; Am Libr Assoc. **Honors/Awds:** Civic Achievement Award, United Way, Las Cruces, 1981; Certificate of Achievement, Dept Army, 1990, 1991; Certificate of Achievement Award, 1992; Certificate of Achievement, Am Libr Asn, 1992; Certificate of Appreciation, Am Biographical Inst, 1995; Kent State Univ Grad Assistanceship; Asn Col & Res Libr, Certificate of Recognition; Certificate of Achievement, US Army, 1997. **Business Addr:** Librarian, US Army Van Noy Library, 5966 12th St Bldg 1024, Fort Belvoir, VA 22060, **Business Phone:** (703)806-3238.

RAMSEY, FREEMAN, JR.
Photographer. **Personal:** Born Oct 8, 1943, Nashville, TN; son of Freeman (deceased) and Rosetta Scott (deceased); married Doretha Pipkin Ramsey, Apr 20, 1968; children: Freeman Ramsey III, Ronald Ramsey, Christine Renee. **Educ:** Tenn State Univ, BS, 1970; Nashville Tech Inst, Nashville, TN, dipl commun & photog, 1983. **Career:** CBS Records, Nashville, TN, recording engr, 1969-82; Ramsey's Photog, Nashville, Tenn, self employed, photogr, 1982-85; Metro Bd Educ, Nashville, TN, transp, 1984-90; The Tennessean, Nashville, TN, staff photogr, 1989-. **Orgs:** Nat Press Photogr Asn, 1989-; Tenn Press Asn, 1989-; Nat Asn Black Journalists, 1989-. **Honors/Awds:** Photographic Achievement, The Tennessean, 1965; Photographic Achievement, The Tennessean, 1966; Feature Picture Award, AP, 1991; Third Place, Feature Picture, NPPA, 1991; Third Place, Sports Feature Photo, AP, 1991; Third Place, Sports Feature Photo, AP, 1991; First Place, News NPPA Awards, 1991, 1993; Second Place & Thirrd Place, News Picture, AP, 1992; Second Place, Southern Short Course in News Photography, 1992; Honorable Mention, 1993; Outstanding Achievement Award, Tennessean, 1993; First Place, News NPPA Awards, 1991, 1993; Honorable Mention, Atlanta Seminar in Photojournalism, 1993; Honorable Mention, Atlanta Seminar in Photojournalism, 1993; Best of Gannett, Second Place, Color Photography, 1994; First Place, Feature Picture, AP, 1994; Best News Picture, Tenn Press Asn, 1994; Gannett Well Done Awards, 1991, 1994; second place, Gordon Parks Photography Competition, 1994; Third Place, NABJ Photog Competition, 1994; First & Second Place, AP Awards, 1994; First Place, News Picture, Penn Press Asn, 1995; Best News Picture Story, AP, 1995. **Military Serv:** USAF, 1966. **Business Addr:** Staff Photographer, The Tennessean, Photo Dept, 1100 Broadway St, Nashville, TN 37203.*

RAMSEY, HENRY, JR.
School administrator, judge. **Personal:** Born Jan 22, 1934, Florence, SC; married Eleanor Anne Mason; children: Charles, Githaiga, Robert, Ismail, Yetunde & Abeni. **Educ:** Univ Calif, Riverside, CA, AB, 1960; Univ Calif Sch Law, Berkeley, CA, LLB, 1963; Harvard Univ Inst Educ Mgt, attended 1992; William Mitchell Col Law, LLD, 1996. **Career:** Judge (retired); Contra Costa Co, CA, dep dist atty, 1964-65; Ramsey & Rosenthal, Richmond CA, partner, 1965-71; Univ Calif Sch Law, Berkeley CA, prof law, 1971-80; Univ Tex, Austin TX, vis prof law, 1971-77; Univ Colo, Boulder CO, vis prof law, 1977-78; Univ N Mex Sch Law, Spec Scholar Prog Am Indians, Albuquerque NM, vis prof law, 1980; State CA, Co Alameda, super ct judge, 1980-90; Howard Univ Sch Law, Wash, DC, dean, 1990-96; Howard Univ, actg vpres & gen coun, 1994-95. **Orgs:** Curric Develop & Supplemental Materials Comt State CA; Calif Bar Asn, 1964-80; Calif Judges Asn; Human Rel Comt City Richmond; bd dir, Re develop Agency; United Bay Area Crusade; bd dir, Am Civil Liberties Union Northern CA; Berkeley City Coun; exec comt

mem, Asn Am Law Sch; Coun Legal Educ Opportunity; Coun Sect Legal Educ & Admiss Bar Am Bar Asn, 1982-; Am Law Inst; Accreditation Comt Sect Legal Educ & Admiss Bar Am Bar Asn; Comn Trial Ct Performance Stands, Nat Ctr State Cts, 1987-95; Blue Ribbon Comn Inmate Population Mgt, 1987-90; Judicial Coun Calif, 1988-; chairperson, Judicial Coun Adv Comt Change Venue, Judicial Coun Calif, 1988-89; Nat Comn Trial Ct Performance Stands; life mem, Nat Advan Asn Colored People; life mem, Am Civil Liberties Union; Am nesty Intl; chair, trustee, Fibre Bd Asbestos Compensation Trust; bd advisor, Charlotte Sch Law. **Honors/Awds:** Bernard S Jefferson Jurist Award, Calif Asn Black Lawyers, 1986; Distinguished Alumnus Award, Univ Calif Alumni Asn, 1987; Fifth Annual Distinguished Service Award, The Wiley Manuel Law Found, 1987; Distinguished Service Award, The Nat Ctr State Cts, 1990; Henry Ramsey Jr Award, Am Bar Asn Law Stud Div, 1996; Boalt Hall Citation Award, 2003; Charles Houston Bar Asn Hall of Fame, 2006; Judge D Lowell & Barbara Jensen Public Service Award, Univ Calif, Berkeley, Sch law, 2006. **Special Achievements:** Author, "Affirmative Action at American Bar Association Approved Law School": 1979-80, Jour Legal Educ, 1980; author, "California Continuing Education of the Bar," chap Calif Criminal Law Procedure & Pract, 1986. **Military Serv:** USAF, 1951-55.

RAMSEY, JEROME CAPISTRANO
Lawyer, executive, association executive. **Personal:** Born Mar 28, 1953, San Bernardino, CA. **Educ:** Univ Calif, BA(hons) 1975, JD, 1978. **Career:** Holland & Hart, atty, 1978-80; US Dept Justice, asst US atty, 1980-82; Mile Hi Cablevision, vpres/gen coun, 1982-86; Paragon Commun, regional vpres, 1986-90; Am Telecommunications, New England Div, pres, 1990-; Time Warner Entertainment, Time Warner Cable, vpres, currently; WUSA New York & Orlando team mkts, pres, currently. **Orgs:** Am Bar Asn, 1978-; Colo & Denver Bar Asn, 1978-; bd mem, New England Cable TV Asn, 1990, chmn, Maine Exec Comt, 1991. **Honors/Awds:** Distinguished Service, US Dept Justice, 1982; Executive Excel the Minority Professional Directory, 1984. **Business Addr:** Vice President, Time Warner Entertainment, Time Warner Cable, 6401 10th Mountain Div Rd Ft Benning, Atlanta, GA 31995-2008, **Business Phone:** (706)687-6109.

RAMSEY, WALTER S.
Executive. **Personal:** Married Grace E Walker; children: Walter S Jr. **Educ:** The City Col NY, BS. **Career:** US Signal Corps, physicist, 1942-43; Standard Eletronics, physicist, 1943-45; Raytheon Mfg Co, proj engr, 1945-46; Sylvania Electric, proj engr, 1946-53; Ramsey Electronics, owner, mgr, consult, 1953. **Orgs:** Adv comt mem, August Martin HS Jamaica NY; bd Queens Child Guid; bd chmn, NAACP Jamaica; Montauk Day Care Ctr; educ chmn, Queens boro Fed Parents Clubs; pres, Jamaica Br NAACP.

RAND, A. BARRY (ADDISON BARRY RAND)
Executive, chief executive officer. **Personal:** Born Nov 5, 1944, Washington, DC; son of Addison Penrod and Helen Matthews; divorced. **Educ:** Rutgers Univ, Camden, NJ; Am Univ, Wash, DC, BS, mktg, 1968; Stanford Univ, MBA, 1972, MA, mgt sci, 1973. **Career:** Xerox Corp, Rochester, NY, from sales rep to regional sales rep, 1968-80, corp dir mkt, 1980-84, vpreseastern opers, 1984-86; Xerox Corp, Stamford,CT, corp vpres, pres US mkt group, 1986, exec vpres opers, Avis Group Holdings Inc, chmn & ceo, 1999-2001; Equitant Inc, chmn & ceo, 2003-05; Campbell Soup Co, bd dir, 2005-; AARP, Ceo, 2009-. **Orgs:** Bd dir, Abbott Laboratories; bd dir, Agilent Technologies; bd dir, AT&T Wireless; bd dir, Equitant Corp; bd dir, Urban Family Inst; bd trustee, Howard Univ. **Honors/Awds:** National Sales Hall of Fame; NAACP Image Award; Malcolm Baldridge Quality Award. **Special Achievements:** AARP's first African-American CEO. **Business Phone:** 800-257-8443.*

RAND, CYNTHIA
Government official. **Educ:** Hampton Univ, BS, math; Fairleigh Dickinson Univ, MS, comput sci. **Career:** Government official (retired); Transp Dept, IRM dir, 1991; US Dept Defense, prin dir info mgt.

RANDALL, ALICE
Writer, songwriter. **Personal:** Born May 4, 1959, Detroit, MI; daughter of George and Bettie; married David Ewing; married Avon Williams II (divorced); children: Caroline Randall Ewing. **Educ:** Harvard Univ, eng & am lit, 1981. **Career:** Author: The Wind Done Gone, 2001; shkin & the Queen of Spades; Co-author, TV Movie Screenplay: "XXX's & OOO's", 1994; songwriter, 1983-; Film & TV companies: Black & White Pictures, She Writes Movies; country songwriter, author, currently. **Orgs:** Harvard-Radcliffe Club; ASCAP; African-Am Hist & Geneal Asn; Metro Hist Comn Nashville; Andrew Jackson Slave Descendent Proj; Family Cemetary Proj. **Honors/Awds:** ASCAP Number One Club, 1994; Al Nueharth Free Spirit Award, 2001; finalist NAACP Image Award, 2002; Literature Award of Excellence, Memphis Black Writers Conf, 2002. **Special Achievements:** Only African-American woman in history to write a Number 1 country song. **Business Addr:** Author, Songwriter, Hougton Mifflin Company, 215 Pk Ave S, New York, NY 10003.

RANDALL, ANN KNIGHT
Educator, librarian. **Personal:** Born in New York, NY; married Julius T; children: Christine Renee. **Educ:** Barnard Col, BA 1963; NY Univ, post grad study 1967; Columbia Univ, DLS, 1977. **Career:** US Social Security Admin NYC, claims adjuster, 1963-64; AUS Bamberg Germany, lib asst, 1964-65; Brooklyn pub libr, libr adult trainee, 1965-67; City Univ NY Queens Col, instr, 1967-69; Brookyn Col, adj lectr,1976-; Columbia Univ, Pratt Inst, Queens Col, Rutgers Univ, teacher part-time, 1970-73; Univ S Educ Resources Info Center ERIC, indexer, 1967-68; Urban Ctr Columbia Univ, libr consult, 1970-; Urban Resources Syst Univ MI, 1973; RR Booker, pub consult, 1973; Brown Univ, asst librn,1982. **Orgs:** YWCA Brooklyn; Acad Pol Sci; Am Libr Asn, 1966-; Asn Study African Am Life& Hist, 1968-; exec bd, Spec Libr Asn NY Group, 1969-71; pres, NU chap Columbia Univ, Beta Phi Mu, 1971-72; N Atlantic Health Sci Libr, 1979. **Honors/Awds:** Publ review & art in jour and book chap; NDEA Fellowship Award for doctoral studies.

RANDALL, MARLENE WEST
Educator, city council member. **Personal:** Born Oct 18, 1934, Norfolk, VA; daughter of James E West and Gladys M Pretlow; married Vernon W Randall, Aug 26, 1958; children: Ricardo C Randall, Veronica L Randall Williams, Michelle D Bryant. **Educ:** Va State Univ, BS, 1954; Columbia Univ, MA, 1968; Univ Va, Sch Law; Old Dominion Univ, admin cert; NOVA Univ. **Career:** Educator (retired); Portsmouth Pub Schs, teacher, 1955-66, reading specialist, 1966-70, asst prin, 1970-76, prin, 1976-89, admin asst, 1989-93; City Portsmouth, VA, vice mayor, currently. **Orgs:** Bd dirs, bd chair, Effingham St YMCA; bd dirs, Am Red Cross; bd dirs, Portsmouth Chamber Com; bd dirs, Her Shelter; bd dirs, Norfolk Portsmouth Empowerment; bd dirs, Metro YMCA; bd dirs, Portsmouth Schools Found; Am Asn Univ Women; New Bethel Baptist Church; nat treas, Jack & Jill Am; Coalition 100 Black Women; Links Inc; Drifters Inc; Portsmouth Moles Inc; Sigma Gamma Rho Sorority; Saturday Evening Bridge Club; Pinochle Bugs Inc. **Honors/Awds:** Humanitarian Award, Portsmouth Public Schools, 1994; Now Black Woman, Natl Drifters Inc, 1994; Community Service Award, NAACP, 1998; Distinguished Service Award, Effingham YMCA, 1999; Strong, Smart, Bold Women, Girls Inc, 1999; YMCA, South Hampton, The Red Triangle, 2002; Humanitarian Award, Nat Coun Community & Justice, 2001. **Business Addr:** Vice Mayor, City of Portsmouth VA, Portsmouth, VA 23705, **Business Phone:** (757)393-8639.*

RANDALL, DR. QUEEN FRANKLIN
School administrator, educator. **Personal:** Born Jan 28, 1935, Pine Bluff, AR; children: Barbara J. **Educ:** Lincoln Univ, BS Ed, 1956; Ind Univ, AM, 1961; Nova Univ, EdD, 1975. **Career:** School administrator, educator (Retired); Lincoln Univ, math instr, 1956-58; Am River Col, math instr, 1962-70, math & engineering dept chair, 1970-72, assoc dean instr, 1972-76; Pioneer Community Col, dean, instructional syst & stud develop, 1976-78, pres, 1978-80; Metrop Comm Col, asst chancellor, 1980-81; El Centro Col, pres, 1981-84; Am River Col, pres, 1984-93; Los Rios Community Col Dist, chancellor, 1993; Lincoln Univ, adj prof. **Orgs:** Alpha Kappa Alpha, 1953-; pres, Soroptimist Club Kansas City MO, 1981; bd dirs, Indust Develop Corp, 1982-85; pres, Delta Kappa Gamma; adv bd, Treescape Dallas, Contact Dallas; Crocker Art Mus; bd dirs, Mercy Healthcare Sacramento; bd dirs, Methodist Hosp Sacramento; bd dirs, The Sacramento Theatre, Co. **Honors/Awds:** Outstanding Educr, YWCA, 1985; Outstanding Alumni, Nova Univ, 1985; Women of Distinction Award, Soroptimist Int Sacramento N, 1986; Dollars & SenseMag's Second Annual Salute to Am Top 100 Bus & Prof Women, 1986.

RANDLE, BERDINE CARONELL
Executive, educator. **Personal:** Born Mar 18, 1929, Lufkin, TX; married Lucious; children: Lydia. **Educ:** Prairie View A&M Univ, BA, 1949; Prairie View A&M Univ, MS, 1955; Univ Houston, post grad. **Career:** Miss Lucy's Acad & Early Childhood Educ Ctr, exec dir, 1969; Friendship Realty Co, owner, 1970-; HI SD Houston, 1957-72; Marlin ISD, phys educ teacher, 1951-57; teacher elem sch, 1951-55; phys educ teacher, 1946, 1948, 1949, 1951; YMCA Waco, dance instr. **Orgs:** Adv bd consult, Clanthe House of Bees Halfway House, 1973-77; vpres, N Forest Sch Bd, 1974-76; vpres, Fontaine Scenic Woods Civic Club, 1976-; golden life mem, Delta Sigma Theta Sor, 1972; life mem, YWCA, 1975; Nat State & Houston Area Asn Educ Young C, 1976-; ACEI, 1974-77; SACUS, 1973-; NAESP, 1973-; AAHPER, 1955-; chrpsn NFTFO, 1976-; AUCW, 1974-77; HALBPWC, 1973-; NALB-PWC, 1973-; chairperson, F SWCC, 1976; AlphaTau chpa, Theta Nu Sigma Nat Sor; charter mem, Diamond Jubilee; Delta Sigma Theta Sorority, Inc, life mem; Nat Coun Negro Women; NAACP; bd dirs, Habitat for Humanity & Delta's Educ Found; Nominated to Prairie View A & M Univ, Sports Hall of Fame, 1994. **Honors/Awds:** Community serv award, 1974; nat coun negro women's award, 1973; outstanding community serv award, 1973; Tex Asn Sch Bd Award, 1975; Kashmere Gdns HS Comm Serv Awd, 1975; Fontaine Scenic Woods Civic Club's Civic Minded Awd, 1973, 1974; Pres Coun on Phys Fitness Awd, 1966; Bd Educ N Forest Sch Dist Awd, 1976; Miss Lucy's Acad Outstading Serv & PTO Awd,1977; ded serv awd, Houston Ind Sch Dist, 1977; Gulf Coast Comm Serv Awd, 1977; ded serv awd Calanthe Hse of Bees, 1977; cert of merit serv Mayor of Houston Gov of TX Hse Spkr Bill Clayton, 1977; achiever award for excellence in education & community service, Houston League of Bus & Prof Women's Club. **Business Addr:** 10620 Homestead Rd, Houston, TX 77016.

RANDLE, CARVER A
Lawyer. **Personal:** Born Jan 12, 1942, Indianola, MS; married Rosie Knox; children: Regina, Carver Jr & Rosalyn. **Educ:** MS Valley State Univ, BS, 1965; Univ MS, JD, 1973. **Career:** Pattonlane High Sch, teacher coach, 1965-67; Wash County Schs, teacher, 1967-68; Quitman Co, spec proj dir, 1968-69; N Miss Rural Legal Serv, staff atty; Randle & McDaniel, partner & prin, currently. **Orgs:** ACSC, 1967-70; Nat Conf Black Lawyers; Miss Nat Bar Asn; cand Mayor, City Indianola, 1968; cand state rep, Miss, 1971; bd dirs, Indianola Fed Credit Unoin; pres, Sunflower Co, Miss Br Nat Asn Advan Colored People; Miss Coun Human Rels, 1977-. **Honors/Awds:** Coach of the Year, N Cent Athletic Conf, 1965-66; Award for outstanding achievements & leadership, Indianola, 1973. **Business Addr:** Partner, Principal, Randle & McDaniel, 130 2nd St, PO Box 546, Indianola, MS 38751-0546.

RANDLE, JOHN
Football player. **Personal:** Born Dec 12, 1967, Hearne, TX; married; children: Brittany. **Educ:** Tex A&M-Univ. **Career:** Football player (retired); Minnesota Vikings defensive tackle, 1990-2000; Seattle Seahawks, defensive tackle, 2001-04. **Honors/Awds:** All-Decade Team, Nat Football League; Hall of Fame, Division II Football; College Football Hall of Fame, 2008.

RANDLE, LUCIOUS A.
Educator. **Personal:** Born Aug 15, 1927, McGregor, TX; married Berdine C Reese; children: Lydia Louise. **Educ:** BS, 1949; MEd, 1953; Univ Tex. **Career:** OJ Thomas High Sch, 1949-57; Charlie Brown High Sch, 1957-58; Worthing High Sch, sci teacher, 1958-62; Attucks Jr High Sch, teacher, part-time prin, 1962-70; Homefinders Real Estate Inc, co broker, 1965-70; Miss Lucy's Acad & Early Childhood Educ Ctr, owner-dir, 1969; Robert E Lee Sr High Sch, Houston Independent Sch Dist, vice prin, 1970; Friendship Realty Co, owner-broker, 1970; Homestead Road Sch Dance, owner, 1971. **Orgs:** NEA; TSTA Houston Prin Asn; Nat Asn Real Estate Brokers; Houston Realtors Asn; Tex Realtors Asn; N Forst Task Force Orgn; Fontaine-Scenic Woods Civic Club; Masonic Lodge; Lions' Club. **Honors/Awds:** Teacher of Year, 1955; Real Estate Salesman of Year, 1965; hon mem FFA Award, 1973; Community Service Award, Nat Coun Negro Women, 1974. **Military Serv:** AUS, signal corps, med br oc classification, 1951-53.

RANDLE, THERESA ELLEN
Actor. **Personal:** Born Dec 27, 1964, Los Angeles, CA. **Educ:** Beverly Hills Col. **Career:** Films: Maid to Order, 1987; Near Dark, 1987; Easy Wheels, 1989; The King of New York, 1990; The Guardian, 1990; Heart Condition, 1990; The Five Heartbeats, 1990; Jungle Fever, 1991; Malcolm X, 1992; CB4, 1993; Sugar Hill, 1994; Beverly Hills Cop III, 1994; Bad Boys, 1995; Girl 6, 1996; Space Jam, 1996; Spawn, 1997; Bad Boys II, 2003; The Hunt for Eagle One,voice, 2006; The Hunt for Eagle One: Crash Point, voice, 2006; "Ink", 2009, "Shit Year", 2009; TV series:"A Different World", 1989; "Seinfeld", 1991; "Duckman: Private Dick/Family Man", 1997; "Livin' for Love: The Natalie Cole Story", 2000; "Partners &Crime", 2003; "Law & Order: Criminal Intent", 2006; "State of Mind", 2007; "Lost & Found", 2007; Passion Fishing, 2007; Helpy Helperpants, 2007; O Rose, Thou Art Sick, 2007. **Business Addr:** Actress, c/o William Morris Agency, 151 El Camino Dr, Beverly Hills, CA 90212, **Business Phone:** (310)859-4000.

RANDLE, WILMA J E. See RANDLE, WILMA JEAN-ELIZABETH EMANUEL.

RANDLE, WILMA JEAN-ELIZABETH EMANUEL (WILMA J E RANDLE)
Journalist. **Personal:** Born Apr 20, 1955, Chicago, IL; daughter of Emanuel Randle and Ruth Helen. **Educ:** Rosary Col, River Forest, IL, BA, hist, commun arts, 1977; Univ Southern Calif, MA, int journ, 1991. **Career:** Chicago Independent Bulletin, news ed, 1977-78; The Maynard Inst Journ Educ, fac, summer prog, 1978, 1986; Muskegon Chronicle, reporter; St Paul Pioneer Press Dispatch, reporter, columnist, 1984-88; Chicago Tribune, bus reporter, 1988. **Orgs:** Nat Asn Black Journalists; Int Woman's Media Found; dir, African Women's Media Ctr, Dakar, Senegal. **Honors/Awds:** Int Women's Media Found Int CNF, delegate, 1990; Univ Southern Calif, Ctr for Int Journalism Fel, 1990; Davenport Bus & Econs Reporting Fel, 1984. **Home Addr:** 1434 W Thome Ave, Chicago, IL 60660.

RANDOLPH, DR. BERNARD CLYDE
Physician. **Personal:** Born May 22, 1922, New York, NY; son of William F and Jessie K Briggs; married Bille Jean Coleman; children: Dana Grace, Bernard C Jr, MD & Paul Allen Esq. **Educ:** City Col NY, BS, 1943; Howard Univ Col Med, MD, 1947. **Career:** Mound City Med Forum, pres, 1963-65; Mo Pan-Med Asn, pres, 1966-67; Talent Rec Coun, Nat Med Asn, chmn, 1972-81; Pvt Pract, physician, currently. **Orgs:** Founder & pres, St Louis Coun Env Health & Safety; past pres, Gamma Chapter Chi Deltu Mu Frat; Phi Beta Sigma Frat; life mem & golden heritage mem, NAACP, Nat Health Comn; chair, St. Louis Br, NCP, Health & Hosp Comn; chair, Health & Hosp Comn; chmn Health Comn, 5th Senatorial Dist Corp & Prof Round Table; Selection Comm,

Dorothy I Height Lifetime Achievement Award, 5th Biennial Symposium on Minorities, the Medically Underserved & Cancer, 1995. **Honors/Awds:** Mission to W Africa Nat Med Asn, 1961; NMA delegate Conference on Hosp Discrimination Pres John F Kennedy, 1963; Practitioner of the Year, Nat Med Asn 1988; Community Service Award, Legal Serv Eastern Mo, 1989; Awards for fifty years of med practice, Howard Univ Med Alumni Asn & Mo State Med Asn. **Military Serv:** USAF, capt, 1952-54. **Business Addr:** Physician, 3737 N Kingshighway, Saint Louis, MO 63115, **Business Phone:** (314)383-1746.

RANDOLPH, LAURA B
Publishing executive. **Personal:** Born Aug 1, 1957, Washington, DC; daughter of Horace and Anna; married Ronny Lancaster. **Educ:** George Wash Univ, BA, 1979; Georgetown Univ Law Ctr, JD, 1987. **Career:** US Dept Health & Human Serv, regulations analyst, 1980-82, health policy specialist, 1982-84, prog analyst, 1984-85, legal assistance specialist, 1985-87; Ebony, journalist & writer, 1987-96, managing ed, 1996-99; Johnson Publishing Co Inc, ed, 1987-. **Orgs:** US Senate/House Press Gallery, 1987; White House Correspondents Asn, 1992-. **Honors/Awds:** Superior Achievement Award, US Dept Health & Human Serv, Secy HHS, 1982; NAACP Image Award, 1996. **Home Addr:** 76 Sheridan St NE, Washington, DC 20011. **Business Addr:** Editor, Johnson Publishing Co, 1750 Pennsylvania Ave NW Suite 1201, Washington, DC 20011, **Business Phone:** (202)393-5860.

RANDOLPH, LEONARD WASHINGTON
Police officer. **Personal:** Born Oct 15, 1954, Newark, NJ; son of Leonard Randolph Sr and LaVera Conover Randolph. **Educ:** Correction Officers Training Acad, Trenton, NJ, 1981; New Jersey State Police Acad, Sea Girt, NJ, drug enforcement, 1981; Correction Offrs Training Acad, Trenton, NJ, hostage negotiations hostage trainer, 1985; Div Criminal Justice, Lawrenceville, NJ, co & state investr, 1991; FBI Training Acad, Gloucester Co Col, Gloucester, NJ, 1993; Middlesex Co Police Acad, Interviewing & Interrogation Techniques, Union, NJ, 1994; Bergen Co Police Acad, NJ Narcotica Task Force, Top Gun Street Survival Training, Mahwah, NJ, 1996; NY State Police Acad, Interviewing & Interrogation Techniques, Albany, NY, 1997. **Career:** NJ Dept Corrections, E Jersey State Prison, correctional officer, 1979-90, Internal Affairs Inc, 1990-, info officer & sgt-at-arms, currently. **Orgs:** Chap deleg, Men & Women Justice NJ Coun Charter Member Nat Black Police Asn, 1988-; chap deleg, Men & Women Justice, Nat Black Police Asn, 1988-; first vpres, Nat Bd Men & Women Justice, 1989-; pres, Men & Women Justice, NJ Chap, 1989-; Social Fel Inc, NJ Grand chap, 1997; Grove Phi Grove; Nat Asn Advan Colored People. **Business Addr:** Senior Investigator, Information Officer and Sergeant-at-Arms, New Jersey Department of Corrections, 168 Frontage Rd, Newark, NJ 07114.

RANDOLPH, LONNIE MARCUS
Lawyer, state government official, judge. **Personal:** Born Aug 7, 1949, Auburn, AL; son of Charles Boyd and Gertha Mae; married Linda Diane, Aug 25, 1973; children: Lakesha & Lonnie Marcus II. **Educ:** Northern Ill Univ, BS, 1973; John Marshall Law Sch, JD, 1978. **Career:** State Ill, asst state's atty, 1978-79; State Ind, dep prosecutor, 1979-81; self employed, atty, 1981-; State Ind, state sen, 1993-98; Lonnie Randolph & Assocs, atty, currently. **Orgs:** Bd mem, NAACP, 1983-; Lions Club, 1983-; Exchange Club, 1983-; adv bd mem, Boys Club. **Honors/Awds:** Talent Award, Northern Ill Univ, 1972; Spark Plug Award, Black Law Stud Asn, 1978; Image Award, Fred Hampton Scholar Fund, 1983. John Marshall Law Sch Service Award, E Chicago, 1991; Recognition Award, NAACP; Ind State Sen, Freshman Legislator of th Year, 1991. **Business Addr:** Attorney, Lonnie M Randolph & Associates, Law Office of Lonnie M Randolph, 1919 E Columbus Dr, East Chicago, IN 46312, **Business Phone:** (219)397-5531.

RANDOLPH, ROBERT LEE
Educator, economist. **Personal:** Born Jan 2, 1926, East St Louis, IL; children: Heather. **Educ:** DePauw Univ, BA, 1948; Univ Ill Urbana, MS, 1954, PhD, 1958; Case Western Reserve Univ, attended 1960; Univ MI, PhD, 1962. **Career:** Springfield Col MA, from instructor to assoc prof, 1958-65, chmn dept, 1960-63, dir evening & summer schs, 1960-64; Job Corps, dep assoc dir, 1965-67; Equal Employment Oppor Commn Wash, dep exec dir, 1967-68; Chicago State Univ, exec vpres, 1969-73; Westfield Col MA, pres, 1973-79; MA State Col Syst, vice chancellor, 1979-81; Ala State Univ, pres, 1981-83; Univ Montevallo AL, prof economics, 1983-. **Orgs:** Vpres Springfield Urban League, 1962-66; pres, Randolph Asn Birmingham AL, Boston 1983-; Am Asn State Colls & Univs; Am Asn Polit & Social Scis; Am Economic Asn; Phi Delta Kappa; Alpha Phi Omega; Kappa Alpha Psi. **Honors/Awds:** Danforth Foundation Award, 1943; State Ill Scholar, 1952-56; Bailey Fel, 1957-58; Carnegie Fel, 1962; Vpres Award, Excellence Pub Serv, US Govt, 1967; Outstanding Alumni Award, Lincoln HS E St Louis, 1973.

RANDOLPH, WILLIE LARRY
Baseball executive, baseball player. **Personal:** Born Jul 6, 1954, Holly Hill, SC; married Gretchen Foster; children: Taniesha, Chantre, Andre & Ciara. **Career:** Baseball player (retired), baseball executive; Pittsburgh Pirates, infielder, 1975; NY Yankees, infielder, 1976-88, asst Gen Mgr, 1993, coach, 1994-2004; Los Angeles Dodgers, infielder, 1989-90; Oakland Athletics, infielder, 1990; Milwaukee Brewers, infielder, 1992; NYMets, infielder, 1992, mgr, 2005-08. **Honors/Awds:** James P Dawson Award, 1976; Silver Slugger Award, 1980; Nat League All-Star Team, 1989; World Series champion, 1977 & 1978; Leadership Award, 100 Black Men, 2005; Sportsman of the Year Award, 2005; Koby Mandell Foundation Humanitarian Award, 2006. **Business Addr:** Manager, New York Mets, Shea Stadium, 123-01 Roosevelt Ave, Flushing, NY 11368, **Business Phone:** (718)507-6387.

RANDOLPH, ZACH (ZACHARY RANDOLPH)
Basketball player. **Personal:** Born Jul 16, 1981, Marion, IN. **Educ:** Mich State Univ. **Career:** Portland Trail Blazers, forward, 2001-07; New York Knicks, 2007-09; Los Angeles Clippers, 2008-09. **Honors/Awds:** NBA's Most Improved Player, 2003-04. **Business Addr:** Basketball Player, Memphis Grizzlies, PO Box 3463, Memphis, TN 38173.*

RANDOLPH, ZACHARY. **See RANDOLPH, ZACH.**

RANDOLPH-JASMINE, CAROL DAVIS
Television news anchorperson, lawyer. **Personal:** Born in St Louis, MO; daughter of John and Clarice; married Frank Jasmine, Jan 1, 1980. **Educ:** Catholic Univ Am, Columbus Sch Law, law degree, 1977; Wash Univ, St Louis, masters degree; Fisk Univ, BA. **Career:** Wash Times, columnist, 1987-88; WUSA TV, talk show host, 1987-90; Gold, Farb, Kaufman, lawyer, 1987-90; O'Toole & Rothwell, lawyer, 1990-93; Court TV, anchor, 1993-. **Orgs:** DC Comn Arts, comnr, 1987-; Women's Mus, adv bd; AFTRA, 1970-; Zonta, 1992-; Links Inc, pres, vpres, 1984-; ACLU, nomination comt, 1988-93. **Honors/Awds:** Honourable doctorate from Bowie University. **Business Addr:** Anchor, Court TV, 600 3rd Ave 2nd Fl, New York, NY 10016, **Business Phone:** (212)692-7851.*

RANDY JACKSON, RANDALL DARIUS. **See JACKSON, RANDY.**

RANGEL, CHARLES BERNARD
Congressperson (U.S. federal government). **Personal:** Born Jun 11, 1930, New York, NY; married Alma Carter, 1964; children: Steven & Alicia. **Educ:** NY Univ, BS, bus admin, 1957; St Johns Univ Law Sch, LLB, 1960, JD, 1968. **Career:** Weaver Evans Wingate & Wright, atty, 1960; pvt law pract, 1960-61; Southern Dist NY, asst atty, 1961-62; NY State Assembly, 72nd Legis Dist Cent Harlem, mem, 1967-70; US House Rep, 18th Dist, rep, 1971-73, 19th Dist, rep, 1973-83, 16th Dist, rep, 1983-93, 15th Cong Dist, rep, 1993-. **Orgs:** House Judiciary Comt, 1973-74; co-founder & chmn, Cong Black Caucus, 1974-75; House Comt Ways & Means, 1975-; chmn, House Select Comt Narcotics Abuse & Control, 1976-93; dean, NY State Cong Deleg, 1993-; Joint Comt Taxation, 1995-; Cong Adv US Trade Rep, 1995-; Pres Export Coun, 1995-; NY Bar Asn; 369th Vet Asn; chmn, House Ways & Means Comt, 2007-; Community Educ Prog. **Military Serv:** AUS, sgt, 1948-52; Bronze Star; Purple Heart; US Korean Presidential Citations; Four Battle Stars. **Business Addr:** Representative, US House of Representatives, 15th District, 163 W 125th St Suite 737, New York, NY 10027, **Business Phone:** (212)663-3900.

RANKIN, DR. EDWARD ANTHONY
Surgeon, college teacher, physician. **Personal:** Born Jul 6, 1940, Holly Springs, MS; son of Robbie Lee and Edgar E Jr; married Dr Frances Espy; children: Tony Jr & Marc. **Educ:** Lincoln Univ, BS, biol, 1961; Meharry Med Col, MD, 1965. **Career:** Walter Reed Gen Hosp, rotating internship, 1965, orthop surg residency, 1970; Howard Univ Sch Med, from asst prof to assoc prof, 1973-89, prof, 1989-; Georgetown Univ Sch Med, assoc prof, 1982-; Providence Hosp, chief orthop surg, 1977-; DC Gen Hosp, actg chief children's orthop, 2000; Sports Med Today, ed bd; ed bd orthop, currently. **Orgs:** Eastern Ortho Asn, 1973; Am Col Surgeons, 1975; deleg bd coun, Am Acad Ortho Surg, 1975, 1982-; Am Orthop Foot & Ankle Soc, 1977; Am Soc SurgHand, 1979; comt mem, Regional Advisors Am Col Surgeons, 1980-; oral examr, Am Bd Ortho Surg, 1980-84, 1993-; Wash Soc Surg Hand, 1983-; comt mem, Regional Advisors Am Acad Ortho Surg, 1984-; Am Ortho Asn, 1988; pres, Metro Wash Soc Surg Hand, 1989; sec tres, pres, Wash Ortho Soc,1989-; vpres & pres, Metro Wash Chap, Am Col Surg, 1989-91; prog chmn, Liberia Proj, Ortho Overseas, 1989; pres, Wash Acad Surg, 1998; bd dir, Am Acad Ortho Surgeons, 1996-98; secy, Am Acad Ortho Surgeons, 2001-04; Lincoln Univ Nat Alumni Asn. **Honors/Awds:** Association's Distinguished Alumni Award, Lincoln Univ Nat Alumni Asn, 1992; Pub Works 2 Chap Award, DC Med Soc Comt Serv, 2002; received number of awards. **Military Serv:** AUS, major, 1965-73; US Naval Acad, army comdr med, 1973; USA, 1971; 12th Evacuation Hosp, Repub Vietnam, chief orthop; 95th Evacuation Hosp, Repub Vietnam, chief orthop; Walson Army Hosp, chief orthop; Bronze Star Medal; Army Commendation Medal. **Business Addr:** Chief Orthopaedic Surgion, Providence Hospital, 1160 Varnum St NE Suite 312, Washington, DC 20017-2110.*

RANKIN, DR. MARC E.
Orthopedic surgeon. **Career:** Rankin Orthop & Sports Med Ctr, orthopedic surgeon, currently. **Business Addr:** Orthopedic Surgeon, Rankin Orthopedic & Sports Medicine Ctr, 1160 Varnum St NE Suite 312, Washington, DC 20017, **Business Phone:** (202)526-7031.

RANKIN, MARLENE OWENS
Foundation executive, executive director. **Personal:** Born Apr 19, 1939, Cleveland, OH; daughter of James Cleveland (Jesse) and Minnie Ruth Solomon; married Stuart McLean, Nov 19, 1961; children: Stuart Owen. **Educ:** Ohio State Univ, Columbus, OH, BSW, 1961; Univ Chicago, IL, MSW, 1978. **Career:** Cook County Dept Pub Aid, Cs Div, Chicago, IL, social worker, 1961-66; Chicago Youth Ctrs & Proj Learn, Chicago, IL, social worker, 1968-69; Chicago Comt Urban Opportunity & Model Cities, Chicago, IL, planning unit coord, 1969-74; Govs Office Human Resources, social serv planner, 1974-75; United Charities Chicago, IL, clin social worker, personnel assoc, dir personnel, 1978-88; Mus Sci & Indust, Chicago, IL, dir human resource mgt, 1988-90; The Jesse Owens Found, Chicago, IL, exec dir, 1990-. **Orgs:** Acad Cert Social Workers, 1980-; bd dirs, The Jesse Owens Found, 1980-; bd mem, OSU Alumni Asn, 1985-90; sustaining mem, bd dirs, Hyde Park Neighborhood Club, 1985-; bd dirs, City Chicago Bd Ethics, 1987-92; Bd dirs, Univ Chicago Sch Social Serv Adminr, 1990-93; chmn, OSU Annual Fund, 1991-95; bd, Sporting Chance Found, 1995-. **Honors/Awds:** Annual Orchid Award, Top Ladies of Distinction, 1992; Distinguished Service Award, OSU, 1993. **Special Achievements:** 100 Women Making A Difference, Today's Chicago Woman, 1992. **Business Addr:** Executive Director, The Jesse Owens Foundation, 333 N Michigan Ave Suite 932, Chicago, IL 60601, **Business Phone:** (312)263-8222.

RANKIN, MICHAEL L
Judge. **Personal:** Born in Holly Springs, MS; married Zinora M Mitchell; children: Lee, John-Michael, Michael Joseph & Everette. **Educ:** Lincoln Univ, Jefferson City, Mo, BA, 1967; Howard Univ Sch Law, JD, 1970. **Career:** US Dept Justice, staff atty; US Attys Off, US Attys Off Felony Trial Div, Wash, DC, dep chief; Dist VI, asst fed pub defender, 1976, actg fed pub defender, spec asst US; Wesley Williams Assocs, pvt pract, 1978-80; presiding judge criminal & spec operations divs Ct; Dist Columbia, asst US atty; Super Ct DC, Wash, DC, judge, Criminal Div, assoc judge, judge, currently. **Orgs:** Master, Charlotte E Ray Am Inn Ct. **Military Serv:** AUS, Rep Viet Nam. **Business Addr:** Judge, Court of the District of Columbia, Moultrie Courthouse, Rm 5630 500 Ind Ave NW Chamber, Washington, DC 20001, **Business Phone:** (202)879-1220.

RANKIN, SHEILA
Businessperson. **Career:** NCR Corp, dir bus opers, dir external reporting & policies, 2003-. **Business Addr:** Director of External Reporting, Policies, NCR Corp, 1700 S Patterson Blvd, Dayton, OH 45479, **Business Phone:** (937)445-1936.

RANN, DR. EMERY LOUVELLE
Physician. **Personal:** Born Mar 9, 1914, Keyestone, WV; son of Emery Rann Sr and Vicie Froe; married Flossie Aurelia Fox; children: Judith Rann Thompson, Emery L III, J D, Lara Diane, Jonathan Cheshire & Flossie Aurelia. **Educ:** Johnson C Smith Univ, BS, cum laude, 1934; Univ Mich, MS, 1936; Meharry Med Col, MD, 1948; Johnson C Smith Univ, ScD, hon, 1981. **Career:** Old N State Med Soc, pres, 1959; Mecklenburg Co Med Soc, v pres 1958; NC Acad Fmly Pract, dist dir, 1981; Imhotep Conf For Hosp Integ, chmn, 1961-63; Mediation Servs Forsyth County, exec dir, currently. **Orgs:** Pres, Nat Med Asn, 1973-74; fel, Am Acad Family Pract, 1975; past chmn, bd trustees, Johnson C Smith Univ; boule sire archon Sigma Pi Phi Fraternity, 1968; life mem, Alpha Phi Alpha. **Honors/Awds:** Award of Merit, Johnson C Smith Univ, 1954, 1968; Doctor of the Year, Old N State, 1961; Charlotte Med Soc, 1972; ZOB merit ZOB Sor, 1981; merit scs award, Family Practice Div NMA, 1984; Southeast Regional Sire Archon, Sigma Pi Phi, 1989-91; initiated into Alpha Omega Alpha Meharry Chap, 1991. **Special Achievements:** First black physician to be accepted, Mecklenburg County Med Soc. **Military Serv:** USNA, capt, 1955-57. **Home Addr:** 203 Todd St, Belmont, NC 28012-3048. **Business Addr:** Executive Director, Mediation Services of Forsyth County, City Plaza Bldg 225 W 5th St Suite 110, PO Box 436, Winston-Salem, NC 27101-0436, **Business Phone:** (336)724-2870.*

RANSBURG, FRANK S.
Educator. **Personal:** Born Jan 29, 1943, Keatchie, LA; married Ivory Bowie; children: Ursula. **Educ:** Southern Univ, BA, 1965; La State Univ, MA, 1970; Loyola Univ, New Orleans, grad, inst polit, 1994. **Career:** Southern Univ, counr, 1965-69, asst dean, 1969, instr, 1969; Jr Div La State Univ, counr, 1969-73; HS Rel La State Univ, asst dir, 1975; Southern Univ, dean stud act, 1969-81, dir, int stud affairs, 1981-87, dir planning, 1987-91, asst to chancellor, 1991-97, vice chancellor stud affairs, 1997-99; Cleo Fields Gov, state campaign mgr; polit consult, 1999; Southern Univ & A&M Col, Baton Rouge, instr, polit sci. **Orgs:** Admin asst, Lt Gov's Off, 1973, 1974; La Comn Campaign Pract, 1974; hon mem, La State Sen, 1974; Am Polit Sci Asn; Southern Polit Sci Asn; Am Asn Univ Profs; Nat Asn Advan Colored People; Am Personnel & Guid Asn; Nat Asn Personnel Workers; Old State

Capitol Bd; pres, Common Cause La; bd chair, La Leadership Inst; FOCUS; Baton Rouge Comn Fear & Violence. **Honors/Awds:** Faculty Award, Southern University, 1970. **Home Addr:** 23294 Gen Gardner Lane, Zachary, LA 70791.

RANSBY, BARBARA
College teacher, community activist, writer. **Personal:** Born May 12, 1957, Detroit, MI; married. **Educ:** Columbia Univ, BA, hist, 1984; Univ Mich, MA, hist, 1987, PhD, hist, 1996. **Career:** Inst African Affairs & Dept Hist, Columbia Univ, res asst, 1982-84; Woodrow Wilson Fel Found, Nat Mellon fel, 1984-86; Univ Mich Rackham Grad Sch Fellow, Michigan Minority Merit fel, 1986-90; Univ Mich, instr, 1986-87, 1989, teaching asst, 1987, res asst, 1988; Museum African Am Hist, curator Nineteenth & Twentieth Century spec proj, 1989-90; Chicago Clergy & Laity Concerned, group trainer, 1992; Crossroads Found, grouptrainer, 1992; DePaul Univ, instr, 1992-95, dir & asst prof, 1995-96; Ancona Sch, consult & group facilitator, 1993; Chicago Hist Soc, consult & panelist, 1993; Mac Arthur Found, consult, 1994; Am Col Testing, consult, 1996; Univ Ill, Dept Hist & Dept African-Am Studies, asst prof, 1996-2002, assoc prof, 2002-; NW Univ, manuscript reviewer, 1997. **Orgs:** Bd mem, Anti-Racism Inst, Clergy & Laity Concerned; bd mem, Chicago Coalition Solidarity Southern Africa; stud mem, Univ Mich, Hist Dept Search Comm; Ed Bd, Jour Race & Class; bd mem, Ella Baker-Nelson Mandela Ctr Anti-Racist Educ, Univ Mich; Asn study Afro-Am Life & Hist; Asn Black Women Historians; Coordinating Comm Women Hist Prof; Orgn Am Historians; co-founder, United Coalition Against Racism; co-founder & co-chairperson, Free S Africa Coordinating Comm. **Honors/Awds:** Women Studies Program fellow, Student Essay Competition Award, 1986; Student Recognition Award for Leadership, Univ Mich, 1987; Annual Peace Award, Women's Action Nuclear Disarmament, 1988; Herman Ausubel Student Award for Achievement in History, Columbia Univ, 1983; Grad Student Research grant, Ford Found & Ctr Afro-Am & African Studies, 1990; Summer Faculty Research Award, DePaul Univ Sch Liberal Arts & Sci, 1993; Office of Social Science Research Seed Fund Initiative, grant, Univ Ill, Chicago, 1996; Gustavas Myer Outstanding Book Award, Simmons Col, 2003; Joan Kelley Prize for best book in women's history, Am Hist Asn, 2003; Letitia Woods Brown Memorial Prize for best book in African American women's history, Asn Black Women Historians, 2003; Lillian Smith Book Award, 2004; CCWH Prelinger Award Winner, 2004. **Special Achievements:** Books: Feminism in Black & White: Reflections on Anita Hill & ClarenceThomas, 1992; The Press for Freedom: African American Newspapers,1827, 1987, 1993; The death penalty in black & white, 1995; Black History Month is a Time To Honor Those Who Shared the Dream, 1997; MIT Self-StudyIs Powerful Lesson For Others In Academia, 1999; Author of numerousarticles & essays. **Business Addr:** Assistant Professor, University of Illinois, Department of African-American Studies, 601 S Morgan St 913 Univ Hall, Chicago, IL 60607-7109, **Business Phone:** (312)996-2961.

RANSIER, FREDERICK L
Lawyer. **Personal:** Born Dec 3, 1949, Brooklyn, NY; son of Frederick L Jr and Doris A; married Kathleen Hayes, Nov 16, 1973; children: Bradley, Charles & Frederick IV. **Educ:** Cent State Univ, BA, polit sci, 1971; Ohio State Univ Col Law, JD, 1974. **Career:** Ohio Atty Gen, ast atty gen, 1974-76; Ransier & Ransier, partner, 1976-; Central State Univ, chair, 1996-2000; Vorys, Sater, Seymour & Pease LLP, Columbus off, partner & atty, currently. **Orgs:** Columbus Bar Asn, 1974-; Nat Bar Asn; Ohio State Bar Asn; Am Bar Asn; law dir, Village Urbancrest, Ohio, 1978-98; comnr, 1987-99, Columbus Munic Civil Serv Comn, pres 1995-2000; panel trustee, Off US Trustee, 1988-; Columbus Bar Found, 1999-; chair, Cent State Univ Bd Trustees; chair, Supreme Ct Ohio, Bd Comnrs Unauthorized Pract Law, 1999-; Columbus City Coun, 2000-; Nat Asn Bankruptcy Trustees; Am Bankruptcy Inst. **Honors/Awds:** Community Service Award, Columbus Bar Asn, 1990; Minority Business Advocate Award, Soc Nat Bank, 1993; Urban Columbus Urban League Equal Opportunity Day Award of Excellence, 1998; Alumnus of the Year Award, Alumni Asn, Cent State Univ, 1999; Presidential Citation, Nat Asn Equal Opportunity Higher Educ, 1999;Col of Law Alumni Community Service Award, Ohio State Univ, 2002. **Business Addr:** Attorney, Partner, Vorys Sater Seymour & Pease LLP, Columbus Office, 52 E Gay St, PO Box 1008, Columbus, OH 43216-1008, **Business Phone:** (614)464-8226.

RANSOM, DERRICK
Football player, consultant. **Personal:** Born Sep 13, 1976, Indianapolis, IN. **Educ:** Univ Cincinnati, BBA & Fin Admin, 1994-98. **Career:** Player (retired), fin Consultant; Kans City Chiefs, defensive tackle, 1998-2002; Ariz Cardinals, def tackle, 2003; Jacksonville Jaguars, def tackle, 2004-05: UBS, financial advisor, 2006-07; AXA Advisors, fin consultant, currently.

RANSOM, GARY ELLIOTT
Judge. **Personal:** Born Dec 23, 1941, New Brunswick, NJ; married Gloria P. **Educ:** Rutgers Univ, BA, Econ, 1965; Univ Pac-McGeorge Sch Law, JD, 1974. **Career:** Judge (retired); Sacramento Cty Pub Defenders Off, asst pub defender, 1974-81; NJ Div Civil Rights, field rep, 1965-66; Ct Appeals-Third Appellate Dist, justice pro tem, 1983; Sacramento Munic Cty Dist, judge, 1981-88; Calif Super Ct, judge. **Orgs:** Bd dir, Planned Parenthood Asn Sacramento, 1978-81; pres, Wiley Manuel Bar Asn, 1981; bd dir, Family Serv Agency Greater Sacramento, 1981-; Calif Judges Asn, 1981-; Sigma Pi Phi, Gamma Epsilon Boule, Prince Hall F&AM thirty third Deg; life mem, Kappa Alpha Psi; bd dir, Easter Seals Soc Gr Sacramento, 1978-; life mem, No Calif Peace Officers Asn; vpres, Calif Asn Black Lawyers, 1981; Int Platform Asn; pres, bd dir, Greater Sacramento Easter Seals Soc, 1988-. **Honors/Awds:** Phi Nu Pi Award, Kappa Alpha Psi Frat, 1981; Sacramento Wardens & Masters Achievement Award, 1982; Earnest E Robinson Jr Award, Black Law Stud Asn Univ Pac, 1982; Bernard S Jefferson Jurist Award, Calif Asn Black Lawyers, 1989; McKusick Award, Friends Outside, 1994. **Military Serv:** USAF, capt, 1966-71, second Lt. **Home Addr:** 1406 Commons Dr, Sacramento, CA 95825.

RANSOM, LETICIA BUFORD
Consultant. **Personal:** Born Dec 25, 1964, Chicago, IL; daughter of Harold G and Mary F West. **Educ:** Dillard Univ, BA, 1987; Roosevelt Univ, Chicago, IL, MBA, 1995. **Career:** Allied Educ Corp, financial aid dir, 1988-90; Motorola, credit analyst,1990-91, field inventory analyst, 1991-92, COF syst support, group analyst, 1992-93, customer oper adminr, 1993-99, price book mgr, 2000-04; Bryn Mawr Community Church, acct, 1995-2001; Chicago Urban League, Anheuser-Busch Scholar & Coors Excellence Prog, educ specialist, 2004-. **Orgs:** Life mem Nat Black MBA Asn, Chicago, 1995-; UNCF Inter Alumni Coun, 1987-;chair, Ebony Fashion Fair, 1995-2001; chair, UNCF Scholar Pageant, 2000; Dist bd dirs, Boy Scouts Am, 1994-; pres, treas, 1995-, Dillard Univ Alumni, Chicago Chap; Motorola Finance Club, 1991-97; pres, Better Investors Through Educ, 1997-2001. **Honors/Awds:** Service Award, Dillard Univ, Steering Comt, Dillard Alumni Campaigns,1993-95; Motorola Worldwide Employee Recognition Award, 1995, 1997;Outstanding Alumni, 1996; President's Outstanding Service Award, 2000. **Special Achievements:** Author: LinkAge, 2000; AgeLess Pain, 2006. **Business Addr:** Education Specialist, Anheuser-Busch Scholarship & Coors Program, Chicago Urban League, 4510 S Michigan Ave, Chicago, IL 60653-3898, **Business Phone:** (773)285-5800.

RANSOM, LILLIE
College administrator, teacher. **Personal:** Daughter of Frank L and Martha Louise; children: Christopher Leslie & Michael Arthur. **Educ:** Oberlin Col, Oberlin, Ohio, BA, 1976; Gallaudet Univ, Wash, DC, MA, 1979; Univ Md, Col Park, MD, PhD, 1996. **Career:** Univ Md, Col Park Scholars Prog (Honors), teacher, 1998-2004; Univ Md, Col Pk Scholars & Am Cultures, fac co-dir & lectr, 1998-2004, interim exec dir & asst dean, 2003; Gallaudet Univ, Commun Studies, assoc prof, 2002, 2004-; Md Sch for the Deaf, pres, 2004-. **Orgs:** Bd trustees & vice chair, Md Sch Deaf. **Business Phone:** (202)651-2731.

RANSOM, DR. PRESTON L
Educator, school administrator. **Personal:** Born Jan 2, 1936, Peoria, IL; son of James and Spezzie; married Mildred D Murphy; children: Patricia Lynn & Michael Murphy. **Educ:** Univ Ill, Urbana-Champaign, BS, 1962, MS, 1965, PhD, 1969. **Career:** Raytheon Co, Bedford, MA, elec engr, 1962-63; Univ Ill, grad res asst, 1963-67, instr 1967-70, asst prof, 1970-72, assoc prof, 1972-88, prof, asst dean & dir, cont engr educ, prof emer, currently; Univ Ill, Paul V Golvin teaching fel, 1967-68; Univ Col London, hon res fel, 1976. **Orgs:** Sr mem, Inst Elec & Electronic Engrs, 1970-; Am Soc Engr Educ, 1972; Optical Soc Am, 1972-; Ete Kappa Nu Honorary Soc. **Business Addr:** Emeritus Professor, University of Illinois Urbana-Champaign, 422 Eng Hall 1308 W Green St, Urbana, IL 61801, **Business Phone:** (217)333-6634.

RASBERRY, ROBERT EUGENE
Clergy, educator. **Personal:** Born in Philadelphia, PA; married Gloria E Hooper; children: Roslyn, Robert, John, Denise. **Educ:** Morgan State Col, AB, 1955; Howard Univ, sch soc work, 1956; NY Univ, MA, 1958; Andover Newton Theol Sch, BD, 1966. **Career:** Clergy, Educator (retired); Big Bros Baltimore, social case worker, 1954-56; Bureau Child Welfare NYC, social investigator, 1956-57; First Baptist, pastor, 1957-59; Friendship Baptist, pastor, 1959-62; Bethany Baptist Church Syracuse NY, pastor; Messiah Baptist, pastor, 1962-65; Mt Calvary Baptist Church Springfield MA, pastor, 1965-73; Springfield Tech Community Col, asst prof, 1969-73; Episcopal Church Atonement Westerfield MA, asst to rector, 1970-72; Bethany Baptist Church Syracuse, pastor; State Dept Correctional Servs, chaplain. **Orgs:** Exec comt, Am Asn Univ Prof; Urban League; Human Righst Comn; Protestant Comn Ministries; bd dir, Syracuse Univ Hill Corp Syracuse Chap OIC's Am; coun rep, NY State Coun Churchs; past exec comt, TABCOM; asn moderator, Pioneer Valley Am Baptist Churchs MA. **Honors/Awds:** Host producer WSYR Words & Music Sunday Morning Syracuse; ten most watchable men Post Standard Newspaper Syracuse, 1977; Nat Forsensic Coun; national honor society Philosophy.

RASBY, WALTER HERBERT
Football player. **Personal:** Born Sep 7, 1972, Washington, DC; married Cortney. **Educ:** Wake Forest Univ. **Career:** Pittsburgh Steelers, tight end, 1994; Carolina Panthers, 1995-97; Detroit Lions, 1998-2000; Wash Redskins, 2001-02 & 2004; New Orleans Saints, 2003; Pittsburgh Steelers, 2004-05; New England Patriots, 2006; New York Jets, 2006.

RASHAD, DR. AHMAD (ROBERT EARL MOORE)
Broadcaster. **Personal:** Born Nov 19, 1949, Portland, OR; married Phylicia Ayers-Allen, Jan 1, 1985 (divorced 2001); children: Condola Phylea; married Sale Johnson, Jan 1, 2007; married Matilda Johnson, Jan 1, 1976 (divorced 1979); children: Maiysha & Ahmad Jr. **Educ:** Univ Ore; Univ Puget Sound, PhD, jour. **Career:** Football player (retired), broadcaster; St Louis Cardinals, 1972-73, Buffalo Bills, 1974-76, Seattle Sea hawks, 1976, Minn Vikings, 1976-82; KMSP-TV, Minneapolis, MN, host monday night football preview show; WCCO-TV, Minneapolis, MN, sports reporter; Real TV, host; NBC Sports, host, studio anchor, game reporter, sportscaster, 1982; NBA Entertainment, exec producer, currently. **Orgs:** Bd trustees, Univ Ore; Omega Psi Phi Fraternity Inc. **Honors/Awds:** MVP award, Pro Bowl, 1979; Emmy Award; University's Pioneer Award; Col Football Hall of Fame, 2007; Honorary Degree of Doctor of Journalism, Univ Puget Sound. **Special Achievements:** Author, Rashad: Vikes, Mikes and Something on the Backside. **Business Addr:** Executive Producer, NBA Entertainment, 450 Harmon Meadow Blvd, Secaucus, NJ 07094, **Business Phone:** (201)865-7700.

RASHAD, JOHARI MAHASIN
Government official. **Personal:** Born Mar 13, 1951, Washington, DC; daughter of Millie Lucerita Adams and Henry Jones; children: Chekesha Wajeehah. **Educ:** Howard Univ, BA, 1976; Univ DC, MBA, 1981; Howard Univ, PhD, 1997. **Career:** US Customs Serv, GS-4, clerk typist, 1977; US Civil Serv Comn, standardization specialist, 1976; Off Personal Mgt, instr, 1980; US Coast Guard, employee develop specialist, 1986; Bur Land Mgt, personnel mgt specialist, 1990; US Off Personnel Mgt, sr human resources specialist, currently; Lutheran Col Wash Semester, instr. **Orgs:** Am Asn Univ Women; Am Soc Training & Develop; Int Commun Asn; Nat Career Develop Asn; Int Asn Career Mgt Professionals; Capitol Hill Seventh Day Adventist Church, Wash, DC. **Honors/Awds:** Exceptional Service Award, Downtown Jaycees, 1984; Outstanding Service Award, Downtown Jaycees, 1985; Directors Service Award, 1986; President's Distinguished Service Award, 1987; Special Achievement Award, Bur Land Mgt, 1992; Board of Directors Award, Metro-DC Chap, ASTD 1998; Volunteer Partnership Award, 1998. **Home Addr:** 430 M St SW Suite 706, Washington, DC 20024-2650, **Home Phone:** (202)484-2171. **Business Addr:** Senior Human Resources Specialist, US Office of Personnel Management, 1900 E St NW, Washington, DC 20415-1000, **Business Phone:** (202)606-1800.

RASHAD, PHYLICIA
Artist. **Personal:** Born Jun 19, 1948, Houston, TX; daughter of Andrew A and Vivian Ayers; married William Lancelot Bowles Jr, Jan 1, 1972 (divorced 1975); children: William Lancelot Bowles III; married Victor Willis, Jan 1, 1978 (divorced 1980); married Ahmad, Dec 14, 1985 (divorced 2001); children: Condola Phyleia. **Educ:** Howard Univ, BFA, 1970. **Career:** Off-Broadway & Broadway actress: Into the Woods; Dream girls; The Whiz;Ain't Supposed to Die a Natural Death; The Old Settler, 2001; Touched byan Angel: The Last Chapter, 2002; Great Women of Television & Comedy, 2003; A Raisin in the Sun, 2008; TV shows: soap opera, One Life to Live; The Cosby Show, 1984-92, 2005, 2007; Cosby, 1996-2000; TV specials: "Uncle Tom's Cabin", 1987; "False Witness", 1989; "Polly", 1989; "Polly Once Again", 1990; "Jailbirds", 1990; "Tough Love", 1994; "Touched by an Angel", 1994-2002; "The Old Settler", 2001; "Bull"; "Murder, She Wrote:The Last Free Man", 2001; "PBS Hollywood Presents", 2001; The Last Chapter, 2002; Character Studies, host, 2005. **Orgs:** Spokesperson, Save the C, 1989-91; spokesperson, Cancer Info Serv, 1990-91; bd dirs, Recruiting New Teachers, 1990-. **Honors/Awds:** Two People's Choice Awards; Image Award, Nat Asn Advan Colored People;Honorary Doctorate of Humanities, Barber-Scotia Col, Concord, NC, 1989; Outstanding Achievement Award, Women Film, 1991; Honoree of the Year, Harvard Found, 1991; Honorary Doctorate, Providence Col, Providence, RI, 1991; Emmy Award, Outstanding Lead Actress in a Comedy Series; Tony Award for Best, 2004. **Special Achievements:** Two Emmy nominations for The Cosby Show; Ace Award nomination for best supporting actress in tv film, Uncle Tom's Cabin. **Business Phone:** (718)392-5600.

RASHEED, FRED
Executive, association executive, president (organization). **Career:** Nat Asn Advan Colored People, co-interim exec dir, Econ Develop Prog, dir; Rasheed Assocs, founder & pres, currently. **Business Phone:** (973)414-8518.

RASHEED, HOWARD S
Executive, educator. **Personal:** Born Feb 3, 1953, Chicago, IL; son of Howard L Lee Sr and Kathlene P Lee; married Barbara; children: Candace, Derick, Hassan & Mikal. **Educ:** Univ West Fla, Pensacola, BS, Mkt, 1978, MBA, Fin, 1979; Fla State Univ, Tallahassee, FL, PhD, bus admin, 1996. **Career:** FSC Bus Develop, fin analyst, 1973-74; AMM Jour, purchasing mgr, 1974-76; Nat Standard Life Ins Co, Pensacola, FL, sales mgr, 1976-79; Southern Bell, acct exec, 1981-84; Ver Val Enterprises, dir fin, 1983-87, exec vpres, fin & admin, 1990, Univ NC-Wilmington, Cameron Sch Bus, Dept Mgt & Mkt, assoc prof, currently; Mgt Training & Educ Consultants Inc, managing dir, 1998-2003; Inst Innovation Inc, Wilmington, NC, chief exec officer, 2003-; Pensacola News

Jour, ed bd. **Orgs:** Dir, Pensacola Pvt Ind Coun, 1982-85; Asn MBA Execs, 1983-87; comnr, Pensacola-Escambia Develop Comn, 1984; dir, Ft Walton Beach Community 100, 1986-; Nat Black MBA Asn, 1987; treas, Haynes Services; founding bd mem, Enterprise Fla Minority Econ Develop Adv Coun; chmn, Pensacola Chamber Com Minority Develop Task Force; 100 Black Men Am; Nat Youth Entrepreneurship; bd trustee, Leadership Pensacola, Charter Graduate. **Honors/Awds:** Outstanding Instructor, Univ W Fla; Outstanding Alumni, Col Bus, Univ W Fla; Emerging Leader of the Year Nominee, Pensacola Chamber Com. **Home Addr:** 16 Neptune Dr, Mary Esther, FL 32569. **Business Addr:** Associate Professor, University of North Carolina at Wilmington, Cameron School of Business, 601 S Col Rd, Wilmington, FL 28403, **Business Phone:** (910)962-3779.

RASHEED, JEROME NAJEE. **See NAJEE, J.**

RASHFORD, DR. JOHN HARVEY
Educator. **Personal:** Born May 10, 1947, Port Antonio Jamaica, West Indies; son of Winifred Jacobs and Hector G; married Grace Maynard. **Educ:** Friends World Col, BA, 1969; City Univ NY, Grad Ctr, MA, PhD, 1982. **Career:** Crossroads Africa, group leader, 1971; City Univ NY, adj lectr; Brooklyn Col, fac, 1974-75; Queens Col, fac, 1977-80; Lehman Col, fac, 1977-82; Rutgers Univ, vis lectr, 1980-82; Col Charleston, prof anthrop, 1983-. **Orgs:** Soc Econ Bot, 1979-; ed bd, SC Hist Soc, 1989-; Phi Kappa Phi, Col Charleston, 1989; Omicron Delta Kappa; Charleston Friends Quaker Meeting; bd dir, Gaylord & Dorothy Donnelley Found. **Honors/Awds:** Distinguished Service Award, Omicron Delta Kappa, 1989. **Special Achievements:** Author: The Past and Present Uses of Bamboo in Jamaica vol 49; Those That Do Not Smile Will Kill Me: The Ethnobotany of the Ackee in Jamaica vol 55. **Home Addr:** 2799 Bohicket Rd, Johns Island, SC 29455. **Business Addr:** Professor of Anthropology, College of Charleston, Department of Sociology and Anthropology, Rm 203 19 St Philip St 66 George St, Charleston, SC 29424, **Business Phone:** (843)953-8188.

RASPBERRY, WILLIAM J
Educator, columnist. **Personal:** Born Oct 12, 1935, Okolona, MS; married Sondra Dodson; children: Patricia D, Angela D & Mark J. **Educ:** Ind Cent Col, BS, 1958; Ind Univ, addn study; George Wash Univ. **Career:** Indianapolis Recorder, reporter, ed, 1956-60; Washington Post, columnist, 1962-2005; Howard Univ, instr jour, 1971-73; WTTG Wash, TV commentator, 1973; Duke Univ Sch Pub Policy, DeWitt Wallace Ctr Media & Democracy, prof, Knight prof pract journ & pub policy studies, currently. **Orgs:** Bd mem, Pulitzer Prize Bd, 1980-86; Grid Iron Club; Nat Press Club; Capitol Press Club; Nat Asn Black Journalists; Wash Asn Black Journalists; Kappa Alpha Psi. **Honors/Awds:** Pulitzer Prize, 1994; Winner of several awards for interpretive & reporting. **Military Serv:** AUS, 1960-62. **Business Addr:** Knight Professor of the Practice of Journalism & Public Policy Studies, Duke University, Terry Stanford Institute of Public Policy, 141 Sanford Inst Bldg 201 Sci Dr, Durham, NC 27708, **Business Phone:** (919)613-7401.

RATCLIFF, WESLEY D
Computer executive. **Personal:** Married Marie. **Educ:** Prairie View Agri & Mech Univ. **Career:** Advan Technol Solutions Inc, ceo & founder, currently; IBM, staff. **Orgs:** Freestone County Exten Serv Beef; Landowners Asn Tex; chairperson, Tex Black Chamber Com. **Honors/Awds:** Recipient Yr, Tex Chapter Orgn & Agr Comt, 2005. **Business Phone:** (214)428-0222.

RATCLIFFE, ALFONSO F (RICK RATCLIFFE)
School administrator. **Personal:** Born Oct 21, 1928, St Louis, MO; son of William Morgan and Alice Elizabeth Carter; married Dolores Corita Potter, Jan 16, 1969. **Educ:** Univ Calif, LA, BA, physics, 1951, MS, eng, 1963, PhD, eng, 1970. **Career:** Ogden Technol, Monterey Park, CA, dir spec proj, 1955-69; Mattel Inc, Hawthorne, CA, staff engr, 1969-73, 1974-75; Audio Magnetics Corp, Gardena, CA, mgr spec proj, 1973-74; Calif State Univ, Northridge, CA, prof eng, 1975-80, assoc dean eng, 1980-81, dean eng, 1981-92, dean emer, currently. **Orgs:** Sr mem, Inst Elec & Electronics Engrs, 1978; fel Inst Advan Eng, 1983; bd mem, Pac Southwest Sect, Am Soc Eng Educ, 1984-86, chair, 1986-87; chmn 1988-90; bd mem, San Fernando Valley Engrs Coun, 1990-91; Am Soc Eng Educ; Nat Soc Prof Engrs; La Coun Black Engrs. **Honors/Awds:** Distinguished Engineer, Tau Beta Pi Eng Hon Soc, 1981; Educator of the Year, Soc Mfg Engrs, Region VII, 1982; Distinguished Professor of Engineering Education Achievements Award, Nat Soc Prof Engrs, 1987. **Military Serv:** AUS, corporal, 1946-48. **Business Addr:** Dean Emeritus, California State University, Department of Engineering & Computer Science, 18111 Nordhoff St EN IOI, Northridge, CA 91330-8295, **Business Phone:** (818)677-4694.

RATCLIFFE, RICK. **See RATCLIFFE, ALFONSO F.**

RATES, REV. NORMAN M
Clergy. **Personal:** Born Jan 1, 1924, Owensboro, KY; married Laura Lynem; children: Sondra & Shari. **Educ:** Kent State Col, BA, 1947; Lincoln Univ, BD, 1950; Oberlin Col, MDiv, 1952; Yale Univ, MAR, 1961; Vanderbilt Univ, DMin, 1974; Oberlin Col, STM, 1953; Harvard Univ, independent study, 1968-69. **Career:** Clergy (Retired); Camac Community Ctr Phila, stud counr, 1947-48; Philadelphia Gen Hosp, asst to protestant chaplain, 1948-49; St Paul Baptist Church, W Chester, PA, asst to pastor, 1949-50; Div Home Missions National Coun Christ of Christ, USA NY FL DE, missionary to agricultural migrants, 1948-56; Morris Col, minister dean of men teachr, 1953-54; Morehouse Spelman Col Pre-Col Prog summers, counr & minister, 1966-67; Central Brooklyn Model Cities Summer Acad Spelman Col summer, counr, 1972; Interdenom Theol Ctr, guest lectr & part-time teacher, 1971; Westhills Presby Church, GA, summer, interim pastor, 1963; Spelman Col, GA Dept of Religion, col minister & assoc chmn, 1954. **Orgs:** National Asn Col & Univ Chaplains; Ministry to Blacks in Higher Educ; Am Asn Univ Prof; Nat Asn of Biblical Instr; Univ Ctr in Ga Div, Teacher of Religion; Petit Juror Fulton Co Superior Ct, 1971, 1973; grand jr Fulton Co Superior Ct, 1972; ministerial standing The United Ch of Christ; Fel Conf on African & African-Am Studies Atlanta Univ Campus; bd mem, Camping Unlimited Blue Star Camps Inc; bd dir, Planned Parenthood Asn Atlanta; chmn, Religious Affairs Com Planned Parenthood Asn Atlanta; Comn on the Ministry The United Church Christ; The Metro Atlanta Christian Coun; Ga-SC Asn United Church Christ SE Conf; Alpha Phi Alpha Frat; bd trustee, Carrie Steele-Pitts Home. **Honors/Awds:** C Morris Cain Prize in Bible, Samuel Dickey Prize in New Testament, Lincoln Univ, 1949; Campus Christian Worker Grant, Danforth Found, 1960-61; Atlanta Univ Ctr Non-Western Studies Prog Grant, Travel & Study Ford Found, 1968-69.

RATHMAN, THOMAS DEAN
Football coach, football player. **Personal:** Born Oct 7, 1962, Grand Island, NE; married; children: 3. **Educ:** Univ NE, attended 1985. **Career:** Football player (retired), football coach; San Francisco 49ers, fullback, 1986-93; Los Angeles Raiders, fullback, 1994; Menlo Coll, offensive coordr, 1996; San Francisco 49ers, running backs coach, 1997-2002; Detroit Lions, running backs coach; Oakland Raiders, running backs coach, 2007-. **Honors/Awds:** Post-season play, 1988, 1989: NFC Championship Game, NFL Championship Game. **Business Phone:** (510)864-5000.

RATLIFF, JOE SAMUEL
Clergy, college teacher. **Personal:** Born Jul 24, 1950, Lumberton, NC; married Doris Gardner. **Educ:** Morehouse Col, BA, hist, 1972; Interdenominational Thel Ctr, Atlanta, MDiv, 1975, DMin, 1976. **Career:** Cobb Mem Church, Atlanta, pastor, 1971-78; Morehouse Col, prof, 1974-77; Brentwood Baptist Church, Atlanta, pastor, 1980-; Interdenominational Thel Ctr, chmn, bd trustees; Morehouse Sch Relig, chmn, bd trustees; Nat African-Am Fel Southern Baptist Conv, founding pres. **Orgs:** Bd trustees, Interdenominational Theol Ctr, Atlanta, 1986-; Cong Black Caucus Found, 2002; Alpha Phi Alpha Fraternity Inc; bd trustees, Morehouse Sch Relig; Joe Samuel Ratliff Lifelong Learning Ctr; Doris Gardner Ratliff Ctr Child Develop; Union Baptist Asn. **Honors/Awds:** Minister of the Yr, Nat Conf Christians & Jews, 1985; Hon Doctor Divinity, Interdenominational Theol Ctr, 1988; Spiritual Enlightenment Award, Turner Broadcasting Systs, 2003; Spiritual Enlightenment Award. **Special Achievements:** Featured in several national media outlets including: CNN; Assoc Press; Wall St Jour; NY Times; USA Today; Black Enterprise; TIME & Houston Chronicle; first African-American pastor to lead the Union Baptist Assn; co-author, Church Planting in the African-Am Community, Southern Baptist Preaching Today; portrait was hung in the Martin Luther King Jr International Chapel Hall of Fame at Morehouse. **Home Addr:** 8202 Frontenac Dr, Houston, TX 77071, **Home Phone:** (713)270-7743. **Business Addr:** Pastor, Brentwood Baptist Church, 13033 Landmark Dr, Houston, TX 77045, **Business Phone:** (713)852-1400.*

RATLIFF, THEO CURTIS (THEOPHILUS RATLIFF)
Basketball player. **Personal:** Born Apr 17, 1973, Demopolis, AL. **Educ:** Univ Wyo, commun. **Career:** Detroit Pistons, forward-ctr, 1995-97; Philadelphia 76ers, 1997-2000;Atlanta Hawks, 2001-03; Portland Trailblazers, forward-ctr, 2004-06;Boston Celtics, 2006-07; Minnesota Timberwolves, 2007-08; Detroit Pistons,2008; Philadelphia 76ers, currently; owner, Rome Gladiators; mem, Natl Basketball Players Assoc. **Honors/Awds:** Defensive Player of the Year Award, NBA, 2002. **Business Addr:** Professional Basketball Player, Philadelphia 76ers, 3601 S Broad St, Philadelphia, PA 19148, **Business Phone:** (215)339-7600.*

RAUCH, DOREEN E.
Lawyer, college administrator. **Personal:** Born Jul 17, 1947, Port-of-Spain, Trinidad and Tobago; daughter of Joseph Fernandes (both deceased) and Stella M B Estrada; married Terry M, Sep 2, 1969; children: Camille M Welch, J Roxanne, Jeanne M & Terry Michael. **Educ:** Univ Cincinnati, BA, 1976; Howard Univ Sch Law, JD, 1984. **Career:** Emerson Law Sch, fac, 1984-89; Univ Mass, instr, 1985-86; Mass Bay Community Col, instr, 1985-86; Murray State Univ, dir equal opportunity & affirm action, 1991-93; Northern Mich Univ, affirmative action officer, 1993-. **Orgs:** Nat Orgn Women, 1990-; Am Asn Univ Women, 1990-; Am Asn Affirmative Action, 1990-; Am Asn Univ Adminrs, 1995. **Honors/Awds:** Am Jurisprudence Award Municipal Law, 1982; Am Jurisprudence Award Criminal Law, 1982; Am Jurisprudence Award Contracts, 1983; AmJuri sprudence Award, Howard Univ, Commercial Paper, 1983.

RAVELING, GEORGE HENRY
Basketball coach, executive. **Personal:** Born Jun 27, 1937, Washington, DC; married Vivian James; children: Mark. **Educ:** Villanova Univ, BS, 1960. **Career:** Univ Iowa, head basketball coach, 1983-86; Wash State Univ, head basketball coach; Villanova Univ, asst basketball coach; Sun Oil Co,marketing anal & sales rep; Converse Rubber Co, promotions rep; former syndicated newspaper columnist Pac NW; conducts ann basketball coaches clinic; Univ Southern Calif, head basketball coach, 1986-94; CBS Sports & FOX Sports Net, color commentator; Nike Worldwide Camps, global basketball sports mkt dir, currently. **Orgs:** Nat Speakers Asn; Sports Illus Speakers Bur; Nat Asn Basketball Coaches;Am Humor Studies Asn; adv bd, Uniroyal Corp, Spaulding Corp, Joseph P Kennedy Found Mentally Retarded, Letterman Coach & Athletic Mags. **Honors/Awds:** Black Hall of Fame, Nat Black Sports Found; Hon Cert Citizenship, Kans City & New Orleans; Pac-8 Coach of Year, 1975; UPI West Coast Coach of the Year, 1975; Coach of the Year, Nat Col, 1977; Distinguished Alumnus &Humanitarian Awards, Villanova Univ; Cert Merit Outstanding Sales, PubRels, & Mkt, Philadelphia Tribune Newspaper. **Special Achievements:** Books: War on the Boards; A Rebounder's Workshop. **Business Phone:** (503)671-2500.

RAVEN, RICKY A
Lawyer. **Educ:** Univ Houston, attended 1983; Univ Houston Sch Law, attended 1986. **Career:** Harris Co Dist Atty Off, 1994-2000; Woodard, Hall & Primm, prin, 1994-2001; Porter & Hedges LLP, partner, currently. **Orgs:** Julia C Hesten House Inc; bd mem, Ronald McDonald House; bd mem, Houston Symphony Orchestra; Houston Golf Asn; bd mem, Univ Tex Health Sci Ctr Develop Bd; Am Bar Asn. **Honors/Awds:** African American Achiever, 1997. **Special Achievements:** First African American partner in the history of the firm. **Business Phone:** (713)226-0663.

RAVENELL, REV. JOSEPH PHILLIP
Clergy. **Personal:** Born Jan 20, 1940, Pinesville, SC; married Mary Jane Frazier; children: Joseph, Phillip, Byron. **Educ:** St Peters Col, BS, hist, 1973; Princeton Theol Sem, MDiv, 1976. **Career:** NJ St Prison, instnl chaplain; Trenton St Col, Col chaplain, 1975-78; US Postal Ser, lett carrier, 1966-75; Samaritan Bapt Ch, pastor, 1979-. **Orgs:** Pres, NJ Chap St Chaplain Orgn, 1978-; AUS Nat Guard Asn, 1978-; Mil Chaplains Asn, 1978-; Am Correctnl Chaplains Asn, 1978-; dir, Com Network Proj, 1979-. **Military Serv:** AUS, lt col, 29 yrs, Good Conduct Medal, 1963. **Business Addr:** New Jersey State Prison, Third Fedr St, Trenton, NJ 08625.

RAVENELL, MILDRED
Educator. **Personal:** Born Dec 1, 1944, Charleston, SC; married William; children: William Samuel & Teressa Emlynne. **Educ:** Fisk Univ, BA, 1965; Howard Univ, JD, 1968; Harvard Univ, LLM, 1971. **Career:** IBM, systs engr, 1968-70; mkt rep, 1970; Boston Univ, asst dean admissions & financial aid, 1971-72; FL State Univ, assoc prof law, 1976-84; Univ VA, visiting assoc prof law, 1984-85. **Orgs:** Phi Beta Kappa; Am Bar Asn; MA Bar Asn; Bethel AME Church; Delta Sigma Theta Sor; Jack & Jill Am Inc; bd dirs, Terrell House Tallahassee; bd trustees, Law Sch Admission coun; Bd Bus Regulation FL.

RAVENELL, WILLIAM HUDSON
Lawyer, educator. **Personal:** Born May 31, 1942, Boston, MA; son of William S and Isabella T; children: William Samuel & Teressa Emlynne. **Educ:** Lincoln Univ, BA, 1963; St Col, Boston, MEd, 1965; Howard Univ, Sch Law, JD, 1968. **Career:** John Hancock Ins Co, analyst, 1968-71; Housing Inspection Dept, admin, 1971-72; St Dept Comm Affairs, dep secy, 1972-75; Fla Dept Comm Affairs, secy, 1975-79; Fla A&M Univ, prof, 1979; Fla Off Atty Gen, special asst, 1979-80; US Dept Transp Fed Hwy Admin, chief coun, 1980-81; St Fla, asst atty gen, 1981-85; Fla A&M Univ, atty, tenured prof, prof, currently. **Orgs:** Chmn, Fla Comn Human Rels, 1975-77; chmn, Fla Manpower Serv Coun, 1975-80; bd dirs, First Union Bank, 1990-; Fla Nat Am Bar Asn; Phi Alpha Delta, Omega Psi Phi, Fla Coun 100; life mem, Nat Asn Advan Colored People. **Honors/Awds:** Most Outstanding Professor. **Business Addr:** Professor, Lawyer, Administrator, Florida A&M University, Rm 112 Tucker Hall, Tallahassee, FL 32307, **Business Phone:** (850)385-8078.

RAWLINS, SEDRICK JOHN
Dentist. **Personal:** Born May 29, 1927, New York, NY; married Alyce Taliaferro; children: Wayne, Mark. **Educ:** Lincoln Univ, AB, 1950; Meharry Med Col, DDS, 1954. **Career:** E Hartford Conn Dentist, pvt prac, 1956-; Conn Savs & Loan, incorporator, 1969-70; Manchester Mem Hosp, 1969-72. **Orgs:** Manchester Human Relations Comn, 1959-; Conn State Bd Parole, 1959-, chmn, 1966-68; Conn Govt Planning Comt Criminal Admin; chmn, correction comt, 1967-69; Conn House Del, 1970; Nat Dent Asn st vpres, 1968-70; Am & Conn Dent Asn; Conn Coun Nat Paroling Authorities; Phi Beta Sigma; pres, Nat Asn Advan Colored People, 1959-60; Bapt; High Noon Club, Hartford, CT. **Honors/Awds:** Recipient human relation award, E Hartford, 1970; serv award, Nat Asn Advan Colored People, 1960. **Military Serv:** USAAF, Dental Corps, 1944-46; AUS, 1954-56. **Business Addr:** 183 Burnside Ave E, Hartford, CT 06108.

RAWLS, DR. GEORGE H
Surgeon. **Personal:** Born Jun 2, 1928, Gainesville, FL; son of Nicholas and Lona; married Lula; children: Yvonne, Bettye Jo & Sherree. **Educ:** FL A&M Univ, 1948; Howard Univ Sch Med, MD, 1952. **Career:** VA Hosp Dayton, surg resddence, 1955-59; OH State Univ, clin instr surgeon, 1957-59; Am Bd Surg, dipl, 1961; pvt surg pract, 1959-93; Ind Sch Med, asst dean, currently; Ind Sch Med, Clin Prof Eme Surg, currently. **Orgs:** Life mem bd, Nat NAACP, 1961-91; fel, Am Col Surgeons, 1963; guest examr, Am Bd Surg, 1977; pres, Ind State Med Asn, 1979; co-chmn & life mem, NAACP; pres, Marion Co Med Soc; Alpha Phi Alpha; bd dirs, Urban League; Children's Mus; past bd dir, Flanner House. **Honors/Awds:** Alpha Phi Alpha Man of the Year, Alpha Phi Alpha, Indianapolis, 1970; Citizen of the Yr Omega Psi Phi, 1971; Citizen of the Year, Federated Clubs, 1976; Sagamore of Wabash, Gov Orr, 1988; Sagamore of Wabash, Governor Bayh, 1990. **Military Serv:** AUS, First lt 1953-55. **Business Addr:** Clinical Professor Emeritus of Surgery, Indiana University, School Medicine, 340 W 10th St Suite 6200, Indianapolis, IN 46202-3082, **Business Phone:** (317)278-3048.

RAWLS, MARK ANTHONY
Insurance executive. **Personal:** Born May 6, 1967, Brownsville, TN; son of Oliver Lee and Mary. **Educ:** Lane Col, Jackson, TN, BS, 1989. **Career:** Dayton-Hudson, Inc, sales consult, 1989-90; Rawls Funeral Home, printer, 1995-; Golden Circle Life Ins Co, asst vpres & dir ins serv, 1993-. **Orgs:** Nat Ins Asn, undersec, 1995-; HCL Talk Show, co-host, 1997-; Nat Asn Advan Colored People, 1997-, vpres, Hagwood Co br, 2000-. **Honors/Awds:** Honor Award, Nat Asn Advan Colored People, 1998, 1999; Junior Achievement Certificate, 1999; United Way, 1998. **Special Achievements:** Editorials, Memphis Tri-State Defender, 2000; Silver Star News, 2000; Mid-South Tribune, 2000; TN Tribune, 2000; Nashville Pride, 2000; Metro Forum Newspaper, 2000; Brownsville-States Graphic Newspaper, 1997-; NAACP, publisher, 1997-; Jerusalem Center for Biblical Studies, 1989; Lane College Poetry Magazine, 1988.

RAWLS, RALEIGH RICHARD
Lawyer. **Personal:** Born Jun 12, 1925, Gainesville, FL; married Annie R Robinson; children: Regina D, Rene N, Renard A, Rodney P. **Educ:** Howard Univ, BA, 1950, LLB, 1956. **Career:** Atty, pvt prac, 1957-; City Ft Lauderdale, pub defender, 1973-. **Orgs:** Braward Co Bar Asn; Nat Bar Asn; life mem, Alpha Phi Alpha; Nat Advan Asn Colored People. **Military Serv:** UUSN, 1943-46. **Business Addr:** 1024 NW 6th St, Fort Lauderdale, FL 33311-8006.

RAWLS BOND, CHARLES CYNTHIA
Insurance executive. **Personal:** Born Feb 10, 1934, Brownsville, TN; daughter of Charles Allen and Maude Crofton; married Maltimore Bond, Aug 27, 1961; children: Jo Zanice, Alan R, Andrea C Bond Johnson, Maude Y. **Educ:** Fisk Univ, BS, 1955; NY Univ, MS, 1956. **Career:** Golden Circle Life Ins Co, personnel dir, 1957, asst secy, pres, 1987-02; Golden Circle Ins Agency, partner, 2001-; Rawls Funeral Syst, pres, currently. **Orgs:** Insouth Bank Bd Dirs; Lane Col Trustee Bd & Tenn Black Health Care Comn; State Bd Educ; Judicial Eval Comn; YMCA Local & Regional Bds; Birth Choice Adv Bd; Delta Sigma Theta Sorority; Jackson Tennessee LINKS; life mem, Haywood County Nat Asn Advan Colored People Br. **Honors/Awds:** Avon N Williams Jr Living Legend Award; Alumni Achievement Award, Fisk Univ. **Business Addr:** Partner, Golden Circle Insurance Agency, 39 S Jackson Ave, Brownsville, TN 38012, **Business Phone:** (731)772-9932.*

RAY, ANDREW
Educator. **Personal:** Born Feb 4, 1948, Centreville, MS; son of Perry and Ruby. **Educ:** Southern Univ, BS, econ, 1969; State Univ NY, MS, educ, 1970; Univ Buffalo, MS, admin, 1982, PhD, admin & policy, 1994. **Career:** Dept St, intern, 1968; US Congress, intern, 1974; Urban League, career educr, 1983; Adolescent Voc Exploration Prog NY, dir; CSD, Rochester Childrens Zone, instr, dean, 1985-, admin, vprin, 1988-96, prin, 1997-2005, admin prin, 2005-. **Orgs:** Chair bd, Baden Fed Credit Union, 1978-; comt mem, YMCA, 1979-; first vice dist rep, Omega Psi Phi, 1984, dist rep, 1986; bd dirs, Omega Scholar Found, 1991; founder, Black Educrs Asn. **Honors/Awds:** Teacher of the Year, City Rochester, 1974; Distinguished Citizen, Urban League, 1980; Administrator of the Year, 1989; Outstanding Mentor, 1991; Outstanding Educator of the Year, NY State, 1991; Charles Terrell Lunsford Distinguished Community Service Award, Urban League, 1997; Educator of the Year, United Church Ministries, 2000; Examplar Award, About Time Mag Inc, 2001; Omega Psi Phi Founders Award, 2001, 2004; Metrop Womens Network Award, 2004; Emanuel Presbyterian Church Award, 2004; Foreign Affairs Scholar, Dept State, Wash, DC. **Business Addr:** Administrative Principal, CSD Rochester Childrens Zone, 131 W Broad St, Rochester, NY 14614, **Business Phone:** (585)262-8456.

RAY, BIG PLAY. **See BUCHANAN, RAYMOND LOUIS.**

RAY, FRANCIS
Nurse, writer. **Personal:** Born Jul 20, 1944, Richland, TX; daughter of Mc Radford Sr and Venora; married William H, Jul 28, 1967; children: Carolyn Michelle. **Educ:** Texas Woman's Univ, BS, nursing, 1967; Am Nursing Asn, Sch Nurse Practr, 1992. **Career:** Parkland Memorial Hosp, staff nurse, 1967-68; Chester Clin & Hosp, LVN Prog, teacher, 1968-71; Dallas City Health Dept, nursing supvr, 1971-82; Dallas Publ Schs, school nurse pract, 1982; The Turning Point Legal Fund, owner, 2001-; Books: Fallen Angel, Odyssey Pub Co, 1992; Forever Yours, Kensington Pub Co, 1994; Spirit of the Season, anthology, Kensington Pub Co, 1994; Undeniable, book, Kensington Pub Co, 1995; The Bargain, Kensington Pub Co, translated Taiwan/Italian, 1995; Only Hers, Kensington Pub Co, 1996; Romantic Times Magazine, p 53, April, 1996; Incognito, Kensington Pub Co, 1997; Today's Black Woman, excerpt of Incognito, 1997; Silken Betrayal, Kensington Pub Co, 1997; Heart of the Falcon, Kensington Pub Co, 1998; Heart of the Falcon, alternate for Doubleday/Literary Book Club, 1998; Forever Yours, 2nd ed for TV movie, Chuck Fries Prod, 1998. **Orgs:** Romance Writers Am, 1984-; Women Writers Color, 1992-; Am Nurses Asn, 1992-. **Honors/Awds:** Yellow Rose Award, North Texas Romance Writers, for Service, 1990; Multicultural Career Achievement Award, Romantic Times Magazine, 1995-96; Outstanding Achievement, Dallas Pub Libr, Polk Wisdom Branch, 1996; Appreciation Award, Texas Black Women's Writers, 1996. Emma Award; The Golden Pen Award; The Atlantic Choice. **Home Phone:** (214)375-5418. **Business Addr:** Owner, The Turning Point Legal Fund, PO Box 764651, Dallas, TX 75376.

RAY, JACQUELINE WALKER
Educator. **Personal:** Born May 14, 1944, Buffalo, NY; married Lacy Ray Jr. **Educ:** State Univ NY, Buffalo, BA, 1965, MSW, 1967; New York Univ, PhD, 1975. **Career:** Columbia Univ Coler Proj, social worker, 1967-68; New York City Housing Authority Model Cities Prog, field supvr, 1968-70; Jersey City State Col, asst prof psychol, 1970-71; City Univ New York, York Col, assoc prof psychol, Dept Psychol, chair, prof emer, currently; urban educ res trainee, City Univ New York, 1982-83; fac fel, City Univ New York, 1989-90. **Orgs:** Am Psychol Assoc; Community Mediation Servs; Queens City Mental Health Soc; Alpha Kappa Alpha; League Women Voters Region II; Ment Health Consult; Job Corps. **Honors/Awds:** Ford Found Study Grant, 1980; fel, City Univ New York, 1982-83. **Special Achievements:** Articles: Journal Gen Educ, 1979, Journal Intergroup Tensions, 1983, Journal Col Stud Personnel. **Business Addr:** Professor Emeritus, York College, City Univ New York, 94 20 Guy Brewer Blvd, Jamaica, NY 11451, **Business Phone:** (718)262-5115.*

RAY, JAMES R, III
Consultant. **Personal:** Born Feb 10, 1963, Brooklyn, NY. **Educ:** John Jay Col, BA, 1988; Long Island Univ, MBA, 1996. **Career:** BEST Adv Group, chief exec officer; da Bag Productions, founder, currently. **Orgs:** Omega Psi Phi Fraternity, 1986-. **Honors/Awds:** Black Achievers in Industry Award, Harlem YMCA, 1991; National Sales Quality Award; Excellence in Iinternational Business, 1996.

RAY, JOHNNY (JOHN CORNELIUS RAY)
Baseball player. **Personal:** Born Mar 1, 1957, Chouteau, OK; married Tammy; children: Jasmine & Johnny Jr. **Educ:** Northeastern Okla A&M, Miami, OK; Univ Ark, Fayetteville, AR. **Career:** Baseball player (retired); Pittsburgh Pirates, infielder, 1981-87; Calif Angels, infielder, 1987-90; Japanese Baseball League, Yakult Swallows, 1991. **Honors/Awds:** Rookie Player of the Year, Sporting News, 1982; National League Silver Slugger Award, 1983; All-Star Team, Am League, 1988.

RAY, DR. JUDITH DIANA
Educator. **Personal:** Born Sep 14, 1946, St Louis, MO; daughter of Arthur Charles Sr and Pauline Malloyd. **Educ:** Harris Stowe Teachers Col, St Louis, MO, ABEd, 1968; Wash Univ, St Louis, MO, MAEd, 1972; Wash State Univ, Pullman, WA, MS, 1979; Univ Minn, PhD, 1996. **Career:** St Louis Bd Ed, teacher, 1968-72; Wash Univ, St Louis, MO, grad teaching, res asst, 1970-79; ARC Milwaukee Pierre Marquette Div, nat field rep, 1972-73; York Col City Univ NY, Jamaica Queens, lectr, 1973-75; Wash State Univ, Sch Vet Med, equine researcher; W Chester Univ Pa, asst prof kinesiology, 1977-. **Orgs:** Vol teacher, ARC, 1960-80; Am Alliance Health PE & Rec & Dance, 1968-80; vol & mem, Am Soc Testing & Mat, 1978-89; Int & Am Soc Biomechanics, 1978-89; Gamma Sigma Sigma, Nat Serv Sor, 1978-80; Phi Delta Kappa W Chester, 1978; Int Soc Biomechanics Sport; Alpha Kappa Alpha; US Fencing Coaches Asn; US Tennis Asn; US Prof Tennis Asn; USPTR, Registry; fac adv, Phi Beta Sigma. **Special Achievements:** Co-author: EEG Analysis of Equine Joint Lameness, 1977; The Effects of Different Ground Surfaces of Equine Joint, 1980; Motion As Analyzed by EEG, Journal of Biomechanics, vol 13, p 191-200, 1980; An Instrument Designed to Quantify Spinal Motion in Athletic Performance, Book of Abstracts Pre-Olympic Congress Intl Congress on Sport Science, Sports Medicine & Phys Edu, 2000-; Sport As a Medium for Upward Social Mobility for Afr Amers in the USA, German Olympic Institute Yearbook, 2001; Sport: An Oppressive or Liberating Force- A Feminist Perspective, International Council of Sports Science & Physical Education, 2002. **Business Addr:** Assistant Professor of Kinesiology, West Chester University of Pennsylvania, Department of Kinesiology, 206 Sturzebecker Health Scis Ctr, West Chester, PA 19383, **Business Phone:** (610)436-2260.

RAY, REV. PATRICIA ANN
Association executive. **Personal:** Born Jan 30, 1950, Bremond, TX; daughter of Leon and Leola Jewel Moody; married Apr 10, 1970; married Billy Clark Ray, Apr 10, 1970; children: Selwin Carroll & Krissa Leola. **Educ:** Anchorage Community Coll, AA, sociology, 1976; Univ AK, Anchorage, AK, bachelors, sociology, 1980; AK Bible Col, Bible Certificate, theology, 1993, AA, theology, 1996; American Baptist Theological Seminary, ThB, 1998. **Career:** Eaton County Library, librarian aide, 1969-70; Montgomery Wards, salesperson, 1970-71; Dr RH Lewis, chairside dental asst, 1969-70; Dr Bob B Bliss, chairside dental asst, 1971-72; Chugach Electric Assoc Inc, service rep, 1972; shiloh assoc minister, currently. **Orgs:** Delta Sigma Theta Sorority, life mem, 1989-; AK State Asn Colored Women's Club, pres, 1986-91; Mother's Christian Fellowship Club, pres, 1987; NW Regional Colored Women's Club, statistician, 1973; Nat Asn Colored Women's Club, youth coord; NAACP, life mem; Tom Thumb Montosorn Parents Teachers asn, pres, 1983; Big Brother Big Sister, big sister, 1980-82; Janet Helen Tolan Gamble & Tony Gamble, Educational Trust Fund, bd dirs, 1998. **Honors/Awds:** AK Black Caucus, Recognition of Excellence, 1988; American Baptist Churches, scholarship, 1998-99; Business Professional Woman, 1997; NW Regional CWC, Outstanding Dedicated Service, 1987; AK State Assn CWC, Woman of the Year, 1986-89; Mother's Christian Fellowship CWC, Mother of the Year. **Special Achievements:** Anchorage Police Dept, chaplain, 1998-; AK Regional Hosp, chaplain, 1997-; Eagle River Meadow Creek, chaplain, 1998-; 6th Avenue Women's Jail, chaplain, 1996-; Workshop Seminar Retreats in Prayer, Discipleship, Evangelism, ushering, Greeting. **Business Addr:** Shiloh Associate Minister, Shiloh Missionary Baptist Church, 855 East 20th Ave, Anchorage, AK 99518, **Business Phone:** (907)276-6673.

RAY, ROSALIND ROSEMARY
Lawyer. **Personal:** Born Jun 29, 1956, Washington, DC; daughter of Walter I Jr and Rosemary W. **Educ:** Georgetown Univ; Harvard Univ, attended 1976; Boston Univ, BA, 1978; Howard Univ, Sch Law, JD, 1990. **Career:** Law Offices of Jack Olender & Howard Univ, Earl B Davis Trial Advocacy, 1988; DC Super Ct, law clerk, 1990-91; Law Off Indus J Daniel Jr, atty, 1991-; Law Off Leonard L Long Jr, atty, 1991-93; Entertainment Resources, asst gen coun, 1992; DC Housing, hearing officer, 1994-. **Orgs:** Nat Bar Asn, asst ed, 1987-; Am Bar Asn, 1987-; Alpha Kappa Alpha Sorority, 1977-; Phi Delta Phi Legal Frat, 1987-; Howard Univ Law Alumni Asn, 1990-. **Honors/Awds:** Merit Scholarship for High Academic Achievement, Howard University, 1988-90. **Special Achievements:** NBA Magazine, 1992. **Home Addr:** 1205 Morningside Dr, Silver Spring, MD 20904, **Home Phone:** (301)384-9155. **Business Addr:** 9039 Silgo Creek Pkwy Suite 707, Silver Spring, MD 20901.

RAY, WALTER I
Executive, writer. **Personal:** Born Sep 2, 1923, Newburgh, NY; son of Walter I Sr and Mary Bingham R Robinson; married Rosemary White; children: Rosalind R & Walter I III. **Educ:** WV State Col, attended, 1943; Howard Univ, BS. 1949. **Career:** Anheuser Busch, Inc, sales/sales supvr, 1958-70, br mgr, 1971-81; Game Prod Inc, vpres, 1982-83; Esoray Publ Co, Bus & Mkt, consult, 1983-85, pres, 1983-; John N Miller Assoc, assoc vpres, 1983-. **Orgs:** Writer, Broadcast Music Inc; consult, DC Gov; life mem, Nat Asn Advan Colored People; Masons Shriners Const; Omega Psi Phi; Nat Capital Parks, 1973; United Black Fund, 1979; Leadership mem, BSA, 1979. **Honors/Awds:** Black Achievers of Industry, 1972; Walter I Ray Jr Day proclaimed in District of Columbia 1981. **Military Serv:** AUS, s/sgt 3 yrs; USA. **Home Addr:** 1205 Morningside Dr, Silver Spring, MD 20904, **Home Phone:** (301)384-9155. **Business Addr:** President, Esoray Publishing Company, 1205 Morningside Dr, Silver Spring, MD 20904, **Business Phone:** (301)384-9155.

RAY, PROF. WILLIAM BENJAMIN
Educator, opera singer. **Personal:** Born in Lexington, KY; son of Mason and Beatric Clifton Smith; married Carrie Walls Kellogg, Sep 1, 1949; children: Alexander Pierre & William Benjamin Jr. **Educ:** Acad Music Vienna Austria; Ky State Col, 1947; Oberlin Col, BA, 1952; Western Reserve Univ, 1953; Univ Heidelberg, Germany, 1981; Boston Univ, Med, 1982. **Career:** Educator (retired); De Paur's Infantry Chorus, featured soloist, 1953-54; Karamu Theater, opera singer, 1954-56; Cleveland Playhouse, opera singer, 1954-56; Frankfurt Opera Frankfurt, Germany, opera singer, 1957; Decca, Intercord, Marcato, BBC, CBS, recording artist, 1960-78; Concert Tour Europ, concert/opera singer, 1983; Peabody Conservatory Music, prof voice, 1982-92; Howard Univ, prof voice, head voice dept, 2000; Int Music Inst, Austria, voice fac. **Orgs:** Founder/pres, Black Theater Prods, 1974-82; Alpha Phi Alpha Fraternity,1947-; Nat Asn Negro Musicians; Gamma Boule Sigma Pi Phi Fraternity, 1993; bd mem, Annapolis Opera Inc; life mem, NCP. **Honors/Awds:** Recipient of Gold Medal, Lions Club Italy, 1978; inducted into Howard Univ, Pi Kappa Lamda Music Soc, 1993; Merit Award for Professional Achievement & Outstanding Service to students, Howard Univ. **Special Achievements:** Actor/singer appeared in 14 different roles in Germany and Austrian Filmand Television, in the German language; appointed as an exclusive American representative to select operatic talent for the Kaleidoscope Production Company, Munich, Germany;

listed in Blacks in Opera by Eileen Southern, Berlin Opera Yearbook by Walter Felsenstein, Black Americans in Cleveland by Russell Davis. **Military Serv:** Engr Sgt 1942-45; Bronze Medal, Purple Heart, Good Conduct, Excellent Marksmanship, ETO Medal, PTO Medal. **Home Addr:** 539 Higgins Dr, Odenton, MD 21113-2001. *

RAYBURN, DR. WENDELL GILBERT
School administrator. **Personal:** Born May 20, 1929, Detroit, MI; son of Charles Jefferson and Grace Victoria Winston; married Gloria Ann Myers; children: Rhonda Reneen & Wendell Gilbert. **Educ:** Eastern MI Univ, BA, 1951; Univ MI, MA, 1952; Wayne State Univ Detroit, EdD, 1972. **Career:** Detroit Pub Sch, teacher, admin, 1954-68; Univ Detroit, asst dir to dir spec proj, 1968-72, assoc dean acad support prog, 1972-74; Univ Louisville, dean, 1974-80; Savannah State Col, GA, pres, 1980-88; Lincoln Univ, pres, 1988-90; Penson Assocs Inc, vpres, secy, treas & sr assoc, currently. **Orgs:** Am Asn Higher Educ; Nat Asn Equal Opportunity Higher Educ; Kappa Alpha Psi; Sigma Pi Phi; dir, Jefferson City Area Chamber Com; Jefferson City Rotary Club; bd dir, Am Asn State Col & Univs; bd trustees, Stephens Col; bd dirs, Capital Region Med Ctr; bd dir, United Way; exec bd, Boy Scouts Am, Great Rivers Coun; dir, Mo Capital Punishment Resource Ctr; bd, Intl Food & Agr Develop, 1988-. **Honors/Awds:** Whitney M Young Jr Award, Lincoln Found, 1980; Distinguished Citizens Award, City Louisville, 1980; Savannah Port Authority, Savannah GA, 1982-87; West Broad St, YMCA, 1986; Communicator of the Year, Pub Rels Soc Am, 1988; United Way of the Coastal Empire, 1988; Executive of the Year, 1989-90, Ink & Quill Chap Prof Secretaries Intl; Rotarian of the Year, Jefferson City Rotary Club, 1990; Distinguished Alumni Award, Wayne State Univ, Detroit, 1993; Commendation Ribbon. **Special Achievements:** Author: Compensatory Educ: Effective or Ineffective, Jour Coun Psychol, 1975. **Military Serv:** AUS, 1952-59. **Business Addr:** Vice President & Secretary, Treasurer & Senior Associate, Penson Associates Inc, 4701 Willard Ave Apt 1735, Chevy Chase, MD 20815-4632, **Business Phone:** (301)951-9418.

RAYE, JOHN. See SMITH, JOHN RAYE.

RAYE, VANCE WALLACE
Lawyer, state government official, judge. **Personal:** Born Sep 6, 1946, Hugo, OK; son of Edgar Allen and Lexie Marie; married Sandra Kay Wilson; children: Vanessa. **Educ:** Univ Okla, BA, 1967, JD, 1970. **Career:** USF, asst staff judge advocate, Beale AFB chief military justice, chief civil law, judge advocate, 1970-74; Calif Atty Gen, civil div, dep atty gen, 1974-80, sr asst atty gen, 1980-82, dep legis secy, 1982-83; Gov Cali, legal affairs secy, adv, legal coun, 1983-89; Sacramento County Superior Ct, judge, 1989-90; Calif Ct Appeal, Third Dist, assoc justice, 1991-; Lincoln Law Sch, prof; Bulla & Horning, atty. **Orgs:** State Bar Calif, 1972-89; Calif Asn Black Lawyers; Nat Asn Advan Colored People; Urban League; former chmn, Staff Adv Coun Nat Governors Asn Comn Criminal Justice & Pub Safety; Gov Emergency Opers Exec Coun, vice chair; peer reviewer, Nat Inst Justice; Sacramento Health Decisions; 100 Black Men Sacramento; Nat Bar Asn; Wiley Manuel Bar Asn; Calif Judges Asn; chmn, Judicial Coun Comt Family Law; criminal justice standards comn, Am Bar Asn; Calif Comn Future Courts; chair, Family Rels Comn; chair legis subcomt, Judicial Coun Appellate Standards Comt; Calif Comn Status African Am Male; Univ Calif, Davis Med Sch Leadership Coun; Calif Coun Judicial Performance. **Honors/Awds:** Pi Sigma Alpha Political Sci Honor Soc; President's Leadership Award, Univ Oklahoma. **Special Achievements:** Publications: Contributor, "California Public Contract Law;" co-author: California Family Law Litigation, 3 volumes. **Military Serv:** USAF capt 4 yrs; Air Force Commendation Medal. **Business Addr:** Associate Justice, California Court of Appeal, 3rd Appellate District, 900 N St Rm 400, Sacramento, CA 95814-4869, **Business Phone:** (916)654-0209.

RAYFIELD, DENISE E
Labor relations manager. **Personal:** Born Jan 13, 1955, New York, NY; daughter of Thomas and Laura Chandler. **Educ:** Temple Univ, Philadelphia, PA, BA, 1976; Fordham Univ, New York, NY, MBA, 1981. **Career:** WR Grace & Co, New York, NY, benefits admin asst, 1977-81; Ziff-Davis Publ Co, New York, NY, benefits mgr, 1981-83; Hearst Corp, New York, NY, asst mgr, employee benefits, 1983-90, mgr, employee benefits, 1990-94, sr mgr, employee benefits, 1994-. **Business Addr:** Senior Manager, The Hearst Corp, 227 W Trade St, Charlotte, NC 28202.*

RAYFORD, BRENDA L.
Administrator, social worker. **Personal:** Born Apr 3, 1940, Dayton, OH; married Kent A; children: Blake Nyette, Valdez Kamau. **Educ:** Cntrl St Univ, BA, sociol, 1962; Wayne St Univ, MSW, 1971. **Career:** Detroit Black United Fund Inc, exec dir; Comp Hlth Svc, soc wkr, 1969; Highland Park Pub Sch Spl Proj, soc work supr, 1967-69; Travelers Aid Soc, soc wkr, 1966-67; Montgomery Co Wlf Dept, soc worker-intake, 1962-66. **Orgs:** Consult Creative Strategies Inc; exec dir, Nat Black United Fund Inc; field work supr Wayne St Univ Sch of Soc Work; chmn, Fund Raising Comn Bus & Professional Wmn Inc New Metro Chap; adv comn, Detroit Pub Sch. **Honors/Awds:** community service award, World Islam W Community, 1978; Who's Who in Black America; WSU Citizen of the Year; the Spirit of Detroit Award. **Special Achievements:** co-author, The Guy Who Controls Your Future, 1970. **Business Addr:** Executive Director, Black United Fund of Michigan Inc, 2187 W Grand Blvd, Detroit, MI 48208, **Business Phone:** (313)894-2200.

RAYFORD, FLOYD KINNARD
Baseball player. **Personal:** Born Jul 27, 1957, Memphis, TN; married Mary Luvenia Hawkins. **Career:** Baseball player (retired); Baltimore Orioles, infielder, 1980 & 1982, 1984-87; St Louis Cardinals, infielder, 1983; New Britain Rock Cats, coach, currently.

RAYFORD, LEE EDWARD
Government official. **Personal:** Born Nov 17, 1935, Fordyce, AR; married La Neal Lucas (died 1990); children: Vickie & Celese; married Billie Knight. **Educ:** Agr Mech & Normal Col, Pine Bluff, AR, BS, 1961; Univ AR, MS, 1963; E Tex State Univ, EdD, 1979. **Career:** Clark County Sch Dist, Las Vegas, adult educ teacher, 1969-74, res teacher, 1973, asst prin; CCSA Las Vegas, site admin, 1970-72; Econ Opportunity Bd, Las Vegas, ESAA prog dir, 1974; State Nev Equal Rights Comn, Las Vegas, exec dir, 1979-80; Redeemer Lutheran Elem Sch, prin, 1998-. **Orgs:** Bd dir, Westside Community Develop; treas bd dir, OIC/A; Nat Asn Advan Colored People, Las Vegas; SW Equal Employment Opportunity Officers; IntAsn Human Rights Agency; Personnel Adv Comn State Nev; Kappa Alpha Psi, Las Vegas; Phi Delta Kappa, Las Vegas; Kappa Delta Psi, Las Vegas; Clark County Asn Sch Adminr; bd dirs, Sheppard Hills Develop. **Honors/Awds:** Publ "Criteria for the Selection of Pub Elementary Sch Principal of the State NV", 1979. **Military Serv:** USAF, a/2c, 1955-59. **Business Addr:** Principal, 1730 N Pecos, Las Vegas, NV 89115.*

RAYFORD, ZULA M.
Educator. **Personal:** Born Aug 5, 1941, Memphis, TN. **Educ:** Langston Univ, BA, 1964; Univ WI, Grad Work, 1971; Nat-19 Louis Col, Evanston, Ill, MEd, 1984. **Career:** YWCA, prog counr, 1964-68; Holy Angels Catholic Sch, teacher, 1968-70; Milwaukee Pub Sch, teacher, 1970-. **Orgs:** NEA; WI Educ Asn; United Milwaukee Educ; Milwaukee Teachers Asn; United Teachers; Northside Neighbourhood Action Group; Recording Sect; Black Educr; Int Masons & OES; bd mem, N Cent Serv Club; State Funded Kindergarten Day Care Prog; adv mem, Milwaukee Pub Sch Alternative Educ. **Honors/Awds:** Rep, NEA Minority Leadership Conf; WI St del, NEA Conv.

RAYNOR, ROBERT G
Lawyer. **Personal:** Born Jul 18, 1954, New Bern, NC; son of Robert G Sr and Cora P. **Educ:** NC Cent Univ, BA, 1977, Sch Law, JD, 1981. **Career:** Harmon & Raynor, Atty Law, lawyer, 1984-87; Pvt Pract, lawyer, 1987-. **Orgs:** KAP Frat Inc, 1973-; bd dirs, Big Brothers-Big Sisters Lower Neuse, 1984-86; NC Asn Black Lawyers, 1984-; Nat Asn Advan Colored People, 1985-; Craven County Voters League, 1985-; secy, Neuse River Develop Authority Inc, 1986-; NC Asn Black Elected Munic Officials, 1986-; trustee, New Bern-Craven County Libr, 1987-; Nat Black Caucus Local Elected Officials, 1988-, parliamentarian, 1999-2001; bd dirs, Wachovia Bank NC; adv bd, Neuse River Community Penalties; Craven County Voters League; trustee, New Bern/Craven County Libr; New Bern Craven County Libr Found. **Honors/Awds:** Robert G Raynor Jr Day Honoree, Craven County Voters League, 1985; Achievement Award, Nat Asn Advan Colored People, New Bern Chap, 1985; Achievement Award, 1985; Drum Major for Justice Award, New Bern Police Dept, 1994; Golden Eagle Business Service Award, Dudley Products Inc, 1997. **Special Achievements:** Elected: Mayor Pro-Tem, City of New Bern, NC, 1987; Board of Alderman, City of New Bern, NC, Second Ward, 1989-93, 1993-97, 1997-01, currently. **Home Addr:** 1511 Spencer Ave, New Bern, NC 28560, **Home Phone:** (252)637-5276. **Business Addr:** Lawyer, 417 Broad St, PO Box 446, New Bern, NC 28563, **Business Phone:** (252)633-5299.

READY, CATHERINE MURRAY
Educator. **Personal:** Born Apr 22, 1916, Richmond, VA; daughter of Etta Johnson Murray and George Murray; married Edward K, Feb 3, 1941; children: Diane C. **Educ:** Hampton Univ, attended 1936; Va Union Univ, attended 1948. **Career:** Richmond City Schs, teacher. **Orgs:** Va Retired Teachers; World Mutual Comt, YWCA; Urban League Guild Greater Richmond; Zeta Phi Beta; Black Hist & Cult Ctr Va. **Honors/Awds:** Community Service Award, YWCA, 1983; Volunteer Service Award, Sr Golfers Va, 1985; Service Award, Urban League Guild, 1986-88; Appreciation Award, 1986; Volunteer Sponsor Award, Martin Luther King, 1992.

READY, STEPHANIE
Television broadcaster, basketball coach. **Personal:** Born Jan 1, 1972, Takoma Park, MD. **Educ:** Coppin State Univ, BS, psychol, 1998. **Career:** Coppin State Univ, women's volleyball coach, 1998-2000, men's basketball asst coach, 2000-01; Greenville Groove, asst coach, 2001-03; Washington Mystics, asst coach; Charlotte Bobcats, television sideline reporter, currently. **Special Achievements:** First woman to coach in men's professional sports. **Business Addr:** Television Sideline Reporter, Charlotte Bobcats, 333 E Trade St, Charlotte, NC 28202, **Business Phone:** (704)688-8600.

REAGON, DR. BERNICE JOHNSON
Composer, museum curator, singer. **Personal:** Born Oct 4, 1942, Dougherty, GA; daughter of Jesse Sr and Beatrice; married Cordell Hull (divorced 1967); children: Toshi & Kwan Tuana. **Educ:** Albany State Col, Albany, Ga, BA, 1959-62; Spelman Col, Atlanta, Ga, BA, hist, 1970; Howard Univ, Wash, DC, PhD, USA hist, 1975. **Career:** Singer, composer, music producer, educator, curator; Albany Movement, mem exec comt, 1961-62; Student Non Violent Coord Comt Freedom Singers, field secy & mem, 1962-63; singer, composer & music producer, 1961-; pub lectr/songtalker, 1962-; Harambee Singers, Atlanta, Ga, founder, 1968, dir, 1968-70; DC Black Repertory Theater, Wash, DC, vocal dir, 1972-77; Ithaca Col, vis lectr African-Am music, 1972; Howard Univ Sch Music, teaching fel, 1973-74; Sweet Honey in the Rock, Wash, DC, founder &artistic dir, 1973-2004; Smithsonian Inst, Wash, DC, folklorist, 1974-76; Skidmore Col, vis scholar African-Am cult hist, 1976; Univ Calif, vis fel African-Am cult, 1977; Smithsonian Inst Mus Am Hist, dir & cult historian program Black Am cult, 1976-88, cur, 1988-93, cur emer, 1993-; Portland State Univ, vis fel women's studies prog, 1980; Am Univ, Wash, DC, distinguished prof hist, 1993-2002, prof emer, 2002-; Spelman Col, Atlanta Ga, William & Camille Cosby Endowed prof fine arts, 2002-04; Sound recordings: We Shall Overcome, 1963; Songs of the South, 1964; Give Your Hands to Struggle, producer & performer, 1975; Sweet Honey In The Rock, 1977; B?lieve I?ll Run On, See What The End?s Gonna Be, 1978; For Somebody to Start Singing, music composer & performer, 1979; Good News, 1981; We All.Everyone of Us, exec producer & performer, 1983; The Other Side & Feel Something Drawing Me On, producer & performer, 1985; River of Life, producer & performer, 1987; Live At Carnegie Hall, co-producer, 1987; All For Freedom, co-producer & performer, 1989; In This Land, co-producer, 1992; Still On The Journey, co-producer, 1993; I Got Shoes, exec producer & performer, 1994; Sacred Ground, co-producer, 1995; Wade in the Water:African American Sacred Music Traditions, producer, compiler & author, 1996; Selections, 1976-88, producer, compiler & performer, 1997; Africans in America, producer, composer & performer, 1998; Still the Same Me, producer & performer, 2001; Alive In Australia, co-producer, 2002; Rutha Harris: I am On the Battlefied, producer, 2004; Temptations of St Anthony, exec producer, composer & librettist, 2006; Books: The African Diaspora: World Family of Black Culture, 1980; Compositions One: The Original Compositions of Bernice Johnson Reagon, 1986; Black American Culture & Scholarship, Contemporary Issues, 1986; We Who Believe in Freedom: Sweet Honey in the Rock Still on the Journey, ed & contrib, 1993; We'll Understand It Better By & By Pioneering African American Gospel Composers,ed & contrib, 1993. **Honors/Awds:** The Martin Luther King Jr Center for Nonviolent Social Change Trumpet of Conscience Award, 1986; Charles E Frankel Prize, 1995; Isadora Duncan Dance Award, 1996; George F. Peabody Award, 1999; Leeway Laurel Award,2000; Heinz Foundation Award, 2003; Hon doctorates: Bates Col, 1991; Old Dominion Univ, 1991; Princeton Univ, 1992; Swarthmore Col, 1993; Williams Col, 1995, Spelman Col, 1997; Boston Col, 1997; St Mary's Col, 2000; Univ Mich, Ann Arbor, 2000; Wesleyan Univ, 2001; Haverford Col, 2001; Colby Col, 2004; Rockford Col, 2005; Gallaudet Univ, 2006. **Special Achievements:** Her "Temptation" completed a run at the Paris Opera House de Garnier (the first African American cast to play in the house since the 19th century). **Business Addr:** Professor Emerita of History, American University, 4400 Massachusetts Ave NW, Washington, DC 20016-8033, **Business Phone:** (202)885-2700.*

REARDEN, SARA B
Lawyer. **Personal:** Born in Edgefield, SC; daughter of Oacy and Mamie Lewis; married Nigel Lauriston; children: Kai Nicole. **Educ:** Howard Law Sch, JD; NC State A&T Univ, BS, Bus Admin with hons. **Career:** Fel NLS, prog staff, 1969-71; Reginald H Smith Comn Law Fel Prog; Neighborhood Legal Serv, Wash DC, managing Comt, atty, 1971-73; Equal Employement Opportunity Comn, atty adv, 1973-74; Equal Employement Opport Comt, supr atty, 1974-79; George Washington Law Ctr Wash DC, part-time asst prof, 1978-82; US Merit Systs Protection Bd, sr appellate atty, 1979-, Equal Employment Div, actg dir, currently. **Orgs:** Howard Law Jour, 1968-69; Admin Bars Supreme Ct SC, 1971, DC, 1973; US Dist Ct DC, 1973, US Ct Appeals DC, 1973; secy, Bd Wash DC, Neighborhood Legal Serv, 1980-; co-chmn bd dir, Neighborhood Legal Serv Prog, Wash DC; Am Bar Asn; Nat Conf Black Lawyers; Nat Asn Black Women Attys; vpres, Howard Law Alumni Asn; Nat Couns Negro Women; pres, first & second yr law class; Coun Legal Educ Opportunity, 1990; Bar US Supreme Ct, 1983; US Ct Appeals Fed Circuit; bd dir, Fed Circuit Bar Asn. **Honors/Awds:** Winner Constance Baker Motley Scholar, 1968; MSPB Merit Awards, 1986-91; Chairmans Award for Extraordinary Performance, 1992; MSPB, Chairmans Award for Legal Excellence, 1999. **Home Addr:** 1012 Nolcrest Dr, Silver Spring, MD 20903. **Business Addr:** Lawyer, Acting Director, Equal Employment Division, US Merit Systems Protection Board,

Office of General Counsel, Rm 818 1120 Vermont Ave NW, Washington, DC 20419, **Business Phone:** (202)653-7171.

REASON, J PAUL
Executive, naval officer. **Personal:** Born Mar 22, 1941, Washington, DC; son of Joseph and Bernice; married Dianne, 1965; children: Reason Jr & Joseph. **Educ:** US Naval Acad, attended 1965; US Naval Post Grad sch, attended 1970. **Career:** Executiver, Naval officer (retired); USN, USS J D Blackwood, 1967; USS Truxtun, 1968-70; USS Enterprise, 1971-75; USS Truxtun, Bur Naval Personnel, assignment officer, naval aide to Pres US, 1976-79; USS Mississippi, exec officer, 1979-81; USS Coontz, USS Bainbridge, commanding officer; Naval Base Seattle, comdr, 1986-88; Cruiser-Destroyer Group One, comdr, 1988-91; US Atlantic Fleet, Naval Surface Force, comdr,1991-94, dep chief opers, 1994-96, comdr chief, 1996-99; Syntek Technol Inc, vpres ship systs, 1999-2000; Metro Machine Corp, Ship Repair Yards, Norfolk, VA, pres, coo, 2000-05, vice chmn & dir, 2005-06; Norfolk Southern Corp dir; Todd Shipyards Corp, dir. **Orgs:** Bd mem, AMGN Inc; bd mem, Norfolk Southern, 2002-; bd mem, Wal-Mart, 2001-06; bd, Metro Machine Corp, 2005-. **Honors/Awds:** Distinguished Service Medal; Legion of Merit; Navy Commendation Medal; The Venezuelean La Medulla Naval Almirante Luis Brion Medal; The Republic of Vietnam Honor Medal; The Navy Unit Commendation; National Defense Service Medal; Armed Forces Expeditionary Medal; The Republic of Vietnam Meritorious Unit Citation; The Republic of Vietname Campaign Medal. **Special Achievements:** First African American to earn a four-star rank in the US Navy. **Military Serv:** USN, 1965-69. **Business Addr:** Board of Directors, Amgen Inc, One Amgen Ctr Dr, Thousand Oaks, CA 91320-1799, **Business Phone:** (805)447-1000.

REAVES, REV. DR. BENJAMIN FRANKLIN
Vice president (organization), minister (clergy). **Personal:** Born Nov 22, 1932, New York, NY; son of Ernest McKinley and Lella Brinson; married Jean Manual, Sep 4, 1955; children: Terrilyn Jackson, Pamela & Benjamin. **Educ:** Oakwood Col, Huntsville, AL, BA, 1955; Andrews Univ, MA, MDiv; Chicago Theol Sem. **Career:** Mich Conf Seventh-Day Adventist, pastor, 1956-68, minister; Westside Hosp, Chicago, IL, counr, 1968-72; Andrews Univ, Berrien Springs, MI, youth pastor, 1972-73, assoc prof, 1973-77; AUS, instr homeletics, 1977-85; Oakwood Col, Huntsville, AL, pres; Adventist Health Syst, vpres mission & ministries, currently. **Orgs:** Vision, 2000; adv bd, Andrews Univ; adv bd, Loma Linda Univ; United Negro Col Fund; Nat Asn Equal Opportunity Higher Educ; Coun Advan Pvt Cols, AL; Huntsville Chamber Com Bd; Rotary club; Urban Ministries Prog; bd dir, UNCF; Chicago Sunday Evening Club. **Honors/Awds:** Distinguished Alumnus Award, Oakwood Col, 1973; Teacher of the Year,Oakwood Col, 1983; Music Humanitarian Award, Oakwood Col, 1984; Outstanding Leadership Award, Oakwood Col, 1986; The Medallion of Distinction. **Special Achievements:** Author of articles in numerous journals such as: Message, Review & Herald, Ministry, Adventist Laymen, Colgiate Quarterly, South African Signs Times. **Business Addr:** Vice President of Mission and Ministries, Adventist Health System, 111 N Orlando Ave, Winter Park, FL 32789, **Business Phone:** (407)647-4400.

REAVES, E. FREDERICKA M
Educator. **Personal:** Born Nov 7, 1938, Washington, DC; married Robert Reeves IV (deceased); children: Reginald & Ricardo. **Educ:** Morgan St U, BS, 1960. **Career:** Jr High Sch, math teacher, 1961; Guam Pub Schs, math teacher, 1964; SanDiego City Sch, math teacher, 1966; Alameda Unified Sch, math teacher, 1967-83; Oakland Unified Sch Dist, 1984-86. **Orgs:** Nat Ed Asn, 1967-; secy, Alameda Nat Asn Advan Colored People, 1967-; bd mem, Alamedans HOPE, 1967-70; adv, Youth Nat Asn Advan Colored People, 1968-75; bd mem, Am Red Cross, 1970; chair, Multicult Inst Impl Article 3.3 CA Ed Code Training Group, 1970-74; Nat Coun Teacher Math, 1970-82; Phi Delta Kapna, 1973-. **Honors/Awds:** PTA Scholar, Fairmont Heights High, 1956; Merit Scholar, Morgan St Univ, 1957. **Home Addr:** 762 Santa Clara Ave, Alameda, CA 94501. **Business Addr:** Insurance Adjuster, 7700 Edgewater Dr, Oakland, CA 94621.

REAVES, REV. FRANKLIN CARLWELL
Social worker, association executive. **Personal:** Born Aug 7, 1942, Mullins, SC; married Willie Dean White; children: Kathy Juanita, Jacquelyn C, Frankie Diana, Anthony "Kenny", Ron, Randy, Dexter & Branden; married Algenia (deceased). **Educ:** Fayetteville State Univ, BS, 1968; NC A&T State Univ, MS, hist, 1974, MS, admin & supv, 1982; LaSalle Ext Univ, LLB 1978; Univ Santa Barbara, PhD; Lutheran Theol Sem, attended. **Career:** Columbus Co Bd Educ, teacher, 1968-; Operation HELP, pres & founder, 1968-; pastor, currently. **Orgs:** Pres, Marion Co Chap Nat Asn Advan Colored People, 1973-76; Am Friends Serv Comn, 1978-84; pres, SC Affiliate of ACLU, 1979-82; Nat Bd Dirs Am Civil Liberties Union, 1982-; pres, Black Educr Leadership Coun, 1984; Pres, Columbus Co Unit NC Asn Educr; pres, NC Region V Leadership Prevocational Planning Coun; Southern Regional Coun; founder, Rev Dr & Mrs Franklin C & Algenia Reaves Found Legal Ministry; Major & Ruth Davis Humanitarian Found; founder & pres, Oper Help Econ Linkage Poor; SC Affil Southern Christian Leadership Conf; Nat Platform Asn. **Honors/Awds:** Honorary Doctorate Humanity, Allen Univ, 1984. **Special Achievements:** Book: An Analysis of Legislative Segregation in Black and White Schools, Public and Private, During the Periods of 1948-54 and 1985-1990, 2007. **Business Addr:** President, Operation HELP, PO Box 534, Mullins, ND 29574.

REAVES, GINEVERA N.
Educator. **Personal:** Born Jan 21, 1925, Greenwood, MS; married Henry Eugene Sr; children: Henry Eugene jr & Naomi Normene (deceased). **Educ:** Rust Col, BA, 1951; Univ Chicago, MA 1954; Univ Tenn; Va State Col; Tex State Col; Tenn State Univ; Southern Univ New Orleans; Ball State Inst. **Career:** Miss Pub Sch, teacher, 1942-64; Rust Col, asst prof, 1964, dir of teacher educ. **Orgs:** Chair person, First Cong Dist Dem Party MS, 1972; alt del Dem Nat Mid-Term Conf, 1974; st exec bd, Dem Party MS; MS Affirmative Action Com, 1975; Phi Delta Kappa; Am Asn Univ Wy; Miss Teacher Asn; Historian Phi Delta Kappa, 1976-77; US Comn Civil Rghts, 1976-77; vpres, Miss Asn Higher Educ; Delta Sigma Theta Sor; Benton Co, Nat Asn Advan Colored People. **Honors/Awds:** Runner-up teacher of yr, Rust Col, 1966; Sargent Shriver Award, alleviating poverty in rural Am 1966; Miss Finer Wmnhd award, Zeta Phi Beta, 1968; teacher of yr, Rust Col, Zeta Phi Beta, 1972; ginevera Reaves Day Benton Co Nat Asn Advan Colored People, 1975.

REAVIS, JOHN WILLIAM
Educator, association executive. **Personal:** Born Oct 30, 1935, Nyack, NY; son of John and Frances; married Doris S Bailey; married Catherine Smith, Aug 31, 1997 (divorced); children: Dawn, John III & Timothy. **Educ:** Fayetteville State NC Univ, BS, 1959; NY Univ, MA, 1965; Univ Rochester, NDEA, inst guid, 1965; State Univ NY, Albany, higher educ. **Career:** Continental Can Co, mach tender, packer, 1953-55, part-time, 1956-59; Grand St Sch, teacher, 1959-61, asst prin, 1967-68; Elem English Negro Hist, adult educ teacher, 1961-62; Montgomery St Sch, elem guidance counr, 1962-67, prin, 1968-69; Cent Admin State Univ NY, coordr spec progs, 1969-72, asst dean, 1972-80; EDPA Grant Garnett Patterson Jr High Sch, consult, 1972-73; State Univ NY, Farmingdale, Educ Opportunity Ctr, asst pres affirmative action, 1980-81, dean, 1981-86, prof, 1986-90; Minority Youth Groups Sports, consult; Col Dormitory, asst; Port Chester Carver Ctr, Port Chester, NY, exec dir; sports statistician; newspaper public relations writer; athletic teams, mgr; Sno-Burners Ski Club NY, adult racing comt chairperson, currently. **Orgs:** Nat Asn Supv & Curric Develop, 1969-; pres bd, dir, Schenectady Carver Community Ctr, 1973-78; adv coun Suffolk Co, BOCES Dist III, 1978-89; Grumman Ski Club, 1980-; vice chmn, Suffolk County Human Rights Comn, 1981-89; educ comn, life member, Nat Asn Advan Colored People, 1981-; chmn draft bd, US Selective Serv Suffolk Co, 1983-89; eastern regional racing coordr, Nat Brotherhood Skiers, 1994-98, nat youth racing dir, 1996-98; pres, Metrop NY Ski Coun Inc; life mem, Omega Psi Phi Fraternity Inc; Phi Delta Kappa; Nat Alliance Black Sch Educ; comt mem, Nat Legis Comn; NY State Teachers Asn; NY State Guid Asn; Fayetteville St Col Alumni Asn; NY Univ Alumni Asn; life mem, PTA; pres, Grand-Montgomery St Schs; pres, Port Chester Town Rye Coun COT Serv; Port Chester Midget Football League; St Francis' AME Zion Church, Stewart; steering comn, Campaign Kids Estchester Co. **Honors/Awds:** Omega Man of Year, 1977-78; Notable American, 1976-77; Dedicated Service, State Univ NY Col, Farmingdale, 1986; Presidential Citation to Distinguished Alumni NAFEO, 1987. **Home Addr:** 325 King St, Port Chester, NY 10573, **Home Phone:** (914)937-6613. **Business Addr:** Adult Racing Committee Chairperson, Sno-Burners Ski & Sports Association Inc, State Off Bldg 263 W 125 St, New York, NY 10027, **Business Phone:** (914)937-6613.

RECASNER, ELDRIDGE DAVID
Basketball player, executive. **Personal:** Born Dec 14, 1967, New Orleans, LA; married Karen, Aug 14, 1993; children: Sydney, Erin, Lauren & Eldridge III. **Educ:** Univ Wash, archit, 1990. **Career:** Basketball player (retired), executive; Louisville Shooters, CBA, guard, 1991-92; Yakima Sun Kings, CBA, 1992-95; Denver Nuggets, 1994-95; Houston Rockets, 1995-96; Atlanta Hawks, 1996-98; Charlotte Hornets, 1999-2001, 2001-02; Los Angeles Clippers, guard, 2001-02; real estate bus, currently. **Orgs:** Nat Basketball Retired Players Asn. **Honors/Awds:** Most Valuable Person, CBA, 1995; CBA, All-League First Team, 1995.

REDD, ALBERT CARTER, SR.
Chaplain. **Personal:** Born Mar 13, 1917, Columbia, SC; son of Curtis and Polly Carter; married Georgia Harrison, Sep 29, 1952 (deceased); children: Althea B & Albert C Jr. **Educ:** Benedict Col, Columbus, SC, BA, 1948; Howard Theol Sem & Sch, Wash, DC, social work & YMCA cert, 1949, MA, 1951; Union Theol Sem, New York, NY, 1954. **Career:** Turner Chapel CME Church, Mt. Clements, MI, pastor, 1958-61; Womack CME Church, Inkster, MI, pastor, 1961-63; Grace CME Church, Detroit, MI, pastor, 1963-67; Cleaves CME Church, Denver, CO, pastor, 1967-74; Vet Admin Med Ctr, Kans City, MO, chaplain, 1974-75; Vet Admin Med Ctr, Augusta, GA, chaplain, 1975-. **Orgs:** Bd trustees, Eden Theatrical Workshop, 1979; bd mem, Soc Concerns, Ga Conf, CME Church, 1980; Augusta Black Hist Comt, 1981; bd trustees, Penn Com Ctr, St Helena, SC, 1986; ministerial adv bd: Ford, GMC, & Chrysler; exec secy, SC Conf Nat Asn Advan Colored People; chair, adv bd, Inter-Civic Coun, Tallahassee, Fl. **Honors/Awds:** Minister of the Year, Denver Area, 1974; Public Service Award, Veterans Admin Hosp, 1978; Superior Performance Award, 1979, 1982, 1984, 1989, Employee of the Year, 1989, Administrator's Hand and Heart Award, Veterans Admin Med Ctr, 1989; Eden Award, Eden Theatrical Workshop, 1990; Golden Rule Award, 1993. **Special Achievements:** First full-time Black chaplain, VA Hospital, Kansas City, MO. **Military Serv:** AUS, Spc 6, 1941-46; received Good Conduct Medal. **Business Addr:** Protestant Chaplain, Veterans Administration Medical Center, 2460 Wrightsboro Road, Augusta, GA 30910-0001, **Business Phone:** (404)724-5116.

REDD, M. PAUL, SR. See Obituaries section.

REDD, ORIAL ANNE
Government official, journalist. **Personal:** Born Apr 19, 1924, Rye, NY; daughter of William A and Ethel Griffin; married M Paul Redd Sr, Sep 4, 1954; children: Paula Redd Zeman & M Paul Jr. **Educ:** Bennett Col, BA, 1946. **Career:** Urban League Westchester, housing specialist, 1970-72, prog dir, 1972-74; Co Human Servs Dept, asst to county, exec for Human Servs, 1974-83, Records & Archives, dep co clerk, 1983-91; Westchester Co Press, vpres, pres & exec ed, 1986-. **Orgs:** Black Democrats Westchester; Zeta Phi Beta; Nat Asn Advan Colored People; bd adv, Equal Justice Am. **Honors/Awds:** Hon Doctorate in Human Letters, Mercy Col; Community Service Award, NY State Black & Puerto Rican Caucus; Government Achievement Award, Nat Asn Minority Bankers; Community Service Award, NY State Conf, Nat Asn Advan Colored People Brs; Government Achievement Award, Westchester Co Bd Legislators; Community Service Award, United Hosp Med Ctr; Woman of the Year, Daughters Isis; Ernest G Lindsay Award, Black Democrats Westchester; Community Service Award, Westchester Community Opportunity Prog; Community Service Award, Operation PUSH Westchester. **Home Addr:** 100 Nyack Pl, Nyack, NY 10960.

REDD, WILLIAM L
Lawyer, educator. **Personal:** Born Sep 3, 1950, Wilcoe, WV; married Marie E; children: Le Marquis & D'Ann. **Educ:** Marshall Univ, BA, 1972; NC Cent Univ Law Sch, JD, 1976. **Career:** Marshall Univ, instr, 1976, prof legal asst technol, currently; Henderson & Redd, atty, 1976-82; Law Off, pvt atty, 1982-. **Orgs:** Grad Chap Omega Psi, 1971; WVa State Bar, 1976-; legal redress officer, Huntington Br, Nat Asn Advan Colored People, 1976-; Legal Redress Comt WVa Conf, 1976-; pres, Black Alumni Inc, 1978-81; pres, Mountain State Bar Asn, 1980-82; pres Cabell Co Dep Sheriff's Civil Serv Comt, 1981-; secy, Cabell Co Comn Crime & Delinquency, 1982-83; chmn bd dirs, Green Acres Found, 1982-84; Marshall Univ Orial Tournament Comt, 1984; vpres, Green Acres Ment Retardation Ctr, 1981-; trustee, First Baptist Church Huntington, 1981-; chmn, Scottie Reese Scholarship Bd First Baptist Church, 1982-; Big Green Scholarship Fund Marshall Univ, 1982-; adv coun, Licensed Practical Nurses Cabell Co, 1982-; chmn, Minority Recruitment Comt Fac & Staff Marshall, Nat Asn Advan Colored People, 1984-. **Honors/Awds:** Prentice Hall Award, NC Cent Univ Sch Law, 1976; Omega Man of the Year Omega, Psi Phi Nu Beta Chap, 1978; Outstanding Black Alumni, Black Alumni Inc Marshall, 1979; Recognition Award, Adbul Temple, 1981; Outstanding Leadership, Mt State Bar Asn, 1982. **Military Serv:** USAR, sp-4, 6 yrs. **Business Addr:** Professor of Legal Assisting Technology, Marshall University, Business Technologies Division, 324 Corbly Hall, Huntington, WV 25755-2725, **Business Phone:** (304)696-3009.

REDDICK, ALZO JACKSON
Government official, educator. **Personal:** Born Nov 15, 1937, Alturas, FL; married Elouise Williams; children: Nesper, Tausha, Alzo J Jr & Jason. **Educ:** Paul Quinn Col, BS, 1960; Fla A&M Univ, ME, 1971; Nova Univ, EdD, 1977. **Career:** High Sch, teacher; Valencia Comn, asst vpres planning; Rollins Col, asst dean, 1970-; State Fla, state rep; Univ Cent Fla, Orlando, dir spec prog, dir defense transition servs, currently. **Orgs:** Pres-elect, SABAP; chmn, Fla Caucus Black Dems; consult, Fla Drug Abuse Trust; adv, Criminal Justice Task Force; bd dir, Youth Prog Inc; bd dir, Additions Orange Co Inc; bd dir, Mid-FL Ctr for Alcoholism; bd dir, Channel No 24 Pub TV; mem, Fla Bur Hist Mus; Youth Comn, chmn dep majority leader, Dem Nat Comn, 1984-86; chmn, Affirmative Action Comn, Fla Dem Party, Orlando Single Mem Dist Task Force; mem, Am Asn Higher Educ, Southern Col Placement Asn; bd dir, Orange Co Additions; bd dir, Better Bus Bur, Brookwood Comn Hosp, Guardian Care Nursing Home; mem, Alpha Phi Alpha, Phi Delta Kappa; chmn, Mercy Drive Neighbors Action; exec comm, 1976-82, chmn, 1980-81, Orange Co Dem; mem, Fla Police Standards Comn, 1980-81; chmn, United Negro Col Fund. **Honors/Awds:** Community Service Award, Wash Shores Asn Rctrn; Community Serv Award, Orange Co Dem Exec Comn, 1981; First Black Legislator Award, Modern Majestic Club 1982; Law Enforcement Most Effective Freshman, 1983; Service& Leadership Award, Jones High Sch, 1983; Appreciation Award, Nat Dem Comn, 1983; Florida Black Business Investment Board Award, 1994; American Electronics Association Legislator of the Year, 1994; Florida Commission on Human Relations Civil Rights Legislative Award, 1994; Florida Funeral Directors Association Legislative Leadership Award, 1996. **Military Serv:**

AUS, 1961-64. **Business Addr:** Director of Defense Transition Services, University Central Florida, 12424 Res Pkwy Suite 168, Orlando, FL 32826-3269, **Business Phone:** (407)882-0326.

REDDICK, LANCE
Actor, musician. **Personal:** Born in Baltimore, MD. **Educ:** Eastman Sch Music, Rochester, compos; Yale Drama Sch, actg. **Career:** Actor, musician, business owner; Wall St Jour, paperboy; Films: The Siege, 1998; Godzilla, 1998; Great Expectations, 1998; I Dreamed of Africa, 2000; Don't Say a Word, 2001; Bridget, 2002; Brother to Brother, 2004; Dirty Work, 2006; Tennessee, 2008; TV series: What the Deaf Man Heard, 1997; Witness to the Mob, 1998; The Fixer, 1998; Falcone, 2000; "The Corner", 2000; "Oz", 2000-01; "Law & Order: Special Victims Unit", 2000-01; "The Wire", 2002-08; "Keep the Faith, Baby", 2002; "Probability", 2003; "Law &Order", 2001-04; "City Hall", 2004; "CSI: Miami", 2005-06; "Vengeance", 2005; "Alliances", 2006; Lost, 2008; Fringe, 2008; New York Undercover; Numb3rs; Oz; The West Wing; Swift Justice; What the Deaf Man Heard; The Wire; YNC Films, owner, 2006-; Album: Contemplations & Remembrances, 2008. **Business Addr:** Actor, c/o Thomas Cushing, Innovative Artists, 1505 10th St, Santa Monica, CA 90401, **Business Phone:** (310)656-5100.*

REDDING, GLORIA ANN
Consultant, school administrator, educator. **Personal:** Born Apr 4, 1952, Courtland, AL; daughter of W D Watkins Sr and Mary Ella Mitchell; divorced; children: Clifford Cannon. **Educ:** Ohio State Univ, BS, home econ, lib studies & family rels human develop, MA. **Career:** Kroger Co, asst mgr, 1975-76; Grocery Prod Group, sales rep, 1976-77;Borden Inc, food serv unit mgr, 1977-79; Advanced Bus Commun, commun consult, 1979-80; WIC Prog, proj asst & nutritionist, 1980-83, pub health educr, 1982-85; Ohio State Univ Young Scholars Prog, regional prog dir, 1988; Ohio Dept Educ, asst dir & ODE GEAR UP coordr, consult, currently. **Orgs:** Vpres, Ohio State Univ Black Alumni Asn; Ohio State Univ Mentor Prog; bd trustee, Neighborhood House Inc; adv coun, Women Infants & C; golden life mem, vpres, 1982, Delta Sigma Theta Sorority Inc; Nat Alliance Black Sch Educr; Olde Orchard Alternative Sch Parents Asn; A Gathering Sisters; women's day chairperson & womens breakfast fel comt, New Salem Missionary Baptist Church, Missionary Soc; mem, NatForum to Accelerate Middle grade Reforms. **Honors/Awds:** Professional Mentor Achievement Award, Ohio State Univ Mentoring Prog, 1989-91; Outstanding Service Award, Ohio State Univ Young Scholars Prog, 1990. **Home Addr:** 300 Caro Lane, Gahanna, OH 43209, **Home Phone:** (614)428-7777. **Business Addr:** Assistant Director & Consultant, GEAR UP Coordinator, Ohio Department of Education, 25 S Front St, Columbus, OH 43215, **Business Phone:** (614)387-2205.

REDDRICK, MARK A
Executive, chief executive officer. **Career:** Phoenix Oil Co, chief exec officer, pres.

REDMAN, JOSHUA (JOSHUA SHEDROFF)
Saxophonist. **Personal:** Born Feb 1, 1969, Berkeley, CA; son of Dewey and Renee Shedroff; married 1997. **Educ:** Harvard Univ, 1991. **Career:** Saxophonist, Recording Artist, Composer; Joshua Redman, 1993; Wish, 1993; Mood Swing, 1994; Spirit of the Moment: Live at the Village Vanguard, 1995; Freedom in the Groove, 1996; Timeless Tales (For Changing Times), 1998; Beyond, 2000; Passage of Time, 2001; Elastic, 2002; Momentum, 2005; Back East, 2007. **Honors/Awds:** First Place, Thelonius Monk InterNat Jazz Saxophonist Comp, 1991; Jazz Times Best New Artist, 1992; Down Beat Readers Poll, Jazz Artist of the Year, 1994; Down Beat Readers Poll, Album of the Year, 1994; Rolling Stone Critics Poll, Best Jazz Artist, 1994 & 1995. **Special Achievements:** Appeared in the Robert Altman film Kansas City. **Business Addr:** Recording Artist, Composer, Wilkins Management, 323 Broadway, Cambridge, MA 02139, **Business Phone:** (617)354-2736.

REDMAN, R
Actor, rap musician. **Personal:** Born Apr 17, 1970, Newark, NJ. **Career:** Albums: Whut? Thee Album, 1992; Dare Iz a Darkside, 1994; Muddy Waters, 1996; Doc's Da Name 2000, 1998; Malpractice, 2001; Red Gone Wild, 2006; Film: Rhyme & Reason, 1997; Ride, 1998; PIGS, 1999; Boricua's Bond, 2000; Backstage, 2000; How High, 2001; "Statistic: The Movie," 2001; TV guest appearances: "The Jamie Foxx Show," 2000; "Stung", writer, 2002; "Method & Red", producer, 2004; "Def Jam Fight for NY," 2004; "Celebrity Rap Superstar", 2007. **Honors/Awds:** Rap Artist of the Year, The Source Mag, 1993; Live Performer of the Year Award, The Source, 2000. **Business Addr:** Recording Artist, Def Jam Records, 825 8th Ave, New York, NY 10019, **Business Phone:** (212)333-8000.

REDMON, ANN LOUISE. See ALI, DR. FATIMA.

REDMON, KENDRICK ANTHONY
Football player. **Personal:** Born Apr 9, 1971, Brewton, AL; married Stephanie; children: Haleigh & Kelseigh. **Educ:** Auburn Univ. **Career:** Ariz Cardinals, guard, 1994-97; Carolina Panthers, guard, 1998-99; Atlanta Falcons, guard, 2000.

REDMOND, DEVERA YVONNE
Executive. **Personal:** Born Dec 6, 1948, Baltimore, MD. **Educ:** Morgan State Univ, BS, 1970; Univ Baltimore, MPA, 1980. **Career:** DR & Assocs, pres/owner, 1986-; US Small Bus Admin, bus spec, 1978-86; URS Group Inc, SB liaison officer, currently. **Orgs:** Bd mem, Salvation Army, Washington, DC; Nineteenth Street Baptist Church; Alpha Kappa Alpha Sorority; trustee, Museum Afr Art; Asn Univ Women; comnr, Com Nat Community Serv, Washington, DC; AT&T Small Bus advisory coun, 1996; chair, Comt Employer Support Guard & Reserve (ESGR), 1998-2004; Secy Defense; Chair Columbia. **Business Addr:** SB Liaison Officer, URS Group Inc, EG&G Technical Services Inc, 200 Orchard Ridge Dr Suite 100, Gaithersburg, MD 20878, **Business Phone:** (301)652-2215.

REDMOND, EUGENE B.
Poet, educator. **Personal:** Born Dec 1, 1937, East St Louis, IL; son of John Henry and Emma Hutchinson; children: Treasure. **Educ:** Southern Ill Univ, BA, 1964; Wash Univ, St Louis, MO, MA, 1966. **Career:** East St Louis Beacon, East St Louis, IL, assoc ed, 1961-62; East St Louis Evening Voice, asst ed, 1962-63; Monitor, East St Louis, IL, contributed, 1963-65, exec ed, 1965-67, ed page & contributing ed, 1967-; Southern Ill Univ Edwardsville, East St Louis IL branch, Exp Higher Educ, teacher & counr, 1967-68, poet residence & dir lang workshops, 1968-69; Oberlin Col, Oberlin OH, writer residence & lectr Afro-Am studies, 1969-70; Calif State Univ, Sacramento, CA, prof eng & poet residence ethnic studies, 1970-85; Eugene B. Redmond Writers Club, East St Louis, IL, co-founder & bd dirs, 1985-; East St Louis Pub Schs, East St Louis, IL, spec asst supt cultural & lang arts, 1985; Wayne State Univ, Detroit, MI, Martin Luther King Jr-Cesar Chavez-Rosa Parks, distinguished visiting prof, 1989-90; Black River Writers Press, founder & publisher; Annual Third World Writers & Thinkers Symposium, coordr, 1972-; Henry Dumas Creative Writing Workshop, coordr, 1974-; Literati Int & Original Chicago Blues Annual, assoc publisher; Southern Ill Univ, prof eng, 1990; prof emer eng currently; Univ Wis, visiting writer residence; Univ MSR-St Louis, visiting writer residence; Southern Univ Baton Rouge, visiting writer residence. **Orgs:** Cong Racial Equality; Am Newspaper Guild; Nat Newspaper Publishers Asn; Nat Asn African Am Educrs; African Asn Black Studies; Calif Asn Teachers Eng; Calif Writers Club; Nat Asn Third World Writers; Northern Calif Black Eng Teachers Asn; founder, Eugene B. Redmond Writers Club, 1986. **Honors/Awds:** Washington Univ Annual Festival of the Arts first prize, 1965; Free Lance magazine first prize, 1966; Literary Achievement Award, Sacramento Regional Arts Coun, 1974; Best of the Small Press Award, Pushcart Press, 1976; Poet Laureate, East St Louis, IL, 1976; Faculty research Award, Calif State Univ, Sacramento, 1976; California Arts Council grant, 1977; Illinois Arts Council grant, 1977-78; National Endowment for the Arts fellowship, 1978; Pyramid Award, Pan African Movement USA, 1993; American Book Award, for collection of poems The Eye in the Ceiling, 1993; Illinois Author of the Year (Ill Asn Teachers Eng), 1989; Pushcart Prize; Lifetime Achievement Award, Pan-African Movement USA. **Special Achievements:** Has authored six volumes of poetry and has edited many more, author of Sentry of the Four Golden Pillars, Black River Writers, 1971, author of Songs from an Afro/Phone, Black River Writers, 1972, author of In a Time of Rain and Desire: Love Poems, Black River Writers, 1973, author of Drum voices: The Mission of Afro-American Poetry, A Critical History, Anchor, 1976, author of Visible Glory: The Million Man March, Southern Ill Univ, 1998. **Military Serv:** US Marines, 1958-61. **Home Addr:** PO Box 6165, East St Louis, IL 62202.

REDMOND, DR. JANE SMITH
College administrator. **Personal:** Born Jul 20, 1948, Cleveland, TN; daughter of V Campbell and Earnestine; children: Gyasi. **Educ:** Knoxville Col, BS, 1970; Univ Tenn, MS, 1979; Ohio State Univ, PhD, 1991. **Career:** Univ Tenn, Knoxville, Prog Off, prog advr, Women's Ctr, dir, Off Minority Stud Affairs Univ Tenn, dir, Minority Stud Affairs, asst vice chancellor, currently. **Orgs:** Bd dirs, United Way Knoxville, 1984-; bd dirs, Knoxville Inst Arts, 1985-; Alpha Kappa Alpha Sorority. **Honors/Awds:** Chancellors Citation, Extraordinary Cot Serv, 1994-; Bronze Woman Candidate, 1996-97. **Special Achievements:** Knoxville's Ten Most Eligible Career Women 1983. **Home Addr:** 8650 Eagle Pointe Dr, Knoxville, TN 37931. **Business Phone:** (865)974-6861.

REDON, LEONARD EUGENE
Executive. **Personal:** Born Nov 4, 1951, St Louis, MO; son of Leonard and Joyce Woodfox (deceased); married Denise Socquet, Aug 26, 1972; children: Jason & Jennifer. **Educ:** Worchester Polytech Inst, Worchester, Mass, BS, chem engineering, 1973. **Career:** Eastman Kodak Co, Rochester, New York, dist serv mgr, 1984-86, prod serv mgr, 1986-87, mkt mgr copy prod, 1987, corp acct exec, 1987-88, asst chmn & pres, 1988-89, dir serv parts mgt, 1989, vpres & dir rochester area opers, currently; Paychex Inc, vpres western opers, currently. **Orgs:** Asn Field Serv Managers, 1984-; bd chmn, Network North Star Inc, 1989-; bd dirs, Ctr Youth Serv, 1989-; Urban League Rochester, 1989-. **Business Addr:** Vice President, Paychex Inc, 911 Panorama Trail S, Rochester, NY 14625-0397, **Business Phone:** (585)385-6666.

REDUS, GARY EUGENE
Baseball player. **Personal:** Born Nov 1, 1956, Athens, AL; married Minnie Diggs; children: Lakesha, Manesha & Nakosha. **Educ:** Athens State Univ, Attended. **Career:** Baseball player (retired); Cincinnati Reds, Outfielder, 1982-85; Philadelphia Phillies, 1986, Chicago White Sox, 1987-88; Pittsburgh Pirates, infielder & outfielder, 1988-92; Texas Rangers, 1993-94. *

REECE, AVALON B.
Educator, counselor. **Personal:** Born Oct 10, 1927, Muskogee, OK. **Educ:** Langston Univ, Bachelors Degree, attended 1948; Univ Southern CA Los Angeles; M Music Ed, 1954; Pepperdine Col Los Angeles CA; Vander Cook Sch Music Chicago, Ill; Northeastern OK State Univ, Standard Cert Phys Ed, 1963, Standard Cert HS Coun, 1967; Southwestern OK State Univ, attended. **Career:** Educator, Counselor (retired); Manuel Training HS, band directress, 1948-66, girls physical educ instructor, 1953-67, activity dir, 1967-70, counselor, 1967-70; EASP, secondary activity coordinator, 1971-73; Muskogee HS, counselor; Oklahoma State Regents Higher Educ, asst secy, 1985. **Orgs:** Life mem, Nat Educ Asn; Am Personal & Guide Asn; Am Sch Coun Asn; Prof Recognition Comt, Am Sch Coun Asn; Asn Non White Concern; Okla Personnel & Guide Asn; Midwest Reg Br Assembly Okla Personnel & Guide Asn; Okla Ed Asn; Human Relations Comn, Okla Ed Asn; Eastern Dist Deans & Coun Okla Educ Asn; Muskogee Educ Asn; Nat League Cities; Okla Muncipal League; Prof Standards Bd State Bd of Ed; Nat Black Caucus Local Elected Officers; Women in Municipal Govt; Area VI Rep Bd Dir; Citizens Adv Coun on Goals Okla Higher Ed; Okla UN Day Com IWY; Human Resource Comt NLC; parlimentarian southwest region Nat Sorority of Phi Delta Kappa- Delta Omicron Chap; Asn Governing Bd; Real Estate Sales Asn; Muskogee City Coun mem Mayor's City Chrtr Revison; bd dir Muskogee City Coun Youth Serv; Mayor's Coun Drug Abuse; WIBC; mem Juvenile Personnel Training Prog; AAUW; Alpha Epsilon Omega Chap Alpha Kappa Alpha Sor; Found Excellence, Top Ladies of Distinction, selection comt. **Honors/Awds:** First black city cnclwmn State of OK; distgshd women Muskogee Serv League; Woman of the Year, Zeta Phi Beta Sorortity, 1975; demo presdtl elector 1976; Patriot of the Month, Muskogee Bicentennial Com, 1976; Key to the City, Gary, IN, 1976; Key to the City, Kansas City, MO, 1979; delegate to the Demo Natl Conv 1980; Honorable Order of Kentucky Colonel; Distinguished Public Service Award, OK Clg of Osteopatic Medicine & Surg 1985; Ambassador of Goodwill Award, Governor Nigh, 1982; Distinguished Public Service Award, The OK Coll of Osteopathic Medicine & Surgery 1985; Awd 35 yr Pin Muskogee Educ Assoc; apptd as Hon Atty General by OK State Atty Genl Michael C Turpen 1986; Achievement Awd, Top Ladies of Distinction, OK chp, 2001; NTU Afr Amer Hall of Fame, 2002; Community Service Awd, Alpha Kappa Alpha, Alpha Epsilon Omega chp, 2002; Human Rights Awd, OK Human Rights Commission, 2002. **Home Addr:** 927 S Main St, Muskogee, OK 74401. *

REECE, GUY L., II
Judge. **Personal:** Born in St Louis, MO. **Educ:** Univ Nebr, BS, bus, 1972; OH State Univ Law Sch, Moritz Col, JD, 1981. **Career:** Colonel (retired), judge; City Columbus, chief labor atty & asst city atty, 1981-89; Franklin Co Munic Ct, judge, 1990-91; Common Pleas Court, Judge, 1992-95; City Jakarta, Indonesia, legal adv, 1995-96, consult, 1996-97; vis judge, 1998; Franklin Co, Bd Elections, dir, 1998-2003; Franklin Co Ct Common Pleas, judge, 2003-04, 2006-; Franklin Co, dir bd Elections, currently. **Orgs:** Nat Asn Advan Colored People; Vietnam Veterans Am; bd trustees, Maryhaven; Metrop Bd YMCA Cent OH; bd trustees, Direction for Youth; deacon, Second Baptist Church; John Mercer Langston Bar Asn; Columbus Bar Asn, Ohio Bar Asn; Am Bar Asn, & Nat Bar Asn. **Honors/Awds:** Dr Martin Luther King Jr Image Award, 2006. **Military Serv:** USAR, Active Duty, 1965-78; Reserve 1979-97; capt, col; Bronze Star; Meritorious Serv Medal with two Oak Leaf Clusters; Army Commendation Medal with five Oak Leaf Clusters. **Business Addr:** Judge, Franklin Co Ct Common Pleas, 369 S High St Ct Room 7A, Columbus, OH 43215, **Business Phone:** (614)462-7200.

REECE, STEVEN
Executive. **Personal:** Born Sep 12, 1947, Cincinnati, OH; son of Edward and Claudia; married Barbara Howard, Sep 12, 1970; children: Alicia Michelle Reece, Steven Reece Jr, Tiffany Janelle Reece. **Educ:** Xavier Univ, BS, commun, 1970; Ohio Bus Col, BA, 1985; Amos Tuck, Dartmouth Col, MBA, 1987; Temple Bible Col, honorary degree. **Career:** Univ Cincinnati's Evening Col, prof; WCPO-TV, TV director; Motown Records, rd mgr for Supremes, Temptations, Stevie Wonder; Cincinnati's 1st Black Mayor Theodore M Berry, exec asst; Kool Jazz festival, assoc producer; Communiplex Serv, pres & founder; Reece & Reece Enterprise, Cincinnati OH, pres & founder, currently; State Comn African American Males, 2007-. **Orgs:** Pres, Oper PUSH; cochmn, Rev Jesse Jackson's Presidential Campaign, Hamilton Co; local chmn, Oper PUSH Int Trade Bureau; mkt chmn, Greater Cincinnati Chamber of Com; jr grand warden, Prince Hall Masons; prom dir, Prince Hall Shriner's Free & Accepted; Trustee Bd & Deacon Bd, New Friendship Baptist Church; founder, Oper Step-Up; Integrity Hall Child Care Center; Communiplex Nat Woman's Sports Hall of Fame; founder, Communiplex & Martin Luther King & Educ and Sports Classic; founder, producer, Cincinnati Public Sch Nat Teleconf. **Honors/Awds:** Cert of Honor, Cent State Univ; CEBA Awd; Cum Laude Hon Soc; Withrow Hall

of Fame; grad of the Leadership Cincinnati, Greater Cincinnati Chamber of Com, 1979; Am Best & Brightest Young Bus & Prof Men, Dollars & Sense Mag, 1987. **Special Achievements:** first Black elected to Cincinnati Advert Club; Radio appearance: "What Are the Issues?"; produced & wrote music for several nationally known musical artist; featured in the Who's Who in Black Cincinnati, 2003-04.

REED, DR. ALLENE WALLACE
College administrator. **Personal:** Born in Harpersville, AL; daughter of Waymon Lether and Eula Bell Davis; married Jesse Reed Jr; children: Jesse III & Gwenderlyn Carol. **Educ:** Univ Cincinnati, BS, 1972, EdM, 1975, PhD, 1980. **Career:** Ben Siegel Realtor, real estate sales assoc, 1956-72; Cincinnati Pub Schs, teacher, 1968-72; Univ Cincinnati, asst to the dean, 1972-73, assoc dean, 1973-75, asst dean dir div social sci, 1975-89, asst dean, grad studies & res, 1990-. **Orgs:** Nat Asn Women Deans, Admins & Counrs; Ohio Asn Women Deans, Admins & Counrs; Asn Continuing Higher Educ; Nat Univ Continuing Educ Asn; The Ohio Conf on Issues Facing Women; Black Fac & Admin Higher Educ; Rainbow Coalition; Nat Polit Cong Black Women; Nat Asn Advan Colored People; Southern Poverty Law Ctr; Citizen's Cable Commun Bd Cincinnati; Citizen's Comn Youth; Woman's City Club Greater Cincinnati; City Cincinnati Police Consortium; vpres, Charter Comt Greater Cincinnati, Ohio Psychol Asn; Delta Sigma Theta; Psi Chi; Nat Polit Women's Caucus, 1988-89; Black Forum; Oper Bootstrap; Counc Grad Studies. **Honors/Awds:** Outstanding Woman's Award, Nat Asn Advan Colored People Nat Office, 1981; Outstanding Contribution to the Black Community, UBAFAS 1981; Image Maker Radio Station WCIN 1984; Citizen for the Day; Enquirer Woman of the Year, Cincinnati Enquirer, 1986; 200 Greater Cincinnatians, Cincinnati Bicentennial Comn, 1988; Portraits of Excellence: 100 Black Cincinnatians, Cincinnati Bicentennial Comn, 1988. **Home Phone:** (513)221-5126. **Business Addr:** Assistant Dean, Research, University of Cincinnati, 305 Braunstein St, PO Box 210627, Cincinnati, OH 45221, **Business Phone:** (513)556-4335.

REED, ANDRE DARNELL
Football player, president (organization). **Personal:** Born Jan 29, 1964, Allentown, PA; married Cyndi; children: Auburn & Andre Jr. **Educ:** Kutztown State Col. **Career:** Football player (retired), exec; Buffalo Bills, wide receiver, 1985-99; Wash Redskins, wide receiver, 2000; Fitness Powerhouse Gym, owner; ESPN2, Cold Pizza, NFL Europe & NCAA football commentator, currently; Andre Reed Enterprises, owner, currently; TV: Football: Who's Got Game, 2006. **Orgs:** Celebrity spokesperson, Big Bros Big Sisters Western NY. **Honors/Awds:** Post-season play: AFC Championship Game, 1988, 1990-91; Pro Bowl, 1988-94; Super Bowl XXV, XXVI, XXVII, XXVIII; Hall of Fame Inductee, Kutztown Univ, 1991; Pro Footballs Hall of Fame, 2005; Buffalo Sports Hall of Fame. **Business Addr:** Owner, Andre Reed Enterprises, 1806 Watermere Lane, Windermere, FL 34786, **Business Phone:** 888-550-6672.

REED, BEATRICE M.
Real estate agent. **Personal:** Born Jan 5, 1916, St Georges, Grenada; died Aug 22, 1999; children: 1 Daughter. **Educ:** Howard Univ Wash DC, BA, 1967. **Career:** NC Mut Ins Co, ins agt, 1940-42; War & Prod Bd US Govt, asst supvr stat sec, 1942-44; DC Br Nat Advan Asn Colored People, admin asst, 1944-46; Unit Pub Workers Am CIO, int rep, 1946-48; Beat M Reed RE Co. **Orgs:** Cam mgr, Camper Congr 4th Congress Dist MD, 1948; pres, Bymarc Inc; past pres, Wash RE Brok Asn, 1975-76; chmn, const & by laws com Nat Asn RE Brok; past pres, chmn, cent Club Nat Asn Negro Bus & Prof Women Club Inc, 1968-71; bd dir, Sub MD Bd Dir; pres, Carib Am Intercul Orgn, 1980. **Honors/Awds:** 1st Black Civ Serv employ to serve as civ serv exam US Civ Serv Commn 1943; 1st Black Wom to be Intnl Rep Labor Un Unit Pub Wrkrs of Am CIO 1946-48; feat in HUD Chal Mag Intnl Wom Yr iss Dept of Hous & Urb Devel 1975; pres of the yr awd Nat Assn of RE Est Brok Inc 1976; pion wom in RE Nat Wom Counc of Nat Assn of RE Brok Inc 1979; awd of recog Nat Assn of RE Brok Inc 1980.

REED, BOBBY. See REED, KWAME OSEI.

REED, BRANDY (BRANDY CARMINA REED)
Basketball player. **Personal:** Born Feb 17, 1977. **Educ:** Univ Southern Miss, attended 1998. **Career:** Minn Lynx, forward, 1998-99; Phoenix Mercury, forward, 1998, 2000-02. **Honors/Awds:** Player of the Yr, Conf USA, 1995-96; first team, All Conf USA, 1995-96; Player of the Week, Conf USA, 1996; Miss Comeback Player of the Yr; Most Val Player, Fla Int Univ Classic.
*

REED, BRANDY CARMINA. See REED, BRANDY.

REED, DR. CHARLOTTE (DR. REV. CHARLOTTE REED PEEBLES)
Educator, colonial administrator. **Personal:** Born Apr 27, 1948, New York, NY; daughter of Thomas L and Lillian M; married Twain M Peebles, Sep 12, 1987; children: Mark D Peebles. **Educ:** Richmond Col, City Univ NY, BA, 1972; Univ Va, MEd, 1977, EdD, 1980. **Career:** New York City Pub Schs, Eng teacher, 1972-76; Charlottesville Pub Schs, behavior modification teacher, 1976-77; Univ Va, project dir, 1977-81; Univ Louisville, asst prof, 1981-87; Alverno Col, asst & assoc prof, 1987-90; Purdue Univ, Calument, assoc prof, 1990-92; Indiana Univ Northwest, dir & assoc prof, 1992-2004, IU Northwest, Exec dir & Prof, 2005-. **Orgs:** Am Educ Res Asn, 1981-; adv bd mem, Int Alliance Invitational Educ, 1982-; Nat Asn Multicultural Educ, 1992-99; Nat Coun Black Studies, 1992-94; comn mem, Asn Teacher Educrs, 1992-99, ATE Resolutions Comt Chair, 2002-05; exec bd mem, Phi Delta Kappa, Chap 1029, 1978-, pres, 1993-96, 2000-01; Co-Chair, Comn Urban Educ, 2008-; sch bd, Sunnybrook Sch Dist, 1999-, vpres, 2000, pres, 2001-; Ill Sch Bd Asn, 1999-. **Honors/Awds:** Fel, Nat Acad Educ, 1983; Cert Commendation Commun Serv, State Ky House Reps, 1984; Gov Ky, Ky Col Comn, 1984; Activism Award, Women Educrs, 1993; Alumni Hall of Fame, Col Staten Island, 1994; Outstanding Service, Phi Delta Kappa, 1994-95, distinguished serv, 2000; Dedicated Serv, Urban Teacher Educ Program, 2001; Leadership Award, Northwest IN Serv Ctr, 1999; FACET Award, 2004. **Special Achievements:** Chapter in Advancing Invitational Thinking, Novak, J (Ed), 1992; "Invitational and Multicultural Perspectives: What Do They Have in Common?"; "Family Stress and Self-Esteem," Denver Univ Law Review, 1992; "Enhancing Self-Esteem in Multicultural Classrooms," Invitational Education Forum, 1992; "Teacher Invitations and Effectiveness," ERIC, 1981; "Overcoming Prejudices: An Invitational Approach," The Urban Review, 1996. **Home Addr:** 19725 Orchard Ct, Lynwood, IL 60411. **Business Addr:** Executive Director, Professor of Urban Education, Indiana University Northwest, Center for Excellence in Teaching & Learning (CETL), 3400 Broadway LC332A, Gary, IN 46408, **Business Phone:** (219)980-6804.

REED, CLARA TAYLOR
Health services administrator. **Personal:** Born in Isola, MS; daughter of Rev N C and Ethel Lee; married Henry. **Educ:** Miss Valley State Univ, pract nurse prog, 1963; Assoc Degree, nursing, 1970, BA, gerontol, 1990. **Career:** Mid-Delta Home Health Inc, chief exec officer, currently. **Special Achievements:** Co is ranked No 83 on Black Enterprise's list of top 100 companies, 1994. **Business Addr:** Chief Executive Officer, Mid-Delta Home Health Inc, 222 Issaquena Ave, Clarksdale, MS 39038, **Business Phone:** (662)624-4910.

REED, CLARENCE HAMMIT, III
Executive, sales manager, salesperson. **Personal:** Born Oct 25, 1957, Amite, LA; son of Clarence Reed and Eunice Paddio Johnson; married Sandra A Reed (divorced 1987); children: Doreal Hayes & Matthew David. **Educ:** Cornell Univ, Ithaca, NY, BS, 1979. **Career:** Eli Lilly & Co, Indianapolis, IN, sales, 1979-81; Solar Resources Am, Columbus, OH, sales mgr, 1982-83; Xerox Corp, Columbus, OH, sales, 1983-86; Reed Enterprises & Develop, Columbus, OH, owner, 1986-; Animed Comput Syst, Oshkosh, WI, sales, 1986-88; CMHC Systems, Dublin, OH, sales rep, 1988-2002, sr sales rep, currently. **Home Addr:** 2332 Vendome Dr, Columbus, OH 43219-1437, **Home Phone:** (614)258-7292. **Business Addr:** Senior Sales Representative, CMHC Systems Inc, 570 Metro Pl N, Dublin, OH 43017, **Business Phone:** (614)764-0143.

REED, CLIFFORD
Educator. **Career:** Loyola Marymount Univ, Theatre Dept, asst prof.

REED, CORDELL
Executive. **Personal:** Born Mar 26, 1938, Chicago, IL; son of Clevon and Carrie Bell; married Bernice; children: Derrick, Brian, Barry, Steven & Michael. **Educ:** Univ Ill, BS, mech eng, 1960. **Career:** Executive (retired); Commonwealth Edison, engr, 1960, nuclear eng dept, mgr, 1975; vpres nuclear oper, sr vpres, ethics officer & chief diversity officer, 1994-97. **Orgs:** Am Nuclear Soc; West Soc Engrs; Nat Tech Asn; trustee, Metrop Comn Church; trustee, Abraham Lincoln Ctr; dir, Independent Bank Chicago; bd dir, LaSalle Bank; bd dir, Walgreen Co; Inst Elec & Electronics Engrs; Nat Acad Eng, 1992; Tau Beta Pi Eng Honor Soc; Urban Fin Serv Asn; Ill Acad Decathlon Asn; Cal-Met Village Sr Citizen Housing; bd dir, John G Shedd Aquarium; Development Fund Black Stud; adv bd, Metrop Family Serv. **Honors/Awds:** Lifetime Achievement Award, 1988; Black Achievers of Industry Recognition Award, YMCA; Tommy Thompson Award, Am Nuclear Soc, 1993.

REED, DR. DAISY FRYE
Educator. **Personal:** Born in Washington, DC; daughter of James Edward and Alberta Ruth Edwards; divorced; children: James S Jr & Kristel M. **Educ:** DC Teachers Col, BS, 1953-56; George Washington Univ, MA, 1957-61; Teachers Col, Columbia Univ, MEd, EdD, 1973-75; Loyola Univ, MRE, 1992-94. **Career:** Washington DC Publ Schs, teacher, 1956-73; Teachers Col Columbia Univ, asst prof, dir teacher corps proj, 1975-76; Publ Sch Syst Va, consult; State Dept Educ, consult; Sch Ed Va Commonwealth Univ, prof, 1976-2000, emer prof teaching & learning, 2000-. **Orgs:** Phi Delta Kappa; Zeta Phi Beta Sorority, 1955-; ATE, 1978-; Asn Teacher Educators Va, 1988-91. **Honors/Awds:** Innovation Award, DC Publ Schs Washington; Minority Stud Scholar, Teachers Col Columbia Univ; Reise-Melton Award for Promoting Cross-Cultural Understanding, Va Commonwealth Univ, 1990-91; Outstanding Service Award, 1991-92; Outstanding Teacher Award, 1994-95; Phi Kappa Phi; Bd Visitors, teaching fellow, 1998-2000; Distinguished Faculty award in Teaching, Va Commonwealth Univ, 2000. **Special Achievements:** Co-Author: Classroom Management for the Realities of Today's Schools; Author of book chapter in J Wood's Mainstreaming; articles published in Action in Teacher Education; NASSP Journal; Middle School Journal; Research Studs: Resilient At-Risk Children; Teaching in Culturally Diverse Classrooms; Overage & Disruptive Students in the Middle School; Social Reconstructionism for Urban Students, 1999. **Home Phone:** (804)745-0080. **Business Addr:** Professor Emeritus, Virginia Commonwealth University, School of Education, Box 842020, Richmond, VA 23284-2020, **Business Phone:** (804)828-1945.

REED, DAPHNE MAXWELL. See REID, DAPHNE ETTA MAXWELL.

REED, DERRYL L
Executive. **Personal:** Born in Chicago, IL; son of Jesse A Jr. **Educ:** Southern Ill Univ, BS, Math, 1970; Univ Chicago, MBA, Mkt/Fin, 1976. **Career:** Chicago Bd Educ, substitute teacher, 1970-77; Am Can Co, sales rep, 1970-73, acct mgr, 1973-75, area mgr, 1975-77, assoc product mgr, napkins, 1977-78, asst product mgr, Aurora Bathroom Tissue, staff, 1978-80; Tetley Inc, product mgr soluble tea products, 1980-83, product mgr tea bags, 1983-85, sr product mgr tea bags, 1985-86, sr product mgr tea products, 1986-87; Heublein Inc, dir mkt prepared drinks, 1987-89; Teachers Ins & Annuity Asn Am, asst vpres ins servs, 1989-94; Ameritech, dir brand mgmt, dir mkt planning & develop, 1994-95, dir mkt, 1995-97, dir multicultural mkt, advert, 1998-2000, dir multicul mkt, SCBDO, 2000-; Derryl L. Reed & Associates, LLC, Chicago Gospel Showcase & Awards, pres & founder, currently. **Orgs:** Bd dirs, Chicago, Nat Am Advan Colored People, 1975; consult partner, Reed & Reed Assocs; bd dirs, Nat Black MBA Asn, 1986-; assoc bd dirs, Tea Asn USA Inc; past chmn, NY Corp Matching Gift Fund Lou Rawls Parade Stars Telethon United Negro Col Fund; Kappa Alpha Psi Frat; Consumer Promotion Comn, Asn Nat Advertisers; nat pres, Nat Black MBA Asn; adv bd mem, Southern Ill Univ Sch Bus, 1992-; bd overseers, Univ Conn, Sch Bus Admin, 1993-95; founding mem, multicultrual mkt comt, radio advertising & sports & events mkt comt, Asn Nat Advertisers; celebrity entertainment comt & prog consult, Spec Olympics World Games, 1995. **Honors/Awds:** A Black Achiever in Industry Award, Am Can Co; Outstanding Service & Achievement Award, Kappa Alpha Psi Frat; MBA of the Year, 1988. **Special Achievements:** Featured in Oct 1985 issue of Black Enterprise Magazine; participant in 2 TV progs, hosted by Phil Donahue; guest speaker, Connecticut Public TV; guest lectr, Univ Conn & Atlanta Univ; honored for outstanding leadership & contrib to bus community, Leonard N Stern Sch Bus, NY Univ; selected An Achiever in History, Am Can Co. **Home Addr:** 3297 Woodview Lake Dr, West Bloomfield, MI 48323. **Business Addr:** President, Founder, Derryl L. Reed & Associates, LLC, Chicago Gospel Showcase & Awards, 3297 Woodview Lake Rd Suite 100, West Bloomfield, MI 48323, **Business Phone:** (586)214-5557.

REED, ESQUIRE JERRILDINE
Lawyer. **Personal:** Born in Jersey City, NJ; daughter of Jesse Henry and Della Mae Anderson; divorced; children: Steven M Adams. **Educ:** Temple Law Sch, JD, 1981. **Career:** Daniel Preminger PC & Hugh Clark Esq, law clerk, 1981-83; Cong Staff Robert A Borski MC, 1983-86; Greater Pa Chamber Com, 1986-90; Rohm & Haas Co, in-house coun, Polit Action Comm, treas, 1990-97; Congressman Chaka Fattah, atty, 1998, spec asst, currently. **Orgs:** Delta Sigma Theta, 1961-2000; NJ Bar Asn, 1990-2000; Am Bar Asn, 1990-2000; Nat Bar Asn, 1990-2000; Barristers Asn Philadelphia, 1990-2000; trustee, Community Col Philadelphia, 1980-92; homeless advocacy, Proj Bar Asn, 1990-96; mentor, Phildelphia Futures, 1990-96. **Honors/Awds:** Robert Kline Acad Achievement, Temple Law, 1981; Small Bus Advocate, Chamber Com, 1989; Volunteer of the Year Award, Rohm & Haas Co, 1995. **Special Achievements:** Author: "Budget Crisis, A Turning Point for the City," Urban League Leadership Inst, 1990; Presentation of "How To Launch a Judicial campaign," Barristers' Assn Conf, 1992; Completion of Pub Affairs Coun Inst Prog, Sr Pub Affairs Prof, 1993-96. **Home Addr:** 6760 Emlen St, Philadelphia, PA 19119, **Home Phone:** (215)843-4360. **Business Addr:** Special Assistant, United States House of Representatives, Fattah Chaka Congressman, 4104 Walnut St, Philadelphia, PA 19104, **Business Phone:** (215)387-6404.

REED, FLORINE. See Obituaries section.

REED, GREGORY J.
Lawyer, executive. **Personal:** Born May 21, 1948, Michigan; son of James and Bertha Mae; married; children: Arian Simone, Ashley Sierra. **Educ:** Mich State Univ, BS, 1970, MS, 1971; Wayne State Univ, JD, 1974, LLM, 1978. **Career:** Price Waterhouse, Tax Specialist, 1976; AHR Packaging Consult Corp, Mich, pres & developer, 1987-; Wayne State Univ, Detroit MI, prof, 1988-89; Mich Bar Continuing Legal Educ, teacher, 1992; Gregory J Reed & Assocs PC, owner & atty, currently. **Orgs:** Chairperson, Martin

Luther King Statue Comt; bd dirs, Mich Asn Community Arts Agencies; Nat Bar Asn; bd, Mich State Univ Found; Omega Psi Phi; comt mem, Am Bar Asn; Am Bar Asn; Accounting Aide Soc Metro Detroit; bd comt, New Detroit Inc; tax and corp advisor BUF; Mich State Bar Taxation & Corp Div; Am Arbitration Asn; bd dir, BESLA Entertainment Law Asn; bd dirs, Mich Asn Community Arts Agencies; State Bar Law Media Comn; adv bd mem, US Internal Revenue Serv; founder, Advan Amateur Athletics Inc, 1986; Gregory J. Reed Scholar Found, 1986-96; chmn, US State Bar Mich Arts Communication Sports and Entertainment Sect, 1987-88; vpres, BESLA, 1992-93; Mich State Univ Found, vice chairperson, 1996-97. **Honors/Awds:** Distinguished Alumni of the Yr Award, Mich State Univ, 1980; Resolution for Achievement State of Mich Senate, City of Detroit; implemented Gregory J Reed Scholarship Foundation 1986; Award for Contributions to the arts Black Music Month, State Mich House of Rep, 1987; govt appointment Martin Luther King Comn Mich, 1989-; 1992 Hall of Fame inductee by BESLA; Nat Book Award, 1994; Keeper of the Word Found, 1994; American Book Award; John Hensel Award, State Bar Mich, 2003; John Henselaward significant contribution to the Art, State Bar Mich. **Special Achievements:** Author: Tax Planning and Contract Negotiating Techniques for Creative Persons; Professional Athletes and Entertainers (first book of its kind cited by Am Bar Asn); This Bus of Boxing & Its Secrets, 1981; This Bus of Entertainment and Its Secrets, 1985; Negotiations Behind Closed Doors, 1987; Economic Empowerment through the church, Am Book Award, 1994; "Quiet Strength," co-author with Rosa Parks; "Dear Mrs Parks," co-author with Rosa Parks; author, Economic Empowerment Supplement book guide; American Book Awd; NCP Image, for outstanding literature. **Business Addr:** Owner, Gregory J Reed & Associates, 1201 Bagley, Detroit, MI 48226.*

REED, ISHMAEL SCOTT
Educator, writer. **Personal:** Born Feb 22, 1938, Chattanooga, TN; son of Henry Lenoir and Thelma Coleman; married Priscilla Rose, Sep 1960 (divorced 1970); children: Timothy & Brett; married Carla Blank; children: Tennessee Maria. **Educ:** St Univ NY, Buffalo, attended 1960; Univ Buffalo, DSc, 1995. **Career:** Educator (retired), Writer; East Village Other, co-founder, 1962; Yardbird Pub Co Inc, Berkeley CA, co-founder, 1971, ed dir, 1971-75; Reed Cannon & Johnson Commns Co, Berkeley, co-founder, 1973; Columbus Fdn, Berkeley, co-founder, 1976; Ishmael Reed & Al Young's Quilt, Berkeley, co-founder, 1980; US cols & Univs, guest lectr num; Univ CA, Santa Barbara, regents lectr, 1988; judge lit competitions, 1980-81; Berkeley Art Comn, chairperson; Univ CA, Berkeley, lectr; am poet, essayist & novelist, currently; Books: Flight to Canada, 1976; Secretary to the Spirits, 1978; Shrovetide in Old New Orleans, 1978; The Terrible Twos, 1982; God Made Alaska for the Indians, 1982; Reckless Eyeballing, 1986; Thirty-Seven Years of Boxing on Paper, 1988; The Terrible Threes, 1989; Airing Dirty Laundry, 1993; Japanese by Spring, 1993; Conversations with Ishmael Reed,1995; A Walk in Oakland, 2003. **Orgs:** Chmn bd dirs, Coordinating Coun Lit Mags, 1975-79, adv bd chmn, 1977-79; Authors Guild of Am, PEN, Celtic Found. **Honors/Awds:** Award, ACLU, 1978; National Endowment for Arts, Writing Fel, 1974; Guggenheim Fellow, 1975; Rosenthal Foundation Award, 1975; American Academy Award, 1975; Michaux Award, 1978. **Home Addr:** 870 53 St, Emeryville, CA 94608. **Business Addr:** Poet, Essayist, Novelist, Ishmael Reed Publishing Company, PO Box 3288, Berkeley, CA 94703.

REED, JAKE (WILLIE REED)
Football player, football executive. **Personal:** Born Sep 28, 1967, Covington, GA; married Vinita; children: Jake Rashann & Jaevin Octavia. **Educ:** Grambling State Univ, criminal justice. **Career:** Football player (retired); Minn Vikings, wide receiver, 1991-99, 2001; New Orleans Saints, wide receiver, 2000, 2002; Intense Football League, Frisco Thunder, owner, 2007-. **Business Addr:** Owner, Intense Football League, Firsco Thunder, 6537 Weber Road, Corpus Christi, TX 78413, **Business Phone:** (409)363-1957.

REED, DR. JAMES W
Physician, endocrinologist, writer. **Personal:** Born Nov 1, 1935, Pahokee, FL; son of Thomas and Chineater Gray Whitfield; married Edna; children: David M, Robert A, Mary I & Katherine E. **Educ:** WV State Col, BS, summa cum laude, 1954; Howard Univ, MD, 1963; resident/internal med Tacoma, WA, 1969. **Career:** Madigan Army Med Ctr, resident & internal, 1966-69; Univ Calif, San Francisco, res fel, 1971; AUS Med Dept, chief med, 1978-81; Univ Tex, Dallas, dir internal med educ, 1982-84; State WA Med Asst Prog, int med consult, 1984-85; Morehouse Sch Med, prof & assoc chmn dept med, 1985-, Grady Hosp, chief endocrinol & chief med serv; Co-auth: The Black Man's Guide to Good Health, Perigee Books, 1994; updated edition, Hilton Publishing, 2000; Hypertension: What Every African Man & Woman should Know About Living with High Blood Pressure, Hilton Publishing, 2002; Living With Diabetes: A Guide for Patients & Parents, Hilton Publ Co, 2005. **Orgs:** Consult med, Tuskegee, Va Hosp, 1982-; med dir, MMA Inc, 1982-; AMA; Am Diabetic Asn; Am Endocrine Soc; bd dir Int, Indisciplinary Soc Hypertension Blacks; pres, Int Soc Hypertension Blacks 1987-; pres, Int Soc Hypertension Blacks; course dir, seventh Int Conf Hypertension Blacks, 1992; lifetime hon trustee, Morehouse Sch Med; fel Am Col Endocrinol. **Honors/Awds:** Master American Col of Physicians; Nat Alumnus of the Year, W Va St Col 1987; Distinguished Alumni Award, NAFECO, 1989; Course Director second Int Conf on Hypertension in Blacks 1987; Lifrtime Achievement Award, COSEC. **Military Serv:** AUS, col, 1962-81; Meritorious Serv Medal, Legion Merit. **Business Addr:** Professor of Medicine, Associate Chair for Research, Morehouse School of Medicine, Department of Med, 720 Westview Drive SW, Atlanta, GA 30310, **Business Phone:** (404)756-5788.

REED, JASPER PERCELL
Educator. **Personal:** Born Mar 2, 1929, Centenary, SC; married Sandra Lee; children: Rosalyn Jackson, Rene Jackson & Valerie Linette. **Educ:** SC State Col, BS, biol, 1957; Pa State Univ, MEd, bio sci, 1968, DEd, bio sci, 1977. **Career:** Educator (retired); Community Col Philadelphia, prof bio, 1965; Temple Univ Med, asst instr, 1957-65; City Univ Syst, NY, evaluator, 1970; Educ Testing Serv, Col Level Educ Prog, test prod, 1970-73. **Orgs:** Kappa Alpha Psi, 1956-; Beta Kappa Chi, 1957; bd deac, White Rock Bapist Church, 1962-; Am Soc Allied Health Prof, 1979; Allied Health Admin, Am Asn State Col & Univ, 1979; Am Soc Pharmacol & Exp Therapeut. **Honors/Awds:** Annual Achievement Award, Philadelphia, Kappa Alpha Psi, 1974. **Military Serv:** AUS, sgt, 1948-54; Bronze Star Combat Medic Badge, Good Conduct, 1948-54. *

REED, JOANN
Educator. **Personal:** Born Mar 28, 1939, Flint, MI; daughter of Robin B Green Owens and Wendell A Owens; married Willie C, Oct 22, 1960; children: Kim F, George & Troy M. **Educ:** Eastern Mich Univ, BS, 1960, MA, 1982. **Career:** Educator (retired); Carman-Ainsworth Sch, teacher educable ment impaired,1963-73; Bassett Sch Dist, inst prog inst lab, 1973-74, teen mother prog coordr, 1973-74; Metro Day Care Ctr, admin, 1975-76; Carman Sch Dist, consult, 1975-95; Ken MacGillivray Buick, salesperson, 1976-77; Flint Comm Sch, admin, 1995-98. **Orgs:** Nat Asn Negro Bus & Prof Womens Club Inc; teach consult, 1977-, asst secy treas, 1981, vpres, 1984, treas, 1988-89, pres, 1985-86, 1989-, Flint Bd Educ; prog develop Mott Comm Col, 1984; Alpha Kappa Alpha Sor; Adahi-Hon Soc; Carman Educ Asn; Nat Roster Black Elected Officials; Greater Flint Afro-Am, Hall Fame, 1985-; Urban Coalition, 1989-; admin, Parent Involvement Advocate, 1995-98. **Honors/Awds:** Educators Award, Zeta Phi Beta Sorority Flint, 1981; Appreciation Award Nat Asn, Negro Bus & Prof Women, 1982. **Home Addr:** 6671 W Oraibi Dr, Glendale, AZ 85345, **Home Phone:** (623)825-0473.

REED, JOE LOUIS
Secretary (office). **Personal:** Born Sep 13, 1938, Evergreen, AL; son of Louis (deceased) and Eula Morgan; married Mollie Perry; children: Irva, Joe & Steven. **Educ:** Ala State Univ, BS, 1962; Case West Resv Univ, MA, 1966. **Career:** Ala Educ Asn Inc, assoc secy, 1969-; Ala State Teachers Asn, exec secy, 1964-69; Ala State Univ, stud act, 1963; Trenholm HS, teacher, 1962; Ala Dem Conf (ADC), chairman, currently; Democratic Party for Minority Affairs, vice chairman, currently. **Orgs:** Loc State & Nat Prof Asn; life mem, NEA; mem exec bd, NCSEA, 1969-75; coord vpres, NCSEA, 1975; pres NCSEA, 1976-; consult, AL Educ Asn Prof Rts & Resp Comn; chmn, DuShane Com Teachers Rights NEA, 1971-; staff adv, Unit Teaching Prof; delg, NEA Conv & Rep Assembly; pres, Ala League Advan Educ Chmn Ala Dem Conf, 1970-; Ala Adv Comn Civil Rights; vchmn, Minorty Affairs Ala Democratic Party, 1974-; chmn, NAACP Comn on Econ, 1969-; del Dem Nat Conv, 1968; Nat co-chmn Com Educr for Humphrey-muskie pres tkt, 1968; city cnclmn City Montgomery, 1975-; Masons; Omega Psi Phi Frat; past chmnof the bd trustees, Ala State Univ. **Honors/Awds:** Abraham Lincoln Award, Nat Educ Asn; addressed Democratic Nat Conv, 1972; initial report, Ala League Advan Educ, "The Slow Death of the Black Educator in Alabama"; pres, jr class, Ala State Univ, 1960-61; pres, student body, Ala State Univ, 1961-62; rated as one of the ten most influential citizens in the State of Alabama. **Military Serv:** AUS, 1956-58. **Business Addr:** 422 Dexter Ave, Montgomery, AL 36101.

REED, KATHLEEN RAND
Sociologist. **Personal:** Born Feb 6, 1947, Chicago, IL; daughter of Johnie Viola Rand Cathey and Kirkland James; divorced. **Educ:** San Francisco State Univ, BA; Univ Md, Col Park, BA, appl biocultural anthrop. **Career:** Ill Supreme Ct Comm on Character & Fitness, Chicago, Ill, investigator & res consult 1970; ETA Public Relations Chicago, Ill, acct exec, 1970-72; WTVS TV 56 (Public TV) Detroit, Mich, public relations & promotion dir, 1972; WJLB Radio Detroit, Mich, pub affairs dir, 1972-74; KH Arnold San Francisco, Calif, bus resource & resource consult, 1974-80; Headquarters Co Subsidiary United Tech, special proj coord, 1980-81; Nat Alliance Bus San Francisco, Calif, admin mgr, 1981-83; Michael St Michael & Corp Leather (self-employed), manufacturing exec & pres, 1983-; Necronomics & Ethnographics, Palo Alto, Calif, pres, 1989; Geog Genetic Systs, pres, 2001; Rand Reed Group, pres & applied biocultural anthropologist & ethnomarketer, currently; Dept Health & Human Serv, grant proposal reviewer. **Orgs:** Pres, Am Futurists Educ Women; World Future Soc; Nat Orgn Women; Women's Inst Freedom Press; World Affairs Coun; Bay Area Urban League; League Women Voters; Nat Women Studies Asn; Nat Coun Negro Women; Commonwealth Club Calif, 1977; Int Aff Com; Women Comn; Media & Public Info Comn; consult & contrib, Black Esthetics, 1972; bd dir, San Francisco Convention & Vis Bur, 1987-90, Urban Coalition West, Phoenix, Ariz 1987-93; chmn, African Am Donor Task Force, 1990-; NIH; inst review bd, Nat Heart, Lung, Blood Inst; panelist, Nat Res Coun Workshop Race & Ethnic Classification; Am Anthrop Asn; Soc Appl Anthrop; Am Asn Geographers; Afro-Am Historical & Geol Soc; Kennedy Inst Ethics, Georgetown Univ. **Honors/Awds:** Nat Asn Negro Bus & Prof Women, Western Region Vol Award, 1977; San Mateo Co Women's Hall of Fame, 1993. **Special Achievements:** Publications/productions: "Femininity" Book Review Women's Review of Books, 1984; "San Francisco Government, The City, The Citizen & Technetronics", 1978; Lectures/Speeches, Univ Calif Davis "The Black Female in Contemporary Society" Afro-American Studies & Women's Studies Combined Session, 1984; Univ San Francisco Lecturer "Women and the Working World", 1978.

REED, KIMBERLEY DEL RIO
Lawyer. **Personal:** Born Jan 7, 1957, Detroit, MI; daughter of William F II and Charlie Johnson; children: William Mandela Matthews. **Educ:** Ky State Univ, BS, 1978; Howard Univ Sch Law, JD, 1981; Wayne State Univ Sch Law, LLM, 1995. **Career:** US Dept Labor, law clerk, 1980-81; UAW Legal Dept, law clerk, 1981-82; Legal Aid & Defender Assoc, dep defender, 1982-92; Am Inst Paralegal Studies, law instr, 1986-87; Mich Paralegal Inst, law instr, 1988-89; Oak Grove Am Church, sunday sch teacher, 1992-; Detroit Recorders Ct, State Judicial Coun, chief legal coun, judicial asst, 1992-. **Orgs:** Life mem, Delta Sigma Theta Sorority Inc, 1975-; Oak Grove Am Church, chancel choir, 1982-; treas, Detroit chap, Ky State Unive Alum Asn, 1987-90; vpres, Detroit chap, Howard Univ Alum Asn, 1987-88; Detroit Alumnae Chap, 1990-; African Am Enrichment Asn, 1990-; consult, Jr Achievement, 1992-. **Honors/Awds:** Outstanding Alumnus, Outstanding Alumnus Mumford High Sch, 1984; Service Award, Ky State Univ Alum Asn, 1991; Service Award Teenlift, Delta Sigma Theta Sorority Inc, 1993; Service Award, Mumford Class of 1974, 1994. **Special Achievements:** Publications: The Exclusionary Rule is There Life After Lean? Vol I Criminal Practice Law Rev 137, 1980; The Economic Impact of Colonialism on the Legal Systems of Cameroon, Cote D'Ivorie and Senegal; Wayne State Law Lib, Masters Essay, 1994; Admitted to the State Bar of MI, 1992. **Business Addr:** Chief Legal Counsel, Judicial Assistant, Recorder, 1441 St Antoine Suite 1069, Detroit, MI 48226, **Business Phone:** (313)224-7073.

REED, KWAME OSEI (BOBBY REED)
Lawyer, clergy. **Personal:** Born Apr 28, 1948, McComb, MS; son of Charles James and Helen Marie Garner; married Rita Wallace Reed MD MPH; children: Nene Wallace Reed & Kojo Wallace Reed. **Educ:** Howard Univ, BA, 1972, Sch Law, JD, 1975; Yale Univ Divinity Sch, Master Divinity, 1979. **Career:** Oberlin Col, Black Studies Dept, instr, 1976-77; Comt Reconciliation, 1979-81; Univ Pittsburgh, 1980-81; North MSP Legal Servs, 1982-83; United Church Christ, Heritage Fel, 1983-87; Legal Servs Northern Va, 1992-93; Potomac Asn Cent Atlantic Conf, United Church Christ, clergy, 1987, assoc conf minister, currently; National Capital Area, exec officer; Oberlin Col, fac; Univ Pittsburgh, Legal Studies Dept, fac. **Orgs:** Founder, Heritage Fel United Church Christ; co-founder, Hope Med Clinic, Accra, Ghana, 1993-98; founding mem, United Church Christ Atty Network, 1996-98; Andrew Rankin Memorial Chap Howard Univ; chmn, Potomac Asn. **Honors/Awds:** Outstanding Contribution to Reston, Va in its First 20 Years, 1985; Calvin Coolidge High School Alumni Award, 1995; Visiting scholar, Yale Law Sch. **Special Achievements:** Yale Law Sch Vis Scholar Res Law & Religion, 1981-82. **Military Serv:** AUS, Sec Lt, 1968-69; Nat Defense Serv Medal, 1969. **Home Addr:** 11651 N Shore Dr Apt 12, Reston, VA 20190-4615. **Business Addr:** Associate Conference Minister, Potomac Association of the United Church of Christ, Atlantic Conference, 916 S Rolling Rd, Baltimore, MD 21228-5318, **Business Phone:** (410)788-4190.

REED, MICHAEL H
Lawyer, teacher, administrator. **Personal:** Born Jan 17, 1949, Philadelphia, PA; married Yalta Gilmore Reed, Aug 12, 1978; children: Alexandra & Michael Jr. **Educ:** Temple Univ, BA, 1969; Yale Univ, JD, 1972. **Career:** Pepper Hamilton LLP, Philadelphia, PA, partner, 1972-; Temple Univ, Sch Law, adj prof; Rutgers Univ, Sch Law, adj prof. **Orgs:** Trustee, Episcopal Hosp, 1986-; chmn, Prof Guid Comt, Philadelphia Bar Asn, 1986; trustee & corp secy, Acad Natural Sci, 1988-; chmn, Pa Bar Asn, Minority Bar Comt, 1988-90; Pa Judicial Inquiry & Rev Bd, 1990-93; bd gov, Pa Bar Asn, 1993-; fel Am Col Bankruptcy; bd dirs & bd adv, Pub Interest Law Ctr Philadelphia; exec bd, Comt Seventy; Chambers USA. **Honors/Awds:** Outstanding Serv Award, Philadelphia Bar Asn, Young Lawyers Sect, 1975; Spec Achievement Award, Pa Bar Asn, 1989; Cert of Hon, Outstanding Alumnus, Temple Univ, Col Arts & Sci, 1995. **Special Achievements:** First person of color to

lead the Pa Bar Asn. **Business Addr:** Partner, Pepper Hamilton LLP, 3000 2 Logan Sq 18th Arch St, Philadelphia, PA 19103-2799.

REED, ROBIN LYNN. See REED-HUMES, ROBI.

REED, DR. RODNEY J
School administrator, educator. **Personal:** Born May 16, 1932, New Orleans, LA; son of Ursul C Desvignes and Edgar J; married Vernell M Auzenne, Aug 5, 1961; children: Karen & Ursula. **Educ:** Clark Col, BA, 1951; Univ Mich, MA, 1956; Univ Calif, Berkeley, PhD, 1971. **Career:** Southern Univ, Baton Rouge, asst prof & asst cond bnds, 1956-61; Oakland Calif Unified Sch Dist, high sch teacher & vice prin, 1961-68; Univ Calif, Berkeley, Urban fel, 1968-70, from asst prof to prof, 1970-90, fac asst chancellor affirmative action, 1980-82, prof emer, 1991-; Pa State Univ, Col Educ, prof & dean, 1990-98, dean emer & prof emer, 1999-. **Orgs:** Am Ed Res Asn, 1970-; ed bd mem, Educ & Urban Soc, 1972-86; pres, Fornax Inc, 1975-88; life mem, Nat Asn Advan Colored People, 1975-; Asn Calif Sch Admin, 1976-90; ed bd, Policy Studies Review Annual, 1976-86; Nat Conf Prof Ed Admin, 1977-94; chair, Ed Comt Bay Area Black United Fund, 1979-82; vice chair & mem bd, Bay Area Urban League, 1980-89; ed bd, Educ Researcher, 1982-90; ed bd, Nat Forum Educ Admin & Supervisors, 1983-; Omega Psi Phi Fraternity; Sigma Pi Phi Frat, 1983-; Am Asn Sch Admin, 1986-94; Phi Delta Kappa, 1971-; Am Educ Res Asn, 1974-; Omicron Tau Theta, Nat Hon Soc, 1990-; ed adv bd, J African Am Male Studies, 1990-94; Cleveland Nat Forest, 1991-2002; treasurer, Exec Comt, Asn Cols & Schs Educ State Universities & Land Grant Cols & Affiliated Pvt Univs, 1992-95; ed bd, Educ ADM Quarterly, 1993-96; mem-at-large, bd dirs, Holmes Partnership, 1994-96; mem-at-large, bd dirs, Am Asn Cols Teacher Educ, 1994-97; bd dirs, Penn Goals, 1994-96 & 2000; Asn Cols & Schs Educ State Universities & Land Grant Cols & Affiliated Pvt Univs, pres, 1995-98; bd dirs, Am Asn Cols Teachers Educ, 1996-98; life mem, Pa State Univ Alumni Asn; life mem, Univ Calif, Berkley, Alumni Asn; Asn Col Educ & Schs Educ State Univs & Land Grant Cols & Affiliated Pvt Univs. **Honors/Awds:** Outstanding Man of the Year, Omega Psi Phi Frat Sigma Iota, 1966; Bronze Award, Bay Area Black United Fund, 1982; Order of the Golden Bear, Univ Calif, Berkeley, 1985-; Recipient Calif State Legislatue Assembly & Senate Resolutions, 1989; Calif Assembly Speakers Plaque, 1989; Alumnus of the Year, Black Alumni Club, Univ Calif Berkeley Alumni Club, 1992; Golden Key, Nat Honor Soc. **Special Achievements:** Author, Expectation & Student Achievement; co-author, (James W Gutherie) Edtl Admin Policy Ldshp Am Ed, Second Edition, 1991; co-author, The Politics of Urban Educ in the US, 1992; co-author, Restructuring Public Schooling: Europe, Canada, America, 1997. **Military Serv:** AUS, specialist 3, 1953-55. **Home Addr:** 6623 Glen Oaks Way, Oakland, CA 94611. **Business Addr:** Dean Emeritus, Professor Emeritus, Pennsylvania State University College of Education, Department of Education Policy Studies, 274 Chambers Bldg, University Park, PA 16802, **Business Phone:** (814)865-1542.

REED, SHEILA A
Editor, journalist. **Educ:** Univ Fla, Gainesville, FL, BSJ, 1981. **Career:** Sarasota Herald Tribune, Sarasota, FL, 1982-83; Gainesville Sun, Gainesville, FL, 1984-86; Florida Times-Union, Jacksonville, FL, 1986-87; St Petersburg Times, St Petersburg, FL, 1987-91, seniority ed, currently; Gannett Suburban Newspaper, White Plains, NY, 1991-94; Lexington Herald-Leader, Lexington, KY, 1994-98; Atlanta Journal-Const. **Orgs:** Nat Asn Black Journalists, 1990-. **Business Addr:** Seniority Editor, St. Petersburg Times, PO Box 1121, St Petersburg, FL 33731, **Business Phone:** (727)893-8452.

REED, DR. THERESA GREENE
Physician, educator. **Personal:** Born Dec 9, 1923, Baltimore, MD; daughter of William James Greene and Theresa Greene Evans; divorced. **Educ:** Va State Col, BS, chem, 1945; Meharry Med Col, MD, 1949; Johns Hopkins Univ, MPH, 1967. **Career:** Physician, Educator (retired); Homer G Phillips Hosp, staff physician, pub health physician, 1950-58, asst clinic dir 1958-66; pvt pract physician, 1950-65; Johns Hopkins Univ & Sinai Hosp, prev med fel, 1966-68, lectr clin pharmacol; US Food Drug Admin, medical officer 1968-92, supvry med officer, 1977-80, 1988-92; Howard Univ, assoc prof community med; Nat Med Asn, historian. **Orgs:** Chmn, Comt Admin & Financial Affairs, Nat Med Asn, 1987-89; pres, Medico-Chirurgical Soc DC, 2001-; Am Col Epidemiol; fel Am Col Preventive Med; Soc Epidemiol Res; Am Soc Microbiol; Am Med Womens Asn; Am Pub Health Asn; Asn Teachers Preventive Med; Am VD Asn; fel City Med Soc; Int Epidemiological Asn; life mem, Alpha Kappa Alpha; secy & treas, Daniel Hale Williams Med Reading Club; Chi Delta Mu Fraternity; Delta Omega; Homer G Phillips Alumni Asn; Xi Zeta Omega Ch; Nat Asn Advan Colored People; Trinity Episcopal Church; pres, African Am Hist & Geneal Soc; ROOTS Users Group; Uncrowned Queens Inst Res & Educ Women Inc. **Honors/Awds:** Public Health Serv Special Recognition Award, 1985; Commendable Service Award, Food & Drug Admin, 1985; Outstanding Serv Award, Nat Med Asn, 1986-87; Pub Health Serv Supvr Serv Award, 1991; Community Serv Award, Am Med Women's Asn, 1992; Equal Opportunity Achievement Award; Distinguished Service Award, Nat Med Asn Region II. **Special Achievements:** The founder and first president of the first Black female medical society in 1963; One of the first members of the St Louis Medical Society; first Black Female Med Epidemiologist; Author of numerous papers in medical journals. **Home Addr:** 11516 Patapsco Dr, Rockville, MD 20852-2454, **Home Phone:** (301)468-6830.

REED, DR. VINCENT EMORY
Educator. **Personal:** Born Mar 1, 1928, St Louis, MO; son of Artie and Velma; married Frances Bullitt. **Educ:** WVa State Col Inst, BS Educ, 1952; Howard Univ, MA, 1965; Wharton Sch Finance & Comn Univ PA, completed inst Colective negotiations; VA St Col, Guidance NDEA Scholarship; Iowa Univ. **Career:** Educator (retired); WV St Col, football coach, 1955; Jefferson Jr HS, teacher, 1956; Anacostia HS, Cardozo HS, Jefferson Jr HS, counr, 1963; Manpower Develop Training Prog DC Pub Schs, asst dir, 1964; Dunbar HS, Wilson HS, asst prin; Woodrow Wilson Sr HS; DC Pub Sch, asst supt personnel, 1969-70; DC Pub Sch, asst supt safety & security, 1970, exec asst, 1970-71, asst supt, 1971-74, assoc supt off state admin, 1974-75, supt, 1975-80; pres US, asst secy elem & secondary educ, 1981-82; The Washington Post, vpres communs, 1982-98. **Orgs:** NAACP, mem Jr Achievement Wash, DC; bd dir, Stonewall Athletic Club; bd dir YMCA; bd dir, Nat Conf Christians & Jews; bd trustees, Univ DC; bdtrustees, Southeastern Univ; bd trustees, Gallaudet Col; bd trustees, Am Univ; found trustee, WV St Col; exec comt Convention & Visitors Ctr; Howard Univ Charter Day Comt; bd dir, Big Brothers Inc; chmn, Sch & Summer Jobs Bd Trade Wash, DC; bd dir, Girl Scouts; bd dir, Boy Scouts; bd dir, Boys' & Girls' Club DC Police Dept; Merit Select Panel US Magistrates; DC chmn, United Way; past mem, Am Asn Sch Personnel Admin; Am Personnel & Guidance Asn; past chmn Area Supts Study Seminar; past bd dir, Goodwill Indust. **Honors/Awds:** Community Service Award, SE Citizens Asn, 1970; Superior Service Award, DC Bicentennial Assembly, 1976; Outstanding Achievement Award, WV State Col, 1976; Outstanding Community Service Award, NAACP, 1977; Distinguished Service Award, Phi Delta Kappa Intl George Washington Univ, 1979; Keynote Speaker, NY State Urban League Convention; Keynote Speaker, Nat Head Start Conf; Keynote Speaker, Seven-State Conf PTA; comn eval qualifications pvt sch admin vocational training DC pub schs; Principal Speaker, Commencement Exercises Univ DC, Southeastern Univ, etc; Honorary degrees, WV State Col, HHD; Southeastern Univ, Doctor Pub Admin; Georgetown Univ, Doct Humane Letters; Univ DC, Doctor Laws; Strayer Col, Doctor Humane Letters;Harris-Stowe Univ, Doctor Humane Letters. **Special Achievements:** Award is given in the name of Dr. Vincent Reed, the distinguished educator. **Military Serv:** AUS, 1st lt. *

REED, WILLIE. See REED, JAKE.

REED, WILLIS
Basketball executive, basketball player. **Personal:** Born Jun 25, 1942, Bernice, LA; married Gale; children: Carl & Veronica. **Educ:** Grambling State Univ, LA, attended 1964. **Career:** Basketball Player (retired), Coach (retired), Basketball Executive; NY Knicks, ctr, forward, 1964-74, head coach, 1977-79; St John's Univ, volasst basketball coach, 1980-81; Creighton Univ, head basketball coach, 1981-82, 1984-85; Atlanta Hawks, asst coach, 1985-87; Sacramento Kings, asst basketball coach, 1987-88; NJ Nets, head coach, 1987-88; basketball & bus develop, vpres, 1989-90; basketball opers, sr vpres, 1990, exec vpres & gen mgr, 1993, sr vpres, 1994-96; New Orleans/Okla City Hornets, vpres basketball oper, currently. **Orgs:** Phi Beta Sigma fraternity. **Honors/Awds:** Rookie of the Year, 1965; All Star Team, 1965-71, 1973; MVP, All-Star game, play offs, 1970; Basketball Hall of Fame, Nat Asn Intercollegiate Athletics, 1970; NBA World Championship Team, 1970, 1973; MVP, play offs, 1973; Nat Memorial Basketball Hall of Fame, 1981; Naismith Memorial Basketball Hall of Fame, 1982. **Special Achievements:** Co-author, The View from the Run, 1971; One of the 50 Greatest Players in NBA History, 1996. **Business Addr:** Vice President of Basketball Operations, New Orleans/Oklahoma City Hornets, Oklahoma Tower, 210 Pk Ave Suite 1850, Oklahoma City, OK 73102, **Business Phone:** (405)208-4800.

REED-CLARK, LARITA DIANE
Financial manager. **Personal:** Born Sep 26, 1960, Chicago, IL; daughter of Henry and Joyce Hinton; widowed 1999. **Educ:** Loyola Univ, Chicago, Ill, BBA, 1982, CPA, Ill, 1983; Kellogg Sch Bus, Northwestern Univ, MS, mgt, 1993. **Career:** KPMG, Chicago, Ill, auditor, 1982-84; McCormick Pl, Chicago, Ill, asst controller, 1982-84, controller, fiscal operations dir, 1984-97, dir finance & admin, 1997-. **Orgs:** Strive Community Serv Orgn, 1997-2000; Nat Asn Black Acct, 1980-; Am Inst CPA's, 1983-; Ill CPA Soc, 1983-; Family Christian Ctr Ch, 1992-; Govt Finance Officers Asn, 1984-. **Honors/Awds:** Named among top black business & professional women, Dollars & Sense Magazine, 1988. **Business Addr:** Director of Administration & Finance, McCormick Place, 2301 S Lake Shore Dr, Chicago, IL 60616, **Business Phone:** (312)791-7000.

REED-HUMES, ROBI (ROBIN LYNN REED)
Administrator, television producer, actor. **Personal:** Born in Mount Vernon, NY; married; children: 2. **Educ:** Hampton Univ, BA, speech & drama, 1980. **Career:** Films: The Falcon & the Snowman, production asst; Best Seller, casting asst; She's Gotta Have It, 1984; Sch Daze, 1988; I'm Gonna Git You Sucka, 1988; Do the Right Thing, 1989; Harlem Nights, 1989; Mo' Better Blues, 1990; Jungle Fever, 1991; Malcolm X, 1993; Soul Food, 1997; Never Die Alone, 2004; The Gospel, 2005; Waist Deep, 2006; Crossover, 2006; TV: "Roc, The Robert Guillaume Show, A Different World, In Living Color, & Good News; Michael Jackson's Music Video, "Remember the Time," casting dir, 1993; "Woo," casting dir, 1998; Wifey, 2007; Others: McClean & DiMeo, casting asst; To The Glory of God, founder, pres; Robin Reed-Humes & Assocs, pres, currently. **Orgs:** Delta Sigma Theta Sorority Inc. **Honors/Awds:** Casting Circle Award, Casting Soc Am, 1993; Emmy-nomination for Only in Am: The Don King Story, 1998; Emmy for casting "The Tuskegee Airmen"; Emmy for casting, Black Hollywood Educ & Resource Ctr. **Business Addr:** Casting Director, Raleigh Studios, 5300 Melrose Ave, Los Angeles, CA 90038, **Business Phone:** (213)871-4440.

REED-MILLER, ROSEMARY E
Businessperson. **Personal:** Born Jun 22, 1939, Yeadon, PA; married Paul E (deceased); children: Sabrina E & Paul D. **Educ:** Temple Univ, AB, hist & anthrop, 1962. **Career:** US Dept Agr, info specialist, 1966-67; jewelry design, crafts develop, jour, Jamaica, WI, & Washington, DC (Womens Wear Daily, Afro-American, et al); Toast & Strawberries Inc, Boutique, owner, 1966-; Howard Univ, Sch Fine Arts & Ecol Awards, adj teacher; TV Shows, 1993; Work Post Home Mag, 1995. **Orgs:** Pres, Task Force Educ & Train Minority Bus ctr, 1973-74; Interracial Coun Bus, 1973; pres, Howard Univ Faculty Wives Asn, 1973; founding group Asn Women Bus Owners, 1974; del White House Conf Small Bus, 1980; Dupont Cir N Bus Asn; DC Barristers Wives Asn; DC Govt Econ Develop Comn, 1983-86; TV shows, Eye Wash, maternity fashions 1985; Woodley House, 1986; Wash Ethical Soc Sch, 1997; Nat Asn Women Bus Owner. **Honors/Awds:** Bus Award Century Club Nat Asn Negro Bus & Prof Women's Clubs, 1973; Bus Serv Award, Wash Black Econ Develop Corp, 1973; delegate White House Conf Small Bus award, delegate White House Comn Entrepreneural Educ, 1973; Business woman of Year, Nat Coun Small Bus Develop Eastern Reg, 1974; Black Acad Develop Alpha Kappa Alpha Sor, 1975; Appreciation Plaque Award Bus & Prof Women's League, 1980; Black Women Sisterhood Calendar Honoree, 1982; Bus Serv Award, Century Club Club, 1983; Econ Develop Bd Mayor's Office, 1983; Bus Serv Award, Howard Univ, Inst Urban Affairs, 1984; Bus Serv Award, Blacks Within Govt, 1984; Comt Serv Award, RSVP Club, 1984; Minority Women's Enterprise Fund, bus Accomplishment, 1995; DC Private Industry Corriel Award, 1996; Nat Theatre Supporter Award, 1996; Am Soc Study African Am History, The Path Toward Enpowerment Award, 1998; Phenomenal Business Women Award, Wash bus guide mag, 2002. **Special Achievements:** Author, The Threads of Time, The Fabric of History: Profiles of African Am Designers & Dressmakers, 2002; radio show, Fashion Bus, Capital Edition WUSA, News WJLA, Inaugural Dressup, Wash Post; ACTCO Theatre graphics, African Coalition. **Business Addr:** Owner, Toast & Strawberries, DuPont Cir 1608 Connecticut Ave NW, 1532 Upshur St, Washington, DC 20009, **Business Phone:** (202)723-9007.

REED PEEBLES, DR. REV. CHARLOTTE. See REED, DR. CHARLOTTE.

REESE, ALBERT
Football player. **Personal:** Born Apr 29, 1973, Mobile, AL. **Educ:** Grambling State Univ. **Career:** Football player (retired) San Francisco 49ers, defensive tackle, 1997; Grand Rapids Rampage, 2003; Dallas Desperados, 2005.

REESE, CALVIN, JR. See REESE, POKEY.

REESE, DELLA (DELLAREESE PATRICIA EARLY)
Actor, composer, singer. **Personal:** Born Jul 6, 1931, Detroit, MI; daughter of Richard Early and Nellie Early; married Vermont Taliaferro (divorced); married Franklin T Lett; children: Deloreese, James, Franklin & Dominique; married Leroy Gray (divorced). **Educ:** Wayne State Univ, attended. **Career:** TV Appearance: The Tonight Show; Merv Griffin Show; Ed Sullivan; McCloud; Police Woman; Twice in a Lifetime; Chico & the Man; Petro celli; Mike Douglas Show; Mahalia Jackson Troupe, performed, 1945-49; solo rec artist, 1957-; Let's Rock, 1958; The Last Minstrel Show, 1978, actress; Jubilee, RCA, Victor Records, ABC Paramount, rec artist; Della Variety Show, hostess, 1969-70; Sahara-Tahoe, Caesar's Palace, Coconut Grove, MrKelly's, Caribe Hilton, Flamingo, performer; Film : Harlem Nights, actress; Distinguished Gentleman, actress; Thin Line Between Love & Hate, actress; Della, Spec Delivery, singer; I Like It Like Dat, singer; Sure Like Lovin' You, singer; Something Cool, singer; Royal Family, 1991-92; IfI Had Known I Was a Genius, actress, 2007; TV series: Beauty Shop, 2005; If I Had Known I Was a Genius, 2007; minister, currently; tv movie roles: Anya's Bell, 1999; Having Our Say: The Delany Sisters' First 100 Yrs, 1999; The Secret Path, 1999; The Moving of Sophia Myles, 2000; "That's So Raven", 2006; "The Young and the Restless", 2009. **Honors/Awds:** Num gold recs; Most Promising Girl Singer, 1957; NAACP, 5 Image Awards; Nat Asn Black-Owned Broadcasters,

Oscar Micheaux Excellence Film Award, 1998; NAACP, Image Award, Outstanding Actress Drama Series, 2002. **Special Achievements:** Author: God Inside of Me; nominee, Grammy award, 1987. **Business Addr:** Actress, William Morris Agency, 151 El Camino Dr, Beverly Hills, CA 90212, **Business Phone:** (310)859-4085.

REESE, REV. FREDERICK D
Clergy, educator. **Personal:** Born Nov 28, 1929, Dallas County, AL; married Alline Toulas Crossing; children: Frederick jr, Valerie, Marvin, Christa & Alan. **Educ:** Alabama State Univ, BS; Atlanta Bible Inst Clark Col, adv study; Southern Univ; Selma Univ; Univ Alabama; Livingston Univ, MEd. **Career:** Ebenezer Bapt Church, Selma AL, pastor, currently; Eastside Jr High & Selma High Sch, prin; Supt educ, admin asst; city councilman. **Orgs:** Nat Educ Asn; Alabama Educ Asn; Dist VI Educ Asn; Phi Beta Sigma; bd dir, YMCA; pres, Dallas County Voters League. **Honors/Awds:** Abraham Lincoln Award; Outstanding Leadership Educr, NEA, Detroit, 1971; Dr Frederick D Reese Parkway, 2000; Teacher of the Year Award, Selma City Teachers Asn; Good Guy Award, Unit Appeal; numerous plaques & certificates for outstanding leadership in education and civil rights. **Special Achievements:** Local leader in 1965 Voters Rights Movement, Selma, organized black teachers for the right to vote, led demonstrations against local newspaper, resp for black clerks and cashiers in stores and banks, organized black citizens for position on Dallas County Dem Executive Committee. **Business Addr:** Pastor, Ebenezer Baptist Church, 1548 Legrande St, Selma, AL 36703, **Business Phone:** (334)875-6526.

REESE, GREGORY LAMARR
Librarian. **Personal:** Born Jul 30, 1949, Cleveland, OH; son of Jasper and Margaret Smith; married Evangeline Bynum, Dec 13, 1975; children: Michael. **Educ:** Morehouse Col, BA, hist, 1975; Case Western Reserve Univ, MLS, 1977. **Career:** Cuyahoga County Pub Libr, librn, 1975-80, br mgr, 1980-85; E Cleveland Pub Libr E, asst dir, 1985-88, exec dir, 1988-. **Orgs:** Past pres, East Cleveland Kiwanis; Cleveland, Area Metropolitan Libr Serv, 1980-; Alpha Phi Alpha Fraternity, 1986-; Cleveland Opera Multicult Awareness Prog, 1988-. **Honors/Awds:** Friend of Literacy Award, Project Learn, 1990; Alumni Fund Chairman, Case Western Reserve, 1981; Jazz Volunteer, Northeast Ohio, 1989; Ohio Librarian of the Year, 1991; Martin Luther King Jr, Altruism Award, East Cleveland Citizens for Sound Government, currently; Librarian of the Year, Ohio, 1992. **Home Phone:** (216)932-7073. **Business Addr:** Director, East Cleveland Public Library, 14101 Euclid Ave, East Cleveland, OH 44112, **Business Phone:** (216)541-4128.

REESE, IKE (ISIAH REESE)
Football player, radio host. **Personal:** Born Oct 16, 1973, Jacksonville, NC. **Educ:** Mich State Univ, commun. **Career:** Football player (retired), Radio host; Philadelphia Eagles, linebacker, 1998-2004; Atlanta Falcons, linebacker, 2005-07; 610WP(AM), 2008-. **Honors/Awds:** Jack Edelstein Memorial Award, 2002; Pro Bowler Selection, 2004. **Business Addr:** Radio Host, Sports Radio 610 WIP, 2 Bala Plz 7 Fl Suite 700, Bala Cynwyd, PA 19004, **Business Phone:** (215)592-0610.

REESE, ISIAH. See REESE, IKE.

REESE, IZELL
Football player. **Personal:** Born May 7, 1974, Dothan, AL. **Educ:** Univ Ala, Birmingham. **Career:** Football player (retired); Dallas Cowboys, defensive back, 1998-2001, 2005; Denver Broncos, 2002; Buffalo Bills, 2003-04.

REESE, MAMIE BYNES
Educator. **Personal:** Born in Gibson, GA. **Educ:** Spelman Col, BS, 1933; Drake Univ, MS, 1948; OH State Univ, adv study; Univ So CA; Simmons Col; Boston Univ. **Career:** Ctr HS, teacher; Des Moines Tech HS; Baker & Burke Counties, home demon agent; Albany State Col, assoc prof dean women. **Orgs:** GA State Bd Pardons & Pardons; past pres, Nat Asn Colored Wom Club Inc; GA Asn Educat; NEA; Sigma Rho Sigma Honor Sor; aux GA Osteop Med Asn; Nat Health Asn, Delta Sigma Theta Sor; Asn Parol Author; Am Correct Asn; World Fed Meth Wom; Hines Mem Butler St Meth Episco Chs; Albany Urban League & Guide; Albnay C C; Govs Spec Coun Fam Plan; Semper Fidel Club; GA Div Am Cancer Soc; comt mem, Girl Scouts Am; num off NAACP. **Honors/Awds:** Couple of year, Albany Chap Zeta Phi Beta Sor Inc, 1958; cit Spelman Col, 1966; outstanding Citizen, Albany State Col Comt Rel Comn, 1966; women conscience award, Nat Coun Women USA, 1969.

REESE, MILOUS J.
Chiropractor. **Educ:** Tex Chiropractic Col, applied kinesiology, 1972, diagnostic roentgenology, 1976; Emerson Col Herbology, MA, herbology, 1978; DHL, Miles Col, 1989; Midwestern Univ, BA; Am Inst Sci, MS, Philosopher; Ohio Christian Col, psychol; Am Non-Allopathic Univ, chiropractic; Emory Univ, Internal Med; McCormick Med Col; Nei Ching Int Chinese Healing Arts, Philosophy; Univ AL, Spec Study Alphine Cult Art & Lang. **Career:** Chiropractor (retired); Chiropractor pvt pract. **Orgs:** Am Fed Physio-Therapists, 1943; Nat Asn Naturopathic Herbalists Am, 1945; cert mem Nat Chiropractic Asn, 1945; founder, Ala Col Drugless Therapy, 1950; Booker T Wash Bus Col 1972; Big Brothers Club, 1975; Nat Psychiatric Asn, 1978; Am Col Chiropractic Orthopedist, 1979; Coun Nutrit Am Chiropractic Asn Inc; Orthopedic Class, 1979; cert mem, Am Coun Orthopedics ACA, 1979; cert holistic practr & life mem, Acad Holistic Practr,; Ala Acupuncture Coun, 1993; Ala State Chiropractic Asn; Jefferson County Chiropractic Soc; Acupuncture Soc Ala; Acupuncture Soc Am Kansas City, MO; Ctr Chinese Med Los Angeles, CA; US Acad Acupuncture; Traditional Acupuncture Found Columbia, MD; First African Appointed US Bd Acupuncture; Kappa Phi Sigma Med Frat; hon mem, Beta Psi Acctg Honor Soc, assoc mem, NY State Chiropractic Soc. **Honors/Awds:** Notary Pub Jefferson County, 1954; Dinner & Plaque Exemplary Serv, Field Med Humanitarian Serv; Cert Expression Gratitude Support, Columbia Inst Chiropractic Dipl Club, 1977; Dedicated Prof Leadership Award, Univ Montevallo, 1985; Cert Mem Gold Lapel Pin-50 years, Nat Col Chiropractic 1989; Plaque Recognition Continued Support Col Develop, Palmer Col Chiropractic, Davenport, IA; Lifetime Achievement Plaque, Chiropractic Asn, 1993; Proclamation Sen Earl Hilliard; Milous Reese Day, proclaimed Birmingham Councilman, Roosevelt Bell; Am Col Chiropractic Specialist; Ala State Chiropractic Asn; Cert Appreciation. **Home Addr:** 2117 18th St Ensley, Birmingham, AL 35218, **Home Phone:** (205)787-6162. *

REESE, POKEY (CALVIN REESE, JR.)
Baseball player. **Personal:** Born Jun 10, 1973, Columbia, SC; children: Naquwan & LaBresha. **Career:** Cincinnati Reds, infielder, 1997-01; Pittsburgh Pirates, 2002-03; Boston Red Sox, infielder, 2004; Seattle Mariners, infielder, 2005; Florida Marlins, 2006; Red Sox, free agt, 2003-06. **Honors/Awds:** NL Gold Glove, 1999-2000; World Series Champion; 3-time Top 10 in stolen bases, 1999-2001; Boston Red Sox, 2004. *

REESE, VIOLA KATHRYN
Social worker. **Personal:** Born Aug 23, 1953, Lexington, TN; daughter of Rev Billy Frank and Willie Mae Smith; married J Monroe Reese Jr; children: Idesha & James III. **Educ:** Tenn State Univ, BS, 1975; Wash Univ, MSW, 1977. **Career:** Children's Ctr for Behav Develop, therapist, 1977-80, satellite coordr, 1980-82, interim clinic dir, 1982-83, family therapist, coordr, 1983-84; RDS Found Inc, exec dir, 1986-; Jackson State Univ, Off VPres Acad Affairs & Stud Life, exec asst to vpres, currently. **Orgs:** Nat Asn Social Workers, 1972-, Nat Asn Black Social Workers, 1972-, Ill Asn Sch Social Workers, 1976-; St Clair Co Comn Difficult C, 1980-84; bd dirs, Coun House, 1981-84; Big Brothers & Big Sisters; pvt consult, 1981-; Bd Mem, Lexington Charter, Optimist Int, 1989-; secy, Caywood PTO, 1988-90; bd mem, E-911, 1989-91; TENA, 1989-90; bd mem, LHCCN, 1990-; PADA, 1991-; SEC, 1992-95; Jonah, 1995; Nat Org Women, 1975-84; Friends LHS, 1997; Delta Sigma Theta Soroity; Comprehensive Emergency Servs; bd, United Assistance, 1999-. **Honors/Awds:** Outstanding Black Col Female, Essence Mag, 1975; University Scholar, Tenn State Univ, 1975; Outstanding Achievement, Big Brothers & Big Sisters, 1982, 1984; Certificate Achievement, CCBD, 1984; Outstanding Parent Volunteer, Caywood PTO, 1989; Outstanding Parent Volunteer, Caywood PTO, 1990; Outstanding Parent Volunteer, 1991, 1992-95; Outstanding Volunteer, 1992; FKIX County Award, 1991; Volunteer Award, Caywood Sch, 1992-93; Outstanding Parent Volunteer, 1993-98; School of Bell Award, 1994-95; Community Service Award, Jackson Girl Scout Coun; Community Service Award, Big Brothers Big Sisters. **Home Addr:** 221 Eastern Shore Dr, Lexington, TN 38351. **Business Addr:** Executive Assistant to the Vice President, Jackson State University, Office of the Vice President for Academic Affairs & Student Life, 7th Fl Admin Tower 1400 Lynch St, Jackson, MS 39217, **Business Phone:** (601)979-2246.

REEVES, ALAN M
Automotive executive. **Career:** Quality Ford Sales Inc, Columbus GA, chief exec officer; Spalding Ford, owner, 1982-; Spalding-Lincoln-Mercury Inc, Griffin, chief exec officer, 1982-; Albany Ford Inc, Albany, chief exec officer, currently. **Honors/Awds:** Company ranked No 25 on Black Enterprise's list of top 100 auto dealerships, 1998. **Business Addr:** Chief Executive Officer, Albany Ford Inc, 410 N Slappery Blvd, Albany, GA 31701, **Business Phone:** (912)883-3100.

REEVES, BRENDA
President (Organization). **Career:** Reeves Automated Off Servs, founder & pres, currently. **Orgs:** Exec Women Int. **Business Addr:** President, Founder, Reeves Automated Office Services, Marquette Bldg 243 W Cong St Suite 350, Detroit, MI 48226-3278, **Business Phone:** (313)961-6657.*

REEVES, CARL
Football player. **Personal:** Born Dec 17, 1971, Durham, NC; married Iris. **Educ:** NC State Univ. **Career:** Chicago Bears, defensive end, 1996-98; Barcelona Dragons, 1971; Carolina Cobras, Arena Football League, offensive line & defensive line, 2000-01.

REEVES, DIANNE
Singer. **Personal:** Born Jan 1, 1956?, Detroit, MI. **Educ:** Univ Colo. **Career:** Clark Terry Band, singer; Co Symphony Orchestra; Monterey Jazz Festival; worked with: Sergio Mendez, Harry Belafonte, George Duke, Herbie Hancock, numerous others; Albums: Welcome To My Love, 1977; Better Days, 1987; I Remember, 1988; Never Too Far, 1990; Dianne Reeves, 1991; Art & Survival, 1993; Quiet After Storm, 1994; The Grand Encounter, 1996; That Day, 1997; The Calling: Celebrating Sarah Vaughan, 2001; A Little Moonlight, 2003; Christmas Time is Here, 2004; Good Night & Good Luck, 2005; Lush Life, featured, 2007; When You Know, 2008. **Honors/Awds:** Grammy award, In the Moment-Live in Concert, 2001; Grammy Awards, 2002-03; fourth Best Jazz Vocal Grammy, 2006. **Business Phone:** (310)659-1700.*

REEVES, JOHN E
Government official, commissioner. **Career:** Southfield City Coun, councilman, 1996; Mich Veterans Mem Pk Comn, comnr, currently. **Orgs:** Kappa Alpha Psi Frat; chmn, bd dirs, Cypriaw Ctr. **Honors/Awds:** Leadership Award, Kappa Alpha Psi Frat. **Special Achievements:** First African American male elected to Southfield City Council. **Military Serv:** AUS, vietnam war, hon discharge. **Business Addr:** Commissoner, Michigan Veterans Memorial Park Commission.

REEVES, JULIUS LEE
Engineer. **Personal:** Born Nov 10, 1961, Detroit, MI; son of Troy Sr and Delores; married Jun 16, 1990. **Educ:** Wayne State Univ, Detroit, BSIE, 1986; Univ Mich, Dearborn, MSIE, 1992, Univ Chicago, MBA, 1991. **Career:** Midwest Aluminum Corp, eng asst, 1983; Kelsey-Hayes, mfg engr, 1984-85; Electronic Data Syst, syst engr, 1985-86; Gen Motors, Warren, engr, 1986-89, bus planner, 1989-92, sr engr, 1992-97, strategic bus planner, 1997-98, prog mgr, 1998-2000, eng group mgr, 2000-. **Orgs:** Phi Delta Psi 1979-, Inst Indust Eng, 1983-, Eng Soc Detroit, 1984-; chap pres, Phi Delta Psi Fraternity, 1984-85; nat pres, Phi Delta Psi Fraternity, 1990-92; vpres, African-Am MBA Asn, 1990-91. **Honors/Awds:** Col of Engineering Deans List, Wayne State Univ, 1984-85; Nat Dean's List, 1984-85; Fellowship, Gen Motors, 1989. **Home Addr:** 3294 Woodview Lake Rd, West Bloomfield, MI 48323-3570. **Business Addr:** Engineering Group Manager, General Motors, Powertrain Division, 777 Joslyn Rd MC 483-720-410, Pontiac, MI 48340-2920.

REEVES, KHALID
Basketball player. **Personal:** Born Jul 15, 1972, Queens, NY. **Educ:** Univ Ariz, attended. **Career:** Basketball player, basketball coach; Miami Heat, guard, 1994-95; Charlotte Hornets, 1995-96; NJ Nets, 1996; Dallas Mavericks, 1996-98; Detroit Pistons, 1998-99; Chicago Bulls, guard, 1999-2000; asst coach, Christ The King RHS, 2006-07; Deportivo Saprissa, Costa Rican League. **Orgs:** YMCA; Spec Olympics. **Honors/Awds:** East Team MVP, McDonalds All-America Game, 1990; NCAA Champions, Ariz Wildcats, 1994. **Special Achievements:** First round pick, No 12, NBA Draft, 1994.

REEVES, LOUISE
Government official. **Personal:** Born Aug 13, 1944, St Louis, MO; married Charles B Mitchell. **Educ:** St Louis Univ, BA, polit sci, 1976; Webster Col, MA, pub admin, 1980. **Career:** SIU Edwardsville IL, fel, 1974; St Louis Agency Training & Employ, dep dir, 1977-; St Louis Met YWCA, dir housing & coun, 1976-77; Consult Neighborhood Serv Inc, assoc dir, 1965-76; Mo State Housing Develop Comn, comnr, 1978-; Freedom Res Inc, pres, 1978-79; Women Comm Serv, dir, 1983-95; Grace Hill Neighborhood Serv, assoc exec dir, 1995-; Jobs & Employ Support Serv, exec dir, 2007-. **Orgs:** Chmn, Monsignour John Schocklee Scholar Comm, 1979-; YMCA & YWCA; St Louis Wom Polit Caucas, 1975-; Coun Negro Women, 1976; Family Support Coun Mem. **Honors/Awds:** YWCA serv (vol) Award, St Louis Met YWCA; 70001 support Award, St Louis Chap 70001 Youth Orgn, 1979.

REEVES, MARTHA ROSE (MARTHA LAVAILLE)
Entertainer, city council member. **Personal:** Born Jul 18, 1941, Eufaula, AL; daughter of Ruby Lee Gilmore and Elijah Joshua. **Career:** The Vandellas, lead singer, 1963-71; Martha Motown Records, leader; albums: Martha Reeves, 1974; The Rest of My Life, 1977; We Meet Again, 1978; Home to You, 2004; Films: Fairy Tales, 1979; TV: "Saturday Night Live", 1975; "The Temptations", 1998; Singles: "Power of Love", 1974; "Wild Night", 1974; "Love Blind", 1977; "Nowhere to Run", 1999; "(Love Is Like A) Heatwave", 2000; "(Love Is Like A) Heat Wave", 2002; "It's Easy to Fall in Love (With a Guy Like You)", 2005; "Dancing in the Street", 2006; Detroit City Coun, coun mem, currently. **Orgs:** AFTRA; AGUA; SAG; Negro Women's Asn; Mt Zion Bapt Ch; Detroit's Metropolitan Church. **Honors/Awds:** Recipient 7 Gold Singles; numerous Grammy nominations; 12 albums; Inducted into Rock & Roll Hall of Fame, 1995. **Special Achievements:** Ranked No 56 on VH1's 100 Greatest Women of Rock N Roll.

REEVES, MICHAEL STANLEY
Executive. **Personal:** Born Oct 2, 1935, Memphis, TN; son of William (deceased) and Grace Stanley (deceased); married Patricia, Jun 27, 1959; children: Michael & Michelle. **Educ:** Roosevelt Univ, BA, 1964; NW Univ, MBA, 1972. **Career:** Peoples Gas,

mkt mgr, 1972-73, customer rel supt, 1973-74, office pres admin asst, 1974-75, customer rels dept gen supt, 1975-77, vpres 1977-87, exec vpres, 1987-. **Orgs:** Dir, Better Bus Bur, 1978-; chmn, Better Bus Bur Chicago & Northern Ill, 1994; exec, Leadership Coun; dir, Shedd Aquarium; adv comt, Local Initiatives Support Corp Chicago; bd mem, Abraham Lincoln Ctr; bd mem, Children's Memorial Hosp; bd mem, Am Heart Asn Metropolitan Chicago; Am Asn Blacks Energy; Am Gas Asn. **Military Serv:** USNA, Signal Corp speclt, 1958-60. **Business Phone:** (312)240-4000.

REGISTER, DR. JASPER C.
Educator. **Personal:** Born Jan 15, 1937, Valdosta, GA; son of Audra Mae Hall and Perry; divorced. **Educ:** Morehouse Col, AB, 1959; Univ KY, MA, 1969, PhD, 1974. **Career:** Stillman Col, instr, 1966-67; Baldwin-Wallace Col, asst prof, 1971-73; Carolina Univ, assoc prof emer sociol, currently. **Orgs:** Am Sociol Assoc, 1974-; Southern Sociol Soc, 1974-; Human Relations Coun, 1980-83; bd dir, Mental Health Assoc, 1984-87, 1989-92. **Honors/Awds:** Research Award, Social Sci Rsch Coun, 1968; Assoc Dan forth Found, 1981-86; Department of Sociology Teaching Excellence Award, 1998. **Military Serv:** AUS, capt, 3 yrs; Occupation Medal, 1962-65. **Home Addr:** 104 Fairwood Lane, Greenville, NC 27834. **Business Addr:** Associate Professor Emeritus, East Carolina University, Department of Sociology, A-416 Brewster Bldg E Fifth St, Greenville, NC 27858, **Business Phone:** (252)328-6883.

REID, ANTONIO (ANTONIO L A REID)
Songwriter, television producer, executive. **Personal:** Born Jun 7, 1956, Cincinnati, OH; son of Emma Reid; married Perri McKissick (Pebbles) (divorced 1995); children: Antonio Jr; married Erica, 2000; children: Addison Kennedy. **Career:** Arista Records, pres, 2000-04; Island Def Jam Music Group, chmn, 2004-; Hitco Music Publ, pres & chief exec officer, currently; Deele, R&B group, singer; albums include: Street Beat; Material Thanz; Eyes Of A Stranger; Producer, songwriter with Kenny Edmonds (Babyface) albums: Bobby Brown; Karyn White; Sheena Easton; Pebbles; Paula Abdul; MAC Band. **Honors/Awds:** Producer of the Year Non-Classical, 1992. **Special Achievements:** Grammy award nomination for song "Every Little Step," 1989; accomplished songwriters producing music which sold a double-platinum album for Bobby Brown, a Grammy nomination for Karyn White, and a Top-10 single for Paula Abdul. **Business Addr:** President, Chief Executive Officer, Hitco Music Publishing, 500 Bishop St NW Suite A-5, Atlanta, GA 30318, **Business Phone:** (404)352-5911.*

REID, ANTONIO L A. See REID, ANTONIO.

REID, CHRISTOPHER (CHRISTOPHER KID REID)
Actor. **Personal:** Born Apr 5, 1964, Bronx, NY. **Educ:** Lehman Col Bronx, attended. **Career:** Librn; filing clerk; theatrical stage worker; free-lance journalist; nanny & tutor; actor, currently; TV Series: "Kid 'n' Play," 1990; "Minor Adjustments," 1996; "Sister, Sister," 1996-97; "Smart Guy," 1997; "The Temptations," 1998; "Border Line," 1999; "VIP," 2000; "That's Life," 2001;"Barbershop," 2005; Videos: Sword of Honor, producer, 1994; Films: House Party, 1990; House Party 2, 1991; Class Act, 1992; House Party 3, 1994; Pauly Shore Is Dead, 2003; War of the Worlds 2: The Next Wave,2008; TV shows: "Your Big Break"; "It's Show time at the Apollo"; Song: "Why Don't You Stay?", 2008. **Honors/Awds:** Eric Gregory Award, 1978; Prudence Farmer Award, 1978 & 1980; Somerset Maugham Award, 1980; Hawthornden Prize, 1980. **Business Addr:** Actor, Endeavor Talent Agency, 9601 Wilshire Blvd Fl 3, Beverly Hills, CA 90210, **Business Phone:** (310)248-2000.*

REID, CHRISTOPHER KID. See REID, CHRISTOPHER.

REID, DR. CLARICE WILLS
Physician, government official. **Personal:** Born Nov 21, 1931, Birmingham, AL; daughter of Noah Edgar Sr and Willie Mae Brown; married Arthur Joseph Reid Jr, Jun 11, 1955; children: Kevin, Sheila, Jill & Clarice. **Educ:** Talladega Col, BS, 1952; Meharry Med Col, med tech, 1954; Univ Cincinnati Sch Med, MD, 1959. **Career:** Physician, government official (retired); Cincinnati, pediatrician pvt prac, 1962-68; Ohio Dept Health, pediat consult, 1964-70; Univ Cinncinati Sch Med, asst clin prof pediat, 1965-70; Pediat Jewish Hosp, Dept Health,Educ & Welfare, dir pediat, 1969-70, Pediat Dept, chmn, 1970; Nat Ctr Family Planning, Health Servs & Mental Health Admin, med consult, 1972-73, dep dir, 1973-76; Howard Univ Col Med, asst clin prof pediat, 1979-94; US Nat Insts Health, Sickle Cell Prog, Div Blood Dis & Resources, actg dir, 1988-89, dir, 1994-98; Am Bridge Asn, vpres. **Orgs:** Nat Med Asn; AAAS; Am Acad Pediat; NY Acad Sci; Am Soc Hemat; chair, Am Bridge Asn Found. **Honors/Awds:** Outstanding Student Faculty Award, Meharry Med Col, 1954; Director Award, NIH; Merit Award, NIH; Special Recognition Award, Pub Health Serv, 1989; Superior Service Award, Pub Health Serv, 1989; Presential Meritoroius Executive Award, Pub Health Serv, 1991. **Special Achievements:** She was included in the Book of Black Heroes, Volume II: Great Women in the Struggle. *

REID, DAPHNE ETTA MAXWELL (DAPHNE MAXWELL REED)
Actor, executive. **Personal:** Born Jul 13, 1948, New York, NY; daughter of Green and Rosalee; married Timothy L; children: Christopher Tubbs, Tim Jr & Tori. **Educ:** Northwestern Univ, BA, 1970. **Career:** Screen Actors Guild, bd mem, 1974-76; Screen Actors Guild, co-chmn, conserv comt, 1977; Daphne Maxwell Inc, pres; Timalove Enterprises Inc, vpres, currently; New Millennium Studios, co-founder, currently; ForReal, exec producer, 2003; TV episodes: "The Duke", 1979; "A Man Called Sloane", 1979; "Coach of the Year ", 1980; "WKRP in Cincinnati", 1980-82; "Hill Street Blues", 1981-85; "The Love Boat", 1982; "Hardcastle and McCormick", 1982; "Simon & Simon", 1983-87; "The Duck Factory", 1984; "Matt Houston", 1984; "Protocol", 1984; "Paper Dolls", 1984; "The A-Team", 1983-85; "Cagney & Lacey", 1985; "The Long Journey Home", 1987; "Frank's Place", 1987; "Murder, She Wrote", 1988; "ABC Afterschool Specials", 1989; "Snoops", 1989; "You Must Remember This", 1992; "The Cosby Show", 1992; "The Fresh Prince of Bel-Air", 1993-96; "Once Upon a Time.. When We Were Colored", 1995; "Sister, Sister", 1996; "Asunder", 1998; "In the House", 1998; "Linc's", 1999; "Alley Cats Strike", 2000; "Crossing Jordan", 2004; "Slavery and the Making of America", 2004; "Eve", 2003-06; "Polly and Marie", 2007. **Orgs:** Bd visitors, Va State Univ, 2008-. **Honors/Awds:** First Commercials, 1967; Ladies Home Jour as 1 of 14 Most Beautiful Women, 1970; Starred in Frank's Place, Snoops, The Tim & Daphne Show, Exposed; Fresh Prince Bel Air; Best New Product Award, Linc's Home Sewing & Crafts Asn, 1993; Norfolk State Univ Hon Degree, 1996; Hon Doctorate Degree, Va Common wealth Univ, 1999. **Special Achievements:** Created and produced videotape package with the McCall Pattern Company,"Suddenly You're Sewing"; created pattern line at the McCall Pattern Company; "The Daphne Maxwell Reid Collection"; First African Am Homecoming Queen, Northwestern Univ, 1967; First African Am on the cover, Glamour Mag, 1969. **Business Addr:** Co-Founder, New Millennium Studios, One Millenium Dr, Petersburg, VA 23805, **Business Phone:** (804)957-4200.

REID, DESIREE CHARESE
Executive. **Personal:** Born Jan 13, 1964, Bronx, NY; daughter of Elsie McDaniels and John Jr; divorced. **Educ:** Seton Hall Univ, BA, 1984; Paralegal Inst, 1988; Adelphi Univ, MBA, 1993; NY Restaurant Sch, prof mgt develop prog, 1998. **Career:** Jordache Enterprises, chargeback supvr, 1985-86; H Cotler Co, exec acct mgr, 1986-92; John Kaldor, acct rec supvr, 1992; Farberware, corp credit mgr, 1994-96. **Orgs:** Co-chmn, Black Stud Union, 1982-83; Delta Sigma Theta Sorority Inc, 1983-; Nat Asn Advan Colored People, 1992-; vol, Mayor Dinkins Re-Election Camp, 1993; Black Filmmaker Asn; Thruway Homeowners Asn; Nat Asn Female Exec; Drama Soc, mem & actress; Nat Asn Credit Mgt. **Honors/Awds:** Martin Luther King Acad Scholar, 1980-84; Business Award, Nat Asn Negro Bus & Prof Women's Clubs Inc, 1996. **Special Achievements:** Dean's List, Nat Hon Soc, 1977-83; founding mem, Martin Luther King Asn Seton Hall Univ, 1981; First & youngest African-Am Corp Credit Mgr, 1994-96; Peter Kump Pastry, cert prog, 1997. **Home Addr:** 3118 Mickle Ave, Bronx, NY 10469-3104. **Business Addr:** President, Ms Reid Enterprises, Baychester Station, PO Box 1061, Bronx, NY 10469, **Business Phone:** (718)379-5347.

REID, DON
Basketball player. **Personal:** Born Dec 30, 1973, Washington, DC. **Educ:** Georgetown Univ. **Career:** Basketball Player (retired); Detroit Pistons, forward, 1995-2000, 2003; Wash Wizards, 2000; Orlando Magic, 2001-02.

REID, DUANE L
Automotive executive. **Personal:** Married Wanda; children: Katie, Alex & Evan. **Educ:** Western Carolina Univ, BS, Bus Admin, 1982. **Career:** Reid Automotive Group, chief exec officer; Rome Ford Lincoln Mercury Inc, pres, currently; Rome City Comnr, 2006. **Orgs:** Vice-Chmn, Greater Rome Chamber Com; bd govs, Rome Area Hist Mus; Rome-Floyd County Planning Comn; bd dirs, Rome Rotary Club; Am Red Cross. **Honors/Awds:** Outstanding Volunteer of the Year; Omega Psi Phi Fraternity Man of the Year. **Special Achievements:** Top 25 African American Influencers. **Business Addr:** President, Rome Ford Lincoln Mercury Inc, 101 Hwy 411 SE, Rome, GA 30161-7270, **Business Phone:** (706)235-4453.

REID, EDITH C.
Cardiologist. **Personal:** Born in Atlantic City, NJ; married John L Edmonds. **Educ:** Hunter Col, BA; Meharry Med Col, MD. **Career:** St Albans NY, pvt practice; Flower & 5th Ave Monroe, clin asst; clin instr& asst physician; New York City Dept Health, physician chest clin Jamaica Hosp, asst visiting physician; assoc attend med; Carter Community Health Ctr, chief med. **Orgs:** Queens Clin Soc Inc; Nat Am Med Asn; Med Soc Queens & NY St; NY Heart Asn; Empire St Soc; Ad Hoc Com; NY Trudeau Soc; Am Geriatric Soc; Ethics Comm; Civic Asn; NAACP; Neighborhood Health Coun; Med Adv Comm NYUniv Bd Regents; fel, New York Acad Med. **Honors/Awds:** Quest hon wives club lunch, 1973; achievement award, Omega Psi Phi, 1974;friends York Col, 1974; outstanding service, Delta Sigma Theta Sor. **Business Addr:** Chief, Carter Community Health Center, 97 04 Sutphin Blvd, Jamaica, NY 11435.

REID, DR. F. THEODORE, JR.
Psychiatrist, educator. **Personal:** Born Nov 22, 1929, New York, NY; married Diane; children: Lynne & Frank. **Educ:** Columbia Univ, Columbia Col, BA, 1950; McGill Univ, Montreal, Can, MD, fac med 1954; King Col Hosp, Brooklyn, attended 1955, psychiat resident, 1957; Va Res Hosp Chicago, chief resident psychiat, 1960. **Career:** Educator (retired); Pvt Prac, psychiatry 1960-; NW Univ, assoc dept psychol neurol, 1966-72; Outpatient Psychiat Clin, 1967-69; Michael Reese Hosp, coord group therapy training, 1969-76; Univ Chicago, Pritzker Sch Med, clin assoc prof psychiat, 1975-76; Maricopa Col Hosp, AZ State Hosp, instr; psychiat residency 1976; Camel back Hosp, assoc, 1977-; Scottsdale Memorial Hosp Family Pract Residency, instr, 1977; Phoenix Indian Hosp, consult, 1977-80; Madden Zone Ctr, dir ctr referral unit, 1966-67; M Reese Hosp Serv, ISPI, chief, 1961-66; Mental Health Assoc, owner. **Orgs:** Fel, Am Ortho psych Asn, 1974-80; Comn Emerging Issues APA 1978-80; bd dirs, Camel back Hosp Found, 1979; dir, Am Group psychother Asn, 1979-82,1983-; cochmn, Inst Comm Am Group psychother Asn, 1974-78; exec comt, Am Group psychiat Asn, 1973-75, 1977-79, 1984-86; life fel, APA. **Honors/Awds:** Distinguished Fel, About Groups Inc. **Military Serv:** USNR, lt med corps 1957-59. **Business Addr:** Owner, Mental Health Associates, 7659 E Wood Dr, Scottsdale, AZ 85260-4039, **Business Phone:** (602)994-1448.

REID, HERMAN, JR. See REID, J. R.

REID, DR. INEZ SMITH
Lawyer. **Personal:** Born Apr 7, 1937, New Orleans, LA. **Educ:** Tufts Univ, BA, 1959; Yale Univ Law Sch, LLB, 1962; Univ Calif, Los Angeles, MA, 1963; Columbia Univ, PhD, 1968. **Career:** Ecole Nat de Droit et d'Admin, lecturer, 1963-64; State Univ New York, New Paltz, asst prof African studies & political sci, 1964-65; Hunter Col, New York, lecturer political sci, 1965-66; Brooklyn Col, from instr to assoc prof political sci, 1966-71; Barnard Col, Columbia Univ, assoc prof, 1971-72, 1976-79; pvt pratice, 1972-76; New York State Div Youth, gen coun, 1976-77; Dept Health Educ & Welfare, dep gen counsel, 1977-79; Environmental Protection Agency, inspector gen, 1979-80; DC Ct Appeals, judge, 1996-. **Orgs:** Past bd, Antioch Univ Bd Trustees; United Church Christ Bd Homeland Ministries. **Honors/Awds:** numerous awards. **Special Achievements:** Numerous articles published. *

REID, IRVIN D
School administrator, educator. **Personal:** Born Feb 21, 1941, Pawleys Island, SC; son of Joseph and Etta Louise; married Pamela Trotman; children: Nicole & Dexter; married Pamela Trotman Reid; children: 2. **Educ:** Howard Univ, BS, MS; Univ Pa, MBA, PhD. **Career:** Montclair State Univ, pres, 1989-97; Wayne State Univ, pres, 1997-. **Orgs:** Nat Conf Christians & Jews; Pres Comn Nat Collegiate Athletic Asn; Detroit 300 Comt; bd trustee, Detroit Med Ctr; Economic Club Detroit; bd mem, Fleet Bank; bd mem, Mack-Cali Real Estate Investment Trust; Alpha Soc; Beta Gamma Sigma; Omicron Delta Epsilon; Phi Kappa Phi; Alpha Kappa Psi. **Honors/Awds:** Technology Utilization Office of the NASA Tree of Life Award; Austrian-American Medal, Austrian- American Coun NA. **Special Achievements:** First African American president of Wayne State Univ. **Business Addr:** President, Wayne State University, Office of the President, 4200 Fac Admin Bldg, Detroit, MI 48202, **Business Phone:** (313)577-2424.

REID, J. R. (HERMAN REID, JR.)
Basketball player. **Personal:** Born Mar 31, 1968, Virginia Beach, VA; married Pansy King, Sep 19, 1991; children: Kaylah & Jaylen. **Educ:** Univ NC, Chapel Hill, NC, commun, 1989. **Career:** Basketball player (retired); Charlotte Hornets, forward, 1989-92 & 1997-98; San Antonio Spurs, 1992-95; New York Knicks, 1996; Charlotte Hornets, 1998-99; Los Angeles Lakers, 1998-99; Milwaukee Bucks, 1999-2000; Cleveland Cavaliers, 2000-01. **Honors/Awds:** NBA All-Rookie Second Team, 1990; Olympic Bronze Medal, 1988.

REID, JANIE ELLEN
Administrator. **Personal:** Born Feb 15, 1950, Pelzer, SC. **Educ:** SC State Col, BS Bus Admin, 1972. **Career:** SC Assoc Stud Finan Aid Admin, mem, 1973-87, secy, treas, 1975-77; JE Sirrine Scholar Adv Bd, mem, 1974-75, chmn, 1980-82; SC Comm Higher Ed, adv bd mem, 1975-78; US Dept Ed Bur Stud Financial Aid, inst appl rev panel mem, 1976; Greenville Tech Col, dean, fin aid dir, currently; Financial Aid, dir, currently. **Orgs:** Instr, New Financial Aid Officer Workshop Southern Asn Stud Fin Aid Admin, 1978-79; charter mem, Greenville Urban League's Early Leadership & Confidence Training, 1978-79; adv bd, SC Student Loan Corp, 1981-83; chmn, adv bd Greenville Urban League's Ed Talent Search Prog, 1982-84; minister, ed Shady Grove Baptist Ch, 1983-85; ed, adv comm SC Appalachian Coun Gov, 1983-89; chmn, Greenville Community Human Rels Comm, 1985. **Honors/Awds:** Citizenship Award, Greenville Civitan Club, 1968; Iota Phi Lambda, Delta Eta Chap 1971-; Annual Pastor's Award, Shady Grove Baptist Ch, 1981, 1982, 1983. **Home Addr:** 405 Old Hundred Rd, Pelzer, SC 29669. **Business Addr:** Director, Dean, Greenville Technical College, PO Box 5616 Sta B, Greenville, SC 29606-5616.

REID, JOEL OTTO
Educator. **Personal:** Born May 17, 1936, Newark, NJ; children: Joel II & Nicol. **Educ:** NY Univ Sch Educ, BS, 1959; Montclair

State Col, MA, 1965; Claremont Grad Sch, Claremont, CA, PhD, 1973. **Career:** Elizabeth Pub Sch System, Elizabeth, NJ, teacher; White Plaines High Sch, counr, teacher, 1962-65; White Plaines Bd Educ, professional recruiter, 1965-67; Nat Teachers Corps, Migrant Univ, Southern Calif, teacher, leader, 1967-68; Claremont Grad Sch, staff mem, 1971-72, Social Sci Dept, prof, 1978; Pasadena City Col, dean continuing educ, 1968-78, prof social sci, 1978, prof emer social sci, currently. **Orgs:** Chmn, Eval Com Western Asn Sch & Col, 1969, 1970 & 1974; Pasadena Educ Asn; Pasadena City Col Fac Asn; NEA; Los Angeles Co Adult Educ Adminr Asn; chmn, bd dirs, Urban League Com Educ Fund Dr; Fair Hsg Comt of Westchester Co, New York; Am Friends Serv Comt on Hsg, Pasadena; coun Neighborhod Youth Ctr. **Honors/Awds:** Two year Scholar Col; Kiwanis Rotary Club Scholar; Valley Settlement House Scholar, West Orange, NJ; Womens Aux Scholar, West Orange, NJ. **Military Serv:** AUS, sp5, 1959-62. **Business Addr:** Professor Emeritus of Social Science, Pasadena City College, 1570 E Colorado Blvd, Pasadena, CA 91106, **Business Phone:** (818)578-7248.*

REID, DR. LESLIE BANCROFT
Educator. **Personal:** Born Nov 7, 1934, Clarendon, Jamaica; son of Walter B Reid; married Norma A Morris; children: Donovan & Diane. **Educ:** Howard Univ, BS, 1968, DDS, 1972. **Career:** Govt Bact Lab Jamaica, med tech, 1953-59; Tia Maria Ltd, Jamaica, chemist, 1959-64; Cafritz Hosp, Wash DC, med tech, 1966-72; Howard Univ Dent Sch, fac mem, 1972-; Reid & Asn, pres. **Orgs:** Bd trustees, Charles County Community Col, l969-76; dir, Reid-& Yip Young DDS PA, 1973-; consult, Ministry Health, Jamaica, 1974; consult, Ministry Health, Guyana, 1976; partner, Eastover Dent Serv, 1979-; consult, Ministry Health Belize Cent Am, 1984; bd trustees, Hospice Charles County, 1985-; staff, Greater Southeast Comn Hosp, 1986-; bd trustees, Warner Pac Col, l989-; clinician, Numerous Dent Conv. **Honors/Awds:** Outstanding Fac, Howard Univ Col Dent Stud Coun, l989. **Special Achievements:** Adaptability of Several Amalgam to Enamel Surface, J Dent Res, 1985; co-auth: A Manual of Fixed Prosthodontics, Howard Univ, 1986; Lab Manual Dent Anat & Occlusion, l988. **Home Addr:** 11865 Federal Sq Suite 102, Waldorf, MD 20601, **Home Phone:** (301)645-2211. **Business Addr:** Faculty Member, Howard University College of Dentistry, 600 W St NW, Washington, DC 20059, **Business Phone:** (202)806-0440.

REID, MALISSIE LAVERNE
Interior designer, real estate agent. **Personal:** Born Aug 23, 1953, Orange, NJ; daughter of Joseph Wilbur Sr and Malissie Elizabeth. **Educ:** Rider Col, BA, polit sci, 1971-75; Prof Sch Bus, ins broker, 1978; NYK Sch Interior Design, 1980-82; Kovats Sch Real Estate, 1987. **Career:** Union Camp Corp, Tax Dept, ade asst, 1975-76; Aetna Life & Casualty, com lines underwriter, 1976-78; Chubb Custom Mkt, specialty lines underwriter, 1978-81; Cigna Ins Co, underwriting mgr, 1981-86; Home Ins Co, underwriting mgr, 1986-87; Reid's Interior Decorators & Upholstery, exec vpres, 1987-; Weichert Realtors, broker, currently. **Orgs:** Bd adjustments, Town Nutley, 1991-; bd dir, Community Ment HTH, 1991-. **Home Addr:** 35 Hopper Ave, Nutley, NJ 07110. **Business Phone:** (973)667-1778.

REID, DR. MILTON A.
Clergy, publisher, businessperson. **Personal:** Born Jan 26, 1930, Chesapeake, VA; son of Mary M Reid and Rev Moses Annias Reid; married Marian Elean Todd, Aug 18, 1952; children: Maravia Nse Ebong, Humphrey T, Michelle A Brown & Milton A Jr. **Educ:** Va Union Univ, AB 1958; Virginia Union Univ School Religions, MDiv,1960; Boston Univ Sch, Liberation Theology, DMin, 1980. **Career:** Minister, Gideon's Riverside Fellowship; Guide Publishing Co, publisher & pres, 1974-87, publisher emer, 1987; Virginia Unit SCLC, Chmn Bd; My Memoirs, author. **Orgs:** Former mem, STOIC Natl Newspaper Publishers Asn; life mem, SCLC; founder, organizer, & past pres, Virginia State Unit, SCLC; past moderator, Bethany Baptist Assn; dir, TRUST Inc; dir, NNPA, 1975-81; life mem, Norfolk Branch, NAACP, 1982-; bd of dirs, Inter religious Found for Community Org, 1972-; chmn, bd of dirs, Gideon Family Life Ctr, 1985-; pres, Faith Village Corp. **Honors/ Awds:** Doctor of Divinity Degree, Virginia Seminary & Col, 1960; Distinguished Leadership Award, Virginia State Conference of NAACP, 1974; Meritorious Service Award, 1974-87; Journal & Guide Citizens Award. **Military Serv:** AUS 82nd Airborne Div, corporal, 1948-52. **Home Addr:** 1909 Arlington Ave, Norfolk, VA 23523, **Home Phone:** (757)545-4312. *

REID, N NEVILLE
Lawyer. **Personal:** Married. **Educ:** Harvard Univ, BA magna cum laude, 1984; Harvard Law Sch, JD, 1987. **Career:** Mayer, Brown, Rowe & Maw LLP, assoc, 1987-96, partner, 1996-; supt, St Mark United Methodist Church Sch, 2005-. **Orgs:** Panel Pvt Trustees, Northern District Ill, 1994-; Am Bankruptcy Inst, 1994-; bd dirs, Good Shepherd Community Servs Org, 1995-; Am Bar Asn Conf Minority Partners Majority/Corp Law Firms, 1996-2000; chmn, Beverly Area Local Dev Corp, 1996; fel, Leadership Greater Chicago, 1997-; Bankruptcy Focus Group. **Honors/Awds:** Harvard Col Scholar, Harvard Univ, 1981; John Harvard Col Scholar, 1982-84; Rhodes Scholar Finalist, 1983. **Business Addr:** Partner, Mayer, Brown, Rowe & Maw LLP, 71 S Wacker Dr, Chicago, IL 60603, **Business Phone:** (312)701-7934.

REID, PAMELA TROTMAN
Educator, college administrator. **Personal:** Born Jun 1, 1946, Bronx, NY; daughter of Louis Hilary and Gloria Legare Trotman; married Irvin Dexter, Aug 27, 1966; children: Nicole Legare & Irvin Dexter. **Educ:** Howard Univ, BS; Temple Univ, MA; Univ Pa, PhD . **Career:** Prof develop psychol; assoc provost & dean academic affairs; interim provost, City Univ New York Grad Ctr; Univ Mich, dir women's studies prog; Univ Mich, prof educ & psychol; Univ Mich, Inst Res Women & Gender, res scientist; Roosevelt Univ, provost & exec vpres, 2004-08, prof; St Joseph Col, provost & exec vpres, 2008-. **Orgs:** Am Psychol Asn. **Honors/Awds:** Several national awards including Distinguished Leadership Award, Distinguished Publication Award, Distinguished Contribution to Research Award. **Special Achievements:** 60 journal articles, book chapters, book reviews and essays; Named among the 100 Distinguished Women in Psychology in 1992. **Business Addr:** Provost and Executive Vice President, Saint Joseph College, 1678 Asylum Ave, West Hartford, CT 06117, **Business Phone:** (860)232-4571.*

REID, ROBERT
Basketball player. **Personal:** Born Aug 30, 1955, Atlanta, GA; married Donna; children: Robert & Keva Rachel. **Educ:** St Mary's Univ, attended 1977. **Career:** Basketball player (retired), basketball coach; Houston Rockets, 1977-88; Charlotte Hornets, 1989-90; Portland Trail Blazers, 1989-90; YakimaSun Kings, coach; Brevard Blue Ducks, head coach, 2004. **Orgs:** Spec Olympics, Big Brothers, hosp groups. **Honors/Awds:** NBA Humanitarian of the Yr Award, 1981. *

REID, DR. ROBERTO ELLIOTT
Educator, physician. **Personal:** Born Nov 12, 1930, Panama, Panama; son of Exley and Ettie; married Joyce. **Educ:** NY Univ, AB, 1954; Case Western Res Univ Sch Med, MD, 1958. **Career:** Philadelphia Gen Hosp, 1959; assoc prof urol, 1973; asst prof urol, 1965-73; Bronx Municipal Hosp, dir urol, 1973; Albert Einstein Col Med, assoc prof urol, 1963-85, prof urol; Weiler Hosp, chief urol; pvt practr, currently. **Orgs:** Coun Am Col Surgeons, 1975-77; New York sec rep, AVAA, 1976; Sigma Pi Phi; Am Urol Asn Inc. **Business Addr:** Surgeon, Eastchester Prof Ctr 1695 Eastchester Rd Suite 306, Bronx, NY 10461, **Business Phone:** (718)904-0222.

REID, RONDA EUNESE
Security guard. **Personal:** Born May 1, 1955, Dayton, OH; married Washington Reid Jr, Sep 26, 1981; children: Darnell & Byron. **Educ:** Sinclair Community Col, Dayton, AS, law enforcement, 1974; Univ Dayton, Dayton, BS, crim justice, 1976; Cent Mich Univ, Mount Pleasant, MS, pub adm, 1992. **Career:** USF, civilian: Wright Patterson AFB, Dayton, res & develop, admin support, 1977-84, security specialist, 1984-86; Gen Elec Co, Cin, security specialist, 1986-88, Jnson Space Ctr, Houston, security specialist, 1988; The Pentagon, security specialist, 1989-. **Orgs:** Nat Classification Mgt Soc, 1985-; vpres, 1984-85, pres, 1985-86, Am Bus Women's Asn, Gem City Chapter; holds one of six seats, USAF Security Career Prog Training & Develop Panel; Blacks Gov, Pentagon Chapter. **Honors/Awds:** Outstanding Performance Rating, 1979; Sustained Superior Performance Award, 1984; Superior Performance Award, 1985; Notable Achievement Award, 1986; Quality Step Increase, 1986; Performance Award, 1987, 1990-92, USF. **Home Addr:** 6132 Surrey Sq Lane Suite 203, Forestville, MD 20747. **Business Addr:** Security Specialist, US Air Force International Affairs Office, The Pentagon, Rm 4C1074, Washington, DC 20330-1010, **Business Phone:** (202)695-6057.

REID, RUBIN J
Real estate agent. **Personal:** Married; children: 2. **Educ:** Va, Grad Col, Bus, 1963; BS, bus admin. **Career:** Glenarden, mayor, vice mayor; Gitelson Neff Assoc Inc, real estate agent; Coldwell Banker Residential Brokerage, sales assoc, currently. **Orgs:** Chmn, Town Council. **Military Serv:** AUS, sargent; Korean Service Medal; Good Conduct Medal; National Defense Serv Medal; Bronze Star; United Nations Service Medal; Republic of Korea Presidential Unit Citiation. **Business Addr:** Sales Associate, Coldwell Banker Residential Brokerage, 1525 Pointer Ridge Pl Suite 101, Bowie, MD 20715, **Business Phone:** (240)245-1860.

REID, TIM
Writer, actor, television producer. **Personal:** Born Dec 19, 1944, Norfolk, VA; son of William Lee Reid and Augustine Wilkins; married Daphne Maxwell, Dec 4, 1982; children: Christopher Tubbs (stepson); married Rita, May 9, 1967 (divorced 1980); children: Tim II & Tori LeAnn. **Educ:** Norfolk State Coll, BS, Bus Mkt, 1968. **Career:** Dupont Corp, mkt rep, 1968-71; Tim & Tom Comedy Team, 1971-75; stand-up comedian; Timalove Enterprises, founder, 1979; United Image Entertainment Enterprises, co-founder, 1990, co-chmn; New Millennium Studios, founder, currently; TV Series: "Easy Does It. Starring Frankie Avalon",1976; "The Marilyn McCoo & Billy Davis, Jr. Show", 1977; "The Richard Pryor Show", 1977; "WKRP In Cincinnati", 1978-82; "Teachers Only", 1983;"Simon & Simon", 1983-87; "Frank's Place", actor & co-executive producer,1987-88; "Snoops", actor & co-creator, executive producer, 1989-90;"Sister, Sister", actor, creator & producer, 1994-; "That 70?s Show", actor, 2007; TV Movies: You Can't Take It With You, 1979; Perry Mason: The Case of the Silenced Singer, 1990; Stephen King's It, 1991; The Family Business, 1991; You Must Remember This, 1992; Race to Freedom: The Underground Rail road, 1994; Simon & Simon: In Trouble Again, 1995; Films: Dead Bang, 1989; The Fourth War, 1990; Once Upon a Time; When We Were Colored, actor & dir, 1995. **Orgs:** Writers Guild Am; Screen Actors Guild; bd dirs, Phoenix House Calif; Norfolk St Univ, Commonwealth Va; bd dirs, Nat Acad Cable Programming; AFTRA; life mem, NAACP. **Honors/Awds:** Emmy Award; Critics Choice Award, 1988; NAACP Image Award, 1988; Best Actor in a Comedy Award, Viewers for Quality Television, 1988; Nat Black Col Alumni Hall Fame, 1991; Directional Award, Ft. Lauderdale Int Film Festival; Best Producer, Houston Int Film Festival; Image Award Nominee for Producer, NAACP; Oscar Micheaux Award, Producer's Guild of America,1999. **Special Achievements:** Involved in efforts to provide scholarship funds for Minority students; organizer, sponsor: Annual Tim Reid Celebrity Tennis Tournament, Norfolk St University Campus; actively involved in anti-drug movement since 1969; testified many times before House and Senate Sub-committees. **Business Phone:** (804)957-4200.

REID, TRACY
Basketball player. **Personal:** Born Nov 1, 1976. **Educ:** Univ NC, BS, commun, 1998. **Career:** Charlotte Sting, 1998-2000; Miami Heat, 2001; Phoenix Mercury, 2002-03; Maccabi Ramat Hen, 2005; Acis-Incosa Leon, 2006-07. C.B. Olesa Espanyo, 2008-. **Honors/Awds:** WNBA Rookie of the Year, 1998; Atlantic Coast Conf, Player of the Year &Player of the Week, 1998, First Team All-ACC -96, 97, 98; ACC player of the Year -97, 98. *

REID, VERNON
Rock musician, guitarist, composer. **Personal:** Born Aug 22, 1958, London, England; divorced. **Educ:** Brooklyn Tech. **Career:** Living Colour, founder & singer, 1984-; Black Rock Coalition 1, co founder; albums: Vivid, 1988; Time's Up, 1990; Biscuits, 1991; Stain, 1993; films: Fresh Kill, 1994; Vintage - Families of Value, 1995; Dr.Hugo, 1998; Ghosts of Attica, 2001; That's My Face, 2001; Paid in Full,2002; Mr. 3000, 2004; Twelve Disciples of Nelson Mandela, 2005; Shadow:Dead Riot, 2006; Guitar Hero III: Legends of Rock, 2007; TV: "Almost Home", 2006. **Honors/ Awds:** With Living Colour: two Grammy Awards, two MTV Music Awds, two Int Rock Awards, 1988-93; Grammy nomination for Best Rock Instrumental, 1996. **Special Achievements:** Named No 66 on Rolling Stone's 100 Greatest Guitarists of All Time. **Business Addr:** Singer, The Black Rock Coalition, Cooper Sta, PO Box 1054, New York, NY 10276.*

REID, WILLIAM J
Executive director. **Career:** Reid Funeral Home, fun dir. **Business Addr:** Funeral Director, Reid Funeral Home, 108 Kershaw St, Cheraw, SC 29520, **Business Phone:** (843)537-7419.

REIDE, ATTY. JEROME L.
Lawyer, educator. **Personal:** Born Apr 23, 1954, New York, NY; son of Leonora E and St Clair E Reide Sr. **Educ:** State Univ NY, New Paltz, BA, 1977; Hofstra Univ Law Sch, JD, 1981;Columbia Univ, Grad Jour Sch, MS, 1982; Mich State Univ, PhD, 1991. **Career:** Am Civil Liberties Union, Access to Justice, 1986-87; Ctr Labor Studies,SUNY, polit sci lectr, 1986-87; Eastern Mich Univ, African Am studies lectr, 1987-88; Detroit City Coun, spec proj asst, 1987-88; Mich State Univ, dean Urban Studies, res asst, 1988-90; NAACP, Spec Contrib Fund Midwest, develop dir, 1990-93, regional dir, 1999-2001, Nat Field Opers, dep dir, 2001-03; Wayne State Univ, Sch Educ, lectr, 1992-93; Wayne County Comn, Chair Ways & Means, legis aide, 1993-94; Wayne State Univ,Interdisciplinary Studies, asst prof, 1994-; Raheem, Eickemeyer & ReidePLLC, 1997-99; Baltimore City Community Col, adj fac, 2004-05; Bowie State Univ, adj fac, 2004-05; Mckinney & Assocs, 2004; State Bar Mich, dir justice initiatives, 2005-07; Law Off Jerome L Reide, PC, currently; coun mem, Am Bar Assoc, 2008-09. **Orgs:** Nat Asn Advan Colored People, 1975-; press aide, Sutton for Mayor, 1977;nat press secy, Black Law Students Asn, 1980-81; press secy, Nat Conf Black Lawyers, 1986-87; Urban League, Mich, 1988-; Urban Affairs Graduate Studies Asn, 1989-90; Dispute Resolution Coord Coun, 1991-95; Boniface CtAction, 1991-95; pres, Global Econ Develop Conf, 1993; exec comt, Wayne State Univ, Ctr Peace & Conflict Studies, 1994; State Bar Mich, 1996; AmBar Asn, 1997-; Wolverine Bar Asn, 1997-; Team Justice, 1997; chair, Civil Rights Comt, IRR Section, Am Bar Asn, 2006-. **Honors/Awds:** Governor Ky, Order Ky Colonels, 1991; Fair Housing Award, Jackson Fair Housing CMS, 1992; Special Tribute, State Legis Mich, 1994; CLL Teaching Excellence Award, Wayne State Univ, ISP, 1997; Freedom Fighter Award,Detroit Branch, Nat Board, Nat Asn Advan Colored People, 1999; Foot Soldier's in the Sands Award, Nat Bd, Nat Asn Advan Colored People, 2007. **Special Achievements:** Author, Justice Evicted, Am Civil Liberties Union, 1987; executive producer & moderator, "The State of Black Mich," 1989-; ed, Mulitcultural Edu Resource Guide, Mich State edu, 1990; exe producer, "Human Rights and Civil Wrongs," Museum of African american History, 1991; writer, "NAACP Ct Economic Development," The Crisis Magazine, 1992; "Human Rights and Natural Disaster, Human Rights Magazine, IRR, ABA, co-editor, 2006. **Business**

Addr: Attorney, Law Office of Jerome L Reide, PC, 120 N Wash Sq Suite 805, Lansing, MI 48933-2012, **Business Phone:** (517)667-0568.

REIDE, SAINT CLAIR EUGENE, JR.
Nurse. **Personal:** Born Aug 24, 1950, Brooklyn, NY; son of Saint Clair E Sr and Leonara E; married Portia Gayle, Dec 29, 1972; children: Saint Clair E, III & Nicole A. **Educ:** Morris High Sch, LPN, 1968; Boro Manhattan Community Col, AAS, 1971; Hunter Col, Bellevue Sch Nursing, BSN, 1974. **Career:** NY Univ Med Ctr, LPN, 1968-71, staff nurse sr, 1971-74; Dept Health, Prison Health Nursing, psy staff nurse, 1974; Dept Vet Affairs, nursing supvr, 1974-. **Orgs:** Trinity Luthern Church, pastoral asst, 1970-, sunday sch supdt, 1993-; Reserve Officers Asn, life mem, 1975-. **Honors/Awds:** Manhattan Community Col, Dean List, 1971; Dept Vet Affairs, St Albans, Employee of the Month, 1987. **Special Achievements:** Portrait Photographer, Owner Creative Photography by Saint studio; American Nurses Assn, certification in Nursing Admin, 1989-93, Gerontological Nurse, 1989-93; USA Goju, karate, Brown Belt, 1972; Radio License Novice, KB2CQA. **Military Serv:** USAR, army nurse corp, lt col, beginning 1975; Army Reserve Component Achievement Medal, 1991; Army Forces Reserve Medal 1985; Nat Defense Serv Medal, 1991. **Home Addr:** 115-02 223 St, Cambria Heights, NY 11411, **Home Phone:** (718)527-7838. **Business Addr:** Nursing Supervisor, St Albans VA - Extended Care Center - Dept of Vet Affairs, 179 St & Linden Blvd Nursing Office 1182, Jamaica, NY 11425, **Business Phone:** (718)526-1000.

REID-MCQUEEN, LYNNE MARGUERITE
Health services administrator, lawyer. **Personal:** Born Jan 26, 1958, Great Lakes, IL; daughter of B Jacquelyne and F Theodore Reid; married Leigh E McQueen, Feb 9, 1985; children: Naima Marguerite & Jared Leigh. **Educ:** Mount Holyoke Col, AB, 1980; Univ Connecticut, Sch Law, JD, 1983. **Career:** State of Conn, Judicial Dept, Supreme Ct, law clerk, 1983-85; NYC Commission on Human Rights, staff atty, 1985-90; State Univ NY Health Sci Ctr, dep dir policy analysis, 1990-. **Orgs:** YWCA Brooklyn, 1991-98, first vip, 1994-96, chair, nominating com, 1993-98; Nat Hth Lawyers Asn, 1990-; Brooklyn Mediation Ctr, pro bono mediator, 1996-; Roosevelt Union Sch Dist. **Business Addr:** Deputy Director for Policy Analysis, State University of New York Health Science Ctr at Brooklyn, Department of Management Services, 450 Clarkson Ave, PO Box 101, Brooklyn, NY 11203, **Business Phone:** (718)270-1464.

REID-MERRITT, PATRICIA ANN
Educator. **Personal:** Born Oct 31, 1950, Philadelphia, PA; daughter of Curtis and Etrulia; married William Thomas Merritt; children: Christina, Brahim, Jeffrey & Gregory. **Educ:** Cabrini Col, BA, 1973; Temple Univ, MA, social work, 1975; Univ Pa, advanced cert, social work educ, 1979, PhD, social work, 1984. **Career:** Pa Gen Hosp, psychiat social worker, 1975-76; Nat Asn Black Social Workers, nat interim exec, 1984-85; Lawnside Public Schs, sch social work consult, 1980-; Stockton State Col, coordr social work, prof, currently; Afro-one, founder. **Orgs:** NJ Black Issues Conv, 1984-; Willingboro Black Bus & Prof Asn, 1985-89; co-founder & chair, Burlington County Inter Orgn Black Leadership Coun, 1986; bd dirs, Asn Black Women Higher Educ, 1986-88; Black United Fund NJ, Burlington County, 1986-; founder & pres, Nat Asn Black Social Workers, SJ; pres, Asn Black Women Higher Educ, Greater Pa, 1986-88; Nat Coun Black Studies, 1993-97. **Honors/Awds:** Citizen of the Year, NJ State Council Black Social Workers, 1983; 100 Pa Women, Pa Publ Group, 1983; Youth Role Model Award, Lawnside Bd Educ, 1984; Commitment to Black Youth Award, Bd Dirs, Afro-One, 1984; Distinguished Alumni Achievement Award, Cabrini Col, 1986; Cert of Honor, General Alumni Asn, Temple Univ, 1987; Civic Award, Links, Inc, Eastern Area Conference, 1989; Outstanding Achievement Award, Coun Black Faculty & Staff, 1989; 25th Anniversary Freedom Award, Nat Asn Advan Colored People, S Burlington Br, 1991. **Special Achievements:** Author: "Sister Power: How Phenomenal Black Women Are Rising to the Top". **Business Addr:** Professor, Coordinator, Stockton State College, Department of Social Work, Jimmy Leeds Rd, PO Box 195, Pomona, NJ 08240, **Business Phone:** (609)652-4609.

REINHARDT, JOHN EDWARD
Educator. **Personal:** Born Mar 8, 1920, Glade Spring, VA; married Carolyn; children: Sharman, Alice & Carolyn. **Educ:** Knoxville Col, BA, 1939; Univ WI, MS, 1947, Phd, 1950. **Career:** VA State Col, prof eng, 1950-56; USIS Manila Philippines, cult affairs officer, 1956-58; Am Cultural Ctr Kyoto Japan, dir, 1958-63; USIS Tehran Iran, cult attach, 1963-66; Off E Asia & Pacific USIA, dep asst, 1966-68; Nigeria, ambassador, 1971-75; Wash DC, asst sec state, 1975; Int Community Agency, dir, 1976-81; US Info Agency, dir, 1977-80; Smithsonian Inst, asst sec, history & art, 1981-84, dir & dirate Int Activities, 1984-87; Univ Vt, prof polit sci, 1987-91, prof emer, 1991-. **Orgs:** Am Foreign Serv Asn, 1969-; Modern Lang Asn; Int Club; Cosmos Club. **Military Serv:** AUS, officer, 1942-46. **Home Addr:** 4200 Massachusetts Ave NW 702, Washington, DC 20016. **Business Addr:** Professor Emeritus, University of Vermont, 50 Univ Pl, Burlington, VT 05405, **Business Phone:** (802)656-3131.

RELAFORD, DESI (DESMOND LAMONT RELAFORD)
Baseball player. **Personal:** Born Sep 16, 1973, Valdosta, GA. **Career:** Philadelphia Phillies, shortstop, 1996-00; San Diego Padres, 2000; NY Mets, infielder, 2001; Seattle Mariners, 2002; Kans City Royals, infielder, 2003-04; Colo Rockies, infielder, 2004; Baltimore Orioles, 2006; Texas Rangers, 2007; free agent, currently. **Orgs:** Founder, Six hole Records. *

REMBERT, DR. EMMA WHITE
School administrator. **Personal:** Born in Quincy, FL; daughter of Zinerva and Jessie. **Educ:** Fla Agri & Med Col, AB, MEd; Syracuse Univ, EdD. **Career:** Pinellas Co, supvr & teacher; Mobilization Youth New York City, supvr clinician; Charles E Merrill Pub, educ consul; Fla Int Univ, prof, asst & dean; Bethune-Cookman Col, prof, chairperson educ; Bowie State Univ, assoc prof. **Orgs:** State organizer, Nat Coun Negro Women; Phi Delta Kappa; Kappa Delta Pi; Pi Lambda Theta; consult & lectr, Ministry Educ-Commonwealth Bahamas; dir, adult educ, Okeechobee Schs Ed & prof consult, Textbook Series C E Merrill Co; pub com Int Reading Asn; manuscript reviewer McGraw Hill & Allyn & Bacon Co; dir, Hemispheric Women's Cong; chairperson, Delta Sigma Theta Fla Coun; Delta Sigma Theta Leadership Acad. **Honors/Awds:** Competence Award, State Florida; International Scholarship-Leadership Awards, Delta Sigma Theta; EPDA Fel, Syracuse Univ; Florida Outstanding Teacher & Educator; CRA Service Award. **Special Achievements:** Book: Alternative Strategies, Kendall Hunt Pub Co. **Home Addr:** PO Box 3382, Fort Pierce, FL 34948.

REMY, DONALD M
Executive, lawyer. **Personal:** Born Feb 8, 1967, Petersburg, VA; son of Donald and Ann; married Monitra C Remy; children: J Alexander & Jason A. **Educ:** La State Univ, BA, 1988; Howard Univ Sch Law, JD, 1991. **Career:** Judge Nathaniel Jones, Judicial Clerk, 1995-96; O'Melveny & Myers, LLP, assoc, 1996-97; US Dept Justice, sr coun policy, dep asst Atty Gen, 1997-2000; Fannie Mae, vpres & dep gen coun, 2000-02, sr vpres, dep gen coun & chief compliance Officer, 2002; Latham & Watkins LLP, partner, currently. **Orgs:** Kappa Alpha Psi, 1987-; Am Bar Asn, 1991-; Nat Bar Asn, 1991-; Blacks Govt, 1991-2000; Wash Bar Asn, 1993-. **Honors/Awds:** One of America's most powerful executives under 40, Black Enterprise, 2005. **Military Serv:** AUS, capt, 1988-95, asst gen coun, 1991-95; Meritorious Service Medal, 1995. **Business Addr:** Partner, Latham & Watkin, 555 Eleventh St NW Suite 1000, Washington, DC 20004-1304.

RENDER, ARLENE
Government official, ambassador. **Personal:** Born Aug 16, 1943, Cleveland, OH; married; children: Jonathan Blake & Kiara Isabella. **Educ:** WVa State Col, BS, 1965; Univ Mich, MPH. **Career:** US Diplomat, 1970-; US Ambassador Gambia, 1990-93; US Ambassador Repub Zambia, 1996-99; US Ambassador Repub Cote d'Ivoire, 2001-04; Spelman Col, dipl-in-residence, 2004-. **Honors/Awds:** Multiple Senior Performance Awards & several Superior and Meritorious Honor Awards; Senior Performance Pay Award. **Business Phone:** (404)270-5526.

RENDER, DR. WILLIAM H
Physician. **Personal:** Born Feb 9, 1950, LaGrange, GA; son of Elizabeth Render; married Barbara Jean; children: Eric & Keyiana. **Educ:** Emory Univ, A Med, 1974; GA State Univ, Pre-med; Meharry Med Col, MD, 1984. **Career:** Dr James B Palmer Atlanta GA, physician asst, 1975-80; Emory Univ Affil Hosp, med resident, 1984-87; pvt pract, Internal Med, 1987-; Fulton County Jail, physician 1987-92, Med dir; Piedmont Hosp, physician, currently; Render's Primary Care Ctr PC, physician, currently. **Orgs:** Atlanta Med Asn; Ga State Med Asn; Southern Med Asn; Am Col Physician; Honor Med Soc; Alpha Omega Alpha, 1984. **Honors/Awds:** Bd Certified, Internal Med. **Military Serv:** USN. **Business Addr:** Physician/Owner, Render, 970 Martin Luther King Jr Dr No 305, Atlanta, GA 30314, **Business Phone:** (404)524-1721.

RENE, ALTHEA (ALTHEA MCCULLERS JOHNSON)
Flutist. **Personal:** Born Dec 25, 1958, Detroit, MI; daughter of Dezie and Barbara McCullers; married; children: Brandon & Stephen. **Educ:** Howard Univ, attended 1981; Wayne County Sheriffs Dept Police Acad, attended 1998. **Career:** Wayne County Sheriffs Dept, police officer, 1992; Althea Rene Productions LLC, flutist, currently. **Orgs:** Band leader, Althea Rene & Co, 1984; band mem, Straight Ahead Female Jazz Group, 1997. **Special Achievements:** Opened for Tony Bennett in Puerto Rico, 1998; performed in Jamaica, 1997. **Business Addr:** Flutist, Althea Rene Productions LLC, PO Box 3073, Spring, TX 77383, **Business Phone:** (281)214-4270.

RENFORD, EDWARD
Executive. **Career:** Executive (retired); Grady Health Syst, pres & chief exec officer; Grady Mem Hosp, pres.

RENFRO, MELVIN LACY
Football coach, football player. **Personal:** Born Dec 30, 1941, Houston, TX; children: 4. **Educ:** Univ Ore. **Career:** Football player, Football coach (retired); Dallas Cowboys, defensive back, scout, 1964-77; Miller Beer Dallas, acct mgr; Los Angeles Express, defensive sec coach; St Louis Cardinals, defensive back coach. **Orgs:** Melvin Renfro Found; Involved in various charitable activities. **Honors/Awds:** Most Valuable Player, E & W Game, 1960; Most Valuable Player, Nat Golden WTrack Meet HS, 1960; Most Valuable Player, Pro-Bowl Nat Football League, 1971. **Special Achievements:** Listed in famous people raised in Houston.

RENFROE, IONA ANTOINETTE
Lawyer. **Personal:** Born Feb 13, 1953, New Orleans, LA; daughter of George and Leona "Maude" Madison. **Educ:** Loyola Univ, New Orleans LA, BA, 1975; Loyola Law Sch, New Orleans LA, JD, 1978. **Career:** TANO Inc, New Orleans LA, tech writer, 1975; Chevron USA Inc, New Orleans LA, landman, 1979-81; La Power & Light, NOPSI, New Orleans LA, corp coun, 1981-. **Orgs:** La State Bar Asn, 1980-; La Martinet Soc, 1980-; New Orleans Asn of Black Women Attorneys, 1984-; corporate dir, Sec Riverland Credit Union, 1985-; US Dist Ct, Eastern Dist La, 1986-; coun bd, Nat Forum Black Pub Admin, New Orleans Chap, 1986-; New Orleans Pro Bono Prog, 1987-; La State Bar Asn Continuing Legal Educ Theme Subcommittee 1988-; dir, New Orleans Children's Bur, 1988-; coun bd, New Orleans Birthright Soc Inc, 1988-. *

RENICK, JAMES C.
School administrator, chancellor (education). **Personal:** Born Dec 8, 1948, Rockford, IL; son of James Renick and Constance Carmachael Renick; married Peggy Gadsden; children: Karinda. **Educ:** Central State Univ, BA, 1970; Kans Univ, MSW, 1972; Fla State Univ, PhD, pub admin, 1980. **Career:** Univ West Fla, prof, 1975-81; Univ S Fla, prof, 1981-83, asst to pres, 1983-85, asst dean & educ chmn, 1985-88, depart chair, 1988-89; George Mason Univ, Fairfax, VA, vice provost, 1989-93; Univ Mich-Dearborn, prof & chancellor, 1993-99; Polit Sci NC Agr & Tech State Univ, chancellor & prof, 1999-06; Am Coun Educ, Wash, DC, sr vpres of prog & res, 2006-. **Orgs:** Trustee, Univ Pshycol Ctr, 1984-; fel Am Coun Educ;chmn, Am Asn Higher Educ Black Caucus, 1985-; Fla Leadership Network, Community of C, 1985-; Fla Inst Govt Policy Coun, 1986-89; exec, comn Coun of Fel Am Coun on Educ, 1987-89. **Honors/Awds:** Leadership Fla Community of C, 1985; vis prog assoc, Smithsonian Inst, 1987; Up & Comers Award, Price Waterhouse, 1987; inducted, Donald K Anthony Achievement Hall of FameCentral State Univ, 1993. **Business Phone:** (202)939-9300.*

RESPERT, SHAWN CHRISTOPHER
Basketball player, athletic director, basketball coach. **Personal:** Born Feb 6, 1972, Detroit, MI; married Lenae; children: Cheyenne & Aaron. **Educ:** Mich State Univ, BA, commun, 1995. **Career:** Basketball player (retired), basketball coach, director; Milwaukee Bucks, guard, 1995-96; Toronto Raptors, 1996-98; Dallas Mavericks, 1998; Phoenix Suns, guard, 1999-2000; Prairie View A&M Univ, asst vol basketball coach; Imola Basketball Club, Italian League, asst coach; Komfort Kronopolus Basketball Club, Polish League, asst coach; Rice Univ, dir basketball opers; NBA Develop League, dir basketball opers; Rockets, dir of player prog, currently. **Orgs:** Goodwill Games, USA Basketball Team. **Honors/Awds:** NCAA Player of the Year, The Sporting News, 1995; Player of the Year, NatlAssn Basketball Coaches, 1995. **Home Addr:** 11122 Desert Springs Cir, Houston, TX 77095, **Home Phone:** (281)304-6016. **Business Addr:** Director of Basketball Operations, NBA Development League, 477 Madison Ave 3rd Fl, New York, NY 10022, **Business Phone:** (212)407-8700.

REUBEN, GLORIA
Actor. **Personal:** Born Jun 9, 1964, Ontario;married Wayne Isaak. **Career:** Films: Immediate Family, 1989; Wild Orchid II: Two Shades of Blue, 1992; The Waiter, 1993; Timecop, 1994; Nick of Time, 1995; MacBeth in Manhattan, 1999; Pilgrim, 1999; David & Lola, 1999; Shaft, 2000; Pilgrim, 2000; Bad Faith, 2000; Happy Here & Now, 2002; Salem Witch Trials, 2002; The Sentinel, 2006; Kettle of Fish, 2006; Padre Nuestro, exec producer, 2007; TV series: "Polka Dot Door", 1971; "CBS Schoolbreak Special", 1987;"Alfred Hitchcock Presents", 1987; "21 Jump Street", 1988; China Beach, 1990; The Flash, 1990-91; "The Young Riders", 1991; "The Round Table",1992; Shadow hunter, 1993; Percy & Thunder, 1993; "Silk Stalkings", 1993; Dead Air, 1994; Confessions: Two Faces of Evil, 1994; "McKenna", 1994; "ER", 1995-2008; Johnny's Girl, 1995; "Homicide: Life on the Street", 1995; "Indiscreet", 1998; "Deep In My Heart", 1999; Sara, 1999; "Sole Survivor", 2000; "The Agency", 2001-02; "Feast of All Saints", 2001; Little John, 2002; The District, 2002; "Law & Order: Special Victims Unit", 2002-06; Salem Witch Trials, 2002; "Little John", 2002;"1-800-Missing", assoc producer, 2003; "Numb3rs", 2005; Life Support, 2007; Positive Voices: Women & HIV, producer, 2007; "Raising the Bar", 2008. **Honors/Awds:** Numerous honors & awards including "Miss Black Ontario", 1986; Screen Actors Guild Award for Outstanding Performance, Ensemble in a Drama Series, 1997; Viewers for Quality Television Awards for Best Supporting Actress, Quality Drama Series, 1997; Screen Actors Guild Award for Outstanding Performance, Ensemble in a Drama Series, 1998; Viewers for Quality Television Awards for Best Supporting Actress, Quality Drama Series, 1998; Screen Actors Guild Award for Outstanding Performance, Ensemble in a Drama Series, 1999. **Special Achievements:** In 1996 she was chosen by People as one of the 50 most Beautiful People in the World; She sang back up for Tina Turner on her

Twenty Four Seven Tour, 2000. **Business Addr:** Actress, c/o Untitled Entertainment, 322 Eighth Ave Suite 601, New York, NY 10001, **Business Phone:** (212)777-1214.*

REUBEN, DR. LUCY J
Educator. **Personal:** Born in Sumter, SC. **Educ:** Oberlin Col, BA, econ; Univ Mich, MBA, 1974, PhD, 1981. **Career:** Ford Motor, finance staff coordr; George Mason Univ, vis assoc prof; Fla A&M Univ, assoc prof; SC State Univ Sch Bus, Marshall B Williams prof & dean; NC Cent Univ, provost & vice chancellor, 2002; Univ Mich Ctr Educ Women, vis scholar, currently; Duke Univ Fuqua Sch Bus, vis prof, currently. **Orgs:** Bd dir, Int Educ Resource Ctr; vis comt, Univ Mich Ross Bus Sch; Black Enterprise Bd Economists; bd dirs, Charlotte Off Fed Res Bank, Richmond; Greater Res Triangle Coun; Asn Advan Col Sch Bus; SC Export Consortium; Providence Hosp; SC World Affairs Coun; Orangeburg County United Way; Orangeburg County Chamber Com; SC Technol Transition Team; Fla Black Bus Investment Bd; pres & bd dir, Metrop Wash Planning & Housing Asn; Nat Asn Urban Bankers, Wash, DC; SC Urban League; YWCA; Hayti Develop Corp, Durham, NC; bd govs, Univ Mich Bus Sch Alumni Soc; life mem, Nat Asn Black MBAs; life mem, Nat Coun Negro Women; life mem, Nat Asn Advan Colored People. *

REUBEN, DR. LUCY JEANETTE
Educator. **Personal:** Born Dec 15, 1949, Sumter, SC; daughter of Odell Richardson and Anna Mays; married Dr John A Cole; children: John Akayomi Cole; children: Kwame Odell Oliver. **Educ:** Oberlin Col, BA, 1971; Univ Mich, MBA, 1974, PhD, 1981. **Career:** Ford Motor Co, financial analyst 1974-75; Earhart Found fel 1978; Ayres fel, Stonier Grad Sch Banking 1982; NC Central Univ, from dean to provost & vice chancellor; SC State Univ, Sch Bus, prof; Fla Agri & Mech Univ, assoc prof finance; George Mason Univ, vis assoc prof finance; Univ Chicago, Nissan fel; Fed Res Syst, vis scholar; Duke Univ, Fuqua Sch Bus, vis prof currently. **Orgs:** Adv bd, Hayti Develop Corp, 1982-84; adv bd, Wash DC Urban Bankers Asn, 1984-; adv bd, Wash DC Women Economists, 1984-; consult, Nat Bankers Asn, 1984-; consult, US Dept Com, 1984-; bd dirs, Metrop Wash Planning & Housing Asn, 1986-; Am Finance Asn; Eastern Finance Asn; Nat Black MBA Asn; Nat Econ Asn; Nat Asn Female Exec; Nat Asn Black MBAs; Nat Coun Negro Women; Nat Asn Advan Colored People; Alpha Kappa Alpha; adv bd, Links, Inc; bd dir, Int Educ Resource Ctr. **Special Achievements:** Twelve publications including "Black Banks, A Survey and Analysis of the Literature" (with John A Cole, Alfred L Edwards, and Earl G Hamilton) Review of Black Political Economy Fall 1985; taught and written in various areas on finance and minority business development; co-edited, authored, co-authored books, articles, and other publications; appeared in television and print media, including The Wall Street Journal, and Black Enterprise magazine. **Business Addr:** Visiting Professor, Duke University, The Fuqua School of Business, 1 Towerview Dr, PO Box 90120, **Business Phone:** (919)660-7661.

REVELLE, ROBERT, SR.
Clergy. **Personal:** Born Jan 6, 1947, Harrellsville, NC; son of Hugh L (deceased) and Carrie L; married Annie M (Adams), Dec 9, 1969; children: Sharon Marie & Robert Jr. **Educ:** Goldey Beacom Bus Col, AA, mgt, 1969-71; Nat Grad Univ, cert, 1973; Wilmington Col, BBA, 1973-78; Eastern Theol Sem, Cert, 1989. **Career:** CDA, Wilmington, planner, consult, 1971-73, admin chief, 1973-74; Community Affairs, dept dir, 1974-75; Community Ctr, supt, 1975-84; Wilmington City, dir, minority bus prog, 1984-87, dep personnel dir, 1987, Delaware State, personnel recruitment specialist, 1994-98; Holy Christian Church Am Inc, pastor, presiding bishop; Robert Revelle Sr. Ministries, pastor, 2000-. **Orgs:** AUS Personnel Sch Personnel Mgt, 1967; Pres, Am Cancer Soc, 1973-75, vpres; pres, vpres, Price Run Child Ctr 1976-84; YMCA Resource Ctr, 1983-84; mem chmn, orgn community Police, Community Coun, Wilmington, 1983-85; Del Minority Bus Med Week, Trade Fair Comn, 1984-87; Del Pvt Indust Coun, 1988-90; ambassador, YMCA Black Achievers Prog, 1989-; pres, Del chap, Nat Forum Black Pub Adminr, 1990-; pres, World Import Visions, Inc 1999-; pres, Robert Revelle Sr. Ministries 1999-; Nat Asn Advan Colored People; Wilmington Small Bus Develop Ctr. **Honors/Awds:** Honor Cert, Freedom Found Valley Forge, 1970; Cert Merit, Am Cancer Soc, 1975; Certificate of Apppreciation, West Center City Community Ctr, 1980. **Military Serv:** AUS spec, E-5, 1966-69; Outstanding Soldier, 1966. **Business Addr:** Pastor, Robert Revelle SR Ministries, 110 W 37th St, Wilmington, DE 19802, **Business Phone:** (302)764-7656.

REVELY, WILLIAM
Clergy, social worker. **Personal:** Born Jan 20, 1941, Charlottesville, VA; son of William Revely Sr (deceased) and Reaver E Carter (deceased); children: Christana Re & Christopher. **Educ:** Howard Univ, BA, 1964, M Div, 1967, MSW, 1971, D Min, 1982. **Career:** Messiah Baptist Church, pastor, 1989-; Mt Gilead Baptist Church, pastor, 1979; Union Baptist Church, pastor, 1965-79; Nara II Aftercare Unit Bureau Rehab, chf, 1973-76; Shaw Residence III (Hlfway House) Bureau Rehab, dir, 1976-77; Howard Univ, Sch Social Work, 1977-79. **Orgs:** Nat Asn Advan Colored People; SCLC; ACA; NABSW; Nat Progressive Baptist Convention; Nat Baptist Convention USA Inc; bd trustees, Shaw Divinity Sch; bd chmn, GOIC, Detroit, 1991; bd dirs, mortuary sci, Univ DC, 1989; Lott Carey Foreign Missions Convention, clergy support comt; Int Found for Educ & Self Help. **Honors/Awds:** Vernon Johns Preaching Award, Sch Religion, Howard Univ, 1967; NIMH Fel, 1967-71. **Special Achievements:** Author of Poetry, 'From the Heart', Foster Publ, 1989. **Home Addr:** 29314 Tiffany Ct, Southfield, MI 48034-4538. **Business Addr:** Pastor, Messiah Baptist Church, 8100 W Seven Mile Road, Detroit, MI 48221, **Business Phone:** (313)864-3337.

REVIS, DR. NATHANIEL W
President (Organization), scientist. **Personal:** Born Jul 27, 1939, Glenridge, NJ; divorced 1993; children: Natalie & Jarrett. **Educ:** Fairleigh Dickinson Univ, NJ, BS, 1962; Univ Louvain, Belgium, Med Sch, 1968; Univ Glasgow, Scotland, PhD, 1972. **Career:** Oak Ridge Realty Holdings Inc, scientist & pres; Oak Ridge Nat Lab & Univ Tenn, asst prof, 1975-81; Univ Glasgow, Dept Cardiol, asst prof, 1972-74; Sci & Techn Resources Inc, pres, currently; Nominating Comt, Oak Ridge Res Inst, chairperson, currently. **Orgs:** Int Soc Biochem, 1972; Am & Int Soc Cardiol, 1975; adv, (brain trust), Cong Black, 1978; adv, Nat Cancer Inst, 1979. **Business Phone:** (865)481-6088.

REVISH, DANIELLE A
Executive director. **Career:** Fashion Group Int Columbus, Inc., regional dir, currently. **Business Addr:** Regional Director, Fashion Group International of Columbus, Inc., 4413 Beech Wood Loop, Dublin, OH 43016.

REVISH, JERRY
Television journalist. **Personal:** Born Mar 15, 1949, Youngstown, OH; son of Dewey and Estelle; married Danielle, Jun 22, 1974; children: Nicole & Jerome II. **Educ:** Youngstown State Univ, 1969; Chapman Col, 1970. **Career:** WBBW Radio, anchor & reporter, 1972-74; WBNS Radio, assignment ed & reporter, 1974-80; WBNS-10 TV, anchor & reporter, 1980-. **Orgs:** NAACP, 1990-; pres, Columbus Asn Black Journalists, 1991-92; bd mem, United Way, Proj Diversity, 1991-. **Honors/Awds:** Best Series, Sigma Delta Chi, 1979; Best Spot, news, feature & doc, Asn Press, 1980-90; Best Spot, news, feature & doc, UPI, 1980-90; 16 Emmy Nominations, 1980-90, 5 Emmy Awards, Nat Acad TV Arts & Sci; Achievement in Journalism Award, Cent Ohio Chap Prof Journalists; Hall of Fame, Ohio Broadcasters, 2005. **Special Achievements:** Two tours Persian Gulf Operation Desert Shield Desert Storm, 1991. **Business Addr:** TV News Anchor, Reporter, WBNS-10TV, 770 Twin Rivers Dr, Columbus, OH 43216, **Business Phone:** (614)460-3950.

REYES, RICARDO A.
Executive. **Career:** Int Transp Solutions Express Inc, sales mgr, 2001-03, pres & chief exec officer, 2003-. **Honors/Awds:** Achievement Award, Black Bus Mag, 2003.

REYNOLDS, ANDREW BUCHANAN
Consultant, vice president (organization). **Personal:** Born Jun 29, 1939, Winston-Salem, NC; son of Andrew Buchanan and Florence Terry; divorced. **Educ:** Lincoln Univ, BA, 1960; NC A&T Univ, BS, 1962; Columbia Univ, cert journ, 1970. **Career:** Bowman Gray Sch Med, Dept Pharmacol, res asst, 1962-63; CORE, dir, 1963; Madigan Gen Hosp, Ft Lewis, WA, radioisotope tech, 1964-65; NC Advan Sch, counr & teacher, 1966-67; PA Advan Sch, curric & develop specialist, 1967-70; WCAU-TV, reporter & producer, 1970-71; September & Assoc, prod dir, 1973-75; New Day Inc, prod dir, 1975; City Seattle, Seattle Dept Parks & Recreation, mgr, mkt & pub rels, 1987-93; Exec Diversity Serv, owner, vpres, 2005; consult, currently; Andy Reynolds & Assocs, owner & prin; Wash State Lottery Comn, chair; King Broadcasting Co, TV news reporter; Executive Diversity Services (EDS), vpres, 2009; SIETAR, pres, 2009. **Orgs:** NAACP, 1978; pres, bd trustees, Educ Opportunity Prog Univ Wash; chmn & ed, Leadership Tomorrow; chmn, WA State Lottery Comn; prog chmn, UNCF Telethon Comn; Pub Defender Asn; Northwest Aids Found; Seattle/King Co Red Cross; Greater Seattle Chamber Com. **Honors/Awds:** Hon, Sigma Delta Chi Features, 1973; First Place, Sigma Delta Chi Spot News, 1975; Third Place, Sigma Delta Chi Doc, 1977; Humbolt Award, 1978; Hon, Puget Sound Pub Rels Soc America, 1983; Outstanding Alumni Award, Leadership Tomorrow, 1992. **Military Serv:** AUS, E-4, 1963-65. **Home Addr:** 3315 37th Ave S, Seattle, WA 98144. *

REYNOLDS, BARBARA A
Columnist, editor. **Personal:** Born in Columbus, OH; daughter of Harvey and Elizabeth Taylor; divorced; children: John Eric. **Educ:** Ohio State Univ, BA, jour, 1967; Howard Univ, Sch Divinity, MA, 1992; United Theol Sem, Dayton, DMin, 1998. **Career:** Cleveland, social worker; Ebony Mag, Chicago, IL, ed, 1968-69; Chicago Tribune, Chicago, IL, reporter, 1969-81; Harvard Univ, Nieman fel, 1976-77; USA Today, Arlington, VA, ed, columnist, 1983-; Reynolds News Serv, pres, currently; Mt Calvary Baptist Church, Wash, DC, minister, currently; Shenandoah Univ, Winchester, VA, Jessie Ball Dupont chair jour, prof, currently. **Orgs:** Chmn, Women's Task Force; Nat Asn Black Journalists, 1991-. **Honors/Awds:** Martin Luther King Jr Drum Major for Justice Award; Outstanding Alumni, Ohio State Univ, 1990; DHL, Ohio State Univ; DHL, Shenandoah Univ, 1995; Journalist of the Year Award, Nat Asn Black Journalists, 1999; Outstanding Achievement Award, Columbia Univ, Sch Jour, MO, 1999. **Special Achievements:** Author: Jesse Jackson, the man, the myth & the movement, 1975; No, I Won't Shut Up: 30 Years of Telling It Like It Is, 1998; Out of Hell and Living Well, 2005. **Home Addr:** 5602 Windsor Ct, Suitland, MD 20746, **Home Phone:** (301)899-1341. **Business Phone:** (301)899-1341.

REYNOLDS, BRUCE HOWARD
Dentist. **Personal:** Born Oct 7, 1935, Chicago, IL; married Ellen Barnes; children: Bruce Jr & Jana. **Educ:** Dillard Univ, BS, 1959; Howard Univ, DDS, 1963. **Career:** Pvt prac, dentist, currently. **Orgs:** Am Dent Asn; Nat Dent Asn; Am Endodontic Soc; Evanston Dent Asn; Dent Consult, IL, Dent Srv NAACP; bd op, PUSH; The Cheesmen Inc. **Honors/Awds:** AUS, medic, 1957-59; USAF, DDS, 1963-65. **Home Addr:** 1012 Darrow Ave, Evanston, IL 60202, **Home Phone:** (847)864-1644. **Business Addr:** Dentist, 1012 Darrow Ave, Evanston, IL 60202, **Business Phone:** (847)864-1644.

REYNOLDS, CHARLES MCKINLEY, JR.
Executive. **Personal:** Born Jan 11, 1937, Albany, GA; son of Johnnie Hadley and Charles McKinley; married Estella Henry, Aug 19, 1956; children: Eric Charles & Gregory Preston. **Educ:** Morehouse Col, BA, 1954; Wayne State Univ, mortuary sci cert, 1962; Albany State Col, mid grades cert, 1964. **Career:** Southside Jr High Sch, Dept Social Studies, teacher & chmn, 1962-65; US Treas Dept, asst examr, 1965-69, nat bank examr, 1969-71; Citizen Trust Bank, vpres 1971, pres, 1971; Atlantic Nat Bank, pres & chief exec officer, 1975-88; Reynolds & Assocs, pres, 1988-. **Orgs:** Bd dirs, Atlantic Nat Bank; bd dirs, Norfolk C C; Jr Achievement Tidewater Inc; Tidewater Area Minority Contractors; exec comt, Greater Norfolk Develop Corp; treas, Norfolk Investment Co Inc; bd visitors, James Madison Univ; treas, bd dirs, Norfolk State Univ Found; corp bd mem & chmn, Audit Comt, SCI Systems Inc; adv bd mem, Norfolk State Univ Bus & Social Work; gerontol adv coun, Hampton Inst; life mem, Alpha Phi Alpha Frat; Sigma Pi Phi Fraternity; Guardsman Inc; Rotary Club; Old Dominion Univ Exec Adv Coun; treas, Bank St Mem Baptist Church; treas, William A Hunton YMCA; Sire Acron, SPP; Cong Racial Equality, 1975; Nat Assoc Minority Contractors, 1984. **Honors/Awds:** Outstanding Achievement Award, Alpha Phi Alpha Gamma Omicron Lambda Chap, 1966; Minority Advocacy of the Year Award, 1984; US Presidential Citation, White House Conf Small Bus; Community Service Award, Madison Sec Sch, 1985; Distinguished Leadership Award, United Negro Col Fund, 1985; McDonald's Black Achievement Award, 1986; First Black Student Awards Banquet, Old Dominion Univ, 1986; Award for Blazing New Horizons in Banking, Delicados Inc, 1986; William A Hunton Heroes Award, 2003. **Military Serv:** US Air Force, A/lc, 1956-60. **Home Addr:** 4504 Kelley Ct, Virginia Beach, VA 23462, **Home Phone:** (757)490-7191. **Business Addr:** President, Chief Executive Officer, Reynolds & Associates, 1430 G St NE, Washington, DC 20002, **Business Phone:** (202)396-8982.

REYNOLDS, DR. EDWARD
Educator. **Personal:** Born Jan 23, 1942; son of Elizabeth; children: Joel. **Educ:** Wake Forest Univ, BA, 1964; Ohio Univ, MA, 1965; Yale Univ, MDiv, 1968; Univ London Sch Oriental & African Studies, PhD, 1972. **Career:** Christ United Presby, assoc pastor, 1982-; Univ Calif, San Diego, asst prof, 1971-74, assoc prof, 1974-83, assoc dir acad affairs, prof hist, prof emer hist, currently; City San Diego, planning comnr, 1989-93. **Orgs:** Vice moderator, Presbytery San Diego, 1993, moderator, 1994; dir, Univ Calif Study Ctr, 1994-96. **Honors/Awds:** Excellence in Teaching Award, Univ Calif, San Diego, 1990-91. **Special Achievements:** Has written books-Trade and Economic Change on the Gold Coast 1974, Stand the Storm A History of the Atlantic Slave Trade 1985, Focus on Africa, 1994. **Business Addr:** Professor Emeritus of History, University of California-San Diego, Department of History, Rm 0104 9500 Gilman Dr, La Jolla, CA 92093-0104, **Business Phone:** (858)534-1996.

REYNOLDS, IDA MANNING
Government official, executive director. **Personal:** Born Sep 8, 1946, Hines, FL; daughter of James Westley and Catherine Mosley; married Wilfred Reynolds Jr, Sep 8, 1984; children: Ronald Jr, Katrina, Joseph Hayes Rawls, Tina, Wilfred Reynolds III. **Educ:** Lincoln Tech Inst, comput sci, 1966. **Career:** Alachua City, FL, benefit & payroll supv, 1963-73, personnel specialist, 1973-79, personnel mgt analyst, 1979-81, dir equal opportunity div, 1981-. **Orgs:** Secy, Local Chap, Am Soc Personnel Admin, 1979; vpres, Cent Fla Conf, Women Missionary, 1980-; state coordr, Am Asn Affirmative Action, 1982; adv bd, Santa Fe Community Col, Human Serv, 1982-; bd dir, Fla Asn Community Prof, 1983-; chairperson, Area XIV Fla Church Women United, 1984-; bd dirs, United Gainesville Community Develop Corp, 1984-; regional pres, Fla Asn Community Rels, 1984-; bd dir, One Church One Child Black Adoption, 1986-; Gov Comn Martin Luther King Commemorative Celebration, 1986; Alachua County Black Adoption Bd; producer/host, Forum Black Social & Econ Issues, 1989-; vpres, Nat Forum Black Pub Admin, 1990-; chap chair, Nat Asn Human Rights Workers, 1990-; vpres, N Cent Fla Nat Forum Black Pub Admin, 1990-; Am Asn Pub Admin & Conf Minority

Pub Admin; bd dirs, Gainesville/Alachua County Martin Luther King Fund Inc; Developed, implemented and coordinated private and public participation in Countywide Annual Conference on Human Rights and Equal Opportunity Law. **Honors/Awds:** Future Bus Leaders Am, 1981; Appreciation Award, Am Cancer Soc, 1981; Outstanding Contrib Reg IV, Am Asn Affirmitive Action, 1982; Outstanding Contrib, Gainesville Job Corps, 1984; Cert of Recognition & Cert of Appreciation, Gov State, FL,1986; Distinguished Serv Award, Alachua County, 1989; Special Recognition Plaque, Ment Health Serv Cent Fla, 1989; Distinguished Serv Award, Gainesville/Alachua County Martin Luther King Jr Found, 1991. **Home Addr:** 2405 NE 65th Terr, Gainesville, FL 32609. **Business Addr:** Director, Alachua County Equal Opportunity Office, 21 E Univ Ave, PO Box 1467, Gainesville, FL 32602.*

REYNOLDS, JAMES
Actor, artistic director, business owner. **Personal:** Born Aug 10, 1946, Kansas City, MO; son of Leonard and Dorothy J Cotton; married Lissa Layng, Dec 21, 1986; children: Jed. **Educ:** Washburn Univ, Topeka KS, BFA, 1970. **Career:** Los Angeles Repertory Theater, managing artistic dir, 1975-82; La Famille Enterprises, pres, 1987-; S Pasadena Repertory Theater, managing artistic dir, 1989-; La Famile Films, S Pasadena, Calif, pres, 1990-; Generations, Burbank, CA, lead actor, 1990-91; Classics Unlimited, S Pasadena, vpres; Free St Productions, ceo & partner, 1996-; Fremont Ctr Theater, artistic dir, currently; Films: Mr. Majestyk, 1974; Fun with Dick & Jane, 1977; The Magic of Lassie, 1978; C.H.O.M.P.S., 1979; TV series: Keeper ofthe Wild", 1977; Devil Dog: The Hound of Hell, 1978; Jennifer: A Woman's Story, 1979; "The Incredible Hulk", 1979; "Time Express", 1979; "Diff'rent Strokes", 1979-80; M Station: Hawaii, 1980; "Days of Our Lives", 1981-2009; "Hotline", 1982; "Generations", 1989; Days of Our Lives' 35th Anniversary, 2000. **Orgs:** Mem adv bd, Topeka Performing Arts Ctr, 1989-; bd dirs, Kans State Hist Soc. **Honors/Awds:** Man of the Year, Nat Jewish Hosp, Nat Asthma Ctr, 1985, 1986, 1987; Volunteer of the Year, Dir Vols Am, 1987; Honorary Citizen, Wichita, Kans, 1988; Business Person of the Year, 1994; Artistic Dir Award, Outstanding Comedy-Actor; Nominated for Emmy for Outstanding Actor Drama Series, 1991; Heroes & Legends Award, 2003; Soap Chat, Best Supporting Actor, 2003; Nominated for Image Awards, 2002, 2004, 2007; Nominated for Day Time Emmy Award, 1991, 2004. **Military Serv:** US Marine Corps, 1964-66.

REYNOLDS, JAMES F.
Administrator. **Personal:** Born Aug 29, 1914, Winston-Salem, NC; married Alice Gertrude Rausch; children: Lanell Rhone, Alice Owens, Micaela Jones, John. **Educ:** Univ Denver, BA, 1962, MA, 1963; Met State Col, DPA, 1980. **Career:** City & Co Denver, race consult, 1963; Univ Colo, teacher, 1967-75; Univ Denver, teacher, 1970-74; United Progress Headstart, pres; Congress Racial Equality, chmn; Colo Civil Rights Comn, dir, 1963-80. **Orgs:** Pres, Black Dir Council, 1980; pres, People People & Sister Cities Int, 1980. **Honors/Awds:** Man of the Year Award, Delta Psi Lambda, 1967; Whitehead Award, ACLU CO Chap, 1978; Martin Luther King Award, Martin Luther King Found, 1980; Award Int Asn, Ofcl Human Rights Agency, 1980. **Military Serv:** USAF, major. *

REYNOLDS, JAMES W.
Government official. **Personal:** Born Jun 25, 1944, Florence, AL; son of Welton and Evelyn M; married Dianne Daniels, Jun 26, 1969; children: Rodney James. **Educ:** Talladega Col, AB, 1966; Alabama A&M Univ, MBA, 1975; Fla Inst Technol,MS, 1980; Grad, AUS Logamp Prog, 1992. **Career:** Government Offical (retired); Florence City Sch, math teacher, 1966; AUS Missile Command, procurement intern, 1966-67, procurement agent, 1970-71; AUS Corps Engineers, contract specialist, 1971-80, br chief, acquisition mgt, 1980-86, dep dir contracting, 1986-91, dir contracting, 1991-2002. **Orgs:** Nat Contract Mgt Asn, chap prog chmn, 1982-83, chap vpres, 1983-84, chappres, 1984-85, chap dir, 1987-89; treasr, Huntsville High Sch PTA, 1986-87;chmn southern region meeting, Talladega Col Alumni, 1989, chap secy, 1991-98; deacon bd secy, Church St Cumberland Presbyterian Church, 1991-96; deacon bd chmn, 1997-98; elder, Church Christ, 2003-; MBR Huntsvile Rehab Bd, 2003-. **Honors/Awds:** Chapter Man of the Year, Omega Psi Phi Fraternity, 1986; Meriterious Civilian Service Award, 2002. **Military Serv:** AUS, sgt, 1967-70; Army Commendation Medal, 1968-69; AUS CEngr, Employee of the Year, 1979. **Home Addr:** 128 Heritage Lane, Madison, AL 35758.

REYNOLDS, JERRY
Basketball coach, basketball player. **Personal:** Born Dec 23, 1962, Brooklyn, NY. **Educ:** Madison Area Tech Col, attended 1982; La State Univ, attended 1985. **Career:** Basketball player (retired), basketball coach; Milwaukee Bucks, guard, 1985-88; Seattle Supersonics, guard, 1988-89; Orlando Magic, guard, 1989-92; Milwaukee Bucks, guard, 1995-96; Webber Int Warriors, Webber Int Univ, assoc head coach, 2005-. **Business Phone:** (863)638-2980.

REYNOLDS, MEL
Congressperson (U.S. federal government). **Personal:** Born Jan 8, 1952, Mound Bayou, MS; married Marisol Reynolds; children: Corean. **Educ:** Roosevelt Univ; Univ Ill; Oxford Univ, Rhodes Scholar, JDS. **Career:** Col prof; US House Rep, dem congressman, IL, 1992-95; House Ways & Means Comt, mem; Rainbow Coalition, consult, 2001-.; Salem Baptist Church, community develop dir, 2001-. **Special Achievements:** first African-Am Rhodes Scholar, IL. **Business Phone:** (773)373-3366.

REYNOLDS, NANETTE LEE
Founder (Originator). **Personal:** Born Feb 22, 1946, Oberlin, OH; married Murphy L Reynolds (deceased); children: Malika, Michon Imani. **Educ:** Howard Univ, BA, 1967; Southern Ill Univ, Carbondale, MS, Educ, 1969; Harvard Univ, EdD, 1978. **Career:** Mass Inst Technol, asst dean stud affairs, 1970-72; Brown Univ, asst dean acad affairs, 1972-74; RI Consortium Continuing Educ Human Serv & Community Welfare, exec dir, 1977-78; Reynolds Group Human Res Consult, managing dir, 1980-81; Fed Coun Domestic Violence Progs, exec dir, 1982-83; Office Mich's Govt, prog specialist educ & civil rights, 1983-85; Mich Dept Civil Rights, exec asst dir, 1985-87, community serv bur, dir, 1987-93, dir & mem Gov's Cabinet, 1993-03 (retired); Reynovations, LLC, founder, 2003-; Grand Valley State Univ, Sr Adv to Pres, 2004-. **Orgs:** Nat Asn Advan Colored People, Delta Sigma Theta Sor Inc; Links; Ele's Place grieving c, bd mem; Greater Lansing UNCF Campaign, co-chair, 1997-98; J Inter-group Rels, adv bd, 1996-. **Honors/Awds:** Ford Fel Black Am, 1975-78; numerous awards and recognition for civil rights work. **Special Achievements:** First African-Am female to head Michigan's Civil Rights Dept; Nat Asn for Equal Opportunity Hon, Distinguished Alumna Historically & Predominately Black Col & Univ, 1994; Hon "Delta Legacy: Women Making a Difference", 1994; Mich Dept Civil Rights Dir's Award, 1987; Listings in "Outstanding Young Women of America" and "Outstanding Black Americans".

REYNOLDS, PAMELA TERESE
Journalist. **Personal:** Born Dec 10, 1963, Los Angeles, CA; daughter of Theodore; married Philip G Roth, Feb 13, 1988 (deceased). **Educ:** Univ Mo, Columbia Sch Jour, BJ (magna cum laude), 1985. **Career:** The Boston Globe, feature writer, reporter & nat reporter, 1987-89, asst arts ed, 1990-91, asst living ed, 1991-. **Orgs:** Sigma Delta Chi, 1984; Young Black Journalists Under 30, 1985; Boston Assoc Black Journalists, 1986; tutor, Literacy Vol MA, 1987. **Honors/Awds:** Nat Achievement Scholar, 1981; Reynolds Scholar Donald W Reynolds Found, 1983; Kappa Tau Alpha Hon Jour Soc, 1985; Best Stud Journalist, New Eng Women's Press Assoc, 1985; Best Fashion Writer of the Year. **Special Achievements:** Won first place in Feature Writing category for two of her articles. **Home Phone:** (617)244-1233. **Business Addr:** Assistant Living Editor, The Boston Globe, 135 William T Morrissey Blvd, Dorchester, MA 02125, **Business Phone:** (617)929-2000.

REYNOLDS, R. J.
Baseball player. **Personal:** Born Apr 19, 1959, Sacramento, CA; children: Fawn Rashelle & Robert IV. **Educ:** Sacramento City Col; Cosumnes River Col. **Career:** Baseball player (retired); Los Angeles Dodgers, outfielder, 1983-85; Pittsburgh Pirates, outfielder, 1985-90; Yokohama Taiyo Whales, outfielder, 1991-92; Kintetsu Buffaloes, 1993; Japanese Baseball League, outfielder, 1991-94; Mexican League, Yucatan Lions, outfielder, 1994. **Honors/Awds:** Gold Glove Award.

REYNOLDS, RICKY SCOTT
Founder (Originator), football player. **Personal:** Born Jan 19, 1965, Sacramento, CA. **Educ:** Wash State Univ. **Career:** Football player (retired), owner; Tampa Bay Buccaneers, defensive back, 1987-93; New Eng Patriots, cornerback, 1994-96; Reynolds Child Develop Ctr, owner, currently. **Business Addr:** Owner, Reynolds Child Development Center, 8474 West Hillsborough Ave, Tampa, FL 33615, **Business Phone:** (813)885-6262.

REYNOLDS, SANDRA MICHELE
Financial manager, founder (originator), investment banker. **Personal:** Born Apr 9, 1964, Chicago, IL; daughter of Odessa O and Mitchell; married James Reynolds Jr, Feb 8, 1992; children: James III, Kendall Marie & Miles Joseph. **Educ:** Stanford Univ, Sch Mgt, AB, 1984; Northwestern Univ, MM, 1987. **Career:** First Chicago Capital Markets, bond broker, vpres, 1985-95; Loop Capital Markets LLC, investment banker, managing dir, 1997-. **Orgs:** AKA Sorority, 1982-; Nat Black MBA Asn, 1985; Asn Investment Mgt & Res, chartered fin analyst, 1994-. **Business Phone:** (312)913-4903.

REYNOLDS-BROWN, BLONDELL
Government official. **Personal:** Born Oct 16, 1952, Sumter, SC; daughter of Whittmore and Sadie Reynolds; married Howard, Aug 24, 1996; children: Andrew & Brielle. **Educ:** Pa State Univ, BS, edu, MS, edu; Univ Pa Community Leadership Prog, graduate. **Career:** Sch Dist Philadelphia, elem sch teacher; Pa State Univ-Philadelphia Recruitment Ctr, assoc dir admin; Philadelphia Urban League, youth proj dir; Philadelphia Opportunities & Industrialization Ctr, dir community affairs & fund develop; State Senator Chaka Fattah, legis dir; State Senator Vincent Hughes, community affairs dir; City Coun Philadelphia, city coun woman, 2000-. **Orgs:** Bd mem, Philadelphia Convention & Visitor's Bur; bd mem, Pa Ballet; bd mem, Wellness Community Philadelphia; bd mem, Philadelphia Cult Fund, 2000-; bd mem, Greater Philadelphia Cult Alliance; bd mem, Fairmont Park Hist Preserv Trust; chair woman, City Coun Comt on Parks, Recreation & Cult Affairs, 2000-; Delta Sigma Theta Sorority; charter class mem, Philadelphia Urban League Leadership Inst. **Honors/Awds:** Fel, Robert Wood Johnson Found Urban Health Initiative; Univ Pa Community Leadership Prog, graduate; Marian Anderson Award, African Am Mus Philadelphia. **Business Addr:** Councilwoman-At-Large, City Council of Philadelphia, City Hall Room 581, Philadelphia, PA 19107, **Business Phone:** (215)686-3438.

RHAMES, IRVING. See RHAMES, VING.

RHAMES, VING (IRVING RHAMES)
Actor. **Personal:** Born May 12, 1959, New York, NY; son of Ernest and Rather; married Valerie Scott (divorced 1999); married Deborah Reed, Dec 25, 2000; children: Rainbow, Freedom & Tiffany. **Educ:** State Univ NY, Purchase, attended; Juilliard Sch Drama, BFA, 1983. **Career:** Stage: The Boys of Winter, 1985; TV Series: Go Tell It on the Mountain,1985; "Miami Vice", 1985-87; Men, 1989; Rising Son, 1990; The Long Walk Home, 1990; When You Remember Me, 1990; Terror on Track 9, 1992; "Philly Heat", 1994; "Suicide Squad"; "ER", 1994-96; Deadly Whispers, 1995; "Don King: Only in America", 1997; American Tragedy, 2000; "UC: Undercover", 2001; "Holiday Heart", 2000; Sins of the Father, 2002; "RFK", 2002; "Lilo& Stitch", 2002; "Little John", 2002; The District:, 2002-03; "Freedom: A History of Us", 2003; Kojak, co-exec producer, 2005; "Mercy Reef", 2006; "Leroy & Stitch", 2006; Aqua man, 2006; Football Wives, 2007; Frank Lucas, 2007, "American Gangster", 2007; Films: Go Tell It on the Mountain, 1984; Native Son, 1986; Patty Hearst, 1988; Casualties of War, 1989; Jacob's Ladder, 1990; Flight of the Intruder, 1991; The People Under the Stairs, 1991; Homicide, 1991; Stop! Or My Mom Will Shoot, 1992; Dave, 1993; Bound by Honor, 1993; The Saint of Fort Washington, 1993; Drop Squad, 1994; Pulp Fiction, 1994; Kiss of Death; 1995, Striptease, 1996; Mission: Impossible, 1996; Dangerous Ground, 1997; Rosewood, 1997; Con Air, 1997; Body Count, 1998; Out of Sight, 1998; Entrapment, 1999; Bringing Out the Dead, 1999; Mission Impossible II, 2000; Baby Boy, 2001; Final Fantasy: The Spirits Within, 2001; Undisputed, 2002; Lilo & Stitch, 2002; Dark Blue, 2002; Sin, 2003; Envy, 2004; Dawn of the Dead, 2004; Back in the Day, co-exec producer, 2005; Mission: Impossible III, 2006; Idle wild, 2006; Animal 2, 2007; A Broken Life, 2007; Ascension Day, producer, 2007; I Now Pronounce You Chuck & Larry, 2007; "A Broken Life", 2008; "Day of the Dead", 2008; "Saving God", 2008; "Phantom Punch", 2009; "The Bridge to Nowhere", 2009; "Evil Angel", 2009; "Echelon Conspiracy ", 2009; "Give 'em Hell, Malone", 2009; "The Tournament", 2009; "The Goods: Live Hard, Sell Hard", 2009. **Honors/Awds:** Golden Globe Awards, Best Actor, Miniseries Movie Made TV, 1998; Locarno International Film Festival Award, 2001. **Business Addr:** Actor, William Morris Agency, 1 William Morris Pl, Beverly Hills, CA 90212, **Business Phone:** (310)859-4000.*

RHEA, MICHAEL
Association executive. **Personal:** Born Oct 3, 1946. **Educ:** UCLA, MBA; Memphis State Univ, Tokyo Univ, LA Writers Workshop, Post grad. **Career:** Met Manpower Comn, Indianapolis, dept adminr, 1973; WLWI TV "Here & Now", host, 1970-74; Econ Develop Corp, mgr, 1970-73; Thomas Ryan Inc Mgt Consult, reg mgr, 1969-70. **Orgs:** Gov's Commn Status & Women, 1973; chmn bd dirs, Youth Market Pl, 1973; pres & chmn bd, People Better Broadcasting, 1973; Jaycees; adv, Black Student Union; adv, Black Arts Workshop; Mayor's Task Force Improve City Govt; Indianapolis Cable Steering Com; Adult Educ Coun Central IN; bd City & State Black Caucus; CORE; Young Rep; Nat Asn Execs & Mgr; Prof Mgrs Club; Artist Am; Midwst Poet's Org; adv Boys Club Am. **Business Addr:** 2101 N Col Ave, Indianapolis, IN 46202.

RHEAMS, LEONTA (LEONTA DEMARKEL RHEAMS)
Football player. **Personal:** Born Aug 1, 1976, Tyler, TX. **Educ:** Univ Houston. **Career:** New Eng Patriots, defensive tackle, 1998; Xtreme Football League, Memphis Maniax, defensive tackle, 2001-. **Business Addr:** Defensive Tackle, Memphis Maniax, 315 S Hollywood St, Memphis, TN 38104, **Business Phone:** (901)515-2000.

RHEAMS, LEONTA DEMARKEL. See RHEAMS, LEONTA.

RHETT, ERRICT UNDRA
Football player, football coach. **Personal:** Born Dec 11, 1970, Pembroke Pines, FL. **Educ:** Univ Fla. **Career:** Football player (retired), Football coach; Tampa Bay Buccaneers, runningback, 1994-97; Baltimore Ravens, 1998-99; Cleveland Browns, running back, 2000; Piper High Sch, running back coach, currently. **Orgs:** Omega Psi Phi Fraternity Inc. **Honors/Awds:** Offensive Rookie of the Year, Nat Football League Players Asn, 1994; Pro Bowl alternate, 1995. **Business Phone:** (754)322-1700.

RHETT, MICHAEL L
Law enforcement officer. **Personal:** Born Dec 1, 1954, Charlottesville, VA; son of Walter P Sr and Bernice N; married Susan G.

Educ: Newberry Col, attended 1973-74; Ohio State Univ, attended 1973-78. **Career:** State Ohio, Nat Resources, pk ranger, 1978-80; Standard Oil Ohio, mgr, 1980-82; City Columbus, Div Police, police officer, 1982-. **Orgs:** Newsletter ed, Fraternal Order Police Conductor, 1982-92; bd mem, Crittenton Family Serv, 1983-, bd chair, 1986-87, bd chair elect, 1993-94; bd mem, Cent Community House, 1992-, bd chair, 1994-95; vpres, Fraternal Order Police, 1992-; bd chair, Cent Community House, 1997-. **Special Achievements:** First black chair of largest United Way agency in Franklin County, Ohio, 1986-87; First black elected board member FOP CCL 9. **Home Phone:** (614)351-0707. **Business Addr:** Police Officer, City of Columbus, Division of Police, 120 Marconi Blvd, Columbus, OH 43215, **Business Phone:** (614)645-4864.

RHETTA, HELEN L.
Physician. **Educ:** Univ Mich, AB; Univ MI Med Sch, MD; Univ MI Sch Pub Health US Dept HEW, MPH, 1976. **Career:** Provident Hosp, intern & resident, 1938-39; physician, 1939. **Orgs:** IL State, Chicago, Med Soc; Am Mgt Asn; Am Pub Health Soc; Delta Sigma Theta; Am Physicians Art Asn. **Honors/Awds:** USPH Fel 1966-67; Superior Serv Award, US Dept HEW, 1972; Nat Asn Col Women Award; Am Physicians Recognition Award; Zeta Phi Beta Woman of the Year.

RHINEHART, JUNE ACIE
Publishing executive. **Personal:** Born Jul 1, 1934, McKeesport, PA; daughter of William Elmer Acie (deceased) and Gladys Cornelia Allen Acie (deceased); married Vernon Morel, Apr 4, 1958 (divorced 1975). **Educ:** Wilson Jr Col, AB, 1962; Roosevelt Univ, Chicago, BA, 1968; Northwestern Univ; Loyola Univ Chicago, Grad Sch Bus, 1972; Loyola Univ Chicago SchLaw, JD, 1980. **Career:** Johnson Publ Co Inc, Chicago, IL, secy, 1955-60, admin asst, 1960-71, vpres, asst to publ, 1971-80, sr vpres & gen coun, 1980, vice chmn & gen coun, 2005. **Orgs:** Adv bd exec prog, Stanford Univ, 1976-78; Roosevelt Univ Alumni Bd; bd trustees, Chic St Univ Found; Alpha Kappa Alpha Sor; Chicago Network; Women's Div Oper PUSH; Chicago Focus. **Honors/Awds:** Achievement Award, Nat Coun Negro Women, 1973; 1000 Successful Blacks. **Business Addr:** Vice Chair, Johnson Publishing Company Inc., 820 S Mich Ave, Chicago, IL 60605, **Business Phone:** (312)322-9200.

RHINEHART, N PETE
Executive, chairperson, chief financial officer. **Career:** A T & T, vpres & chief financial officer, currently; USATF, chmn audit comt, currently. **Business Addr:** Chairman, USATF, 1 RCA Dome Suite 140, Indianapolis, IN 46225, **Business Phone:** (317)261-0500.

RHINES, JESSE ALGERON
Educator. **Personal:** Born Jul 30, 1948, Washington, DC; son of Jacinto and Julia Marie Watson Barbour. **Educ:** Antioch Col, BA, pol comm, 1974; NYU, film prod cert, 1983; Yale Univ, MA, afro-am studies, 1983; UCLA, MA, polit sci, 1986; Univ CA, Berkeley, PhD, ethnic studies, 1993. **Career:** YMCA World Ambassador Hong Kong, Japan, South Korea, 1975; Congressman R Dellums, leg intern, admin aide, 1975-76; Mayor, New Haven, leg affairs officer, 1978-89; U-Skate Rollerskates, founder, 1979-81; Opers Crossroads Africa Inc, Mali group leader, 1980; IBM Corp, systs eng, 1981-83; State NY Mortgage Agency, comput systs analyst, 1989-90; Cineaste Mag, asst ed, co-ed, Race Contemp Cinema Sect, 1992-; Eugene Lange Col, instr, 1993; Rutgers Univ, African Am & African Studies Dept, asst prof, 1993-. **Orgs:** Black Filmmaker Found; Independent Feature Project; Nat Asn Advan Colored Peope; Soc Cinema Studies; fel, Nat Coun Black Polit Scientists, 1976; fel, Am Polit Sci Asn, 1976. **Honors/Awds:** Ideals of the Center Award, Yale Afro-Am Cult Ctr, 1981; Outstanding Young Man of America, Jaycees, 1982; Distinguished Scholarship Award; Dona & Albert R Broccoli Found Scholarship, 1997. **Special Achievements:** Publications: Black Film, White Money: African American Entrepreneurship & Employment in the American Film Industry, dissertation, 1994; "Integrating the Hollywood Craft Uniions," Cineaste, 1994; "Stimulating a Dialogue Among African American Viewers: An Interview with Daresha Kyi," 1994; Black Film, White Money-(book), Rutgers Univ Press, 1996; numerous others. **Home Addr:** 219 W 16th St Suite 1A, New York, NY 10011-6028. **Business Addr:** Assistant Professor, Rutgers University, African American & African Studies Department, 249 University Ave, Newark, NJ 07102, **Business Phone:** (973)824-2457.

RHOADES, DR. SAMUEL THOMAS
School administrator. **Personal:** Born Aug 11, 1946, Raleigh, NC; children: Audria Michelle Humes. **Educ:** NC Cent Univ, BA, psychol, 1967, JD, 1973. **Career:** Durham Col, coun & cooperative ed, 1973-77; St Paul's Col, spec asst/fed progs, 1977-; Nat Asn Title III Admin, Va Union Univ, parliamentarian, 1978, pres, spec asst pres, currently. **Orgs:** Treas, Phi Alpha Delta Law Fraternity, 1975; Am Legion, Omega Psi Phi Fraternity, Beauty Dunn Lodge F&A Masons. **Honors/Awds:** Law J NC Cent Univ, 1972; Honor Graduate, NC Cent Univ, 1972; Omega Man of the Year, Omega Psi Phi Fraternity, 1977; Honorably Discharge Military Veteran. **Military Serv:** AUS, sgt, E-5, 2 yrs. **Business Addr:** Special Assistant to President, Virginia Union University, Title III Administration, 1500 N Lombardy St, PO Box 399, Richmond, VA 23220.

RHODEMAN, CLARE M.
Educator. **Personal:** Born Jul 21, 1932, Biloxi, MS; married Thomas Johan; children: Rennee Maria, Thomas Johan & Nichole Irene. **Educ:** Xavier Univ, New Orleans, BA, 1953; Xavier Univ, MA, 1957. **Career:** Elem, Jr High & Sr High teacher & Sr High coun; Nicholas Jr HS Biloxi Municipal Separate Sch Syst, Jr HS coun; MTA BEA, coordr, 1973-74. **Orgs:** MS Personel & Guide Asn; prof Standards Com; chmn guide Com 6th dist MS Teacher Asn; Nat Educ Asn; Cath 67, sec 67-71, vpres, 1971-72 Biloxi Interparochial Sch Bd; Our Mother Sorrows Cath Ch; Parish Coun; MS Gulf Coast Alumnae Chap, Delta Sigma Theta Sor; Biloxi Nat Asn Advan Colored People; bd dir, Harrison Co Devl Comn; Harrison Co Community Action Prog; Harrison Co United Found; Dem Party; vol worker, Mothers March Birth Defects, Heart Fnd & PTA. **Home Addr:** 392 Fayard St, Biloxi, MS 39530.

RHODEN, DWIGHT
Choreographer, artistic director. **Personal:** Born Jan 1, 1962?, Dayton, OH. **Career:** Dayton Contemporary Dance Co, dancer, 1976-82; Les Ballets Jazz de Montreal, dancer, 1982-86; Alvin Ailey Am Dance Theatre, dancer, 1987-94; Complexions, co-founder, artistic dir & choreographer, 1994-. **Honors/Awds:** New York Found Arts Award, 1998; Choo San Gho Award, 2001; Apex Award, Alvin Ailey School, 2006. **Special Achievements:** Hailed by the New York Times as "One of the most sought out choreographers of the day". **Business Addr:** Artistic Director, Complexions, 7 WTC 250 Greenwich St 41st Fl, New York, NY 10007, **Business Phone:** (212)777-7771.*

RHODEN, DR. RICHARD ALLAN
Scientist. **Personal:** Born May 8, 1930, Coatesville, PA; son of Dorothy Rhoden; married Stephanie Auroa Thompson; children: Richard Jr. **Educ:** Lincoln Univ, BA, 1951; Drexel Univ, MS, 1967, PhD, 1971. **Career:** Scientist (retired); Naval Air Develop Ctr, res chemist, 1972; Environ Protection Agency, environ scientist, 1972-75; Nat Inst Occupational Safety & Health, res pharmacologist, 1975-82; Nat Inst Health, health scientist adminr, 1982-89; Am Petrol Inst, health scientist, 1989-97. **Orgs:** Exec secy, subcomt toxicol, exec comt, Sci adv bd, US Environ Protection Agency, 1979; Environ Studies Inst Adv Comm, Drexel Univ, 1980-84; Alpha Omega Chap, Omega Psi Phi Frat Inc, 1992-97; Am Chem Soc; Soc Toxicol; Am Indust Hygiene Asn; Fel AAAS; Fel Am Inst Chemists. **Honors/Awds:** Omega Man of the Year, Alpha Omega Chap, 1996-97. **Home Addr:** 430 Oglethorpe St NW, Washington, DC 20011-2149.

RHODES, ARTHUR LEE, JR.
Baseball player. **Personal:** Born Oct 24, 1969, Waco, TX. **Career:** Baltimore Orioles, pitcher, 1991-99; Seattle Mariners, pitcher, 2000-03; Oakland Athletics, pitcher, 2004; Cleveland Indians, pitcher, 2005;Philadelphia Phillies, 2006; Seattle Mariners, pitcher, 2008; Florida Marlins, pitcher, 2008; Cincinnati Reds, pitcher, 2009-. *

RHODES, AUDREY B.
Executive, educator, physician. **Educ:** Bowling Green State Univ, MS, 1976; Med Col Ohio, Toledo, MD, 1980; FAAFP. **Career:** Univ SC, asst prof family & prev med, 1992-; HOPE for Kids, state proj dir, 1994; SC Acad Family Physicians, pres, 1996; SC Dept Ment Health, CM Tucker Jr Ctr, med sect chief, 1996; SC Dept Ment Health, staff physician& clin asst prof, currently; Palmetto Health & Univ SC Sch Med, residency family med, currently; Palmetto Health, clin fac, currently. **Orgs:** Am Acad Family Physicians; pres, South Carolina Chapter. **Special Achievements:** First African American and second female to be installed as president ofSouth Carolina Academy of Family Physicians. **Business Addr:** Clinical Faculty, Palmetto Health, 1330 Taylor St, Columbia, SC 29220, **Business Phone:** (803)296-5010.

RHODES, HON. C ADRIENNE
Consultant, journalist. **Personal:** Born Jul 16, 1961, Camden, NJ; daughter of Lawrence Wilmer and Adele Clark Polk. **Educ:** Pratt Inst, Sch Art & Design, 1980; State Univ New York FIT, AAS, 1984, BS, 1989; New York Univ, Sch Film, Video & Broadcasting, 1994. **Career:** New York Times Mag Group, circulation & promotion serv asst, 1980-82; Diane Von Furstenberg Inc, pub rels mgr, 1982-84; United Negro Col Fund, mgr media rels, 1984-86, asst dir commun, 1986-89, dir commun, 1989-93; Daily News LP, dir commun & media rels, 1993-98, vpres& dir commun, consult, currently; instr, Columbia Univ, 1994-; New York State Consumer Protection Bd, chairwoman & exec dir, currently. **Orgs:** Senator, Student Govt Asn, Pratt Inst, 1979-80; PRSA Young Professionals Comn, NY Chap, 1983-84; assoc mem, New York Asn Black Journalists, 1986; Pub Rels Soc Am, Nat Chap, 1987-89; mkt chmn, Nat Asn Black Journalists, 1989; co-founder, Black Pub Rels Soc Greater New York, 1990; US Comn Minority Bus Develop, Media & Perception Task Force, 1991; Nat Black Women's Polit Caucus, media & entertainment comn, 1993-; chair, 1989-99, adv bd, 1993-, New York Urban League; Publisher's Liasion, Harlem Y Steering Comt, 1994; chair, World Women Leaders Conf, 1999; chair, exec dir, New York Consumer Protection Bd, 2001. **Honors/Awds:** CEBA Award of Merit, World Inst Black Community, 1986; Outstanding Women in Public Relations, Black Pub Rels Soc-Los Angeles Chap, 1991; ANDY Award for Outstanding Tv Advertising, Advertising Club New York, 1991; Gold Medal, Int Film Festival, 1991; CEBA Award of Excellence, World Inst Commun, 1991; Certificate of Special Merit for an Outstanding Example of Graphic Arts, Asn Graphic Arts, 1992; Silver edal Award for Outstanding Advertising, Art Dirs Club, 1992; Advertising Women of New York, ADDY Award for Outstanding Television Advertising, 1992; Pratt Black Alumni Award, 1996; Governor's Martin Luther King Living the Dream Award, 1998. **Special Achievements:** First African American woman appointed as vice president in the news paper New York Daily News. **Business Addr:** Consultant, Daily News LP, 450 W 33rd St, New York, NY 10001, **Business Phone:** (212)210-2100.

RHODES, EDWARD THOMAS, SR.
Executive. **Personal:** Born Mar 20, 1933, Cumberland, MD; son of John Henry and Ella Harrison Burgee; married Ovetta Lyles Williams (divorced); children: Shari & Edward Jr. **Educ:** Kenyon Col, BA, 1955. **Career:** W-PAFB, contract negotiator, 1958-61; GSFC, sr procurement analyst, 1961-64; FWPCA, dept of the int, dir div gen serv, 1964-71; EPA, dir contract mgt div, 1971-75, dept asst adv, 1975-78; HEW dept asst sec grants & procurement mgt, 1975, dept asst sec grants & procurement, 1978-80, dep assoc dir, admin off of personnel mgt, 1980-86; Wash metro Area Transist Authority, dir, 1986-92; Sectek Inc, pres, 1992-. **Orgs:** Past mem, Nat Bd of Adv; Nat Contract Mgt Asn; past mem bd, Regents Inst Cost Analysis; past pres, Nat Asn of Black Procurement Prof; past dir, Procurement Roundtable. **Honors/Awds:** Meritorious Service Award, Distinguished Service Award, Dept Interior, 1967; Award for Achievement in Public Admin, Wm Jump Mem Found, 1969; Silver Medal Super Service, EPA, 1972; Meritorious Service Award, OPM. **Military Serv:** AUS, SPC-4, 1955-57. **Business Phone:** (703)435-0970.

RHODES, GERALD (JERRY RHODES)
Executive. **Personal:** Born in Linden, NJ. **Educ:** Stevens Inst Technol, Hoboken, NJ, BS, eng; Columbia Univ, NY, MS, bus admin. **Career:** Gen Foods Corp, White Plains, NY, mkt mgr; Citibank, NY, pvt banking group, vpres, Citiphone Sales Ctr, vpres, bus mgr, vpres mkt; Sprint, Kans, MO, vpres emerging markets & vpres of mkt; Aerial Comun, Chicago, vpres & chief mkt officer, 1996-99; Peco Energy Co, vpres, 1999-; Exelon Energy, pres, 1999-. **Business Phone:** (215)841-4000.

RHODES, JACOB A
Association executive. **Personal:** Born Nov 30, 1949, Brownsville, TN; son of Franklin A and Mary J; married; children: Jalena. **Career:** Butler St YMCA, pres & chief exec officer, 2000-; YMCA Greater Rochester, pres/chief exec officer, dir. **Special Achievements:** Author: Managing in a Changing Environment, 1982; "Management Styles of 30 CEOs," Jun 1990. **Business Phone:** (404)659-0915.

RHODES, JEANNE
Executive. **Personal:** Born in Monongahela, PA; widowed; children: Joseph Simmons Scott & Margaret Herndon. **Educ:** Duffs Bus Sch; Univ Pitts; Duquesne U. **Career:** Philadelphia Tribune, vpres pub rltns. **Orgs:** Bd mem, Am Red Cross; life mem, exec com, Grad Hosp Aux; bd mem, Inglis Hse Home Incurables; bd mem, Philadelphia Tribune Co; bd trustee, Ruth W Hayre Schlrshp Found; Sponsers Scholar Club; La Cabaneetas Eastern SeaBd Dinner Club; Finesse Bridge; DCR Birthday Club; bd mem, Philadelphia 76; bd trustee, Dowingtown Agr & Indust Sch; spec Dept Labor; pres, p sec, Pitts Br, NAACP; chmn bd, Lemington Home Aged; nat pres, Iota P Hi Lambda; mem bd, Civil Light Opera Pittsburgh; hon bd mem, Tribune Charities; Adv comn, Afro-am Mus; bd mem, YWCA Belmont Br; Philadelphia Bicentennial Comn; Cenntennial Com for Lucretia Mott, 1980; Bethesda United Presbyterian Ch; adhoc com Floyd Logan Archives Temple U; treas, S St W Bus Asn 1979; lay mem, Fee Disputes Com Philadelphia Bar Asn, 1979. **Honors/Awds:** Service Award, Philadelphia Tribune Charities, 1973; Bicentennial Achivement Award, AME Ch, 1976; Appreciaiton Award, Bicentennial Comn PA; recoganisation award, Police Athletic Leg, 1977; Service Award, ARC, 1978; Distinguished Service Award, Downingtown A&I Sch, 1979; 50th Anniversary Leadersihp Award, Iota Phi Lambda Sor, 1979.

RHODES, JOHN K
Government official, consultant. **Personal:** Born Mar 18, 1965, San Francisco, CA; son of Gus and Lillian. **Educ:** Univ Nev-Las Vegas, BS, 1987, post grad, 1989; Univ Nebr-Lincoln, 1983-84. **Career:** Univ Med Ctr, personnel, 1989; Clark County, agent, 1989-94; John K Rhodes Consult, pres, 1991-; N Lasvegas Coun, Councilman. **Orgs:** Life mem, Omega Psi Phi Frat, 1988-; founding mem, Committed 100 Men Helping Boys, 1991-; City Las Vegas, Task C, 1992; bd mem, Lied Discovery Mus, 1992-93; bd mem, DARE Inc, 1992-93; Bd Equalization, 1995-. **Honors/Awds:** Banquet Awardee, Nat Asn Advan Colored People, 1993; cong recognition, US Cong, 1992; Give Me The Ballot Award,

MLK, 1994; cert spec recognition, US Senate, 1994. **Business Addr:** President, John K Rhodes Consulting Inc, 3028 Diana Dr, North Las Vegas, NV 89030, **Business Phone:** (702)649-0860.

RHODES, KARL DERRICK
Baseball player. **Personal:** Born Aug 21, 1968, Cincinnati, OH. **Career:** Gulf Coast League, 1986; Fla State League, batting, 1988; Houston Astros, 1990-93; Chicago Cubs, 1994-95; Boston Red Sox, 1995; Kintetsu Buffaloes, 1996-2003; Yomiuri Giants, Japanese Cent League, 2004-05; Orix Buffaloes, 2007-.

RHODES, DR. PAULA R
Educator, lawyer. **Personal:** Born Jul 18, 1949, New Orleans, LA; daughter of Leroy and Marie Richard. **Educ:** Am Univ, BA, 1971; Harvard Univ, JD, 1974. **Career:** Legal Serv Corp, atty, demonstration proj mgr, 1977-79; Howard Univ Sch Law, assoc prof, 1979-90; Mid Atlantic Legal Educ, prof, 1980; Univ San Diego Law Sch, vis prof, 1983-84; Univ Bridgeport, vis prof, 1985; Univ Denver Col Law, Denver, CO, vis prof, 1989-90, prof & dir, LLM Am & Comp Law Prog, 1990-. **Orgs:** Dist Columbia Bar Asn; Am Bar Asn; Am Soc Int Law; former vice chair, Am Friends Serv Comt; African Am UN Comt; Transafrica; Finance Comt, Mountainview Friends Meetings; Soc Am Law Teachers; Sam Carey Bar Asn; Am Soc Int Law; Consortium Human Rights Develop; Supreme Court CO Gender Fairness Judicial Educ Ads Comt; bd, DC Chap Fed Bar Asn, 1980-87; Nat Coun, 1980-81; chmn, Sturm Col Admis & Fin Aid Comt; Co-chmn, Univ Denver Fac Color Asn. **Special Achievements:** Various Conf including Am Friends Serv Comt Consult on Korea Los Angeles, CA, 1983, "Meeting the Corporate Challenge" Washington DC 1984; Pub: "Expanding NGO Participation in Intl Decision Making", "Devel of New Business Opportunities for Minorities in the Synthetic Fuels Program"; "Energy Security Act and its Implications for Economic Devel," Howard Law Journal 1981, "We the People and the Struggle for a New World," WSA Constitution Human Rights 1987. **Business Addr:** Professor, University of Denver, Sturm College of Law, 2255 E Evans Ave, Denver, CO 80208, **Business Phone:** (303)871-6258.

RHODES, RAY
Football executive, football coach. **Personal:** Born Oct 20, 1950, Mexia, TX; married Carmen; children: Detra, Candra, Tynesha & Raven. **Educ:** Tex Christian Univ; Univ Tulsa. **Career:** Football player (retired), Football coach, football executive; NY Giants, wide receiver & defensive back, 1974-79; San Francisco 49ers, defensive back, 1980, asst sec coach, 1981-82, defensive backfield coach, 1983-91, defensive coordr, 1994; Green Bay Packers, defensive coordr, 1992-93, headcoach, 1999; Philadelphia Eagles, head coach, 1995-98; Wash Redskins, defensive coordr, 2000; Denver Broncos, defensive coordr, 200-02; Seattle Seahawks, defensive coordr, 2003, spec projs, defense, 2005; Houston Texans, asst defensive backs coach, 2008-. **Honors/Awds:** Super Bowl XXIX, 1995; NFL Coach of the Year Award, 1996. **Special Achievements:** One of only a few African Am NFL coaches, third in NFL history. **Business Addr:** Assistant Defensive Backs Coach, Houston Texans, 2 Reliant Pk, Houston, TX 77054, **Business Phone:** (832)667-2000.

RHODES, DR. ROBERT SHAW
Physician. **Personal:** Born Mar 3, 1936, Orangeburg, SC; son of John D and Emma W; married Gwendolyn M; children: Robin, Robert Jr, Nekole Smith & Candace Smith. **Educ:** Meharry Med Col, MD, 1962; Hubbard Hosp, Internship, 1962-63; Meharry Med Col, Resident, 1963-67; Vanderbilt Univ Sch Med, fel, 1967-70; Univ Mich Sch Pub Health, MPH, 1981-83. **Career:** Meharry Med Col, head div hemat, 1972-78; Multiphasic Screening Lab, dir, 1973-78; Hubbard Hosp, med dir, 1975-78; Hydra-matic Div GMC, assoc med dir, 1978-80, med dir, 1980-82; Health Serv & Safety, div dir, 1982-87; Gen Motors Corp, Detroit W Med Region, regional med dir; pvt pract, currently. **Orgs:** Chairperson, Sickle Cell Adv Comn, 1977-81; Mich Occup Med Asn; chmn, Med Audit Comn Beyer Hosp, 1980-83; ed comm Nat Sickle Cell Found, vpres, 1983-84; pres, elect; exec bd, Wolverine Coun BSA, house deleg, 1988-90, bd dirs, 1990; Am Col Occup Med; pres, ACOEM, 1997-98. **Military Serv:** USMC, maj, 1967-70; AUS, Army Commendation Medal, 1970; AFIP, Cert Meritorious Achievement, 1970. **Business Addr:** Physician, 7393 Whittingham Way, West Bloomfield, MI 48322, **Business Phone:** (248)788-1290.

RHODES, RODRICK
Basketball coach, basketball player. **Personal:** Born Sep 24, 1973, Jersey City, NJ; children: Ro. **Educ:** Univ Ky; Univ Southern Calif. **Career:** Basketball player (retired), basketball coach; Houston Rockets, guard-forward, 1997-98; Vancouver Grizzlies, guard, 1998-99; DallasMaverick, 1999-2000; prof leagues, player, Cyprus, Greece, Philippines, France & Puerto Rico; St Edward's Univ, asst coach; Idaho St Univ, asst coach, 2006-07; Univ Mass, asst to coach & dir player personnel; Selton Hall Univ, Administrative Asst coach, Currently. **Honors/Awds:** USA Today Nat Championship, 1988. **Business Phone:** (973)761-9000.

RHONE, SYLVIA M
Executive. **Personal:** Born Mar 11, 1952, Philadelphia, PA; daughter of Marie Christmas and James; married. **Educ:** Univ Pa, Wharton Sch Bus & Com, MA, 1974. **Career:** Bankers Trust, 1974; Buddah Recs, admin asst, promotions coordr; Atlantic Recs, Nat Black Music Promotion, dir, 1985, Black Music Opers, vpres/gen mgr, sr vpres, 1988; EastWest Rec Am, chairperson, chief exec officer, 1991; Atco-EastWest label, chief exec officer, 1991-94, chairperson; Elektra/EW Co, chair, 1994; Elektra Entertainment Group, chief exec officer; Universal Rec, exec vpres, 2004-; Motown Rec, pres, 2004-. **Special Achievements:** First African American woman to head a major record company when she was named Chief Executive Officer & President of Atlantic's new East West Records America division. **Business Addr:** President, Motown Records, 1755 Broadway 6th Fl, New York, NY 10019, **Business Phone:** (212)373-0750.

RHYMES, BUSTA (TREVOR SMITH, JR.)
Actor, rap musician. **Personal:** Born May 20, 1972, Brooklyn, NY; son of Trevor Smith Sr and Geraldine; children: Tahiem II (deceased). **Career:** The Leaders of The New Sch, mem; Group Albums: Future Without A Past, 1991; T.I.M.E The Inner Mind's Eye: The Endless Dispute With Reality, 1993; Solo Albums: The Coming, 1996; When Disaster Strikes, 1997; Extinction Level Event (The Final World Front), 1998; Anarchy, 2000; Genesis, 2001; It Ain't Safe No More, 2002; The Big Bang, 2006; TV series appearances: Cosby, 1997; TV movies: The Oz, 2002; Film appearances: Higher Learning, 1994; Extinction Level Event (The Final World), 1998; Shaft, 2000; Finding Forrester, 2000; Halloween: Resurrection, 2002; The Punisher, 2003; Waiting, 2003; The Neptunes Present: Dude We're Going to Rio!, 2003; Death of a Dynasty, 2003; Full Clip, 2004; Strong Arm Steady, 2004; Busta Rhymes: Everything Remains Raw, 2004; Def Jam Fight for NY, 2004, The Game: Documentary, 2005. **Special Achievements:** Rapped on "Scenario" with Tribe Called Quest, 1991; "Chim Chim Badass Revenge," with Fishbone, 1996; "Hit 'Em High," with Method Man, Coolio, LL Cool J, and B-Real, 1996; "Rumble In The Jumble," with Tribe Called Quest & the Refugee All-Stars, 1997; nominee, Best Live Performer, BET Hip Hop Awards. **Business Addr:** Rapper, J Records, 745 Fifth Ave Fl 6, New York, NY 10151, **Business Phone:** (646)840-5600.

RIBBINS, GERTRUDE. See Obituaries section.

RIBBS, WILLIAM THEODORE, JR. (WILLY T RIBBS)
Race car driver. **Personal:** Born Jan 3, 1956, San Jose, CA; son of William T Sr and Geraldine Henderson; married Suzanne, Nov 22, 1979; children: Sasha Wanjiku. **Educ:** San Jose City Col, San Jose, CA, 1975. **Career:** Car racing (retired); formula ford circuit, driver 1977; formula atlantic events; sports 2000 events; neil deatley trans-Am team, driver 1984; ford motors sports, 1984-85; digard & brooks racing, 1986; racing driver dan gurneys all Am racers, Santa Ana, CA, 1987. **Orgs:** Nat Sporting Clays Asn. **Honors/Awds:** Dunlop Star Tomorrow Champion Europe, 1977; International Driver of the Year Europe, 1977; British Sports Writers Award, 1977; Trans-Am Rookie of the Year, 1983; winner of Trans-Am series opener in Phoenix (10 victory in 25 Trans-Am starts), 1985; Norelco Driver Cupt Award winner; Proclamation Willy T Ribbs Day City of Miami, 1984, City of Atlanta, 1984; City of St Petersburg, 1987; Interamerican Western Hemisphere Driving Champion, 1984; All American Drivers Award, Motorsports Press Assoc, 1984-85; Norelco GTO Driver of the Year, Phillips Business systems, l988; Norelco GTO Driver of the Year; SCCA; Trans American All Time Money Earner, l988; first bl to compete in Indianapolis 500, 1991. **Special Achievements:** First African American to qualify and compete in the Indianapolis 500; First African American to compete in NASCAR's Winston Cup series; First African American to compete in CART/Indy Car Championship in partnership withentertainer, Bill Cosby; First and only African American to test for Formula 1 Grand Prix team in Estroil, Portugal. *

RIBBS, WILLY T. See RIBBS, WILLIAM THEODORE, JR.

RIBEAU, DR. SIDNEY
College president. **Personal:** Married Paula Whetsel; children: 3. **Educ:** Wayne State Univ, BS; Univ Ill, MS, PhD, interpersonal commun. **Career:** Calif State Univ, prof commun studies, 1976-87, dean undergrad studies; Calif State Polytech Univ, Pomona, vpres acad affairs, 1992-95; Bowling Green State Univ, pres, 1995-. **Orgs:** Trustee, Teachers Ins & Annuity Asn; presidents coun, Nat Col Athletic Asn; chair, Inter Univ, Coun Presidents.; Toledo Urban League; Toledo Symphony; The Andersons Inc; Convergys Corp; Worthington Indust. **Honors/Awds:** Distinguished Alumnus Award, Wayne State Univ; Distinguished Alumnus Award, Univ Ill; Scholarly recognition, Natl Commun Asn; Presidents Award, Nat Asn Stud Personnel Adminr. **Business Addr:** President, Bowling Green State University, Presidents Office, 220 Mcfall Ctr, Bowling Green, OH 43403, **Business Phone:** (419)372-2211.

RIBEIRO, ALFONSO
Actor, television director. **Personal:** Born Sep 21, 1971, New York, NY; son of Michael and Joy Ribeiro; married Robin Stapler, Jan 20, 2002 (divorced); children: Sienna. **Educ:** Univ Calif & Valley Prof Sch Los Angeles. **Career:** Films: Seek & Hide, 2004; Love wrecked, 2005; TV series: "Oye Willie", 1980; "Silver Spoons", 1984-87; "Magnum, P.I.", 1986; Mighty Pawns, 1987; Christmas, 1988; "CBS School break Special", 1988; Out on the Edge, 1989;"A Different World", 1990; "The Fresh Prince of Bel-Air", 1990-96; "Bill Nye, the Science Guy", 1994; Kidz in the Wood, 1996; "In the House", 1995-99; "Spider-Man", 1996-97; "Extreme Ghostbusters", 1997; "One on One", 2002; "The Brothers Garcia", 2002; "The Rerun Show", 2002; "Cedricthe Entertainer Presents", 2003; "All of Us", dir, 2004-07; "One on One", dir, 2005-06; "Cuts", dir, 2006; "Eve", dir, 2006; "Meet the Browns", dir, 2009; Game Show Network, "Catch 21", host, 2008-. **Orgs:** Say No to Drugs: Hands Across Am. **Honors/Awds:** Hollywood Press Club's Rising Star Award, 1985; Image Award, Nat Asn Advan Colored People, 1996 & 1998. **Special Achievements:** Two-time winner of the Toyota Pro/Celebrity Race in 1994 & 1995. **Business Addr:** Actor, c/o United Paramount Network, 11800 Wilshire Blvd, Los Angeles, CA 90025, **Business Phone:** (310)575-7000.*

RICANEK, CAROLYN WRIGHT
Government official. **Personal:** Born Mar 10, 1939, Washington, DC; married Karl; children: Lloyd O Taylor, Carooq M Taylor, Carmen T Harris, Demetrius A & Karl II. **Educ:** Federal City Col, attended 1976; George Mason Univ, 1979. **Career:** K&R Plumbing Heating Co, vpres, 1969-87; ANC Comnr, 7C, First elected, 1976-85, chair person, 1986-87; Phelp Career Ctr, chmn, 1982-87; Marshall Heights Community Develop Corp, asst treas, 1983-85, financial secy, 1983-87; Adv Neighborhood Comn, vchmn. **Orgs:** Chmn, HD Woodson Athletic Booster Club, 1976-79; Deanwood Civic Asn, 1970-85; Metropolitan Women Dem Club, 1980-85; asst coordr, Garden Resource Orgn, 1983-85; Majestic Eagles Minority Entrepreneur Inc. **Honors/Awds:** Cert of appreciation, Houston Elem Sch, 1979; Outstanding Citizen, Coun Willie Hardy, 1979-80; cert of award, HD Woodson Sr High/Community Servs, 1982; cert of appreciation, Phelps Car Dev Cent, 1983-84; First Elected Comm Mayor Marion Barry, 1985. **Home Addr:** 1220 47th Place NE, Washington, DC 20019. **Business Addr:** Vice Chairman, Advisory Neighborhood Commission, 4651 NHB Place NE, Washington, DC 20019.

RICARD, REV. JOHN H
Bishop. **Personal:** Born Feb 29, 1940, Baton Rouge, LA; son of Maceo and Albanie St Amant. **Educ:** Tulane Univ, New Orlenas, LA, MA 1970; The Catholic Univ, Wash, DC, PhD, 1983; Josephite Col Sem, Newburgh, NY; St. Joseph's Sem, Wash, DC. **Career:** Archdiocese Baltimore, auxiliary bishop, 1984-96; Diocese Pensacola-Tallahassee, bishop, 1997-. **Orgs:** Chmn, Domestic Policy Comt, USA Conf Cath Bishop. **Business Addr:** Bishop, Diocese of Pensacola-Tallahassee, 11 N B St, Pensacola, FL 32501, **Business Phone:** (850)435-3500.

RICARDO, JAIME. See NIX, RICK.

RICE, REV. ALLEN TROY
Football player, clergy. **Personal:** Born Apr 5, 1962, Houston, TX. **Educ:** Wharton Co Jr Col; Ranger Jr Col; Baylor Univ. **Career:** Football player (retired), clergy; Minn Vikings, running back, 1984-90, spiritual leader; Green Bay Packers, running back, 1991; Joy Temple Apostolic Church, fel; Together We Stand Christian Church, founder, 1996-, sr pastor, currently. **Honors/Awds:** Played in NFC Championship Game, 1987. **Business Phone:** (281)403-0373.

RICE, DR. CONDOLEEZZA
Government official. **Personal:** Born Nov 14, 1954, Birmingham, AL; daughter of John Wesley (deceased) and Angelena Ray (Deceased). **Educ:** Univ Denver, BA, 1974, Grad Sch Int Studies, PhD, polit sci, 1981; Univ Notre Dame, MA, polit sci, 1975. **Career:** US Dept State, intern, 1977; Rand Corp, intern, 1980; polit sci consult, 1980; Stanford Univ, asst prof polit sci, 1981-87, assoc prof, 1987-93; prof, provost, 1993-; asst dir arms control prog, 1981-89; Nat Security Coun, dir, sr dir Soviet & E European Affairs, 1989-91; George W Bush presidential campaign, nat security consult, 2000; Nat Security Coun, natl security adv, 2001-05; US Secy State, 2005-09; univ Stanford, prof, polit sci, currently. **Orgs:** Trans Am Corp; bd mem, Hewlett Packard; Carnegie Corp; Carnegie Endowment Int Peace; Nat Coun Soviet & E European Studies; Mid-Peninsula Urban Coalition; bd dirs, Chevron Corp; Charles Schwab Corp; William & Flora Hewlett Found; Univ Notre Dame; Int Adv Coun, JP Morgan; San Francisco Symphony Bd Gov; founding bd mem, Ctr New Generation; vpres, Boys & Girls Club Peninsula; fel Am Acad Arts & Sci. **Honors/Awds:** Walter J. Gores Award, 1984; Honorary doctorates: Morehouse Col, 1991;Univ Ala, 1994; Univ Notre Dame, 1995; Nat Defense Univ, 2002; Miss Col Sch Law, 2003; Univ Louisville, 2004; Mich State Univ, 2004; School of Humanities and Sciences Dean's Award, 1993; Award for Excellence in Teaching, Stanford Univ; President's Award, Nat Am Advan Colored People Image Awards, 2002. **Special Achievements:** First African-American Secretary of State; First African-American chief acad & budget officer & second-ranking off behind the pres, Stanford Univ,1993-99; auth: The Gorbachev Era; co-auth: Germany Unified & Europe Transformed; ranked as the most powerful woman in the world by Forbes magazine in 2005 &

number two in 2006; ranked among the world's 100 most influential people by Time magazine in 2006. **Business Addr:** Political Science Professor, Stanford University, Stanford, CA 94305.

RICE, DR. CONSTANCE WILLIAMS
Social worker, school administrator, business owner. **Personal:** Born Jun 23, 1945, Brooklyn, NY; daughter of Beulah Marshall Williams and Elliott Williams; married Norman Blann, Feb 15, 1975; children: Mian A. **Educ:** Queens Col, BA 1966; Univ Wash, MA, pub admin, 1970, PhD, higher educ admin, 1974; Carnegie Mellon Univ, Sr Exec Mgt, 1983. **Career:** State Bd, prog asst; Shoreline Community Col, chairperson; Corp Comn METRO, mgr; US West, Seattle, WA, adv bd, 1981-; Pub Rels/Mgt Firm, pres, 1984-89; Sec Pac Bank, Seattle, WA, bd dir, 1985-; Community Col Dist VI,vice chancellor; N Seattle Community Col, pres; Seattle Community Col, srv pres, currently; CWR Inc, pres, currently; NW News Coun, founder; Shoreline Community Col, Ethnic Studies Dept, chair; dir, Ctr Urban Studies, Western Wash Univ. **Orgs:** Vpres, Seattle King Co United Way, 1983-84; pres-elect, Seattle Chap 101 Black Women, 1984-85; trustee, Seattle Found, 1984-92; bd mem, Am Soc Pub Admin, 1984; pres, Seattle Chap, Links Inc, 1985-86; asst exec dir, Wash Educ Asn, 1987-88; bd gov, Shoreline Community Col Found; past bd mem, Fred Hutchinson Cancer Res Found; vice chair, King Co Open Space Commn, 1989; bd mem, King Co Chamber Com, 1989-96; rotary, Evergreen State Col; bd dirs, Seafirst, 1992-96; bd dirs, Bonneville Broadcast GRP, 1993-96; founder & dir, Seattle Desmond Tutu Peace Found USA, 2000-; managing dir, Prev & Family Support Casey Family Found, Seattle, 2002; Nat Sci Found Traineeship; exec dir, Desmond Tutu Peace Found. **Honors/Awds:** Professional Director Award; Kellogg Grant; NW Outstanding Young Woman, 1983-86; Women Entrepreneur of The Year runner-up, 1985; White House Small Bus deleg, 1986; Top 25 Influential Women, (Seattle), The Seattle Weekly, 1986; Dorothy Bullitt Award, Women's Funding Alliance, 1991; Woman of Distinction Award, Nat Coun Jewish Women's; Torch of Liberty & Distinguished Community Service Award, B'Nai B'rith; Special Individual Award, Njeri Temple; Seattle First Citizen Award, 1993, honorary doctorate, Seattle Univ, 2002. **Special Achievements:** First African American woman to receive a doctorate in higher educ admin from the Univ Wash, Sch Educ; one of the 25 most powerful women in Seattle; Seattle's First Citizen of 1993. **Business Addr:** Senior Vice Chancellor, Seattle Community College, 1500 Harvard Ave, Seattle, WA 98122, **Business Phone:** (206)587-4100.

RICE, EDWARD A.
Computer executive, artist. **Personal:** Born Apr 8, 1929, Richmond, VA; married Josie Wigfall; children: Patricia, Edward & Audrey. **Educ:** VA Union Univ, BS, 1949; Columbia Univ, MA, 1952; Univ Conn, MBA, 1963. **Career:** Air Force Units, admin, 1951-56; Aerospace Med Div, Wright-Patterson AFB, res sci, 1956-61; USAF Nuclear Engineering Ctr, Wright-Patterson AFB, asst dir, 1966-71; Central State Univ, Wilberforce OH, asst prof, chmn bus admin, 1967-89; Edward Rice Trust, Dayton, OH, CEO, 1989-; CAPCOM, pres, 1989-96; Guilin Gallery, dir, 1996-. **Orgs:** Alpha Phi Alpha 1948-; Res Fac & Sch Aerospace Med, San Antonio, 1962-66; Yellow Springs Bd Educ, 1972-; Pres, Green County Joint Voc Sch Bd, 1973-74; Ohio Bus Teachers Asn; Miami Valley Consortium; Midwest Bus Admin Asn; Am Nuclear Soc; Am Asn Univ Profs. **Honors/Awds:** USAFR Medal; Nat Defense Service Medal; Korean Service Medal; UN Service Medal; Air Force Commendation Medal. **Military Serv:** USAF, maj retired, 1951-71.

RICE, EMMETT J.
Government official. **Personal:** Born in Florence, SC. **Educ:** CCNY, BBA 1941, MBA, 1942; Univ Calif, Berkeley, PhD, 1955. **Career:** Univ Calif, Berkeley, res asst econs, 1950-51, teaching asst, 1953-54; Cornell Univ, asst prof econ, 1954-60; Fed Reserve Bank, economist, 1960-62; Central Bank Nigeria Lagos, advr, 1962-64; Off Develop Nations Dept Treasury, dep dir, actg dir, 1964-66; World Bank, exec dir, 1966-70; Mayor's Econ Develop Comn Wash, 1970-71; Nat Bank Wash, sr vpres, 1972-79; Fed Reserve Bank Wash, govr, 1979.

RICE, FLORENCE
Consumer advocate. **Personal:** Born Mar 22, 1919, Buffalo, NY; daughter of Hubert and Amy; children: Joyce Garrett. **Career:** ILGW, 1948-62; Consumers Edu Coun, founder & dir, 1963-; League Autonomous Bronx Orgs for Renewal, consumer educ consult, 1966; Malcolm King Col, instr consumer educ; 30 Minutes with Florence M Rice, Channel 34, host, currently. **Orgs:** Founder & nat pres, Nat Black Consumers, 1973-; trustee, Harlem Community Law Office; bd dir, Community Nutrition Inst; adv comn, New York State Pub Utility Law Project; New York Senate Consumer Adv Community; adv comm, New York Urban League, Manhattan Chap; secy, New York City Black Republicans; nat standards comn, Am Bankers Asn; vpres, New York City Independent Black Women's Political Caucus; New York City Mayor's Adv Coun Consumer Affairs; pres, Harlem Consumer Educ Coun, currently. **Honors/Awds:** Sojourner Truth Award; Ophelia DeVore Award for Community Service; Consolidated Edison Better Business Award; Frederick Douglas Award, Urban League; Josephine Shaw Lowell Award; Woman of the Year, New York Republican Club, 1997. **Special Achievements:** US Delegation to World Congress of Int Women's Year, Berlin, official mem; UN Cong Non-Govt Orgs, rep; initiated Son-in-Law Day. **Business Addr:** Founder, President, Harlem Consumer Education Council Inc, Triboro Sta 550 W 155th St, PO Box 1165, New York, NY 10032, **Business Phone:** (212)283-7011.

RICE, FRED, JR.
Law enforcement officer. **Personal:** Born Dec 24, 1926, Chicago, IL; married Thelma Martin; children: Lyle & Judith. **Educ:** Roosevelt Univ, BS, 1970, MS, pub admin, 1977. **Career:** Law enforcement officer (retired); Chicago Police Dept, mem, 1955, sgt, 1961, lt, 1968, capt, 1973, dist comdr, 1970-78, Area Four, dep chief patrol, 1978-79, chief patrol div, 1979-83, supt police, 1983-87. **Orgs:** Stud Nonviolent Coord Comn; Police Oversight Bd. **Honors/Awds:** Numerous awards for contributions to community. **Special Achievements:** Chicago's first black Police Superintendent. **Military Serv:** AUS, 1950-52.

RICE, FREDRICK LEROY
Lawyer. **Personal:** Born Feb 26, 1950, Indianapolis, IN; son of Willie B and Marion I; married Ellen M, Aug 10, 1974; children: John F & Edward C. **Educ:** Beloit Col, BA, 1972; Ind Univ Sch Law, JD, 1977. **Career:** Landman & Beatty, assoc atty, 1977-82; UAW Legal Serv Plan, staff atty, 1982-83; Indianapolis Pub Sch, gen coun, 1983-90; State Ind, gen coun, 1990; Indianapolis Pub Sch, gen coun, 1990-96; Ind Supreme Ct, Disciplinary Comn, staff atty, 1996-. **Orgs:** Bd, ITC; pres, Waycross; bd mem, Ment Health Asn Marion County; bd governors, Indianapolis Bar Asn; atty, bd mem, Nat Sch Bds Asn Coun Sch; Ind State Bar Asn; Marion County Bar Asn. **Business Addr:** Staff Attorney, Indianapolis Supreme Ct Disciplinary Comn, 115 W Washington St Suite 1165 S Tower, Indianapolis, IN 46204, **Business Phone:** (317)232-1807.

RICE, GLEN A.
Basketball player. **Personal:** Born May 28, 1967, Jacksonville, AR; married Cristina Fernandez, Jan 1, 1997; children: Glen Anthony Jr, G mitri, Brianna & Giancarlo. **Educ:** Univ Mich, Ann Arbor, attended 1989. **Career:** Basketball Player (retired); Miami Heat, guard, 1989-95; Charlotte Hornets, 1995-98; Los Angeles Lakers, 1998-2000; NY Knicks, 2000-01; Houston Rockets, 2001-03; Los Angeles Clippers, 2003-04. **Honors/Awds:** Nat Collegiate Athletic Asn Champions, Michigan Wolverines, 1989; MVP, All-Star Game, 1997; Mr Basketball, 1985; 3 Point Champion, 1995; NBA Second Team, 1997. **Special Achievements:** NBA Draft, First round pick, #4, 1989.

RICE, HORACE WARREN
Manager, lawyer, college teacher. **Personal:** Born Feb 14, 1944, Huntsville, AL; son of John W and Lucy E Rice; divorced; children: Tasha M. **Educ:** Chicago City Col, AA, 1964; Ala A&M Univ, BS, 1966; Univ Toledo, JD, 1972. **Career:** Chicago Legal Asst C Found, atty, 1972-75; Univ Ala-Huntsville, prof, 1976-82; Ala A&M Univ, prof, 1976-; self-employed, player rep, sports agent, 1977-84; self-employed, arbitrator & mediator, 1977-; Ala A&M Univ, prof Bus Law & Ethics, currently. **Orgs:** Am Arbit Asn; Acad Legal Studies Bus; Am Mgt Asn; Soc Profs Dispute Resolution. Nat Football League. Ohio State Impasse Plan. **Honors/Awds:** Appointed to Arbitration Panel, Ohio State Impass Panel, 1985; Am Arbitration Ass, Nat Panel, 1980; Fed Mediation & Conciliation Serv, Nat Panel, 1982; United States Postal Serv, Nat Panel, 1983; Citizens Ambassador Prog, US State Dept, educr, Europe, Russia, Africa, 1988-89. **Special Achievements:** Zoning: A Substantive Analysis, AAMU Fac Res Jour, 1978; "LaborArbitration: A Viable Method of Dispute Resolution," Am Bus Law Assn Jour,1983; "Class Actions Under the 1964 Civil Rights Act," AAMU Fac Res Jour,1989; "What Consumers Should Know About Installment Buying," BusNewsletter, 1980; published 23 arbitration cases in Bureau of NatlAffairs, Commerce Clearinghouse, Labor Relations Reporter, LaborArbitration In Govt. listed in Who's Who International, 1998. **Home Addr:** 3100 Dyas Dr NW, Huntsville, AL 35810, **Home Phone:** (205)852-8406. **Business Addr:** Professor, Alabama A&M University, Depart of Business Administration, Rm 315 C 4900 Meridian St, Normal, AL 35762, **Business Phone:** (256)372-4816.

RICE, J DONALD, JR.
President (Organization), chief executive officer. **Educ:** Kettering Univ, BS, eng; Harvard Business Sch, MBA. **Career:** Merrill Lynch & Co, founding mem; Rice Financial Products Co, pres, chmn & chief exec officer, currently; Apex Pryor Securities, chmn & chief exec officer, currently. **Honors/Awds:** Entrepreneur of the Year, Nat Asn Securities Profs, 2002; One of the 75 Leading African-American professionals working on Wall Street, Black Enterprise Mag, 2006. **Business Addr:** Chairman, Chief Execuitve Officer, Rice Financial Products Co, 17 State St 40th Fl, New York, NY 10004, **Business Phone:** (212)908-9200.*

RICE, JERRY LEE
Football player. **Personal:** Born Oct 13, 1962, Crawford, MS; son of Brick Mason; married Jackie; children: Jaqui Bonet, Jerry Jr & Jada Symone. **Educ:** Miss Valley State Univ, 1981-85. **Career:** Football player (retired); San Francisco 49ers, wide receiver, 1985-2000, 2006; Oakland Raiders, 2001-04; Seattle Seahawks, 2004; Denver Broncos, 2005. **Orgs:** Phi Beta Sigma Fraternity Inc. **Honors/Awds:** NFC Rookie of the Year, UPI, 1985; NFC Offensive Rookie of the Year, Nat Football League Players Asn, 1985; NFL Player of the Year, Sports Illustrated, 1986, 1987, 1990, 1993; Most Valuable Player, 1996; NFL Player of the Year, Sporting News, 1987, 1990; Most Valuable Player, Super Bowl XXIII, 1989; Len Eshmont Award, 1993; NFL Offensive Player of the Year, 1993; Col Football Hall of Fame, 2006. **Special Achievements:** First non-kicker in NFL history to score 1000 points in his career. Career touch downs record holder; most 100-yard games for a receiver; co-hosts the radio talkshow "The Afternoon Blitz"; co-host on NBC 11's Sports Sunday; co-authored two books about his life: Rice and Go Long: My Journey Beyond the Game and the Fame.

RICE, JIM (JAMES EDWARD RICE)
Baseball player, athletic coach. **Personal:** Born Mar 8, 1953, Anderson, SC; married Corine Gilliard; children: Chauncy Brandon & Carissa Jacinda. **Career:** Baseball player (retired), Athletic coach, commentator; Boston Red Sox, outfielder, 1974-89, Roving, batting coach, 1992-94, instructional batting coach, 2001-, analyst; Hitting Instr, 1995-2000; New England Sports Network, commentator, 2003-; So Bank & Trust Co, Greenville, SC, public rels rep. **Orgs:** Hon chmn, Jimmy Fund, Fund raising Arm Dana-Farber Cancer Inst, Boston, 1979; Red Sox Orgn. **Honors/Awds:** All-Star Team, Am League, 1977, 1978, 1979, 1983, 1984, 1985, 1986;co-winner Tucson Pro-Am Gold Tournament, 1977; AL Player of the Year, Sporting News 1978; Joe Cronin Award, 1978; T A Yawkey Award, Sox MVP, Boston Writers, 1983; UPI & AL All-Star Team 1984; Boston Red Sox Hall of Famer, 1995; inductee, Baseball Hall of Fame, 2009. **Special Achievements:** Fortieth mem of Ted Williams Mus & Hitters Hall of Fame. **Business Addr:** Instructional Batting Coach, Boston Red Sox organization, Boston Red Sox Community Relations, 4 Yawkey Way, Boston, MA 02215, **Business Phone:** (617)585-0300.

RICE, JUDITH CAROL
Government official. **Personal:** Born Jul 30, 1957, Chicago, IL; daughter of Fred and Thelma. **Educ:** Northern Ill Univ, 1976; Loyola Univ, BA, 1981; John Marshall Law Sch, JD, 1988. **Career:** Cook County, staff asst, 1982-88, asst state's atty, 1988-89; City Chicago, dir ade adjudication, 1990-92, parking adr, 1992-93, revenue dir, 1993-95, exec asst Mayor, 1995-96, comnr Chicago Dept Water, 1996-1999, head Chicago Dept Transp, 1999-2000, city treas, 2000-. **Orgs:** assoc bd mem, Chicago Bar Asn; March Dimes; bd mem, STEP Sch, Sch Treatment C Emotional Prob, 1996-. **Special Achievements:** First woman commissioner of two of the biggest infrastructure agencies in City of Chicago government. **Business Addr:** Treasurer, City Chicago, 121 N LaSalle St Rm 206, Chicago, IL 60602, **Business Phone:** (312)744-3356.*

RICE, LEWIS, JR.
Police officer. **Personal:** Married Karen; children: 4. **Educ:** St John's Univ, BS, criminal justice. **Career:** Drug Enforcement Admin, 1974-84, Miami, Fla, supervisory spec agt, 1984-97, Detroit, Mich, spec agt-in-charge, New York, NY, head, currently. **Orgs:** Nat Asn Black Law Enforcement; Drug Enforcement Admin, Career Bd; NY Law Enforcement Exploring Prog; chair, Boy Scouts Am; chmn emer, Law Enforcement Explorer's; Fed Law Enforcement Found, vpres global security, currently. **Honors/Awds:** Achievement Award, Nat Asn Black Law Enforcement, 1997; Senior Executive Service Award, Drug Enforcement Admin, 1997; Alumni of the Year Award, St John's Univ, 1997; Nat Demand Reduction Award, 1998; honoree, New York's Finest Found, Ann Chiefs' Night Gala, 1999. **Special Achievements:** One of two African Americans heading DEA field offices. **Business Addr:** Head, Drug Enforcement Administration, 99 10th Ave, New York, NY 10011, **Business Phone:** (212)337-3900.

RICE, LINDA JOHNSON
Publishing executive. **Personal:** Born Mar 22, 1958, Chicago, IL; daughter of John H Johnson and Eunice W Johnson; married S Andre, Jan 1, 1984 (divorced 1994); children: Alexa Christina; married Mel Farr Sr, 2004. **Educ:** Univ Southern Calif, Los Angeles, BA, journalism, 1980; Northwestern Univ, J L Kellogg Grad Sch, Evanston, MBA, 1987. **Career:** Johnson Publ Co Inc, Ebony Mag, fashion ed, 1980-85, vpres, 1985-87, pres & chief exec officer, 2002-, chmn, 2006-. **Orgs:** Nat Asn Black Journalists; bd dirs, Kimberly-Clarke, Omnicom; bd dir, Viad Corp; bd dir Magazine Publishers Am; bd dirs, Bausch & Lomb; bd trustees, Univ Southern Calif; adv bd, Nat Underground Railroad Freedom Ctr; adv bd, Women's Bd Art Inst Chicago; Nat Asn Advan Colored People; Econ Club Chicago; Commercial Club Chicago; Exec Club Chicago; Nat Mus African Am Hist & Cult. **Honors/Awds:** Women Power Award, Nat Urban League; Tower Power Award, Trumpet Awards; Crain's Chicago Bus 40 Under 40 Award; From Whence We Came Award, All State Insurance Co, 1999; Alumni Year Award, Kellogg Grad Sch; Phenomenal Woman Award, 2000. **Special Achievements:** Named one of Chicago's 100 Most Powerful Women & one of the Top 10 Women in Media by the

Chicago Sun-Times; first African American woman to be named CEO of a company listed among the top five of the Black Enterprise. **Business Addr:** Chairman, Chief Executive Officer, Johnson Publishing Company Inc, 820 S Mich Ave, Chicago, IL 60605, **Business Phone:** (312)322-9200.

RICE, LOIS DICKSON
Executive, educator. **Personal:** Born Feb 28, 1933, Portland, ME; daughter of David A and Mary D; married Alfred B Fitt (deceased); children: Susan E & Emmett John Jr. **Educ:** Radcliffe Col, AB, 1954; Brown Univ, LLD, 1981; Bowdoin Col, LLD, 1984;Radcliffe Col, Phi Beta Kappa grad. **Career:** Nat Scholar Serv Fund Negro Students, dir, 1955-58; Col Entrance Exam Bd, dir, 1959-62; Ford Found, educational specialist, 1963-64; Col Entrance Exam Bd, dir 1973-74; Col Entrance Exam Bd, vpres, 1974-81; Int Multi foods & HSB Group; Control Data Corp, sr vpres govt affairs, 1981-91; Brookings Inst, guest scholar, currently. **Orgs:** Bd dir, Beauvoir Sch, 1970-76; bd dir, C TV Workshop, 1970-73; bd dir, Fund Improvement Post Sec Educ, 1972-75; bd trustees, Urban Inst PotomacInst; Carnegie Coun Policy Studies Higher Educ; Community Acad Affairs, Am Coun Educ, 1974-76; DC Community Post Sec Educ, 1974-76; nat adv bd, Inst Study Educ Policy, 1974; chmn, Afro-Am Studies, Harvard Univ, 1974-77; Govt Temporary State Comn Future Post sec Educ, NY, 1976-77; trustee, Stephens Col, 1976-78; President's Foreign Intelligence Bd, 1993-95; trustee, Ctr Naval Anal, Mgt Leadership Tomorrow, Pub Agenda, currently. **Honors/Awds:** Distinguished Service Award, HEW, 1977. **Special Achievements:** Numerous publications. **Business Addr:** Guest Scholar, Brookings Institute, 1775 Mass Ave NW, Washington, DC 20036, **Business Phone:** (202)797-6000.

RICE, DR. LOUISE ALLEN
Educator. **Personal:** Born Jan 1, 1941?, Augusta, GA; daughter of Elnora Allen and Willie Allen; married Wilson L, Apr 4, 1965; children: Wilson L Jr & Robert Christopher. **Educ:** Tuskegee Univ, BS, 1963; Columbia Univ, Teachers Coll, MA, 1969; Univ Ga,PhD, reading educ, 1979. **Career:** Washington High Sch, eng teacher, 1963-66; Lucy Laney High Sch, eng teacher, 1966-68; Paine Col, instr & reading specialist, 1968-71; Lansing Sch Dist, instr & reading specialist, 1971-72; Paine Col, assoc prof, 1972-77; Paine Col, asst acad dean, 1979-81; Lamar Elem Sch, instr leadteacher, 1981-84; Augusta St Univ, assoc dir admis, 1984-88; Augusta St Univ, asst prof educ & reading, 1988-2003; Augusta St Univ, assoc prof learning support, 1989-2003; Minority Adv Prog, coordr, 1998-2003; Augusta St Univ, assoc prof reading, assoc prof reading emer, currently. **Orgs:** Adv bd, Richmond County Bd Educ, 1982-; bd dirs, CSRA Econ Opportunity Authority Inc, 1984-; dir southern region, Delta Sigma Theta Sor Inc, 1986-91; Educ Comn, Augusta Human Rels Comn, 1989-90; chair, NatLeadership Acad, Delta Sigma Theta Sorority Inc, 1996-00; nat pres, DeltaSigma Theta Sorority, 2004-. **Honors/Awds:** Black Womanhood Speaker's Award, Paine Col, 1983; Distinguished Service Award, Augusta Pan-Hellenic Coun, 1984; Urban Builders Award, Augusta Black History Comn, 1985; Outstanding Commission Services, Leadership and Achievement Certificate, Am Asn Univ Women, 1986; Educator of the Year, Lincoln League, Augusta, 1988; Distinguished Leadership Award, United Negro College Fund, 1990; Woman of the Year, Augusta Alumnae Chap, Delta Sigma Theta Sorority, 1991; Nat Soc Delta Sigma Theta Sorority Inc, 1992-96; Citizen of the Year, Augusta Chap, Nat Social Workers, 1999. **Business Addr:** Associate Professor Emeritus of Reading, Augusta State University, Department of Learning Support, 2500 Walton Way, Augusta, GA 30910, **Business Phone:** (706)737-1685.

RICE, DR. MITCHELL F
Educator. **Personal:** Born Sep 11, 1948, Columbus, GA; son of Joseph M and Clarice Mitchell; married Donna Artis; married Cecelia Hawkins Rice (deceased); children: Colin C Rice, Melissa E Rice, Van Artis & Michael Overton. **Educ:** Los Angeles City Col, AA, 1969; Calif State Univ, Los Angeles, BA, 1970, MS, 1973; Claremont Grad Sch, PhD, 1976. **Career:** Bonita Unified Sch Dist, pub sch teacher, 1971-76; Prairie View A&M Univ, asst prof, 1976-77; Southwest Tex State Univ, assoc prof polit sci, 1977-85; Am Coun Educ fel acad admin, 1983-84; Nat Res Coun Ford Found Postdoctoral fel, 1984-85; Rockefeller Found Postdoctoral fel, 1985-86; Los Angeles State Univ, prof pub admin & pol sci, 1985-97; Tex A&M Univ, Bush Sch Govt, prof polit sci, currently; Tex A&M Univ, Race & Ethnic Studies Inst, dir, currently; ed chief, Jour Pub Mgt & Social Policy. **Orgs:** Pres, chair-elect & nat chair, Conf Minority Pub Admin; Am Polit Sci Asn; Nat Conf Black Polit Scientists; Am Soc Pub Admin; pres & owner, Mgt Develop & Training Consult Serv, 1980-; Am Pub Health Asn; elected fel, Nat Acad Pub Admin, 1999; pres, Southeastern Conf Pub Admin. **Special Achievements:** Co-author of Contemporary Public Policy Perspectives and Black Amers Greenwood Press 1984; co-author "Health Care Issues in Black America," Greenwood Press 1987; "Black Health Care, An Annotated Bibliography," Greenwood Press 1987; co-author, Blacks and American Government, Kendall Hunt 1987; author, "Diversity and Public Organizations," Kendall Hunt, 1996; co-author, "Public Policy and The Black Hospital," Greenwood Press, 1995. **Business Addr:** Professor of Political Science, Texas A&M University, Bush School of Government & Public Service, Office 1039, 4220 TAMU, College Station, TX 77843-4220, **Business Phone:** (979)845-0966.

RICE, NORMAN BLANN
Executive, mayor. **Personal:** Born May 4, 1943, Denver, CO; son of Otha Patrick and Irene Johnson Powell; married Constance Williams, Feb 15, 1975; children: Mian A. **Educ:** Univ Wash, BA, commun, 1972, MPA, 1974. **Career:** KOMO TV News, news asst & ed, 1971-72; Seattle Urban League, asst dir, media action proj monitor, 1972-74; Puget Sound Coun Govts, exec asst & dir of govt serv, 1974-75; Rainier Nat Bank, mgr corp contribs, soc policy coord, 1976-78; City of Seattle, coun mem, 1978-83, pres, 1983-90, mayor, 1990-97; Fed Home Loan Bank of Seattle, pres & chief exec officer, 1998-2004; Capital Access LLC, vice chmn; Univ Wash, Daniel J Evans Sch Public Affairs, distinguished visiting practr, currently. **Orgs:** Am Soc Pub Admin; life mem, NAACP; Pi Alpha Alpha. **Honors/Awds:** Outstanding Pub Citizen, Nat Asn Social Workers, 1991; Nat Award Leadership on Behalf of Neighborhoods, Nat Neighborhood Coalition; Isabel Coleman Pierce Award, YWCA, King Co chairperson; Mark F Cooper Leadership Award, Wash Coun Crime & Delinquency; Distinguished Community Serve Award, Alpha Kappa Alpha; Faces of Courage Award, NW Coalition Against Malicious Harassment; Civic Leadership in the Arts Award, Corp Coun for the Arts. **Special Achievements:** Seattle's first & only African-American mayor. **Business Addr:** Distinguished Visiting Practitioner, University of Washington, Parrington Hall Rm 228, PO Box 353055, Seattle, WA 98195-3055, **Business Phone:** (206)221-3893.

RICE, DR. PAMELA ANN
Counselor, educator. **Personal:** Born Jun 27, 1956, Baltimore, MD; daughter of Rev Shirley Carrington and Edward Rice. **Educ:** VA State Univ, BS, 1977; Coppin State Col, Med, 1980; The Johns Hopkins Univ, Advanced degree, 1982; The Am Univ, Wash, DC, Ed.D, 1982, 1988. **Career:** Anne Arundel Community Col, Psychol Dept, adj instr, 1994-94; Essex Community Col, Criminal Justice Dept, adj instr, 1983-94; instr, Psychol Dept, Prince George's Community Col, 1989-90; Coppin State Univ, res asst, 1989-90; Howard Univ, Sch Educ, res fel, 1989-89; Md Dept Juvenile Serv, Juvenile Counr, 1978-91; Baltimore City Pub Sch Syst, substitute teacher, 1977-78; Youth Incentive Entitlement Prog, Comprehensive Employment & Training Act, worksite supvr; Rice Coun Serv, counr, currently. **Orgs:** VA State Alumni Asn, Baltimore Metro Chapter, 1980-, Am Asn Coun & Develop, 1980-, Alpha Kappa Alpha Sorority, 1982-. **Honors/Awds:** Special Service Award, Dept Probation, 1998; United States Parole Comn Award, 1996; Post-Doctoral Minority Scholar's Fellowship Service Award, Howard Univ, 1989; Two Thousand Notable Women Award, 1986; Outstanding Young Women Award, 1986; Personalities of the South Award, 1986; International Directory of Distinguished Leadership Award, 1986; Citation of Honor, Nat Fedn of Bus & Profssional Women's Clubs, 1984; Graduate Award, Coppin State Col, 1980; Recipient, US Am Asn for Play Therapy. **Home Addr:** 3708 Campfield Rd, Baltimore, MD 21207.

RICE, RONALD
Football player. **Personal:** Born Nov 9, 1972, Detroit, MI. **Educ:** Eastern Mich Univ, criminal justice. **Career:** Football player (retired), Detroit Lions, defensive back & safety, 1995-2001. **Orgs:** Founder, Ron Rice Found, 1999. **Honors/Awds:** Walter Payton Man of the Year Award, Nat Football League, 2000.

RICE, SIMEON
Football player, founder (originator). **Personal:** Born Feb 24, 1974, Chicago, IL. **Educ:** Univ Ill, speech communs, 1996. **Career:** Ariz Cardinals, defensive end, 1996-2000; Tampa Bay Buccaneers, defensive end, 2001-06; Denver Broncos, 2007-08; T3K-Thermal 3000, 2004; Nat Football League Network, media day corres, 2005; free agent, currently. **Orgs:** Founder, Lucid Dream Entertainment. **Honors/Awds:** Defensive Rookie of the Month, 1996; Defensive Player of the Month,Northern Football Conf, 2001, 2002; Alumni Defensive Lineman of the Year,Nat Football League, 2002; Defensive Player of the Week, Northern Football Conf, 2003. **Special Achievements:** Featured on the cover of The Sporting News, 2003; named to The Sporting News 2003 NFLocos 100 Best Players List; hosted Simeon Rice Back-2-Sch Workout prog with Fair Play Found, The Univ Area Community Develop Corp Inc & Buchanan Mid Sch, 2004; hosted The Simeon Rice Back-2-School Workout program for 50 at-risk youth at the University Center Complex in Tampa in 2004. **Business Addr:** Co-founder, Lucid Dream Entertainment Group, 3816 W Linebaugh 210, Tampa, FL 33618, **Business Phone:** (813)374-3825.

RICE, SUSAN
Gov't Official, Diplomat. **Personal:** Born Nov 17, 1964, Washington, DC; daughter of Lois Dickson Fitt and Emmett J. Rice; married Ian Cameron, Sep 12, 1992. **Educ:** Standford Univ, BA, 1986; New College, Oxford, earned a M.Phil, 1988; D.Phil, 1990. **Career:** Foreign policy aide to Michael Dukakis during the 1988 presidential election; management consultant at McKinsey & Company, in the early 1990s; during the Clinton administration as the Natl Security Council from 1993-97;Dir for Intl Organizations and Peacekeeping, 1993-95; Special Assistant to the President and Senior Dir for African Affairs, 1995-97; Assistant Secretary of State of African Affairs, 1997; managing dir and principal at Intellibridge, 2001-02; senior fellow in Foreign Policy and Global Economy and Development program at Brookings Institution; foreign policy adviser to John Kerry, 2004;United States Ambassador to the United Nations, 2009-. **Orgs:** Serve on the boards of the Natl Democratic Institute, The U.S. Fund for UNICEF; board of directors of the Atlantic Council, Bureau of Natl Affairs, Partnership for Public Service, the Beauvoir Natl Cathedral Elementary School; adv bd of Freeman Spogli Institute for Intl Studies at Stanford Univ; member of the Council on Foreign Relations and the Aspen Strategy Group. **Honors/Awds:** Awarded a Rhodes Scholarship; recipient, Walter Frewen Lord prize, Royal Commonwealth Society, 1990; Association prize, Chatham House British Intl Studies, 1992; Samuel Nelson Drew Memorial award (co-recipient), NSC, 2002; inducted into Stanford's Black Alumni Hall of Fame in 2002. **Special Achievements:** Third woman ambassador to the UN; youngest assistant secretaries of state ever. **Business Addr:** Press and Public Diplomacy Section, United States Mission to the United Nations, 140 East 45th St, New York, NY 10017, **Business Phone:** (212)415-4062.*

RICE, SUSIE LEON
Government official. **Personal:** Born Dec 28, 1922, Corona, AL; married Robert Calvin Rice; children: Brenda Sue Wright. **Educ:** Ohio State Univ, BS, educ, 1948; Western Res Univ, MA, educ, 1953; John Carroll Univ, Cert, elem admin & guid, 1968; Cleveland State Univ, continued studies, 1975. **Career:** Government officical (Retired); Cleveland Bd Educ, elem teacher, 1948-69, jr/sr high guid counr, 1969-78; Woodmere Ohio, city coun woman, 1978-83. **Orgs:** Bd mgt, Glenville YWCA, 1962-68; bd dirs, Valley YMCA-YWCA, 1969-75; pres, Lambda Phi Omega Chap, Alpha Kappa Alpha Sorority Inc, 1980-81. **Honors/Awds:** Outstanding Volunteer Service Award, Valley YM-YWCA Bd Dirs, 1975; Professional Honors Achievements Pi Lambda Theta Cleveland State Univ, 1977. **Home Addr:** 3707 Avondale Rd, Beachwood, OH 44122.

RICE, WILLIAM ARNOLD
Radiologist. **Career:** Am Radiol Servs at Northpointe, radiologist; Pvt Prac, radiologist, currently. **Orgs:** Am Bd Radiol. *

RICE, WILLIAM E.
Government official. **Personal:** Born Dec 18, 1933, Huntsville, AL; married Delores; children: Duane, Donald & Marvin. **Educ:** Ala Univ, BS, 1955; De Paul Univ, grad stud, 1971. **Career:** Mich Employee Secy Comn, prog coordr, 1955-62; Bur Labor Statist, regional employee anal, 1962-65, asst regional dir, 1967-70, dep regional dir, 1970-71, regional comnr, 1971; OEO Chicago, asst regional mgr admin, 1965-67. **Orgs:** Am Statist Asn; Am Soc Pub Admin; Chicago Guid Asn; Indust Rels Res Asn; Exec Club Chicago; chmn, Adv Comt, Roosevelt Univ, Sch Pub Admin; chmn, Econ & Manpower Develop Adv Comt, Chicago Urban League; chmn, Res Comt Chicago Construction Coordr Comt; Adv Comt Current Develop; Young Men's Christian Asn Col. **Honors/Awds:** Recipient outstanding vc award, Chicago US Dept Lib, 1964. **Special Achievements:** Authored number of articles on regional library market and analysis. **Military Serv:** AUS, 1956-58; USAR, 1958-62. **Business Addr:** 230 S Dearborn, Chicago, IL 60604.

RICH, BETTY
Ballet director, television show host. **Personal:** Born May 30, 1938, Philadelphia, PA; daughter of Samuel and Bertha Richburg; widowed; children: Larry Williams (Rick). **Career:** Children Hour Show, WOAV-TV, Philadelphia, PA; Paul Whiteman Teen Club, WFIL-TV; Ted Mack Amateur Hour; numerous other tv appearances; appeard at the Liborio, the Copacabana, San Juan's Condado Beach Hotel, the Jungle Room; toured SE US for Dept Labor, vocalist, Job Corps Ctrs; Step Toledo tv show, host, assoc producer, 6 years; ballet teacher, currently. **Honors/Awds:** Step Toledo Salutes Betty Rich, 1991; Ghanian Foundation Award, 1997; Award for Dedicated Service to Children, Redeemer Lutheran Church, 1998; Award to Betty Rich House of Ballet, Dr King's 17th Annual Oratorical Contest, 2001; numerous other awards. **Home Addr:** 1805 Oakwood Ave, Toledo, OH 43607. **Business Addr:** Ballet Teacher, Betty Rich House of Ballet, 1805 Oakwood Ave, Toledo, OH 43607, **Business Phone:** (419)537-1284.

RICH, ISADORE A
Counselor, school administrator. **Personal:** Born in Montgomery, AL; son of Lydia Rich. **Educ:** Ala State Univ, BS, eng, 1967, MEd, 1970. **Career:** Ala State Univ, counr; Stillman Col, counr; Ky State Univ, Early Admission students, counr, basketball team, acad advisor, coordr athletics, Upward Bound Prog, tutorial coordr, currently. **Orgs:** Am Personnel & Guid Asn; Nat Asn Acad Advisors Athletics; Southern Asn Col & Employers; Nat Asn Col & Employers; Alpha Phi Omega Service Frat; Phi Delta Kappa Educ Fraternity. **Honors/Awds:** Outstanding Young Man of America; Man of Achievement Award; Teacher of the Year, State Ga; Distinguished Service Award, Ky State Univ; Staff Employer of the Month, Ky State Univ; Athletes Service Award; Outstanding Advisor Award, APA, Beta Nu Chap; Gov Brereton C Jones, KY Colonels, 1994. **Special Achievements:** Professional Consult-

ant; Kentucky State University Marching Band, halftime announcer, special events coordinator; articles: "The Urge to Conform," Off to College Journal, Feb 1979; "Coaching and Academic Counseling: A Case of Role Strain," Black Excellence, Nov/Dec 1991; "Hasty Conclusion: The Freshman College Athlete," Black College Today, 1999; Advisors, "Athletes Team up to Close the Educational Gap," Blacks Issues in Education, 2001; "Faculty Adopt Coach Role in Classroom," Black Issues in Higher Education, 2003; NCAA News. **Business Addr:** Career Counselor/Academic Advisor for Athletics, Kentucky State University, 400 E Main St, Frankfort, KY 40601, **Business Phone:** (502)597-6063.

RICH, MATTY (MATTHEW STATISFIELD RICHARDSON)
Movie director, video producer, writer. **Personal:** Born Nov 6, 1971, Brooklyn, NY. **Educ:** Tisch Sch Arts, New York Univ, film; John Jay Col Criminal Justice. **Career:** Films: Straight Out of Brooklyn, writer, producer, dir & actor, 1991; The Inkwell, dir, 1994; 187 Ride or Die, dir & writer, 2005; auth, Short-term & Long-term Thinking, 1991; Blacks N Progress Prod, film prod cofounder & owner, currently; 187 Ride or Die, dir, 2005. **Honors/Awds:** Special Award, Sundance Film Festival, 1991. **Business Addr:** Filmmaker, William Morris Agency, 151 S El Camino Dr, Beverly Hills, CA 32767, **Business Phone:** (310)859-4000.

RICH, STANLEY C
Police officer. **Personal:** Born Feb 25, 1920; married Coralie. **Educ:** Morris Brown Col, AB; Wayne State Univ, MA. **Career:** Detroit, Mich Police Dept, second dep comnr; Detroit Health Dept, jr acct, 1947-50; Mayor's Com Human Resources Develop, sr acct, 1964-65, 1967; Small Bus Develop Ctr, adminr, 1965-67; chmn police trial bd equal employ officer small & minor bus enter officer for police dept. **Orgs:** Kappa Alpha Psi Fraternity; United Community Serv Met Detroit; bd dir, St Peter Claver Community Ctr.

RICH, WILBUR C
Educator. **Personal:** Born Sep 28, 1939, Montgomery, AL; son of Lydia and Savage; married Jean; children: Rachel & Alexandra. **Educ:** Tuskegee Inst, BS, 1960; Univ Ill, EdM, 1964, PhD, 1972. **Career:** Univ Wis, Dept Ment Health, IL, counr asst admin, 1965-67; Ment Health CT, asst dir, 1969-72; Columbia Univ, asst prof polit sci; Wayne State Univ, fac; Univ IL Urbana, vis asst prof; Wesleyan Univ, Middletown, CT, vis lectr; Univ Mich, vis prof; Wellesley Col, prof polit sci, currently. **Orgs:** Pres, Northeastern Polit Sci Asn, 1999-2000; pres, Urban Sect, Am Polit Sci Asn, 2006-; vpres, New Eng Polit Sci Asn, 2006-; Am Soc Pub Admin; Nat Conf Black Polit Sci; Am Pol Sci Asn; Alpha Phi Alpha; Chi Gamma Iota; Phi Delta Kappa; Am Soc Pub Admin; Urban Affairs Asn; Am Educ Res Asn; Eastern Educ Res Asn; Eastern Commun Asn; Nat Conf Black Polit Scientists. **Honors/Awds:** Career Development Chair Award, Wayne State Univ, 1989. **Special Achievements:** Author: The Polits Urban Personnel Policy, 1982; Coleman Young & Detroit Polits, 1989; Black Mayors & Sch Polits, 1996; The Politics of Minority Coalitions, 1996. **Military Serv:** USAF, 1961-65. **Business Addr:** Professor of Political Science, Wellesley College, Department of Political Science, 106 Cent St, Wellesley, MA 02481, **Business Phone:** (781)283-2184.

RICHARD, ALVIN J.
Educator. **Personal:** Born Oct 14, 1932, New Orleans, LA; married Arlene Lecesne; children: Terrence, Kent & Wendy. **Educ:** Xavier Univ LA, BS, 1955, MA, 1967; Univ Ill, EdD, 1972. **Career:** Orleans Pre Sch Bd, teacher, 1957-65; Xavier Univ, asst dean of men,1965-66, dean of men, 1966-70, dir univ admin, 1972-75, dir recruitment,1972-, dean of admins & financial aid, 1975-, dean grad sch & dir grad admissions grad sch, currently; Univ Ill, staff asst, 1970-72; Ford Found, fel, 1972; S Univ New Orleans, assoc prof, 1973. **Orgs:** Consult, Consortium Admin & Financial Admin, 1974-; Am Asn Col Reg & Admis Officers; Southern Asn Col Regs & Admin Officers; La Asn Col Regs & Admin Officers; Nat Asn Col Deans Regs & Admin Officers; Am Soc Allied Health Profs; bd mem, Young Adults Sports Asn; Met Area Com; Strng Com Am Found Negro Affairs. **Business Addr:** Dean Graduate School, Xavier University, 1 Drexel Dr, New Orleans, LA 70125, **Business Phone:** (504)483-7487.

RICHARD, DR. ARLENE CASTAIN
Physician. **Personal:** Born Mar 1, 1955, St Martinville, LA; daughter of Joseph Soban and Mary Luna Louis; married Donald Ray, Apr 6, 1974; children: Dawnia, Donald Jr, Sterlyn, Arlen & Orlando. **Educ:** Univ Southwestern La, BS, BA, acct, (Cum Laude), 1977; Howard Univ Col Med, MD, 1983. **Career:** Earl K Long Mem Hosp, internship, 1983-84; Univ Med Ctr, LSU staff physician, 1985; Howard Univ Hosp, family practice resident, 1985-87; pvt pract, currently. **Orgs:** Alpha Kappa Alpha Sor, 1974-, Am Med Asn. **Home Addr:** 605 Ducharme Rd, Opelousas, LA 70570. **Business Addr:** Physician, Richard Medical Clinic, 507 N Market St, Opelousas, LA 70570, **Business Phone:** (337)948-1212.

RICHARD, FLOYD ANTHONY
Obstetrician, gynecologist. **Personal:** Born May 5, 1952, Opelousas, LA; married Robin; children: Keiana, Floyd II, Jonathan. **Educ:** Southern Univ, BS, 1973; Meharry Med Col, MD, 1981. **Career:** Conoco Oil, process control chemist, 1973-74; The Upjohn Co, asst res chemist, 1976-77; Meharry Med Col, asst prof dept Obstets & Gynec, 1985; Cent N Ala Health Servs, chief dept Obstets & Gynec; pvt pract, Nashville, TN, currently. **Orgs:** Chmn, youth div Second Ward Voters League, 1976. **Honors/Awds:** Upjohn Award Gynecologist & Obstetrician, 1981; Outstanding Young Men of America, 1982; Gynecologic Laparoscopist Award, 1984; AOA Med Hon Soc.

RICHARD, DR. HENRI-CLAUDE
Physician. **Personal:** Born Feb 12, 1944, Port-au-Prince, Haiti; son of Theophile and Christiane; children: Maurice. **Educ:** Howard Univ Col Lib Arts, BS, 1968; Howard Univ Col Med, MD, 1972. **Career:** Ireland Army Hosp, radiologist, 1977-87; Breckenridge Mem Hosp, radiologist, 1980-94; Pk duValle Health Ctr, radiologist, 1992; Radcliff Radiol Serv, radiologist, currently. **Orgs:** Am Med Asn; Ky Med Asn; Hardin Co Med Asn; Radiol Soc N Am; Am Col Radiol; Am Inst Ultrasound Med; Falls City Med Soc; Inter-Am Col Physicians & Surgeons. **Home Addr:** 1548 Redbud Circle, Radcliff, KY 40160. **Business Addr:** Physician, Radcliff Radiology Services, 650 W Lincoln Trail Blvd, Radcliff, KY 40160-2602, **Business Phone:** (270)351-4342.

RICHARD, STANLEY PALMER (THE SHERIFF)
Football player. **Personal:** Born Oct 21, 1967, Miniola, TX. **Educ:** Univ Tex. **Career:** Football player (retired); San Diego Chargers, def back, 1991-95; Wash Redskins, def back, 1995-98.

RICHARDS, DELEON MARIE
Actor, singer. **Personal:** Born Sep 18, 1976, Lake Forest, IL; daughter of Robert Leon Jr and Deborah Y Wallace; married Gary Sheffield, Feb 5, 2000; children: Jaden Amir & Christian Emari. **Educ:** Steve Scott, Goodman Theatre; Northwestern Univ, Music Dept; Sherwood Conservatory. **Career:** TV series: "Brewster Place", 1990; "Legends from the Land of Lincoln";"Patti LaBelle Gospel Special"; "Ebony/Jet Showcase"; "March of Dimes Telethon"; "McDonald Gospel Fest"; "Kelly & Co"; Theatre appearances:Polly & the Dinosaurs, World Book Encyclopedia Musical; Albums: DeLeon,1985, Don't Follow the Crowd, 1987, Christmas, 1988, We Need to Hear from You, 1989; New Direction", 1992; Straight From the Heart, 2001; Here In Me; My Life; Videos: DeLeon in Concert; "When", 1993; The Mighty Clouds of Joy; Contributed musical input for Nancy Reagan's anti-drug film, "IBelieve in Me," 1986; cast, The Women of Brewster Place, 1990. DeMari Publishing and Entertainment, Inc, Pres. **Honors/Awds:** Participated in the Chicago Gospel Fest at the age of 5, 1982; Grammy Nomination (youngest artist ever to be nominated), 1986; GMWA Award, 1988;Stellar Nomination, 1991; GMWA Award. **Special Achievements:** Youngest artist ever signed to a major Gospel label; Youngest person ever to be nominated for a Grammy; One of the Most Outstanding Role Models in America. **Business Addr:** Gospel Singer, Word Records, 4800 W Waco Dr, Nashville, TN 37219.

RICHARDS, EDWARD A
Military leader. **Personal:** Born Dec 15, 1930, Trenton, NJ; married Barbara; children: Edward Jr & Denise. **Educ:** Univ Calif, Los Angeles; Washburn Univ; Bellvue Col; Univ Md; Mgt Schs; USAF Sr NCO Acad. **Career:** Military leader (Retired); USAF, chief mgmt & br, 1950-80; Golden Nugget Hotel/Casino, security, 1980; Grand Hotel/Casino, asst dir security, currently. **Orgs:** Disabled Am Veterans, 1990; Life mem, African Sergeant Asn; Human Rels Coun; Enlisted Adv Coun; served Complaints NCO;Am Asn Retired People, AARP. **Honors/Awds:** Received numerous decorations most important AF commendation, 1962; Two Oak Leaf Clusters, 1968, 1974. **Military Serv:** USAF, chief sgt, 1950.

RICHARDS, GEORGE
Vice president (Organization). **Career:** Comerica Bank, banking ctr mgr, personal banker; Southeast Mich Banking Ctr, Comerica Bank, sr vpres, currently. **Business Addr:** Senior Vice President, Comerica Bank, Southeast Michigan Banking Centers, MC 7805 500 Woodward Ave, Detroit, MI 48226, **Business Phone:** (313)964-4125.*

RICHARDS, DR. HILDA
School administrator. **Personal:** Born Feb 7, 1936, St Joseph, MO; daughter of Togar Young-Ballard and Rose Avalynne Williams Young-Ballard; married Alfredo (divorced). **Educ:** St John's Sch Nursing, St Louis, grad, nursing, 1956; CUNY, BS cum laude, 1961; Columbia Univ, Teachers Col, MEd, 1965, EdD, 1976; NY Univ, MPA, 1971; Inst Educ Mgt Harvard Univ, cert, 1981. **Career:** City Hosp, Adolescent Psychiatric Unit, head nurse; Harlem Rehab Ctr, Dept Psychol, Div Rehab Serv, coordr clin serv, 1965-69; Harlem Hosp Ctr, dept chief, 1969-71; Medgar Evers Col, dir nursing prog, 1971-76, from assoc prof to prof, 1971-76; Acad Admin Am Coun Educ, fel, 1976-77; City Univ NY, assoc dean acad affairs, 1976-79; Ohio Univ Col Health & Human Serv, dean, 1979-86; Ind Univ, PA, provost & vpres acad affairs, 1986-93; Ind Univ NW, chancellor & pres, 1993-2001, chancellor emer & prof emer, 2001-. **Orgs:** Bd mem, 1974-77, 1983-84, 1988-91, first vpres, 1984-88, pres, Nat Black Nurses Asn; exec comm, Am Coun Educ, 1982-85; bd mem, AVANTA Network, 1984-; bd mem, Ind Co Comm Action, 1986-91; Pa Nurses Asn, 1986-; Econ Develop Comn, 1986-; bd mem, Citizen's Ambulance Serv, Indiana Co, 1987-; Asn Black Women Fac, 1988-; Asn Black Women Higher Educ, 1988-; exec comm, Pa Black Conf Higher Educ, 1988; NAACP, life mem, exec comm, Ind Chapter, 1988-; Am Nurses Asn; Am Asn Higher Educ; Am Pub Health Asn; Nat Asn Allied Health Prof; Nat Women's Studies Asn; bd mem, Big Brothers/Big Sisters, 1989-; Pa Acad Prof Teaching, bd mem, 1990-; Am Asn Univ Adminr; Am Asn Univ Women; Asn Black Nursing Fac Higher Educ; Asn Black Women Fac; Pa Nurses Asn; Phi Delta Kappa; Sigma Theta Tau; ACE Comn Minorities Higher Educ, Diversity & Social Change; Zonta Club Ind County; bd dirs, Sta 56-TV; Active NW Satir Inst, Execs Coun, NW, IN; Urban League, 1993; NW Ind Forum, 1993; Bank One Regional bd, Merrillville, IN,1994; Meth Hosp Inc, Gary, 1994; Lake Area United Way, 1994; Boys & Girls Clubs, NW, IN; NW Kiwanis. **Honors/Awds:** Martin Luther King Grantee, NYU, NYC, 1969-70; Recipient, Rockefellow Found Award, Am Coun Educ, WA, 1976-77; Grant Found Grantee, Harvard Inst Educ Mgt, Cambridge, MA, 1981; Black Achiever Award, Black Opinion Mag, 1989; Outstanding Woman of Color, 1990, Special Recognition Award, 1991, Am Nurses Asn Inc; Distinguished African/American Nurse Educator, Queens County Black Nurses Asn, Queens borough Comm Col, 1991; Athena Award, Bus &Prof Women's Club Ind, 1991; Lifetime Achievement Award, Asn Black Nursing Fac, 1996; Dr, Medgar Evers College, City University of New York; 100 Most Influential Black Americans, Ebony magazine, 1999-2003. **Special Achievements:** Co-author of "Curriculum Development and People of Color: Strategies and Change," 1983, editor of "Black Conf on Higher Education Jour, 1989-93; First female and first African-American academic dean at Ohio University; First black graduate of St. Johns School of Nursing in St. Louis. **Business Addr:** Chancellor Emeritus, Professor Emeritus, Indiana University Northwest, 3400 Broadway, Gary, IN 46408-1101, **Business Phone:** (219)980-6500.

RICHARDS, JAIME AUGUSTO, III
Actor. **Personal:** Born Aug 28, 1973, Washington, DC. **Educ:** Univ Southern Calif. **Career:** Films: Good Burger, 1997; Any Day Now, 2000; Paved with Good Intentions, 2006; TV Series: "Undressed", 1999; "Moesha", 2000; "Running Mates", 2000; "Critical Assembly", 2003; "CSI: Miami", 2004; "Angel", 2004; "Conviction", 2006; "The 4400", 2006; "Raising the Bar", 2008. **Orgs:** Make-A-Wish Found. **Honors/Awds:** Won numerous scholarships & grants. **Special Achievements:** Named No 10 of the Top Ten Sexiest Men of the Buffy. **Business Addr:** Actor, c/o Rising Stars, PO Box 99, China Spring, TX 76633, **Business Phone:** (254)836-0273.

RICHARDS, JOHNETTA GLADYS
Educator. **Personal:** Born Jul 18, 1950, Brooklyn, NY; daughter of Leo Richards and Nettie James. **Educ:** Va State Col, BA, 1972; Univ Cincinnati, MA, 1974, PhD, 1987. **Career:** Northeastern Univ, adj instr Afro-Am hist, 1971; Univ Cincinnati, danforth fel, 1972-73, lecturer Am hist, 1976-77; Univ Calif, Santa Barbara, lectr Afro-Am hist, 1977-78, Ctr Black Studies, Dissertation fel, 1977-78; Nat Fel Fund, Atlanta, GA, Doctoral fel, 1978-79; Trinity Col, asst prof hist, 1979-84; State Univ Fresno, Women's Studies Calif, assoc prof, 1984-88; San Francisco State Univ, assoc prof black studies, prof black studies, currently. **Orgs:** Phi Alpha Theta Nat Hon Fraternity Historians, 1974-; Asn Study Afro-Am Life & Hist, 1978-; Nat Asn Advan Colored People, Hartford, CT, 1979-80; life mem, Asn Black Women Historians, 1983-; chair, Far Western Region Asn Black Women Historians, 1986-88; nat dir, Asn Black Women Historians, 1990-92; Am Hist Asn, Pac Coast Br; life mem, African Am Mus Libr, Oakland. **Business Addr:** Professor of Black Studies, San Francisco State University, Black Studies Department, 1600 Holloway Ave, San Francisco, CA 94132, **Business Phone:** (415)338-7589.

RICHARDS, LAVERNE W.
School administrator. **Personal:** Born Jun 19, 1947, Gaffney, SC; divorced; children: Brant, Jerrel. **Educ:** San Jose State Col, BA, 1969; Univ CA Berkeley, Teach Cert, 1970; Univ Houston TX, MEd, 1974, Mid Mgt Adminr, 1981. **Career:** Oakland Unified Sch Dist, teacher, 1969-72; Delta Sigma Theta Inc, prog asst, 1972; El Paso ISD, teacher, 1974-76; Houston ISD, teacher, 1972-74, 1977-85, asst prin; T M Fairchild Elem, prin, currently. **Orgs:** Fine arts chmn, Delta Sigma Theta Ft Bend, 1984; coordr, United Way Clifton Middle Sch, 1985-87; coordr, United Negro Col Fund, 1985-87; finance comt Houston Assoc Sch Adminrs, 1985-; TX Assoc Sec Sch Prins, 1985-; phi Delta Kappa, Assoc Supervision & Curriculum 1985-; Urban League Guild, 1986-; scholarship chmn, Human Enrichment Life Prog, 1987; Human Enrichment Life Prog, 1986-; Exec bd mem, Windsor Village Elem Vanguard Parents Asn, 1983-85; HISD Instructional Adv Comn Houston, 1984. **Honors/Awds:** Young Black Achiever of Houston, Human Enrichment Life Programs Inc, 1986. **Business Addr:** Principal, T M Fairchild Elementary, 8701 Delliah, Houston, TX 77033-3827, **Business Phone:** (713)732-3472.

RICHARDS, LEON
School administrator, educator. **Personal:** Born Jun 7, 1945, Montgomery, AL; son of Carrie Mae Smith and John; married

Pauline Sakai, Dec 31, 1969; children: Kayin Takao & Kalera Toyoko. **Educ:** Ala State Univ, BS, (summa cum laude), 1968; Univ Hawaii-Manoa, MA, 1970, PhD, 1974; MA, ESL, 2000. **Career:** Univ Hawaii, EW Ctr, Honolulu, HI, res asst, 1970-71, 1974-75; Leeward Community Col, Pearl City, HI, staff develop specialist, 1975-77; Kapiolani Community Col, Honolulu, HI, asst dean instr, 1977-81, actg provost, 1983-84, 2002, dean instr, 1983-, interim chancellor, currently, Honda Int Ctr, exec dir, currently, sr acad dean, currently. **Orgs:** Vpres, Hawaii Asn Staff, Prog & Orgn Develop, 1978-90; Nat Comn Black Polit Scientist, 1979-; Nat Coun Resource Develop, 1980-. **Honors/Awds:** Alpha Kappa Mu Scholastic Hon Soc, 1966-68; Sigma Rho Sigma Scholastic Honorary Soc Hist Majors, 1966-68; summer inresidence fel, Nat Ctr Res Voc Educ, 1979; Am Coun Educ Fel Acad Admin, 1981-82; EWt Ctr fels, 1993-97; Field Study fel, Peking Univ. **Home Addr:** 98-363 Puaalii St, Aiea, HI 96701. **Business Addr:** Executive Director, Senior Academic Dean, Kapiolani Community College, Honda International Center, 4303 Diamond Head Rd, Honolulu, HI 96816, **Business Phone:** (808)734-9519.

RICHARDS, LORETTA THERESA
Religious educator. **Personal:** Born Apr 8, 1929, New York, NY; daughter of David A and Mary Cornelius Richards Edwards. **Educ:** Col Mt St Vincent, New York, NY, BA, 1954; Cath Univ, Wash, DC, MA, 1960; Catechetical Inst, Yonkers NY, MRS, 1984. **Career:** St Aloysius Sch, New York NY, teacher, 1954-55, 1957-61; St Thomas Sch, Wilmington NC, teacher, 1955-57; Cathedral High Sch, New York NY, teacher, 1961-64; FHM, New York NY, sch supvr, 1964-74, congregation pres, 1974-82; St Aloysius Parish, New York NY, pastoral assoc, 1982-90, congregation pres, 1990-98, vpres, 1998-2006. **Orgs:** Pres, Nat Black Sisters Conf, 1985-89; vpres, 1989-91, congregation minister, Nat Black Catholic Congress; Nat Forum Catechumenate, 1990-; Vicariate Coun Cent Harlem; congregation minister, Franciscan Fed, currently. **Honors/Awds:** Doctor of Pedagogy, New York Col Podiatric Med, 1981; Doctor of Humane Letters, Col New Rochelle, 1997. **Home Addr:** Handmaids Of Mary Convent, 15 W 124th St, New York, NY 10027, **Home Phone:** (212)289-5655.

RICHARDS, WILLIAM EARL
Executive, secretary of the navy. **Personal:** Born Oct 19, 1921, New York, NY; son of John Earl Jr and Camily Deravaine; married Ollun Sadler, Sep 16, 1949; children: William Jr. **Educ:** Washburn Univ, BA; NY Univ, Additional Study; Officer Cand Sch, AF Spec Weapons Sch. **Career:** KS Dept Soc & Rehabilitation Serv, comn income maintenance & med asst, 1973-83 (retired); Lipsett Steel Co, gen supt, 1946-49; Progressive Life Insurance agent, 1949-51; NAACP, staff dir, legislative agent, 1972; KS Comn Alcoholism, 1972-73; Richards Et Cie, pres; Myers and Stauffer CPA's, sr consultant; Cottonwood Technology Corporation, Kansas City KS, pres, 1988-93; Topeka Human Relations Commission, commissioner, vchmn. **Orgs:** Washburn Alumni Asn; Retired Officers Asn; Assn AUS; Military Order World Wars; Alpha Phi Alpha; SPP; life mem, NAACP; Euclid Lodge; Kaw Valley Consistory; 33 Degree Mason; pres, Topeka Branch NAACP; Topeka Knife & Fork Club. **Honors/Awds:** KS Governor Certificate Meritorious Serv; Whitney M Young Jr Service Awd, Boy Scouts of America. **Military Serv:** AUS, lt col; Asiatic-Pacific Campaign Medal; Nat Defense Medal Oak Leaf Cluster; Korean Serv Medal; 2 Battle Ser Starr; AF Expeditionary Serv Medal; Vietnam Serv Medal; Battle Star; Armed Forces Res Medal Device; United Nat Serv Medal; Legion Merit, Army Commend Ribbon Pendant; Oak Leaf Cluster; Good Conduct Medal; Amer Campaign Medal; Battle Serv Star. *

RICHARDS, WINSTON ASHTON
Educator. **Personal:** Born Mar 7, 1935, Chaguanas, Trinidad and Tobago; son of Edward Ivan and Leanora Nimblett; married Kathleen Marie Hoolihan Richards, Apr 4, 1964; children: Ashton, Winston, Marie, Michael, Bridgette, Mary, Patricia & Edward. **Educ:** Marquette Univ, Milwaukee, Wis, BS, 1959, MS, 1961; Univ Western Ontario, London, Ontario, MA, 1966, PhD, 1970. **Career:** Aquinas Col, Grand Rapids, Mich, instr, 1961-62; Wayne State Univ, Detroit, Mich, lectr, 1962-64; Univ Western Ont, grad asst, 1964-69; Penn State Univ, Capitol Col, Middletown, Pa, assoc prof math & statist, 1969-; Univ West Indies, Trinidad, from vis sr lectr to sr lectr, 1980-82; Stanford Univ, Dept Statist, vis prof, 1995-97. **Orgs:** Treas, 1987, pres, 1989-90, 1992-93, Harrisburg Chap, Am Statist Asn; Math Asn Am; Inter Am Statist Inst; Inst Statisticians; Int Statist Inst; Pa Black Conf Higher Educ. **Honors/Awds:** Nat Math Hon Fraternity, Pi Mu Epsilon, 1960; Fel IST Statisticians, 1985; Recognition Award, Harrisburg Chap, Pa Soc Prof Engrs, 1987; Appreciation Award, Black Studs Union Penn State Univ, 1989-90; Recognition Award, Harrisburg Chap, Am Statist Asn, 1990; Recognition Award, Philadelphia African Am Alumni Asn Pa State Univ, 1990; Miembro Honario, La Sociedad Venezolana de Biometria y Estadistica, 1994; Fel, Am Statist Asn, FASA, 1997; Excellence in Teaching Award, James A Jordan, Jr Award, 1997. **Home Addr:** 2100 Chestnut St, Harrisburg, PA 17104. **Business Addr:** Associate Professor of Mathematics, Pennsylvania State University, The Capital College, W256 Olmsted Bldg, Penn State HBG, Middletown, PA 17057, **Business Phone:** (717)948-6090.

RICHARDS-ALEXANDER, BILLIE J.
Consultant, executive. **Personal:** Born in Austin, TX; daughter of Johnnie M Barber Bacon and Roy A Bacon; married Castomal Alexander Sr, Jun 6, 1987; children: Roy, Dianne & Reginal. **Educ:** Huston Tillotson Col, Austin, Tex, BS, 1962; Univ Tex, Austin, attended 1963; Scarritt Col, Nashville, attended 1966; Univ Tex, Arlington, Mass, attended 1974; London Sch Bus, London, Eng, attended 1986. **Career:** Ebenezer Baptist Church, Austin, dir educ, 1960-61; Dunbar High Sch, Temple, Tex, teacher, 1961-64; Bethlehem Ctr, from asst dir to dir, 1965-73; Fed Home Loan Bank Bd Ctr Exec Develop, urban prog coordr, 1972-73; Neighborhood Housing Serv Dallas Inc, exec dir, 1973-78; Dallas Fed Savings & Loan Asn, Urban Lending Dept, vpres/dir, 1978-80, sr vpres, 1980-87; Int Bus fel, 1986; Billie Richards & Assocs, pres, 1987-; Dallas County, housing adminr, 1988; prin, Sch Urban & Pub affairs. **Orgs:** AKA, Alpha XI Omega Chapter. **Honors/Awds:** Woman of the Year, United Action Women's Affiliate Dallas Black Chamber Com, 1978; Community Affairs Award, Com 100, 1978; Trailblazer Award, S Dallas Bus & Prof, Women's Orgn, 1979; Int Bus Fel, 1986. **Special Achievements:** First Black Female Vice President of a major financial institution in the Southwest, 1978; First African American Female Senior Vice President, 1980. **Home Addr:** 1517 Bar Harbor Dr, Dallas, TX 75232. **Business Addr:** President, Billie Richards & Associates Inc, 1517 Bar Harbor Dr, Dallas, TX 75232.

RICHARDSON, ALBERT DION
Executive, president (organization). **Personal:** Born Dec 14, 1946, New York, NY; son of Robert L McKinney and Onolda Jacquelyn McKinney; married Beverly V A, Jan 15, 1984; children: Dara & Erika. **Educ:** Mercer Co Community Col, Trenton, NJ, attended 1973. **Career:** Richardson Environ Contracting, pres, 1986-. **Orgs:** Nat Asn Minority Contractors, 1986-. **Military Serv:** USMC, E-5, 1965-71. **Business Phone:** (609)386-8884.

RICHARDSON, ALFRED LLOYD
Engineer, vice president (organization). **Personal:** Born Jan 17, 1927, Kerens, TX; married Georgia E Murphy; children: Paul G, Yllona, Victor. **Educ:** Prairie View A&M Univ, 1950; Univ So CA, 1952. **Career:** CA Div of Hwys, jr civil engr, 1950-52; LACFCD, chief eng asso chief eng asst, 1952-65; PCFC Sls Eng Inc, proj engr, 1963-71, vpres coop tech servs, dir fnd tech servs, 1971-76. **Orgs:** Pres, LA Coun Black Prof Engrs, 1969-71; Lic Prof Engr CA; Engrs Coun Prof Devel, 1970-84; So CA Eng Soc Comt Manpower Training, 1970-71; chmn, ASCE LA; secy, Human Resources Devel Comt, 1971-77; ASCE Nat Comt Minority Progs, 1975-79; asso mem, Structural Engrs Asn CA; adv Nat Soc Black Eng Stud 2nd Annual Nat Conf CA Poly Univ ,1975-76; Eng Prof Adv Coun Calif State Univ; Int Soc Soil Mech & Fnd Engrs; fel Am Soc Civil Engrs; fel Inst Advan Eng. **Military Serv:** AUS, 1946-47; comndg officer, 1947-53.

RICHARDSON, ANDRA VIRGINIA
Magistrate. **Personal:** Born Apr 16, 1954, Detroit, MI; daughter of James Law and Odessa Law; married William Lee, Sep 22, 1984 (divorced); children: Brittney Leigh & Chelsea Anne. **Educ:** Wayne State Univ, BS, 1984; Wayne State Univ Law Sch, JD, 1987. **Career:** Delta Airlines, reservation sales agent, 1977-86; Oakland County, prosecutor, asst prosecuting atty, 1988-90; 52nd Dist Ct-1st Div, magistrate, 1990-; Eastern Mich Univ, adj prof, 1998-; part-time law pract, currently. **Orgs:** Exec bd & chair, Oakland County Chap Child Abuse & Neglect Coun, 1990-94; bd dirs, Girl Scouts Am, 1991-94; exec bd, rec secy, Top Ladies Distinction Inc, 1993-95; exec bd, parlimentarian, Jack & Jill Am Inc, 1993-95; pres, Top Ladies, 1995-97; Doll League, 1998-; Legis Liaison, 1998-; Wolverine Bar Asn; Asn Black Judges Mich. **Honors/Awds:** Outstanding Business & Prof Award, Dollars & Sense Mag, 1993; Prof Woman of the Year, Nat Asn Negro Bus & Prof Women Club Inc, 1993. **Business Addr:** Magistrate, 52nd District Court -1st Division, 48150 Grand River Ave, Novi, MI 48374-1222, **Business Phone:** (248)305-6511.

RICHARDSON, ANTHONY W.
Dentist. **Personal:** Born Mar 15, 1957, New York, NY; son of Archie Richardson and Harriet Boyd Brooks; children: Solunda Yvette, Sherie Odetta, Toni Charisse. **Educ:** Bucknell Univ, BS 1979; Fairleigh Dickinson Univ Sch Dent Med, DMD 1983. **Career:** Montefiore Hosp & Med Ctr, gen pract resident, 1983-84; Fairleigh Dickinson Univ Sch Dent Med, asst dir minority affairs, 1984-86, asst prof, 1984-87, asst dir admis, 1986-87, asst dir prog grads nonapproved dent sch, 1986-87, dir minority affairs, 1986-87; Con-Court Dent Assocs, Bronx, NY, owner, 1989-. **Orgs:** Charter mem, Phi Beta Sigma Fraternity Iota Gamma Chap, 1977; Am Assoc Dent Sch; Acad Gen Dentistry; Nat Dent Asn; NJ Commonwealth Dent Soc; adv bd, Health Careers Prog Montclair State Col, 1983-90; chapter adv Phi Beta Sigma Fraternity Xi Omicron Chap 1984, 1985; Phi Beta Sigma Fraternity; Greater Metrop NY Dent Soc; US Coast Guard Auxillary; bd dirs, Fordham Hill Owners Corp, 1998-01. **Honors/Awds:** NY State Governor's Citation, 1975; Outstanding Serv Cert, Nat Dent Asn, 1982, 1983; NJ Soc Dentistry C Award, 1983; NJ Commonwealth Dent Soc Award 1983; Outstanding Young Men Am, 1986. **Business Addr:** Owner, Con-Court Dent Assocs, 840 Grand Concourse Suite 1BB, Bronx, NY 10451, **Business Phone:** (718)585-1616.*

RICHARDSON, ANTONIO. **See RICHARDSON, TONY.**

RICHARDSON, CLINT DEWITT, JR.
Basketball player. **Personal:** Born Aug 7, 1956, Seattle, WA; married Vicki; children: Tiffany Jade. **Educ:** Seattle Univ, attended 1979. **Career:** Basketball player (retired); Philadelphia 76ers, guard, 1979-85, Ind Pacers, guard, 1985-87; dir & coach, CYO athletics, currently.

RICHARDSON, DAMIEN
Football player. **Personal:** Born Apr 3, 1976, Los Angeles, CA. **Educ:** Ariz State Univ. **Career:** Carolina Panthers, defensive back, 1998-2004; Az state Sun Devils, currently. **Honors/Awds:** All-conference honor, 1997.

RICHARDSON, DERUTHA GARDNER
Educator. **Personal:** Born May 3, 1941, Muskogee, OK; married Alfred; children: Allyn Christopher & Adrian Charles. **Educ:** Muskogee Jr Col, OK, AA, 1960; NE State Col, Tahlequah, OK, BS 1962, masters degree, 1964. **Career:** School Adminstrator (retired); Atty C P Kimble, part-time private legal sec, 1955-70; L'Ouverature High Sch, teacher sec, 1962-63; Mountain High Sch, secondary bus teacher, 1963-65; Cent High Sch, first black sec business teacher, 1965-66; Taft St C Home Matriculation Sch, exec sec &t eacher, 1966-67; Muskogee County Head Start, sec book keeper, 1966-68; Muskogee High Sch, first black bus dept head & teacher co ord; YWCA Connells St Col, adult bus teacher, 1975-77; Antique Store, owner, currently. **Orgs:** Zeta Phi Beta Sorority Inc, WA 1973-74; treas, Alpha Lambda Zeta Sorority,1975-80; pres, Eastern Dist Oklahoma Educ Asn 1977-78. **Honors/Awds:** First black teacher yr, Muskogee Educ Asn, 1977; teacher yr finalist, Oklahoma Educ Asn, 1977; Black Heritage hon, Mt Calvary Baptist Church, Muskogee, 1977; first black fourth place & second runner-up plaques, Oklahoma Teachers, 1978-80; outstanding teachers plaque, Du Bois School Reunion, 1980; author Dear Teacher, Carlton Press, NY 1980; Recipient of over 35 Awards, state, regional and national. **Special Achievements:** First black teacher in Muskogee Public Schools; Published author of three books. **Business Addr:** Assistant Principal, West Junior High School, 6400 Mathew Dr, Muskogee, OK 74401.

RICHARDSON, DESMOND
Dancer. **Personal:** Born Jan 1, 1969?, Sumter, SC. **Educ:** Alvin Ailey Am Dance Ctr, attended 1986. **Career:** Alvin Ailey Am Dance Theater, prin dancer, 1986-94; Frankfurt Ballet, 1994-96; Am Ballet Theatre, prin dancer, 1997-98; Broadway Musical Fosse, 1998; Swedish Opera Ballet; Wash Ballet; Teatro at La Scala; San Francisco Ballet; COMPLEXIONS Contemp Ballet, co-artistic dir, currently; NY City Dance Alliance, guest fac, currently. **Honors/Awds:** Presidential Scholar Award for the Arts, 1986; Bessie Award, 1992; Tony Award Nomination for Fosse, 1999. **Special Achievements:** First African-American principal dancer at Amer Ballet Theatre. **Business Addr:** Co-Artistic Director, COMPLEXIONS Contemporary Ballet, c/o Darby & Darby PC, 7 World Trade Ctr, 250 Greenwich St, New York, NY 10007, **Business Phone:** (212)777-7771.*

RICHARDSON, DONNA
Personal trainer, executive director. **Personal:** Born Jan 1, 1962; married Tom Joyner, Jul 29, 2000. **Educ:** Hollins Col, health educ. **Career:** Aerobics instr, 1980; Donnaerobics, 1984; Stay Fit Plus, 1989; ESPN, co-host fitness Pro show, 1992; Donna Richardson LLC, owner, currently. **Orgs:** founder, StayFit Kids; spokesperson, Am Heart Asn; mem, Women's Sports Found Bd trustees; adv bd mem, Boys & Girls Clubs Am. **Special Achievements:** Presidential appointee of President George W. Bush's Council on Physical Fitness and Sports; The author of the best-selling book Let's Get Real: Exercise Your Right To A Healthy Body, 1998; selected by the "Oprah Winfrey Show" as one of the Top 5 Fitness Video Instructors; Also selected by Fitness Magazine as one of their Top 10 Movers And Shakers; has lectured in 40 countries and has been a featured motivational speaker with several national tours including God's Leading Ladies, Sisters In The Spirit and the Pantene Total You. Also entered the Guinness Book of World Records for creating the world's largest line dance, with over 50,000 participants. Has done numerous TV shows. **Business Addr:** Owner, Donna Richardson LLC, 13760 Noel Rd Suite 750, Dallas, TX 75240, **Business Phone:** 800-475-6399.*

RICHARDSON, DR. EARL STANFORD
College administrator. **Personal:** Born Sep 25, 1943, Westover, MD; son of Phillip; married Sheila Bunting; children: Eric. **Educ:** Univ Md, Eastern Shore, BA, 1965; Univ Pa, MS, 1973, EdD, 1976. **Career:** Univ Md, Eastern Shore, exec asst to the chancellor, dir career planning & placement, 1970-75, acting dir admis & reg, 1970-71, exec asst to chancellor, 1975-82; Univ Penn, grad asst sch study coun, 1973-74; Univ Md Syst, asst to pres, 1982-84; Morgan State Univ, pres, 1984-. **Orgs:** Alpha Kappa Mu Hon Soc Int, 1964-65; pres, bd dir, mem, Somerset City Head Start

Prog, 1974-; chap pres, Alpha Phi Alpha Fraternity Inc, 1976-79; pres, Panhellenic Coun Eastern Shore, 1977-79; consult, Col Placement Serv, 1979; Sigma Pi Phi Fraternity Gamma Boule; Md State Bd Higher Educ, 1984-; Goldseker Found, 1985-; Life Bridge; NIH; Baltimore Vision 2030 Comt; Am Coun Educations Comn Int Educ; Goldseker Found; adv bd, Md Educ Coalition; Educ Testing Serv; bd dir, Nat Black Col Alumni Hall Fame Found, 1994; Nat Asn Equal Opportunity Higher Educ; bd mem, Baltimore Symphony Orchestra; bd mem, Greater Baltimore Comt; Alvin Ailey Dance Theater Found Md; Md Bus Round table Educ. **Honors/Awds:** Fel Ford Found, NY, 1972-75; Phi Kappa Phi Hon Soc Int, 1979-; fel Kellogg Found, NY, 1980-83. **Special Achievements:** Written several articles of proposals to merge historically Black institutions with white institutions and on inter-institutional cooperation in higher education. **Military Serv:** USAF, capt, 4 yrs; Commendation Medal, 1970. **Business Addr:** President, Morgan State University, 1700 E Cold Spring Lane 409 Truth Hall, Baltimore, MD 21251, **Business Phone:** (443)885-3200.

RICHARDSON, EDDIE PRICE, JR.
Publisher, editor. **Personal:** Born Mar 29, 1936, Carrollton, MS; son of Eddie Price and Helen; married Katherine Etta Shorter, Apr 5, 1958; children: Karen Lorriane Munds, Angela Renea. **Educ:** Univ Md, human rels, 1958; McNease State Col, sociol, 1968; Lubbock Christian Univ, 1969. **Career:** Univ S Fla, 1954-64; E P Richardson & ASC, mgt consult, 1970-; Lubbock Opports Industrialization Ctr, exec dir, 1970-74; Wyatt's Cafeteria, asst mgr, 1974-76; Lubbock Black Chamber Entrepreneurs, founder, pres, 1977-91; Lubbock Southwest Digest, co-publ & ed, 1977-. **Orgs:** Organizer, June Tenth Celebration Comt, 1981; organizer, Martin Luther King Celebration, 1983; organizer, E Lubbock Develop Asn, 1987; W Tex Black Heritage & Cultural Ctr, founder, 1987; founder, E Lubbock Cent Core Develop Project, 1988; organizer, W Tex Farmers Ctr & Cultural Project, 1988; E Lubbock Affordable Home Res Project, 1991. **Honors/Awds:** Journalism Award, NCP, 1992; Merit Award, Nat Newspaper Award, Advertisement Original, 1983, 1984, 1985; NBC KCBD TV, Electronic Media Assoc, Best Talk Show Host, 1989. **Military Serv:** USF, m sgt, 1954-58, 1958-64; Nat Defense, 1954; Good Conduct; various unit citations, 1958; Bronz Star, 1964. **Business Addr:** Co-Publisher, Lubbock Southwest Digest, 510 E 23rd St, Lubbock, TX 79404.*

RICHARDSON, ELAINE POTTER. **See KINCAID, JAMAICA.**

RICHARDSON, ELISHA R
Educator, dentist. **Personal:** Born Aug 15, 1931, Monroe, LA; married Pattye Whyte (deceased); children: Scott, Jonathan & Mark. **Educ:** Southern Univ, BS, 1951; Meharry Med Col, DDS, 1955; Univ Ill Med Ctr, MS, 1963; Univ Mich & Harvard Univ, attended 1973; Univ Mich, PhD, 1988. **Career:** Sch Dentist, Dept Orthdont, assoc dean & chmn,; Meharry Med Col, Sch Dent, dir res, 1969-78, dean, 1988-92, prof & chmn, Regional Res Ctr, dir, 1992-; Hbrd Hosp, pres med & dent staff, 1971-72; Univ Colo, Div Orthodont, prof & chmn, 1985-. **Orgs:** Chmn, Orthodont Am Asn Dent Sch, 1972-73; pres,Craniofacial Biol, 1978-79; pres elect chmn bd, Nat Dent Asn, 1980; Am Asn Orthdnontist; Am Soc Dent C; Int Asn Dental Res; Am Asn Dental Schs; AAAS; Craniofacial Biol Group; Meharry Alumni Asn; Univ Ill Orthdont Alumni Asn; Am Pub Health Asn; Am Col of Dentists, Alpha Phi Alpha; Nat Asn Advan Colored People; Nashville Urban League; YMCA; Nashville Symphony Asn; Civitan Internat; pres, Nat Dent Asn, 1981; chmn, Coun Educ Am Asn Orthodontists, 1987. **Special Achievements:** One of the 100 Most Influential Black Americans by Ebony Magazine, 1981. **Military Serv:** USAF, capt, 1955-60. **Business Addr:** Director, Meharry Medical College, Regional Research Center, School of Dentistry, 1005 DB Todd Blvd, PO Box 33-A, Nashville, TN 37208, **Business Phone:** (615)771-6365.

RICHARDSON, ERNEST A.
Consultant. **Personal:** Born Aug 2, 1925, New York, NY; married Olive; children: Brenda. **Educ:** Columbia Univ, New York, BA, 1952; New York Univ, MBA, 1958. **Career:** Schnly Indust, acct, 1952-60; Int Pearl Corp, controller, 1960-66; St Regis Corp, mgr minority affairs. **Orgs:** Bd chmn, New York City Task Force Youth Motivation; nat chmn, Nat Urban Affairs Coun; indust chmn, Fisk Univ Cluster; bd adv, Tenn State Univ Cluster; adv com, Nat Task Force Youth Motivation; Black Corp Caucus; adv com, Nat Urban League Skills Bank. **Honors/Awds:** Executive of the Year, Asn Meeting Planners, 1983; Crusade Award, Am Cancer Soc, 1985; Merit Award, St Regis, 1985; Certificate of Appreciation, Nat Urban Affairs Coun, 1987. **Military Serv:** USMC, staff sgt, 1943-46 & 1950-51. **Home Addr:** 18630 Mangin Ave, Jamaica, NY 11412.

RICHARDSON, FRANK
Politician, artist. **Personal:** Born Jan 14, 1950, Baltimore, MD. **Educ:** Md Inst Col Art, AA; Towson St Col, Baltimore, BFA. **Career:** Third World Prep Sch Art, headmaster, 1975; News Am, 1976-; Baltimore's Black Art's Mus, dir, 1976; Enoch Pratt Free Libr Br 17, painter; Phase's Gallery, 1977; Ebony Collective, 1977; Democratic Party, City Coun Baltimore, coun mem, currently. **Orgs:** Black Cult Endowment, 1974; artist fel prog, Md Arts Coun, 1977; Nat Soc Pub Poets. **Special Achievements:** Art show, Univ Ife Bookshop Ltd, Nigeria; African-Am Day Parade, 1976. **Business Addr:** Council Member, City Coun Baltimore, Apt 1A 2624 St Paul St, Baltimore, MD 21218, **Business Phone:** (410)889-8058.

RICHARDSON, FREDERICK D
Government official. **Personal:** Born Sep 4, 1939, Nymph, AL; son of Frederick and Helen; married Ruby, 1959; children: Lawanda Lawson, Lisa & Frederick III. **Educ:** Carver State Voc Col, 1969; Bishop State Community Col, 1971; Univ South Ala, BA, polit sci & hist, 1974. **Career:** Mobile Infirmary Hosp, housekeeper; US Postal Serv, substitute lett carrier, mgr sta & br opers, 1992-; City Mobile, city coun mem dist 1, currently. **Orgs:** Nat League Cities, 1997-; Ala League Cities, 1997-; World Conf Mayors; bd chair, Hist Mus Mobile; Bd Zoning Adjust; exec bd mem, Mobile Tricentennial Inc; Nat Coalition Justice & Equality, nat coord; Exploreum. **Special Achievements:** Author of books: "The Genesis & Exodus of Now", 1978, 1996; "The Stone Street Baptist Church, AL's 1st", 1806-1982; author of plays: "The Birth of a Church". **Home Addr:** 1803 S Indian Creek Dr, Mobile, AL 36607, **Home Phone:** (334)473-3268.

RICHARDSON, GEORGE C
Legislator. **Personal:** Born Feb 19, 1929, Newark, NJ. **Educ:** USAF Admin Sch, grad; Jersey City Tech. **Career:** NJ Gen Assembly, asst minority leader, 1961-. **Orgs:** Chmn, NJ Black Legis Caucus; NJ State Narcotics Div Comn, Inst & Agency; Com Transp & Pub Utilities Sub-Comn Hwy & Com Taxation; pres, Periscope Asn; pres & founder, Nat Comt Declare War Drugs. **Military Serv:** USAF, Korean War. **Business Addr:** Assistant minority leader, New Jersey General Assembly, 21 N Main St, Cape May Court House, NJ 08210, **Business Phone:** (609)465-0700.

RICHARDSON, GILDA FAYE
Government official. **Personal:** Born May 8, 1926, Wichita Falls, TX; married James; children: Linda Moore & Michael Cooper. **Educ:** Southern Univ, attended 1945; Lansing Bus Univ, attended 1946; Mich State Univ, attended 1972. **Career:** Beurmann/Marshall Adv Agency, com photogr, 1965-68; Lansing Sch Dist, pres, 2006. **Orgs:** Bd mem, YWCA, 1967-85; bd mem/guild chairperson, Lansing Urban League,1968-77; mem bd, Lansing Family Health Ctr, 1972; Housing Ast Found, 1973-74; Office Econ Opportunity, 1973-74; Capital Area United Way, 1973-78; secy/bd United Negro Col Fund, 1974-77; mem/secy, 1975-85, pres, 1988, Lansing Bd Ed; Nat Asn Advan Colored People. **Honors/Awds:** Community Service, Nat Asn Negro Bus Prof Women, 1967; Dedicated Service Award, Lansing Urban League, 1973; Dedicated Service Award, Ingham City Comn, 1979; Diana Award Community Service, YWCA, 1980; Multicultural Award Lansing Sch Dist, 1982. **Home Addr:** 3024 Colchester, Lansing, MI 48906. **Business Addr:** Elected Official Secretary, Lansing School District, 519 W Kalamazoo, Lansing, MI 48933.

RICHARDSON, GLOSTER V.
Sports manager, football player, football coach. **Personal:** Born Jul 18, 1942, Greenville, MS; son of Rev Willie Sr and Mary Alice Tompkins; married Bettye Neal, Dec 27, 1966; children: Glasetta & Maury. **Educ:** Jackson State Col, 1965. **Career:** Football player (retired), football coach; Kans City Chiefs, 1967-70; Dallas Cowboys, 1971; Cleveland Browns, 1972-74; instr phys ed; dir & organizer, touch football, Chicago pub Sch, 1990. **Orgs:** Better Boys Found; NFL Retired Players Assn; Mt Carmel high sch Fathers Assn; vpres, Rainbow Bench, 1991-92. **Honors/Awds:** Played in 3 Super Bowl Championships; Football Hall of Fame, Jackson State Univ; NFL Alumni Award, NFL Alumni Assn, 1990-91. **Home Phone:** (312)721-1172.

RICHARDSON, HENRY J.
Educator. **Personal:** Born Mar 24, 1941, Indianapolis, IN; married Renee Poussaint. **Educ:** Antioch Col, AB, 1963; Yale Law Sch, LLB, 1966; Univ Calif, Sch Law, LosAngeles, LLM, 1971. **Career:** Govt Malawi Cent Africa, int legal adv, 1966-68; Maxwell Afro-Asian, fel,1966-68; Maxwell Writing, fel, 1968-69; Univ Calif, Los Angeles, African Studies Ctr, fac africanist law, 1969-71; Univ Calif, Los Angeles, Ford LLM fel, 1969-71; Ind Univ, Sch Law, from asst prof to assoc prof,1971-74, fac res fel, 1973; Northwestern Univ Sch Law, vis assoc prof law,1975-76; Nat Security Coun, staff, 1977-79; Temple Univ, Beasley Sch Law, prof law, currently. **Orgs:** AID Res Team Law & Social Change, 1971; chmn, Int Legal Educ Africa, 1973;exec coun, Am Soc Int Law, 1975-; adv comt, ITT Inter Nat Fel Prog; Am Soc Int Law Working Group Info Systs; chmn, Nat Conf Black Lawyers Task Force Int Affairs; rep, UNNGO; Ind Bar; Nat Conf Black Lawyers; World Peace Through Law Ctr, Sect Int Legal Ed; World Peace Through Law Conf. **Honors/Awds:** Maxwell Afro-Asian Fellowship, 1966-68; Maxwell Writing Fellowship, 1968-69; UCLA-Ford LL.M Fellowship, 1969-71; 1973 Summer Faculty Research Fellowship, Indiana University; Vis Scholar, Temple University Law School, March 1979; Friel-Scanlan Award for Best Faculty Scholarship, Temple Law School, 1997. **Special Achievements:** Author of numerous publications in various legal journals on International Law, African Law & Black People; Henry J Richardson III Award, Temple Univ, named in honor. **Business Addr:** Professor of Law, Temple University, Beasley School of Law, 1719 N Broad St, Philadelphia, PA 19122-2585, **Business Phone:** (215)204-7861.

RICHARDSON, JEROME (POOH RICHARDSON)
Basketball coach, basketball player. **Personal:** Born May 14, 1966, Philadelphia, PA. **Educ:** Univ Calif, Los Angeles, 1989. **Career:** Basketball player (retired), head coach, business owner; Minn Timberwolves, guard, 1989-92, Ind Pacers, guard, 1992-94; Los Angeles Clippers, guard, 1994-99; Maywood Laguneros, Am Basketball Asn, head coach, 2005-. **Honors/Awds:** NBA All-Rookie First Team, 1990. **Business Addr:** Head Coach, Maywood Laguneros, American Basketball Association, 4801 E 58th St, Maywood, CA 90270, **Business Phone:** (323)562-5570.

RICHARDSON, JOHNNY L.
Executive. **Personal:** Born Jul 14, 1952, Cleveland, MS; married Mary Goins; children: Teria D; Rapahelle K. **Educ:** Ripon Col WI, BA, econ, 1974. **Career:** Miller Brewing Co, pricing analyst, 1974-75, merchandising rep, 1975-77, area mgr, 1977-82, reg merchandising mgr, 1982. **Orgs:** Vpres, Nat Urban League, 1981-82; Chicago Merchandiser Exec Club, 1982; grad instr, Dale Carnegie Inst, 1984; dir, Park Ridge Jaycees, 1984-85; Ripon Col Alumni Bd, 1984-87. **Honors/Awds:** Dir of the Yr, Chicago S End Jaycees, 1980; Pres Award, Merit Chicago South-End Jaycees 1982.

RICHARDSON, JOSEPH
Business owner, executive. **Personal:** Born Apr 23, 1940, Kansas City, MO; son of Joseph and Genevieve; married Jacquel. **Educ:** Lincoln Univ, BA, social, 1964; Augsburg Col, Minneapolis, MN, MA, 1989. **Career:** JR & Assocs Inc, pres, 1980; The Toro Co, dir employees relations mgr, 1979-80, corp mgr manpower planning, 1978-79, corp training mgr, 1977-78, corp employment mgr, 1976-77; Mgt Recruiters, acct exec, 1973-76; John Tschohl & Assocs, vpres, 1972-73; Butler Mfg Co, div employee relations mgr, 1970-72; Butler Mfg Co, copr employment rep, 1968-70; Pan Hellenic Coun, pres, 1978-; Minneapolis Coun of Ex-offender Employ, pres, 1979-; Honeywell Inc, sr human resources rep, 1984; Metrop State Univ, community fac mem, currently. **Orgs:** Twin City Personnel Asn, Vietnam Serv; vpres, Gamma Xi Lambda Alpha Phi Alpha Frat, 1977. **Honors/Awds:** Medal-AUS Commedation Medal; Pres Citation Oak Leaf Cluster AUS. **Military Serv:** AUS, capt, 1964-68. **Business Addr:** Community Faculty Member, Metropolitan State University, College of Management, 1501 Hennepin Ave, Minneapolis, MN 55403.

RICHARDSON, DR. LACY FRANKLIN
Executive. **Personal:** Born Apr 8, 1937, Lynhurst, VA; son of Roxie E Richardson Burgess and Lacy Richardson; married Regina L Crick, Mar 1, 1980; children: Darnel, Tina, Dori & Alexander. **Educ:** Ohio Christian Col, BTh, summa cum laude, 1972; Univ Pittsburgh, BA, cum laude, 1976, MSW, 1977; Bible Philos Int Sem, PhD, summa cum laude, 1984. **Career:** US Steel, laborer, 1955-64; Westinghouse Air Brake, tester, 1964; Auburn & Assocs, design draftsman, 1964-68; Kaiser Engs, design draftsman, 1968-72; Mt Zion Baptist Church, West Newton, PA, pastor, 1971-74; Mon Yough Community Servs Inc, dir consult & educ, 1972-85, human resources dir, 1985-; First Baptist Church, Donora, PA, pastor, 1974-78; St John Baptist Church, Wilmerding, PA, pastor, 1979-81; Metrop Baptist Church, Northside, Pittsburgh PA, pastor, 1981-; Dept State Bur Prof & Occup Affairs, pastor. **Orgs:** Bd dirs, Govs Justice Comn; bd dirs, Auberle Home Boys; bd dirs, Coun & Tutoring Serv; McKeesport Area Sch Dist, Parents Adv Coun; Baptist Ministers Conf Pittsburgh & vicinity; vpres, Northside Pastor's Alliances; Nat Asn Advan Colored People; bd dirs, Res & Planning Comt, Mon Valley Health Ctr; Boy Scouts Am, Long Range Study Membership Comt. **Honors/Awds:** Humanitarian Award for Outstanding Achievement, Mon-Yough Community Serv Inc, 1985; Humanitarian Award, Parents Adult Mentally Ill, 1986; Outstanding Employee Award, Mon-Yough Community Serv Inc, 1986; Outstanding Service Award, Auberle Homes Boys, 1987. **Home Addr:** 1501 Libr St, McKeesport, PA 15132, **Home Phone:** (412)673-1750. **Business Addr:** Pastor, Metropolitan Baptist Church, 1225 R St NW, Washington, FL 20009, **Business Phone:** (202)238-5000.

RICHARDSON, LATANYA
Actor. **Personal:** Born Jan 1, 1949?, Atlanta, GA; married Samuel L Jackson; children: Zoe. **Educ:** Spelman Col, BA, theater, 1974; New York Univ, MA, drama. **Career:** Film appearances: Hangin' with the Homeboys, 1991; The Super, 1991; Fried Green Tomatoes, 1991; Lorenzo's Oil, 1992; Juice, 1992; Malcolm X, 1992; Sleepless in Seattle, 1993; The Last Laugh, 1994; When a Man Loves a Woman, 1994; Losing Isaiah, 1995; Lone Star, 1996; Julian Po, 1997; Secrets, 1998; Loved, 1998; US Marshalls, 1998; The Fighting Temptations, 2003; Freedom land, 2006; Blackout, 2007; All About Us, 2007; Tv series: "One Life to Live", 1968; "Life Choice", 1991; "Frannie's Turn", 1992; "Sisters of Mercy", 1992; "Midnight Run for Your Life", 1994; "Private Lives", 1994; "A Memory Play", 1994; "Cutting Edges", 1995; "Heavin' Can Wait", 1995; "Betrayal", 1997; "Call Him Johnny", 1998; "Judg-

ing Amy", 1999; "100 Centre Street",2001; "Chapter Sixty-Two", 2003; tv movies: The Nightman, 1992; Shameful Secrets, 1993; Losing Isaiah, 1995; The Deliverance of Elaine, 1996; Introducing Dorothy Dand ridge, 1999; Within These Walls, 2001; "100 Centre Street", 2002; "Boston Public", 2003. **Honors/Awds:** Frederick D. Patterson Award, United Negro Col Fund. **Business Phone:** (310)281-4868.*

RICHARDSON, LAURA
Congressperson (U.S. federal government). **Educ:** UCLA, Bachelors Degree; USC, Masters Degree. **Career:** Councilwoman; State Government Official; Congressperson. **Orgs:** Committee on Science and Technology. **Special Achievements:** Served local, state, and federal government branches in less than one year's time. **Business Addr:** 2233 Rayburn House Office Building, Washington, DC 20515, **Business Phone:** (202)225-7924.*

RICHARDSON, DR. LEO
Government official, executive director. **Personal:** Born Dec 19, 1931, Marion, SC; son of Ethel Richardson and Isiah Richardson; married Mary Jane Frierson; children: Sandra Jane, Alfred Leo & Beverley Lynette. **Educ:** Morris Col, BS, 1954; Tuskegee Univ, MA, 1961; State Univ New York, Buffalo, PhD, 1985. **Career:** Morris Col, head football & basketball coach, 1961-64; Savannah State Col, head football & basketball coach, 1964-71; State Univ New York, Buffalo, head basketball coach & adminr, 1972-84; SC Dept Social Servs, asst to comnr 1984-86, dep comnr, 1986; South Carolina Inst Poverty & Deprivation, exec dir, currently. **Orgs:** Nat Asn Basketball Coaches, 1971-78; Nat Asn Basketball Coaches Clin Comt, 1974-76; Buffalo Urban Caucus, 1974-78; Black Educr Assoc Buffalo, 1975-76; PUSH Inc, 1976; Nat Assoc Basketball Coaches Res Comn, 1976-78; Comt Action Orgn, educal task force comt, 1977-84; Buffalo Pub Schs, task force on discipline chmn, 1979; sports adv comt chmn, 1979-80; bd dirs, Nat Asn Advan Colored People, 1979-82; pres, Housing Assistance Ctr Niagara Frontier, Inc, 1979-82; chmn, Dept Educ, adv comm for single parents/homemakers & sex equity pgms 1985; bd trustees, Francis Burns United Methodist Church, 1985; Leadership Columbia, 1986; Alpha Phi Alpha Frat; Morris Col Bd Trustees; Leadership SC Bd Regents. **Honors/Awds:** Community Service Staff Award, Univ Buffalo Community Adv Coun, 1983; Community Service Award, Black Educrs Niagara Frontier, 1984-85; Man Year Award, Alpha Phi Alpha, 1987. **Military Serv:** AUS specialist third class. **Home Addr:** 241 King Charles Rd, Columbia, SC 29209. **Business Addr:** Executive Director, South Carolina Institute on Poverty and Deprivation, 2219 Two Notch Rd, PO Box 86, Columbia, SC 29202, **Business Phone:** (803)256-7219.

RICHARDSON, LEON
Manager. **Personal:** Born Dec 1, 1964, Nashville, GA; son of Joe Lee King; married Alfreda, Aug 24, 1991; children: Demetrius Leon. **Educ:** Stillman Col, BA, 1987. **Career:** Shaw Industs, prod supvr, 1987, human resources supv, 1993, training mgr, 1990, regional human resources mgr, 1997, corp employee resources mgr, currently. **Orgs:** Kappa Alpha Psi, dean pledges, 1985; Big Brother Big Sister, 1997; Dr MLK Comt Serv, 1997. **Honors/Awds:** Stillmam CLG, Dean's List, 1984-86. **Business Addr:** Manager, Shaw Industries Inc, 616 E Walnut Ave, Dalton, GA 30721, **Business Phone:** (706)278-3812.

RICHARDSON, LEROY
Manager. **Personal:** Born Aug 21, 1964, Brooklyn, NY. **Career:** NBA, referee, currently. **Orgs:** Mentor, speaker, Tidewater Detention Ctr, Chesapeake, VA; Youth Ministries New First Baptist Church, Portsmouth, VA; Nat Basketball Referees Asn. **Honors/Awds:** Sailor of the Year, Training Group Atlantic, 1991-92; United States Navy Sailor of the Year, Damneck, VA, 1991-92; Navy Achievement Medal-Surface warfare qualification, 1992-93; Officiated 2003 NBA All-Star Saturday Game and 2003 Japan Games; Officiated the 2000 Schick Rookie Game. **Military Serv:** USN, 12Yrs. **Business Addr:** Member, NBA Referee, National Basketball Referees Association, The Willard Offices, 1455 Pennsylvania Ave NW Suite 225, Washington, DC 20004, **Business Phone:** (202)638-5090.

RICHARDSON, LINDA WATERS
Consultant, executive. **Personal:** Born Nov 21, 1946, Philadelphia, PA; daughter of Lester Waters and Bertha Stovall; married Albert J Pitts; children: Aissia, Tarik, Monifa & Mariama. **Educ:** Overbrook HS, Bus, 1964; New Hampshire Col, MS, 1990. **Career:** BEDC Inc, asst dir, 1971-73; Peoples Fund, coord, 1973-74; Philadelphia Clearing House, dir, 1974-81; Black United Fund, exec dir, 1982-89, pres & chief exec officer, 1989-. **Orgs:** Nat Black United Fund, 1983-89; Willingboro Home & Sch, 1986; adv comt, Episcopal Community Serv; Interfaith Revolving Loan Fund; Women in Philanthropy; Asn Black Found Execs. **Honors/Awds:** Merit Chapel 4 Chaplains, 1985; Community Leadership Award, Comm Leadership Seminars, 1985; Minority Mental Health Advocacy Task Force Award, 1989. **Business Phone:** (215)236-2100.

RICHARDSON, LITA RENEE (LITA SPENCER)
Manager, lawyer. **Personal:** Born Nov 24, 1964, San Diego, CA; daughter of Victor and Barbara Nason; married Leonard, Dec 5, 1993; children: Abi Olajuwon & Lauren. **Educ:** Rice Univ, BA, 1986; Univ Houston, Bates Sch Law, JD, 1988. **Career:** Judge Michael O'Brien, law clerk, 1986-88; Brown, Collett & Pryce, atty, 1990-91; Reed & Assoc, atty, 1992-97; Magic Johnson Mgt Group, ent vpres, 1997-. **Orgs:** La County Bar Assoc, 1990-; Alpha Kappa Alpha Sorority, 1983-; State Bar Calif, 1990-; Black Child Development Inst, 1992-; Black Women Lawyers Assoc, 1990-; Women Film, 1998-. **Special Achievements:** Manage the careers of over 20 television & film personalities; NASA Space Ctr, student intern, 1981. **Business Phone:** (310)247-2033.

RICHARDSON, LONNEAL
Administrator. **Career:** Salvation Army Midland Div, St Louis, MO, comdr, currently.

RICHARDSON, LOUIS M, JR.
Government official, clergy. **Personal:** Born Nov 7, 1927, Johnstown, PA; son of Lewis and Leatha Elizabeth Hemphill; married Allie; children: April, Louis III, Emmett, Alan T, Hope C, Peter & Holly A. **Educ:** Livingstone Col, BA, 1955; Hood Theol Sem NC, BD, 1958. **Career:** First AME Church, minister, 1964-; NJ State Employ Serv, counr, 1967-70; Paterson Bd Educ, vpres, 1969-74; OIC, pres, 1970-71; Martin Luther King Comm Ctr, dir, 1970-73; Paterson CETA Prog, dir, 1973-76; City Paterson City Hall, affirmative action coordr; Varick Mem A M E Zion Church, pastor. **Orgs:** Paterson Rotary No 70, 1970-74; pres, Alpha Phi Alpha Frat. **Honors/Awds:** Citizenship Award, Paterson Teachers Asn, 1971. **Business Addr:** Pastor, Varick Memorial A. M. E. Zion Church, 120 Atlantic St, Hackensack, NJ 07601, **Business Phone:** (201)343-8240.

RICHARDSON, DR. LUNS C
Educator. **Personal:** Born Apr 29, 1928, Hartsville, SC. **Educ:** Bendict Col, AB, 1949; Columbia Univ Teachers Col, MA, 1958. **Career:** Denmark Tech Educ Ctr, dean, 1949-64; St Helena HS, prin, 1964-66; Wilson HS, prin, 1966-67; Benedict Col, staff & acting pres, 1967-73; Voorhees Col, vpres, 1973-74; Morris Col, pres, 1974-. **Orgs:** Chmn, Com Res & Spec Proj, Southern Assoc Cols & Schs; bd dirs, SC State C C; bd dir Sumter C C; Wateree Comt Actions Bd; adv bd, Citizens & Southern Bank Sumter; Omega Psi Phi Frat, NAACP, NEA, AAHE, Am Acad Polit & Social Sci, SC Educ Assoc, Sumter Co Econ Develop Admin Com, Sumter Human Rels Coun; NAACP; Alpha Kappa Mu Honor Soc; Phi Delta Kappa.; SC Higher Educ Tuition Grants Comn. **Honors/Awds:** Hon Ped D Benedict Col; Hon LHD Morris Col; Citation Links Inc, 1973; Citation Voorheez Col BD Trustees, 1974; Outstanding Alumnus Award, Benedict Col; Outstanding Alumnus Award, Columbia Univ, Teachers Col; Order of the Palmetto, conferred Gov Beasley, 1996; SC Black Hall of Fame, 1997; named one 60 "20th Century Press Who Have Influenced Higher Edu Landscape," Black Issues Higher Educ, 1999. **Business Addr:** President, Morris College, 100 W College St, Sumter, SC 29150-3599, **Business Phone:** (803)934-3200 Ext 3211.

RICHARDSON, DR. MADISON FRANKLIN
Surgeon. **Personal:** Born Dec 26, 1943, Prairie View, TX; son of Dr William; married Constance; children: Kelly, Kimberly & Karen. **Educ:** Howard Univ, BS, 1965, MD, 1969; Am Bd Otolaryngol, Cert. **Career:** Walter Reed Hosp, chief, head & neck surg, 1974-76; Martin Luther King Hosp, chief head & neck surg, 1977-; Voice Inst Beverly Hills; Otolaryngol Specialist, pvt pract, currently. **Orgs:** Bd chair, Los Angeles Urban League, 1984-87; pres, Charles Drew Med Soc, 1984-85; chief surg serv, Daniel Freeman Hosp, 1986-87; pres bd chair, Nat Urban League, 1986; Calif Medical Bd, 1987-; bd dir, Charles Drew Med Sch, 1988; bd dir, Salerni Collegium; Alpha Omega. **Honors/Awds:** Member of Distinction, Los Angeles AME Church, 1982; Meritorious Award, La NAACP, 1983; Distinguished Alumnus, Howard Univ, 1987; Appointee of Governor to California Medical Board, 1988. **Military Serv:** AUS, Lt col, 1968-77. **Business Addr:** Surgeon, Otolaryngology Specialist, 8500 Wilshire Blvd Suite 908, Beverly Hills, CA 90211-3107, **Business Phone:** (310)360-9520.

RICHARDSON, MARY MARGARET
School administrator. **Personal:** Born Feb 19, 1932, Christian County, KY. **Educ:** Ky Community Col, Hopkinsville, AA, 1970; Valdosta State Col, BSN, 1973; Med Col Ga, MSN, mental health & psychol nursing, 1974; Univ Southern Miss, EdD, 1994. **Career:** Educator (retired); Brooks Hosp, officer nurse, 1952-72; Western Ky State Ment Hosp, clin nurse, 1956-71; Jennie Stuart Mem Hosp, pvt duty nurse, 1970-71; Col Manor Hosp, part time head nurse, 1974-75; Univ N Ala Florence, Sch Nursing, asst prof, 1974-75; Med Col, Grad Sch Nursing, Augusta, GA, asst prof, 1975; Valdosta State Col, asst prof nursing, 1975-78, assoc prof nursing, 1978-80, asst dir nursing, dept head, undergrad studies, asst dean. **Orgs:** Nat League Nursing; Am Nursing Asn; Ga League Nursing; Ga Nurses Asn; Ky Fed LPN; Am Asn Univ Prof; Am Asn Univ Women; task force leader, Fac Develop Proj, SREB Valdosta State; Sigma Theta Tau, Epsilon Pi Chap. **Honors/Awds:** Fed Traineeship Scholar, 1973.

RICHARDSON, MATTHEW STATISFIELD. **See RICH, MATTY.**

RICHARDSON, MUNRO CARMEL
Consultant, executive. **Personal:** Born Jul 24, 1971, Pittsburgh, PA; son of Frederick and Dianna; married Teresa Hu, Sep 9, 1995; children: Melina & Kera. **Educ:** Univ Kans, BA, 1993; Harvard Univ, MA, 1995; Oxford Univ, masters, philos, 1996. **Career:** Sen Nancy Kassebaum, legis asst, 1996-97; Sen Joseph Biden, Foreign Rels Comn, prof staff mem, 1997-98; Greater Kans City Community Found, mgr community leadership, 1998-2000; Inner City Consul Group, managing dir, 2000-01; BCT Partners Inc, founding mem & pres; Kauffman Scholars Inc, deputy dir; Kauffman Legacy Found, dir, currently. **Orgs:** NAACP; bd dirs, United Inner City Serv, 2000-; City Plan Comn, City Kans City, MO, 2000-01; bd secy, Hispanic Econ Develop Corp, 2000-; bd, Int Rels Coun, 2000-; Phi Beta Kappa. **Honors/Awds:** National Achievement Scholar, Nat Merit Corp, 1989; Golden Key, Golden Key Nat Hon Soc, 1992; Rhodes Scholar, Rhodes Trust, 1994; Up and Comers Award, Junior Achievement of Greater Kansas City, 2000. **Business Addr:** Director, Ewing Marion Kauffman Found, 4801 Rockhill Rd, Kansas, MO 64110, **Business Phone:** (816)932-1000.

RICHARDSON, NOLAN
Basketball coach, basketball player. **Personal:** Born Dec 27, 1941, El Paso, TX; married Rose; children: Madalyn, Bradley, Nolan III, Yvonne (deceased) & Sylvia. **Educ:** Univ Tex, El Paso, BA, 1964. **Career:** Basketball player (retired), basketball coach; Texas Western, forward, 1960-64; Bowie High Sch El Paso, TX, coach; Western Tex Jr Col; Univ Tulsa, head coach, 1981-85; Univ Ark, head basketball coach, 1985-2002; Panamanian National Team, head coach, 2005-07; Mexican National Team, head coach, 2007-. **Orgs:** Bd dir, Am Red Cross; chmn, Easter Seal. **Honors/Awds:** Nat Coach of the Year, 1994. **Special Achievements:** First black student to attend El Paso's Bowie High School; Second African-American coach to win the NCAA title, 1994; only head coach to win a Junior College National Championship, the NIT, and the NCAA Tournament.

RICHARDSON, ODIS GENE
Writer, educator. **Personal:** Born Nov 29, 1940, Lakes Charles, LA; son of Lucky Sip and Estella Scott; children: Ron Pressley & Odis G II. **Educ:** Univ Tampa, BS, 1965; Chicago State Univ, MA, 1971; Roosevelt Univ, MS, 1983; Northwestern Univ, postgrad studies. **Career:** Educator (retired), writer; Boy Scouts Am, exec, 1965-66; Dept Pub Assistance, social caseworker, 1966-67; Chicago Pub Sch, teacher, 1967-, free lance writer, currently. **Orgs:** Chicago Debate Comn(CRS), 1998, Small Schs Movement, DuSable Urban Ecol Sanctuary Bd; pub rels chmn, Ill Speech & Theatre Asn, 1985-86; pres bd dirs, Maranatha Youth Ministries, 1985-87; fel, Northwestern Univ, 1986; IL Coun Exceptional C; dir, Richardson Special Educ Consultants; Phi Beta Sigma, Phi Delta Kappa, Chicago Urban League, NAACP; deacon South Shore Bible Baptist Church; Emergency Land Fund; bd dirs, Chicago Citizens Schs Comt, 1987-89; fel, Golden Apple Found, life mem, 1986-89; res linker, Chicago Teacher's Union, Educ Res & Develop; vol proj Image, Man-Boy Conf,1988-89; precinct captain, Fourth Ward Reg Dem, 1981-; teacher sponsor, PAPPA Club, Pan African Pen Pal Asn, 1988-89; writer & diarist, Catalyst Magazine-Chicago Sch Reform, 1990-91; bd dirs, Don Nash Community Ctr; bd dirs, Marantha Youth Ministries Head Start. **Honors/Awds:** DuSable Man of the Year, DuSable High Sch, Chicago, 1985; S Shore Outstanding Community Vol, 1986; Golden Apple Award, 986; Leadership, Ill Coun Exceptional C, 1989; Vol, DuSable Mus African-Am Hist, 1987; Vol Award, Pace Inst, Cook County (Jail) Dept Corrections, 1979; Celebration of Excellence in Teaching-Organizer, 1991; Blum-Kolner Outstanding Teacher Award, Univ Chicago; Small Schools Award, 1996. **Special Achievements:** Featured on the Home Show (Natl TV); Student Cultural Exchange Program; Proposal Writer School granted over 1 million dollars from proposals; Educator of the Month-Jan 91, Coca Cola Bottling Co, 1991. **Military Serv:** USAF, A/2C admin spec 4 yrs; Distinguished Airman Award. **Home Addr:** 8108 S Eberhart, Chicago, IL 60619, **Home Phone:** (773)846-9473.

RICHARDSON, OLYMPIA SCOTT. **See SCOTT, OLYMPIA RANEE.**

RICHARDSON, OTIS ALEXANDER
Executive. **Personal:** Born Jan 16, 1943, Newport News, VA; son of Mildred C and Carey D; married Corrine Foots, Dec 4, 1965; children: Otis Alexander II & Shamagne Nicole. **Educ:** Hampton Univ, BS, acct & finance, 1965; Pace Univ, MBA, exec mgt, 1978; Kennedy-Western Univ, PhD, bus admin, 1999. **Career:** Johnson & Johnson, nat sales mgr, 1979-80, dir sales planning & develop, 1980-82, dir prof markets, 1982-83, dir new prod develop, 1983-85, group product dir, 1985-86; Oral Health USA Inc, pres & chief exec officer, 1986-. **Orgs:** Nat Asn Accts, 1965-72; Am Acad Dent Group Practices, 1981-89; steering comt, Nat Asn Dent Labs, 1985-86; corp sponsor, Nat Dent Asn, 1986-92; Dent Group Mgt Asn, 1987-90. **Honors/Awds:** Clinician Commerative Award, Nat Dent Asn, 1983; Clinician Commerative Award, MAC Dent Technol, 1985. **Special Achievements:** Numerous articles and seminars including Clinical Marketing Techniques for Dental Labs, 1984-86; Practice Building for Dental Groups, 1980-84; "Make That Dental Center Your New Account," Dental Lab Review, 1986; State of Art-Dental Restoratives, 1990; Presentation & Seminar, Use of Color in Dentistry, 1991. **Military Serv:** AUS, Capt, 1966-68. **Home Addr:** 32 Coventry Circle, Piscat-

away, NJ 08854, **Home Phone:** (732)572-4308. **Business Addr:** President, Chief Executive Officer, Oral Health USA Inc, 44 Stelton Rd Suite 200, Piscataway, NJ 08854, **Business Phone:** (732)424-3435.

RICHARDSON, POOH. See RICHARDSON, JEROME.

RICHARDSON, RALPH H
Lawyer. **Personal:** Born Oct 12, 1935, Detroit, MI; son of Ralph Onazime and Lucinda Fluence; divorced; married Arvie Yvonne (deceased); children: Traci, Theron (deceased), Cassandra Jo Williams, Arvie Lyn Williams & Tanya Elaine Hunter. **Educ:** Wayne St Univ, BA, 1964; Wayne St Law Sch, JD, 1970. **Career:** City Detroit, clerk, pub aid worker, 1956-65; Ford Motor Co, sr labor rel rep, 1965-70, wage admin, 1966, labor rel rep, 1967; Citizens Urban Opportunity Fund, dir, 1970; Brown Grier & Richardson PC, sr partner, 1970-71; Richardson & Grier PC, sr partner, 1971-73; Stone & Richardson PC, labor arbitrator & sr partner, 1973-. **Orgs:** Wolverine Bar Asns; Am Arbitration Asn; Mich Trial Lawyers Asn; Am Judicial Soc; MI Criminal Defense Lawyers; Phi Alpha Delta, Kappa Alpha Psi; Smithsonian Inst; Nat Geographic Soc; Recorder's Ct Bar Asn; Labor Arbitrators; Am Arbitration Asn; Thirty-Third degree Mason; Grtr Detroit Chamber Com; Palmer Woods Asn; Econ Club Detroit; Renaissance Club; Detroit Bar Asn, Nat Bar Asn, State Bar Mich, Am Bar Asn, Am Trial Lawyers Asn, MI Asn Prof, Boy Scouts Am, Jr Vice Polemarch Northern Reg; appointed by Gov to serve on bd appeals for Hosp Bed Reduction in SE Mich 1982; appointed spec asst atty Gen by Frank J Kelley, Atty Gen for State Mich 1984; exec bd, Detroit Golden Gloves Inc; bd dir, Legal Aid & Defenders Asn 5; past master, Hiram Lodge #1 1986; comdr-in-chief, Wolverine Consistory #6 1988; Marracci Temple #13, past potenate, past imperial potentate, imperial legal adv, Shriners, 1988; David Leary Lodge #6, GEM, knight templar, 1989; Optomist Club, 1990-; Mich State Bar Fellow, 1990-; past eminent comdr, Eureka Comdry #1 Knights Templars, 1995; past most eminent grand comdr, Grand Comdry Knights Templars for State MI, 1997; past grand sr deacon most worthy Grand Lodge Stat MI, Prince Hall Affiliation (PHA). **Honors/Awds:** Cert of Appreciation Native Am Strategic Serv, 1976; MI State Bar Young Lawyers Sect Prison Project Service Award, 1977; Award of Merit Mother Waddles Perpetual Mission, 1979; Distinguished Recognition Award, Detroit City Coun, 1981; Spirit of Detroit Award, 1981, Honored Citizen Award, Mayor Coleman Young, Distinguished Detroit Citizen Award, 1981; Office of the City Clerk James Bradley, 1981; life membership, NAACP, 1983; contributing supporter Golden Heritage (NAACP), 1989; appointed to committee on Child Care Homes by City Council member Mehaffey, 1988-89; honorary special agent, office of Inspector General, US Printing Office, 1997. **Military Serv:** AUS, sp4, 1958-60. **Business Addr:** Labor Arbitrator, Sr Partner, Stone & Richardson PC, 2910 E Jefferson Ave, Detroit, MI 48207-4208, **Business Phone:** (313)393-6700.

RICHARDSON, RHONDA KAREN
Government official. **Personal:** Born Dec 8, 1956, Louisville, KY; daughter of Charles Robert and Dorothy Bryant. **Educ:** Fisk Univ, Nashville, TN, BA, psychol; Univ Louisville, JD, 1987. **Career:** City Louisville, 10th Ward alderman, 1990-; pvt pract, atty, currently. **Business Addr:** Attorney, Private Practitioner, 934 S 6th St, Louisville, KY 40203-3318, **Business Phone:** (502)584-8861.

RICHARDSON, ROBERT EUGENE
Lawyer. **Personal:** Born Jul 16, 1941, Kansas City, MO; son of Joseph and Genevieve; married Shirley Ann Durham; children: Kerri L & Patrick G. **Educ:** Rockhurst Col, KC, MO, 1962; Georgetown Univ, Wash, DC, AB, 1972; Georgetown Univ Law Sch, JD, 1975. **Career:** Georgetown Univ, asst exec vpres, 1970-74; US Gen Serv, asst legal policy coordr, 1975-76; US Dept Justice, trial atty, 1976-78; US Dept Justice, spec asst asst atty gen, 1978; Civil Div US Dept Justice, sr trial atty, 1979-85; Howard Univ, exec asst vpres legal affairs & gen coun, 1985-86, pvt pract, atty, 1986-94; US Dept Veterans Affairs, atty. **Orgs:** Alpha Phi Alpha Fraternity. **Honors/Awds:** Academic Fellow Whitney M Young, 1973-75. **Military Serv:** AUS, capt, 1963-70; USAR, 1970-84. **Home Addr:** 1371 Underwood St NW, Washington, DC 20012, **Home Phone:** (202)726-3131.

RICHARDSON, ROGER GERALD
School administrator, educator. **Personal:** Born Dec 23, 1953, Chicago, IL; son of Eddie and Ella Brown. **Educ:** Univ Wis-Stout, BA, psychol, 1976, cousel & guid, 1979; New York Univ, PhD, higher educ admin & planning. **Career:** Univ Wis-Stout, coordr, educ & culturals enrichment ctr, 1976-79, dir, black stud servs, 1979-80; Col Human Ecol, Cornell Univ, admin mgr, counr, 1980-84, acting dir, coun servs, assoc dir minority educ affairs & state progs 1984-85; Dartmouth Col, asst dean residential life, 1986-88; NY Univ, dir, African-Am Stud Serv, 1988-; Ithaca Col, dir off multicultural affairs, 2000-, assoc vpres acad & stud affairs, dean first-yr experience; educ policy fel, Inst Higher Educ Leadership, Wash, DC. **Orgs:** Am Asn Higher Educ; Col Stud Personnel Asn; Nat Asn Stud Personnel Adminr; One Hundred Black Men Inc; chmn, Affirmative Action Task Force; Educ Opprtunity Adv Bd, Cornell; Chancellor's Task force on Diversity Conflict Stud Life Comt, New york Univ. **Honors/Awds:** Outstanding Alumni Award, 1992. **Business Addr:** Associate Vice President & Dean, Director of Office of Multicultural Affairs, Ithaca College, Student Affairs Campus Life, 324 Egbert Hall 953 Danby Rd, Ithaca, NY 14850.

RICHARDSON, SALLI (SALLI ELISE RICHARDSON)
Actor. **Personal:** Born Nov 23, 1967, Chicago, IL; married Dondre T Whitfield, Jan 1, 2002; children: Parker Richardson Whitfield. **Career:** Kuumba Workshop, actor; Film appearances: Mo' Money, 1992; Prelude to A Kiss, 1992; How U Like Me Now, 1993; Sioux City, 1994; Posse; A Low Down Dirty Shame, 1994; Once Upon a Time When We Were Colored, 1996; The Great White Hype, 1996; Rude Awakening, 1998; Butter, 1998; Lillie, 1999; Book of Love, 2002; The Antwone Fisher Story, 2002; Baby of the Family, 2002; Biker Boyz, 2003; tv guest appearances: Roc, 1991; Star Trek: Deep Space Nine, 1993; New York Undercover, 1994; Stargate SG-1, 1997; The Pretender, 1998; "The Jamie Foxx Show," 1999; "True Women," 1997; "Gargoyles," 1994-96; Rude Awakening, 1998; Family Law, 1999-2002; TV films: I Spy Returns, 1994; Lily in Winter, 1994; Soul of the Game, 1996; True Women, 1997; "Rude Awakening", 1998; Antwone Fisher, 2002; "CSI: Miami", 2003; "NYPD Blue", 2004; "1-800-Missing", 2005; "The War at Home", 2005; "Eureka," 2006; "Bones," 2006; "I Am Legend,: 2007; Co Host: "Midnight Soul", 2007. **Business Addr:** Actress, Craig Dorfman & Associates, 6100 Wilshire Blvd Suite 310, Los Angeles, CA 90048, **Business Phone:** (323)937-8600.

RICHARDSON, SALLI ELISE. See RICHARDSON, SALLI.

RICHARDSON, TIMOTHY L
Association executive. **Personal:** Born Jul 28, 1958, Los Angeles, CA; son of Irving Berlin and Christeale Dandridge; children: Camille & Bradley. **Educ:** West Los Angeles Col, AA, 1980; Chapman Univ, Orange, CA, BS, bus admin & mkt, 1986. **Career:** Boys & Girls Club Tustin, CA, prog dir, 1980-85; Boys & Girls Clubs Am, N Hollywood, CA, Olympic Sport Prog, coord, 1985-89, New York, NY, Atlanta, GA, Nat Prog Servs, asst dir, 1989-94, dir, 1994-96, sr dir, 1997-; Sports Spirit Newspaper, founding ed, 1987-90. **Orgs:** Exec comt, US Table Tennis Asn, 1986-91; deleg, US Olympic Acad XI, 1987; bd mem, USS Olympic Comt, 1989-; Athlete Identification & Develop Comn, 1990-93, bd dirs, Women's Sports Found, 1990-95; head US deleg, Int Olympic Acad, Olympia Greece, 1992; panelist, Nat Strategic Planning Forum, 1993; Educ Comt, 1993-; consult, Asn Better Zambian Youth Proj, 1993; asst envoy, Centennial Olympic Games, 1996; assoc, Cult Enrichment Found; Pres Coun Phys Fitness & Sports; consult, Jackie Joyner Kersee Youth Found; consult, Southern Christian Leadership Conf; consult, Inkanta Freedom Party Youth Brigade. **Honors/Awds:** Coach of the Year, Nat Youth Sports Coaches Asn, 1983; Womens Sports Found President Award, 1995. **Special Achievements:** NIKE Kids Movement Summit, organizer, 1993; Secured a $3 million congressional grant to serve children of Desert Storm war; author, Boys and Girls Club Guide to Military Outreach; negotiated with US Air Force, Marine Corps & Navy to convert on-base youth centers into Boys and Girls Clubs, 1995-96; Nike Youth Sports Summit, organizer, 1996; NIKE PLAY Daily, Nat Youth Fitness Prog, cocreator & proj mgr; US Information Agency. **Business Addr:** Senior Director Program Service, Boys & Girls Clubs of America, National program services, 1230 W Peachtree St, Atlanta, GA 30309, **Business Phone:** (404)815-5759.

RICHARDSON, TONY (ANTONIO RICHARDSON)
Football player. **Personal:** Born Dec 17, 1971, Frankfurt, Germany; son of Ben Richardson. **Educ:** Auburn Univ, BEd, 2000; Webster Univ, MBA, 2004. **Career:** Kansas City Chiefs, running back, 1995-2005; Minn Vikings, running back, 2006-07; New York Jets, forward back, 2008-; Off season Player, Dallas Cowboys, 1996. **Orgs:** Derrick Thomas Acad; founder, Rich Spirit Found, 2000; chmn, Buck Buchanan Spec Olympics Sports Festival, 2000; Good Guys Sports, The Sporting News, 2002, 2003, 2004; exec comt, Nat Football League Players Asn. **Honors/Awds:** Nominated for NFL Man of te Year Award, 2002; Arthur S Arkush Humanitarian of the Year, Pro Football Weekly, 2003; second-team All-Pro hons, AP, 2004; Distinguished Citizen Award, Nat Conf Community & Justice, 2005; Pro Bowl, 2007. **Special Achievements:** Spokesperson for various prog. **Business Addr:** Forward Back, New York Jets, 1000 Fulton Ave, Hempstead, NY 11550-1099, **Business Phone:** (516)560-8100.

RICHARDSON, VALERIE K.
Financial manager, manager. **Personal:** Born Aug 5, 1955, Oakland, CA; daughter of Clyde Sr and Clarice; married Victor E Richardson II, Feb 14, 1981; children: Whitney K & Victor E III. **Educ:** San Jose State Univ, BA, 1981. **Career:** Ketchum Communs, res asst, 1978-81; Mc Kesson CRP, project mgr, 1982-86; Mervyn's CRP, media/mkt planner, 1986-87; Pacific Gas & Electric CPN, mkt analyst, 1988-, evaluation/qual control specialist, 1991-2007; KEMA Inc, sr prin consult, 2007-. **Orgs:** Am Asn Blacks in Energy; Am Mkt Asn; chair, Vermont Pub Serv Bd.

RICHARDSON, WALTER T.
Clergy. **Personal:** Born Jul 2, 1948; son of Walter H and Poseline M Richardson. **Career:** St Thomas Univ, adj prof; Miami-Dade Police Dept, chaplain; Home Missionary Baptist Church, Perrine, FL, sr pastor, 1983-. **Special Achievements:** Author, Going through Samaria, 1999. **Business Addr:** Senior Pastor, Sweet Home Missionary Baptist Church, 17201 SW 103rd Ave, Miami, FL 33157.

RICHARDSON, WAYNE MICHAEL
Lawyer. **Personal:** Born Sep 22, 1948, Philadelphia, PA. **Educ:** Cheyney State Col, BA, 1970; Temple Univ Law Sch, JD, 1976. **Career:** Pa Dept Educ, regional legal coun, 1976-83; Pa State Syst Higher Educ, chief legal coun, 1983-95; Rutgers Univ, Dept Gen Servs, asst coun, 1995-96; Fairleigh Dickinson Univ, gen coun & secy, currently. **Orgs:** Alpha Phi Alpha Fraternity Inc, 1968-; bd dir, Nat Asn Col & Univ Attys, 1977-. **Honors/Awds:** Distinguished Service Award, Bd Trustees, Pa Fac Health & Welfare Trust Fund, 1995; Distinguished Service Award, Comn Univs, Pa State System Higher Educ, 1995; Distinguished Service Award, United Cerebral Palsy Asn Capital Area, 1996; Citation, Nat Asn Col & Univ Attys, 2002. **Home Addr:** 688 Cranbury Cross Rd, North Brunswick, NJ 08902-2806. **Business Addr:** General Counsel, Secretary, Fairleigh Dickinson University, Office of General Counsel, 1000 River Rd H-DH3-03, Teaneck, NJ 07666, **Business Phone:** (201)692-7071.

RICHIE, DR. BETH E.
College teacher. **Educ:** Cornell Univ, Ithaca, NY, BSW, 1979; Wash Univ, St Louis, MO, MSW, 1980; Grad Sch & Univ Ctr, City Univ New York, New York, NY, PhD, sociol, 1992. **Career:** Inter Am Univ, San Juan, Dept Sociol, adj instr, 1983-84; City Univ NY, Hunter Col, Prog Community Health Educ, from adj instr to instr, 1984-91, Prog Community Health Educ, from asst prof to assoc prof, 1992-98,Undergrad Prog Community Health Educ, prog dir, 1993-94; Winston Churchillfel, 1987; New Sch Social Res, Grad Fac Polit & Social Sci, NY, vis fac, 1993; Univ Ill, Chicago, IL, Women's Health Policy fel, 1994, Ctr Res Women & Gender, fel, 1994-95, Depts Criminal Justice & Gender & WomenStudies, assoc prof, 1998-2002, Great Cities Inst, fac scholar, 2001-02, Dept African-Am Studies, head & assoc prof, 2002- 03, Dept African-AmStudies, head & prof, 2003-. **Orgs:** Ctr Fathers, Families & Pub Policy; Chicago Found Women; Chicago Black Feminist Network; mentor, Women Community Serv, US Dept Health & Human Servs, Violence Against Women Grants Review Panel; Mortar Bd Honor Soc,1979; nominated, Asn Outstanding Black Women, 1985. **Honors/Awds:** Flora Rose Award, Cornell Univ, 1980; Vision Award, Violence Intervention Prog, 1998; Audre Lorde Leadership Award, 2000; Women Year Award, Chicago Nat Orgn Women, 2003; Advocacy Award, Vagina Monologues, 2004. **Business Phone:** (312)355-2468.*

RICHIE, LEROY C.
Lawyer, executive. **Personal:** Born Sep 27, 1941, Buffalo, NY; son of Leroy C and Mattie Allen; married Julia C Thomas, Jun 10, 1972; children: Brooke, Darcy. **Educ:** City Col NY, BA, 1970; NY Univ Sch Law, JD, 1973. **Career:** White & Case NY, atty, 1973-78; Fed Trade Comns NY Off, dir, 1978-83; Chrysler Corp, asst gen coun, 1983-84, assoc gen coun, 1984-86, vpres & gen coun, 1990-97, bd dirs, 1998-; Infinity Inc, bd dir, 1999-; Intrepid World Commun, pres, 1998-99; Capitol Coating Technol Inc, chmn & chief exec officer, 1999-00; Q Standards World Wide Inc, chmn & chief exec officer, 2000-; Kerr-McGee Corp, dir, 1998-, chair audit comt, 2003-; bd dirs, J.W. Seligman & Co, 2000-; Digital Ally, lead outside dir, 2005-. **Orgs:** Chmn, Vis Nurse Asn; chmn, Highland Park Develop Corp; bd mem, Marygrove Col; bd mem, St Josephs Hosp, Pontiac; bd mem, Detroit Bar Found; gen coun, US Golf Asn; secy, Detroit's Mus African American Hist; officer, Detroit Black Chamber Com. **Honors/Awds:** Valedictorian, City Col NY, 1970; Arthur Garfield Hays Civil Liberties Fellow, NY Univ Law Sch, 1972. **Special Achievements:** Only African American in the top ranks of the giant Detroit automaker, Chrysler Corp; first African American to serve as general counsel to the Executive Committee of the US Golf Asn. 1992. **Military Serv:** AUS, sp4, 4 yrs. **Business Addr:** Lead Outside Director, Digital Ally Inc., 4831 W 136th St Suite 300, Leawood, KS 66224, **Business Phone:** (913)814-7774.*

RICHIE, LIONEL BROCKMAN, JR.
Songwriter, actor, singer. **Personal:** Born Jun 20, 1950, Tuskegee, AL; son of Lionel Brockman Sr (deceased) and Alberta Foster; married Diane Alexander, Dec 25, 1995 (divorced 2004); children: Miles Brockman & Sofia; married Brenda Harvey, 1975 (divorced 1993); children: Nicole. **Educ:** Tuskegee Univ, attended 1974. **Career:** The Mystics; The Commodores; Brockman Music, Los Angeles, CA, pres; Songs: "Truly", writer & producer, 1982; "All Night Long", 1983; "Hello", 1984; "Say You, Say Me", writer & producer, 1985, "Are We Done Yet?", 2007; "Lady", writer & producer; "All Night Long", writer & producer; "Can't Slow Down"; writer & producer; "Dancing on the Ceiling", writer & producer; "Easy", writer & producer; "Three Times a Lady", writer & producer; "Still", writer & producer; "Sail On", writer & producer; "Am the Beautiful", composer, 2001; "Undercover Brother", composer, 2002; "House of 1000 Corpses", composer, 2003; "Grattis Victoria", composer, 2004; "80s", composer, 2005; Films: Endless Love, songwriter & composer; Scott Joplin, actor, 1977; Thank God It's Friday, actor, 1978; Live Aid, actor, 1985; We Are the World, 1985; The Preacher's Wife, actor, 1996; Pariah,

actor, 1998; Albums: Time, 1998; Renaissance, 2000; Encore, 2002; Just for You, 2004; Coming Home, 2006; Are We Done Yet?, 2007; Baby Mama, 2008; Tropic Thunder, 2008; Duplicity, 2009; Transformers: Revenge of the Fallen, 2009. **Orgs:** United Negro Col Fund; Am Soc Composers, Authors & Publishers; Nat Acad Recording Arts & Sci; Am Acad Motion Picture Arts & Sci; Nat Asn Song writers. **Honors/Awds:** Three Platinum Albums; 4 Gold Albums; American Award, 1979, 1982, 1983, 1984, 1985 & 1987; People's Choice Award for Best Song, 1979, 1980, 1982, 1983 & 1986; Best Young Artist in Film, 1980; Nat Music Publications Award, 1980, 1981 & 1984; People's Choice Award for Best Composer, 1981; Grammy Award, 1982, 1985 & 1986; American Movie Award, 1982; Image Award, NAACP, 1983; Black Gold Award, 1984; Man of Year, Children's Diabetes Foundation, 1984; Alumnus of Year, United Negro Col Fund, 1984; Writer of Year, ASCAP, 1984, 1985 & 1986; Publisher of Year, ASCAP, 1985; ABAA Music Award, 1985; Honorary Degree in Music, Tusee Univ, 1986; Academy Award, 1986; Golden Globe Award, 1986; Entertainer of Year Award, NAACP, 1987; Pop Award, ASCAP, 1987; American Music Academy Award, 1987; Favorite Male Vocalist, Soul/R&B Award, Am Music Acad, 1987; Star, Hollywood Walk of Fame, 2003; Golden Note Award, ASCAP, 2008; George & Ira Gershwin Lifetime Achievement Award, Univ Calif, Los Angeles, 2008. **Special Achievements:** Grammy nominee 18 times.

RICHIE, WINSTON HENRY
Association executive, dentist, real estate agent. **Personal:** Born Sep 18, 1925, Jersey City, NJ; son of Dr William F and Celeste Strode; married Beatrice, Sep 5, 1953; children: Winston, Jr, Beth E, Laurel L, Anne C. **Educ:** Adebert Col Western Res Univ, BS, 1948; Western Res Univ, DDS, 1952. **Career:** Dentist (retired); E Suburban Coun Open Communities, exec dir, 1984-90; self-employed dentist, 35 yrs; Realty One, real estate agent, currently. **Orgs:** Am Dent Asn; Cleveland Dent Soc; Ohio State Dent Asn; Elder Fairmount Presbyterian Church, 1972-75; pres, Fair Housing Inc; Shaker Heights City Coun, 1972-; Shaker Heights City Coun, 1972-84, vice mayor, 1977. **Honors/Awds:** Distinguished Service in Open Housing Award, Cuyahoga Plan Cleveland; invited to Australia to represent the Ford Foundation & Harvard Univ discussing racial integration in the USA; 2007 Honr Roll, Dartmouth Col. **Military Serv:** USN, seaman 2nd cl, 1944-46. *

RICHMOND, DELORES RUTH
Real estate agent. **Personal:** Born May 28, 1951, Chicago, IL; daughter of Arthur Lee Freeman and Mamie Elizabeth McBride Freeman; married Larson, Oct 18, 1980; children: Tesha Elizabeth, Dwayne L & Nicole L. **Educ:** Chicago Col Com, Chicago, Ill, 1975-76; Prairie State Col, Chicago Heights, Ill, 1980-81; Real Estate Educ Sch, South Holland, Ill, cert, 1985; Sch Ministry, lic & ordained minister, 1985; Real Estate Educ Sch, Homewood, Ill, realtor broker's cert, 1989; US Fed Gov Courses, credited state Ill, 28 hrs. **Career:** Ill Dept Ins, agent & producer; US Fed Govt, Chicago, Ill, adminr, 1970-79; Continental Bank, Matteson, Ill, asst supr, 1981-84; TV 38 Christian Sta & Radio, Chicago, Ill, studio audience coordr, 1984-87; Century twenty one Dabbs & Assoc, Homewood, Ill, broker, asso relocation dir, 1985; Richmond GMAC Real Estate, owner & pres, currently. **Orgs:** Homewood Full Gospel Church, 1981-; Nat Asn Advan Colored People, 1982-; pres, Today Is Your Day, 1984-, bd dir, Century twenty one Dabbs & Assoc, 1986-; Jack & Jill, 1988-; publicity dir, Women's Coun Realtors, 1988-; UNCF, 1989-; pres, Rich Star Inc, 1990; Ill State Chap WomenNPower, state pres, currently; Asn West-South Suburban Chicago; bd dir, Prof Stand & Grievance Comt; Ill Asn Realtors; Greater Northwest Ind Asn Realtors; Ind Asn Realtors; Nat Asn Realtors; Notary Pub-State Ill; Grad Real Estate Inst GRI; Women's Coun Realtors. **Honors/Awds:** Bronze, Silver, and Gold medals, Ill Asn Realtors, 1986-94; Centurian Award, Nat Century 21, 1986-91; Appreciation Award, Ford Motor Co, 1987, 1988, 1989; Kizzy Award, Kizzy Scholar Fund Found, 1989; has received hundreds of other real estate awards. **Special Achievements:** Stockbroker Series 6 & 22, Lic, 1992. **Home Addr:** 20223 St Andrews Dr, Olympia Fields, IL 60461, **Home Phone:** (708)503-0797. **Business Addr:** Owner, President, Richmond GMAC Real Estate, 3309 Vollmer Rd, Flossmoor, IL 60422, **Business Phone:** (708)647-9200.

RICHMOND, MITCH (MITCHELL JAMES)
Basketball player, basketball executive. **Personal:** Born Jun 30, 1965, Ft Lauderdale, FL; son of Ernell O; married Juli, Jan 1, 1993; children: Phillip, Jerin & Shane. **Educ:** Moberly Area Jr Col; Kans State Univ, BA, soc sci, 1988. **Career:** Basketball player (retired), Basketball executive; Golden State Warriors, guard, 1988-91, spec asst, scout, currently; Sacramento Kings, guard, 1991-98; Wash Wizards, guard, 1998-2001; Los Angeles Lakers, guard, 2001-02. **Orgs:** Founder, Solid As a Rock Found, 1992; bd mem, Nat Comm Prevent Child Abuse. **Honors/Awds:** NBA Rookie of the Year, 1989; US Olympic Team, bronze, 1988; NBA All-Rookie Team, 1989; NBA All-Star, 1993-98; NBA All-Star Game Most Valuable Player, 1995; Spec Friend Award, Nat Comt Prevent Child Abuse; US Olympic Team, gold, 1996. **Special Achievements:** Hosted the NBA Live 95 Sega Genesis Celebrity Basketball Tournament, 1995. **Business Phone:** (510)986-2200.

RICHMOND, MYRIAN PATRICIA
Government official. **Personal:** Born Sep 28, 1942, Birmingham, AL; divorced; children: Brian & Kevin. **Educ:** Lane Col, BA 1965; Atlanta Univ, 1971-72. **Career:** Beauford City Sch, teacher, 1967-69; The Onyx Corp, consult, 1973-75; WAOK Radio, writer/reporter, 1973-76, news dir, 1976-78; Fulton City Govt, info officer, beginning 1978, deputy dir, dept info & public affairs, currently. **Orgs:** Alumna Leadership, Atlanta 1980-; TV show host, GA Public TV, 1981-84; consult, Martin L King Ctr, 1982-84; Atlanta Asn Black Journalists, 1984-85; bd mem, Neighborhood Arts Ctr, 1984-85. **Honors/Awds:** Media Woman of the Year, Nat Asn Media Women, 1975; Essence Woman Essence Mag, 1975; SCLC Achievement Award, Nat SCLC, 1983; GA Black Women Honoree, GA Coaltion of Black Women, 1984-85. **Business Addr:** Deputy Director, Fulton County Government, Department of Info & Public Affairs, 141 Pryor St SW, Atlanta, GA 30303, **Business Phone:** (404)730-8307.

RICHMOND, RODNEY WELCH
Labor activist, vice president (organization). **Personal:** Born Jul 25, 1940, Washington, DC; son of Vernon and Ella Welch; married Joyce Reeves, Jun 24, 1981; children: Inga, Anthony & Ronda. **Educ:** Howard Univ, Wash, DC, BA, 1977; Am Univ, Wash, DC, 1984-85; Univ Dist Columbia, Wash, DC, 1986. **Career:** Wash Metropolitan Transit Authority, Wash, DC, bus operator, 1962-86; Amalgamated Transit Union, Wash, DC, int vpres, 1986-. **Orgs:** Reserve Civil Sheriff, Civil Sheriff's Office, 1989-. **Military Serv:** AUS, SP/4, 1958-61. **Home Addr:** 5573 Stillwater Dr, New Orleans, LA 70128, **Home Phone:** (504)245-1377. **Business Addr:** International Vice President, Amalgamated Transit Union, 5025 Wisconsin Ave NW, Washington, DC 20016, **Business Phone:** (202)537-1645.

RICKMAN, RAY
State government official, business owner, association executive. **Personal:** Born Nov 25, 1948, Galatin, TN; son of James Bailey and Betty Richards. **Educ:** Eastern Mich Univ, Ypsilanti, attended 1968; Wayne State Univ, Detroit, BA 1971. **Career:** US Congressman John Conyers, Detroit, chief asst, 1971-74; Jeff Chalmers Non-Profit Corp, exec dir, 1974-77; Harmony Village Non-Profit Corp, exec dir, 1977-79; Mass Medicaid Handicapped Prog, dir, 1979; Police Abuse Housing Issues, lectr; Providence Human Rels Comn, exec dir, 1979-; Affirmative Action, consult; Mass Housing Finance Agency, equal opportunity officer, 1982-85; Cornerstone Books, owner, 1985-; Gen Assembly RI, state rep, 1986-96; Shades-Talk Show, host, producer, 1986-; RI Secy State, dep Secy State Admin, 2001-03; Adopt A Doctor, chmn, currently. **Orgs:** Pres, Friends Belle Isle, Detroit, 1974-78; bd mem Langston Hughes Ctr 1986-89; bd mem, ACLU RI, 1979-80; bd mem, Nat Asn Advan Colored Perople, RI Chap, 1980-82; comnr, Providence Historic Dist Comn, 1986-; bd mem, RI Hist Soc, 1989-; Affirmative Action/Equal Opportunity Dir, City Providence, 2003-. **Honors/Awds:** City of Providence-Resolution, 1987; Talk Show Host of the Year, 1988; Numerous awards City of Detroit, County of Wayne, State of Mich & Civ Org. **Special Achievements:** Many op-ed articles in Detroit Free Press, Detroit News, Providence Journal, Maine Times, 1971-. **Home Addr:** PO Box 2591, Providence, RI 02906-0591, **Home Phone:** (401)861-7244. **Business Addr:** Chairman, Adopt A Doctor, 150 Chestnut St, Providence, RI 02903, **Business Phone:** (401)861-7244.

RICKS, MIKHAEL (MIKHAEL ROY RICKS)
Football player. **Personal:** Born Nov 14, 1974?, Galveston, TX. **Educ:** Stephen F Austin State Univ. **Career:** Football player (retired); San Diego Chargers, wide receiver, 1998-2000; Kans City Chiefs, 2000-01; Detroit Lions, 2002-03; Dallas Cowboys, Inactive/practice squad member, 2004.

RICKS, MIKHAEL ROY. See RICKS, MIKHAEL.

RICKSON, GARY AMES
Artist, poet. **Personal:** Born Aug 12, 1942, Boston, MA; married; children: Mary Pendeton, Kianga Akua, Tianee Rayna & Alea Sekua. **Educ:** Ministry Degree, 1964. **Career:** Boston African Am Artist, pres, 1964-68; Harvard Radio Boardcast Corp, artist-poet, 1974-84; artist, currently. **Orgs:** Roxbury Boys Club, 1970; Cult adv, Roxbury YMCA, 1984-85; Boston Urban Gardeners, 1984-; pub rels Boston African Am Artists, 1985-. **Honors/Awds:** Outstanding Roxbury Citizen Award, Black Bros Assoc, 1970; Nat Endowment Grant, 1970; Champ of Black Youth Award, Roxbury Boys Club, 1970. **Special Achievements:** Began Mural Movement in Boston in 1968, author of the Black Artist Bible 21st Century Artist, 1998. **Home Addr:** 107 Dewitt Dr, Roxbury, MA 02119. **Business Addr:** Artist, Gary A. Rickson Studio, 107 DeWitt Dr, Roxbury, MA 02120, **Business Phone:** (617)445-2823.

RICO, DR. TRACEY
Physician, artist. **Educ:** Bd cert emergency & pediat emergency med. **Career:** Physician & artist, currently; Quilts: Aunt Jemima's Debut; Our Glory; A Talisman for the Coffled; Mammy's Cakewalk, 2002; Bamboozled, 2002; Beth Israel Hosp, emergency care physician; Maimonides Med Ctr, pediat emergencies physician; Brooklyn Hosp, emergency residency; pvt pract, currently; Jade Rico Designs, owner & atrist, currently. **Business Addr:** Artist, Owner, Jade Rico Designs, 138 Court St Suite 390, Brooklyn, NY 11201.

RIDDICK, EUGENE E
Engineer. **Personal:** Born Jan 23, 1938, Lee Hall, VA; son of James Wesley Riddick and Gertrude Burks Reid; married Evelyn G McNeese, Sep 8, 1962; children: Eric. **Educ:** Howard Univ, BSME, 1961; State NJ, Prof Engrs lic, 1970; State Ky, PE lic, 1989; State Wyo, PE lic, 2003; Canadian PE, Ont, 2003. **Career:** Gibbs & Cox Inc, asst engr, 1963-64; MW Kellogg, sr engr, 1964-70; Badger Engrs Inc, mgr, fired heaters, 1970-74, mgr, piping eng, 1974-79, mgr, eng aux, 1979-82, mgr, heat transfer, 1982-95; Kinetics Technol Intl Corp, mgr, heat transfer group, 1995-99; Technip USA, mgr mech group & task force chmn, 1999-. **Orgs:** Am Soc Mech Engrs, 1972-; chmn, Am Petrol Inst Mfg & Contractors S/C on Fired Heaters, 1984-94; treas, First Parish Unitarian Church, 1980-82, chmn, Art Comt, 1980-87. **Honors/Awds:** Black Achiever of 1989, Boston YMCA, 1989; Raytheon Black Achievers Alumni, 1990-95; Certificate of Appreciation, Am Petrol Inst, 1994, 1999. **Military Serv:** AUS, first lt, 2 yrs. **Home Addr:** 14161 Heathervale Dr, Chino Hills, CA 91709-5902. **Business Addr:** Manager Mechanical Group, Technip USA Corp, 555 W Arrow Hwy, Claremont, CA 91711, **Business Phone:** (909)447-3788.

RIDEAU, IRIS
Business owner. **Personal:** Born in New Orleans, LA; divorced; children (previous marriage): Renee; married Jimmy Rideau, Jan 1, 1957. **Career:** The Rideau Insurance Agency, owner, 1967-99; Rideau Retirement Planning Consultants Inc, owner; Rideau Securities Firm, owner, 1982; Rideau Vineyards, owner, 1997-. **Orgs:** Chmn, Mayor's Affirmative Action Comt, 1973-76. **Honors/Awds:** Business Innovator of the Year, Black Enterprise, 2004. **Special Achievements:** Part time model for Victoria's Secret; featured in numerous magazines. **Business Addr:** Owner, Rideau Vineyard, 1562 Alamo Pintado Rd, Solvang, CA 93463, **Business Phone:** (805)688-0717.

RIDEAU, WIBERT
Journalist, editor, photographer. **Personal:** Born Feb 13, 1942, Lawtell, LA. **Career:** ABC-TV, DayOne corresp, 1993-94; Fresh Air, WHYY-FM, corresp, 1994-95; The Angolite mag, ed, 1976-. **Orgs:** Angola Human Rels Club, pres, 1997-. **Honors/Awds:** Charles C Clayton Award, Southern Ill Univ Sch Jour, 1977; Robert F Kennedy Jour Award, RFK Found, 1979; Silver Gavel Award, Am Bar Asn, 1979; The George Polk Award, Long Island Univ, 1980; The Sidney Hillman Award, Sidney Hillman Found, 1982; Golden Eagle Award, Coun on Int Non-Theatrical Events, 1995; Acad Award, Doc Feature, Sundance Film Fest, 1998. **Special Achievements:** Auth: "The Wall Is Strong: Corrections In Louisiana", USL, 1989, Second Edition, 1991, Third Editon, 1996; "Life Sentences: Rage & Survival Behind Bars", Times Books, 1992; "Unforgiven" by Amy Bach, 2002. **Business Addr:** Editor, The Angolite Magazine, Louisiana State Penitentary, Angola, LA 70712, **Business Phone:** (504)655-4411.*

RIDENHOUR, CARLTON DOUGLAS
Rap musician, writer, journalist. **Personal:** Born Aug 1, 1960, Roosevelt, NY. **Educ:** Adelphi Col, NY. **Career:** New York, bike messenger; Public Enemy, rapper, 1987-; Fox News Channel, commentator & corresp, 1998-; MP3 & file sharing technol, pub supporter, 2000; Albums: Lies, 1984; Check Out the Radio, 1984; Yo! Bum Rush The Show, 1987; It Takes A Nation of Millions to Hold Us Back, 1988; Fear Of A Black Planet, 1990; Apocalypse '91: The Enemy Strikes Black, 1991; Greatest Misses 1986-92, 1992; Muse Sick n Hour Mess Age, 1994; Autobiography of Mistachuck, 1996; Revolverlution, 2002; How You Sell Soul To A Soulless People Who Sold Their Soul?, 2007; Songs: "Fight The Power", 1989; "911 Is A Joke"; "Don't Believe The Hype", 1988; Film appearances: Rhyme & Reason, 1997; Anthem, 1997; Voices of the Voiceless, 2001; Underground Poets Railroad, 2003; Grand Theft Auto, 2004; Wake Up, 2004; TV Series: "In Living Color", 1991; "Johnny Bravo", 1997; Movie compositions: Less Than Zero, 1987; Do the Right Thing, 1989; Mo' Money, 1992; CB4, 1993; Shadow Boxing, 1993; An Alan Smithee Film: Burn Hollywood Burn, 1997; He Got Game, 1998; Bulworth, 1998; Bamboozled, 2000; Paid in Full, 2002. Race, Reality, 1997. **Special Achievements:** MTV "Enough Is Enough" antidrugs/antiviolence program, spokesperson, 1993; MTV News, reporter for Republican Convention; co-author of Fight The Power: Rap, Race, Reality, 1997. *

RIDENOUR, LIONEL
Executive. **Career:** Arista Recs, exec vpres; La Face Recs, co-founder; Virgin Recs, exec vpres urban music, currently. **Business Addr:** Executive Vice President, Virgin Records, 150 Fifth Ave, New York, NY 10011, **Business Phone:** (212)786-8300.

RIDER, ISAIAH
Basketball player. **Personal:** Born Mar 12, 1971, Oakland, CA. **Educ:** Univ Nev, Las Vegas, attended 1993. **Career:** Basketball

player (retired); Minn Timberwolves, guard, 1993-96; Portland TrailBlazers, 1996-99; Atlanta Hawks, 1999-2000; Los Angeles Lakers, 2000-01; Denver Nuggets, guard-forward, 2001. **Honors/ Awds:** Espy Award, ESPN, 1995.

RIDGEL, DR. GUS TOLVER
School administrator. **Personal:** Born Jul 1, 1926, Poplar Bluff, MO; son of Herford S Ridgel and Lue Emma Davis Ridgel; married Gertrude Cain; children: Betty Bolden. **Educ:** Lincoln Univ, BS, 1950; Univ Mo, Columbia, Mo, MA, 1951; Univ Wis, Madison, PhD, 1956. **Career:** Fort Valley State Col, Ft Valley, Ga, head dept bus, 1952-58; Wiley Col, Marshall, Tex, dean acad affairs, 1958-60; Kentucky State Univ, Frankfort, KY, dean, Sch Bus, 1960-84; Cent State Univ, Wilberforce, OH, vpres, acad affairs, 1972-74; Southern Univ, Baton Rouge, vpres acad affairs, 1985; Kentucky State Col, vpres admin affairs, currently. **Orgs:** Adv bd, Repub Savings Bank, 1983-86; LA Univ, Marine Consortium Coun, 1986-. **Honors/Awds:** Gus T Ridgel Minority Grad Fel, Univ Mo, Columbia, 1988. **Special Achievements:** First African-American student to earn a graduate degree at University of Missouri-Columbia. **Military Serv:** AUS, CPL, 1945-46. **Home Addr:** 312 Cold Harbor Dr, Frankfort, KY 40601-3082, **Home Phone:** (502)291-6919. *

RIDGEWAY, DR. BILL TOM
Educator, zoologist. **Personal:** Born Aug 26, 1927, Columbia, MO; married Leta M Baker; children: Mark B, Myra Chesser & Beth A. **Educ:** Freidns Univ Wichita KS, AB, 1951; Wichita Univ KS, MS, 1958; Univ MO Columbia, PhD, 1966. **Career:** Wichita St Univ, grad res asst, 1956-58; SW Col Winfield KS, asst prof zool, 1958-66; Univ Mo, Columbia, asst prof zool, 1966; Eastern Ill Univ, prof zool, 1966-95, Afro-Am Studies Studies, dir, 1971-73, prof emer,1995-; Ill Dept Conserv, contract res sci, 1970-; Univ Md, Natural Resources Inst, res assoc, 1974, vis prof, 1976. **Orgs:** Regional dir, Alpha Phi Alpha, 1969-77; treas, Concerned Citizens Charleston Assoc, Nat Asn Advan Colored People, 1975-; prog officer, 1981, presiding officer, 1985, Midwest Conf Parasitologists; Spec Ministries Comn, 1982, Soc Concerns Comn Episcopal Diocese Springfield; pres, Rotary Club Charleston, 1986. **Honors/Awds:** Graduate Fellowship in Zoology, Wichita State Univ, 1957; NSF Fellowship, Univ Wash Marine Sta, 1960; NSF Fellowship, Univ Mich Biol Sta, 1961-62; Research Fellowship in Zoology, Univ Mo, Columbia, 1963-66. **Military Serv:** AUS, 1945-47. **Business Addr:** Professor Emeritus, Eastern Illinois University, 600 Lincoln Ave, Charleston, IL 61920-3099, **Business Phone:** (217)581-5000.

RIDGEWAY, WILLIAM C.
Executive. **Personal:** Born Sep 24, 1942, Selma, AL; married Charlotte A Nicholson; children: Traci L & Kristina L. **Educ:** Tenn State Univ, BSEE, 1965. **Career:** Chevy Motor Div, auto engr, 1965-67; IBM Corp, jr component engr, 1967-68, assoc component engr, 1968-69, sr assoc component engr, 1969-72, staff component engr, 1972-73, proj engr, 1973-76, proj mgr. **Orgs:** IBM Golf Club; IEEE; vpres, Sr Class Tenn St Univ.

RIDLEY, DR. ALFRED DENNIS
Educator. **Personal:** Born Jun 23, 1948, Kingston, Jamaica; married Pamela; children: Andrew & Jon. **Educ:** Middlesex Univ, England, dipl elec & electronic eng, 1969; Univ West Indies, Trinidad, MSc, elec eng, 1977; Clemson Univ, SC, PhD, eng mgt,1982. **Career:** Jamaica Public Serv Comn, mgr syst planning, 1970-79; Int Atomic Energy Agency, fel, 1977; Clemson Univ, lectr, 1979-82; OAS, fel, 1980; George Mason Univ, asst prof decision sci, 1982-84; Howard Univ, asst prof info systs & anal, 1984-87; Fla A&M Univ, Sch Bus & Indust, assoc prof mgt scioper res & statist, prof oper res mgt & global logistics, currently. **Orgs:** Eng Mgt Consult, 1983-. **Honors/Awds:** Jamaica Ind Govt Scholar, 1965; JPS Co Scholar, 1974; Fulbright Senior Specialist Award, Kharkov Univ, Ukraine, 2004. **Special Achievements:** Publications: "Economic conductor size under load growth conditions, constrained by load limited life times", 1978; "A spectral analysis of the power market in South Carolina", 1981; "Fourcast-multivariate spectraltime series analysis & forecasting", 1984; "Promoting Management Science" PBS TV course, 1986; "Moving Window-Spectral Method", p 192, Sept/Oct1984; "Application of a Spectral Analysis algorithm (MWS) to time series analysis of automobile demand," Refereed Proceedings, Washington operations research management science annual symposium, p 139, 1987; "Competing with Global Quality Control", "Journal of Business Strategies", Vol 7, No 2, p 125, Fall 1990; "Counterbalancing another approach to forecasting," Journal of Business Forecasting, Vol 10, No 3, p 8, Fall 1991; "Spectral Forecasting and the Financial Market," Technical Analysis of Stocks & Commodities, Vol 11, No 1, p 84, 1993; "Combining Negatively Correlated Forecasts," Technical of Analysis of Stocks, Commodities, Vol11, No 5, p 66, 1993; "Variance Stabilization: A Direct yet Robust Method," Journal: Review of Business, Vol 15, No 1, p 28, Summer/Fall1993; "Optimal Window Length for MWS Forecasting," Technical Analysis of Stocks and Commodities, Vol 12, No 3, p 70, March 1994; "CounterbalancingUsing Unequal Weights," Production Planning and Control, Vol 5, No 2, March/April 1994; "A Model-free Power Transformation to Homoscedasticity,"Intl Journal of Production Economics, 1994; Preprints: "The Global Univariate Moving Window Spectral Method," Supercomputer Computations Research Institute, Feb 1994; "Antithetic Forecasting from a Lognormal history," Supercomputer Computations Research Inst, 1994; "Combining Global Antithetic Forecasts," Intl Trans in Operational Research, 1995; "Optimal Weights for combining Antithetic Forecasts, Computers & Industial Eng, 1996; "Antithetic Log Normal/Normal Random Variables, "On the Sum of Weights: antithetic forecasting," ITOR, Vol 15, No 4, p 341, 1998; "Internet Learning Ctr for Time Series Analysis & Forecasting, "www.polaris.net, 1996; " Optimal Antithetic Weights for Lognormal Time Series Forcasting," C & OR, Vol 26, No 3, p 189, 1998; "Combining Heteroscedastic Antithetic Forecasts," C & IE. **Business Addr:** Professor Operations Research Management, Global Logistics, Florida A&M University, School of Business and Industry, Rm 410W 1 SBI Plz, Tallahassee, FL 32307-5200, **Business Phone:** (850)412-7730.

RIDLEY, DR. CHARLES ROBERT
Educator. **Personal:** Born Aug 6, 1948, Philadelphia, PA; married Iris Rochelle Smith; children: Charles & Charliss. **Educ:** Taylor Univ, BA, 1970; Ball State Univ, MA, 1971; Univ Minn, PhD, coun psychol, 1978. **Career:** Veterans Admin Hosp, psychol intern, 1974-76; Ind Univ, asst prof, 1977-79, dir Training, 1993-99, Dept Coun & Educ Psychol, from assoc prof to prof, 1990-; assoc dean, Res & Univ Grad Sch, 1999-; Univ Md Col Park, asst prof, 1979-80; Personnel Decisions Inc, consult psych, 1980-83; Fuller Theol Sem Grad Sch Psych, from asst prof to assoc prof, 1983-90. **Orgs:** Bd mem, Urban League Marion, IN, 1971-73; Am Psych Asn, 1977-. **Honors/Awds:** Rsch Grant Spencer Found 1978; "Clinical Treatment of the Nondis closing Black Client, A Therapeutic Paradox" Amer Psych 1984. **Special Achievements:** Published numerous books and articles between 1984-95.

RIDLEY, JOHN
Television writer, television producer. **Personal:** Born Jan 1, 1967?; married Gayle Yoshida, Feb 14, 1998; children: 2. **Educ:** NY Univ, east asian lang & cult. **Career:** Writer, producer & director; Films: U Turn, screenplay & producer, 1997; Cold Around the Heart, writer & dir, 1997; Three Kings, writer, 1999; Undercover Brother, screenplay & exec producer, 2002; Those Who Walk in Darkness, writer, 2003; Undercover Brother: The Animated Series, writer & exec producer, 2004; Justice League, writer, 2004; Bobby, co-producer, 2006; Street Kings, producer, 2008; TV series: "The John Larroquette Show", writer, 1993; Martin, writer, 1993-94; "The Fresh Prince of Bel-Air", writer, 1994; "Team Knight Rider", writer, 1997; Trinity, writer, 1998; "Third Watch", writer, 1999-2001; The Chang Family Saves the World, producer, 2002; I Got You, exec producer, 2002; "Platinum", dir, writer & exec producer, 2003; "Barbershop", exec producer, 2005; Novels: Stray Dogs, 1997; Love Is a Racket, 1998; Everybody Smokes in Hell, 1999; A Conversation with the Mann, 2002; Those Who Walk in Darkness, 2003; What Fire Cannot Burn, 2006; The Authority: Human On The Inside; MSNBC, "Morning Joe", contibr, currently. **Business Addr:** Author, Alfred A Knopf Inc, 1745 Broadway, New York, NY 10020, **Business Phone:** (212)782-9000.

RIDLEY, DR. MAY ALICE
School administrator. **Personal:** Born in Nashville, TN; widowed; children: Donald G Jr & Yvonda P. **Educ:** Tenn State Univ, BS, 1959, MS, 1967; Univ Pittsburgh, PhD, 1982. **Career:** Metro Pub Sch, teacher, 1962-84; Univ Pittsburgh, asst prof, 1975-76; Tenn State Univ, adjunct prof, 1982-; Tenn State Dept Educ, Off Civil Rights, dir civil rights, 1984, exec dir off civil rights, currently. **Orgs:** Tenn State Bd Educ, 1981-; chair, Spec Schs Community, Tenn State Bd Educ, 1982-83; Metro Nashville Human Rels Comt; St Vincent de Paul Church; Alpha Kappa Alpha Sorority; Phi Delta Kappa Ed Frat; bd mem, Links Inc; Jr League Nashville; second vpres, Societas Docta Inc; Phi Alpha Theta Honor Soc. **Honors/ Awds:** Alumnus of the Year, Tenn State Univ, 1978-79; Award of Appreciation from Nashville Mayor, 1979; Humanitarian Award, Tenn State Univ, 1985; Tenn Colonel State Honor. **Home Addr:** 2024 Jordan Dr, Nashville, TN 37218, **Home Phone:** (615)244-4090. **Business Addr:** Executive Director, Tennessee State Department of Education, Office of Civil Rights, 26th Fl William Snodgrass Tower 312 8th Ave N, Nashville, TN 37243, **Business Phone:** (615)532-4982.

RIFE, ANITA
College teacher. **Personal:** Born Jan 10, 1946, Des Moines, IA; daughter of Charles R (deceased) and Mary C (deceased); married Donald Rife (divorced 1971); children: Donnyta, Donald & Charles. **Educ:** Metropolitan State Col, Denver, 1977; Univ Northern Colo, Greeley, BA, 1979, MA, 1988; Southern Illinois Univ Carbondale, PhD, 1997. **Career:** KARK-TV, Little Rock, producer & resr, 1982-86; Univ Northern Colo, Greeley, teaching asst, 1986-88, asst prof, 1995-98; Southern Illinois Univ, Carbondale, teaching & res asst, 1988-89; UN Secretariat, NYC, project mgr & pub info officer, 1992-93; Pa State Univ, State Col, asst prof, 1998-2003; consult, Fleming-Rife Cons, State Col, 2003-04; Lock Haven Univ Pa, assoc prof, 2004-05; Clark Atlanta Univ, dir Mass Media Arts Ctr Excellence, 2005-, chair mass media arts, Clark Atlanta Univ, 2005-. **Orgs:** Nat Womens Studies Asn, 1987-89; Colo Womens Studies Asn, 1987-89. Asn Educrs Journ Mass Commun, 1989-; Black Grad Stud Asn, 1989-90; Alpha Kappa Alpha Sorority, Gamma Kappa Omega Chapter, 1991; Asn Educ Jour & Mass Commun. **Honors/Awds:** Graduate Student Council Award, Study British Broadcast London, Eng, UNC, 1987; Marcus Garvey Cultural Center, UNC Greeley Co, study BBC in London, England, 1987; Illinois Consortium for Education Opportunity, Fellowship SIU, 1989-; Graduate Dean's Fellowship, 1989; Fred L McDowell Award, Outstanding Scholar, SIU-C, 1990.

RIGGINS, JEAN
Executive. **Career:** Capitol Records, vpres & gen mgr, 1983-93; Arista Records, Black Music, sr vpres, 1993-96; Universal Records, exec vpres & gen mgr, pres, currently; Label, Black Music, pres, currently. **Orgs:** YWCA, New York, 1999. **Honors/ Awds:** The Shero Hall of Fame Inductee, Nat Asn Black Female Execs Music & Entertainment, 2002. **Business Addr:** President, Universal Records, Black Music, 1755 Broadway 7th Fl, New York, NY 10019, **Business Phone:** (212)373-0600.

RIGGINS, LESTER
Educator, administrator. **Personal:** Born Dec 8, 1928, Marshall, TX; son of John and Effie; married Marvell; children: 6. **Educ:** Fresno State Col, BA, Hist, 1951, Ind Univ, MBA, 1962; DC Univ, MS, 1974; USC, DPA prog, 1984. **Career:** Educator, Administrator (retired); Calif State Univ, asst, prof; State Calif, chief dep dir, 1976; Grank Skill Ctr, counsr; California Matrix Inc, owner. **Orgs:** Blue Key Honor Soc, 1950-51; Am Personal & Guid Asn, 1971-75; Sen, CSUF1971-75; coord, Ethnic Studies, CSUF, 1971-76; Bass-Black Advocates State Serv, 1977-83; cent vpres, BA-PAC 1979-; pres, Fannie Lou Hamer Dem Club, 1987-; lifetime mem, Urban League, Sacto, 1987; pres, Civil Serv Bd, Sacramento City, 1994-; Am Legion Post 511; Educrs Africa Asn; Res Officer Asn; Woodlin Lodge 30 Prince Hall Masons; Black Polit Coun; Sacto Chap, Nat Asn Advan Colored People; Victoria Consistory No:25; Menelik Temple No:36; Calif Dem Coun Black Caucus, Phi Gamma Mu Phi Sigma; Fresno Dem Coalition; Affirmative Action Comn Sacto Unified Sch Dist; Affirmative Action Comm City Sacto; AARP; pres, Harry S Truman Dem Club; pres, Harold C Washington Dem. **Honors/Awds:** Outstanding ROTC Cadet, 1951; Troy Award, 1974; Advocates Award, 1977; LABBA Presidents Award, 1979-81; Nominee Community Award, Human Rights, Fair Housing Comn, Sacramento CA. **Special Achievements:** Alpha Man of the Year, 1985; Outstanding Democratic Activist 1988. **Military Serv:** AUS, buck sgt, 1946-48, 1951-71. **Home Addr:** 6783 Middlecoff Way, Sacramento, CA 95822.

RIGGS, HON. ELIZABETH A
Judge. **Personal:** Born Jan 2, 1942, Camden, NJ; children: Luke, Michael & Adam. **Educ:** Bennett Col, BA, 1963; Rutgers Univ Sch Law, JD, 1973. **Career:** San Diego Co Dist Atty, dep dist atty; State Calif, dep atty gen, 1977-79; El Cajon Judicial Dist, judge municipal ct, 1979-84, presiding judge, 1984-86, judge, 1985; Calif Judicial Col, inr, felony sentencing, 1986; Hastings Trial Advocacy Summer Sch, 1983-86; State Calif Munic Ct El Cajon Dist, judge, currently. **Orgs:** Dir, YWCA Greensboro NC, 1964-65; Camden City OEO; crd, Neighborhood Youth Corp; dir, Head Start, 1966-68; Rutgers Univ Proj, Talent Search, 1968-70; Citizens Adv Bd, Rutgers Univ, 1970-73; Calif State Bar, 1974-; chmn, MNY Affairs Comn San Diego City Bar, 1978-79; bd dir, Black Atty Asn; Legal Aid Soc Lawyers Club, 1977-79; San Diego Co Black Atty's Asn, 1974-; Calif Asn Black Lawyers, 1976-; Dimensions, 1977-; Speakers Bur San Diego Co Nat Conf Negro Women; Mayors Comn Status Women; dimensions & charter 100 Prof Womens Asn; Nat Asn Women Judges; Calif Judges Asn; Co Women's Network; Soroptimist Int; Nat Bar Asn; Earl B Gilliam Bar Asn; bd dir, Urban League, 1989-91. **Honors/Awds:** Woman of the Year, San Diego Tribune, 1974; Black Achievement Award In Law, 1980; Delta Epsilon Chap Kappa Alpha Psi Award in Law, 1980; Distinguished Service Award Black Student Union Grossmont College, 1981; Distinguished Service Award, 1982; Women's Criminal Defense Appreciation Award, 1983; Valuable Service Award, 1983; California Women Government Law & Justice Award; Commission Appreciation Award, Earl B Gillian Bar Asn, 1984; NAWJ, Moderator; Alice Paul Award, Nat Women's Polit Caucus, 1986. **Special Achievements:** Only African American woman judge ever appointed or confirmed in the history of San Diego County. **Home Addr:** 4346 Caminito De La Escena, San Diego, CA 92108. **Business Addr:** Judge, State of California Municipal Court El Cajon District, 250 E Main St, El Cajon, CA 92020-3941, **Business Phone:** (619)441-4336.

RIGGS, DR. ENRIQUE A
Dentist. **Personal:** Born Jun 3, 1943, Panama City, Panama; son of Eric and Winifred; married Carol S Morales DDS; children: Myra Christine. **Educ:** Central State Univ, Wilberforce, Ohio, BA, Psychol, 1968; State Univ NY, Albany, MS, Coun, 1971; Howard Univ, Col Dentistry, DDS, 1978; Sydenham Hosp, NFCC, Cert, 1980; Iona Col, MBA, Fin Cert Int Bus, 1997. **Career:** State Univ NY, Albany, EOP counr, 1968-71; Hudson Valley Community Col, EOP dir, 1971-72; Pvt Practice, gen dentist, 1978-; NY City Health & Hosp Corp, Sydenham Hosp, resident, 1979-80; NYSA-ILA Med Ctr, gen dentist, 1980-84; NYS Dept Corrections, dent dir, 1984-90; Coun's Ambulatory Health Care Ctr, exec dir, 1991-92; Am Arbitration Asn, arbitrator, 1993-; small Bus Stock Exchange Am, vchair. **Orgs:** Alpha Phi Alpha, 1964-; Nat & Am Dent As-

socs, 1973-; bd dirs, Uptown Chamber Com, 1978-; dir, Central State Univ, Gen Alumni Asn, 1978-91, 100 Black Men, 1980-; bd dirs, Health Systs Agency, 1979-82; Acad Gen Dentistry, 1980-88; dir, Save Amateur Sports, 1981-82; bd gov, Small Bus Stock Exchange Am, 1983-; vpres, C&E Assocs, 1983-; nominating comt, Howard Univ, AA, 1985; chmn, Central State Univ, Centennial Football Classic Comn, 1987; dir, NY Urban League, 1986-88; NYUL Finance Comn, 1986-88; pres, Central State Univ, Gen Alumni Asn, 1987-91; vchmn, bd dir, Small Bus Stock Exchange Develop Corp; bd dirs, Am Asn Securities Dealers; bd dirs, Am Cancer Soc; bd dirs, The New York Foundling Hosp; Zeta Boule Sigma Pi Phi; Prince Hall F&AM. **Honors/Awds:** Table Clinic Award, DC Dental Soc & Howard Univ, Col Dentistry, 1974; Oral Cancer Fellowship Memorial Sloan-Kettering Hosp, 1976; Distinguished Alumni Award, NAFEO, 1988; Alumnus of the Year, Central State Univ, 1988. **Military Serv:** AUS Reserve, Col, 24 yrs. **Home Addr:** 25 Kathwood Rd, White Plains, NY 10607. **Business Addr:** Dentist, 40 W 135th St Suite 1E, New York, NY 10037, **Business Phone:** (212)281-5500.

RIGGS, GERALD ANTONIO
Football player. **Personal:** Born Nov 6, 1960, Tullos, LA; children: Gerald Riggs Jr. **Educ:** Ariz State Univ, attended. **Career:** Football player (retired); Atlanta Falcons, running back, 1982-88, Wash Redskins, running back, 1989-91. **Honors/Awds:** Post-season play: Pro Bowl, 1985-87. **Special Achievements:** Pro Bowl selection, 1985, 1986, & 1987; All-Pro selection, 1984 & 1985. *

RIGSBY, ESTHER MARTIN
School administrator. **Personal:** Born in Port Gibson, MS; daughter of Alex L Martin (deceased) and Annie M Wilson Martin (deceased); married John D; children: Reginald, Atty Delbert, Mark & Kenneth. **Educ:** Alcorn State Univ, BS, 1954; Ind Univ, MS, 1959; Mass State Univ, doctoral study, 1983; Univ Mass, additional study, 1980; Univ Southern Mass, doctoral study, 1985. **Career:** Jackson Pub Sch, teacher, 1960-; chmn, eng & j teacher, 1960-, Alcorn State Univ, adj instr, 1965; Alpha Kappa Alpha Sor Inc, regional dir, currently. **Orgs:** MS Ed Asn, 1960-; Nat Educ Asn, 1975-; Nat Asn Advan Colored People, 1975-; Nat Coun Negro Women, 1977-; liaison coord Jackson Coun & Nat Coun Eng Teachers, 1979; Jackson Urban League, 1980-; admin bd, New Hope Baptist Church, 1982-85; nat bd mem, Alpha Kappa Alpha Sor Inc, 1982-; supt adv coun, Jackson Pub Sch, 1984-85; YWCA, 1985; Opera South Guild, 1985; Links Inc, 1987. **Honors/Awds:** Service Award, Alpha Kappa Alpha Sor Inc, 1975-85; Award Loyal Alumnae, Alcorn State Univ, 1977; Service Award, Nat Coun Negro Women, 1981; Service Award, Women Prog, 1981. **Home Addr:** 5952 Hanging Moss Rd, Jackson, MS 39206-2147. **Business Addr:** Southeastern Regional Director, Alpha Kappa Alpha Sorority Inc, 6616 Trace Dr, Jackson, MS 39203, **Business Phone:** (601)948-1946.

RIJO, JOSE ANTONIO (JOSE ANTONIO RIJO ABREU)
Baseball player, baseball executive. **Personal:** Born May 13, 1965, San Cristobal, Dominican Republic; married Teddy; children: 1. **Career:** Baseball player (retired), baseball executive; NY Yankees, pitcher, 1984; Oakland Athletics, pitcher, 1985-87; Cincinnati Reds, pitcher, 1988-95, 2001-02; Wash Nationals, spec asst to gen mgr, 2009. **Honors/Awds:** World Series champion, 1990; World Series MVP, 1990; Tony Conigliaro Award, 2002. **Special Achievements:** Rijo had a supporting role in the 2008 baseball film Sugar.

RIJO ABREU, JOSE ANTONIO. See RIJO, JOSE ANTONIO.

RILEY, ANTONIO
State government official. **Personal:** Born Aug 22, 1963. **Educ:** Carroll Col, BA. **Career:** Milwaukee Mayor's Off, staff asst; Wisc State Assemblyman, Dist 18; Wisc State Capital, state rep, 1992-2002; Wis Housing & Econ Develop Authority, exec dir. **Orgs:** YMCA; Transcenter for Youth; Greater Milwaukee Am Red Cross; Ctr Policy Alternatives; chmn Milwaukee Westside Health Care Asn; comn chmn, Milwaukee Metrop Sewerage Dist; chmn Dem Leadership Coun; Midtown Neighborhood Asn; adv bd, Dem Leadership Coun. **Business Phone:** (608)266-7884.

RILEY, BARBARA P
Librarian. **Personal:** Born Nov 21, 1928, Roselle, NJ; daughter of Charles Carrington Polk and Olive Bond Polk; married George Emerson, Feb 23, 1957 (deceased); children: George Jr, Glenn & Karen; married William F Scott, Oct 6, 1990 (divorced 1998). **Educ:** Howard Univ, AB, 1950; NJ Col Women, BS, 1951; Columbia Univ, MS, 1955; Catholic Univ; Jersey City State Col; Rutgers Univ; Kean Col. **Career:** Librarian (retired): FL A&M Univ, asst librn, 1951-53; Morgan, asst librn, 1955; US Dept Defense, lib, 1955-57; SC State Col, asst librn, 1957-59, 1960; Univ WI, asst lib, 1958-59; Atlanta Univ, circulation acquisitions librn, 1960-68; Union Co Tech Inst, lib, 1968-82; Union Co Col, librn, Scotch Plains campus, 1982-92, Plainfield Campus, librn, 1992-95. **Orgs:** Asst dir, Union Co Anti-Poverty Agency, 1968; Just-A-Mere Lit Club; ALA Black Lib Caucus; Alpha Kappa Alpha Sor; Bd Educ, Roselle, NJ, 1976-78; bd dirs, Union Co Psychiat Clin, 1980-83; Urban League Eastern Union Co; bd dirs, Roselle, NAACP 1984-88; bd dirs, Pinewood Sr Citizens Housing, 1982-85; NJ Coalition 100 Black Women, 1983-90; NJ Black Librns Network, 1983-, bd dir, 1986; bd dir, Black Womens Hist Conf, 1986-89; Links Inc. **Home Phone:** (908)241-5036.

RILEY, CLAYTON. See Obituaries section.

RILEY, DOROTHY WINBUSH
Writer, school administrator. **Personal:** Born in Detroit, MI; daughter of Jack Winbush and Odessa; married Robert (divorced); children: Schiavi, Ted, Robert, Tiaudra & Martay. **Educ:** Wayne State Univ, BS, 1969, MSLS, 1972; MSGC, 1983; Eastern Mich Univ, Admin certif, 1986. **Career:** Administrator (retired), writer; Detroit Bd Educ, teacher, 1969-87, principal, 1987-2003. **Orgs:** Delta Sigma Theta; Nat Asn Advan Colored People; Hartford Missionary Bapt Church; Nat Asn Black Sch Educr; Metrop Detroit; Asn Black School Educr; Nat Asn Elem Sch Principals; Nat Coun Teachers Eng; Asn Curric & Sch Develop; Booker T Washington Bus Asn. **Honors/Awds:** Educator Award, Milken Foundation, 1994. **Special Achievements:** Author: My Soul Looks Back Less I Forget, 1993; The Complete Kwanzaa, 1994; Black Man in the Image of God; Black Woman in the Image of God; Like A Second Layer of Skin; My Soul Is a Witness Less I Forget, 2008.

RILEY, EDWARD THEODORE. See RILEY, TEDDY.

RILEY, ERIC
Basketball player. **Personal:** Born Jun 2, 1970, Cleveland, OH. **Educ:** Univ Mich, attended 1993. **Career:** Basketball player (retired); Houston Rockets, ctr, 1993-94; Los Angeles Clippers, 1994-95; Minn Timber wolves, 1995-96; Dallas Mavericks, 1997-98;Boston Celtics, 1998-99; San Antonio Spurs, ctr, 2001-02. *

RILEY, HON. EVE MONTGOMERY
Judge. **Personal:** Born Oct 8, 1955, Sedalia, MO; daughter of Ralph and Neppie Elizabeth Gerhardt; married Joel Younge, Aug 6, 1988; children: Max Sebastian & Cruz Dylan. **Educ:** Fisk Univ, Nashville, TN, attended 1974; Carthage Col, Kenosha, attended 1975; Roosevelt Univ, Chicago, IL, BA, 1976; Valparaiso Univ Sch Law, Valparaiso, IN, JD, 1978; Fontbonne Col, Clayton, MO, MBA, 1995. **Career:** US Off Spec Coun, Wash, DC, law clerk, 1979-80, staff atty, 1980-82; US Merit Systs Protection Bd, Philadelphia, PA, admin judge, 1982-87; Support Ctr Child Advocates, Philadelphia, PA, exec dir, 1987; St Louis Univ Sch Law, St Louis, MO, instr, 1988-89; St Louis, MO, atty law, 1988-94; Nat Asn Advan Colored People, St Louis Br Lawyer Referral Serv, dir, 1993-94; Social Security Admin, admin law judge, 1994-, hearing off chief admin law judge, currently. **Orgs:** Nat Asn Women Bus Owners, 1987-89; pres, Fed Bar Asn, St Louis Chap, 1988-90; leader, Girl Scout Coun Greater, St Louis, 1989-; Delta Mu Delta Hon Soc, EOR Bus Admin, 1994; Mission Coun, 1999-; C Work Comn, 1997-; ed, Greater St Louis Suzuki Asn Newsletter, 1999-; Color Justice, Nat Asn Women Judges, 2001; Ladue Chapel Presby Church. **Business Addr:** Hearing Office Chief Administrative Law Judge, Social Security Adminstration, Office of Disability Adjudication & Review St Louis, 200 N Broadway Suite 900, Saint Louis, MO 63102, **Business Phone:** (314)588-7534 Ext 3050.

RILEY, GLENN PLEASANTS
Television producer. **Personal:** Born Jan 17, 1960, Milwaukee, WI; son of Robert and Annie Pleasants; married Felice Ligon Riley, Jun 7, 1987. **Educ:** Milwaukee Area Tech Col, Milwaukee, WI, AAS, 1980; Univ Wis-19Milwaukee, Milwaukee, WI, 1986. **Career:** WITI TV6 Inc, Milwaukee, WI, traffic log keeper, 1980-81; WMVS/WMVT TV, Milwaukee, WI, prod specialist, 1982-; Milwaukee Area Tech Col, instr, currently. **Orgs:** Nat Asn Black Journalists, 1987-; Wis Black Media Asn, 1988-; Wis Broadcasters Asn. **Business Addr:** Instructor, Milwaukee Area Technical College, 1200 S 71st St, Milwaukee, WI 53233, **Business Phone:** (414)271-1036.

RILEY, KENNETH J.
Football coach, football player. **Personal:** Born Aug 6, 1947, Bartow, FL; married Barbara Moore; children: Kimberly, Ken II & Kenisha. **Educ:** Fla A&M Univ, BS, health & phys educ, 1969; Univ N Fla, MEd, admin, 1974. **Career:** Football player, Football coach (retired); Cincinnati Bengals, corner back, 1969-83; Green Bay Packers, asst coach, 1984-86; Fla A&M Univ, football coach, 1986-93; athletic dir, 1994-2003. **Orgs:** Bd dir, Big Brothers Polk County; Alpha Phi Alpha Frat; Mt Gilboa Bapt Church; consult Fla A&M Nat Alumni; adv bd, Nat Football League; adv comt, NCAA. **Honors/Awds:** Distinguish Alumni Award, Fla A&M Univ, 1988; Hall of Fame, Polk County Sch Bd, 1992; Polk County Hall Fame, 2000. **Military Serv:** AUS Reserve, Sgt.

RILEY, LIZ (LIZ RILEY HARGROVE)
Executive director. **Career:** Duke Univ, The Fuqua Sch Bus, asst dean & dir admissions, currently. **Business Addr:** Assistant Dean, Director of Admissions for The Duke MBA Daytime program, Duke University, Fugua School of Business, 1 Tower View Dr, Durham, NC 27708, **Business Phone:** (919)660-1956.*

RILEY, ROSETTA MARGUERITTE
Automotive executive. **Personal:** Born Oct 25, 1940, Kansas City, MO; divorced; children: Courtney Elizabeth. **Educ:** California State Univ, Los Angeles, BS, 1968; UCLA, MA, 1969. **Career:** Bendix Corp, Detroit, MI, mgr bus planning, mkt mgr; Gen Motors, Detroit, MI, Prod Team, mgr qual, Rochester NY Prods Div, qual improv mgr, Buick Oldsmobile Cadillac Group, Detroit, MI, mgr opers planning, Cadillac Motor Car Division, Detroit MI, dir, currently. **Orgs:** Zeta Phi Sorority, 1964-; life mem, Nat Asn Advan Colored People, 1984-89; United Found, 1984-; Detroit Inst Arts, 1987-; Am Soc Qual Control; Gen Motors Key Exec Tenn State Univ. **Home Addr:** 5928 Naneva Ct, West Bloomfield, MI 48322, **Home Phone:** (248)626-1842. **Business Phone:** 800-222-1020.*

RILEY, SHAUNCE R
Counselor, educator. **Personal:** Born Mar 23, 1970, Savannah, GA; son of William Jr and Mary; married Karla W, Oct 13, 2001. **Educ:** Savannah State Univ, BBA, CIS & MAN with Teacher's Certification, 1996; Central Mich Univ, MA, Educ, 2002. **Career:** Savannah State Univ, Off Human Resources, records coordr, 1996-99, Ctr Stud Develop, staff asst, 1999-2001, Stud Support Servs, prog spec, 2001-, freshman experience instr, 2001-. **Orgs:** Southeastern Asn Educ Opport Prog; Ga Col Personnel Asn; Phi Beta Lambda; Savannah State Univ, 2002 Homecoming Comt, chairperson, 2002-03. **Home Addr:** Rt 1 Box 149-2LA7, Hardeeville, SC 29927, **Home Phone:** (843)748-5074. **Business Addr:** Program Specialist/ Student Advisor, Savannah State University, 3219 Col St Whiting Hall Rm 238, PO Box 20489, Savannah, GA 31404, **Business Phone:** (912)353-3236.

RILEY, TEDDY (EDWARD THEODORE RILEY)
Television producer, songwriter, musician. **Personal:** Born Oct 8, 1966, Harlem, NY; children: 3. **Career:** Jazz Singer: Guy, 1988; High Hat, 1989; The Future, 1990; Juice, l992; Dangerous, 1992; Bobby, 1993; Eleven, 1993; recording appears on Heavy D's album Peaceful Journey; Solo: "D-O-G Me Out"; "Let's Chill"; "Long Gone"; "No Diggity"; has produced, written & played for: Bobby Brown, Stevie Wonder, Boy George, Kool Moe Dee, Michael Jackson; BLACKSTREET, 1994-; Little Man Rec, owner, currently; writer: New Jack City, 1991; Madonna: Truth or Dare, 1991; CB4, 1993; Blankman, 1994; Get on the Bus, 1996; The Rugrats Movie, 1998; Music of the Heart, 1999; Love & Basketball, 2000; The 40 Year Old Virgin, 2005; Wild Hogs, 2007; Actor: New Jack City, 1991. **Honors/Awds:** Grammy Award for Best Rhythm and Blues Performance by a Duo or Group, 1998. **Special Achievements:** Debut recording, Guy, sold over 2 million copies. **Business Addr:** Owner, Little Man Records, PO Box 45636, Seattle, WA 98145.

RILEY, VICTOR ALLAN
Football player. **Personal:** Born Nov 4, 1974, Swansea, SC. **Educ:** Auburn Univ. **Career:** Football player (retired); Kansas City Chiefs, tackle, 1998-2001; New Orleans Saints, tackle, 2002-04; Houston Texans, tackle, 2005. **Honors/Awds:** Rookie of the Year, 1998; Mack Lee Hill Award winner, 1998.

RILEY, DR. WAYNE JOSEPH
Health services administrator, physician. **Personal:** Born May 3, 1959, New Orleans, LA; son of Emile Edward Jr and Jacqueline Cerf; married Charlene Dewey MD; married Charlene M Dewey; children: Erin Elizabeth & Alexis Camille. **Educ:** Yale Univ, BS, anthrop, 1981; Tulane Univ, New Orleans, LA, MPH, Health Mgt, 1988; Morehouse Sch Med, MD, 1993; Am Bd Internal Med, dipl, 1996; Rice Univ, Jesse H Jones Grad Sch Mgt, MBA, Execs Prog, 2002. **Career:** Off Mayor, New Orleans, from admin asst to the mayor, 1981-86, from exec asst to the mayor, 1986; Off Pub Health, LA, health serv planner, 1987-88; Alpha Omega Alpha Stud res fel, 1991; Morehouse Sch Med, Minority AIDS Educ Proj, proj asst, consult; Baylor Col Med, asst prof med, 1996-, asst dean, 2001-, Health Affairs Govt Rels, vpres, vice dean; Ben Taub Gen Hosp, asst chief med; Rice Univ, Jesse H Jones Grad Sch Mgt, adj prof; Tex Med Ctr, vpres, vice dean health affairs & govt rels, assoc prof med; Baylor Col Med, Dept Med, staff, 2000-04, vpres & vice dean, 2004-06; Meharry Med Col, pres & chief exec officer, 2006-; Michael E DeBakey Veteran Affairs Med Ctr, attending physician & staff. **Orgs:** Am Col Physicians, Nat Med Asn; Kingsley Trust Asn Yale Univ, 1981-, Yale Alumni Asn LA, 1981-88; bd dirs, LA Youth Sem, 1984-86; NAACP, Am Med Stud Asn, AMA, Stud Nat Med Asn; exec dir, LA Independent Fedn Electors Inc, 1985-88; pres, Tulane Univ Black Prof Stud Asn, 1987-88; sec, treas, Yale Alumni Asn LA, 1988; Lectr, Adolescent Health Concerns Proj, Emory Univ 1989; fel, NMF/Prudential Foundation AIDS Educ & Pub Policy, 1990; Eta Lambda Chap, Alpha Phi Alpha Fraternity Inc; Nat coordr, Standing Comm Minority Affairs, AMSA, 1990-91; Stud Govt Asn, Morehouse Sch Med, vpres, 1990-91, pres, 1992-93; class pres, Class 1993, Morehouse Sch Med; adv, Boy Scouts Am Health Explorer's Post, 1990-93; AUC Stud Leadership Forum, 1992-93; bd dirs, Cath Charities, Diocese Galveston-Houston, 2002-; Nat Black MBA Asn, 2003-; Harris County Hosp Dist Med Bd, 2003-06. **Honors/Awds:** Hall of Fame Inductee, LA Youth Sem, 1986; partic, Metrop Leadership Forum, New Orleans, 1987; St Vincent dePaul Scholar, 1989-93; Fac Excellence Award, Fulbright & Jaworski LLP, 2002; "Physician of theYear? Award, Ben Taub Gen Hosp, 2004; Distinguished Alumnus Award, Nat Asn Equal Opportunity Higher Educ, 2006. **Special Achievements:** First African American corporate officer in Baylor's one hundred plus year history. **Busi-**

ness Addr: President, Chief Executive Officer, Meharry Medical College, Off President, 1005 Dr DB Todd Jr Blvd, Nashville, TN 37208, **Business Phone:** (615)327-6904.

RILEY, WILLIAM SCOTT
Police officer. **Personal:** Born Sep 24, 1940, Chester, PA; son of Benjamin and Leanna; married Deloris L; children: Kimberly, Kelly & William S Jr. **Educ:** Eastern Carolina Col, attended 1961; Lincoln Univ, MS, human servs, attended. **Career:** Police officer (retired); City Chester, Police Dept, police officer, liaison to mayor. **Orgs:** Bd mem, Delaware Co Selective Serv Bd, 1987; bd mem, Del Co Democratic Exec Bd, 1987; polit chmn, Cult Develop Coun Del Co, 1990-; bd mem, Chester Community Prev Coalition, 1990-; pres, Chester Police Athletic League; chair, bd trustees, Providence Bapt Church, 1990-98; comdr, Charles Horsey Post 300, Am Legion, 1995-98; fed adv bd, Chester-Upland Schl Dist, 1998. **Honors/Awds:** Outstanding Community Service Award, Chester Scholarship Comn, 1983; Eva Lou Winters Johnson Freedom Awards, Chester Br, Nat Asn Advan Colored People, 1985; Citizen of the Year, Omega Psi Phi Fraternity Inc, Epsilon Pi Chap, 1993; Westend Ministerial Fellowship's Presidential Award for Youth Service, 1993; The American Legion's Past Commander's Award, 1996. **Military Serv:** USMC, corpl. **Home Addr:** 918 Lloyd St, Chester, PA 19013.

RINGGOLD, FAITH
Artist, writer, painter (artist). **Personal:** Born Oct 8, 1930, New York, NY; daughter of Andrew Jones and Willi Jones; married Robert Earl Wallace, Nov 1, 1950 (divorced 1956); children: Michelle Wallace & Barbara Wallace; married Burdette, May 19, 1962. **Educ:** City Col NY, BS, 1955; City Col NY, Grad Sch, MA, 1959. **Career:** Am Asn Univ Women, Sculpture fel, 1976; Nat Endowment Arts, sculpture fel, 1978; artist & writer; Univ Calif, San Diego, prof art, prof emer, currently; Wilson Col, artist-in-residence. **Honors/Awds:** Nat Endowment for the Arts Award, 1978; Wonder Woman Foundation Award, 1983; Warner Communications Candace Award, 100 Black Women, 1984; honorary doctor of fine art, Moore Col Fine Art, 1986; doctor of fine art, Wooster Col, 1987; John Simon Guggenheim Foundation Award, 1987; La Napoule Foundation Award, 1990; Honorary Doctor of Fine Art, Massachusetts Col Art, 1991; Honorary Doctor of Fine Art, City Col New York, 1991; Gold Award for Illustration, Parent's Choice, 1991; ALA Notable Children's Book, Tar Beach, 1991; Honorary Doctor of Fine Arts, Brockport State Col, 1992; Best Children's Book Award, The NY Times, 1992; Coretta Scott King Award; Booklist Editor's Choice, Aunt Harriet's Underground Railroad Sky, 1993; Reading Magazine Award, Parenting Mag, 1993; Picture Book Award, Jane Addams Peace Asn, 1993; Honorary Doctorate, Calif Col Arts & Crafts, 1993; Honorary Doctorate, Brockport State Univ, 1993; Nat Endowment for the Arts travel award, 1993; Woman's Caucus for the Arts Honors Award, Outstanding Achievement in the Visual Art, NY, 1994; Honorary Doctor of Fine Arts, Rhode Island Sch Design, 1994; Honors Award for Outstanding Achievement in the Visual Arts, Women's Caucus Arts, 1994; Art Start for Children Award, Guggenheim Museum C's Prog, 1994; Recognition Award, New York State Fibers Asn, 1994; Townsend Harris Medal, City Col, Alumni Asn, 1995; Key to the City, Lake Charles, LA, 1995; Parent's Choice Award, 1996; Honorary Doctor of Fine Arts, Parsons Sch Design, 1996; Honorary Doctor of Fine Arts, Russell Sage Col, 1996; Honorary Degrees: Russel Sage, Troy, NY, 1996; Parsons Sch Design, NYC, 1996; Wheelock Col, Boston, 1997; Molloy Col, NYC, 1997; New Jersey Artist of the Year Award, NJ Ctr Visual Arts, 1997. **Special Achievements:** Author & illustrator of Tar Beach published by Crown press, 1991, Dinner at Aunt Connie's House, 1993, Talking to Faith Ringgold, 1995, We Flew Over the Bridge: Memoirs of Faith Ringgold, 1995, Bonjour Lonnie, 1996, My Dream of Martin Luther King Jr," 1996, solo exhibits include ACA Gallery, NYC, 1998, Exhibition Dancing at the Louvre: Faith Ringgold's French Collection and Other Story Quilts, The New Mus of Contemp Art, NYC, 1998-2000, group exhibits include The Art of the American Negro, Harlem Cultural Council, NYC, 1966, Cairo Biennial, Aknaton Gallery, Egypt, Cairo, Alexandria, Arman, Jordon, 1994, Damascus, Syria, 1995, Doha & Gala, Bahrain, 1996, Sewing Comfort Out of Grief-OK Bombing, 1996-98, A Shared Experience: 100 yrs at the Mac Dowell Colony, NYC, 1997, collections: ARCO Chemical, Philadelphia, Fort Wayne Museum of Fine Art, Ind, Harold Washington Library Center, Chicago, public Art For Public Schools, PS 22 Brooklyn, NY, Spenser Mus, Lawr, Kansas, 20 year retrospective exhibition at Studio Museum in Harlem 1984, Aunt Harriet's Underground Railroad in The Sky, Crown Press, 1992. **Business Addr:** Professor Emeritus, University of California, The Visual Arts Department, 9500 Gilman Dr, La Jolla, CA 92093-0327, **Business Phone:** (858)534-2860.

RIPPY, RODNEY ALLEN
Actor. **Personal:** Born Jul 29, 1968, Long Beach, CA; son of Fred and Flossie Hubbard. **Educ:** Cerritos Col, AA, bus admin, 1991; Calif State Univ. **Career:** Actor; cameraman; Films: Blazing Saddles, 1974; Oh, God! Book II, 1980; Checking the Gate, 2003; TV: "The Light at the Threshold", 1973; "Marcus Welby, M.D.", 1973; "The Harlem Globetrotters Popcorn Machine", 1974; "Medical Center", 1974; "The Odd Couple", 1975; "The Six Million Dollar Man", 1975; "Police Story", 1976; "The Hunter Hunted", 1980; "Vega$", 1980; "Parker Lewis Can't Lose", 1990-92; The Rodney Allen Rippy Show, host; Bow Tie Productions, partner, currently; RAR Entertainment, founder, currently. **Business Addr:** Founder, RAR Entertainment, PO Box 250153, Glendale, CA 91225, **Business Phone:** (323)665-9006.

RISBROOK, DR. ARTHUR TIMOTHY
Businessperson, physician, administrator. **Personal:** Born Dec 21, 1929, Brooklyn, NY; son of Belleville Timothy and Ruby Isolene Wilkinson; married Ida Marie Slaughter, Jun 8, 1957; children: Donna Michelle & Deborah Nicole. **Educ:** City Col, NY, BS, 1955; Meharry Med Col, MD, 1961; Bank Dirs Sch, Montreal, attended, 1973; CW Post Col, nursing home admin course, 1980. **Career:** Trida Travel Serv, owner; Hempstead Sch Dist, chief physician; Nassau Co Drug Abuse & Addiction Ctr, founder dir, med servs; Mercy Hosp, physician; Holly Patterson Home Aged, physician; Hempstead Gen Hosp, physician; Nassau Co Med Ctr, physician, 1965-; Chapin Nursing Home, med dir; Holly Patterson Geriat Ctr, med dir; P&R Advert Co, founder, 1974; Greater Harlem Nursing Homes, med dir, 1976-84; Marcus Garvey Nursing Homes, med dir, 1977-84. **Orgs:** AMA; Nat Med Asn; Empire State Med Asn; Nassau/Suffolk Clin Asn; Clin Soc New York Diabetes Asn; Am Thoracic Soc; Nassau Co Med Soc; Aer Cancer Soc; founder, Topic House Drug Abuse Prog, 1966; life mem, Nat Asn Advan Colored People; New York State Bd Prof Med Conduct; NY Statewide Adv Coun; Dept Soc Serv; bd dir, Nassau Prof Rev Org; chmn, Sub-Comn Medicaid Serv NY Statewide Adv Comt Soc Servs; Caduceus Med Hon Soc; exec comt, Nassau Co Med Ctr; chmn bd, Vanguard Nat Bank, 1972-74; pres med/dent staff, Nassau Co Med, 1972-74; Am Med Dir Asn, 1990-; NY Med Dir Asn, 1990-; elder, Mem Presbyterian Church, Roosevelt NY, 1995-. **Honors/Awds:** Trail Blazer Award for Founding Vanguard National Bank, Mayor's Comt; Man of Year Award, Westbury Bus & Prof Women; Achievement Award, Brooklyn Bus & Prof Women, 1973; President's Award, Meharry Med Col; Dr Martin Luther King Award; Pioneer in Humanitarianism, New York State & Nassau Co Human Rights Comns, 1993. **Military Serv:** AUS, artillery, capt, 1950-54; Purple Heart, 3 Battle Stars. **Home Addr:** 175 Maple Ave, Westbury, NY 11590-3169.

RISCOE, ROMONA A
Association executive, president (organization). **Personal:** Born Sep 18, 1959, Brooklyn, NY; daughter of Alfonso Riscoe and Mary Crawford. **Educ:** Univ Pittsburgh, 1977-81; Antioch Univ, BA, human serv admin, 1986. **Career:** Abraxas Found, Abraxas Group, mkt liaison, fac dir, regional dir, vpres; NJ state Aquarium, dir, visitor servs & com rels; Philadelphia Multicultural Affairs Cong, exec dir; Riscoe & Associates, pres, currently. **Orgs:** Am Soc Exec Asn; Nat Coalition Black Meeting Planners; African Am Travel & Tourism Asn; Meeting Planners Int; Philadelphia Urban League; Philadelphia Int Airport Bd; bd mem, Black Family Reunion Cult Ctr; Philadelphia Conv & Visitors Bur Bd; pres, African Am Mus. **Honors/Awds:** Hospitality Award, Philadelphia Hotel Asn, 1996; Hospitality Sales & Marketing Association Award, 1996; Share the Heritage Award, 1997; Minority Business Award, Nat Coalition Black Meeting Planners, 2007. **Special Achievements:** Appointed to serve as delegate to the White House Conference on Travel & Tourism. **Business Addr:** President, Riscoe & Associates, 4548 Market St, Philadelphia, PA 19139, **Business Phone:** (215)895-4073.

RISHER, JOHN ROBERT, JR.
Lawyer. **Personal:** Born Sep 23, 1938, Washington, DC; son of John R and Yvonne G Jones Peniston; married Carol Adriane Seeger, Jun 9, 1974; children: John David, Michael Temple, Mark Eliot & Conrad Zachary. **Educ:** Morgan State Univ, BA, 1960; Univ S CA, JD, 1962; John F Kennedy Sch, Harvard Univ, attended 1977. **Career:** US Dept Justice, staff atty, 1965-68; US Dept Justice, spec asst US atty, 1966-68; Arent Fox Kintner Plotkin & Kahn PLLC, 1968-74, partner, 1975-76, pvt pract atty, 1978-; Dist Columbia Govt, corp coun, 1976-78. **Orgs:** Exec comt, Nat Capital Area Civil Liberties Union, 1969-71; chmn, Montgomery Co Civil Liberties Union, 1970-71; chmn, Nominating Comt DC Bd Elections & Ethics, 1974-76; DC Jud Conf, 1975-; bd dir, DC Pub Defender Serv, 1975-76; bd dir, chmn, DC Comt Licensure Pract Healing Arts, 1976-78; Jud Conf DC Cir, 1976-; Adv Comt Rules & Evidence Super Ct DC, 1976; DC Law Rev Comt, 1976-78; Jud Planning Comt, 1976-81; dir & sec, Jewish Soc Serv Agency, 1979-85; DC Bar AD-Hoc Comn Transfer Felony Prosecutorial Jurisdiction, 1979-81; dir, Am Jewish Commmunity, DC Chap, 1981-90; dir, Greater Wash Jewish Commmunity Ctr, 1982-91; pres, DC Jewish Comn Ctr, 1985-87; bd dir, DC Jewish Community Ctr, 1986-; Dist Columbia Comn Admis, 1986-92; bd dir, United Jewish Appeal Fed, 1988-; trustee, Exec Comt, Supreme Ct Hist Soc, 1990-; bd dirs, Wash Civic Symphony, 1992-; secy, DePriest Fifteen, 1994-; fel, Am Bar Asn, 1995-; bd dirs, Frederick B Abramson Mem Fed, 1995-; bd dirs, Smithsonian Inst Wash Coun, 1997. **Military Serv:** AUS, capt, 1963-65. **Home Addr:** 3311 Cleveland Ave NW, Washington, DC 20008, **Home Phone:** (202)333-4454. **Business Phone:** (202)857-6452.

RISON, ANDRE PREVIN
Football player. **Personal:** Born Mar 18, 1967, Flint, MI; married; children: Andre Jr. **Educ:** Mich State Univ, attended. **Career:** Football player (retired); Indianapolis Colts, wide receiver, 1989; Atlanta Falcons, 1990-94; Cleveland Browns, 1995; Green Bay Packers, 1996; Jacksonville Jaguars, 1996; Kans City Chiefs, 1997-99; Oakland Raiders, wide receiver, 2000; Toronto Argonauts, CFL, wide receiver, 2004-05. **Honors/Awds:** Pro Bowl, 1990, 1991, 1992 & 1993; Kans City Chiefs, Most Valuable Player, 1997.

RISON, DR. FAYE
Educator. **Personal:** Born Feb 25, 1942, Nacogdoches, TX; daughter of Rebecca and Archie; children: Sondra R Scott. **Educ:** Univ Colo, MA, 1970, PhD, generalist, 1984. **Career:** Univ Colo Med Ctr, psychiat nurse, 1965-67; NW Team Dept Health Hosp, Denver, CO, psychiat nurse, 1967-71; Metro State Col, from asst prof to assoc prof, 1971-98, prof human serv; Colo Tech Univ, adj prof, currently; Christmas Project Toys Kids, founder. **Orgs:** Bd mem, Nat Orgn Human Serv, 1980-84; Am Civil Liberties Union; Delta Sigma Theta; Black Womens Network; Denver Sister Cities; Black Women with Advanced Degrees. **Honors/Awds:** Doct Fellowship, Univ Colo, 1980-82; Outstanding Faculty Award Human Service, 1979-82; Sertoman of the Year, 2000; Sertoma International Tribune Award, Presidents Award, 2001; In the Black Smart Women, 2001. **Home Addr:** 8792 E Kent Pl, Denver, CO 80237. **Business Addr:** Adjunct Professor, Colorado Technical University, 4435 N Chestnut St, Colorado Springs, CO 80907, **Business Phone:** (719)598-0200.

RIST, SUSAN E
Lawyer. **Personal:** Born in Chicago, IL; daughter of Seward Sr (deceased) and Irma Tatum (deceased); married Steve F Sbraccia, Sep 9, 1989. **Educ:** Principia Col, Elsah, IL, BA; Boston Univ, Boston, MA, MS; Suffolk Univ, JD, 1995. **Career:** KAAY Radio, Little Rock, Ark, news anchor, reporter, 1978-80; WHDH Radio, Boston, Mass, news anchor, reporter, 1980-82; WLVI-TV, Boston, Mass, news anchor, reporter, 1982-85; WBOS Radio, Boston, Mass, news anchor, 1985-87; WHBQ-TV, Memphis, Tenn, news reporter, 1987; WBZ Radio, Boston, Mass, news anchor, reporter, 1987-95; Emerson Col, Boston, Mass, broadcast jour instr, 1987-92; Suffolk Co Dist atty Off, asst dist atty, 1995-. **Orgs:** Nat Asn Black Journalists, 1989-95; Soc Prof Journalists, 1990-95; Black Law Students Asn, 1992-95; Am Trial Lawyers Asn, 1994-; Mass Bar Asn, 1995-. **Honors/Awds:** Harold Goodwin Best Trial Advocate Award, 1994. **Home Addr:** 29 Irving St, Newton, MA 02459-1611, **Home Phone:** (617)243-0205. **Business Addr:** Assistant District Attorney, Suffolk County District Attorney, One Bulfinch Pl, Boston, MA 02114, **Business Phone:** (617)619-4000.

RITCHIE, JOE (JOSEPH EDWARD RITCHIE, II)
Journalist, educator. **Personal:** Born Jul 10, 1949, Oak Hill, WV; son of Joseph E Sr and Dorothy; married Louise Reid, Jun 23, 1979; children: Jabari Russell & Akin Zachary. **Educ:** Calvin Col, Grand Rapids, MI, AB, 1970; Ruprecht-19 Karl Univ, Heidelberg,W Ger, 1972; Ohio State Univ, Columbus, OH, MA, Ger, 1973, MA, jour, 1975. **Career:** Woodrow Wilson fel, 1970; Ohio State Univ, Columbus, OH, grad teaching asst, 1972-75; Wash Post, Wash, DC, reporter, 1975-77; Duke Univ, Wash, postdoctoral fel, 1981; Fla A&M Univ, prof & Knight chair jour, 1990-. **Orgs:** Nat Asn Black Journalists; Soc Prof Journalists; bd dir, Am Coun Ger, 1984-; adv bd mem, Pew Ctr Civic J, Jim Batten Prize for Excellence in Civic Jour, 1996-2002; mem rules & referees comn, US Team Handball Fedn; treas, Black Col Commun Asn. **Honors/Awds:** French-Am Found Young Leader. **Home Addr:** 1001 Lasswade Dr, Tallahassee, FL 32312-2862. **Business Addr:** Professor, Knight Chair in Journalism, Florida A&M University, Division of Journalism, Tucker Hall Suite 305, Tallahassee, FL 32307, **Business Phone:** (850)599-3880.

RITCHIE, DR. LOUISE REID
Newspaper executive, educator. **Personal:** Born Jul 10, 1951, Niskayuna, NY; daughter of Antoinette Lyles and Lester Frank Reid Sr; married Joseph E Ritchie II, Jun 23, 1979; children: Jabari Russell & Akin Zachary. **Educ:** Harvard Univ, Radcliffe Col, Cambridge, MA, AB, govt, 1973; George Washington Univ, Wash, DC, M Phil, psychol, 1982, PhD, 1986. **Career:** Assoc Press, Atlanta, Ga, Nashville, TN, reporter, 1974-76; The Wash Post, Wash, DC, reporter, 1976-77; Detroit Urban League, Detroit, MI, dir, substance abuse prev, 1987; Detroit Free Press, columnist, 1987-92, exec asst to publ, 1990-92; self-employed prof pub speaker, 1987-; Wayne State Univ, instr, 1988-92; Knight-Ridder Inc, human resources consult, 1993-94; Fla Agri & Mech Univ, assoc prof, 1994-; Fla Inst Leadership Excellence, Fla Agri &Mech Univ, founding dir, 1998-; Media & Graphic Arts, Fla A&M Univ, Tallahassee, Fla, assoc prof jour, currently. **Orgs:** Delta Sigma Theta Sorority, 1984-; Hartford Memorial Baptist Church; Mich Prof Speakers Asn; Sorosis Arts & Literacy Club; Nat Speakers Asn; mem bd dir, Radcliffe College Club, Wash, DC, 1985-86; Samaritan Hospital Substance Abuse Committee, 1987; Wayne County Juvenile Court Substance Abuse Comt, 1988; Childrens Ctr Perinatal Health Comt, 1988; mem admis comt, Harvard Univ, 1989-92; vice chmn, community adv bd, WTVS-TV, Detroit, MI, 1989-90; Newspaper Asn Am Diversity, sub comt co-chair, 1992-95; Class secretary, Radcliffe Col. **Honors/Awds:** Navy Health Prof Scholar, 1979; Woman Who Makes Things Happen Award, Detroit Chap Nat Coun Negro Women, 1987; Celebrate Literacy Award, Metropolitan Detroit Reading Coun, 1988; Celebrate

Literacy Award, Oakland County Reading Asn, 1989; Martin Luther King Community Service Award, Southfield, MI, 1990; Distinguished Graduate Award, Niskayuna High Sch, New York, 1990; Woman of the Year for Journalism, Hartford Memorial Baptist Church, 1991; Honorary Doctorate in Community Svc, Eastern Mich Univ, 1992; Award of Excellence, Knight-Ridder, 1992; Kellogg Nat Fel, 1995. **Military Serv:** USNR, O-3, Lt, 1979-86.

RITTER, THOMAS J.
Executive. **Personal:** Born Dec 24, 1922, Allendale, SC; married Betty Davis; children: Eva, Jephrey. **Educ:** E Bapt Col, BS, divinity, 1959; Morris Col, DD honorary, 1968; E Bapt Col, DD, 1969; Temple Univ, Dr Humane Letters, Pentecostal Theol Sem, 1970. **Career:** Ritter Bros Med Equip Sales Co, partner, 1947-49; ins, 1949-55; Second & Macedonia Bapt Ch, pastor, 1958; Dept of Welfare, PA, caseworker, 1959-60; N Philadelphia Youth Community & Employ Serv, exec dir, 1960-63; Opportunities Industrialization Ctr Inc, exec dir, 1963. **Orgs:** Bd mem, Franklin Inst; Philadelphia Nat Bank; E Bapt Col; Albert Einstein Med Ctr; Pathway Sch; Area Manpower Planning Coun; PA Industrial Develop Auth; Contact Philadelphia; pres, Coun of Am Inst of Mgt; Acad for Career Educ Mem, Philadelphia Partnership; Mayor's Com of Twelve; Baptist Ministers Conf of Philadelphia & vincinity; Greater Philadelphia C of C; Governor's adv coun on Housing; Crime Comn of Philadelphia; adv Coun Vocational Educ Sch Dist of Philadelphia; Am Inst of Mgmt; Philadelphia Baptist Keystone Asn; Lower KY Environ Ctr; Bd of Dir, Philadelphia Martin Luther King Jr. Assoc Nonviolence Inc & Philadelphia Gas Works. **Honors/Awds:** Cit com No-fault Ins; recipient OIC, Decade of Progress Award, 1974; distinguished cit award, US Civil Serv Comn, 1972; outstanding serv award, Bronze Asn for Cult Adv, 1971; humanitarian award, World Alliance of Holiness, 1970; award of achievement Philadelphia Tribune Charities, 1967; outstanding alumni award, E Bapt Col, 1964; Margaret Van Dyne Award, outstanding scholar & christian devotion, 1959; NAACP, Community Service Award; City of Philadelphia Citation Award. **Military Serv:** AUS, 1942-45. **Business Addr:** Opportunities Industrialization Center Inc, 1415 N Broad St, Philadelphia, PA 19122-3323.

RIVERA, EDDY
Lawyer. **Personal:** Born Jul 23, 1938, St Croix, Virgin Islands of the United States; son of Margot M and Adelo; married Gloria Maria Rojas, Feb 26, 1967; children: Lisette M, Julia I, Eddy Jr & Vanessa M. **Educ:** Interam Univ San German PR, 1960; Univ PR San Juan, BBA (cum laude), 1963, JD, 1972. **Career:** VI Properties Inc, chief acct, 1966-69; Govt VI, asst atty gen, 1973-76, VI Bd Educ, 1976-78, senator, 1979-80; pvt pract atty; CRC Law List Co Inc, atty, currently. **Orgs:** PR Bar Asn, 1973; bd mem, Camp Arawak Youth Serv Orgn, 1974-76; pres, Hispanos Unidos VI Inc, 1974-78, 1992-; bd educ, Govt VI, 1976-78; Virgin Islands Bar Asn, 1976; pres, Full Gospel Bus Men's Fel Int, 1981-86; Am Bar Asn, 1981-96; Asn Trial Lawyers, 1982-94. **Military Serv:** AUS, pfc, 1963-65. **Home Addr:** 231 Judiths Fancy Christiansted, St Croix, Virgin Islands of the United States 00823, **Home Phone:** (809)773-7097. **Business Addr:** Attorney, CRC Law List Company Inc, 1168 King St Sunny Isle Christiansted Suite 2, PO Box 7430, St Croix, Virgin Islands of the United States 00823, **Business Phone:** (340)773-5756.

RIVERA, LANCE
Executive, writer. **Career:** Untertainment Records, ceo & label co-founder, currently; Writer: The Perfect Holiday, 2007; Producer: Life Support, 2007. **Special Achievements:** Formed co with Notorious BIG; artists include: Lil Kim, Lil Cease, Junior MAFIA, Charli Baltimore. **Business Phone:** (718)390-3928.

RIVERA, MAXWELL
Singer. **Personal:** Born May 23, 1973, Brooklynn, NY; son of Puerto Rican and Trinidadian. **Career:** The Coffee Shop, waiter; Albums: Maxwell's Urban Hang Suite, 1996; MTV Unplugged, 1997; Embrya, 1998; Now, 2001; BLACK summers' night, 2009; Singles: "Til the Cops Come Knockin", 1996; "Ascension (Don't Ever Wonder)", 1996; "Sumthin', Sumthin'", 1996; "Whenever, Wherever, Whatever", 1997; "Luxury: Cococure", 1998; "Matrimony: May be You", 1998; "Each Hour Each Minute Each Second Each Day:Of My Life", 1998; "Let's Not Play the Game", 1999; "Fortunate", 1999; "Get to Know Ya", 2000; "Lifetime", 2001; "This Woman's Work", 2001. **Honors/Awds:** Soul Train Awards, 1996 & 2000; Billboard Music Award, 1999. **Business Phone:** (212)833-8000.*

RIVERO, MARITA
Librarian. **Personal:** Born Nov 25, 1943, West Grove, PA; daughter of Manuel and Grace Rivero; divorced; children: Raafi Muhammad. **Educ:** Tufts Univ, BS, 1964; Wharton Sch Bus, exec mgt prog, 1981; Stanford Bus Sch, exec mgt prog, 1994. **Career:** WGBH, producer, 1970-76; consultant; WPFW, vpres, 1981-88; WGPH, vpres, 1988, gen mgr, radio & TV, 2005-, producer, currently. **Orgs:** Nat Fed Community Broadcasters, 1982-86; NPR, Distribution/Interconnection Bd, 1985-88; Public Radio Int, 1990-2002; Kolcrobiley Inst, Ghana, 1992-; Partnership, 1996-; chair, Mus African Am Hist, 1996-; Inst Contemporary Art; Urban League Eastern Mass, 1999-. **Honors/Awds:** Vision Award, Women Film, 2000; Peabody Award, Univ Ga, 2000; Acad Women Achievers, YWCA, 2001; Honarary Doctor of Arts, Pine Manor Col, 2002; other community & professional awards. **Special Achievements:** Helped build an educational institution in Ghana. **Business Addr:** General Manager for Radio & Television, Producer, WGBH, 125 Western Ave, PO Box 200, Boston, MA 02134, **Business Phone:** (617)300-2429.

RIVERS, ALFRED J.
Executive. **Personal:** Born Sep 18, 1925, Crisp, GA; married Vera Stripling; children: Gwendolyn Thrower, Gregory Rivers, Glenda. **Educ:** LUTC, 1976; TN State Univ. **Career:** NC Mutual Ins Co; Gillespie Selden Comn Devel Ctr, dir, vpres, 1972-77; Middle Flint Planning APDC, dir, 1973-77; Crisp Cordele & C C, dir, 1973-77; Cordele City Comn, vchmn, 1972-77. **Orgs:** NAACP; Local Am Legion; Cancer Soc. **Military Serv:** AUS, capt, 1943-46.

RIVERS, D ADOLPHUS. See CHICAGO, DENOVIOUS ADOLPHUS.

RIVERS, DOROTHY
Administrator. **Personal:** Born Aug 14, 1933, Chicago, IL; divorced. **Educ:** John Marshall Law Sch, 1951; Northwestern Univ, BA, 1959. **Career:** Michael Reese Hosp & Med Ctr, exec adminstr, dept of psychtry; Nelson Prods Inc, vp. **Orgs:** Founder, chwmn, Women's Div Chicago Ec Develop Corp; founder, mem, The XXI of Michael Reese Hosp; chwmn, 1st, 2nd & 3rd Midwest Regional Conf on Bus Opport for Women; vp, bd dir Chicago Ec Develop Corp; bd dir, Chicago Fin Dev Corp; chairperson, Vanguard of Chicago Urban Leag; chairperson, exec adv bd Big Buddies Yth Serv, 1964-; Bravo Chap Lyric Opera; bd dir, Oper PUSH Found; womens bd United Negro Col Found; Chicago Chap of Links. **Honors/Awds:** Recip Vol Serv Award, Chicago Ec Develop Corp, 1973; Vol Serv Award, Gov of IL, 1967; Lady of the Day Award, Radio Sta WAAF & WAIT; cert of ldrshp Met YMCA 1975;cert merit, Chicago Heart Asn, 1975; M F Bynun Comm Serv Award, 1975.

RIVERS, GLENN ANTON
Basketball player, basketball coach. **Personal:** Born Oct 13, 1961, Maywood, IL; married Kristen Campi; children: Jeremiah. **Educ:** Marquette Univ, Milwaukee, attended 1983. **Career:** Basketball Player (retired), Coach; Atlanta Hawks, guard, 1983-91, Los Angeles Clippers, 1991-92, NY Knicks, 1992-95; San Antonio Spurs, 1995-96; Orlando Magic, head coach, 1999-2003; NBA on ABC, commentator; Boston Celtics, head coach, 2004-. **Orgs:** All-Star Adv Coun. **Honors/Awds:** FIBA World Championship, MVP, 1982; NBA Coach of the Year, 2000. **Business Phone:** (617)854-8000.

RIVERS, JESSIE
Administrator. **Educ:** Wayne State Univ. **Career:** Camp Gilman, supvr; Mich Reformatory, dep warden; Mich Parole Bd, staff; Egeler Correctional Facil, warden; Ryan Regional Correctional Facil, warden.

RIVERS, JOHN MILTON. See RIVERS, MICKEY.

RIVERS, JOHNNY (JOHN HENRY RAMISTELLA)
Singer. **Personal:** Born Nov 7, 1942, New York, NY. **Career:** Rivers Music, pres; Imperial Records, rcrdng artst, 1963-; Albums: At The Whisky A Go-Go, 1964; Meanwhile, 1965; ".and i know you want to dance", 1966; Rewind, 1967; Realization, 1968; Touch Of Gold, 1969; Homegrown, 1971; Blue Suede Shoes, 1973; Last Boogie In Paris, 1974; The Very Best Of, 1975; Wild Night,1976; Outside Help, 1979; Borrowed Time, 1980; Not A Through Street, 1983; Memphis Sun, 1991; Last Train To Memphis, 1998; Back at the Whisky, 2000; Reinvention Highway, 2004; Last Boogie in Paris: The Complete Concert, 2007; Shadow of the Moon, 2009. Soul CityRecords, LA, owner, 1967-; Soul City Prods, Johnny Rivers Mus. **Orgs:** First hit Record Memphis. **Honors/Awds:** Louisiana Music Hall of Fame, 2009. **Business Addr:** Singer, Soul City Records, 3141 Coldwater Canyon Lane, Beverly Hills, CA 90210.

RIVERS, JOHNNY
Chef. **Personal:** Born Oct 5, 1949, Orlando, FL; son of Johnnie Mae; married Shirley Capers; children: Johnny Jr, Djuan, Dwain, Tanya & Zina. **Educ:** Johnson & Wales Univ, Doctor Culinary Arts (hon). **Career:** Cherry Plz Hotel, cook; Mission Inn Country Club, chef, 1963-64; Flountainbleu Miami FL, chef, 1968; Palmer House, chef, 1969; Walt Disney World Co, exec chef, beginning 1970, corp exec chef, 1989-95; JR Intl Enterprises Inc, chef & restaurateur, 1995-; Johnny Rivers' Smokehouse Express, owner, currently; Darden Restaurants, consult; Smokehouse & BBQ Co, Chef & Owner, currently; McArthur Dairy, chef, currently. **Orgs:** Pres, Cent Fla Chef Asn, 1974-75; host, World Chef Congress, 1984; pub rels, Am Culinary Fed, 1984-85; Orange City Sch Bd, 1985; Cent Fla Community. **Honors/Awds:** Acad Chefs Am Culinary Fed, 1976-77; Award of Gratitude, Brown Col, 1979; Chef of the Year, Cent Fla Chef Asn, 1980; Chef Professionalism Award, Am Culinary Fedn, 1992; Orlando Mag Golden Palm Awards; Fla Trend's Golden Spoon Awards; Orlando Sentinel Foodie Awards. **Special Achievements:** TV appearance: "Good Morning Am"; "Today Show"; "Oprah Winfrey Show"; "Live! With Regis & Kathie Lee"; publ including: Time mag; Natl Restaurant News; Redbook; Southern Living; Bon Appetit; Chef mag; Food Arts; Better Homes & Gardens; Ebony mag; Cooked for U.S. Presidents Nixon, Ford, Carter, Reagan and Clinton, and for South African President Nelson Mandela. **Business Phone:** (407)293-5803.

RIVERS, LEN
Athletic coach. **Educ:** Springfield Col, attended 1957. **Career:** Coach (retired); Franklin Township High Sch, head football coach; NJ Nets, dir community affairs; Univ Conn, coach; Univ Princeton, coach; Univ Montclair, coach; Lakewood, athletic dir, 7yrs; Ocean County All Stars, coaching staff. **Orgs:** Chmn, football comt, NJ State Interscholastic Athletic Asn.

RIVERS, LOUIS
Educator. **Personal:** Born Sep 18, 1922, Savannah, GA; married Ligia Sanchez; children: Luisa, Liana, Loria, Leigh. **Educ:** Savannah State Col, BS, 1946; New York Univ, MA, 1951; Fordham Univ, PhD, 1975. **Career:** WV State Col, instr, 1951-52; Southern Univ, instr, 1952-53; Tougaloo Col, asst prof, 1953-58; New York Tech Col, prof; Andrew Mellon creative writing fel, 1984; The City Univ New York, emer, currently. **Orgs:** Natl Writers Club; Dramatist Guild; Speech Commun Asn; Col Lang Asn; Phi Delta Kappa; Kappa Delta Pi. **Honors/Awds:** John Hay Whitney Theater 1957; Outstanding Teacher Plaque, Kappa Delta Pi, 1983. **Military Serv:** US Corps Engrs pvt, 1942. **Business Addr:** Professor of Writing, Speech, New York City Tech College, 300 Jay St, Brooklyn, NY 11201.

RIVERS, MICKEY (JOHN MILTON RIVERS)
Baseball player. **Personal:** Born Oct 31, 1948, Miami, FL. **Educ:** Miami-Dade Community Col, attended 1969. **Career:** Baseball Player (Retired); California Angels, outfielder, 1970-75 (Retired); New York Yankees,outfielder, 1976-79; Texas Rangers, outfielder, 1979-84. **Honors/Awds:** American League pennant, 1976, 1977, 1978; World Series champion, 1977,1978; All-Star, Am League, 1976; Rangers Player of the Yr, 1980. **Military Serv:** AUS, 1970-71; US Air Force Reserves, 1971. *

RIVERS, DR. ROBERT JOSEPH, JR.
Physician, educator. **Personal:** Born Nov 14, 1931, Princeton, NJ; married Ruth Lewis; children: Michael, Scott, Wendy & Robert D. **Educ:** Princeton Univ, AB (Cum Laude), 1953; Harvard Med Sch, MD, 1957. **Career:** Educator, physician (retired); Pvt pract, vascular surg, 1965-86; Univ Rochester Sch Med & Dentist, prof clin surg 1984-89; assoc dean for minority affairs, 1984-89. **Orgs:** Trustee, Princeton Univ, 1969-77; bd trustees, Rochester Savings Bank, 1972-83; chief, Div Vascular Surg, The Genesee Hosp, 1978-85. **Honors/Awds:** President's Citation Medical Society of the State of NY, 1971; Distinguished Alumni Service Award, Asn Black Princeton Alumni, 1982; Outstanding Service Award, Nat Asn Med Minority Educr Inc, 1989. **Military Serv:** USN, lt; USNR, 1959-61. **Home Addr:** 164 Highland, Williamsburg, VA 23188-7467, **Home Phone:** (757)565-4193. *

RIVERS, RON. See RIVERS, RONALD LEROY.

RIVERS, RONALD LEROY (RON RIVERS)
Football player. **Personal:** Born Nov 13, 1971, Elizabeth City, NJ; married Myla; children: Malia. **Educ:** Fresno State Univ. **Career:** Football player(retired); Detroit Lions, running back, 1995-99; Atlanta Falcons, running back, 2000. **Honors/Awds:** Special Teams Most Valuable Player, Detroit Lions, 1995.

RIVERS, TOM. See WAGONER, J ROBERT.

RIVERS, VALERIE L
Lawyer, government official. **Personal:** Born Nov 25, 1952, Birmingham, AL; daughter of Eddie. **Educ:** Tuskegee Inst, BS, 1975; Southern Univ Sch Law, JD, 1980. **Career:** Wayne County Community Col, asst dir human resources, 1976; Gov Off Consumer Protection State La, investigator 1979-80; B'ham Area Legal Serv, staff atty cand, 1981; Birmingham City Coun. **Orgs:** Phi Alpha Delta Law Frat Int, 1978-; adv comn, minor recruiter, Big-sister, 1983-; bd dir Big Bros/Big Sisters Gr Birmingham, 1985-88; Am Soc Pub Admin, 1981-; Nat Forum Black Admin, 1983-. **Honors/Awds:** First & past justice AP Tureau Chap Phi Alpha Delta Law Frat int & founding mem Chapter 1978; Reginald Heber Smith Comm Lawyer Fellowship, 1980-81; Hon Mayor of Pritchard, AL, 1980; exec in residence Birmingham-Southern Coll, 1983; Govt & Politics Black Women Bus & Prof Asn, 1984. **Special Achievements:** Birmingham, city council admin-first Black and first female to hold this position. **Home Addr:** 1908 Huntington Circle, Birmingham, AL 35214. **Business Addr:** Council Administrator, Birmingham City Council, 710 N Nineteenth St, Birmingham, AL 35203.

RIVERS, VERNON FREDERICK
School administrator. **Personal:** Born Jul 25, 1933, Peekskill, NY; married Audrey Cherry; children: Gregory, Pamela & Karen.

Educ: State Univ NY, BS, Educ, 1955; Teachers Col, Columbia Univ, New York, Grad Work, 1960; City Col, New York, Grad Work, 1963; State Univ New York, New Paltz, MS, Educ, 1971. **Career:** School Administrator (Retired); Peekskill New York Sch System, teacher, 1957-61; Irvington New York Sch System, teacher, 1961-68; Elmsford New York Sch Syst, prin, 1968-72; Elmsford Sch System, fed funds coordr, 1971-72; Ossining New York Sch System, teacher adult educ, 1975; Brewster Sch Syst, prin, 1972-88, dir professional serv, 1988-91. **Orgs:** Kappa Alpha Psi Fraternity, Inc; AARP; bd dir, Salisbury Wicomico Arts Coun; Deer's Head Hosp; Ward Mus Wild fowl Art; bd dir, Mid-Delmarva Family YMCA; bd dir, Inst Retired Persons/SSU; vice chmn, Diocese Easton, Md; Sigma Pi Phi; Westchester County Football Officials & Coaches Asn; Tri-County Asn Black Admin. **Honors/Awds:** Vanguard Award, Peekskill NAACP, 1959; Certificate of Appreciation, Elmsford Comt, 1972; Certificate of Appreciation, Lions Club Yorktown & Rotary Club Brewster, 1974; Certificate of Appreciation, Yorktown Area Jaycees, 1978; Cert Safety & Good Medal. **Special Achievements:** First black teacher & principal in each school system employed. **Military Serv:** AUS, PFC, 1955-57.

ROACH, DELORIS
Public relations executive, president (organization), business owner. **Personal:** Born Apr 15, 1944, Pine Bluff, AR; children: Yvette Guyton, Frank, Anthony & Monica. **Educ:** Univ Calif, Berkeley, BA, Jour, 1975; San Francisco State Univ, MA, Radio & TV, 1979. **Career:** KQED-TV Educ TV, admin asst, 1979-81; KQED-TV Educ Films, researcher, 1981-82; New Images Prod Inc, prod coordr, 1982-84; Fleming Co Inc, advertising coordr; Emery Unified Sch Dist, mem, bd of trustees; TLW Pub Rels, Inc, pres & owner, currently. **Orgs:** Consult, CA Schs Bd Assoc, 1979; CA Sch Bds Assoc, Alameda Co Sch Bds Assoc, 1979, CA Black Sch Bd Mem Assoc, 1981. **Honors/Awds:** Outstanding Citizen Award, Emery ville Neighborhood Assoc, 1981; Disting Service Award, Alameda Co Sch Bds Assoc, 1984. **Business Addr:** President, Owner, TLW Pub Rels Inc, 340 2 Travis Blvd Suite 167, Fairfield, CA 94533, **Business Phone:** (707)208-9479.

ROACH, PROF. HILDRED ELIZABETH
Educator. **Personal:** Born Mar 14, 1937, Charlotte, NC; daughter of Howard and Pearl Caldwell. **Educ:** Fisk Univ, Nashville, Tenn, BA, 1957; Juilliard Sch Music, New York, 1959; Yale Univ, New Haven, Conn, MM, 1962; Univ Ghana, 1969. **Career:** Tuskegee Inst, Tuskegee, Ala, fac, 1957-60; Fayetteville State Col, Fayetteville, NC, fac, 1962-66; Howard Univ, Washington, DC, fac, 1966-67; Virginia State Col, Petersburg, Va, fac, 1967-68; Univ DC, Washington, DC, prof, 1968-. **Orgs:** Alpha Kappa Alpha; Music Educators; Nat Black Music Caucus; NAACP; NANM;Phi Beta Kappa. **Honors/Awds:** Ford Found Scholar, 1953-57; scholar, Omega Psi Phi, 1953-57; Theodore Presser Award, 1956; Yale Merit Award, 1982; Lockwood Concerto Competition, Yale, 1961. **Special Achievements:** Author, Black American Music: Past & Present, Krieger, 1985, 1992, 2nd ed., 1994. **Business Addr:** Professor, University of the District of Columbia, Department of Music, 4200 Connecticut Ave NW B46W Room A05A, Washington, DC 20008, **Business Phone:** (202)274-5810.

ROACH, LEE
Association executive, teacher, business owner. **Personal:** Born Jan 3, 1937, Rock Hill, SC. **Educ:** Lincoln Univ, BA, 1960; Bryn Mawr Col, MSW, 1969; Cornell Univ. **Career:** Restaurant, owner, mgr, 1955-74; teacher, 1960-66; Health & Welfare Coun, asst dir, 1966-67; Grad Sch Soc Work, Bryn Mawr, comn orgn instr, 1970-71; Health Adminr Prog, 1972; Regional Comprehensive Health Planning Coun Inc, sep assoc dir; Equestrian Acad.

ROACH, MAXWELL LEMEUL
Musician, educator. **Personal:** Born Jan 10, 1924, Newland, NC; son of Alphonse and Cressie; married Mildred Wilkinson; children: Daryl & Maxine. **Educ:** Manhattan Sch Music, compos, 1952. **Career:** Jazz clubs, drummer; Univ Mass, Amherst, Dept Music & Dance, fac, 1972-; Debut Rec, co-founder. **Orgs:** Jazz Artists Guild; Omega Psi Phi Fraternity. **Honors/Awds:** Winner, Down Beat poll, 1955, 1957, 1958, 1959, 1960, 1984; Mac Arthur Foundation "genius" grant; French Grand Prix du Disque; International Percussive Art Society's Hall of Fame; Down beat Magazine Hall of Fame; Harvard Jazz Master; eight honorary doctorate degrees. **Special Achievements:** First to be given a Mac Arthur Foundation "genius" grant, cited as a Commander of the Order of Arts and Letters in France.

ROAF, WILLIAM LAYTON (WILLIE ROAF)
Football player. **Personal:** Born Apr 18, 1970, Pine Bluff, AR; son of Andree Layton. **Educ:** La Tech Univ. **Career:** Football player (retired); New Orleans Saints, tackle, 1993-2001; Kans City Chiefs, offensive tackle, 2002-05. **Honors/Awds:** NFC Offensive Lineman of the Year, Nat Football League Players Asn, 1994; Offensive Lineman of the Year, Nat Football League Alumni Asn, 1995; Louisiana Sports Hall of Fame, 2009.

ROAF, WILLIE. See ROAF, WILLIAM LAYTON.

ROANE, REV. GLENWOOD P, SR.
Lawyer. **Personal:** Born Jul 26, 1930, Virginia; married Lucie Porter; children: Karen, Glenwood Jr & Rosemary. **Educ:** VA State Col, BS, 1952; Howard Univ, JD, 1957; Fletcher Sch Law, Postgrad, 1970-71. **Career:** Teacher, 1957-59; USVA, adjudicator & atty rev, 1960-62; USN, negotiator, 1962-65; USAID, Liberia, officer, 1966-68, Ghana, asst dir, 1968-70, Vietnam, asst dir, 1974-75, Cairo, officer, 1976, Kenya, dir; Louis Arthur Grimes Law Sch, Liberia, instr, 1967-68; Reg Pop Off, dir, 1971-73; Agency Int Develop Off Equal Opportunity Prog, dir, 1977-78; Va State Univ, diplomat residence, 1980-83; Peterson & Basha, PC Law Firm, coun atty; Second Congregational United Church Christ, pastor, 2002-03; Sloan & Swedish, pvt pract, currently. **Orgs:** Interim pastor, Shiloh Baptist; assoc pastor, Purity Baptist Church, 1976-; pastor, 1st Baptist Church Vienna, VA, 1977-; pres, first Baptist, Warrenton, VA; vice chair bd, Zoning Appeals, Vienna, VA, 1992-2000; atty, bar mem VA, Dist Columbia & Tenn; Va State Bar Asn; Old Dominion, McLean Bar Asn; Nat Bar Asn; trustee, Phelps-Stokes Fund; trustee, Service & Develop Agency AME Church. **Honors/Awds:** Superior Performance Award, 1962; Merit Honor Award EOE Efforts, 1976; Fairfax County Citizen of the Year, 1985; Human Rights Award, 1985. **Military Serv:** AUS, first lt, 1952-54. **Home Phone:** (901)758-8006. **Business Addr:** Attorney, Sloan & Swedish, 107 Pleasant St NW, Vienna, VA 22180, **Business Phone:** (703)938-2944.

ROANE, DR. PHILIP RANSOM
Educator, virologist. **Personal:** Born Nov 20, 1927, Baltimore, ME; son of Philip Ransom and Mattie Brown Roane; married Vernice Haynes Roane, Aug 1, 1981; children: Crystal Reed & Donald H Reed. **Educ:** Morgan State Col, BS, 1952; Johns Hopkins, ScM, 1960; Univ MD, PhD, virol, 1970. **Career:** Johns Hopkins, Dept Microbiol, asst prof, 1960-64; Microbiol Assocs Inc, virologist, 1964-72, dir quality control, 1967-72; Howard Univ, asst prof microbial, 1972-79, asst prof oncol, 1977-, grad assoc prof, 1979-. **Orgs:** Am Asn Immunologists; Virol Study Sect NIH; Am Soc Microbiol; NIH Virol Study Sect, 1976-80; Dept Army Viral & Rickettseal Diseases Review Group, 1979-81; Sigma Xi; res publs field virol. **Honors/Awds:** Kaiser Permanente Award for Distinguished Teaching, 1979; Inspirational Leadership Award, Pre-Clinical Prof, 1982; Merit Award at the Outstanding Instructor in Microbiology, Howard Univ Grad Student Coun, 1982; Certificate of Appreciation, Med Col Class, 1987; Kaiser Permanente Award for EXcllence in Teaching, 2004. **Military Serv:** USAAF, 1946-47. **Business Addr:** Associate Professor, Howard University, Department of Microbiology, 520 W St NW, Washington, DC 20059, **Business Phone:** (202)806-6284.

ROBBINS, AUSTIN DION
Football player. **Personal:** Born Mar 1, 1971, Washington, DC. **Educ:** Univ NC. **Career:** Football player (retired); Los Angeles Raiders, 1994; Oakland Raiders, defensive tackle, 1995, 2000; New Orleans Saints, 1996-99; Green Bay Packers, defensive tackle, 2000; Free agt, Green Bay Packers, currently.

ROBBINS, CARL GREGORY CUYJET
Executive, manager. **Personal:** Born Feb 2, 1948, Philadelphia, PA; son of Leon Wallace Robbins Sr and Agnes Cuyjet; married Sydney, Aug 20, 1977; children: 5. **Educ:** Univ Pa, BA, 1970; Univ Pa, The Wharton Sch, MBA, 1980. **Career:** The Vanguard Group Inc, inst mkt, mgr consult rels, currently. **Honors/Awds:** NAt Achievement Scholar, 1966-70. **Business Addr:** Manager of Consultant Relations, The Vanguard Group Inc, 100 Vanguard Blvd, Malvern, PA 19355, **Business Phone:** (610)669-2703.

ROBBINS, HERMAN C.
School administrator. **Personal:** Born Jul 23, 1928, Ft Gibson, OK; children: Kelly, Beverly, Carol, Jacquelyn Shirley, Gerald, Ronald & Herman Jr. **Educ:** Langston Univ, BS, 1951; OK State Univ, MS, 1952; Univ Tulsa, post grad study, 1969. **Career:** Tulsa Jr Col, vpres bus & aux servs; Tulsa Jr Col, evening prog, assoc dean, 1974-75; Tulsa Jr Col, bus serv div, chmn, 1971-74; Tulsa Jr Col, mid-mgt coordr, bus instr, 1970-71; Hanna Lumber Co, mgr, 1965-70; Nanna Lumber Co, gen hardware, dept head, 1960-65; Hanna Lumber Co, floor salesman, 1953-60; Hanna Lumber Co, bldg engr, 1947-53; Hanna Lumber Co, dir, 1965-70; Multi Fab Mfg Corp, dir, 1968-71; Tulsa Jr Col Found Inc, financial agt, 1976-. **Orgs:** Turstee, treas First Bapt Ch, 1965-; bd mem, Hutcherson Br YMCA, 1965-; exchequer Kappa Alpha Psi Frat, 1970-; bd mem, ARC, 1976-; bd mem, Childrens Med Ctr, 1978-; Gov Coun Phys Fitness, 1980-; Nat Conf Christians & Jews, 1980-.

ROBBINS, JESSICA DOWE
Physician. **Personal:** Born Sep 19, 1956, Birmingham, AL; daughter of Jesse and Janie Dowe; married Gilbert, May 28, 1986; children: Janaya Alyce. **Educ:** Dillard Univ, BA, 1978; Howard Univ, PhD, 1983; Univ Louisville, MD, 1996, MD, 1999. **Career:** Procter & Gamble Labs, toxicologist, 1986-87; Hoescht Roussel Pharmaceuticals, mgr scientific affairs, 1987-89; Marion Merrell Dow Pharmaceuticals, mgr clinical pharmacokinetics, 1989-92; Correctional Medical Services, chief medical officer, 1999-; Full Circle Family Practice, pres & ceo, 2000-; pvt pract, currently. **Orgs:** Full Circle Med Soc, 1999-; Jefferson County Med Soc, indigent comt, 1999-; New Zion Baptist Church, double degree mem, 1999; Green Castle Baptist Church, Sunday Sch teacher, 2001; Humana Quality Improvement Comt, 2001-02; Health Care Excel QA Comt, 2002. **Home Addr:** 3108 Ridgemoor Ct, Prospect, KY 40059, **Home Phone:** (502)228-5348. **Business Addr:** Physician, 1009 N Dixie Ave, Elizabethtown, KY 42701, **Business Phone:** (270)765-4361.

ROBBINS, KEVIN F
Lawyer, district court judge. **Personal:** Born Nov 17, 1958, Detroit, MI; son of Robert J and Beryl E Claytor. **Educ:** Univ Mich, Ann Arbor, Mich, BA, 1980; Thomas M Cooley Law Sch, Lansing, Mich, JD, 1984. **Career:** City Detroit, Detroit, Mich, Law Dept, asst corp coun, 1985-89; Kmart Corp, Troy, Mich, pub liability atty, 1989; 36th Dist Ct, judge, currently. **Orgs:** Nat Minority Coun Demonstration Prog; Asn Defense Trial Coun; Am Corp Coun Asn; Detroit Bar Asn; Wolverine Bar Asn; mediator, 36th Dist Detroit; mediator, Mich Mediation Asn Wayne Co; Greater Christ Baptist Church; life mem, Nat Asn Advan Colored People; Detroit Pub Sch, asst gen coun; Davenport Univ, lectr bus law. **Honors/Awds:** Faculty Commendation Award, Am Inst Paralegal Studies, 1990. **Business Addr:** Chief Judge, Court Administrator, Michigan's 36th District Court, 421 Madison Ave, Detroit, MI 48226, **Business Phone:** (313)965-8719.

ROBBINS, LEONARD
Housing developer, architect, executive director. **Personal:** Born Nov 3, 1955, Okaloosa County, FL; son of Bonzie and Elizabeth Eady; married Celia King Robbins, May 26, 1985. **Educ:** Syracuse Univ, archit, 1979; NY Univ, Dipl, construct mgt, 1987; Upsala Col, small bus mgt, 1989. **Career:** City Syracuse, Dept Bldgs, architect, 1979-81; Syracuse NHS, rehab specialist, 1981-82; NHS E Flatbush, Brooklyn, NY, construct specialist, 1982-85; Creative Restoration Consult Inc, vpres & owner, 1984-91; NHS NY City Inc, neighborhood dir, 1985-87; LR construct Mgt, Maplewood, NJ, sole owner, 1990-; Unified Vailsburg Serv, Newark, NJ, dir housing develop, 1991-98; Housing & Community Develop Network NJ, dir housing develop, 1998-. **Orgs:** Bldg Trades Asn, 1988; Nat Asn Home Builders, 1989-90; Builders Asn Metrop NJ, 1989-90; Newark Community Develop Network. **Honors/Awds:** Certificate, NY State, Construct Code, 1981; Certificate, HUD Default Coun HUD, 1984; Safety Certificate, OSHA, New York Bldg & Construct Indust Coun, 1986; Recognition, McCreary Report, WNEW-TV Channel 5, NY, 1988; Recognition, Entrepreneur Ser, WWOR-TV Channel 9, NY, 1989. **Home Addr:** 90 Plymouth Ave, Maplewood, NJ 07040, **Home Phone:** (973)763-3677. **Business Addr:** Director, Housing & Community Development Network of New Jersey, 145 W Hanover St, Trenton, NJ 08618, **Business Phone:** (609)393-3752.

ROBERSON, HON. DALTON ANTHONY
Judge. **Personal:** Born May 11, 1937, Mount Vernon, AL; son of Drue and Sarah Ann Williams; married Pearl Janet Stephens; children: Portia & Dalton Jr. **Educ:** Mich State Univ, BA, JD; Detroit Col Law, BA, JSD. **Career:** State Mich, social worker, 1964-68; Wayne City, asst prosecutor, 1969-70; US Dist, atty, 1970-71; Harrison Friedman Roberson, criminal defense lawyer, 1970-74; Recorders Ct City Detroit, judge, exec chief judge, currently. **Orgs:** Mich State Bar Asn, 1969; Wolverine Bar Asn, 1969; Criminal Defense Lawyers Asn, 1970-74; Mich Civil Rts Comn, 1972-73; chmn, Mich Civil Rts Comn, 1973-74; Mich Judges Asn, 1974-; bd mem, State Mich, 1989-; chmn, Asn Black Judges Mich; bd mem, Detroit Br, Nat Asn Advan Colored People; exec comn, Combines Wayne Circuit/Recorders Ct; mem exec comt, Mich Judges Asn. **Honors/Awds:** Judge of the Year Award, Nat Conf Black Lawyers, 1991. **Military Serv:** USAf, a/1c 1954-58. **Business Addr:** Executive Chief Judge, Recorder's Court for the City of Detroit, 1441 St Antoine St, Detroit, MI 48226-2384, **Business Phone:** (313)224-2444.

ROBERSON, F ALEXIS H
Administrator. **Personal:** Born Sep 20, 1942, Aiken, SC; daughter of F M Gomillion Hammond and T A Hammond; divorced; children: Alan. **Educ:** Howard Univ, Wash, DC, BA, 1963, MA, educ, 1974; Univ DC, Wash, DC, post grad. **Career:** Opportunities Industralization Ctr, dir remedial educ, 1967-70, curric specialist, 1970-73, dep dir, 1973-80; dep dir, 1980-82, dir, 1983-86, Dept Recreation, Dept Employ Serv, Wash, DC, dir, 1987-, pres & chief exec officer, currently; DC Water & Sewer Authority, prin, currently. **Orgs:** Comnr, Wash DC Bd Appeals & Rev, Comn Post-Secondary Educ; chairperson, bd dir, US Youth Games; Links Inc; Girl Friends Inc; Wash Chap, Nat Asn Advan Colored People; Zion Baptist Church; Govt Rep, Wash DC Wage-Hour Bd; Pvt Indust Coun; pres, Wash Metrop Area Chap; Nat Forum Black Pub Admin, 1987-; bd dirs, DC Water and Sewer Authority. **Honors/Awds:** The President's Award, Wash Chap, Nat Asn Advan Colored People, 1986; Top 100 Black Bus & Prof Women, Dollars & Sense Mag, 1988. **Business Addr:** President, Chief Executive Officer, Opportunities Industrialization Center, 3031-B Martin L King Jr Ave SE, Washington, DC 20032, **Business Phone:** (202)373-0050.

ROBERSON, GLORIA GRANT
Educator, librarian. **Personal:** Born Feb 6, 1945, East Meadow, NY; daughter of William Grant and Lillie Cofield Grant; married Clifford, Oct 31, 1965; children: Gloriane, Cynthia & Clifford. **Educ:** Adelphi Univ, Garden City, NY, BS, 1980, MS, 1987; Long Island Univ, Brookville, New York, MLS, 1984. **Career:** Adelphi

Univ, Garden City, NY, asst prof, 1975, prof & librn, currently; Hofstra Univ, Hemp, NY, adj asst prof, 1980. **Orgs:** Corresp secy, Acad & Spec Libr Nassau County Libr Asn, 1989-90; Am Asn Univ Professors. **Honors/Awds:** Person of the Year Award, Third World Stud Asn, 1990; Septima Clark Commitment to Service Award, 1995; Bench by the Road Award, 2003; Book Award, 2004. **Business Addr:** Professor, Adelphi University, Swirbul Library, PO Box 701, Garden City, NY 11530.

ROBERSON, LAWRENCE R
Consultant, executive. **Personal:** Born Aug 26, 1946, Birmingham, AL; son of Mack and Ressie. **Educ:** Ala A&M Univ, BS, 1967; Ind Univ, MBA, 1970; Col Financial Planning, Cert Financial Planner, 1986. **Career:** IBM, systs engr, 1967-68, financial analyst, 1969; Ford Motor Co, supvr financial analysis, 1973-83; Wealth Mgt Group Inc, pres, founder & sr portfolio mgr, currently. **Orgs:** Inst Cert Financial Planners, 1983-; Int Asn Financial Planning, 1984-; dir, Int Exchange Coun, 1986-. **Honors/Awds:** White House Fel Prog Regional finalist, 1983-84. **Business Addr:** President, Founder, Wealth Management Group Inc, 220 W Cong 2nd Fl, Detroit, MI 48226, **Business Phone:** (313)223-2500.

ROBERSON, SANDRA SHORT. See SHAKOOR, DR. WAHEEDAH AQUEELAH.

ROBERSON, VALERIE R
Educator. **Educ:** Bradley Univ, BS, psychol; Roosevelt Univ, master degree, adult educ; Ill State Univ, PhD. **Career:** City Cols Chicago Dist Off, assoc vice chancellor acad affairs & adult educ, 1994-2004; Olive-Harvey Col, interim vpres, 2004-06, pres, 2006-. **Orgs:** Numerous memberships including S Chicago Chamber Com; S Chicago YMCA; Int Stevenson Found; Ill Coun Community Col Adminrs. **Business Addr:** President, Olive-Harvey College, Rm 1107 D1 10001 S Woodlawn, Chicago, IL 60628, **Business Phone:** (773)291-6313.

ROBERTS, DR. ALFRED LLOYD
School administrator. **Personal:** Born Dec 18, 1942, Austin, TX; son of James Roberts and Ellen Woodfork Arnold; married Billie Kerl, Feb 17, 1968; children: Alfrelynn, Latasha & Alfred Jr. **Educ:** Prairie View Agri & Mech Univ, BS, 1963; Tex Agri & Mech Univ, MEd, 1966,PhD, 1973. **Career:** Dallas Independent Sch Dist, teacher, 1965-69, elem prin, 1969-71, dir community relations, 1971-75; E Oak Cliff Sub Dist, Dallas Pub Sch, dep asst supt, adminr sub-dist III, exec dir, 1975-89, asst supt personnel, 1989-93, exec dir alternative cert, exec dir crisis prev, currently. **Orgs:** Nat Educ Asn; Phi Delta Kappa; Dallas Sch Adminr Asn; Alpha Phi Alpha; St Luke Comn United Methodological Church; Hist Preserv League; YMCA; Tex Alliance Black Sch Educr; nat pres, Nat Alliance Black Sch Educr; Dallas Regional Alliance Black Sch Educr. **Business Addr:** Executive Director of Crisis Prevention, Dallas Public Schools, 3700 Ross Ave, Dallas, TX 75204-5491, **Business Phone:** (972)925-3700.

ROBERTS, ANGELA DORREAN
Administrator, vice president (organization). **Personal:** Born Nov 21, 1960, Chicago, IL; daughter of Betty Williams and Morris Peoples; married Marvin James, Oct 3, 1992; children: Anjai G Shields. **Educ:** Calif State Univ, BA, commun. **Career:** Weiss, Jones & Co, data processing mgr, 1979-85; Acad Students, Univ Calif, Los Angeles, comput operations mgr, 1985-89; Housing Authority City Los Angeles, MIS dir, 1989; AltaMed Health Serv Corp, vpres admin serv & chief info officer, currently. **Honors/Awds:** Outstanding Service Award, City Los Angeles, 1992; The Innovations in Technology Award, Nat Asn Housing & Redevelopment Officials; The Career Service Award, Housing & Urban Develop Dept. **Business Addr:** Vice President Administrative Services, Chief Information Officer, AltaMed Health Services Corp, 5427 Whittier Blvd, Los Angeles, CA 90022, **Business Phone:** (323)869-5450.

ROBERTS, BIP
Baseball player, media executive. **Personal:** Born Oct 27, 1963, Berkeley, CA. **Educ:** Chabot Col. **Career:** Baseball player (retired), Media executive; San Diego Padres, infielder,1986-91, 1994-95; Cincinnati Reds, 1992-93; Kansas City Royals, 1996-97; Cleveland Indians, 1997; Detroit Tigers, 1998; Oaklands Atheltics, 1998; Comcast Sports Net, co-host, currently. **Honors/Awds:** National League All-Star, 1992. **Special Achievements:** Co-host for the San Francisco Giants pre-game telecasts. **Business Phone:** (215)336-3500.

ROBERTS, BRETT
Baseball player. **Personal:** Born Mar 24, 1970, Portsmouth, OH. **Career:** Cincinnati Reds, baseball player; Minn Twins, prof baseball player, 1993.

ROBERTS, BRYNDIS WYNETTE
School administrator, lawyer. **Personal:** Born Sep 4, 1957, Sylvania, GA; daughter of Roy Heyward and Josie Spencer Walls; children: Jennifer Yvonne & Jessica Kathleen. **Educ:** Wesleyan Col, Macon, GA, BA, magna cum laude, 1978; Univ GA, Athens, Ga, JD, cum laude, 1981. **Career:** State Law Dept, Atlanta, GA, asst atty gen, 1981-87; Univ GA, Athens, GA, vpres legal affairs, 1987-99; Jenkins & Roberts LLC, partner, currently; Pvt Pract, atty, currently. **Orgs:** Jenkins & Roberts LLC, 1981; Nat Asn Col & Univ Atty's, 1986-92; GA State BRD Accountancy, 1988-; Sch & Col Law Sect, State Bar, sec. 1988-89; Classic City Pilot Club, 1991-92; Wesleyan BRD Trustees, 1991. **Honors/Awds:** Outstanding Woman Law Stud, GA Asn Women Lawyers, 1981; Business & Professional Women Young Careerist, DeKalb Business & Prof Women, 1985. **Business Phone:** (404)522-6386.

ROBERTS, CECILIA
Insurance executive. **Career:** Majestic Life Ins Co, chief exec officer. **Special Achievements:** Company is ranked 14 on Black Enterprise's list of top insurance companies, 1994.

ROBERTS, CHARLES L.
Executive director. **Personal:** Born May 25, 1943, Farmerville, LA; married Charlesetta Shoulders; children: Traci & Channa. **Educ:** Ky State Univ, BS; Univ Louisville, MS; Univ Ga. **Career:** City Louisville, dir sanitation; Met Parks & Recreation Bd, asst dir, 1970-74; Louisville Sch Dist, teacher, 1964-70. **Orgs:** Am Pub Works Asn; Mgmt Planning Coun; State Reg Crime Coun; Nat Asn Advan Colored People; Omega Psi Phi. **Honors/Awds:** Outstanding Citizen Award, 1973. **Business Addr:** 400 S 6 St, Louisville, KY 40202.

ROBERTS, CHERYL DORNITA LYNN
Educator, basketball coach, physician. **Personal:** Born Jul 31, 1958, Martinsburg, WV; daughter of Dorothy J Davenport and Shelby L Roberts Sr. **Educ:** Shepherd Col, BS, 1980; Univ DC, MA, 1984. **Career:** Edgemeade Md, recreation specialist, 1980-81; Univ DC, asst coach, en's basketball, 1981-85; Vet Affairs Med Ctr, recreation therapist, 1985-87, vocational rehabilitation specialist, 1987-88, asst chief, Domiciliary Care Prog, 1988-94, educ specialist, 1994-, Twelveth Nat Veterans Golden Age Games, coord, 1997-98; Jefferson High Sch, head coach girls basketball, 1995; West Virginia Sec Sch, coach, currently. **Orgs:** Bd dir, Focus, 1991-96, treas, 1992; Delta Sigma Theta Sor Inc; Golden Life; Shepherd Col Alumni Asn; life mem, Nat Asn Advan Colored People; adv, Employees Asn, Va Med Ctr; Mandela Chap Blacks Govt. **Honors/Awds:** Outstanding Performance in Educational Civic & Professional Sports Accomplishments, Serenity 7th Day Adventist Church, 1990; Team Excellence Award, Va Med Ctr, 1992; Special Contribution Award, 1994; Employee of the Month, 2003. **Special Achievements:** TV Appearances Good Morning Am 1981, 1982; NY Times Feature Article Sports World Specials, 1984. **Home Addr:** 329 W German St, PO Box 217, Shepherdstown, WV 25443, **Home Phone:** (304)876-2277. **Business Addr:** Basketball coach, West Virginia Secondary School, 2875 Staunton Turnpike, Parkersburg, WV 26104-7219, **Business Phone:** (304)485-5494.

ROBERTS, DEBORAH
Television journalist. **Personal:** Born Sep 20, 1960, Perry, GA; daughter of Ruth and Ben Roberts; married Al Roker, Sep 16, 1995; children: Leila & Nicholas. **Educ:** Univ Ga, attended 1982. **Career:** WTVM-TV, Columbus, GA, reporter, 1982-84; WBIR-TV, Knoxville, TN, gen assignment reporter, 1984-87; WFTV-TV, Orlando, FL, bur chief, NASA field anchor & weekend news co-anchor, 1987-90; NBC News, Atlanta, Miami, gen assignment corresp, 1990-92; Dateline NBC, corresp, 1992-95; ABC, 20/20, news corresp, 1995-; Lifetime Television, Lifetime Live, host, currently. **Orgs:** Manhattan Soc. **Honors/Awds:** Distinguished Alumnus Award, Univ Ga, 1992; Orlando Sentinal Award, Top Local Female Anchor; Clarion Award. **Special Achievements:** Earned a Sports Emmy nomination for her coverage of the 1992 Olympics; cited as top local female anchor by the Orlando Sentinel. **Business Addr:** News Correspondent, 20/20, ABC, 77 W 66th St, New York, NY 10023, **Business Phone:** (212)456-7777.

ROBERTS, EDGAR
Executive, county government official. **Personal:** Born Aug 8, 1946, Valdosta, GA; son of John and Fannie Mae Davis; married Mary Catherine Gardner, Dec 12, 1965; children: Tia Charlotte, Sherri Latrell & Carla Maria. **Educ:** Temple Bus Sch, Wash, DC, 1964-66; Cent Bus Sch, Valdosta, GA, 1969-70; Ga Military Col, Valdosta, GA, 1971-72. **Career:** Elcona Mobile Homes, Valdosta, GA, receiving clerk, 1969-71, 1972-73, purchasing mgr, 1973-76; self employed, Valdosta, GA, minit mkt mgr, 1971-72; A-1 Construction Co Inc, Valdosta, GA, pres/treasr, 1976-; Lowndes County, GA, dist I comnr, 2004-; Thomas Chapel Baptist Church, Valdosta, GA, pastor & visionary, currently. **Orgs:** Trustee, Valdosta State Col Found, 1988-; chmn, Valdosta State Col Minority Found, 1988-; vpres, Minority Bus Group Valdosta, 1989-; bd dirs, First State Bank & Trust, 1989-; adv bd, Supt Lowndes Co Schs, 1989-; bd dirs, Leadership Lowndes, 1989-; pres & owner, James Scott & Son Funeral Home Inc, 1989-; exec bd, Valdosta-Lowndes Co Chamber Com, 1990-; bd dirs, Art Comn, 1990-; VSC Sch Bus, 1990-; mem bd, Gov's Comn Economy & Efficiency State Govt, 1990-; bd dirs, GAME (Ga Asn Minority Entrepreneurs), 1991-; Home Builders Asn Ga. **Honors/Awds:** Distinguished Serv Award, Nat Asn Home Builders US, 1983-84; Appreciation Dedicated & Outstanding Participation, Valdosta/Lowndes County Zoning Bd Appeals, 1984-90; Outstanding Business of the Year, US Dept Com, Minor Bus Develop Agency & Columbus Min Bus Develop Ctr, 1984; Minority Small Business of the Year, 1987; Appreciation Award, US Dept Com Minority Bus Develop Agency, 1990; Atlanta Region Minority Construction Firm of the Year, Minority Bus Develop Asn, 1990; Appreciation of Service in the Field of Business, Black History Action Comt, 1990. **Military Serv:** US Marine Corps, E-5, 1966-68, awarded the Purple Heart by President Lyndon Johnson. **Business Addr:** District I Commissioner, Lowndes County, 325 W Savannah Ave, Valdosta, GA 31601, **Business Phone:** (229)671-2455.

ROBERTS, EDWARD A
School administrator, lawyer. **Personal:** Born Jun 17, 1950, Brooklyn, NY; married Yuklin B John. **Educ:** City Col NY, BA, econ, 1979; St. John?s Univ Law Sch, JD. **Career:** City Col NY Off Dean Studies, asst higher educ officer, 1975-76; City Univ NY, bd trustees, 1976-80; Univ Stud Senate City, Univ NY, chmn, 1976-80; 902 Auto Inc, asst dir, 1980; NY State Div Housing & Community Renewal, supv assoc atty, 1984-89; Bedford Stuyvesant Community Legal Serv, dep dir & housing dir, 1989-91; pvt law pract, atty, 1991-. **Orgs:** City Col Pres Policy Adv Comt, 1976-77; pres, Carter's Action Review Comn, 1977; exec mem, Comn Pub Higher Educ, 1977-79; NY State Higher Educ Serv Corp, 1978; Gov's Task Force Higher Educ, 1979; NY State Bar Asn; Brooklyn Chapter Nat Asn Advan Colored People; Asn Strategic Progress Trinidad & Tobago. **Honors/Awds:** Outstanding Enlisted Man Award, AUS, 1972; Award of merit, Bronx Community Col, 1979. **Special Achievements:** First student-voting member of the CUNY Board of Trustees. **Military Serv:** AUS, e-5, 1971-73. **Business Addr:** Attorney, 3009 Glenwood Rd, Brooklyn, NY 11210, **Business Phone:** (718)421-4300.

ROBERTS, DR. ESTHER PEARL
Psychiatrist, physician. **Personal:** Born Nov 9, 1942, Little Rock, AR; daughter of Marion T and S O Roberts; divorced; children: Ashley & Marion. **Educ:** Fisk Univ, BA, 1964; Meharry Med Col, MD, 1968; Columbia Univ, MPH, 1972. **Career:** US Dept State, physician & psychiatrist, 1980-. **Orgs:** Am Psychiatric Asn, 1978-; Am Col Psychiatrists, 1986-; Nat Med Asn, 1980-; Am Occup Med Assoc; Royal Soc Med, London, 1997-. **Honors/Awds:** fels, American Psychiatrist Assoc, 1998.

ROBERTS, GRADY H., JR.
College teacher, administrator. **Personal:** Born Feb 8, 1940, Pittsburgh, PA. **Educ:** Central State Univ, Wilberforce, OH, BS, 1963; Univ Pittsburgh, MSW, 1965, MPH, 1971, PhD, 1974. **Career:** College teacher (retired); Madigan Gen Hosp Tacoma WA, clinical soc work officer, social work serv, 1965-67; Western Psychiatric Inst & Clinic, psychiatric social worker, 1967-69; Univ Pittsburgh Sch Social Work, dir admins, asst prof, 1969-03. **Orgs:** Asn Black Soc workers; Coun Soc work Ed; Nat Asn Soc Workers; Alpha Phi Alpha; Nat Asn Advan Colored People. **Military Serv:** AUS, capt, 1965-67; AUSR, maj, 1985.

ROBERTS, GREGORY G
Government official. **Personal:** Married; children: 4. **Educ:** Cent Mich Univ, attended. **Career:** Metrop Detroit Youth Found's Learning Ctrs Achievement, dir; Wayne County's Dept Community Justice, dep dir; Congresswoman Carolyn Cheeks Kilpatrick, dist dir; State Mich, Off Faith Based Community Initiatives, assoc dir, dir, 2005-. **Business Phone:** (313)456-0020.

ROBERTS, HARLAN WILLIAM, III
Physical therapist. **Personal:** Born Jan 12, 1931, Wilmington, DE; divorced; children: Teala Jeanne, Harlan David. **Educ:** Univ Pa, BS, MSW, 1976. **Career:** United Methodist Action Prog, suprv, 1968-69; Family Serv Northern DE, counr, 1969-74; Univ Pa Family Maintenance Orgn, coordr, 1975-76; Mental Health-Child Protective Serv Md, clin therapist. **Orgs:** Bd mem, Del OIC, 1970-74; bd mem, Family Asn Am, 1971-74; exec bd, Wilmington DE Chap Nat Asn Advan Colored People, 1971-82; vpres, Wilmington United Neighborhood, 1973-74; vpres & pres, Red Clay Consolidated Sch Bd, 1981-85. **Honors/Awds:** Harriet Tubman Del Chapter Harriet Tubman, 1984. **Military Serv:** AUS, capt, 8 yrs; US Ranger, Counted Intellegent Corp. **Home Addr:** 221 N Cleveland Ave, Wilmington, DE 19805.

ROBERTS, JACQUELINE JOHNSON
Consultant, state government official. **Personal:** Born Apr 30, 1944, Dermott, AR; daughter of Gertrude Colen Johnson and Ocie; married Curley Roberts, Aug 16, 1964; children: Lisa LaVon, Curlee LaFayette & Dwyane Keith. **Educ:** Ark AM&N Col, BS, 1967, elem educ teaching cert, 1968, libr sci, 1970. **Career:** Bradley Elem, Warren, AR, teacher, 1967-68; Ark AM&N Col Libr, shipping & receiving, 1969-74; B&W Tobacco Co, sales rep, 1979-83; Dancy Oil Co, off mgr, 1983-85; St John Apartments, mgr, 1986-89; State Ark, state rep, 1991-99; Camden-El Dorado, dist consult, currently. **Orgs:** Bd mem, Asn Community Orgs Reform Now, 1986-; secy, Jefferson Co Black Caucus, 1987-; Ark Democratic Party, Filing Fee Comn, 1988-90; Nat Comn Preserve Social Security, 1988-90; Pine Bluff Downtown Develop, Spec Events Comn, 1990-; Pine Bluff Chamber Comm, Membership Comm, 1990-; Urban League Ark,

1991-. **Honors/Awds:** Certificate of Honor for Community Service, Top Ladies Distinction, 1990; Recognition of Outstanding Achievement, Ark State Press & Cent Ark Asn Black Journalist, 1991; Certificate of Recognition, Female Black Action Inc, 1991. **Business Addr:** Consultant, PO Box 2075, Pine Bluff, AR 71613-2075, **Business Phone:** (870)536-1723.

ROBERTS, JANICE L (JANICE LYNN ROBERTS)
Government official. **Personal:** Born Dec 31, 1959, Pine Bluff, AR; daughter of James C and Deloris Diane Strivers. **Educ:** Univ Ark Pine Bluff, Pine Bluff, Ark, BA, econ, 1981; Univ Southern Calif, Los Angeles, Calif, MPA, 1989; New York Univ, Baruch Col, New York, NY, MPA, 1991; Nat Urban Fel, New York, NY, urban studies, 1991. **Career:** US Dept Agr, Soil Conserv Serv, economist, 1979-85; AUS Corps Engr, Los Angeles, Calif, economist, 1985-90; World Port Los Angeles, Port Los Angeles, Los Angeles, Calif, exec dir spec assist, 1990-; Ark State Electoral Coalition, legis analyst & head lobbyist; City Pine Bluff Coun, ward four, rep, currently. **Orgs:** Nat Asn Female Exec, 1982-; treas, Delta Sigma Theta Sorority, 1987-; asst chairperson, stud adv, Los Angeles Chap, Nat Forum Black Pub Adminrs, 1987-; Am Asn Port Authorities, 1990-; SRI Int Asn, 1990-. **Honors/Awds:** Adv, United States Congional Adv Bd, US Congional Off, 1982; Fed Exec Bd Fel, Univ Southern Calif, 1987; Outstanding Young Women of America, US Rep Dale Bumper, 1989. **Business Addr:** Representative Ward 4, City of Pine Bluff, 4903 W 13th Ave, Pine Bluff, AR 71603, **Business Phone:** (870)879-1846.

ROBERTS, JANICE LYNN. See ROBERTS, JANICE L.

ROBERTS, JOHN CHRISTOPHER
Automotive executive. **Personal:** Born Sep 12, 1944, Boston, MA; son of Lillian G and John Warren; married Joan Clarke, Dec 28, 1968; children: John Michael, Jason Martin & Kristen Renee. **Educ:** GMI Eng & Mgt Inst, BSME, 1967; Xavier Univ, MBA, 1970. **Career:** Gen Motors, Inland Div, eng mrg, 1962-79, Hydramatic Div, mgr exp, 1981-89, dealer develop trainee, 1989-91; Ford Motor Co, sr prod planner, 1979-81; Roberts Buick Saab GMC Truck Inc, pres, 1991-; Best Buick Saab Gmc Truck, dealer, currently. **Orgs:** Pres, Miami Valley section, 1972-76; treas, MI Alumni Asn, 1976-86; dir, Wolverine Coun, Boy Scouts, 1981-89; treas, GMI Alumni fed, 1982; Haverhill Coun, 1992-; dir, Bethany Home bd, 1992-; Gen Motor Dealer Asn, 1991-; Soc Automotive Engrs; Geo Tech Develop Adv Comt, 1986-89; Soc Plastics Engrs; Rotary Int; Nat Asn Minority Automobile Dealers; bd dir, Merrimac Valley Red Cross; Northern Essex Community Occup Adv Coun; bd dirs, ESRA Inc; nat adv bd, Gen Motors Youth Educ Syst. **Honors/Awds:** Distinguished Alumni Award, GMI Eng & Mgt Inst, 1986; Minority Business Award, Mass Black Caucus, 1995. **Home Phone:** (978)689-7958. **Business Addr:** Dealer, Best Buick Saab Gmc Truck, 901 S Main St, Haverhill, MA 01835, **Business Phone:** (508)373-3882.

ROBERTS, DR. JONATHAN
Hospital administrator. **Career:** Louisiana State Univ, Health Scis Ctr, Healthcare Servs Div, CAO, currently. **Business Addr:** Chief Academic Officer, Louisiana State University, Health Sciences Center, Healthcare Services Division, 8550 United Plz Blvd, Baton Rouge, LA 70809-2256, **Business Phone:** (225)922-0798.

ROBERTS, KAY GEORGE
Musician, educator. **Personal:** Born Sep 16, 1950, Nashville, TN. **Educ:** Fisk Univ, Nashville, Tenn, BA; Yale Univ, New Haven, Conn, MM, MMA, DMA. **Career:** Ensemble Americana, Stuttgart, Germany, music dir & founder, 1989-; Artemis Ensemble, Stuttgart, Germany, conductor, 1990-; German Acad Exchange Serv, res grant, 1990, 1992 & 1998; String Currents, music dir & founder, 1994-; Harvard Univ, res fel, 1997-2003; W E B DuBois Inst Afro-Am res fel, 1997-2003; Univ Mass, Lowell, conductor-univ orchestra, dir string proj, prof music, currently; New Eng Orchestra, founder, currently. **Honors/Awds:** Distinguished Alumni of the Year Award, Nat Asn Equal Opportunity Higher Educ, 1987; Distinguished Black Women Award, Black Women Sisterhood Action, 1998; Black Achievers Award, Greater Boston YMCA, 1988; Cultural Specialty Music (Egypt), US State Dept, 1988; Outstanding Achievement in the Performing Arts, League of Black Women, 1991; Distinguished Alumna, USN/PDS Univ Sch, Nashville/Peabody Demonstration Sch, 1991; Nat Achievement Award, Nat Black Music Caucus, 1993; Certificate of Special Recognition, US house Representatives, 2001; Presidential Professor, Univ Mich, 2003; "President's Public Service Award", Univ Mass, 2007. **Special Achievements:** First woman to earn the Doctor of Musical Arts degree in conducting from Yale University . **Business Addr:** Professor, Department of Music, 35 Wilder St Suite 3 Durgin Hall 219, Lowell, MA 01854.

ROBERTS, KIM (KIM ROBERTS HEDGPETH)
Executive. **Personal:** Born May 28, 1957, New York, NY; daughter of Howard and Doris Galiber. **Educ:** Harvard Univ, BA, 1978; Georgetown Univ law Ctr, JD, 1981. **Career:** San Francisco exec dir, 1987-92; nat exec dir, 1992-98; Harvard Univ, dir labor & employee relations; 1981-87; Am Fed TV & Radio Artists (AFTRA), nat exec dir, currently. **Orgs:** Mayors Film Adv Coun, San Francisco, 1990; San Francisco Labor Coun, delegate, 1989-92; NY Cent Labor Coun, deleg, 1986-87; NAB, 1992-98; Governors African-Am Adv, CMS, 1999-. **Special Achievements:** First African-American to serve as chief executive of a major entertainment union. **Business Phone:** (212)532-0800.

ROBERTS, LILLIAN
Executive, social worker. **Personal:** Born Jan 2, 1928, Chicago, IL; daughter of Henry Davis and Lillian Henry; divorced. **Educ:** Univ Ill, attended 1945; Roosevelt Univ, Labor Sch, attended 1960; Col New Rochelle, hon degree, 1973. **Career:** Lyng-in-Hosp, nurse aide, operating room technician, 1945-58; Chicago AFSCME, Dist Coun 19, 34, labor organizer, ment health employees, 1958-65; Dist Court 37, AFSCME Div Dir, Hosp Div, New York City, 1965-67, assoc dir, AFSCME, AFL-CIO, New York City, 1967-81; New York State Comnr Labor, appointed, 1981-86; Total Health Systems, sr vpres, 1987-90; Cigna, consult, 1991-; Dist Coun 37, Polit Action Comt, chairperson, exec dir, currently. **Orgs:** Nat Med Fel; nat exec bd, Jewish Labor Community, Am Jewish Congr; adv bd, Resources Children Spec Needs Inc, Philip Randolph Inst; bd dirs, Col New Rochelle; Am Dem Action; Nat Asn Advan Colored People New York Br; hon mem, Delta Sigma Theta Sorority; hon mem, AFSCME, New York City, Clerical Employees Union, Local 1549. **Honors/Awds:** Roy Wilkins Award, Nat Asn Advan Colored People; Benjamin Potoker Award, New York State Employees Brotherhood Comt; Achievement Award, Westchester Minority Contr Asn; Histadrut Humanitarian Award, Am Trade Coun Histadrut; Good Govt Award, New York State Careerists; Adam Clayton Powell Govt Award, Opportunity Indust Ctr, 1982; Honorary Award, Hispanic Women's Ctr; Friends of Education Award, Asn Black Educr New York, 1983; Frederick Douglass Award, New York Urban League; Labor Award, Adj Fac Asn Nassau Community Col, 1984. **Special Achievements:** A Salute to America's Top 100 Black Business and Professional Women 1985. **Business Addr:** Chairperson, District Council 37, Political Action Committee, 125 Barclay St, New York, NY 10007, **Business Phone:** (212)815-1550.

ROBERTS, LORRAINE MARIE
Consultant. **Personal:** Born May 12, 1930, Philadelphia, PA; daughter of Adele Pettie and Willie Pettie; children: Kevin M & Harlan K. **Educ:** Hampton Univ, BS, 1952; Bucknell Univ, exchange stud; Columbia Univ, MA, 1954. **Career:** Bowling Green Bd Educ VA, teacher, 1952-53; Rochester City Sch Dist-,teacher, 1956-64; NYS Univ System State Educ Dept, adj prof; Poughkeepsie NY City Sch Dist, coordr, Bus Educ, teacher, chmn, Occup educ, 1966-96,SED Curric OE & Tech Studies Comn, co-chmn, 1992-95; CDOS, consult, 1996-98. **Orgs:** BTA; EBTA; NBEA; PPSTA; NYSUT; AFL-TA; Bd trustees, YWCA, Dutchess Co,1970-75; bd mem, secy, United Way Dutchess County, 1973-80; chmn, Cent Alloc Div United Way Dutchess Co, 1979-80; basileus, Iota Alpha Omega Chap, Alpha Kappa Alpha Sor, 1969-71; Bethel Missionary Baptist Ch; AFSPoughkeepsie; United Way; Nat Advan Asn Colored People; bd, Dutchess County & Dominica Partnership Am, 1984-92; bd, Friends GreaterPoughkeepsie Libr Dist, 1988-94; pres, Bus Teachers Mid-Hudson, 1989-92;Bus Educ Div NYS Educ Dept; pres, Dutchess Co Historical Soc, 1996-99; bd,treas, DC Girl Scouts, 1993-99; Vassar Warner, 1999-01; KAD; ERVK; chmn,Poughkeepsie Day Sch, Diversity Comt, 2002-. **Honors/Awds:** Outstanding Occupational Educ, NYS Educ Dept, 1989; Outstanding Business Teacher, NYS, 1994; Outstanding educ, Dutchess Beulah Baptist Ch, 1992; YWCA Award, Salute Women, 1993; Martin Luther King Honoree, 1997;presidents Award, Marist Col, 1998; Eleanor Roosevelt Candle Award, 1999;Contributing writer, Pougnkeepsie Journal Millenum Series, 2000; DCHS Award, 2000. **Special Achievements:** Invisible People, co-author; Untold Stories: A Historical Overview of the Black Community in Poughkeepsie (Dutchess County Historical Society Yearbook), 1987. **Business Addr:** Chairman, Poughkeepsie Day School, Diversity Committee, 260 Boardman Rd, Poughkeepsie, NY 12603, **Business Phone:** (845)462-7600.*

ROBERTS, LYNNETTE DAURICE
City planner. **Personal:** Born Oct 8, 1971, East Orange, NJ; daughter of Gale Bennett and Gus Roberts. **Educ:** Trenton State Col, BA, polit sci, 1994; GA Inst Tech, masters, city planning, 1996; GA State Univ, real estate cert, 1996. **Career:** City East Orange Dept Planning Col Assoc, 1993-94; GA Inst Tech Community Serv Grad Intern, 1995-96; Buckhead Coalition/BellSouth Mobility Intern Planner, 1996-98; Fulton County, sr land use planner, Dept Environment & Community Develop Planner, 1998-; "His Will - Destiny Praise", asst dir & prod mgr. **Orgs:** Am Planning Asn, 1995-96, 2000-; GA Planning Asn, 1995-96, 2000-; Toastmasters Int, 1999-2000; Am Inst Certified Planners, 2001-; Destiny Metropolitan Worship Church, lead service programmer & producer. **Special Achievements:** Worked with Buckhead Coalition to install 911 Call boxes, 1999; American Inst Certified Planners Exam, certified, becoming only African-Am female in Fulton Co Dept Environment & Community Develop with this certification, 2001. **Business Addr:** Senior Planner III, Fulton County, American Institute of Certified Planners, 141 Pryor St Suite 5001, Atlanta, GA 30303, **Business Phone:** (404)730-8023.

ROBERTS, MARCUS
Pianist, educator. **Personal:** Born Aug 7, 1963, Jacksonville, FL. **Educ:** Fla State Univ. **Career:** Jazz pianist, composer, arranger, educator; Albums: J Mood, 1986; Standard Time, Vol. I, 1987; Live at Blues Alley, 1988; The Majesty of the Blues, 1989; Crescent City Christmas Card, 1989; Standard Time, Vol II, 1991; Thick in the South: Soul Gestures in Southern Blue, 1991; Uptown Ruler: Soul Gestures in Southern Blue, 1991; Levee Low Moan: Soul Gestures in Southern Blue, 1991; Blue Interlude, 1992; Tribute to John Coltrane "A Love Supreme", 1994; Live at the Village Vanguard, 1999; Higher Ground, 2006; 2002 Winter Olympic Games, artist-in-residence, 2002; Fla State Univ, Housewright Scholar, 2003-04, asst prof jazz studies, currently. **Honors/Awds:** Young Artist's Award, Nat Asn Jazz Educr, 1982; First Prize, Thelonious Monk Int Jazz Competition, 1987; National Academy of Achievement Award, 1995; Helen Keller Personal Achievement Award, Am Fedn Blind, 1998; Commissioning Award, Chamber Music Am, 2001; Jacksonville Jazz Hall of Fame, 2003; Commissioning Award, NC Asn Jazz Educr, 2004; Commissioning Award, Am Soc Composers, Authors & Publishers, 2005. **Business Addr:** Pianist, c/o Marcus Roberts Enterprises Inc, PO Box 320159, Boston, MA 02132, **Business Phone:** (617)323-2658.

ROBERTS, MARGARET MILLS
Pathologist, educator. **Personal:** Born Dec 5, 1936, Pittsburgh, PA; daughter of Everett and Isabelle; married Vernard T Sr; children: Vernard Jr & Sharon Renee. **Educ:** Fisk Univ, attended 1957; Ohio State Univ, BA, 1962, MA, 1964, PhD, 1966. **Career:** prof (retired); Children's Hosp, founder & dir speech path & audiol, 1966-95; Ohio State Univ, adj asst prof, 1972-94; MMR Consults, 1995. **Orgs:** Fel, Am Speech-Lang-Hearing Asn, 1980-96; Elected legis counr, vpres various comts, Crittenton Family Servs Bd, 1976-85, 1987-; bd mem, Develop Disabilities, 1982-89; chair, Ohio Bd Speech Path & Audiol, 1984-91; Ohio State Univ Alumni Adv Coun, 1985-93; pres, Ohio Speech & Hearing Asn, 1993. **Honors/Awds:** Community Service Award, Alpha Kappa Alpha, 1972; Community Service Award, Delta Sigma Theta, 1986; Outstanding Alumni Award, Ohio State Univ Alumni Asn, 1991. **Home Addr:** 2365 Bellevue Ave, Columbus, OH 43207, **Home Phone:** (614)445-6398.

ROBERTS, MARGARET WARD
Educator. **Personal:** Born Jul 18, 1934, Chapel Hill, NC; daughter of James S and Margaret S Skinner. **Educ:** Va State Col, BS, 1960; Old Dominion Univ, spec edu, 1975; reading cert, 1988. **Career:** Educator (retired); Portsmouth Sch Syst, state remedial teacher. **Orgs:** Prog develop, Work Incentive Prog; Chesapeake Chap Pinochle Bugs Inc; vpres, Norfolk Chap, Delicados Inc; chairperson, literacy proj, teacher yr comt, Portsmouth Reading Coun; Va Reading Asn; Portsmouth Educ Asn; Nat Educ Asn; Dem Women; Asn Supervision & Curric Develop; Delta Sigma Theta; Grace Episcopal Church; Jack & Jill Mother, Chesapeake Chap; Coalition Black Women, Tidewater Chap; Urban League Hampton Rd; bd mem, Boys & Girls Club Hampton Roads; co-ordr, Safety & Crime Prev, Level Green Civic League; Proj (AIMS), Activ Intergrate Math & Sci. **Honors/Awds:** Honorary Citizen, City Chesapeake, VA. **Special Achievements:** Dedicated Supporter of Reading & Mathematics Programs in Portsmouth Public Schools; Selected by Portsmouth Public School System to Participate in Workshop For Teachers of Upgraded Groups; Dedicated & Invaluable Services Rendered to Project Lead's Partnership Forum, Norfolk, VA. **Home Phone:** (804)424-3613.

ROBERTS, MICHAEL V.
Executive, businessperson. **Personal:** Born Oct 24, 1948, St Louis, MO. **Educ:** Linden wood Col, BS; St Louis Univ, Law Sch, JD, 1974; Hague Acad Int Law,Hague Holland, Cert; Int Inst Human Rights, Strasbourg France, Cert. **Career:** Roberts Roberts & Assoc, pres, chmn & chief executive officer, 1974-; St Louis Brd Aldermen, officer, 1977-85; Alamosa PCS Holding, brd dir; ACME Commn, brd dir; Roberts Broadcasting Co, owner, 1989-. **Orgs:** Kappa Alpha Psi Fraternity; Phi Delta Phi Legal Frat; MO Athletic Club; St Louis Coun World Affairs; St Louis Arts & Educ Coun; Cert PADI Scuba Diver's Assn; bd mem, Better Family Life; bd mem, Home Shopping Network; All Saints Episcopal Church; leader, Am Youth Found; alt comnr, St Louis Land Reutilization Authority; trustee, Intl Counc Shoppin Centres; chmn, Natl Assn Black hotel Owners, Operators & Developers; brd dir, Natl Assn Black Owned Broadcasters. **Honors/Awds:** JCCA tennis champion; Danforth Found Fellowship; Morehouse Col Dist Leader; Ernst 7 Young Enterpreneur of the Year Award, 2006; Trumpet Award for Business, 2009. **Special Achievements:** Black Enterprise's Top 100 Industrial & Service companies list, ranked 94,2000; Author of the book, "Action Has No Season: Strategies And Secrets To Gaining Wealth And Authority"; He Has been the feature story for many magazines; Has been a guest speaker at various renowned stages. **Business Addr:** President, Chief Executive Officer, The Roberts Companies, 1408 N Kings Hwy Suite 300, Saint Louis, MO 63113, **Business Phone:** (314)367-4600.*

ROBERTS, NYREE
Basketball player. **Personal:** Born Mar 10, 1976. **Educ:** Old Dominion Univ, elem educ, 1998. **Career:** Houston Comets, ctr, 1998-00; Wash Mystics, ctr, 1999-2000; Cleveland Rockers, ctr, 2002; Tenn Titans; Los Angeles Sparks; Lady Monarchs; Paghiakos Greece, currently. **Honors/Awds:** Player of the Yr, Colonial Athletic Assn, 1997-98; All CAA First Team twice; ODU Sports Hall of Fame 2008. *

ROBERTS, PAQUITA HUDSON
Educator. **Personal:** Born Mar 2, 1938, Andrews, SC; children: Craig, Tali, Paquita. **Educ:** SC State Col, BA, 1961; Newark State Col, MA, 1967. **Career:** Hosp Ctr Orange, speech pathologist, 1964-67; Newark Bd Educ, 1968-69; Mt Carmel Guild, prog dir, 1969-75; NJ Dept Educ, educ prog specialist; Learning Resource Ctrs North, Presch Consult, currently. **Orgs:** Consult, Orange Head Start, Intercoastal Bus Assocs, Barnett Hosp Speech & Hearing Div, CH Aston Assocs; adv bd, RAP NY Univ Coun Exceptional C, 1979-; vpres, chairperson bd educ Christian St Marks AME Church. **Honors/Awds:** Special Education Fellow, NJ Dept Educ; Professional Recognition, NJ Division Early Childhood Award, 1986. **Business Addr:** Preschool Consultant, Learning Resource Centers North, 240 So Harrison St 6th Fl, East Orange, NJ 07018, **Business Phone:** (973)414-4491.

ROBERTS, RAY
Football player, football coach. **Personal:** Born Jun 3, 1969, Asheville, NC; married Beth, May 8, 1993. **Educ:** Univ Va, BS, communs, 1991. **Career:** Football player (retired), Football coach; Seattle Sea hawks, tackle, 1992-95; Detroit Lions, 1996-2001; Interlake High Sch, Bellevue, WA, coach; Lake Washington High, Kirkland, WA, coach, currently. **Business Phone:** (425)828-3371.

ROBERTS, ROBIN
Television journalist. **Personal:** Born Nov 23, 1960, Pass Christian, MS; daughter of Lawrence and Lucimarian. **Educ:** Southeastern La Univ, BA, commun, 1987. **Career:** WDAM-TV, Hattiesburg, Miss, sports anchor, 1983-84; WLOX-TV, Biloxi, Miss, 1984-86; WSMV-TV, Nashville, Tenn, 1986-88; WAGA-TV, Atlanta, Ga, sports anchor & reporter, 1988-90; V103, radio host, 1988-90; ESPN, sportscaster, 1990, contribr, 1990-2005; ABC News, Good Morning America, reporter, 1995-2005, co-anchor, 2005-. **Orgs:** Arthur Ashe Athletic Asn; Women's Sports Found. **Honors/Awds:** Numerous honors & awards including Daughters of the American Revolution Television Award of Merit, 1990; Women at Work Broadcast Journalism Award, 1992; Excellence in Sports Journalism Award for Broadcast Media, Northeastern Univ Ctr Study Sport Soc & Sch Jour, 1993; Distinguished Achievement Award in Broadcasting, Univ Ga Di-Gamma Kappa, 1996; Media Award, New Eng Women's Fund, 1998; "Louisiana Legend", La Pub Broadcasting, 2001; Hall of Fame, Women's Inst Sport & Educ Found. **Special Achievements:** Book: From the Heart: Seven Rules To Live By, 2007. **Business Addr:** News Anchor, ABC TV Network, 190 N State St Suite 1100, Chicago, IL 60607, **Business Phone:** (312)899-4250.

ROBERTS, DR. RONA DOMINIQUE
Educator. **Personal:** Born Dec 18, 1969, Christiansted, VI; daughter of Robert D Roberts and Constance E Roberts. **Educ:** Duquesne Univ, BA, 1992, MS, 1994; Univ Southern Miss, PhD, 2004. **Career:** Duquesne Univ, asst dir, 1992-94; Marietta City Schs, Woods-Wilkins Ctr, teacher, 1995-2000; Hickory Hills Elem Sch, asst prin to admin asst curric & opers; Marietta City Sch, Admin Asst Special Serv, currently. **Orgs:** Ga Asn Educrs, 2003-; Cobb Educ Consortium. **Honors/Awds:** GEM Award, Marietta Kiwanis; Outstanding new Employee, Teacher of the Year (WWC), Outstanding Employee, Marietta City Schools; Academic Achievement, Univ Southern Miss. **Special Achievements:** Dancer's Mural at WWC, 1998; Two Dancers at WWC, 1999; Fairies & Flowers Mural at WWC, 2000; Span Lang Proficiency. **Home Addr:** 1642 Ashmar Lane, Marietta, GA 30064. **Business Addr:** Administrative Assistant for Curriculum & Operations, Hickory Hills Elementary School, 250 B Howard St, Marietta, GA 30060, **Business Phone:** (770)427-4631.

ROBERTS, ROY J.
Educator. **Personal:** Born Jul 1, 1940, Carthage, TX; son of Baker and Thelma Hicks; married Barbara Brown; children: William & Ronan. **Educ:** Willey Col, BS, 1964; Yeshiva Univ, attended 1969; State Univ New York, Stony Brook, 1969-70; Adel phi, 1973-74. **Career:** John Marshall High Sch, physics instr, 1964-66; E Islip, New York, math teacher, 1966-67; Bellport New York, math teacher, 1967-70; Long Island Asn Black Counrs, treas, 1969; Dowling Col, upward bound proj dir, affirmative action community, chairperson, 1973-77. **Orgs:** Bayshore Control Islip, Nat Asn Advan Colored People, 1966-; Cits United Betterment Educ, 1967-; NEA, 1968-; Bellport fel, 1968-; Vol Bellport Ambulance Co, 1968-; Minority Educr Asn Long Island, 1974-; treas, Asn Equality & Excellence Educ, 1979-. **Home Addr:** 180 Baiting Pl Rd, Farmingdale, NY 11735. **Business Addr:** Project Director, Dowling College, Oakdale, NY 11769.

ROBERTS, ROY S.
Vice president (organization), automotive executive. **Personal:** Married. **Educ:** Western Mich Univ, BBA; Harvard PMD Prog. **Career:** Navistar Int, vpres & gen mgr, 1988-90; Gen Motors Corp, staff, 1977-92; Gen Motors Assembly Plant, N Tarrytown, NY, mgr; GM Flint Automotive Div, MI, vpres personnel, 1988; Cadillac Motor Car, gen mfg mgr, 1990-91; Pontiac Gen Motors Corp Div, vpres & gen mgr, 1992-98; Gen Motors Corp, N Am Vehicle Sales, Serv & Mkt, group vpres, 2000 (retired); M-Xchange.com, staff, 2000-; Reliant Equity Investors LLC, managing dir, currently. **Orgs:** Exec Comt, Nat Urban League; Nat Boy Scout; bd Trustees, Western Mich Univ; bd Trustees, Morehouse Sch Med; Volvo Heavy Truck; bd dirs, Air Road Express; bd dirs, Saginaw Power Train Inc; bd dirs, Abbott Labs, currently; bd dirs, Burlington Northern Sante Fe Pac, currently; bd dirs, Aspen Inst, currently. **Honors/Awds:** Hon Doctorate, Fla A&M Univ, Grand Valley State Col, Paine Col; American Success Award. **Business Addr:** Managing Director, Reliant Equity Investors LLC, 401 N Mich Ave Suite 550, Chicago, IL 60611, **Business Phone:** (312)494-0300.

ROBERTS, SALLY-ANN. See CRAFT, SALLY-ANN ROBERTS.

ROBERTS, DR. SAMUEL KELTON
Educator. **Personal:** Born Sep 1, 1944, Muskogee, OK; son of Foster Roberts and Hattie Harper Roberts; married Valerie Hermoine Fisher; children: Samuel Kelton Jr & Franklin. **Educ:** Univ de Lyon France, dipl, 1966; Morehouse Col, BA, 1967; Union Theol Sem, MDiv, 1970; Columbia Univ, PhD, 1974. **Career:** Fund Theol Educ, Protestant fel, 1967-70; New York Mission Soc, summer proj dir, 1967-70; Columbia Univ, fel, 1970-72; S Hempstead Cong Church, pastor, 1972-73; Pittsburgh Theol Sem, asst prof, 1973-76; Union Theol Sem, asst prof religion & soc, 1976-80; VA Union Univ, dean; Va Union Univ Sch Theol, prof christian ethics & dir doctor ministry prog; Union Theol Sem & Presbyterian Sch Christian Educ, Anne Borden & E Hervey Evans prof theol & ethics, currently. **Orgs:** Am Acad Rels; Soc Sci Study Rel; Soc Study Black Relition; Am Theol Soc, 2003. **Honors/Awds:** Merril Overseas Study Award, Morehouse Col, 1965-66. **Special Achievements:** Author, George Edmund Haynes, 1978; African American Christian Ethics & In the Path of Virtue: The African American Moral Tradition. **Business Addr:** Anne Borden & E Hervey Evans Professor of Theology & Ethics, Union Theological Seminary & Presbyterian School of Christian Education, 3401 Brook Rd, Richmond, VA 23227, **Business Phone:** (804)355-0671.

ROBERTS, TARA LYNETTE
Publisher. **Personal:** Born Feb 5, 1970, Atlanta, GA; daughter of Melvin Murphy and Lula Roberts. **Educ:** Mount Holyoke Col, BA, 1991; New York Univ, MA, 1994. **Career:** New York Univ, publ fel, 1991-93; Scholastic Books, asst ed, 1992-93; Essence Mag, ed asst, 1993-94, lifestyle ed, 1994-97, online ed, 1997, contributing writer; Heart & Soul, lifestyle ed, 1998; Syracuse Univ, instr, 1999-2000; Fierce Mag, publisher, 2001-; Cosmo Girl, sr ed, 2007-; AOL Living, staff; Ed: Am I the Last Virgin? Teen African Reflections On Sex & Love. **Orgs:** Alpha Kappa Alpha Sorority Inc, 1989-; Black Filmmaker Found, 1991-94; comt mem, Mount Holyoke Col Alumnae Quarterly, 1995-; Nat Asn Female Execs, 1996-. **Honors/Awds:** Scripps Howard Found Scholarship, 1989; Travel Grant, Coun Int Educ Exchange, 1991; Student Service & Leadership Award, Mount Holyoke Col, 1991; Entertainment Award for article in Essence, New York Asn Black Journalists; Service to Syracuse University Award, Nat Asn Negro Bus & Prof Women's Clubs; New York Public Library chose Am I the Last Virgin' as one of the best books for teenagers in 1998. **Business Addr:** Senior Editor, CosmoGIRL Magazine, 300 W 57th St Fl 20, New York, NY 10019, **Business Phone:** (212)649-3851.

ROBERTS, DR. TERRENCE JAMES
Psychologist, educator. **Personal:** Born Dec 3, 1941, Little Rock, AR; son of William Roberts and Margaret Gill Thomas; married Rita Anderson, Mar 8, 1962; children: Angela Rayschel & Rebecca Darlene. **Educ:** Calif State Univ Los Angeles, Los Angeles, Calif, BA, 1967, MSW, 1970; Southern Ill Univ, Carbondale, Ill, PhD, 1976. **Career:** Southern Ill Univ, Carbondale, Ill, asst prof, 1972-75; Pacific Union Col, Angwin, Calif, asst prof, 1975-78; St Helena Hosp, Deer Park, Calif, dir, mental health, 1975-85; Univ Calif Los Angeles, Los Angeles Calif, asst dean, 1985-93; Antioch Univ, chair, Masters Psychol Prog, 1993; Terrence J. Roberts & Assoc, ceo, currently. **Orgs:** Am Psychol Asn, 1980-; Asn Black Psychologists, 1985-88; bd mem, African Am Cultural Inst, 1988-; bd mem, Eisenhower Inst World Affairs, 1991-; bd mem, Economic Resources Corp, 1995-; bd mem, Winthrop Rockefeller Found, 1998-. **Honors/Awds:** Civil Rights Award, NAACP Legal Defense & Educ Fund, 1982; Spingarn Medal, NAACP, 1958; SCLC Women "Drum Major for Justice Award," 1995; Congressional Medal of Freedom. **Special Achievements:** One of "The Little Rock Nine". **Home Phone:** (626)296-8441. **Business Addr:** Chief Executive Officer, Terrence J. Roberts & Associates, Los Angeles, CA.

ROBERTS, TRISH
Basketball coach. **Personal:** Born Jun 14, 1955, Monroe, GA. **Educ:** N Ga Col; Emporia State Col; Cent Mich Univ, MA; Univ Tenn, attended 1979. **Career:** Cent Mich Univ, Women's Basketball, asst coach; Univ ME, Women's Basketball, coach; Univ Mich, Women's Basketball, head coach; State Univ NY, head coach, currently. **Orgs:** Black Caucus Asn; Women's Basketball Coaches Asn. **Honors/Awds:** World Univ Team, 1979; Hall of Fame, Emporia State Col, 1994; Women In Sports & Educ Hall of Fame, 1996; Inductee, Women's Basketball Hall of Fame, 2000; Coach of the Year, State NY Div I, 2000; Olympic Medalist. **Special Achievements:** US Olympic Women's Basketball Team, 1976; USA Nat Women's Basketball Team, 1978. **Business Addr:** Head Coach-Women, State University of New York, 006 Gymnasium, Stony Brook, NY 11794-3503.

ROBERTS, TROY
Journalist. **Personal:** Born Sep 9, 1962, Philadelphia, PA; son of Robert and Ellen. **Educ:** Univ Calif, Berkeley, AB, 1984. **Career:** KPIX-TV, mag show host; KATV-TV, corresp; WCBS-TV, anchor, corresp, 1990-93; CBS News, anchor "Up to the Minute" 1993-94, anchor Morning News, 1994-96, corresp Evening News, 1996-; 48 Hours, corresp, 1998-. **Orgs:** Nat Asn Black Journalists; Harlem YMCA; Big Brothers Am. **Honors/Awds:** Nat Emmy Award, Olympic Park Bombing, 1997. **Business Addr:** Correspondent, 48 Hours CBS-TV, 524 W 57th St, New York, NY 10019, **Business Phone:** (212)975-4290.*

ROBERTS, VICTORIA A
Judge. **Personal:** Born Nov 25, 1951, Detroit, MI; daughter of Grace and Manuel. **Educ:** Mich Univ, BA, 1973; Northeastern Univ Sch Law, JD, 1976. **Career:** Mich Court Appeals, res Atty, 1976-77; Lewis, White, Clay & Graves, assoc, 1977-85; Am Motors Corp, sr litigation atty, 1983-85; Goodman, Eden, Millender & Bedrosian, 1988-93, partner, 1992-95, managing partner, 1995-98; Eastern Dist Mich, US Dist Ct judge, 1998-. **Orgs:** Am Bar Asn, 1989-, House Delegs, 1990-97; tate Bar MI,1976-; Wolverine Bar Asn, 1976-; Women Lawyers Asn MI, Wayne Region, 1976-; Nat Bar Asn; Am Arbitration Asn; Mich Trial Lawyers Asn; Am Trial Lawyers Asn; bd dir, Fair Housing Ctr Metro Detroit, 1985-91, chairperson, 1986-89; State Bar Mich, 1976-; bd dirs, State Bar Mich Found, 2002-; North Rosedale Pk Civic Asn; Detroit Inst Arts Founders Soc. **Honors/Awds:** Wolverine Bar Asn, Outstanding Mem Yr, 1986, Commendations Awards, US Dept Justice, 1986, 1987; First in Leadership Award, Women Lawyers Asn, Wayne Region, 1987; Distinguished Serv Award, Fair Housing Ctr Metrop Detroit, 1987, 1994; Mem of Year, Region VI, Nat Bar Asn, 1990-91; Award, Lansing Black Lawyers Asn, 1994; Trailblazer Award, 1991; Univ Detroit Mercy Black Law Studs Asn, Distinguished Serv Award, 1996; State Bar Mich Young Lawyers Section, Recognition as First African Am Female Pres State Bar Mich, 1996; Lansing Black Lawyers Asn, Recognition contribs to pract law, 1994; Fair Housing Ctr Metrop Detroit, Distinguished Serv Award, 1987, 1994; Nat Bar Asn, mem yr award, Region VI, 1990-91; State Bar Mich, Champion Justice Award, 1999; Roberts P Hudson Award, 2001; Honary Degree Laws, Northeastern Univ, 2004; Augustus Straker Award, Wolverine Bar Asn, 2004; Guardian Justice Award, American-Arab Anti-Discrimination Comt, 2005; President's Award, Wolverine Bar Asn, 2006. **Business Addr:** Judge, Eastern District of Michigan, 231 W Lafayette Rm 123, Detroit, MI 48226, **Business Phone:** (313)234-5230.

ROBERTS, REV. WESLEY A
Clergy, educator. **Personal:** Born Jan 3, 1938, Jamaica, WI; son of Ignatius and Rayness Wong; married Sylvia Y Forbes; children: Paul, Carolyn, Suzanne & Michael. **Educ:** Waterloo Lutheran Univ, BA, 1965; Toronto Baptist Sem, MDiv, 1965; Westminster Theol Sem, ThM, 1967, DDIV, 2002; Univ Guelph, MA, 1968, PhD, 1972. **Career:** Gordon-Conwell Theol Sem, asst prof black studies, 1972-73, asst prof Christian Thought, 1974-75, assoc prof Church Hist, 1977-84, asst dean, acad prog, 1980-84, prof Church Hist, 1984-85; Peoples Baptist Church, Boston, MA, interim pastor, 1980-82, sr pastor, 1982-; Gordon Col, Wenham, MA, adj prof Hist, 1974. **Orgs:** Soc Study Black Religion; Am Soc Church Hist; Conf Faith & Hist; The Assoc Theol Schs, US & Canada, 1980-84; Black Ministerial Alliance Greater Boston, 1994-. **Special Achievements:** Articles: Eerdman's Handbook Amer Christianity, Eerdman's Handbook of the Hist Christianity, Fides et Historia; Ontario Grad Fel Govt Ont, 1968-70; Gov Canada, Canada Coun Doctoral Fel, 1970-72; Author: Chap on Cornelius VanTil in Reformed Theol in Am, Wm B Eerdman, 1985, in Dutch Reformed Theol, Baker Bookhouse, 1988; Martin Luther King Jr & March on Washington, in Christian Hist Magazine, 1989; Rejecting the "Negro Pew," in Christian Hist Mag, 1995. **Home Addr:** 1 Enon Rd, Wenham, MA 01984. **Business Addr:** Senior Pastor, Peoples Baptist Church of Boston, 134 Camden St, Boston, MA 02118, **Business Phone:** (617)427-0424.

ROBERTS, WILLIAM HAROLD
Football player, football coach. **Personal:** Born Aug 5, 1962, Miami, FL. **Educ:** Ohio State Univ. **Career:** Football player (retired), Football coach; New York Giants, guard,1984-94; New England Patriots, 1995-96; New York Jets, 1997, asst coach, 1999-2001.

ROBERTSON, ANDRE LEVETT
Baseball player. **Personal:** Born Oct 2, 1957, Orange, TX; married Lanier Hebert; children: Ryan Andre, Chrystina Ulyssa & Jace Christian. **Educ:** Univ Tex, BBA, mgt. **Career:** Baseball player (retired); NY Yankees, shortstop, 1981-85; Dupont De Nemours EI & Co, staff. **Honors/Awds:** Athlete of the Century in Baseball; American League Championship Series, 1981; World Series, 1981. **Home Addr:** 3190 Chasse Ridge Dr, Orange, TX 77632.

ROBERTSON, DR. BENJAMIN W
Clergy, school administrator. **Personal:** Born Apr 6, 1931, Roanoke, VA; son of Clarence and Anna Mary Holland; married

Dolores Wallace; children: Benjamin W Jr. **Educ:** Va Theol Sem, BTh, 1951; Va Union Univ, AB, 1954; Va Sem & Col, MDiv, 1956, DD, 1959, DMin, 1968; Union Baptist Sem, LLD, 1971; Richmond Va Sem, LLD, 1982; Va Union Univ, HLD, 1997. **Career:** Cedar St Memorial Baptistist Church God, pastor 1955-; Radio Station WLEE, radio preacher 1961-; Nat Progressive Baptist Cong, teacher, 1962-; Radio Station WANT, 1965-; Robertson's Kiddie Col, pres, 1968-; First Union Baptist Church, Chesterfield, pastor; Piney Grove Baptist Church, pastor; Richmond Va Sem, pres, 1981; Va Theol Sem & Col, Lynchburg, VA, pres, 1980-81; BWR Ministries & Seminary, pres, currently. **Orgs:** Bd dirs, Commonwealth Va Girl Scouts, 1960-69; treas, Baptist Ministers Conf, 1960-70; founder, Progressive Nat Baptist Conv, 1961; teacher leaders, PNBC, 1961-81; Brookland Br, YMCA, 1963-75; Rich Met Blood Serv, 1963-68; Rich Br, NAACP, 1964-68; dean preaching, Va Theol Sem, 1965-75; vpres, Lott Carey Baptist Foreign Missionary Conv, 1976-83; Xi Delta Lambda Chap Alpha Phi Alpha Frat Inc; founder & pres, Richmond Va Sem, 1981-, State Bd Psychol, 1996-2000; Va State Bd Psychol; Va State Bd Health Prof; Va State Bd Radio Broadcasters. **Honors/Awds:** FOX Channel 35, television ministry; appointed to Brown v Bd of Education 50th Anniversary Pres Commission, 1954-04, 2002; Beta Gamma Lambda Chap Alpha Phi Alpha Frat Inc 1968; Minister of Year, Hayes-Allen VTS&C, 1975; Humanitarian Award, Rich Com Hosp, 1975; Afro-Amererican Award, Superior Public Serv without Thought of Gain, 1981; Lifetime Achievement Award, Va Baptist State Convention, 2000; recognized Dean of Virginia's Pastors, 2000; Outstanding Service to Humanity, Commander's Medallion, 2001. **Special Achievements:** Author, Just As He Promised; Led By The Spirit of God, 2000. **Home Addr:** 8901 Strath Rd, Richmond, VA 23231. **Business Phone:** (804)648-8919.

ROBERTSON, CARDISS. See COLLINS, CARDISS H.

ROBERTSON, CHARLES E, JR.
Administrator, consultant. **Personal:** Married Angela; children: Kendall. **Educ:** Southern Univ, BS, bus mgt, 1986; Mountain State, mgt develop, 1987; Dale Carnegie Mgt Sem, 1990; Am Hotel & Motel Asn, Cert Security & Loss Prev Mgt, 1990. **Career:** Harmony Ctr, Baton Rouge, La, counr, 1982; Capitol House Hotel, Baton Rouge, La, mgt trainee prog, 1984-86; Copper Mountain Resort, Copper Mountain Co, mgr, 1986-94; Denver Parks Recreation Dept, dep mgr parks, 1994; CER & Assocs, pres, currently; Univ Colo, Off Pres, comn mem, currently. **Orgs:** Utility Consumers Bd; Summit County Chamber Com Statesmen Comt; Nat Coalition Black Meeting Planners; Religious Conf Mgt Asn; Soc Govt Meeting Planners; Phi Beta Sigma Frat; Nat Brotherhood Skiers; Young Adults Positive Action; comn mem, Univ Colo Syst. **Business Phone:** (303)860-5600.

ROBERTSON, DEWAYNE
Football player. **Personal:** Born Oct 16, 1981, Memphis, TN. **Educ:** Univ Ky, gen studies. **Career:** New York Jets, defensive tackle, 2003-07; Denver Broncos, defensive tackle, 2008-. **Business Addr:** Defensive Tackle, Denver Broncos, 7505 S Potomac St, Englewood, CO 80112, **Business Phone:** (303)649-9777.

ROBERTSON, DOLORES W.
Educator. **Personal:** Born Jul 11, 1934, Richmond, VA; married Benjamin W, Mar 6, 1955; children: Benjamin W Jr. **Educ:** VA Union Univ, BA, 1957; VA Commonwealth Univ, attended; Univ VA,attended. **Career:** Educator (retired); Robertson's Kiddie Col, founder, pres, 1958-80; BW MemChoir, mentor, 1980; Bellevue Elem Sch, teacher; Whitcomb Elem Sch, teacher, 1989. **Orgs:** Richmond Educ Asn; Eastern Star #79 East End; Minister' Wives Richmond &Vicinity; Int Ministers' Wives & Widows; Nat Asn Advan Colored People;Southern Christian Leadership Conf; Progressive Nat Baptist Conv Inc;chairperson, Deaconess Bd,; secy, Educ Tutorial Prog,; bd dir, BWR Ministries & Seminary; co-founder, Nat Christian Educ Conv; hon mem, execbd, Richmond Va Seminary. **Honors/Awds:** Mother of The Year, Royal Ushers, 1956; Outstanding Achievement Award, Richmond VA Seminary, 1986; Woman of The Year, Cedar St Baptist Church God, 1990; Woman of the Year, Richmond VA Seminary Publ. **Special Achievements:** Contributor, Led By The Spirit of God, 2000. **Home Addr:** 8901 Strath Rd, Richmond, VA 23231, **Home Phone:** (804)795-1111.

ROBERTSON, EVELYN CRAWFORD
School administrator. **Personal:** Born Nov 19, 1941, Winchester, TN; son of Evelyn and Pearl; married Hugholene Ellison; children: Jeffrey Bernard & Sheila Yvette. **Educ:** Tenn State Univ, BS, 1962, MA, 1969; Southwest MO State Univ, NDEA Cert, 1970. **Career:** Sch Adminr(retired); Allen White High Sch, teacher/coach, 1962-68; AllenWhite Elem Sch, prin, 1969; Cent High Sch, asst prin, 1970-74; Western Ment Health Inst, asst supt, 1974-79, 1983-91; Nat T Winston Develop Center, supt, 1979-83; Tenn Univ, Dept Ment Health & Ment Retardation, comnr, 1991-95; Bank Bolivar, dir, 1991-; SW Tenn Develop District, exec dir; WestStar Alumni Coun, 2006-09. **Orgs:** Pres, Hardeman Co Teachers Asn, 1973; chmn, Whiteville Civic League,1976-79; chmn bd, Hardeman Co Develop Serv Ctr, 1977-78; bd mem, Am Heart Asn affil, 1980-; pres, Bolivar Civitan Club, 1981; vpres, Whiteville Bus Enterprise Inc, 1982; chmn, Admin Div, SEAAMD, 1983; consult, Hardeman Ment Health Asn, 1983; bd dir, Quinco Ment Health Ctr; bd dir, NADO. **Honors/Awds:** Outstanding Young Educator, Hardeman Co Jaycees, 1976; EC Robertson Day given by citizens in honor, 1983. **Home Addr:** 2665 Newsom Rd, Whiteville, TN 38075.

ROBERTSON, KAREN A
Librarian. **Personal:** Born in Montclair, NJ; daughter of Joesph C and H June Hawkins. **Educ:** Morgan State Univ, Baltimore, MD, BA, 1966; Atlanta Univ, Atlanta, GA,MSLS, 1967; Univ Baltimore, MBA, 1983. **Career:** Prince George's County, Hyattsville, MD, ref librn, 1967-68; Morgan State Univ, Baltimore, MD, chief ref librn, 1968-80, dir libr, 1980-. **Orgs:** Alpha Kappa Alpha Inc, 1964-; Md Libr Asn, 1974-; Am Libr Asn, 1975-. **Business Addr:** Director of Library Services, Morgan State University, Soper Library, 1700 E Cold Spring Lane, Baltimore, MD 21239-4098.

ROBERTSON, MARCUS AARON
Football player. **Personal:** Born Oct 2, 1969, Pasadena, CA; married Holly, Jun 27, 1992; children: Morgan Ashley. **Educ:** Iowa State Univ. **Career:** Houston Oilers, defensive back, 1991-96; Tennessee Oilers, 1997-98; Tennessee Titans, 1999-00; Seattle Seahawks, 2001-02, Tennessee titans, sec coach, currently. **Honors/Awds:** First-Team All-Pro, Assoc Press, Sporting News, 1993; Ed Block Courage Award, 1994.

ROBERTSON, MARILYN A
Physician. **Personal:** Born Dec 19, 1959, Curacao; daughter of David and Nina; married Curtis E Fisher, Aug 3, 1985; children: Michael, Christopher, Matthew & Christian. **Educ:** Hofstra Univ, MA, 1984; Med Col PA, MD, 1989. **Career:** Nassau County Med Ctr, staff physician, 1990-93, part time staff physician, 1993-97; staff physician, 1990-93; KMLT Gynec Assoc, assoc physician, 1993-96; Hempstead Gynec Obstet Assoc, physician, 1995-96; pvt pract, 1996-; Franklin Hosp Med Ctr, physician, acting dir obstet, dir womens health ctr, 2000-, chief gynec, currently. **Orgs:** Philadelphia Med Soc, 1985-89; AMA, 1993-; vpres, Coalition Comm Develop, 1995-97; Am Col Obstetricians & Gynecologists, 1995-; Franklin Hosp Med Ctr, 1998-. **Honors/Awds:** Distinguished Service Award, Hofstra Univ Alumni Assn, 1997; Annual Award for Excellence, NY State Governor George Pataki, 2001; Woman of the Year, Town of Hempstead, 2001. **Business Addr:** Chief Gynecology, Franklin Hospital Medical Center, 900 Franklin Ave, Valley Stream, NY 11580, **Business Phone:** (516)538-1932.

ROBERTSON, OSCAR PALMER
Executive, basketball player, businessperson. **Personal:** Born Nov 24, 1938, Charlotte, TN; son of Henry Bailey and Mazell Bell; married Yvonne Crittenden, Jun 25, 1960; children: Shana Robertson Shaw, Tia & Mari. **Educ:** Cincinnati Univ, BS, bus, 1960. **Career:** Basketball player & guard (retired), pres, chief exec officer; Cincinnati Royals NBA, guard, 1960-70; Milwaukee Bucks NBA, 1970-74; Oscar Robertson Construct, pres & chief exec officer, 1975-; Avondale Town Ctr, Cincinnati, developer, 1981; ORCHEM Inc, pres, chief exec officer & owner, 1981-; TV sports announcer; Oscar Robertson & Assocs, pres, 1983-; Oscar Terrace (affordable housing units), Indianapolis, IN, developer/owner, 1989; Orpack-Stone Corp, pres & chief exec officer, 1990-; Oscar Robertson Media Ventures, 1998-; Oscar Robertson Document Mgt Servs, 2000-; Oscar Robertson Foods, pres, currently; OR Solutions, pres, currently. **Orgs:** Pres, Nat Basketball Players Asn, 1964-74; St Dept Tour Africa, 1971; World Championship Team, 1971; Nat Asn Advan Colored Poeple Sports Bd, 1987; trustee, Ind High Sch Hall Fame, 1984-89; trustee, Basketball Hall Fame, 1987-89; nat dir, Pepsi Cola Hot Shot Prog; pres, NBA Retired Players Asn, 1993-99; bd mem, Countrywide Savings & Loan, 2000-; Nat Basketball Hall Fame; Ind Basketball Hall Fame. **Honors/Awds:** Gold Medal, Olympic Games, 1960; Most Valuable Player Award, All Star Game, 1961; NBA Most Valuable Player Award; Rookie of the Year Award, 1961; NBA champion, 1971; Basketball Hall of Fame, 1979; Olympic Hall of Fame, 1984; Nat Award, Boys Clubs Am, 1987; Statue in his Honor, Univ Cincinnati Campus, 1994; Col Player of the Year Award, Oscar Robertson Trophy, 1998; William Howard Taft Medal, Univ Cincinnati, 2003; DHL, Univ Cincinnati, 2007. **Special Achievements:** Author & publisher: Play Better Basketball, 1968; named one of the Greatest Athletes of the 20th Century, Sports Illustrated, 1999; Named Ind Living Legend, 1999; Named one of the 50 Greatest Athletes of the Century, ESPN, 1999; Author: The Art of Basketball, 1999; The Big O: My Life, MyTimes, My Game, 2003. **Military Serv:** AUS, pvt first class, 1960-67. **Business Addr:** Owner, ORCHEM Inc, 4293 Mulhauser Rd, Fairfield, OH 45014, **Business Phone:** (513)874-9700.

ROBERTSON, QUINCY L.
School administrator. **Personal:** Born Jul 30, 1934, Wedowee, AL; son of Jessie and Viola Wilkes; married Dollie Williams; children: Stephanie. **Educ:** Tenn State Univ, BA, 1955, MA, 1957. **Career:** School Administrator (retired): Richmond County Bd Educ, guidance counr, 1959-68; Paine Col, dir of upward bound, 1968-69, bus mgr, 1970-83, Admin & Fiscal Affairs, vpres, 1983. **Orgs:** Bd dir, USO, 1964-68; comn, Richmond Cty Personnel Bd, 1973-78; chmn, Thankful Baptist Church Trustee Bd, 1977-85; vpres, Frontiersman, 1984-85; bd dir, EIIA, 1985-; bd dir, Univ Hosp; bd mem, Richmond County Hosp Authority; bd mem & treas, The Gertrude Herbert Art Inst; bd mem, Sun Trust Nat Bank; bd mem, Augusta Rescue Mission; Am Asn Affirmative Action, 1982-; Nat Asn Black Public Admin, 1983-; Nat Asn Human Rights Workers, 1986-; DeKalb Co Nat Asn Advan Colored People; den leader, Boy Scouts Am, 1992-. **Honors/Awds:** Man of the Year, Thankful Baptist Church, 1969; Admin of the Year, Paine Col, 1973-74; Citizen of the Year, Alpha Phi Alpha Frat, 1984; Outstanding Young Men of America, 1984; Distinguished Service Award, Univ Ga, 1985; Community Service Award, Black Pages Magazine, 1990; Minority Business Advocate of the Year, 1991. **Military Serv:** AUS, spec 4 1957-58; Good Conduct Medal, Expert Rifleman, Honorable Discharge. **Home Phone:** (706)821-8232.

ROBERTSON, QUINDONELL S.
Educator. **Personal:** Born in Dallas, TX; married J William. **Educ:** BA, 1954, MA, 1970. **Career:** Educator (retired); Dallas Independent Sch Dist & Sch Sec, educr, 1957-58, educ cluster coord, 1984. **Orgs:** Am Asn Univ Women, 1986; master educr, Am Bd Master Educr, 1987; NEA; Tex St Teacher Asn; Classroom Teachers Dallas; Tex Classroom Teacher; Tex Asn Teacher Educ; Amigos. **Honors/Awds:** Sigma Gamma Rho; Tex Col; Tex St Univ Alumni Asn; life mem, YWCA; charter mem, Dallas Urban League Guild; pres, Top Ladies Distinction Inc; bd dir, Dallas Pan Hellenic Coun; mem, Phi Delta Kappa. **Special Achievements:** Cup for chartering Arlington Tex, Sigma Gamma Rho, 1983; Gold Charm for serving 3 yrs as pres of Sigma Gamma Rho, 1985-88; Gold Teacher of The Year, 1990-91; Yellow Tea Rose Award, SW Region Sigma Gamma Rho, 1992; Region Sigma Gamma Rho Service Award, 1992; 9 plaques for leadership & service; 1 silver tray for leadership & service; Gavel for leadership; 2 trophies for leadership & service; Medallion for YWCA Quota Buster.

ROBESON, PAUL, JR.
Writer, television producer, lecturer. **Personal:** Born Nov 2, 1927, Brooklyn, NY; son of Paul Leroy and Eslanda Goode; married Marilyn Paula Greenberg, Jun 19, 1949; children: David Paul (deceased) & Susan. **Educ:** Cornell Univ, BSEE, 1949. **Career:** Sch Indust Technol, instr, 1949-52; Othello ASC, chief exec officer, 1953-56; Int Physical Index, exec ed, partner, 1957-70, freelance translator from Russian, 1971-89; Prog Corp Am, lectr, 1990-96; Books: Celebration of Paul Robeson, Shubert Theater, 1988; producer, Odyssey of Paul Robeson, compact disc, Omega Record Group, 1992; Auth, Paul Robeson Jr Speaks to America, Rutgers Univ Press, 1992; The Undiscovered Paul Robeson, John Wiley & Sons, 2001. **Orgs:** The Players Club, 1997-. **Honors/Awds:** Cornell Univ, Tau Beta Pi Honor Society, 1949; Eta Kappa Nu Honor Society, 1949; Alpha Phi Alpha Fraternity; Founders Award of Excellence, 1991; Cornell Univ Athletics Hall of Fame, 1998. **Military Serv:** USAAF, corporal, 1946-47.

ROBICHAUX, JOLYN H.
Executive. **Personal:** Born May 21, 1928, Cairo, IL; widowed; children: Sheila, Joseph. **Educ:** Chicago Teacher Col, AB, 1960; PA State Univ Ice Cream Tech, Cert. **Career:** Retired: State Dept Tour of Africa, spec nutritions consult 1956; Betty Crocker Home Serv Dept of Gen Mills, 1960-65; Cook Cty, jury comm 1971-72; Baldwin Ice Cream Co, owner 1971-92. **Orgs:** Bd dir, Chicago United Way, 1984. **Honors/Awds:** Elected 1 10 Outstanding Black Bus Leaders Black Book, 1973; Community Service Award, Chicago S End Jaycees, 1973; Black Excellence Award, Bus by PUSH, 1974-75; Achievement Award, So IL Council, 1974; Achievement in Bus World Black Women, Iota Phi Lambda, 1974; Bus Woman Year, Cosmopolitan C C, 1976; Disting Alumna Award, Chicago State Univ, 1984; Par Excellence Award, PUSH Bus Woman Year, 1984; Nat Minority Entrepreneur of the Year, Univ S Dept Com presented by Vice Pres George Bush, 1985. *

ROBIE, CLARENCE W.
Business owner. **Career:** B & S Elec Supply Co Inc, owner & pres, 1980-. **Orgs:** Greater Atlanta Elec League. **Business Addr:** Owner, President, B & S Electrical Supply Company Inc., 4505 Mills Pl SW, PO Box 44769, Atlanta, GA 30336, **Business Phone:** (404)696-8284.

ROBINET, HARRIETTE GILLEM
Writer. **Personal:** Born Jul 14, 1931, Washington, DC; daughter of Richard Avitus and Martha Gray; married McLouis Joseph, Aug 6, 1960; children: Stephen, Philip, Rita, Jonathan, Marsha & Linda. **Educ:** Col New Rochelle, BS, 1953; Catholic Univ Am, MS, 1957, PhD, 1962. **Career:** Children's Hosp, Wash DC, bacteriologist, 1953-54; Walter Reed Army Med Ctr, Wash, DC, med serologist, 1954-57, research bacteriologist, 1958-60; Xavier Univ, New Orleans LA, instructor biol, 1957-58; US Army, Quartermaster Corps, civilian food bacteriologist, 1960-62; freelance writer, 1962-; Books: Jay & the Marigold, 1976; Ride the Red Cycle, 1980; Children of the Fire, 1991; Mississippi Chariot, 1994; If You Please, pres Lincoln, 1995; Washington City is Burning, 1996; The Twins, The Pirates & The Battle of New Orleans, 1997; Forty Acres & Maybe a Mule, 1998; Walking to the Bus Rider Blues, 2000; Missing From Haymarket Square, 2001;

Twelve Travelers, Twenty Horses, 2002. **Orgs:** Soc Childrens Book Writers & Illustrators; Nat Writers; Soc Midland Authors; Sisters Crime; Mystery Writers Am. **Honors/Awds:** Carl Sandburg Children's Literature Award, Wash City, Burning, 1997; Children's Literature Award, Friends Am Writers, Children Fire, 1991; Notable Children's Trade Books Social Studies: Miss Chariot, 1994; Children of the Fire, 1991; Books for the Teen Age, NYC Librarians: Mississippi Chariot; Children's Literature Award, "The Twins, the Pirates and the Battle of New Orleans," Society of Midland Authors, 1998; Scott O'Dell Award, children's historical fiction, 1999; Walking to Bus Rider Blues nominated for an Edgar, Mystery Writers, Jane Addams Peace Award Honor Book. **Home Addr:** 409 S Elmwood Ave, Oak Park, IL 60302, **Home Phone:** (708)524-0227.

ROBINSON, ALBERT ARNOLD
Salesperson. **Personal:** Born May 2, 1937, Lawrenceville, VA; married Mary Elizabeth Wright; children: Terence, Todd, Trent, Tevis, Lisa. **Educ:** VA State Univ, BS, 1958; Central State Univ, BS, 1968; East Calif Univ, attended 1977. **Career:** salesperson (retired); US Army, commissioned officer, 1958-78; Ford Motor Co, manufacturing supvr, 1978-80; Bechtel Power Corp, supvr reprographics, 1980-84; Nat Reproductions Corp, sales rep, 1984-85; Eastern MI Univ, mgr serv opers, special asst vpres bus & finance, 1985-02. **Orgs:** Trustee, Second Baptist Ch; Ypsilanti& Willow Run Br NAACP; councilman, Ypsilanti City Coun; Ann Arbor & Ypsilanti Bus & Prof League; Emanon Club; Beta Kappa Chi Honorary Scientific Frat, 1958; Kappa Phi Kappa Hon Educ Frat, 1958. **Honors/Awds:** Meritorious Serv Medal. **Military Serv:** AUS, lt col; Legion Merit, Bronze Star, Army Commendations, Parachutist Badge, 1958-78. **Home Addr:** 918 Pleasant Dr, Ypsilanti, MI 48197.

ROBINSON, ALBERT M.
Association executive. **Personal:** Born Oct 1, 1958?; married Jane B Carter; children: Albert Jr & Kimberly. **Educ:** VA State Col, BS; Rutgers Univ; Rider Col. **Career:** United Progress Inc, exec dir; Dept Comm Affairs NJ, relocation officer; Trenton House Auth, mgr; Lockerman High Sch Denton, teacher; Trenton Br NAACP, pres. **Honors/Awds:** Brotherhood award, Jewish Fed; outstanding & community service award, 1970; Trenton Public Service Award, 1968; outstanding achievment community affairs, NAACP, 1971; pol action council award, 1967. **Military Serv:** AUS, 1942-46.

ROBINSON, ALCURTIS
Insurance executive. **Personal:** Son of Eris Sr. and Corean Skinner. **Educ:** Harris Teachers Col, AA, 1960; Purdue Univ, Prof Mgt Inst, 1976. **Career:** Mutual Omaha-United Omaha, St Louis, MO, salesman, 1967-69, sales training instr, 1969-70, dist mgr, 1970-73; Mutual Omaha-United Omaha, Omaha, NE, assoc dir mgt training, 1973-75, asst vpres career develop & mgt training, 1975-77, second vpres, 1977-82, vpres career develop & pub affairs, 1982-85, vpres pub serv & minority affairs, 1985-, vpres minority & community affairs, 1988-; Ins Indust Designation, registered health underwriter, currently. **Orgs:** NAACP, Baltimore, MD; bd mem, Nat Assoc Sickle Cell Disease Inc; Black Executive Exchange Prog, Nat Urban League, Inc, NY; Nat Alliance Business; Career develop advisory comm, Nat Urban League; develop dir, United Negro Col Fund Drive; chmn, public employees retirement bd, State of Nebraska; chmn, bd dir, Christian Urban Educ Serv; Urban League of Nebraska; pres Omaha Sch Found, 1990-91; bd dir, YMCA of Omaha. **Honors/Awds:** Distinguished Alumni Award, Harris-Stowe State Col, 1992; Distinguished Eagle Award, Nat Eagle Leadership Inst, 1997; Af-Am award, Western Heritage Museum, Omaha, 1998; Otto Swanson Spirit of Service Award, Nat Conference for Comm and Justice, 2000. **Military Serv:** AUS, 1963-65. **Business Addr:** Vice President, Mutual of Omaha Insurance Company, Mutual of Omaha Plz, Omaha, NE 68175, **Business Phone:** (402)342-7600.*

ROBINSON, ALFREDA P.
School administrator, dean (education). **Personal:** Born May 7, 1932, Charlotte, NC. **Educ:** Upsala Col, BA, 1954; Rutgers Sch Social Work, attended 1957; Union Grad Sch, doctoral cand. **Career:** School administrator(retired), Dean(retired); Financial Aid Douglass & Cook Col, Rugers Univ, dir; Essex Co Probation Dept, sr probation officer; NJ Bur C Serv Nat, case worker; Rutgers Univ Grad Sch Bus & Admin, asst dean in charge stud serv; Rutgers Grad Sch Mgt, dean in charge stud serv. **Orgs:** Proj comt mem, Delta Sigma Theta; Nat Scholar & Stand Comn, NJ Alumnae Chap; corr secy, ed, Eastern Asn Stud Financial Aid Admin; Counman, Nat Coun Stud Financial Aid; NJ Asn Stud Financial Aid Admin; Counman, Col Entrance Exam Bd; Mid States Regional Counman Pub & Guid Comn; Upper Div Scholar Rev; NJ Alumnae Chap; vpres, bd trustees, St Timothy House. **Honors/Awds:** Community Serv Award, Sigma Gamma Rho, 1979; Serv Award, Rutgers Black MBA Asn, 1979; Alfreda P Robinson Award.

ROBINSON, DR. ANDREW
Educator. **Personal:** Born Feb 16, 1939, Chicago, IL. **Educ:** Chicago State Univ, BA, 1966; Roosevelt Univ, MA, 1970; Northwestern Univ, PhD, 1973. **Career:** Chicago Pub Schs, teacher, 1966-69; Chicago Urban League, educ dir, 1970-73; Univ IL, visiting instr, 1972-73; Urban & Ethnic Educ, Asst dir; Pub Inst Chicago, supt, 1973-74; Chicago City Cols, adminr, 1974-75; Univ KY, asst prof, assoc dir Ctr urban educ; Univ North Florida, first interim pres, 1980-82. **Orgs:** Phi Delta Kappa; Am Asn Sch Admins; Am Asn Teacher Educ; Nat Alliance Black Sch Educators; Prog Planning Comt Am Assoc Col Teacher Educ. **Military Serv:** Mil serv, 1962-63.

ROBINSON, ANGELA YVONNE
Television journalist. **Personal:** Born Jul 14, 1956, Atlanta, GA; daughter of Ann Roberts Robinson and Johnny Robinson (deceased). **Educ:** Syracuse Univ, Syracuse, NY, BS, public communications, television/radio broadcasting, 1978. **Career:** WAGA-TV, Atlanta, GA, production assistant, 1978-83; WTTG-TV, Washington, DC, general assignment reporter, talk show host, news anchor, news editor & reporter, 1983-94; WXIA, co-anchor, 1994-97; In Contact, co-exec producer, host, currently. **Orgs:** Member, National Assn of Black Journalists; mem, Washington Chapter, National Council of Negro Women, 1989-; Atlanta Assn of Black Journalists; Natl Assn of Black Journalists Region 4 Hall of Fame; Atlanta Press Club; United Negro Coll Fund; Advisory bd, SI Newhouse School of Communication, Syracuse Univ; 100 Black Men of Atlanta Inc; Success Circle; Natl Academy of Television Arts & Sciences; Outstanding Young Women of America; bd mem, Fund for Southern Committee. **Honors/Awds:** Emmy Awards, National Academy of Television Arts and Sciences, 1980; United Press International Award, 1980, Editing Award, 1981; Emmy Award Nominee, National Academy of Television Arts and Sciences, 1986, 1989, 1990; Outstanding Enterprise Reporting, Associated Press International; Award of Distinction, George Aman, 1989; National Association of Black Journalists Award, 1990; Associated Press Award, Sports Feature, 1990, Feature/Humor Interest, 1991; National Association of Black Journalists Award, 1991-92; Omega Psi Phi Fraternity Inc, Public Service Award, 1992; Atlanta Assn of Media Women; Chancellor's Citation, Syracuse Univ, Distinguished Achievement in Journalism; Angela Y Robinson, Student Scholarship, Syracuse Univ; Atlanta Business League: 100 Women of Vision; Several Awards of Excellence, National Assn of Black Journalists; Southern Regional Emmy Awards, News Anchor, 1995, Best Newscast & Olympic Special, 1996, Special Series, 1997; Atlanta Association of Black Journalists Pioneer Award, Special Reports, 1995, 1997; Southern Regional Emmy Awd; Absolute Africa Awd, Absolute Inc & Women Looking Ahead magazine. **Special Achievements:** News Anchor, Southern Regional Emmy Awards, 1995; is noted in Who's Who Among African Americans and Outstanding Young Women of America. *

ROBINSON, ANN GARRETT
Educator. **Personal:** Born Jun 8, 1934, Greenville, NC; married Charles; children: Angela Carol & George Carl. **Educ:** NC Cent Univ, BA, 1954; Wayne State Univ, MA, 1957; Nova Univ, EdD, 1975; Yale Univ, res fel, 1986. **Career:** NC Bd Corrections, 1956-57; Cent State Hosp, clin psychol, 1958-64; LaRue Carter Hosp, clin psychol, 1958-64; Augusta State Hosp, clin psychol,1958-64; Yale Univ Child Study Ctr, res asst, 1968-70; Trinity Col, Hartford, asst prof psychol, 1970-72; Gateway Community Col, prof psychol, 1972-99, prof emer, psychol, 2000-; freelance writer, 1983-; New Haven Register, newspaper columnist, 1985-; Robinson Behavioral Sci Consult, New Haven, co-owner. **Orgs:** Bd dir, S Cent Conn Mental Health Planning Reg, 1974-77; NEA, Am Psychol Asn; bd deaconnesses, Immanuel Baptist Church; Alpha Kappa Alpha; Black Educrs Asn; Afro-Am History Bd; Jack & Jill Am Inc; regional vpres, N EPsi Beta Inc; Nat Honor Soc Psychol; pres-elect, Nat Coun, Psi Beta Inc; chairlady, Immanuel Baptist Church, bd deaconesses, 1985. **Honors/Awds:** Nannie H Burroughs Award Outstanding Black Educator of New Haven, 1974; Presidential Citation Award, SCCC, 1977; Community Service Award, New Haven; Church of Christ National Youth Conference Award, 1986; Most Scholarly Award, SCCC, 1987; Most Influential Professor, SCCC Student Government Award, 1987; Professional Woman of the Year, Elm City Business & Prof Women. **Special Achievements:** Author: "Clouds & Clowns of Destiny", "Behind Krome Detention Center Walls", "Are the Doors to Higher Education Starting to Close", "Heroic Women of the Past, The Three Wives of Booker T Washington"; contributed articles to the New Haven Register, as well as to other newspapers. **Business Addr:** Professor Emerita, Gateway Community College, 60 Sargent Dr, New Haven, CT 06511, **Business Phone:** (203)285-2000.*

ROBINSON, ANTHONY W
Executive. **Personal:** Born Dec 11, 1948, Clarksville, TN; son of Charles C and Eva Mae Childs; married Yvonne Davis, Aug 30, 1980; children: Charles Anthony & Camille A. **Educ:** Morgan State Col, BS, 1970; Wash Col Law, Am Univ, JD, 1973. **Career:** US Equal Employment Opportunity Comn, legal coun, 1972-75; Law Firm Singleton, Dashiell & Robinson, Baltimore, MD, co-founder, 1975; Spec Coun US Congressman Parren J. Mitchell, 1976-86; Minority Bus Enterprise Legal Defense Educ Fund, pres, 1984-; Md State Inmate Grievance Comnr, chmn. **Honors/Awds:** Advocate Recognition Award, Minority Human Bus Enterprise, 1995; Nat Conf Blak Mayors, 1995; Recognition Award, NMSDC, 1996; Advocate of the Year, Minority Bus Report, 1996. **Special Achievements:** The Affirmative Action Debate edited by George E Curry, 1996; Various Citation include: US Department of Transportation; National Minority Supplier Development Council; American Contract Compliance Association; National Federation of Black Public Administrators; Baltimore's Monumental City Bar Association; Boston's Office of Minority Business Development Agency. **Military Serv:** AUS, Lt, 1972-78. **Home Addr:** 8134 Scotts Level Rd, Baltimore, MD 21208. **Business Phone:** (301)583-4648.

ROBINSON, BARRY LANE
Government official. **Personal:** Born Jun 5, 1943, White Plains, NY; divorced; children: 2. **Educ:** State Univ Buffalo, BA, 1980. **Career:** Johnson & Johnson, salesman, 1974-75; Attica Correction Ctr, corrections officer, 1975-79; Masten Park Secure Ctr, child care worker, 1979-; Erie County, County Legislator, First Vice Chair, 1982-85. **Orgs:** NAACP, 1985; Ellicott Dist Concerned Taxpayers, 1985; Oper PUSH. **Honors/Awds:** Mr Black America, 1981; Dale Carnegie Award, Pub Speaking & Univ; training course, NY State Police. **Military Serv:** AUS, sp & 5 trans, 1966-80; Honorable Discharge.

ROBINSON, BEVERLY JEAN
Publishing executive. **Personal:** Born Dec 15, 1957, Bath, NY; daughter of George Wesley and Alice Jackson; married Christopher K Chaplin, Aug 30, 1981; children: Christopher & Khalif. **Educ:** Dowling Col, Oakdale, NY, BA (magna cum laude), 1979; New Sch Social Res, New York, NY, master, 1988. **Career:** Random House Inc, New York, NY, advert asst, 1979-82, Ballantine Publ Group, New York, NY, publicity coord, 1982-87, publicity mgr, 1987-90, asst publicity dir, 1990-93, assoc, dir press rels, 1993-99, dir publicity, currently, free lance publicist & consult writer. **Orgs:** Women Communs, 1983-85. **Honors/Awds:** Excellence in Publicity Award, Lit Mkt Pl, 1991. **Special Achievements:** Member of the team that founded One World, the first multicultural imprint at a major publishing house, 1992. **Home Addr:** 135 Clinton St Suite4V, Hempstead, NY 11550. **Business Addr:** Director of Publicity, Random House Inc, Ballantine Publishing Group, 1745 Broadway, New York, NY 10019, **Business Phone:** (212)572-2717.

ROBINSON, CARL CORNELL
Lawyer. **Personal:** Born Sep 21, 1946, Washington, DC; son of Louis W and Florence A. **Educ:** Univ Mich, BS, aero eng, 1969; Golden Gate Univ, MBA, 1974; Univ Calif, Los Angeles, JD, 1977. **Career:** O'Melveny & Myers, atty, 1977-84; Robinson & Pearman LLP, atty & partner, 1984-. **Orgs:** Dir, Univ Calif Los Angeles Law Alumni Asn, 1977, 1997; dir, San Fernando Valley Neighborhood Legal Serv, 1981-91, chair, 1982-86; dir, Univ Calif Los Angeles Pub Interest Law Found, 1982-89, chair, 1982-84; vpres, Nat Black MBA Asn, Los Angeles, 1985; Legal Serv Trust Fund Comn CA, 1985, Judicial Eval Comn Los Angeles Co Bar Asn, 1986, 1988, 1990, 1994, 1998, 2000; dir, Nat Asn Securities Prof, 1986-94; dir, John M Langston Bar Asn, 1987-94; dir, Western Ctr Law & Poverty Inc, 1988-94. **Military Serv:** USAF, capt, 1969-74. **Home Addr:** 3924 S Sycamore Ave, Los Angeles, CA 90008, **Home Phone:** (323)290-2926. **Business Addr:** Partner, Attorney, Robinson & Pearman LLP, 810 S Flower St Suite 1215, Los Angeles, CA 90017, **Business Phone:** (213)627-9060.

ROBINSON, CARL DAYTON
Pediatrician. **Personal:** Born Jun 14, 1942, Tallulah, LA; son of Bernie Dayton and Emily Parker; married Sandra Lawson, Aug 14, 1965; children: Michael, Carla. **Educ:** Howard Univ, BS, 1964, MD, 1968; Tulane Univ Sch Pub Health, MPH, 1977. **Career:** Letterman Army Med Ctr, cheif prenatal/infant serv, 1971-73; Flint Goodridge Hosp, dir sickle cell prog, 1973-78; Genetic Disease Ctr, med dir, 1978-81; Tulane Univ Med Sch, clin asst prof pediat, 1973-; Robinson Med Grp, pres, 1978-; APTECH Inc, pres, 1978-; LA Health Corp, pres , 1984-; C Hosp, New Orleans, pres med staff, 1986-88; Develop Ctr Am, New Orleans, LA, pres, 1990-; Key Mgt, Birmingham, AL, vpres & med dir, 1990-; Kids First Prytania, pediatrician, currently. **Orgs:** Nat Sickle Cell Adv Comn, 1976-78; Reg Med Prog, LA, 1976-78; LA Comn Prenatal Care, 1977-81; vpres, SE LA Med Quality Review Found, 1979-81; secy, Dept Health & Human Resources, LA, 1984; life mem, Alpha Phi Alpha; mem, Am Publ Health Asn; pres, Orleans Parish Sch Bd, 1990; fel, AmAcad Pediat; fel Int Col Pediat. **Special Achievements:** Book : "Dr. Carl Robinson's Basic Baby Care", 1998. **Military Serv:** AUS, major, 1971-73. *

ROBINSON, CAROL EVONNE
Journalist. **Personal:** Born Sep 15, 1959, Sacramento, CA; daughter of Herbert Allen and Claudia Cleatus Buford. **Educ:** Univ Calif, Davis, Calif, BA, 1983; Cosumnes River Col, Sacramento, Calif, 1984-86; Summer prog, Minority Journalists, Berkeley, Calif, 1988. **Career:** Meracor Mortgage, Sacramento, Calif, asst loan closer, 1986-87; Calif Personnel Serv, Sacramento, Calif, word processor, 1988; Bellingham Herald, Bellingham, Wash, educ writer, 1988-89; Daily Republic, Fairfield, CA, educ writer, 1989; Calif Energy Comn, info officer & editor, currently. **Orgs:** Nat Asn Black Journalists, 1989-; Sacramento Black Journalists Asn, 1990-; Soc Prof Journalists, 1989-. **Honors/**

Awds: First Place, Government Reporting, Society of Professional Journalists, Northwest Chapter, 1989. **Home Addr:** 2118 60th Ave, Sacramento, CA 95822, **Home Phone:** (916)427-0399. **Business Addr:** Information Officer, Editor, California Energy Commission, PO Box 188372, Sacramento, CA 95818-8372, **Business Phone:** (916)654-5015.

ROBINSON, CAROL W.
Librarian. **Personal:** Born Dec 4, 1953, New Rochelle, NY; daughter of Richard Word and Dorothy Clark; married Curtis Robinson (died 1982); children: Ujima, Zakiyyah, Saliym. **Educ:** Atlanta Univ, GA, attended 1973; Northeastern Univ, Boston, MA, BA, 1976; Pratt Inst, Brooklyn, NY, attended 1982; Queens Col, Flushing NY, MLS, 1984. **Career:** Libr Cong, Wash, DC, libr intern, 1973; MIT Hist Collections, Cambridge, MA, mus intern, 1974-76; Coopers & Lybrand, Wash, DC, libr asst, 1976-78; Wash, DC Pub Schs, Wash, DC, teacher, 1978-80; Mt Vernon Pub Libr, Mt Vernon, NY, librn, 1981, asst dir, actg dir, 1997. **Orgs:** Westchester Libr Asn, 1981-; Am Libr Asn, 1982-; NY Black Librarians Caucus, 1984-; Black Caucus Am Libr Asn, 1990-; vpres, Sons & Daughters African Unity Inc; NY Libr Asn, 1994-; chair, African Am Librarians Westchester, 1994-; adv bd, Jr League Montclair, 1999-; Women's History Proj, 1999-. **Honors/Awds:** Phi Alpha Theta, Zeta-Tau Chapter, 1975-; Beta Phi Mu, Beta Alpha Chapter, 1985-. **Business Phone:** (973)744-0500.*

ROBINSON, CARRIE C. See Obituaries section.

ROBINSON, CATHERINE
Educator. **Personal:** Born Sep 11, 1904, Petersburg, VA; widowed; children: Lynne, McDonald II & Valarie. **Educ:** RI Col, Univ RI. **Career:** Family & Bus Rel Serv, field interviewer, 1959-63; So Prov Proj Univ RI Coop Exten Serv, asst home econ ldr, 1963-75; TV Series Home Econ & Other Areas, hostess 2 yrs. **Orgs:** Bd dir, Opportunity Ind Ctr; Women's Coun United Way; Civil Rights Comn RI Adv Comn US Comn Civil Rights; bd dir BlackHeritage Soc; founder, Scitamard Players, 1937. **Honors/Awds:** Community leader award, United So Providence Block Club, 1971; Community Service Award, 1973; Citation Distinguished Service, Univ RI Coop Exten Serv, 1974; RI Heritage Hall Fame, 1975.

ROBINSON, DR. CECELIA ANN
Educator. **Personal:** Born May 28, 1948, Dallas, TX; married Kenneth E. **Educ:** Prairie View A&M Univ, BA, 1969; Univ Mo, Columbia, MEd, 1971, education spec, 1971; Univ Kans, EdD, 1986. **Career:** Univ MO, epda fel, 1970-71; Prairie View A&M Univ, Eng Inst, 1972; Oak Park HS, Eng teacher, 1972-79; Penn Valley Community Col, Eng instr, 1976-79; Univ Oxford Eng, Eng Speaking Union fel, 1976; Maple Woods Community Col, Eng instr, 1979-2008; William Jewell Col, Prof Eng currently. **Orgs:** Ed bd, Collegiate Eng Handbook, 1999-2000; Delta Kappa Gamma; Delta Sigma Theta Inc; Sigma Tau Delta; Pi Lambda Theta; MO Asn Teachers Eng. **Honors/Awds:** Pkwy Baptist Church Distinguished Prof Award, William Jewell, 1996; Excellence in Teaching Award, Northland Chamber Com, 1996; Anne Robb Townsend Women Excellence Award, 1996; AT&T Leadership Coun Award Human Relations work,1993, 1994; Liberty Outstanding Citizen Award, 1995; Liberty Sertoma Outstanding Serv, Mankind Award, 2000; Joe Wally Award for Community Serv, Liberty Fel Concerned, 2003; Outstanding Missourian Award, MO House Rep, 2004; Look North Award, Clay County Econ Develop Coun, 2004; Evelyn Wasserstrom Social Justice & Community Serv Award, Kans City Southern Christian Leadership Conf, 2004. **Business Addr:** Professor, William Jewell College, Department English, 500 College Hill, Liberty, MO 64068, **Business Phone:** (816)781-7700.

ROBINSON, CHARLES
School administrator. **Personal:** Born Mar 19, 1940, Philadelphia, PA; married Bernice Ann Baker; children: Deborah Ann & Lesly Denise. **Educ:** Cheyney State Univ, BS, 1966. **Career:** Philadelphia Dept Recreation, dec leader, 1962-66; Philadelphia Pub Schs, teacher, 1966-75, admin asst, 1975-84, teacher, 1984-85; Friends & Family Serv, supvr, 1997-2005. **Orgs:** Scout master, Troop 713, 1968-74; chmn, Edgewater Pk Twp Juvenile Conf Comt, 1970-85; bd educ, Edgewater Pk Twp, 1977-87; adv bd, Burlington Co Voc Tech, 1978-85; pres, bd trustees, Edgewater Pk Football Asn, 1981-83; vpres, Burlington Co Sch Bds Asn, 1982-86; NJ Sch Bd Asn, vpres, 1984-85, bd dirs, 1988-91; vpres, NJ Sch Bd Asn. **Military Serv:** AUSR, sgt, E-5, 6 yrs.

ROBINSON, CHARLES E
Social worker. **Personal:** Born Aug 31, 1926, Indianapolis, IN; married Ann Garrett; children: Angela & George. **Educ:** Ind Univ, BS, 1950, MSW, 1952. **Career:** Robinson & Robinson Behavioral Sci Cons, co-partner; Hallie Q Brown Settlement House St Paul, group soc worker, 1952-54; Cent State Hosp, psychiatric social worker, 1954-64; Ind Bd Sch Comm, sch social worker, 1964-68; CMHC, dir social work; Yale Univ Dept Psychiatry, asst clin prof soc work psychiatry, currently. **Orgs:** Bd deacons Immanuel Baptist Church; Ind Alumni Asn; Jr C of C; Acad Cert Soc Workers; Nat Asn Soc Worker; treas, bd dir, Newhallville Comm Action, 1971-73; nat bd mem Family Serv Asn, 1973-; pres, New Haven Family Serv Asn Am, 1974-78. **Honors/Awds:** Outstanding Community Service Award, United Newhallville Org. **Military Serv:** AUS, 1945-47. **Business Addr:** Assistant Clinical Professor, Yale University, Department of Psychiatry, 34 Pk St, New Haven, CT 06510.

ROBINSON, CHARLES S
Actor. **Personal:** Born Apr 13, 1945, Houston, TX. **Career:** Television credits include: "Night Court"; "Love & War"; "Home Improvement Ink"; "Buddy Faro", 1998; film credits include: Together Brothers; Sugarhill, 1974; Black Gestapo, 1975; Uncle Joe Shannon; Apocalypse Now; The River; Set It Off, 1996; Land of Fire, 1997; Scam, 2001; Antwone Fisher, 2002; Jackson, 2002; Break A Leg, 2003; Cold Case, 2005; plays include: My Sweet Charlie; Spoon River Anthology; The Night Thoreau Spent in Jail; Othello; Television Film credits include: Set This Town on Fire, 1973; A Killing Affair, 1977; The Trial of Lee Harvey Oswald, 1977; Rehearsal for Murder, 1982; Haywire, 1980; Crash Course, 1988; Murder C.O.D, 1990; Project: ALF, 1996; Land of the Free, 1997; The Last Dance, 2000; Miss Lettie& Me, 2002; Santa, Jr, 2002; Secret Santa, 2003, Mercy Street, 2005, River's End, 2005; TV episodes: "McBride: Requiem", 2006; "Still Standing", 2006; "How I Met Your Mother", 2006; "Mercy Street", 2006; "The Game", 2007; "McBride: Dogged", 2007; "The Riches", 2007; "Steam", 2008; "Jackson", 2008. **Business Phone:** (310)277-7779.

ROBINSON, CHARLOTTE L.
Consultant, educator. **Personal:** Born Jun 13, 1924, Long Island, NY; widowed; children: Barry & Cherylyn. **Educ:** BA, 1948; MA, 1967; Univ Pa, PhD, 1976. **Career:** Philadelphia Pub Sch Systs, asst dir curric & instr multimedia instrnl resources; City Univ NY, consult; Sears Roebuck & Co Phila, consult. **Orgs:** Phi Delta Epsilon; Am Women Radio & TV; Media Adv Comn Commonwealth Pa; Asn Educ Commun & Tech; Pa Learning Resources Asn; Philadelphia Unique Commun Proj, 1974. **Home Addr:** 702 St Georges Rd, Philadelphia, PA 19119. **Business Phone:** (215)247-3629.

ROBINSON, CHRIS
Basketball player. **Personal:** Born Apr 2, 1974, Columbus, GA. **Career:** Vancouver Grizzlies, guard, 1996-98; Sacramento Kings, guard, 1997-98. **Honors/Awds:** Conf Player of the Year, Sun Belt, 1995; All-Conf Hons, 1995.

ROBINSON, CLEO PARKER
Dancer, business owner. **Personal:** Born Jan 1, 1948?, Denver, CO; daughter of Jonathan and Martha Parker; married Tom, 1971. **Educ:** Colo Women's Col, BS, psycho & dance. **Career:** Univ Colo, instr; Cleo Parker Robinson Dance Ensemble, founder, 1970-. **Orgs:** Vpres, Int Assn Blacks Dance; brd dir, Denver Ctr Performing Arts; Nat Coun Arts. **Honors/Awds:** Govenor's Award for Excellence in the Arts, 1974; Honorary doctorate, Univ Denver, 1991; Blacks in Colo Hall of Fame, 1994; Coming Up Taller Award, Pres's Comt Arts & Humanites, 2000; choreography fellowships, Colorado Council on the Arts; Lifetime achievement award Business & Professional Women Aurora Chapter; Oni Award, International Black Woman's Congress. **Business Addr:** Founder, Cleo Parker Robinson Dance, 119 Pk Ave W, Denver, CO 80205, **Business Phone:** (303)295-1759.*

ROBINSON, CLIFFORD RALPH
Basketball player. **Personal:** Born Dec 16, 1966, Buffalo, NY. **Educ:** Univ Conn, attended. **Career:** Basketball player (Retired); Portland TrailBlazers, forward, 1989-97; Phoenix Suns, 1997-2000; Detroit Pistons, 2001-03; Golden State Warriors, 2003-05; New Jersey Nets, 2004-07. **Honors/Awds:** NBA Sixth Man Award, 1993; NBA All-Star, 1994; All Defensive Second Team Twice, 2000, 2002.

ROBINSON, CRYSTAL
Basketball player, basketball coach. **Personal:** Born Jan 22, 1974, Atoka, OK; daughter of Billy and Nancy. **Educ:** SE Okla State Univ, health & phys educ, 1996. **Career:** Basketball player, (retired), Wash Mystics, asst coach, 2007-; coach Colo Xplosion, forward, 1996-98; NY Liberty, forward, 1999-05. **Orgs:** Big Bros Big Sisters. **Honors/Awds:** Most Valuable Player, US Olympic Festival, 1993; Most Valuable Player, Nat Tournament; ABL Rookie of the Year Award, 1996,1997; National Association Intercollegiate Athletics Hall of Fame, 2003; Tournament MVP honors. **Business Addr:** Professional Basketball Player, Washington Mystics, 627 N Glebe Rd Suite 850, Arlington, VA 20005, **Business Phone:** (202)266-2200.*

ROBINSON, CURTIS
Educator. **Personal:** Born May 12, 1934, Wilmington, NC; married Joan Elenor Williams; children: Debra D, Milton C & Cheryl A. **Educ:** Morgan State Univ, BS, 1960; Howard Univ, MS, 1968; Univ MD, PhD, 1973. **Career:** Lincoln HS, NC, sci & math teacher, 1960-61; Williston Sr HS, NC, sci & math teacher, 1961-62; Radiation Biol Lab, Smithsonian Inst, Rockville, MD, res biologist, 1962-69; Edinboro Univ, PA, prof, 1973, prof emer, currently. **Orgs:** Alpha Phi Alpha, 1959-; Am Society Plant Physiologists, 1970-; Nat Educ Asn, 1973-; Asn Pa State Col Biologists, 1973-; NAACP, 1975; Am Asn Univ Professors, 1978-. **Military Serv:** AUS, spec-3, 3 yrs. **Home Phone:** (814)734-4332. **Business Addr:** Professor Emeritus, Edinboro University of Pennsylvania, Biology & Health Sciences, Edinboro, PA 16444-0001.

ROBINSON, DAMIEN DION
Football player. **Personal:** Born Dec 22, 1973, Dallas, TX; married Michele; children: Zoya & Zariah. **Educ:** Univ Iowa. **Career:** Football player (retired); Tampa Bay Buccaneers, defensive back, 1998-2000; New York Jets, 2001-02; Seattle Seahawks, 2003-04.

ROBINSON, DAVID MAURICE
Clergy, basketball player. **Personal:** Born Aug 6, 1965, Key West, FL; son of Ambrose and Freda; married Valerie Hoggatt, Jan 1, 1991; children: David Maurice Jr, Corey & Justin. **Educ:** US Naval Acad, math, 1987. **Career:** Basketball player (retired), clergy; Naval Acad, 1983-84, 1986-87; San Antonio Spurs, ctr, 1989-2003; US Olympic Basketball Team, 1988, 1992,1996; Oak Hills Church, staff, 2004-. **Orgs:** Funder, David Robinson Found, 1992-. **Honors/Awds:** John R Wooden Award, 1987; Naismith Award, 1987; All-NBA Third Team, 1990; NBA All-Defensive Second Team, 1990; NBA Rookie of the Year, 1990; NBA All-Rookie First Team, 1990; Schick Pivotal Player Award, 1990; NBA All-Star, 1990-98; NBA Most Valuable Player, 1995; Selected as one of the50 Greatest Players in NBA Hist, 1996; NBA Champion, 1999, 2003; Tex Sports Hall of Fame, 1999; NBA Sportsmanship Award, 2001; Prize in Philanthropic Leadership, Simon Found, 2004; 10-time NBA All-Star, Elec to the U.S. Olympic Hall of Fame Class of 2008, 2008; Basketball Hall of Fame Class of 2009, 2009. **Special Achievements:** Film: Forget Paris, 1995; Like Mike, 2002. **Business Addr:** Staff, Oak Hills Church, 19595 IH-10 W, San Antonio, TX 78257-9508, **Business Phone:** (210)698-6868.

ROBINSON, DAWN (DAWN TSHOMBE)
Songwriter, singer, actor. **Personal:** Born Nov 28, 1968, New London, CT. **Career:** Films: Another 48 Hrs., 1990; Conceiving Ada, 1997; Batman Forever, 1995; Tank Girl, 1995; Life, 1999; Shaft, 2000; The Last Request, 2006; TV series: "Saturday Night Live", 1992; "A Different World", 1993; Roc, 1993; "SeaQuest DSV", 1995; Albums: Born to Sing, 1990; Remix to Sing, 1991; Funky Divas, 1992; Runaway Love EP, 1993; EV3, 1997; Best of En Vogue, 1998; The Very Best of En Vogue, 2001; Hold On & Other Hits, 2005. **Honors/Awds:** Platinum, Born to Sing, 1990; Grammy nominations, Nat Acad Rec Arts & Sci, best short video, "Free Your Mind", rock duo or group; Funky Divas, r&b duo or group. **Business Addr:** Singer, c/o David Lombard, Lombard Management, 4859 W Slauson Ave, Los Angeles, CA 90056, **Business Phone:** (213)962-8016.*

ROBINSON, DEANNA ADELL
Manager. **Personal:** Born Jul 31, 1945, Chicago, IL; married Willie. **Educ:** MI State Univ, BS, 1967. **Career:** Palmer House Hilton Hotel, conv serv mgr. **Orgs:** Nat Coalition Black Meeting Planners, 1986. **Home Addr:** 9842 S Bensley, Chicago, IL 60617, **Home Phone:** (312)978-3147. **Business Addr:** Assistant Director Convention Service, Palmer House-Hilton Hotel, 17 E Monroe St, Chicago, IL 60690, **Business Phone:** (312)726-7500.

ROBINSON, DENAUVO M.
Manager. **Personal:** Born Apr 10, 1949, Quincy, IL. **Educ:** Northeast MO St Univ, BS, 1971; MA, 1971; Northern IL Univ, EdD, 1977. **Career:** Western IL U, Macomb, counr, 1971-72; Drexel U, dir Spec Serv; Northern IL Univ CHANCE Dekalb, IL, counr, 1972-74, assoc dir, 1974. **Orgs:** APGA; ANWC; IGPA; IANWC; NIU; APGA; NAACP; Civil Liberties Union.

ROBINSON, EDDIE JOSEPH, JR. (EDWARD JOSEPH ROBINSON, JR.)
Football player. **Personal:** Born Apr 13, 1970, New Orleans, LA; married Tonja. **Educ:** Ala State Univ, BS, chem, 1993. **Career:** Football player (retired); Houston Oilers, linebacker, 1992-95;Jacksonville Jaguars, linebacker, 1996-97; Tenn Oilers, 1998; Tenn Titans,1999-2001; Buffalo Bills, 2002. **Orgs:** Omega Psi Phi Fraternity. **Honors/Awds:** Second round draft pick, 1992.

ROBINSON, EDITH
Executive. **Personal:** Born Dec 31, 1924, Buffalo, NY; married James C. **Educ:** Wilberforce Univ, BS, 1946; State Univ NY, MSW. **Career:** Erie Co Dept Social Servs, caseworker, unit supvr, dist supvr, asst dep comnr, dep Comnr, 1947-81; Pub Welfare, caseworker, sr caseworker, unit supvr, dist supvr, 1947-77; State Univ Col SEEK Prgm, adj prof, 1969-70. **Orgs:** Past pres, Nat asn Social Workers ACSW; exec bd, NY State Welfare Conf, 1970-72; chmn, Nat Field Adv Coun Alexandria Am Red Cross, 1977-78; vchmn, Greater Buffalo Chap ARC; pres, Am Lung Asn NY, 1977; vpres, pres elect, Zonta Club Buffalo, 1970; YWCA, 1972; Links Inc; Commun Adv Coun, State Univ NY Buffalo; vchmn, secy, Nat Am Res Cross; Buffalo Philharmonic Soc; Samaritan Coun ctr; pres, Bry Lin Hosp; Interima Home Health Care; Admissions Comt United Way Buffalo; Golden Soror, Alpha Kappa Alpha Sorority Inc. **Honors/Awds:** Alumna of year, Wilberforce Univ,

1967; outstanding service award, Bronze Damsels, 1968; womans service award, Buffalo Urban Ctr, 1971; communication service award, Buffalo Urban League, 1975. **Business Addr:** Member, Xi Epsilon Omega Chapter, PO BOX 1861, AMHERST, NY 14226-7861.

ROBINSON, REV. EDSEL F
Clergy, real estate agent. **Personal:** Born May 5, 1928, Wrightsville, GA; son of Rev Jasper and Tressie; married Pearlie Haynes; children: Edsel Jr & Desiree. **Educ:** Morris Brown Col, BMus, 1959; Turner Theol Sem, BD; Interdenominational Theol Ctr; Turner Theol Sem Interdenominational Theol Ctr Atlanta, Hon DD cand, 1980. **Career:** EF Robinson Realty Co, pres; Augusta Athens Dist, AME Church, dir music; Turner Chapel African Methodist Episcopal, dir music, currently . **Orgs:** Nat Asn Advan Colored People; Young Men Chrisitian Award; African Methodist Episcopal Ministers' Union; Southern Christian Leadership Conf; Empire Real Estate Bd; Oper Breadbasket, mgt broker Veterans Admin, 1970-73; Nat Asn Real Estate Brokers, 1974; Organizer Doraville Community Orgn, 1974. **Honors/Awds:** Salesman of the Year, 1971-72; Special Award for Outstanding Service to African Methodist Episcopal Church; recipient E F Robinson Day Proclamation for Outstanding Contribution to the city & people of all races, City of Doraville GA, 1976; Outstanding Georgia Citizen, 1995. **Home Addr:** 3322 Rabun Dr SW, Atlanta, GA 30311. **Business Addr:** Music Director, Turner Chapel African Methodist Episcopal, 492 N Marietta Pkwy, Marietta, GA 30060, **Business Phone:** (770)422-6791.

ROBINSON, EDWARD A.
Educator. **Personal:** Born Jun 13, 1935, Gary, IN; married Lavada Hill; children: Edward Allen & Arlen Yohance. **Educ:** Howard Univ, BA, 1959; Univ Chicago, MAT, 1970; Northwestern Univ, PhD, 1974. **Career:** Carver High Sch, Chicago, instr, 1959-60; Harlan High Sch, Eng Dept, instr & chmn, 1960-69; Wendell Phillips & Summer High Sch, Chicago, instr, 1961-64; NDEA Inst, Univ Chicago, summer participant, 1965; Univ Chicago, experienced teacher fel, 1969-70; Northeastern Ill Univ, asst prof; LakeForest Col, IL, eng instr, 1970-72; Chicago Bd Educ High Sch, eng consul, 1970-72; Ford Found, fel, 1973-74. **Orgs:** Nat Urban League, 1968-74; S Shore Valley Community Orgn, 1969-74; Operation PUSH, 1972; Faulkner Sch Asn, 1974-75; Faulkner Sch Father's Club, 1974-75. **Special Achievements:** Author of numerous publications; TV series: "The Giants" & "The Common Men", narrator, 1967; "Like It Was the black man in America", teacher & host, 1969. **Military Serv:** AUS, 1953-55. *

ROBINSON, EDWARD ASHTON
Lawyer. **Personal:** Born Jan 1, 1949?, Hammond, LA. **Educ:** Grambling Univ; State Univ, NY; Rutgers Univ. **Career:** pvt practice, atty, 1979-; Baton Rouge La, chief adminr, state atty gen. **Honors/Awds:** Outstanding young man, La Jaycees, 1977.

ROBINSON, PROF. ELLA S.
Educator, school administrator. **Personal:** Born Apr 16, 1943, Wedowee, AL; daughter of Less Scales and Mary Ella MacPherson Scales; married John William, May 9, 1980 (deceased); children: John William Jr. **Educ:** Ala State Univ, BS, 1965; Univ NE, MA, 1970, PhD, 1976. **Career:** Univ Ill, asst prof, 1975-77; Atlanta Univ, asst prof, 1977-79; Univ Nebraska-Lincoln, prof Eng, 1979; Tuskegee Univ, assoc prof; Concordia Col-Selma, head humanities & fine arts dept, currently. **Orgs:** MLA, 1974-87; chair, afro-lite session SMLA, 1985-86; life time mem, Nat Asn Advan Colored People, 1986-; Ala African Am Poet Heritage Room, Bennet Martin Libr, 1989; CLA; NCTE; Ala Media Prof, pres, 2006-. **Special Achievements:** Painted 85 oils & acrylics; author, Selected Poems, 1995; To Know Heaven,1996; Love the Season and Death, 1996; Heritage: Tuskegee Poems a Celebration, 1997; numerous articles. **Home Phone:** (334)270-8785. **Business Addr:** Head of Humanities, Concordia College Communications, 1804 Green St, Selma, AL 36701, **Business Phone:** (334)874-5755.

ROBINSON, EUGENE HAROLD
Editor, writer. **Personal:** Born Mar 12, 1954, Orangeburg, SC; son of Harold I and Louisa S; married Avis Collins, Sep 23, 1978; children: Aaron E & Lowell E. **Educ:** Univ Mich, BA, 1974. **Career:** Harvard Univ, Nieman fel, 1988; San Francisco Chronicle, reporter, 1975-80; Wash Post, city hall reporter, 1980-82, asst city ed, 1982-84, city ed, 1984-87, S Am corresp, 1988-92, London corresp, 1992-94, foreign ed, 1994-, assoc ed, currently; Books: Coal to Cream: A Black Man?s Journey Beyond Color to an Affirmation of Race, 1999; Last Dance in Havana, 2004. **Orgs:** Nat Asn Black Journalist, 1987-; Coun Foreign Rels, 1995-. **Special Achievements:** Several journalism awards. **Home Addr:** 5302 N 18th St, Arlington, VA 22205. **Business Addr:** Associate Editor, Washington Post, 1150 15th St NW, Washington, DC 20071, **Business Phone:** (202)334-7400.

ROBINSON, EUGENE KEEFE
Football player, radio broadcaster, football coach. **Personal:** Born May 28, 1963, Hartford, CT; married Gia; children: Brittany & Brandon. **Educ:** Colgate Univ, BS, comput sci. **Career:** Football player (retired), Football coach, Radio broadcaster; Seattle Seahawks, defensive back, 1985-95; Green Bay Packers, 1996-97; Atlanta Falcons, 1998-99; Carolina Panthers, safety, 2000; Inter Mix Rec, co-owner; Panthers Radio Network, radio analyst, currently; Charlotte Christian Sch, coach. **Honors/Awds:** Man of the Year Award, Nat Football League; Bart Starr Award, 1999. **Business Phone:** (704)358-7000.

ROBINSON, EUNICE PRIMUS
Counselor, teacher. **Personal:** Born Oct 17, 1935, Hardeeville, SC; married DeWitt T Jr; children: Janice, De Witt III, Glenn. **Educ:** Savannah State Col, BS, elem educ, 1953; Univ SC, MEd, 1972. **Career:** Hardeeville Elem Sch, teacher 1953-55; SC State Col, counr 1955-59; Allen Univ, counr, dir student activities 1959-63; Rosenwald Elem Sch, teacher, 1965-67; Benedict Col, dean women & counr, 1968-71; Aiken County Pub Schs, transp supvr; Midlands Tech Col, counr. **Orgs:** Nat Dirs Orientation Asn; founder & adv, Afro Am Club Midlands Tech Col, 1972-; team mother, Pony League, Dixie Youth League Baseball Prog, 1972-75; secy, Fairwald Elem Sch Parent Teacher Asn, 1974-; treas, Fairwald Middle Sch Parent Teacher Asn; secy, Altar Guild, St Luke's Epis Church, 1974-; secy, Omega Psi Phi Frat Wives, 1974-75; Scholar Found Booker T Wash, 1975; Zeta Phi Beta Sorority; SC Pers & Guid Asn, 1975; Episcopal Diocese Upper SC, Bena Dial Scholar, chairperson, 2004-. **Honors/Awds:** Mother Of The Year, Zeta Phi Beta Sorority, 1959; Counselor Most Seen by Students, Midlands Tech Col, 1973; Mother of The Year, Afro-Am Club, Midlands Tech Col, 1975. **Business Addr:** Midlands Technical College, PO Drawer Q, Columbia, SC 29250.*

ROBINSON, FRANK
Baseball executive, baseball player. **Personal:** Born Aug 31, 1935, Beaumont, TX; son of Frank and Ruth Shaw; married Barbara Ann Cole; children: Frank Kevin & Nichelle. **Career:** Cincinnati Reds, farm system teams, 1953-56, player, 1956-65; Santurce Cangrejeros PR, mgr; Baltimore Orioles, out fielder, 1966-71, mgr, 1988-91, asst gen mgr; Los Angeles Dodgers, player, 1972; Calif Angels, 1973-74; Cleveland Indians, mgr, 1974-76; Rochester Red Wings, mgr, 1978; San Francisco Giants, mgr, 1981-84; Ariz Fall League, dir baseball opers; Montreal Expos, mgr, 2002-04; Wash Nationals, mgr, 2005-06; ESPN, analyst, 2007; MLB comnr off, spec asst, currently. **Honors/Awds:** Nat League Rookie of Year, Baseball Writers Asn, 1956; Most Valuable Player, 1961 & 1966; World Series Most Valuable Player Award, 1966; American League Triple Crown, 1966; 11 All Star games; Hall of Fame at Coopers town, 1982; Nat Baseball Hall of Fame, 1982; American League Manager of the Year Award, 1989; Presidential Medal of Freedom, 2005; Jackie Robinson Society Community Award, George Wash Univ, 2007. **Special Achievements:** Baseball's first African American manager with the Cleveland Indians, 1974; first African American manager in the National League with the San Francisco Giants; My Life Is Baseball, author, 1968; only player to win League MVP honors in both the National and American Leagues. **Business Addr:** Special Assitant, Major League Baseball, Office of the Commissioner of Baseball, 245 Pk Ave 31st Fl, New York, NY 10167.

ROBINSON, FRANK J.
Educator, clergy. **Personal:** Born Nov 18, 1939, Montgomery, TX; married Reecie (deceased); children: Lady Robinson Nelson, Portia Elaine, Frank J Jr & Gusta Jovon. **Educ:** Tex Southern Univ, BS, 1964. **Career:** Bowid Dance Studio, Houston, instr dramatics; Houston Community Col, instr; Urban Theatre, tech dir; Assured Blessing Ministry Church 39, tech dir; Cent Conv Tex Brotherhood, treas; Greater St Matthews Baptist Church, clergyman; Greater Second Baptist Church, asst pastor. **Orgs:** Chmn, Tex State Conf Br, Nat Asn Advan Colored People; vpres, Alpha Mu Omega; W End Civic Club. **Military Serv:** USMCR, 1957-68. **Business Addr:** Clergyman, Greater St Matthews Baptist Church, 7701 Jutland, Houston, TX 77027, **Business Phone:** (713)673-2726.

ROBINSON, DR. GENEVIEVE
School administrator, educator. **Personal:** Born Apr 20, 1940, Kansas City, MO; daughter of James L and Helen Williams. **Educ:** Mt St Scholastica Col, BA, hist, 1968; N Mex Highlands Univ, MA, hist, 1974; Catholic Univ Am, attended 1979; Boston Col, PhD, hist, 1986. **Career:** Lillis High Sch, hist teacher, 1969-73 & 1974-75, hist dept chairperson, 1970-73, admin & curric dir, 1974-75; Donnelly Community Col, instr, 1976-78; Boston Col, instr, 1983; Boston Col, Gasson fel, 1984-85; Rockhurst Univ, instr, 1985-86, asst prof, 1986-91, assoc prof, 1991-2002, dir hon prog, 1990-2001, chair dept hist, 1994-2001 & 2003-09, prof, 2002-. **Orgs:** Phi Alpha Theta; Kappa Mu Epsilon; Orgn Am Historians; Immigration Hist Soc; Pi Gamma Mu; Ethical Rev Bd, 1988-; Rockhurst Col, presidential grant, 1988; bd dirs, Notre Dame de Sion Schs, 1990-95; regional rep, Nat Asn Women Catholic Higher Educ; St Monica Sch Bd, 1999-2002; hon mem, Sigma Delta Pi. **Honors/Awds:** Distinguished Alummni Award, NMex Highlands Univ, 2000. **Business Addr:** Professor, Chair, Rockhurst University, Department of History, 1100 Rockhurst Rd, Kansas City, MO 64110-2508, **Business Phone:** (816)501-4108.

ROBINSON, GEORGE ALI
Administrator. **Personal:** Born Apr 16, 1939, Americus, GA; married; children: Ali, Omari & Khalid. **Educ:** Shaw Univ, AB, 1965, MDiv, 1975; Neotarian Col, DD, 1976; Metanoia Univ, PhD, 1981. **Career:** Black Bus Awareness Mag, ed; US Dept Justice Col, community rel spec; Ridgeway Baptist Church, pastor; Raleigh, social worker; DHEW, prog analysis staff; A&G Enterprises Raleigh, pres; MKT Pol Camp, consult; HEW, soc sci analyst; Chris Ed Black Relig Conv, Black Theol Mason, lectr; Georgian For Two Party State, chief exec officer, currently. **Orgs:** Consult, AMEC Press; PUSH; ASPA. **Special Achievements:** Author, Metanoia Convention, The need for the Black Church, Republican Council of Georgia. **Military Serv:** AUS, sgt, 1957-62. **Home Addr:** 251 Mem Ter SE, Atlanta, GA 30316. **Business Addr:** Chief Executive Officer, Georgian For Two Party State, 2936 Glenwood Ave SE, Atlanta, GA 30317, **Business Phone:** (404)289-0590.

ROBINSON, GLENN A
Basketball player. **Personal:** Born Jan 10, 1973, Gary, IN; son of Jesse Mack and Christine Bridgeman. **Educ:** Purdue Univ. **Career:** Milwaukee Bucks, forward, 1994-2002; Atlanta Hawks, 2002-03; Philadelphia 76ers, 2003-04; San Antonio Spurs, 2005. **Honors/Awds:** Naismith Award; 1994; John Wooden Award, 1994; NBA All-Rookie Team, 1995; Nat Col Basketball Player of the Year; 1995, NBA All-Rookie Team; 1996; NBA All-Star Team. **Special Achievements:** Selected in first round, first pick of NBA draft, 1994.

ROBINSON, GLORIA
Government official. **Career:** HUD, asst secy, 1997-98; City Detroit, Planning, Community & Econ Develop dept, dir. *

ROBINSON, HAROLD OSCAR
Educator, clergy. **Personal:** Born Apr 21, 1943, Trenton, NJ; son of Oscar and Emma; married Alice Steele, Sep 21, 1991; children: Kheesa & Harold Jr. **Educ:** Rutgers Univ, BA, 1973, MEd, 1974, EdD Cand, 1978; Hood Theol Sem, MDiv, 1998. **Career:** African Methodist Episcopal Zion Church, assoc minister, 1996-2000; Cabarrus County Schs, dir diversity task force, 1997-99; Shaw Univ, adj prof humanities; Livingstone Col, dir career coun, 1998-99; AL Brown HS, teacher, 1999-; First Cong United Church Christ, pastor, 2000-; Carolinas Med Ctr, Chaplain Resident, 2002-03. **Orgs:** Pres, Nat Asn Advan Colored People, Cabarrus County br, 1991-93; bd visitors, Barbara Scotia Col, 1993-00; Community Bldg Task Force Community, 1997-98; bd dir, Historic Cabarrus, 1998-01. **Honors/Awds:** History Book Award, NC Soc Historians, 1993; Heritage Award, Livingstone Col, 1997. **Special Achievements:** Contributor Revival of Hope, 1992; Editor, A History of African Americans in Cabarrus County, NC, 1992; Contributor, Encyclopedia of African-American Education, 1996. **Military Serv:** AUS, 1964-66; USAR, 1976-78. **Home Addr:** 3735 Rock Hill Church Rd, Concord, NC 28027, **Home Phone:** (704)786-9550.

ROBINSON, DR. HARRY, JR.
Museum director, chief executive officer. **Educ:** Southern Univ, bach deg; Atlanta Univ, masters, lib sci; Univ Illinois, PhD; Getty Museum Management Inst, attended 1984. **Career:** Bishop Col, libr dir, assoc dean acad affairs, spec asst pres & vpres develop; Mus African-Am Life & Cult, dir; African Am Mus, pres & chief exec officer, currently; Good Street Baptist Churc, librarian, currently. **Orgs:** Soc SW Activ; Am Libr Assn; pres, African Am Mus Assn; Dallas Theater Ctr; Dallas Arboretum & Botanical Soc; Booker T Washington High Sch Visual & Performing Arts; SW Black Arts Festival; brd trustees, Dallas Mus Art; brd dirs, Friends Dallas Pub Libr; bd mem, South fair Comm Devp Corporation; bd mem, Natl Museum & Lib Brd. **Special Achievements:** Editor of The Lives and Times of Black Dallas Women, 2002. **Business Addr:** President, Chief Executive Officer, African American Museum, 3536 Grand Ave, PO Box 150157, Dallas, TX 75315-0157, **Business Phone:** (214)565-9026.*

ROBINSON, HARRY G
City planner, educator, architect. **Personal:** Born Jan 18, 1942, Washington, DC; son of Gwendolyn Herriford Robinson and Harry G Robinson Jr; married Dianne O Davis; children: Erin K, Leigh H & Kia L. **Educ:** Howard Univ, BArch, 1966, MCP, 1970; Harvard Univ, MCP, urban design, 1972. **Career:** DC Redevelop Land Agency, archit planner, 1968-72; Woodrow Wilson Found, Martin Luther King Jr fel, 1969-70; US DOT, urban transp res fel, 1969-70; Univ DC, prof, 1969-70, 1971-74; Morgan State Univ, chmn & prof, 1971-79; TRG Consult, prin, 1976-; Howard Univ, dean arch & planning, 1979-95, vpres, 1995-99, prof, prof & dean emer, currently. **Orgs:** Am Inst Cert Planners, 1974-; Am Inst Arch, 1976-; pres, DC Bd Exam & Reg Arch, 1983-89; pres, Nat Coun Archit Regist, 1992-93; chmn, US Comn Fine Arts, 1995-; prof adv, Goree Mem & Mus, Dakar, Senegal, 1995-97; pres, Nat Archit Accrediting Bd, 1996-97; prof adv, Nat Underground RR Freedom Ctr, Cincinnati, OH, 1996-99; trustee & secy, Nat Bldg Mus; trustee, Cooper-Hewitt Nat Mus Design; founder & dir, African-Am Archit Initiative; dir; Arch Adventure/City Pl; chmn, UNESCO Int Comn GOREE Mem & Mus; trustee, Idea Pub Charter Sch; trustee, Booker T Washington Charter Sch; Int Adv Bd, IIBC, Tokyo, Japan; dir, Vietnam Veterans Mem Fund; master mason, Prince Hall Free & Accepted Masons; Comt Preserv White House; White House Hist Asn; trustee, John F Kennedy Ctr

Performing Arts; chmn, Pa Ave White House Pres Comt; Comt 100 Fed City; dir, Chauncey Group Int; hon mem, Trinidad & Tobago Institute Archit; hon mem, Mexican Soc Architects. **Honors/Awds:** Faculty Gold Medal in Design, Howard Univ, 1965; Silver Medal, Tau Sigma Delta, Hon Soc, 1988; Whitney M Young Jr Citation; Richard T Ely Distinguished Educator, Lambda Alpha Int Land Econ Soc; The Centennial Medal, Wash Chap AIA, 2003; Architect of the Year, DC Coun Eng & Archit Soc, 2004. **Special Achievements:** Author of the award winning third history of Howard University, THE LONG WALK: The Placemaking Legacy of Howard University and producer of the TELLY recognized documentary by the same name. **Military Serv:** AUS, 1st lt; Purple Heart, Vietnam Service Ribbion, 1966-68; Ranger Tab; Bronze Star. **Business Addr:** Professor, Dean Emeritus, Howard University, School of Architecture and Design, Rm 218 2366 6th St NW, Washington, DC 20059, **Business Phone:** (202)806-5585.

ROBINSON, HENRY
Government official, mayor. **Personal:** Born Oct 2, 1936, Port Royal, SC; married Jannie Middleton; children: Elizabeth, Tracy & Stephanie. **Career:** Town Port Royal, coun mem & mayor protempore, 1999-. **Orgs:** Pres, Community Ctr Port Royal; second vpres, Dem Party Port Royal Prec. **Honors/Awds:** Outstanding Community Service. **Business Addr:** Council Member & Mayor Pro Tempore, Town of Port Royal, 632 Ft Frederick Circle St, Port Royal, SC 29935.

ROBINSON, JACK, JR.
Lawyer. **Personal:** Born Mar 20, 1942, Chicago, IL; son of Jack Sr and Clara L Jones; married Flora G; children: Jacqueline, Craig, Christopher. **Educ:** Chicago Teachers Col, BE, 1963; Chicago Kent Col Law, JD 1970. **Career:** Lawyer (retired); Miller & Pomper, atty, 1970-71; Argonne Nat Lab, atty, 1971-97. **Orgs:** Nat Bar Asn; Cook County Bar Asn; Omega Psi Phi Fraternity. *

ROBINSON, JACK E
Publisher, editor, president (organization). **Personal:** Born in Indianapolis, IN; son of Jack and Billie; divorced; children: Jacqueline, Errol & Sarah. **Educ:** Boston Univ, AA, BS, 1955; Boston Col, majors educ & bus, 1957. **Career:** Wash Globe, ed, publ; Park Dale Nursing Home; Burton Nursing Home; Compact Advt; Burton Realty Trust; Am Bus Mgt; Consolidated Liquors; Am Beverages Corp; Robinson Construct Corp; Universal Distributing; Compact Corp; Apex Construct Co, Boston, MA, ceo; Nat Asn African Americans, pres & ceo, 1975-. **Orgs:** Pres, Commonwealth Rep Club; pres, Nat Asn Advan Colored People, 1975-; Sportsmen Tennis Club; State Enterprises; Nat Asn Minority Contractors; Real Estate Owners Asn; bd dirs, Voluntary Action Ctr; ABCD; Circle Asn; pres, Am Motorist Asn; Omega Psi Phi Frat; Phi Epsilon Kappa Frat; Bay State Golf Club; pres, Oak Bluffs Tennis Club; Alliance Safer Greater Boston; pres, Nat Asn Advan Colored People, 1973-84. **Honors/Awds:** Civil Liberties Union Adv Com Man of Year, Construct Engineering News Mag; Man of Year, Boston Bldg Dept; Savenergy Award, Dir US Dept Com; Builder Of The Year, City Boston, 1972; Excellence Award, US Dept Com, 1972. **Military Serv:** AUS. **Home Addr:** PO Box 255, Boston, MA 02130. **Business Phone:** (215)235-6488.

ROBINSON, JAMES EDWARD
Executive. **Personal:** Born Aug 31, 1943, Asheville, NC; married Shirley Byrd; children: Geno Nigel, Tajuana Yvette, Tanya & Aisha Monique. **Educ:** Taylor Sch Broadcast Tech, AA, 1969; Elkins Inst Broadcasting, cert, 1971. **Career:** Model Cities Agency, pub info asst, 1971-74; City Asheville, pub info officer, 1974-76; Radio Sta WBMU-FM, pres, gen mgr, 1975-. **Orgs:** Nat Asn Black Owned Broadcasters; NC Soc Pub Rel Dirs. **Military Serv:** AUS, 82nd airborne div, 9 yrs.

ROBINSON, JAMES L
Architect, entrepreneur, city planner. **Personal:** Born Jul 12, 1940, Longview, TX; son of W L and Ruby Newhouse; divorced; children: Kerstin G, Maria T, Jasmin Marisol, Ruby Nell, Kenneth & James L Robinson Jr. **Educ:** Southern Univ, BArch, 1964; Pratt Inst, MCP, 1973. **Career:** Herbst & Rusciano AIA, architect, 1964; Carson Lundin & Shaw, architect, 1965; Kennerly Slomanson & Smith, architect, 1966-68; Carl J Petrilli, architect, 1968-69; James L Robinson PC, architect, 1970-84; Robinson Architect PC, architect, 1984, ceo, 1989; 55C Construct Corp, owner, currently. **Orgs:** Independent Platform Asn; former Bd Dirs, Boys Clubs Am; arbitrator, Am Arbitration Asn, 1979. **Honors/Awds:** National Housing Award, Design & Environ, 1976; Bard Award, Fulton Ct Complex 1977. **Military Serv:** AUS, pfc, 1966; Good Conduct Medal, 1966. **Business Addr:** Owner, 55C Construction Corp, 55C Delancey St, New York, NY 10002, **Business Phone:** (212)966-7828.*

ROBINSON, JAMES WAYMOND
Physician. **Personal:** Born Nov 6, 1926, Wilmington, NC; son of Addie Best Robinson and Sam Robinson; married Carol Blackmar, Sep 18, 1979. **Educ:** NC Col, Durham, BS, 1950; Meharry Med Col, MD, 1960; internship, 1960-61; resident, 1961-65. **Career:** Physician (retired); Joint Dis N Gen Hosp, asst attending physician; Beth Israel's Methadone Maintenance Treatment Prog, assoc chief; Beth Israel's Methadone Maintenance Treatment Prog Harlem Unit, unit dir, 1965-75; Arthur C Logan Memorial Hosp, assoc attending physician, 1965-79; Harlem Hosp, asst attending physician, 1965-92. **Orgs:** Med Soc State & Co NY; Omega Psi Phi Fraternity; ASIM; NYSSIM; NYCSIM. **Special Achievements:** Author: "Methadone Poisoning, Diagnosis & Treatment"; "Methadone Treatment of Randomly Selected Criminal Addicts". **Military Serv:** AUS, corporal, 1945-46.

ROBINSON, DR. JAMUIR MICHELLE
Association executive. **Educ:** MSW, MPH, PhD. **Career:** Nat Cancer Inst, Cancer Prev, fel, Off Educ & Spec Initiatives, currently. **Business Phone:** (301)496-8640.*

ROBINSON, JANE ALEXANDER
Clinical psychologist. **Personal:** Born Jan 17, 1931, Chicago, IL; daughter of Cornelius and Janie Burruss-Goodwin; divorced; children: David, Amorie, Richard. **Educ:** BS, 1952, MS, 1963; Univ Detroit, PhD, 1977. **Career:** Detroit Pub Schs, elem teacher, 1957-63; Southfield Bd Educ, sch psychol, 1964-68; Detroit Bd Educ, sch psychol, 1968-97; Pvt prac, clinical psychol. **Orgs:** Founder & secy, Mich Asn Black Psychol, 1968-70, pres, 1975-76; Psi Chi Nat Hon Soc Psychol, Univ Detroit Chap. **Honors/Awds:** Award for Organisation Leadership, Nat Asn Black Psychol, 1976; "Self-Esteem, Racial Consciousness & Perception of Difference Between the Values of Black & White Americans", 1977. **Business Addr:** Clinical Psychologist, Fisher Bldg, 3011 W Grand Blvd Ste 1710, Detroit, MI 48202.*

ROBINSON, JEANNETTE
School administrator. **Personal:** Born in Atlanta, GA; daughter of Reginald and Mary; children: Yolanda C Wade. **Educ:** Essex Co Col Newark, AS 1975; Rutgers Univ, BS 1977; Fairleigh Dickinson Univ, MBA, 1980. **Career:** Newark Educ Inst, adminr 1973-80; Dept Planning & Econ Develop Div Employment Training, contract mgt supvr, 1980-83; Essex County Col, Newark, dir human resources, 1983-. **Orgs:** Arbitrator Better Bus Bur NJ 1982-; NJ Educ Asn, NJ Asn Equality & Excellence Educ, Asn Black Women Higher Educ, Delta Sigma Phi Frat, Nat Asn Col & Univ Personnel Admin. **Honors/Awds:** Publications "People Just Like You: A Guide for the Employer of the Handicapped" 1982, "People Just Like You: A Guide for the Teacher of the Handicapped" 1982. **Home Addr:** 317 Lilac Dr, Union, NJ 07083. **Business Addr:** Director, Human Resources, Essex County College, Human Resources Dept, 303 Univ Ave Rm 5112, Newark, NJ 07102.

ROBINSON, JEFFREY
Executive, educator, consultant. **Personal:** Born Sep 13, 1971, East Orange, NJ; son of Ronald and Doreen; married Valerie Mason, Aug 12, 2000. **Educ:** Rutgers Univ, Rutgers Col, BA, urban studies, Col Eng, BS, Civil Eng, 1995; Ga Inst Technol, MS, Civil Eng Mgt, 1995; Columbia Univ, Grad Bus, PhD, 2002. **Career:** MBS Enterprises, LLC, founder & bd mem, 1993-2001; Law Engineering, staff engr, 1995; Merck & Co, Inc, proj engr, 1996-98; BCt Partners, founding mem & partner, 2001-; Stern Sch Bus, NY, asst prof mgt, 2003-. **Orgs:** Nat vice chair, Nat Soc Black Engrs, 1995-96, Nat Conv Chair, 1996-97; Nat Black MBA Asn, 1998-; PhD Proj Doctoral Studs Asn, 1998-. **Honors/Awds:** James Dickson Carr Awards, Rutgers Univ, 1989; Cap & Skull Honors, 1994. **Home Addr:** 1939 Eutaw Place, Baltimore, MD 21217. **Business Addr:** Partner, BCT Partners, 105 Lock St, Newark, NJ 07103, **Business Phone:** (973)622-0900.

ROBINSON, JIM C
College teacher. **Personal:** Born Feb 9, 1943, Ackerman, MS. **Educ:** Calif State Univ, BA, 1966, MA, 1968; Stanford Univ, MA, 1972, PhD, 1973. **Career:** San Jose St Col, teacher; Calif State Univ, Long Beach, assoc prof black studies, spec asst vpres acad affrs, dean fac & staff affairs, prof, currently. **Orgs:** Nat Alliance Black Sch Educrs; Am Asn Univ & Prof; dir regents, Progs W Am Asn Higher Educ; chmn, Asn Black Fac & Staff Calif; Mayor's Task Force Fiscal Mgt & Control, Compton. **Business Addr:** Professor, California State University, 1250 Bellflower Blvd, Long Beach, CA 90840, **Business Phone:** (562)985-5561.

ROBINSON, JOHN E
Executive, president (organization). **Personal:** Born Jul 12, 1942, Hollywood, AL; son of John Karie and Anna Naomi Ellison Edwards; divorced; children: Dana L. **Educ:** Clark Col, BA, 1979; Atlanta Univ, MBA, 1979. **Career:** Soc Savings Bank, asst br mgr, 1964-69; Wesleyan Univ, asst personnel dir, 1969-73; WSC Corp, admin vpres, 1973-77; Aetna Life & Casualty, adminr; Aetna Inc, mkt consult, currently. **Orgs:** Past pres, Beta Sigma Lambda Chapter Alpha Phi Alpha, 1981-; Sigma Pi Phi, 1983-; Univ Club Hartford, 1983-95; producer, host talk show, WVIT Channel 30, 1983-; bd mem, Greater Hartford Business Develop Ctr, 1984-; bd mem, Trinity Col, Comm Child Center 1986-94; bd mem, Univ Club Scholarship Fund; chmn,Youth Prog Serv Comt, YMCA, 1992-95; life mem, Alpha Phi Alpha; Craftery Art Gallery, 1994-99; bd mem, Catholic Charities, Catholic Family Services, 2001-02. **Honors/Awds:** Outstanding Business Student, Clark Col, 1979; Leadership of Greater Hartford Chamber of Commerce, 1982; founded a network group F-200, 1983; The Pinnacle Men Award, 1994. **Home Addr:** 485 High St Suite E, New Britain, CT 06053, **Home Phone:** (860)224-9492. **Business Addr:** President, Chief Executive Officer, RJ Enterprises LLC, 485 High St, New Britain, CT 06053, **Business Phone:** 800-224-9492.

ROBINSON, JOHN F.
Executive, chief executive officer. **Personal:** Born May 3, 1944, Brooklyn, NY; children: Timothy. **Educ:** AAS; BBA; New York City Community Col; Baruch Col Off Serv. **Career:** F Chusid & Co, off serv dir, 1966-68; Cancer Care Inc, dir, 1968-76; NewYork Educ & Training Consortium Inc, pres, exec dir; Nat Minority Bus CounInc, pres & chief exec officer, currently. **Orgs:** Am Mgt Asn; Soc Advan Mgt; chmn, Alliance Minority Bus Orgn Inc; bd Harlem YMCA; pres, bd dirs, Serv Underserved, 1989-92; pres, Minority Bus Exec Prog Alumni Asn; Small Bus Admin Adv Coun. **Special Achievements:** Published several management articles in the monthly and quarterly journals of the American Management Association. **Home Addr:** 8043 Utopia Pkwy, Jamaica, NY 11432. **Business Phone:** (212)693-5050.

ROBINSON, JOHN G
Executive. **Personal:** Born Feb 22, 1942, Birmingham, AL; son of Johnny G Sr and Addie B; married Yvonne R Young, Feb 29, 1980; children: Brittany Ann. **Educ:** Miles Col, BA, 1963; Univ Minn, attended, 1968. **Career:** Executive (retired); Magnetic Peripherals Inc, staff, employee rels & training mgr, 1975-79, remote site personnel mgr, 1979-80, div personnel mgr, 1980-82; Control Data Corp, compen consult, 1971-75, human resources mgr, 1986-86; ETA Systs Inc, human resources mgr, 1986-89; John Robinson & Assocs, pres, 1989-93; Co Anoka, diversity coordr, housing opers mgr, 1993-2005. **Orgs:** Life mem, Alpha Pi Alpha Fraternity, 1961-; Minneapolis Vikings Pub Rel Game Staff, 1968-93; Twin City Personnel Asn, 1986-89; fund distrib comt, United Way Minneapolis, 1992-98; Minneapolis Asn Human Rights Workers, 1993-; bd dir, Law Enforcement Opportunities, 1995-; Nat Asn Pub Sector Equal Opportunity Officers, 1996-. **Honors/Awds:** Inducted into Miles Col Hall of Fame, 1980; Distinguished Chapter Service Award, Alpha Pi Alpha Fraternity, 1982. **Military Serv:** USY, security agency, 1965-67. **Home Addr:** 14620 Carriage Lane, Burnsville, MN 55306, **Home Phone:** (952)892-7837.

ROBINSON, JOHN L.
Television broadcaster. **Personal:** Born Dec 15, 1930, Atlantic City, NJ; son of John and Beatrice Johnson; married Louise J Lambert (died 1995); children: Tracy R Crew, Jefrey L Robinson; married Anita B. Johnson. **Educ:** Lincoln Univ, attended 1949; Xavier Univ, attended 1950; TV Workshop, NY, 1955. **Career:** Television broadcaster (retired); Crosley Broadcasting Corp, film librarian, 1955-62; WTEV-TV, film dir, 1962-65, prod mgr, 1965-68, prog mgr, 1968-79. **Orgs:** Corporator, New Bedford Five Cents Savings Bank, 1970-; RI Broadcasters Asn, 1970-79, treas, 1975-76; Mass Broadcasters Asn, 1970-79; Nat Asn TV Prog Execs, 1970-79; Human Rels Comm, New Bedford, MA 1975-76; Gov Coun Civil Rights RI; vpres, New Bedford Br, Nat Asn Advan Colored People; Nat Asn Advan Colored People. **Honors/Awds:** Humanitarian Award, NAACP, New Bedford, MA, 1970; Marian Award, 1980. **Military Serv:** USAF staff & sergeant, 1951-55; Occupation Medal, Japan; Korean Service Medal; United Nations Service Medal; Nat Defense Service Medal; Good Conduct Medal. **Home Addr:** 111 Brandt Island Rd, Mattapoisett, MA 02739. *

ROBINSON, JOHN M.
Executive, president (organization), chief executive officer. **Personal:** Born May 22, 1949, Philadelphia, PA; son of Marvin and Janie Hines; married Alisa Ramsey, Mar 12, 1988; children: Faith Caryn. **Educ:** Edward Waters Col, 1971; Dartmouth Univ, Amos Tuck, 1991. **Career:** SI Handling Syst, sales engr, 1971-76; Black Diamond Enterprises Ltd, founder & pres, 1978-; Edward Waters Col, vis prof, 1989. **Orgs:** Nat Asn Advan Colored People; Soc Mfg Engrs; Omega Psi Phi; Int Mat Mgt Soc; Opers Crossroads African Inc; Minorority Bus Educ Legal Defense Fund. **Honors/Awds:** Small Bus of the Year, Maryland Deed, 1989. **Business Phone:** (610)559-7370.

ROBINSON, JOHNATHAN PRATHER
Executive, vice president (organization). **Personal:** Born Apr 7, 1953, Cleveland, OH; son of Verdix and Robbie Luster; married Deborah Lynn Turner, Apr 12, 1980; children: Rikki Lauren & Jorie Patrice. **Educ:** Northwestern Univ, Evanston, IL, BS, radio tv film, 1975. **Career:** Nat Talent Assocs, Chicago, IL, asst mgr, 1975-77; Wash Nat Ins Co, Evanston, IL, mkt asst, 1977-80; WorldBook Childcraft Int, Chicago, IL, proj supvr, 1980-81; Kemper Financial Servs, Chicago, IL, sales prom specialist, 1981-82; ShopTalk Publ Inc, Chicago, IL, vpres, 1982-90; Burrell Consumer Prom Inc, Chicago, IL, sr vpres, managing dir, 1990-92; Career Television Network Inc, vpres mkt, sales; Topica Inc, sr vpres sales & mkt, currently. **Orgs:** Omega Psi Phi Fraternity Inc, 1972-; servs comn, bd dir, Howard/Paulina Develop Corp, 1989-; steering comt, Promotional Mkt Asn Am, 1990-. **Special Achievements:** Editor: Who's Who in American Beauty, 1990. **Home Addr:** 1440 W Birchwood, Chicago, IL 60626. **Business Addr:** Senior Vice President of Sales & Marketing, Topica Inc, 685 Market St Suite 300, San Francisco, CA 94105, **Business Phone:** (415)344-3878.

ROBINSON, JONTYLE THERESA
Writer, educator, curator. **Personal:** Born Jul 22, 1947, Atlanta, GA. **Educ:** Clark Col, BA, Spanish, 1968; Univ GA, MA, art history, 1971; Univ MD, PhD, contemporary Caribbean & Latin Am art history, 1983. **Career:** Univ GA, Study Abroad Prog fel, res asst, 1970; Philander Smith Col, chairperson, 1971-72; Univ MD, Eastern Shore, instr, 1972-75; Emory Univ, instr, 1978-83, asst prof, joint appointment AFA & AFR Studies Prog/art history, 1983-86, designer, AFA & AFR studies/art history, Summer Study Abroad Prog, Haiti, Jamaica, 1984, 1986, Haiti, The Dominican Repub, Puerto Rico, 1985; WVA State Col, assoc prof, 1986-87; Smithsonian Inst & Archives Am Art, res retrospective exhibition, catalogue raisonne, Am painter Archibald John Motley Jr, 1986-88; Kenkeleba Gallery, res fel, co-curator, 1987-88; Winthrop Col, assoc prof, 1989; Spelman Col, Depart Art, assoc prof, cur & prof, currently. **Orgs:** Nat exec secy, Nat CNF Artists, 1971-72; DST; Phi Kappa Phi Nat Hon Soc. **Honors/Awds:** Amoco Faculty Award, 1992. **Special Achievements:** Author, works include: Archibald John Motley Jr, Chicago Historical Society, 1991; "Archibald John Motley Jr: Painting Jazz and Blues," paper, College Art Association, Chicago, Feb 13-15, 1992; "Archibald John Motley Jr: The Artist in Paris, 1929-30," paper, AFAs and Europe INT CNF, Paris, Feb 5-9, 1992; review: "Black Art-Ancestral Legacy: The AFR Impulse in AFA Art," AFR Arts Magazine, Jan 1991; judge: Contemporary Art Exhibition, Nat Black Arts Festival, Atlanta, 1988; consult: Archibald John Motley Jr Exhibition, Your Heritage House, Detroit, 1988; curator: "VH-4 Decades: The Art of Varnette P Honeywood," Spelman Col, 1992; numerous other television/public lectures, tours, panels, publications. **Business Phone:** (404)223-7672.

ROBINSON, REV. JOSEPH
Clergy. **Personal:** Born Jul 28, 1940, Orangeburg, SC; married Lizzie Miller; children: Jonathan, Joseph C & Jason. **Educ:** Claflin Col, Orangeburg, SC, BA, 1964; Interdenominational Theol Ctr, Atlanta, BD, 1967, MDiv, 1973. **Career:** Morris Brown Col, chaplain, 1965-66; Turner Theo Sem, teacher, 1966-67; Woodbury, NJ, Campbell AME, chmn, 1967-68; St of NJ, social worker, 1967-68; St Johns AME Church, Brooklyn, minister, 1968-72; Grant AME Church Boston, minister, 1972-78; Bethel AME Church, Freeport, NY, minister, 1978-86; Bethel AME Church, New Haven, CT, minister, 1986; Trinity AME Church, pastor, currently. **Orgs:** Phi Beta Sigma; bd dir, Mass Coun Churches; Family Serv Div Prof Couns Staff Boston; pres bd dir, Brightmoor Terr Inc, Boston; Minstl All Greater Boston; vchmn trustee bd, New England Annual Conf AME Ch; delegate, Gen Conf AME Ch Atlanta, 1976; pres, Nat Asn Advan Colored People Freeport/Roosevelt Br, 1978-79; comnr, Human Rels Coun Freeport; trustee, NY Annual Conf; bd examiners, NY Annual Conf; coordr, First Dist Episcopal Headquarters; bd dirs Liberty Park Housing; chmn bd, Paul Quinn Fed Credit Union; trustee, NY Annual Conf, AME Church, 1976-; Self Help, First Episcopal Dist, 1989; NF Housing Authority, hearing officer; bd dir, Christians & Jews in Am. **Honors/Awds:** School Award, Phi Beta Sigma, 1964; Jackson Fisher Award, 1964; Scholar Award, Intrdenmntl Theol Ctr, 1966-67; Turner Memorial Award, 1967; Mortgage Reduction Citation; 19 years ahead of time Leadership Award, Macedonia AME Church, 1986. **Special Achievements:** Morehouse Coll, Martin Luther King Col of Ministers, Religious Emphasis Week, speaker. **Home Phone:** (215)289-8444. **Business Addr:** Pastor, Trinity African Methodist Episcopal Church, 2502 N 27th Street, Philadelphia, PA 19132, **Business Phone:** (215)229-5619.

ROBINSON, JOSEPH WILLIAM
Architect, president (organization). **Personal:** Born in Georgetown, SC; married Willie Louise Taylor; children: Joseph William Jr, Jeffrey Leonardo & Janice Burns. **Educ:** Hampton Univ, BS, 1949. **Career:** JW Robinson & Assocs Inc, pres, currently. **Orgs:** Dir, Am Inst Architects, Atlanta Chap; dir, Nat Orgn Minority Architects; Nat Coun Archit Regist Bds; Atlanta Bus League Leadership; secy, Ga World Cong Ctr, Bd Gov; Butler St YMCA, 1982-90; West End Merchants Com Develop Asn; Phi Beta Sigma Fraternity Inc. **Honors/Awds:** Nat Hampton Alumni, Lambda Sigma Chap Leadership Atlanta, 1974; Catalyst Award, Southeastern Region, Int Conf Bldg Officials, 1975; Outstanding Leadership, Atlanta Bus League, 1984; Lay Fellowship Service Award, Big Bethel Am Church, 1987; Trailblazer Award, 1999. **Business Addr:** President, J W Robinson & Associates Inc., 1020 Ralph David Abernathy Blvd SW, Atlanta, GA 30310, **Business Phone:** (404)753-4129.

ROBINSON, DR. JOYCE RUSSELL
Educator. **Personal:** Born Jul 15, 1950, Palmer Springs, VA; divorced; children: William Russell. **Educ:** Bennett Col, BA, 1971; NC Cent Univ, MA, 1982; Emory Univ, PhD, 1991. **Career:** NC Public Sch Syst, instr, 1972-84; Univ Tenn, Knoxville, teaching assoc, 1984-87; St Augustine's Col, assoc prof, assoc dir, Bush-Hewlett Writing Across the Curriculum, 1987-96; NC State Univ, Meredith Col, adj prof, 1994-95; Fayetteville State Univ, project dir, assoc prof, African Am & womens lit, 1996-. **Orgs:** Asn Dept Eng, 1992; Col Lang Asn, 1993-; Nat Coun Teachers Eng, 1993-95; asst secy, John Chavis Soc, 1997; Sankore Charter Sch, 1999. **Honors/Awds:** Writing Teacher of the Year, St Augustines Col, 1993, Faculty Research Award, 1996; Fayetteville State Univ Res & Publ, 1998, 1999. **Special Achievements:** Publication: "Elizabeth Laura Adams," African American Writers, pg 1745-1945, 2000; implemented first courses in Womanism and Feminist literature, Fayetteville State University, 1997; sponsored "Communiversity" appearance by Amiri Baraka, 1997; co-sponsored "Communiversity" appearance by Nikki Giovanni, 1999; The Cocoa Club, founder 1994; JASA, founder, 1999; created and hosted weekly TV lecture series in African American literature, St Augustine's Coll, 1993; initiated the Anna J Cooper Society, St Augustine's Col. **Business Addr:** Associate Professor, Fayetteville State University, Rm 132 Butler Bldg 1200 Murchison Rd, Fayetteville, NC 28301-4298, **Business Phone:** (910)672-1589.

ROBINSON, KENNETH
Government official. **Personal:** Born Dec 10, 1947, Chicago, IL; son of Seayray Govan and Henry Lee; married Etta D Clement, Jun 7, 1987. **Educ:** Ill State Univ, BA, bus admin, 1975. **Career:** Am Hosp Supply Corp, tax acct; Abbott Labs, staff tax admin; Ill Dept Revenue, revenue auditor; Lake County Community Action, econ develop coordr, admin dir; City N Chicago, city treas, currently. **Orgs:** Pres, Five Points Econ Develop Corp, 1981-; bd mem, Lake County Urban League, 1981-; bd mem, N Chicago Plan Comt, 1982-; sch bd mem, Dist 64 No Chicago, 1984-; bd mem, Lake City Pvt Indust Coun, 1994;Treasurer of the 911 Board, Treasurer of the Police Pension Fund. **Military Serv:** AUS, sp/4, 2 years. **Home Addr:** PO Box 1181, North Chicago, IL 60064-8181. **Business Addr:** City Treasurer, City of North Chicago, 1850 Lewis Ave, North Chicago, IL 60064, **Business Phone:** (847)596-8628.

ROBINSON, KENNETH EUGENE
Educator. **Personal:** Born Mar 9, 1947, Hannibal, MO; married Cecilia. **Educ:** William Jewell Col, BS; Northwest Mo State Univ, MS, educ; Univ Mo, Kans City, ed spec, 1980. **Career:** Liberty Sr High Sch, psychol & sociol instr, 1972-80; Moberly Pub Schs, social studies instr, 1969-71; Liberty Pub Schs, asst football & head track coach, 1972-80; Clay Co Juv Justice Center, detention officer, 1977-78; Franklin Life Ins, ins agent, 1979-80; State Farm Ins Co, agent, currently. **Orgs:** Parks & Recreation Bd Liberty MO, 1977-80; pres, elect Liberty CTA,1978-79; pres, Liberty Teachers Asn, 1979-80; Minority Studies Task Force, William Jewell Col, 1979-80; campaign chmn, United Way Liberty Pub Schs, 1979; Pub Rels, Com MSTA, 1980. **Business Addr:** Agent, State Farm Insurance, 7605 NW Roanridge, Kansas City, MO 64151, **Business Phone:** (816)587-8330.

ROBINSON, DR. KITTY KIDD (WILLIE MAE KIDD)
Educator. **Personal:** Born Jan 7, 1921, West Point, MS; widowed. **Educ:** Tenn State Univ, BS, 1949; De Paul Univ, MEd, Supvis & Admin, 1960; NW Univ, PhD, 1974. **Career:** Educator (Retired); Chicago Pub Sch, pr teacher, 1956-66; Univ Chicago, Recipient Independent Workshop fel, 1967; Chicago State Univ, prof, early child educ, 1967-76; asst dean. **Orgs:** Chmn, Asn Child Educ, 1974; pan mem, Coop Urban Teacher Educ Work shp; Am Asn Univ Prof; Nat Educ Asn Int; Asn Child Educ Int; Ill Asn Supv &Current Devel; Nat Coun Teaching Eng Res Asn; bd mem, Asn Mammequins; Nat Reading Conf; Chicago Urban League; S Shore Community Serv; Women Mobil Change; PUSH; Asn Mannequins; Trophy Sch Fund Bd Jeffery-Yates Neighbour base oper, Shore Patrol; past pres, 79th St Block Club; Widows Club; Peace Corps Adv Coun. **Honors/Awds:** City Sch Community Serv Award, Phi Delta Kappa Educ Hon Soc.

ROBINSON, LARRY
Basketball player. **Personal:** Born Jan 11, 1968, Bossier City, LA. **Educ:** Centenary Col La. **Career:** Wash Bullets, 1990-91; Golden State Warriors, 1991; Boston Celtics, 1991-92; Rapid City Thrillers, 1991-92; Wash Bullets, 1992-93; Houston Rockets, 1993-94; Vancouver Grizzlies, 1997-98; Cleveland Cavaliers, 2001; Atlanta Hawks, 2001; NY Knickerbockers, forward-guard, 2002.

ROBINSON, LAWRENCE D.
Physician. **Personal:** Born Sep 20, 1942, Baltimore, MD; married; children: one. **Educ:** Univ Pittsburgh, BS, 1964; Howard Univ, MD, 1968. **Career:** Martin L King Jr Hosp; Johns Hopkins Hosp, intern, 1968-69; res, 1969-70; Sinai Hosp Baltimore, chief res, 1970-71; US Army Ped Dir Sicle Cell Dis Prog, 1971-73; Charles R Drew Postgrad Med Sch UCLA Immunology Fellowship; Allergys & Immunology, asst prof pediatrics, dir. **Orgs:** Nat Med Asn; Science Adv Com, Nat Asn Sickle Cell Dis; Bd, Cert by Am Bd Ped; Bd Allery & Immunology, 1975; Am Thoracic Soc; Am Acad Ped; mem bd, Am Lung Asn LA; Immunization Action Comn, 1978-80; co-chmn, Nat Immunization Prog LA. **Special Achievements:** Has written & present many pub at meet of Am Ped Soc Atlantic City, Am Ped Soc Wash; contributing editor Essence Mag; presented papers to Am Acad of Allergy. **Business Addr:** 1523 West Avenue J, Lancaster, CA.

ROBINSON, LEARTHON STEVEN, SR.
Lawyer. **Personal:** Born May 8, 1925, Pittsburgh, PA; son of Learthon Steven and Mamie Miller; married Beulah Beatrice Brown, Aug 26, 1950; children: Deborah L Flemister, Learthon S Jr, Iris R Rodgers, Michael J & Denise E Baba. **Educ:** Univ Pittsburgh, BA, 1948; Univ Wis, grad study, 1950; Cleveland-Marshall Sch Law, Cleveland State Univ, JD, 1952. **Career:** Ohio Civil Rights Comn, judicial hearing officer, 1964-65; Warren, Ohio Law Dept, city prosecuter, 1967-71, first dep law dir, 1971-; Montford Point Marines Asn, Inc nat off, gen coun; Pvt Pract, atty, currently. **Orgs:** Omega Psi Phi Fraternity, 1947; Nat Asn Advan Colored People, 1973; life mem, Nat Bar Asn, 1980; pres, PA-OH Blk Lwyrs Asn Inc, 1981-; pres, Shenango Vly Serv Inc, 1985; comt mem, Pub Rel Spkrs Bur Trumbull Co Bar Asn, 1985; Ohio Bar Asn; Am Bar Asn; DC Bar Asn; bd trustees, Goodwill Indust Warren Youngstown Area, 1986-89; life mem, life mem, Montford Point Marine Asn Inc, 1993. **Honors/Awds:** Congressial Citation & Proclamation Exemplary Prof Serv, City Warren Ohio, 1971-87; Man of the Year, Urban League Warren Trumbull Chap, 1976; Community Service Award, Trumbull Co, Nat Asn Advan Colored People, 1982; Outstanding Leadership, 17th Cong Dist Caucus, 1984; Nat Semper Fidelis Award for Outstanding Service, Montford Point Asn Inc, 1994; Hall of Fame, Nat Bar Asn, 1995; Iwo Jima Medal, 1995. **Military Serv:** USMC, gnry sgt, 1942-46; Honorably Discharged; 4 mjr cmpgns, Award 4 battle stars, 1942-46; Pres Unit Citation, WWII Vctry Medal, 2 Purple Hrts, Navy Commendation for Bravery in Combat, Asiatic-Pacific Medal in Combat, Japanese Occupation Medal, Marine Corps Service Medal. **Home Addr:** 4119 Chevelle Dr SE, Warren, OH 44484. **Business Addr:** Attorney, 179 W Mkt St, Warren, OH 44481, **Business Phone:** (330)395-7405.

ROBINSON, DR. LUTHER DABNEY
Physician, educator. **Personal:** Born Dec 22, 1922, Tappahannock, VA; son of William H and Fannie E; married Betty Boyd; children: Jan, Barry & Vance. **Educ:** VA State Col, BS, 1943; Meharry Med Col, MD, 1946. **Career:** Mercy Hosp Phila, intern, 1946-47; Lakin State Hosp Lakin WV, staff, 1947-49; Freedmen's Hosp Wash, psychiat residency, 1953-54; St Elizabeths Hosp, 1954-55; St Elizabeths Hosp, staff, 1955-; Howard Univ Col Med, clin instr, 1956-68, vis lectr, assoc prof emer psychiat, currently; Gallaudet Col, lectr, 1968-; Geo Wash Univ, clin assoc prof, 1969-; Georgetown Univ Sch Med, fac mem, 1974-; St Elizabeths Hosp Wash, supt, 1975; Howard Univ Hosp, psychiat, currently. **Orgs:** Medico Chirurgical Soc; Med Soc DC; Wash Psychiat Soc; AMA; nat chmn, Commn Med & Audiol 7th World Cong; World Fedn Deaf Originated Mental Health Prog Deaf St Elizabeths Hosp, 1963; co-founder, AA Prog St Elizabeths Hosp; life mem, Am Psychiat Asn. **Honors/Awds:** DSc, Gallaudet Col, 1971; Edw Miner Gallaudet Award, 1974; Meritorious Achievement Award, Nat Med Asn. **Special Achievements:** First African-American director of the prestigious St Elizabeth's Hosp in Washington. **Military Serv:** AUS, capt, 1949-52. **Business Addr:** Psychiatrist, Howard University Hospital, 2041 Ga Ave NW Suite 5B02, Washington, DC 20012, **Business Phone:** (202)865-6611.

ROBINSON, MALCOLM
Administrator, lawyer. **Personal:** Born Jan 1, 1948, Chicago, IL; married; children: Brian. **Educ:** Ottowa Univ, KS, BA, speech commun, 1970; Univ Kansas, JD, 1975. **Career:** Alliance Am Insurers, corp coun, 1975-79; Scor Reinsurance Co, vpres & corp coun, 1979-84; Robinson, West & Gooden law firm, co-founder & sr managing partner, 1984-2002; Robinson & Hoskins LLP, co-founder & partner, 2002-. **Orgs:** Pres, Nat Bar Asn, 2002-; vpres finance, Nat Bar Asn, 1998-2001; State Bar Tex; Dallas Bar Asn; Former dir & mem, J.L. Turner Legal Asn; Col State Bar Tex; pres, Dallas Black Chamber Com, 1990, 1991, 1992; former chmn & bd dir, Dallas Conv & Visitors Bur; former dir, N Tex Comn; former chmn, bd trustees, State Bar Tex Ins Trust; former chmn, Greater Dallas Crime Comn; former mem, Dallas Citizens Coun; Am Bar Asn. **Special Achievements:** First African American named chairman of the Dallas Conv and Visitors Bureau. **Business Addr:** Co-founder, Partner, Robinson & Hoskins LLP, 400 S Zang Blvd Suite 920, Dallas, TX 75208, **Business Phone:** (214)941-0717.

ROBINSON, DR. MALCOLM KENNETH
Physician, surgeon. **Personal:** Born Nov 22, 1961, Philadelphia, PA; son of James H and Soiesette Furlonge; married Alyssa Shari Hayworde, May 8, 1999; children: James H Robinson III. **Educ:** Harvard, AB, 1983, MD, 1987. **Career:** Harvard Med Sch, instr, 1994-2000, asst prof, 2001-; Dana Farber Cancer Inst, consulting surgeon & physician, 1995-; Mass Gen Hosp, asst surgeon, 1997-; Nutritional Restart Ctr, sr res consult, 1998-2000; Faulkner Hosp, attending surgeon, 1998-; West Roxbury Veterans Admin Hosp, attending surgeon, 1999-; Brigham & Women's Hosp, dir, Metabolic Support Services, 2000; pvt pract, currently; Editor, JPEN Journal for Parenteral & Enteral Nutrition, New England Journal of Medicine, Archives of Surgery, Journal of American Col of Surgeons, Journal of Women's Health & Topics in Clinical Nutrition. **Orgs:** Amer Med Asn, 1984-; MA Med Soc, 1984-; Am Asn Acad Surg, 1995-; Soc Black Acad Surgeons, 1995-; Soc Surg Alimentary Tract, 1996-; Boston Surgical Soc, 1998-; Am Obesity Asn, 1999-; Boston Obesity Nutrition Res Ctr, 2000-. **Honors/Awds:** Nat Insts Health, Nat Res Service Award, 1990-92; Maurice Shils Research Award, Am Society for Parenteral & Enteral Nutrition, 1996, 1997. **Special Achievements:** Published numerous articles. **Home Addr:** 183 Mt Vernon St, West Newton, MA 02465, **Home Phone:** (617)965-5636. **Business Addr:** Physician, 75 Francis St, Boston, MA 02115, **Business Phone:** (617)732-8272.

ROBINSON, MALCOLM S
Lawyer. **Educ:** Ottawa Univ, Ottawa, KS, BS, speech communs, 1970; Univ Kansas Sch Law, Lawrence, Kansas, JD, 1975. **Career:** Alliance Am Insurers, Chicago, IL, corp coun, 1975-79; Scor Reinsurance Co, Dallas, TX, corp coun & vpres, 1979 -84; Robinson West & Gooden, PC, fka Robinson & West, Dallas, TX, sr managing partner & co-founder, 1984-2002; Robinson & Hoskins LLP, atty, co-founder & partner, 2002-. **Orgs:** Dallas Bar Asn Found; Dallas Bar Asn; State BarTex; vpres, Nat Bar Asn, 1998-2001; pres, Nat Bar Asn, 2002; Am Bar Asn; J L Turner Legal Asn; Dallas Black Chamber Com; Greater Dallas Crime Comn. **Business Phone:** (214)941-0717.

ROBINSON, MARCUS
Football player. **Personal:** Born Feb 27, 1975, Ft Valley, GA. **Educ:** Univ SC. **Career:** Football player (retired); Chicago Bears, wide receiver, 1997-2002; Baltimore Ravens, wide receiver, 2003; Minn Vikings, wide receiver, 2004-09; Detroit Lions, 2007. **Orgs:** Founder, Marcus Robinson Foundation.

ROBINSON, MAURICE C
Lawyer. **Personal:** Born Mar 4, 1932, St Andrew, Jamaica; son of Herbert Ulysses and Mildred Anastasia Magnus; married Hazel Thelma Chang Robinson, Nov 24, 1990; children: Mark Wayne, Janet Marie & Wade Patrick. **Educ:** Univ Col West Indies, BA 1954. **Career:** Manton & Hart, assoc, 1959-64, partner, 1964-77; secy, Air Jamaica Ltd 1968-69; Air Jamaica Ltd, legal officer, 1970-80; Eric Fong-Yee Eng Co Ltd, chmn, Pub Utility Comn, 1972-76; Myers, Fletcher & Gordon, consult, 1977-. Ericsscon Jamaica Ltd, staff. **Orgs:** Chair, Victoria Mutual Bldg Soc; dir Travel Planners Ltd; Dyoll/Wataru Coffee Co Ltd; dir, Security Adv & Mgt Servs Ltd; bd dir, Victoria Mutual Investments Ltd; Inst Trade Mark Agts; bd dir, Victoria Mutual Property Servs Ltd; bd dir, Victoria Mutual Ins Co Ltd; bd dir, Restaurant Assoc Ltd, Burger King Franchise; assoc mem, Int Trademark Asn. **Honors/Awds:** Full University Colours for Field Hockey, 1953. **Business Addr:** Consultant, Myers, Fletcher & Gordon, 21 East St, PO Box 162, Kingston, Jamaica, **Business Phone:** (876)922-5860.

ROBINSON, MELVIN P.
Entrepreneur. **Personal:** Born Feb 12, 1935, Atlantic City, NJ; son of Warren and Marcella Derry; children: Tiffany & Michael Ribando. **Educ:** Villinova Univ, Villinova Pa, 1954. **Career:** Melvin P Robinson Pipe Organs, owner, 1965-. **Orgs:** Am Inst Organ Builders, 1990-. **Business Addr:** Owner, Melvin P Robinson Pipe Organs, 12 Irving Pl, Mt Vernon, NY 10550, **Business Phone:** (914)699-5862.

ROBINSON, DR. MILTON J
State government official. **Personal:** Born Aug 16, 1935, Asbury Park, NJ; married Sadie Pinkston; children: Valerie & Patricia. **Educ:** Univ Mich, BS, 1958; Columbia Univ, MA, 1962; Univ Mich, MSW, 1966, PhD, 1980. **Career:** Battle Creek Urban League, exec dir, 1966-69; Flint Urban League, exec dir, 1969-70; Dept Civil Rights State Mich, exec dir, 1970-72; State Mich, parole bd mem, 1972-, exec sec parole & review bd, currently; Wayne State Univ Sch Social Work, adj prof, 1975-, GMI Engineering & Mgt Inst, admis & corp rels consult; Kettering Univ, Off Multicultural Stud Initiatives, consult to the pres, currently. **Orgs:** Kappa Alpha Psi Frat; bd mem, United Neighborhood Ctrs Am, 1972-; pres, Cath Youth Orgn, 1978-; Lions Int, 1979-; bd mem, Detroit Metro Youth Prog, 1985-. **Honors/Awds:** Community Service Award, City Battle Creek, 1969; Outstanding Professional Service Award, Flint Urban League, 1978; Outstanding Contrib to Continuing Judicial Educ, Mich Judicial Inst, 1979; Meritorious Service Award, Catholic Youth Orgn, 1984; Certificate of Achievement, Nat Coun Juvenile & Family Court Judges, 1986. **Military Serv:** AUS, Sp 4, 1958-60. **Business Addr:** Consultant to the President, Kettering University, Office of Multicultural Student Initiatives, 1700 W Third Ave, Flint, MI 48504-4898, **Business Phone:** (810)762-9521.

ROBINSON, DR. MURIEL F COX
Physician. **Personal:** Born Nov 6, 1927, Columbus, OH; daughter of Veola and Henry W; divorced. **Educ:** Ohio State Univ, attended 1948; Meharry Med Col, MD, 1952. **Career:** Homer G Phillips Hosp, affiliated w/Wash Univ Sch Med, psychiatry resident, 1953-56; St Louis Munic Child Guidance Clin, staff psychiatrist, 1956-57; Napa State Hosp, staff psychiatrist, 1958; Richmond Mental Health Ctr, staff psychiatrist, 1959-75; E Oakland Mental Health Ctr, staff psychiatrist, 1976-79; pvt psychiat pract, psychiatrist, 1960-79; Calif Youth Authority, staff, 1979-92; Locum Tenens Group, 1992-94. **Orgs:** North Richmond Neighborhood House; mem, Am Psychiatric Asn 1957-; mem, Black Psychiatrists Am; Nat Asn Advan Colored People Sacramento, 1987-; life mem, Am Psychiatric Asn, 1991-; AMA, 1957-; mem, AAAS, 1989-; mem, Nat Med Asn, 1960-.

ROBINSON, MYRON FREDERICK
Association executive. **Personal:** Born Dec 15, 1943, Youngstown, OH; son of Virginia L Robinson-Robinson and Romeo Robinson; married Brenda King, Dec 15, 1987; children: Myron Rodney & Myra Michele. **Educ:** Ohio State Univ, Youngstown, OH, BA; Univ of Pittsburgh, Pittsburgh, PA; Univ of Wisconsin; National Urban League Executive Development Training. **Career:** Association executive (retired); Urban League New Haven Ct; Urban League, Madison, Wi, Urban League-Greater Cleveland, pres & chief exec officer, 1972-2008. **Orgs:** Bd dirs, Am Fed Bank; bd dirs, YMCA; Greenville SC, Rotary Club; The Govs Task Force Reducing Health Cost; Bd dirs, Christ Episcopal Church.

ROBINSON, NINA
Public relations executive. **Personal:** Born Jul 17, 1943, Stamford, CT; daughter of Henry Scott (deceased) and Olga Larionova Scott (deceased); married Lawrence Donniva, Jul 28, 1962 (divorced); children: Lawrence Damian & Lauren Danielle. **Educ:** New York Univ, New York, NY, attended 1961-62. **Career:** New York Urban League, New York, NY, adminr, Brownstone Prep, 1968-72; Newark Bd Educ, Newark, NJ, staff trainer, researcher, 1972-74; Chad Sch, Newark, NJ, adminr, 1974-82; New York Times Co, New York, NY, coordr pub rels & media, 1983-. **Orgs:** A Better Chance, 1980-83; bd mem, Newark Bd Educ, 1982-83; New York Black Journalists, 1992-93; exec bd, Fund Raising Chairwoman, 1992-; Newark Citizen Educ Comt; bd mem, Newark Beth Israel Hosp, CDC, 1998-. **Honors/Awds:** Miss Manhattan, 1961. **Special Achievements:** Contributing writer, New York Times, New Jersey Edition. **Business Addr:** Coordinator of Public Relations Media, The New York Times Company, 229 W 43rd St, New York, NY 10036, **Business Phone:** (212)556-1234.

ROBINSON, PATRICIA
Executive. **Personal:** Born Apr 18, 1951, Miami, FL; children: Lennard & Patrice. **Educ:** Miami-Dade Community Col, AA, 1981; Barry Univ, BS, 1983. **Career:** Dade City Circuit Ct, ct calendar clerk, 1974-77; Dade County Dept Human Resources, admin officer, 1977-83, newsletter asst ed, 1983-87, adminr, 1987-89; Thomas & Doyle Real Estate Inc, assoc realtor, 1979-85; ERA Empress Realty Inc, assoc realtor, 1985-86; Coldwell Bankers, referral agent, 1986-87. **Orgs:** Nat Forum Black Pub Admin; Iota Phi Lambda Sor; Nat Asn Advan Colored People; trustee, bd chair, Valley Grove MB Church; Nat Assoc Life Underwriters; Barry Univ, Alumni Asn; Florida Real Estate Coun; Nat Asn Female Exec. **Honors/Awds:** Employee of the Year, Dept Human Resources Off Admin, 1985; Honored for Outstanding Business Achievement, 1989; National Quality Award; National Sales Achievement Award; Million Dollar Round Table Qualifier. **Business Addr:** Financial Advisor Representative, MetLife Financial Services, 1 Alhambra Plz Suite 1, Coral Gables, FL 33134.

ROBINSON, PETER LEE, JR.
Artist, graphic artist, consultant. **Personal:** Born Jan 16, 1922, Washington, DC; married Romaine Frances Scott. **Educ:** Howard Univ, AB, 1949. **Career:** USN, supr illustrator, 1957-62; Nat Aeronautics & Space Admin, dir, visual info officer, 1962-77; fine artist, graphics designer, consult. **Orgs:** Dir, founder, HEM Rsch Inc Past Inc; pres, treas DC Art Asn; past v pres Soc of Fed Artists & Designers, Fed Design Council; US State Dept "Arts for the EmbassiesProg"; speaker Rice Univ, 1969, 16th Int Tech Commission Conference, 1969; Morgan State Col, 1969; 19th Int Tech Commission Conference, 1970; NAIA, 1971; 19th Int Tech Commission Conference, 1972; 1st Indust Graphics Int Conference, 1974; 4th Tech Writing Inst, 1974, Nat Conf of Artists, 1980. **Honors/Awds:** Award of Excellence in Visiting Comm Soc of Fed Artists & Designers 1961; Meritorious Civilian Serv Award, 1960; Apollo Achievement Award, 1969; NASA Exceptional Serv Medal, 1973; NASA Outstanding Performance Award, 1975; NASA Spaceship Earth Award, 1975. **Military Serv:** USAAC, 1943-46. *

ROBINSON, DR. PREZELL RUSSELL
School administrator, government official. **Personal:** Born Aug 25, 1922, Batesburg, SC; son of Clarence and Annie; married LuLu Harris, Apr 9, 1950; children: JesSanne. **Educ:** St Augustine's Col Raleigh NC, AB, 1946; Bishop Col, LLD, 1951; Cornell Univ NY, MA, 1951, EdD, 1956. **Career:** Voorhees Sch & Jr Col Denmark SC, instr French/math/sci, 1948-54; Univ Nairobi Kenya, vis prof, 1973; Univ Dar es Salaam Tanzania, vis prof, 1973; Haile Selassie I Univ Addis Ababa Ethiopia, vis prof, 1973; Univ Guyana, vis prof, 1974; Cornell Univ Ithaca NY, fel, 1954-56; St Augustines Col, prof sociol, 1956, dean, 1956-64, exec dean, 1964-66, actg pres, 1966-67, pres, 1967-95, pres emer & instr anthrop, 1995-; alt rep gen assembly UN, 1996. **Orgs:** Phi Kappa Phi; Delta Mu Delta; Alpha Kappa Mu; Phi Delta Kappa; Am Social Soc; NC Social Soc; Am Acad Polit Sci; So Social Soc; Am Asn Advan Sci; Study Negro Life & History, Am Acad Pol & Soc Sci; bd dir, Wachovia Bank & Trust Co; state bd ed, NC; exec comt, NC Asn Col & Univ; bd dir Nat Asn Equal Oppty Higher Ed; bd dir, Tech Asst Consortium Improve Col Serv; pres, United Negro Col Fund, 1978-80; bd dir, Occoneechee Cty BSA; pres, Nat Assoc Equal Opportunity Higher Educ, 1981-84; bd dir, C C; pres, Cooperating Raleigh Cols, 1981, 1986-88; exec comt, Asn Episcopal Col, Omega Psi Phi; 47th Gen Assembly, UN, pub mem ambassador, 1992; Alternative Rep US UN,1992; vice chmn, NC State Bd Educ; African Am Cult Complex, currently; Pres's Comt Race Rels. **Honors/Awds:** Recipient Fulbright Fellow to India, 1965; Tar Heel of the Week Raleigh News & Observer, 1971; Recognition for Services Rendered Award 2nd highest Award from Liberia, 1971; Outstanding Service Award, Alpha Phi Alpha,1977; Citizen of the Year Award, Omega Psi Phi, 1979; Silver Anniversary Award, NC Community Col Syst, 1989. **Special Achievements:** Appointed by Pres George Bush as public mem ambassador to the General Assembly of United Nations in 1992 & re-appointed to the same post by Pres Clinton; author of more than 21 articles in professional journals. **Military Serv:** AUS, World War II. **Home Addr:** 821 Glascock St, Raleigh, NC 27604. **Business Addr:** President Emeritus, St Augustines College, 1315 Oakwood Ave, Raleigh, NC 27610, **Business Phone:** (919)516-4237.

ROBINSON, R DAVID, SR.
Football player, executive. **Personal:** Born May 3, 1941, Mount Holly, NJ; son of Leslie H and Mary E Gaines; married Elaine Burns, Mar 22, 1963; children: Richard, David & Robert. **Educ:** Penn State Univ, BS, 1963. **Career:** Football player (retired), business executive; Green Bay Packers, linebacker, 1963-72; Wash Redskins, linebacker, 1973-74; Schlitz Brewing Co, Youngstown Ohio, dist sales mgr; Mars Dist Co, exec vpres, 1984; Superior Beverage Akron, MARS Div, vpres; Pro Football Hall Fame, secy & trustee, currently. **Orgs:** Nat Football League Players Asn; Nat Football League Player rep, 1967-70; vpres, Players Asn, 1968-70; YMCA; Big Bros; bd dirs, Pro Football Hall Fame, 1990. **Honors/Awds:** Liberty Bowl, 1960; All Am, 1962; Hula Bowl, 1962; All Star Game, 1963; All Pro, 1965-69; MVP Pro Bowl, 1968. **Special Achievements:** First Black Linebacker in National Football League; First black Gator Bowl, 1961. **Business Addr:** Secretary, Trustee, Pro Football Hall of Fame, 2121 George Halas Dr NW, Canton, OH 44708, **Business Phone:** (330)456-8207.*

ROBINSON, DR. RANDALL S
Educator. **Personal:** Born Nov 26, 1939, Philadelphia, PA; married Janice Whitley; children: Randall & Ginger. **Educ:** Ohio State Univ, BS, 1961; Univ Pa, MS, 1965; Temple Univ, EdD, 1972. **Career:** Philadelphia Bd Educ, teacher, 1961-65; Summer Sch Improv Proj, 1967; Educ Mat Co, project coordr, res & develop, 1968-69; Temple Univ, adjunct prof, 1968-69, consult & group leader annual summer workshop lang arts; Tioga Community Youth Coun, educ consul disruptive youth, 1971; Rowan Univ, NJ, Dept Elem & Early Childhood Educ, assoc prof, prof, prof emer, currently; Egg Harbor Sch System, NJ, consult. **Orgs:** Wash Twp Bd Educ, 1973-76; Curric Rev Comt; early childhood educ & curric develop comt mem, Glassboro State Col; Dept Tenure & Recontracting Comt; Urban Educ Curric Develop Comt; fac adv, Black Cult Leg; counr, Adv Upward Bound Stud; counr & adv, Martin Luther King Scholars Fac; Glassboro State Fedn Col Teachers; Nat Coun Social Studies; Negotiations Comt; Wash Twp Educ; Curric Comt; Balanced Group Wash Twp. **Honors/Awds:** Plaque, Tioga Community Youth Coun, 1973. **Business Addr:** Professor Emeritus, Rowan University, Department of Elementary & Early Childhood Education, 201 Mullica Hill Rd, Glassboro, NJ 08028, **Business Phone:** (856)256-4500.

ROBINSON, DR. RANDALL S.
Association executive, lawyer, educator. **Personal:** Born Jul 6, 1941, Richmond, VA; son of Doris Griffin and Maxie Cleveland; married; children (previous marriage): Anike & Jabari; married; children: Khalea. **Educ:** Va Union Univ, BA, sociol, 1967; Harvard Law Sch, JD, 1970. **Career:** US Rep Diggs, admin asst; Ford fel; Trans Africa, founder & exec dir, 1977-2006, pres, 2001; lawyer; activist; nationalist & adminr; Pa State Univ, Dickinson Sch Law, distinguished scholar in residence, currently. **Honors/Awds:** MLK Public Service Award, Ebony Mag. **Special Achievements:** Author, The Debt; Author, Defending the Spirit: A Black Life in America,2001; First African-Am network tv news anchor.

ROBINSON, RENAULT ALVIN
Police officer, government official, consultant. **Personal:** Born Sep 8, 1942, Chicago, IL; son of Robert Robinson and Mabel; married Annette Richardson; children: Renault Jr, Brian, Kivu & Kobie. **Educ:** Roosevelt Univ, BS 1970, MS, urban studies, 1971; Northwestern Univ, Urban Fellow 1973. **Career:** Chicago Police Dept, police officer & vice detective, 1965-83; Chicago Housing Authority, chmn brd dirs, 1979-87, chmn brd commissioners, 1983-87; ASI Personnel Serv Inc, sr mgt assoc, 1989-; Renault Robinson Staffing Assocs, pres, currently. **Orgs:** Exec dir, Afro Am Police League, 1968-83; co found, chmn brd dir, Afro-Am Police League, 1983-; Natl Am Advan Colored People; Chicago Urban League; Natl Forum Black Pub Admin; natl inform officer, Natl Black Police Assn. **Honors/Awds:** Subject of "The Man Who Beat Clout City", 1977; Renault A Robinson Award, named in honor, Natl Black Police Assn, 1979; Youth Award, John D Rockefeller III Found, 1979; over 50 awards from government, business & community organizations. **Business Addr:** President, Renault Robinson Staffing Associates, 111 W Wash St Suite 1815, Chicago, IL 60602, **Business Phone:** (312)236-6169.

ROBINSON, ROBERT G
Health services administrator, educator. **Personal:** Born Aug 11, 1943, New York, NY; son of Robert Garl and Dorothy May Wilson. **Educ:** City Col NY, BA, 1967; Adelphi Univ, MSW, 1969; Unv Cal, Berkeley, MPH, 1977, PhD, 1983. **Career:** Health service administrator (retired), educator; Adelphi Univ, chap, asst prof, 1969-76; REACH, Inc, psychotherapist, 1973-75; Univ Cal, Berkeley, staff, 1977-84; Am Cancer Soc, prin investr, 1983-85;

Nat Cancer Inst fel, Cancer Control Sci Asn, 1985-88; Fox Chase Cancer Ctr, assoc mem, 1988-90, dir cot planning & develop, 1990-92; Ctrs Dis Control, assoc dir prog develop; Emory Univ, Sch Pub Health, adj prof, 1997. **Orgs:** Nat Black Leadership Initiative Cancer Philadelphia, 1988-93; bd, Uptown Coalition Tobacco Control & Pub HTH, 1989-93; bd, Stop Teenage Addiction Tobacco, 1990-; nat ed bd, Jour Health Care Poor & Underserved, 1990-; Am Pub Health Asn; Nat Med Asn; AAAS; ed adv bd, An Int Jour, 1992-; Nat African Am Tobacco Prev & Control Network, 1999-. **Honors/Awds:** Cot Health Award, Am Med Women's Asn, 1990; COT Service Award, Nat Asn Health Serv Execs, 1990; PEN Heritage Award, Commonwealth PEN, 1992; Outstanding Leadership, Uptown Coalition Tobacco Control & Pub HTH, 1992; Outstanding Leadership Award, Nat Black Leadership Initiative Cancer, 1992; Presdential Citation, Am Asn Health Educr, 2000. **Special Achievements:** Pathways to Freedom, video, 1990; "Cancer Awareness Among AFAs," 1991; "Pathways to Freedom," guide 1992; "Smoking & AFAs," pubation Henry J Kaiser Found, 1992; "Report Tobacco Policy Group," Tobacco Control: An International Journal, 1992; CDC ASTDR Hon Award, Serv to Pub, 1995; NCCDPHP, Outstanding Performance in INT HTH, 1996; Presial Citation Award, Amn Asn HTH Educators, 2000.

ROBINSON, ROBERT LOVE, JR.
Accountant. **Personal:** Born Apr 21, 1961, Madera, CA; son of Robert L Sr and Evelyn Barnes. **Educ:** Univ Pac, BS, 1982. **Career:** Price Waterhouse, auditor, 1982-85; Sun Diamond Growers Calif, internal auditor, 1985-86; Grupe Co, Stockton, Calif, sr acct, 1986-89, mgr, acct oper, 1989-92; Delta Syst Associate, staff consult, 1993-. **Orgs:** Calif State Soc CPA's, 1985-; adv, Sacramento Valley Chap Nat Asn Black Acct, 1985-; pres, Sacramento Valley Chap Nat Asn Black Acct, 1989; Univ Phoenix Alumni Asn, 1986-. **Honors/Awds:** Award of Excellence, Grupe Co, 1990. **Home Addr:** 7023 Germanna Ct, Stockton, CA 95219-3117, **Home Phone:** (209)477-1525. **Business Addr:** Staff Consultant, Delta Systems Associate, 2295 Gateway Oaks Dr Suite 165, Sacramento, CA 95833, **Business Phone:** (209)473-6060.

ROBINSON, ROBIN
Journalist, television news anchorperson. **Personal:** Born Aug 4, 1957, Chicago, IL. **Educ:** Jour, BA, 1981. **Career:** KGTV, McGraw Hill, 1978-81; KMGH-TV, McGraw Hill, reporter, 1981-83; WBBM-TV, CBS, anchor, 1983-86; WFLD-TV, Fox News, anchor, 1986-. **Orgs:** Chicago Asn Black Journalists, 1985-; bd mem, S Central comm Serv, 1993-; Child Abuse Prev Serv, spokeswoman, 1995. **Honors/Awds:** Emmy Awards on Art Achievement, San Diego Chap, 1980; Emmy Awards on Art Achievement, Nat Acad TV Arts & Sci, Chicago Chap, 1985-87, 1993, 1997. **Business Addr:** Anchor, WFLD-TV, Fox-News, 205 N Michigan Ave, Chicago, IL 60601-5911, **Business Phone:** (312)565-5532.*

ROBINSON, RONNIE W
Executive. **Personal:** Born Dec 26, 1942, Louisville, KY; son of Lawrence and Donetta L Smith; married Veronices Gray, Jul 14, 1973; children: Kelli & Ronnie Jr. **Educ:** Ky State Univ, Frankfort, KY, BS, 1964. **Career:** ICI Am Inc, Charlestown, Ind, mgr ballistics lab, 1965-71, mgr EEO, 1971-73, mgr employ, 1973-77; Johnson & Johnson, Chicago, Ill, mgr personel admin, 1977-82; Hart Schaffner & Marx, Chicago, Ill, dir human resources admin, 1982-88, vpres human resources & admin, sr vpres human resources & admin, currently. **Orgs:** Bd mem, Soc Human Resources Profs, 1982-83; bd mem, Cosmopolitan Chamber Com, 1983-; Chicago Urban Affairs Coun, 1983-; chmn, Human Resources Comt, Ill State Chamber Com, 1986-87; personnel comt, Chicago Youth Ctr, 1986-; bd mem, Duncan YMCA, 1987-. **Home Phone:** (312)881-4961. **Business Addr:** Senior Vice President of Human Resources & Administration, Hart Schaffner & Marx, 101 N Wacker Dr, Chicago, IL 60606, **Business Phone:** (312)372-6300.

ROBINSON, ROSALYN KAREN
Lawyer. **Personal:** Born Dec 5, 1946, Norristown, PA; daughter of James H (deceased) and Patricia. **Educ:** Dickinson Col, Carlisle, PA, AB, 1968; Boston Col, Law Sch, Newton, MA, JD, 1973. **Career:** Chemical Bank NY, NY, mgt trainee, officer's asst, 1968-70; Hon Doris M Harris, Ctr Common Pleas, law clerk, 1973-74; Philadelphia Dist Atty's Off, asst dist atty, 1974-79; Pa Dept Aging, chief coun, 1979-83, Gen Coun, dep gen coun, 1983; Commonwealth Pa, Ct Common Pleas, first Judicial Dist, judge, currently. **Orgs:** Treas, Barrister's Asn, 1973-; Philadelphia Bar Asn, 1973-; Pa Bar Asn, 1982-; Am Bar Asn, 1979-83; cls chmn, Dickinson Col Annual Giving, 1984; vpres, Dickinson Col Alumni Coun, 1974-80; Pa Coalition 10 Black Women, 1984-; Harrisburg Chap Links Inc, 1984-; Bd Trustees, Dickinson Col, 1985-; Alpha Kappa Alpha Sorority Inc, Rho Theta Omega Chap, 1990-. **Special Achievements:** One of 79 to watch in 1979, Philadelphia Mag, 1979. *

ROBINSON, DR. RUFUS E
Dean (Education), educator. **Personal:** Born Feb 9, 1941, Baton Rouge, LA; son of Beatrice Jackson. **Educ:** Southern Univ, BA, hist; Webster Univ, MA, pub admin; Howard Univ, PhD, orgn commun. **Career:** Howard Univ, assoc dir off career serv; Johnson C Smith Univ, Charlotte, NC, asst vpres instnl advan; Strayer Univ, Columbia Campus, campus dean, currently. **Military Serv:** USAF, 1964-69.

ROBINSON, RUMEAL JAMES
Basketball player. **Personal:** Born Nov 13, 1966, Mandeville, Jamaica. **Educ:** Univ Mich, attended 1990. **Career:** Basketball player (retired); Atlanta Hawks, guard, 1990-92, NJ Nets, 1992-93; Charlotte Hornets, 1993-94; CBA, Rapid City Thrillers, 1994-95; CBA, Shreveport Crawdads, 1995; CBA, Conn Pride, 1995; Portland TrailBlazers, 1995-97; Los Angeles Lakers, 1996; Phoenix Suns, 1996-97; Detroit Pistons, guard, 1997; European League, KK Zadar, 2001-02; Fortitudo Pallacanestro Bologna, Italy, 2002. **Honors/Awds:** NCAA Championship, 1989; second Team All Am, 1990; Silver Medal, Pan Am Games, 1995. **Special Achievements:** First round pick, No 10, NBA Draft, 1990.

ROBINSON, S YOLANDA
School administrator, educator. **Personal:** Born Oct 1, 1946, Gilliam, WV; daughter of Rudolph V and Lucy M; children: Chad Heath. **Educ:** Franklin Univ, attended 1965; Univ Mass, attended 1981. **Career:** Midwest Inst Equal Educ, admin assist, 1971; Inst Black Community Res & Develop, res coordr, 1980-81; Ohio State Univ, admin secy, 1980-81, prog coordr, 1998; Ohio Youth Advocate Prog, instr; Head Start, family wellness mgr; All Women One Cause, lay health advoc; Columbus Col & Post, writer; Ohio State Univ, Dept Black Studies Extension Ctr, Nat Conf Chair, currently. **Orgs:** Conf chair, Nat Coun Black Studies, 1978-; vpres, Ohio Black Polit Assembly, 1978-81; pres, founder, Cardinal 9 to 5, 1985-86; Ohio State Univ Affirmative Action Comt, 1985; bd mem, Call VAC, 1990; pres, African-Am Triumphs Consortium, 1992-; Columbus Black Women's Health Proj. **Honors/Awds:** President's Award, Nat Coun Black Studies, 1988; Distinguished Diversity Enhancement Award, Ohio State Univ, 1988; Coalition of 100 Black Women, Mwanawake, 1992. **Special Achievements:** Editor: "Research Profiles," OSU Dept of Black Studies, 1982; International Business and Professional Women, 1990; Blue Chip Profile, 1992. **Business Addr:** National Conference Chair, Ohio State University, Department Black Studies Extension Center, 905 Mount Vernon Ave, Columbus, OH 43215, **Business Phone:** (614)253-4620.

ROBINSON, DR. SAMUEL
School administrator. **Personal:** Born Dec 18, 1935, Memphis, TN; son of Omar R Sr (deceased) and Sarah; married Hugh Ella Walker; children: Debra & Charlotte. **Educ:** Tenn State Univ, BS 1956, MS, 1958; Ind Univ, EdD, 1974. **Career:** Lincoln Inst, dean ed, 1964-66; Lincoln Sch, prin, 1967-70; Shawnee High Sch, prin, 1970-73; Lincoln Found, exec dir, 1974-; pres; Bellarmine Univ, exec-in-residence, currently. **Orgs:** Nat exec dir, Phi Beta Sigma Ed Found, 1980-; Sigma Phi Phi, 1983-; bd mem, Presbyterian Health Ed & Welfare Asn, 1982-, Black Achievers Asn, 1980-, Asn Black Found Exec, 1974-, Louisville Presbyterian; chmn, KY Humanities Coun, 1984-; Kentucky Ctr Arts, 1988-; Ky State Bd Educ, 1991; bd trustees, Bellarimme Col, 1990; Outstanding Community Serv, Nat Conf Christians & Jews, 1993; KY Bd Educ; Ky Civilian Aide Sec Army. **Honors/Awds:** Recipient Outstanding Young Man Award, Louisville C C, 1963; Outstanding Young Educator Award, Shelbyville Jr C C, 1966; Disting Service Award-,Zeta Phi Beta, 1974; Outstanding Citizen Award, Louisville Defender, 1975; Comt Service Award, Alpha Kappa Alpha, 1976; Social Action Award, Phi Beta Sigma; Outstanding Black Achiever Award, Louisville, 1980; Distinguish Citizen Award, Alpha Kappa Alpha, 1980; Man of the Year, Sigma Pi Phi, 1986; Achiever of the Year, Black Achievers Asn, 1987; Berea Col Community Service Award, 1986. **Military Serv:** AUS, sp4, 1958-60. **Business Addr:** Executive in Residence, Bellarmine University, 2001 Newburg Rd, Louisville, KY 40205, **Business Phone:** (502)452-8131.

ROBINSON, SANDRA HAWKINS
Lawyer. **Personal:** Born Jul 17, 1951, Lynchburg, VA; daughter of William Sterlon and Mary Alice Baker; divorced; children: Mary Alysia. **Educ:** Oberlin Col, BA, 1973; Howard Univ Grad Sch, attended 1973-75; Catholic Univ Sch Law, JD, 1982. **Career:** Robinson & Robinson, partner, atty, 1985-87; FDL Election CMS, sr atty, 1987-90; Jack H Olender & Assoc PC, sr trial atty, 1990-. **Orgs:** Prog coord, Nat Asn Black Women Attys, 1985-; Nat Bar Asn; Am Bar Asn; pres, Trial Lawyers Asn, Metropolitan Wash; Mar Trial Lawyers Asn; Wash Bar Asn; bd gov, Asn Trial Lawyers Am; vpres, Civil Justice Found; pres, Women's Bar Asn Found; fac, Nat Inst Trial Advocacy; master, Charlotte E Ray Am Inn Ct; pres, Pub Justice Found. **Honors/Awds:** Star of the Bar, Women's Bar Asn; Distinguished Black Woman in the 23rd Annual Scholarship Calendar, Black Women Sisterhood Action; The Pursuit of Justice Award, Am Bar Asn; Presidential Award, Wash Bar Asn; Trial Lawyer of the Year, Trial Lawyers Asn; Charlotte E Ray Award, Greater Wash Area Chap, Women's Div, Nat Bar Asn; Marie Lambert Award, Am Asn Justice Women's Caucus; Presidential Award, Nat Bar Asn; Alumna of the Year, Black Law Students Asn, Catholic Univ Columbus Sch Law. **Home Addr:** 1359 Kalmia Rd NW, Washington, DC 20012, **Home Phone:** (202)291-7057. **Business Addr:** Senior Trial Attorney, Jack H Olender & Associates PC, 888 17th St NW Fl 4, Washington, DC 20006, **Business Phone:** (202)879-7777.

ROBINSON, DR. SANDRA LAWSON
Physician, health services administrator. **Personal:** Born Mar 22, 1944, New Orleans, LA; daughter of Alvin J Lawson and Elvera Martin; married Carl Dayton (divorced); children: Michael David & Carla Marie. **Educ:** Howard Univ Col, Liberal Arts, Wash, DC, BS, 1965; Howard Univ Col Med, Wash, DC, MD, 1969; Health Care Admin, Tulane Univ Sch Pub Health & Tropical Med New Orleans, LA, MPH, 1977; Pediat Intrnshp Childrens Hosp, Nat Med Ctr Dist Columbia, 1969-70; Pediat Resdnc Chldrens Hosp Nat Med Ctr Dist Columbia, 1970-71; Pediatric Residency Fel Ambulatory Care, Univ CA, San Francisco, San Francisco Gen Hosp, 1971-72. **Career:** Neighborhood Health Clin New Orleans, med dir, 1973-77; Ambulatory Care/Outpatient Serv Charity Hosp, dir, 1977-81; Minority Afrs LA State Med Ctr, coordr, 1979; Ambulatory Care Serv Childrens Hosp, dir, 1981-84; LA State Univ & Tulane Univ Sch Med, clin asst prof pediat; Tulane Univ Sch Pub Health & Trop Med, adj asst prof; Dept Health & Human Resources, sec/comnr, 1984-88; Robinson Med Group, vpres, 1988-96; Children's Med Care, pres affil office; C Hosp Med Pract Corp, physician, 1996-. **Orgs:** Med consult to Learning Disabilities Teams Pilot Proj Mission Area Sch Unified Sch Dist,San Francisco, 1971-72; team pediat Family Clin San Francisco Gen Hosp; Med Adv & Sickle Cell Anemia Res Found San Francisco; med consult of Sch & Behavoir Unit Mt Zion Hosp San Francisco, CA; Prvt Practice of Peds San Francisco 1972-73; Proposal Dev Comprehensive Health Serv New Orleans Parish Prison Inmates 1974; Common Health Problem Manual Neighborhood Hlth Clinics 1974; Coordination Preventive Med Prog Nat Med Asn Convention 1974; Ross Roundtable Upper Resp Dis, 1974; Proj Anal Paper New Orleans Neighborhood Health Clinics, 1975; bd mem, Kingsley House, 1976-79; bd mem, Family Serv Soc, 1976-79; consult, Westington Corp Headstart Prog, 1976-80; bd mem, New Orleans Area Bayou River Systms Agcy, 1977-82; Plan Dev Com Health Systms Agency, 1978-82; Comn Use Human Subjects Tulane Univ; bd mem, Urban League Greater New Orleans, 1967-82; bd mem, Isidore Newman Sch, 1978-88; bd admin, Tulane Univ; Robert Wood Johnson "Coverny Kid", nat adv bd, 1998-. **Honors/Awds:** Howard Univ Alumni Region V Award; Black Org for Leadership Develop Outstanding Community Service Award; Woman of the Year, Nat Asn Black Social Workers, 1987; The Scroll of Merit, Nat Med Asn Award, 1988. **Business Addr:** Physician, Children's Hospital Medical Practice Corporation, 298 Henry Clay Ave, New Orleans, LA 70118, **Business Phone:** (504)896-9827.

ROBINSON, SHARON
Writer, baseball executive. **Personal:** Born in Connecticut; daughter of Jackie Robinson and Rachel. **Educ:** Howard Univ, attended 1973; Columbia Univ, attended 1976; Univ Pa, Sch Nursing, post-master's cert. **Career:** Nurse midwife; PUSH, dir, 1985-90; Yale Univ Sch Nursing, asst prof; Major League Baseball, vpres educ programming, currently. Books: Stealing Home: An Intimate Family Portrait by the Daughter of Jackie Robinson, 1996; Jackie's Nine: Jackie Robinson's Value to Live, 2002; Promises to Keep: How Jackie Robinson Changed America, 2004; Safe at Home, 2006. **Orgs:** Vice chmn, Jackie Robinson Found, 1976-; bd trustess, Am Col Nurse-Midwives Found; nat adv comm, Robert Wood Johnson Found, 1998-; United Negro Col Fund & A Better Chance. **Honors/Awds:** Hon degree, Medaille Col, 1998; Hon degree, Dowling Col, 2004; Hon degree, Monmouth Col, 2005. **Business Addr:** Vice President, Educational Programming, Major League Baseball, 12 E 49th St Fl 24, New York, NY 10017, **Business Phone:** (212)826-0808.

ROBINSON, SHARON PORTER
Association executive, chief executive officer, president (organization). **Personal:** Children: one. **Educ:** Univ Ky, Lexington, BA, eng, 1966, MA, curriculum & instruction, 1976, EdD, admin & supv, 1979. **Career:** classroom teacher; Nat Educ Assoc, dir instruction & prof develop, 1980-89, dir res & develop; Jefferson County Educ Consortium, assoc dir; Ky Desegregation Training Inst, grad asst; Nat Bd Prof Teaching Stands, consult; US Dept Educ, Off Educ Res & Improvement, asst secy educ; Educ Testing Serv, vpres state & fed rels, sr vpres & chief oper officer; Am Asn Col Teacher Educ, pres & chief exec officer, currently. **Honors/Awds:** Alumni Hall of Fame, Univ Ky, 1991. **Special Achievements:** First African Am to fill the res & planning post within the Depart of Educ. First African-American woman to serve as the American Association of Colleges for Teacher Education's chief executive officer. **Business Phone:** (202)293-2450.*

ROBINSON, SHAUN
Television news anchorperson, actor. **Personal:** Born Jul 12, 1962, Detroit, MI; daughter of Joanne Oglesby and Wylie. **Educ:** Spelman Col, English/Mass Communs. **Career:** WISN-TV, Milwaukee, Wisc, anchor, reporter; KEYE-TV, Austin Tex, anchor,reporter; WSVN-TV, Miami, Fla, anchor, reporter; Access Hollywood, weekendanchor, currently; TV: "Bruce Almighty", "America's Sweethearts", "Dr.Dolittle 2", "Everybody Hates Chris", "Studio 60 on the Sunset Strip","DIRT", "Charmed", "She Spies", "The Parkers", "The Proud Family", "Half &Half", "Days

of our Lives" & "Any Day Now"; Operation Shock and Awe.. some, 2008; "The Morning Show with Mike & Juliet", 2009. **Orgs:** Nat Asn Black Journalists; Am Fed TV & Radio Artists; Screen Actors Guild. **Honors/Awds:** Media Award, Am Heart Assn; Commendation Award, Am Women in Radio & TV;Austin Bus Journal, Profiles in Power; EMMY, A Grand Night in Harlem, WNBC. **Special Achievements:** Presenter, 15th Annual Soul Train Awards, 2001; Presenter, 16th AnnualSoul Train Awards, 2002; Host, Pre-Show, 59th Golden Globe Awards, 2002;Host, Pre-Show, 75th Annual Academy Awards, 2003. **Business Addr:** Weekend Anchor/Weekday Correspondent, Access Hollywood, 3000 W Alameda Ave, Burbank, CA 91523, **Business Phone:** (818)526-7000.

ROBINSON, SHERMAN
Executive, consultant. **Personal:** Born Sep 16, 1932, Piqua, OH; son of Sherman and Anna Lou; married Beverly J Clark; children: Tod, Tina & Tracy. **Educ:** Cent St Col, attended 1952-53; Ohio Univ, attended 1953-56, attended 1958-59. **Career:** Western Fixture Co, equip dealer, 1959; JG Richards & Assocs, draftsman, designer, vpres, 1961; Saylor, Rhoads Equip Co, designer, draftsman, 1969-70; Sherman Robinson Inc, pres & owner, 1970-. **Orgs:** Past pres, Keystone Optimist Club, 1972-73; bd dirs, Food-service Consults Soc Int, 1992-95; consult, Food Facilities Soc; assoc mem, AIA Rippledale Optimist Club. **Honors/Awds:** Optimist International Award, Keystone, Indianapolis, Ind Chap, 1972-73; Volume Feeding Award, INSTITUTIONS magazine, 1975; Client of the Year Award, Indianapolis Bus Develop Found, 1979; Honorable Mention Award, Constructions Specif Inst, 1982; Outstanding Achievement Award, Ct Leadership Develop, 1983; Governor's Reception Award, Outstanding Bus Develop African Am Community, Indiana Black Expo, 1992-95; Black Businessman Entrepenuer Award, The Links, 1997. **Special Achievements:** Numerous Certificates of Appreciation for speaking engagements and other donated services. **Military Serv:** AUS, sp3, 1956-58. **Business Addr:** President, Owner, Sherman Robinson Inc, 708 Bungalow Ct, Indianapolis, IN 46220, **Business Phone:** (317)257-4485.

ROBINSON, SMOKEY (WILLIAM ROBINSON, JR.)
Executive, musician, business owner. **Personal:** Born Feb 19, 1940, Detroit, MI; son of William Sr; married Frances Glandney; married Claudette Rogers, Nov 7, 1959 (divorced 1985); children: Berry William, Tamla Claudette & Trey. **Educ:** Jr Col. **Career:** Detroit Nightclub, performer; Motown Rec Corp, singer, 1959-60, v pres, 1961-88; Smokey Robinson & The Miracles, rec artist, 1957-72; solo recartist, 1972-; Big Time, exec producer, 1977; "An Evening With Smokey Robinson", 1985; Albums: The Miracles: Hi; We're the Miracles, 1961; Shop Around, 1962; Doin' Mickey's Monkey, 1963; The Fabulous Miracles, 1964; Going to a Go Go, 1964; Away We Go, 1965; Make It Happen, 1968; Spec Occasion, 1969; Time Out, 1970; Four in Blue, 1970; Smokey & the Miracles, 1971; The Miracles, 1977; solo albums: Renaissance, 1973; Smokey, 1973;Pure Smokey, 1974; A Quiet Storm, 1974; City of Angels, 1974; Love Machine, 1975; Smokey's Family Robinson, 1975; Power of the Music, 1977; Deep in My Soul, 1977; Love Breeze, 1978; Warm Thoughts, 1980; Being with You, 1981; Yes It's You, 1981; Touch the Sky, 1983; Essar, 1984; Intimate, 2000; Our Very Best Christmas, 1999; Food for the Spirit, 2004; The Live Collection, 2004; Motown Legends: Shop Around, 2004; Motown Legends: Being With You, 2004; My World: The Definitive Collection, 2005; Legends, 2006; Timeless Love, 2006; Soul Legends, 2006; Gold, 2006; Time Flies When You're Having Fun, 2009; 50th Anniversary Collection, 2006; "American Idol", guest judge, 2003; SFGL Foods Inc, owner & dir, 2004-. **Orgs:** Great Am Smokeout. **Honors/Awds:** Rock & Roll Hall of Fame, 1986; Songwriters Hall of Fame, 1986; Grammy Award for "Just to See Her," 1987; Kennedy Center Honor, 2006; DMus, Howard Univ, 2006; DMus, Berklee Col Music, 2009. **Special Achievements:** Author, Smokey: Inside My Life, 1989. **Business Phone:** (818)500-0420.

ROBINSON, STEVE
Basketball coach. **Personal:** Born Oct 29, 1957; married Lisa; children: Shauna Kiaya, Tarron & Denzel. **Educ:** Radford Univ, BS, health & phys educ, 1981, MS, counsel, 1985. **Career:** Radford Univ, asst coach, 1983-86; Cornell Univ, asst coach, 1986-88; Univ Kans, asst coach, 1988-95, 2002-03; Univ Tulsa, head men's basketball coach, 1995-97; Florida State Univ, head men's basketball coach, 1997-2005; Univ NC, asst coach, currently. **Orgs:** NABC. **Honors/Awds:** Outstanding Young Men of America, 1986; Radford Univ Sports Hall of Fame, 1997; Ferrum Univ Sports Hall of Fame, 1998; Basketball Coach of the Year, Western Athletic Conf, Mountain Div, 1996-97; WAC Mountain Division Coach of the year. **Special Achievements:** First African American coach at Florida State Univ; Only African American coach in the Atlantic Coast Conference. **Business Addr:** Assistant Coach, University of North Carolina, 440 W Franklin St, Chapel Hill, FL 27516, **Business Phone:** (919)962-2211.

ROBINSON, SYLVIA. See BARAKA, AMINA.

ROBINSON, THELMA MANIECE
Educator. **Personal:** Born May 1, 1938, Tuscaloosa, AL; married. **Educ:** Ala State Univ, BS, 1960; Univ Ala Tuscaloosa, MA, 1970, EdS. **Career:** TVA, personnel clerk, examining officer; Florence Bd Educ, guid counr; Coffee High Sch, sr guid counr. **Orgs:** Am Personnel & Guid Asn; Am Sch Counr Asn; AL PGA & AL SCA; St sec for ALPGA; Nat Educ Asn; AEA; Florence Educ Asn; pres, Delta Sigma Theta Sororoty; Ala Asn Univ Women; Florence League Women Voters; Lauderdale Co Chap, ARC, treas; vpres, Muscle Shoals Asn Ment Health; Ala Coun Asn. **Honors/Awds:** Chosen Outstanding Sec educr, 1974.

ROBINSON, THOMAS DONALD
Health services administrator, chief executive officer, vice president (organization). **Educ:** Marshall Univ, BBA, 1964; Georgia State Univ, MHA, 1977. **Career:** Welch Emergency Hosp, adminr, 1977-80; Pkwy Regional Med Ctr, asst adminr, 1980-84; Newport News Gen Hosp, adminr, 1984-85; Tyrone Hosp, chief exec officer, 1985-92; Penn St Univ, Continuing Educ Faculty, 1988-; Quoram Health Resources, Robinson Group, Pittsburgh Office, group, vpres. **Orgs:** Bd Tyrone Salvation Army, 1986; pres, Tyrone Rotary Club, 1986; pres, Tyrone Area Chamber Com, 1987; bd Blair County United Way, 1987; pub affairs comm Hospital Assoc Western PA, 1987; reg adv bd, Mellon Bank; Blair County Human Servs bd; adv bd, Mc Dowell Co Bus; adv bd, Marshall Univ. **Honors/Awds:** Fel, Am Col Healthcare Execs, 1981.

ROBINSON, VERNEDA
Manager, president (organization). **Personal:** Born Dec 17, 1960, Memphis, TN; daughter of Rev CL Bachus and Wilma; married Curtis Robinson, Mar 30, 1991; children: Bria & Bryan. **Educ:** Washburn Univ, BBA, 1985; Webster, Univ, MA, 1992, MBA, 1995. **Career:** Western Resources Inc, vp customer serv, 1990-94; Miss Gas Energy, vp customer serv & acct, 1994; V Robinson & Co Inc, pres & chief exec officer, 1995-2001; Swope Community Enterprise Serv, chief operating officer, 2001-. **Orgs:** Bd mem, Jr Achievement Middle Am; bd mem, Gem Theater;, bd mem, Kans City Pub TV; bd mem, Negro Leagues Baseball Mus; Nat Asn Women Bus Owners; Kans City friends Alvin Riley; Greater Kans city Coun; Minority Supplier Coun; bd dir, YouthNet. **Honors/Awds:** 'New Business of the Year', Minority Enterprize Develop, 1997. **Special Achievements:** Featured by Fox 4 News, Women On the Move Segment, 1997. **Business Addr:** Chief Operating Officer, Swope Community Enterprises, 4001 Blue Pkwy Suite 270, Kansas City, MO 64130-2807, **Business Phone:** (816)923-5800.

ROBINSON, VIRGIL, JR.
Banker. **Educ:** Grambling State Univ; Univ Oklahoma-Norman; Am Inst Banking. **Career:** Liberty Bank & Trust, exec vpres; Jefferson Guaranty Bank Metairie, sr vpres; Dryades Savings Bank, pres & chief exec officer. **Orgs:** Bd dir, La Recovery Authority; La Bd Regents; Am Inst Banking; Bur Govt Res; New Orleans & River Region Chamber Com; New Orleans Found; Urban League Greater New Orleans.

ROBINSON, DR. WALKER LEE
Educator, neurosurgeon. **Personal:** Born Oct 13, 1941, Baltimore, MD; son of Wilma L Walker and Edward F Robinson; married Mae Meads, Apr 9, 1966; children: Kimberly Yvette & Walker Lee Jr. **Educ:** Morgan State Col, BS, 1962; Univ Md, MD, 1970; Univ London, attended, 1975; Univ Rochester, attended. **Career:** Univ Md Med Sch, Baltimore, MD, from asst prof to assoc prof, 1976-97, acting chmn. Div Neurosurg, 1989-92; Nat. Cancer Inst, consult, Md., 1985-91; Seton Hall Sch Grad Med Educ, Pediat Neurosurgeons, head; Carle Clin Asn & Carle Found Hosp, Urbana, Ill, Div Neurol Surg, head; Carle Spine Inst, bd cert neurosurgeon, currently; prof neurosci, Seton Hall Univ Sch Grad Med Educ. **Orgs:** Pres, Clarence S Green, Md neurosurg Soc, 1984-87; bd dirs, Urban Cardiol Res Ctr, 1986-91; pres, Baltimore Urban Serv Found, 1986-87; bd dirs, Variety Club Baltimore, 1988; pres, Black Fac & Staff Asn, Univ Md, 1989-90; Am Soc Pediat Neurosurg, Univ Md Med Systems, Cancer Comt, 1989-94; Int Soc Pediat Neurosurg; fel, Am Col Surgeons; fel, Am Acad Pediat; Am Soc Pediat Neurol; Am Med Asn; Am Asn Neurosurgeons; Congress Neurol Surgeons. **Honors/Awds:** Paul Harris fel, Rotary Int, 1989; Honoree, AFRAM Expo-City Baltimore, 1988 & 1997; Distinguished Alumnus Award, Fund Educ Excellence, 1991; Living Legend Honoree, African Am heritage Soc, 1995; fel, Stroke Coun, Am Heart Asn; fel, Am Col Surgeons; fel, Am Acad Pediat; consult, NIH, NCI, CDC. **Business Addr:** Neurosurgeon, Carle Spine Institute, 602 W University, Urbana, IL 61801, **Business Phone:** (217)383-6555.

ROBINSON, WENDY RAQUEL
Actor, movie producer. **Personal:** Born Jul 25, 1967, Los Angeles, CA; married Marco Perkins, Jan 1, 2003. **Educ:** Howard Univ, BA. **Career:** Actror; TV series: "MANTIS", 1994; "Me & the Boys", 1994; "The Steve Harvey Show", 1996-2002; "Baby Blues", 2000-02; "A Baby Blues Christmas Special", voice,2002; "Cedric the Entertainer Presents", 2002; "Heroes of Black Comedy", 2002; "All of Us", 2004-05; "Girlfriends", 2006; "The New Adventures of Old Christine", 2006; "Family Guy", 2007; "The Game", 2006-08; Films: The Walking Dead, 1995;A Thin Line Between Love & Hate, 1996; Ringmaster, 1998; Miss Congeniality, 2000; Two Can Play That Game, 2001; Mind Games, 2003; With or Without You, 2003; Reflections: A Story of Redemption, 2004; Squirrel Man, 2005; Rebound, 2005; Something New, 2006; Angels Can't Help But Laugh, 2007; Keys, producer, 2007; Contradictions of the Heart, 2009; Amazing Grace Conservatory, founder & artistic dir, currently. **Honors/Awds:** Nominee for Image Award 6 times. **Business Phone:** (323)732-4283.*

ROBINSON, WILL
Basketball coach, athlete, educator. **Personal:** Born Jun 3, 1911, Wadesboro, NC. **Educ:** West Va State Col, attended; Univ Mich, Master's Degree. **Career:** Sports manager (retired); Cass Tech High Sch, teacher; Miller High Sch, teacher; Pershing High Sch, teacher; Ill State Univ, educr & coach; Detroit Pistons, admin asst gen mgr, asst pres basketball oper. **Honors/Awds:** Mich Sports Hall of Fame, 1982; Mich Jewish Sports Hall of Fame, 1995; Alvin N Foon Award, 1995; The Mich High Sch Coaches Hall of Fame; The W Va State Hall of Fame; The Ill State Hall of Fame; The Upper OH Valley Dapper Dan Hall of Fame; The Afro-Am Sports Hall of Fame; Mich High Sch Basketball Hall of Fame. **Special Achievements:** First African Am head coach in top coll basketball.

ROBINSON, WILLIAM
Government official, real estate agent. **Personal:** Born Jun 30, 1920, Harrisburg, PA; son of Saddie and Earnest; married Beatrice S; children: Paula, Evelyn & Nancy. **Educ:** Lincoln Univ, BA; Pa State Exten Courses, acct; Air Force & Army, mgt courses. **Career:** US Civil Serv Air Force & Army, supply & logistics mgt; real estate sales, currently. **Orgs:** Former mem, Harrisburg City Coun; former mem, Vestry St Stephens; Cathedral Dioces Cent Pa; Bd Realtors Pa; Nal Asn Realtors; Harristown Bd Dirs; Comn Ministry Episcopal Dioces Cent Pa; life mem, NAACP; life mem, Omega Psi Phi; lay dep, 1985/1988, Gen Nat Conv Episcopal Church; bd mem, Pa Coun Churches; trustee, Lincoln Univ, Pa. **Home Phone:** (717)236-6759. **Business Addr:** Real Estate Agent, 2309 Edgewood Rd, Harrisburg, PA 17104, **Business Phone:** (717)236-6759.

ROBINSON, WILLIAM, JR. See ROBINSON, SMOKEY.

ROBINSON, WILLIAM ANDREW
Administrator, physician. **Personal:** Born Jan 31, 1943, Philadelphia, PA; son of Colonial and Lillian; married Jacqueline E Knight; children: William Jr & David. **Educ:** Hampton Inst, BA, 1964; Meharry Med Col, MD, 1971; Johns Hopkins Sch Hygiene & Pub Health, MPH, 1973; Nat Bd Med Examiners, dipl. **Career:** George W Hubbard Hosp, Nashville, emergency rm physician, 1972; US Food & Drug Admin, reviewing med officer, 1973-75; Health Resources & Servs Admin, med officer, 1975-80, dep bur dir, 1980-87, chief med officer, 1987-89; Pub Health Serv, Off Minority Health, dir, 1989-91; Health Resources & Serv Admin, chief med officer, 1991-, actg adminr, 1993-94, Ctr Qual, dir, 1997-. **Orgs:** Delta Omega Hon Pub Health Soc, 1993; Am Pub Health Asn; Sr Execs Asn; Fed Physicians Asn; Am Acad Family Physicians, Nat Med Asn; AMA. **Honors/Awds:** Special Recognition Award, Pub Health Serv, 1980; Sr Exec Serv Award, US Govt, 1984; HRSA Administrators Award for Excellence, 1987; Distinguished Alumnus of Medicine, Meharry Med Col, 1991; Hildrus Poindexter Memorial Award, 1994. **Military Serv:** AUS, Med Serv Corps, capt, 1964-67; Nat Defense Medal; Army Commendation Medal, 1967. **Home Addr:** 16608 Frontenac Terr, Rockville, MD 20855, **Home Phone:** (301)869-1165. **Business Addr:** Chief Medical Officer, Center for Quality Director, Health Resources & Services Administration, Rm 7-100 5600 Fishers Lane, Rockville, MD 20857, **Business Phone:** (301)443-0458.

ROBINSON, WILLIAM EARL
Government official, consultant. **Personal:** Born Nov 18, 1940, Morton, MS; son of P B and Gladys; divorced; children: Jacqueline & William E II. **Educ:** Miss Valley State Univ, Soc Sci & Pol Sci, 1962. **Career:** Consultant (retired), Government official; N Las Vegas Chamber Com, hon dir, 1972-82; N Las Vegas City, Councilman, 1983-; N Las Vegas, Mayor Pro Tempore, currently; Sch Success Monitor; Clark County Sch Dist, outreach consult. **Orgs:** N Las Vegas Redevelop Adv Comm; hon dir, N Las Vegas Chamber Com, 1973-80; Founding mem, N Las Vegas Pop Warner Football, 1973-80; Gaming policy comn State Nev, 1973-81, 1975-81; pres, N Las Vegas Jaycees, 1974; chmn, N Las Vegas Fair Show Family Yr, 1975-76; US & Int Jaycees; chmn, Libr, Pks & Recreation Adv Bd, 1977-80; dir, Nev Jaycees Chaplin, Nev Nat, 1976-78; life mem, US & Int Jaycees JCI Senator, 1977; S Nev Comn Gov Job Training Bd; Nat League Cities Community & Econ Develop, 1983-88; Nev Develop Authority Alt Bd, 1983-97; Chmn, Real Property Adv Bd; Econ Opportunity bd, 1983-97, exec mem, 1997-04; chmn, Clark Co Health Dist, 1983-97; chmn, Crime Prevention Task Force, 1984-97; N Las Vegas Housin Authority, 1985-;secy pres, vpres, Nev League Cities, 1987-88; bd mem, N Las Vegas Lib, 1995-; Nev Develop Authority exec bd, 1997-; exec mem, econ Opportunity bd, 1997-04; Las Vegas conv & Visitor's Authority bd, 2001-; chmn, bd dirs, N Las Vegas Dem Club; chmn, Crime Prevention Task Force; Clark co Health Dist; Environ Quality Policy Review bd; Job Training bd; N Las Vegas Lib Dist; bd, Southern Nev Dist bd Health & Southern Nev Comn;

bd mem, N Las Vegas Redevelopment Agency; past pres, Nev League Cities & Municipalities; Community & Econ Develop Comt Small Cities Nat League Cities, currently; Las Vegas Convention & Visitor's Authority Bd Mem, 2001-; mem, Work Force Investment Bd; mem, Criminal Justice Advisory Comn. **Honors/Awds:** Jaycee of the Year, N Las Vegas Jaycees, 1972, 1974, 1975; Man of the Yr, N Las Vegas Jaycees, 1974, 1976; Who's Who Outstanding Young Men of Am, 1976; Public Official of the Year, NV League Cities, 1989. **Business Phone:** (702)633-1336.

ROBINSON, WILLIAM PETERS, JR.
State government official. **Personal:** Born Oct 14, 1942, Washington, DC; son of William P Sr and Agnes R Watson Butler; married Sylvia F Thompson, 1966; children: William P III, Trevor J, Justin M & Danica A. **Educ:** Morehouse Col, BA, 1964; Harvard Univ, LLB, 1967. **Career:** Commonwealth's Attorney's Off, asst, 1968-70; asst atty gen, 1970-72; Mason & Robinson Ltd, partner, 1972-78; Robinson, Eichler, Zaleski & Mason, partner, 1978-; State Va, Dist 90, state rep, 1981-. **Orgs:** Va State Legis Black Caucus; Friends Norfolk Juvenile & Domestic Rels Ct; Norfolk City Dem Comt & Conf Southern Legislators; Indus Develop Authority Norfolk; Tidewater Area Bus & Contractors Asn; Twin City Bar Asn; Norfolk-Portsmouth Bar Asn; Old Dominion Bar Asn; Va State Bar Asn; Va Trial Lawyers Asn; Asn Trial Lawyers Am; Southeastern Va Adv Coun Arts; Va Asn Black Elected Officials; Va House Delegates. **Special Achievements:** Author: "Handling Narcotic Cases," Law Enforcement Training Manual, 1979.

ROBINSON-IVY, JACQUELINE
Banker, vice president (organization). **Career:** Northern Trust Bank, vpres, currently. **Honors/Awds:** School Leadership Award. **Business Addr:** Vice President, Northern Trust Bank, 50 S LaSalle B-7, Chicago, IL 60675, **Business Phone:** (312)630-6000.

ROBINSON-JACOBS, KAREN DENISE
Journalist. **Personal:** Born Aug 21, 1956, Chicago, IL; daughter of Dymple Orita McIntyre and S Benton; married Ralph M. **Educ:** Univ Ill, Champaign, IL, BS, jour, 1979; Univ Wis, Milwaukee, Milwaukee, WI, 1985. **Career:** The Champaign News-Gazette, Champaign, IL, reporter, 1977-80; Milwaukee Jour, Milwaukee, WI, asst metro ed, asst state ed, n suburban ed & reporter, 1980-89; Los Angeles Times, Los Angeles, CA, asst metro ed, 1989-91, Times New Media Unit, assoc ed; Dallas Morning News, contributor, currently. **Orgs:** Bd dirs, Black Journalists Asn Southern Calif, 1991-; vpres, Wis Black Media Asn, 1982-89; bd dirs, Hansberry Sands Theatre Co, 1986-89; Delta Sigma Theta Sorority, 1976-; vol, United Negro Col Fund, 1988-; chairperson, Minority Ed Caucus: Los Angeles Times, 1990-. **Honors/Awds:** Black Achiever Award, YMCA, 1986. **Home Phone:** (818)769-1970. **Business Addr:** Contributor, Dallas Morning News, PO Box 655237, Dallas, TX 75265, **Business Phone:** (214)977-8222.

ROBINSON PEETE, HOLLY
Actor, singer, writer. **Personal:** Born Sep 18, 1964, Philadelphia, PA; daughter of Matt Robinson and Dolores; married Rodney Peete, Jun 10, 1995; children: Rodney James, Ryan Elizabeth, Robinson James & Roman. **Educ:** Sarah Lawrence Col. **Career:** Films: Howard the Duck, 1986; This Is the Life; TV series: Booker, 1989-90; ABC TGIF, 1990; 21 Jump Street, 1987-91; Hanging W/ Mr Cooper, 1992-97; For Your Love, 1998; One on One, 2001-02; My Wonderful Life, 2002; Like Family, 2003-04; The Honeymooners, 2005; Three's Co, 2005; Hello Larry, 2006; Anything But Love, 2006; Fired Up, 2006; Love Inc, 2005-06; Football Wives, 2007; Matters of Life & Dating, 2007; TV movies: Dummy, 1979; The Jacksons: An American Dream, 1992; Killers in the House, 1998; After All, 1999; Good Day Live, 2004; Earthquake, 2004; Love Inc, 2005; Speed-Dating, 2009. **Orgs:** Owner, HollyRod Found. **Special Achievements:** Proud Hands, 2008. **Business Addr:** Actress, William Morris Agency, 1 William Morris Pl, Beverly Hills, CA 90212, **Business Phone:** (310)859-4000.

ROBINSON-WALKER, MARY P.
Executive, dancer. **Personal:** Born in Pittsburgh, PA; daughter of William and Eula; divorced. **Educ:** Iron City Col; Rose Demars Legal Sec Sch; French Inst; Henry George Sch Social Socs; Hunter Col. **Career:** Executive, dancer (retired); Am Comn Africa, secy, 1960-64; Artist CivilRights Asst Fund, spec proj dir, 1965-66; Savings Bank Asn NY, sec,1967-68; Metro Applied Res Ctr, secy, 1968-70; Black Econ Res Ctr, adminasst, 1970-76; Pearl Bailey Review, Phillip-Fort Dancers, prof dancer,dance instr; Ctrs Reading & Writing, NY Pub Libr. **Orgs:** Emcee Comn Discrimination Housing; bd dir, Harlem Philharmonic Soc, 1969-;co-chmn, Am Red Cross, Harlem Div, 1974-; admin asst, 21st Century Found;Cent Baptist Church, 1993-.

ROBISON, LOUIS
Educator. **Personal:** Born Sep 9, 1950, Miami, FL; son of Rudolph Robison and Joanne Miller; married Yvette McIntosh, Jul 10, 1982; children: Louis Audra, Shoneji, Carta & Maureik. **Educ:** Florida A & M Univ, BS, 1972; Fisk Univ, MA, 1974; Univ South Florida, EdD, 1997. **Career:** Sch Board of Sarasota Co, principal, 1976-96, 2000-01; Correctional Services Corp, vice pres, 1996-99; The LAYR Group, pres & chief exec officer, 2000-. **Orgs:** Phi Delta Kappa, 1986-; Florida A & M Alumni Assoc, life member, 1995-; Omega Psi Phi Fraternity Inc, 1986-; Sigma Pi Phi Fraternity Inc, membership chair. **Honors/Awds:** Sarasota Jaycees, Outstanding Young Educator, 1986; Omega Psi Phi Fraternity, Omega Man of the Year, 1996; Riverview High School, First Among Equals, 2001. **Special Achievements:** Author: Effects of One-on-One Mentoring on African American Middle School Males, 1997.

ROCHE, JOYCE M
Marketing executive. **Personal:** Born in New Orleans, LA. **Educ:** Dillard Univ, BS, math educ, 1970, hon degree; Columbia Univ, MBA, 1972; Stanford Univ, Sr Exec Prog Grad, 1991; North Adams State Col, hon degree. **Career:** Carson Inc, pres & coo, 1996-98; Southern New England Telecommunications Corp, dir, 1997-98; AT&T Inc, dir, 1998-2000;Anheuser-Busch Companies Inc, dir; Federated Dept Stores Inc, dir; Tupperware Corp, dir; Girls Inc, pres & chief exec officer, 2000-. **Orgs:** Corp Governance & Nominating Comt & Pub Policy & Environ Affairs Comt. **Honors/Awds:** 21 Women of Power & Influence in Corp Am, 1991; 40 Most Powerful Black Executives, Black Enterprise, 1994; Business Week, Top Managers to Watch, 1998; Legacy Award, Black Enterprise, 2006; Distinguished Alumna Award, Columbia Univ Women in Bus, 2007. **Special Achievements:** Featured on the cover of Fortune, 1997.

ROCHESTER, GEOF
Executive. **Personal:** Born Sep 20, 1959, St Michael, Barbados; son of Edric G Rochester and Elma I Rochester. **Educ:** Georgetown Univ, BS, BA, 1981; Univ Pa, Wharton Sch, MBA, 1985. **Career:** Procter & Gamble, sales, Folgers Coffee, 1981-83, prod mgr, Bain de Soleil, Oil Olay, Clearasil, 1985-89; Marriott Hotels, dir bus transient mkt, 1989-90; Radisson Hotels, sr vpres mkt, 1990-95; Comcast Cable Commun Inc, sr vpres sales & mkt, 1995-98; Tivo, vpres mkt, 1999; ISun Networks, chief mkt officer; Showtime Networks, sr vpres mkt; World Wrestling Entertainment, exec vpres, currently. **Orgs:** Bd gov, Georgetown Univ Alumni, adv coun, 1990-92; bd dirs, Hoya Hoop Club, 1990-92. **Business Phone:** (203)352-8600.

ROCHESTER, DR. MATTILYN T
School administrator. **Personal:** Born May 14, 1941, Chester, SC; married Enoch B Rochester, Aug 18, 1963; children: Enoch B II & Mattilyn C. **Educ:** Bennett Col, BS, 1962; Glassboro State, MA, 1966; Temple Univ, PhD, 1985. **Career:** Sch Administrator (retired); John T Williams Jr High Sch, math teacher, 1962-63; Burlington City Dist, fifth grade teacher, 1964-76; Perry L Drew Sch, asst prin, 1976-77; Wilbur Watts Middle Sch, vice prin, 1977-79; Robert Stacy Sch, prin, 1979-82; Captain James Lawrence Sch, prin, 1982-86; Burlington City Sch Dist, high sch prin, 1986-90. **Orgs:** Am Asn Sch Admin; NJ Asn Sch Admin; Camden County Asn Sch Admin; Asn Supv & Curriculum Develop; Nat Congress Parents & Teachers Asn; Phi Delta Kappa; gen bd, Nat Coun Churches Christ,; Burlington Kiwanis Club; Acad Advan Teaching Mgt; Nat Supt Acad; Am Asn Sch Admin; exec secy, Woman's Home & Overseas Missionary Soc, African Methodist Episcopal Zion Church. **Honors/Awds:** Principal, Supervisor & Adminstrator Award, NJ Sch Dist, District Superintendent's Award, Letter of Elgibility, Pa Sch Dist.

ROCHON, LELA (LELA ROCHON QUINONES)
Actor. **Personal:** Born Apr 17, 1964, Los Angeles, CA; daughter of Samuel and Zelma; married Antoine Fuqua. **Educ:** Calif State Univ, BA, communs. **Career:** Fred Amsel & Associates Inc, modeling: Spudette Bud Lite TV com; dancer: music videos for Lionel Richie, Luther Vandross, & Levert; Tv appearances: "The Cosby Show"; "Amen'; "Facts of Life"; "21 Jumpstreet"; "A Bunny's Tale"; "The Division, 2001'; films: Harlem Nights, 1989; Boomerang, 1992; Waiting to Exhale, 1995; The Chamber, 1996; Gang Related, 1997; The Big Hit, 1998; Knock Off, 1998; Why Do Fools Fall in Love, 1998; Any Given Sunday, 1999; Labor Pains, 2000; First Daughter, 2004; Running Out of Time in Hollywood, 2006; Balancing the Books, 2008. **Business Phone:** (310)550-4000.

ROCK, CHRIS (CHRISTOPHER JULIUS ROCK, III)
Actor, comedian, singer. **Personal:** Born Feb 7, 1965, Andrews, SC; son of Julius (deceased) and Rosalie; married Malaak Compton, Nov 23, 1996; children: Lola Simone & Zahra Savannah. **Career:** Actor, producer, director, singer; Films: Beverly Hills Cop II, 1987; I'm Gonna git You Sucka, 1988; Comedy's Dirtiest Dozen, 1989; New Jack City, 1991; Boomerang, 1992; Beverly Hills Ninja, 1997; CB4, co-producer, 1993; Panther, 1995; The Immortals, 1995; Sgt. Bilko, 1996; Lethal Weapon 4, 1998; Dogma, 1999; Spin Doctor, 2000; Nurse Betty, 2000; Down to Earth, exec producer, 2001; AI, 2001; Pootie Tang, producer, 2001; Osmosis Jones, 2001; Jay & Silent Bob Strike Back, 2001; Bad Company, 2002; You'll Never Wiez in This Town Again, 2002; Head of State, producer & dir, 2003; Paparazzi, 2004; The Longest Yard, 2005; I Think I Love My Wife, producer & dir, 2007; You Don't Mess with the Zohan, 2008; TV series: "Saturday Night Live", 1990-93; In Living Color", 1993-94; Ike Turner & Hooch, 1993; Dirty Dozens Tournament of Champions, 1994; "Happily Ever After: Fairy Tales for Every Child", 1995; The Moxy Show", 1995; "Billboard Music Awards", host, 1996; "The Chris Rock Show," 1997-2001; "Chris Rock: Bigger & Blacker"; "given star on Hollywood Walk of Fame", 2003; Exec producer: Chris Rock: Big Ass Jokes, 1994; Chris Rock: Bring the Pain, 1996; "The Chris Rock Show", 1997; Chris Rock: Bigger & Blacker, 1999; Best of the Chris Rock Show, 1999; Chris Rock: Never Scared, 2004; Chris Rock: Kill the Messenger, 2008; Good Hair, 2008; Everybody Hates Chris, 2009; Albums: Born Suspect, 1992; Roll with the New, 1997; Death at a Funeral (post production). **Honors/Awds:** Numerous honors & awards including CableAce Award, 1995 & 1997; Emmy Award, 1997 & 1999; Grammy awards for best spoken album, 1998 & 2000, forbest comedy album, 2006; Blockbuster Entertainment Award, 1999; AmericanComedy Award, 2000; ShoWest Awards, Comedy Star of the Year, 2001;presented star on Hollywood Walk of Fame, 2003; Black EntertainmentTelevision Comedy Awards, 2005; Kid's Choice Awards, USA, 2006. **Special Achievements:** Author of Rock This!, 1998. **Business Addr:** Actor, Writer, Director, c/o Home Box Office Inc, 1100 Avenue of the Americas, New York, NY 10036, **Business Phone:** (212)512-1000.*

ROCKETT, DAMON EMERSON
Executive. **Personal:** Born Nov 13, 1938, Chicago, IL; married Darlene Sykes; children: Deborah & Sean Damon. **Educ:** Drake Univ, BS/BA, 1960. **Career:** Allstate Ins Co, claims super, 1964-69; City Harvey, comn pub health & safety; Ill Bell Telephone Co, bus off mgr, 1969-80, phone ctr mgr, 1980-81, staff-assessment ctr, 1981-82, community rels mgr; S Suburban Col, acad skills adv, transition adv, currently. **Orgs:** Pres, Harvey Rotary Club, 1971-80; S Suburban Human Rels Comt, 1973; bd mem & policy comn chmn, Thornton Commiunity Col, 1975-79; bd mem, CEDA, 1980; YMCA Task Force, 1984; Rotary Club Park Forest, 1984-; S Suburban Asn Com & Indust, 1984-; S Suburban Mayors & Managers Asn, 1984-; bd mem, Red Cross, 1985; chmn, African Relief Campaign 1985; Nat Asn Advan Colored People; adv bd mem, W Haywood Burns Inst, currently. **Honors/Awds:** Ten Outstanding Young People, Harvey Jaycees, 1975; Outstanding Citizen, UHURU Black Student Orgn, Thornton Community Col, 1979; Outstanding Citizen, S Suburban Chamber Com & Indus, 1979. **Business Addr:** Academic Skills Advisor, South Suburban College, 15800 S State St, South Holland, IL 60473-1200, **Business Phone:** (708)596-2000.

ROCKWELL, KARYN. See PARSONS, KARYN.

RODDY, HOWARD W
Health services administrator, administrator, vice president (organization). **Personal:** Born Feb 28, 1950, Nashville, TN; son of Howard Walden and Marie Bright; married Donna Norwood; children: Howard Carthie & John Travis. **Educ:** Austin Peay State Univ, BS, chem, 1971; East TN State Univ, MS, environ health admin, 1974. **Career:** Chattanooga-Hamilton Co Health Dept, environmentalist, dir vector control proj, 1971-76; Alton Park/Dodson Ave Comm Health Ctrs, asst admin planning/evaluation, 1976-81; Chattanooga Hamilton Co Health Dept, adminr/dir, 1981-98; Mem Health Care Syst, vpres, Healthy Comm Initiative, currently. **Orgs:** Am Pub Health Asn, 1977-98; Ten Pub Health Asn, 1981-; bd, Chattanooga-Hamilton County Air Pollution Control Bur, 1983-96; treas, Leadership Chattanooga Alumni Asn, 1985-89; bd exec comm., Chattanooga Area Urban League, 1986-93; bd, United Way Greater Chattanooga, 1987-92, 1995-97; pres, Friends the Festival Inc, 1991-92; pres, Tenn Pub Health Asn, 1991-92; bd ber, Chattanooga Venture, 1991-96; bd, East TN Area Health Educ Ctr, 1991-97, pres, 1993-95; First vpres, Southern Health Asn, 1995, 1998; 100 Black Men Am Inc-Chattanooga Chapter, 1992-; pres, Develop Corp, Orchard Knob, 1995-99; bd ber, Volunteer Community Sch, 1993-96; Chancellor's roundtable Univ Tenn Chattanooga, 1991-94; bd, Univ Chattanooga Found, 1997-; bd, Community Found Greater Chattanooga; bd chair, Alexian Brothers Community Serv Adv Bd, 1998-02; bd, Chattanooga Trust Pub Land, 1998-, bd, First Things First, 1999-; bd, Friends Chickamauga & Chattanooga Nat Military Park, 2000-; bd, YMCA Metro Chattanooga, 2000-; adv bd, Salvation Army Chattanooga, 2000-; bd, Tenn Valley Fed Credit Union, 2000-; bd, Allied Arts Greater Chattanooga, 2001; bd, E Tenn State Univ Found, 2002-; bd, Alexian Brothers Southeast, 2003-; bd, Regional Health Coun, 2003-. **Honors/Awds:** Omega Man of the Year, Kappa Iota Chapter Omega Psi Phi Frat Inc, 1981; Omega Citizen of the Year, 1992; Honorary Staff Mem State Tenn 28th Dist Adv Comm, 1982; Distinguised Service Award, Tenn Pub Health Asn, 1997; MD Pub Health Career Award, R H Hutcheson, Sr, 1995; Creating Healthier Communities Fellow, Health Forum/Am Hosp Asn. **Business Addr:** Vice President, Memorial Health Care System, 2525 deSales Ave, Chattanooga, TN 37404, **Business Phone:** (423)495-8686.

RODEZ, ANDREW LAMARR
Police chief. **Personal:** Born Oct 9, 1931, Chicago, IL; married Patricia Lander; children: Angelina, Andy, Rita. **Educ:** Va Union Univ, AB; Nebr Ill State Univ, MA; Mich State Univ, PhD; FBI Nat Acad NW Traffic Inst, dipl. **Career:** Off-The-Street-Boys Club, group worker, 1956-57; Cook County Welfare Dept, case

worker, 1957-58; Evanston Police Dept, police officer, 1958; Chicago Bd Educ, teacher, 1958-64; Benton Harbor, chief police, 1973-79; Benton Harbor Area Sch Dist, asst prin, 1979-82; Maywood Police Dept, chief police, 1982-. **Orgs:** Pres, Task ForceYouth Motivation, 1970; charter mem, vpres, Nat Org Black Law Enforcement Reg IV, 1984; Kappa Alpha Psi; NW Univ Traffic Inst Alumni; FBI Nat Acad Alumni Asn; Phi Delta Kappa Ed; Ill Asn Chiefs Police; West Suburban Chiefs Police; Nat Asn Advan Colored People. **Honors/Awds:** All CIAA Football &Track, 1951-52; Negro Col All-Am, 1952; Outstanding Alumni Award, Kappa Alpha Psi, 1968; Outstanding Citizen Award, Nat Asn Advan Colored People, 1970; Model Cities Award, 1974; Bicent Award Lake Mich Col, 1976. **Business Addr:** Chief of Police, Maywood Police Dept, 125 S 6th Ave, Maywood, IL 60153.

RODGERS, ANTHONY RECARIDO, SR.
Law enforcement officer. **Personal:** Born Apr 2, 1951, Jacksonville, FL; son of Clara Lee Maddox Washington and Clarence; divorced; children: Anthony Jr, Martisha, Edward & Eric. **Educ:** Fla Jr Col, Jacksonville, Fla, 1971-72; NE Fla Criminal Justice Educ & Training Ctr, 1973. **Career:** Duval Co Sheriffs Off, Jacksonville, Fla, sch attendance officer, abandoned property officer, cert radar operator, Dep Sheriff, field training officer, 1973-, honor guard, 1973-, sch resource officer, 1990-; PAL officer, 1996-. **Orgs:** Jacksonville Urban League, 1973; pres, Jacksonville Brotherhood Police Officers Inc, 1978; pres, Bliss Sertoma Club, 1979; treas, Viking Athletic Booster Club Raines High Sch, 1980; pres, Jacksonville Brotherhood Police Officers Inc, 1981-91 Jacksonville Job Corps Community Rels Coun, 1983; Moncrief Improv Asn, 1984; JUST US Comn Community Prob, 1986; Fla Community Col Jacksonville Adv Bd New Direction, 1987; charter mem, 100 Black Men Jacksonville, 1992; bd dirs, NE Fla Community Action Agency Inc, 1992; pres, Edward Waters Col, Tiger Athletic Booster Club, 1994; pres, Jacksonville Br, Nat Asn Advan Colored People, 1995-96, vpres; vpres, Southern Region Nat Black Police Asn, 1996. **Honors/Awds:** Community Service Award, Oper Respect, 1981; Outstanding Service Award, NW Jacksonville Sertoma Club, 1984; Community Service Award, NE Fla Community Action Agency, 1984; Achievement Award, Nat Black Police Asn Southern Region, 1985; Charlie Sea Police Officer of the Year, Jacksonville Brotherhood Police Officers, 1988; Community Service Award Role Model, El Bethel El Divine Holiness Church, 1989; Sallye Mathis Community Service Award, Jacksonville Br, Nat Asn Advan Colored People, 1989; Principal's Alumni Award, William M Raines Sr High Sch, 1990; Southern Region Achievement Award, Nat Black Police Asn Inc, 1991; Coalition for Respect, First Civil Rights Award, 1992; Civil Rights Award, Jacksonville Br, Nat Asn Advan Colored People, Rutledge Pearson, 1996. **Home Addr:** 5720 Oprey St, Jacksonville, FL 32208. **Business Addr:** Deputy Sheriff, Duval County Sheriffs Office, Police Mem Bldg 501 E Bay St Suite 204, Jacksonville, FL 32202, **Business Phone:** (904)630-0500.

RODGERS, DR. AUGUSTUS
Educator. **Personal:** Born Jan 27, 1945, Columbia, SC; son of William Augustus and Susanne Gaymond; married Claudia Taylor; children: Christopher Augustus, Mark Adejolah & Shaundra Ave. **Educ:** Benedict Col, Columbia, SC, BA, 1965; NY Univ, New York, NY, MSW, 1969;Univ SC, Columbia, SC, PhD, 1977; Luthern Theol Southern Sem, Columbia,SC, M.Div, 1988. **Career:** SC Dept Ment Health, psychiat worker, 1965-71; Univ SC, Columbia, SC,assoc prof, prof, prof emer, currently. **Orgs:** Dir, Nat Black Family Summit, 1986-; vice basileus, Omega Psi Phi Fraternity, Omicron Phi Chapter; Phi Delta Kappa; Nat Asn Social Work; Coun Social Work Educ (CSWE). **Honors/Awds:** Order of the Palmetto. **Home Addr:** PO Box 11446, Columbia, SC 29211. **Business Addr:** Professor Emeritus, University South Carolina, College of Social Work, 1731 College St Room 205, Columbia, SC 29208.

RODGERS, BARBARA LORRAINE (BARBARA RODGERS DENNIS)
Television journalist. **Personal:** Born Sep 27, 1946, Knoxville, TN; daughter of Jackson Rodgers and Anna Connor Rodgers; married James Dennis, Sep 2, 1972. **Educ:** Knoxville Col, Knoxville, TN, BS, business education, 1968; SUNY at Buffalo, Buffalo, NY, 1976; Univ Chicago, Chicago, IL, 1986. **Career:** Eastman Kodak Co, Rochester, NY, public affairs researcher, computer programmer, 1968-71; Educational Opportunity Center, Rochester, NY, department head/instructor, 1971-76; WOKR-TV, Rochester, NY, anchor/reporter/show host, 1972-79; KPIX-TV, San Francisco, CA, anchor & reporter, 1979-. **Orgs:** Co-founder, past president, board mem, treasurer, Bay Area Black Journalists Assn, 1981-; board mem, World Affairs Council of North CA, 1990-; board mem, Regional Cancer Foundation, 1989-; board mem, Western Center for Drug Free Schools and Communities, 1987-90; quarterly chair, The Commonwealth Club of California, 1990; mem, Alpha Kappa Alpha Sorority, 1966-. **Honors/Awds:** Emmy, North California Chapter/Nat'l Academy of Televison Arts & Sciences, 1980-88; William Benton Fellowship in Broadcast Journalism, University of Chicago, 1985-86; Eugene Block Journalism Award, 1990; Miss Knoxville College, 1968. **Business Addr:** Anchor, Reporter, CBS 5 & KPIX-TV, 855 Battery St, San Francisco, CA 94111.*

RODGERS, CAROLYN MARIE
Writer, teacher. **Personal:** Born Dec 14, 1945, Chicago, IL; daughter of Bazella Colding and Clarence. **Educ:** Univ Ill, Navy Pier, 1960-61; Roosevelt Univ, Chicago, Ill, BA, 1981; Univ Chicago, MA, 1984. **Career:** Columbia Col, Chicago, Ill, Afro-Am lit instr, 1969-70; Malcolm X Col, Chicago, Ill, writer-in-residence, 1971-72; Ind Univ, Bloomington, Ind, vis prof Afro Am lit, 1973; Roosevelt Univ, Chicago, Ill, writer-in-residence, 1983; Chicago State Univ, Chicago, Ill, lectr, 1985; Eden Press, Chicago, Ill, editor & publ, currently; Columbia Col, Eng & poetry workshop instr; Poets & Writers, Inc, poet, currently; Poems: Paper Soul, 1969, Songs of a Blackbird, 1970, How I Got Ovah, 1975, The Heart as Evergreen, 1978, Echoes, From a Circle Called Earth, 1988, A Little Lower Than The Angels, 1988, Morning Glory, 1989, Eden & Other Poems, 1987, We're Only Human, 1994, A Train Called Judah, 1996, The Girl with Blue Hair, 1996, The Salt of The Earth: The Book of Salt, 1999; The Chosen. **Orgs:** Black Am Culture; Delta Sigma Theta. **Honors/Awds:** Poet Laureate, Soc Midland Authors, 1970; Nat Endowment for the Arts, 1970; PEN, 1987. **Home Addr:** 12750 S Sangamon, Chicago, IL 60643. **Business Addr:** Poet, Writer, Poets & Writers, Inc, PO Box 804271, Chicago, IL 60680, **Business Phone:** (212)226-3586.

RODGERS, REV. CHARLES
Clergy. **Personal:** Born Jul 28, 1941, Memphis, TN; married Gloria Dickerson; children: Adrian, Victor, Allison & Carlos. **Educ:** Attended LeMoyne Owen Coll; Arkansas Bapt College; International Coll of Bible Theology, bachelor of biblical studies; Midwest Theological Seminary, master of pastoral studies, div. **Career:** Memphis Press-Scimitar, staff writer, 1969; Covington Church God Christ, pastor, 1969-97; Memphis Publ Co, recruiting & job coun, 1973-74; Central Tenn Jurisdiction Church God Christ, second asst to Bishop 1982-89; New Dimensions Ministries, pastor, 1985-; Fifth Jurisdiction Tenn Church God Christ, admin asst to bishop, 1989-97; bishop, 2003-. **Orgs:** Bd dir, Memphis Teen Challenge; Int Church God Christ, 1972-84; Shelby United Neighbors, 1973-74; dir, News Serv Church God Christ Int Conv, 1981-87; chmn, Impact Fel Int. **Honors/Awds:** Man of Year, Congressman H Ford, 1976; Cert Outstanding & Meritorious Serv, 1976; numerous civic & religious awards. **Business Addr:** Pastor, New Dimensions Ministries, 3607 Frayser-Raleigh Rd, Memphis, TN 38128-5377, **Business Phone:** (901)377-1195.

RODGERS, DERRICK ANDRE
Football player. **Personal:** Born Oct 14, 1971, Memphis, TN; married Kareff, Jun 1, 2001; children: Elasia. **Educ:** Ariz State Univ. **Career:** Football player (retired); Miami Dolphins, linebacker, 1997-2002; New Orleans Saints, linebacker, 2003-04. **Honors/Awds:** NFL Defensive Rookie of the Year, Sports Illustrated, 1997.

RODGERS, EDWARD
Judge. **Personal:** Born Aug 12, 1927, Pittsburgh, PA; married Gwendolyn; children: 3. **Educ:** Howard Univ, BA, polit sci, 1949; Fla A&M Univ Law Sch, LLB, 1963. **Career:** Judge (retired); Palm Beach Co Sch Sys, teacher; asst co Solicitor; Cities W Palm Beach & Riviera Beach Fla, prosecutor ad litem; City W Palm Beach, judge ad litem; Pvt Atty; Palm Beach Co Bd, circuit ct judge, 1995. **Orgs:** Bd dir, Cancer & Soc; Masons; Vis Nurses Asn; Ment Health Asn; PB Community Found; Urban League; Palm Beach County Bar Asn; Nat Bar Asn. **Honors/Awds:** Nat Jefferson Award. **Special Achievements:** First Black county prosecutor in Palm Beach County; First black judge. **Military Serv:** USN pharmacist mate 3/c 1944-46. *

RODGERS, HORACE J.
Lawyer. **Personal:** Born Dec 10, 1925, Detroit, MI; married Yvonne Payne; children: Kimberly, Pamela. **Educ:** Univ Mich, BA, 1948; Univ Mich, Sch Law, JD, 1951. **Career:** Asst US Atty; Fedn Housing Admin, reg atty; Standard Mortgage Corp & Bert L Smokler & Co, vpres; Premier Mortgage Corp, founder & chmn bd; Rodgers & Morgenstein Attys, partner, currently. **Orgs:** Adv bd, Govt Nat Mortgage Asn; Com Visitors, Univ Mich, Law Sch; past adv bd mem, Fedn Nat Mortgage Asn; Nat Corp Housing Partnerships; chmn, Nat Urban Affairs Comt, MBA; dir, Nat Bank Southfield; life mem, Nat Asn Advan Colored People; Alpha Phi Alpha; Sigma Pi Phi; chmn, Class Officers & Leaders Coun, Univ Mich Alumni Asn; dir, Univ Mich, Alumni Asn; trustee & vice chancellor, Episcopal Diocese, MI; pres, St Luke's Episcopal Health Ministries; vpres, Canterbury Health Care Inc; dir, vpres, Cranbrook Acad Arts. **Honors/Awds:** Distinguised Service Award, Univ Mich Alumni Asn. **Military Serv:** AUS, 1944-46. **Business Addr:** Partner, Rodgers & Morgenstein Attorneys, 24445 NW Hwy Suite 214, Southfield, MI 48075.*

RODGERS, JOHNATHAN A.
Executive, president (organization), chief executive officer. **Personal:** Born Jan 18, 1946, San Antonio, TX; son of M A Rodgers and Barbara; married Royal Kennedy, Sep 27, 1975; children: David & Jamie. **Educ:** Univ Calif, Berkeley, BA, jour, 1967; Stanford Univ, MA, Commun, 1972. **Career:** TV network executive; Sports Illus, reporter, 1960; Newsweek Mag, assoc ed, 1972-73; WNBC-TV, writer-producer, 1973-74; WKYC-TV, Cleveland, OH, reporter, 1974-75; WBBM-TV, Chicago, IL, asst news dir, 1976-78; KCBS-TV, Los Angeles, CA news dir, exec producer & sta mgr, 1978-83, sta mgr,1982-83; CBS News, exec producer, 1983-86; WBBM-TV, chicago, gen mgr & vpres, 1986-90; CBS TV Stas Div, pres, 1990-96; Discovery Networks, pres, 1996-2002; NIKE Inc, bd dirs, 2006-; Procter & Gamble Co, dir; TV One LLC, pres & chief execofficer, currently. **Orgs:** Alpha Phi Alpha; bd mem, Univ Calif. **Honors/Awds:** Vanguard Award, 2005. **Military Serv:** AUS, sgt, 1969-71. **Business Addr:** President, Chief Executive Officer, TV One LLC, 1010 Wayne Ave 10th Fl, Silver Spring, MD 20910, **Business Phone:** (301)755-0400.

RODGERS, NAPOLEON
Banker. **Career:** Comerica Bank, Detroit, MI, first vpres.

RODGERS, NILE GREGORY
Music producer, musician. **Personal:** Born Sep 19, 1952, New York; married. **Career:** Musician & music producer; Sesame Street Band, session guitarist; Boys, group mem; Chic, group mem; Ear Candy Rec, co-pres; Let's Dance, producer, 1983; Nile Rodgers Prodn Inc, pres, currently; A lbums with Chic: Chic, 1977, C'est Chic, 1978; Risque, 1979; Real People, 1980; Take It Off, 1981; Soup for One, 1982; Tongue in Chic, 1982; Believer, 1983; Chic-Ism, 1992; Dance, Dance, Dance: The Best of Chic, 1992; Live at the Budokan, 1999; Solo albums: Adventures in the Land of the Good Groove, 1983; B Movie Matinee, 1985; (with Out loud) Out Loud, 1987; Chic Freak & More Treats, 1996; Productions: Norma Jean, 1978; We Are Family, 1979; King of theWorld, 1980; Love Somebody Today, 1980; diana, 1980; I Love My Lady, 1981;Koo Koo, 1981; Let's Dance, 1983; Situation X, 1983; "Invitation ToDance", 1983; Trash It Up, 1983; "Original Sin", 1984; Like a Virgin,1984; "The Reflex", 1984; "The Wild Boys", 1984; Flash, 1985; She's TheBoss, 1985; Here's to Future Days, 1985; Do You, 1985; When The Boys MeetThe Girls, 1985; Home of the Brave, 1986; Notorious, 1986; Inside Story,1986; Inside Out, 1986; L Is For Lover, 1986; "Moonlighting Theme", 1987;"Route 66", 1987; Cosmic Thing, 1989; Slam, 1989; Decade: Greatest Hits,1989; So Happy, 1989; Workin' Overtime, 1989; Family Style, 1990; Move ToThis, 1990; The Heat, 1991; "Real Cool World", 1992; Good Stuff, 1992;Black Tie White Noise, 1993; Your Filthy Little Mouth, 1994; Azabache,1997; Us, 1997; Samantha Cole, 1997; On & On, 1998; Everything is Cool,1998; Su Theme Song, 1998; Just Me, 2001; Dellali, 2001; "We Are Family", 2001; Only A Woman Like You, 2002; Shady Satin Drug, 2004; Astronaut, 2004; Evolution, 2007. **Honors/Awds:** Numerous honors including Named top singles producer, Music Week, 1985; Named number one pop singles producer, Billboard, 1985; Grammy Award,1986; Dance Music Hall of Fame, 2005; Lifetime Achievement Award; Heroes Award, Nat Acad Rec Arts & Sci. **Business Addr:** Musician, Warner Brothers Records, 75 Rockefeller Plz Suite 1, New York, NY 10019, **Business Phone:** (212)275-4600.*

RODGERS, PAMELA E
President (Organization), automotive executive. **Personal:** Born May 8, 1958, Detroit, MI; daughter of Horace J and Yvonne S. **Educ:** Univ Mich, BA, Econ, 1980; Duke Univ, MBA, Finance, 1983. **Career:** Ford Motor Co, Car Prod Develop, financial analyst, 1984-86, dealer cand, 1988-90; Heritage Ford Flint Inc, pres, 1990-92; Harrell Chevrolet, gen mgr, 1992-93; Ford Motor Co, All Am Ford, dealer cand, 1992; Flat Rock Chevrolet Oldsmobile Inc, pres, 1993-96; Internet Corp, bd dir; Gen Motors Fixed Opers Adv Bd, bd mem; Rodgers Chevrolet Inc, pres & owner, 1996-. **Orgs:** Secy, Nat Asn Minority Automobile Dealers; bd, Gen Motors Minority Dealer Asn; bd, Family Serv Wayne City; pres, Flat Rock Rotary Club; Big Brothers Big Sisters; Detroit Metro Chevrolet Dealer Asn; Links; Nat Women Auto Asn; Girlfriends; New Detroit Coalition; Southeastern Mich Community Found; Detroit Med Ctr Harper Hosp; Downtown Develop Authority; Merrill Palmer Inst, Wayne State Univ; Univ Mich Dean's Adv Coun. **Honors/Awds:** Special Tribute, State Mich, 1992; Kizzy Award, 1997; Dealer of the Year, Gen Motors; Professional Achievement Award, 2006 . **Business Addr:** President, Owner, Rodgers Chevrolet Inc, 23755 Allen Rd, Trenton, MI 48183, **Business Phone:** (734)676-9600.

RODGERS, SHIRLEY MARIE
Manager. **Personal:** Born Dec 29, 1948, Saginaw, MI. **Educ:** MI State Univ, 1970, BA 1984. **Career:** Manager, Administrator (retired); Blue Cross Mich, serv rep, 1970-71; Mich State Univ, tutor for athletic dept, 1970-71; Lansing Sch Dist, comm relations liaison, 1972, tutor, 1972; Mich State Univ, prog coordr Teach-a-Brother, 1972-73, prog coordr National Jr Tennis League, 1973; Meridian 4 Theaters, cashier, 1973; Lansing Sch Dist, clerk, Personnel Dept 1975-76, payroll clerk IV, 1976-81, acad secy to dir of adult & continuing educ, 1981-82, acad secy to dep supt, 1982-94, payroll supervisor. **Orgs:** Zeta Phi Beta Sor Inc Mich State Univ, 1970; Lansing Asn Educ Secretaries, 1976-82; Mich Democratic Party, 1980-; Ingham Co Democratic Party, 1980-; bd dir, Mich State Univ Black Alumni Inc, 1980-; Ingham Co Sch Officers Asn 1981-; bd trustees, Lansing Comm Col, 1981-93; State Adv Coun for Voc Educ, 1983-84; Gr Lansing Mich State Univ Black Alumni Chap, 1983-; Mich State Univ Alumni Asn 1984; Nat Asn Advan Colored People, 1985; mem, State Coun Voc Educ, 1985. **Honors/Awds:** Citizen of the Year in Education, Phi Beta Sigma Frat Inc, 1985; Black Distinguished Alumni, Mich State

Univ, 1989; Governors Award, Outstanding Local Elected Official, 1989; Certificate of Recognition, Am Citizens for Justice, Detroit Chapter.

RODGERS, VINCENT G
Educator. **Personal:** Born Feb 17, 1958, St Louis, MO; son of Bennie and Frances; married Padmini Srinivasan, Dec 23, 1989. **Educ:** Univ Dayton, BS, physics, 1980; Syracuse Univ, MS, theoretical particle physics, 1982, PhD, theoretical particle physics, 1985. **Career:** Univ Dayton, Res Inst & Wright Paterson Air Force Base, res asst & numerical analyst, 1979-80; Univ Fla, Gainesville, FL, Inst Fundamental Theory, postdoctoral res assoc, 1985-87; State Univ New York, Stony Brook, NY, Inst Theoretical Physics, res assoc, 1987-89; Univ Iowa, asst prof, 1989-95, assoc prof, 1995-2004, prof, 2004-. **Orgs:** Nat Soc Black Physicists, 1990-; NSBP Electronic Network Monitor, 1993-2002; NSBP Newsletter Editor, 1996-98; Am Physical Soc; Am Asn Physics Teachers, 2004-. **Honors/Awds:** Chester Davis Fel, Univ Ind, 1985; Outstanding Graduate Research Award, Sigma Xi, Syracuse Chap, 1985; Old Gold Summer Fel, Univ Iowa, 1990-91; Stellar Achievement Award, St. Louis, Am Newspaper, 1992; Outstanding Teaching Certificate, Univ Iowa Counl Teaching, 1994; UI Faculty Development Award, Fall, 1996; Eduard Bouchet Award, Nat Conf Black Physics Students, MIT, 1997; Fellow of the Nat Society of Black Physicists, 2001; UI Faculty Development Award, Fall, 2002. **Business Addr:** Professor, University of Iowa, Department of Physics & Astronomy, 513 Van Allen Hall, Iowa City, IA 52242-1479, **Business Phone:** (319)335-1219.

RODGERS, WILLIAM M., JR.
Engineer. **Personal:** Born Dec 22, 1941, Friars Point, MS; son of William M Rodgers Sr and Leanna Felix (deceased); married Venora Ann Faulkerson; children: William III, Melita Elizabeth & Steven Eric. **Educ:** Tenn State Univ, BS, 1963; Dartmouth Col, MS, 1970. **Career:** Nat Inst Health, Md, mathematician, 1963-64; Electronic Data Processing Div, Honeywell Inc, Va, systs analyst, 1964-66; Data Analysis Ctr Itek Corp, Va, sr scientific programmer, 1966-67; Bell Telephone Labs, New Jersey, tech staff mem, 1968; Exxon Refinery Tex, systs analyst, 1970-75; Lockheed Elect Co Inc, Tex, staff engr, 1975-77; Xerox Corp, mgr computer graphics requirements & appl, 1977-82, project mgr, CAD/CAM acquisition, 1982-83, mgr, CAD/CAM acquistion & integration, 1983-87, CAD/CAM strategy & planning, 1987-88, principal engr, 1988-. **Orgs:** Asn Computing Machinery; Soc Prof Engrs; Dartmouth Soc Engrs; Dartmouth Alumni Org; Dartmouth Soc Engrs Stud Exec Comt, 1969-70. **Honors/Awds:** Univ Counr Tenn State Univ, 1961-62; 'University Scholar Award'; Sears Roebuck Scholar, 1959; conducted presentation on large scale CAD/CAMAcquisitions, NCGA, 1989; conducted presentation on CAD/CAM system acquisition, related topics, Univ Wis, 1985, Rochester Inst Tech, 1987. **Business Addr:** Principal Engineer, Xerox Corporation, Advanced Systems Tools for Product Development, 800 Phillips Rd, Pittsford, NY 14534, **Business Phone:** (716)422-3253.

RODGERS-ROSE, LAFRANCES AUDREY
Association executive. **Personal:** Born Jul 19, 1936, Norfolk, VA; daughter of Carroll M and Beulah Smith; married Vattel T, May 29, 1960 (divorced); children: Henry D & Valija C. **Educ:** Morgan State Univ, BA, 1958; Fisk Univ, MA, 1960; Univ Iowa, PhD, 1964. **Career:** State Olaf Col, asst prof sociol, 1964-69; Case Western Reserve Univ, asst prof sociol, 1970-72; Educ Testing Serv, res sociologist, 1972-73; Princeton Univ, African Am studies, lectr, 1973-88; Int Black Womens Cong, founder & pres, 1983-99, chief exec officer, 2000-; Drew Univ, 1988-94. **Orgs:** Delta Sigma Theta Sorority, 1963-; Am Sociological Asn, 1971-; pres, Asn Black Sociologists, 1975-76; chap pres, Black Child Develop Inst, 1979-81; Nat Black United Fund, 1994-; pres, Asn Social & Behavorial Scientists, 1995-96; Asn Study Classical African Civilizations, 1998-; Univ Louisville, Plight Black Men African Diaspora, 2007. **Honors/Awds:** Mayor Proclamation, City Newark, NJ, 1985; Fannie Lou Hamer Award, US Organization, 1995; InterNat Leadership Award, Nat Orgn Black Elected Legis Women, 2000; WEB DuBois Award, Asn Social & Behav Scientists, 2001; James E Blackwell Founders Award, Asn Black Sociologists, 2003. **Special Achievements:** Author of The Black Woman, 1980, co-author of Black Male and Female Relationships, 1985, River of Tears, 1993, Every Black Woman Should Wear a Red Dress, 2003. **Business Addr:** Founder, Chief Executive Officer, International Black Women, 555 Church St Suite 102, Norfolk, VA 23510, **Business Phone:** (757)625-0500.

RODMAN, DENNIS KEITH
Basketball player, business owner, actor. **Personal:** Born May 13, 1961, Trenton, NJ; son of Philander and Shirley; married Michelle Moyer, May 13, 2003; children: 2; married Carmen Electra, Nov 14, 1998 (divorced); children: DJ & Trinity; married Annie Bakes, Sep 28, 1992 (divorced 1993); children: Alexis. **Educ:** Cooke Co Jr Col, attended 1983; South eastern Okla State Univ, attended 1986. **Career:** Basketball player (retired), business owner; Dallas-Ft Worth Airport, janitor, 1978; Detroit Pistons, forward, 1986-93; San Antonio Spurs, 1993-95; Chicago Bulls, 1995-98; Los Angeles Lakers, 1998-99; Dallas Mavericks, forward, 1999-2000; Rodman Underground Inc, owner, currently; Lingerie Football League, comnr, 2005; Torpan Pojat, 2005; Brighton Bears,2005; Dennis K Rodman Inc, owner, currently; Films: Double Team, actor,1997; Simon Sez, actor, 1999; Coming Attractions, actor, 2006, The Minis,2008; TV series: "Soldier of Fortune Inc", 1997; "Cutaway", 2000;"Stripper's Ball", 2003; "Lingerie Bowl", 2006. **Honors/Awds:** NBA All-Defensive Team, 1989-93, 1996; NBA Defensive Player of the Yr, 1990, 1991; NBA All-Star, 1990, 1992; IBM Award for all around contributions to team's success, 1992; Golden Raspberry Award. **Special Achievements:** Author: Bad As I Wanna Be, 1996; Walk on the Wild Side, 1997; Words from the Worm: An Unauthorized Trip through the Mind of Dennis Rodman, 1997; I Should Be Dead by Now, 2005; first NBA player in history to win five championships with two different teams. **Business Phone:** (972)335-7114.

RODMAN, JOHN
Computer executive, president (organization). **Career:** Fed Info Exchange Inc, pres, currently. **Business Addr:** President, Federal Information Exchange Inc, 1849 Sawtelle Blvd Suite 543, Los Angeles, CA 90025-7011, **Business Phone:** (310)444-1431.

RODMAN, MICHAEL WORTHINGTON
Banker. **Personal:** Born Sep 29, 1941, Indianapolis, IN; son of Hubert E Dabner and Faye R Dabner; married Kaaren, Oct 23, 1965; children: Michael H, Heather L. **Educ:** Ind Univ, BS, edu, attended MBA, 1990. **Career:** Midwest Nat Bank, asst cashier, 1972-74; INB Nat Bank, br mgr & asst vpres, 1974-81, AVP, CRA officer, 1981-86, vip, sr compliance officer, 1986-; NBD Neighborhood Revitalization Corp, pres, 1986-. **Orgs:** Ind Sch Bd, secy, 1994, pres, 1996; Ardyth Burkhart Series; Ind Housing Policy Study Comn, 1989-; Indianapolis Urban League, edu com chair, 1992-; 100 Black Men, 1991-; Frontiers, 1991-; Volunteer Action Ctr. **Honors/Awds:** ABA, Presidential Citation, 1986; United Way, Outstanding Service Award, 1984; CLD, Outstanding Achievement in Business, 1983; HOURS Award for COT Service, INB Nat Bank, 1979.

RODNEY, KARL BASIL
Founder (originator), publisher, chief executive officer. **Personal:** Born Nov 29, 1940, Kingston, Jamaica; married Faye A; children: Michele, Denine & Karlisa. **Educ:** Hunter Col CUNY, BA, Econ, 1966, MA, 1970. **Career:** Equitable Life Assurance Soc US, analyst, project mgr, div mgr, 1967-82; New York Carib News, publ, ceo, co-founder, currently. **Orgs:** Chmn, Caribbean Educ & Cult Inst, 1976-; dir, Martin Luther King Jr Living Dream Inc NY, 1985-; bd mem, mem exec comt, New York United Way, currently; bd mem, mem exec comt, United Way Int, currently; chmn, Am Found Univ West Indies, currently; bd mem, New York Urban League, currently; bd mem, exec comt, Greater Harlem Chamber Com, currently. **Honors/Awds:** Community Serv Award, 1980; WA Domingo Award, 1980; Excellence in Ethic Journ Harlem Week, 1985; Black Journalist Award, Pepsi-Cola NY, 1986; Award of Excellence, Caribbean Tourism Orgn, 2005. **Home Addr:** 525 Baldwin Pl, Mamaroneck, NY 10543, **Home Phone:** (914)698-5582. **Business Addr:** Publisher, Chief Executive Officer, New York Carib News, 28 W 39th St, New York, NY 10018, **Business Phone:** (212)944-1991.

RODNEY, DR. MARTIN HURTUS
Dentist. **Personal:** Born Mar 4, 1909; son of Charles and Blanche McKenzie; married Olga Eskimo Hart. **Educ:** Howard Univ, Wash, DC, pre-dent, 1934; Meharry Med Col, DDS, 1938. **Career:** Dentist (retired). **Orgs:** Nat Dent Asn; Baltimore City Dent Asn; past pres, Md Dent Asn; Fellow, Acad Gen Dent; Chi Delta Mu Fraternity; Omega Psi Phi Fraternity; OKU Nat Hon Soc; life mem, Nat Advan Asn Colored People; Douglass Memorial Ch, Baltimore City; bd mem & past pres, AARP; Queen Anne's Comn Aging, 1994. **Honors/Awds:** Louise Charlotte Ball Award, Ball Fed, 1938; Guggenheim Dental Scholarship Award, Guggenheim Found, 1938-39; Dentist of the Year Award, Md Acad Gen Dent, 1973; Recognition Award, Md Dent Soc, 1975; President's Award, Meharry Med Col, 1938-87; Meharry National Alumni Association Award, 1993. **Special Achievements:** Book: My Journey to Success. **Home Phone:** (410)643-6783. *

RODRIGUEZ, ARGELIA VELEZ
Educator. **Personal:** Born Nov 23, 1936, Havana, Cuba; daughter of Pedro Velez; married Raul (divorced); children: Raul P & Argelia M. **Educ:** Marianao Institute, BS, BA, 1954; Univ Havana Sch Sci, DSc, math, 1960. **Career:** Marianao Inst, Havana, Cuba, instr, asst prof, math & physics, 1957-61; Tex Col, asst prof math, chmn dept, 1962-64; Bishop Col, dir, lectr, NSF Summer Prog Advan High Sch Students Math, 1964, instr, Modern Math NSFI n-Serv Inst Sec Sch Teachers, 1964-68, Educ Prof Develop Act-Teachers Training Develop, coord, 1970-73, prof math, 1972-77, dept head math & sci, 1978-78, dir, Coop Col Sch Sci-Nat Sci Found, coordr, Math Proj Jr High Sch Teachers, coordr, 1972-74, Coop Doc Prog Math Educ Houston, assoc dir, 1973-74; Minority Institutions Science Improvement Program, Washington, DC, prog mgr, 1979-80; US Dept Educ, prog dir, 1980-, Robert C. Byrd Honors Scholarship program, head, sr prog officer, DC Col Access Prog, exec dir. **Orgs:** AAAS; DC Am Math Soc Providence; Nat Coun Teachers Math; DC Tex Acad Sci, Austin; Math Asn Am, DC; mem comn, Affirmative Acton Conf Bd Math Sci; Am Asn Univ Prof, DC; Asn Univ Women, DC; Young Women Christ Asn, Dallas; Cuban Cath Asn, Dallas; speaker, Annual Conv Nat Coun Teacher Math, NC Sec, Nov,1972; bd dirs, Dallas Br, Am Asn Univ Women, 1973-; chmn, Int Rel Com Am Asn Univ Women, 1973-; dir, NSF Minority Inst Sci Improvement Proj, 1976-78; dir, NSF Pre-Col Teacher Develop Math Proj, 1977-78. **Honors/Awds:** NSF Fel, 1965; Computer Assisted Instructor Fel, 1967-68; Liason rep to the Am Asn of Univ Women, Bishop Col, 1970-72. **Special Achievements:** First black woman to have earned her doctorate from the University of Havana in Cuba.

RODRIGUEZ, DORIS L.
Association executive. **Personal:** Born Mar 8, 1927, New York, NY; married Jules S; children: Anna, Julio & Louis. **Educ:** Queens Col. **Career:** Litman Dept Store NY, comparison shopper, interpretor, 1946-48; Pvt Nurse, 1948-51; Manhattan Gen Hosp, obstet nurse, 1951-58; Bilingual Adv Dists 27 & 28; Originals Jamaica Inc, Urban Ctr, exec dir. **Orgs:** Assoc, St Marys Sch Girls & Convent, 1950; Musical Art Group, 1950; 103rd Precinct Comm Coun, 1969; Concerned Parents Day Care Ctr, 1969; Queensboro Coun Soc Welfare, 1971; bd dir, Youth Consult Serv, 1972-; exec bd mem, PTA Manlius Mil Acad; Adv Coun Reimbursable Funds, Dist 27 & 28 City wide; Queens Child Guid Comn; founding mem, Ida B Wills Sch; Christ Ch Sag Harbor, NY.

RODRIGUEZ, RUBEN
Executive. **Career:** Motown Records, NE regional mkt & promotions mgr; Casablanca Records, staff; Columbia Records, sr vpres; sr vpres, Elektra Records; Pendulum Records, founder, pres & chief executive officer, 1991-; Ruben Rodriguez Entertainment Inc, owner, currently. **Honors/Awds:** Joseph Papp Racial Harmony Award, Found Ethnic Understanding, 2003. **Business Addr:** President, Rubin Rodriguez Entertainment Inc, 96 Linwood Plaza Suite 354, Fort Lee, NJ 07024, **Business Phone:** (201)363-1461.

ROEBUCK, GERARD FRANCIS
Entrepreneur. **Personal:** Born Sep 26, 1953, New York, NY; son of Gladys Johnson and Waldamar; married Sharon Jeffrey, Nov 4, 1985; children: Jared & Jashaun. **Educ:** City Col New York, New York, NY, BA, 1978; Pratt Inst, Brooklyn, NY, MLS, 1980. **Career:** New York Pub Libr, New York, NY, supv librn, 1980-89; Black Expo USA, New York, NY, founder & chmn, 1987-; New York City Bd Educ, New York, NY, media dir, 1989-90. **Orgs:** Nat Asn Mkt Developers, 1989-; NAACP; bd dir, OLMEC Toy Corp; Atlanta Chamber Com; Black Librn Caucus. **Honors/Awds:** Class Leader, Xavier Summer Prog Higher Achievement Prog; Promoter of the Year, New York City Promoters Orgn, 1981. **Special Achievements:** concert & rap group promoter. **Business Phone:** (404)892-2815.

ROEBUCK, JAMES RANDOLPH
State government official. **Personal:** Born Feb 12, 1945, Philadelphia, PA; son of James Randolph Sr and Cynthia Compton; married Cheryl Arrington. **Educ:** VA Union Univ, BA, 1966; Univ VA, MA, 1969, PhD, 1977. **Career:** Drexel Univ, lectr hist, 1970-77, asst prof hist, 1977-84; City Philadelphia, Off Mayor, legal asst, 1984-85; Pennsylvania House Reps, rep gen assembly, 1985-. **Orgs:** Philadelphia Coun Boy Scouts Am; Child Crisis Treatment Ctr; NAACP; Univ VA Alumni Asn; bd deacons, Mt Olivet Tabernacle Baptist Church; PA Higher Educ Assistance Agency; Philadelphia Community Col; PA Hist & Mus Comn; PA Legis Black Caucus; PA Hist & Museum Comn. **Honors/Awds:** Recognition Award, United Negro Col Alumni, 1978; Chapel of the Four Chaplians Legion of Honor Award, 1980; Conestoga District Award of Merit, Boy Scouts Am, 1983; Silver Beaver Award, 1986; Achievement Award, VA Union Univ Alumni, 1986; Citation, Nat Asn Equal Opportunity Higher Educ, 1987; fel grant, Foreign Affairs Scholars Prog, Wash, DC; Southern Fel Fund, Atlanta, GA; Mutual Educ Exchange Grant, US Off Educ & Fulbright Prog, Wash, DC; Nat Endowment for the Humanities Grant; German Federal Republic Grant. **Home Addr:** 4712 Baltimore Ave, Philadelphia, PA 19143, **Home Phone:** (215)724-2227. **Business Addr:** Representative, Pennsylvania House of Representatives, 208 K Leroy Irvis Office Bldg, PO Box 202188, Harrisburg, PA 17120-2188, **Business Phone:** (717)783-1000.

ROEBUCK-HAYDEN, MARCIA
Publishing executive. **Career:** Scott Foresman Publ, Res & Curric, ed dir, English as a Second Lang, Adult Basic Educ, ed vpres, currently. **Business Addr:** Editorial Vice President, English as a Second Language Basic Adult Education, Scott Foresman Publications, 1900 E Lake Ave, Glenview, IL 60025, **Business Phone:** (708)729-3000.

ROGERS, ALFRED R
Public utility executive. **Personal:** Born Apr 7, 1931, Hartford, CT; son of John and Oretta; married Alice. **Educ:** Univ Conn, BA, 1953, JD 1963; Am Inst Real Estate Appraisal; Rensselar Polytech Inst Conn; Univ Mich, Pub Utilities Exec Prog, 1982; Edison Electric Inst, Pub Utilities Exec Prog. **Career:** Bur Rights Ways Conn Dept Transp, chief pub utilities sect, 1957-64; Hartford Elec Light Co Legal & Real Estate Dept, sr land agent, 1964-69; Hartford Electric Light Co, mgr, 1970-85; Northeast Utilities Central Region, vpres, 1985-. **Orgs:** Pres & sec, Bd Educ,

Hartford, 1965-73; state treas, Conn Asn Bds Educ, 1966-69; Govt Adv Coun Voc Educ, 1967-71; Govt Clean Air Task Force, 1967-69; exec bd, Long River Coun BSA, 1973-; adv bd, Salvation Army, 1973-; corporator, Newington Childrens Hosp, 1975-; dir, Hartford Hosp, 1982-; trustee, Young Men Christian Asn, 1990-; trustee, Boys Club Hartford; dir, Mech Savings Bank Hartford; trustee, St Joseph Col, West Hartford. **Military Serv:** AUS, second Lt, 1953-56; Commendation Medal.

ROGERS, DR. BERNARD ROUSSEAU
Physician. **Personal:** Born Jan 17, 1944, Winston-Salem, NC; married Linda Hargreaves, May 21, 1986. **Educ:** NC Central Univ, BS, 1966; Meharry Med Col, MD, 1971; Univ Minn, MN, residency, radiation oncol, 1973-76. **Career:** Youngstown Hosp, intern & resident pathol, 1971-72; Pvt Practice, physician, currently; Oncol Servs, dir, brachytherapy, 1991-; Chesapeake Regional Cancer Ctr, Charlotte Hall, Md, med dir; Regional Cancer Ctr, Bon Secours-Holy Family Hosp, currently. **Orgs:** Am Med Asn, 1976-; Am Col Radiol, 1977-; Am Endocurietherapy Soc, 1985-; Am Soc Therapeutic Radiologists & Oncologists, 1976-; Am Brachytherapy Soc. **Home Addr:** 50 Dana Ave, Auburn, ME 04210, **Home Phone:** (207)784-3731. **Business Addr:** Physician, 400 Highland Ave, Lewistown, PA 17044, **Business Phone:** (717)248-5411.

ROGERS, CARLOS DEON
Basketball player. **Personal:** Born Feb 6, 1971, Detroit, MI. **Educ:** Univ Ark-Little Rock; Tenn State Univ, attended 1994. **Career:** Basketball player (retired); Golden State Warriors, forward-ctr, 1994-95; Toronto Raptors, 1995-98; Portland Trail-Blazers, 1998-99; Houston Rockets, 2000-01; Ind Pacers, forward-ctr, 2002. **Special Achievements:** First round pick, No 11, NBA Draft, 1994.

ROGERS, CHARLES
Football player. **Personal:** Born May 23, 1981, Saginaw, MI. **Educ:** Mich State Univ. **Career:** Detroit Lions, wide receiver, 2003-05; free agent, currently. **Honors/Awds:** All State Honoree Thrice; Biletnikoff award, 2002; Consensus All American, 2002.

ROGERS, CHARLES D
Artist, educator. **Personal:** Born Jan 5, 1935, Cherokee County, OK; son of Henry and Alberta Lay; divorced; children: Warren Donald. **Educ:** Calif State Col, BA, 1964; Ohio State Univ, MA, 1971; Univ Nc, Greensboro, NC, MFA, 1977. **Career:** Artcraft Studios, Los Angeles, com designer 1964-69; Watts Summer Festival, Watts, CA, co-dir 1967-69; Vanguard Studios, Van Nuys, CA, com designer, 1970; Bennett Col, Greensboro, NC, produced Harlem Renaissance, 1972; Johnson C Smith Univ, Charlotte, Nc, assoc prof arts, 1972-, art prog dir, currently. **Orgs:** Black Arts Coun, Los Angeles, CA; Charlotte Guild Artists, 1980-; Nat Conf Artists, 1986-. **Honors/Awds:** Teaching Fellow Award, Ohio State Univ, Columbus, 1970; Teaching Fel, African Am Inst, 1974; Scholar in Residence, New York Univ, 1993. **Special Achievements:** Author of Prints by American Negro Artists & Black Artists On Art. **Home Addr:** 3322 Anson St, Charlotte, NC 28209. **Business Addr:** Associate Professor, Johnson C Smith University, Department of Arts, 100 Beatties Ford Rd, Charlotte, NC 28216, **Business Phone:** (704)378-1000.

ROGERS, CHARLES LEONARD
Aerospace engineer. **Personal:** Born Jul 27, 1951, Decatur, AL; son of Felix M E and Estelle Holmes; married Ramona, Oct 22, 1988. **Educ:** Northern Ill Univ, BS, 1976; West Coast Univ, MS, 1986. **Career:** Commonwealth Edison, tech staff engr, 1976-80; Lockheed Martin Astronaut, chief launch opers, 1988-97; Athens/MSLS Launch Opers, pres, mgr, 1997-. **Orgs:** Nat Mgt Asn. **Honors/Awds:** Martin Marietta, Jefferson Cup, 1992; Black Engr Mag, Cert Recognition, 1992; Dollars & Sense Mag, Am's Best & Brightest, 1993. **Military Serv:** AUS. **Home Addr:** 161 Galaxy Way, Lompoc, CA 93436, **Home Phone:** (805)733-3228. **Business Addr:** Manager Launch Operations, Lockheed Martin, Bldg 8500, PO Box 1681, Vandenberg AFB, CA 93437-1681, **Business Phone:** (805)734-8232.

ROGERS, CHRIS
Football player. **Personal:** Born Jan 3, 1977, Washington, DC. **Educ:** Howard Univ. **Career:** Minn Vikings, defensive back, 1999; Seattle Seahawks, corner back, 2001-03.

ROGERS, DAVID WILLIAM
Television journalist, meteorologist. **Personal:** Born Feb 2, 1959, Cleveland, OH; son of David Louis and Thelma Elizabeth Grahma; married; children: David & Chloe. **Educ:** Temple Univ, Philadelphia, PA, jour, 1983. **Career:** WCAU-TV, Philadelphia, Pa, news producer, 1979-85; WBBJ-TV, Jackson, Tenn, news anchor, 1985-86; WTVR-TV, Richmond, Va, 1986-87; WJBK-TV, Detroit, Mich, weather anchor, 1987-; KYW-TV, seasoned weatherman; WKYC-TV3, chief meteorologist; CBS-2, meteorologist; WVIR-TV NBC29, morning weekend & part-time noon show meteorologist, currently. **Orgs:** YMCA, 1979; Nat Asn Advan Colored People, 1989; Nat Asn Black Journalists, 1985; proj coord, United Negro Col Fund, 1986; Westland Cultural Soc, 1987; Muscular Dystrophy Asn, 1987; bd dirs, Children's Aid Soc.

Honors/Awds: Award of Outstanding Achievement, United Negro Col Fund, 1986; Barrier Awareness Award, Am Asn Handicapped Persons, 1987; Award of Appreciation, Am Cancer Soc, 1988; Numerous Emmy Awards in the Anchor Weathercaster category. **Special Achievements:** Various articles published in the Philadelphia Inquirer, 1979-81. **Business Addr:** Meteorologist, WVIR-TV NBC29, 503 E Market St, Charlottesville, VA 22902, **Business Phone:** (434)220-2900.

ROGERS, DR. DECATUR BRAXTON
School administrator. **Educ:** Tenn State Univ, BS, mech eng; Vanderbilt Univ, MS, eng mgt, MS, mech eng, PhD, mech eng. **Career:** Fed City Col, fac; Prairie View A&M Univ, fac; Fla St Univ, prof, dean; Tenn St Univ, Col Eng, Technol & Comput Sci, Nashville, TN, dean, 1988-, prof mech eng, currently. **Orgs:** Am Soc Eng Educ; Am Sos Mech Engrs; NAMEPA; Nat Soc Prof Engs; Nat Asn Advan Colored People; Phi Delta Kappa; Pi Tau Sigma; Mech Eng Hon Soc; Tau Beta Pi; Nat Eng Hon Soc; Phi Kappa Phi. **Business Addr:** Dean, Professor of Mechanical Engineering, Tennessee State University, College of Engineering Technology & Computer Science, 3500 John A Merritt Blvd, Nashville, TN 37209-1561, **Business Phone:** (615)963-5401.

ROGERS, DESIREE
Government Official, Public Relations. **Personal:** Born Jun 16, 1959, New Orleans, LA; daughter of Joyce Glapion and Roy Glapion; married John W. Rogers, Jr. (divorced); children: Victoria. **Educ:** Wellesley College, BA, 1981; MBA from Harvard Business School. **Career:** Appointed by governor Jim Edgar to run the Illinois State Lottery, 1990-97; VP of corp communications for Peoples Energy (PE), 1997; Chief Marketing Officer of Peoples Energy, 2000; Senior VP of Customer Service; Senior VP of Peoples Energy, 2001; Allstate Financial; Pres of Peoples Gas and North Shore Gas, 2004; White House Social Secretary, 2009-. **Orgs:** Board of Directors, Allstate Life Insurance Co., Equity Residential, and Blue Cross Blue Shield of Illinois; Vice-chairman of the Lincoln Park Zoo and The Museum of Science and Industry; The Chicago Children's Museum; The Young Presidents Organization; member of the Commercial Club of Chicago; The Chicago Network; Member of the 2016 Chicago Olympic Cultural committee. **Special Achievements:** Named twice as queen of the Zulu Social Aid and Pleasure Club; survivor of breast cancer, 2003; First female Af Am to hold the post of Pres of both Peoples Gas and North Shore Gas; "Top 50 Most Powerful Black Af Am Business Women", Black Enterprise Magazine, 2006; featured in Vogue Magazine; "Top 25 Women to Watch", Crain's Chicago Business, 2007; "Top 75 Most Powerful Blacks in Corp Am", Black Enterprise Magazine, 2005; First Af Am to hold the position of White House Social Secretary. **Business Addr:** The White House, 1600 Pennsylvania Ave., NW, Washington, DC 20500, **Business Phone:** (202)456-1414.*

ROGERS, DESIREE GLAPION
Executive, president (organization). **Personal:** Born Jun 16, 1959, New Orleans, LA; daughter of Joyce and Roy; children: Victoria. **Educ:** Wellesley Col, polit sci, 1981; Harvard Univ, MBA, 1985. **Career:** AT&T, custom serv mkt mgr; Levy Organizations Lobby Shop Div, dir develop; Mus Opers Consult Asn, pres; Ill State Lottery, dir; Peoples Energy, sr vpres; Peoples Energy, sr vpres, pres peoples gas & N shore gas, currently. **Orgs:** WTTW Channel 11, Mus Sci & Indust; Lincoln Park Zoo; Ravina; Econ Club Chicago; Executives Club Chicago. **Honors/Awds:** League Black Women, Black Rose Award; Harvard Grad Sch Bus Admin, COGME Fel. **Business Addr:** President of Peoples Gas & North Shore Gas, Peoples Energy, 130 E Randolph Dr, Chicago, IL 60601, **Business Phone:** (312)240-4567.

ROGERS, EARLINE S
Senator (U.S. federal government), educator, consultant. **Personal:** Born Dec 20, 1934, Gary, IN; daughter of Earl Smith and Robbie Hicks Smith; married Louis C Rogers Jr, Dec 24, 1956; children: Keith C Rogers & Dara Dawn. **Educ:** Ind Univ, Bloomington, IN, BS, 1957, MS, 1971. **Career:** Educator (retired), senator; Gary Community Sch Corp, teacher, 1957-95; Gary City Coun, pres/coun mem, 1980-82; Ind House Representatives, rep, 1982-90; Ind State Senate, Dist 3, asst minority leader, asst minority whip, senator, 1990-; educ consult, currently. **Orgs:** Am Fedn Teachers; Black Prof Women; Bus Prof Women; Campagne Acad; Drug Free Ind, Lake County; Hoosier Boys Town; Ind State Teachers Asn; Nat Asn Advan Colored People; Nat Coun Negro Women; Urban League; Young Women's Christian Asn. **Special Achievements:** First woman elected president of Gary Common Council. **Business Addr:** Senator, Indiana State Senate, Senate District 3, 200 W Wash St, Indianapolis, IN 46204-2785, **Business Phone:** (317)232-9491.

ROGERS, ELIJAH BABY
Executive, president (organization), chief executive officer. **Personal:** Born Nov 2, 1939, Orlando, FL; married Jean Doctor. **Educ:** SC State Col, BA, 1962; Univ SC, 1965; Howard Univ, MSW, 1967, MA, 1972. **Career:** SC Dept Corrections, supvr soc work serv, 1967-69; Wash Bur Nat UrbanLeague, asst dir, 1968-70; Nat Urban League, sr field rep, 1969; Bowie MD, asst mgr, chief staff 1970-71; Richmond VA, asst city mgr, 1972-

74; Berkeley CA, asst city mgr, mgr, 1974-76; City Berkeley, city mgr, 1976-79; DC, Wash, DC, city adminr, 1979-83; Grant Thornton, asst managing partner, 1983-88; Delon Hampton & Assoc, chief operating officer, pres &ceo, 2001, sr advisor, currently. **Orgs:** Young Prof Task Force, 1971-72; mem adv comt, Sch Soc Work 1972-73; Special Task Force Minorities, 1973-74; bd dir, Great Richmond Transit Co, 1973-74; adj prof, Urban Studies, 1973-74; chairperson Minority Exec Placement Bd, 1975-; Comn Mgt Labor Rel, 1976; adv comt, Econ Develop Nat Inst Advan Studies, 1977; transp steering comt, Nat League Cities, 1977; bd dirs, Met Wash Coun Govs, 1980; vice chmn, Wash Metropolitan Airports Authority, 1986-88; bd trustees, The Found Nat Capital Region, 1993; chmn, Wm Bd Fitzgerald Scholar Fund, 1994-; Chmn, Mayor's Blue Ribbon Panel Health Care Reform, 1994; Mayor-Elect Marion Barry's Fin Transition Team, 1994; secy, Federal City Coun Bd Wash Trustees, 1998; Nat Asn Soc Workers; Acad Cert Soc Workers Inc; City Mgt Assoc; fel, Int City Mgt. **Honors/Awds:** Outstanding Service Award, Gavel Club #29, 1969; Distinguished Alumnus Award, 1979; Howard Univ, Sch Soc Work, Community Services Award; National Association for Equal Opportunity in Higher Education Award, 1984; "Hallof Fame" Award, Nat Forum for Black Pub Adminr, 1994. **Special Achievements:** ICMA/COG Minority Internship Prog Dept Urban Studies, Howard Univ, Reflect" ICMA Newsletter, 1971; "A Career in Municipal Govt for Blacks-WhyNot?" Publ Mgt, 1972; "The Minority Exec-Which Way ICMA" Publ Mgt 1975; SC St Col. **Business Addr:** Senior Advisor, Delon Hampton & Associates, 800 K St NW Suite 720 N Lobby, Washington, DC 20001, **Business Phone:** (202)898-1999.

ROGERS, GEORGE
School administrator. **Personal:** Born Jan 8, 1947, Chicago, IL; son of George II and Gertrude Ellington; married Rita F Guhr; children: Tara M & Bret Z. **Educ:** Wilson City Col, AA, 1967; Bethel Col, BS, 1969; Wichita State Univ, MEd, 1972; Univ AR, PhD. **Career:** Bethel Col, track coach, 1969, dir athletics, asst to coach, assoc prof phys ed, 1997; Whitewing Construct, secy & treas & estimator, 2003-, chief exec officer, currently. **Orgs:** Newton Jaycee's, 1970; bd dir, FARM House, 1975; pres, USD No 373 Sch Bd, 1987-88, 1994-95; pres, Harvey Co Rural Water Dist 3, 1987-88; bd dir, Meadowlark Homestead Inc, 1996; bd dir, Mirror Inc, 1996; Kappa Alpha Psi Fraternity; First Step Indust; Nat Asn Stud Personnel Adminr. **Honors/Awds:** Coach of the Year, NAIA Area 3 Track Coach, 1975; Athletic Administrator of the Year, Kansas, NAIA, 1989-90. **Home Addr:** 3219 Royer W Dr, Newton, KS 67114. **Business Addr:** Chief Executive Officer, Treasurer, Whitewing Construct Inc, 1410 E 12th Ave, PO Box 1045, Newton, KS 67114, **Business Phone:** (316)283-8180.

ROGERS, DR. GEORGE
Educator. **Personal:** Born Sep 23, 1935, McKeesport, PA; married Emalyn Martin; children: Cheryl Jeanne Mincey, Rhea Avonne & Emalyn Cherea. **Educ:** Langston Univ, BS, educ, 1961; Cent State Univ, MS, educ, 1968; Univ Kans, EdD, 1971. **Career:** Ala A&M Univ, asst prof, 1968-71; Wichita State Univ, assoc prof, 1971-83; Langston Univ, vpres acad, 1983-86, prof special asst to the pres, 1986-. **Orgs:** Phi Delta Kappa 1969; Alpha Phi Alpha Frat, 1970; pres, George Rogers & Asns, 1972-; Sigma Pi Phi Frat, 1986. **Honors/Awds:** Ford Found fel, 1969-70; Honor Graduate Univ Kans, 1971; Distinguished Young Black American, Incentive Asn, Tallahasse, FL, 1972. **Military Serv:** AUS, SP-3, 3 yrs. **Home Addr:** 10201 C N Finely Rd, Oklahoma City, OK 73120. **Business Addr:** Professor, Special Assistant to President, Langston University, Langston, OK 73050.

ROGERS, GWENDOLYN H
Executive director. **Career:** Equal Bus Opportunity Comn, exec dir; Columbus City Coun, Ohio, legis analyst, currently. **Special Achievements:** First African American female executive director of the EBOC, Columbus. **Business Phone:** (614)645-7380.

ROGERS, JOHN W.
Executive, chairperson, chief executive officer. **Personal:** Son of John W Sr and Jewel Lafontant; married Desiree Glapion. **Educ:** Princeton Univ, BS, econ, 1980. **Career:** Ariel Capital Mgt LLC, founder, chmn & chief exec officer, 1983-; Aon dir, 1993, Chmn Audit Comt, chief investment officer, currently; Ariel Fund & Ariel Appreciation Fund, lead portfolio mgr, currently; William Blair & Co, broker; Exelon Corp & McDonalds Corp, dir, currently. **Orgs:** Bd dirs, Chicago Urban League; Family Focus; bd dirs, Chicago Symphony Orchestra; bd dirs, Lake Forest Col; bd dirs, Am Nat Bank; bd dirs, Aon Corp; bd dirs, Burrell Communs Group; Chicago Park Dist; bd dir, First Chicago NBD Corp; bd dir, First Nat Bank Chicago; bd dir, Invest Comt; dir, John S & James L Knight Found; trustee, Rush-Presbyterian-St Lukes Med Ctr; invest adv, Ariel Invest Trust. **Honors/Awds:** Hon Degree, Columbia Col, 1996. **Special Achievements:** Fourty Leaders of the Future, Time Magazine, 1994. **Business Addr:** Chairman, Chief Executive Officer, Ariel Capital Management LLC, Ariel Mutual Funds, 200 E Randolph Dr Suite 2900, Chicago, IL 60601, **Business Phone:** (312)726-0140.

ROGERS, JOHN W, SR.
Judge. **Personal:** Born Sep 3, 1918, Knoxville, TN; son of Mary Turner Rogers; married Jewel Lafontant Mankarious (deceased);

children: John Jr. **Educ:** Chicago Teacher Col, BEd, 1941; Univ Chicago, LLD, 1948. **Career:** Judge (retired); Circuit Ct Cook County, judge, 1977-2001. **Orgs:** Admitted Ill Bar, 1948; former mem, bd trustees, Met Sanitary Dist Greater Chicago; former treas & gen coun, Sivart Mortgage Co Chicago; admitted practice US Supreme Ct; former mem, bd dir, Chicago Coun Human Rels; former bd mem, Ada S McKinley; Chicago Bar Asn; Cook County Bar Asn; Judicial Coun; Nat Coun Juv & Family Court Judges; Ill Coun Juv & Family Court Judge's Asn. **Honors/Awds:** Congressional Black Caucus Award, Recognition of Courageous Leadership and Discipline in the Air and on the Ground during World War II, 1991. **Military Serv:** USSA, original 99th Squadron, fighter pilot, capt, WW II; Air Medal.

ROGERS, ESQ. JOYCE Q
Executive, chief executive officer. **Personal:** Born in Indianapolis, IN. **Educ:** Ind State Univ, BS, 1979; Ind Univ Sch Law, PhD, 1996. **Career:** Caseworker & family counr; Family & Social Servs Admin, dir contract mgt; Ind Black Expo Inc, chief operating officer, 2001-04, pres & chief exec officer, 2004-; Ivy Tech Community Col, vpres develop, 2007-. **Orgs:** Indianapolis Bar Asn. **Business Phone:** (317)925-2702 Ext 3043.*

ROGERS, JUDITH ANN WILSON. See ROGERS, JUDITH W.

ROGERS, JUDITH W (JUDITH ANN WILSON ROGERS)
District attorney, judge. **Personal:** Born Jan 1, 1939?, New York, NY. **Educ:** Radcliffe Col, Ba, cum laude, 1961; Harvard Law Sch, LLB, 1964; Univ Va Law Sch, LLM, 1988; DC Sch Law, hon doctorate. **Career:** DC, asst US atty, 1965-68; US Dept Justice, Criminal Div, trial atty, 1967-71; San Francisco Neighborhood Legal Assistance Found, staff atty, 1968-69; Cong Comn Orgn, gen coun, 1971-72; DC Govt, off asst mayor, legis prog coordr, 1972-74; DC Govt, Legis Mayor, spec asst, 1974-79; DC Govt, Intergovernmental Rels, asst city adminr, 1979; DC, corp coun, 1979-83; DC Ct Appeals, assoc judge, 1983-88, chief judge, 1988-93; US Ct Appeals, DC Circuit, judge, 1994-; Juvenile Ct, DC, law clerk. **Orgs:** Phi Beta Kappa. **Honors/Awds:** Woman Lawyer of the Year, Women's Bar Asn, 1990; Distinguished Public Service Award; Chairman's Special Award, Nat Bar Asn. **Business Addr:** Judge, United States Court of Appeals, District of Columbia Circuit, 333 Constitution Ave NW, Washington, DC 20004, **Business Phone:** (202)216-7260.

ROGERS, ORMER, JR.
Government official. **Personal:** Born Jul 23, 1945, Mount Vernon, TX; son of Ormer Sr and Susie; married Helen Pettis, Sep 27, 1983. **Educ:** Dallas Baptist Univ, BCA, 1977; Abilene Christian Univ, MS, 1978; Mass Inst Technol, attended, 1990. **Career:** Post Master (retired); USS Postal Serv, dir, customer serv, 1983-86, opers prog analyst, 1986-87, field dir, mkt, 1987-88, drr, city opers, 1988-91, field dir, opers support, 1991, dist mgr, postmaster, 1991-92, area mgr, Great Lakes, 1992, dist mgr, Kansas City. **Orgs:** Fed Exec Bd, 1991-93; Rotary Chicago, 1992-93; Univ Ill, Chicago, Dept Med, develop coun, 1992-93; Combined Fed Campaign, chair, 1993; LifeSource, bone marrow donor com, 1992-93; United Way, Crusade Mercy, minority outreach com, 1992-93. **Honors/Awds:** Service Achievement Award, Abilene Christian Univ, 1978; Regional Postmaster General Award for Excellence, USS Postal Serv, 1989, 1991, 1992. **Military Serv:** USY, ssg, 1965-68; Bronze Star, Army Commendation Medal, Combat Infantry Badge, Sr Parachutist Wings, Good Conduct, Vietnam Campaign Medal, Vietnam Serv Ribbon, Unit Citation.

ROGERS, REV. DR. OSCAR ALLAN
Clergy, school administrator. **Personal:** Born Sep 10, 1928, Natchez, MS; son of Oscar Sr and Maria; married Ethel Lee Lewis; children: Christopher, Christian & Christoff. **Educ:** Tougaloo Col, AB, 1950; Harvard Divinity Sch, STB, 1953; Harvard Univ, MAT, 1954; Univ Ariz, EdD, 1960; Univ Wash, attended 1969. **Career:** Natchez Jr Col, dean & registr, 1954-56; AR Baptist Col, pres, 1956-59; Jackson State Univ, dean studs & prof soc sci, 1960-69, dean grad sch, 1969-84; Bolton-Edward United Methodist Church, pastor, 1961-84; Claflin Col, pres, 1984-94. **Orgs:** Dir, Orangeburg Chamber Comn, 1987-90; Phi Delta Kappa. **Honors/Awds:** DHL, Okla City Univ, 1992; Alumni Award, Harvard Divinity Sch, 2003. **Special Achievements:** Author: My Mother Cooked My Way Through Harvard With These Creole Recipes, 1972; Mississippi, The View From Tougaloo, 1979. **Military Serv:** USN, stm 3/c, 1946-47.

ROGERS, RODNEY RAY
Basketball player, entrepreneur. **Personal:** Born Jun 20, 1971, Durham, NC; married Tisa; children: Roddreka & Rydeiah. **Career:** Basketball Player (retired), entrepreneur; Denver Nuggets, forward, 1994-95; Los Angeles Clippers, forward, 1995-99; Phoenix Suns, forward, 2000-02; Boston Celtics, forward, 2002; New Jersey Nets, forward, 2003-04; New Orleans Hornets, forward, 2004-05; Philadelphia 76ers, 2005; RRR Trucking Inc, owner, currently. **Honors/Awds:** Atlantic Coast Conference Player of the Year in 1993; NBA Sixth Man of the Year, 2000. **Special Achievements:** NBA Draft, first round, ninth pick, 1993.

ROGERS, ROY
Basketball player, basketball coach. **Personal:** Born Aug 19, 1973, Linden, AL; married Trish; children: Jasmine & Jordan. **Educ:** Univ Al, BS, Mkt Mgt, 1995. **Career:** Basketball player (retired), basketball coach; Vancouver Grizzlies, forward, 1996-97; Boston Celtics, 1997-98; Toronto Raptors, 1998; Denver Nuggets, 2000; Russia, Italy, Greece & Poland, 2000-04; Huntsville Flight, asst coach, 2005; Tulsa 66ers, asst coach, 2006-07; Okla Storm, head coach, 2007-. **Business Phone:** (580)237-8769.

ROGERS, SAM
Football player. **Personal:** Born May 30, 1970, Pontiac, MI; married Leslie; children: Sam Jr, Aaron, Ariel & Armani Lee. **Educ:** Univ Colo. **Career:** Football player (retired); Buffalo Bills, linebacker, 1994-2000; San Diego Chargers, 2001; Atlanta Falcons, 2002-03; free agent, currently.

ROGERS, SHAUN
Football player, artist. **Personal:** Born Mar 12, 1979, LaPorte, TX; son of Ernie. **Educ:** Univ Tex. **Career:** Detroit Lions, 2001-07; Cleveland Browns,2007-. **Honors/Awds:** NFC Defensive Player of the Week Award; Mel Farr Rookie of the Year; Pro Bowl sel, 2005, 2006 & 2008. **Special Achievements:** Appeared in com advert, The Lion King, 2003. **Business Addr:** Professional Football Player, Detroit Lions Inc, 222 Republic Dr, Allen Park, MI 48101, **Business Phone:** (313)216-4056.

ROGERS, VICTOR ALVIN
Clergy, educator. **Personal:** Born Oct 2, 1944, St Peter, Barbados; son of Grafton Simmons and Violet; married Gloria Bock, Feb 4, 1984; children: Nicholas, Paul, Matthew. **Educ:** Univ W Indies, LTH, 1971; Laurentian Univ, BA, 1973; Jackson State Univ, MA, sociol, 1977; Miss State Univ, PhD, sociol, 1987. **Career:** Diocese Barbados, St Paul's Church, cur, 1969-70, St Philip's Parish Church, cur, 1970-71; Diocese Long Island, St Philip's Episcopal Church, 1973-74; Diocese MSP, St Mark's, rector, 1974-83; St Luke's Episcopal Church, rector, 1983-; Southern Con State Univ, asst prof, 1992, adj prof, currently. **Orgs:** Bd mem, Downtown Coop Ministry, 1986; bd mem, Habitat Humanity, 1988; bd mem, Soc Increase Ministry, 1992. **Honors/Awds:** Outstanding Community Serv, Aldermanic Cit. **Special Achievements:** Co-author with VV Prakassa Rao, Sex, Socio-Economic Status and Secular Achievement Among High School Students, The Researcher, Vol 9 winter, p 25-36. **Business Addr:** Adjunct Professor, Southern Connecticut State University, 501 Crescent St, New Haven, CT 06511.

ROGERS-GRUNDY, ETHEL W.
Educator, insurance executive. **Personal:** Born Dec 3, 1938, Macclesfield, NC; daughter of Russell Wooten and Martha Pitt; married Sherman Grundy (deceased); children: Duane A Rogers & Angela S. **Educ:** St Augustines Col, BA, 1960; Temple Univ, MEd, 1970; Cath Univ Am, addnstudy; Univ Md. **Career:** Educator, insurance executive, (retired); St Augustines Col, NC, asst dean stud, 1965-66; Johnston Co Sch, Smithfield, NC, asst dir headstart, 1966-67; Woodson St High Sch, chmn bus dept, 1972-74; Fed City Col Wash, adj prof, 1975; Franklin Life Ins Co, agency mgr; DC Bd Educ, coordr off. **Orgs:** Delta Phi Epsilon, 1969; Eastern Bus Teacher Asn; Nat Bus Educ Asn; DC Bus Educ Asn; charter pres, Prince Georges Co Alumnae Chap Delta Sigma Theta,Inc; pres, Md Coun Deltas; secy, St Augustines Col Nat Alumni Asn; mem bddir, Lung Asn Southern Minn Inc; Alpha Zeta Chap Delta Phi Epsilon; Prince Georges Co, MD; Nat Asn Advan Colored People; Womens Polit Caucas Prince Georges Co, MD; Pan Hellenic Coun Prince Georges Co, MD. **Honors/Awds:** Female Business Leader of the Year, Md Chamber Com, 1976; Female Business Leader of the Year, Franklin Life Ins Co, 1981, 1983. **Home Addr:** 145 Leonard Lane, Harrisburg, PA 17111, **Home Phone:** (717)545-3174.

ROGERS-JONE, KELIS
Singer, songwriter. **Personal:** Born Aug 21, 1979, Harlem, NY; daughter of Kenneth and Eveliss; married Nas, Jun 8, 2005. **Career:** Singer & songwriter; R&B trio Black Ladies United, 1994-96; backup singerfor Gravediggaz' recording Fairytalz, 1997; Virgin Records, 1998-; Albums: Kaleidoscope, 1999; Wanderland, 2001; Tasty, exec producer, 2003; KelisWas Here, 2006; The Hits, 2008; After Ten So Good, 2009. **Honors/Awds:** NME Award, Best R&B Singer, 2001; Q magazine Award, Best Video ("Caughtout There"), 2003; Winner, Brit Award, Nominee, Grammy Awards, Twice. **Business Addr:** Singer, Songwriter, c/o Virgin Records, 338 N Foothill Rd, Beverly Hills, CA 90210, **Business Phone:** (310)278-1181.*

ROGERS-LOMAX, DR. ALICE FAYE
Educator, physician. **Personal:** Born Jan 20, 1950, Darlington, SC; daughter of James Rogers and Alice McCall Rogers; married Michael W, May 5, 1979; children: Lauren & Whitney. **Educ:** Holy Family Col, BA, 1972; Philadelphia Col Osteop Med, DO, 1976; HPCOM, Pediat Residency, 1977-79. **Career:** Philadelphia Col Osteop Med, asst prof pediat, 1979-80, chmn, divambulatory pediat, 1981-; NY Col Osteop Med, vis lectr, 1980; Sch Nursing Univ Pa; adjunct clin preceptor, 1981-; Osteop Med Ctr Philadelphia, chmn,div ambulatory pediat, 1981-89; Lomax Med Assoc, Philadelphia, Pa, pvtpediat pract, 1989-. **Orgs:** Am Osteop Asn, 1976-; Am Col Osteop Ped, 1977-; Pa Osteop Med Soc, 1979-; Stud Admis Comn, 1982-, Philadelphia Pediat Soc, 1983-; Ambulatory Pediat Asn, 1983-; Osteop Med Ctr 1982-86; Med Soc Eastern Pa, 1987-; Am Acad Pediat. **Honors/Awds:** Beta Beta Beta Nat Biol Hon Soc, 1972; Legion Honor, mem, Chapel Four Chaplains, Philadelphia, 1983. **Business Addr:** 300 N 52nd St, Philadelphia, PA 19139-1518, **Business Phone:** (215)472-1500.

ROGERS-REECE, SHIRLEY
Executive, school administrator, vice president (organization). **Personal:** Born in Carson, CA. **Career:** McDonald's Corp, restaurant mgr, 1981, area supvr, 1982-83, opers consult, 1983-85, McDonalds Hamburger Univ, prof, 1986-87, training mgr, 1987-88, opers mgr, 1988-90, field serv mgr, 1990-91, dean, 1991-94, Indonesia, dir opers, 1995-97, gen mgr, 1997, Worldwide Training, Learning & Develop, vpres, currently. **Honors/Awds:** McDonald's President's Award; Revlon Kizzy Award, Outstanding Women of America. **Business Addr:** Vice President of Worldwide Training Learning & Development, McDonalds Corporation, 2111 McDonald, Oak Brook, IL 60523, **Business Phone:** (630)623-3000.

ROHADFOX, RONALD OTTO
Executive. **Personal:** Born Mar 12, 1935, Syracuse, NY; son of Otto and Rita; children: Renwick, Roderick, Reginald & Rebekah. **Educ:** Ind Inst Technol, BSCE, 1961; Woodbury Univ, MBA, 1980; Century Univ, PhD, 1984. **Career:** Anal Construct Co, pres; Rohadfox Construct Control Servs Corp, chief exec officer, pres, currently. **Orgs:** Kappa Alpha Psi, 1960, Am Soc Civil Engrs, 1969, fel, 1996; Am Pub Works Asn, 1977, Soc Mkt Prof Serv, 1982; Nat Asn Minority Contractors, 1985. **Honors/Awds:** Republican Inner Circle, 1985; NC Transp Board, Appointment, 1991-92. **Special Achievements:** One of the Top 100 Black Successful Businessmen, Black Enterprise Magazine, 1974. **Business Addr:** President, Rohadfox Construction Control Services Corp, 411 W Chapel Hill Rd, Durham, NC 27701, **Business Phone:** (919)682-5741.

ROHE, BERNIE
Designer, executive. **Personal:** Married Uli Rohe. **Career:** Model, 1975; Bernie NY Inc, pres & chief designer, 1991-. **Special Achievements:** Featured in Essence Mag, Black Enterprise Mag; TV Show, "B. Smith with Style". **Business Phone:** (212)764-3320.*

ROHR, LEONARD CARL. See Obituaries section.

ROJAS, DON
Entrepreneur, journalist. **Personal:** Born Jan 1, 1949; married Karen Codrington; children: 3. **Educ:** Univ WI Madison, jour & commun. **Career:** Afro Am newspaper, asst ed; Nat Urban League, asst dir commun; Grenadian Prime Minister Maurice Bishop, press secy, 1979-83; Nat Granadian newspaper, ed chief, 1979-83; NY Amsterdam News, exec ed & asst publ, 1990; NAACP, communs dir, 1993; Pacifica station WBAI, gen mgr; Communs New Tomorrow LLC, founder, pres & chief exec officer, 1996-. The Black World Today, chief exec officer, currently. **Orgs:** Int Orgn Journlists, exec, 1980. **Honors/Awds:** Webby Award, The Black World Today, 1998; Silicon Alley Dozen, 1999; Outstanding Contribution for Journalism, Inst Caribbean Studies. **Business Addr:** Founder, President, Chief Executive Officer, The Black World Today, 729 E Pratt St Suite 500, Baltimore, MD 21202, **Business Phone:** (410)521-4678.

ROKER, AL. See ROKER, ALBERT LINCOLN.

ROKER, ALBERT LINCOLN (AL ROKER)
Television broadcaster, writer. **Personal:** Born Aug 20, 1954, Queens, NY; married Deborah Roberts, 1995. **Educ:** State Univ New York, Oswego, BA, commun. **Career:** WTVH-TV, Syracuse, NY, weekend weatherman, 1974; WNBC, New York, weekend weathercaster, 1983; CNBC, meteorologist & talk show host; Al Roker Prod Inc, founder & owner, 1992-; CNBC Today Show, weatherman, 1996-; Author: Don't Make Me Stop This Car: Adventures in Fatherhood; Big Bad Book of Barbecue; Hassle-Free Holiday Cookbook, 2003. **Honors/Awds:** Emmy Awards; 1997 Daytime Emmy Award nominee, Outstanding Game Show Host; hon doctorate, State Univ New York, Oswego.

ROLAND, BENAUTRICE, JR.
Manager. **Personal:** Born Dec 11, 1945, Detroit, MI; married Brenda Thornton; children: Michele S & Michael L. **Educ:** Univ Detroit, BS, Finance, 1972; Wharton Grad Sch Univ PA, MBA, Finance, 1974. **Career:** Morgan Guaranty Trust NY, eurocurrency trader, 1974-75; Ford Motor Co,financial analyst, 1975-79; MI Bell Tele Co, staff supr, 1979-. **Orgs:** Bd dirs, Univ PA Alumni Club MI; co-chmn, Secondary Sch Com. **Military Serv:** USAF, sgt, 1964-67.

ROLISON, NATE (NATHAM MARDIS ROLISON)
Baseball player. **Personal:** Born Mar 27, 1977, Hattiesburg, MS. **Career:** Minor League: Marlins, 1995, 2001; Kane County, 1996; Brevard County, 1997, 2001; Portland Sea Dogs, 1998-99, 2001; Calgary Cannons, 2000-02; Tacoma Rainiers, 2002; Colombus

Clippers, 2003; Major League : Fla Marlins, infielder, 2000; Seattle Mariniers, 2002; Chicago White Sox, infielder, 2004. *

ROLLE, DR. ALBERT EUSTACE
Surgeon. **Personal:** Born Aug 3, 1935, Miami, FL; son of Jerod and Bessie; married Josephine James; children: Allyson & Jonathan. **Educ:** Fla A&M Univ, AB, 1954; Univ Pittsburgh, BS, 1960; Univ Pittsburgh Sch Med, MD, 1965. **Career:** Surgeon (retired); Georgetown Univ Med Ctr, clin asst prof surg, 1972; DC Bd Police/Fire Surgeons, surgeon, 1973-78; Capital Area Permanent Med Group, gen surgeon, 1985. **Orgs:** Kappa Alpha Psi Frat 1952-; Fel Am Col Surgeons, 1973-; DC Med Soc, 1970-; past master, Fel Lodge 26, F & AM, PHA 1973-; Wash Acad Surg, 1975-. **Honors/Awds:** Physicians Recognition Award, Am Med Asn, 1972; Outstanding Performance Award, Metro Police Dept Bd Police Surgeons 1977. **Military Serv:** Retired. Lt Col USAF Med Corps. **Home Addr:** 600 Riverbend Rd, Fort Washington, MD 20744, **Home Phone:** (301)839-1484.

ROLLE, FRANKIE SHANNON
Educator. **Personal:** Born Nov 25, 1924, Jacksonville, FL; daughter of Frank and Mary Isham; married William, Oct 27, 1952; children: Melodie, Zachary, William jr & Jeanette. **Educ:** Florida A&M Univ, BS, 1946; Ind Univ, MS, 1960. **Career:** Educator (retired); Dade County Pub Schs, physical educ instr, guidance counr, 1946-87. **Orgs:** Pres, FAMU Alumni Asn, Miami Chap, 1970-72; basileus, Zeta Phi Beta Sorority, BTZ Chap, 1979-83; pres, Dade County Community Action Agency, 1980-99; scholar chair, Phi Delta Kappa Fraternity, 1982-83; pres, Gold Coast Chap, 1987-88; exec bd, Nat Asn Advan Colored People, Miami Br; trustee bd, Black Archives & Historical Soc, 1990; bd chair, Helen B Bentley Family Health Ctr, 1994-98; treas, Coconut Grove Negro Women's Club, 1998. **Honors/Awds:** FL A&M Univ Sports Hall of Fame, 1979; Award for Outstanding Community Serv, King Club's Lifetime Achievement Award, Nat Asn Negro Bus & Prof Women's Club, 1988; Distinguished Alumni Award, 1988; Living Legend Award, FAMU, 1998. **Special Achievements:** Nat Convention of Aging, rep, 1995; G W Garner Middle Sch Gymnasium named Frankie Shannon Rolle Gymnasium, 1995; Coconut Grove Human Resource Center re-named Frankie Shannon Rolle Neighborhood Serv Ctr.

ROLLE, JANET
Vice president (Organization), executive, manager. **Personal:** Born Dec 25, 1961, Mount Vernon, NY; daughter of William Sr and Barbara Rolle; married Mark Keye, Apr 14, 1995; children: 1. **Educ:** State Univ NY, Purchase, BFA, 1984; Columbia Bus Sch, MBA, mkt & film, 1991. **Career:** HBO, spec asst chmn, 1991-92, mgr, multiplex mkt, 1992-93, dir mkt & sales prom; MTV Networks, Programming enterprises & bus develop, vpres; Am Online Inc, Am Online Black Voices serv, vpres & gen mgr; BET Networks, exec vprs & chief mktg officer, 2007-. **Orgs:** Black filmmaker found, 1990-; NY women film & TV, 1991-; NY Coalition 100 Black Women, 1992-; mentor, Harlem YMCA Mentoring Prog, 1993-; chairperson, Multicultural Participation Comn US Tennis Asn; mem, bd adv, City At Peace NY. **Honors/Awds:** Black Achievers in Industry, Harlem YMCA, 1993. **Business Phone:** (202)608-2000.

ROLLINS, AVON WILLIAM, SR.
Government official, executive director. **Personal:** Born Sep 16, 1941, Knoxville, TN; son of Ralph Kershaw and Josephine Rollins Lee; married Sheryl Clark, Sep 28, 1974; children: Avon Jr, Avondria F. **Educ:** Knoxville Col; Univ Tenn. **Career:** Stud Nonviolent Coord Comn, nat exec; Southern Christian Leadership Conf, spec asst; Tenn Valley Authority, mgr; Rollins & Assocs Inc, pres & chief exec officer; Beck Cult Exchange Ctr Inc, exec dir & chief exec officer, currently. **Orgs:** One of co-founders, former nat exec, SNCC Raleigh NC, 1960; asst to the late Rev Dr Martin Luther King Jr; bd dir, Mgt Comn Knoxville Int Energy Exposition, 1982; chmn, Magnolia Fed Savings & Loan Asn; adv, former chmn & founder, TVA Employees Minority Invest Forum; Chancellors Asn; The Univ Tenn; Pres, Round Table Knoxville Col; chmn emeritus, former chmn of bd; founder, Greater Knoxville Minority Bus Bur Inc; former chmn, pres, Knoxville Comm Coop, former mem, Nat Rural Cable TV Task Force; co-founder, Greater Knoxville Urban League; co-founder, former mem bd dir, Knoxville Opportunity Indust Ctr Inc. **Honors/Awds:** Tenn 94th Gen Assembly; Untiring Serv Humanity, US Dept Com; Bus Advocate of the Year, Nashville Bus Devt Ctr, 1987, 1993; Nat Asn of Human Rights Workers, dedication of 47th Annual Conf to Rollins, 1994; Nat Civil Rights Museum, named annual Heritage Award after Rollins; Nat Asn Black Legislatures, Nation Builder Award, 1994; Nat Bus League Award; Leadership & Achievement Award, Booker T Wash Found; Outstanding Lard, Top Ladies of Distinction Inc, 1995; numerous other awards. **Special Achievements:** Publications include: "Minority Economic Development/Problems & Opportunity"; "The Tennessee Black Economy", 1972-; numerous other articles on the civil rights struggle and minority economic development; song entitled "Avon Rollins" recorded by MAtt Jones depicting Rollins' involvement in civil rightts movement. **Business Addr:** Cheif Executive Officer, Director, Beck Cultural Exchange Center Inc., 1927 Dandridge Ave, Knoxville, TN 37915-1997, **Business Phone:** (865)524-8461.*

ROLLINS, ETHEL EUGENIA
Social worker. **Personal:** Born Feb 16, 1932, Paris, TX; daughter of Elisha and Julia; married Edward C; children: Vyla LeJeune & Rojeune Bali. **Educ:** Jarvis Christian Col, BA, 1954; Univ Pittsburgh, MSW, 1958. **Career:** Social worker (retired); Dayton Children Psychol Hosp & Child Guidance Clinic, psychol soc worker, 1958-62; Family & Childrens Serv Asn Dayton, psychol soc worker, 1964-65; Denver County Pub Sch Psychol Serv, sch social worker, 1965-68; Ft Logan Mental Health Ctr, Denver, psychol soc worker, 1972-95; Denver Univ, assoc prof soc work, 1975. **Orgs:** Colo Christian Home Bd, Colo Christian Home for Children, Denver, 1970-75; human servs, adv bd, Metro State Col, Denver, 1979-84, chap, 1984-; week compassion comn, Christian Ch Disciples Christ Indianapolis, 1975-80; adv bd, Mother to Mother Ministry, 1978-80; bd & comn mem, Habitat for Humanity, 1979-80; leg & social concerns, Colo Coun Church, 1980-82; sec Colo coun Churches, 1981-82; chmn, Outreach Christian Church Disciples Christ Colo, WY Reg Outreach on Reg Needs, 1982-83; activist Peace/Justice Movement/Nuclear Freeze Movement, 1982-84; evaluator, Annual Ethnic Youth Leadership Conf, United Methodist Church, 1986-91; Info & Servs, Christian Church (Disciples of Christ) Gen Assembly, volunteer/layministry /vice chair person, 1997; team mem, Anti-racism ProreCouniation Initative, Central Rocky Mountain region Christian Church, 2001-02. **Honors/Awds:** Hon Award for Leadership State Fair, TX 4-H Club, 1949; "Student Contributing Most to the Religious Life of Campus" Award, Jarvis Christian Col, 1952; Outstanding Leadership Award, Col Christian Home, 1971-75; Rojeune, Edward & Ethel appeared as family on KCNC NBC Affil Denver CO, 1983; discussing film "The Day After"; Outstanding Member, Chair, Human Services Dept/Human Serv Educ Org, 1988. **Special Achievements:** Author, "Changing Trends in Adoption", Nat Conf Social Welfare, 1971. **Home Addr:** 2439 S Dahlia Lane, Denver, CO 80222.

ROLLINS, JUDITH ANN
Sociologist, educator, writer. **Personal:** Born in Boston, MA; daughter of Edward B and Edith F. **Educ:** Howard Univ, BA, 1970, MA, 1972; Brandeis Univ, PhD, 1983. **Career:** Fed City Col, instr, sociol, 1972-77; Boston Col, instr, sociol, 1977-83; Northeastern Univ, asst prof, sociol, 1983-84; Simmons Col, from asst prof to assoc prof, 1984-92; Wellesley Col, Africana Studies, assoc prof, sociol, 1992-95, prof, 1995-; Books: Journal of Social Relations, 1987; Readings, 1988; Women's Studies International Forum, 1989; Gender & Society, 1990; American Journal of Sociology, 1991; McGill's Literary Annual, 1992; Sage, 1993; Women's Review of Books, 2002. Written: Between Women: Domestics & Their Employers, 1985; All is Never Said: The Narrative of Odette Harper Hines, 1995; chapter, At Work in Homes, American Ethnological Society Monograph, no. 3, 1990; Articles: Black World, 1974; Phylon, 1986; Actes la Recherche En Sciences Sociale, 1990; Abafazi, 1991; Journal of Women's History, 1993. **Orgs:** Am Sociol Asn; Asn Black Sociologists; Soc Study Soc Probs; Delta Sigma Theta Sorority; Asn Soc & Behav Scientists; Caribbean Studies Asn. **Honors/Awds:** Social Issues Dissertion Award, Soc Psychological Study Soc Issues, 1984; Jessie Bernard Award, Am Sociological Asn, 1987; research grant, Am Philosophical Soc, 1987. **Special Achievements:** Author of numerous articles. **Business Addr:** Professor, Wellesley College, Africana Studies & Sociology, 106 Cent St, Wellesley, MA 02481, **Business Phone:** (781)283-2569.

ROLLINS, LEE OWEN
Executive. **Personal:** Born Dec 22, 1938, Kansas City, KS; married Rosalie D; children: Lori, Linda, Larry, Lonny, Lyle. **Educ:** Univ NE, psychol, 1963. **Career:** Flintkote Co Los Angeles CA, mkt rep, 1963-66; San Diego Gas & Elec, license negotiator, 1966-68, employ rep, 1968-78, mgr employ, 1979. **Orgs:** Outstanding Kappa Man ETA Chap Univ of NE, 1960; vpres, transportation SD Jr C C, 1970-74; dir, Southeast Rotary, 1974-79; chmn, Affirmative Action Com WCPA, 1975-78; vpres, campus rels Soc Advancement Mgt, 1979-; Bd mem, Western Col Placement Asn, 1975-80; dir, Amigos del Serv, 1979-80. **Honors/Awds:** Community Service Award, Nat Alliance Bus, 1968; Outstanding Service Award, Urban League, 1979. **Business Addr:** 101 Ash St, San Diego, CA 92101.

ROLLINS, DR. RICHARD ALBERT
Educator, clergy. **Personal:** Born Nov 30, 1927, Philadelphia, PA; married Audrey J King. **Educ:** Lincoln Univ, BA, 1952; Union Theol Sem, MDiv, 1955; Boston Univ Sch Theol, STM, 1960; Claremont Schl Theoly, RelD, 1969. **Career:** Bishop Col, chmn, Div Rel, 1958-67, assoc dean, admin, 1969-70, dean, 1970-77, vpres & prof relig, 1977-83, exec asst pres, dean chapel, 1983-89; Nat Baptist Conv Am, liaison officer, 1989-. **Orgs:** Chmn, Moorland Br, YMCA, 1969-85; Nat Urban League; Nat Asn Advan Colored People; Nat Campus Ministry Asn, Acad Relig; Tex Alcohol & Narcotics Asn; bd dir, Dallas YMCA. **Honors/Awds:** Teacher Award, Danforth Found, 1960-62; Fel Award, Ford Found, 1967; Dallas Citizenship Award, Radio Sta KNOK, 1970. **Military Serv:** AUS, corpl, 2 yrs. **Home Addr:** 630 Woodacre Dr, Dallas, TX 75241. **Business Addr:** Liaison Officer, National Baptist Convention of America, 777 S RL Thorton Freeway Suite 205, Dallas, TX 75203, **Business Phone:** (214)946-8913.

ROLLINS, SONNY. See ROLLINS, WALTER THEODORE.

ROLLINS, TREE
Basketball player, basketball coach. **Personal:** Born Jun 16, 1955, Winter Haven, FL; married Michelle; children: Nicolas, Undria, Kendall Rollins & Katreesa. **Educ:** Clemson Univ, attended 1977. **Career:** Basketball player (retired), basketball coach; Atlanta Hawks, ctr, 1977-88; Cleveland Cavaliers, 1988-90; Detroit Pistons, 1990-91; Houston Rockets, 1991-93; Orlando Magic, ctr, 1993-96, asst coach, 1996-99; Greenville Groove, coach; Ky Colonels, pres & gen mgr; NBA Pre-Draft Camp, head coach; Wash Wizards, asst coach; Ind Pacers, asst coach, 2000; Greenville Groove, head coach, 2006; Wash Mystics, asst coach, 2006, interim head coach, 2007-. **Honors/Awds:** NBA All-Defensive Second Team, 1983; NBA All-Defensive First Team, 1984. **Special Achievements:** Orlando Magic, player & asst coach; NBA Player, 18th season; Third oldest active player behind Robert Parrish & Moses Malone, 1994-95; Atlanta Hawks Career Record, most games played 814; blocked shots 2,283; defensive rebounds 4,092. **Business Addr:** Interim Head Coach, Washington Mystics, 627 N Glebe Rd Suite 850, Arlington, VA 22203, **Business Phone:** (202)266-2200.

ROLLINS, WALTER THEODORE (SONNY ROLLINS)
Composer, musician. **Personal:** Born Sep 7, 1930, New York City, NY; son of Valborg and Walter; married Lucille Pearson, 1959; married Dawn Finney, 1956 (divorced). **Career:** Pianist, saxophonist, tenor; Rec, 1949, Recorded with Bud Powell, Dizzy Gillespie, Max Roach, Clifford Brown & Thelonious Monk; discography contains 71 recordings, 1997; Albums: Sonny Rollins Quartet, 1951; Sonny &the Stars, 1951; Sonny Rollins with the Modern Jazz Quartet, 1951; Mambo Jazz, 1951; Moving Out, 1954; Sonny Rollins Plays Jazz Classics, 1954; Sonny Rollins Quintet, 1954; Taking Care of Business, 1955; Work Time, 1955; Saxophone Colossus, 1956; Sonny Rollins Plus Four, 1956; Three Giants, 1956; Tenor Madness, 1956; Rollins Plays for Bird, 1956; Sonny Boy, 1956; Tour de Force, 1956; Sonny Rollins, Vol. 1, 1956; Alternate Takes, 1957; Way Out West, 1957; Sonny Rollins, Vol. 2, 1957; Wail March, 1957; Sonny's Time, 1957; Newk's Time, 1957; Night at the Village Vanguard, 1957; Sonny Rollins Plays/Jimmy Cleveland Plays, 1957; European Concerts, 1957; Sonny Side Up, 1957; Sonny Rollins On Impulse, 1966; East Broadway Run Down, 1966; Don't Stop the Carnival, 1978; This Is What I Do, 2000; Without a Song: The 9/11 Concert, 2001; Sonny Please, 2006; Road Shows, 2007. **Honors/Awds:** Numerous honors & awards including Guggenheim Fellow, 1972; Hall of Fame, Downbeat Mag; hon Doctorate, Music Bard Col, 1992; hon doctorate fine arts, Wesleyan Univ, 1998; hon doctorate music, Long Island Univ, 1998; hon doctorate, fine arts, Duke Univ, 1999; Lifetime Achievement Award, Tufts Univ, 1996, hon doctorate music, New England Conserv, 2002; hon doctorate Music Berklee Col Music, 2003 & Polar Music Prize, 2007. **Special Achievements:** The city of Minneapolis, Minnesota officially named 31 October 2006 after Rollins in honor of his achievements and contributions to the world of jazz. **Home Addr:** Rte 9G, Germantown, NY 12526, **Home Phone:** (518)537-6112. **Business Addr:** Composer, Rte 9G, PO Box 175, Germantown, NY 12526, **Business Phone:** (518)537-6112.

ROMAIN, PIERRE R
Executive. **Personal:** Born Sep 24, 1967, Nyack, NY; divorced. **Career:** JP & Associates Advert, pres; Harolds Evergreen Restaurant, partner & dir mkt, 1990-91; Giraldi Entertainment, vpres; Pierre Romain Inc, chief exec officer & producer, currently; Workout Partners Fitness Inc, chmn & chief exec officer, currently. **Business Phone:** (212)564-0177.

ROMANS, ANN
Educator, association executive. **Personal:** Born Apr 3, 1929, Wetumpka, AL; daughter of Tumpa Riley Varner (deceased) and John Varner; married Lawrence Jones, Mar 9, 1960 (divorced); children: Anthony L Jones & Annetta Romans Williams. **Educ:** Knoxville Col, Knoxville, Tenn, BA, educ, 1952; Univ Tenn, Knoxville, Tenn, spec educ; Case-Western Res Univ, Cleveland, OH, 1965; John Carroll Univ, Cleveland, OH, comput educ, 1985, master's degree, 1996. **Career:** Cleveland Sch Bd, Cleveland, OH, counr, teacher/sub teacher, 1952; Comedian, Cleveland, OH, 1979; Help Educate Serv, Cleveland, OH, dir, 1979-; Cleveland Black Writers, Cleveland, OH, pres, 1986-; Cleveland Cablevision, producer, TV host, currently. **Orgs:** St Mark's Presbyterian Church, 1948-; Alpha Kappa Alpha Sorority, 1951-; Polit Black Caucus, 1973-; 21st Dist Caucus, 1973-; US Adv Community, Congressional Security Coun. **Honors/Awds:** 21st District Caucus Community Award; Miss Galaxy Black Pageant, Ohio dir, 1968; Comedy Award, Cleveland Comedy Club, 1989; Wave Comm Award; American Poets Award; res fel, Ford Foundation. **Special Achievements:** World Traveler. **Business Addr:** Director, HES, PO Box 22016, Beachwood, OH 44122, **Business Phone:** (216)321-9477.

ROMEO, LIL. See MILLER, PERCY ROMEO, JR.

ROMES, CHARLES MICHAEL
Football player. **Personal:** Born Dec 16, 1954, Verdun, France; married Redalia; children: Twila Redalia. **Educ:** NC Central Univ.

Career: Football player (retired); Buffalo Bills, cornerback, 1977-86; San Diego Chargers, 1987; Seattle Seahawks, 1988.

ROMNEY, EDGAR O.
Labor activist. **Personal:** Born Feb 9, 1943, New York, NY; son of Edward Romney Sr and Ida Johnstone; married Gladys Talbot, Oct 20, 1972; children: Juliette, Monique, Nicola & Edgar Jr. **Educ:** Hunter Col, Queens, NY, attended 1975; Empire State Labor Col, attended 1982. **Career:** Local 99, ILGWU, New York, NY, organizer & bus agent, 1966-75; Local 23-25, ILGWU, New York, NY, dir orgn, 1976-78, asst mgr, 1978-83, mgr & secy, 1983; ILGWU, New York, NY, exec vpres, 1989-; UNITE!, exec vpres, 1995; UNITE HERE, secy-treas; Workers United, secy-treas, pres. **Orgs:** Bd dirs, Am Labor ORT Fedn, 1986-; bd dirs, Garment Indust Develop Corp, 1987-; nat secy, A Philip Randolph Inst, 1987-; bd dirs, NY Urban League, 1987-; bd dirs, NY State Dept Labor Garment Adv Coun, 1988-; bd dirs, Bayard Rustin Fund, 1989-; co-chair, NY Labor Comt Against Apartheid, 1989-94; Brain trust on Labor Issues, 1991-; second vpres, NY Labor Coun AFL-CIO, 1992-; co-chmn, NY Comt African Labor Solidarity, 1994-; Cong Black Caucus. **Honors/Awds:** Recognition Award, Negro Labor Comt, 1984; Nelson Mandela Award, Coalition Black Trade Unionists, 1984, 1989; Achievement Award, NAACP, NY Br, 1987; Roberto Clemente Appreciation Award & Hispanic Labor Comt, 1987; NAACP Man of the Year Award, NAACP, 1987; Recognition Award, China town, YMCA, 1988; Outstanding Leadership in Labor & Community Service, Borough of Manhattan Community Col, 1989; Leadership Award, Am ORT Fedn, 1989; Outstanding Service & Commitment & Hispanic Labor Comt, 1989; Distinguished Service Award, AFL-CIO, 1990. **Special Achievements:** First African-American to head an American labor federation. **Business Addr:** President, Workers United, 31 W 15th St 3rd Fl, New York, NY 10011, **Business Phone:** (917)832-1558.

RONEY, RAYMOND G
Educator, publisher. **Personal:** Born Jul 26, 1941, Philadelphia, PA; son of Wallace and Rosezell Harris; married Ruth A Westgaph; children: Andre. **Educ:** Cent State Univ, BA, polit sci, 1963; Pratt Inst, MS, libr sci, 1965; Cath Univ, post grad, 1985. **Career:** Howard Univ Libr, supr ref dept, 1965-66; Nat League Cities/US Conf Mayors, dir libr serv, 1966-70; Wash Tech Inst, dir libr serv, 1970-78, chmn med tech dept, 1971-78; Univ DC, dep dir learning resources, 1978-83; El Camino Col, assoc dean learning resources, 1984, dean instrnl serv, 1988-; Libr Mosaics Mag, publ, 1989-; Yenor Inc, pres & publ, 1989-. **Orgs:** Pres, Shepherd Park Citizens Asn, DC, 1972-74; exec bd, Paul Community Sch, 1974-83; bd mem, COLT, 1978; Phi Delta Kappa, 1980; pres, Coun Lib/Media Tech, 1983; United Way Adv Bd, 1988-; dir, Calif Libr Employees Asn, 1988; libr adv bd, Afro-Am Mus, CA, 1989-; long range planning comt mem, Calif Libr Asn, 1988-91, mem comt, 1989-91; prog planning comt mem, CARL, 1989-91; bd mem, Learning Resources Asn Calif Community Col, 1994-; pres, Cent State Univ S CA Alumni Chap, 1999-. **Honors/Awds:** Outstanding Achievement, Bright Hope Baptist Church, 1963; Grass Roots Award, DC Fed Civic & Citizens Asn, 1975; Outstanding Achievement, Shepherd Park Citizens Asn, 1975; Administrative Excellence Award, INTELECOM, 1993; ADR of the Year Award, Calif Asn Post Secondary Educ & Disabilities, 1997; Special Friend Award, El Camino Alumni Asn, 2000. **Business Addr:** President, Publisher, Yenor Inc, PO Box 5171, Culver City, CA 90231, **Business Phone:** (310)645-4998.

ROOKS, SEAN LESTER
Basketball player, basketball coach. **Personal:** Born Sep 9, 1969, New York, NY. **Educ:** Univ Ariz, attended 1992. **Career:** Basketball player(retired), basketball coach; Dallas Mavericks, ctr, 1992-94; Minn Timberwolves, 1994-96; Atlanta Hawks, 1996; Los Angeles Lakers, 1996-99; Dallas Mavericks, 1999-2000; Los Angeles Clippers, 2000-03; Orlando Magic, 2003-04; New Orleans Hornets, ctr, 2003-04; Bakersfield JAM, interim head coach, asst coach, 2008-. **Business Addr:** Assistant Coach, Bakersfield JAM, 1400 Norris Rd, Bakersfield, CA, CA 93308, **Business Phone:** (661)716-4526.

ROPER, BOBBY L.
School administrator. **Personal:** Born Jan 1, 1930, Chicago, IL; son of William and Irvia Carter; children: Reginald. **Educ:** Chicago Teachers Col, BEd, 1959; Chicago State Univ, MS, 1966. **Career:** Principal (retired); Chicago Pub Sch, master teacher, 1962-64, adjustment teacher, 1965-68, asst prin, 1968-71; Lawndale Comm Acad, prin. **Orgs:** Bd dir, Lawndale Homemakers, 1970-75; bd dir, Chicago Youth 1975-; bd dir, Marcy New berry 1982-83. **Military Serv:** USY, corporal, 1954-56.

ROPER, DEIDRE (DEIDRE LATOYA ROPER)
Rap musician, business owner. **Personal:** Born Aug 3, 1971, New York, NY; children: Christenese. **Career:** Rap Group Salt-N-Pepa, mem, currently; She Things Salon & Day Spa, owner, currently; Films: Stay Tuned, 1992; Kazaam, 1996; TV includes: Sinatra: "The 6th Annual Soul Train Music Awards", 1992; "Saturday Night Live", 1994; "80 Years My Way", 1995; "Wrestlemania XI", 1995; Comedy Central Roast of Flavor Flav, 2007; The Salt-N-Pepa Show, 2007; The Surreal Life, 2005; Behind the Music, 2005; Singer:"Juice", 1992; "Space Jam", 1996; beauty salon, owner, 1997. **Special Achievements:** Co-wrote a song for Kazaam, 1996. **Business Phone:** (718)276-5212.*

ROPER, DEIDRE LATOYA. See ROPER, DEIDRE.

ROPER, RICHARD WALTER
Executive. **Personal:** Born Sep 20, 1945, Deland, FL; son of Henry and Dorothe; married Marlene Peacock; children: Jelani & Akil. **Educ:** Rutgers Univ, BA, 1968; Princeton Univ, MPA, 1971. **Career:** NJ Dept Higher Educ, Trenton, NJ, asst to vice chancellor, 1968-69; Dept Transp & Planning Greater London Coun, London, res asst, 1971; Mayor's Educ Task Force, Off Newark Studies, Newark, NJ, staff coordr, 1971-72; NJ Dept Insts & Agencies, Div Youth & Family Servs, Trenton, NJ, 1972-73; Greater Newark Urban Coaltion, NJ Educ Reform Proj, Newark, NJ, dir, 1973-74; Mayor Kenneth A Gibson, Newark, NJ, legis aide, 1974-76; Off Newark Metrop Studies, Newark, NJ, dir, 1976-78; US Dept Com, Off Secy, Wash, DC, dir, 1979-80, spec asst intergovernmental relations; Woodrow Princeton Univ, Wilson Sch Pub & Int Affairs, lectr pub & int affairs, dir, 1980-88, asst dean grad career servs & govt rels, 1988-92; Port Authority NY & NJ, dir, Off Econ & Policy Anal, 1992; Off State & Local Govt Assistance, dir; Roper Groups, founder & pres, currently; Grad Career Serv & Govt Relations, asst dean. **Orgs:** Bd trustees, Newark Pub Radio; Gov Taskforce Child Abuse & Neglect, 1984-; NJ Child Life Protection Comn; bd dirs, NJ Pub Policy Res Inst; bd trustees, exec comt mem, Boys' & Girls' Clubs Newark, NJ; bd dir, Asn Black Princeton Alumni; bd dirs, Greater Jamaica Develop Corp, NY; bd overseers, Rutgers Univ Found; adv comt, Ctr Govt Servs, Rutgers Univ; adv bd, New Jersey Nat Ctr Pub Productivity; dir, Prog NJ Affairs; exec dir, Coun NJ Affairs. **Honors/Awds:** Distinguished Princeton Alumni, 1992; New Jersy Nat Asn Advan Colored People Service Award, 1990; New Jersy Legal Services Recognition Award, 1989. **Special Achievements:** Wrote several articles including: "Building One New Jersey," New Jersey Reporter, February 1990; "New Jersey's Crunch: Better to Take the Hit Now," Commentary, Asbury Park Press, April 1990; "Florio's Fiscal Plan Makes Sense," coauthor, Trenton Times, October 1990; "The 1991 Legislative Election in New Jersey: An Analysis," Black Issues Convention Quarterly, December 1991; "An Analysis of Changes in Population, Education and Income for African-Americans in New Jersey: 1980-90 (Northern Counties)", New Jersey African-Americans and the 1980 Census, New Jersey Public Policy Research Institute, Inc, February, 1994. **Home Addr:** 12 Rutgers St, Maplewood, NJ 07040. **Business Addr:** Founder, President, The Roper Group, 550 Broad St Suite 601, Newark, NJ 07102, **Business Phone:** (973)286-2780.

ROSCOE, WILMA J.
Association executive. **Personal:** Born Aug 24, 1938, Kershaw, SC; daughter of Chalmers Harris and Estelle Harris; married Alfred D Roscoe Jr (deceased), Jul 6, 1963; children: Alfred D Roscoe III, Jenae V, Jeneen B. **Educ:** Livingstone Col, Salisbury, NC, BS, 1960. **Career:** Howard Univ, Wash, DC, admissions asst, 1963-69; Fayetteville State Univ, Fayetteville, NC, dir tutorial prog, 1969-74; Nat Asn Equal Opportunity Higher Educ, Wash, DC, 1975, sr vpres & chief exec officer, Interim Pres & Chief Exec Officer, currently. **Orgs:** Am Personnel & Guidance Asn; Nat Coalition Black Meeting Planners; Delta Sigma Theta. **Honors/Awds:** Distinguished service award, Nat Asn Equal Opportunity Higher Educ, 1986; Honorary degrees: Miles Col, AR Baptist Col, Livingstone Col; Nat Bus League Award; Outstanding Service Award, Langston Univ; Outstanding Service Award, Denmark Tech Col. **Business Addr:** Interim President, Chief Executive Officer, National Association Equal Opportunity Higher Education, 8701 Georgia Ave Suite 200, Silver Spring, MD 20910, **Business Phone:** (301)650-2440.*

ROSE, ALVIN W.
Educator. **Personal:** Born Feb 14, 1916, New Haven, MO; married Helen Cureton. **Educ:** Lincoln Univ, BA 1938; Univ IA, MA 1942; Univ Chicago, PhD 1948; Sorbonne Paris, post-doctoral study 1952. **Career:** Fisk Univ, prof of Sociology, 1946-47; NC Col, prof, 1948-56; Wayne State Univ, prof, 1956-72; Dept of Sociology Wayne State Univ, chmn, 1968-72; Univ of Miami, prof, 1972-; visiting prof & lectr at numerous Col & univ. **Orgs:** Am Social Assn; Soc for Study of Social Problems; Am Assn of Univ Prof; Intl Soc for Scientific Study of Race Relations; So Social Soc; AmAcad of Political & Social Sci; Phi Delta Kappa Social Sci Soc; Alpha Kappa Delta Social Soc; Nat Assn of Intergroup Relations Officials; FL Social Soc; African Studies Assn; NAACP; mem bd of Govs Museum of Sci; bd dir United Nations Assn; chmn Intergroup Relations Sect Soc for Study of Social Problems; mem Univ of Miami Com on Salaries Rank & Promotion; mem Univ of Miami Grad Com on Degrees & Acad Prog; Univ of Miami Faculty Com for Afro-Am Studies; mem exec com Univ Cntr for Urban Studies; Author of Numerous Publications.

ROSE, ANIKA NONI
Actor. **Personal:** Born Sep 6, 1972, Bloomfield, CT. **Educ:** Am Conserv Theater. **Career:** Films: King of the Bingo Game, 1999; From Justin to Kelly, 2003; Temptation, 2004; Surviving Christmas, 2004; Dream girls, 2006; One Part Sugar, 2007; Razor, 2007; Just Add Water, 2007; The Princess and the Frog, 2009; TV: "100 Centre Street,"2001; "Third Watch," 2002; "Caroline, or Change", 2004; The Startet Wife,2007; The No 1 Ladies' Detective Agency, 2008-09; Episode dated 23 April 2009, 2009; "Tavis Smiley", 2009; stage: Valley Song, 1998; Threepenny Opera, 1999; Tartuffe, 1999; Footloose (musical), 2000; Carmen Jones, 2001; Caroline, or Change, 2003-04; Cat on a Hot Tin Roof, 2008. **Honors/Awds:** Tony Award for Best Performance by a Featured Actress in a Musical, 2004; Lucille Lortell Award; Theatre World Award; Clarence Derwent Award; Los Angeles Critic's Circle Award; Ovation Award; Obie Award; Drama-Logue Ensemble Award. **Business Addr:** Actress, c/o Don Buchwald & Associates, 10 E 44th St, New York, NY 10017, **Business Phone:** (212)867-1070.*

ROSE, BESSIE L
Electrical engineer. **Personal:** Born Mar 2, 1958, Lafayette, LA; daughter of Andrew and Iritha Stevens. **Educ:** Southern Univ, Baton Rouge, BSEE, 1980. **Career:** Naval Air Rework Faci, Pensacola, co-op stud, 1976-78; Xerox, Rochester, summer intern, 1979; Commonwealth Edison, Chicago, elec engr, 1980-. **Orgs:** Alpha Kappa Alpha, 1977-; Nat Black MBA Asn, 1990-; League of Black Women, 1990-. **Special Achievements:** Section Engr (responsible for defining, developing and implementing an entirely new dept on quality control). **Home Phone:** (312)955-4245. **Business Addr:** Section Engineer, Commonwealth Edison Co, 1319 S 1st Ave, Maywood, IL 60153, **Business Phone:** (708)450-5267.

ROSE, JALEN
Basketball player, broadcaster, executive. **Personal:** Born Jan 30, 1973, Detroit, MI; son of Jimmy Walker. **Educ:** Univ Md, Univ Col, BS, mgt studies. **Career:** Basketball player (retired), broadcaster, executive; Denver Nuggets, guard, 1994-96; Indiana Pacers, 1996-2002; Chicago Bulls, 2002-04; Toronto Raptors, 2003-06; NY Knicks, guard-forward, 2006; Phoenix Suns, 2006?07; ESPN, studio analyst & broadcaster, 2007-; Three Tier Entertainment, chief exec officer & founder, 2007-. **Orgs:** Founder, Jalen Rose Found; Make-a-Wish Found. **Honors/Awds:** NBA Most Improved Player Award, 1999-2000; Fox Sports Net Bull of the Year, 2002-03; CDW Chicago Bulls Player of the Year, 2002-03; Chicago Bulls Lubin Award, 2003; NBA Community Assist Award, 2003; Magic Johnson Award, Prof Basketball Writers Asn, 2003; NBA Community Assist Award Winner, 2005; NBA Eastern Conference Player of the Week, 2005. **Special Achievements:** One of America's Leading Individual Donor Black Philanthropists by Black Enterprise Magazine.

ROSE, MALIK JABARI
Basketball player. **Personal:** Born Nov 23, 1974, Philadelphia, PA. **Educ:** Drexel Univ, attended 1996. **Career:** Charlotte Hornets, forward, 1996-97; San Antonio Spurs, 1997-2005; Malik Philly Phamous, owner, 2003; NY Knicks, forward, 2005-. **Honors/Awds:** NBA Community Assist Award, 2003; Tommy Award. **Business Addr:** Professional Basketball Player, New York Knicks, Madison Sq Garden, 2 Pa Plz, New York, NY 10121-0091, **Business Phone:** (212)465-6471.

ROSE, RACHELLE SYLVIA
Social worker. **Personal:** Born Aug 19, 1946, Chicago, IL. **Educ:** DC Teachers Col, BS, 1974; Howard Univ Grad Sch Social Work, MSW, 1976. **Career:** Lic clin social worker, currently. **Orgs:** Kappa Delta Pi; Nat Teachers Honor Soc, Howard Univ; Nat Asn Social Workers; Calif Soc Clin Social Workers; Alpha Kappa Alpha Sorority, Mu Lambda Omega Chapt, Culver City, Calif.

ROSE, SHELVIE, SR.
Educator, government official. **Personal:** Born Jan 5, 1936, Covington, TN; married Odessa White; children: Delores, Shelvie Jr, Saundra, Kelda La Trece & Kenny. **Educ:** Tenn State Univ, BS; Memphis State Univ. **Career:** Aquatics, pro boy scout instr, 1959-63; Tipton County Pub Sch Syst, instr, 1959, alderman, District 1, bd mem, currently; Tipton County Bd Educ, health & driver educ instr; Tipton County, Dist 1, comnr. **Orgs:** Finance & admin, Alderman Community; General Welfare-Pub Rel; bd control, Tipton County Pub Works; Tipton County Voters Coun; bd mem, Tenn Voters Coun. **Business Addr:** Alderman District, City Covington, 200 W Wash, Covington, TN 38019, **Business Phone:** (901)476-8791.

ROSE, TRICIA
Educator. **Personal:** Born in Harlem, NY. **Educ:** Yale Univ, BA, Sociol, 1984; Brown Univ, MA, PhD (am civilization), 1993. **Career:** Princeton Univ, Afro-Am Rockefeller Found fel, 1993-94; NY Univ, Goddard fel, 1996; Ford Found fel, 1996-97; Univ Calif Santa Cruz, prof Am studies; NPR, expert commentator; Brown Univ, prof africana studies, currently. **Honors/Awds:** American Book Award, Before Columbus Foundation, 1995; Golden Dozens Teaching Award, New York Univ, 1998. **Special Achievements:** Author of Black Noise: Rap Music and Black Culture in Contemporary America, Wesleyan Press, 1994; co-editor, with Andrew Ross, of Microphone Fiends: Youth Music &

Youth Culture, Routledge, 1994; Black Noise, which made the Village Voice's top 25 books of 1994; Hip Hop Theorist" by The New York Times and a "Ph.Diva" by Essence magazine. **Business Addr:** Professor of Africana Studies, Brown University, Department of Africana Studies, 155 Angell St, PO Box 1904, Providence, RI 02912, **Business Phone:** (401)863-3558.*

ROSEMAN, JENNIFER EILEEN
Manager. **Personal:** Born Sep 6, 1952, Spokane, WA; daughter of Jerrelene Hill Williamson and Sam Williamson; married Larry Roseman Sr, May 13, 1983; children: Larry Jr & Maya. **Educ:** NY Univ, NY, BA, jour, 1974; Gonzaga Univ, Spokane, Wash, MA, orgn leadership, 1989. **Career:** New York Daily News, NY, intern, 1973-74; The San Diego Union, San Diego, Calif, reporter, 1974-78; The Spokesman-Review, Spokane, Wash, ed/ed writer, 1978-92; Ct Col Spokane, dir commun & develop, vice chancellor, instl advancement, 1992-2000; Sisters Providence, Mother Joseph Province, dir Commun & Develop, 2001-. **Orgs:** Spokane Public Library, trustee; Wash Comn for the Humanities; Casey Family Partners-Spokane. **Honors/Awds:** Distinguished Journalism Award, Ncp, San Diego br, 1977; African-Am Pioneer Award, Links Inc, Spokane chp, 1995; Woman of the Year, Spokane Falls Ct Col, Asn Women Students, 1998; Trailblazer Diversity, Comm Col Spokane, 2000; Woman of the Year, Soroptimist Club, 2001; Ct Activist Award, Ncp, Spokane br, 2002. **Business Addr:** Communications Director, Sisters of Providence, Mother Joseph Province, 9 E 9th Ave, Spokane, WA 99202, **Business Phone:** (509)474-2306.

ROSEMOND, DR. MANNING WYLLARD, JR.
Dentist. **Personal:** Born May 20, 1918, Toccoa, GA; married Edrose Smith; children: Manning III. **Educ:** Calif Univ, AB, 1940; Atlanta Univ, MS, 1949; OH State Univ, DDS, 1956. **Career:** Pvt pract, dentist, currently. **Orgs:** Pres Adv Bd; pres, 1973-74, chmn bd, pres elect, 1972-73, vpres, 1971, 1972, exec bd, 1967-71; pres, Forest City Dental Study Club, 1973-74; founder, Buckeye State Dental Asn, 1974; dir, Jane Adams Dental Clin, 1977-; pres, CRC Enterprises; pres, Romac Co; Omega Psi Phi, Nat Asn Advan Colored People, Frontiers Intl; holder, pvt pilots license; Aircraft Owners & Pilots Asn; Am Dental Asn, OH Dental Asn; Pres, Max's Aerial Photographic Serv. **Military Serv:** AUS, first lt, 1942-46, 1950-52; Bronze Star. **Home Addr:** 15858 Forest Hills Blvd, Cleveland, OH 44112, **Home Phone:** (216)932-4318.

ROSENTHAL, ROBERT E
Real estate developer, executive. **Personal:** Born Apr 9, 1945, Phillips, MS; son of Inez and J R Rosenthal; divorced; children: Robert E Jr. **Educ:** Univ Fla, attended 1967; Jackson State Univ, BS, 1971; Jackson State Univ, Grad Work, 1973. **Career:** Whitten Jr High Sch, Jackson, teacher 1972; PO Jackson, EEO coun, 1974; PO Dist Jackson, staff mgr, 1976; PO US Postmaster, 1978; Mid-South Rec Inc, vpres, co-owner, 1978-94; mgt & mkt consult artists & rec cos; Who's Who in Black Music, ed, 1986; Who's Who in Music, ed, 1987; Programming Radio, ed, 1987; Rosenthal & Maultsby Music Res Int, nat pub rels mgr young Black Programmer Coalition & The Black Music Asn; Philadelphia Int Rec, mkt & nat pub rels mgr; Corps Engrs, staff mgr/equal employ oppurtunity officer; Int Trade Inc, vpres, pres, currently; Richboy Entertainment Inc, operational mgr; Rosenthall Group, real estate developer, investor & chief operating officer, currently. **Orgs:** Miss Teachers Asn; Nat Bus League; Nat Asn Postmasters; Nat Asn Advan Colored People; NAREB Realist; Urban League; Jackson State Univ Alumni; Nat Coun Affirm Action; Minority Bus Brain Trust Cong Black Caucus, 1982-83, 1984, 1986 & 1987-; Rock Music Asn; Young Black Programmers Coalition. **Honors/Awds:** Best All Around Student Award, Rosa Scott High Sch, Madison, Miss, 1963; Music Scholar, Jackson State Univ, 1964. **Military Serv:** USAF, 1968; Good Conduct Medal. **Home Phone:** (601)918-9035. **Business Addr:** President, International Trade Inc., PO Box 1051, Vicksburg, MS 39181, **Business Phone:** (601)918-9035.

ROSHELL, PAMELA P (PAMELA JOHNSON)
Association executive. **Educ:** Columbia Col; Clark Atlanta Univ, PhD. **Career:** AARP SC, state dir, state pres. *

ROSHELL, WIN C
President (Organization), chief executive officer. **Personal:** Born in Chattanooga, TN. **Educ:** Morehouse Col, mkt, 1992. **Career:** Walt Disney World; After Five Prof Networking Assn, founder, pres & chief exec officer, 2000-; Merck, sales rep, currently. **Honors/Awds:** Minority Small Bus Champion of the Year, US Small Bus Admin, 2005; SBA award. **Special Achievements:** Nominated for Statewide Award, Univ GA Small Bus Develop Ctr; Share-A-Smile Dent Health Scholar Prog. **Business Phone:** (478)476-9946.*

ROSS, ADRIAN
Football player, football coach, president (organization). **Personal:** Born Feb 19, 1975, Santa Clara, CA. **Educ:** Colo State Univ, BS, animal sci. **Career:** Football player (retired), football coach; Cincinnati Bengals, linebacker, 1998-2004; Sacramento State Univ, asst defensive line, 2006; free agt, currently. **Orgs:** Pres, Maddbacker Found, currently; Make A Wish Found Sacramento & Northern Calif. **Business Addr:** President, Maddbacker Foundation, 4660 Natomas Blvd 120-57, Sacramento, CA 95835, **Business Phone:** (916)273-6340.

ROSS, DR. ANTHONY ROGER
School administrator. **Personal:** Born Jan 28, 1953, Jamaica, NY; son of Esther Ross and Abram Ross; children: Jamal & Shama. **Educ:** St Lawrence Univ, BA, sociol, 1975, MEd Counseling, 1978; Northern Ariz Univ, EdD, 1984. **Career:** Utica Col Syracuse Univ, counr higher educ opportunity prog, 1975-76; St Lawrence Univ, dir higher educ opportunity prog, 1976-81, asst basket ball coach 1977-80; Northern Ariz Univ, asst assoc dean, 1983-84, dean students, 1985, adj prof, 1986-, asst vpres, student serv, 1989; Wichita State Univ, assoc to the pres, interim vpres student affairs, 1994-99; Edison Sch Inc, vpres develop, Calif State Univ, assoc prof, 2000-, vpres, student affairs currently. **Orgs:** Pres, Higher Educ Opportunity Prog Prof Org, 1976-81; Am Asn Coun& Develop, 1978-; Am Col Personnel Asn, 1978-; pres, Higher Educ Opportunity Prog, 1979-80; bd, 1992-94, Nat Asn Student Personnel Admin, 1980-; NatAsn Advan Colored People, 1982-; coach, Youth League Basketball & Soccer, 1982-; coach, Big Brothers of Flagstaff 1983-; coach, Buffalo Soldiers of Flagstaff 1984-; Blacks Prog Higher Edu, 1985-; bd dirs, Coconino Community Guidance Ctr, 1986; comnr, Flagstaff City Parks & Recreational Comn, 1986-92; pres, Ariz Asn Student Personnel Administrators, 1990-91. **Honors/Awds:** Athlete of the Year, St Lawrence Univ, 1975; Hall of Fame, St Lawrence Univ, 1986; Distinguished Alumni Award, Northern Ariz Univ, 1989; Americas Best & Brightest Young Business & Professional Men, Dollars & Sense Magazine, 1992; Distinguished Service Award, Ariz Alliance Black School Educr, 1992; Pillar of the Profession, Nat Asn Student Personnel Adminr, 2006; Outstanding Commitment to Leadership and Service Award, Am Knowledge Community, Nat Asn Student Personnel Adminr, 2006; Professional Achievement Award, Nat Asn Presidential Assts Higher Educ, 2006. **Business Addr:** Vice President, Division of Student Affairs, California State University, 5151 State University Dr SA 108, Los Angeles, CA 90032, **Business Phone:** (323)343-3100.

ROSS, DR. CATHERINE LAVERNE
Executive director, educator. **Personal:** Born Nov 1, 1948, Cleveland, OH; married Dr Thomas Daniel; children: 2. **Educ:** Kent State Univ, BA, history & sociol, 1971; Cornell Univ, MA, Reg Planning, 1973; Cornell Univ, PhD, city & reg planning, 1979; Univ Calif, Berkeley, post-doctorate work. **Career:** Am Soc Planning Officials, Ford Found fel, 1971-73; Reg Planning Comn, Cleveland, grad asst, 1972; Daton Dalton Little Newport Shaker Hights, OH, transp planner, 1973-74; Cornell Univ, res asst officer transport, 1975-76; Cornell Univ, Rockefeller Found fel, 1975; Ga Inst Tech, asst prof, 1976-83, assoc prof, 1984-89, prof, 1990, vice provost acad affairs, assoc vpres acad affairs, Transport Res & Educ Ctr, co-dir & Col Architecture's PhD Prog, dir, Ctr Qual Growth & Regional Develop, dir Harry West chair, currently; Atlanta Univ, asst prof, 1977-79; Ga Tech Eng Exp Sta, consult, 1979; Comn Serv Admin Atlanta, consult res, 1979. **Orgs:** AAAS, 1978; Black Women Academicians, 1979; policy analyst, Am Planning Asn, Wash, DC, 1979. **Honors/Awds:** Outstanding Women, Essence Mag, 1974. **Special Achievements:** The college's first endowed faculty member; First executive director of the Georgia Regional Transportation Authority. **Business Phone:** (404)385-5130.

ROSS, CATHYE P
President (Organization). **Educ:** Univ Southern Miss, bus admin degree, 1983; Millsaps Col, MBA. **Career:** Trustmark Nat Bank, mgr; Hinds Co Econ Develop Dist, asst dir opers, 1990-93; Grand Casino Biloxi, vpres guest servs, vpres mkt opers, currently, bd dirs, currently. **Orgs:** Co-comt chair, Hartley Educ Fundraiser, Tabernacle Baptist Church; comt mem, Silver Cloud Dist, Pine Burr Area Coun, Boy Scouts Am; bd trustees, Walter Anderson Mus Art; Leadership Gulf Coast; leadership bd, Coast Community Bank; bd dirs, Lynn Meadows Discovery Ctr. **Honors/Awds:** Best Citizen Award, Univ Southern Miss; Presidential Award, Grand Casino Biloxi. **Business Addr:** Vice President Of Marketing Operations, Board of Director, Grand Casino Biloxi, 280 Beach Blvd, Biloxi, MS 39530, **Business Phone:** (228)436-2946.

ROSS, DR. DENISE ELIZABETH
Educator. **Personal:** Born Jan 1, 1971?, Ohio. **Educ:** Spelman Col, BA, eng, 1993; Columbia Univ, Teachers Col, MA, spec edu Stud with Behavior Disorders, 1995, PhD, 1998. **Career:** Columbia Univ, Teacher's Col, visiting asst prof psychol & educ, asst prof, psychol & educ currently. **Special Achievements:** Publ: Education and Training in Mental Retardation & Developmental Disabilities.

ROSS, DIANA (DIANE ERNESTINE EARLE ROSS)
Actor, singer. **Personal:** Born Mar 26, 1944, Detroit, MI; daughter of Fred Ross and Ernestine; married Arne Naess Jr, Oct 23, 1985 (divorced 2000); children: Ross Arne Naess & Evan; children: Rhonda Ross Kendrick; married Robert Ellis Silberstein, Jan 20, 1971 (divorced 1977); children: Tracee Joy & Chudney. **Career:** The Primettes, mem; The Supremes, mem; Diana Ross & The Supremes, lead singer, 1960-68; Hit Singles: "Where Did Our Love Go,"; "Baby Love,"; "Come See About Me,"; "Stop! In the Name of Love,"; "Back in My Arms Again,"; "I Hear A Symphony,"; "Reflections,"; "Love Child,"; "Someday We'll Be Together"; solo performer, 1970-; Albums: Diana Ross; Everything is Everything; Ross; Why Do Fools Fall in Love; Silk; Take Me Higher;Voice of Love, 2000; Take Me Higher, 2000; Gift of Love, 2000; Sing Motown, 2000; Stop! In the Name of Love, 2000; 20th Century Masters - The Millennium, 2000; Love From Diana Ross, 2000; Chain Reaction, 2000; Classic: The Universal Master Collection, 2000; The Motown Anthology, 2001; Life & Love: The Very Best of Diana Ross, 2001; Best of Diana RossImport, 2001; Best of Diana Ross, Vol 1, 2001; Stolen Moments: The Lady Sings Jazz & Blues, 2002; Stolen Moments: The Lady Sings Jazz & Blues, 2002; Diana Ross (1970), 2002; Reach Out & Touch: The Very Best of Diana, 2002; No 1's, 2003; To Love Again, 2003; Diana, 2003; Too Cool for Christmas, 2004; Ultimate Collection, 2004; Legends, 2006; The Definitive Collection, 2006; Blue, 2006; I Love Yoy, 2006; Films: Lady Sings the Blues, 1972; Mahogany, 1975; The Wiz, 1978; The Making and Meaning of We Are Family, 2002; ATL, 2006; TV: "An Evening with Diana Ross", 1977; "Diana", 1981; "Daria", 2000; "The Wire", 2003;"Shminiya, Ha-", 2006; "Everybody Hates Chris", 2006; "The Sopranos",2007; TV movie: Double Platinum, 1999; Diana Ross Enterprises Inc, pres; Anaid Film Prods; RTC Mgt Corp; Chondee Inc; Ross town; Rossville Music Publ Co; Soundtrack: Maid in Manhattan, 2002; Juwanna Mann, 2002; Bridget Jones's Diary, 2001; Chicken Little, 2005; Talk to Me, 2007. **Orgs:** Rhythm & Blues Found, 2003-. **Honors/Awds:** Grammy Award for Best Female Vocalist, 1970; Billboard, Cash Box, & Rec World Awards for Best Female Vocalist, 1970; Female Entertainer of the Year, Nat Asn Advan Colored People, 1970; Cue Award, 1972; Tony Award, 1977; Rock 'n' Roll Hall of Fame, 1988; Lifetime Achievement Award, MIDEM, 1994; Walk of Fame Award, Black Entertainment TV, 1999; Heroes Award, Nat Acad Rec Arts & Sci, 2000; Legendary Female award from the Capitol Gold Legends Award, 2003; Kennedy Center Honors, 2007. **Special Achievements:** Nominated for 12 Grammy awards; nominated for Best Actress for Lady Sings the Blues, Academy Award, 1972; honoured by the Guinness Book of World Records in 1993 as the most successful female singer of all time; Female Entertainer of The Century, Billboard Mag; two stars on the Hollywood walk of fame, one for her work with The Supremes and one for her solo career;one of only 7 African-American actresses to receive the Best Actress Oscar nomination. **Business Phone:** (972)250-1162.

ROSS, DIANE ERNESTINE EARLE. See ROSS, DIANA.

ROSS, DR. EDWARD
Cardiologist. **Personal:** Born Oct 10, 1937, Fairfield, AL; son of Carrie Griggs Ross and Horace Ross; married Catherine I Webster; children: Edward, Ronald, Cheryl & Anthony. **Educ:** Clark Col Atlanta, Ga, BS, 1959; IN Univ Sch Med, MD 1963; Am Bd Internal Med, dipl, 1970; Am Soc Hypertension, cert, clin specialist hypertension, 1999. **Career:** Edward Ross, MD, Inc, pres & chief exec officer, 1970-; Med Cardiovasc Data, Inc, pres & chief exec officer, 1982; Pvt pract, cardiologist; Methodist Hosp Ind, dir cardiovasc patient care progs, chief cardiovasc med, 1989-95, 2001-; Methodist Hosp Indianapolis, dir cardiovasc serv, 1990-, physician, currently; Winona Hosp, chief, Cardiovasc Dis, 2000; dir, Intervential Cardiol, 2000-; Clarian Health, Cardiologist, currently. **Orgs:** Cent Ind Comprehensive Health Plannning Coun; med dir, Martindale Health Ctr, 1968-71; clin asst prof, Ind Univ Schl Med 1970-75; apt Nat Cent Health Serv Res & Develop, 1970; bd dir, Cent Ind TB & Resp Diseases Asn, 1971-74; Comprehensive Health Plannning Coun Marion County, 1972-73; Secy, Div Nat Med Asn, 1972-73; NMA pres Hoosier State Med Asn, 1980-86; bd dirs, Asn Black Cardiologists, 1990-92; Sire Archorn alpha eta Boule (Indpolis Ind) Sigma Pi Phi Fraternity, 2006-; Am Soc Angiol, 2003-; Marion County Med Soc; Ind State Med Asn; Royal Soc Prom Health (London); Am Col Physicians; Aesculapean Med Soc; Nat Med Asn; Am Col Cardiol; Am Col Angiol; Ind State Med Asn; Coun Sci Assembly. **Honors/Awds:** Nat Federation Health Scholarship, 1955; Fellowship, Woodrow Wilson, 1959; Certificate of Merit Scientific Achievements in Biology, 1959; Ind Heart Asn, 1961-62; Dept of Cardiology, Research Fellow in Cardiology Dept Med, 1968-70; chief fellow int med, Ind Univ, 1969-70; Fel, Int Col Angiol, 1971-; Fellow Royal Soc for the Promotion of Health, 1974; Fel, Am Col Angiol; Fellow, Am Col Cardiol; Treasurer, Int Col Angiol, 2007. **Special Achievements:** Lifetime Achievement award in Cardiology, Center for Leadership Development Of Indianapolis,IN, 2003. **Military Serv:** USAAF, capt, Certificate of Appreciation SAC 1966-68. **Business Addr:** Methodist Cardiology Physician, Methodist Hospital, 1801 N Senate MPC 1 Suite 310, Indianapolis, IN 46202.

ROSS, EMMA JEAN
School principal. **Personal:** Born Sep 6, 1945, Independence, LA; daughter of Isaac E Sr and Lillie Leola Brown. **Educ:** Southern Univ, BS, 1970; Southeastern La Univ, MA, guid & coun, 1974, MA, admin, supv, 1979. **Career:** Wash Parish Sch, libm, 1970-84, guid counr, 1984-, Lic Prof Counr, 1990-; Varnado High Sch, prin, 1993-. **Orgs:** Theta Theta Zeta, 1974-; La Sch Counr's Asn, 1989-; La Coun Asn, 1989-; La Asn Multi-Cultural Develop, 1989-. **Home Addr:** 27344 Hwy 21, Angie, LA 70426, **Home Phone:**

(985)986-2491. **Business Addr:** Principal, Varnado High School, 25543 Washington St, Angie, LA 70426, **Business Phone:** (985)732-2025.

ROSS, FRANK KENNETH
Certified public accountant. **Personal:** Born Jul 9, 1943; son of Ruby and Reginald; married Cecelia M Mann; children: Michelle & Michael. **Educ:** Long Island Univ, BS, 1966, MBA, 1968. **Career:** Peat, Marwick, Mitchell & Co CPA, partner, 1966-73, 1977-87; Ross, Stewart & Benjamin, PC, CPA, pres & owner, 1973-76; KPMG LLP, partner, 1977-2003, Mid-Atlantic Audit & Risk, managing partner, 1996-2003; Howard Univ, vis prof, 1982-, Ctr Acct Educ, dir, Middle Sch Math & Sci, treas, currently; Wash DC Off & Midatlantic Area, managing partner, 1996-. **Orgs:** First nat pres & founder, Nat Asn Black Acct, 1969-70; Am Inst CPA's, 1969-; treas, Ellington Fund, 1982-; Bd Counr, Col Bus & Pub Mgt, Univ Dist Columbia, 1983-; treas, Wash Urban League, 1986-; bd adv, Howard Univ Sch Bus, 1990-; pres, bd mem, Iona Sr Serv; vpres, Corcoran Mus & Sch Art, 1994-, treas; bd dir, KPMG, 1993-96, 1998-; mgt comt, 1996-98; bd adv, George Washington Univ Sch Bus & Pub Admin, 1996-; trustee, Hoop Dreams Scholar Fund, currently; trustee, Corcoran Gallery Art; Gore, 2000; mem bd, Pepco Holdings, 2004-; United Negro Col Fund Wash & Baltimore Bd. **Honors/Awds:** Black Achievers in Industry, YMCA Greater NY, 1980; Outstanding Achievement Award, Wash DC Chap NABA, 1984; Distinguished Service Award, NABA, 1985; Accountant of the Year, Beta Alpha Psi, 1994; Alumni of the Year, Long Island Univ, 1998; DHL, Long Island Univ, 2001. **Home Addr:** 10130 Darmuid Green Dr, Potomac, MD 20854. **Business Addr:** Treasurer, Professor, Howard University, Middle School of Mathematics and Science, 405 Howard Pl NW, Washington, DC 20059, **Business Phone:** (202)806-7725.

ROSS, KEVIN ARNOLD
Lawyer. **Personal:** Born Apr 22, 1955; married Gornata Lynn Cole; children: Kelly Alexis & April Whitney. **Educ:** Dartmouth Col, BA, 1977; Emory Law Sch, JD, 1980. **Career:** Kilpatrick & Cody, summer legal clin, 1979; Long & Aldridge, assoc atty, 1980; Hunton & Williams, managing partner, 1992; Kaj Pub Affairs Group, pres; Attache Pub Affairs, staff; Kevin Ross Pub Affairs Group, owner, pres, currently. **Orgs:** Vol Lawyer Arts, 1981-84; secy, vpres, pres elect, Gate City Bar Asn, 1982-85; vpres, Am Diabetes Asn, 1982-84; State Licensing Bd Used Car Dealers, 1984-89; State Bar Ga. **Special Achievements:** Leader Under 30, Ebony Mag, 1985. **Business Phone:** (404)572-6622.

ROSS, LEE ELBERT
Educator, college administrator. **Personal:** Born Mar 16, 1958, Shorter, AL; son of Geneva Trimble and Silas Bates Ross Sr; married Leslie Ann, Aug 31, 1985; children: Christopher Daniel & Alexander Nelson. **Educ:** Niagara Univ, BA, 1981; Rutgers Univ, Grad Sch Criminal Justice, MA, 1983, PhD, 1991. **Career:** New York State Sentencing Guidelines Comn, res asst, 1982; NY State Sentencing Guidelines Comn, 1984; New Jersey Admin Off Cts, res intern, 1984; Kean Col, Political Sci Dept,lectr, 1984; US Treas Dept, customs officer, 1984-91; Bloomfield Col, Dept Sociol, lectr, 1991; Univ Wis-Milwaukee, from asst prof to assoc prof, criminal justice, 1991-98, field placement coordr, 1994-97, Col Arts & Sci, internship coordr & supvr, 1999-2003, Criminal Justice Dept, assoc prof & dept chmn, 1999-2003; Univ Cent Fla, Dept Criminal Justice & Legal Studies, grad coordr, 2004-05, hon maj coordr, 2003-, asso prof criminal justice, 2003-, provost fel & assoc prof, 2005-. **Orgs:** Am Soc Criminol, 1984-; Acad Criminal Justice Scis, 1991-; Nat Orgn Black Law Enforcement Exes, 1991-; Am Civil Liberties Union, bd mem, 1992-; ed & bd mem, J Crime & Justice, 1996-98. **Honors/Awds:** Patricia Roberts Harris Fel, State Univ New Jersey, 1981-84; Michael J Harasmik Fel, 1982-83; WIS Teaching Fel, 1996; Distinguished Undergraduate Teaching Award, Univ Wis-Milwaukee, 1998; provost fel, Univ Cent Fla, 2005. **Special Achievements:** African Am Criminologists: 1970-1996, 1997; "School Environment, Self-Esteem & Delinquency,", J Crime & Justice, 1995; "Religion, Self-Esteem & Deliquancy," J Crime & Justice, 1996; "Religion & Deviance: Exploring the Impact.," Sociological Spectrum, 1992; "Black, Self-Esteem & Delinquency:.," Justice Quarterly, 1992; Expert witness in areas of Crime Causation Theory. **Home Addr:** 7045 N Braeburn Lane, Milwaukee, WI 53209-2609. **Business Addr:** Provost Fellow, Associate Professor, University of Central Florida, School of Social Welfare, 4000 Cent Fla Blvd, PO Box 161600, Orland, FL 32816-1600, **Business Phone:** (407)823-2000.

ROSS, LINDA TRACEY. See ROSS, TRACEY.

ROSS, MARTHA ERWIN
Entrepreneur. **Personal:** Born Jun 4, 1944, Tyler, TX; daughter of Carvie Earnest Sr and Miner Mae Jackson; married Lamont W, Oct 27, 1961; children: Stetron Proncell & Trelitha Rochelle Ross Bryant. **Educ:** Bus degree secretarial sci, 1967; Bellevue Univ, mgt degree, hons, 1994. **Career:** AT&T, secy, 1964-66, pub rels, 1966-80, network sales support info rep, 1980-85; United Way Midlands Western/Central, region mkt mgr, loaned exec, 1986-88, customer serv training tech, 1988-91; OSHA safety inspector, 1991-94, materials auditor, 1994-; Qual Nutri & Painting Contractors, pres, 1985; Youth Motivation Task Force, mkt mgr, 1991; Midwest Market Place, owner, currently. **Orgs:** Urban League Nebr, 1970-; Urban League Guild, 1970-; ambassador, United Way the Midlands, 1978-86; auctioneer, 1985, ambassador, 1985-86, Nebr Pub TV; COC, 1985-; YMCA Youth Camp Campaign, 1985-86; Church Christ, numerous auxiliaries. **Honors/Awds:** Top 10 in Jefferson Award, KETV Channel 7, 1988; United Way, Loaned Exec Honor, Commercial Div, 1988; Top ambassador, NPTV, 1987, 1988; Top Honors, Annual Campaign, Chamber of Commerce, 1988-89; Urban League of Nebraska, Top Honors, Membership Drive, 1987-89; Omaha Opportunities Industrialization Ctr Honors, 1992, 1993. **Home Addr:** 5741 Tucker Circle, Omaha, NE 68152.

ROSS, N. RODNEY
Graphic artist, photographer. **Personal:** Born Jun 28, 1957, Indianapolis, IN; son of Virginia Cottee Ross and Norman Ross. **Educ:** Indiana University, Herron School Art, BFA, 1982. **Career:** Noble Industries, Indianapolis, IN, art dir, 1984-87; Poster Display Co, Beach Grove, IN, graphic artist, 1987-91; Ross Concepts, Art Dept, Indianapolis, IN, pres, 1982-90; Career Com, Advertising Design, prof, 1990-92; Turner, Potts & Ross, Indianapolis, IN, vice pres, currently. **Orgs:** Youth leader/counselor, Community Outreach Ctr, 1985-; mem, Central IN Bicycling Assn, 1988-; African Based Cultures Study Group of Indianapolis, 1989-; Indy Rennaissance, African-American Artists Network, 1990-. **Honors/Awds:** Addy Award, 1992. **Business Addr:** Vice President, Turner, Potts & Ross, 2825 Thornton Lane, Indianapolis, IN 46268-1257.*

ROSS, OLIVER CALVIN
Football player. **Personal:** Born Sep 27, 1974, Culver City, CA; married Billie. **Educ:** Iowa State Univ. **Career:** Dallas Cowboys, 1998; Philadelphia Eagles, tackle, 1999-2000; Pittsburgh Steelers, 2000-04; Arizona Cardinals, 2005-07; New England Patriots, 2008; Arizona Cardinals, 2009-. **Business Phone:** (508)543-8200.*

ROSS, OLIVER CALVIN, III
Football player. **Personal:** Born Sep 27, 1974, Culver City, CA; married Billie. **Educ:** Iowa State Univ. **Career:** Dallas Cowboys, tackle, 1998; Philadelphia Eagles, 1999; Pittsburgh Steelers, 2000-04; Arizona Cardinals, 2005-07; New England Patriots, guard, 2008; Arizona Cardinals, Offensive lineman, 2009-.

ROSS, PHYLLIS HARRISON
Educator, psychiatrist. **Personal:** Born Aug 14, 1936, Detroit, MI; married Edgar. **Educ:** Albion Col, Albion, MI, BA 1956; Wayne State Univ, Detroit, MD, 1959; Kings Co Hosp, Brooklyn, internship, 1960. **Career:** Physician pediat, adult & child psychiatry, 1959-; NY Hosp, Cornell Med Col, residency-pediat, 1960-62; Jacoby Hosp Albert Einstein Col Med,residency-adult & child psychiat, 1962-66; NY Med Col, prof psychiat, emer prof psychiat & behavioral health sci, currently; Metropolitan Hosp,Community Mental Health Ctr, dir, chief psychiat, Med Bd, pres; State Univ NY, Empire State Col, bd dir, 1972-79; Bank St Col, bd dir, 1972-79; C's TV Workshop, bd dir, 1976-; Black Psychiatrists Greater New York & Assoc founder & managing dir, currently. **Orgs:** Pres, Black Psychiatrists Am, 1976-78; Med Review Bd, NY State Comn Corrections, 1976-; Minority Adv Comt, ADAMHA, 1978-; chair, Social Servs Bd, NY Soc Ethical Cult. **Honors/Awds:** Achievement Award, Greater NY Links, 1973; Distinguished Alumnus Award,Albion Col, 1976; Leadership in Medicine Award, Susan Smith McKinney Steward Med Soc, 1978; Award of Merit, Public Health Asn New York City,1980; Lifetime Achievement Award, Am Psychiat Asn; Solomon Carter Fuller Award, 2004. **Special Achievements:** Author of "Getting It Together A Psychology Textbook", 1972; Author of "The Black Child A Parents Guide" 1973. **Business Addr:** Founder, Managing Director, The Black Psychiatrists of Greater New York and Associates, 331 W 57th St Suite 522, New York, NY 10019, **Business Phone:** (212)969-0417.

ROSS, REV. RALPH M
Clergy, educator. **Personal:** Born Dec 23, 1936, Miami, FL; son of Effie Mae Ross and Leroy Ross; married Gertrude; children: Sharlene, Lydia, Ralph, Ray, Simona & Randall. **Educ:** BA, 1961; BD, 1965; MDiv, 1970; DMin, 1988. **Career:** Beth Salem United Presb Church, Columbus, GA, minister, 1965-66; Eastern Airlines Atlanta, ramp agent, 1965-66; Mt Zion Baptist Church, Miami, assoc minister, 1966-68, pastor/teacher, 1990-; Urban League Miami, field rep 1967-68; Knoxville Col, campus minister, 1968-70, dean stud; UT Knoxville, lectr relig dept 1969-; NC A&T State Univ, dir, relig activities 1978-86, asst dean student devel 1986-90. **Orgs:** Theta Phi Hon Soc, 1965; bd dir, Blacks Higher Educ, Knoxville; Knoxville Interdenominational Christian Ministeral Alliance; life mem, Alpha Phi Alpha; Nat Asn Advan Colored People; Baptist Ministers Coun & Faith In The City; ROA; Historic Mt Zion Missionary Baptist Church; AACCC. **Honors/Awds:** YMCA Best Blocker Award, Knoxville Col, 1959; Rockefeller Fellowship Award, 1964. **Special Achievements:** Named first African-American captain in the US Naval Reserve Chaplains Corps. **Military Serv:** USNR, Chaplains Corps capt. **Business Addr:** Pastor/Teacher, Historic Mount Zion Missionary Baptist Church, 301 NE 9th St, Miami, FL 33136, **Business Phone:** (305)379-4147.

ROSS, TRACEE ELLIS (TRACEE JOY SILBERSTEIN)
Actor. **Personal:** Born Oct 29, 1972, Los Angeles, CA; daughter of Robert Silberstein and Diana. **Educ:** Brown Univ, 1994; William Esper Acting Studio. **Career:** Mirabella Mag, fashion ed; New York Mag, fashion ed; Films: Far Harbor, 1996; Sue, 1997; A Fare to Remember, 1998; Hanging Up, 2000; In the Weeds, 2000; I-See-You.Com, 2006; Daddy's Little Girls, 2007; Labor Pains, 2009; TV series: "The Dish", 1997; "Race Against Fear", 1998; "Lyricist Lounge Show", 2000; "Girlfriends", actor & dir, 2000-07; "Trial & Errors", 2005; "In Too Deep", 2006; Life Support, 2007. **Honors/Awds:** BET Comedy Award, 2005; Image Award, 2007, 2009. **Business Addr:** Actress, c/o International Creative Management, 10250 Constellation Blvd, Los Angeles, CA 90067, **Business Phone:** (310)550-4000.*

ROSS, TRACEY (LINDA TRACEY ROSS)
Actor. **Personal:** Born Feb 27, 1959, Brooklyn, NY; married Kashif (divorced); children: Bryce. **Educ:** Rutgers Univ. **Career:** Films: Best Defense, 1984; The Cotton Club, 1984; Solar Eclipse, 1995; Mr.Payback: An Interactive Movie, 1995; Small Time, 1996; Cold Around the Heart, 1997; Unconditional Love, 1999; TV Series: Jacqueline Susann's Valley of the Dolls, 1981; Miss Black America Pageant, 1985; Braker, 1985; "Ryan's Hope", 1985-87; Mayflower Madam, 1987; "The Cosby Show", 1989; "Doctor Doctor", 1991; "Roc", 1991; Lies of the Twins, 1991; "On Our Own", 1994; "Bay watch Nights", 1996; "Passions", 1999-2008; "Providence", 2002; "House of Payne", 2008. **Honors/Awds:** Miss New Jersey Pageant, 1975; winner in the Spokes model category in the television series "Star Search"; Image Award, 2007. **Special Achievements:** First $100,000 Star Search spokes model in 1980s. **Business Addr:** Actress, c/o NBC Viewer Relations, 30 Rockefeller Plz, New York, NY 10112.

ROSS, WILLIAM R
Association executive. **Career:** Off of Neighborhood Com Revitalization, vice chair; Booker T Wash Bus Asn, exec dir, pres & chief exec officer, currently. **Business Phone:** (313)875-4250.*

ROSS, WINSTON A
Social worker. **Personal:** Born Dec 2, 1941; son of Reginald Ross and Ruby Swanston Ross; married Rosalind Golden. **Educ:** NY City Community Col, AAS, 1961; NY Univ, BS, 1963; Columbia Univ Sch Social Work, MS, 1971; Adelphi Univ Sch Social Work, Doctoral Candidate. **Career:** New York Dept Social Serv/Preventive Serv/Bureau Child Welfare, caseworker, supv, 1966-73; St Dominic's Home, Blauvelt NY, exec supv, 1973-74; Graham Home & Sch, Hastings NY, social work supv, 1975-76; Wiltwyck Sch, Yorktown NY, unit dir, 1976-78; Westchester Community Opportunity Prog Inc, exec dir, currently. **Orgs:** Chmn trustee bd, Metropolitan AME Zion Ch, 1969-; pres, Yonkers, NY Branch NAACP, 1971-78; dir, Westchester Regional NY Conf NAACP, 1977-; co-chmn, 5th Ann Whitney M Young Conf on Racism & Del Human Serv, NASW, 1978-83; chmn, Westchester Div, NY Chap NASW, 1979-80, secy, 1981-83; chmn, Minority Affairs Comn, NY NASW, 1979-84; chmn, Career Guid Adv Coun, Educ Oppor Ctr Westchester, 1979-85; chairperson, Nat Nominations & Leadership Comn, NASW, 1984-; Statewide Adv Coun, NYS Div Human Rights, 1984-; NY Bd Social Work, 1987-. **Honors/Awds:** Freedom Fighter Award, Yonkers NAACP, 1978; Eugene T Reed Medalist, NY Conf NAACP, 1983; Social Worker of The Year, West Div NASW, 1982; Citizen of The Year, Omega Psi Phi Frat, Beta Alpha Alpha Chap, 1983. **Military Serv:** AUS, supt 4th class, 1963-66; National Social Worker of the Year, 1989; National first vpres, NASW, 1989-91, first vpres, NACAA, 1992-94. **Home Addr:** 5 Rte 202, Yorktown Heights, NY 10598. **Business Addr:** Executive Director, Westchester Community Opportunity Program Inc, 2269 Saw Mill River Rd Bldg 3, Elmsford, NY 10523, **Business Phone:** (914)592-5600.

ROSSER, DR. JAMES M.
School administrator, educator. **Personal:** Born Apr 16, 1939, East St Louis, IL; son of William M and Mary E Bass; children: Terrence. **Educ:** Southern Ill Univ, Carbondale, BA, 1962, MA, 1963, PhD, 1969. **Career:** Holden Hosp, diag bacteriologist, 1961-63; Health Educ & Coordr of Black Am Studies, instr, 1968-69; Eli Lily & Co, res bacteriologist, 1963-66; Southern Ill Univ, mem grad fac, 1967-70; Univ KS, ten assoc prof & assoc vice chancellor, 1970-74; State Univ NJ, Dept Higher Ed, vice chancellor, 1974-79, acting chancellor, 1977; Calif State Univ, Los Angeles, pres, 1979-, prof health care mgt, currently; NIH, consultant. **Orgs:** Bd gov, Am Red Cross, 1986-91; bd dirs, FEDCO Inc, 1987-2001; adv bd mem, Blue Cross Calif, 1989-; bd dirs, Hispanic Urban Ctr, Los Angeles, CA,1979-; bd dir, Am Coun on Educ, 1979-; bd dir, LA Area Coun, Boy Scouts Am, 1979-; bd dir, Community TV Southern CA KCET, 1980-89, 1998-; bd dirs, Los Angeles Urban League, 1982-95; bd dirs, Southern Calif Edison, 1985-; bd dirs, Los Angeles Philharmonic Asn, 1986-99; bd dirs, Am for the Arts,1985; adv coun mem, Nat Sci Found Directorate for Educ & Human Resources,1989-96; bd dirs, Nat Health Found, 1990-98; LA's Best Avd Comn, 1988-; bd dirs, Calif Chamber Comn, 1993-; bd dirs, United Calif Bank, 1993-2002; bd trustees, The Woodrow Wilson Nat Fel Found, 1993-; vice chair, Am Asn State Cols & Univs-Steering Comn or the Coun Urban & Metrop Cols & Univs,1993-96; CA Coun on Sci & Technol, 1998-; hon mem, Rotary Club LA, 1998-

;TEXACO & CHEVRON Task Force on Equality and Fairness, 1999-2002; Los Angeles Adv Alliance, Pasadena Tournament Roses, 2000-; bd dir, LA Alliance for Stud Achievement, 2001-; The Audubon Ctr Campaign Adv Comn,2001-; The CA Community Found, 2003-; Calif Dept Educ; Pacific Coun Int Policy. **Honors/Awds:** Cert of Merit, City of Los Angeles Human Rels Comn, 1982; Alumni Achievement Award, Southern Ill Univ, 1982; Leadership Award, Dept of Higher Educ & EOP Fund, State of NJ, 1989; Medal of Excellence, Golden State Minority Found, 1990; Teacher Education: The Linchpin in a Changing Soc Order, Southern Ill Univ, 1986; Strategic Planning and Mgt Methodology for Responsible Change, J of Libr Admin, 1990; Hon Mention, Outstanding Support of Teacher Educ, Am Asn of Cols for Teacher Educ, 1992; Watts Found Comn Trust, Ed Award, 1995; Distinguished Alumnus, Southern Ill Univ, 2000; DHL, Southern Ill Univ, Carbondale, 2003; Hon Doctorate, Pepperdine Univ, 2005. **Business Addr:** President, California State University, 401 Golden Shore, Long Beach, CA 90802-4210, **Business Phone:** (562)951-4000.

ROSSER, DR. PEARL LOCKHART
Physician. **Personal:** Born Dec 27, 1935, Miami, FL; married Samuel B; children: Charles. **Educ:** Howard Univ, BS, 1956, MD, 1960. **Career:** Freedman's Hosp, intern, 1960-61, pediat resident, 1961-63; Howard Univ, Col Med, prof pediat, 1964-85; consult, Develop Pediat, currently; pvt pract, currently. **Orgs:** Fel, AmAcad Pediat; Am Pediat Soc; Soc Res Child Develop; Asn C Learning Disabilities; Nat Coun Black Child Develop. **Special Achievements:** Co-editor "The Genetic Metabolic & Devel Aspects of Mental Retardation," 1972; author of numerous other articles and chapters in professional textbooks. **Home Addr:** 2222 Westview Dr, Silver Spring, MD 20910, **Home Phone:** (301)589-2456. **Business Addr:** Physician, 2222 Wview Dr, Silver Spring, MD 20910, **Business Phone:** (301)589-2456.

ROSSER, SAMUEL BLANTON
Physician. **Personal:** Born Jul 13, 1934, Tallapoosa, GA; married Pearl; children: Charles. **Educ:** Clark Col, BS 1954; Wayne State Univ, MS 1956; Howard Univ Col Med, MD 1960. **Career:** Physician (retired); Freedmen's Hospital, resident general surgeon, 1961-66; C's Hosp Nat Medical Ctr, resident, 1970-72; Howard Univ Col Med Pediat Surgery, assoc prof, 1972-02. **Orgs:** Asn Former Interns & Residents Howard Univ Hosp; fel Am Col Surgeons; Am Acad Pediat; Am Pediat Surg Asn. **Special Achievements:** First African American certified in pediatric surgery. **Military Serv:** AUS, nat guard, major. **Home Addr:** 2222 Westview Dr, Silver Spring, MD 20910. *

ROSS-JONES, DONNA. See JONES, DONNA L.

ROSS-LEE, BARBARA
School administrator. **Personal:** Born Jan 1, 1942?; married Edmond Beverly; children: 5. **Educ:** Wayne State Univ, BA, MA; Mich State Univ, Col Osteop Med, DO, 1973. **Career:** Mich State Univ, assoc dean, 1993; Ohio Univ Col Osteop Med, dean, 1993-2000; NY Inst Technol, dean sch life sci & allied health & vpres, health sci & med affairs, 2001-02, NY Col Osteopathic Med, dean, currently. **Orgs:** Am Osteop Asn, 1974-; Am Col Osteop Gen Practrs, 1982-; Ingham County Osteop Soc, 1984-; Nat Asn Med Minority Educrs, 1985-; Osteop Gen Practrs Mich, 1985-; Am Asn Family Practrs, 1986-; Mich Asn Family Practrs, 1986-; Nat Acad Pract, 1986-; Acad Osteop Dirs Med Educ, 1988-91; AMA, 1989-; pres, Nat Osteop Med Asn, 1992-; Ohio Osteopathic Asn, 1993-; fac mem, Phi Kappa Phi Hon Soc, 1994. **Honors/Awds:** Distinguished Alumni Award, Wayne State Univ, 1994; Women's Health Award, Blackboard African-Am Bestsellers, Inc, 1994; Magnificent 7 Award, Bus & Prof Women USA, 1994; Inductee, Ohio Women's Hall of Fame, 1998; Distinguished Service Award, Okla State Univ, 1998; honorary doctorate, NYIT, 1998; Distinguished Alumni Award, Mich State Univ, 2000; NBNA Trailblazer Award, National Black Nurses Asn, 2003. **Special Achievements:** First African American woman to head an American medical school, editor of the Journal of the American Osteopathic Association annual education edition. **Military Serv:** USN Reserve, capt. **Business Addr:** Vice President, New York Institute of Technology, Health Sciences and Medical Affairs, Rockefeller Bldg Room 107, Old Westbury, NY 11568-8000, **Business Phone:** (516)686-3828.

ROSSUM, ALLEN
Football player. **Personal:** Born Oct 22, 1975, Dallas, TX; married Angela; children: Trinity Amaia, Talia Alyse, Alexa & Avian. **Educ:** Univ Notre Dame, BS, mkt & comput application. **Career:** Philadelphia Eagles, defensive back, 1998-99; Green Bay Packers, defensive back, 2000-01; Atlanta Falcons, defensive back, 2002-06; Pittsburgh Steelers, 2007; San Francisco 49ers, 2008-. **Orgs:** Founder, Allen Rossum Healthy Kids Found. **Honors/Awds:** NFC Special Teams Player of the Week, 1999-2000; National Fatherhood Award, 2005; Pro Bowler Alternate, 2000; Pro Bowler Selection, 2004; Falcons' All Time Career Return yards Leader; Falcons' all time career kick off return yards. **Business Phone:** (415)656-4900.*

ROTAN, DR. CONSTANCE S.
Educator, attorney general (u.s. federal government). **Personal:** Born Apr 19, 1935, Baton Rouge, LA; married James Rotan Jr (died 2003); children: Kevin & Michael. **Educ:** Southern Univ,BA, 1956; Howard Univ Grad Sch, MA, 1968; Howard Univ Sch Law, JD, 1967. **Career:** Educator (retired); US Dept Justice, gen trial atty, 1968-70; United Planning Orgn, ast gen counsel, 1970-72; Howard Univ Sch Law, ast dean,asst prof, 1972-75; Howard Univ, exec ast vpres admin, 1975-87, Univ secy, bd trustees secy, 1987-92, vpres admin, 1989-92; Board Chair, The Horizon Foundation, 2003-. **Orgs:** Nat Bar Assoc; Kappa Beta Pi Int Legal Sor; Alpha Kappa Alpha; Assoc Am Law Sch; Nat Assoc Col & Univ Attnys; US Dist Ct DC; US Ct Appeals DC;dean, Howard Univ Chap Kappa Beta Pi Int Legal Sor, 1963-64; cochmn, Comn Age Majority DC; DC Bar; Phi Sigma Alpha; founding mem, officer Waring & Mitchell Law Soc; Pub Assoc Foreign Serv. *

ROULHAC, DR. EDGAR EDWIN
School administrator. **Personal:** Born Sep 28, 1946, Chicago, IL; son of Portia Goodloe and Edgar Elijah; married Patricia Gayle Johnson. **Educ:** Southern Ill Univ Carbondale, BS, 1969, MS, 1970, PhD, 1974; Johns Hopkins Univ Sch Pub Health, MPH, 1975, postdoctoral studies, 1975; Harvard Univ, attended 1987. **Career:** Southern IL Univ Sch Med, prof health care planning, 1972-74; Towson State Univ, prof health sci, 1975-78; Johns Hopkins Univ, dean studs, 1978-86; asst provost, 1986-93, provost's off, vice provost, 1993-, interim vpres, 1994-95. **Orgs:** Kappa Alpha Psi Fraternity, 1965-; Hon Educ Phi Delta Kappa, 1972-; Hon Educ Kappa Delta Pi, 1972-; vpres, MD Soc Med Res, 1981-84; Hon Pub Health Delta Omega, 1982-; Sigma Pi Phi, 1986-; Sigma Pi Phi Fraternity, 1986-,AAHE, APHA, BCHW, SOPHE; adv bd, Drew-Meharry-More house Med Sch Cancer Prev Consortium, 1987-99; trustee, Provident Hosp Baltimore, 1978-82; gov bd, Cent MD Health Systs Agency, 1976-80; Dunbar-Hopkins Health Partnership; Elijah Cummings & Jerold C Hoff berger Youth Prog Israel; mem, Maryland Asn of Higher Education; mem, the Am Public Health Asn. **Honors/Awds:** Postdoctoral fellow, Johns Hopkins Univ Sch Pub Health, 1975; Acad PubHealth Recognition Award, Asn Schs Pub Health, 1985; Meritorious Service Award, Johns Hopkins Minority Med Fac Asn, 1986; Meritorious Service Award, Johns Hopkins Alumni Asn Exec Comt, 1983. **Business Addr:** Vice Provost for Academic Services, Johns Hopkins University, Office of the Provost, 207 Garland Hall 3400 N Charles St, Baltimore, MD 21218, **Business Phone:** (410)516-6049.

ROULHAC, JOSEPH D.
Judge. **Personal:** Born Aug 18, 1916, Selma, AL; son of Robert D and Minerva; married Frances; children: Delores. **Educ:** Stillman Col, cert, 1936; Lincoln Univ, AB, 1938; Univ Pa, MA, 1940, JD, 1948. **Career:** Judge (retired); Lincoln Univ, instr, 1938-39; Ft Valley St Col, instr, 1940-41; Summit City OH, asst county pros, 1957-63; Akron Munic Ct, judge. **Orgs:** OH, Nat, Am Bar Asn; Am Judicature Soc; Ohio Munic Judges Asn; trustee, Baldwin Wallace Col & Stillman Col; Nat Asn Advan Colored People; Veterans Foreign Wars; Am Leg; Phi Beta Sigma Dist Serv Chapt; Phi Beta Sigma; fel, Akron Bar Asn. **Special Achievements:** First African American municipal judge in Akron, Ohio. **Military Serv:** M sgt 1942-46. **Home Addr:** 381 Sun Valley Dr, Akron, OH 44333. *

ROULHAC, DR. NELLIE GORDON
Educator. **Personal:** Born Jun 5, 1924, Washington, DC; daughter of Levi Preston Morton Gordon and Agnes Pauline Lee Gordon; married Christopher M Roulhac Jr, Aug 1, 1944; children: Christopher M III & Yvonne Agnes Roulhac Horton. **Educ:** Cheyney State Univ, BA, 1944; Teachers Col, Columbia Univ, MA, 1946; Univ PA; Temple Univ, cert special educ; Univ Sarasota, EdD, 1978. **Career:** Westmoreland Co, VA, prin sch, 1945; Albany St Col, Albany, GA, instreng, 1949; Memphis Pub Sch, classroom teacher, 1954; Sch Dist Penn, supvr special educ, 1971-83. **Orgs:** Nat Found Infantile Paralysis, 1954; pres, Nat Jack & Jill Am, 1954-58; nat sec, Delta Sigma Theta Sorority Inc, 1954-58, Personnel Comn, chair; pres, Bd Trustees Pennhurst St Sch & Hosp, Spring City, PA, bd trustees Pennhurst, 1970-80; United Cerebral Palsy Asn Philadelphia & Vicinity, 1974-80; pres, Jack & Jill Am Found, 1975-78; founder, Thirty Clusters; Links Inc Philadelphia Chap; chair, Eastern Area Links Inc; chair, Servs Youth Comn; organizer, Friends Combs Col Music, 1978; bd trustees, Combs Col Music, 1979-83; bd mem, charter mem, Friends Moore Col Art; comnrMayor's Commn for Women, 1984-91; bd trustees, Free Libr Philadelphia, 1985-96; steering comt mem, Am Foun Negro Affairs, 1987; Inauguration & Investiture COM City Philadelphia, 1988; Nat Asn Parliamentarians, 1993. **Honors/Awds:** Gold Medalist, Alice Coachman, Olympic Champion, 1948, 1993; Century Club Awards, 1966-69; First Prize, Best Student Teaching, Cheyney St Univ; Meritorious Service Volunteer Instructor; Outstanding Service FieldSpecial Education Division Philadelphia PA 1982; Sadie T M Alexander Award, Philadelphia Alumnae Chap, Delta Sigma Theta Sorority Inc, 1988; Outstanding Service Award, Jack & Jill of Am, 1988; Honorary Chair, Greater Philadelphia March Dimes, 1990; Citation, City Philadelphia City Coun, 1994; Humanitarian Service Award, Liberian Child Rehab Network, 1995. **Special Achievements:** Author, "Seventeen Days of Jimmie" 1981; author History of Jack and Jill of America Inc 1990: "Work, Play, and Commitment: The First Fifty Years Jack and Jill of America, Inc;" author, "Jumping Over the Moon," biography.

ROULHAC, HON. ROY L.
Judge. **Personal:** Born Mar 27, 1943, Marianna, FL; son of J Y Rolack and GeHazel Gibson; children: Sheryl LaSonya McGriff. **Educ:** Wayne State Univ, BS, bus mgt, 1970; Univ Detroit Sch Law, JD, 1975. **Career:** Wayne County Prosecutors Off, asst prosecutor, 1976; Mich Dept State,admin law judge, 1977-; Mich Dept Labor, admin law judge, 1979-94; MichDept Consumer & Indust Serv, staff, 1995. **Orgs:** Pres, Mich Asn Admin Law Judges, 1982-84; bd dir, Nat Alliance Against Racist & Polit Repression, 1985-94; treas, Am Asn Jurist, 1987-89; Omega Psi Phi, 1987-; pres, Asn Black Judges Mich, 1988-89; pres, Admin Law Sect, State Bar Mich, 1989-90; bd dir& secy, Music Hall Ctr Detroit,1988-98; pres, Fred Hart Williams Gen Soc, 1992-98; ed, FHWGS Newsletter,1994-98; founder, Roulhac Family Asn, 1990; ed & publ, Roulhac Quarterly,1990-; founder, Gilmore Acad, Jackson Co Training Sch Alumni Asn, 1996; ed & publ, Gilmore Acad, CTS Newsletter, 1996-; Labor & Employment Law Sect Coun, State Bar Mich, 1994-, chair, 2001-02. **Honors/Awds:** Admin Law Judge of the Year, Mich Asn Admin Law Judges, 1986; Certificate of Appreciation, Off Gov, 1989. **Military Serv:** USAR, Livonia, MI; Wash DC Nat Guard; first lt, 1964-70. **Business Addr:** Administrative Law Judge, State of Michigan CIS Employment Relations, 1200 6th Ave Fl 14, Detroit, MI 48226-2418, **Business Phone:** (313)256-3540.

ROUNDFIELD, DANNY THOMAS
Basketball player. **Personal:** Born May 26, 1953, Detroit, MI; married Bernadine Owens; children: Corey & Christopher. **Educ:** Cent Mich Univ, BS, 1975. **Career:** Basketball player (retired), bus exec; Ind Pacers, 1975-78; Atlanta Hawks, 1978-84; Detroit Pistons, 1984-85; Wash Bullets, 1986-87; Earth Tech, mgr; Camp Dresser & McKee Inc, currently. **Honors/Awds:** First Team All-Pro, Nat Basketball Asn, 1980; First Team All-Defense, Nat Basketball Asn, 1980; 30th Team All-Star, Nat Basketball Asn, 1980. *

ROUNDTREE, DOVEY (DOVEY JOHNSON ROUNDTREE)
Lawyer, clergy, army officer. **Personal:** Born Apr 14, 1914, Charlotte, NC. **Educ:** Spelman Col; Howard Law Sch, attended, 1950. **Career:** Lawyer, Clergy, Army officer (retired); Military officer, civil rights activist, lawyer, ordained minister; lawyer, criminal, civil; co-coun, 1955; African Methodist Episcopal Church, ordained minister. **Orgs:** Gen Coun, Nat Coun Negro Women. **Honors/Awds:** Margaret Brent Award, Am Bar Asn, 2000. **Military Serv:** AUS, commissioned officer, teacher, 1942-45; Women's Auxiliary Army Corps.

ROUNDTREE, DOVEY JOHNSON. See ROUNDTREE, DOVEY.

ROUNDTREE, RALEIGH CITO
Football player. **Personal:** Born Aug 31, 1975, Augusta, GA. **Educ:** SC State Univ. **Career:** San Diego Chargers, guard, 1997-2001; Ariz Cardinals, 2002-03; Edmonton Eskimos, offensive line, 2006-07.

ROUNDTREE, RICHARD
Actor. **Personal:** Born Jul 9, 1942, New Rochelle, NY; son of John and Katheryn; married Karen; children: Kelly, Nicole & Morgan Elizabeth. **Educ:** Southern Ill Univ. **Career:** Barney's, suit salesman; model; Stage Appearances: Negro Ensemble Co; Kongi's Harvest Man; Better Man; Mau-Mau Rm; The Great White Hope; Shaftin Africa; Recorded song: St Brother; Films: What Do You Say To A NakedLady?, 1970; Shaft, 1971; Shaft's Big Score, 1972; Parachute to Paradies, Embassy, 1972; Charley One-Eye, Earthquake, 1974; Man Friday, 1975; Diamonds, 1975; Escape to Athena, 1979; An Eye for an Eye, 1981; The Winged Serpent, 1982; The Big Score, 1983; City Heat, 1984; Killpoint, 1984; Portrait of a Hitman, 1984; A Time to Die, 1991; Amityville: A New Gen, 1993; Ballistic, 1995; Once Upon a Time When We Were Colored, 1996; George of the Jungle, 1997; Shaft, 2000; Antitrust, 2001; Shoot, 2001; Corky Romano, 2001; Al's Lads, 2001; Boat Trip, 2002; Wild Seven, 2006; Ladies of the House, 2008; Speed Racer, 2008; Lincoln Heights, 2008; What Do You Say to a Naked Lady?, 2009; TV appearances: "The Merv Griffin Show"; "Search for Tomorrow"; "The New Yorkers"; "Inside Bedford-Stuyvesant"; "The Dean Martin Show, Shaft", 1973-74; "Outlaws", 1987; "413 Hope St", 1997; "Having Our Say: The Delany Sisters' First 100 Years", 1999; "Joe & Max", 2002; "The Rise & Fall of Jim Crow", 2002; "As the World Turns", 2002-03; "The Closer", 2005; "Painkiller Jane, Painkiller Jane", 2005; "Blade: The Series", 2006; "Grey's Anatomy", 2006; "Heroes", 2006; "Close to Home", 2006; "Heroes",2006; "Final Approach", 2007; "Lincoln Heights", 2007; "Point of Entry", 2007; advocate, currently. **Orgs:** Negro Ensemble Co. **Honors/Awds:** Golden Globe Nominee for Most Promising Newcomer-Male, 1972; MTV Movie Award for Life time Achievement, 1994. **Special Achievements:** Ranked No 62 on Premiere Magazine's 100 Greatest Movie Characters of All Time in 1971. **Business Phone:** (310)273-0744.

ROUNTREE, ELLA JACKSON
Educator, elementary school teacher. **Personal:** Born Feb 27, 1936, Griffin, GA; widowed. **Educ:** Ft Valley State Col, BS, 1957;

Western Conn State Col, MS, 1973. **Career:** Ala State Elem Sch, 1957-60; Moore Elem Sch, 1960-63; Grassy Plain Sch,teacher, 1963-. **Orgs:** Danbury City Coun, 1973-77; Danbury City Coun 6th Ward, 1973-; Bethel Educ Asn; Conn Educ Asn; Nat Educ Asn; Phi Lambda Theta; Nat Hon & Prof Asn Educ; Nat Asn Adv Colored People; Alpha Kappa Alpha Sorority; Waterbury Chap, LINKS; Mt Pleasant, AMEZ Church. **Honors/Awds:** Outstanding Elem Teacher of Am, 1974. **Business Addr:** 241 Greenwood Ave, Danbury, CT 06810.

ROUSE, JACQUELINE ANNE
Educator. **Personal:** Born Feb 1, 1950, Roseland, VA; daughter of Fannie Thompson. **Educ:** Howard Univ, attended 1972; Atlanta Univ, Atlanta, MA, 1973; Emory Univ, Atlanta, PhD, 1983. **Career:** Pal, Beach Jr Col, Lake Worth, sr instr, 1973-80; Ga Inst Teachers, Atlanta, guest lectr, 1983; Morehouse Col, Atlanta, assoc prof, 1983; Am Univ Smithsonian Inst, Landmarks, prof hist, 1989-91; Ga State Univ, prof hist & Dept African Am Studies, adj fac, currently; Univ Pretoria, South Africa, Hist & Hist Preserv Dept, lectr, 2004; Lincoln Col; Oxford Univ, Oxford, England, 2003. **Orgs:** Asst ed, Jour Negro Hist, 1983-89; adv, ref Harriet Tubman Historial & Cult Mus, Macon, 1985; panelist, Am Asn Univ Women, 1985-; prin scholar, Steering Comt, Nat Conf Women Civil Rights Movement, 1988; panelist, Jacob Javits Fellowship, Dept Educ, 1989; nat vice dir, Asst Black Women Historians, 1989-; vpres, Asn Social & Behav Scientists, 1989-; consult, adv, Atlanta Hist Soc, 1989; historian consult, Apex Collection Life & Heritage, 1989. **Honors/Awds:** FIPSE, Curriculum on Black Women's History, Spellman Col, 1983-84; NEH Summer Grant Col Teachers, 1984; UNCF Strengthening the Humanities Grant, 1985; Distinguished Scholar in Residence, 1993-94; Governor's Humanities Award, 2002; Southern Regional Educational Board's Faculty Mentor of the Year, 2007. **Business Addr:** Professor, Georgia State University, Department of History, PO Box 4117, Atlanta, GA 30302-4117.

ROUSSELL, NORMAN
Educator. **Personal:** Married Dorothy McCullum; children: Michael K. **Educ:** Dillard Univ, BA, 1960; Fisk Univ, MA, 1965; Wayne State Univ, EdD, 1974. **Career:** Educator (retired); Orleans Parish Sch Systs, chmn sci dept, 1960-66; Dillard Univ, assoc dean students, 1969-75; Charles S Mott Fel, 1972; Loyola Univ, dir title III, 1976-79, exec asst pres, 1979-86, vpres admin; Dillard Univ, fac improvement grant, 1973, assoc vpres. **Orgs:** Bd trustees, NO Museum of Art, 1973-86; Am Asn Higher Educ, 1977-86. **Military Serv:** USAF staff sgt 4 yrs; Korean Serv Medal, Good Conduct Medal. **Home Addr:** 7441 Bullard Ave, New Orleans, LA 70128. *

ROUTTE-GOMEZ, ENEID G
Journalist. **Personal:** Born May 16, 1944, Long Island, NY; daughter of Jesse Wayman and Maud Gomez. **Educ:** Univ Mo, Sch Journ, multicultural mgmt prog, 1984; Univ Puerto Rico. **Career:** San Juan Star, San Juan, PR, editor & spec writer, 1964-94. **Orgs:** Pres, Caribbean Women's Network, 1984-; dir, Displaced Homemakers Coun Region II, 1990-; dir & ex-pres, Overseas Press Clubs Puerto Rico, 1975-; Nat Asn Black Journalists, 1984; Puerto Rico Endowment for the Humanities, 1990. **Honors/Awds:** Numerous civic and press awards. **Business Addr:** Editor, Special Writer, San Juan Star, PO Box 9020058, Old San Juan, Puerto Rico 00902.

ROUX, DR. VINCENT J
Physician. **Personal:** Born Apr 27, 1937, New Orleans, LA; son of John and Beatrice Grammer; married Lois Milton; children: Bridgette, Vincent Jr & Denise. **Educ:** Xavier Univ, BS, 1961; Howard Univ Col Med, MD, 1965; Nat Bd Med, Bd Examiners, Dipl, 1966; Am Bd Surg, Cert, 1971; Am Col Surgeons, fel, 1975. **Career:** Montreal Neurol Inst, extern, 1964; Freedmen's Hosp, intern, 1966; Howard Univ Col Med, resident gen surgeon, 1966-70, Dept Surg, asst prof, chief resident, 1969-70, assoc dean/clin affairs, 1972-75, Dept Comn Health Practices, clin instr, 1972, med dir, assoc dean alumni & pub affairs, currently. **Orgs:** AMA; Nat Med Asn; Am Col Surgeons; Med Chirurgical Soc DC; chmn/bd dir, DC Chap United Way, 1974-76; mem/bd dir, Nat Cap Med Found; mem, DC C C. **Honors/Awds:** Daniel Hale Williams Award, 1966; Physician's Recognition Award, AMA,1969; Charles R Drew Memorial Award, 1965; 1st Annual Clarence Sumner Green Award, 1965. **Special Achievements:** Publisher: "The Stimulation of Adenosine 3', 5' Monophosphal Prodn by Antidiuretic Factors", "The CV Catheter, An Invasive Therapeutic Adj" 1977. **Military Serv:** AUS, specialist 3rd cl E-4, 1955-58. **Business Addr:** Associate Dean Alumni, Public Affairs, Howard University College Of Medicine, 520 W St NW 2041 Georgia Ave, Washington, DC 20059, **Business Phone:** (202)806-6270.

ROWAN, MICHAEL TERRANCE
Hospital administrator, chief executive officer. **Personal:** Born in Indianapolis, IN; son of Charles and Odessa. **Educ:** Miami Univ, Ohio, BA, 1980; Univ Mich, health services admin, 1982. **Career:** Dist Columbia Gen Hosp, admin extern, 1981; Univ Penn Hosp, admin resident, 1982-83, Transport Serv Dept, dir, 1982-83; St Vincent's Hosp, outpatient admin, Dept Psychiatry, 1983-84; St Vincent Med Ctr, asst vpres, 1985-87; Memorial Med Ctr, vpres, admin, 1987-92; Sarasota Memorial Hosp, exec vpres & chief operating officer, 1993; Humility Mary Health Care Corp, Youngstown, Ohio, pres & chief exec officer; St John Health, vpres & chief operating officer; Catholic Health Initiatives, exec vpres & chief operating officer, 2004-; St Vincent Med Ctr, Toledo; Saint Vincent's Hosp, NY; Wash Univ Sch Med, adj instr. **Orgs:** Am Col Healthcare Execs, 1981-; health div chmn, United Way, Coastal, GA, 1991; bd mem, Am Heart Asn, Southwest FL, 1994-; bd mem, Savannah Area Chamber Com, Southside, 1989-92; bd mem, Sarasota Family Coun Ctr, 1994-; bd mem, JH Floyd Sunshine Manor Nursing Home, 1994-. **Honors/Awds:** Nat Asn Pub Hosp fel, 1989. **Business Phone:** (303)298-9100.*

ROWE, ALBERT P
Clergy. **Personal:** Born Sep 22, 1934, Columbia, SC; married Dorothy Collins. **Educ:** Morgan St Col, BA, 1958; Crozer Theol Sem, 1962; Princeton Theol Sem, 1969, ThM; Eastern Bapt Theol Sem, DMin, 1982. **Career:** Cent Baptist Church, pastor, 1962-68; Calvary Baptist Church, pastor 1968-; Paterson Bd Edu, comnr, 1977-82; Paterson City Coun, councilman at large, 1982-90, pres, 1989-90; Calvary Baptist Comn Ctr, founder & pres; Cavalry Baptist Housing Develop Corp; Calvary Baptist Comn Health Ctr. **Orgs:** Vpres, Nat Asn Advan Colored People, Wilmington, DE, 1966-68; vpres, Passiac Valley United Way, 1974-82, 1978-82; bd trustee, Barnett Mem Hops, 1980-84; bd trustee, Passaic-Bergen County Urban League, 1990-96; bd trustee, Nat Coun Churches; chmn, PNBC Home Mission Bd; Paterson Boys Club; Paterson YMCA; Alpha Phi Alpha. **Honors/Awds:** Nominated Young Man of the Year, Wilmington JC'S, 1967; Distinguish Service Award, Calvary Baptist Church, 1973; Community Service Award, Paterson Nat Asn Advan Colored People, 1974. **Special Achievements:** Official observer, first free election, South African, Nelson Mandella elected president; named African chief Nii Addo Ayee, Accrea Ghana Council of Chiefs; preaching missions to Russia, Cuba, Ghana, Puerto Rico, Haiti & Kenya. **Military Serv:** AUS, Lt, 1958-59. **Business Addr:** Pastor, Calvary Baptist Church, 575 E 18th, Paterson, NJ 07504, **Business Phone:** (973)278-1849.

ROWE, AUDREY
Educator. **Personal:** Born Nov 4, 1946, New York, NY; divorced. **Educ:** Fed City Col, BA, 1971; George Washington Univ, pub admin; John F Kennedy Sch Govt, Harvard Univ, Fel Inst Polits. **Career:** Nat Asn Advan Colored People, asst dir, 1967-68; SASA House Sum Prog, consult, 1969; CPB dir Womens Activ; Nat Yough Alternative Proj, consult; Child Defense Fund, educ specialist/child advocate; Nat Welfare Rights Orgn, spec asst to exec dir, 1972; Proj New Hope, ed dir, 1972-72; Nat Womens Pol Caucus, nat vice chairperson, 1973-75, nat chairperson,1975-77; Nat Comn Observance Int Womens Yr, commr; Womans Adv Com Sec Lbr, 1973; Rockefeller Found, Equal Opportunity Div, consult, 1988-91; Dept Social Servs CT, comnr; Nat Urban League Inc, exec vpres; Affiliated Comput Serv Inc, sr vpres pub affairs, 2005-. **Orgs:** Nat Coun Negro Women, 1967; chairperson, Juvenile Justice Adv Group DC; founder, DC Womens Pol Caucus, 1972; pres bd, Movement Econ Justice, 1974; bd mem rep, Womens Task Force; bd mem, Womens Campaign Fund; DC Comm Mgt; chair, Nat Comn Family Foster Care; bd mem, Joint Ctr Polit & Econ Studies; bd mem, Am Pub Welfare Asn; bd mem, Child Welfare League Am. **Honors/Awds:** Organic Award DC Black Economic Union Commission; Sojourner Truth Award, 1974. **Business Addr:** Senior Vice President, Affiliated Computer Services Inc, 2828 N Haskell Ave, Dallas, TX 75204, **Business Phone:** (214)841-6111.

ROWE, SR. CHRISTA F
Nun, educator. **Personal:** Born Jun 10, 1959, Clearwater, FL; daughter of Peter John Rowe Sr and Theresia Roberson. **Educ:** Int Religious Studies, Dublin, Ireland, 1979-80; San Diego Community Col, 1982; Hillsborough Community Col, Tampa, FL, AA, 1986; St Leo Col, St Leo, FL, BSW, 1988; Boston Col, MEd, 1998; Hawkstone Ctr Spirituality & Renewal, Shrewsbury, England, 2000. **Career:** Holy Family Cath Church, San Diego, CA, sec, 1980-82; St Lawrence Cath Church, Tampa, FL, pastoral minister, 1983-87; Diocese St Petersburg, Off Black Cath Ministries, St Petersburg, FL, assoc dir, 1988-90; Diocese St Petersburg, St Petersburg, FL, columnist, 1988-90; Diocese St Petersburg, Tampa, FL, productions coordr, innervision radio prog, 1988-90; Our Lady Queen Peace Church, New Port Richey, FL, dir religious educ, 1990-96; Sisters St Clare, New Port Richey, FL, formation dir, 1996-98; St Joseph's Parish, St Petersburg, FL, pastoral assoc & dir religious educ, 1998-99; Sacred Heart Oratory, Wilmington, DE, dir outreach, 2000-. **Orgs:** Fools Jesus Mime & Pantomine Clown Troup, 1976-79; vocations promoter, Sisters St Clare, 1986-91; Nat Asn Social Workers, 1987-89; Campaign Human Devt, 1988-91; Nat Asn Black Cath Adminrs, 1988-89; Liturgical CMS Diocese, St Petersburg, 1991-94; Vocations Team, Sisters St Clare, 1992-96, Regional Team, 1992-95; regional Counr, 2003-. **Honors/Awds:** Outstanding Academic Performance Award, 1987. **Home Addr:** 1105 W 8th St, Wilmington, DE 19806. **Business Addr:** Director of Outreach, Sacred Heart Oratory, 917 N Madison St, Wilmington, DE 19801, **Business Phone:** (302)428-3658.

ROWE, JIMMY L.
Association executive. **Personal:** Born Dec 6, 1932, Haskell, OK; married; children: Dianna, Leonardo, James, Kimberly & Michael. **Educ:** SC State Col, BA, Industrial Educ, 1956. **Career:** Trans Oppor Prog Pico Rivera, CA, training coordr, 1967-68, asst dir, 1968-71, acting dir, 1971-72; Sons Watts Own Recog Proj, dir, 1971-74. **Orgs:** Tulsa Personnel Asn; Nat Asn Pretrial Release Asn; Com Rel Comn Employ Com; dir, coalition LA Model Ctys; Tulsa Urban League; asst pastor & minister christian ed St Luke Bapt Ch; youth minister, Doublerock BCCompton, CA; Truevine BC Hawthorne, CA; NAACP; Black Econ Union LA; Mexican Am Political Asn. **Honors/Awds:** Received Resolution Los Angeles City Coun Outstand Leadership. **Military Serv:** AUS Signal Corp, 1956-58.

ROWE, MARILYN JOHNSON
Consultant. **Personal:** Born Nov 9, 1954, Batesburg, SC; married Thaddeus E Rowe Jr; children: Brandolyn & Alesia. **Educ:** Univ SC, BA, Educ, 1977. **Career:** SC Human Affairs Comn, sr equal employ opportunity consult; Olive Branch Baptist Church, dir music. **Orgs:** Am Asn Affirmation Action, 1979-; Nat Asn Human Rights Worker,1979-; Tau Beta Sigma USC, 1976; vol, Metro Community Rels Coun, 1989-90. **Honors/Awds:** Employee of the Year, SC Human Affairs Comn, 1990. **Business Addr:** Senior Consultant, South Carolina Human Affairs Commission, PO Box 4490, Columbia, SC 29240.

ROWE, DR. NANSI IRENE
Executive, lawyer. **Personal:** Born May 6, 1940, Detroit, MI; children: Leslie Anika-Ayoka. **Educ:** Detroit Inst Tech, BBA, 1965; Wayne State Univ, JD, 1973; Payne Seminary, MDiv, attended. **Career:** City Detroit Corp, corp coun, dep corp coun, 1974-78; Detroit Econ Growth Corp, vpres, gen coun, secy to bd dir, 1979-82; EO Constructors Inc, pres, chairperson bd, 1980-; Nansi Rowe & Assoc PC, pres, chief coun, partner, atty, 1982-. **Orgs:** Secy, treas, Wayne Cnty Com Col Found; secy, gen coun, Detroit Eco Growth Corp; bd mem, Southeastern Mich Transit Auth; former bd mem, Homes Black C; bd mem, United Community Serv, 1978-81; State Bar Mich; Am Arbitration Asn; NAACP; Inner-City Bus Improvement Forum, Southeastern Mich Bus Develop Ctr; Am Bar Asn; Detroit Bar Asn; life mem, Nat Bar Asn; former bd mem, Southeastern Mich Transit Authority; former bd mem, Brent Gen Hosp. **Honors/Awds:** AME Church, ordained elder; Business Woman of the Year, Nat Asn Prof Women, 1976; Woman of the Year, United Coun Churches, 1981. **Business Addr:** Attorney, Nansi Rowe & Associates, 719 Griswold Suite 820, Detroit, MI 48226-3360, **Business Phone:** (313)628-0777.

ROWE, RICHARD L.
Executive. **Personal:** Born Sep 21, 1926, New York, NY; married Mercedes L Walker; children: Delena Pugh, Patricia Anderson, Richard Jr. **Educ:** City Col, B Indust Mgt; City Univ, MBA. **Career:** Executive (retired); Port Authority of NY & NJ, asst mgr operating personnel personnel dept, 1968-70, mgr equal opportunity prog personnel, 1970-72, mgr operating personnel, 1972-76, mgr employee relations, 1976-78, asst dir aviation dept, 1978-83, general mgr JFK Intl Airport, 1983-95. **Orgs:** Kappa Alpha Psi Fraternity; Int Pub Mgt Asn Human Resources; Nat Asn Adv Colored People ; Port Authority NY. **Honors/Awds:** NI Distinguished Service Medal; IPMA-HR, Honorary Life mem. **Home Addr:** 501 Webster Ave, New Rochelle, NY 10801, **Home Phone:** (914)235-7374. *

ROWELL, VICTORIA LYNN
Actor. **Personal:** Born May 10, 1960, Portland, ME; married Radcliffe Bailey, Jun 27, 2009; married Tom Fahey, Jan 1, 1989 (divorced 1990); children: Maya; married Wynton Marsalis; children: Jasper. **Career:** Films: Distinguished Gentleman, 1992; Full Eclipse, 1993; Secret Sins of the Father, 1993; Dumb & Dumber, 1994; One Red Rose, 1995; Barb Wire, 1996; Eve's Bayou, 1997; Secrets, 1997; Dr Hugo, 1998; A Wake in Providence, 1999; Fraternity Boys, 1999; Black Listed, 2003; Motive, 2004; Midnight Clear, 2005; A Perfect Fit, 2005; Home of the Brave, 2006; Polly & Marie, 2007; Of Boys & Men, 2008; Tv series: "The Young & The Restless", 1990-98, 2000, 2002-; "Diagnosis Murder", 1993; "Feast of All Saints", 2001; TV movies: "Full Eclipse", 1993; "Secret Sins of the Father", 1994; "Without Warning", 2002; "A Town Without Pity", 2002; "Noah's Arc", 2006; Polly and Marie, 2007; "All of Us", 2007; Plays: Drucilla Winters, 1990; Feast of All Saints, 2001. **Orgs:** Founder & pres, The Rowell Foster Children's Postive Plan, 1990-; ambassador, St Lucian Bd Tourism, 1995; spokesperson, Child Welfare League Am, 1992; spokesperson, Annie E Casey Found; mem, Sigma Gamma Rho Sorority, Inc. **Honors/Awds:** Best Actress in a Daytime Drama, Nat Asn Advan Colored People, 1993; SoapOpera Awards Scene Stealer, 1994; Image Award for Outstanding Actress in aDaytime Drama Series, 1995, 1996, 1997, 1998, 1999, 2001, 2003, 2004,2005; Doctorate of Humane Letters, Univ Southern Maine, 2006. **Special Achievements:** Full Scholarship Recipient of the American Ballet Theatre School of NYC;American Ballet Theater II, NYC; Guest Teacher, resident of the Elma LewisSchool of Fine Arts/Mass; Guest resident teacher of the Roxbury Ctr of thePerforming Arts, Roxbury, Mass. **Business Addr:** Founder, President, The Rowell Foster Children Positive Plan, Rm 651 425 Shatto Pl, Los Angeles, CA 90020, **Business Phone:** (323)857-1717.

ROWLAND, KELLY TRENE (KELENDRIA TRENE ROWLAND)
Singer, actor. **Personal:** Born Feb 11, 1981, Atlanta, GA. **Career:** Albums: Destiny's Child, 1998; The Writing's On the Wall, 1999;

Survivor, 2001; Eight Days of Christmas, 2001; Dilemma; Stole, 2002; Train On a Track, 2003; Here We Go, 2005; Ms Kelly, 2007; TV appearance: "The Hughleys", 2002; "Born to Diva", 2003; "Am Dreams", 2003; "Eve", 2003; "Girlfriends", 2003; "Wild n Out", 2003; Girlfriends3, 2006; The 20th Annual Soul Train Music Awards, 2006; The British Soap Awards 2008: The Party, 2008; Episode dated 26 May 2008, 2008; "TRL Italy", 2008; "So You Think You Can Dance", 2009; Ode to la Mode, 2009; It's in the Cards, 2009; Blood, Sweat and Sparkle, 2009; Films: Freddy vs Jason, 2003; The seat Filler, 2004; Soundtrack appearance: Down to earth, 2001; monaLisa Smile, 2004; Album appeareances: Seperated (Remix), 1999; Oh Why, 2003; How I Feel, 2005; Solo Albums: Simply Deep, 2002; R&B group, ling: A Planet Rock, 2007, "This Morning", 2009; Two of 12 Voted Off, 2009; "So You Think You Can Dance", 2009. **Honors/Awds:** Grammy Awards, 2002; Ebel award, 2003; Capital FM Awards, 2003; TMF Awards, 2003; Billboard R&B/Hip-Hop Awards, 2003; Soul Train Lady of Soul Awards; Image Award, Nat Asn Advan Colored People; Artist Direct (ADOMA) Awards. **Business Phone:** (212)833-8000.*

ROXBOROUGH, MILDRED BOND
Association executive, consultant. **Personal:** Born Jun 30, 1926, Brownsville, TN; daughter of Ollie S and Mattye Tollette; married John W II. **Educ:** NY Univ, Wash Square Col, BA, 1947; Columbia Univ, MA, 1953; Univ Paris; Univ Mexico. **Career:** Executive (retired), consultant; Nat Asn Advan Colored People, nat field secy, 1954-58, dir, Life Mem Prog, 1958-63, admin asst to exec dir, 1963-67, exec ast to exec dir, 1967-75, asst dir, 1975-78, dir opers, 1978-84, dep dir progs, 1984-86, dir develop, 1986-97, consult, 1997-; InterGroup Corp, dir, 1987-2006. **Orgs:** Nat Asn Advan Colored People, 1958-; bd dir, Intergroup Corp; former vice chair, bd dirs, chair, Personnel Comm, Am's Charities; former chair, Personnel Comm Morningside Retirement & Health Inc. **Honors/Awds:** James Weldon Johnson Medal; Medgar Wiley Evers Award; Ams Charities Distinguished Service Award. **Business Addr:** Development Consultant, NAACP, 39 Broadway Suite 2220, New York, NY 10006, **Business Phone:** (212)344-7474.

ROY, JAN S
Executive. **Personal:** Born Jan 19, 1954, Evanston, IL; daughter of Bedford McCowan; married Anthony E Roy, Jun 11, 1980; children: Harrison & Erica. **Educ:** Harold Wash Col, AS, hospitality mgt, 1991; Roosevelt Univ, BS, hospitality mgt, 1997. **Career:** Ramada Hotel, conv sales mgr, 1987-89; Sheraton Int Hotel, conv sales mgr, 1989-91; Am Med Asn, sr rep, 1991-94; McCormick Place Conv Ctr, mgr sales prom, 1994-96; Chicago Conv Bur, dir corp sales, 1996-. **Orgs:** Bd mem, NEWH Network of Exec Women in Hospitality, 1995-96; adv bd mem, Harold Wash Coll, 1996-; Meeting Prof Int, bd mem, 1997-. **Honors/Awds:** Franklin Honor Soc, 1997. **Business Addr:** Director, Chicago Convention and Tourism Bureau, 2301 S Lake Shore Dr, Chicago, IL 60616, **Business Phone:** (312)567-8500.

ROY, JOHN WILLIE
Automotive executive. **Career:** Southland Chrysler-Plymouth, pres, currently. **Special Achievements:** CPN is ranked No. 93 on Black Enterprise magazine's list of top 100 auto dealers, 1998. **Business Addr:** President, Southland Chrysler-Plymouth, 223 Goodman Rd E, Southaven, MS 38671-9521.*

ROYAL, ANDRE TIERRE
Football player. **Personal:** Born Dec 1, 1972, Northport, AL; children: Tierra. **Educ:** Univ Ala. **Career:** Carolina Panthers, linebacker, 1995-97, Indianapolis Colts, 1998-99.

ROYAL, DONALD
Basketball player, basketball coach. **Personal:** Born May 2, 1966, New Orleans, LA. **Educ:** Notre Dame Univ, attended 1987. **Career:** Basketball player (retired), basketball coach; Minn Timberwolves, 1989-90; San Antonio Spurs, 1991-92; Orlando Magic, 1992-96; Charlotte Hornets, 1996; Pensacola Tornados, 1987-88; Cedar Rapids Silver Bullets, 1988-89; Tri-City Chinook, 1991-92; Brevard Blue Ducks, asst head coach, 2002. **Business Addr:** Assistant Head Coach, Brevard Blue Ducks, c/o Brevard County Sport Management Group, 100 Hive Dr, PO Box 410064, Melbourne, FL 32941-0064, **Business Phone:** (321)751-2583.

ROYE, MONICA R HARGROVE
Lawyer. **Personal:** Born Feb 7, 1955, Atlanta, GA; daughter of Bettye Forston and Ernest Crawford; divorced; children: Stephen Paul. **Educ:** Dartmouth Col, Hanover, BA, 1976; Univ Mich Law Sch, Ann Arbor, JD, 1979. **Career:** Kutak Rock & Huie, Atlanta, paralegal, 1976; IBM Legal Dept, Armonk, summer law clerk, 1978; US Dept Justice, Antitrust Div, trial atty, 1979-83; USAir Inc, Arlington, VA, from atty to asst gen coun, assoc gen coun, currently. **Orgs:** Henry & Mayme Sink Scholarship Fund, 1986-91; Celestial Echoes, 1986-91, assoc pastor, 1993-96; Lomax Am Zion Church; secy, USAM Corp, 1988-96; judicial coun, Am Zion church; Bicentennial Revival COM, 1996. **Honors/Awds:** Outstanding Performance Award, US Dept Justice, 1980. **Home Addr:** 1330 Kingston Ave, Alexandria, VA 22302, **Home Phone:** (703)370-1418. **Business Addr:** Associate General Counsel, US Airways Inc, 2345 Crystal Dr, Arlington, VA 22202, **Business Phone:** (703)872-5300.

ROYE, ORPHEUS
Football player. **Personal:** Born Jan 21, 1973, Miami, FL. **Educ:** Fla State Univ, criminal justice. **Career:** Pittsburgh Steelers, defensive end, 1996-99; Cleveland Browns, defensive end, 2000-07; Pittsburgh Steelers, defensive end, 2008-, free agent, NFL, currently. **Honors/Awds:** Super Bowl Champion XLIII. **Business Phone:** (412)323-1200.*

ROYSTER, DON M, SR.
Executive, banker. **Personal:** Born Mar 12, 1944, Baltimore, MD; married Vertie M Bagby; children: Don M Jr & Denise C. **Educ:** Morgan State Univ, attended 1962-63; Agr & Tech Univ NC, attended 1963-64; Nat Col, BA, 1970; Am Col, CLU, 1976; Life Off Mgt Assoc, FLMI, 1977. **Career:** Wash Nat Ins Co, asst vpres, 1967-85, adminr, 1985-89, mkt serv officer, 1989-92, vpres opers; Atlanta Life Ins Co, pres, chief operating officer, 1992-93, pres/chief exec officer, 1993; United Insurance Co Am, sr vpres, 1998-2000, pres Career Agency Div, pres, 2000-; Reliable Life Ins Co, pres, 2001-. **Orgs:** Chicago Chap Chartered Life Underwriters, 1976-92; Chicago Chap FLMI, 1977-92; Chicago Asn Health Underwriters, 1979-92; vpres, Ment Helath Asn Evanston, dir, 1981-83; chair, Evanston Human Rels Comn, counr, 1981-84; secy, Sweet Auburn Area Improv Asn Atlanta, bd dirs, 1992-; dir, Martin Luther King Jr, Ctr Nonviolent Social Change, bd adv, 1992-; bd dir, Atlanta Bus League, 1993-; bd dirs, Cent Atlanta Progress, 1993-; dir, bd visitors, 1993-, Clark Atlanta Univ; bd visitors, Emory Univ, 1994-; dir, Ga Inst Technol; exec adv bd, Ivan Allen Col, 1994-; bd dirs, Life Insurers Conf, 1994-. **Honors/Awds:** Hispanic Achievement Award, 1980. **Business Addr:** President, United Insurance Company of America, 1 E Wacker Dr, Chicago, IL 60601, **Business Phone:** (312)661-4500.

ROYSTER, PHILIP M
Educator, writer. **Personal:** Born Jul 31, 1943; married Phyliss M; children: Rebecca Suzanne, Francesca Therese, Barbara Kaye Hammond & Tara Lynn Hammond. **Educ:** Univ Ill, 1962; Detroit Univ, BA, 1965, MA, 1967; Roosevelt Univ, Black Cultures Sem, 1969; Loyola Univ, PhD, am & brit lit, 1974. **Career:** Loyola Univ, asstship, 1967-68, fel, 1968-69, teacher, 1969-70; Fisk Univ, Eng Dept, instr, 1970-74, asst prof, 1974-75; State Univ NY Albany, Dept African/Afro-Am Studies, asst prof, 1975-78; Syracuse Univ, Dept ARO Studies, assoc prof, 1978-81; Kans State Univ, Dept Eng, assoc prof, 1981-85, Am Ethnic Studies Prog, coordr, 1984-88, prof, 1985-88; Bowling Green State Univ, Dept Ethnic Studies, prof, 1987-92, asst chmn, 1990-91; Univ Ill, Chicago, Dept Eng, prof, 1991-, Dept African Am Studies, prof, 1991-, African Am Cultural Ctr, dir, 1991-. **Orgs:** Bd mem, Soc New Music, 1979-81; African-Am Drum Ensemble, 1987-; Asn Black Cultural Ctrs, 1991-, Nat Steering Comn, 1991-, Const laws Subcomn, 1991-; Hon Soc Phi Kappa Phi, 1992-; Ill Comn Black Concerns Higher Educ, 1992-; Univ Ill Chicago Black Alumni Asn, 1992-; Popular Cult Asn, 1976-; Modern Lang Asn; Col Lang Asn; Nat Coun Black Studies; Nat Asn Church God Summit Meeting Task Force; chairperson, Emerald Ave Church God, Hist Comn. **Honors/Awds:** Arthur J Schmitt Scholarship, DePaul Univ, 1967; Study Grant, Fisk Univ, 1971, 1974; Senate Research Committee Grant, Syracuse Univ, 1979; Mellon Found, Mellon Proj, 1980; Faculty Research Grant, Kans State Univ, 1981, 1982; The Seaton Third Poetry Award, 1983; Faculty Research Committee Basic Grant Award, Bowling Green State Univ, 1988, Certificate of Appreciation, Black Stud Union & Bd Black Cultural Activ, 1988. **Special Achievements:** Books: "The Rapper as Shaman for a Band of Dancers of the Spirit: U Can't Touch This," The Emergency of Black and the Emergence of Rap Special Issue of Black Sacred Music: A Journal of Theomusicology, pages 60-67, 1991, "The Sky is Gray: An Analysis of the Story," American Short Stories on Film: A Series of Casebooks, Langenscheidt-Longman, "The Curse of Capitalism in the Caribbean: Purpose and Theme in Lindsay Barrett's Song for Mumu," Perspectives in Black Popular Culture, The Popular Press, pages 22-35, 1990; Literary & Cultural Criticism: "In Search of Our Fathers' Arms: Alice Walker's Persona of the Alienated Darling," Black American Literature Forum, 20.4, 347-70, 1986; "The Spirit Will Not Descend Without Song: Cultural Values of Afro-American Gospel Tradition," Folk Roots: An Exploration of the Folk Arts & Cultural Traqditions of Kansas, Ed Jennie A Chinn, Manhattan: Univ for Man, 19-24, 1982; "Contemporary Oral Folk Expression," Black Books Bulletin, 6.3, 24-30, 1979; "A Priest and a Witch Against the Spiders and the Snakes: Scapegoating in Toni Morrison's Sula," Umoja 2.2, 149-68, 1979; "The Bluest Eye: The Novels of Toni Morrision," First World, 1.4, 34-44, 1977; Suggestions for Instructors to Accompany Clayers' and Spencer's Context for Composition, Co-authored with Stanley A Clayes, New York: Appleton-Century-Crofts, 1969; Books of Poetry: Songs and Dances, Detroit, Lotus Press, 1981; The Back Door, Chicago, Third World Press, 1971; Photography: A Milestone Sampler: Fifteenth Ann Anthology, Detroit, Lotus Press, "Samuel Allen," 10, "Jill Witherspoon Boyer," 22, "Beverley Rose Enright," 40, "Naomi F Faust," 44, "Ray Fleming," 50, "Agnes Nasmith Johnston," 56, "Delores Kendrick," 68, "Pinkie Gordon Lane," 74, "Naomi Long Madgett," 80, "Haki R Madhubuti," 86, "Herbert Woodward Martin," 92, "May Miller," 104, "Mwatabu Okantah," 110, "Paulette Childress White," 122, 1988; Master Drummer & Percussionist: "Earth Blossom," The John Betsch Society, Strata-East Recording Co, #SES-19748, 1975; Received a four and a half star review in Downbeat, 24-26, May 1975; "A White Sport Coat and a Pink Crustacean," Jimmy Buffet, Dunhill ABC, DSX 50150, 1973; "Hanging Around the Observatory," John Hiatt, Epic KE 32688, 1973; "We Make Spirit (Dancing in the Moonlight)," John Hiatt, Epic, 5-10990, ZSS 157218, 1973; "Backwoods Woman," Dianne Davidson, Janus, JLS 3043, 1972; "The Knack," The Interpreters, Cadet LP 762, 1965. **Business Addr:** Director, African American Cultural Center, Professor of African American Studies, University of Illinois, Department of African American Studies, 209 Addams Hall MC 020 830 S Halsted St, Chicago, IL 60607-7030, **Business Phone:** (312)413-2705.

ROYSTER, SCOTT ROBERT
Executive. **Personal:** Born Jul 17, 1964, New Haven, CT; son of Robert and Jean Royster. **Educ:** Duke Univ, BA, 1987; Harvard Univ, MBA, 1992. **Career:** Chemical Venture Partners, analyst, 1987-90; Capital Resource Partners, prin, 1992-94; TSG Capital Group, prin, 1995-96; Radio One Inc, exec vpres & chief financial officer, 1996-. **Orgs:** Bd mem, Telemedia, 1999-; bd mem, Netscan iPublishing, 1999-; bd visitors, Duke Univ, 2000-. **Business Addr:** Executive Vice President, Chief Financial Officer, Radio One Inc, 5900 Princess Garden Pkwy 7th Fl, Lanham, MD 20706, **Business Phone:** (301)429-2642.

ROYSTER, DR. VIVIAN HALL
College administrator. **Personal:** Born Feb 21, 1951, Monticello, FL; daughter of Emma L and Henry; married Charles (divorced); children: Renee Gwendolyn-Juanita. **Educ:** Fla A&M Univ, Tallahassee, FL, BS (magna cum laude), 1973; Atlanta Univ, Atlanta, GA, MSLS (summa cum laude), 1974; Fla State Univ, Tallahassee, FL, PhD candidate, 1990. **Career:** Atlanta Univ GSLIS, educ fel, 1973-74; Fla State Univ, Tallahassee, FL, assoc univ librarian, 1974-80; Univ Md, East Shore Princess Anne, MD, admin librarian, 1980-83; Fla A&M Univ, Tallahassee, FL, assoc dir, Title III prog, 1982-84, assoc prof foreign lang, 1984-86; Fla A&M Univ Libraries, Tallahassee, FL, univ librarian & head acquisitions dept, 1986-2003; Del State Univ, dean libr, 2003-. **Orgs:** Am Libr Asn, 1976-; Am Libr Asn Black Caucus, 1978-; financial secy, Fla A&M Univ Friends Black Archives, 1988-; secy & bd dir, Asn Col & Res Libr, Fla Chap, 1989-; libr adv bd, Bond Comm Br Libr-Leon County Pub Libr Syst, 1989-; steering comm mem, E A Copeland Scholar Dr, Fla A&M Univ Found, 1989-. **Honors/Awds:** Alpha Beta Beta Alpha Undergrad Libr Science Honor Soc, FAMU, 1972; Undergraduate Advisor Awards, Alpha Kappa Alpha Sorority, Inc, 1974-80; Grant Award Of Black America, Nat Endowment Humanities, MD, 1980-82; Doctoral Fellowship Award, State Fla Bd Regents, 1984; Beta Phi Mu Grad Honor Soc, libr sci; Professional Develop Grant-in-Aid, Fla A&M Univ, 1988, 1993, 1994. **Special Achievements:** Selected as Host, Florida Governor's Conference on the White House Conference on Library & Information Services, 1990. **Business Addr:** Dean of Libraries, Delaware State University, W.C. Jason Library, 1200 N Dupont Hwy, Dover, DE 19901, **Business Phone:** (302)857-6176.

ROYSTON, EVELYN ROSS
Business owner, consultant. **Personal:** Born Dec 14, 1959, Victoria, MS; daughter of Ethel M Brown; married Jan 13, 1989; children: Gariel Brownlee & Natasha Brownlee. **Educ:** Tenn State Univ, attended 1981; State Tech Inst, Memphis, attended 1999. **Career:** Construction Code Enforcement, plans & permit reviewer, 1984-94; Royston Construct Consults, pres, 1994-. **Orgs:** Asn Construct Inspectors, 1996-; Better Bus Bur, 1999-. **Honors/Awds:** Iris Award, HER Bus News, 1999; Business Award, Small Minority Bus, 2000. **Home Addr:** 1712 Belledeer Dr E, Cordova, TN 38016, **Home Phone:** (901)757-3725. **Business Addr:** President, Royston Construction Consultants Inc, 1712 Belledeer Dr E, Corodova, TN 38016, **Business Phone:** (901)757-3725.

ROZIER, CLIFFORD GLEN
Basketball player. **Personal:** Born Oct 31, 1972, Bradenton, FL; married Diane. **Educ:** Univ NC; Univ Louisville. **Career:** Basketball Player (retired); Golden State Warriors, ctr-forward, 1994-97; Toronto Raptors, 1996-97; Minn Timberwolves, ctr-forward, 1997-98; US Basketball League, Brevard Blue Ducks, 2000. **Honors/Awds:** First round pick, NBA Draft, 1994.

ROZIER, GILBERT DONALD
Executive, association executive. **Personal:** Born Oct 19, 1940, West Palm Beach, FL; married Juanella Miller; children: Ricardo & Rellisa. **Educ:** Benedict Col, BA, 1963; Southern Conn State Col, MA, Urban Studies, 1973. **Career:** W Side YMCA NYC, youth worker 1963-66; W Main St Comm Ctr, prog dir, 1966-67; Stamford Neighborhood Youth Corp, dir, 1967-74; Urban League of S Weston Fairfield, asso dir, 1970-74; Urban League Union CO, pres, 1974; Urban League of S Weston, exec dir; Kentucky Fried Chicken Restaurants, franchise owner & pres, currently. **Orgs:** Secy, Conn State Fedn Demo Clubs, 1974; pres, AFLO Am Dem Club, 1979; life mem, Kappa Alpha Psi; bd trustees, Benedict Col; trustee, Stamford Bethel AME; bd mem, Stanford Planning. **Honors/Awds:** Outstand Young Man of the Year; Outstanding Young Men of America, 1973; Outstanding Citizen Union Co New Jersey Human Resources, 1979; Outstanding Citizen St John Lodge 14, Stamford, CT, 1980. **Business Addr:** President, Kentucky Fried Chicken, 356 Strawberry Hill Ave, Stamford, CT 06902, **Business Phone:** (203)348-6048.

RUBIN, CHANDA
Tennis player. **Personal:** Born Feb 18, 1976, Lafayette, LA; daughter of Edward Rubin and Bernadette. **Career:** Pro tennis

player, 1991-. **Honors/Awds:** Orange Bowl, 1988; Nat Championship, 1988, 1989; Wimbledon Jr Singles,1992; ATA Athlete of the Yr, 1995; USTA Female Athlete of the Yr, 1995; Pan Am Games, silver medal, bronze medal, 1995; Most Caring Ahtlete, USA Weekend magazine, 1997; Arthur Ashe Leadership Awd, 1997; Player Who Makes A Difference Award, Family Circle & Hormel Foods, 2002; winner, Eastbourne, 2002; Winner, 2003 Madrid, 2003. **Business Addr:** Professional Tennis Player, United States Tennis Association, 70 W Red Oak Lane, White Plains, NY 10604-3602.*

RUBIO, JACQUELINE
Army officer. **Personal:** Born Nov 25, 1961, Hempstead, NY; divorced; children: Joseph, Justin & Jessica. **Educ:** Morgan State Univ, attended 1981; Fayetteville Community Col, attended1986; Miller Motte Bus Col, attended 1991; Forsyth Tech Community Col, attended 1993. **Career:** AUS, instr, 2000-. **Orgs:** Greeter & usher, City Refuge Christian Church, 1997-. **Military Serv:** AUS, res, 1984-90, 1992-97, reserves, 1997-. **Business Addr:** Staff, U.S. Army, Staff Sergeant Rubio 88M30, Ft Drum, NY 13603, **Business Phone:** (315)772-5996.

RUCKER, ALSTON LOUIS
Banker. **Personal:** Born Aug 29, 1949, Greenwood, SC; son of Thomas L (deceased) and Annie (deceased); married Shirley Gordon, Jul 12, 1975; children: Montrice Ginelle, Aaron Louis. **Educ:** SCA State Col, BA, bus admin, 1971. **Career:** LaSalle Bank FSB, savings rep, 1973-81, retirement account specialist, 1981-84, human resources mgr, 1984-85, asst secy, 1985-86, br mgr, 1986-87, br officer, 1987-91, asst vpres, 1992. **Orgs:** SCA State Col, Chicago Chap, 1975-; prog speaker, Chicago Asn Com & Ind, Youth Motivation Prog, 1981-; Lillydale Progressive Missionary Baptist Church, 1985-; Dolton Sch Dist 149, PTA, 1990-; Thornton High Sch, District 205, PTA, 1992; bd mem, Teen Living Programs Inc, 1993-; bd mem & treas, The Harvey 100 Club Inc, 1995-. **Honors/Awds:** Chicago South Side YMCA, Black & Hispanic Achievers, 1991; America's Best & Brightest Young Business & Professional Men, 1992; Branch Administration Certificate of Achievement, LaSalle Bank, FSB, 1994.

RUCKER, CLYDE
Vice president (Organization). **Educ:** Univ Colo, BA; Cent Mich Univ, MS. **Career:** Arby's, staff; KFC, staff; Burger King Corp, staff, 1994-00; vpres US franchise oper, 2000-03, sr vpres diversity capability & bus develop, 2003-04, sr vpres diversity capability & bus develop & chief staff, sr vpres & chief support officer, 2004-05, sr vpres global commun & external affairs, 2005-07; Quiznos, exec vpres & chief admin officer, 2007-. **Orgs:** Bd trustees, Fla Memorial Univ. **Honors/Awds:** Corporate Executive of the Year; Top 100 Blacks in Corporate America, Black Professionals Mag, 2005-06; Most Influential Who's Who in Black S Fla. **Business Addr:** Executive Vice President, Chief Administrative Officer, Quiznos, 1475 Lawrence St Suite 400, Denver, CO 80202, **Business Phone:** (720)359-3300.*

RUCKER, DARIUS
Guitarist, singer. **Personal:** Born May 13, 1966, Charleston, SC; married Beth Leonard; children: Carey. **Educ:** Univ SC. **Career:** Lead vocalist/guitarist, Hootie & the Blowfish, formed, 1986; released self-financed EP, Kootchypop, 1991; platinum album Cracked Rear View, 1994, features hit single "Hold My Hand"; released Fairweather Johnson, 1996; Musical Chairs, 1998; Take 2, 2000; Albums: The Return of Mongo Slade, 2001; Back to Then, 2002; Learn to Live, 2008; Singles: Message in a Bottle, 1999; "God's Reasons", 2007; Don't Think I Don't Think About It, 2008; Films: Shallow Hal, 2001; TV series: "The Daily Buzz", 2005; "I Married", 2004. **Honors/Awds:** Two Grammy Awards, including best new group, for Cracked Rear View. **Special Achievements:** Ranked in Golf Digest's "Top 100 in Music", 2006. **Business Phone:** (212)833-8000.

RUCKER, RALEIGH
Clergy. **Career:** Ga State Patrol, chaplain; Ga State Nat Orgn Black Law Enforcement, Chaplain, currently; GA chapter, chaplain; GA Bur Invest, chaplain; Raleigh Rucker Funeral Home, proprietor, currently; chief adv, Monticello Police Dept, currently. **Special Achievements:** First African Am chaplain for the GA Bureau of Investment.

RUCKER, DR. ROBERT D.
Judge, lawyer. **Personal:** Born Jan 1, 1952?, Canton, GA; married Jacqueline Pace; children: 3. **Educ:** Ind Univ, BA, 1974; Valparaiso Univ Sch Law, JD, 1976; Univ Va Law Sch, ML, judicial process, 1998. **Career:** Lake County, IN, dep prosecutor, 1979-85; City Gary, IN, dep city atty, 1987-88; pvt prac, 1985-90; Ind Ct Appeals, judge, 1991-99; Ind Supreme Ct, judge, 1999-. **Orgs:** Bd dirs, Ind Trial Lawyers Asn; Bd Dirs, Northwest Ind Legal Serv Orgn; Nat Bar Asn; Marion County Bar Asn; fel Indianapolis Bar Asn; Ind State Bar Asn; vice chair, Ind Comn Continuing Legal Educ; Am Bar Asn; Ind Judges Asn. **Special Achievements:** First black appointed to Ind Ct of Appeals. **Business Addr:** Judge, Indiana Supreme Court, 315 Ind State House, Indianapolis, IN 46204, **Business Phone:** (317)232-1930.

RUCKS, ALFRED J
Engineer. **Personal:** Born Oct 20, 1935, Bellwood, TN; son of Alfred and Horty. **Educ:** Tenn A&I State Univ, BSEE, 1958. **Career:** Engineer (retired); Defense Atomic Support Agency, 1958-62; White Sands Missile Range, electronics engr, 1962-85, EEO counr, 1973-85, chief safety engineering br, 1985-93. **Orgs:** IEEE, 1959-; assoc mem, NSPE; trustee, N Mesquite St Church Christ, 1962-; chmn, Minority Housing Bd City Las Cruces NM, 1968-80; pres, NM State NAACP, 1970-86; chmn, Reg VI NAACP, 1974, 1979, 1984; nat bd dir, NAACP, 1981-87; pres, Dona Ana County NAACP, 1990-; State NM, Martin Luther King Comn, 1985-86; Las Cruces Community Develop Bd, 1990-; NM Private Ind Counc, 1994-. **Honors/Awds:** Commanders Award White Sands Missile Range, 1975, 1982, 1993; NM NAACP Award, 1972, 1979, 1986, 1992; Nat Merit Acad Award, 1973; Region VI award, 1990; City Las Cruces, NM Award, 1980; NM Gov, 1975, 1985, 1993; Omega Psi Phi, NMSU chap, Citizen of the Year Award, 1992; Hispanic Leadership and Development Program Award, 1993; NMSU 'African-American Citizen of the Year', 1993; Tennessee NAACP, 1994. **Home Phone:** (505)524-2906.

RUDD, CHARLOTTE JOHNSON
Educator, administrator. **Personal:** Born Jul 4, 1948, Columbus, OH; daughter of James W and Helen; divorced; children: Toyia Lynn. **Educ:** Ohio State Univ, BS, 1970, MS, 1985. **Career:** Columbus Pub Schs, jr high eng teacher, 1970-73, Drop Out Prev Proj: Move Ahead, coordr, 1973-79, middle sch reading/lang arts teacher, 1980-83, Human Relations, staff develop supt, 1983-85, middle sch asst prin, 1985-91, Effective Schs Process, dist adminr, 1991-; Ohio Avenue Elem Sch, prin, currently. **Orgs:** Mortar bd, Ohio State Univ, 1970; co-founder, Doris L Allen Minority Caucus-OEA, 1974; PRIDE Inc group develop stud self-esteem & leadership, 1974; Treas, Minority Caucus, 1974-76; exec comm, Ohio Educ Asn, 1978-83; dept & team leader, Franklin Alternative Middle Sch, 1979-83; Phi Delta Kappa, 1979; bd mem, Prof Develop Comm, 1979-83, Nat Educ Asn, 1981-83; Ohio House Rep, 1983-90; Nat Alliance Black Sch Educrs, 1989-93; designer, Staff Develop Model Sch Improvement, 1984; child abuse & neglect adv bd, Comn Inter professional Educ & Practice, Ohio State Univ; comm clothes dr, House Rep Miller's, 1992-93. **Special Achievements:** Start-up model for middle & high schools, Effective Schools Process, 1992-93. **Business Addr:** Principal, Ohio Avenue Elementary School, 505 S Ohio Ave, Columbus, OH 43205, **Business Phone:** (614)365-6130.

RUDD, DWAYNE
Football player. **Personal:** Born Feb 3, 1976, Batesville, MS. **Educ:** Univ Ala. **Career:** Minn Vikings, linebacker, 1997-2000; Cleveland Browns, 2001-02; Tampa Bay Buccaneers, 2003; free agent, currently.

RUDD-MOORE, DOROTHY
Composer, singer. **Personal:** Born Jun 4, 1940, New Castle, DE; married Kermit. **Educ:** Howard Univ Sch Music, BA, music theor & compos (magna cum laude), 1963; Am Conserv Fontainebleau, France, dipl, 1963. **Career:** Best works: Dark Tower, 1970; Harlem Sch Arts, teacher piano & music theory, 1965-66; NY Univ, teacher music hist appreciation, 1969; Bronx Community Col, teacher music histappreciation, 1971; pvt piano, voice, sight-singing & ear-training teacher, 1968-. **Orgs:** Founder, Soc Black Composers, 1968; bd mem, 1986, mem, Am Composers Alliance, 1972-; Broadcast Music Inc, 1972-; composer mem rec panel, Nat Endowment Arts, 1986 & 1988; NY State Coun Arts, 1988-90; NY Singing Teachers Asn; NY Women Composers. **Honors/Awds:** Lucy Moten Fellowship, 1963; Grant, Am Music Ctr, 1972; Grant, NY State Coun Arts, 1985. **Home Addr:** 33 Riverside Dr, New York, NY 10023. **Business Addr:** Composer, c/o Rud/Mor Publishing Co, 33 Riverside Dr, New York, NY 10023, **Business Phone:** (212)787-1869.

RUDOLPH, DAVID ERICSON
Public relations executive. **Personal:** Born Oct 7, 1966, Detroit, MI; son of Grover and Thelma. **Educ:** Mich State Univ, BA, criminal justice, 1989; Fla State Univ, MA, int affairs, 1994. **Career:** Detroit Pistons, Player Progr, coordr, 1994-95; D Erickson & Assocs Pub Rels, pres & ceo, 1995-99, consult, currently; Caponigro Pub Rels Inc, sr acct exec. **Orgs:** Bd dir, Detroit Club, 1994; bd dir, Non Profit PR Network, 1998-99; vol, Detroit Grand Prix Asn, 1998-99; off vol, Ford Montreux Jazz Festival; bd dir, Sphnix Org, currently; Piston-Palace Found; Corp Commun & Community Rels Dept, Palace Sports & Entertainment. **Home Addr:** 5027 Greenway St, Detroit, MI 48204, **Home Phone:** (313)834-7117. **Business Addr:** Board of Director, Sphinx Organization, 400 Renaissance Ctr Suite 2550, Detroit, MI 48243, **Business Phone:** (313)877-9100.

RUDOLPH, MAYA. **See RUDOLPH, MAYA KHABIRA.**

RUDOLPH, MAYA KHABIRA (MAYA RUDOLPH)
Actor, television actor. **Personal:** Born Jul 27, 1972, Gainesville, FL; daughter of Dick and Minnie Riperton (deceased); children: Pearl. **Educ:** Univ Calif, Santa Cruz, BA, photog, 1994. **Career:** The Rentals (music group), keyboard player & backup singer, 1994-96; The Groundlings (comedy troupe), Los Angeles, Calif, cast member, 1996-99; actress & comedienne, 1999-; TV serials: "Liver Let Die", 1996; "Chicago Hope", 1996-97; "Action"; "City of Angels", 2000; "TV Funhouse", 2001;"Saturday Night Live", 2000-; Films: Gattaca, 1997; The Devil's Child, 1997; A Glance Away, 1999; Chuck & Buck, 2000; Duets, 2000; Duplex, 2003; 50 First Dates, 2004; Wake Up, Ron Burgundy: The Lost Movie, 2004; A Prairie Home Companion, 2006; Idiocracy, 2006; Shrek The Third, Voice, 2007; Prop 8: The Musical, 2008; Away We Go, 2009. **Honors/Awds:** Vogue Fashion Awards, 2002; Nominee, Golden Satellite Award, 2005, Image Awards, 2007, Best Ensemble Cast, 2006. **Special Achievements:** Voted No 20 on Entertainment Weekly's list of Funniest People in America in April 2004. **Business Addr:** Actor, c/o Saturday Night Live, 30 Reockefeller Plz, New York, NY 10012, **Business Phone:** (212)315-9016.*

RUFFIN, JANICE E.
Psychologist, nurse. **Personal:** Born Dec 6, 1942, Cleveland, OH. **Educ:** Ohio State Univ Sch Nursing, BS, 1964; Rutgers The State Univ Col Nursing, MS, psychiat nurs, 1967; City Univ NY Grad Ctr, MPhil, 1984, PhD, clin psychol, 1985. **Career:** Conn Mental Health Ctr, New Haven, CT, dir nursing, 1974-77; Yale Univ Sch Nursing, asst prof grad prog psychiat nursing, assoc prof 1975-77; City Col City Univ NY, lectr dept psychol, 1978-80; Bronx Psychiatric Ctr, psychologist Highbridge out-patient clin, 1980-85; Baruch Col Off Counseling & Psychol Serv, psychologist, 1985-, dir 1986-94, dir, stud health serv, 1990-. **Orgs:** Sigma Theta Tau, 1968-; bd dir, NY Black Nurses Asn, 1971-74; chmn, 1969-71, mem, 1971-72, Comn Nursing Soc Crisis; Affir Action Task Force, 1972-76; ed bd, Perspectives Psychiat Care, 1973-83; Historian Nat Black Nurses Asn, 1972-82; bd dir, Nat Black Nurses Asn, 1972-74; chmn, 1971-72 & vpres, 1972-73, Oper Success Nursing Educ; bd dir, Inst Comm Organ & Personal Effectiveness, 1974-77; Nurse Training Rev Comn, NIMH, 1974-78; AK Rice Inst, 1979. **Honors/Awds:** Certificate & Gold Medal Ohio State Univ Sch Nursing, 1970; Certificate of Excellence, Am Nurses Asn, 1975; Certificate in Psychiatric Mental Health Nursing, Am Nurses Asn, 1975; Award Nat Asn Negro Bus & Prof Women's Clubs, 1977; Dedicated Professional Service Award, Nat Asn Negro Bus & Prof Womens Clubs, 1977; excellence in psychology, City Col, City Univ NY, 1987. **Special Achievements:** Author: Affirmative action programming for the nursing profession through the American Nurses' Association, 1975; A Strategy for change : papers presented at the conference held June 9-10, 1979, Albuquerque, New Mexico; An exploratory study of adult development in black, professional women, 1985.

RUFFIN, JOHN
Executive director, educator. **Personal:** Born Jun 29, 1943, New Orleans, LA; married Angela Beverly; children: John Wesley, Meeka & Beverly. **Educ:** Dillard Univ, BS, 1965; Atlanta Univ, MS, 1967; Kans State Univ, PhD, 1971; Harvard Univ, PhD, 1977. **Career:** Southern Univ Baton Rouge, biol instr, 1967-68; Atlanta Univ, asst prof,1971-74; AL Agri & Mech Univ, assoc prof, 1974-75; NC Central Univ, prof biol, 1978-86, chmn biol, dean coll of arts & sci, 1986-90; NIH Office Res Minority Health, dir; Nat Ctr on Minority Health & Health Disparities, dir, 1990-. **Orgs:** Consult, NIH, 1978-; consult, Bd Sci & Tech, 1983-; consult, ADAMHA, NIMH,1984. **Honors/Awds:** Samuel L. Kountz Award; NIH Directors Award; National Hispanic Leadership Award; Beta Beta Beta Biological Honor Society Award; Department of Healthand Human Services Special Recognition Award; US Presidential Merit Award; Martin Luther King Legacy Award, 2007. **Business Addr:** Director, National Center on Minority Health & Health Disparities, 6707 Democracy Blvd Suite 800, Bethesda, MD 20892-5465, **Business Phone:** (301)402-1366.*

RUFFIN, JOHN H
Judge. **Personal:** Born Dec 23, 1934, Waynesboro, GA; son of John H Ruffin Sr and Anna Davis; married; children: Brinkley. **Educ:** Morehouse Col, BA, 1957; Howard Univ, LLB, 1960. **Career:** Ruffin & Watkins, Augusta, GA, partner, 1961-63; Ruffin & Brown, Augusta, GA, partner; Augusta Judicial Circuit, super court judge, 1986-94; Ga Ct Appeals, chief judge, 1994-. **Orgs:** Nat Bar Asn; Augusta Bar Asn; Nat Lawyers Guild; Ga Asn Criminal Defense Lawyers; State Bar Ga; Bars Supreme Ct Ga; US Supreme Ct, US Ct Appeals 11th Circuit & US Dist Cts Southern & Middle Dists Ga. **Special Achievements:** First African-Am Super Court Judge, Augusta Judicial Circuit; first African-Am mem, Augusta Bar Asn; third African-Am & first African-Am, Chief Judge, Ct Appeals Ga. **Business Addr:** Chief Judge, Georgia Court of Appeals, 47 Trinity Ave Suite 501, Atlanta, GA 30334, **Business Phone:** (404)656-3450.

RUFFIN, JOHN WALTER
Executive, president (organization), chief executive officer. **Personal:** Born Jun 15, 1941, Moncure, NC; son of John Sr and Theima Harris; married Dorothy L Walton; children: Jonathan & Jehan. **Educ:** Morgan State Univ, AB, 1963; Cornell Univ, MS, 1970. **Career:** Pantry Pride Inc, vpres, 1980-85; Sunao Broadcasting Co Inc, pres, gen mgr, 1986-92; Bus Equipment Co, pres, chief exec officer, 1988-91; Paradies Airport Shops, partner, consult; JD Ruffin Assoc Inc, consult, pres & chief exec officer, currently. **Orgs:** Chmn bd, Urban League Broward, 1984-87; adv bd, Barnett Bank, 1985-87; chmn, Broward Employ & Training, 1986; chmn, Coral Springs Econ Develop Found, 1995-97; 33rd Degree Mason, 1996; pres, Sigma Pi Phi Fraternity, Alpha Rho Boule,

1997; chmn, Broward Alliance, 2006-07. **Honors/Awds:** Special Recognition by US Congress, 1985; Senator Lawton Chiles Commendation Outstanding Citizen, City Fort Lauderdale, 1986; Great Achievement, Nat Asn Advan Colored People Broward, 1986; State Top Ten Awards, Nat Bus League. **Business Addr:** President, Chief Executive Officer, J D Ruffin Associates Inc, 3111 N Univ Dr, PO Box 8589, Coral Springs, FL 33075, **Business Phone:** (954)341-6667.

RUFFIN, PAULETTE FRANCINE
Military leader, educator. **Personal:** Born Dec 13, 1956, Alexandria, VA; daughter of Paul and Rosetta Payton; divorced; children: M Joshua, D Christopher. **Educ:** Lehigh Univ, Bethlehem, Pa, BS, 1978; Univ NC, Chapel Hill, NC, MA, 1987. **Career:** Military Leader, Educator (retired); AUS, Ordnance Sch, Aberdeen Provin Ground, Md, stud basic course, 1978; Stud Officer Co, Aberdeen Provin Ground, Md, exec officer, 1978-79; Mil Acad, West Point, NY, admissions officer, 1979-80; 9th INF Div, Ft Lewis, WA, asst secy to the gen staff, 1980-85; Mil Acad, West Point NY, assoc prof, 1987-90; 41st Area Spt Group, Panama, Log Oper, mat off, exec off, 1990-93; Army Mat Command HQ, spec asst commanding gen, speechwriter, 1994-96, Georgetown Univ, dir Army ROTC, 1996-99; Army Times Publ Co, media rels & prog mgr. **Military Serv:** AUS, LTC, 1978-00; Army Commendation Medal, 1979, 1985; Army Achievement Medal, 1983-84, 1993; Meritorious Service Medal, 1990, 1993-00; Legion Merit, 1996-99. **Home Addr:** 8126 Clifforest Dr, Springfield, VA 22153, **Home Phone:** (703)913-1997. *

RUFFIN, RONALD R.
Government official. **Personal:** Born Jul 23, 1947, Saginaw, MI; son of William and Catherine; married Verlie M Ruffin, Oct 31, 1970; children: Tulani M, Omari A. **Educ:** Mich State Univ, BS, 1970; Atlanta Univ, MA, 1990. **Career:** Lakeside Labs, pharmaceut rep, 1970-73; Ayerst Labs, pharmaceut rep, 1973-77; CYSP (Ceta), exec admin, 1977-78; City Detroit, mgr, Neighborhood City Halls, 1978-81, exec admin, Municipal Parking Dept, 1981-94; Wayne Co Comm Col, part-time instr, 1990-; City Detroit, dir munic parking dept, 1994-. **Orgs:** Nat Asn Advan Colored People, 1965-; Kappa Alpha Psi Fraternity, 1967-; Motown Athletic Club, 1982-; Municipal Parking Asn, 1983-; Prince Hall F & A Masons, 1993-; Detroit Zoological Soc, 1993-; Inst & Municipal Parking Cong, 1994-; Mus African Am Hist, 1995. **Special Achievements:** Developed a Practitioner's Manual: Total Fitness for Law Enforcement Officers, 1989; First appointed African-American Parking Dir, City of Detroit, 1994. **Business Phone:** (313)967-1600.*

RUFFIN-BARNES, WENDY YVETTE
Insurance agent. **Personal:** Born Jan 10, 1961, Ahoskie, NC; daughter of Audrey H and Linzy M; married Roy T Jr, Apr 6, 1985; children: Mia. **Educ:** Univ NCA, Chapel Hill, BA, 1982; Old Dominion Univ, 1987-88. **Career:** Brown's & Williamson Tob Corp, sales rep, 1982-91; State Farm Ins, agt, 1991-. **Orgs:** Kappa Alpha Sorority Inc, 1980-; exec comt, Rotary, 1994-; chair, Hertford Economic Develop Comt, 1994-; treas, Alpha vice chair, Roanoke Chowan Assoc Life Underwriters, 1995-; vice chair, Hertford Co Schs Job Ready, 1997-; chair, Hertford Co Wellness Ctr, 1997-; bd mem, Wachovia Bank NC, 1998-. **Honors/Awds:** Service Above Self, Alpha Kappa Alpha Sorority Inc, 1997. **Business Addr:** Insurance Agent, State Farm Insurance, 101 S Acad St, Ahoskie, NC 27910, **Business Phone:** (252)332-4458.

RUFFINS, REYNOLD
Illustrator, designer. **Personal:** Born Aug 5, 1930, New York, NY. **Educ:** 1951. **Career:** Cooper Union, 1951; Sch Visual Arts, instr, 1967-70; Dept Visual Commun Col Visual & Performing Arts Syracuse Univ, vis adj prof, 1973; Queens Col, Vis Distinguished Prof, 1989-90, prof, currently. **Orgs:** Soc Publ Designers; Soc Illus. **Honors/Awds:** Best Illustration Award, NY Times Book Rev, 1973; Bologna (Italy) Children's Book Fair 1976; Am Inst Graphic Arts Art Dir Club; CA mag Award; Soc Illus Award;Professional Achievement Award, Cooper Union, 1972; 200 Years Am Illus NY Hist Soc; outstanding achievements, integrity, and commitment excellence educ, NYC, 1991; The Youth Friends Award, 1991; Augustus St. Gaudens Award, 1993; Coretta Scott King Award, 1997. **Special Achievements:** His designs and illustrations have been internationally recognized in group show exhibitions at the Louvre, Paris, Milan, Tokyo and at the Society of Illustrators Annual Shows, AIGA shows, Art Directors Club of New York and many other corporate shows. **Business Addr:** Dept of Fine Arts, Parsons School of Design, 66 Fifth Ave, New York, NY 10011.

RUFFNER, RAY P.
Insurance executive, real estate appraiser. **Personal:** Born Aug 11, 1946, Washington, DC; married Patricia Smith; children: Damien Earl. **Educ:** Wash Lee HS, Grad 1964; Acct Corresp Course, 1967. **Career:** Larry Buick Ar & VA, body & fender mech, 1969-71; United Co Life Ins Co, ins sales, 1971, ins sale & mgmt, 1971-77; Ruffner & Assocs Inc, ins sales & mgt, sole proprietor, pres, 1977-. **Orgs:** Investor, Real Estate, 1973-. **Honors/Awds:** Renovating homes for low income, 5 town homes currently in progress, 1985; Public Service to High Sch & Col, 1984. **Military Serv:** USMC E-5 4 yrs; NCO Awd, 1966. **Home Addr:** PO Box 8, Camden, SC 29020-0008. **Business Addr:** President, Sole proprietor, Ruffner Associates Inc, 87 W Lee Hwy Suite 27, PO Box 290, Warrenton, VA 20186.

RUNDLES, JAMES ISAIAH
Government official. **Personal:** Born Jul 9, 1920, Jackson, MS; married Mattie Singleton. **Educ:** Tougaloo Southern Christian Inst, BA, 1940; Univ HI Honolulu, 1945; Johnson Sch Bus, Bus Ed, 1949. **Career:** Radio WOKJ & Jackson, MS, news dir, 1954-60; Pittsburg Courier & Chicago & Defender, civil rights reporter, 1960-71; Govt Miss, exec asst, 1972-76; City Jackson, MS, exec asst mayor, 1977-. **Orgs:** Assoc ed, The Jackson Advocate & Newspaper, 1946-50; Founder, Rundles & Asn Pub Rels Consult, 1960-71; Nat pub affairs, dir, Montford Pt Marines Asn, 1960-66; adv comn, rels Div US Justice Dept, 1972-76; bd dir, Miss Bar Legal Asn, 1973-76; bd dir, Am Red Cross; bd dir, Boys Clubs Am. **Honors/Awds:** Black Journalism Award, Nat Project Media Asn, 1975; Humanitarian Endeavors, Miss Independent Beauticians Asn, 1975; Outstanding & Dedicated Service, Govt Coun Minority Affairs, 1975; efforts achivement, humanities Nine Iron Golf Asn, SE, 1979. **Military Serv:** USMC, sgt maj, 1942-45; Presidential Unit Citation, (Iwo Jima) 1945.

RUNNELS, BERNICE M.
School administrator. **Personal:** Born Aug 29, 1925, Memphis, TN; daughter of Ben Bradd and Susie Bradd; married Ike (deceased); children: Patricia Teague, Isaac Jr, Reginald & Maurice. **Career:** Pembroke Dist 259, pres, bd mem, 1963-2003. **Orgs:** Three Rivers Div Ill Bd Asn, 1975-83. **Honors/Awds:** State Bd Educ. **Special Achievements:** One of the community's outstanding volunteers by the Junior League of Kankakee. **Home Addr:** PO Box 149, Hopkins Park, IL 60944.

RUPAUL. **See CHARLES, RUPAUL ANDRE.**

RUSH, BOBBY (BOBBY LEE RUSH)
Congressperson (U.S. federal government). **Personal:** Born Nov 23, 1946; married Carolyn Thomas. **Educ:** Roosevelt Univ, BA, 1974; Univ Ill, MA, 1994; McCormick Theol Sem, theol studies, 1998. **Career:** Ins salesman; Chicago City Coun, 1983-92; US House Rep, rep, congressman, 1993-. **Orgs:** Congressional Black Caucus; Iota Phi Theta Fraternity Inc; Chicago City Coun. **Military Serv:** AUS, 1963-68. **Business Addr:** Congressman, US House of representatives, 2416 Rayburn HOB, Washington, DC 20515, **Business Phone:** (202)225-4372.

RUSH, BOBBY LEE. **See RUSH, BOBBY.**

RUSH, EDDIE F.
Basketball executive. **Personal:** Born Sep 19, 1961, Columbus, GA. **Educ:** Ga State Univ, 1983. **Career:** Nat Basketball Asn, referee, currently. **Special Achievements:** Only NBA refree to have officiated the last game of the NBA Finals for the last four seasons 2005-08. **Home Addr:** PO Box 490838, Atlanta, GA 30349. *

RUSH, OTIS
Guitarist, singer. **Personal:** Born Apr 29, 1934, Philadelphia, PA; son of O C Rush and Julia Boyd. **Career:** Albums: I Can't Quit You Baby, 1958; Chicago: The Blues Today!, 1966; Door To Door, 1969; Mourning in the Morning, 1969; Screamin' & Cryin', 1974; Cold Day In Hell, 1975; So Many Roads, 1976; Right Place, Wrong Time, 1976; Troubles Troubles, 1978; Groaning the Blues, 1980; Tops, 1989; Blues Interaction -Live In Japan 1986, 1989; His Cobra Recordings, 1989; Ain't Enough Comin' In, 1994; Any Place I'm Going, 1998; The Essential Otis Rush, 2000; All Your Love I Miss Loving, 2005; Live At Montreux 1986, 2006; Live & From San Francisco, 2006. **Honors/Awds:** Grammy Award, Best Traditional Blues Album, 1999. **Business Addr:** Musician, c/o Bates Mayer Inc, 714 Brookside Lane, Sierra Madre, CA 91024, **Business Phone:** (626)355-9201.*

RUSH, SONYA C
Manager. **Personal:** Born Aug 23, 1959, Columbia, LA; daughter of Walter C and Shirley Cross. **Educ:** Ga Inst Tech, BChE, 1981; Univ Mich, MBA, 1983. **Career:** Black Execu Exchange Prog, vis prof; Philip Morris USA, opers analyst, 1983-88, supt-mfg, 1988-90, MBA assoc, 1990-92, sr planning analyst, 1992, asst brand mgr, 1992-93, assoc brand mgr, 1993-97, sr brand mgr; consult, currently. **Orgs:** Allocations mem, United Way; adv Jr Achievement; Nat Coalition 100 Black Women; Alpha Kappa Alpha Sor; The Friends Art; Leadership Metro Richmond; bd mem, Greenwich House; exec comt mem, Ga Tech Alumni Asn; Pan Hellenic Coun; Nat Soc Black Engrs; Harlem Small Bus Initiative Pilot; Black Exec Exchange Prog; Leadership Metro Richmond. **Honors/Awds:** President's Award, Philip Morris USA, 1989. **Home Addr:** 1005 Abercorn Dr SW, Atlanta, GA 30331-7514. **Business Addr:** President, The Georgia Tech Black Alumni Organization, 190 N Ave, Atlanta, GA 30313.

RUSHEN, PATRICE LOUISE
Composer, singer. **Personal:** Born Sep 30, 1954, Los Angeles, CA; daughter of Allen Roy and Ruth L; married Marc St Louis, Jan 4, 1986. **Educ:** Univ Southern Calif, Los Angeles, music educ, piano performance, 1976. **Career:** Albums: Prelusion, 1974; Before the Dawn, 1975; Shout It Out, 1976; Let There Be Funk: The Best Of Patrice Rushen, 1976; Patrice, 1978; Pizzazz, 1979; Posh, 1980; Straight from the Heart, 1982; Now, 1984; Anthology of Patrice Rushen, 1985; Watch Out, 1986; The Meeting, 1990; Anything But Ordinary, 1994; Haven't You Heard - The Best of Patrice Rushen, 1996; Signature, 1997; The Essentials: Patrice Rushen, 2002; Singles: "Haven't You Heard," "Never Gonna Give You Up," "Don't Blame Me," "Remind Me," "Feels So Real," "Forget Me Nots"; TV Series: "The Women Brewster Place"; "The Midnight Hour," CBS-TV, musical dir, conductor & arranger, 1990; musical dir & arranger for John Lithgow's Kid-Size Concert Video; For One Night, 2006; Films: Without You I'm Nothing, Hollywood Shuffle; Just a Dream, 2002; Composed: for Robert Townsend & His Partners in Crime Part I, II, III, IV, HBO; Pacific Bell radio campaign, 1988; Kid's Talk; musical dir of's highest honor, Emmy Awards, 1991, 1992; musical dir for "Comic Relief V," 1992; rec artist, composer, currently. **Honors/Awds:** Nat Acad Recording Arts & Scis, Best R&B Vocal Performance, "Forget Me Nots," 1982, Best R&B Instrument, "Number One," 1982; Songwriter's Award, "Watch Out," Am Soc Composers, Auth & Publ, 1988; Image Awards TV Spec, Nat Asn Advan Colored People, 1989-90; 48th Annual Grammy Awards, 2006. **Special Achievements:** First African-American Women to music direct for Emmy Awards.

RUSHING, BYRON D
State government official, educator. **Personal:** Born Jul 29, 1942, New York, NY; son of William and Linda Turpin; divorced; children: Osula Evadne. **Educ:** Roxbury Community Col, AA, 1989; Episcopal Divinity Sch, attended 1994; Harvard Col, attended; Mass Inst Technol, attended. **Career:** Northern Stud Movement, community organizer, 1964-65; Community Voter Regist Proj, dir, 1964-66; Comn Church & Race MA Coun Churches, field dirm 1966-67; Ctr Inner-City Change, adminr, 1969-70; Mus Afro-Am Hist, pres, 1972-84; Commonwealth Mass, House Rep, state rep, 1983-; Episcopal Divinity Sch, adj fac, 1991-. **Orgs:** Pres, Roxbury Hist Soc, 1968; lay dep, Gen Conv Episcopal Church, 1974; chaplain, Gen Conv Episcopal Church, 1994; treas, St John's/St James Episcopal Church, 1975-; co-chair citizens adv comn, Roxbury Heritage Pk, 1985-; Roxbury Hist Soc; Episcopal Network Econ Justice; Shirley Eustis House Asn; Unitarian Universalist Urban Ministry; Episcopal Church Archives. **Honors/Awds:** Human Rights Campaign Fund Award, 1985; Bay State Banner 20th Anniversary Celebration, 1985; Public Official of the Year, Boston Teachers Union, 1987; hon degree, Roxbury Community Col, l989; Action for Boston Community Development Award, 1992; hon degree, Episcopal Divinity Sch, 1994. **Business Addr:** State Representative, The Commonwealth of Massachusetts, Rm 481 State House, Boston, MA 02133, **Business Phone:** (617)722-2180.

RUSK, REGGIE
Football player. **Personal:** Born Oct 19, 1972, Galveston, TX. **Educ:** Univ Ky. **Career:** Footbal player (retired); Tampa Bay Buccaneers, corner back, 1996-97; Seattle Seahawks, corner back, 1997; San Diego Chargers, corner back, 1999-2000; pres, Platinum Limousines Inc, currently.

RUSS, BERNARD
Football player. **Personal:** Born Nov 4, 1973, Utica, NY. **Educ:** Ariz Western JC, WVa. **Career:** New England Patriots, linebacker, 1997-99. **Honors/Awds:** Rookie of the year, 1997.

RUSS, TIMOTHY DARRELL
Actor. **Personal:** Born Jun 22, 1956, Washington, DC; son of Walter H and Josephine D; children: Madison Camille. **Educ:** Ill State Univ, Bloomington, Ill, post grad theater; St Edwards Univ, BS, theater, psych, 1978. **Career:** Films: Crossroads, 1986; Fire with Fire, 1986; Death Wish 4: The Crackdown, 1987; Spaceballs, 1987; Pulse, 1988; Bird, 1988; Eve of Destruction, 1991; Night Eyes II, 1992; Mr Saturday Night, actor & dir, 1992; Dead Connection, 1994; Star Trek: Generations, 1994; East of Hope Street, 1998; The Cabinet of Dr. Caligari, 2005; Unbeatable Harold, 2006; The Oh in Ohio, 2006; Live Free or Die Hard, 2007; TV series: "The Twilight Zone, 1985-87; "Amazing Stories", 1986; Samaritan: The Mitch Snyder Story, 1986; Casebusters, 1986; The Highwayman, 1987; Timestalkers, 1987; "The Highwayman", 1988; Roots: The Gift, 1988; Police Story: Cop Killer, 1988; Who Gets the Friends?, 1988; "The People Next Door", 1989; "The Fresh Prince of Bel-Air", 1990-92; "Freddy's Nightmares", 1990; "CopRock", 1990; The Bakery, 1990; Dead Silence, 1991; The Heroes of Desert Storm, 1991; "Tequila & Bonetti", 1992; Journey to the Center of the Earth, 1993; "Sea Quest DSV", 1993; "Star Trek: Deep Space Nine", 1993-95;"Hangin' with Mr. Cooper", 1993-94; "Living Single", 1993; "Murphy Brown", 1993; "Dark Justice", 1993; "Star Trek: The Next Generation", 1993; "Melrose Place", 1994; Bitter Vengeance, 1994; "Monty", 1994; "Star Trek-Voyager", 1995-2001; "Any Day Now", 2002; "ER", 2005; "Unfabulous", 2005; "General Hospital", 2006; "Navy NCIS: Naval Criminal Investigative Service", 2006; "Twenty Good Years", 2006; "General Hospital", 2006-07; "Hannah Montana", 2007; "Without a Trace", 2007; "Samantha Who?", 2007-09; "iCarly", 2007-09; Stage appearances: Romeo & Juliet; Barrabas; Dream

Girls; As You Like It; Twelfth Night; Cave Dwellers. **Orgs:** Nat Asn Advan Colores People Hollywood Br, 1986. **Honors/Awds:** Sony Innovator Award, 1991; Image Award, theater, Nat Asn Advan Colored People, 1987; New York International Independent Film & Video Festival Feature Film Award for Best Urban Drama, 1998. **Business Phone:** (323)655-1313.*

RUSSELL, BEVERLY A.
Librarian, manager. **Personal:** Born Jan 15, 1947, Riverside, CA; daughter of James H (deceased) and Hazel M Hawkins. **Educ:** CA State Col, BA, 1971; CA State Univ, MS, 1973. **Career:** Riverside Public Libr, libr asst, 1974; CA State Dept Rehab, librn, 1978; Magnavox Res Labs, libr tech, 1978-84; Burbank Unified Sch Dist, bookroom librn, 1986-90; Social Vocational Servs, cot supvr, 1990-94; Pleasant Valley State Prison, libr Tech asst, currently. **Orgs:** Alpha Kappa Alpha 1973-; Intl Black Writers & Artists 1983-; Black Advocates State Serv Calif, 1995-; Calif Asn Black Correctional Workers, 1995-. **Honors/Awds:** Co-auth, On Being Black, 1990, Bearers of Blackness, poetry published February 1987 by Guild Press MN; co-author of Three Women Black, Guild Press 1987; published in Roots and Wings, An Anthology of Poems for African-American Children, published by New York City Schools 1988; Published in River Crossings, Voices of the Diaspora, Int Black Writers & Artists, 1994. **Home Addr:** 250 Truman St Suite 250, Coalinga, CA 93210. *

RUSSELL, BILL (WILLAM FELTON RUSSELL)
Broadcaster, basketball player. **Personal:** Born Feb 12, 1934, Monroe, LA; son of Charles and Katie; married Didi Anstett, Jun 8, 1977 (divorced); married Rose Swisher, 1956 (divorced); children: 3. **Educ:** Univ San Francisco, BA, 1956. **Career:** Basketball player (retired), broadcaster; Boston Celtics, ctr, 1956-69,coach, 1966-69, consult, 1999-; NBC-TV, sportscaster, 1969-8, CBS,1980-83; Seattle SuperSonics, head coach, 1973-77; The Superstars, co-host, 1978-79; Sacramento Kings, head coach, 1987-88, dir player personnel, 1988-89; IMG Speakers Bureau, speaker, currently. **Orgs:** Bd mem, Nat Mentoring Partnership. **Honors/Awds:** Olympic Gold Medal for basketball, Int Olympic Comt, 1956; Podoloff Cup, Nat Basketball Asn, 1958, 1961, 1962, 1963, 1965; Most Valuable Player, US Basketball Writers, 1960-65; MVP All-Star Game, 1963; Named "Sportsman of the Year", Sports Illustrated, 1968; NBA 25th Anniversary All-Time Team, 1970; Inducted into Basketball Hall of Fame, 1975; Second Wind: The Memoirs Opinionated Man, 1979; NBA 35th Anniversary All-Time Team, 1980; Greatest Player in the Hist of the NBA, Prof Basketball Writers Asn Am, 1980; NBA 50th Anniversary All-Time Team, 1996' FIBA Hall of Fame, 2007. **Special Achievements:** Author: Go up for Glory, MacMillan, 1966; Second Wind, Random House, 1979; Nothing but A Man, 1999; Russell Rules; 11 Lessons on Leadership from the Twentieth Century's Greatest Winner, 2002; 50 Greatest Players in NBA History, 1996; guest-starred on the television series Miami Vice as a corrupt judge named Ferguson; first player in NBA history to average more than 20 rebounds per game for an entire season; Appeared as an actor in films. **Business Phone:** (617)854-8000.

RUSSELL, BRYON DEMETRISE
Basketball player. **Personal:** Born Dec 31, 1970, San Bernardino, CA; married Kimberli; children: Kajun. **Educ:** Calif state Univ, criminal justice, 1993. **Career:** Utah Jazz, forward, 1993-02; Wash Wizards, guard-forward, 2002-03; Los Angeles Lakers, forward, 2003-04; Denver Nuggets, forward, 2004-06; IBL: L.A. Lightening, Forward, 2007-. *

RUSSELL, CHARLIE L.
Administrator, educator, playwright. **Personal:** Born Mar 10, 1932, Monroe, LA; son of Charlie Sr and Katie; children: Michael R, Katheryn K & Joshua. **Educ:** Univ San Francisco, BS, eng, 1959; New York Univ, MSW, 1967; Univ Calif, San Diego, MEA, 1986. **Career:** City Col NY, asst prof, 1969-74; Film: Five on the Black Hand Side, writer, 1973; NY Univ, asst prof, 1975-77; Am Place Theatre, writer-in-residence, 1976; Nat Black Theatre, writer-in-residence; Afro-Am Theater Conta Costa Col, dir. **Orgs:** Harlem Writers Guild, 1963-70; Founder, Onyx Players. **Honors/Awds:** Image Award, Best Film script Nat Asn Advan Colored People, 1975; Playwright Award, Rockefeller Found, 1976. **Special Achievements:** Published plays, "Five on the Black Hand Side", "The Incident at Terminal Ecstasy Acres", film script "Five on the Black Hand Side", published novellas, short stories, author of The Worthy Ones, 2002. **Military Serv:** AUS, PFC, 1953-55. **Home Addr:** 1413 Neilson St, Berkeley, CA 94702, **Home Phone:** (510)528-7025.

RUSSELL, DEREK DWAYNE
Football player. **Personal:** Born Jun 22, 1969, Little Rock, AR; children: Nicolis. **Educ:** Univ Ark. **Career:** Football player (retired); Denver Broncos, wide receiver, 1991-94; Houston Oilers, 1995-96; TennesseeOilers, 1997.

RUSSELL, DIAN BISHOP
Media executive. **Personal:** Born Sep 24, 1952, Rich Square, NC; daughter of Paul A Jr. and Genora Tann; married Larry Russell, Sep 21, 1971; children: Tammy, Paula, Letitia. **Educ:** Fayetteville State Univ, Fayetteville, NC, BS, 1976; NC Central Univ, Durham, NC, MLS, 1980, NC educ admin cert, 1985; Durham City Sch, Durham, NC, NC mentor cert, 1988. **Career:** T S Cooper Elementary, Sunbury, NC, librarian, 1974-77; Durham County Sch, NC Testing Consortium, Durham, NC, testing clerk, 1978; Durham County Library, Proj LIFT, Durham, NC, special asst to the dir, educ brokering, 1979; Durham City Sch, Durham, NC, lead teacher, summer comput progs, 1986-89, media coordr, 1980-, site coordr for summer enrichment, 1990; Baskerville Elementary Sch, Media Specialist, currently. **Orgs:** Assoc rep, 1985-, past treas, 1987, past secy 1988, Durham City Educ; special registration comnr, Durham County Bd Elections, 1988-; treas, Eta Beta Zeta Chapter, Zeta Phi Beta Sorority, 1990-; past vice pres, Eta Phi Beta Chapter, Zeta Phi Beta, 1985; directress, Union Baptist Youth Choir, 1985-. **Honors/Awds:** Durham City Schools Superintendent's Creative Teaching Award, 1985; Gold Star Awards, Final Four Teacher of Year, 1987, Women in Achievement, Durham City Sch, 1989. **Business Addr:** Media Specialist, Baskerville Elementary School, 1100 Stokes Ave, PO Box 2246, Rocky Mount, NC 27801, **Business Phone:** (252)451-2880.

RUSSELL, DOROTHY DELORES
Publishing executive. **Personal:** Born Sep 11, 1950, Hayti, MO; daughter of Carrie Vianna Lewis Rus and Jimmie Sr. **Educ:** Southeast MO State Univ; Three Rivers Comm Col; Lincoln Univ. **Career:** Univ Ark CES, clerk steno I, 1973-76; Dept Natural Resources, clerk steno II, 1976-78; Mo Exec Off, secy receptionist, 1978-79; Mo Patrol State Water, admin secy, 1979-80; Community Rev Newspaper, ed, writer, photogr, 1983-84; Pemiscot Publ Co, copysetter, circulation & classified mgr, 1989-. **Orgs:** Former asst, 4-H Leader; former bd mem & vpres, Community Rev Paper expired, 1983-84; missionary Church Jesus Christ Congregation; organized Southeast Mo Black Writers Club, 1989. **Honors/Awds:** Certificate of Apppreciation, Univ Mo Extension Prog, Pemiscot County, 1983; Certificate of Apppreciation, Hayti Junior High Sch, 1985; Certificate of Apppreciation, Educ & Pub Serv, Cent Star Chap #114, Order Eastern Star, 1988; Certificate of Apppreciation, St James Word Faith, 1988. **Home Phone:** (314)359-1452. **Business Addr:** Circulation Manager, Pemiscot Publishing Co, PO Box 1059, Caruthersville, MO 63830-1059, **Business Phone:** (314)333-4336.

RUSSELL, GEORGE A
Theorist, composer, bandleader. **Personal:** Born Jun 23, 1923, Cincinnati, OH; son of Joseph and Bessie Sledge; married Alice Norbury, Aug 4, 1981; children: Jock Millgardth. **Educ:** Wilberforce Univ, OH, 1943. **Career:** Lectr: Harvard Univ, Tufts Univ, New Music Gallery Vienna, Sibelius Acad Helsinki; Sch Jazz Lenox, MA, 1959-60; Swedish Labor Orgn, 1965; Fesitval Arts Finland, 1966-67; Lund Univ Sweden, Vaskilde & Summerschule, 1971; New Eng Conserv Music, Boston, MA, prof jazz studies, 1969-2003, distinguihsed artist in residence emer, currently; Nat Endowment Arts Wash DC, panel, 1975; George Russell Living Time Orchestra, conductor, 1977-. **Orgs:** Inter Soc Contemp Musicians; Norwegian Soc New Music; Am Fedn Musicians Local 802; adv coun, MA state Coun Arts; adv bd, 3rd St Music Sch Settlement; foreign mem, Swedish Royal Acad Music. **Honors/Awds:** Nat Endowment for the Arts Award, 1969; Nat music award, 1976; George Russell Day, Gov MA, named in honor, 1983; Grammy nomination, 1958, 1985; Guggenheim fel; NEA Fel, 1969, 1978, 1982; Jazz Master Award, Afro-Am Museum Philadelphia, PA, 1985; Jazz Master Award, Nat Endowment for the Arts,1990; British Music Award, 1989; Jazz Master Award, New Eng Found, 1996; Guardian Award; John and Catherine Macarthur Fel, 1989-95; Kennedy Ctr Living Jazz Legend Award, 2007. **Special Achievements:** Author of George Russell's Lydian Chromatic Concept of Tonal Organization, 1953, 1959, 2001; numerous recordings, US & abroad; performances in Europe, Japan and in the US with the George Russell Living Time Orchestra. **Business Addr:** Composer, Concept Publishing, 258 Harvard St Suite 296, Broolkine, MA 02446, **Business Phone:** (617)522-1242.

RUSSELL, GEORGE ALTON, JR.
Banker. **Personal:** Born in Boston, MA; married Faye Sampson; children: Martin Bakari. **Educ:** Clark Univ, BA, 1972; NY Univ, MBA, 1974. **Career:** Urban Bus Assistance Corp, pres 1972-74; State St Bank & Trust Co, vpres, 1979-84; City Boston, treas, chief financial officer; Freedom Nat Bank NY, chief exec, pres & chief exec officer; State St Corp, dir community affairs, exec vpres, currently; OneUnited Bank, bd dir, currently. **Orgs:** Dir, Dimock Comn Health Ctr, 1983-; bd mem, Boston Indus Develop Finance Author, 1984-; treas-custodian, State Boston Retirement Syst, 1984-; Boston Arson Comn, 1984-; custodian, Boston Pub Sch Teachers Retirement Fund, 1984-; Bus Asn Club, 1984-; Govt Finance Officers Asn, 1984-; MA Collector-Treas Asn, 1984-; trustee, Boston Concert Opera; corp, Boston Sci Mus dir Organization New Equality, 1985-; trustee, United Methodist Church, 1985-; chmn, Urban League Eastern Mass; Fin Serv Acad; bd advisors, African Presidential Archives & Res Ctr, Boston Univ. **Honors/Awds:** Professor Achievement Award, Boston Urban Bankers Forum, 1984; Ten Outstanding Young Leaders Award, Boston Jaycees, 1985; Professional Achievement Award, Boston Urban Banker's Forum, 1985; Industrial Service 100, Freedom Nat Bank NY, Black Enterprise, 1990. **Business Phone:** (323)290-4848.

RUSSELL, HERMAN JEROME
Chairperson, executive. **Personal:** Born Dec 23, 1930, Atlanta, GA; married Otelia; children: Donata, Michael & Jerome. **Educ:** Tuskegee Inst, BS, 1953. **Career:** City Beverage Co Inc, Atlanta GA, pres, chmn bd; Atlanta Enquirer Newspaper Inc, chmn bd dir; Enterprise Investments Inc, chmn bd; Concessions Int Inc, pres, chmn bd; GA Southeastern Land Co Inc, pres & chmn bd; Paradise Apts Mgt Co Inc, pres; HJ Russell Plastering Co & Constr Co, prs & chief exec officer, 1952-2003; HJ Russell & Co, chief operating officer, chmn, currently. **Orgs:** Chmn bd, DDR Int Inc, Atlanta, GA; bd dir, World Cong Ctr Authority, Atlanta, GA; chmn bd dir, Cit Trust Co Bank; bd dir, YMCA; mem bd trustees, Morris Brown Col; life mem, Nat Asn Advan Colored People; Nat adv bd GA Inst Tech; African Meth Episcopal Church; mem bd trustees, African Episcopal Church; chmn bd Russell/Rowe Commun Inc; bd dir, Prime Cable Inc; mem bd dir, First Atlanta Corp; past pres, Atlanta C C; mem bd dir, GA C C, Central Atlanta Prog, Tuskegee Inst. **Honors/Awds:** Nat Asn of Market Developers Award, 1968; Meritorious Business Achievement Award, Atlanta Community Rels, 1969; Equal Opportunity Day Atlanta Urban League, 1972; African Method Episcopal Outstanding Business of the Year, 1973; Winter Conference Award, Affil Contractor Am Inc, 1973; Disting Service Award, Empire Real Estate Bd, 1973; Black Enterpise Magazine Annual Achievement Award, 1978; Junior Achievement Award (Bus & Youth), 1979; Nat Alumni Award, Tuskegee Inst. **Business Addr:** Chairman of the Board, H J Russell & Co, 504 Fair St NW, Atlanta, GA 30313.

RUSSELL, JACKSON
President (Organization). **Educ:** Univ Mich, MA, social psychol, PhD, urban technol, & environ planning. **Career:** Decision Info Resources Inc, pres, currently. **Business Addr:** President, Decision Information Resources Inc, 2600 Southwest Freeway Suite 900, Houston, TX 77098, **Business Phone:** (713)650-1425.

RUSSELL, JAMES A., JR.
Educator. **Personal:** Born Dec 25, 1917, Lawrenceville, VA; son of J. Alvin and Nellie P.; married Lottye J Washington; children: Charlotte R Coley, James A III. **Educ:** Oberlin Col, BA, 1940; Bradley Univ, MS, 1950; Univ Md, EdD, 1967; St Paul's Col, LLD, 1984. **Career:** Educator (retired); Norfolk Naval Shipyard, electrician 1941-42; US Naval Training Sch, instr, 1942-45; St Paul's Col, asst prof, 1945-50; Hampton Univ, prof & div dir, 1950-71; St Paul's Col, pres, 1971-81; Va Community Col Sys, dir instr prog, 1981-82; WVa State Col, prof & div chmn, 1982-86, Interim pres, 1986-87; West Va Community Col, interim pres, 1988-89. **Orgs:** Pres, Peninsula Coun Human Rels, 1962-65; Richmond Metro Authority, 1981-82; sen warden & vestryman, St James Episcopal Church, 1982-; mem/bd dirs, West Va Pub Radio, 1988-; jury comnr, Kanawha County, 1990-. **Honors/Awds:** Space scientist McDonnell Douglas Astronautics, 1968; Nat Asn for Equal Opportunity Study Group Republic of China, Taiwan, 1979; Hon Degree LLD, St Paul's Col, 1984; Distinguished Alumnus Award, Bradley Univ 1984. **Home Addr:** 811 Grandview Dr, Dunbar, WV 25064. *

RUSSELL, JEROME
Executive, president (organization). **Personal:** Born Jan 1, 1962; son of Herman J; married Stephanie Marie Beasley; children: Herman III, Sydney, Mori & Kelsey. **Educ:** Ga State Univ, BS, bus admin, 1985; Cert Com Invest Mgr; Cert Property Mgr. **Career:** City Beverage Co, mgr; Gibraltar Land Inc, proj mgr, 1989; HJ Russell & Co, exec vpres, 1992-94, chief operating officer, 1995, pres russell new urban, currently. **Orgs:** Zoo Atlanta; Citizens Trust Bank; Ga Affordable Housing Coalition; Atlanta Urban League; Concessions Int; Metro Atlanta YMCA; Cent Atlanta Progress; Urban Land Inst; Atlanta Rotary; Atlanta Chamber Com; 100 Black Men Atlanta. **Business Addr:** President of Russell New Urban, HJ Russell & Company, 504 Fair St SW, Atlanta, GA 30313, **Business Phone:** (404)330-1000.

RUSSELL, JOHN PETERSON
College administrator. **Personal:** Born Aug 26, 1947, Cora, WV; son of Johnnie P Sr and Mary Louise Thompson; married Gail P Davis, May 31, 1968; children: Kim & Janelle. **Educ:** Bluefield St Col, BS, 1970; WVa Col Grad Studies, MA, 1975; VPI & SU, CAGS, 1978. **Career:** Nathaniel Macon Jr High Sch, sec teacher, 1970-71; Omar Jr & Logan HighSch, sec teacher, 1971-74; Southern WVa Community Col, counr, 1974-76, dean students, 1979-81, asst dean students, dir financial aid, 1986-87; Walters St Community Col, Morristown, TN, coordr training, 1987-, Coun & Testing Ctr, exec dir, currently. **Orgs:** Chmn, bd dir New Employment for Women, 1981-; mem appt Amer Friends Serv Comm Relation Comm, 1982-; mem elected, Amer Friends Serv Exec Comm 1983-; polemarch, Knoxville Chapter, 1989-, field deputy, Eastern Region, 1990-, Kappa Alpha Psi Fraternity; chmn, community relations comt, Am Friends Serv, 1985-86; Kappa Alpha Psi, Polemarch S Cent Province, 1994; chmn, Kappa Alpha Psi Social Actions Comt. **Honors/Awds:** Community Service Award, Mechanicsville Community Develop Corp, 1991; Bronze Man of the Year, Iota Phi Lambda Bus & Professional Sorority. **Home Addr:** 1608 Blackwood Dr, Knoxville, TN 37923. **Business Addr:** Executive Director, Walters State Community College, Counseling & Testing Center, Rm 207 500 S Davy Crockett Pkwy Col Ctr, Morristown, TN 37813-6899, **Business Phone:** (423)585-6800.

RUSSELL, JOSEPH J.
Educator. **Personal:** Born Apr 11, 1934. **Educ:** VA State Col, BS, 1960; Ind Univ, MS, 1968, EdD, 1970. **Career:** Richmond Soc Serv Bur, soc worker, 1960-64; Richmond Pub Sch, vis teacher, 1964-67; Ind Univ, chmn, 1972; Ohio State Univ, dir, 1970-72, vice provost, 1989-94; Global Team America, Inc, 1995-. **Orgs:** Adv comt, Urban Affairs, 1973-; adv comt, Univ Div, 1974-; standing comt, Bloomington Campus, 1974-; faculty hearing officer, 1974-; chmn, Afro-Am Conf Group, IHETS, 1974-; Ind State Adv Bd, 1974-; Student Life Study Comn, 1977; chmn, Dept Afro-Am Studies; exec dir, Nat Coun Black Studies. **Honors/Awds:** Commission Serv Award, Second Baptist Church, 1976; Outstanding Educr Award, Phi Beta Sigma 1976; Serv Appreciation Plaque, NM Black Studies Consortium, 1977; Nat Develop & Leadership Award, Nat Coun Black Studies, 1977; Distinguished Alumni Service Award, 2008. **Special Achievements:** Num Presentation & Papers; OSU African American Student Affairs Council of Honor, 1995; 100 Most Influential Friends for 1977. **Military Serv:** USAF, airman, 1954-58.

RUSSELL, KEITH BRADLEY
Ornithologist. **Personal:** Born Aug 13, 1956, Augusta, GA; son of John Raphael and Barbara Elaine Jefferson. **Educ:** Cornell Univ, Ithaca, NY, BS, biol, 1977; Clemson Univ, Clemson, SC, MS, zool, 1981. **Career:** Acad Natural Sci, Philadelphia, PA, collection mgr, 1982-92; Birds N Am Inc, asst ed; Audubon Pa, Fairmount Park Outreach coordr, 2006-. **Orgs:** Del Valley Ornith Club, 1973-; Nat Audubon Soc, 2003-. **Home Addr:** 6222 McCallum St, Philadelphia, PA 19144. **Business Addr:** Fairmount Park Outreach Coordinator, Audubon Pennsylvania, 100 Wildwood Way, Harrisburg, PA 17110, **Business Phone:** (215)844-2810.

RUSSELL, LEON W
Government official. **Personal:** Born Nov 3, 1949, Pulaski, VA. **Educ:** E Tenn State Univ, BS, 1972; E Tenn State Univ Sch Grad Studies, attended 1974. **Career:** Tenn State House Reps, legis intern & asst, 1973; E Tenn State Univ Dept Polit Sci, grad teaching asst, 1972-73; Tenn Municipal League, mgt intern & res asst, 1974; Ky Comn Human Rights, field rep, 1975-77; Pinellas County Govt Off Human Rights, affirmative action, equal employ opportunity officer, 1977-85, human rights equal employ opportunity officer, 1985-. **Orgs:** Charter mem, Beta Zeta Alumni Chap, Alpha Kappa Lambda Frat; nat bd dirs, Nat Asn Human Rights Workers; Int City Mgt Asn; bd dirs, OIC Suncoast; Clearwater Br, NAACP; pres, Fla State NAACP Conf Branches; E Tenn State Univ Alumni Asn; Allocations Comm bd dirs United Way Pinellas County; bd dirs Fla Asn Comn Rels Prof; bd dirs, Fla Asn Equal Opportunity Prof, Inc; Am Soc Pub Admin; nat bd dirs, NAACP, 1990-98. **Honors/Awds:** Pi Gamma Mu Nat Social Sci Honor Soc. **Business Addr:** Human Rights, EEO Officer, Pinellas County Government, 400 S Ft Harrison 5th Fl, Clearwater, FL 33756.

RUSSELL, DR. LEONARD ALONZO
Dentist. **Personal:** Born Dec 27, 1949, Paris, KY; son of Joseph Bailey and Celia Russell. **Educ:** Easter Ky, BS, Indust, 1971; Cent State, BS, biol, 1978; Case Western Reserve Univ, DDS, 1982. **Career:** Pvt pract, dentist, currently. **Orgs:** Nat parliamentarian Student Nat Dental Assoc, 1981-82; mem, Am Acad General Dent, 1981-; mem, Ohio Dental Assoc, 1982-; pres, Forest City Dent Soc, 1986-87; Am Den Asn; Nat Dent Asn; Cleveland Dent Soc; Ohio Acad Gen Dent. **Honors/Awds:** Leonard A Russell Award, Kappa Alpha Psi Frat, 1971; Kenneth W Clement Award, Cleveland City Coun, 1981; Outstanding Young Man America, US Jaycees, 1984. **Home Addr:** 2204 South Taylor Rd, Cleveland Heights, OH 44118, **Home Phone:** (216)321-3462. **Business Addr:** Physician, 2204 S Taylor Rd, Cleveland Heights, OH 44118, **Business Phone:** (216)321-3462.

RUSSELL, M. CAMPY (MICHAEL CAMPANELLA RUSSELL)
Executive director, basketball coach. **Personal:** Born Jan 12, 1952, Jackson, TN; married Robyn; children: Allex, Mandisa, Oyin, Saki & Michael II. **Educ:** Univ Mich, attended 1974. **Career:** Basketball player (retired), Director; Cleveland Cavaliers, 1975-80,1984-85, NY Knicks, 1975-82, 1985; Cleveland Cavaliers, outer mkt event specialist, currently; Cleveland Cavaliers, dir alumni rels, currently, Cleveland Cavaliers Youth Prog, trainer, currently; WOIO & WUAB TV, Cleveland, basketball analyst, currently. **Honors/Awds:** Athlete of year, Pontiac-Waterford Times, 1978-79; pro of year Cleveland Touchdown Club, 1978-79; Michigan Hall of Honor, 2002. **Special Achievements:** Co-host, "Cavaliers' pregame show". **Business Phone:** (216)420-2165.

RUSSELL, MARK
Newspaper executive, newspaper editor. **Educ:** BJ, 1984. **Career:** Plain Dealer; Wall St Jour; Orlando Sentinel, managing ed, 2004-. **Honors/Awds:** Recognition, Mo Sch Jour, 2004. **Business Addr:** Managing Editor, Orlando Sentinel, 633 N Orange Ave, Orlando, FL 44114, **Business Phone:** (407)420-5467.

RUSSELL, MICHAEL
Chief executive officer. **Personal:** Born in Atlanta, GA; son of Herman; married Lovette Twyman; children: 2. **Educ:** Univ Va, BS, civil eng; Ga State Univ, MBA. **Career:** HJ Russell & Co, field engr, proj mgr & head bus develop, exec vpres, chief exec officer, 2003-. **Orgs:** Kennesaw Univ Found; Nat Asn Minority Contractors; Va Eng Found; Ga State Athletic Asn Bd; pres, Asn Builders & Contractors Ga; Metro Chamber Exec Comt; bd dir, Commerce Club; bd trustees, Univ Va Eng Sch; Children's Healthcare Found bd; 100 Black Men Atlanta. **Business Addr:** Chief Executive Officer, H J Russell & Company, 504 Fair St SW, Atlanta, GA 30313, **Business Phone:** (404)330-1000.*

RUSSELL, MICHAEL CAMPANELLA. See RUSSELL, M. CAMPY.

RUSSELL, MILICENT DE
School administrator. **Personal:** Born Jul 10, 1950, Chicago, IL; daughter of Robert Richard and Mildred Iles; married Clifford M, Aug 29, 1970; children: Clifford, Corey & Kimberly. **Educ:** Chicago State Univ, BS, educ, 1972; Roosevelt Univ, MA, admin & sup, 1984; Nova Univ, EdD, early middle & childhood, 1989. **Career:** Chicago Bd Educ, teacher, 1972-90, acting asst prin, 1985-86, asst prin, 1990-96, prin, 1996-; Kennedy King Col, lectr, 1988-89; Woodlawn Org, consult, 1992. **Orgs:** Roosevelt Univ, alumni, 1984-; NAEYC, 1986-89; coord, Parent Volunteer Prog, 1988-89; secy, Local School Coun, 1989-; Nova Univ, alumni, 1989-; CAEYC, 1992; Asn Sup & Curriculum Develop, 1992. **Special Achievements:** Author: "Increased Home and School Involvement of Parents of Primary Grade Students," 1989; "Improved Math Skills of Second Grade Students," Resources in Educ, 1988. **Business Addr:** Principal, Chicago Pub Sch, 125 S Clark St, Chicago, IL 60603, **Business Phone:** (773)553-1000.

RUSSELL, SANDRA ANITA (SANDI RUSSELL)
Jazz singer, teacher, writer. **Personal:** Born Jan 16, 1946, New York, NY; daughter of James Oliver and Gazetta. **Educ:** Syracuse Univ, AB, music, 1968; NY Univ, grad studies, 1969; Hunter Col, grad studies, 1971. **Career:** NY Bd Educ, teacher, 1968-76; jazz vocalist, 1977-81; San Francisco Clothing Co, mgr, 1981-84; writer & jazz vocalist, 1984-; Durham Univ, Eng, vocal instr, 2005-. Albums: Sweet Thunder; co-author, several books. **Honors/Awds:** CP Memorial Award, CP Memorial Fund, 1990; Author's Foundation Award, Soc Authors, 1991; Northern Arts Award, 1993; Guest of Honor, Univ Angers, France, Int Conf Orality in Short Fiction, 2005. **Special Achievements:** Drama. Essay: "Minor Chords/Major Changes," in Glancing Fires, ed Lesley Saunders, Women's Press, London, 1987; author, Render Me My Song: African-American Women Writers, Pandora Press St Martins, NY, 1990, updated ed, 2001; theatrical performance, "Render Me My Song' One-Woman Show in Words and Song," 1990; contrib ed, The Virago Book of Love Poetry, London/NY, 1990; Sister, short story in Daughters of Africa, ed, Busby, London, Cape Pantheon, NY, 1992; recorded album, 'Incandescent,' 2001, (Freedom Song); recorded album, 'Sweet Thunder', 2007. Lyricist: 'Feet on the Ground', 'Given Time', 2007; Mark Rowles Music; 'ELLA!' - one woman theatrical show: conceived, researched, written and performed, 2009-. **Home Addr:** 11 Tenter Terr, Durham City DH1 4RD, United Kingdom, **Home Phone:** (191)386-0092.

RUSSELL, WESLEY L.
Executive. **Personal:** Born Nov 6, 1938, Camp Hill, AL; son of Cordie Mae Mennifield and Pearlie L; married Geraldine K; children: Derek, Dante, Deirdre & Derwin. **Educ:** Tuskegee Inst, BS, 1963; San Diego State Univ. **Career:** General Dynamics Electronics Systems Inc, assoc engr, 1963, elec engr, 1964, sr elec engr, 1968, mgr, tactical syst sect head, 1984-, prog mgr, 1990-. **Orgs:** Nat Mgt Asn. **Honors/Awds:** Letter of Commendation in support of initial operational evaluation of P5604 Secure Telecommunication Terminals, Tinker AFB Okla, 1974; Numerous extraordinary achievement awards. **Home Addr:** 3927 Country Trail, Bonita, CA 91902. **Business Addr:** Program Manager, General Dynamics Electronics Systems Inc, MZ 6164-P, PO Box 509008, San Diego, CA 92150-9008.

RUSSELL, WILLAM FELTON. See RUSSELL, BILL.

RUSSELL-MCCLOUD, PATRICIA
Orator, writer. **Personal:** Born in Indianapolis, IN; married Bishop E Earl McCloud. **Educ:** Ky State Univ; Howard Univ Sch Law, JD. **Career:** Broadcast Bur Fed Commun Comn, Wash, DC, chief complaints br; Russell-McCloud & Assoc, pres & owner, currently; Auth: A IS FOR ATTITUDE: An Alphabet for Living, 2006. **Orgs:** Nat parliamentarian, Alpha Kappa Alpha Sorority Inc; pres, Links Found Inc; pres, The Links Inc; Am Entertainment Int Speakers Bur Inc. **Honors/Awds:** Elks Oratorical Award; Outstanding Entrepreneur in Georgia, Women Looking Ahead News Mag, 1996. **Special Achievements:** One of the top five business motivators in America, Black Enterprise Mag; 100 Most Influential People, EBONY Mag, 1998-2002; featured in a number of national publications including Black Enterprise, EBONY & ESSENCE. **Business Addr:** President, Professional Orator, Russell-McCloud & Associates, PO Box 310043, Atlanta, GA 31131, **Business Phone:** (404)691-9841.

RUTH, JAMES A
Judge. **Personal:** Born Jan 1, 1956, Palatka, FL. **Educ:** Fla State Univ, BS, criminol, 1979, MS, pub admin, 1980; Fla State Univ Col Law, JD, 1984. **Career:** Off Pub Defender, invest intern; Fla Dept Corrections, Dade Correctional Inst, counr & instr, 1980-81; Broward Co Juv Restitution Prog, criminal justice coun, 1981-82; Off State Atty, Fourth Judicial Circuit, Jacksonville, FL, div chief, 1985-91; Duval Co Courthouse, judge, 1991-. **Orgs:** Vol & sponsor, Tots-N-Teens Theater Inc; bd mgt, YMCA; Fla Coun Co Ct Judges; Jacksonville Bar Asn; DW Perkins Bar Asn; Fla Bar Found; Modern Soc Free & Accepted Masonry; Fla Army Nat Guard Offrs Asn; Northside Busmen's Club. **Honors/Awds:** Outstanding Alumni Award for Achievement, Fla State Univ, 1992; Leadership Jacksonville, 1992; Various Achievement Awards, Fla Army Natl Guard, 1982, 1983, 1987, 1988, 1989, 1991, 1992; Outstanding Community Serv Award, Tots-N-Teens Theater Inc, 1990; Northeast Fla Community Action Agency Award for Vol Serv, 1987, 1989, 1990, 1991, 1992; Outstanding Serv Award, Natl Black Law Stud Assn, 1984; Track Scholar, Fla State Univ, 1974; Elected Circuit Rep, Fla Conf Co Ct Judges, 1994; Adv Comm Selectee, Fla Times Union, 1993; Meritorious Service Medal; Global War on Terror Expeditionary Medal; FL Distinguished Service Cross. **Military Serv:** USAR, Bronze Star. **Business Addr:** Judge, Duval Co Courthouse, 330 E Bay St Rm 301, Jacksonville, FL 32202, **Business Phone:** (904)630-2568.

RUTHERFORD, HAROLD PHILLIP, III
School administrator. **Personal:** Born Sep 3, 1951, New York, NY; son of Steve and Ethel Leona Hollinger; married Vancenia Dowdell; children: Paitra. **Educ:** John Carroll Univ, AB, 1974; Ky State Univ, MA, 1977. **Career:** Ky State Univ, asst dean, 1976-80; City East Cleveland, vice-city mgr, 1980-83; RDR Mgmt Consult, exec dir, 1982-85; Fort Valley State Col, dir develop, 1985-; Woodrow Wilson Nat fel, 1985-86; Mgt Develop Prog, Harvard Univ, 1986; Univ State NY, Regents fel, 1988-89. **Orgs:** Consult, E Cleveland Sch Bd, 1980-83; consult, City Maywood, Ill, 1982-85; Sigma Pi Phi Fraternity, 1983; Portage Co Nat Asn Advan Colored People, 1984; bd mem, Record & Assocs, 1984-86. **Honors/Awds:** Management Award Certificate, Wharton Sch, 1986. **Business Addr:** Executive Director of Development, Fort Valley State College, 805 State Col Dr, Fort Valley, GA 31030, **Business Phone:** (912)474-2593.

RUTLEDGE, DR. ESSIE MANUEL
Educator, sociologist. **Personal:** Born in Midway, AL; daughter of Ollie M Jordan Jones and Algie L Manuel Sr (deceased); married Albert C; children: Jeffrey A. **Educ:** Fla A&M Univ, BA, 1958; Univ Wis, Madison, MA, a1965; Univ Mich, PhD, 1974. **Career:** Sixteenth St Jr High Sch, St Petersburg, social studies teacher, 1958-61; Gibbs & St Petersburg Jr Col, instr, 1961-67; Macomb County Community Col, asst prof sociol, 1968-71; Univ Mich, Flint, asst prof sociol, 1974-76; Western Ill Univ, Afro-Am Studies, chairperson, 1976-84, from asst prof sociol to prof sociology, 1976-2006, prof emer, 2006-; Gerontological Soc AME, Prog Appl Gerontlogy, post doctoral fel, 1989. **Orgs:** Pi Gamma Mu Nat Social Sci Honor Soc, Florida A&M Univ, 1965; Am Sociol Asn, 1967-, memship chmn, 1970-84, pres, 1985-86, exec officer, 1996-99; Asn Black Sociologists; Comt Status Women Am Sociol Asn, 1978-80; Ill Counc Black Studies, 1979-; adv bd, McDonough Co Health Dept, 1979-81; Ch Women United, 1980; Equal Opportunity & Fair Housing CMS City Macomb, Ill, 1986-; exec bd, Univ Professionals Ill, local 4100, 1990-97; publications comt, Sociologists Women Soc, 1993-96; Southern Sociol Soc, 1992, honors comt, 1995-98. **Honors/Awds:** Rackham Fel, Univ Mich, 1971-74; Award for Service to Enhance Position of Women Western Orgn for Women, Western Ill Univ, 1979; Inducted into Gamma Lambda Chapter, Honorary Order of Omega, 1990; Faculty Excellence Award,Western Ill Univ, 1991; Blue Key Fraternity, Hon Fac, Western Ill Univ, 1993; Affirmative Action Directors Award, Western Ill Univ, 2006. **Special Achievements:** Published numerous articles on Black Women, Role Knowledge, Black Husbands & Wives, Separatism, Black Families, racism, socialization, and suicide in the following books, documents, and journals: The Black Woman, ERIC Documents, Reflector, Genetic Psychology Monograph, Journal of Negro History, Marriage and Family Therapy, Contemporary Sociology, Journal of Comparative Family Studies, Minority Voices, Ethnic Issues in Adolescent Mental Health. **Business Addr:** Professor Emeritus, Western Illinois University, Department of Sociology, Morgan Hall 404 1 Univ Cir, Macomb, IL 61455, **Business Phone:** (309)298-1056.

RUTLEDGE, GEORGE
Automotive executive. **Career:** Rutledge Chevrolet Oldsmobile, chief exec officer, currently. **Special Achievements:** company is listed No 11 on Black Enterprise's list of top 100 auto dealers, 1994. **Business Phone:** (217)728-4338.

RUTLEDGE, JENNIFER M (JENNIFER MERDITTE RUTLEDGE)
Management consultant. **Personal:** Born Sep 12, 1951, White Plains, NY; daughter of James and Elizabeth. **Educ:** Mich State Univ, BS, indust psychol, 1973; Pace Univ, Lubin Sch Bus, MBA, 1982. **Career:** Allstate Ins, personnel, 1973-76; Nat Asn Advan Colored People Legal Defense & Educ fund, dir personnel, 1976-79; Nat Coun Negro Women, nat coord work exp prog, 1979-80; Girls Clubs Am Inc, NE Serv Ctr, dir, 1983-86; Delphi Consult Group Inc, partner, 1984-, partner & vpres, currently. **Orgs:** Bd mem, Westchester Urban League, 1976; bd mem, Afro-Am Cult

Asn, 1976; bd mem, vpres Afro-Am Civic Asn, 1978; Nat Asn MBA's; guest lectr, Bus & Prof Women's Clubs; Meeting Planners Int; bd mem, Lubin Grad Sch Bus Alumni Asn, Pace Univ; bd mem, Support Network Inc, 1988-; bd mem, Greenwich Girls Club, 1989-; Delta Sigma Theta; bd mem, Yonkers Pvt Indust Coun Affiliated Nat Ctr Non-Profit Bds Mem-Res Bd Adv-ABI; bd mem, Westchester Community Found, 1996-; bd mem, Alzheimer's Asn, 1999-; Nat Asn Female Exec; assoc fel Am Mgt Asn; Meeting Planners Int. **Honors/Awds:** Business Woman of the Year, Afro-Am Civic Asn, 1987; Professional of the Year, Westchester Chap Negro Bus & Prof Women's Club Inc, 1993; Honoree of the Year, Nat Conf Community & Justice, 1997. **Special Achievements:** Contributing writer to several publications and has been cited in numerous articles. **Business Addr:** Partner, Vice President, Delphi Consulting Group Inc, 399 Knollwood Rd Suite 108, White Plains, NY 10603, **Business Phone:** (914)684-2400.

RUTLEDGE, JENNIFER MERDITTE. See RUTLEDGE, JENNIFER M.

RUTLEDGE, ROD
Football player. **Personal:** Born Aug 12, 1975, Birmingham, AL; son of Wallace and Rose. **Educ:** Ala Univ. **Career:** Football player (retired); New England Patriots, tight end, 1998-2001; Houston Texans, tight end, 2002. **Honors/Awds:** Rookie of the year, 1998; Lifter of the Year.

RUTLEDGE, DR. WILLIAM LYMAN
Surgeon. **Personal:** Born Jun 27, 1952, Little Rock, AR; children: Rodney B, Estelle A, Jessica M. **Educ:** Tex Southern Univ, BA, 1975; Meharry Med Col, MD, 1979. **Career:** Ark Surg Assocs, pres, 1984; Cancer Control Outreach Ctr, Little Rock, gen practice, currently; gen surgeon, ark, currently. **Orgs:** Alpha Omega Alpha Honor Med Soc, 1978; Nat Med Asn, 1979; dist comnr, Boy Scouts Am, 1986; secy, Scott Hamilton Dr Med Clin Inc, 1986; exec bd, Urban League; minority advr bd, Univ Ark Med Sci Campus.

RYAN, AGNES C.
Lawyer. **Personal:** Born Sep 17, 1928, Houston, TX; widowed; children: 3. **Educ:** Howard Univ, BA, 1947; Fordham Univ, Juris Doc, 1950. **Career:** Legal Aid Bureau, lawyer, 1951-52; pvt pracice, lawyer, 1952-53; Legal Aid Bureau, staff lawyer; supervisory lawyer. **Orgs:** Chicago Bar Asn; Am Bar Asn; bd mem, Bartelme Homes. **Honors/Awds:** Educational Award, Elks, 1971. **Business Addr:** Supervisory Lawyer, Legal Aid Bureau, 14 E Jackson Blvd, Chicago, IL 60604.

RYAN, MARSHA ANN
Executive. **Personal:** Born Mar 12, 1947, New Orleans, LA; married Cecil James; children: Michelle & Marisa. **Educ:** Fisk Univ, BA, 1968; Tenn State Univ, teacher cert, 1970. **Career:** Neely's Bend Jr High Sch, teacher, 1970-71; Gen Elec Co, data processing instr, 1971; Xerox Ed Prod Div, area sales rep, 1973; Singer, area sales mgr, 1974; Ore Dept Transp, affirmative action & officer, 1977-78, career develop anal, 1975; Ore Motor Vechicles Div, prog develop, 1978-79; Ore Dept Human Resources, dir prog anal, 1979-80; Ore Adult & Family Serv Dir Multnomah Reg Off, prog exec bd, supvr pre-admis screening & resource unit, 1980; Ore Dept Transp Serv Employ Prog, mgr, 1984. **Orgs:** Am Asn Affirmative Action; Gov Tri-Co Affirmative Action Asn; Affirmative Action Officers Asn; adv coun, Wash Co Dept Aging Servs; adv coun, Wash Co Retired Sr Vol Prog; adv bd, Portland Community Col Prof Skills Prog.

RYAN-WHITE, JEWELL
Television producer, executive, president (organization). **Personal:** Born May 24, 1943, Columbus, MS; daughter of Larry A Sr and Martha; divorced; children: Donald Andre White. **Educ:** Alcorn A&M Col; Joliet Jr Col; Olive Harvey Col; IL State Univ; Rueben Cannon Master Series, screenwriting. **Career:** Ill Bell Tel Co, opr investr dial serv admin, 1967-76; Community Workers Am Loca 5011, pres, 1972-86; Am Cable systems Midwest, comm TV, 1985-88, pub rel, promotions coord, 1987; NCP Image Awards, television comm, 1990-92; Calif Sch Employees Asn, CBS prog analyst; Am Film Inst, admin campus oprs, 1989-91; Nat Asn Advan Colored People Image Awards, TV Comm, 1990-92; Marla Gibbs Crossroads Arts Acad, adminr, 1991-; Turner Broadcast Syst, Trumpet Awards, script supvr, 1993-98; Clark Atlanta Univ, sr assignment mgr, CAU-TV News 3, adj fac, 1994-97; Olympic Games Atlanta Comm, internship placement coord, mgr prof comm outreach, 1996; independent producer, currently; US Dept Community, Bureau Census, partnership specialist, 1999-; Off Labor-Mgt Progs, ed, currently. **Orgs:** Nat Black Commun Coalition, nat pres, 1975-85; State Ill Lit Coun, Govrs Grievance panel; Coalition Black Trade Unionists; Urban League; Oper PUSH; Vol Parent Guardian Angel Home; St John Vianney Cath Church; SCLC; Cath Educ Asn; Smithsonian Asn; personnel & pub policy comts Nat Campaign Human Dev, 1985-87; bd dirs, Joliet Jr Col MNY, Intercult Affairs, 1985-87; Women in Cable, 1986-87; comnr, 1986, cbd 1987 Housing Authority Joliet; Nat Asn Housing & Redevelop Officials, 1986-87; bd dirs, Sr Serv Ctr, 1987; bd dirs, Sr Companion Prog, 1987; chmn, EEO/AA Comm, Nat Fedn Local Cable Progrs, 1988-90; Nat Asn Advan Colored People, Beverly Hill/Hollywood Chap, 1989-90; Los Angeles Urban League, 1989-92; master plan comt, City Los Angeles Cult Arts; Los Angeles Black Educ Comn, 1989-93; vpres bd dir, arbitrator, Nat Bd Arbitrators, 1989. **Honors/Awds:** Scholarship in Clothing, 1961; Award Salesclerking RE Hunt HS, 1961; Award Newly Elected Officers Training Sch CWA, 1973; Certificate Merit IL Bell Tele Co, 1974; Award of Appreciation CWA, 1976; United Way Will Co, 1977; City of Hope COPE, 1977; Pace Setter Award, City of Hope, 1979; Crusade Award, Am Cancer Soc, 1980; Citizen of the Month, City of Joliet, 1982; Certificate of Achievement, Pro-Skills, 1986, Achievement Award, 1986, American Ambassador Award, 1986; Award of Appreciation Campaign Human Develop Joliet Catholic Diocese, 1986; Award of Appreciation, Nat Campaign Human Dev Wash DC, 1987; Award for Cable Excellence, Cable Television Admin & Mkt Soc, 1987; 3 Awards for overall contribution to field of adult educ/illiteracy, Joliet Jr Col, 1987; Public Speaking American Cable Systems Midwest 1987; named to Nat Bd Consumer Arbitrators, 1989; NFLCP, Jewell Ryan-White Cultural Annual Diversity Award. **Home Addr:** 8575 Pineview Lane, Jonesboro, GA 30238. **Business Addr:** Editor, Office ofLabor-Management Programs, 1350 Pennsylvania Ave NW Suite 324, Washington, DC 20004, **Business Phone:** (202)727-4999.

RYCE, SUNDRA L
President (Organization). **Personal:** Born in Buffalo, NY. **Educ:** State Univ NY Col, Buffalo, BS, bus studies; Medaille Col, Buffalo, MS. **Career:** SLR Contracting Serv Co Inc, pres & chief exec officer, currently. **Orgs:** Bd trustees, Western NY Pub Broadcasting Asn; bd trustee, Buffalo Urban Develop Corp; bd dirs, Buffalo State Col Found Bd; bd dirs, Western NY Health Syst. **Honors/Awds:** Minority Small Bus Person of the Year, US Small Bus Admin, Buffalo, 2002; Inner City 100 Award, 2003; Entrepreneur of the Year Leadership Award, YWCA, 2003; Top 21 Women, Business Women First. **Special Achievements:** "10 Women Making History in Erie County", Erie County Executive, Joel Giambra. **Business Addr:** President, Chief Executive Officer, SLR Contracting & Service Company Inc, 260 Mich Ave, Buffalo, NY 14203, **Business Phone:** (716)896-8148.

RYCRAW, EUGENIA (EUGENIA MILLER-RYCRAW)
Basketball player, basketball coach. **Personal:** Born Dec 6, 1968; married Richard; children: Robert, Mia, Richard & Janelle. **Educ:** Calif State-Fullerton, BA, psychol, 1994. **Career:** Basketball player (retired), basketball coach; Japan Airlines, basketball player, 1991-93; Los Angeles Sparks, ctr, 1997; Calif State-Fullerton,asst coach, 1993-94, currently. **Honors/Awds:** All-Am, Kodak; Player of the Year, Big West Conference, 1990-91; Player of the Week, Sports Illus, 1991; Titan Athletics Hall of Fame, 2005. **Special Achievements:** The only basketball player in California State Fullerton history to score more than 2,000 points; Set new NCAA record for career blocks, 428. **Business Addr:** Assistant Coach, California State Fullerton, California State University, 800 N State College Blvd, PO Box 34080, Fullerton, CA 92831-3599, **Business Phone:** (714)278-3480.

S

SAADIQ, RAPHAEL (CHARLIE RAY WIGGINS)
Singer, business owner. **Personal:** Born May 14, 1966, Oakland, CA. **Career:** Tony Toni Tone, vocalist, co-founder; D'Angelo albums, co-producer; Albums: Instant Vintage, 2002; All Hits at the House of Blues, 2003; Ray Ray, 2004; Songs: "Ask of You", 1995; "Get Involved", 1999; "Be Here", 2002; "Rifle Love", 2004; "I Want You Back", 2005; Pookie Entertaiment, founder, currently. **Special Achievements:** Five Grammy Award nominations, 2003. **Business Addr:** Founder, Pookie Entertainment, 4850 Vineland Ave, PO Box 241, N Hollywood, CA 91601.*

SAAR, BETYE IRENE
Artist, designer, educator. **Personal:** Born Jul 30, 1926, Los Angeles, CA; daughter of Jefferson Brown and Beatrice Brown; divorced; children: Lesley, Alison, Tracye. **Educ:** Univ Calif, BA, 1949; Calif State Univ, Long Beach; Univ Southern Calif; Calif State Univ. **Career:** Whitney Mus Modern Art, solo exhib, 1975; Studio Mus Harlen, solo exhib, 1980; Monique Knowlton Gallery, NY, solo exhib, 1981; Jan Baum Gallery, LA, solo exhib, 1981; Quay Gallery, San Francisco, 1982; WAM & Canberra Sch Art, Australia, solo exhib, 1984; Ga State Univ Gallery, 1984; Mus Contemp Art, LA, solo exhib context, 1984; MIT Ctr Gallery, 1987; J Paul Getty Fund for the Visual Arts fel, 22nd Annual Artist Award, 1990; Savannah Col Art & Design, distinguished lectr, 2000; solo exhibitions: Connections: Site Installations, 1989; Sanctified Visions, 1990; Sentimental Souvenirs, 1991; Signs of the Times, 1992; Betye Saar: The Secret Heart, 1993; Limbo, 1994; Personal Icons, 1996; Tangled Roots, 1996; Ritual & Remebrance, 1997; Workers & Warriors: The Return of Aunt Jemima, 1998; Crossings, 1998; A Women's Boat: Voyages, 1998; Betye Saar: As Time Goes By, 2000; In Service: A Version of Survival, 2000; Betye Saar: Personal Icons, 2002; Betye Saar: Colored-Consider the Rainbow, 2002; Crocker Art Museum, Sacramento, CA, 2006; group exhibitions: Secrets, Dialogues, Revelations: The Art of Betye & Alison Saar, 1990-91; 500 Years: With the Breath of Our Ancestors, 1992; In Out of the Cold, 1993; Generation of Mentors, 1994; The US Delegation Fifth Biennial of Havana, 1994; The Art of Betye Saar and John Otterbridge, 1994, 1995; Bearing Witness, 1996; Three Outdoor Installations, 1996; The Amer Century: Art & Culture, 1900-00, 1999; Uncommon Threads: Contemp Artists & Clothing, 2001; Contemp Romanticism, 2001; Some Assemblage Required, 2002; Layers of Meaning, 2003. **Honors/Awds:** Award, Nat Endowment Arts, 1974, 1984; James Van Der Zee Award, Brandywine Workshop, 1992; Distinguished Artist Award, Fresno Art Mus, 1993; honorary doctorates: Calif Col Arts & Crafts, 1991, Otis/Parson, 1992, San Francisco Art Inst, 1992, Mass Col Art, 1992, Calif Inst Arts, 1995; Visual Arts Award, Flintridge Found, 1997; National Artist Award, Anderson Ranch Art Ctr, 1999; Living Artists Award, Calif Art Educ Asn, 1999; Pioneer Award, IAM, 2000. *

SABREE, CLARICE S
Administrator. **Personal:** Born Oct 25, 1949, Camden, NJ; daughter of Roy McClendon and Clara Ingram; divorced; children (previous marriage): Zahir, Anwar, Ameen & Hassan (divorced); children: Zahir, Anwar, Ameen & Hassan. **Educ:** Rutgers Univ Camden, BA, 1978. **Career:** Lawnside Bd Educ, teacher 1978-80; Camden Bd Educ, elem teacher, 1980-82; DMC Energy Inc, energy conserv specialist, 1983-87; CAPEDA, energy analyst, 1987-88; Energy Conserv, supvr monitors, 1988-; NJ Dept Community Affairs, Div Housing & Community Resources, Off Low-Income Energy Conserv, adminr, prog supvr, 1993-; jazz vocalist, poet, african dance perfomances. **Orgs:** Res Intl Black Dolls, 1979; bd mem, S African Freedom Comt; owner, Cult Concepts Trenton, African Art, Wearing Apparel; bd mem, Nat State & Community Serv Prog. **Honors/Awds:** Outstanding Volunteer, Headstart Camden, 1978; Dark Images Award, 1992; Homelessness Prevention Award, 1993; Jim Gardner Weatherization Award, Nat State & Community Serv Prog; State of NJ Teamwork & Partnership Award, 2005; James Gardner Service Award, The Nat State & Community Serv Prog, 2006. **Special Achievements:** Self published book of poetry titled Spoken Words of a Ghetto Girl Turned Intl Woman. **Home Addr:** 1406 S Broad St, Trenton, NJ 08610, **Home Phone:** (609)989-7298. **Business Addr:** Supervisor, Office of Low-Income Energy Conservation, New Jersey Department of Community Affairs, Division of Housing & Community Resources, 101 S Broad St, PO Box 811, Trenton, NJ 08625, **Business Phone:** (609)984-3301.

SADDLER, ELBERT M
Psychologist. **Personal:** Born Aug 17, 1948, Philadelphia, PA; son of Elbert and Jeannette; married Joyce, May 17, 1975; children: Elbert III, Bradley & Amanda; married Joyce. **Educ:** Rutgers Univ, BA, 1975; Temple Univ, MEd, 1980, PhD, 1985. **Career:** City Philadelphia, voc coun; Eastern Col, adj asst prof; St Joseph's Col, adj asst prof; Temple Univ, adj asst prof; W Chester Univ, assoc prof psychol, 1985-, Coun Ctr, psychologist, 1985-. **Orgs:** Am Psychol Asn; PA Psychol Asn; Omega Psi Phi; Nat Asn Develop Edu; founder, Chi Alpha Epsilon Nat Honor Soc, 1990-. **Honors/Awds:** Outstanding Service, Nat Asn Develop Educ, 2000; Education Equity Award, Pa Human Rels Comn. **Military Serv:** USN Reserve, E3, 1968-70. **Business Addr:** Associate Professor, West Chester University, 129 Lawrence Center, West Chester, PA 19383-4120, **Business Phone:** (610)436-2301.

SADDLER, JOSEPH. See GRANDMASTER FLASH.

SADLER, DONNIE LAMONT
Baseball player. **Personal:** Born Jun 17, 1975, Gohlson, TX. **Career:** Boston Red Sox, second baseman-shortstop, 1998-2000; Cincinnati Reds, 2001; Kans City Royals, 2001-02; Tex Rangers, 2002-03; Ariz Diamondbacks, 2004; Chicago White Sox, shortstop, 2004; Ariz Diamondbacks, 2007; Milwaukee Brewers, 2008; Pacific League: Triple-A Tucson, 2007. *

SADLER, DR. KENNETH MARVIN
Dentist. **Personal:** Born in Gastonia, NC; son of Edward Dewitt Sadler Sr and Mildred Jackson; married Brenda Arlene Latham MD; children: Jackson Lewis Ezekiel & Raleigh DeWitt Samuel. **Educ:** Lincoln Univ, BA, 1971; Howard Univ Col Dent, DDS, 1975; Golden Gate Univ, MPA, 1978. **Career:** Howard Univ Col Dent, instructor & coordr, 1972-76; US Army Dental Corps, captain & dentist, 1975-78; Kenneth M Sadler DDS, pres, admin dir, 1978-. **Orgs:** Omega Psi Phi, life mem, 1969; Am Dental asn, 1975-; Acad Gen Dent, 1976-; Lincoln Univ, chmn, bd trustees, 1983-; Old North State Dental Soc, chmn peer review comt, 1986; bd dir, Old Hickory Coun Boy Scouts Am, 1988-; Lewisville Town Coun, mayor pro tempore, 1991-; Am Asn Dental Sch, consultant, 1991; vpres, BSA, Old Hickory Coun, 1990; Forsyth Technical Cmnty Clg, bd trustees; Winston-Salem Forsyth County Appearance Comn, 1992-98; Winston-Salem Forsyth County Industrial Financing Pollution Control Authority. **Honors/Awds:** Int Col Dent Award, 1975; The Am Assn Endodontics Award, 1975; US Army, dental diploma-gen pract, 1976; Acad Gen Dent, Master, 1996; Recognition Cert, Chicago Dental Soc, 1989; Plaque-Appreciation, Fifth Dist Dental Soc, 1989; Lecture/Table Clinic, Chicago Mid-winter Meeting, 1989; Table Clinic, Thomas P Hin-

man Dental Meeting, 1989, 1996; United Way Forsyth County, chmn budget review panel, 1991; Forsyth County Dental Hygiene Soc, lecturer, 1991; NAFEO, Distinguished Alumni of the Year, 1986; Citizenship Award, 1996, NCDS; Mastership Acad Gen Dent; Silver Beaver Award, OHC BSA; Fellow, American Col Dentists, 1995; Fel Acad Dent Int; Fel Int Col Dentists; Distinguished Alumni Award, Howard Univ Col Dentistry, 2000. **Special Achievements:** Presentations include: DC Dental Soc; Howard Univ, Post-grad Seminar; Pellican State Dental Soc; Nat Dental Soc; Forsyth County Dental Assistant Soc; Lincoln Univ, Chemistry Dept; Am Acad Dental Group Practice; Palmetto State Dental Med Pharmaceutical Assn; author: "Resin Bonded Retainers," Journal of Nat Dental Assn, 1984; Acad Gen Dentistry, 2003. **Military Serv:** AUS Reserves, col, 1978-2003; Commendation Medal with 2 Oak Leaf Clusters; Army Achievement Medal. **Business Addr:** President, Administrative Director, Kenneth M Sadler DDS & Associates, 201 Charlois Blvd, Winston-Salem, NC 27103, **Business Phone:** (336)718-1834.

SADLER, DR. WILBERT L
Educator. **Personal:** Born in Atlanta, GA; son of Willie Mae Sanford and Wilbert Sr; married Carolyn Johnson; children: Anthony Lee, Wilbert Bryant & Crystal Yolanda. **Educ:** Paine Col, BS, 1970; Morgan State Univ, MS, 1972; Boston Univ, EdD, 1981; Univ Pa, Post Doctorate study, 1981; Columbia Univ, post doctorate study, 1988. **Career:** Morgan State Col, instr, 1970-74; Boston Univ, grad asst, 1974-76; Livingstone Col, asst prof, 1976-82, adj prof, 2001-; Winston-Salem State Univ, assoc prof, 1982-92, prof, 1992-2001, prof emer, 2001-. **Orgs:** Pinehurst Comm Club, 1976-; Asn Col & Univ Profs; Nat Asn Advan Colored People; life mem, Alpha Upsilon Alpha, NC Col Read; life mem, Col Reading Asn; Int Reading Asn; Alpha Kappa Mu Hon Soc; Beta Mu Lambda; life mem, Alpha Phi Alpha Frat Inc; coordr, ELE; bd trustees, Rowan Pub Libr; Alpha Upsilon Alpha, Nat Reading Honor Soc, 1989-90; Phi Delta Kappa, Nat Educ Hon Soc, 1989-90. **Military Serv:** AUS, sp/4, 2 yrs. **Business Addr:** Professor Emeritus, Winston-Salem State University, Education Department, Martin Luther King Jr Dr, Winston-Salem, NC 27101, **Business Phone:** (919)750-2694.

SAFFOLD, OSCAR E.
Physician. **Personal:** Born Feb 20, 1941, Cleveland, OH. **Educ:** Fisk Univ, BA 1963; Meharry Med Col, MD, 1967. **Career:** George W. Hubbard Hosp, intern, 1967-68; Tufts Univ Sch Med, asst resident dermatologist, 1968-72; Boston City Hosp, chief resident dermatologist, 1972-73; Case Western Res Med Sch, Dept Dermat, assoc clin prof; Mid-Florida Dermat Assocs, physician, currently. **Orgs:** Secy, Dermat Sect, Nat Med Asn, 1975-; Univ Hosp Cleveland, 1973-; mem, Mass State Bd; Ohio State Bd; Am Bd Dermat, 1974; mem, Am Acad Dermat; Am Soc Dermat Surg; Am Med Asn; Cleveland Acad Med; Cleveland Dermat Asn; Nat Med Asn; Ohio State Med Asn. **Business Addr:** Physician, Mid-Florida Dermatology Associates, 7652 Ashley Park Ct Suite 305, Orlando, FL 32806.*

SAFFOLD, SHIRLEY STRICKLAND
Judge. **Personal:** Married Oscar E Saffold; children: Sydney. **Educ:** Cent State Univ, BA; Cleveland-Marshall Col Law, JD. **Career:** Cleveland Munic Ct, judge, 1987-94; Legal Aid Soc, Criminal Div, staff atty; Cuyahoga County Ct Common Pleas, judge, 1995-. **Orgs:** Nat Bar Asn; Nat Asn Women Judges; past pres, resolutions comt, pres, Am Judges Asn. **Honors/Awds:** Judge of the Year, Dew Ward Club. **Special Achievements:** First African Am woman to serve in an exec position in the Am Judges Asn. **Business Addr:** Judge, Cuyahoga County Commons Pleas Court, 1220 Ontario St Ct Rm 21B, Cleveland, OH 44114, **Business Phone:** (216)443-7000.*

SAFFORE, LATEEF
Oncologist, research scientist. **Personal:** Married Yetunde Aranmolate. **Educ:** MS. **Career:** Cleveland Clin Found, res oncologist scientist, 2003, Dept Cancer Biol, Lerner Res Inst, lead res technologist, currently. **Business Phone:** (216)444-8196.

SAGERS, RUDOLPH, JR.
Marketing executive. **Personal:** Born Feb 14, 1955, Chicago, IL; married Carol Hillsman; children: Ryan Christopher. **Educ:** Univ Ill, BS, 1978; Univ Cincinnati, MS, 1980. **Career:** Veterans Admin, mgt analyst trainee, 1979-80, mgmt analyst, 1980-81, health systems specialist, 1981-84; Int Bus Mach, mkt rep, 1984; Edge Technol Resources Inc, currently. **Orgs:** Amer Col Hosp Adminrs, 1982, MI Health Coun, 1982, Am Health Planning Assoc, 1983, Soc Hosp Planning, 1983, Black Data Prof Assoc, 1986-. **Honors/Awds:** Outstanding Young Man of America Award, 1983; Veterans Admin Achievement of Service Award, 1983; Veterans Admin Superior Performance Award, 1983; Veterans Admin Special Contribution Award 1984; Medical Ctr Director's Commendation of Excellence Award; Branch Manager Award, Int Bus Mach, 1985,86; National 100% Sales Club Award, Int Bus Mach, 1985-86. **Business Addr:** Edge Technological Resources Inc, 230 West Cermak Rd Suite 2A, Chicago, IL 60616, **Business Phone:** (312)842-4617.*

SAILOR, ELROY
Secretary (Office). **Personal:** Born Oct 26, 1969, Detroit, MI; son of Rev DeAnna and Clarence. **Educ:** Morehouse COL, BA, political sci, 1990; MIC State UNIV, cert, pub policy, 1994; Wayne State UNIV, master's, urban planning, 1998. **Career:** Governor John Engler, ast to governor, 1991-93, re-election campaign, deputy political dir, 1993-94; US Senate Spencer Abraham, spec ast, 1995-; House Republican Conf, dir. **Orgs:** Exec bd mem, US Senate Black Legislative Staff Caucus, 1995-96; co-host, "Youngbloods" NAT Empowerment TV, 1995-96; pres & owner, The Sailor CPN Vending Machines, 1996-; Fellowship Chapel, 1990-; volunteer, COTS - Homeless Shelter, 1991-92; Black Farmers & Agriculturalists asn. **Honors/Awds:** Detroit News, Detroit's Five Future Leaders, 1995; MPLP MIC St UNIV, Fellowship, Pub Policy Prog, 1994. **Special Achievements:** Entered Morehouse COL at age 16, 1986. *

SAINTE-JOHNN, DON
Radio broadcaster, executive. **Personal:** Born Jul 9, 1949, Monroeville, AL; son of Walter Johnson and Nell B Henderson; married Brenda L Hodge; children: W Marcus & J'Michael Kristopher. **Educ:** La City Col, attended 1968; Calif State Univ, Long Beach, attended 1969; San Francisco State Univ. **Career:** XEGM Radio, San Diego, prog dir, 1968-69; KWK, St Louis, prog dir, 1969-71; KYUM Yuma AZ, sports dir, 1969; Aradcom Prod, St Louis, pres, 1970-71; WJPC Radio, Chicago, am air personality, 1971-74; KFRC RKO Broadcasting Inc, air personality; KSFM-FM, Sacramento, air talent; KQLL-FM, air talent. **Orgs:** Nat Asn Radio-TV Ammoun; Calif Real Estate; bd mem, E Bay Zool Soc; Bay Area March Dimes Superwalk, Nat Acad TV Arts & Sci, Am Fed TV & Radio Art; Alpha Epsilon Rho; SC Broadcaster Asn,; bd dir, Paul J Hall Boys Club; athletic dir, St Davids Sch; bd mem, Diocesan Boys Athletic Coun Oakland; basketball coach, Richmond Police Activ League, El Sobrante Boys Club, St Davids Schs. **Honors/Awds:** Most Outstanding Radio Student, La City Col, 1967; Billboard Air Personalities of the Year, 1973, 1974; Honored as Concerned Spon for Chicago Pin-Killers Bowl Club, 1974; Air Personality of the Year, Billboard Mag, 1974, 1975; Air Personality on Pop Radio Award, Black Radio Exclusive Mag, 1980. **Business Addr:** Air Talent, KQLL-FM, 2625 S Mem, Tulsa, OK 74129.

SAINT JAMES, SYNTHIA
Illustrator, writer, artist. **Personal:** Born Feb 11, 1949, Los Angeles, CA. **Educ:** Los Angeles Valley Col, Dutchess Community Col. **Career:** Artist; first commissioned paintings, 1969; Inner City Cult Ctr, first one-woman show, 1977; Musee des Duncans, Paris, group exhibition; House Seagram comn Black Hist Month, 1989; Terry McMillan's Waiting to Exhale, int ed, cover art designer,1992; Atelier Saint James, owner, currently. **Orgs:** Panel, Paul Getty Trust Fund Visual Arts, 1992. **Honors/Awds:** Prix de Paris, 1980; Gentlemen Concerned Service Award, AIDS Found,1995; Greeting Card Artist Award, UNICEF, 1995; Parents Choice Silver Honor, 1996; Oppenhem Gold Award; Nappa Gold Award; Woman of the Year in Education, Los Angeles County Comn Women, 2004. **Special Achievements:** Designed the Kwanzaa stamp commissioned by the US Postal Service, 1997, Coretta Scott King Honor, illustrator, has own signature line of clocks, illustrator of 13 children's books, including three which she authored, 4 activity books, cookbook; has also written two books of poetry and prose. **Business Addr:** Owner, Atelier Saint James, PO Box 27683, Los Angeles, CA 90027, **Business Phone:** (323)993-5722.*

SAINT-JEAN, OLIVIER. **See ABDUL-WAHAD, TARIQ.**

SAINT-LOUIS, RUDOLPH ANTHONY
Lawyer. **Personal:** Born Dec 28, 1951, Port-au-Prince, Haiti; son of Libner and Georgette; married Elizabeth H Saint; children: Shaundri, Melissa & Yolanda. **Educ:** St Joseph's Col, BA, 1973; Univ Wis, Law Sch, Madison, JD, 1976. **Career:** Wis Dept Ind, Unemploy Div, hearing examr,1976-77; ICC, atty, adv, 1977-81; US Atty Off spec, asst US atty, 1980-81; ICC, SBA, staff atty, 1981-83; ICC, OPA, actg dir, 1983, staff atty, 1983; US Dept Transp, staff atty, currently. **Orgs:** Chair Employee Bd Educ, ICC; Fed Bar Asn, agency rep, 1980; pres, ICC Toastmasters, 1988 & 1990; pres, In-Com-Co Club, 1991-95; pres, Low Frequency Radio Astron, 1993-95. **Honors/Awds:** Cot Service Award, 1990 & 1991; EEO Award, ICC, 1991. **Home Addr:** 6500 Killarney St, Clinton, MD 20735, **Home Phone:** (301)856-7174. **Business Addr:** Staff Attorney, US Department of Transportation, Surface Transportation Board, 1925 K St NW Rm 848, Washington, DC 20423, **Business Phone:** (202)565-1590.*

SALAAM, ABDEL R
Executive, choreographer. **Personal:** Born Jan 1, 1950. **Educ:** Herbert H Lehman Col, BFA prog, 1973; Univ Ife, Nigeria, cert, 1979. **Career:** Ailey Dance Co, dancer; Joan Miller Chamber Arts/Dance Players; Fred Benjamin Dance Co; Ron Pratt's Alpha Omega 1-7 Theatrical Dance Co; Otis Salid's New Art Ensemble; Chuck Davis Dance Co, assoc artistic dir; Am Contemp Ballet Co, guest artist; Contemp Chamber Dance Theater, guest artist; Forces of Nature Dance Theatre Co, co founder, exec artistic dir & choreographer, 1981-; Nat Endowment for the Arts, choreographers fel, 1991-93, 1994-96. **Orgs:** Lehman Black Stud Orgn. **Honors/Awds:** Dance Africa Award, Brooklyn Acad Music, 1987; Carla Sayrce Alumni Award, Lehman Col City Univ NY, 1989; Morani Shujaa Award, Lehman Col City Univ NY, 1990; Monarch Merit Award, Nat Coun Arts & Cult, 1993; Silver Anniversary Award, Lehman Col City Univ NY, 1994; Better Family Life Lifetime Achievement Award, 2000; Entertainment Award, Best Musical Show in the World Within a Theme Park, 2004. **Home Addr:** 14 Mount Morris Pkwy, New York, NY 10027. **Business Addr:** Artistic Director, Forces of Nature Dance Theater Company, 14 Mount Morris Pkwy, New York, NY 10027, **Business Phone:** (212)289-2057.

SALAAM, DR. ABDUL (LEO MCCALLUM)
Dentist. **Personal:** Born Aug 18, 1929, Newark, NJ; son of Roosevelt McCallum and Katie Allen McCallum; married Khadijah, May 14, 1954; children: Sharonda Khan, Valerie Best, Robert, Darwin & Abdul II. **Educ:** Wash Sq Col, NY Univ, BS, 1952; Columbia Univ Sch Oral Dent Surgery, DDS, 1956; Acad Gen Dent, FAGD, 1973. **Career:** Specialty Promotions Co Inc, founder, 1959; Inst Grad Dent, postgrad instr, 1966-72; Books & Things, owner, 1969; Lincoln Dental Soc Bulletin, ed, 1972; Guaranty Bank, Chicago, IL, bd dir, 1976; Muhammad Ali Investment Corp, treas, 1988-90; Inst Gen Semantics, guest lectr, 1988-; Am Muslim Jour, newspaper columnist; Construct Systs Inc, chmn; First Africa Capital Investment Corp, Chicago, IL, treas, 1988-; pvt pract dent, currently. **Orgs:** Am Dent Asn, 1956-; pres, Specialty Promo Co Import Export, 1959-; Am Equilibration Soc, 1963-; pres, Commonwealth Dent Soc, NJ, 1964; Pierre Fauchard Soc; orgn pres, Nation Islam, 1976; bd dirs mem, Am Muslim Jour, 1982-84; pres, bd dir, New Earth Child Care Community Network, 1984-88; rep, Chicago Dent Soc Dialogue Dent, 1987-89; pres-elect, Kenwood Hyde Park Br Chicago Dent Soc, 1987-88; bd dir, Masjid Al' Fatir 1987-; bd dirs, Chicago Dent Soc, 1993-96. **Honors/Awds:** Man of the Year, Commonwealth Dental Soc, NJ, 1966; Dentist of the Year Award, Lincoln Dent Soc, Chicago, IL, 1989; Named in Honor, Dr Abdul Salaam Day, Mayor's Office, City Newark, NJ, 1989. **Special Achievements:** First African American in the Columbia University School of Oral & Dental Surgery school; First African American to import & distribute an English translation of the Holy Quran; Contributor of Archival Film & Consultant to "Malcolm X, An American Experience," TV Documentary. **Military Serv:** AUS, Med Corp pvt first class, 1947-48. **Business Addr:** Dentist, Abdul Salaam DDS, 1502 E 63rd St, Chicago, IL 60637, **Business Phone:** (773)496-5138.

SALAAM, EPHRAIM MATEEN
Football player. **Personal:** Born Jun 19, 1976, Chicago, IL; son of Malikah. **Educ:** San Diego State Univ, child develop, 1998. **Career:** Atlanta Falcons, tackle, 1998-01; Denver Broncos, 2002-03; Jacksonville jaguars, offensive tackle, 2004-05; Houston Texans, offensive tackle, 20062008; Detroit Lions, 2009-. **Orgs:** EMS Found. **Honors/Awds:** Bronze Panther academic award. **Business Addr:** Professional Football Player, Detroit Lions, 222 Republic Dr, Allen Park, MI 48101.*

SALAAM, RASHAAN IMAN
Football player. **Personal:** Born Oct 8, 1974, La Jolla, CA; son of Sultan Salaam and Khalada. **Educ:** Univ Colo. **Career:** Football player (retired); Chicago Bears, running back, 1995-97; Oakland Raiders; Cleveland Browns,1999; Green Bay Packers, 1999; Memphis Maniax (XFL), 2001; San Francisco 49ers, 2003; Toronto Argonauts Football Club (CFL), 2004. **Honors/Awds:** Heisman Trophy, 1994; Doak Walker Award, 1994. *

SALLEY, JOHN THOMAS
Basketball player, television show host. **Personal:** Born May 16, 1964, Brooklyn, NY; son of Quillie and Mazie Carter; married Natasha, 2001; children: 3. **Educ:** Ga Tech Col Mgt, 1988. **Career:** Basketball player (retired), TV show host; Detroit Pistons, power forward, 1986-92; Miami Heat, power forward, 1992-95; Toronto Raptors, power forward, 1995-96; Chicago Bulls, power forward, 1996; Panathinaikos BC,1996; Los Angeles Lakers, 2000; Funkee's Enterprises, pres; 100.3 The Beat, "The John Salley Block Party," 2005-06; Fox Sports Network, "The Best Damn Sports Show Period", currently;"One on One",2005; "HE's a lady",2005; "Stranded with a star, who would you choose?",2205; "Rescue Me", 2006; "Fast cars & superstars: Th Young guns celebrity Race", 2007, "Shaken not Stirred"; 2008-09; "Comedy Central Roast Of Larry The Cable Guy",2009; Hollywood Fame, co-owner, 2006-;Films: Bad Boys, 1995; A Fare to Remember, producer, 1998; Bad Boys II, 2003; The Ultimate Christmas Present; Eddie, 2003; Mr.3000, 2004; Hair Show, 2004; Rebound, 2005; Confessions of a Shopaholic, 2009. **Orgs:** Be The Best You Can Be; Metro Youth Found; Cancer Assn; Omega Phi Psi; NBA Stay Sch, Hepatitis B Campaign; comnr, Am Basketball Assn, 2006-. **Honors/Awds:** Unsung Hero Award; I Have a Dream Award. **Business Addr:** Host, Fox Sports Net, The Best Damn Sports Show Period, 10201 W Pico Blvd Bldg 101 Suite 5420, Los Angeles, CA 90035, **Business Phone:** (310)369-1000.

SALLEY, LAWRENCE C.
Commissioner. **Career:** Westchester County Dept Transp, transp comnr, currently. **Business Addr:** Transportation Commissioner, Westchester County Department of Transportation, 148 Martine Ave, White Plains, NY 10601.*

SALMON, DR. JASLIN URIAH
Educator. **Personal:** Born Jan 4, 1942, Darliston, Jamaica; son of Leaford and Jane Sylent; married Dr Anita Hawkins; children: Ja-

net Felice & Jennifer Renee. **Educ:** Olivet Nazarene Univ, BA, 1969; Ball State Univ, MA, 1970; Univ Ill, Chicago, PhD, 1977. **Career:** Ball State Univ, teaching asst, 1969-70; George Williams Col, asst prof sociol, 1970-76; Triton Col, prof sociol, 1976-77, 1977-79; Human Resource Develop Govt Jamaica, dir, 1977-79; Triton Col, dir ctr parenting, 1985-88; Office Prime Minister Jamaica, dir adv, 1997-; The Jamaica Red Cross, vpres, 2002, Poverty Eradication Prog, nat coordr, pres, 2005-. **Orgs:** Social worker,Dept Ment Health IL, 1968-69; dir, HOPE, 1973-75; dir & mem, Chicago Forum, 1971-72; chmn, Academic Senate George Williams Col, 1974; consult, Parenting Women & Minorities; pres, NAACP Oak Park, Ill Branch, 1989-94. **Honors/Awds:** Teacher of the Year, George Williams Col, 1973; author, "Black Executives in White Business" 1979. **Home Addr:** Lot 3 Woodlands Red Hills, PO Box 1, St Andrews 60303-0586, Jamaica. **Business Addr:** President, Jamaica Red Cross Headquarters, 76 Arnold Rd, Kingston 5, Jamaica, **Business Phone:** (876)984-7860.

SALMOND, JASPER
Executive. **Personal:** Born Jul 5, 1930, Camden, SC; son of James and Dora James; married Thelma Brooks, May 25, 1954; children: Jeryl Gerald Salmond & Jenita LaZelda Salmond. **Educ:** Benedict Col, BA (magna cum laude), educ, 1954; Columbia Univ, Teachers Col, MA, educ admin, 1960; Atlanta Univ, cert, Sch Systs Admin, 1963; Univ SC, exten course. **Career:** Executive (retired); Richland Co Sch Dist One, from sch teacher to prin, 1954-72; Wilbur Smith Assocs Inc, prin assoc, United Nations contact, proj develop, community involvement planning, sr mktg coordr, vpres, 1972. **Orgs:** Pres & parliamentarian, Benedict Col Nat Alumni, 1960-98; vpres, SC Elem Sch Prins, 1971-72; chmn, Terrific Kids Prog, 1975-99; bd comm, Midlands Tech Col, 1975-91; comn secy, Midlands Tech Col, 1989-90; secy, 1990-2003, vpres, 1995-96, pre-elect, 1997, pres, 1998, bd dirs, 1992-2000, SC Sch Bds Asn; regional rep, Afro-Am Coalition Comm, Asn Community Col Trustees, 1990-91; bd comnrs, 1990-, chmn, 1993-94, parliamentarian, 1998, chairperson finance & facilities comm, 1995-97, Richland Co Sch Dist One; bd dirs, Rep Nat Bank, 1992-94; regional officer, completing distinguished toastmasters requirements, Toastmasters Int, 1993-; bd dirs, 1993-2000, chmn, 1996-97, Guardian Ad Litem; bd dirs, technol comm, 1994-98, Mortgage bd, 1998-, Carolina First Bank; chairperson exec coun & exec comm, Greater Columbia Chamber Com, 1996-98; bd dirs, 1996-2005, treas, Palmetto Health Systs; Alpha Phi Alpha Fraternity; Alpha Psi Lambda Chap; chap chmn, Am Red Cross; chmn, Conv Plenary Presenter; pres & exec comm mem, Columbia Kiwanis Club; NEA, Nat Prin Asn; life mem, NAACP; Richland County Sch; bd trustees, Richland Memorial Hosp; bd dir, Pledged Alpha. **Honors/Awds:** Man of the Year, Alpha Psi Lambda Chap, 1976, 1992; Outstanding Alumnus, Dedicated Serv Bd Trustees, Benedict Col, 1980; Meritorious Service, 1989, Outstanding Service as Commissioner, 1991, African-Am Asn, Midlands Tech Col; Achievement Award, Alphas Columbia, 1992; Service Award, Columbia Chamber Com; Level III School Boardmanship Inst Training Award, 1992; Lula J Gambrell Award, Top Distinguished Alumnus, 1995; Order of the Palmetto, SC, Governors, 2002; Global Vision Award, Columbia World Affairs Coun, 2003; numerous others. **Military Serv:** AUS, mil police, corporal, 1954-56; Good Conduct Medal. **Home Addr:** 4035 Coronado Dr, Columbia, SC 29203, **Home Phone:** (803)765-2795.

SALMONS, JOHN. See SALMONS, JOHN RASHALL.

SALMONS, JOHN RASHALL (JOHN SALMONS)
Basketball player. **Personal:** Born Dec 12, 1979, Philadelphia, PA. **Educ:** Miami Univ. **Career:** Philadelphia 76ers, forward, 2002-06; Sacramento Kings, Guard, 2007-09; Chicago Bulls, 2009-. **Honors/Awds:** Big E Sportsmanship Award, 2002; Most Valuable Player hons; MostOutstanding Player, Boston Reebok pro summer league, 2003. *

SALONE, MARCUS
Judge. **Personal:** Born Apr 28, 1949, Chicago, IL; son of Herbert Spencer and Anna Rae; married Valee Glover, Oct 29, 1976; children: Lisa Michelle & Andrea Valee. **Educ:** Univ Ill, Chicago Circle Campus, BA, 1974; John Marshall Law Sch, JD, 1981. **Career:** Cook Co State's Atty's Off, asst, 1981-83; Salone, Salone, Simmons, Murray & Assocs, 1983-91; Circuit Ct Cook Co, assoc judge, 1991-. **Orgs:** Life mem, Kappa Alpha Psi Fraternity, 1987-; bd dirs, Cook Co Bar Asn, 1988-; bd dirs, Ancona Montessori Sch, 1988-90; bd dirs, John Howard Asn, 1994-. **Honors/Awds:** Meitorious Service Award, Cook Co Bar Asn, 1988; Judiciary Service Award, Cook Co Bar Asn, 1991; Monarch Award, Alpha Kappa Alpha Sorority, 1992. **Military Serv:** AUS, Spc4, 1969-71; Vietnam campaign award; service award. **Home Addr:** 6830 S Bennett, Chicago, IL 60649. **Business Addr:** Associate Judge, Circuit Court, Cook County Judicial Circuit, Richard J Daley Ctr, 50 W Wash St Rm 1001, Chicago, IL 60602, **Business Phone:** (312)603-2600.

SALTER, KWAME S
Executive, vice president (organization). **Personal:** Born Jan 31, 1946, Delhi, LA; son of Reva Daniels and Samuel Leon (deceased); married Phyllis V Harris, Jan 31, 1987; children: Kevin-Jamal, Keri-JaMelda & Matthew-Harrison. **Educ:** Wis State Univ, Whitewater, EdB (magna cum Laude), 1968; Univ Wis, Madison, MA, educ admin, 1970. **Career:** Milwaukee Pub Sch Bd Educ, teacher, 1968-69; Wis State Univ, Whitewater, acad counr, 1968-70; Univ Wis, Madison, proj asst, 1969-70; Univ Wis, Madison, Afro-Am Cult Ctr, exec dir, 1970-73, Ford Found, fel educ, 1970; Dane Co Parent Coun Inc, exec dir, 1976-86; Bd Educ Madison Metrop Sch Dist, pres, 1982-86; Oscar Mayer Foods Corp, dir employ pub rels; Kraft/Oscar Mayer Foods Corp, vpres human resources, sales & customer serv, 1986-. **Orgs:** Pres, Exec Coun Cult Interaction & Awareness Inc, 1973; vpres, Nat Asn Advan Colored People, Madison Chap, 1974-75; Madison Downtown Optimist Serv Club, 1977; pres, Common Touch Inc, 1977-; Admin Mgt Soc, 1978-; vpres, Madison Metrop Sch Dist Bd Educ, 1980; Phi Delta Kappa 1980-; chmn, Wis State Adv Comn US Civil Rights Comn, 1985-87; chmn, Stud Readiness Comt, Governor's Comn 21st Century; African-Am Alumni Asn; Nat Career Develop Asn. **Honors/Awds:** Outstanding Leader & Educator, Kappa Phi Chap, Omega Psi Phi Fraternity Inc, Milwaukee, 1979; State Leaders 80's Wis, Milwaukee Jour Newspaper, 1980; Outstanding Recent Alumni Award, Univ Wis, Whitewater, 1986; State of Wisconsin Public Interest Award. **Business Addr:** Vice President for Human resources, Sales & Customer Service, Kraft/Oscar Mayer Foods Corporation, 910 Mayer Ave, Madison, WI 53704, **Business Phone:** (608)241-3311.

SALTER, ROGER FRANKLIN
Executive, president (organization). **Personal:** Born Jul 15, 1940, Chicago, IL; married Jacqueline M Floyd; children: Dawn, Roger J, Marc CPres, Sanmar Fin. **Educ:** Chicago Teachers Col, BE, 1962; DePaul Univ. **Career:** Ins Sales, asst mgr, 1964; Chicago MetAsrnc Co, second ldng agt, 1962-63; Mutual Benifit Life, agt, 1965-70; Blkbrn Agency Mutual Benifit Life, asst gen agt, 1970-74; Sanmar Financial Planning Corp, pres, currently. **Orgs:** dir, sec second vpres, first vpres S Side Br Chicago Assn of Life Underwriters; exec dir, Fin for S Shore Comm; pres, Ekrsll Nghrs Comm Grp; bd dir, Mile Sqr Health Ctr; mem, NAACP; Chicago Urban League; Natl Bus League; Chicago Area Coun Boy Scouts of Am; Omega Psi Phi Frat; life mem, Mlln Dllr Rnd Tbl, 1972-; fourth Blk in US. **Honors/Awds:** Man of Yr, 1965-67; Natl Qulty Award Ins Sales, 1971; 10 Outst Bus Award Jycs, 1972. **Business Addr:** President, Sanmar Financial Planning Group, 1327 W Washington Blvd Suite 102, Chicago, IL 60607, **Business Phone:** (708)422-6600.

SALTER, SAM
Singer. **Personal:** Born Feb 16, 1978, Los Angeles, CA. **Career:** Albums: It's On Tonight, 1997; The Little Black Book, 2000; Strictly For Da Bedroom, 2008; Singles: "After 12, Before 6", 1997; "There You Are/It's on Tonight", 1998; "Tell Me", 1996; "Never Make a Promise", 1997; "In My Bed", 1997; "We're Not Making Love No More", 1997; "Once My Shit (Always My Shit)", 2000; The Little Black Book, 2002. **Business Addr:** Vocalist, c/o Red Zone Entertainment, 400 Galleria Pkwy SE Suite 1500, Atlanta, GA 30339, **Business Phone:** (678)244-1100.*

SALTERS, DR. CHARLES ROBERT
School administrator. **Personal:** Born Nov 1, 1943, St Stephen, SC; son of Willie D and Marie Izzard; married Vivian Governor, Apr 13, 1968; children: Bobvita Shawntrea & Dorian Mont. **Educ:** SC State Col, Orangeburg, SC, BS, 1965; Atlanta Univ, Atlanta, GA, MA, 1971; Morgan State Univ, Baltimore, MD, MS, 1977; Univ Md, College Park, EDd, 1985. **Career:** State Md, Henry Welcome fel, 1984; Atlanta Bd Educ; Morgan State Univ, asst dean grad studies & res, mentor, currently; . **Orgs:** Nat Sci Found, 1970-71; Alpha Phi Alpha Fraternity Inc, 1973; Phi Delta Kappa, 1982; Union Bethel AME Church, 1984; Alpha Lamba Delta, 1990; Golden Key, 1995. **Honors/Awds:** Dr. Charles Salters Special Achievement Award, honor. **Military Serv:** AUS, capt, 1965-68; Meritorious Service Award, 1967. **Business Phone:** (443)885-3333.

SAM, SHERI (SHERI LYNETTE SAM)
Basketball player. **Personal:** Born May 5, 1974, Lafayette, LA. **Educ:** Vanderbilt Univ, attended 1996. **Career:** San Jose Lasers, guard, 1996; Orlando Miracle, 1999; Miami Sol, 2000-03; Seattle Storm, forward-guard, 2004; Charlotte Sting, guard, 2005-06; Indiana Fever, Forward, Guard, 2007; Detroit shock, Panionios, currently. **Business Addr:** Professional Basketball Player, Indiana Pacers, Conseco Fieldhouse, 1 Conseco Ct 125 S Pennsylvania St, Indianapolis, IN 46204, **Business Phone:** (317)917-2500.*

SAM, SHERI LYNETTE. See SAM, SHERI.

SAMARA, NOAH AZMI
Executive. **Personal:** Born Aug 8, 1956, Addis Abeba, Ethiopia; son of Ibrahim Azmi and Yeshiemebet Zerfou; married Martha Debebe, May 6, 1989; children: Leila & Gideon. **Educ:** E Stroudsburg Univ, East Stroudsburg, Pa, BA, 1975-78; Univ Calif, Los Angeles, Calif, hist; Georgetown Univ, Wash, MS, Int Bus Diplomacy, 1985; Georgetown Univ Sch Law, JD, 1985. **Career:** Law Offices Rothblatt & Millstein, Wash, DC, law clerk, 1981-84; Geostar Corp, Wash, DC, staff atty, 1984-86, dir internal affairs, 1986-88; Robbins & Laramie, Wash, DC, coun, 1988-89; Venable, Baetjer & Howard, Wash, DC, coun, 1989-90; WorldSpace Inc, Wash, DC, chmn & chief exec officer, 1990-. **Honors/Awds:** Pacem In Terris; Commander, Order of the Lion, Senegal. **Business Addr:** Chairman, Chief Executive Officer, WorldSpace Incorporated, One Worldspace 8515 Georgia Ave, Silver Spring, MD 20910, **Business Phone:** (301)960-1200.

SAMKANGE, TOMMIE MARIE (TOMMIE MARIE ANDERSON SAMKANGE)
Educational psychologist. **Personal:** Born Aug 1, 1932, Jackson, MS; daughter of Harry and Marie Hughes; widowed 1988; children: Stanlake jr &, Harry M. **Educ:** Tougaloo Col, BS, 1953; Ind Univ, MS, 1955, PhD 1958. **Career:** Tougaloo Col, asst prof, 1955-56; African Pub Rels, Harare, Zimbabwe, psychologist, market researcher, 1959-64; Tuskegee Inst, assoc prof, 1964-67; Tenn St Univ, assoc prof, 1967-71; Harvard Univ, Cambridge, Mass, sr tutor, 1971-74; Harvard Univ, Afro-Am Studies Dept, lect headtutor, 1971-74; Tufts Univ, asst prof, 1974-76; Northeastern Univ, lect, 1979; Ministry of Educ & Cul, Zimbabwe, chief educ officer, psychol, special educ & early childhood educ, 1981-94, dir, 1994-; Govt Zimbabwe, chief educational psychologist, 1981-94; Chinyaradzo Children's Home, Zimbabwe, bd dirs, 1982; Moleli Sec Sch, Selous, Zimbabwe, bd govt, 1988; Stnlk Smkng, prof; Salem St Col, asst dir minority affairs; Ranche House Col, Harare, chairperson, 1992-96; Nyatsime Col, Chitungwiza, Zimbabwe, fac, 1995; Proposed S African Method Univ, fac, 1997. **Orgs:** Am Psychol Asn; League Women Vtrs; Health Prof Coun Zimbabwe; Zimbabwe Psychol Asn; Ranche House Col Citizenship. **Honors/Awds:** Mellon Found Grant, 1977; Fellow Am Asn Advan Sci; Consortium of Doctors, Women of Color in the Struggle, 1993. **Home Addr:** The Castle Chiremba Rd PO Hatfield, Harare 00000, Zimbabwe.

SAMPLE, HERBERT ALLAN
Journalist. **Personal:** Born Mar 19, 1961, Los Angeles, CA; son of Herbert Warner and Ramona Adams; married Kathy R Yarrell, Oct 13, 2002. **Educ:** Pepperdine Univ, Malibu, CA, 1981; Calif State Univ, Sacramento, CA, BA, govt, journ, 1983. **Career:** Los Angeles Times, reporter, 1983-85; Sacramento Bee, reporte, capitol bur, 1986-91, 1992-93, Bay Area Correspondent, 2001, writer, currently; Dallas Times Herald, chief capitol bur, 1991; McClatchy Newspapers, Wash Bur, reporter, 1993-2000. **Orgs:** Vpres, Black Journalists Asn Southern Calif, 1985; pres & founder, Sacramento Black Journalists Asn, 1988-; Nat Asn Black Journalists, 1986-2000; Wash Asn Black Journalists, 1993-2000, pres, 1999; Bay Area Black Journalists Asn, 2001-. **Business Addr:** Writer, The Sacramento Bee, 4100-10 Redwood Rd Suite 221, PO Box 15779, Oakland, CA 94619, **Business Phone:** (510)382-1978.

SAMPLE, JOE
Musician, activist. **Personal:** Born Feb 1, 1939, Houston, TX; children: Nicklas. **Educ:** Tex Southern Univ, piano. **Career:** The Crusaders; pianist; solo artist, 1978-; Albums: Fancy Dance, 1969; Rainbow Seeker, 1978; Carmel, 1979; Voices In The Rain, 1980; The Hunter, 1982; Roles, 1983; Oasis, 1989; Spellbound, 1989; Ashes To Ashes, 1990; Invitation, 1993; Do You Feel That?, 1994; Old Places, Old Faces, 1996; Sample This, 1997; The Song Lives On, 1999; Moulin Rouge, 2001; The Pecan Tree, 2002; Soul Shadows, 2004; Feeling Good, 2007. **Special Achievements:** Has recorded with Miles Davis, Joni Mitchell, Mahalia Jackson, Michael Franks, Al Jarreau, Marcus Miller. **Business Addr:** Composer, Musican, Patrick Rains & ASC, New York, NY 10025.

SAMPLE, WILLIAM AMOS (BILL SAMPLE)
Writer, baseball player, broadcaster. **Personal:** Born Apr 2, 1955, Roanoke, VA; son of William T and Nora; married Debra Evans; children: Nikki, Ian & Travis. **Educ:** James Madison Univ, BS Psychol, 1978. **Career:** Baseball player (retired), Broadcaster; Tex Rangers, outfielder 1978-84;NY Yankees, 1985; Atlanta Braves, 1986; ESPN, broadcaster, studio analyst,color analyst, 1991-93; Baseball Weekly, USA Today, writer; AtlantaBraves, TV & radio broadcaster, 1988-89; Universal 9 WWOR-TV, broadcaster,1990; Seattle Mariners, TV broadcaster, 1992; Calif Angels, radio anal-,play by play broadcaster, 1993-94; Pennant Chase-Baseball Inside Out,Phoenix Comn, 1996; Maj League Baseball Radio, talk show host, reporter,writer, 2001-. **Orgs:** Major League Baseball Players Asns Licensing Comt, 1986-87; consult, Major League Baseball-Umpire Rev Bd, 1995. **Honors/Awds:** Man of the Year, Tex Rangers Womens Club, 1984; Topps All-Rookie Team,1979; 5th in American League Stolen Bases, 1983; Outfielder on Topps Major League All-Rookie Team; Hall of Fame, Inaugural Roanoke-Salem Baseball, 1992. **Special Achievements:** Articles published in the New York Times, "Views of Sport," 1987; Article published in Sports Illustrated, "The Point After," 1987; Articles published in The National Sports Daily, 1990; Voice used for voice-over in industrial films. Movie consultant, "Joe Torre: Curveballs Along the Way,"Show time Network Inc, 1997. **Business Addr:** Writer, Reporter, MLB Advanced Media, 75 9th Ave 5th Fl, New York, NY 10011, **Business Phone:** (512)434-1542.

SAMPLES, BENJAMIN NORRIS. See Obituaries section.

SAMPLES, JARED LANIER
Government official. **Personal:** Born Jan 22, 1965, Atlanta, GA; son of Cadmus Allen and Dorothy Burns. **Educ:** Ga State Univ,

BS, 1989. **Career:** Atlanta Housing Authority, Atlanta, GA, weatherization specialist, 1982; NW Perry Recreation Ctr, Atlanta, GA, youth counr, 1985; Ga State Univ, handicapped serv counr, 1988; Metrop Atlanta, Rapid Transit Authority, Atlanta, GA, intern, 1989; Atlanta City Coun, council mem, Dist 9, 1996; campaign mgr, 2003. **Orgs:** Bd mem, Bd Comnrs-Atlanta, Housing Authority; bd mem, Bd Dirs, Econ Opportunity Atlanta; bd mem, Atlanta Police Citizen Rev Bd; vpres, Perry Homes Tenant Asn. **Honors/Awds:** Martin Luther King Tribute Speaker Award, J C Harris Elem Sch; 50 Most Young Promising Black Am, Ebony Mag; Lt Colonel, Aide De Camp, Former Gov Joe Frank Harris; Proclamation Outstanding Community Serv, State Ga. **Business Addr:** Councilmember, Atlanta City Council, 55 Trinity Ave SW, Atlanta, GA 30303.

SAMPSON, REV. DR. ALBERT RICHARD
Clergy. **Personal:** Born Nov 27, 1938, Boston, MA; son of Paul and Mildred Howell; divorced. **Educ:** Shaw Univ, BA, 1961; Governor's State Univ, MA, 1973; McCormick Theol Sem, DIV, 1977; Union Baptist Theol Sem, Ddiv, 2000. **Career:** Newark New Jersy Poor People's Campaign, proj dir; Zion Baptist Church Everett MA, pastor; Fernwood United Methodist Church, sr pastor, currently. **Orgs:** Spokesman Ministers Action Comn Jobs, 1985-92; pres, Nat Black Farmers Harvest & Bus Corp, 1989; speaker, Million Man March, 1995; consult, Poverty prog, Syracuse NY, Wilmington DE, Indianapolis IN, Boston MA; founder, Black Churches Coun; int vpres, training Allied Workers Int Union; vice chmn, Mayor Harold Washington's First Source Task Force; vpres, Roseland Clergy Asn; biblical scholar, Original African Heritage Bible; chmn, Million Man March MAPCO, Metro Area, planning corp, Chicago; nat field secy, Nat African Leadership Summit; bd mem, Univ Ill Col Urban Bus; chaplain, World Conf Mayors. **Honors/Awds:** Christian Award, 1981; Westside People for Progress Award, 1983; South Shore Chamber of Commerce Award, 1983; Martin Luther King Jr Award, Int Black Writer's Asn, 1983. **Special Achievements:** Organized Dr Martin Luther King's low income cooperative housing program entitled 221d3, the only one of its kind in the nation; traveled fact finding mission to Angola, South Africa, Israel, Lebanon, Kenya, Tanzania, Zaire, Caribbean, Bermuda; publ: From Africa to the Americas: One God for One People, 1979, The Market Place from 1990-2000, Professional Agricultural Workers Conference, 1990; Only Christian Minister Traveled 18 African Countries, Friendship Tour with the Honorable Minister Louis Farrakhan; Featured Jet Magazine, Minority Builders Magazine, Chicago Sun-Times, Chicago Tribune. **Home Addr:** 10056 S Parnell, Chicago, IL 60628. **Business Addr:** Senior Pastor, Fernwood United Methodist Church, 10057 S Wallace, Chicago, IL 60628, **Business Phone:** (773)445-7125.

SAMPSON, DR. CALVIN COOLIDGE
Educator, editor. **Personal:** Born Feb 1, 1928, Cambridge, MD; son of Robert Henry (deceased) and Hattie Mae Stanley (deceased); married Corrine Delores Pannell, 1953; children: Cathleen Dale & Judith Gail. **Educ:** Hampton Inst Univ, BS, Chem, 1947; Meharry Med Col, MD, 1951. **Career:** Episcopal Hosp Philadelphia PA, asst dir lab, 1956-58; Freedmen's Hosp Howard Univ, dir lab, 1958-75; Howard Univ Col Med, asst prof Path, 1958, prof pathol, emer prof pathol; J Nat Med Assn Wash DC, ed, 1978, ed emer, currently. **Orgs:** Vpres bd trustees, Hosp for Sick Children Wash DC, 1979-85. **Honors/Awds:** 105 scientific articles published in med journals. **Military Serv:** AUS, col, 1953-76. **Home Addr:** 1614 Varnum Pl NE, Washington, DC 20017. **Business Addr:** Editor Emeritus, National Medical Association, 1012 Tenth St NW, Washington, DC 20001, **Business Phone:** (202)347-1895.

SAMPSON, CHARLES
Entertainer. **Personal:** Born Jul 2, 1957, Los Angeles, CA; married Marilyn; children: Laurence Charles & Daniel. **Educ:** Cent Ariz Col. **Career:** Rodeo Cowboys Asn circuit, prof, 1977; Presidential Command Performance Rodeo, 1983; bull rider, 1994; Berkshire Farm Ctr & Serv Youth, mentor, Therap Riding Prog, asst dir, currently. **Honors/Awds:** World Champion Bull Rider, 1982. Championships: Sierra Circuit, 1984, Turquoise Circuit, 1985-86, Copenhagen & Skoal, 1992, Calgary Stampede, Pendleton (OR) Round-Up, Grand Nat Rodeo, Calif Rodeo, Del Rio bull-riding buckle, Rodeo Superstars; Prof Rodeo Hall of Fame, 1996. **Special Achievements:** First African American World Champion Bull Rider; was hired by Timex to promote the durability of their watches; signed endorsement contract with Wrangler jeans; appeared 10 times in Nat Finals Rodeo. **Business Addr:** Assistant Director for the Therapeutic Riding Program, Berkshire Farm Center and Services for Youth, 13640 Rte 22, Canaan, NY 12029, **Business Phone:** (518)781-4567.

SAMPSON, DR. HENRY THOMAS
Engineer. **Personal:** Born Apr 22, 1934, Jackson, MS; son of Henry T and Esther Sampson; divorced; children: Henry III & Martin. **Educ:** Purdue Univ, BS, Chem Engineering, 1956; Univ Calif, Los Angeles, MS, Engineering, 1961; Univ Ill, Urbana, MS, Nuclear Engineering, 1965, PhD, Nuclear Physics, 1967. **Career:** US Naval Weapons Ctr, China Lake, CA, res chem engr 1956-61; res consult several documentary films; Pioneer Black Filmmakers, lectr; Aerospace Corp, El Segundo, CA, proj engr, 1967-81, dir Planning & Opers, dirate Space Test Prog, 1981-. **Orgs:** AAAS; Am Nuclear Soc; Omega Psi Phi; fac adv comn, Nuclear Eng, 1976-. **Honors/Awds:** US Naval Educ Fel, 1962-64; Atomic Energy Comn (AEC), Fel, 1964-67; several patents engineering devices, 1957-65; Scarecrow Press, 1977; Black Image Award, Aerospace Corp, 1982; 'Blacks in Engineering, Applied Science, and Education Award', Los Angeles Counc Black Prof Engrs, 1983. **Special Achievements:** Author, "Blacks in Black & White-A Source Book on Black Films 1910-50", "Blacks in Blackface, A Source Book on Early Black Musical Shows", Scarecrow Press, 1980, "The Ghost Walks, A Chronological History of Blacks in Show Business 1863-10", Scarecrow Press, 1987, "Blacks in Black and White", Scarecrow Press, 1995; That's Enough Folks: Black Images in Animated Cartoons, Scarecrow Press, 1998; Swingin on the Ether Waves: A Chronological History of African Americans in Radio & Television Programming, 1925-1955; Co-invented the Gamma-Electric cell, 1971. **Home Addr:** PO Box 648, El Segundo, CA 90245. **Business Addr:** Director of Planning and Operations, Aerospace Corporation, Directorate of Space Test Program, 2350 E El Segundo Blvd, El Segundo, CA 90245-4691, **Business Phone:** (310)336-5000.

SAMPSON, JAMES S.
Executive. **Career:** Sampson Assocs, managing dir. **Business Phone:** (510)531-4237.*

SAMPSON, KELVIN
Basketball coach. **Personal:** Born Oct 5, 1955, Laurinburg, NC. **Educ:** Pembroke State Univ, BA, physical educ & polit sci, 1978; Mich State, MS, coaching admin, 1980. **Career:** Basketball player (retired), basketball coach; Pembroke State, guard, 1974-78; Michigan State Univ, asst coach, 1979-80; Montana Tech, coach, 1981-85; Wash State Univ, asst coach, 1985-87, head coach, 1987-94; UnivOkla, head coach, 1994-2006; Ind Univ, coach, 2006-07. **Orgs:** USA Basketball Men's Collegiate Comt, 1997-2000. **Honors/Awds:** Frontier Conference Coach of the Year, 1983, 1985; Pac 10 Coach of the Year, 1991; District 14 Coach of the Year, 1991, 1993; Basketball Coach, US Olympic Festival, 1993; Big Eight Coach of the Year, 1995; Asniated Press Coach of the Year, 1995, 2002; Nat coach of the year, 1995, 2002;USBWA Nat Coach of the Year, 1995; Basketball Weekly Nat Coach of the Year, 1995; Montana Tech Hall of Fame, 1996; Pembroke State Athletic Hall of Fame, 1998; Col Hoops Insider Big 12 Coach of the Year, 2000, 2001; NABC Nat Coach of the Year, 2002; Chevrolet Nat Coach of the Year, 2002; Bucks Roster,ass coach, 2008-. **Business Phone:** 877-428-2825.

SAMPSON, MARVA W
Executive, association executive. **Personal:** Born Sep 4, 1936, Hamilton, OH; daughter of Willie Ray Sudbury (deceased) and Isiah Wells (deceased); married Norman C, Sep 29, 1956; children: Raymond & Anthony. **Educ:** Miami Univ; Univ Dayton, MPA, 1976. **Career:** Executive (retired); Hamilton Ohio City Sch System, pvt secy, 1954-58, off mgr, 1958-59; Citizens Coun Human Rels, coord secy, 1966-70; City Middletown, dept community develop, relocations officer, 1964-66, dir dept human resources, 1971. **Orgs:** Bd dir, YMCA, 1971; Ohio Munic League, 1978; bd trust, ASPA 1978; pres, Pi Alpha Alpha, 1979; pres, Ctr Forensic Psychiatry, 1979-80; choir dir, pianist 2nd Baptist Church; exec bd mem, Arts Middletown; bd trustees, Cent Ohio River Valley Asn; exec comt mem, Butler County C Serv Bd; pres, Middletown Area Safety Coun; secy/coordr, Middletown Job Opportunity Inc; exec comm mem, Middletown Area United Way; Nat Asn Social Workers; Ohio Pub Health Asn; Human Serv Coun; Friends Sorg; Ohio Parks & Recreation Asn; Nat Parks & Recreation Asn; Am Soc Pub Admin; Human Resources Comt; Int Personnel Mgt Asn; ecec mem, State Ohio, Alcohol & Drug Addiction Serv Bd. **Honors/Awds:** Cert Merit, Serv C C, 1968; Lady of the Week, Woman of the Year, WPFB Radio Sta, 1970; Red Triangle Award, YMCA 1971-76; Outstanding Citizens Award, Knights Social Club, 1972; Community Center Selective Award; Leisure Professional Cert, Ohio Parks & Recreation Asn, 1992-95; NAACP & Southside Community Image Award, NAACP, 1994; Volunteer of the Year, Middletown United Way, 1996; JC Penney Golden Rule Award, 1997; Woman of the Year, Butler County, 1997. **Home Addr:** 6366 W Alexandria Rd, Middletown, OH 45042. **Business Phone:** (513)425-7840.

SAMPSON, RALPH
Basketball coach, basketball player. **Personal:** Born Jul 7, 1960, Harrisonburg, VA; married; children (previous marriage): 1; married Aleize Rena Dial (divorced 2003); children: 4. **Educ:** Univ Va, BA, speech Comm, 1983. **Career:** Basketball player (retired), basketball coach; Univ Va, ctr basketball player; Houston Rockets, 1984-88; Golden State Warriors, 1988-89; Sacramento Kings, 1990-91; Washington Bullets, 1991-92; James Madison Univ, asst coach, 1992; minor league, Richmond, Va, coach. **Honors/Awds:** John R. Wooden Award, 1982-83; NBA Rookie of the Year, 1984; NCAA Player of the Year; All Am; Rookie of the Year; MVP, All Star, 1985; mem, 36th & 37th NBA All Star Team; Virginia Sports Hall of Fame, 1996. *

SAMPSON, ROBERT R
Pharmacist. **Personal:** Born Oct 17, 1924, Clinton, NC; son of Frank J and Annie Curry; married Myrtle B; children: Frank R Sampson. **Educ:** Fayetteville State Univ, Fayetteville NC, 1942-43; Howard Univ, Wash, DC, BS, Pharm, 1946-50. **Career:** Sampson's Pharm, owner. **Orgs:** Pres NC, Old N St Pharm Soc; mem-at-large, NPhA; Incorp Chap Stockholder Gateway Bank; Am Pharm Asn; Nat Asn Retail Druggists; Greensboro Med Soc; Greensboro Soc Pharm; Omega Psi Phi Frat; Nat Pharm Asn; UMLA; Greensboro C of C. **Military Serv:** AUS, combat infantry. **Home Addr:** 4608 Splitrail Ct, Greensboro, NC 27406, **Home Phone:** (336)697-1220. **Business Addr:** Owner, Sampson, 1502 E Market St, Greensboro, NC 27401, **Business Phone:** (336)272-3131.

SAMPSON, RONALD ALVIN
Advertising executive. **Personal:** Born Nov 13, 1933, Charlottesville, VA; son of Percy and Lucile Mills Martin; married Norvelle Johnson Sampson, Aug 8, 1959; children: David, Cheryl. **Educ:** DePaul Univ, BS, commerce, 1956. **Career:** advert exec (retired); Ebony Mag, advert sales rep, 1958-63; Foote Cone & Belding Advert, merchandising supvr, 1963-66; Tatham Laird Kudner Advert, partner & mgt supvr, 1966-78; Am Asn Advert Agencies, advisor, 1972; Burrell Advert, exec v pres, 1978-81, sr v pres, exec vp development; D'Arcy MacManus Masius Advert, sr vp, 1981-89; Chicago United, deacon; Burrell Commun Group, dir develop. **Orgs:** v pres, bd dir, Community Renewal Soc, 1973-93; co-chair, Protestants Common Good; Am Advert FED Diversity Comn; Chicago Forum. **Military Serv:** AUS, sp 4, 1956-58. *

SAMPSON, THOMAS GATEWOOD
Lawyer. **Personal:** Born Oct 4, 1946, Durham, NC; son of Daniel and Claretta; married Jacquelyn Sampson MD, Jun 5, 1968; children: Thomas G II & Alia J. **Educ:** Morehouse Col, BA, 1968; Univ NC, Sch Law, JD, 1971. **Career:** Thomas, Kennedy, Sampson & Patterson, managing partner & atty, 1971-, sr prtner, currently; Int Bus fel, 1983; Ga State Law Sch, adj prof law, 1985-93; Ga State Univ Col Law, adj prof law, 1986-93; instr, Atlanta Col Trial Advocacy; instr, Nat Inst Trial Advocacy; Logan E Bleckley Inn Ct, master; Logan Inn Am Inns Ct, master. **Orgs:** NC & Ga Bar Asn; regional dir, Nat Bar Asn, 1974-75, mem, curently; vpres, Atlanta Coun Younger Lawyers, 1974-75; pres, Gate City Bar Asn, 1977; second vpres, Atlanta Legal Aid Soc, 1979; vice-chmn, State Bar Disciplinary Bd, 1984; Ga Supreme Ct Comn Racial & Ethnic Bias; Chief Justice's Comn Professionalism, 1990-94; chmn, State Bar Ga Client's Security Fund, 1991; bd dirs, Atlanta Bar Asn, 1992-93; inducted, Am Bd Trial Advocates, 1993; bd gov, State Bar Ga, 1994-; Ga Supreme Ct Comn Racial & Ethnic Bias, 1994-96; vice-chair, Judicial Nominating Comn State Ga, 1999-. **Honors/Awds:** Man of the Year, Omega Psi Phi, Psi Chap, 1991; Best Lawyers in America, 1991-; Listed in Best Lawyers, Atlanta Mag, 2000 & 2002. **Business Phone:** (404)688-4503.

SAMUEL, ANTOINETTE ALLISON
Chief executive officer. **Educ:** Chatham Col, BA; Tex Southern Univ, Ctr Asn Leadership, Cert Assoc Exec. **Career:** Employee Asst Prof Asn, chief exec officer, currently; Am Soc Pub Admin, exec dir, currently. **Orgs:** Employee Asst Prof Asn; UN Asn; Am Soc Asn Execs, 2005-06.

SAMUEL, DAVID
Executive. **Educ:** State Univ NY; Harvard Bus Sch. **Career:** GTE Corp, staff; Digital Equipment Corp, staff; Informix Software, staff; AT&T Solutions, consult; AT Kearney, consult; Boston Edison Co, vpres customer care; NSTAR Electric & Gas Corp, vpres info serv & chief info officer; IBM Corp, Global Energy & Utilities, gen mgr, currently. **Orgs:** Edison Electric Inst; Am Gas Asn; Bd dirs, Whittier State Health Ctr, Roxbury, MA; New Vision Found, Framingham, MA. **Business Addr:** General Manager, IBM Corporation, Global Energy & Utilities, 1 New Orchard Rd, Armonk, NY 10504-1722, **Business Phone:** 877-426-6006.*

SAMUEL, JASPER H
Executive. **Personal:** Born Dec 13, 1944, Brooklyn, NY; son of Frederick and Ruby. **Career:** Jasper Samuel Printing Co, pers, currently. **Orgs:** NCP. **Military Serv:** USF, lt, 1966. **Business Phone:** (212)239-9544.

SAMUEL, LOIS S.
Educator, social worker. **Personal:** Born May 26, 1925, Boston, MA; widowed; children: David & Judith. **Educ:** Simmons Col, BS; Columbia Univ Sch, SSW. **Career:** Educator (retired); Leake & Watts Childrens Home, soc worker, 1947-49; Youth Consult Serv, soc worker 1949-51; New York City Bd Educ Bureau,child guid, 1955-73, supvr, 1973-79; Dist 29 Drug Abuse Prevention & Educ Prog, dir, 1971-79; Queens High Sch Unit, clinical supvr, 1979-85. **Orgs:** Acad Cert Social Workers; Nat Asn Social Workers; Nat Asn Black Social Workers; br pres, NAACP, 1972-76; Community Adv Coun; Hemp stead Sch Bd; bd mem, Wndhm C Serv; trustee, Congreg Ch S Hempstead; Delta Sigma Theta Sorority; past pres, Nassau Alumni Chap. **Honors/Awds:** Simmons Honor Soc Num Publs in Field.

SAMUEL, SEAL HENRY OLUSEGUN OLUMIDE ADEOLA
Singer. **Personal:** Born Feb 19, 1963, London, England; son of Francis Samuel and Adebisi Samuel; married Heidi Klum, May

10, 2005; children: Henry Guenther Ademola Dashtu & Johan Riley Fyodor Taiwo. **Educ:** Degree archit. **Career:** Albums: Seal, 1991; The Acoustic Session, 1991; Violet: Acoustic EP, 1991;Seal II, 1994; Human Being, 1998; Seal IV, 2003; Seal: Best 1991-2004,2004; Live in Paris, 2005; One Night to Remember, 2006; System, 2007; Livein Hattiesburg, 2008; Soul, 2008. **Honors/Awds:** Grammy awards for Record, 3; Song, Pop Male Vocal, 1995. **Business Addr:** Vocalist, Warner Brothers Records, 75 Rockefeller Plz, New York, NY 10020-1604, **Business Phone:** (212)275-4600.*

SAMUELS, ANNETTE JACQUELINE

Consultant, educator. **Personal:** Born Jul 27, 1935, New York, NY; daughter of Mattie Annette Lindsay Duke and Fred Douglas Duke Jr; divorced; children: Linda, Shelly, Angelique (deceased), Micheal, Douglas & Melvin. **Educ:** NY Univ; New Sch Social Res; Sch Visual Arts; Am Univ; Harvard Univ,JFK Sch Govt, Cambridge, MA, MPA, 1989. **Career:** Essence Mag, fashion ed, 1969-70; Family Circle Mag, asst fashion ed, 1970-71; Tuesday Publ, sr ed, 1972-73; Continental Group, coor dr environ affairs, 1973-74; Community News Serv, exec ed, 1974-76; freelance jornalist, 1976-77; NY State Chamber, Women's Div, assoc dir pub info, 1977-79; White House, asst pres press secy, 1979-81; City Wash, Mayor's Off, press secy mayor, 1981-87, pub affairs/rels consult, 1990-92; HarvardUniv, JFK Sch Govt, Cambridge, MA, sr exec fel, 1987; DC Comn Women, exec dir, 1992-94; Eastern Ill UNiv, Dept Jour, asst prof, assoc prof, 1996-. **Orgs:** Women Wash; Women Community Inc; Coalition 100 Black Women; Capital Press Club; adv, Eastern Ill Univ Chap, Nat Asn Black Journalists. **Honors/Awds:** Community Service Award, Nat Asn Media Women, 1976. **Special Achievements:** First African-American and first woman to serve as a spokesperson for a US president (Jimmy Carter). **Business Addr:** Associate Professor, Eastern Illinois University, Department of Journalism, 2521 Buzzard Hall 600 Lincoln Ave, Charleston, IL 61920-3099, **Business Phone:** (217)581-6003.

SAMUELS, BOB. See SAMUELS, ROBERT J.

SAMUELS, BRYAN

Executive director. **Educ:** Univ Notre Dame, BA, econs; Univ Chicago, MA, public policy. **Career:** Human Serv Dept, asst; Ill Dept C & Family Serv, dir, 2003-06.

SAMUELS, CHARLOTTE

Educator. **Personal:** Born May 27, 1948, Philadelphia, PA. **Educ:** Cent State Univ, BS, 1969; Temple Univ, MEd, 1973; Supervisory certif; prin certif. **Career:** Educator (retired); Sch District Philadelphia, mathematics chairperson, 1969-99, cluster Facilitator; Prentice-Hall, math consult, 1999; acad consult, Proj GRAD, 2008-09; Mathematics Academic Consult, Proj GRAD USA, currently. **Orgs:** Assoc Supervision & Curriculum Develop, Nat Coun Teachers Math, Assoc Teachers Math Philadelphia & Vicinity, Black Women's Educ Alliance, Assoc Prof & Exec Women, Joint Ctr Political Studies, COBBE; mem, NAACP, Big Sisters Am, Campaign Comm for State Rep Dwight Evans; vol Victim Crime Prog mem, Nat Forum for Black Public Administrators Philadelphia Chapt; Nat Asn Univ Women; Mathematics, Sci Leadership Congress. **Honors/Awds:** Civil Affairs Award for Distinguished Services. **Military Serv:** AUS Reserves Sp5 3 yrs.

SAMUELS, EVERETT PAUL

Executive. **Personal:** Born Aug 27, 1958, Tulsa, OK; son of Chester R and Gwendolyn Verone Busby; married Patricia Ann Harris, Sep 4, 1982; children: Everett Paul II & Paige Noelle. **Educ:** Central State Univ, BS, 1980. **Career:** Westin Hotel, Tulsa, OK, hotel mgt, 1980-82; Xerox Corp, sr mgt rep, 1983-84, mkt exec, 1984-85, acct exec, 1985-86; Progressive Mgt Assocs, exec vpres, 1985-; EPS Mgt Servs, Tulsa, OK, pres & owner, 1989-; Dean Witter, vpres, 1991-. **Orgs:** Tulsa Pub Sch, 1982-; bd dirs, Tulsa Econ Develop Corp, 1984-, pres 1987-90; asst treas, bd trustees, Friendship Baptist Church, 1985-, asst secy, Deacon Bd, 1986-; bd mem, Sickle Cell Anemia Found, 1987-; bd mem, Gilcrease Hills Homeowners Asn, 1989-; bd mem, N Tulsa Heritage Found, 1990-; Phi Mu Alpha Fraternity; Nat Asn Advan Colored People; vol, United Negro Col Fund. **Honors/Awds:** Outstanding American Award, Outstanding Young Americans. **Home Addr:** 1814 N Xenophon Ave, Tulsa, OK 74127. **Business Addr:** President, EPS Management Services, PO Box 27671, Tulsa, OK 74149-0671, **Business Phone:** (918)585-8749.

SAMUELS, DR. LESLIE EUGENE

Government official. **Personal:** Born Nov 12, 1929, St Croix, Virgin Islands of the United States; son of Henry Francis Samuels and Annamartha Venetia Ford; married Reather James; children: Leslie Jr, Venetia, Yvette & Philip. **Educ:** NY Univ/Carnegie Hall Music Sc, BM, 1956; Blackstone Sch Law, LLB, JD, 1975; Columbia Pac Univ, MBA, PhD, 1985. **Career:** Van Dyke Studios, concert artist 1956-66; NY Dept Housing Preserv & Develop, dir city serv, 1966-; NY State, bandmaster, 1967-76; comman rep, dist leader, 86th AD, Bronx County, NYC, 1969-73; MAS IST TEC, Sloan Mgt Rev, 1986; Samuels Inst, pres & chief exec officer, 1993-; Summitt Univ LA, prof/mentor, 1994; St Martin's Col & Sem, prof/mentor, 1995; Col Philos & Educ, pres

& chief exec officer, 1997-. **Orgs:** Penthouse Dance & Drama Theatre, 1949; Comm bd mem Astor Home Children, 1975-; Am Mgt Asn, 1984-; bd chmn, Samuels & Co Inc, 1985-; NY/NJ Minority Purchasing Coun, 1986, Nat Black MBA Asn, 1986-; Harvard Bus Rev Harvard Grad Sch Bus Admin, 1987; Int Traders, 1988-90; task force mem Repuban Presial Task Force, 1989; Smithsonian Assocs, 1989-90; Nat Repuban Senatorial Comt, 1994. **Honors/Awds:** Performance Role of Dr Herdal in Henrik Ibsen's Master Builder, 1950; Concert Artist Tenor Carnegie Hall, 1951-; Mem of cast in Langston Hughes', Simply Heavenly 1957; Marketing Thesis Columbia Pacific Univ 1984; Presidential Merit Award, Republican Presidential Task Force, 1989. **Military Serv:** AUS, pvt first class 2 yrs. **Home Addr:** 2814 Bruner Ave, Bronx, NY 10469. **Business Addr:** President, Samuels Institute For Historical Research Of Christian Principles, 2814 Bruner Ave, Bronx, NY 10469.

SAMUELS, ROBERT J (BOB SAMUELS)

Executive. **Personal:** Born Aug 14, 1938, Philadelphia, PA; son of Hubert and Lorraine; divorced; children (previous marriage): Robert Jr, Anthony & Christopher; married Lillie; children: 5. **Educ:** Am Inst Banking; New York Inst Credit, New York Univ; Rutgers Univ, Stonier Grad Sch Banking. **Career:** First Pa Bank, mgr, 1964-69; Manufacturers Hanover Trust Co, New York, credit investr, 1969-71, asst secy, 1971-73, asst vpres, 1973-75, Global Finance Inst Group, vpres, 1975-92; Samuels-Glass Consultancy Group, owner, currently. **Orgs:** Pres, Nat Asn Urban Bankers; dir, New York Urban League; chmn, United Negro Col Funds New York Corp Matching Gifts Prog; vis prof, Nat Urban League Black Exec Exchange Prog; trustee, New York State Higher Educ Serv Corp, 1987; chair, HESC Audit Comt; bd mem, Aaron Davis Hall; chair, New York City Bd Educ Adopt-a-Class Corp Adv Comt; founder, Tampa Bay Men's Cancer Task Force, 1992; chmn, Nat Prostate Cancer Coalition, 1996. **Honors/Awds:** Philadelphia's Outstanding Jaycee, 1968; Robert J Samuels Founder's Award, Nat Asn Urban Bankers, named in honor, 1984; Outstanding Citizen Award, United Negro Col Fund, 1987; Roy Wilkins Humanitarian Award, NAACP, 1988; listed in "Who's Who in Black America". **Special Achievements:** Likeness placed in the Baltimore Great Blacks in Wax Museum, 1998. **Military Serv:** USAF, 1956-60. **Home Phone:** (212)932-9825. **Business Addr:** Owner, Samuels-Glass Consultancy Group LLC, 5620 FishHawk Crossing Blvd Suite 241, Lithia, FL 33547, **Business Phone:** (813)784-1460.

SAMUELS, RONALD S

Lawyer. **Personal:** Born Jun 17, 1941, Chicago, IL; son of Lena and Peter; married Melva; children: 4. **Educ:** Chicago State Univ, BA, 1964; John Marshall Law Sch, JD, 1969. **Career:** Chicago Bd Educ, teacher, 1964-69; Atty, 1969-70; Leadership Coun Metro Open Housing, chief trial lawyer, 1970-73; Cook Co States Atty Off, chief fraud div, 1974-77; Ronald S Samuels & Assoc, partner & atty, currently. **Orgs:** Nat Bar Asn; Cook Co Bar Asn, Chicago, IL; State Bar Asn; Am Bar Asns; dir, Legal Opportunities Scholar Prog; chmn, Consumer Task Force; Chicago Urban League; Kappa Alpha Psi Alumni Chap; CSU Alumni Asn; PUSH. **Honors/Awds:** American Jurisprudence Award; William Ming Award; Richard E Westbrooks; PUSH Outstanding Public Service; Distinguished Service Award, Nat Bar Asn. **Home Addr:** 9957 Winchester, Chicago, IL 60643. **Business Addr:** Attorney, Partner, Ronald S Samuels & Associates, 29 S Lasalle Suite 434, Chicago, IL 60602, **Business Phone:** (312)263-6600.

SAMUELS, DR. WILFRED D

Educator. **Personal:** Born Feb 7, 1947, Puerto Limon, Costa Rica; son of Noel L Samuels Sr and Lena Jones Samuels; married Barbara Fikes, Jun 1980; children: Michael Alain Fikes-Samuels & Detavio Ricardo Fikes-Samuels. **Educ:** Univ Calif, Riverside, Calif, BA, end & black studies, 1971; Univ Iowa, MA, 1974, am studies, PhD, am studies, 1977. **Career:** Univ Colo, Boulder, Colo, asst prof, 1978-85; Col Arts & Sci, Univ Calif, Los Angeles, fel, 1982 & 1983; Ford Found, fel, 1984 & 1985; Benjamin Banneker Hon Col, Prairie View AM, TX, assoc prof, 1985-87; Univ Utah, Salt Lake City, UT, assoc prof eng & ethnic studies, 1987-, African Am Studies Prog, dir, currently,Ethnic Studies Prog, actg coordr, currently. **Orgs:** Popular Cult; Modern Lang Asn; exec bd, Am Lit Asn; pres, African Am Lit & Cult Soc. **Honors/Awds:** Outstanding Teacher Award, 1978-84; NEH Symposium Grants, 1980, 1984 & 1989; Ramona Cannon Award for teaching Excellence in the Humanities, 1992; Student's Choice Award, 1993; Distinguished Teaching Award, Univ Utah, 1994; Distinguished Teaching Award Campus-wide teaching Award. **Special Achievements:** General editor, "A Gift of Story and Song: An Encyclopedia on Twentieth Century African American Writers"; published essays, book reviews, and interviews on African American literature. **Business Addr:** Associate Professor of English and Ethnic Studies, Director of the African American Studies Program, University of Utah, Department of English, Rm 3500 Eng Lang & Commun Bldg 255 S Cent Campus Dr 3407 LNC, Salt Lake City, UT 84112, **Business Phone:** (801)581-3288.

SAMUELSSON, MARCUS

Chef. **Personal:** Born Jan 1, 1970?, Ethiopia, Sweden. **Educ:** Culinary Inst Go, UMLteborg, attended. **Career:** Georges Blanc

Lyon, asst chef, 1992-94; Aquavit Restaurant, exec chef & co-owner, currently. **Honors/Awds:** Best Chef: New York City, James Beard Found, 2003; James Beard Found, best "Rising Star Chef", 1999; World Econ Forum, "Global Leaders for Tomorrow". **Business Addr:** Executive Chef, Co-Owner, Aquavit, 65 E 55th St, New York, NY 10022, **Business Phone:** (212)957-8884.*

SANCHEZ, DR. SONIA BENITA

Educator, writer. **Personal:** Born Sep 9, 1934, Birmingham, AL; divorced; children: Morani, Mungu & Anita. **Educ:** Hunter Col, BA, 1955; NY Univ, 1957; Wilberforce Univ, PhD, 1972. **Career:** Educator (retired); San Francisco State Col, instr, 1966-67; Univ Pittsburgh, instr, 1968-69; Rutgers Univ, asst prof, 1969-70; Manhattan Community Col, asst prof, 1970-72; Amherst Col, assoc prof, 1973-75; Temple Univ, prof eng & womens studies, Laura Carnell chair, 1975-99. **Orgs:** Pa Coun Arts; contrib ed, Black Scholar & J African Studies; adv bd, SISA, MADRE & WILPF. **Honors/Awds:** PEN Writing Award, New York City, 1969; NEA Recipient, Wash, DC, 1978-79; Lucretia Mott Award, Nat Endowment Arts, 1984; American Book Award, 1985; Honorary Doctorate, Trinity Col, 1987; Governor's Award for Excellence in the Humanities, 1988; Freedom, Peace & Freedom Award, Women Int League Peace, 1989; Honorary Doctorate, Baruch Col, 1993; Freedom Award 2000; Lindback Award; American Book Award, Homegirls & Handgrenades; Outstanding Arts Award, Pa Coalition 100 Black Women; Community Service Award, Nat Black Caucus State Legis. **Special Achievements:** Author of: Homecoming, It's a New Day, We a Baddddd People, Love Poems, I've Been a Woman: New and Selected Poems, A Sound Investment and Other Stories, Homegirls and Handgrenades, Under a Soprano Sky, Wounded in the House of a Friend; edited two anthologies: We Be Word Sorcerers: 25 Stories by Black Americans and 360 Degrees of Blackness Coming at You; author of play "Sister Sonji" Joseph Papps Public Theatre, New York; author, Does Your House Have Lions?, 1997; author, Like the Singing Coming Off the Drums, 1998.

SANDERS, ANUCHA BROWNE (ANUCHA CHIOGU BROWNE)

Vice president (Organization). **Career:** NY Knicks, mkt exec, 2000, sr vpres mkt & bus opers, 2002-06. *

SANDERS, ARCHIE, JR.

Government official. **Personal:** Born Sep 6, 1937, Hughes, AR; married Bernice Dawkines; children: Tommy, Willie C, Bonnie, Archie III, Theresa & Diann. **Career:** Adult educ adv coun, 1972-73; Bonner Springs, KS, councilman. **Orgs:** Jaycees, Police Reserve, Fire Dept; bd dir, C & D Ctr; treasure, NCP; bdsupvr, Wyandotte County Soil Conservation; pres, Bonner Springs, city coun, 2003. **Honors/Awds:** Achievement Awd, Nat Advan Asn Colored People, 1971. *

SANDERS, BARBARA A.

Automotive executive. **Personal:** Born in New Orleans, LA; daughter of Arma L Atkins Miles and Otis Miles; married Joe Sanders Jr. **Educ:** Southern Univ, BS, 1969; Rutgers Univ, MS, 1972; Ind Exec Prog, Cert, 1982; Harvard Univ, PMD Prog Cert, 1985. **Career:** Gen Motors Corp, composites mat dept head, 1979-81, composites processing mgr, 1981-83, CAD/CAM dir, 1983-85, artificial intelligence dir, 1985-87, advan mfg engineering dir, 1987-89, prog mgr, 1989-90; Truck & Bus Baltimore Assembly Plant, Paint Syst, Gen Motors Tech Ctr, Advanced Engineering Staff, dir, 1991-; Delphi Corp, dir eng, currently. **Orgs:** Engineering Soc Detroit, 1981-86; mem, Soc Mfg Engrs, 1983-86; key exec, GM/Southern Univ Key Inst Prog, 1984-86; chairperson entrepreneurs comt, Minority Tech Coun Mich, 1985-89; class sec, Harvard Univ PMD-49, 1985-87; mem, Women Econ Club. **Honors/Awds:** Outstanding Alumni, Southern Univ Alumni Detroit Chap, 1982, 86; Distinguished Alumni, Nat Asn Equal Opportunity, 1986; numerous articles/presentations in Tech Area, Lasers, CAD/CAM, AI, Composite Materials, 1979-86; Honorary Doctorate, Southern Univ, 1988; US Black Engr of the Year, 1988; Lifetime Achievement Award, Soc Plastics Engrs Automotive Div, 2006. **Special Achievements:** Dollars & Sense magazine as an honoree at the Tribute to African-American Business and Professional Men & Women, as well as being selected by Professional Engineer's magazine's Top 20 Minority Engineers of the 1980s. **Business Addr:** Director, Delphi Corporation, 5725 Delphi Dr, Troy, MI 48098-2815.*

SANDERS, BARRY

Football player. **Personal:** Born Jul 16, 1968, Wichita, KS; son of William and Shirley; married Lauren Campbell, Nov 11, 2000; children: 4; children: Nigel. **Educ:** Okla State Univ, attended 1989. **Career:** Football player (retired); Detroit Lions, running back, 1989-98. **Orgs:** Pro Football Hall Fame. **Honors/Awds:** Kick returner, 1987, running back, 1988, Sporting News Col All-Am Team; Heisman Trophy winner, 1988; Maxwell Award, 1988; Col Football Player of the Year, 1988, Sporting News NFL Rookie of the Year, 1989, Sporting News; NFL All-Star Team, Sporting News, 1989; NFC Most Valuable Player, NFL Players Asn, 1991; Pro Bowl, 1989, 1990, 1991, 1992, 1993, 1994, 1995, 1996, 1997, 1998; NFL MVP, 1992, 1998; Offensive Player of the Year, Asn Press, 1994; Player of the Year, NFL, 1998. **Special**

Achievements: He was ranked 2 in ESPN's list of the Top 25 Greatest College Football Players Ever.

SANDERS, BRANDON CHRISTOPHER
Football player. **Personal:** Born Jun 10, 1973, San Diego, CA. **Educ:** Univ Ariz. **Career:** Football player (retired); New York Giants, defensive back, 1997-99; Amsterdam Admirals, 2001.

SANDERS, REV. DR. CHERYL J
Religious educator, clergy. **Personal:** Married Alan Carswell; children: Allison & Garrett. **Educ:** Swarthmore Col, BA, math; Harvard Univ Divinity Sch, MDiv, ThD. **Career:** Church God, Anderson, IN, clergy; Howard Univ Sch Divinity, prof, 1984-; Third St Church God, Wash, DC, sr pastor, 1997-. **Honors/Awds:** Hon DDiv, Asbury Col, Wilmore, KY, 2002; Hon DDiv, Anderson Univ, 2007. **Special Achievements:** Author over 50 articles & several books including: Empowerment Ethics for a Liberated People, Fortress, 1995; Saints in Exile: The Holiness-Pentecostal Experience in African American Religion and Culture, Oxford, 1996; Ministry at the Margins, InterVarsity Press, 1997; ed: Living the Intersection, Fortress, 1995.

SANDERS, CHRIS
Football player. **Personal:** Born May 8, 1972, Denver, CO; married Stacie; children: Chris Jr. **Educ:** Ohio State Univ. **Career:** Houston Oilers, wide receiver, 1995-96; Tenn Oilers, 1997-98; Tenn Titans,wide receiver, 1999-01; coach, Christ Presbyterian Aca, 2005-08; Athletics councilor, montgomerybell academy, 2008-.

SANDERS, DEION LUWYNN
Athlete. **Personal:** Born Aug 9, 1967, Fort Myers, FL; married Pilar Biggers, May 21, 1999; children: Shilo, Shedeur & Shelomi; married Carolyn Chambers (divorced 1998); children: Diondra & Deion Luwynn Jr. **Educ:** Fla State Univ, attended 1988. **Career:** Baseball player (retired), football player (retired), TV host; MLB Career: NY Yankees, outfielder, 1989-90; Atlanta Braves, outfielder, 1991-94; Cincinnati Reds, 1994-95, 1997, 2001; San Francisco Giants, 1995; NFL Career: Atlanta Falcons, defensive back, 1989-93; San Francisco 49ers, 1994; Dallas Cowboys, 1995-99; Wash Redskins, 2000; Baltimore Ravens, 2004-05; Nat Women's Basketball League, Dallas Fury, asst coach, 2004; CBS Sports, "The NFL Today", feature reporter/contribr, commentator, 2001-04, studio analyst, currently; ESPN Radio, host; NFL Network, "NFL Game Day", host, currently; AFL, Austin Wranglers, owner, 2006-. **Orgs:** Potters House Church. **Honors/Awds:** Jim Thorpe Award; Pro Bowl, 1991, 1992, 1993, 1994, 1995, 1996, 1997, 1998; NFL Defensive Player of the Year, 1994; NFC Defensive Back of the Year, NFL Players Asn, 1997. **Special Achievements:** Appeared in numerous television commercials for Nike, Pepsi, Burger King, Pizza Hut & American Express. **Business Addr:** Owner, Austin Wranglers, Arena Football League, 2209 W Braker Lane, Austin, TX 78758.

SANDERS, DORI
Farmer, writer. **Personal:** Born Jan 1, 1934, York, SC. **Career:** Peach farmer; Clover, auth, 1990; Her Own Place, auth, 1993; Dori Sanders Country Cooking: Recipes & Stories from the family farm stand, 1995; Promise Land: a Farmer Remembers, 2004. **Honors/Awds:** Lillian Smith Book Award, 1990; Dori Sanders' Country Cooking. **Special Achievements:** Featured in Gourmet magazine, 2004; Southern Lady magazine, 2004. **Business Addr:** Farmer, Sander, 2275 Filbert Hwy, Filbert, SC 29745-9777.

SANDERS, FRANK VONDEL
Football player. **Personal:** Born Feb 17, 1973, Fort Lauderdale, FL; married Tracy. **Educ:** Univ Auburn. **Career:** Arizona Cardinals, wide receiver, 1995-02; Baltimore Ravens, 2002-03; WJOX radio, host.

SANDERS, DR. GEORGE L.
Physician. **Personal:** Born Jul 4, 1942, Vidalia, GA; son of Felton Sanders (deceased) and Eva Mae Sanders (deceased); married Frances; children: G Eldridge & Cleaver. **Educ:** Morehouse Col, 1965; Univ Miami Sch Med, 1969; Jackson Memorial Hosp, intern 1970, resident, 1974, fel cardiol, 1976; Air War Col, grad, 1992. **Career:** Pvt pract, phy internal med & cardiol; USF, Eglin AFB, Cardiopulmonary Lab, dir. **Orgs:** Life mem, Phi Beta Sigma Frat; Phi Delta Epsilon; bd dir, Spectrum Prog Inc, 1977; Univ Miami Sch Med, assoc clin prof, vpres, Greater Miami Heart Asn; Am Col Physicians; med dir, N Shore Med Ctr Cardiol, 1985-90; lifemem, NCP. **Honors/Awds:** Am Col Cardiol, fel, 1992; Am Bd Internal Med, Dipl; Student of the Year, Phi Beta Sigma, 1966; Student Award, Nat Med Asn, 1976; Nat Med Found, fel, 1965-69. **Military Serv:** USY, capt, 1970-72; USAF, lt col, Commendation Medal, 1992; AUS, Commendation Medal, 1972.

SANDERS, GLADYS N.
Educator. **Personal:** Born Jun 27, 1937, Martinez, GA; daughter of Rile Nealous and Rebecca; married Robert B Sanders, Dec 23, 1961; children: Sylvia Lynne, William Nealous. **Educ:** Ottawa Univ; Univ Kans; Atlanta Univ; Paine Col, Augusta, GA, BA, 1959. **Career:** Educator (retired); Columbia County Ga Pub Schs, math teacher, 1959-61; Richmond County Ga Pub Schs, math teacher, 1961-62; Macmillan Pub Co Inc, nat math consult, 1991; Lawrence KS Pub Schs, math coordr, teacher, 1973-98; Univ Kans, 1999. **Orgs:** Vice chair, Nat Bd Prof Teaching Stand, 1992-99; Coun Chief State Sch Officers, Interstate New Teacher Assessment Consortium, 1993; Kans State Dept Educ, Writing Team Qual Performance Accreditation, 1994, Rev Team Kans Math Assessment, 1996, Kans Curric Stand Comt, 1997-98, Kans Math Stand Comn, 1997-99; NCTM-NCATE, 1996-99; reviewer, Technology Challenge Grants, 1997; team leader, US Dept Educ. **Special Achievements:** Co-wrote: Probability & Statistics, 1997, Geometry and Spatial Sense, 1996, Mathematics Benchmark Assessments, Lawrence Public Schools, 1996; wrote: Families Thinking Mathemathically, 1997, A Parent Handbook for Elementary School Mathematics, Lawrence Public School, 1995; co-author, UGSMP Transition Mathematics, 1992. *

SANDERS, GLENN CARLOS
Consultant, computer engineer. **Personal:** Born May 24, 1949, Bastrop, TX; son of Charles Sanders, Sr and Marjorie Sanders; married Catherine McCarty; children: Chandra & Brian. **Educ:** Texas Southern Univ, attended, 1969; Calif Baptist Col, BS, 1987; CNE (certified netware Engr), 1995. **Career:** Zales Jewelers Inc, asst mgr, 1973-76; TRW Info Serv, Programmer analyst, 1976-80; Riverside Co Data Processing, data base analyst, 1980-83; Transamerica Life Co, sr systs programmer, 1983-95; Sandcastle Enterprises, consult, 1995-. **Orgs:** Phi Beta Sigma, 1968-; Planetary Soc, 1985-; vpres, Southwestern Info Mgt Users Group, 1986-88; bd mem, Parents Against Gangs, 1989-92. **Honors/Awds:** Nat Student Merit Qualifying Test Commended Candidate; Who's Who in Am High Sch Stud, 1967; First Place State Extemporaneous Speaking Competition, 1967; Second Place State Debate Competition 1967; Deans List Freshmen Year, TX Southern Univ, 1968; Top DivSales Zales Jewelers, 1973. **Military Serv:** USN, machinist mate, Third class 2 yrs. **Business Addr:** Lan Administrator, Riverside County, 4080 Lemon St 10th Fl, Riverside, CA 92501, **Business Phone:** (909)275-3755.

SANDERS, DR. GWENDOLYN W.
School administrator. **Personal:** Born Dec 17, 1937, St Louis, MO; daughter of Adolph Fisher and Burnette B Harris Fletcher; married Gordon B; children: Darrell F, Romona R Sanders Fullman & Jocelyn M. **Educ:** St Louis Univ, BS, 1956; Harris Teachers Col, BA, 1962; St Louis Univ, MEd, educ syst urban educ & admin, 1967; Nova Univ, EdD; Univ Delaware, Col Urban Affairs, PhD, prog; Harvard Grad Sch Educ, psychol & pluralism; George Wash Univ, educ outcomes. **Career:** Pvt Phy St Louis, med tech, 1956-59; Harris Teachers Col, St Louis, lab asst, 1959-62; St Louis Pub Sch, master teacher, 1962-68; Lincoln Pub Sch, teacher, 1966-68; St Peters Cathedral-Wilmington Pub Sch, teacher dir, 1968-70; Opportunity Indust Ctr, teacher, 1969-70; City Demonstration Agency, educ consult & planner, 1969-72; Del Tech & Comm Coll, planning coordr, 1972-73; Univ Del, instr, 1973-75; Del Tech & Comm Col, dean stud serv, 1973-89, dean develop, 1989-92; Springfield Col, Sch Human Serv, adj prof; Wilmington Col, MEd, coun & clin supvr; Family & Workplace Connection, Childcare Provider, educr & trainer; Wesley Col, Nat Training Inst Child Care Health, consult; Univ NC, Chapel Hill, consult. **Orgs:** Delta Sigma Theta; Nat Women's Polit Caucus; United Way Critical Issues Taskforce; adv bd, Headstart; vpres, Educ Comt, Nat Asn Advan Colored People; consult, US Dept Justice; pres, Northeast Coun Black Am Affairs; bd mem, Nat Coun Black Am Affairs, Am Asn Community & Jr Col; consult, NJ Dept Higher Educ, Middle States Comn Higher Educ; reader & evaluator, US Dept Higher Educ; vpres, Brandy wine Prof Asn, Am Acad Cosmetic Dentistry, 1980-; Denver Ctr Performing Arts; NAFSA; Am Asn Health Educ; NCRD; People People Int; exec bd, Del Acad Youth; field reader, Okla Bd Regents; rep,Nat Coun Early Childhood Develop; bd dir, Col Resource Ctr; bd mem, Metro Urban League. **Honors/Awds:** Outstanding Community Service Award, Alliance Ministers Bus & Agencies, 1988; Outstanding Community Service Award, Delaware Head Start, 1988; Outstanding Achievers Award-Education, BPA, 1989. **Special Achievements:** Developed bi-lingual bi-cultural day care center, 1970, developed and initiated ESL Prog, Delaware Tech, 1976, developed freshman orientation course, human potential and career & life planning courses, developed and initiated career centers Stanton and Wilmington campuses, developed, implemented & coordianted Springfield College Academic Support Center, Wilmington Campus. **Business Addr:** Owner, G & G Enterprise, 507 Wyndham Rd N Hills, Wilmington, DE 19809, **Business Phone:** (302)762-0422.

SANDERS, HANK (HENRY SANDERS)
State government official, lawyer, senator (u.s. federal government). **Personal:** Born Oct 28, 1942, Baldwin County, AL; son of Sam and Ola Mae Norman; children (previous marriage): Charles, Maurice, Rosie & Jennifer; married Rose M Gaines, Jan 23, 1970; children: Malika A, Kindaka J & Ainka M. **Educ:** Talladega Col, BA, 1967; Harvard Law Sch, JD, 1970. **Career:** Stucky Lumber Co, saw mill worker, 1960-61; Honeywell, elec tech, 1962-63; Reginald Heber Smith fel, 1971; Chestnut Sen, Sanders Sanders & Pettway, atty, 1972-; Ala State Senate, sen, 1983-. **Orgs:** Co-founder & pres, Ala Lawyers Asn, 1972; co-founder & pres, Campaign News, 1982; co-founder & pres, Ala New S Coalition, 1988-90, 1997-2000; co-founder & chmn, Nat Voting Rights Mus & Inst, 1992-95; co-founder & former bd mem, 21st Century Youth Leadership Monument, 1985-95; co-founder & former chmn, Coalitions Alabamians Rebuilding Educ, 1992-98; Nat Conf Black Lawyers; pres, Harvard Black Law Studs Asn. **Honors/Awds:** Catherine Waldell Award, 1964; Felix Frankfuther Award, Harvard Law Sch,1967; Second Annual Nat Award for Outstanding Service, Nat Asn Landowners, 1979; Outstanding Senator, 1986; New South Leadership Award, 1989; Lawyer of the Year, Nat Conf Black Lawyers, 1990; Martin Luther King Community Service Award, 1996; Alabama Legislator of the Year Award, Ala Nursing Homes Asn, 1998; Nation Builders Award, Nat Caucus Black State Legislators, 1999; Inducted into African Hall of Fame, Durban, S Africa,2002; Ala New S Coalition All World Leader Award. **Home Addr:** 1 Imani Way, PO Box 1290, Selma, AL 36702, **Home Phone:** (334)875-1395. **Business Addr:** Senator, Alabama State Senate, 1405 Jeff Davis Ave, PO Box 1305, Selma, AL 36702, **Business Phone:** (334)875-9264.

SANDERS, DR. ISAAC WARREN
School administrator. **Personal:** Born Aug 9, 1948, Montgomery, AL; son of Hurley W Sr and Bertha Lee McKenize; married Cora Allen, May 29, 1975; children: W Machion, Christin Machael & Bryant Allen. **Educ:** Tuskegee Inst, BS, 1971; Cornell Univ, MS, rural sociol, 1973; Kans State Univ, PhD, 1984; Columbia Univ, New York NY, post grad cert, 1988. **Career:** Grad Fel, Cornell Univ, 1971-73; Ft Valley State Col, instr res assoc, 1973-75; Claflin Col, fed relations officer, 1975-76; Ala State Univ, dir fed relations, 1976-82; Woodrow Wilson Nat Fellowship Found, vpres, 1984-86; Nat Action Coun Minorities Eng, dir, 1986-90, vpres, 1990-91; Kellogg Nat fel, Kellogg Found, 1990-93; Tuskegee Univ, Tuskegee, AL, vp emss, 1991-96; Ala State Univ, exec asst pres, staff asst bd trustees, 1996-97; Stillman Col, vpres, assoc prof; E Stroudsburg Univ Pa, vpres, 2000-, exec dir, E Stroudsburg Univ Found, currently. **Orgs:** Nat Soc Fund raising Execs 1980-; bd mem, Greater Trenton NJ Mental Health,1984-; vice pres & bd mem, Optimist Club Lower Bucks, PA, 1985-; pres-,Tuskegee Univ Philadelphia Area Alumni Asn, 1986-; assoc dir, NE Region Tuskegee Alumni Assoc 1986-; Kappa Alpha Psi; bd dir, NAACP Bucks Co, PA,1989; Tuscaloosa Rotary Club 1998-; pres, Tuscaloosa Exchange Club, 1998-; Phi Delta Kappa; Golden Key Int Honor Soc. **Honors/Awds:** United Negro Col Fund Mind Fire Award, 1982, Martin Luther King Community Service Award, ESU, 2006 . **Business Addr:** Vice President, Executive Director, East Stroudsburg University, 200 Prospect St, East Stroudsburg, PA 18301-2999.

SANDERS, JAMES WILLIAM
Clergy. **Personal:** Born Sep 17, 1929, Union, SC; married Ruby Lee Corry; children: Jewette LaVernae, James William Jr, Ruzlin Maria. **Educ:** Benedict Col Columbia SC, BA, 1951; A&T State Univ Greensboro NC, MEd, 1961; Friendship Col Rock Hill SC, DD, 1973; Morris Col, LHD, 1991. **Career:** Bethel Baptist Church, minister, 1949-; Union SC, elem sch prin, 1961-65, HS asst prin, 1965-72; Union Co Educ Asn, treas, 1964-69; Union SC Adult Educ Prog, co coordr, 1970-72; Island Crek Baptist Church, pastor, 1971-; J & R Fine Jewelers, owner. **Orgs:** pres, NAACP Cherokee Co Gaffney SC, 1962-68; Pres, Cherokee Co Black Ministers Alliance, 1965-79; exec bd mem, Appalachian Coun Govts, 1972-; Mayor's Human Rels Comn Gaffney SC, 1972-; Gov's Task Force Study Health Needs State SC; moderator, Co Baptist Asn, 1973-; chmn, Area Agency Aging 6 county region, 1979-; finance committeeman, Nat Baptist Conv Am, 1979-; vpres, Cherokee Co Dem Party, 1978-; Planning & Zoning Comn, City Gaffney, 1980-; Election Comn Cherokee Co, 1980-; bd mem, Habilitation Serv Cherokee Co Inc, 1981-; vice chmn, Cherokee Co Comn Food & Shelter Emergency Fund, 1984-; trustee bd mem, Morris Col, Sumter, SC, 1986-94; trustee bd mem, South Carolina State Univ, Orangeburg, SC, 1993-; exec bd mem, Financial Corp, 1988-; vchair, trustee bd, South Carolina State Univ, 1996; chair, South Carolina Appalachian Coun Govt, 1996. **Honors/Awds:** Leadership Award, Boy Scouts Am, 1960; Human Service Award, Comt Action Prog, 1971; Citizen of the Year Award, Phi Alpha Chap Omega Psi Phi Frat Inc, 1975; Palmetto Gentleman's Award, State South Carolina, 1980; House of Representatives Award, State South Carolina, 1994; State Senate Award, State South Carolina, 1994; Hall of Fame, NAACP, Cherokee County Chapter, 1996; Cherokee County Chamber of Commerce Hall of Fame, 2003. *

SANDERS, JASMINE
Media executive. **Personal:** Born Oct 21, 1967, Chattanooga, TN; daughter of Joseph and Joyce; children: Joey. **Educ:** Middle Tenn State Univ, BS, 1990. **Career:** Phoenix Commun, midday on-air personality, 1990-93; Brewer Broadcasting, morning show host, 1993-95; Gaylord Entertainment, engr, 1995-98; Dickey Brothers Broadcasting, midday on-air personality, 1998-2001; Cumulus Broadcasting, mkt & promotions dir, 2001; WNPL-Nashville, morning show host; ARPR, E Coast div, head, 2004-. **Orgs:** Delta Sigma Theta Sorority, 1986-. **Honors/Awds:** Girls Inc, 1 of 10 Most Influential Black Women, 1994; YMCA Black Achievers, 1997. **Business Addr:** Head, AR PR Marketing, East Coast Division, **Business Phone:** (323)330-0555.

SANDERS, JOSEPH STANLEY
Lawyer. **Personal:** Born Aug 9, 1942, Los Angeles, CA; son of Hays and Eva; married Melba Binion, Mar 17, 1984; children:

Edward Moore, Justin Hays, Alexandria Thedarin & Chelsea Winifred. **Educ:** Whittier Col, BA 1963; Magdalen Col Oxford Univ, BA/MA 1965; Yale Law Sch, LLB 1968. **Career:** Yale Univ Transitional Year, dir pro tem & instr 1967-68; Western Ctr on Law & Poverty Los Angeles, staff atty 1968-69; Lawyer's Com for Civil Rights Under Law LA, exec dir 1969-70; Wyman Bautzer Finell Rothman & Kuchel Beverly Hills, assoc 1969-71; Rosenfeld Lederer Jacobs & Sanders Beverly Hills, partner 1971-72; Sanders & Tisdale LA, partner 1972-77; Sanders & Dickerson Los Angeles, atty partner 1978-94; Barnes, McGhee & Pryce, Law Off J Stanley Sander, sr patner, currently. **Orgs:** Co-founder Watts Summer Festival 1966; Am Bar Asn 1969-; bd dirs W LA United Way 1970; LA World Affairs Coun 1971-; trustee Ctr for Law in Pub Interest 1973-80; bd trustees Whittier Col 1974-; bd dir Econ Resources Corp 1974-; Mayor's Com on Cultural Affairs 1975-; bd dir Am Red Cross LA 1975-; bd dir Arthritis Found So CA Chap 1976-; co-chmn CA Dem Party Rules Comm 1976-; pres LA Recreation & Parks Comt1986-93; LA orial Coliseum Comm 1980-; dir Black Arts Coun; Langston Law Club LA Co Bar Asn; chmn United Way Task Force on Minority Youth Employ 1985-; NCAA Found, bd trustees; Mus Contemporary Art, Los Angeles. **Honors/Awds:** Rhodes Scholar; 1st Team NAIA All-Am Football 1961; Small Col NAIA Discus Champion 1963; Ten Outstanding Young Men American Award 1971; Fifty Distinguished Alumni Award Los Angeles City Sch Bicentennial 1976. **Special Achievements:** Pub "I'll Never Escape the Ghetto" Ebony Mag 1967, "Rhodes Scholar Looks at South Africa" Ebony Mag 1970. **Home Addr:** 2015 Wellington Rd, Los Angeles, CA 90016, **Home Phone:** (323)737-6334. **Business Addr:** Senior Patner, Law Office J Stanley Sanders, 2015 Wellington Rd, Los Angeles, CA 90016-1824, **Business Phone:** (323)737-6334.

SANDERS, DR. KAREN ELEY
School administrator. **Personal:** Born Sep 8, 1962, Newport News, VA; daughter of Alvin Eley and Margaret; married Reliford Jr, Jul 6, 1991; children: Reliford (Theo) III & Micaela Karynne Eley. **Educ:** VA State Univ, BS, 1986, MS, 1992; Univ Ark, Fayetteville, EdD, 2000, Appalachian State Univ, Develop Educ Specialist, 2003. **Career:** Univ Ark, Boyer Ctr Stud Serv, dir, 1992-97, Minority Edu Serv, dir, 1997-2001; Va Tech, Ctr Acad Enrichment & Excellence, dir, 2001-; Va Tech, asst provost, 2004-. **Orgs:** Nat Acad Advising Asn, 1993-; Phi Beta Kappa, 1995-; Delta Sigma Theta Sorority Inc, 1997-; Va Asn Develop Educ, 2001-; Nat Asn Develop Educ, 2001-; Nat Col Learning Ctr Asn, 2002-, Am Asn Blacks Higher Educ, 2000-. **Honors/Awds:** Dr Martin Luther King Jr Fac Staff Award, Univ Ark, 1999-2000; Outstanding Dissertion, Am Asn Higher Educ, Black Caucus, 2000; Woman of the 21st Century, Alpha Kappa Alpha, Phi Alpha Omega chapter, 2001; Services to Students Recognition, Va Tech Black Caucus, 2002; Outstanding Contributions in Campus and Community Outreach, Va Tech Black Caucus, 2003; Executive of the Year, New River Valley Int Asn Admin Profs, 2004-05. **Business Addr:** Assistant Provost for Academic Support, Virginia Tech, 110 Femoyer Hall (0276), Blacksburg, VA 24061, **Business Phone:** (540)231-5499.

SANDERS, LARRY KYLE
Educator. **Personal:** Born Oct 16, 1970, Hammond, LA; son of Frank and Shirley. **Educ:** Southern Univ, BA, jour, 1993, MA, mass communications, 1994. **Career:** Wiley Col, instr, 1997, dir mass commun, 1999;Alcorn State Univ, instr Mass Commun, currently. **Orgs:** Am Asn Univ Profs, 1997-; Nat Asn Advan Colored People, 1997-; Int Commun Asn, 1997-; Asn Educ Jour & Mass Commun, 1997-; Nat Asn Black Journalists, 1997-; life mem, Southern Univ Alumni Fedn; Alpha Phi Alpha, 1998. **Honors/Awds:** Southern Univ Media Club Award, Southern Univ, 1994; Journalist's Award, Dow Jones Newspaper Fund, 1998. **Special Achievements:** Contributed to: Southern Univ Digest, articles and poems, 1988-94; Southern Univ Yearbook, poem, 1991; The Morning Advocate, article, 1991; Clark Atlanta Univ Panther, poem, 1996; Howard Univ Hilltop, poem, 2001. **Home Addr:** 144 N Shields Lane Apartment E 8, Natchez, MS 39120, **Home Phone:** (985)514-0421.

SANDERS, LAURA GREEN
Executive. **Personal:** Born Nov 14, 1942, Victoria, TX; daughter of Althea McNary Green and Cluster Green; married Willie Sanders; children: Laresee Sanders Harris. **Educ:** Victoria Junior Col, attended 1968; Tex State Mgt Develop Ctr, Managers Prog, 1986. **Career:** Tex workforce solutions, exec dir, currently. **Orgs:** African Am Chamber Com, Victoria; Victoria Hispanic Chamber Com; Victoria Area Chamber Com; DeWitt County Chamber; Calhoun County Chamber; Victoria Financial Educ Coalition; Golden Crescent Pvt Indust Coun; FW Gross Alumni; Victoria Prof Women's Group; bd dirs, Victoria County Sr Citizens; Univ Houston-Victoria Presidents Adv Coun; Women In Partnership Progress; Int Asn Personnel Employment Serv; Tex Pub Employee Asn; Mt Nebo Baptist Church. **Honors/Awds:** Outstanding Women in Texas Awards, State Tex, 1995. **Business Addr:** Executive Director, Texas Workforce Solutions of the Golden Crescent, 120 S Main Suite 501, PO Box 1936, Victoria, TX 77902, **Business Phone:** (361)576-5872.

SANDERS, LINA
Educator. **Personal:** Born Apr 9, 1937, Johnston County, NC; children: Gary & Gretchen. **Educ:** BS, 1964. **Career:** Educator (retired); Johnson Co Bd Educ, teacher; Smithfield Jr High Sch, teacher; John Tech Inst Sec, part-time instr. **Orgs:** Secy, Nat Asn Univ Women; pres, NC Asn Educ; NEA; Asn Classroom Teachers; chairperson, Polit Act Comt Educ; parliamentarian, Dist 2 ACT; NCAE Comn Foreign Benefits & Spec Serv; NCAE Prof Negoti Comn; Nat Asn Advan Colored People; NC All City Times-NC Asn Educrs; Johnston Co Bd Elections; secy & treas, Johnston Co Industs. **Honors/Awds:** Outstanding Elementary Teacher of America, 1973; Teacher of the Year, Smithfield Jr High Sch, 1975-76; Human Relation Nominee, NC Asn Educrs, 1977. **Home Phone:** (919)934-2376.

SANDERS, DR. LOU HELEN
Librarian, college teacher. **Personal:** Born Mar 2, 1951, Bolton, MS; daughter of Eddie and Irene Singleton; divorced; children: Nicol. **Educ:** Jackson State Univ, Jackson, Miss, BA, 1973, EdS, 1981; Univ Mich, Ann Arbor, Mich, AMLS, 1974; Univ Pittsburgh, Pittsburgh, Pa, PhD, 1989. **Career:** Jackson State Univ, Jackson, Miss, reserve & asst cir libr, 1974-76, sci technol div lib, 1976-77, instr libr sci, 1977-87, asst prof lib sci, 1983-87, dean libraries, prof educ, currently. **Orgs:** MSP Libr Asn, 1974-; Am Libr Asn, 1974-, educ bibliog instr, 1990-92; Univ Mich Alumni Asn, 1977-, African Am life mem; Jackson State Univ Alumni Asn; Southeastern Libr Asn, 1979-; Alpha Kappa Alpha, 1983-; Am Soc Info Sci, 1988-; Beta Phi Mu, 1989-; chair, State Miss Libraries Dir Coun, 1990-; ASIS, Information Analysis & Evaluation, vchair, 1990, chair, 1991. **Honors/Awds:** Phi Kappa Phi, 1976; Provost Develop Fund Scholar, Univ Pittsburgh, 1988; Atlanta Univ FIPSE Internship, 1985-88. **Special Achievements:** Author: Faculty Status of Academic Librarians in Four Year State-Supported Colleges and Universities, Univ Microfilms, International, 1989; "Staff Training Programs for State and Local Government for Publication," Document to the People, vol, 17, 1989; reviewed in: "Social Responsibility in Librarianship: Essays on Equality," RQ, 1990; "Faculty Status for Academic Librarians," Encyclopedia of Library and Information, vol 48, Marcel Dekker, 1991; "The Commitment of a Dean at a Predominately Black University," The Black Librarian in America Revisited, 1994. **Business Addr:** Professor of Education, Jackson State University, Department of Educational Leadership, Rm 217 Joseph H Jackson Bldg, PO Box 18829, Jackson, MS 39217, **Business Phone:** (601)979-2351.

SANDERS, LOUIS
Clergy, educator. **Educ:** NC AT & T State Univ, BS, soc sci; City Univ NY, MS, MA; Union Theol Sem, NY, MDiv. **Career:** Anderson High Sch, Camden, NC, teacher; Camden County High Sch, teacher; Tuckahoe Bd Educ, teacher, 1968-98; Saint Charles Am Methodist Episcopal Church, sr pastor, currently. **Orgs:** Past pres, Rockland County Ministerial Alliance; Rockland County Headstart; Rockland County Girl Scout Coun; Fresh Start Found; Francis Ellis Acad, Ghana. **Special Achievements:** First Black teacher in Camden County High School. **Military Serv:** USAF, chaplain, lt col. *

SANDERS, MELBA T.
Vice president (Organization), executive. **Educ:** Calif State Univ, Dominguez Hills, BS, polit sci & psychol, 1986; Fashion Inst Design & Merchandising, merchandising & mkt. **Career:** Berkhemer Clayton Inc, vpres & co founder, currently. **Business Addr:** Co founder, Vice President, Berkhemer Clayton Inc, 221 S Figueroa St Suite 240, Los Angeles, CA 90012, **Business Phone:** (213)621-2300.*

SANDERS, MICHAEL ANTHONY
Basketball player. **Personal:** Born May 7, 1960, Vidalia, LA; married Crystal Tate; children: Lamar & Kendra. **Educ:** Univ Calif, Los Angeles, BA, History, 1982. **Career:** Basketball player (retired); San Antonio Spurs, 1982-83, Philadelphia76ers, 1984-88; Cleveland Cavaliers, 1988-99, 1992-93; Ind Pacers, 1989-92; Adirondack Wildcats, coach, 2003; The Milwaukee Bucks, asst coach; 2005-07. **Honors/Awds:** Named CBA Rookie of Yr; Western Reg NCAA MVP; Louisiana Hall of Fame, 2000. *

SANDERS, PATRICIA ROPER
Consultant. **Personal:** Born Dec 23, 1945, Tulsa, OK; daughter of Rev Anderson and Harold M; married C Edward; children: Lark Nanette & Thomas Bradford. **Educ:** Lincoln Univ, BA, 1966; PRSA, accreditation, 1977. **Career:** US Senate Cand, dir res & policy info, 1970-71; Blue Cross Hosp Serv St Louis, sr vpres PR community rels pub affairs & spec events, 1971-73; AT&T, sr vpres PR community rels pub affairs & spec events; Western Elect Co, St Louis, managing com affairs spec, 1973-77; Philip Morris Indust Milwaukee, mgr communs, 1977-78, vpres int PR opers; Rhopar Report/RHOPAR, pres/publ, 1978-85; PR Assocs, 1979-86; TRB Speakers Agency, pub rels consult, 1986-90; Int Black Network Exchange, dir, 1990; Int Bus Consult, dir, 1990-; Transatlantic Link, founder; P&E Assoc, sr consult, currently. **Orgs:** Dir pub rel & adv bd mem, UNCF OIC Sherwood Forest St Louis, 1974-77; bd adv, Lincoln Univ, Jefferson City, MO, 1975-77; Panel Judges Coro Found, St Louis, 1976; chmn, Steering Comt Comn Pride Expo Milwaukee, 1977; Pub Rel Soc Am, 1977-80; bd dir, Chicago Forum, 1979; bd mem, Winnie Mandella Women's Ministries, 1987; The Links; exec dir & co-founder, RMBD, 1990-92; Alpha Kappa Alpha; pres, NPFR, currently. **Honors/Awds:** Distinguished Service Awards, 1974-77; Golden Phoenix Award, 1983; CA Gov honored Woman of the Year, 1985. **Special Achievements:** Author: Pub Relations for Small Bus; producer, moderator/host: "A Woman's Place," WYMS; "Focus on Black Bus Woman," KJLH; "Ask Me," KACD, 1977-80; "Living Positively"; Black Wallstreet, producer, 1990; African Heritage World Celebration, spec events coordr, 1995. **Business Addr:** Senior Consultant, P&E Associates, 14902 Preston Rd Suite 404-744, Dallas, TX 75254, **Business Phone:** (972)517-1254.

SANDERS, PRENTICE EARL
Police chief, writer. **Personal:** Born in Texas. **Educ:** Golden Gate Univ, BS, criminal justice; MS, pub admin. **Career:** Police chief (retired), author; San Francisco Police Dept, staff, 1964, investr, homicide investr, 1971, inspector, asst police chief, police chief, 2002-03; Book: The Zebra Murders, 2006. **Orgs:** Officers Justice. **Honors/Awds:** Washington High School Hall of Merit. **Special Achievements:** First black police chief of the San Francisco Police Department. **Business Addr:** Author, Arcade Publishing, 116 John St Suite 2810, New York, NY 10038, **Business Phone:** (212)475-2633.

SANDERS, REGINALD LAVERNE
Baseball player. **Personal:** Born Dec 1, 1967, Florence, SC; married Wyndee, Dec 23, 1994; children: Cody, Carigon, Cooper & Carson. **Career:** Cincinnati Reds, outfielder, 1991-98; San Diego Padres, 1999; Atlanta Braves, 2000; Ariz Diamondbacks, 2001; San Francisco Giants, 2002; Pittsburgh Pirates, 2003; St Louis Cardinals, 2004-05; Kans City Royals, 2005-. **Honors/Awds:** Midwest League Most Valuable Player, 1990; NL All-Star Team, 1995. **Business Phone:** (816)504-4040.

SANDERS, DR. RELIFORD THEOPOLIS
Psychologist. **Personal:** Born Sep 30, 1961, Kansas City, MO; son of Reliford Sanders Sr and Elizabeth Barber; married Karen Eley, Jul 6, 1991; children: Reliford III & Micaela. **Educ:** Benedictine Col, BA, 1983; Univ ILL, MA, 1987, PhD, 1997. **Career:** Univ Ark, licensed psychologist, 1991-2001; pvt pract, licensed psychologist, 2001-. **Orgs:** Asn Black Psychologists; Am Psychological asn; United States Tennis asn; Alph Phi Alpha Fraternity Inc.

SANDERS, RHONDA SHEREE
Journalist, writer. **Personal:** Born Jun 25, 1956, Montgomery, AL; daughter of Isaac Sanders and Marie Williams Hamilton. **Educ:** Univ Mich, Ann Arbor, MI, BA, 1978, MA, 1979; Wayne State Univ, Detroit, MI, 1990-. **Career:** Flint Jour, Flint, MI, reporter, 1980-, j staff writer, currently. Author: Bronze Pillars: An Oral History of African American in Flint, 1996. **Orgs:** Mid-Mich Asn Black Journalists, 1982-92; Nat Asn Black Journalists, 1987-. **Honors/Awds:** Media Award, Nat Asn Media Women, 1983, 1990; Wade McCree Memorial Award, Justice Award Media, 1989; Press Award, Mich Press Asn, 1989. **Business Addr:** Journal Staff Writer, Flint Journal, 200 E 1st St, Flint, MI 48502.

SANDERS, RICKY WAYNE
Football player. **Personal:** Born Sep 30, 1962, Temple, TX; married Michelle; children: Ashlynn & Richard Wayne. **Educ:** SW Tex State Univ. **Career:** Football player (retired); Houston Gamblers (USFL), 1984-85; Wash Redskins, wide receiver, 1986-93; Atlanta Falcons, wide receiver, 1994-95. **Honors/Awds:** Most Valuable Player, Palm Bowl, 1982; Most Valuable Player, Wash Redskins, 1988.

SANDERS, ROBER LAFAYETTE
Engineer, scientist. **Personal:** Born Feb 14, 1952, Raleigh, NC. **Educ:** NC State Univ, BSEE, 1973; Univ Ariz, Phoenix, MBA, 1983; MIT, MSEE, 1976. **Career:** IBM, program mgr, currently. **Orgs:** Vpres, IEEE, 1973, 1986; ACME, 1973-; Am Physicists, 1973-; basileus Omega Psi Phi Frat, 1982-90; pres, Scholastic Aptitude, 1983-; treas, Tucson Black Forum, 1985-87; treas, Tucson Democratic Party, 1986-87; Black Engrs Am, pres, 1989-; State NAACP, pres, 1983-90; Br NAACP, pres, 1983-90; Optimist Club, vpres, 1985-91. **Honors/Awds:** Outstanding Young Man, Jaycees, 1985, 1986; 'Engineer of the Year', BEA, 1986; Man of the Year, Omega Psi Phi, 1986; Citizen of the Year; Omega Psi Phi, Asst KF, 1994. **Home Addr:** 429 N St SW, Washington, DC 20024, **Home Phone:** (202)484-4407. **Business Addr:** Program Manager, IBM Corp., 9221 Corporate Blvd, Rockville, MD 20850, **Business Phone:** (301)640-4294.

SANDERS, DR. ROBERT B
Biochemist, consultant, educator. **Personal:** Born Dec 9, 1938, Augusta, GA; son of Robert Sanders and Lois Jones Sanders; married Gladys Nealous; children: Sylvia Sanders Schneider & William. **Educ:** Paine Col, Augusta, GA, BS, 1959; Univ Mich, Ann Arbor, MI, MS, 1961, PhD, 1964; Univ Wis, Madison, PhD, 1966. **Career:** Battelle Memorial Inst, vis scientist, 1970-71; Univ Tex Med Sch, Houston, vis assoc prof, 1974-75; Nat Sci Found, prog dir, 1978-79; Univ Kans, Lawrence, from asst prof to prof, 1966, assoc dean, The Grad Sch, 1987-96, assoc vice chancellor, Res Grad Studies & Pub Serv, 1989-96, coordr minority Grad Stud

Support, 1996-99, prof emer, cuurently. **Orgs:** Bd dir, United Child Develop Ctr, 1968-93; consult, Interx Res Corp, 1972-80, Nat Res Coun 1973-77, Nat Inst Health 1982, Nat Sci Found, 1983-94, Dept Educ 1993-97, 2003; bd Higher Educ, United Meth Church, 1976-80; Asn Cent States, 2006-; Am Soc Biochem & Molecular Biol; Am Soc Pharmacol & Exp Therapeut; Am Asn Univ Prof; Sigma XI; Am Lung Asn USA Nationwide Assembly, 2006-. **Honors/Awds:** postdoctoral fel, Am Cancer Soc, 1964-66; fel, Battelle Mem Inst, 1970-71; postdoctoral fel, Nat Inst Health, 1974-75; more than 57 research grants. **Special Achievements:** Published more than 60 scientific articles. **Military Serv:** AUS, e-4, 1955-62; Hon Discharge. **Home Addr:** 5738 Longleaf, Lawrence, KS 66049-5802. **Business Addr:** Professor Emeritus Biochemistry, University of Kansas, Department Molucular Biosciences, 2045 Haworth Hall, 1200 Sunnyside Ave, Lawrence, KS 66045-7534, **Business Phone:** (785)864-4301.

SANDERS, ROBIN RENEE
Government official. **Personal:** Born in Hampton, VA. **Educ:** Hampton Univ, BA communs; Ohio Univ, MA, int rels & Africa studies, MS, communs & jour. **Career:** Nat Security Coun, dir, African Affairs, 1997-99; US Dept State, Off Pub Diplomacy, dir, 2000-02, Repub Congo, US ambassador, 2002-05, US ambassador, Nigeria, 2005-. **Orgs:** Alpha Kappa Alpha Sorority; Coun Foreign Rels; Women Int Security; DC Chamber Com; Operation Hope; dir, Nat Security Coun. **Honors/Awds:** State Dept Superior Honor Awards; State Dept Meritorious Honor Awards. **Business Addr:** Ambassador, Republic of the Congo, 4891 Colo Ave NW, Washington, DC 20011, **Business Phone:** (202)726-5500.

SANDERS, SALLY RUTH
Registered nurse, social worker. **Personal:** Born Jun 1, 1952, Tyler, TX; married Donald Ray Sanders; children: Carla, Candace, Christopher. **Educ:** Tex Eastern Sch Nursing, Tyler Jr Col, dipl nursing asst, 1975, 1974; Univ Tex Tyler, BSN, 1984. **Career:** Relief Health Care Servs, dir, 1985-86; Triage, head nurse; Progressive Health Care, asst admin, 1986-. **Orgs:** Historian Diabetes Asn, 1984-85; asst dir, Marche Incorp, 1986-; Negro Bus & Prof Women's Org; Rose Bud Civitan Club, Civitan; dir, Sanders Community Health Servs. **Honors/Awds:** Woman of the Year, UTHCT, 1985. **Business Addr:** Nurse Clinician, Assistant Administration, Progressive Health Care, PO Box 2003, Tyler, TX 75710.*

SANDERS, STEVEN LEROY
Financial manager. **Personal:** Born Oct 26, 1959, Philadelphia, PA; son of Willie E and Elouise Tooten; married Kelly DeSouza, Jun 3, 1989; children: son. **Educ:** Howard Univ, Wash, DC, BBA, 1982. **Career:** Aetna Life & Casualty, Pittsburgh, PA, employee benefit rep, 1982-85; Mellon Bank, Philadelphia, PA, credit analyst, 1985-86; Hunt & Sanders Financial Adv, Philadelphia, PA, partner & founder 1986-; MDL Capital Mgt, pres & chief exec officer; Your Money Matters Prog, New York, NY, Citibank Master Card & Visa lectr, 1989-; First Genesis Financial Group, chmn & chief exec officer, 2005-. **Orgs:** Bd dirs, Freedom Theatre, 1990-; bd dirs, Help Line, 1984-85; Bus Educ Adv Comt, 1987-89; pres, Howard Univ Alumni, Pittsburgh Chap, 1984-85; Scout Master Troop 629, Boy Scouts Am, 1986-88; African Am Chamber Com; Greater Philadelphia Chamber Com; Pennsylvania Acad Fine Arts; Howard Univ Eli Inst Bd Entrepreneurship; United Bank Philadelphia, To Our Children's Future With Health. **Honors/Awds:** Leaders Club, The New England, 1990; Chairperson of the Month, Vectors Pittsburgh, 1985; Nat Speaker-Citibank Master Card & Visa Money Matters for Young Adults, 1989-. **Special Achievements:** Black Enterprise Top 100 Asset Managers List, company ranked No 9, 2000; author of "Money Matters for Young Adults. **Home Addr:** 13 Stockton Dr, Voorhees, NJ 08043. **Business Phone:** (610)886-1947.

SANDERS, WESLEY, JR. See Obituaries section.

SANDERS, WILLIAM E
Clergy, executive, military leader. **Personal:** Son of George and Veala M. **Educ:** Morehouse Col, Atlanta, Ga, BA, 1971; Union Theol Sem NY, Mdiv. **Career:** Military leader (retired), clergy; NY Army Nat Guard, chaplain; Ohio Army Nat Guard, chaplain; 37th Armor Brigade, brigade chaplain; Third Baptist Church, Toledo, Oh, assoc Minister; Calvary Baptist Church, Jamaica, NY, asst pastor; Bethany Baptist Church, Brooklyn, NY, asst pastor; William E Sanders Family Life Ctr, staff; Lee Road Baptist Church, pastor & bd dir, 1977-. **Orgs:** Nat Asn Advan Colored People; chair, Cleveland Baptist Asn. **Special Achievements:** First Black chaplain to serve in the Ohio Army National Guard. **Military Serv:** AUS. **Business Addr:** Pastor, Lee Road Baptist Church, 3970 Lee Rd, Cleveland, OH 44128.*

SANDERS, DR. WOODROW MAC
Educator. **Personal:** Born Aug 4, 1943, Luling, TX; son of Alburnice Stewart and R V; divorced; children: Rodrigo R, Justin W & Jennifer M. **Educ:** Univ Alaska; Univ ND, 1964-66; TX A&I Univ Kings ville, BA, 1970; TX A&I Univ Corpus Christi, MS, 1977; Univ N Tex, Denton, TX, PhD, 1992; Social Work Licenses, 1993. **Career:** Bee Co Col, Bee ville, TX, counr & instr, 1978-81; Nueces Co Mental Health/Mental Retardation Ctr, dir outpatient serv, 1972-78; Gateway Wholesale Sporting Goods, asst mgr, 1971-72; USN Counseling & Asst Cntgr Corpus Christi, TX, consult assn psychologist, 1973-78; Univ TX Austin, inst Alcohol Studies, 1977; S TX Housing Corp, bd pres, 1978; South western Bell Telephone Co, Laredo, TX, mgr engineering, 1981-89; Bee County Col, Beeville, TX, counr/instr, 1989-91; TX Dept Health-Social Work Servs, part time instr Bee County Col. **Orgs:** Sdv bd mem, Nueces House TX Youth Coun, 1977-78; bd mem, Coastal Bend Bus & Indsl Devel Inc, 1977-; NAACP; US Rifle Marksmanship Team USAF, 1962-64; vpres 7 bd dirs, Children's Heart Institute Tex, 1985-; Texas Asn Telecommunication Engineers, 1981-89; Southwest Asn Student Special Servs Prog, 1989-; Tex Asn Coun & Develop, 1989-91. **Honors/Awds:** Presidential Unit Citation USAF, 1965; Republic of Vietnam Medal of Valor USAF, 1966; Youth Serv Award Corpus Christi Police Dept, 1967; Award for Ser in Drug Abuse - Prevention, Coastal Bend Council of Govts Drug Abuse Adv Com Corpus Christi, 1976-77; fellowship TX Research Inst of Mental Sci Houston, 1978. **Military Serv:** USAF, staff sgt, 1961-66. **Home Addr:** 341 Merrill Dr, Corpus Christi, TX 78408, **Home Phone:** (361)888-5707. **Business Addr:** Instructor, Texas Department of Health-Social Work Services, 1322 Agnes St, Corpus Christi, TX 78401, **Business Phone:** (512)888-7762.

SANDERSON, RANDY CHRIS
Executive, consultant. **Personal:** Born Dec 23, 1954, St Louis, MO; married Toni M Harper. **Educ:** Univ Mo, St Louis, BS, 1977. **Career:** May Dept Stores, mgr & dir, 1979-81; May Dept Stores, Calif, advert controller, 1981-84; Caldor Inc, asst controller, 1987-89; Lord & Taylor, div controller, 1989-91; May D&F, vpres & controller, 1991-93; Famous Barr Dept Store, vpres controller, 1993-96; Dollar Gen, vpres controller, 1996-2001; Millennium Digital Media, vpres contoller, 2003-06; INROADS, vpres-consumer prods, health & retail industs, 2006-08; consult, currently. **Orgs:** Chmn, Nat Alumni Assoc Inroads, 1985-87; 100 Black Men Greater St. Louis; bd dirs, Mathews Dickey Boys & Girls Club. **Honors/Awds:** John C Willis Award, Nat Asn Black Accountants, 1976.

SANDIDGE, KANITA DURICE
Executive, chairperson. **Personal:** Born Dec 2, 1947, Cleveland, OH; daughter of John Robert Jr and Virginia Louise Caldwell. **Educ:** Cornell Univ, BA, 1970; Case Western Reserve Univ, MBA, 1979. **Career:** Executive (retired), Chairperson; AT&T Network Systems, acting sect chief, 1970-72, sect chief cost control, 1972-78, dept chief data processing & acct. 1978-79, dept chief acct anal, 1979-80, admin mgr, 1980-83, sales forecasting & anal mgr, 1983-86, planning & develop mgr, 1986-87, admin serv dir, 1987-89, div staff dir, 1990; NY/NJ Minority Purchasing Coun Inc, chairperson, currently. **Orgs:** Beta Alpha Psi Acct Hon, Am Mgt Asn, The Alliance AT&T Black Mgrs, Nat Black MBAs, Nat Asn Female Exec; life mem, Nat Asn Advan Colored People; black executives exchange prog NUL, 1986-; bd dir, E-W Corporate Corridor Asn, Ill, 1987-90, Quad County Urban League, Ill, 1988-90. **Honors/Awds:** Harlem YMCA Black Achiever in Industry, 1981; Tribute to Women & Industry Achievement Award YWCA, 1985. **Home Addr:** 10 Trade Winds Dr, Randolph, NJ 07869.

SANDIDGE, DR. ONEAL C
Clergy. **Personal:** Born in Lynchburg, VA; son of Hattie and Wardie; married Janice Oliver; children: Jermaine Oneal & Ieke Monique. **Educ:** Lynchburg Col, BA, 1977; Howard Univ Divinity Sch, MA, Christian educ, 1986; Columbia Univ, MA, 1988; Drew Univ, DMin, 1992; Capella Univ, PhD cand Higher Educ, currently. **Career:** Pastor, 1979-86; Madison County Public Sch, teacher; Campbell County Pub Sch, teacher; Petersburg Pub Sch, teacher, 1982-90; Piedmont Va Community Col, teacher, 1989-90; author; workshop leader; preacher; Beulah Heights Bible Col, assoc prof, 1994-96; Luther Rice Sem, teacher, 1995-96; Conv Ave Baptist Church, minister christian educ, 1997-98; Alexandria Pub Sch, teacher, 1999-; Defiance Col, prof, 1999-; Trinity Episcopal Sch Ministry Sem, adj prof; Md Pub Sch, Eng teacher, 2000-06; Liberty Univ, Lynchburg, VA, prof relig, 2006; Nat Bible Col & Seminary, fac, currently. **Orgs:** Member numerous prof orgns. **Honors/Awds:** Merrill Fellowship, Harvard Univ, 1992-93; Achievement Award for Outstanding Leadership, Lynchburg Col Alumni, 1993; Memphis Writer's Award; Award for Christian education of the the year, 2004; LABBE Award, Los Angeles Book Expo. **Special Achievements:** Books published by National Baptist USA, Inc: Beyond the Classroom; Strategies for the Director of Christian Edu in the African Church; Teacher Training in the African American Church, I'm Stuck! Help Me Start a Youth Ministry in the African American Church; Articles Published: book review, "Black Religious Leaders-Conflict in Unity," The Journal of Black Scholar, Sept 1991; "Tracing Gospel Roots with Professor Thomas Dorsey," Score Gospel Magazine, Jan/Feb 1992; "Black History," Virginia Education Association Journal, Feb 1992; "The Uniqueness of Black Preaching," The Journal of Religious Thought, Howard University, 1992; "Glancing at Curriculum," June 1995, "Whosoever Will Come," Dec/Jan 1995-96, Journal of Church School Today; Informer Journal, four articles, 1999; "Twelve Teaching Tips for Church Educators," 2000; "Back to the Basics: Teaching Teenagers at Home and at School," 2000; "Assessing Your Students," 2001; "Can Your Students Read Scripture Without Knowing the Vocabulary," 2001. **Business Addr:** Undergraduate College Dean, National Bible College & Seminary, 6700 Bock Rd, Fort Washington, MD 20744, **Business Phone:** (301)567-9500.

SANDIFORD, ORPHIA
Administrator, scout. **Career:** Mass State Police, dir recruitment, 2003. *

SANDLER, JOAN D
Association executive. **Personal:** Born Oct 2, 1934, New York, NY; divorced; children: Eve & Kathe. **Educ:** City Col NY; Univ Mexico. **Career:** Bloomingdale Family Serv, teacher dir, 1963-66; Metro Appl Res Ctr, res, 1966-68; Dept Cult Affairs, prog specialist, 1968-72; Black Theatre Alliance, exec dir, 1972-77; Senghor Found, staff, 1977-80; Metro Mus Art, assoc mus educ charge comn educ; Nat Endowment Arts, regional dir; Romau Bearden Found, exec dir. **Orgs:** Panelist & consult, Nat Endowment Arts, 1971-74; consult, NY State Coun Arts, 1972-; adv, VISIONS KCET/TV Pub Broadcasting Corp, 1974; theater panel, Theater Develop Fund; bd dirs, Nat Coun Women; bd dirs, Children Arts Carnival; Opportunity Resources; adv, Gov's Task Force; bd dirs, First Am Cong Theatre, NSINGHA; Nat Coalition 100 Black Women; Am Mus Asn; Mus Educr Roundtable. **Honors/Awds:** Audelco Award, 1973.

SANDOVAL, DOLORES S.
Educator. **Personal:** Born Sep 30, 1937, Quebec. **Educ:** Inst Chicago, art, 1958; Univ Mich, BSD, 1960; Ind Univ, MS, 1968, PhD, 1970; Harvard Univ, Educ Mgt Iem, 1975. **Career:** State Univ Col, Buffalo, assoc prof, 1970-71; Univ Vt, assoc prof, educ,1971; Mid E studies, co-chair, 1994-, asst to pres, human resources, 1972-77; fel, Challenges to Unity: The European COT, 1995, Maastricht, 1995; Univ Vt, emer fac, Currently. **Orgs:** Fel, NAT Endowment Humanities Summer on African Cult, 1987; Bd mem, Pub Access Govt TV Channel 17 (VT), 1991-95; Fel, Univ New Mexico Col Fine Arts, Nat Arts Proj, Daring To Do It, 1993-94; Bd mem, Sister Cities, Burlington, VT Arad (Israel & Bethlehem), 1995-96; Pres, Vt & Honduras, 1997-; Partners AMEs. **Honors/Awds:** Elected Democratic candidate for Congress from VT, 1990; Primary candidate, 1988; fel mem bd trustees, 1976-82; Rhode Island Sch Design, 1981, Univ Senate, Univ Vt, chair, 1981-82; Contributions to Duke Ellington Concert & Speech Series Award, Black Am Heritage Fund NY, 1989-92. Malone Fel Arab and Islamic Studies in Tunisia, summer, 1989; Malone Alumni Fel Jordan, Israel, Palestine and Syria, summer, 1991. **Business Addr:** Emeriti Faculty, University of Vermont, 16 Colchester Ave, Burlington, VT 05405-0001, **Business Phone:** (802)656-3131.

SANDOZ, JOHN H
Judge. **Career:** Judge (retired); Los Angeles County, judge; Los Angeles Super Ct, judge.

SANDRIDGE, JOHN SOLOMON
Artist, physician. **Personal:** Born in Gadsden, AL; son of Edward (deceased) and Lucille; married Frances, Feb 7, 1975; children: Peter, Priscilla & David. **Educ:** Fesperman Sch Naturopathic Med, ND, 1983. **Career:** Artist, author & physician; Creative Displays, supvr; Gadsden City Bd Educ, teacher; Luvlife Collectibles Inc, ceo, founder & pres; Dr. John's Natural Health Prods, formulator, currently; Self-Healing Ministries Inc, founder & pres, currently; Trees Of Wealth Inc, founder & pres, currently; THE SYSTEM, designer & formulator; Simply Results Inc, consult & physician, currently. **Orgs:** Pres, Carver Theatre; Sandridge Mus Living Hist. **Honors/Awds:** Numerous honors and awards including Key to Birmingham, Gadsen, Rainbow City, Fairfield, Ala; Certificate of Appreciation, Gov Ala, 1982; Certificate of Appreciation, Black Bus Asn, 1983; National Vendors Award, JC Penney's, 1993; Outstanding Citizen's Award, Roberta Watts Med, 1993. **Special Achievements:** First African-American to be licensed by The Coca-Cola Company to create a series of paintings incorporating an African-American theme. **Business Addr:** Consultant, Physician, Simply Results Inc, 3100 Lorna Rd Barbizon Bldg Suite 301, Birmingham, AL 35216, **Business Phone:** (205)979-3933.

SANDS, GEORGE M.
Consultant. **Personal:** Born Jan 15, 1942, Port Chester, NY; married Mary Alice Moxley; children: Jeffrey & Kenneth. **Educ:** Western Mich Univ, BS, 1964; Hunter Col Sch Social Work, MSW, 1970. **Career:** Cage Teen Ctr Inc, exec dir, 1972-78; Empire State Col, lectr, 1981-;West chester Comm Col, adj prof, 1973, assoc prof, 1988-; Sands Assocs, owner, dir, 1978-. **Orgs:** Educ chmn, Middletown NAACP; Am Soc Personnel Admin; bd dirs, Michael Schwerner Found, 1970-72; personnel chmn, Middletown Bd Educ, 1976-82; consult, trainer, Stony Brook Univ, 1977-; bd mem, Orange Co Pvt Indus Coun, 1983-; trainer, Cornell Univ Sch Indust Labor Rels. **Honors/Awds:** Teacher of the Yr, West chester Comm Col, 1982; Service Award, Middletown Bd Educ, 1982. **Business Addr:** Director, Sands Associates, 1204 Spinnaker Dr, North Myrtle Beach, SC 29582-6810, **Business Phone:** (914)692-6296.

SANDS, JERRY LEIGH
Athletic coach. **Personal:** Married Torrie Lynn Gant. **Career:** Univ Ark Pine Bluff, linebacker coach & spec teams coordr,

currently. **Business Addr:** Linebacker Coach, University of Arkansas Pine Bluff, 1200 N Univ Dr, Pine Bluff, AR 71611, **Business Phone:** (870)575-8000.*

SANDS, PROF. MARY ALICE
School administrator. **Personal:** Born Oct 20, 1941, Indianapolis, IN; daughter of Frank O Moxley and Velma Goodnight Moxley; married George M; children: Jeffrey & Kenneth. **Educ:** State Univ Iowa, attended 1960; Western Mich Univ, BS, 1964; Bank St Col Ed, MS Ed, 1982. **Career:** School administrator (retired); Bronx Municipal Hosp Ctr, asst chief, 1965-70; Harlem Hosp OT Dept, supvr clinical ed, 1971; Rockland Community Col, chair OTA Prog, 1973-77; Orange Cty Community Col, chair, full prof, OTA Prog, 1977-01, prof emer currently; Founder & Co-Owner Occup Therapy Plus. **Orgs:** Nat Asn Advan Colored People; Alpha Kappa Alpha; Am OT Asn; AOTA Prog Adv Comm, 1983-86; mem bd dirs, Orange Cty Cerebral Palsy Asn, 1984-87; chair, NY State Bd Occupational Therapy, 1986-89; mem bd dir, Horton Med Ctr,1998-00; chair, Am Occup Therapy Asn Comn Educ, 1989-92. **Honors/Awds:** Award of Merit, Pract NY State OT Asn, 1985; Service Award, Am Occup Therapy Assoc, 1992; Certificate of Appreciation, Hudson-Taconic District NYSOTA, 1992; Fel Am Occup Therapy Assn, 1994. **Special Achievements:** Contributing author, Willard & Spackman's Occupational Therapy, 1997, 2003. **Home Addr:** 1204 Spinnaker Dr, North Myrtle Beach, SC 29582. *

SANDS, ROSETTA F
School administrator. **Personal:** Born in Homestead, FL; daughter of John H and Annie Pickett Harriel; married Charles H, Jun 9, 1956 (divorced); children: Michael H Sands. **Educ:** Harlem Hosp Sch Nursing, New York, Dipl, 1954; Univ Md Sch Nursing, Baltimore, Md, BSN, 1966, Univ Md-Col Park, MS, 1970; Johns Hopkins Univ, Baltimore, Md, postgraduate study, 1970-77; The Union Graduate Sch, Cincinnati Ohio, PhD, 1980. **Career:** Univ Md Sch Nursing, Baltimore Md, instr med & surg, nursing, 1970-71, asst prof, registered nursing prog, 1971-83, team coordr, 1971-74, asst dean, 1974-79; Tuskegee Univ, Tuskegee Inst Ala, dean & assoc, 1983-87; The William Paterson Col, Wayne, NJ, dean & prof, 1987-93; Stud Retention In Acad Nursing, nurse consult, 1993-. **Orgs:** Trustee Nat Sorority House, 1976-79; Chi Eta Phi Sorority for Nurses; Sigma Theta Tau Intl Honor Society for Nursing, 1969; Peer Review Panel, Special Project Grants, Dept Health & Human Servs, 1976-85; Task Force on Teaching Culturally Diverse Studs, 1977-82; Phi Kappa Phi Honor Society, 1977; pres, bd of trustees, Provident Hosp, 1978-81; bd of dir, Md Blue Cross, 1980-83; Md Adv Comt, US Civil Rights Comt, 1981-83; pres, Md Nurse Asn, 1981-82; bd of dir, Am Asn Cols Nursing, 1986-88; Zeta Phi Beta Sorority Inc; bd trustees, United Hosps Medical Ctr, 1993-96. **Honors/Awds:** Cert Recognition Leadership in Nursing, Univ Md Nursing Faculty, 1976; Community Serv Nomination for Mary E Mahoney Award, Resolution, Md Senate, 1979; Prof Leadership in Nursing, Award, Chi Eta Phi Sorority, Gamma Chap, 1980; Superior Leadership as Pres Bd Trustees, Provident Hosp Bd Trustees, 1981; Finer Womanhood Award for Work with Youth in Health Careers, 1981; 'Excellence in Professional Achievements Award', Black Nurses Asn Baltimore, 1983; Dr Rosetta Sands Mentorship Award, Coppin State Univ, established, 2001. **Special Achievements:** Author, Consumer Perception of the Expanded Role of the Nurse, Glowing Lamp, 1973; The 1985 Resolution and the Nursing Shortage, Md Nurse, 1981; Cultural Conflict in Nurse, Client Interactions, Videocassette, 1983; Enhancing Cultural Sensitivity in Clinl Practice, 1987; The Predictive Potential of Social Variables for Black Studs, Performance on NCELX, 1988; Predictive Potential of Social Variables for Black Nursing Students' Performance on the National Council Licensure Examination, 1988; Hosp Governance: Nurse Trustee Vis-A-Vis Nurse Exec, Nursing Mgmt, 1990; Black Nurses As Mentors: Linking The Past With Our Future, The Glowing Lamp, 1990. **Home Addr:** 4406 Norfolk Ave, Baltimore, MD 21216. **Business Addr:** IMS, Consultants, 4406 Norfolk Ave, Baltimore, MD 21216, **Business Phone:** (410)448-3563.

SANDY MILLER, JONES
Association executive. **Educ:** Northwestern's Kellogg Sch Bus, MBA. **Career:** The Quaker Oats Co, mkt mgr; Segmented Marketing Services Inc, founder & chmn, 1978-. **Business Addr:** Founder, Chairman, Segmented Marketing Services Inc, 4265 Brownsboro Rd Suite 225, Winston-Salem, NC 27106-3425, **Business Phone:** (336)759-7477.

SANFORD, MARK
Executive. **Personal:** Born Nov 24, 1953, St Louis, MO; son of Levi; children: Tifani Iris, Marcus L Alexander. **Educ:** Wash Univ, BA, 1975; St Louis Univ, MHA, 1981. **Career:** St Louis Univ Med Ctr, staff assoc, 1981-82; St Mary's Hosp, vpres, 1982-89; People's Health Ctrs, dir opers, 1989-. **Orgs:** Am Col Healthcare Execs, 1981-; bd mem, Black Music Soc; St Louis Chap Black MBA's, 1985-; youth chmn, UNCF Telethon; bd mem, African-Am Chamber Com; 100 Black Men; past pres, Nat Black MBA Asn St Louis Chapter; Nat Soc Fund Raising Exec, 1992; nat conf chmn, Nat Conf NBMBAA; bd mem, Am Heart Asn; bd mem, Nat Black MBA; bd mem, BABAA. **Honors/Awds:** MBA of the Year, St Louis Chapter, Nat Black MBA Asn, 1988; EA Shepley Award. **Business Addr:** Director of Planning and Development, People's Health Centers, 5701 Delmar blvd, Saint Louis, MO 63112, **Business Phone:** (314)367-7848.

SANKOFA, MIKA'IL. See LOFTON, MICHAEL.

SANTIAGO, O. J. (OTIS JASON SANTIAGO)
Football player. **Personal:** Born Apr 4, 1974, Ontario. **Educ:** Kent State Univ, attended 1996. **Career:** Atlanta Falcons, tight end, 1997-99; Dallas Cowboys, tight end, 2000;Cleveland Browns, tight end, 2000-02; Minnesota Vikings, 2002; Oakland Raiders, tight end, 2003, 2006-07; Denver Broncos, 2004; New England Patriots, tight end, 2006; free agent, currently.

SANTIAGO, OTIS JASON. See SANTIAGO, O. J.

SANTIAGO, ROBERTO
Journalist, writer. **Personal:** Born Jun 30, 1963, New York, NY; son of Francisca Castro and Fundador. **Educ:** Oberlin Col, BA, hist/creative writing, 1985. **Career:** McGraw Hill Inc, NY, corporate writer, 1985-87; Times Mirror Inc, NY, sports writer, 1987-88; Emerge Magazine, NY, staff writer, 1989-92; The Plain Dealer, columnist, 1992; Miami Herald, sr staff writer, currently; Books: Our Times 2, Bedford Books, 1991; The Contemporary Reader, Harper Collins, 1992. **Orgs:** Mystery Writers Am; The Newspaper Guild. **Honors/Awds:** Int Am Press Assn, Award for Commentary, 1991; Guest Lecturer: Rutgers Univ; Princeton Univ; Vassar Clg; Oberlin Col; CBS-TV; Columbia Univ; Trenton State Co. **Business Addr:** Senior Staff Writer, Miami Herald, 1 Herald Plz, Miami, FL 33132, **Business Phone:** (305)350-2111.

SANTISIMA, LANGSTON FAIZON. See LOVE, FAIZON.

SANTOS, EDWIN J
Executive. **Personal:** Married Paula; children: Erica, Steven & Michael. **Educ:** Bryant Univ, BS, 1981. **Career:** FleetBoston Financial Corp, chief auditor; Citizens Financial Group Inc, exec vpres & gen auditor, 2004-. **Orgs:** Bd trustee, Roger Williams Med Ctr; vice chmn & br trustee, Bryant Univ; bd dir, Crossroads RI; Bd Delta Dent; Rock Hill Sch, Bd Trustee, co-vpres, 2007-. **Business Addr:** Executive Vice President, General Auditor, Citizens Financial Group Inc, 1 Citizens Plz, Providence, RI 02903, **Business Phone:** (401)282-3735.

SANTOS, HENRY JOSEPH
Educator, pianist. **Personal:** Born Aug 29, 1927, Lewistown, ME; son of Beulah Benjamin Santos and Henry Santos; married Leola Waters. **Educ:** Boston Univ Sch Fine & Appl Arts, BA Music; Harvard Univ, Grad Study; Boston Univ, pvt study piano Alfredo Fondacaro, 1952-60, MA, Music, 1980. **Career:** Perkins Sch Blind, 1956-70; Henry Santos Piano Summer Piano Inst High Sch Stud, founder; Bridgewater State Col, asst prof music to prof music, prof emer, currently. **Orgs:** Music Ed Nat Conf; Nat Entertainment Conf Am; Asn Instr Blind; adv bd, Fuller Art Mus; support panel mem, Rhode Island Arts Coun, 1987, 1989; vis mem, Blue Ribbon Comn, Rhode Island Arts Coun, 1991. **Honors/Awds:** Piano recitals chamber music prog in major cities of NE US & Europe; chosen instr perf Albert Schweitzer Fest, 1950; rec cits Achievement Award, Cape Verdean Benef Soc, 1968; semi-fin 1st Louis Moreau Gottschalk Int Competition Pianists & Comp, Dillard Univ, 1970; performance of classical music for piano by Afro-Am Composers; TV prog Say Bro, 1971; prog WGBH Performance European & Afro-Am Composers for Piano, 1972; lectr recital, St Eastern Reg Conf, Music Educ Nat Conf, 1973; Ethnic Herit Task Force of Commonwealth of MA by Gov Francis Sargent, 1974; grant, MA Council on Arts & Humanities for Trade Europe & Afro-Am music progs for elem & sec sch child Bridgewater St Col, 1974; compositions: Androscoggin Pines, 1983, Sonata for Piano, 1985, Massin G Major, 1987, Two Dances for Piano, 1988, Healing Song, 1988, Movement for Piano Brass Quintet, 1990, Songs of Innocence, 1990; Henry Santos Scholar, Bridgewater State Col, named in honor. **Military Serv:** AUS, 418th Army Bad, pvt, 1946-47. **Home Phone:** (508)947-9909. **Business Addr:** Professor Emeritus, Bridgewater State College, Department of Music, 131 Summer St, Bridgewater, MA 02325, **Business Phone:** (508)531-1000.

SANTOS, MATHIES JOSEPH
Educator. **Personal:** Born Jan 10, 1948, Providence, RI; son of Matthew J and Rosemarie Lopes; married Michelina Doretto, Sep 6, 1969; children: Chiara & Mathies-Kareem. **Educ:** Brown Univ, Providence, RI, BA, 1977; Rhode Island Col, Providence, RI, BA, 1982. **Career:** Educator (retired); Rhode Island Col, Providence, RI, fin aid officer, 1978-80; State Rhode Island, Dept Educ, consult, 1980-82, project dir, 1983-85, Gov's Office, sr policy analyst, 1985, Dept Admin, exec asst, 1985-90, spec asst to comnr educ; Lippitt for Mayor, Providence, RI, campaign mgr, 1982. **Orgs:** CRP mem, Delta Dental Rhode Island; Brown Univ Third World Alumni Activities Comn; bd mem, Rhode Island Col Alumni Asn; mem, Rhode Island Black Heritage Soc; Nat Asn Advan Colored People; Gov's Adv Comt Refugee Resettlement Mgt; trustee, The Wheeler Sch. **Military Serv:** Rhode Island Air Nat Guard, Capt, beginning 1982; Air Force Achievement Medal; sr air weapons dir; military aide-de-camp to the gov, beginning, 1985.

SAPP, LAUREN B
Librarian. **Personal:** Born Jul 13, 1937, Smithfield, NC; daughter of Lee and Senoria Burnette; children: Corey, Christopher & Cheston Williams. **Educ:** NC Cent Univ, Durham, NC, BA, 1967; Univ Mich, Ann Arbor, Mich, AMLS, 1971; Fla State Univ, Tallahassee, FL, Adv MS, 1979, PhD, 1984. **Career:** Voorhees Col, Denmark, NC, instr librn, 1971-74; Fla State Univ, Tallahassee, FL, librn, 1974-84; NC Cent Univ, Durham, NC, vis prof, 1985-96; Duke Univ, Durham, NC, librn, 1984-96; Univ NC Chapel Hill, adjunct prof, 1993-95; Fla A&M Univ, Tallahassee, Fl, dir libr, 1996-. **Orgs:** Am Libr Asn; Black Caucus, LAMA, ACRL; chair, docs caucus, Fla Libr Asn, 1982; chair, docs Secy, NC Libr Asn, 1988-89; secy, State & Local docs Task Force GODORT, 1987-88; ACRL Int Rels Comn, 1994-98; Beta Phi Mu Honor Soc, 1980-; Lama Cult Diversity Comn, 1997-2001; Lama Publs Comn Fund Raising & Financial Develop Sec, 1997-; treas, Libr Dir Asn, 1998-. **Honors/Awds:** EEO Fell, bd Regents, State Fl, 1978-79, 1982; Title II Fell, Univ Mich, 1970-71; Women Achievement Award, YWCA, Durham, NC, 1988; Star Award, Perkins Libr, Duke Univ, 1989, 1991. **Home Addr:** PO Box 6326, Tallahassee, FL 32314, **Home Phone:** (850)514-1817. **Business Addr:** Director of Libraries, University Librarian, Florida A & M University, 307 Coleman Libr, 1500 S Martin Blvd, Tallahassee, FL 32307, **Business Phone:** (850)599-3370.

SAPP, PATRICK
Football player. **Personal:** Born May 11, 1973, Jacksonville, FL. **Educ:** Clemson Univ. **Career:** Football player (retired) San Diego Chargers, linebacker, 1996-97; Ariz Cardinals, 1998-99; Indianapolis Colts, 2000. **Honors/Awds:** Rookie of the Year, 1996.

SAPP, WARREN CARLOS
Football player, executive. **Personal:** Born Dec 19, 1972, Florida; son of Annie Roberts; married JaMiko Vaughn, 1998; children: Mercedes & Warren Jr. **Educ:** Univ Miami, attended 1994. **Career:** Football player (retired), Executive; Tampa Bay Buccaneers, defensive tackle, 1995-2003; Oakland Raiders, defensive tackle, 2004-07; Showtime Networks Inc, studio analyst, 2008-. **Orgs:** Nat Football League Network. **Honors/Awds:** Lombardi Award, 1994; Big East Defensive Player of the Year, 1994. **Special Achievements:** First round/12th overall NFL draft pick, 1995. **Business Addr:** Studio Analyst, Showtime Networks Inc, 1633 Broadway, New York, NY 10019, **Business Phone:** (212)708-1600.*

SARDIN, JAMES
School administrator. **Career:** Miss Dept Educ, assoc supt, currently.

SARGEANT, LARRY
Executive. **Educ:** Rutgers Univ, attended 1976; Brown Univ, AB. **Career:** Seattle-King County Legal Aid, staff atty, 1976; State Wash, asst atty; Pac NW Bell Tel Co, Seattle, WA, atty; US WEST, vpres Fed Regulatory; US Telecom Asn, vpres, Law & Gen Coun, currently. **Orgs:** DC Bar Asn; Wash State Bar Asn; Fed Commun Bar Asn; Nat Bar Asn. *

SARGENT, VIRGINIA HIGHTOWER
Executive, consultant. **Personal:** Born Jun 24, 1963, South Boston, VA; daughter of Virginia Maude Dixon Hightower and Obey Hightower; divorced; children: Ashley. **Educ:** Pace Univ, BA com, 1993; Baruch Col, Nat Urban Fel MPA, 2000; George Washington Univ, CPM, 2002; Univ Phoenix, Doctorate, bus admin, 2006. **Career:** ABC-TV/Disney Inc, ed 1993-99, DC govt commun, dir 2000-03, healthcare dir mkt & pr 2003-05; Univ Md Univ Col, adjunct bus prof; Daily Business Blessing.com, Publ, spiritual bus consult, currently. **Orgs:** Pres & founder, Young Readers Network, 1995-; bd dir, Proj Ctrl NYC. **Honors/Awds:** President's Service Award, 1997; Volunteerism in Children Award, 1997; NYC Principal for a Day, 1998, 1999, 2000; Silver Inkwell Award, Int Asn Bus Communicators, 2002; Aegis Award, 2002. **Special Achievements:** Ed, Spiritual Expressions, 2005; creator, Reeedy Readercize; 7-time marathon runner. **Business Addr:** Publisher, Business Coach, Daily Business Blessing.com, 549 Brummel Ct NW, Washington, DC 20012, **Business Phone:** (202)722-2788.

SARKODIE-MENSAH, DR. KWASI
Librarian. **Personal:** Born Jun 13, 1955, Ejisu, Ashanti, Ghana; son of Thomas Kwaku Mensah and Margaret Akua Barnieh; divorced; children: Kofi, Kwame & Nana Akua. **Educ:** Univ Complutense, dipl, 1978; Univ Ghana, BA (w/Hons), 1979; Clarion Univ, MSLS, 1983; Univ Ill, PhD, 1988. **Career:** Ahmadiyya Sec Sch, teacher, 1979-80; Origbo County High Sch, teacher, 1980-82; Clarion Univ, grad asst, 1982-83; Univ Ill, grad asst, 1984-86; Xavier Univ La, head pub serv, 1986-89; Northeastern Univ, libr instr coordr, 1989-92; Boston Col, chief ref librn, 1992-95; Commonwealth Mass, ct interpreter, 1992-; Boston Col Libr, mgr instr servs, 1995-; US Atty Gen's Off, Boston, consult, African lang;

Col Advancing Studies, Boston Col, fac, 1996-. **Orgs:** Am Libr Asn, 1984-; Northeastern Univ Comn to Improve Col Teaching, 1989-92; adv bd mem, Mass Fac Develop Consortium, 1992-; Multicultural Network, 1992-; chair, ACRL/IS Diverse Comn, 1993-95; Boston Col, Martin Luther King Com, 1993-; ACRL/IS Com on Educ for Libr Instrs; bd mem, African Pastoral Ctr, Archdiocese Boston; Benjamin E Mays Mentor, 1995-, fac adv, Ignacio Volunteers, 1997-, Boston Col; liaison comt, Libr Instr Roundtable, 1999-2001; lectr, St Malachy's Parish, 1999-. Archdiocese Boston, Cardinal's Advisory Bd Member. **Honors/Awds:** Univ Ghana, Scholar, 1975-79; Scholar to study abroad, Span Govt, 1978; Best Teacher, Origbo County High Sch, 1981, 1982; Top 20 Articles in Libr Instruction, Res Strategies, 1986; Fel, Univ Ill, 1986-87; Certificate for Outstanding Achievement in Multicultural Education in Boston County, 1993; Bill Day Award, 1995, Annual Teaching, Advising & Mentoring Grant, 1999-00, County Service Award, 2001, Boston Col; Rev John R Trzaska Award, 2001. Leadership Award, Boston Col AHANA Community, 2007; Massachusetts State Lottery Community Champion Award, 2008. **Special Achievements:** Auth works include: Making Term Paper Counseling More Meaningful, 1989; Writing in a Language You Don't Know, 1990; The Int Ta: A Beat from a Foreign Drummer, 1991; Dealing with International Students in a Multicultural Era, 1992; Paraprofessionals in Reference Services: An Untapped Mine, 1993; ed: Library Instruction Roundtable Newsletter, 1991-92; consul: Northeastern Univ Project Hist Black Writing, 1990-; The Int Student in the US Acad Libr: Building Bridges to Better Bibliographic Instruction; Nigerian Americans, 1995; Human Aspect of Reference in the Era of Technology, 1997; Using Humor for Effective Library Instruction, 1998; International Students US Trends, Cult Adjustments, 1998; Reference Services for the Adult Learner, 1999; Research In The Electronic Age; How To Distinguish Between Good & Bad Data, 1999; "The Difficult Patron Situation: A Window of Opp to Improve Library Service", Catholic Literary World, 2000; "The International Student on Campus: History, Trends, Visa Classification & Adjustment", Teaching the New Libr to Today's Users, 2000; Helping the Difficult Library Patron: New Approches to Examining & Resolving a Long-Standing & Ongoing Problem, 2002; Managing the twenty first Century Reference Department, 2003. **Business Addr:** Manager Instructional Services, Boston College Libraries, 312 O, Chestnut Hill, MA 02467-3810, **Business Phone:** (617)552-4465.

SARMIENTO, SHIRLEY JEAN
Arts administrator, educator, playwright. **Personal:** Born Nov 28, 1946, Buffalo, NY; daughter of John C Laughlin and Claudia Hall Laughlin; divorced; children: Tolley Reeves & William Jr. **Educ:** Medaille Col, BS, 1980; Canisius Col, attended 1983; New York State Univ, Buffalo, am studies & women's studies, 1988; New York State Univ, Buffalo, MA, 2000. **Career:** Offender Aide & Restoration, coord family support mgr, 1982-83; Night People (homeless), worker, 1985-86; Buffalo Bd Educ, sub teacher; Jesse Nash Health Ctr, family life prog; Gowanda Psychiatric Ctr, Western New York Peace Ctr, rep & peace educator; New York State Univ, Buffalo, lectr, 1989; St Ann's Community Ctr, Learning Club, dir, 1990; Langston Hughes Inst, ct advocate; Buffalo Urban Arts, co-founder & producer, currently; Screenplay: Tolley's Place, The Meeting, Black n Blue Theatre, Yolley's Place. **Orgs:** Family advocate, Western New York Peace Ctr Learning Disabled Asn; founder, An African Am Artist Agenda, 1994. **Honors/Awds:** Certificate Head Start; Certificate Offender Aid & Restoration; Award, New York State Arts Coun, 1999; Achievement Award, Housing & Urban Develop Coop Rental Asst Corp, 2001. **Special Achievements:** Editor, Drumbeats: An Urban Arts Anthology, 1996. **Military Serv:** USY Reserves, spec-4, 1977-80; 2 Appreciation Awards. **Home Addr:** 205 Marine Dr Suite 4D, Buffalo, NY 14202. **Business Addr:** Founder and Producer, Buffalo Urban Arts, 2495 Main St Suite 500, Buffalo, NY 14214, **Business Phone:** (716)833-4450.

SARREALS, E. DON
Scientist, businessperson. **Personal:** Born Sep 22, 1931, Winston-Salem, NC; married Florence B Coleman; children: Cheryl Lynn & Esquire. **Educ:** City Col NY, BS, Meteorol, 1957; NY Univ, MS, Meteorol, 1961. **Career:** Nat Weather Serv Forecast Off, NYC, supr radar meteorologist, 1961-69; WRCTV Nat Broadcasting Co, TV meteorologist, 1969-75; Storm Finders Inc, pres & cons meteorologist, 1969-76; Nat Weather Serv Headquarters, dissemination meteorologist, 1976-80; MD Ctr Pub Broadcasting, TV meteorologist, 1976-81; NEXRAD Proj, NOAA/NWS, chief, Oper, 1981-92; Fed Coordr Meteorol, asst fed coordr, NOAA/NWS, 1992-97; E Don Sarreals Inc, pres, 1988; business currently. **Orgs:** Prof mem, Am Meteorol Soc, 1955-; lectr & meterol, City Col NY, 1957-69; chmn bd dir, 157th St & Riverside Dr Housing Co Inc, 1966-68; lectr,Smithsonian Inst Wash DC, 1972; Nat Acad Sci Comt Common Disasters & Media, 1977-75; Montgomery Ctr Sch Community Sec Sch, 1976-78; Nat Tele Communs Info Agency's Teletext Comn, 1978-80; Nat Weather Asn, 1980-; bd mem, D Rumaldry Homes Asn, 1984-; subcomt, Natural Disaster Reduction, 1994-; Nat Sci & Technol Coun & Comt Environ & Natural Resources. **Honors/Awds:** Ward Medal, Meteorol City Col NY, 1957; Teaching Fellowship, CCNY 1957; Community Service Award, River Terrace Men's Club New York City, 1969; Service Awards, NWS, 1964-65, 1980, 1984; publ NWS Forecasting Handbook #2NWS 1978; Next Generation Weather Radar (NEXRAD) Operators Concept 1983, Product Description Document, 1984, second edition 1987; "NEXRAD Products" 23rd Amer Meteorological Soc Con on Radar Meteorology, 1986; "NEXRAD Operational Capability" proceedings of 1987 annual meeting of the Nat Weather Asn; "NEXRAD Products and Operational Capability" proceedings of 25th Aerospace Sciences meeting Amer Inst of Aeronautics & Astronautics, 1987. **Military Serv:** AUS, cpl; Natl Defense Serv Ribbon; Good Conduct Medal 1953-55. **Home Addr:** 6300 Contention Ct, Bethesda, MD 20817.

SARTIN, JOHNNY NELSON, JR.
Television journalist. **Personal:** Born Nov 29, 1960, Hattiesburg, MS; son of Corean Anderson and Johnny N Sartin Sr; married Natalie Renee Bell, Jun 9, 1990. **Educ:** Univ Southern Miss, Hattiesburg, MS, BS, 1982. **Career:** WLOX-TV, Biloxi, MS, TV news photojournalist, 1982-86; WKRG-TV, Mobile, AL, TV news photojournalist, 1986-88; KFOR-TV, Oklahoma City, OK, TV news photojournalist, 1988-. **Orgs:** Alpha Phi Alpha Fraternity Inc, 1979-82; Nat Press Photographers Asn, 1984-; Nat Asn Black Journalists, 1988-; Okla City Black Media Assocs, 1990-. **Honors/Awds:** Award of Excellence/Photojournalism, Nat Asn Black Journalists, 1989, 1990. **Business Addr:** Television Photojournalist, KFOR-TV, 444 E Britton Rd, Oklahoma City, OK 73120, **Business Phone:** (405)478-6333.

SATCHELL, ELIZABETH (LIZ SATCHELL)
Educator, radio broadcaster, television writer. **Personal:** Born in Eastville, VA; daughter of Abe Peed and Alice Watson; children: Troi Eric. **Educ:** Drake Col Bus, attended 1969; Kean Univ, BS, MPA; Radio Sales Univ, Radio Advert Bur, dipl, 1988; New Jersey Realty Inst, dipl, 1989. **Career:** CBS/WCAU-TV Channel 10, sales asst, 1970-75; CBS/WCAU-TV Channel 10, newsprod asst, 1975-77; CBS/WCAU-TV Channel 10, newswriter & reporter, 1977-79; WNJR Radio, dir pub rel & news editorials, 1979-80; WNJR Radio, prog dir, 1980-81; WNJR Radio, vpres & prog dir, 1981-82; WNJR Radio, vpres & station mgr, 1982-; Realty World Prof Assoc, Scotch Plains, NJ, realtor assoc, 1989; Kean Univ, Ctr Integration Math & Sci; Kean Univ, Reform Teacher Educ Proj, adminr, currently. **Orgs:** Bd dir, Future Devel Group, 1986; bd dir, New York Market Radio Braodcasters Asn, 1989; Nat Asn Broadcasters; Nat Asn Black Owned Broadcasters; Radio Advert Bur; Greater Newark Chamber Com; Pi Alpha Alpha Honor Soc; Am Soc Pub Admin; Nat Women's Polit Caucus; Am Acad Broadcasting. **Honors/Awds:** Black Achiever Business & Education, YM-YWCA Newark & Vicinity, 1982. **Home Addr:** 948 West 8th St, Plainfield, NJ 07060.

SATCHELL, ERNEST R
Chairperson, educator. **Personal:** Born Jul 29, 1941, Exmore, VA; married Elsa Martin; children: Kwame & Keita. **Educ:** Towson State Col, MEd, 1971; Md State Col, BS; St Joseph's Col, Philadelphia. **Career:** Boeing Vertol Corp, Philadelphia, commercial art dir; Va Hosp, Philadelphia, art the rapist; Univ MD, Eastern Shore, Depart Fine Arts, prof, chmn & instr ceramics, currently. **Orgs:** Nat Conference Artists; Ant Art Educ Assoc; Md State Teachers asn; NEA; Alpha Phi Alpha; bd dir, Somerset Co Art asn; Union Baptist Church, Comm on Higher Educ. **Honors/Awds:** Pennsylvania State Univ, 1971; One-man Show, Academy of the Arts, Easton, MD, 1974; Exhibits: Towson State Col, 1974. **Military Serv:** USS Forrestal, 1968. **Business Addr:** Chairman, University of Maryland, Department of Fine Arts, 11868 Acad Oval, Princess Anne, MD 21853, **Business Phone:** (410)651-2200.

SATCHER, DR. DAVID
Government official, health services administrator. **Personal:** Born Mar 2, 1941, Anniston, AL; son of Wilmer and Anna; married Nola; children: Gretchen, David, Daraka & Daryl. **Educ:** Morehouse Col, BS, 1963; Case Western Res Univ, MD, PhD, 1970. **Career:** Strong Mem Hosp, Univ Rochester, resident, 1971-72; King-Drew Med Ctr, dir, 1972-75; Charles Drew Post grad Med Sch, Macy fac fel, 1972-75; King-Drew Sickle Cell Ctr, assoc dir, 1973-75, asst prof, interim chmn, 1974-75; Univ Calif Los Angeles, Sch Med, asst prof, 1974-76, resident, 1975-76; King-Drew Med Ctr, Morehouse Col, Sch Med, Dept Family Med, prof, chmn; Meharry Med Col, pres, 1982-93; Ctr Dis Control, head, 1994-97; asst secy for Health, Surgeon Gen, PHS, 1998-2002; Morehouse Sch Med, Nat Health Ctr, head, 2002-, interim pres, currently; Nat Cancer Inst, Ctr Reduce Cancer Health Disparities, proj investr. **Orgs:** Med dir, Second Baptist Free Clin; Am Acad Family Physicians, Am Soc Human Genetics; bd dir, Soc Teachers Fam Med, Joint Bd Family Pract Ga, Phi Beta Kappa chap Delta, 1977; Alpha Omega Alpha Hon Med Soc; AAAS; Am Cancer Soc; AMA; Am Health Asn; Nat Med Asn; NAACP; Urban League; bd dirs, First Am Bank Nashville; vis comn mem, Univ Ala, Sch Med; bd trustees, Carnegie Found Advan Teaching; Inst Med; Nat Acad Sci; Alpha Omega Alpha. **Honors/Awds:** Outstanding Morehouse Alumnus Award 1973; Award for Med Ed for Sickle Cell Disease, 1973; Macy Found Fac Fellow Community Med, 1972-73; Dudley Seaton Memorial Award Outstanding Alumnus, Case Western Res Univ, 1980; Nathan B Davis Award, Am Med Asn, 1996; John Stearn Award for Lifetime Achievement in Medicine, NY Acad Med; American Black Achievement Award in Business and the Professions, Ebony Mag, 1994; Breslow Award in Public Health, 1995; Surgeon General's Medallion; Bennie Mays Trailblazer Award, 2004; Jimmy & Rosalyn Carter Award, 2004. **Special Achievements:** First African-American man to be appointed surgeon general; numerous publications.

SATCHER, DR. ROBERT
Medical scientist, surgeon, astronaut. **Personal:** Born Sep 22, 1965, Hampton, VA; married Jun 28, 1997; children: Daija & Robert III. **Educ:** Mass Inst Technol, BS, chem eng, 1986, PhD, chem eng, 1993; Harvard Med Sch, MD, health scis & technol div, 1994. **Career:** Mass Inst Technol, Cambridge, MA, postdoctoral res, 1993-94; Univ Calif, San Francisco, CA, internship gen surg, 1994-95, postdoctoral res fel, 1997-98; Univ Calif, San Francisco, CA, resident orthop surg, 1995-2000; Univ Calif Berkeley, CA, postdoctoral res fel, 1997-98; Univ Fla, Gainesville, orthop oncol fel, 2000-01; Robert H Lurie Comprehensive Cancer Ctr, Inst Bioengineering & Nanotechnology Advan Med, Northwestern Univ, asst prof, orthopaedic surg, currently, The Feinberg Sch Med, Dept Orthopaedic surg, asst prof, currently, Univ Fla, Musculoskeletal Oncol, fel; EI DuPont deNemours & Co Inc, Wilmington, Del, internships; NASA, Lyndon B Johnson Space Ctr, astronaut, 2004-. **Orgs:** Founder & dir Sarcoma Conf, The Robert H Lurie Comprehensive Cancer Ctr, Feinberg Sch Med, Northwestern Univ; Black Alumni MIT; vice chmn, Orthop Res Soc; Hinton-Wright Biomed Soc Steering Comt, Harvard Med Sch; Tau Beta Pi Eng Honor Soc. **Honors/Awds:** DuPont Eng Scholar, 1982-86; Monsanto Award, Mass Inst Technol, 1985; Zimmer Investigator Award, 1997-98. **Special Achievements:** Selected by NASA in May 2004. **Business Addr:** Assistant Professor, Department of Orthopedic Surgery, Northwestern University Medical Center, 675 N Saint Clair St Fl 13, Chicago, IL 60611, **Business Phone:** (312)908-7937.*

SATCHER, ROBERT LEE
Educator, administrator. **Personal:** Born Sep 18, 1937, Anniston, AL; son of Wilmer and Anna Curry; married Marian Hanna; children: Serena, Robert Jr, Rodney & Robin. **Educ:** Ala State Univ, BS, 1959; Ariz State Univ, MS, 1963; Ore State Univ, PhD, 1971; Univ Mo; Okla Univ; Tufts Univ; Tex A&M Univ; MIT. **Career:** Booker T Washington HS, sci & math inst, 1959-62; Ala State Univ, inst, chem, phys science, 1963-65; Hampton Inst, chief planning officer, instr to assoc prof, chem, 1965-79; Tororo Women Col, Uganda, E Africa, prof chem, sci adv, 1973; Voorhees Col, exec vp, acad dean, prof chem, 1979-82; Fisk Univ, interim pres 1984, acad dean & provost, prof chem, 1982-88; St Paul's Col, acting pres & provost, 1988-89, vpres, acad affairs & provost, 1988-92, prof chem, 1988, interim pres, pres, 2007-. **Orgs:** Fel, acad admin Am Coun Educ, 1975-76; consult, USOE/AIDP, Univ Asn, Wash, DC, 1975-78; Moton Inst Capahosic Va, 1977; external eval, Tenn State Univ, 1977-81; Comn Cols SACS, Atla GA, 1978-86; Norfolk State Univ, 1980-83; eval Title III, US Dept Educ WA, 1980-; Pres, Conf Acad Deans Southern States, SACS, 1990; Oper Push; Nat Asn Advan Colored People; SCLC; Am Nuclear Soc; AKM Nat Honor Soc; BKX Nat Hon Sci Soc; Nat Inst Sci; AAAS; Soc Col & Univ Planning; AIR. **Honors/Awds:** Fel grants, US Atomic Energy Comn, Ford Found, 1968-71; Ford Found fel, 1969-71; Rockfeller Found, 1975-76; NIH grantee, 1972-77; Citizen of the Year, Zeta Omicron Chap, Omega Psi Phi, 1977; Change Mag, 1978; Silver Beaver, BSA, 1988; Outstanding Service Award, Epsilon Gamma Chapter; Outstanding Service Award, Omega Psi Phi, 1992; Outstanding Service Award, CIC, Wash, DC, 1992. **Special Achievements:** Author of many books & articles; Omega Man of the Year, Omicron Omega Chapter, Omega Psi Phi, 1990. **Business Addr:** President, Saint Paul's College, 115 College Dr, Lawrenceville, VA 23868.

SATTERFIELD, PATRICIA POLSON
Supreme court justice. **Personal:** Born Jul 10, 1942, Christchurch, VA; daughter of Thea A Polson and Grady H Polson; married Preston T, Aug 29, 1966; children: Danielle Nicole. **Educ:** Howard Univ, BME, 1964; Ind Univ, MM, 1967; St Johns Univ Sch Law, JD, 1977. **Career:** Sewanhaka High Sch Dist, vocal music teacher, 1968-77; UCS Coun Off Ct Admin, asst dep coun, sr coun, 1978-90; Unified Ct Syst State of NY, judge, 1991-94, New York State Supreme Ct, actg supreme ct justice, 1994-98, supreme ct justice, 1998-. **Orgs:** St John's Univ, Cult Diversity Comm, Sch Law, 1991-; bd dir, law alumni, 1991-; co-chair, bd dirs, Queens Women's Network, 1983-90; bd dirs, Human Resources Ctr St Albans, 1990-; Asn Women Judges, 1991-; Metrop Black Lawyers Asn, 1988-; Queens Co Bar Asn, 1989-; pres, Jack & Jill Am Inc Queens Co, 1978-87; St Albans Congregational Ch, United Ch Christ, 1996-; pres, Greater Queens Chapt Links Inc, 1998-. **Honors/Awds:** Alva T Starforth, Outstanding Teacher of the Year, 1976; Outstanding Community Leader of the Year, Alpha Kappa Alpha, Epsilon Omega Chap, 1991; Ascension to Bench, Queens Co Women's Bar Assn, 1991. **Special Achievements:** First Black female judge elected in Queens Co, NY, 1990. **Business Addr:** Supreme Court Justice, New York State Supreme Court, 11th Judicial District, 88-11 Sutphin Blvd, Jamaica, NY 11435, **Business Phone:** (718)298-1095.

SATTERWHITE, DR. FRANK JOSEPH
Executive. **Personal:** Born Oct 3, 1942, Akron, OH; son of Arthur and Ethel Gindraw; married; children: Frank Jr, Kuntu, Onira & Kai. **Educ:** Howard Univ, BA, Educ, 1965; Southern IL Univ, MS, col admin, 1967; Stanford Univ, PhD Col Admin, 1975. **Career:**

Col Entrance Exam Bd, asst dir, 1968-71; Oberlin Col, asn dean, 1971-72; Ravenswood Sch Dist, asst supt, 1972-76; Community Develop Inst, pres, 1978-; W.K.Kellogg Found, Kellogg Nat fel, 1986-89. **Orgs:** Councilman, EPA Municipal Coun, 1974-78; mem, Narobi Secretarat, 1979-85; planning comn, SMC Planning Comn, 1980-83; mem, BAPAC, 1981-85; mem, Mid-Peninsula Urban Coalition, 1982-85; councilman, EPA City Coun, 1983-85. **Honors/Awds:** Community Serv, EPACCI, 1983; Community Serv, EPA Chamber comt, 1983; Champion, OICW, 1985. **Home Addr:** 2275 Euclid Ave, East Palo Alto, CA 94303. **Business Addr:** President, Community Development Institute, PO Box 50099, East Palo Alto, CA 94303, **Business Phone:** (650)327-5846.

SAULNY, CYRIL
Association executive. **Personal:** Married LaVerne. **Educ:** Xavier Univ, La, attended 1983. **Career:** NAACP, New Orleans chap, pres, 2000. **Home Addr:** 860 Hidalgo St, New Orleans, LA 70124.

SAULSBERRY, CHARLES R.
Lawyer. **Personal:** Born Sep 4, 1957, Goshen, AL; son of Asia William and Ruby Lee; married Dana Scott Saulsberry, Jun 28, 1986; children: Kara, Kalyn. **Educ:** Harvard Univ, AB, 1979; Northwestern Univ, Sch Law, JD, 1982. **Career:** Winston & Strawn, summer assoc, 1980-81, assoc, partner, 1982-92; Parker, Chapin, Flattau & Klimpl, summer assoc, 1981; Thompson & Mitchell, partner, 1992; Blackwell Sanders Peper Martin, partner; St Louis Black Leadership Roundtable, Interim Chief Exec Officer, currently. **Orgs:** Bar Asn Metrop, St Louis; Chicago Coun Lawyers, secy, bd, 1985-86; Cabrini Green Legal Assistance Found, bd, 1985-86; Minority Legal Educ Resources Inc, secy, bd, 1986-87; Am Bar Asn; Ill State Bar Asn; Nat Basketball Asn; Chicago Bar Asn; Cook County Bar Asn; Nat Asn Securities Prof. **Honors/Awds:** Outstanding Student, Coun Legal Opportunities Comn, 1979; Earl Warren Scholar, Earl Warren Found, 1979. **Special Achievements:** Bond counsel to city of Chicago on $489,735,000, O'Hare International Terminal special revenue bonds, 1990; underwriters' counsel on over $1.9 billion housing bonds for Illinois Housing Development Authority, 1984-91. **Business Addr:** Partner, St. Louis Commerce Magazine, 1 Metrop Sq Suite 1300, Saint Louis, MO 63102, **Business Phone:** (314)444-1104.*

SAULSBY, LINDA E. See GASTON, LINDA SAULSBY.

SAULTER, GILBERT JOHN
Executive. **Personal:** Born Apr 20, 1936, Seattle, WA; son of Bernice Saulter and Gerald Saulter; married Mae Frances; children: Bradford, Melonie, Daryl. **Educ:** Univ WA, BSEE, 1962; UCLA, Univ WA; Harvard Univ, sr mgt prog, 1988, registered prof engr, 1969. **Career:** exec (retired); Boeing Co, engr aid, 1958-62; Northrop, 1962-65; Itek, 1965-67; Sundstrand Data Control, 1967-71; US dept Labor, saf engr, 1971-74, area dir, 1974-76, reg admin NE Region, 1976-78, reg admin, SW Region, 1978-95; engineering consul; Desoto City Planning and Zoning Commission, comnr, 1996-98, councilman, 1998-01. **Orgs:** Chmn, YMCA Youth Comn; Indian Guide prog, 1970; vchmn, adv comm Boy Scouts Am, 1970-74; NAACP; Kappa Alphi Psi; pres, Nw Counc Black Prof Engrs; Opportunity Industrialization Ctr, 1985-88; Classical Guitar Soc, 1986-87; Family Place, 1987-90; US delegate Petroleum Conf, Lagos, Nigeria, 1985; chief, US delegate Int Labor Organization Geneva, Switzerland, 1986; chmn, Dallas & Ft Worth Combined Fed Campaign, 1989-91; chmn, DFW Fed Exec Bd, 1993-94; head, US delegation NAFTA Joint Tech Conf Safety Health Petrochemical Industry, Edmonds, Canada, 1994. **Honors/Awds:** Honor, Roll Univ WA, 1961, 1962; Merit Award, Northrop Corp, 1963, 1965; Merit Award, ITEK Corp, 1967; Trail Blazer Award, SO Dallas Bus Prof Women's Club, 1983; Outstanding Exec Award, 1985, 1989, 1990, 1991; Presidential Rank Meritorious Exec, 1992. **Military Serv:** National Guard, honorable discharge, 1962. *

SAUNDERS, BARBARA ANN
Tour guide, administrator. **Personal:** Born Jun 5, 1950, Roanoke, VA; married Byron Creighton. **Educ:** Hampton Univ, VA, BA, Fine Arts 1972. **Career:** Amer Security Bank, WA DC, cust serv rep, 1973-75; GA Film & Videotape Office, pr specialist, 1976-80; freelance writer; freelance commercial voice-over talent, 1985-; GA Dept Ind, Trade & Tourism, acct asst, 1975-76, pr program crd, 1980-90; tour & travel develop asst dir, 1990-94; tourism mktg consult, 1994; Southern int Press ctr, 1996; The Arthur M Blank Family Found, prog associate, 2002, prog officer, currently. **Orgs:** Women In Film-Atlanta 1977-79; pres, Sigma Gamma Nu Social Club, Hampton Univ, 1971; Women In Film-Atlanta. **Business Addr:** Program Officer, Arthur M Blank Family Foundation, 3223 Howell Mill Rd NW, Atlanta, GA 30327, **Business Phone:** (404)367-2100.

SAUNDERS, DAVID J
Executive, chief executive officer. **Personal:** Born Jun 28, 1951, Washington, DC; married Sharon; children: David Jr, Santosha & Michael. **Educ:** Univ Toledo, BA, bus, attended; Carnegie Mellon Univ, Grad Sch Indus Admin, attended. **Career:** Burroughs Corp, 1971; Sara Lee, vpres & gen mgr, serv oper, 2000; Venue Int Professionals Inc, co-founder & chief exec officer, currently. **Orgs:** Bd dirs, Dist Columbia Chamber Com; Int Trade Comt; Int Travel Tourism Comt; Black Presidents' Roundtable Asn; Nat Bd Dirs Blacks Govt; Africa Travel Asn. **Honors/Awds:** Outstanding Leadership Award, ATA, 1999. **Business Addr:** Chief Executive Officer, Co-Founder, Venue International Professionals Inc, PO Box 1872, Clinton, MD 20735, **Business Phone:** (301)856-9188.

SAUNDERS, DORIS E.
Educator, school administrator, editor. **Personal:** Born Aug 8, 1921, Chicago, IL; daughter of Alvesta Stewart Evans and Thelma C Rice Evans; divorced; children: Ann Camille, Vincent Ellsworth III. **Educ:** Roosevelt Univ, BA, 1951; Boston Univ, MS, Journ 1977, Ma Afro-Am Studies, 1977; Vanderbilt Univ, ABD, hist, 1984. **Career:** Educator (retired); Johnson Publishing Co Chicago, ed sp libr, 1949-60, dir, book div, 1960-66, 1972-78; Chicago Daily Defender, columnist, 1966-70; The Plus Factor & Inf Inc, pres, 1966-72; Chicago State Univ, dir comm rels, inst develop, 1968-70; Univ Ill, Chicago, staff assoc, off chancellor, 1970-72; Chicago Courier Newspaper, columnist, 1970-72; Gerri Major, Black Society, Johnson Publishing Co, co-author, 1976; Jackson State Univ, prof of jour, 1978-96, prof mass commun, 1985-96, acting chair, 1990, chair, 1991-96; Ancestor Hunting, pres; Kith & Kin Geneolgical Newsletter, publ, 1985-00. **Orgs:** adv com, Fed Reserve Bd, 1968-71; adv com, Dept Labor Bureau Census, 1972-80; consult, Lilly Endowment, 1978-91; vpres, Black Col Commun Asn, 1994-96. **Honors/Awds:** Outstanding Women Communicators, Nat Black Media Coalition, 1994. *

SAUNDERS, DR. ELIJAH
Physician, educator. **Personal:** Born Dec 9, 1934, Baltimore, MD; married Sharon; children: Kevin, Donna, Monzella, Veronica & Kyle. **Educ:** Morgan State Col, BS, 1956; Univ MD Sch Med, MD, 1960. **Career:** Univ MD, Hosp, intern 1960-61, asst res, 1961-63; Univ MD Hosp, fel, 1963-65; Provident Hosp, chief cardiol 1966-84, dir, 1968, chief, 1969-71, actg chief, 1973-75; MD Gen Hosp, asso cardiol, 1965-84; Univ MD, Sch & Hosp, instr, 1965-84, prof, Hypertension div, 1984-; pvt pract, 1965-. **Orgs:** Num pos; Am Heart Asn: Cent MD Chapter, MD Affil, Nat Dallas; chmn, Nat Scholarship Fund; Unit Ch Jesus Christ Apost; Med & Chirurgi Fac MD; AMA; Pres Med Staff, Provident Hosp, 1966-74; admsns com Univ MD, 1970-75; Ed Bd, Spirit; trste bd, 1st Un Ch Jesus Christ Apost; chmn, steer com Hyperten Contr Prog; chmn, Adv Coun MD on Related end right factors; Hyperten Contr Prog; MD Soc Cardiol; Am Col Physician; Fel Am Col Cardiol; Fel Am Col Angiol; num other asns & com. **Honors/Awds:** Author/producer numerous film strips; num appear on TV & radio; num lect; Bronze Service Medal; Presidential Award, 1975, Silver Distinguished Service Medal, 1976, Am Heart Asn; Pres Plaque Cent MD Heart Asn, 1975; House Resol 15 Del Webs, 1976; founder, Heart House; fel, Am Col Cardiol, 1976; Distinguished Leadership Plaque MD High Blood Pressure Coordinating Coun, 1982; Outstanding Achievement in Health Care Award, Black Nurses Asn Baltimore, 1985; Marcus Garve Memorial Found Plaque, 1987; Louis B Russell Award, Award of Merit, Am Heart Asn, MD Affiliate, 1991; Honoree, Nat Kidney Found MD, 1994; Keynote Speaker, Egyptian Hypertension League & Israel Hypertension Comt Prog, 1994; Community Service Award, Baltimore City Med Soc, 1996; Louis B Russell Award, Am Heart Asn, 1998; Lifetime Achievement Award, Consortium for Southeastern Hypertension Control, 1998; Morgan State University Hall Fame, 1998; Community Service Award, NCP, 1999; honorary doctorate, Med Univ SC, 1999; Alumni Hall of Fame Award, Morgan State Univ, 2000; Plaque featuring special report "The Doctor Are In," Black Enterprise, 2001. **Military Serv:** AUS, NG maj, 1960-66. **Home Phone:** (410)363-0482. **Business Addr:** Professor of Medicine, Cardiology, Hypertension, University of Maryland Professional Building, 419 W Redwood St Suite 620, Baltimore, MD 21201, **Business Phone:** (410)328-4366.

SAUNDERS, DR. ELIZABETH ANN
Educator, executive director. **Personal:** Born Apr 12, 1948, Centralia, IL. **Educ:** Freed Hardeman Univ, AA, 1967; Memphis State Univ, BS, 1969, MEd, 1979, E Tenn State Univ, EdD. **Career:** Haywood High Jr Div, Brownsville, instr eng & reading lab, 1970-76; Anderson Grammar Sch, Brownsville, instr reading, 1976-77; Haywood High Sch, Brownsville, Tenn, instr eng & reading, 1977-78; Freed Hardman Col, Henderson, Tenn, acad advr & instr, 1978-; Freed-Hardeman Univ, prog dir, prof educ, currently, dir grad studies, currently. **Orgs:** HEA/WTEA/TEA/NEA, 1970-78; Tenn Asn Super & Curriculum Develop, 1978-; Int Reading Asn, 1979-; Am Pers & Guid Asn, 1980; Nat Asn Advan Colored People; Alpha Kappa, 1969-; comn chmn, FHC Women's Club & Student Relations Comn, Fac Self-Study Comn, 1979-; teacher, Lucyville Church Christ. **Honors/Awds:** Scholar, Freed Hardeman Col, 1966; elected rep, Tenn Educ Asn, Gen Assembly, 1975; Certificate, Appalach State Univ, Boone, NC, 1980. **Business Addr:** Director of Graduate Studies, Professor of Education, Rm Gardner Ctr 02a Freed-Hardeman University, 158 E Main St, Henderson, TN 38340, **Business Phone:** (731)989-6087.*

SAUNDERS, JERRY
Association executive, executive. **Personal:** Born Apr 23, 1953, Columbus, OH; son of Earl and Rosalie; married Gayle Saunders; children: Jerry Jr. **Educ:** Ohio Wesleyan Univ Upward Bound, completion cert, 1971; Oberlin Col, BA, 1975; Ohio State Univ, attended 1976. **Career:** Futon Corp, draftsman, 1976-77; Las Vegas Dealers Basketball Team, player, 1977-79; Ohio Wesleyan Univ, assoc dir of Upward Bound, 1979-80; JC Penney Ins, ins adjuster, 1980-87; Waiters & Assocs, vpres, 1990-; Eldon W Ward YMCA, exec dir, 1988-97; UCAN Networks, owner, 1997; Africentric Personal Develop Shop Inc, Pres & chief exec officer, Columbus, Ohio, 1997-. **Orgs:** Unique Community & Neighborhood Networks, 1989-; Columbus Urban League, 1991-95; chmn of trustee bd, Flintridge Baptist Church, 1979-; adv bd, Columbus Pub Schs, 1991-; prog dir, MVP Basketball Camps, 1989-; prog coordr, Make the Right Choice, 1992-; chmn, Blue Chip Mag Awards Gala, 1992-; chmn, 100 Black Men, Cent Ohio. **Honors/Awds:** Columbus Pub Sch Golden Ruler Award; Who's Who in Black Cent Ohio; 100 Black Men of Cent, Ohio, 2002; Mentor of the Year; Columbus Urban League Award of Excellence; City Year of Columbus Moccasin Award for community serv; 2005 Community Service Award, New Salem Missionary Baptist Church; Outstanding Community Service Award; 20 various plaques & certificates for community serv. **Business Addr:** Chief Executive Director, President, Africentric Personal Development Shop, 1409 E Livingston Ave, Columbus, OH 43205, **Business Phone:** (614)253-4448.

SAUNDERS, JOHN EDWARD
Executive director, state government official. **Personal:** Born Jan 17, 1945, Bryn Mawr, PA; son of John Edward and Eleanor Smith; married Vivian E Williams (deceased); children: John Edward IV, Jason Elliott & Shanna Marie. **Educ:** Cent State Univ, BS, bus admin, 1968; LaSalle Col & Univ PA, Social Serv Agency Mgt Educ & Develop Prog, cert, 1982; IBM Comm Exec Sem, cert, 1982; Lincoln Univ, MA, human serv admin, 1983; Duke Univ, Sanford Inst Pub Policy, Strategic Leadership Sem, 1993. **Career:** Dun & Bradstreet Inc, credit analyst, 1972-76; Urban League Philadelphia, prog dir, 1976-78, sr vpres, 1978-83; Urban League Greater Hartford Inc, pres & chief exec officer, 1983-88; Hartford Health Network Inc, chmn, 1984-88; Almada Lodge Times Farm Camp Corp, bd mem, 1985-; Oper Fuel Inc, chmn, 1986-97; State Conn, dep labor comnr, 1988-97; Nat Forum Black Pub Adminr, exec dir, 1997-. **Orgs:** Fel Am Leadership Forum Hartford, 1985; corporator, St Francis Hosp, 1986-96; bd mem, Conn Prison Asn, 1986-92; bd mem, World Affairs Coun, 1986-90; bd mem, Conn Law Enforcement Found, 1987-90; trustee, Watkinson Sch, 1987-; bd mem, Sci Mus Conn, 1988-96; trustee, Watkinson Sch, 1988-96; bd mem, Salvation Army, 1990-; trustee, IST Living, 1992; vice chmn, Am Lendership Forum, 1992; Hartford Rotary Club; Asn Black Social Workers; Conn Civil Rights Coord Community; Tuscan Lodge 17; F&AM; Pulmonary Hypertension Asn. **Honors/Awds:** Hon LLD, Briarwood Col, 1983; ML King Jr Award, Hand Hand Inc, Philadelphia, 1984. **Military Serv:** AUS specialist 6, 3 1/2 yrs; Bronze Star; Army Commendation w/OLC; Air Medal; Vietnam Serv & Campaign Medal. **Business Addr:** Executive Director, National Forum Black Public Administrators, 777 N Capitol St NE Suite 807, Washington, DC 20002, **Business Phone:** (202)408-9300 Ext 106.

SAUNDERS, JOHN P
Television show host, broadcaster. **Personal:** Born Feb 2, 1955, Ontario. **Educ:** Western Mich Univ, 1976; Ryerson Univ, 1977. **Career:** CKNS Radio, news dir, 1978; CKNY-TV, sports anchor, 1978-79; ATV News, anchor, 1979-80; ESPN, host basketball & hockey, 1986-; Toronto Raptors, Play-by-play announcer, 1995-2001; ABC Sports, host football & baseball, currently; ESPN, journalist, currently. **Special Achievements:** Emmy Nominee, 1994, 1996. **Business Phone:** (860)766-2000.

SAUNDERS, KIM D
President (Organization), chief executive officer. **Educ:** Wharton Sch Finance, BS, econs; Univ Pa, BS, com. **Career:** City First Bank, Washington, DC, exec vpres & chief lending officer; Greater Richmond Chamber Com, bd mem; Va Biotech Res Pk Corp, bd mem; Consolidated Bank & Trust Co, pres & chief exec officer, currently. **Orgs:** Va Fair Housing Bd; bd mem, Saint Catherine's Sch; bd mem, World Affairs Coun; bd mem, Bon Secours Richmond Health Syst. **Business Addr:** President, Chief Executive Officer, Consolidated Bank & Trust Co, 320 N First St, Richmond, VA 23219, **Business Phone:** (804)771-5200.*

SAUNDERS, DR. MEREDITH ROY
Ophthalmologist. **Personal:** Born Apr 15, 1930, Mason City, IA; son of Albert J and Edna Marie; divorced; children: Meredith Jr, Desda C, Brita B & Alaire M. **Educ:** Mason City Jr Col, AA, 1949; Univ Iowa, BA, 1952, MD, 1956. **Career:** Pvt practice, ophthalmologist. **Orgs:** AMA; NMA; AAO. **Honors/Awds:** 'Class of Gold', Nat Med Asn. **Home Phone:** (515)274-4790. **Business Addr:** Ophthalmologist, 2101 Wown Pkwy, West Des Moines, IA 50265, **Business Phone:** (515)225-2566.

SAUNDERS, RAYMOND
Artist, educator. **Personal:** Born Oct 28, 1934, Pittsburgh, PA. **Educ:** Carnegie Inst Technol, BFA, 1960; Calif Col Arts & Crafts, MFA, 1961. **Career:** Calif State Univ, prof, 1962-89; Guggenheim fel, 1976; Calif Col Arts & Crafts, prof, 1989-; Solo exhibi-

tions: "New Works", Stephen Wirtz Gallery, 1999; Cooley Memorial Art Gallery, Reed College, Portland, 2000; "Paintings & Works on Paper", Stephen Wirtz Gallery, 2001; "Raymond Saunders", Centre Jerome Cuzin a AUCH, France, 2002; Gallery Resche, Paris, France, 2004. **Honors/Awds:** Schwabcher Frey Award, San Francisco Mus Modern Art, 1961; Atwater Kent Award, 1970; Granger Memorial Award, Pa Acad Fine Arts, 1975; National Endowment for the Arts Awards, 1977, 1984; Visual Arts Award, S Eastern Ctr Contemp Art, 1989; Distinguished Faculty Award, Calif Col Arts & Crafts, 1996-97. **Business Addr:** Professor of Painting, Drawing, California College of Arts & Crafts, 1111 8th St, San Francisco, CA 94107-2247, **Business Phone:** (415)703-9500.*

SAUNDERS, VINCENT E
Financial manager. **Personal:** Born Jan 28, 1954, Chicago, IL; son of Vincent E Saunders Jr and Doris Elaine; married Lynette Smith, Sep 23, 1984 (divorced); children: Vincent IV, Asia Imani & Evan Paul. **Educ:** Howard Univ, Wash, DC, BA, 1976; Inst Financial Educ, Chicago, IL, cert, 1980; Dept Defense, Equal Opportunity Mgt Inst Grad, 1988; Univ Ill, Chicago, IL, 1989; Keller Grad Sch Mgt, Chicago, IL, MBA, 1997. **Career:** Citibank, FSB, sr financial serv Rep, asst br mgr, 1978-86; Drexel Nat Bank, Retail Banking, dept mgr & vpres, 1986-89; Midway Airport Concessionaires, off admin & info syst, mgr, 1989-97; Environ Protection Agency, fin specialist, 1997-2001, admin officer, 2001-02, budget analyst, 2002-05, div budget coordr, 2005-. **Orgs:** Fin secy, Alpha Phi Alpha Fraternity, 1986-88; bd mem, Elliot Donnelley Chicago Youth Ctr, 1986-89; asst scout master, Boy Scouts Am, 1998-2001; Toastmasters Int, CTM, 1999-2003; Chicago chap, Nat Black MBA Asn; New Kemet Harambe Chap, Blacks Govt; chap treas, Chicago Chap Tuskegee Airman Inc; life mem, Nat Guard Asn US. **Honors/Awds:** Outstanding Young Men of America, US Jaycees, 1981; Bronze Medal Superior Fin Serv, EPA, 2000. **Special Achievements:** Up Coming Bus & Professionals, Dollars & Sense Magazine, 1989. **Military Serv:** Ill Air Nat Guard, major, 1983-99, Wing Human Rels, officer, 1986-93, comdr 126 serv Flight, 1993-97; Outstanding Airman Award, Aberdeen Proving Award, MD, 1983; Outstanding Unit Award, 1984, 1989, 1993; Logistics Group, exec officer, 1997-99; Officer Commendation Medal, 1993; Meritorious Service Medal, 1997, 1999. **Home Addr:** 9718 S Indiana Ave, Chicago, IL 60628. **Business Addr:** Budget Analyst, Environmental Protection Agency, 77 W Jackson Blvd, Chicago, IL 60606, **Business Phone:** (312)353-9077.

SAUNDERS, WILLIAM
Commissioner. **Personal:** Born Feb 14, 1935; married Henrietta; children: William Jr, Sharon, Loretta, Kathleen, Byron, Gary, Alphea, Myra, Clinton & Tamara. **Educ:** Southern Bus Col, bus mgt, 1974; Southern Ill Univ, voc educ, 1978. **Career:** Pub Serv Comn SC, First Dist, comnr, 1994-2004, chmn, 2000-02. **Orgs:** Pres, SC Broadcasters Asn, 1988; Nat Asn Broadcasters; Nat Asn Regulatory Utility Comt; Nat Water Comt; founding mem, Trident Urban League; Wesley United Methodist Church; founder & exec dir, Comt Better Racial Assurance; bd gov, Col Chas Bus Sch; Rotary Intl Breakfast Club; pres, YMCA, 1991; bd visitors, Charleston Southern Univ; Black Hall Fame; Admin Law-Fair Hearing, Univ NV. **Honors/Awds:** Broadcasters Hall of Fame; Malcolm D Haven Community Service Award; Harvey Gantt Award; Outstanding Service Award, Nat Asn Advan Colored People; Public Service Award, Arabian Temple No 139; Outstanding Service in the Arts Award, Links Inc; Outstanding Service Award, Delta Sigma Theta Sorority. **Special Achievements:** Featured in national media including The Today Show, New Yorker magazine, Black Enterprises, National Geographic, Redbook, The Washington Post & New York Times. **Military Serv:** AUS, staff sgt, 1951-54.

SAUNDERS, WILLIAM JOSEPH
Association executive, educator. **Personal:** Born Oct 14, 1924, Washington, DC; son of Edgar Eugene and Sara Mennah Hill; married Gladys Mae Gray, Apr 19, 1947; children: Lois Camille & Ada Delores. **Educ:** Howard Univ, Wash, DC, BS, 1948, MS, 1952. **Career:** DC Pub Sch, Wash, DC, asst supt, 1952-81; National Alliance Black Sch Educr, NABSE, Wash, DC, exec dir, 1982-93; Sci Serv Inc, spec asst to pres, 1993-96. **Orgs:** Pres, DC Sch Mens Club, 1982-89; vpres, Vis Nurses Asn, 1983-89; Whittle Channel One Adv Comt; Radio Shack Tech Adv Comt, 1988-2000; pres, Educr Leadership Consortium, 1990-93. **Military Serv:** AUS, First sgt, 1943-46. **Home Addr:** 1335 Tewkesbury Place NW, Washington, DC 20012.

SAUNDERS-HENDERSON, MARTHA M.
Educator, school administrator, museum director. **Personal:** Born Dec 18, 1924, Spartanburg, SC; daughter of Milderd Ruth Clemons and Alix Pinky; married Mark Henderson Jr, Nov 3, 1941; children: Sondra Jo Ann Jones, Woodrene Ruth, Markette Harris, Mark III & AlexisLillian Marion. **Educ:** Burlington City Col, AA, 1978, AS, 1979; Southern Ill Univ, BS, 1982; Cent Mich Univ, MBA, 1983; Rutgers Univ, doctoral. **Career:** Gov Island Nursery Sch, dir, 1963; Girls Scouts Far East Okinowa, coordr, 1965; NJ, PA Dept Ed, consult, 1970; Merabash Mus, pres, vp & mus exec,1970-; Spec Serv Sch, NJ, instr, 1983-84; Beverly City Sch, instr, NJ,1984; Merabash Mus, dir prog teaching spec sch, 1986-87, instr, 1989; Burlington County Col, Pemberton, NJ; African Am Preservation, Hist Sites & Hist African Am, consult. **Orgs:** Bd trustee, Merabash Mus, 1969-85; Burlington Co Cult & Heritage, NJ, 1975; consult, New Jersey Art Asn, 1977-78; Burlington City Col, NJ, 1980-84; hon mem, Sigma Gamma Rho Sorority, 1986; consult, Burlington Co Cult & Heritage Ft Dix Black Hist Prog; Burlington Col Alumni Hall of Fame; Union Co Col Fund Raising; Community Alert, WNET/Thirteen Comt Affairs Dept; African Am Mus Asn, Contemporary Educ Arts & Cult Res Black C. **Honors/Awds:** Outstanding Service, New Jersey Dept Educ, 1979; Recognition, New Jersey Comn, 1980; Black Arts & History, 1981; Hall of Fame, Burlington City Col, 1984; Award of Recognition, New Jersey Hist Comn; Certificate for Outstanding Service, Public Nat Bus & Prof Women's Club New Jersey; Spec Recognition Award, Afro-One Dance, Drama & Drum Theatre Inc, 1989; Appreciation for Service Award, Burlington County Cult & Heritage Comn; Service Award for Outstanding Contributions in Cultural Arts; Neighborhood Leadership Initiative Comt Found New Jersey. **Home Addr:** 59 Emerald Lane, Willingboro, NJ 08046. **Business Addr:** President, Merabash Museum, PO Box 752, Willingboro, NJ 08046, **Business Phone:** (609)877-3177.

SAVAGE, DR. ARCHIE BERNARD, JR.
School administrator. **Personal:** Born Nov 12, 1929, Memphis, TN; son of Mattie Hester and Archie; married Susan; children: Carl, Karen & Barbara. **Educ:** Univ Denver, BA, 1966; Univ MD, MEd, 1971, PhD, 1976. **Career:** School administrator (Retired); US Counter intelligence Spec Agent, 1951-73; Co ord Inst Res Univ Denver, 1973-76; Utah State Univ, Logan, UT, asst dir affirmative action prog, 1976-79; Cent Conn State Univ, New Britain, CT, dir affirmative action, 1980-86; Univ Conn Health Ctr, Farmington, CT, dir diversity & affirmative action, 1981-95; New Britain Hosp Spec Care, dir; ABS Enterprises, pres. **Orgs:** New Britain Gen Hosp 1981-; Asn Black Cardiologists, 1984-90; chmn, NB Comt On Human Rights & Opportunities, 1984-89; pres, Rotary Club New Britain, 1991-92; chmn & bd trustees, YMCA New Britain, 1995-2002; Kappa Alpha Psi Fraternity; bd dir, CTS Global Investments Inc. **Honors/Awds:** Paul Harris Fel, Rotary Int; Henry C Minton Fel, Sigma Pi Phi Fraternity. **Military Serv:** Bronze Star, 1971, Army, Navy & Air Force Commendation Medal, 1973. **Home Addr:** 299 Steele St, New Britain, CT 06050, **Home Phone:** (860)224-0270. **Business Addr:** President, ABS Enterprise, PO Box 877, New Britain, CT 06050, **Business Phone:** (860)224-0270.

SAVAGE, DENNIS JAMES
State government official. **Personal:** Born Jun 28, 1944; children: Dennis Jr. **Educ:** Cheney Univ, BA, sec educ, 1966; Temple Univ, post grad. **Career:** Chester, PA, teacher; Wilmington Sch Dist, teacher; Proj 70001, DE, teacher & coordr; 70001 Ltd, vpres; St bd educ, 2003; Del Off Community Serv, dir, currently. **Orgs:** Del Adv Coun Career Voc Educ; Christina Sch Dist Bd Educ. **Business Addr:** Director, Delaware Office of Community Services, Carvel State Office Bldg 820 N French St 4th Fl, Wilmington, DE 19801-3509.

SAVAGE, DR. EDWARD W, JR.
Physician. **Personal:** Born Jul 7, 1933, Macon, GA; son of Edward Warren and Mildred Eleanor; married Carole Avonne Porter, Jun 6, 1958; children: Cheryl, Racheal & Edward III. **Educ:** Talladega Col, AB, 1955; Meharry Med Col, MD, 1960; St Louis Univ, postgrad, 1955; State Univ NY, USPHS; Fel, Downstate Med Ctr, 1967-69. **Career:** State Univ NY Downstate Med Ctr, from asst instr to instr, 1964-69; Univ IL Med Ctr, asst prof, 1969-73; Charles R Drew Postgrad Med Sch, assoc prof, 1973-80, chief, Div Gyncol, 1983; King/Drew Med Ctr, med dir; Univ CA, adj assoc prof, 1977, prof, 1986; Charles R Drew Postgrad Med Sch, adj prof, currently; Pvt Pract, physician. **Orgs:** Numerous hosp appointments; various committees, Univ IL, Martin Luther King Hosp, Chas Drew Postgrad Med Sch; Task Force on the Assessment of Quality Health Care Am Col Ob/Gyn, 1977-80; consult ob/gyn Albert Einstein Eval Unit Dept of Health Educ & Welfare, 1973-76; consult ob/gyn Drew Ambulatory Care Review Team Dept Health Educ & Welfare, 1973-76; consult ob/gyn State of CA Health Care Evaluation Sect Alternative Health Systems Div, 1975-77; consult, The Albert F Mathieu Chrioepithelioma Registry S CA Cancer Ctr, 1975; consult, Dept Health & Human Serv 1980; consult, Ob/Gyn Nat Inst Health, 1981; certi Am Bd Obstet & Gynecol, 1969; certif Spec Competence Gynecol Oncol, 1974; ed bd, J Nat Med Asn,1981; specl reviewer Ob/ J Am Med Asn, CHEST. **Honors/Awds:** Dean's list Meharry Med Col, 1960; USPHS Postdoctoral Fel Gynecologic Cancer, 1967-69; Best Doctors in Am 1st Ed. **Special Achievements:** numerous publs abstracts & presentations including Savage EW Matlock DL Salem FA & Charles EH "The Effect of Endocervical Gland Involvement On the Cure Rates of Patients with CIN Undergoing Cryosurgery" Gynecol Oncol 14, 194-198 1982; Savage E W "Cesarean Hysterectomy Abstracts of Semelweiss Waters" OB Conf Dec 30 1981; "Treatment of Cervical Intraepithelial Carcinoma" Meharry Med Coll Ob/Gyn Grand Rounds Nashville TN June 16 1983. **Military Serv:** USAF, med corps capt, 1961-63. **Home Addr:** 3660 E Imperial Hwy, Lynwood, CA 90262, **Home Phone:** (310)631-9988. **Business Addr:** Adjunct Professor of Obstetrics and Gynecology, Charles R. Drew University of Medicine and Science, 1731 E 120th St, Los Angeles, CA 90059, **Business Phone:** (323)563-4800.

SAVAGE, FRANK
Executive, chairperson, chief executive officer. **Personal:** Born Jul 10, 1938, Rocky Mount, NC; son of Frank and Grace Vivian Pitt; married Lolita Valderrama, Feb 1, 1980; children: Eric, Brett, Mark, Antoine, Grace & Frank. **Educ:** Howard Univ, BA, 1962; Johns Hopkins Sch Advan Int Studies, MA, 1968. **Career:** Citibank, Int Div, staff, 1964-70; Equico Capital Corp, pres, 1970-73; TAW Int Leasing, exec vpres, 1973-75; Equitable Life Assurance, vpres, 1976-85, sr vpres, 1987; Alliance Capital Mgt Int, exec vpres, 1985-86, vice chmn, 1986-92, chmn, 1992-2002; Savage Holdings LLC, chmn emer, & chief exec officer, 2002-. **Orgs:** Trustee, Johns Hopkins Univ, 1977-; Coun Foreign Rels, 1982-; dir, Boys Choir Harlem, 1985-; dir, Essence Commun, 1988-; dir, Lockheed Corp, 1990-; bd trustee, Inst Int Educ, 2001; dir, NY Philharmonic. **Honors/Awds:** Outstanding Alumnus Award, Howard Univ, 1982; Honorary Doctorate Degree in Humane Letters, Hofstra Univ; Honorary Doctorate of Humanities, Howard Univ. **Business Addr:** Chairman, Chief Executive Officer, Savage Holdings LLC, 1414 Ave of the Americas, New York, NY 10019, **Business Phone:** (212)750-7400.

SAVAGE, HORACE CHRISTOPHER
Executive, clergy. **Personal:** Born Jul 30, 1941; children: Christopher, Nicholas & Carter. **Educ:** VA State Col, BA, 1968; Northwestern Univ, Evanston Il, MA & PhD, 1977. **Career:** USN Naval Shipyard, Past, personnel mgt spec, 1968-70; Sesame St Eval Proj Ed Testing Serv, 1969; Northwestern Univ, research asst, 1968-69; Northwestern Univ, teaching asst, 1969-70; teaching interns, 1970-71; EMarie Johnson & Assoc Chicago, staff, 1970-72; Chicago read Mental Health Ctr Chicago, 1971-72; NW Univ, visiting lectr ed, 1971-72; Lake Forest Col Ill, lectr psychol, 1971-72; Howard Univ Wash DC, lectr asst vice pres & dir research & eval, 1972; George Mason Univ, Fairfax, VA, assoc prof clinical psychol; Pvt Pract, 1973. **Orgs:** Eastern region chmn, Nat Asn Black Psychol; Am Psychol Asn; Am Asn Univ Profs; Int Transactional Analysis Asn; Am Correctional Asn; Am Ed Res Asn; Nat & Coun Black Child Develop; Phi Delta Kappa Prof Ed Frat; Am Asn Advan Sci; MD Pry Asn; DC Asn Black Psychol; DC Psychol Asn; Am Mgt Asn; bd psychol Examiners, Wash, DC. **Honors/Awds:** Univ Scholarship, Northwestern Univ, 1970; summer research fellowship Princeton, 1970; Martin Luther King Jr Woodrow Wilson Fellowship, 1970; WEB Dubois Award, 1968; Alpha Mu Gamma National Foreign Language Honor Soc; Beta Kappa Chi Nat Sci Honor Soc. **Special Achievements:** Has written many papers and publications in his field and conducted many workshops. **Military Serv:** USAF, 3 yrs.

SAVAGE, DR. JAMES EDWARD
Psychologist. **Personal:** Born Jul 30, 1941, Norfolk, VA; son of James and Thelma; divorced; children: Jeffrey, Itayo & James. **Educ:** Norfolk State Univ, Norfolk, VA, BA, 1968; Northwestern Univ Evanston, IL, MA, 1970, PhD, 1971. **Career:** Inst Life Enrichment, dir, 1979-; James E Savage, Jr & Assoc Ltd, pres, 1978-. **Orgs:** Past eastern reg chmn, Nat Asn Black Psychologists, 1971; Int Transactional Anal Asn, 1972-; Am Psychol Asn, 1972-. **Honors/Awds:** Martin Luther King Jr/Woodrow Wilson Fel, Woodrow Wilson Fel Found, 1968-70; Educational Testing Serv Summer Res Fel Princeton, NJ, 1970. **Military Serv:** USAF E-3. **Business Addr:** President, James E Savage Jr & Associates Ltd, 7852 16th St NW, Washington, DC 20012, **Business Phone:** (202)291-5008.

SAVAGE, JANET MARIE
Executive. **Personal:** Born Nov 12, 1960, Chicago, IL; daughter of Howard T and Ruth F; married John Fellows, Sep 1, 1991; children: Jared & Rachel. **Educ:** Stanford Univ, BA, 1982; Harvard Law Sch, JD, 1985. **Career:** Wilson, Sonsini, Goodrich & Rosati, 1985-89; The Walt Disney Co, 1989-92; KCAL TV, 1992-95; Twentieth Century FOX TV, vpres, 1995-2001. **Orgs:** Co-founder & pres, Comt Sports & Entertainment Law, Harvard Law Sch. **Home Addr:** 2346 Veteran Ave, Los Angeles, CA 90064, **Home Phone:** (310)478-8689. **Business Addr:** Vice President, Twentieth Century FOX Television, PO Box 900, Beverly Hills, CA 90213-0900, **Business Phone:** (310)369-2934.

SAVAGE, DR. VERNON THOMAS
Psychologist. **Personal:** Born Sep 13, 1945, Baltimore, MD; son of Theodore Savage and Mary Williams Savage; married Frances Sommerville, Dec 16, 1970; children: Tonya, Nakia, Bariki & Jabari. **Educ:** Hagerstown Community Col, Hagerstown, MD, AA, 1971-73; Syracuse Univ, Syracuse, NY, AB, 1974; Univ Ill, Urbana, IL, MA, 1976, PhD, 1981. **Career:** C Psychiatrist Ctr, Eatontown, NJ, clin intern, 1978-79; Oberlin Col, Oberlin, OH, clinical psychologist, 1979-83; Swarthmore Col, Swarthmore, PA, assoc dean students, 1983-87; Towson State Univ, Towson, MD, psychologist/senior counselor, 1987; John Hopkins Univ, Coun Ctr, assoc dir & dir outreach, currently. **Orgs:** Black Fac Adminr & Staff Asn, 1987-; Am Psychol Asn, 1989-. **Honors/Awds:** National Honor Fraternity for American Junior Colleges, Phi Theta Kappa, 1972; Ford Foundation, Upper Div Scholar, 1973; Traineeship, United State Pub Health Admin, 1974. **Military Serv:** USMC, Pfc, 1962-68. **Business Addr:** Associate Director, Director of Outreach, Johns Hopkins University Counseling Center, 358 Garland Hall, Baltimore, MD 21218, **Business Phone:** (410)516-8278.

SAVAGE, WILLIAM ARTHUR
College administrator. **Personal:** Born in Chicago, IL; son of John and Marie; children: William Jr & Michelle. **Educ:** Univ Ill, Urbana-Champaign, BS, 1969; Ill State Univ, Normal, MS edu, 1973, ABD. **Career:** Edu Asst Prog, Chicago, Ill, instr & counr, 1969-70; Ill State Univ, Normal, asst dir & coordr academic support servs, High Potential Stud Prog, 1970-75, lectr history, 1971-73, advisor & coordr, Academic Advisement Ctr, 1975-77, affirmative action, 1977-80; Univ Ill, Urbana-Champaign, asst chancellor, dir, 1980-91; Univ Pittsburgh, asst chancellor, dir affirmative action, currently. **Orgs:** Am Asn Affirmative Action; Col & Univ Personnel Asn; Nat Asn Advan Colored People; Pa Black Coun Higher Edu; Three Rivers Youth. **Honors/Awds:** Educ Hon, Kappa Delta Pi; Phi Delta Kappa. **Business Addr:** Assistant to the Chancellor, Director of Affirmative Action, University of Pittsburgh, 901 William Pitt Union, Pittsburgh, PA 15260, **Business Phone:** (412)648-7860.

SAWYER, ALFRED M.
Executive. **Personal:** Born Aug 8, 1934, Enterprise, OK; married Bertha L; children: Alfred Jr, Allen M & Alecia M. **Educ:** USAF Inst, 1959. **Career:** Gen Serv Dept, dir EO; NM Human Rights Com, dep dir; NM Human Rights Comn, civil rights investigator, 1969; NM St Office Econ Opportunity, econ develop, 1970; EEO NM St Planning Office, spec asst gov, 1971-74; Albuquerque Black Econ League, exec dir, 1976-79. **Orgs:** Bd mem, Albuquerque Black Econ Leag, 1975-77; bd dir, Albuquerque C C, 1977-79; organizer consult, NM Human Rights Citizens Comn; pres, Chaves Co Neighbourhood Asn, 1966-67; vpres, Roswell Br NAACP, 1966, pres, 1967; Roswell Urban Renewal Housing Comn, 1967-68; sec Chaves Co Employing Handicapped Comn, 1968-69; pres, Roswell Youth Res develop, 1968-69; panel judges, Annual St DECA Leadership Conf, 1971; adv comn, Title ISecondary Educ, 1970-71; recruitment comn mem, Upward Bound Proj, 1970-71; steering com mem, Chaves Co Red Cross, 1970-71; adv com mem, Home Educ Livelihood, 1971; bd mem, pres, Sickle Cell Coun NM, 1971-72; Black Leadership Conf, 1971-73; Minority Bus Opportunity Comn, 1973-78; Black Merit Acad, 1974; vpres, NM Conf of Brs NAACP, 1975-76; pres, Albuquerque NAACP, 1975-76; bd mem, Gov's Black Task Force, 1976; vpres, NM NAACP, 1976; bd mem Albuquerque Fed Org, 1977; Job Corps Friends Comn, 1977. **Honors/Awds:** Certificate outstanding achivement black committee Black Merit, Acad AL Chap, 1973; citizen of the year award, NM Black Leadership Conf, 1974; certificate of achivement in economic development, Albuquerque Black Con Leag, 1974; certificate of nobility, Sec St NM, 1975; certificate of appreciaiton, Black Student Union Univ AL, 1976; USAF longevity service Award, USAF; certificate of nobility, Sec St NM, 1980. **Military Serv:** USAF, a 2 & c, 1956-60. **Business Addr:** Director of EO, General Services Department, State of New Mexico, Santa Fe, NM 87503.

SAWYER, DEBORAH M.
Consultant. **Personal:** Born May 11, 1956, Columbus, OH; daughter of Betty P. **Educ:** Emory Univ, polit sci & biol, 1978; Eastern New Mex Univ, petrol microbiol, 1982. **Career:** URS Consultants, asst & midwest opers mgr, 1986-88; The Ohio Environ Protect Agency , environ scientist II, solid, toxic & hazardous waste mgt div, 1986-89; Beling Consultants Inc, sr vpres, bd mem, opers mgr, 1988-90; Environ S/E Inc, opers mgr, toxic & hazardous waste mgt div, 1990-91; Environ Design Int Inc, founder, pres & chief exec officer, 1991-. **Orgs:** Chicago Region Cert Hazardous Mat Mgrs, 1988-; bd mem, Joseph Corp, 1992-; Womens Bus Develop Ctr, 1992-; bd mem, Suburban Black Contractors Asn, 1993-; Evanston Bus Adv Comn, 1993-; Chem Indust Coun Ill, 1994-; pres, Nat Asn Women Bus Owners, Chicago Chap, 1996-97; Consulting Engrs Coun Ill, 1996-; Rice Campus Adv Bd; Chicagoland Chamber Com; Bradley Univ Col Eng; Ill Inst Technol. **Honors/Awds:** Small Minority Bus of the Yr Region 5, Small Bus Asn, 1994; Small Bus Award, Bank Am, 1995; Woman of Achievement, Bank Am, 1996; Entreprenuer of the Yr, Nat Asn Women Bus Owners, 1996. **Business Phone:** (312)356-5400.*

SAWYER, GEORGE EDWARD
Lawyer. **Personal:** Born May 7, 1919, Mobile, AL; married Maxine; children: Cynthia, Donald, Geoffrey & Michael. **Educ:** A & I State Col, AB, 1947; Univ Southern Calif, MA, 1952, PhD, 1955. **Career:** Huston-Tillotson Col, dean, 1947-56, prof speech drama; A&I State Univ, Tenn, bd dir & Nat Space Hall Fame, former vpres; Coun Pres Tex Sr Col & Univ, vchmn; Southern Asn Col & Sch, trust; Fed Facilities & Equip Grants Prog Tex Col & Univ sysyem, adv comn; Tex Southern Univ, pres, 1968-. **Orgs:** Bd mem, Standard Savs Asn. **Special Achievements:** publ articles on black acad & stud dissent black col campuses. **Business Addr:** 206 Reed Bldg, Richmond, IN 47374.

SAWYER, RODERICK TERRENCE
Lawyer. **Personal:** Born Apr 12, 1963, Chicago, IL; son of Celeste C Taylor and Eugene. **Educ:** DePaul Univ, BS, finance, 1985; Ill Inst Technol Chicago, Kent Col Law, JD, 1990. **Career:** SNN Inc, dba S's Lounge, pres, 1986-; Ill Com Comn, ade law judge, 1991-; Law Off Steven G Watkins Assoc, partner, 1992-. **Orgs:** Park Manor Neighbors Asn, 1985-; Phi Alpha Delta Law Fraternity, 1990-; 6th Ward Dem Orgn, pres, 1990-92; Chicago Bar Asn, 1990-; CCBA-ARDC Liaison Comt, 1992-; Ill State Bar Asn. **Home Addr:** 7229 S Prairie Ave, Chicago, IL 60619, **Home Phone:** (773)488-0228. **Business Phone:** (773)846-0011.

SAWYER, TALANCE
Football player. **Personal:** Born Jun 14, 1976, Bastrop, LA. **Educ:** Univ Nev, Las Vegas. **Career:** Football player(retired); Minn Vikings, defensive end, 1999-2003.

SAWYER, WILLIAM GREGORY
School administrator, dean (education). **Personal:** Born Nov 6, 1954, Columbus, OH; son of William Wesley Sawyer. **Educ:** Eastern Mich Univ, Ypsilanti, MI, 1972; Mount Union Col, Alliance, OH, BA, 1976; Eastern New Mex Univ, Portales, NM, MA, 1978; Univ N Tex, Denton, TX, PhD, 1986. **Career:** Amarillo Col, Amarillo, TX, comun instr, 1978-80; Univ N Tex, Denton, TX, teaching fel, 1980-83, hall dir, 1983-85, coordr interculture serv, 1985-86, from asst dean stud to dean stud, 1986-90; Fla Gulf Coast Univ, chief stud affairs officers & dean students, 1995; Calif Univ Channel Islands, vpres, 2002-. **Orgs:** Minority Caucus Advisor Unit, 1985-; adv, Progressive Black Stud Org Univ N Tex, 1985-; Tex Asn Black Prof, 1988-92; bd mem, Tex State Sickle Cell Found; pres, Tex Asn Col & Univ Personnel Adminr, 1991-92, pres elect, 1990-91, vpres, 1989-90, minority comm chair, 1987-89. **Honors/Awds:** Top Professor, Mortar Bd Honors Soc, 1987-92; Outstanding Contributions to the Minority Community, Tex Woman's Univ; Outstanding Service to the African Community, Progressive Black Stud Org; Texas Award for Outstanding Vision & Leadership in Education. **Home Addr:** 1201 SW 44th St, Cape Coral, FL 33914-6389. **Business Addr:** Vice President for Student Affairs, California Staet University Channel Islands, One University Dr, Camarillo, CA 93012, **Business Phone:** (805)437-8400.

SAWYERS, DORRET E
Educator. **Personal:** Born Jul 27, 1957, Clarendon, Jamaica; daughter of W McTaggart; married P Sawyers, Dec 17, 1994; children: Brian, Kareem & Akilah. **Educ:** Col Arts, Sci & Technol, dipl, 1979; Tuskegee Univ, BS, 1984; Univ Mo-Columbia, MPA, 1987. **Career:** Knox Col, lectr, 1979-81; Tuskegee Univ, stud asst, 1982-84; Univ Mo, fiscal analyst, 1985-91; Fla Int Univ, Stud Support Serv, dir, 1992-. **Orgs:** Fla Asn Women Educ; Nat Alliance State Pharm Asn. **Business Addr:** Director, Florida International University, Division of Student Affairs, 11200 SW 8th St GC 216, Miami, FL 33199, **Business Phone:** (305)348-2797.

SAXTON, PAUL CHRISTOPHER
Government official. **Personal:** Born Dec 14, 1970, Cleveland, OH; son of Cay and Madison. **Educ:** KY State Univ, BA, Criminal Justice, 1998, MPA, pub admin, 1999. **Career:** Cabinet Families & Children, policy analyst, 1999-; Tomball Col, dir Res Develop & Grant Admin, currently. **Business Addr:** Director, Tomball College, 30555 Tomball Pkwy, Tomball, TX 77375, **Business Phone:** (281)351-3300.

SAYERS, GALE EUGENE
Football player, entrepreneur. **Personal:** Born May 30, 1943, Wichita, KS; married Linda McNeil, Jun 10, 1962 (divorced 1973); married Ardythe Elaine Bullard, Dec 1, 1973; children: Gale Lynne, Scott Aaron, Timothy Gale, Gaylon, Guy & Gary. **Educ:** Kans Univ; NY Inst Finance. **Career:** Football Player (retired), entrepreneur; Chicago Bears, running back, 1965-72; Kansas Univ, asst to athletic dir; Southern Ill Univ, athletic dir, 1981; Chicago Daily News, columnist; Comput Supplies by Sayers, vpres, mkt; Sayers Comput Source, chmn & chief exec officer, 1982-; Sayers 40 Inc, founder, pres & chief exec officer, currently. **Orgs:** Co-chmn, Legal Defense Fund, Sports Comt, NAACP; coordr, Reach Out Prog,Chicago; hon chmn, Am Cancer Soc; comnr, Chicago Pk Dist; Kappa Alpha Psi;Triad Hosp; Am Century Funds; Marklund; Cradle Soc. **Honors/Awds:** Most Courageous Player Award, Pro Football Writers Am, 1970; Pro Football Hall of Fame, 1977; Chicago's Entrepeneurship Hall of Fame, Univ Ill, 1999; Technical & Communications Entrepeneurs of the Year, Ernst & Young,1999; Ranked number 21 on The Sporting News' list of the "100 Greatest Football Players". **Special Achievements:** Company is ranked No 26 on Black Enterprise mag's 1997 list of Top 100 Black businesses; Author, autobiography, I Am Third. **Business Addr:** President, Chief Executive Officer, Sayers 40 Inc, 1150 Feehanville Dr, Mount Prospect, IL 60056, **Business Phone:** (847)391-4040.

SCAFE, JUDITH ARLENE
Executive. **Personal:** Born May 14, 1961, Detroit, MI; daughter of Julious O and Mary A. **Educ:** Mich State Univ, telecommun, 1984; Wayne State Univ, comput sci, 1986, small bus mgt coursework, 1991; Central Mich Univ, pursuing MPA, 1991. **Career:** WDTB News Radio, reporter, 1983-84; MCI Commun, corp acct exec, 1985-86; Detroit Public Schs, substitute teacher, 1987-88; The Polimage Group Inc, proj coordr, 1988-90; Wayne County HTH & community Serv, prog coordr, 1988-92; Detroit City coul, spec proj asst, 1989-; WTVS Channel 56, City Youth, proj mgr, 1992. **Orgs:** Planning comn, United Commun Serv, 1988-92; bus united, Officers & Youth, 1988-; comnr, Detroit City Coun Youth Comn, 1989-; New Detroit Inc, 1990-92; adv, Mumford Area Youth Assistance, 1990-; Detroit Urban league, 1991-92; Nat Asn Black Journalists, 1992-; Am Red Cross, 1992-. **Special Achievements:** Speaker, Creating Caring Communities Conf, Mich state Univ, 1992; "50 Leaders of Tommorrow," Ebony Magazine, 1992; Dress a Doll for Christmas, Goodfellows org, 1992; New Detroit Inc, Spec Recognition for Dropout Prevent, 1991-92; Spec Recognition Volunteerism, Phoenix Optimist Club, 1990; Barden Cablevision, Spec Recognition Producing, 1989.

SCAGGS, DR. EDWARD W.
Management consultant. **Personal:** Born Mar 4, 1932, East St Louis, IL; children: Jonathan, Gregory, Helen, Keith, Edward Jr & Patricia Jean. **Educ:** Ill State Normal Univ, BS, 1956; Univ Ill, MS, 1958; Kans State Univ, PhD, 1975. **Career:** Self-employed, consult; PATCO, spec exec dir; Ten Cities DOL-HEW, exec dir; Univ Kans, asst prof; Training Corp Am, exec dir; Social Dynamics Inc; Poland Springs Eco Sys Corp, lang dir; St Paul Sch Midwest Theol Sem; Western Auto Co; Milgrams Food Chains; Builder's Assoc; Impact Studies Inc; Wichita Fallas Tex Govt, currently. **Orgs:** Kans City C of C, KS City Human Rel Menorah Med Ctr, Skill Upgrading Inc, Al Nellum Asn, Al Andrews & Co; dir, KC Sch Dist Bd; exec bd, Mo Sch Bds Asn; adv bd, Mo Voc Educ Bd; adv bd, Urban League; adv bd, YMCA Careers; adv bd, Niles Home C. **Honors/Awds:** Published numerous articles and manuals. *

SCALES, ALICE MARIE
Educator. **Personal:** Born Nov 3, 1941, Darling, MS. **Educ:** Rust Col, BS, elem educ, 1963; Univ Mass, EdD, Reading & Lang Arts Educ, 1971; Southern Univ, MEd, elem educ, 1966. **Career:** John Hyson Elem Sch, teacher, 1963-65; Brookfield Elem Sch, remedial reading teacher, 1966-67; Ware Sch System, reading specialist, 1966-69; Hadley Sch System, reading specialist, 1969-70; Univ Mass, instr & dir; Westfield State Col, instr, 1970-71; Indiana Univ, asst prof educ, 1971-72; Int Col Cayman Islands, adj prof educ; Univ Pittsburgh, from asst prof educ to assoc prof educ, 1972-97, prof, instr & learning, 1997-, Dept Instr & Learning, assoc chair. **Orgs:** Consult, Carnegie-Mellon Action Proj, Carnegie Mellon Univ; ESAA Sch; Banneker Contracted Curric Ctr; Int Reading Asn; Am Personnel & Guid Asn; NAACP; Nat Asn Black Psychologists; Alpha Kappa Alpha; Nat Alliance Black School Educr; Am Educ Res Asn; Nat Coun Teachers Eng; Black Women's Asn Inc; Aging & Intergenerational Reading; Am Asn Adult & Continuing Educ; Phi Delta Kappa; Am Asn Univ Prof; Am Educ Res Asn. **Honors/Awds:** USA Presidential Citation, 1980; Cert Appreciation, PA Asn Adult & Continuing Educ, 1985; City of Pittsburgh Award, 1987; Distinguished Service Award, Negro Educ Rev, 1997; Henry Highland Garnet Society Award, 2006. **Special Achievements:** Publications: "Efficient Reading for Minorities Implications for Counselors", "Strategies for Humanizing the Testing of Minorities", "College Reading & Study Skills An Asses-Perscriptive Model", "A Comm Operated After Sch Rdg Prgm", "Preparing to Assist Black Children in the Rdg Act". **Business Addr:** Professor, University of Pittsburgh, School of Education, 5115 Wesley W Posvar Hall, Pittsburgh, PA 15260.

SCALES, JEROME C.
Dentist. **Personal:** Born Nov 21, 1942, Birmingham, AL; son of J C and Annie Fancher Mason; married Sandra Wills Scales, Aug 17, 1973; children: Lia, Jerome III, Marc. **Educ:** Fla State Univ, attended 1962; Univ Dayton, attended 1964; Tenn State Univ, BS, 1969; Meharry Med Col, DDS, 1973; Univ Ala Sch Dent, cert pediat dent, 1975. **Career:** US Postal Serv, letter carrier, 1965-66; Veterans Admin Hosp, dent intern, 1972; Meharry Medical Col, stud res asst, 1970-73; Univ Ala Sch Dent, clinical assoc prog, 1975-; pediat dent, 1975-. **Orgs:** Phi Beta Sigma Fraternity, 1976-; vpres, 1977, treas, 1978-90, Ala Dent Soc, Zone I, Birmingham; pres, vpres, Birmingham Pediatric Dent Asn, 1981-84; bd deacons, Tabernacle Baptist Church, 1982; adv bd, Am Straight Wire Orthod Asn, 1983-84; pres, 1989-90, vpres, 1988-89, Ala Soc Pediat Dent; pres, Ala Dent Soc, 1989-91; Nat Dent Asn; Am Dent Asn; Am Acad Pediat Dent; Am Orthod Soc; Ala Dent Asn; Southeastern Soc Pediat Dent; Birmingham Dist Dent Asn; Meharry Med Col Alumni Asn; Tenn State Univ Alumni Asn; bd dir, Dent Examiners of Ala, 1997-02. **Honors/Awds:** Nominated for Martin L King Jr Award, Meharry Medical Col, 1973; best graduate student, Univ Ala Sch Dent, 1975; Certificate in Straight Wire Orthodontics, Straight Wire Technique Found, 1978, 1980; plaque, services as pres, Ala Soc Pediatric Dentistry, 1990. **Military Serv:** USAF, 1960-64; Airman of the Month, 1964; Good Conduct Medal, 1962; Unit Citation Medal, 1962. **Business Addr:** Pediatric Dentist, 623 8th Ave W, Birmingham, AL 35204.*

SCALES, DR. MANDERLINE ELIZABETH WILLIS
Educator. **Personal:** Born Mar 14, 1927, Winston-Salem, NC; daughter of Shakepeare Pitts and Roxanne Pitts; married Robert Albert, Apr 9, 1955; children: Albert Marvin. **Educ:** Spel man Col, AB, 1949; Univ Pittsburgh, MEd; Univ Valencia, Spain; Univ NC, Greensboro, PhD. **Career:** Winston-Salem State Univ, prof soc sci spanish; Winston-Salem Forsyth Co,Schs Forsyth Tech Inst, teacher; Asn Classroom Teachers, past pres; Dist &State Levels Foreign Lang Teachers NCTA, chmn; Forsyth PTA Enrich Proj, chmn; Forsyth Co YWCA, dir bd; Winston-Salem Nat Coun Negro Women. **Orgs:** Past Loyal Lady Ruler Golden Circ; OES; Delta Sigma Theta Sor; bd dirs, Delta Fine Arts Proj; trustee,

Shiloh Baptist Church; pres, Union RJ Reynolds Fellowship study Spain; dir, Shilohian St Peter's Corp Family Ctr, 1984-02; pres, Top Ladies Distinction Inc, 1986-89; past nat pres, Nation Women Achievement Inc; Chamber Com; Allocations Community & Project Blueprint, United Way; Chair Community Develop, Legacy 2000 Forsyth County; YWCA; pres & convener, Nat Coun Negro Women Inc; pres, Spelman Col Alumni Chap. **Honors/ Awds:** Outstanding Woman in Civic & Comm Winston-Salem, 1974; Commandress of Year, Nat Organ Daughters Isis; Hall of Justice, Community Forsyth County; Leadership Award, United Negro Col Fund. **Special Achievements:** Past Nat Adv COM for NASA classroom of the Future; Honored by 1981 classof Winston-Salem Univ; organizer of the collegiate Group WSSU & the Regional and Nat Levels; COT Leader Award by Winston-Salem Chronicle. **Home Addr:** 4000 Whitfield Rd NE, Winston-Salem, NC 27105, **Home Phone:** (336)767-4003. **Business Addr:** Convener, National Council of Negro Women Inc, 633 Pennsylvania Ave NW, Washington, DC 20004, **Business Phone:** (202)737-0120.

SCALES, DR. PATRICIA BOWLES
Executive, president (organization). **Personal:** Born Dec 13, 1939, Matinsville, VA; daughter of Tommy B Bowles and Irene Martin Bowles (deceased); married Vesharn Nathaniel, Sep 27, 1969. **Educ:** Va State Univ, BS, 1963; Trinity Col, MA, 1975; George Wash Univ, EdD, 1984. **Career:** MTI Const Co Inc, vpres, 1978-83; Liberty Constr Inc, pres, ceo, 1983-. **Orgs:** Pres, Torchbearers Circle Shiloh Baptist Church, 1981-89; life mem, Nat Coun Negro Women, 1983-; White House Conf Small Bus, 1986; Md Productivity Award Comn, 1986-89; Md Apprenticeship & Training Coun, 1986-87; bd dir, Africare, Inc 1989-96; The Woman's Nat Democratic Club, 1990-91; vice chair, Bowie State Univ Found Inc, 1994-; YMCA Urban Prog Ctr, Wash DC; bd visitors, Bennett Col. **Honors/Awds:** Achievement Award, National Counl Negro Women, 1986; Achievement Award, One of Am Top 100 Bus & Professional Women, Dollars & Sense Mag, 1986; Proclamation for Achievement from Prince George's County Council, MD, 1987. **Home Addr:** 12506 Pleasant Prospect Rd, Mitchellville, MD 20716, **Home Phone:** (301)249-9582. **Business Addr:** President, Chief Executive Officer, Liberty Construction Inc, 6029 Dix St NE Suite 201, Washington, DC 20019, **Business Phone:** (202)399-1500.

SCALES, ROBERT L.
Politician. **Personal:** Born Sep 14, 1931, Wedeowee, AL; married Marcia. **Educ:** Allied Inst Tech, master machinist; Univ Ill. **Career:** Maywood, village trust fourth dist; Tool & Die Maker Am Can Co; Am Fed Labor & Congress Indust Orgn, work men's compen rep; United Steel Workers Am, grieve com, 1972. **Orgs:** Bd dir, Proviso Day Care Ctr; past bd mem, Proviso-Leyden Coun Comn Action; Asn Dean Polit Educ Operation PUSH; Oper PUSH; Nat Black Caucas Loc Elected Off; Political orgn voter registered & Voter Educ; First Baptist Church Melrose Pk; Maywood Comn, 1972 pres elec; demon vote splitting; initiated comn wide newsletter Black Men Pushing, oper PUSH. **Honors/Awds:** Maywood, village trust fourth dist; Tool & Die Maker Am Can Co; Am Fed Labor & Congress Indust Orgn, workmen's compen rep; United Steel Workers Am, grieve com, 1972. **Military Serv:** AUS, 1952-54.

SCALES-TRENT, PROF. JUDY
Lawyer, educator, college teacher. **Personal:** Born Oct 1, 1940, Winston-Salem, NC; daughter of William J Trent Jr and Viola Scales Trent; children: Jason B Ellis. **Educ:** Oberlin Col, BA, French, 1962; Middlebury Col, MA, French, 1967; Northwestern Univ, JD, 1973. **Career:** Equal Employ Opportunity Comn, supvr atty, 1973-76, spec asst vice chmn, 1977-79, spec asst gen coun, 1979-80, appellate atty, 1980-84; SUNY Buffalo Law Sch, assoc prof law, 1984-90, prof law, 1990-, Floyd H & Hilda L. Hurst Fac Scholar, currently; Senegal grant, 2000-01. **Orgs:** DC Bar; New York State Bar; US Ct Appeals Fourth, Fifth, Sixth, Seventh, Nineth & Eleventh Circuits; Am Bar Asn; bd dir, Park Sch Buffalo, 1985-88; bd dir, Nat Women & Law Asn, 1987-91; bd visitors, Roswell Park Mem Cancer Inst, 1991-96; bd gov, Soc Am Law Teachers, 1992-95. **Honors/Awds:** Haywood Burns Award, 2004, Trailblazer Award, 2000, 2007, Northeast People Color Legal Scholar Conf. **Special Achievements:** Articles published: "A Judge Shapes and Manages Institutional Reform: School Desegration in Buffalo," 12 NYU Review of Law and Social Change 19 (1989)' "Black Women and the constitution: Finding our Place, Asserting our Rights," 24 Harvard Civil Rights-Civil Liberties Law Review 9 (1989)' "Women of Color and Health: Issues of Gender, Power and Community," 43 Stanford Law Review 1357, 1991; "The Law as an Instrument of Oppression and the Culture of Resistance," in Black Women in America: An Historical Encyclopedia 701, 1993; "On Turning Fifty," in Patricia Bell-Scott, ed Life Notes 336, 1994; "Equal Rights Advocates: Addressing Legal Issues of Women of Color," Berkeley Women's Law Jnl, 1998; "African Women in France: Immigration, Family, and Work," Brooklyn Jnl of Internatl Law, 1999; Book published: Notes of a White Black Woman: Race, Color, Community, 1995; listed in Who's Who Among African-Americans. **Business Addr:** Professor of Law, State University of New York Buffalo Law School, 519 O'Brian Hall North Campus, Amherst Campus, Buffalo, NY 14260-1100.

SCANLAN, AGNES BUNDY
Executive. **Educ:** Smith Col, BA, 1979; Georgetown Univ Law Ctr, JD, 1989. **Career:** US Sen Budget Comt, legal coun; Fleet Boston Financial Corp, sr vpres, 1994-99, chief privacy officer, 1999, managing dir, chief compliance officer, 2002-04; Bank Am, regulatory rels exec, 2004; Goodwin Procter LLP, Bus Law Dept, coun, 2005-, Financial Serv Prac, mem, currently. **Orgs:** Chairwoman, Fed Res Bd Gov Consumer Adv Coun; pres, Int Asn Privacy Prof; chair, Compliance Mgt Subcomt, Am Bar Asn; trustee, Bd Smith Col; vice chair & trustee, Bd Bryant Univ; chair, Risk Mgt Comt, Bridge Over Troubled Waters; Boston C Mus; Bars Supreme Ct Pa; Superior Ct the Dist Columbia. **Honors/ Awds:** Bostons Power Women, CBS Boston affiliate WBZ, 2004; IAPP Synomos Vanguard Award, 2004. **Special Achievements:** Frequent speaker on government & regulatory relations, ethics, privacy & risk management matters at industry seminars, professional conferences & academic institutions. **Business Addr:** Counsel, Goodwin Procter LLP, 53 State St Exchange Pl, Boston, MA 02109, **Business Phone:** (617)570-1161.

SCANTLEBURY-WHITE, VELMA PATRICIA
Surgeon. **Personal:** Born Oct 6, 1955, Barbados; daughter of Delacey and Kathleen; married Harvey White, Nov 4, 1989; children: Akela, Aisha. **Educ:** Long Island Univ, Brooklyn Campus, BS, 1977; Columbia Univ, Col Physicians & Surgeons, MD, 1981. **Career:** Harlem Hosp, intern & resident gen surg, 1981-86; Univ Pittsburgh, fel, transplantation surg, 1986-88; asst prof, surg, 1988-94, assoc prof, 1995-. **Orgs:** diplomat, Am Col Surgeons, 1982-90; Am Med Asn, 1987, 1991-; Nat Med Asn, 1989-; P & S Minority Alumni Asn, 1981-; Gateway Med Soc, 1991-; Am Col Surgeons, 1994; Am Soc Transplant Surgeons, 1994; African Am Outreach Comt; Nat Kidney Found Western Pennsylvania. **Honors/Awds:** Distinguished Daughter of PA, 1996; Carlow Col "Women of Spirit" Award, 1997; Celebration Excellence Award, Triangle Corner Ltd, 1992; WPTT & Duquesne Light, Outstanding African Am Contribution, 1992; Annual Award, Outstanding Young Women Am, 1988; Outstanding Service Award, Harlem Hosp Ctr, 1988; "Gift of Life" Award, Nat Kidney Found, 1998. **Special Achievements:** New Onset of Diabetes in FK 506 versus Cyclosporine treated kidney transplant recipients, 1991; "The Results of Kidney Transplantation in African Americans Using Tacrolimus", 1997; Reproduction After Transplantation, 1991; Pregnancy and Liver Transplantation, 1990; Successful Reconstruction of Late Portal Vein Stenosis, 1989; Beneficial Effect of Dopamine on Function of Autotransplanted Kidney, 1984. **Business Addr:** Associate Professor Surgery, University of Pittsburgh Falk Clinic, 3601 5th Ave Suite 4C, Pittsburgh, PA 15213-2583, **Business Phone:** (412)692-6110.

SCANTLING, WAYNE LAMAR
Engineer. **Personal:** Born Mar 21, 1954, Greensboro, NC; son of Johnny and Ann; married Wendi, 1984; children: Whitney. **Educ:** NC A&T State Univ, BS, mech engineering, 1977; Univ Central Fla, MS, mech engineering, 1999. **Career:** NASA Langely Res Ctr, 1972-77; Raytheon Electronics, corp engr, 1977-80; Lockheed Martin, staff engr, 1980-93; Walt Disney World, sr project engr, currently. **Orgs:** Vpres, SECME, NSBE-Orlando Chap, 1994-96; pres, NCA&T CEN Fla Alumni, 1992-94. **Honors/ Awds:** Martin Marietta, Spot Award, 1985; misc achievement awards. **Special Achievements:** Nasa High Number TM-X; published various articles in: NSBE Bridge Mag, Black Enterprise, ASEE Prism Mag, ASME Mech Engr Mag. **Home Addr:** 7273 Branchtree Dr, Orlando, FL 32835, **Home Phone:** (407)291-9482. **Business Addr:** Senior Project Engineer, Walt Disney World, PO Box 10000, Lake Buena Vista, FL 32830, **Business Phone:** (407)824-7260.

SCARBOROUGH, CHARLES S.
Educator. **Personal:** Born May 20, 1933, Goodman, MS; married Merion Anderson; children: Charles II & James II. **Educ:** Rust Col, AB, 1955; Northwestern Univ, MS, 1958; Mich State Univ, PhD, 1969. **Career:** Alcorn A&M Col, instr, 1957-59; Mich State Univ, grad teacher asst, 1959-63, instr, 1963-69, asst prof, 1969-72, asst dir, 1971-73, assoc prof, 1972, dir, 1973. **Orgs:** Am Men & Women Sci; Acad Affairs Admin; Sigma Xi; Am Asn Advan Sci; Asn Gen & Liberal Studies; consumer info comm, Mich State Univ Employee Credit Union; chmn elect, Mich State Univ Black Fac & Admin Group. **Honors/Awds:** Dr. Charles S. Scarborough Endowed Scholarship, named in honor, Mich State Univ. *

SCHENCK, FREDERICK A
Executive. **Personal:** Born May 12, 1928, Trenton, NJ; son of Frederick A Schenck Sr and Alwilda McLain Schenck; married H Quinta Chapman, Jan 25, 1974. **Educ:** Howard Univ, attended, 1948-50; Rider Col, BS, Com, 1958, MA, 1976. **Career:** NJ Dept Labor & Indust, personnel officer, 1960-64; NJ Office Econ Opportunities, chief admin serv, 1966-68; NJ Dept Community Affairs, chief pub employ career develop prog, 1966-68, dir admin, 1967-72; NJ Dept Inst & Agy, dir div youth & family serv, 1972-74; NJ Dept Treas, dep dir admin Div purchase & property, 1974-77; US Dept Com, reg rep sec commerce, 1977-78, dep under secy, 1978-79; Resorts Int Casino Hotel, Atlantic City NJ, sr vpres admin; Cunard Line Ltd, New York, NY, vice pres, 1988-92; Bur Nat Affairs Inc, dir, currently; self employed mgt consult, Secaucus, NJ, 1995-. **Orgs:** Govs Task Force Serv Disabled, 1986-87; bd trustees, Sammy Davis Jr Nat Liver Inst, 1990-; bd, Bur Nat Affairs Inc; adv bd, Rider Col. **Military Serv:** USN, Seaman 1st Class, 1946-48. **Business Addr:** Director, The Bureau of National Affairs Inc, 1231 25thSt Nw, Washington, DC 20037, **Business Phone:** (202)452-4200.

SCHEXNIDER, DR. ALVIN J
School administrator. **Personal:** Born May 26, 1945, Lake Charles, LA; son of Alfred and Ruth Mayfield; married Virginia Y Reeves. **Educ:** Grambling State Univ, BA, 1968; Northwestern Univ, MA, 1971, PhD, 1973. **Career:** Owens-IL Inc, asst dir personnel, 1968; Northwestern Univ, Norman Wait Harris fel, 1971-72; Ford Found, fel, 1972; Woodrow Wilson Found, fel, 1973; Southern Univ, asst prof, 1973-74; Syracuse Univ, asst prof, 1974-77; Fed Exec Inst, sr prof, 1977-79; Va Commonwealth Univ, assoc dean, 1979-84, vice provost undergrad studies, 1987-95; Univ NC Greensboro, asst vice chancellor, 1984-87; Winston-Salem State, chancellor, 1996-2000; Wake Forest Univ Sch Med, Off Health Policy Develop, dir; Norfolk State Univ, interim exec vpres, 2002, exec vpres, 2003-, interim pres, 2005-. **Orgs:** Am Pol Sci Asn; Am Soc Pub Admin; Nat Conf Black Polit Sci; Alpha Phi Alpha, 1965-; fel Inter- Univ Seminar Armed Forces & Soc, 1975-; consult, Va Munic League, 1980; pres, Va Chap, Am Soc Pub Admin, 1983-84; gov commiss Va Future, 1982-84; adv bd, Greensboro Nat Bank, 1986-87; bd visitors, Va State Univ, 1986-87; Sigma Pi Phi, 1989-; State Bd Educ, 1990-94; vice chair, Gov Adv Comn Revitalization Virginia's Cities. **Honors/Awds:** Outstanding Young Men Am US Jaycees, 1978; J Sargent Reynolds Award, Am Soc Pub Admin, 1980. **Military Serv:** AUS, sgt, 1968-70. **Business Addr:** Interim President, Executive Vice President, Norfolk State University, School of Education, 700 Pk Ave, Norfolk, VA 23504.

SCHMIEGELOW, TONI D
Executive. **Educ:** Univ Pa, BA, sociol; Columbia Univ Educ Coun, MA. **Career:** US Dept Housing & Urban Develop, Off Multifamily Housing Develop, sr proj mgr, dir cong rels, field dir, currently. **Business Addr:** Field Director, US Department of Housing & Urban Development, McNamara Fed Bldg 477 Michigan Ave, Detroit, MI 48266, **Business Phone:** (313)226-7900.

SCHMOKE, KURT LIDELL
Mayor, business owner. **Personal:** Son of Murray and Irene; married Patricia; children: Gregory & Katherine. **Educ:** Yale Univ, BA, 1971; Oxford Univ, MA, 1973; Harvard Univ, JD, 1976. **Career:** Piper & Marbury Baltimore, atty, 1976-77, 1981-82; White House Domestic Policy Staff, asst dir, 1977-78; City Baltimore, asst US atty, 1978-82, state's atty for Baltimore City, 1982-87, mayor, 1987-99; Wilmer, Cutler & Pickering, partner, 1999-2002; Howard Univ, Washington, DC, Dean of the Sch Law, 2003-. **Orgs:** Admitted Md Bar, 1976; Govs Comn Prison Overcrowding, MD Criminal Justice Coord Coun, Task Force to Reform the Insanity Defense. **Honors/Awds:** National Literacy Award, 1992.; Rhodes Scholar; Honorary Degree, Western MD Col; Honorary Degree, Univ Baltimore; Honorary Degree, Bard Col; Honorary Degree, Bowie State Univ; Honorary Degree, Goucher Col; Honorary Degree, Gov's State Univ; Honorary Degree, Morgan State Univ. **Special Achievements:** First black man elected mayor of Baltimore, Maryland. **Business Phone:** (202)806-8000.

SCHOOLER, DR. JAMES MORSE
Educator. **Personal:** Born Mar 22, 1936, Durham, NC; son of Frances W Williams and James Morse Schooler Sr; married Mignon I Miller, Aug 10, 1968; children: Wesley G & Vincent C. **Educ:** Wittenberg Col, BA, 1957; Univ Wis, MS, 1959, PhD, 1964. **Career:** Harvard Med Sch, res fel, Dept Physiol, 1964-66; Tuskegee Inst, asst prof, 1966-70; Duke Univ, asst prof physiol, 1970-75; NC Cent Univ, prof chem; Duke Univ, adj assoc prof, 1975-. **Orgs:** Am Chem Soc; Am Asn Advan Sci; Am Physiol Soc; BSA; Durham Com Black Affairs Educ Subcom; Trust White Rock Baptist Church; Sigma Xi; Beta Kappa Chi; Phi Lambda Upsilon; Phi Alpha Theta; Alpha Phi Alpha. **Honors/Awds:** Hillside HS Alumni Award, 1970. **Business Addr:** Adjunct Associate Professor, Duke University, 2138 Campus Dr, Durham, NC 27708, **Business Phone:** (919)684-8111.

SCHOONOVER, BRENDA BROWN
Ambassador. **Personal:** Born in Baltimore, MD. **Educ:** Morgan State Univ, BA; Howard Univ, grad studies. **Career:** Ambassador (Retired); Peace Corps, Philippines, vol, 1961; Bur European & Canadian Affairs, chief personnel, 1988-91; Off Joint Admin Serv, US Embassy, Brussels, Belgium, admin Officer & deputy dir, 1992-96, dep chief, 2001-04; US Ambassador Togo, 1998-2000. **Orgs:** Alpha Kappa Alpha Sorority; Peace Corps Alumni Asn; Peace Corps All-Vol Conf, Pagala, Togo. **Honors/Awds:** Superior Honor, State Dept.

SCHULTERS, LANCE A.
Football player. **Personal:** Born May 27, 1975, Guyana; married Sherrice; children: Kayanna & Unique. **Educ:** Nassau Comm Col; Hofstra Univ, sociol, 1998. **Career:** San Francisco 49ers, defensive back, 1998-2001; Tenn Titans, 2002-04; Miami

Dolphins, safety, 2005 & 2007; Atlanta Falcons, defensive back, 2006; New Orleans Saints, 2008. **Orgs:** Founder, Lance Schulters Found, 2001. **Honors/Awds:** Defensive Player of the Week; Ed Block Courage Award, 2001. **Business Addr:** Professional Football Player, New Orleans Saints, 5800 Airline Dr, Metairie, VA 70003, **Business Phone:** (504)733-0255.

SCHULTZ, MICHAEL A
Movie director, movie producer. **Personal:** Born Nov 10, 1938, Milwaukee, WI; son of Leo and Katherine Frances Leslie; married Lauren Jones, Dec 6, 1965; children: 2. **Educ:** Univ Wis; Marquette Univ, BFA. **Career:** Director & producer; Theater direction includes: Waiting for Godot, 1966; Song of the Lusitanian Bogey, 1968; Kongi's Harvest; God Is a (Guess What?); Does a Tiger Wear a Necktie?; The Reckoning, 1969; Every Night When the Sun Goes Down, 1969; Eugene O'Neill Memorial Theatre, directed plays by new playwrights, 1969; Operation Sidewinder; Dream on Monkey Mountain, 1970, 1971; Woyzeck, 1970; The Three Sisters, 1973; Thoughts, 1973; The Poison Tree, 1973; What the Winesellers Buy, 1974; The New Theater for Now, director, 1974; Films: Together for Days, 1972; Honeybaby, Honeybaby, 1974; Cooley High, 1974; Billie Holliday, 1974; Honeybaby, 1974; Car Wash, 1976; Greased Lightning, 1977; Which Way Is Up?, 1977; Sgt Pepper's Lonely Hearts Club Band, 1978; Scavenger Hunt, 1979; Carbon Copy, 1981; Bustin' Loose, 1983; The Last Dragon, 1985; Krush Groove, producer & dir, 1985; Disorderlies, dir & co-producer, 1987; Livin' Large, 1991; Phat Beach, exec producer, 1996; The Adventures of Young Indiana Jones: Tales of Innocence, 1999; Woman Thou Art Loosed 2004; The Adventures of Young Indiana Jones: My First Adventure, 2007; TV series: To Be Young, Gifted, & Black, 1972; Toma, 1974; The Rockford Files, 1974; Ceremonies in Dark Old Men, 1975; "Starsky & Hutch", 1975; What's Happeining!!, 1976; Benny's Place, 1982; For Us the Living: The Medgar Evers Story, 1983; Earth, Wind & Fire in Concert, 1984; The Jerk, Too, 1984; The Spirit, 1987; Timestalkers, 1987; Rock 'n' Roll Mom, 1988; Tarzan in Manhattan, 1989; Hammer, Slammer, & Slade, 1990; Jury Duty: The Comedy, 1990; "Picket Fences", 1992-95; Day-O, 1992; "L.A. Law", 1993; "The Adventures of Brisco County Jr.", 1993; Young Indiana Jones & the Hollywood Follies, 1994; "Diagnosis Murder", 1995; Shock Treatment, 1995; "Sisters", 1995-96; "Chicago Hope", 1996-98; "Promised Land", 1996; Young Indiana Jones: Travels with Father, 1996; The Practice, 1997-2001; "Ally McBeal", 1997-2001; "JAG", 1997-2002; Killers in the House, 1998; "Family Law", 1999; "Felicity", 1999; "Wasteland", 1999; "Ally", 1999; My Last Love, 1999; "That's Life", 2000; "City of Angels", 2000; "City of Angels", 2000; Charmed, 2000-01; "Boston Public", 2000-03; "Philly", 2001; "L.A. Law: The Movie", 2002; "Everwood", dir & producer, 2002-05; "Jack & Bobby", 2004-05; "Cold Case", 2005; "Pepper Dennis", 2006; "Gilmore Girls", 2006; "October Road", 2007; "Lincoln Heights", 2007; The O.C., 2007; "Dirty Sexy Money", 2007; "Brothers & Sisters", 2007-08; "Women's Murder Club", 2008; "Eli Stone", 2008. **Honors/Awds:** Obie Award for best direction, Song of the Lusitanian Bogey, 1968; Tony nomination & Drama Desk Award, Does a Tiger Wear a Necktie, 1969; Technical Grand Prize, Cannes Film Festival, 1977; Oscar Micheaux Award, Black Filmakers Hall Fame, 1991; Best Film Award, Am Black Film Festival, 2004; Best American Film, Santa Barbara Int Film Festival, 2004; Black Reel Award, 2005; Christopher Award, Ceremonies of Dark Old Men. **Business Phone:** (310)859-4000.*

SCHUMACHER, BROCKMAN
Educator, air force officer. **Personal:** Born Aug 26, 1924, St Louis, MO; married Doris Goodman; children: Brockman Jr, Douglass William, Andrew Jason. **Educ:** State Univ IA, BA, 1949; Wash Univ, MA, educ, 1952, PhD, 1969. **Career:** Educator, Air Force officer (retired); St Louis State Hosp, dir rehab serv, 1957-66; Halfway House Psychiat Patients, dir res & demon, 1959-62; Webster Col, asst prof soc scis, 1966-67; Southern Ill Univ, coordr rehab couns training prog rehab inst, 1968; Human Devel Corp, dir comprehen manpower progs, 1968; Counc on Rehab, pres, 1971-97. **Orgs:** bd dir, Nat Rehab Asn, 1971-; Ill Ment Health Plann Bd, 1970-73; chmn com, Accreditation of rehab couns training progs, Am Rehab Couns Asn, 1972-; Ill bd of Ment Health Commnrs, 1974-. **Honors/Awds:** St Louis Ment Health Asn Citation for community service in mental health, 1963; Ed Problems Uniue to the Rehab of Psychiat Patients, St Louis Hosp, 1963; Award for service, Human Devel Corp, 1968; NRA Certifiacte of appreciatopn for service on bd of dirs, 1971-73; Am Rehab Couns Asn; Nat Asn Non-White Rehab Wkrs; Nat Task Force for Rehab of the mentally ill, Dept of Health Educ & Welfare; Intens Serv for the Disadvataged, Ill Div of Voc Rehab, 1972. **Military Serv:** USAF, 1943-46. **Home Addr:** 609 S Skyline Dr, Carbondale, IL 62901. *

SCHUTZ, ANDREA LOUISE
Executive. **Personal:** Born Feb 15, 1948, Natchez, MS; married Simuel (divorced); children: Kobie & Kareem. **Educ:** Tougaloo Col, BA; Tuskegee Inst, attended 1966; Yale Univ, attended 1967; Princeton Univ, MA, 1971. **Career:** Adams-Jefferson Improve Corp, tutorial dir, 1969; Educ Found, consult, 1970; DC Redevel Land Agy, urban renewal asst, 1970; Urban Opinion Surveys Mathematica Inc, res assoc, 1971; NJ Municipal & Co Govt Study Com, researcher interviewer, 1971; Princeton Univ, asst to dean grad sch, 1972-75; Mathematica Inc, personnel dir, 1975-77, vpres, 1978-84; Lenox Inc, dir human resources, 1984-88; Educ Testing Ser, Human Resources, vpres, 1988-97; Mgt Due Diligence Inc, pres & chief exec officer, founding prin, 1997-; Mackenzie & Co, Lawrence, KS, prin consult; Surv Admin & Survey Opers, Mathematica Policy Res, oper, surv assoc; Adams County Redevelopment Asn, assoc; Southern Educ Found, consult; Dist Columbia Redevelopment Land, consult. **Orgs:** Alpha Kappa Alpha Sorority Tougaloo Col, pres, 1966-67; Asn Black Princeton Alumni, 1979-; Tougaloo Col Alumni Asn, 1979-; bd mem, Princeton NJ YMCA; Nat Asn Advan Colored People Legal Defense & Educ Fund; bd trustees, Hun Sch Princeton; bd trustees, Granville Acad; Am Compensation Asn; Soc Human Resource Mgt. **Honors/Awds:** Hon mention, Danforth Found, 1969; hon mention, Woodrow Wilson Found, 1969; "Admin Issues in Establishing & Operating a Nat Cash Assistance Program" Joint Econ Com US Congress Princeton, NJ 1972; frequent speaker at Nat conferences. **Business Addr:** President, Chief Executive Officer, Management Due Diligence Inc, 301 N Harrison St Suite 250, Princeton, NJ 08540-3512, **Business Phone:** (609)683-4980.

SCIPIO, LAURENCE HAROLD
Physician, executive. **Personal:** Born Aug 15, 1942; married JoAnn Wilson; children: Kia Nicole, Courtney Lauren. **Educ:** Howard Univ, Col Liberal Arts, BS, 1970; Howard Univ Col Med, MD, 1974. **Career:** Voc Rehab, physician, 1979-82; Birt & Howard PA, physician/urologist, 1979-80; Pvt Pract, urologist, 1980-; Northwest Community Health Care, urol consult, 1983-; Constant Care Community Health Ctr, urol consult, 1984-; Liberty Med Ctr Inc, staff; Md Gen Hosp, staff; Bon Secours Hosp, staff; Mercy Hosp, staff; N Charles Gen Hosp, staff; St Mary's Parish, pastoral Coun pres, currently. **Orgs:** Md Urol Asn; Med & Chirurgical Fac State Md, Baltimore City Med Soc; Monumental City Med Soc, 1980-; West Baltimore Community Health Ctr; Care First; Knights Columbus. **Home Addr:** 1649 Westchester Ct, Annapolis, MD 21401.

SCONIERS, HON. ROSE H
Judge. **Career:** NY State Supreme Ct, judge, currently. **Orgs:** NY Bar Found; Judicial Comn Minorities; emer mem col coun, State Univ NY, Buffalo. **Honors/Awds:** Outstanding Black Woman of Justice, N Region Black Polit Caucus, 1984; Lawyer of the Year Award, Nat Bar Asn, Buffalo Chap, 1984; Frank F Hughes Memorial Award, African-Am Police Asn, 1988, Community Service Award, 1992; Sojourner Truth Award, Nat Asn Negro Bus & Prof Women's Clubs Inc, 1993; Woman of the Year Civil Rights Award, Omega Psi Phi Fraternity Inc, 1996; Outstanding Achievement Award, YWCA, 1996; Buffalo Humanitarian Award, Urban League, 1997; Judiciary Award, Univ Buffalo Law School Alumni, 2000; Western New York Women's Hall of Fame, 2001. **Home Phone:** (716)876-2019. **Business Addr:** Judge, New York State Supreme Court, Part 31 - 8th fl, 50 Delaware Ave, Buffalo, NY 14202, **Business Phone:** (716)845-9495.

SCOTT, ALBERT J
State government official, association executive, chairperson. **Personal:** Married Diann Scott. **Educ:** Armstrong State Col. **Career:** Ga House Reps, Dist 2, rep, 1976-82; Ga State Senate, Dist 2, sen, 1982-90, comnr labor, 1990-92; Ga Ports Authority, bd dir, chairperson, currently. **Orgs:** Goodwill Indust; Boy Scouts Coastal Empire; Hospice Operating Bd; Nat Asn Advan Colored People; King Tisdale Inc; Beach Inst; chmn, Pub Utilities Comt; Consumer Affairs Comt; Appropriations Comt; Union Camp Corp; Hodge Mem Day Care Bd; Hospice Savannah Found Inc; bd mem, BB & T Community Bank Bd. **Military Serv:** AUS, 1966-68. **Business Addr:** Chairperson, Georgia Ports Authority, PO Box 2406, Atlanta, GA 31402, **Business Phone:** (912)964-3811.

SCOTT, ALBERT NELSON
Government official. **Personal:** Born Nov 27, 1916, Richmond, VA; married Annie Mae Smith; children: Maxine Gill, Albert N Jr, Luana Webster, Duane, Leona, Barbara, Charlene Jones, Eugene & Cynthia Henry. **Educ:** Fayette Co Schs WVa. **Career:** Local Union 2325 Coal Mine, vpres, 1971; Mine Comm, chmn, 1971-79; Beckley City Council, city councilman, 1979-. **Orgs:** Head, deacon Holiness Church of Jesus, 1965-; Raleigh Co Commitment Comm for Democratic Party, 1970; Recreation Bd, 1971; Citizens Adv Comt, 1972; WVa Planning Asn, 1979-84; Am Legion Post 70, 1982; St Comn, 1982-84; Nat Asn Advan Colored People, 1985; appt mem Beckley Urban Renewal Auth 1985. **Honors/ Awds:** Working With Youths Beckley City Youth, 1981-82; Cert of Appreciation Quad Counties OIC Inc, 1982; ground breaking Water Pollution Control Proj, 1984. **Military Serv:** AUS, staff sgt, 1941-45; Good Conduct Medal. **Business Addr:** City Councilman, Beckley City Council, 820 S Fayette St, Beckley, WV 25801.

SCOTT, ALEXIS (M ALEXIS SCOTT)
Publisher, chief executive officer. **Personal:** Born in Atlanta, GA; children: 2. **Career:** Atlanta Jour-Const, vpres/community affairs; Cox Enterprises Inc, reporter to vpres & dir diversity; Atlanta Daily World, publ & chief exec officer, currently. **Orgs:** St Jude's Recovery Ctr; Kenny Leon's True Colors Theater Co; Atlanta Hist Ctr; High Mus Art; Atlanta Conv & Visitors Bur & Cent Atlanta Progress; Atlanta Workforce Develop Agency; presiding officer, First Congregational Church, 1982-92; Nat Asn Advan Colored People. **Honors/Awds:** Media Woman of the Year Award, Nat Asn Media Women, 1983; Commentary Award, Atlanta Asn Black Journalists, 1983; Bronze Woman of the Year in Professions, Iota Phi Lambda Sorority, 1984; Citizen of the Year Award, Southwest Hosp & Med Ctr, 2001; Media of the Year Award, Ga Legislative Black Caucus, 2001; Atlanta Regional Minority Media Firm of the Year Award, Minority Enterprise Develop Agency, US Dept Com, 2002; Heritage Award, Frank Ski Kids Found, 2002; Citizen of the Year Award, Southwest Hosp & Med Ctr, 2002; Media of the Year Award, Ga Conf, Nat Asn Advan Colored People, 2002; DHL, Argosy Univ, Atlanta, 2003; President's Award, Atlanta Br, Nat Asn Advan Colored People, 2004; Imperial Court Daughters of Isis Hall of Fame Award, 2004; TD Jake's Megafest Phenomenal Woman Award, 2004; Georgia Press Association Award for Column writing, 2004; Millennium Pacesetter Award, Atlanta Bus League, 2005. **Business Addr:** Publisher, Chief Executive Officer, Atlanta Daily World, 145 Auburn Ave NE, Atlanta, GA 30303, **Business Phone:** (404)659-1110.*

SCOTT, DR. ALICE H
Librarian. **Personal:** Born in Jefferson, GA; daughter of Frank D Holly and Annie Colbert Holly; married Alphonso, Mar 1, 1959; children: Christopher & Alison. **Educ:** Spelman Col, Atlanta, Ga, AB 1957; Atlanta Univ, Atlanta, Ga, MLS 1958; Univ Chicago, PhD, 1983. **Career:** Librarian (retired); Brooklyn Pub Libr, NY, librn, 1958-59; Chicago Pub Libr, libr I, Woodlawn Br, 1959-61, libr Hall Br 1961-67, libr Woodlawn Br, 1968-73, dir, Woodson Regional Libr, 1974-77, dir commun rel, 1977-82, dep comnr, 1982-87, asst comnr, 1987-98. **Orgs:** Former coun mem, Am Libr Asn, 1982-85; Ill Libr Asn. **Honors/Awds:** Beta Phi Mu Libr Hon Soc, 1958-; CIC Doctoral Fel, Univ Chicago 1974. **Home Addr:** 6723 S Euclid, Chicago, IL 60649.

SCOTT, ANTHONY R
Police chief. **Educ:** Loyola Univ, BA, bus admin, BA, criminal justice; FBI Nat Acad. **Career:** Holyoke Police Dept, chief police, 2001-. **Orgs:** Quad Cities Metrop Enforcement Group; Quad Cities Gang Task Force; Ill Quad Cities Law Enforcement Group; Quad Cities Coun Police Chief's; Ill Asn Chief's Police; Agenda Black Quad Citizens; Land Lincoln Chap, Nat Org Black Law Enforcement Execs, past pres; FBI Nat Acad Assocs; Int Asn Chief's Police; & FBI Law Enforcement Exec Develop Sem Assocs. **Honors/Awds:** Outstanding Law Enforcement Professional of America, 1990; Who's Who in Law Enforcement, 1990; Charles E Dunbar Jr Career Civil Service Award; Martin Luther King Jr Community Relations Award; City Employee of the Year, Rock Island, 1996; Law Enforcement Professional for the State of Illinois, Ill Bar Asn, 2001; Paul Harris Fellow Award, Rotary Found. **Special Achievements:** First African-American appointed Chief of Police in Holyoke, MA. **Business Addr:** Chief of Police, Holyoke Police Department, 138 Appleton St, Holyoke, MA 01040, **Business Phone:** (413)536-6431.*

SCOTT, ARTIE A.
Insurance executive. **Personal:** Born Mar 23, 1946, Americus, GA; daughter of Lee Decie Anthony and Cicero Anthony; divorced; children: Shujwana Smith, Gabriel Omari. **Educ:** Albany State Col, attended 1968; Fla Int Univ, BA, 1974; Ins Inst Am, HIAA, attended 1980, 19; Life Off Mgt Inst, attended 1993; Corp Mgt Sch, attended 1991. **Career:** ILA Welfare & Pension Fund, admin clerk & examr, 1970-76; Equitable Life Assurance Soc, examr, supvr, 1976-86; Alexander & Alexander, Turner & Shepard, supvr, asst mgr, 1986-88; Nationwide Life Ins Co, mgr, 1988-. **Orgs:** Am Bus Women's Asn, 1984-90; vpres, secy, Action Alliance Black Prof, 1987-; Nationwide's Civic Activities Rep, 1990-; United Negro Col Fund Ann Walk-A-Thon, 1991-. **Honors/Awds:** Ohio House Reps, Community Clothes Dr, 1992; chmn, United Way Employee Campaign Dr, 1988; Action Alliance Black Prof, Homeless Shelter Dr, 1991, 1992. **Special Achievements:** Contributing writer, "How to File a Claim," The Total Manager Mag, 1992; Song Dedication Ceremony for educ wing of Tabernacle Baptist Church, 1987; Soar Award recipient, Excellence Customer Serv, 1993-94. **Home Addr:** 1472 Fahlander Dr N, Columbus, OH 43229, **Home Phone:** (614)847-4282. **Business Phone:** (614)249-6279.

SCOTT, DR. BASIL Y
Administrator. **Personal:** Born Jan 18, 1925; son of Iris and James; married Luna Lucille Edwards; children: Karen & Brian Y. **Educ:** City Col New York, BA, 1948; Columbia Univ, MA, 1949; Siena Col, MBA, 1952; Syracuse Univ, PhD, 1962. **Career:** Administrator (retired); State Univ New York, adj prof, 1959-68; New York State, Dept Motor Vehicles, staff, 1960-70, admin dir, 1970-77, dep comnr, 1977-78, Dept Educ, dep comnr, 1978-83; Kutztown Univ, adj prof, 1984-86, vpres admin & finance, 1995. **Orgs:** Bd dir, Blue Shield Northeastern New York, 1971-81, chmn bd dir, 1978-81; secy, Nat Motor Vehicle Safety Adv Coun, 1975-77; bd gov, Albany Med Ctr, 1975-81; bd dir, Kutztown Univ Found, 1983-89; bd dirs, Concern Prof Serv C, Youth & Families, 1995-, bd pres, 1997-99; bd trustees, Alvernia Col, 1999-; bd trustees, Reading Berks County YMCA, 2001-; Facilities & Technol Comn, 2003-. **Honors/Awds:** Phi Beta Kappa, 1948; pres, Nat Hwy Safety Adv Comn, 1969-72 & 1977-80. **Military Serv:** AUS, corpl, 1943-46. **Home Addr:** 1927 Meadow Lane, Wyomissing, PA 19610.

SCOTT, BENJAMIN
Executive, consulting engineer. **Personal:** Born Nov 30, 1929, Maringouin, LA; son of Harry and Sarah; married Doretha; children: Benjamin E Scott Jr & Daryl D. **Educ:** Pasadena City Col, AA, 1954; Pac State Univ, BS, 1959; Univ Calif, Los Angeles, MS, 1969. **Career:** US Dept Defense, Res & Develop Lab, elec engr, 1959, proj engr 1974; Benjamin Scott Assocs & Co Inc, consult engr, 1974-. **Orgs:** Chmn, Pasadena Nat Asn Advan Colored People, 1967; chmn, Pasadena Urban Coalition, 1968; chmn, Watts Comm Action Comn, 1970. **Honors/Awds:** Medal Freedom, Nat Asn Advan Colored People Pasadena Urban Coalition & Core, 1966; Medal Achievement, Pres Wm Tolbert Jr, 1972; Congratule Achievement, Pres Richard M Nixon 1972. **Special Achievements:** Played Important Key Role in the peace process in South Africa, 1987-93. **Military Serv:** AUS, m/sgt, 5 Yrs; Silver Star, 1950. **Home Addr:** 1004 E Woodbury Rd, Pasadena, CA 91104. **Business Addr:** Consulting Engineer, Benjamin Scott Associates & Company Inc, 1004 E Woodbury Rd, Pasadena, CA 91104-1315, **Business Phone:** (626)798-0486.

SCOTT, DR. BEVERLY ANGELA
Government official. **Personal:** Born Aug 20, 1951, Cleveland, OH; daughter of Winifred M Jones Smith and Nathaniel H Smith; married Arthur F, Dec 31, 1986; children: Lewis K Grisby III. **Educ:** Fisk Univ, BA, polit sci, 1972; Howard Univ, PhD, pub admin, 1977. **Career:** Tenn State Univ, asst prof, 1976; Metrop Transit Authority, Harris County, TX, asst gen mgr, 1978-83; Minority Contractors Asn, exec dir, 1983-84; A O Phillips & Assocs, consult, 1984-85; New York City Metrop Transit Authority, asst vpres, 1985-89, vpres, admin & personnel, 1989; RI Pub Transit Authority, gen mgr; Sacramento Regional Transit Dist, gen mgr & chief exec officer, 2002-07; Metrop Atlanta Rapid Transit Authority, gen mgr & chief exec officer, 2007-. **Orgs:** Am Pub Transit Asn; US Dept Transp; Am Pub Transp Asn; Nat Bus League; Women Transp Sem; RI Prof Engineers Soc; Sierra Club; Conf Minority Transp Officials; Nat Forum Black Pub Admin; Urban League. **Honors/Awds:** Numerous awards & honors including Ford Found fel, 1972-76; Carnegie Found fel, 1977-78; Outstanding Black Woman Award, Black Media, 1984; Numerous citations from varoius organizations including, US Dept Transp, Am Pub Transp Asn, Nat Bus League, Women's Transp Sem, RI Prof Engineers Soc, Sierra Club, Conf Minority Transp Officials, Nat Forum Black Pub Administrators, Urban League & City Year.

SCOTT, BOBBY. See SCOTT, ROBERT CORTEZ.

SCOTT, BRENT
Basketball player, basketball coach. **Personal:** Born Jun 15, 1971, Jackson, MI. **Educ:** Rice Univ. **Career:** Basketball Player (retired), Basketball Coach; Anwil Wloclawek; Zaragoza; Bandalona; Murcia; PAOK; Udine; Reggio Cal; Real M; Tau; Forli; Larissa; Rice; Olitalia Forli, 1995-96; Ind Pacers, 1996-97; Viola Reggio Calabria, 1998-99, 2000-01; Snaidero Udine, 2001-02; AEK Athens, 2006-07; Rice Univ, asst backetball coach, 2007-. **Honors/Awds:** All-USBL First Team.

SCOTT, BYRON
Basketball coach, television news anchorperson. **Personal:** Born Mar 28, 1961, Ogden, UT; married Anita; children: Thomas, LonDen & DeRon. **Educ:** Ariz State Univ, attended 1983. **Career:** Los Angeles Lakers, prof basketball player, 1983-93, 1996-97; Ind Pacers, 1993-95; Vancouver Grizzlies, 1995-96; Pananthinaikos, Greece, 1997-98; Sacramento Kings, asst coach, 1998-2000; NJ Nets, head coach, 2000-03; New Orleans Hornets, head coach, 2004-; ABC NBA telecasts, studio analyst. **Orgs:** The Byron Scott Childrens Fund. **Honors/Awds:** NBA Champions, Los Angeles Lakers, 1985, 1987, 1988; NBA Coach of the Year, 2007-08. **Business Addr:** Head Coach, New Orleans Hornets, 1250 Poydras St Fl 19, New Orleans, LA 70113, **Business Phone:** (504)593-4700.*

SCOTT, CARSTELLA H.
Government official. **Personal:** Born Apr 6, 1928, Thomasville, AL; married Percy Scott Sr; children: Rosia B Grafton, Percy Jr, Maxine , Veronia, Geraldine, Katherine YParham, Christine & Roderick. **Educ:** Ruth's Poro Beauty Col, BS; Southern Beauty Cong, MA, PhD, 1984. **Career:** Englewood Elem Fairfield, pres, 1957-67; Law Comn Ala, mem, 1980-; Ala Gov Comn, mem, 1983-; Fairfield Dem Women, v pres; Ala Voter Educ, mem, 1985; Fairfield City Coun, council woman; Fairfield Ala PTA, pres. **Orgs:** Pres, Missionary Circle Shady Grove, CME Church, 1973-; Nat Asn Advan Colored People, Zeta Phi Lambda Sorority, Christian Women Am, 1980; execbd mem, Ala Modern Beauticans, Chamber Com, Fairfield, 1982. **Honors/Awds:** Nine Year Serv Award, CME Church, Birmingham Conf, 1984; Nominating Comn,Women's Missionary Coun; Mother of the Yr, Fairfield Sch Syst. **Home Addr:** 537 Valley Rd, Fairfield, AL 35064. *

SCOTT, CHAD OLIVER
Football player. **Personal:** Born Sep 6, 1974, Capitol Heights, MD. **Educ:** Univ Md, kinesiol sci. **Career:** Pittsburgh Steelers, corner back, 1997-2004; New England Patriots, corner back, 2005-07; free agent, currently. **Honors/Awds:** Joe Greene Award, 1997; All-Rookie team, Assoc Press, 1997. *

SCOTT, CHARLES E
Real estate agent. **Personal:** Born Dec 4, 1940, Macon, GA; divorced; children (previous marriage): Erica & Derek; married Francenia D Hall (divorced). **Educ:** Morris Brown Col, BS, 1963. **Career:** Atlanta Bd Educ, music teacher, 1963-65; IBM Corp, sales rep, 1968-71; Charles E Scott & Assoc, realtor, appraiser, owner, 1971-. **Orgs:** Appraisal Inst Cand, 1977-; pres, Nat Soc Real Estate Appraisers Inc, Local Satellite Chap, 1980; secy, Children's Psychiat Ctr, 1979-. **Military Serv:** AUS, E-4, 1966-68. **Business Addr:** Owner, Charles E Scott & Associates, 931 NE 79th St, Miami, FL 33138, **Business Phone:** (305)757-7111.

SCOTT, CHARLES E
Photojournalist. **Personal:** Born Jul 23, 1949, Houston, TX; son of Garret and Marie Johnson; married Consulla Gipson; children: Tracy, Tamara & Christopher. **Educ:** Univ Houston, Houston, TX, 1968-71. **Career:** KUHT, Houston, TX, 1971-72; Independent Filmmaker, Houston, TX, 1971-73; KPRC-TV, Houston, TX, news camera mgr, 1972-; Video Seminars Inc, Houston, TX, pres, 1990-. **Orgs:** NABJ, 1987-; founding mem, HABS, 1987-; NPPA, 1972-85. **Honors/Awds:** Spec Recognition, HABS, 1988; Unity Awards in Media, Lincoln Univ, 1984; UPI Tex, Texas UPI Broadcaster, 1983; PAT Weavor, MDA, Muscular Dystrophy Asn, 1980; Film Grant, ACT/Pub Television, 1973; Insite photographer of the week. **Home Addr:** 619 Kenwood St, Houston, TX 77074, **Home Phone:** (713)453-0847. **Business Addr:** Photojournalist, KPRC-TV, 8181 Southwest Fwy, Houston, TX 77074, **Business Phone:** (713)778-4906.

SCOTT, PROF. CHARLOTTE HANLEY
Educator. **Personal:** Born Mar 18, 1925, Yonkers, NY; daughter of Charlotte Hanley and Edgar Hanley; married Nathan A Scott Jr, Dec 21, 1946; children: Nathan A III MD & Leslie Ashamu. **Educ:** Barnard Col, AB, 1947; Am Univ, attended 1949-53; Univ Chicago Sch Bus, MBA 1964; Allegheny Col, LLD 1981. **Career:** Nat Bureau Econ Res, NY, res assoc, 1947-48; RW Goldsmith Assoc, res assoc, 1948-55; Univ Chicago Sch Bus, economist, 1955-56; Fed Res Bank Chicago, economist, 1956-71, asst vpres, 1971-76; Univ Va, McIntire Sch Com, profemer, currently. **Orgs:** Pres, Women's Bd Chicago Urban League, 1967-69; trustee, Barnard Col, Columbia Univ, 1977-81; Charlottesville Bd Nations Bank, 1977-93; vicechmn 1981, Consumer Adv Bd Fed Res, chmn, 1982; Gov's Comn Va Future,1982-84; Va Comn Status Women, 1982-85; treas, Va Women's Cult Hist Proj, 1982-85; bd dirs, Nations Bank Va, 1989-95; gov bd, Charlottesville /Albemarle Found, 1993-; treas, Region XV, Episcopal Diocese, 1999-. **Honors/Awds:** Outstanding Woman, Alpha Gamma Pi, Chicago 1965; Alumni Medal, Columbia Univ, 1984; Public Service Citation, Univ Chicago, 1990; hon mem, Golden Key Nat Honor Soc, 1990. **Home Addr:** 250 Pantops Mountain Rd, Charlottesville, VA 22911. **Business Addr:** Professor Emeritus, University of Virginia, McIntire School of Commerce, Carruthers Hall S Entrance 1001 N Emmet St, Charlottesville, VA 22903-4833, **Business Phone:** (434)924-4122.

SCOTT, DARNAY
Football player. **Personal:** Born Jul 7, 1972, St Louis, MO. **Educ:** San Diego State Univ. **Career:** Football player (retired); Cincinnati Bengals, wide receiver, 1994-99, 2001; Dallas Cowboys, wide receiver, 2002.

SCOTT, DAVID
Government official, founder (originator), chief executive officer. **Personal:** Born Jun 27, 1946, Aynor, SC; married Alfredia Aaron, 1969; children: Dayna & Marcye. **Educ:** Fla A&M Univ, BA, 1967; Univ PA, Wharton Sch Bus, MBA, 1969. **Career:** GA House Representatives, rep, 1974-82; Dayn-Mark Advert, founder, ceo, 1979-2002; GA State Sen, sen, 1982-2002; US House Representatives, US rep, 2002-. **Orgs:** Fin Servs Comt; co-chairman of the Democratic Study Group on Nat Security. **Business Addr:** US Representative, US House of Representatives, Washington Congressional Office, 417 Cannon House Off Bldg, Washington, DC 30236, **Business Phone:** (202)225-2939.*

SCOTT, DR. DEBORAH ANN
Physician. **Personal:** Born Oct 2, 1953, New York, NY; married Ralph C Martin II. **Educ:** Princeton Univ, BA, 1975; Howard Univ, MD, 1979. **Career:** Howard Univ Hosp, dermat fel, 1982-83; Roger Williams Gen Hosp, dermat fel, 1983-86; MIT, staff physician, 1986-96; Harvard Community Health plan, 1993-; Beth Israel Deaconess Med Ctr, 1996-; Brigham & Women's Hosp, assoc physician & instr, currently; Laser & Skin Healthcare Syst, dir, currently. **Orgs:** NE Med Soc, 1983-87, Am Acad Dermat, 1986-, New England Med Soc, 1986, New England Dermatological Soc, 1987. **Honors/Awds:** Alpha Omega Alpha Hon Soc, 1979. **Home Addr:** 154 Moss Hill Rd, Jamaica Plain, MA 02130. **Business Phone:** (617)732-9300.

SCOTT, DENNIS EUGENE
Basketball player, radio host. **Personal:** Born Sep 5, 1968, Hagerstown, MD. **Educ:** Ga Inst Tech, Atlanta, GA, 1987. **Career:** Basketball player (retired), basketball executive, host; Orlando Magic, forward, 1990-97; Dallas Mavericks, 1997-98; Phoenix Suns, 1998; NYKnicks, 1999; Minn Timberwolves, 1999; Vancouver Grizzlies, 1999-2000; 3-D Entertainment Inc, pres; Atlanta Vision, gen mgr, 2005-; FSN, studio analyst; Atlanta Hawks, radio analyst, currently. **Honors/Awds:** Inductee, Ga Tech Hall of Fame; Player of the Year, ACC; Player of the Year, Asn Press Nat. **Business Addr:** Radio Analyst, Atlanta Hawks, Centennial Tower, 101 Marietta St NW Suite 1900, Atlanta, GA 30303, **Business Phone:** (404)878-3800.

SCOTT, DR. DONALD LAVERN
Government official, military leader. **Personal:** Born Feb 8, 1938, Hunnewell, MO; son of William E and Beatrice Dant; married Betty Jean, Mar 3, 1962; children: Jeffrey & Mel. **Educ:** Lincoln Univ, BA, graphic arts, 1960; Troy State Univ, MA, 1982. **Career:** Military leader (retired), Government Official; AUS, brig gen, 1960-91; Res &Natl Guard units south eastern US & Virgin Islands, 1988-91; City Atlanta, chief operating officer, chief staff, 1991-93; Ameri Corps Nat NCCC, Corp Nat Serv, dir, 1993-96; Dep Librn Cong, 1996-. **Orgs:** Kappa Alpha Psi Fraternity, 1960-; NAACP, 1991-; 100 Black Men, Atlanta Chap, 1991-94; Am Libr Assn, 1993-; Black Caucus Am Libr Assn, 1997-; Hon Doctor Law, Lincoln Univ, 1992. **Special Achievements:** Speak Vietnamese, 1965; Air Force War Col, Leadership Thesis, 1981. **Military Serv:** AUS, brig gen, 1960-91; Defense Superior Award, Bronze Star (6 Awards). **Business Addr:** Deputy Librarian of Congress, Library of Congress, 101 Independence Ave SE, Mail Stop 1010 Off LM608, Washington, DC 20540, **Business Phone:** (202)707-5215.

SCOTT, DONNELL
Executive, interior designer, chief executive officer. **Personal:** Born Oct 25, 1947, Orange, NJ; son of Walter and Katherine Robinson; married Bessie Beckwith, Aug 5, 1972; children: Darrin B. **Educ:** NC Cent Univ, Durham, NC, BA, polit sci, 1970; Seton Hall Univ, S Orange, NJ, MA, Am studies, 1973; Nova SE Univ, EdD, Orgn leadership. **Career:** Int Bus Mach Corp, 1976-80; NC Central Univ, Durham, NC, dir exec MPA (EMPA), currently; NC Central Univ, Dept Public Admin, adjunct prof; On Point Consulting Group, pres; At the Window, Sea Bright, NJ, pres, 1980-; WS Exterminating Inc, chief exec officer, currently. **Orgs:** United Black Families Freehold Twp, 1976-; 100 Black Men of Am, 1989-. **Business Addr:** Chief Executive Officer, WS Exterminating Inc, 26 Orange Rd, Montclair, NJ 07042-2110, **Business Phone:** (973)746-7460.

SCOTT, DR. ELSIE L
Manager, police officer. **Personal:** Born in Lake Providence, LA; daughter of John H and Alease Truly; married Irving Joyner, 1983 (divorced). **Educ:** Southern Univ, BA, 1968; Univ Iowa, MA, 1970; Atlanta Univ, PhD, 1980. **Career:** St Augustines Col, dir Criminal Justice Prog, 1977-79; NC Cent Univ, asst prof, 1979-80; Howard Univ, asst prof & res assoc, 1981-83; Nat Org Black Law Enforcement Exec, prog mgr, 1983-85, exec dir, 1985-91; NY Police Dept, dep scomnr training, 1991, asst exec dir corp support, currently. **Orgs:** Pres, Nat Conf Black Polit Scientists, 1980-81; secy, Rev John H Scott Memorial Fund, 1980; panelist, Comn Status Black Am Nat Res Coun, 1986-88; adv bd, Nat Inst Against Prejudice & Violence, 1987-93; Nat Org Black Law Enforcement exec bd, 1991-93; Am Soc Criminol. **Honors/Awds:** Achievement Award, 100 Black Women, 1988; African American Women Distinction, Guardian Assoc, 1991; Black Comn Crusade C, Working Comt, 1992; Louisiana Black History Hall of Fame, 1993. **Special Achievements:** Violence Against Blacks US, 1979-81, Howard Univ, 1983; co-author, Racial & Rel Violence, NOBLE, 1986. **Business Addr:** Assistant Executive Director, Metropolitan Police Department, 300 Indiana Ave NW, Washington, DC 20001, **Business Phone:** (202)737-4404.

SCOTT, COL. EUGENE FREDERICK
Publisher. **Personal:** Born Oct 14, 1939, Miami, FL; son of Eugene Scott Sr and Bertha; married Patricia; children: Eugene Jr, Jacqueline, Gregory, Michael & Leta. **Educ:** Univ Okla; Fla A&M Univ, BS. **Career:** Chicago Defender, gen mgr, 1990, publ, 2000-01; Chicago Defender Charities, pres, currently; Sengstacke Enterprises, exec asst. **Orgs:** Omega Psi Phi; Nat African Am Military Museum, chair; Armed Forces Comt; Nat Newspaper Publ's Asn. **Honors/Awds:** Boy Scouts, Silver Beaver, 1987. **Military Serv:** AUS, 2nd Lt, col & post comdr, 1962-90; Legion of Merit, Bronze Star. **Home Addr:** 20724 Corinth Rd, Olympia Fields, IL 60461, **Home Phone:** (708)748-6231. **Business Addr:** President, Chicago Defender Charities, 700 E Oakwood Blvd 5th Fl, Chicago, IL 60653, **Business Phone:** (773)536-3710.

SCOTT, GILBERT H, SR.
Executive, consultant. **Personal:** Born Sep 7, 1946, Richmond, VA; son of Charles and Vernell Green Dickerson; married Brenda Patterson, Apr 26, 1969; children: Gilbert H Jr & Cecily R. **Educ:** Hampton Univ, BS, econ, 1968; Stanford Univ, exec mkt mgr prog, 1995. **Career:** Va Elec & Power Co, sales rep, 1970-71; Xerox Corp, Va, sales rep, gen mgr & vpres, 1971-96; Bartech Group, pres & chief operating officer; Hurshell Assoc, pres & chief exec officer, currently; Mass Inst Technol, guest lectr; Sloan Grad Sch, guest lectr. **Orgs:** Vice chmn & exec mem, President's Cabinet, Univ Calif; corp adv bd, George Washington Univ; San Luis Obispo. **Honors/Awds:** Community Involvement, Asn Black Military Officers, 1987. **Military Serv:** AUS, second lt, Fort Carson, Colo, 1968-69, first Lt, Vietnam, 1969-70; Two Bronze Stars for Valor, Vietnamese Cross of Galantry. **Business Addr:**

President, Chief Executive Officer, Hurshell Associates, 10731 Hunters Place Dr, Vienna, VA 22181-2843, **Business Phone:** (703)716-7501.

SCOTT, DR. GLORIA DEAN RANDLE
School administrator. **Personal:** Born Apr 14, 1938, Houston, TX; married Will Braxton. **Educ:** Ind Univ, BA, 1959, MA, 1960, PhD, 1965, LLD, 1977. **Career:** School Adminr(retired); Inst Psych Res, res assoc genetics, 1961-63; Marian Col, col prof, 1961-65; Knoxville Col, prof, 1965-67; NCA Tex Southern Univ, prof, 1967-76, asst to pres, 1967-68, prof, 1976-78; Nat Inst Educ, head post secondary res, 1973-75; NCA Tex Southern Univ, Planning & Inst Res, dir, 1973-76; Clark Col, prof, 1978-86, vpres,1978-86; Grambling State Univ, prof, 1987; Bennett Col, pres, 1987-2001; Scotts Bay Enterprises, owner, currently; G Randle Serv, pres, currently. **Orgs:** Bd dirs, Southern Educ Found, 1971-76; pres, G Randle Serv, 1975-; owner, Scotts Bay Courts, 1972-; consult, Ford Found, Southern Educ Found, 1967-72, 76; sec, Corp PREP, 1966-82; vpres, Girl Scouts USA, 1972-75, pres, 1975-78; bd dir, Nat Urban League, 1976-82; mem & chw, Defense Community Women Servs, 1979-81; chair bd dirs, Nat Scholar Fund Negro Studs, 1984-85; contributing ed, Good Housekeeping, 1985; adv bd, Historically Black Cols, 1988-92; vchair, PRSs Advisory HBCU Bd, 1976-83; vpres, United Meth Ch Black Col Fund, 1995-97, pres, 1997-99; nat bd dir, UNCF, 1990-97; head delegation, Women INT Forum, Beijing, China,1995; Delta Sigma Theta Sorority, currently. **Honors/Awds:** Woman of the Year, YMCA, 1977; Kizzie Image Award, 1979; Honarary Degrees, Ind Univ, 1977; NCA Governor's Award-Women, 1990; Drum Major for Justice Award, SCLC, 1994; Texas Woman of Achievement, Girl Scouts San Jacinto-Coun, 1997; numerous honarary degrees. **Special Achievements:** First African-American to get a degree in zoology from Indiana Univ; First African-American to head the Girl Scouts of the USA. Author, "A Historically Black College Perspective". **Home Addr:** 539 CRS 1142, PO Box 900, Riviera, TX 78379, **Home Phone:** (361)297-5307. **Business Addr:** President, Owner, G. Randle Services, 539 S County Rd Suite 1142 Rt 1, PO Box 53B, Riviera, TX 78379.

SCOTT, HATTIE BELL
Real estate executive. **Personal:** Born May 28, 1945, Fort Motte, SC; daughter of Cassie Keith Weeks and Jesse Weeks; married Leonard Henry, Jun 17, 1966; children: Allen Leonard & Gregory Walter. **Educ:** Allen Univ, attended 1965. **Career:** Long & Foster, Camp Springs, Md, realtor assoc, 1977-81, sales mgr, 1981-88, Waldorf, Md, sr vpres & regional mgr, 1988-. **Orgs:** Prince Georges' County Bd, Realtors Distinguished Sales Club, 1978; Prince Georges' County Fair Housing Comt, 1980-; Women's Coun, Prince Georges' County Bd Realtors, 1982-; mem, Prince Georges' County Bd Realtors Polit Action Comt, 1987-, chmn, 1989; Prince Georges' County Arts Coun, 1990-. **Honors/Awds:** Manager of the Year, 1984, Rookie of the Year, 1978. **Home Addr:** 5221 Cottonwood Dr, Lothian, MD 20711, **Home Phone:** (301)627-1953. **Business Addr:** Senior Vice President, Regional manager, Long & Foster Realtors, 3165 Crain Hwy Suite 100, Waldorf, MD 20603, **Business Phone:** (301)932-4700.

SCOTT, HELEN K. See SCOTT, DR. HELEN MADISON MARIE PAWNE KINARD.

SCOTT, DR. HELEN MADISON MARIE PAWNE KINARD (HELEN K SCOTT)
Executive. **Personal:** Born in Washington, DC; daughter of David and Helen T; married Victor F; children: Lenise Sharon & Monique Sherine. **Educ:** Wash Univ, BMT, 1963; Howard Univ, BA, 1971, MA, 1973; Grant Col, PA, pub admin. **Career:** Univ West Indies, distinguished vis prof, 1971-72; Howard Univ, liaison pres, 1971; Dr Joyce Ladner, res asst, 1972-74; Dept Comm Plan, asst prof, 1973-74; Howard Univ, Sch Social Work, adj prof, 1973-74, Sch Commun, asst admin, prof, from adj asst to mgr Cramton Aud; TV, writer, co-star, 1973; Travel Way Found, prof soc plan & policy; RLA Inc, vpres, dir Zambia (HIRD) Proj Lusaka, Zambia; Licensure Real Estate, Wash DC; LICSW Social Work, Wash DC; Am Psychol Asn, prog adminr, currently. **Orgs:** Int Manpower Dev Sem, 1972, 1974; consult, Soc Planning Cong Black Caucus, 1973; Nat Inst Ment Health Maint & Tuition, 1973; Chi Lambda Phi; State Calif Child Care Conf, 1973; Phi Beta Kappa 1973; Com Human Settlements, 1976; state organizer, Nat Coun Negro Women, 1973; coord, 7th World Law Conf, 1975; Am Ded Radio & TV Artists; Am Planning Asn; Am Soc Plan Off, Delta Sigma Theta Sorority; Nat Acad Sci; Nat Asn Soc Workers; Nat Asn Col & Univ Concern Mgt; Nat Asn Advan Colored People; Southern Christian Leadership Conf; Nat Asn Black Educrs; Nat Asn Educ Young C; Coun Except C, Int City Mgt Asn; Howard Univ Alumni Asn; bd dirs, Freedom Bowl Alumni Comn, Asn Black Psychologists; Caribbean Am Intercult Org Inc; Caribbean Festivals Inc; Phi Delta Kappa. **Honors/Awds:** National Endowment for Arts Scholarship, 1971; Outstanding Human Service, Howard Univ MS Proj, 1971; Bureau of Standard Award for Outstanding HS Student in Mathmatics & Science; Southern California Film Institute Award, 1973; Emmy Award, TV Show, 1973; Rockefeller Foundation Award, 1973. **Home Phone:** (301)330-0131. **Business Addr:** Program Administrator, American Psychological Association, 750 1st St NE, Washington, DC 20002-4242, **Business Phone:** (202)336-5500.

SCOTT, HOSIE L
Clergy, college administrator. **Personal:** Born May 31, 1943, Clopton, AL; married Ruth. **Educ:** Kean Col, BA, MA; Brookdale Community Col. **Career:** Jersey Cent Power Co, Sayreville, NJ, technician, 1967-68; NC Mutual Life Ins Co, Newark, NJ, life underwriter counr & debit mgr, 1968-70; Red Bank YMCA, exec youth prog dir, 1970-72; Brookdale Community Col, Lincroft, NJ, coordr affirm action & personnel admin, 1972-; chaplain minister, currently. **Orgs:** NJ Col & Univ Personnel Asn; Monmouth Ocean Co Prof Personnel Dir Asn; dir affirm action, NJ Prof; Nat Coun Black Am Affairs; Am Asn Community Jr Col; past mem, Life Underwriters Asn, 1968-70; Asn Prof Dir YMCA, 1970-72; BANWY'S YMCA, 1970-74; Am Soc Notaries; Greater Red Bank Nat Asn Advan Colored People; bd dir, Union Co Urban League, NJ; chmn, Affirm Action Adv Comt Brookdale Col, NJ; chmn, Matawan Twp Drug Coun, NJ; adv bd, EOF Brookdale Col; Dept Higher Educ Affirm & Action Comn; adv com mem, Inst Appl Humanities Brookdale Community Col; Dr M Luther King Observance Com; exec com mem, Monmouth Co NJ Bicentennial; past pres Tri-Community Club Matawan NJ; exec comt, African Am Arts & Heritage Festival. **Honors/Awds:** Outstanding Certificate of Leadership & Achievement Award, Dept Army, 1967; Fitness Finders Award, Nat YMCA, 1972; Outstanding Leadership Award, New Shrewbury, NJ Kiwanis 1972; Recipient Matawan Twp Tri-Community Club Distinguished Service Award, 1973; Service Award Greater Red Bank Nat Asn Advan Colored People, 1973. **Business Addr:** Coordinator Affirm Action, Personnel Administration, Brookdale Community College, 765 Newman Springs Rd, Lincroft, NJ 07738.

SCOTT, HUBERT R.
Executive. **Personal:** Born Sep 24, 1919, Athens, GA; married Betty DuMetz; children: Hubert, Wayne. **Educ:** Morehouse Col, BS, 1942; Atlanta Univ, MS, 1947; Univ MI, Addl Stud. **Career:** Pilgrim Health & Life Ins Co, actuary, 1947-68, 2nd vice pres & sec treas, 1968-, . **Orgs:** Tech secy chmn actuary statistician Nat Ins Asn, 1953-59; treas, NAACP, 1958-66; bd dir, chmn Personnel Comt YMCA, 1956-; bd dir, Shiloh Orphanage, 1956-; Civil Serv Comn, 1968-73. **Honors/Awds:** Citizen of year, YMCA, 1956; citizen of year, Kappa Alpha Psi, 1968. **Military Serv:** AUS, s & sgt, 1942-45.

SCOTT, HUGH B
Judge. **Personal:** Born Apr 29, 1949, Buffalo, NY; son of Edward Nelson and Anne Braithwaite (deceased); married Trudy Carlson, Jun 9, 1973; children: Hugh B Jr & Everett N. **Educ:** Niagara Univ, Lewiston, NY, BA, 1967-71; State Univ New York, Buffalo Law Sch, JD, 1974. **Career:** Co Erie Dept Law, asst co atty, 1974-75; City Buffalo Dept Law, asst corp coun, 1975-77; Dept Justice, Buffalo, NY, asst US atty, 1977-79; NY State Dept Law, Buffalo, NY, asst atty gen, 1979-83; Univ Buffalo Law Sch, Amherst Campus, lectr, 1980-; NY State Off Ct, Buffalo City Ct, judge, 1983-; US Magistrate Judge, 1995-. **Orgs:** Vice chmn, Urban League Buffalo, 1980; Alpha Kappa Boule, 1983-; bd dirs, Univ Buffalo Law Alumni Asn, 1988-; bd mgrs, Buffalo Mus Sci, 1989-; adv coun, TransAfrica Buffalo, 1990-; bd trustees, Canisius Col, chair adv bd, Off Multicultural Prog; bd trustees, Catholic Health Syst; bd mem, Nat Fedn Just Communities; bd dir, Erie Co Bar Asn Aid Indigent Prisoners Soc; dean's adv bd, Buffalo Law Sch; bd mem, Community Found Greater Buffalo; Second Circuit Judicial Conf Planning & Prog Comt. **Honors/Awds:** Lifetime Achievement Award, Rochester Black Bar Asn; Citation Award, Nat Conf Community & Justice; One Hundred Black Men of Buffalo Community Service Award; YMCA of Buffalo Toast of Buffalo Community Service Award; Law Review Distinguished Service Award, Buffalo Law Sch; Distinguished Alumnus Award, UB Law Alumni Asn; William Wells Brown Award, Afro-American Hist Asn; Judges & Police Executives Community Service Award; Man of the Year Award, Nat Asn Negro Bus & Prof Women's Clubs; Greater Buffalo Council on Alcoholism and Substance Abuse Service Award; Attorney General Robert Abrams Alumnus Award; Caritas Metal, Niagara Univ. **Special Achievements:** First African-American Assistant United States Attorney for the Western District of New York. **Home Addr:** 9 Woodley Rd, Buffalo, NY 14215, **Home Phone:** (716)833-5923. **Business Addr:** Judge, Western District of New York, Buffalo City Court, 25 Delaware Ave Suite 600, Buffalo, NY 14202, **Business Phone:** (716)847-8282.

SCOTT, DR. HUGH J.
Educator. **Personal:** Born Nov 14, 1933, Detroit, MI; married Florence I Edwards; children: Marvalisa & Hugh. **Educ:** Wayne State Univ, BS, educ, 1956, MS, educ, 1960, specialist cert educ admin, 1964; Mich State Univ, EdD, 1966. **Career:** City Detroit, teacher, 1956-65; Mich St Univ, instr, 1965-66; Detroit Great Cities Sch Improvement Proj, asst dir, 1965, asst prin, 1966-67, asst dep supt sch community rels, 1967-68; Wash, supt sch, 1970-73; Howard Univ, prof educ, 1973-75; Hunter Col, City Univ New York, dean prog educ, 1975-2000, prof emer, 2000-; Pace Univ, dir & hon scholar residence, 2004-. **Orgs:** Phi Delta Kappa, 1960-; Nat Asn Advan Colored People, 1967-70; bd dirs, Detroit Soc Black Educ Adminr, 1968-70; Am Asn Sch Adminr, 1969-; Nat Alliance Black Sch Educr, 1970-; Chevel & conf, 1974-. **Honors/Awds:** Distinguished Service Certificate, Phi Delta Kappa, 1969; Distinguished Alumni Award, Mich St Univ, 1970; Hall of Fame, Nat Alliance Black Sch Educr, 1990; Distinguished Service President's Medal, 1993; President's Medal for Distinguished Service, Hunter Col, City Univ New York, 1993; Lifetime Achievement Award, Nat Alliance Black Sch Educr, 1996. **Special Achievements:** First Black school superintendent in Howard University; Author of The Black Superintendent: Messiah or Scapegoat?, Howard University Press, 1980; published numerous articles. **Military Serv:** AUS, pfc, 1956-58. **Business Addr:** Scholar in Residence, Director, Pace University, One Pace Plz, New York, NY 10038, **Business Phone:** (212)346-1200.

SCOTT, JACOB REGINALD
Executive. **Personal:** Born Jun 2, 1938, New York, NY; married Merri Hinkis; children: Elaine Beatrice & Lisa Anne Scott White. **Educ:** Lincoln Univ, BS, psychol, 1960; Inst African De Geneve, Geneva Switz, dipl african studies, 1971. **Career:** US State Dept Foreign Serv, Ethiopia, econ & comn officer, 1966-68; Seagram Africa, sales mkt dir, 1971-80; Seagram Overseas Sales NY, mkt dir Africa, 1982-83, vpres Africa, 1984-91; Seagram Europe & Africa, vpres Africa, 1992-94, vpres external affairs, 1995-. **Orgs:** Montclair Alumni Chap, Kappa Alpha Psi, 1981-83; founding mem & dir, Seagram South Africa Pty Ltd, 1994-. **Home Addr:** 3650 Environ Blvd, Lauderhill, FL 33319. **Business Addr:** Vice President External Affairs, Seagram Europe & Africa, Seagram House, 57 Mandeville Pl, London W1M 5LB, United Kingdom.

SCOTT, JAMES HENRY
Executive. **Personal:** Born Dec 22, 1942, St Louis, MO; married Cora Sabeta Dillon; children: James H. **Educ:** Villanova Univ, BE, 1965; Wash Univ, St Louis, MBA, 1970. **Career:** Guyana, S Am, Peace Corps volunteer, 1966-68; Citibank, acct officer, 1970-72; Gulf & Western Ind Inc, asst vpresfin, 1972-73; Morgan Guaranty Trust Co NY, vpres; Bank Morgan Labouchere NY, vpres; The White House, 1978-79. **Orgs:** Ed chief, The Circuit, 1964-65; co-found & sec, AFRAM Enterprises Inc,1968-73; asst treas, Greater NY Coun Boy Scouts Am; NY Urban League; Acad Polit Sci.

SCOTT, JENNIFER J (JENNIFER SCOTT WILLIAMS)
Engineer. **Personal:** Married Leon M Williams. **Educ:** Georgia Inst Technol, BEE, 2001. **Career:** NASA, Johnson Space Ctr, space shuttle flight controller, currently. **Business Addr:** Space Shuttle Flight Controller, NASA Johnson Space Center, NASA Langley Research Center Attn: Jennifer J Scott, Hampton, VA 23681-2199, **Business Phone:** (757)864-1000.*

SCOTT, JILL
Singer, songwriter, actor. **Personal:** Born Apr 4, 1972, Philadelphia, PA. **Career:** Singer-songwriter, poet, 2000-; Vocalist, songwriter; albums: In Too Deep, 1999; Who Is Jill Scott?: Words & Sounds Vol 1, 2000; Save the Last Dance, 2001; Down to Earth, 2001; Experience: Jill Scott 826, 2001; Brown Sugar, 2002; Love Don't Cost a Thing, 2003; Beautifully Human: Words & Sounds Vol 2, 2004; Beauty Shop, 2005; Block Party, 2005; Something New, 2006; stage appearance: Rent, Canadian touring cast; songs: "Gettining In the Way", 2000; "A Long Walk", 2001; "He Loves Me (Lyzel In E Flat)", 2002; "Golden", 2004; "Whatever", 2005; "Cross My Mind", 2005; "Daydreamin", 2006; films: Hounddog, 2007; Why Did I Get Married, 2007; TV: Broadway's Best, 2002. **Orgs:** Founder, Blues Babe Found. **Honors/Awds:** Best Urban & Alternative Performance, 2005; Best R&B/Soul Album, Solo: Who is Jill Scott? Words and Sounds Vol 1, 2001; Best R&B/Soul Female Album: Who is Jill Scott? Words and Sounds Vol 1, 2001. **Business Phone:** (310)453-1400.

SCOTT, DR. JOHN SHERMAN
Writer, educator. **Personal:** Born Jul 20, 1937, Bellaire, OH; son of Beauta and George; married Sharon A Riley, 1982; children: Jon-Jama & Jasmin Evangelene. **Educ:** SC State Univ, BA, 1961; Bowling Green State Univ, MA, 1966, PhD, 1972. **Career:** Bowling Green State Univ, OH, prof ethnic studies & resident-writer, 1970, prof emer, currently; dir, Ethnic Cultural Arts Program; dir, Nathan Hale Auditorium, 1987. **Orgs:** Consult, Toledo Model Cities Prog, 1969-72; Eugene O'Neill Memorial Theatre Ctr, 1970-; consult, Toledo Bd Educ; NY Dramatists League, 1971-; Speech Comm Asn, 1966-73; Frank Silvera Writer's Workshop, 1973-. **Honors/Awds:** Karma & The Goodship Credit, Richard Allen Ctr, 1978-79; Governor's Award for the Arts, State of Ohio, 1990; produced play (TV), CURRENTS, 1991, produced docu-drama (TV), Hats & Fans, 1991, PBS. **Special Achievements:** Pub articles Players Black Lines; plays performed, Off-Broadway, NYC; Ridea Black Horse, Negro Ensemble Co, 1972. **Military Serv:** AUS, pfc, 1961-64. **Business Addr:** Professor Emeritus, Bowling Green State University, 1830 Destiny Ln 107, Bowling Green, OH 43403-0001, **Business Phone:** (419)372-2531.

SCOTT, JOSEPH M
Banker, president (organization). **Personal:** Born Apr 2, 1945, Vicksburg, MS; son of Pierre A Sr and Carrie Albert; divorced; children: Bettina Harding & Patrick. **Educ:** Grambling State Univ, BS, 1967; Eastern Mich Univ, MA, 1974. **Career:** Government official (retired); National Bank Detroit, asst br mgr, 1967-68; First of Am Bank, 1971-98; First Independence National Bank, pres. **Orgs:** Adv bd, Detroit Med Ctr NW; United Way Community Servs; Leadership Detroit Alumni Asn; Urban Bankers Forum;

Detroit Urban League; Detroit Economic Growth Corp; Sothfield Economic Develop Corp. **Honors/Awds:** Spirit of Detroit Award, 1995. **Military Serv:** Army, sp/5, 1968-70. **Home Addr:** 28051 Golf Pointe Blvd, Farmington Hills, MI 48331, **Home Phone:** (248)489-9089.

SCOTT, JOSEPH WALTER
Educator. **Personal:** Born May 7, 1935, Detroit, MI; son of William Felton Scott and Bertha Colbert Scott; married; children: Victor, Valli & Velissa. **Educ:** Central Mich Univ, BS, 1957; Ind Univ, MA, sociol, 1959, PhD, sociol & anthrop 1963. **Career:** Univ KY, asst prof sociol, 1965-67; Univ Toledo, prof sociol, 1967-70; Univ Notre Dame, Black Studies Prog, dir, 1970-72, assoc prof sociol, 1970-75, prof sociol & anthrop, 1978-85; Univ Ibadan, vis prof sociol, 1972-73; Univ Wash, Am Ethnic Studies prof, 1985-97 & 1990-98, African Ethnic Studies, chair, 1985-90, prof sociol, prof emer sociol, currently. **Orgs:** Am Sociol Asn, 1958-; fel Inst Health, 1962-63; N Cent Sociol Asn, 1963-; Asn Black Sociologists, 1969-; State Dem Convention, 1970-; Rockefeller fel, Nigeria, 1972-73; fel Am Coun Educ, NW Univ, 1975-76; pres, N Cent Sociol Asn, 1983-84; pres, Asn Black Sociologists, 1996-97; consult, War Poverty Prog Ind; Sunday Sch teacher Braden Meth Church Toledo; bd mem, Mt Zion Baptist Church Ethnic Sch; bd mem, Inner-City Devel Educ Action (IDEA); Rainbow Coalition Organizer SB Ind; Nat Asn Advan Colored People; Pi Kappa Delta; Kappa Delta Pi. **Honors/Awds:** Leadership Award, Mil Police Officers Basic Sch, 1963; Fulbright Scholar Argentina, 1967, 1969; Outstanding Graduate Award, Carnegie Mellon Univ; Outstanding Student Senator Award; Athletic Scholarship Award, Carnegie Mellon Univ; Centennial Award, Cent Mich Univ, 1992-93; G Pritchy Smith Multicultural Educator Award, Nat Asn Multicultural Educ; Ford Foundation Lecturer Award, Nigeria. **Special Achievements:** Publisher of numerous books and articles. **Military Serv:** USMPC capt 1963-65; ROTC Distinguished Mil Stud, 1956-57. **Home Addr:** 4814 49th Ave S, Seattle, WA 98118, **Home Phone:** (206)722-2376. **Business Addr:** Emeritus Professor of Sociology, University of Washington, Department of Sociology, 102M Savery, PO Box 353340, Seattle, WA 98195-4380, **Business Phone:** (206)543-2376.

SCOTT, JUDITH SUGG
Executive, lawyer. **Personal:** Born Aug 30, 1945, Washington, DC; daughter of Irvin D Sugg and Bernice Humphrey; married Robert C, Jan 2, 1988; children: Carmen & Nichole. **Educ:** Virginia State Univ, Petersburg VA, BS, Bus Admin; Swarthmore Col, Swarthmore PA, post-bachelor degree; Catholic Univ Sch Law, Washington DC, JD. **Career:** Commonwealth VA, asst atty gen, 1975-76; Va Housing Develop Authority, sr coun, 1976-82; Gov Va, sr coun, 1982-85, gen coun, 1985-91; Old Dominion Univ, dir, 1991-98; Portfolio Recovery Assoc, exec vpres & gen coun, 1998-. **Orgs:** Am Bar Asn; Va State Bar; Norfolk & Portsmouth Bar Asn; chmn, Govs War Drugs Task Force; fel, Rockefeller Found. **Honors/Awds:** Outstanding Woman Award, Iota Phi Lambda; Named Virgina Woman of Achievement; Virginia's Outstanding Woman Attorney. **Business Phone:** (757)519-9300.

SCOTT, JULIE
Planner. **Career:** Eli Lilly & Co, planner, currently. **Home Addr:** 11325 Bear Hollow Ct, Indianapolis, IN 46229. **Business Addr:** Planner, Eli Lilly & Co, Lilly Corp Ctr, Indianapolis, IN 46285.*

SCOTT, DR. JULIUS S, JR.
School administrator. **Personal:** Born Feb 26, 1925, Houston, TX; son of Julius Sebastian and Bertha Bell; married Ianthia Ann; children: Julius III, David K & Lamar K. **Educ:** Wiley Col, Marshall Tex, BA, 1945; Garrett Theol Seminary, Evanston Ill, BD, 1949; Brown Univ, Providence RI, MA, 1964; Boston Univ, Boston Mass, PhD, 1968. **Career:** Mass Inst Technol, Cambridge Mass, Meth campus minister, 1960-61; Wesleyan Found, Houston Tex, chair united ministries, 1961-63; Southern Fellowships Fund, Atlanta Ga, asst dir, 1967-69; Spelman Col, Atlanta Ga, spec asst pres, 1972-74; Paine Col, Augusta Ga, pres, 1970-82; Division of Higher Educ, Bd Higher Educ, Nashville Tenn, assoc gen secy, 1982-88; Paine Col, Augusta Ga, pres, 1975-82 & 1988-94; Albany State Col, interim pres; Wiley Col, Marshall Tex, pres, 1996-2002; interim pres, Philander Smith Col, Little Rock, Ark, currently. **Orgs:** Am Sociol Asn; Am Asn Univ Profs; Black Methodists Church Renewal; Soc Educ Reconstruction. **Honors/Awds:** Citizen of Year Award, Augusta Chap Assoc Social Workers, 1982; Distinguished Alumnus Award, Boston Univ, 1987; Alumni Hall of Fame, Wiley Col, 1988. **Home Phone:** (404)737-6063. **Business Addr:** Interim President, Philander Smith College, 1 Trudie Kibbe Reed Dr, Little Rock, AR 72202, **Business Phone:** (501)375-9845.

SCOTT, DR. KENNETH RICHARD
Educator. **Personal:** Born Apr 17, 1934, New York, NY; son of Howard Russell and Emma Eugenia Doby; married Elizabeth Willette Miller, Jun 30, 1956; children: Russell William & Preston Richard. **Educ:** Howard Univ, Wash, BS, pharmacy, 1956; State Univ NY, Buffalo, MS, pharmaceut chem, 1960; Univ Md, Baltimore, PhD, organic chem, 1966. **Career:** State Univ NY, Buffalo, fel grad asst, 1956-60; Univ Md, Baltimore, terminal predoctoral, 1965-66; Howard Univ, Wash, instr, 1960-66, from asst prof to assoc prof, 1966-76, prof & interim chmn, 1976-, dir grad studies, currently; Fulbright fel, 1989-90. **Orgs:** Pres, Howard Univ Chap, Rho Chi Pharm Hon Soc, 1963-64; pres, Howard Univ Pharm Alumni Asn, 1972-74; pres, Howard Univ Chap, Sigma Xi Sci Soc, 1975-77; Epilepsy Found Am, 1982-83; bd dirs, Epilepsy Found Am, 1983-89; ed adv bd, Transactions Pharmaceut Scis, 1987-; Rho Chi; Am Chem Soc; Soc Neuroscience; Am Epilepsy Soc. **Home Addr:** 9816 Cottrell Terr, Silver Spring, MD 20903-1917. **Business Addr:** Professor & Interim Chairman, Director of Graduate Studies, Howard University, College of Pharmacy, Dept Pharmaceut Sci, Rm 319A Cooper Hall 2300 4th St NW Chauncey, Washington, DC 20059, **Business Phone:** (202)806-7288.

SCOTT, LARRY B.
Writer, actor, executive. **Personal:** Born Aug 17, 1961, Harlem, NY. **Educ:** John Bowne, dipl, 1978. **Career:** Films: Karate Kid, 1984; Revenge of the Nerds, 1984; That Was Then This Is Now, 1985; Space camp, 1986; Iron Eagle, 1986; Inside Adam Swit; Extreme Prejudice, 1987; Revenge of the Nerds Part II, 1994; A Hero Ain't Nothing But a Sandwich, 1978; Thieves; Diablo II, 2000; The Cheapest Movie Ever Made, 2000; Diablo II: Lord of Destruction, 2001; 100 Kilos, 2001; Judge Koan, 2003; Getting Played, 2005; Business Johnson, 2007; TV series: "Onein a Million", 1978; "Rag Tag Champs", 1978; "Roll of Thunder Hear My Cry", 1978; "The Jerk Too", 1984; "Grand Babies", 1985; "Children of Times Square", 1986; "The Liberators", 1987; "All for One"; "The Trial of Bernard Goetz"; "Magnum PI", 1985; "Super Force", 1990; "A Mother's Testimony", 2001; "Meter Maids Need Love, Too", 2002; "The Parkers", 2002,; Theater: Back to Back; Eden; The Wizard of Oz; The Tempest; Stainless Steele; radio series & writer; dir: Funny Futher muckers in Concert, Volume 1, 2001, Funny Futher muckers in Concert, Volume 2, 2001;producer: Funny Futhermuckers in Concert, Volume 1, 2001, Funny Futhermuckers in Concert, Volume 2, 2001, The Cheapest Movie Ever Made, 2000; Television appearance0: Barney Miller, The Jeffersons, Seinfeld, St, Elsewhere, Martin; LBS Productions, owner. **Honors/Awds:** Best Supporting Actor, Virgin Islands Film Festival; Outstanding Achievement in Theatre, Ensemble Perf, 1980; LA Drama Critics Award. **Business Addr:** Actor, c/o Harris & Goldberg, 1999 Ave of the Stars Suite 2850, Los Angeles, CA 90067, **Business Phone:** (213)553-5200.

SCOTT, DR. LEONARD STEPHEN
Dentist. **Personal:** Born Feb 28, 1949, Indianapolis, IN; son of Nathaniel and Bernice Katherine Covington; married Christine Tyson; children: John, Bryant, Nathan, Leonard, Lynna & Melanie, Katherine. **Educ:** Ind Univ Med Ctr, attended 1976; Ind Univ Sch Dent, DDS, 1973. **Career:** Leonbea Inc, pres; Tyscot Inc Recording Co, pres; pvt dent pract; Rock Community Church, pastor. **Orgs:** Amer Dental Asn; Indianapolis Dist Dental Soc; Ind State Health Facility Admin; Ind Dental Asn; Omega Psi Phi Frat; NAACP; tst Christ Ch Apostolic; bd dir, sec Christ Ch Apostolic; AO Dental Frat; Nat Acad Recording Arts & Sciences; pres, Gospel Excellence Ministries Inc; faculty mem, Aenon Bible Coll. **Honors/Awds:** Fel, Acad Gen Dent. **Home Addr:** 3402 Schofield Ave, Indianapolis, IN 46218-1136, **Home Phone:** (317)923-3343. **Business Addr:** Pastor, Rock Community Church, 5501 E 71st St Track No 4, Indianapolis, IN 46220, **Business Phone:** (317)257-2688.

SCOTT, DR. LINZY, JR.
Physician. **Personal:** Born Jul 4, 1934, Newark, NJ; son of Linzy Scott Sr and Ruby; divorced; children: Gina Ann & Linzy III. **Educ:** Lincoln Univ, BA, 1957; Fisk Univ, MA, 1959; Howard Univ, MD, 1963; NJ Orthop Hosp, residency; Columbia Presbyterian Hosp, residency. **Career:** NJ NG, hq phys, 1964-68; NJ Col Med, instr, 1968-70; Crippled Children's Hosp, lectr phys, 1968-70; Holy Family Hosp, phys, 1970-75; SW Comm Hosp, chairperson disaster prog, 1970-76; Hughes Spalding Pav, phys, 1970-76; SW Comm Hosp, initiator pain clin, 1977; GA State Med Asn, clin studies, 1977; SW Comm Hosp, chief ortho, 1970-78; Morris Brown Col, orthop physician, 1970-; New Jersey Rehabil Comn, orthop consult, 1970-; Metropolitan Insurance Co, orthop consult, 1982-; Dept Surg, Morehouse Med Sch, currently, family practice, currently; SW Ortho Assoc, pres, currently. **Orgs:** Am Med Asn; Atlanta Med Asn; Atlanta Ortho Soc; Eastern Ortho Soc; Nat Med Asn; diplo Am Bd Orthop Surgeons; fel, Am Acad Orthop Surgeons; fel, Am Acad Cerebral Palsy; founder, Gladden Memorial Orthopedic Soc, 1967; Southwest Comm Hosp, founder, Pastoral Prog. **Honors/Awds:** Am Acad Cerebral Palsy, Residency fel, 1967-68; Olympic Team Physician, 1981; Gold Medalist Nat Amateur Basketball Team, physician, 1983; Benjamin E Mays Appreciation Award, 1983; Am Med Asn Negotiation Award; Howard Univ Alumni Soc; Am Acad Family Physicians, 1983; Am Bd Orthopedic Surg, Cert; numerous other awards and honors. **Special Achievements:** Inventor, Scott Spiral Knee Brace, 1980. **Military Serv:** NJ NG, capt med corps, 1964-68. **Business Phone:** (404)752-5545.

SCOTT, M ALEXIS. See SCOTT, ALEXIS.

SCOTT, MARIAN ALEXIS
Newspaper publisher, journalist. **Personal:** Born Feb 4, 1949, Atlanta, GA; daughter of William Alexander III and Marian Willis; married Marc Anthony Lewis (divorced 1973); married David L Reeves, Mar 16, 1974; children: Cinque Scott Reeves & David L Reeves Jr. **Educ:** Barnard Col, attended 1968; Spelman Col, attended 1990; Leadership Atlanta, 1991; Regional Leadership Inst, 1992. **Career:** Atlanta Const, Atlanta, Ga, reporter, 1974-78, copy ed, 1978; Columbia Univ Sch Journ, Michelle Clark fel, 1974; Atlanta Jour-Const, Atlanta, Ga, ed, Intown Extra, 1979-81, asst city ed, 1982-84, ed/dir, video ed, 1984-86, vpres community affairs, 1986-93; Cox Enterprises, dir diversity, 1993-97; Atlanta Daily World Inc, chmn, pres, 1997-; Atlanta Daily World Newspaper, publ, 1997-. **Orgs:** Atlanta Chap, Nat Asn Media Women, 1985-87; chair, Nat Asn Advan Colored People Youth Achievement Acad, 1987-90; chair, Exodus/Cities Schs, 1990-91; steering comt mem, Ga Partnership Excellence Educ, 1990-91; adhoc comt chair, Multi-Cult Audience Develop, High Mus Art, 1990-91; vice chair, Friends Spelman, 1990, 1991; vice chair, High Mus Art, bd dirs, 1991-93; chair, Friends Spelman, 1992-94; chair, Atlanta C's Shelter, 1995-96; pres, Atlanta Press Club, 2000-01. **Honors/Awds:** Sch Bell Excellence Educ Reporting, Ga Asn Educr, 1977; Distinguished Urban Journ Award, Nat Urban Coalition, 1980; Nat Media Woman of the Year, Nat Asn Media Women, 1983; Top 100 Bus & Prof Women, Dollars & Sense Mag, 1986; Acad of Women Achievers, YWCA, 1989; Pioneer Black Journalist Award, Atlanta Asn Black Journalists, 1998; Citizen of the Year Award, SW Hosp, 2001; Media of the Year Award, Ga Legis Black Caucus, 2001; Grimes Fel, Cox Family Enterprise Ctr, Kennesaw Univ, 2001; Imperial Court Daughters of Isis Hall of Fame Award, 2004; TD Jake's Megafest Phenomenal Woman Award, 2004. **Special Achievements:** Appointed by Mayor Shirley Franklin to the bd Atlanta Workforce Development Agency, 2003; named Among 20 Women Making A Mark on Atlanta, Atlanta Mag, 1998. **Business Addr:** Publisher, Journalist, Atlanta Daily World, 145 Auburn Ave E, Atlanta, GA 30305, **Business Phone:** (404)659-1110.

SCOTT, DR. MARVIN BAILEY
Educator, administrator, politician. **Personal:** Born Mar 10, 1944, Henderson, NC; son of Robert B and Gertrude Bailey; married Dr Carol A Johnson, Oct 15, 1967 (divorced 1988); children: Robert B & Cinda P; married Dr Dulce M, Jun 10, 1995; children: Alex Costa & Marvin B Scott Jr. **Educ:** Univ Allahabad, India; Johnson C Smith Univ, BA, psychol, 1966; Univ Pittsburgh, MEd, 1968, PhD, 1970; Martin Univ, Hon Doctorate Laws, 2004. **Career:** Boston Univ Sch Educ, assoc prof dean, 1970-79, asst Provost, 1979-80; Univ Mass, Off Pres, ACE fel, 1979-80; ATEX Comput, dir humRRO, 1980-82; St MA, asst chancellor prof, 1983-86; St Paul's Col, Lawrenceville, VA, pres, 1986-88; Marvin B Scott Assocs, pres, 1988-89; Lilly Endowment, educ prog officer, 1991-; Butler Univ, spec asst pres, assoc dean educ, chair sociol & criminol dept, prof sociol, currently. **Orgs:** Numerous memberships including vpres, Bd Int Visitors; vpres, Minuteman Coun BSA; bd dirs, Black Media Coalition, Wash, DC; Old Dominion Area Coun Boy Scouts Amer; secy & exec bd mem, Cent Intercoll Athletic Asn; Community Adv Bd, Brunswick Correctional Ctr, Lawrenceville; 100 Black Men Indianapolis; bd dirs, Indianapolis Civie Theater; bd dirs, Crossroad Coun, Boy Scouts Am; bd dirs, Martin Luther King, Mult-Serv Ctr; ct expert, Boston Desegregation Case, 1975-82; NAACP Sch Desegration Cases, 1981-84; Kappa Alpha Psi; Phi Delta Kappa; Alpha Kappa Mu; Alpha Kappa Delta; Phi Kappa Phi; Nat Coun Humanities. **Honors/Awds:** Distinguished Service Award, Kappa Alpha Psi, 1978; Am Coun Educ Fel Acad Admin, 1979-80; Silver Beaver Award, Boy Scouts Am, 1984; Paul Revere Patriots Award; Honorary Doctorate of Law, Martin Univ. **Special Achievements:** Host of radio talk show, WRKO, Boston, 1982-86; host of "Central VA Focus" TV program, WPLZ, Richmond, VA, 1987-88; author of books, The Essential Profession, Five Essential Dimensions of Curriculum Design, and Schools on Trial; author of chapter in The Future of Big-City Schools; Ran for Congress in the 10th congressional district in Indiana; candidate for US Senate, 2004. **Home Addr:** 7567 Sycamore Grove Ct, Indianapolis, IN 46260, **Home Phone:** (317)259-1102. **Business Addr:** Professor, Butler University, Department of Sociology, Jordan Hall 371 4600 Sunset Ave, Indianapolis, IN 46208, **Business Phone:** (317)940-9464.

SCOTT, MARVIN WAYNE
Educator. **Personal:** Born Jan 21, 1952, Philadelphia, PA; son of Albert and Maloy; married Marcia Annette Simons, Nov 23, 1973; children: Thembi L & Kori A. **Educ:** E Stroudsburg Univ, BA, 1973; Ohio State Univ, MA, 1974; Univ NC, Greensboro, EdD, 1986. **Career:** Miami Dade Community Col, asst prof, 1974-78; Howard Community Col, assoc prof, 1979-87; Univ Md, asst prof, 1987-. **Orgs:** Scholar comt, Md Asn Health, Phys Educ, Recreation & Dance, 1980, 1984; Comt investigate greater involvement, EDA Am Alliance Health, Phys Educ, Recreation & Dance, 1981; Nom Comt, Nat Asn Sport & Phys Educ, 1982; curric consult, Hampton Inst, 1982, Maryland State Dept Educ, 1982; prog eval, Univ Md, Batlimore, 1984; Am Asn Univ Women annual conf. **Honors/Awds:** Social Action Award, Omega Psi Phi Fraternity; Human Rights Celebration Lectr, E Stroudsburg Univ. **Special Achievements:** Published books like: "Miami Dade South Basketball Motion Offense", 1978, "In Persuit of the Perfect Job, A Philosophical Fable", 1979. **Business Addr:** Assistant Profes-

sor, Department of Kinesiology, University of Maryland, Rm 2347 HHP Bldg, College Park, MD 20742-2611.

SCOTT, DR. MARY SHY
Association executive, music patron, consultant. **Personal:** Born in Atlanta, GA; daughter of Robert and Flora; married Alfred; children: Alfredene Scott Cheely, Arthur Robert & Alfred Jr. **Educ:** Spelman Col, AB, 1950; NY Univ, MA, 1969; NY Univ; GA State Univ. **Career:** Atlanta Pub Schs, music specialist, 1950; Alpha Kappa Alpha Sorority Inc, S Atlantic regional dir, nat vpres, 1986-90, int pres, 1990-94, Int Comt, mem; independent educ consult, currently. **Orgs:** Chair, Nat Arts Alpha Kappa Alpha Sorority Inc, 1978-82; Music Educrs Nat Conf, 1985; GA Music Educators Asn, 1985; steward, Allen Temple AME Church, 1985-; pres, Peachtree Chap LINKS Inc, 1987; bd dirs, SCLC, 1986-88; Top Ladies Distinction Inc; bd dir, United Negro Col Fund, 1990-94; vpres, Educ Advan Found, Alpha Kappa Alpha Inc; protocal chair,Azalea City Chap LINKS Inc, 1995-; City Atlanta, Human Rels Comn, 2001-. **Honors/Awds:** Basilius Award, Alpha Kappa Alpha, 1978; Golden Dove Award, Kappa Omega Chap, Alpha Kappa Alpha, 1980; Negro Heritage Bronze Woman of the Year,Fine Arts Iota Phi Lambda Sor, 1980; Meritorious Service Award, Omega PsiPhi, 1987; Keys to the Cities of: Pansacola, Thomasville, Columbus, GA,Orlando, Augusta, Selma, Long Beach, and Kansas City; Mary Shy Scott Dayin Kansas City, Macon, Fulton Co, Charleston, SC & Miami; Hon Citizen of: Columbus, GA, Huntsville, Jacksonville, Little Rock, Baltimore, & State AL; Hon Lt, State of Alabama, 1988; LHD, Miles Col, 1992; OUIDAH 1992 Award, Presented by Pres NO Soola of Benin, 1993; Portrait of Sweet Success, A Living Legend Award, Intergenerational Resource Ctr, Atlanta, GA, 1994. **Special Achievements:** Co-author: And These Came Forth, drama, 1980; rec: Kappa Omega Chorus In Concert, Mark Rec, 1980. **Home Addr:** 2781 Baker Ridge Dr NW, Atlanta, GA 30318. **Business Addr:** Independent Educational Consultant, 2781 Baker Ridge Dr NW, Atlanta, GA 30318.

SCOTT, MELVINA BROOKS
Insurance agent, government official, executive director. **Personal:** Born Mar 19, 1948, Goodman, MS; daughter of Sabina Walker and Shed; widowed; children: Johnny F Jr, James T & Kateea P. **Educ:** Hawkeye Inst Tech, grad life underwriting assting; Univ Northern Iowa, BA, social work, 1976, masters prog, currently; Wartsburg Col, cert, mgt by objective, community law, affirmative action & substance abuse, 1985. **Career:** Prudential Ins Co, dist agent, 1977-81; Black Hawk Co Dept Corresp Serv, probation officer, 1976-77; Minority Alcoholism Coun, 1975-76; Area Educ Agency VII, media clerk, 1968-75; polit consult, 1978-86; Cutler Cong, polit counr; All State Ins, 1981-85; Waterloo Comm Schs, 7th grade basketball coach, 1985-93; Nagle Cong, polit counr, 1986; Congressman David Nagle, caseworker & staff asst, 1987-93. **Orgs:** Chairperson, dem party Black Hawk Co, 1974-78; youth adv & vpres, Black Hawk Co Nat Asn Advan Colored People, 1976-80; vpres bd, Logandate Coop Daycare, 1977-78; civic comm, memberships C of C Com Delta Sigma Theta, 1977-79; pres, United Sister Black Hawk Co; polit action coun mem, Life Underwriters Asn, 1978-; comm develop, Comm Funding CMS, 1980-86; Layman Orgn Payne AME Ch; Payne AME; comm mem, Minority Drug Coun Int Women's Year Comm Del to Houston; co mem, Third Dist Affirmative Action Comm; ward leader, Dem Party Cent Comm, 1980-86; vice chairperson, Iowa Black Caucus; bd treas, NHS, 1983-86; Mayor Review Comm Streets, 1988-89; Mayor Review Comm Area Econ Develop, 1989; exec bd mem, YWCA, 1990-96; affirmative action chairperson, Iowa Dem Party; founding mem & exec dir, African Am Hist & Cult Mus; pres, United Sisters & Regional Networkers Together Inc. **Honors/Awds:** Service Award, Boys Club Waterloo, 1977; National Sale Achievement Award, 1978, 80. **Home Addr:** 413 Oneida St, Waterloo, IA 50703. **Business Addr:** Full Time Student, University of Northern Iowa.

SCOTT, MICHAEL W
Association executive, president (organization). **Personal:** Married Diana. **Educ:** Fordham Univ, BA, urban planning. **Career:** Pyramid West Develop Corp, vpres; Lawndale People's Planning & Action Coun, dir community develop, 1978-82; Chicago Bd Edu, bd mem, 1980-81; Dept Special Events, deputy dir; Spec Asst Mayor, dir; City Chicago's Off Cable Commun, chief cable admin; Prime Cable, gen mgr; AT&T Broadband, vpres local govt affairs; Comcast Corp, vpres regulatory affairs; Pyramidwest Develop Corp, vpres; Michael Scott & Assocs LLC, pres, currently; Chicago Pk Dist Bd, pres; Chicago Bd Edu, pres; Pub Bldg Comn Chicago, Comnr, 2002-; YMCA USA, bd mem, 2006-. **Orgs:** Coun Great City Sch; Chicago Olympic Comt; Mount Sinai Hosp; Better Boys Found; Chicago Hist Soc. **Business Addr:** Board Member, YMCA of the USA, 101 N Wacker Dr, Chicago, IL 60606, **Business Phone:** 800-872-9622.

SCOTT, DR. MONA VAUGHN
Educator. **Personal:** Born in Jackson, MS; daughter of Birel and Nora (deceased); married Dr Richard; children: Monika, Sean & Malaika. **Educ:** Col Pacific, BA; Univ Pacific, MA; Stanford Univ, PhD, 1977. **Career:** Scotts Int Res & Educ Consult Orgn, exec dir researcher; Univ Calif Dent Sch, teacher, minority admis comn, consult, 1969; Dental Sch Univ San Francisco, Gen Admis Comt, consult, 1969; Nat Med Asn, res cons; Golden State Med Asn, res cons; Black Repertory Group, exec dir; Wash Sch Psychiat, dir res soc servs; George Wash Univ, dir res soc servs, 1966; Minortiy Allied Health League Concentration Motivation, founder, dir consult, 1970-75; Family Background & Family Lifestyles Minorities San Francisco, dir res, 1971-73. **Orgs:** Calif Teachers Eng Speakers Other Languages; dir, SIRECO; Bay Area Asn Black Psychologists; Nat Asn Advan Colored People; ORCHESIS; Honor Soc Nat Modern Dance. **Honors/Awds:** Tulley Knowles Scholarship Philosophy Inst; Mary R Smith Scholarship; Outstanding National Meth Student Scholarship; National Meth Scholarship; Ambassadors Award, Comm Serv Wash, DC; Women of Year Award, Delta Theta Nu, 1964; Dept Behavioral Technical Award, Westinghouse. **Special Achievements:** Auth: The Efficacy of Tuition-Retention Programs for Minorities, 1968; White Racism & Black Power, 1969; co-auth: Algerian Interview with Kathleen Cleaver, 1972; Institutional Racism in Urban Schools, 1975.

SCOTT, NELSON
Fashion model. **Personal:** Born in Bronx, NY. **Career:** Ads: Guess, Banana Republic, Benetton; Ralph Lauren, runway show. **Business Phone:** (212)242-1500.

SCOTT, NIGEL L.
Lawyer. **Personal:** Born Aug 23, 1940; married Monica Chasteau; children: Duane, Omar, Rion. **Educ:** Howard Univ, BS, Chem, 1970; Howard Univ Sch Law, JD, 1973. **Career:** Eastman Kodak, patent atty, 1973-75; Atty, pvt pract, 1975-79; Scott & Yallery-Arthur, atty, 1980-. **Orgs:** DC PA & US Patent Bars, 1975-; exec dir, Nat Patent Law Asn, 1979-; pres, Trinidad & Tobago Asn, Wash DC, 1977-79; adv Human Rights Comn, Montgomery County, 1980; . **Business Addr:** Attorney, Scott & Yallery-Arthur, 7306 Ga Ave NW, Washington, DC 20012.*

SCOTT, OLYMPIA RANEE (OLYMPIA SCOTT RICHARDSON)
Basketball player, basketball coach. **Personal:** Born Aug 5, 1976, Los Angeles, CA; daughter of Jacqueline; married Al Richardson; children: BreAzia Ranee. **Educ:** Stanford univ, Sociology, 1998. **Career:** Basketball coach (retired), basketball player; Utah Starzz, 1998-99; Detroit Shock, ctr-forward, 2000-01; Ind fever, ctr-forward, 2001-02, 06-; Charlotte Sting, ctr-forward, 2004; William Smith College, head coach, 2004; Sacramento Monarchs, ctr, 2005; Col of the Sequoias, asst coach; Phoenix Mercury, ctr, 2007. **Honors/Awds:** Kodak All-Am, regional pick; Boost/Naismith Award; AP All-Am, 1997-98. *

SCOTT, REV. OTIS, SR.
Educator, clergy. **Personal:** Born Sep 19, 1919, Lynchburg, SC; son of Ed Scott and Emma Green Scott; married Wilhelmenia Dennis; children: Myrtle Scott Johnson, Otis Jr & Linda Scott Norwood. **Educ:** Morris Col, BA; Columbia Univ, MA; Univ SC. **Career:** Mt Nebo, Jerusalem & Barnettesville Baptist Churches, pastor, 1952-70; Mt Moriah Baptist Church, pastor, 1970-; Sumter County, councilman, 1993-; Sumter County Sch Dist #2, teacher; Vet Job Training, instr; Lower Lee Sch, teacher, basketball coach; Delaine Elem Sch, teacher; Ebenezer Jr High Sch, Sumter County Educ Asn, teacher; Mulberry Baptist Church, pastor. **Orgs:** Councilman, Nat Asn Counties, 1984-; councilman, Sc Asn Counties, 1984-; bd mem, Hillcrest High Sch Found, 1988-; bd mem, Minority Scholar Comn, Sumter Sch Dist 17, 1989-; Asn Classroom Teachers; Sc Educ Asn; bd dir, NEA Boylan Haven-Mather Acad; bd dir, Proj T Sq; Sumter County Econ Opportunity; Day Care Ctr; Sumter Co Dem Party; pres, Voters Precinct #1; Notary Pub; master mason Prince Hall Affil; Nat Asn Advan Colored People; Shriner; field worker Morris Col; clerk Wateree Asn LD; moderator Lynches River Union; clerk Sunday Sch Conv; instr, Ann Inst Mt Moriah Asn; Nat Prog Conv; Rembert Horatio Comn; built churches Lee Co Clarendon Do; Order Eastern Star, Cathall Chapter 315; Nat Asn County Sci Asn Counties; Santee Lynches Regional Coun govt; bd mem, Rural Transp & Public Rd. **Honors/Awds:** Distinguished Alumnus Award, Morris Col, 1988; Special Recognition Award, Morris Col, 1989; Special Recognition Award, NCP, 1992. **Military Serv:** USAF, 1941-45.

SCOTT, DR. OTIS L
Educator, administrator. **Personal:** Born Dec 27, 1941, Marion, OH; son of William and Harriett Booker; married Willie Vern Hawkins, Mar 2, 1963; children: William F, Byron O & David A. **Educ:** Univ Md; Eastern Wash State Col, Cheney, WA; Central State Col, Wilberforce, OH; Calif State Univ, Sacramento, BA, 1971, MA, 1973; Union Grad Sch, Cincinnati, OH, PhD, 1982. **Career:** Calif State Univ, Sacramento, CA, prof, 1974-, actg dean, assoc dean, Col Soc Sci & Interdisciplinary Studies, dean, currently . **Orgs:** Sacramento Area Black Caucus, 1974-; Nat Coun Black Studies, 1979-; Nat Asn Ethnic Studies, 1985-; Nat Conf Black Polit Scientists, 1989-; pres, 1998, Nat Asn Ethnic Studies, 1996-98. **Honors/Awds:** CSUS Exceptional Merit Award, 1984; Cooper-Woodson Medal of Honor, 1996; John L Livingston Award, 1998. **Special Achievements:** Journal article, Ethnic Studies Past and Present Explorations in Ethnic Studies Vol 11, No 2, 1988; Journal article, Coping Strategies of Women in Alice Walkers Novels Explorations in Ethnic Studies, Vol 10, No 1, 1987; Co-Project Director, Beyond the Canon, 1990-; Author, The Veil: Perspectives on Race & Ethnicity in the US, West Publishing Co, 1994; co-author, Teaching From A Multicultural Perspective, Sage, 1994; editor, Lines, Borders and Connections, Kendall Hunt, 1997; co-author, Anatomy of Genocide, Thomas Mellen, 2001; honored as the 2006 outstanding faculty initiate at the annual banquet of Phi Kappa Phi. **Military Serv:** Air Force, SSGT, 1960-68. **Business Addr:** Associate Dean, Professor of Ethnic Studies and Government, California State University Sacramento, College of Social Sciences and Interdisciplinary Studies, Ethnic Studies Dept, 6000 J St, Sacramento, CA 95819-6013.

SCOTT, PORTIA ALEXANDRIA
Journalist. **Personal:** Born Jun 9, 1943, Atlanta, GA; daughter of C A Scott. **Educ:** Howard Univ, BA, 1964; Atlanta Univ, MA, 1972. **Career:** Atlanta Daily World, managing ed, 2005. **Orgs:** Nat Asn Negro Business & Professional Women; Nat Asn Media Women; Nat Fed Bus Prof Women; NAACP; Church Women United Atlanta;; Nat Fed Republican Women; M L King Jr Nat Historic Site Advisory Commn, chairwoman, 1987-92; pres, Bush Advisory Bd Historically Black Col & Univ, 1990-. **Honors/Awds:** Numerous civic & communications awards; Southern Bell, Black History Calendar, "Women of Achievement," 1990-91; Republican Nominee for 5th District Congressional Seat, Ga, 1986; Atlanta Bus League, Most 100 Influential African-American Women, 1995, 1996. **Home Addr:** 209 Winters Pk Dr, Atlanta, GA 30360, **Home Phone:** (770)613-0513. **Business Addr:** Magazine Editor, Atlanta Daily World, 145 Auburn Ave NE, Atlanta, GA 30303, **Business Phone:** (404)659-1110.

SCOTT, QUINCY, JR.
Clergy. **Personal:** Born Jan 11, 1944, Norfolk, VA; son of Josephine D; married Col Constance L, Feb 6, 1972; children: Toya Williams & Quincy III & Derek. **Educ:** Shaw Univ, BA, 1965; Vanderbilt Univ, MDiv, 1973; Boston Univ, MEd, 1976; Howard Univ, DMin, 1979. **Career:** Shaw Univ, chaplain dean, 1995-; Army Chaplain Sch, assoc prof; Pentagon, Wash, chaplain; Second Infantry Div, S Korea, div chaplain; Walter Reed Army Med Ctr; staff chaplain; Edgehill United Methodist Church; Norfolk Pub Recreation. **Orgs:** Alpha Kappa Mu Honor Soc; Kappa Alpha Psi Fraternity; Nat Asn Advan Colored People; Retired Officers Asn; Nat Theol Fraternity; Military Chaplains Asn; life mem, Shaw Alumni Asn. **Honors/Awds:** Man of the Year, Norfolk Women Dnl, 1996; The Legion of Merit, US Government . **Military Serv:** AUS Chaplains Corp, col, 1968-95; Bronze Star for Valor, 1970, MSM, 1984, Vietnam Service Cross, 1970. **Home Phone:** (919)557-2141. **Business Addr:** Dean of the Chapel, Shaw University, Thomas J Boyd Chapel, 118 E S S, Raleigh, NC 27601-2399, **Business Phone:** (919)546-8454.

SCOTT, R LEE
Executive. **Personal:** Born Oct 8, 1943, Hollywood, AL; son of Lee J (deceased) and Jannie; married Mae Frances Kline; children: Ronald & Lynne. **Educ:** Univ Conn, BA, 1966; Univ Hartford, MBA, 1977; Cornell Univ, exec dev prog, 1984; Northwestern Univ, attended consumer strategy, 1989. **Career:** Aetna Life & Casualty Ins, sr underwriter, 1966-70; Southern New Eng Telecom, dist staff mgr int auditing, 1970-87, dist mkt mgr, consumer prod, 1987-, dir legislative affairs, currently; Univ Hartford, adj prof, 1978-; Univ New Haven, adj prof. **Orgs:** Alpha Phi Alpha Frat, 1968-; Sigma Pi Phi Frat 1981-; pres, Scott & Assocs, 1983-; New Britain Nat Asn Advan Colored People; bd dir, Indian Hills Country Club Newington CT. **Honors/Awds:** Certificate of Recognition, Nat Alliance Businessmen, 1973; Outstanding Young Man, Am Nat Jaycees, 1978, 1980; Distinguished Minority, Grad Univ Conn, 1984. **Special Achievements:** Articles like: "Make Your Class Room Time Count," Minority Educ Philadelphia 1980, preprinted by Northern Michigan Univ in career newsletter 1980; case study Personnel Assessment Ctrs in Collaboration in Organization, Alternatives to Hierarchy by William A Kraus, Human Sciences Press NY 1980. **Home Addr:** 27 Hillside Pl Apt 25, New Britain, CT 06051-2571. **Business Addr:** Director Legislative Affairs, Southern New England Telecommunications, 55 Trumbull St, Hartford, CT 06111, **Business Phone:** (203)947-7034.*

SCOTT, RICHARD ELEY
Judge. **Personal:** Born Dec 25, 1945, Kilgore, TX. **Educ:** Prairie View A&M Univ, BA, 1968; Univ Tex, JD, 1972. **Career:** Pvt pract atty, 1972-; Tex Stand Rep Eddie B Johnson, legal asst, 1973; Austin Community Col, part-time instr, 1973; Travis Co Tex, justice of the peace, 1975-. **Orgs:** Nat Asn Advan Colored People; State Bar Tex, 1972; Del Dem Nat Conv, 1972; Travis County Jr Bar Asn, 1973; Nat Bar Asn, 1975; comt chmn adm State Bar Tex, 1976; E Austin Youth Found Coach, 1976; sponsoring comt, Austin Urban League, 1977; Rishon Lodge Suite 1, 1977. **Business Addr:** Judge, Travis County, 1811 Springdale Rd Suite 110, Austin, TX 78721, **Business Phone:** (512)854-7700.

SCOTT, ROBERT CORTEZ (BOBBY SCOTT)
Congressperson (u.s. federal government). **Personal:** Born Apr 30, 1947, Washington, DC; son of C Waldo and Mae Hamlin. **Educ:** Harvard Col, BA, 1969; Boston Col Law Sch, JD, 1973. **Career:** Atty at law; Va Gen Assembly, del, 1978-83; Va House Representatives, state rep, 1983-93; US House Rep, congressman,

1993-, Currently. **Orgs:** Newport News Old Dominion Bar Asn, 1973-; pres, Peninsula Bar Asn, 1974-78; golden heritage life mem, NAACP, 1976-; pres, Peninsula Legal Aid Ctr Inc, 1976-81; chmn, 1st Congional Dist Dem Com, 1980-85; vchmn, Va Dem Black Caucus, 1980; del, Nat Dem Convention, 1980; Hampton Inst Annual Fund Com; bd mem, Peninsula Asn Sickle Cell Anemia; Peninsula Coun Boy Scouts Am; March Dimes; Alpha Phi Alpha, Sigma Pi Phi. **Honors/Awds:** Outstanding Leader Hampton Roads Jaycees, 1976; Man of the Year, Zeta Lambda Chap Alpha Phi Alpha Frat, 1977; Distinguished Community Service, Kennedy-Evers-King Memorial Found, 1977; Outstanding Achievement, Peninsula Nat Asn Negro Bus & Prof Women, 1978; Brotherhood Citation Nat Conf Christians & Jews, 1985; Public Health Recognition Award, Va Pub Health Asn, 1986; Outstanding Legislator Award, Va Chapt & Amer Pediat Soc, 1986; hon doctorate govt sci degree, Commonwealth Col, 1987; Nat Humanitarian Hero Award, 2004; Virginia Fire & Emergency Services Award, 2005; NAMI Exemplary Legislator Award, 2006; Honorary Degree, Norfolk St Univ, 2007; Good Scouter Award, 2007; Distinguished Lifetime Award, 2007; Norvleate Downing-Gross Achievement Award, 2007; Distinguished Citizen of the Year Award, Va Peninsula Chamber Commerce, 2008. **Military Serv:** MA Army Nat Guard, 1970-73; AUSR 1973-76. **Business Phone:** (202)225-8351.

SCOTT, ROBERT JEROME
Media executive. **Personal:** Born Feb 2, 1946, San Francisco, CA; son of Robert and Mary Helen Harris Weeks; divorced; children: Siiri Sativa & Jeremy Harrington. **Educ:** Wayne State Univ, attended 1964-71. **Career:** Studio Theatres Detroit, supvr, 1968-69; Detroit News, staff photographer, 1969-71; Optek Photographic, owner & photographer, 1971; Detroit Free Press, staff photographer & jazz critic, 1971-79; Mich Dept Com, dir mich film off, 1979-85; WTVS/Channel 56, dir proj mkt, 1985-87, vpres community develop, 1987-91, vpres govt rels & support; WRCJ, sta mgr, 2005-. **Orgs:** New Detroit Inc, comt racial & econ justice, 1986-88; bd dirs, Theatre Grottesco, 1987-90; Governors Arts Awards Comt, 1989-92; bd dirs, Concerned Citizens Arts Mich, 1991-92. **Honors/Awds:** Michigan Emmy Award, Nat Acad TV Arts & Sci, 1987. **Special Achievements:** Director & Executive Producer of various Television shows including "Senzinina: What Have We Done to Deserve This?", 1987; "Back to Detroit: The Future", 1987; "Spectrum, The Series on Arts in Michigan", 1987-90; "Governors' Arts Awards Program", 1989-92; "1991 Montreux Jazz Festival", 1991-92. **Home Addr:** 14518 Abington Rd, Detroit, MI 48227. **Business Addr:** Station Manager, WRCJ, 123 Selden St, Detroit, MI 48201, **Business Phone:** (313)494-6400.

SCOTT, RUBY DIANNE
Media executive, consultant. **Personal:** Born Sep 19, 1951, New Rochelle, NY; daughter of Carmen Saunders and Clemmie Scott; married Raymond Williams, May 15, 1978. **Educ:** Boston Univ, BS, jour, 1973; Northwestern Univ Mgt Training Ctr, 1985; Northwestern Univ, Advan Exec Prog, 1998. **Career:** Boston Globe, intern asst news ed, 1972-77; Chicago Tribune, copy ed to op-ed page ed, 1977-93; Tribune Publ, dir ed resources & diversity, 1993-99; Tribune Co, dir diversity recruiting, 1998-2001; Nomadic Consult, sr consult, 2001-. **Orgs:** Nat Asn Black Journalists, 1984-; Nat Asn Minority Media Exec, 1993-; Am Soc Newspaper Editors Diversity Comn, 1994-; Media Diversity Managers, 1995-; Newspaper Asn Am, recruitment & youth develop comn, 1997-. **Honors/Awds:** Outstanding Professional Performance, Chicago Tribune, 1983; YMCA Black & Hispanic Achievers Bus & Indust, 1993. **Special Achievements:** Sisters of Struggle, mentor, 1993-; co-chair, Tribune Diversity Steering Comm, 1995-. **Business Addr:** Senior Consultant, Nomadic Consulting Inc, 200 E Ohio St Suite 300, Chicago, IL 60611, **Business Phone:** (312)664-1732.

SCOTT, RUTH ELAINE HOLLAND
Management consultant, executive, government official. **Personal:** Born Aug 13, 1934, Albion, MI; daughter of Robert Holland and Edna; married William G; children: Greg, June & Chrystal. **Educ:** Albion Coll, BA (cum laude), social work, 1956; Kent State Univ, ME, couns, 1961; Buffalo State, EdD, 1968; SUNY, cert, educ admin, 1981; Alfred Univ Honors Causa, DHL, 1997. **Career:** Cleveland Pub Schs, teacher, 1956-61; W Valley Cent Sch, NY, teacher, 1961-62; Arcade Cent Sch, NY, teacher, 1964-66; Educ Serv BOCES Cattaraugus Co, consult, 1966-70; City Sch Dist Rochester, consult nursing prog, 1971; Wilson Jr High Sch, reading lab coordr, 1974; City Sch Dist Rochester, adv specialist & human rels, 1975-77; Ford Found, consult, 1976-78; Community Savings Bank Rochester, personnel compliance coordr, 1977-, regional mgr; City Rochester, city councilwoman-at-large, coun pres, 1986-; Scott Assoc Inc, pres, ceo, 1989-; Multicultural Inst, Portland, develop multi-cultural workshops, 1993-. **Orgs:** Bd dirs, WXXI, 1976-87; Friends Rochester Pub Libr, 1976-87; adv coun, Women's Career Ctr, 1977-; adv bd, WHEC TV-10; chairperson, Nat League Cities Community & Econ Develop, 1987; bd, Monroe County Water Authority; treas, Leadership Am Alumni Bd, 1990; bd mem, New Futures Initiative, NLC's Women Munic Govt bd pres, Rochester Community Found, 1991-96; exec secy, Rochester Area Found, pres, 1992; Phi Delta Kappa. **Honors/Awds:** Championship Debater Albion Col, 1952; Outstanding Alumni Award, Albion Col, 1975; Chamber Civic Award, Leadership Am Class, 1989; Exemplar Award, 1997; Senate Woman of Distinction Award, 2005; Outstanding Citizen-Politician-Christian Worker, Black Student Caucus local Col Divinity; Volunteer Service Award, Cert Martin Luther King Jr Greater Rochester Festival CMS. **Special Achievements:** Served as Rochester Community Savings Bank's first Community Reinvestment officer; One of the Women Builders of Communities and Dreams, honored by YWCA; One of five businesswomen, honored by prestigious Athena Award comm significant contrib bus & community. **Business Addr:** President, Chief Executive Officer, Scott Associates Consulting, Inc, 30 Arvine Heights, Rochester, NY 14611, **Business Phone:** (716)328-4770.

SCOTT, SAMUEL
Engineer. **Personal:** Born Feb 2, 1946, San Francisco, CA; married Christine Mary Harrington; children: Stephany & Sybil. **Educ:** Wayne State Univ, attended 1968. **Career:** Univ Mich Soc Res Study, coord personal, 1967-68; Studio Theaters Detroit, supvr, 1968-69; Detroit News, photo, 1969-71; Optek Photographics, dir & photo, 1971-72; Detroit Free Press, photo & jazz critic, 1972-79; Off Film & TV Serv Mich Dept Com, dir present. **Orgs:** Mich Press Photo Asn, 1972-80; exec off, Mich Film & TV Coun; Nat Asn Film Comn, 1980. **Honors/Awds:** Honorable mental Michigan Press Photo, 1976-79; public service award, Wayne Co Bd Comnrs, 1979. **Business Addr:** 2021 Jefferson Davis Hwy Crystal City, Arlington, VA 22202.

SCOTT, SERET (SERET SCOTT WILLIAMS)
Administrator. **Personal:** Born Sep 1, 1947, Washington, DC; daughter of John William and Della Beidleman Scott; married Amos Augustus, Mar 20, 1976; children: Anang. **Educ:** NYU Sch Arts, attended 1969; Rutgers Univ, attended 1989. **Career:** Sundance Theatre Lab, dir, 1989-95; Buffalo's Studio Arena Theatre, dir, 1993-95; San Diego's Old Globe Theatre, dir, 1993-2000; New Haven's Long Wharf Theatre, dir, 1994-97; Costa Mesa's S Coast Repertory, dir, 1996, 1999; NYC's Vivo Flamenco, dir, 1999. **Orgs:** Fox Found, 1988-; Soc Stage Dirs & Choreographer's, 1990-; Nat Endowment Arts, 1994-95; Nat Found Advan Arts, 1996,1999. **Honors/Awds:** Drama Actress Desk Award/Broadway, NY Theatre Critics, 1974. **Special Achievements:** Director: American Stage Premiere, The Joy Luck Club, 1997; World Premiere, Mud, River, Stone, 1997; World Premiere, Leaving The Summerland, 2000.

SCOTT, SHAWNELLE
Basketball player. **Personal:** Born Jun 16, 1972, New York, NY. **Educ:** St John's Univ. **Career:** Cleveland Cavaliers, ctr, 1996-98; San Antonio Spurs, 2000-01; Denver Nuggets, 2001-02.

SCOTT, STEPHEN L
President (Organization), businessperson. **Career:** Scott-Hilliard-Kosene, Inc, pres & partner, currently. **Orgs:** Indianapolis Adv Comn Indust Develop; Greater Indianapolis Chamber Com.

SCOTT, STUART
Television sportscaster, actor. **Personal:** Born Jul 19, 1965, Chicago, IL; married Kimberley, Mar 1, 1993; children: 2. **Educ:** Univ NC, BA, speech commun & radio, tv & motion pictures, 1987. **Career:** WPDE-TV, Florence, SC, news reporter & weekend sports anchor, 1987-88; WRAL-TV, Raleigh, NC, news reporter, 1988-90; WESH-TV, Orlando, FL, sports reporter & anchor, 1990-93; ESPN, "Sports Center", anchor, 1993-, "Sunday NFL Countdown", 1999-2001; "Monday Night Countdown", 2002-05; "ET", 2009; Films: Enchanted, 1998; He Got Game, 1998; The Kid, 2000; Drumline, 2002; Love Don't Cost a Thing, 2003; Mr 3000, 2004; Herbie Fully Loaded, 2005; TV series: "NFL Primetime", 1987; Monday Night Countdown, 1993; "Arli$$",1999-2000; Jim Brown: All American, 2002; "She Spies", 2003; Relatively Speaking: Joe Dumars, 2003; "Soul Food", 2003; "Dream Job", 2004; Naughty or Nice, 2004; "Last Call with Carson Daly", 2004-05; In the Game, 2005; I Love the Holidays, 2005; "I Love the '70s: Volume 2", 2006; David Blaine: Drowned Alive, 2006; "I Love Toys", 2006; "The 2007 NBA Finals", 2007; 2007 80th Annual Scripps National Spelling Bee, 2007; "I Love the New Millennium", 2008; "Black to the Future", 2009. **Orgs:** Alpha Phi Alpha Fraternity. **Business Addr:** Anchor, ESPN Inc, ESPN Plz, Bristol, CT 06010, **Business Phone:** (860)766-2000.

SCOTT, SYREETA
Founder (Originator), beautician. **Educ:** Hampton Univ, math. **Career:** Duafe Holistic Hair Care, founder, owner & stylist, currently. **Orgs:** Treas, Blues Babe Found; vol, Temple Univ, Pan African Studies Community Educ Prog. **Business Addr:** Stylist, owner, Duafe Holistic Hair Care, 2947 W Girard Ave, Philadelphia, PA 19130-1119, **Business Phone:** (215)232-6850.

SCOTT, TIMOTHY VAN
Ophthalmologist. **Personal:** Born Jul 12, 1942, Newport News, VA; son of William H and Janet H; married Karen Hill Scott; children: Van, Lanita, Kevin, Amara. **Educ:** Fisk Univ, BA 1964; Meharry Med Col, MD, 1968; Hubbard Hosp Nashville Ophthal Res, rotating internship, 1969; Thomas Jefferson Univ Hosp Philadelphia, 1972; HEED Ophthalmic Found Fel, Glaucoma Jules Stein Eye Inst, Univ Calif Los Angeles, 1973. **Career:** Pvt pract; Ophthal Martin Luther King Jr Gen Hosp, chief div, 1973-82; Glaucoma Serv Jules Stein Eye Inst, Univ Calif Los Angeles, consult, 1973-; Glaucoma Serv Harbor Hosp, Torrance, CA, 1973-79; Ophthalmologist Kaiser Hosp, Torrance, CA, staff, 1972-73; Am Bd Ophthal, dip, 1973-; Charles R Drew Postgrad Med Sch, asst prof surg; Ophthal Univ Calif Los Angeles, Sch Med, assoc prof. **Orgs:** Am Asn Ophthal; Nat Asn Res & Interns; Soc HEED Fels; Omega Psi Phi Frat. **Honors/Awds:** Outstanding Young Men of America, 1974. **Business Addr:** 1001 Potrero Ave Rm 4M31, San Francisco, CA 90301.*

SCOTT, TODD CARLTON
Football player. **Personal:** Born Jan 23, 1968, Galveston, TX. **Educ:** Southwestern La univ. **Career:** Minnesota Vikings, 1991-94; New York Jets, 1995; Tampa Bay Buccaneers, 1995-96; Kansas City Chiefs, 1997. **Honors/Awds:** Pro Bowl, 1992.

SCOTT, VERONICA J.
Educator, physician. **Personal:** Born Feb 8, 1946, Greenville, AL; daughter of C B Jr and Mary Loys Greene. **Educ:** Howard Univ, BS, 1968; Albert Einstein Col Med, MD, 1973; UCLA Sch Pub Health, MPH, 1978. **Career:** Beth Israel Hosp, intern res med, 1973-75; UCLA preventive med resident, 1976-78, West Los Angeles VAMC, geriatric med fel, 1978-80; Birmingham VAMC, chief geriatrics sect, 1980-88; UAB/Med Ctr Aging, asst dir, 1980-; Meharry Consortium Geriatric Educ Ctr, dir, 1990-; Meharry Med Col, ctraging, assoc prof, currently; Geriatric Res Educ & Clin Ctr, assoc dire duc & prog eval, currently. **Orgs:** Am Geriatric Soc, 1978-; Geriatric Soc Am, 1978-; AMR Soc Aging, 1978-; Am Pub Health Asn, 1978-; comt mem, Jeff Co Long Term Care Ombudsman Comt, 1982-84; chmn, Vis Nurses Asn, 1983; VNA Med Adv Comt, co-chairperson, 1983-; Mayors CMS Status Women, 1984-87; charter mem, Asn Heads Acad Progs Geriatrics, 1991-; NA Res Task Force Aging, 1992-. **Honors/Awds:** Govenor's Award, ITTG, Govenor G C Wallace, 1984; National Science Foundation Research Award, 1965-68; Geriatric Medicine Academic Award, Nat Inst Aging, 1982-87; Associate Inv Award, W Los Angeles VAMC, 1980. **Home Addr:** 1701 Old Hickory Blvd, Brentwood, TN 37027, **Home Phone:** (615)373-3688. **Business Addr:** Director, Meharry Medical College, 1005 D B Todd Jr Blvd, Nashville, TN 37208, **Business Phone:** (615)327-6862.

SCOTT, VIRGIL M.
Executive. **Career:** Anderson Commun, pres & ceo. *

SCOTT, WERNER FERDINAND
Marketing executive. **Personal:** Born Feb 27, 1957, Pfungstadt, Germany; son of Arthur Jr and Irene Schaffer. **Educ:** New Mexico State Univ, Las Cruces, BBA, 1979. **Career:** Xerox Corp, Albuquerque, sales rep mgr, 1979-82, dist reg mgr, 1982-85; Advantage Mkt Group Inc, founder, pres & ceo, 1985-; Advantage Lifestyle LLC, property owner, currently. **Orgs:** Supporter, United Negro Col Fund, 1988-91; chmn, Dallas Int Sports Comn, 1989-90, bd mem, 1990-91; Nat Asn Advan Colored People, 1990-91; founding mem, Open Doors Found; Academies Excellence; Ctr Study Sports Soc. **Honors/Awds:** Presidents Club Winner, Xerox Corp, 1980-85; Quest for Success Award, Dallas Black Chamber, Morning News, 1991. **Military Serv:** AUS, 1st Lt, 1979-87. **Business Phone:** (972)869-2244.

SCOTT, WESLEY ELLINGTON
Physician. **Personal:** Born Mar 23, 1925, Memphis, TN; married Virginia Smith, Dec 14, 1946; children: Stephany Scott Boyette. **Educ:** Meharry Med Col, MD, 1950. **Career:** Orthop surgeon, 1954-84; pvt pract, currently. **Orgs:** Omega Psi Phi Fraternity, 1950-; Am Acad Orthop Surgeons, 1960-; fel, Am Col Surgeons, 1961-; NAACP, 1969-. **Honors/Awds:** Man of the Year, NAACP, Freeport, NY, 1959. **Special Achievements:** Certified private pilot: single engine-land, single engine-sea, multi-engine-land, helicopter, instrument rating. **Military Serv:** USAF, capt, 1943-46, 1950-53; Asiatic-Pac, Victory Medal, 1946. **Home Addr:** 2614 Princess Lane, Missouri City, TX 77459, **Home Phone:** (281)261-0262. **Business Addr:** Physician, 2614 Princess Lane, Missouri City, TX 77459, **Business Phone:** (281)261-0262.

SCOTT, WILL
Social worker, college teacher. **Career:** Stephen F Austin State Univ, Sch Social Work, prof & social worker, currently. *

SCOTT, WINDIE OLIVIA
Lawyer. **Personal:** Born in Mobile, AL; daughter of Clifford A and Vivian Pugh Scott. **Educ:** Calif Polytech Univ, BA, polit sci, 1974; Univ CA, Juris Dr, 1977. **Career:** Wiley Manuel Bar Asn, pres, 1984; Calif Asn Black Lawyers, bd mem, 1984-85; Centro de Legal-Sacramento, bd mem, 1984-85; State Calif, tax coun III, 1995-, Off State Controller, sr staff coun, 1987-95; Calif State Workforce Investment Bd, chief coun, currently. **Orgs:** State Bar Calif, 1979-; Nat Bar Asn, 1980-; treas, Pan Hellenic Coun, 1982-84; Black Women's Network; City Bar Sacramento, 1984-85; elected mem, County Bar Coun, 1989-92; vpres, Calif Asn Black Lawyers, 1989; pres, Women Lawyers Sacramento, 1989; exec comt, State Bar Conf Dels, 1990-93; chair, Mayor's City Affirmative Action Adv Coun, 1991-94; pres, Alpha Kappa Alpha Soror-

ity, 1992; pres, Sacramento County Bar Asn, 1997. **Honors/Awds:** Pres Award, Wiley Manuel Bar Asn, 1985; Ernest L Robinson Jr Award, McGeorge Black Law Studs Asn, 1985; Outstanding Women Award, Nat Coun Negro Women, 1988; Outstanding Woman of the Year, Gov/Law Sacramento, YWCA, 1990; Unit Award, Wiley Manuel Bar Asn, 1990; Mayor's Community Serv Award, 1995. **Special Achievements:** Sacramento 100 Most Influential Blacks, 1984; 25 Blacks to Watch in 1989, Observer Newspapers, 1989. **Business Addr:** Chief Counsel, California State Workforce Investment Bd, 777 12th St Suite 200, Sacramento, CA 95814, **Business Phone:** (916)324-3425.*

SCOTT-CLAYTON, PATRICIA ANN
Lawyer. **Personal:** Born Oct 6, 1953, Chicago, IL; daughter of Verna Scott and Merle; divorced; children: Robynn. **Educ:** Northwestern Univ, BA, 1975; Georgetown Univ Law Ctr, JD, 1978, ML Tax, 1986. **Career:** Dept Justice, Tax Div, trial atty, 1978-85; IRS, sr atty, 1985-89, employee plans litigation coun, 1989-93, sect chief, employee benefits & exempt orgns, 1991-93; Pension Benefit Guaranty Corp, assoc gen coun, 1993-97, dep gen coun, 1997-. **Orgs:** Secy, Parents Asn, 1993-94; bd dirs, Essential Theatre, 1993-96; bd trustees, Sheridan Sch, 1994-97, chmn, 1996-97; chmn, Pension Benefit Guaranty Corp, 1995; travel coord, 1996-98, Fundraising Comn, chmn, 1997-98, DC Jrs Volleyball Club; parents rep, Sidwell Friends Sch, 1997-99; bd dirs, Peak Performance Volleyball Club & Peak Performance Sports Acad, 1998-99; Wash Univ Parents Coun, 2000-. **Honors/Awds:** Attorneys General's Award, Dept Justice, 1979; Special Achievement Awards, IRS, 1990, 1992, 1993. **Special Achievements:** Author: Tax Qualification of Tax Sheltered Annuities, The Tax Lawyer, Fall 1995. **Home Phone:** (301)434-1825. **Business Addr:** Deputy General Counsel, Pension Benefit Guaranty Corp, Office of General Counsel 1200 K St NW Suite 340, Washington, DC 20005, **Business Phone:** (202)326-4020.

SCOTT-HERON, GIL
Musician, poet, writer. **Personal:** Born Apr 1, 1949, Chicago, IL; son of Giles and Bobbie. **Educ:** Fieldston Sch Ethical Cult, Lincoln Univ, attended 1967; Johns Hopkins Univ, MA, Creative Writing, 1972. **Career:** Poet, musician & author; Johns Hopkins Univ, fel; Creative Writing FedCity Col, Wash, DC, teacher; Midnight Band; Albums: Small Talk at 125th &Lenox, 1970; Pieces of a Man, 1971; Free Will, 1972; Winter in America, 1974; The First Minute of a New Day, 1975; From South Africa to SouthCarolina, 1975; It's Your World (Live), 1976; Bridges, 1977; Secrets,1978; The Mind of Gil Scott-Heron, 1979; 1980, 1980; Real Eyes, 1980;Reflections, 1981; Moving Target, 1982; The Best of Gil Scott-Heron, 1984;The Revolution Will Not Be Televised, 1988; Tales of Gil Scott-Heron & HisAmnesia Express, 1990; Glory: The Gil Scott-Heron Collection, 1990;Minister of Information, 1994; Spirits, 1994; The Gil Scott-HeronCollection Sampler: 1974-75, 1998; Ghetto Style, 1998; Evolution &Flashback: The Very Best of Gil Scott-Heron, 1999; Gil Scott-Heron & Brian Jackson - Messages (Anthology), 2005; The-Count Upcoming & Rising, 2007; Malik & the OG's - Rhythms of the Diaspora, 2009. Books: The Vulture (novel), 1970; Small Talk at 125th & Lenox (poems),1970; The Nigger Factory (novel), 1972; The Mind of Gil Scott-Heron, 1979;So Far, So Good (poems), 1988; Now and Then: The Poems of Gil Scott-Heron, 2001. Films: Black Wax, 1982; Word Up, 2005. **Honors/Awds:** Langston Hughes Creative Writing Award, Lincoln Univ, 1968. **Business Addr:** Writer, Poet, c/o Third World Press, 7822 S Dobson Ave, Chicago, IL 60619, **Business Phone:** (773)651-0700.

SCOTT-JOHNSON, ROBERTA VIRGINIA
Government official, educator. **Personal:** Born in West Virginia; married Jesse; children: Robert Jerome Patterson, Rex Lenear Patterson, Carolyn Marie Patterson & Terrence Jerome. **Educ:** Bluefield Col, BS, bus admin; Univ Mich, MA, guid & couns, 1966; Univ Edinborough, 1979. **Career:** Elkhorn High Sch, WVa, dir com ed; Saginaw City Sch Dist, teacher, counr; Econ Develop Corp, Buena Vista Township, dirship, township trustee, 1978-84, township treasurer. **Honors/Awds:** Outstanding Service Award, Jessie Rouse Sch, 1970-80; Honorary Award, Buena Vista Township, 1980. **Home Addr:** 4636 S Gregory, Saginaw, MI 48601. **Business Addr:** Township Treasurer, Teacher, Buena Vista Char Township, Saginaw City Schools, 1160 S Outer Dr, Saginaw, MI 48601.

SCOTT-WARE, BARBARA ANN (BARBARA ANN WARE)
Activist. **Personal:** Born Feb 17, 1955, Brooklyn, NY; daughter of Marion Bertha James and Dudley Fairfax; married Morris Ware, 1991; children: Michele C Ware & Morris Ware Jr; married Keith Brandon (divorced). **Career:** Lady Di Construct, Lady Di Prod, gen contractor; Citizens Advocate Employ & Housing, ceo, currently. **Orgs:** Asn Gen Contractors, 1985; vpres, NYS, Nat Orgn Women, 1985; Corporate bd mem, Asn Minority Enterprises, 1986; bd chair, Long Island Affirmative Action, 1987; bd mem, Long Island Prepared Recruitment Prog, 1987; bd mem, Alliance Majority & Minority Contractors; New York State Asn Minority Contractors; Long Island Womens Equal Opportunity Coun, 1989; trustee, Roosevelt Pub Libr, 1996. **Honors/Awds:** Outstanding Amongs Blacks, Community Service Award, 1984; Certificate of Appreciation, Long Island Womens Equal Opportunity Coun, 1984; Certificate of Achievement, NYS Dept Energy, 1987; Womens Bus Develop & Savvy Mag, 1987; Essence Mag, 1988; LI Historic Women Award, LI Hist Found, 1997. **Special Achievements:** Founder of Project Alive, lecturer on Business For World National TV, Washigton, DC, 1980, Poet of "So Where Does It All Go," poem published in Europe, 1987, "Hope Is the Enemy of Love," 1989.

SCRANTON, BRENDA A.
Vice president (Organization). **Educ:** Loyola Marymount Univ, BA; Calif State Univ, MA. **Career:** Bronx Community Col, vpres stud develop, 2002-. **Business Phone:** (718)289-5869.*

SCRIBNER, ARTHUR GERALD, JR.
Manager, engineer, chief executive officer. **Personal:** Born Nov 19, 1955, Baltimore, MD; son of Arthur Gerald Scribner Sr and Elizabeth Worrell; children: Lamara Chanelle, Arthur Gerald III & Milton Thomas. **Educ:** Univ Md Baltimore, BA (Magna Cum Laude), 1981, BS (Magna Cum Laude), 1981; Johns Hopkins Univ Sch Eng, MS (Cum Laude), 1987. **Career:** Scribner Consult Inc, pres, 1985; MD Med Labs, pathol asst, 1986; Inner Harbor Sounds Inc, producer, 1986; US Dept Defense, sr syst anal & engr, 1982; A G Scribner & Assocs, pres, 1988; The Consortium Inc, pres & ceo, 1988. **Orgs:** Tenor & soloist Univ MD Chamber, 1978-81; pub rel consult Vivians Fashions NY, 1980-; asst instr, Univ MD, 1980-81; talent coordr, Baltimore Citywide Star Search, 1985-86; vpres, Metropolitan Entertainment Consortium Inc, 1985. **Honors/Awds:** Superior Achievement Award, Inter prof Studies Inst, Univ MD, 1982; Black Engineer of the Year, Nat Security Agency, 1993. **Home Addr:** 6820 Parsons Ave, Gwynn Oak, MD 21207, **Home Phone:** (410)653-1886.

SCRIVENS, JOHN J
Administrator, educator. **Personal:** Born in Tampa, FL. **Educ:** Fla A & M Univ, BS, 1972; Univ Fla, MS, pharm, 1976; Univ S Fla, PhD, pub health, 1994. **Career:** V.A. Hosp, Miami, clin pharmacist; Tampa Gen Hosp, clin coordr; Centro Espanol Hosp, dir pharm; USF Psychiat Ctr Tampa, dir; Veterans Admin Hosp, residency, 1997; Fla A & M Univ, assoc prof & dir, Tampa Pharm Pract div, currently. **Orgs:** Am Pharmaceut Asn; Am Soc Health-Systems Pharmacists; tres, Nat FAMU Pharm Alumni Coun. **Honors/Awds:** Faculty Mentor Nat Role Model Award, 2004; Research and Publication Achievement Award, Asn Black Health-Syst Pharmacists, 2005. **Military Serv:** USAF, 4 yrs. **Business Addr:** Associate Professor, Director, Florida A & M University, College of Pharmacy & Pharmaceutical Sciences, 3500 E Fletcher Ave Suite 133, Tampa, FL 33613.

SCROGGINS, BOBBY
Artist, college teacher. **Personal:** Born in Kansas City, MO. **Educ:** Kans City Art Inst, BFA, 1976; Southern Ill Univ, Edwardsville, MFA, 1980. **Career:** Univ Ky, head ceramics dept, 1990-96, assoc prof, 1996-; Ky Gov Sch Arts, visual art fac. **Orgs:** Dir-at-large, Nat Coun Educ Ceramic Arts, 1993-95; Northwest Acad Arts, Donegal, Northern Ireland, chmn, 2003-04. **Honors/Awds:** First Place Purchase Award, Atlanta Life Ins Co Nat Art Competition. **Special Achievements:** First African American artist to construct a monument in state of Missouri.

SCROGGINS, TRACY
Football player. **Personal:** Born Sep 11, 1969, Checotah, OK. **Educ:** Univ Tulsa. **Career:** Football player (retired); Detroit Lions, defensive end, 1992-2001.

SCRUGGS, BOOKER T., II
Educator, college administrator. **Personal:** Born Oct 2, 1942, Chattanooga, TN; son of Mabel Humphrey and Booker T; married Johnnie Lynn Haslerig, Oct 26, 1968 (divorced); children: Cameroun. **Educ:** Clark Col, BA, 1964; Atlanta Univ, MA, 1966. **Career:** Col Administrator (retired), educator; Howard High Sch, social sci teacher, 1966; Community Action Agency, coordr res & reporting, 1966-70;WNOO Radio, prog moderator, 1973-82; Univ Tenn Chattanooga, asst dir Upward Bound, 1970-91, instr sociol, prog dir, currently, adj fac mem, currently. **Orgs:** Alpha Phi Alpha, Adult Educ Coun; former mem bd, Chattanooga Elec Power Bd, 1975-85; life mem, Nat Asn Advan Colored People; Chattanooga Gospel Orchestra; bd mem, Methodist Student Ctr, Univ Tenn, Chattanooga; chair mem, Wiley Methodist Church; pres, Tenn Asn Spec Prog, 1991-93; vpres, Brainerd High Sch PTA, 1989-90; Chattanooga Clarinet Soc; Maxtiam Trio; Spectrum Jazz Ban; Bethlehem-Wiley United Methodist Church. **Honors/Awds:** Jaycees Presidential Award Honor, 1974; Man of the Year, Alpha Phi Alpha, 1986; M.L. King, Jr. Birthday Celebration Community Service Award. **Special Achievements:** TV host, public affairs producer: "Point of View"; Recorded Gospel Albums:To God Be The Glory, Let Not Your Heart Be Troubled, My Tribute, Salute tothe Duke; Recorded Live Concert: "A Musical Garden". **Business Addr:** Sociology Instructor, University of Tennessee, 213 Race Hall 615 McCallie Ave, Chattanooga, TN 37403, **Business Phone:** (423)755-4691.

SCRUGGS, CLEORAH J.
Educator. **Personal:** Born Aug 20, 1948, Akron, OH; daughter of Cleophus and Deborah Scruggs. **Educ:** Univ Akron, Ohio, BA, elem educ, 1970, MA, elem educ, 1977, admin cert, 1984. **Career:** Educator (Retired); Flint Bd Educ, instr, 1970-2000; GED instr, 1974; Charles Harrison Mason Bible Col, instr, 1975-76; Mott Adult High Sch, Flint, Mich, workshop presenter; Scruggs & Assoc Educ Consulting Serv, founder. **Orgs:** United Teachers Flint, 1987-, precinct delegate, 1990, 1994; Mich Educ Asn; Nat Educ Assoc; Nat Alliance Black Sch Educ; Silver Soror, Sorority Inc; Flint Community Schs, Supt's Advisory Coun Way; United Negro Col Fund; Univ Akron, Alumni Asn; Nat Asn Advan Colored People. **Honors/Awds:** Comm Serv Award, Humane Soc, McCree Theater, Religious/Comm Orgn, 1975,1988, 1990; Identification of Beginning Teachers Problems, Univ Akron,1977; Nominee Teacher of the Year, 1987; Excellence Award, MEA IPD, Commitment Educ & Diversity, 1993; Multicultural Diversity Award, MEA Concerns Comm, 1994; Social Studies Educator of the Year, Mich Coun for the Social Studies, 1995; Dr Martin Luther King Jr Award, NEA, 2000; Childrens Champion Award, Priority Children, 2001; Alumni Award, Univ Akron, 2002; Int Understanding Award, MEA, 2002. **Home Addr:** 1963 Laurel Oak Dr, Flint, MI 48507-6038.

SCRUGGS, FREDRO. See STARR, FREDRO.

SCRUGGS, PROF. OTEY MATTHEW
Educator. **Personal:** Born Jun 29, 1929, Vallejo, CA; son of Otey and Maude; married Barbara Fitzgerald; children: Jeffrey. **Educ:** Univ Calif, Santa Barbara, BA, 1951; Harvard Univ, MA, 1952, PhD, 1958. **Career:** Univ Calif, Santa Barbara, from instr to assoc prof, 1957-69; Syracuse Univ, prof, hist, 1969-94, chair, dept hist, 1986-90, emer, 1994-. **Orgs:** Asn Study Afro Am Life & Hist; ed Bd, Afro-Am NY Life & Hist 1977-; Orgn Am Historians; bd dir, Onondaga Historical Asn, 1988-92. **Honors/Awds:** Chancellor's Citation for Exceptional Academic Achievement, Syracuse Univ. **Military Serv:** USNR, 1948-57. **Home Addr:** 5125 5th Ave Apt A3, Pittsburgh, PA 15232, **Home Phone:** (412)683-7459. **Business Addr:** Professor Emeritus, Syracuse University, Department of History, 145 Eggers Hall, Syracuse, NY 13244-1020.

SCRUGGS, SYLVIA ANN
Educator, social worker. **Personal:** Born Jun 18, 1951, Akron, OH; daughter of Cleophus and Deborah. **Educ:** Univ Akron, BS, 1976; Case Western Res Univ, MS, 1990. **Career:** Univ Akron, clerk typist, 1974-77; Akron Children's Medical Ctr, ward secy 1977-78; Akron Urban League, edur, 1978-82; Hawkins Skill Ctr, edur, 1983; Depart Human Services, income maint III, 1984-. **Orgs:** Counrs asst South High Sch, 1969; Big Sister & Tutor Univ Akron, 1970; NAACP, 1981-82; precinct comt Community Third Ward, 1981; youth leader, Youth Motivation Task Force 1982; Nat Asn Social Workers, 19901 vol, Project Learn, 1990; vol, Battered Women's Shelter, 1991. **Home Addr:** 1066 Orlando Ave, Akron, OH 44320. **Business Addr:** Income Maintenance III, Department of Human Services, 47 N Main St, Akron, OH 44308.

SCRUGGS-LEFTWICH, YVONNE (YVONNE SCRUGGS-PERRY)
Executive, educator, advocate. **Personal:** Born Jun 24, 1933, Niagara Falls, NY; married Edward V Jr; children: Cathryn D Perry, Rebecca S Perry-Glickstein, Tienne Davis & Edward III. **Educ:** NC Cent Univ, BA, polit sci, 1955; Free Univ Berlin, German Hochschule fur Politik, cert, 1956; Univ Minnesota, MAPA, 1958; Univ Penn, PhD. **Career:** Fullbright fel, Germany, 1952-53; Univ Penn, Wharton Schs HRC, fac, 1970-74; Howard Univ, Dept City & Regional Planning, prof, 1974-77, Presidents Urban & Regional Policy Group, exec, 1977-78, Dept Housing & Urban Develop, Community Planning & Develop, dep asst secy, 1977-79, prof, 1979-81; NY State Div Housing & Community Renewal, regional dir, 1981-82; NY State Div Housing & Community Renewal, staff, 1982-85; YEL Corp, CSC Inc & Harlem USA Inc, chief operating officer, & bd chair, 1984-90; City Philadelphia, dep mayor, 1985-87; Pryor, Govan, Counts & Co Inc, sr consulting vpres, 1987-88; George Washington Univ, prof, 1987-99; Urban Policy Inst & Nat Policy Inst, Joint Ctr Polit & Econ Studies, dir, 1991-96; Black Leadership Forum Inc, exec dir & chief operating officer, 1996-2005; Nat Labor Col, prof, 2005-. **Orgs:** Bd mem, World Affairs Coun, 1970-73; Philadelphia Coun Community Advan, 1970-74; vpres, Penn Housing Fin Corp, 1974; trustee, Cornerstone Equity Adv; Nat Coun Negro Women; Nat Asn Advan Colored People; Greater Washington Urban League; vpres & trustee, Milton S Eisenhower Found; pres, Women Distinction; Nat Polit Cong Black Women; founding pres, Geneva B Scruggs Community Health Ctr; Am Inst Planners; comnr, Mobile Homes Community; vpres, Asn Collegiate Schs Planning. **Honors/Awds:** SAIS Scholar, Johns Hopkins Univ, 1956-57; Elks Oratorical Scholar, 1951-55; Howard University Graduate Student Council Award, Grad Educators, 1975; Leadership Award, Nat Coun Negro Women, 1975; Outstanding Contribution to Graduate Education, Howard Univ, 1975; Faculty Research Award, Howard Univ, 1976; Outstanding Achievement Award, Dept Housing & Urban Develop, Howard Univ, 1979; Life and Culture of the Black Community Award, Howard Univ Inst Urban Affairs & Res, 1980; Diana Donald Award, Am Inst Physics. **Special Achievements:** First African American female elected speaker of assembly of New York State Youth-in-Government; First Fulbright fellow from Buffalo, NY; First Fulbright fellow from North Carolina Central Univ; First African American Fulbright fellow from the State of North

Carolina; First African American appointed as housing commissioner for New York State; Bronze Jr Olympic medalist; Author over 100 professional and journal articles and books. **Business Phone:** (301)431-5452.

SCRUGGS-PERRY, YVONNE. See SCRUGGS-LEFTWICH, YVONNE.

SCURLOCK, MICHAEL LEE (MIKE SCURLOCK)
Football player, football coach. **Personal:** Born Feb 26, 1972, Tucson, AZ; married Michaela; children: 3. **Educ:** Univ Ariz, BA. **Career:** Football player (retired), Football coach; St Louis Rams, defensive back, 1995-98; Carolina Panthers, 1999; Westminster Catawba Christian Schs, head coach, athletic dir, currently. **Honors/Awds:** Ram Attitude Award, 1998. **Business Addr:** Athletic Director, Westminster Catawba Christian School, Catawba Campus 2650 India Hook Rd, Rock Hill, SC 29732, **Business Phone:** (803)366-4119.

SCURLOCK, MIKE. See SCURLOCK, MICHAEL LEE.

SCURRY, FRED L
Lawyer. **Personal:** Born Dec 16, 1942, London, OH; divorced; children: Jeriah. **Educ:** Central State Univ, BS, 1966; Howard Univ Law Sch, JD, 1969. **Career:** Clarence J Brown MC, staff, 1967-69; IRS, 1972-74; Pvt prac, atty, 1974-; London, city solic, 1976-79. **Orgs:** Columbus OH Bar Asn; Madison Co Bar Asn; Ohio State Bar Asn. **Military Serv:** AUS, capt, 1970-72. **Business Addr:** Lawyer, 229 Toland St, London, OH 43140, **Business Phone:** (740)852-4133.

SEA, HOUSTON. See HOUSTON, SEAWADON L.

SEABROOK, REV. BRADLEY MAURICE
Clergy. **Personal:** Born Mar 12, 1928, Savannah, GA; son of Bradley and Katie Lue Carpenter; married Minnie Lucile Long, May 14, 1951; children: Criss, Lilla, Tina & Lisa. **Educ:** Fla Int Univ, Miami, FL, BT, indust technol, 1979. **Career:** Clergy (Retired); Aircraft Engine Mechanic, USAF, Eglin AFB, FL, 1955-58, 1961-68; Naval Aviation Engineering Serv Unit, Philadelphia, PA, 1968-83. **Orgs:** Past commander, Am Post 193 Pensacola, FL, 1956-58; sir knight, 4th Degree, Deluwa Assembly, 1971; life mem, Nat Asn Advan Colored People, 1975; Knights Columbus-5658, Past Grand Knight, 1975-76; dir, Off Black Cath Ministry, 1986-2003. **Honors/Awds:** Knight of the Year, Knights of Columbus Coun-5658, 1974-75; Sustained Superior Performance Award, Dept Navy, NAESU, 1983; Ordination to the Diaconate, Diocese Pensacola-Tallahassee, 1980; George Wash Honor Medal, 1995; Community Volunteer Award, Nat Asn Advan Colored People Pensacola Branch, 1995. **Military Serv:** USN, 1946-48; USAF, 1951-55. **Home Addr:** PO Box 702, Cantonment, FL 32533.

SEABROOK, JULIETTE THERESA (TERRY SEABROOK)
Real estate agent, business owner. **Personal:** Born Jan 27, 1954, Charleston, SC; daughter of Luther and Eva Wilson; children: Gerren. **Educ:** Howard Univ, BA (Cum laude), 1975; Univ Md Law Sch, JD, 1978. **Career:** US Dept Health & Human Servs, staff atty, 1979-85; The Space Co, owner & broker-in-charge, 1986-. **Orgs:** Charleston County Planning Bd, 1993-96; adv bd, First Union Nat Bank, 1994-; adv bd, Charleston County Human Servs Comn, 1994-; adv bd, Charleston Local Citywide Develop Corporation, 1994-95;adv bd, The Community Found, 1995. **Honors/Awds:** The Space Co, Black Enterprise Mag, Nov, 2006. **Special Achievements:** The Space Company featured in Black Enterprise Magazine November, 2006. **Home Addr:** 220 3rd Ave, Charleston, SC 29403, **Home Phone:** (843)577-6428. **Business Addr:** Owner, Real Estate Broker, The Space Company, 82 1/2 Spring St, Charleston, SC 29403, **Business Phone:** (843)577-2676.

SEABROOK, TERRY. See SEABROOK, JULIETTE THERESA.

SEABROOKS, NETTIE HARRIS
Government official, executive. **Personal:** Born Feb 22, 1934, Mount Clemens, MI; daughter of Ivan Joseph and Katherine Marshall Davis Harris; children: Victoria D & Franklyn E. **Educ:** Marygrove Col, BS, chem; Univ Mich, MLS. **Career:** Detroit Pub Libr, Technol Dept, chem librn; Tenn State Univ, instr; Gen Motors, Pub Rels Staff Libr, librn, Corp Res Opers, mgr, Pub Affairs Info Servs, dir, GM Chev-Pont, Canada Group, dir govt & civic affairs, GM N Am Passenger Car Platforms, dir govt rels; City Detroit, dep mayor, chief admin officer, 1994-97, chief operating officer & chief of staff, 1998; Detroit Inst Arts, sr assoc officer to dir, chief operating officer, 2002-. **Orgs:** Bd mem, Mus African-Am Hist; Detroit Inst Arts Friends African & African-Am Art; Detroit Med Ctr; Karmanos Cancer Inst; Detroit Med Ctr. **Honors/Awds:** Hon DHL, Marygrove Col, 1995; Hon DHL, Univ Detroit, Mercy. **Business Addr:** Chief Operating Officer, Detroit Institute of Arts, 5200 Woodward Ave, Detroit, MI 48202, **Business Phone:** (313)833-4005.

SEABROOKS-EDWARDS, MARILYN S.
Government official. **Personal:** Born Mar 3, 1955, Allendale, SC; married Ronald Burke Edwards. **Educ:** Univ SC Saik Regional Campus, attended 1975; Ga Southern Col, AB, 1977; US Dept Agr, attended 1984; Baruch Col/City Univ NY, MPA, 1984. **Career:** City Savannah Housing Dept, spec proj coordr, 1981-83, prog coordr, 1984-85; Dept Human Serv, spec asst to the dir, 1983-84, prog analyst, 1985-; Exec Office of the Mayor Office of the Secy of the DC, chief admin officer, 1987, chief technol officer, currently. **Orgs:** Secretary WVGS Radio Board Georgia So College 1976 & 1977; social studies teacher Jenkins County School System 1977-78; financial counselor City of Savannah Housing Department 1978-81; instructor YMCA 1983; memship YMCA 1983-85; memship Washing Urban League 1984-85; memship Natl Forum for Black Public Admin 1984-85; memship Intl City Management Assn 1984-85; sec Wash DC Chap natl Forum for Black Public Admin; bd mem Notary Public Bd for the Dist of Columbia; hearings compliance officer Exec Office of the Mayor. **Honors/Awds:** John Phillip Sousa Award, 1973; Psi Alpha Theta, Ga Southern Col, 1975-77; Outstanding Young Women of Am, 1982-83; Nat Urban Fel, 1983-84. **Business Phone:** (202)727-2277.

SEALE, BOBBY
Actor, activist. **Personal:** Born Oct 22, 1936, Dallas, TX; married Artie; children: Malik Kkrumah Stagolee. **Educ:** Merritt Col, attended. **Career:** Black Panther Party for Self-Defense, chmn, former minister of info & co-founder, 1966-74; Temple Univ, teacher; Advocates Scene, founder, 1974-; Films: Rude Awakening, actor, 1989; Malcolm X, actor, 1992; A Lonely Rage, actor, 2006; Reach Cinema Prod, creator & dir, currently. **Orgs:** Afro-Am Asn. **Special Achievements:** Author: Seize the Time: The Story of the Black Panther Party and Huey P Newton, Random House, 1970; A Lonely Rage: The Autobiography of Bobby Seale, 1978; Barbeque with Bobby, 1987. **Military Serv:** USAF, 3 yrs. **Business Addr:** Creator, Director, Reach Cinema Productions Inc., PO Box 26712, Elkins Pk, PA 19027.

SEALE, SAMUEL RICARDO
Football player, scout. **Personal:** Born Oct 6, 1962, Barbados; married Elizabeth; children: Sam Jr, Samir & Shi-Ann. **Educ:** Western State Col. **Career:** Football player (retired), scout; Los Angeles Raiders, 1984-87, 1992; San Diego Chargers, cornerback, 1988-91; Los Angeles Rams, cornerback, 1993; Green Bay Packers, col scout, 1995-. **Honors/Awds:** Western State Col Hall of Fame, 2002. **Business Addr:** College Scout, Green Bay Packers, Lambeau Field Atrium 1265 Lombardi Ave, PO Box 10628, Green Bay, WI 54304, **Business Phone:** (920)569-7500.

SEALLS, ALAN RAY
Meteorologist, educator. **Personal:** Born in New Rochelle, NY; son of Albert and Josephine Reese; married. **Educ:** Cornell Univ, Ithaca, NY, BS, 1985; Fla State Univ, Tallahassee, FL, MS, 1987; Am Meteorol Soc, cert; Nat Weather Asn, cert. **Career:** Fla State Univ, Tallahassee, FL, grad asst, 1985-87; WALB-TV, Albany, GA, meteorologist, 1987-88; WTMJ Inc, Milwaukee, WI, meteorologist, 1988-92; Columbia Col, prof meteorol; WGN-TV, meteorologist; WMAQ-TV, meteorologist; Univ S Ala, instructor meteorol; WKRG-TV, chief meteorologist, currently. **Orgs:** Am Meteorol Soc, 1984-; Nat Weather Asn, 1987-; Nat Asn Black Journalists, 1989-; Nat Asn Advan Colored People, 1989-. **Honors/Awds:** Distinguished Man of the Year, 1990; Black Achiever, Metrop Young Men's Christian Asn, Milwaukee, 1990-91; Award for Excellence, Mobile Press Club, 2 years; Best Weather Anchor, Ala Asn Press Broadcasters Asn, 2001, 2003. **Special Achievements:** Nominee for an Emmy in 2003 and in 2007. **Business Addr:** Chief Meteorologist, WKRG-TV, 555 Broadcast Dr, Mobile, AL 36606.

SEALS, GEORGE E.
Executive. **Personal:** Born Oct 2, 1942, Higginsville, MO; married Cecelia McClellean. **Educ:** Univ MO. **Career:** Trader, Chicago, bd of trade; WA Redskins, Chicago Bears, & KC Chiefs, former football player; Chicago Bd Options Exchange Bd. **Orgs:** Better Boys Found; Chicago PUSH; bd of regents Daniel Hale Williams Univ 1967; All Pro Team. **Business Phone:** (312)435-3500.

SEALS, GERALD
Government official, administrator. **Personal:** Born Sep 22, 1953, Columbia, SC; son of Janet Kennerly; married Carolyn; children: Gerald II & Jelani-Akil; married Kanet. **Educ:** Univ SC, BA, 1975; Univ Denver, MA, 1976; Southern Ill Univ, Carbondale, MS, ABT, 1978. **Career:** Carbondale City, IL, admin intern, 1977-78; Village Glen Ellyn IL, asst to village admin, 1978-81; Village Glendale Heights, from asst village mgr to village mgr, 1981-84; Springfield City, from asst city mgr to city mgr, 1984-88; Corvallis City, city mgr, 1988; Greenville County, SC, county adminr. **Orgs:** Vice chmn bd, Intergovt Risk Mgt, 1982-83; chmn DuPage, Reg IV Sub-Region Regionalization Comn, 1982-84; chmn bd, Intergovt Risk Mgt Agency, 1983-84; bd mem, Springfield Civic Theatre, 1985-88; bd mem, Springfield OIC 1985-; bd dir, Clark County Transp Coordinating Comn, 1985-88; State Ore Structural Code Adv Bd, 1988-; Corvallis/Benton County United Way, 1989-; bd mem, Nat Forum for Black Pub Adminr, 1989-. **Honors/Awds:** Academy Fellowship, Univ Denver, 1975-76; Academy Fellowship, Southern Ill Univ, 1976-78; Image Award, Fred Hampton Scholarship Fund, 1983; Certificate of Conformance, Govt Finance Officers Asn, 1984; A Face of 1984 Article Springfield News Sun, 1984. **Home Addr:** 230 NE Powderhorn Dr, Corvallis, OR 97330.

SEALS, MAXINE LANE
School administrator, executive. **Personal:** Born in Trinity, TX; married Frank Seals; children: Thaddeus & Cedric. **Educ:** Houston Community Col, attended; Tex Southern Univ, attended. **Career:** Southwestern Bell Telephone Co, mgr; Gulf Coast Sch Bd, bd dirs, 1984-85; N Forest Independent Sch Dist Sch Bd, mem, currently; Continental Airlines, reservation group sales, currently; North Forest Independent Sch Dist, bd, 1994-2007. **Orgs:** Fontaine Scenic Woods Civic Club; pres, Tex Caucus Black Sch Bd Mems, 1984-85; dir, Gulf Coast Sch Bd Asn, currently; N Forest Bd; life mem, Nat Asn Advan Colored People; mem bd dir, Northeast Young Men Christian Asn; bd officer, Settegast Health Clinic Coun; Fontaine Scenic Woods Civic Club. **Honors/Awds:** Hon membership, Order Eastern Star, Starlight Grand Chap. **Business Addr:** Sales Agent, 5106 Nolridge, Houston, TX 77016, **Business Phone:** (713)633-5125.

SEALS, RAYMOND BERNARD
Football player, football coach. **Personal:** Born Jun 17, 1965, Syracuse, NY; married Jamesetta (deceased). **Career:** Football player (retired), coach; Tampa Bay Buccaneers, defensive end, 1989-93; Pittsburgh Steelers,1994-96; Carolina Panthers, 1997; Madison High Sch, coach, currently. **Honors/Awds:** High School Football Coach of the Year, National Football League, 2009.

SEALS, RUPERT GRANT
School administrator, educator. **Personal:** Born Aug 6, 1932, Shelbyville, KY; married Georgetta Angela Lynem; children: Rupert La Wendell, Rori LaRele, Regan Wayne & LaRita Angela. **Educ:** Fla Agr & Tech Univ, BS, hon, 1953; Univ Kent, MS, 1956; Wash State Univ, PhD, 1960. **Career:** Fla Agr & Tech Univ, instr dairy, 1954-55, dean prof sch agr & home econ, 1969-74, int prog, 1989-94; Wash State Univ, res asst dairy mfg, 1955-59; Tenn State Univ, asso prof dairy chem biochem, 1959-64; Iowa State Univ, res assoc food tech, 1964-66, asst prof food tech, 1966-69; USDA, coordrspec prog SEA/CR, 1974-76; Col Agr Univ Nev, Reno, assoc dean, 1976; Univ Nev, Reno, prof, biochem, 1982-87, prof emer, 1987-; Univ Ariz, Pine Bluff, interim dir develop, 1988-89. **Orgs:** Alpha Kappa Mu Honor Soc Fla Agr & Mech Univ, 1951; Sigma Xi Wash State Univ, 1958; chmn, Am Fair Housing Bd Am, IA, 1967-69; pres, Men First Methodological Church, IA, 1967-68; Expert state comt policy, NASULGC, 1971-73; Overseas liaison com Am Counc Educ, Wash, DC, 1971-77; dir, FAMU Agr Res & Educ Ctr, Inst Food & Agr Sci Univ Fla, 1972-74; Alpha Phi Alpha; Gamma Sigma Delta Honor Soc, 1979; Alpha Zeta Honor Soc, 1979. **Honors/Awds:** Named Distinguished Alumnus, Fla Agr & Mech Univ, 2000; Named Distinguished Graduate, Wash State Univ, 2003; Lifetime Achievement Award, Nat Asn Advan Colored People, 2008. **Special Achievements:** Published numerous articles. **Military Serv:** USAR, e-6, 8yrs. **Business Addr:** Professor Emeritus, University of Nevada, 1664 N Va St, Reno, NV 89557, **Business Phone:** (775)784-1110.

SEALS, THEODORE HOLLIS
Journalist. **Personal:** Born Oct 26, 1950, Chicago, IL; son of Jack H and Costello C. **Educ:** Yale Univ, BA, 1973. **Career:** Chicago Courier, ed writer, 1969-73, assoc ed, 1973-74; Chicago Sun-Times, reporter, 1974-78; C-BREM Commun Corp, corp secy, 1983-, sr ed, currently. **Orgs:** Monitor, Comt Decent Unbiased Campaign Tactics, 1987; 6th Ward Econ Develop Comt; Block Club, pres, 1994-98; Community Policing Strategy Movement. **Special Achievements:** Editor, Evelyn, Vantage Press, 1995; author, The Discovery, Godfrey, The Demon Killer; freelance writer, work has appeared in Chicago Crusader, Chicago Defender, Chicago Tribune, Heritage, newsletter of American Jewish Committee. **Home Addr:** 7228 S Rhodes Ave, Chicago, IL 60619. **Business Addr:** Corporate Secretary, Senior Editor, C-BREM Communications Corp, 7228 S Rhodes Ave, Chicago, IL 60619-1704, **Business Phone:** (773)783-5833.

SEALY, JOAN RICE
Physician. **Personal:** Born Apr 23, 1942, Philadelphia, PA; daughter of John K Rice Jr and L Beverly Daniels Rice; divorced; children: Desa, Denice. **Educ:** Univ Chicago, BA, 1964; George Wash Univ, MD, 1968. **Career:** Wash Hosp Ctr, internship, 1968-69; Yale Univ Med Ctr, res psychiatric, 1969-72; pvt pract, psychiatrist; George Wash Univ Med Sch, assoc clin prof, currently; Providence Hosp, psychiatrist. **Orgs:** Am Psychiatric Asn; Wash Psychiatric Soc; DC Med Soc. **Business Phone:** (202)994-2987.

SEAMS, FRANCINE SWANN
Entertainer, business owner. **Personal:** Born Sep 15, 1947, Ronceverte, WV; daughter of John Calvin Sr and Virginia Caroline; married Michael Hugh, Dec 18, 1971; children: Scott Calvin & Coy Jvon. **Educ:** WVa State Col, 1967; Marshall Univ, 1976. **Career:** C&P Tel Co, serv supvr, 1970-77; Diamond State Tel, mkt advr, 1977-83;AT&T Info Systs, supvr, 1983-85; Aerobicize, co-owner, educ dir, 1983-87; Fitness Specialists, dir educ, 1988-

92; State Delaware, telecommunications consult, 1986-; Christina Sch Dist, adult continuing educ, fitness, 1987-; Body Seams, Fitness Specialists, owner, dir, 1987-. **Orgs:** Gold certified mem, Am Coun Exercise, 1986-; educ comt, Gov's Coun Lifestyles & Fitness, appointee, 1989-; educ comt, Gov's Coun Drug Abuse,appointee, 1989-; solicitor & presenter, Am Heart Asn Dance for Heart,1989-; chair, IDEA, Asn Fitness Prof, Task Force AFA Fitness Participation, 1990-; chair, City Hope Nat Workouts, Delaware Workouts,1992-; planner & presenter; United Cerebral Palsy Workouts, 1992-. **Honors/Awds:** Gold Certification, Am Coun Exercise, 1986; Avia Outstanding Achievers,Avia Outstanding Professional Achievement Award, 1987; Randal, winner's cup, over 40 cycle racers, 1990; Educator Honor Roll, Christina Sch Dist, Bd Educ, 1992. **Special Achievements:** Developed new exercise technique: board bounding, 1990; wrote, 40-hour Fitness Instructor Course, 1990; founded IDEA Task Force on AFA Fitness Participation, 1990; wrote ", An Instructor's Guide to Board Bounding", 1991; developed data and delivered, "Black, Bold, Beautiful-Make it Fit,"series, 1992. **Business Addr:** Owner, Body Seams The Fitness Specialists, 237 Crystal Ct, Newark, DE 19713, **Business Phone:** (302)368-7721.*

SEARCY, LEON, JR.
Football player, football coach. **Personal:** Born Dec 21, 1969, Washington, DC; married Joycelyn; children: Malika-Maya & Kenya Imani. **Educ:** Univ Miami, FL, BS, sociol, 1992. **Career:** Football player (retired), Football coach; Pittsburgh Steelers, offensive tackle, 1992-95; Jacksonville Jaguars, 1996-2000; Baltimore Ravens, 2001; Miami Dolphins, 2002; Fla Int Univ, offensive line asst coach, 2004-06. **Orgs:** Founder, Leon Searcy Jr Found; spokesman, Kidney Found; Jacksonville Bone Marrow Donor Registry. **Honors/Awds:** First-team All-America honors, Football Writers Asn Am; second-team All-American, The Sporting News, 1991.

SEARCY, LILLIE
Executive director. **Educ:** Lesley Col, grad. **Career:** Mattopan Family Serv Ctr, exec dir, currently. **Orgs:** Mattapan Community Develop Corp; bd mem, Blue Hill Ave Coalition; Mattapan Bd Trade; Mattapan Re-Zoning Adv Comm; Action Boston Community Develop Inc. **Business Phone:** (617)298-2045.

SEARS, COREY (COREY ALEXANDER SEARS)
Football player. **Personal:** Born Apr 15, 1973, San Antonio, TX. **Educ:** Miss State Univ. **Career:** Football player (Retired); St Louis Rams, defensive tackle, 1998; Arizona Cardinals, 1999-2000; Houston Texans, 2002-04.

SEARS, COREY ALEXANDER. See SEARS, COREY.

SEATON, SANDRA CECELIA
Educator, playwright. **Personal:** Born Sep 10, 1944, Columbia, TN; daughter of Albert S Browne and Hattye Evans Harris; married James, Nov 9, 1965; children: Ann, James Jr, Amanda & Jeremy. **Educ:** Univ Ill, BA, 1971; Mich State Univ, MS, creative writing, 1989. **Career:** Author, plays: The Bridge Party, 1998; The Will, 1999; Do You Like Philip Roth?, 2001; Room & Board, 2002; Sally, 2003; Libretto for Song Cycle by Composer William Bolcom: From the Diary of Sally Hemings, 2001; Cent Mich Univ, prof english, 1990-2004. **Orgs:** Dramatist's Guild; BMI; Society Study Midwestern Lit; Theater Commun Group; Asn Fac & Staff Color; MI Education Asn; Nat Education Asn; African Am Bridge Club. **Honors/Awds:** Theodore Ward Playwriting Prize for NY Works by African-American Playwrights, for The Bridge Party, 1989; Educator of the Year, Phi Delta Kappa, 1993; Kellogg Found Research Grant, 1994; Consultant Libr Congress, 1996-96; Writer-in-Residence, Hedgebrook, 1997, Dorset Writers Colony, 1998; Ragdale, 2002; Yaddo, 2002; New York State Writers Inst, 2003. **Special Achievements:** numerous scholarly publications.

SEATON, DR. SHIRLEY SMITH
School administrator, educator. **Personal:** Born in Cleveland, OH; daughter of Kibble Clarence Smith and Cecil Stone Smith Wright; married Lawrence Seaton, Oct 2, 1965; children: Eric Dean. **Educ:** Howard Univ, Wash, DC, BA, 1947, MA, 1948; Case Western Res Univ, Cleveland, OH, MA, 1956; Inst Universitario di Studi Europei, Turin, Italy, cert, adv study, 1959; Univ Akron, Akron, OH, PhD, 1981; Beijing Normal Univ, Beijing, China, 1982; post doctorate. **Career:** Cleveland Bd Educ, teacher, 1950-58, asst prin, 1959-65, prin, 1966-76; WEWS-TV, Cleveland, OH, teacher, 1963-67; US Govt, Dept Educ, educ specialist, 1965; Cleveland State Univ, adj prof, 1977-85; Basics & Beyond Educ Consults, dir; John Carroll Univ, liason, community affairs, 2004-06. **Orgs:** Nat Alliance Black Sch Edur; Nat Coun Social Studies; Nat Asn Sec Sch Principals; Asn Supervision & Curric Develop; pres, Metrop Cleveland Alliance Black School Educr, 1981-; Coalition 100 Black Women, 1991-; Phi Delta Kappa 1979-; Fulbright Asn; bd mem, Western Res Hist Soc; bd mem, Retired & Sr Vol Prog; Am Asn Univ Women. **Honors/Awds:** Fulbright grant to Italy, 1959, China, 1982; Martin Luther King Outstanding Educator Award, 1989; Outstanding Educator Awards, Cleveland City Coun & Ohio State Legis; Martin Luther King Humanitarian Award, Governor Ohio, 1992. **Home Addr:** 13825 Cedar Rd 102, Cleveland Heights, OH 44118. **Business Addr:** Liason Community Affairs, John Carroll University, 20700 N Pk Blvd, University Heights, OH 44118, **Business Phone:** (216)397-1604.

SEAVERS, CLARENCE W.
Executive, army officer. **Personal:** Born Aug 15, 1919, Sandusky, OH; married Juanita Jackson (died 1999). **Educ:** Bowling Green Extension, Univ HI. **Career:** exec (retired); Erie Co Health Dist, bd mem, beginning, 1968; Erie Huron CAC, treas; Erie County Bd Elections, bd mem. **Orgs:** OH Off Consumers Coun, 1989; trustee, Providence Hosp, 1989; trustee, YMCA, 1989; LEADS, 1984; chmn, Goodwill Industries, 1984; chmn, Youth Advisory Comn, 1985; Downtown Merchants Inc, 1986; Chamber Com, 1987; trustee, Stein Hospice Inc, 1992; bd mem, Second Harvest Inc, 1993; bd mem, Black Culture Awareness; bd mem, Bayshore Counseling Serv, 2001; trustee, Firelands Regional Medical Ctr, 2002; The Rotary found Rotary Int, 2003; life time mem, NCP; Sandusky Medical Col Ohio Area health educ Ctr, 2003; St. Stephen's AME; bd mem, Stein Hospice; Am Legion. **Honors/Awds:** Outstanding Citizen's Award, State Ohio, 1983; Community Service Award, Progress Lodge, 1985; Gold Award, United Way, 1989; OH Veteran's Hall of Fame, 2000; Paul Harris fellow; Good Conduct Medal, 1943. **Military Serv:** AUS, tech, sgt, 1943; Asiatic Pacific Medal, 1944. *

SEAY, DAWN CHRISTINE
Sales manager. **Personal:** Born Jan 23, 1964, Washington, DC; daughter of Ewart and Marjorie Russell; married Geoffrey V Seay, Oct 11, 1989; children: Alexandra & Ashton. **Educ:** Univ Cent Fla, BA, jour, 1986. **Career:** Wash Hilton & Towers, guest serv, 1986-87; hospity Parteners, sales mgr, 1987-89; Philadelphia Hilton & Towers, nat sales mgr, 1989-93; Philadelphia Conven Bur, conven sales, 1993-, dir, currently. **Orgs:** Assoc mem, Nat Coalition of Black Meetings Planners, 1989-; bd mem, Hospitality Sales & Mkt Asn, chapter, 1990-93; chair educ comm, Multicult Affairs Cong, 1994-. **Home Phone:** (215)763-0439. **Business Addr:** Director, Philadelphia Convention & Visitors Bureau, 1515 Market St Suite 2020, Philadelphia, PA 19102, **Business Phone:** (215)636-4401.

SEAY, NORMAN R
School administrator. **Personal:** Born Feb 18, 1932, St Louis, MO. **Educ:** Stowe Teachers Col, BA, 1954; Lincoln Univ, MEduc, 1966. **Career:** Work-Study Coord St Louis Bd Educ, teacher, 1954-65; Dist OEO Officers, dir, 1965-67; Concentrated Employ Prog, dir, 1967-70; Dept Health, Educ & Welfare, equal employ opportunity specialist; Social Serv, dep gen mgr, 1970-71, proj dir, 1971-73; Univ Mo, Retirees Asn, Off Equal Opportunity, bd dir, 2006-. **Orgs:** Co-chair, Racial Polarization Task Force, 1988-; co-chair & vpres, Educ Adv Comt, 1989-; Bd Adult Welfare Serv; exec bd, MO Asn Soc Welfare; Pub Improv Bond Issue Screening Comt; chmn bd dirs, Yeatman-Cent City Foods Inc; Patrolman CC Smith's C Educ Trust Fund Comt. **Honors/Awds:** Distinguished Citizen Award, St Louis Argus Newspaper, 1974; Most Distinguished Alumni Award, Harris-Stowe State Col, 1989; Outstanding Community Service, Gamma Omega Chap, Alpha Kappa Alpha; Outstanding Service, Dist St Louis Black Police Asn; Valiant Leadership, Alpha Zeta Chap Iota Phi Lambda Sor Inc; Cert Achievement United Front Cairo, IL; Outstanding Aid Law Enforcement, St Louis Police Dept; Community Service Award, St Louis CORE; Outstanding Community Service, Northside Church Seventh-Day Adventists; Outstanding Civic Work, True Light Baptist Church; Merit Service Award, HDC Credit Union. **Military Serv:** AUS, 1955-57. **Home Addr:** 3032 James Cool Papa Bell Ave, Saint Louis, MO 63106, **Home Phone:** (314)533-2635. **Business Addr:** Board of Director, University of Missouri, Retirees Association Office of Equal Opportunity, 1 Univ Blvd, Saint Louis, MO 63121-4400, **Business Phone:** (314)516-5000.

SEBHATU, DR. MESGUN
Educator. **Personal:** Born Jan 6, 1946, Monoxeito, Eritrea, Ethiopia; married Almaz Yilma; children: Emnet M Sebhatu & Temnete M Sebhatu. **Educ:** Haile Selassie I Univ, BSc, physics, 1969; Clemson Univ, PhD (physics), 1975. **Career:** NC State Univ, visiting asst prof, physics, 1975-76; Pensacola Jr Col, asst prof physics, 1976-78; Winthrop Col, from asst prof physics to assoc prof physics, 1978-91; NSF res grant, 1990-91; Mich State Univ, King-Chavez-Parks, visiting prof physics, 1991-92; Winthrop Univ, prof physics, 1992-. **Orgs:** Catholic Church, 1946-; Nat Soc Black Physicists; Am Phys Soc; Am Asn Physics Techers. **Honors/Awds:** Kavli Institute Theoretical of Physics scholar, University Calif, Santa Barbara, 2002-04. **Special Achievements:** Published articles Ill Nuovo Cimento, Acta Physica Polonica, Physics Teacher Etc; reviews physical science and physics books for major publishers; Listed in "Who's Who". **Business Addr:** Professor of Physics, Pre-Engineering Advisor, Winthrop University, Department of Chemistry and Physics, 101 Sims Bldg, Rock Hill, SC 29733, **Business Phone:** (803)323-2113 Ext 235.

SEBREE, MINNIE
Business owner, executive. **Personal:** Born in Mound Bayou, MS. **Career:** Aunt Minnie's Food Serv Inc, owner, currently. **Business Addr:** Owner, Aunt Minnie's Food Service Inc, 12265 Williams St Suite B, Perrysburg, OH 43551.

SEBREE-BROWN, CLAUDIA
Executive. **Personal:** Daughter of Minnie. **Career:** Aunt Minnie's Food Serv Inc, vpres, currently. **Business Addr:** Vice President, Aunt Minnie's Food Service Inc, 12265 Williams St Suite B, Perrysburg, OH 43551.

SEE, LEE. See SEE, DR. LETHA A.

SEE, DR. LETHA A (LEE SEE)
Educator, social worker, psychotherapist. **Personal:** Born Jan 23, 1930, Poteau, OK; daughter of Truppy Sanders Smith and Edward Sanders; married Colonel Wilburn R See; children: Terry L. **Educ:** Langston Univ, BA, 1956; Univ Okla, EdM, 1957; Univ Ark, MSW, 1972; Univ Wis, post masters, 1976; Bryn Mawr Col, PhD, 1982. **Career:** Univ Ark, asst prof, 1972-77; Child Welfare Serv, agency head, 1977-80; Atlanta Univ, adj prof, 1982-83; Univ Ga, assoc prof, 1983-98, prof emer, currently; Univ WI-Madison, Title III fel, 1987. **Orgs:** US deleg Soviet Union World Cong Women, 1987; Peoples Republic China, Australia Social Welfare; Acad Social Workers. **Special Achievements:** Published over 75 articles including: "Migration and Refugees", Nat Asn Human Rights, 1986-87; Cosmological Paradigm, Australian Social Welfare, 1986; Author for the books like: "Tensions & Tangles" 1987; Black Folk Healing, Sage Publisher, 1990; Inequality in America, Garland Press, 1991; co-auth & ed, Human Behavior in the Social Environment. **Home Addr:** 909 Otter Way, Marietta, GA 30068-4244, **Home Phone:** (770)971-1051. **Business Addr:** Professor Emeritus, University of Georgia, 240A Riverbend Rd, Athens, GA 30602-1511, **Business Phone:** (706)542-5286.

SEELE, PERNESSA C.
Educator, chief executive officer, founder (originator). **Personal:** Born Oct 15, 1954, Lincolnville, SC; daughter of Charles and Luella. **Educ:** Clark Col, BS, 1976; Atlanta Univ, MS, 1979. **Career:** Res NY Univ, res asst, 1981-84; Drake Univ Bus Sch, instr, 1987; Interfaith Hosp, AIDS coordr, 1987-89; Narcotics & Drug Res, assoc AIDS trainer, 1988-89; NY City Health & Hosps, Drug Addiction Prog, admin, 1989-92; Balm In Gilead, founder & chief exec officer, 1989-, Currently; HCCI, vpres, 1992-94. **Orgs:** Bd mem, Harlem United, 1993-95; bd mem, AIDS Action Coun, 1996; AIDS Action Comt, 1998. **Honors/Awds:** State of Michigan Special Tribute, 1997; President Award, Manhattan Borough, 1996; Community Works Award, Harlem Women Making Difference, 1997, 1998; Bishop Carl Bean Visionary Award, Unity Fellowship Church, 1998; Guest of President's Fifth state of the Union Address, 2006; Time Magazine's Top 100 Americans, 2006; Featured speaker at the XVII International Conferences on AIDS, Mexico City, 2008. **Special Achievements:** Author, The Church's role in HIV Prevention, 1995; AIDS and Spirituality,International Catholic Child Bur, 1996; National Black Church Week ofPrayer, Fed; Jessye Norman Sings for the Healing of AIDS, exec producer,1996. **Business Addr:** Founder, Chief Executive Officer, The Balm In Gilead Inc, 130 W 42nd St Suite 450, New York, NY 10036-7802, **Business Phone:** (212)730-7381.

SEGAR, LESLIE
Radio host, actor, dancer. **Personal:** Born in Queens, NY; daughter of Leo and Ella. **Educ:** Springfield Col, BS, exercise physiol & sports med, MA; Howard Fine Actg Sch, Los Angeles, Calif, scene study; Herbert Bergdoff Actg Acad, New York, NY, technique & scene study i provisational & Scene; Flushing YMCA, Flushing, NY, gymnastics & rhythmic gymnastics. **Career:** Emmis Broadcasting, Hot 97 Radio, New York, dj; CBS Radio, V103, Atlanta, dj; Sirius Satellite Radio, Hot Jamz-National, Afternoon Drive, dj; Emmis Broadcasting, Power 106, Big Boy Morning Show, dj; Chancellor Media,1000.3 The Beat-Los Angeles, dj; Radio One, Steve Harvey Morning Show, Los Angeles, dj; Premiere radio Networks, Hollywood 360, entertainment reporter clear channel affil; Films: House Party 2, 1991; Malcolm X, 1992;Who's the Man?, 1993; New Jersey Drive, 1995; Hav Plenty, 1997; An Alan Smithee Film: Burn Hollywood Burn, 1998; 3 A.M., 2001; 142 John Street, 2008. TV series: Rap City, 1993-2000; "My Coolest Years", 2004; Made You Look: Top 25 Moments of BET History, 2005; Big Lez Enterprises Inc, owner. **Orgs:** Screen Actors Guild; Am Fedn TV & Radio Asn. **Special Achievements:** Set up fitness training program for SWV, Heavy D, Andre Harrell, Puff Daddy; Choreographed & danced in videos by Whitney Houston, Michael Jackson, Bobby Brown, Salt-n-Pepa, Mary J Blige. **Business Addr:** Actress, c/o Talent Agency, 6310 San Vincente Blvd Suite 200, Los Angeles, CA 90048, **Business Phone:** (323)965-5600.

SEGREE, E RAMONE
Fund raising consultant. **Personal:** Born Aug 23, 1949, Chicago, IL; son of Eustas Matthew and Blanche Hill; married Carmen Montague, Aug 18, 1984; children: Ashton Montague & Tara Montague. **Educ:** Calif State Col, BA, 1972; Penn State Univ, Middletown, PA, MPSSC, 1979. **Career:** PEN NCP, Harrisburg, PA, exec dir, 1980-82; USX CRP, Pittsburgh, pub & goval affairs rep, 1982-83; Ketchum Inc, Pittsburgh, campaign dir, 1983-84; United Way SW PEN, Pittsburgh, PA, div & proj dir, 1984-86; Univ Pittsburgh, PA, sr dir develop, 1986-89; Pittsburgh Pub Theater, Pittsburgh, vpres develop; Salem State Col, vpres inst advan & found exec dir; Meharry Med Col, sr vpres inst advan; Roger Williams Univ, Univ Advan, vpres, currently; Segree As-

soc, pres. **Orgs:** Pres bd, Hill House Asn, 1991-; founder & co-chr, Pittsburgh Black & Jewish Dialogue, 1984-; secy, Nat Found Bd, Nat Soc Fundraising Execs, 1994-; chair, performing arts cmsing, Three Rivers Arts Festival, 1992; Minority Theater Panel, Penn Coun the Arts, 1993; bd mem, Pittsburgh Youth Symphony Orchestra, 1991; bd mem, Pittsburgh Community TV Programming Trust, 1987; chmn, Corps & Founds Comt, St Edmunds Acad, 50th Anniversary Capital Campaign. **Honors/Awds:** Service Award, Kappa Alpha Psi Fraternity, Harrisburg Alumni Chapter, 1980; Community Leadership Award, 100 Black Men of Pittsburgh, 1988; Service & Achievement Award, Univ Pittsburgh African Heritage Classroom Comt, 1988; Coun Fund-Raisers Citation, 1989; Pittsburgh Continuing Our Traditions Award, 1992; Certified Fund Raising Exec, Nat Soc Fund-Raising Exec, 1990; Honorary AS Degree, Community Col Allegheny County, 1992; Distinguished Alumni Award, Community Col Allegheny County, 1992. **Military Serv:** AUS & PA Nat Guard, SPC-5, 1969-75; Adv Med Training Honors Grad, 1969. **Business Phone:** (401)253-1040.

SEIDENBERG, MARK
Banker. **Career:** Time Savings & Loan Asn, San Francisco, CA, chief exec officer. **Business Addr:** Time Savings and Loan Association, 100 Hegenberger Rd Suite 110, Oakland, CA 94621-1447.

SEIGLER, DEXTER
Football player. **Personal:** Born Jan 11, 1972, Avon Park, FL. **Educ:** Univ Miami. **Career:** Seattle Seahawks, defensive back, 1996-97; Amsterdam Admirals, corner back, 1999. **Special Achievements:** First-Team All-Big East honors, 1993; All-Star NFL Europe. 1993; All-Star NFL Europe, 1998.

SELBY, CORA NORWOOD
Educator, secretary (government). **Personal:** Born Jul 15, 1920, Nassau, DE; daughter of Martha L Maull and Clarence Page; married Paul M Selby, May 26, 1945 (deceased); children: Paul MN, Clarence PN, Clyde LN, Adrian Selby LeBlanc, Terence RN. **Educ:** Del State Col, BS, 1940; Univ DE, MEd, 1959; Del State Col, Dover, DE, BS, 1940; Univ Del, Newark, DE, MEd, 1948-1959. **Career:** Educator, Secretary (Government) (retired); State Bd Educ, Dover, Laurel teacher specialist, 1941-87; Ross Point Sch Dist, teacher, 1941-64, reading teacher, 1964-65, spl educ teacher, 1965-66, 2nd grade teacher, 1966-69; Indian River Sch Dist, Millsboro, ABE Inst; Headstart Follow-through Prog, fac adv, 1969-80; Migrant Educ Prog, teacher, 1981-87; Sussex Technol, ABE-GED teacher, 1991-95; Sussex County, secy, currently. **Orgs:** LEA, DSEA, NEA Teacher Educ Org, 1941-; United Methodist Church, cert lay speaker, 1980-; secy, DE State Col, 1980-, vpres, Peninsula Delaware Conf Coun on Ministries, UM Church, 1985-; life mem, Nat PTA, 1986-; chaplain Alpha Delta Kappa State Chap, 1986; bd trustees; pres, Laurel Sr Ctr, 1987-; Gov's Comn Post-Sec Educ; AARP-DRSPA, SCRSPA, 1987; Phi Delta Kappa; secy, bd dirs, Carvel Garden Housing; Laurel Hist Soc; lay leader, Peninsula Delaware Conf, UM Church; state & nat PTA youth coun; Comn Archives & Hist, Peninsula Del Conf; Comn Area Episcopacy Peninsula Del Conf; Del Div Literacy, 1988-; Child Placement Review Bd, 1992-; First State Community Action, policy coun, 2000-; pres, Carvel Gardens Housing, bd dir, 2000-; Laurel Exchange Club, 2000; Laurel Chamber Com, 2000; vol, Read Aloud; Math Magic; pres, Sussex County Sch Personnel Asn, 2001; pres, Laurel Sr Ctr, 2001. **Honors/Awds:** Pres's Award for Vol Serv, DAACE, 1982; First Lady of Yr, Psi Chap Beta Sigma Phi, 1983; Outstanding Educr in DE, Nat Asn Univ Women, 1983; Laurel Sch Dist gifted & talented teacher, 1980; Teacher of the Yr, Laurel Sch Dist, 1985-86; Outstanding Alumnus DE State Col NAFEO, 1985-86; DHL, Del State Col, 1987; Alumni Queen, Del State Col, 1988; Outstanding Vol, Gov Del, 1990; Citizen of the Yr, Town of Laurel, Del, 1990; Delegate to Del State Conference on Libraries & Info, Lieutenant Gov, 1991; Preservation of Afro-Am Cultures, Hall of Fame, 1993; Martin Luther King Jr Award, Peninsula DE Conf Comn Religion & Race, 1994; Community Relations DSUAA Hall of Fame, 1995; Pres's Award, DAACE, 1995; Rural Adult Educr, 1997; Order of St Barnabas, 2000; Distinguished Elem African-Am Teacher of 20th Century; Intl Woman, 2000. **Home Addr:** Rd 62, Laurel, DE 19956. **Business Addr:** Secretary, Sussex County, PO Box 874, Ocean View, DE 19970, **Business Phone:** (302)537-4198.*

SELBY, MYRA C
Lawyer, judge. **Personal:** Born Jul 1, 1955, Saginaw, MI; daughter of Ralph and Archie; married Bruce Curry, Aug 12, 1978; children: Lauren & Jason. **Educ:** Kalamazoo Col, BA, 1977; Univ Michigan Law Sch, JD, 1980. **Career:** Seyfarth, Shaw, Fairweather & Geraldson, assoc, 1980-83; Ice, Miller, Donadio, & Ryan, partner, 1983-93; State Ind, dir health care policy, 1993-94; Ind Supreme Ct, justice, 1995-99; Ice Miller LLP, atty & partner, currently. **Orgs:** Bd dir, Nat Health Lawyers Asn; Am Inn Cts; Am Law Inst; fal Am Bar Asn; The Chicago Med Sch, Finch Univ Health Sci, 1993-94; pres & bd dir, Alpha Nursing Home; Am Hosp Asn; bd dir, Flanner House; bd dir, Indianapolis Ballet Theatre; bd trustees, Indianapolis Mus Art; bd adv, Indiana Univ, Indianapolis; bd adv, Purdue Univ, Indianapolis; chair, Ind Supreme Ct Comn Race & Gender Fairness; Stanley K Lacy Leadership Selection Comt; bd develop comt, Big Sisters Cent Ind, 1995. **Honors/Awds:** A Breakthrough Woman Award, Stanley K Lacy Leadership Series Class XIII, 1989; Coalition of 100 Black Women, 1990; Leadership Initiative, Indianapolis Chamber Com, 1992-94; Antoinette Dakin Leach Award, Indianapolis Bar Asn, 1997; listed in The Best Lawyers in America; featured in Indiana's Trailblazing Women, 2000; Touchstone Awards, Girls Inc, 2001. **Special Achievements:** First woman and the first African American to sit on the bench of the state's highest court.

SELF, FRANK WESLEY
Accountant, manager. **Personal:** Born Nov 2, 1949, Junction City, KS; son of Wilma Pollet and Nolan; married Shirley M Brown Self, Aug 28, 1969; children: Frank E & Shelley M. **Educ:** Univ Colo, Denver, CO, BS, acct, 1976; State Colo, Denver, CO, CPA, cert, 1979. **Career:** Ashby, Armstrong & Johnson, Denver, CO, mgr, 1977-82; Am TV & Commun Corp, Englewood, CO, dir, 1982; Time Warner Cable, dir invest acct. **Orgs:** Am Inst CPAs, 1981; Colorado Soc CPAs, 1981; Nat Asn Black Accts, 1978; Korean Tong Soo Do Karate Asn, 1989; Nat Asn Minorities Cable, 1985. **Honors/Awds:** Am Best & Brightest, Dollars & Sense, 1989; Young Bus & Prof Men. **Military Serv:** AUS, E-4, 1971-73. **Home Addr:** 17 Heritage Hill Rd, Norwalk, CT 06851, **Home Phone:** (203)846-4517.

SELLARS, HAROLD GERARD
Banker, administrator, vice president (organization). **Personal:** Born May 27, 1953, Vass, NC; son of Frank Alfred Sellars and Bessie Mae Johnson Sellars; married Clara Scott, Oct 7, 1978; children: Dwight & Dwayne. **Educ:** NC Cent Univ, Durham, NC, BA, bus admin, Cum Laude, 1978. **Career:** United Carolina Bank, Whiteville, NC, sr vpres; Br Banking & Trust Co, vpres; Mechanics & Farmers Bank, Durham, NC, sr vpres, currently, lending adminr, currently. **Orgs:** Bd mem, Bankers Educ Soc Inc, 1985-95; adv bd, NC Small Bus Admin Adv Coun, 1990-95; bd mem, NC Rural Economic Development Center, 1990-97; bd mem, NC Small Bus Tech & Develop Centers, 1989-97; bd edu, Whiteville City Schs, 1996-98; bd mem, Self Help Ventures Fund; bd mem, Durham's Partnership C. **Honors/Awds:** founding chmn & bd mem, Columbus County Partnership C. **Military Serv:** AUS, Spec 4, 1972-75. **Home Addr:** 4 Wateroaks Ct, Durham, NC 27703. **Business Addr:** Senior Vice President, Mechanics & Farmers Bank, PO Box 1932, Durham, NC 27702, **Business Phone:** (919)687-7800.

SELLERS, JACQUELINE H
Lawyer. **Educ:** Howard Univ, BA; Detroit Col Law, JD. **Career:** Lewis & Munday, pres & chief exec officer; Clark Hill PLC, pract group leader, Litigation Mgt group, & mem, Detroit off, currently. **Orgs:** Am Bar Asn; Defense Res Inst; Nat Bar Asn; Straker Bar Asn; Wolverine Bar Asn; bd dir & exec secy, Forgotten Harvest; Augustus Straker Bar; fel State Bar Mich; Renaissance Chapter the Links Inc. **Business Phone:** (313)965-8377.*

SELLERS, WALTER G.
Association executive. **Personal:** Born Jul 25, 1925, Ann Arbor, MI; son of Walter and Leona; married Irene; children: Victoria, Walter III, Ronald. **Educ:** Central State Univ, BS, 1951. **Career:** Retired: Central State Univ, admin positions, from special asst to pres, 1951-93. **Orgs:** Xenia City Bd Educ, 1968-; past pres, Xenia Kiwanis Club, 1971-72; bd dirs, Am Alumni Coun, 1972-73; OH Sch Bds Tenure Study Comn, 1973; lt governor, Kiwanis Intl, 1974-75; bd trustees, Am Alumni Council & Am Col Pub Rel Asn, 1974-; past pres, OH Asn Col Admissions Counrs; Coun Admissions Officers State Asst Col Univ OH; OH HS Col Rel Comn; Midwestern Adv Panel Col Entrance Exam Bd; OH Sch Bds Asn Comn; OSBA Governance Comn; exec bd, Xenia YMCA; bd dirs, Xenia Sr Citizens; pres, OH Sch Bd Asn, 1981-82; governor, OH Dist Kiwanis Intl, 1984-85; comn chmn, Kiwanis Intl; trustee, Kiwanis International, vice pres, 1994-97, pres, 1997-. **Honors/Awds:** Alumnus of Year, CSU Gen Alumni Asn, 1972; Hon mem, SW Region OH Sch Bds Asn, 1973; FM Torrence Award, Outstanding Community Serv, 1980; Hon LND, Central State Univ, 1988. **Special Achievements:** First African-Am president of Kiwanis International; Alumni Bldg, Central State Univ, named the "Walter G Sellers Alumni Center", 1988; had a senior citizen apartment building named in his honor. **Military Serv:** USN, 1944-46. *

SENBET, PROF. LEMMA W
Research scientist, educator. **Personal:** Born in Ethiopia; son of Wolde; divorced. **Educ:** Haile Sellassie I Univ, Addis Ababa, BBA, 1970; UCLA, Los Angeles, MBA, 1972; SUNY/Buffalo, Buffalo, NY, Phd, 1975. **Career:** Northwestern Univ, visiting assoc prof, 1980-81; Univ Wis-Madison, assoc prof, 1980-83, prof & Dickson Bascom prof, finance, 1983-87; Charles Albright chair & prof, finance, 1987-90; Distinguished Res Visitor, London Sch Econ; World Bank, consult, 1989-; Univ Md, Robert H Smith Sch Bus, William E Mayer chair prof, finance, 1991-, Dept Finance, chair, 1998-2006; African Economic Res Consortium, consult, 1994-; Int Monetary Fund, consult, 1996-; United Nations, consult, 1996-97 & 2002-03. **Orgs:** Pres, Western Finance Asn, 1989-90; bd dirs, Am Finance Asn; edial bd, Jour Finance; ed bd, Jour Financial & Quant Anal; edial bd, Financial Mgt, exe ed; ed bd, Jour Banking & Finance, 1995-99; chair, FMA Doctoral Panel; bd dirs, Fortis Mutual Funds, 1999-2002; Financial Economists Roundtable, 2000-. **Honors/Awds:** Chancellor's Gold Medal, Haile Sellassie I Univ, Emperor Haile Sellassie, 1970; Teaching Excellence, Univ Md, 1994. **Special Achievements:** Ranked third among world-wide contributors to the Journal of Finance, 1975-86. **Business Addr:** William E Mayer Chair Professor of Finance, Chair of Finance Department, Robert H Smith School of Business, 4437 Van Munching Hall, College Park, MD 20742, **Business Phone:** (301)405-2242.

SENEGAL, NOLTON JOSEPH, SR.
Lawyer, religious leader. **Personal:** Born Mar 15, 1952, Lafayette, LA; son of Willie Floyd; married Patricia Dianne Frank-Senegal; children: Nolton Joseph Jr, Ansia Nicole, Terrence Jamal. **Educ:** Southern Univ, BS, bus & social studies, 1973, MS, admin, supv, 1975; Southern Univ Law Sch, JD, 1984. **Career:** St Landry Parish Police Jury, 1975-77; Diocese Lafayette, 1975-77; Lafayette Regional Voc Tech Sch, 1977-81; Lafayette Parish Sch Bd, 1977-81; Acadiana Legal Serv Corp, dir, 1985-, sr atty; Farmworkers Legal Assistance Proj, dir, currently; Mother of Mercy Catholic Church, Rayne, Deacon, 2000-. **Orgs:** Alpha Phi Alpha Frat, 1977-; Phi Delta Kappa Law Frat, 1982-; pres, Stud Bar Asn Law Ctr, 1983-84; chair, Minority Involvement Sect LSBA, 1993-95; pres, Acadia Parish Sch Bd; Fed Rel Network, Nat Sch Bds Asn, 1996-. **Special Achievements:** First African American to serve as president of the Acadia Parish School Board; first vice president of LA School Bds Assn, 1997-99. **Home Addr:** 413 Sect St, PO Box 564, Rayne, LA 70578, **Home Phone:** (318)334-5759. **Business Phone:** (337)334-3516.*

SERAILE, JANETTE GREY
Lawyer. **Personal:** Born Oct 24, 1945, New York; daughter of Sarah Edwards Grey and Maurice W; married William; children: Garnet Tana, Aden Wayne. **Educ:** Lake Forest Col, 1967; Col Law Sch, attended 1972. **Career:** Edwards Sisters Realty Asn, asst mgr, 1967-70; Chance & White, law asst, 1970-72; Bedford Stuyvesant Restoration Corp, atty, 1972-83; Pvt pract, 1983-. **Orgs:** NY County Lawyers Asn. **Business Addr:** Attorney, 740 St Nicholas Ave, New York, NY 10031-4002.*

SERGEANT, CARRA SUSAN
Association executive, educator. **Personal:** Born Jul 16, 1953, New Orleans, LA; daughter of James Bernard Sergeant and Susan Caralita Craven Sergeant. **Educ:** Dillard Univ, New Orleans, LA, BA, 1976; Univ Cent Ark, Conway, AR, MS, 1978. **Career:** Ind Univ Pa, Ind, PA, residence dir, 1978-80; Ind Coun Against Rape, Indiana, PA, dir, 1979-80; Ga Inst Technol, Atlanta, GA, area coord, 1980-85; Metrop Develop Ctr, New Orleans, LA, active treat mgr, 1985-89; Los Angeles State Univ, Eunice, LA, coord support serv, 1989-90, coord Upward Bound, 1990-, asst dir acad assistance prog & counr, currently. **Orgs:** Vpres, New Orleans Chap, Nat Orgn Women, 1987-89, pres, 1988-89; regional newsletter ed, Southwest Asn Stud Assistance Prog, 1989-91; comt chair, La Asn Stud Assistance Prog, 1990-, secy, 1991-, pres, 1995; Nat Asn Women Educ. **Honors/Awds:** Cited Community Serv, New Orleans Mayor's Office, 1989. **Special Achievements:** Quoted in Article on Date Rape, Ebony Magazine, 1990. **Business Addr:** Assistant Director Academic Assistance Programs, Louisiana State University Eunice, 2048 Johnson Hwy, Eunice, LA 70535, **Business Phone:** (318)457-7311.

SERGENT, ERNEST, JR.
Physicist, business owner. **Personal:** Born Feb 9, 1943, New Orleans, LA; married Claudette Ruth Brown; children: Sandra Michelle, Ernest III & James Richard. **Educ:** Southern Univ New Orleans, BS Math & Physics, 1970; Univ MI Ann Arbor, MS Physics, 1972. **Career:** Univ Mich, fel, 1970-72; Univ Mich Geol Dept, res assoc, 1972-74; Gen Motors Res Ctr, jr physicist, 1973; 3M Co, advan physicist, 1974-75, adv prod control engr, 1975-79, sr physicist, 1979; Sergent Enterprises, owner, currently. **Orgs:** Afro-Am Art Soc 3M Co; bd dir, Cottage Grove Jaycees, 1978-79; Cottage Grove Human Serv Community; Cottage Grove Baseball/Softball Div; Soc Automotive Engrs; Community Vol Serv. **Military Serv:** AUS sp-4 1961-64; Good Conduct Medal. **Home Addr:** 9119 79th St S, Cottage Grove, MN 55016. **Business Addr:** Owner, Sergent Enterprises, 9119 79th St S, Cottage Grove, MN 55016-2214, **Business Phone:** (651)459-8052.*

SERMON, ERICK (ERICK ONASSIS)
Rap musician. **Personal:** Born Nov 25, 1968, Bayshore, NY. **Career:** Singer, producer & writer; Albums: Strictly Business, 1988; Unfinished Business, 1989; Business Never Personal, 1992; No Pressure, 1993; Business as Usual, 1994; Double or Nothing, 1995; Back in Business, 1997; El Nino, 1998; Out of Business, 1999; Erick Onasis, 2000; Music, 2001; React, 2002; Chilltown, New York, 2004; Singles: Hittin' Switches, 1993; Stay Real,1993; Bomdigi, 1995; Welcome, 1996; Why Not, 2000; I'm Hot, 2001; Love Iz, 2002; Feel It, 2004; Street Hop, 2004; Producer: Reservoir Dogs, 1999; Da Heat wave, 2000; So Fly, 2005; Goldmine, 2006; We Mean Business, 2008; Films, lyricist; Juice, 1992; Who's the Man?, 1993; A Low Down Dirty Shame, 1994; Die Hard: With a Vengeance, 1995; The Show, 1995; Don't Be a Menace, 1996; Rhyme & Reason, 1997; Side, actor, 1998; Blade, 1998; Black & White, 1999; The Corruptor, 1999; In Too Deep,

1999; Nutty Professor II The Klumps, 2000; Rush Hour 2, 2001; Barber Shop, 2002; Honey, 2003; Beef II (doc), 2004; Syriana, 2005; Rock The Bells, 2006; 2008. **Business Addr:** Recording Artist, Universal Motown Records, 1755 Broadway 6th Fl, New York, NY 10019, **Business Phone:** (212)373-0750.*

SERWANGA, WASSWA KENNETH
Football player. **Personal:** Born Jul 23, 1976, Kampala, Uganda. **Educ:** Univ Calif, Los Angeles. **Career:** Football player (Retired); San Francisco 49ers, defensive back, 1999; Minn Vikings, 2000-01; LosAngeles Avengers, defensive back, 2003; Wash Mutual Business Banking, vpres, currently. **Honors/Awds:** Rookie of the Year, 1999.

SESSION, JOHNNY FRANK
Government official. **Personal:** Born Mar 2, 1949, Panama City, FL; son of Karetta Baker Alexander and Jake; married Linda Tibbs, May 11, 1969; children: Tomeka, Johnny Frank Jr & Marcus. **Educ:** Gulf Coast Jr Col, Panama City, FL, AA, 1970; Fla A&M Univ, Tallahassee, FL, BS, 1973. **Career:** Deloit, Haskins & Sells, Ft Lauderdale, FL, staff acct, 1973-75; City Hollywood, Hollywood, FL, staff acct, 1975-77, sr acct, 1977-81, controller, 1981-84; City Tallahassee, Tallahassee, FL, controller, 1984, sr financial mgr. **Orgs:** Govt Finance Officers Asn; chap pres, Nat Asn Black Accountants; Fla Inst Cert Pub Acct; Am Inst Cert Pub Acct. **Honors/Awds:** Award for financial reporting, Govt Financial Officer Asn, 1985; WORD Award, Fla A&M Univ Alumni Asn, 1987; Distinguished Service Award, Nat Asn Black Accountants, Tallahassee Chap, 1988. **Home Addr:** 2806 Sweetbriar Dr, Tallahassee, FL 32312. **Business Addr:** Senior Financial Manager, City of Tallahassee, 300 S Adams St, Tallahassee, FL 32301, **Business Phone:** (850)891-8867.

SESSOMS, ALLEN LEE
School administrator, physicist. **Personal:** Born Nov 17, 1946, New York City, NY; son of Albert Earl and Lottie Beatrice Leff; married Csilla Manette von Csiky, Apr 18, 1990; children: Manon Elizabeth & Stephanie Csilla. **Educ:** Union Col, BS, maths, 1968; Univ Wash, MS, physics, 1969; Yale Univ, DSc, Physics, 1972. **Career:** Brookhaven Nat Lab, res, 1972-73; European Org Nuclear Res, (CERN), res, 1973-75; Harvard Univ, assoc prof physics, 1974-81; Alfred P Sloan Found, fel, 1977-81; US Dept State, Bur Oceans & Int Environ & Sci Affairs, sr tech adv, 1980-82, Bur's Off Technol & Safeguards, dir, 1982-87, Sci & Technol Affairs, counr, 1987-89; Univ Mass, exec vpres, 1993-95, vpres acad affairs, 1994-95; US Dept State, US Embassy Mexico, dep chief mission, 1991-93, minister counsr polit affairs, 1989-91; Queens Col, CUNY, pres, 1995-00; Harvard Univ, JFK Sch Gov, vis prof, 2000-03; Del State Univ, pres, currently. **Orgs:** Chair, US Dept Energy, 1996-, sec energy adv bd, 1996-; Am Phys Soc; MR Asn Advan Sci, 1973-; NY Acad Sci; 100 Black Men, 1995-. **Honors/Awds:** Tree of Life Award, Jewish Nat Fund, 1996; Meritorious & Superior Honor Awards, State DPT; Medal of Highest Honor, Soka Univ, Japan, 1999; Wilbur Lucius Cross Medal, Yale Grad Sch Asn, 1999; Officier dans l'Ordre des Palmes Academiques, 1999; Seikyo Culture Award, Japan, 1999. **Special Achievements:** Author of over 30 scientific publications in professional journals and US government policy papers. **Business Phone:** (302)857-6001.

SESSOMS, DR. FRANK EUGENE
Physician. **Personal:** Born Oct 24, 1947, Rochester, PA; son of Frank L and Catherine; married Sandra Scalise, Jun 18, 1988. **Educ:** Bradley Univ, 1966; Harvard Univ, Intensive Summer Studies prog, 1968; TN State Univ, BS, 1970; Meharry Med Col, MD, 1974. **Career:** Procter & Gamble, food products technical brand specialist, 1969; US Dept Agr, summer researcher animal health div, 1970; Procter & Gamble Miami Valley Labs, summer researcher,1971; Meharry Med Col, student researcher, 1971-74; St Margaret's Memorial Hospl, internship & residency in family pract, 1974-77; Samuel Goldwyn Found, fel, 1971-74; St John's Gen Hosp, dir emergency serv, 1977, Diplo Am Bd Family Pract, 1977, 1983; med consult psychiat dept; Pvt Pract, physician, 1979-; Univ Pittsburgh Family Med & Proc, prof; W Penn Allegheny Health System, physician, 1998-. **Orgs:** Vpres, stud coun, Tenn State Univ, 1969-70; class pres, Meharry Med Col, 1970-71; vpres, Pre-Alumni Coun, Meharry Med Col, 1973-74; Congressional Black Caucus Health Brain Trust, 1974-; mem bd, Homewood Brushton YMCA, 1979-83; chmn bd Pittsburgh Black Action Methadone Maint Ctr, 1985-86; Nat Med Asn; med dir, Bidwell Drug & Alcohol Prog; pres, Alpha Phi Alpha, 1998-; NAACP; Urban League, AMA; Penn Med Soc; Undersea Med Soc; Nat Asn Health Serv Executives; Pittsburgh Chap 100 Black Men; Frontiers Int; bd govs, Tenn State Univ Student Union; Univ Counselors Tenn State Univ; Alumni Bd Mgmt, Meharry Med Col; Chi Delta Mu Fraternity; Am Corner, 1987-; Gateway Med Soc; Allegheny County Med S; pres, Meharry Nat Alumni Asn, 1993-95; comnr PA, Gov Com on African Am Affairs, 1992-; participant, President's Intercultural Task Force on Healthcare Reform, 1994; Guest Lectr, CCAC, 1994; Pittsburgh Pub School's Restructing Task Force, 1992-93; Comt African Am Student's; Bd Mgt, Meharry Med Col, 1995-. **Honors/Awds:** Fel, NY Acad Sci; patent holder High-Protein Fruit-Flavored Fat Stablized Spread 1969; Pre-Alumni Council Awd 1974; Hon Sgt-at-Arms, Tenn House Representatives, 1974; Presidential Citation Nat Asn for Equal Opportunities in Higher Educ, 1984; fel, Am Acad Family Pract. **Special Achievements:** Publisher: "Effects of Ethane 1,1 Dihydorxy Diphospanate "EHDP" on the Collagen Metabolism in the Rat" 1971 (Procter & Gamble Res Lab); scientific articles "Uses of the Soybean and Their Prospects for the Future," TN State Univ Dept of Bio-Chemistry 1970. **Military Serv:** USAF, Award for Valor & Heroism, 1968. **Home Addr:** 2777 Shamrock Dr, Allison Park, PA 15101-3146. **Business Addr:** Physician, 211 N Whitfield St 590, Pittsburgh, PA 15206, **Business Phone:** (412)363-6560.

SESSOMS, GLENN D
Executive, vice president (organization). **Personal:** Born Oct 20, 1953, Norfolk, VA; son of Clarence and Geraldine; married Linda, Jul 14, 1979; children: Daryn, Justin & Adea. **Educ:** Va State Univ, BS, 1976. **Career:** Johnson & Johnson, 1976-82; Fed Express Corp, 1983-88, managing dir, 1988-94, vpres, 1994-, chief diversity officer, currently. **Orgs:** Omega Psi Phi Fraternity, 1975; bd dir, Leadrship Memphis. **Honors/Awds:** VSU Sports Hall of Fame; Small Coll All-Am; 2 Fed Express 5 Star Awards. **Home Addr:** 341 Riveredge Dr W, Cordova, TN 38018, **Home Phone:** (901)754-4144. **Business Addr:** Board of Directors, Leadership Memphis, 119 S Main St Suite 425, Memphis, TN 38103, **Business Phone:** (901)278-0016.

SETTLES, DARRYL STEPHEN
Restaurateur, executive. **Personal:** Born Mar 30, 1961, Augusta, GA; son of David Jr and Rebecca. **Educ:** Carnegie-19Mellon Univ, attended 1978; Univ Tenn, Knoxville, attended 1981; Va Polytech Inst & State Univ, BS, 1984. **Career:** Gen Elec Co, 1979-81; Digital Equip Corp, engr, 1984-85, sales acct mgr, 1985-90; Commonwealth Mass, assoc comnr, 1991-; D'Ventures Unlimited Inc, pres, 1990-; Bob the Chef's Jazz Cafe, owner; Bob's Southern Bistro, owner & pres, currently. **Orgs:** Bd mem, Mass Restaurant Asn, 1992-; Boston Fellows, 1991-; lead Boston, Nat Conf Community & Justice, 1991-; Greater Boston Convention & Tourism Bur, 1991-; bd mem, Kids Fund, Boston Med Ctr; organizer, BeanTown Jazz Festival. **Honors/Awds:** America's Best & Brightest Young Business and Professional Men, Dollars & Sense Magazine, 1992; Entrepreneur of the Year, City Boston, 1997. **Business Addr:** Owner, President, Bob's Southern Bistro, 604 Columbus Ave, Boston, MA 02118, **Business Phone:** (617)536-6204.*

SETTLES, TRUDY Y
Government official. **Personal:** Born Jun 3, 1946, Springfield, OH; daughter of Nathaniel and Ruth Dennis. **Educ:** Cent State Univ, Wilberforce, OH, BS, 1968. **Career:** City Dayton, Dayton, OH, 1971-75; RL Polk & Co, Wash, DC, office assoc, 1975-76; Southern Calif Gas Co, Wash, DC, secy, 1976-82, govt affairs asst, 1982-94; Senate Judiciary Subcomt Immigration, staff asst, 1995-97; Columbia Gas Transmission, adv asst chief exec officer, 1997-; Wilberforce Univ, Wilberforce, OH, secy pres. **Orgs:** Rules comt, Wash Energy Affiliates, Desk Derrick Clubs, 1983-86, corresp secy, 1986, bd dir, 1986-88, chmn, program comt, finance comt, pres, 1992-93; secy, DC Metrop Chap Am Asn Blacks Energy, Wash, 1990-92. **Business Addr:** Assistant to the chief Executive Officer, Columbia Gas Transmission Corp, 12801 Fair Lakes Pkwy, Fairfax, VA 22033, **Business Phone:** (703)227-3200.

SEUNAGAL, DEBORAH EVANS
Librarian. **Personal:** Born Sep 30, 1959, Detroit, MI; daughter of Thomas and Irene Parks; married; children: 1. **Educ:** Univ Mich, AB, 1981, AMLS, 1983; Wayne State Univ, cert archival admin, 1992; Preserv Intensive Inst, Univ Calif at Los Angeles, 1994. **Career:** Dickinson, Wright, et al, law librn, 1983-84; Wayne Co Libr, librn, 1985-88; Detroit Pub Libr, field archivist, 1988-95, librn III/specialist, 1995-99; Southfield Pub Libr, adult serv librn, 2001; info search coach, currently. **Orgs:** Am Asn Law Libraries, 1983-84; Spec Libraries Asn, 1983-84; Fred Hart Williams Genealogical Soc, 1989-97; Mich Libr Asn, 1987-88; Oral Hist Asn, 1988-89; pres, Deborah Evans Asn, 1990-94; Am Libr Asn, 1992-94; Detroit Asn Black Storytellers, 1994-97; bd large, Fred Hart Williams Geneal Soc, 1995-96, vpres, 1996-97; Int Platform Asn, 1995-97. **Honors/Awds:** Margaret Mann Award, Univ Mich, Sch Infor & Libr Studies, 1983, Edmon Low Award, 1983; Cert Appreciation, Mich Geneal Coun, 1991; Libr Mich, Librn's Prof Cert, 1991; Scholar form Calif State Libr to attend Preserv Intensive Inst, 1994. **Special Achievements:** Presented paper: "MIC in Perspective," Local Hist Conf, 1991; MIC Archival ASN Spring Conf, panelist, 1992; published video reviews, Libr Journal, 1992; MIC AFA Symposium, Detroit MIC, conf co-chair, 1995; Developer & presenter: AFA Internet Resources Workshops, Detroit Pub Libr, 1996-97.

SEVILLIAN, CLARENCE MARVIN
Educator. **Personal:** Born Apr 23, 1945, Buffalo, NY; married Madeline Carol Cochran; children: Clarence II & Nicole Ren. **Educ:** Fla Agr & Mech Univ, BS, 1966; Eastern Mich Univ, MEd, admin, 1974. **Career:** Hoxey Job Corp Ctr, Cadillac, resident, counr, 1966-68; Saginaw Foundries, purchase agt, 1968-70; N western High Sch, Flint, staff spec; Bryant Jr High Sch, instrumental music teacher, 1970-74; Beecher Community Sch, dep prin. **Orgs:** Rec keeper Saginaw Alumni, Kappa Alpha Psi; Mich Educ Asn; NEA; United Teacher of Flint; Mich Sch Band & Orchestra Asn; Music Edur Nat Conf; Adv Bryant Band & Orchestra Parents Asn. **Honors/Awds:** Outstanding Secondary Educator of America, 1974; Outstanding Young Man of America, 1974. **Special Achievements:** First vice president of Unity Urban Community Development & Rehabilitation Corporation.

SEWELL, EDWARD C
Executive, real estate developer. **Personal:** Born Aug 18, 1946, Hanover, MD. **Educ:** Bowling Green Univ, BA, (magna cum laude) Omicron Delta Kappa; Ind Univ, MBA (magna cum laude). **Career:** Xerox Corp, financial analyst, 1970-72; Irwin Mgt Co, asst pres, real estate developer, 1972-75; Crocker Nat Bank, vpres real estate planning, 1975-78; J P Mahoney & Co, real estate developer, 1978-; Prof Sports Ctr, pres sports agent, 1983-. **Orgs:** Vice chmn & founder, Judge Joseph Kennedy Scholar Found Bay Area Minorties; fel, Consortium Grad Study Mgt, 1968-70. **Home Addr:** 1238 Cole St, San Francisco, CA 94117-4322.

SEWELL, EUGENE P
Association executive. **Personal:** Born Jun 20, 1962, Detroit, MI; son of Solomon and Carrie; married Adrienne, Oct 8, 1988; children: Christopher, Alexandria & Maya. **Educ:** Wayne State Univ, BA, 1984; Univ Detroit Mercy, MA, 1996. **Career:** City of Detroit, asst dir, 1988-94; Univ Detroit Mercy, mgr, community rel, 1994-2000; 100 Black Men Greater Detroit Inc, exec dir, 2000; St. Peters Home for Boys, pres, currently; Mkt Plus Co, pres & chief exec officer, currently. **Orgs:** Bd mem, Detroit Neighborhood Housing Serv, 1994-; adv bd, Detroit Compact, 1995; exec comt, Nat Kidney Found, 2000; NW Neighborhood Health Empowerment Ctr, 2001-; bd mem, Franklin Wright Settlement, 2001-. **Honors/Awds:** Key to the City, City of Detroit Mayor's Office, 1989. **Home Addr:** 6129 Yorkshire Rd, Detroit, MI 48224. **Business Addr:** President, St. Peter Home for Boys, 16121 Joy Rd, Detroit, MI 48228, **Business Phone:** (313)846-6942.

SEWELL, ISIAH OBEDIAH
Government official. **Personal:** Born Nov 20, 1938, Lexington, SC; son of Joseph Preston and Annie Bell Sligh; married Julia Smith, Dec 24, 1962; children: Kevin, Kendra & Keith. **Educ:** SC State Col, BSEE, 1961; George Wash Univ, attended 1972. **Career:** US Dept Navy, elec engr, 1964-71, head utilities, 1971-75; US Dept Energy, Wash, DC, gen engr, 1975-84, hbcu liason, 1984-92; coordr minority educ progs, 1986-92; Innovative & Univ Progs, staff dir, 1992-95. **Orgs:** Past secy, trustee bd Ward Memorial AME, 1975-; Fed Task Force Nat Power Grid Study, 1979; Lawrence Berkeley Nat Lab/Mendez Educ Found Sci Consortium, 1986-92; chmn, Fed Agency Sci & Tech Bd, 1986-92; past pres, Athenians Inc Wash DC; past pres, Wash Chap SC State Col Nat Alumni; Alpha Phi Alpha, Alpha Kappa Mu. **Honors/Awds:** Disting Military Grad, 1961; Civic Award-Serv Sci & Technol, Carnegie Corp NY, 1989; Outstanding Black Engrs Govt, Black Engr Mag, 1989; SC State Coll Distinguished Alumni, Nat Asn Loyal Opportunity Higher Educ, 1991. **Military Serv:** AUS, First Lt, 3 years. **Home Addr:** 7000 97th Ave, Seabrook, MD 20706.

SEWELL, LUTHER JOSEPH
Executive, consultant, founder (originator). **Personal:** Born Aug 9, 1936, Chattanooga, TN; son of Luther Sewell and Minnie P Sloan; married Wilma Johnson, Jan 19, 1968; children: Luther J III & Lela J. **Educ:** Tenn A&I Univ, attended 1956, Duquesne Univ, 1958, Monterey Peninsula Col, 1960, Allegheny Community Col, Univ Ariz, 1969; Trinity Hall Col & Sem, grad, 1971. **Career:** Talk Magazine, publ, 1962-; Luther J Sewell Inc, founder, 1962-; Bus & Job Develop Corp, consult, market analyst, community develop coord, 1964-70;Mellon Nat Bank, consult, 1965-71; Allegheny County Civil Serv Comn, secy,1973-; Trans World Airlines, Pennsylvania Lottery, consult, currently. **Orgs:** Bus & Job Develop Corp, 1963; Am Mkt Asn, 1968-72; former vpres, LoendiLit & Social Club, 1969; review comt, Community Chest Allegheny County,1971-73; bd dirs, Pittsburgh Goodwill Indust, 1972-; Mendelssohn Choir,1972-; former partner, vpres, A & S Securities Syst Inc, 1973-74; bd dirs Pittsburgh Chapter Nat Asn Advan Colored People, 1973-; Pittsburgh Press Club; Gateway Center Club. **Honors/Awds:** Young Businessman of Year, AME Gen Conf, 1965; Economic Development Award,Urban Youth Action Inc, 1972; Communications Award, Pittsburgh Club United, 1972; Martin Luther King Award, Music & Arts Club Pittsburgh,1972; Red Cross Volunteer Award, 1973; Black Achievers Award, Ctr Ave YMCA, 1973; Publishers Award, Black Polit Action Asn, 1988; Business Award, Federal Exec Bd, 1989. **Military Serv:** AUS sp4 1958-62.

SEWELL, STEVEN EDWARD
Football player, football coach. **Personal:** Born Apr 2, 1963, San Francisco, CA; married; children: Samuel, Caleb & Calah. **Educ:** Univ Okla, BA, organizational commun, 1986. **Career:** Football player (retired), football coach; Denver Broncos, running back, wide receiver, 1985-92; Grandview High Sch, asst football coach, offensive coordr; Colo State Univ, Pueblo Football Prog, running backs coach, 2008-. **Orgs:** Youth Found.

SEYMORE, STANLEY
Executive. **Personal:** Born Jul 2, 1951, Bronx, NY; son of Charles Bernard Clark and Ertha Mae Reese; married Julia A Williams,

Feb 12, 1977; children: Kadeem Toure. **Educ:** Brooklyn Col, Brooklyn NY, BA, 1980. **Career:** Blue Cross Blue Shield, New York, oper auditor, 1974-79, syst coord, 1979-81, programmer, 1981-84; Morgan Guaranty Trust, New York, prog analyst, 1984-86; New York Times, New York, syst mgr, 1986-. **Orgs:** Black Data Processing Asn; Am Payroll Asn. **Honors/Awds:** Member of Year, New York Chap, Black Data Processing Asn, 1987. **Military Serv:** USAF, sgt, 1970-74. **Business Addr:** Systems Manager, New York Times, 229 W 43rd St 7th Fl, New York, NY 10036, **Business Phone:** (212)556-1577.

SEYMOUR, BARBARA L.
Lawyer, secretary (office). **Personal:** Born in Columbia, SC; daughter of Leroy Semon and Barbara Youngblood; divorced. **Educ:** SC State Univ, BS, bus admin, 1975; Georgetown Univ Law Ctr, JD, 1979; Harvard Univ Grad Sch Bus, Cambridge, MA, MBA, 1985. **Career:** Texaco Inc, White Plains, tax atty, 1979-98; Equilon Enterprises LCC, Off Chief Financial Officer/Gen Coun, exec asst, 1998-99, asst corp secy & counr, 1999; Warner & Assocs PLLC, Houston, TX, lawyer, currently. **Orgs:** Tax Sect, Am Bar Asn, 1979-; Leadership Houston, 1989; Sickle Cell Asn Tex Gulf Coast, treas, 1986-88, pres, 1988-90; Leadership Am, 1990-; IRS Comn's Adv Group, 1995-97; Houston Area Urban League, dir, 1995-, vpres, 1998-; Sandra Orgn Dance Co, dir, 1999-; Houston Chap Links, vpres, 1996-; Alpha Kappa Omega Chap, Alpha Kappa Alpha, 1996-; Found Main St, dir, 1999-; Nat Bar Asn; Houston Bar Asn; Houston Lawyers Asn; Bd mem, Making Main St Happen; bd mem, Houston Grand Opera. **Honors/Awds:** Distinguished Business Alumnus, SC State Univ Sch Bus, 1991; Foremost Fashionable, Alpha Kappa Alpha, 1994; Eagle Award, Nat Eagle Leadership Inst, 1995. **Special Achievements:** One of 50 Outstanding Young Leaders, Ebony Magazine, 1983; Author: The 1980 Crude Oil Windfall Profit Tax, Howard Law Journal, 1980. **Business Addr:** Lawyer, Warner & Associates PLLC, 4200 Montrose Blvd Suite 360, Houston, TX 77006, **Business Phone:** (713)807-1007.*

SEYMOUR, CYNTHIA MARIA
Clergy. **Personal:** Born Sep 1, 1933, Houston, TX; married Oliver W; children: Michael Dwight Sweet, Wendell Raynard Sweet & Eugene LaValle Sweet Jr. **Educ:** John Adams Sch Bus, bus cert, 1965. **Career:** Gamma Phi Delta Sor, western regional dir soror, currently. **Orgs:** Vpres, San Francisco 49ers Toastmistress, 1981-83; financial grammateus, Gamma Phi Delta Sor Regional, 1982-86; Nat Asn Advan Colored People; Nat Coun Negro Women; Jones Memorial United Methodist Church; adv, Young Adult Fel; secy, Joseph P Kennedy Found; bd dirs, Eleanor R Spikes Memorial; secy, Finance Comt, Jones Memorial United Methodist Church, 1986-. **Honors/Awds:** Outstanding Salesperson Lion's Club, 1976, 1982; Certificate of Appreciation, Gamma Phi Delta Sor, 1983; Certificate of Appreciation, Jones Memorial United Methodist Church, 1984, 1986; Certificate of Honor City & County of San Francisco, 1985; Woman of the Year Western Region, Gamma Phi Delta Sor, 1987; Certificate of Appreciation, City of Detroit. **Home Addr:** 2535 Ardee Lane, South San Francisco, CA 94080. **Business Addr:** Director, Gamma Phi Delta Sorority, 2657 W Grand Blvd, Detroit, MI 48202-1203, **Business Phone:** (313)873-2691.

SEYMOUR, LAURENCE DARRYL
Surgeon. **Personal:** Born Feb 1, 1935, Memphis, TN; children: Lauren Juanita, Eric Lawrence. **Educ:** Tenn State Univ, BS, 1957; Howard Univ, MD, 1961. **Career:** City St Louis Hosp, intern, 1961-62; resident, 1962-66; Boston Univ, instr urol, 1966-68; Univ Tenn, Memphis, clinical assoc urol, 1969-; Med Clinic Inc, vpres, 1971-. **Orgs:** Trustee Collins Chapel Hosp Memphis, 1972; Am Bluff City Med Asns; Alpha Kappa Mu; Beta Kappa Chi; Omega Psi Phi; Mason; bd dirs, Boys Club Memphis, 1969-; Sigma Pi Phi Fraterniry; Memphis Unologic Soc; fel, Int Col Surgeons; fel, Am Asn Clinical Urologists. **Military Serv:** USNR, lt comdr, 1966-68. **Business Addr:** Vice President, Medical Clinic Inc, 1325 Eastmoreland Suite 435, Memphis, TN 38104.*

SHABAZZ, KALEEM
Association executive, government official. **Personal:** Born Jul 17, 1947, Atlantic City, NJ; son of Theodus Jowers Sr and Edna Evans Jowers; married Yolanda Dixon, Jul 3, 1973; children: Anjail. **Educ:** Cheyney Univ, Cheyney, Pa, 1965-68; Rutgers Univ, New Brunswick, NJ, BA, 1971; Rutgers Univ, Camden, NJ, courses towards masters, 1987-88. **Career:** Co Atlantic City, NJ, welfare care worker, 1979-81, info Atlantic, 1981-83, bus coordr, 1983-85, dir community develop, 1985-87; City Atlantic City, Atlantic City, NJ, aide city coun pres, 1987-89; Atlantic City Art Ctr, secy, actg exec dir, exec dir, currently; Nat Conf Christians & Jews, dir; Atlantic City, dep mayor, currently. **Orgs:** Chmn, Minority Community Leaders Adv Bd, Rutgers Univ, 1987-; chmn, Inst Rev Bd Inst Human Develop, 1989-; United Negro Col Fund, 1989-; Atlantic City Chamber Com; Atlantic City Hotel & Lodging Asn. **Honors/Awds:** Community Service Award, Bus & Prof Women, 1984; Meritorious Service, Youth Orgn, 1990; Outstanding Community Service Award, Stockton State Col Coalition, 1991; Selection to ACT, Regional Leadership Training Prog. **Special Achievements:** Raised over $7500 to benefit children in Atlanta, Ga; frequent lecturer in local high schools and colleges Intro Group Relations, Prejudice Reduction; developed, organized and implemented Black/Jewish retreat 2 day session of over 20 African-American and Jewish Leaders to engage in dialogue, exchange and group dynamics around issues affecting both groups. **Home Addr:** 1258 Monroe Ave, Atlantic City, NJ 08401, **Home Phone:** (609)344-2590. **Business Addr:** Executive Director, Atlantic City Art Center, NJ Ave & Boardwalk, PO Box 1061, Atlantic City, NJ 08401, **Business Phone:** (609)347-5837.

SHACK, WILLIAM EDWARD, JR.
Automotive executive, business owner, consultant. **Personal:** Born Feb 4, 1943, Woodward, AL; married Lois D Webster; children: William Edward III, Nicole, Vincent W & Christina. **Educ:** Clark Col, attended 1961-62. **Career:** Thrifty Drug & Discount, mgr, 1966-72; Ford Motor Co, mgr, 1972-75; B & W Rent A Car, owner, 1974-75; Miramar Lincoln-Mercury, San Diego, Future Ford Banning, pres, owner 1983-; Cooper Hill Homes, Yucca Valley, CA, pres, 2002; Miramar Lincoln Mercury Yucca Valley Ford Future Ford, pres & owner; Shack-Woods & Assocs, Long Beach, CA, chief exec officer, currently; Shack-Findlay Honda, co-owner, currently. **Orgs:** Dir, United Way, 1977-83; Yucca Valley Lions, 1977-84; dir, Inland Area Urban League, 1977-83; pres, Black Ford Lincoln Mercury Dealer Coun, 1979, 1982 & 1985; pres, PUSH Int Trade Bur, 1985; dir, Jackie Robinson YMCA, San Diego; comnr, San Diego City & County Int World Trade Comn; bd trustees, Clark Atlanta Univ. **Honors/Awds:** Distinguished Achievement Award, Ford Motor Co, 1977-84; Gold Award United Way, 1979-80; Founder Milligan Mem Scholar, 1980; Gold Award, Urban League 1980-82; Johnson Publishing Distinguished Businessman Award, 1984. **Military Serv:** USAF, E-4, 1961-64. **Business Addr:** Co-Owner, Shack Findlay Honda, 933 Auto Show Dr, Henderson, NV 89014, **Business Phone:** (702)568-3500.

SHACKELFORD, BILL. See SHACKELFORD, WILLIAM G.

SHACKELFORD, GEORGE FRANKLIN
Manager. **Personal:** Born Jun 3, 1939, Baltimore, MD; son of George and Doris; married Barbara Janice; children: Shawn, Terrence, Kymberly, Tanya & George. **Educ:** Univ Md, prog mgt develop; Harvard Univ. **Career:** Amoco Oil Co, dir acquistions, gen mgr, lubricants, bus mgr, light oils,capital investment mgr, mgr advert & consumer affairs, dir mktg res, dirmkt strategies, mgr spec acct, dist mgr; mgr mdsg, spec proj develop, pricing spec, fld sales mgr, term mgr, territory mgr, equip clerk, mail boy, 1965. **Military Serv:** AUS, 1962-65. **Home Addr:** 55 Stratham Circle, North Barrington, IL 60010.

SHACKELFORD, LOTTIE HOLT
Executive. **Personal:** Born Apr 30, 1941, Little Rock, AR; daughter of Curtis Holt (deceased) and Bernice Linzy Holt; divorced; children: Russell, Karen & Karla. **Educ:** Broadway Sch Real Est, Diplm 1973; Inst Polit, Fel, 1975; Philander Smith Col, BA (cum laude), 1979; JFK Sch Gov Harvard Univ, Fel, 1983; Shorter Col, DHL, 1987; Philander Smith Col, DHL, 1988. **Career:** Urban League Greater Little Rock, educ dir, 1973-78; AR Regional Minority Coun, exec dir, 1982-92; Overseas Private Investment Corp, dir, 1994-; Global Usa Inc, sr exec vpres, currently. **Orgs:** Pres, S Reg Coun 1980-; vice chmn, AR Dem St Comm, 1982-90; bd mem, Nat League Cities, 1984-86; vice chmn, Dem Nat Comn, 1989-92; reg dir, Nat Black Caucus Locally Elected Official; bd dir, Urban League; bd mem, Womens Pol Caucus; Delta Sigma Theta Sorority; Links Inc. **Honors/Awds:** Outstanding Community Serv, HOPE NLR, 1977; Trailblazer Award, Delta Sigma Theta Sorority, 1977; Outstanding Citizen Philander Smith Alumini Award, 1982; Outstanding Citizen Business & Professional Women, 1984. **Special Achievements:** One of the Distinguished Men and Women in US, Esquire Magazine, 1987. **Business Addr:** Senior Executive Vice President, Global USA Inc, 2121 K St NW Suite 650, Washington, DC 20037, **Business Phone:** (202)296-2400.

SHACKELFORD, WILLIAM G (BILL SHACKELFORD)
President (Organization), consultant. **Personal:** Born Mar 30, 1950, Chicago, IL; married Renee Nuckols; children: Dionne Deneen, Lenise Yvonne & Andre' Tarik. **Educ:** Clark Col, BS, physics, 1971; Ga Inst Tech, MS, applied nuclear sci, 1974; Wake Forest Univ Babcock Ctr Mgt Develop, formal mgt training. **Career:** Babcock & Wilcox Navl Nuclear Fuel Div, VA, quality control engr, 1972-73; Clark Col, assoc res phys dept, 1973-74, coop gen sci prog phys dept; Nat Ctr Atmospheric Res Co, visiting res, 1975; Cent Intel Agency, analyst, 1975-77; Nuclear Assurance Corp, proj mgr, 1977-79; Atlanta Univ Ctr, dir dual degree engineering prog, 1980-86; Knox Consults, mkt mgr, 1986-87; pres & founder, IEC Enterprises Inc, currently. **Orgs:** Chmn, Spectrum Club Comm, 1974; Leadershp Ga Partic, 1982; bd dir, Atlanta Camp Fire; regional pres & nat membership chmn, Nat Asn MNY Engineering Prog ADRs; Soc Human Resource Mgt; pres, Am Soc Training & Develop, 1997-. **Honors/Awds:** Beta Kappa Chi Nat Hon Soc Joint Mtng, 1971; Judge DeKalb Co Dist Sci Fair, 1974-75, 1978-84; Roster Listee, Blacks Physics Second Awds Ceremony Outstanding Black Physics, 1975; First Prize, paper presented Nat Sci Found. **Special Achievements:** Author of the book "Minority Recruiting.Building the Strategies and Relationships for Effective Diversity Recruiting," published in the Society of Human Resources Management (SHRM) Journal, the Journal of Staffing and Recruiting, Bureau of National Affairs, Resources Management, Recruiting Trends and he Black Collegian. **Home Addr:** 5439 Golfcrest Circle, Stone Mountain, GA 30088. **Business Addr:** President, Founder, IEC Enterprises Inc, 4319 Covington Hwy Suite 209, Decatur, GA 30035, **Business Phone:** (404)289-9692.

SHACKLEFORD, CHARLES EDWARD
Basketball player. **Personal:** Born Apr 22, 1966, Kinston, NC. **Educ:** NC State Univ. **Career:** Basketball player (retired); NJ Nets, forward-ctr, 1989-90; Phonola Caserta, Italian League, 1990-91; Philadelphia 76ers, 1992-93; Minn Timberwolves, 1994-95; Charlotte Hornets, 1999.

SHADE, DR. BARBARA J.
Educator. **Personal:** Born Oct 30, 1933, Armstrong, MO; daughter of Murray K Robinson and Edna Bowman; married Oscar DePreist; children: Christina Marie, Kenneth E & Patricia Louise. **Educ:** Pittsburg State Univ, BS, 1955; Univ Wis Milwaukee, MS, 1967; Univ Wis Madison, PhD, 1973. **Career:** Univ Wis, Dept Afro-Am Studies, asst prof, 1975; Dane Co Head Start, exec dir, 1969-71; Milwaukee Wis Pub Schs, teacher, 1960-68; Consult, parent Develop Regn, V, 1973-75; Dept Pub Instr Wis, urban educ consult, 1974-75; Univ Wis Parkside, assoc prof & chmn div educ, prof & dean emer, currently. **Orgs:** Delta Sigma Theta Sor, 1952-; Am Psychol Asn; bd pres, St Mary's Hosp Med Ctr, 1978; vpres, Priorities Dane Co United Way, 1979; Asn Black Psychologists, Am Educ Res Asn. **Honors/Awds:** Postdoctoral Fel, Nat Endowment Humanities, 1973-74. **Business Addr:** Emeritus Teacher Education, University of Wisconsin Parkside, 900 Wood Road, PO Box 2000, Kenosha, WI 53141-2000, **Business Phone:** (262)595-2345.

SHADE, DR. GEORGE H, JR.
Physician. **Personal:** Born Jan 4, 1949, Detroit, MI; son of George H Shade Sr and Julia M Bullard; married Carlotta A, Jul 24, 1976; children: Carla N & Ryan M. **Educ:** Wayne State Univ, BS, 1971, MD, 1974, Residency Training - Obstet & Gynec, 1974-78. **Career:** Wayne State Univ Affiliated Hosps, chief resident gynec, 1977-78; Southwest Detroit Hosp, chief gynec, 1981-84; Detroit Receiving Hosp, vchief gynec, 1982-87; Wayne State Univ Sch Med, clinic instr gynec, 1983-87, clinic asst prof, 1987-; Detroit Riverview Hosp, dir resident educ gynec, 1991-, chief obstet & gynec dept, 1995-; OHEP, course instr, 1996-98; Mich State Univ, asst clinical prof, 2000; Phy Leadership Coun St John Health Sys, chmn, 2001-; Sinai-Grace Hosp, vpres, 2005-; pvt pract, currently. **Orgs:** Am Med Asn; Nat Med Asn; Mich State Med Soc; Wayne County Med Soc; Detroit Med Soc; bd dirs, Detroit-Macomb Hosp Corp, 1996-; bd dirs, Wayne State Univ Alumni Asn, 1983-87; bd, Omnicare Health Plans. **Honors/Awds:** Am Legion Scholar Award; 'David S Diamond Award for Obstetrics and Gynecology'; Chrysler Youth Award; Outstanding Senior Residence Award, Obstetrics and Gynecology; Boy Scouts of America, Eagle Scout Award; Detroit Medical Society, Service Award; American Society for Laser Medicine and Surgery, fellow; American Coll of Physician Execs, fel; Am Col Obstet & Gynecs, fellow. **Special Achievements:** Presentations: "Paradoxical Pelvic Masses," Hutzel Hospital, 1986; "Viral Infections in Obstet & Gynec," Detroit Riverview Hospital, 1992; "Urinary Stress Incontinence," Detroit Riverview Hospital, 1992; "Pelvic Endometriosis: Diagnostic Challenges," Henry Ford Hospital, 1993; "Endoscopy in Modern Gynecology," The Detroit Medical Society, 1995. **Home Addr:** 31555 Franklin Fairway, Farmington Hills, MI 48334, **Home Phone:** (248)626-8481. **Business Addr:** Physician, 26400 W 12 Mile Rd Suite 140, Southfield, MI 48034, **Business Phone:** (248)352-8200.

SHADE, SAM
Football player, football coach. **Personal:** Born Jun 14, 1973, Birmingham, AL. **Educ:** Univ Ala. **Career:** Football player (retired), football coach; Cincinnati Bengals, defensive back, 1995-98; Wash Redskins, 1999-2002; pres & ceo, Shade Holdings, LLC, 2004-; corner backs coach, financial consultant, Wealth Mgt Partners, LLC, 2006-. Samford football prog, 2009-. **Honors/Awds:** Redskins' Unsung Hero Award, 2000.

SHAKESPEARE, EASTON GEOFFREY
Consultant, president (organization). **Personal:** Born Mar 20, 1946, Kingston, Jamaica; son of Easton G and Leone Williams-Phillips; married Maria A, Apr 20, 1968; children: Christopher G & Collin M. **Educ:** The Col Arts, Sci & Technol, 1960; Senera Col, 1969; The Col Ins, 1992; The Am Co, CLU, CHFC, 1993. **Career:** Island Life Ins Co-Kingston Jamaica, rep, 1974-77; The Guardian Life Ins Co, group rep, 1978-87; ERA Realtors, real estate assoc, 1990-91; Easton Shakespeare & Assoc, ins broker, 1987-; FF&G Inc, Newark, NJ, vpres & treas, 1991-93; Fin Supermarket Ins Sch, partner & instr, 1992-; Capital Employee Benefit Servs Inc, pres, 1993-97; EMCC Marketing Corp, pres, 1997; Blue Cross & Blue Shield Asn, currently. **Orgs:** Am Soc Chartered Life Underwriters & Chartered Fin Consult, 1983-; NJ Soc CLU's & ChFC, 1985-; NY Soc CLU & CHFC, 1983-85; Monmouth County, NJ Bd Realtors, 1990-; Nat Asn Life Underwriters, 1988; Nat Asn Health Underwriters; Soc Fin Servs

Prof. **Honors/Awds:** Health Ins Asn Am-HIAA Group Ins, 1982; Int Quality Award, Life Ins Mkt & Res Asn, 1975. **Business Addr:** Manager, Blue Cross and Blue Shield Association, PO Box 55, Lithonia, GA 30058, **Business Phone:** (404)312-4141.

SHAKIR, DR. ADIB AKMAL
School administrator. **Personal:** Born Jun 15, 1953, Richmond, VA; married Annette Goins; children: Ameenah N & Yusuf S. **Educ:** Morehouse Col, BA (cum laude), 1976; Norfolk State Univ, MA, Educ, 1980; Fla State Univ, PhD (coun & human systs), 1985. **Career:** Fla A&M Univ, instr psychol, 1981-83; Bethune-Cookman Col, dir coun ctr, 1983-85, asst to pres govt affairs, 1985-86, interim vpres acad affairs & dean fac, 1986-88; Tougaloo Col, pres, 1988-94; Norfolk State Univ, exec asst to pres, 2007-, asst prof psychol; Cassidy & Assocs, srvpres mgt consult; Educ Consult LLC, owner & pres; Mattox Woolfolk LLC, sr consult. **Orgs:** E Cent FL Consortium Higher Educ Indust; Nat Coun Black Studies; Nat Asn Black Psychologists; N FL Chap Asn Black Psychologists; bd dirs, Miss Mus Art; bd dirs, United Negro Coll Fund; bd dirs, Amistad Res Ctr; Asn Black Psychologists; 100 Black Men; Sigma Pi Phi Fraternity. **Honors/Awds:** Presidential Leadership Award, Knight Found, 1991. **Special Achievements:** US President's Bd Advisors on Historically Black Colleges and Universities, 1992-2000. **Home Addr:** PO Box 1504, Daytona Beach, FL 32115. **Business Addr:** Executive Assistant, Assistant Professor Psychology, Norfolk State University, 700 Pk Ave, Norfolk, VA 23504.

SHAKOOR, ADAM ADIB
Lawyer. **Personal:** Born Aug 6, 1947, Detroit, MI; son of Harvey Caddell and Esther Caddell; married Gayle Lawrence; children: Sahir, Lateef, Keisha, Malik, Khalidah, Koya, Kareena & Jelani. **Educ:** Univ MI, Labor Sch, cert Local Union Admin, 1969; Wayne State Univ, cert Local Union Admin, 1969, BS 1971, MEd 1974, JD, 1976; King Abdul Aziz Univ Saudi Arabia, cert, 1977. **Career:** Wayne Co Community Col, Detroit MI, prof bus law & black studies, 1971-93; US Dept Housing & Urban Develop, Grand fel, 1971-73; SE MI Coun Govt, Grad fel, 1971-73; 36th Dist Ct, Detroit MI, chief judge; Common Pleas Ct Judge, Wayne Co, judge, pub adminr, 1981-89; Marygrove Col, Detroit MI, prof real estate law, 1984; City Detroit, dep mayor & chief admin officer, 1989-93; Reynolds, Beeby & Magnuson, PC, managing partner, 1994-97; Shakoor Grubba & Miller, PC, partner & founder, 1997-; Cluster Leaders Mgt Group, chmn. **Orgs:** Consult community affairs, New Detroit Inc, 1973-74; pres, Black Legal Alliance, 1975-76; founding mem, Nat Conf Black Lawyers Detroit Chap, 1975; club pres, Optimist Club Renaissance Detroit, 1982-83; pres, Asn Black Judges MI, 1985-86; Detroit Alumni Chap, Kappa Alpha Phi; pres bd, Boysville Inc, 1994; founder, Nat Day Freedom Inc, 1996. **Honors/Awds:** Scholar, Nat Bar Asn, 1975; Certificate of Distinction, Comt Student Rights, 1979; Certificate of Merit Exceptional Achievement, Govt Affairs MI State Legis, 1980. **Business Addr:** Partner, Founder, Shakoor Grubba & Miller PC, 615 Griswold Suite 1800, Detroit, MI 48226-3989, **Business Phone:** (313)961-2720.

SHAKOOR, DR. WAHEEDAH AQUEELAH (SANDRA SHORT ROBERSON)
School administrator, government official. **Personal:** Born Feb 11, 1950, Washington, DC; married; children: Barella Nazirah. **Educ:** Wilberforce Univ, attended 1971; Univ Cincinnati, BS, 1973; Univ DC, MEd, 1980; Trinity Col, attended 1984; Wash Univ, Doc,Edn,2006. **Career:** Cin Recreation Comn, prog dir, mentally retarded, 1973; Cin Pub Sch, teacher spec educ, 1973-74; Univ Islam, teacher, elem educ, 1974-75; Charles County Schs, teacher spec educ, 1976-79; Dist Columbia Pub Schs, teacher, dept chairperson spec educ, 1979-85; Cardoza High Sch, teacher, dir Eng Lang dept, currently. **Orgs:** Counc Exceptional C, 1971-84; coach Spec, Olympics, 1974-77; Marshall Hts Civic Assn, 1981-84; adv neighborhood, comn, DC Govt, 1981-83; Capitol View Civic Assn, 1981-85; consult brd educ, Sis Clara Muhammad Sch, 1981-85; exec bd mem, Marshall Hts Community Devel Org, 1981-84; educ pres, Wash Saturday Col, 1982-85; pres, Bilal Entr Inc, 1983-85; Friends DC Youth Orchestra, 1985-. **Honors/Awds:** Outstanding Service, DCPS Eastern HS, 1981. **Special Achievements:** Doc Dissertation :"Alternative Assessments for Determining the English Language Proficiency Level of English Language Learners". **Home Addr:** 3510 Sunflower Pl, Bowie, MD 20715, **Home Phone:** (301)860-0316. **Business Addr:** Director, English as Second Language Department, Cardozo High School, 1300 Clifton St NW, Washington, DC 20009.

SHAMBERGER, JEFFERY L
Automotive executive. **Personal:** Married Regina; children: Jason & Jessica. **Educ:** Wilberforce Univ, BS, 1971. **Career:** Shamrock Ford-Lincoln-Mercury, owner, currently. **Business Addr:** Owner, Shamrock Ford-Lincoln-Mercury, 829 Tecumseh Rd, Clinton, MI 49236, **Business Phone:** (517)456-7414.

SHAMBORGUER, NAIMA
Singer. **Personal:** Born in Detroit, MI; daughter of Julian Thomas and Cleopatra Davis Jones; married George L G, Oct 6, 1975; children: Michael Julian Griffin, David William Griffin & James Keith Griffin. **Educ:** Peralta Jr Col, attended 66; Highland Park Community Col, attended 1970; Wayne State Univ, attended 1976, attended 1985. **Career:** Vernor Pre-Sch, head teacher, 1968-72, 1977-79; Story Book Nursery, head teacher & dir, 1972-73; Grand Circus Nursery, head teacher supvr summer, 1974; Greenfield Peace Lutheran Sch, prog dir, 1979-80; Action Head Start, parent involvement coordr, 1980-85; Detroit, Montreux Jazz Festival, performer, 1980-96; Clark & ASC, psychologist asst, 1986-93; Skyline Club,performer, 1988-89; Renaissance Club, house performer, 1989-; Shambones Music, owner, currently; Recordings: Naima's Moods; A Blossom Sings; Negre Con Leche; Tirbute to Louis Armstrong; Hope for Christmas; Songs: "A Blossom Sings"; "Land of Illusion"; "Puerto Vallarta"; "Music In The Air"; "Willy Nilly"; "Yesterday's Everyday"; "I Will Never Walk Away". **Orgs:** Performer, Montreux Jazz Festival, 1980-2000; performer, Skyline Club,1988-89; house performer, Renaissance Club, 1989-; bd mem, Jazz Alliances MIC; bd mem, Ctr Musical Intelligence; Int Asn Jazz Educrs; Jazz Vocal Coalition. **Honors/Awds:** Spirit of Detroit Award, City Detroit, 1984; Outstanding Service Award,Societies Culturally Concerned, 1992; Best Jazz Video, BET Jazz Discovery,1994; Artisans Award, Friends Sch C's Festival, 1995; Special Volunteer,Nat Soc Fund Raising Exec, 1997; Creative Art Grant, Art serve, MI. **Special Achievements:** Michigan Heart Assn Fund raiser, Opening act for Phyllis Diller/ Ruda Lee,1988, Michigan Cancer Foundation Fund raiser, Opening act for Lainie Kazan,1988, Vocal Workshop, Technique and Song, 1989-, voted number 1 female vocalist by the Southeastern Jazz Assn Musicians Poll, 1989, Featured Black History Month WEMU, Eastern Michigan University Radio, co-wrote" Sands of Love", "The Only Blessing That I Have Is You", "It's Good to be home Again", performances with: Steve Turre, Geri Allen, Michigan Jaxx Masters Marcus Blegrave, Donald Walden, Harold Mckinney, Wendell Harrisoin, Teddy Harris, Jr, Marion Hayden, James Carter, Rayse Biggs,George (Sax Man) Benson Donald Byrd, Kenny Burrell, Berry Harris, Rodney Whittaker, Ken Cox, Charlie Gabriel and Lewis Smith, Jonny Turdell, Jimmy Wilkins, Erine Rodgers and the African American Black Caucus Band. **Business Addr:** Owner, Shambones Music, 19760 Hartwell Ave, Detroit, MI 48235, **Business Phone:** (313)863-7168.

SHAMMGOD, GOD
Basketball player. **Personal:** Born Apr 29, 1976, New York, NY. **Educ:** Providence Col, attended. **Career:** Wash Wizards, guard, 1997-98; La Crosse Bobcats, guard, 1999-2000; BrokCzarni Slupsk, 2000-01; Fla Sea Dragons, 2001-02; Zhejiang Horses,2001-02; Al Ittihad (KSA-D1), guard, 2001-02; Zhejiang Horses, 2002-03; Zhejiang Wanma Cyclones, 2003-04; Al Ittihad, guard, 2004; Shanxi Yujun,China; Portland Chinooks, 2009. **Honors/Awds:** Most Valuable Player, Arab Club Championships, 2004; Saudi Arabia League Champion, 2004.

SHAMSID-DEEN, WALEED
Executive. **Personal:** Born Jul 31, 1972, Brooklyn, NY; son of Edith and Lawrence; married; children: 3. **Educ:** Fla A&M Univ, BS, 1994. **Career:** Supreme Fish Delight, vpres, 1994-2001; Youth Vibe Inc, chmn & founder, 1996-; Abdur-Rahim Enterprises Inc, managing partner; AVF Inc, managing partner, 2001-; Shamsid-Deen & Assocs, pres, currently. **Orgs:** Rotary Int; S Dekalb Bus Asn; Leadership Dekalb; adv bd, DeKalb Co Develop; S DeKalb Bus Asn; Youth VIBE, founder. **Honors/Awds:** Outstanding Citizen, GA Secy State, 2003; Rotary Serv Above Self, 1998; People to Watch Award, SDBA, 1999; Community Service Award, The Winning Circle, 1999; Youth Vibe Award, SDBA, 2000; Young Adult of the Year Award, Muslim Soc, 2001; Youth Summit Award, Islamic, 2001; Economics Award, UJAAMA Collective, 2002; Amercian Leader Under 30, Ebony Mag, 2003; Business Man of the Year, S Decatur Bus Asn, 1998. **Business Addr:** President, Shamsid-Deen & Associates, 5240 Snapfinger Pk Dr Suite 125, Decatur, GA 30035, **Business Phone:** (770)593-8900.

SHAMWELL, RONALD L
Educator, executive director. **Personal:** Born Nov 8, 1942, Philadelphia, PA; married Jean; children: Nathan & Monique. **Educ:** Winston-Salem St Univ, BS, 1969; Temple Univ, MSW, 1973. **Career:** Philadelphia Sch, teacher, 1970-71; asst exec dir, 1973; Antioch Col, instr, 1974; Wharton Ctr, exec dir, 1974; Community Col Philadelphia, adj prof, currently. **Orgs:** Asn Black Social Workers; Nat Fed Settlements; bd mem, Urban Priorities; chmn bd, N Cent Dist Youth & Welfare Coun; Del Valley Asn Dirs Vol Prog; bd mem, Comm Concern #13; Rotary Club; consult, Temple Univ Massiah Col; consult, Antioch Col; chmn, Youth Task Force N Cent Philadelphia; Philadelphia Chap Oper Breadbasket. **Honors/Awds:** Honor Award, Temple Univ; Merit Award, Antioch Col.

SHANGE, NTOZAKE (PAULETTE WILLIAMS)
Poet, playwright, writer. **Personal:** Born Oct 18, 1948, Trenton, NJ; daughter of Paul T and Eloise. **Educ:** Barnard Col, BA, Am studies (cum laude) 1970; Univ Southern Calif, MA, 1973. **Career:** Mills Col, teacher; Sonoma St Univ, teacher; Medgar Evers Col, teacher; Univ Calif, Berkeley, teacher, 1972-75; Univ Houston, drama instructor, 1983-; Plays: For Colored Girls Who Have Considered Suicide When the Rainbow Is Enuf, 1976; Sassafrass: A Novella, 1976; A Photograph: Lovers-in-Motion, 1977; Nappy Edges, 1978; Boogie Woogie Landscapes, 1979; Spell #7, 1979; Three Pieces, 1981; Cypress & Indigo, 1983; A Daughter's Geography, 1983; From Okra to Greens, 1984; Betsey Brown, 1985; Ridin' the Moon in Texas, 1988; Daddy Says, 1989; If I Can Cook, You Know God Can, 1998; Float Like a Butterfly: Muhammad Ali, 2002; Ellington Was Not a Street, 2003; Poems: "I Live inMusic", 1994; "Whitewash", 1997; "How I Come By This Cryin' Song", 2006. **Orgs:** Poets & Writers Inc; New York Feminist Art Guild; Inst Freedom Press; fel Guggenheim Found; fel Lila Wallace-Reader's Digest Fund. **Honors/Awds:** Outer Critics Circle Award, 1977; Obie Award, 1977; Audelco Award, 1977; Frank Silvera Writers Workshop Award, 1978; Pushcart Prize. **Business Addr:** Instructor, University of Houston, Department of Drama, 4800 Calhoun Rd, Houston, TX 77004, **Business Phone:** (713)743-2611.

SHANK, SUZANNE
Businessperson. **Personal:** Born 1962; married; children: Devin, Camryn. **Educ:** The Georgia Institute of Technology, BA in Civil Engineering; Univ of Pennsylvania, MBA in Finance. **Career:** President and CEO (Partner) of Siebert Brandford Shank & Co., LLC.; design engineer with a General Dynamics Electric Boat Division. **Orgs:** Board Member of the Municipal Securities Rulemaking Board; member of the National Association of Securities Professionals. **Special Achievements:** Board member of Detroit Regional Chamber, Detroit Institute of Arts, Governing Council, New Economic Initiative, CAMERA (Caribbean American Mission for Education Research in Action); named one of the "50 Most Powerful Black Women in Business" (Feb, 2006), and one of the "75 Most Influential Blacks on Wall Street" (Oct 2005 and Oct 2006),by Black Enterprise Magazine; recognized by Crain's Detroit Business as one of the 40 outstanding leaders under 40, as the Natl Entrepreneur of the year by Madame CJ Walker Center and by the Women's informal Network (Detroit and Wayne County); spearheaded the Detroit Summer Finance Institute internship program, 2000; founding member of Michigan Women in Finance; founding VP of WAVE, a local initiative assisting needy residents with water bills. **Business Addr:** Siebert Brandford Shank & Co, 660 Woodward Ave 2450, Detroit, MI 48226-3528, **Business Phone:** (313)496-4500.*

SHANKS, JAMES A
Mayor. **Personal:** Born Feb 7, 1912, Tutwiler, MS; son of T A Shanks and Dora; married Willye B Harper. **Educ:** Miss Valley State Col, BS, Ed, 1958; Univ St Louis, 1961; Miss State Univ, attended 1964-65. **Career:** Coahoma County Sch System, teacher, 1938-77; Town Jonestown, mayor, 1973-, alderman, 1973. **Orgs:** Deacon/supt & teacher, Met Baptist Church, 1942; secy & treas, Nat Asn Advan Colored People, 1944; MACE, 1944; Elks Club 1946; exec comt, Dem Party County & Dist, 1974; asst prog, Elderly Housing Inc/Manpower Proj, Clarksdale, MS, 1978. **Honors/Awds:** Outstanding Achievement Pub Serv Award, Miss Valley State Col, Itta Bena, 1977; Miss Internal Develop System, Govt Miss, 1978.

SHANKS, TRINA R. **See WILLIAMS, DR. TRINA RACHAEL.**

SHANKS, WILHELMINA BYRD
Executive. **Personal:** Born Jul 19, 1951, Atlanta, GA; daughter of T J Watkins Sr and Annie Beatrice Byrd; divorced; children: Harold Jerome Jr. **Educ:** Morris Brown Col, Atlanta, GA, BA, 1973; Georgia State Univ, Atlanta GA, 1974. **Career:** Rich's, Atlanta GA, sales mgr, 1973-75, buyer, 1975-78; Jordan Marsh, Fort Lauderdale FL, div mgr, 1978-80; Macy's South, Atlanta GA, merchandise mgr, 1980-84, store mgr, 1984-, vpres, 1986-, vice pres & admin, 1986-90; Foley's, Dallas, TX, vpres & gen mgr, 1990-92; Ashford Mgt Group, Atlanta, geo, retail acct exec, 1992-94; Shanks & Assoc Exec & Temp Placement Servs, pres, 1994-; Atlanta Com Olympic Games, dir merchandising, 1996; Reebok Int, vpres apparel forecasting & inventory mgt, 1996-98; Class A Consults, exec consult, 1998-2000; Atlanta Pub Schs, English teacher, 2000. **Orgs:** Bd dirs, Family Life Serv, 1986; Am Bus Women's Asn; ex bd, Romar Acad; AKA; Hundred Black Women, Atlanta Chapter; bd dir, Bethel Acad Advan Career Training; mem, Nat Coalition Black Women. **Honors/Awds:** English Award, Teachers Guild, 1973; Outstanding Leadership Award, Junior Achievement, 1974; Outstanding Business Leaders, Nat Asn Advan Colored People, 1989. **Business Addr:** Member, National Coalition of 100 Black Women, 1925 Adam C Powell Jr Blvd Suite 1L, New York, NY 10026, **Business Phone:** (212)222-5660.

SHANNON, REV. DAVID THOMAS. **See Obituaries section.**

SHANNON, HON. JOHN WILLIAM
Army officer. **Personal:** Born Sep 13, 1933, Louisville, KY; son of John and Alfreda Williams; married Jean Miller, Apr 21, 1956; children: John W Jr. **Educ:** Cent State Univ, BS, 1955; Shippenburg Col, MS, 1975, AUS War Col, Carlisle, PA, 1975. **Career:** AUS, col, 1955-78, Off Sec, Army, Wash, cong liaison officer, 1972-74, Dept Dir Manpower & Reserve Affairs Off, asst secy defense LA, 1975-78, Dept Army Wash, dep dir manpower & res affairs, 1978-81, Off Asst Secy Defense Legis Affairs, spec asst manpower res affairs & logistics, 1978-81, dep under secy, 1981-84, asst secy installations & logistics, 1984-89, under secy army, 1989-93. **Orgs:** Kappa Alpha Psi Fraternity. **Honors/Awds:**

Legion of Merit; Bronze Star; Combat Infantry Badge; Distinguished Civilian Service Award, Dept Army; Secretary of Defense Award for Outstanding Public Service; Defense Superior Service Award; Roy Wilkins Meritorious Service Award. **Military Serv:** AUS, 1955-93.

SHANNON, MARIAN L H
Counselor. **Personal:** Born Oct 12, 1919, Escambia County, FL; daughter of Lacey Sinkfield Harris and James Henry Harris; married TJ. **Educ:** Hampton Inst, BS, 1944; Univ Miami, MEd, 1964. **Career:** Counselor (retired); Dade County Pub Sch, sch counr; Dade County Pub Sch, Stud Serv Guid & Testing, chairperson; Booker T Washington Jr High Sch; Curr Writer Fed Proj, "Self Concept", "Images in Black" & "Counseling the Minority Student"; Bus Educ Courses Social Studies Courses, teacher & test chmn. **Orgs:** Miami Chap March Dimes Found; vpres, Black Archives Hist & Res Found, S Fla; 1987-91; proj coordr, Thedore R Gibson Oratorical/Declamation Contest, 1989-; participant, Intergenerational Proj Dade Pub Schs, 1993-97; phylacter, Fla State Leadership Conf, Zeta Phi Beta Sorority Inc, 1995-03; historian emer, Southeastern Region, Zeta Phi Beta Sorority Inc; sr adult ministry, Greater Bethel Am, 1996; Hist Beta Tau Zeta Chap, 1999-03; couns & res consult senior citizens and youth. **Honors/Awds:** EWD Waters Col, hon doctor, 1954; Outstanding Cit, Omega Psi Phi Frat, 1967; Meritorious Service Award Outstanding Zeta, Zeta Phi Beta Sorority, 1965, 1970; Outstanding Service Award, Prof Orgns 1971-73; Shannon Day, Miami City & Dade County, 1984; Zeta Hall of Fame, Fla, 1986; Educator Trail Blazer Award, Delta Sigma Theta Sorority, 1990; Dade County Woman of Impact Honoree; Dade County Co Women Award, 1995. **Home Addr:** 2191 NW 58 St, Miami, FL 33142-7816.

SHANNON, ODESSA M.
County government official, executive director. **Personal:** Born Jul 4, 1928, Washington, DC; daughter of Gladys McKenzie and Raymond McKenzie; divorced; children: Mark V & Lisa S. **Educ:** Smith Col, BA, 1950. **Career:** EEOC, dep dir field serv, 1979-81; prog planning & eval, dir, 1981-82; nat prog dir, 1982-84; Off Res, exec asst; Bur Census, comp syst analyst; Baltimore Pub Sch, teacher; spec asst to county exec, 1984-86; Montgomery County, MD, human serv coord & planning, dir, 1986-89; dep dir family resources, 1990-94; Montgomery County Md Off Human Rights, exec dir, 1994-, dir human rights comn, currently. **Orgs:** Elected mem bd ed, Montgomery County, MD, 1982-84; regional bd dir, Nat Conf Christians & Jews, 1980-89; Local Coun; United Way; Alpha Kappa Alpha Sor; Nat Asn Advan Colored People; chmn bd dir, Regional Inst Children & Adolescents; bd dir, Montgomery County Arts Coun; chmn bd, Coalition Equitable Representation Govt, 1986-; bd dir, Montgomery Housing Partnership; bd dir, Nat Polit Cong Black Women, 1985-86; bd dir, Nat Coalition 100 Black Women, Montgomery County, 1989-; bd dir, Round House Theatre, 1990-92; bd dir, Metropolitan Boys & Girls Clubs, 1990-92; bd dir, Christmas April, 1989-; bd dir, Positive Shades Black; founder, Montgomery County Human Rights Hall of Fame, 2001. **Honors/Awds:** Outstand Public Service, Am Asn Pub Admin, 1984; Exceptional Achievements, Nat Asn Advan Colored People Legal Def & Ed Fund, 1984; Outstanding Public Service, AKA, 1984; Kappa Alpha Psi, 1982; Alpha Phi Alpha, 1978; Omega Psi Phi, 1977; Outstanding Achievements in Human Rights, Tex State, NAACP, 1983; International Book of Honor, 1986; Hall of Fame, Int Prof & Bus Women, 1994; Woman of Distinction, Comn Women, 1997; Leadership Montgomery, 1997; Archives of Women of historical importance, Montgomery County, comm Women, 2002. **Special Achievements:** First African American woman to have been elected to a policy-making political position in Montgomery County, first woman to hold the post of Special Assistant to the Montgomery County Executive, is honored as One of Nine Montgomery County Women at Women of Achievement Gala, 2006. **Home Addr:** 13320 Bea Kay Dr, Silver Spring, MD 20904. **Business Addr:** Executive Director, Montgomery County Human Rights Commission, 21 Maryland Ave Suite 330, Rockville, MD 20850, **Business Phone:** (240)777-8450.

SHANNON, ROBERT F
Educator, army officer. **Personal:** Born Jul 15, 1920, Montgomery, AL; married Eloise Wynn; children: Robert, Yolanda, Valerie & Charles. **Educ:** AL State Teachers Col, BS, 1940; Wayne State Univ, MA, 1955, EdS, 1974. **Career:** Neighborhood Serv Org, group worker, 1954-64; Detroit Bd Educ, teacher, 1964-65, job upgrading & Couns, 1965-67; elem staff coord, 1967-68; admin, 1968-; Detroit Bd Educ In-Sch Neighborhood Youth Corps, proj dir. **Orgs:** Deacon Tabernacle Bapt Ch, 1961; subcom, Juvenile Delinq State of MI, 1968-71; bd dir, Met Detroit Soc Black Educ Adminrs, 1971; trustee, Detroit Coun Youth Serv, 1971-; educ com, Detroit Urban League, 1972-73; pres bd trust, Afro-Am Mus Detroit, 1974. **Honors/Awds:** Outstanding Service, Wash Sch PTA, 1963; Outstanding Man of Year, Tabernacle Bapt Ch, 1964; Youth Service Award Hannan Br, YMCA, 1969-71; Crisis Team Intervention Sch-Comm Unrest Social Casework, 1971. **Military Serv:** AUS, pvt first class, 1943-46. **Business Addr:** 10100 Grand River, Detroit, MI 48204.

SHANNON, SYLVESTER LORENZO
Clergy. **Personal:** Born May 25, 1935, Pelham, GA; son of J Powell and Maude Kelly; married Doris Brooks Shannon, Dec 28, 1957; children: Glenn Leroy, Keith Lester, Theresa LaVonne. **Educ:** Florida A&M Univ, AB & BS, 1955; Duke Univ Divinity Sch. BDiv & MDiv, 1966, ThM, 1973; Univ Kans, PhD, 1974. **Career:** US Army, staff chaplain, 1966-81; Laconia Assocs, pres & chief exec officer, 1979-99; Thyne Memorial Presbyterian Church, pastor, 1987-90; Siloam Presbyterian Church, sr pastor, 1990-01; chaplain, Pentagon. **Orgs:** chmn bd, Living Water Ministries Int, 1979-; convention chaplain, Alpha Phi Alpha Frat, 1979-97; pres, Duke Divinity Sch, Nat Alumni Coun, 1992-93; candidate gen pres, Alpha Phi Alpha Fraternity. **Honors/Awds:** Eagle Scout, 1948; House of Reps Scholarship, 1951-55; Mary Reynolds Babcock Scholarship, 1963-66; Legion of Merit, 1968. *

SHARP, CHARLES LOUIS
Executive, educator. **Personal:** Born May 19, 1951, Madisonville, KY; son of Macindy and Charlie. **Educ:** Millikin Univ, BS, mkt mgt, 1973; Wash Univ, MBA, mkt mgt, 1975; Univ Wis-Madison, Madison, Wis, PhD, mkt, 1996. **Career:** RJ Reynolds Tobacco Co, Winston-Salem, NC, asst brand mgr & mkt asst, 1975-77, Camel Flavor Brands, Salem Lights, brand mgr, 1977-80, brand mgr spec mkts, 1980-83, prom mgr, 1984-89, group mgr financial control & admin, 1986-89; Southern Ill Univ, Edwardsville, Ill, part-time instr, 1974-75; Winston-Salem State Univ, Div Bus & Econs, from part-time instr to instr, 1982-90; Univ Louisville, Sch Bus, instr, 1990; Upper Iowa Univ, adj prof, 1992; Univ Wis-Madison, Wis, Sch Bus, teaching asst, 1991-96; Univ Louisville, Col Bus & Pub Admin, asst prof, 1997-. **Orgs:** Big Brother & Big Sister, 1983-87; Young Men Christian Asn, 1984-; treas, Civic Develop Coun, 1987; Entrepreneurship Fac Res Team, 1996-99; Int MBA Team, 1999-2002; MBA Prog Comt, 1999-2003; Hon & Awards Comt, currently; fac adv, Alpha Kappa Psi Prof Bus Frat, Omicron Phi Chap; fac adv, Stud Mkt Asn; Fac Grievance Rev Comt; fac lectr, Proj BUILD; Integrated MBA Comt, currently; Stud Recruitment & Retention Comt, currently; Am Mkt Asn; Asn Consumer Res; Acad Mkt Sci. **Honors/Awds:** Gen Motors Scholar; HF Bird Scholar-Athlete Award; Scholar, Millikin Univ;Gen Motors Fel, Washington Univ; Nat Consortium Educ Access Fel; AdvanOpportunity Fel; Outstanding Teacher Award, EMERGE Prog, Univ Wis; Red &Black Athletes 2003 Awards Banquet; Undergrad Teacher of the Year Award,Col Bus, 2004; Womens Field Hockey Honorary Game Coach, 2004; CertAppreciation, Black Exec Exchange Prog, Am Mkt Asn; Numerous honors,awards & scholarships. **Special Achievements:** Published numerous articles including "Big Brother Has A Deal For You: TheEthics of M-Commerce", "Future External Reference Prices: You Better BuyNow", Soc Mkt Advances Conf, 2001; "The Best Undergraduate MarketingEducation Program: An Assessment", Mkt Educ Rev, 2002; "Making GradingEasier: The Use of Rubrics in Grading Written Cases", "InstitutionalProductivity in the Scholarship of Teaching: A Study of MarketingEducation Journal Publications", Mkt Educ Rev, 2003; "Valuing The OptionTo Fire Your Customer: An Integrative Marketing/Finance Exercise", MktEduc Rev, 2004; "Racial Identity and Art Consumption", Acad Mkt Sci AnnualConf, 2005. **Home Addr:** 129 Gardiner Lake Rd, Louisville, KY 40205. **Business Addr:** Assistant Professor of Marketing, University of Louisville, College of Business, Rm 153, Louisville, KY 40292, **Business Phone:** (502)852-7565.

SHARP, DR. J ANTHONY
Consultant, school administrator. **Personal:** Born Dec 27, 1946, Norfolk, VA; son of James A and Viola Brown; married Khalilah Z, Jan 1975 (divorced 1986); children: Tahmir T & Aleem S. **Educ:** Norfolk State Univ, Norfolk, undergrad study, 1968-70; Long Island Univ, NY, BA, polit sci, 1971; New York Univ, New York, MA, polit sci, 1972; Yavapai Community Col, Prescott, AA, gen educ, 1982; Univ Miami, Coral Gables, PhD, higher educ. **Career:** USF, aircraft mech, 1964-68; Embry-Riddle Aero Univ, flight instr & flight supvr, 1978-81; Hawthorne Aviation, contract & charter pilot, 1982-83; Elizabeth City State Univ, adj instr airway sci, 1986; Hampton Univ, asst prof airway sci, 1986-89; Fla Mem Col, Div Airway & Comput Scis, chp, 1989-94; Nova Southeastern Univ, prof technol, 1994-96; Ohio State Univ, Dept Aviation, chmn, 2005-; consult currently. **Orgs:** Aircraft Owners & Pilot Asn, 1976-; pres, Nat Asn Minorities Aviation, 1976-; Tuskegee Airmen Inc, 1987-90; Univ Aviation Asn, 1989-; Negro Airmen Int, 1990-; 100 Black Men S Fla, 1991-; Am Inst Aeronautics & Astronautics, 1989-; bd mem, Magnet Educa Choice Asn Inc, Dade County, 1992; Nat Asn Advan Colored People. **Honors/Awds:** Arizona Flight Instructor of the Year, Scottsdale, AZ, 1980. **Military Serv:** USF, sgt, 1964-68; US Armed Forces Air Medal, 1968. **Business Addr:** Chairman, Ohio University, Department of Aviation, 751 Columbia Rd, Albany, OH 45701, **Business Phone:** (740)597-2626.

SHARP, JAMES ALFRED
Executive. **Personal:** Born May 28, 1933, New York, NY; married Tessie Marie Baltrip; children: Owen, Jacqueline H, James A III & LaTanya M. **Educ:** Univ Calif San Diego; John F Kennedy Sch. **Career:** US Senate, Senator Donald Riegle Jr, mgr state serv; City Flint Mich, mayor, 1983-87; City Mgt Corp, vpres community & govt affairs, 1988-98. **Orgs:** Bd dir, Oakland Univ Found; chmn, Detroit Inst Art, 1998-2000, bd dir, currently. **Military Serv:** US Marine Corps, sgt; Served in Korea, Cuba, Vietnam; Vietnam Cross of Gallantry; 3 Navy Commendation Medals for Valor; Purple Heart. **Business Phone:** (248)386-4242.

SHARP, JEAN MARIE
School administrator. **Personal:** Born Dec 31, 1945, Gary, IN. **Educ:** Ball State Univ, BA, 1967; Ind Univ, MA, teaching, 1969; Columbia Univ, Teachers Col, EdM, 1975, EdD, 1976. **Career:** Froebel HS Gary, IN, teacher, 1966-68; W Side HS Gary, IN, dept chmn & teacher, 1969-72; Doctoral Prog Educ Leadership, Ford Found fel, 1973-76; Gen Asst Ctr, Columbia Univ, field specialist, 1976; Off Human & Develop Serv, special asst to asst secy, 1977; Rockefeller Found fel, 1977; Montclair Bd Educ, dir pupil, 1978-, asst supt admin serv, 1978. **Orgs:** Am Asn Sch Admin, 1980; Black Child Develop Inst, 1980; Kappa Delta Pi, 1980; coord, 1st & 2nd Ann Black Representation Orgn Symp, 1973-74; Uhuru-Sasa Sch Brooklyn, 1975; vpres, Nu Age Ctr Harlem, 1979-. **Honors/Awds:** Outstanding Young Women of the Year, United Fedn Women, 1971; Stud Senate Award, Columbia Univ, NY, 1974. **Business Addr:** Director, Montclair Board of Education, 22 Valley Rd, Montclair, NJ 07042.

SHARP, SAUNDRA
Writer, movie director, actor. **Personal:** Born Dec 21, 1942, Cleveland, OH; daughter of Faythe McIntyre and Garland Clarence. **Educ:** Bowling Green State Univ, Bowling Green, Ohio, BS, 1964; Los Angeles City Col, Los Angeles, Calif, attended 1980-84, 1989. **Career:** Plays: "Black Girl", "To Be Young, Gifted & Black," "Hello, Dolly!"; Playwright: "The Sistuhs"; Voices Inc, Los Angeles, CA, head writer, 1988; Black Film Review, former asn ed; Black Anti-Defamation Coalition, newsletter, ed; publ & ed: The Black History Film List; Poets Pay Re Too, 1989; Books: Typing in the Dark, 1991; From The Windows of My Mind, 1970; In the Midst of Change, 1972; Soft Song, 1978; Black Women For Beginners, 1993; TV series: "The Jeffersons", 1977; The Greatest Thing That Almost Happened, 1977; "Wonder Woman", 1977-79; Minstrel Man, 1977; "Good Times", 1978; "Charlie's Angels", 1978-80; "Barnaby Jones", 1978-79; Night Cries, 1978; Lou Grant, 1978; "The White Shadow", 1979-81; Hollow Image, 1979; "The Incredible Hulk", 1980; "Different Strokes", 1981; "Benson", 1981; "NBC Special Treat", 1984; "St. Elsewhere", 1984-87; "Knots Landing", 1985; "T.J. Hooker", 1985; Films: The Learning Tree, 1969; Back Inside Herself, producer, writer & dir, 1984; Picking Tribes, dir, ed, writer & producer, 1989; The Healing Passage: Voices from the Water, exec producer, writer & dir, 2004; Dilemma, producer, 2006. **Orgs:** Black Am Cinema Soc; Reel Black Women; Atlanta African Film Soc; co-founder, Black Anti-Defamation Coalition. **Honors/Awds:** First place film production, Black American Film Soc, 1984 & 1989; First Place, San Francisco Poetry Film Festival, 1985; Heritage Magazine Award for outstanding journalism, 1988; Paul Robeson Award, Newark Black Film Festival, 1989; Artist Grant, Calif Arts Coun, 1992; Best Script Award, Black Filmmakers Hall of Fame, 1992; Poet of Los Angeles' Watts Towers Arts Center, 2006-07. **Business Addr:** Actress, c/o Allen & Associates, 5417 Whitesept Ave, North Hollywood, CA 91607, **Business Phone:** (213)462-6565.

SHARPE, DR. AUDREY HOWELL
Educator, school principal, physician. **Personal:** Born Dec 14, 1938, Elizabeth City, NC; daughter of Simon and Essie Griffin; married Willie M, Aug 7, 1964; children: Kimberly Y. **Educ:** Hampton Inst, BS, 1960; Northwestern Univ, MA, 1966; Ball State Univ, Ed.D,1980. **Career:** Educator (retired); State Ind Ft Wayne, speech & hearing therapist, 1960-62; State Ill Dixon, hearing & speech specialist, 1962-64; Ft Wayne, speech & hearing therapist, 1964-65; Univ Mich C Psychiatric Hosp Ann Arbor, educ diagnostician lang pathologist, asst prin, 1965-68; E Wayne St Ctr Ft Wayne, Head start dir, 1968-69; Purdue Univ, lecturer educ, 1968-69; E Allen Co Sch, Title I teacher, 1973-74, Title I coordr, 1974, prin; Village Woods Jr High, asst prin, 1980-81; Village Elem Sch, prin 1981-84; Sch & Community Rels, dir, 1994-96; Hoagland Sch, prin, 1996-98. **Orgs:** Am Speech & Hearing Asn, 1961-74; Asn C with Learning Disabilities, 1968; bd dir, Three Rivers Asn C with Learning Disabilities, 1969-72; DST; Alpha Kappa Mu; Kappa Delta Pi; Morrow Presbyterian Ch Morrow, Ga; Delta Sigma Theta Sorority; Leadership, Ft Wayne; bd dir, YWCA, 1984-87; Jr League. **Honors/Awds:** Woman of the Year, DST, 1973; Florene Williams Service Award, 1986; EDR of the Year, Phi Beta Sigma, 1987; Dual Service Award, 1988; Service Award, KAP Fraternity, 1984-85. **Special Achievements:** Author: "Another View of Affective Education: The Four H's-Honesty,Humaneness, Humility, and Hope", Principal, Fall 1985; "Language Training in Headstart Programs", ISHA, Spring 1969; "Pass Me That Language Ticket", Principal, Spring 1986; "Physical Education, A No Frills Component to the Elementary Curriculum", Principal, Fall 1984; guest columnist: Fort Wayne News-Sentinel; Frost Illustrated. **Home Addr:** 5415 Emily Cir, Ellenwood, GA 30294-4327. *

SHARPE, DR. CALVIN WILLIAM
Lawyer, educator. **Personal:** Born Feb 22, 1945, Greensboro, NC; son of Mildred Johnson and Ralph David; married Janice McCoy Jones; children: Kabral, Melanie & Stephanie. **Educ:** Clark Col, BA, philos & relig, 1967; Oberlin Col, Post-Baccalaureate psychol, 1967-68; Northwestern Univ, Law Sch, JD, 1974; Chicago Theol Sem, MA, philos, relig & polit sci, 1996. **Career:** Hon Hubert L Will US Dist Ct, law clerk, 1974-76; Cotton Watt Jones King & Bowlus Law Firm, assoc, 1976-77; Nat Labor Rels Bd,

trial atty, 1977-81;Univ Va, Law Sch, asst prof, 1981-84; Wake Forest Univ, vis assoc prof law, 1982-83; Case Western Res Univ, vis assoc prof law, 1983-84, assoc prof law, 1984-88, prof law, 1988-, John Deaver Drinko-Baker & Hostetler chair, 1990-, assoc dean acad affairs, 1991-92, John Deaver Drinko-Baker & Hostetler prof law, 1999-, Ctr Interdisciplinary Study Conflict & Dispute Resolution, dir, currently; Ariz State Univ Col Law (Tempe), scholar residence, 1990; George Wash Univ, Nat Law Ctr, DC, vis prof, 1991; DePaul Univ Col Law, distinguished vis prof, 1995-96; Chicago-Kent Col Law,vis scholar. **Orgs:** Labor, Am Arbitration Asn, 1984-; bd trustees, Cleveland Hearing & Speech Ctr, 1985-89; OH State Employment Rels Bd Panel Neutrals, 1985-;chair-evidence sect, Asn Am Law Schs, 1987; exec bd, Pub Sector Labor Rels Asn, 1987-89; Fed Mediation & Conciliation Serv Roster Arbitrators, 1987-;OH Health Care Employees Asn Dist, 1199, 1987-92; AFSCME/OCSEA, 1987-92;Fedn Police, 1988-92; State Coun Prof Educr OEA/NEA, 1989-; Youth Serv Subsid Adv Bd Comnr, Cuyahoga Co, Ohio, 1989; Nat Acad Arbitrators, 1991-;Asn Am Law Schs Comn Sect & Annual Meeting, 1991-94; convener & first chair, Labor & Employment Law Sect IRRA, 1994-96; Univ Minn Panel Arbitrators, 2000-; Phoenix Employ Rels Bd Panel Neutrals; Los Angeles City Employee Rels Bd Panel Neutrals; Permanent Arbitrator State Ohio; Am Bar Asn. **Special Achievements:** First National Artra Scholar; Publisher: Two-Step Balancing & the Admissibility of Other Crimes Evidence, A Sliding Scale of Proof, 59 Notre Dame Law Review 556, 1984;.Proof of Non-Interest in Representation Disputes, A Burden Without Reason,. 11 Univ Dayton Law Review 3, 1985; Collective Bargaining,Univ of Toledo Law Review, 1987; .NLRB Deferral to Grievance-Arbitration,A General Theory,. 48 Ohio St LJ No 3, 1987; Introd, The Natl War Labor Bdand Critical Issues in the Develop of Modern Grievance Arbitration, 39Case W Res L Rev No 2, 1988; A Study of Coal Arbitration Under the Natl Bituminous Coal Wage Agreement-Between, 1975, 1991, vol 93, issue 3, Natl Coal Issue, W Va Law Review; .The Art of Being A Good Advocate,. Dispute Resolution Journ, January 1995; .Judging in Good Faith -Seeing Justice Marshall's Legacy Through A Labor Case,. 26 Ariz State LJ 479 (1994);.From An Arbitrator's Point of View—The Art of Being a Good Advocate;.Dispute Resolution Journ, 1995; Book Review: Edward J Imwinkelreid, Evidentiary Distinction: Understanding the Federal Rules of Evidence, 1993; & Arthus Best, Evidence & Explanations, 1993; 46 J Legal Ed 150,1996; book chp, Seniority, pub in Common Law of the Workplace, 1998; the Nalt Labor Relations Act,. Berkeley Jnl of Employ & Labor Law, 1999;co-auth, book, Understanding Labor Law, 1999; .Judicial Review of Arbitration Awards Under the New S Afr Labour Relations Act of 1995, CaseW Res J Intl, 2001; numerous others. **Business Addr:** John Deaver Drinko-Baker & Hostetler Professor, Director, Case Western Reserve University, 11075 E Blvd, Cleveland, OH 44106, **Business Phone:** (216)368-5069.

SHARPE, FELIX
Personal: Married Lisa Webb Sharpe. **Career:** Detroit City, aide to mayor; archiveher's staff, ending, 1999; DeMaria Bldg Co, dir bus develop & govn rels; Strategic Staffing Solutions, vpres bus develop, currently. **Orgs:** Detroit Regional Chamber of Com. **Business Phone:** (313)965-1110.

SHARPE, SHANNON
Television show host, football player. **Personal:** Born Jun 26, 1968, Chicago, IL. **Educ:** Savannah State Univ, criminal justice. **Career:** Football player (retired), Television show host; Denver Broncos, tightend, 1990-99 & 2002-03; Baltimore Ravens, 2000-01; CBS TV Network, studio analyst, 2004-. **Honors/Awds:** Super Bowl Champion. **Special Achievements:** Played in World Series of Poker, 2005; appeared in SIRIUS NFL Radio's Movin' The Chains & writes a column on NFL.com. finalists, Pro Football Hall of Fame, 2009. **Business Phone:** (954)351-2120.

SHARPE, V RENEE
Consultant. **Personal:** Born Oct 24, 1953, Jackson, TN; daughter of Vermon Huddleston Cathey and Marvin Cathey. **Educ:** Memphis State Univ, Memphis, TN, BBA, 1974, MBA, 1979; State Tech Inst, Memphis, TN, AAS, 1976. **Career:** Transamerica Ins, Los Angeles, CA, proj leader, 1979-81; FedEx, Memphis, TN, tech consult, 1981-2001. **Orgs:** Stud tutor, Neighborhood Christian Ctr, 1982-95; Asn Female Execs, 1986-95; pres, Memphis chap, Black Data Processing Assoc, 1989-90; NAACP, 1989-90; Nat corr secy, Black Data Processing Assoc, 1991-92; Allocations Comt, United Way Greater Memphis.

SHARPER, DARREN
Football player, talk show host. **Personal:** Born Nov 3, 1975, Richmond, VA; son of Harry and Pauline; children: Amara. **Educ:** Col William & Mary, BA, sociol, 1997. **Career:** Green Bay Packers, defensive back, 1997-2004; Minnesota Vikings, 2005-08;color commentator, 2004-07. New Orleans Saints, 2009-. **Honors/Awds:** First-team All-Yankee, 1994; 1995; 1996, Hall of Fame, Col William & Mary, 2008. All-Pro selection, 2000, 2002, 2005, 2007. Pro Bowl selection, 2000, 2002, 2005, 2007. **Business Addr:** Safety, NEW ORLEANS SAINTS, 5800 Airline Dr, Metairie, LA 70003, **Business Phone:** (504)733-0255.

SHARPLESS, MATTIE R
Federal government official. **Personal:** Born Jul 1, 1943, Hampstead, NC. **Educ:** NC Cent Univ, BA, bus educ, MBA, bus admin & econs. **Career:** USDA Foreign Serv, Off Agr Affairs, Geneva & Bern, Switzerland, US Mission Europe Union, Brussels, Belgium, Rome, Italy, Paris & France, Foreign Agr Serv, acting adminr, spec asst dep under secy, currently; US Ambassador, currently. **Honors/Awds:** Numerous performance awards & citations including the prestigious Presidential Meritorious Service Award, 1998; Presidential Distinguished Service Award, 2001. **Business Phone:** (202)690-1177.

SHARPP, NANCY CHARLENE
Social worker. **Personal:** Born in Pine Bluff, AR; married Tilmon Lee; children: Tilmon Monroe. **Educ:** Wayne State Univ, BA, 1961; Govs State Univ, MA, 1976. **Career:** Ill Dept Corrections Juvenile Div, supvr, admin, 1966-79; Ill Dept C & Family Servs, mgr support servs, 1979-81, case review admin, 1981-; W Maywood Park Dist, pres bd commrs. **Orgs:** Panelist Panel Am Women, 1968-72; founder & pres, Chicago Area Club-Nat Asn Negro Bus & Prof Womens Clubs, 1977-82; founder, Ascension Manhood, 1982; life mem, Nat Asn Negro Bus Prof Womens Clubs; comdr, W Maywood Park Dist, 1981. **Honors/Awds:** Nat Presidents Award, Nat Asn Negro Bus & Prof Womens Clubs, 1977; Sperry-Hutchins Community Serv Award, Sperry-Hutchins Corp & NANBPW, 1981; Community Image Award, Fred Hampton Mem Scholarship Fund Inc, 1983. **Business Addr:** President Bd of Commissioners, West Maywood Park District, 16th & Washington, Maywood, IL 60153.

SHARPTON, AL. See SHARPTON, REV. ALFRED CHARLES.

SHARPTON, REV. ALFRED CHARLES (AL SHARPTON)
Activist, politician, clergy. **Personal:** Born Oct 3, 1954, Brooklyn, NY; son of Alfred C Sharpton Sr and Ada Richards; married Kathy Jordan, Oct 31, 1985; children: Dominique & Ashley. **Educ:** Brooklyn Col, attended 1975. **Career:** SCLC Oper Breadbasket, NY, youth dir, 1969-71; Nat Youth Movement Inc, founder, pres, 1971-86; singer James Brown, rd mgr, 1973-80; Wash Temple Church God Christ, jr pastor; Nat Action Network Inc, founder, pres, 1991-. **Orgs:** Founder & dir, Nat Youth Movement, 1971-88; nat coordr, Nat Rainbow Coalition's Minister Div, 1993-; assoc minister, Bethany Baptist Church, Brooklyn, 1994-; co-founder, Second Chance, 1999. **Honors/Awds:** Man of the Year Award, Omega Psi Phi Fraternity; Fel Award, Goldsmith Col, London, England, 1991; Man of the Year, Caribbean-Am Lobby, 1992; Community Service Award, SCLC, Buffalo Chap,1992; Key to the City, City Orange, 1993; Man of the Year, NY State Cult Soc, 1993; Ecumenical Freedom Fighter Award, 1998; Hennessy Priviledge Award, 2003. **Special Achievements:** State Senate candidate, 1978; first African-American Senate candidate in NY hist, US Senate Dem Primary, NY State, 1992; US Senate NY Dem Primary received 27% of statewide vote, 90% of black statewide vote; Go and Tell Pharaoh: The Autobiography of Al Sharpton, 1996; NYC Mayoral candidate, 1997; presidential candidate, 2004; cameo appearances in the movies: Cold Feet, Bamboozled & Mr. Deeds; TV shows: "New York Undercover," "Law & Order: Special Victims Unit," "Girlfriends," "My Wife and Kids," "Boston Legal," Spike TV reality television show, "I Hate My Job," host; nomination for the US presidential election, 2004. **Business Addr:** President, National Action Network Inc, 1941 Madison Ave Suite 2, New York, NY 10035, **Business Phone:** (212)987-5020.

SHARPTON, DENISE
Public relations executive. **Personal:** Born Jul 18, 1958, Vero Beach, FL; daughter of Raymond. **Educ:** Fla A&M Univ, attended 1978; Fla State Univ, BS, 1979. **Career:** KKDA Radio, news anchor, pub affairs host; SHARP/PR, pres, currently. **Orgs:** Chmn, Multi-Ethnic Heritage Found. **Honors/Awds:** Businesswoman of the Year, Iota Phi Lambda, 1993.

SHATTEEN, WESTINA MATTHEWS
Executive. **Personal:** Born Nov 8, 1948, Chillicothe, OH; daughter of Wesley Smith Matthews; married Alan. **Educ:** Univ Dayton, BS, 1970, MS, 1974; Univ Chicago, PhD, 1980. **Career:** Mills Lawn Elem Sch, Yellow Springs, OH, teacher, 1970-76; Stanford Res Inst, Menlo Park, CA, admin asst, 1976-77; Chicago Community Trust, Chicago, IL, sr prog officer, 1982-85; Merrill Lynch, dir, philanthropic programs, 1985-97, first vpres, global diversity, 1997-2000, sr vpres, community develop serv, 2000-01, first vpres, community leadership, global pvt client group, 2001-03, Merrill Lynch, first vpres, community leadership, chief financial officer, 2003-. **Orgs:** Bd mem, Exec Leadership Coun; New York Bd Educ, 1990-93; trustee, Univ Dayton; pres, New York Women's Forum, 2006-. **Honors/Awds:** Hon Doctorate Humanities, Carlow Col, 2000; Honarary Degree, Doctor Humane Letters, Metrop Col New York; Kizzy Award, Black Women Hall of Fame Foundation, 1985; Donald H. McGannon Award, New Urban League, New York, 1994; Woman of Distinction Award, Girl Scout Council of Greater New York, 1998; Corporate Leadership Award, Brooklyn Center for the Performing Arts, 2001; Urban Angel Award, New York Theological Seminary, 2004. **Special Achievements:** Author of Have A Little Faith.the faith of a mustard seed, 2003, Have A Little Faith for Women Fully Grown, 2004, Have A Little Faith in the Midst of Relationships, 2005; first black woman elected a trustee of the Merrill Lynch Foundation. **Business Addr:** Managing Director, Merrill Lynch & Co Inc, 4 World Financial Ctr 15th Fl, 250 Vesey St, New York, NY 10080, **Business Phone:** (212)449-5679.

SHAVERS, CHERYL L.
Chairperson, scientist, chief executive officer. **Personal:** Born in Phoenix, AZ; married Joe Agu, Jan 1, 1984; children: Cecily. **Educ:** Ariz State Univ, BS, chem, 1976, PhD, Solid State Chem, 1981. **Career:** Motorola, prod engr, 1976; Libr Cong, US Patent & Trademark Off Dept Comn, registered patent agt, 1984-; Aspen Inst, Henry Crown fel, 1998; Under Secy Comn Technol, US Dept Comn, staff, 1999; Bit Arts, chair, 2001-; Global Smarts Inc, chairwoman & chief exec officer, 2001-; Hewlett-Packard, process engr; Wiltron Co, microelectronics sec mgr; Varian Assocs, thing films appln mgr; Intel Corp, Technol & Mfg Group, genmgr advan technol oper; ATMI Inc, dir, 2006-. **Orgs:** US-Israel Sci & Technol Comn; bd dir, US-Israel Sci & Technol Found;co-chair, Technol Subcomt, US-Egypt Partnership Econ Growth; Technol Comt, US-China Joint Mgt Comt; US-Japan Joint High Level Comn; Media Tech Capital Partners; Am Red Cross; Am Vacuum Soc. **Honors/Awds:** Inter Nat Network of Women in Technology Hall of Fame, 1996; Honorary Master Degree Engineering Management, Calif Poly tech State Univ, 1996; Col Liberal Arts & Science Hall of Fame, Ariz State Univ, 1997; Presenter of the Year, San Francisco Bay Area Chap of the Nat Black MBA Asn, 1998. **Business Addr:** Chairwoman, Chief Executive Officer, Global Smarts Inc, 3333 Bowers Ave Suite 130, Santa Clara, CA 95051, **Business Phone:** (408)844-9099.

SHAW, DR. ANN
College teacher. **Personal:** Born Nov 21, 1921, Columbus, OH; daughter of Pearl Daniel and Sarah Roberts; widowed; children: Valerie, Leslie Jr, Rebecca & Dan. **Educ:** Univ Redlands, AB, 1943, LHD, 1971; OH State Univ, MA, 1944; Univ Sothern Calif, MSW, 1968. **Career:** Univ Calif Los Angeles, teacher; LA Job Corps Ctr Women, exec asst, 1965-66; LA City Sch, teacher, 1949-51; Cent St Col, asst prof, 1946-48; Va Union Univ, instr; Founders Savings & Loan Assoc, chmn bd, 1986-87. **Orgs:** Bd mem, The California Community Found, The California Med Ctr Found; appointed to serve on Calif Joint Select Task Force on the Changing Family; alumni asn; Univ Sothern Calif; OH St & Redlands Univ; PTA; Nat Coun Negro Women; Nat Asn Advan Colored People; mem, YWCA World Serv Coun; pres, Wilfandel Club; bd dir, Lloyds Bank Calif, 1978-85; charter mem, Am Women Int. **Honors/Awds:** Agency leadership awards & com Womens Div United Way; cert merit, Assn Study Negro Life & Hist, 1964; Univ Redlands, 1964; Woman of the Year LaSentinel Newspaper, 1964; Royal Blue Book; Nat Asn Advan Colored People Legal Defense & Educ Fund Award, Black Women of Achievement, 1985; BigSisters Los Angeles Award, 1986; Calif Senate Woman of the Year Award, Senatorial Dist 30, 1987; United Way's Highest Honor The Gold Key Award; The Athena Award, YWCA, 1989; Community Serv Award, YWCA, 1989; The Key Council Award, California Afro-Amer Museum, 1989; Calif Welfare Archives, Lantern of Hope Award, Calif Med Ctr Community Leadership, 1997; Distinguished Aluma Award, USC, 2001. **Home Addr:** 1650 S Victoria Ave, Los Angeles, CA 90019.

SHAW, BERNARD
Television news anchorperson. **Personal:** Born May 22, 1940, Chicago, IL; son of Edgar and Camilla Murphy; married Linda Allston, Mar 30, 1974; children: Amar Edgar & Anil Louise. **Educ:** Univ Ill, Chicago Circle, hist, 1963. **Career:** Television News Anchorperson (retired); WYNR/WNUS-Radio, Chicago IL, reporter, 1964-66; Westinghouse Broadcasting Co, Chicago IL, reporter, 1966-68; corresp, WA, DC, 1968-71; Columbia Broadcasting System, WA, DC, tv reporter, 1971-74, corresp, 1974-77; Am Broadcasting Co, Miami, FL, corresp & chief Latin Am bur, 1977-79; Cable News Network, WA, DC, tv news anchor, 1980-2001, chief anchor. **Orgs:** Nat Press Club; Sigma Delta Chi; fel Soc Prof Journalists. **Honors/Awds:** Hon Doctorate, Marion Col, 1985; Distinguished Service Award, Cong Black Caucus, 1985; Lowell Thomas Electronic Journalism Award, 1988; Golden Award for Cable Excellence, Nat Acad Cable Programming; Best New Anchor, 1988; Journalist of the Year, Nat Asn Black Journalists, 1989; George Foster Peabody Broadcasting Award, 1990; Golden Award for Cable Excellence, Nat Acad Cable Programming, ACE, 1991; Gold Medal, Int Film & TV Festival; Nat Headliner Award; Overseas Press Club Award; Best Newscaster, 1991; Cultural Journalistic Award, Eduard Rhein Found, 1991; President's Award, Italian Government, 1991; David Brinkley Award for Excellence in Communications, Barry Univ, 1991; Chairman's Award for Outstanding Journalistic Excellence, NAACP, 1992; Best Newscaster of the Year, Award for Cable Excellence, 1992 & 1993; Honor Medal for Distinguished Service in Journalism, Univ Mo, 1992; Emmy Award, Nat News &Documentary Competition, 1992; Best Newscaster, 1993; Dr Martin Luther King Jr Award for Outstanding Achievement, Cong Racial Equality, 1993; Dr Martin Luther King Jr Award for Outstanding Achievement, Cong Racial Equality, 1993; Hon Doctor of Humane Letters Degree, Univ Ill, 1993; William Allen White Medallion for Distinguished Service, Univ Kans, 1994; Nat Headliner Award, Nat Conf Christians & Jews-Miami Region, 1994; Hon Doctorate, Northeastern Univ, 1994; Emmy Award,

Instant Coverage of a Single Breaking News Story, 1996; Edward R Murrow Award, Best TV Interp or Documentary on Foreign Affairs, 1996; Paul White Life Achievement Award, 1996; Best Newscaster of the Year, Award for Cable Excellence, 1996; Trumpet Award, 1997; Chicago Journalists Hall of Fame, 1997; Tex McCrary Award for Journalism; Congressional Medal of Honor Society; Broadcasting &Cable Hall of Fame, 1999; Hubert M Humphrey 1st Amendment Freedom Prize, Anti-Defamation League, 2001; Pioneer in Broadcasting Award, Nat Asn Black Owned Broadcasters, 2001; Edward R Murrow Lifetime Achievement Award, Washington State Univ, 2001. **Special Achievements:** Held exclusive interview with Saddam Hussein, Operation Desert Storm, October 1990; presidential debate moderator, second debate in Los Angeles,1988; named to top ten outstanding business and professional honorees list, 1988; Bernard Shaw Endowment Fund established, Univ of IL Foundation, 1991; Democratic presidential candidates' debate moderator, third debate, 1992; first correspondent/anchor to break the news of Jan17, 1994, Los Angeles earthquake; anchored CNN's live coverage of President Bill Clinton's first Economic Summit from Tokyo, 1993; moderated vice presidential debate, 2000. **Military Serv:** USMC, 1959-63.

SHAW, BOOKER THOMAS
Judge, educator. **Personal:** Born Sep 14, 1951, St Louis, MO; married Jane; children: 3. **Educ:** Southern Ill Univ, Carbondale, BA, govt, 1973; Catholic Univ Am, DC, JD, 1976; MO Bar, 1976; Nat Judicial Col, attended 1983; Am Acad Judicature, attended 1989. **Career:** Fed Trade Comn, law clerk, 1974; Columbus Comm Legal Servs, Wash, DC, law clerk, 1975-76; Circuit Atty Off, asst circuit atty, 1976-83; MO, assoc judge, circuit judge, 1983-2002; Eastern Dist Ct Appeals, MO, judge, 2002-; Eastern Dist Ct Appeals, MO, judge, 2006-; Emory Trial Tech Prog; Nat Inst Trial Advocacy; Miss Bar CLE prog; Wash Univ Sch Law, adj prof trial advocacy, currently. **Orgs:** Mound City Bar Asn; Metro Bar Asn; St John AME Church; trustee; Nat BarAsn; Second Presbyterian Church. **Honors/Awds:** Scholar Award in Music, Southern Ill Univ, 1970-72; Spirit of St Louis Scholar Award, 1975; Am-Jur Bk Award, 1976; Distinguished Service, Mound City Bar, 1983; Distinguished Service, Circuit Atty, St Louis, 1983; Outstanding Service, Black Law Studs, Wash Univ, 1989; Outstanding Service, Judicial Coun, Nat Bar Asn, 1992. **Business Addr:** Adjunct Professor, Washington University School of Law, 1 Brookings Dr, PO Box 1120, St Louis, MO 63130-4899, **Business Phone:** (314)935-6400.

SHAW, BRIAN K
Basketball coach, basketball player. **Personal:** Born Mar 22, 1966, Oakland, CA. **Educ:** St Marys Col, attended 1985; Univ Calif, Santa Barbara, attended 1988. **Career:** Basketball player (retired), basketball coach; Boston Celtics, guard, 1988-89, 1990-92; Il-Messaggero, Italy, 1989-90; Virtus Roma, 1989; Miami Heat, 1992-94; Orlando Magic, 1994-97; Golden State Warriors, 1997-98; Philadelphia 76ers, 1998; Portland Trailblazers, 1998; Los Angeles Lakers, guard, 1999-2003, asst coach, 2004-. **Honors/Awds:** NBA All-Rookie Second Team, 1989. **Business Addr:** Assistant Coach, Los Angeles Lakers, 555 N Nash St, El Segundo, CA 90245, **Business Phone:** (310)426-6000.

SHAW, CARL BERNARD
Restaurateur, entrepreneur, teacher. **Personal:** Born Jan 4, 1964, Detroit, MI; son of Cyrus and Louise. **Educ:** Eastern Mich Univ, bus & info syst, 1990. **Career:** Detroit Pub Schs, adult educ teacher, 1985-87; Automatic Data Processing, sr comput operator; Stroh Brewey Co, bus analyst, 1987; Cafe Mahogany Inc, pres. **Orgs:** Alpha Phi Alpha Fraternity Inc, 1984.

SHAW, CHARLES ALEXANDER
Judge. **Personal:** Born Dec 31, 1944, Jackson, TN; son of Alvis and Sarah; married Kathleen Marie Ingram, Aug 17, 1969; children: Bryan Ingram. **Educ:** Harris-Stowe Col, BA, 1966; Univ Mo, MBA, 1971; Catholic Univ Am, JD, 1974. **Career:** Berlin Roisman & Kessler, law clerk, 1972; Dept Justice, Law Enforcement Asst Admin, law clerk, 1972-73; Off Mayor, DC, assigned DC pub sch, hearing officer, 1973-74; Nat Labor Rels Bd, Enforcement Litigation Div, DC, atty, 1973-76; Lashly-Caruthers-Thies-Rava & Hamel, atty, 1976-80; Danforth Found, St Louis Leadership fel, 1978-79; Dept Justice, E Dist Mo, asst US atty, 1980-87; State Mo, circuit judge, 1987-94; US Dist Judge, judge, currently. **Orgs:** Chairperson, Labor Mgt Rels Comn, Am Bar Asn Young Lawyers Div, 1976-77; Mound City Bar Asn, 1976-; Mo state vice chairperson, Econ Law Sect, Am Bar Asn, 1976-77; United Negro Col Fund, 1978-80; commr, Lawyers Fee Dispute Comn, St Louis Met Bar Asn, 1979-80; Am Bar Asn; MO Bar Asn; DC Bar Asn; MO State & Corp Comn; Nat Asn Advan Colored People; Catholic Univ Law Sch Alumni Asn; Harris-Stowe Col Alumni Asn; bd mem, St Louis Black Forum, 1979-80, bd trustees, St Louis Art Mus, 1979-80, 1992-96; Sigma Pi Phi Fraternity, 1988-; St Louis Metro Amateur Golf Asn, 1993-; Asn Guardsmen, 1994-. **Honors/Awds:** Distinguished Service Citation, United Negro Col Fund, 1979; St Louis Public Schools Law & Education Service Award, 1984; Wellston School District Service Award, 1987-; Distinguished Alumni Award, Harris Stowe State Col, 1988; BLSA Distinguished Alumni Award, Catholic Univ, 1994; Catholic Univ Alumni Achievement Award, 2001. **Business Phone:** (314)244-7480.

SHAW, CURTIS MITCHELL
Lawyer. **Personal:** Born Apr 13, 1944, Jacksonville, TX; married Ann (divorced); children: Caja, Curtis Jr & Alexis. **Educ:** Univ NM, BS, 1967; Loyola Univ, LA, JD, 1975. **Career:** Pvt Pract, atty; Musical Entertainers & Motion Picture Personalities, rep; Denver Pub Schs, educr. **Orgs:** Dir, Num Motion Picture & Prod Co; Los Angeles Unified Sch Dist Bd; Hollywood Chamber Com; Los Angeles Co Bar Asn; Langston Law Club; Am Bar Asn; Beverly Hills Bar Asn.

SHAW, FERDINAND
Educator. **Personal:** Born May 30, 1933, McDonough, GA; children: Mark & Gail. **Educ:** Ohio State Univ, BS, nursing, 1955; Boston Univ, MS, 1957; Union Grad Sch, PhD, 1980. **Career:** Cincinnati Gen Hosp, staff nurse/asst head nurse, 1955-56; Ohio State Univ, instr/asst prof, 1957-73; Ohio State Univ Sch Nursing, assoc prof, 1973. **Orgs:** Consult & rev panel mem, Div of Nursing Dept HEW, 1965-74; bd mem, Sex Info & Educ Coun US, 1971-74; adv comt, Am Nurses Asn RN Maternity Fel Prog, 1973-; 2nd vpres, Am Nurses Asn, 1974-76; chair, Am Nurses Asn Comn Human Rights, 1976-; consult, Womens Res Staff Nat Inst Educ Dept HEW,1975. **Honors/Awds:** Mortarboard Award, Ohio State Univ, 1970; Centennial Award, Ohio State Univ Sch Nursing, 1970; Award for Contribution to Organization, Nat Black Nurses Asn, 1974-77; Fel, Am Acad Nursing; Am Nurses Asn, 1979. **Business Addr:** 830 K St Mall, Sacramento, CA 95814.

SHAW, HAROLD (HAROLD LAMAR SHAW)
Football player. **Personal:** Born Sep 3, 1974, Magee, MS. **Educ:** Southern Miss Univ. **Career:** New England Patriots, 1998-2000; Grand Rapids Rampage, 2001-02; New England Surge, running back, 2007-. **Business Phone:** (508)791-6373.*

SHAW, HAROLD LAMAR. **See SHAW, HAROLD.**

SHAW, HENRY
Automotive executive. **Career:** Knox Ford Inc, chief exec officer, currently. **Special Achievements:** Co is ranked No 80 on Black Enterprise's list of top 100 Auto Dealers, 1994, ranked No 57, 1998.

SHAW, LEANDER JERRY, JR.
Judge. **Personal:** Born Sep 6, 1930, Salem, VA; son of Leander J Sr and Margaret W; children: Sean, Jerry, Sherri, Dione & Dawn. **Educ:** WVa State Col, BA, 1952; Howard Univ, JD, 1957. **Career:** Judge (retired); Fla A&M Univ, asst prof, 1957-60; pvt pract, atty, 1960-69; Duval Co, asst pub defender, 1965-69, asst state atty, 1969-72; pvt pract, Jacksonville, Fla, atty, 1972-74; Fla Indust Rels Comt, comt, 1974-79; State Fla 1st Dist Ct Appeal, judge, 1979-83; Fla Supreme Ct, justice, 1983-2003, chief justice, 1990-92. **Orgs:** Chmn, bd elections, Am Bar Asn, FL Bar Asn, Nat Bar Asn, FL Gov Bar Asn; dir, FL Bar Found; adv, Judicial Admin Comn, State Traffic Ct Rev Comn; chmn, State Ct Restructure Comn; FL Assoc Vol Agencies Caribbean Action, Most Worshipful Union Grand Lodge Free & Accepted Masons FL PHA Inc, Alpha Phi Alpha; Tallahassee Bar Asn; Am Judicature Soc; Nat Ctr State Ct; Appointment Mayor Jacksonville; police adv comn, Human Rels Coun; Jacksonville Jetport Authority; bd chmn, Jacksonville Oppotunities Industrialization Ctr, offender, Res Adv Comn; FL Standard Jury Instrs, Civil Comn; adv, Ethnic Bias Study Comn, Guardian Ad Litem Prog; chmn, FL Sentencing Guidelines Comn, Gov Chiles' Criminal Justice Task Force; second vpres, Conf Chief Justices; bd visitors, FL State Univ, Col Law; bd dirs, Nat Ctr State Ct; Am Judicature Soc; Judicial Fel Prog Supreme Ct US. **Honors/Awds:** Dedication to Justice, FL Chap Nat Bar Asn, 1977; Community Service, Jacksonville Bar Asn, 1978; Exemplary Achievement in Judicial Service, State Fla Nat Bar Asn, 1984; Hon Doctor of Laws Degrees; WV State Col, 1986; Wash & Lee Univ, 1991; Nova Univ, 1991; hon pub affairs degree, Fla Int Univ, 1990; Fla Humanist of the Year Award, St Petersburg FL, 1991; Ben Franklin Award, St Petersburg, FL, 1992. **Special Achievements:** First African American to head the high court of Florida. **Military Serv:** AUS, Lt, 1952-54.

SHAW, MARTINI
Clergy. **Personal:** Born Nov 6, 1959, Detroit, MI; son of Melton and Joyce. **Educ:** Wayne State Univ, BS, psychol, 1983, BA, biol, 1983; McCormick Theol Sem, MDiv, 1988; Seabury-Western Theol Sem, cert Anglican Studies, 1988. **Career:** Detroit Pub Schs, teacher, 1983-85; St Johns Church, asst to rector, 1988-90; St Thomas Church, rector, 1990; South Diocesan Deanery, dean, 1999; The African Episcopal Church, St. Thomas, rector, currently. **Orgs:** Alpha Pi Alpha, 1985-; Chicago Urban League, 1986-; bd dir, vpres, Chase House Child Care, 1988-; Exec bd, NAACP, 1988-; chair, Church Fedn Chicago, Ecumenical Affairs, 1988-90; Cook County Democrats, 1990-; Ill Comn Afr Am Males, 1992-; diocesan secy, Union Black Episcopalians, 1993; chair, Desegregation Monitoring, Chicago educ bd. **Business Addr:** Rector, The African Episcopal Church St. Thomas, 6361 Lancaster Ave, Philadelphia, PA 19151, **Business Phone:** (215)473-3065.

SHAW, MELVIN B
School administrator, executive. **Personal:** Born Dec 23, 1940, Memphis, TN; married Pearl; married Gwendolyn (divorced); children: Remel, Dana, Randall & Renee. **Educ:** Lane Col, BS, 1962; Univ Memphis, MBEd, 1968; Harvard Bus Sch, Ed Mgt, 1970. **Career:** Shelby City Bd Ed, teacher, 1962-68; Lane Col, dir develop, 1968; Tex Asn Develop Cols, exec dir; United Negro Col Fund, vpres mkt; Shaw & Co, founder; Great Urban Escape, co-founder; Saad & Shaw, founder & prin, currently. **Orgs:** Omega Psi Phi, 1959; bd, Asn Fundraising Prof Golden Gate Chapter; adv coun, MultiCultural Alliance; Develop Exec Roundtable. **Honors/Awds:** Teacher of the Year, Geeter High Sch; Honorary Doctor of Humanities degree, Lane Col. **Business Addr:** Founder, Principal, Saad & Shaw, 360 Grand Ave Suite 170, Oakland, CA 94610.

SHAW, NANCY H.
Executive director. **Personal:** Born Sep 24, 1942. **Educ:** Jarvis Christian Col Hawkins TX, BA, 1965. **Career:** Flanner House, res asst, 1965-66; VISTA Training Prog, counr, 1966; Manpower Training Prog, employ counr, 1966-67; Bd Fundamental Educ, adminr asst dir & educ, 1967-68, mgr adminr servs, 1968-69, special asst pres, 1969-70; Indianapolis Bus Dev Fed, vpres; Comn Action Against Poverty, vpres; Ind Civil Rights Comn, dep dir, 1970-71; Human Rights Comn Indianapolis & Marion Co, exec dir, 1971-. **Orgs:** Comp Health Planning Coun; Citizens Comn Full Employ; bd dirs Comn Serv Coun Gr Indianapolis; racism com Episcopal Diocese So Ind; All Saints Epi Sch; bd mem, YMCA of Greater Indianapolis. **Business Addr:** Associate, Lilly Eli & Co, Lilly Corporate Ctr Drop 1017, Indianapolis, IN 46285.

SHAW, SEDRICK
Football player. **Personal:** Born Nov 16, 1973, Austin, TX; son of Charles and Sandrea. **Educ:** Univ Iowa. **Career:** Football player (retired); New England Patriots, running back, 1997-98; Cincinnati Bengals, running back, 1999; Cleveland Browns, running back, 1999.

SHAW, DR. SPENCER GILBERT
Librarian, consultant, educator. **Personal:** Born Aug 15, 1916, Hartford, CT; son of Eugene D and Martha A Taylor Shaw. **Educ:** Hampton Univ, BS,1940; Univ Wis, Sch Librarianship, BLS, 1941; Univ Chicago, Grad Libr Sch, advanced studies, 1948-; Univ Wis, LittD, 1992. **Career:** Hartford CT, br librarian, 1940-43, 1945-48; Brooklyn Pub Libr prog coord, storytelling spec, 1949-59; Queens Col, vis fac, 1958-60; Nassau Co NY Libr Syst, consult pub lib serv, 1959-70; Univ Wash, vis fac, 1961; Drexel Univ, vis fac, 1962; Syracuse Univ, vis fac, 1964; Kent State Univ, vis fac, 1965; Univ MD, vis fac, 1968; Univ Ill, vis fac, 1969; Univ HI, vis fac, 1969-70; Univ Wash, prof, 1970-86, prof emer, 1986-; Univ AK, Anchorage, vis fac, 1974; Univ Wis, Madison-,vis fac, 1979; Univ NC, vis fac, 1992; Univ NTex, vis fac, 1990-93. **Orgs:** Beta Phi Mu, 1949; Am Libr Asn, 1950-; Wash Lib Media Asn, 1970-; Int Reading Asn, 1970-; Wash Lib Asn, 1970-; Nat Coun Teachers Eng,1970-; Pacific Northwest Lib Asn, 1978; Black Heritage Soc Wash State, Inc, 1988-; Am Asn Homes & Serv Aging, 1994-98. **Honors/Awds:** Distinguished Alumnus Award, Hampton Univ, 1960; Spencer G Shaw Res Storytelling Collection, Invergargill Pub Lib, NZ, 1978; Grolier Found Award, 1983; Certificate of Apppreciation, Univ Wash, Grad Sch Libr & Info Sci, 1986; Black Librarians Puget Sound Plaque, 1986; President Award, Wash Libr Asn, 1986; Recog Cert, King County Co, Seattle, 1986; Distinguished Serv Award, Black Caucus, Am Libr Asn, 1988; First Distinguished Alumnus Award, Sch Libr & Info Studies, Univ Wis-Mad, 1990; Am Cult Specialist, New Zealand, US Info Agency, 1990; Leadership in Profession, Black Caucus ALA, 1992; Distinguished Serv Profession, 1992; Trustee of the Year, Wash Asn Homes Aging, 1995; Nancy Blankenship Pryor Award, Wash State Libr & The Wash State Comn Humanities, 1996; Nordstrom Community Serv Award, 1997; Distinguished Serv Award, Asn Libr Serv C, 1998; Lifetime Achievement Award, Black Caucus, Am Libr Asn, 2005. **Special Achievements:** Narrator of films: "Ashanti to Zulu: African Traditi," Weston Woods Studio, 1976, "Why the Sun and Moon Live in the Sky," ACI Films, 1977; Recording: "Sounds of Childcraft," Field Enterprises, 1974; Author of articles like: Notable Black American Women, 1992; Musical Story Hours: Using Music with Storytelling and Puppetry, 1989; A Sea of Upturned Faces, 1989; Libraries and Storytelling; the Art and Craft of Spencer G Shaw, 1995; Storytelling for Everyone; a Three Day Lecture Series by Spencer G Shaw in Toyonaka Japan, 1996. **Military Serv:** USY, lt, 1943-45. **Home Addr:** 29 Revere Dr Apt 3, Bloomfield, CT 06002-2649. **Business Addr:** Professor Emeritus, University of Washington, Grad Sch Libr & Info Sci FM-30, Seattle, WA 98195, **Business Phone:** (206)543-1794.

SHAW, TALBERT OSCALL
Educator. **Personal:** Born Feb 28, 1928; married Lillieth H Brown; children: Patrick Talbert & Talieth Andrea. **Educ:** Andrews Univ, BA, 1960, MA, 1961, BD, 1963; Univ Chicago, MA, 1968, PhD, 1973. **Career:** Educator (retired); Oakwood Col, prof chris ethics, 1965-72, dean stud; Col Lib Arts Morgan State Univ Baltimore, dean; Sch Religion Howard Univ, acting dean & assoc prof ethics, 1972-81; Cath Univ Am, vis prof, 1973-74; Bowie State Col, vis prof, 1974; Princeton Theo Sem, vis prof, 1975; Shaw Univ, pres emer, currently. **Orgs:** Exec bd, Nat Com Prev Alcoholism; exec com, Wash Theo Consortium; exec com, Howard Univ; fac mem, Soc Study Black Religions; Am Acad Religion; Am Soc Chris Ethics, 1972. **Honors/Awds:** Voted

distinguished teacher of yr, Howard Univ Sch of Religion, 1974; Talbert O Shaw endowment Fund, NC Community Found, named in honor. **Business Addr:** President Emeritus, Shaw University, 118 East South St, Raleigh, NC 27601, **Business Phone:** (919)546-8200.

SHAW, TERRANCE
Football player, football coach. **Personal:** Born Jan 11, 1973, Marshall, TX; married Shawneeque Bowers; children: Ashley & Terrance Jr. **Educ:** Stephen F. Austin State Univ. **Career:** Football player (retired), coach; San Diego Chargers, corner back, 1995-99; Miami Dolphins, 2000; New England Patriots, 2001; Oakland Raiders, 2002-03; Minn Vikings, 2004; Titans, youth league coach, currently. **Orgs:** Phi Beta Sigma Fraternity. **Special Achievements:** Second round/34th overall NFL draft pick, 1995.

SHAW, THEODORE MICHAEL
College teacher, lawyer. **Personal:** Born Nov 24, 1954, New York, NY; son of Theodore Shaw (deceased) and Jean Audrey Churchill Shaw (deceased); married Cynthia E Muldrow; children: T Winston & Zora Jean. **Educ:** Wesleyan Univ, BA, 1976; Columbia Univ Sch Law, JD, 1979. **Career:** US Dept Justice, Civil Rights Div, trial atty, 1979-82; NAACP Legal Defense Fund, asst coun, 1982-87, western regional coun, 1987-90, assoc dir-coun, 1993, dir coun & pres, 2004-; Columbia Univ Sch Law, adj prof, 1993-; Univ Mich Sch Law, asst prof law, 1990-93. **Orgs:** Bd mem, Greater Brownsville Youth Coun, 1982-; bd trustees, alumni elected trustee, 1986-89, charter mem, 1992-2003, vice chmn bd, 1999-2003, Wesleyan Univ; bd mem, Poverty & Race Res Action Coun, 1990-; bd mem, Archbishop's Leadership Proj, 1994-; Haywood Burns Chair Civil Rights, CUNY Law Sch, 1997-98; adv bd mem, Europ Roma Rights Ctr, Budapest, Hungary, 1998-; bd mem, Nat Res coun Bd Testing & Assessment Farrlest, 1999-; Nat Bar Asn; Am Bar Asn. **Honors/Awds:** US Dept Justice, Civil Rights Div, Spec Commendation, 1981; Aspen Inst Fel Law & Soc, 1987; Twentyfirst Century Trust Fel Global Interdependence, London Eng, 1989; Salzburg Sem Fel, Salzburg, Austria, 1991; Civil Trial Lawyer of the Year,Langston Bar Asn, 1991; Outstanding Attorney of the Year, Metropolitan Black Bar Asn, 1998; Distinguished Alumni Award, Columbia Law Sch, Black Am Law Students Asn, 1997; Recognition Award, 1990, Distinguished Service Award, 1991, Wesleyan Univ, Black Alumni Coun Alumni; A Leon Higginbotham Jr Memorial Award, Nat Bar Asn Young Lawyers Div; Lawrence A Wein Prize, Columbia Univ; Baldwin Medal, Wesleyan Univ. **Special Achievements:** Led Delegation of NAACP Legal Defense Fund Lawyers to South Africa to present seminars on constitutional litigation, 1994, 1995; Consulted with Spanish Senate Judiciary Comn & Judiciary on Jury Systems, Madrid, Spain, 1994. **Home Addr:** 63 Lefferts Place, Brooklyn, NY 11238, **Home Phone:** (718)783-6937. **Business Addr:** Director-Counsel, President, NAACP Legal Defense & Educational Fund Inc, 99 Hudson St 16th Fl, New York, NY 10013, **Business Phone:** (212)965-2210.

SHAW, TODD ANTHONY. **See TOO SHORT, A.**

SHAW, WILLIAM
Clergy. **Personal:** Born Jan 1, 1934?, Marshall, TX; married Camellia, 1957; children: Tim. **Educ:** Bishop Col, BA; Union Theological Seminary, MA; Colgate Rochester Divinity Sch, DMin. **Career:** White Rock Baptist Church, Philadelphia, pastor, 1956-; Pa Baptist St Conv, pres, 1978-82; Opportunities Industrialization Centers, exec dir Nat Baptist Conv, USA, pres, 1999-. **Orgs:** Bd mem, Community Legal Serv Philadelphia; Medical Ctr Univ Penn; Presbyterian Hosp Med Ctr; Philadelphia Airport Adv Bd; mem, Greater Philadelphia Urban Affairs Coalition & Martin Luther King Fellows Black Studies. **Business Addr:** Pastor, White Rock Baptist Church, 3400 Fayetteville St, Durham, NC 27707, **Business Phone:** (215)474-1738.*

SHAW, DR. WILLIE G.
Athletic director. **Personal:** Born Mar 29, 1942, Jackson, TN; married Brenda Joyce Robinson; children: Stacey Alexis & Daricus. **Educ:** Lane Col, BS, 1964; Univ TN Knoxville, MS, 1968; Middle TN State Univ, DA, 1975; Memphis State Univ, 1984. **Career:** New York Astronauts, 1964-65; Lane Col, asst football coach, 1965-71, basketball coach, 1976-79; City of Jackson TN, gymnastics instr, 1976-79; Lane Col Nat Youth Sports Prog, proj activity dir, 1976-80; Lane Col, dir of athletics; North Carolina Central Univ. **Orgs:** Chmn, south reg Natl Collegiate Athletic Assoc Div III Basketball Comm, 1977-; Natl Coll Athletic Assoc Comm on Committees, 1979-81; proj admin, Lane Coll Natl Youth Sports Prog, 1980-; bd mem, Jackson-Madison Cty Airport Auth Bd of Dir, 1980-; natl chmn, Natl Coll Athletic Assoc Div III Basketball comm, 1981-; bd chmn, Jackson Housing Auth Anti-Crime Comm, 1982. **Honors/Awds:** State Fellow, Middle TN State Univ, 1972,73. **Special Achievements:** Coll div Basketball Scoring Leading Natl Assn of Inter coll Athletic Natl Coll Athletic Assn, 1962,64; Basketball All Amer Natl Asn of Inter coll Athletics Asn Press United Press Intl, 1963-64. **Home Addr:** 149 Commanche Trail, Jackson, TN 38305.

SHAWNEE, LAURA ANN
Manager. **Personal:** Born Sep 18, 1953, Merced, CA. **Educ:** Univ Santa Clara, BA, 1975; Stanford Univ, cert. **Career:** NASA Ames Res Ctr, Col recruitment coordr, 1975-83, personnel mgr, 1975-84, handicapped prog mgr, 1982-84, dep chief off equal opportunity prog, mgr informal educ prog, educ div, strategic commun & develop, currently. **Orgs:** Admin asst, 1975-, church treas, 1975-, Cumming Temple Christian Methodist Episcopal Church; pres, Missionary Soc, 1985; Nat Asn Minority Engineering Prog Adminr, 1985-; Community Life & Witness, 1986; Christian Methodist Episcopal Church; bd dir, Imperative Comt to Eliminate Racism, 1987; Mid Peninsula YWCA; Nat Asn Female Exec. **Honors/Awds:** Achievement Award, Bank Am 1971; Agency Group Achievement Award, Summer Med Stud Intern Prog NASA, 1976; Special Achievement Award, NASA, 1980. **Business Addr:** Manager, NASA Ames Research Center, Education Division Strategic Communications & Development, Moffett Field, CA 94035-1000.

SHEAD, KEN (KENNETH W SHEAD)
Executive. **Personal:** Born in St Louis, MO. **Educ:** St Benedicts Col, bus admin. **Career:** Xerox; Exxon; Sperry/Unisys; Iqmedia Inc, chief exec officer; Drew Pearson Co, founder, 1985-, pres. **Orgs:** Nat Minority Develop Coun. **Honors/Awds:** Top 30 African American Executives, Black Enterprise mag, 1993; Company of the Year, Black Enterprise, 1994. **Special Achievements:** Company is ranked 79 among list of top 100 companies, Black Enterprise mag, 1992.

SHEAD, KENNETH W. **See SHEAD, KEN.**

SHEALEY, RICHARD W
Banker, president (organization), chief executive officer. **Career:** First Independence Nat Bank, pres & ceo, 1995; Faulkner/Haynes & Assocs Inc, financial dir, currently. **Business Addr:** Financial Director, Faulkner/Haynes & Associates Inc, 4365 Dorchester Rd Bldg 100 Suite 107, Charleston, SC 29405, **Business Phone:** (843)884-3554.*

SHEARD, REV. JOHN DREW
Clergy. **Personal:** Born Jan 1, 1959, Detroit, MI; son of John H and Willie Mae; married Karen Clark, Jun 16, 1984; children: Kierra V & John Drew II. **Educ:** Wayne State Univ, BS, 1982, MED, 1988. **Career:** Detroit Pub Sch, teacher, 1982-93; Mich Dept Health, supvr, 1985-86; COGIC, Greater Emmanuel Inst, sr pastor, 1988-, dist supt, 1994-, spec asst to Bishop, 1996-2005, AIM Convention exec sec, 1995-2005, youth dept int pres, 1997-2000; AIM Convention, Chmn, 2005-, 1st admin asst to Bishop, 2005-. **Orgs:** Exec dir, Southern Christian Leadership Cou, 1985-87; supvr, Mich Youth Employment, 1985-86. **Honors/Awds:** Mich Chptr Pastor of the Year, SCLC, 2006; J Barett Lee Award, Martin Luther KIng, Jr. Board of Preachers, 2008. **Business Addr:** Senior Pastor, Greater Emmanuel Institutional COGIC, 19190 Schaefer Hwy, Detroit, MI 48235, **Business Phone:** (313)864-7170.

SHEARIN, KIMBERLY MARIA
Journalist. **Personal:** Born Apr 1, 1964, Baltimore, MD; daughter of Matthew and Mary James Withers. **Educ:** St Mary's Col, St Mary's City, MD, BA, english, 1986; Boston Univ, Boston, MA, MS, jour, 1987. **Career:** The Associated Press, Providence, RI, staff reporter, 1985, 1987-89; New Haven Regist, New Haven, CT, staff reporter, 1989-. **Orgs:** Mem, Nat Asn of Black Journalists, 1987-. **Honors/Awds:** National Dean's List, 1983, 1985; helped launch St Louis Sun newspaper, 1989. **Home Phone:** (410)931-9544. **Business Addr:** Reporter, New Haven Register, 40 Sargent Dr, New Haven, CT 06511, **Business Phone:** (203)789-5714.

SHEATS, MARVIN ANTHONY
Consultant. **Personal:** Born Nov 22, 1958, Detroit, MI; son of Marvin and Evelyn Flacks. **Educ:** Wayne County Community Col, lib arts, 1981; Comput Skills Training Ctr, cert, comput oper, 1985; EDS, cert, comput oper, 1986. **Career:** Electronic Data Syst, comput operator, 1985-87; Wayne County Pub Serv, comput operator, 1988-92; Mac Training & Design Inc, vpres, owner, consult, currently. **Orgs:** MacGroup Detroit, vpres, 1990-. **Honors/Awds:** Achievement Award, Comput Skills Training Ctr, 1992. **Business Phone:** (313)557-0750.

SHEDD, KENDRICK DWAYNE. **See SHEDD, KENNY.**

SHEDD, KENNY (KENDRICK DWAYNE SHEDD)
Football player, police officer. **Personal:** Born Feb 14, 1971, Davenport, IA. **Educ:** Northern Iowa Univ. **Career:** Football player (retired), Police officer; New York Jets, wide receiver, 1993-96; Oakland Raiders, wide receiver, 1996-99; Wash Redskins, 2000; San Leandro Police Dept, law enforcement officer, currently. **Business Addr:** Law Enforcement Officer, San Leandro Police Department, 835 E 14th St, San Leandro, CA 94577-3767, **Business Phone:** (510)577-0663.

SHEDROFF, JOSHUA. **See REDMAN, JOSHUA.**

SHEFFEY, DR. RUTHE T.
Educator. **Personal:** Born in Essex County, VA; married Vernon R; children: Illona Cecile Sheffey Rawlings & Renata Gabrielle Sheffey Strong. **Educ:** Morgan State Univ, BA, 1947; Howard Univ, MA, 1949; Univ Pa, PhD, 1959. **Career:** Howard Univ, grad asst eng, 1947-48; Claflin Col, instr eng & french, 1948-49; Morgan State Col, asst prof to assoc prof, 1959-70; Morgan State Col, Eng Dept, chairperson, 1970-74; Morgan State Col, Dept Eng, prof,1975-. **Orgs:** Communications Comt, United Fund Md, 1972-74; Maryland Coun Humanities, 1990-96; Col Eng Asn; Col Lang Asn; Modern Lang Asn; Nat Coun Teachers Eng; Eighteenth Century Studies Asn; Middle Atlantic Writers Asn; vpres, Langston Hughes Soc; founder & pres, Zora Neale Hurston Soc; ed, Zora Neale Hurston Forum; Asn Study Aro Life & Culture; Kings Kids Mentor,Heritage United Church Christ; Mayor's Coun Women's Rights; delegate, White House Conf Women Econ Equals; Morgan State Univ Alumni Asn, Howard Univ Alumni Asn, Univ Penn Alumni Asn; comnr & vice chair, Baltimore Co Human Rels Comn; Md state delegate, Paula Hollinger's Scholar Award Panel. **Honors/Awds:** Creative Achievement Award, Col Lang Asn, 1974; Award Community Serv,United Fund, 1975; Community Serv Award, Jack & Jill Am, 1979; Distinguished Alumni Citation, Nat Asn Equal Opportunity, 1980;Achievement Award, African-Am History & Culture, 1984; Distinguished BlackWoman Am, Towson State Univ, 1984; Morgan State University Women Award, 1985; Alumna of the Year, Howard Univ, Baltimore Chapter, 1987; Faculty Member of the Year Award, Md Asn Higher Educ, 1994; Hall of Fame, Morgan State Univ, 1998. **Special Achievements:** Author of numerous books, articles, and reviews. **Business Addr:** Professor of English, Morgan State University, 1700 E Cold Spring Lane 202 Holmes Hall, Baltimore, MD 21251, **Business Phone:** (443)885-3165.

SHEFFIELD, GARY ANTONIAN
Baseball player. **Personal:** Born Nov 18, 1968, Tampa, FL; married Deleon Richards, 1999; children: Ebony, Carissa & Gary Jr. **Career:** Milwaukee Brewers, infielder, 1988-92; San Diego Padres, third baseman, 1992-93; Fla Marlins, 1993-98; Los Angeles Dodgers, 1998-2001; Atlanta Braves, 2002-03; New York Yankees, right fielder, 2004-06; Detroit Tigers,2007-09. **Orgs:** The Gary Sheffield Found, 1995-; Sheff's Kitchen. **Honors/Awds:** NL All Star Team, 1992-2000; NL Batting Champion, 1992; San Diego Hall of Champions, 1992; Pro Star of the Year, 1992; Sporting News Major League Player of the Year, 1992; ESPY: Breakthrough Athlete, 1993; Silver Slugger Award, 1992, 1996, 2003, 2004, 2005; NL All Star Team, 2003-05. **Special Achievements:** Natl League, batting champion, 1992, all-star team mem, 1992; holdsMarlins all-time record for most home runs and highest batting average,1997. **Business Addr:** Professional Baseball Player, Detroit Tigers, 2100 Woodward Ave, Detroit, MI 48201, **Business Phone:** (313)962-4000.

SHEFFIELD, REV. HORACE L
Baptist clergy, association executive. **Personal:** Son of Horace Sheffield Jr. **Career:** Nat Action Network, Mich Chap, pres; Natl Asn Black Orgn, chief exec officer; New Galilee Missionary Baptist Church, pastor, currently. **Orgs:** Del, Dem Nat Conv, 2004; Detroit Asn Black Orgn. **Home Addr:** 12048 Grand River Ave, Detroit, MI 48204, **Home Phone:** (313)491-0003. **Business Addr:** Pastor, New Galilee Missionary Baptist Church, 11241 Gunston St, Detroit, MI 48213, **Business Phone:** (313)521-1248.

SHEFTALL, DR. WILLIS B., JR.
School administrator. **Personal:** Born Dec 12, 1943, Macon, GA. **Educ:** Morehouse Col, BA, 1964; Atlanta Univ, MA, 1969; Ga State Univ, PhD, 1981. **Career:** Ala State Univ, instr econ, 1969-71; Atlanta Univ, res assoc, 1978-80; Ga State Univ; Morehouse Col, asst prof of econ, 1976-81, prof, 2002-07, sr vpres acad affairs, pres, 1998; Hampton Univ, chmn econ dept, 1981-82, dean Sch business; bd dir, Piedmont Med Ctr, 2001. **Orgs:** Consult, City Atlanta, State Ga; Commonwealth Va; Gen Serv Admin; 1977-82;Am Econ Assoc; Nat Econ Assoc; Int Assoc Black Bus Ed; Assoc Social & Behavioral Sci; past pres, Nat Urban League; Nat Advan Asn Colored People. **Special Achievements:** Published articles in the areas of local public finance & urban economics; Merrill Foreign Study Travel Scholar 1968-69. **Military Serv:** USN quartermaster 3rd class 1964-66.

SHEHEE, RASHAAN
Football player. **Personal:** Born Jun 20, 1975, Los Angeles, CA. **Educ:** Univ Wash. **Career:** Football player (retired), Kans City Chiefs, running back, 1998-99; X treme Football League, Los Angeles X treme, running back, 2000. **Orgs:** Youth Friends Prog. **Honors/Awds:** Rookie of year, 1998.

SHELBY, KHADEJAH E.
Government official. **Personal:** Born Feb 15, 1929, Dayton, OH; daughter of Eloise Evans and Artman; divorced; children: Elizabeth Diane Lugo. **Educ:** Baldwin-19Wallace Col, Berea, OH, 1949; NCA Univ, grad, 1986; Wayne State Univ Prof Mgt & Develop Sch, Am Asn Zool Parks & Aquariums, 1989. **Career:** NY Univ Med Ctr, exec asst, 1958-69; City Detroit, adr, 1975-82, Zool Parks Dept, dep dir, 1982-. **Orgs:** Fel, Am Asn Zool Parks & Aquariums, 1982-; Friends African Art, 1972-; Detroit Inst Arts, Founders Soc, 1972-; Nat Asn Advan Colored People. **Honors/Awds:** Wayne State Univ, Golden Key Honor Soc, 1989-; Outstanding Freshman, Baldwin-Wallace Col, 1947. **Business Addr:** Deputy Director, Detroit Zoological Parks Department, 8450 W Ten Mile Rd, PO Box 39, Royal Oak, MI 48068-0039.

SHELBY, DR. REGINALD W
Physician. **Personal:** Born Aug 6, 1920, Memphis, TN; son of Charles H and Grace Irving; married Jay; children: Cathi & Reginald Jr. **Educ:** LeMoyne-Owen Coll Memphis TN, BS, 1940; Meharry Med Col, 1950; NY City Hosp, Post-Grad Training, 1950-57; Int Col Surgeons, Fel, 1959; Am Bd Surg, Chicago, Ill Mem, 1967; Am Brd Surg Chicago Ill re-Certified, 1980. **Career:** Pvt pract, 1959-; Ashtabula County Med Ctr, chief surgeon, 1987. **Orgs:** Bd dir, Western Res Health Plan, Ashtabula County Health Serv, 1987; bd dir, Ashtabula County Health Dept, 1987; past pres, Ashtabula County Med Soc; past chief, staff Ashtabula County Med Ctr; past mem, Ashtabula City Bd Health; bd dir, Mary Chatman Comm Ctr; past asst, Coroner Ashtabula County; mem, Comm Action County-wide Sickle-Cell Screening; fel, Pan-Am Soc Med; OH State Med Asn; Ashtabula County Med Asn, Kappa Alpha Psi; life mem, Nat Asn Advan Colored People; bd dir, Ashtabula Co Metro Housing Auth. **Honors/Awds:** Meharry Founders Circle Award, 2000; 50 Year Member Award, OH State Med Asn, 2000. **Military Serv:** AUS, 1942-46; WWII Pacific Theatre m/sgt New Guinea, Philippines, Japan. **Home Addr:** 4243 S Ridge E, PO Box 1172, Ashtabula, OH 44004.

SHELL, ARTHUR
Football coach, football player. **Personal:** Born Nov 26, 1946?, Charleston, SC; son of Arthur Sr and Gertrude; married Janice; children: Arthur III & Christopher. **Educ:** Maryland State-Eastern Shore Col, BS, indust arts educ, 1968. **Career:** Football player (retired), football coach; Oakland Raiders, player, 1968-81; Los Angeles Raiders, 1982; Los Angeles Raiders, coach, 1983-94; Kansas City Chiefs, offensive line coach, 1995-96; Atlanta Falcons, 1997-2000; NFL, sr vpres for football opers & develop, 2001-05. Oakland Raiders, head coach, 2006-07. **Orgs:** Alpha Phi Alpha. **Honors/Awds:** Football Hall of Fame, 1989; played in Pro Bowl, 1972-78, 1980; first black head football coach in NFL; Pro Football Weekly Coach of Year, 1990; Asniated Press, Coach of the Year, 1991.

SHELL, DR. JUANITA
Educator, psychologist. **Personal:** Born Apr 21, 1939, Winston Salem, NC; daughter of Douglas and Sallie Sanders; married Alonza Peterson, Dec 24, 1961; children: Lisa & Jason. **Educ:** City Col New York, BA, 1971; Grad Ctr City, Univ New York, PhD, 1977, postdoctoral prog psychoanal & psychother, cert, 1991. **Career:** Fel, Black Analyst Inc, 1975-76; Brooklyn Com Counl Ctr, staff psychol, 1976-84; Brooklyn Col, adj prof 1976-78; New York Univ, Bellevue Med Ctr, staff psychol, 1978-, clin asst prof, currently; pvt pract, psychoanalyst, currently. **Orgs:** Am Psychol Asn, 1975-; Mayors Adv Sub-comt Mental Retard & Dev Disabilities, 1978-; chairperson, Health Comn Community Bd dist 4, 1979-81; NYAcad Sci, 1981-; vpres, Metrop Chap Jack & Jill Am, 1984-86, pres, 1987-89, 1990-; cofounder, Metrop Jack & Jill Alumnae Inc, 1990-; consult, Shelter & Arms Child Serv, 1984; New York Univ, Bellevue Psychiatric Soc; New York State Div Women Comt; trustee, Schomburg Corp; secy, bd dirs, Coun Greater Harlem Inc, 1994-99. **Honors/Awds:** Governor's Award, Excellence Mental Health, 1997. **Special Achievements:** Article:"A Study of Three Brothers with Infantile Autism" J Am Acad Child Psychcol, 1984; "The Reactions of Black Children to the Atlanta Child Murders," 1988; co-wote "Values of Post Partum Women From The Inner City: An Exploratory Study," J Child & Family Studies, 1997. **Business Addr:** Clinical Assistant Professor, New York University Medical Center, School of Medicine Psychiatry, New Bellevue 22 20W40 462 First Ave, 20W40, New York, NY 10016, **Business Phone:** (212)562-4509.

SHELL, THEODORE A.
Dentist. **Personal:** Married Juanita Hamlin; children: Gail & Theodore Jr. **Educ:** Miles Mem Col, AB; Wayne State Univ, MBA; Calif Lutheran Univ, Am Col Life Underwriters. **Career:** Great Lakes Mutual Ins Co, debit mgr, asst mgr & mgr, 1934-44; Great Lakes Mutual Life Ins Co, exec vpres, 1944-59; Golden State Minority Found,various offices, pres; Golden State Mutual Life Ins Co, vice chm bd, 1960-. **Honors/Awds:** Olive Crosthwait Award, Chicago Ins Asn; Special Service Award, Nat Ins Asn, 1973. **Business Addr:** Dentist, 4328 Wover Pl NW, Washington, DC 20016, **Business Phone:** (202)363-2446.

SHELTON, BRYAN
Tennis player, athletic coach. **Personal:** Born Dec 22, 1965, Huntsville, AL; married Lisa; children: Emma & Benjamin. **Educ:** Ga Inst Technol, BA, indust eng, 1989. **Career:** Prof tennis player (retired), athletic coach; Prof tennis player, 1989-97; MaliVai Wash, coach; US Tennis Asn, nat coach, 1998-99; Ga Tech Athletic Asn, womens tennis team, head coach, currently. **Honors/Awds:** Athletic Hall of Fame, Ga Tech, 1993; Hall of Fame, Ga Tennis, 2002; Huntsville-Madison County Hall of Fame Inductee, 2006; USTA/ITA National Coach of the Year, 2007. **Special Achievements:** First African-American to win an ATP event. **Business Addr:** Head Coach, Georgia Tech Athletic Association, Georgia Tech Athletics Womens Tennis, 150 Bobby Dodd Way NW, Atlanta, GA 30332-0455, **Business Phone:** (404)894-0458.

SHELTON, CHARLES E
Newspaper executive. **Personal:** Born Oct 5, 1945, New York, NY; son of Edward and Fredrine Bolden; married Sylvina Robinson, Oct 10, 1964; children: Helen, Charmaine & Mia. **Educ:** Northeastern Univ, Boston, Mass, attended 1963-65; Pace Univ, attended 1984; Stanford Univ, grad sch, attended 1991; Dartmouth, Tuck Exec Prog, 1994. **Career:** New York Times, New York, NY, budget analyst, 1967-79, consumer mkt rep, 1979-81, city circulation mgr, 1981-83, metro circulation mgr, 1983-87, metrop home delivery dir, 1987-88, single copy sales dir, 1988-89, dir, 1989, group dir, sales & opers, 1992, vpres circulation, vp distrib, 1995-98, vpres human resources workforce develop, 1998-. **Orgs:** Soc Human Resources Mgt. **Honors/Awds:** Black Achiever Award, Harlem YMCA br, 1982. **Business Phone:** (212)556-1234.

SHELTON, CORA R.
Counselor, social worker. **Personal:** Born Mar 5, 1925, Monroe, MI; married Jean C Mitchell; children: Deborah, Mark, Janice. **Educ:** Wayne State Univ Detroit, attended 1960; Wayne County Community Col, attended 1969; Univ Mich, Detroit, attended 1972. **Career:** Detroit State & Rys, transp equipment operator, 1946-73; Met Life Ins Co, sales rep, 1973-79; Kent Barry Eaton Connecting Ry Inc, corp dir, pres gen mgr, 1979. **Orgs:** Dist rep, Div 26 Street car & Bus Oper, 1960-62; vice chmn, City-Wide Polit Action Group, 1961-63; pres, St Cecelia Church Dad's Club, 1968-70; Nat Fedn Independent Bus, 1979; Southcentral Mich Transp Planning Comn, 1980. **Honors/Awds:** Man of the year award, Nat Life Underwriters, 1974.

SHELTON, DAIMON
Football player. **Personal:** Born Sep 15, 1972, Duarte, CA; married Stephanie; children: Aliya. **Educ:** Sacramento State Univ; Fresno City Col, rctrn admin, 1994. **Career:** Jacksonville Jaguars, running back, 1997-00; Chicago Bears, 2001-02; Buffalo Bills, full back, 2004-07; SanJose Saber Cats,currently. **Honors/Awds:** Co-Most Valuable Player, Cent Valley Conf, 1994.

SHELTON, HAROLD TILLMAN
Physician. **Personal:** Born May 4, 1941, Lake Charles, LA; married Dolores Hayes; children: Keith, Sherry & Stephanie. **Educ:** McNeese State Univ, BS, 1970; LA State Univ Med Sch, MD, 1974; LA State Univ Med Ctr, internship, 1975; La State Univ Med Ctr, New Orleans, residency gen surg, 1975-79. **Career:** Pvt Pract, gen surg, 1979-; La State Univ, Med Ctr, clin instr, 1980. **Orgs:** Regional dir, Region III Ctr Nat Med Asn, 1973; cand group Am Col Surgeons, 1979; diplo, Am Bd Surg,1980; AMA; LA State Med Soc; Calcasieu Parish Med Soc, 1979; staff mem, Lake Charles Memorial Hosp & St Patrick Hosp, 1979. **Special Achievements:** Publisher: "Evaluation of Wound Irrigation by Pulsatile Jet & Conventional Methods" Annals of Surg, Feb 1978. **Business Addr:** General Surgeon, 511 Hodges St, Lake Charles, LA 70602, **Business Phone:** (337)309-1428.

SHELTON, HARVEY WILLIAM
Administrator. **Personal:** Born Jan 18, 1936, Charlottesville, VA; married Mary Etta; children: Renee & Harvey Jr. **Educ:** Va State Univ, BS, 1960; NC State Univ, cert pub policy, 1967; NC State Univ, Adult Educ 1969; VPI & SU, EdD Adult & Continuing Educ, 1976. **Career:** Administrator (Retired); Pittsylvania Co Va, extension agent, 1963-69; VPI & SU, area resource develop agent, 1969-70; Comn Resource Develop VPI & SU, prog leader 1970-78; Comn Resource Devel & Energy MD Coop Ext Serv, asst dir, 1978-86; MD Cooperative Extension Serv, asst dir, 1986-93. **Orgs:** Fel, Kellogg Found, 1966-67; Big Brothers Assoc, 1971-73; Adult Educ Asn USA, 1972-80; fel, Ford Found, 1974-75; Phi Kappa Phi Hon Soc, 1975-80; Boy Scout Coun, 1976-78; treas, Roanake Nat Asn Advan Colored People, 1976-78; chmn, prof improv comt, Comn Develop Soc Am, 1979-83; MD Assoc Adult Educ, 1980. **Honors/Awds:** Epsilon Sigma Phi Outstanding Achievement Award, Va Pol Inst & State Univ, 1978; US Senator MacMathis Award, 1983; Community Develop Soc Serv Award, 1985. **Military Serv:** AUS, lt 1961-63; Army Commendation Medal.

SHELTON, HELEN C
Executive. **Educ:** Dartmouth Col, BA, hist & govt; Boston Univ, MS, jour & commun. **Career:** WRKS-FM Radio, NY, promotions & pub rels positions; HR Develop Inst, dir pub affairs; Seventeen Mag, promotions & pub rels positions; City Chicago, Dept Cult Affairs, app position; Ruder Finn Inc, exec trainee, Ruder Finn Arts & Commun Counrs, exec vpres, currently. **Orgs:** Bd mem, The Support Network Inc; founding mem, Pi Theta Chap, Delta Sigma Theta Sorority Inc; bd mem, ReadNet Inc. **Honors/Awds:** 40 Under 40 Award, The Network Jour, 2004; Outstanding Woman in Communications Award in Public Relations, Ebony Mag, 2006. **Business Addr:** Executive Vice President, Ruder Finn Arts & Communications Counselors, 301 E 57th St, New York, NY 10022, **Business Phone:** (212)593-6443.*

SHELTON, HILARY O.
Federal government official, civil rights activist. **Personal:** Born in St. Louis, MO; married Paula Young Shelton; children: Caleb Wesley, Aaron Joshua, Noah Ottis. **Educ:** Howard University, Political Science; University of Missouri, Communications; Northeastern University in Boston, Legal Studies. **Orgs:** Federal Policy Program Director, The United Methodist Church's General Board of Church and Society; Federal Liaison/Asst. Director to the Government Affairs Dept. of the UNCF; Director to the Washington Bureau, NAACP. **Honors/Awds:** National NAACP Medgar W. Evers Award for Excellence; American Arab Anti-Discrimination Committee's Excellence in Advocacy Award; The Religious Action Center's Civil Rights Leadership Award; NCADP 30th Anniversary Award, 2006; Congressional Black Caucus' Chairman's Award. *

SHELTON, JOHN W
Executive. **Personal:** Born Dec 16, 1958, Buffalo, NY; son of John and Joyce Hargrave; married Martha Zehnder Shelton, Jun 8, 1986; children: John Bradford & Nicholaus Edwin. **Educ:** Valparaiso Univ, Valparaiso, Ind, BBA. **Career:** MGM Grand Hotel, Las Vegas, Nev, reservations, 1981-82; Flamingo Hilton Hotel, Las Vegas, Nev, front off, 1982-83; Hyatt Regency Oakland, Oakland, Calif, sales mgr, 1984-87; Hyatt Regency Atlanta, Atlanta, Ga, sales mgr, 1987-88; Hyatt Regency Flint, Flint, Mich, dir sales, 1988-90; Zehnder's Frankenmuth, Frankenmuth, Mich, dir sales, vpres sales & mkt, currently. **Orgs:** Chmn, Soc Govt Meeting Planners, 1987; Big Brothers/Big Sisters E Bay, 1987; Rotary Int, 1989; Nat Coalition Black Meeting Planners; Mich Soc Asn Execs; Mental Illness Res Asn. **Honors/Awds:** Nat Nominations & Elections Comn, Soc Govt Planners, 1988; Hyatt Hotels Career Develop, Hyatt Hotels Corp, 1988, 1989. **Business Addr:** Vice President of Sales & Marketing, Zehnder of Frankenmuth, 730 S Main St, Frankenmuth, MI 48734.

SHELTON, JOSEPH B, JR.
Executive, construction manager. **Personal:** Born Oct 12, 1946, Vicksburg, MS; son of Charlene (deceased) and Joseph B (deceased); married Valeria D Bledsoe, Nov 10, 1973; children: Robert Waites Jr, Tamara, Joseph III & Jonathan. **Educ:** Hampton Inst, BS, bldg construct eng, 1969. **Career:** Darin & Armstrong, field engr, 1969-70, coordr, 1970-75, proj engr, 1975-78, proj mgr, 1978-84; Walbridge Aldinger Co, proj mgr, 1984-91, proj dir, 1991, vpres, currently. **Orgs:** Eng Soc Detroit, 1976-; admis comn, St Gerard's Church, vpres, 1989-92; vpres, St Gerard's Sch, sch bd, 1987-90; pres, N Huntington Block Club, 1982-88. **Honors/Awds:** Minority Achiever in Industry, Young Men's Christian Asn, 1980. **Home Addr:** 20310 Huntington Rd, Detroit, MI 48219, **Home Phone:** (313)592-0134. **Business Addr:** Vice President, Walbridge Aldinger Company, 703 Woodward Ave Suite 300, Detroit, MI 48226-2521, **Business Phone:** (313)963-8000.*

SHELTON, MILLICENT BETH
Administrator, executive, screenwriter. **Personal:** Born Jan 29, 1966, St Louis, MO; daughter of Mildred E and Earl W. **Educ:** Princeton Univ, BA, eng, 1988; New York Univ, MFA, 1993. **Career:** Forty Acres & a Mule Filmworks, wardrobe asst, 1988; Cosby Show, wardrobe asst, 1988-89; Idolmakers Films & Fat Productions, dir, 1989-92; Fat Film Productions, pres & dir, 1992; dir: Cavemen, 2007; Girlfriends, 2007; Lincoln Heights, 2007; The Loop, 2007; Everybody Hates Chris, 2006-07; Big Day, 2006; My Name Is Earl, 2006; The Bernie Mac Show, 2005; Barbershop, 2005; Dance Like We Do, 2005. **Honors/Awds:** Nancy Susan Reynolds Award, Ctr Pop Options, 1992; Thirty Under Thirty Award, Urban Profile Mag, 1992; WTC Johnson Scholarship, New York Univ, 1989; Image Award, Bernie Mac Show, 2001. **Special Achievements:** Directed videos for: Salt-N-Pepa, MC Lyte; wrote, directed, Ride, 1998.

SHELTON, O L
State government official. **Personal:** Born Feb 6, 1946, Greenwood, MS; son of Idell McClung and Obie; married Linda Kay; children: Eric, Shron, Jaimal & Kiana. **Educ:** Lincoln Univ, AB, 1970. **Career:** Mo Exten Serv, St Louis, youth specialist, 1972-82; Mo State Legis, state rep, 1983-. **Orgs:** William Community Sch Bd; chmn, Ville Area Neighborhood Housing Asn Inc; chmn, St Louis Dem Cent Comn; Early Childcare Develop Corp. **Home Addr:** 4273 W Dr Martin Luther King, St Louis, MO 63113. **Business Addr:** Representative, Missouri House of Representatives, 201 W Capitol Ave Rm 407B, Jefferson City, MO 65101, **Business Phone:** (573)751-2198.

SHELTON, REUBEN ANDERSON
Lawyer. **Personal:** Born Dec 6, 1954, St Louis, MO; son of Sedathon and Elizabeth; married D; children: Christian & Heather. **Educ:** Univ Kans, BS, jour, 1977; St Louis Univ Sch Law, JD, 1981; Wash Univ, MBA, 1991. **Career:** US Dist Ct, law clerk, 1978-83; Legal Serv Eastern Mo, atty, 1980-81; Husch, Eppenberger, Donohue et al, litigation atty, 1983-84; Union Electric Co, in house atty, 1984-; Kappa Alpha Psi, Past Province Polemarch, gen coun, currently. **Orgs:** Kappa Alpha Psi Fraternity Inc, 1974-; chair atty comn, United Negro Col Fund, 1983-; task force dir, Bar Asn Metro St Louis, 1984-; pres, Mound City Bar Asn, 1985-86; dir, Childhaven Autistic Childcare, 1986-, YMCA 1986-; CRWLC Comn, Mem Intake Comt. **Honors/Awds:** Law Student of the Year, St Louis Chap, Black Am Law, 1981; Lifetime Achievement Award. **Home Addr:** 5155 Westminster Pl, Saint Louis, MO 63108, **Home Phone:** (314)367-2340. **Business Phone:** (314)694-8998.

SHELTON, ROY CRESSWELL, JR.
School administrator, electrical engineer. **Personal:** Born Jun 30, 1941, Toledo, OH; son of Celestine B Campbell and Roy C; mar-

ried Patricia Lee Little, Apr 24, 1976; children: Kevin Lamont, Kelly Marie, Roy C III, James Phillip & Katherine Celestine. **Educ:** Cent State Univ, pre-engineering, 1959-61; Univ Toledo, BSEE, 1964, MSEE, 1967; Univ Detroit, doctorate engineering, 1969-72, 1991. **Career:** Lawrence Technological Univ, assoc prof, elec engineering, chair, Dept Eng; Badgett Indust Inc, proj mgr, currently. **Orgs:** Nat Soc Black Engrs, fac adv, 1983-; Tau Beta Pi, 1963-; Eta Kappa Nu, 1964-. **Honors/Awds:** Black Educator of the Year, Peace Corps, 1990.

SHELTON, ULYSSES
State government official. **Personal:** Born Jul 1, 1917; married Pearl; children: Charles & Frederick. **Educ:** Mastbaum Voc Sch. **Career:** Pa House Rep 181 Dist, dem mem, 1960-80; US Congressman Bradley, former magistgrate's clerk, dept rec, clerk, aide; beer distribr; Yorktown Civic Asn, club owner. **Orgs:** N Philadelphia Model City Prog. **Military Serv:** USAF. **Business Addr:** Owner, Yorktown Civic Association, 1132 W Jefferson St, Philadelphia, PA 19122.

SHEPARD, BEVERLY RENEE
Journalist, lawyer. **Personal:** Born Nov 30, 1959, Jacksonville, NC; daughter of Odis and Ruth Pearson. **Educ:** Univ NC, Chapel Hill, NC, BA, journ, 1982, JD, 1985. **Career:** Virginian-Pilot, Norfolk, VA, reporter, 1985; Manheim Interactive Inc, dir mkt, exec dir, currently. **Orgs:** Nat Asn Black Journalists; Hampton Roads Black Media Profs. **Honors/Awds:** Team winning First Place In A Series for project concerning the Year of the Child, Va Press Asn, 1990; First Place, news writing, Va Press Women's Asn, 1990; The Virginian-Pilot/Ledger-Star, Second Place, overall news coverage among staff, 1990; Hon Mention, News Writing, Nat Fed Press Women, 1990; Algernon Sydney Sullivan for all-around excellence to an undergraduate female: Order of the Valkyries for scholastic achievement; Soc Hellenas for contributions to sorority life; Holderness Moor Court, UNC Law Sch. One of three selected from 60 competitors to fill the 27-member team, 1983; Winner, Regional Team Competition, Black Law Studs Asn. **Home Phone:** (804)490-4572. **Business Addr:** Director of Marketing, Executive Director, Manheim Interactive Inc, 6205 Pachtree Dunwoody Rd, Atlanta, GA 30328, **Business Phone:** (678)645-2377.

SHEPARD, GREGORY
Executive. **Personal:** Born Mar 7, 1961, Trenton, NJ; son of George Jr and Evelyn M. **Educ:** Rensselaer Polytech Inst, BS, elec eng, 1983; Wharton Sch, Univ Pa, MBA, 1985. **Career:** Shepard-Patterson & Assocs, chief exec officer, 1986-95; Britton Financial Group, Investment Banking, prin, 1995-97; US Web Page Co, chief exec officer, 1997-. **Orgs:** Alpha Phi Alpha, 1982-; chmn, Osayande Partners, 1991-; pres, Rensselaer Alumni Club Wash, DC, 1992-; chmn, Leadership Congress 21st Century, 1994-. **Honors/Awds:** Leadership fel, Johnson & Johnson, 1983; Dir Award, Rensselaer Polytech Inst, 1994. **Special Achievements:** Pvt Pilot Cert, 1993.

SHEPARD, LINDA IRENE
Business owner, consultant. **Personal:** Born Dec 13, 1945, St Louis, MO; daughter of Woodie McCune and Dorothy Alice McCune; widowed; children: Monica Shepard, Adrienne Fitts & Alton Fitts III. **Educ:** Merritt Col, Oxford Calif, AA, 1972; Mills Col, Oakland Calif, BA, 1975. **Career:** Assemblyman Bill Lockyear, San Leondio Calif, dist secy, 1975-76; Jimmy Carter Pres, Atlanta Ga, dir campaign oper, 1976; BART, Oakland Calif,affirmative action officer, 1976-85; Mayor Lionel Wilson, Oakland Calif, campaign mgr, 1985-86; AC Transit, dir human resources; Superior Consult, owner, 1985-88. **Orgs:** Nat Coun Negro Women; Nat Asn Advan Colored People. **Honors/Awds:** Outstanding Business Achievement Award, Nat Coun Negro Women, 1987. **Home Addr:** 25800 Industrial Blvd, Hayward, CA 94545, **Home Phone:** (510)786-9024.

SHEPHERD, BENJAMIN ARTHUR
Educator. **Personal:** Born Jan 28, 1941, Woodville, MS; married Ann Marie Turner; children: Benjamin III & Amy Michelle. **Educ:** Tougaloo Col, BS, 1961; Atlanta Univ, MS, 1963; Kansas State Univ, PhD, 1970. **Career:** Atlanta Univ, teacher, 1962-63; Tougaloo Col, instr, 1963-65; Kansas State Univ, teacher asst, 1966-69; Southern Ill Univ, asst prof, 1970-73, assoc prof, 1973-75, asst dean grad sch, 1973-74, asst chmn, zoo, 1976-79, prof zoo, assoc vpres, acad affairs & res, 1979, vpres, acad affairs & res, 1988, vpres, acad affairs & provost, 1992-96, prof emer, currently. **Orgs:** Omega Psi Phi Fraternity; Am Soc Zoologists; Am Asn Anatomists; Ill Acad Sci; New York Acad Sci; AAAS (AAAS); Sigma Xi; Soc Study Reproduction; NAACP; life mem, Tougaloo Alumni Asn. **Honors/Awds:** Mason Senior Achievement Award Biology, Tougaloo Col, 1961; Reg Fellowship, Atlanta Univ, 1962; Best Graduate Teacher Assistant, Kansas State Univ, 1968; ACE Fellowship, LSU, Baton Rouge, 1978-79; Omega Man of the Year, Tau Upsilon chapter, 1979. **Special Achievements:** Numerous publications in field. **Home Addr:** 4009 Old US Hwy 51 S, Makanda, IL 62958-2201. **Business Addr:** Professor, Southern Illinois University, Department of Zoology, Life Science Bldg II 354C, Carbondale, IL 62901-6501, **Business Phone:** (618)453-4516.

SHEPHERD, BERISFORD
Drummer. **Personal:** Born Jan 19, 1917, Honduras; married Pearl E Timberlake (died 1996); children: Roscoe, Synthia, Keith. **Career:** Jimmy Gorham's Orchestra Phila, drummer, 1932-41; Benny Carter, 1941-42; AUS Bands, 1943-46; Cab Calloway, 1946; Buck Clayton Sextet, 1947; Earl Bostic Philadelphia, 1950-52; Bill Doggett Combo, freelancer, 1952-59; Mr Kicks & Co, Am Be Seated, Jerico Mim Crow, Here's Love; Sy Oliver Orchestra, 1964; Honky-Tonk, co-writer; Berisford San Francisco, owner, designer & builder fine furniture; N Peninsula Wind & Percussion Ensemble, 2nd Trombone; John Cordoni, Big Band, drummer; Charles Brown Combo, West Coast Only, "sub" drummer. **Orgs:** Pres, Friendly World Sound Swoppers; hon mem, Friendly Fifty. **Honors/Awds:** Men of Distinction, British Publ. **Business Addr:** Owner, Fine Furniture by Berisford of San Francisco, 195 Elmira St, San Francisco, CA 94124, **Business Phone:** (415)468-4426.

SHEPHERD, ELMIRA
Accountant. **Personal:** Born Sep 9, 1959, Birmingham, AL; daughter of Fred and Cordell Johnson. **Educ:** Lakeshore Clerical Training, Birmingham, AL, clerical cert, 1980; Booker T Washington Jr Col, Birmingham, AL, attended 1987; Southern Jr Col, Birmingham, AL, BBA, 1989. **Career:** Church sch teacher, Bethel African Methodist Episcopal Church, 1983-91; YMCA, Birmingham, AL, tutor, 1984-85; Lakeshore Hosp Work Lab, Birminham, AL, microfilm aide, 1984-85; Goodwill Industs, Birmingham, AL, book sorter, 1986-88; Div Four Inc, Birmingham, AL, bookkeeper, 1991. **Honors/Awds:** Valadictorian, Southern Jr Col, 1990. **Home Addr:** 13 14th St N, Birmingham, AL 35203. *

SHEPHERD, GRETA DANDRIDGE
School administrator, educator. **Personal:** Born Aug 15, 1930, Washington, DC; daughter of Philip J and Bertha Johnson; married Gilbert A (deceased); children: Michele M Murchison. **Educ:** Miner Teachers Col, Wash, DC, BS, 1951; DC Teachers Col, Wash, DC, MA, 1961. **Career:** Educator, school administrator (retired); DC Pub Schs, teacher, 1951-66, from asst prin to prin, 1966-72; Int Christian Univ, Fulbright/Hayes Fel, 1965; EOrange Pub Schs, NJ, supt, 1980-82; Plainfield NJ, supt schs 1982-84; NJ St Dept Educ, county supt schs; Essex County Voc Schs, NJ. **Orgs:** Alpha Kappa Alpha Sorority, 1950; assoc, CFK Ltd Found, 1971; pres elect, CADRE Found, 1975-; bd dir, YWCA Oranges, 1975-98; bd trustees, EastOrange Pub Libr, 1981-83; bd trustees, Mercer Co Community Col, 1984-; fed policy comm mem, Am Asn Sch Admin, 1984-; Phi Delta Kappa, 1987-; bd trustees mem, Univ DC, 1994-. **Honors/Awds:** Woman of the Year, NJ Chap Zeta Phi Beta, 1983; 5 Point Education Award, NJ Chap Delta Sigma Theta Sorority, 1984; Award Recognition, Cong Black Caucus Educ, 1984; Educator of The Year, Northeast Coalition Educ Leaders Inc, 1988; Distinguished Alumni Award, Nat Asn Equal Opportunity Higher Educ; Gubnertorial Appointee, NJ Educational Opportunity Fund. **Special Achievements:** NJ State Assembly Citation; Person of the Decade, Black New Jersey Magazine. **Home Addr:** 6 Linden Ave, West Orange, NJ 07052.

SHEPHERD, LESLIE GLENARD
Football player. **Personal:** Born Nov 3, 1969, Washington, DC. **Educ:** Temple. **Career:** Football player (retired); Wash Redskins, wide receiver, 1994-99;Cleveland Browns, 1999; Miami Dolphins, 2000.

SHEPHERD, DR. LEWIS A
Educator. **Educ:** EdD. **Career:** Greater Pleasant Hill Baptist Church, pastor; Ouachita Baptist Univ, asst to pres spec prog & univ compliance officer, currently. **Honors/Awds:** President Award. **Business Addr:** Assistant to President for Special Programs, Ouachita Baptist University, 410 Ouachita St, PO Box 3779, Arkadelphia, AR 71923, **Business Phone:** (870)245-5000 Ext 5234.

SHEPHERD, MALCOLM THOMAS
Executive, consultant, president (organization). **Personal:** Born Sep 27, 1952, Chicago, IL; son of Christine and Chester; married Thelma Jones, Nov 25, 1970; children: Monica, Malcolm Jr, Marlon, Maxwell & Makalen. **Educ:** Jackson State Univ, Jackson, Miss, BA, 1976, MPA, 1981; Bernard M Baruch Col, New York, NY, MPA, 1985. **Career:** State New York Mortgage Agency, New York, NY, spec asst pres, 1984-85; Dept Econ Develop, Jackson, Miss, financial consult, 1985-88; Governor's Off, State Miss, Jackson, Miss, econ develop policy analyst, 1988-89; Madison Madison Int, Jackson, Miss, mgr, 1989-93; MTS Ltd Inc, Jackson, Miss, pres, 1993-. **Orgs:** Nat Asn Advan Colored People, 1977; Nation Urban Fel, 1985-; pres, Miss Chap-Nat Bus League, 1990-91; chmn, JSU-Small Bus Develop Ctr, 1990-91; Nat HUD Fel. **Honors/Awds:** Annie Divine Community Service Award, Jackson State Univ, 1984. **Military Serv:** USMC, corporal, 1970-72. **Home Addr:** 773 Woodlake Dr, Jackson, MS 39206. **Business Addr:** President, MTS Ltd Inc, PO Box 2542, Jackson, MS 39207-2542, **Business Phone:** (601)366-0290.

SHEPHERD, ROOSEVELT EUGENE
Educator, chairperson. **Personal:** Born Oct 31, 1933, Elkridge, WV; married Vivian L Diggs; children: Nathetha Chamelle Shepherd. **Educ:** Kentucky State Col, BS, bus admin, 1955; Univ Louisville, certified police sci, Southern Police Inst, 1969; Mich State Univ, MS, criminal justice, 1971; Univ PA, MGA, Govt admin, 1979. **Career:** Educator, chairperson (retired); Cincinnati Div Police, police officer (patrolman specialist sgt lt), 1956-71; Cincinnati, Ohio, secy consult, 1971-72; Pa Depart Community Affairs, Harrisburg, community serv consult, (police mgmt), 1972-76; Shippenburg Univ, assoc prof criminal justice & dept chairperson, 1976-99. **Orgs:** Prog chmn, Harrisburg-Riverside Optimist Club, 1977-79; Acad Criminal Justice Sci, 1978-; City Harrisburg, PA, Civil Serv Comt; dist dir, PA, Black Conference Higher Educ, 1979-80; bd dirs, Dauphin Co Pretrial Serv Agency; Omega Psi Phi, 1953-; Reserve Officers Asn, ROA, 1968-; Phi Delta Kappa Int, 1977-; consult: Pa Depart Community Affairs; Md Transp Authority; Pa Human Relations Comn. **Honors/Awds:** Law Enforcement Exec Develop Fel, LEAA, US Depart Justice, 1970. **Military Serv:** AUS, spec 4, 1956-58; Good Conduct Medal; Soldier of the Month Award; AUS Reserves, chief warrant officer, 1958-83. **Home Addr:** 497 Kelker St, Oberlin, PA 17113, **Home Phone:** (717)939-4468.

SHEPHERD, SHERRI EVONNE. See SHEPHERD-TARPLEY, SHERRI.

SHEPHERD, VERONIKA Y
Government official. **Personal:** Born Apr 9, 1947, Cincinnati, OH; daughter of Carl Nathenial Oliver and Leola Oliver Gibson (deceased); married David Louis, Dec 3, 1981; children: Kevin, Willie, Bryan, Athena & Deja Dewberry. **Educ:** Ohio State Univ, Columbus, AA, 1975. **Career:** Government official (retired); State Ohio, Columbus, training coordr, 1974-75, head start admin coordr, 1975-79, grants adminr, 1979-82, CCA/CSA/state adminr, 1982-84, geriatric admin specialist, 1985, personnel adminr, 1985-86; Village Urbancrest, mayor, 1987-91. **Orgs:** First vice chair, Nat Chap Black Mayors Inc, Black Women Caucus, 1990-91; Unicare Develop Bd, Village Urbancrest, 1990-94; Southwestern City Sch Dist Bus Comput Prog Adv Comt, Hayes Tech High Sch, 1990-91; Franklin County Headstart Policy Comt, 1991-93; Franklin County Right From Start Community Forum Bd, 1991-93; comnr, State Ohio Women Res Policy Comn, 1991-93; Mid-Ohio Regional Planning Bd, 1991-94; pres, Ohio Chap Black Mayors, Inc; first vpres, Columbus Metropolitan Area Community Action Orgn. **Honors/Awds:** Public Service Award, President Jimmy Carter, 1982; Ohio Community SectAward Legis & Community Leadership, 1984; Governor Award Pub Serv, Govr Ohio, 1984; Woman of the Year Award, The United Methodist Church, 1986; County Action Community Ctr Award, Vol Serv, 1987-91; Sisterhood Award, Unselfish Serv & Committment Bethune Tradition, Clark County Sect, Nat Coun Negro Women, 1990.

SHEPHERD-TARPLEY, SHERRI (SHERRI EVONNE SHEPHERD)
Actor, television actor. **Personal:** Born Apr 22, 1970, Chicago, IL; married Jeff Tarpley, Mar 10, 2001 (divorced 2006); children: Jeffrey Charles Tarpley. **Educ:** Trade col. **Career:** Films: King of the Open Mic's, 2000; Pauly Shore Is Dead, 2003; Cellular, 2004; Guess Who, 2005; Beauty Shop, 2005; Who's Your Caddy, 2007; Push, 2008; Madagascar: Escape 2 Africa, 2008; Precious: Based on the Novel Push by Sapphire, 2009; TV Series: "Cleghorne!", 1995; "Claude's Crib", 1997; "Holding the Baby", 1998; Rewind, 1997; "The Jamie Foxx Show", 1998-2000; "Everybody Loves Raymond", 1998-2001; "Suddenly Susan", 1996; "Emeril", 2001; "Wednesday 9:30 (8:30 Central)", 2002; "Less Than Perfect", 2002-06; "Holla", 2002; "Joan of Arcadia", 2003; "Kim Possible", 2004-07; "Brandy & Mr.Whiskers", 2005-06; "Capitol Law", 2006; The View", 2008; "The Wedding Bells", 2007; "30 Rock", 2007-09. **Honors/Awds:** BET Comedy Award Nominee for Outstanding Supporting Actress in a Comedy Series for: "Less Than Perfect" (2002), 2005; 2 Emmy Award Nominee for Outstanding Talk Show Host for: "The View" (1997), 2008 & 2009. **Business Addr:** Actress, c/o AKA Talent, 6310 San Vicente Blvd Suite 200, Los Angeles, CA 90048, **Business Phone:** (323)965-5600.*

SHEPPARD, DONALD
Association executive. **Personal:** Born Nov 26, 1950, Houston, TX; son of L K and Blanche; married Donna Marie, Jul 1996; children: Ahmad, Wali, Aisha, Jamilah, LaChande & LaLyssa. **Educ:** Tex A&I Univ; Houston Community Col, AA, 1976; Texas Southern Univ, BA, social work, 1979; Univ Chicago, Sch Social Serv Adm, AM, 1988. **Career:** Pub Welfare Coalition, prog coord, 1987-88; Tex Southern Univ, asst prof, social work, 1988-91; Houston Endowment, grant officer, currently. **Orgs:** Coun on Founds, 1993-; Conf Southwest Founds, 1993-; Asn Black Found Exec, 1995-; Nat Asn Social Workers; Nat Asn Black Social Workers; Phi Beta Sigma Fraternity Inc. **Honors/Awds:** President's Award, NAACP, Houston Br, 1998. **Military Serv:** USAF, sgt, 1970-74. **Business Addr:** Grant Officer, Houston Endowment Inc, 600 Travis Suite 6400, Houston, TX 77008, **Business Phone:** (713)238-8100.

SHEPPARD, STEVENSON ROYRAYSON
Government official, school administrator. **Personal:** Born Jan 10, 1945, Bunkie, LA; married Diana Lewis; children: Stephen & Steven. **Educ:** Grambling State Univ, BS, 1967; Southern Univ, MEd, 1974; Northwestern State Univ, MA, 1976. **Career:** Rapides Parish Sch Syst, teacher, 1967; Aroyelles Parish Sch Syst, teacher & coach, 1968; Aroyelles Progress Action Comt, athletics dir,

1968; Sheppard & Jones Reading Clinic, dir; Town Bunkie, alderman-at-large. **Orgs:** Wm Progressive Lodge No 217, 1975; chmn bd, Amazon Baptist Church, 1982; dir & vpres, Zach & Shep's Skate-Arama Inc, 1983. **Home Addr:** PO Box 647, Bunkie, LA 71322. **Business Addr:** Alderman at Large, Town of Bunkie, Walnut St, Bunkie, LA 71322.

SHEPPHARD, DR. CHARLES BERNARD
Civil rights activist, business owner, educator. **Personal:** Born Sep 26, 1949, Port Gibson, MS; married Brenda Joyce Stone; children: Charles Kwame & Tenopra Me. **Educ:** Alcorn State Univ, BS, 1970; Southern Univ, JD, 1973; MS Col, JD, 1977. **Career:** Shepphard & Assoc, consult; Alcorn State Univ, prof hist & polit sci, 1977; MS House Rep, 1980-; Fayette Chronicle Newspaper, owner, publisher; Alcorn State Univ, exten specialist, CRD specialist, currently. **Orgs:** Am Hist Asn; Southern Growth Policy Bd; Am Mgt Asn; Int Affairs Asn; chmn, Nat Asn Advan Colored People-Fair Share Comt; chmn, Local Polit Party Activities; coordr, Polit Sci Internship Prog, Black Polit Sci Soc. **Honors/Awds:** Outstanding Young Men Award; Progressive Young Legislator of Miss. **Home Addr:** 163 Cemetery Rd, Lorman, MS 39096.

SHERIDAN, EDNA
Contractor, lawyer. **Personal:** Born Feb 20, 1951, Huntsville, AL; daughter of Willie Ed Fletcher and Beulah Ford; divorced; children: Daryl Andrae & Renita LaKaye Kimbrough. **Educ:** Ala A&M Univ, BS, 1980, MBA, 1982; Fla Inst Technol, MS, 1993. **Career:** Contract specialist for over 20 years; USAR, sr instr, 1976-; AUS Corps Engrs, chief contracting div, currently, contracting officer, currently. **Orgs:** Pres, Alpha Kappa Alpha Sorority Inc, Rho Chi Omega Chap, 1994-97, South Eastern Region, cluster coordr, 1999-2002; bd mem, Am Red Cross, Madison/Marshall Co Chap, 1996-; Nat Contract Managers Asn, 1999-; pres, Fun-Set Social & Charity Club, 1999-2002; life mem, Nat Asn Advan Colored People; bd mem, Calhoun Community Col Ctr Polit Cult. **Honors/Awds:** South Eastern Region President of the Year, Alpha Kappa Alpha, 1995; 20 Distinguished Men, Community Serv/Leadership, 1996; Resolution, Leadership, City Huntsville, 1997; Resolution, Community Leadership, City Madison, 1997; Leadership Award, Women Studies Group, 1997; Presidential Excellence Award, Nat Asn Advan Colored People, Madison County Br, 1998; Resolution, Community Leadership Award, State Ala; South Eastern Region Member of the Year, 1998; Woman of the Year, AUS Corp Engrs, Huntsville Ctr, 2000. **Home Addr:** 3238 Delicado Dr NW, Huntsville, AL 35810. **Business Addr:** Chief of Contracting Division, Contracting Officer, US Army Corps of Engineers, 4820 Univ Sq, Huntsville, AL 35816, **Business Phone:** (540)665-2025.

SHERIFF, THE. See RICHARD, STANLEY PALMER.

SHERMAN, BARBARA J. (BARBARA J SHERMAN-SIMPSON)
Stockbroker, financial manager, vice president (organization). **Personal:** Born Jul 20, 1944, Los Angeles, CA; daughter of Ernest Sherman and Estelle Sherman; married Mike O Simpson, 1989. **Educ:** Calif State Univ, Northridge, CA, 1961; Mesa Community Col, Mesa, AZ, 1971; Ariz State Univ, Tempe, AZ, bus admin, 1974. **Career:** Merrill Lynch, Phoenix, AZ, acct exec, 1975-77; Dean Witter, Sun City, AZ, acct exec, 1977-80; Merrill Lynch, Sun City, AZ, acct exec, 1980-84; Prudential Securities, Sun City, AZ, first vpres, investments, 1984-. **Orgs:** Ariz Bd Realtors, 1972-; Stockbroker's Soc, 1975-; The City PhoenixMayor's Comn Status Women, 1979-82; Valley Big Sisters, 1983-86;chairperson, Black Republican Coun-Phoenix, 1985; Black Jewish Coalition, 1986-; Ariz state chairperson, United Negro Col Fund, 1987-88; bd mem, Am Red Cross Cent Ariz Chap, 1988-. **Honors/Awds:** Woman of the Year in a Non-traditional role, Delta Sigma Theta, Inc, Phoenix, AZ Chapter, 1983; numerous performance awards, Merrill Lynch and Prudential-Securities; 100 of the most promising Black women in corporate America, Ebony Mag. **Military Serv:** USAF, E-5, 1963-71. **Business Addr:** Vice President Investments, Prudential Securities Inc, 17220 N Boswell Blvd, Sun City, AZ 85373-2000, **Business Phone:** (623)876-4800.

SHERMAN, C A (TONY SHERMAN)
Artist, sculptor. **Career:** Tex Comn Arts, comnr; Tony Sherman's Gallery, owner, artist & sculptor, currently. **Orgs:** Tex Arts Comn. **Special Achievements:** First African American and professional artist appointed as commissioner of the Texas Commission of the Arts. **Business Addr:** Owner, Artist, Tony Sherman's Gallery, 2420 Cartwright Rd Suite C, Missouri City, TX 77489-6000, **Business Phone:** (281)499-9958.

SHERMAN, EDWARD FORRESTER
Photographer. **Personal:** Born Jan 17, 1945, New York, NY; married Audrey Johnson; children: Edward F. **Educ:** Amsterdam Photographic Workship, 1960; Bronx Community Col, 1964; Univ S Marine Corps, 1966; New Sch Soc Res Spring, 1969; Brooklyn Col, 1973. **Career:** Freelance photogr, 1962-65; still photogr, USMC, 1965-67; Photo-Lab Tech, 1968-69; New Dimensions Assocs, dir, 1968; Freelance Photogr, 1969; Photographic Prog, dir, 1970; Comm Corp Lower W Side, art instr, 1972; NCA New Jour, assoc ed, 1973. **Orgs:** Co-chmn, Collective Black Photogrs, 1971; chmn, Benin Enterprises Inc, 1975. **Military Serv:** USMC, sgt.

SHERMAN, RAY
Football coach. **Personal:** Born in Berkeley, CA; married Yvette; children: Alana & Erica. **Educ:** Laney Jr Col; Fresno State Univ; San Jose State, educ, 1975. **Career:** Mich State Univ, coaching staff, 1974, 1976-77; Univ Calif, coaching staff, 1975, 1985; Wake Forest Univ, coaching staff, 1978-80; Purdue Univ, coaching staff, 1982-85; Ga Univ, coaching staff, 1986-87; NY Jets, offensive coordr; Houston Oilers, running backs coach, 1988; Minn Vikings, quarterback coach; Titans Radio, wide receivers coach, 2004-07; Green Bay Packers, wide receivers coach, 2005; Dallas Cowboys, coach, 2007-. **Orgs:** Am Football Asn.

SHERMAN, THOMAS OSCAR, JR.
Administrator, engineer. **Personal:** Born May 29, 1948, Elberton, GA; son of Thomas Sr and Edna Murray; married Joyce Chestang, May 12, 1973; children: Alfred, Morris & Katherine. **Educ:** NC A&T State Univ, BSEE, 1971; Golden Gate Univ, MBA, 1979. **Career:** USAF SAC, ATC, capt ewo instr, 1971-80; 129th Commun Flight Calif Air Nat Guard, oper officer, capt, 1980-83; Ford Aerospace, sr syst engr, 1980-83, mgr comput syst, 1983-84, mgr TREWS engrg, 1984-88, SDDS/TREWS Prog Mgr, 1988-90; 129th Info Syst Flight Calif Air Nat Guard, comdr, major, 1983-87; 129 Mission Support Squadron Calif Air Nat Guard, comdr, lt col, 1987-94; Loral SRS, Ridgecrest, Calif, dir E W prog, 1990-91, dep engineering dir, 1991-95; 129th Support Group, col, comdr, 1994-98; Lockheed Martin SRS, chief engr, dir, 1996-. **Orgs:** Asn Old Crows, 1976-; Nat Guard Air Force Asn, 1980-; Union Baptist Church Ridgecrest Calif; adult bible teacher, Union Baptist Church, 1987, choirmem, Union Baptist Church, 1986-94; chmn, Kiwanis Club Ridgecrest, Calif, 1990-91; adult bible teacher, mem, Emanual Baptist Church, 1994-. **Honors/Awds:** Distinguished ROTC Grad, NC A&T State Univ, 1971. **Military Serv:** USAF/ANG, col, 1971-98; AF Commendation Medal, National Defense Ribbon, Coast Guard Outstanding Unit Ribbon, AF Outstanding Unit Ribbon, Longevity Service Ribbon, Armed Forces Research Medal, Air Force Training Ribbon, Government Outstanding Unit Ribbon, Meritorious Service Medal, Senior Navigator Wings. **Home Addr:** 1100 Creek Ridge Ct, Roseville, CA 95747-7912. **Business Addr:** Chief Engineer, Director, Lockheed Martin Western Development Labs, Systems Engineering Laboratory, 1260 Crossman, Sunnyvale, CA 94089, **Business Phone:** (408)734-6500.

SHERMAN, TONY. See SHERMAN, C A.

SHERRELL, CHARLES RONALD, II
Executive, broadcaster, president (organization). **Personal:** Born May 10, 1936, Gary, IN; son of George Wesley Sherrell Jr and Beatrice Mariner Sherrell; married Trutie Thigpen, Nov 25, 1969. **Educ:** Mexico City Col, Mexico, BA, 1958; Roosevelt Univ, Chicago IL, MA, 1963; Univ Chicago, PhD, 1975. **Career:** Gary Pub Schs, Gary IN, foreign lang teacher, 1961-65; United States Steel, Gary IN, foreman, 1965-67; Globe Trotter Commun, Chicago IL, sales mgr, 1967-71; Bell & Howell Schs, Chicago IL, vpres, 1971-74; Mariner Broadcasters Inc, Chicago IL, pres, 1974-. **Orgs:** Radio Advert Bur, 1974-; pres, Am Soc Linguists, 1978-80; chmn mem comt, Black Hisp Asn, 1979-84; reading educ comn, New Fronteirs Inc, 1981-82; chmn, Nat Asn African-Am Anthropologists, 1983-85; chmn, cable TV comn, 901 Condo Bd Asn, 1987-89; pres 1988-90, chmn, 1990-, Nat Asn Black-Owned Broadcasters Inc. **Honors/Awds:** Distinguished Alumnus Award, Univ Chicago Alumni Asn, 1979; Humanitarian Award, American Ling Soc, 1980; Humanitarian Award, New Frontiers Inc, 1981. **Military Serv:** AUS, 1959-61. **Home Addr:** 901 S Plymouth Ct Apt 106, Chicago, IL 60605, **Home Phone:** (312)461-9247. **Business Addr:** President, Mariner Broadcasters Inc, 15700 Campbell Ave, Harvey, IL 60426, **Business Phone:** (708)331-7840.

SHERRILL, WILLIAM HENRY
Educator. **Personal:** Born Dec 6, 1932, North Carolina; married Gloria; children: William Jr, Adrienne Budd, Erick, Sharon & Karen. **Educ:** Shaw Univ, AB, 1954; Univ Pa, 1959; Univ Mich, MA, 1960; Univ Calif, PhD, 1972; SF State Col, attended 1965. **Career:** LH Foster High Sch, teacher, 1954-59; Berkeley High Sch, teacher counr, 1960-67; SF State Col, lectr, 1965-69; Univ Calif, dir, 1967-72; Howard Univ, dean. **Orgs:** Afro-Am Educs Asn; Am Asn Collegiate Registrants & Admin Officers; Am Coun Higher Educ; Am Personnel & Guidance Asn; Calif Couns & Guidance Asn; Calif Teachers Asn; Col Entrance Exam Bd; Berkeley Teachers Asn; No Calif Couns & Guidance Asn; Nat Asn Berkeley Counr; Nat Asn Col Deans Registrars Admins Officers; Nat Asn Col Admin Couns; Nat Asn Foreign Stud Affairs; Consortium Univ Wash Metro Area; Wash Area Admis Asn; DC Orgn Admin &Financial Aid Personnel; Proj BOOST, 1968; Upward Bound, 1968; Monterey Co Counr Asn, 1968; Am Col Test Adv Bd, 1968-72; Educ Testing Serv, 1969; Educ Opportunity Prog, 1968-72; Col Entrance Exam Bd Proj Access, 1969; Nat Merit Scholarship Selection Comn, 1971-72; Nat Achievement Scholarship Section Comn, 1969-70; Nat Teamsters Scholarship Selection Comn; W Reg Scholarship Selection Comn 1972.

SHERROD, REV. CHARLES M
Chaplain, clergy. **Personal:** Born Jan 2, 1937, Petersburg, VA; son of Raymond and Martha Walker Sherrod Gibson; married Shirley M; children: Russia & Kenyatta. **Educ:** Va Union Univ, AB, 1958; Va Union Univ, Sch Rel, BD 1961; Union Theol Sem, STm, 1967; Univ Ga, Cert Community Develop. **Career:** Interdenominational, minister, 1956-; SNCC, Field Secy, 1961-67; SW Ga Proj, dir 1961-87; New Community Inc, dir, 1969-85; City Albany, city comnr, 1976-90; Ga State Senate, 1996; Ga State Prison, Homerville, Ga, chaplain, currently. **Orgs:** First SNCC Field Organizer, 1961; Freedom Ride Coord Comn, 1963; pres, SW Ga Proj, 1967-85; bd, NAACP, 1970-85; US Govt OEO, 1974; Fel Inst Policy Studies, 1974; consult, Nat Coun Churches, 1978; bd, Slater King Ctr, 1975-85; bd, SW Ga Planning Comn, 1978-85; bd mem, Fed Southern Coop, 1979-87; Ga Coalition Housing, 1983-85. **Honors/Awds:** Omega Man of the Year, Lambda Chap, Richmond, 1958; Hons Civil Rights, Nat Lawyers Guild, 1985; Delegate, Nat Dem Party Conv, 1984. **Home Addr:** 201 Garden Hill Dr, Albany, GA 31705. **Business Addr:** Chaplain, Homerville State Prison, 700 Reddick St, PO Box 337, Homerville, GA 31634, **Business Phone:** (912)487-3052.

SHERROD, EZRA CORNELL
Executive. **Personal:** Born Jul 25, 1950, Wilson, NC; son of John and Mary Hester Worsely; married Charlotte Pye Sherrod, Aug 23, 1975; children: Derrick Cornell. **Educ:** Lear Siegler Inst, AA, 1971; Univ DC, BA, 1977; proj mgt seminars, 1980; People & Resources Mgt Seminars, 1986. **Career:** Woodard & Lothrop, comput specialist, 1970-72; Int Bus Serv Inc, proj mgr, 1972-80; Automated Datatron Inc, proj mgr, 1980-86; Sherrod Security Co, pres, owner, 1986; Wilkins Systs Inc, facil mgr, 1986-; Hecht's, comm sales, prof sales exec, 1990-91; Advantage Mortgage Serv, vpres, 1993-. **Orgs:** pres, hist club Univ DC, 1974-76; Univ DC Alumni, 1984; Minority Bus Comn, 1986; Evangel Assembly Church Camp Springs MD; Bus Network Wash DC; Phys & Ment Self-Improv Prog. **Honors/Awds:** Diamond Club Mem, Top Sales Level Hecht's, 1991. **Special Achievements:** Top Five Managers of Year Automated Datatron Inc, 1985; Author letter of intro "Saga of Sidney Moore," 1985; Top candidate for major exec position involving a major computer network w/Wilkins Systems Inc, 1987. **Home Addr:** 808 Kirkwood Rd, Waldorf, MD 20602.

SHERWOOD, O PETER
Lawyer. **Personal:** Born Feb 9, 1945, Kingston, Jamaica; son of Leopold and Gloria Howell; married Ruby Birt; children: 1. **Educ:** Brooklyn Col, BA, 1968; NY Univ Sch Law, JD, 1971. **Career:** NY Civil Ct, law secy to Hon Fritz W Alexander II 1971-74; NAACP Legal Def & Educ Fund Inc, asst coun, 1974-84; NY Univ Sch Law, adj asst prof law, 1980-87; State NY Ethics Comn, solicitor gen, 1986-91; City New York, corp coun, 1991-93; Kalkines, Ark, Zall & Bernstein, partner, 1994-2002; Appellate Practice II Circuit, NY State Bar Asn, lectr, 1996; NYS Ethics Comn, comnr, 1998-2003; NY State Judicial Inst Professionalism Law, 1999-; Manatt, Phelps & Phillips, litigation partner, 1994-. **Orgs:** Trustee, NY Univ Law Ctr Found; 100 Black Men; Metro Black Bar Asn; Nat Bar Asn; secy, Asn Bar City New York, 1992-97; New York City Procurement Policy Bd, 1991-94; NY State Bar, 1972; arbitrator, Am Arbitration Asn; Bd Deleg, NY State Bar Asn; Fed Bar Asn; Inns Ct; Am Acad Appellate Lawyers; panelist, Ctr Policy Rev, Panel Distinguished Neutrals; Comt Gen Aptitude Test Battery, Nat Res Coun, 1987-90; Law Ctr Found, NY Univ Sch Law. **Business Addr:** Litigation Partner, Manatt, Phelps & Phillips LLP, 7 Times Sq, New York, NY 10036, **Business Phone:** (212)830-7288.

SHERWOOD, WALLACE WALTER
Lawyer, college teacher, educator. **Personal:** Born Oct 6, 1944, Nassau, Bahamas; son of Walter and Tereceta. **Educ:** St. Vincent Col, BA, 1966; George Washington Univ, JD, 1969; Harvard Univ, LLM, 1971. **Career:** Legal Serv, staff atty, 1969-71; Mass Comn Against Discrimination, comnr, 1971-73; Roxbury Defenders Comt, exec founding dir, 1971-73; OEO, gen coun, 1973-74; Lawyers Comn Civil Rights Under Law, exec div, 1974-76; Pvt Prac, atty, 1976-; Northeastern Univ Col Criminal Justice, adj assoc prof, asst prof, assoc prof, chair, currently, prof criminal justice, currently; Community Legal Assistance Off, staff atty; Boston Off Lawyers Comt Civil Rights Under Law, exec dir. **Orgs:** Mass Bar Asn, 1969-; Boston Bar Asn, 1969-; Mass Coun Pub Justice. **Honors/Awds:** Dulles Fulbright Award, Nat Law Ctr, 1969; Teacher of The Year, Col Criminal Justice, 1987. **Business Addr:** Professor of Criminal Justice, Northeastern University College of Criminal Justice, Rm 401D 204 Churchill Hall 360 Huntington Ave, Boston, MA 02115.

SHIELDS, DR. CLARENCE L
Physician. **Personal:** Born Jul 19, 1940, Helena, AR; married Barbara Wilson; children: Brian, Christopher & Angela. **Educ:** Loyola Univ, Los Angeles, 1962; Creighton Univ Sch Med, Omaha, MD. **Career:** Univ Calif, Los Angeles Med Ctr, surg intern, 1966-67; Southwestern Orthop Med Group, orthop surg, 1973; Daniel Freeman Hosp, staff, 1973; Los Angeles Rams, assoc physician 1973-; Viewpark Community Hosp, staff, 1973; Martin Luther King Hosp, staff, 1973; Charles Drew Sch Med, clin prof, 1973-; Rancho Los Amigos Hosp, staff, 1976; Los Angeles Dodgers, Los Angeles Lakers, Los Angeles Kings, Calif Angels,

orthop consult, currently; Univ Southern Calif Sch Med, clin prof, 1976-; Kerlan-Jobe Orthop Clin, pvt pract, currently. **Orgs:** AMA; Am Orthop Soc Sports Med; Am Bd Orthop Surg; Am Acad Orthop Surgeons; dipl, Nat Bd Med Examrs; bd dirs, Western Orthop Asn, 1979; Los Angeles Co Med Asn; Charles Drew Med Soc; Calif Med Asn; Western Orthop Asn; chmn, Orthop Rev Comm, 1978-, orthop Comm & Credential Comn, Centinela Hosp; adv bd, 1973-, chmn, Fel Comm, 1973-; Nat Athletic Health Inst; Alpha Omega Alpha; Herodicus Soc; Calif Orthop Asn; Pan Pac Surg Asn; Am Col Sports Med; Int Soc Knee; Int Arthroscopy Asn; Arthroscopy Asn North Am. **Honors/Awds:** Numerous academic awards from organizations like: Alpha Omega Alpha, Herodicus Soc, Am Orthopedic Soc. **Special Achievements:** Authored more than 40 publications, 5 book chapters, 1 book, and 3 editorials and has been a facilitator for over 200 lectures. **Military Serv:** USAF, capt, gen med officer, 1967-69. **Business Addr:** Physician, Kerlan-Jobe Orthop Clinic, 6801 Pk Terrace Dr, Los Angeles, CA 90045, **Business Phone:** (310)665-7200.

SHIELDS, CYDNEY ROBIN
Manager. **Personal:** Born Feb 24, 1957, Jamaica, NY; daughter of Waddel and Sylvia; divorced. **Educ:** Ind Univ Penn, BA, Eng, 1980; Univ Md, Masters Degree Technol Mgt & MBA. **Career:** Lockheed Mgt Info Systs, internal auditor, analyst, 1982-84, control mgr, 1984-87, regional office mgr, 1987-; Claims Admin Corp, div mgr audit serv, 1989; Coventry HealthCare, dir; Verizon Business, IT Sox Compliance, mgr, 2004-. **Orgs:** Delta Sigma Theta, 1977-; founder, Black Women Who Win, 1986-; vpres, Am Bus Women's Asn, 1988-; Black Women's Adv Bd, 1989-; Nat Comn Working Women Wider Opportunities Women, 1992-; Nat Asn Female Execs; mem, Project Mgt Inst; ISACA; Women Technol. **Honors/Awds:** 100 Heroes Award; IT Strategic Pillar Award; Woman of the Year award, Am Bus Women's Asn, Wash, DC chap. **Special Achievements:** Co-author, Work, Sister, Work: The Right Moves on Your New Job, Women in Business, 1991; Why Black Women Can't Get Ahead, 1992; Managing Your Writing, Mgt World, 1992; Mounting a Career Climb, Career Focus Magazine, 1992; Author: Career Decisions: the Art of Soaring to the Top. **Home Phone:** (301)590-0119. **Business Addr:** IT Manager, Verizon Business, 140 W St, New York, NY 10007, **Business Phone:** (301)517-2165.

SHIELDS, REV. DEL PIERCE
Radio host, clergy. **Personal:** Born Apr 29, 1933, New York, NY; son of Judge and Daisy Hite; divorced; children: Leslie, Allyson, Cydney, Cynthia & Stacy. **Educ:** Nat Theol Sem, BS, 1978, MA, 1982, MDiv, 1984; Univ Santa Barbara, PhD, 1989. **Career:** WLIB, radio host, 1965-68; Independent Network-WLIB, WRVR, WWRL, radio host, 1968-70; Jemmin Inc, asst vpres, 1970-77; Avant-Garde Broadcasting Inc, vpres & gen mgr, 1975-77; Zion Gospel Church, sr pastor, 1980-; Unity Broadcasting WWRL, Morning Fel host, 1986-91, Drivetime Dialogue commentator; Zion Gospel Church, pastor, sr pastor. **Orgs:** Exec vpres, 1971-73, exec dir, 1974-78, Nat Asn TV & Radio; Church God Christ, Inc, 1999. **Honors/Awds:** Blanton Peale, Grad Inst, 1981. **Special Achievements:** Moments in Meditation, 1991-92. **Home Addr:** 112-11 Dillon St, Jamaica, NY 11433, **Home Phone:** (718)658-2420.

SHIELDS, KAREN BETHEA (KAREN LOUISE BETHEA-SHIELDS)
Lawyer. **Personal:** Born Apr 29, 1949, Raleigh, NC; daughter of Bryant W and Grace Louise; married Kenneth R Galloway, 1971 (divorced 1976); married Linwood B, Dec 1, 1984. **Educ:** E Carolina Univ, AB, psychol, 1971; Duke Univ, Sch Law, JD, 1974. **Career:** Paul Keenan Rowan & Galloway, partner, 1974-77; Loflin Loflin Galloway & Acker, partner, 1977-80; 14th Judicial Dist Durham Co, judge, 1980-85; Karen Bethea-Shields law firm, sole practitioner, 1986-; atty & counr-at-law, currently; Juvenile Crime Prev Coun, atty. **Orgs:** Am Bar Asn; Nat Conf Black Lawyers; judiciary coun, NBA, Nat Judicial Col; ACL; fac mem, Nat Inst Trial Advocacy; trial pract instr, training lawyers; Nat Col Criminal Defense Lawyers NACDA; Nat Asn Women Judges; Am Judicature Soc; guest lectr & workshop panel mem, Nat Acad Trial Lawyers, Toronto, Can, 1982; Nat Judicial Col Search & Seizure & Grad Evidence Spec Sessions, 1983; fac mem, Women Trial Lawyers Advocacy Clin, San Francisco, CA, 1984; Int Platform Asn, 1988-89; NCW, 1989; vice chairperson, Educ Comn, Durham Comn Affairs Black People, 1989-; bd mem, Edgemont Community Ctr, 1990-; bd mem, Hayti Develop Corp; bd mem, Durham Community Shelter HOPE. **Honors/Awds:** Joann Little Defense Team, 1974-75; Lawyer of the Year, Nat Conf Black Lawyers, 1976; Outstanding Service Award, Raleigh Chap, Delta Sigma Theta, 1977; Certificate of Appreciation, NC State Asn Black Social Workers, 1979; Outstanding Young Woman of the Year, 1983; Distinguished Achievement Award, Nat Asn Advan Colored People, 1981; Runner-up, NEXT Mag, 100 Most Powerful People for the 80's; Certificate for 1982, NC Juvenile Ct Judges, 1984; Outstanding Service, Community Service, Excellence in Education, Sister Clara Muhammad Schs Educ Fund NC, 1989. **Special Achievements:** First Black female and first female Dist Court Judge in Durham County, second Black female judge in North Carolina. **Home Addr:** 3221 Apex Hwy, Durham, NC 27713, **Home Phone:** (919)361-0228. **Business Addr:** Attorney, 123 Orange St, PO Box 6, Durham, NC 27702, **Business Phone:** (919)682-0383.

SHIELDS, REV. LANDRUM EUGENE
Clergy. **Personal:** Born Mar 17, 1927, Winston-Salem, NC; son of Samuel Jennings and Joanna Mary Berry; married Marjorie, Jun 11, 1955; children: Landrum Jr, Sharyn, Laurita & Andrea. **Educ:** Lincoln Univ, AB, 1949; Oberlin Grad Sch Theol; Howard Univ Sch Religion, BD, 1954; Christian Theol Sem, MRE, 1960. **Career:** Witherspoon Presby Church, clergyman; United Presby Chuch, 1985; Central State Hosp; Ind Univ, assoc fac; Ind Central Col, instr; Indianapolis YMCA, youth & adult secy; Howard Univ, chaplain; First Congregational Church, pastor; Covenant Community Church, clergyman & pastor, currently. **Orgs:** Pres, bd comnr, Indianapolis Pub Schs; bd dir, Comt Serv Coun; Whitewater Presbytery United Presby Church; Marion Co Tax Adjustment Bd; Indianapolis Mayor's Task Force on Communications; UNICEF Indianapolis Com; bd dir, United Way Cent IN; bd dir, Am Red Cross; bd dir, Flanner House; Indianapolis Pub Sch Bd; chaplain, Indianapolis Police Dept; chaplain, Indianapolis Int Airport; bd dir, United Way Cent Indiana; bd dir, Little Red Door; bd dir, Am Red Cross. **Honors/Awds:** Human Relations Role of Honor, Indianapolis; Recorder Newspaper, 1968; Award of Merit, So Cross #39 F & A M; Award for Outstanding Leadership & Dedication, Am Cancer Soc, Indianapolis, 1972-73; 50th Ann Distinguished Alumni Award, Christian Theol Sem; Father of Year Award, Greyhound Corp, 1976; Chaplain for A Day US Senate, 1977; Distinguished Hoosier. **Home Phone:** (317)283-1627. **Business Addr:** Pastor, Clergyman, Covenant Community Church, 5640 N Cooper Rd, Indianapolis, IN 46208, **Business Phone:** (317)298-7868.

SHIELDS, VINCENT O.
Administrator. **Personal:** Born Feb 20, 1924, Chillicothe, MO; married Edna Gilbert. **Educ:** Lincoln Univ, Attended 1948. **Career:** Chillicothe MO, us post office, fireman, laborer, 1948-73; Fed Hwy Admin, equal opportunity; Office Civil Rights Fed Hwy Admin Reg 7, dir, 1985; Mayor's Citizen Adv Comt Minority Housing Chillicothe, chmn, 1970; Chillicothe Housing Authority, pres; MO State Conf NAACP, pres, 1968-73. **Orgs:** Bd mem, Hope Haven Ind, 1968; pres, Livingston Ct Human develop Corp, 1969-73; Am Legion Post 25 Veterans Foreign Ward; pres, KC Chillicothe Br, 1954-73; chmn, EEO Adv Comt Green Hills Comn Action, 1970-71; chmn, Housing Urban develop, 1972; pres, Plaque Outstanding Dedicated & Loyal Leadership; Bd Mem, KS City Br NAACP. **Honors/Awds:** Award for Outstanding Service, Green Hill Human develop Corp, 1971; Award Regional IV, NAACP, 1976. **Military Serv:** AUS, Inf, 1943-45.

SHIELDS, WILL HERTHIE
Football player. **Personal:** Born Sep 15, 1971, Fort Riley, KS; married Senia; children: Soloman, Sanayika & Shavon. **Educ:** Univ Nebr, BA, commun. **Career:** Football player (retired); Kansas City Chiefs, guard, 1993-06. **Orgs:** Bd mem, Marillac Ctr C; spokesperson, United Way, 2003-06; founder, WilltoSucceed Found. **Honors/Awds:** Outland Trophy, 1992; Mack Lee Hill Award, 1993; Arthur S Arkush Humanitarian of the Year Award, Pro Football Weekly, 1999; The Citizenship Through Sports Award, Citizenship Through Sports Alliance, 2000; Good Guysin Sports, The Sporting News, 2000, 2002, 2004; Extra Effort Award, Nat Football League, 2002; Mid-Am Educ Hall of Fame; Walter Payton Man of theYear, 2003; Tribute to a Champion Award, Midwest Leukemia & Lymphoma Soc,2004; Kans City Spirit Award, 2004; Byron Whizzer White Humanitarian Award, 2004; Henry B Iba Citizen-Athlete Award, 2006; state Lineman of the Year, Daily Oklahoman. **Business Addr:** Founder, Will to Succeed Foundation, PO Box 26104, Overland Park, KS 66225-6104.

SHIELDS-JONES, ESTHER L M
Consultant, executive. **Personal:** Born in Beatrice, AL; daughter of Marshall A Montgomery Sr (deceased) and Annie Gertrude Ishman Montgomery; widowed; children: Reginald A & Darryl K. **Educ:** Tuskegee Univ, Tuskegee Inst, Ala, BS, 1963, dietetic internship, 1966-67; Tex Southern Univ, Houston, Tex, MS, 1976; Univ Minn, Minneapolis, Minn, nutrit admin, 1989. **Career:** Veterans Admin Hosp, Tuscaloosa, Ala, clinical dietician, 1976-78; Jefferson County Health Dept, Birmingham, Ala, nutrit consult, 1978-84; Elba Gen Hosp, Elba, Ala, dir dietary serv, 1984-85; Univ Ala, Birmingham, Ala, clin instr, 1985-86; Hillhaven Corp, Nashville, Tenn, staff dietician, 1985-87; Beverly Enterprises Inc, Atlanta, Ga, dietary consult, 1987-91; Consult Dietician Community Dialysis Ctrs, Salem Nursing Home & Rehab Ctr, Ala Dialysis Inc, 1993-96; Prof Directions, Consult Dietician Group, 1996-; Healthcare Partners, Med Group, nutrit educr, 1996; Inglewood Unified Sch Dist, Food Serv Dept, dir foof serv; pvt practice, dietician, currently. **Orgs:** Am Dietetic Asn, 1968-; Ala Dietetic Asn, 1967-; Delta Sigma Theta Sorority, Birmingham Alumnae Chap, 1984-; Consult Dietitians Health Care Facilities, 1988-; Top Ladies Distinction, Birmingham Metrop Chap, 1989-. **Honors/Awds:** Outstanding Dietitian Nominee, Birmingham Dietetic Asn, 1982. **Military Serv:** AUS, lt col, 1990. **Business Phone:** (323)299-9026.

SHIFFLETT, LYNNE CAROL
Administrator. **Personal:** Born in Los Angeles, CA; daughter of James Hubbard and Carolyn Ellen Larkin. **Educ:** Govt, Polit Sci, LA State Col, BA; Univ Wis, MA. **Career:** NBC, admin; Neighborhood Adult Participation Proj, Watts Ctr Dir; Sch Workers, Univ WI, instr; Commun Rel Social Develop Comn, Milwaukee Co, urban planner, 1969-71; KMOX-TV, cbs, news writer, 1971-72, news producer, 1972-73; Columbia Univ Summer Prog Broadcast Jour Minority Groups, consult & tchr 1973; WNBC-TV NewsCenter 4, weekend news producer, 1973-75, NBC Loan Community Film Workshop, trng dir & tchr, 1975, WNBC-TV news field, producer & writer, 1975-85; Shifflett Gallery, art dir, 1985-; Sr news writer, KCOP Television News, 1989-91; tchr, English & Soc Studies, Horace Hann Middle Sch, LA, 2000-, faculty adv, Chess Club; House representatives, congressman, 2002-. **Orgs:** Fellowship Opers Crossroads Africa; delegate 8th Nat Conf US Nat Com UNESCO, 1961; Cert Comn Leadership Sch Pub Admin USC, 1966; bd dir, Triad Inc, 1977; bd dir, Henry St Settlement , 1978; adv comn Edwin Grould Serv Children, 1985; Golden Life Mem, Delta Sigma Theta Sorority; AmWomen in Radio & TV; Nat Acad Television Arts & Sci; Nat Asn Black Journalists. **Business Addr:** Art-Director, Shifflett Gallery, 8033 Sunset Blvd No 877, PO Box 19159, Los Angeles, CA 90028, **Business Phone:** (323)737-6900.*

SHINE, THEODIS
Educator. **Personal:** Born Apr 26, 1931, Baton Rouge, LA; son of Theodis Wesley and Bessie Herson. **Educ:** Howard Univ, Wash, DC, BA, 1953; Univ IA, 1958; Univ Calif, Santa Barbara, CA, PhD, 1973. **Career:** Dillard Univ, New Orleans, LA, instr drama & eng, 1960-61; Howard Univ, Wash, DC, asst prof drama, 1961-67; Prairie View A&M Univ, Prairie View, TX, prof & head dept drama, 1967, Dept Musin & Drama, adj Prof, currently. **Orgs:** Omega Psi Phi; Nat Theatre Conf, Nat Conf African Am Theatres; Southwest Theatre Asn; Tex Educ Theatre Asn; bd mem, Tex Non-Profit Theatres; Am Theatre Asn. **Honors/Awds:** Brooks-Hines Award for Playwriting, Howard Univ; Delta Sigma Theta Award-Teaching; Beanie Award-Teaching. **Special Achievements:** plays include "Plantation," Contribution, "The Woman Who Was Tampered with in Youth," "Shoes", " Three Fat Batchelors"; author of over sixty television scripts for series "Our Street". **Military Serv:** AUS, 1955-57. **Home Addr:** 10717 Cox Lane, PO Box 2082, Dallas, TX 75229. **Business Addr:** Adjunct Professor, Prairie View A & M University, Department of Music and Drama, PO Box 2779, Prairie View, TX 77446-0519, **Business Phone:** (936)857-2817.

SHIPE, JAMESETTA DENISE HOLMES
Journalist. **Personal:** Born May 30, 1956, Knoxville, TN; daughter of James Edward and Lavonia Thompson; married Abie, Oct 10, 1987; children: Kristen Janan. **Educ:** Univ Tenn, BS, Commun & Jour, 1980; Cooper Bus Sch, AS (Cum Laude) Bus, 1982; Tenn Inst, Electronics, 1989-90. **Career:** FBI Office Cong & Pub Affairs, writer, pub release rep, 1982-83; Martin-Marietta Energy Syst Inc, Comp Electronics Servs, customer rels rep, 1983-. **Orgs:** Sigma Delta Chi Soc Prof Journalists, 1975-, Pub Rels Soc Am, 1977; pub affairs, press consult, Knoxville Women's Ctr, 1979-80; Phi Beta Lambda Soc Bus, 1982; Smithsonian Inst, 1987-; NAACP, 1988-. **Honors/Awds:** PTA Scholar Knoxville Chap, 1974-75; Minority Scholar Am Newspaper Pub Asn, 1976-78; Dean's List, Univ Tenn, 1980. **Home Addr:** 206 Northwestern Ave, Oak Ridge, TN 37830. **Business Addr:** Public Relations Assistant, Martin Marietta Energy Systems, Y-12 Plant, PO Box 2009, Oak Ridge, TN 37831, **Business Phone:** (615)574-6528.

SHIPLEY, REV. ANTHONY J
Clergy, educator. **Personal:** Born May 19, 1939, New York, NY; son of Oscar and Lillian Hawkins; married Barbara McCullough, Sep 3, 1960; children: Cornelia Jean. **Educ:** Drew Univ, BA, 1961; Garrett Sem, DMin, 1964; Adrian Col, DD, 1974; Am Mgt Asn, pres course, 1975. **Career:** Christ United Methodist Church, coun dir, 1971-82, Detroit W Dist, supt, 1982-, Gen Bd Global Ministry, dep gen secy, 1992, sr pastor, 1994-; Scott Church, pastor, 1987-; Garrett Evangelical Theol Sem, adj prof; Church Admin N MS Pastors Sch, lectr; Harvard Univ, fel, 1999. **Orgs:** Delegate, Gen Conf United Methodist, 1980; consult, NCJ Urban Network; bd dir, Adrian Col; chmn, Develop Comn Nat Black United Fund; Presidents Asn Am Mgt Asn; Inst Adv Pastoral Studies; pres, Nat Fel Conf Coun; dir, Detroit Coun Churches; Mich State United Ministries Higher Educ; Nat Bd Higher Educ & Min; mgt consult, Charfoos Christenson Law Firm; bd dir, Methodist Theol Sch, OH; founder, McKenzie High Sch/Adrian Col Bound Prog; bd dir, Barton McFarland Neighborhood Asn; cert trainer, Cuvy Leadership Ctr, 7 Habits Highly Effective People; chair bd, U-Snap-Back Community Develop Corp; chair, Phoenix Dist Boy Scouts Am. **Special Achievements:** Author: The Care & Feeding of Cliques in the Church, Interpreter Mag 1975, The Self Winding Congregation, Interpreter Mag 1975, Everybody Wants to Go to Heaven But Nobody Wants to Die, Christian Century 1976, The Council on Ministries as a Support System, Letter Ctr for Parish Developmet, Long Range Planning in the Local Church, MI Christian Advocate, Something for Nothing, MI Christian Advocate, Fable of Disconnection, MI Christian Advocate. **Home Addr:** 19505 Canterbury Rd, Detroit, MI 48221. **Business Addr:** Senior Pastor, Christ United Methodist Church, 15932 E Warren, Detroit, MI 48224, **Business Phone:** (313)882-8547.

SHIPMAN, SHELDON R.
Clergy, executive. **Personal:** Born in Durham, NC; son of F George. **Educ:** Univ NC-Charlotte, BS; Hood Theol Sem, MDiv;

Va Union Univ, Samuel DeWitt Proctor Sch Theol, PhD. **Career:** IBM Corp, news reporter & acct mgr sales; Silvanus Enterprises, vpres & secy; Greenville Mem African Methodist Episcopal Zion Church, pastor, currently. **Orgs:** United Way; Urban League; Nat Asn Advan Colored People; Kappa Alpha Pai Fraternity Inc; UNCC. **Honors/Awds:** Outstanding Young Men of America, Kappa Alpha Pai Fraternity Inc. **Business Addr:** Pastor, Greenville Memorial African Methodist Episcopal Zion Church, 6116 Montieth Dr, Charlotte, NC 28213.*

SHIPP, ETHELEEN R
Columnist, educator. **Personal:** Born Jun 6, 1955, Conyers, GA; daughter of Johnny Will Shipp Sr and Minnie Ola Moore. **Educ:** Georgia State Univ, BA, jour, 1976; Columbia Univ, MS, jour, 1979, JD, 1980, MA, hist, 1994. **Career:** The NY Times, nat corresp, legal corresp; asst metrop ed, 1980-93; NY Daily News, columnist, 1994-2006; Columbia Univ Grad Sch Jour, asst prof, 1994-2005; Wash Post, ombudsmen, 1998-2000; Hofstra Univ, Dept Jour Media Studies & Pub Rels, distinguished prof, 2005-. **Orgs:** Nat Asn Black Journalists, 1983-; NY Asn Black Journalists, 1986-. **Honors/Awds:** Pulitzer Prize, 1996. **Special Achievements:** Co-author, Outrage: The Story Behind the Tawana Brawley Hoax, Bantam, 1990. **Business Addr:** Distinguished Professor, Hofstra University, Department of Journalism Media Studies and Public Relations, 405 NAB, Hempstead, NY 11549-1000, **Business Phone:** (516)463-5426.

SHIPP, HOWARD J., JR.
Educator, athletic coach. **Personal:** Born Oct 2, 1938, Muskogee, OK; married Jeanetta Combs; children: Jackie. **Educ:** Langston Univ, BS, 1962; Northeastern State Col, MS, 1966; Okla State Univ, post grad. **Career:** Muskogee Pub Schs, teacher football coach; Douglas HS Okla City, teacher football coach; Northeast HS Okla City, asst prin; Prof Baseball Player, 1958-59; Prof Barber, 1966-71; Okla State Univ, Univ Coun Serv, counr, 1971-05. **Orgs:** Okla City Classroom Teacher Asn; Okla City C C; Okla Educ Asn; Nat Asn Educ; Am Pub Gardens Asn; Nat Asn Advan Colored People; Okla Coun Pub Affairs, Bd Community Action Prog Still water, OK; treas, Mid Scope; chmn, Minority Scholar Comt; Inst Scholar Comt; fac advr, Okla State Univ, Afro-Am Soc; sponsor, Kappa Alpha Phi. **Honors/Awds:** Recipient Black Gold Award, Alpha Phi Alpha Epsilon Epsilon Chap, 1972-73. **Special Achievements:** Co-coordinated Book, "Techniques for the Low-Achiever in Science".

SHIPP, DR. MELVIN DOUGLAS
Educator. **Personal:** Born Aug 10, 1948, Columbus, GA; son of Gene T and Doris O; married Dr Michele Pierre-Louis; children: Gael & Elizabeth. **Educ:** Ind Univ Sch Arts & Sci, BS, 1970; Ind Univ Sch Optom, OD, 1972; Harvard Univ Sch Pub Health, MPH, 1980; Univ Miss, Sch Pub Health, DrPH, 1996. **Career:** USNR, capt, 1972-2001; Naval Hosp Port Hueneme, CA, chief optom serv, 1972-76; Univ Ala, Birmingham, asst prof, 1976-83, dir optom technician prog, 1976-79, asst dean clin serv & dir clin, 1980-86, from assoc prof to prof, 1983-2004; Senator Donald W Reigle Jr, health legis asst, 1989-90; Robert Wood Johnson Health Policy, 1989-90; OH State Univ, prof & dean, 2004-. Pew Health Policy Doctoral fel. **Orgs:** Panelist, Nat Asn Minority Med Educr, 1994; Am Acad Optom; Am Optom Asn; Am Pub Health Asn; bd mem, Asn Sch & Col Optom; Bur Health Professions; Food & Drug Admin; Nat Bd Examiners Optom; Nat Eye Inst; Nat Optom Asn; Prevent Blindness Am; Transp Res Bd. **Honors/Awds:** Commissioner's Special Citation, Food & Drug Admin, 1983; Certificate of Commendation, USNR, 1984; Optometrist of the Year, 1986; Founder's Award, Nat Optom Asn, 1989; Navy Commendation Medal, 1992; President's Award, Southern Coun Optometrists, 2000; Inductee, Nat Optometry Hall of Fame, 2002; Koch Medal, Am Acad Optom, 2003. **Military Serv:** USNR, 1971-2001; Nat Defense Medal; Armed Forces Reserve Medal; Meritorious Mast 61st Marine Amphibious Unit USCM, 1978; Bell Ringer Award, REDCOMNINE, Navy Commendation Medal, 1992. **Business Addr:** Dean, Professor, Ohio State University, College of Optometry, 338 W 10th Ave, Columbus, OH 43210-1280, **Business Phone:** (614)292-3246.

SHIPP, PAMELA LOUISE
Psychologist. **Personal:** Born Feb 18, 1947, St Louis, MO; daughter of Mall B and Lovia L Falconer. **Educ:** Colo Col, BA, 1969; George Wash Univ, MA, 1973; Denver Univ, PhD, 1985. **Career:** Irving Jr HS, dean studs, 1975-77, counr, 1977-83; Southern Ill Univ, Coun Ctr, therapist, 1983-84; Palmer HS, counr, 1984-85; Colo Col, therapist, 1985-; Pikes Peak Psychol Ctr, therapist, 1985-; Leadership Peak, fac; Founds Coaching, fac; Pub Sch Adminr; Bus Mgt Consult; Exec Coach; Denver Univ, Grad Prog Couns Psychol, adj prof, currently; Ctr Creative Leadership, sr prog assoc, currently. **Orgs:** Alumni, Kappa Kappa Gamma Sorority, 1966-87; Am Psychol Asn, Div 16, 1985-87; consult, Ctr Creative Leadership, 1986-; pres, Asn Black Psychol, Denver/Rocky Mountain Chap, 1986-87; bd dirs, Boys & Girls Club Pike Peaks Region, 1988-91; bd dirs, World Affairs Coun, Colo Springs, 1988-91; mem adv bd, El Pomar Found, bd dirs, Colo Springs C's Mus; Colo Springs Human Rels Bd. **Honors/Awds:** NAACP Community Service Award, Nat Asn Advan Colored People. **Special Achievements:** Author: Counseling Blacks: A Group Approach; The Personnel and Guidance Journal, Oct. 83; Managing Diverse Work Teams: Leaders in Action, Jan/Feb 01, Vol. 20; Building Communities For Tomorrow, One Person At A Time, 2002; recognized in Who's Who in Black Colorado Springs; featured in the Gazette Telegraph's Women at the Top. **Home Addr:** 1510 Witches Willow Lane, Colorado Springs, CO 80906, **Home Phone:** (303)579-6878. **Business Phone:** (719)633-3891.

SHIPPY, JOHN D
Government official. **Personal:** Born in Gaffney, SC; son of John H and Hattie M Gibbs; married Carmen L Richardson; children: Angela A, Tamar S & Stearmen R. **Educ:** USAF, cert master instr, 1975; Culver-Stockton Col, Canton, Mo, BA, Polit Sci, 1978; Webster Univ, St Louis, Mo, MA, personnel mgt, 1986; St Mary's Univ; Our Lady Lake Univ; AHMA, cert convention serv Mgr, 1988; Dept State Administrative Offrs Crs. **Career:** USAF officer (retired); USF, MacDill AFB, cook, 1964-65; MACV, Compound, Pleiku AB, Vietnam, cook, 1965-66; High Wycombe Air Station, England, storeroom supvr, 1967-69; 12th TFW Alert Facility, Cam Ranh Bay AB, Vietnam, supvr, 1969-70, Offr's op en mess, suv, 1970-71; 4th TFW Hosp, Seymour Johnson AFB, shift supvr, 1970; Bien Hoa AB, Vietnam, shift suv, 1970; Lackland AFB, military training inr, 1971-76; Royal Saudi Air Force, info progr, 1976-77, military training instr, 1977-79; Offutt AFB, serv opers off, 1979-81; Air Force recruitment off, 1981-83; Off Recruitment Branch, chief, 1983-85; Kunsan AB, Korea, serv opers officer, 1985-86; Cent Tex Col, Pacific Div, human Rels mgt instr, 1985-86; Kelly AFB, Base Servs Div, chief, 1986-88; Royal Air Force, 20th Serv Squadron, Upper Hayford, Eng, comdr, 1988-91, spec asst, 1991-93; Army Air Force Exchange Serv Hq, planning officer, USAF off, Dept State, Foreign Serv Off, 1994; US Am Embassy, Lima Peru, currently. **Orgs:** Veterans Foreign Wars, 1972-; Air Force Asn, 1978-; Vietnam Veterans Am; Am Legion Servs Soc; Hq AAFES Food Inspection & Eval Prog; Servs Soc, 1985-; Retired Off Asn, 1985-; vpres, Black Awareness Comt, 1990-91; bd Govs, Hq AAFES Officers' Club, 1991-92. **Honors/Awds:** Master Instructor, USAF, 1976; Master Drill Instructor, USAF, 1976; Instructor of the Quarter, USAF, 1976; Best Recruiting Group in Nation, USAF, 1983; Best Innkeeper, USAF, 1986. **Military Serv:** USAF, Major, 1964-93; Meritorious Serv Medal, 1986, 1988, 1992, Air Force Commendation Medal (6 Awards), Vietnam Serv Medal.

SHIRLEY, DR. CALVIN HYLTON
Physician. **Personal:** Born Jan 28, 1921, Tallahassee, FL; son of Edwin S and Stella Gertrude; married Jeanette Lindsey (deceased); children: Calvin H Jr, John W, Jasmin Denise, Cedric H & Carmen Anita. **Educ:** Fla A&M Col, Tallahassee, pre-med, 1942; Boston Col Physicians & Surgeons, MD, 1947. **Career:** Physician (retired); JC & SB Property Develop Corp, owner/mgr; Pvt Pract, physician, 1947-2000. **Orgs:** Pres, Broward Co Med Dental & Pharm Asn Fla, 1955-59; adv exec bd mem, FL State Bur Comprehensive Med, 1969; past Grand Asst Med Dir IBPO Elks of the World; med dir FL State Sickle Cell Found, 1979; active mem, AMA, Nat Med Asn; past pres, Kappa Alpha Psi Alumni Chapt; solo accompanist playing trumpet with St Christopher Episcopal Church Choir; 1st trumpet player with the Broward Comm Col Symphony Orchestra. **Honors/Awds:** FL State Distinguished Serv Awd Gov FL, 1976; So Provincial Achievement Award, So Provincial Kappa Alpha Psi Fraternity Inc, 1977; Doctor of the Year Award, Caducean Soc Greater Ft Lauderdale, 1985. **Military Serv:** USN, hosp corpsman, 1944-46; Asiatic Pacific Campaign.

SHIRLEY, GEORGE IRVING
Opera singer, educator. **Personal:** Born Apr 18, 1934, Indianapolis, IN; son of Irving Ewing and Daisy Shirley; married Gladys Lee Ishop, Jan 1, 1956; children: Olwyn & Lyle. **Educ:** Wayne State Univ, BS, 1955, grad study, 1956; Univ Northern, Iowa, DHL. **Career:** Detroit Bd Edu, music teacher, 1955-56; Univ Md, voice prof, 1981-87; Univ Mich, Joseph Edgar Maddy distinguished Univ prof voice, dir Vocal Arts Div, 1987-, Joseph Edgar Maddy distinguished Univ emer prof voice, currently. **Orgs:** Nat Asn Teachers Singing; Am Guild Musical Artists; AFTRA; Nat Asn Negro Musicians; Wayne State Univ Alumni Asn; Univ Mich Musical Soc, adv bd; Alpha Phi Alpha; Phi Mu Alpha; Phi Kappa Phi; Omicron Delta Kappa; Pi Kappa Lambda. **Honors/Awds:** Nat Arts Club Award, 1960; Grammy Award, for performance in recording Mozart's Cosi Fan Tutte, 1968; Named one Distinguished Teachers, Univ MD, 1985-86; Alumni Achievement Award, Wayne State Univ; Black Alumni Achievement Award, Wayne State Univ; Honorary doctorates: Montclair Col,1984; Wilberforce Univ, 1987; Lake Forest Col, 1988; Univ Northern Iowa, 1997. **Special Achievements:** Appeared in over 80 opera productions; first African-American tenor and second African-American male to sing leading roles with the Metropolitan Opera. **Military Serv:** First African Am member AUS Chorus, Ft Myer, VA, Mil Dist Wash, 1956-59. **Business Addr:** Director Vocal Arts Division, Joseph Edgar Maddy Distinguished University Emeritus Professor of Voic, University of Michigan, School of Music Theatre & Dance, 1100 Baits Dr, Ann Arbor, MI 48109-2085, **Business Phone:** (734)764-5595.

SHIRLEY, DR. OLLYE BROWN
Association executive. **Personal:** Born in Mound Bayou, MS; married Aaron. **Educ:** Tougaloo Col, BA, eng; Miss Col, MA, 1969; Jackson State Univ, EdS, 1978; Univ Miss, PhD, 1988. **Career:** Vicksburg Citizens' Appeal, ed; Lanier High Sch, coordr & consult, currently; Jackson Pub Schs, Jackson Med Mall Quantum Opportunities Prog, staff, currently. **Orgs:** Nat Sch Bds Asn; bd dir, First Am Bank; MS Museum Nat Sci Found; Jackson chapter, vpres, Serv Youth dir, The Links Inc. **Honors/Awds:** Goodman, Chaney, Schwerner Award, 1989; Medgar Evers Award, Nat Asn Advan Colored People, 1999. **Business Addr:** Coordinator, Jackson Pub Schools, S Concorse Suite 201, PO Box 11508, Jackson, MS 39283, **Business Phone:** (601)713-2814.

SHIVER, JUBE
Journalist. **Personal:** Born May 30, 1953, South Boston, VA; son of Jube Shiver Sr and Mildred Leigh; married Tadasha Culbreath-Shiver, Nov 18, 1989. **Educ:** Syracuse Univ, Syracuse, NY, BS, 1975; Antioch Sch Law, Wash, DC, JD, 1978; Univ Southern Calif, Los Angeles, CA, MA, 1988. **Career:** Wilmington News-Journal, Wilmington, DE, staff writer, 1977-79; Wash Star, Wash, DC, staff writer, 1979-81; Wash Post, Wash, DC, staff writer, 1981-82; USA Today, Arlington, VA, staff writer, 1982-83; Los Angeles Times, Los Angeles, CA, staff writer, 1983-, Wash, DC, nat corresp, jornalists, currently. **Orgs:** Wash Asn Black Journalists; Nat Asn Black Journalist. **Honors/Awds:** Wash/Baltimore Newspaper Guild Award, 1981; Int Journ, fel Univ SC, 1987; Los Angeles Press Club Award, 1992. **Special Achievements:** Author, Horizons East, 1974. **Business Addr:** Journalists, Los Angeles Times, 1875 I St NW Suite 1100, Washington, DC 20006, **Business Phone:** (202)861-9238.

SHIVERS, AUDRA BARRETT. **See BARRETT, AUDRA.**

SHIVERS, P DERRICK (PETER DERRICK SHIVERS)
Media executive. **Personal:** Born Oct 30, 1964, Kansas City, MO; son of Isiah and Alice L Perry. **Educ:** Maplewoods Community Col, attended 1984; Penn Valley Community Col, AS, 1986; Univ MSR Kans City, attended 1988. **Career:** PDS Universal Entertainment Group Inc, pres, 1989-92; Paradigm Entertainment, consult, 1990-; PDS Communs Inc, chmn, chief exec officer, 1992-; SS Gear Int Ltd, vpres, gen mgr, 1994. **Orgs:** BMI, 1989; Am Soc Composers, Authors & Publ, 1989; Nat Asn Record Merchants, 1990; Nat Asn Ind Record Distributors, 1990; RIAA, 1991; UCC, 1991. **Honors/Awds:** Outstanding Achievement, Black Bus Asn, 1990-91. **Special Achievements:** Image Magazine, Kans City, Entertainment Indust Top Ten, 1990. **Business Phone:** 800-473-7550.

SHIVERS, PETER DERRICK. **See SHIVERS, P DERRICK.**

SHIVERS, S. MICHAEL
Government official, business owner, scientist. **Personal:** Born Mar 20, 1935, Madison, WI; son of Dimetra C Taliaferro and Stanley M; married Jacklyn Lee Gerth; children: Steven Michael, David Wallace & Julie Ann. **Educ:** Univ Wis, BS, 1958. **Career:** Government, business owner, scientist (Retired); City Madison, alderman17th dist, 1971-73, 1975; soil scientist, entrepreneur & politician. **Orgs:** Wis Soc Prof Soil Scientists, 1958-78; Equal Opportunities Comn; Bd Pub Works; City Parks Comn; Transp Comn; Legis Comn; Madison Water Utility, Health Comn; Dane County Parks Comn; Common Coun Orgn Comn; City-County Bldg Comn; Nat Asn Advan Colored People; Urban League; City County Liaison Comn; City MATC Liaison Comn; sr mem, Madison Common Coun. **Honors/Awds:** Distinguished Service Award, N Madison Jaycees, 1977-78.

SHOCKLEY, ALONZO HILTON, JR.
Educator. **Personal:** Born Sep 3, 1920, Milford, DE; married Kay Marilyn Falke; children: Novella Shockley Randolph, Cheryl Shockley Durant & Alonzo Hilton III. **Educ:** Del State Col, BS, 1943; Mich State Univ, MA, 1947; New York Univ, advan cert ad & supv, 1956. **Career:** Educator (retired); Brooks HS, sci teacher, 1948; Dept Pub Instr, prin, elem & jr high, 1948-58; DE State Col, res asn, 1958-60; Cent Sch Dist 4, teacher, 6th grade, 1960-62; Union Free Sch Dist, prin, 4-6 grades, 1962-63; New York State Educ Dept, assoc adminr, 1964-65; Nassau Co Health & Welfare Coun, educ coordr, 1965-66; Freeport Pub Schs, dir state fed progs, 1966. **Orgs:** Pres, New York Univ Alumni, 1984-85, bd dirs, 1973-; allocation comn, United Way Long Island, 1977-; New York State Coun Supt Fed Legis Comt, 1976-; Nat Educ Asn; Asn Childhood Educ Int; Educ Res Asn New York; Nassau County Elem Principles Asn; New York Teachers Asn; Long Island Nat Conf Christians & Jews; coun pres, United Nation Asn; Am Asn Sch Adminr; New York Coun Sch, Supt, legis corps mem, 2000; Asn Supv & Curric Develop. **Honors/Awds:** Afro Am Republican Cert Award, Long Island Coun, 1973; Meritorious Service Award, Recog Dedicated Serv Adminr Compensatory Educ New York State, 1972; Alumni Meritorious Service Award, 1988. **Military Serv:** AUS, Thirty seventh Special Service, 1942-45. **Home Addr:** 49 Gaymore Rd, Port Jefferson Station, NY 11776-1353.

SHOCKLEY, ANN ALLEN
Librarian, educator, writer. **Personal:** Born Jun 21, 1927, Louisville, KY; daughter of Bessie L Allen and Henry Allen; married William, Jan 1, 1949 (divorced); children: William L &

Tamara A. **Educ:** Fisk Univ, BA, 1948; Case Western Reserve Univ, MSLS, 1959. **Career:** Del State Col, freelance writer, 1959-60, asst lib, 1959-66, assoc lib,1966-69, African Am Collections, cur, currently; Univ Md, Eastern Shore, lib, 1969, assoc lib pub serv & dir oral hist, Libr Admin Devel Inst fel, 1974, cur, currently; Fisk Univ, assoc lib spec collections & univ archivist, assoc prof lib sci, 1970-98, cur, 1999-. **Orgs:** Authors Guild; Am Lib Asn Black Caucus; Tenn Archivists. **Honors/Awds:** Additional Awards, Cent High Sch, Louisville, KY, 1944; Short Story Award, Asian Am Writers Workshop, 1962; Faculty Research Grant, Fisk Univ, 1970; ALA Black Caucus Award, 1975; First Annual Hatshepsut Award for Literature, CVOBW, 1981; Martin Luther King Black Author's Award, 1982; Susan Koppelman Award for Best Anthology, Popular & Am Cult Asn, 1989; Outlook Award, 1990; Achievement Award for Extraordinary Achievement in Professional Activites, Black Caucus Am Libr Asn, 1992; 1/2 Success Recognition Award Librarian/Author, 1997. **Special Achievements:** History of Public Library Services to Negroes 1900-55; Loving Her, Bobbs-Merrill Inc, 1970; Living Black American Authors, 1973; A Handbookfor Black Librarianship, 1977; The Black and White of It, Naiad Press, 1980; Say Jesus and Come to Me, Avon Books, 1982; Afro-American WomenWriters 1746-1933: An Anthology and Critical Guide, G K Hall, 1988; author, paperback, New Am Libr, 1989. **Home Addr:** 5975 Post Rd, Nashville, TN 37205. **Business Addr:** Curator, Fisk University, 1000 17th Ave N, Nashville, TN 37208-3051, **Business Phone:** (615)329-8500.

SHOEMAKER, VERONICA SAPP
Clergy, government official. **Personal:** Born Jun 23, 1929, Ft Myers, FL; daughter of Henry L Sapp and Lillian Sapp; children: Mattie, Bennie & Duane E (deceased). **Educ:** Edward Waters Col, Jacksonville, FL, attneded 1951; Edison Comm Col, Ft Myers, FL, attended 1972. **Career:** Fla Health & Rehab Servs, foster care home, 1974-83; Sunland Develop Ctr, resident training instr; City E Ft Meyers, city councilwoman-at-large, 1982-2002; Veronica Shoemaker Florist, owner & designer, 1974-. **Orgs:** Area dir, Southwest Fla State Conf, Nat Asn Advan Colored People; vol prog, Lee County RSVP Comn; Hispanic Am Soc; mem bd, Lee County Cemetary; sch bd mem, Lee County Sch Bd ESAA Comn; bd mem, charter mem Dunbar Merchants Asn Inc; Greater Ft Myers Chamber Com; Fla Conf C & Youth; Lee County Charter Comn; Lee County Hosp Study Comn; Lee County Human Rels Comn; past chmn, Lee County Bi-Racial Comn; Lee County Ment Health Asn; past pres, Dunbar HS & Elem PTA; past mem, Lee County Coun PTA; past pres & charter mem, Dunbar Little League; past charter Ebony Parent Club; past mem, Dunbar Easter Club; past charter mem, vpres, Fla Women's Polit Caucus; past charter mem, Southwest Fla Women's Polit Caucus; past mem Lee County League Women Voters, Overall Econ Devel Comm; pres & charter mem, Dar Improvement Asn 1979-; bd dir, Nat League Cities, Goodwill Indust, Metro Org, SW Fl League Cities, Women in Munic Govt; founder & dir, Source Light & Hope Develop Ctr Inc, 1988; pres, Veronica S Shoemaker Charity Serv Inc. **Honors/Awds:** Woman of the Year, Zeta Phi Beta; SROP for Comm Serv Plaque; Nat Asn for the Advancement of Colored People Award FL; Presidential Award, Dunbar Little League; Honor & Award, Edison Comm Col Black Student Union; High Honor Heart of Gold Gannett Found; Martin Luther King Jr Human & Civil Rights Award, FTP & Nat Educ Asn, 1992. **Special Achievements:** Honored 3 Mile Street Named "Veronica S Shoemaker" Blvd, 2002; Shoemaker Lane, 1998; first black council member. **Home Addr:** 3054 Mango St, Fort Myers, FL 33916. **Business Addr:** Owner, Veronica Shoemaker Florist, 3510 Martin Luther King Blvd, Fort Myers, FL 33916, **Business Phone:** (239)332-1802.

SHOFFNER, GARNETT WALTER (GUS SHOFFNER)
Counselor. **Personal:** Born Jul 12, 1934, Greensboro, NC; son of Robert and Hortense; married Doris Cole, Feb 1, 1958; children: Joseph, Robin & Debra. **Educ:** Bellevue Col, BS, 1972; Univ Nebr, MPA, 1975; Creighton Univ, MS, 1988. **Career:** Employee Develop Ctr, Enron Corp, dir, 1979-87; Great Plains Coun Ctr, counr, 1988-90, dir, 1990-. **Orgs:** Bd vpres, Nova Therapeut Community; bd mem, Sarpy County Ment Health; bd mem, Bryant Res Community Ctr; steering comt, Omaha Temp Organizing; Rotary Intl; Nat Asn Advan Colored People; Urban League; Family Life Ministry, Creighton Univ, 1990-. **Honors/Awds:** Great American Family Midlands, State Nebr, 1990. **Military Serv:** USAF, TSgt, 1952-72. **Business Addr:** Counselor, Co-owner, Great Plains Counsel Center, 205 N Galvin Rd Suite B, Bellevue, NE 68005-4852, **Business Phone:** (402)292-7712.

SHOFFNER, GUS. **See SHOFFNER, GARNETT WALTER.**

SHOFFNER, JAMES PRIEST
Chemist, counselor. **Personal:** Born Jan 14, 1928, New Madrid, MO; married Cornelia Dow; children: Stuart, Karen, Andrew. **Educ:** Lincoln Univ, BS, 1951; DePaul Univ, MS, organic chem, 1956; Univ Ill Med Ctr, PhD, organic chem, 1965. **Career:** Chemist (retired), Counselor; Post Off, Chicago; CPC Internat, res chmn, 1956-61; UOP Inc, res chemist, 30 yrs; Inst Sci Educ & Sci Commun Columbia Col, adj prof, 2004; Am Chem Soc Depart Diversity Prog, consult, currently. **Orgs:** Am Chem Soc; Catalysis Soc; Chicago Chem Club; Ill Acad Sci; Nat Counr Am Chem Soc; chmn, Chicago Am Chem Soc, 1976-77; bd mem, NW Suburban SCLC; Dist 59 Sch Community Coun; Omega Psi Phi. **Honors/Awds:** Black Achievers Award, YMCA, 1975; Encouraging Disadvantaged Students into Careers in the Chemical Sciences Award, Am Chem Soc, 2002; 30 year councilor plaque, Am Chem Soc, 2004. **Special Achievements:** Pub Papers in Num Sci Jours Patents; first in 1968 to chair (with Dr. Joe Arrigo) the pilot of Project SEED. **Military Serv:** AUS, tech-5, 1946-47. **Business Addr:** Counsilor, American Chemical Society, Department of Diversity Programs, 1155 16th Street NW, Washington, DC 20036, **Business Phone:** (202)872-6243.*

SHOPSHIRE, DR. JAMES MAYNARD
Educator, clergy. **Personal:** Born Oct 7, 1942, Atlanta, GA; son of James Nathaniel and Esther Pickett; married Berlinda Kay Brown; children: James Jr, Anika Diarra & Ekerin Ayobami; married. **Educ:** Clark Col, BA, 1963; Gammon Theol Seminary Interdenominational Theol Ctr, BD, 1966; Northwestern Univ, PhD, 1975. **Career:** Interdenominational Theol Ctr, asst prof, 1975-80, chair of church & soc dept, 1978-80; Wesley Theol Seminary, Washington, DC, assoc prof, 1980-83, assoc dean, 1980-85, prof, relig, 1983-. **Orgs:** Minister Bethlehem United Methodist Church, 1964-66, Burns United methodist Church, 1966-71, Ingleside-Whitfield United Meth Church, 1974-75. **Honors/Awds:** Rockefeller Doctoral Fel Fund, Theol Educ, 1971-72; United Methodist Church, Crusade Scholar, 1973-74. **Business Addr:** Professor, Wesley Theological Seminary, Department of Sociology, 4500 Massachusetts Ave NW, Washington, DC 20016, **Business Phone:** (202)885-8616.

SHORT, KENNETH L
Educator. **Personal:** Born Aug 21, 1943, Chicago, IL. **Educ:** Howard Univ, BSEE, 1966; State Univ New York, Stony Brook, MS, 1969, PhD, 1972. **Career:** State Univ New York, Stony Brook, Dept Elec Sci, 1968, asst prof, 1985; Nat Eng Consortium Inc, Schmitt Scholar fel, 1974; Stony Brook Univ, Dept Elec & Comput Engineering, dir, prof, currently. **Orgs:** Inst Elec & Electronic Engrs, 1964-; NY State Soc Prof Engrs, 1970-; NY Karate Asn, 1970-. **Honors/Awds:** Chancellors Award, Excellence Teaching, State Univ New York, Stony Brook, 1985; Presidents Award, Excellence Teaching, State Univ New York, Stony Brook, 1985; Frederick Emmons Terman Award, 1987; Deans Award for Extraordinary Service, Col Engineering, State Univ New York, 1994; Excellence in Teaching Award, Col Engineering, 1994; Award of Honor for Excellence in Teaching, Elec Engineering Dept, State Univ New York, 1997. **Special Achievements:** Published 14 articles. **Business Addr:** Professor, Stony Brook University, Department of Electrical & Computer Engineering, Light Engineering Bldg 229, Stony Brook, NY 11794-1400, **Business Phone:** (631)632-8403.

SHORT, LESLIE
Businessperson, chief executive officer. **Career:** J. Men's Tokyo, owner; Montel Williams Show, assoc producer; Thirteen/WNET, music Coordr; Macy's Dept Store, special events mgr; K.I.M. Media, pres & ceo, 1999-; FUBU, pres mkt, advert & public rels, currently. **Orgs:** Adv bd mem, CMO Coun. **Business Addr:** President, Chief Executive Officer, K.I.M. Media LLC, 24 W 45th St Suite 2, New York, NY 10036, **Business Phone:** (212)869-4996.

SHORTY, VERNON JAMES
Health services administrator. **Personal:** Born Dec 17, 1943, New Orleans, LA; son of Adries and Earl (deceased); divorced; children: Angelique & Chyna. **Educ:** Southern Univ New Orleans, BA, Hist, 1972, BA Sociol, 1973; Tulane Univ New Orleans, Fel Cert, 1974; Admin Drug Abuse Progs, Southern Univ Baton Rouge, MS, 1992. **Career:** Desire Narcotic Rehab Ctr Inc, exec dir, 1970-; LA State Univ, adj instr, 1970-72; CADA Desire Fla, outreach admin asst, 1970-72; Southern Univ Syst adj prof, 1973-. **Orgs:** Consult Technician Veterans Admin, 1973-; co-chmn, First Nat Drug Abuse Conf, 1974; chmn, LA Asn Prog Dirs, 1974-86; NIDA AIDS Outreach Demonstration Res Proj, 1989-92; prin investr, Phi Alpha Theta Soc. **Honors/Awds:** Nyswander-Dole Award, 1994; Social Justice Award, Nat Black Policemen Asn. **Special Achievements:** Published "A Situation of Desire" Org & Adm of Drug Treatment Prog 1974; HTLV III Study Research, Triangle Inst, 1985-86; America's Unsung Heroes 1988; Kool Achiever Awards Nominee; Part of Research Team, frequent isolation & molecular identification human T-Cell Leukemia Virus Type-2 1988; Part of Research Team, High rate of HTLV-II infection in Seropositive IV Drug Abusers in New Orleans 1989. **Military Serv:** USN, E-4 2 yrs; USN Reserves 4 yrs. **Home Addr:** 4760 Franklin Ave, New Orleans, LA 70122. **Business Addr:** Executive Dir, Desire Narcotics Rehabilitation Center Inc, 4116 Old Gentilly Rd, New Orleans, LA 70112, **Business Phone:** (504)945-8885.

SHOTWELL, ADA CHRISTENA
Educator. **Personal:** Born Sep 5, 1940, Helena, AR; married Roy Edward. **Educ:** Southern Univ, Baton Rouge, BA, 1961; Univ Calif, Berkeley, teaching cert,1962; Memphis State Univ, MEd, 1974, Univ Miss, PhD, 1986. **Career:** Clover Park Sch Dist, teacher, 1964-67; Memphis City Sch, teacher,1968-75; State Tech Inst, dept head, develop studies, 1976-78; State Tech Inst, teacher, 1975; State Tech Inst Memphis Correctional Ctr, div head, correctional educ, 1978-; SW Tenn Comm Col, Liberal studies & educ, prof, dean, currently. **Orgs:** AVA, 1976-; TVA, 1976-; ATEA, 1976-; TTEC, 1976-; WTEA, 1976-; MACBE,1976-; Nat Asn Black Amns Vocational Educ, 1979-80; chapter, bd dirs-,Black Black Crime Task Force, 1985; NAACP, 1985; PUSH, 1985; Pierian Soc. **Honors/Awds:** Outstanding Young Woman of America, 1976; Citizen of the Week, WLOK Radio Station, 1978; Teacher of The Year, Correctional Educ Asn, Region III,1978; Tennesse Correctional Educator of the Year, Tenn Asn, 1978; Profv Quarter Quarterly Jour Corrections, Quality Commitment Award Winner, Univ Memphis, 2001; Outstanding Service Award, ACTE, 2002. **Business Addr:** Dean, Liberal studies and education, Southwest Tennessee Community College, Macon Whitehead 43 Union C-202F, Memphis, TN 38101.

SHOWELL, HAZEL JARMON
Educator. **Personal:** Born Apr 5, 1945, Macon, GA; children: Angela & Patrick. **Educ:** Del State Col, BA, English, 1968; Univ Bridgeport, MA, guid, 1973. **Career:** Univ Del, consult staff leadership, 1975; Dept Pub Instr, state supt,adult educ, 1976-; Wm Henry Middle Sch, Dover, DE, teacher humanities,1968-73, assoc prin, 1973-76; State Va, consr & evaluator, 1978; State Del, cons & police training, 1979; Groves Adult High Sch, Middletown, DE, prin, currently; Del Coalition Literacy Inc, dir, currently. **Orgs:** Delta Sigma Theta, 1968; Women Vision Daring to Venture, Delta Sigma Theta Sor, Dover, DE, 1974; pres, Peninsula Sect Nat Coun Negro Women, 1976-79;chairperson, Social Justice Comn, NAPCAE, 1978; Dir, Comnof Affiliate Organizations (CAO), AAACE Leadership. **Honors/Awds:** Teacher of the Year Award, Capital Sch Dist, Dover, DE, 1972; Outstanding Young Women in America, 1978; White House Conference on Families, State Del, 1979-80. **Business Addr:** Principal, Groves Adult High School, 504 S Broad St, Middletown, DE 19709, **Business Phone:** (302)378-5037.

SHOWELL, MILTON W.
Military leader. **Personal:** Born Apr 19, 1936, Baltimore, MD; married Alberta Graves; children: Keith & Kimberly. **Educ:** Morgan St Col, BS, 1958. **Career:** Logistic Vietnam, mgr med serv, 1966-67; Korea, 1971-72; AUS Europe, implemented race rels prog; Seminars Drug Abuse; Author Book; Dept Def Race Relations Inst, grad; Patrick AFB, FL, 1974. **Special Achievements:** First African American to win All Europe Winner Toastmaster's Dist Speech Contest, 1975. **Military Serv:** AUS, major, 1961-.

SHOWS, MARK D
Chief executive officer. **Career:** New Detroit Real Estate Management LLC, managing partner & chief exec officer. **Business Addr:** Managing Partner, Chief Executive Officer, New Detroit Real Estate Management LLC, 14648 Ohio St, Detroit, MI 48238.*

SHROPSHIRE, HARRY W.
Financial manager, consultant. **Personal:** Born Apr 13, 1934, Asbury Park, NJ; married Kathleen Rae Nelson. **Educ:** Moravian Col, BS, econs & bus admin, 1957; Advan Training Mgt Prog, cert, 1972; Foreign Affairs Exec Studies Prog, cert, 1974; Financial & Econ Analysis, 1976. **Career:** Emerson Radio & Phonograph Corp, NJ, acct, 1957-62; Hess Oil & Chemical Corp, NJ, acct, 1962-65; US Dept State AID, auditor, 1965-70, acct mgr,1970-75; foreign serv controller, 1975-86; Self-employed, financial mgt consult, 1986-. **Orgs:** Asn Govt Accountants, 1966-; Am Mgt Asn, 1976-. **Honors/Awds:** Certificate of Appreciation for Cooperation in Equal Opportunity Program, Dept State AID, 1974. **Military Serv:** USNR, 1952-60. **Business Addr:** Consult, 592 Trout Lake Dr, Bellingham, WA 98226, **Business Phone:** (360)676-4683.

SHUFORD, HUMPHREY LEWIS
School administrator, dean (education). **Personal:** Born Nov 18, 1945, Wetumpka, AL; son of Robert and Cora; divorced; children: M Shondia & Monique. **Educ:** Ala A&M Univ, BS, 1969; Troy State Univ, advan studies, attended 1973; Univ Southern Ala, advan studies, attended 1974; Auburn Univ, advan studies, attended 1976; Ala State Univ, MS, 1978. **Career:** Atmore State Tech Col, coordr stud personnel; Jefferson Davis St Jr Col; part time Sociol Inst; Jefferson Davis Community Col, dean extended servs. **Orgs:** Ala Col Personnel Asn, 1980-86; Ala Counsr Asn, 1980-86; Atmore State Tech Col Educ Asn, vpres, 1982-84, pres 1984-86; vpres, pres, Progressive Civic Club, 1982-83; vpres 1983, pres, 1985, Atmore Alumni Chap, Kappa Alpha Psi; bd mem, Atmore Chamber Com; Ala Educ Asn, 1986; Nat Educ Asn, 1986; Am Asn Coun, 1986, Ala Dem Conf, Hermon Lodge No 260; vice chmn bd, Escambia County Sch Bd, Atmore, AL. **Honors/Awds:** Achievement Award, Progressive Club, 1979; Polemarch Award, 1981, Achievement Award, Atmore Alumni Chap Kappa Alpha Psi, 1981; Achievement Award, State Testing Prog, 1982; Special Service Award, Atmore Alumni Chap Kappa Alpha Psi, 1982; Southern Province Achievement Award, Kappa Alpha Psi, 1986; Chapter of the Yr Award, Kappa Alpha Psi Frat, 1986. **Home Addr:** PO Box 902, Atmore, AL 36504. *

SHULER, ADRIENNE
Basketball player, basketball coach. **Personal:** Born Apr 24, 1969, Bowman, SC. **Educ:** Univ Ga, social work. **Career:** Basketball

player (retired), basketball coach; Univ Ga, point guard, 1987-91; Wash Mystics, guard, 1998; Ind Fever; Marshall Univ, grad asst coach; Okaloosa-Walton Comm Col, asst coach; Furman Col, asst coach; Appalachian State Univ, Appalachian Mountaineers, head coach, 2002; Lady Pirates, asst coach, currently. **Business Phone:** (559)637-1250.

SHUMATE, GLEN
Executive. **Personal:** Born Sep 9, 1958, Sandusky, OH; son of John Wesley and Annie Ruth Henson; children: Darrin Wesley. **Educ:** Univ Toledo, Toledo, Ohio, BS, Stud Serv, 1982. **Career:** Univ Toledo, Toledo, Ohio, activities coordr, 1980-82, counr asst, 1982-83; Burlington Northern, Holland, Ohio, operations agent, 1983-84; Cimmaron Express, Genoa, Ohio, opers mgr, 1984-86; Hillcrest Hosp, Mayfield, Ohio, mgr patient support serv, 1986-88; Cleveland Ind, dir community rels, 1988-95; Cleveland Conv & visitors Bur, vpres tourism develop, 1995-. **Orgs:** Rainbow Hosp, Sickle Cell Anemia Advi Bd, 1989-95; coordr, United Way Campaign, 1990-93; bd mem, Esperanza Inc, 1991-95; Children's Mus Cleveland, 1997-02. **Honors/Awds:** Glen Shumate Award, Black Faculty/Staff, Univ Toledo, 1981; Leadership Award, Black Student Union, 1981; Unemployment 9th Cong Dist, Cong Record, 1982; Eastern Campus Honors List, Cuyahoga Community Col, 1987; Hispanic Hertiage Award of Excellence, City Cleveland, 1993; Humanitarian Award, Nat Orgn Black Law Enforcement Executives, 1994; Leadership Cleveland, 2000. **Business Addr:** Vice President of Tourism Development, Cleveland Convention & Visitors Bureau, 50 Public Sq, Cleveland, OH 44113, **Business Phone:** (216)621-4110.

SHUMPERT, TERRANCE DARNELL
Baseball player. **Personal:** Born Aug 16, 1966, Paducah, KY. **Educ:** Univ KY. **Career:** Baseball player (Retired); Kans City Royals, infielder, 1990-94; Boston Red Sox, 1995; Chicago Cubs, 1996; San Diego Padres, 1997; Colorado Rockies, 1998-02; Omaha Royals, ending 2001; Tampa Bay Devil Rays, 2003. *

SHURNEY, DR. DEXTER WAYNE
Physician. **Personal:** Born Jul 15, 1958, Loma Linda, CA; son of Dr Green and Juanita; married Wanda Whitten, Oct 10, 1982; children: Simone & Cameron. **Educ:** Loma Linda Univ, BS, 1979; Howard Univ Col Med, MD, 1983; Univ Detroit/Mercy, MBA, 1990. **Career:** Westland Med Ctr, surgical staff physician, 1986-90; Blue Cross/Blue Shield, case mgmt dir, 1987-90, Network, HMO, med dir, 1990-92, planning sr assoc med dir, 1992-95, vp corp med dir, 1996; American Healthways Inc, vpres & nat bus med dir, currently. **Orgs:** Am Med Asn, 1988-; Hospice Southeast Mich, bd, 1995-; Mich AIDS Fund, bd, 1995-; Mich Environ Coun, bd, 1997-; Journal Mgr Care, editorial bd, 1997-; Drug-Free Mich Comn, steering comt, 1997-; Fed Int Health Funds, adv panel, 1998-; Kids Immunization Initiative Detroit/Southeast Mich, co chair, 1998-. **Honors/Awds:** Detroit Med Soc, Community Service Award, 1998. **Home Addr:** 1497 W Boston Blvd, Detroit, MI 48206, **Home Phone:** (313)865-0987.

SHUTTLESWORTH, FRED L
Clergy. **Personal:** Born Mar 18, 1922, Montgomery County, AL; widowed; children: Patricia, Ruby, Fred jr & Carolyn. **Educ:** Selma Univ, BA; Ala State Col, BS, 1955; Birmingham Baptist Col, LlD, 1969; Cincinnati Baptist Bible Col, hon doctorate, 1971. **Career:** Clergy (Retired); Greater New Light Baptist Church Cincinnati, founder, pastor, 1966-2006. **Orgs:** Founder, Ala & Christian Movement Human Rights, 1956-69; bd mem, SCLC, secretary, interim pres, 2004; former aide Dr Martin Luther King, Jr; founder, Housing Found. **Honors/Awds:** Spec Citation Nat Conm for Rural Sch, 1961; Human Relation award, Press Club, 1962; Special Award, Back Our Brothers Inc, 1963; Rosa Park Award, 1963; Excellence Award, PUSH 1974; Martin Luther King Civil Rights Award, Progressive National Baptist, 1975; Founder Award, SCLC, 1977.

SIDBURY, HAROLD DAVID
Executive. **Personal:** Born Sep 15, 1940, Hampstead, NC; married Vivian Ann Radd; children: Timothy, Channeta, Felicia, Colette, Harold Jr, Jarvis & Ingar. **Educ:** Cape Fear Tech, attended 1960, Kittrell Col, attended 1966. **Career:** African Methodist Episcopal Church, pastor, 1966-87; Gen Contractor, 1974-87; SCC Construction Co, pres, currently. **Orgs:** Chmn, Coun Bd Educ Pender co, 1960-85; E Gate Masonic Lodge No 143, 1965-; chmn bd trustees, Grand United Order Salem, 1978-85, chmn bd dirs, 1985-87. **Honors/Awds:** Appreciation Award, Neighborhood Housing Develop Wilmington Chap, 1979; Designing & Building Award, Grand United Order Salem Bldg, 1982; Most Outstanding Minister of Year, Black Caucus Robeson Co, 1984. **Home Addr:** 800 Hwy 17 N, Hampstead, NC 28443, **Home Phone:** (910)270-2603. **Business Phone:** (919)762-5353.

SIEVERS, ERIC SCOTT
Football player. **Personal:** Born Nov 9, 1957, Urbana, IL. **Educ:** Univ Md, 1980. **Career:** Football Player (retired), football coach, executive; San Diego Chargers, tight end, 1981-88; Los Angeles Rams, 1988; New Eng Patriots, tight end, 1989-90; Langley High freshmen team, asst football coach;General Motors Corporation, mgr, 2008; Lindsay Cadillac, sales mgr, currently. **Orgs:** Numerous memships including Arlington Better Sports Club, 1991; Wash-Lee High 2002. **Honors/Awds:** Numerous awards including Maryland's Offensive Lineman of the Year; Outstanding Senior Award; AV Williams Award, 1980; played in AFC Championship Game, post-1981 season. **Business Addr:** Sales Manager, Lindsay Cadillac of Alexandria, 1525 Kenwood Ave, Alexandria, VA 22301, **Business Phone:** (703)998-6600.

SIFFORD, CHARLIE
Golfer. **Personal:** Born Jun 2, 1922, Charlotte, NC. **Career:** Pvt golf instr, Singer Billy Eckstine, 1947-53; prof golfer. **Orgs:** Deerwood Country Club. **Honors/Awds:** Achievement Award, 2001; World Gold Hall of Fame, 2004. **Special Achievements:** Author, Just Let Me Play, autobiography, 1992; First Black to achieve success on the PGA tour; first Black to win the PGA Sr Championship, 1975; first black elected to World Gold Hall of Fame, 2004. **Military Serv:** AUS, 1943-46.

SIGLAR, RICKY ALLAN
Football player, business owner. **Personal:** Born Jun 14, 1966, Albuquerque, NM. **Educ:** San Jose State Univ, 1986-88. **Career:** Football player (retired), business owner; San Francisco 49ers, tackle, 1990; Kans City Chiefs, 1993-96, 1998; New Orleans Saints, 1997; Carolina Panthers, 1998; Tri-Union & Associates, owner. **Orgs:** Chmn, Kans City Ambassadors, 2006-; Caring Athletes Touching Children's Hearts. **Home Addr:** 10408 Eden Dr NE, Albuquerque, NM 87112, **Home Phone:** (505)296-5110.

SIGLER, I. GARLAND
Executive. **Personal:** Born Dec 7, 1932, Bessemer, AL; married Bertha; children: Glenn Garland, Ennis Stevenson. **Educ:** Pennsylvania State Univ; Temple Univ. **Career:** SE PA Transportation Authority, ino agent, 1960-; Philadelphia HS Girls, instr, 1967-; Sigler Travel Serv & Ticket Agency, pres; Comn Serv Ctr, exec dir, 1970-; Teamster Local 161 Intl Brotherhood Teamster, vice pres, 1972-. **Orgs:** Children's pgm dir Nat Med Assoc, 1971; pres, Transit Roundtable Philadelphia; pres, York 15 Home Assoc; life mem, NAACP; dir, N Philadelphia Br, 1972-73. **Honors/Awds:** Mason of year, Prince Hall Mason Tuscan Morning Star Lodge 48, 1968; community service award, NAACP, 1971; service award, Nat Dairies Corp.

SIGUR, WANDA ANNE ALEXANDER
Engineer. **Personal:** Born May 26, 1958, New Orleans, LA; daughter of Alvin Maurice and Louella Clara Boyd; married Michael Gerard, Feb 14, 1981; children: Michael Jr & Gregory. **Educ:** Rice Univ, Houston, TX, BS, mech & materials sci, engineering, 1979; Tulane Univ, MBA. **Career:** Gen Electric, Houston, TX, lab technician, 1977-79; Martin Marietta Manned Space Systems, New Orleans, LA, sect chief, 1979-; Lockheed Martin Corp, mgr, Design & Analysis, 1996, dir, Engineering & Technol Labs, 2000, vpres, External Tank Project, currently. **Orgs:** Treas, Am Inst for Aerospace & Astronaut, 1988-90; Soc for the Advancement Materials & Process Engineering, 1983-90. **Honors/Awds:** R&D Investigator Award, Martin Marietta Corp, 1986; Author Award, Martin Marietta Corp, 1987; Author Award, AIAA, 1988; Technology Disclosure Award, US Patent and Technology Disclosure Office, 1989; Principal Investigator of the Year, Martin Marietta Corp, 1989. **Home Addr:** 6828 Glengary Rd, New Orleans, LA 70126, **Home Phone:** (504)246-4825. **Business Addr:** Vice President, External Tank Project, Lockheed Martin Corporation, 1401 Del Norte St, Denver, CO 80221-6910.

SIKES, DR. MELVIN PATTERSON
Educator, psychologist. **Personal:** Born Dec 24, 1917, Charleston, MO; son of Kimmie and Dorthy E; married Zeta Lorraine Bledsoe. **Educ:** NC Col Durham, BA (cum laude), 1938; Univ Chicago, MA, 1948, PhD, 1950. **Career:** Educator (retired); Wilberforce Univ Ohio, dean, 1950-52; Bishop Col Marshall Tex, dean, admin, 1952-55; Va Hosp Houston TX, clinical psych, 1960-69; Univ Tex, Austin, prof educ psych, 1969, prof emer; Zeta Assoc Inc, dir, currently. **Orgs:** Am Psychol Asn, 1950-; Nat Educ Asn; Tex Psychol Asn; Int Psychol Asn; Nat Asn Advan Colored People; Kappa Alpha Psi; 32 Deg Mason, Shriner. **Honors/Awds:** Meritorious Service Award, Am Psychol Asn; Harper and Rowe The Admin of Injustice; res grant; Living with Racism (with Joe Feagin) Beacon Press. **Military Serv:** USAF, second lt, 1943-45; Amer Theatre Medal Sharpshooter. **Business Addr:** Director, Zeta Associates Inc., 8703 Point W Dr, Austin, TX 78759.

SILAS, DENNIS DEAN
President (organization). **Personal:** Born Jul 4, 1954, Beulah, MS; son of Flossie Bowie; married Brenda, Jun 24, 1978; children: Angela Denise. **Educ:** Delta State Univ, BS, 1976, masters, 1981. **Career:** Drew High Sch, sci teacher, 1976-92; Hunter Mid Sch, prin, 1992-94; Drew Sch Dist, technol coordr, asst supt, 1994, supt. **Orgs:** Friends Libr, 1988-2000; MAE, 1992-94; MECA, 1993-2000; chap pres, Phi Delta Kappa, 1994-2000; Miss Prof Educr, 1997-2000; pres bd dir, Miss Prof Educr, currently. **Honors/Awds:** Star Teacher, Miss Econ Coun, 1981, 1982, 1988 & 1992; SERVE, Prog Excellence, 1990; Administrator of the Year, Drew Sch Dist, 1995; Spotlight School, Miss Dept Educ, 1999; Exemplery Program Award, Nat Rural Educ Asn, 2000. **Home Addr:** 117 Morgan St, Cleveland, MS 38732.

SILAS, PAUL THERON
Basketball coach, basketball player. **Personal:** Born Jul 12, 1943, Prescott, AZ; married Carolyn; children: Paula & Stephen. **Educ:** Creighton Univ, Omaha, NE, attended. **Career:** Basketball Player, basketball Coach (retired); St Louis Hawks, forward, 1964-68, Atlanta Hawks, 1968-69, Phoenix Suns, 1969-72, Boston Celtics, 1972-76, Denver Nuggets, 1976-77, Seattle Supersonics, forward (retired), 1977-80; San Diego Clippers, head coach, 1980-83; NJ Nets, asst coach, 1985-86; New York Knicks, asst coach, 1989-92; Phoenix Suns, asst coach, 1995-97; Charlotte Hornets, asst coach, 1997-99, head coach, 1999-2003; Cleveland Cavaliers, head coach, 2003-05; ESPN, analyst. **Honors/Awds:** NBA All-Star Team, 1972 & 1975; NBA All-Defensive Team.

SILAS-BUTLER, JACQUELINE ANN
Lawyer. **Personal:** Born Aug 20, 1959, Middletown, OH; daughter of Frank and Elizabeth Peterson; married Lawrence Berry Jr, Jun 14, 1986. **Educ:** Ohio State Univ, BA, 1981; Univ Akron Sch Law, JD, 1984. **Career:** Parms, Purnell, Stubbs & Gilbert, law clerk, 1982-83; Jones Day Reavis & Poque, law clerk, 1983-84; Akron Metro Housing Auth, legal intern & Hearing officer, 1983-84; Summit Co Prosecutor's Off, asst prosecuting atty, 1984-87; Parms Purnell Gilbert & Stidham, assoc, 1985-86; Robinson Smith & Silas Law Firm, atty & partner, 1986-87; Akron Metropolitan Housing Authority, Akron, OH, chief legal coun, 1987-89; Pvt Pract, atty, 1989-91; Univ Akron Sch Law, assist admis dir, 1990, adj prof; Summit County Juvenile Ct, ct referee, 1991-; Summit County Domestic Rels Ct, magistrate; Proj GRAD Akron, exec dir, currently. **Orgs:** Vip, Black Law Students Asn, 1981-84; Akron Alumnae Chap, Dst Sorority, 1984-, pres, 1990-; Akron Barristers Club 1984-; vip, 1985-87, pres, 1987-90; bd mem, Akron Area YWC, 1987-90; Akron Br, Nat Asn Advan Colored Peopel; Young Lawyers Comn, 1986-87; Akron Bar Asn, 1986-91; Nat Bar Asn. 1986-91; Nat Asn Black Women Atty, 1986-90; OH State Bar Asn, 1986-90; Bus Network Connection, 1986-88; bd mem, secy, E Akron Ct House, 1986-88; bd mem, Western Res Girl Scout Coun, 1989-; Junior League of Akron, 1989-; bd mem, Akron Summit Community Action Agency, 1991-; Wesley Temple AME Zion Church; bd mem, Summit County Am Red Cross, 1992-; NCW, 1992-. **Honors/Awds:** Member of the Year, Black Law Students Asn, 1984; Senior Award, Black Law Students Asn, 1984; Delta Service Award, DST Inc, Akron Alumnae Chap, 1989; Community Service Award, DST Inc, 1988. **Home Addr:** 2081 Larchmont Rd, Akron, OH 44313, **Home Phone:** (216)867-4889. **Business Addr:** Executive Director, Project GRAD Akron, 65 Steiner Ave, Akron, OH 44301, **Business Phone:** (330)761-3113.

SILBERSTEIN, TRACEE JOY. See ROSS, TRACEE ELLIS.

SILER, BRENDA CLAIRE
Public relations executive. **Personal:** Born Oct 3, 1953, Washington, DC; daughter of Helen G and Floyd Howard. **Educ:** Spelman Col, BA, eng, 1975. **Career:** Natl Ctr Voluntary Action, resource specialist, 1978-79; United Way Metro Atlanta, comm assoc, 1979-82; Rafshoon Shivers Vargas & Tolpin, acct exec, 1982; Siler & Assocs, owner pres, 1982-83; Am Red Cross Metro Atlanta Chap, asst dir, pub rel, dir, chap commun, dir, external communs, 1983-89; AARP, communs rep, 1989-94; Coun Competitiveness, dir communs, 1994-99; Am Speech-Lang-Hearing Assn, dir Pub Rels, 1999; United Negro Col Fund, nat dir commun & mkt, 2006-. **Orgs:** Chairperson, 1980, publicity chair, 1983, prof standards chair, 1984, Atlanta Asn Black Journalists; pub comn, Minority Bus Awareness Week, 1982; Bronze Jubilee Task Force, WETV, 1982-83; chaplain, Nat Asn Media Women, Atlanta, 1983; adv coun, United Way's Vol Atlanta, 1983-; second vpres, Nat Asn Media Woman, 1984-85; team capt, High Mus Mem Comt, 1985; bd mem, 1985-86, vpres, 1987, Atlanta Women's Network; Nat Asn Mkt Developers; Int Asn Bus Communicators, Atlanta Chap, vpres, int bd dir-at-large, int chairwoman, 1998-99; Capital Press Club, 1995-; Speech-Language-Hearing Asn. **Honors/Awds:** Gold Award for Annual Report Writing, United Way, 1980; Outstanding Achievement in Public Relations, Nat Asn Media Women, 1980; Outstanding Young Women in America, 1981; President's Award, Nat Asn Media Woman, 1983-85; Chairman's Award, Atlanta Asn Black Journalists, 1984; hon mention for Annual Report Writing, Am Red Cross Commun Excellence, 1987; hon mention for Exhibits, Am Red Cross Commun Excellence, 1989; Outstanding Atlanta Hon, 1989; President's Award, Int Asn Bus Communicators, 1990; Award of Merit for Press Kits, Pub Rels Soc Am, Georgia Chap. **Special Achievements:** First African American woman to be named chairwoman of the International Association of Business Communicators; contributed a chapter titled, "Research and Evaluation on a Shoestring" for the PR News guidebook titled, "Lessons Learned in the PR Trenches," 2004. **Home Addr:** 1400 E W Hwy Suite 1020, Silver Spring, MD 20910. **Business Addr:** Director, United Negro College Fund, 8260 Willow Oaks Corp Dr, PO Box 10444, Fairfax, VA 22031-8044, **Business Phone:** (703)205-3454.

SILER, DR. JOYCE B
Educator. **Personal:** Born Aug 1, 1945, Siler City, NC; daughter of Juanita Womble and Ross; married Lloyd G Flowers; children: Rashad Flowers. **Educ:** NC Central Univ, BS, 1967; Hunter Col, MS, 1976; Manhattan Col, MBA, 1983; Columbia Univ, Teachers Col, EdD, 1991. **Career:** Barnard Col, secy, 1967-68; NY City Housing Authority, housing asst, 1968-70; Model Cities Admin,

prin prog spec, 1970-74; Medgar Evers Col, asst prof, chair & dir, Bus Admin, assoc prof, currently. **Orgs:** Secy, John W Saunders Scholar Com Conv Church, 1985-94; corresp secy, Women's auxiliary bd, 1986; vpres prog, Delta Pi Epsilon Alpha Xi Chap 1988-91; historian, Col Bus Educr Asn BEA, 1989-90; ML Wilson Boys' Club Harlem; state adv, Phi Beta Lambda, 1989-; editorial bd, Collegiate Press, 1990-; bd trustees, Belle Zeller Scholar Trust Fund, Prof Staff Cong City Univ NY, 1992-; chairperson, NY State, Phi Beta Lambta, 1993. **Honors/Awds:** Fannie Lou Hamer Award, Women's Hist Month, Ctr Women's Devel, 1990. **Special Achievements:** Author of articles Computer Software Evaluation Model for Education, Advice for Business Women. **Home Addr:** 700 Columbus Ave 11G, New York, NY 10025. **Business Phone:** (718)270-5121.

SILVA, OMEGA C. LOGAN
Physician, president (organization). **Personal:** Born Dec 14, 1936, Washington, DC; daughter of Louis Jasper and Mary Ruth Dickerson; married Harold Bryant Webb, Nov 28, 1982; children: Frances Cecile Silva. **Educ:** Howard Univ, BS (Cum Laude), 1958, chem, MD (with honors), 1967. **Career:** Physician, President (Organization) (retired); NIH, chemist, 1963; Veterans Admin Med Ctr, intern med, 1967-68, resident 1968-70, res assoc, 1971-74, clin investr, 1974-77, asst chief endocrinol, Diabetic Clin, chief, 1977-96; Howard Univ, aasoc prof to prof oncology, 1977-97; George Washinton Univ, from asst prof to prof med, 1975-97, prof emer med, 1999. **Orgs:** Fel endocrinol, George Washington Univ, 1970-47; consult, FDA Immunol Panel, 1981-89; pres, Howard Univ Med Alumni, 1983-88; VA Adv Comn Women Veterans, 1983-88; gen res support review comt, NIH, 1984-89; pres, Am Med Womens Asn Br I, 1987-88; Am Med Women's Asn, vpres progs, 1997-99, pres elect, 1999-00, pres, 2000-02; bd trustees, Howard Univ, 1991-97; bd dirs, Health Care Coun; Nat Capital Area, 1995-. **Honors/Awds:** Letter of Commendation from the Pres of the United States 1984; Alpha Omega Alpha Hon Med Soc, Howard Univ, 1990; Distinguished Alumni Award, Howard Univ Col Med, 1997. **Special Achievements:** First women president, Howard Univ Medical Alumni, 1983-88; The first African American to be awarded a Clinical Investigatorship in the Department of Veterans Affairs; the lead author of the first description of the production of calcitonin from human small cell cancer of the lung. **Home Addr:** 354 N St SW, Washington, DC 20024. *

SILVER, DR. JOSEPH HOWARD
Educator, administrator. **Personal:** Born Oct 19, 1953, Goldsboro, NC; son of Joel Sr and Augusta King; married Rosalyn Smalls, Aug 14, 1976; children: Crystal & Joseph H Jr. **Educ:** St Augustine's Col, BA, 1975; Atlanta Univ, MA, 1977, PhD, 1980. **Career:** Kennesaw State Col, Marietta, GA, prof polit sci, 1977-83, dir minority affairs & prof, polit sci, 1983-85; Ga bd regents, Atlanta, GA, asst vice chancellor acad affairs, 1985-97; Savannah State Univ, vpres acad affairs, 1997-, prin investr, 2003-. **Orgs:** Pres, Kathryn R Woods Scholar Fund, 1987-; pres, St Augustine's Col Alumni Asn, 1988-; pres, bd dirs, Girls Inc Cobb County, 1990-92; pres, Nat Conf Black Polit Scientists, 1990-92; nat bd dir, Girls Inc; Am Red Cross Metro Chap, 1991-. **Honors/Awds:** Presidential Award for Distinguished Service at Kennesaw Col, 1983; Educator of the Year, Cobb County NAACP, 1984; Outstanding Educator, Kennesaw Jaycees, 1985; Leadership Cobb, 1986; Leadership Georgia, 1988; Selected to Leadership Atlanta, 1990; Excellence in Education Award, Savannah State Col Nat Alumni Assn, 1991; Man of the Year, St Anthony's Church; Alpha Phi Alpha, Carter G Woodson Freedom Award, 1993; Outstanding Educator, Kathryn Woods Found, 1993; Living the Dream, MLK Support Group, 1994; Girls Inc, Youth Advocacy Award, 1995. **Business Addr:** Vice President for Academic Affairs, Savannah State University, Office of Academic Affairs, Colston Admin Bldg Rm 204, PO Box 20411, Savannah, GA 31404.

SILVER-PARKER, ESTHER
Executive. **Educ:** NC Cent Univ, BA, polit sci; Columbia Univ, MA, jour; Penn State Univ, Exec Mgt Prog. **Career:** Essence mag, journalist; Review Polit Econ, journalist; New World Outlook, journalist; NY telephones, pub rels officer; AT&T, entry level pub rels position, vpres corp affairs, found pres; Wal-Mart Stores Inc, vpres, diversity rels, 2003-. **Orgs:** Int Womens Forum. **Honors/Awds:** Black Achiever in Industry Award, Harlem YMCA, 1998; honarary doctorate, Benedict Col; 2007 Humanitarian award, Just Communities. **Business Addr:** Vice President for Diversity Relations, Wal-Mart Stores Inc, 702 SW 8th St, Bentonville, AR 72716-8611, **Business Phone:** (479)277-2065.

SIMEUS, DUMAS M
Executive. **Personal:** Born Jan 1, 1940?, Haiti; son of Mecene and Bonne Simeus. **Educ:** Fla Agri & Mech Univ; Howard Univ, Wash DC, BS; Univ Chicago, MBA, 1972. **Career:** TLC Beatrice Int Holdings Inc, pres & ceo, 1982-94; Simeus Foods Int, chmn & founder, 1996-; Rockwell Int, financial analyst; KB Home, financial analyst; Bendix, Latin Am Opers, dir; Hartz Pet Food, gen mgr; Atari, exec staff. **Orgs:** Bd mem, Greater Dallas Chamber Com; TGI Friday's; bd mem; Nat Org Advan Haitians; Dallas Forth Worth Minority Bus Develop Coun; pres, Simeus Found. **Honors/Awds:** Entrepreneur of the Year, Ernest & Young, 1999; Distinguished Alumni Award, Univ Chicago Grad Sch Bus, 2003; Horatio Alger Award. **Business Addr:** Chairman, Founder, Simeus Foods International Inc, 812 S 5th Ave, Mansfield, TX 76063, **Business Phone:** 888-772-3663.

SIMIEN, TRACY ANTHONY
Football player, football coach. **Personal:** Born May 21, 1967, Sweeny, TX. **Educ:** Tex Christian Univ. **Career:** Football player (retired), coach; Pittsburgh Steelers, 1989; New Orleans Saints, 1990; Kansas City Chiefs, 1991-97; San Diego Chargers, 1999; Cologne Centurions, coaching staff, 2007. **Orgs:** Established the Simien for Seniors Found.

SIMMELKJAER, DR. ROBERT T
Lawyer, school administrator. **Personal:** Born in New York, NY; son of Lenora and Carl; married Gloria J Foster; children: Robert Jr & Mark Allen. **Educ:** City Col NY, BS, polit sci, 1962, MA, polit sci, 1964; Columbia Univ, Teachers Col, EdD, educ admin, 1972, Bus Sch, MBA, bus admin, 1977, Pub Admin, PhD; Fordham Univ Sch Law, JD, 1978. **Career:** Inst Educ Develop, exec asst to pres, 1969-71; NY City Bd Educ, prin, 1971-74; City Col NY, prof ed admin, 1974-79, dean gen studies & vice provost acad admin, 1979-86; atty & arbitrator; Gov Adv Cms Black Affairs, exec dir, 1986-88; NY Transit Authority, admin law judge, 1988-90; Joint Cms Integrity Pub Schs, dep chief coun, 1989-90; Inst Mediation & Conflict Resolution, pres, 1991-. **Orgs:** PERC, OCB, 1977-; minority sch fin network, Urban League & Nat Asn Advan Colored People, 1980-83; bd dir, Inst Mediation & Conflict Resolution, 1980-84; NY Task Force Equity & Excellence; Urban Coalition Local Sch Develop, 1980-83; bd dirs, Inst Mediation & Conflict Resolution, 1980-92; vice chmn, Personnel Appeals Bd, US Acct Off, 1981-84; speaker, consult US Info Agency, 1981-84; consult, NY Univ Sch Bus, 1982-83; bd dirs, Nat Acad Arbitrators, 1988-; consult, Ford Found, Nat Sch Finance Proj; Bar Asn City NY; DC Bar Asn. **Honors/Awds:** NY State Regents Scholarship, 1957; US OE Ed fellowship, 1969-70; Great Cities res fel, 1971. **Special Achievements:** Chapter in a Quest for Ed Opportunity in a Major Urban School District, The Case of Washington DC, 1975; Finality of Arbitration Awards, The Arbitration Forum, Fall, 1989; State Aid to Substantially Black School Districts, in Crisis and Opportunity Report NY; Federal Civil Service Law and Procedure, Wash, DC, 1990: two chapters on collective bargaining and arbitration; author: From Partnership to Renewal, Evolution of an Urban Ed Reform, The Ed Forum, 1979; State Aid to Substantially Black School Districts, Crisis and Opportunity; Collective Bargaining Impasses in Federal Civil Service Law and Procedures, BNA, 1990. **Business Addr:** President, Inst Mediation & Conflict Resolution Inc, 384 E 149th St Suite 330, Bronx, NY 10455, **Business Phone:** (718)585-1190.

SIMMONS, ANNIE MARIE
Educator, dean (education). **Personal:** Born Jul 25, 1949, Henderson, TX; daughter of Lonnie Marie Henderson and Roscoe Jr; children: Shirley N Lawdins. **Educ:** North Tex State Univ, BA, psychol, 1970, MEd, 1972, attended 1974; TXSouthern Univ, attended 1975 & 1979. **Career:** NTSU Couns Ctr, counr, 1970-72; Favor's Pre-Sch, asst dir, 1970-72; GearyElem Sch, para prof, 1972-74; Galveston Col, asst dean. **Orgs:** Psi Chi, 1968-; Tex Jr Col Teacher's asn, 1974-; League Women Voters,1976-; Electa Chapter Order Eastern Star, 1979-; pres, Black LadiesDistinction, 1980-81; pres, Alpha Kappa Alpha Sor, 1983-85; pres, GISD BdTrustees, 1989-91, 1995-97; Phi Delta Kappa, 1990-; facilitator &co-founder, Save Our C/Galveston, 1990-; Gulf Coast Apollo Links Inc;Galveston Col Found, bd dir. **Honors/Awds:** Outstanding Grammateus-Beta Phi Omega Chap of Alpha Kappa Alpha, 1978;Outstanding Achieve Galveston Comt, 1979; cert of appreciation, Epsilon MuChap Alpha Kappa Alpha Outstanding Alumni, 1972-82; Galveston Fire DeptTraining Acad most popular vis instr, 1979-81; pres, BLOD, 1980-81;Distinguished Service Award Galveston Jaycees, 1981; Sigma Gamma RhoOutstanding Black Galvestonian, 1982; Certificate of appreciation, NoonOptimist Club Galveston, 1982; NTSU/TWU Black Alumni Assn Quality Life,1982; Outstanding Citizen of the Year, Gamma Phi Lambda Chap Alpha PhiAlpha Frat, 1982; elected to Galveston Independent Sch Dist Bd Trustees,1982-85; NAACP Galveston Br Juneteenth Image Award, 1983; OutstandingWomen of America, 1983; appointed to Gov's Commn for Women, 1983-85; GovTX Markite; Exceptional Service Award, Galveston Col, 1995; CommencementSpeaker, Galveston Col, 1994; Brazosport Col, 1995. **Home Addr:** 3525 Ave O, Galveston, TX 77550. **Business Addr:** Board Director, Galveston College, Galveston College Found, 4015 Ave Q, Galveston, TX 77550, **Business Phone:** (409)763-6551.

SIMMONS, ANTHONY LAMONT
Football player. **Personal:** Born Jun 20, 1976, Spartanburg, SC. **Educ:** Clemson Univ. **Career:** Football player (retired); Seattle Seahawks, linebacker, 1998-2004. **Honors/Awds:** Rookie-of-the-Year; ACC 50-Year Anniversary team.

SIMMONS, BELVA TERESHIA
Journalist. **Personal:** Born Jul 2, 1927, Jacksonville, FL. **Educ:** Spelman Col, attended 1947; Lincoln Univ, attended 1952. **Career:** St Louis Argus, feature ed; US Sen Const Rights, prof staff, 1955-69; Am Nat Red Cross, pub rels writer, 1970-73; KMOX-TV, community rels coordr, 1973-78; Anne Beers Elem Sch Jour, dir/instr, 1981-83; ANC 7B Newsletter, ed/writer, 1981-; DC Community Schs, Sound Off, ed. **Orgs:** Nat Asn Advan Colored People; League Women Voters. **Honors/Awds:** Alumni Achievement Award, Lincoln Univ Sch Jour, 1975; Distinguished Service, Human Develop Corp, 1978; Community Service Award, ANC & Southeast Neighbors Inc, 1981; pres, Hillcrest Community Civic Asn. **Home Addr:** 901 NJ Ave NW, Washington, DC 20001.

SIMMONS, BOB
Football coach. **Personal:** Born Jun 13, 1948, Livingston, AL; son of Fred and Annabelle; married Linda Davidson; children: Brandon, Nathan & Lelanna. **Educ:** Bowling Green Univ, BS, phys educ, 1971, MS, stud personnel, 1972. **Career:** Bowling Green Univ, receivers coach, 1974-77; Univ Toledo, outside linebackers coach, 1977-79; WVa Univ, linebackers coach, asst coach, 1977-88; Colo Univ, asst coach, 1988-94; Okla State Univ, football coach, 1995-2000; Big XII Conf, vol consult, 2001; Notre Dame, 2002-04; Univ Wash, 2005-07. **Honors/Awds:** Big XII Conference Coach of the Year; Salt & Light Award, 1998; Distinguished Citizen Award, Boy Scouts Am, 1998.

SIMMONS, BRIAN
Football player. **Personal:** Born Jun 21, 1975, New Bern, NC. **Educ:** Univ NC, BS, sociol. **Career:** Cincinnati Bengals, linebacker, 1998-06; New Orleans Saints, 2007-08; freeagent, currently. **Orgs:** Univ NC 15player Leadership Comm; hon chmn, Greater Cincinnati Northern Ky Walk Am, 2002. **Honors/Awds:** AFC Defensive Player of the Week, 2005; Walter Camp Foundn. first All Am honors .

SIMMONS, DR. CHARLES WILLIAM
School administrator. **Personal:** Born Jun 17, 1938, Baltimore, MD; son of Floyd Mays and Vivian Jordan; married Brenda Leola Hughes; children: Dominic, Natalie Bohannan, Wanda Williams, Anthony, Kojo, Rashida & Tacuma. **Educ:** Antioch Univ, Baltimore MD, AB, 1972; Union Grad Sch, Cincinnati OH, PhD, admin of higher educ, 1978; Harvard Univ, Cambridge, MA, 1984. **Career:** Int Brotherhood of Teamsters, Baltimore, MD, field rep, 1964-67; Baltimore City Health Dept, Baltimore, MD, dir of health, educ & community orgn, 1967-74; Antioch Univ, Baltimore, MD, Homestead Montebello Ctr, co-dir, 1972-80; Sojourner-Douglass Col, Baltimore, MD, pres & founder, 1980-. **Orgs:** NAACP, African-Am Empowerment Project; bd dir, secy & bd mem, Nat Asn Equal Opportunity Higher Educ; co-founder & bd mem, Left Bank Jazz Soc; Coun Advan Experiential Learning; Asn Community Based Educ; Greater Baltimore Comt. **Honors/Awds:** President Award, Black Women's Polit Leadership Caucus, 1988; Leadership Award, Historically Black Cols & Univ, 1988; Pace Setter Award, African-Am Heritage Inc, 1989; City of Baltimore Presidential Citation, Pres Baltimore City Coun, 1997; Public Service Award, The Peace With Justice Comn, 1999. **Military Serv:** USMC, sgt, 1955-60. **Business Addr:** President, Sojourner-Douglass College, 500 N Caroline St, Baltimore, MD 21205, **Business Phone:** (410)276-0306.

SIMMONS, CLAYTON LLOYD
Law enforcement officer, circuit court judge. **Personal:** Born Sep 11, 1918, New York, NY; son of William Arthur (deceased) and Florence Albertha Forde (deceased); married Angela L Petioni; children: Janet, Sandra, Angela & Rene. **Educ:** Columbia Univ, BS 1954, MS, 1969. **Career:** New York City Dept Probation, probation officer, supervising probation officer, proj coordr, equal employment opputunity officer, 1960-82; freelance pianist & keyboardist, 1983-; Upjohn Health Care Serv, contract social worker, 1984-85; ABC Home Health Florida Inc, social work consult, 1987-89; Best Western Hotel, pianist 1988-92; Eighteenth Judicial Circuit, circuit court judge, currently. **Orgs:** NNat Coun Crime & Delinquency, 1962-83; chmn, bd dirs, Youth Activities Community Inc, 1972-82; Rockland County, NY, Bd Commissioners Sewer Dist No 1, 1974-78; bd dirs, Columbia Univ Sch Social Work 1977-80; Rockland County, NY, Bd Governors Health Facilities, 1977-79; jr warden, St Paul's Episcopal Church, 1977-82; vice chmn, Spring Valley, New York Dem Community, 1978-80; bd trustees, Village Spring Valley, NY, 1979-82; pres, Martin Luther King Jr Multi-Purpose Ctr Inc, 1980-82; Vestry St Stephen's Episcopal Church, Silver Spring Shores FL 1984-88, 1995-; Comn Church Soc Cent Fla Episcopal Diocese 1984-88; pres, St Stephen's Episcopal Church Men's Club, Ocala, Fla, 1987, 1988 & 1991; second vice comdr Post 284 Am Legion, Belleview, Fla, 1988. **Honors/Awds:** Plaque, Club Personality Magnificent Job, Pres Spring Valley Nat Asn Advan Colored People, 1973-79; Cert Merit, Roberto Clemente Social & Cult Club Inc, 1974; Plaque, Carlton & Surrey Apts serv tenants, 1977; Guardsman Award, Nat Guard Bur, 1977; Distinguished Serv Award, Rockland County, 1977, 1979 & 1982; Plaque for Outstanding Leadership & Intensified Struggle Minorities, First Baptist Church, 1978; Certificate of Apppreciation, Off Dist Atty Rockland County, 1980; New York State Senate Achievement Award, 1981; Cert Merit, New York State Assembly, 1981; Plaques, Outstanding Serv Village Spring Valley, NY, 1982; Plaque, Outstanding & Dedicated Serv Nat Asn Advan Colored People & Community, Nat Asn Advan Colored People, 1982; Plaque, Haitian-Am Cult & Social Orgn Serv Community, 1982;

Certificate of Apppreciation, 26th Cong Dist, 1982; Cert Merit, Spring Valley, NY, Youth Coun Nat Asn Advan Colored People, 1982; Martin Luther King Jr, Multi-Purpose Ctr Inc, 1982; Award Clock, Black Dem Comt Men, 1982; Plaque, Black Polit Caucus Rockland County, NY, 1984; Cert Participation, Am Legion Post 284 Bellview, Fla, 1986; Cert Appreciaton, Off Gov State Fla, 1986. **Military Serv:** AUS, staff sgt, 1942-45. **Business Addr:** Circuit Court Judge, Eighteenth Judicial Circuit, Seminole County Courthouse, 301 N Pk Ave, Sanford, FL 32771, **Business Phone:** (407)665-4048.

SIMMONS, CLYDE
Football player. **Personal:** Born Aug 4, 1964, Lanes, SC; married Sandra; children: Jaison, Corey & Janaya. **Educ:** Western Carolina, BA, indust distrib, 1996. **Career:** Football player (retired); Philadelphia Eagles, defensive end, 1986-93; Ariz Cardinals, 1994-95; Jacksonville Jaguars, 1996-97; Cincinnati Bengals, 1998; Chicago Bears, 1999-2000. **Orgs:** Omega Psi Phi Fraternity Inc. **Honors/Awds:** Pro Bowl selection, 1991, 1992; First-Team All-Pro selection, 1991, 1992.

SIMMONS, CRAIG, SR.
Executive. **Personal:** Born Sep 2, 1962, Riverside, NJ; son of William and Joan; married Dail St Claire, Jul 5, 1986; children: Rachel & Craig. **Educ:** Amherst Col, BA, 1984; Doshisha Univ, exchange stud. **Career:** First Boston Corp, analyst, corp finance, 1984-85; Sumitomo Bank NY, asst treas, pub finance, 1985-87; Lehman Bros, asst vpres, int sales, 1987-90; Kankaku Securities Am Inc, vpres, fixed income, 1990-96; Cantor Fitzgerald Co, vpres; Ashland Capital Holdings, vice chmn, currently. **Orgs:** Campership steering comt, Boy Scouts Am, 1987-; vpres bd dirs, One Hundred Black Men Inc, 1989-; bd vestry, St Bartholomew's Church, 1994-; adv bd, St Bartholomew's Community Preschool, 1994-; adv bd, Nat Asn Advan Colored People, 1994-95; vpres bd dir, Fifth Ave Tower Condominium, 1994-97. **Honors/Awds:** Outstanding Bus & Prof Award, Dollars & Sense Mag, 1993. **Business Addr:** Vice Chairman, Ashland Capital Holdings L.L.C, 380 Lexington Ave 11th Fl, New York, NY 10168, **Business Phone:** (212)587-7666.

SIMMONS, EARL
Rap musician, actor. **Personal:** Born Dec 18, 1970, Baltimore, MD; married Tashera; children: Tacoma & Xavier. **Career:** Columbia Rec, rapper; Sony BMG, currently; Bloodline Rec, founder; Def Jam Rec; Albums: "It's Dark and Hell is Hot", 1998; "Flesh of My Flesh, Blood of my Blood", 1998;". And Then There Was X", 1999; "The Great Depression", 2001; "Grand Champ", 2003; "Year of the Dog.Again", 2006; "Walk With Me Now", "You 'll Fly with Me Later", 2009; Films: Belly, 1998; Romeo Must Die, 2000; Exit Wounds, 2001;Cradle 2 The Grave, 2003; Never Die Alone, 2004; DMX: Soul of a Man, 2006; Lords of the Street, 2008; Last Hour, 2008; Death Toll, 2008; The Bleeding, 2009. songs; "Born Loser", 1993; " Time To Build", 1995; "Usual suspects", 1997; "Money, Power & Respect", 1998; "We Got This", 1998; "Dog & A Fox", 1999; "Scenario 2000", 1999; "Tales from the Darkside", "Get it Right", 2000; "Scream Double R", 2001; "Walk with Me", 2001; "Most High", 2002; "Deeper", "What's Really Good?"; 2003; "Lets Get Crazy", "Put Your Money", 2004; "Get Wild", 2005; "Innocent Man", 2006; "Gonna Get Mine", 2007; "Bad Boys", 2008; "Intro", 2008; "Who's Real", 2009. **Honors/Awds:** American Music Award, Favorite Rap/Hip-Hop Artist, 2000. *

SIMMONS, DR. ELLAMAE
Physician. **Personal:** Born Mar 26, 1919, Mt Vernon, OH; daughter of G L Simmons and Ella Cooper Simmons; divorced; children: Delabian, Diana, Daphne & Debra. **Educ:** Hampton Inst, RN, 1940, MA, 1950; Meharry Med Col, grad student, 1955; Howard Univ, MD, 1959; Ohio State Univ, BS, l948; Ohio State Univ, MA, l958. **Career:** Physician (retired); Practiced nursing at various hosps, 1940-42, 1950-51; Bellevue Hosp, med social worker, 1951-53; Wayne Co Hosp, intern; Univ Co Med Ctr, resident, 1962-63; Nat Jewish Hosp, resident chest med & allergy 1963-65; Kaiser Found Hosp, allergist. **Orgs:** AMA; Admissions Com Univ CA Sch Med, 1974-79; CA & San Francisco Med Soc; John Hale Med Soc; Am Acad Allergy; Am Med Womens Asn, CA; Mutual Real Estate Investment Trust; No CA Med Dental Pharmaceut Asn; Univ CA, San Francisco Sch Med Admissions Com, 1974-79; NAACP, Urban League. **Honors/Awds:** Certifcate of Recognition, CA State Senate & CA Legislature Assembly, 1990; Women of Distinction, Soroptomist Int, 1995; Award for Didication & Commitment to Service, Martin Luther King Family Health Ctr, 1994. **Military Serv:** AUS, Nurse Corps, 1st Lt, 1942-46.

SIMMONS, ESMERALDA
Lawyer, school administrator, executive. **Personal:** Born Dec 16, 1950, Brooklyn, NY; daughter of Frank V and Esmeralda Benjamin; children: Marques Akinsheye, Ewansiha Elias. **Educ:** Hunter Col, CUNY, BA, 1974; Brooklyn Law Sch, JD, 1978. **Career:** NY Col Law Dept, hons atty, civil rights employ unit, 1978-79; US Dist Ct US Dist Judge Henry Bramwell, law clerk, 1979-80; US Dept Educ Office Civil Rights, reg civil rights atty, 1980-82; NY Dept Law Atty Gen's Office, asst atty gen, 1982-83; NY State Div Human Rights, first dep comnr, 1983-85; Medgar Evers Col, Ctr Law & Social Justice, exec dir, currently. **Orgs:** Nat Conf Black Lawyers, 1975-; Nat Bar Asn, 1979-; pres, Bedford Stuyvesant Lawyers Asn, 1981-84; legal comt chair, Coalition Community Empowerment, 1983-91; bd dirs, Metro Black Bar Asn, 1984-91; vice chair, NY City Districting Comn, 1990-92; bd mem, Fund City NY, 1990-00; NYC Bd Ed, 1993-94; Appl Res Ctr, 1997. **Honors/Awds:** Partner in Educ Award, NY City Bd Educ, 1981; Appreciation Award Central Brooklyn Mobilization, 1982; Lawyer of the Year, Bedford Stuyvesant Lawyers Asn Inc, 1984; Imani Award, Weusi Shule Parents Coun, 1984; Professional of the Year, Nat Asn Negro Bus & Prof Womens Clubs Inc, 1986; Harriet Tubman Award, Fannie Lou Hamer Collective, 1987; Woman on the Move, Concerned Women of Brooklyn, 1988; Leadership Award, Asian Americans for Equality, 1990; Leadership in Civil Rights Award, UN Fund, Brooklyn Chap, 1990; Women for Racial and Economic Equality, Fannie Lou Hamer Award, 1991; council member Annette M Robenson, Spirited Leadership Award, 1992; Ellen Luriel Award, 1992; Magnolia Award, Magnolia Tree Earth Ctr, 1992. **Business Phone:** (718)270-6297.*

SIMMONS, FRANK
Automotive executive. **Career:** Hill Top Chrysler Plymouth, pres, currently. **Orgs:** Chrysler Minority Dealer Asn; bd mem, Volunteers Am. **Business Addr:** President, Hilltop Chrysler & Plymouth Inc, 940 N Beckley St, Lancaster, TX 75146, **Business Phone:** (972)230-2300.

SIMMONS, FREDDIE SHELTON WAYNE
Social worker. **Personal:** Born Jun 14, 1966, Allendale, SC; son of Ella Mae Simmons. **Educ:** Univ SC, Columbia, SC, BS, psychol, 1988, Grad Sch Columbia, SC, attended 1997. **Career:** Univ SC, Col Pharm, res asst, 1986-87; SCA Prog, asst line, Off Lt Gov Nick Theodore, data entry specialist, 1987-88; SCA Dept Social Serv, social servs specialist II, 1988-93, self sufficiency case mgr, 1996-; Carolina Boys Home, prog dir, 1999-2000; Verizon Wireless Corp, corp employee trainer, 2001-. **Orgs:** Bd Social Work, licensed baccaulaureate, social work, 1989; bd mem, SCA State Employees Asn, Allendale Chap, 1989-93; adult choir, pres, Macedonia Christian Methodist Episcopal Church, Sunday Sch, 1996-, supt, 1998-, trustee, 1998-. **Honors/Awds:** Meritorious Biology Society, Omni Biol Soc, 1982; Honor Student, Psi Chi Honor Society, Univ SC, Columbia, 1986; Outstanding College Students of America, Outstanding College Student Award, 1987; Outstanding Young Americans, Outstanding Young American Award, 1998. **Home Addr:** 2020 Memorial Dr, Cayce, SC 29033, **Home Phone:** (803)796-8347. **Business Addr:** Corporate Employee Trainer, Verizon Wireless Corporation, 398 Barnvell, Columbia, SC 29204, **Business Phone:** (803)400-4000.

SIMMONS, GERALDINE CROSSLEY
Lawyer. **Personal:** Born Feb 17, 1939, Chicago, IL; daughter of Ivey Moore and Hosea H Crossley Sr; divorced; children: Stacey Elizabeth. **Educ:** Roosevelt Univ, BA; John Marshall Law Sch, JD, 1981. **Career:** Scott Foresman & Co, dir copyrights/ permission contracts, 1965-80; Ill Appellate Ct, judicial law clerk, 1981; US Ct Appeals 7th Circuit, staff atty, 1981-83; Wash, Kennon, assoc, 1983-84; pvt pract, 1984-; Roosevelt Univ Paralegal Prog, instr, 1985-86. **Orgs:** Cook County Bar asn; Am Bar asn; Women's Bar asn; Black Women Lawyers asn; Ill State Bar asn; Nat Bar asn; Chicago Bar asn; Sojourner's Political Action Committee; Alpha Gamma Phi; State Literacy Advisory Bd; past pres, John Marshall Law Sch Alumni asn; Pkwy Community House. **Honors/Awds:** Nathan Burkan Copyright Competition, John Marshall Law Sch, 1979; Law Review, John Marshall Law Sch, 1981; Distinguished Serv Award, Cook County Bar Assn, 1985, 1995, 1996, 1997; Businesswoman of the Year, Pkwy Community Ctr, 1986; Distinguished Service Award, John Marshall Law Sch, 1990; Nat Bar Assn Award, 1996. **Home Phone:** (773)994-2600.

SIMMONS, HENRY OSWALD, JR.
Actor. **Personal:** Born Jul 1, 1970, Stamford, CT; son of Henry and Aurelia; married Lauren Sanchez (divorced 2003). **Educ:** Franklin Pierce Col, BA, bus, 1992. **Career:** Films: Above the Rim, 1994; On the Q.T., 1999; Snow Days, 1999; A Gentlemen's Game, 2001; Taxi, 2004; Are We There Yet?, 2005; Something New, 2006; Madea's Family Reunion, 2006; The Insurgents, 2006; South of Pico, 2007; World's Greatest Dad, 2009; TV series: "Saturday Night Live", 1994; "The Cosby Mysteries",1994; "New York Undercover", 1994-95; "One Life to Live", 1997; "Another World", 1997-99; "NYPD Blue", 2000-05; Spartacus, 2004; Lackawanna Blues, 2005; "Pepper Dennis", 2006; "Shark", 2006-08; "The Cleaner", 2009; Georgia O Keeffe, 2009. **Honors/Awds:** Grand Jury Prize, Am Black Film Festival, 2007. **Business Addr:** Actor, c/o Gersh Agency Inc, 232 N Canon Dr, Beverly Hills, CA 90210, **Business Phone:** (310)274-6611.*

SIMMONS, DR. HOWARD L
School administrator, educator. **Personal:** Born Apr 21, 1938, Mobile, AL; son of Eugene and Daisy. **Educ:** Spring Hill Col, BS, sec educ & span, 1960; Ind Univ, MAT, slavic lang & lit, 1965; Fla State Univ, PhD, design & mgt postsecondary educ, 1975. **Career:** St Louis Community Col, fac; Northampton Community Col, fac; Lafayette Col, fac; Lake Shore High Sch, FL, span & eng instr, 1960-61; Cent High Sch, AL, russ & span instr, 1961-63; Ind Univ, NDEA fel, 1963-64; Forest Park Community Col, MO, chmn foreign lang dept, 1964-69; Northampton County Area Community Col, PA, dean instrnl serv, 1969-74; Fla State Univ, EPDA fel, 1973-75; Comm Higher Educ, Middle States Asn, assoc dir, 1974-88, exec dir, 1988-95; Ariz State Univ, Div Educ Leadership & Policy Studies, prof & assoc dean, 1995-99, prof emer, 2000-; Morgan State Univ, Dept Advan Studies, prof & chmn, currently. **Orgs:** Bd mem, St Louis Teachers Credit Union, 1965-69; consult, 1969-; staff assoc, Am Asn Community & Jr Col, 1972-73; Phi Delta Kappa, 1972-; fel Am Coun Exercise; fel Asn Am Indian Physicians; fel Am Coun Educ, 1972-73; bd dirs, Am Asn Higher Educ, 1974-75; Kappa Delta Phi, 1974-; sr researcher & visiting scholar, Nat Ctr Postsecondary Governance & Finance Res Ctr Ariz State Univ, 1986-87; consult, Asn Dominican Univ Chancellors, Santo Domingo, 1987-; exec bd, Am Asn Higher Educ Black Caucus, 1989-92; Ariz State Bd Behavl Health Examiners, 1996-99; Coun Chiropractic Educ Comm Accreditation, 1999-; Accreditation Comm Acupuncture & Oriental Med, 2002-; adv coun, Am Psychol Asn, BEA, 2003-; Asn Study Higher Educ, 2000-; pub mem & chairperson, Accreditation Comn Acupuncture & Oriental Med, 2003-; secy, Nat League Nursing Accreditation Comn, 2005-. **Honors/Awds:** Grad Made Good Distinguished Alumnus, Fla State Univ, 1988; First Annual Diversity Award, Am Asn Higher Educ Caucuses, 1992; LHD, Sogourner-Douglas Col, MD, 1995; HHD, King's Col, PA, 1998; ETS-HBCU Research Scholar, 2003-. **Special Achievements:** Keynote speaker on future of higher education in Puerto Rico, Angel Ramos Foundation, 1987, published study "Involvement and Empowerment of Minorities and Women in the Accreditation Process," 1986, various articles in professional journals. **Business Addr:** Professor, Chairman, Morgan State University, Department of Advanced Studies, Rm 325 Jenkins Behavioral Sci Bldg 1700 E Cold Spring Lane, Baltimore, MD 21251, **Business Phone:** (443)885-1969.

SIMMONS, ISAAC TYRONE
Manager. **Personal:** Born Aug 9, 1946, Birmingham, AL; married Jamesena Hall. **Educ:** Knoxville Col, BS, math, 1968; Univ Tenn, MS, math educ, 1970. **Career:** Robertsville Jr HS, teacher, 1970-71; Atlanta Area Tech Sch, teacher, 1978-83; Ben Hill UMC Santuary Choir, vpres, 1983; Sylvan Learning Ctr, tutor, 1999; Grievance Review Comt, adj instr, 1999-; City Atlanta, syst & programming mgr; Ga Military Col, asst prof, dept coordr, currently. **Orgs:** Data Processing Mgr Asn, 1979-85; pres, City Atlanta Toastmasters, 1980-85; Am Mgt Asn, 1983-85. **Business Addr:** Assistant Professor, Department Coordinator, Georgia Milaitary College, Department Business & Information Technology, 6280 Bryant St, Union City, GA 30291, **Business Phone:** (770)306-6401.

SIMMONS, JAMES, JR.
Chief executive officer, president (organization). **Personal:** Born in Houston, TX. **Educ:** Kellogg Grad Sch Mgt; Tuck Sch Bus, Dartmouth, minority bus exec prog. **Career:** Total Premier Serv Inc, chmn & ceo, 1982-. **Orgs:** Prairie View A & M Univ; Tex Southern Univ; bd mem, Am Petrol Inst. **Honors/Awds:** Ranked as No 1 largest minority-owned bus, Houston Chronicle newspaper. **Business Addr:** Chairman, Chief Executive Officer, Total Premier Services Inc, 2211 Norfolk Suite 1100, Houston, TX 77098, **Business Phone:** (713)610-1100.*

SIMMONS, JAMES RICHARD
Administrator. **Personal:** Born Mar 1, 1939, Chicago, IL; son of Phyllis Isbell Jones and Oscar Lee; married Judith Marion Albritton; children: James Jr & David. **Educ:** Grinnell Col, BA, 1961; Univ Chicago, Sch Social Serv Admin, MA, 1964; Brandeis Univ, Heller Sch Advanced Soc Policy, MM, 1984. **Career:** Ill Youth Comn, caseworker & team moderator, 1964-66; Ill Children's Home & Aid Soc, caseworker & psychotherapist, 1966-69; Volunteers Am, state & exec dir & dir children's serv, 1969-71; Chicago United Inc, vpres & admin, 1984-. **Orgs:** Nat Asn Social Workers, 1964-72; Acad Cert Social Workers, 1966-72; delegate ill, White House Conf C, 1970; Nat Asn Black Social Workers, 1973-75; vpres, Grinnell Col Alumni Bd, 1973; bd mem, Planning Consortium C, 1973-75; bd mem, Ill Child Care Asn, IL, 1975-76; Nat Socail Welfare Sec Vol Am, 1980; Nat Asn Black MBA's, 1986; pres, Hellen Sch Alumni, Brandeis Univ, 1986-. **Honors/Awds:** Minority Advocate-IL, US Small Bus Admin, 1989. **Home Phone:** (773)262-5984. **Business Addr:** Vice President, Chicago United Inc, 300 E Randolph St E Pedway Dr, PO Box 11, Chicago, IL 60601-5083, **Business Phone:** (312)977-3060.

SIMMONS, PROF. JOHN EMMETT
Educator. **Personal:** Born Feb 6, 1936, St Petersburg, FL. **Educ:** Morehouse Col, BS, 1957; Syracuse Univ, MS, 1961; CO State Univ, PhD, 1971. **Career:** Educator (retired); Western Col Women, asst prof biol, 1965-68; Res FndWash Hosp Ctr, res assoc, 1968-70; CO State Univ, asst prof physiol,1971-72; Trinity Col, assoc prof biol, 1972-82, prof biol, 1982-97, prof emer biol, 1997-. **Orgs:** Soc Neuroscience; Endocrine Soc. **Honors/Awds:** Fulbright Scholar, Gezira Univ, Wad Medani, Sudan, Africa, 1982-83. **Home Addr:** 31 Woodland St Apt 5-P, Hartford, CT 06105, **Home Phone:** (860)522-6810. **Business Addr:** Professor

Emeritus of Biology, Trinity College, 300 Summit St, Hatford, CT 06106, **Business Phone:** (860)297-2000.

SIMMONS, JOSEPH JACOB, III
Judge, government official. **Personal:** Born Mar 26, 1925, Muskogee, OK; son of Jacob Jr and Eva Flowers; married Bernice Elizabeth Miller, Jan 30, 1947; children: Joseph Jacob IV, Bernice Garza, Mary Agnes Simmons, Jacolyn Simmons-Reade & Eva Frances Simmons-O. **Educ:** Univ Detroit, attended 1942-44; St Louis Univ, BS, 1949. **Career:** Amerada Hess Corp, vpres govt rels, 1970-82; Dept Interior, under secy, 1983-84; Interstate Com Comn, comnr, 1984-85, vchmn, 1985-86, comnr, 1987-95; Surface Transp Bd, vchair, 1995-97; Simmons Co, pres, 1997-. **Orgs:** Youth dir, Nat Asn Advan Colored People, 1950-55; Prof Am Asn Petrol Geologists, 1958-; comnr, Statue Liberty Ellis Island Comn, 1983-; Nat Acad Sci Bd Mineral & Energy, 1984-91; Dept Interior Outer Continental Shelf Adv Bd, 1984-. **Honors/Awds:** Public Service Award, Am Asn Petrol Geologists, 1984; The JJ Simmons III Boardroom, Surface Transp Bd, 2000; Spec Act Service Award; Outstanding Performance Award; Distingusihed Service Award, Dept Interior. **Military Serv:** AUS, sgt, 2 yrs. **Home Addr:** 2736 Unicorn Lane NW, Washington, DC 20015.

SIMMONS, JOYCE HOBSON (JOYCE ANN HOBSON-SIMMONS)
Accountant. **Personal:** Born Aug 1, 1947, Port Jefferson, NY; daughter of Nathan Edward Sr and Ada Rebecca Townes; married Leroy Jr, Feb 21, 1978; children: Leroy III (stepson) & Victor. **Educ:** Essex Cty Comm Col, attended 1971; Indian River Comm Col, AA, 1973; Am Inst Banking, Basic Cert, 1973; Fla Atlantic Univ, BBA, 1975. **Career:** Port NY Authority, personnel dept, police recruitment, world trade ctr, bldg construct dept, toll collector, 1969-71; First Nat Bank & Trust Co, auditor com loan dept, supv proof dept, 1971-75; Homrich Miel & Mehlich, staff acct, 1976-77; Westinghouse Comn Develop Group, staff supvr, 1977; JA Hobson Acct & Tax Serv, sole proprietor, 1978-95; Fla Dept Educ, dirbus & citizens partnerships, dir, 1995-97, Div Admin, dir, 1997. **Orgs:** Stuart/Martin City Chamber Com, 1980-82, 1992-95; pres, Am Bus Women's Asn, 1981-82; Martin Co Sch Bd, 1982-86, 1990-95; chmn, Martin City Sch Bd, 1982-86, 1993-94; dir, Girl Scouts Am Palm Glade Coun, 1982-86; FAU Alumni Asn, 1982-88, IRCC Adv Coun Acct & Fin, 1984-86, Martin Cty 4-HFound, 1984-86; bd trustees, IRCC, 1987; dir, C Serv Coun, 1988; dir, United Way Martin Co, 1990-95; Grad Leadership Martin Co, 1991-92; treas, 1992-93, pres-elect, 1993-94, pres, 1994-95, Fla Sch Bd Asn; Martin Mem Found Hosp Comm Coun, Am Acct Asn; pres, 1993-94, South Fla Consortium SchBd; Martin County Econ Coun, Republican Club, Exec Comt Coun 100; Fla Comn Community Serv Found; Fla Educ Found, 1997. **Honors/Awds:** Women of the Year, Am Bus Women's Asn, 1982; Outstanding Service, LegisSubcomt Fla Sch Bd's Asn, 1986; Community Service Award, Phi Delta Kappa, 1993; Leroy Collins Award, Fla Asn Community Col, 1991; Martin County Women Distinction, Palm Glades Girl Scout Coun Inc, 1993; Commissioner's Award for Exemplary Teamwork, 1996; Black Achiever Award, Tallahassee Br, Nat Asn Advan Colored People, 1996; Dept Educ Qual Improv Team Award, 1999. **Home Addr:** 2322 Tina Dr, Tallahassee, FL 32301, **Home Phone:** (904)216-1702. **Business Addr:** Director, Florida Department of Education, 325 W Gaines St Suite 1532, Tallahassee, FL 32399, **Business Phone:** (850)245-0445.

SIMMONS, JUANITA
Business owner. **Personal:** Born Oct 4, 1950, Columbus County, NC; daughter of Raymond and Ethel; children: Karen Y Simmons. **Educ:** York Col, attended 1993. **Career:** Mind Body Soul Connection, pub tv producer, 1995; Goldman Sachs, client rep, 2000; Salmon Smith Barney, staff; Body Connections Health Club, chief exec officer, 2000-. **Orgs:** Founder & vpres, Women Maintenance Club, 1999; dir, Neighborhood Housing Serv New York. **Business Addr:** Owner, Body Connections Health Club, 18820 linden blvd, Saint Albans, NY 11412, **Business Phone:** (718)723-4060.

SIMMONS, KELVIN
Executive, government official. **Career:** Kansas City Coun mem; Mo Dept Econ Develop, dir; Mo Pub Serv Comn, chmn; Swope Community Builders, pres & chief operating officer, 2005-06; A M Develop LLC, chief exec officer, 2006-. **Business Addr:** Chief Executive Officer, A M Development LLC, 2928 S Brentwood Blvd, St Louis, MO 63119, **Business Phone:** (314)963-1212.*

SIMMONS, KENNETH H
Architect, planner, educator. **Personal:** Born Jun 28, 1933, Muskogee, OK; divorced; children: Margot Eva, Kenneth II, Annette & Jalia. **Educ:** Harvard Col, AB, 1954; Univ Calif, Berkley, BArch, 1964. **Career:** Housing & Community Develop Prog, coordr; San Francisco Econ Opportunity Coun, 1964; Bay Group Architects & Planners, princ, 1965; Arch Renewal Com, coordr, 1966; Hunts Point Neighborhood Proj Urban Am Inc, exec dir, 1967; Univ Calif-Berkeley, Dept Archit, assoc prof, 1968-; Com Design Collaborative Architects & Planners, prin, 1989; Miller, Simmons & Grant Design Group, Architects & Urban Planners, partner, 1991-; Univ Calif-Berkeley, prof emer archit, currently. **Orgs:** Am Planning Asn; Am Inst Certified Planners; Int Cong Archit & Townplanning; Architects Designers and Planners for Social Responsibility; Bay Area Black Architects; Nat Orgn Minority Architects; African Studies Asn; Asn Concerned Affairs Scholars; TransAfrica; Wash Office Africa; Bay Area Anti-Apartheid Network; Greenpeace; Nat Asn Arab Am; San Francisco African Hist & Cult soc; World Affairs Coun N Calif; Joint Ctr Polit & Econ Studies; Harvard Club, San Francisco. **Business Addr:** Professor Emeritus of Architecture, University of California, Berkeley, Department of Architecture, 232 Wurster Hall, Berkeley, CA 94720-1800, **Business Phone:** (510)642-4942.

SIMMONS, KIMORA LEE
Fashion Designer. **Personal:** Born May 3, 1975, St. Louis, MO; daughter of Joanne (Perkins) Kyoko Syng and Vernon Whitlock, Jr.; married Russell Simmons, 1998 (divorced 2008); children: Ming Lee, Aoki Lee; children: Kenzo Lee Hounsou. **Educ:** Attended Univ of California, Los Angeles. **Career:** Model, 1989-; Baby Phat CEO and Head of Design, 1999-; Feb 2007 launched Simmons' Barbie doll; launched couture line, KLS, Fall 2007-;launched four perfumes, Goddess, Golden Goddess, Seductive Goddess, and Baby Phat Fabulosity; Diamond Diva jewelry line 2004-. **Orgs:** Established the Kimora Lee Simmons Scholarship Fund at Lutheran High School North; active member of youth advocacy organizations Amfar, The G&P Foundation, Keep a Child Alive, and Hetrick-Martin Institute; on the Board of Directors at Rush Philanthropic. **Honors/Awds:** Tony Award, for Russell Simmons Def Poetry Jam (executive producer), 2003. **Special Achievements:** Book, Fabulosity: What It Is and How To Get It; presented by the mayor with the key to the city and March 18 2008 was named "Kimora Day" in St. Louis. **Business Addr:** Phat Fashions, LLc, 512 7th Avenue, 29th Floor, New York, NY 10018, **Business Phone:** (212)391-3100.*

SIMMONS, MAURICE CLYDE
Marketing executive. **Personal:** Born Feb 15, 1957, Washington, DC; son of Clyde T and Ada Blaylock; married Vicki Baker, Sep 1988; children: Marcus, Shaun. **Educ:** Dartmouth Col, AB, 1979; Univ Pa Wharton Sch, MBA, 1986. **Career:** Procter & Gamble, sales rep, 1979-81, dist field rep, 1981-82, unit mgr, 1982-84; McNeil Consumer Prod Co, from asst prod dir to prod dir, mgr, customer support; Johnson & Johnson CFT, mkt mgr, currently. **Orgs:** Nat Black MBA Asn, Philadelphia Chap, 1984-; reg coordr, Black Alumni Dartmouth, 1984, 1987; pres, Wharton Black MBA Asn, 1985; co-chmn prog develop, Nat Black MBA, 1987 Conf Comn. **Home Addr:** 5963 Woodbine Ave, Philadelphia, PA 19131-1206. *

SIMMONS, NORBERT
Executive. **Career:** First Commonwealth Securities Corp, pres & ceo, currently; Ballys Casino Lakeshore Resort, owner, currently. **Special Achievements:** Black Enterprise's Top 100 Industrial & Service Companies, ranked 24, 1999. **Business Addr:** Owner, Bally Casino Lakeshore Resort, 1 Stars & Strips Blvd, New Orleans, LA 70126, **Business Phone:** (504)248-3200.

SIMMONS, PAUL A.
Judge. **Personal:** Born Aug 31, 1921, Monongahela, PA; son of Perry C and Lilly D; married Gwendolyn; children: Paul Jr, Gwendolyn, Anne. **Educ:** Univ Pittsburgh, 1946; Harvard Law Sch, 1949. **Career:** Judge (retired); Pa RR, employee, 1941-46; SC Col Law, prof law, 1949-52; NC Col Law, prof law, 1952-56; gen pract, 1956-58; Clyde G Tempest, 1958-70; Hormell Tempest Simmons Bigi & Melenyzer, law partner, 1970-73; Common Pleas, Wash County, PA, judge, 1973-78; US Dist Ct, W Dist Pa, judge, 1978-90. **Orgs:** Am Bar Asn; Am Trial Lawyers Asn; Am Judicature Soc; Pa Bar Asn; Wash County Bar Asn; NC State Bar; Nat Asn Advan Colored People; Ind Benevolent Protective Order Elks World; Pa Human Rel Comn; Commonwealth Pa Minor Judiciary Educ Bd; Bethel AME Church; Alpha Phi Alpha; bd dir, Mon Valley United Health Serv; past grand atty, State Pa Most Worshipful Prince Hall Grand Lodge F&AM, PA. **Honors/Awds:** Two Human Rights Awards, Nat Asn Advan Colored People; Meritorious Community Service Award, Most Worshipful Prince Hall Grand Lodge; Lifetime Achievement Award, Pa Bar Asn, Minority Bar Comt, 1992; Hall of Fame, Nat Bar Asn, 1994. **Special Achievements:** First African-American in Pennsylvania to sit regularly as a Common Pleas Orphans Court judge; first African-American to become a U.S. District Judge for the Western District of Pennsylvania (1978; he was President Carter's first African-American judicial nominee). In 1965, was the first African-American to run statewide for a judicial office in Pennsylvania, and in 1975 was appointed judge of the Court of Common Pleas of Washington County (nominated by both parties in 1975 and elected to a full term). *

SIMMONS, RON
Wrestler, football player. **Personal:** Born May 15, 1958, Warner Robins, GA. **Educ:** Fla State Univ. **Career:** Football Player (retired), Wrestler; Cleveland Browns, NFL, 1981; Tampa Bay Bandits, USFL, 1984; Memphis Showboats, 1985; Professional wrestler: Extreme Championship Wrestling, 1994-95; World Wrestling Entertainment, 1996-. **Honors/Awds:** College Football Hall of Fame, 2008. **Special Achievements:** First African American to win the WCW World Heavy weight Championship, & was thus the first officially recognized African American world heavy weight champion. **Business Addr:** Professional Wrestler, World Wrestling Entertainment, 1241 E Main St, Stamford, CT 06902, **Business Phone:** (203)352-8600.

SIMMONS, RUSSELL
Executive, music producer. **Personal:** Born Oct 4, 1957, Queens, NY; son of Daniel Simmons; married Kimora Lee, Dec 20, 1998; children: Ming Lee & Aoki Lee. **Educ:** City Col NY, Harlem Br, sociol. **Career:** Rush Producers Mgt, owner; Rush Model Mgt, partner; Krush Groove, film co-producer; Tougher Than Leather, film co-producer; Rush Artist Mgt, owner, Phat Fashion, developer, Russell Simmons' Def; Def Jam Rec, co-founder, owner, 1985-; Comedy Jam, producer HBO, 1992-; Nutty Prof, coproducer, 1996; Waist Deep, 2006, exec producer; Hip-Hop Summit Action Network, founder; Russell Simmons Music Group, owner, 2005-; Rush Commun, chmn & chief exec officer, currently. **Business Addr:** Chairman, Chief Executive oficer, Rush Communications Inc, 512 7th Ave Suite 43-45, New York, NY 10018-4603, **Business Phone:** (212)840-9399.

SIMMONS, DR. S DALLAS
School administrator, management consultant. **Personal:** Born Jan 28, 1940, Ahoskie, NC; son of Yvonne Martin; married Mary A, Feb 10, 1963; children: S Dallas jr & Kristie Lynn. **Educ:** NC Cent Univ, BS, 1962, MS, 1967; Duke Univ, PhD, 1977. **Career:** NC Cent Univ, dir data processing, 1962-64; Norfolk State Univ, dir data processing, 1964-66; NC Cent Univ, asst prof bus admin, 1967-71, asst chancellor, 1971-77, vice chancellor univ rels, 1977-81; St Paul's Col, pres, 1981-85, VA Union Univ, pres, 1985; Dominions Bd Dirs, mem; Dallas Simmons & Assocs, pres & ceo, currently. **Orgs:** Durham C of C, 1971-81; liaison officer, Moton Col Serv Bureau, 1972-; competency testing comn, NC State Bd Educ, 1977-81; exec comn, Cent Intercollegiate Athletic Assoc, 1981-, coun pres, 1981-, bd dir, 1981-, fin comn, 1984-85; Brunswick C of C, 1981-85; bd dir, VA Polytech Inst & State Univ, 1982-83; bd trust, NC Cent Univ, 1983-85; conf comm, Nat Assoc Equal Opportunity Higher Educ, 1983, chmn leadership awards comm, 1984-85, bd dir, 1985; exec comm, NC Cent Univ, mem bd trust, 1983-85; mem bd dir, Pace Am Bank, 1984-; US Zululand Educ Found, 1985; exec bd, John B McLendon Found Inc, 1985; exec com mem bd dir, UNCF; Am Mgt Asn; Kappa Alpha Psi; Data Processing Mgt Assoc; Doric Lodge No 28 Free & Accepted Masons; Kappa Alpha Psi, Tobaccoland Kiwanians; Sigma Pi Phi Frat Alpha Beta Boule; Optimist Club; Am Assoc Sch Admin; Am Assoc Univ Admin; The Downtown Club. **Honors/Awds:** Kappa of the Month, Kappa Alpha Psi Fraternity, 1981; Citizen of the Year, Omega Psi Phi Fraternity, 1983-84; Black Am Achievers, 1983-84; Business Associate of the Year, B&G Charter Chap, ABWA, 1984. **Home Phone:** (804)353-6949. **Business Addr:** President, Chief Executive Officer, Dallas Simmons & Associates, 314 Burnwick Rd, Richmond, VA 23227.

SIMMONS, SHIRLEY DAVIS
Government official. **Personal:** Born Sep 3, 1941, Vaughn, MS; married Princeston G; children: Brenda S Gooden, Vernadette S Gipson, Princeston Jr, Katrina & Makeba. **Educ:** Tougaloo Col, cert AA; Jackson State Univ, cert; Mary Holmes Col, cert. **Career:** Nat Coun Negro Women, first vpres, 1978; Nat Asn Advan Colored People, chmn redress, 1980-82; Women Progress, publicity chmn, 1982; Madison-Yazoo-Leake Health Clinic, chmn personnel, 1984; Madison County Sch, sect, currently. **Orgs:** Coordr, Summer Feeding Prog, 1979; coordr, Energy Assistance, 1984;Project Unity, 1985; Madison County Sch Bd, 1984-. **Honors/Awds:** Outstanding Contribution to Youth Award, Project Unity, 1983. **Home Addr:** Rte 3, PO Box 327, Canton, MS 39046. **Business Addr:** School Board Member, Madison County School, 3903 Hwy 16 E, Canton, MS 39046, **Business Phone:** (601)859-2991.*

SIMMONS, STEPHEN LLOYD
Restaurateur. **Personal:** Born Aug 4, 1958, Boston, MA; son of Herbert and Sylvia; married Elizabeth Simmons, May 14, 1994; children: Alexander Charles. **Educ:** City Col San Francisco, hotel restaurant mgt, 1984. **Career:** Stanford Ct Hotel, roundsman, 1980-83; Campton Place Hotel, chef de cuisine, 1983-86; Casa Madrona Hotel, exec chef, 1986-88; SS Monterey Cruise Ship, exec chef, 1988-89; One Mkt Restaurant & Lark Creck Inn, chef, partner, 1989-94; Bubba's Diner, owner, chef, currently. **Orgs:** Bd mem, Full Circle Progs, 1993-96; bd mem, City Col Adv Bd, 1992-. **Honors/Awds:** 100 Black Men, Top Black Chefs, 1993; James Beard House, Rising Star Chef, Am Cuisine, 1989; Cornell Univ, Cross Country Dining Prog, 1989. Celebrated Chef World Pork Expo, Nat Pork Producers Coun, 1999. **Special Achievements:** Published Recipes include : Detroit Free Press, 1984-95, San Jose Mercury News, San Francisco Chronicle, Marin Independent Jour; presently working on cookbook; Nat Pork Producers Coun announced Stephen Simmons, chef and owner as a Celebrated Chef at the 1999 World Pork Expo in June. **Business Addr:** Owner, Bubba's Diner, 566 San Anselmo Ave, San Anselmo, CA 94960, **Business Phone:** (415)459-6862.

SIMMONS, DR. SYLVIA Q. (SYLVIA JEANNE QUARLES SIMMONS)
Educator. **Personal:** Born May 8, 1935, Boston, MA; daughter of Lorenzo C Quarles and Margaret M Thomas Quarles; married

Herbert G Simmons Jr, Oct 26, 1957; children: Stephen, Lisa & Alison. **Educ:** Manhattanville Col, BA, 1957; Boston Col, MED, 1962, PhD, 1990. **Career:** ABCD Headstart Prog, soc serv suprv, 1965; Charles River Park Nursery Sch, Montessori, teacher, 1965-66; Boston Col, reg sch mgt, 1966-70; Harvard Univ, assoc dean admis & financial aid, fac arts & sci, 1974-76; Radcliffe Col, assoc dean admis, financial aid & womens educ, dir financial aid, 1972-76; Univ Mass Cent Off, assoc vpres acad affairs, 1976-81; Mass Higher Educ Asst Corp, sr vpres, 1982-; Am Stud Assistance Corp, exec vpres, 1992-95, pres, 1995-96, chief exec officer; Boston Univ, lectr educ, assoc trustee; Mount Ida Col, trustee, currently; Am Stud Assistance Serv Corp, pres; Boston Univ, lectr educ, currently; Exec Serv Corps New Eng, consult, currently, The Educ Resources Inst Inc, vice chair, currently. **Orgs:** Exec Coun Nat Assoc Stud Fin Aid Admin; vpres, Eastern Assoc Fin Aid Admin; Mass Asn Col Minority Admin; consult, Dept HEW Off Educ Reg I; consult, Col Scholar Serv, Mass Bd Higher Educ; Rockefeller Selection Comn Harvard Univ; Delta Sigma Theta Nat; bd mem, Family Serv Assoc Boston, Wayland Fair Housing, Concerts Black & White, pres, Newton Chap Jack & Jill Inc, Boston Chapter Links Inc, Boston Manhattanville Club; bd trustees, Manhattanville Col; bd trustees, Rivers Co Day Sch; bd mem, Cambridge Mental Health Asn; bd trustees, Simons Rock Col; N Shore CC, chmn bd trustees; pres, William Price Unit Am Cancer Soc; bd dir, MA Div1-90, Am Cancer Soc; bd trustees, Boston Col; mem bd, Mass Found Humanities, 1990-91; bd trustees, Merrimack Col; bd overseers, Mt Ida Col; bd dirs, Grimes-King Found; bd trustees, Regis Col; bd mem, Anna StearnsFound; bd dir, Exec Serv Corps. **Honors/Awds:** Women Politics; Outstanding Young Leader Boston Jr Chamber Commerce, 1971; Boston College Bicentennial Award, 1976; Black Achiever Award, 1976; President's Award, Mass Educ Opportunity Prog, 1988; Human Rights Award, Mass Teachers Asn, 1988; Recognition of Contributions to Higher Education, Col Club, 1988; Educator of the Year, Boston Chap Asn Negro Bus & Prof Women's Club, 1989; Sojournore Daughters, 25 AFA Women Who Have Made A Difference, 1990; Honorary Degree, St Joseph's Col, 1994; Bishop James Healey Award, 1997; Honorary Degree, Merrimack Col. **Home Addr:** 19 Clifford St, Roxbury, MA 02119, **Home Phone:** (617)445-5014. **Business Addr:** Trustee, Mount Ida College, 777 Dedham St, Newton, MA 02459, **Business Phone:** (617)928-4500.

SIMMONS, THELMA M

Manager. **Personal:** Born Aug 10, 1942, Bastrop, LA; daughter of Charlie Cross and Leona Averitt Cross; married Arthur (divorced 1985); children: R Stevonne, Eric & Brenda. **Educ:** Western WA State Col, Bellingham, human resources, 1979. **Career:** Pacific Northwest Bell, Seattle, supvr, mgr, 1965-76, staff mgr, 1976-79, mgr, operator serv, 1979-82, exec asst, 1982-84; AT&T, Seattle, carrier selection mgr, 1984-85; AT&T, Oakland, CA, regional diversity mgr, 1985-88; AT&T, San Francisco, CA, regional compensation mgr, 1988-. **Orgs:** Lifetime mem, Nat Asn Advan Colored People, 1965-; Delta Sigma Theta, 1979-; Seattle Women's Comm, 1981-83; chairperson, human resource comm, Oakland Pvt Indust Coun, 1987-. **Honors/Awds:** Future Black Leaders of the 80's, Black Elected Officials, Wash State, 1980; Certificate of Appreciation, Mayor of Oakland, 1990. **Business Addr:** Regional Compensation Manager, Human Resources, AT&T Western Region, 795 Folsom St Rm 400, San Francisco, CA 94107, **Business Phone:** (415)442-2255.

SIMMONS, TONY DEANGELO

Football player. **Personal:** Born Dec 8, 1974, Chicago, IL. **Educ:** Univ Wis-Madison, BS, construct admin. **Career:** New England Patriots, wide receiver, 1998-2000; Barcelona Dragons, 2001; Indianapolis Colts, 2001; Cleveland Browns, 2001; Houston Texans, 2002; New York Giants, 2002; British Columbia Lions, 2005-07. **Honors/Awds:** Rookie of the year, 1998; Direct TV NFL Play of the Week Award, 2000.

SIMMONS, WILLIE

Banker, chief executive officer, manager. **Personal:** Born May 23, 1939, Meridian, MS; son of Gussie (deceased) and Willie (deceased); married Vernocia Neblett; children: Michael Anthony & Kevin Lawrence. **Educ:** Military Police Officer, advan course, 1970; Univ Tampa, BS (sr honors), 1975. **Career:** AUS, police officer, 1958-78; Ingalls Memorial Hosp, dir security, 1978-80; First Chicago Security Serv Inc, chmn & chief exec officer, 1985-; First Nat Bank Chicago, mgr protection & security, 1980-85, dir corp security, 1985-. **Orgs:** Pres, IL Security Chiefs Asn, 1982; speaker Project We Care, 1982-; chmn, Deacon Bd Truevine MB Church, 1982-; Am Soc Industl Security, 1984-; chmn, Bd Christian Educ Truevine MB Church, 1985-; vice chmn, Crime Stoppers Plus, 1986-; Int Org Black Security Execs; chair, BAI Security Comm, 1992. **Honors/Awds:** Outstanding Service Award Hospital Security, 1980; Outstanding Service Award, IL Security Chiefs Asn, 1980, 1981; Award of Excellence, 1986, First Chicago Corp; Appreciation Award, 1988, Nat Asn Asian-Am Profs, 1986; Mayor Richard J Daley Police Medal Honor, 1994. **Military Serv:** AUS, major 20 yrs; Bronze Star, Meritorious Svcs, Vietnam Serv 1958-

78. **Business Addr:** Director/First Vice President, Chicago NBD Corp, One First Natl Plz, Chicago, IL 60670, **Business Phone:** (312)732-3343.

SIMMONS-EDELSTEIN, DEE

Executive. **Personal:** Born Jul 1, 1937, New York, NY; daughter of Gertrude Dobson and Tonsley Dobson; divorced. **Educ:** City Col New York, attended. **Career:** Fashion commentator; Grace Del Marco, prof com model, vpres & exec dir; WNJR-AM, NJ, Dee Simmons Radio Show, host; Nat Shoes, New York City, statist bookkeeper; mag cover girl; New York Images & Voices, host, currently; Dee Luxe Talent Productions, owner; Dee Simmons TV Show, producer & host, currently; talent agent, 2001-; Ophelia DeVore Assocs Inc, vpres, currently. **Orgs:** Am Fedn TV & Radio Asn; Nat Asn Women Media; 100 Coalition Black Women; Affairs Comt Freedom Fund Dr; NAACP; Nat Dr Cerebral Palsy Telethon. **Honors/Awds:** Pharmaco Products Award for first model of color to do TV commercial, 1962; Ms Empire State, 1962; Model of the Year, 1963; Ms Beaux Arts for Schaefer Brewery, 1962-63; Special Achievevment Award, 1973; hon award, United Negro Col Fund; Community Service Award, Antinarcotic Rehab Pgm; New York Evvy Fashion Award, 1994; Ophelia DeYore & Florence M Rice Positive Image Award, 1994; Host of New York Images & Voices; Models of the South Convention Award, 1994. **Special Achievements:** Producer and host of an educational video on modeling in the new millennium. **Business Addr:** Vice President, Executive Director, Ophelia DeVore Associates , Inc., Empire State Bldg, 350 5th Ave Suite 3108, New York, NY 10118, **Business Phone:** (212)629-6400.

SIMMS, ALBERT L

Clergy. **Personal:** Born Jan 21, 1931, Claremont, WV; son of Robert T Simms; divorced; children: Div. **Educ:** Appalachian Bible Inst, grad; Southern Baptist Sem Ext Sch, attended, 1973; Hilltop Baptist Ext Sem, grad, 1976; N Gate Bible Col, BA. **Career:** First Baptist Church, Harlem Heights, pastor; Newcastle Southern Baptist Church, pastor, currently. **Orgs:** Int Governor Club, 2000-; past treas, New River Valley Missionary Baptist Asn; asst dir, Hill Baptist Ext Sem; historian, New River Valley Baptist Asn; Hist Comn WV Baptist State Conv; chair, Dist Asn New River Educ Com; adv bd, Hill Top Baptist Ext Sem; WV Baptist Minister Conf; past vpres, Fayette County Community Action; Crippled Children Div Asn, Huntington; youth counr, active in Bible Integrated camps & 4H camps. **Honors/Awds:** Award of Merit, Profiles Christian, 1972; Int Man of the Yr, Intl Biographical, 2000, 2001; Int Diploma of Honor. **Special Achievements:** Selected one of Outstanding People of 20th Century, Int Biographical, 1999; inducted Int Directory of Distinguished Leadership Hall of Fame, 2000. **Home Addr:** 216 Broadway Ave, Oak Hill, WV 25901. **Business Addr:** Pastor, Newcastle Southern Baptist Church, 19 Stampede St, Newcastle, WY 82701, **Business Phone:** (307)746-4231.

SIMMS, BILL. See SIMMS, WILLIAM E.

SIMMS, CARROLL HARRIS

Artist, educator. **Personal:** Born Apr 29, 1924, Bald Knob, AR; son of Tommie Wesley Sims and Rosa Hazel Harris (deceased). **Educ:** Cranbrook Art Acad, BFA, 1950, MFA, 1960. **Career:** Educator (retired); Toledo State Ment Hosp, 1948-49; Detroit Art Inst Art Sch, 1950; Tex Southern Univ, prof art, 1950-87. **Orgs:** Assoc life mem, Inst African Studies, Univ Ibadan, Nigeria; Tex Southern Univ Group Study Abroad Proj Nat Univ Haiti Port-au-Prince Henriquez Padre Urena Nat Univ Santo Domingo Dominican Repub, West Indies, 1981 East,West, Contemporary Am Art July, 1984; sec, 1987-91, Houston Municipal Art Comm Houston TX; Dallas Mus Fine Arts 1952, 1953; Am Soc African Cult; life mem, Inst Int Educ; life mem, Slade Soc Univ Col London, England; Tex Asn Col Teachers; adv panel, Tex Comm Arts & Humanities 1972-79; Nat Humanities Fac, 1975-77; volunteer, Tex Southern Univ Select Comt/Recruitment Stud. **Honors/Awds:** First Award Toledo Mus Fine Arts, 1949-50; Purchase Award, Cranbrook Mus Art, 1953; Fulbright fel, 1954-56; scholarship, Swedish Inst Stockholm Survey Contem Ceramic Pottery, 1964; Tex Southern Univ Award; cert Recog Exemplory Representing Afro-Am Artistic & Cult Expression Second World Black & African Festival Arts, 1977; contrib author "Black Art in Houston, The TX Southern Univ Experience" Tex A&M Univ Press 1978; cited "Black Artists/South 1800-1978" Huntsville Mus Art Al, 1979; Carroll Sims Day, Mayor City Houston, 1977; exhibition "African-Amer Artists" 1978; Griot Award Southern Conf Afro-Am Studies Inc, Houston 1984; "He's Got the Whole World In His Hands" bronze sculpture permanent collection new Calif Afro-Amer Mus LA CA; Alpha Kappa Omega Chap Alpha Kappa Alpha Sor Inc Ed, Outstanding Achievement in Visual Arts; Sculpture bronze permanent collection Tex Southern Univ title "A Tradition of Music", 1986; Tex Southern Univ dedicated a sculpture plaza to Carroll Harris Simms, 1996. **Special Achievements:** Forerunners and Newcomers: Houston's Leading AFA Artists, 1989-; Our Commonwealth: Our Collections, Works from Traditionally Black Colleges and Universities. Cited in numerous books, articles, illustrations and periodicals; numerous exhibitions and sculpture commissions.

SIMMS, JAMES EDWARD

Secretary (Government), clergy. **Personal:** Born Dec 14, 1943, Richmond, VA; married Emmajane Miller; children: Rachael,

Eboni, James. **Educ:** VA Union Univ, BA, 1967; Pittsburgh Theol Sem, MDiv, 1972, Dr ministry, 1974. **Career:** Pittsburgh Human Rels Comn, exec dir, 1972; Allegheny County Comn Col, stud serv coord, 1973; Chatham Col, instr, 1974; Comn Release Agency, exec dir, 1974; Comn Action Pittsburgh Inc, neighborhood admin, 1977; City Pittsburgh, Off Mayor, asst exec secy. **Orgs:** Chmn, United Negro Col Fund Telethon, 1983; pastor, St Paul Baptist Church; pres, Am Baptist Theol Sem; chmn, Munic Campaign United Way; Nat Forum Black Pub Admin; pres, Homer S Brown Alumni Asn Va Union Univ; pres, bd dirs, Hill House Community Serv Inc; bd dirs, Hill House Asn; bd dirs, Vol Action Ctr; bd dirs, Action Housing; Bd Garfield Jubilee Housing Inc; pres, Allegheny County Coun. **Honors/Awds:** Varsity Lett Inter-Col, Football VA Union Univ, 1965-67; Distinguished Serv Award, Conf Minority Pub Admin, 1978; Polit Awareness Award, Young Republican Coun, 1979; Civil Rights Award, Hand in Hand Inc, 1980. *

SIMMS, DR. MARGARET CONSTANCE

Economist. **Personal:** Born Jul 30, 1946, St Louis, MO; daughter of Frederick T and Margaret E. **Educ:** Carleton Col, Northfield, MN, BA, 1967; Stanford Univ, MA, 1969; Stanford Univ, PhD, 1974. **Career:** Univ of CA, Santa Cruz, acting asst prof 1971-72; Atlanta Univ, asst prof Sch of Business 1972-76; Atlanta Univ, Econ Dept, assoc prof & dept chair 1976-81; The Urban Inst, sr rsch assoc 1979-81, dir minorities & social policy prog 1981-86; The Joint Center for Political Studies, dep dir of rsch, 1986, drr of research programs, 1991-97, vpres for research, 1997, sr vpres res, 2003-. **Orgs:** Editor, The Review of Black Political Econ, 1983-88; Nat Econ Asn, 1971-, pres, 1978-79; bd mem, Coun Econ Priorities, 1979-85; Inst For Women's Policy Res, bd mem, 1991-99, bd chair, 1993-98; Partners for Democratic changes, bd, 1999-; Fed Adv Panel Fin Elem & Secondary Educ, 1979-82. **Honors/Awds:** Selected Publs ed. Black Economic Progress: An Agenda for 1990s, with Julianne M Malveaux, Slipping Through the Cracks, The Status of Black Women 1986, with Kristin A Moore & Charles L Betsey, Choice & Circumstance, Racial Differences in Adolescent Sexuality & Fertility (New Brunswick, NJ, Transaction Books, 1985); Economic Perspechives on Affirmative Action, 1995; Young Black Men in Jeopardy, 1994. **Home Addr:** 212 G St NE, Washington, DC 20002. **Business Addr:** Senior Vice President, Joint Center for Political and Economic Studies, 1090 Vermont Ave NW, Washington, DC 20005, **Business Phone:** (202)789-3500.

SIMMS, ROBERT H

Consultant, executive. **Personal:** Born Oct 2, 1927, Snowhill, AL; son of Harry and Alberta; married Aubrey Watkins, Nov 27, 1953; children: Leah Aliece Simms-Graham & David Michael. **Educ:** Xavier Univ, BS 1949; Tuskegee Inst; NY Univ, Advanced Study; Univ Miami; Univ MA. **Career:** Macon Co Bd Educ, teacher, 1949-50, 1952-53; Dade Co Bd Educ, teacher, 1953-65; Small Bus & Develop Ctr, exec dir, 1965-66; Comm Rel Bd Metro Dade Co, exec dir, 1967-83; Bob Simms Assoc Inc, pres & chief exec officer. **Orgs:** Creator Inner City & Minority Experience Defense Depts Race Rels Inst, 1972; founder, Miami Varsity Club; Orange Bowl Com; Kappa Alpha Psi; Sigma Pi Phi; trustee, trustee emer currently, Univ Miami. **Military Serv:** AUS, sgt e5, 1950-52.

SIMMS, STUART OSWALD

Government official, lawyer, politician. **Personal:** Born Jul 17, 1950, Baltimore, MD; married Candace Otterbein; children: Marcus & Paul. **Educ:** Dartmouth Col, BA, 1972; Harvard Law Sch, JD, 1975. **Career:** Baltimore City, dep's state atty, state's atty; Baltimore state's attorney, 1987-95; US Attny's Off US Courthouse, atty; Md Dept Juvenile Servs, secy, 1995-97; Md Dept Pub Safety & Correctional Servs, secy, 1997-2003; Brown, Goldstein, Levy LLP, partner & atty, currently; mem, Dem Party, currently. **Orgs:** Pres, Black Alumni Asn, 1979-81; co-chair, Md Mentoring Partnership; NatAsn Advan Colored People; Baltimore Educ Scholar Trust; Baltimore Mus Art;Sinai Hosp; Baltimore Zool Soc; Am Bar Asn; Md State Bar Asn; Monumental City Bar Asn; bd mem, Gilman Sch; bd mem, Baltimore Symphony Orchestra; Baltimore City Bar Asn. **Honors/Awds:** Nelson A Rockefeller Distinguished Service Award, Rockefeller Ctr, Dartmouth, 1998; Daniel Webster Distinguished Service Award, Dartmouth Club Washington, DC, 2003. **Business Addr:** Partner, Attorney, Brown, Goldstein & Levy LLP, 120 E Baltimore St Suite 1700, Baltimore, MD 21202, **Business Phone:** (410)962-1030.

SIMMS, WILLIAM E. (BILL SIMMS)

Insurance executive, business owner. **Personal:** Born Aug 23, 1944, Indianapolis, IN; son of Frank T Sr (deceased) and Rosa Lee Smith (deceased); married Maxine A Newman, Jul 3, 1971; children: Terry Denise Reddix-Simms & Randall L. **Educ:** Univ Southern Calif, Los Angeles Calif, BS, bus admin, 1971, MBA, mkt, 1976. **Career:** Transamerica Occidental Life, Los Angeles, Calif, mgr, 1969-77, vpres reinsurance mkt 1980-84, vpres sales/ admin, 1984-86, vpres reinsurance, 1987, sr vpres reinsurance, 1988; Lincoln Nat Reinsurance Co, Fort Wayne, Ind, second vpres, 1977-80; Transamerica Life Co, reinsurance div, pres, currently; Carolina Panthers, owner, currently. **Orgs:** Pres & chief exec officer, 100 Black Men Am, 2001-; Calif Life Ins Co Asn; Los Angeles Jr Chamber Com; Nat Urban Leauge; bd trustees, Los Angeles Summer Games Found; Los Angeles Open Gulf Found;

adv bd, United Negro Col Fund. **Special Achievements:** Second African American member of the exclusive Augusta National Golf Club, 1995. **Military Serv:** USAF, staff sgt, 1963-67. **Business Phone:** (704)358-7000.

SIMON, AMY ELLIS
Salesperson, Businessperson. **Educ:** Univ of Michigan, BA, 1994. **Career:** Managing Dir and Head of the Multi-Product Sales Team at Merrill Lynch. **Orgs:** Co-founder of the Global Market's and Investment Banking's Women's Leadership Council; member of Employee Diversity Council; contact person for the Three Sisters Scholarship Foundation. **Special Achievements:** Named "Top 40 Under 40", Crain Magazine, 2004; named one of the"50 Most Powerful Women in Business", Black Enterprise Magazine. **Business Addr:** Merrill Lynch & Co., Inc., 4 World Financial Center, 250 Vesey Street, New York, NY 10080, **Business Phone:** (212)449-1000.*

SIMON, COREY JERMAINE
Football player. **Personal:** Born Mar 2, 1977, Pompano Beach, FL; married Natasha, Mar 3, 2001; children: Corey Jr. **Educ:** Univ Fla, info studies. **Career:** Football player(retired); Philadelphia Eagles, defensive tackle, 2000-04; Indianapolis Colts,defensive tackle, 2005-06; Tenn Titans; 2007. **Orgs:** Founder, Corey Simon Success Ctr. **Honors/Awds:** Howie Long Tough Guy Team, 2000; Pro Football Weekly AllNFL Rookie Team, 2000; Pro Football News All NFL Rookie Team, 2000; Football Digest Top 16Rookies, 2000; NFL Defensive Rookie of the Month, 2000; Football Digest All NFL, 2001; Pro Bowl, 2003. **Special Achievements:** Finalist, Lombardi Award, Outland Trophy.

SIMON, DR. ELAINE
Beautician. **Personal:** Born Nov 30, 1944, St Johns, Antigua-Barbuda; daughter of Rosalyn Richards Jarvis and Hubert Phillips; divorced; children: Denise, Francine & Sheldean. **Educ:** Bay Col Baltimore, Baltimore Md, AA, 1976; Univ Baltimore, attended 1978; Nat Beauty Culturist League, Wash, DC, Doctorate, 1987; Catinsville Community Col, Cert, 1982; Cent State Univ, Columbus, Ohio, Cert, 1985; Coppin State Col, Cert, 1985. **Career:** Bay Col Md, lounge mgr, 1985-76; Johnsons Product Co, lectr, technician, 1979-85; Touch Paris Coiffure, owner, mgr, 1978-. **Orgs:** Pub rels dir, Nat Beauticulturist League, Baltimore, Md, 1978-89; exec dir, Nat Black Women Consciousness Raising Asn, 1980-89; pub rels dir, Master Beautician Asn, 1982-89; educ dir, Md State Beauty-Culture Asn, 1982-89; pub rels dir, Theta Mu Sigma Nat Sorority, Zeta Chap, 1985; exec, pres & CEO, currently, Caribbean Am Carnival Asn Baltimore. **Honors/Awds:** Civil Rights Humanitarian Award, Md Spec Inaugural Comn, 1981; Governor's Citation, Gov Md, 1983; Resolution, City Coun Baltimore, 1989; Booker T Washington Citation Honor, Bus League Baltimore, 1989; Econ Stress Threaten Black Salon, shop talk mag, 1983; "Pocket News Paper," 1983; Business Award, Mayor Baltimore City, 1994; Nat Black Women Consciousness Raising Asn Inc; nat exec dir, Baltimore Response Asn; admin adv, Rosa Pryor Music Scholarship Fund. **Home Addr:** 20 N Kossuth St, Baltimore, MD 21229. **Business Addr:** President, Chief Executive Officer, Caribbean American Carnival Association of Baltimore, 1906 N Charles St, Baltimore, MD 21218, **Business Phone:** (410)230-2969.

SIMON, DR. KENNETH BERNARD
Surgeon. **Personal:** Born Sep 29, 1953, San Francisco, CA. **Educ:** Univ Ariz, Tucson, BS, 1976; Meharry Medical Col, MD, 1980; Am Bd Surg, Specialty Cert, 1986; Am Bd Surg, Recertification Gen Surg, 1995; Am Bd Surg, Cert Vascular Surg, 1995; Kennesaw State Univ, MBA, 1999. **Career:** DC Gen Hosp, staff surgeon/instr surg, 1985-86; Univ Alberta Hosps, resident cardiac surg, 1986-87; Univ Miss, Jackson, Miss, asst prof surg, 1987-90; Va Hosp, Jackson, Miss, staff surgeon, 1987-90; Cleveland Clin, Cleveland, Ohio, fel vascular surg, 1991-; Va Hosp, chief surg serv; Univ Miss Med Ctr, asst prof surg, 1992-; Health Care Financing Admin, med officer; pvt pract, currently. **Orgs:** NMA; Am Col Surgeons; Asn Acad Surgeons; Nat Med Asn; Asn Va Surgeons. **Honors/Awds:** Kim Meche Scholar, Univ Ariz, 1974-75. **Home Addr:** 1500 E Woodrow Wilson Dr, Jackson, MS 39206, **Home Phone:** (601)982-0128. **Business Addr:** Surgeon, 1500 E Woodrow Wilson Dr, Jackson, MS 39206, **Business Phone:** (601)982-0128.

SIMON, LONNIE A
Clergy. **Personal:** Born Mar 23, 1925, East Mulga, AL; son of William and Tempie Haywood; married Florence, May 14, 1949; children: Janet Write, Lonita Ross, Kenneth & Cynthia Layton. **Educ:** Youngstown Col, attended 1959; Central Bible Col, attended 1963; Am Baptist Theol Sem, attended 1975; Trinity Theol Sem, enrolled master theol prog, Newburgh, IN, 1983-. **Career:** Elizabeth Baptist Church, 1954-59; US Post Off, Youngstown, OH, letter carrier, 1955-65; Jerusalem Baptist Church, 1960-62; New Bethel Baptist Church, 1962-95; Eastern Ohio Baptist Asn, moderator, 1968-76; Youth Ext Unit Am Baptist Theol Sem, instr. **Orgs:** Missionary Guyana South Am, 1968, 1976; Youngstown Bd Educ, 1972-75; co-chmn, Inter-Racial Clergy Dialogue, 1982-97; comnr, Ohio Socially Disadvantaged Black Males, 1990; adv bd, Ohio Dept Econ Develop, 1991-; Downtown Kiwanis; Moderator Northern Ohio Baptist Asn, 1993-97; Mayor's Bi-Centennial Comt, 1996; Song leader exec bd mem, Lott Carey Baptist Foreign Mission Conv; past pres, Int Ministerial Alliance; past pres, Youngstown Coun Churches; past pres, Youngstown Urban League; past vpres, Youngstown Br, Nat Asn Advan Colored People; former mem, Health & Welfare Coun; former mem, Mayor's Human Rels Comn. **Honors/Awds:** Observer All African Coun Churches, Partners Ecumenism, 1987; Committee Member Award; Ohio Commission Martin Luther King Holiday, 1989; National Leadership Award, 1991; Martin Luther King Award, State of Ohio, 1995. **Special Achievements:** Published: An Anthology, "Songs of Simon" 1993. **Military Serv:** USN, third class officer's steward, 1943-46.

SIMON, MATT
Athletic coach. **Career:** Eastern NMex Univ, Graduate Asst, 1977; Borger High Sch, Borger, Tex, Asst Coach, 1978; Univ Tex-El Paso, Tight Ends, Linebackers, 1979-81; Univ WA, Running Backs, Kicking, 1982-91; Univ NMex, Offensive Coordr, 1992-93; Univ North Tex, head football coach, 1994-97; Baltimore Ravens, Running Back Coach, 1999-05; San diego chargers, Running Back Coach, 2007. *

SIMON, MILES JULIAN
Basketball player, basketball coach. **Personal:** Born Nov 21, 1975, Stockholm, Sweden; son of Walter Simon. **Educ:** Univ Ariz, attended 1998. **Career:** Basketball player (retired), basketball coach; Orlando Magic, guard, 1998-99; Maccabi Ra'anana, 2000-01; Mabo Livorno, 2001; Univ Ariz, Ariz Daily Wildcats, guard; Dakota Wizards, 2001-03;Univ Ariz, Ariz Daily Wildcats, asst coach, 2005-08. **Honors/Awds:** All-Am, 1997-98; Most Outstanding Player award, NCAA Tournament, 1997;Player of the Week; CBA Newcomer of the Year.

SIMONS, EGLON E
Advertising executive. **Personal:** Born Mar 7, 1946, Bermuda, Bermuda; son of Edward H and Ivy S; married Renee V H, Nov 29, 1969; children: Kimberly, Cameron & Kourtney. **Educ:** City Col New York, 1968; Harvard Bus Sch, MBA, 1976. **Career:** CBS Inc, sales & mkt vpres, 1976-90; Cablevision, Rainbow Ad Sales Co, exec vpres, 1990; NY Interconnect, sr vpres & gen mgr, 2002; Rainbow Ad Sales Co, sr vpres opers, currently. **Orgs:** Omega Psi Phi Fraternity; bd dirs, Westchester ARC, 1994-2002; bd dirs, Nat Down Syndrome Soc, 1998-2003. **Military Serv:** NY Nat Guard, capt, 1971-80. **Business Addr:** Executive Vice President, Cablevision Systems Corp & Rainbow Advertising Sales Co, 530 5th Ave 6th Fl, New York, NY 10036, **Business Phone:** (212)382-6100.

SIMONS, RENEE V H
Executive, consultant. **Personal:** Born May 27, 1949, New York, NY; daughter of Charles Leroy Moore and Phyllis Harley Phipps; married Eglon Simons, Nov 29, 1969; children: Kimberly, Cameron & Kourtney. **Educ:** Hunter Col, New York, NY, BA, 1971; Fordham Grad Sch Educ, New York, NY, MS, educ, 1974; Columbia Grad Sch Bus, New York, NY, MBA, 1978. **Career:** Gen Foods, White Plains, NY, asst brand mgr, Kool-Aid, 1978-80; Am Can James River, Greenwich, Conn, brand mgr, Dixie Northern, 1980-83; Seven-Up, St Louis, Mo, brand mgr, 1983-85; Philip Morris USA, NY, exec asst exec vpres, 1985-86, brand mgr, 1986-89; Philip Morris Mgt Corp, NY, dir, special proj, 1989-91, group dir mkt, 1991, Trade Mkt, Sales Promotions & Info, dir, 1991-93, Mkt, dir consumer mkt serv, 1993-94, Mkt, dir media, 1994-98; Chase Manhattan Bank, vpres, Corp Mkt & Commun, 1998-2000, sr vpres, ETECH Mkt & Commun, 2000-01; JP Morgan Chase, managing dir, Mkt & Commun; Harley Simons Group, founder; Clear Peak Communications, consult, currently. **Orgs:** Delta Sigma Theta Sorority, 1968-; Links, 1990-; pres, bd dirs, vpres bd trustees, Ad Club NY. **Honors/Awds:** Fel, COGME, 1976-78; Black Achievers Award, YMCA, 1981-82; Outstanding Professional Women in Advertising Award, Dollars & Sense, 1989; 21 Women of Power & Influence, 1991. **Business Addr:** Consultant, Clear Peak Communications, 167 W 21st 3rd Fl, New York, NY 10011, **Business Phone:** (646)336-7566.

SIMPKINS, CUTHBERT O.
Dentist, state government official. **Personal:** Born Jan 13, 1925, Mansfield, LA; married Elaine J. Shoemaker; children: four. **Educ:** Wiley Col; Tenn State Univ; Meharry Med Col, DDS, 1948; Harvard Med Sch, med degree; Downstate Med Ctr, Brooklyn, NY. **Career:** Boston Univ, res fel; Naval Med Res Inst, Bethesda, Md, res fel; Dentist pvt pract; La House Reps, Trauma & Critical Care, Prof & Chief; pvt pract, currently. **Orgs:** Nat Soc Dental Practitioners; Nat Dental Asn; Acad Gen Dentistry; Am Analgesic Soc; Am Dental Asn; NY State Dental Soc; Queens County Dental Soc; Queens Clinical Soc; Alpha Phi Alpha Fraternity; charter mem, Inst Continuing Dental Educ Eleventh Dist; Biracial Comn; fourth vpres, Southern Christian Leadership Conf; Sigma Pi Phi Fraternity. **Honors/Awds:** First Civil Rights Award, 1970, President's Appreciation Award, 1975; Martin Luther King Award, Outstanding Contributions Civil Rights Movement, 1989; Southern Univ Leader of the Year Award, 1988-89; Civil Rights Award, Nat Dental Asn, 1970; Distinguished Service Award, New Elizabeth Baptist Church, 1989; Meharry Medical College President's Award, 25 Years Serv Mankind, 1973; Dedication to Mankind Award, Airport Park Adv Coun, 1989; La State Beauticians Award, Achievement Civil Rights, 1989; Arthritis Humanitarian Award, recipient, 1992; Founders Day Award, York Col, New York, 1993; Bill of Rights Award, 1994. **Military Serv:** USAF, Capt, 1951. **Business Addr:** Dentist, Private Practitioner, 4001 Lakeshore Drv, Shreveport, LA 71109, **Business Phone:** (318)635-2382.

SIMPKINS, J. EDWARD
Educator. **Personal:** Born Oct 18, 1932, Detroit, MI; married Alice Marie Mann; children: Edward & Ann Marie, Evelyn. **Educ:** Wayne State Univ, BA, 1955, ed.M, 1961; Harvard Univ, CAS, 1969, ed.D, 1971. **Career:** High Sch Eng J Hist, teacher, 1956-65; Detroit Fedn Teachers, exec vpres,1965-68; Harvard Univ fel; Hist Dept, Tufts Univ, lectr, 1968-71; fac & exec dir, Ctr Urban Studies, Harvard Grad Sch Educ, asst & dean, 1970-71; Penn Pub Schs, chief negotiator, 1971-72; Wayne State Univ, Ctr Black Studs, 1972-74, Col Educ, dean, 1974. **Orgs:** Am Arb Asn; Ind Rel Res Asn; Woodrow Wilson Found; Phi Delta Kappa; pres, Asn Study Afro Am Life & History State Mich. **Honors/Awds:** Human Rights Award, 1968; Spirit of Detroit Award, 1974; Martin Luther King Award. **Military Serv:** USNA, pvt, 1956-58. *

SIMPKINS, LUBARA DIXON
Basketball player, basketball coach, founder (originator). **Personal:** Born Apr 6, 1972, Ft Washington, MD. **Educ:** Providence Col, BA, mkt & art, 1994. **Career:** Chicago Bulls, forward, 1994-97, 1998-2000, 2006; Golden State Warriors, 1997-98; Makedonikos, 2000-01; Atlanta Hawks, 2001-02; Maroussi, 2001-02; Rockford Lightning, 2001-02; Criollos Caguas, 2001-02; Unics Kazan, 2002-03; Lietuvos Rytas, 2003-04; Leones Ponce, 2003-04; Dakota Wizards, 2004-05; Plus Pujol Lleida, 2004-05; Alaska Aces, 2004-05; Blue Stars, 2005-06; Bamberg, 2005-06; Next Level Performance, Inc., founder, pres & head trainer, currently. **Honors/Awds:** Washington, D.C. Area Championship, 1987, 1989 & 1990; Gold Medal, Olympic Festival, 1991; NBA Championship, 1996, 1997, 1998.

SIMPKINS, WILLIAM JOSEPH
Military leader. **Personal:** Born Dec 30, 1934, Edgefield, SC. **Educ:** NC A&T State Univ, BS 1956; Univ Md; Baylor Univ, MHA, 1969. **Career:** A121 Evc Hosp Repub Korea, exec officer, 1969-70; Mcdonald Army Hosp Ft Eustis Va, exec officer, 1970-71; HQ AUS Off Surgeon Gen, asst chief personnel serv, 1971-75; Eisenhower Med Ctr Ft Gordon, chief/personnel div troop comdr, 1975-78; AUS Med Command Korea, exec officer, 1978-79; Walter Reed Army Med Ctr, col AUS dir personnel & comm activ, 1979-83; US Army Med Dept Personnel Support Agency Off Surgeon Gen, comdr, 1983-. **Orgs:** Nat Asn Health Serv Exec, 1971-80; US Mil Surgeons Asn; Am Hosp Asn; Keystone Consistory 85 Free & Accepted Masons; Nat Asn Advan Colored People; Alpha Phi Alpha Fraternity Inc. **Honors/Awds:** Legion of Merit, Off Surgeon Gen HQ, AUS; Bronze Star Medal Repub Vietnam; Meritorious Serv Medal, Ft Gordon GA; Meritorious Serv Medal, Repub Korea. **Military Serv:** AUS col 1956-. **Business Addr:** AUS Medical Deparment Personnel Sup Agency, Office of the Surgeon Genl, 1900 Half St SW, Washington, DC 20024.

SIMPSON, CARL WILHELM
Football player. **Personal:** Born Apr 18, 1970, Vidalia, GA. **Educ:** Fla State, bachelor's degree in criminol. **Career:** Football player(retired); Chicago Bears, defensive tackle, 1993-97; Ariz Cardinals, defensive tackle, 1998-99; Las Vegas Outlaws XFL, 2001.

SIMPSON, CAROLE
Journalist. **Personal:** Born Dec 7, 1940, Chicago, IL; daughter of Lytle Ray and Doretha Viola Wilbon; married James Edward Marshall, Sep 3, 1966; children: Mallika Joy & Adam. **Educ:** Univ Ill, 1960; Univ Mich, BA, 1962; Univ Iowa, 1965. **Career:** Northwestern Univ's Medill Sch, jour instr; WTTW, commentator; WCFL Radio, news reporter, 1965-68; WBBM Radio, reporter, 1968-70; WMAQ-TV, news reporter, 1970-74; NBC News, news corresp; ABC News, news corresp, weekend anchor; ABC News Women's Adv Bd, chair; Carole Simpson Leadership Inst African Women's Ctr Dakar, Senegal, 1998; ABC News, sr corresp, 1982-; World News Tonight Sunday, anchor, currently. **Orgs:** Radio-TV Corresps Asn; Theta Sigma Phi; Nightline, S Africa; chair, ABC News Women's Adv Bd; vice chair, Int Women's Media Found; bd dirs, Nat Comn Working Women; bd trustees, Radio & TV News Dirs Found; Nat Acad Scis' forum Future C & Families; Nat Press Found. **Honors/Awds:** Media Jour Award, AMA; Outstanding Woman in Communs, YWCA Metro Chicago,1974; Journalist of the Year, Nat Asn Black Journalist, 1992; Star Award, Am Women Radio & TV; Carole Simpson scholar, Radio-TV News Dirs Found; Trumpet Award, Turner Broadcasting; Emmy Award, ABC News; Milestone in Broadcasting Award, Nat Comn Working Women; Leonard Zeiden berg First Amendment Award, Radio-TV News Dirs Found; Nat Organization of Women Legislators Nat Media Award; Joseph Medill Distinguished Journalism Award, Chicago Hist Soc. **Business Addr:** Senior Correspondent, ABC News, 1717 DESALES ST NW, Washington DC, WA 20036.

SIMPSON, DARLA
Basketball player. **Personal:** Born Apr 11, 1969. **Educ:** Univ Houston. **Career:** Atlanta Glory, forward, 1997-98; Colo Xplo-

sion, forward, 1998; Sacramento Monarchs, 2002; Houston Jaguars, ctr, 2003-04. **Honors/Awds:** All-tournament team hons. *

SIMPSON, DR. DAZELLE DEAN
Physician. **Personal:** Born Aug 28, 1924, Miami, FL; married George Augustus Simpson Sr; children: George Jr, Gregory & Gary. **Educ:** Fisk Univ, BA (magna cum laude), 1945; Meharry Med Col, MD, highest honors, 1950. **Career:** Pvt pract physician, currently. **Orgs:** Bd trustees Meharry Med Col, 1977-; diplomate Am bd Pediatrics, 1957; fel Am Acad Pediatrics; 'Alumnus of Year', Meharry Col, 1974; chmn (pediatric sec), Nat Med Asn, 1975-77; nat pres, Meharry Alumni Asn, 1976-77; life mem, NAACP; Delta Sigma Theta Sor Head Start Consult Force on Pediatric Educ, 1974-78; Task mem, Am Acad Ped; mem, bd dirs, Miami Childrens Hosp, 1988. **Honors/Awds:** Contributing editor, Current Therapy, 1980. **Special Achievements:** First Black pediatrician in Florida. **Home Addr:** 3619 Percival Ave, Miami, FL 33133, **Home Phone:** (305)759-0591. **Business Addr:** Physician, 150 NE 42 St, Miami, FL 33127, **Business Phone:** (305)573-1443.

SIMPSON, DIANE JEANNETTE
Counselor, social worker. **Personal:** Born Sep 20, 1952, Denver, CO; daughter of Arthur H Simpson and Irma Virginia Jordan Simpson; children: Shante Nicole. **Educ:** NE Wesleyan Univ, BS, 1974; Univ Denver Grad Sch Social Work, MSW, 1977. **Career:** Girl Scouts Mile Hi Coun, summer asst, 1971-77; Denver Public Sch, social worker asst, 1974-75, social worker, 1977-; Univ Denver Grad Sch Soc Work, field instr, 1984; Adoption Home, study work Denver, Dept Human Services. **Orgs:** Mem Nat Assoc Black Soc Workers, 1980-86, Nat Asn Social Workers; sec bd trustees, Warren Village Inc, 1982-83; nominations & personnel comm, Christ United Methodist Ch, 1981-84; mem, Denver Chap Black Genealogy Org, 1981-87; chairperson minority adult recruitment team Girl Scouts Mile Hi Coun, 1982-84; mem, Black Women's Network, 1983-86; nat coun delegate Girl Scouts, 1984-87; chairperson planning comm, Creative Ctr for Children, 1984, adv bd, 1984-86, Christ United Meth Ch; mem, traveler, Denver Sister Cities Inc, 1984; admin bd, staff, parish relations, Coun Ministries Christ United Methodist Church, 1984-87; vpres, United Methodist Women, Christ United Methodist Ch, 1989-91; Education Scholarship Comm Shorter African Methodist Episcopal Ch; Shorter AME Ch, Breast Cancer Support Ministry, 2001-; Denver Child Fatality Review Bd, 1998-. **Honors/Awds:** Selectee to Ghana West Africa Girl Scouts of the USA/Oper Crossroads Africa 1974; Crusade Scholar Bd of Global Ministries, United Methodist Church 1976-77; Spec Mission Recognition United Methodist Women, United Methodist Church 1982; Elizabeth Hayden Award for Outstanding Serv Girl Scouts Mile Hi Council 1983; Young Alumni Loyalty Awd NE Wesleyan Univ 1985; Woman of the Year Award Aurora Area Business & Professional Women's Org 1986; Excellence in Education Award, Black Educators United, Denver Public Schools, 1990. **Business Addr:** Social Worker, Denver Public Schools, 900 Grant St, Denver, CO 80204, **Business Phone:** (303)322-5080.

SIMPSON, DONNIE
Radio host. **Personal:** Born Jan 30, 1954, Detroit, MI; son of Calvin and Dorothy; married Pamela; children: Donnie Jr & Dawn. **Educ:** Univ Detroit, BA, communs. **Career:** WJLB Detroit, air personality, 1969-77; WKYS Washington, radio host & prog dir, 1977-93; Black Entertainment TV, host, "Video Soul"; WRC-TV, sports anchor, 1981; BET, host Video Soul, 1983; WPGC Radio, on-air personality, 1993-. **Orgs:** Supporter, United Negro Col Fund, Donnin Pam Simpson Scholar Fund; Hon Chmn; NatBlack Family Reunion. **Honors/Awds:** Program Dir of the Year, Billboard Mag, 1982; Superstar of the Year, The Nat Urban Coalition, 1989; Personality of the Year, Billboard Mag, 1999; BET Walk of Fame, 2004. **Special Achievements:** TV series: "Video Soul", actor, 1983-00. **Business Addr:** Radio Host, WPGC 95.5, 4200 Parliament Pl Suite 300, Lanham, MD 20706, **Business Phone:** (301)918-0955.

SIMPSON, FRANK B.
School administrator, army officer. **Personal:** Born Dec 21, 1919, Jewett, TX; son of Herman W and Annie Matson; married Estelle Martin, Dec 28, 1945; children: Rosetta S Hassan, Oliver B. **Educ:** Kentucky State Univ, BS, 1942; Univ Kentucky, MS, 1956; Univ Kentucky & Univ Louisville, postgrad. **Career:** School administrator (retired); Todd Co & Christian Co, high sch prin, 21 yrs; Hopkinsville Sch Syst, asst supt, 1967-69; Jefferson Co Sch System, asst supt, 1969-80. **Orgs:** KEA, NEA, KASA; pres, 3rd Dist Teachers Asn; 2nd Dist Prin Asn; KY HS Athletic Asn; Gov Commn High Educ, 1967-70; Gov Adv Comn Local Govt, 1969-71; life mem, Nat Asn Advan Colored People, Urban League; Alpha Phi Alpha Fraternity; Mason; Gov Comm Improving Educ, 1978-86; Sigma Pi Phi Frat Boule Louisville Chpt; bd mem, USO; steward Miles Meml CME Ch; vpres, pres, KSU Nat Alumni Asn; pres, KSU Found; pres, State Bd Athletic Control; past pres, E 41 Athletic Asn. **Honors/Awds:** Man of Year, Alpha Phi Alpha Gamma Epsilon Lambda, 1966; Distinguished Alumni Award, 1970, Distinguished Service Award, 1981, Meritorious Service Award, 1984, President Club Award, 1984, KY State Univ; Lucy Hart Smith-Atwood S Wilson Award, KY Educ Asn, 1974; Distinguished Alumni Award, Nat Asn Black Cols, 1989; Award, KEA Comn Human Rights Comm on Black Hist, which wrote "Kentucky Black Heritage," used in Ky schls; Trailblazer Award, Univ Ky. **Military Serv:** AUS, staff sergeant, 1942-46. *

SIMPSON, HARRY L
Association executive, executive director. **Personal:** Born Mar 21, 1950, Birmingham, AL; son of Calvin and Dorothy; married Rosalind, Apr 27, 1985; children: Daren, Ramon & Rosalind Rolack. **Educ:** Oakland Community Col, assoc degree, ment health, 1986; Wayne State Univ, attended. **Career:** Eastwood Community Clins, acting prog dir, 1985-89; Mich Dept Pub Health, HIV/AIDS Sect, pub health consult, 1989-94; Community Health Awareness Group, exec dir, 1994-, dir training, currently; Nat Inst Drug Abuse, consult. **Orgs:** Minority adv comt, MSU Community HIV/AIDS & Ment Health, 1991-93; bd secy, Midwest DS Prev Proj, 1991-94; bd mem, Southeastern Mich HIV/AIDS Coun; bd mem, Community Health Outreach Workers; adv mem, Southeastern Mich Regional Community Planning Coun; task force mem, Metro Detroit Substance Abuse AIDS Prev; comt co chair, Statewide Community Prevention Planning Group; past pres, Community Health Outreach Workers. **Honors/Awds:** Price Fellow, Ctrs Dis Control & Prev (CDC), 1996; Join Together Fellow, Boston univ Sch Pub Health, 1997; Spirit of Detroit Award, 1997; Greater Detroit Area Recovery is Possible Award, Nat Coun Alcoholism & Drug Dependence, 1998; Comm Service Award, ACSEM, 1998; Testimonial Resolution, Detroit City Council, 1998. **Military Serv:** AUS, specialist, 1968-72; Purple Heart, Army Accomodation Medal/Valor. **Business Addr:** Executive Director, Community Health Awareness Group, 3028 E Grand Blvd, Detroit, MI 48237, **Business Phone:** (313)872-2424.

SIMPSON, INDIA ARIE
Songwriter, singer. **Personal:** Born Oct 3, 1975, Denver, CO; daughter of Ralph Simpson and Marie Simpson. **Educ:** Savannah Col Arts & Design, jewelry making. **Career:** India.Arie Band, singer & songwriter, currently; Albums: Acoustic Soul, 2001; Voyage to India, 2002; Brown Sugar, 2002; I Am Not My Hair, 2005; Testimony Vol 1, 2006; Testimony Vol 2, 2008; Films: Radio, 2003; Shark Tale, 2004; "The Tyra Banks Show," 2005; Singles: "Ready For Love," 2006; TV Series, "Motown Christmas", 2002; "Act of contrition", 2003; "American Dreams", 2003. **Honors/Awds:** Nominated 8 Grammy Awards, for Acoustic Soul, 2001; won 2 Grammy awards for "Little Things" & Voyage to India, 2003. **Business Addr:** Recording artist, Universal Motown Records, 1755 Broadway Fl 6, New York, NY 10019-3743, **Business Phone:** (212)841-8600.

SIMPSON, JAMES ARLINGTON. See SIMPSON, NORVELL J.

SIMPSON, JOHN O
School administrator, school superintendent. **Personal:** Married Rita; children: John. **Educ:** W Chester Univ, BA, music educ, 1970, MA, vocal pedagogy, MEd, 1975; Univ Del, educal leadership, 1981; Univ Mich, PhD, educ policy, 1983. **Career:** Newark, DE, Philadelphia, music teacher; Wash, asst jr high prin, 1984-86, elem prin, 1986-88; Okla City, 29 pub elem sch, dir, 1988-91; N Chicago Pub Schs, supt, 1993; Ann Arbor Bd Educ, supt, 1993-. **Orgs:** Rotary Club; bd dirs, Hands-On Mus, Washtenaw Co Red Cross, Univ Musical Soc; Am Asn Sch Adminr; Nat Asn Black Sch Educrs; Mich Asn Sch Adminrs. **Business Addr:** Superintendent, Ann Arbor Public Schools, 2555 S State St, Ann Arbor, MI 48104, **Business Phone:** (734)994-2200.

SIMPSON, DR. JOHN RANDOLPH
Educator, college administrator. **Personal:** Born Jun 27, 1946, Elloree, SC; son of Arthur and Geneva; divorced; children: Stephanie C Simpson. **Educ:** Tuskegee Univ, BS, 1972; Atlanta Univ, MA, 1973; Ohio State Univ, PhD, 1981. **Career:** Social Security Admin, claims rep, 1974-77; Ky State Univ, dir govt rels, 1977-78; Univ SC, Beaufort, assoc prof, 1978-86; SC State Univ, dean & prof, 1986; Philander Smith Col, dean acad affairs, 2005-06. **Orgs:** Kappa Delta Pi, 1977; Phi Kappa Phi, 1980; Gamma Sigma Delta, 1981; Southern Sociol Soc, 1982-; Asn Behav & Social Scientists, 1986-; Rural Sociol Soc, 1988-. **Special Achievements:** Graduated in the top 10 of class, 1981. **Military Serv:** AUS, SP/5, 1966-69. **Home Addr:** 420 Hodges Dr NW, Orangeburg, SC 29118, **Home Phone:** (803)531-2176.

SIMPSON, LORNA
Artist. **Personal:** Born Aug 13, 1960, Brooklyn, NY; daughter of Elian and Eleanor; divorced; children: Zora Simpson Casebere. **Educ:** NY Sch Visual Arts, BFA, 1982; Univ Calif, San Diego, MFA, 1985. **Career:** Group exhibits: Whitney Mus Am Art; Studio Mus, Harlem, 1989; solo exhibits: Mus Modern Art, NY, 1990; Cameos & Appearances, Whitney Mus Am Art, 2002; Am Fedn Arts traveling show, Mus Contemp Art, 2006. **Orgs:** Fel Nat Endowment Arts, 1985. **Honors/Awds:** Louis Comfort Tiffany Award, 1990; Col Art Asn grant, 1994; Am Art Award, Whitney Mus, 2001. **Special Achievements:** First African American woman to have works exhibited at the Venice Biennale, Venice, Italy, 1990. **Business Phone:** (305)375-3000.*

SIMPSON, MERTON DANIEL
Executive, artist. **Personal:** Born Sep 20, 1928, Charleston, SC; married Beatrice Houston (divorced); children: Merton Daniel Jr & Kenneth Charles. **Educ:** NY Univ, Attended; Cooper Union Art Sch. **Career:** Merton D Simpson Gallery Inc, pres & owner, Currently; artist, currently. **Orgs:** Red Cross Exchange Exhibit Paris & Tokyo, 1950; Intercultural Club, 1951; SC Cultural Fund, 1951; Gibbes Art Gallery, 1956; Curatorial Counc Studio Mus Harlem, 1977-. **Honors/Awds:** Publ Young Am Painters, 1954; Am Negro Art, 1960; contemporary Artists of SC, 1970; The Afro Amer Artist, 1973; numerous exhibits, permanent collections; Studio Museum of Harlem Award, 2002. **Special Achievements:** Numerous publications. **Military Serv:** USAF artist 1951-54. **Home Phone:** (212)686-6735. **Business Addr:** Owner, President, Merton Simpson Gallery, 38 W 28th St 5th Fl, New York, NY 10001, **Business Phone:** (212)686-6735.

SIMPSON, NORVELL J. (JAMES ARLINGTON SIMPSON)
Administrator. **Personal:** Born Mar 25, 1931, Rochester, NY; son of Frank Douglas and Martha Perlina Jentons; married Alice Elizabeth Saxton Simpson, Jul 11, 1953; children: Gary A, Sharon R, Leslie A. **Educ:** Park Col, BA, Econ, Bus admin, 1970; Univ CO, MA, Cand Guid, Couns, 1981. **Career:** adminr (retired); USAF, sr mstr sgt, 1949-71; Pikes Peak Comm Action Prog, exec dir, 1972-79; El Paso City co, dir comm serv dept, 1974-79; TRW/EPI, prop control & serv mgr, bus adminr, 1979-86; colo Springs Public Schools Dist 11, human relations adminstrator, external affairs & affirmative action coordr, 1986-94. **Orgs:** exec bd, United Way Pikes Peak Reg, 1978-93; Sch Dist 11, 1975-85; CO Assoc Sch Bd, 1983-84; comm Colo Sprngs Human Rel, 1973-79; Alpha Phi Alpha; Kadesia Shrine Temple; Jr Achievement bd dirs, Citizen's Goals Colo Springs comt; youth employ advisory comt; Pikes Peak Mental Health Advisory comt; Clean Air Task Force; Colo Martin Luther King Jr State Holiday Comn; Colo State educ Accountability comt. **Honors/Awds:** Citizen of the Year, Alpha Phi Alpha, 1979, 1981, 1982; Omega Psi Phi, 1978; TRW Leadership Award, TRW, 1979; The Colorado Education Association Lion II Award, The Norvell Simpson Community ctr. **Military Serv:** USAF, sr mstr sgt, 1949-71. *

SIMPSON, O. J. (ORENTHAL JAMES SIMPSON)
Football player, actor. **Personal:** Born Jul 9, 1947, San Francisco, CA; son of James Lee and Eunice Durden; married Nicole Brown (Deceased) (divorced); children: Sydney & Justin. **Educ:** San Francisco City Col, attended 1967; Univ Southern Calif, attended 1969. **Career:** Football player, (retired); Buffalo Bills, halfback, 1969-78; San Francisco 49'ers, 1978; Films: Why, 1973; The Towering Inferno, actor, 1974; The Klansman, actor, 1974; Killer Force, actor, 1975; Cassandra Crossing, actor, 1976; Capricorn I, actor, 1977; Firepower, actor, 1978; Hambone & Hilly, actor, 1983; The Naked Gun, actor, 1989; The Naked Gun 21/2, actor, 1991; No Place to Hide, actor, 1993; Naked Gun 33 1/3: The Final Insult, actor, 1994; Orenthal Prods, owner & exec producer of several TV prods; ABC-TV Sports, 1969-77; Monday Night Football, sports color commentator, 1983-86; Rose Bowl color commentator, 1979, 1980; 1976 Summer Olympics, color commentator; NBC-TV Sports, 1978-82, NFL Live, co-host, 1989; 1984 Summer Olympic Sports spec events; TV Series: Goldie & the Boxer, exec producer, 1979; Detour to Terror, exec producer, 1980; Goldie & the Boxer Go to Hollywood, exec producer, 1981; Cocaine & Blue Eyes, exec producer, 1983; Cocaine & Blue Eyes, 1983; Student Exchange, 1987; Frogmen, 1994. **Honors/Awds:** Col of San Francisco, All Am, 1965-66; USC, All Am, 1967-68; world rec 440 yd relay team, 1967; Heisman Trophy winner, 1968; UPI & AP, col athlete of the yr, 1968; voted col player of the decade ABC Sports, 1970; Named Am Football League All Star Team 1970; named collegiate athlete of the decade, 1972; Pro Bowl, 1972, 1974-76; AFC most valuable player, 1972, 1973, 1975; Most yds gained in a season, 1973, 2003; Most games in a season with 100yds or more 11 1973; Most rushing attempts in a season 332, 1973; Hickok Belt recipient, 1973; NFL most valuable player, 1975; Most yds gaine drushing in a game 273, 1976; Most yds rushing gained in a game; named NFL Player of the Decade, 1979; Col Football Hall of Fame induction, 1983; Pro Football Hall of Fame induction, 1985.

SIMPSON, ORENTHAL JAMES. See SIMPSON, O. J.

SIMPSON, RALPH DEREK
Basketball player. **Personal:** Born Aug 10, 1949, Detroit, MI; married Joyce McMullen. **Educ:** Mich State Univ, attended 1973. **Career:** Basketball player (retired); Denver Rockets, 1970-74; Denver Nuggets, 1974-76, 1977-78; Detroit Pistons, 1976-77; Philadelphia 76ers, 1978-79; New Jersey Nets, 1979-80.

SIMPSON, SAMUEL G.
Clergy, writer. **Personal:** Born Dec 6, 1931, Jamaica, West Indies; married Lola Campbell; children: Erica, Stephen, Kim. **Educ:** BRE, 1967; MDiv. **Career:** Jamaica, civil servant treas, 1955-59; Bronx Baptist Church, NY, pastor, 1964-74; Southern Baptist Churches, Bronx, pastor dir; Carib News, weekly column writer; Wake-Eden Community Baptist Churches, pastor; Bronx Baptist Church, pastor, currently. **Orgs:** Exec bd mem, Alumni Yr, Northeastern Bible Col, 1974; pres, E Tremont Church Coun; vpres, Coun Church Bronx Div; vpres, Meterop NY Baptist Asn; vpres, Baptist Conv NY; chmn, Nominating Comt, Coun Chairs, NY City Sec Comt Planning Bd No 6 Bronx; treas, Twin Parks

Urban Renewal Bronx; Honeywell Baptist Chapel; Grace Baptist Chapel; Shepherds Restoration Corp. **Honors/Awds:** Award Bapt Conv, MD; Air Jamaica Nat Airlines Award; Alumni of the Yr, Northeastern Bible Col; Man of the Yr, Bronx Coun Churches. **Special Achievements:** Books: What God did for Me; Architect of Hope; To Dream the Impossible Dream; Wake Eden Community Baptist Churches. **Business Addr:** Pastor, Bronx Baptist Church, 331 E 187th St, Bronx, NY 10458.

SIMPSON, STEPHEN WHITTINGTON
Lawyer. **Personal:** Born Mar 14, 1945, Philadelphia, PA; married Audrey C Murdah; children: Stephen Jr & Christopher Lindsey. **Educ:** Harvard Univ, AB, 1966; Univ Pa, JD, 1969. **Career:** Pa Super Ct, law clerk 1969-70; Dechert, Price & Rhoades, atty, 1970-73; Goodrs Greenfield, atty, 1973-77; Suns Co Inc, chief coun, 1978-87; Vance, Jackson, Simpson & Overton, atty, currently. **Orgs:** Am Bar Asn; Philadelphia Bar Asn; Barristers Club. **Home Addr:** 239 W Allens Lane, Philadelphia, PA 19119. **Business Addr:** Attorney, Vance, Jackson, Simpson & Overton, 1429 Walnut St Fl 8, Philadelphia, PA 19102-3218, **Business Phone:** (215)665-8082.

SIMPSON, VALERIE
Singer, songwriter, restaurateur. **Personal:** Born in New York, NY; married Nicholas; children: Nicole. **Career:** Motown Records, Songwriter & singer Nick Ashford; songs: Diana Ross; Marvin Gaye & Tammi Terrell; Ray Charles; Chaka Khan; Gladys Knight & the Pips; Sugar Bar Restaurant, co-owner, 1996-. **Business Addr:** Co Owner, Sugar Bar, 254 W 72 St, New York, NY 10023, **Business Phone:** (212)579-0222.*

SIMPSON, DR. WILLA JEAN
Manager. **Personal:** Born May 15, 1943, Little Rock, AR; married Earl Henry; children: Desiree, Jill & Earla. **Educ:** Kennedy King Col, AA, 1969; Chicago State Univ, BS, 1974; Governors State Univ, MA, 1975; Fielding Inst, PhD, 1981. **Career:** Golden Gate Consult, child family therapist, 1981-; Malcolm X Col, Chicago, Ill, instr, 1981-84; Dept Army Savanna Ill, educ spec, 1984; BCDI Chicago affil, rec secy, 1982-85; AUS Dept Defense Rock Island Arsenal, child develop serv coordr; Fort Hood Army Base, child develop serv coordr, 1987-; AUS Materiel Command, Youth Serv die, 1991-93; US Dept HTH & Human Serv, Ed Prog Specialist, 1993-2003; Trinity Col, adj prof, 1995-2003. **Orgs:** Handicap coordr, Dept Human Srv Chicago Ill, 1982-83; spec needs mgr, Ebony Mgt Asn Chic, 1980-82; dep dir, CEDA Chicago, 1976-78; Nat Black Child Develop Inst, 1982-00; Nat Phi Delta Kappa Inc, 1983; pres, Golden Gate Bd Dir, 1971-81; Pi Lam Theda, 1985-; Nat Asn Ed Young C; Potomac Hosp Cancer Support Group, 1995-00; chmn, Dale City Christian Support Group, 1993-00; Nat Polit Cong Black Women, Prince William Chap, 1995. **Honors/Awds:** Biog study Black Educ PhD Dissertation GGDCC Pub, 1981; Service Award, Harris YWCA Chic, 1974, Holy Cross Child Care Ctr, 1984, Gldn Gate Day Care Ctr Chic, 1984; Special Act Award, Rock Island Arsenal, 1985; Exceptional Performance Award, Rock Island Arsenal, 1986; ACYF Service Award, Early Head Start Team, 1997; Holy Family Cath Church Outreach Award, 2000; presenter, Nat Asn Ed Young Conf, 2000; 2001, 2003; Nat Black Child Develop Inst, 2000, 2001, 2002. **Home Addr:** 10726 S King Dr, Chicago, IL 60628.

SIMPSON-MITCHELL, SANDRA
Executive. **Personal:** Born Oct 4, 1955, Laurel, MS; daughter of Charles and Annie; divorced; children: Charles & Justin. **Educ:** Southern Univ, BS, 1977; Univ Wis, MBA, 1980. **Career:** Peak, Marwick & Mitchell asst acct, 1977-79; Gen Mills, asst producer mgr, 1980-82; HBO, vpres, 1998-82, sr vpres, 1999-, gen mgr, affil sales, currently. **Orgs:** Delta Sigma Theta, 1974-; Nat Asn Minorities Cable, 1980-; TV bd mem, Mkt Soc Cable TV & Telecommunications Indust, 1987-. **Honors/Awds:** Consortium fel, 1979. **Business Addr:** Senior Vice President, General Manager, HBO, Affiliate Sales, 1100 Ave Americas, New York, NY 10036, **Business Phone:** (212)512-1208.

SIMPSON-TAYLOR, DR. DOROTHY MARIE
Educator. **Personal:** Born Jun 25, 1944, Pickens, MS; daughter of Willie Andrew and Mary Jane Young; married Harold J, Nov 26, 1965; children: Harold Duane & Robert Lance. **Educ:** Univ Neb, Omaha, BGS, urban studies, 1972, MS, guid & coun, 1974; Univ Denver, Phd, coun psychol, 1988. **Career:** Pikes Peak Coun Ctr, ment health therapist, 1978-83; Iowa State Univ, psychol intern, 1984-85; Va Veterans Readjustment Ctrs, team leader & coun, 1985-88; Univ Northern Colo, asst prof, coun psychol, 1988-90; Ind State Univ, asst prof, africana studies, 1990, asst pres, Ethnic Diversity, 1995. **Orgs:** Gov affairs, Ind Asn Blacks Higher Edu, 1991-93; prog review bd, Ind State Bd Health, 1991-93; Vigo County AIDS Task Force, 1991-93; steering com, Wabash Valley Critical Incident Stress Debriefing Team, 1992-93; Nat Asn Black Psychologists; Nat Black Storytellers Asn. **Honors/Awds:** Fullbright Hayes Scholar, 1993; Nat Asn Advan Colored People Community Service Award, 1993. **Military Serv:** USF, a-1C, 1963-66. **Home Addr:** 1819 S 8th St, Terre Haute, IN 47802, **Home Phone:** (812)235-0139.

SIMPSON-WATSON, DR. ORA LEE
Educator. **Personal:** Born Jul 7, 1943, East Chicago, IN; children: Ronald Damon & Kendyl Joi. **Educ:** Ball State Univ, BA, 1965; Purdue Univ, MA, 1969, PhD, 1977. **Career:** Dallas Independent Sch Dist, dir learning, 1977-80, dean instr, 1981-83; Dallas County Community Col, N Lake Col, div chair 1983-. **Orgs:** Sch bd trustee, Dallas Independent Sch Dist; Nat Asn Black Sch Educs; Alpha Kappa Alpha; Links Tex Asn Sch Bd; consult Rep Suri Name, 1986; Child Care, Dallas, 1986. **Business Addr:** Div Chair Humanities, North Lake College, 5001 N Mac Arthur Blvd, Irving, TX 75038.

SIMS, BARBARA MERRIWEATHER
Judge. **Personal:** Born in Buffalo, NY; daughter of Frank and Carmelita; married William; children: Frank William & Sue Cynthia. **Educ:** State Univ Col Buffalo, BS; State Univ NY, Buffalo Law Sch, JD. **Career:** Erie Co Off, asst dist atty, 1964-68; State Univ NY, Buffalo, asst to pres, 1969-74, Law Sch, lectr; City Buffalo Parking Violations Bur, hearing officer, 1975-77; City Ct Buffalo, city ct judge, 1977-. **Orgs:** Nat Bar Asn; Women's Polit Caucus; nat vpres, Nat Asn Black Women Attys, 1975-80; Erie Co Bar Asn; pres, Women Lawyers W NY; bd dir, Nat Asn Advan Colored People; bd dir, BC/BS W NY; United Fund Nat Fund Birth Defects; Nat Asn Negro Bus-Prof Women Buffalo Chap; deleg, Nat Women's Year Conf Houston, 1977; African Am Community Builders. **Honors/Awds:** Recipient Community Service Award, 1968; Fight for Freedom Award, 1968; Distinguished Achievement Award, 1968; Distinguished Service Award, Grand United Order Odd fellows, 1978. **Special Achievements:** Chosen as one of 100 Black Women in Chicago Convention, 1972, first African American women to receive a law degree at UB, first African American women Assistant District Attorney in Erie County. **Home Phone:** (716)881-1322. **Business Addr:** Counsel, Buffalo Criterion Weekly Newspaper, 623-625 William St, Buffalo, NY 14206, **Business Phone:** (716)882-9570.

SIMS, CALVIN GENE
Journalist. **Personal:** Born Dec 17, 1963, Compton, CA; son of Calvina Odessa Borders and Lonnie Gene. **Educ:** Yale Univ, New Haven, CT, BA, 1985. **Career:** The New York Times, New York, NY, reporter, 1985, ed producer, 2003, dir tv develop, 2005-; Poynter Fel, jour, 1985; Am univ, consult, 2002-04; Ford Found, vice chair, prog officer, currently. **Orgs:** Fel, Am Asn Advan Sci, Mass Media, 1984; Scroll & Key, 1985-; staff worker, Coalition Homeless, 1985-87. **Honors/Awds:** New York Times Publisher's Award, 1990. **Business Phone:** (212)556-1234.

SIMS, CARL W
Newspaper editor. **Personal:** Born Apr 29, 1941, Washington, DC; married Barbara Lindsey; children: 1. **Educ:** Howard Univ, 1962; Univ Minn, 1987. **Career:** Peace Corps Sierra Leone, vol, 1962-63; Wa Post, reporter, 1965-70; Boston Globe, copy ed, 1970; Bay State Banner Boston, ed, 1970-72; Newsweek, assoc ed, 1973-74; Minneapolis Star Tribune, nat ed, asst ed, 1992. **Orgs:** Capital Press Club, 1966-69, Harvard Club Minn; Nat Asn Black Journalists, 1990-. **Honors/Awds:** Nieman Fel, Harvard Univ 1972-73. **Business Addr:** National Editor, Minneapolis Star Tribune, 425 Portland Ave, Minneapolis, MN 55488.

SIMS, DELORIS
Entrepreneur. **Career:** Legacy Bank inc, pres & ceo, currently. **Orgs:** Wisc African-Am Women Ltd, 1997; founder, Wis African-Am Womens Ctr. **Business Addr:** Chief Executive Officer, President, Legacy Bank Inc, 2102 W Fond du Lac Ave, Milwaukee, WI 53206, **Business Phone:** (414)343-6900.*

SIMS, DR. EDWARD HACKNEY
Surgeon, physician. **Personal:** Born Sep 5, 1944, Atlanta, GA; children: Jessica Carolyn. **Educ:** Morris Brown Col, Atlanta, BS, 1965; Meharry Med Col, Sch Med, MD, 1972. **Career:** King/Drew Med Ctr, chief gen surg, 1983-87; Pvt Practice, currently. **Military Serv:** USAF, E-4, 3 yrs. **Home Addr:** 3625 Martin Luther King J, Lynwood, CA 90262-3509, **Home Phone:** (310)631-9073. **Business Addr:** Physician, Surgeon, 3625 E Martin Luther King Suite 9, Lynwood, CA 90262, **Business Phone:** (310)631-9073.

SIMS, ESAU, JR.
Executive. **Personal:** Born Apr 14, 1953, Barberton, OH; son of Esau Sr and Eleanor; married Sarah Harris, Dec 1972; children: Esau Jaques, Rashawn & Jeffrey. **Educ:** National Col Educ, BS, 1972. **Career:** Arthur Treacher's Fish 'n Chips, dist mgr, 1973-75, area mgr, 1975-78, asst dir, franchise oper, 1978-79; Burger King, dist mgr, 1979-83, area mgr, 1985, vpres opers, 1989, vpres, franchise sales & serv div. **Orgs:** Vpres, Swift Creek Athletic Asn, 1986-92; vpres, Chesterfield County Athletic Asn, 1991; chair, trustee, Spring Creek Baptist Church, 1992-93. **Business Addr:** Vice Pres, Franchise Sales, Services, Burger King Corp, 9200 Arboretum Pkwy Suite 104, Richmond, VA 23236, **Business Phone:** (804)649-7604.

SIMS, GENEVIEVE CONSTANCE
Lawyer, educator. **Personal:** Born Nov 4, 1947, Baltimore, MD; daughter of Joe and Fannie. **Educ:** NC State Univ, BA, 1969; Univ Southern Calif, MPA, 1976; NC Cent Univ, JD, 1986; North Carolina State Bd Elections & the Bd Summit House Raleigh, currently. **Career:** Off State Personnel, NC State Govt, econ analyst, 1969-72; US Civil Serv Comn, personnel mgt specialist, 1972-76; Off Mgt & Budget Exec Off Pres, mgt analyst, 1976-77; US Civil Serv Comn, special asst comnr, 1977-78; Merit Sys Protection Bd, special asst, 1979-81; NC State Univ, Raleigh,NC, asst prof, 1982-93; NC Cent Univ, Durham, NC, vis instr, 1982-92; Genevieve C Sims Law Off, lawyer, 1987-. **Orgs:** Bd dir, YWCA Wake County; bd adjustments, Wake County; NC Bar Asn; bd, United Black Fund Wash, 1976-81; chmn, bd dir, Shelley Sch; bd dir, NC Asn Black Lawyers, 1989-92; bd, NC Acad Trial Lawyers, 1995-2000; NC State Bd Elections; bd dir, Summit House Raleigh, 1996-2001; NC State Bar; SC Bar; Wake County Bar Asn. **Honors/Awds:** Award, NC Special Olympics, 1982. **Business Addr:** Lawyer, Offices of Genevieve C Sims PC, 4024 Barrett Dr Suite 204, Raleigh, NC 27609, **Business Phone:** (919)834-7775.

SIMS, GRANT
Administrator. **Career:** AAA Michigan, asst vpres. *

SIMS, HAROLD RUDOLPH
Executive, writer. **Personal:** Born Jul 25, 1935, Memphis, TN; son of Benjamin Webster and Geraldine Rayford; married Lana Joyce Taylor, Jun 25, 1962; children: Douglass D & Kimberly J. **Educ:** Southern Univ, BR, LA, BA (cum laude), 1957; Johns Hopkins Univ, Baltimore, Grad Study 1962; Univ Poona, Poona, India, cert, 1956; Geo Washington Univ, MS, 1967; King Memorial Col, DHL, 1977. **Career:** Office Econ Opportunity Exec Office Pres White House, exec sec, 1967-69; Nat Urban League, dep exec dir, 1969-71, exec dir, pres, 1971-72, actg dir; Johnson & Johnson, vpres, 1972-79; Sims & Assoc/Sims Int, pres, 1979-; Sound Radio WNJR, ceo, gen mgr, pres, 1984-92; MLK Jr NJ Comn, Office Gov, exec dir, 1985-86; Ebony Mag, sr acct exec, 1986-87; Uni-Med Consult, chmn, exec comt, beginning 1992; Centennial Concepts. **Orgs:** Adv bd, Princeton Univ, 1971-82; vpres, Oper PUSH, Eastern Region, 1972-74; bd dir, Martin Luther King Jr Ctr, 1972-, sr int adv & UN rep, 1972-96; chair, Friends Cong Black Caucus, 1973-78; bd trustees, St Louis Univ, 1974-84; pres, Nat Asn Mkt Develop, NY Chapter, 1974-76; bd dirs, Near E Found, 1976-; int bd adv, African-Am Inst, 1976-; nat adv bd, Nat Sci Found, 1977-82; pres, Sims-Sutton Indust Develop Group, 1982-; exec vpres, Gibson-Wonder Film Co/Jos P Gibson Found, 1983-; comnr, NJ MLK Jr Comn, 1984-86; co-founder, King-Luthuli S African Transformation Ctr, 1989-; Sharon Baptist Church, deacon, 1989-; AUS Spec Forces Asn, 1996-; life mem, Alpha Phi Alpha Fraternity; Nat Asn Advan Colored People. **Honors/Awds:** Cert, urban fel, Yale Univ, New Haven, CT, 1969; Doctor of Humane Letters, Award of Merit, Nat (South) African Chamber Com, 1978; Outstanding Graduate-First Century, Southern Univ, 1980; Forty Living Legends Award, Nat Asn Mkt Develop, 1996; Southern Univ Alumni Hall of Fame, 1999; NJ State MLK Jr Achievement Award, 2000. **Military Serv:** AUS, Major, 1957-67; Bronze Star, Army Commendation Medal w/Oak Leaf Cluster, 1963, 1967, Purple Heart, 1964, Army Parachutist Badge, 1963; Vietnam Service Medal, 1965; Joint Staff Campaign, Certs of Achvmnt 1957-67. **Home Addr:** 1 Lincoln Place Suite 27K, North Brunswick, NJ 08902. **Business Addr:** President, Sims & Associates Consultants, 1 Lincoln Pl, North Brunswick, NJ 08902, **Business Phone:** (732)940-9918.

SIMS, JOHN LEONARD
Computer executive, president (organization). **Personal:** Born Jul 1, 1934, Wilmington, DE; son of Thomas A and Ella Gibbs; married Shirley (Horton) Sims, Jun 14, 1962; children: John Jr, Kevin & Joe. **Educ:** Delaware State Col, Dover DE, BS, 1962; Ohio State Univ, Columbus OH, Grad Work; Columbia Univ, New York NY, Mgt Training Courses. **Career:** Computer executive, President (retired); E I Du Pont de Nemours Co Inc, mgt positions, chemist; Champion Int Corp, mgt positions, govt rels; Digital Equip Corp, Maynard, MA, corp mgr EEO/AA, 1974-75, dir manf personnel, 1975-81, corp staff mgr, 1981-84, vpres personnel, 1984-87, vpres strategic resources, 1987-93; John L. Sims Consul, pres, currently. **Orgs:** Bd dirs, The Boston Bank Com, 1983-; bd govs ASTD, 1987-; chmn, Freedom House, 1987-; bd govs, Boston Chamber Com, 1992-; Nat Nat Asn Advan Colored People; The Boston Pvt Indust Coun; exec leadership coun, Northeast Human Resources Asn; bd trustees, The Nat Urban League; SBI Roundtable Fla A&M. **Honors/Awds:** Award for Contributing, Nat Urban League, 1988; Award for Service, Freedom House; Award for Service, Alpha; Award for Achievements, Several Colleges and Minority Organizations; Image Award, Nat Asn Advan Colored People. **Special Achievements:** Top 25 Most Powerful Black Managers, Black Enterprise Magazine, 1988. **Military Serv:** AUS, Corps, 1955-57.

SIMS, JOSEPH WILLIAM
School administrator. **Personal:** Born Feb 14, 1937, Detroit, MI; married Constance A Williams; children: Nicole & Andre. **Educ:** Mich State Univ, BA, 1961, MA, 1962; Univ Mich, PhD, 1972. **Career:** Southwestern High Sch, Flint, MI, span teacher, 1962-62, fr teacher, 1967-68; AC Spark Plug, Flint, MI, supvr, 1965-67; Flint Community Sch, Flint, MI, from asst prin to prin, 1968-75; Oakland & Berkeley Sch Dist CA, Rockefeller intern, 1975-76; Prairie State Col, Chicago Heights, IL, vpres stud serv, 1976-83. **Orgs:** Am Asn Higher Educ; Nat Asn Stud Personnel Admin; Alliance Black Sch Educ; Ill Coun Community Col Admin; Ill Col

Personnel Asn; Nat Defense Educ Act Grant US Govt, 1968; Mott Found Grant, Charles S Mott Found, Flint, MI, 1970-71. **Honors/Awds:** Superintendency Training Grant, Rockefeller Found, NY, 1975-76; Distinguished Service Award, Detroit City, 1975. **Military Serv:** USAF, sgt, 1954-58.

SIMS, KEITH
Football player, foundation executive. **Personal:** Born Jun 17, 1967, Baltimore, MD; married Tia; children: Cairo & Storm. **Educ:** Iowa State Univ, BS, indust technol. **Career:** Football player (retired); Miami Dolphins, guard, 1990-97; Wash Redskins, 1997-2000. **Orgs:** Franchise owner, Dunkin Donuts.

SIMS, LOWERY STOKES
Museum director. **Personal:** Born Feb 13, 1949, Washington, DC; daughter of John Jacob Sr and Bernice Banks. **Educ:** Queens Col, BA, 1970; Johns Hopkins Univ, MA, 1972; City Univ NY, MA, philosphy, 1990, PhD, 1995. **Career:** Metro Mus Art, asst mus educr, 1972-75; Queens Col Dept Art, adj instr, 1973-76; Sch Visual Arts, instr, 1975-76, 1981-86; Metro Mus Art, assoc curator, 1979-95, curator, 1995-99; Studio Mus Harlem, exec dir, 2000-. **Orgs:** Col Art Asn, 1983-; Am Sect Int Art Critics Asn, 1980-; coun mem, NY State Coun Arts, 1987-92; bd, Col Art Asn, 1994-97; bd, Tiffany Found, 1995-97; adv bd, Ctr Curational Studies, 1995-; Asn Art Critics. **Honors/Awds:** DHL, Md Inst Col Art, 1988; Frank Jewett Mather Award, Col Art Asn, 1991; Lifetime Achievement Award in the Arts, Queens Mus Art, 1998; Honorary Doctorate, Parsons Sch Design, 2000; Honorary Doctorate, Arts, Atlanta Col Art, 2002; Honorary Doctorate, Col New Rochelle, 2003; Honorary Doctorate, Brown Univ, 2003. **Special Achievements:** One of Crain's Mag Top 100 Minority Executives, 1998, 2003; One of 50 Women Who Have Changed the World, Essence Magazine, 2003. **Business Addr:** Executive Director, The Studio Museum in Harlem, 144 W 125th St, New York, NY 10027, **Business Phone:** (212)864-4500.

SIMS, MILLICENT JEANNINE
Government official. **Personal:** Born Jun 30, 1958, Chicago, IL; daughter of James Gaither and Millie; married Charles R Sims, Aug 11, 1985; children: Charles R. **Educ:** OH State Univ, BS, microbiol, 1980. **Career:** OH Dept Health Lab, analytical chemist, 1981-86; OH Environ Protection Agency, environ specialist, 1986-88, dist admin, 1994-; Sims Construction Co Inc, co officer & mgr, 1988-94; OH Environ Protection Agency, dist adminr, currenlty; My Gift Card Co, owner. **Orgs:** Alpha Kappa Alpha, 1978-; bd trustees, officer, Columbus Neighborhood Housing Serv Inc, 1985-2000; bd trustees, officer, Livingston Park Neighborhood Improvement Asn, 1985-; bd mem, Susan G Komen Breast Cancer Found, Columbus Race Cure, 1993-96; bd mem, officer, African Am Cancer Support Group, 1995-; bd mem, Am Cancer Soc, 2000-; patient advocate, Nat Cancer Inst, Consumer Advocates Res & Related Activities, 2001-. **Home Addr:** 601 S Ohio Ave, Columbus, OH 43205. **Business Addr:** District Administrator, Ohio Environmental Protection Agency, Central District Office, 3232 Alum Creek Dr, PO Box 1049, Columbus, OH 43207, **Business Phone:** (614)728-3784.

SIMS, NAOMI R
Writer, executive, fashion model. **Personal:** Born Mar 30, 1949, Oxford, MS; married Michael Alistair Findlay; children: Pip. **Educ:** NY Univ, attended 1967. **Career:** Model (retired), Business Owner, Writer; Fashion Model, 1967-73; Fashion & Beauty, freelance writer; Naomi Sims Beauty Prods Ltd, founder, 1985-. **Orgs:** Bd dirs, Northside Ctr Child Develop Harlem; Nat Asn Advan Colored People; Womens' Firm Inc, 1977; Sickle Cell Anemia; NY State Drug Rehab Prog; Play Schs Asn, NY. **Honors/Awds:** Model of the Year Award, 1969 & 1970; New York City Board of Education Award, 1970; Women of Achievement Leadership, Home Jour, 1970; International Best Dressed List, 1971-73, 1976 & 1977; Women of Achievement, Am Cancer Soc, 1972; Top Hat Award, New Pitts Courier, 1974; Women of the Country, 1977; Modeling Hall of Fame, 1977. **Special Achievements:** Published numerous articles and books on modeling, fashion & beauty. **Business Phone:** (631)243-1000.

SIMS, PETE
Executive. **Personal:** Born May 11, 1924, El Dorado, AR; widowed. **Educ:** Atlanta Col Mil Sci, 1950. **Career:** El Dorado Housing Authority, pres, 1970-; Sims Enterprises, pres, 1973-; AR Fun Dirs & Mrtcns Asn, pres, 1974; Sims Mortuary Inc, pres, currently; NFDMA AR St Funeral Dirs, past pres dist gov. **Orgs:** Bd mem, Nat Funeral Dirs & Morticians Inc; Nat Funeral Dirs Asn; Ark Off Asn; Nat Asn Advan Colored People; Oper PUSH; DeSota Area Coun Boys Scouts; Past Ex-Ruler, IBPOE W; Chamber Com, El Dorado, Ark; chmn, First Baptist Church; Nat Ex-Ruler Coun Elks; past state pres, Ark State Elk Asn; Past Dist, Gov, Dist VI; Exchange Club; past bd mem, State Bd Burial Asn; Ark Funeral Dirs Asn; N E La Funeral Dirs Asn; past pres, Booker T Wash Alumni Asn. **Honors/Awds:** Outstanding Citizen Award, United Way, 1969; Personality of the South Award, 1977; Public Service Award, Boys Club Am, 1979; Outstanding Public Service, Boys Club Movement, 1979; Sales Award, Guaranty Nat Ins Co, 1980; Elk of the Year, 1982; Century Member Award, Boy Scouts Am, 1983; Outstanding Contribution to Elkdom, 1988; US Small Busi-

ness Administration for Successful Community Outreach Activity, 1994; Business Man of the Year, Omego Psi Phi, Kappa Chi Chap, 2002; Business Man of the Year, Searchers USA Inc, 2002; Elk Community Service Award, 2002. **Military Serv:** AUS, m/Sgt WW II. **Business Addr:** President, Sims Mortuary Inc, 432 Liberty St, PO Box 967, El Dorado, AR 71730, **Business Phone:** (870)862-4266.

SIMS, RIPLEY SINGLETON
Educator. **Personal:** Born Jul 5, 1907, Mobile, AL; married Dorothy Revalion. **Educ:** Talladega Clge, AB, 1931; Northwestern Univ, MA, 1939; Univ Chicago, attended 1942. **Career:** Teacher math, 1931-32; pvt high sch, prin, 1932-38; Univ Chicago, res asst, 1940-42; USAAF, math-electricity instr, 1942-46; USAF Inst, educ spec, 1946-54, head educ div, 1954-68; assoc dep dir acad prog; Educ Consult. **Orgs:** Am Assoc Higher Educ; Adult Educ Assoc; Am Educ Res Assoc. **Honors/Awds:** University Extension Associate Award for Achievement. **Special Achievements:** Contrb articles to prof J; author "An Inquiry into Correspondence Educating Processes". **Military Serv:** USAAF, civilian instr, 1942-46.

SIMS, RONALD CORDELL
Government official. **Personal:** Born Jul 5, 1948, Spokane, WA; son of James M and Lydia Williams; married Cayan Topacio, May 30, 1987; children: Douglas, Daniel & Aaron; married Topacio. **Educ:** Cent Wash State Univ, Ellensburg, WA, BA, psychol, 1971. **Career:** Wash State Atty Gen, Seattle, WA, investr, 1971-72; Fed Trade Comn, Seattle, WA, sr investr, 1972-78; City Seattle, WA, dir, 1978-81; Wash State Senate, Olympia, WA, leadership coordr, 1981-86; King Co Coun, Seattle, WA, counman, 1986, exec, currently; US dep sec of Dep of Housing and Urban Devp, 2009-. **Orgs:** Pres comn on trade/investment policy in Asia; Seattle Human Rights Comn, 1984-86; volunteer, Meany Middle Sch; lay minister, Operation Night watch; former pres, Rainier Dist Youth Athletic Asn; bd dirs, Planned Parenthood; bd mem, Families First Children's Home Soc. **Honors/Awds:** World Affairs Fellow, James Madison Found, 1986-87; Humanitarian of the Year Award, Progressive Animal Welfare Soc, 1993. **Special Achievements:** Most powerful post yet attained by an African American in Washington. **Home Addr:** 3227 Hunter Blvd S, Seattle, WA 98144. **Business Addr:** Deputy Secretary, U.S. Department of Housing and Urban Development, 451 7th St S W, Washington, WA 20410, **Business Phone:** (202)708-1112.

SIMS, PROF. RONALD R
Educator, consultant. **Personal:** Born Apr 27, 1949, Steubenville, OH; married Serbrenia J Sims, Apr 25, 1986; children: Nandi, Dangaia & Sieya. **Educ:** Univ Steubenville, BA, 1971; Univ MD, Baltimore, MSW, 1972; Case Western Reserve Univ, PhD, 1981. **Career:** Auburn Univ, Montgomery, prof, 1981-86; consult, currently; Col William & Mary, Sch Bus, prof, Floyd Dewey Gottwald sr prof bus admin orgn behavior, currently. **Orgs:** Acad Mgt, 1981-; ABSEL, 1983-97. **Honors/Awds:** Outstanding Faculty Award, State Coun Health Va, 2000. **Special Achievements:** Published books: Accountability & Radical Change in Public Organizations, 1998; Reinventing Training & Development, 1998; Keys to Employee Success in the Coming Decades,1999; The Challenge of Front-line Management: Flattened Organizations in the New Economy, 2000; Organizational Success through Effective Human Resources Management, 2002; Ethics & Corporate Social Responsibility: Why Giants Fall, 2003; Managing School System Change: Charting a Course for Renewal, 2004; Leadership: Succeeding in the Private, Public and Not-for-profit Sector, 2005. **Military Serv:** AUS, ltcol, 1972-97. **Business Addr:** Floyd Dewey Gottwald Sr Professor of Business Administration, College of William & Mary, Graduate School of Business, Rm Tyler 318A 102 Richmond Rd, PO Box 8795, Williamsburg, VA 23187-8795, **Business Phone:** (757)221-2855.

SIMS, THEOPHLOUS ARON
Pharmacist, school administrator. **Personal:** Born Mar 17, 1939, Jefferson, TX; married Nancy Jayne Wattley; children: Theophlous Jr & Shannon D. **Educ:** Tex Southern Univ, BS, pharmacol, 1961; Doc Pharmacy Certification, Nat Asn Retail Druggists. **Career:** Forth Worth Independent Sch Dist 4, secy, currently; pharmacist, currently. **Orgs:** Nat Asn Retail Druggist; life mem, Kappa Alpha Psi; Alpha Phi Alpha, 1983; bd mem, Tex Enterprise Found, 1984; adv comt, Tex Girls Choir, 1984; NIH, 1984-; Ft Worth Metrop Black Chamber Com; Nat Asn Sch Bd; Rolling Hills Civic League Club; Tarrant County Health Planning Coun; Campus Dr United Methodist Church; Kappa Alpha Fraternity; Chi Delta Mu Medical Fraternity; Tex Pharmaceutl Asn; Am Pharmaceutl Asn; Tarrant County Pharmaceut Asn. **Honors/Awds:** Black Achievers Award, 1980; Outstanding Business Award, Fannie Brooks Heath Club, 1984; Texas Southern University Shining Star, Tex Southern Univ, 1985; Quest for Success Award, 1985; Fort Worth Black Achiever's Award; Outstanding Achiever in the Community, Texas Sickle Cell Anemia Asn; Outstanding Alumni Award, Col Pharma & Health Scis, Tex Southern Univ; Intercultural Services Citation from the Univ N Tex; Community Service and Involvement Honoree, Dallas Pharmacy Asn; Excellence in the African American Community, Cowan United Methodist Church. **Special Achievements:** Honored with naming of T. A. Sims Elementary School. **Home**

Addr: 4421 Kingsdale Dr, Fort Worth, TX 76119. **Business Addr:** School Board Member, Secretary, Fort Worth Independent School District 4, 100 North Univ Dr, Fort Worth, TX 76107-1360.

SIMS-DAVIS, EDITH R.
School administrator. **Personal:** Born Dec 24, 1932, Marion, LA; daughter of Rich Louis Robinson and LuEllen Nelson; married Samuel C, Jun 15, 1984; children: Cynthia Laverne Sims & William Sims Jr. **Educ:** AM&N Col, BS, 1955; Tuskegee Inst, MS, 1960; Univ Buffalo, PhD, 1962; Chicago State Univ, Chicago, Ill, attended 1966. **Career:** Merrill High Sch, teacher, 1955-59; Englewood High Sch, 1961-66; counr, 1966-68; Fenger High Sch, fac, 1968-69; Calumet High Sch, asst prin, actg prin, 1969-71; Caldwell & McDowell Sch, prin, 1971-82; Corliss High Sch, prin, 1982-96; Bryn Mawr Col, interim prin; Sch Bd, consult, currently. **Orgs:** Delta Sigma Theta Sorority, 1953-; Univ Ark Alumni Asn, 1969-; Samuel B Stratton Asn, 1980-; Chicago Bd Educ; Ill Prin Asn; Chicago Prin Asn; Ella Flagg Young Chap Nat Alliance Black Sch Educations; Nat Coun Admin Women Educ; Chicago Urban League; Beta Kappa Chi Sci Frat; Nat Coun Negro Women; Metrop Cluster. **Honors/Awds:** Univ Ark Alumni Asn, Pine Bluff "Miss Alumni", 1955; Alpha Kappa Mu Nat Honor Soc; Roseland Comt Grit Award, 1986; Outstanding Chicago Prin Award Dist 33, 1986; Outstanding Prin Award, Supt Sch Chicago Bd Educ, 1986; Distinguished Alumni Award, Univ Ark, Pine Bluff, 1987; Whitman Award, Excellence Educ Mgt, Whitman Corp, 1990; Phi Delta Kappa Award, 1992. **Home Phone:** (312)649-1425. **Business Addr:** School Board Consultant, 21 E Huron St, Chicago, IL 60611, **Business Phone:** (312)649-1425.*

SIMS-PERSON, LEANN MICHELLE
Banker. **Personal:** Born Aug 14, 1972, Fort Worth, TX; daughter of William and Mildred; married Marc A, Jul 27, 1996; children: Austin Person. **Educ:** Tex Christian Univ, BBA, 1994; Tex Wesleyan Univ, MBA, 2000. **Career:** Chase Bank Tex (formerly Tex Com Bank), human resources recruiter, 1994-, asst vpres, currently; songwriter. **Orgs:** Financial asst, Delta Sigma Theta Sorority, 1992; youth teacher & choir mem, Campus Drive United Methodist Church; bd mem, Minority Leaders & Citizens Coun, 1996-99; Young Bankers Asn, 1996-2000; Consumer Skills Comm, Tex Agr Exten Serv, 1996-2000; Finance Comm, Neighborhood Housing Serv, 1997-99; United Way, Increasing Self-Sufficiency Community, 1998-2000; Heritage Coun, FW Conv & Visitors Bur, 1998. **Honors/Awds:** 50 Future Leaders, Ebony Mag, 1994; Doer's Award, City Ft Worth, 1997.

SIMTON, CHESTER
Librarian. **Personal:** Born Jan 28, 1937, Longstreet, LA; son of Jim Simton and Umie Lee; married Peggy I Nabors, Jul 4, 1978; children: Annelle M & Mary Lee; married Dorothy M Powell, Jun 27, 1959 (divorced 1977); children: Jessica & Jennifer. **Educ:** Univ Calif, Berkeley, BS, 1976, MLS, 1977; Matanuska Susitna Community Col, Palmer, AK; Norton Sound Col, Nome, AK; Univ Anchorage, Anchorage, AK. **Career:** Matanuska Susitna Borough Sch Dist, Palmer, AK, librn media, 1973-; Nome Pub Sch Dist, Nome, AK, libr & media specialist, 1980-83; King Cove City Sch Dist, King Cove, AK, libr & media specialist; Wasilla Pub Libr, dir, currently. **Orgs:** Media Round Table, Alaska Libr Asn, 1987-88; Diversified Occupation Palmer High Sch, 1987-90; Teachers Right Comt, Exec Bd, NEA Alaska, 1989-; multicultural chair, State of Alaaska, 1992-93. **Home Addr:** PO Box 3429, Palmer, AK 99645, **Home Phone:** (907)745-7233. **Business Addr:** Director, Wasilla Public Library, 391 N Main St, Wasilla, AK 99654, **Business Phone:** (907)376-5913.

SINBAD. (DAVID ATKINS)
Actor, comedian, talk show host. **Personal:** Born Nov 10, 1956, Benton Harbor, MI; son of Donald Atkins and Martha; married Meredith Fuller, Jan 1, 1985 (divorced 1992); children: Paige & Royce. **Educ:** Univ Denver, attended,1974-78. **Career:** Actor, currently; Opening act for music groups such as the Pointer Sisters, Kool & the Gang; Actor: The Redd Foxx Show; The Cosby Show; ADifferent World; Hollywood Squares; The Sinbad Show, 1994; Cosby; Show time at the Apollo, host; Films: House guest, 1995; withPhil Hartman, 1995; Cherokee Kid; Jingle All the Way with Arnold Schwarzenegger, 1996; Hansel & Gretel, 2002; Leila, 2006; Stompin, 2007; Slacker Cats, 2007, Cuttin Da Mustard,2008; VIBE, tv talk show,host. **Honors/Awds:** Star Search, seven time winner. **Special Achievements:** Author, Sinbad's Guide to Life. **Military Serv:** USAF, 1983.

SINCLAIR, BENITO A
Engineer. **Personal:** Born Aug 18, 1931, Colon, Panama; son of Arthur Donovan and Isabel Darshville; married Helen Rahn Sinclair, Sep 7, 1963; children: Marcia Yvette & Shana Elida. **Educ:** Calif Polytechnic State Univ, San Luis Obispo, CA, BS, archit eng, 1957. **Career:** B A Sinclair & Assoc Inc, Los Angeles, CA, pres & chief exec officer, 1964-. **Orgs:** Dir, Structural Engrs Asn Calif, 1982-84; Los Angeles city comnr, Building & Safety, 1984-94; founding mem, pres, Los Angeles Coun Black Prof Engrs; founding mem, pres, Calif Asn Minority Consult Engrs; Nat Asn Black Consult Engrs; Am Soc Civil Engrs; Am Coun Eng Companies; Earthquake Eng Res Inst. **Honors/Awds:** Distinguished Alumnus, Calif Polytech Univ Arch Engr, 1969;

Outstanding Contributions to Community, Am Soc Civil Engrs, 1976; Excellence in Design, AM Inst Architects, 1984; Tom Bradley Terminal, LAX, Prestressed Conc Inst, 1987; Special Honoree, Los Angeles Coun Black Prof Engrs, 1987. **Special Achievements:** First Black Graduate from School of Architecture and Environmental Design, Calif Polytechnic State Univ, 1957. **Business Addr:** President, Chief Executive Officer, B A Sinclair & Assoc Inc, 5601 W Wash Blvd, PO Box 29339, Los Angeles, CA 90016, **Business Phone:** (213)933-5581.

SINCLAIR, CLAYTON
Lawyer. **Personal:** Born Jul 4, 1933, Wadesboro, NC; married Jeanette B. **Educ:** Univ Maine, BA, 1955; Howard Univ Law Sch, LLB, 1960. **Career:** O'Donald & Schwartz NYC, atty, 1960-68; NY State Banking, Dept NYC, asst coun, 1968-69; Scott Paper Co, 1969-70; Goodis, Greenfield & Mann Phila, atty, 1970-71; Patterson Parks & Franklin Atlanta, atty, 1971-76; Sinclair & Dixon, sr partner, 1976-; pvt pract atty, currently. **Orgs:** Am Bar Asn; Nat Bar Asn; Atlanta Bar Asn; GA Trial Lawyers Asn; State Bar Ga. **Business Addr:** Attorney, 5095 Dublin Dr SW, Atlanta, GA 30331.

SINCLAIR, MICHAEL GLENN (MIKE SINCLAIR)
Football player, football coach. **Personal:** Born Jan 31, 1968, Galveston, TX; married Betty, May 25, 1991; children: Michael, Michaela & Johnnie Glenn. **Educ:** Eastern NMex Univ, BS, phys educ. **Career:** Football player (retired), Football coach; Seattle Seahawks, defensive end, 1991-2001; Sacramento Surge, 1992; Philadelphia Eagles, defensive end, 2002; W Tex A&M Univ, asst coach defensive line, 2005-06; Hamburg Sea Devils, defensive line coach, 2007; Montreal Alouettes, defensive line coach, currently. **Honors/Awds:** Steve Largent Award, 1998. **Business Addr:** Defensive Line Coach, Montreal Alouettes, 4545 Pierre-de-Coubertin CP 65 Succursale M, Montreal, QC, Canada H1V 3L6, **Business Phone:** (514)253-0008.

SINCLAIR, MIKE. See SINCLAIR, MICHAEL GLENN.

SINDLER, MICHAEL H.
Executive director. **Personal:** Born May 15, 1943, District of Columbia; married Louise Bates. **Educ:** Georgetown Sch Foreign Serv, BS, 1965; Georgetown Law Sch, JD, 1968. **Career:** DC Legislation & Opinions Div, asst corp coun, 1969-73; Motor Vehicles DC, asst dir, 1973-74, spl asst dir, 1974-. **Orgs:** Washington Bar Asn; DC Bar Asn; Fed Bar Asn; DC Munic Officers Club, 1973-. **Honors/Awds:** American Jurisprudence Award. **Business Addr:** 301 C St NW, Washington, DC 20001.

SINGH, DR. RAJENDRA P
Educator, dentist. **Personal:** Born May 6, 1934, Mnagar; married Sneh P; children: Ram C & David A. **Educ:** Agra Univ, BSci, 1952; King George's Dent Col & Hosp, BDS, 1964; Guggenhiem Dent Ctr, Cert Clin Dent, 1966; Univ Pittsburgh, Grad Studies Endodontics, 1975; Ohio State Univ, ScD, 2000. **Career:** King George's Dent Hosp, house surgeon, 1964-65; Murry & Leonie Dent Clin fel dent staff, 1965-66; Howard Univ Col Dent, instr, 1969-77, asst prof, 1977-. **Orgs:** Res assoc, oral surgery, NJ Col Dent, 1966-69; Am Dent Asn, 1970-; Am Asn Endodontists, 1975-; lectr, Adv Sci, 1978-79; Black Brotherhood Week Key Jr High 1983; nominee, judge Montgomery County Debating Contest, 1985; Wash DC Dent Soc, 1977; Edward C Penne Endodontic Club, 1978; official deleg, Citizen Ambassador Prog-People People Int; Am Col Dent, fel; Am Soc Laser Med & Surg. **Honors/Awds:** Outstanding Clinical Teacher, Stud Coun Col Dent, 1973-74; Louise C Ball Fellowship Award, Col Dentists, 1974-77; Outstanding Faculty Award, Stud Coun Dent, 1973, 1989. **Special Achievements:** Author: "Endodontic Considerations of Tricanaled Mand Premolar," Journal of MAR Dental Assn, 1987; "Evaluation of Optimal Site Maxi Teeth," thesis, Library of Congress, 1977. **Home Addr:** 8822 Sleppy Hollow Lane, Potomac, MD 20854.

SINGLETARY, DEBORAH DENISE
Artist, consultant. **Personal:** Born Apr 27, 1952, Brooklyn, NY; daughter of Peter and Doris. **Educ:** Hunter Col, attended, 1973. **Career:** Elva McZeal Comput Learning Ctr, instr, 1996-; Mama Found Arts, prog coordr, 2001-; Vision Carriers, painter & multimedia artist, pres, currently. **Orgs:** Coord coun, Entitled Black Women Artists, 1999-; Nat Coun Artists, 2000-. **Honors/Awds:** Exemplary Service Award, US Dept Justice Off USA, 2001; Award, Art Matters Inc. **Special Achievements:** Artwork in permanent collection of Schomburg Ctr for Research in Black Culture; exhibition in Black NY Artists of the 20th Century, Schomburg Ctr; illustrations in NY Magazine; One Woman Exhibition, Langston Hughes Community Library & Cultural Ctr; creator, facilitator, Free the Closest Artist! & Liberation Arts! workshops. **Home Addr:** 360 Clinton Ave Suite 1R, Brooklyn, NY 11238. **Business Addr:** President, Painter & Multi-Media Artist, Vision Carriers, 360 Clinton Ave Suite 1R, Brooklyn, NY 11238, **Business Phone:** (718)398-4616.

SINGLETARY, INEZ M.
Government official. **Personal:** Born Jul 1, 1923, New York, NY; daughter of Edison Maloney and Adina; married Samuel P; children: Shauna K Singletary Alami & Samuel P III. **Educ:** Hunter Col, BA, MA. **Career:** PS 99 Bronx, sch teacher, 1947-64; Ferris Ave Neighborhood Ctr, exec dir,1965-68; White Plains Comm Action Prog Inc, exec dir, 1968-69; Day Care Coun Westchester Inc, exec dir, 1969-81; Col New Rochelle, Grad Sch Educ,prof; W County Dept Comm Ment Health, dir comm rel, currently. **Orgs:** Invaluable Serv Comt Yonkers Child Care Assn Yonkers NY, 1975; ch per, spec events, Child Care Coun Westchester Inc; co found & pres, NY State Child Care Cord Coun Inc; bd mem, Oak Lane Child Care Ctr Inc; Child Place Plz Albany NY; ch per, Westchester Women's Coun; Task Force Worship; ch per admin brd, Pleasant ville United Meth Church; ch per, Brd Women's News. **Honors/Awds:** Outstanding Serv Humanity, Church Our Savior United Meth Church Yonkers NY, 1971; Woman of the Year, County Westchester, 1979; Sojourner Truth Award, Natl Assn Negro Bus & Prof Women Inc West County Club, 1981. **Business Addr:** Director of Community Relations, West County Department Committee for Mental Health, 112 E Post Rd, White Plains, NY 10601, **Business Phone:** (914)995-5250.

SINGLETARY, REGGIE LESLIE
Executive, football player. **Personal:** Born Jan 17, 1964, Whiteville, NC; son of Dan Arron and Notredane Pridgen; married Janice Jeffires, May 21, 1988; children: 2. **Educ:** NC State Univ, attended. **Career:** Football player (retired), employee; Philadelphia Eagles, guard & offensive tackle, 1986-90; Gen Elec, Burlington, staff, currently. **Honors/Awds:** Dick Christy Award, NC State Univ, 1985; All Rookie Team Defense, NFL, 1986. **Home Addr:** 3434 N NC 49, Burlington, NC 27217, **Home Phone:** (336)578-3614. **Business Addr:** Staff, General Electric Company, 510 E Agency Rd, West Burlington, IA 52655-1649, **Business Phone:** (319)753-8400.

SINGLETON, ALSHERMOND GLENDALE
Football player. **Personal:** Born Aug 7, 1975, Newark, NJ. **Educ:** Temple Univ, BS, sport recreation mgt. **Career:** Tampa Bay Buccaneers, linebacker, 1997-2002; Dallas Cowboys, linebacker, 2003-06; free agent, currently.

SINGLETON, BENJAMIN, SR.
Police officer, business owner. **Personal:** Born Dec 17, 1943, Summerville, SC; son of Clement Addison Sr and Catherine Fludd; married Dorothy Abraham, May 2, 1964; children: Benjamin Jr. **Educ:** Voc Training, Columbia SC, Cert, 1977-81; Atlanta Univ, Criminal Justice Inst, Miami FL, Cert, 1985. **Career:** Dorchester County Sheriffs Dept, St George SC, lt, deputy sheriff, 1971-; Knights ville Dry Cleaners, Summer ville SC, owner, 1986. **Orgs:** Life mem, Cannan United Methodist Church, United Methodist Mens Club; New Eden Lodge 32, 1984; Nat Asn Advan Colored People, 1985;, The Upper Dorchester Civic Club, 1985; vpres, Palmetto State Law Enforcement Office Asn, 1985-87, pres, 1987-89; The First Congressional Dist Black Caucus, 1986-90; SC Attorney General Adv Bd State Grand Jury, 1988-92, Univ SC Police Census, 1988-92. **Honors/Awds:** Sponsor, Ann sr Citizens Dinner Tri-County; Co-Sponsor, Dixie League Baseball Team Community, 1967-; Co-Founder, The Berkeley-Dorchester Chap PSLEOA, 1977; Outstanding Servs, Palmetto State Law Enforcement, 1982; Sponsor, Dixie League Baseball Team, 1984; Speaker varied church youth groups on law enforcement, 1985-90; Community Serv, Berkeley-Dorchester Chap, 1989.

SINGLETON, CHRIS
Football player, sports manager. **Personal:** Born Feb 20, 1967, Parsippany, NJ. **Educ:** Univ Ariz, sociol maj, 1989. **Career:** Football player (retired), New Eng Patriots, outside linebacker, 1990-93; Miami Dolphins, 1993-96; Vanderbilt Univ, asst equipment mgr/football, currently. **Honors/Awds:** Two-time All-Pac 10 selection; Second-team All-Am, Sporting News, 1989. **Business Addr:** Assistant Equipment Manager/Football, Vanderbilt University, Vanderbilt Athletic Department, 2601 Jess Neely Dr, Nashville, TN 37212, **Business Phone:** (615)322-4117.

SINGLETON, CHRISTOPHER VERDELL
Baseball player, media executive. **Personal:** Born Aug 15, 1972, Martinez, CA; married LaShunda Gray. **Educ:** Univ Nev. **Career:** Baseball player (retired), Media Executive; Chicago White Sox, outfielder, 1999-2001; Baltimore Orioles, ctr fielder, 2001; Oakland Athletics, ctr fielder, 2003; Pittsburgh Pirates, 2004; Tampa Bay Devil Rays, ctrfielder, 2005; Chicago White Sox, commentator, 2006-07, color analyst, 2006-08; ESPN, baseball tonight, currently.

SINGLETON, ERNIE
Executive, president (organization). **Personal:** Born in New Orleans, LA. **Career:** Radio Sta, New Orleans, host; Radio Sta, Jackson ville, host, music dir, prog dir, morning newsman; Fantasy, Mercury Recs, regional prom mgr; Casablanca Recs, regional prom mgr, nat prom dir; Poly Gram Recs, nat prom dir, 1978-83; Warner Brothers Recs, sr vpres, Reprise Recs Prom, staff head, 1987; Urban & Jazz Music Prom, v pres, Black Music Div, pres, 1990-; MCA Recs, Black Music Div, black music prom nat dir. **Orgs:** Young Black Prgm Coalition, 1989; Founding mem. 1990. **Honors/Awds:** Bobby Poe Executive of the Year Award, 1985; Award of Excellence, Young Black Programmers Coalition, 1987; Executive of the Year, Urban Network, Impact, Black Radio Exclusive, 1990.

SINGLETON, HAROLD, III
Financial manager. **Personal:** Born Apr 11, 1962, Chicago, IL; son of Harold Singleton Jr and Ruth Ann Singleton; married Saundra R, Mar 18, 1989; children: James D Butler, Juliana L Singleton & Deana J Singleton. **Educ:** Ill Inst Technol, BS, chem eng, 1983; Univ Chicago, MBA, finance, 1989. **Career:** Atlantic Richfield Co, assoc chem engr, 1980-83; RR Donnelley & Sons, mfg supvr, 1984-90; First Chicago Corp, corp banking officer, 1990-93; Zaske Sarafa & Assoc, managing analyst, 1993-95; Fifth Third Bank NW Ohio, sr portfolio mgr, 1995-96; Brinson Partners Inc, partner, 1996-2000; Metropolitan West Capital Mgt, sr vpres, 2000-; UBS Global Asset Mgt, exec dir, currently; Perspectives Charter Sch, Oper & Finance Comt, bd dir, currently. **Orgs:** Nat Black MBA Asn, 1990-; Nat Asn Securities Prof, 1992-; Asn Investment Mgt & Res, 1993-; Orange Co Soc Investment Mgr, 2000-; bd dir, Loretto Hosp Found, currently; Investment Analyst Soc Chicago. **Honors/Awds:** Chartered Financial Analyst, Asn Investment Mgt & Res, 1995. **Home Addr:** 5320 Chariton Ave, Los Angeles, CA 90056, **Home Phone:** (323)291-9410. **Business Addr:** Board of directors, Executive Committee, Perspectives Charter School, 1930 S Archer Ave, Chicago, IL 60616, **Business Phone:** (312)225-7400.

SINGLETON, HAROLD DOUGLAS
Clergy, president (organization). **Personal:** Born Dec 10, 1908, Brunswick, GA; son of Joseph and Annie King; married Mary; children: Mercedes, Harold Jr, Alvin, Kenneth, Marilyn, Dwight. **Educ:** Oakwood Col, 1928; Union Col; 7th Day Advent Sem. **Career:** Clergy (retired); Pastor, 1929-42; S Atlantic Conf SDA, pres, 1946-54; NE Conf SDA, pres, 1954-62; N Am Black SDA Prog, dir, 1962-75; clergyman, state man. **Honors/Awds:** The First President of South Atlantic Conference. *

SINGLETON, HARRY M
Lawyer, real estate agent. **Personal:** Born Apr 10, 1949, Meadville, PA; son of Rose A Fucci and GT; divorced; children: Harry Jr & Leah. **Educ:** Johns Hopkins Univ, BA, 1971; Yale Law Sch, JD, 1974. **Career:** Houston & Gardner Law Firm, assoc, 1974-75; Consult, Am Enterprise Inst, 1975; Off Gen Coun/Fed Trade Comn, atty, 1975-76; Covington & Burling Law Firm, assoc, 1976-77; Com Dist Columbia, US House Reps, dep minority coun, 1977-79, minority chief coun & staff dir, 1979-81; Off Congional Affairs, US Dept Com, dep asst secy, 1981-82; US Dept Ed, asst secy, 1982-86; Harry M Singleton & Assocs Inc, pres, 1986-91; Pvt Pract, atty, 1991-; Remax Allegiance, chief exec officer. **Orgs:** Pres bd trustees, Barney Neighborhood House, 1978-80; corp bd dirs, C's Hosp Nat Med Ctr, 1984-88; bd dirs, DC Chap, Republican Nat Lawyers Asn, 1990-91; bd dirs, Coun 100 Black Republicans, 1991-92; DC Black Republican Coun, 1991-93, chmn, 1992-93; Repuban Nat Hisp Assembly DC, 1991-93; DC Republican Comt, 1991-; Republican Nat Comt man, DC, 1992-2000; Republican Nat Comt Exec Coun, 1993-95; Republican Nat Comt, Resolutions Community, 1997-2000; Lions Club, Dist 22-C, 1991-97; Nat chmn, Republican Nat African-Am Coun, 1993-2000; chmn, DC Chap Republican Nat African-Am Coun, 1993-2000; Boys & Girls Clubs Greater Wash, 1994-97. **Honors/Awds:** Distinguished Honorary Alumnus Award, Langston Univ, 1984. **Business Addr:** Attorney, 2300 N St NW Suite 600, Washington, DC 20037, **Business Phone:** (202)291-1781.

SINGLETON, ISAAC, SR.
Clergy. **Personal:** Born Mar 31, 1928, Tallulah, LA; married Pearl B; children: Gloria Hayes, Isaac Jr, Charles, Barbara Edward, Valerie Gaffin, Willie D. **Educ:** Lincoln Christian Col, BA, 1962; Bearea Sem, M Div, 1983. **Career:** Lebanon Baptist Dist Assoc, moderator, 1963-75; Joliet Chapter Oper PUSH, pres, 1974-; Joliet Reg Chamber Com, vpres, 1978-80; Oper Push, nat bd, 1979-; Russell St Church, East St Louis, Ill, pastor; Colette St Church, Danville, Ill, pastor; Mt Zion Baptist Church, pastor, currently. **Orgs:** Pres, PUSH, 1974-; adv bd, Children & Family, Ill, 1980-, chmn, 1986-; vpres, Baptist Gen Congress Chris Ed, 1980-; chmn regional bd, Children & Family, 1983-; pres, Metropolitan Alliance Coun. **Honors/Awds:** Dr Divinity Miller, Univ Plainfield, NJ, 1969; Honor Citizen New Orleans, 1978. **Military Serv:** US-AAF, sgt, 1945-47; Good Conduct. **Business Addr:** Pastor, Mt Zion Baptist Church, 402 Singleton Pl, Joliet, IL 60436, **Business Phone:** (815)723-9445.*

SINGLETON, DR. JAMES LEROY, JR.
Podiatrist. **Personal:** Born Jul 20, 1944, Beaufort, SC; married Maxine; children: Daphne, Andrea & Krystal. **Educ:** Va Union Univ, BS, 1967; Va State Col, 1969; Ohio Col Podiatric Med, DPM, 1973; Sidney A Sumby, resident, 1973-74. **Career:** Richmond Pub Sch System; pvy pract, currently. **Orgs:** Am Podiatry Asn; Mich State Podiatry Asn; dipl, Nat Bd Podiatry Examiner; Va Podiatry Soc; staff mem, Sidney A Sumby Mem Hosp; Norfolk Community Hosp; Med Ctr Hosp; Chesapeake Gen Hosp; Noble Mystic Shrine; 32nd degree Mason; OH Royal Arch Mason; Eureka Lodge 52 Most Worshipful Prince Hall; Alpha Phi

Alpha Frat; bd dir, Jamson Bible Inst. **Honors/Awds:** Christian Physician Award, Jamson Bible Inst, 1975; Podiatric Award, Ohio Col, 1973; Nat Fed, March Dimes, 1974; Pa Podiatry Asn, Surg Seminar, 1972; Pres's Award, 1966. **Home Addr:** 1098 Cascade Blvd, Chesapeake, VA 23324, **Home Phone:** (757)543-4833. **Business Addr:** Physician, 1098 Cascade Blvd, Chesapeake, VA 23324, **Business Phone:** (757)543-4833.

SINGLETON, JAMES MILTON
Government official. **Personal:** Born Aug 10, 1933, Hazelhurst, MS; married Allie Mae Young; children: James Jr & Jacquelyn. **Educ:** Southern Univ Baton Rouge LA, BS; Xavier Univ, New Orleans, health planning; Loyola Univ; Univ Okla. **Career:** Government official (retired); Orleans Parish Sch Bd, teacher, 1956-70; Nat Urban Health, New Orleans, consult, 1970-71; City New Orleans Mayors Off, spec consult health, 1971-78; City New Orleans, city councilman, 1978, council pres. **Orgs:** Pres, Cent City Econ Corp, 1965-78, Total Comm Action Inc, 1975; chmn, Dryades St YMCA; chmn, Heritage Aq Adv Comm, Bd, LA Health Plan, Total Comm Action Inc, prime mover BOLD. **Honors/Awds:** President Award, Total Comm Action Inc, 1976; President Award, Dryades St,YMCA, 1977. **Military Serv:** AUS, lt col, 16 yrs.

SINGLETON, JOHN (JOHN DANIEL SINGLETON)
Screenwriter, movie director. **Personal:** Born Jan 6, 1968, Los Angeles, CA; son of Danny and Sheila Ward; married Akosua Busia, Jan 1, 1999 (divorced 1997); children: 5. **Educ:** Univ Southern Calif, Sch Cinema-TV, BA, 1990. **Career:** Films: Boyz N the Hood, writer & dir, 1991; Poetic Justice, producer, 1993; Beverly Hills Cop III, 1994; Higher Learning, producer, 1995; Rosewood, 1997; Woo, exec producer, 1998; Shaft, producer, 2000; Baby Boy, producer & music supvr, 2001; Too Fast Too Furious, dir, 2003; How to Get the Man's Foot Outta Your Ass, 2003; Four Brothers, dir, 2005; Hustle & Flow, producer, 2005; Black Snake Moan, producer, 2006; Illegal Tender, producer, 2007; Videos: "Remember the Time," 1995; Columbia Studios, internship. **Honors/Awds:** New Generation Award, 1991; NYFCC Award, Best New Director, 1991; ShoWest Award, Screenwriter of the Year, 1992; Special Award, Directorial Debut of the Year, 1992; MTV Movie Award, Best New Filmmaker, 1992; Oscar nominee, Best Original Screenplay, Best Dir, both for Boyz N the Hood, 1992; Career Achievement Award, 2001; Star on the Walk of Fame, Motion Picture, 2003; Image Award, Outstanding Directing in a Feature Film/Television Movie, 2006. **Special Achievements:** Youngest person & first African American nominated for Best Director Acad Award, 1992; author of articles: "The Fire This Time," Premiere, 1992; Coolin' with Spike, Essence, 1991; Movie Too Fast Too Furious, Biggest Box Office Opening for an African American Director. **Business Phone:** (310)288-4545.

SINGLETON, JOHN DANIEL. See SINGLETON, JOHN.

SINGLETON, KATHRYN T
Executive. **Personal:** Born May 15, 1951, Orange, TX; daughter of Gertie M and Lester B Sr (deceased); married Lonnie M Cane, Apr 18, 1992. **Educ:** Incarnate Word Col, BS, 1973; State Univ New York, MS, 1977. **Career:** Highsmith Rainey Memorial Hosp, dir, Med Rec Dept, 1973-76; Henry Ford Hosp, asst dir, Med Rec Dept, 1978-79; Univ Wis, asst prof, 1978-80; Holy Cross Hosp, adr, Med Rec Dept, 1980-82; Tascon Inc, pres & ceo, 1982-. **Orgs:** Am Med Rec Asn; exec bd mem, DIS Med Rec Asn; chmn, Hosp Coun Med Rec DRR's Div, NAT Capitol Area; MAR DRR's Div; fac senate mem, Univ Wis; Alpha Kappa Alpha Sorority; chmn, Metrop Baptist Church, New Mem Orientation Prog. **Honors/Awds:** Young Comunity Leadership Award, 1989-91. **Special Achievements:** New Technologies Affecting Medical Records, J Am Med Rec Asn, 1987; Portable Information Technology, J Am Med Rec Asn, 1987. **Business Addr:** Chief Executive Officer, Tascon Inc, 1803 Research Blvd Suite 305, Rockville, MD 20850-3155, **Business Phone:** (301)315-9000.

SINGLETON, KENNETH WAYNE
Baseball player, television broadcaster. **Personal:** Born Jun 10, 1947, New York, NY; married Suzanne Molino; children: 4. **Educ:** Hofstra Univ, Hempstead, NY. **Career:** Baseball player (retired), commentator; New York Mets, outfielder, 1970-71; Montreal Expos, outfielder, 1972-74; Baltimore Orioles, outfielder, 1975-84; Sports Network Canada, analyst; New York Yankees, YES Network, commentator, currently. **Honors/Awds:** American League All-Star Team, 1977, 1979, 1981; Roberto Clemente Award, 1982; World Series champion, 1983. **Business Phone:** (646)487-3600.

SINGLETON, LEROY, SR.
Funeral director. **Personal:** Born Oct 8, 1941, Hempstead, TX; son of Oscar Singleton (deceased) and Rosie Lee Singleton-Moore; married Willie E Franklin, Apr 25, 1977; children: LaRonda K, Leroy Jr, Kaye, Erica, Kareen & Garard W. **Educ:** Prairie View A&M Univ, Prairie View, TX, BS, 1968; Prairie View A&M Univ, Prairie View, TX, MEd, 1971; Commonwealth Sch Mortician, Houston, TX, dipl, mortuary sci, 1982. **Career:** Dallas ISD, Dallas, TX, teacher, 1968-69; Prairie View A&M Univ, Prairie View, TX, assoc teacher, 1971-75; Singleton Funeral Home, Hempstead, TX, owner, mgr, 1982-; mayor, Hempstead, TX, 1984-; Singleton Trucking, owner & mgr, 1975-82. **Orgs:** Am Legion Post 929; 1966-; charter mem, Lion Tamer, Lion's Club, 1972-; Lone Star Masonic Lodge No 85; 1980-; Tex State Review Bd, 1986-89; Appraisal Licensing & Cert Bd, 1991-94; Independent Funeral Dirs Asn, Texas Independent Funeral Dirs Asn; Kiwanis Int; Nat Conf Black Mayors, World Conf Mayors; Am Personnel & Guidance Asn; Am Col Personnel Asn; Admin Stud Personnel; Piarie View Alumni Asn; Asn for Counr Educ & Supv; Am Sch Counr Asn; Tex Admin Stud Personnel; Phi Delta Kappan; Omega Psi Phi Fraternity Inc; Tex Coalition Black Democrats; Nat Asn Advan Colored People. **Honors/Awds:** Plaque, Boy Scouts Am, 1985; Plaque, Vocational Guidance Serv, 1986; Houston Chap Community Serv Award, Nat Tech Asn; Outstanding Serv Award, First Black Mayor Hempstead, TX. **Special Achievements:** First Black Mayor, Lone Star Lodge No 85, 1985. **Military Serv:** USN, E-4, 1962-65; Navy Unit Citation, 1964; Expeditionary Serv Medal. **Home Addr:** PO Box 344, Hempstead, TX 77445. **Business Addr:** Manager, Owner, Singleton Funeral Home, 616 7th St, Hempstead, TX 77445, **Business Phone:** (979)826-2425.

SINGLETON, NATE
Football player, athletic trainer. **Personal:** Born Jul 5, 1968, New Orleans, LA. **Educ:** Grambling State Univ. **Career:** Football player (retired), trainer; San Francisco 49ers, wide receiver, 1993-96; Baltimore Ravens, 1997; Mackie Shilstone's PEP Prog, athletic trainer, currently. **Honors/Awds:** Newcomer of the Yr, Grambling Univ; Bayou Classics Most Valuable Player, 1991; NFL Superbowl Champion. **Business Phone:** (504)842-9503.

SINGLETON, RICKEY
Executive. **Personal:** Born Nov 13, 1959, Chicago, IL; son of Isaac and Juanita; married Diane, Aug 4, 1995; children: Sean Marcus, Corey & Taranikqa. **Educ:** Word Faith Sch Ministry, DDiv, 1996. **Career:** South End Conservatory Music, owner/teacher, 1979-84; Word Faith Fel, sr pastor, 1984-96; WEMG-FM Radio, owner/gen mgr, 1993-96; Grace Church Int, sr pastor, 1996-; Richards Ice Cream, chief exec officer, 2000-; King Richard's Deli, chief exec officer, 2002-. **Orgs:** Pres & ceo, Covenant Entrepreneur's Network, 1997-. **Honors/Awds:** Entrepreneur of Year Award, CE Enterprises, 2000. **Special Achievements:** Author: ABC's of Faith, 1986; God Wants You to be an Entrepreneur, 1999; How I Dealt With Monster in My House, 2000; Power to Create Wealth & New Money, 2002; Owner of first FM Radio station owned by Black Church in a major media market in America. **Business Addr:** Pastor, Grace Church International, 13957 S Marquette, Burnham, IL 60633-1914, **Business Phone:** (708)891-4800.

SINGLETON, ROBERT
Association executive, educator. **Personal:** Born Jan 8, 1936, Philadelphia, PA; married Helen; children: Robby, Damani & Malik. **Educ:** Univ Calif, BA, 1960, MA, 1962, PhD, 1983. **Career:** Pac Hist Rev Univ Calif, asst ed, 1958-60; Univ Calif, res asst, 1961-63; Inst Indus Rels Univ Calif, chief res, 1963-64; John Hay Whitney fel, 1963; US Labor Dept, res economist, 1964-66; US Dept Labor Grant support dissertation, 1966; Educ Asn Inc, Wash, consult; Univ Calif, res economist 1967-69; Afro-Am Studies Ctr Univ Calif, dir, prof, 1969-70; Univ Calif, economist, 1969-71; Robert Singleton & Asn, pres, 1979-; Loyola Marymount Univ, prof econs, 1980-, chmn econs, currently. **Orgs:** Founding dir, Univ Calif Los Angeles, Ctr Afro-Am Studies, 1969-71; Social Sci Res Coun, Comt Afro-Am Studies, 1969-75; mem bd dir, Am Educ Finance Asn, 1969-78; founder, chmn J Black Studies mem, bd dir, Am Civil Liberties Union, Southern Calif Chap, 1970-72; Am Econ Asn, 1979-; Western Econ Asn, 1980-; Western Regional Sci Asn, 1986-; Econ Asn, 1988-; Int Atlantic Econ Soc, 1985-; past pres, Univ Calif Los Angeles, Nat Asn Advan Colored People; past chmn, Santa Monica Venice Congress Racial Equality; Chancellors Adv Com Discrimination, Am Civil Liberties Union, Soc Sci Res Coun Com Afro-Am Studies; consultant staff Senate Select Subcom, OP-EN; HEW; Urban Educ Task Force; Nat Urban League Educ Task Force; Nat Asn Planners. **Home Phone:** (323)291-2672. **Business Addr:** Professor, Loyola Marymount University, Economics Department, 1 LMU Dr Suite 4200, Los Angeles, CA 90045-2659, **Business Phone:** (310)338-7373.

SINGLEY, ELIJAH
Librarian. **Personal:** Born Jan 29, 1935, Bessemer, AL; son of Daniel and Singley; married Yvonne Jean; children: Jennifer. **Educ:** Miles Col, AB, 1958; Atlanta Univ, MS, 1963; Sangamon State Univ, MA, 1980. **Career:** Librarian (retired); Va State Col, asst ref librarian, 1960; Ala State Univ, library dir, 1963-71; Lincoln Land Community Col, asst librarian, 1971. **Orgs:** Alpha Phi Alpha Frat; Am Numismatic Asn; Nat Urban League; Ill Sociolog Asn; Ill Libr Asn; White House Conf Libr & Info Serv, 1978-79; Nat Asn Advancement Colored People. **Honors/Awds:** Sports Hall of Fame, Miles Col, Birmingham, Ala, 1981. **Military Serv:** AUS, spec 4th class, 1960-63; Good Conduct Medal; Nat Defense Service Medal. **Home Addr:** 2301 S Noble Ave, Springfield, IL 62704. *

SINGLEY, YVONNE JEAN
School administrator, vice president (organization). **Personal:** Born Jun 18, 1947, Gary, IN; daughter of William Webb and Mary Williams; married Elijah Singley, May 24, 1980; children: Jennifer. **Educ:** Univ Memphis, BA, latin, 1969; Univ Ill, Urbana, MUP, 1974, doctoral studies, educ admin. **Career:** Ind Univ-Northwest, social researcher, 1969-72; Opportunities Indust Ctr, Manpower Training, CETA, educ coordr, 1974-75; Div Voc Rehab, Prog Eval Unit, methods & procedures adv, 1975-78; Ill Dept Pub Aid, Title XX Prog, social service planner, 1978-79; Ill Bd Educ, Acad & Health Affairs, asst dir, 1979-87; Ill Co Col Bd, sr dir stud & inst develop, 1987-; Diversity Works Inc, vpres, currently; Univ Ill, Grad Col, grad fel. **Orgs:** Bd mem, Springfield Urban League, 1977-80; bd mem, Springfield League Women Voters, 1979-84; pres, Access Housing, 1981-86; YMCA, 1985-91; bd mem, Springfield Jr League, 1987-88; vol, Springfield Magical Event, 1991; Kappa Delta Pi, Int Honor Soc, 1995; co-founder, Ill Comt Black Concerns Higher Educ; Am Asn Women Community Cols, State Exec Comt; Phi Theta Kappa Honor Soc; regional dir nat bd, Am Asn Women Community Cols. **Honors/Awds:** Nat Leadership Development Award, AAWCJC, 1991 & 1992; Honorary Membership Award, Ill Co Col Fac Asn, 1991; Program Award, Ill Asn Personalized Learning, 1992; Phi Theta Kappa Honor Soc, 2001. **Home Addr:** 2301 Noble Ave, Springfield, IL 62704. **Business Addr:** Vice President, Diversity Works Inc, 44 E Main St Suite 508, Champaign, IL 61820-3649, **Business Phone:** (217)378-5135.

SINKFORD, REV. WILLIAM GEORGE
Clergy, association executive. **Personal:** Born Jun 15, 1946, San Francisco, CA; son of William Johnson and Kathryn Love; divorced; married Maria Sinkford, Apr 23, 2005; children: William James & Danielle Shay. **Educ:** Harvard Col, BA, 1968; Starr King Sch Ministry, MDiv, 1995; Hon DHumane Letters, Tufts Univ, 2002; Hon D, Meadville/Lombard Theol Sch, 2003. **Career:** Various mgt positions, 1970-80; Sinkford Restorations Inc, 1981-92; Co-ed, Creating Safe Congregations: Toward Ethnic Right Rels; Unitarian Universalist Asn, dir, Congregational Dist Exten Servs, Pres, 2001-. **Honors/Awds:** Black Achievers Industry Award, Harlem YMCA. **Special Achievements:** First African Am pres of Unitarian Universalist Asn. **Business Phone:** (612)722-0040.

SINKLER, DR. GEORGE
Educator. **Personal:** Born Dec 22, 1927, Charleston, SC; son of Moses and Mary; married Albertha Amelia Richardson, Aug 19, 1949; children: Gregory, Kenneth & Georgette Alberta. **Educ:** Augustana Col, Rock Island, IL, BA, 1953; Columbia Univ, MA, 1954, EdD, hist, 1966. **Career:** Augustana Grad Fel, 1953; Bluefield State Col, instr, 1954-55; Prairie View A & M Col, instr assoc prof, 1955-65; John Hay Whitney Opportunity fel, 1958; Danforth fel, 1961, 1964; Morgan State Univ, prof hist, 1965-88, prof emer hist, 1988-; Jackson State Col, vis prof, 1969, post doctoral fel, 1972-73; Frostburg State Univ, vis prof, 1969; Youngstown State Univ, vis prof, 1969; Baltimore Community Col, vis prof, 1972. **Orgs:** Loch Raven United Church, 2000-; Am Hist Asn; Orgn Am Historians; Am Asn Univ Professors; Phi Beta Kappa; Phi Alpha Theta; Kappa Delta; Kappa Delta Pi. **Honors/Awds:** Mr Friendship, 1953; NEH Summer Stipend Col Teacher, 1980. **Special Achievements:** Books: "Racial Attitudes of American President", Doubleday, 1971; articles in OH Hist, Vol 77, 1968; Ind Mag Hist Vol 65, 1969; newspapers Afro-Am Baltimore 1972; Amsterdam News 1976; publication: "What History Tells Us About Presidents and Race" Afro-American Feb 19, 1972; "Blacks and American Presidents" New York Amsterdam News Summer, 1976. **Military Serv:** USN first class stewards mate, 1946-49; Particiapted Navy Golden Gloves; Good Conduct Medal. **Home Addr:** 821 Beaumont Ave, Baltimore, MD 21212. **Business Addr:** Professor Emeritus, Morgan State University, 1700 E Cold Spring Lane, Baltimore, MD 21251, **Business Phone:** (443)885-3185.

SINNETTE, DR. CALVIN HERMAN
Physician. **Personal:** Born Aug 30, 1924, New York, NY; son of Norman J and Frances; married Elinor Kathleen DesVerney; children: Caleen S Jennings & Darryle S Craig. **Educ:** City Col NY, BS, 1945; Howard Univ Col Mede, MD, 1949. **Career:** Physician (retired); Univ Ibadan & Zaria Univ, prof pediat, 1964-70; Columbia Univ, prof pediat, 1970-75; Univ Nairobi Kenya, prof pediat, 1975-77; Sch Med Morehouse Assoc, dean clin affairs, 1977-79; Howard Univ, from asst to vpres health affairs, 1979-88, asst vpres health affairs, 1988-91; emer prof pediat, currently. **Orgs:** Nat Med Asn, 1977; Alpha Omega Alpha, 1978; bd dirs, Trans Africa, 1981-89; Nat Minority Golf Scholar Asn. **Honors/Awds:** Magnificent Prof Award, Howard Univ Col Med, 1996; Leadership Award, Arthur Ashe Athletic Asn, 1998. **Military Serv:** USAF, capt, 2 1/2 yrs. **Home Addr:** 1016 S Wayne St Apt 409, Arlington, VA 22204, **Home Phone:** (703)521-2515.

SINNETTE, ELINOR DESVERNEY
Librarian, college teacher. **Personal:** Born Oct 8, 1925, New York, NY; daughter of James C DesVerney and Elinor Adams Calloway; married Dr Calvin H Sinnette, Nov 19, 1949; children: Caleen Sinnette Jennings, Darryle Sinnette Craig. **Educ:** Hunter Col City Univ NY, AB, 1947; Pratt Inst Sch Libr Serv, MLS, 1959; Columbia Univ Sch Libr Serv, DLS, 1977. **Career:** Librarian (retired); NY City Pub Libr, librarian, 1947-54; NY City Bd Educ, sch librarian, 1960-65; Inst African Studies, Univ Ibadan, Nigeria,

lectr, Ist Librarianship, 1965-69; Ahmadu Bello Univ, Zaria, Nigeria, lectr, 1969-70; Howard Univ, Moorland-Spingarn Res Ctr, 1980; Black Bibliophiles & Collectors, ed. **Orgs:** Oral Hist Asn, Oral Hist Mid Atlantic Region; Black Caucus Am Libr Asn. **Honors/Awds:** Distinguished Serv Award, 92nd Inf Div, World War II Asn, 1986; Forrest C Pogue Award, OHMAR, 1991; BCALA Prof Achievement Award, 1992; Inducted Hall of Fame, Hunter Col, City Univ NY, 2001. **Special Achievements:** Auth: W.E.B. Du Bois Anthology by the Editors of Freedomways, Beacon Press, 1970; Arthur Alfonso Schomburg, Black Bibliophile and Collector, A Biography, The New York Public Library and Wayne State Univ Press, Detroit MI, 1989; Preservers of Black History, Wash, DC, Howard University Press, 1990; Oral History, publ in The Harvard Guide to Afa History, 2001; The Brownies Book; A Pioneer Publication for Children in Black Titan. **Home Addr:** 1016 S Wayne St Apt 409, Arlington, VA 22204-4435. *

SIZEMORE, ANDRIA LYNETTE HALL. See ANDRIA, HALL in the Obituaries section.

SKEENE, LINELL DE-SILVA
Physician. **Personal:** Born Nov 6, 1938, Brooklyn, NY. **Educ:** Temple Univ, BA, 1959; Meharry Med Col, MD, 1966. **Career:** Maimonides Med Ctr, attending surgeon; Metro Hosp, 1971-72; NY Med Col, instr surgeon, 1971-72. **Orgs:** AMA; Am Med Women's Asn; NY St Med Soc; Nat Coun Negro Women; Nat Advan Asn Colored People. **Honors/Awds:** Outstanding Young Women of Am, 1974. **Business Addr:** 25 Dunhill Rd, New Hyde Pk, NY 11040, **Business Phone:** (718)240-6504.

SKELETON, DEBRA RENEE WILSON. See WILSON, DEBRA.

SKINNER, BRIAN
Basketball player. **Personal:** Born May 19, 1976, Temple, TX; son of James Skinner and Gladys; married Rebecca, Jan 9, 1998. **Educ:** Baylor Univ, environ studies, 1998. **Career:** Los Angeles Clippers, forward, 1998-01; Cleveland Cavaliers, forward-center, 2001-02; Milwaukee Bucks, 2002-03, 2006-07; Philadelphia76ers, forward-center, 2004-05; Sacramento Kings, 2004-05; Portland Trail Blazers, 2006; Phoenix Suns, 2007-08; Los Angeles Clippers, free agt, currently. **Honors/Awds:** World Championships, gold medal, 1996; World University Games, gold medal, 1997. **Business Phone:** 888-895-8662.*

SKINNER, BYRON R
College administrator. **Career:** Univ Maine Augusta, pres, 1983-85.

SKINNER, EUGENE W.
Educator. **Personal:** Born Jul 25, 1931, Bristow, VA; son of Harrison E Sr and Doris Thomas; married Rosamond Anderson; children: Inez India, Eugene Jr, Carl Edward & Paul Wesley. **Educ:** VA Union Univ, BS, 1957; Howard Univ, MS 1967; Am Univ MD, Advan studies. **Career:** Educator (retired); Lynchburg VA, science teacher, coach; Fairfax County Sch Bd, sci supvr; Va Union Univ, asst coach, 1958; Luther Jackson HS, chmn sci dept, 1959-60, asst football coach & asst baseball coach, 1959; Vernon HS, chmn sci, 1960-67; Fort Hunt HS, asst prin, 1981-85; Hayfield Sec Sub Sch, prin. **Orgs:** Nat Asn Advan Colored People; Urban League; Fairfax Hosp Assoc; pres, Randall Civic Assoc, 1969-; founder & pres, Psi Nu Chap Omega Psi, 1971; pres, Va Union Athletic Alumni Assoc; Manassas Elks; Focus Club; Dept Progressive Club; Fairfax Retired Teachers Asn, 1988; Fairfax Retired Coaches & Administrators Asn, 1989. **Honors/Awds:** Outstanding Sci Teacher, 1961; Omega Man of the Year, Psi Nu Chap, 1971; Top Ten Class Leadership Sch; Scroll Honor, Psi Nu Chap, 1981; 25 Year Certificate of Award, Omega Psi Phi, Va Union Univ, 1989. **Military Serv:** AUS sfc 1953-55.

SKINNER, DR. EWART C.
Educator. **Personal:** Born Jan 2, 1949. **Educ:** Univ Hartford, Hartford, CT, 1969; Tarkio Col, Tarkio, MO, BA, 1971; Am Univ Cairo, Cairo, Egypt, MA, 1974; MI State Univ, East Lansing, MI, PhD, 1984. **Career:** Self-employed media consult, Trinidad & Tobago, 1975-79; UNESCO, Trinidad& Tobago, West Indies, 1987; MI State Univ, East Lansing, MI, instr, 1983-84; Purdue Univ, West Lafayette, IN, asst prof, 1984-; Caribbean Mass Media Systems & Int Media, specialist; Bowling Green State Univ, assoc prof Telecommunications, currently. **Orgs:** Int Asn Mass Communs Res; Int Commun Asn; Int Peace Res Asn; Semiotics Soc Am; Asn Educ Jour & Mass Commun; Caribbean Studies Asn. **Special Achievements:** Poet. "Empirical Research on Mass Communication and Cultural Domination in the Caribbean." In Humphrey Regis (Ed.) Culture and Mass Communication in the Caribbean. Gainsville, FL: University of Florida Press. **Business Addr:** Associate Professor of Telecommunications, Bowling Green State University, 323 West Hall, Bowling Green, OH 43403-0001, **Business Phone:** (419)372-2531.

SKINNER, ROBERT L, JR.
Airline executive. **Personal:** Born Oct 5, 1941, Chicago, IL; son of Willie Louise Jemison and Robert L Sr. **Educ:** Chicago City Col, Chicago IL, attended, 1959-61; Univ Wis, Madison WI, attended, 1963; Northeastern Univ, Boston, MA, attended, 1979. **Career:** Am Airlines, Chicago IL, passenger serv rep, 1965-66, passenger serv mgr, 1966-69, sales rep, 1969-77, Boston, MA, supvr flight serv, 1977-80, Chicago IL, acct exec, 1980-84, mgr conv & co meeting sales, 1984-88, Rochester, MN, gen mgr, 1987-91, gen mgr, Indianapolis, IN, 1991-96; Atlanta, GA, gen mgr, 1996-2001; Conv/Co Meeting Sales, Chicago, Ill, specialist, 1984-87. **Orgs:** Bd dir, Rochester Conv & Visitors Bur, 1989-91; Chicago Soc Asn Exec; Chicago Area Meeting Planners Int. **Military Serv:** USAF, Airman First Class, 1961-64. **Home Addr:** 175 N Harbor Dr Suite 3904, Chicago, IL 60601-7348, **Home Phone:** (312)819-0366.

SKIPPER, CLARENCE
Restaurateur. **Personal:** Born Jul 5, 1971, Lafayette, LA; son of Philomena and Clarence Skipper; children: Travion. **Educ:** Southern Univ, A&M Col, BS, Comput Sci. **Career:** JC Penney Life, Systs analyst, 1994-96; Neiman Marcus, programmer analyst, 1996; Midwest Consult, contract programmer, 1996-97; Systware, contract programmer, 1997-98; chief exec officerle Cafe, owner, currently.

SKLAREK, NORMA MERRICK (NORMA MERRICK-FAIRWEATHER)
Architect. **Personal:** Born Apr 15, 1928, New York, NY; daughter of Walter and Amelia Willoughby; married Cornelius Welch, Oct 12, 1985; children: Gregory Ransom, David Fairweather & Susan. **Educ:** Columbia Univ, BArch, 1950. **Career:** Architect (deceased); Skidmore Owings Merrill, archit, 1955-60; New York Col, arch faculty mem, 1957-60; Gruen Assoc, dir arch, 1960-80; UCLA, arch fac mem, 1972-78; Welton Becket Assocs, vpres, 1980-85; Own architectural firm, 1985-89; Siegel-Sklarek-Diamond, prin; The Jerde Partnership, prin, 1989-92. **Orgs:** Commr Calif Bd Arch Examrs, 1970-; vpres, CC & AIA 1973-; fel, Am Inst Architects, 1980; dir, USC Arch Guild, 1984-87; master juror NCARB; CA Architects Bd; chair, AIA Nat Ethics Coun. **Honors/Awds:** Professional Achievement Award, YWCA Los Angeles, 1987, 1989; Keynote Speaker Award YWCA Cincinnati, 1990; Whitney M Young Jr Award, Am Inst Architects, 2008. **Special Achievements:** First African Woman Licensed as an architect in the US; First Arican female Fellow of AIA; First African-American woman director of architecture at Gruen and Associates in Los Angeles.

SLADE, CHRIS. See SLADE, CHRISTOPHER CARROLL.

SLADE, CHRISTOPHER CARROLL (CHRIS SLADE)
Football player. **Personal:** Born Jan 30, 1971, Newport News, VA; married Talisa Marie; children: Soreah. **Educ:** Univ Va. **Career:** Football player(retired); New Eng Patriots, linebacker, 1993-2000; Carolina Panthers, linebacker, 2001. **Honors/Awds:** Defensive Most Valuable Player, 1776 Quarterback Club, 1994; Pro Bowl Alternate, 1995; Pro Bowl Selection, 1997.

SLADE, DR. JOHN BENJAMIN
Physician. **Personal:** Born Dec 20, 1950, Columbus, OH; son of John Benjamin Slade Sr and Betty Buckner; married Rischa Ann Williams, Mar 8, 1980; children: Danielle & Alana. **Educ:** US Air Force Acad, BS, 1972; Case Western Res Univ, MD, 1978. **Career:** USAF, Beale AFB, Family Practice Clinic, chief, 1981-84, David Grant Med Ctr, Travis AFB, family practice staff, 1984-86, Iraklion Air Sta, Crete, Greece, chief, hosp servs, 1986-88, Sch Aerospace Med, fel, hyperbaric med, 1988-89, David Grant Med Ctr, Travis AFB, chair, Dept Hyperbaric Med, 1989-96, chief med staff, 1996-97; Hyperbaric Med, Doctors Med Ctr, San Pablo, CA, assoc med dir, med dir, currently; Northbay Ctr Wound Care, hyperbaric physician. **Orgs:** Am Acad Family Pract, 1981-; Aerospace Med Asn, 1989-; Wound Healing Soc, 1990-; treas, Undersea & Hyperbaric Med Soc, pres, 1999-2000; Hyperbaric Oxygen Ther & Educ Comt. **Military Serv:** USF, col, 1972-97, retired; Meritorious Service Medal, 1988; Legion of Merit, 1997. **Home Addr:** 131 Blackwood Ct, Vacaville, CA 95688-1058. **Business Addr:** Medical Director, Hyperbaric Medicine, Doctors Medical Center, 131 Blackwood Ct, Vacaville, CA 95688-1058, **Business Phone:** (510)235-3483.

SLADE, KAREN E
Executive. **Personal:** Born Oct 18, 1955, Cleveland, OH; daughter of Charles and Violette Gohagan. **Educ:** Ky State Univ, BS, 1977; Pepperdine Univ, MBA, 1991. **Career:** Xerox Corp, sr acct exec, 1978, mkt consult, proj mgr, dealer sales mgr, regional sales mgr, 1988-89; Taxi Productions Inc, vpres & gen mgr, 1989, KJLH-FM, Radio, sr vpres & gen mgr, currently. **Orgs:** Bd mem, Urban League, 1989-95; MOSTE, mentoring program w/junior high school students, 1989-; Black Media Network, 1989-; Nat Asn Black Owned Broadcasters, 1989-. **Honors/Awds:** Peabody Award, 1992; Image Award, Recognition of Broadcast Achievement, NAACP, 1993. **Business Addr:** Senior Vice President, General Manager, Taxi Productions Inc., KJLH-FM, 161 N La Brea Ave, Inglewood, CA 90301, **Business Phone:** (310)330-2200.

SLADE, PHOEBE J.
Sociologist, educator. **Personal:** Born Oct 17, 1935, New York; married Robert H; children: Robert & Paula. **Educ:** Columbia Univ, EdD, 1976, MA, 1960; Jersey City State Col, BS, 1958; Bellevue Nursing Sch, RN, 1957; Hunter Col, 1954. **Career:** Educator (retired); New York City Dept Health, public health nurse, 1959-61; New Jersey State Dept Health, consult, 1961-63; Jersey City State Col, asst prof, 1963-74, assoc prof, 1975-77, prof, 1977, chair, sociol & anthrop dept, 1985, prof emer, currently; Hunter Col, lectr, 1965-71, chmn, health scis dept, 1968-69; asst dir, dorm, 1966-67. **Orgs:** Jersey City State Col Fac Asn, 1963-; Asn NJ Col Fac, 1963-; Delta Sigma Theta, 1954-; Am Pub Health Asn, 1962-; Nat Coun Family Rels, 1966-; Tri-State Coun Family Rels, 1968-; Royal Soc Health, London, England,1969-; Nat Educ Asn, 1972-; Bd Ethics, Teaneck, 1976-; Jersey State Col,1975-; Archdiocean Bd Educ, 1976-; vpres, Hawthorne's PTA, 1977; Afro-Amer Comm Polit Act, 1985; Mayors Spl Task Force Res, Teaneck, 1985; Teaneck & Together, 1973-; Mayors Task Force Ed, Jersey City, 1972-; Jersey City Bd Ed, 1971-74; Jersey City Pub Lib, 1970-74; Jersey City Com Criminal Justice, 1970-75; ANSSCF; HCEA; Nat Geog Soc; Mus Nat Hist; New Jersey State Bd Human Servs, 1991-; Nat Asn Advan Colored People, 1960-; Zonta Int, 1994-. **Honors/Awds:** Pi Lamda Theta, National Scholastic Organization for Women in Education,1967; Citation Award, Comm Civil Rights Met, New York, 1963; Jersey City Public Library, Board of Trustee's Service Award, 1975; Tribute to Mother's Award, Hudson County Sickle Cell Anemia Asn, 1989; Teaneck Pioneer Recognition Award, Teaneck Centennial Comt 100, 1995. **Special Achievements:** Author: "Evaluating Today's Schools: Relevancy of the Open Classroom," NJE Pac, May 1978; co-author: The Complete Guide to Selected Health and Health Related Careers, 1980. **Home Phone:** (201)833-9269. **Business Addr:** Professor Emeriti, Jersey City State College, Department of Sociology, 2039 Kennedy Blvd, Jersey City, NJ 07305-1527, **Business Phone:** (201)200-2552.

SLADE, DR. PRISCILLA DEAN
School administrator. **Personal:** Children: Al & Maurice. **Educ:** Miss State Univ, BS, bus admin; Jackson State Univ, MS, prof acct; Univ Tex, Austin, PhD, acct. **Career:** Tougaloo Col, asst prof acct, 1979-80; Jackson State Univ, MPA coordr, 1980-81; Univ Tex, asst acct instr, 1981-85; FL A&M Univ, asst prof acct, 1985-91; Tex Southern Univ, assoc prof acct, 1991, chair Acct Dept, 1991-93, Jesse H Jones Sch Bus, dean, 1993-99, actg pres, 1999, pres, currently. **Orgs:** Bd mem, Quality Review Oversight Bd State TX; bd mem, Finance Comn, Houston Area Urban League; bd mem, Am Asn Col Sch Bus; Am Acct Asn; Am Asn Univ Women; Am Coun Educ; Am Soc Women Acct; Beta Alpha Psi; Coun Pub Univ Pres & Chancellors; Nat Asn Equal Opportunity Higher Educ; Prof Black Women's Enterprise; bd dirs, Fed Reserve Bank-Houston Br; Greater Houston Partnership; Houston 2012 Found; Houston Technol Ctr; INROADS Houston Inc.; Jr Achievement; The Houston Forum; YMCA the Greater Houston Area; HISD HU-LINC Governing Bd; The Telecom Opportunity Inst. **Honors/Awds:** Recognition Awd, 1998; Texas Health Care Financing Admin & the Health Resources and Service Admin, Houston Headliners of the Century Awd, Houston Area Urban League, 1999; Appreciation Awd, Black Male Initiative, 1999; Young Eagles Award, Prof Black Women's Enterprise, 1999; Enchancing Black Leadership Award, Nat Black MBA Asn, Inc, 1999; Outstanding Leadership & Service Appreciation Award, Col of Pharmacy & Health Scis, 1999; Appreciation Awd, The Nat Asn Math Inc, 1999; Founding Partner Award, Greater Houston Partnership for Quality Edu, 2000; Impact Awd, Wheeler Ave Baptist Church Women's Guild, 2000; Special Recognition Award, Texas South Central, 2000; honored by the City of Yazoo, MS, 2000; Impact Award, Wheeler Avenue Baptist Church Women's Guild, 2000; honored by Jackson State Univ Houston Alumni Chap, 2000; Women of Excellence Award, Suburban Sugar Land Women, 2000; Women on the Move, Executive Women on the Move, 2000; Spirit of Fredom Award, Alpha Kappa Alpha Sorority Inc, 2000; Value Vision Recognition Awd, TSU Stud Government Asn, 2000; Wall of Fame Honoree, St. James Sch, 2000; honored by the Wesley Found, 2000; Sisterhood Speaker, St. Emmanuel Missionary Baptist Church, 2000; Soaring Eagle Awd, Tougaloo Col, 2000; Commendation of Leadership & Participation in Gold Coast Classic, Councilman George Stevens, City of San Diego, 2000; Appreciation Award, TSU Stud Govt Asn, 2000-01; Outstanding Woman of Achievement, YWCA of Houston, 2001; honored by the Federal Reserve Bank of Dallas, 2001; Achiever's Award, Houston Bus & Prof Men's Club, 2001; Woman of the Year, Nat Asn of Negro Bus & Prof Women's Club, 2001; Appreciation Award, Kay On-Going Education Ctr, 2001.

SLASH, JOSEPH A
President (Organization), executive, accountant. **Personal:** Born Aug 25, 1943, Huntington, WV; son of Joseph Autumn and Clara Rose; married Meredith; children: Alexandria Dawson & Adrianne Letetia. **Educ:** Marshall Univ, BBA, 1966. **Career:** Sears Roebuck & Co, comptroller asst, 1966; Arthur Young & Co, audit mgr, 1968-78; City Indianapolis, Ind, dep mayor, 1978-89; Indianapolis Power & Light Co, Indianapolis, Ind, vpres, 1989; Indianapolis Urban League, pres & chief exec officer, 2002-. **Orgs:** United Way Greater Indianapolis; Ind Asn CPA's Adv Forum, 1976-78; Am Inst CPA; Ind Asn CPA; bd dir, Indianapolis Chap Ind Asn CPA; Kappa Alpha Psi; Alpha Eta Boule; Sigma Pi Phi; bd dirs, United Way Cent Ind, 1985-; exec comt, Comn Downtown, 1991-; exec comt, Ind Sports Corp, 1991-; co-chair, IndyCounts community; Ind Humanities Coun; bd dir, Greater

Indianapolis Progress Comn; adv bd, Marshall Univ Lewis Sch Bus. **Honors/Awds:** Kappa of the Month, Kappa Alpha Psi, 1978; Outstanding Black Alumni, Marshall Univ, 1986; Professional Achievement Award, Ctr Leadership Develop, 1987. **Home Addr:** 1140 Fox Hill Dr, Indianapolis, IN 46208. **Business Addr:** President, Chief Executive Officer, The Indianapolis Urban League, 777 Ind Ave, Indianapolis, IN 46202, **Business Phone:** (317)693-7603.

SLATER, JACKIE RAY
Football player, executive. **Personal:** Born May 27, 1954, Jackson, MS; married Annie; children: Matthew. **Educ:** Jackson State Univ, BA; Livingston Univ, MS. **Career:** Football player (retired), executive; Los Angeles Rams, offensive tackle, 1976-94; St Louis Rams, offensive line, 1995; Slater Enterprises LLC, owner, currently. **Orgs:** Rams Speakers Bur; Pro Football Hall Fame. **Honors/Awds:** Walter Payton Phys Educ Award, Jackson State Univ; All-NFC & All-NFL second team, UPI, 1983, 1985; All-NFC, Football News, 1985; Pro Bowl, 1983, 1985-89. **Special Achievements:** First recipient of Walter Payton Physical Education Award, Jackson State University. **Business Addr:** Owner, Slater Enterprises LLC, 9203 Bent Spur Lane, Houston, TX 77064, **Business Phone:** (281)469-0818.

SLATER, REGGIE
Basketball player. **Personal:** Born Aug 27, 1970, Houston, TX; married Katie; children: Aliya & RJ. **Educ:** Univ Wyo, attended 1992. **Career:** Basketball Player (retired); Argal Huesca, Spain, forward, 1992-93; Denver Nuggets, free agent, 1994-95, 1996; Portland Trail Blazers, 1995; Dallas Mavericks, 1996; Chicago Rockers, CBA, 1995-96, 1996-97; Toronto Raptors, 1996-99; Minn Timberwolves, 2000-01, 2002-03; Atlanta Hawks, 2001-02.

SLATER, RODNEY E
Government official. **Personal:** Born Feb 23, 1955, Tutwiler, MS; son of Earl Brewer and Velma Brewer; married Cassandra Wilkins; children: Bridgette & Josette. **Educ:** Eastern Mich Univ, BS, 1977; Univ Ark, JD, 1980; Howard Univ, hon doctorate. **Career:** State Atty Gen Off, asst atty, 1980-82; Ark Gov Bill Clinton, staff spec asst, 1983-85, exec asst, 1985-87; Ark State Univ, dir govt rels, 1987; US Fed Hwy Admin, fed hwy adminr, 1993-96; Secy Transp, 1997; Ark Hwy & Transp, comnr; Patton Boggs LLC, partner & atty, currently. **Orgs:** Campaign mgr, Gov Bill Clinton's Staff, 1982-86; Ark State Hwy Comn, 1987-92; pres, W Harold Flowers Law Soc; founding mem, Ark Children's Hosp Community Future; former bd mem, GW Carver YMCA Little Rock; John Gammon Scholar Found Ark; former bd mem, United Cerebral Palsy Cent Ark; vol & supporter, Boy Scouts Am; Gyst House; March Dimes; Sickle Cell Anemia Found; Thurgood Marshall Scholar Fund; United Negro Col Fund; Eastern Ark Area Coun; bd dirs, Ark Advocates C & Families; secy-treas, Ark Bar Asn; Comn Ark Future; bd mem, John Gammon Scholar Found Ark; Fed Judge Henry Woods, mem Eastern Dist Ark Comn Bicentennial US Const. **Honors/Awds:** Elton Rynearson Grid Scholar Award, 1976; Eastern Michigan Univ Top Ten Student Award, 1977; Eastern Mich Univ Nat Championship Forensics Team, 1977; Lamplighter Award, Balck Leadership Forum, 1998; President's Award, Nat Bar Asn; George Collins Award, Nat Black Caucus; Albert Schweitzer Leadership Award, Hugh O'Brian Leadership Foun. **Special Achievements:** First African American member of the Arkansas Highway Commission; First African American Federal Highway Administrator; named on 100 Most Influential Black Americans, Ebony mag. **Business Addr:** Parnter, Attorney, Patton Boggs LLC, 2550 M St NW, Washington, DC 20037, **Business Phone:** (202)457-6000.

SLATON, GWENDOLYN C
Librarian. **Personal:** Born Jun 19, 1945, Philadelphia, PA; daughter of George Alexander Childs and LaFronia Delorial Dunbar Childs; married Harrison Allen, Sep 17, 1966; children: Kimberly Dawn & Leigh Alison. **Educ:** Pa State Univ, PA, BA, hist, 1970; Seton Hall Univ, NJ, MA, educ, 1975; Rutgers Univ, NJ, MLS, 1982. **Career:** Essex County Col, Newark, NJ, staff, 1970-, librn, 1976-81, libr admin, 1981-97, dir & assoc dean, learning resources, 1997-. **Orgs:** Bd dirs, Family Serv Child Guidance Ctr, 1977-83; adv bd, Youth Ctr, S Orange-Maplewood, 1983-89; exec bd, Essex-Hudson Regional Libr Coop, 1986-91; sec, Maplewood Cult Comn, 1986-91; Delta Sigma Theta Sorority, 1966-; Delta Sigma Theta Sorority, N Jersey Alumnae Chap, 1982-, pres, 1993-95; Mid-Atlantic Innovative Users Group. **Home Addr:** 620 Prospect St, Maplewood, NJ 07040, **Home Phone:** (973)763-3668. **Business Addr:** Associate Dean, Director, Essex County College, 303 Univ Ave, Newark, NJ 07102, **Business Phone:** (973)877-3233.

SLAUGHTER, CAROLE D.
School administrator. **Personal:** Born Jul 27, 1945, Chattanooga, TN; daughter of Preston Jones and Rebecca Jones; married Thomas F Slaughter Jr; children: Kelli & Eric. **Educ:** Douglass Col, Rutgers Univ, BA, 1972; Princeton Univ, MA, 1975. **Career:** Educ Testing Services, assoc examr, 1974-79, grad record exams assoc prog dir & dir develop, 1979-86, coll & univ prog, prog dir, 1986-87, off corp Secy, dir, 1987. **Orgs:** Chairperson ETS Comt Personnel Equity, 1983-85; chair person, League Women Voters Women's Rights Study Group; Highland Park NJ Sch Bd. **Honors/Awds:** Ford Foundation Fel, 1972-76; Test Preparation Specialist.

SLAUGHTER, ATTY. FRED L.
Educator, lawyer. **Personal:** Born Mar 13, 1942, Santa Cruz, CA; married Kay Valerie Johnson; children: Hilary Spring & Fred Wallace. **Educ:** Univ Calif, Los Angeles, BS, 1964, MBA, 1966; Columbia Univ, JD, 1969. **Career:** Spec asst chancellor, 1969-71; Practicing atty, 1970-; Sch Law, Univ Calif, Los Angeles, asst dean, lectr, 1971-80; assoc campus advocate, 1971-72; real estate broker, 1974-. **Orgs:** La Co, Calif St Am Bar Asn; US Fed Cts, Calif St Cts; life mem, UCLA Alumni Asn. **Business Addr:** Attorney, PO Box 3522, Santa Monica, CA 90408-3522, **Business Phone:** (310)393-3522.

SLAUGHTER, DR. JOHN BROOKS
School administrator. **Personal:** Born Mar 16, 1934, Topeka, KS; son of Reuben Brooks and Dora; married Ida Bernice Johnson, Aug 31, 1956; children: John II & Jacqueline Michelle. **Educ:** Kans State Univ, BS, elec eng, 1956; Univ Calif Los Angeles, MS, eng, 1961; Univ Calif, PhD, eng sci, 1971. **Career:** Gen Dynamics Convair, electronics eng, 1956-60; Naval Elec Lab Ctr, 1960-75, div head, 1965-71, dept head, 1971-75; Appl Physics Lab Univ Wash, dir, 1975-77; Nat Sci Found, asst dir, 1977-79; Wash State Univ, acad vpres & provost, 1979-80; Nat Sci Found, dir, 1980-82; Univ MD Col Park, chancellor, 1982-88; Occidental Col, pres, 1988-. **Orgs:** Pres, Zeta Sigma Lambda Chap Alpha Phi Alpha, 1956-60; bd mem, San Diego Urban League, 1962-66; San Diego Transit Corp, 1968-75; bd dir, Comm Credit Co, 1983-88; bd mem, Monsanto CPN, 1983-; AAAS, 1984-; bd mem, Baltimore Gas Elec Co, 1984-88; bd dirs, Sovran Bank, 1985-88; Med Mutual Liability Insurance Soc, Md, 1986-88; Nat Collegiate Athletic Asn, chmn President's comn, 1986-88; bd mem, Martin Marietta Corp, 1987; bd dir, Int Bus Mach, 1988-; bd mem, Avery Dennison, 1989-; bd mem, Atlantic Richfield, 1989-; bd govrs, LA World Affairs Coun, bd 1990-96; Town Hall Calif, 1990-94; bd dir, Northrop Grumman & Solutia Inc, 1993-; pres & chief exec officer, Nat Action Coun Minorities Eng, 2000-; Inst Elec & Electronic Engrs; Am Acad Arts & Scis; Tau Beta Pi Hon Eng Soc; Eta Kappa Nu Soc. **Honors/Awds:** Distinguished Alumnus of the Year Award, Univ Calif Los Angeles, 1978; Distinguished Service Award, NSF, 1979; Service in Engineering Award, Kans State Univ, 1981; Distinguished Alumnus of the Year Award, Univ Calif-San Diego, 1982; Topeka High Sch Hall of Fame, 1983; First US Black Engineer of the Year Award, 1987; Medal of Excellence, Univ Calif Los Angeles, 1989; Hall of Fame, Am Soc Eng Educ, 1993; Kansan of the Year, Kans Native Sons Daughters, 1994; Martin Luther King Jr National Award, 1997; Arthur M Bueche Award, NAE, 2004. **Business Phone:** (914)539-4010.

SLAUGHTER, PETER
Physician. **Personal:** Born May 15, 1928, Detroit, MI; married Geraldine; children: Chevon, Karen, Tracy. **Educ:** Wayne Univ, BS 1955; Univ MI, MD 1963. **Career:** Samaritan, med dir; Clinical Opers, Dmic Prescad, dir; Pvt Pract, Pediat, currently. **Orgs:** Fel Am Acad Ped; Detroit Ped Soc. **Honors/Awds:** Am Acad Pediat, 1973; Spec Achievement Galen's Hon Soc, 1961. **Military Serv:** AUS sfc 1950-52. **Business Addr:** Medical Dir, Samaritan, 10201 E Jefferson, Detroit, MI 48221.

SLAUGHTER, WEBSTER
Football player. **Personal:** Born Oct 19, 1964, Stockton, CA. **Educ:** San Joaquin Delta Col, San Diego State Univ. **Career:** Football player (retired); Cleveland Browns, wide receiver, 1986-91; Houston Oilers, 1992-94; Kans City Chiefs, 1995; New York Jets, 1996; San Diego Chargers, wide receiver, 1998. **Honors/Awds:** Pro Bowl,1989 & 1993; All Pro Bowl, 1989.

SLAUGHTER-DEFOE, DR. DIANA T.
Psychologist, educator. **Personal:** Born Oct 28, 1941, Chicago, IL; daughter of John Ison Slaughter and Gwendolyn Malva Armstead; married Michael, Sep 16, 1989 (divorced). **Educ:** Univ Chicago, BA (with Honors) 1962, MA, 1964, PhD, 1968. **Career:** Univ Chicago, Grad Sch Educ, res assoc, 1966-67, asst prof behavioral sci human devel educ, 1970-77; Howard Univ Sch Med, instr psychiat, 1967-68;Yale Univ, Sch Med, Child Study Ctr, asst prof psychiat, 1968-70;Northwestern Univ, from asst prof to prof, 1977-97; Univ PA, Graduate Sch Educ, Constance E Clayton prof urban educ, 1998-. **Orgs:** Inst Int Educ New York & Inst African Studies, Univ Ghana, 1972; elected chairperson, Black Caucus Soc Res Child Devel, 1979-81; Nat Adv Bd Child Abuse & Neglect, 1979-81; elected mem, Governing Coun Soc Res Child Devel,1981-87; Soc Res Child Devel Study Tour Peoples Republic China, 1984; Am psych Asn; Soc Res Child Devel; Am Educ Res Asn; Nat Asn Black Psych;Groves Conf Family; Delta Sigma Theta; Nat Assoc Educ Young C; bd ethnic &minority affairs, Am Psycholog Asn, 1986-88, bd scientific affairs,1995-97; Comt Child Develop Res & Pub Policy, Nat Res Coun, 1987-92; bd dir, Ancona Sch, Chicago IL, 1989-91; adv panel, Head Sta Bureau, ACF,1988-; bd vistors, Learning, Research & Develop Ctr, currently. **Honors/Awds:** First Pi Lambda Distinguished Research Award for Most Outstanding Thesis,1969; First Black Scholar Achievement Award, Black Caucus, Soc Res Child Develop, 1987; Received many awards, 1987; Elected Fellow, Am Psycholog Assn, 1993; Distinguished Contributions Research Pub Policy, Am Psychol Asn, 1994; Distinguished Research Award, Pi Lambda Theta; Lifetime Professional Achievement Citation, Univ Chicago, 2007. **Special Achievements:** Published books, Visible Now: Blacks in Private Schools (Greenwood Press)1988, & Black Children & Poverty: A Developmental Perspective (Jossey-Bass Press) 1988. **Business Phone:** (215)573-3947.

SLAUGHTER-TITUS, REV. LINDA JEAN
Clergy. **Personal:** Born Aug 5, 1948, Albany, GA; daughter of Howard Mitchell and Burniece Jackson-Thomas (deceased); married Phylemon Depriest, Dec 21, 1991; children: Henry Lee Slaughter Jr, Duane Dushaun Slaughter & Faouly-Sekou. **Educ:** Highland Park Community Col, AA, 1979; Wayne State Univ, BA, 1989; United Theol Sem, MDiv, 1997. **Career:** Golden State Ins, agent, 1973-82; Merrill Lynch Brokers, acct asst, 1982-85; Thoburn United Methodist Church, pastor, 1985-90; Jefferson Ave United Methodist Church, pastor, 1990-91; Oak Park Faith United Methodist Church, pastor, 1991-97; Cass Cot United Methodist Church, assoc pastor, 1995-97; Henderson Memorial United Methodist Church, pastor, 1997; Berkley First United Methodist Church, pastor, currently. **Orgs:** Black Psychol Alumni, Wayne State Univ, 1985-; bd dir, Oakland County Nat Asn Advan Colored People, 1992-97; ABATEJWA, Nat Asn, 1995-; Black United Fund Mich, CTOB 100, 1997-; Mich Emmaus; Bd dir, Nat Black Methodist Church Renewal; chair, Women's Concern, Pastor's Inst. **Special Achievements:** First Black Female licensed in Health/Life/Property/Casualty in Michigan, 1983; First Black Chair Annual Conf on Religion/Race, Detroit, 1980-84; New Church Developers, 1989; Mediation Certification, 1996. **Business Addr:** Pastor, Berkley First United Methodist Church, 2820 W 12 Mile Rd, Berkley, MI 48072, **Business Phone:** (248)399-3698.

SLEDGE, CARLA
Government official. **Personal:** Born Jul 20, 1952, Detroit, MI; daughter of Thomas Griffin Sr and Zephrie; married Willie F, Jul 20, 1974; children: Arian Darkell & Ryan Marcel. **Educ:** Eastern Mich Univ, BA, 1978, MA, 1981; Wayne State Univ, BS, acct, 1989. **Career:** Taylor Bd Educ, teacher, 1974; Deloitte & Touche LLP, audit mgr, 1982-95;Metropolitan Youth Found, instr, 1986; Wayne County, Mich, chief dept financial officer, 1995-2002, chief financial officer, 2002-. **Orgs:** Treas, Mich Munic Finance Officers Asn, 1995-; Black Caucus, 1995-;Women's Network, 1995-; Spec Rev Comt, 1996-; Am Inst Cert Pub Accountants, 1996-; Asn Govt Accountants, 1996-; Mich Inst Cert Pub Accountants, Mem Standing Comt, 1996-; bd dir, COBRA Comt, 1997-; mem,co-chair, 1998-, Nat Asn Black Accountants Inc; pres, Govt Finance Offices Asn; Mem Comt, Women's Econ Club, 1999-; treas, Children's Outreach, 1999-; trustee, Rochester Col, 2000. **Honors/Awds:** Outstanding Professional Achievement in Govt, Nat Asn Advan Colored People, 1996-97; Nat Achievement in Govt, 1999; Outstanding Cert Pub Acctin Government Award. **Special Achievements:** The 30 Most Influential Black Women in Metro Detroit, Women's Informal Network, 1999. **Home Addr:** 24550 N Cromwell Dr, Franklin, MI 48025, **Home Phone:** (248)737-6929. **Business Addr:** Chief Financial Officer, President of the Government Finance Officers Association, Wayne County, Department of Management & Budget, 600 Randolph St 3rd Fl, Detroit, MI 48226, **Business Phone:** (313)224-0420.

SLEDGE, PERCY
Singer. **Personal:** Born Nov 25, 1940, Leighton, AL; married Rosa; children: 12. **Career:** Albums: When A Man Loves a Woman, 1966; Tender Love, 1966; Baby Help Me,1967; Cover Me, 1967; Take Time to Know Her, 1968; My Special Prayer, 1969; Stop The World Tonight, 1971; Rainbow Road, 1972; Sunday Brother, 1972; Sunshine, 1973; I'll Be Your Everything, 1974; When a Man Loves a Woman, 1987; Blue Night, 1994; Wanted Again, 1998; Shining Through the Rain, 2004. **Honors/Awds:** When A Man Loves A Woman named one of Best 100 Singles in Last 25 Yrs,Rolling Stone mag, 1988; Career Achievement Award, R&B Fndn, 1989; MostPerformed Song of the Yr, BMI, 1993; 5 gold records; 2 platinum records;Inducted into the Rock and Roll Hall of Fame, 2005; Louisiana Music Hall of Fame, 2007; inductee, Delta Music Museum. **Business Addr:** Singer, Artists International Management, 9850 Sandalfoot Blvd Suite 458, Boca Raton, FL 33428.*

SLEET, GREGORY M
Judge. **Personal:** Born Jan 1, 1951, New York, NY; married Mary G Sleet. **Educ:** Hampton Univ, BA, 1973; Rutgers Univ Sch Law, JD, 1976. **Career:** Defender Asn Philadelphia, asst pub defender, 1976-83; Pvt prac lawyer, Philadelphia, PA, 1983-90; Dept Justice, Del state, dep atty gen, 1990-92; coun, Hercules Inc, 1992-94; US Dist Ct Del, dist atty, Judge, 1994-. **Orgs:** Del Bar Asn; Penn Bar Asn; New York State Bar Asn; Am Bar Asn; Nat Bar Asn. **Honors/Awds:** Freedom Fund Distinguished Service Award, NAACP, 1994. **Special Achievements:** First African-American US attorney for Delaware. **Business Addr:** Judge, US District Court, District of Delaware, 844 N King St, J Caleb Boggs Fed Bldg Rm 4324, Wilmington, DE 19801-3570, **Business Phone:** (302)573-6470.

SLIE, SAMUEL N
Educator, clergy. **Personal:** Born Jun 8, 1925, Branford, CT; son of Robert and Hannah Brown. **Educ:** Springfield Col, Mass, BS,

1949; Wilberforce Univ, Ohio, attended; Yale Divinity Sch, Roman Cath Though, 1963; New York Sem, Doctor Ministry, 1985. **Career:** YMCA, southern area staff, 1952-55; Stud Christian Movement, United Church Christ, staff, 1955-63; Yale Univ, assoc pastor & lectr in higher educ, 1965-, Church Christ, assoc pastor, 2004-; Southern Conn State Univ, dir united ministry higher educ, 1976-86; Downtown Cooperative Ministry, New Haven, coordr, 1986-94. **Orgs:** United Church Christ Task Force World Hunger, 1972-73; corp mem, United Church Bd World Ministries, 1973-81; past pres, Nat Campus Ministers Asn, 1973-74; Theol Community Worlds Alliance YMCA's, 1981-86; treas, Conn United Nations Asn USA, 1984-92; Adv coun Nat Ecumenical Stud Christian Coun, 1984-86. **Honors/Awds:** Distinguished Service Award, Alpha Phi Omega, Gamma Eta Chap, Springfield Col, 1949; International Distinguished Service Award, Nat YMCA, Boston, 1981; Elm-Ivy Award Contribution Town-Govt Rels, Mayor New Haven & Pres of Yale Univ, 1985; Distinguished Educational Service Award, Dixwell Community House, 1989; Man of the Year, Nat Negro Prof & Bus Women, New Haven Chapter, 1991; Distinguished Alumnus Award, Yale Divinity Sch, 1993. **Special Achievements:** Articles: "The New Naionall Ecumenical Journal", 1981; "The Black Church" "Identity in the United Church of Christ," Theol, 1990. **Military Serv:** AUS, 92nd infantry division staff sargent, 1943-46; Mediteranean & European Theatre Medals; Two Battle Stars; Combat Infantry Medal. **Home Addr:** 188 W Walk, West Haven, CT 06516. **Business Addr:** Associate Pastor, Yale Univ, Church of Christ, 300 College St, PO Box 209078, New Haven, CT 06511-8960, **Business Phone:** (203)432-1128.

SLOAN, EDITH BARKSDALE
Clergy, government official. **Personal:** Born Nov 29, 1940, New York, NY; married E Ned; children: Douglass Ned. **Educ:** Hunter Col, BA, 1960; Cath Univ Am, JD, 1974. **Career:** Coun Stand Travel, mgr info off, 1960-61; US Peace Corps Philippines, 1962-64; Eleanor Roosevelt Human Rel NY Urban League, intern, 1964-65; US Comn Civil Rights, pub info specialist, 1965-68; Nat Comn Household Emp, exec dir & counr, 1969-75; DC Off Consumer Protection, dir, 1976-77; US Consumer Prod Safety Comn, 1978-83; Unity Church, minister, 1992. **Orgs:** PA Bar Asn, 1974; DC Bar Asn, 1977; Community Adv Comn, Howard Univ Cancer Res Ctr; Women's Div Nat Bar Asn, Inst Women Today; adv com, Nat Ctr Policy Rev; bd dir, Lupis Found; founder, Black Am Law Stds Asn; Catholic Univ; Delta Sigma Theta Inc; bd mem, Greater Wash Res Ctr, Nat Consumers League, Pub Voice. **Honors/Awds:** Adam Clayton Powell Award, 1974. **Special Achievements:** Named One of 75 Outstndng Black Women in Public Service, 1974; subject of NBC-TV Documentary "a woman is " 1974. **Home Addr:** 1639 Primrose Rd NW, Washington, DC 20012.

SLOAN, MACEO KENNEDY
Financial manager. **Personal:** Born Oct 18, 1949, Philadelphia, PA; son of Maceo Archibald and Charlotte Kennedy; married Melva Iona Wilder; children: Maceo S & Malia K. **Educ:** Morehouse Col, BA 1971; Ga State Univ, MBA, 1973; NC Central Univ Law Sch, JD, 1979. **Career:** NC Mutual Life Ins Co, investment analyst trainee, 1973-75, investment analyst, 1975-77, asst treas, 1977-78, asst vpres, 1978-83, treas, 1983-85, vpres, treas, 1985-86; NCCU Sch Law, adj visiting prof, 1979-86; Study Seminar Financial Analysts, workshop review leader, 1980-; Moore &Van Allen Attorneys Law, couns, 1985-86; NCM Capital Mgt Group Inc, pres & ceo, 1986; Sloan Financial Group Inc, chair, pres & ceo; NCM Capital, chmn, ceo & chief investment officer, currently. **Orgs:** Fin Analysts Fedn, 1974-; Durham Chamber Com, 1974-; vpres NC Soc of Fin Analysts, 1977-78; bd visitors NCCU Sch Law, 1979-86; NC State Bar, 1979-;bd dirs Mechanics & Farmers Bank, 1979-; bd dirs, Nat Ins Asn, 1980-; bd dirs, United Way of Durham, 1980-89; vice chmn, treas, Urban Ministries of Durham, 1983-88; Univ Club, 1986-; The Georgetown Club, 1988-; founder & chair, Nat Investment Managers Asn. **Honors/Awds:** Outstanding Service as Pres Better Business Bureau, 1980; Freedmon Guard Award, Durham Jaycees, 1981; Outstanding Leadership Award, United Way Durham, 1984; Resolution in Appreciation, The Durham City Coun; Cert Serv. **Special Achievements:** Featured on "Bridge builders," 1998. **Business Addr:** Chairman, Chief Executive Officer & Chief Investment Officer, NCM Capital, Sloan Financial Group, 2634 Durham-Chapel Hill Blvd, Durham, NC 27707-2875, **Business Phone:** (919)688-0620.

SLOCUMB, HEATHCLIFF
Baseball player. **Personal:** Born Jun 7, 1966, Jamaica, NY; son of Karl Paul and Mattie Louise; married Deborah, Mar 4, 1986 (deceased); children: Jessica & Heather. **Career:** Baseball Player (retired); Chicago Cubs, pitcher, 1991-93; Cleveland Indians, pitcher, 1993; Philadelphia Phillies, pitcher, 1994-95; BostonRed Sox, pitcher, 1996-97; Seattle Mariners, pitcher, 1997-98; Baltimore Orioles, pitcher, 1999; St Louis Cardinals, pitcher, 1999-2000; San Diego Padres, pitcher, 2000. **Honors/Awds:** Winner, All-Star Game, 1995. *

SLOCUMB, JONATHAN
Comedian. **Educ:** Oakwood Col, Huntsville, AL, BS, broadcast jour. **Career:** TV series: "Def Comedy Jam"; "The Big One's Back: The Sanford & Son Reunion"; "When the Funk Bites the Dust", 1997; "Jamie Foxx Presents Laffapalooza", 2003; Album: Laugh Yo Self 2 Life. **Special Achievements:** Co-hosted the Annual Stellar Awards for two consecutive years and 28th Annual NAACP Image Awards. **Business Phone:** (615)748-8000.*

SMALL, DR. CLARA LOUISE
Educator. **Personal:** Born May 17, 1946, Plymouth, NC; daughter of Tarlton and Doris Skinner (deceased). **Educ:** NC Cent Univ, BA, 1969, MA, 1971; St John's Col, MA, 1974; Univ Del, PhD,1991. **Career:** Saint Paul's Col, hist instr, 1970-72; Chambers Child Develop Ctr, HeadStart teacher, 1972-73; Lincoln Univ, hist instr, 1973-77; Salisbury Univ, hist prof, 1977-. **Orgs:** Chancellor, North Eastern Region, bd trustees, 1991-, Pi Gamma Mu; adv,Phi Alpha Theta, 1977-2003; historian, Buffalo Soldiers, Thomas E Polk Sr.Chapt, 1999-; Princess Anne Chap Links Inc, 2002-; bd mem, Lower Eastern Shore Heritage Comt; bd mem, Pemberton Manor. **Honors/Awds:** Faithful Service Award, international organization, 1991; Comn Coordinate Study, Commemoration, & Impact of Slavery's History & Legacy in Md, Md Gov Off, 2001-; Frank H Morris Humanitarian Award, 2005. **Special Achievements:** Author: A Reality Check: Brief Biographies of African-Americans on Demarva, 1998. **Business Addr:** Professor of History, Salisbury State University, Department of History, 1101 Camden Ave Holloway Hall 333, Salisbury, MD 21801, **Business Phone:** (410)543-6000.

SMALL, ERIC
President (government), chief executive officer, executive. **Educ:** Georgetown Univ, BS, finance; Boston Col, Arthur D Little Sch Mgt, MSM. **Career:** Aurthur D Little Inc, mgt consult; Aetna Life & Casualty, sr invest dir; SBK-Brooks Invest Corp, former pres & chief exec officer, exec vpres, currently. **Orgs:** Pres Coun. **Honors/Awds:** Weatherhead 100 Award, 1999. **Special Achievements:** Bank listed No 9 on Black Enterprise's list of top investment banks, 1998,No 5, 1999, No 8, 2000, ranked as the top co-underwriter of municipal bonds in Ohio & among the top 50 in the US.

SMALL, ISADORE, III
Salesperson. **Personal:** Born Apr 27, 1944, Pontiac, MI; married Earline Olivia Washington; children: Michael, Brian & Vanessa. **Educ:** Univ Mich, BS, Elect Engr, 1967; Wayne State Univ, MBA, 1981. **Career:** Cutler-hammer Inc, Milwaukee Wis, design engr, 1967-74; Detroit Mich, sales engr, 1974-82; Eaton Corp Southfield Mich, sales mgr, 1982-83; Eaton Corp Grand Rapids Mich, sales engr, 1984. **Orgs:** Soc Automotive Engrs, 1966-67; Asn Iron & Steel Engrs, 1974-84; Elect Mfg Rep Asn, 1979-; state youth dir, Church God Wis, 1969-74; Alpha Pi Omega Fraternity, 1966-67; chmn, bd trustees, Metrop Church God, 1974-84; chmn, Bus Assembly; Men Church God, 1983-90; Kentwood Sch Legis Comt, parent adv, 1986-91; church coun chmn, Orchard View Church God, 1987-93; chmn, Div Church Exten, 1988-94; Nat Div Church Exten, Church God, 1994-. **Honors/Awds:** Electronic Patent US Patent Off, 1972, 1974; Eaton Soc Inventors, 1980; Man of the Year, 1984. **Home Addr:** 4233 Shaffer SE, Kentwood, MI 49512.

SMALL, ISRAEL G.
Manager. **Personal:** Born Feb 26, 1941, Rincon, GA; married Jenetha Jenkins. **Educ:** Savannah St Col, BS, 1963; GA S Col, Grad Study; Ft Valley St Col; Univ GA; Comm Planning & Evaluation Inst, Wash DC. **Career:** Bur of Pub Dev, Savannah, dir, hum serv, 1985; City Savannah, model cities admin; Model Cities Prog, 1970; asst city mgr, currently. **Orgs:** Kappa Alpha Psi; GA Tchrs Ed Asn; Nat Ed Asn; Am Tchrs Asn; YMCA; Savannah Drug Abuse Adv Cncl; NAACP; People United to Save Humanity; completed training in Municipal & Comm Planning. **Military Serv:** AUS e-5 1966-68. **Business Addr:** Assistant City Manager, City Savannah, 6 E Bay St, PO Box 1027, Savannah, GA 31401.*

SMALL, KENNETH LESTER
Association executive. **Personal:** Born Oct 1, 1957, New York, NY; son of Julius and Catherine Johnson; divorced 1998; children: Catherine Louise. **Educ:** Fordham Univ, BA, 1979; Long Island Univ, MA, 1981. **Career:** Long Island Univ, res asst, 1979-80, adj prof, 1995; Bur Labor Statistics, US Dept Labor, economist, 1980-81; The NY Pub Libr, info asst, 1981-84; Nat Urban League, New York, NY, prog evaluator, 1984-86; Nat Urban League Inc, asst dir, 1985-86, exec asst, 1986-89, strategic planner, 1986-95, assoc dir, res & evaluation, 1994-95; Citizen Advice Bur, dev dir, 1995-; KTL Asn, prin consult, 1990-; Sphinx Communs Group, assoc consult, 1989-95. **Orgs:** NY Urban League; Nat Econ Asn, 1990-; Co-op Am; Friends Black Scholar; Hunger Action Network New York State, bd mem, 1993-99, 2001-02; Nat Coalition Blacks for Reparations Am, 1993-99; Nat Urban League Guild, 1999-; Imani House Int, 1998; Urban League Essex County; bd mem, Bethex Fed Credit Union, 1999-; Nat Electronic Communs Network, bd mem, 2001-02. **Honors/Awds:** Connolly Sch Grad Assistantship, Long Island Univ, 1979-80; HW Wilson Scholar, Pratt Inst, 1990. **Home Addr:** 3520 Tryon Ave Suite 704, Bronx, NY 10467, **Home Phone:** (718)881-5265. **Business Addr:** Development Director, Citizens Advice Bureau of New York, 2054 Morris Ave, Bronx, NY 10453-3538, **Business Phone:** (718)365-0910.

SMALL, LILY B.
Educator. **Personal:** Born Sep 1, 1934, Trelawny, Jamaica; married Sylvester; children: Dale Andrew & Donna Marie. **Educ:** Calif State Univ, Fresno, BA, eng, 1970, MA, eng, 1971; Univ Pac, Stockton, EdD, curriculum & instr, 1976. **Career:** Calif State Univ, Fresno, assoc prof & affirmative action coordr, 1972, Univ Affirmative Action, dir, 1977-82, acad specialist, 1977-82, from assoc prof ethnic studies prog to prof ethnic studies prog, 1978-2003, dir proj enhancement,1989-90 & 1992-93, Ethnic Studies Prog, chair, 1990-98, prof emer ethnic studies prog, 2003-; Stockton Univ Sch Dist, Stockton, reading specialist, 1973-74; Ministry Educ, Kingston, Jamaica, teacher. **Orgs:** Am Asn Affirmative Action; Am Asn Univ Women; San Joaquin Reading Asn; chap secy, Phi Kappa Phi, 1978-80; teacher, supvr, Sun School Church of God; Black Faculty & Staff Asn; Nat Acad Honor Soc; Human Rels Comn, Calif State Univ, Fresno, 1995-96; Athletic Behavior Review Comt, 1995-96; founder & pres, FCPW Investment Club. **Honors/Awds:** Cited in Whos Who in the West and Mid-West, 1973; Community Service Award, Church Living God & Living Heritage Drama Group, 1999; Rosa Parks Award for Service and Dedication to the African American Community, 1999; Human Relations Commission Community Recognition Award, City of Fresno, 1999; Honorary Member Award, Africana Students United, 2003. **Special Achievements:** Nominated for the Fresno Bee/Channel 30/YWCA Top Ten Business/Professional Women of the Year, 1994. **Business Addr:** Professor Emeritus, California State University, Fresno, Ethnic Studies Program, 2225 E San Ramon, McF 215, Fresno, CA 93740, **Business Phone:** (559)278-5418.*

SMALL, STANLEY JOSEPH
School administrator. **Personal:** Born Jun 1, 1946, Weeks Island, LA; married Dorothy Collins; children: Keith V, Keisha L & Kory K. **Educ:** Southern Univ Baton Rouge, BS, math & sci, 1968, MS, admin & supv, 1973. **Career:** New Iberia Middle Sch, teacher, 1968-70, asst prin; Anderson Middle Sch, teacher, 1970-81, prin, 1992; Iberia Parish Coun, elected parish off, 1984; Lee Street Elem Sch, prin, 1989-92. **Orgs:** Nat Educ Asn, 1969-85; pres, Neighborhood Community Serv Coalition, 1978-85; Los Angeles Asn Educ/Polit Action Comt, 1979-85; chmn, Human Serv Comt Iberia Parish Coun, 1984; NACO Human Serv Steering Comt, 1984; Parish Bd Comt Action Agency, 1984. **Honors/Awds:** Outstanding Teacher of the Year, Asn Classroom Teachers, 1978. **Special Achievements:** Developed and implemented motivation program for students New Iberia Middle School in 1981. **Home Addr:** 816 Francis St, New Iberia, LA 70560.

SMALL, SYDNEY L.
Executive. **Personal:** Born Feb 18, 1941, Brooklyn, NY. **Educ:** Pace Univ, BA, 1961. **Career:** Unity Broadcasting Network Inc, exec vice pres & co-found; Nat Black Network NYC, vice chmn, 1973; Unity Broadcasting Network PA Inc WDAS AM & FM Phila, PA; ABC, bus mgr, 1963-69; Time Inc, 1969-71; Unity Broadcasting Network Inc, exec vpres; Queens Inner Unity Cable Syst NYC, pres; NBN Broadcasting Inc, pres, chmn; American Urban Radio Network, pres, currently. **Orgs:** Intl Radio & TV Soc; Nat Asn Broadcaster; Nat Asn Black-Owned Broadcaster; NAACP; NY Urban League; bd dir, World Insto Black Comn Inc, 1978; New York C Comn Com, 1979; pres, World Inst Black Commun, 1986; pres, Nat Assoc Black Owned Broadcasters, 1987. **Special Achievements:** Company ranked 87 on Black Enterprise's list of top 100 industrial & service companies, 1998. **Military Serv:** AUS, 1961-63. **Business Addr:** President, American Urban Radio Network, 432 Park Ave S 14th Fl, New York, NY 10016, **Business Phone:** (212)883-2100.

SMALL, TORRANCE RAMON
Football player. **Personal:** Born Sep 6, 1970, Tampa, FL; married Denise; children: Devante & Kayla. **Educ:** Alcorn State Univ, gen studies, 2000. **Career:** Football player (retired); New Orleans Saints, wide receiver, 1992-96; St.Louis Rams, 1997; Indianapolis Colts, 1998-99; Philadelphia Eagles, 1999-2000; New Eng Patriots, wide receiver, 2001. *

SMALL, WILLIAM
Administrator. **Personal:** Born Dec 5, 1940, Elizabeth, NJ; married Carolyn; children: William & Michael. **Educ:** Howard Univ, AB, 1962; Howard Univ, JD, 1965. **Career:** Contract Admin, dir, 1975-; William Paterson Col, dir acad serv, 1971; William Patterson Col, asso prof, 1970; Newark St Col, instr, 1970; CAFEO, dep dir, acting exec dir, 1969; Union Co Legal Serv Corp, chief investigator, 1968-69; Domar Buckle Mfg Corp, laborer, 1959; Astro Air Prod Corp, laborer, 1960-61; Western Elec Corp, laborer, 1962; Union Co Legal Serv Corp, 1968-69; Polit Sci Soc; The Promethean vpresSummer Serv Corp, pub & circulation mgr, 1969; Title 1, asv com; Plans for Progress Task Force on Youth Motivation, part; Mayors Task Force. **Orgs:** Bd trustees, Urban League of Eastern Union Co; Concern Inc; adv, various comn based youth groups; SPS conflict mgt educ consult firm. **Honors/Awds:** Outstanding Achievement Award, Fed Jurisdiction; Outstanding Service Award, William & Paterson Col Student Govt Asn; Service Award, Nat Headquarters Boy Scouts Am, 1974-75; Outstanding Trainee, Univ Co 3re BCTBde; Outstanding Trainee, postwide competition; National Defence Service Medal; Vietnamese Service Medal; Vietnamese Campaign Medal; Good Conduct Medal; Army Commedation Medal. **Military Serv:** Military Serv, E-5, 1956-67. **Business Addr:** Dean of Social Sciences, William Patterson College, 300 Pompton Rd, Wayne, NJ 07470.

SMALLEY, PAUL
Manager. **Personal:** Born Dec 8, 1935, Gay Head, MA; married; children: Polly, Patrick. **Career:** Comn Rel NE; Gen Dynamics, 1958-69; Adv Com OIC Nat Tech V. **Orgs:** Chmn, OIC Reg I; chmn, Deep River Dem Town, 1980-82; v chmn, Reg Bd Ed, 1973-79; CT NAACP St Bd Fin; mem bd dir, Urban League Gr Hartford; min adv bd chmn, WFSB-TV-3. **Military Serv:** USMC, 1954-75.

SMALLS, CHARLEY MAE
Scientist. **Personal:** Born Oct 22, 1943, Charleston, SC; daughter of Charles A Smalls Sr and Ida Mae White (deceased). **Educ:** Knoxville Col, BS, 1965; Univ Md, MS, Zool, 1972. **Career:** Med Univ SC, Dept Anat, lab technician, 1965-68; Johns Hopkins Univ, Dept Path, res technician, 1968-70; Dept Zoology, Univ Md, grad asst, 1970-72; Dept Anat Milton S Hershey Med Ctr, res asst, 1973-79; US EPA, EPA asst, 1980-81, environ scientist, 1981-88, HMC/EPA Environ Monitoring Lab, environ radiation specialist, 1988-90, environ radiation specialist, 1990-94, div health physics. **Orgs:** Capital Presb Church, deacon, 1986-90, elder, 1992-; Microscopy Soc Am; Pa Alliance for Environ Educ; Susquehana Valley Health Physics Soc; Alpha Kappa Alpha Sorority. **Honors/Awds:** CM Smalls & MD Goode, 1977; "Ca2 Accumulating Components in Dev Skeletal Muscle" J Morph, 1977; Bronze Medal, US Environ Protection Agency, 1980, 1988; 'Award for Excellence', Commonwealth Pa, Dept Environ Protection, 2001. **Home Addr:** 1901 Herr St, Harrisburg, PA 17103.

SMALLS, DIEDRE A
Executive. **Career:** Grey Global Group, vpres & group mgt supvr. **Orgs:** New Prof Theatre. **Honors/Awds:** Outstanding Women in Marketing & Communication, Ebony Mag, 2003. **Special Achievements:** featured in various magazines including EBONY, ESSENCE.

SMALLS, DOROTHY M.
Educator. **Personal:** Born Jan 2, 1920, Georgetown, SC; divorced; children: Eleanor J, Carla S, Lois D. **Educ:** SC State Col, BS, 1940, MS, 1960; Univ SC; Univ Chicago. **Career:** Bd End Georgetown, eng teacher; JB Beck Elem Georgetown, elem sch teacher; Kensington Sch Georgetown, reading consultant; Wm C Reavis Sch Chicago, teacher; Beck Jr High Sch Georgetown, teacher eng, reading. **Orgs:** United Teaching Prof; Pee Dee Reading Coun; Nat Coun Reading; pres, SC State Alumni; secy, GC Educ Asn; pres, Dis Missions; Nat Asn Advan Colored People; Voter Regist; Home Missions.

SMALLS, EVELYN F
President (Organization), chief executive officer. **Career:** United Bank Philadelphia, sr vpres, 1993-2000, pres & chief exec officer, 2000-. **Business Addr:** President, Chief Executive Officer, United Bank of Philadelphia, 30 S 15th St Suite 1200, Philadelphia, PA 19102, **Business Phone:** (215)351-4600 Ext 105.*

SMALLS, DR. JACQUELYN ELAINE
Consultant, pathologist. **Personal:** Born Nov 16, 1946, Charleston, SC; daughter of Charles Augustus Sr and Ida Mae White (deceased); married Willard Goodnight Jr, Oct 12, 1991. **Educ:** Hampton Inst, BA, 1968; Pa State Univ, MA, 1976; Howard Univ, MS, 1980, PhD, 1984. **Career:** Grad fel, Pa St Univ, 1970, 1971 & 1973; fel, Howard Univ, 1978-83; York City Pub Sch, speech pathologist, 1968-78; Blast IU 14, coordr, 1975-76; Pub Sch Prog, consult, prog evaluator, 1982; DC Pub Schs, speech pathologist, 1982; Mentally Retarded C & Adults, consult, 1987; Functional Commun Assocs Inc, partner. **Orgs:** Consult, Nat Educ Asn, 1975; Philadelphia Pub Sch, 1982; Am Speech Lang & Hearing, 1982; Sgt Memorial Presbyterian Church, 1983. **Honors/Awds:** Distinguished Am. **Special Achievements:** MD Licensure, 1995.

SMALLS, MARCELLA E
Executive, administrator. **Personal:** Born Sep 30, 1946, McClellanville, SC; children: Marcus. **Educ:** Voorhees Col, attended 1963-65; Durham Col, BA, 1968. **Career:** South Santee Germantown Action Group, fin secy, 1980-83; SC Charleston Chap Nat Sec Asn, name tag comnr, 1982; South-Santee Comm Ctr, bd dir, 1983; Howard AME Church, asst secy, 1982-; Amoco Chem Co, acct; Sewee Santee CDC, adminr, currently. **Orgs:** Treas, Amoco Chem Recreation Club, 1983; secy, trustee Bldg Fund Howard AME Church; fin adv, Jr Achievement Cainhoy HS, 1986-87; chmn, March Dimes, Amoco Chem Co, 1989-91; March Dimes Ad Bd, Charleston Chap, currently; treas, PTA, St James Santee Elem Sch, McClellanville, SC; past chmn, Qual Awareness Recognition Subcomt; Amoco Cooper River Wellness Focus Comn, Amoco Bonner & Moore; COMPASS implementation team mem. **Honors/Awds:** Employee of the Month, Jan 1989; Opportunity for Improvement Winner, 1991. **Home Addr:** 1940 Hill Rd, McClellanville, SC 29458. **Business Addr:** Administrator, Sewee to Santee CDC, PO Box 26, McClellanville, SC 29458, **Business Phone:** (843)887-4453.

SMALLS, MARVA
Executive. **Educ:** Univ SC, BA, MA, pub admin. **Career:** Gov Richard Riley, SC Pvt Indust Coun, staff dir; Congressman Robin Tallon, chief staff; Nickelodeon, Nick Nite, Network Rels, sr vpres, Pub Affairs, exec vpres & chief staff, currently. **Orgs:** Nat Asn Advan Colored People; Nat Dem Inst; Northside Ctr Child Develop; Big Bros Big Sisters Am; Nat Bank SC; SC Educ TV Endowment Comn; Univ SC Educ Found; Nat Alumni Coun; Bd Noggin; Exec Leadership Coun; Alpha Kappa Alpha Sorority; Trinity Baptist Church. **Honors/Awds:** George C Peabody Award; Golden CableAce Award. **Business Addr:** Executive Vice President, Chief Staff, Nickelodeon, 1515 Broadway 38th Fl, New York, NY 10036, **Business Phone:** (212)258-8000.

SMALLS, O'NEAL
Educator. **Personal:** Born Sep 7, 1941, Myrtle Beach, SC. **Educ:** Tuskegee Inst, BS, 1964; Harvard Law Sch, JD, 1967; Georgetown Univ, LLM, 1975. **Career:** Am Univ, assoc prof, 1969-76; Syst & Appl Sci Corp, bd dir, 1974-85; George Washington Univ Sch Law, prof law, 1976-79; Am Univ, prof law, 1979-88; Univ SC Sch Law, prof, 1988, distinguished prof emer law, currently. **Orgs:** Harvard Law Sch Res Comn, 1966-67; asst dir, Harvard Law Sch Summer Prog Minority Stud, 1966; dir admis & chmn Comt Admis & Scholars, Am Univ, 1970-74; DC, Nat Am Bar Asns; serv comn & bd trustees, Law Sch Admis Coun Princeton, 1972-76; adv comn, Legis Serv Plan Laborers Dist coun Wash DC, 1973-75; bd dir, Syst & Appl Sci Corp, 1974-85; bd chmn, Frewood Found,1987-; chmn bd dir, Skyanchor Corp; exec bd, DC Bapt Conv; pres & chmn bd, Freedoms Found, Myrtle Beach, SC, currently. **Special Achievements:** Articles "Class Actions Under Title VII", Am Univ Law Rev, 1976; "The Path & The Promised Land", Am Univ Law Rev, 1972; booklets "New Directions, An Urban Reclamation Program for the Dist of Columbia", 1982; "Manhood Training An Introduction to Adulthood for Inner City Boys Ages 11-13",1985. **Military Serv:** AUS, capt, 1967-69. **Business Addr:** Distinguished Professor Emeritus of Law, University of South Carolina, School of Law, 701 Main St, Columbia, SC 29208, **Business Phone:** (803)777-4155.

SMALLWOOD, DR. CATHERINE
Educator, television show host. **Personal:** Born in East St Louis, IL; daughter of Charles Junior and Lela Bell; widowed; children: Gayle Shields & Cynthia (deceased). **Educ:** San Francisco Stat Univ, BA, 1974; Union Inst, Cincinnati, Ohio, PhD, 1976. **Career:** Antioch Univ, adj prof, 1974-77; San Francisco City & County, Comn StatusWomen, exec dir, 1975-80; Urban Health Inst, exec dir, pres, 1980-; SanFrancisco St Univ, Sch Social Work, Sch Extended Educ, asst prof, 1991-; Christian Free Radio Oakland, 93.7FM, producer, host, "Black Pathways-Your Mental Health", 1998; KBST TV, Channel 37, producer, host, "Black Mental Health", 1998-99; KVEN, TV, Channel 26, host & producer, "Pathways", 1999-. **Orgs:** Founder & chair, Cindy Smallwood Med Educ Found, 1973-; alumni, San Mateo County Grand Jury Asn, 1977-78; assoc mem, Inst Multicultural Res & SocialWork Pract, 1992-; chair, Black Repertory Theater, Audit Comt, 1995-; lifetime mem, NAACP, San Mateo Br, Exec Comt, 1995-; pres, Top Ladies Distinction, San Francisco Chapt, 1997-; lifetime mem, Calif Parent Teacher's Asn. **Honors/Awds:** San Mateo County Women's Hall of Fame Award, 1985; Calif St Assembly Commendation, 1985; San Francisco Bd Supvrs Commendation, 1994; Distinguished Grandmother Award, African Am Community Entrustment, Affinity Group & United Way, 1999. **Special Achievements:** Co-authored: Quasi-Mortiside, Self Destructive Behavior: Reversing the Cycle in the African-American Community, Pittsburgh, Pa, Dorrance Publ, 1977; Black on Black Homicide: The National Medical Association's Responsibilities, J Nat Med Asn, Norwalk, Conn, 1986; Calif Community Action Prog Training & Tech, manual, 1974; featured columnist, Sun Reporter. **Home Addr:** 817 Juno Lane, Foster City, CA 94404.

SMALLWOOD, RICHARD
Gospel singer, musician. **Personal:** Born Nov 30, 1948, Atlanta, GA. **Educ:** Howard Univ, grad, ethnomusicology; Howard Univ Divinity Sch. **Career:** Gospel vocalist, pianist, composer: Richard Smallwood Singers, founder,1977; Vision, mem; Albums with Richard Smallwood Singers: Richard Smallwood Singers, 1982; Psalms, 1984; Textures, 1986; Vision, 1988; ortrait, 1990; Testimony, 1992; Live at Howard Univ,1993; Albums with Vision: Adoration: Live in Atlanta, 1996; Rejoice, 1997; Healing: Live in Detroit, 1999; Persuaded: Live in D.C., 2001; Journey: Live in New York, 2007; Compilations: Gospel Greats, 1994; Memorable Moments, 1999; Praise & Worship Songs of Richard Smallwood With Vision, 2003; Quintessential Collection, 2007; "Center of My Joy", 2007; Run To Him, 2008; Metrop Baptist Church, assoc minister, currently; Metrop Music Ministry Metrop Baptist Church, artist-in-residence, currently. **Honors/Awds:** Numerous honors & awards including Distinguished Achievement Award, Howard Univ; Stellar Award for Choir of the Year, 2000; Stellar Award for Traditional Male Vocalist of the Year, 2000; Stellar Award for Traditional Choir of the Year, 2000; Stellar Award for Choir of the Year, 2003; Gospel Music Hall of Fame, 2006. **Business Addr:** Gospel Vocalist, c/o The Alliance Agency, 1035 Bates Ct, Hendersonville, TN 37075, **Business Phone:** (615)822-5308.

SMALLWOOD, WILLIAM LEE
School administrator, city council member. **Personal:** Born Sep 2, 1945, York, PA; son of Vera Horton and Herman L; married Janis M Rozelle; children: Yolanda M Sherrer, Aundrea L & Liza D. **Educ:** USAF Personnel Tech Sch, Personnel Cert, 1963; LaSalle Exten Univ, Acct Cert, 1968; Penn State Univ, Continuing Ed, 1971; Empire State Col-State Univ NY, Distance Learning, 1983. **Career:** US Civil Serv, acct clerk, 1967-68; LIAB Aircraft Corp, admin, 1968-69; WJ Grant Co, credit mgr, 1969-70; Caterpillar Inc, track press operator-material handler, 1970-71; Community Progress Coun Inc, bus mgr, 1971-74; Pa Dept Community Affairs, admin Officer, 1974-79; York City Coun, 1977-80, pres, 1984-, councilman, currently; York Co Off Employment & Training, exec dir, 1979-80; Crispus Attucks Asn Inc, housing financial coor, 1980-88. **Orgs:** Founder, Minority Bus Asn Inc, 1983-; bd mem, Leadership York, 1983-87; Off Minority Bus Develop, 1992-; pres, William C Goodridge Bus Resource Ctr, 1993-; York Co Industrial Dev Corp, 1994-; S Pershing Community Develop Corp, 1994-. **Honors/Awds:** Resolution for Service, City of York, PA, 1980; Certificate of Merit, Crispus Attucks Asn Inc, 1985; Pres's Salute, Nat Conf on Sch & Col Colla, 1991; Awarded Honorable Mention, Nat Univ Continuing Educ Asn, 1991; Public Service Award, Minortiy Bus Asn Inc, 1992. **Special Achievements:** The second black man elected to serve the York City Council. **Military Serv:** USAF, E-4, AIC, 1963-67; Air Force Longevity Serv Medal 1967; Vietnam Serv Medal, 1967. **Home Phone:** (717)845-1901. **Business Phone:** (717)771-4068.

SMEDLEY, ERIC ALAN
Football player. **Personal:** Born Jul 23, 1973, Charleston, WV. **Educ:** Ind Univ. **Career:** Buffalo Bills, defensive back, 1996-98; Indianapolis Colts, safety, 1999. **Honors/Awds:** Rookie of the Year, 1996.

SMILEY, DR. EMMETT L
Dentist. **Personal:** Born Jun 14, 1922, Montgomery, AL; son of George Washington Smiley (deceased) and Hattie Dabney Smiley (deceased); married Mary Jo Carter, Aug 14, 1953; children: Lynn S Hampton, Karen J, Kim A & George Wesley. **Educ:** AL State Univ, BS, 1945; Prairie View Univ, Hempstead, Tex; Univ Florence, Florence Italy; Meharry Med Col, DDS, 1950. **Career:** Pvt pract, dentist, 1950-. **Orgs:** Pres, Ala Dental Soc, 1964-66; exec bd, Ala Dental Soc, 1966-; pres, Capitol City Med Soc, 1968-70; Nat Dental Asn; Mid-century Dental Asn; Ewell Neil Dental Soc; Delta Dental Care Inc; adv bd Urban League; mem, Montgomery Area C C; Mayors Com on Comm Affairs, 1964-70; Montgomery Improvement Asn; Alpha Phi Alpha Frat past pres; Cligue Social Club past pres; Cleveland Ave Branch YMCA; Century Club mem; mem, Phi Boule. **Honors/Awds:** Listed in AL Dept of Archives History under "Men of Prominence"; Service Award, Alabama Dental Soc, 1990. **Military Serv:** AUS, Corporal, 1942-45. **Home Addr:** 4601 Lawnwood Dr, Montgomery, AL 36108, **Home Phone:** (205)263-7418. **Business Addr:** Physician, 1031 Oak St, Montgomery, AL 36108, **Business Phone:** (334)263-7418.

SMILEY, JAMES WALKER, SR.
Government official. **Personal:** Born May 19, 1928, Selma, AL; son of David Sr. and Sophia Deanna Bonner; married Lillian; children: James W Jr, Gloria Jean, Jacqueline, Carolyn Smiley-Robinson. **Educ:** Evening Col, 1968; Univ Cincinnati. **Career:** government official (retired); US Postal Serv, line foreman, 1967-68, exec secy, 1968-69, gen foreman, 1969-74, opers mgr, 1974-78, mgr mail distrib, 1978-81, dir mail processing, 1981-85; Woodlawn, OH, councilman, 1980-81 & 1983-87; Village Woodlawn, Woodlawn, OH, adminr, 1989-92. **Orgs:** Nat Asn Advan Colored People; Nat Asn Postal Supervisors; nat vpres, Nat Phoenix Asn Postal Mgrs, 1983-l985; bd dirs & pres, Cincinniti Hypertension Educ, 1989-95; pres, Ideal Investment Club. **Honors/Awds:** Superior Accomplish Award, US Postal Serv, 1969; Dedicated Service, Nat Asn Postal & Fed Employees, 1981; Outstanding/Dedicated Service, Nat Phoenix Asn Postal Managers, 1983. **Military Serv:** RA sfc 5 years; World War II Victory, Good Conduct, 1946-52. **Home Addr:** 1122 Prairie Ave, Cincinnati, OH 45215. *

SMILEY, TAVIS
Television journalist. **Personal:** Born Sep 13, 1964, Biloxi, MS; son of Joyce M and Emory G. **Educ:** Ind Univ, attended 1986. **Career:** Mayor Tomilea Allison, asst mayor, 1984-85; Pat Russell, coun pres & coun aide, 1987; Southern Christian Leadership Conf, LA, special asst exd, 1978-88; Mayor Tom Bradley, ade aide, 1988-90; self-employed; The Smiley Report, radio & tv commentator, 1990-2001; BET Tonight, host, 2001; ABC TV, spec corresp, 2001-; Tavis Smiley (talk show), chief exec officer, 2004-. **Orgs:** Chmn, Opers Comt, LA's Young Black Profs, 1988-90; adv bd, Inner City FND Excellence Edu, 1989-91; bd dir, Challengers Boys & Girls Club, 1989-; bd dir, Los Angeles Black CLG Tour, 1991-; KAP; adv bd, Martin Luther King Jr Ctr Non-violent Soc Change, 1992-93; adv bd, After Class Scouting, Scouting USA, 1991; steering comt, United Way Greater Los Angeles, 1989-90. **Honors/Awds:** Outstanding Business & Professional Award, Dollars & Sense Mag, 1992; Hall of Fame, Vanity Fair, 1996; PRS Image Award, NCP, 2000; Image Award, Best News Talk or Info Series, 1999; Mickey Leland Humanitarian Award, Nat Asn Minorities Commun, 1998. **Special Achievements:** US Debate Team, "International Dialogue," 1986; Author: Straight Talk About the Wrongs of The Right, Anchor & Doubleday. **Business**

Addr: Organiser, The Smiley Group Inc., The Tavis Smiley Show, 3870 Crenshaw Blvd Suite 391, Los Angeles, CA 90043-1208, **Business Phone:** (323)290-4690.

SMILEY-ROBERTSON, CAROLYN
Systems analyst, counselor, consultant. **Personal:** Born Aug 26, 1954, Cincinnati, OH; daughter of James W and Lillian Anderson; married Tommie L, Nov 19, 1983; children: Kevin James & Michael John. **Educ:** Wellesley Col, BA, 1976. **Career:** Western Southern Life Ins, programmer, 1976-78; AT&T, systems develop specialist, 1978-83, mgr, systems analyst, 1984-85, mgr, info mgmt, 1985-96, dist mgr, 1996-2002; Village Woodlawn, coun mem, 1978-84; Village Evendale, Pres of Council, 2003-; consultant, currently. **Orgs:** Woodlawn Bd Zoning Appeals, 1978-82; Woodlawn Planning Comn, 1978-84;trustee, Woodlawn Community Improvement Corp, 1981-; econ consult, VillageWoodlawn, 1984-. **Honors/Awds:** Ambassador, Village Woodlawn, 1980; vice mayor, Village of Woodlawn, 1982;YMCA Black Achiever, Cincinnati, OH, 1983. **Home Addr:** 9620 Otterbein Rd, Cincinnati, OH 45241. **Business Addr:** President of Council, Village of Evendale, 10500 Reading Rd, Evendale, OH 45241, **Business Phone:** (513)563-2244.

SMIRNI, ALLAN DESMOND
Lawyer. **Personal:** Born Aug 27, 1939, New York City, NY; son of Donald and Ruby; married Barbara; children: Amie. **Educ:** City Univ NY, Brooklyn Col, BA, 1960; Univ Calif, Law Sch, Berkeley, JD, 1971. **Career:** Brobeck Phleger & Harrison, assoc atty, 1971-74; Envirotech Corp, asst gen couns, asst secy, 1974-81; TeleVideo Systems Inc, chief couns & secy, 1982-86; Memorex Corp, vpres, gen couns & secy, 1987-89; Pyramid Technology Corp, Siemens Pyramid Info Systems Inc, vpres, gen coun, secy, 1989-. **Orgs:** State Calif Job Training & Develop, 1970-72; State Bar Calif, 1972-; Charles Houston Bar Asn, 1972-; Am Soc Corp Secy, 1976-; trustee, Envirotech Found, 1978-81; Am Asn Corp Coun, 1982-; trustee, TeleVideo Found, 1983-; Soc Corp Secretaries & Governance Prof. **Military Serv:** USAF capt; AF Commendation Medal, 1966. **Home Addr:** 1363 Lennox Dr, Sunnyvale, CA 94087. **Business Phone:** (408)428-8486.

SMITH, AL FREDRICK
Football player, president (organization). **Personal:** Born Nov 26, 1964, Los Angeles, CA; married; children: 3. **Educ:** Utah State Univ, BS, sociol, 1987; Tennessee State Univ, MS, sports admin. **Career:** Football player (retired), dir; Houston Oilers, linebacker, 1987-96; Tenn Titans, dir player develop & pro personnel; Masterplan Group, dir player personnel & partner football opers, currently. **Honors/Awds:** Pro Bowler: 1991, 1992.

SMITH, DR. ALBERT E
College administrator. **Personal:** Born Oct 24, 1932, Sioux Falls, SD; son of Ethel Johnson Smith and Calvert Smith; married Sadie Burris, Jan 27, 1956; children: Albert Clayton, Robbin Renae & Angela E. **Educ:** NC A&T State Univ, Greensboro NC, BS, 1956; George Williams Col, Downers Grove Ill, MS, 1963; Univ Pittsburgh, Pittsburgh Pa, PhD, 1984. **Career:** Knoxville Col, Knoxville Tenn, dir stud ctr & head baseball coach, 1964-66; NC A&T State Univ, Greensboro NC, dir intercol athletics & memorial stud union, 1968-71; Univ Pittsburgh, Pittsburgh Pa, exec asst dir intercol athletics & lectr, 1971-75; Eastern Mich Univ, Ypsilanti Mich, dir intercol athletics & assoc prof educ, 1975-76; NC A&T State Univ, Greensboro NC, vice chancellor develop & univ rel, 1976-86; SC State Col, Orangeburg SC, pres, 1986; Florida Memorial Univ, pres, currently. **Orgs:** Chmn, coun pres, SC State Col & Univ; adv comt, Off Advan Pub Black Col; adv bd, Gov's Agr & Rural Econ Develop Task Force; comnr, Commn Future SC; bd dir, SC Heart Asn, First Nat Bank Orangeburg, City Indust Develop Comn, SC Bus Week. **Honors/Awds:** Inventor, Desk Ornament, 1982; Inventor, Combined Clock & Advert Display, 1984; NC A&T Sports Hall of Fame, NC A&T State Col & Univ, 1988; Hall of Fame, Mid-Eastern Athletic Conf; Second Ann Golden Achievement Award, Afro-Am Hist Club, George Wash Carver High Sch. **Special Achievements:** "A Plan for the Development of the Afro-American Cultural and Entertainment Complex, Univ of Pittsburgh, Pittsburgh PA," 1974; "Reach for Progress," Greensboro Business, (Greensboro Chamber of Commerce Publication) Greensboro NC, 1968; Weekly Sports Column, Carolina Peacemaker, Greensboro NC, 1968. **Military Serv:** AUS, 2nd lt. **Business Addr:** President, Florida Memorial University, 15800 Northwest 42nd Ave, Miami, FL 33054, **Business Phone:** (305)626-3600.

SMITH, ALFRED J., JR.
Educator. **Personal:** Born Jul 9, 1948, Montclair, NJ; married Judith Moore. **Educ:** Boston Univ, BFA, 1970, MFA, 1972. **Career:** Natl Ctr Afro-Amer Art, instr art, 1969-72; Boston Univ Afro-Amer Center,dir cult affrs, 1970-71; Howard Univ, assoc art, 1972, prof & chair, currently; Norfolk Correct Inst, instr art, 1970-72; Boston Univ, asst instr, 1970-72. **Orgs:** Nat Conf Art. **Honors/Awds:** Boston Univ, "Educ to Africa Assn" African Amer Inst Teachers Assist grant, 1970-72; Boston Univ, art award, 1967-68, 1970; comm from City Boston in "Grtr Walls & Spaces" compet 1972; partic in num exhib; Natl Endow grant for crafts, 1975. **Home Addr:** 10901 Little Patuxent Pkwy, Columbia, MD 21044, **Home Phone:** (410)772-4800. **Business Addr:** Professor, Chair, Howard University, Department of Art, 2455 Sixth St NW, Washington, DC 20059, **Business Phone:** (202)806-7047.

SMITH, BISHOP ALFRED M
Clergy. **Personal:** Born Sep 7, 1930, Detroit, MI; son of Bishop Alfred (deceased) and Minnie J; married Roberta Williams; children: Daryl Michael, Beverly Gail Otis & Marsha Renee Brown. **Educ:** Detroit Bible Col, 1956; Univ Mich, attended; Wayne State Univ, attended. **Career:** Indiane Ave COGIC, asst pastor, 1957; Shiloh Chapel COGIC, founder, pastor, 1962-; Penecostal Tabernacle COGIC, 1972; Gen Motors Corp, 1988; Sunday Sch, supt, 1970, bd elders, chair, 1971, admin asst, 1975, sr admin asst, 1995. **Orgs:** Exec secy, Great Lakes Jurisdiction COGIC, 1966-93; Church God Christ, Nat Registration Dept; Nat Ways & Means Comn; Nat Standards & Jurisdiction Extension Comn; Gen Assembly Exec Comn; Nat Constitutional Comn; Am Mgt Asn; coordr, United Found Gen Motors Corp, 1972-83; United Way Mich, Finance Allocation Comn, 1978-80. **Business Addr:** Pastor, Shiloh Chapel Church of God in Christ, 14841 Eastburn Ave, Detroit, MI 48205, **Business Phone:** (313)527-5400.

SMITH, ALICE
School administrator. **Educ:** Fort Valley State Col, BA, French Lit, 1968; Atlanta Univ, MA, French Lit, 1969; Yale Univ New Haven, Conn, Intensive Lang & Lit, 1970; Mich State Univ, French Lit, 1971-72; Sorbonne, Paris, France, Modern French Lit, 1972-73; Columbia Univ New York, German Lang, 1973; Univ Mass, PhD, French Lit, 1978. **Career:** Hawkinsville HS, instr, 1967; Fort Valley State Col, instr 1969-71; Univ Mass, teaching asst, 1973-77, placement counr, 1979-80, dir resource ctr, 1979-81, asst dir, placement servs, 1979-. **Orgs:** Mem Alpha Kappa Mu Nat Hon soc, Alpha Kappa Alpha, Phi Delta Kappa, 1980. **Honors/Awds:** Academic Scholarship, Paris France, 1966; Nat Defense Scholarship, Fort Valley State Col, 1964-68; The Atlanta Univ Fellowship, 1968-69; Nat Fellowships Fund, 1976-78. **Business Addr:** Assistant Director, Placement Services, University of Massachusetts, Amherst, MA 01003, **Business Phone:** (413)545-0111.

SMITH, ALLEN JOSEPH, SR.
School administrator. **Personal:** Born Mar 10, 1936, Chicago, IL; divorced; children: Allen J Jr, Wendy M, Anthony R. **Educ:** Roosevelt Univ, BA, 1960, MA, 1966; Nova Univ, EdD, 1981. **Career:** Chicago Bd Educ, teacher, 1960-67, adult educ teacher, 1964-67, counr, 1967-69, guidance coordr, 1969-82, dir bur guidance, 1982-. **Orgs:** Bd dirs, Parliamentarian Asn Multicultural Couns & Develop, 1978-82, 1985-86; bd dirs, Human Resource Develop Inst, 1984-. **Honors/Awds:** Distinguished Volunteer Award, UN Col Fund, 1984; Educator of the Year, Phi Delta Kappa, 1984; Special Appreciation Award, ANWC, 1985; Certification of Appreciation, Nat Beta Club, 1985.

SMITH, DR. ALONZO NELSON
Educator. **Personal:** Born Oct 11, 1940, Washington, DC; son of Alonzo de Grate and Marie Wright Smint; married Susan T Cramer; children: Anne Marie & Alexander. **Educ:** Georgetown Univ, BS, foreign serv, 1962; Howard Univ, MA, african hist,1967; Univ Calif, Los Angeles, PhD, afro am hist, 1978. **Career:** Los Angeles City Col; Black Studies Ctr Claremont Col, lectr, 1970-75; Cal Poly State Univ, inst hist, 1976-77; Univ Nebr, asst prof, 1978-86; Hampton Univ; Nat Consult Systs, writer, researcher, 1986-89; Africare, Sierra Leone, prog dir, 1991-92; Montgomery Col, Rockville, MD, prof, currently; Smithsonian Nat Mus, assoc curator, 1994-2005. **Orgs:** Omaha Nat Assn Advan Colored People, 1985; Cent Comm Nebr State Dem Party,1985; vpres, Urban League, Nebr, 1989. **Special Achievements:** Article: Afro-Ams and the Presidential Election, 1948; Western J of Black Studies, 1984. **Military Serv:** Peace Corps, W Africa, 1962-64.

SMITH, ALPHONSO LEHMAN
School administrator, dean (education), college teacher. **Personal:** Born Feb 27, 1937, Memphis, TN; divorced; children: Angela, Anthony & Audrey. **Educ:** Fisk Univ, 1957; Ohio State Univ, BS, 1959, MS, 1964. **Career:** Wright State Univ, math instr, 1964-68, asst prof math, 1970-93, asst dir affirmative action fac, 1972-73; dir affirmative action progs, 1973; pres of fac, 1987-91, asst dean, Col Sci & Math, 1991-93, prof emer, 1993. **Orgs:** Fel NSF, 1956-72; Pi Mu Epsilon, 1958-; Phi Beta Kappa, 1960-; Am Math Soc, 1961-; chmn, Ohio Affirmative Action Officers Asn, 1973-; Yellow Springs Title, IX Adv Comt, 1976-77; United Way, 1982-87; Phi Kappa Phi, 1992-. *

SMITH, ANDRE RAPHEL
Conductor (Music). **Personal:** Born in Durham, NC. **Educ:** Univ Miami, BM, trombone; Yale Univ, MA; Curtis Inst Music; Julliard Sch Music. **Career:** New York Philharmonic, asst conductor; St Louis Symphony Orchestra, asst conductor, 1991-94, "In Unison? prog, dir; Philadelphia Orchestra, asst conductor, 1994-2000; Neubrandenburger Philharmonie, guest conductor, 2005; Wheeling Symphony, music dir, currently; New York Philharmonic, guest conductor. **Orgs:** In Unison. **Honors/Awds:** Order of the Long Leaf Pine, NC Senate, 2001; Honorary Commendations, Cities of Philadelphia & St Louis; Honorary Doctorate, W Liberty State Col, 2004; Distinguished Alumnus Award, Yale Univ, 2006. **Business Addr:** Music Director, Wheeling Symphony, 1025 Main St Suite 307, Wheeling, WV 19102-4223, **Business Phone:** (304)232-6191.

SMITH, ANDREW W.
School administrator, singer. **Personal:** Born Aug 24, 1941, Lexington, KY; married Yvonne Bransford; children: Antron William, Avrom Willon & Ahira Yvonne. **Educ:** Ky State Univ, Frankfort, Ky, BS, 1964; Roosevelt Univ, Chicago, M Mus,1970. **Career:** Chicago Brd Educ, teacher, 1964-70; City Markham, dir urban develop, 1971, actg city mgr, 1972-74; Markham Roller Rink Markham, Ill, asst mgr &co-owner, 1972-79; Met Opera, opera singer, 1976-; Opera Orchestra New York, 1979-; Ky State Univ, Dept Music, asst prof, prof & dir, currently. **Orgs:** Opera singer New York City Opera, 1977-79; Houston Grand Opera; Mich Opera; Boston Opera; Atlanta Symphony; Grand Park Summer Festival; Art Park Music Festival; Chicago Sinai Congregation Cantorial Soloist 7 Yrs; Kappa Alpha Phi. **Honors/Awds:** Winner Of Chicago land Music Festival, 1965; WGN Audition Air Met Audition; Emmy Award, 1977; Tony Award. **Home Addr:** 2712 Whiteberry Dr, Lexington, KY 40511. **Business Addr:** Professor, Director, Kentucky State University, Department of Music, 400 E Main St, Frankfort, KY 40601, **Business Phone:** (502)597-6611.

SMITH, DR. ANN ELIZABETH
School administrator. **Personal:** Born Aug 17, 1939, Poplar Bluff, MO; daughter of Leland G (deceased) and Hallie W (deceased). **Educ:** Lincoln Univ, BA, 1960; Univ Iowa, MA, 1962; Union Inst, PhD, 1974. **Career:** Eng Cent High Sch, instr, 1960; E Ill Univ, instr, 1962-66; Univ Ind Black Theatre, lectr, 1971; Northeastern Ill Univ, vpres acad affairs, actg vpres, Speech & Performing Arts, assoc prof, 1975-77, asst to pres, 1969-75, instr, 1966-69; Prudential Ins Co, sales mgr, 1978; Endow Inc, Chicago, IL, vpres, 1978-88; Univ Ill, Chicago, assoc chancellor community affairs, 1988, asst chancellor, dir community rels; Gamaliel Found, pres, currently. **Orgs:** Consult, Dramatic Art; Delta Sigma Theta Sorority, 1957; prod coordr, Orgn Black Am Cult, 1967-; consult, Women's Prog Reg Off HEW & HUD, 1972-73; nat policy bd mem, Union Grad Sch, 1972-75, chairperson, 1974-75; City Col, Commuters & Community Houses; Improving Col & Univ Teaching, 1974; bd mem, League Black Women, 1976-80; bd mem, PUSH Womens Benefit Bd, 1979-90; bd trustees, Univ Ill, 1985-88; bd mem, Chicago Access Corp, 1989-; bd mem, Gamaliel Found, 1990. **Honors/Awds:** International Women's Year Award, Nebr Ill Univ, 1975; PUSH Excellence Award, 1977; Legionaire Award, Prudential Ins Co, 1978-79; Presidential Citation, Prudential Ins Co, 1979; Million Dollar Roundtable Prudential Ins Co, 1980; HDL, Lincoln Univ, 1987; Top 100 Black Business & Professional Women, Dollars & Sense Mag, 1988; Lincoln Univ, honorary doctorate. **Special Achievements:** First African American women to be elected to the board of trustees. **Home Addr:** 505 N Lake Shore Dr, Chicago, IL 60611. **Business Addr:** President, Gamaliel Foundation, 203 N Wabash Ave Suite 808, Chicago, IL 60601, **Business Phone:** (312)357-2639.

SMITH, ANNA DEAVERE
Playwright, actor, educator. **Personal:** Born Sep 18, 1950, Baltimore, MD; daughter of Deavere Young and Anna. **Educ:** Beaver Col, BA; Am Conserv Theatre, MFA, 1976. **Career:** Actress, writer, educator & director; Carnegie-Mellon Univ, Pittsburgh, Pa, asst prof theater, 1978-79; Yale Univ, New Haven, Conn, vis artist, 1982; NY Univ, New York, teacher actg, 1983-84, univ prof; Performance Studies Tisch Sch Arts, art & pub policy affiliate; Nat Theatre Inst, vis teacher, 1984-85; Am Conserv Theatre, master teacher actg, 1986; Univ Southern Calif, Los Angeles, asst prof actg; Lincoln Ctr Inst, teaching artist; Writings: On the Road (play), 1983; Aye, Aye, Aye, I'm Integrated (play), 1984; Piano (play), 1989; Fires in the Mirror: Crown Heights, Brooklyn, & Other Identities (play), 1993; Twilight: Los Angeles, 1994; Talk to Me: Listening between the Lines, 2000; House Arrest: A Search for American Character in & around the White House, Past& Present (play), 2003; Films: Soup for One, 1982; Unfinished Business,1987; Dave, 1993; Philadelphia, 1993; The American President, 1995; The Human Stain, 2003; The Manchurian Candidate, 2004; Cry_Wolf, 2005; Rent, 2005; The Kingdom, 2007; Rachel Getting Married, 2008; TV series: "All My Children", 1970; Fires in the Mirror, writer, 1993; "The West Wing", 2000-06; "The Practice", 2000; "Presidio Med", 2002; Expert Witness, 2003; Life Support, 2007; "Nurse Jackie", 2009; Twilight: Los Angeles, writer & producer, 2000. **Orgs:** Dramatists Guild; Am Fedn TV & Radio Artists; Screen Actors Guild; Actors Equity Asn. **Honors/Awds:** Genius award for theater work, John D & Catherine T Mac Arthur Found, 1996; WAFCA Award, 2003; Black Reel Award, 2004. *

SMITH, ANNE STREET
Social worker. **Personal:** Born Mar 19, 1942, Spartanburg, SC; daughter of Willie L Amos and Sallie McCracken Amos; married Douglas M Smith, May 11, 1991; children: Michael D Street, Jerome Smith, Jared Smith. **Educ:** Howard Univ, BA, 1964, MSW, 1969; Ctr Group Studies, 1974. **Career:** Dept Human Resources, social worker, 1969-72; Howard Univ Hosp Psychol & Social Serv Dept, social worker/instr, 1972-80; Howard Univ Hosp Social

Work Serv Dept, assoc dir, 1980-86; Howard Univ Hosp, Wash DC, dir social servs, 1986-93; Sabbatical Leave, 1993-94; Howard Univ Hosp, social worker, 1994-. **Orgs:** Gamma Sigma Sigma Nat Service Sorority, 1963-; realtor assoc, Jackson Realty, 1989-91; corresp secy bd dir, Ionia R Whipper Home Inc, 1984-85; recording secy, DC Hook-Up Black Women, 1980-84; Nat Asn Social Workers, 1969-; Soc Hosp Social Work Dirs Am Hosp Asn, 1986-93; Am Pub Health Asn, 1986-; Nat Inst Mental Health. **Honors/Awds:** Training Student, Nat Inst Mental Health, 1967-69; Fellowship Grant, Nat Endowment for Humanities, 1980; Prestigious Meritorious Award, DC Hook-Up Black Women, 1983. **Business Addr:** Social Worker, Howard University Hospital, 2041 Georgia Ave NW Rm 2023, Washington, DC 20060.*

SMITH, ANTHONY
Football player. **Personal:** Born Jun 28, 1967, Elizabeth City, NC. **Educ:** Univ Ala, commun. **Career:** Los angeles/Oakland Raiders, defensive end, 1991-97.

SMITH, ANTHONY EDWARD
Manager. **Personal:** Born Nov 14, 1961, Harvey, IL. **Educ:** Univ Ill, Urbana, BS, eng, 1983. **Career:** Owens-Corning Fiberglas, eng intern, 1981-82; Ill Bell Tel Co, asst mgr, 1983-86, area mgr, 1986-. **Orgs:** Am Youth Found, 1978-; pres, Black Stud Union Univ Ill, 1980-81; Ill Soc Gen Engrs, 1982-83; Rotary Int Harvey Club, 1986-; Nat Black MBA Assoc. **Honors/Awds:** Larson Award, Univ Ill, 1983. **Special Achievements:** US Black Engr High Tech Jobs in Midwest 1987.

SMITH, ANTHONY TERRELL. See TONE-LOC.

SMITH, ANTOWAIN DRURELL
Football player. **Personal:** Born Mar 14, 1972, Millbrook, AL. **Educ:** Univ Houston, kinesiol. **Career:** Buffalo Bills, running back, 1997-2000; New Eng Patriots, 2001-03; Tenn Titans, 2004; New Orleans Saints, running back, 2005; Houston Texans, 2006.

SMITH, ARTHUR D.
School administrator. **Personal:** Son of Augusta Banks and Adolphus; divorced. **Educ:** Kent State Univ, BS, 1957, MA, 1962; Yale Univ, PhD, 1973. **Career:** Yale Univ, Transitional Prog, dir, 1968-70; Yale Child Study Ctr, Baldwin-King Prog, dir, 1970-73; Yale Univ, asst dean, 1973-74; Northwestern Univ, assoc prof, 1974-78; Northeastern Univ, dean, 1979-80, assoc provost, 1981-86, dir planning, 1986, dir opers, 1992. **Orgs:** Educ consult, Am Friends, 1974-; chmn bd, Northcare, 1976; assoc provost, Northeastern Univ, 1980-; prog vol evaluator, United Way Boston, 1979-80. **Honors/Awds:** John Hay Fellow, John Hay Whitney Found, 1964; Branford College Fellow, Yale Univ, 1972.

SMITH, ARTHUR L, JR. See ASANTE, DR. MOLEFI KETE.

SMITH, AUBREY CARL
Manager. **Personal:** Born Mar 12, 1942, Clarksdale, MS; son of Aubrey Carl Sr and Mattye Alice Johnson; married Marie Joyce Smith, Jun 17, 1967; children: Nicole Denise & Aubrey Brian. **Educ:** Univ Ill, Chicago, attended 1963; Thornton Community Col, Harvey, AA, sci, 1968; Ill Inst Technol, Chicago, BA, chem, 1972. **Career:** Manager (retired); A B Dick Co, Niles, toner chemist, 1972; Arco Petrol Prod Co, Harvey, anal chemist, 1974, lubricants chemist, 1983, supvr, health, safety & environ protection, 1985; Argonne Nat Lab, Argonne, supvr, waste mgt operations, 1986, lab environ compliance officer, 1988, mgr, waste mgt operations, 1988, dep building mgr, environ compliance rep, 1990-92, building mgr, environ compliance rep, 1992-. **Orgs:** Am Chem Soc, 1983-; Am Soc Lubrication Engs, 1983-85; Soc Automotive Eng, 1983-85; Chicago Nat Safety Coun, 1983-85; Am Soc Testing Materials, 1983-85. **Honors/Awds:** Elected to Dwight D Eisenhower High School Hall of Fame, Blue Island, IL; Selected by Ebony and Jet Magazines "Speaking of People" Sections, 1989; First black person to hold the following positions at Argonne Nat Laboratory: Laboratory Environmental Compliance Officer; Manager, Waste Management Operations. **Military Serv:** AUS, specialist E-4, 1964-66; Vietnam Good Conduct Metal.

SMITH, AUDREY S
Executive, educator. **Personal:** Born Feb 24, 1940, Upper Marlboro, MD; daughter of Frank Spriggs and Mary Henry Spriggs; married Lynn H (divorced 1983); children: Michael & Lisa Miller. **Educ:** Hampton Univ, Hampton, VA, 1957-61; Roger Williams Col, Bristol, RI, BS, 1976; Univ Col, Univ Md, Col Park, MD. **Career:** Brown Univ, Providence, RI, training asst, 1971-73, dir employment & employee rels, 1973-75, from assoc dir personnel, to dir personnal, 1975-81; Montgomery Col, Rockville, MD, dir personnel, 1981-89; Princeton Univ, Princeton, NJ, vpres human resources, 1989-. **Orgs:** Urban League, 1963-; Col & Univ Personnel Asn, 1975-; ACE, 1975-; NIP, 1975-; comt status women, Princeton Univ, 1989-; Multicultural Studies Proj, 1990-; Am Coun Educ; Nat Identification Prog. **Business Addr:** Vice President Human Resources, Princeton University, 1 New S, Princeton, NJ 08544, **Business Phone:** (609)258-3300.

SMITH, BARBARA
Writer. **Personal:** Born Nov 16, 1946, Cleveland, OH. **Educ:** Mount Holyoke Col, BA, 1969; Univ Pittsburgh, MA, 1971; Univ Conn, ABD, 1981. **Career:** Univ Mass, instructor, 1976-81; Barnard Col, instructor, 1983; NY Univ, instructor, 1985; Univ Minn, vis prof, 1986; Hobart William Smith Col, vis prof, 1987; Mount Holyoke Col, vis prof, 1988; Kitchen Table Women Color Press, dir, 1981-95; Books: This Bridge Called My Black: Writings by Radical Women of Color, 1981; All the Blacks Are Men, But Some of Us Are Brave: Black Women's Studies, 1982; Home Girls: A Black Feminist Anthology, 1983; Yours in the Struggle: Three Feminist Perspectives on Anti-Semitism & Racism, 1984; The Truth That Never Hurts: Writings on Race, Gender, & Freedom, 1998. **Orgs:** Mem/founder, Combahee River Collective, 1974-80; artist-in-residence Hambidge Ctr for the Arts & Sci, 1983, Millay Colony Arts, 1983, Yaddo, 1984, Blue Mountain Ctr, 1985; bd dir, NCBLG, 1985-88; mem, NAACP, Black Radical Congress, Feminist Action Network, Nat Writers Union. **Honors/Awds:** Outstanding Woman of Color Award, 1982; Women Educator's Curriculum Award, 1983; Books, "Conditions, Five The Black Women's Issue," co-ed, 1979; "But Some of Us Are Brave, Black Women's Studies," co-ed, 1982; "Home Girls, A Black Feminist Anthology," ed, 1983; "Yours in Struggle, Three Feminist Perspectives on Anti-Semitism and Racism," co-author 1984; The Readers' Companion to US; Women's History, co-ed, 1998; The Truth That Never Hurts: Writing on Race, Gender and Freedom 1968-98, 1998; Stonewall Award, for Service to the Lesbian and Gay, 1994; Scholar-in-Residence, Schomburg Ctr for res in Black Culture, 1995-96; Fel, Bunting Inst Radcliffe Col, 1996-97; Rockefeller Fel, Humanities Ctr, Lesbian & Gay Studies, City Univ, NY, 1998-99. **Home Addr:** 15953 Whitcomb Rd, Cleveland, OH 44110, **Home Phone:** (216)541-6262.

SMITH, BARBARA
Restaurateur. **Personal:** Born Aug 24, 1949; daughter of William H and Florence; married Donald Anderson, Jan 1, 1988 (divorced); children: Dana; married Dan Gasby. **Educ:** John Robert Powers Modeling Sch, 1967. **Career:** Former model, TV host; B Smith's restaurant, owner, 1986-; TV culinary hostess, 1997; B Smith Restaurant Group, owner, 1998-; B Smith Style Home Collection, 2001-; B Smith Jewelry Collection, currently; TV shows: "The Oprah Winfrey Show", ABC's "Good Morning America", "The View" & NBC's "Today". **Orgs:** Trustee, Culinary Inst Am; Feminist Press; founding mem, Times Sq Bus Improv Dist. **Honors/Awds:** First Black Woman on Cover, Mademoiselle, 1976. **Special Achievements:** B Smith's Entertaining and Cooking for Friends, Artisan, 1995; hosted the lifestyle television show B Smith with Style; graced the covers of 15 magazines including Mademoiselle 's first ever featuring an African-American woman; author of two tabletop books on entertaining the host of B. Smart Tips for a Better Life heard on New York 's WBLS-FM, and a columnist for Soap Opera Digest. **Business Phone:** (212)315-1100.

SMITH, DR. BARBARA WHEAT
School administrator, educator. **Personal:** Born May 28, 1948, Mobile, AL; daughter of Sidney W Wheat and Rosetta W Wheat; divorced; children: Daryl E, Yuri J, Afra S & Mastaki A. **Educ:** Tuskegee Univ, BA, 1969; Univ Wis, MA, 1972, PhD, 1982. **Career:** Univ Wis, Sch Nursing, Equal Opportunities Prog, dir, 1973-75, acad adv, 1976, col Agr & Life Sci, 1978-80, asst dean, 1991-; BJ Smith Co Inc, Mobile, pres, 1982-88; Us Census Bur, Mobile Ala, recruiting operations mgr, 1990; Searcy Hosp, psychiatric rehab counr, 1990-91. **Orgs:** Nat Asn Minorities Agr; Nat Resources & Related Sci; historian, Madison Metrop Links Inc; bd dirs, State Ala Ment Health Technicians; bd dirs, Progressive League Inc; bd dirs, Nat Assault Illiteracy; coop bd adv, Asn Women Agr; Nat Conf Black Mayors, Guyana, South Am; Am Ethnic Sci Soc; Nat Coun Negro Women; Ala state prs; Delta Sigma Theta Sorority. **Honors/Awds:** Delta Sigma Theta Sorority Service Award, 1974; Vilas Fel, 1975; Advance Opportunity fel, 1976-78; Pi Lamba Theta, 1976; Nat Soc Minorities Agr Nat Resources & Related Sci, Appreciation Awards, 1993, 1994; Advising Role to Student Clubs, 1993; Distinguished Leadership Award, 1994; Dean Students, Student Orgn Service Appreciation Award, Univ Wis, Madison, 1994; Governor's Service Appreciation Award, State Ala; Univ Wis Admin Develop Prog; Parents Minority Students Adv Coun; Highlighted in articles appearing in the spring issue of Home Address & Wisconsin Week. **Special Achievements:** Numerous Articles published including, Wisconsin Agricultural and Life Sciences Alumni Association, vol 7, no 3, Fall 1978; "Proceedings of the North Central Teaching Symposium", Univ Wis, Madison, June 24-26, 1991; "The Black Collegiate Magazine", 4th edition, 1992; The New Times Newspaper Vol, no 7. **Business Addr:** Assistant Dean, University of Wisconsin, College of Agricultural & Life Sciences, 116 Agriculture Hall 1450 Linden Dr, Madison, WI 53706, **Business Phone:** (608)262-3003.

SMITH, BEN (BENJAMIN J SMITH)
Football player. **Personal:** Born May 14, 1967, Warner Robbins, GA; son of Bennie Joe. **Educ:** Univ Ga, social work; Northeastern Okla A&M Univ. **Career:** Football player (retired); Philadelphia Eagles, free safety, 1990-93; Denver Broncos, 1994; Ariz Cardinals, defensive back, 1995-96. **Honors/Awds:** Defensive MVP hons, 1989.

SMITH, BENJAMIN J. See SMITH, BEN.

SMITH, BEVERLY EVANS
Business owner. **Personal:** Born Apr 12, 1948, Massillon, OH; daughter of Louie Edward and Willa Dumas; married Stephen J, Aug 28, 1970; children: Brian S & Stacy N. **Educ:** Bowling Green State Univ, OH, BS, 1970; Kent State Univ, OH, M.Ed, 1973; Babson Col, Wellesley, MA, Exec Develop Consortium, 1987; St Catherine's Episcopal Church, cert Stephen Minister, 1991. **Career:** Garfield High Sch, teacher, speech, 1971-72: Kent State Univ, Kent, OH,asst dir, Financial Aids, 1972-74, dir, Upward Bound, 1974; Georgia State Univ, Atlanta, GA, asst dean, Student Life, 1976-78; Southern Bell, Atlanta, GA, staff mgr, 1978-83; AT&T, Atlanta GA, dist mgr, 1984-96; Delta Sigma Theta, Wash DC, exec dir, 1988-90; HR Group, prin & vpres, sr partner, currently; Riverside Bank, adv bd; Chattahoochee Tech Col, bd dir. **Orgs:** Past exec dir, Delta Sigma Theta Sorority, 1967; past pres, Jack & Jill, N Suburban Atlanta Chap, 1981-84; state commr, Ga Clean & Beautiful Comn, 1984-88; chair, Adult Educ, St Cathrine's Episcopal Church, 1986-88; CobbCounty Ga governing bd, Leadership Cobb, 1987-91; Project Mgt Inst,1987-89; Asn Chief Exec Coun, 1988-89; bd mem, Women Meaningful Summit,1989; adv bd, United Way, Cobb County, 1991-95; bd dir, Girls Inc, 1992-94; chairperson, Leadership Cobb, 1997-98; Cobb Exec Women, 1998-; adv bd, Riverside Bank; bd trustees, chair, Strategic Planning Comn,Bowling Green State Univ; Soc Human Resource Professionals; exec bd, Atlanta Human Resources Asn. **Honors/Awds:** Outstanding Freshman & Senior Woman, Bowling Green State Univ, 1967, 1970; Mortar Bd Honor Soc, 1969; Omicrom Delta Kappa Honor Soc, 1977; Georgia Woman of the Year in Business, Cobb County Georgia, 1984; Outstanding Business Professional, Washington DC Business Professional Asn, 1988; Salute to Women Achievement Award, YWCA, 1995. **Business Addr:** Senior Partner, The HR Group, PO Box 680634, Marietta, GA 30068-0011.

SMITH, BOB (ROBERT D SMITH)
Businessperson, artist. **Personal:** Born Apr 3, 1932, Chicago, IL; son of Henry D and Lois Etta Bullock; married Rosemary Booker, Aug 24, 1952; children: Laura Susan, David Bernard & Stacy Donnell. **Educ:** East Los Angeles Col, LA, Calif, AA, 1952; Calif Sch Art, Los Angeles, Calif, 1948; Art Ctr Sch Design, Los Angeles, Calif, BPA, 1958. **Career:** Merville Studios, Los Angeles, Calif, illusr, 1959-60; ACP Graphic Art Studio, Los Angeles, Calif, illusr, 1960-62; freelance illusr, Los Angeles, Calif, 1962-67; Tri-Arts Studio, Los Angeles, Calif, illusr, 1967-75; freelance Illusr, Los Angeles, Calif, 1975-; Blacksmiths Cards & Prints, Altadena, Calif, owner, pres, 1980-. **Orgs:** Los Angeles Soc Illusr, 1958-; Graphic Arts Guild; adv comn, Los Angeles Trade Tech Col. **Honors/Awds:** CEBA Award of Distinction, World Inst Black Commun, Graphics Annual Int Annual Advert & Ed Art, 1979-80; Best Black & White Illustration, Soc Illusr, 1960; Exhibitor, Int Exhib Media Arts Commun Arts Mag, 1976, 1978, 1979. **Military Serv:** AUS, Sgt, 1952-54. **Home Addr:** 1024 Royal Oaks DR Apt 908, Monrovia, CA 91016-5405, **Home Phone:** (213)681-1446. **Business Addr:** Owner, Blacksmiths Cards & Prints, PO Box 623, Altadena, CA 91003.

SMITH, BOBBY (ROBERT EUGENE SMITH)
Baseball player. **Personal:** Born May 10, 1974, Oakland, CA. **Career:** Tampa Bay Devil Rays, 1998-02; Milwaukee Brewers, 2003; NY Yankees, 2003;Chicago White Sox, 2003-04; Oakland Athletics, 2005. **Honors/Awds:** Topps Rookie All-Star Third Baseman, 1998. *

SMITH, BOBBY ANTONIA
Government official. **Personal:** Born Feb 12, 1949, West Palm Beach, FL; daughter of Will and Ida Mae; divorced; children: Antonia & Erika. **Educ:** Fla A&M Univ, BS, 1970; Fla State Univ, MPA, 1972; Nova Univ, attended 1983. **Career:** Broward County Sch Dist, Pompano Beach, FL, instr, 1970-73; Fla Dept Community Affairs, Tallahassee, FL, local govt spec II, 1973-75; Fla WPB, asst county adminr, 1975; Fla Wildlife Unlimited Inc, pres, currently. **Orgs:** Nat Asn Advan Colored People; Urban League Palm Beach County. **Honors/Awds:** Public Service Award, Fla A&M Univ, 1979. **Business Addr:** President, Florida Wildlife Unlimited Inc., PO Box 2523, Wauchula, FL 33873, **Business Phone:** (863)767-0930.

SMITH, BRIAN R
Engineer. **Career:** Gen Dynamics Land Systs, biomechanical engr. *

SMITH, BRUCE BERNARD
Football player, businessperson. **Personal:** Born Jun 18, 1963, Norfolk, VA; married Carmen; children: Alston. **Educ:** Va Tech, sociol. **Career:** Football Player(retired), businessperson; Buffalo Bills, defensive end, 1985-99; Wash Redskins, defensive end, 2000-03; Bruce Smith Enterprise, LLC, founder, currently. **Honors/Awds:** Outland Trophy, 1985; AFC Defensive Player of

the Year, NFLPA, 1985; Pro Bowl MVP, 1987; UPI AFL-AFC Player of the Year, 1987, 1988, 1990, 1996; George Halas Trophy, Newspaper Enterprise Asn, 1990, 1993; NFL Defensive Player of the Year, 1990, 1996; Ed Block Courage Award, 1992; Independence Bowl Hall of Fame, 1996; Mackay Award, 1996; Virginia Tech Hall of Fame, 2005; Col Football Hall of Fame, 2006.

SMITH, BRUCE L
Automotive executive, president (organization). **Personal:** Born Oct 15, 1962, McKeesport, PA. **Educ:** Carnegie-Mellon Univ, BS, Mech eng, 1985; Harvard Univ, MBA, 1989. **Career:** Delphi, Gen Motors maintenance supvr, 1985-86, mfg eng, 1989, mfg gen supvr, 1989-90; ITT, mgr mfg syst, 1993-94, exec asst ceo, 1994-95, plant mgr, 1995-97; Diesel Technol Co, pres & ceo; Am Nat Can, dir mfg; Piston Automotive LLC, vpres; United Plastics Group Inc, pres & chief operating officer, currently. **Military Serv:** Air Force, cadet, 1980-81. **Business Addr:** President, Chief Operating Officer, United Plastics Group Inc, 900 Oakmont Lane Suite 100, Westmont, IL 60559, **Business Phone:** (630)321-5500.

SMITH, BUBBA (CHARLES AARON SMITH)
Football player, actor. **Personal:** Born Feb 28, 1945, Orange, TX; son of Charlie Smith; divorced. **Educ:** Mich State Univ, Sociology, 1966. **Career:** Football player (retired), actor; Baltimore Colts, defensive lineman, 1967-71; Oakland Raiders; defensive lineman, 1973-74; Houston Oilers, defensive lineman, 1975-76; Television: Blue Thunder, actor, 1984; Half Nelson, actor, 1985; Film: The New Batch, 1990; MacGyver, actor, 1991; The Naked Truth, actor, 1992; My Samurai, actor, 1992; Fist of Honor, actor, 1993; Silenzio dei prosciutti, actor, 1994; Drifting School, actor, 1995; Sabrina, the Teenage Witch, actor, 1997; Down 'n Dirty, actor, 2000; The Flunky, actor, 2000; Sports Geniuses, actor, 2000; Full Clip, actor, 2004; The Coach, actor, 2004; Negermagasinet, actor, 2005; Television: Who's the Boss?, 1991; Coach, 1992; Family Matters, 1993; Police Academy; Married with Children, 1994; ESPN Sports Century, 2002-05. **Orgs:** Vol Young People in LA Area. **Honors/Awds:** All American, MI State, 1965, 1966; All American Team Sporting News, 1966; AFC All Star Team Sporting News, 1970, 1971; player Super Bowl, 1969, 1971; player AFC Championship, 1973, 1974; First Team All Pro, 1971; Second Team All Pro Twice, 1968, 1970.

SMITH, C MILES
Television journalist. **Personal:** Born Apr 2, 1950, Atlanta, GA; son of Margaret N and C Miles; married Jul 19, 1975 (divorced); children: Calvin Miles III, Nina Patrice & Che Lena. **Educ:** Morehouse Col, BS, 1979. **Career:** WGST-AM, News Radio 640, talk show host; Radio One Corp magnate Cathy Hughes, Radio One 1450 am, talk show host; Talk How You Like Underground Posse On Line Show, host, currently; Radio Diary, host, currently. **Orgs:** Omega Psi Phi, Psi Chapt, Morehouse, 1969. **Business Addr:** Host, Radio Diary, PO Box 71061, Washington, DC 20024, **Business Phone:** (301)808-0833.

SMITH, DR. CALVERT H.
College president, educator. **Educ:** PhD. **Career:** Morris Brown Col, pres; Cincinnati Pub Schs, dep supt, 1992; Univ Cincinnati, Col Educ, Criminal Justice & Human Serv, adj prof, prof emer, currently; Winston-Salem State Univ, brd visitors, currently. **Orgs:** Pres, Cincinnati Br NAACP, 2002-. **Business Phone:** (513)556-3646.

SMITH, CARL WILLIAM
Administrator. **Personal:** Born Jun 8, 1931, Raleigh, NC; married Pearl Mitchell Wilson; children: Wanda, Wendi. **Educ:** St Augustine Col, BA, 1954; NC Cent Univ, MSC, 1962; Univ WI-Madison, attended 1965; Exec Prog Univ NC-Chapel Hill, Cert, 1981. **Career:** Administrator (retired); CE Perry HS, asst prin & teacher, 1954-55; St Augustine's Col, adminr& instr, 1955-60; Consult, PPG Indust, 1969-71; NC Cent Univ, asst chmn & fac, 1961-72; Univ NC-Chapel Hill, asst to the provost, 1972-95. **Orgs:** Am Mgmt Asn; Am Mktg Asn; Am Asn Higher Educ. **Honors/Awds:** Alpha Phi Alpha Frat Inc; Alpha Kappa Mu; Fel Nat Urban League 1968. **Special Achievements:** First black administrator appointed to the provost's office. **Military Serv:** USAF airman 1949. **Home Addr:** 5825 N Beaver Ln, Raleigh, NC 27604. *

SMITH, DR. CARLOS F
Physician. **Educ:** Monmouth Col, Monmouth, IL, BA, 1990; Dr William M Scholl Col Podiatric Med, Chicago, IL, BS, 1994, DPM, 1994; Univ Texas Health Sci Ctr, San Antonio, Tx, internship, 1995; Bellaire Med Ctr, Harris Co Podiatric Surg Prog, Houston, Tx, residency PSR-1924, 1997; Am Bd Podiatric Orthop & Primary Podiatric Med, dipl; Am Bd Podiatric Surg, diplomate. **Career:** Dr William M Scholl Col Podiatric Med, Dept Med & Surg, from clin fac, asst prof, 1997-; Ill Masonic Med Ctr, Dept Surg, clin fac, 1997-; pvt pract, 1997-; Dr. William M Scholl Coll Podiatric Med, Off Minority Student Affairs, actg dir, 1997-2001; Mt Sinai Hosp Med Ctr, Dept Surg, clinical fac, 1998-; Loyola Univ Med Ctr, Dept Orthop Surg & Rehab, lectr, 1999-; Centers for Foot & Ankle Care, chief exec officer & med dir, currently. **Orgs:** Am Diabetes Asn; Am Podiatric Med Asn; Ill Podiatric Med Asn; Durlacher Podiatric Hon Soc, 1991; pres, Cook Co Podiatric Med Asn, 1998-; alumni bd, Monmouth Col, 1998-; bd dirs, Nat Podiatric Med Asn, 1999-; bd trustees, Monmouth Col, 2001-; fel, Am Coll Foot & Ankle Surgeons; fel, Am Coll Foot & Ankle Orthop & Med. **Honors/Awds:** Scholl Col Half-Tuition Scholar, 1991-92; Philip R Brachman & Alumni Scholar, 1992-93; Ill State Podiatric Med Full-Tuition Scholar, 1993-94. **Special Achievements:** listed in Whos Who Among Students In American Universities and Colleges.

SMITH, CAROL BARLOW
Government official, chairperson. **Personal:** Born Mar 9, 1945, Atlanta, GA; married Douglas; children: Eric Douglas. **Educ:** Ark Bus Col; Wayland Baptist Univ, BA (cum laude), 1996. **Career:** Gr Anchorage Area Comm Action Agency Northwest Rep Women's Caucus, pub info specialist; BLM Anchorage, asst to chief br field surveys; City Anchorage, eeo officer; Municipality Anchorage, affirmative action compliance officer & personnel specialist, currently. **Orgs:** Int Asn Official Human Rights Agencies; bd dir, Ark Presswomen; Coun Drug Abuse; Coun Planned Parenthood; bd dir, Citizens Consumer Protection; YWMU; pres, New Hope Baptist Ch; mem bd comnrs, Ark State Human Rights Comn; 2nd vpres, Nat Asn Advan Colored People; Ark Presswomen; Anchorage Bicentennial Comn; chmn, Ark State Human Rights Comm, 1976; Anchorage Equal Rights Asn; chairperson, Nat Asn Advan Colored People, Freedom Fund Banquet, 1972; vice chairperson, Ark State Human Rights Comn. **Honors/Awds:** Business Leader of the Day, 1974; Outstanding Student Award, Wayland Baptist Univ. **Business Addr:** Personnel Specialist, Municipality of Anchorage, 632 W 6th Ave Suite 620, Anchorage, AK 99501, **Business Phone:** (907)343-4896.

SMITH, CAROL J (CAROL J HOBSON)
Consultant. **Personal:** Born Dec 24, 1923, Houston, TX; daughter of Richard T Andrews Sr and Julia Augusta Somerville; divorced; children: Julius W Hobson Jr & Jean M Hobson. **Educ:** Prairie View, BA, 1944; Howard Univ, MA, 1948. **Career:** Howard Univ, grad fel, 1944-45, 1947-48; US Off Educ, dep act asst comn spec concern, 1971-74; US Dept Educ Off Postsecondary Educ, liaison minorities & women in higher educ, 1974-84, prog deleg nat adv comt black higher educ & black cols & univs, 1976-82; US Dept Educ Off Higher Educ Progs, Div Stud Serv, dir, 1984-86; Howard Univ, Wash, DC, conf coordr, 1989-90; pvt pract, consult, currently. **Orgs:** Elder Church Redeemer Presbyterian; adv consult, NAFEO Educ Braintrust, Congressional Black Caucus; vpres, B May's Res Ctr. **Honors/Awds:** Superior Service Award, US Off Educ, 1970; Certificate for Outstanding Performance, US Dept Educ Off Postsecondary Educ, 1979; Achievement Award, Nat Alliance Black Sch Educs, 1982; Leadership Award, Higher Educ Nat Asn Equal Opportunities Higher Educ, 1983; Honored, Nat Coun Educ Opporortunities Asn, 1986; Phenomenal Woman Tribute, 1997. **Business Addr:** Consultant, 4801 Queens Chapel Ter NE, Washington, DC 20017, **Business Phone:** (202)529-1445.

SMITH, CAROLYN LEE
Executive. **Personal:** Born Nov 14, 1942, Lakewood, NJ; daughter of Davis Lee and Arline Erwin Knight; married Vernon, Oct 16, 1965 (deceased); children: Soniab & Angela. **Educ:** Howard Univ, BA, 1965; Univ Md, MBA, 1994. **Career:** United Planning Orgn, specialist, 1965-66; Cooper & Lybrand, audit mgr, 1971-77, nat inst comm dev, vpres financial mgt, 1972-73; DC Dept Fin & Revenue, 1979-82, dir govt dc, tres, 1977-79; Coopers & Lybrand, audit mgr, 1982-85, dir, mgmt consult 1985-86, Pricewaterhouse Coopers, partner 1986-. **Orgs:** Past pres, Met Wash DC Chapt; Greater Wash Bd Trade, 1983-; treas, Pub Access Bd, 1985-87; chmn, DC Bd Accountancy, 1985-88; bd gov DC Inst CPAs, 1985-87; mem, DC Retirement Bd 1988-92; chmn, DC Retirement Bd, 1990-92; Nat Asn Black Accts. **Honors/Awds:** Meritorious Service Awards, DC Govt, 1979,80; Outstanding Achievement Award, Nat Asn Minority CPA Firms, 1979; Proclamation from the Mayor of the District of Columbia for Outstanding Service 1982. **Business Addr:** Partner, Pricewaterhouse Coopers, 1616 N Ft Myer Dr, Arlington, VA 22209, **Business Phone:** (703)465-6967.

SMITH, CARSON EUGENE
School administrator. **Personal:** Born Dec 23, 1943, Louisville, KY; son of Fred Eugene and Louise Bernadine Carson; married Gleneva McCowan, Dec 26, 1965; children: Mark, Shanna, Angela & Andrew. **Educ:** Ky State Univ, BA, Hist & Pol Sci, 1965; Univ Ky, MA, Pol Sci, 1972, Dissertation Stage, 1973. **Career:** Office for Policy & Mgmt State Govt, policy adv for higher educ, 1973-74; Coun on Higher Educ, coordr for fin planning, 1974-77; Univ Ky, asst budget dir 1977-80; Univ Mo, asst dir budget, 1980-83; Ky State Univ, Frankfort, Ky, vpres, admin servs, fin & admin; Univ Ky, Col Medicine, Lexington, Ky, bus mgr; State Univ New York, Canton, vpres, Admin Servs, 2001-. **Orgs:** Central Assoc Col & Univ Bus Officers, Southern Assoc Col & Univ Bus Officers, Nat Assoc Col & Univ Bus Officers, EDUCAUSE, Alpha Phi Alpha 1962-. **Honors/Awds:** Who's Who in the South and Southwest, Who's Who Among Black Americans, Outstanding Young Men of America. **Military Serv:** USAF (Personnel Quality Control/Data Processing), capt, 4 yrs. **Home Phone:** (502)227-2850. **Business Addr:** Vice President for Administrative Services, State University of New York, 34 Cornell Dr, Faculty Office Bldg Rm No 612, Canton, NY 13617, **Business Phone:** (315)386-7103.

SMITH, CEDRIC DELON
Football player, football coach. **Personal:** Born May 27, 1968, Enterprise, AL; married Nicole; children: Cole, Chandler & Canyon. **Educ:** Univ Fla, BS, 1990, rehabilitative coun, 1993. **Career:** Football player (retired), Football coach; Univ, 1986-89; Fla MinnVikings, running back, 1990; New Orleans Saints, 1991; Wash Redskins, 1994-95; Ariz Cardinals, 1996-97; Mental Hosp, Gainesville; Denver Broncos, asst strength & conditioning coach, 2001-06; Kansas City Chief, strength & conditioning coach, 2007-. **Home Addr:** Parker, CO 80134. **Business Addr:** Strength & Conditioning Coach, Kansas City Chief, One Arrowhead Dr, Kansas City, MO 64129, **Business Phone:** (816)920-9300.

SMITH, CHARLES AARON. See SMITH, BUBBA.

SMITH, CHARLES CORNELIUS
Basketball player. **Personal:** Born Aug 22, 1975, Fort Worth, TX. **Educ:** Nmex State Univ. **Career:** Miami Heat, guard, 1997-98; Los Angeles Clippers, 1998-99; Rockford Lightning, 1999-2000; Amatori Basket Udine, 2000-01; San Antonio Spurs,2001-02; Portland Trail Blazers, 2002-03, 2005-06; Makedonikos Kozani, 2003; Virtus Bologna, 2003-04; Scavolini Pesaro, 2004-05; Denver Nuggets, 2006; Efes Pilsen Istanbul, 2006, 2008-; Real Madrid, 2006-08; Efes Pilsen Istanbul, 2008-. **Honors/Awds:** Alphonso Ford Top Scorer Trophy, 2005; 2007 ULEB Cup Final MVP; Turkish National Championship, 2009.

SMITH, CHARLES DANIEL
Association executive, chief executive officer, basketball player. **Personal:** Born Jul 16, 1965, Bridgeport, CT; son of Charles D Smith and Dorthy J Childs Lee. **Educ:** Univ Pittsburgh, attended 1988. **Career:** Basketball player (retired), asn exec, chief exec officer; Los Angeles Clippers, ctr-forward, 1988-92; NY Knicks, ctr-forward, 1992-96; San Antonio Spurs, ctr-forward, 1996-97; Charles Smith Educ Ctr, Bridgeport, CT, owner, founder; Players Capital Mgt, co-founder; Fluid Sports & Entertainment, chief exec officer; NBA Players Asn, regional rep, currently. **Orgs:** Founder, Charles D Smith Jr Foundation, 1989; NBPA Found. **Honors/Awds:** NBA All-Rookie First Team, 1989; member US Olympic team, 1988; Services Appreciation, 5th Cent LA YMCA, 1989; Outstanding Servman, Assemblywoman Maxine Waters, 1990; Key to City, City Bridgeport, 1990. **Business Addr:** Regional Representative, National Basketball Players Association, 2 Penn Plz Suite 2430, New York, NY 10121, **Business Phone:** (212)655-0880.

SMITH, CHARLES EDISON
Educator. **Educ:** California Polytech Univ, BS, 1965; Georgetown Univ, Wash, DC, JD, 1972; Duke Univ, LLM, 1983. **Career:** US Patent & Trademark Off, Wash, DC, patent examr, 1967-69; Xerox Corp, Patent Atty, 1972-75; Bechtel Corp, Patent Atty, 1975-78; Golden Gate Univ, asst prof law, 1977-79; Con Edison, consult, 1987-; NC Cent Univ SchLaw, Durham, NC, prof law, currently. **Orgs:** Arbitrator, Am Bar Asn, 1979-, St reporter (NC), ABA LP Laws, 1986-; Delta Theta Phi Law Frat, 1970-; comnr, NC Statutes Comn, 1987-; atty vol, AIPLA Inventor Consult Serv, 1985-; St reporter (NC), ABA LLC Act, 1993-. **Honors/Awds:** Fel Grant, Duke Univ, 1982-83; Am Jurisprudence Award, Lawyers Coop Publishers. **Military Serv:** AUS, Spec E-5, 1960-63; Good Conduct Medal, Expert Marksman, 1963. **Home Addr:** 105 Get-a-Way Lane, Bahama, NC 27503. **Business Addr:** Professor, North Carolina Central University School of Law, 1512 S Alston Ave, Durham, NC 27707.

SMITH, DR. CHARLES F.
Educator. **Personal:** Born Jan 5, 1933, Cleveland, OH; son of Charles Frank Smith Sr and Julia Anna W; married Lois Thompson; children: Carolyn Adelle & Charles Frank III. **Educ:** Bowling Green State Univ, BS, 1960; Kent State Univ, EdM, 1963; Harvard Univ, Grad Sch Ed, CAS, 1965; Mich State Univ, EdD, 1969. **Career:** Elem Sch Teacher Lorain, OH, 1960-62; Peace Corps Field Training Ctr, Puerto Rico, acad dir, 1962-63; Peace Corps, Wash, DC, spec asst, 1963; Flint Pub Schs, asst dir elem educ, 1965-66; Mich State Univ, instr educ, 1966-68; Boston Col, Teacher Corps Prog, dir, 1968, instr, 1968, Lynch Sch Educ, assoc prof educ, assoc prof emer, 1996-. **Orgs:** Danforth Asn, 1974; bd dir, Nat Coun Social Studies Supvrs Asn; bd dir, Mass Coun Social Studies; Am Asn Univ Prof; Am Asn Col Teachers; Am Asn Sch Adminrs; Asn Supervision & Curric Develop; Dept Elem Sch Prins; Nat Coun Social Studies; Phi Delta Kappa emer, 1998; chmn, Newton, Mass Area Welfare Bd; vchmn, Black Citizens Newton, Mass; founder & chmn, Coun Black Fac, Staff & Adminrs Boston Col. **Honors/Awds:** Vis scholar, Univ Mich, 1988; vis scholar, Atlanta Univ, 1991; vis scholar, Yale Univ, 1995; April 30 was declared "Charles Smith Day" by Newton Mayor Thomas Concannon, 1997. **Special Achievements:** He was the first African-American professor on campus to receive tenure in Boston College; Numerous fellowships representing the US in humanitarian goodwill missions, including Jamaica, BWI, 1953; W Germany, 1954; Canada, 1957; French Cameroon, 1958;

Nigeria, 1960; ed goodwill tours, including Egypt, 1990; Russia, 1995; China, 1996; Australia, 1997; New Zealand, 1997. **Military Serv:** AUS Med Corps, staff sgt; active duty, Austria & Italy, 1954-56; inactive duty, OH, 1956-62. **Business Addr:** Professor Emeritus, Boston College, Lynch School of Education, Campion Hall 140 Commonwealth Ave, Chestnut Hill, MA 02467, **Business Phone:** (617)552-4246.

SMITH, CHARLES HENRY, III (CHUCK SMITH)
Football player, radio host. **Personal:** Born Dec 21, 1969, Athens, GA; married Mynique; children: 3. **Educ:** Univ Tenn. **Career:** Football player (retired), radio host; Atlanta Falcons, defensive end, 1992-99; Carolina Panthers, 2000; Ryan Cameron Morning Show, co-host; Fox Sports Net, host; Media One Cable Network, host; Frank & Wanda Morning Show, co-host & sports dir; WQXI AM, Sports Radio 790 The Zone, radio host; fitness trainer, Defensive Line Inc, currently. **Honors/Awds:** Most Valuable Player, Senior Bowl; Best Defensive Lineman, Atlanta Falcon Fans; NFL Quarter back Award; NFLUnsung Hero Award, 1998; Howie Long Tough Guy Award. **Business Phone:** (404)237-0079.

SMITH, CHARLES LEBANON
Administrator. **Personal:** Born Apr 30, 1938, Neptune, NJ; married Muriel Lyle; children: Stacey, Romy, Kecia. **Educ:** Albright Col Reading PA, BA, psychol, 1960. **Career:** US Dept Labor, Labor Mgt Serv, compliance officer, 1966-70, sr compliance officer, 1970-74, field liaison officer, 1974-75, dep asst reg adminr, 1975-77, asst reg adminr, 1977-78, reg adminr, 1978-89, Off asst, sec adminr & mgt, regional adminr. **Orgs:** So Fed Labor Rels Prof; Indust Rels Res Asn; Omega Psi Phi Frat Inc; former chmn, NJ Black Heritage Festival 1978-79; Monmouth Men's Club. **Business Addr:** Deputy Assistant for Secretary, Office of the Assistant Secretary for Administration & Management, US Department of Labor, Frances Perkins bldg, 200 Const Ave NW, Washington, DC 20210, **Business Phone:** (866)487-2365.*

SMITH, CHARLES LEON
Automotive executive. **Personal:** Born Feb 7, 1953, Charleston, WV; son of James Smith and Frances Elizabeth Brown; married Emma Ruth Witten, Feb 26, 1977; children: Charles & Andrew. **Educ:** W Va Wesleyan Col, Buckhannon, WV, BS, bus adminr, 1972-76; W Va Sch Banking, Charleston, WV, banking degree, 1979-83; Nat Automobile Dealers Asn Dealer Acad, 1985-86; Ford Motor Co. Dealer Acad Prog, Detroit, MI, 1986-88. **Career:** CL Smith Enterprises, Clarks Summit, PA, pres & owner, 1977-; Kanawha Banking & Trust, Charleston, WV, vpres loans, 1978-85; Ford Motor Co., Detroit, MI, dealer cand, 1985-88. **Orgs:** Treas, Charleston Prof & Bus Club, 1978-85; bd mem & treas, Charleston Housing Bd, 1979-83; bd dirs, Optimist Club, 1980-85; W Va State Senate Small Bus Adv Bd, 1982-85; selective serv bd mem, Charleston, WV, 1982-85; adv bd mem, W Va State Community Col, 1982-85; vpres, Lackawanna Valley Auto Dealers Asn, 1988-; Black Ford Lincoln Mercury Dealers Asn, 1988-; Kiwanis Club, 1990; Scranton Chamber Com. **Honors/Awds:** Black Enterprise 100 Top Black Auto Dealers, Black Enterprise, 1989; Outstanding Achievement Award, Ford Motor Credit Co., 1989.

SMITH, DR. CHARLES U.
Educator. **Personal:** Born in Birmingham, AL; married; children: Shauna. **Educ:** Tuskegee Inst, BA, 1944; Fisk Univ, MA, 1946; WA State Univ, PhD, 1950; Univ Mich, attended 1958. **Career:** Fla A & M Univ, adj prof sociol, 1966, grad dean, 1974, emer distinguished prof, currently. **Orgs:** Pres, Southern Sociol Soc; Am Sociol Asn, 1960-; Nat Soc Study Educ, 1973-; Am Acad Polit Soc Sci, 1969-; WFSU TV adv Com, 1973-; ed bd, Jour Soc & Behavioral Sci, 1973-; state committeeman, 1975; Leon Co Dem exec comm, 1969-; bd dir, Leon Co CAP, 1972-; bd advr, Fla Ment Health Inst; pres, Conf Deans Black Grad Schs; Coun Grad Sch US; Conf Southern Grad Schs; ed bd, Negro Ed Review 1976-; ed, Fla A & M Res Bulletin, 1960-; consult, SC Comm Higher Educ, 1984. **Honors/Awds:** Plaque, Serv Dept Sociol, 1970; Col Athletics, 1966; Cert Serv State Fla, 1965, 1972; Silver Mental Health Service, 1966; Gold Medallion, 1970; Fla delegate White House Conf, 1960, 1965, 1970, 1971; DuBois Award Scholarship Service, 1973; Fla A & M Univ Merit Achievement Award, 1973; plaque Sociol, 1974; FAMU Martin Luther King Leadership Award, 1995; Distinguished Career Award, Southern Sociol Soc, 1997; Received honors from various societies like: Sigma XI, Alpha Kappa Delta, Pi Gamma Mu,Alpha Kappa Mu, Phi Delta Kappa, Sigma Rho Sigma, Phi Kappa Phi, Lambda Alpha Epsilon; DuBois-Johnson-Frazier Award, Am Sociol Asn, 2000. **Special Achievements:** Author, editor, co-author: 14 books, 8 monographs, approximately 80 scholarly and research journals, 10 book reviews, 12 copyrighted songs and lyrics.

SMITH, CHARLIE CALVIN
Educator. **Personal:** Born Jun 12, 1943, Brickeys, AR; son of Charlie and Estella; married Earline Williams. **Educ:** AM & N Col Pine Bluff AR, BA, history, 1966; AR State Univ Jonesboro, MSE, social sci, 1971; Univ AR Fayetteville, PhD, US history, 1978. **Career:** AR State Univ, asst prof history 1978-; AR State Univ, instr history, 1970-78; Lee Co Pub Sch Marianna AR, Soc Studies teacher, asst football coach, 1966-70; Ark State Univ, assoc prof history, 1982-86, asst dean, 1986-2002, presidential distinguished prof heritage studies, 2003-. **Orgs:** Comt mem, AR Endowment Humanities, 1975-77; gov appointee bd mem, AR Student Loan Asn, 1975-76; gov appointee bd mem, AR Historic Preservation Prog, 1979-84; Jonesboro Rotary Club, 1987-; pres, Southern Conf Afro-Am Studies, 1988-. **Honors/Awds:** Presidential Fellow, Ark State Univ, 1982; Outstanding Black Faculty Member & Teacher, Black Student Body ASU, 1984-86, 1988. **Special Achievements:** Publications: "The Oppressed Oppressors Negro Slavey Among the Choctaws of OK" Red River Valley History Review vol 2 1975; published "The Civil War Letters of John G Marsh" Upper OH Valley History Review 1979; published"The Diluting of an Inst the Social Impact of WWII on the AR Family" AR History Quarter (spring) 1980; published biographical sketches of AR Governors J Marion Futrell & Homer M Adkins AR Endowment for theHumanities 1980; "LC Bates: Newsman and Civil Rights Activist," in Negro History Bulletin, Oct-Dec 1982; War and Wartime Changes: The Transformation of AR, 1940-45, Univ AR Press, 1987; "The Civil RightsLegacy of President Ronald Reagan," in Western Jnl of Black Studies,summer 1990; "The Houston Riot of 1917 Revisited," in Houston Review, fall1991; "Serving the Poorest of the Poor: Black Med Practitioners in the ARDelta," in AR Historical Quarterly, autumn 1998; "Wiley Jones: Real Estate Entrepreneur, Public Transportation, Entertainment, Sportsman," in Ency of African Am Business History, Greenwood Press, 1999. **Business Addr:** Presidential Distinguished Professor, Arkansas State University, PO Box 1990, State University, AR 72467, **Business Phone:** (870)910-8279.

SMITH, CHARLOTTE (CHARLOTTE DANIELE SMITH)
Basketball player. **Personal:** Born Aug 23, 1973; daughter of Ulysses and Falonda. **Educ:** Univ NC, attended 1995. **Career:** San Jose Lasers, forward, 1996-99; Charlotte Sting, 1999-04; US SportsMgt, 2001-02; univ nc, asst coach, 2002-03; wash mystics, 2005; indianafever, 2006. **Honors/Awds:** Most Outstanding Player, 1994; female Player of Yr, 1995; Best Play of the Yr; conference championships; Valuable Player, 1994, 1995. *

SMITH, CHARLOTTE DANIELE. See SMITH, CHARLOTTE.

SMITH, CHELSI
Fashion model, actor. **Personal:** Born Aug 23, 1973, Deerpark, TX. **Career:** Actress & fashion model, currently; Films: Playas Ball, 2003; One Flight Stand, 2003; Miss Teen USA 2006 pageant, judge; Host: "Beyonce: Family & Friends Tour", co host. **Honors/Awds:** Miss Galveston County USA, 1994; Miss Congeniality, 1994; Miss USA, 1995; Miss Universe, 1995. **Special Achievements:** First American woman of biracial origin to win the Miss Texas USA, Miss USA, and Miss Universe titles, was the sixth Miss USA to be crowned Miss Universe, and the seventh woman from Seventh Texas Woman to be crowned Miss USA;the first & only Miss USA to win Miss Congeniality in the Miss USA competition; Co-wrote & recorded her first single,"Dom Da Da". **Business Phone:** (310)859-4000.

SMITH, CHESTER B.
Government official. **Personal:** Born Jul 1, 1954, Mound Bayou, MS. **Educ:** Tufts Univ, BA, 1976; Northwestern Univ, MBA, 1977, JD, 1980. **Career:** Delta Capital Corp, vpres, 1980-84; vis prof, Black Exec Exchange Prog, 1981-83; dir, New Memphis Dev Corp, 1981-84; founder, Ctr Econ Growth, 1982; Pro-Mark Inc, financial consult, 1984-85; Pvt Practice, attorney, 1983-86; US Dept Com Minority Bus Develop Agency, asst dir, 1986-. **Orgs:** consult, Proj Bus, 1982-85; Miss State Bar Asn, 1982-87; consult, Tenn Valley Authority, 1985-86. **Honors/Awds:** Jr Achievement Award, 1983-85; Distinguished Serv Award, Nat Bus League, 1986; Exec Forum Dept Com, 1987. **Home Addr:** PO Box 2746, Arlington, VA 22202. *

SMITH, CHRIS G
Basketball player. **Personal:** Born May 17, 1970, Bridgeport, CT. **Educ:** Univ Conn, 1992. **Career:** Basketball player (retired); Minn Timberwolves, guard, 1993-95. **Honors/Awds:** Bronze Medal, FIBA World Championship, 1990.

SMITH, CHUCK. See SMITH, CHARLES HENRY, III.

SMITH, CLARENCE O.
Music publisher, publishing executive. **Personal:** Born Mar 31, 1933, Bronx, NY; son of Clarence and Millicent Fry; married Elaine Goss, Jun 22, 1963; children: Clarence & Craig. **Educ:** Baruch Sch Bus, attended 1961. **Career:** Prudential Ins Co Am, NY, spec rep, 1963-69; Investors Planning Corp, NY, regist rep, 1966-69; Essence Commun Inc, NY, co-founder & pres, 1969-2002, pres emer, 2003-; Avocet Travel LLC, chmn & chief exec officer; You Entertainment LLC, founder & chmn, chief exec officer, currently; Records: CD Love Pages, 2005. **Orgs:** Chmn, African Am Mkt & Media Asn, 1991; dir-at-large, Advert Coun; Am Mgt Asn; bd dirs, Cosmetic, Toiletry & Fragrance Asn; African Am Task Force Media-Advert Partnership Drug-Free Am. **Honors/Awds:** Annual Achievement Award, Black Enterprise Mag, 1980; Black Achievement Award, The Equitable Assurance Soc US, 1985; Prin's Award, Henry Highland Garnet Sch Success, 1988-89; Communicator of the Year, Nat Asn Mkt Developers, 1990; Meritorious Service Award, UNCF, 1990; President's Award, One Hundred Black Men Am, 1995; A G Gaston Lifetime Achievement Award, Black Enterprise & Nations bank Entrepreneurs Conf, 1997; Fred Luster Sr Image Award, Luster Prod Black Heritage Found, 1997. **Military Serv:** AUS, spl 4th class, 1957-59. **Business Addr:** Chief Executive Officer, Chairman, YOU Entertainment LLC, 304 Pk Ave S Fl 10, New York, NY 10010.

SMITH, CLIFFORD (METHOD MAN)
Rap musician, actor, music director. **Personal:** Born Apr 1, 1971, Hempstead, NY. **Career:** Wu-Tang Clan, rapper; Group albums: Enter the Wu; Wu-Tang Forever, 1997; Solo Albums: Tical, 1995; Blackout, 1999; Blackout (Bonus Track), 2003; Films: Batman Forever, 1995; High School High, 1996; Space Jam, 1996; Hav Plenty, 1997; Soul in the Hole, 1997; Copland, 1997; Belly, 1998; Bulworth, 1998; In Too Deep, 1999; Shaft, 2000; Boricula's Bond, 2000; How High, 2001; Save the Last Dance, 2001; The Fast and the Furious, 2001; Pootie Tang, 2001; How High, 2001; Paid in Full, 2002; All About the Benjamins, 2002; My Baby's Daddy, 2004; Soul Plane, 2004; Venom, 2005; The Wackness, 2008; Meet the Spartans, 2008; TV series: "Wonderland", 2000; "Oz", 2001; "Boston Public", 2003; "The Fairly OddParents", 2004; "The Wire", 2003-09; "CSI: Crime Scene Investigation", 2006-08; "Burn Notice", 2008. **Honors/Awds:** Grammy Award, 1996. *

SMITH, CLIFFORD C.
Physician. **Personal:** Born in Waterloo, IA; divorced; children: 2. **Educ:** Univ Iowa, attended 1946; Meharry Med Col, MD, Nashville, TN. **Career:** Physician (retired), director; McGregor clinic, physician, 2003; McGregor nursing home, med dir. **Honors/Awds:** Practr of the Yr, Nat Rural Health Asn, 1998; street named as "Dr. Clifford Smith Appreciation Day".

SMITH, DR. CLIFFORD V., JR.
School administrator. **Personal:** Born Nov 29, 1931, Washington, DC; son of Clifford V Sr; married Nina Marie Singleton; children: Sharon, Debra & Patricia. **Educ:** St Univ Iowa, BS,Civil & Sant engg, 1954; John Hopkins Univ, MS, Sant engg & water res, 1960, PhD, radiological sci & sant engg, 1966. **Career:** Pa Dept Health, chief engr water supply sect, 1959-61; Univ Conn, asst prof, 1961-63; Johns Hopkins Univ, res & teaching asst, 1963-65; Univ Mass, asst prof, 1965-66; Tufts Univ, asst prof, 1966-68; Dorr-Oliver Inc,Stamford, CT, sanitary technol mgr, 1968-70; City Col NY, asst prof, 1970-72; US Environ Protection Agency, admin, 1972-74; Bech tel Corp,Advan Technol Div, exec engr, prog mgr & bus develop mgr; Ore State Syst Higher Educ, spec asst to chancellor; Univ Wis-Milwaukee, chancellor & pres, 1986-90; Ore State Univ, vpresadmin; Gen Elect Found, pres, 1997;Inst Int Educ Inc, trustee, currently. **Orgs:** New Eng Health Physics Soc; Am Water Works Assn; Water Pollution Control Fed; Int Assn Water Pollution Res; treas, Kappa Alpha Psi; Radiation Adv Comt US; US NASA Adv Coun; Energy Res Adv Bd, US Dept Energy; UI Found Bd Dir; President's Club; Col Eng Develop Coun; pres, G E Found. **Honors/Awds:** Gold Medal, Environ Protection Agency; Distinguished Alumni Award forAchievement, Univ Iowa. **Special Achievements:** Published numerous articles.

SMITH, CONRAD P. See Obituaries section.

SMITH, REV. CONRAD WARREN
Clergy. **Personal:** Born May 10, 1919, St Thomas, Virgin Islands of the United States; son of Conrad V (deceased) and Florence Stevens (deceased); married Marjorie Estella Weston, Jun 10, 1957; children: Conrad, Arlene Smith Lockridge, Craig & Riise Richards. **Educ:** Lincoln Univ, BA, 1941; Howard Univ, Sch Med, MD, 1944; Harvard Univ, Sch PH, MPH, 1952; El Semnario Episcopal del Caribe, Cert, theol, 1975. **Career:** Clergy (retired); Knud-Hansen Hosp, chief pediatrics, 1955-75; Gov VI, comnr health; Episcopal Diocese VI, St Ursula Church, vicar. **Orgs:** Past pres, secy, VI Med Soc; Am Med Asn; Pan Am Med Asn; chaplin, Alpha Phi Alpha Fraternity; bd dir, VI Veterinary Med. **Honors/Awds:** C Warren Smith Pediatric Wing, St Thomas Hosp, 1984; VI Boy Scouts Annual Award Distinguished Serv, 1986; Physician of the Year Award, The VI Med Soc, 1986. **Special Achievements:** Physician for the Virgin Islands Olympic Teams in the Caribbean and World Olympics; Developed public health services in the Virgin Islands; Publication: Tables of Maximum Breathing Capacities in Female Children; Numerous publications of public health reports on the Virgin Islands & Ciguatera. **Military Serv:** AUS, first lt, 1943-44, Cert Med; Good Conduct Medal. **Home Phone:** (809)775-1225.

SMITH, DANTE TERRELL. See MOS DEF.

SMITH, DANYEL
Writer, journalist. **Personal:** Born Jan 1, 1966?, Oakland, CA. **Educ:** Univ Calif, Berkeley, 1986-89; Northwestern Univ, Medill Sch Jour fellowship, 1996. **Career:** Freelance music writer, 1989-91; SF Weekly, music ed, 1991-93; Billboard mag, R&B ed, 1993; NY Times, music writer, 1994; Vibe, music ed, 1994-96, ed-in-chief, 1997-99; Time, writer, 1999; Vibe, ed chief, 2006-; Books:

More Like Wrestling, 2003; Bliss, 2006. **Business Addr:** Editor-in-Chief, VIBE, 215 Lexington Ave, New York, NY 10016, **Business Phone:** (212)448-7300.*

SMITH, DARRIN ANDREW
Football player. **Personal:** Born Apr 15, 1970, Miami, FL. **Educ:** Univ Miami, Fla, BS, bus mgt, 1991, MS, mkt, 1993. **Career:** Football player (retired); Dallas Cowboys, linebacker, 1993-96; Philadelphia Eagles, 1997; Seattle Seahawks, 1998-99; New Orleans Saints, 2000-04; bondsman, NC, currently. **Orgs:** Founder & pres, Int Asn Black Millionaires. **Honors/Awds:** Super Bowl, XXVIII & XXX; Miami Sports Hall of Fame, 2006.

SMITH, DARRYL C.
Manager, lecturer. **Personal:** Born Aug 1, 1966, Maryland; married Pheorma N Davis, Sep 21, 1991. **Educ:** Towson Univ, BS, cum laude, 1989; Univ MO, Sch Jour, MA, Journ & Media Mgt; Univ MO, Sch Law, JD. **Career:** Mo Supreme Court Office State Cts admin, mgr; WJHU FM, opers mgr,1988-90; WETA FM, ops mgr, 1990-91; KL UM-FM/KJLU FM, gen mgr, 1991-; Univ W Florida, lectr, currently. **Orgs:** Am Mensa; Commn Arts Graduate Prog. **Business Addr:** Lecturer of Communication & Arts, University of West Florida, 11000 Univ Pkwy Bldg 36, Pensacola, FL 32514, **Business Phone:** (850)474-2064.

SMITH, DAWN C F (DAWN CAROL FABIOLA SMITH)
Marketing executive. **Personal:** Born Dec 23, 1960, London, England; daughter of George and Mavis Collier; married Elbert Robertson, Nov 3, 1990. **Educ:** Brown Univ, BA, 1982; Univ Mich, MBA, 1985. **Career:** Black Student's Guide Col, co-managing ed, 1982; MBA Consortium fel, 1983-85; Gen Mills, market res internal, 1984; Colgate Palmolive, asst brand mgr, 1985-87; Kraft Inc, assoc brand mgr, 1987-88; Jacobs Suchard, brand mgr, 1988-90; Citicorp's Diners Club, Corp Travel Div, dir mktg, 1990-. **Orgs:** Nat Black MBA Asn, 1983-; Nat Alumni Schs Prog, Brown Univ, 1985-. **Honors/Awds:** National Black MBA Scholar, 1984. **Home Phone:** (312)373-7850. **Business Addr:** Director, Citicorp Diners Club, 8430 W Bryn Mawr Suite 700, Chicago, IL 60631, **Business Phone:** (773)380-5160.

SMITH, DAWN CAROL FABIOLA. See SMITH, DAWN C F.

SMITH, DEBBIE A.
Association executive. **Personal:** Born Apr 12, 1959, Washington, DC. **Educ:** The Catholic Univ, US, BA, 1981; Howard Univ, MBA, 1985. **Career:** Xerox, mktg rep, 1985-87; Riggs Nat Bank, credit lecding officer, 1987-90; Signet Bank, credit lecding officer, 1990-93; US House Reps, staff dir small bus, sub comt, 1993-94; The Nat Asn Invest Co, vpres, 1994-95; The Nat Asn Urban Bankers, exec dir; Discovery Commun, named vpres diversity & human resorces serv; Walter Kaitz Found, exec dir; Discovery Commun, Human Resource Dept, currently. **Orgs:** Mayor's Congressional Affairs Advisory, Wash, DC, 1991-; adv bd, Orgn New Equality, 1996. **Honors/Awds:** Pioneer Award, Orgn New Equality, 1997. *

SMITH, DEHAVEN L
Lawyer. **Personal:** Born Aug 10, 1928, Baltimore, MD; married Gertrude Jackson; children: Rubye. **Educ:** Va Union Univ, AB, 1949; Univ Md, Sch Law, JD, 1958. **Career:** Williams, Smith & Murphy, atty; pvt pract atty, currently. **Orgs:** Am Bar Asn; Nat Bar Asn; Monumental City Bar Asn; Baltimore City Bar Asn Judicature Soc; World Peace Law Comn; Nat Asn Advan Colored People. **Military Serv:** AUS 1950-52. **Business Addr:** Attorney, 1212 Winston Ave, Baltimore, MD 21239-3411.

SMITH, DENNIS
Football player. **Personal:** Born Feb 3, 1959, Santa Monica, CA; married Andree; children: Tiffany Diamond & Armani Joseph. **Educ:** Univ Southern Calif, attended 1980. **Career:** Football player (retired); Denver Broncos, safety, 1981-94. **Orgs:** Make-A-Wish Found; Covenant House. **Honors/Awds:** Most Inspirational Player, 1992; Ring of Fame, 2001; Colorado Hall of Fame, 2006.

SMITH, DENVER LESTER
Insurance agent. **Personal:** Born Sep 21, 1946, Detroit, MI; son of Henry L and Hattie M. **Career:** Denver L Smith Ins Agency Inc, pres, currently. **Business Addr:** President, Denver L Smith Insurance Agency Inc, 28475 Greenfield Rd, Southfield, MI 48076, **Business Phone:** (248)559-9833.

SMITH, DETRON NEGIL
Football player. **Personal:** Born Feb 25, 1974, Dallas, TX. **Educ:** Tex A&M Univ. **Career:** Football player (retired); Denver Broncos, running back, 1996-2001; Indianapolis Colts, fullback, 2002-04. **Honors/Awds:** Pro Bowl, 1999. **Special Achievements:** Denver Broncos Super Bowl XXXII Champions, 1997; 1998.

SMITH, DIANE L
Government official. **Personal:** Born Nov 2, 1962, Hartford, CT; married LaMont Andrews, Oct 1996; children: Derek L. **Educ:** Univ Conn, BA, 1986; Trinity Col, attended. **Career:** State Conn, Office Policy & Mgt, policy & prog analyst, 1988-92, mgr bus devel, 1992-93; Dept Econ Devel, spec projs mgr, 1993-96; Dept Econ & Community Develop, devel specialist, 1996-98, exec dir, 1998-. **Orgs:** Hartford Neighborhood Support Collab, Steering comt, 1996-; bd mem, Greater Hartford Bus Devel Ctr, 1997-99; bd mem, Waterbury Partnership 2000, 1998-2000; bd mem, Literacy Vols Greater Hartford, 1999-; Hartford Studies Proj Trinity, Col Steering Comt. **Honors/Awds:** Natl Devel Coun, Econ Develop Finance Prof, 1994. **Home Addr:** 226 Deerfield Rd, Windsor, CT 06095, **Home Phone:** (860)687-1903. **Business Addr:** Director, Community, Housing Development, Department of Economic & Community Development, 505 Hudson St 4th Fl, Hartford, CT 06106, **Business Phone:** (860)270-8223.

SMITH, DOLORES J
Executive. **Personal:** Born Feb 10, 1936, Lockport, IL; daughter of Ernest Gill Jones and Mira Ellen Bills Jones-Spinks; married Paul R; children: Kathleen, Robert, Debra, Alan, Paul II & Dolores II. **Educ:** Roosevelt Univ, BS, 1979; Ohio Univ Athens OH, MA, 1983; Gestalt Inst Cleveland, post-grad studies orgn & systs develop, 1989. **Career:** Smith's Office Serv, owner/mgr, 1959-65; Suburban Echo Reporter, advertising mgr, 1965-67; Jewel Cos Inc, area personnel mgr, 1967-79; Bausman Assocs, mgt consult, 1979-80; WTTW Chicago, dir admin serv, 1980-82; Ohio Univ, instr/grad asst, 1982-83; Columbia Col Chicago, instr, 1983-; NBC WKQX Radio, producer/host, 1983-86; DJ Smith Enterprises, pres, 1983-. **Orgs:** Exec comm bd dir, Midwest Women's Ctr, 1977-87; Gov Adv Coun Employ & Training, 1977-82; Nat Asn Advan Colored People, Soc Human Resources Mgt; Soc Training & Develop; trustee, Wieboldt Found, 1982-92; bd dirs, Women & Foundations Corp Philanthropy, 1984-88; exec comm bd dir, Lambda Alpha Omega Chap; Alpha Kappa Alpha Sorority, 1986-87; Soc Intelletual Educ, Training & Res. **Honors/Awds:** Corp Public Broadcasting Scholar, Ohio Univ, 1982-83. **Home Addr:** 1150 N Lake Shore Dr Suite 7F, Chicago, IL 60611. **Business Addr:** President, DJ Smith Enterprises, 10 S 17th Ave, Maywood, IL 60153, **Business Phone:** (708)343-4499.

SMITH, DR. DONALD HUGH
Educator. **Personal:** Born Mar 20, 1932, Chicago, IL; son of William H and Madolene; divorced. **Educ:** Univ Ill, AB, 1953; DePaul, MA, 1959; Univ Wis, PhD, 1964. **Career:** Baruch Col, prof, chmn, dept educ, prof dir, 1970-97, assoc provost, profemer, currently; Chicago Pub Sch, teacher, 1956-63; Ctr Inner City Studies Northeastern Ill Univ, asst prof, asso prof, dir, 1964-68; Univ Comm Educ Prog Univ Pitts, prof, dir, 1968-69; Nat Urban Coalition Wash DC, exec asso, 1969-70. **Orgs:** Nat Adv Counc Voc Educ, 1968-70; Inter Am Cong Psychol, 1972-; Nat Study Comn Teacher Educ, 1972-75; Exec dir, Chancellor's Task Force SEEK City Univ NY, 1974-; adv Doctoral Prog Educ Admin Atlanta Univ, 1975; founder,NY Alliance Black Sch Educ, 1981; pres, Nat Alliance Black Sch Educr,1983-85; chmn, Black Fac City Univ NY, 1989-92; adv Martin Luther King JrCtr Social Change; chmn, task force NY State Dropout Prob; bd dir, NY Serv Older People; consult, numerous sch & univ; adv bd, African Heritage Studies Asn; founding mem, Bd Educ People African Ancestry; chair, New York City Bd Educ Comn Stud African Descent. **Honors/Awds:** Recipient, Chicago Bd Educ Fel, 1962; Univ Wis Fel, 1963; del White House Conf Disadvantaged, 1966; Distinguished Leadership Award, Nat Alliance Black Sch Educr, 1986; Award for Distinguished Service, NY State Black &Puerto Rican Legis, 1986. **Military Serv:** AUS, 1954-55. **Home Addr:** 250 W 103rd St Apt 4A, New York, NY 10025. **Business Addr:** Professor Emeritus, Bernard M Baruch College, 1 Bernard Baruch Way, New York, NY 10010, **Business Phone:** (646)312-1000.

SMITH, DONALD M
Executive. **Personal:** Born Jul 12, 1931, Elgin, IL; married Jeanette M; children: Tracy & Tiffany. **Educ:** Purdue Univ, BA, 1956, MA, 1961. **Career:** Hills McCanna, shop supt, 1960-69; Hemmenns Auditorium, gen mgr, 1969-80; Rockford Metro Ct, oper mgr, 1980-. **Orgs:** Int Asn Aud Mgr, 1964; Am Legion, 1969-; founder, Performing Arts Young People, 1969-80; founder, Elgin Area Arts Coun, 1969-80; Prince Hall Masons, 1980-. **Military Serv:** AUS, USAF, sgt, 5 yrs; Bronze Star, Korean Service Medal, Far East Campaign Medal, 1949.

SMITH, DR. DOROTHY LOUISE WHITE
Educator. **Personal:** Born Sep 28, 1939, Memphis, TN; daughter of Theodore and Classy Ellie Mae; married Carl, Nov 26, 1958; children: Carlton Edward Smith & Sharian Smith Lott. **Educ:** Philander Smith Col, nat methodist scholar, 1959; Cuyahoga Community Col, attended 1964; Case-19Western Res Univ, BA, eng, 1966; Calif State Univ,MA, eng, 1969; Univ Southern Calif, EdD, educ leadership & intercult educ, 1992. **Career:** Educator (retired); Glenville High Sch, instr eng, 1966-67; Millikan High Sch, instr eng, 1969-70; Long Beach City Col, prof eng, 1970-73; San Diego City Col, instr eng & African Am lit, 1973-97; Women Inc; San Diego Unified Sch Dist, bd educ, 1981-88; San Diego St Univ Sch Teacher Educ, 1989-91; San Diego Pub Sch Bldg Corp; educ consult; Grio Press, writer & pres; Books: My face to the rising Sun, 1999. **Orgs:** Alpha Kappa Alpha Sorority, 1958-; adv comt mem, Allensworth St Hist Pk, 1977-86; Del Assembly Calif Sch Bds Asn, 1981-88; Asn Calif Urban Sch Dist, 1982-87; CSBA Curric & Res Task Force, 1983-85; Del Assembly, Nat Sch Bds Asn, 1983-85; Steering Comt, Coun Urban Bds Educ, 1985-88; Calif Middle Grades Task Force, 1986-87; pres, bd dirs, San Diego Sch Success, 1989-98; Ctr City Develop Comt, Martin Luther King Promenade, 1991-; Ctr City Develop Corp Black Hist Dist Adv Comt; City San Diego Ethics Comt, 2001-; chair, City San Diego Ethics Comn, 2003-05; adv comt, Univ San Diego Sch Leadership & Educ Sci, 2004-. **Honors/Awds:** Phi Kappa Phi Honor, 1969; Distinguished School Board Award, 1984; Woman of the Year Award, 1984; County of San Diego Proclamation, 1984, 1988; Salute to Black Women Achievement Award, 1984; Distinguished Public Service Award, Alpha Kappa Alpha, 1985; Woman of Achievement Award, 1985; Special Commendations, City San Diego; Urban League Award; Women in Government Tribute to Women, 1985; Phi Delta Kappa Community Service Award, 1988; Samaritan of the Year Award, 1988; Literacy Award, Int Reading Asn, 1989; Magnet Schools Leadership Award, 1989; Phi Delta Kappa Honor, 1990-; Outstanding Faculty Award, Sch Teacher Educ, San Diego State Univ, 1990; Founder's Award, 1995; Tribute to Living African American History Award; 100 African American Role Models Award; Distinguished Faculty Award, San Diego City Col, 1997; Salvation Army Women of Dedication, 2000; Distinguished Educator Award, San Diego Historian society, 2001; Service Award, United Negro Col Fund, 2003; Martin Luther King Community Leadership Award, 2006.

SMITH, DOROTHY O.
Mayor, government official. **Personal:** Born May 28, 1943, Lawrence County, AL; daughter of James Samuel Owens Sr (deceased) and Cornelia Swoope Owens; divorced; children: Derra S Jackson, Leo Smith Jr, Kathleen S Goodlaw. **Educ:** John C Calhoun, Decatur, Bus, 1969. **Career:** S Cent Bell, Decatur, network, 1971; City Hillsboro, Hillsboro, mayor, 1986-00. **Orgs:** Secy, Black Mayors Conf, 1988; Nat Black Women Mayors Caucus, 1988; Martin Luther King Jr Profiles Courage, ADC, Lawrence County Chap, 1988. **Honors/Awds:** Award for Church Secy, 1987; Award, Lawrence County Ext Serv, 1989; Award, The Lawrence County Chamber Com, 1989; Numerous Community Service Awards. *

SMITH, DOUG (DOUGLAS SMITH)
Basketball player. **Personal:** Born Sep 17, 1969, Detroit, MI. **Educ:** Univ Mo. **Career:** Basketball player (retired); Dallas Mavericks, forward, 1992-95; Boston Celtics, forward, 1996; Great Lakes Storm, Continental Basketball Asn, 2004-05. **Honors/Awds:** Bronze Medal, FIBA World Championship, US Nat Team, 1990.

SMITH, DOUGLAS. See SMITH, DOUG.

SMITH, DOUGLAS M
Journalist. **Personal:** Born Apr 18, 1942, Hampton, VA; son of Samuel R and Virginia Jones; married Shirley Thomas, May 11, 1991 (divorced); children: Jerome & Jared; married Anne Street. **Educ:** Hampton Univ, Hampton, VA, BA, math, 1964. **Career:** Newsday, Garden City, NY, reporter & ed, 1970-77; New York Post, New York, NY, reporter & ed, 1977-78; Newark Bd Educ, Newark, NJ, pub rels specialist, 1978-79; Howard Univ Hosp, Wash, DC, ed & writer, 1980-85; USA Today, Arlington, VA, reporter & tennis writer, 1986-; Hampton Univ, Dept Mass Media Arts, journalist-in-residence, 1993-94. **Orgs:** Am Tennis Asn, 1979-86; US Tennis Asn, 1979-88; US Tennis Writers Asn, 1990-; Nat Asn Black Journalists, 1990-; pres, USTWA, 1990-92, vpres, 1994-95. **Honors/Awds:** Appreciation Award, Am Tennis Asn, 1985; Lifetime Achievement Award, US Tennis Asn, 1988; Media Person of the Year, Women's Int Tennis Asn, 1989; Great Am Tennis Writing Award, Tennis Week, 1990; Deadline Writer of the Year, Tennis Week, 2000. **Special Achievements:** Co-author with Zina Garrison of My Life as a Tennis Pro, 2001. **Military Serv:** AUS, capt, 1964-70; Bronze Star w/"V" Device; Army Commendation Medal; Purple Heart; Vietnam Service & Campaign Medals. **Business Phone:** (703)854-8050.

SMITH, DR. EARL BRADFORD
Social worker, teacher. **Personal:** Born Sep 28, 1953, St Louis, MO; married Treva Talon. **Educ:** Thiel Col, BA, Psych, Sociol, 1977; Marywood Col, MSW, 1979; Univ Pittsburgh, PhD, cand educ. **Career:** Vet Admin Hosp, social work assoc, 1976-78; Lackawanna Cty Child & Youth Serv, social worker II, 1979-82; Susquehanna Human Serv, human resources spec; Pittsburgh Bd of Educ, sch social worker; Point Pk Univ, adj fac; Univ Phoenix, adj prof; Robert Morris Univ, West Allegheny Sch Dist, adj fac & adminr, currently. **Orgs:** Nat Asn Social Workers; lector, St Peters Cathedral Soc, 1977-82; lector, St Benedicts & St Marys Lectureship Soc. **Honors/Awds:** Dance Awards, Modern Dance-Jazz Performances. **Military Serv:** USMC, corpl; Expert Rifleman, 1972-74. **Home Addr:** 1616 Meadville, Pittsburgh, PA 15214. **Business Addr:** Administrator, Adjunct Faculty, West Allegheny School District, Robert Morris University, 6001 Univ Blvd, Coraopolis, PA 15108, **Business Phone:** (412)262-8200.

SMITH, EDDIE D., SR.
Clergy. **Personal:** Born Jun 8, 1946, Macon, GA; son of Rev Jack Smith Jr (deceased) and Mattie Mae; married Verlene Fields; children: Charlitha S Austin, Edwanna L, Eddie Jr, Corey, Alvy.

Educ: Ft Valley State Col, BS, 1968, MS, 1971; Universal Bible Col, Alamo, TN, D Div. **Career:** Bibb Co Sch, teacher, 1968-82; Macedonia Missionary Baptist Church, pastor, 1972-; City Macon, counman, 1975-78; Bibb Co, bd educ, 1985-. **Honors/Awds:** Cert of Appreciation, Bibb Co Voter's League, 1977; Dr E D Smith Day Proclamation, City Macon, 1977; Citizens Award, Macon Courier, 1977; Nat Alumni Cert of Achievement, Ft Valley State Col, 1978; 3 Yr Service Award for City Coun, City Macon, 1979; Medgar Malcolm Martin's Award, SCLC, 1979; dir, Disting Am, 1981; Minister of the Day GA State Legis, 1981. **Business Addr:** Pastor, Macedonia Missionary Baptist Church, 928 Anthony Rd, Macon, GA 31204.*

SMITH, DR. EDGAR EUGENE
Educator. **Personal:** Born Aug 6, 1934, Hollandale, MS; son of Augusta McCoy and Sam; married Inez Wiley; children: Edwin D, Anthony R, Stephen S & Gregory S. **Educ:** Tougaloo Col, Tougaloo, BS, MS, 1955; Purdue Univ, Lafayette, IN, MS, 1957, PhD, Biochem, 1960. **Career:** Purdue Univ, Dept Biochem, Lafayette, IN, res asst, 1955-58, teaching asst, 1958-59; Nat Found fel, Purdue Univ, Lafayette, IN, 1958-59; Harvard Med Sch, Boston, MA, res fel surg biochem, 1959-61, res assc surg biochem, 1961-68; Beth Israel Hosp, Boston, MA, assoc surg res, 1959-68; Boston Univ Sch Med, Boston, MA, from asst prof surg chem to assoc prof surgchem, 1968-73; Univ Mass Med Ctr, provost & assoc prof, 1974-83; Robert Wood Johnson Health Policy fel, Inst Med, 1977; Univ Mass, syst vpres, 1983-91, prof emer, 1991-; Nellie Mae, vpres, 1991-93; Tougaloo Col, actgpres, 1995, consult, 1993-97, sr adv pres, 2002, Search Comn, chair, trustee emer, currently; MS AHEC, founding dir, 1998-2000. **Orgs:** Trustee, Tougaloo Col, 1968-90; trustee, Metco Scholar Fund, 1969-86; trustee, Morehouse Sch Med, 1976-89; gov bd, Rob Wood Johnson Health Policy Fel Prog, 1978-85; Am Soc Biol Chemists; consult, NIH; trustee, Alcohol Bev Med Res Found, 1982-94; bd dir, Planned Parenthood, MA, 1984-90; Am Asn Higher Educ; chief acad officer, Nat Forum Syst; Nat Asn State Univ & Land-Grant Col Coun Acad Affairs; Am Soc Biol Chemist; Am Chem Soc; AAAS; NY Acad Sci; Am Asn Cancer Res; fel Am Inst Chem; Boston Cancer Res Asn; Sigma Xi; Phi Lambda Upsilon; Nat Chem Hon Soc; Am Pol SciAsn; Nat Asn Minority Media Exec; chmn, Deans Adv Hoc Com Black GradStudents; admin comt, Sch Med; chmn, Black Fac Caucus; ed bd, Centerscope; comnr, Am Cancer Ins Grant; liaison, Div Med Sci Biochem. **Honors/Awds:** Research Cancer Development Award, Nat Cancer Inst, 1969-74; Alumnus of Year, Tougaloo Col, 1969; Award Outstanding Achievement Field Biochem, Nat Consortium Black Prof Develop, 1976; Health Award, Boston Br, Nat Asn Advan Colored People, 1977; Human Relations Award, Mass Teachers Asn, 1977; Old Master, Purdue Univ, 1978; Distinguished Alumnus, Nat Asn Equal Opportunity Higher Educ; Distinguished Leaders Health Care, 1978; Directory Distinguished American, 1981; ScD, Morehouse Sch Med, 1989; ScD, Univ Mass, Amherst, 2000; DHL, Tougaloo Col, 2002. **Home Addr:** 5934 Paddock Pl, Jackson, MS 39206. **Business Addr:** Trustee Emeritus, Tougaloo College, Edward Blackmon Admin Bldg 500 W Co Line Rd, Tougaloo, MS 39174, **Business Phone:** (601)977-7730.

SMITH, EDITH B
Manager. **Personal:** Born Jan 18, 1952, Norfolk, VA; daughter of Elijah J Billups and Nannie Ruth Winstead Codrington; married Joseph, Aug 1970 (divorced 1988); children: Kelley N. **Educ:** Norfolk State Univ, Norfolk, BA, 1970-74. **Career:** The Virginian-Pilot, Norfolk, VA, reporter, 1972-80; WHUR Radio, Wash, DC, promotions dir, 1981-84; Mondale-Ferraro Campaign, Wash, advan press person, 1984; WDCU-FM Radio, Wash, gen mgr, 1985. **Orgs:** Capitol Press Club, 1994-95. **Honors/Awds:** Nat Black Media Coalition, for achievements in broadcasting, 1994. **Business Addr:** General Manager, WDCU-FM Radio, 4200 Connecticut Ave NW Bldg 38 Rm A-03, Washington, DC 20008, **Business Phone:** (202)274-5090.

SMITH, DR. EDWARD NATHANIEL, JR.
Physician, educator. **Personal:** Born Jul 28, 1955, Elizabeth City, NC; son of Edward Nathaniel Sr and Georgia Long; married Mona LaMothe, Nov 26, 1983; children: Edward N III & Arianne LaMothe. **Educ:** Morehouse Col, BS, 1976; Howard Univ Col Med, MD, 1980; Am Bd Radiol, cert. **Career:** US Pub Health Serv, med officer, 1980-82; Emory Univ Sch Med, clin assoc, 1982-84; Howard Univ Hosp, radiol resident 1984-87, asst prof radiol, 1988-. **Orgs:** Omega Psi Phi Frat, 1974-; Am Cancer Soc, 1980-; bd dirs, Omega Diversified Investment Corp, 1982-; Piney Br Sligo Civic Orgn, 1984-; Nat Med Assoc Radiol Sect, 1985-, vice chairman; Radiol Soc N Am, 1985-; Am Roentgen Ray Soc, 1988-; Am Col Radiol, 1989-; Am Heart Asn, 1990-; bd dirs, Homemaker Health Aide Serv, Wash, DC, 1992-; Soc Cardiovascular & Inerventional Radiol, 1991-. **Honors/Awds:** Delta of Georgia, Phi Beta Kappa, 1976. **Business Addr:** Assistant Professor, Howard University Hospital, Department of Radiol, 2041 Ga Ave NW, Washington, DC 20060, **Business Phone:** (202)865-1571.

SMITH, ELAINE MARIE
Government official. **Personal:** Born Nov 30, 1947, Mobile, AL; children: Vernon Leon York Jr. **Educ:** Ala A&M Univ, BS; Merced Col, AA, 1972. **Career:** USAF, staffing asst, 1976-77, personnel staffing spl, 1977-78; AUS Corps Engrs, staffing asst, 1978, affirmative action recruiter, 1978-. **Orgs:** Youth Motivation Task Force, 1980-86; vpres, secy Blacks Govt, 1980-86; secy, Carver State Tech Col Adv Bd, 1982-86; Southern Col Placement Asn, 1982-86; Southeastern Federal Recruiting Coun, 1982-86; Black Execs Exchange Prog, 1986. **Honors/Awds:** Outstanding Young Woman of Am, 1981; Quality Salary Increase US Corps Engrs, 1984; Sustained Super Performance Award, US Corps Engrs, 1982, 86. **Business Addr:** Affirmative Action Recruiter, US Army Corps of Engineers, PO Box 2288, Mobile, AL 36628.

SMITH, DR. ELEANOR JANE
School administrator. **Personal:** Born Jan 10, 1933, Circleville, OH; daughter of John A Lewis (deceased) and Eleanor J Dade Lewis; married Paul M Smith Jr, Dec 27, 1972; children: Teresa Marie Banner. **Educ:** Capital Univ, BSM, 1955; Ohio State Univ, 1966; The Union Grad Sch//UECU, PhD, 1972. **Career:** School administrator (retired); Bd Educ, Columbus, Ohio, 2nd-6th grad teacher, 1956-64; Bd Educ, Worthington, Ohio 6 & 7th grad teacher, 1964-69; Univ Cinn, prof, Afro-Am Studies 1972-82; vice provost Fac & Acad Affairs; Smith Col, dean instnl affairs, 1988-90; William Paterson Col, vpres acad affairs & provost, 1990-94; Univ Wis-parkside, chancellor. **Orgs:** Asn Black Women Historians, Nat co-founder & co-director, 1978-80; Nat Coun Black Studies, 1982-88; Nat Asn Women Educ, 1986-; Am Asn Higher Educ; Am Coun Educ; Am Asn State Cols & Univs. **Honors/Awds:** Historical Presentation, Black Heritage, History, Music & Dance written & produced, 1972-; numerous publications; YWCA Career Women of Achievement, 1983; Capital Univ, Alumni Achiev Awd, 1986.

SMITH, REV. ELIJAH (WYRE SMITH)
Clergy. **Personal:** Born Dec 28, 1939, Peach County, GA; son of Samuel Lee and Ola Mae John; married Janet Broner, Jun 7, 1987; children: Audrey Maria Diamond, Elijah Jr, Sonja A, Avice D, Richard A, Mark A, D'ete Smith, LaShaunda R Thomas, Velecia Thomas. **Educ:** Turner Theol Sem, dipl theol, 1975. **Career:** Blue Bird Body Co, utility man, 1964-66; Robins Air Force Base Ga, electronic repairman, 1966-75; Eastman Circuit Eastman Ga, pastor, 1967-71; Allen Chapel & Mountain Creek AME Churches, pastor, 1971-84; D&S Florist, owner, 1974-76; St John AME Church, pastor; Eastern Dist Southwest Ga, Sixth Episcopal Dist African Methodist Episcopal Church, presiding elder to sr presiding elder, currently. **Orgs:** Columbus & Phoenix City Ministerial Alliance, 1984-; Masonic Lodge 134 Powersville Ga, 1965-; Columbus Branch Nat Asn Advan Colored People, 1984-; Pub Affairs Coun, Columbus, 1984-;AME Church Ministers Alliance Columbus; S Columbus Exchange Club 1989; A J McClung YMCA; Columbus Urban League Inc. **Honors/Awds:** Oscar Maxwell Award, Man of the Yr, Americus Boy Scouts, 1978; Minister of the Yr, Black Youth Action, 1979; Tomorrow's Leaders Award, Ga Power, 1979; Outstanding Public Service Award, Sumter Co Bd Gov of C of C, 1980; Outstanding Service & Dedication Award, Kent Hill Youth Devel Prog, 1984; Distinguished & Devoted Service Award, Americus-Sumter Co Nat Asn Advan Colored People, 1984; Community Service Award, Mayor City Americus, 1984; Service Award, Chief Police Americus, Ga, 1984; Outstanding & Dedicated Service Award, Americus Police Dept & Comm Americus & Sumter Co, 1984; Devoted Leadership Service to St John & Community, St John AME Church, 1989; The Martin Luther King Sr, Minister's Community Service Awd, PUSH, 1991; Pastor of the Year, The Sons of Allen of the Southwest Ga Ann Conf AME Church, 1992; Pastor of the Year, Lay Orgn Southwest Ga, Ann Conf AME Church, 1992. **Home Addr:** 1938 Armory Dr, Americus, GA 31709-2110. *

SMITH, DR. ELMER G, JR.
Physician. **Personal:** Born May 22, 1957, Chicago, IL; son of Elmer and Joyce; married Ingrid S P, Jun 4, 1983; children: Brittany Francoise, Harrison Monfort, Samantha Dominique & Alexander Jean-Marc. **Educ:** Univ Ill-Chicago, BS, 1980; Howard Univ Col of Med, MD, 1983. **Career:** Norwalk/Yale Hosp, resident physician, 1983-86; Northwestern Med Sch, clinical med instr, 1989; Northwestern Mem Hosp, active attending, 1990; Cook County Hosp, med consult, 1988-93, dir ambulatory screening, 1993-; pvt pract, currently. **Orgs:** Alpha Phi Alpha Frat Inc, 1980-; Am Med Asn, 1980-; Am Col Physicians, 1985-; Ill State Med Soc, 1986-; Chicago Med Soc, 1986-; pres, Am Cancer Soc, Ill Div, Austin Unit, 1987-89; Soc Gen Internal Med, 1991. **Honors/Awds:** VPres, Pub Relations, Sr Class, Howard Univ, 1982-83; Psychiatry Res Award, Howard Univ Col Med, 1983; Dipl Am Bd Internal Med, 1986; Chicago's Caring Physicians Award, Metropolitan Chicago Health Care Council, 1987; Cook County Hosp, Acute Pharyngitis, 1989, syphilis, 1990; WVAZ, Heat Syndromes, 1991. **Special Achievements:** Round Table Moderator, Hypertension Mgt, 1993; Cook County Hosp, Hypertension, 1991. **Home Addr:** 4351 Booth Calloway Rd Suite 311, North Richland Hills, TX 76180, **Home Phone:** (817)595-4949. **Business Phone:** (817)595-4949.

SMITH, ELSIE MAE
Nurse. **Personal:** Born Feb 27, 1927, Erin, OK; daughter of Isadore Brooks and Laura Latour; married James Almer Jr, Oct 15, 1949; children: Dr James, Dr Roger, Dr Margo & Melanie. **Educ:** St Marys Sch Nursing, St Louis, MO; Am Int Col. **Career:** Nurse (retired) Bay State Med Ctr, gastroenterol, staff RN, 1973-90. **Orgs:** Links, Greater Springfield Chapter Inc; docent, Museum Fine Arts, Springfield, MA; cooperator, Springfield Museum & Libr Asn; pres, 1980-82, Springfield Chap Girl Friends; bd dirs, secy, Springfield Girls Club Family Ctr; bd dirs, Connecticut Valley Girl Scouts; pres, Springfield Alpha Wives, 1961-63; world traveler; vol, Housing Habitant; vol, Springfield Tech Community Col, Tutor students foreign taking Eng; African Hall Steering Comt, Sci Museum, Springfield, MA; Cooperator Bay State Med Ctr; Comt St Michaels Cathedral. **Honors/Awds:** Achievement Award, McKnight Neighborhood; Cert Training, Springfield Libr & Museum Asn, 1989. **Special Achievements:** United Church Christ, Travel Nurse to 3 Countries West Africa, for col student & others. **Home Addr:** 96 Dartmouth St, Springfield, MA 01109.

SMITH, EMMITT J
Football player, television broadcaster. **Personal:** Born May 15, 1969, Pensacola, FL; son of Emmitt Smith Jr and Mary; married Patricia Southall, Apr 22, 2000; children: 4. **Educ:** Univ Fla, BA, pub recreation, 1996. **Career:** Football player (retired), Analyst; Dallas Cowboys, running back, 1990-2002; Ariz Cardinals, running back, 2003-04; NFL Network, NFL Total Access, analyst, 2005-07; ESPN, NFL analyst, 2007-; EJSmith Enterprises LLC, owner, currently. **Orgs:** Make a Wish Found; founder, Emmitt Smith Charities Inc; founder, Emmitt Smith Scholar Prog; spokesperson, Just Say No Anti-Drug Campaign, 1986; Phi Beta Sigma. **Honors/Awds:** Surpassed the 1,000-yard rushing mark earlier than any other player in Col football hist; Freshman of the Yr, UPI, Sporting News, 1987; Pro Bowl, 1991, 1992-98; Miller Lite NFL Player of the Yr, 1993; Nat Football League, Most Valuable Player Award, 1993; Super Bowl XXVIII Most Valuable Player, 1993; Four NFL Rushing Titles; holder of numerous Cowboys & NFL records; all-time NFL leading rusher; Two consecutive Jim Thorpe Football Awards; Bert Bell Award, 1993. **Special Achievements:** Co-author: Autobiography, The Emmitt Zone, Crown Pub, 1994; first Dallas Cowboy Player to lead the league in rushing; football field named and holiday created in his hon, Escambia HS, Pensacola, FL, 2003.

SMITH, ERNEST HOWARD
Physician, cardiologist. **Personal:** Born Nov 9, 1931, Bethlehem, PA. **Educ:** Lincoln Univ, AB cum laude, 1953; Howard Univ, MD, 1957. **Career:** C Hosp Philadelphia, DC Gen Hosp, resident pediatrist; C Hosp Philadelphia, Henry Ford Hosp Detroit, fel pediat cardiolUSPHS Cheyenne Sioux Reservation Eagle Butte SD, med officer incharge, 1958-61; Henry Ford Hosp, staff pediat cardiologist, 1965-71; Detroit, priv prac pediat cardiol, 1964-68; Univ Calif, Los Angeles, assoc prof pediatKing Charles R Drew Med Sch, Los Angeles, CA, asst prof pediat, dir pediat cardiologist & head community pediat, 1972-04; Martin Luther King General Hosp, assoc prof pediat cardio, currently. **Orgs:** Catalytic Community Asn, Detroit, 1968-70; S Cent Planning Coun, Los Angeles, 1973-; SE Mental Health Liason Coun, 1973-; Cit Youth Employ, 1973-; organist, Pilgrim Congregational Ch Eagle Butte, SD; Christ United Church Christ, Detroit; Hartford Ave Baptist Church Detroit; First Baptist Church Warrenton, VA; St Pauls Baptist Church, Bethlehem, PA; accompanist, Lincoln Univ Glee Club, PA. **Honors/Awds:** Quinland Prize For Biology, Lincoln Univ, 1953; Award, Kappa Alpha Psi Mu Chap, 1953; President's Award, S Cent Planning Coun, 1974; Education Fraternity Award, Phi Delta Kappa, 1975. **Special Achievements:** Cheyenne Sioux Tribal Citation 1961. **Business Addr:** Associate Professor, Martin Luther King General Hospital, 12021 S Wilmington Ave, Los Angeles, CA 90059.

SMITH, ESTELLA W
Executive. **Educ:** Univ Bloomington, BS; Memphis State Univ, MS, PhD. **Career:** Executive (Retired); Duquesne Light Co, dir invest & bank rels, community rels mgr, 1991, pub affairs, gen mgr; Univ Pittsburgh, asst prof; Memphis State Univ, instr; Heritage Nat Bank, ceo. *

SMITH, DR. ESTUS
Foundation executive. **Personal:** Born Oct 13, 1930, Crystal Springs, MS; son of David and Margaret; married Dorothy Triplett; children: Donald Gregory. **Educ:** Jackson State Univ, BS, 1953; Ind Univ, MME, 1961; Univ Iowa, PhD, 1970; Eastman Sch Music, addn studies. **Career:** Foundation Executive (retired); Jackson State Univ, dean, vpres acad affairs, prof music, 1973-84; Kettering Found, vpres & chief operating officer. **Orgs:** Univ Iowa Alumni Asn; fel, Am Coun Higher Educ, 1969; former chmn Comn, Miss Humanities; former bd trustees, Dept Archives & Hist State Miss; past pres, vpres, Southern Conf Deans Fac & Acad; past chmn bd dir, State Mutual Fed Savings & Loan Asn; past pres, Opera/S Co; Nat Asn Advan Colored People; Omega Psi Phi; Phi Delta Kappa; Phi Kappa Phi; Beta Beta Beta; bd trustees, Centerville/Wash Township Educ Found, 1990-; Sigma Pi Phi Frat; Alpha Lamba Delta; Phi Kappa Phi Frat; Kappa Psi Frat; trustee, Dayton Found, 1990-; St George's Episcopal Church; bd trustees, bd dirs, Knowledge Works Found, 1999-; chmn bd, Cent State Univ, 2002-; emer mem, Bd Dirs, African Am Community Fund. **Honors/Awds:** Numerous awards including Episcopalian Outstanding American, 1970; Outstanding Alumni & Scholar, 1970; Outstanding Educator of America; Jackson State University Sports Hall of Fame, 1980; Archon of the Year, Sigma Pi Phi Frat, 1988. **Military Serv:** AUS. **Home Addr:** 398 Grassy Creek Way, Centerville, OH 45458.

SMITH, EUGENE. See Obituaries section.

SMITH, EUGENE
Executive. **Personal:** Born Aug 13, 1938, Alquippa, MT; married Jacquelyn; children: Charmaine, Deborah, Carlton. **Educ:** Geneva Col; Univ Duquesne. **Career:** Aliquippa Water Authority, asst mgr, gen mgr. **Orgs:** Bd mem, vpres, Alquippa Pub Sch Dist; bd mem, Beaver Co Hosp Authority; mem bd dir, PA Minority Bus develop Comn; US Mil Selection Com; Zion Hope Lodge; St Cyprian Consistory; Sahara Temple. **Honors/Awds:** Man of the Year Award, Negro Bus Prof Women Beaver Co. **Business Addr:** General Manager, ALIQUIPPA MUNI WATER AUTH, 160 Hopewell Ave, Aliquippa, PA 15001, **Business Phone:** (724)375-5525.

SMITH, EUGENE DUBOIS
Athletic director. **Personal:** Born Dec 18, 1955, Cleveland, OH; son of Theodore and Elizabeth DuBois; married Paula Griffin, May 6, 1977; children: Nicole Dawn, Lindsey Rose & Summer Denise. **Educ:** Univ Notre Dame, IN, BBA, 1977. **Career:** Univ Notre Dame, IN, asst football coach, 1977-81; IBM, South Bend, IN, mkt rep, 1981-83; Eastern Mich Univ, Ypsilanti, MI, from asst athletic dir to athletic dir, 1983-93; Iowa State Univ, athletic dir, 1993-2000; Ariz State Univ, athletic dir, 2002-, exec dir intercollegiate athletics, 2003-. **Orgs:** Bd mem, Nat Collegiate Athletic Asn Track & Field Rules Comt, 1987-89; Nat Asn Advan Colored People; Ypsilanti Chap, 1988-; bd mem, Chamber Com, Ypsilanti, MI, 1989-; exec bd, Nat Assoc Collegiate Dirs Athletics, 1990-. **Business Addr:** Athletic Director, Arizona State University, Univ Dr Mill Ave, Tempe, AZ 85287-7906, **Business Phone:** (480)965-6360.

SMITH, FERNANDO DEWITT
Football player. **Personal:** Born Aug 2, 1971, Flint, MI; children: Quantiash & Tyna. **Educ:** Jackson State Univ. **Career:** Football player (retired), Minn Vikings, defensive end, 1994-97, 2000; Jacksonville Jaguars, defensive end, 1998; Baltimore Ravens, defensive end, 1999; St Louis Rams, defensive end, 2000.

SMITH, FRANCES C
Funeral director. **Personal:** Born in Williamston, NC; daughter of Leo Cherry (deceased) and Omenella Riddick Cherry; married Alfred J Smith Jr; children: Randy & Trent. **Educ:** McAllister Sch Embalming; Am Acad Sch Embalming, grad studies. **Career:** Smith Funeral Home, owner & funeral dir, currently. **Orgs:** Gov Comn Qual Educ State NJ, 1991-; NJ State Bd Mortuary Sci; Elizabeth Develop Co; Garden State Funeral Dirs; past pres, Urban League Guild; past matron, Lincoln Chap OES; pres, Union Co Unit Nat Asn Negro Bus & Prof Women's Clubs; past pres, Women's Scholar Club Elizabeth; Elizabeth Bd Educ; Soroptimist Int Eliz; Union Co Asn Women Bus Owners. **Honors/Awds:** Achievement Award, Urban League Eastern Union Co; Professional Woman of the Year Award, NJ Unit Nat Asn Negro Bus & Prof Women's Clubs; Appreciation Award, Elizabeth Br Nat Asn Adv Colored People, 1980; Business Woman of Year Award, Union Co Nat Asn Negro Bus Women & Prof Women's Clubs. **Special Achievements:** First Black Board Member in Egenolf Day Nursery in Elizabeth & Presently on advisory board of nursery; Honored by receiving 'Key to City' by Mayor and the first Black woman to receive such an honor. **Business Addr:** Owner, Director, Smith Funeral Home, 45 Cherry St, Elizabeth, NJ 07202, **Business Phone:** (908)352-1855.*

SMITH, FRANK
Executive director, government official, chief executive officer. **Personal:** Born Sep 17, 1942, Newnan, GA. **Educ:** Morehouse Col, attended 1959; Union Inst, Ohio, PhD, 1980. **Career:** SNCC, organizing & registering African Am voters, 1962-68; City Wash, DC, city councilman; Dist Columbia City, coun, 1982-98; African Am Civil War Mem, chmn bd, exec dir & chief exec officer, 1998-. **Orgs:** Chair, Civil War Found. **Honors/Awds:** Man of the Year Award; DC Pub Schs, Outstanding Bus & Educ Partnership; Summer Youth Employ Prog, Civil War Mem, Outstanding Leadership. **Business Addr:** Chief Executive Officer, Executive Director, African American Civil War Memorial, 1200 U St NW, Washington, DC 20009, **Business Phone:** (202)667-2667.

SMITH, FRANKIE L.
Football player. **Personal:** Born Oct 8, 1968, Fort Worth, TX. **Educ:** Baylor Univ. **Career:** Miami Dolphins, defensive back, 1993-95; San Francisco 49ers, 1996-97; Chicago Bears, safety, 1998-2001.

SMITH, FRONSE WAYNE, SR.
Executive, painter (artist). **Personal:** Born Aug 11, 1946, Chicago, IL; son of Elmer and Floy; married Germaine, Jan 20, 1972; children: Alonda Fleming, Lehia Franklin, Fronse Jr, Gamal-Azmi & Julius. **Educ:** Univ Ill, Chicago, BS, chem, 1970; Grand Valley State Univ, MBA, int new ventures, 1980. **Career:** Glidden Co, qual control technician, 1965-67; DeSoto Inc, res chemist, 1968-75; W-L Co, Parke Davis Div, Paints, analytical chemist, 1977-81; Warner Lambert Co, Pharmaceut, sr buyer, 1981-83; purchasing mgr, 1983-88; Sterile Prod, purchasing agent, 1988-92; May Day Chemical Co Inc, gen mgr, chem distrib, 1992-96; BPS Int Ltd,

Consults Africa Chem Procurement & Bus Match-making, pres. **Orgs:** Deacon & elder, Hope Reformed Church, 1977-96; Steward, Bethel AME Church, 1982-83; master mason, Prince Hall, FAM, Tyrian Widows & Sons Lodge 34, 1987; co-founder, Holland Coalition, People Color, 1989; nat assoc mem, Nat Asn Purchasing Mgr; Univ Ill, Chicago, Black Alumni Asn; life mem, Univ Ill Alumni Asn. **Honors/Awds:** Certified Volunteer, State Mich, Dept Corrections, 1979-82. **Special Achievements:** Eagle scout, 1961; Contributor, "Dew Freeze Vacuum, Wet Adhesion Test," Journal of Coatings Technology, 1973; amateur painter & exhibitor in Holland, MI, 1981. **Home Addr:** 601 Douglas Ave, Holland, MI 49424, **Home Phone:** (616)396-1082.

SMITH, G ELAINE
Association executive. **Career:** Am Baptist Churches USA, pres, 1996-97, vice chair, currently. **Orgs:** Tenn Bar Asn; PA Bar Asn; NJ Bar Asn; Alpha Kappa Alpha Sorority; Death Penalty Initiative; mem, The Const Proj. **Honors/Awds:** Hon Doctorate, Ottawa Univ. **Special Achievements:** First African American female president of the American Baptist Churches USA. **Business Phone:** (202)580-6920.

SMITH, GEORGE BUNDY
Judge. **Personal:** Born Apr 7, 1937, New Orleans, LA; married Alene Jackson; children: George Jr & Beth. **Educ:** Inst d'Etudes Politiques Paris, CEP Inst, 1958; Yale Univ, BA, 1959; Yale Law Sch, LLB, 1962; NYU, MA, polit sci, 1967, PhD, 1974; Univ Va Sch Law, LLM, 2001. **Career:** New York City Civil Ct, judge, 1975-79; Supreme Ct State NY, justice, 1980-86; Supreme Ct, Appellate Div State NY, first dept assoc justice, 1987-92; NY State Ct Appeals, assoc judge, 1992-2006; Fordham Univ Law Sch, adj prof law; NY Law Sch, adj prof law, 2001; Chadbourne & Parke LLP, partner, currently. **Orgs:** Chartered Inst Arbitrators; Am Arbitration Asn; trustee, Horace Mann-Barnard Sch, 1977-99; mem bd dirs, Metrop Black Bar Asn, chmn bd, 1984-88; Phillips Acad, 1986-90; vpres, Asn Bar City New York, 1988-89; pres, Harlem Lawyers Asn; commr, NY State Ethics Comn Unified Ct Syst, 1989-2001; Judicial Friends; Nat Bar Asn Judicial Coun. **Honors/Awds:** William Brennan Award for Outstanding Jurist, NY State Asn Criminal Defense Lawyers, 2007; Honorary Doctor of Laws, Fordham Univ Sch Law, 2004; honorary PhD, Albany Law Sch Union Univ, 2006; Honorary Doctor of Laws, Brooklyn Law Sch, 2008. **Home Addr:** 549 W 123 St Apt 13 F, New York, NY 10027. **Business Addr:** Partner, Chadbourne & Parke LLP, 30 Rockefeller Plz, New York, NY 10112, **Business Phone:** (212)408-1054.

SMITH, GEORGE EDMOND
Educator. **Career:** Family Pract Physician; Hahnenmann Sch Med, Philadelphia, asst clin prof, Family Med, currently. **Orgs:** Am Cancer Soc Inc; Am Diabetes Asn; Am Heart Asn Inc. **Business Addr:** Assitant Clinical Professor, Hahnenmann School of Medicine, Philadelphia, PA.*

SMITH, HON. GEORGE S.
Government official. **Personal:** Born Jan 6, 1940, Terry, MS; children: George Jr, Tosha, Eric & Carol. **Educ:** Utica Jr Col, AA; Jackson State Univ. **Career:** Gov Miss, sr staff, 1966; State Medicaid Comt, comt mem, 1966; State Bldg Comn, supvr, 1979; Hinds Cty Dist Five, supvr, 1979-, pres 1984-; Smith Enterprises, owner & operator, 1965-. **Orgs:** TC Almore Lodge 242; Jackson Chap Nat Bus League; Jackson Urban League; Natl Assn Advan Colored People; brd dir, Smith-Robertson Comn; Metrop Young Men Christian Assn; Goodwill Indust; Cent MS Planning & Develop Dist Adv Coun Aging; Ctr S Indust Develop Group; Jackson Chamber Com; 100 Black Men Jackson; Hinds County Pvt Indust Coun; vice chmn, Natl Assn Counties; Nat Assn Black County Officials; Natl Urban Leag; Mississippi Consortium for Intl Dev; Hinds County Private Ind Coun; Americ Red Cross; Operation Heartbeat of the Am Heart Asn. **Honors/Awds:** Jackson St Univ/Natll Alumni, Spec Recog Award for Outstanding Achiev in Govt, 1986; Trailblazer Award; Proven Leader through the New Millennium, MAS Mag, 2000; Elliott Fel- Governing in the Global Age, George Wash Univ, 2002; Hinds Community College, Utica Campus, Distinguished Alumnus Award, 2003. **Special Achievements:** First black appointed to the State Building Commission; First black to be senior staff member to Governor of Mississippi; First black to be appointed as commn of State Med Commn; One of two blacks to be elected as supervisor of Hinds County Dist Five 1979, re-elected supvr,1983; First black to serve as president of Hinds County Board of Supervisors, 1984. **Business Addr:** President, Supervisor, Hinds County Board of Supervisors, PO Box 686, Jackson, MS 39205, **Business Phone:** (601)968-6795.

SMITH, GEORGE WALKER
Clergy. **Personal:** Born Apr 28, 1929, Hayneville, AL; married Elizabeth; children: Anthony, Carolyn, Joyce. **Educ:** Knoxville Col, BS, 1951; Pittsburgh Theol Sem, MDiv. **Career:** Golden Hill United Presby Church, minister; Nat Sch Bd Asn, 1st vpres; The Catfish Club, found, currently. **Orgs:** App to serv CA Ad Hoc Comn; secy treas, Nat Sch Bd Asn; app, CA Savs & Loan Leag; past pres, Coun Great City Schs; San Diego Bd Educ; one founders dir vpres Pacific Coast Bank; served various capacities

various org; Kappa Alpha Psi; Soclia Club; charter mem, San Diego Chap Alpha Pi Boule; Sigma Pi Phi. **Honors/Awds:** Received various honors & awards; Annual Civic Service Award, 2004. **Business Addr:** Founder, The Catfish Club, 610 Gateway Ctr Way Suite G, San Diego, CA 92102, **Business Phone:** (619)266-7278.*

SMITH, GERALD B
Chief executive officer. **Educ:** Tex Southern Univ, BBA, finance. **Career:** Westcap Corp, sr vpres & dir mkt; Underwood Neuhaus & Co, sr vpres & dir; Pennzoil Corp, dir, currently; Charles Schwab Mutual Funds, dir, currently; Cooper Industries, dir, currently; Smith, Graham & Co Investment Advisors LP, chmn & chief exec officer, currently. **Orgs:** Mus Fine Arts Houston; bd mem, MD Anderson Cancer Ctr; Houston Mus African-Am Cult; Greater Houston Partnership; Adv Bd, Tex Southern Univ Sch Bus; METRO Bd, City Houston, 2004-; chair, Audit Comt, ONEOK Partners. **Business Addr:** Chairman, Chief Executive Officer, Smith Graham & Co Investment Advisors LP, 6900 JP-Morgan Chase Tower 600 Travis St, Houston, TX 77002, **Business Phone:** (713)227-1100.*

SMITH, DR. GERALD LAMONT
Educator, college administrator. **Personal:** Born Apr 8, 1959, Lexington, KY; married Teresa, Sep 20, 1986; children: Elizabeth & Sarah. **Educ:** Univ Ky, BA, 1981, MA, 1983, PhD, 1988. **Career:** Univ Ky, teaching asst, 1985-86, instr, 1986-88, asst prof hist, 1993-, African American Studies & Res Prog, dir, 1997-; Univ Memphis, asst prof, 1988-93; pastor, Farristown Baptist Church Berea, Kentucky; dir, African Am Studies and Res Prog, 1997-2005; General hist African Am, writer, currently. **Orgs:** Nat Fac Scholar; Greater Lexington Chamber Com, Minority Bus Develop Adv Bd, 1999; Univ Ky Libr Assocs, Exec Comt, 1999; Univ Press KY Comt; assoc minister, Consolidated Baptist Church; bd trustees, Lexington Hist Mus; Ky Hist Mus; bd dir, Univ Ky Athletic Asn. **Honors/Awds:** Outstanding Young Man of America, 1983; YMCA Black Achievers, 1996; induction into the Martin Luther King Jr Collegium of Scholars, 2000; Keyto the City of Winchester, 2000; Evelyn Black Award, UK Black Stud Union, 2005; Kentucky Hall of Fame, Henry Clay High Sch, 2006. **Special Achievements:** Author: A Black Educator in the Segregated South: Kentucky's Rufus Batwood, 1994; article: "Martin Luther King Jr and the War on Poverty", 1999; "The Duty of the Hour: African American Communities in Memphis, 1862-1923", 1996; "Unhidden Transcripts of Resistance: Memphis and African American Agency, 1862-1920", 1995, 1996; Natl Faculty Scholar, 1997; ed:Black America Lexington, Ky, 2002; co-ed: The Papers of Martin Luther King Jr: Advocate of the Social Gospel. **Business Addr:** Associate Professor of History, University of Kentucky, Department of History, 1307 Patterson Off Tower, Lexington, KY 40506-0027, **Business Phone:** (859)257-3593.

SMITH, GERALD WAYNE
Television director, television show host. **Personal:** Born Jul 26, 1950, Detroit, MI; son of Jacob M and Antoinette T Howard; divorced; children: Adanna Nekesa Smith. **Educ:** Highland Park Community Col, Highland Park, Mich, attended 1968-69; Univ Detroit, Detroit, Mich, BA (magna cum laude), 1974, grad studies, 1974-75; Am Soc Indust Security, Detroit Chapter, cert, 1983; Real Estate Inst, Sch Continuing Educ, NY Univ, New York, NY, Cert, 1984; Crittenton Real Estate Inst, Chicago, Ill, Cert, 1984; Nat Soc Fund Raising Execs, Detroit, Mich, cert, 1990; Wayne State Univ, Detroit, Mich, attended 1991. **Career:** New Detroit Inc, Detroit, Mich, admin serv asst, 1968-69; City Detroit Model Neighborhood Agency, Detroit, Mich, community organizer, 1969-71; Wayne Co Community Col, Detroit, Mich, instr, 1972-80; Wayne Co Circuit Ct, Probation Dept, Detroit, Mich, social serv worker, 1974-75; Wholesale Distribution Ctr, Citizens Dist Coun, Detroit, Mich, adminr, 1976-80; Detroit Econ Growth Corp, develop assoc, 1980-85; Wayne State Univ, Dept Africana Studies, asst prof, 1980; TV/Radio Host, "Back to Back," Detroit Pub TV/WQBH AM 1400, 1992; Comcast Cable Commun Inc, area dir corp affairs, currently. **Orgs:** Bd mem, Big Brothers/Big Sisters, 1997; secy, bd dirs, Cent Educ Network, Chicago, Ill, 1996-97; chmn, Detroit Cable Commun Comt, 1994-; chmn, Friends African Art, 1988-90; trustee, Detroit Inst Arts, 1988-90; Move Detroit Forward, 1980-; Arab-Am Community Ctr; bd govs, Nat Acad TV Arts & Scis, 2001-; President's Regional Adv Bds. **Honors/Awds:** Numerous honors and awards including Spirit of Detroit Award, 1978; Afro-American Benefactor's Award, 1980; Crime Prevention Citation, 1982; Mayor's Award of Merit, 1982; Wayne County School District Merit Awards, 1984, 1985; Michigan Legislative Resolution, 1986; Michigan Senate Tribute, 1986; Certificate of Appreciation, Literacy Vols Am, 1986; Certificate of Appreciation, Greater Detroit Community Outreach Ctr, 1986; Carter G Woodson Award, Educator of the Year, Creative Educ Concepts, 1987; Certificate of National Recognition, 7 Mile-Livernois Project, US Dept Housing & Urban Develop, 1986; Arab Community Center for Economic & Social Services Award, 1990; Haitian American Award, 1990; Black Educator of the Year, US Peace Corps, 1990; author, Arab-American Directory, 1990; Spirit of Detroit Award, 1991; MI Minority Women's Network, Man of the Year, 1993; Public Television's Gold Award, 1993; Commitment of Youth Award, W K Kellogg Found, 1994; Emmy nominations, 1995, 1996 & 1997;

Testimonial Resolution, City of Detroit, 1999; Spirit of Detroit Award, 1999. **Business Addr:** Area Director of Corporate Affairs, Comcast Cable Communications Inc, 12775 Lyndon St, Detroit, MI 48227, **Business Phone:** (313)646-4202.

SMITH, GERALDINE T
Social worker. **Personal:** Born Sep 14, 1918, Cave Spring, GA; daughter of Dallas C and Cora L Johnson Turner; divorced; children: Karen T Smith Watts (deceased). **Educ:** Hunter Col, BA 1943; Columbia Univ, MA 1947; Smith Col, Sch Social Work, MSS, 1952. **Career:** Social worker (retired); Bureau Child Welfare, social worker, 1952-57; Pittsburgh Pub Schs, social worker, 1957-58; Western Psychiatric Inst, sr psychiat social worker, 1958-68; Univ Pittsburgh, asst prof, 1965-87; Neighborhood Psychiat Unit & Counseling Serv, 1966-68; Western Psychiatric Inst, Univ Pittsburgh, dir social work, 1968-75; Pittsburgh Model City Agency, consult, 1968-69; CMH/MRC, asst dir of educ, 1975-78; Dixmont State Hosp Social Serv, consult, 1973-74; Pittsburgh Model Cities Agency, consult, 1968-69; WPIC Hill Satellite Ctr, Western Psych Inst, Univ Pittsburgh, dir, 1979-87. **Orgs:** Secy adv bd, New Opportunities for the Aging, 1984; Nat Asn Social Workers; Acad Certified Social Workers; Coun Social Work Educ; Nat Conf Social Welfare; Soc Hosp Social Work, dir; United Mental Health Allegheny County; bd mem, Bethesda Ctr, 1988-94. **Home Addr:** 1710 Swissvale Ave, Pittsburgh, PA 15221. *

SMITH, GLORIA DAWN
Hospital administrator, vice president (organization). **Personal:** Born Oct 2, 1947, Jones, LA; daughter of Alvin and Hazel; divorced; children: Lawonda & Orlando. **Educ:** Univ San Francisco, BS, 1982; Golden Gate Univ, MBA, 1989-90. **Career:** Real Estate Consult, 1984-87; Stanford Univ, human resources mgr, 1968-85; Children's Hosp Stanford, dir personnel, 1985-88; Woodland Mem Hosp, vpres human resources, 1988-91; Children's Hosp, Oakland Calif, dir personnel, 1991-93; Univ Health Center Tyler, vpres human resources, 1993-. **Orgs:** Bureau Nat Affirs Forum, 1995-97; Parkinsonian, Tyler, TX, 1994-; Child Care Comn City of Woodland, Ca, 1990-91; YMCA, Bd Dir, Woodland, Calif, 1989-91; Neighborhood Housing, Menlo Park, Calif, pres, 1980-82; Nat Asn Advan Colored People, 1995; Democratic Cent Comt, 1990-91; Prof Woman Asn, 1995. **Home Phone:** (817)232-2085. **Business Phone:** (903)877-7748.

SMITH, DR. GLORIA RICHARDSON
Nurse, vice president (organization), educator. **Personal:** Born Sep 29, 1934, Chicago, IL; married Leroy. **Educ:** Wayne Univ, BS, 1955; Mich Univ, MPH, 1959; Univ CA, Cert, 1971; Univ OK, MA, 1977; Union Experimenting Col & Univ, PhD, 1979. **Career:** Vice president (retired), nurse; Detroit Vis Nurse's Asn, pub health nurse, 1955-56; sr pub health nurse, 1957-58; asst dist off supvr, 1959-63; Tuskegee Inst, asst prof, 1963-66; Albany State Col, 1966-68; Okla State Health Dept, dist nurse supvr, 1968-70; medicare nurse consult, 1970-71; Univ Okla Col Nursinf Health Sci Ctr, dean & prof, 1975-83; MI Dept Public Health, dir 1984; Wayne State Univ Col Nursing, dean & prof nursing, 1988; W.K. Kellogg, MI, vpres prog, 2002. **Orgs:** Bd dirs, St Peter Claver Community Credit Union, 1961-63; Mayor's Comt Study Immigrants Detroit, 1963; bd dirs, YMCA, 1972-; Black Nurses' Caucus1973; Am Asn Col Nursing; comt mem, Am Acad Nursing; Nat Black Nurses Asn; steering comt mem, bd dir, Midwest Alliance Nursing, 1977-80; Nat Student Nurses Asn; bd dir, Nat League Nursing; Okla State Nurses Asn; Am Nurses Asn; Okla Pub Health Asn; Wayne State Alumni Asn; Nursing Alumni Asn; Sigma Gamma Rho Sorority; Sigma Theta Tau; Int Greek Coun; Inter agency Community Health Serv Task Force; steering comt, Human Rels Coun, Greater Okla City; hon mem, Chi Eta Phi Sor, 1984; Nat Acad Sci, 1997-. **Honors/Awds:** Outstanding Service Award, Franklin Settlement, Detroit, 1963; Outstanding Sigma of the Year, 1963; Key to the City Miami Beach, 1974; Leaders in Education, 1975; Certificate of Recognition, Nat Black Nurses Asn, 1976; Certificate & Plaque, Sigma Gamma Rho, 1977; Hall of Fame, Sigma Gamma Rho Sorority, 1974; Community Service Award for Leadership; Soul Bazaar Coordinator Clara Luper, 1980; Plaque of Appreciation, Pres Banowsky Univ Okla, 1983; Plaque of Appreciation, Asn Black Personnel, 1983; Honorary Recognition Award, Okla Nurses' Asn, 1984; Distinguished Alumni Award, Wayne State Univ, 1984; Distinguished Scholar, Am Nurses Found, 1986; Distinguished Leadership Award, Comn Grad Foreign Nursing Sch Int, PA, 2003; Distinguished Black Woman Award, Black Women Sisterhood Action,2007; Henry M. Turner Legacy of Freedom Award, Afro-American Civil War Mus Found, 2007. **Special Achievements:** First Speaker, Katherine Faville Distinguished Lecturer Series, Wayne State Univ, 1975; One of 60 new members elected to the Institute of Medicine of the National Academy of Sciences in 1997.

SMITH, GORDON ALLEN
School administrator, association executive. **Personal:** Born May 8, 1933, Detroit, MI; married Patricia Evon Ware; children: Dorel, Gordon, Brian, Stephanie. **Educ:** Wayne State Univ, BS, 1966; Northern Ill Univ, MS, 1969; No IL Univ, EdD, 1977. **Career:** Detroit & Pub Sch, teacher 1965-68; Detroit, public aid worker, 1968; Northern Ill Univ, counr, 1970-73, asst to pres, 1973-75; Ill Affrm Action Officers Asn, Dekalb Human Rel, Commr, 1973-75; Ill Commn on Human Rel, comnr, 1974; Inland Steel Recruitment Com; Nat Asn Affrm Act Officers; Ill Off Educ, affirmative action officer; Village of Sherman, bd mem, currently. **Military Serv:** AUS, 1954-56. **Business Addr:** Board Member, Village of Sherman, 401 St Johns Dr, Sherman, IL 62684, **Business Phone:** (217)496-2621.

SMITH, GREG
Radio host. **Personal:** Born Mar 25, 1964, Bay Springs, MS; son of Jim and Adelia Barnes; children: Greg Jr, Donovan & Berkeley. **Educ:** Ariz State Univ, BA, broadcasting, 1986. **Career:** KTAR/K-Lite Radio, dir res & sales promotion, 1986-91; AccessLife.com, consult, 2000-01; On a Rol Commun, radio prog, founder & host, 1992-; Strength Coach, host, currently. **Orgs:** Nat Asn Black Journalists; Pres's Comm on Employ People with Disabilities, Communs Subcomt; Media Adv Bd, Am Asn People Disabilities; bd dirs, Nat Asn Alcohol, Drugs, & Disabilities, Inc; Nat Speakers Asn, 2002. **Honors/Awds:** Twenty Leaders Award in the Disability Community, Access Ctr for Independent Living, 20 Yrs, 2000; Second Place award for commentary about the movie Toy Story 2, Pub Radio News Dirs Inc, 2000. **Business Phone:** 877-331-7563.

SMITH, DR. GREGORY ALLEN
Gynecologist, obstetrician. **Personal:** Born Sep 12, 1952, Detroit, MI; married Jennifer; children: Amber & Camille. **Educ:** Mich State Univ, BS, 1974; Howard Univ, MD, 1978. **Career:** Wayne State Univ, resident, 1978-82; AMI Doctors Med Ctr, chief, 1987-88; Assoc Women's Care Tulsa, pres; pvt pract, currently. **Orgs:** Nat & Amer Med Assoc, Okla State Med Soc, Tulsa Co Med Soc; adv bd, Sickle Cell Anemia Rsch Found, Okla. **Honors/Awds:** Diplomate Amer Bd of Obstetrics-Gynecology. **Home Addr:** 1910 S Jamestown Ave, Tulsa, OK 74112, **Home Phone:** (918)747-7002. **Business Phone:** (404)522-4888.

SMITH, GREGORY ROBESON, SR.
Clergy, executive. **Personal:** Born Sep 22, 1947, Philadelphia, PA; son of Louis and Bennie Ryan; married Brenda Lee Galloway Smith, Jun 28, 1969; children: Gregory Robeson Jr, Avery Vaughn, Whitney DeAnna. **Educ:** Livingstone Col, BA, 1969; Univ Wis, MBA, 1972; Union Theol Seminary, MA, 1985; Columbia Univ. **Career:** Lever Brothers, prod mgr, 1975-77; Revlon Inc, mkt mgr, Group I Classic Revlon, mkt mgr, 1977-80; Polished Ambers, 1977-79; Classic Revlon, 1979-80; Joseph E Seagram & Sons Inc, nat prod mgr, 1980-82; Nat Coun Churches, Church World Serv, dir disaster relief, 1983-88; Mt Hope AME Zion Church, pastor, 1986-; Antonovich Inc, dir mkt, 1988-91; African Develop Found, pres & chief exec officer, 1991-95; Mother AME Zion Church, sr pastor, currently. **Orgs:** Omega Phi Psi Fraternity Inc; Beta Alpha Alpha Chap. **Honors/Awds:** No 17, Holy Royal Arch Masons, King David Consistory; No 3, ASSR 33 Degree Mason; Delegate, 14th Session of the World Methodist; White House Fellow, Nat Finalist, 1976. **Special Achievements:** Author, thesis: "Ghetto as a Marketing Segment,"; "Towards a more Perfect Union between the AME, AME Zion, and CME Denominations,"; AME Zion Church, youngest person in history, elected in 1976. **Business Addr:** Pastor, The Mother A.M.E. Zion Church, 140 6 W 137th St, Harlem, NY 10030, **Business Phone:** (212)234-1545.*

SMITH, GUY LINCOLN
Executive. **Personal:** Born Mar 16, 1949, New Orleans, LA; son of Guy Lincoln III and Laura Louise Orr; married Marjorie Whaley Russell, Jun 19, 1971; children: Abigail, Guy & Laura. **Educ:** Bowling Green State Univ, 1968; Univ Tenn, attended 1970; Am Univ, attended 1971; US Dept Agr Grad Sch, attended 1971. **Career:** Knoxville Jour, reporter, 1967-68, asst city ed, 1968-70; Appalachian Regional Comn, Wash, DC, asst dir info, 1970, dir info, 1970-72; City Knoxville, press secy, 1972-76; Miller Brewing Co, Milwaukee, WI, mgr corp affairs, 1976-79; Seven-Up Co, St Louis, MO, vpres corp affairs; Philip Morris Co Inc, vpres corp affairs, 1985-90, sr pub rels, pub rels officer, 1992; Tobacco Itute, Commun Comt, chair; Hill & Knowlton Int Pub Rels, chief operating officer, 1992-93; Smith Worldwide Inc, 1994-96; President Clinton, spec adv, 1998-99; Hawthorn Group, 1999-2000; Diageo, exec vpres, 2000-05; Intelli-Check Inc, dir, 2005-. **Orgs:** Bd dirs, Laumeir Int; bd dirs, Jackie Robinson Found; bd dirs, Opera Theatre St Louis; chmn, Barrier Island Trust; hon battalion chief, Fire Dep New York; chmn, Compensation Comt, Intelli-Check Inc; Corporate Governance & Nominating Comt, Intelli-Check Inc. **Honors/Awds:** Excellence in News Writing Award, William Randolph Hearst Found, 1970; Award for Communication Excellence to Black Audiences, Black Commun Inst, 1982. **Business Phone:** (516)992-1900.

SMITH, GWENDOLYN ILOANI
Association executive, president (organization), chief executive officer. **Educ:** Colgate Univ, BA; Univ Hartford, MBA. **Career:** Aetna Inc, managing dir; Smith Whiley & Co, pres & chief exec officer, currently. **Orgs:** Bd Trustees Colgate Univ; life mem, Nat Asn Advan Colored People; chairperson, Audit Comt. **Business Addr:** President, Chief Executive officer, Smith Whiley & Company, 242 Trumbull St, Hartford, CT 06103, **Business Phone:** (860)548-2513.

SMITH, H RUSSELL
Entrepreneur, lawyer, founder (originator). **Personal:** Born Oct 8, 1957, Detroit, MI; son of Oliver H and Mildred A. **Educ:** Univ Mich, BBA, 1979; Northwestern Univ, MBA, MM, 1983, JD, 1983. **Career:** Dykema, Gossett, atty, 1983-85; Burroughs crp & Unisys, atty, 1985-87; Growth Funding Ltd, atty, consult, 1987-88; H Russell Smith Esq, atty, 1988-89; Lewis, White & Clay PC, sr atty, 1989-92; Blacks Factor Inc, pres & founder, 1992-. **Orgs:** Wolverine Bar Asn; Detroit Bar Asn; Mich Bar Asn. **Business Phone:** (313)862-7287.

SMITH, HALE
Editor, educator, composer. **Personal:** Born Jun 29, 1925, Cleveland, OH; son of Hale and Jimmie Anne Clay; married Juanita R Hancock; children: Hale Michael, Marcel Hancock, Robin Alison & Eric Dale. **Educ:** Cleveland Inst Music, BM, 1950, MM, 1952. **Career:** Univ Conn, prof emer music; freelance composer & arranger, 1945-; CF Peters Corp, 1962-; Edward B Marks Mus Corp, educ consult, 1962-63; Frank Music Corp, 1963-65; Sam Fox Music Publ, 1967-71; CW Post Col, adj & assoc prof, 1969-70; orchestrator & consult, Black Music Repertory Ensemble, Ctr Black Music Res, Columbia Col Chicago. **Orgs:** Freelance consult to Performers, Composers, Diverse Music Publishing Firms; consult Copyright Infringement; lectr numerous col throughout the US; Am Music Ctr, dr; former mem Bd Gov, Am Comp All; Composers Recording Inc, bd dirs; former pres Freeport Arts Coun; Freeport Bd Ethics; New York State Coun For The Arts, bd mem, 1993-97. **Honors/Awds:** BMI Student Composers Award, 1952; Cleveland Arts Prize, 1973; Distinguished Scholar Xavier Univ New Orleans La; American Academy Institute Arts & Letters Award, 1988; Honorary Doctorate Music, Cleveland Institute Music, 1988; numerous commns maj perf & publ. **Military Serv:** Military Serv, private, 1943-45. **Home Addr:** 225 Pine St, Freeport, NY 11520, **Home Phone:** (516)868-9798.

SMITH, HAROLD GREGORY
Clergy. **Personal:** Born in Chicago, IL; son of Harold and Mable Lee Cline Smith Jenkins. **Educ:** Bradley Univ, BS, 1974; Nashotah House Theol Sem, MDiv, 1980. **Career:** Am Nat Red Cross, prog develop, 1974-76; US Pres Exec Off, staff writer, 1976-77; Church Holy Cross, rector, 1980-85; St Simon Episcopal Church, rector, 1985-88; St Simon Cyrene, rector, 1988-90; St Timothy Episcopal Church, rector, 1990-93; Church Holy Redeemer, rector, 1993-; Church St Luke, rector. **Orgs:** Bd mem, Rochester Soc Prev Cruelty C, 1985-88; bd mem, Oregon-Leopold Day Care ctr, 1988-90; Judicial Process Comn; bd mem, Bishop Sheen Ecumenical Housing Found; bd mem, Episcopal Church Home; bd mem, Am Cancer Soc, Rochester Chapter; bd mem, Am Heart Asn, Rochester Chapter; vol, Proj Open Hand; chair, The Place Ministry; Chaplain, Col State House Representatives; econ adv bd, comnr, Denver City. **Home Phone:** (404)816-2916.

SMITH, HAROLD TELIAFERRO
Lawyer. **Personal:** Born Apr 10, 1947, Miami, FL; son of Harold and Mary; divorced; children: Katrell & Talia. **Educ:** Fla A&M Univ, BS, math, 1968; Univ Miami Law Sch, JD, 1973. **Career:** Dade County Pub Defenders, atty; Dade County Attys Off, Long & Smith PA, H T Smith PA, atty, 2001, pres, currently. **Orgs:** Kappa Alpha Psi Fraternity, 1983-; chair, Coalition Free S Africa, 1985-90; exec comt, Miami Dade Br, Nat Asn Advan Colored People, 1990-; co-spokesperson, Boyscott Miami Campaign, 1990-93; co-chair, Miami Partners Progress, 1993-; secy, Inroads/Miami, 1993-; Community Partnership Homeless, 1993-94; pres, Nat Bar Asn, 1994-; Nat Bar Asn. **Honors/Awds:** Service Award, Nat Conf Black Lawyers, 1991; Charles Whited Spirit of Excellence Award, Miami Herald, 1993; Best Lawyers in America, 1995-96. **Special Achievements:** Wrote numerous articles for publication and gave hundreds of speeches and seminars. **Military Serv:** AUS, first lt, 1968-70; Bronze Star (valor), Vietnam Service. **Business Addr:** President, H T Smith PA, 1017 NW 9th Ct, Miami, FL 33136, **Business Phone:** (305)324-1845.

SMITH, HEMAN BERNARD
Lawyer, educator. **Personal:** Born Aug 20, 1929, Alexandria, LA; son of Heyman and Rosa; married Ina Jean Washington, Dec 26, 1952; children: Heman III, Lanie C & Paula Barnes. **Educ:** Univ Md, attended 1958-60; Univ Pac, McGeorge Sch Law, JD, 1971. **Career:** Smith, Hanna, de Bruin & Yee, Sacto, partner & sr attorney, 1971-78; Smith & Yee, Sacto, partner, 1978-84; Smith & Assoc, Sacto CA, sr attorney,1984; Univ Northern Calif, L P Sch Law, Sacto, exec dean & founder, 1988; Univ Northern Calif, L P Sch Law, dean studs; Univ Northern Calif, Lorenzo Patino Law Sch, founder, emer fac, currently. **Orgs:** Bd mem, Am Red Cross, Sacto, 1980-87; Minority Steering Comt Calif Youth Authority, 1985-87; Wiley Man Bar Asn, 1988-; Calif State Bar Asn; bd trustees, Sacramento Urban League; Nat Asn Advan Colored People; arbitrator, Sacramento Co Bar Asn Atty Client Dispute. **Military Serv:** USAF, 1948-69. **Home Addr:** 6370 Havenside Dr, Sacramento, CA 95831, **Home Phone:** (916)422-6296. **Business Addr:** Emeritus Faculty, University of Northern California, Lorenzo Patino School of Law, 1012 J St, Sacramento, CA 95814, **Business Phone:** (916)441-4485.

SMITH, DR. HENRY THOMAS
Physician. **Personal:** Born Mar 31, 1937, Portsmouth, VA; son of Julius; married Diane; children: Robert & Alicia. **Educ:** Howard Univ, wash, DC, BS, 1957; Univ Rochester, Sch med & dent,

Rochester, NY, MD, 1961. **Career:** Minn Gen Hosp, Minneapolis, MN, intern, 1961-62; Hennepin County Gen Hosp, Minneapolis, MN, med resident, 1964-67; Hennepin Co Med Ctr, asst dir, chronic dialysis unit, 1967-69; Pilot City Med Ctr, Minneapolis, MN, physician, 1969-71; Modern Med Jour, assoc editor, 1970-72; Geriatrics Jour, abstract editor, 1970-72; Nephrology Modern Med Jour, consult, 1975-77; Park Nicollet Medical Ctr, Minneapolis, MN, 1971-94; Univ Minn, Sch Med, Minneapolis, MN, assoc clinical prof to clinical prof, 1975-95; Hennepin Fac Assocs, HFA Div Internal Med, Minneapolis, MN, dir, 1994-; Hennepin Fac Assocs, Minneapolis, MN, Clinics med dir, 1996-. **Orgs:** Nephrol Fel, Hennepin County Gen Hosp, Minneapolis, MN, 1967-69; Sister Kenny Inst, 1972-75; Minn Heart Asn, 1974-76; pres, Nat Kidney Found Upper Midwest, 1982-84; Minneapolis Soc Internal Med; Nat Med Asn; Am Soc Hypertension; Fel Am Col Physicians; Am Heart Asn, Minn Affiliate, bd dirs; Nat Kidney Found Upper Midwest, med adv bd; Hennepin Fac Assocs, chief HFA Div internal med; Hennepin County Med Ctr, exec comt; Univ Minn Health System, bd govs; Minn Med Asn, bd trustees; Turning Point Community Health Care Ctr, bd dir, 1997-99; Am Med Asn; Am Soc Internal Med; Minn Asn Black Physicians; Minn State Med Asn. **Honors/Awds:** Cert Internal Med, 1969, Nephrol, 1974; Phi Beta Kappa; 'Commanding General Award for Medical Service', 1964; 'Award of Excellence', Communities Color, 1997; Best Doctors in America: Central Region, 1996-97; President's Award, Minn Med Asn, 1999; Best Doctors in America, 2000; Laureate Award, ACP-ASIM, Minn chap, 2001; designated specialist in hypertension, ASH, 2001; Minority Service Award, Minn Asn, 2002; Top Doctors list: Minneapolis - St. Paul Mag annual survey, 2003. **Special Achievements:** Author, Modern Medicine Practice Guide, VIAGRA: Study to Assess the Effectiveness and Safety of Viagra in Men with Erectile Dysfunction Who Are Taking 2 or More Blood Pressure Medications. **Military Serv:** AUS, Capt, 1962-64; Kenner Army Hosp, 1964; commanding officer; Med Detachment, Camp Ames, Korea, 1962-63. **Home Addr:** 6717 Cahill Rd, Edina, MN 55439. **Business Addr:** Medical Director, Hennepin Faculty Associates, Internal Medicine, 825 S 8th St Suite 206, Minneapolis, MN 55404, **Business Phone:** (612)347-3627.

SMITH, HERMAN BRUNELL, JR.
Consultant. **Personal:** Born Feb 12, 1927, Mansfield, OH; married Annie Mae Lavender, Dec 26, 1951; children: Gregory B., Terri Lynne. **Educ:** Knoxville Col, Knoxville, TN, BA, 1948; Univ Wisconsin, Madison, WI, MS, 1955, PhD, 1960. **Career:** Consultant (retired); Southern Educ Found, Atlanta, GA, consult, 1966-68; Nat Asn Land Grant Cols, Washington, DC, dir, 1968-74; Univ Arkansas, Pine Bluff, AR, pres, 1974-81; Atlanta Univ, Atlanta, GA, vpres, 1981-82; Kettering Found, Dayton, OH, consult, 1982-88; Univ Georgia, Athens, GA, consult to pres, 1985-88; Jackson State Univ Jackson, MS, interm pres, 1991-92. **Orgs:** Vpres, West End Rotary Club; pres, Knoxville Col Nat Alumni Asn, 1988-91. **Honors/Awds:** Distinguished Alumnus, Univ Wisconsin Alumni Asn, 1988; Outstanding Service Award, City Knoxville, TN, 1986; Outstanding Service Award, Sigma Pi Phi, 1986; Outstanding Service Award, Phi Delta Kappa, Atlanta Univ, 1989; Doctor Laws Degree, Stillman Col, Tuscaloosa, Alabama, 1991; Sch Educ Alumni Achievement Award, Univ Wisconsin, Madison, 1992. **Military Serv:** AUS, 1st lt, 1951-53. *

SMITH, HOWLETT P.
Musician. **Personal:** Born Feb 28, 1933, Phoenix, AZ; son of Howard Lowell and Josephine Cox; married Judith Celestin; children: Juliette, Rachel, Mark, April, Sandra & Peter. **Educ:** Univ Ariz, BM, 1955. **Career:** Composer, pianist, singer, arranger, vocal coach, music teacher, whistler, performer & instr; Inter-Cult Awarness Prog, LA Unifiead Sch dist, church pianist, organist & numerous pub appearances; lectr & demonstrations concerning use jazz in church; Songs: Me & Bessie, dir; A Candle in the Dark, composer; Raven Records, pianist, currently; Piano & Vocals: Funny Side Up; Ugly Woman; Sin Around Here; Pennies From Heaven; Gail, All About Love; Equal Opportunity Lover; Chitlins in the Whitehouse; Ebonically; He Sho' Did Preach; Are We Havin' Fun Yet?; Truth; Gender Bender Blues; Would Anybody Care?; Almost Human; Tired of Bein' White; You Punched A Hole In My Dreams; I Used To Be Colored; Shoes & Laughin' To Keep From Cryin'. **Orgs:** Life mem, Psi Mu Alpha; Univ Ariz Alumni Asn; Kappa Psi; Newman Club;Camino Col Fac. **Honors/Awds:** Named Mr Newmanite, Univ Ariz, 1955; Hall of Fame. **Special Achievements:** Composer of popular & religious works, numerous recording tapes/CDs, featured performer at Bob Burns Restaurant, Santa Monica, CA, for 20years, listed in April 1994 issue of LA Mag as "One of the reasons toremain in LA", composer of special masses, musicals, and cantatas; appearances in TV and movies, The Sch for the Deaf & Blind, Tueson, AZ, 2002, awarded a Scroll of Recognition from the Los Angeles County Bd of Supvrs for cultural & humanitarian contributions to the greater Los Angeles area community, 2002. **Business Addr:** Pianist, Raven Records, 1821 Wilshire Blvd, Santa Monica, CA 90403.

SMITH, DR. IAN
Physician, journalist, writer. **Personal:** Married Shelby. **Educ:** Harvard Col, BA, 1992; Columbia Univ, MS, 1993; Dartmouth Med Sch, attended; Chicago Univ, Pritzker Sch Med. **Career:** Albert Einstein Col Med Hosp, surg intern, orthopedics; NBC News Network NewsChannel 4, NY, med corresp; NY Daily Men's Health Mag, med columnist; WNBC's Today in NY, reporter; Newsweek Mag, med columnist; The Blackbird Papers, 2004; VH1's Celebrity Fit Club, med/diet expert; NPR's Tavis Smiley Show & nationally Syndicated The View, commentator, currently; Celebrity Fit Club, med diet expert, currently; 50 Million Pound Challenge, founder, currently. Author: The Fat Smash Diet, The Blackbird Papers, 2004, Dr. Ian Smith's Guide to Medical Websites, The Take-Control Diet. **Orgs:** Bd mem, New York City Mission Soc; bd mem, Cancer Res Found Am; bd mem, Am Coun on Exercise; bd mem, N Shore-Long Island Jewish Res Inst; bd mem, Henry H. Kessler Found, Building with Books. **Honors/Awds:** Nat Acad TV Arts & Sci, 2001; The Blackbird Papers BCALA fiction Honor Book Award winner, 2005; Trauma: Life in the ER, NY Asn Black Journalists; BCALA Fiction Honor Book Award Winner, 2005. **Special Achievements:** Featured in several publ including: People, Ebony, Cosmopolitan, JET, Univ Chicago Med on the Midway. **Business Addr:** Medical Contributor, The View, PO Box 765, New York, NY 10150.

SMITH, IRVIN MARTIN
Football player. **Personal:** Born Oct 13, 1971, Trenton, NJ. **Educ:** Univ Notre Dame, mkt. **Career:** Football player (retired); New Orleans Saints, tight end, 1993-97; San Francisco 49ers, tight end, 1998; Cleveland Browns, tight end, 1999.

SMITH, J. ALFRED, SR.
Clergy, college teacher. **Personal:** Born May 19, 1931, Kansas City, MO; son of Amy; married Joanna Goodwin; children: J Alfred Jr, Craig, Anthony, Amy Jones, Shari Rigmaiden, Ronald Craig. **Educ:** Western Baptist Col, BS, elem educ, 1952; Mo Sch Relig, Univ Mo, Columbia, BD, 1959; Pac Sch Relig, Berkeley, CA, attended 1962; Inter-Baptist Theol Ctr, TX, Church & Community, ThM, 1966; Am Baptist Sem W, attended 1970, ThM, 1972; Golden Gate Baptist Theol Sem, DMin, 1975; Hampton Univ, lectr, 1979; ABSW, DHL, 1990. **Career:** Senior pastor (retired). Licensed minister, 1948-; ordained minister, 1951-; Am Baptist Sem W, actg dean, 1975-87, prof, 1975-; Grad Theol Sem, prof; Fuller Theol Sem, vis prof; Allen Temple Baptist Church, sr pastor, 1970-06. **Orgs:** Pes, Baptist Pastors/Ministers Conf, Oakland & Easy Bay, 1986-; pres, Progressive Nat Baptist Conv, 1986-88; bd dirs, Metrop YMCA; bd bir, Nat Coun Churches; bd dirs, Cong Nat Black Churches; Bread World; Nat Conf Black Seminarians; Howard Thurman Educ Trust; Bishop Col Renaissance Campaign; adv bd, Howard Univ Sch Divinity; adv bd, United Theol Sem; adv bd, Univ Calif, Berkeley, county; rep, Am Baptist Churches USA; founding chairperson, Bay Area Black United Fund; AFRICARE; APA. **Honors/Awds:** Man of the Yr Award, Golden West Mag, LA, 1976; Award for Outstanding Accomplishments, Grass Roots Level New Oakland Community, 1976; Man of the Yr Award, Sun-Reporter/Metro Reporter, 1976; Recognition Distinguished Serv, Boy Scouts Am, 1986; Bishop Col Renaissance Campaign; Earl Lect, Pac Sch Relig, 1989; Hay Lect, Drake Univ, 1989; Addressed United Nations S African Apartheid, 1989; Outstanding Citizen of the Yr, Oakland Tribune; Martin Luther King Int Chapel, Morehouse Col; Prince Hall, Free & Accepted Masons, Elevated 33rd Degree; Three awards named in honor. **Special Achievements:** Co-author, works include: Giving to a Giving God: Basic Bible Sermons; The Study Bible, Holman Bible Publishing; Preaching As a Social Act; Guidelines for Effective Urban Ministry; listed in Ebony Magazine as one of the fifteen greatest African American preachers in America. *

SMITH, DR. J. CLAY, JR.
Lawyer, government official, educator. **Personal:** Born Apr 15, 1942, Omaha, NE; son of John Clay Smith Sr and Emily V Williams; married Patti Jones; children: Stager, Michael Laurel, Michelle Lori & Eugene Douglas. **Educ:** Creighton Univ Omaha, NE, AB, 1964; Howard Law Sch, Wash, DC, JD, 1967; George Wash Law Sch, Wash, DC, LLM, 1970, SJD, 1977. **Career:** Educator (retired), Lawyer, Government offical; AUS Judge Advocates Gen Corp, capt lawyer, 1967-71; Arent Fox Kintner Plotkin & Kahn Wash, DC,assoc, 1971-74; Fed Commun Comn, Cable TV Bureau, dep chief, 1974-76, assoc gen coun; Fed Communs Comn, assoc gen counr, 1976-77; Equal Employment Opportunity Comn, us comnr, 1977-82, acting chmn, 1981-82; Howard Univ Sch Law, prof law, 1982-86, dean & prof law, 1986-88, prof, 1988-2004. **Orgs:** NE Bar Assoc, 1967; Howard Law Sch Alumni Asn, 1967-; Dist Columbia Bar, 1968; pres bd dirs, Wash Bar Asn, 1970; US Supreme Ct, 1973; adv pres, Nat Bar Asn, 1973-; Nat Asn Advan Colored People, 1975-; Urban League, 1975-; founder, Wash Bar Asn, 1978; nat pres mem, Fed Bar Asn, 1979; Utility Spec Pub Serv Comm, 1982-84; Am Bar Asn, 1982-; mem ed bd, ABA Compleat Lawyer, 1984-87; Adv Comm, DC Bar Exam; bd mem, Nat Lawyers Club; planning comm Task Force Black Males, Am Psyh Asn, 1986-90; Am Law Inst, 1986-88; chairperson, Nat Bar Asn Comm Hist Black Lawyers; legal coun Elderly Policy Bd, 1986-88; Verizon Consumer Adv Bd, 2000-; dir, Nat Lawyers Comt Civil Rights Under Law, currently. **Honors/Awds:** Ollie May Cooper Award, 1986; C Francis Strad ford Award, 1986; Outstanding Alumni Achievement Award, Howard Univ, 1981; Outstanding Alumni Achievement Awards, Creighton Univ, 1989; Outstanding Alumni Achievement Awards, George Wash Univ, 1990; National Book Award, Nat Conf Black Political Scientist, 1995; Distinguished Faculty Author Award, 2001 & 2002. **Special Achievements:** First Black Governor of Boys State (NE and nation) in 1959, has published Fed Bar Assn Natl Pres Messages, Fed Bar News, CIVICS LEAP, Law Reason & Creativity, Mgng Multi-ethnic Multi-racial Workforce Criminal, Chronic Alcoholism — Lack of Mens Rea — A Dfns Pblc Intoxication 13 Howard Law Journal, An Investment in a New Century, Wash Afro Am; The Black Bar Assn & Civil Rights, A Black Lawyer's Response to the Fairmont Papers, Memoriam: Clarence Clyde Ferguson, Jr, Harvard Law Rev, Forgotten Hero- :Charles H Houston, Harvard Law Rev, Justice & Juris prudence & The Black Lawyer, Notre Dame Law Rev, Emancipation: The Making of The Black Lawyer, 1844-1944, Rebels in Law: Voices in History of Black Women Lawyers, 1998, Served on the transition team of president Clinton and Vice president PGore, 1992, first African American elected as national president, Fed Bar Asn in 1980-81. **Military Serv:** AUS, capt. **Business Addr:** Director, National Lawyers Committee for Civil Rights Under Law, 1401 New York Ave NW Suite 400, Washington, DC 20005, **Business Phone:** (202)662-8600.

SMITH, J THOMAS
Lawyer, broadcaster, consultant. **Personal:** Born in Wayne County, MI; son of Marjorie and Louis. **Educ:** Univ State New York, BS, 1988; Vermont Col, Norwich Univ, MA, 1988; Univ San Jose (Costa Rica), PhD, 1995; Tex Southern Univ, Thurgood Marshall Sch Law, JD, 1999; Calif Coast Univ, PsyD, 2005. **Career:** Mind Science Primer, author, 1986; Columist, "Ask the Doctor", Majic the Magazine, KMJQ Com, 1999-2002; "Ask the Doctor", NPR Syndicated, "Sisters & Friends", radio program, 1997-2001; Houston Community Col System, assoc campus dir/ instr, 1982-87; City Univ Los Angeles Sch Law, interim dean, 1989-90; Atlanta Metropolitan Col, 1990-91; Dr. J Thomas Smith & Assoc, pres/chief exec officer, 1991-; Columbia/HCA Spring Branch Med Ctr, dir John Lucas Treat & Rec Ctr, 1991-93; Texas Southern Univ, Sch Cont Ed, adj prof, 1993-97; Prairie View A & M Univ, dir coun & multicultural servs, 1993-97; KMJQ-FM, air talent, 1994-; Anderson & Smith, PC, law clerk, 1998-2000. **Orgs:** Phi Alpha Delta Legal Fraternity, 1997-; Nat Bd Certified Counselors, Examination Comm, 1994-99; Am Mental Health Counselor asn, bd dir, CCMH, liaison, 1993-96; Nat Asn Alcoholism & Drug Abuse Counselors; Screen Actors Guild; Am Fed TV & Radio Artists, Ethnic Minority Comm, chair, 1983-87; Nat Comm on Mental Health, bd dirs, 1995-96; State Bar Tex, Law Student Div, campus dir, 1999-2000; United Clergy Religious Science; Am Bar asn; Fed Bar asn; Houston Bar asn; Am Immigration Lawyers asn. **Honors/Awds:** Black Radio Exclusive, Air Personality of the Year on Pop Radio, 1983. **Business Addr:** Attorney, Counselor at Law, Law Offices of J Thomas Smith JD PhD, 2855 Mangum Rd Suite 525, PO Box 681113, Houston, TX 77092, **Business Phone:** (713)529-9372.

SMITH, JACK. See SMITH, JOHN L, JR.

SMITH, JAMES, JR.
Labor relations manager. **Personal:** Born Nov 10, 1932, Beckley, WV; married V Anne; children: Byron A. **Educ:** Spokane Falls Community Col, AAS, 1978; Fort Wright Col, BS, mgt, 1981. **Career:** USAF, security police, 1953-70, training admin, 1970-75; City of Spokane, personnel tech, 1978-81, asst personnel dir, 1981-83, personnel dir, dir human resources, currently. **Orgs:** Chmn bd, Nat Mgt Asn, 1983-87; Nat Forum Black Pub Admin, 1983-; Alpha Phi Alpha Fraternity, 1983-; pres, Pine State Athletic Club, 1984-87; bd dir, NFBP, 1985; pres, WA Coun Pub Admin, 1987-; bd dir, Asn Negotiators & Contr Adminr. **Honors/Awds:** Superior Service Award, City Spokane, 1985. **Military Serv:** USAF msgt 1953-75; Commendation Medal; Good Conduct Medal. **Business Addr:** Director of Human Resources, City of Spokane, 808 W Spokane Falls Blvd, Spokane, WA 99201, **Business Phone:** (509)755-2489.

SMITH, DR. JAMES ALMER, JR.
Physician, educator. **Personal:** Born May 30, 1923, Montclair, NJ; son of James A and Carrie Elizabeth Moten; married Elsie Brooks, Oct 15, 1949; children: James A III, Roger M, Margo A & Melanie K. **Educ:** Howard Univ, BS, 1947, MD, 1948. **Career:** Homer G Phillips Hosp, intern, 1948-49, res psychiat, 1949-51; Wash Univ,child psychiat, 1952-53; Ment Hygiene Clin Group Co, 1953-55; Hartley Salmon Child Guidance Clin, staff psychiat, 1955-60; Children's Serv Conn, 1956-60; Juv Ct, Hartford, consult, 1956-61; Bay State Med Ctr, asst vis psychiat, 1960; Childrens Study Home, consult, 1960; Springfield Child Guidance Clin, assoc psychiatrist, 1960-83; Tufts Sch Med, asst clin prof, 1977; Kolburne Sch New Marlborough, med dir. **Orgs:** Human Rel Comn Springfield, 1961-62; Am Psychiat Asn; fel Am Ortho Psychiat Asn; Bd Negro Catholic Scholar Fund, 1980-; Am Asn Psychoanalytic Physicians Inc; Am Soc Psychoanalytic Physicians fel, 1987-; Sigma Pi Phi. **Honors/Awds:** Am Acad Human Serv Award, 1974-75; Community Leaders & Noteworthy Americans Award, 1978; Int Directory Distinguished Psychotherapists, 1981,1982; Dr Anthony L Brown Award, WW Johnson Ctr, 1987. **Military Serv:** AUS MC, capt, 1953-55. **Home Addr:** 96 Dartmouth St, Springfield, MA 01109.

SMITH, DR. JAMES ALMER, III
Psychiatrist. **Personal:** Born May 24, 1950, St Louis, MO; married Sandra Wright; children: Anthony, Jason & Brian. **Educ:**

Howard Univ, BS, 1972, MD, 1976. **Career:** Harlem Hosp Ctr, intern, 1976-77; Walter Reed Army Med Ctr, resident, 1977-80; AUS Ft Bragg, in-patient chief psychologist, 1980-81, out-patient chief psychologist, 1981-82; Central Prison Dept Corrections, staff psychologist, 1982-85, clinic dir, 1985-87; NC Dept Corrections, clinic dir mental health; pvt pract, currently. **Orgs:** Out-patient psychologist, Wake Co Alcoholism Treatment Ctr, 1983-87; bd dirs, Drug Action Wake Co, 1986-87; pres, La Scruggs Med Soc, 1989-91, 1993-; criminal adjuctant prof, Duke Med Ctr, 1989-91; Duke Med Ctr, Dept Psychiatry, consulting assoc; Healthy Wake Co 2000, chair. **Military Serv:** AUS, LtC, 9 yrs; AUS, Army Commendation Medal, 1986; gov Coun Alcoholism, 1991; LtC, 1977-91. **Home Addr:** 209 Worham Dr, Raleigh, NC 27614. **Business Addr:** Physician, 1055 Dresser Ct, Raleigh, NC 27609, **Business Phone:** (919)876-3130.

SMITH, JAMES CHARLES
Computer executive. **Personal:** Born Jul 27, 1936, Winnfield, LA; son of Annie Lee Rush; divorced; children: Rodney D, Michael D, Wanda T & Donna M Murphy. **Educ:** Southern Univ A & M Col, BA, 1960; St Mary's Univ, MBA, 1971; GE Mgt Develop Inst, attended 1985. **Career:** AUS, Mil Award Br, chief, 1977-79, Comput Syst Cmd, dir personnel & admin, 1979-81; Gen Electric Co, sr syst engr, 1981-83, mgr, 1983-86; Syst Eng & Mgt Assocs Inc, founder, pres, chief exec officer, 1986-. **Orgs:** Omega Psi Phi Fraternity, KRS, Basielus, 1985-87; INROADS-Greater Wash Inc, 1991-92; Adv Bd, George Washington Univ, 1992-93; comnr, Va Govs Comt Defense Conversion, 1992; Va Gov's Task Force Workforce, 2000, 1992-93; NASA Minority Bus Resource Adv Coun, 1993-94; bd dir, Va Venture Fund Found, 1993-94; bd dir, DC Math Sci Tech Inst, 1993; Kauffman Found. **Honors/Awds:** Chapter Man of the Year, Omega Psi Phi Fraternity, 1984; Chapter & District Citizen of the Year, Omega Psi Phi Fraternity, 1988, 1990; Mentor of the Year, N Va Minority Bus Asn, 1989; Small Bus of the Year, Defense Comt Agency, 1989; Outstanding Vendor Award, Teledyne Brown Engr, 1989; New Bus of the Year, Fairfax Co Chamber Com, 1990; Jump Start Recognition, Wash Tech Mag, 1990, 1991; Entrepreneur of the Year, Merrill Lynch Inc, Ernst & Young & Wash Bus Jour, 1991. **Special Achievements:** Responsible for convincing Pres Jimmy Carter to award the Pres Unit Citation to the 761st Tank Battallion, 1978; Top 10 Fastest Growing Govt Contractors, Govt Comput News, 1989, 1992; First African American to be appointed by Gov L Douglas Wilder to the three member Bd of Vistors, Gunston Hall, home of Geoorge Mason, author of the US Constitution, 1990; Testified before Congress on efforts to be made to involve more minorities in math, sci & tech, 1991, 1992; Profiled on the CBS local affiliate's TV show "Success Stories", 1991, 1992; Fast 50 Fastest Growing Companies, Wash Tech Mag, 1992-93; Inc 500 Fastest Growing Co, Inc Mag, 1993; Top 100 Black Owned Cos in US, Black Enterprise Mag, 1994; Company ranked no 80 on Black Enterprise's list of top 100 industrial/service companies, 1998. **Military Serv:** AUS, lt col, 1960-81; Legion of Merit, 1981; Bronze Star, 1968; 2 Meritorious Service Medals, 1973, 1974; Joint Service Commendation Medal, 1976; 2 Army Commendation Medals, 1965, 1967; National Defense Service Medal, 1968; Vietnamese Gallantry Cross, 1968; Vietnamese Service Medal, 1968; 4 Armed Forces Expeditionary Medals, 1965-73; Expert Infantry Man Badge, 1962; Sr Parachutist Badge, 1966. **Business Addr:** President, Chief Executive Officer, Systems Engineering Management Associates Inc, 2800 S Shirlington Rd Suite 750, Alexandria, VA 22206, **Business Phone:** (703)845-1200.

SMITH, JAMES DAVID. See Obituaries section.

SMITH, JAMES RUSSELL
Government official, air force officer, insurance executive. **Personal:** Born May 2, 1931, Tupelo, MS; married Madie Ola; children: Rickey Young, Robert Young, Anita Young, Bonita Tate, Valeria Wedley & Richard. **Educ:** Jackson State Jr Col, BA, 1979. **Career:** Airforce Officer, government official insurance executive (Retired); USAF, Commun CGN, supvr, 1951-72, Air Refueling Tech, supvr 1951-72; Golden Circle Life Ins Co, salesman, 1972-85. **Orgs:** Pres, Humboldt Chap Nat Asn Advan Colored People, 1975-80; bd mem, Humboldt City Schs, 1982-85. **Military Serv:** USAF, tsgt, 1951-72; Air Medal 2 oak leaf clusters, 1967; USAF oak leaf cluster, 1968; retired 1972. **Home Addr:** 301 S 3rd Ave, Humboldt, TN 38343.

SMITH, JAMES TODD (L L COOL J)
Rap musician, actor. **Personal:** Born Jan 14, 1968, Queens, NY; married Simone; children: Najee, Italia, Samaria & Nina. **Career:** Def Jam, music arranger & rap artist, 1985-; Discography: Radio, 1985; Bigger and Deffer, 1987; Walking With A Panther, 1989; Mama Said Knock You Out, 1990; 14 Shots To The Dome, 1993; Phenomenon, 1997; GOAT, 2000; Todd Smith, 2006; Exit 13, 2007; Movies: Krush Groove, 1985; The Hard Way, 1991; Toys, 1992; Out of Sync, 1995; Deep Blue Sea, 1999; In Too Deep, 1999; Any Given Sunday, 1999; Charlie's Angels, 2000; Kingdom Come,2001; Roller ball, 2002; Deliver Us From Eva, 2003; SWAT, 2003; Mind hunters, 2004; Slow Burn, 2005; Edison, 2005; Last Holiday, 2006; The Deal, 2008 Television: "In the House", 1995-98; "House M.D.", 2005; 30 Rock", 2007; The Man, producer, 2007; "NCIS: Los Angeles", 2009. **Honors/Awds:** MTV Video Music Award for Best Rap Video, 1991; Grammy Award for Best Rap Solo performance, 1992; Best Rap Artist, 1996, 1997; MTV Video Music Vanguard Award, 1997; Outstanding Hip-Hop/Rap Artist, NAACP Image Awards, 2001; Outstanding Male Artist, NAACP Image Awards, 2003; Billboard Award; Source Foundation Image Award, 2003; 10 Soul Train Awards; 15 New York Music Awards. **Special Achievements:** Author of I Make My Own Rules, 1997; Was named the 10th greatest hip hop MC of all time by MTV. **Business Phone:** (212)229-5200.*

SMITH, DR. JANE E
Educational consultant, executive director. **Personal:** Born Jul 27, 1946, Atlanta, GA. **Educ:** Spelman Col, BA, sociol; Emory Univ, MA, sociol; Harvard Univ, PhD. **Career:** Spelman Col, asst prof sociol & dir freshman studies, 1975, Ctr Leadership & Civic Engagement, exec dir, 2004-; Atlanta Univ, asst vpres develop; INROADS, Atlanta & Detroit, managing dir, 1981-94; Martin Luther King Ctr Noviolent Social Change, dir develop, 1991-94; Carter Ctrs Atlanta Project, dir, 1994-98; Nat Coun Negro Women Inc, pres & chief exec officer, 1998-2002; Bus & Prof Women & USA, chief exec officer, 2002. **Honors/Awds:** Roy Wilkins Image Award, Nat Asn Advan Colored People, Atlanta Chap, 1997; Honorary Doctorates, Spelman Col & Tex Col. **Business Phone:** (404)681-3643.

SMITH, JANET K
Government official. **Career:** New Castle County Police Dept, police officer, lt, capt, 1973, maj, 1997. **Special Achievements:** First African American female to become captain in New Castle County.

SMITH, JANET MARIA
Publisher. **Personal:** Born in Bluefield, WV; daughter of John H and Edith P; divorced; children: Tiffany A & Taashan A. **Educ:** Franklin Univ, 1984-87. **Career:** J M Smith Commuss, pres; The Blue Chip Profile Inc, publ & chief exec officer. **Orgs:** Columbus Asn Black Journalists, co-chair, regional conf, 1992; Nat Asn Market Developers; Columbus Urban League; NCP, Columbus. **Special Achievements:** Publisher, Blue Chip Profile, resource guide for African American, annual, 1991; Founder, Blue Chip Awards, honoring African Americans, 1992. **Business Addr:** Chief Executive Offier, The Blue Chip Profile Inc, 4313 Donlyn Ct, Columbus, OH 43232, **Business Phone:** (614)861-0772.

SMITH, JANICE EVON
Association executive, public relations executive. **Personal:** Born Feb 21, 1952, Warsaw, NC. **Educ:** NC A&T State Univ, BS, 1974; OH State Univ, MA, 1975. **Career:** Greensboro Daily News-Record, reporting intern, 1974; The Charlotte News, daily newspaper reporter, 1975-79, reporter & ed, 1980; Nat Urban League Wash Opers, comn assoc, 1981-83; DC Off Human Rights, spec asst dir; Greater Wash Urban League Inc, chief staff & gala coordr, currently. **Orgs:** Chmn, Dist III NC Press Women's Assoc, 1977; publicity chmn & bd dir, Charlotte Mecklenburg Afro-Am Cult Ctr, 1978-80; forum coord, Wash Assoc Black Journalists, 1982; Capital Press Club, 1982-85; NAACP, 1983-84; comn chmn, Nat Capital Chap Pub Rels Soc Am, 1986-87. **Honors/Awds:** Outstanding Young Women of America, 1982; Serv Cert Recognition, Nat Capital Chap Pub Rels Soc Am, 1986. **Business Addr:** Chief of Staff, Gala Coordinator, Greater Washington Urban League Inc, 3501 14th St NW, Washington, DC 20010, **Business Phone:** (202)265-8200.

SMITH, JERALDINE WILLIAMS
Executive, lawyer. **Personal:** Born Jan 14, 1946, Tampa, FL; married Walter L; children: Salesia Vanette & Walter Lee II. **Educ:** Univ Fla, BS, Jour, 1967; Atlanta Univ, MBA, 1970; Fla State Law Sch, JD, 1981. **Career:** Freedom Savings, bank mgr, 1973-75; Digital Equip Corp, admin mgr, 1975-77; Fla Dept Ins, lawyer 1983-; Capital Outlook Weekly Newspaper, pub, 1983-91. **Orgs:** Am Bar Asn; Fla Bar Asn; Nat Newspaper Pub Asn; Fl Press Asn. **Honors/Awds:** William Randolph Hearst Nat Newspaper Awards Winner, 1967; Businesswoman of the Year, Iota Phi Lambda, 1971. **Home Addr:** 2122 E Randolph Circle, Tallahassee, FL 32312.

SMITH, JERMAINE
Football player. **Personal:** Born Feb 3, 1972, Augusta, GA. **Educ:** Univ Ga. **Career:** Green Bay Packers, defensive tackle, 1997-2000; New Jersey Hit men, 2001; Las Vegas Outlaws, 2001; Georgia Force, 2002-03; Orlando Predators, 2004; Georgia Force, Defensive Lineman, 2005-. **Special Achievements:** Ranked first in club history in career sacks with 26.0 and ranks second for sacks in a single-season with 7.5, 2007. **Business Addr:** Defensive Line, Georgia Force, 4400 Falcon Pkwy, Flowery Branch, GA 30542, **Business Phone:** (770)965-4344.

SMITH, DR. JESSE OWENS
Educator. **Personal:** Born Dec 5, 1942, Comer, AL; son of Victor C and Lena Mae Corbitt; married Rhoda Lee Crowe, Aug 22, 1987; children: Rhonda, Karla & Seaton. **Educ:** Calif State Univ, Los Angeles, BA, 1971; Univ Chicago, IL, MA, 1973, PhD, 1976. **Career:** Univ Wis, Oshkosh, WI, prof, 1974-76; San Diego State Univ, San Diego, prof, 1977-84; Calif State Univ, Fullerton, prof, 1984-. **Orgs:** Nat Conf Black Polit Scientists, 1972-; Nat Coun Black Studies, 1976-; Am Polit Sci Asn, 1976-; Calif Black Fac & Staff Asn, 1978-; Nat Asn Advan Black Studies. **Military Serv:** AUS, E-4, 1962-64. **Business Addr:** Professor, California State University, 800 State Col Dr, Fullerton, CA 92831, **Business Phone:** (714)278-2011.

SMITH, DR. JESSIE CARNEY
Educator, librarian. **Personal:** Born Sep 24, 1930, Greensboro, NC; daughter of James Ampler Carney and Vesona Bigelow Graves; divorced; children: Frederick Douglas Jr. **Educ:** NC A&T Univ, BS, home econ, 1950; Cornell Univ, attended 1950; Mich State Univ, MA, child develop, 1956; George Peabody Col Teachers, MA, libr sci, 1957; Univ Ill, PhD, libr sci, 1964. **Career:** Nashville City Schs, teacher, 1957; Tenn State Univ, head cataloger & instr, 1957-60, coordr libr serv, asst prof, 1963-65; Univ Ill, teaching asst, 1961-63; Fisk Univ, univ librn & prof, 1965-, univ libr, prof, fedrel officer, dir, fed progs, 1975-77, William & Camille Cosby prof humanites & librn, currently; Vanderbilt Univ, Dept Libr Sci, lectr, 1969-, vis prof, 1980-84; Ala A & M Univ, assoc prof, consult, 1971-73; Univ TN Sch Libr Sci, vis lectr, 1973-74; Atlanta Univ, Workshop Intern Prog Librns Predominately Negro Col, assoc dir, 1969, 1970; Fisk Univ, Inst Selection Orgn & Use Materials & About Negro, dir, 1970; Develop Collections Black Lit, dir, 1971; African-Am Mat Proj, coordr, 1971-74;Internship Black studies Librarianship, dir, 1972-73; Mini-Inst Ethnic Studies Librarianship, dir, 1974; Internship Ethnic Studies Librarianship, dir, 1974-75; Res Prog Ethnic Studies Librarianship, dir, 1975; Libr Study, Tenn Higher Educ Comn, dir, 1975-76; Inst Ethnic Geneal Librns, dir, 1979; Race Rels Collection Proj, dir, 1980-81; Images Black Artifacts, dir, 1980-81; Learning Libr Prog, dir, 1980-84; I've Been Mountain Top: A Civil Rights Legacy, dir, 1984-86; Chicago Renaissance Proj, dir, 1988-89. **Orgs:** Episcopacy Comt, United Methodist Church, 1984-88; Metro Hist Comn, Nashville, 1984-88; Nat Comt Bicentennial Scholars Prog, United Methodist Church, 1985-87; adv coun, Black Col Libr Improvement Proj, Southern Educ Found, 1985-; bd dir, C Int Educ Ctr, 1986-; bd dir, Hist Nashville, 1986-89; Tenn Adv Coun Libr, 1990-; chair, bd dir, Coop Col Libr Ctr,1990-99; bd trustee, Gammon Theol Sem, 1998-; bd trustee, Fisk Univ,2000-; Am Libr Asn; Tenn Libr Asn; SE Libr Asn; Asn Col & Res Lib ALA; Lib Admin Div ALA; Lib Educ Div ALA; Am Asn Univ Profs. **Honors/Awds:** Martin Luther King Jr Black Authors Award, 1982; Academic or Research Librarian of the Year Award, Asn Col & Res Libr, Am Libr Asn, 1985; Distinguished Scholars Award, United Negro Col Fund, 1986; Distinguished Alumni Award, Dept Libr Sci, Peabody Col Vanderbilt Univ, 1987; Distinguished Alumni Award, Grad Sch Libr & Info Sci, Univ Ill, 1990; Certificate of Commendation, State Tenn, 94th Gen Assembly, House & Senate Concurring, 1985. **Special Achievements:** He became the first African American to earn a Ph.D. in library science from the University of Illinois.Writings includes: A Handbook for the Study of Black Bibliography, 1971, Ethnic Genealogy: A Research Guide, 1983, Images of Blacks in Amer Culture: A Reference Guide to Info Sources, 1988; Black Heroes, ed, 2001; Black Firsts: 4,000 Ground-Breaking & Historical Events, 2003; Notable Black American Women: Book III, 2003. **Business Addr:** William and Camille Cosby Professor in the Humanities, Librarian, Fisk University, 1000 17th Ave N, Nashville, TN 37208-3051, **Business Phone:** (615)329-8500.

SMITH, JIMMY LEE, JR.
Football player. **Personal:** Born Feb 9, 1969, Detroit, MI; married Sandra; children: Jimmy III. **Educ:** Jackson State Univ, BS, bus mgt, 1992. **Career:** Player (retired); Dallas Cowboys, wide receiver, 1992-94; Philadelphia Eagles, wide receiver, 1994; Jacksonville Jaguars, 1995-2005. **Orgs:** Hon chmn, Chairs Wolfson Childrens Hosp, 1999. **Honors/Awds:** Mackey Award, 1996; Vol of the Year, Am Lung Asn & Thoracic Societies Fla, Ga & SC, 1999; Pro Football Hall of Fame. *

SMITH, DR. JOANNE HAMLIN
School administrator. **Personal:** Born Oct 19, 1954, Pittsburgh, PA; daughter of Robert E and Helen Rogers; married James E Jr, May 17, 1986. **Educ:** Edinboro Univ Pa, BS, elementary educn, 1976; Wichita State Univ, MEd, Counseling and student Personnel, 1979; Kans State Univ, PhD, stud personnel admin, 1986. **Career:** McPherson Col, dir housing & asst stud servs, 1976-86; Ariz State Univ,asst dir residence life, 1986-91; Southwest Tex State Univ, dir residence life, 1992-2000, assoc vpres stud affairs, 2000, dir residence life, interim vpres stud affairs, asst prof coun & guid, vpres stud affairs, currently. **Orgs:** Phi Delta Kappa, 1976-; certified counr, Nat Brd Certified Counrs, 1980-; treas, pres elect & pres, Ariz Col Personnel Assn, 1986-91; Am Col Personnel Asn, 1986-; Southwest Assn Col & Univ Housing Officers, 1986-; Southwest Assn Col & Univ Housing Officers, pres, 1999-2001. **Honors/Awds:** Award for Outstanding Contributions, NASPA Region IV W, 1978; Women Helping Women Honoree, Soroptomist Int, 1979. **Home Addr:** 13438 Forum Rd, Universal City, TX 78148-2801, **Home Phone:** (210)945-9089. **Business Addr:** Vice President for Student Affairs, Southwest Texas State University, 601 Univ Dr, San Marcos, TX 78666, **Business Phone:** (512)245-2152.

SMITH, JOCK MICHAEL
Lawyer. **Personal:** Born Jun 10, 1948, Manhattan, NY; married Yvette Smiley Johnson; children: Janay M. **Educ:** Tuskegee Inst,

BS, hist, 1970; Univ Notre Dame Law Sch, JD, 1973. **Career:** US Customs Ct, clerk, 1970; Police Youth Involvement Prog, instr, 1972; Nat Urban League, legal asst, 1972-73; Nat Asn Advan Colored People, Civil Rights Proj, gen coun, 1973; City Camphill, Ala, judge, 1985-86; Camp Hill, Ala, city judge, 1987-89; Ala Dept Environ Mgt, admin law judge, 1993-94; Scoring Life Inc, Motivational Speaking Co, pres, founder, 1995-; Macon Co Comn, Tuskegee, atty; Cochran, Cherry, Given & Smith PC, sr partner, atty, 1998-. **Orgs:** Alpha Phi Alpha Fraternity, 1968-; vpres, Stud Govt Asn, 1969-70; chmn, Notre Dame Law Sch Chap, Black Am Law Stud Asn, 1972-73; pres, Ala Lawyers Asn, 1983-84; Ala Trial Lawyers Asn, 1983-; Nat Bar Asn, 1983-; bd dirs, Montgomery Co Trial Lawyers Asn; exec comt, ATLA; pres, Macon Co Bar Asn, 1989-91; Ethics Comt, Ala State Bar, 1996-97; NY State Bar, 2002-; legal advisor, Nat Asn Advan Colored People. **Honors/Awds:** Awarded Honor Roll Cert of 3 consecutive yrs, 1967-70; Citation for Achieving Highest Average in Major 38, Dept Hist, Tuskegee Inst, 1968-70; Luther H Foster Award, Outstanding Performance, 1969-70; Alpha Phi Alpha Award, 1969-70; Awarded 3 yr scholar for continuing acad achievement; 3 yr Academic Scholarship, Notre Dame Law Sch; Outstanding Young Man of America, 1977; Honorary Doctor of Divinity Degrees, Pentecostal Bible Col, 1987; Justice Award, Nat Bar Asn Conv, 2005. **Special Achievements:** Co-author for: Summer Youth Educ Legal Rights Career Guidance Citizen Awareness, 1972; Author: "Serving the Last of These," pub in Success Briefs for Lawyers, 2001; Climbing Jacob's Ladder, 2002. **Home Addr:** 2712 Lansdowne Dr, Montgomery, AL 36111-1712. **Business Addr:** Attorney, Senior Partner, Cochran, Cherry, Givens & Smith P.C., 306 N Main St, PO Box 830419, Tuskegee, AL 36083, **Business Phone:** (334)727-0060.

SMITH, JOE (JOSEPH LEYNARD SMITH)
Basketball player. **Personal:** Born Jul 26, 1975, Norfolk, VA; married Yolanda; children: Alanna, Jamie & Cameron. **Educ:** Univ Md, attended 1995. **Career:** Golden State Warriors, forward, 1995-98; Philadelphia 76ers, 1997-98; Minn Timberwolves, 1998-2000, 2001-03; Detroit Pistons, 2000-01; Milwaukee Bucks, forward, 2003-06; Denver Nuggets, 2006; Philadelphia 76ers, forward, 2006-07; Chicago Bulls; 2007-08; Cleveland Cavaliers, 2007-08, 2008-09; Oklahoma City Thunder, 2008-09; Atlanta Hawks, currently. **Orgs:** Joe Smith Found. **Honors/Awds:** James A Naismith Award, Col Player of the Yr, 1995; Celebrity Video Game Championship, Nat Basketball Asn Live, 1995; All-Rookie first team, Nat Basketball Assn, 1996; Adolph Rupp Award. **Special Achievements:** Film appearance: Rebound. **Business Addr:** Professional Basketball Player, Atlanta Hawks, Centennial Tower 101 Marietta St NW Suite 1900, Atlanta, GA 30303, **Business Phone:** (404)878-3800.*

SMITH, DR. JOE LEE
School administrator. **Personal:** Born May 29, 1936, Cocoa, FL; married Altamese Edmonson; children: Chyrell, Trina, Sharon & Twila. **Educ:** Fla A&M Univ, BS, 1959, MEd, 1963; Univ Fla, Rank 1-A, EdS, 1973, Doctorate Ed Admin & Supv Higher Educ, 1974. **Career:** Brevard City Pub Sch, instr, 1959-63; Ft Lauderdale Broward City Pub Sch, instr, 1963-67; Miami Dade Community Col, instr, 1967-69; Cocoa High Sch, asst prin, 1969-70; Brevard Community Col, dir stud activities, 1970-72, dir placement, 1974-75, dir coop educ placement & follow-up, 1975-77, dean stud serv, Ambassador, currently; Univ Fla, res asst assoc dir inst res coun, 1972-73. **Orgs:** Phi Delta Kappa, 1963; Omega Psi Phi Frat, 1969; vchmn, Rockledge City Coun; Fla Assoc Community Col, 1974; sunday sch teacher, Zion Orthodox Primitive Baptist Ch. **Honors/Awds:** Citizen of the Year, Alpha Phi Alpha Frat, 1972; Outstanding Educator Am, 1975. **Special Achievements:** Recreation ctr named Joe Lee Smith Recreation Ctr 1973; Article "27 Stepsto Better Discipline", 1974. **Business Addr:** Ambassador, Brevard Community College, 1519 Clearlake Rd, Cocoa, FL 32922, **Business Phone:** (321)433-7306.

SMITH, DR. JOHN ARTHUR
Educator, physician. **Personal:** Born Aug 25, 1937, Cincinnati, OH; son of John Douglas and A Malvena Campbell; divorced; children: Ann, Janis, Gwen & Jill. **Educ:** Miami Univ, AB, 1958; Univ Cincinnati, MD, 1964. **Career:** SUNY Downstate, physician, 1971-72; Ind Univ Sch Med, prof, 1972, prof emer radiol, currently; Harvard Univ, vis prof, 1978; Univ Wis, vis prof, 1992; Riley C Hosp, Pediat Radiol, prof, dir. **Orgs:** Kappa Alpha Psi, 1957; mem & deleg, NMA, 1969-; bd, Indianapolis Boys Club, 1979-85; Alpha Eta Boule, 1979-; mem & chmn, Soc Pediat Radiol, 1983. **Special Achievements:** contributor 3 books; numerous articles prof j. **Military Serv:** USAF, capt, 2 yrs; USAFE, consult & radiologist, 1968-70. **Home Addr:** 2885 W 131st, Carmel, IN 46032. **Business Addr:** Professor Emeritus of Radiology, Indiana University Hospital, 550 N Univ Blvd, Indianapolis, IN 46202, **Business Phone:** (317)274-1866.

SMITH, JOHN B., SR.
Publisher. **Personal:** Married; children: 3. **Educ:** Morehouse Col, BS; Atlanta Univ, MA, admin, MA, math. **Career:** NNPA, chmn, 1961-; Black Press Archives, chmn; The Atlanta Inquirer, publ & exec officer, currently. **Orgs:** Chmn, Nat Newspapers Publ Asn, currently; Omega Psi Phi. **Honors/Awds:** Publisher of the Year', NNPA, 1992, 1994; 'Alumni of the Year', Morehouse Col, 1993. **Business Addr:** Publisher, Chief Executive Officer, The Atlanta Inquirer, NNPA, 947 Martin Luther King Jr Dr NW, PO Box 92367, Atlanta, GA 30314-2367, **Business Phone:** (404)523-6086.

SMITH, JOHN L, JR. (JACK SMITH)
School administrator, educator. **Personal:** Born Sep 14, 1938, Bastrop, LA; son of John L Sr and Julia S; married Juel Shannon, Aug 4, 1972; children: Kenneth, Babette, Angela, Gina, Lisa, Michael & Eva. **Educ:** Lincoln Univ, BME, 1959; Univ Ind, MME, 1961, performance certi, 1961; Univ Mo, Kansas City, DMA; Harvard Univ, post-doctoral study, 1992. **Career:** Black Liberated Arts Ctr, Inc, founder, pres, 1969; Langston Univ, Fine Arts Series, dir, 1969-72, Music dept, chair, 1969-72; Univ S Fla, Music dept, acting asst chair, 1973-74, asst dean, coordr adv, 1977-86, acting dean, 1986-88, Fine Arts Col, dean, 1988-98; Fisk Univ, pres, 1999-2001. **Orgs:** Bd dir, Hillsborough County Arts Coun, 1986-; bd dir, African Arts Coun, 1988-90; bd dir, The Fla Orchestra, 1989-; comn arts, Nat Asn State Univs & Land Grant Cols, 1989-92; chair, Community Cultural Diversity & Inclusion Arts, 1989-92; bd trustee, Fla Cultural Action & Educ Alliances, 1990-; The Mayor's Task Force Arts, 1991-92; chair, Fla Higher Educ Arts Network, 1992-94; pres, Int Coun Fine Arts Deans, 1997-98; Pi Kappa Lambda. **Honors/Awds:** Commencement speaker, Ringling Sch Art & Design, 1991; Education Award, Start Together Progress, Inc, 1989; Human Rights Award, Tampa, Hillsborough County Human Rights Council, 1990; Alumni Achievement Award, Univ MSR, 1989. **Special Achievements:** National Endowment for the Arts, Grant for USF Jazz Artists' Residence Program, 1981-89; University of South Florida, Equal Opportunity Award, 1985; Summary of USF's Black Composers' Project in the Black Perspective in Music, 1983; Doctoral Diss Abstract, Missouri Journal of Research in Music Education, 1979; Florida Orchestra Brass Quintet, 1978-. **Military Serv:** USN, petty officer, 2nd class, 1962-66.

SMITH, JOHN RAYE (JOHN RAYE)
Public speaker, chief executive officer, president (organization). **Personal:** Born Jan 30, 1941, Gibson, LA; son of Paul and Vera Phillips; married Rosie King, Aug 25, 1962; children: Michelle & Dexter Renaud. **Educ:** Southern Univ, Baton Rouge, La, BS, 1964; Columbia Univ, NY, jour, 1967;Wash Jour Ctr, Wash, DC, 1968. **Career:** Albany Springfield High Sch, Albany, LA, instr, gen scis, chem, biol,1963-64; US Dept Agri, Alexandria, LA, Mc-Minniville, OR, soil conversationist, 1964-66; Valley Migrant League, voc counr, Dayton, OR,1966-67; Moses Lakes Job Corps Ctr, Moses Lakes, WA, 1967-68; KREM-TV,Spokane, WA, King TV-Seattle, WA, WNBC-TV, New York, NY, WTTG-TV,Washington, DC, TV reporter/anchor-producer, 1968-79; US Census Bur, Wash,DC, 1979-83; Majestic Eagles Inc, pres, chief exec officer, founder,1983-; John Raye & Associates, pres, ceo, founder, 1983-; regional Dir, Compro Tax. **Orgs:** Dir, funds secure Majestic Eagles headquartes bldg. **Honors/Awds:** Author, The ABC's Of Starting Your Own Business, Think Your Way to Success and Prosperity, audio cassette tape, 1986; Born to Win: Success and Prosperity Now!, 1990, exec producer, BusLine - The TV Prog, 1988; Producer: Portrait of a Queen: The Legacy of Ethel L Payne, 1987; Exec producer, Making Money in the 90's: How to Get Your Share, 1991. **Business Addr:** President, Chief Executive Officer, Majestic Eagles Inc, 2029 Rhode Island Ave NE, Washington, DC 20018, **Business Phone:** (202)635-0154.

SMITH, JOSEPH EDWARD
Chemist, dentist. **Personal:** Born Sep 13, 1938, Jacksonville, FL; married Mildred; children: Daryl, Ivan & Jomila. **Educ:** Allen Univ, BS, 1960; Howard Univ, Col Dent, DDS, 1970. **Career:** Dentist self; Jacksonville Health Ctr, 1974-76; Boston Univ, Grad Sch Dent, asst prof, 1970-74; Roxbury Health Ctr, chemist, 1966-67; Smith & Smith Dent Assocs, FL, Chief Dent, currently. **Orgs:** US Bur Mines, 1964-66; secy, treas, Denticare Prepaid Dent Plan FL, 1976-77; dir, Denticare Prepaid Dent Plan, 1976-77; Small Bus men's Serv Asn, 1976-77; Nat Dent Asn; Am Dent Asn; FL Dent Asn; VI Dent Asn; New Bethel AME Ch; stewart, pres Kenneth White Gospel Chorus; 3rd Sunday supt Sunday Sch; dir, Northside Boys Club; bd mem, Youth Congress Sickle Cell Anemia Prog; life mem, NAACP; Jacksonville Opt Ind Ctr, 1976-77; Ribault Jr HS, 1975. **Military Serv:** AUS, E-5, 1961-63. **Home Addr:** 3905 Ernjo Rd, Jacksonville, FL 32209. **Business Addr:** Chief Dentist, Smith & Smith Dental Associates, 1190 W Edgewood Ave No B, Jacksonville, FL 32208, **Business Phone:** (904)764-4549.

SMITH, JOSEPH F.
Government official. **Personal:** Born Aug 22, 1945, Jacksonville, FL; son of Hazel Hall and Joe; married Mary Townsend, Oct 15, 1974; children: Joseph Cordell & Karina Sharon. **Educ:** T Valley State Col, BA, 1967; Howard Univ, JD, 1970; Fort Valley State Col, Fort Valley, GA, BA, 1967; Howard Univ, Sch Law, Wash, DC, JD, 1970. **Career:** WRC/NBC, Consumer Guidelines, moderator, 1971-74; Consumer Liaison Div Of Consumer Affairs Dept HUD, dir; Nat Consumer Info Ctr, producer & exec dir; WRC/NBC, It's Your World, exec producer & moderator; Am Univ, prof;Howard Univ, prof; numerous consumer manuals, econ & polit articles, ed & lct pub; Dept Housing & Urban Develop, Wash, DC, dir inter governmental affairs, 1980-85, dir econ analysis & eval, 1985-89, dep dir, off policy, 1989, dep off healthy homes & lead hazard control. **Orgs:** Fed Trade Comn, 1968-; Mem & consult, Off Consumer Affairs, 1969-; Cong Staff; Black Caucus; Housing & Urban Dev; Social Rehab Serv; OEO 1970-;Atty Gen Off MA, DC & WI, 1970-74; Nat Inst Educ Law & Poverty, 1970; AmBar Asn, 1971; Nat Legal Aid & Defender's Asn, 1972; Consumer Adv Comm Fed Enery Off, 1972-74; NY NV Consumer Off, 1973-74; Ohio C of C, 1973; Office Gov, 1973-; Cost Living Coun Asn, 1974; Nat Asn Atty Gen; Asn Home Appliances Mfg, 1974; Alpha Phi Alpha; NAACP; Consumer Fedn Am; Nat Conf Black Lawyers; Howard Univ Law Sch Alumni Asn; secy, Class 23 Fed Exec Inst, 1984-86; treas, Reid Temple AME, 1987-. **Honors/Awds:** Certificate of Merit, 1989, Outstanding Executive, 1988, Federal Executive Institute Award, 1995, Dept Housing & Urban Develop. **Business Addr:** Director, Office of Executive Services, Department of Housing and Urban Development, 451 7th St SW, Washington, DC 20410-4500.

SMITH, JOSHUA ISAAC
Executive. **Personal:** Born Apr 8, 1941, Garrard County, KY; married Jacqueline Jones; children: Joshua I II. **Educ:** Central State Univ, BS, Biol & Chem, 1963; Univ Akron Sch Law, grad studies, 1967-68; Univ Delaware, asn mgt, 1975; Central MI Univ, grad studies, bus mgt, 1977. **Career:** Plenum Publ Corp, mgr databook div, 1969-70; Am Soc Info Sci, exec dir, 1970-76; Herner & Co, vpres, 1976-78; The MAXIMA Corp, pres & ceo, 1978-2000; The Coaching Group, chmn & managing partner, currently; Caterpillar, bd, currently. **Orgs:** Chmn, United Way Fundraising Campaign, 1984; chmn bd, Nat Bus League Montgomery Co; mem bd dirs, Int Asn Studs Bus Mgt & Econs; Minority Bus Enterprise Legal Defense & Educ Fund; Nat Urban Coalition; dir, TN Tech Found; Citizens Adv Comt for Career & Voc Educ; Corp Round Table; mem adv bd, Grad Sch Libr & Info Sci Univ TN; mem adv bd, NC Cent Univ Sch Libr Sci; Am Asn Advan Sci; Am Libr Asn; Am Soc Info Sci; Black Presidents Roundtable Wash; Engineering Index Inc; Info Indust Asn Long Range Planning Comn; Nat Bus League Montgomery Co. **Honors/Awds:** Minority Businessperson of the Year, Small Bus Admin; Distinguished Corporate Award, US Dept Com Minority Bus Develop Agency; Special Recognition Award for Valuable Commitment, US Dept Com Minority Bus Develop Agency. **Special Achievements:** Numerous publications. **Business Phone:** (301)589-9800.*

SMITH, DR. JOSHUA L.
Educator. **Personal:** Born Dec 11, 1934, Boston, MA; son of Joshua Smith and Lorina A Henry Smith. **Educ:** Boston Univ, BA, 1955; Harvard Grad Sch Educ, MAT, 1959, EdD, 1967. **Career:** Pittsburgh Pa, admin asst supt sch, acting vice prin, 1966-68; Ford FND, prog officer, asst program off, proj specialist, 1968-74; City Col, City Univ, New York, prof educ, 1974-76, dean, sch educ, 1976-77; Boro Manhattan Community Col, acting pres, 1977-78, pres, 1978-85; St Calif Community Cols, chancellor, 1985-87; Brookdale Community Col, pres, 1987-90; Baruch Col, CUNY, Dpt Educ, prof, 1990-, interim chmn, 1992-; New York Univ, chmn, dir, Prog Higher Educ & Ctr Urban Community Col Leadership, prof emer, currently. **Orgs:** Bd trustees, Pub Educ Asn, 1974-; bd trustees, Mus Collab Inc, 1974-; bd trustees, Nat Humanities Fac, 1974-; chmn, NAACP Task Force Qual Educ, 1977-; AACJC Comn Govt Affairs, 1978-; rep, CUNY Big City Community Col Pres & Chancellors, AACJC, 1978-; New York Co Local Develop Corp Inc, 1980; bd dir, AACJC, 1980; vice chmn, Joint Comn Fed Rel AACJC/ACCT, 1982, chmn, 1983; bd dir vice chmn, 1983-84, bd dir chmn, AACJC, 1984-85; bd overseers, Univ St New York Regents Col Degrees & Exam, 1985-; golden heritage mem, NAACP; bd deacons, Riverside Church, NY, 1977-82, bd trustees, 1988-; bd trustees, Excelsior col, currently. **Honors/Awds:** Phi Delta Kappa Award of Achievement for Outstanding Service to the Field of Educ, AL A&M Univ, 1972; Distinguished Service Award, Bilingual Vol Am, 1973; Distinguished Service Award, Harlem Prep Sch, 1973-75; Award of Appreciation, Support Develop S Leadership Develop Prog, So Region Coun, 1974. **Military Serv:** USAF, capt, 1955-58. **Home Addr:** 315 W 70th St, New York, NY 10023, **Home Phone:** (212)721-4063. **Business Addr:** Professor Emeritus, New York University, 100 Wash Square E, New York, NY 10003.

SMITH, JUANITA
Government official. **Personal:** Born Jun 28, 1927, St Petersburg, FL; daughter of Ruffin Sr and Annabelle Momoan; married Thomas H, Apr 13, 1956; children: Carol Tracey. **Educ:** Gibbs Jr Col, elem educ; Tuskegee Inst, indust arts, 1947; Fla Int Univ, BS polit sci, 1974. **Career:** AL Lewis Elem Sch, teacher; Homestead Jr HS, teacher; Dade County Bd Pub Instruction, teacher, 1967-; Fla City, comnr, currently. **Orgs:** Dade County Crime Comm Court Aide; Am Red Cross; United Heart Fund; Dade County Cancer Soc; March Dimes; Dade County Comn Action Ctr; Dade County Dept Pub Health; Hills borough Co Juvenile Home; vpres, Dade County Voters League; vpres, A L Lewis PTA; adv bd, Protestant Christian Comm Serv Agency; adv bd, Fla City Parks & Rec; chair person Public Relation Bd A L Lewis Elem Sch; Comm Block Club; Nat Coun Negro Women; Crime Stoppers; Children's Libr Club; youth leader, welfare worker Seventh Day Adventist Church; bd mem, Greater Miami Urban League, 1984-; bd mem, Community Health S Dade County, Inc, 1985-; Nat Asn Advan Colored People, 1986-; bd mem, Dade County League Cit-

ies, 1987- treas, 1992. **Honors/Awds:** Woman of the Year, Links Inc 1985; Award of Appreciation, Naval Security Group Activity, 1985; Certificate & Award of Service, Dade County Community Action Ser 1985; Woman of the Year, Zeta Phi Beta, 1985; Woman of the Year, Bethel Seventh Day Adventist Church. **Home Addr:** 706 NW 3rd St, Florida City, FL 33034.

SMITH, DR. JUDITH MOORE (JUDI MOORE LATTA)
Educator. **Personal:** Born Aug 3, 1948, Tallahassee, FL. **Educ:** Hampton Inst, BS, 1970; Boston Univ, MA, 1971; Univ Maryland, PhD, 1999. **Career:** Cambridge High & Latin Sch, instr eng, comt, 1971-72; Univ DC, Dept Commun, 1972-80, Van Ness Campus Fac Senate, chairperson, 1977-78, asst prof communicative & performing arts, FM Radio Proj, communs cons, bd mem's newsletter, 1978-80; African Heritage Dancers & Drummers, lead dancer, 1973-; WAMU-FM Radio, prod, writer, series host, 1977-78; Howard Univ, Dept Radio, Tv & Film, from asst prof to assoc prof, 1984-2000, prof, 2000-, dept chair, 2000-02, dep gen mgr, 2002-03; interim gen mgr, 2003-, Grad Cert Women Studies, co-dir, currently. **Orgs:** Bd dir Friendship House, 1975-; Nat Coun Negro Women, 1977; Nat Commun Asn; Am Fed Television & Radio Artists; People's Community Baptist Church;Am Studies Asn. **Honors/Awds:** Faculty Service Award, Univ DC student body, 1972-74; Outstanding Young Women of America, 1978; Corporation for Public Broadcasting Documentary Gold Award 1982, 1986, 1987, 1989, 1995; Peabody Award, 1983; Gabriel Awards, 1987; Best of Gannett Community Service Award, 1990; Metropolitan Area Media Award, 1991; Outstanding Faculty Research Award, Howard Univ, 1995; Angel Award, 1995; Award for Advancement of Learning Through Broadcasting, Nat Educ Asn, 1995; George Foster Peabody Award, 1995; American Asn of University Women Graduate Award, 1999; Bode Dissertation Award, Univ Md, 1999. **Business Addr:** Professor, Interim General Manager, Howard University, Department of Radio Tv & Film, C B Powell Bldg, Washington, DC 20059, **Business Phone:** (202)806-7927.

SMITH, JUDY SERIALE
Government official, social worker. **Personal:** Born Mar 10, 1953, Lafayette, LA; daughter of Joseph Seriale and Vernice Bellard; married Sylvester Lee Smith Jr, Dec 10, 1974; children: Sylvester Lee III & Joseph Seriale. **Educ:** Grambling State Univ, BA, social worker, 1974. **Career:** S Cent Ark Community Action, Camden, Ark, community serv coordr, 1980-84; PAC Inc, exec dir, 1984-2002; state legislator, Ark; Ark Minority Health Comn, exec dir, 2002-07; Dept Workforce Educ/Ark Re-habilitation Serv, transition serv dir, 2007-. **Orgs:** Sigma Beta Omega Chap Alpha Kappa Alpha Sorority Inc; bd mem, Ouachita County Emergency Food & Shelter Bd, 1986-; bd mem, Women's Crisis Ctr Camden, 1988-; SAU Tech Br Adv Bd, 1988-; bd mem, Ark Child Abuse Prevention, 1989-; regional coordr, Ark Drug Free Youth, 1990-. **Honors/Awds:** Delegate to Japan, ACYPL, 1992; Top Ten Legislative Hall of Fame, 1993; Ark Democrat Gazette; Ark Bus Weekly, Woman of Distinction, Top 100 Women in Ark; Flemming fel, Leadership Inst, 1995. **Business Addr:** Transition Service Director, Arkansas Department of Workforce Education, Luther Hardin Building, Three Capitol Mall, Little Rock, AR 72201, **Business Phone:** (501)682-1500.

SMITH, KATRINA MARITA
Chiropractor. **Personal:** Born Oct 1, 1958, Kosciusko, MS. **Educ:** Palmer Junior Col; East Carolina Univ; Univ Northern Iowa; Palmer Col Chiropractic, DC 1984. **Career:** Pvt practice, chiropractor, currently; Forth Worth Independent Sch Dist, sch bd mem, secy, currently; Thrive Chiropractic Wellness Ctr, currently; Diamond Hill Jarvis High Sch, Asst Prin, currently. **Orgs:** Sigma Phi Chi, 1984; Intl Chiropractic Asn 1984; Am Chiropractic Asn, 1984; secy, Black Chiropractic Asn, 1984. **Military Serv:** US Marine Corps, corporal, 4 yrs; Meritorious Mast, Good Conduct Medal. **Business Phone:** (604)730-0111.

SMITH, KEITH DRYDEN
School administrator. **Personal:** Born Jun 8, 1951, New York, NY; son of Keith Dryden Sr and Marion B Sutherland; married Heather Y Duke; children: Mitchell Duke & Ally Megan Lusk. **Educ:** State Univ NY, BA, 1973; Syracuse Univ, MS, 1978. **Career:** Red Creek Cent Sch, sci teacher, 1974-75; Syracuse Univ, Utica Col, HEOP counr, 1975-77, HEOP coordr acad & supportive serv, 1977-79, HEOP dir, 1979-81; State Univ NY, Plattsburgh, lectr Afro-Am studies, 1984-86, EOP dir, 1981-92; State Univ NY, Cortland, lectr African-Am studies, Educ Opportunity Prog, dir, 1992-. **Orgs:** Am Asn Univ Prof, 1975-81; United Univ Profs, 1981-; secy affirmative action comt, State Univ NY, Plattsburgh, 1983-85; inst planning comt mem, State Univ NY Off Spec Prog, 1985-87; human rights chair, Col Stud Personnel Asn NY Inc, 1986-87; certified mediator, Unified Ct Syst NY, Community Dispute Resolution Prog, 1987-; secy & dir, State Univ NY, Coun Educ Opportunity Prog, 1988-90; sen, State Univ NY, Plattsburgh, 1990-92; chmn, State Unvi NY, Plattsburgh Pres Adv Comt Affirmative Action, 1990-92; affirmative action comt mem, State Univ NY, Cortland, 1992-98; curric rev comt, State Univ NY, 1992-95; chair, State Univ NY, Cortland Affirmative Action Comt, 1993-95; State Univ NY, Cortland, Stud Support Comt, 1992-93, 1994-95; treas, Coun Educ Opportunity Prog Dir, 1994-95; Affirmative Action comt chair, State Univ NY, Cortland, 1993-98; secy & bd dirs, State Univ NY, Cortland Child Ctr, 1997-99, treas, bd dir, 1999-2004. **Special Achievements:** Co-author collaborator: Report of Work Group on Multicultural Fair Treatment, Toward A More Equitable, Inclusive and Diverse Academic Community, SUNY Cortland, 1992; Co-Author, Report of SUNY Cortland President's Task Force on the Recruitment and Retention of Ethnic Minority Students, 2000; Appointed to Task Force on Creation of Ethnic Study, Dept at SUNY, Cortland, 2003; Conference Planning Committee for SUNY-wide conference on the retention of students of color 2004-05. **Home Addr:** 100 Halseyville Rd, Ithaca, NY 14850. **Business Addr:** Director Educational Opportunity Program, State University of New York, D-116 Cornish, PO Box 2000, Cortland, NY 13045, **Business Phone:** (607)753-4808.

SMITH, KELLITA
Actor, entertainer, pesticide applicator. **Personal:** Born May 29, 1969, Chicago, IL. **Educ:** Santa Rosa Jr Col, AA, polit sci, 1989. **Career:** Films: House Party 3, 1993; The Crossing Guard, 1995; Q: The Movie, 1999; Retiring Tatiana, 2000; Kingdom Come, 2001; Hair Show, 2004; Fair Game,2005; King's Ransom, 2005; Roll Bounce, 2005; Feel the Noise, 2007; Three Can Play That Game, 2007; Conspiracy X, 2009; TV appearances: Martin, 1994-95; "Sister,Sister", 1995; "Malcolm & Eddie", 1997; "The Jamie Foxx Show", 1997-99; "Masquarade", 2000; "The Bernie Mac Show", 2001-06; "Nash Bridges", 2001; "NYPD Blue", 2001; "The Bernie Mac Show", 2001-06; Theatre performance: Tell It Like It Tiz; No Place To Be Somebody; Feelings; Strange Fruit, owner, 2001-. **Honors/Awds:** Best Supporting Actress, NAACP Theatre Award; nominee, NAACP Theatre Award for Best Actress; Outstanding Lead Actress in a Comedy Series, Bet Comedy Awards, 2004 & 2005; Nominee, Image Award, 2003, 2004, 2005 & 2006. **Business Addr:** Actress, c/o Fox Broadcasting Co, 10201 W Pico Blvd, Los Angeles, CA 90035, **Business Phone:** (310)369-1000.*

SMITH, KEVIN L
Executive. **Career:** SC Security Inc, Charlottesville, pres, currently. **Business Addr:** President, SC Security Inc, 125 Riverbend, Charlottesville, VA 22901, **Business Phone:** (434)293-8164.

SMITH, KEVIN REY
Football player, vice president (organization). **Personal:** Born Apr 7, 1970, Orange, TX. **Educ:** Tex A&M Univ. **Career:** Football player (retired), Vice president; Dallas Cowboys, defensive back, 1992-99; First Plus Financial Group, vpres, currently. **Business Addr:** Vice President, First Plus Financial Group, 3965 Phelan Blvd Suite 209, Beaumont, TX 77707.

SMITH, LAFAYETTE KENNETH
Executive, administrator. **Personal:** Born Dec 17, 1947, Memphis, TN; son of Joseph and Elizabeth Berniece Hodge. **Educ:** Howard Univ, Washington, DC, BS, 1971; Bernard M Baruch Col, New York City, NY, MPA, 1984. **Career:** Opportunities Industrialization Ctr, Washington, DC, job placement specialist, 1972-75, job placement supvr, 1975-76, prog supvr, 1976-78, br mgr, 1978-81, prog coordr, 1981-82; Chicago Pub Schs, Chicago, IL, spec asst gen supt, 1982-83; Washington DC Govt, Dept Human Serv, Contracts Div, asst chief, 1984-87; Youth Serv Admin, contract adminr, 1987-91; DC Dept Human Servs, Washington, DC, sr contract specialist, 1993-98; DC Off Contracting & Procurement, supv contract specialist, 1999, contracting officer, currently. **Orgs:** Nat Asn Advan Colored People, 1970-; Howard Univ Alumni Asn, 1971-; Big Brothers, Washington, DC, 1975-82; Prince Georges County, Pvt Indust Coun, 1979-81; State Md Occup Info, 1980-81; bd mem, Washington DC Pub Schs, 1980-82; scout master, Boy Scouts Am, 1981-81; Am Soc Pub Admin, 1982-; Chicago Urban League, 1982-83; Baruch Col Alumni Asn, 1984-; Nat Forum Black Pub Admin, 1985-; bd mem, Nat Urban Fels Alumni Asn, 1986-; Concerned Black Men Inc, 1986-95. **Honors/Awds:** Ten year Service Award, Nat OIC Am, OIC, 1982; Outstanding Young Men of America, US Jaycee, 1983; Appreciation Award, Concerned Black Men, Washington, DC Chap, 1995. **Home Addr:** 2400 16th St NW Suite 423, Washington, DC 20009, **Home Phone:** (202)232-4464. **Business Addr:** Contracting Officer, District of Columbia, Office of Contracting & Procurement, 1 Judiciary Sq 441 4th St NW Suite 700, South Washington, DC 20001, **Business Phone:** (202)724-4014.

SMITH, LAMAR
Football player. **Personal:** Born Nov 29, 1970, Fort Wayne, IN. **Educ:** Northeastern Okla A&M Jr Col; Univ Houston. **Career:** Football player (retired); Seattle Seahawks, running back, 1994-97; New Orleans Saints, 1998-99, 2003; Miami Dolphins, 2000-01; Carolina Panthers, 2002; coaching internship program with NFL Europe, 2007.

SMITH, LARRY
Basketball coach, basketball player. **Personal:** Born Jan 18, 1958, Rolling Fork, MS; married Belinda; children: Larry Jr, Tiffany & Torri. **Educ:** Alcorn State, BS, Recreation Admin; MS, Athletic Admin. **Career:** Basketball player (retired), basketball coach; Golden State Warriors,1980-89; Houston Rockets, 1989-92; San Antonio Spurs, 1992-93; Houston rockets, asst coach, 1993-03; Los Angeles Lakers, asst coach; Atlanta Hawks, asst coach; Albuquerque Thunderbirds, asst coach, 2004-05; Anaheim Arsenal, head coach, 2006-07; Austin Toros, asst coach, 2006-07; Los Angeles Sparks, asst coach, 2008; Alcorn State Univ, head coach, currently. **Business Phone:** (601)877-6100.

SMITH, LASALLE, SR.
Law enforcement officer. **Personal:** Born Oct 13, 1947, Lithonia, GA; son of Ollie Tuggle and Link; married Evelyn Peek, Dec 25, 1966; children: LaSalle Jr, Evita & Erika. **Educ:** Modern Sch Music, Wash, DC, 1966; LaSalle Exten Univ, Chicago, Ill, 1968; Dekalb Community, Clarkston, Ga, 1977; Brenau Col, Gainesville, Ga, 1985. **Career:** Fed Bur Invest, Wash, DC, finger print sect, 1965-66; Atlanta Police Dept, patrol squad, 1968, detective, 1971, police sgt, 1973-74, police lt, 1974-80, Off Mayor, Atlanta, exec protection comdr, 1980-84, Off Comnr Pub Safety, Internal Affairs Unit, comdr, 1984-86, Off Chief Police, comdr numerous task forces, 1986-90, Chaplaincy Corp, dir, 1991-98; Ga Security Prof LLC, pres & chief exec officer, currently. **Orgs:** Nat Orgn Black Law Enforcement Exec, 1984-; Nat Forum Black Pub Adminr; Nat Black Police Asn; Fulton County Task Force Drugs & Crime; Wings Hope Anti-Drug & Anti-Gang Task Force; Ga Asn Chiefs Police; Beautiful Blessings Christian Ministries. **Special Achievements:** Guest lecturer & instructor for a number of agencies & organizations throughout the United States. **Home Phone:** (404)987-7586. **Business Addr:** President, Chief Executive Officer, Georgia Security Professionals LLC, 8075 Mall Pkwy Suite 101-354, Lithonia, GA 30038, **Business Phone:** (770)605-9937.

SMITH, LAWRENCE JOHN, JR.
Executive. **Personal:** Born Dec 20, 1947, New York, NY; son of Jeanne Henderson and Lawrence John; married Ernestine Randall, Nov 27, 1985; children: Karyn Jennifer & Lawrence John III. **Educ:** Univ Notre Dame, Notre Dame, Ind, BBA, 1969; Harvard Bus Sch, Boston, Mass, MBA, 1971. **Career:** Honeywell Info Syst, Waltham, Mass, sr financial analyst, 1972-74; Digital Equip Corp, Maynard, Mass, prod line controller, 1974-79; Pizza Hut Inc, Wichita, Kans, US Controller, 1979-81; Wang Lab Inc, Lowell, Mass, chief exec officer software subs, 1982-89; Transnational Mgt Asn, Grafton, Mass, pres & managing dir, 1989-90; Venture Capital Inst, trainer; Mass Ind Fin Agency, Boston, Mass, chief financial officer, 1990-94; TM Group, pres, 1994-; Babson Col, adj fac mem, currently; Inner Circle Logistics Inc, Net-Centric Supply Chain Software & Serv, chief financial officer, mem bd, currently. **Orgs:** MENSA, 1982-; Harvard Bus Sch Asn Boston, 1988-; trustee, Dimock Community Health Ctr, 1990-; trustee, Boston Opera Theatre, 1990-; dir, N Am Consult Inc, 1994-; Harvard Club Boston, 1990-; dir, Metro W Med Ctr, 1994-. **Honors/Awds:** Minority Business Advocate of the Year, Boston MBDC, 1993. **Home Addr:** 46 Hinckley Rd, Milton, MA 02186-1634, **Home Phone:** (617)696-2261. **Business Addr:** Chief Financial Officer, Inner Circle Logistics Inc, Frederiksted, PO BOX 3171, St Croix, VI 00841, **Business Phone:** (340)244-3345.

SMITH, LEE ARTHUR
Baseball player, basketball coach. **Personal:** Born Dec 4, 1957, Shreveport, LA; married Diane. **Educ:** Northwestern State Univ, Natchitoches, LA. **Career:** Baseball player (retired), baseball coach; Chicago Cubs, pitcher, 1980-87; Boston Red Sox, pitcher, 1988-90; St Louis Cardinals, 1990-93; NY Yankees,1993; Baltimore Orioles, 1994; Calif Angels, 1995-96; Cincinnati Reds,1995-96; Cincinnati Reds, 1996; Montreal Expos, 1997; San Francisco Giants, pitching instr, 2000; South Africa Nat Baseball Team, pitching coach, 2006. **Honors/Awds:** Nat League All-Star Team, 1983, 1987, 1990-95; Nat League Rolaids Relief Man of the Year, 1991-92; American League Rolaids Relief Man of the Year,1994; TSN Fireman of the Year.

SMITH, LEO GRANT
Educator, association executive. **Personal:** Born Jun 21, 1940, Atlanta, GA; married Mildred Louise Hoke; children: Wendy & Kimberly. **Educ:** BA, 1962, MA, 1971; EdS, 1982. **Career:** Hamilton High Sch, teacher, 1962-68; Chamblee High Sch, asst prin, 1968-72; Gordon High Sch, DeKalb City Bd Ed, prin. **Orgs:** Vpres, Ga Asn Sec Prin, 1973-74; DeKalb Asn Sec Sch Prin, Gordon High PTA, Venetian Hills Elem PTA; vpres, DeKalb Admin Asn, 1975; Pomona Pk Neighborhood Asn, currently. **Honors/Awds:** Administrator of the Year, Am Sch Counsr Asn. **Home Addr:** 1941 Fort Valley Dr, Atlanta, GA 30311, **Home Phone:** (404)768-2872. **Business Addr:** Member, Pomona Park Neighborhood Association, 1941 Fort Valley Dr SW, Atlanta, GA 30311, **Business Phone:** (404)375-0971.

SMITH, LEONARD PHILLIP
Football player. **Personal:** Born Sep 2, 1960, New Orleans, LA. **Educ:** McNeese State Univ; Fla State Univ. **Career:** St Louis Cardinals, 1983-87; Phoenix Cardinals, 1988; Buffalo Bills, safety, 1988-91. **Honors/Awds:** Played in AFC Championship Game, 1988 season; McNeese Hall of Fame.

SMITH, LEROI MATTHEW-PIERRE, III
Social worker. **Personal:** Born Jan 11, 1946, Chicago, IL; son of Norma and LeRoi Jr; children: Le Roi IV. **Educ:** Idaho State Univ,

BA, psychol, 1969, M.Ed; WA State Univ, PhD, psychol, 1977. **Career:** Idaho State Univ, lectr, 1969-70; WA State Univ, lectr, 1970-71; Evergreen State Col, prof, 1971-81; Port Seattle, dir, Diversity Programs; Thomas Edison State Col, mem fac, currently. **Orgs:** Bd dir, Thurston Mason Co Ment Health, 1974-81; Nat Asn Black Psychologists, 1974-80; Tacoma-Pierce Co OIC, 1979-81; consult, Seattle Pub Schls, 1976-85; Am Soc Personnel Admin, 1981-; Am Psychol Asn. **Honors/Awds:** US Dept Educ, 1969; Nat Sci Found, 1976; Danforth Found, 1978; Fellowship, Lilly Found, 1981. **Home Addr:** PO Box 2903, Blaine, WA 98231-2903. **Business Addr:** Faculty Member, Thomas Edison State College, 101 W State S, Trenton, NJ 08608-1176, **Business Phone:** (609)984-1181.

SMITH, LILA
Scientist. **Personal:** Born in Memphis, TN. **Educ:** Lemoyne Col, BS, Math, 1957; Howard Univ, MS, Physics, 1959. **Career:** Fla A&M Univ, asst prof physics, 1959-62; LeMoyne Col, asst prof Math, 1962-63; US Atomic Energy Comn, sci analyst, 1963-76; Tech Info Ctr US Dept Energy, chief conserv & solar br, 1976-83, chief nuclear eng & physics br, OSTI & USDOE. **Orgs:** Pres & charter mem, Blacks Govt Oak Ridge Chap, 1984; vpres, Region IV Blacks Govt Inc, 1984-; vpres, Xi Iota Omega Chap Alpha Kappa Alpha Sor, 1985; Am Solar Energy Soc Inc; Nat Forum Black Pub Admis; Altrusa Inc, Oak Ridge Chap; Nat Asn Advan Colored People; Fed Employed Women Inc; Negro Bus & Prof Women's Clubs; mem TN Coun Human Rels; Oak Valley Baptist Church; Toastmasters Int. **Honors/Awds:** Sigma Pi Sigma Physics Soc; Equal Employ Opportunity; adv bd, US Atomic Energy Comn, Oak Ridge, 1968-77; personnel security bd, US Dept Energy, 1974-81; publ incl Geothermal Resources Bibliog 1975-76; Solar Energy Update Abstr J, 1975; Achievement Award, Outstanding Accomplishments Sci & Civic Affairs Jack & Jill Am, 1976; Spec Achievement Award, EEO US Energy Res & Develop Admin, 1978.

SMITH, LONNIE
Baseball player. **Personal:** Born Dec 22, 1955, Chicago, IL; married Pearl; children: Yaritza LaVonne & Eric Tramaine. **Career:** Baseball player (retired); Philadelphia Phillies, 1978-81; St Louis Cardinals, 1982-85; Kans City Royals, 1985-87; Atlanta Braves, 1988-92; Pittsburgh Pirates, 1993; Baltimore Orioles, 1993-94. **Honors/Awds:** Rookie of the Year, The Sporting News & Baseball Digest, 1980; World Series champion, 1980, 1983 & 1985; St Louis Man of the Year, Baseball Writers Asn Am, 1982; Nat League All-Star Team, 1982.

SMITH, LORETTA GARY
Banker, vice president (organization). **Personal:** Born Mar 27, 1949, Detroit, MI; daughter of Luther (deceased) and Doris Gary; married William J, Apr 17, 1983; children: Stacey Espie, Stephanie & Ashley. **Educ:** Univ Detroit-Mercy, bus admin. **Career:** JL Hudson, clerk, 1966-67; Comerica Inc, vpres, pub affairs, 1968-. **Orgs:** Detroit & Pontiac Neighborhood Housing Serv Inc, bd dirs; Habitat Humanity, Metro-Detroit, bd dirs; Univ Detroit Mercy, Leadership dev inst, adv bd mem; Cornerstone Schs, partner, tutor; Tri City Dev Corp; New Mt Hermon Baptist Church; United Negro Col Fund, adv bd mem. **Honors/Awds:** Minority Achiever, YMCA Metrop Detroit, 1993; Award of Recognition, Detroit Neighborhood Housing Serv; Pioneer Supporter Award, Black Caucus Fund Mich, 1993; Certificate of Appreciation, Minority Technology Coun Mich Inc, 1994; Spirit of Detroit Award, City of Detroit. **Home Addr:** 19345 Santa Rosa, Detroit, MI 48221, **Home Phone:** (313)345-2152. **Business Addr:** Vice President Public Affairs, Comerica Inc, 500 Woodward Ave, PO Box 75000, Detroit, MI 48275-3352, **Business Phone:** (313)222-6987.

SMITH, LOUIS. See Obituaries section.

SMITH, LOVIE LEE
Football coach. **Personal:** Born May 8, 1958, Gladewater, TX; married MaryAnne; children: Mikal, Matthew & Miles; married MaryAnne; children: Mikal, Matthew & Miles. **Career:** Big Sandy High Sch, defensive coordr, 1980; Cascia Hall Prep, head coach, 1981-82; Tulsa, linebackers coach, 1983-86; Univ Wis, 1987; Arizona State Univ, linebackers coach, 1988-91; Univ Ky, linebackers coach, 1992; Univ Tenn, defensive backs coach, 1993-94; Ohio State Univ, defensive backs coach, 1995; Tampa Bay Buccaneers, linebackers coach, 1996-2000; St. Louis Rams, defensive coordr, 2001-03; Chicago Bears, head coach, 2004-. **Orgs:** Founder, Lovie Smith MaryAnne Smith Found; Am Diabetes Asn. **Honors/Awds:** AP Nfl Coy, 2005; PFW Nfl Coy, 2005. **Business Addr:** Head Coach, Chicago Bears, 1000 Football Dr, Lake Forest, IL 60045.*

SMITH, DR. LUTHER EDWARD
Educator, clergy. **Personal:** Born May 29, 1947, St Louis, MO; son of Luther and Clementine; married Helen Pearson; children: Luther Aaron & Nathan. **Educ:** Wash Univ, AB, 1969; Eden Theol Sem, MDiv, 1972; St Louis Univ, PhD, 1979. **Career:** E St Louis Welfare Rights Org, coordr, 1970-72; Educ Black Urban Ministers, exec coordr, 1972-79; Lane Tabernacle CME Church, asst pastor, 1972-79; St Louis Univ, Black Church Leaders Prog, coordr, 1975-79; Emory Univ, Candler Sch Theol, prof church & community, currently. **Orgs:** Northside Team Ministries, 1973-79; vpres, Mo Asn Soc Welfare St Louis Div, 1973-79; Metrop Ministerial Alliance, St Louis, 1975-79; Urban Churches Community Develop Prog, 1978-79; Urban Training Org, Atlanta, 1980-; Inst World Evangelism, 1982-; Int Soc Theta Phi, 1987; Omicron Delta Kappa, 1991; Families First, 1992; Eden Theol Sem. **Honors/Awds:** Service Award, St Louis & Mid St Louis City Jaycees, 1975; Inducted Martin Luther King Jr Collegium Scholar, Morehouse Col. **Special Achievements:** Co-author, actor: "What's Black," televised KFTC, 1970, "Earth Day," televised PBS, 1970; "Howard Thurman, the Mystic as Prophet," 1992; "Intimacy & Mission: Intentional Community as Crucible for Radical Discipleship". **Home Addr:** 1956 Mountain Creek Dr, Stone Mountain, GA 30087. **Business Addr:** Professor of Church & Community, Emory University, Candler School of Theology, Bishops Hall, Atlanta, GA 30322, **Business Phone:** (404)727-4176.

SMITH, DR. MARIE EVANS
Child psychologist. **Personal:** Born Oct 21, 1928, Philadelphia, PA; daughter of Frederick and Mamie Pace; married Charles N; children: Dianne S Partee, Dionne S Jones & Deborah S Smith. **Educ:** Temple Univ, BS, 1972; Antioch Univ, MEd, 1974; Kensington Univ, PhD, 1985. **Career:** Greentree Sch, teacher, 1960-65; Inst Human Potential, asst dir, 1965-70; Parkway Day Sch, perceptual motor spec, 1970-74; Hahnemann Med Col & John F Kennedy Ment Health Ctr, instr & supvr, 1974-; John F Kennedy Ment Health/Ment Retardation Ctr, PA clin psychologist 1974-, site dir, 1988-; Int Biog Asn, fel 1989. **Orgs:** Pres, Wellesley Civic Asn, 1965-; Temple Univ Alumni Asn, 1973-87, Antioch Univ Alumni Asn, 1974-87; ment health consult, Sch Dist Philadelphia, 1974-; Coun Int Visitors Museum Civic Ctr, 1983-87; Coun Asn Greater Philadelphia, 1985-, Nat Geog Soc, 1985-; mem at large, NAACP, 1985-; Afro-Am Hist Cult Museum, 1985-87; bd mem, Am Black Women's Heritage Soc, 1986-87; Zeta Phi Beta, 1986-; consult & child psychologist, Minority Ment Health Advocacy Task Force; founding mem, Am Legion Aux Henry Hopkins Post 881; Urban League Philadelphia, 1990-; Nat Polit Cong Black Women, 1989-; Philadelphia Museum Art, 1990; fel & diplomate, Am Bd Med Psychotherapist, 1990; golden life mem, Zeta Phi Beta Sorority, 1990. **Honors/Awds:** Legions of Honor Membership Chapel of Four Chaplains Award, 1965; Service to Children Award, parkway Day Sch, 1974; Certificate of Service Award, Hahnemann Med Col, 1980; Certification of African Cultures, Am Forum Int Study, 1981; Certificate of Merit, Sch Dist Philadelphia, 1983; Recognition of Achievement, Providence Baptist Church, 1985; John F Kennedy Community Service Award, Philadelphia PA, 1985, 1986; Certificate of Achievement, Behavioral Ther Temple Univ; Womens Hist Month NJ Black Women's Educ Alliance, 1989; Recognition of Service, John F Kennedy Ment Health/Ment Retardation Ctr, 1988; Top Ladies of Distinction, 1995. **Home Addr:** 518 Wellesley Rd, Philadelphia, PA 19119. **Business Addr:** Site Director, John F Kennedy Mental Health-Poplar Guidance Clinic, Mental Retardation Center, 321 W Girard Ave, Philadelphia, PA 19123, **Business Phone:** (215)235-6250.

SMITH, MARIE F
Association executive. **Personal:** Born Mar 12, 1939, East St Louis, IL; daughter of David and Christina Ford; married Richard Stanley, Dec 13, 1986. **Educ:** Fisk Univ, BS, biol & premed studies; Stanford Univ, pub affairs. **Career:** Social Security Admin, dir manpower mgt & orgn planning, off mgr & mgt analyst; Women's Initiative Prog, spokesperson, nat pres, 2004-06; real estate consult; freelance writer. **Orgs:** Bd dir, AARP, Nat Legis Coun, chair; Maui Vol Ctr; Maui Adult Day Care Ctr; Interfaith Vol Caregivers; pres, African Am Heritage Found Maui; local chap, Nat Asn Retired Fed Employees; Zonta Int, Wash, DC; adv bd, County Off Aging; comnr, Status of Women, Gov Hawaii. **Honors/Awds:** Woman of Excellence Award, Comn Status Women; Circle of Women Award, County Comt Status Women; Commissioner's Citation, Social Security Admin. **Special Achievements:** Cited by Ebony magazine as one of America's 100 most influential African American leaders; listed in Who's Who in American Women, 2004. *

SMITH, MARK
Football player. **Personal:** Born Aug 28, 1974, Vicksburg, MS. **Educ:** Auburn Univ. **Career:** Football player (retired); Ariz Cardinals, defensive end, 1997-2000; Cleveland Browns, defensive tackle, 2001-02.

SMITH, MARQUETTE
Football player. **Personal:** Born Jul 14, 1972, Casselberry, FL; married Dontonya; children: Whitney. **Educ:** Univ Cent Fla, BS, Communs, 1994. **Career:** Football player (retired), football coach: Carolina Panthers, running back; Rhein Fire, NFL Europe; Winnipeg Blue Bombers, CFL; Shreveport Knights, RFL; Green Bay Bombers, IFL; Iowa Barnstormers, AFL; Lacrosse Knight Train, NIFL; Carolina Stingrays, NIFL; alma mater, running backcoach, 2000; Winter Springs High Sch, offensive coordr, 2001; ghostriders, Head Coach & Dir of Football Opers, currently; First Step Adolescence Servs, Dir of Opers. **Honors/Awds:** Second team All-Am honors, 1995; honorable mention selection, Orlando Sentinel's 25th Anniversary Football Team. **Business Addr:** Head Coach, Director of Football Operations, Osceola ghostriders, 1515 Michigan Ave, Kissimmee, FL 34744, **Business Phone:** (407)210-2383.

SMITH, MARVIN PRESTON
Police officer, vice president (organization). **Personal:** Born May 5, 1944, Grand Rapids, MI; son of Maxine and Isaiah; divorced; children: Micheal, Debbie, Tracey, Preston & Marika D. **Educ:** Jackson Ct Col, cert, Mich law enforcement, 1975. **Career:** Police officer (retired), Vice President; Grand Rapids Police Dept, police officer, 1975-92; Grand Rapids Bd Educ, bldg safety rep; Proj Re-Hab Com Alternative Prog, resident counr, 1992, residential supv; Recovery Rd LLC, vpres, currently. **Orgs:** Pres, Officers Shield, 1988-; deleg, Nat Black Police Officer Asn, 1989-; Wealthy St Ctr, 1990-. **Home Phone:** (616)452-2039. **Business Addr:** Vice President, Recovery Road LLC, 3036 Perry Ave SW, Wyoming, MI 49519, **Business Phone:** (616)350-9360.

SMITH, MARY ALICE. See ALICE, MARY.

SMITH, MARY LEVI
College president. **Personal:** Born Jan 30, 1936, Hazlehurst, MS; daughter of William Levi and Byneter Markham; married LeRoy; children: Darryl, Angela Williams & Danee. **Educ:** Jackson State Univ, BS, 1957; Univ Ky, MA, 1964, EdD, 1980. **Career:** Tenn Elem Grade Schs, teacher, 1957-64; Tuskegee Inst, asst dir reading clin, 1964-70; Ky State Univ, assoc prof educ, 1970, chair, dept educ, 1981-83, Col Appl Sci, dean, 1983-88, vpres acad affairs, 1988-89, interim pres, 1989-90, spec asst to pres, prof of educ, 1990-91, pres, 1991-98, pres emer & fac emer, currently. **Orgs:** Comnr, Comn Cols Southern Asn Cols & Schs, 1992-97; bd dir, Nat Asn State Univs & Land Grant Col; Nat Asn Equal Opportunity Higher Ed; Am Asn Cols Teacher Educ; United Way Frankfort; Frankfort & Franklin Co Comt Educ, Govt Servs Ctr Common wealth Ky; Am Coun Educ Comt Women Higher Educ; Nat Bd Examrs, Nat Coun Accreditation Teacher Educ; Delta Sigma Theta Sorority; bd mem, Capital City Mus; St John AME Church; Ky Hist Soc; Nat Asn Advan Colored People. **Honors/Awds:** Outstanding Faculty of the Year, Ky State Univ, 1986; Outstanding Alumnus Award, Jackson State Univ, 1988; Torchbearers & Trail bearers Award, 1989;Women of Achievement Award, Young Women's Christian Asn Lexington, 1990; Woman of the Year Award, Nat Asn Advan Colored People, Frankfort Chap,1990; Citizens Award, Delta Sigma Theta, Frankfort Alumnae Chap, 1990; Alumni Hall of Fame, Univ Ky, 1992; Professional Achievement Award, Louisville Defender; Woman of Achievement Award, Frankfort Bus & Prof Women, 1994; Inducted to Hall of Distinguished Alumni by Ky State Univ, 1995. **Special Achievements:** First Female President of Kentucky State University; author, In Spite of the Odds: Using Roadblocks, Potholes, & Hurdles as Stepping Stone to Success.

SMITH, MARZELL
Educator. **Personal:** Born Aug 14, 1936, Conehatta, MS; married Albertine. **Educ:** Jackson State Col, BS, 1958; TN A&I State Univ, M.Ed, 1964; Univ Miami, 1969; Univ Miami, Ed.D, 1973. **Career:** FL Sch Desegregation Univ Miami, staff consult, 1970-; Univ Miami, fel, 1969-70; GN Smith Elem Sch, asst prin, 1966-69; Jim Hill Jr Sr HS,teacher, 1964-66; Allen Carver Jr Sr HS, 1958-64; Douglas Elem, coordr, 1971-72; Monreo Co Sch Syst; Alachua Co, 1972; Collier Co; Dept Found FL Atlantic Univ, 1975. **Orgs:** Am Educ Res Asn; Nat Asn Sch Adminr; BSA; Nat Asn Sec Sch Prin; Col Hill Bapt Ch; Jackson Bd Cert Officials; Phi Delta Kappa; SW Officials Asn; Kappa Alpha Psi Frat; Urban League; MTA-JTA-CTA; Miami Chap Nat Alliance Black Sch Edr; FL Asn Dist Sch Supt; So Asn Black Adminstrv Personnel; Univ Miami Black Faculty Adminr; bd dir, Miami Black Arts Gallery &Workshop; Dept Adminr Curriculum & Instr; NEA; Nat Alliance Black Sch Educ; Poverty Law Ctr; NAACP; unpub papers "An OD Analysis of Aw Soc Serv Orgn"; "Discipline Problems Pub Jr HS blueprints action"; "the politaction strategies dr martin luther king jr implications & applications"; "the role of Hallucinogenic Plants in Early Am Colonial & European Witchcraft"; "Discipline Problem Three Pub FL Sr HS implications &applications"; "Conflict Intervention Strategies Pub Sch Syst FL Applications". **Military Serv:** AUS, pvt.

SMITH, DR. MAXINE ATKINS
Association executive, social worker, secretary (organization). **Personal:** Born Oct 31, 1929, Memphis, TN; daughter of Joseph Atkins (deceased) and Georgia Rounds Atkins; married Vasco A Smith Jr; children: Vasco III. **Educ:** Spelman Col, Atlanta, Ga, AB, biol, 1949; Middlebury Col, Middlebury, Vt, MA, Fr, 1950. **Career:** Executive (retired); Prairie View A&M Univ, Prairie View, Tex, instr fr, 1950-52; Fla A&M Univ, Tallahassee, Fla, instr fr, 1952-53; LeMoyne Col, Memphis, Tenn, asst prof fr & eng 1955-56; Memphis Br Nat Asn Advan Colored People, exec secy, 1962-95; Memphis Sch Bd, bd pres, 1991-92. **Orgs:** Delta Theta Sorority Inc; Memphis Alumnae Chap; Nat Smart Set Inc, Memphis Chap; Links Inc, Memphis Chap; bd dirs, Dem Voters Coun; temp chmn, Memphis Alliance Community Orgn; exec bd, Memphis Com Community Rels; bd dir, Memphis Br Nat Asn Advan Colored People, 1957; chmn, Memphis Br Nat Asn Advan Colored People, 1958-61; coord & partcipated Freedmon Move-

ment, 1960-61; dir, Nat Asn Advan Colored People Annual Regist Campaigns; bd dir, Voter Ed Proj Inc, 1971; adv bd, Tri-State Defender 1983; hon chrprsn LeMoyne-Owen Col, 1983; bd dir, Lorraine Civil Rights Mus, 1984; bd trustee Leadership, Memphis, 1985; chaired Nat Asn Advan Colored People's Nat Spingarn Award Comt, 1985; pres, Memphis Bd Educ, 1991; exec comt, Mayor's Task Force Educ, 1990-; Tenn Bd Regents; nat bd of dirs, exec secretary emeritus, Nat Asn Advan Colored People; Memphis Smart Set; Memphis Chap Jack & Jill Am. **Honors/Awds:** More than 160 awards including Woman of year, Trinity CME Chrch; Achievement Award, Omega Psi Phi Frat; one of ten outstanding young, Am Pagaent Mag; woman of year Civil Rights, YWCA; Annual Merit Award, Memphis Br NAACP, 1960; Humanitarian of the Year, Alpha Pi Chi Sorority, Alpha Beta Chap, 1964; woman of action award, Alpha Kappa Alpha Sorority, 1969; outstanding citizen of year, Omega Psi Phi Frat, 1969; one of 5 citizens Nat NAACP Outstanding NAACP Leadership, 1970; Outstanding Citizen Award, Frontier Int Inc, 1970; Distinguished Citizen Award for contributions & leadership, Mallory Knights, 1960; Outstanding leadership in field civil rights, Longview Seventh-Day Adventist Church; Cited civil rights actvity Ward Chapel, AME Church 1971; Achievement Award in Public Service, OIC, 1973; Achievement Award, Middlebury Col Alumni Asn, 1985; Plaque for outstanding community sereta Epsilon, Omega Chap Alpha Kappa Alpha Sorority, 1972; Black history week plaque of recognition, Beulah Baptist Chruch, 1972; Kappa Alpha Psi Plaque for Meritorious Service to Community Area Human Rights; LeMayne Owen Col, hon doctorate, 1996; Richard R Green Award, Coun Great City Schs, 1997; Memphis City Schs Hall of Fame, 1998; Freedom Award, Nat Civil Rights Mus,2003. **Home Addr:** 1208 E Pkwy S, Memphis, TN 38114. *

SMITH, MICHAEL
Sports manager. **Personal:** Born Feb 5, 1955, Memphis, TN. **Career:** Basketball coach (retired), basketball referee; MBCC Church League, coach; Nat Basketball Asn, referee, currently. **Orgs:** Nat Basketball Referees Asn. **Honors/Awds:** Schick Rookie Game, 1997; McDonalds High School All-American Game, 1999; Mexico Challenge, 2000; NBA Europe Games, 2003. **Special Achievements:** Volunteered to work with Mid-South Junior Golf Association, 1996-99. **Business Addr:** NBA Official, National Basketball Referees Association, c/o Perennial Strategy Group, The Willard Offices 1455 Pa Ave NW Suite 225, Washington, DC 20004, **Business Phone:** (202)638-5090.

SMITH, MICHAEL JOHN
Basketball player. **Personal:** Born Mar 28, 1972, Washington, DC. **Educ:** Providence Col. **Career:** Basketball player (retired); Sacramento Kings, forward, 1995-98; Vancouver Grizzlies, 1998-99; Wash Wizards, 2000-01.

SMITH, MILDRED B.
Educator, elementary school teacher. **Personal:** Born Feb 3, 1935, South Carolina; divorced. **Educ:** SC State Col, BS; Mich State Univ, MA, PhD. **Career:** Curric coordr, elem teacher; elem dir; vis lectr; consr; Flint Bd Educ, elem dir. **Orgs:** Bd dir, First Independence Nat Bank Detroit; bd regents, Eastern Mich Univ. **Special Achievements:** Auth: Home & Sch Focus on Reading, 1971; co-auth: Reading Systems & Open Highways, 1971-74.

SMITH, MONICA LAVONNE
Editor, journalist. **Personal:** Born Jan 26, 1966, New Haven, CT; daughter of Hulee Evans and Erma J. **Educ:** Va State Univ, BA, 1988. **Career:** Comtex Scientific Corp, copy ed, 1989-90, sr ed, 1990-. **Orgs:** NAB, 1990-; Nat Asn Negro Bus & Prof Womens Clubs Inc, 1990-; NCP, Greater New Haven Br, election supvr comn; Hill Neighborhood Tutoring Prog, 1991-. **Business Phone:** (203)358-0007.

SMITH, MORRIS LESLIE
Research scientist. **Personal:** Born May 29, 1933, Camden, NJ; son of William E and Tamar H; married Alice Marie Gray; children: Morris G, Wesley E & Stephen J. **Educ:** Mich State Univ, BS, 1959; Temple Univ, MBA, 1978. **Career:** Magna Bond Inc, res chemist, 1959-61; EL Conwell Inc, analytical chemist, 1961; Scott Paper Co, Philadelphia, res chemist, 1961-65, sr res project chemist, 1965-74, sect leader, 1974-78, sr res leader, 1978, technol mgr; The ML Smith Group Inc, pres, currently. **Orgs:** Pres, Echelon Branch Camden Co, YMCA, 1983-86; exec large Int Soc African Scientists, 1984-; chmn, Camden Co, YMCA, bd dir, 1990-; chmn, Southern New Jersey Annual Conf United Methodist Church, TV Mins Comm, vice chr, bd pensions; treas parade marshal Lawnside 4th of July Comm Inc; pres, United Methodist Homes New Jersey Found; New Jersey Supreme Ct Commt Minority Concerns, 1996; vice chmn, Southern NJ Annual Conf United Methodist Church, Bd Pensions. **Military Serv:** AUS, 1955-57; Honorable Discharge. **Home Addr:** 307 Tillman Ave, Lawnside, NJ 08045, **Home Phone:** (609)546-8733.

SMITH, NATHANIEL
Executive. **Career:** Ver-Val Enterprises, Fort Walton Beach, FL, pres, 1979-. **Business Addr:** President, Ver-Val Enterprises, 646 Anchors St, PO Box 4550, Fort Walton Beach, FL 32566.

SMITH, NEIL
Football player, sports team owner. **Personal:** Born Apr 10, 1966, New Orleans, LA; married Sheri; children: Joshua, Nesha & Ne. **Educ:** Univ Nebr. **Career:** Football player (retired), sports team co-owner; Sporting News Coll All-Am Team, defensive lineman, 1987; Kans City Chiefs, defensive end, 1988-96; Denver Broncos, defensive end, 1997-99; San Diego Chargers, 2000; Kans City Brigade Arena Football League, vpres expansion, co-owner, currently. **Orgs:** Nat spokesman, Yes I Can Foundation. **Honors/Awds:** Pro Bowl, 1991-97; Super Kans Citian Award, S KC Chamber Com; Outstanding Learning Disabled Achievers Award, Lab Sch Wash; Ed Block Courage Award, 1994; 10 Outstanding Ams Award, US Jr Chamber Com, 1996; Super Bowl, Denver Broncos, 1998; Chiefs' Hall of Fame, 2006; Missouri Sports Hall of Fame, 2008. **Business Phone:** (913)248-6250.

SMITH, DR. NELLIE J.
Educator. **Personal:** Born May 15, 1932, Meridian, MS; daughter of Booker T Johnson and Nettie B Johnson; married Levi, Jan 1, 1963; children: Bobby, Paula, Perry & Joseph. **Educ:** Rust Col Holly Spring, BS, 1954; KS State Teachers Col, Emporia, KS, grad prog bus; Univ NDak, MS, 1956, PhD, 1973. **Career:** Rust Col, secy pres, 1954-55; Int Brothers Teamsters, clerical worker,1960-62; Rust Col, bus instr, 1962-63; Harris High Sch, bus instr, 1963-64; MS Valley State Col, asst prof, 1964-70; Rust Col, chair person div bus, 1970-2002, prof bus educ, 1970-. **Orgs:** Nat Coun Negro Women; mem, Social Bus Educ Asn, UMC, 1942-, Cappella Choir Rust Col 1950-55; voice recital MS Valley State Col, 1969; choral union,Univ NDak, 1971-73, Nat Bus Educ Asn, Delta Pi Epsilon, Pi Omega Pi, PhiBeta Lambda; Marshall Co Election Comn, 1993-97; Miss Arts Comn, 1994-98; app gov, Pvt Industry Cou, & Comn Temp Assistance Needy Families, 1997-2001; adv, Adult Pathway Program; Asbury United Methodist Church; Marshall Co Republican Women's Group. **Special Achievements:** First black clerical worker, 1960-62. Pub poem "Life Its Mystery &Struggles" set to music 1969; publ 6 articles, 4 shorthand tests, 1973, "How to Use Fortran Arithmetic Operators" 1973, typewriting speed test, 1973; author: Doctoral Dissertation, "A Comparative Analysis of National Employment Patterns as Perceived by Minority and Non-minority Bachelor Degree, Bus Educ, Grad 1972," 1973. First black to integrate U.S.teamsters union. **Business Addr:** Professor of Business & Secondary Education, Rust College, 150 Rust Ave, Holly Springs, MS 38635, **Business Phone:** (601)252-8000.

SMITH, NICK
Television show host. **Educ:** Emerson Col. **Career:** WPRI, photogr & truck operator; E! Entertainment TV, entertainment reporter & host; Weather Channel; World News Now, "Live! With Regis & Kelly," host; ABC, host; WTVD-TV, host; FOX 29, "Good Day Philadelphia," co-anchor, 2005-06; KGO-TV, ABC7 News team, host & reporter, 2006-07; ABC, "American Inventor", host, 2007-. **Military Serv:** AUS, Ger. **Business Addr:** Host, ABC TV, Seven Lincoln Sq, New York, NY 10023, **Business Phone:** (212)877-0588.*

SMITH, NORMAN RAYMOND
Publisher. **Personal:** Born Nov 17, 1944, New Orleans, LA; married Patricia A; children: Corey Norman & Christopher Jude. **Educ:** Southern Univ, New Orleans, BA, Hist, 1964; Commonwealth Col Sci, Mortuary Sci, 1966. **Career:** Treme Improv Polit Soc, pres & chmn bd, 1970-; Upper Pontalba Bldg Comn, mem, 1980-88; LA Black Culture Commn, exec bd mem, 1984-88; Forget-Me-Knots Inc, pres & chmn bd, currently; Treme Cult Enrichment Progs, secy. **Orgs:** New Orleans Embalmers Asn, 1966-; fel, Loyola Univ Inst Polit, 1979; Armstrong Park Adv Comn, 1983-88; grand knight, Knights Peter Claver-Thomy Lafon Coun 240, 1986-89; treas, Greater New Orleans Black Tourism Ctr, 1986; exec dir, Treme Community Educ Prog, 1996-. **Special Achievements:** Publisher of "Etches of Ebony Louisiana," annual Black LA history caldenar, 1983-, incl current issue 1995. **Military Serv:** AUS sgt 1967-69; Good Conduct Medal, Vietnam Campaign Medal. **Home Addr:** 1615 Saint Philip St, New Orleans, LA 70126. **Business Addr:** President, Forget-Me-Knots Inc, PO Box 7332, New Orleans, LA 70186.

SMITH, OBRIE
Association executive, president (organization). **Educ:** Lincoln Univ, BS, MA. **Career:** NC A&T Found Inc, chairperson, bd dir & pres, currently. **Orgs:** Vpres & bd mem, Waukesha County Nat Asn Advan Colored People; bd mem, United Way; Nat Hispanic Univ; Milwaukee Enterprise Ctr; Charlotte Meckleburg Ministries. **Military Serv:** AUS, 1965-67. **Home Addr:** 1338 Manicott Dr, Matthews, NC 28105. **Business Addr:** President, Board Director, North Carolina A&T Foundation Inc, 200 N Benbow Rd, Greensboro, NC 27411, **Business Phone:** (336)433-5560.

SMITH, ORLANDO. See SMITH, TUBBY.

SMITH, OSCAR A, JR.
Executive. **Career:** Community Foods Inc, chief exec officer & owner, currently. **Honors/Awds:** CPN, ranked 18, BLK Enterprise mag list of top 100 indust & serv companies, 1992. **Business Phone:** (410)235-9800.*

SMITH, OTIS
Football player, football coach. **Personal:** Born Oct 22, 1965, New Orleans, LA; married Sandy; children: LaKeitha, Chanel, Ciara & Chloe. **Educ:** Univ Mo. **Career:** Football player (retired), Football coach; Philadelphia Eagles, defensive back, 1991-94, asst sec coach, 2008-; New York Jets, 1995, 1997-99; New England Patriots, 1996, 2000-02, asst coach, 2006-07; Detroit Lions, 2003. **Honors/Awds:** Defensive Player of the Week; Kyle Clifton Good Guy Award, 1998; Super Bowl champion (XXXVI). **Business Addr:** Assistant Secondary Coach, Philadelphia Eagles, 1 Novacare Way, Philadelphia, PA 19145, **Business Phone:** (215)463-2500.

SMITH, REV. OTIS BENTON, JR.
Clergy. **Personal:** Born Nov 5, 1939, Lexington, KY; son of Otis B Sr (deceased) and Hattie Bibbs (deceased); married Bertha Odessa Stevenson; children: Otis III, Patrick Tyrone & Kenise Lynette. **Educ:** Central State Univ, BS, 1960; Southern Baptist Theol Sem, MDiv, 1969; Univ N Ala; Certi Continuing Educ, 1985; Selma Univ, DDiv, 1991. **Career:** Nat Jewish Hosp, Pediatric Sect, recreation supvr & counr, 1964-65; E Moline State Hosp, recreation supvr, 1965-66; WV Hosp Dayton, recreation spec, 1966; Fifth St Baptist Church, Louisville, asst pastor, 1966-69; First Baptist Church, pastor, 1969-; Sch Religion N Ala Baptist Acad-Courtland Ala, instr, 1970-73; N Ala Bapt Ministers Conf, lectr & Secy, 1976-79; Ala Bapt State Conv Ministers Seminar, lectr, 1980-. **Orgs:** Exec mem, bd dir, Muscle Shoals Area Mental Health, 1971-2001; conv mem, bd trustees, Selma Univ, 1973-86; exec mem, Colbert Lauderdale Comn Action Agency, 1973-79, bd dir; pres, Muscle Shoals Baptist SS & BTU Congress, 1981-90; vice moderator, Muscle Shoals Baptist Dist Asn Ala, 1983-85; vice chmn, Muscle Shoals Area Mental Health Ctr, bd dir, 1983-85; chmn, Riverbend Mental Health Ctr, 1985-87, bd dirs; adv coun, Shoals Community Col, 1987-; asst sec, Nat Baptist Conv, USA INC, 1988-94; gen secy, Ala State Missionary Baptist Conv, 1995-; asst secy, Nat Baptist Conv USA Inc, 2000-; Nat Asn Advan Colored People; Kappa Alpha Psi; Ala Baptist State Conv; NBC Inc. **Honors/Awds:** Minister of the Year, Nat Asn Advan Colored People, Muscle Shoals, AL, 1976; Minister of the Year, Alpha Pi Chap Omega Psi Phi, 1979; Special Cert Recognition, Tri County Branch, Nat Asn Advan Colored People, 1979; Citizen of the Year, Alpha Pi Chap Omega Psi Phi, 1983; Cert Merit, 1984; Minister of the Year, Top Hatters Club Inc, 1987. **Special Achievements:** First Black member & board directors in Shoals Hospital from 1980 to 1982. **Military Serv:** AUS, Lt, 1960-64; Commendation Medal. **Home Addr:** 1022 Hemlock St, PO Box 544, Tuscumbia, AL 35674. **Business Addr:** Pastor, First Baptist Church, 611 S High St, Tuscumbia, AL 35674, **Business Phone:** (205)383-8818.

SMITH, OTIS FITZGERALD
Basketball player, basketball executive. **Personal:** Born Jan 30, 1964, Jacksonville, FL. **Educ:** Jacksonville Univ, FL, attended 1986. **Career:** Basketball player (retired), basketball exec; Denver Nuggets, 1986-87; Golden State Warriors, prof basketball, 1988-89; Orlando Magic, dir community rels, 1997-99; Golden State Warriors, dir community rels, 1999-2002, exec dir basketball opers, 2002-03; Orlando Magic, asst gen mgr, 2005-06, gen mgr, 2006-. **Orgs:** Founder & pres, Otis Smith Kids Found. **Business Addr:** General Manager, Orlando Magic, 8701 Maitland Summit Blvd, Orlando, FL 32810, **Business Phone:** (407)916-2400.

SMITH, OZZIE
Baseball player, business owner, broadcaster. **Personal:** Born Dec 26, 1954, Mobile, AL; son of Clovis and Marvella; married Denise Jackson (divorced 1996); children: Osborne Earl Jr, Dustin & Taryn. **Educ:** Calif Poly tech State Univ, attended 1977. **Career:** Baseball player (retired), broadcaster, business owner; San Diego Padres, shortstop, 1978-81; St Louis Cardinals, shortstop, 1982-96; CNN News Group, baseball analyst, 1999-2002; Nat Baseball Hall Fame, educ ambassador, currently; Ozzie's Restaurant & Sports Bar, owner, currently. **Orgs:** Red Cross, Multiple Sclerosis, March Dimes & Annie Malone C Home; pres, Coun Drug Abuse; nat spokesman, CPR. **Honors/Awds:** Golden Glove Awards, 1980-92; St Louis Baseball Man of Year, 1982; Father of the Year, Nat Father's Day Comt; Nat League All-Star Team, 1982, 1984-87; Silver Slugger Award, 1987; Lou Gehrig Memorial Award, 1989; Branch Rickey Award, 1994; Roberto Clemente Award, 1995; Alabama Sports Hall of Fame, 1997; Missouri Sports Hall of Fame, 1997; Nat Baseball Hall of Fame, 2002; St. Louis Walk of Fame, 2003. **Special Achievements:** In 1999 he ranked number 87 on The Sporting News' list of .the 100 Greatest Baseball Players. **Business Addr:** Owner, Ozzie's Restaurant & Sports Bar, 645 Westport Plz, St Louis, MO 63146, **Business Phone:** (314)434-1000.

SMITH, PATRICIA GRACE
Executive. **Personal:** Born Nov 10, 1947, Tuskegee, AL; daughter of Douglas Jones Sr and Wilhelmina R Griffin Jones; married J Clay Smith Jr, Jun 25, 1983; children: Stager C, Michelle L, Michael L & Eugene Grace. **Educ:** Wesleyan Col, acad exchange prog, 1964; Univ Mich, acad exchange prog, 1965; Tuskegee Inst, BA, eng, 1968; Auburn Univ, grad courses masters prog eng, 1971; Harvard Univ Grad Sch Bus Admin, Broadcast Mgt Dev Course, 1976; George Wash Univ, telecommunication policy course, 1984; Fed Exec Inst, 1997. **Career:** Tuskegee Inst, instr dept eng, 1969-71; Curber Assoc, prog mgr, 1971-73; Nat Asn Broadcasters, dir placement, 1973-74, dir comm affairs, 1974-77;

Group W Westinghouse Broadcasting Co WJZ TV, from assoc producer to producer, 1977-78; Sheridan Broadcasting Network, dir affil relations & programming, 1978-80; FCC, Off Pub Affairs, chief consumer assist & small bus div, 1980-92, assoc managing dir pub info & ref serv, dep dir policy, 1992-94; US Dept Transp, Off Com Space Transp, assoc managing dir, 1994-95; FAA Off, assoc admin com space transp, actg assoc adminr, 1995-98, assoc adminr, 1998-. **Orgs:** Am Women Radio & TV, 1973-77; interim chairperson, Int Broadcasting Comm Nat Asn TV & Radio Artists, 1974; Cert Prog Commun Mgt & Tech, 1974-76; vice chairperson, Nat Conf Black Lawyers Task Force Commun, 1975-81; Trustee Nat Urban League, 1976-81; Jour & Commun Adv Coun Auburn Univ, 1976-78; comm, Comm Cancer Coord Coun, 1977-84; Adv Bd, Black Arts Celebration, 1978-83; Ala State Soc, 1984-92; Wash Urban League, 1983-87; Nat Asn Advan Colored People, 1983-; commnr, Dist Columbia Comn Human Rights, 1986-87, chairperson, 1987-91; bd adv, Salvation Army, 1992-2001; bd dirs, Broadcasters Club; Nat Adv Comm Women Commun Inc; Lambda Iota Tau Int Hon Soc. **Honors/Awds:** Sustained Superior Performance Award, 1981-91; National Performance Review Award, 1994; Distinguished Alumnus Award, Tuskegee Univ, 1996; C Alfred Anderson Award Recipient, 2002. **Home Addr:** 4010 16th St NW, Washington, DC 20011. **Business Addr:** Associate Administrator, Commercial Space Transportation FAA, US Department of Transportation, 7th & Independence Ave SW Rm 331, Washington, DC 20591, **Business Phone:** (202)267-7793.

SMITH, PAUL
Clergy. **Personal:** Born Sep 20, 1935, South Bend, IN; married Frances Irene Pitts; children: Kathleen, Heather, Krista. **Educ:** Talladega Col, AB 1957; Hartford Sem, MDiv, 1960; Eden Theological Sem, DMin, 1977. **Career:** Clergy (retired); WA Univ, assoc vice chancellor, 1974-78; Morehouse Col, vpres, 1978-79; Columbia Theological Sem, adjunct prof, 1979-; Candler Sch Theology, adjunct prof, 1979-; Hillside Presbyterian Church, pastor; Henry St First Presbyterian Church, sr minister. **Orgs:** Trustee Presby Sch Christian Educ, 1981-; consult, Howard Thurman Educ Trust, 1982; bd mem, Child Serv Family Coun, 1983-; Metro Fair Housing Serv Inc, 1981-; Leadership Atlanta, 1981; Coun Atlanta Pres; State Adv Comt US Civil Rights Comn, 1977-83. **Honors/Awds:** NEH Recepient, 1982; pub Unity, Diversity, Inclusiveness, 1985; book J Knox Press Theology Computerized World, 1985-86; Women United in Philanthropy.

SMITH, REV. PERRY ANDERSON, III
Clergy. **Personal:** Born May 16, 1934, Mound Bayou, MS; son of Perry and Elease Wilson; married Constance. **Educ:** Howard Univ, BA, 1955, Howard Univ, Divinity Sch, MDiv, 1958. **Career:** First Baptist Church Inc, sr pastor, 1958-; Comt Action PG County, MD, exec dir, 1965-69; Nat Civil Serv League, assoc dir, 1969-72; Univ Md, chaplain, 1975-82. **Orgs:** Treas, Prog Nat Baptist Conv, 1974-76, auditor, 1978-80; bd dir, Nat Asn Advan Colored People, Prince George's County, MD; bd dir, Minster Blacks Higher Educ; vpres, Nat Conf Black Churchmen; adv bd mem, Family Serv Prince George's County; Ministries to Blacks in Higher Educ; Concerned Clergy Prince George's County. **Honors/Awds:** Martin Luther King Jr Award, Black Student Union, Univ Md Col Park, 1976; Hester V King Humanitarian Award, 1985; Brotherhood/Sisterhood Award, NCCJ, 1998; The Benjamin E Mays Award, Howard Univ Div Sch; Outstanding Community Serv, Prince George's County, Maryland Nat Asn Advan Colored People; Outstanding Community Serv, Progressive Baptist Laymen of Washington DC; Outstanding Community Serv, Frontiers Int; Outstanding Community Serv, Metropolitan Washington Health & Welfare Coun; Outstanding Serv, Univ Md, Nat Asn Advan Colored People; Outstanding Serv, DC Women Ministers Asn; Outstanding Serv, Community Action Prince George's County Md; Achievement Award, Combined Communities Action, Prince George's County, Maryland; Metropolitan Serv Award, Iota Upsilon Lambda Chapter, Alpha Phi Alpha Fraternity, Inc. **Home Addr:** 2908 Native Dancer Ct, Mitchellville, MD 20721. **Business Addr:** Senior pastor, First Baptist Church Inc, 4009 Wallace Rd, Brentwood, MD 20722, **Business Phone:** (301)277-4742.

SMITH, PHILIP GENE
Manager, educator. **Personal:** Born Mar 3, 1928, Chicago, IL; son of Ruth Smith McGowan and S David Smith; married Elaine J Kehrer; children: Philip G Jr & Kelyn M. **Educ:** Ky State Col, BA, 1949; Chicago Teachers Col, BE, 1953; Antioch Sch Law, MA, 1982. **Career:** Danville IL Human Rels Commmunity, dir, 1976-77; Detroit Human Rights Dept, comn admin coordr, 1977-86; Voters Organized Educate, dir, 1986-; Highland Pk Community Col, Highland Park, MI, instr polit sci, 1987-96; Ga Perimeter Col, Clarkston, GA, prof, 1997-. **Orgs:** Polit ed, Dollars & Sense Mag, 1976-; precinct deleg, Mich Dem Conv 1980-88; chmn, Mich Progressive Dem Orgn, 1988-96; Ga Progressive Dem Orgn, 1996-; Kappa Alpha Psi; Mich Asn Human Rights Workers; pres, Ethnic Educ Res Corp. **Honors/Awds:** Fred Hampton Scholarship Fund Image Award, 1986; 1st annual Frederick Douglass Award, Hope & Magnolia United Methodist Churches, Southfield MI, 1988; Hall of Fame, Tilden Tech High Sch, 1994. **Special Achievements:** Published articles "One Step Forward/Two Steps Backwards-An Analysis of Progressive Politics", Independent Press, Detroit MI, 1989; "The Life and Times of Thurgood Marshall", Dollars & Sense, 1992; "The Historical Significance of the Black Power Management Movement", Dollars & Sense, 2000. **Military Serv:** AUS, pvt E-II, 1 yr. **Home Addr:** 955 Hargett Ct, Stone Mountain, GA 30083. **Business Addr:** Professor, Georgia Perimeter College, Department of Economics, Rm E2406 2101 Womack Rd, Dunwoody, GA 30338, **Business Phone:** (770)274-5150.

SMITH, DR. PHILLIP M.
Educator. **Personal:** Born Jan 24, 1937, Vulcan, WV; son of Robert and Bernice Whaley; married Gloria J; children: Phillip Jr & Jeffrey M. **Educ:** WVa State Col, BS, zool, 1958; City Univ NY, MA, 1969; Educ Admin, dipl; Hofstra Univ, attended 1970; Univ MA, EdD, 1987. **Career:** New York City Dept Welfare, Childrens counr, 1958-59; New York Dept Parks, recreation leader, 1959-60; New York City Dept Hosp, recreation & dir, 1960-; Wilkyck Sch Boys, child care specialist, supvr, 1962-66; Neighborhood Youth Corps, curriculum specialist, 1965-66; Roosevelt Jr & Sr High Sch, sci teacher, 1966-69, dir adult educ, 1969-70, dir reading prog, 1969-70, asst prin, 1969-79, Multi-level Alternative Prog, dir, 1973-74, prin, 1979-88; Roosevelt Sch Dist, dist dir supporting servs, 1988-92; St John's Univ, Queens, adjunct prof; Five Towns Col, trustee bd, currently. **Orgs:** Life mem, Nat Asn Advan Colored People; life mem, Kappa Alpha Psi; Nat Asn Black Sch Educrs; Nat Asn Sec Sch Prin; Sch Adminr Asn NY State; Roosevelt Adminrs Asn; vpres, exec bd, Long Island Asn Supervision & Curriculum Develop, 1988-; vpres, pres, exec bd, PLUS Group Homes Inc, 1980; adv bd, House Good Coun, 1987-; exec comt, Nassau Suffolk Sch Bd Asn, 1995-; trustee, Uniondale Sch Bd, 1991-. **Honors/Awds:** Fifteen Years Service Award, Health & Hosp Corp; listed in Whos who among students in American Colleges and Universities; listed in Whos who in American Education; listed in Whos who among Black Americans. **Special Achievements:** Cover photo for feature article "Black tennis" Tennis Mag, 1974. **Business Addr:** Trustee, Five Towns College, 305 N Service Rd, Dix Hills, NY 11746-6055, **Business Phone:** (631)424-7000.

SMITH, QUENTIN P
Educator. **Personal:** Born Jul 30, 1918, Huntsville, TX; son of Ione and Paige; divorced. **Educ:** Chicago Univ, MA, 1947; Ind Univ, MS, 1956. **Career:** Educator (retired); W Side HS Gary, from educator & guid counr to prin; Gary Comm Sch Corp, exec dir sec ed. **Orgs:** Vpres, Am Fedn Teachers, 1957; Community Pks Gary, 1964; pres, Gary Human Rels Community, 1966; pres, Urban League Ind, 1967; bd trust, Calumet Col, 1968-; pres, Gary City Coun, 1969; adv bd, Bank Ind, 1970-; Gary Redev Community, 1970-72; St Josephs Calumet Col, 1973; Lk Co Bd Pub Welfare, 1973; Ind Coun Educ, 1974; lectr, Urban Studies, Ind Univ, NW, 1974. **Honors/Awds:** Gary Jaycees Good Govt Award, 1971; NEA Teacher in Politics, 1970. **Military Serv:** USAF, 1st lt, 1942-45. **Business Phone:** (219)881-5401.

SMITH, DR. QUENTIN TED
Educator, health services administrator. **Personal:** Born May 1, 1937, Seaford, DE; son of Carlton and Elizabeth Holland; married Marjorie McCoy, Jun 19, 1967; children: Candace, Jason & Michael. **Educ:** Fisk Univ, AB, 1961; Howard Univ, MD, 1967. **Career:** Univ Chicago, Woodrow Wilson fel, 1961-62; Howard Univ, Nat Med fel, 1963-67; WMHC Fulton City, dir, 1974-75; Ment Health Grady Hosp, dir outpatient child & adolescent, 1977-82; Ridgeview Inst, pvt practice & dir child & adolescent serv & supr psychiat residents & child fel; Emory Univ, assoc prof; Morehouse Sch Med, prof clin psychiat, currently, dir third psychiatry clerkship & fourth yr child & adolescent psychiat elective; Cork Inst, Black Alcohol Studies, vice chair psychiat educ & med dir. **Orgs:** Fel Am Psychiatric Asn, 1971-; Am Acad Child Psychiat, 1974-; Public Affairs Comt, Ga Psychiat Asn, 1986-95; Ridgeview Inst, Peer Review Subcommittee, Nominating Comt; Morehouse Sch Med, Stud Acad Affairs & Prom Comt, Residency Training Comt, Stud Appeals Comt; Children's Trust Fund Comt State Ga; Clin Adv Comt, Ridgeview Inst; 100 Black Men Atlanta Inc, Community Involvement Comt; Am Orthopsychiatric Asn; Doctors Med Stud Educ Psychiat; Am Coun Alcoholism Psychiatrists Alcohol & Addictions; Nat Med Asn; Ga Psychiat Physicians Asn; Ga Coun Child & Adolescent Psychiat; Black Psychiatrists Am; Guate Educ Biomed Sci Coun; pres, Atlanta Chap Black Psychiatrists Am. **Honors/Awds:** Phi Beta Kappa, Fisk Univ, Nashville, TN, 1961; Beta Kappa Chi, 1961; Man of the Year Award, Fisk Univ, 1961, Community Service Award, 2000. **Business Addr:** Professor of Clinical Psychiatry, Morehouse School of Medicine, 720 Westview Dr SW Suite 212, Atlanta, GA 30310.

SMITH, REGINALD D
Educator. **Personal:** Born Feb 21, 1918, Baltimore, MD; married Euzelle Patterson; children: Andrea, Pamela, Patrice & Regi. **Educ:** Hampton Inst, BS, 1940; A&T Col Greensboro NC State Univ, Raleigh, attended. **Career:** Hampton Inst, staff, 1940-42; Chapel Hill City Schs, teacher, 1942-80, asst prin, 1970-80, vice prin, 2004, prof emer, currently. **Orgs:** Civitan Chapel Hill; Chapel Hill Planning Bd, 1959-65; bdalderman, 1965-74; Triangle J Council Govts, 1970-74; Mem NCAE; NEA; NASSP; NC League & Municipalities. **Honors/Awds:** NC Hamptonian of Year, 1969; mayor pro-tem Chapel Hill, 1969-74; Chapel Hill Father of Year, 1970; Masonic Distinguished Service Award, 1971; Outstanding Service Award, Ment Health Asn, 1983; Martin Luther King Community Service Award, 1988; Outstanding Service Award, Am Cancer Soc, 1991; Outstanding Senior Citizen, Chapel Hill Jaycees, 1991-92; Sertomian of Year Award, Chapel Hill Cariboro, 1993. **Military Serv:** CAC, sgt, 1944-46.

SMITH, REV. REGINALD EDWARD
Clergy. **Personal:** Born Jan 10, 1967, Detroit, MI; son of Major E and Edith; married Tracy Geneen, Jul 20, 1991; children: Tkhari Gamal, Tyre Gavon-Major & Tavis Geremiah. **Educ:** Ala State Univ, BS, 1991; Va Union Theol Sem, MDiv, 1997; Univ Mich, Dearborn. **Career:** Union Grace Missionary Baptist Church, pastor, currently. **Orgs:** Alpha Phi Alpha Fraternity Inc, 1989; mem comt, Coun Baptist Pastors Detroit & Vicinity; exec dir, Union Grace Community Develop Corp; exec mem, Kingdom Builders Pastor & People Int Conf. **Business Addr:** Pastor, Union Grace Missionary Baptist Church, 7729 Rosa Parks Blvd, Detroit, MI 48206-2699, **Business Phone:** (313)894-2500.

SMITH, REGINALD KEITH
School administrator. **Personal:** Born Mar 3, 1960, Kenansville, NC; son of Rayford and Willie Lucille Miller; married Lisa L Nelson, Apr 14, 1990. **Educ:** NC Cent Univ, Durham, NC, BA, 1982; Univ Del, Newark, DE, MPA, 1984. **Career:** Dept Health & Human Serv, Rockville, MD, pub health analyst, 1981; State NC Gov's Off, Durham, minority affairs asst, 1982; Univ Del, Newark, dorm residence dir & nutrition monitor, 1982; NC Cent Univ, Durham, adj asst prof, spec asst & internship coordr, 1984-87; Durham County Govt, NC, asst county mgr, 1987-88; NC Univ, Durham, bus opers mgr; Pub Educ Network, Durham Pub Schs, Durham, NC, interim exec dir, currently. **Orgs:** Parliamentarian & pub rels chairperson, NCCU Alumni Asn, 1984-88; zone chmn, Durham Scouting Roundup, 1984, 1986; bd dirs, Salvation Army Boys Club; Youth Serv Adv Comm, 1985-; contributing founder, Acad Help Ctr, 1986-89. **Honors/Awds:** Second-Mile Award, NCCU Public Admin Prog, 1981-82; Public Service Fellow, US Dept Educ, 1982-84; Youth for Energy Independence and Histadrut, Israel US Youth Delegate, 1983; Rockefeller Fellow, Duke UNC Women Studies, 1985-86. **Home Addr:** 3200 Victor Ave, Durham, NC 27707. **Business Addr:** Interim Executive Director, Durham Public Schools, Durham Public Education Network, 4235 University Dr, Durham, NC 27707, **Business Phone:** (919)683-6503.

SMITH, DR. RICHARD ALFRED
Physician. **Personal:** Born Oct 13, 1932, Norwalk, CT; son of Julius and Mabel; married Lorna Carrier; children: Dirk Devi, Rik Balakrishna, Erik Dibnarine, Blake Andrew & Quintin Everett. **Educ:** Howard Univ, BSc, 1953, MD, 1957; Columbia Univ, Sch pub health, MPH, 1960. **Career:** US Pub Health Serv, med dir, 24 yrs; Peace Corps Nigeria, 1961-63; Wash DC, deputy med dir, 1963-65; Dept Health & Human Serv, Office Int Health, chief office planning, 1965-67; MEDEX Prog, Univ Wash, prof & dir, 1968-72; The MEDEX Group, Sch Med, Univ Hawaii, clin prof & dir, 1972-, primary care & health specialist, currently. **Orgs:** Fel, Am Col Preventive Med, 1961-; Am Pub Health Asn, 1963-; Inst Med Nat Acad Sci, 1972-; consult World Health Org, 1972-. **Honors/Awds:** William A Jump Award, Dept Health, Educ & Welfare; Gerard B Lambert Award, Lambert Found, 1971; Rockefeller Public Service Award, Princeton Univ, 1981; Outstanding Service Award, Region IX, Dept Health & Human Servs for Leadership in Developing the Physician Asst & Nurse Practitioners Movement USA, 1992. **Business Addr:** Clinical Professor, Director, University of Hawaii, John A. Burns School of Medicine, 95-390 Kuahelani Ave, Mililani, HI 96789, **Business Phone:** (808)533-6492.

SMITH, DR. ROBERT. **See Obituaries section.**

SMITH, REV. ROBERT, JR.
Clergy. **Personal:** Born Oct 5, 1951, Pensacola, FL; son of Robert Sr and Ollie Mae Hale; married Cynthia Perkins, Dec 23, 1972; children: Sherique, Conderidge & Terique. **Educ:** Lawson St Jr Col, Birmingham, AL; Jefferson St Jr Col, Birmingham, AL; Miles Col, Birmingham, AL; New Orleans Baptist Theol Sem, New Orleans, LA, MDiv. **Career:** New Bethel Baptist Church, Detroit, MI, pastor, 1984-; Eastern Star Baptist Church, Birmingham, AL, pastor; Mt Tabor Baptist Church, Brent, AL, pastor; First Baptist Church, Mason City, Birmingham, AL, pastor; Bethel Baptist Church, Pratt City, Birmingham, AL, pastor; recording artist. **Orgs:** Chmn, Mayor Young's, 1989; Re-election Comm; bd mem, Greater Opportunities Industrialization Ctr; Continuing steering comt, Nat Bank Detroit; Detroit Econ Club; prog coordr, SCLC, Detroit Chap; vpres, Detroit Chap Nat Asn Advan Colored People. **Honors/Awds:** Councilman David Eberhard Outstanding Community Award, 1989; Outstanding Achievement Award, 1982; Sermon Album of the Year, Singing Preacher of the Year, WENN Radio & Clergy That Care, 1982; SCLC Minister of the Year Award, 1992. **Business Addr:** Pastor, New Bethel Baptist Church, 8430 C L Franklin Blvd, Detroit, MI 48206, **Business Phone:** (313)894-5788.

SMITH, ROBERT CHARLES
Educator. **Personal:** Born Feb 12, 1947, Benton, LA; son of Martin and Blanch Tharpe; married Scottie Gibson Smith, Aug 31,

1972; children: Blanch & Jessica Scottus-Charles. **Educ:** Los Angeles City Col, CA, AA, 1967; Univ Calif, Berkeley, BA, 1970; Univ Calif, Los Angeles, CA, MA, 1972; Howard Univ, Wash, DC, PhD, 1976. **Career:** Columbia Univ, New York, NY, res assoc, 1976-80; SUNY Col, Purchase, asst prof, 1975-80; Howard Univ, Wash, DC, assoc prof, 1980-89; Prairie View A&M, Prairie View, TX, prof, 1989-90; San Francisco State Univ, San Francisco, CA, prof, 1990-. **Orgs:** Fel Ford Found, 1973-76; Am Polit Sci Asn, 1976-; Acad Polit Sci, 1976-; Nat Conf Black Polit Sci; Nat Cong Black Fac, 1988-; CA Black Fac, 1990-. **Honors/Awds:** Distinguished PhD Alumni Award, Howard Univ, 1998. **Special Achievements:** Co-author of American Politics & the African American Quest for Universal Freedom and the Encyclopedia of African American Politics and the Race, Class and Culture: A Study in Afro-American Mass Opinion; Racism in the Post-Civil Rights Era: Now You See It, Now You Don't; We Have No Leaders: African Americans in the Post-Civil Rights Era; African American Leadership; and Contemporary Controversies and the American Racial Divide. **Business Addr:** Professor, San Francisco State University, Political Science Department, 1600 Holloway Ave, San Francisco, CA 94132.

SMITH, ROBERT D. See SMITH, BOB.

SMITH, ROBERT EUGENE. See SMITH, BOBBY.

SMITH, DR. ROBERT H.
College administrator, chancellor (education). **Career:** Southern Univ, Shreveport, LA, exec, chancellor, 1987-92.

SMITH, REV. DR. ROBERT JOHNSON
Educator, clergy. **Personal:** Born Sep 26, 1920, Chicago, IL; married Jennie Mae; children: Estelle, Everett, Renee & Robert II. **Educ:** Morehouse Col, AB, 1937; Theol Sch, BD, STM, DMin; Bryn Mawr Col, MSW; Morehouse Col & VA Col, DD. **Career:** High St Church, minister, 1946-56; Va Hosp, chap, 1945-54; Salem Baptist Church, sr minister, 1956-96, pastor emer, 1997-; Philadelphia Sch Dist, counr, 1960-85; Penn Human Rels Comn, comnr. **Orgs:** Chmn bd trustees, Berean Inst; bd mem, Abington Mem Hosp Va Col; Rotary Int; Omega Psi Phi; Acad Certified Soc Workers. **Military Serv:** AUS, maj & chap, 1941-45. **Business Addr:** Pastor Emeritus, Salem Baptist Church, 610 Summit Ave, Jenkintown, PA 19046.

SMITH, ROBERT LONDON
Political scientist, educator. **Personal:** Born Oct 13, 1919, Alexandria, LA; son of Daniel C and Lillie Roberts; married Jewel Busch; children: Jewel Smith Feist, Robert London Jr, Karl Busch. **Educ:** Yale Univ, dipl, 1944; Air Univ, dipl, 1952; Col St Joseph, BA, 1954; Univ Okla, MA, 1955; Am Univ Wash, DC, PhD, 1964. **Career:** Aerospace Res Wash, asst dept chief staff material, 1960-62; Off Sci Res Wash, asst exec dir, 1963-65; Nat Acad Sci, dir AFOSR post doctoral res prog, 1964; Univ Ark, assoc prof & dept head, 1965-67; Univ Ark, dean col bus econ & govt, 1968-70, prof & head dept polit sci, 1970-80; Governor's Cabinet State Ark, comnr dept health & social serv, 1983-84; Univ Ark, prof polit sci emer, 1984. **Orgs:** Nat Acad Polit Sci, 1957; Nat Inst Social & Behav Sci, 1961; AAAS, 1964; Nat Inst US in World Affairs, 1964; Am Polit Sci Asn, 1965-80; educ comnr, Ark C of C, 1967; Men of Achievement, Cambridge, England, 1974; Res & Adv Study Coun, Univ Ark, 1968-70; Acad Coun Univ Ark, 1968-70; committeeman-at-large, Nat Coun Boy Scouts Am, 1970-72; AK Govt Employment Comn; pres, Fairbanks USO Coun; bd dirs, Artic First Fed Savings & Loan Asn; corporator, Mt McKinely Mutual Savings Bank; Governor's Cabinet, Rotary, Fairbanks Chap, 1981-84. **Honors/Awds:** Nat Polit Sci Honor, Frat Pi Sigma Alpha, 1962; Silver Beaver Award, Boy Scouts Am, 1970; Outstanding Educator Award, Nat Asn Advan Colored People, 1970; Outstanding Professor, Univ Ark, 1974-75; Outstanding Educator of America, 1975; National Social Science Honor, Pi Gamma Mu, 1962. **Military Serv:** USAF, lt col, 25 yrs; Commendation Medal Meritorious Serv, 1956.

SMITH, DR. ROBERT P., JR.
Educator, college teacher. **Personal:** Born Oct 12, 1923, New Orleans, LA; son of Robert Sr (deceased) and Leola Mitchell (deceased); married Arlette Marie Carlton, Nov 27, 1954; children: Arlette Therese. **Educ:** Howard Univ, BA, 1948; Univ Chicago, MA, 1950; Univ Bordeaux, France, attended 1953; Univ PA, PhD, 1969. **Career:** DEU CEF Univ de Bordeaux, France, Fulbright fel, 1952-53; Talladega Col, instr fr span & german, 1953-54; Fisk Univ, asst prof fr & span, 1954-58; John Hay Whitney Found fel, 1958-59; Rutgers Univ, instr, asst prof, assoc prof, Fr Dept, chmn, 1965-73, assoc dean acad affairs, 1973-79, prof, 1984-89; prof emer, 1987-; NEH Summer grant, 1981. **Orgs:** Treas, Col Lang Asn, 1986-98; Alpha Phi Alpha; Am Asn Univ Prof; Am Asn Teachers Fr; Mod Lang Asn; African Lit Asn; Col Lang Asn. **Special Achievements:** Published articles in French Review, College Lang Assn Journal, Langston Hughes Review, Le Petit Courier, Celacef Bulletin, World Literature Today, Celfan Review. **Military Serv:** USAF, sgt, 1943-45. **Home Addr:** 3263 Morning Glory Rd S 914, Philadelphia, PA 19154. *

SMITH, ROBERT SCOTT
Football player, football executive. **Personal:** Born Mar 4, 1972, Euclid, OH. **Educ:** Ohio State Univ. **Career:** Football player (retired), Football executive; Minn Vikings, running back, 1993-2000; Nat Football League Network, analyst, currently. **Orgs:** Founder, Robert Smith Found. **Honors/Awds:** Ohio's Mr. Football Award, 1988 & 1989. **Special Achievements:** Ohio State buckeyes starting tailbacks, 1990; made a cameo in the TVseries Mystery Science Theater 3000, Antagonist; Book: The Rest of the Iceberg, saw publication, 2004; appearing as a guest on the ESPN news program Outside the Lines, The Mole People. **Business Phone:** (212)655-5665.

SMITH, ROBERT W.
Automotive executive. **Career:** Bob Smith Chevrolet Inc, Louisville, KY, chief exec. **Business Addr:** Chief Executive, Bob Smith Chevrolet Inc, 10500 Westport Rd, Louisville, KY 40222, **Business Phone:** (502)425-9993.

SMITH, ROBIN (ROBIN A SMITH)
Association executive. **Educ:** Harvard Bus Sch. **Career:** One to One Partnership, exec dir, 1992-93, vpres local mobilization, currently; Beacon Group, LLC, admin dir, 1997-; Goldman, Sachs & Co, corp financial assoc. **Orgs:** Bd dirs, Dreyfus Corp. **Special Achievements:** First African American female, & youngest mem to serve on the Dreyfus Corp bd of dirs. **Business Phone:** (212)339-9112.

SMITH, ROBIN A. See SMITH, ROBIN.

SMITH, ROD. See SMITH, RODNEY MARC.

SMITH, ROD (RODERICK SMITH)
Football player. **Personal:** Born May 15, 1970, Texarkana, AR; children: Devin, Roderick Jr & Vanessa. **Educ:** Mo Southern State Col. **Career:** Football player (retired); Denver Broncos, wide receiver, 1995-2008. **Orgs:** Spokesman, Ann Denver Broncos Community Blood Dr. **Honors/Awds:** Harlon Hill Award; Inducted school's Athletics Hall of Fame, 2003; nominated NFL's Walter Payton Man of the year, 2004; College Football Hall of Fame, 2009.

SMITH, RODERICK. See SMITH, ROD.

SMITH, RODNEY MARC (ROD SMITH)
Football player, manager. **Personal:** Born Mar 12, 1970, St Paul, MN. **Educ:** Notre Dame, BA, econs; Pfeiffer Univ, MBA. **Career:** Football player (retired), Manager; New England Patriots, defensive back,1992-94; Carolina Panthers, 1995-98; Minnesota Vikings, 1996; Green Bay Packers, 1998; ESPN Regional, Studio Analyst, currently. **Orgs:** Advisory Bd mem, Point Lake & Golf Club. **Honors/Awds:** New England Rookie of the Year, 1992. **Business Addr:** ESPN Regional, ESPN Regional, 11001 Rushmore Dr, Charlotte, NC 28277, **Business Phone:** (704)973-5000.*

SMITH, RODNEY STACEY
Athlete. **Personal:** Born Apr 13, 1966, Washington, DC. **Educ:** Bachelors, criminal justice, 1988; Western New England Col, attended 1989. **Career:** US Olympic Team, Wrestling Team, athlete, 1992, 1996; Olympics, Sydney, Australia, asst coach, 2000; Western New England Col, asst coach, currently. **Military Serv:** AUS, 1992. **Business Phone:** (413)796-2200.*

SMITH, ROGER LEROY
Electrical engineer. **Personal:** Born May 15, 1946, New York, NY; divorced; children: Kim M, Lisa R, Shawnee L. **Educ:** Criminal Justice Nassau Community Col, AA, 1975. **Career:** US Customs Bur, 1971-74; FAA, air traffic controller 1974-76; Fed Aviation Admin & Flight Inspec, electronic technician 1976-; US customs, sec & patrol off skymarshal. **Honors/Awds:** Comm pilot only black airborne technician FAA Flight Inspec Div; First All Black Flight Insp Crew. **Military Serv:** USN, 2nd class petty, officer, 1966-69; vietnam serv medal.

SMITH, DR. ROLAND BLAIR
School administrator. **Personal:** Born Mar 21, 1946, Washington, DC; son of Roland B Sr and Annie Louise; married Valerie V Peyton; children: Rovelle Louise & Roland Blair III. **Educ:** Bowie State Col, BA, soc anthrop, 1969; Univ Notre Dame, attended 1970; Ind Univ Sch Pub & Environ Affairs, MPA, 1976; Univ Notre Dame, attended 1980; Harvard Univ, EdD, 1988. **Career:** Bowie St Col, Sociol-Anthrop Dept, fac asst, 1968-69; US Senate, intern res asst, 1970; PSC South Bend Ind, dir youth employment, 1970-71; City S Bend, Ind, Pub Serv Careers Off, job coach, 1970-71, Summer Youth Employment Prog, dir, 1971, Mayor's Manpower Planning Coun, Systs Coordr, 1971-73; MAPC South Bend Ind, manpower systs coord, 1971-73; Univ Notre Dame Proj Upward Bound, asst dir, 1973-76, dir, 1976-80; Ctr Educ Opportunity, dir, 1980-83, 1986-92; Harvard Grad Sch Educ, admin intern & researcher, 1983-84, acad counsr, 1984-86, Off Asst Dean, grad asst, 1984-86, teaching, 1985; Univ Norte Dame, South Bend, Ind, from asst dir to dir, Upward Bound, 1973-83, 1986-88, from asst prof to assoc prof specialist fac urban studies, 1976-96, Inst Urban Studies, Ctr Educational Opportunity, founding dir, 1980-83, 1986-96, exec asst to the pres, freshman writing instr, 1989-92, concurrent assoc prof sociol, 1991-96, Urban Inst Community & Educ Initiatives, dir, 1992-95; Rice Univ, Houston, assoc provost, 1996-, lectr educ, 1996-2000, Mellon Mays Undergraduate Fel Prog, prin investr & coordr, 1998-, adj prof educ, 2000-; consult. **Orgs:** Lambda Alpha Nat Anthrop Honor Soc, 1969; Field reader DHEW US Office Educ, 1977; bd dirs, Mid-Am Asn Educ Opportunity Prog Personnel, 1979-81; pres, Ind Asn Educ Opportunity Prog Personnel, 1979-80; ed bd, Harvard Educ Rev, 1984-; exec bd, Youth Serv Bur St Joseph County IN 1972-77; pres, S Bend Br, Nat Asn Advan Colored People, 1975-76; Ind Adv Com US Civil Rights Comn 1979-83; Phi Delta Kappa Harvard Chapter, 1986; vpres, Private Indust Coun St Joseph County, 1990-92; exec comt Community Educ Round Table, 1988-91; chair, prog comt, Minority Bus Develop Coun, 1990-92; MLK Fed Holiday Comm, 1993-94; chair, Nat Asn Presidential Assist Higher Educ, 1994-95; bd dirs, Harvard Alumni Asn, 1995-; vice chair, Black Caucus, Am Asn Higher Educ, 1995-97, chair, 1997-99; bd visitors, Bowie State Univ, 1998-; bd dirs, Houston INROADS, 1997-; bd dir, Houston Nat Black MBA Asn, 1999-; bd dir, Life Gift Organ Donation Ctr, 2000-; bd dir, Am Conf Acad Deans; Martin Luther King, Jr Fed Holiday Comn. **Honors/Awds:** MD State Senatorial School Award, 1968; Distinguished Service Award, United Negro Fund, 1974; Outstanding Achievement Award, Kappa Alpha Psi South Bend Alumni Chap, 1976; President Citation, Bowie State Col, 1977; Distinguished Alumni Award, Ind Univ South Bend Sch Pub & Env Aff, 1983. **Business Addr:** Adjunct Professor, Associate Provost, Rice University, Department of Sociology, Rm 313A Lovett Hall 6100 S Main St, PO Box 3, Houston, TX 77005-1892, **Business Phone:** (713)348-5688.

SMITH, DR. ROULETTE WILLIAM
Educator. **Personal:** Born Jan 19, 1942, New York, NY; married Norma Abe (divorced 1990); children: Nicole Michelle & Todd Roulette. **Educ:** Morehouse, BS, 1961; Stanford, MS, 1964; MS, 1965; PhD, 1973; Univ CA San Francisco, further study, med, 1980. **Career:** Stanford Univ, res asst, 1966-70; asst prof, 1970-75; Univ CA Santa Barbara; Bureau Educ Res & Develop, Univ CA Santa Barbara, specialist assoc dir, 1970-74; Inst Postgraduate Interdisciplinary Studies, Palo Alto, CA, dir, 1984-; San Jose State Univ, asst dir, testing & eval, 1997-99; California State Univ, Dominguez Hills, Testing Off, head, 1999-03; Inst Trans personal Psychol, assoc prof, res faculty, 2001-. **Orgs:** Pres, Humanized Tech & Inc, 1973-; editor Instructional Sci, 1971-83; assoc editor, Health Policy & Educ, 1979-83; sales mgr, Stanford European Auto, 1970-74; Consult Rand Corp, 1970-74; Value Engineering Co, 1973; consult, Asn Support Grad Students, 1995-. **Business Addr:** Associate Professor, Institute of Transpersonal Psychology, 744 San Antonio Rd Suite 15, Palo Alto, CA 94303, **Business Phone:** (650)493-4430.

SMITH, RUFUS HERMAN
Government official. **Personal:** Born Jun 23, 1950, Loudon, TN; married Patricia Ann Howse; children: Rufus H Jr, Courtney Danielle. **Educ:** Ten State Univ, BS, 1972; Univ Ten, Knoxville, MS, 1978. **Career:** TN Valley Authority, equal opportunity staff, 1978-83; US Dept Energy, equal opportunity mgr, 1983, diversity progs mgr & Employee Concerns Mgr, currently. **Orgs:** Mgr, affirmative action prog Fed employees & direct minority educ assistance progs, including specifically related historically black cols & univs. **Honors/Awds:** APA. **Business Addr:** Diversity Programs Manager and Employee Concerns Manager, United States Department of Energy, Oakridge Operations, 200 Admin Rd, PO Box 2001, Oak Ridge, TN 37831, **Business Phone:** (865)576-0885.*

SMITH, SHERMAN, SR.
Manager, government official, teacher. **Personal:** Born Apr 26, 1957, Earle, AR; married Odessa Pitchford; children: Margual & Sherman Jr. **Educ:** Draughon Bus Col, assoc bus mgt, 1977. **Career:** Earle Jr High Sch, sub-teacher 1977-78; Halstead Indus Prod, store room supvr, 1981; Arkan Munic League, Earles city, mayor. **Orgs:** Youth dept pres Earle Church God Christ; pres Student Govt, 1976-77; Alderman City Earle, 1983; minister gospel Earle Church God Christ, 1983. **Honors/Awds:** Cert income tax preparer cert HR Block, 1978. **Home Addr:** 215 Alabama St, Earle, AR 72331.

SMITH, SHEVIN JAMAR
Football player. **Personal:** Born Jun 17, 1975, Miami, FL; married; children: 3. **Educ:** Fla State, BA, finance. **Career:** Football player (retired), Tampa Bay Buccaneers, defensive back, 1998-99; St Louis Rams, safety; Tampa Bay Storm, wide receiver & defensive back, 2004; high sch teacher,currently.

SMITH, SHIRLEY HUNTER
Entrepreneur, consultant, educator. **Personal:** Born Sep 22, 1940, Macon, GA; daughter of E Willie Hunter Sr; married Charlie Haskins Smith, Jul 30, 1972 (deceased); children: David Asher. **Educ:** Morris Brown Col, BS, 1962; Fisk Univ, Nat Sci Found, MS, 1967; City Col New York, prof dipl, 1972; NY Univ, PhD, 1983; Hunter Col/CUNY, MS, 2001; Columbia Univ Bus Sch, exec mgt not-for-profit cert prog, 2001-02; Harvard Univ, Col Admissions Inst, 2003. **Career:** Carver High Sch, Columbus, GA,

physics/gen sci teacher, 1962-66; Morris Brown Col, Atlanta, GA, asst prof, sci ed, asst dir teacher training, 1967-68; IS 201, NY, gen sci teacher, 1969-74; NY Pub Schs, asst prin/teacher, 1974-88; NYC Bd Educ, Central Bd, Off Appeals & Reviews, hearing officer, 1988-92; Medgar Evers Col/CUNY, dir SEEK, 1993-95; Hostos Community Col/CUNY, asst dir coun, 1995-97; Bronx Community Col/CUNY, dir coun & col discovery, 1997-99; NJ Pub Schs, asst supdt, dir sci, 1999-2000; US Dept Educ, Settlement Col Readiness Trio, dir/consult, currently; Sch Admin & Supervision/Training Prins, assoc adjunct; UFT Teacher's Ctr; SUNY/Stony Brook; Col New Rochelle. **Orgs:** Delta Sigma Theta Sorority, Inc; Am Coun Asn; Kappa Delta Pi; Nat Sci Teachers Asn; AAAS; NY Acad Scis; Black Psychologist Inst, NYC, dir Clinic Educ; Jack & Jill Am Inc; Asn Supervision & Curric Develop; Am Asn Univ Women; Phi Delta Kappa; NACAC; NASACAC; bd trustees, UMEZ; Manhattan/Bronx Mental Health Coun; co-chair, Youth Comn, Community Bd #2 Manhattan; mentor, Int House Women in Leadership; United Univ Profs; NYS comnr, Educ Parent Adv; bd mem, Lewis H Latimer Fund; Manhattan Borough Pres's Educ Adv Panel. **Honors/Awds:** Ford Found Col Fac Fel, 1968-70; Cited in 104th Session, US Cong Record, 1995; NY City's Mayor's Award for Volunteers, CASA, 1998; NY City-Wide Headstart Policy Coun, Community Rep Award, 1998; NY State Dept Educ, Comnr appointed SURR review team, 1999; US Dept Educ, reader, proposals grant funding, 1999; CORO Leadership, NY, 2000-01. **Special Achievements:** Published: Survey of Recruiting: Employment Practices at Western Electric Co", NYC, Aug 1968; "Public Assistance Comprehensive Educ" ERIC/UCLA, June 1998; "Three Year College Discovery Plan for the Millenium" ERIC/UCLA, Sept 1998; "Career and Placement Services Survey" ERIC/UCLA Clearinghouse Comm Colleges, Oct 1998; "Student Devel: Restructuring for Bronx 2000" ERIC/Univ NC, Greensboro, Oct 1998. **Business Addr:** Director/Consultant, Settlement College Readiness, Washington Houses Community Center, 98th St & 3rd Ave, New York, NY 10029, **Business Phone:** (212)828-6138.

SMITH, SHIRLEY LAVERNE
Government official, manager. **Personal:** Born Apr 2, 1951, Midlothian, VA; daughter of Walter and Thelma Draper. **Educ:** Va Commonwealth Univ, BS, 1973. **Career:** Internal Revenue Serv, clerk/tax examiner, 1974-79, tax rep/tax specialist, 1979-81, EEO specialist, 1981-84, EEO officer, 1984-88, recruitment coordr, 1988-92, personnel mgt specialist, 1992-94, IRS Workers Compensation Ctr, mgr, 1994, chief, currently. **Orgs:** NE Region Undergrad Chap Coor Sigma Gamma Rho, 1986-88; Nat Coun Negro Women; NE regional dir, 1988-92, int secy, 1992-94, grand anti-grammateus, Sigma Gamma Rho Sorority, 1992-; int bd dirs, Sigma Gamma Rho Sorority, 1986-92; Federally Employed Women; Int Training Commun Clubs; Urban League Guild; YWCA; Nat Asn Advan Colored People; Richmond Jazz Soc; Asn Improv Minorities-IRS. **Honors/Awds:** IRS Communication Award, 1981; IRS Performance Award, 1984; Nat Achievement Award, Sigma Gamma Rho Sorority, 1984; Certificate of Apppreciation, Richmond Urban League, 1982 & 1984; Certificate of Apppreciation, NE Region Sigma Gamma Rho Sorority, 1984; Richmond Youth Serv Recognition Award, 1985; IRS Performance Award, 1987-. **Home Addr:** 14421 Tanager Wood Trail, Midlothian, VA 23114. **Business Addr:** Chief, Internal Revenue Service, 1111 Constitution Ave Nw, Washington, DC 20224, **Business Phone:** (202)622-5000.

SMITH, STANLEY G.
Lawyer, manager. **Personal:** Born Jul 21, 1940, Brooklyn, NY; married Ruth Grey; children: Craig, Carl. **Educ:** Seton Hall Univ, JD, 1970; Rutgers Univ, BA, Acct. **Career:** Fed Prog Newark Housing Develop Corp, atty; RCA, 1964-68; Fidelity Union & Trust Co, fed asst, code enforcer, financial analyst, 1968-70; City Newark, NJ, asst corp coun, 1972; Seton Hall Univ Sch Law, prof; Newark Housing Develop & Rehabilitation Corp, pres, chief exec officer; Lofton Lester & Smith, atty law partner, 1985; Urban Develop Res Inc, pres; Smith & Forbes, atty, currently. **Orgs:** Nat Bar Asn; concerned legal asn mem, bd dirs, Neighbourhood Health Serv Corp, 1972; bd dirs, Voice Newspaper, 1971-72; vpres, Phi Sigma Delta 1960; New Jersey State Bar Asn, 1990-91. **Honors/Awds:** State Scholarship, Rutgers Univ, 1957; Honarary Scholarship, NJ Bell Elks Club. **Business Addr:** Attorney, Smith & Forbes, 1032 S Ave Suite 242, Plainfield, NJ 07062, **Business Phone:** (908)755-0001.*

SMITH, STEVEN DELANO
Basketball player, broadcaster, executive. **Personal:** Born Mar 31, 1969, Highland Park, MI; son of Donald Smith and Clara Bell Smith; married Millie; children: Brayden & Davis. **Educ:** Mich State Univ, attended 1991. **Career:** Miami Heat, guard, 1991-94, 2004-05; Atlanta Hawks, 1995-99, announcer, currently; Portland Trail Blazers, 1999-2001; San Antonio Spurs, 2001-03; New Orleans Hornets, 2003-04; Charlotte Bobcats, 2004-05; Fox Sports, color analyst, currently; Steve Smith Scholar Fund, owner, currently. **Orgs:** Bd Dirs, Nat Bd Reading Fundamental; Boys & Girls Club; Nat Alumni Bd Mich State Univ; Nat Develop Bd Mich State Univ. **Honors/Awds:** Miami Heat, Most Valuable Player, 1993; J Walter Kennedy Citizenship Award, 1998; Michigan State University Athletics Hall of Fame, 2001; Joe Dumars Sportsmanship Award, 2002; World Sports Humanitarian Hall of Fame, 2006. **Special Achievements:** Tribute by holding "Steve Smith Day" in September 2001.

SMITH, STEVIN L
Basketball player. **Personal:** Born Jan 24, 1972, Dallas, TX. **Educ:** Ariz State Univ, attended 1994. **Career:** Turkey, prof basketball player; France, prof basketball player; Continental Basketball Asn, prof basketball player; Dallas Mavericks, guard, 1996-97; France League, 2000-03; Israeli League, 2004; MBC Dynamo Moscow, Russia, 2005-06; Italian Serie A League, Legea Scafati, 2006-07; PBC Lukoil Akademik Sophia, 2007-. **Business Addr:** Professional Basketball Player, PBC Lukoil Akademik Sophia, Postoyanstvo 67A, 1111 Sofia, Scafati, Bulgaria.

SMITH, SUNDRA SHEALEY
Health services administrator. **Personal:** Born Feb 9, 1948, Birmingham, AL; daughter of John Shealey (deceased) and Eddie Griggs Harrell; married Marcellus L Jr, Sep 9, 1978; children: Sonja Q & Stephanie M. **Educ:** Tuskegee Inst, Tuskegee AL, BS, 1970; Southern Ill Univ, Carbondale IL, MS, 1973; Univ Ala, Birmingham AL, MPH, 1984. **Career:** Progressive Enterprises, Birmingham, AL, owner, 1976-80; Ala Christian Col, Birmingham, AL, instr, 1981-83; Univ Ala, Sch Pub Health, Birmingham, AL, med researcher, 1982-84; Lawson State Jr Col, Birmingham, AL, instr, 1983-86; Geriatric Med, coordr, 1984-86; Birmingham Reg Plan Comn, Birmingham, AL, mgr, Medicaid Waivers, 1987-90; AIDS Task Force Ala Inc, exec dir. **Orgs:** Nat Asn Negro Bus & Prof Womens Clubs Inc, 1974-; gov, SE Dist; Omicron Omega Chap, Alpha Kappa Alpha Sorority; secy, Birmingham Rose Soc; arbitrator, Birmingham Better Bus Bur, 1981-; Am Pub Health Asn, 1982-; Ala Pub Health Asn, 1986-; Ala Geront Soc, 1986-; Brown & Williamson, Kool Achiever Awards Screening Comt, 1986-89; Birmingham News Adv Bd, 1986-88; Birmingham League Women Voters, 1988. **Honors/Awds:** Club Service Award, Metro Birmingham Club, Nat Asn Negro Business & Prof Women, 1986; Paper Presentation, Southern Geront Asn Mkt, 1986; Service Award, St Marks Episcopal Church, 1987; District Service Award, Nat Asn Negro Bus & Prof Women, 1989; Appreciation Award, Better Bus Bur, 1989. **Home Addr:** 1569 Fairway View Dr, Birmingham, AL 35244, **Home Phone:** (205)985-7360.

SMITH, SYMUEL HAROLD
Executive. **Personal:** Born Jun 1, 1922, Port Tampa City, FL; divorced; children: Cynthia D, Celeste D & Carmen D. **Educ:** St Louis Univ, St Louis, AA, pub admin, 1943; Wash Univ St Louis, BS, Bus Finance, 1961, MS, hosp admin, 1965. **Career:** City St Louis Dept Health, 1950-52; Homer G Phillips Hosp, St Louis, asst adminis, 1952-63; Flint-goodridge Hosp New Orleans, adminis resi & adminis asst, 1964-65; Bronx Muni Hosp Ctr Bronx, asst admin, 1965-66; NY State Dept Health NY, hosp admin consult, 1966-67; Edgecombe Rehab Ctr NY State Narcotic Addiction Control Community NYC, dir, 1967-68; Morisania City Hosp Bronx, exec dir, 1968-74; Wayne Co Gen Hosp Mich, exec dir, 1974-78; Detroit Gen Hosp, dir hosps & Chief exec officer, 1978; Milwaukee Co Inst & Dept WI, dir beginning 1978; ARS-MARK Group Ltd, ceo & founder, 1986-; Group Limited, Sales & Consult, pres, Currently. **Orgs:** Omicron Chap, 1970; Am Hosp Asn; fel, Am Pub Health Asn; Am Col Hosp Admin; Nat Asn Health Serv Execs; vpres, Hosp Exec Club NY; exec comt, Greater Detroit Area Hosp Coun; MI State Arbit Comt; Hosp admin consult, City St Louis MO; NAACP; Gov Coun Pub Gen Hosp; secy, AHA; Cita Chi Eta Phi Sorority Inc. **Honors/Awds:** Cita Morrisania, City Hosp Employees Coun, 1971; cita Morrisania City Hosp Comm Licensed Prac Nurses of NY Inc, 1971; cita Employees of Morrisania City Hosp, 1971. **Special Achievements:** Man of the year, South Bronx NAACP, 1971; author, Contrasting the Virtual Sphere, with Reality an Faith. **Military Serv:** USY SSGT 1943-46. **Home Addr:** 3460 N Dousman, Milwaukee, WI 53212, **Home Phone:** (414)962-1381.

SMITH, TANGELA NICOLE
Basketball player. **Personal:** Born Apr 1, 1977, Chicago, IL. **Educ:** Univ Iowa, cult studies & sports, 1998. **Career:** Sacramento Monarchs, forward, 1998-04; Turkish league crown, Botasspor squad, 2001; Korean league, Shinsegae Coolcats, 2002; Studio 5027,co-owner, currently; Charlotte Sting, forward & ctr, 2005; Phoenix Mercury, forward, currently. **Honors/Awds:** Bronze Medal, US Olympic Festival, 1995; silver Medal, R William Jones Cup, 1997; All Am hon mention, Assoc Press; All Big Ten first team; Big Ten Player of The Year Award, 1998; WNBA All Star Charlotte, 2006. **Business Addr:** Co owner, 5027 Studio, 579 Main Str, Palmetto, GA 30268, **Business Phone:** (770)463-4129.*

SMITH, TARIK
Football player, football coach. **Personal:** Born Apr 16, 1975, Agoura, CA. **Educ:** Univ Calif, Los Angeles. **Career:** Dallas Cowboys, running back, 1998; Concord High Sch, coach.

SMITH, THELMA J
Executive. **Career:** Ill Serv Fed Savings & Loan Asn Chicago, Chicago, Ill, pres, chief exec, 1984-. **Orgs:** Chicago Theol Sem; Community Renewal Soc; bus adv coun, NC Mutual Univ Ill; Chicago Network; Links, Inc, Chicago Chap; Ill Serv Fed Savings & Loan Asn; bd trustees, Chicago Sunday Evening Club; equal opportunity adv coun, Chicago Area Ill Nat Guard & Comm Ctr Influence; bd trustees, Chicago Acad Sci; prin, Chicago United; Union League Club; Congregational Church Park Manor. **Honors/Awds:** Black Rose Award, 1989; Top Ladies Distinction, 1993; Fedn Leadership Award, Ora Higgins Youth Fed, 1993; Lovejoy Award, 1995; Nat Asn Advan Colored People Freedom Fund Dinner Award; Black Book's Nat Bus & Prof Award; Top 100 Black Business & Prof Women's Award, Dollars & Sense Mag. **Special Achievements:** Bank listed 14 on Black Enterprise's list of top African American-owned banks, 1998. **Business Addr:** President, Chief Executive Officer, Illinois Service Federal S&L Association, 4619 S King Dr, Chicago, IL 60653, **Business Phone:** (773)624-2000.

SMITH, THOMAS LEE, JR.
Football player. **Personal:** Born Dec 5, 1970, Gates, NC. **Educ:** Univ NC. **Career:** Football player(retired), Buffalo Bills, defensive back, 1993-99; Chicago Bears, 2000; Indianapolis Colts, 2001.

SMITH, DR. TOMMIE
Athlete, lecturer, activist. **Personal:** Born Jun 6, 1944, Clarksville, TX; son of Richard and Dora Smith; married Delois Jordan. **Educ:** San Jose State Univ, BA, soc sci, MA, sociol, hon doctorate, alma mater,2005; MS, phys educ & soc. **Career:** Athlete (retired), football player, lectr; Cincinnati Bengals, wide receiver; Prof Athlete, sprinter; Santa Monica Col, fac mem; Delo 2K Enterprise, educr & lectr, currently. **Honors/Awds:** Top ranked 200-m, 220-yds Man in the World Track & Field News 1967-68;World Olympic Record Mexico City 1968; Olympic Gold Medalist, sprinter, 1968; California Black Sports Hall of Fame, 1996; Bay Area Hall of Fame, 1999; Sportsman of the Millennium Award, 1999; inductee, Bay Area Hall of Fame, 1999; inductee, San Jose State University Sports Hall of Fame, 1999; Commendation, Recognition and Proclamation Awards, 2000-01; Honorary Doctorate Degree, Humane Letters, San Jose State University, 2005. **Special Achievements:** Silent gesture is captured in the HBO TV documentary: Fists of Freedom,1999. Held more world records simultaneously (11) than any other athletein track & field Hist San Jose State Univ; Still holds World Track & FieldRecords in 3 individual events; Currently working on book to precede movieof his life. **Home Phone:** (818)618-0553. **Business Addr:** Educator, Lecturer, DELO2K Enterprises, PO Box 870010, Stone Mountain, GA 30087, **Business Phone:** (818)618-0553.*

SMITH, TOMMIE M
President (Organization). **Personal:** Born Jun 19, 1919, Pulaski, TN; married Eugene W; children: Joe W London. **Educ:** Univ Louisville, 12 Hrs "Sucessful Mgmt Indpendent Bus". **Career:** President (retired) Tommie's Health Salon Inc, pres, 1989. **Orgs:** Chmn, Voter Regist NAACP, 1963-64; Am Massage & Therapy Assoc Inc, 1965; chair, Political Action Comt NAACP, 1972-76; precinct capt 141-A, 1974-84; comn KY Colonel, 1974; life mem NAACP; mem River City Bus & Prof Club 1977; Older Women's League 1982; pres, KY Chap Massage Therapy Asn, 1983-87. **Honors/Awds:** Cert of Merits & Apprections Louisville Urban League Comn Vol Serv, 1961, Ketuckiana Recruiting Serv, 1971, Jefferson Cty Bd Ed, 1974, Govnr Comn State Health Planning Coun; Woman Achievement River City Bus & Prof Women's Club, 1979; Achiever Award Achievers AKA, 1980; Black Women for Political Action Award, 1986; Jefferson County Democrat Award, 1986. **Special Achievements:** first black owners of health salon in Louisville, Ky; first black mem Better Bus Bureau 1965; first black chairman 33rd Legislative District Dem, 1984.

SMITH, TONI COLETTE (TONI COLETTE SMITH-ALSTON)
Government official. **Personal:** Born Oct 31, 1952, Columbus, OH. **Educ:** Ohio State Univ, BA, 1974, mgt courses; Ohio State Univ, Columbus, attended 1976; Univ Dayton, MS, 1993. **Career:** Ohio State Human Servs, consult, 1974-75; Franklin County Human Servs, caseworker, 1976-79, supvr, 1979-86, adminr, 1986-91, asst dep dir, dep dir; Columbus State Community Col, instr, 1990-91; Human Servs, dep dir, 1996-; Best, Inc, bus consult & vpres, 1998-; Tex Lottery Comn, mkt dir, 2000-. **Orgs:** Corresponding secy, Am Asn Univ Women, 1988-; vpres, Berwick Civic Asn, 1989-91, pres, 1991-; pres, exec bd, Syntaxis Residential Care for Youth, 1990-92, 1996-98; admis exec bd, United Way, 1990-. **Honors/Awds:** Franklin County Human Servs, SUV Year, 1983. **Home Addr:** 6740 Temperance Point St, Westerville, OH 43082. **Business Addr:** Market Director, Texas Lottery Commission, 6740 Temperance Pt St, Westerville, OH 43082, **Business Phone:** (614)891-6645.

SMITH, TONY
Basketball player. **Personal:** Born Jun 14, 1968, Wauwatosa, WI. **Educ:** Marquette Univ, Milwaukee, WI, attended 1990. **Career:** Basketball player (retired); Los Angeles Lakers, 1990-95; Miami Heat, 1995-96; Phoenix Suns, 1996; Miami Heat, 1996; Charlotte Hornets, 1997; Milwaukee Bucks, 1998; Atlanta Hawks, guard, 2000-01; Phoenix Eclipse, 2002. **Honors/Awds:** Marquette's Hall of Fame, 2006.

SMITH, TORRANCE
Football player. **Personal:** Born Sep 4, 1970, Tampa, FL; married Denise; children: Kayla. **Educ:** Alcorn State Univ. **Career:** New

Orleans Saints, wide receiver, 1992-96; St Louis Rams, 1997; Indianapolis Colts, 1998; Philadelphia Eagles, 1999-.

SMITH, TREVOR, JR. See RHYMES, BUSTA.

SMITH, TUBBY (ORLANDO SMITH)
Basketball coach. **Personal:** Born Jun 30, 1951, Scotland, MD; married Donna; children: GG, Saul & Brian. **Educ:** High Point Col, BS, health & phys educ, 1973. **Career:** Va Commonwealth Univ, asst coach, 1979-86; Univ SC, asst coach, 1986-89; Univ KY, 1989-91; Univ Tulsa, men's basketball coach, 1991-95; Univ GA, men's basketball coach, 1995-97; Univ KY, head basketball coach, 1997-2007; Univ MN, Golden Gophers, head coach, 2007-. **Honors/Awds:** Henry Iba Award, 2003; Naismith Col Coach of the Year, 2003; Jim Phelan Coach of the Year, 2005. **Special Achievements:** First African American head coach at the Univ GA-Athens; guided the Univ Tulsa's Golden Hurricane to the Sweet 16 in the NCAA men's basketball tournament; first African American coach at the Univ KY; first African American & first rookie coach to win a championship at KY.

SMITH, VASCO A.
Commissioner, association executive. **Personal:** Born Aug 24, 1920, Harvard, AR; son of Florence E and Rev Vasco A; married Georgia Maxine Atkins; children: Vasco A III. **Educ:** LeMoyne Col, BS, 1941; Meharry Med Col, DDS, 1945; TN Bapt Sch Religion, LHD, 1978; Tex Col, ScD, 1983; LeMoyne-Owen Col, DSc, 1992. **Career:** Commissioner (retired), Association executive; pvt pract, dentist 1946-95; Memphis Br Nat Asn Advan Colored People, bd mem, 1955; Tri-State Bank Memphis, bd mem, 1970-, bd dirs, currently; Shelby Co Govt, comnr, 1972-95. **Honors/Awds:** Merit Award, Nat Asn Advan Colored People, 1961; Citizen of Yr, Omega Psi Phi Frat, 1968; Leadership Award, IBPOE of W, 1969; Citation Mallory Knights, 1969; Pres Award, Meharry Med Col, 1970; Achievement Award, OIC, 1973; Citation Cong Record, 1975; Pub Serv Award, Memphis Urban League, 1975; Merit Award, Tenn A&I Univ, 1979; Civil Rights Award, Nat Dental Asn, 1980; Merit Award, W Tenn, 1980. **Military Serv:** USAF, capt, 1953-55. **Home Addr:** 1208 E Pkwy S, Memphis, TN 38114, **Home Phone:** (901)454-9825. **Business Addr:** Board of Directors, Tri State Bank of Memphis, 180 S Main St, Memphis, TN 38103, **Business Phone:** (901)525-0384.*

SMITH, VERNEL HAP
Government official. **Personal:** Born Nov 12, 1924, Waycross, GA; divorced; children: Randy & Kevin. **Educ:** Ohio State Univ, BS, MA. **Career:** US & Overseas Social Welfare, admin, lectr, teacher, trainer; City Oakland, CA, mgr recreation serv, 1966-74, dir off pk & recreation, 1974-. **Honors/Awds:** Outstanding & Dedicated Service Award, Nat Recreation & Pk Asn Ethnic Minority Soc, 1984.

SMITH, VERNICE CARLTON
Football player. **Personal:** Born Oct 24, 1965, Orlando, FL; married Era; children: Alexandria, Vernice Jr & Mitchell. **Educ:** Fla A&M Univ. **Career:** Phoenix Cardinals, ctr, 1990-92; Chicago Bears, 1993; Wash Redskins,1993-95; St Louis Rams, 1997.

SMITH, VERNON G
State government official. **Personal:** Born Apr 11, 1944, Gary, IN; son of Albert J and Julia E; married Phoebe Downs. **Educ:** IN Univ, BS, 1966, MS, 1969, EdD, elem educ & elem admin, 1978, post-doctoral work, 1990. **Career:** Gary Urban League's Oper Jobs, asst dir, 1966; Gary, IN Pub Sch Syst, teacher, 1966-71, resource teacher, 1971-72; OEO's Oper Sparkle, asst dir, 1967; John Will Anderson Boys Clb, staff asst, 1967-68; Ivanhoe Sch Gary, IN, asst prin, 1972-78; City Gary, IN, 4th dist councilman, 1972-90; Nobel Sch Gary, IN, prin, 1978-85; Williams Sch Gary IN, prin, 1985; Ind House Rep, rep, 1990-; Ind Univ Northwest, adj prof, 1992, assoc prof educ, currently. **Orgs:** Pres & tres, Gary Downtown Merchants Asn; Gary Brnch NAACP; IN Univ Alumni Asn; mega Psi Phi Frat; founder & pres, IU Gents Inc; founder & pres, IU Dons Inc; founder & sponsor, Focus Hope; founder & sponsor Young Citizens League; founder sponsor, Youth Ensuring Solidarity; Phi Delta Kappa Frat; pres, Gary Comt Mental Health Bd; deacon, trustee, & teacher, Pilgrim Baptist Church; pres, Gary Common Coun, 1976, 1983-84, vpres, 1985, pres, 1986; chmn, Gary, IN, City-wide Festivals Comt Inc; Handgun Control Inc; Gary Reading Coun-IN State Reading Asn; IN Asn Sch Principals; founder, Northern IN Asn Black Sch Educrs; founder & bd pres, African-Amn Achievers Youth Corps Inc; bd trustees, Criminal Justice Inst; Gov's Comn Drug Free IN; chmn, IN Comn Social Status Black Males; founder & sponsor, Vernon Stars. **Honors/ Awds:** Omega Psi Phi 10th Dist Citizen of Year, 1972, 1989; Omega Man Year, 1974; Gary Jaycees, Good Govt Award, 1977; Club FAB Outstndg Achvmnt citation Ebony mag most eligible bachelor, 1977; Club FAB Outstndg Achvmnt Citation, 1978; Gary Downtown Merchants Businessman of Year Award, 1979; Young Democrat's outstanding Service Award, 1979; Mahalia Jackson Special Achievement Award, 1980; Alpha Chi Chap Citizen of Year Award, Omega Psi Phi, 1980; Appreciation Award, Gary Community Mental Health Ctr, 1981; GOIC Dr Leon H Sullivan Award, 1982; Youth Award, 1983; Outstanding Citizen of NW IN & Outstanding Educ Award, Info Newspaper, 1984; Blaine Marz Tap Award, Post Tribune, 1984; 10th Year Service Award, 1985; Focus Hope Dedication in Action Award, 1987; Gary Educator for Christ Administrator Leadership Award, 1988; Omega Psi Phi Citizen of the Year, 10th District, 1989; Froebel High Scl Alumni Appreciation Award; Phi Delta Kappa Northwest IN Chapter 25 Year Award; IU Northwest Alumni Asn Chiefs Police Appreciation Award; Methodist Hosp Child & Adolescent Prog Mr G's Service Award; IUSAA Founding Member Award; Gary Community Schs Presenter's Award; Omega Psi Phi's Omicron Rho Appreciation Award, 1991; IU Northwest Alumni Asn Chiefs Police Appreciation Award; Methodist Hosp Child & Adolescent Prog Appreciation Award; Brothers Keeper Appreciation Award; IN Asn Elem & Middle Schl Principals Service Award, 1992; Northwest IN Black Expo's Senator Carolyn Mosby Above & Beyond Award, 1995; Gary Community Sch Corp, Parent Involvement Program Presenters Award; Nat Coun Negro Women In The Bethune Tradition Award, 1996; Froebel High Scl Alumni Appreciation Award; IN Chapt Nat Asn Social Workers, Citizen of the Year; Pittman Square Sch Appreciation Award, 1997; recipient of over 125 awards & citations. **Home Addr:** 4333 Broadway, Gary, IN 46409, **Home Phone:** (219)887-2046. **Business Addr:** State Representative, Indiana House of Representatives, 200 W Washington St, Indianapolis, IN 46204, **Business Phone:** (317)232-9600.

SMITH, VIDA J
Meeting planner. **Personal:** Born in Lynchburg, VA; daughter of Leo Jones and Mary. **Educ:** Central State Univ, 1976; Univ Dist Columbia. **Career:** Nat Black Media Coalition, dir, black radio projects/meeting planner; Delta Sigma Theta, meeting planner, currently. **Orgs:** NCBMP; GWSAE; Nat Coalition Black Meeting Planners; ASAE. **Honors/Awds:** Meeting Planner of the Year, Coalition of Black Meeting Planners, 1996; Meeting Prof To Watch, Convention South mag, 2001, 2003. **Business Addr:** Meeting Planner, Delta Sigma Theta Sorority, 1707 New Hampshire Ave NW, Washington, DC 20009, **Business Phone:** (202)986-2400.

SMITH, VINSON ROBERT
Football player, broadcaster. **Personal:** Born Jul 3, 1965, Statesville, NC; married Anne Oliver; children: Jayme, Payton & Christian. **Educ:** E Carolina, BS, commun, 1989. **Career:** Football player (retired), Broadcaster; Atlanta Falcons, linebacker, 1988; Dallas Cowboys, 1990-92, 1997; Chicago Bears, 1993-96; New Orleans Saints, 1998-99; JPC LOC, owner, currently; Game Day broadcaster, currently. **Orgs:** Big Brothers & Big Sisters; United Way. **Honors/Awds:** Ed Block Award, Nat Football League; Most Valuable Player, New Orleans Saints, 1998; College Most Valuable Player, 1986, 1987.

SMITH, VIRGIL CLARK
Judge. **Personal:** Born Jul 4, 1947, Detroit, MI; son of Virgil Columbus and Eliza Boyer; married Elizabeth Little; children: Virgil Kai, Adam Justin & Anthony Langdon. **Educ:** Mich State Univ, BA, Polit Sci, 1969; Wayne State Law, JD, 1972. **Career:** Justice Wade McCree US Appeals Ct, stud clerk; Wayne Co Legal Servs, legal adv, 1972-73; Model Cities Drug Clinic; Corporations Coun City Detroit; Mich House Reps, state rep, 1977-88; Mich State Senate, sen, Dem flleader, 1988-2001; The Third Judicial Circuit Mich, Family Div Juv Sect, presiding judge, chief judge, 2009-. **Orgs:** Former finance, Family Law, Criminal Law & Corrections, and Reapportionment Cmtes; Law Revision Cmsn; Legislative Black Caucus;appropriations, sub committes on Capital Outlay, Regulatory &Transportation; Families Mental Health & Human Svcs, judiciary,legislative Coun. **Honors/Awds:** Legislator of Yr, Police Officers Assn Mich & Mich Judges Assn, 1996. **Business Addr:** Chief Judge, The Third Judicial Circuit Michigan, Juvenile Division Family Division, Lincoln Hall of Justice 1025 E Forest, Detroit, MI 48207, **Business Phone:** (313)224-5261.

SMITH, VIRGINIA M.
Educator. **Personal:** Born May 9, 1929, El Dorado, AR; daughter of Henry Burks and Annie Burks; widowed; children: Marcia Green Hamilton, Gregory Green & Dana Paul Green. **Educ:** Am&N Col, BA, 1950; Univ Ill, MEd, 1955; Univ Ark, attended 1963. **Career:** Educator (retired); Ark Pub Sch, teacher, 1950-60; Southern Univ, asstprof, 1963-65; El Dorado, counr, 1965-70; Henderson State Univ, personneldean, 1971-81, dir spec serv disadvantaged stud, 1982-86; Ark Baptist Col,teacher, admin asst pres, 1986-95. **Orgs:** Local Bd Church Women United, 1998; mem, bd dir, Clark Co Community Found, 2002; mem chmn, Clark Co Retired Teachers Asn, 2002; Delta Sigma Theta; Nat Asn Advan Colored People; Arka delphia Women's Develop Coun; life mem, UAPB Alumni Asn. **Honors/Awds:** Teacher of the Year, Ark Baptist Col, 1989-90. **Special Achievements:** First black staff member in Henderson St University, 1971. **Home Addr:** 110 S Austin, PO Box 274, Arkadelphia, AR 71923, **Home Phone:** (870)246-3240.

SMITH, VOYDEE
Banker. **Personal:** Born Feb 14, 1949, Barton, FL; son of Voydee and Fannie Colson; married Saundra Johnson, Jan 23, 1981; children: Daryl, Allen, Eric, Jason & Steven. **Educ:** NC AT&T State Univ, BS, 1973. **Career:** US Dept Treasury, asst bank examr, Off Controller Currency, nat bank examr, 1973-85; IDL Bank Wash, sr vpres, loan admin, 1985-95; Consolidated Bank & Trust Co, sr vpres & loan adminr, 1995-. **Orgs:** IDL Bank, mgt comt, 1986, Loan Officers Comn, chmn, 1985, loan & discount comt, 1985; Wash Area Bankers Asn, 1987; Nat Bankers Asn, 1989; bd mem, Richmond Metrop Bus League. **Business Addr:** Senior Vice President, Loan Administrator, Consolidated Bank & Trust Company, 320 N 1st St, Richmond, VA 23240, **Business Phone:** (804)771-5200.

SMITH, REV. DR. WALLACE CHARLES
Clergy, educator. **Personal:** Born Nov 6, 1948, Philadelphia, PA; married G Elaine Williams; children: Christen Ann. **Educ:** Villanova Univ, BA 1970; Eastern Bapt Sem, MDiv, 1974; Eastern Bapt Sem, DMin, 1979. **Career:** Calvary Baptist Church, Chester, PN, minister, 1974-85; Eastern Baptist Sem, dir alumni affairs & asst dir field educ, 1979-; Prog Nat Baptism, home mission bd, 1979; Eastern Baptist Theological Sem, asst prof practical theology, 1979-85; First Baptist Church-Capitol Hill, Nashville, TN, minister, 1985-91; Vanderbilt Divinity Sch Practice Ministry, prof, 1988-91; Shiloh Baptist Church, Wash, DC, pastor, 1991-, sr minister, currently. **Orgs:** Exec bd, Chester Br NAACP, 1974-; pres, Chester Clergy Asn, 1977-79; pres, Chester Comm Improvement Proj, 1979-; mem bd, Eastern Baptist Sem; Gen Coun Baptist World Alliance; chmn, Spl Comn Baptists Against Racism; 1994 Class Leadership Wash; bd mem, Interfaith Coun Wash Vicinity, United Black Fund Nat Capitol Area United Way, Adv Bd Riggs Nat Bank; chmn, Proj Koinonia DC Baptist Convention; Progressive Nat Baptist Convention, USA, Inc; trustee, Bd Home Missions. **Honors/Awds:** Distinguished Community Service Award, Anti-Defamation League B'nai Brith, 1994; Honorary doctorate, Alderson-Broaddus Univ W Va, 1997. **Special Achievements:** Contributing editor of The Pulpit Digest, has written numerous articles, including guest editorials for the Washington Post, is the author of a book, The Church in the Life of the Black Family, published by Judson Press, Valley Forge, Pennsylvania. **Business Addr:** Pastor, Senior Minister, Shiloh Baptist Church, 1507 9th St NW, Washington, DC 20001-3318, **Business Phone:** (202)232-4200.

SMITH, DR. WALTER L
Educator. **Personal:** Born May 14, 1935, Tampa, FL; children: John, Andre, Salesia & Walter II. **Educ:** Gibbs Jr Col, AA; Fla A&M Univ, BA, biol & chem, 1963, MEd, admin & supv, 1966; Fla State Univ, PhD, higher educ admin, 1974. **Career:** Educator (retired); Nat Educ Asn, assoc regional dir, 1969-70; Fla Educ Asn, admin asst, 1970, asst exec secy, 1970-73; Hillsborough Community Col, colegium dir, 1973, dean employee rels, 1973-74, provost, 1974; Roxbury Community Col, pres, 1974-77; Fla A&M Univ, pres, 1977-85; Univ Malarui, Chancellor Col, Nat Championship Team, head baseball coach, 1985-86; Univ Fla, vis prof, 1995-2002; Educ Develop S Africa, int team leader; Funda Community Col, S Africa, founding rector. **Orgs:** Chairperson, Fla Supreme Ct Judicial Nominating Comt, 1980-83; bd dir, Am Asn State Col & Univs, 1980-83; chmn, State Bd Educ Adv Comn, 1982-85; bd dirs, Nat Asn Equal Opportunity HE, 1982-84; Fla Supreme Ct Article V Comn, 1983; US Dept Interior, 1984; Urban League, 1992-95. **Honors/Awds:** Red-X Award Cape Kennedy, Int Bus Mach Corp, 1966; Scholarly Distinction Award, Nat Urban League, 1974; Meritorious Service Award, Am Asn State Col & Univs, 1984; Jackson Memorial Award, Asn Classroom Teachers, 1984; Fulbright Senior Scholar, 1985; President's Award, Nat Conf Black Mayors. **Military Serv:** AUS, sp-5, 3 yrs; Good Conduct Medal, 1953-56; President Achievement Award, 1999; Commendation Medal; Nat Defense Medal. **Home Addr:** 1940 Cypress St, Tampa, FL 33606.

SMITH, WAYMAN F, III
Executive, vice president (organization). **Personal:** Born Jun 18, 1940, St Louis, MO; son of Wayman Flynn and Edythe; married; children: Kymberly Ann. **Educ:** Wash Univ, 1957-59; Monmouth Col, BS, 1962; Howard Univ, JD, 1965. **Career:** Executive, vice president (retired); Mo Comn Human Rights, dir concilliation, 1966-68; Law Firm Wilson Smith Smith & McCullin, partner, 1969; St Louis City Coun, three-term alderman; City St Louis, munic ct judge, 1973-75; Anheuser-Busch Companies Inc, vpres corp affairs, 1980-2000. **Orgs:** Bd alderman, City St Louis, 1975-; bd dirs, Anheuser-Busch Companies Inc, 1981-00; coordr, Lou Rawls Parade Stars fund-raising telethon which benefits The United Negro College Fund; bd admis, US Dist Ct Eastern Dist Mo; ABA; Nat Bar Assoc; Mound City Bar Assoc; Bar Asn Metro St Louis; bd trustees, Howard Univ. **Honors/Awds:** Distinguished Alumni Award, Howard Univ & Monmouth Col, 1983. **Home Addr:** 3910 Lindell Blvd, Saint Louis, MO 63108. *

SMITH, WAYNE FRANKLIN
Association executive. **Personal:** Born Feb 17, 1951, Providence, RI; married Debra Petrarca; children: Marah Elizabeth Ann. **Educ:** BA, 1977. **Career:** Vietnam Veteran Readjustment Coun Ctr, counr; Vietnam Veterans Am, dir mem, 1987-91; Vietnam Veterans Mem Fund, dir develop, 1991-; Black Revolutionary War Patriots Found, pres; Black Patriots Found Inc, exec dir, pres; human rights advocate, currently. **Orgs:** Bd dirs, Nat Veterans Legal Serv Proj; bd dirs, Friends Vietnam Veterans Mem; bd dirs, Vietnam Veterans Am Found; Nat Asn Advan Colored People.

Special Achievements: Vietnam Veterans of America Foundation, co-recipient of Nobel Peace Prize, 1997; guest appearances on numerous telvesion news and radio programs, including CBS News, ABC News, NBC Nightly News, C-SPAN, CNN, BBC, and National Public Radio; subject in documentaries "Black American Participation in the US Military"; "Fields of Armor and Race Relations During the Vietnam War". **Military Serv:** AUS Med Corp, spec 4, 1968-71; Combat Medic Badge; Army Commendation Medal, Vietnamese Cross of Gallantry, Vietnam Campaign.

SMITH, WILL
Actor, singer, movie producer. **Personal:** Born Sep 25, 1968, Philadelphia, PA; son of Willard Sr and Caroline; married Sheree Zampino, May 9, 1992 (divorced 1995); children: Willard III; married Jada Pinkett, Dec 31, 1997; children: Jaden & Willow Camille Reign. **Career:** Actor, producer, writer, dir & singer; Member duo DJ Jazzy Jeff & the Fresh Prince, 1986; Albums include: Rock the House, 1987, 1989; He's the DJ, I'm the Rapper, 1988; Andin This Corner,1989; Homebase, 1991; Solorapper: Big Willie Style, 1997; Willennium, 2000; Lost & Found, 2005; Actor, Seven Pounds, 2008; Hancock, 2008; Producer: Show Time, exec producer, 2002; Ride or Die, exec producer,2003; "All of Us", exec producer, 2003-07; Saving Face, 2004; The Seat Filler, exec producer, 2004; ATL, 2006; Films: Where the Day Takes You,1992; Made in America, 1993; Six Degrees of Separation, 1993; Bad Boys,1995; Independence Day, 1996, Men in Black, 1997; Enemy of the State,1998; Wild Wild West, 1999; Welcome to Hollywood, 2000; The Legend of Bagger Vance, 2000; America: A Tribute to Heroes, 2001; Ali, 2001; Men in Black 2, 2002; Bad Boys II, 2003; I, Robot, exec producer, 2004; Hitch, producer, 2005; The Pursuit of Happyness, producer, 2006; I Am Legend, 2007; Hancock, producer, 2008. **Honors/Awds:** Grammy Award; Numerous honors and awards including 2 Oscar nominations, 3 ASCAP awards,3 Blockbuster Entertainment awards, 4 Blimp awards, 2 Teen Choice awards,People's Choice award and Razzie award. **Special Achievements:** First hip-hop artist to be nominated for an Academy Award. **Business Phone:** (310)288-4545.

SMITH, WILLIAM FRED
Manager. **Personal:** Born Mar 22, 1938, Savannah, GA. **Educ:** Savannah State Col; Calif State Univ. **Career:** Manager (retired); Litton Guidance & Control Sys, mgr, affirmative action, 1972-76; EEO Computer Sci Corp, corp mgr, 1976-78; Litton Date Syst, mgr affirmative, 1978-80; Bunker Ramo Corp, mgr personnel, 1980; Contel Federal Syts, dir, human resources, 1986-91; GTE, dir, human resources, 1991-94. **Orgs:** Valley Pref Employee Comm; Kappa Alpha Psi Frat; PMAA; LA Basin EEO; Nat Asn Advan Colored People; Employ Mgt Asn; Soc for Human Resources Mgt; bd dir, Westlake Village Chamber Com; Nat Employee Serv & Recreation Asn; Human Relation Comn; West Covina City, 1970-74; Aerospace indust, EEO Comn, 1970-93; personnel mgt asn, Aztian, 1974-93; Soc for Human Resources Mgt, 1980-94; Calif Chap Family Motor Coach Asn, 1980-; Employ Mgt Asn, 1984-; JTPC/Private Indust Coun, Ventura Co, CA, 1987-94; community police adv bd, Los Angeles Police Depart, 1994-; adv bd, Thousand Trails NACO/Leisure Time, 2001-. **Honors/Awds:** Selective syst bd mem adv appointed by Pres, 1971; Community Service Award, 1971; Community Service Award, Los Angeles Co Human Relations Comn, 1972; National Media Women Communication Award, 1973; appointed to Calif Gov Comm Employ Handicapped, 1978; San Fernando Concerned Black Womens Award, 1979; invited to White House by Pres Carter, 1980; Society of Black Engineers, Calif State Univ Northridge, 1980. **Home Addr:** 10611 Ledeen Dr, Lake View Terrace, CA 91342.

SMITH, WILLIAM FRENCH (DAP SMITTY)
Engineer. **Personal:** Born Nov 30, 1941, Bay City, TX; son of William Sr and Willie Mae Perry; married Sylvia Knight, Feb 4, 1977; children: William III & Maurice. **Educ:** Tuskegee Univ, BS, 1964; Wash Univ, St Louis, MO, Grad Study, 1970. **Career:** Boeing Co, Huntsville, AL, equipment engr, 1964-67; McDonnell Douglas Corp, St Louis, MO, plant design engr, 1967-69; St Louis County Govt, project engr, 1969-72; E I DuPont de Nemours & Co Inc, div engr, Wilmington, DE & Victoria, TX, 1972-74; Westinghouse Corp, Millburn, NJ, engineering mgr, 1974-76; Denver Pub Schs, building safety engr, 1976-, project adminr, 1977-, energy conservationist, 1978-; Tuskegee Univ, Denver, CO, mgr hazardous materials, 1985-88, environ safety engr, 1988-, safety engr, mgr environ safety, 1992-; Wm French Smith Consulting, chief exec officer, currently. **Orgs:** Bd dir, Denver Opportunity Ind Ctr, 1979-80, Nat Comn Future Regis Col; Mayor's Citizens Adv Comn Energy, 1980-; Am Soc Safety Engrs, Colo Asn Sch Energy Coordrs, Am Asn Blacks Energy, treas, Denver Pub Schs Black Admin & Supvs Asn; Colo Environ Health Asn, Nat Asbestos Coun, Colo Hazardous Waste Mgmt Soc, Colo Hazardous Materials Asn, Nat Asn Minority Contractors, Rocky Mountain Hazardous Materials Asn, Tuskegee Univ Alumni Asn; vpres, Rocky Mountain Poison & Drug Ctr, 1990-; vpres, Hazardous Materials Asn; Colo Emergency Planning Comn; Colo Alliance for Environ Educ; Nat Black Environ Asn; Denver Emergency Planning Comn; Sr Citizens Adv Bd; City Lakewood, CO, bd Appeals; Community Rels Rep Fed Emergency Mgmt Agency; bd mem, Colo Alliance Environ Educ. **Honors/Awds:** Black Engineer of the Year, Career Community Group Inc, 1990, 1991, 1992; Registered Environ Assessor; Certified Environmental Inspector; Juanita Gray Community Service Award; President's Award on Energy Conservation. **Military Serv:** USNR, 1978-80. **Business Addr:** Safety Engineer & Energy Czar, Special Project Manager, Denver Public Schools, 102 S Balsam St, Denver, CO 80226-1344, **Business Phone:** (303)575-4126.

SMITH, WILLIAM GENE
Banker. **Personal:** Born Jan 23, 1955, Windsor, NC; son of James L (deceased) and Mattie S; children: Byron Eugene & Antoine A. **Educ:** NCA Cent Univ, BA, 1977; Univ NC, Sch Banking, mid mgt, 1985. **Career:** First Union, br mgr, 1977-81, asst consumer bank mgr, 1984-85, Durham, consumer bank mgr, 1985-88, Raleigh, consumer bank mgr, 1988-90, regional consumer bank exec, 1990-92, Durham, city area exec, 1992-2001; Mutual Community Savings Bank, pres & chief exec officer, 2001-. **Orgs:** In-Roads, 1986-92; bd mem & treas, NCCU Found, 1990-; treas & bd mem, Wake Opportunities; chmn, NC Cent Univ Bd Trustees; adv bd chair, Nat Asn Urban Bankers; bd mem, Greater Durham Chamber Com; bd mem, Durham Black Achievers Prog; bd mem, United Way; Phi Beta Sigma; Alpha Tan Blvd; 100 Black Men Am. **Honors/Awds:** Consumer Banking Manager of the Year, 1986; Consumer Credit Sales Manager of the Year, First Union Nat Bank, 1993; Outstanding Chapter Member, NC Asn Urban Bankers, 1994; Positive Image Award, Pee Dee Newspaper Group, 1996. **Special Achievements:** Dollars & Sense Magazine, honored as one of Americas Best and Brighest Executive, 1992. **Home Addr:** 2021 Matilene Ave, Durham, NC 27707, **Home Phone:** (919)596-8858. **Business Addr:** President, Chief Executive Officer, Mutual Community Savings Bank, 315 E Chapel Hill St, Durham, NC 27701-3317, **Business Phone:** (919)688-1308.

SMITH, WILLIAM JAMES
Lawyer. **Personal:** Born Mar 5, 1946, Fresno, CA; married Alice; children: Danielle, Nicole. **Educ:** Univ Calif Los Angeles, BA, polit sci, 1968; Univ Calif Los Angeles Sch Law, JD, 1972. **Career:** Trust Admin Union Bank, Univ Calif Los Angeles football; Nat Labor Rels Bd, atty; Brundage Reich & Pappy Labor Spec, atty; Pigford v. Glickman, class coun, currently; W J Smith & Assoc, partner, currently. **Orgs:** Nat Conf Black Lawyers; bd dirs, Black Law Journ; Los Angeles Bar Asn; Calif Bar Asn; Langston Law Club; Pro Bono Cases Labor Law; Col Labor & Employ Lawyers. **Honors/Awds:** Outstanding employ lawyers in Calif, Calif Law Bus. **Business Addr:** 13130 L St Suite E, Fresno, CA.

SMITH, WILLIAM XAVIER
Banker. **Personal:** Born Dec 9, 1934, Livingston, AL; son of Daisy Jones and Elijah; married Cynthia Wright, Jun 1, 1990; children: Molina, Xavier Gerard, Dianna & April. **Educ:** Bryant Col, BS, 1960; AIB basic & standard cert, cert 1974; Univ Wis, Sch Bank Admin, diploma, 1975. **Career:** Liggett Drug Co, jr acct, 1960-62; Wonstop Auto Serv, acct, 1962-63; US Treas Dept, intl revenue agent, 1963-67; GAC Corp, tax research supvr, 1967-70; Unity Bank & Trust, asst treas, 1970-72; Peoples Bank Virgin Islands, vpres cashier, 1972-77; Am State Bank, vpres oper, 1977-82, pres & dir, 1982-; Gateway Nat Bank, St Louis, Mo, pres/dir 1990; Community Bank of the Bay, staff, vpres & compliance officer, currently. **Orgs:** Dir/treas, Boy Scouts Am, Virgin Islands, 1974-77; pres, Greenwood Chamber Comn, 1984-; dir, Tulsa Comn Action Agency, 1985-; dir, Monsanto, YMCA, St Louis, Mo, 1991-. **Military Serv:** USAF, airman first class, 1954-57. **Home Phone:** (314)367-6916. **Business Addr:** Vice President, Compliance Officer, Community Bank of the Bay, 1750 Broadway, Oakland, CA 94612, **Business Phone:** (510)433-5403.

SMITH, WILLIE B
Educator. **Personal:** Born Mar 30, 1941, Doddsville, MS; daughter of Cato Willis and Flora; married Reubin, Dec 25, 1975; children: Wilton Reubin. **Educ:** MS Valley State Univ, BS, elem educ, 1961; Delta State Univ, MEd, elem educ, elem supervision, 1969; AL A&M, adult educ cert, 1976. **Career:** Caohoma Community Col, basic adult teacher; Ruleville Cent High Sch, teacher, 1961-67; Friars Point Elem Sch, teacher, 1967-91; New Bethel HOP, teacher, 1998-. **Orgs:** NAACP, 1972-91; sunday sch teacher, New Bethel Baptist Church, 1976-00; prog comt, chair, Delta Sigma Theta Sorority, 1996-; jr matron, Heroines of Jericho, 1986-00; vpres, Women Missionary Society, 1998-00. **Honors/Awds:** School Spirit Award, Delta Indust Inst Sch, Honor Award Valedictorian, 1958; OETA Awards, Outstanding Elem Teachers Am, Washington, DC, 1972-75; Service Award, Friars Point PTA, 1990; Who's Who Among America's Teachers Award, Educ Communs Inc, 1990; Community Service Award, Friars Point Day Comt, 1993; Service Award, Delta Indust Inst Alumni Asn, 1996. **Home Addr:** PO Box 434, Clarksdale, MS 38614, **Home Phone:** (662)627-5333. **Business Addr:** Teacher/tutor, librarian (After School Program), New Bethel H.O.P. (Helping Other People), 101 18th St, Clarksdale, MS 38614, **Business Phone:** (662)624-5373.

SMITH, WILSON WASHINGTON, III
Fashion designer, executive. **Personal:** Born Oct 2, 1957, Portland, OR; son of Wilson Jr. **Educ:** Univ Oregon, Sch Architect, BArch, 1980. **Career:** Skidmore, Owings & Merrill, architect, 1981-82; self-employed, map designer & freelance architect, 1982; Portland Gen Elec, CAD, 1982-83; Planning Bur, urban planner, 1983; NIKE, Inc, interior designer, 1983-86, prod designer footwear, 1986-90, sr prod designer & creative dir, 2003-. **Orgs:** Music minister & worship coordr, Portland Foursquare Church, 1987-; coordr, Worship Servants, Portland, 1989-; S Lake Foursquare Church, Lake Oswego, Ore, music minister, currently. **Honors/Awds:** Outstanding Business & Professional Award, Dollars & Sense Mag, 1993; One of America's Top Black Designers, Black Enterprise Mag. **Special Achievements:** Appeared in numerous television series including 20/20, Presentation on NIKE Design, 1988; Breakfast Club, FX Network, "NIKE Design", 1994; "How'd They Do That", Presentation on NIKE Design, 1994; Music Director Summit, 1991, (6000 Youth, 3 day, 1988), National Four Square Youth Convention, 1988; Creator of many athlete-endorsed products including Andre Agassi's signature line, 1997; First dedicated Senior Footwear Designer for Brand Jordan; Collaborating with Michael Jordan created the industry leading Air Jordan 16 & 17, 2003. **Home Phone:** (503)690-2188. **Business Addr:** Senior Product Designer, Creative Director, NIKE Inc, 1 Bowerman Dr MJ4, Beaverton, OR 97005, **Business Phone:** (503)671-6453.

SMITH, WYRE. **See SMITH, REV. ELIJAH.**

SMITH, ZACHARY
Chef. **Personal:** Born Jul 1, 1951, Detroit, MI; son of Jame Z and Leola; married Donna J Alex, Jan 14, 1988; children: Chelsea & Christina. **Career:** Battery Point, chef; Hyatt Regency, San Francisco, sous chef; Benbow Inn, exec chef; Lansdowne, exec chef; Restaurant OneTwentyThree, exec chef; Zachary Cafe, owner, currently. **Orgs:** Chef Asn. **Special Achievements:** Cooking demonstration Baccat Sch; 4-star rating, Restaurant OneTwentyThree, in Restaurants Detroit, 6th edition, by Molly Abraham. **Business Addr:** Owner, Zachary Cafe, 9415 Hwy 64, Zachary, LA 70791, **Business Phone:** (225)654-3354.

SMITH-ALSTON, TONI COLETTE. **See SMITH, TONI COLETTE.**

SMITH-CROXTON, TEARETHA. **See SMITH-CROXTON, TERRI.**

SMITH-CROXTON, TERRI (TEARETHA SMITH-CROXTON)
Executive. **Career:** JD & Assoc Inc, Arlington, TX, pres & chief exec officer, currently. **Orgs:** Links Inc, chaplain; League Women Voters; WIB. **Honors/Awds:** Quest for Success, 1989; Leader of the Year, 1994; Trail Blazer, 1995. **Business Addr:** President, Chief Executive Officer, JD & Associates Inc, 609 E Main St, PO Box 202391, Arlington, TX 76006-8391, **Business Phone:** (817)265-4721.

SMITH-EPPS, E. PAULETTE
Librarian. **Personal:** Born Mar 6, 1947, Atlanta, GA; daughter of William Chauncey Sr and Viola Williams (deceased); married William Given Epps Sr, May 5, 1979. **Educ:** Spelman Col, Atlanta, GA, BA, 1968; Atlanta Univ, Atlanta, GA, MSLS, 1971. **Career:** Librarian (retired). Atlanta Univ, Atlanta, GA, circulation librn, 1972-73; Atlanta-Fulton Pub Libr, Atlanta, GA, ref librn, 1973-76, br mgr, 1976-82, asst br servs admin, 1982-86, br servs admin, 1986-91, cent libr admin, 1991-92, proj mgr, 1992, outreach servs advr, 1992-95, learning assistance bus officer, 1995-96, pub servs adminr, 1996-97, asst dir pub servs, 1997-00. **Orgs:** Spelman Col Alumnae Asn, 1968-; Clark Atlanta Univ Alumni Asn, 1971-; Metro-Atlanta Libr Asn, 1971; Am Libr Asn, 1974-; Black Caucus Am Libr Asn, 1976-; Episcopal Diocese Atlanta. **Home Addr:** 5160 Bruce Pl SW, Atlanta, GA 30331, **Home Phone:** (404)349-0607. *

SMITHERMAN, CAROLE
Judge, educator, lawyer. **Personal:** Born Sep 25, 1952, Birmingham, AL; daughter of Jerry Catlin and Thelma Catlin; married Rodger Smitherman; children: Rodger, Tonya, Mary & Crystal. **Educ:** Spelman Col, BBA, polit sci, 1973; Miles Law Sch, JD, 1979. **Career:** Miles Law Sch, prof, 1982-; pvt pract atty; State Ala, Jefferson County, circuit ct judge, 1991-93; Birmingham City Coun, dist 6 rep, 2001-, coun pres, 2005-. **Orgs:** Founder, Children Village; Econ Develop & Educ Comt; Birmingham Bar Asn; Nat Asn Advan Colored People; bd dirs, Police Athletic Teams, 1989. **Honors/Awds:** Recipient of numerous honors and awards for public service. **Special Achievements:** First African-American woman deputy district attorney, State of Ala, 1982, first appointed woman judge, City of Birmingham, 1986, first appointed African-Am woman circuit ct judge, 1991. **Business Phone:** (121)303-1111.

SMITHERMAN, DR. GENEVA
Educator. **Personal:** Born in Brownsville, TN; daughter of Harry Napoleon; married Jeff R Donaldson; children: Robert Anthony. **Educ:** Wayne State Univ, BA, 1960, MA, 1962; Univ Mich, PhD, 1969. **Career:** Detroit Pub Schs, teacher, 1960-66; Eastern Mich Univ, instr, 1965-71; Wayne St Univ, instr, 1965-71; Wayne St Univ, asst prof; Harvard Univ, Afro-Am studies, lectr, 1971-73; Univ Mich, adj prof, 1973; Wayne St Univ, prof, 1973-; Mich St

Univ, univ distinguished prof eng, currently. **Orgs:** Oral History Comt, Afro Museum, 1967-68; Exec Comt Conf Col Composition, 1971-73; chmn, Black Literature Sec, Midwest Language Asn, 1972; judge, Scholastic Writing Awards Contest, 1975; Modern Language Asn Comt, Minorities, 1976-77; founding mem, African-Am Heritage Asn, 1976; adv bd, Ethnic Awareness Project, 1977-78; Nat Coun Teachers Eng, 1979-82; dir, African Am Language & Literacy Prog, Mich St Univ, currently. **Honors/Awds:** Dean's List of Honor Students, Wayne St Univ; Award for Scholarly Leadership in Language Arts Instruction, 1980; W E B DuBois Scholarship Award, Phylon Soc, Wayne St Univ; Zora Neale Hurston Anthropology Award, Ctr Black Studies, Wayne St Univ; James B Hamilton Award, Mid-Am Assn Educ Opportunity Prog Personnel, 1994; Exemplar Award, Conf Col Composition & Commun, 1999; Distinguished Faculty Award, Mich St Univ,2000; David H Russell Research Award, Nat Coun Teachers Eng, 2001. **Special Achievements:** Published many books. **Business Addr:** University Distinguished Professor of English, Michigan State University, 201 Morrill Hall, East Lansing, MI 48824, **Business Phone:** (517)353-7243.*

SMITHERMAN, RODGER M
Lawyer, government official, senator (u.s. federal government). **Personal:** Born Mar 2, 1953, Montgomery, AL; son of Ralph and Mary; married Carole Smitherman, Nov 29, 1980; children: Rodger II, Tonya, Mary & Crystal. **Educ:** Univ Montevallo, BBA, 1976; Miles Law Sch, JD, 1986. **Career:** Southern Jr Col, Dean Students; State Alabama, state senator, 1994-. **Orgs:** Elder, Westimister Presby Church; bd dirs, Western Area YMCA; youth & govt coach, W End High Sch; adv bd, Camp Birmingham; Vulcan Kiwanis; Birmingham Tip Off Club; vol basketball coach, Amateau Athletic Union; Police Athletic Team; Birmingham Bar Asn. **Honors/Awds:** Vulcan Award, City Birmingham; Distinguished Service Award, Police Athletic Teams; Service Award, Dist 18; Service Award, Westminister Presby Church. **Home Addr:** 928 Center Way SW, Birmingham, AL 35211. **Business Addr:** Senator, Alabama State Senate, 18th District (Jefferson), 2029 Second Ave N, Birmingham, AL 35203, **Business Phone:** (205)322-0012.

SMITHERS, ORAL LESTER, JR.
Engineer. **Personal:** Born Jul 12, 1940, Columbus, OH; son of O Lester Smithers Sr and Mildred H; married Priscilla; children: Sheila & Lisa. **Educ:** Ohio State Univ, BCE, 1963; Sacramento State Col, MEngr, Mech; Central Mich Univ, MA, 1982; Mass Inst Technol, Cambridge, MA, MS, 1985. **Career:** Aerojet Gen Corp, design engr, 1963-68; USF, aerospace engr, 1968-85; Dept Air Force, Wright Patterson Air Force Base, F-16 dir eng 1985-89, dir flight syst eng 1989-92; Wright Lab, deputy dir, 1992-97, dir eng 1997-. **Orgs:** Ohio Soc Prof Engrs, Am Asn Aeronaut & Astronaut; Clark & Champaign County Soc Prof Engrs; bd dirs, Armed Forces Communs & Electronics Asn; Clark State Col Bd trustees; Clark County, Springfield Planning Comn; past mem, steward bd, St Andrews AME Church; New N St AME Church; Omega Psi Phi Fraternity. **Honors/Awds:** Meritorious Civil Service Award, Air Force Sys Command; Civil Engineering Hon, Chi Epsilon; Sloan Fel, MIT, 1984-85; 4th District Man of the Year, Omega Psi Phi Fraternity, 1984; Senior Engineer of the Year, USAF Aeronaut Systems, 1989, Senior Exec Service Asn; Exceptional Civilian Service Award, 1993; Air Force EEO Management Award, 1995; Distinguished Alumni Award, Ohio State Univ, 1998; Prof Distinguished Exe Award, 2000. **Home Addr:** 15 Bobwhite Dr, Enon, OH 45323. **Business Addr:** Director of Engineering, Wright Patterson AFB, Aeronautical Systems Center, Dayton, OH 45433, **Business Phone:** (937)255-3208.

SMITHERS, PRISCILLA JANE
Association executive. **Personal:** Born Jan 2, 1942, Parkersburg, WV; daughter of Robert D and Mildred Burke; married O Lester Jr; children: Sheila & Lisa. **Career:** Mountain State Col, exec secy, 1960; Cont Cable Springfield, comn serv dir, prod, hostess weakly TV show, 1973-78; City Springfield, city clerk, 1978-87; United Way, Springfield, campaign assoc, 1987-91, Alcohol, Drug & Mental Health Bd, exec dir, 1991-96; Clark Co Family Coun, exec dir, 1995-96; United Way, Springfield, dir resource develop. **Orgs:** Chmn, Civil Serv Comn, City Springfield, 1973-78; bd dir, United Way, 1976-87; OH Munic Clerks Asn, 1978-87; bd dirs, Alcohol Drug Mental Health Bd, 1986-91; vpres, Wittenberg Univ & Col Leadership Acad Alumni, 1988-90; Springfield Rotary Club, 1993-; cent comt, Clark Co Republican Party, 1994-; mediation bd, City Springfield, 1994-; Key Corp, Bank Comn Adv Comt, 1995-; Enon Hist Soc, 1995-. **Honors/Awds:** Citizen of the Year, Fraternity Int, 1978; Citizen of the Year, Black Women Leadership Caucus, 1979; Black History Award, St John Miss Church, 1990; Community Leadership Award, Springfield Comn Leadership Alumni Asn, 1990; Nat Citizen of the Year, Omega Phi Psi, 1994; Employee of the Year, ADMH, 1994. **Home Addr:** 15 Bobwhite Dr, Enon, OH 45323. **Business Addr:** Director of Development, United Way of Clark & Champaign Counties, 616 N Limestone St, Springfield, OH 45503, **Business Phone:** (513)324-5551.

SMITH-GASTON, LINDA ANN
Executive, administrator. **Personal:** Born Jan 17, 1949, Kingstree, SC; daughter of George and Frances Latimer Montgomery; married Anthony R (divorced); children: Taylor Aderemi Humphries & Leigh Jamila Gaston. **Educ:** Univ Calif Los Angeles, BA, 1970; Calif State Univ, MA, 1984. **Career:** KTTV-TV, Los Angeles, CA, host, 1978-80; Drew PostGrad Med Sch, Los Angeles, CA, prog specialist, 1979-80; Consumer Credit Counrs, Los Angeles, CA, counr, 1981-82; ARCO, Los Angeles, CA, consumer affairs specialist, 1982-84; Southern Calif Gas Co, Los Angeles, CA, sr consumer affairs specialist, 1984-. **Orgs:** Chairperson, KCET Community Adv Bd, 1988-90; pres, Soc Consumer Affairs Profs Bus, 1989; bd mem, Los Angeles County Comn Local Govt Serv, 1990-; bd mem, Nat Coalition Consumer Educ, 1991-; state coordr, Calif Agenda Consumer Educ, 1990-. **Honors/Awds:** Achievement Award, YWCA Los Angeles, 1987. **Business Phone:** (213)689-3176.

SMITH-GRAY, CASSANDRA ELAINE
Government official. **Personal:** Born Mar 7, 1947, Detroit, MI; married Charles A Gray; children: David Charles. **Educ:** Wayne State Univ, BS, 1971. **Career:** Detroit Pub Sch, ed, 1970-74; City Detroit Youth Dept, dir, 1974-76; City Detroit Bd Assessors, assessor, 1976-82; City Detroit Neighborhood Serv,exec dir; Detroit Housing Comn, dir, currently. **Orgs:** Nat Asn Negro Bus & Prof Women; campaign mgr, Mayor Young's Re-election,1981; bd mem, Mayor's Anti-Crime Project, 1982; trustee, Ctr Humanist Studies, 1983-; bd mem, Wayne City Child Care Coun, 1983-; state cent mem alternate, Mich Democratic Party 1982-; life mem, Nat Adavn Asn Colored People; det campaign mgr, Mondale-Ferrarro Campaign, 1984. **Honors/Awds:** First Black Woman Assessor Cert, MI, 1979. **Business Addr:** Director, Detroit Housing Commission, 1301 E Jefferson, Detroit, MI 48207, **Business Phone:** (313)877-8639.*

SMITH-GREGORY, DEBORAH P.
Educator, journalist. **Personal:** Born May 6, 1951, Dayton, OH; daughter of Mae Mack Pridgen and John Pridgen; married Carl; children: Rahsaan & Hakim. **Educ:** Univ Calif, Berkeley, Calif, cert Jour; Seton Hall Univ, S Orange, NJ, BS, eng, hist, sec educ; Montclair State Col, Montclair, NJ, post grad studies. **Career:** Newark Bd Educ, Newark, NJ, educr, 1974-; NJ Afro-Am newspaper, Newark, NJ, reporter, 1985-88, resident ed, 1988-89; NJ Perspectus News Mag, 1989-93; DP Smith Assoc, Pub Rels, Publ Co, pres, 1994-. **Orgs:** Nat Asn Advan Colored People, 1989-; Nat Asn Black Journalists, 1989-; Garden State Asn Black Journalists, 1990-; pres, bd dir, United Acad, 1990-. **Honors/Awds:** Commendation, Newark City Coun, 1987; Media Woman of the Year, YWCA/Orange, NJ, 1990. **Home Addr:** 800 S 11th St, Newark, NJ 07108, **Home Phone:** (973)733-2260.

SMITH-HENDRICKS, CONSTANCE KASANDRA. **See HENDRICKS, DR. CONSTANCE SMITH.**

SMITH NELSON, DR. DOROTHY J.
Educator. **Personal:** Born Jun 24, 1948, Greenville, MS. **Educ:** Tufts Univ, BA, 1970, MEd, 1971; Southern Ill Univ, Carbondale, PhD, 1981. **Career:** Miss Valley State Univ, acad affairs, asst vpres & acad skills parlor, dir, 1971-99; Southern Ill Univ, Carbondale Off Stud Develop, coordr stud develop, 1979-81; Frisby-Smith-Nelson Rentals, property mgr, 1999-. **Orgs:** Bd mem, Nat Asn Advan Colored People, 1982-84; Post Doctoral Acad Higher Educ, 1979-; fin sec, Les Modernette Social Club; Int Reading Asn; Southern Ill Univ Alumni Asn; Concerned Educrs Black Students; SE Regional Reading Conf; Alpha Kappa Alpha; Progressive Art & Civic Club, Miss Reading Asn; Nat Asn Develop Educrs; Miss Asn Develop Educrs; unexpired term, State Bd Community & Jr Colleges, 2002-08. **Honors/Awds:** Clark Doctoral Scholar Award for Research, Southern Ill Univ; Education Award, Nat Asn Advan Colored People; Education Achievement Award, Progressive Art & Civic Club; Outstanding Young Women of America; MVSA Presidential Citation for Outstanding Services and Financial Support, 1998; Diversity Award/Black History Month, 1998; Preeminence Award, Miss Valley State Univ, 2003. **Home Addr:** 646 S Main St, Greenville, MS 38701, **Home Phone:** (662)332-7075.

SMITH-SMITH, PEOLA
School principal, president (organization). **Personal:** Born in New Orleans, LA; married. **Educ:** MSED. **Career:** Sch Principal (retired), pres; Middle Sch Principal; The Nat Asn Negro Bus & Prof Women's Clubs, nat pres, currently. **Orgs:** Nat Asn Negro Bus & Prof Women's Clubs Inc; Delta Sigma Theta Sorority; Nat Coun Negro Women. **Honors/Awds:** Many Congressional Citations, several community service awards & plaques. **Special Achievements:** Listed in "100 Most influential Black Americans",Ebony, 2004, 2005, 2006, 2007; 100 Most Influential in Education in NJ, The City News of Newark, NJ. **Business Addr:** President, National Association of Negro Business & Professional Women, 1806 New Hampshire Ave NW, Washington, DC 20009, **Business Phone:** (202)483-4206.*

SMITH-SURLES, DR. CAROL DIANN
School administrator. **Personal:** Born Oct 7, 1946, Pensacola, FL; children: Lisa Ronique & Philip. **Educ:** Fisk Univ, BA, 1968; Chapman Col, MA, 1971; The Univ Mich, PhD, 1978. **Career:** Santa Barbara County, social worker, 1968-69; Allan Hancock Col, instr,1971-72; Univ Mich, personnel rep, 1971-77; Univ Cent Fla, dir eeo, 1978-84, exec asst to the pres, 1982-84, assoc vpres, 1984; Calif St Univ, vpres admin & Bus affairs, 1992-94; Tex Woman's Univ, pres, 1994-99; Eastern Ill Univ, pres, 1999-. **Orgs:** Nat Asn Advan Colored People, Urban League; mem bd trustees WMFETV & FM radio, 1984-; bd mem, Orlando Human Rels Bd, 1984-; pres, Orlando Leadership Coun Orlando Chamber Com, 1985; bd dir, First St Bank, Denton, TX, 1995-. **Honors/Awds:** Phi Lambda Theta Honor Soc, 1977-; Outstanding Scholars Award Delta Tau Kappa Int Social Sci Hon Soc, 1983. **Business Addr:** President, Eastern Illiois University, 600 Lincoln Ave, Charleston, IL 61920-3099.

SMITH-TAYLOR, REV. DONNA LYN
Clergy. **Personal:** Born Jan 1, 1949, Detroit, MI; daughter of Roger Brook Smith and Georgia O. **Career:** Carl Byoir & Assocs Inc, supvr, acct payable, acct adminr, 1978-85; Memorial Baptist Church, asst pastor, admin asst, 1985-88; Kenilworth Baptist Church, pastor, 1988-90; Empire Baptist State Conv, Empire Chronicle Newspaper, asst ed, currently; New Progressive Missionary Baptist Church, pastor; Shiloh Baptist Church, pastor, currently. **Orgs:** Recording secy, Central Hudson Baptist Asn, 1989-; asst fin secy, Empire Baptist State Conv, 1989-; Black Ministerial Alliance, 1991-. **Honors/Awds:** Cert Recognition, The Thomas Whitfield Co, 1978; Certificate of Apppreciation, Detroit Renaissance Found, IFF, 1981, 1982; Certificate of Apppreciation, Harlem Hosp, Pastoral Care, 1987; Certificate of Apppreciation, St Clara COGIC, 1991. **Special Achievements:** First female elected to parent body office of Central Hudson Baptist Association, 1991; first female to pastor an African-American Baptist Church in Kingston, NY; First African-American to pastor Kenilworth Baptist Church, 1988; original member of The Thomas Whitfield Co., gospel recording/ministering choir based in Detroit, MI. **Business Addr:** Pastor, Shiloh Baptist Church, 90 N Wash St, Tarrytown, NY 10591, **Business Phone:** (914)631-4197.

SMITH-WHITAKER, AUDREY N.
School administrator. **Personal:** Born Mar 6, 1953, Chicago, IL; daughter of Erron and Anita; married Horace Edward Jr. **Educ:** Wellesley Col, BA, 1974; Univ Maine, Orono, MEd, 1978. **Career:** Zayre Corp, personnel admin exec recruiter, 1974-76; Univ Maine, Orono, intern teacher corps, 1976-78; Wellesley Col, admis counr, 1978-79, fromasst to assoc dir admis, 1979-85; Morgan State Univ, res coordr, 1984; NatAsn Independent Schs, Admis & Financial Aid Serv, dir, 1985-87; RadcliffeCol-Radcliffe Seminars, Cambridge Mass, recruiter/acad adv, 1987-88; SunFinancial Group, Wellesley Hills, Mass, registered rep, 1987-88; Mass Better Chance, Col Bd-Northeast Regional Off, educ consult, 1987-88; Digital Equipment Corp, corp contributions progs mgr, currently. **Orgs:** Nat Assoc Col Admission Counrs, 1978-, New England Assoc Black Admission Counrs Inc, 1978-, Assoc Black Admission & Financial Aid Officers the Ivy League & Sister Schools Inc, 1976-, New England Assoc Col Admission Counrs, 1979-; Black achiever Black Achievers Inc Boston Mass, 1981-; founding mem Wellesley Black Alumnae Network 1981-; Sch Volunteers Boston1982-; eval team mem New England Assoc Schs & Col Secondary Schs, 1983-;consult Tri-Lateral Coun 1984; adv Coun The Educ Resources Inst 1985-;Urban League Eastern Mass, 1986-; bd mem, Girl Scouts Patriots Trail Coun1986-; adv Coun, Educ Records Bureau; mem, Links Inc 1989-. **Honors/Awds:** Black Achiever, Black Achiever Asn Inc, Boston, 1981; Outstanding Admin Black Grad Wellesley Col, 1982. **Home Phone:** (508)875-3916. **Business Phone:** (508)493-4277.

SMITTY, DAP. **See SMITH, WILLIAM FRENCH.**

SMOOT, CAROLYN ELIZABETH
Consultant, school administrator. **Personal:** Born Sep 24, 1945, Logan, WV; daughter of Edward Hickman; married Douglas B, Jan 27, 1967; children: Caroline Trucia. **Educ:** WVa State Col Inst, BS, 1967; WVA Col Grad Study Inst, MPA, 1975. **Career:** Packard Bell Electric Corp, residential adv, 1967-68; Teledyne Econ Develop Co, dept head placement serv, sr instr, 1968-72, 1972-76; W Va State Col Inst, part-time instr, 1975-77; Thiokol Corp, mgr placement &rec dept, 1976-77; W Va Dept Employ Security, comnr, 1977-78;Nemderoloc/Medlock Co Inc, corp consult, 1979-80; mgt consult &researcher, 1981-84; W Va State Col, staff assoc off develop, 1982-83; Mgt& Training Corp, dir Educ & Training, 1984-; Stonewall Jackson Middle Sch, hist teacher, currently. **Orgs:** Guest lectr, Various Civic, Social & Comm Orgn Topics Relating Changing Role Women Placement; Delta Sigma Theta Sorority; Phi Delta Kappa Sor; Nat Women's Polit Caucus; WV Women Polit Caucus; asst, Durbar W Va Chapter Blue Birds Inc; homeroom mother, Dunbar Elem Sch; bd dir, Multi-cap; Nat Am Advan Colored People; Am Voc Asn, 1984-; W Va Adult Educ Asn, 1984-; WVa Voc Educ Asn, 1984-; W Va Human Resources Asn, 1984-87; bd dir, Pvt Indust Coun Kanawha County, 1984-; pres & first vpres, Charleston Bus &Prof Club, 1983-86; bd dir, Shawnee Comm Ctr, 1984-87; polit action chmn, Bus & Prof Club, 1987-; bd dirs, Kanawha Countyeriff Dept, 1990-. **Special Achievements:** Featured in Ebony Magazine, "The Problems of Women Bosses", 1977,participant in the first White House Conf on Balanced Natl Growth &Economic Development, 1978, appointed West Virginia Ambassador of GoodWill, 1981, participant in the White House Conf on Science & Technology, 1985, several TV appearances. **Home Addr:** PO

Box 222, Institute, WV 25112. **Business Addr:** Teacher, Stonewall Jackson Middle School, 812 Pk Ave, Charleston, WV 25302.

SMOTHERS, RONALD
Executive. **Career:** Fastaurants, Inc, Los Angeles, CA, president & chief exec officer. **Business Addr:** President, Chief Executive Officer, Fastaurants Inc, 3700 Coliseum St, Los Angeles, CA 90016.

SMOTHERS, RONALD ERIC
Journalist. **Personal:** Born Sep 3, 1946, Washington, DC; married Brenda. **Educ:** Hobart Coll, BA, 1967. **Career:** Comm News Serv, ed, 1969-72; Newsday, 1968-69; WA Post, 1967-68; New York Times, reporter, currently. **Business Addr:** Reporter, The New York Times, 111 Mulberry St, Newark, NJ 07102, **Business Phone:** (973)623-3904.

SMOTHERSON, REV. MELVIN
Clergy. **Personal:** Born Nov 6, 1936, Hattiesburg, MS; son of Melvin and Estella S Rogers; married Geraldine Jackson, Jun 23, 1957; children: Charles, Bwayne, Pamela & Darren. **Educ:** Brooks Bible Col, Cert, 1965; Mont Baptist Col, BA, 1974; Central Baptist Theol Sem, DD, 1975; Webster Col, MA, 1980. **Career:** First Baptist Church, Creve Coeur, pastor, 1963-71; Baptist State Sunday Sch & BTU Cong, historian, 1974-75; Ministers Union Greater, St Louis, vpres, 1977-79; Wash Tabernacle Baptist Church, pastor, 1971-80; Cornerstone Instnl Baptist Church, pastor, 1980. **Orgs:** Attended various conf & conv assoc with Bapt Church, 1963-67; grand jr warden/grand chaplain, dep grand master, Most Worshipful Prince Hall Grand Lodge; hon mem, Mich Grand Lodge F&AM; exec comt, NAACP; Most Worshipful Grand Master-MWPHGL Mont, 1988-90; dep imperial chaplain, Ancient Egyptian Arabic Order, Nobles of the Mystic Shrine N & S Am & Jurisdiction 1985-. **Honors/Awds:** Various awards & certificates from NAACP & sororities 1965-74; Minister of the Year Award, Baptist Church, 1973; Certificate of Merit, NAACP, 1974; Doctor of Divinity, Central Baptist Theological Seminary, 1975; Citizen of the Year Award, George Washington Carver Assoc, 1979; Citizen of the Year Award, Grand Chap OES; speaker in Trinidad WI, Seoul Korea, Rome, Italy, 1987-88; Knight Grand Commander of Humanity Republic of Liberia, 1989; Chief of Bbandi Tribe Lofa District, Monrovia, Liberia. **Business Addr:** Pastor, Cornerstone Institutional Baptist Church, 4700 Washington Blvd, Saint Louis, MO 63108, **Business Phone:** (314)367-8000.

SMYRE, CALVIN
State government official, executive. **Personal:** Born May 17, 1947. **Educ:** Ft Valley State Univ, BS, bus admin. **Career:** Executive, state representative; Synovus Financial Corp, Columbus Bank &Trust Co, asst vpres & mkt officer, 1976-84, Synovus Financial Corp, asst vpres, vpres corp admin, 1984-90, sr vpres & asst to chmn community affairs, 1990-99, exec vpres corp affairs, 1999-; Ga House Rep, Dist 132, rep, 1974-; Synovus Found Inc, chmn & chief exec officer, currently. **Orgs:** Deleg, Dem Nat Party Conf, 1978; chmn, Ga Legis Black Caucus, 1979-80; deleg, Dem Nat Conv, 1980; pres, Ga Asn Black Elected Officials, 1982-88;secy, Nat Black Caucus State Legisrs; bd trustees, Morehouse Sch Med, Med Col Ga Found, Jack D Hughston Sports Med Hosp Found, Columbus Mus, Fort Valley State Col Found; bd chair, River Center Board, 2002-04. **Honors/Awds:** Ten Best Legislators, Atlanta Jour-Const, 1980; Nat Legislator of the Year, 1985 & 2005; Citizen of the Year, Columbus, Ga; 100 Most Influential Georgians, Ga Trend Mag, 2003. **Special Achievements:** First African American from Georgia elected to the Democratic National Committee. **Military Serv:** AUS, 1970-73. **Business Addr:** Executive Vice President, Synovus Financial Corp, PO Box 120, Columbus, GA 31902, **Business Phone:** (706)649-2311.

SMYTHE, VICTOR N.
Librarian. **Personal:** Son of Constantine (deceased) and Agnes L Scott (deceased). **Educ:** NY Univ, BA, psychol, 1964; Columbia Univ Sch Jour, 1984, Sch Libr Serv, MS, 1984; Modern Archives Inst, Nat Arch, Wash, DC, cert, 1989. **Career:** Librarian (retired); Int Circulating Exhibitions, Mus Mod Art, New York, NY, spec asst; Daniel Yankelovich Inc, field supvr; Post Exchange Servs, US Fort Clayton, internal auditor; S Bronx Proj, community liaison; Brooklyn Col, Dept Educ Serv, chief admin officer; NY Pub Libr, librn; Schomburg Cr Res Black Culture, heritage proj, archivist, librn, 1989; Art & Artifacts Div, Schomburg City, curator. **Orgs:** Am Libr Asn; Arch Roundtable Metrop NY; Mid-Atlantic Regional Arch Conf; dir, Caribbean/Am Media Studies Inc; dir, Coalition Caribbean Interests; bd mem, exec dir, 1990-97, chmn exec comt, 1982-97, Ethiopian Orthodox Church; dir, Western Hemisphere Abyssinian Cultural Ctr, 1993-97. **Home Addr:** 327 St Nicholas Ave, New York, NY 10027. *

SNEAD, DR. DAVID LOWELL
School superintendent. **Personal:** Born Oct 15, 1943, Detroit, MI; son of Herman and Edith; married Sharon McPhail, May 27, 1995; children: Deborah, David II, Brandon, Erika & Angela. **Educ:** Tuskegee Univ, BS, 1968; Univ Mich, MA, Urban Educ, 1970, PhD, Educ Admin, 1984. **Career:** Detroit Pub Sch, sec sch educ cent off supvr, 1985, from asst prin to prin, 1985-93, interim asst supt, 1993, exec dep interim gen supt, 1993, gen supt, 1993-97; Madison Tech High Sch, headmaster; Waterbury Pub Schs, CT, supt, 2000-. **Orgs:** Am Assn Sch Admin; Detroit Police Athletic League; bd mem, Health Alliance Plan, 1990-92; brd trustees, New Detroit Inc, 1994; Metro Detroit Alliance Black Sch Educr, 1994; brd trustees, exec comt, Coun Great City Sch, 1994; commun adv brd, Jr League Detroit, 1994. **Honors/Awds:** Man of the Year & Award of Merit, Alpha Phi Alpha, 1994; Michigan Superintendent of the Year, Mich Assn Sch Admin, 1994; Outstanding Leadership & Service Award, Mich Coun Deliberation Scholar Found, 1994; Editorial Award, Bus United With Officers Youth, 1994; Septima Clark Natl Editorial Award, Southern Christian Leadership Conf, 1995. **Special Achievements:** Author: Dissertation, The Effects of Increased Grade Point Standards for Student Athletes, Univ of Mich Press, December 1984; Recommended Public School Finance Reforms, Detroit Free Press, March 1988; From Coach to Admin, It's All The Same, Secondary Education Today, Vol 29, No 3, Spring 1988; Educ Career Directory, Teaching in Urban Sch, Gale Research Copyright Inc, 1994. **Military Serv:** AUS, personnel admin specialist, 1961-64. **Home Addr:** PO Box 43625, Detroit, MI 48243-0625. **Business Addr:** Superintendent, Waterbury Public Schools, 236 Grand St, Waterbury, CT 06702, **Business Phone:** (203)574-8000.

SNEAD, DR. WILLIE T, SR.
Clergy. **Educ:** Calif Baptist Univ, Riverside, CA, BS, bus admin; Golden Gate Theol Sem, Mill Valley, CA, MDiv & MS. **Career:** Greater Temple of God Missionary Baptist Church, pastor, currently. **Orgs:** Nat Missionary Baptist Conv Am; Nat Asn Advan Colored People; former bd mem, CNBC; former vice chmn, bd dir, Southern Calif Affil CNBC; Police Booster Club; former co chmn, Calif Comt Environ Justicel; moderator emer, Pacific District Missionary Baptist Asn. **Honors/Awds:** Pastor of the Year; Moderator of the Year; Religious Broadcast of the Year. **Business Addr:** Pastor, Greater Temple of God Missionary Baptist Church, 1404 Firestone Blvd, PO Box 512096, Los Angeles, CA 90051-0096, **Business Phone:** (323)582-7344.

SNEED, GREGORY J
Executive. **Career:** Forty Acres & Mule Filmworks Inc, pres, coo, 1996-; Twentieth Century Fox Int, finance & admin, vpres; HBO, vpres, asst controller; Rainbow Media Holdings, vpres financial planning.

SNEED, MICHAEL
Association executive. **Personal:** Married; children: 3. **Educ:** Macalester Col, Minnesota, BA; Dartmouth Col, Tuck Sch, MBA. **Career:** McNeil Consumer Prod, group prod dir, 1991-95, vpres, Nutrit Europe, managing dir, 1998-2000, Nutrit Worldwide, pres, 2000-02; Personal Prod Co, global pres, chmn; Johnson & Johnson Consumer Co, mkt asst, mkt mgr, group chmn, currently. **Orgs:** Med Devices & Diag Group Operating Comt; bd mem, Family Serv Asn Bucks Co, Pa; bd trustees, Macalester Col. **Business Addr:** Group Chairman, North America, Johnson & Johnson Consumer Companies, 1 Johnson & Johnson Plz, News Brunswick, NJ 08933, **Business Phone:** (732)524-0400.

SNEED, PAULA A
Executive. **Personal:** Born Nov 10, 1947, Everett, MA; daughter of Thomas E and F Mary Turner; married Lawrence P Bass, Sep 2, 1978; children: Courtney J Bass. **Educ:** Simmons Col, BA, 1969; Harvard Univ, MBA, 1977; Johnson & Wales Univ, DBA, 1991. **Career:** Outreach Prog Prob Drinkers, educ supvr, female coordr, 1969-71; Ecumenical Ctr, dir plans, prog develop & eval, 1971-72; Boston Sickle Cell Ctr, prog coordr, 1972-75; Gen Foods Corp, from asst prod mgr to assoc prod mgr, 1977-80, prod mgr, 1980-83, prod group mgr, 1983-85, category dir, 1985-86, vpres consumer affairs, 1986-90, sr vpres, Foodservice Div, pres, 1990-91, Desserts Div, exec vpres & gen mgr, 1991-94; Kraft Foods, sr vpres mkt servs, 1995-99; chief mkt officer, 1999, E Com Div, pres, 1999-2000, group vpres, E-com & Mkt Servs, pres, 2000-04, Global Mkt Resources & Initiatives, exec vpres, 2005-. **Orgs:** Am Asn Univ Women, 1980-96; Coalition 100 Black Women, 1982-92; Nat Asn Negro Bus & Prof Women, 1983-95; adv coun to dean, Howard Univ Bus Sch, 1991-96; bd dir, Westchester/Fairfield Inroads, 1993-; bd dir, Hercules Inc, 1994-2002; Exec Leadership Coun, 1994-; bd dir, Airgas Inc, 1999-; bd trustees, Chicago C's Mus, 2000-; bd trustees, IL Inst Tech, 2000-; bd trustees, Simmons Col, 2001-; bd dirs, Charles Schwab Corp, 2002-. **Honors/Awds:** Black Achiever, Harlem YMCA, 1982; MBA of the Year Award, Harvard Bus Sch Black Alumni Orgn, 1987; Benevolent Heart Award, Graham-Windham, 1987; Academy of Women Achievers, NY YWCA, 1990. **Special Achievements:** listed in "Top 100 Black Women in Corp America," Ebony Mag, 1990, 1991; "Very Important Prestigious Woman," Corp Achievers, Dollars & Sense Mag, 1990, 1993; listed in "21 Most Influential African American Women in Corp America," Black Enterprise Mag, 1991, 1997; listed in "40 most influential African American in Corp America," 1993; listed in "Breakthrough 50" Exec Female Mag; 1992 America's 50 Most Powerful Woman Managers, 1994; "25 Most Influential Mothers Working," Mother's Mag, 1998; Most Influential African American in Corp America, Fortune Mag, 2002. **Home Addr:** 1755 Paddock Lane, Lake Forest, IL 60045. **Business Addr:** Director, Charles Schwab & Co Inc., 5190 Neil Rd Suite 100, Reno, NV 89502-8532.

SNELL, JOAN YVONNE ERVIN
Administrator. **Personal:** Born Apr 5, 1932, Waxahachie, TX; married Clarence L Sr; children: Tyrone, Clarence Jr. **Educ:** Draughons Bus Col, attended 1950; Prairie View A&M Col, BA. **Career:** Int Bus Mach Corp, field eng admin specialist; City Lubbock, Parks & Recreation Dept, chair. **Orgs:** Bd dir, YWCA, 1956-66; exec secy, Nat Asn Advan Colored People, 1973-75; secy, New Hope Bapt Chap, 1952; secy, Nat Asn Advan Colored People; Gov Com Higher Educ; dir, New Hope Bapt Chap Youth Dept; secy, W Tex Bapt Dist Asn; secy, Women BM & E Conv Tex; Mayor's Com & C C. **Honors/Awds:** Outstanding IBM Means Serv Award, 1968. **Special Achievements:** First black secretary & elementary school principal, 1952; First black secretary of Lubbock City Hall, 1954; First black to be hired in International Business Machines Corporation; First black woman nominated woman of the year, 1969; First black elected official of City Lubbock, 1970, 1972.

SNELL, JOHNNA
Business owner, designer. **Career:** Originalz creative custom jewelry, jewelry designer & owner, 2003-. **Orgs:** Youth mkt dir, Am Heart Asn, 2002-. **Business Addr:** Jewelry Designer, Owner, Originalz Creative Custom Jewelry, 7030 Church Wood Lane, Huntersville, NC 28078, **Business Phone:** (704)968-3868.*

SNIPES, LOLITA WALKER
Writer, opera producer, playwright. **Personal:** Born in Atlanta, GA; married. **Educ:** Ga State Univ, Atlanta, BA, bus, mkt; Valencia Col, Film & Theater Prod Technol Prog, Orlando, FL. **Career:** Hollywood Pictures; Epic Rec; Atlantic Rec; Good God A'Mighty!, writer, producer & dir; Universal Funny-Bone!, writer, producer & dir; Yes-Amen, writer, producer & dir; God Don't Like Ugly!, writer, producer & dir; Xenon Pictures & Universal Studios, FL, producer; book: Peace in passing: how to find peace in the passing of someone you love, Roman Publ Inc, 2000; Upscale Mag, ed. **Honors/Awds:** National Association Advanced Colored People IMAGE Awards. **Business Addr:** Author, Roman Publishing Inc, PO Box 692651, Orlando, FL 32869.

SNIPES, WESLEY
Actor. **Personal:** Born Jul 31, 1962, Orlando, FL; married Jan 1, 1985 (divorced 1990); children: Jelani. **Educ:** SUNY, Purchase, theatre & dramatic art, 1985. **Career:** Actor, theatre appearances include: Execution of Justice; The Boys of Winter; Death & the King's Horseman; TV: "Wild Cats", 1985; "Sts of Gold"; Michael Jackson's "Bad" video; Major League; HBO's "Vietnam War Story"; Mo "Better Blues"; King of New York; Jungle Fever, 1991; New Jack City, 1990; White Men Can't Jump, 1992; Waterdance, 1992; Passenger 57, 1992; The Rising Sun, 1993; Demolition Man, 1993; Drop Zone, 1994; To Wong Foo; Thanks for Everything; Julia Newmar; Waiting To Exhale; Murder At 1600, 1997; One Night Stand, 1997; US Marshals, 1998; Down In The Delta, 1998; Blade, 1998; Liberty Stands Still, 2002; Zigzag, 2002; Blade II, 2002; Undisputed, 2002; Godforsaken, 2003; John Doe, 2004; prod, actor: The Big Hit; co-prod: Art of War, 2000; Disappearing Acts, HBO, 2000; Amen Ra Films, founder: The Marksman, 2005; The Detonator, 2006; Chaos, 2006; The Contractor, 2007. **Honors/Awds:** Image Award for Outstanding Lead Actor in a Motion Picture, 1993; Image Award for Outstanding Lead Actor in a TV Movie or Mini-Series, 1997; Volpi Cup for Best Actor, 1997; Received a Star on the Hollywood Walk of Fame, 1998; Blockbuster Entertainment Award for Favorite Actor, Horror, 1999; ACE Award, Best Actor, performance in HBO spec, Vietnam War Story; Won Victor Borge Schola, rattend SUNY, Purchase; Best Actor, Venice Film Fest. **Business Addr:** Actor, William Morris Agency, 151 El Camino Dr, Beverly Hills, CA 90212, **Business Phone:** (310)859-4085.

SNODDY, ANTHONY L
Executive. **Educ:** Eastern Mich Univ, indust technol grad, 1973. **Career:** Gen Motors Corp, mats & purchasing mgt; Exemplar Mfg Co, pres, chmn & chief exec officer, 1991-. **Orgs:** Bd mem, Mich Minority Bus Develop Coun; Nat Asn Indust Technol. **Honors/Awds:** Outstanding Industrial Technologist, Nat Asn Indust Technol, 1998. **Special Achievements:** Black Enterprise's Top 100 Industrial/Service Companies, company ranked 38, 1998; company ranked 6, 1999. **Business Phone:** (734)483-5070.

SNOOP DOGG, U (CORDOZAR CALVIN BROADUS, JR.)
Rap musician. **Personal:** Born Oct 20, 1971, Long Beach, CA; son of Vernell Varndo and Beverly; married Chante Taylor, Jun 14, 1997; children: Corde & Cordell. **Career:** Rap musician, currently; 213, mem with Nate Dogg & Warren G; vocalist on Dr Dre's album, The Chronic, 1993; solo music career, albums include: Doggy Style, debut album, 1993; Murder Was the Case, 1994; Tha Dogfather, 1996; Da Game Is to Be Sold Not to Be Told, 1998; Top Dogg, 1999; The Last Meal, 2000; films include: Ride, 1998; Urban Menace, 1999; The Wrecking Crew, 1999; Baby Boy, 2001; Training Day, 2001; Bones, 2001; The Wash, 2001; Old Sch, 2003; You'll Never Weiz in This Town Again, 2003; Starsky & Hutch, 2004; autobiography: Tha Doggfather: The Times, Trials, & Hardcore Truths of Snoop Dogg, 1999; "Distant Shores", 2005; Racing Stripes, 2005; Boss'n Up, 2005; Korn Makes a Video, 2005; The Tenants, 2006; Hood of Horror,

2006; "Arthur et les Minimoys", 2006, Monk, 2007, The Boondocks: Macktastic, 2007; Snoopadelic Films, owner, 2005-. **Orgs:** Deion Sanders Primetime Shootout, 1994. **Honors/Awds:** Billboard Music Charts, No 1 Album, December 1993; MTV Music Awards, presenter, 1993; Soul Train Music Award, 1995. **Business Addr:** Rap Musician, Firstars Artist Management, 14724 Ventura Blvd, Penthouse, Sherman Oaks, CA 91403, **Business Phone:** (818)461-1701.

SNOW, ERIC
Basketball player. **Personal:** Born Apr 24, 1973, Canton, OH; married DeShawn; children: EJ, Darius & Jarren. **Educ:** Mich State, attended. **Career:** Seattle Supersonics, guard, 1995-98; Philadelphia 76ers, 1998-2004; Cleveland Cavaliers, guard, 2005-. **Honors/Awds:** Big Ten Defensive Player Yr; Sportsmanship Award, NBA, 1998-99; NBA Sportsmanship Award, 2000; Good Guys, Sporting News, 2002-04; J Walter Kennedy Citizenship Award, Prof Basketball Writers Asn, 2005; Community Contrib Award, Nat Basketball Players Asn, 2005. **Business Addr:** Professional Basketball Player, Cleveland Cavaliers, 1 Ctr Ct, Cleveland, OH 44115-4001, **Business Phone:** (216)420-2000.

SNOW, KIMBERLY
Marketing executive. **Career:** Mecca USA, prod mgr, dir mkt, currently. **Business Addr:** Director of Marketing, Mecca USA, 31 W 34th St, New york, NY 10001-3009, **Business Phone:** (212)563-1233.

SNOW, PERCY LEE
Football player. **Personal:** Born Nov 5, 1967, Canton, OH. **Educ:** Mich State Univ, criminal justice, 1989. **Career:** Football Player (retired); Kans City Chiefs, linebacker, 1990-92; Chicago Bears, 1994. **Honors/Awds:** first team All-Big Ten, 1987; Sporting News first team All-Am, first team All-Big Ten, 1988; first team All-Am & All-Big Ten, Lombardi Award, 1989; Dick Butkus Award, 1989; Big Ten Defensive Player of the Yr, 1989.

SNOWDEN, FRANK WALTER
Scientist. **Personal:** Born Nov 5, 1939, New Orleans, LA; divorced. **Educ:** Xavier Univ, New Orleans, BS, 1960; Howard Univ, Wash, DC, 1963; Univ New Orleans, PhD, 1975. **Career:** US Dept Agri, Southern Regional Res Lab, stud trainee, 1957-60, chemist, 1960-73, res chemist, 1963-73; Howard Univ, teaching fel, 1960-63; Univ New Orleans, res & teaching, 1970-73; 3M Cent Res Lab, sr res chemist, 1973-78, sr tech serv engineer, 1973-83, global prof serv specialist, 1983-90; Med Video Prod, Video J Ophthamol, med ed, 1990-93; Univ Minn, Inst Technol, Chem Engineering & Material Sci Dept, asst prof, 1991-93, Gen Col, fel, 1993-97, Chem Engineering & Material Sci Dept, prof, 1997-, Multicultural Undergraduate Res Prog, dir, 1997-2001, Pres Distinguished Fac Mentor Prog, dir & chair, 1997-2001, Educ & Human Resources, assoc dir, 1998-, sr tech serv engr, assoc dir, Educ & Human Resources, currently; Kirby Puckett & Jackie Robinson Found Scholarship Comt, chair; Community Scholars Prog, dir, 1998, 2000-; Acad Prog Excellence Engineering & Sci, Dir, 2000-. **Orgs:** Am Chem Soc, 1960-; Am Pub Transit Asn, 1977-93; Comnr Mr Met Transit Comn Twin Cities, 1977-93; Alpha Phi Alpha Frat Inc. **Honors/Awds:** Volunteer of the Year, Sci Mus Minn, 1998; Award of Excellence, 3M/Vision Care Lab. **Special Achievements:** Several Patents, Research Publications & Presentations. **Home Addr:** 9812 Cove Dr, Minnetonka, MN 55305-5800. **Business Addr:** Professor, Director of Education & Human Resources, University of Minnesota, Materials Research Science and Engineering Center, 401 Amundson Hall 421 Washington Ave SE, Minneapolis, MN 55455, **Business Phone:** (612)626-2207.

SNOWDEN, GAIL
Banker, vice president (organization). **Personal:** Born Jul 5, 1945, New York, NY; daughter of Muriel Sutherland and Otto; divorced; children: Leigh Trimmier. **Educ:** Radcliffe Col, BA, 1967; Simmons Col, Grad Sch Mgt, MBA, 1978; Hon Degrees: Bridgewater State Col, 1997, Simmons Col, 1997, Babson Col, 1998. **Career:** First Nat Bank Boston, br officer, 1971-76, br credit officer, 1977-79, loan officer, 1980, asst vpres, 1981-83, vpres, 1984-86, div exec, 1986-88, sr credit officer, 1989-90; dir, Boston First Banking/Bank of Boston, 1990-92; Fleet Boston Financial Corp, pres, 1992-, exec vpres & managing dir, currently. **Orgs:** Nat Asn Bank Women, 1971-; treas, Radcliffe Club Boston, 1976; asst dir, Boston Urban Bankers Forum, 1979-80; conf steering comm, Simmons Grad Prog Man Alumnae Asn, 1979-80; steering comm family Govt Comm C & Family, 1980; vpres, Nat Asn Urban Bankers, 1984-85; vpres, The Boston Found. **Honors/Awds:** Banker of the Yr, Nat Asn Urban Bankers, 1989; Outstanding Alumna, Simmons Grad Sch Mgt, 1989; Big Sister, Women of Achievement, 1992; Bus Advocate of the Yr, Small Bus Admin, Minority 1992; Prof Women's Award, Dollars & Sense Mag, 1992. **Business Addr:** Executive Vice President, Managing Director, Fleet Boston Financial Corp, 100 Fed St, Boston, MA 02110, **Business Phone:** (617)434-5105.

SNOWDEN, GILDA
Educator, artist. **Personal:** Born Jul 29, 1954, Detroit, MI; daughter of Clara Perry and Dr John Thomas; married William Guy Boswell II, May 29, 1987; children: Katherine Snowden Boswell. **Educ:** Wayne State Univ, Detroit, MI, BFA, MA, MFA. **Career:** Wayne State Univ, Detroit, MI, instr, 1979-85; NEA/Arts, fel, Midwest, 1990; Ctr Creative Studies, Detroit, MI, prof, currently. **Orgs:** Dir, Willis Gallery, 1983-84; exhib comt, Detroit Focus Gallery, 1984-91; dir, Detroit Repertory Theatre Gallery, 1987-; Nat Conf Artists. **Honors/Awds:** Fellowship, NEA/Arts Midwest, 1990; Grant, MI Council of The Arts, 1982, 1985, 1988, 1990. **Business Addr:** Professor, College Creative Studies, Fine Arts Department 201 E Kirby, Detroit, MI 48202-4034, **Business Phone:** (313)664-7400.

SNOWDEN, PHILLIP RAY
Engineer. **Personal:** Born Dec 9, 1951, Shreveport, LA; son of Harold Phillip and Nevada Swift; married Mary Ann Robinson, Jul 6, 1974; children: Tamara Sheniki & Tariot-Phillip Ramona. **Educ:** La Tech Univ, Ruston, BSEE, 1974; Xavier Univ, Cin, MBA, 1976. **Career:** Gen Electric Co, Stamford, corporate mgt trainee-Engr, 1974-78; Gen Motors Corp, Detroit, engr, 1978-83; Kent State Univ, Warren, technol, energy instr, 1981-82; Entergy Corp, New Orleans, engr-nuclear safety. **Orgs:** Chmn, Comput Soc Inst Electronic Engrs, New Orleans Sect, 1990-; pres, La Chap Am Asn Blacks in Energy, 1991-; pres elect, Nat Asn Acct, New Orleans Chap, 1991; pres elect, Your Metropolitan Bus & Civic Club, 1991. **Honors/Awds:** Salutatorian, Hopewell High Sch, 1969; Peak Performer Award, La Power & Light, Waterford 3, 1989; Black Achievers Award, Dryades YMCA, 1989.

SNOWDEN, RAYMOND C.
Insurance executive, business owner. **Personal:** Born Aug 5, 1937, McNary, AZ; son of Loretta Hockett Banks and Clarence; married Bettye (divorced); children: Joni, Brian & Eric. **Educ:** AA, psychol, 1962. **Career:** Safe way Stores Inc, La, store mgr, 1965-67; Continental Assurance Co, assoc mgr, 1969; Trans america Occidental Life, 1971; Ray Snowden Insurance, owner, currently. **Orgs:** Pres, Kiwanis Club SW La, 1976-77; Inglewood Calif C C; Salvation Army Youth Adv Coun, 1978; Life Underwriters Asn; dir, Inglewood C C, 1978-80; pres, Crenshaw-Imperial Sect Inglewood C C, 1978-80; citizen adv com, Centenila Hosp, 1980-86; pres, Inglewood C C, 1982-84; pres, Imperial-Crenshaw Kiwanis Club, 1982-83; lt governor, Kiwanis Int, 1991-92; New Testament Church, Los Angeles, Calif, trustee bd chmn, 1978-; bd chmn, New Testament Church Trustee, 1978-2000. **Honors/Awds:** First black gen agent, Trans america Occidental Life Calif, 1971; New Agency of Year Award, Trans america Occidental Life Calif, 1972; featured in issue Sports Illus in Occidental Life's adver June 11, 1974; Kiwanis Int Award Community Serv, 1974; Commendation Inglewood City Coun Community Serv, 1984. **Business Addr:** Owner, Ray Snowden Insurance, 6245 Bristol Pkwy Suite 161, Culver City, CA 90230, **Business Phone:** (310)671-3202.

SNOWDEN, SYLVIA FRANCES
Artist, educator. **Personal:** Born Apr 21, 1944, Raleigh, NC; daughter of George; divorced; children: Shell Snowden Butler & John Malik Butler. **Educ:** Howard Univ, Wash, DC, BA, MFA; Grants People Inc, Cult Alliance, Wash, DC, Marketing Arts & People, cert; Skowhegan Sch Painting & Sculpture, Skowhegan, Maine, cert. **Career:** Yale Univ, Norfolk, Conn, lectr & instr, 1991-92; Brandywine Workshop, Philadelphia, vis artist, 1994; Corcoran Gallery art, vis artist, Wash, DC, 1995; Howard Univ, vis artist, 1995; Hirshhorn Mus & Sculpture Garden, Figurative Painting, Teresia Bush, Wash, DC, panelist, 1997; Phillips Mus Art, Lancaster, PA, panelist, 2004; Cornell Univ, artist-in-residence, panelist. **Honors/Awds:** DC Comn Arts & Humanities Grants; Lois Jones Pierre-Noel Award, Water Color; First Pl Award, Oil Painting, Skowhegan Sch; First Pl Award, Painting, Asn Black Arts E; Lois M Jones Award, Recognition, Fondo del Sol Gallery. **Special Achievements:** Pub: "Images of Shattered Youth", The Washington Times, Joanna Shaw-Eagle, 2000; "Life & Death & Malik", The Washington Post, 2000; "Black Abstract Artist Showcase Shared Traits", The Patriot News, Zachary Lewis, 2004; "Black Abstraction in Lancaster", The Philadelphia Inquirer, Edward Sozanski, 2004. **Home Addr:** 465 M St NW, Washington, DC 20001, **Home Phone:** (202)347-5576.

SNYDER, GEORGE W
Journalist, writer. **Personal:** Born Dec 6, 1944, New Orleans, LA. **Educ:** Mich State Univ, BA, 1966. **Career:** The Canadian Press, Toronto, feature ed, 1967-68; Yukon Terr British Columbia, licensed prospector, 1968-70; San Francisco Chronicle, reporter; KPIX TV, KGO TV, writer, producer & reporter; Sacramento Union; Associated Press, News Indian Country; The Modest Bee, staff writer, currently. **Orgs:** San Francisco & Black Media Asn; adv bd, Sonoma Co Fish & Wildlife, 1986-; vpres, Urban Creeks Coun Sonoma Chap, 1988-; Comm Art Worksho; Calif Indian Basketweavers Asn. **Special Achievements:** Author of "Peyote Moon" 1973. **Home Addr:** PO Box 464, Occidental, CA 95465. **Business Addr:** Staff Writer, The Modest Bee, 1325 H St, Modesto, CA 95354, **Business Phone:** (209)578-2000.

SNYDER, VANESSA W
Editor, writer. **Personal:** Born Oct 19, 1964, Washington, DC; daughter of Alvin and Dorothy Williams; married Deron K, Sep 29, 1990; children: Sierra Ngozi & Sequoia Elon. **Educ:** Univ Md, BS, 1996; Walden Univ, MS, 2007. **Career:** Gannett News Serv, ed/writer, 1989-99; Gospel Today, contributing ed/writer, 1996-; Excellence Mag, writer, ed, teacher, 1999-; Lee County Govt, teacher, 2005; Author: "50 Ways To Put Christ Back In Christmas". **Orgs:** Nat Asn Black Journalists. **Business Addr:** Teacher, Lee County Government, PO Box 398, Fort Myers, FL 33902-0398.*

SOARES, BEA T.
High school principal. **Career:** Guild, prin; Gray Elementary Sch, prin, 1999; William K Moore Elem Sch, prin, 2000-07. **Business Addr:** Principal, William K. Moore Elementary School, 491 N Lamb Blvd, Las Vegas, NV 89110.

SOARIES, REV. DR. DEFOREST BLAKE, JR.
Clergy, public speaker, state government official. **Personal:** Born Aug 20, 1951; son of DeForest B Sr and Mary M; married Donna; children: Malcolm & Martin. **Educ:** Fordham Univ, BA; Princeton Theol Sem, MDiv; United Theol Sem, DMin. **Career:** Kean Col, Union, NJ, vis prof; Shiloh Baptist Church, assoc pastor, 1987-90; First Baptist Church-Lincoln Gardens, sr pastor, 1991-; NJ Secy State, 1999-2002; US Election Assistance Comn, chmn, comnr, 2003-05; Fed Home Loan Bank NY. pub dir, currently. **Orgs:** Chmn bd, First Baptist Community Develop Corp; nd dirs, New Era Bank; judicial Vols Prog, NJ Superior Ct, 1993. **Honors/Awds:** Numerous awards for his leadership and community service including Youth At Risk-Pathway Award, Kappa Alpha Psi Frat Inc, 1994; MLK Award, Elizabeth City State Univ, 1994. **Special Achievements:** New Jersey's 30th Secretary of State making him the first African American male to serve as a Constitutional officer of the State; Author, My Family is Driving Me Crazy, 1991; Seven Bridges to the Promise Land, 1995; published numerous articles. **Business Addr:** Public Director, Federal Home Loan Bank of New York., 101 Pk Ave Suite 5, New York, NY 10178, **Business Phone:** (212)949-0220.

SOBERS, WAYNETT A., JR.
Executive, consultant. **Personal:** Born Feb 15, 1937, Bronx, NY; son of Athlene Ghyll and Waynett; married Yvonne C Barrett, Aug 23, 1969; children: Loren, Julian & Stephanie. **Educ:** City Col NY, BS, 1959; Sobelsohn Sch Ins, 1965; Baruch Col, MBA,1972; Gen Motors Dealer Develop Acad, 1987-88. **Career:** Meteorologist, 1959-69; WA Sobers Assoc Inc, pres 1965-69; Johnson Publ Co, advertising rep, 1969-71; Black Enterprise Mag, Mkt Serv, mgr,1971-73, Advertising & Mkt, vpres, 1973; EGG Dallas Broadcasting Inc, vpres, 1977; BCI Marketing Inc, pres; Earl G Graves Ltd, exec vpres, 1980-87, vpres corp commun, 1998; Sobers Chevorlet Inc, pres, gen mgr, 1988-90; Wayvon Consulting, sr consult & owner, 1990-; Bedford Stuyvesant Restoration Corp, exec vpres, 1995-97; Energy Leadership Index,Master Practitioner & Cert Prof Coach, currently. **Orgs:** Pres, Chappaqua Ridge Assn, 1977; secy, Chappaqua Rotary Club, 1992-95, vpres, 1995-96; former dir, Equitable Variable Life Ins Co; Am Mgt Assn; Am Mkt Assn; City Col New York Alumni Assn; City Col New York Black Alumni Assn; Bernard M Baruch Col Alumni Assn; bd mem & treas, NatAsn of Black Owned Broadcasters NABOB; bd mem, St Peters Union Free School District; bd mem, St Peters School Bd Education, Peekskill, NY. **Honors/Awds:** Salesman of the Year, Ebony, 1971; Exemplary Service Award, St Luke's Epis Church, 1976; Broadcaster of the Year, Nat Assn Black-Owned Broadcasters, 1984. **Military Serv:** USN Reserves, lt, 1959-66. **Business Addr:** Master Practitioner, Coach, Energy Leadership, 149 Ave Common Suite 202, Shrewsbury, NJ 07702.

SOCKWELL, OLIVER R, JR.
Executive director. **Personal:** Born Jul 27, 1943, Washington, DC; son of Janet and Oliver; married Harriet E; children: Kristine, Brian & Jason. **Educ:** Howard Univ, BS, Physics, 1965; Columbia Univ, grad Sch Bus, MBA, finance, 1972. **Career:** Bell Syst, commun engr, 1965-67; IBM, mkt rep, 1967-70; Smith Barney & Co, investment banker, 1972-74; Sallie Mae, Stud Loan Mkt Asn, vpres mkt, 1974-83, sr vpres oper, 1983-84, exec vpres finance, 1984-87; Construct Loan Insurance Corp, pres & chief exec officer, 1987-97; Columbia Univ, Grad Sch Bus, exec residence, 1997-; RR Donnelley & Sons Co, dir; Liz Claiborne Inc, dir, 2002-. **Orgs:** Bd mem, Lizz Claiborne Inc; bd mem, Columbia Univ Grad Sch Bus; bd mem, RR Donnelley & Sons; bd mem, Eugene Lang Entrepreneurial Initiative Fund; bd mem, Atlas Performing Arts Ctr; bd mem, Gail Spot; Mgt Leadership Tomorrow. **Home Addr:** 1685 Myrtle St NW, Washington, DC 20012, **Home Phone:** (202)829-0837. **Business Phone:** (201)869-0371.

SODEN, RICHARD ALLAN
Lawyer. **Personal:** Born Feb 16, 1945, Brooklyn, NY; son of Hamilton David and Clara Elaine Seal; married Marcia LaMonte Mitchell, Jun 7, 1969; children: Matthew Hamilton & Mark Mitchell. **Educ:** Hamilton Col, AB 1967; Boston Univ Sch Law, JD, 1970. **Career:** Hon Geo Clifton Edwards Jr US Ct Appeals 6th Circuit, law clerk, 1970-71; Boston Col Sch Law, fac, 1973-74; Goodwin Procter LLP, assoc, 1971-79, partner, 1979-. **Orgs:** Chmn, emer, trustee, Judge Baker Guidance Ctr, 1974-; pres, United S End Settlements, 1977-79; adv coun, Suffolk Univ Sch Mgt, 1980-; fac, Mass Continuing Legal Educ, 1980-; MA Black

Lawyers Asn, pres, 1980-81; pres, Mass Black Lawyers Asn, 1980-81; Adv Task Force Securities Regulation, Secy State Commonwealth Mass, 1982-; adv comn, Legal Educ Supreme Judicial Co Mass, 1984-; co-chmn, Lawyers Comt Civil Rights Under Law, 1991-93; Mass Minority Bus Develop Comn; Boston Bar Asn, pres, 1994-95; bd visitors, Boston Univ Goldman Sch Grad Dentistry; trustee, Boston Univ, 1995-; house deleg, Am Bar Asn, 1995-97, chair, Standing Comn on Bar Activities & Servs, 1998-; chmn, Boston Munic Res Bur, 1996-98; pres, Greater Boston Coun, Boy Scouts Am, 1997-99; Am Bar Found; pres, United S End Settlements. **Honors/Awds:** Silver Beaver Award, Boy Scouts Am; Community Youth Service Award, Heritage Dist, Boy Scouts Am; Theodore L Storer Award, Boy Scouts Am; Silver Shingle Award, Boston Univ, Sch Law; Community Service Award, Mass Bar Asn; UNICEF-Boston Local Hero Award; Camille Cosby World Children Medallion. **Special Achievements:** Author of the chapter on acquisitions in Massachusetts Business Lawyering. **Home Addr:** 42 Gray St, Boston, MA 02116, **Home Phone:** (617)423-4546. **Business Addr:** Partner, Goodwin Procter LLP, Exchange Pl 53 State St, Boston, MA 02109-2881, **Business Phone:** (617)570-1533.

SOGAH, DR. DOTSEVI YAO
Educator. **Personal:** Born Apr 19, 1945, Tegbi, Ghana; son of Fiawosinu Kwawudzo and Ahiati K; married Monica Adzo Selormey; children: Senanu, Dodzie & Esinam. **Educ:** Univ Ghana, Legon Accra Ghana, BSc, 1970, BSc, 1971; Univ Calif, Los Angeles, MS, 1974, PhD, 1975. **Career:** Univ Calif, Santa Barbara, postdoctoral fel, 1975-77; Univ Calif, res assoc, 1977-80, vis prof, 1978-80; DuPont Co, res chemist, 1981-83, group leader, 1983-84, res supvr, 1984-90, res mgr, 1990-91, consult; Columbia Univ Spring, vis prof, 1984; Cornell Univ, Ithaca, NY, prof, 1991-; Revlon, consult; Toxgon, consult; Vistacon-J&J, consult. **Orgs:** Bd dir, Am Chem Soc Delaware, Wilmington, 1982-84, chmn comt, 1984-85; chmn proj comt, ISAS, 1985-; pres, Int Soc African Sci, 1987-90; vis comtmem, Lehigh Univ Chem Dept, 1989-; pres, Int Soc African Scientists; NY Acad Sci; Sigma Xi Res Soc; AAAS. **Honors/Awds:** Bayer-Mobay Award & Lect, Cornell Univ, 1988; Distinguished CUMIRP Lect, Univ Mass, 1989; Distinguished Service Award, State Del, 1991; Percy Julian Award, Nat Org Prof Advan Black Chemists & Chem Engrs. **Special Achievements:** He invented the Process for Preparing Living Polymers, which was hailed as the invention of the century. **Business Addr:** Professor, Cornell University, Department of Chemistry, 760A Spencer T Olin Lab, Ithaca, NY 14853-1301, **Business Phone:** (607)255-4205.

SOLIUNAS, FRANCINE STEWART
Lawyer, educator. **Personal:** Born Feb 14, 1948, Chicago, IL; daughter of Wilborn Stewart and Juanita Jeanette Harris; married Jonas, Nov 17, 1973; children: Lukas (deceased) & Mikah. **Educ:** DePaul Univ, Chicago, IL, BS, math, 1970; DePaul Univ Col Law, Chicago, IL, JD, 1973. **Career:** Lawyer (retired), Educator; State Appellate Defender, Chicago, IL, staff atty, 1974-76; Equal Employment Opportunity Comn, Chicago, IL, supervising atty, 1976-80; Ill Bell Telephone Co, Chicago, IL, sr atty, 1980-88, sr dir labor relations, 1988-90, sr atty labor, 1990-92; Ameritech, counsel employ, sr dir labor rels, labor-related litigation & arbit, 1992-2000; Cook County, asst state atty; Kent Col Law, prof law, asst dean strat & prof develop & Inst law & Workplace, exec dir, currently. **Orgs:** Cook Co Bar Asn, 1972-; Iowa State Bar Asn, 1974-86; Sickle Cell Anemia Vol Enterprise, 1980-; Nat Bar Asn, 1982-; trustee, St Thomas Theol Sem,1985-88; vpres, Sickle Cell Anemia Vol Enterprise, 1985-87; dir, DePaul Univ President's Club, 1986-; Chicago Bar Asn Judicial Eval Comn, 1987-; bd dir, DePaul Univ Col Arts & Scis Adv Coun, 1987-; dir, S Cent Community Serv, 1988-2000. **Honors/Awds:** Outstanding Corporate Achiever, YMCA-Chicago Tribune, 1987; Distinguished Alumni, DePaul Univ, 1988; Black Rose Award, League Black Women, 1988; Leadership Greater Chicago, 1994; Leadership America, 1995; DePaul Alumni Award, 1999. **Special Achievements:** Hundred Most Influential Black Women in Corporate America, Ebony Magazine, 1990. **Business Addr:** Assistant Dean for Strategy & Professional Development, Executive Director of Institute for Law & the Workplace, Kent College of Law, Rm 807 565 W Adams St, Chicago, IL 60661-3691, **Business Phone:** (312)906-5286.

SOLOMON, BARBARA J.
Educator. **Personal:** Born Sep 10, 1934, Houston, TX; daughter of Willie Bryant and Malinda Edmond Bryant Stinson; married Donald; children: Hugo, Edmund, Jeffrey & Marcia. **Educ:** Howard Univ, BS, psychol, 1954; Univ Calif, Berkeley, MSW, social welfare, 1956; Univ Southern Calif, PhD, social work, 1966. **Career:** Alameda Co Med Inst, clin social worker, 1956-57; Va Hosps, Houston & Los Angeles, clin social worker, 1957-63; Univ Tex, Sch Social Work, field instr, 1958-60; Univ Calif, Los Angeles, Sch Social Welfare, field instr, 1962-63; Univ Southern Calif, Sch Social Work, prof, 1966-77, vice provost grad studies & dean grad sch, 1988-93, vice provost fac affairs & minority affairs, 1993-98, vice provost fac diversity, Stein/Sachs prof mental health, prof emer, currently; Chinese Univ, visiting examiner, Dept Social Work. **Orgs:** Nat Asn Social Workers; Coun Social Work Educ; Coun Grad Schs; Am Asn Higher Educ; bd dir, Greater LA Partnership Homeless; Sickle Cell Found; Calif Pediat Ctr; United Way LA; Alpha Kappa Alpha; bd mem, Links Inc. **Honors/Awds:** USC highest honor, the Presidential Medallion; Rosa Parks Award, Los Angeles chapter, Southern Christian Leadership Conference; USC Associates Award for Teaching Excellence. **Special Achievements:** First African American ever to hold a deanship at University of South Carolina; Books: Black Empowerment Social Work in Oppressed Communities, New York Columbia Univ Press, 1976; held the David Lawrence Stein/Violet Goldberg Sachs Professorship of Social Work. **Home Addr:** 5987 Wrightcrest Dr, Culver City, CA 90232. **Business Addr:** Professor Emeritus, University of Southern California, School Social Work, Rm 202 Admin Bldg, Los Angeles, CA 90089-4015, **Business Phone:** (213)740-5883.

SOLOMON, DAVID
Government official. **Personal:** Born May 19, 1944, Wilmington, NC; son of Vester and Helen Spaulding; divorced. **Educ:** NC A&T State Univ, Greensboro, NC, BS, 1966; St Louis Univ, St Louis, Mo, MBA, 1976. **Career:** McDonnell Douglas, St Louis, Mo, supvr, 1970-72; Monsanto, St Louis, Mo, supvr, 1972-85; self-employed, Mt Laurel, NJ, pres, 1985-88; NC Dept Econ & Community Develop, Raleigh, NC, dir, MBDA, 1988-91; NC DPT Transp, drr civil rights, 1991-93; US Dept Housing & Urban Dev, Wash DC, EO specialist, 1994-96; US Dept Transp, FTA, regional civil rights Officer, currently. **Military Serv:** USAF, capt, 1966-70. **Business Addr:** Regional Civil Rights Officer, US Department of Transportation, Federal Transit Administration Office of Civil Rights, 55 Broadway Suite 920, Cambridge, MA 02142, **Business Phone:** (202)366-6718.

SOLOMON, DONALD L.
Executive. **Personal:** Born Feb 13, 1932, Birmingham, AL; married Clarice; children: Donald Jr, Walter Lynn, Gerald. **Educ:** Miles Col, BA; Life Ins Mgt Course; LUTC; OH State Univ; Savannah State Col, US Armed Forces Inst; Univ CA. **Career:** Booker T Washington Ins Co, sr vpres mkt, currently. **Orgs:** Indus develop bd dirs Birmingham; Omega Psi Phi Frat; Triune Lodge 430 FAM. **Honors/Awds:** Blount Award, Nat Ins Asn, 1972-73; Merit Award, Booker T Wash Ins Co; Manager of Year, Nat Ins Asn. **Military Serv:** ssgt, 1958. **Business Addr:** Senoir Vice President, Booker T Washington Insurance Co, 2724 35th Ave N, Birmingham, AL 35207, **Business Phone:** (205)458-3767.

SOLOMON, FREDDIE LEE
Football player. **Personal:** Born Aug 15, 1972, Gainesville, FL. **Educ:** SC State Univ. **Career:** Football player (retired); Philadelphia Eagles, wide receiver, 1995-98; Cleveland Browns, 1999.

SOLOMON, JIMMIE LEE
Baseball executive. **Personal:** Born Jan 1, 1947, Thompsons, TX; son of Jimmie and Josephine; married; children: Tricia. **Educ:** Dartmouth Col, BA, hist (hon), 1978; Harvard Law Sch, JD, 1981. **Career:** Baker & Hostetler, atty, 1981-90, partner, 1990-91; Major League Baseball, Minor League Opers, dir, 1991-95, exec dir, 1995-2001, sr vpres baseball opers, 2001-05, exec vpres, 2005-. **Business Phone:** (212)931-7800.

SOMERSET, LEO L., JR.
Executive. **Personal:** Born Aug 27, 1945, Memphis, TN. **Educ:** Memphis State Univ, BBA, 1968; Ind Univ, MBA, 1973. **Career:** Citicorp Real Estate Inc & Citibank NA, vpres, 1973-83; Colwell Financial Corp, vpres, 1983-. **Honors/Awds:** Noyes Fel Consortium Grad Study, Mgt Ind Univ, 1971. **Military Serv:** USAF, 1st lt, 3 yrs; Honorable Discharge.

SOMERVILLE, DR. ADDISON WIMBS
Educator, psychologist. **Personal:** Born Aug 6, 1927, Greensboro, AL; son of Ernest and Ellen Wimbs; married Carolyn Coffey; children: Christopher; married Carolyn C; children: Laurene, Ernest & Christopher. **Educ:** Howard Univ, BS, psychol, 1948, MS, psychol, 1950; Ill Inst Tech, PhD, psychol, 1963. **Career:** Crownsville State Hosp MD, clin psych intern, 1950; Tech Valley Frg Army Hosp PA, chief clin psych, 1950-52; W Charlotte High Sch NC, gdnc dir, 1953-54; Elgin State Hosp Elgin, IL, staff psychologist, 1954; IIT Inst Psychol Serv, clin & consult psych, 1954-58; Dept Pupil Appraisal Wash, DC, sch psych, 1958-59; Francis W Parker Sch Chicago, chief sch psychol, 1959-64; Govt Virgin Islands St Thomas, asst dir planning mental health, 1964-65; Calif State Univ, prof psych, 1965-96, proj dir, NIMH, 1971-79, prof emer, 1996-, consult, 1982-94, adjunct prof, 1985-90; pvt pract, Somerville & Somerville Assocs, 1975-2005; Sacramento Valley Chap, Calif Asn Marriage & Family Therapists, acad liaison, 1986-92; CSUS, Chemical Dependency Studies, cert acad coordr, 1990-94. **Orgs:** Alpha Phi Alpha Fraternity Inc, 1945-; Am Psychol Asn, Div 12, 17, 29, 45, 53; Western Psychol Asn; Calif State Psychol Asn, 1988-94, chair, comtmulti-ethnic diversity, 1989-91; MCE Rev Comt, 1995-2001. **Honors/Awds:** Dipl, Am Bd Professional Psych Inc, 1971; Cert Sex Therapist & Sex Educ, Am Asn Sex Educrs, Counrs & Therapist 1977-; Approved Fel, Sex Educ Intl Coun Sex Educ & Parenthood, Am Univ, 1981; Exceptional Merit Service Award, Calif State Univ, 1984; fel & dipl, Am Bd Med Psychotherapists, 1988; Exceptional Merit Service Award, Calif State Univ, 1988; dipl, Am Bd Sexol, 1989; clin supvr, Am Bd Sexol, 1990; life fel, Soc Personality Assessment, 1990; The Honor Society for Int Scholars, Phi Beta Delta; Omicron Chap, CSUS; Outstanding Teaching Award, 1992-93. **Special Achievements:** Licensed Marriage, Family & Child Therapists, 1967; Licensed Psychologists, 1971; Licensed Educational Psychologist, 1971; published numerous articles; nominated for APA Education and Training Board Award for Distinguished Contribution to Education and Training in Psychology, 1988; Certified addiction specialist, Am Acad Health Care Providers in the Addictive Disorders, 1992-; Bd certified Diplomate, Fellow Prescribing Psychologists Register Inc. **Military Serv:** AUS, sgt, 1950-52. **Business Addr:** Professor Emeritus, California State University, Department of Psychology, 6000 J St, Sacramento, CA 95819-6007.

SOMERVILLE, PATRICIA DAWN
Manager. **Personal:** Born Nov 24, 1956, Leonardtown, MD; daughter of James Mitchell Norris and Agnes Elizabeth Stevens. **Educ:** Univ Md, Princess Anne, MD, 1978; Howard Univ, Wash, DC, BS, physical therapy, 1980; Troy State Univ, Troy, Ala, MS, mgt, 1983. **Career:** St Francis Hosp, Columbus, Ga, cardiac physical therapist, 1980-81; US Army Infantry Ctr, Fort Benning, Ga, admin, 1981-84; Headquarters, Communications-Electronics Command, Fort Monmouth, NJ, personnel mgr, 1994-. **Orgs:** Alpha Kappa Alpha Sorority. **Honors/Awds:** Most Studious Student, University of Maryland, 1976. **Business Addr:** Personnel Mgmt Specialist, Communications-Electronics Command (AMSEL-PT-PL-3), Fort Monmouth, NJ 07703, **Business Phone:** (732)532-8700.

SOMMERVILLE, JOSEPH C.
Educator, college teacher. **Personal:** Born Dec 28, 1926, Birmingham, AL; married Mattie Cunningham; children: Joseph Jr & Barry C. **Educ:** Morehouse Col, BS, 1949; Univ Mich, MS, 1956, EdS, 1966, PhD, 1969. **Career:** Douglass & Woodson Sch, Inkster, MI, prin, 1961-68, teacher, 1949-61; Wayne Co Intermediate Sch Dist, Asst Ctr, staff develop specialist, 1968-70; Univ Toledo, prof educ, dir admin internships, 1970-75; Univ Toledo, Col Educ, prof, 1970-92, prof emer, 1992-; Ohio AARP, pres, 1996; Dept Educ Leadership, dept chair, prof admin & supv. **Orgs:** State pres, Ohio AARP; Asn Sch Curric Develop; Phi Kappa Phi; pres, bd trustees, Toledo-Lucas Co Libr; West moreland Asn; Phi Delta Kappa; Sigma Pi Phi Fraternity; scholar comt chmn, Omega Psi Phi. **Honors/Awds:** Citation Outstanding Serv, Wayne Co; Speaker many National & local Professional Conferences. **Special Achievements:** Author several articles in natl & state journals & books. **Military Serv:** AUS, s/sgt, 1945-46. **Home Addr:** 1919 Richmond Rd, Toledo, OH 43607. **Business Addr:** Emeritus Professor, University of Toledo, 2801 W Bancroft, Toledo, OH 43606-3390.

SOREY, HILMON S
Executive, association executive. **Personal:** Born Jan 14, 1935, Bascom, FL; son of Hilmon S Sorey Sr and Bricy Wilson; married Martha; children: Carla-Maria & Hilmon III; married Martha Braden, Dec 23, 1983; children: Megan & Mollie. **Educ:** Fla A&M Univ, BS, 1957; Univ Chicago, MBA, 1969. **Career:** Executive, Association Executive (retired): Fla A&M Univ Hosp, adminr, 1965-67; Cleveland Metro Gen Hosp, assoc dir, 1969-71; Michael Reese Health Plan, fed exec, 1971-75; Kellogg Sch, HHSM Prog, Northwestern Univ, prog dir, 1976-87; Hilmon S Sorey Assoc, pres, 1987-90; Hawthorn Mellody Inc, pres & chief exec officer, 1990-93; Northwestern Memorial Hosp, vpres community rels & vpres support servs, 1993-97; Fla Black Bus Investment, pres. **Orgs:** The Traffic Club of Chicago; Coun Logistics Mgt; Am Col Healthcare Execs; Nat Asn Health Serv Execs. **Military Serv:** AUS, 1st Lt, 1958-60. **Home Addr:** 1425 Oldfield Dr, Tallahassee, FL 32312.

SOSA, SAMUEL PERALTA
Baseball player, executive. **Personal:** Born Nov 10, 1968, San Pedro de Macoris, Dominican Republic; married Sonia; children: Keysha, Kenia, Sammy Jr & Michael. **Career:** Baseball Player (retired), Executive: Tex Rangers, right fielder, 1989, 2007; Chicago White Sox, outfielder, 1989-91; Chicago Cubs, 1992-2004; Baltimore Orioles, right fielder, 2005; Sammy Sosa Restaurant, owner, currently; free agent, currently. **Orgs:** Founder, Sammy Sosa Charitable Found. **Honors/Awds:** Gene Autry Courage Award, 1998; Nat League Most Valuable Player Award, 1998; Sportsman of the Year, Sports Illustrated, 1998; Sportsman of the Year, Sporting News, 1998; Roberto Clemente Man of the Year Award, 1998; Hank Aaron Award, Nat League, 1999; Players Choice Man of the Year, 1999; USA Today Nat League MVP; Outstanding Player of the year; Louisville Slugger Silver Slugger; Baseball Digest Player of the Year. **Special Achievements:** Hit 66 home runs in 1998; selected three times to Nat League All-Star team; first player in major league hist to hit 60 home runs twice. **Business Addr:** Free Agent, 1060 W Addison St, Chicago, IL 60613-4397.

SOULCHILD, MUSIQ (TALIB JOHNSON)
Singer, songwriter. **Personal:** Born Sep 16, 1977, Philadelphia, PA. **Career:** Performed with The Five Spot; Wilhemina's, Mama's Boys; Albums: Aijuswannaseing, 2000; Juslisen, 2002; Soulstar,

2003; Luvanmusiq, 2007; "Radio", 2008; Singles: "Just Friends", 2000; "The Klumps", 2000; TV: "One World Jam", 2002; "Who knows", 2004; special apperence, The Game, 2007. **Honors/Awds:** Numerous honors and awards including Best Male R&B Artist, Best New Artist, BET, 2001; Source Award, R&B Artist of the Year, 2001; NAACP Image Award, Outstanding New Artist, 2001; Soul Train Award, Best R&B Single,2002; NAACP Image Award, Best Song, 2002; Billboard R&B/Hip-Hop Awards; Top R&B/Hip-Hop Artist. **Special Achievements:** Grammy nomination, Best Male R&B Vocal Performance, 2002. **Business Addr:** Singer, Songwriter, c/o Universal Music Group, 2220 Colorado Ave, Santa Monica, CA 90404, **Business Phone:** (310)865-5000.*

SOUTH, LESLIE ELAINE (LESLIE ELAINE JACKSON)
Judge. **Personal:** Born Jan 4, 1949, Chicago, IL; daughter of Mildred Nash and Wesley; married Arthur Jackson, Jul 5, 1981; children: Wesley Jackson & Christopher Jackson. **Educ:** Loyola Univ Chicago, BA, 1976; Northwestern Univ, JD, 1978. **Career:** Cook Co State atty, asst prosecutor, 1978-82; Chicago Transit Authority, 1984-88; State Ill, Circuit Ct Cook Co, assoc judge, 1988, judge 1992-. **Orgs:** Bd mem, Ill Judicial Coun, 1988-, chmn, AFA Hist Month Comn, 1988-; Ill Judges Asn, 1988-; S Suburban Bar Asn, 1989-; Womens Bar Asn, 1992-; Ill State Bar Asn, 1992-. **Honors/Awds:** Distinguished Sfs, Black Prosecutors' Asn, 1991; Judicial Sfs, Ill Judicial Coun, 1992. **Home Addr:** 1412 Heather Hill Cresent, Flossmoor, IL 60422, **Home Phone:** (708)957-5524. **Business Addr:** Judge, State of Illinois, Apellate Court, 160 N LaSalle St Suite N-1607, Chicago, IL 60601, **Business Phone:** (312)793-5450.

SOUTH, WESLEY W.
Media executive. **Personal:** Born Mar 23, 1914, Muskogee, OK; son of Elijah and Mayme Waterford; married Mildres Lynell Nash, May 18, 1946; children: Leslie Elaine South. **Educ:** Northwestern Univ, BS & BA. **Career:** Chicago Defender, 1950-51; Johnson Publishing Co, ed staff, Ebony Mag, assoc ed, 1951- 56; Chicago Am, columnist, 1957-61; NOW Mag, pub ed, 1961-62; Chicago Courier, ed, 1964-68; Radio Sta WVON, pres. **Orgs:** Bd mem, NAACP, 1961-68; Chicago Urban League, 1967-71; co-fed, People United Save Humanity, PUSH, 1971-76; bd mem, vice chmn, PUSH; bd mem, Afro-Am Patrolmen's League. **Military Serv:** AUS, corp, 1943-45.

SOUTHERLAND, ELLEASE (EBELE OSEYE)
Educator, writer. **Personal:** Born Jun 18, 1943, Brooklyn, NY; daughter of Ellease Dozier and Monroe Penrose. **Educ:** Queens Col City Univ New York, BA, 1965; Columbia Univ, MFA, 1974. **Career:** Dept Social Serv, New York City, caseworker, 1966-72; Columbia Univ, New York City, instr eng, 1973-76; Borough Manhattan Comm Col City Univ New York, adj asst prof black lit, 1973-; Pace Univ, New York City, prof eng,1975. **Orgs:** Harlem Writers Guild; Schomburg Soc; Asn Study Classical African Civilizations; Nat Asn Advan Colored People; MLA; NCTE Black Caucus; Acad Am Poets; fel, Inst African Studies Univ Nigeria. **Honors/Awds:** John Golden Award for Fiction, Queens Col City Univ New York, 1964; Gwendolyn Brooks Poetry Award, Black World, 1972; Woman of the Year, Delta Beta Zeta Chapter, Zeta Phi Beta Sorority, New York, 1989. **Special Achievements:** Author of novella White Shadows, 1964, author of poetry collection The Magic Sun Spins, Paul Breman, 1975, author of autobiographical novel Let the Lion Eat Straw, Scribner, 1979, wrote the novel "A Feast of Fools", Africana Legacy Press, 1998, Opening Line: The Creative Writer, Eneke Publications, 2000, contributor of stories, essays, and poems to anthologies and periodicals. **Business Addr:** Professor, Pace University, Department of English, 1 Pace Plz Room 1507, New York, NY 10038.

SOUTHERN, HERBERT B.
Architect. **Personal:** Born May 21, 1926, Washington, DC; son of Albert and Mildred R; married Mary Ann. **Educ:** Howard Univ, BS, Arch, 1950; Cath Univ, addn grad archit study. **Career:** Newark, NJ, draftsman, 1951-53; Architect, pvt practice; Southern Assocs, architect, currently. **Orgs:** Am Inst Architects; NJ Soc Arch; bd dir, Harmonia Savings Bank; Nat Advan Asn Colored People; Urban League; chmn, Piscataway, NJ Planning Bd; City architect design Rahway Pub Libr, 1967. **Honors/Awds:** . **Military Serv:** AUS, sgt, 1943-46. **Business Addr:** Architect, Southern Assocs Architects, 571 E Hazelwood Ave, Rahway, NJ 07065.*

SOUTHERN, JOSEPH
Educator. **Personal:** Born Nov 21, 1919, Indianapolis, IN; son of John and Mary; married Eileen; children: April Southern Reilly, Edward Joseph. **Educ:** Lincoln Univ, BS, 1941; Univ Chicago, MBA, 1945. **Career:** Prairie View State Col, asst registr, 1941-42; Southern Univ, asst prof, 1944-45; Alcorn Col, bus mgr, 1945-46; Claflin Univ, bus mgr, 1946-49; KY State Col, prof, 1950-53; Community Fin Corp, NY, mgr, vpres, 1953-57; NY Pub Sch, teacher, 1957-71; LaGuardia Col, City Univ NY, prof, 1971-85. **Orgs:** Pres, Fedn Res Afro-Am Creative Arts Inc, 1971-; co-founder & mgt ed, The Black Perspective Music, 1973-; Asn Study Afro-Am Life & Hist; Kappa Alpha Psi; life mem, Nat Asn Advan Colored People; scout leader, Boy Scouts Am. **Honors/Awds:** Award Boy Scouts Am, 1960.

SOUTHGATE, MARTHA
Writer, educator. **Personal:** Born Jan 1, 1960, Cleveland, OH; married; children: 2. **Educ:** Goddard Col, Plainfield, VT, MFA creative writing, 1994; Radcliffe Col, Harvard Univ, Cambridge, MA, radcliffe pub procedures course, 1985; Smith Col, Northampton, BA, Anthrop (cum laude), 1982. **Career:** Goddard Cols, MFA writing prog, adj prof, 2003-04; New York Univ, sch continuing & prof studies, adj prof, 2003; Eugene Lang Col, New York City, assoc chair writing dept, 2004-05; Brooklyn Col, MFA writing prog, adj assoc prof, 2006-;Articles: "Another Way to Dance"; "The Fall of Rome". **Honors/Awds:** Coretta Scott King Genesis Award, Best First Novel; NY Found Arts grant; fel, MacDowell Colony & Va Ctr Creative Arts; Alex Award, Am Libr Asn, 2003. **Business Addr:** Adjunct associate professor, Brooklyn College, 2900 Bedford Ave, New York, NY 11210, **Business Phone:** (718)951-5000.

SOWELL, JERALD
Football player. **Personal:** Born Jan 21, 1974, Baton Rouge, LA; married Kim; children: Jillian & Jordyn. **Educ:** Tulane. **Career:** New York Jets, running back, 1997-2005; Tampa Bay Buccaneers, running back, 2006; free agent, currently. **Special Achievements:** Kid Reporter of the Week Program with The Star Ledger. clothing model for the JWO Fashion Show that raised more than $20,000 for St. Marys Children and Family Services.

SOWELL, MYZELL
Lawyer. **Personal:** Born Nov 16, 1924, Detroit, MI; married Robin Hamilton. **Educ:** Wayne State Univ, BBA, 1953; Detroit Col, LlB, 1952. **Career:** Gen law pract, specialist criminal law, 1953-67; Legal Aid & Defender Asn Detroit, Defender Off, chief defender, 1968-80; Gerald K Evelyn firm, lawyer; Pvt Pract, atty, currently. **Orgs:** Detroit Bar Asn; State Bar Mich; Wolverine Bar Asn; Nat Bar Asn; Am Bar Asn; Nat Lawyers Guild; pres, Mich Asn Criminal Defense Attys; Nat Legal Aid & Defender Asn; referee, Civil Rights Comt; bd dir, Homes Black C; Nat Asn Advan Colored People; Urban Alliance; Mayor's Comt Civil Disturbance; Booker T Wash Businessmens Asn; by-laws comn, Detroit-Wayne Co Criminal Justice Syst Coordr Co; Judiciary & Correc Comn, New Detroit Inc; Mich Comn Law Enforcement & Criminal Justice Task Force Adjudication; Comn Min Prog, Comn Visitors Law Sch, Wayne State Univ Law Sch; bd dirs, Wayne State Fund, Wayne State Univ; Wayne Co Jail Adv Comn; bd regents, Nat Col Criminal Defense Lawyers & Pub Defenders. **Honors/Awds:** Lect, Prosecuting Attys Asn Mich; lect, Nat Def Col; lect, Northwestern Univ Law Sch, Criminal Law; lect, Yale Univ Law Sch; lect, Nat Dist Attys Col. **Military Serv:** AUS, sgt, 1943-45. **Business Addr:** Attorney, 645 Griswold St Suite 2000, Detroit, MI 48226, **Business Phone:** (313)964-3960.

SOWELL, THOMAS
Educator. **Personal:** Born Jun 30, 1930, Gastonia, NC; married Alma Jean Parr; children: 2. **Educ:** Harvard Univ, Cambridge MA, AB, econ, 1958; Columbia Univ, NY, AM, econ, 1959; Univ Chicago, IL, PhD, econ, 1968. **Career:** US Dept Labor, economist, 1961-62; Rutgers Univ, instr, 1962-63; Howard Univ, lectr, 1963-64; Am Tel & Telegraph Co, econ analyst, 1964-65; Cornell Univ, asst prof, 1965-69; Brandeis Univ, assoc prof, 1969-70; Univ Calif Los Angeles, assoc prof, 1970-74, prof econ, 1974-80; Urban Inst, WA, DC, proj dir, 1972-74; vis prof, Amherst Col, 1977; Uinv Calif Los Angeles, Prof Economics, 1974-80. **Orgs:** Fel Ctr Advan Study Behavioral Sci, Stanford, CA, 1976-77; sr fel HooverInst, Stanford Univ, CA, 1977 sr fel Rose & Milton Friedman Pub Policy,1980; consult, Urban Coalition, Rockefeller Found, Urban Inst. **Honors/Awds:** Stanford Univ, Senior Fellow, 1980-; Author numerous works in field, incl Civil Rights: Rhetoric of Reality?, Morrow, 1985, Education: Assumptions versus History, Hoover Inst, 1986, Compassion versus Guilt, and Other Essays, Morrow, 1987, A Conflict of Visions: Ideological Origins of Political Struggles, Morrow, 1987; contributed to numerous periodicals; National Humanities Medal, 2002; Bradley Prize, 2003. **Military Serv:** US Marine Corps, 1951-53. **Business Addr:** Rose and Milton Friedman Senior Fellow on Public Policy, Hoover Institution, Stanford University, 434 Galvez Mall, Stanford, CA 94305.

SPAIN, HIRAM, JR.
Lawyer, administrator. **Personal:** Born Aug 22, 1936, Conway, SC; son of Hiram and Gladys; married Doris; children: Hiram, Nicole. **Educ:** SC State Col, BS, 1961; Howard Univ, JD, 1971; Columbia Inte Sem, Master Divinity degree. **Career:** Teacher, 1961-68; legal intern, Greenville, 1971-72; Off Gov John C West, SC, proj dir, 1972-74; Columbia Urban League, chief exec officer, 1974-. **Orgs:** Nat Asn Black Soc Workers; Delta Theta Phi Lavy Fraternity; Delta Psi Omega; consult, HEW, 1977; NABSW Bus Conf, 1975; Nat Asn Advan Colored People; Kappa Alpha Psi; Masons; Columbia Black Lawyers Asn; Notary Pub, SC; Delta Psi Omega; Health Policy Coun, Gov John W, 1974; Nat Coun Urban League; Gethsemane Baptist Asn; pastor, St Mark Baptist Church, Columbia, 1999-; first exec secy, Baptist Educ & Missionary Convention SC, 2000. **Honors/Awds:** Outstanding Soldier, Bussac, France, 1956; Outstanding Business Student Award, UBEA, 1961; Outstanding Employee Award, NCIC, 1971. **Special Achievements:** First black bureau chief of the South Carolina Department of Social Services; recognized by Who's Who in American Colleges and Universities of the South, in the South East, in Black America. **Military Serv:** AUS, 1954-57. **Business Addr:** Executive Assistant, State Department of Social Services, 1520 Confederate Ave, PO Box 1520, Columbia, SC 29202.*

SPAND, REV. DR. MARGOT
Association executive. **Career:** The Women Color Found & Health Ministries Inc, mem & bd dir. **Business Addr:** Member, Board of Directors, The Women of Color Foundation & Health Ministries Inc, PO Box 3835, Southfield, MI 48037, **Business Phone:** (248)569-3532.

SPANN, PAUL RONALD
Clergy. **Personal:** Born Nov 7, 1943, Ann Arbor, MI; son of Paul Leon and Ruth Ann Green; married Jacqueline Graves, Jan 4, 1976; children: Shannon Lyn MacVean-Brown & Seth David. **Educ:** Kalamazoo Col, BA, 1965; Univ Rochester, 1966; Episcopal Divinity Sch, MDiv, 1970. **Career:** St Timothy's Church, asst, 1970-71; Church Messiah, rector, 1971; St Cyprian's Episcopal Church, consult & spiritual dir, 1996; Licensed PRH educr, 1998; Christ Church Spirituality Ctr, dir, currently; CREDO, spirituality fac; Ecumenical Theol Sem, Detroit, adj. **Orgs:** Past pres, founder, vpres, Island view Village Develop Corp, currently; standing comt, Diocese Mich, 1988-92; nat secy, Christian Community Develop Asn, 1989-93; Union Black Episcopalians, 1976-. **Honors/Awds:** Fel, Woodrow Wilson Found, 1965-66; Malcolm Dade Lectureship, St Cyprian's Episcopal Church, 1989; Econ Justice Comn Award, Diocese Mich, 1993. **Special Achievements:** Sojourners Liturgy Mag, "Wholeness & Community," July 1991, "Oblivion & the Ghetto", 1987, Chapter on "Co-operative Housing" in book, Making Housing Happen, 2007, Chalice Press. **Business Addr:** Director, Christ Church Spirituality Center, 61 Grosse Pointe Blvd, Grosse Pointe Farms, MI 48207, **Business Phone:** (313)885-4841.

SPARKS, PHILLIPPI DWAINE
Football player. **Personal:** Born Apr 15, 1969, Oklahoma City, OK; married Jodi; children: Phillippi Jr & Jordin. **Educ:** Glendale Community Col; Ariz State Univ. **Career:** Football player (retired); New York Giants, defensive back, 1992-99; Dallas Cowboys, cornerback, 2000. **Orgs:** Sigma chi fraternity, Ariz State Univ.

SPARROW, RORY DARNELL
Basketball player, baseball manager. **Personal:** Born Jun 12, 1958, Suffolk, VA. **Educ:** Villanova Coll, BS. **Career:** Basketball player (retired); NJ Nets, 1980-81; Atlanta Hawks, 1981-82; New York Knicks, 1982-88; Miami Heat, 1988-90; Sacramento Kings, 1990-91; Chicago Bulls, 1991-92; Los Angeles Lakers, 1992; NBA, prog mgr, 1994. **Orgs:** Founder Rory D Sparrow Found. **Honors/Awds:** All Big-5 First Team; All-Dist Team, US Basketball Writer's; Eastern Atl Assoc All-Tour Team.

SPAULDING, AARON LOWERY
Investment banker. **Personal:** Born Mar 16, 1943, Durham, NC. **Educ:** NC Cent Univ, Durham, attended 1964; Wharton Grad Sch Finance & Com Univ Pa, Philadelphia, attended 1968. **Career:** Re-Con Serv Inc, dir & co-founder, 1968; JFK Ctr Performing Arts, comptroller, 1972-74; Boyden Bd Dirs Servs, exec dir, 1974; B&C Assoc Wash, dir bus develop & consult, 1974; Exec Off Pres The White House, assoc dir pres personnel off, 1974-77; Salomon Brothers Inc, vpres, 1977. **Orgs:** Pres, Wharton MBA Asn; res asst, Dept of Industry & the Placement Off, Univ Pa. **Honors/Awds:** Outstanding Academic Achievement Award, NC Cent Univ, 1964. **Military Serv:** USN, supply corps officer & mil social aide, 1969-72.

SPAULDING, JEAN GAILLARD
School administrator. **Personal:** Born Feb 23, 1947, Birmingham, AL; divorced; children: Chandler & Courtney. **Educ:** Barnard Col, AB, 1968; Duke Univ Sch Med, MD, 1972. **Career:** Duke Univ Med Ctr, Dept Psychiat, adj fac, 1990-92, vice chancellor health affairs, 1998-, assoc consulting prof, currently; pvt psychiat pract, 1977-; WNCU Public Radio, co-host of weekly radio show, 1997-; WTVD Newschannel 11, consult, 1997-; Duke Endowment, trustee, currently. **Orgs:** Alpha Omega Alpha Honor Soc; Am Psychiatric Asn; AMA; Nat Med Asn; Am Asn Psychiat Servs C; Am Col Forensic Examrs; NC Neuro-Psychiatric Asn; NC Coun Child Psychiat; Durham-Orange County Med Soc; NC Med Soc; Old N State Med Asn; Josiah Charles Trent Memorial Found, bd dirs, 1990-, vpres, 1995-; Res Triangle Found, bd trustees, 1993-97; bd dirs, Wachovia Bank NC, 1995-. **Honors/Awds:** Physician's Recognition Award, AMA. **Special Achievements:** First African American woman to attend Duke's School of Medicine; "Delayed Psychiatric Casualties from the Vietnam Conflict," Mental Health and Behavioral Science, Vol. XVIII, No. 3, August 1976; "Anniversary Reactions," Psychosomatics, Vol. XVII, No. 4, 1976, pp 210-12; "Grief: Normal or Abnormal?" North Carolina Medical Journal, Vol. 39, No. 1, January 1978, pp. 31-34. **Business Addr:** Trustee, The Duke Endowment, PO Box 3644, Durham, NC 27710, **Business Phone:** (919)668-3326.

SPAULDING, LYNETTE VICTORIA
Lawyer. **Personal:** Born Dec 21, 1954, Bronx, NY; daughter of Gertie Mae and Aaron M. **Educ:** SUNY Stony Brook, BA, 1976; Syracuse Univ Col Law, JD, 1979. **Career:** Syracuse Univ Law Sch, secy, 1976-79; Bristol Lab, law clerk, 1977-79; Reginald Heber Smith Comn, lawyer fel prog, 1979; Legal Aid Soc Westchester Co, atty, 1979-, Criminal Div, sr atty & dep bur chief, 1987-.

Orgs: Treas, Nat Asn Advan Colored People, Stony Brook, 1975-76; comn chairperson, Black Am Law Stud Asn, 1976-79; justice, Judicial Bd, Syracuse Univ Col, 1976-79; bd dirs, Nat Asn Black Women Attys, 1978-82; Moot Court Bd, Col Law, 1979; chairperson & bd trustees, Divine Light USDA Church, 1985-; Black Lawyers Westchester Co, 1997; New York State Bar; New York State Defenders Asn. **Honors/Awds:** Special Recognition, BALSA & Womens Law Caucus Law Day, 1977; Frederick Douglass Moot Court, BALSA Nat, 1979; Black Boys Westchester Asn; NY Criminal Defenders Asn. **Special Achievements:** Subject of article in Defender's Digest. **Business Addr:** Senior Attorney, Deputy Bureau Chief, Legal Aid Society of Westchester, Criminal Division, 1 N Broadway, White Plains, NY 10601, **Business Phone:** (914)286-3400.

SPAULDING, ROMEO ORLANDO
Firefighter, president (organization). **Personal:** Born Aug 27, 1940, Whiteville, NC; son of Ralph and Sarah George; married Annette Richardson, Jan 23, 1962; children: Valerie G, Bernardine E, Alva G, Karen R & Kevin R. **Educ:** Howard Univ, Wash, DC, math, 1958-62; Univ DC, Wash, DC, fire serv, 1969-70; Univ Md, Col Park, MD, Nat Staff & Command Sch, attended 1981. **Career:** Kenwood Golf & Country Club, Bethesda, MD, food serv, 1958-59; Columbia Hosp Women, Wash, DC, procurement, 1959-65; DC Fire Dept, Wash, DC, dir, community rels/lt, 1965-92. **Orgs:** Supt, Sunday Sch Bethel Bible Church, 1976-; treas, PG County PTA, 1976-80; pres, Progressive Fire Fighter Asn, 1981-85; exec bd mem, Nat Black Leadership Roundtable, 1981-90; pres, 1988, exec dir, Int Asn Black Prof Fire Fighters, 1996-02. **Honors/Awds:** Cong Commendation, US Cong, 1985; Community Service Award, DC Govt, 1986 & 1987; Firefighter of the Year, Firehouse Mag, 1989; National School Volunteer of the Year, 1989; Christian Man of the Year, Bethel Bible Church, 1989.

SPAULDING, WILLIAM RIDLEY
Government official. **Personal:** Born in Clarkton, NC; married Dolores Hinton; children: Angelyn Flowers, Michelle & Deirdre. **Educ:** Howard Univ, BS, mech eng, 1947. **Career:** DC Pub Schs, instr, 1947-52; Howard Univ, instr, 1950-60; Nat Security Agency, engr, 1952-74; Univ DC, instr, 1980; City Council, councilman; DC Courts, Dept Admin Serv, dir, adminr. **Orgs:** Chair, Ft Lincoln Found; bd mem, Kidney Found; bd mem, Am Heart Asn; chair, Talent Search Inc. **Honors/Awds:** Producer, Metro Talent Search, 1978-85. **Business Addr:** Councilman, City Council, 14th E Sts NW, Washington, DC 20004.

SPEAKS, RUBEN L.
Bishop. **Career:** Bishop (retired); African Methodist Episcopal Zion church, sr bishop. **Honors/Awds:** 100 most influential black Americans & organization leaders. *

SPEARMAN, LARNA KAYE
Engineer. **Personal:** Born May 7, 1945, Kokomo, IN; married Sarah Jewell Busch; children: Angela, Derek. **Educ:** Purdue Univ, BS, 1967; Ind Univ Law Sch, 1971. **Career:** Detroit Deisel Allison, engr, 1967-71; Mayor, coordr, 1976-77; Eli Lilly & Co, supr, 1971-76, personnel; Nat Asn Civilian Oversight Law Enforcement, secy. **Orgs:** Guest lectr, Nat Crime Prevention Inst; Sch Police Adminr, Univ Lousiville; vchmn, Human Rights Comn Indianapolis & Marion Co; secy, Indianapolis Settlements Inc; bd mem, Indianapolis Chap Nat Advan Asn Colored People; Indianapolis Black Rep Coun; Indianapolis Police Merit Bd, 1970-74; Minority Contractors Adv Coun, 1970-71. **Honors/Awds:** Distinguished Service Award, Indianapolis Jaycees, 1977; Outstanding Young Hoosier Award, IN Jaycees, 1977; Citz Award, Police League Ind, 1977. **Business Addr:** Secretary, National Association for Civilian Oversight of Law Enforcement, 638 E Vermont St, Indianapolis, IN 46202, **Business Phone:** (866)462-2653.

SPEARS, ANGELENA ELAINE
Journalist. **Personal:** Born Jun 28, 1955, Lansing, MI; daughter of George and Louise Owens; married Charles Spears, Apr 19, 1980; children: Carmen, Jason, George & Lydia. **Educ:** Northwestern Univ, BAS, 1978. **Career:** Reading Eagle/Times, correspondent, 1996-; Spears-Harambee Co, owner, currently. **Orgs:** Bd mem, Cent PA African Am Mus, 1999-; Bethel AME Church. **Home Addr:** 420 Lincoln Dr, Wernersville, PA 19565.

SPEARS, HENRY ALBERT
Executive director, insurance agent. **Personal:** Born Jun 4, 1928, Montgomery, AL; son of Dan Spears and Jettie Bennett; married Kathleen Stanford, Aug 18, 1947; children: Vicki Regina Glass, Henry A Jr & Kathy Evangeline Cobbs. **Educ:** Ala State Col Lab Sch, Grad (valedictorian), 1946; Ala State Univ, BS, sec ed, 1950, MeD, 1955; Springfield Col, Grad Study 1959; NY Life Career Course & NASD Regist Rep Courses, 1974. **Career:** St Jude's Educ Inst, Montgomery AL, teacher auto mech, 1949-50; G W Carver High Sch, sci & math teacher, 1950-55; Carver Adult Sch, instr, 1954-55; Montgomery YMCA, exec secy, 1955-63, 1968-69; Ala State Col, dir col rels, 1963-68; Ala State Univ, vpres develop, 1969-72; NY Life Ins Co, field underwriter, 1972-93, retired agt's contract 1993-; RHU designation 1979-, NYLIFE Securities, Inc, regist rep, 1986-2001; Ala State Univ Found, exec dir, currently. **Orgs:** Emancipation Proclamation Comt, pres, 1957-58, 1971-72; Montgomery Athletic Boosters Club, 1973-98; Montgomery & Nat Asn Life Underwriters, 1973-96; adv bd, Cent Ala Home Health Serv Inc, 1974-89; bd dirs, adv bd, Ala State Univ Found, Inc 1974-94, chmn bd, 1992-94, exec dir, 1994-; trustee, Lomax-Hannon Jr Col, 1978-93; bd mem, Montgomery Co Bd Educ 1976-, chmn bd, 1988-92, vice chmn bd, 1996-98; bd dirs, adv bd, Goodwill Industries, 1983-; bd mem, Omega Life Memshp Found, 1986-92; Nat Sch Bds Asn, 1988-96; dist rep, 7th Dist, Omega Psi Phi Fraternity Inc, 1989-92; Comt "100" Montgomery Area Chamber Com, 1990-92; Red Cross Three Gallon Plus Donor Club, 1991-; treas, AL Caucus Black Sch Bd Members, 1991-; elected Honary life bd member, Montgomery Metropolitan YMCA, 1995; comt, Omega Psi Phi Frat Inc, 1998-2002; past pres, Dist IV & former bd member, & completed Master Level 10th year Sch Bd Acad, 2002; Supreme Coun; former basileus, KRS & KF Sigma Phi Chap Omega Psi Phi Fraternity; Alpha Kappa Mu, Beta Kappa Chi, Phi Delta Kappa; former steward & past trustee, Mt Zion AME Zion Church Inc; life mem, Nat Educ Asn; Elks So Pride Lodge 431; W Montg Masonic Lodge 921; 33 degree Mason; PH Consistory 19; Montgomery Chap NAACP; Dem Party/Club; Ala Dem Conf; steering comt, Coun Urban Bds Ed; chmn, Int NAACP; Ala Asn Sch Bds; life mem 599 Omega Psi Phi Fraternity Inc; bd exec dir, Cleveland Ave Br YMCA. **Honors/Awds:** Distinguished Serv & Prestige award, Ala State Univ, 1972; Outstanding Serv Montgomery Area United Appealm, 1973; Outstanding Alumni Award, Ala State Univ Centennial, 1974; Omega qualified each year as a "Star Club Member" through a notable sales record with NY Life Ins, 1973-81; Outstanding Leadership in the Montgomery Urban League, 1979-81; Health Ins Leader 5 yrs, RHU 1979; Citizen of the Year Award, Sigma Phi Chap, 1982; 40 Yrs of Serv Plaque YMCA, 98; Nationl Sales Achievement Award 10 yrs; Nat Quality Award 6 yrs; Health Ins Quality Award 5 yrs; Leading Producers Roundtable Health Ins 3 yrs; Reg Prof Disability Income & Health Ins Underwriter, RHU, Mt Zion AME Zion Church, honoree for 35 yrs of service, 1988; Man of the Year Award, Omega 7th Dist, 1992; Masters Honor Roll mem of the Ala Asn of Sch Boards Acad. **Home Addr:** 2069 Wabash St, Montgomery, AL 36108-4152, **Home Phone:** (334)263-1221. **Business Addr:** Executive Director, Alabama State University Foundation, PO Box 1046, Montgomery, AL 36101-1046, **Business Phone:** (334)229-4950.

SPEARS, MARCUS (MARCUS DEWAYNE SPEARS)
Football player. **Personal:** Born Sep 28, 1971, Baton Rouge, LA. **Educ:** Northwestern State Univ. **Career:** Football Player (Retired); Chicago Bears, linebacker, 1996; Kans City Chiefs, 1997-2003; HoustonTexans, 2004. **Orgs:** Omega Psi Phi Fraternity.

SPEARS, MARCUS DEWAYNE. See SPEARS, MARCUS.

SPEARS, RICHARD JAMES
Real estate agent, executive. **Personal:** Born Mar 5, 1962, Holyoke, MA; son of James Spears and Janet Spears; married Sheri Spears, Sep 22, 1990; children: Armand & Brandon. **Educ:** Syracuse Univ, BS, 1984; NYU, diploma, re-investment analysis, 1990. **Career:** Gold Coast Realty, project dir, 1987-90; Powerhouse Realty, pres, 1990-. **Orgs:** Alpha Phi Alpha, 1981-; pres, pres, 100 Black Men NJ, 1998-2000; NJ Asn Real Estate Brokers, 1998-2001; bd mem, Big Brothers/Big Sisters, Essex Co, 1999-. **Honors/Awds:** Who's Who in Real Estate, 1984; Outstanding Young Men of America, 1984; NAREB Million Dollar Sales Club, 1998. **Special Achievements:** 100 Most Influential, City News, 1998; Top 20 African-American Business People, NJ Bus News, 1999; Contributor, NJ Star Ledger; Jersey Jour; Bergen Record; Black Collegian Mag. **Business Addr:** President, Powerhouse Realty LLC, 2274 John F Kennedy Blvd Suite 1, Jersey City, NJ 07304, **Business Phone:** (201)333-1800.

SPEARS, SANDRA CALVETTE
Marketing executive. **Personal:** Born Aug 9, 1964, Pontiac, MI; daughter of Calvin and Sandra Wilkerson Lockett. **Educ:** Eastern Mich Univ, Ypsilanti, MI, BS, 1986. **Career:** Total Health Care Inc, Detroit, MI, mkt rep, 1987-89, mkt develop coord, 1989, new provider & mkt develop coord, 1989-90, acct exec, 1990, asst pub mkt mgr, 1994-. **Orgs:** Nat Asn Advan Colored People, 1986; Booker T Wash Bus Asn, 1986; Eastern Mich Univ Alumni Asn, 1986; Nat Asn Health Serv Exec, 1987; Southeastern Mich Health Exec Forum, 1987. **Honors/Awds:** Top Sales Achiever, Total Health Care, 1987-90. **Home Addr:** 27240 Winterset Circle, Farmington Hills, MI 48334-4065, **Home Phone:** (313)354-8408. **Business Addr:** Assistant Public Marketing Manager, Total Health Care Inc, 3011 W Grand Blvd, Detroit, MI 48202, **Business Phone:** (313)871-7805.

SPEARS, STEPHANIE
Consultant. **Personal:** Born Dec 9, 1949, San Francisco, CA; daughter of Richard McGee and Thadyne Black; married John, Jul 22, 1972; children: Mikele Adriana & Julian Richard. **Educ:** Univ Calif, Berkeley, BA, 1972. **Career:** Scenery United Ltd Tours, travel consult, 1968-82; Empire Tours, retail off mgr, 1982-83; Blue World Travel, travel consult, 1983-88; Adventure Express & Rascals Paradise, opers mgr, 1988-98; Blue World Travel, dir opers, 1998-, treas. **Orgs:** Pres, San Francisco Women In Travel, 1995-97; Travel Agent Adv Bd, Govt Bahamas, 1996-99; pac gov, Int Fed Women's Travel Org, 1997-99; bd mem, AFA Hist & Cult Soc, 1997-99. **Special Achievements:** Portion of essay published in Travel Guide for AFA Women, 1997. **Home Addr:** 3450 Wyman St, Oakland, CA 94619, **Home Phone:** (510)536-6707. **Business Addr:** Director, Blue World Travel Corp, 50 1st St 411, San Francisco, CA 94105, **Business Phone:** (415)882-9444.*

SPEARS JONES, PATRICIA KAY (PATRICIA JONES)
Arts administrator, educator, poet. **Personal:** Born Feb 11, 1951, Forrest City, AR; daughter of Lee and Lillie B Dodd. **Educ:** Rhodes Col, BA, commun, 1973; Vermont Col, MFA, 1992. **Career:** Poet & writer, 1974-; Samuel French Inc, mgr amateur leasing, 1974-77; Coord Coun Lit Mag, grants progs dir, 1977-81; Freelance journalist: Essence, Village Voice, Poetry Proj Newsletter, 1978-; Heresies Colctive Inc, managing coordr, 1982-83; Poetry Proj St Mark's Church, prog coordr, 1984-86; Massachusetts Coun Arts & Humanities, prog specialist, 1987-; Film News Now Educ, prog dir, 1990-91; New Mus Contemp Art, develop assoc, 1991-94, dir planning develop, 1994-96; Auth Read Aloud, proj dir & consult, 1996-98; Local Initiatives Support Corp, develop officer, 1998-; Naropa Univ, fac; Sarah Lawrence Col, fac; Parsons Sch Design & Poetry, teacher, currently. **Orgs:** Vpres, Nat Asn Third World Writers, 1979-82; consult, CCLM, 1981; dir, Mabou Mines 1984-86; Poetry Soc Am, 1984-, NY Asn Black Journalists, 1985-86; panelist, New York Found Arts, 1986; bd dirs, Poetry Proj, 1991; juror, Judith's Room Emerging & Outstanding Women Poets Series, 1991; fel Poetry, Nat Endowment Arts, 1993; PEN Am Ctr; Authors Guild; Poets House Friends Comm; panelist, Lit Prog, NY Coun Arts, 1993-94; Breadloaf, fel, 1996; residency, VIR Ctr Creative Arts, 1996; residency, Millay Colony Arts, 1998; judge, Pen Poetry Translation Prize, 2002. **Special Achievements:** Publication of "Mythologizing Always," Telephone Books CT, 1981, author of The Weather That Kills, Coffee House Press, Minneapolis MN, 1995; co-editor, Ordinary Women: Poems by New York City Women; author, "Mother," 1994; poem selected for best American Poetry, 2000; Poetry after 911, 2001. **Business Addr:** Development Officer, Local Initiatives Support Corp (LISC), 733 3rd Ave, New York, NY 10017, **Business Phone:** (212)455-9832.

SPEED, JAMES H, JR.
President (Organization), chief executive officer. **Educ:** NC Cent Univ, BS, 1975; Atlanta Univ, MBA, 1979; Deloitte & Touche, cert pub acct, 1979. **Career:** Hardee's Food Systs Inc, sr vpres, chief fin officer & treas; NC Mutual, consult, sr vpres & chief fin officer; NC Mutual, pres & chief exec officer; NC Mutual Life Ins Co, pres & chief exec officer, currently. **Orgs:** Am Inst Cert Pub Acct; Inst Mgt Acct; Nat Asn Black Accts; bd dirs, RBC Centura Funds Inc; comn, Bus Laws & the Econ; NC Pub Schs Adminr Task Force. **Business Addr:** President, Chief Executive Officer, North Carolina Mutual Life Insurance Co, 411 W Chapel Hill St, Durham, NC 27701, **Business Phone:** (919)682-9201.*

SPEEDE-FRANKLIN, WANDA A.
School administrator. **Personal:** Born Aug 1, 1956, Bronx, NY; married Melvin L; children: Ihsan K. **Educ:** Princeton Univ, BA, 1978, cert prof African-Am Studies, 1978; N western Univ, MA, 1980. **Career:** Princeton Univ, res asst comput ctr, 1974-78, asst dir third world ctr, 1974-78; N western Univ, grad fel, 1978-79; Chicago Metro History Fair, assoc dir progs & opers, 1980-82; Nat Asn Independent Schs, dir, minority affairs & info serv, 1982-87; Mass Bay Transp Authority, asst dir admin pub affairs, 1987-88; Newton Metco Prog, dir; Needham Pub Schs, dir. **Orgs:** Trustee, Proj Match Minority Stud Talent Search Agency, 1984-; Nat Asn-Black Sch Educr; Am Asn Affirmative Action; Nat Asn Negro Women; bd mem,Metro Coun Equal Opportunity, 1985-. **Special Achievements:** Co-Author, Visible Now: Blacks in Private Schools, Greenwood Press, 1988.

SPEIGHT-BUFORD, DR. VELMA R
School administrator. **Personal:** Born Nov 18, 1932, Snow Hill, NC; daughter of John Thomas Speight and Mable Edwards Speight; married William M; children: T Chineta Kennedy Davis. **Educ:** A&T State Univ, NC, BS, 1953; Univ Md, MEd, guid, 1965; PhD, coun personnel serv, 1976. **Career:** Adminr(retired), asn exec; Kennard High Sch, teacher, 1954-60; Morgan State Col, NSF fel, 1956; Univ Md, NSF fel, 1957; Va State Col, NDEA fel, 1963; Kennard High Sch, Queen Anne's Co High Sch, counr, 1960-68; Queen Anne's County High Sch, co-ordr guid dept, 1966-68; Nat Defense Educ Act Inst Disadvantaged Youth; Univ Md, Eastern Shore Br, staff consult, 1967; Family Life & Sex Educ, Caroline, Kent, Queen Anne's & Talbot County, curriculum res specialist, 1969; Univ Md, Johns Hopkins Univ, vis prof & assoc prof; Univ Md, Equal Opportunity Recruitment Prog, dir, 1972; Md State Dept Educ, Compensatory Urban & Suppl Prog, asst supr, 1969-72, specialist guid, 1972-76, adminr, 1976, asst state supt, 1982-86; Univ Md, Eastern Shore, Princess Anne, Dept Couns Educ, chair, 1986-87; East Carolina Univ, Greenville, NC, Dept Couns & Adult Educ, chair, 1987; Univ Md Eastern Shore, Dept Educ, chair, 1989-93; NC A & T State Univ, dir alumni affairs, 1997; bd trustees, 1998-, chmn bd trustees, 2005-. **Orgs:** Life mem, Md State Teachers Asn; Nat Educ Asn; pres, Queen Anne's County Teacher Asn & Educ Asn; Md Asn Counr Educ &

Supv; Md Sch Counr Asn; Am Personnel & Guid Asn; Md Asn Curriculum Develop, Am Asn Sch Bus Officials; Delmarva Alumni Asn, A&T State Univ; Study Group Mothers Prevent Dropouts; teacher, Summer Courses Black Stud; organizer & chmn, Youth Group Study Problems Integration; Queen Anne's, Kent & Talbot County Comn Action Agency Bd; Md & Nat Cong Parents & Teachers; NAACP; organizer & chmn, Parent Educ Group Communication Rather Than Confrontation; chmn, Christian Social Rels Comt, Weslyan Serv Guild; Asn Sup & Curriculum Develop; Am Asn Coun & Develop; Asn Counr Educ & Sup; Nat Career Develop Asn; Sch Counr Asn; Am Rehabilitation Coun Asn; Asn Meas & Evaluation Coun & Develop; Asn Multicultural Coun & Develop; Md Asn Coun & Develop; Md Career Develop Asn; Md Asn Multicultural Coun & Develop; organizer, Black Churches Educ Excellence, 1987-. **Honors/Awds:** Woman of the Year, Negro Bus & Prof Women's Orgn; Alumni Achievement Award, A&T State Univ, 1974; Phi Delta Kappa; Alumni Excellence Award, A&T State Univ, 1982; Presidential Citation to Distinguished Alumni, Nat Asn Equal Opportunity Higher Educ, 1985; Minority Achievement Award, Md State Teachers Asn, 1988; Teacher of the Year, Univ Md Eastern Shore, 1992; Administrator of the Year, NC A&T State Univ, 1997. **Special Achievements:** Author of "Improving the Status of the Culturally Different and Disadvantaged Minority Students" in Gifted Programs, 1988-89. **Home Addr:** 11 Carissa Ct, Greensboro, NC 27407, **Home Phone:** (336)454-8125.

SPEIGHTS, NATHANIEL H
Lawyer. **Personal:** Born Nov 24, 1949, Bellaire, OH; son of Nathaniel H and Ollie; married Grace E, May 21, 1984; children: Ashley & Nathaniel IV. **Educ:** Col Wooster, Ohio, BA, 1972; Univ Miami, Fla, JD, 1975. **Career:** Speights & Mitchell, partner, atty, currently. **Orgs:** Pres, Wash Bar Asn. **Home Addr:** 3130 Rittenhouse NW, Washington, DC 20015, **Home Phone:** (202)362-4713. **Business Addr:** Attorney, Speights & Mitchell, 2600 Va Ave NW, Washington, DC 20037, **Business Phone:** (202)337-9800.

SPEIGINER, GERTHA
School administrator. **Personal:** Born Apr 28, 1917, St Louis, MO; married Louis Sol; children: Delores, Doris, Deborah, Darlene, Delanya, Desiree, Delicya & Dauphne Delauna. **Educ:** Mt San Antonio Col. **Career:** Studio Girl Cosmetic, rep; Calif Polytech Univ, lectr, 1972-73; Mt San Antonio Col, Community Ctr, dir, 1970-74. **Orgs:** Pres, Pomona Parents Coun, 1965-68; past pres, Parents Understanding, 1967-71; pres, Pomona Valley Br, Nat Asn Advan Colored People; vpres, So Area Conf, Nat Asn Advan Colored People, 1974-76; charter mem, treas, Pomona Day Sch; bd mem YWCA; Outreach Prog YMCA; Pasadena Legal Aid Bd; Pomona Legal Aid; Nat Asn Colores Women. **Honors/Awds:** Plaque for outstanding Black community service, 1971; Certificate Merit for continuous service community; plaque dedicated service to community Pomona Valley Branch.

SPELLER, CHARLES K.
Orthopedic surgeon. **Personal:** Born Feb 25, 1933, Windsor, NC; married Virginia. **Educ:** NC Cent Univ, 1954; Meharry Med Col, 1966. **Career:** Monmouth Med Ctr, Long Branch, NJ; Ill Masonic Hosp; Columbia Univ NY, internship. **Orgs:** Harris County Med Soc; Houston Med Forum; Nat Med Asn; Nat Trauma Soc; Sovereign Grand Insp Gen, 33rd & last deg Ancient & Accept Scottish Rite, Free masonry Gen Corp, 1954-56. **Business Addr:** Surgeon, 5445 Almeda Rd Suite 302, Houston, TX 77004.*

SPELLMAN, ALONZO ROBERT
Football player, boxer. **Personal:** Born Sep 27, 1971, Mount Holly Township, NJ; married Lizzie. **Educ:** Ohio State Univ. **Career:** Football player (retired), mixed martial arts fighter; Chicago Bears, defensive end, 1992-97; Dallas Cowboys, 1999-2000; Detroit Lions, 2001; Las Vegas Gladiators, 2006; Mixed martial arts fighter, currently. **Business Addr:** Mixed Martial Arts Fighter, Chicago, IL 48101.

SPENCE, DONALD DALE
Dentist. **Personal:** Born Dec 6, 1926, Philadelphia, PA; married Theresa Seltzer; children: Kenneth, Donna, Rosalynn, Melanie. **Educ:** Morris Col, Atlanta, attended 1950; Howard Univ Sch Dentist, DDS, 1960. **Career:** Staff, Baptist Univ, Sacred Heart Hosp; bd dir, Pensacola C C; Pvt pract dentist, currently. **Special Achievements:** Apptd by Gov Reubin Asken to Escambia County Sch Bd and is the highest ranking Black Official NW Florida in 1975. **Business Addr:** Dentist, 2280 N 9th Ave, Pensacola, FL 32593.

SPENCE, REV. JOSEPH SAMUEL, SR.
Lawyer, educator. **Personal:** Born Dec 20, 1950; son of Olive Maud Bambridge and Kenneth John; married Attorney Sheila M; children: Joseph Jr, Joselyn Maria, Jonathan Clarence & Parrish Spence. **Educ:** Pikes Peak Col, AA; Univ MD, BSc; Webster Univ, MA; Washburn Univ Law Sch, Topeka, KS, JD; Brunnel Univ W London, Brunnel, England, int comparative law. **Career:** Century 21 Real Estate, realtor assoc, 1978-80; AUS, capt, 1980-86; Riley County Dist Atty's Off, 1987; City Topeka Atty's Off, 1988-89; Kans State Senate, 1988-89; Milwaukee Area Tech Col, instr, 1991-; Spence Law Offices, Milwaukee, 1992-; Bryant & Stratton Col, instr, currently. **Orgs:** Founder & chapter pres, Lambda Alpha Epsilon Criminal Justice Fraternity, 1974; Alpha Phi Alpha; Rep-at-large Frederick Douglass Ctr Manhattan KS, 1986-87, WSBA Washburn Law Sch, 1986-87; Kiwanis Int, 1986-87; marshal Phi Alpha Delta Law Fraternity, 1986-87; founder & charter pres, NAACP Manhattan KS, 1986; founder & legal adv, Lex Explorer, Washburn Law Sch, 1988; assoc minister, St Mark AME Church; chairperson, Legal Redress Comt NAACP KS, 1987-89; Manhattan KS Chamber Com, 1987-89; Manhattan KS Am Red Cross, 1988-89; Comnr-at-large, Am Bar Asn, 1987-89; Christian Lawyers Asn, 1987-; Christian Legal Soc, 1987-; Ams United Seperation Church & State, 1987-; Am Bar Asn, 1989-; Nat Bar Asn, 1992-; Am Trial Lawyer Asn, 1993-; Wis Acad Trial Lawyers; Nat Voc Tech Honor Soc, 1999; dist comnr, Boy Scouts Am, 2000. **Honors/Awds:** Disting Military Student, 1979, Disting Military Grad, 1980 Howard Univ ROTC; Earl Warren Scholar, NAACP Legal Defense Fund, 1986-89; various awards for public speaking; Daughters of America Revolution Award, 1980; Distinguished Graduate, Air Assault Sch, 1974; Distinguished Graduate, Logis Automated Mgmt Sch, 1982; Expert Shooting Qualification; Jurcyk-Royle Oral Advocacy Competition; 1988; Certificate of Commendation, Am Bar Asn, 1989; Certificate of Merit, Washburn Law Clin, 1988; Meritorious Service Medal, Pres US, 1997; Good Shepherd Award, Boy Scouts Am, 2000; Army Achievement Medal, Secy Army. **Special Achievements:** Written numerous articles in his newspaper columns You and The Law and Your Financial Investments, and has appeared on radio talk shows regarding various subjects. His recent appearance was on Black Nouveau in Milwaukee, Wisconsin regarding his book "A Trilogy of Poetry, Prose, and Thoughts For The Mind, Body, and Soul". **Military Serv:** AUS, co cmdr capt, 8 yrs; USAR, maj, 1986-; Expert Infantry Badge, Airborne Air Assault Overseas Serv Ribbon, Army Achievement, NCO Develop, Army Servs, Good Conduct; Nat Defense Ribbon; Command & Gen Staff Col grad; Multi-Nat Force & Observer Ribbon. **Business Addr:** Instructor, Bryant & Stratton College, 310 W Wisconsin Ave, Milwaukee, WI 53203.

SPENCER, ANTHONY LAWRENCE
Government official. **Personal:** Born Aug 10, 1946, New York, NY; son of Gladys Harrington; married Jeanette Butler; children: Anthony. **Educ:** City Col NY, 1975; Cmd & Gen Staff Col, 1984. **Career:** Inst for Mediation & Conflict Resolution, spec asst to pres, 1970-74; State Charter Revision Comm NYC, asst to dir community rels, 1973-74; J P Stevens & Co, tech sales rep, 1975-79; New York Dept State, spec asst to sec state, 1979-85, dep dir gov black affairs adv comm 1985; State New York Banking Dept, proj dir; Black United Fund NY, vpres corp develop & govt affairs. **Orgs:** Pres, stud body City Col New York, 1972-73; vpres, Christmas Tree in Harlem, 1981; bd mem, ML Wilson Boys Club Harlem, 1982-; vpres, Community Bd 9 New York, NY 1983-84; Men Who Cook; bd dirs, Harlem Little League; bd dirs, New York Urban League; vpres community develop & evaluation, Nat Black Leadership Comn AIDS. **Honors/Awds:** Distinguished Service Citation, United Negro Col Fund 1981. **Military Serv:** UASF; AUS 33 yrs; NDSM/AFOUA/SOGB/AFGCM/ARCOM/ARCAM; New York Army National Guard, Lt Col, 1990. **Home Addr:** 470 Lenox Ave Suite 8E, New York, NY 10037.

SPENCER, BRENDA L
Industrial engineer, administrator. **Personal:** Born Jul 7, 1951, Youngstown, OH; daughter of Walter and Flonerra; children: Ebony Ayana. **Educ:** Ky State, BS, Ind Engineering, 1978; Malone Col, BA, bus, 1986. **Career:** General Motors, acct, 1973-76; BL Unlimited Engineering & Consult Corp, owner; Republic Steel, indus engr; ITT Tech Inst, dir placement, 1987, dir career serv, 2003. **Orgs:** Nat youth leader, Nal Asn Negro Bus & Prof Women, 1978-80; nat dir, Youth & Young Adults, 1980-82; nat vpres, Prof Women & Young Adults, 1982-85; treas, Kappa Nu Zeta, 1983-85; treas, Zeta Phi Beta, 1983-85; mem chmn, Am Inst Engrs, 1983-84; Nat Coalition Black Meeting Planners; Religious Meeting Planners Convention; Leadership Mahoning Valley. **Honors/Awds:** Voluntary Leader Nat March Dimes, 1980; Leadership Nat March Dimes, 1982; Good Housekeeping 100 Young Women Promise, 1985. **Home Addr:** PO Box 5814, Youngstown, OH 44504. **Business Addr:** Director of Placement, ITT Technical Institute, 1030 N Meridian Rd, Youngstown, OH 44509, **Business Phone:** (330)270-1600.

SPENCER, COLLINS
Television news anchorperson. **Personal:** Married; children: 1. **Educ:** Howard Univ, broadcast mgt. **Career:** Fox News, news correp; CNN, "CNN Headline News," anchor; WSB-TV, "Channel 2 Action News This Morning" & "Channel 2 Action News at Noon," anchor, 2005-. **Business Addr:** Anchor, WSB-TV, 1601 W Peachtree St NE, Atlanta, GA 30309, **Business Phone:** (404)897-7825.

SPENCER, DONALD ANDREW
Broker, educator. **Personal:** Born Mar 5, 1915, Cincinnati, OH; married Marian; children: Donald & Edward. **Educ:** Univ of Cincinnati, AB, 1936; Univ of Cincinnati, BE, 1937; Univ of Cincinnati, ME, 1940. **Career:** Broker, Educator (retired); Cincinnati Public Sch, teacher 1936-54; Donald A. Spencer & Assocs, pres, 1945-83. **Orgs:** Admin & Finance Comn W OH & Lexington Conf Meth Church, 1946-57; estab Beta Eta Chptr Kappa Alpha Psi Frat Univ Cincinnati Campus 1949; trustee OH Council of Churches; orgnzr, 1st pres Comm on Relig & Race 1960-65; PAC Com 1967-75; pres, Housing Bd Appeals, 1970-95; pres & bd trustees, OH Univ, 1974-83; Nat Asn Real Estate Brokers; Organizer, First Midwinter Conf. **Honors/Awds:** President Award, Cincinnati Br NAACP, 1975; Cincinnati Park Board Award, 1992; Service to Cincinnati, Tri-Centennial Time Capsule, 1988; Charles P Taft Civic Gumption Award, 1997; Great Living Cincinnatians, Cincinnati USA Regional Chamber, 2005. **Special Achievements:** Publ First Nat Song Book for Kappa Alpha Psi Frat 1951; First African American broker with the Cincinnati Board of Realtors.

SPENCER, FELTON LAFRANCE
Basketball player. **Personal:** Born Jan 5, 1968, Louisville, KY. **Educ:** Univ Louisville. **Career:** Basketball player (retired); Minn Timber wolves, ctr, 1990-93, 1999; Ut Jazz, 1993-96; Orlando Magic, 1996; Golden State Warriors, 1996-99; San Antonio Spurs, 1999-2000; New York Knicks, 2000-02. **Honors/Awds:** NBA Draft, 1990 .

SPENCER, GREGORY RANDALL
Executive. **Personal:** Born Dec 31, 1948, Washington, PA; son of William H and Anna Mae; married Janet O, Sep 8, 1973; children: Tammy Michelle & Michael Randall. **Educ:** Univ Pittsburgh, BA, 1980; St Francis Col, MA, 1984. **Career:** US Steel, gen mgr human resources, 1971-93; AMSCO Int Inc, vpres human resources, 1993-94; Equitable Resources Inc, sr vpres & chief admin officer, 1994-2003; bd dirs, Minority Enterprise Corp, 1997; Randall Enterprises LLC, pres & chief exec officer, currently. **Orgs:** Chmn, African Am Chamber Com Western Pa; bd dirs, Pittsburgh Found; Leadership Pittsburgh, 1997; bd dirs, Inst Transfusion Med, 1998-; bd trustees, Robert Morris Univ; bd trustees, St. Paul AME Church; bd dirs, Urban League Pittsburgh. **Honors/Awds:** Black Achiever Award, Eastern Stars, 1980; Outstanding Young Man of America, US Jaycees, 1980; Black Trailblazer Award, Renaissance Publ, 1997; Achievement in Business Award, Omega Psi Phi, 1999; WQED-Duquesne Light Community Service Award. **Special Achievements:** Fifty Future Leaders of America, Ebony Mag, 1978. **Military Serv:** USAF, sgt, 1968-71. **Home Addr:** 1020 Devonshire Rd, Pittsburgh, PA 15217. **Business Addr:** President, Chief Executive Officer, Randall Enterprises LLC, 1401 Forbes Ave Suite 201, Pittsburgh, PA 15219, **Business Phone:** (412)281-6903.

SPENCER, JAMES R
Judge. **Personal:** Born Jan 1, 1949?, Florence, SC; married Margaret. **Educ:** Clark Col, Altanta, GA, BA, 1971; Harvard Law Sch, JD, 1974; Howard Univ, MDiv, 1985. **Career:** Dist Columbia, asst US atty, 1978-81; Eastern Dist Va, asst US dist atty, 1983-86, US Dist judge, 1986-2004, chief judge, 2004-. **Orgs:** Omega Psi Phi; Sigma Pi Phi; Phi Beta Kappa; Alpha Kappa Mu. **Special Achievements:** First African American to be nominated to become the US district judge in the eastern district of Virginia. **Military Serv:** AUS, JAG Corps, capt, 1975-78; AUS, Reserves, mil judge, 1981-86. **Business Addr:** Chief Judge, United States District Court, 1000 E Main St No 307, Richmond, VA 23219-3525, **Business Phone:** (804)916-2700.

SPENCER, JIMMY
Football player, football coach. **Personal:** Born Mar 29, 1969, Manning, SC. **Educ:** Univ Fla. **Career:** Football player (retired), Football coach; New Orleans Saints, defensive back, 1992-95; Cincinnati Bengals, 1996-97; San Diego Chargers, 1998-99; Denver Broncos, corner back, 2000-03; Denver Broncos, asst defensive backs coach. 2005-06.

SPENCER, LARRY LEE
Administrator, executive director. **Personal:** Born Jan 1, 1948?, Columbus, OH; son of Hezekiah and Elizabeth; children: Tangelia Spencer Palmer, Mark, Sharese. **Educ:** Franklin Univ, BS, bus admin, 1983. **Career:** Franklin C Dept Human Servs, contract negotiator, 1976-88; Ohio Dept Mental Health, mgt analyst, 1988; United Way Franklin C, sr mgr, Proj Diversity, proj dir, currently. **Orgs:** bd mem, Leadership Worthington, 1991-; outreach comt mem, Nat Black Programming Consortium, 1991-; Dept Health, Minority AIDS Comt, 1992-; bd mem, Westside/Eastside Child Care Ctr Asn, 1988-90; Mental Health State Afro Centric Conf Planning Comt; Worthington Community Multicultural Comt; Worthington Community Rels Comn, 1994-; chair, Players Theatre Advisory Comt. **Honors/Awds:** Most Valuable Volunteer, Players Theatre, 1991; Time to Care Community Award, WBNS-TV, Channel 10, 1992; Second Century Initiative Award, United Way Am, 1991; Walter Eng Award, 1990. **Special Achievements:** Researched and presented: "An Account of Underground Railroad Activity," which focused on Columbus and Worthington area, to community groups; information has been incorporated into a black history course in the Worthington Schools. **Military Serv:** AUS, sergeant, 1968-70. **Business Addr:** Project Director, United Way Franklin County, 360 S 3rd St, Columbus, OH 43215, **Business Phone:** (614)227-2740.*

SPENCER, LITA. See RICHARDSON, LITA RENEE.

SPENCER, PROF. MARGARET BEALE
Educator, psychologist. **Personal:** Born Sep 5, 1944, Philadelphia, PA; daughter of Junius Alton and Elizabeth Rebecca Beale; mar-

ried Charles L, Jun 13, 1967; children: Tirzah Renee, Natasha Ann & Charles Asramon. **Educ:** Temple Univ Col Pharm, BS, 1967; Univ Kans, MA, psychol, 1970; Univ Chicago, PhD, 1976. **Career:** Univ Kans Med Ctr, regist pharmacist, 1967-69; Univ Chicago, res proj dir, 1974-77; Morehouse Sch Med, clin assoc prof, 1982-89; Emory Univ, fac, 1977-93; Univ Pa, endowed chair, bd overseers, prof educ, 1993-. **Orgs:** Consult/comt, Found Child Develop, 1981-85, trustee, 1997-; consult, Fulton County, Georgia Health Dpt, 1983-89; bd exec comt, Fulton County Black Family Proj, 1983-88; bd, South DeKalb County, YMCA, 1984-86; W T Grant Found, 1986-93; Nat Black Child Develop Inst, bd mem, 1986-92; Ctr Successful Child Develop, 1986-88; comt chmn, Soc Res Child Develop, 1987-89; trustee & bd mem, White-Williams Found, 1994-; ed rev bd mem, J Appl Develop Psychol, 1992-; edl rev bd mem, Cambridge Univ Press, Develop & psychopath, 1994-; bd sci affairs, The Am Psychol Asn, 1991-94; ed adv bd, C, Youth & Change: Sociocultural Perspectives, 1994-; adv bd, Ctr Study Context, Generations, & Ment Health, 1994-; adv bd, Ctr Youth Develop & Policy Res; bd mem, Acad Educ Develop, 1993; adv bd, CRESPAR, 1997; dir, Ctr Health, Achievement, Neighborhood, Growth & Ethnic Studies (CHANGES); dir, W E B Dubois Collective Res, U Penn. **Honors/Awds:** Grant Res Support, Spencer, Ford, Commonwealth and WT Grant Found, 1984-87; Award for Service, DeKalb County, GA, YMCA, 1985; Outstanding Service Award, Delta Sigma Theta Sorority, Decatur Alumnae Chap, 1986; Fel Status, Div 7, 15, 45, Am Psychol Asn. **Special Achievements:** Author: Beginnings: The Affective and Social Development of Black Children, LEA Publishing, 1985; Ethnicity and Diversity: Minorities No More, LEA, in press; Over 75 published articles and chapters. **Home Addr:** 737 Cornelia Place, Philadelphia, PA 19118, **Home Phone:** (215)242-9507. **Business Addr:** Professor of Education and Psychology, University of Pennsylvania, Graduate School of Education, 3700 Walnut St, Philadelphia, PA 19104-6216, **Business Phone:** 877-736-6473.

SPENCER, MARIAN ALEXANDER
Activist. **Personal:** Born Jun 28, 1920, Gallipolis, OH; married Donald A, 1940; children: Donald Jr & Edward Alexander. **Educ:** Univ Cincinnati, BA, eng, 1942. **Career:** Community servant & civil rights activist, currently. **Orgs:** Life mem, Nat Asn Advan Colored People; Chairperson, Human Resources Comn, Urban Develop Planning Zoning & Housing Comn, vice chairperson, Law Comn, City Planning Comn, Cincinnati City Coun; life mem, Alpha Kappa Alpha Sor; pres, Cincinnati Chap Links Inc; pres, Woman's City Club; Greater Cincinnati Occup Health Ctr Bd; adv bd, WGUC Radio Sta; pub rels comn & personnel comn, Planned Parenthood; Mt Zion United Methodist Church; vpres, Housing Opportunities Made Equal Bd; chairperson, sub comt, Discipline Task Force, Cincinnati Pub Schs; bd mem, Ctr Voting & Democracy. **Honors/Awds:** Career Woman of Achievement Award, YWCA, 1984; Community Activist Award, A Phillip Randolph Inst Greater Cincinnati, 1992; Jacob E Davis Volunteer Award, Greater Cincinnati Found, 1993; Glorifying the Lions Club, Urban League, 1994; Award recipient, Center Voting & Democracy, 1995; Brotherhood Award, Nat Conf Christians & Jews; Woman of the Year Award, Cincinnati Enquirer; Black Excellence Award, PUSH; Ethelrie Harper Award, Cincinnati Human Rels Comn; Distinguished Alumna Award, Alumna Asn Univ Cincinnati; State of Ohio Award, ACLU. **Special Achievements:** Recognized by the Cincinnati Post as one of the 12 Most Influential Women in the City of Cincinnati, recently inducted into the OH Women's Hall of Fame, first African American woman elected to the Cincinnati City Council, only woman ever to serve as president of Cincinnati Branch, NAACP, honored by Black Careeer Women. **Home Addr:** 940 Lexington Ave, Cincinnati, OH 45229.

SPENCER, DR. MICHAEL GREGG
Engineer, college teacher. **Personal:** Born Mar 9, 1952, Detroit, MI; son of Thomas and Laura Lee; divorced; children: Thomas Lewis. **Educ:** Cornell Univ, Ithaca, NY, BS, 1974, MEE, 1975, PhD, 1981. **Career:** Gen Electric, Syracuse, NY, co-op engineer, 1972, 1973; Bell Lab, Whippany, NJ, mem tech staff, 1974-77; Howard Univ, Wash DC, asst prof, 1981-85, assoc prof, 1985, prof, currently, dept Elecl Engineering, Materials Science Research Ctr Excellence, dir, 1987-; SIMNET Lab, co-dir, 1987-; Cornell Univ, Col Eng, asst dean, prof, 2005-. **Orgs:** Officer, Nat Soc Black Engineers, 1977-; Nat Science Found proposal review comm, 1984-, advi coun Elec Engineering & computer systems, 1988, adv comm for materials research, 1989-; mem, Am Vacuum Soc, 1985-; officer, Electron Device Soc Inst Electrical & Electronics Engineers, 1987-. **Honors/Awds:** Presidential Young Investigator Award, Nat Science Found, 1985; Allen Berman Research Publication Award, Naval Research Lab, 1986; Outstanding Faculty Award, White House Initiative on Historically Black Col & Univ, 1988; Distinguished Vis Scientist, JPL, 1991-92; Cert Recognition, NASA, 1992. **Business Addr:** Professor, Cornell University, Department of Electrical & Computer Engineering, 418 Phillips Hall, Ithaca, NY 14853, **Business Phone:** (607)255-6271.

SPENCER, ROZELLE JEFFERY
Chief executive officer, president (organization), executive. **Personal:** Born Jul 3, 1936, Memphis, TN; son of William Arthur and Octavia McCormack; married Winifred L Jones, Jul 5, 1968; children: Jeffrey C & Derrick C. **Educ:** DePaul Univ, 1956-59; Northeastern Ill Univ, BA, 1990, MA, attended 1990-91. **Career:** Santa Fe Railroad, trans rep, 1956-64; Trans World Airlines, employment supvr, 1964-70; Aaro Medicar Transport, pres, 1976-85; Hyde Park Self Storage Inc, pres, 1990-; Aaron Brothers Moving System, Inc, pres, ceo, currently. **Orgs:** Chicago Coun Foreign Rels; Asn African Historians; Task Force Black Polit Empowerment; Southside Community Art Ctr; Nat Asn Guardsmen. **Home Addr:** 10706 S Seeley Ave, Chicago, IL 60643, **Home Phone:** (773)233-3627. **Business Addr:** President, Chief Executive Officer, Aaron Brothers Moving Systems Inc, 4034 S Michigan Ave, Chicago, IL 60653, **Business Phone:** (312)268-1700.

SPENCER, SHARON A
Physician, educator. **Personal:** Born in Birmingham, AL; daughter of Otis Sr and Annie M Rice. **Educ:** Birmingham Southern Col, Birmingham, AL, BS, chem, 1979; Univ Ala Sch Med, Birmingham, AL, MD, 1983. **Career:** Univ Ala, Birmingham, Birmingham, AL, asst prof, 1989-; Univ Ala Hosp, clin dir, currently. **Orgs:** Am Bd Radiol; Therapeutic Radiol, 1988. **Honors/Awds:** Phi Beta Kappa, 1979. **Business Addr:** Assistant Professor, University of Alabama at Birmingham, Department of Radiation Oncology, Wallace Tumor Inst 115, 1824 6th Ave S, Birmingham, AL 35233, **Business Phone:** (205)934-2760.

SPENCER, TRACIE MONIQUE
Singer, actor. **Personal:** Born Jul 12, 1976, Waterloo, IA. **Career:** Albums: Tracie Spencer, 1988; Make the Difference, 1990; Love High, 1998; Tracie, 1999; The Longest Yard, 2005. Film; A Tale of Two Sisters, 2004. TV Episodes : "ZDF Hit parade", 1988, "It's Show time at the Apollo", 1989; "Family Matters", 1993; "VH-1 Where Are They Now?", 2002. **Honors/Awds:** Martin Luther King Christian Leadership Award. **Special Achievements:** Has appeared on "The Arsenio Hall Show" and "Star Search"; toured with New Kids on the Block and Kid N' Play. **Business Addr:** Singer, c/o Capitol Records Inc, 1750 N Vine St, Hollywood, CA 90028, **Business Phone:** (213)462-6252.*

SPICER, KENNETH, SR.
Government official, president (organization), chief executive officer. **Personal:** Born Aug 21, 1949, Jacksonville, FL; son of Reba Spicer McKinney; married Patricia A Baker, May 25, 1972; children: Kenneth, Sherry & Michelle. **Educ:** Bethune-19 Cookman Col, BS, bus admin, 1971; Univ Mass, MS, pub affairs, 1990; North eastern Univ, PhD, law policy & soc, 1993; Harvard Univ, JFK Sch Govt, attended 1994. **Career:** S Fla Employ Training Consortium, Miami, dir pub serv employ, 1980, diropers, 1980-81; Dade County JMH/Community Ment Health Ctr, Miami, FL, dir opers & finance, 1981; Dade County Haitian Am Community Health Ctr, Miami, FL, exec dir, 1982-85; Off City Mgr, Tallahassee, FL, dir minority bus enterprise, 1985-86; EOCD, Off Secy, Boston, MA, asst to cabinet secy affirmative action, 1986-91, Bur Neighborhood Serv & Econ Opportunity, Div Neighborhood Serv, dir, 1991-99; Mass Dept Housing County Develop, assoc dir, 1999; Ctr Health & Develop, pres & chief executive officer, currently. **Orgs:** Alpha Phi Alpha Fraternity, 1971-; founding mem, Boston Chap, Nat Forum Black Pub Admin Inc; Equal Opportunity, diversity consult, Oxf am Am, Boston Off. **Honors/Awds:** Appreciation Award, Boston Chap, Nat Forum Black Pub Admin, 1989; Appreciation Award, State Mass, 1989; Gov Quality Control Comt, 1993; Urban Edge Community Serv Award, 1994; Self Sufficiency Award, Mass County Action Prog Exec Dir Assn, 1998; Grove HAV CDC Supporter of the Year Award, 1999; Recognition Award, Chelsea's Comn Hosp Affairs, 1999. **Business Addr:** Chief Executive Officer, President, Center for Health and Development Inc, Ten Winter Place 3rd Fl, Boston, MA 02108, **Business Phone:** (617)357-0224.*

SPICER, OSKER, JR.
Journalist. **Personal:** Born Apr 12, 1949, Memphis, TN; son of Rosa Hall Spicer Sias; married Marion Wilson, Jul 31, 1970; children: Aki L. **Educ:** Lincoln Univ, Jefferson City, MO, jour major, 1967-69; Morehouse Col, Atlanta, GA, BA, 1972; Columbia Univ, New York, NY, summer prog minority journalists, 1973; Atlanta Univ, Atlanta, GA, grad studies Afro-Am studies, 1984. **Career:** Atlanta Daily World, Atlanta, GA, reporter & night city ed, 1970-72, 1976-77; Pittsburgh Courier, Pittsburgh, PA, city ed, 1974-75; WCLK Radio, Atlanta, GA, producer-announcer & news dir, 1976-81; Clark Col, Atlanta, GA, jour instr, 1978-81, 1984; Charlotte News-Observer, Charlotte, NC, reporter, 1982-84; The Democrat, Tallahassee, FL, reporter & columnist, 1984-87; The Oregonian, Portland, OR, copy ed & columnist, 1987-. **Orgs:** Morehouse Alumni Asn, 1972-; Inst Jour Educ, 1973-; bd mem, local chap, Soc Prof Journalists, 1980-; Asian-Am Journalists Asn, 1988-; bd mem & charter mem, Portland Asn Black Journalists, 1990-; NABJ, Region X, dir, currently; Int Fedn Journalists, 1990-; IRE; bd mem, W Coast Regional Dirs, Nat Asn Black Journalists, 1995-97; nat bd mem, chap pres, 9th & 10th Cav Asn The Buffalo Soldiers. **Honors/Awds:** Producer of the Year, WCLK Radio, 1979; Journalistic Excellence, Tallahassee Chamber, 1986-87. **Military Serv:** USMC Reserves, 2nd Lt, 1969-71. **Business Addr:** Copy Editor-Columnist, The Oregonian, 1320 SW Broadway, Portland, OR 97201, **Business Phone:** (503)221-8570.

SPIGHT, BENITA L
Executive. **Personal:** Born Apr 21, 1963, Detroit, MI; daughter of James Easterling Jr and Margaret Louise Lindsey McCray; married Brian Wesley, Apr 15, 1989; children: Richard Allen II & Brandon Noah. **Educ:** Univ Mich, attended 1985, Sch Bus Admin, cert completion, 1990; Univ Denver, Publ Inst, cert completion, 1991. **Career:** Consolidated Data Tech, Dearborn, MI, clerical supvr, 1986-88; Thomson Gale Group Inc, Detroit, MI, sr credit & acct serv rep, 1988-90, data entry supvr, 1990-93, mgr, 1993-95, Corp Team & Work Redesign, trainer, 1993-98, Int Thomson Publ, leadership trainer & facilitator, 1995-, HR mgr corp redesign implementation, 1996-99, dir, ed serv, 1999-2002, vpres ed serv; Cengage Learning, exec dir global rights & permissions, currenlty. **Orgs:** Nat Asn Advan Colored People, Univ Mich Br, 1982-83; Data Entry Mgt Asn, 1990-93; Detroit Zoological Soc, 1992-; Asn Work Process Improvement, 1993-95; Am Soc Training & Develop, 1998-; AIIM 2000-; N Am Serials Interest Group, 2002-. **Honors/Awds:** Scholarship recipient, Publ Inst, Univ Denver, Gale Research, 1991. **Business Addr:** Executive Director Global Rights, Permissions, Cengage Learning, PO Box 6904, Florence, KY 41022-6904, **Business Phone:** 800-824-5179.

SPIGNER, DR. CLARENCE
Educator, research scientist. **Personal:** Born Mar 19, 1946, Orangeburg, SC; son of Willie and Carrie McDonald. **Educ:** Santa Monica Col, Santa Monica, CA, AA, social studies, 1976; Univ Calif,Berkeley, CA, AB, sociol, 1979, MPH, behav sci, 1982, DrPH, behav sci, 1987. **Career:** Nat Health Serv, London, Eng, researcher, planner, 1982-83; Univ Calif,Berkeley, CA, fitness supvr, 1983-86, teaching asst, fel, lectr, 1984-88,Chancellor's fel, 1987; Univ Ore, Eugene, OR, asst prof, 1988-94; Univ Wash, Dept Health Servs, assoc prof, 1996-, MIRT Prog, co-dir, currently, adj assoc prof, Am Ethnic Studies, currently. **Orgs:** Phi Beta Kappa Honor Soc, 1979-; evaluator, Am Heart Asn, Marin, CA,1981-82; Bd mem, Woman space, 1989-91; steering comt mem, Clergy & Laity Concerned, 1990-94; Friars Sr Honor Soc, Univ Ore, 1990; Univ Ore, Substance Abuse Adv Bd, 1990-92, Affirmative Action Task Force, 1990-, chair, Coun Minority Educ, 1990-91; chair, Spec Comn Minority Fac, Univ Wash, 1996-99; chair, Minority Int Res Training Prog, 2002-. **Honors/Awds:** Henrik Blum Distinguished Service Award, Univ Calif, Berkeley, 1987;Outstanding Faculty Award, Off Multicultural Affairs, Univ Ore, 1990;. **Special Achievements:** African Americans, democracy, and biomedical and behavioral research:contradictions or consensus in community-based participatory research? IntQ Community Health Educ. 1999-2000; 19(3):259-84; Race, class, and violence: research and policy implications, Int J Health Serv. 1998;28(2):349-72. Review. **Military Serv:** USAF, sgt, 1964-68. **Business Addr:** Associate Professor, Adjunct Associate Professor, University of Washington, Department of Health Services, H692 Health Sci Bldg 1959 NE Pac St, PO Box 357660, Seattle, WA 98195-7660, **Business Phone:** (206)616-2948.

SPIGNER, DR. DONALD WAYNE
Physician. **Personal:** Born Feb 14, 1940, Tyler, TX; son of Jessie Lee McCauley and Kermit; married Carol Wilson; children: Nicole Adeyinka & Danielle Khadeja. **Educ:** Univ CA Riverside, BS, 1962; Univ CA San Francisco, MD 1966; Los Angeles City Govt Hosp, Internship, 1967;bd cert, Acad Family Pract. **Career:** US Peace Corp, physician, 1967-69, med dir, Africa Div, 1969-70; Pilot City Health Ctr, proj dir, 1970-73; Univ MN Sch Med, assoc prof, 1973-75; Univ MN Sch Pub Health, lectr 1973-75; Hamilton Health Ctr; med dir, 1975-87; Comm Med Assoc, pres; Univ PA Hershey Med Ctr, assoc prof, 1975-; City Harrisburg, city health officer, 1977-80; Keystone Peer Rev, part-time reviewer 1986-; Blue Shield PA, med dir. **Orgs:** PA Med Soc Liability Ins Co, bd mem; Consult Africa Care, 1975-85; partner 3540 N Progress Assoc, 1980-; Boys Club, 1982-; partner, Keystone Assocs, 1984-; pres, Dauphin Cty Med Soc, 1984-; Dauphin City MH/MR Bd, 1984-86; St Paul Baptist Church; Adv Bd PA State Univ, Harrisburg Campus; PA State Bd Podiatry bd dir, S Cent Pa Sickle Cell Coun, currently. **Special Achievements:** Selected to represent Univ of CA Riverside on Project India, 1961; video tape on African/Amer Folk medicine, 1977. **Military Serv:** USPMS, US Pub Health Serv Surgeon, 1967-69. **Home Addr:** 2406 Valley Rd, Harrisburg, PA 17104, **Home Phone:** (717)234-9425. **Business Addr:** President, Community Medical Association, 3601 N Progress, Harrisburg, PA 17110, **Business Phone:** (717)652-7266.

SPIGNER, MARCUS E
Government official. **Career:** US Postal Serv, postmaster, currently. **Orgs:** PHA-Masons; treas, Sabre League No 7. **Honors/Awds:** Excellence Award for Western Area, 1999. **Special Achievements:** First African American postmaster in the state of Idaho. **Military Serv:** Idaho National Guard. **Business Addr:** Postmaster, United States Postal Service, 141 N Palmetto Ave, Eagle, ID 83616.

SPIKES, DR. DELORES R.
College president. **Personal:** Born Aug 24, 1936; daughter of Lawrence Granville Richard and Margaret Patterson Richard; married Hermon. **Educ:** Southern Univ, BS, maths, 1957; Univ Ill, MS, maths, 1958; Louisana State Univ, PhD, 1971. **Career:** Mossville High Sch, Calcasien Parish, teacher, 1958; Southern Univ, asst prof & prof; Southern Univ, Baton Rouge, asst to chancellor, exec vchancellor & chancellor academic affairs, 1882-85; Southern Univ A&M Systs, pres, pres emer, currently; Univ Md, Eastern Shore,pres, pres emer, currently. **Honors/Awds:** George

Washington Carver Public Service Hall of Fame Lect, 1993; Most influential Black women in America. **Business Phone:** (410)651-2200.

SPIKES, IRVING
Football player. **Personal:** Born Dec 21, 1970, Ocean Springs, MS; married Stacey, Sep 11, 1994; children: Ices & Irving Jr. **Educ:** Ala Univ; La Univ, Monroe. **Career:** Football player (retired); Miami Dolphins, running back, 1994-97.

SPIKES, TAKEO GERARD
Football player. **Personal:** Born Dec 17, 1976, Sandersville, GA; son of Jimmie and Lillie; children: Jakai. **Educ:** Auburn Univ. **Career:** Cincinnati Bengals, linebacker, 1998-2002; Buffalo Bills, 2003-06; Philadelphia Eagles, 2007; San Francisco 49ers, 2008-. **Honors/Awds:** Georgia Player of the Year, Atlanta Jour-Const; Defensive Player of the Year, Football News, 1997. **Business Addr:** Linebacker, San Francisco 49ers, 4949 Centennial Blvd, Santa Clara, CA 95054, **Business Phone:** (415)656-4900.

SPINKS, MICHAEL
Boxer. **Personal:** Born Jul 13, 1956, St Louis, MO; married Sandy (deceased); children: Michelle. **Career:** Boxer (retired); prof boxer, 1976-88. **Orgs:** Intl Boxing Hall Fame. **Honors/Awds:** Nat Golden Gloves Championship Light Middleweight, 1974; Nat Golden Gloves Championship Middleweight, 1976; Gold Medalist, Olympics, 1976; Light-Heavyweight Champion, World Boxing Asn, 1981; Light Heavyweight Champion, World Boxing Coun, 1983-85; Heavyweight Champion, Int Boxing Fedn, 1985; Int Boxing Hall of Fame, 1994; World Boxing Hall of Fame, 1995. **Special Achievements:** Film appearance: Speed Zone!, 1989; Comedy Cent Presents: The NY Friars Club Roast of Rob Reiner, 2000; Howard Stern, 2005.

SPIRES, GREG (GREGORY TYRONE SPIRES)
Football player. **Personal:** Born Aug 12, 1974, Mariana, FL; married Alzadia Jordan; children: Leila & Gregory. **Educ:** Fla State Univ. **Career:** New Eng Patriots, defensive end, 1998-2000; Cleveland Browns, 2001; Tampa Bay Buccaneers, linebacker & fullback, 2002-07; Oakland Raiders, 2008; free agent, currently. **Honors/Awds:** District Player of the year; All-Region hons; SuperBowl Champion.

SPIRES, GREGORY TYRONE. See SPIRES, GREG.

SPIVA, DR. ULYSSES VAN
Educator. **Personal:** Born May 6, 1931, New Market, TN; son of Samuel and Mary Ruth Spiva-Chandler; married Olivia A; children: Vanessa, Valerie & Bruce. **Educ:** Tenn State Univ, Nashville, BS, math & physics, 1954; Case Western Res Univ, Cleveland, Ohio, MA, 1964; Stanford Univ, Palo Alto, Calif, PhD, educ admin & polit sci, 1971. **Career:** Sch Health Sch Serv, Sch Educ Fla, interim dean, exec asst pres, asst dean; Stanford Univ, Grad Sch Educ, Nat Follow Through Prog, US Off Educ, spec asst to dean; Ohio Pub Sch, Cleveland, eve sch prin & math dept chmn; Union Grad Sch, adj prof; Nova Southeastern Univ, Ft Lauderdale, Fla, Doctoral Prog Educ Leadership, sr nat lectr, 1974-2000, prof emer; Darden Col Educ, prof educ leadership & coun & dean emer, currently; bd dir, Norfolk Kiwanis Inc; HR 200 Men Inc; Cleveland, math teacher, dept chair & adult sch prin; Amherst Col, math coordr; Dartmouth Col Summer ABC Prog, math coordr; US Off Educ, Washington Policy fel; Fla Int Univ, Sch Educ, asst dean & asst prof, exec asst to pres, Sch Health & Social Serv, interim dean, Div Continuing Educ, actg dean, Div Sponsored Res & Training, dir, assoc exec vpres; Old Dominion Univ, prof educ leadership & serv, dean, 1979-84, dean emer; chmn, Legis Comt; Southeastern Tidewater Opportunity Prog, Bd Dir, pres. **Orgs:** Life mem Alpha Phi Alpha Fraternity; Stanford Alumni Asn; bd trustees, Bd Educ, Va Beach Pub Sch Syst; dir, Va Beach Found, 1990-; pres, Va Asn Col Teacher Educ; dir, Nat Sch Bd Asn, 1990-92; mem bd dir, Va Sch Bd Asn; chair, Coun Urban Bd Educ. **Honors/Awds:** Leadership & Eagle Award in Pedagogy, John F Kennedy HS, Alpha Phi Alpha Fraternity, 1969; Phi Delta Kappa Hon Soc. **Special Achievements:** Published 3 books & numerous papers. **Business Addr:** Professor Emeritus of Educational Leadership & Services & Dean Emeritu, Old Dominion University, 108 Alfred B Rollins Jr Hall, Norfolk, VA 23529.

SPIVEY, DR. DONALD
Educator. **Personal:** Born Jul 18, 1948, Chicago, IL; married Diane Marie; children: 2. **Educ:** Univ Ill, BA, hist, 1971, MA, hist, 1972; Univ Calif, PhD, hist, 1976. **Career:** Univ Ill, dept elem educ, res asst, 1971-72; Univ Calif, dept hist teaching asst, 1972-74; Sacramento CA, music instr, 1972-74; Univ Calif, Davis, lectr hist, 1975-76; Wright State Univ, asst prof hist, 1976-79; Univ Mich, vis asst prof hist, 1978-79; Univ Conn, from assoc prof to prof hist, 1979-90, dir, Inst African-Am Studies, 1990-; Am Coun Learned Societies, res grant, 1980; Univ Conn, res found grant, 1983-84; Univ Miami, chair dept; Univ Miami, prof hist, currently. **Orgs:** President's Comm Human Relations, Univ Conn, 1984-85; Asn Study Afro-Am Life & Hist; Orgn Am Historians; Am Historical Asn; Popular Cult Asn; Southwest Social Sci Asn; Nat Coun Black Studies; Southern Historical Asn; N Am Soc Hist Sport; bd trustees, Conn Historical Soc; Conn Acad Arts &Sci; Phi Beta Kappa; Phi Kappa Phi. **Honors/Awds:** Bolinga Dist Teacher-Scholar Award, Black Fac Wright State Univ, 1978; Ronald McDonald House Award for Distinguished Community Service, 1998; Excellence in Teaching Award, Univ Miami, 2002; Recipient of numerous recognitions. **Special Achievements:** Published: Publishing Schooling for the New Slavery, Black Indust Educ (1868-1915), 1978; Union and the Black Musician: The Narrative of William Everett Samuels and Chicago Local 208 (1984); The Politics of Mis education, Booker Washington Inst of Liberia (1928-84), 1986. **Business Addr:** Director, University of Connecticut, Institute for African-American Studies, Rm 610 Ashe, Storrs, CT 06268.

SPOONER, ALLAN M.
Career: Detroit Pub Sch, bd, 2005-; St John Hosp & Med Ctr, vpres bus develop, currently. **Business Addr:** Vice President of Business Development, St John Hospital and Medical Center, 28000 Dequindre, Warren, MI 48092, **Business Phone:** (313)343-4000.*

SPOONER, RICHARD C.
Lawyer. **Personal:** Born Jul 3, 1945, New York, NY. **Educ:** NY Univ, BA, 1970; Fordham Univ Sch Law, JD, 1975. **Career:** Community Develop Agency, dir prog plan, 1970-71; Human Resources Admin NYC, spec asst to gen coun, 1972-75; Carroll & Reid, assoc, 1975-77; Chem Bank, vpres & sr coun. **Orgs:** Am Bar Asn, 1977-; Nat Bar Asn, 1979-; bd dir, 1980-84, gen coun, 1981-85, int vpres, 1983, Urban Bankers Coalition; vpres finance, MetroBlack Bar Asn, 1985. **Business Addr:** Vice President, Counsel, Chemical Bank, 380 Madison Ave, New York, NY 10016.

SPOONER, RICHARD EDWARD
Military leader. **Personal:** Born Sep 15, 1946, Dayton, OH; son of Marie and Lavoy Spooner; married Cora, Jun 4, 1969; children: Angela & Tracey. **Educ:** USAF Acad, Colo, BS, Engineering, 1969; Univ Utah, MS, human resource mgt, 1977. **Career:** Director(retired), military leader; Mather Air Force Base, Calif, student, navigator training, 1970-71; Castle Air Force Base, Calif, student, combat crew training, 1971; Barksdale Air Force Base, La, KC-135 navigator, 1971-73; George Air Force Base, Calif, F-4 weapons systems officer training, 1973-74; Ubon Airfield, Thailand, F-4 weapons systems officer, 435th Tactical Fighter, 1974; Udorn Royal Thai Air Force Base, Thailand, F-4 squadron instruct weapons systems officer, 13th Tactical Fighter Squadron, 1974-75; Royal Air Force Station, Lakenheath, Eng, chief training, weapons systems officer, 1975-76; Luke Air Force Base, Ariz, chief acad scheduling, 1976-78, squadron asst oper officer/F-4, 1978-79; Andrews Air Force Base, Md, wing electronic warfare officer, F-105, 1979-81, F-4 navigator instruct, 1981-84, F-4 weapons systems officer, 1984-86, asst opers officer, 1986-88, F-4 flight commander/instruct weapons systems officer, 1988-89, dep commander support, 1989-91, dep commander support, 113th Fighter Wing, 1991-93, dep commanding general, 1993-2000; Lockheed Martin, dir, 1995-2003; Nat Guard Bur, dir, 2003-. **Orgs:** Tuskegee Airmen Inc; Air Force Asn; Nat Mil Intel Asn. **Honors/Awds:** Black Engineer of the Year Nominee, 1990/1992; Who's Who/Black Engineers of America, Howard Univ, 1972. **Military Serv:** Air National Guard, major gen, 1970-.

SPRADLEY, FRANK SANFORD
Educator. **Personal:** Born Oct 7, 1946, New Rochelle, NY; son of Frank Spradley and Mary Williams Baker; married Patricia Jones, Aug 23, 1972; children: Ayinde, Omolara, Ife & Naima. **Educ:** Southern Ill Univ, Carbondale, IL, BS, acct, mkt, 1970; Brooklyn Col, New York, NY, MA, educ, 1975, admin, supv advan cert, 1981; Fordham Univ, New York, NY, Doctoral Cand. **Career:** Bd Educ, PS 137K, Brooklyn, NY, teacher, 1970-81, prin, 1981-; Shaw Univ, NC, instr curric writer, 1972; Col New Rochelle, New York, NY, adj prof, 1989-; Bd Educ, Brooklyn, NY, instr new teacher workshops, human relation courses. **Orgs:** Polit chmn, Nat Alliance Black Sch Educr; treas, Coalition Concerned Black Educr; Coun Supvr & Adminr. **Honors/Awds:** Outstanding Teacher Award, 1975; Outstanding Administrator Award, 1987; Rachel Jean Mitchelle Leadership Award, 1987; Excellence Education Award, 1988. **Home Addr:** 117-15 224th St, Jamaica, NY 11411. **Business Addr:** Principal, Bd of Education, 121 Saratoga Ave, Brooklyn, NY 11233, **Business Phone:** (718)495-7817.

SPRADLING, MARY ELIZABETH MACE
Librarian, book editor. **Personal:** Born Dec 31, 1911, Winchester, KY; daughter of Minor Jeremiah and Ella Nora; married Louis Lee, Aug 8, 1936 (died 1964). **Educ:** Ky State Col, AB, 1933; Atlanta Univ, BLS, 1958; Rutgers Univ, certificate, 1971. **Career:** Librarian (retired), Books Editor; Pub Schs Ky, SC, teacher, 1933-37; Shelbyville Sch, teacher libr, 1944-47; Pub Libr, librn, 1948-57; Kalamazoo Pub Lib, Young Adult Dept, 1957-76; Gale Res Co, bibliographer & compiler. **Orgs:** Family Serv Orgn Community Coun, Louisville Area Girl Scouts Bd; Kalamazoo Coun Human Rels, Kalamazoo YWCA Pub Affairs Comt; Kalamazoo County Community Serv Coun; Kalamazoo Youth Comt, Kalamazoo Coun Churches; Kalamazoo County Libr Bd, Mayor's Adv Comt Problems Law Enforcement; Kalamazoo County Bi-Centennial Comt; King Mem Fund Bd Secy; Soc, Kalamazoo Br NAACP; bd trustees, Nazareth Col; Delta Kappa Gamma Soc Epsilon Chap; Kalamazoo Alumnae Chap Delta Sigma Theta Sor; asst supt, Friendship Home; chmn, Librarian's Sect, Ky Negro Educ Asn; Ky chmn, Asn Young People's Librarians; Mich LibrAsn Recruiting Comt; YASD Comt "Recent Adult Books for Young People"; Book Bait Comt, Ala; guest lectr, Dept Librarianship Western Mich Univ; bd dirs, Young Adult Serv Ala; Lib Asn Coun; contributor, PREVIEWS Magazine; keynote speaker, Ind Libr Asn YART, Stud Libr Workshop, Western Mich Univ. **Honors/Awds:** Adero Sisterhood Award, Black Educators Kalamazoo; Kalamazoo NAACP Freedom Fund Humanitarian Award, 1984. **Special Achievements:** Citations Midwest Region, Delta Sigma Theta Sor Inc, Kalamazoo Alumnae Delta Sigma Theta Sorority; "There Is No Such Book", Top of the News June, 1965; Afro Am Quiz, 1976; "Black Librarians in KY" 1980; Listed in Notable Black Women Nancy Ellin 1984.

SPRAGGINS, DR. STEWART
Administrator. **Personal:** Born May 17, 1936, Pheba, MS; married Jean Caldwell; children: Renee Ericka & Stewart II. **Educ:** Mary Holmes Col, AA, 1958; Knoxville Col, BA, 1962; Fairfield Univ, MA, 1972. **Career:** YMCA Greater Bridgeport, exec mem & phys educ, 1962-70; YMCA Greater OK City, metro outreach exec, 1970-72; YMCA Oranges, exec dir, 1972-74; YMCA Greater NY, exec dir, 1974-77; JP Stevens & Co Inc, dir comn affairs, 1977-. **Orgs:** Chmn, Counc Concerned Black Exec; exec comt,Edges Group Inc; treas, Nat Urban Affairs Counc Inc; mem, Corp Coordinators Vols Counc Inc; bd mem, Mary Holmes Col, 1983; bd mem, NY March Dimes, 1983; bd mem, Accent Mag, 1984; bd mem, Inst NJ, 1984. **Honors/Awds:** Outstanding Black American, Nat Asn Advan Colored People & City of Bridgeport, 1968; Past State President Elks of North America & Canada, 1969; Board Member of the Year, OK City Comt Action Prog 1970; Dr Humane Letters Miles Col, 1983. **Military Serv:** AUS, pvt 1 yr. **Home Addr:** 18 Maplewood Ave, Maplewood, NJ 07040. **Business Addr:** Director Community Affairs, J P Stevens & Co Inc, 1185 6th Ave, New York, NY 10036.

SPRATLEN, THADDEUS H
Consultant, educator. **Personal:** Born May 28, 1930, Union City, TN; son of John B Spratlen and Lela C Dobbins; married Lois Price, Sep 28, 1952; children: Pamela, Patricia, Paula, Thadd Price & Townsand Price. **Educ:** Ohio State Univ, BS, 1956, MA, 1957, PhD 1962. **Career:** Howard Univ, Sch Bus Admin, visiting res prof, 1986-87; Univ Wash, assoc prof, 1972-75, prof, assoc dir, Black Studies Prog, 1979-80, acting dir, Afro-Amer Studies, 1980-81, prof emer, 2002-, Bus & Econ Develop Prog, fac dir, 1995-; Univ Calif Los Angeles, 1969-72; W WA State Col, inst, asst prof & assoc prof, 1961-69; Univ Calif Los Angeles, consult, adjunct & assoc prof, 1972-75; Univ Calif, Berkeley, lectr, 1965; Ethnic Studies Prog, W WA State Coll, acting dir, 1969; Black Economists Devel Proj, dir, 1970-74. **Orgs:** Nat Econ Asn; Caucus Black Economists; Amer Marketing asn; Wa State Adv Comm Minority Bus, 1974-76; Beta Gamma Sigma, 1956; US Census Adv Comm Amer Marketing asn, 1975-81; United Negro Col Fund, Lectr, 1971, 1974. **Honors/Awds:** John Hay Whitney Fel, 1958-59; Frederick Douglass Scholar Award, Natl Council for Black Studies, Pacific Northwest Region, 1986; Andrew V Smith Faculty Development Award, 1993, 1999; Dean's Citizenship Award, 2004; Special Distinguished Award. **Military Serv:** AUS, first lt, 1952-54; enlisted pvt to corp, 1948-51. **Home Phone:** (206)365-0956. **Business Addr:** Professor Emeritus, Faculty Director, University of Washington, Michael G Foster School of Business, 210 Mackenzie St, PO Box 353200, Seattle, WA 98195-3200, **Business Phone:** (206)543-4778.

SPRAUVE, DR. GILBERT A.
Educator. **Personal:** Born Jun 9, 1937, St Thomas, Virgin Islands of the United States; son of Eunice and Gehardt; married Alvara Eulalia Ritter (divorced); children: Masserae, Margaret, Janine & Singanu. **Educ:** Brooklyn Col, BA, 1960; Univ Puerto Rico, BA; Univ Southern Calif, MA,1965; Princeton Univ, PhD, 1974; Univ Madrid, dipl de cultura espanola. **Career:** Lyce Donka Guinea, Span, Eng teacher, 1960-61; Albert Acad Sierra Leone, French, Spanish teacher, 1961-63; LA City Schs CA, French, Spanish teacher, 1963-67; Rockefeller Found grad black studies fel, 1971-74; Third Constitutional Conv VI, del, 1977; Smithsonian Inst, Festival Am Folklife, VI Sect, gen adv & res, 1990, Off Folklife Prog, sr vis scholar, 1990-91; Col VI, assoc prof modern lang, prof modern lang, currently; 14th LegVirgin Islands, sen at-large, vpres. **Orgs:** VI Bd Educ, 1978-; adv bd mem, Caribbean Fishery Mgt Coun, 1979-. **Special Achievements:** Published "The Queue" The Literary Review 1974; authorship of numerousarticles & monographs on Virgin Islands language & cultural history. **Business Addr:** Faculty Member For Summer Institute, Culture and Communication, University of the Virgin Islands, 2 John Brewer, St Thomas, Virgin Islands of the United States 00802, **Business Phone:** (340)693-1150.

SPREWELL, LATRELL
Business owner, basketball player. **Personal:** Born Sep 8, 1970, Milwaukee, WI; children: Aquilla, Sher, Page, Latrell II, Ray & Billy. **Educ:** Three Rivers Community Col, attended; Univ Ala, social work. **Career:** Golden State Warriors, guard, 1992-97; New

York Knicks, 1999-2003; Minn Timberwolves, guard, 2003-05; Sprewell Racing, owner, currently. **Orgs:** Make-A-Wish Found; Starlight Found. **Honors/Awds:** MetLife Community Assist of the Month Award, 1999. **Business Addr:** Owner, Sprewell Racing, 1001 S San Gabriel Blvd, San Gabriel, CA 91776, **Business Phone:** (626)309-1771.

SPRIGGS, EDWARD J
Government official, administrator. **Personal:** Born May 22, 1947, Minneapolis, MN; married A Pearl Spriggs, Jan 21, 1983; children: Lesley D. **Educ:** Univ Calif, San Diego, BA, econ, 1970; New York Univ Sch Law, JD, 1975. **Career:** Int Corp Law, pvt pract; US Foreign Serv, coun; US Dept Housing & Urban Develop, community develop rep, 1970-72; Arnold & Porter, assoc atty, 1975-79; US Agency Int Develop, E Africa Affairs, dir, 1982-85, regional legal adv, 1986-88, asst general coun for Africa, 1988-94, mission dir, Namibia, 1994-98, regional dir for Southern Africa, Gabon, Botswana, 1998; Univ Calif, San Diego, assoc vice chancellor resource admin, 2001-, int assoc vice chancellor resource admin, 2007. **Orgs:** Nat Bar Asn, 1975-; Int Law Section, 1975-; Am Soc Int Law, 1975-; DC Bar Asn, 1975-. **Honors/Awds:** Root-tilden Scholar, New York Univ, 1972-75; Distinguished Unit Citation, USAID, 1987; Performance Pay Award, 1989-98; Superior Honor Award, 1995; Administrator's Implementation Award, 1996. **Special Achievements:** "Involuntary Sterilization: An Unconstitutional Menace to Minorities and the Poor," NYU Rev L & Soc Change, 1975. **Business Phone:** (858)534-3475.

SPRIGGS, MARCUS
Football player. **Personal:** Born May 30, 1974, Hattiesburg, MS. **Educ:** Univ Houston. **Career:** Football player(retired); Buffalo Bills, tackle, 1997-2000; Miami Dolphins, 2001-02; Green Bay Packers, offensive tackle, 2003.

SPRIGGS, WILLIAM
Economist, educator. **Educ:** Williams Col, BA, 1977; Univ Wis-Madison, MA, econs, 1979, PhD, econ, 1984. **Career:** UN Develop Prog, NY, Prog Policy Div, intern, 1976; US Agency Int Develop, Wash, DC, Africa Bur, intern, 1978; NC A&T State, Univ Greensboro, NC, Dept Econs,asst prof, 1984-83; Norfolk State Univ, Norfolk, VA, Dept Mgt & Dir, Honors Prog, asst prof, 1984-90; Econ Policy Inst, Wash, DC, economist, 1990-93; Nat Commn Employ Policy, Wash, DC, dir, designate, 1993-94; Joint Econ Comt, US Congress, Wash, DC, sr economist, 1994-97; Econs & Statist Admin, US Dept Commerce, Wash, DC, sr adv & economist, 1997-98; Off Gov Contract & Minority Bus Develop, US Small Bus Admin, Wash, DC, sr adv, 1998-2004; Econ Policy Inst, sr fel, 2005-; Howard Univ, Dept Econs, prof & chair, 2005-. **Orgs:** Nat Sci Found Minority grad fel, 1979-84; co-pres, Am Fed Teachers, Local 3220 AFL-CIO, Madison, WI, 1980-81; Nat Neighborhood Asn, 1999-2003; pres, Nat Econs Asn; Org Prof Black Economists; Black Enterprise mag bd Economists; Time Mag Bd Economists; Nat Acad Social Ins; bd, Congressional Black Caucus Inst Leadership & Polit Educ. **Honors/Awds:** Harold Graves Essay Prize, Univ Wis-Madison, Dept Econs, 1980; Nat Econs Asn Dissertation Award, 1985; Chairman's Award, Congressional Black Caucus, 2003. **Special Achievements:** Has numerous publications, has presented at several international conferences, and has done consulting work for various state, local, and international agencies; Frequent guest on various television and radio news programs. **Business Addr:** Professor, Chair, Howard University, Department of Economics, 2400 4th St NW ASB-B Bldg Rm 302, Washington, DC 20059, **Business Phone:** (202)806-6717.

SPRINGER, ASHTON, JR.
Manager, television producer. **Personal:** Born Nov 1, 1930, New York, NY; son of Julia and Ashton; married Myra L Burns; children: Mark & Chesley. **Educ:** Ohio State Univ, BS, 1954. **Career:** Little Theatre Group, New York, NY, managing dir, Helen Hayes Theatre, 1979-85; No Place To Be Somebody, co-producer; Bubbling Brown Sugar, Broadway musical, co-producer; Theatre Mgt Assoc Inc, gen mgr, pres, currently. **Orgs:** Pres, Motor Car Asn, 1966-70; League NY Theatres & Prdcrs; Asn Theatrical Press Agents & Mgrs. **Honors/Awds:** One World Award, No Place To Be Somebody NAACP, 1971; Philadelphia Playgoers Award, Spec Achievement Theatre, 1977; Pulitzer Prize, No Place To Be Somebody, 1970; nomination, Tony Awards, best play, A Lesson From Aloes, 1980-81; nomination, Tony Award, best musical, Bubbling Brown Sugar, 1975-76; Drama Critics Award, best play, A Lesson From Aloes, 1980-81; Life Achievement Award, Nat Black Arts Festival, Atlanta, Ga, 1988; produced on Broadway the following shows: Whoppee, Eubie, A Lesson From Aloes, Cold Storage, All Night Strut, Going Up; Institution Builder, Nat Black Theatre Festival. **Special Achievements:** One of Broadway's first Black producers. **Home Addr:** 255 Storer Ave, New Rochelle, NY 10801, **Home Phone:** (914)235-8779. **Business Phone:** (212)262-1678.

SPRINGER, ERIC WINSTON
Lawyer. **Personal:** Born May 17, 1929, New York, NY; son of Owen W and Maida S; married Cecile Marie Kennedy; children: Brian, Christina. **Educ:** Rutgers Univ, AB, 1950; NY Univ Sch Law, LLB, 1953. **Career:** Justice NY State Supreme Ct, law clerk, 1955-56; Univ Pittsburgh, res assoc, 1956-58, asst prof law, 1958-64, assoc prof law, 1965-68, dir compliance EEOC, 1967; Aspen Systs Corp Pittsburgh, vpres, dir, publ, 1968-71; Horty, Springer & Mattern PC, partner, 1971-82, prin, 1982-, coun, currently. **Orgs:** Trustee Emer, Presby Univ Hosp, 1967; NY Bar; PA Bar; dir, Duquesne Light Co, 1977; ABA, NBA, Allegheny City Bar Asn; Nat Asn Advan Colored People; Allegheny County Bar Asn; Neurol Disorders & Stroke Coun; nat adv; Montefiore Univ Hosp, Pittsburgh, Pen, trustee; Univ Pittsburgh Med Ctr, trustee; Estes Park Inst; Am Col Hosp Exec; Am Acad Hosp Attys; fel Am Pub Health Asn; Univ Pittsburgh Med Ctr. **Honors/Awds:** Nat Bar Asn, Hall of Fame, 1993; Hon Fel, Am Col Healthcare Execs, 1978. **Special Achievements:** Author, "Group Practice and the Law", 1969; Ed, "Nursing and the Law", 1970; "Automated Medical Records and the Law" 1971; contributing editor of monthly newsletter "Action-Kit for Hospital Law" 1973. **Military Serv:** AUS 1953-55. **Business Addr:** Counsel, Horty Springer & Mattern PC, 4614 Fifth Ave, Pittsburgh, PA 15213-3663.*

SPRINGER, GEORGE CHELSTON
Administrator, educator. **Personal:** Born Nov 9, 1932, La Boca, Canal Zone, Panama; son of Bertley Nimrod and Edna Ethel Westerman; married Gerri Brown, Oct 11, 1980; children: Rosina Francesca Springer Audette, Linda Inez Springer-Broderick & George C Jr; married Phyllis Hall, Dec 17, 1955 (divorced 1979). **Educ:** Canal Zone Jr Col, La Boca, Canal Zone, AA, 1952; Teachers Col Connecticut, New Britain, CT, BS, 1954; Cent Connecticut State Univ, New Britain, CT, 1955-75. **Career:** Fafnir Bearing Co, New Britain CT, hardener, 1955-57, 1959; AUS, occup ther tech, 1957-59; Consol Sch Dist, New Britain, CT, teacher, 1959-79; Connecticut Fedn Teachers, Berlin, CT, pres, 1979-; Am Fedn Teachers, vpres, 1988-2001, northeast regional dir, currently. **Orgs:** SDE Educ Equity Comm, 1979-; vpres, Connecticut State AFL-CIO, 1979-; pres, New Britain Chapter NAACP, 1982-86; secy & treas, Legis Electional Action Prog, 1982-; vpres, United Labor Agency, 1983-; adv coun, CSU Ctr Educ Excellence, 1986-; Connecticut Coalition Literacy, 1986-; bd trustees, Connecticut Law Sch Found, 1987-; bd dir, Connecticut Civil Liberties Union, 1987-; bd overseers, Regional Lab Educ Improvement Northeast & Islands, 1988-; vpres, Am Fedn Teachers, 1988-; fel, Am Leadership Forum, 1988-; co-chairperson, Sixth Dist Fedn Priorities Proj, 1988-; AFT Human Rights Comm; AFT Pub Employees Prog & Policy Coun; AFT's Task ForceUnion-Sponsored Prof Develop; pres, New Britain Fedn Teachers; Nat Comn Afri-Am Educ; bd mem & chmn, Educ Comm Amistad Am Inc; vpres, John C Rogers Afri-Am Cultural Ctr Inc. **Honors/Awds:** Man of the Year, St James Baptist Church, 1984; John P Shaw Award (Outstanding Serv to Community), New Britain NAACP, 1984; Meritorious Service Award, UNCF, 1987; Educators of Distinction Award, Connecticut Coalition of 100 Black Women, 1988; Carl Huroit Award (Grassroot Politics, Progressive Issues, Coalition Building), LEAP, 1989; Harriet Tubman Award (Achievement in Pursuit of Social Justice), Connecticut NOW, 1989. **Military Serv:** AUS, Sp-4, 1957-59. **Home Addr:** 15 Brookside Rd, New Britain, CT 06052-1522. **Business Addr:** Northeast Regional Director, American Federation of Teachers, 555 New Jersey Ave NW, Washington, DC 20001.

SPRINGER, LLOYD LIVINGSTONE
Clergy. **Personal:** Born Apr 28, 1930; son of Oscar (deceased) and Olive; married Ottwritta L Philips, May 2, 1970; children: Addison. **Educ:** Codrington Col, GOE Dipl, 1963; New York Theol Sem, STM, 1975; New York Univ, MA, 1982. **Career:** Clergy (Retired); St Martin Episcopal Church, asst, 1971-73; St Edmund Episcopal Church, rector, 1973-2000; Episcopal Mission Soc House Holy Comforter, chaplain, 1980-86; Bronx Lebanon Hosp, part time chaplain. **Orgs:** Pres, Mt Hope Housing Corp, 1987-96; North West Bronx Clergy & Comn Orgn; pension comt, Ecumenical Comn, New York diocese. **Honors/Awds:** Bronx Borough President's Award; Vestry Appreciation Award, St Edmund Episcopal; Appreciation Award, Mt Hope Organization & Community; Bronx Community Board Award, New York; Honored Citizen New York State; Immigrant's Alien Award. **Home Addr:** 1358 N Normandy Blvd, Deltona, FL 32725.

SPRINGS, LENNY F
Executive, executive director. **Personal:** Born Apr 25, 1947, Edgefield, SC. **Educ:** Voorhees Col, BS, 1968. **Career:** Greenville Urban League, proj dir, 1976-79, dep dir, 1979-82, exec dir, 1982-83; Southern Bank, comn rels officer, 1983-85; First Union Corp, sr vpres, corp rels div, currently; Wachovia Corp, sr vpres strategic partnership, dir supplier diversity, currently. **Orgs:** Nat bd, Nat Asn Advan Colored People, 1976-, chair, Spec Contrib Fund bd trustees; Bd dirs, Boy Scouts Southern Region; pres admin, US Dept Treas Bank Secrecy Adv Group; vice chair, SC Human Affairs Comn; pres, founder, & bd mem, Charlotte Chap, Hundred Black Men Am; bd mem, Cent Carolina Urban League; Southeast Reg Bd Nat Alliance Bus; Bus Policy Review Coun; bd dirs, Carolinas Minority Supplier Develop Coun Inc; pres, Voorhees Col Nat Alumni Asn; Nat Urban Bankers Asn; bd visitors, Barber-Scotia Col; bd visitors, Johnson C Smith Univ; bd trustees, Elizabeth City State Univ; bd dirs, Fla Mem Col; bd dirs, SC State Univ Found; bd dirs, Spirit Square. **Honors/Awds:** Outstanding Young Men of America, 1973 & 1979; Legal Award for SC, Nat Asn Advan Colored People, 1980; Greenville Branch Award, Nat Asn Advan Colored People, 1984. **Military Serv:** AUS, sgt E-5 2 yrs; 2 Bronze Stars; Air Medal. **Home Addr:** 10911 Tavernay Pkwy, Charlotte, NC 28273, **Home Phone:** (704)594-9260. **Business Addr:** Director of Supplier Diversity, Wachovia Corporation, Wachovia Bank National Association, Two Wachovia Ctr 301 S Tryon St, Charlotte, NC 28288, **Business Phone:** (704)374-6807.

SPRINGS, SHAWN
Football player. **Personal:** Born Mar 11, 1975, Williamsburg, VA; son of Ron. **Educ:** Ohio State Univ, BS, sociol, 2003. **Career:** Seattle Sea hawks, defensive back & corner back, 1997-2003; Wash Redskins, corner back, 2004-08; New England Patriots, corner back, 2008-. **Honors/Awds:** Big Ten Defensive Player of the Year, 1996, Twice in First Team All Big Ten, 1995-96. **Special Achievements:** NFL Draft, First round pick, Rank 3, 1997; speaker, The Wash Post's ann All-Met dinner, 2004. **Business Addr:** Cornerback, New England Patriots, 2 Patriot Place, Foxborough, MA 02035, **Business Phone:** (508)203-2100.

SPRINKLE-HAMLIN, SYLVIA YVONNE
Librarian. **Personal:** Born Apr 25, 1945, Winston-Salem, NC; daughter of Arthur William Henry Sprinkle, Jr and Thelma Norwood Holtzclaw; married Larry Leon, Aug 29, 1981. **Educ:** Winston-Salem State Univ, Winston-Salem, NC, BS, educ, 1967; Clark Univ, Atlanta, GA, MLS, libr sci, educ admin, 1968; Cheyney State Univ, Cheyney, PA, inst advan study, 1976; Univ NC Chapel Hill, Chapel Hill, NC, cert county admin, 1987. **Career:** Philadelphia Pub Schs, Philadelphia, PA, info specialist, 1973-77; Fashion Two Twenty Cosmetics, Winston-Salem, NC, studio owner, 1977-81; Winston-Salem State Univ, Winston-Salem, NC, asst librn, 1978-79; Forsyth County Pub Libr, Winston-Salem, NC, head, children's outreach, 1979-80, asst dir-exten, 1980-84, dep libr dir, 1984; Forsyth County Pub Libr, dir, currently. **Orgs:** Bd mem, Nat Black Theatre Festival, 1989; secy, NC Black Repertory Co, 1989-; dir large, mem comt, NC Libr Asn, 1989-91; vpres, Nat Women Achievement, 1989-91; nat planning chair, Nat Conference African Am Librarians, 1990-92; pres, Youth Opportunity Homes Inc, 1990-93; pres, Black Caucus Am Libr Asn, 1996-; bd mem, Coun Status of Women; bd mem, Winston-Salem State Univ Diggs Gallery; pres, BCALA, NC. **Honors/Awds:** Annette Lewis Phinazee Award, NC Cent Univ, 1986. **Home Phone:** (336)924-8477. **Business Addr:** Library Director, Forsyth County Public Library, 660 W 5th St, Winston-Salem, NC 27101, **Business Phone:** (336)703-3016.

SPROUT, FRANCIS ALLEN
Artist, educator. **Personal:** Born Mar 5, 1940, Tucson, AZ. **Educ:** Univ Ariz, Tuscon, BFA, 1967; Univ Calif, San Diego, MFA, 1972; Univ Calif, Los Angeles, MA, african studies, 1990. **Career:** Artist & educator, currently; Ford Found fel, 1971-72; Univ Denver, Denver, asst prof painting & drawing, 1972-75; Metrop State Col, Denver, Colo, 1976-87; Fac Inst Africa, Hamline Univ, St Paul, fel, 1978; Ariz State Univ, Phoenix, fac assoc, 1987-90; State Univ NY, Purchase, 1991-95; Manhattanville Col, Purchase, NY, 1993-2004; Pratt Inst, Brooklyn, NY, adj assoc prof, 1995-2004; Indian River Community Col, Ft Pierce, Fla, 2004-; Vero Beach Mus Art, instr, 2005-. **Orgs:** Alliance Contemp Art Denver Art Mus, 1980; African Studies Asn, 1984; grant rev panel, Coun Arts & Humnts, 1984-85. **Military Serv:** USNG, first lt 6, yrs. **Business Phone:** (772)360-5108.

SPRUCE, KENNETH L
Educator. **Personal:** Born Mar 6, 1956, Toledo, OH; son of George Spruce Jr and Helen E Jordan Spruce; divorced; children: Sierra Monique. **Educ:** Univ Cincinnati, Cincinnati, OH, BA, 1980; Am Univ, Wash, DC, attended 1981; Univ Toledo, Toledo, OH, MPA, 1982; Clark Atlanta Univ, Atlanta, GA, PhD cand, 1991-. **Career:** Univ Toledo, Toledo, OH, grad teaching asst, 1981-82; Toledo J Newspaper, Toledo, OH, columnist writer-reporter, 1982-85; State Ohio, Bur Employment Serv, Toledo, OH, personnel counr, 1983-91; Morris Brown Coll, Polit Sci Prog, Atlanta, GA, adj instr, 1993; Clark Atlanta Univ, Polit Sci Dept, grad teaching asst, 1993-94; Floyd Col, Rome, GA, asst prof polit sci, 1993-97, assoc prof, 1998-. **Orgs:** Nat Conf Black Polit Scientists, 1990-95; Am Polit Sci Asn, 1992-95; Am Asn Univ Prof, 1994-95; Georgia Polit Sci Asn, 1994-95. **Honors/Awds:** Seven Hundred One Work-Study Scholarship, US Dept of Housing & Urban Dev, 1980-81; Grad Teaching Assist, Univ Toledo, 1981-82; Merit Award, Best Editorial Nominee, Nat Newspaper Publ Asn, 1986; Community Service Award, Nominee, Black Stud Union, Univ Toledo, 1987; Recipient, Ford Foundations Fellowship, 1992-93; Selected Collegiate Scholastic All-American, 1993. **Business Phone:** (706)802-5000.

SPRUELL, SAKINA P.
Editor. **Personal:** Born Jun 19, 1970, Jersey City, NJ; married Carroll Charles Cole. **Educ:** Rutgers Univ, BA, 1993. **Career:** WBLS, res dir, 1993; WHYY Nat Pub Radio, weekend news anchor; Home News Tribune, staff writer; CNN Headline News NJ Local Ed, reporter & producer; freelance writer; Black Enterprise, bus news ed, 2000, sr ed, currently. **Orgs:** Vpres, Rutgers African Am Alumni Alliance, 1998; bd of dir, Achievement in Radio

Awards, 1999; Nat Asn Black Journalists, 1999-; Soc Bus Ed & Writers, 2000-. **Business Addr:** Senior editor, Black Enterprise, 130 5th Ave 10th Fl, New York, NY 10011.*

SPRUILL, JAMES ARTHUR
Educator, actor. **Personal:** Born Sep 28, 1937, Baltimore, MD; married Lynda; children: Robert Patton & Joshua. **Educ:** Goddard Col, AB, 1968; Boston Univ, MFA, 1975. **Career:** Boston Univ Sch Arts, tenured assoc prof, 1975-; Emerson Col, asst prof,1970-74; Goddard Col, vis prof, 1971-72; Boston State Col, vis prof,1972-75; Theatre Co Boston, acted, production, dir, 1967-75; Boston Univ, acting & directing prof, currently, Sch Theatre, assoc prof; Films: Inherent Darkness & Enlightenment, 2002; Alma Mater, Turntable, actor,2005; Headspace, 2005. **Orgs:** Pres & co-founder, New Africian Co Inc, 1968-; bd trustees, Metro CulturalAll; New England Theatre Conf; sr mem, Actors Equity Asn; AFTRA; SAG; pastmem Theatre Advis Panel MA Coun Arts & Human, Martin Luther King Fellow Boston Univ, 1968; reg cit, New Eng Theatre Conf, 1970; Nat Conf African Am Theatre; past chair, Boston Univ Fac Coun; founding mem, Nat Conf African Am Theatre. **Honors/Awds:** Insight Award, Roxbury Action Prog, 1975; Vernon Blackman Drama Award,1990; Elliot Norton Award, 1991; cited for direction of the Colored museum by George C Wolfe, Boston, 1994; Distinguished Faculty Award, Boston Col,2003. **Business Addr:** Acting and Directing Professor, Boston University, 855 Commonwealth Ave, Boston, MA 02115, **Business Phone:** (617)353-3673.

SPRUILL, ROBERT I.
Executive. **Personal:** Born Jul 10, 1947, New Bern, NC. **Educ:** NC Cent Univ, BS, 1970. **Career:** WAFRM FM Community Radio Workshop Inc, pres & founder. **Orgs:** Nat Asn of Educ Broadcasters; NC Asn Broadcasters. **Honors/Awds:** First black owned & controlled educ radio station Am; Featured, Ebony Magazine, 1973.

SPURLOCK, DOROTHY A
Administrator. **Personal:** Born Mar 18, 1956, Kalamazoo, MI; daughter of Della A Watson Spurlock and Jimmie Spurlock Sr. **Educ:** Western Mich Univ, Kalamazoo, Mich, BS, pub admin, 1979, MA, commun, 1983. **Career:** Western Mich Univ, Kalamazoo, Mich, mgr, employ serv, sr compensation analyst & coordr, legisl affairs, 1979-84; Popcorn Station, Kalamazoo, Mich, owner & mgr, 1984-88; Urban League Greater Muskegon, Muskegon, Mich, exec dir, 1988-89; Nu-Way Consulting Inc, Kalamazoo, Mich, vpres oper, 1989; Eastern Mich Univ, assoc dir, off res develop; Univ Toledo, dir, res & sponsored progs, 2002-. **Orgs:** Coun mem, City Kalamazoo, 1983-87; Nat Coun Univ Res. **Honors/Awds:** Woman of the Year, NOW, 1983. **Business Addr:** Director, University of Toledo, Office of Research, 2801 W Bancroft St, Toledo, OH 43606, **Business Phone:** (419)530-2227.

SPURLOCK, DR. JAMES B
Public relations executive. **Personal:** Born Jan 20, 1936, Roanoke, VA; married Nancy H; children: James B III, Deborah G & Kenneth L. **Educ:** A&T State Univ, BS, 1959; Personnel Adm Personnel Mgt, diploma, 1960, 1962; Mgt Training Course, attended 1968; Univ MI, BA, Advanced Mgt Prog, 1970. **Career:** Mgr (retired); AT&T, public relations mgr, treas; Norfolk State Univ Found Inc, pres, currently. **Orgs:** VA State C C; bd deacons, First African Baptist Ch; Roanoke City Sch Bd; bd visitors, James Madison Univ; Richmond Metro COC; Richmond NAACP; Richmond Urban League; RAPME; dir, C W Anderson Male Chorus; past vpres, Norfolk State Univ found bd; bd visitors, Radford Univ; Outstanding Serv Bd Dir VA Col Placement Asn; Outstanding Comn Ldr Burrell Memorial Hosp; Sigma Rho Sigma Nat Honor Soc, treas. **Honors/Awds:** Outstanding Citizen's Award; Father Year Inter-Faith Comm Choir; Cert Merit, City Council Roanoke; Cert Recog, Nat Alliance Busman Serv, Youth Motivation Task Force; Cert appreciation, State Dir Selective Serv; The Army Commendation medal; Vietnam Serv medal, Good Conduct medal. **Special Achievements:** Publ articles, "Obsolescence or Change"; "Recruiting the Qualified Minority Grad", author. **Military Serv:** AUS, capt, 1960-68. **Home Addr:** 7802 Antionette Dr, Richmond, VA 23227. **Business Addr:** President, Norfolk State University Foundation Inc, 700 Pk Aenue Suite 410, Norfolk, VA 23504, **Business Phone:** (804)266-1573.

SPURLOCK, LANGLEY AUGUSTINE
Association executive, executive. **Personal:** Born Nov 9, 1939, Charleston, WV; son of Langley A and Eunice P. **Educ:** WV State Col, BS (magna cum laude), 1959; Wayne State Univ, PhD 1963. **Career:** Wayne State Univ, NIH predoctoral fel, 1961-63; Harvard Univ, NIH Postdoctoral fel, 1966; Brown Univ, assoc prof chem, 1969-73; Alfred P Sloan fel, 1973-75; Am Coun Educ, asst pres, 1973-76; US Dept HEW, HEW fel, 1976-77; Nat Sci Found, sr staff assoc, 1977-82; CHEMSTAR Div, 1982-94, vpres, 1994-; Chem Mfg Asn, dir. **Orgs:** Am Chem Soc; Am Soc Asn Execs; Am Asn Advan Sci; Phi Lambda Upsilon Hon Chem Soc; Soc Sigma Xi; Beta Kappa Chi Hon Sci Soc; Alpha Kappa Mu Hon Sch Soc; Delta Phi Alpha Hon German Soc; Kappa Alpha Psi. **Honors/Awds:** Cert Asn Exec, 1989-. **Special Achievements:** Author 34 publications & 3 patents. **Business Phone:** (703)741-5000.

SPURLOCK, LAVERNE BEARD
Educator. **Personal:** Born Feb 23, 1930, Richmond, VA; daughter of Joseph C and Mabel M Matney; married Charles T, Jun 10, 1956; children: Carla S Harrell. **Educ:** VA State Col, BS, 1950; Columbia Univ, MA, 1954; Univ VA, advan study, 1974; VPI & SU Blacksburg, VA, EdD, 1984. **Career:** Educator (retired); Richmond Pub Schs, Guidance Dept, co ordr, 1970-91; Maggie L Walker HS, teacher, 1951; John Marshall HS, guid dept head, 1970-86; Richmond Pub Schs, supvr guidance, 1986-91. **Orgs:** VA Asn Non-White Concerns; past pres, VA Sch Counr Asn; past dir, educ & vpres educ Richmond Personnel & Guidance Asn; VPGA; vol listener Youth Emergency Servs; bd mem, Richmond Area Psychiatric Clinic; past mem, Bd Christian Educ Ebenezer Bapt Ch; Personnel Com Ebenezer Bapt Ch; trustee, Ebenezer Bapt Ch; past pres, Richmond Alumnae Chap Delta Sigma Theta; past first vpres, Richmond Chap Nat Coalition 100 Black Women; secy, Henrico Area Mental Health Serv Bd, Human Rights Comn; past project dir, SECME; past pres, VIR Heroes, Inc; Pi Lambda Theta; past assoc dir, AVID; Delicadas Inc; The Moles; The Links, Inc; bd dir, Partnership Future, currently. **Honors/Awds:** Boss of the Year, Am Bus Women's Asn, 1989; Delta Sigma Theta, Richmond Alum Chap, EDUC Award; APGA, Counselor of the Year, honorable mention. *

SPURLOCK, OLIVER M
Judge. **Personal:** Born Feb 28, 1945, Chicago, IL; son of Thomas L and Anna P; divorced; children: Stacey, Brandon & Marc. **Educ:** Univ Ill, BA, 1969; Northwestern Univ Law Sch, JD, 1972. **Career:** Cook County State's Atty, asst, 1972-75; pvt pract, atty, 1975-88; Cook County Circuit Ct, assoc judge, 1988, Criminal Ct, judge.

SPURLOCK, RACQUEL
Basketball player. **Personal:** Born May 25, 1973. **Educ:** La Tech, 1996. **Career:** Basketball player (retired); Houston Comets, ctr, 1997. **Honors/Awds:** Gold medal, United States Jones Cup, 1994.

SPURLOCK-EVANS, KARLA JEANNE
School administrator, college administrator. **Personal:** Born Jun 30, 1949, Willimantic, CT; daughter of Odessa Fuller and Kelly M; married Booker, Jul 1, 1978; children: Mariama Ifetayo & Booker Theodore Jr. **Educ:** Barnard Col, AB, magna cum laude, 1971; Emory Univ, MA, 1972. **Career:** State Univ New York, Albany, asst prof, 1975-77; Haverford Col, dir minority affairs & assoc dean, 1977-80; Lake Forest Col, asst dean students 1981-85; Northwestern Univ, assoc dean students, dir Afro-Am student affairs; Trinity Col, dean multicultural affairs & dir affirmative action, 1999-. **Orgs:** Bd mem, Assoc Advancement Creative Musicians, 1981-83; Ill Col Personnel Asn; Ill Community Black Concerns Higher Educ; Nat Asn Women Deans Adminr & Coun; ed bd, Chicago Reporter; Nat Asn Stud Personnel Adminrs. **Honors/Awds:** Grad Fel John Hay Whitney Found, 1971-72; Grad Fel, Danforth Found, 1971-75. **Business Addr:** Dean of Multicultural Affairs, Director of Affirmative Action, Trinity College, 300 Summit St, Hartford, CT 06106, **Business Phone:** (860)297-2000.

SQUIRE, CAROLE RENEE
Judge. **Personal:** Born Jul 21, 1953, Springfield, OH; daughter of Robert Hutchins and Reva; married Percy, Mar 18, 1978; children: Reva Marie & Deidra Renee. **Educ:** Ohio State Univ, BA, 1974; Ohio State Univ Col Law, JD, 1977. **Career:** Franklin Co Domestic Rels Ct, juvenile unit, asst prosecutor, juvenile unit magistrate, 1991-94; Off Ohio Atty Gen, asst atty gen; pvt law pract family law area; Am Univ, col instr; Off Gen Coun Navy, atty advisor, contracts; Youth Alternative Proj, asst dir; Ohio Legal Rights Serv, staff atty; Phonics READ, founder; Franklin Co Ct, Div Domestic Rels & Juvenile Br, judge, currently. **Orgs:** Community Mediation Serv, 1988-92; Former Youth Advocate Serv, 1989-92; Seal Ohio Girl Scout Coun, 1991-93; Columbus Bar Found, 1992; Asn Female Exec, 1993; Art Child Safe Am, 1999-; Shiloh Baptist Church; Nat Conf Black Lawyers; Ohio State Bar Asn; Nat Asn Juvenile Ct Judges; Women Lawyers Franklin Co. **Business Addr:** Judge, Franklin County Court, 373 S High St 6th Fl, Columbus, OH 43215-4598, **Business Phone:** (614)462-5223.

STAATS, DR. FLORENCE JOAN
School administrator. **Personal:** Born Nov 18, 1940, Newark, NJ; daughter of Jay M and Florence Wheatley. **Educ:** Parsons Sch Design cert, 1961; New York Univ, BS, 1968; Pratt Inst, MFA, 1970; Columbia Univ Teachers Col, EdD, 1978. **Career:** Newark Pub Libr, exhibit artst, 1965-68; Essex Co Col, fine arts instr,1972-78, asst prof, coordr Art prog, 1978-81; Dutchess Comm Col, asst dean, 1982-84, asst pres 1984-; Bloomfield Col, assoc dean, 1985-86; Rockland Community Col, assoc dean, 1986-88; NY African Am Inst SUNY, acting dir, 1988-89; Ulster County Community Col, dir, COPE, proj coordr, 1989-99, Res & Proj Develop, pres; FJS Designs, creatice dir, currently. **Orgs:** Bd dir, Clearwater Inc 1983-; rep, ACE/NIP Instnl Am Coun Educ Mid Hudson Chap, 1983-; exec bd, dir, Ulster Co Coun Arts, 1983-85; creative dir, pres, Arts Connection, 1984-; pres, Arts & Commun Network Inc, 1985-; bd dir, Creative Res African Am Life, 1986-; exec bd, chairperson, UlsterCounty Nat Asn Advan Colored People Educ Comt; Rosendale Environ Comn; bddir, vpres, Ulster Arts Alliance; bd dir, Ulster County Girl Scouts,2000-; Ulster County Off Agung, exec adv Comt, 2002. **Honors/Awds:** NEH Grant Black Exprnc Am, 1977; OE Grant Fulbright G7 Community Col Sem Poland, 1974; CBS EEC Award for Market Planning, 1984; Summer Res Grant, NY African Am Inst, 1987; Grant Award, New York State Coun Arts, 1989; Martin Luther King Jr Award for Community Service, Ulster County Multi Serv, 1995; Recycled Design Award, Hudson Valley Material & Exchange, 2002. **Business Addr:** Creative Director, FJS Research & Designs, PO Box 254, High Falls, NY 12440, **Business Phone:** (914)687-0767.

STACKHOUSE, JERRY DARNELL
Basketball player. **Personal:** Born Nov 5, 1974, Kinston, NC; son of George Stackhouse and Minnie; married Ramirra Marks, Dec 24, 2000; children: Jaye, Alexis & Antonio. **Educ:** NC Univ, BA, 1999. **Career:** Philadelphia 76ers, forward-guard, 1995-97; Detroit Pistons, 1997-2002; Washington Wizards, 2002; Rehab Inst Mich, bd trustee; Dallas Mavericks, 2004-08; Memphis Grizzlies, 2009-; free agent currently. **Honors/Awds:** NBA All-Rookie Team, 1996; NBA All-Star, 2000, 2001.

STAFFORD, DERRICK
Manager. **Personal:** Born Nov 29, 1956, Atlanta, GA. **Educ:** Morehouse Col, attended 1979. **Career:** US Postal Serv, delivery, supv; labour rel; human resources; mkt; Nat Basketball Asn (NBA), referee, currently. **Orgs:** Exec bd mem, Nat Basketball Referees Asn, currently; chmn, I Can Do Anything Found, currently. **Honors/Awds:** NBA All-Star Game, 2002. **Special Achievements:** Officiated the McDonalds Championship game in Paris, France and the Legends All-Star Game in Orlando, 1997; volunteered at the Zion Hill Baptist Church. **Business Addr:** Referee, National Basketball Referees Association, c/o Perennial Strategy Group, 1455 Pennsylvania Ave NW Suite 225, Washington, DC 20004, **Business Phone:** (202)638-5090.

STAFFORD, DON
Law enforcement officer. **Personal:** Born Dec 14, 1934, Rusk, TX; son of L V Mitchell and Chilton; married Geraldine Doughty, Apr 5, 1985. **Educ:** Butler Col, Tyler, TX, BS, 1956. **Career:** Law Enforcement offficer (retired); Dallas Police Dept, Dallas, TX, asst chief police, 1982-88, dist chief, exec asst chief, 1988-91. **Orgs:** Black Chamber Com; Urban League; Int Police Asn; Blacks Law Enforcement. **Honors/Awds:** Certificate Civic Achievement, Dallas Police Dept, 1977; Dallas Mayor, Texas Peace Officers' Asn, Interdenominational Ministers Alliance; Outstanding Texan Award, Governor's Office State Texas. **Special Achievements:** Promoted to the Rank of Sergeant, 1966; One of the first African American to ever hold a Supervisor Rank in the History of the Dallas Police Dept. **Military Serv:** USAF, A/2C, 1956-60; Received plaque for Outstanding Officer the Month, Air Police. **Home Addr:** 2913 S Houston Sch Rd, Lancaster, TX 75146, **Home Phone:** (214)372-6457.

STAFFORD, EARL W
Executive. **Career:** Universal Systs & Tech Inc, chief exec officer & chmn, currently. **Business Addr:** Chief Executive Officer, Chairman, Universal Systems & Technology Inc, 4th Fl 5870 Trinity Pkwy, Centreville, VA 20120-1907, **Business Phone:** (703)502-9600.

STAFFORD-ODOM, TRISHA
Basketball coach, basketball player. **Personal:** Born Nov 11, 1970, Los Angeles, CA; married DeWayne Odom; children: Amari & Trajen. **Educ:** Univ Calif, Berkeley, attended 1992. **Career:** Basketball player (retired), basketball coach; San Jose Lasers, forward,1997-98; Long Beach Stingrays, 1998; Houston Comets, 2001; Miami Sol,forward, 2002; Westchester High Sch, head girls' basketball coach; UnivCalif, Los Angeles, UCLA Bruins, head women's basketball coach, 2005-. **Orgs:** Co-founder, Play Mode Found Inc. **Business Addr:** Head Women, University of California, UCLA Bruins, JD Morgan Ctr, PO Box 24044, Los Angeles, CA 90024-0607, **Business Phone:** (310)825-8699.

STAGGERS, FRANK EUGENE
Physician. **Personal:** Born Aug 23, 1926, Charleston, SC; widowed; children: Frank Jr, Barbara, Michael. **Educ:** Va State Col, BS 1949; Meharry Med Col, MD 1953. **Career:** Physician urol (retired); USN Hosp, asst chief urol, 1961-63; USN, resd, 1957-60; USN Hosp, intern, 1953-54. **Orgs:** Am Med Asn; ACCMA; NMA; Western Sect AUA; Med Staff & Survey Com CA Med Asn; Calif Blue Shield Policy Com; Geriatrics Com; Golden State Med Soc; St Luke's Soc; Nursing Educ Adv Com Merrie & Laney Col; Sigma Pi Phi Frat; Kappa Alpha Psi; Beta Kappa Chi Nat Hon Sci Coc; Golden State Med Asn Calif; Med Asn Liasion Com; Carcinoma Prostate UC Med Ctr; chair, Calif Med Asn found, currently. **Special Achievements:** Publ "Treatment of the Undescended Testis With Especial Reference to Pathological Anatomy" Jour Urology 1960. **Military Serv:** AUS, comdr, 1945-45; AUSNR, 1947-53; USN, 1953-63; USNR, 1963-73. **Business Addr:** 5900 Shattuck Ave, Ste 203, Oakland, CA 94609.

STAGGERS, ROBIN L (ROBIN CHANDLER-STAGGERS)
Manager. **Personal:** Born Jan 24, 1958, Chicago, IL; daughter of Robert L Chandler and Ollie M Williams; children: Barrett Chandler & Davia Anaia. **Educ:** Roosevelt Univ, BS, BA, 1986, paralegal cert, 1992. **Career:** Quaker Oats Co, community affairs, coordr, 1981-86; Chicago Transit Authority, legal exec, asst gen

coun, 1986-95, human resources analyst, 1995; Il Dept Children & Family Serv, actg dep dir, dep dir, chief staff, currently. **Orgs:** Lead coordr, Sweet Holy Spirit FGBC, Wedding Coordrs Ministry, 1993-. **Business Addr:** Chief of Staff, Illinois Department of Children and Family Services, 100 W Randolph St 6-200, Chicago, IL 60601, **Business Phone:** (312)814-6800.

STAHNKE, WILLIAM E.
Banker. **Career:** First Texas Bank, Dallas, pres & chief exec, 1987-97; BOK Financial.

STALEY, DAWN (DAWN MICHELLE STALEY)
Basketball coach, basketball player. **Personal:** Born May 4, 1970, Philadelphia, PA. **Educ:** Univ Va, attended 1992. **Career:** Basketball player (retired), basketball coach, exec; played prof basketball, Brazil, Spain, France, 1992-95; Philadelphia Rage, guard, 1996-98; Charlotte Sting, guard, 1999-2004; Charlotte Sting, guard, 2000; Temple's Univ, head coach, 2001-; USA Basketball Sr Nat Team, asst coach; Univ South Carolina, womens head basketball coach, 2008-. **Orgs:** Founder, Dawn Staley Found. **Honors/Awds:** Honda-Broderick Award, 1991; USA Basketball Female Athlete of the Year,1994; Entrepreneurial Spirit Award, Women's Nat Basketball Asn, 1995; Gold medal, Olympics, 1996; Kodak, All Am, named three times; ABL, All-Star Games, starter, 1997, 1998; Woman One Award, 2005; Wanamaker Award, 2005;Community Leadership Award, 2006; Henry P Iba Citizenship Award, 2007; voted for Big Five Coach of the Year; Virginia Sports Hall of Fame inductee, 2008. **Business Phone:** (215)204-7000.

STALEY, DAWN MICHELLE. See STALEY, DAWN.

STALEY, DUCE
Football player, broadcaster. **Personal:** Born Feb 27, 1975, Columbia, SC; son of Tena Staley; children: Shakia & Damani Zihir. **Educ:** Univ SC, sociol. **Career:** Philadelphia Eagles, running back, 1997-2003; Pittsburgh Steelers, running back, 2004-06; Gamecock Sports Radio Net, sideline reporter, currently; 107.5FM sports Radio, show host, currently. **Orgs:** Eagles Youth Partnership, Philadelphia; First Steps Prog; Variety Club; Direct Care Kids; founder, Catch 22 Found. **Honors/Awds:** ADDY Award, 2001. Neighborhood MVP Award, 2004.

STALEY, KENNETH BERNARD
President (organization), chief executive officer, executive. **Personal:** Born Dec 31, 1948, Philadelphia, PA; son of Kinzy Staley and Bernice Staley; married Shelia Keeys, Apr 26, 1975; children: Tabbatha, Christina & Harrison. **Educ:** Villanova Univ, BSCE, 1971; Miller Theol Sem, MDiv, 1975, DD, 1978; Am Asn Marriage & Family Therapist, clin, 1983. **Career:** Jos A McCollum Inc, engr training, 1966-69; RV Rulon Co, field engr, 1969; United Engrs & Constructors Inc, field engr, 1971-72; Kinzy Staley & Sons Inc, vpres, 1972-90, pres/ceo, 1992-93; Summer Sch, prin, 2003; Covenant Group Inc, pres, currently. **Orgs:** Bd mem, Kinzy Staley & Sons Inc, 1972-; bd mem, Christian Res & Develop,1980-; bd mem, Mendenhall Ministries, 1981-; steering comn, Philadelphia Leadership Found, 1985-; bd mem, Greater Germantown Develop Corp, 1988-89; Fel Christian Athletes, PA state bd, 1992; steering comm, Billy Graham Crusade Philadelphia, 1992; Nat Soc Prof Engrs; Asn Cost Engrs; Am Arbitration Asn; Am Ceramic Soc; Am Concrete Inst; Alpha Phi Alpha. **Honors/Awds:** Outstanding Young Man in America, US Jaycees, 1980, 1981, 1983. **Business Addr:** Principal, Covenant Consulting Corp, 1130 Lakeside Ave, Philadelphia, PA 19004, **Business Phone:** (215)549-7271.

STALEY, VALERIA HOWARD
Librarian. **Personal:** Born May 5, 1925, Georgetown, SC; married Frank Marcellus Staley Jr; children: Frank Howard, Elisa Claire. **Educ:** Talladega Col, BA, 1945; Univ Chicago, BLS, 1946. **Career:** Librarian (retired); Fla Agr & Mech Univ, ref librn, 1946-49; Howard High Sch, sch librn, 1949-57; Orangeburg Co Libry, SC, librn; SC State Col, reference & information specialist, 1958-85. **Orgs:** Chmn, Orangeburg Co Libr Comn ,1969-; bd dirs, Orangeburg Co Arts Festival; Am Libr Asn; Southeastern Lib Asn; life mem, SC Libr Asn; Am Asn Univ Profs; Phi Delta Kappa Frat; Black Caucus Am Library Asn; Churchwomen United; past pres, Links; past pres, Delta Sigma Theta sor; Jeddah Ct Daughters Isis; life mem, Eastern Stars; life mem, VFW Auxiliary Post 8166; past pres, Jack & Jill Am; past pres, state vpres, Nat Asn Aadvan Colored People; chapel, Am Methodist Episcopal Church; bd dirs, SC State Mus Found; SC Dept Social Serv; Foster Care Review Bd; adv bd, Orangeburg Salvation Army. **Honors/Awds:** Distinguished Service Award, SC State Libr; SC Governors' Service Award, 1998; Order of the Palmetto. *

STALKS, LARRIE W.
Government official. **Personal:** Born Sep 28, 1925, Newark, NJ; married Frederick. **Educ:** Rutgers Univ; New York Univ. **Career:** Cent Planning Bd City Newark, former secy; Dept Health & Welfare City Newark, dir, 1966-70; Cent Planning Bd City Newark, exec secy; Congressman Hugh J Addonizio, home dist secy; Essex County Register Deeds, mem. **Orgs:** Bd trustees, Cent Ward Girls Club; Edmund L Houston Found Rutgers Univ; Essex Co Youth House; pres, Metro Urban Social Serv; vpres, OMEGA Investment Corp; counr, Municipal Career women Newark; founder, secy, Newark Comn Housing Corp; secy, Peoples Develop Corp; former pres, Esqui-Vogues Northern, NJ; past vpres, Shanley Ave Civic Asn; past life mem, chmn, Nat Advan Asn Colored People, Newark Br; past state bd dir, Nat Advan Asn Colored People State Conf; past pub affairs chmn, Negro Bus & Prof Womens Club; past Ed, Citizenship; chmn, Newark Chap Coun Negro Women; Nat Planning Asn; Am Soc Planning Officials; vchmn, Newark Cent Ward; co-chmn, Newark Essex Co Meyner, Governor Club; Essex Co Rep Young Dem Conv; Newark Liaison All Co Campaigns; founder, onizer, adv Cent Ward Young Dem; Congressional Liaison Kennedy Air-Lift; exec dir, Hugh Jaddonizio Civic Asn; Minorities Affairs; chmn, Dem Party Co State. **Honors/Awds:** Community Service Award, Afro Am Newspaper, 1952; Achievement Award, Iota Phi Lamba, 1956; Achievement Award, Frontiers Am, 1957; Newark Br Nat Advan Asn Colored People Service Award, 1960; Associaiton Service Award, Stephen P Teamer Civic, 1962; Achievement Award, Negro Bus & Prof Women,1963; Service Award, Metro Civic Asn, 1965; Service Award, ILA Local 1233,1965; Ballantine Award, 1965; Laura Grant Award, 1965; Woman of the Year, Deomart Enterprises, 1965; Appreciation Award, Cent Planning Bd, 1967;Outstanding Women, Iota Phi Chap Sorority, 1968; Service Award, S Ward Little League, 1968; Achievement Award, Am Negro Assembly, 1968; Achievement Award, Municipal Career women Newark, 1968; Abraham Yecies Award, 1972; Service Award, After Hours Magazine, 1974. *

STALLING, RONALD EUGENE
Police officer. **Personal:** Born Mar 11, 1946, Daytona Beach, FL; son of Lloyd George and Helen Katherine Bolden; married Paulette Marian Robinson Stalling, Jul 23, 1973; children: Kali, Dana. **Educ:** Southeastern Univ, Wa, DC, 1970; Am Univ, Wa, DC, 1974. **Career:** US Dept State, Wa, DC, admin asst, 1964-66, 1968-70; US Secret Serv, Wa, DC, fed law enforcement officer, 1970-02. **Orgs:** Nat Black Police Asn, 1989-; secy, Alliance Black Fed Officers Inc, 1989-. **Honors/Awds:** Sustained Superior Performance Award. **Military Serv:** AUS, E-4, 1966-68; service awards of Vietnam service; Master parachutists jmp mstr & instr.

STALLINGS, REV. GEORGE AUGUSTUS
Clergy. **Personal:** Born Mar 17, 1948, New Bern, NC; son of George Augustus Sr and Dorothy. **Educ:** St Pius X Sem, BA, philos, 1970; Univ St Thomas Aquinas, STB, 1973; Univ St Thomas Aquinas, MA, pastoral theol, 1974; Pontifical Univ St Thomas Aquinas, STL, 1975. **Career:** Ordained Roman Cath priest, 1974; Our Lady Queen Peace, Wash, DC, assoc pastor, 1974-76; St Teresa Avila, Wash, DC, pastor, 1976-88; Arch diocese Wash, DC, dir evangelism prog, 1988-89; Imani Temple African-Am Cath Congregation, founder, 1989-, pastor, 1989, bishop, 1990-91, sr pastor, archbishop, 1991-; SKS Press, pres & chief exec officer, currently. **Orgs:** Nat co-pres, Am Clergy Leadership Conf. **Honors/Awds:** Award for Meritorious Service, Mayor Wash; Golden Boy, Boy's Club Richmond, 1972; Outstanding Teaching Award, JL Francis Elem Sch, 1983-86; Doctor Sacred Theol, Eastern Theol Sem, Lynchburg, VA, 1993. **Special Achievements:** Featured on international television and radio programs, and in print media, since the founding of Imani Temple African-American Catholic Congregation, Stallings? appearances include the Oprah Winfrey Show, Larry King Live, 50 Minutes, the Phil Donahue Show, CNN, the British Broadcasting Network (BBC) and the Mario Costanza Show in Rome, Italy. **Business Phone:** (202)388-8155.

STALLINGS, GREGORY RALPH
Educator. **Personal:** Born Dec 28, 1957, Richmond, VA; son of Steward B Sr; married Mitzi Keyes (divorced); children: Brittny Jean. **Educ:** The Col William & Mary, BA, geol, 1980; Univ Va, MA; Va Commonwealth Univ, MA; Va State Univ, MA. **Career:** Boys Club Richmond, unit dir, 1980-81; Richmond Pub Schs, teacher, 1981-86, coord intervention progs, 1986-88, instrnl leader, 1988-91, teacher specialist, 1991-95. **Orgs:** Col adv, Theta Rho Chap, Alpha Phi Alpha, VA Commonwealth Univ; dir educ affairs, Xi Delta Lambda, Alpha Phi Alpha, 1985-87; treas, pres male usher bd & chmn trustee bd, First Union Baptist Church; basketball coach Recreation Dept; pres, Xi Delta Lambda Alpha Phi Alpha, 1988-90; area dir, VACAPAF; instr, VA Ctr Educ Leadership. **Honors/Awds:** Outstanding Teaching Award, JL Francis Elementary Sch, 1983-86; Xi Delta Lamba, Alpha Man of the Year, 1992; Teacher of the Year, Patrick Henry Elementary Sch, 1997-98; finalist for Teacher of the Year, Richmond Public Schs, 1997-98; finalist REB Award, 1997; Richmond Public Schools' 2006 Teacher of the Year, Richmond Pub Sch, 2006. **Special Achievements:** First Black "Golden Boy" Boy's Club of Richmond, 1972.

STALLINGS, HENRY E
Artist, state government official, business owner. **Personal:** Born Dec 30, 1950. **Educ:** Western Mich Univ, BA; Detroit Col Law, JD. **Career:** Artist; Art gallery & picture framing shop owner; Mich State Senate, Dist 3, sen, 1995; Art On The Ave, owner, currently. **Business Addr:** Owner, Art on the Ave, 19132 Livernois Ave, Detroit, MI 48221, **Business Phone:** (313)863-4278.

STALLINGS, JAMES RAIFORD
Administrator. **Personal:** Born Oct 9, 1936, Augusta, GA; married Geneva Butler; children: Sylvia B & James R. **Educ:** Allen Univ, BS, 1959; So IL Univ, MS, 1968. **Career:** Richmond Co Bd Educ, math teacher, 1959-71; C&S Nat Bank, loan officer & asst br mgr, 1971-75; Augusta Col, dir financial aid, 1975. **Orgs:** Nat Bankers Asn, 1971-75; Bank PAC, 1973; Alpha Phi Alpha; hon mem, Ga Asn Stud Fin Aid Adminr; Nat Asn Stud Fin Aid Adminr; Southern Asn Stud Fin Aid Adminr.

STALLINGS, RAMONDO ANTONIO
Football player. **Personal:** Born Nov 21, 1971, Winston-Salem, NC. **Educ:** San Diego State. **Career:** Cincinnati Bengals, defensive end, 1994-97; Edmonton Eskimos, 2000; LosAngeles Xtreme, defensive end, 2001-. **Business Phone:** (213)749-9498.

STALLS, DR. M
Educator, manager. **Personal:** Born Oct 22, 1947, Metropolis, IL; daughter of Robert A and Freda Mae Houston; children: Robert C Goodwin. **Educ:** Southern Ill Univ, BA, 1970, MS, 1976, PhD, 1991, MSW, 2002. **Career:** Ill Dept C & Family Servs, child welfare worker, 1970-75; Ill Farmers Union, manpower coordr, 1976-78; Southern Ill Univ Carbondale Sch Tech Careers, res & serv coordr, 1978-80; Ctr Basic Skills, coord supple inst, develop skills supt inr, vis asst prof, Black Am studies, develop skills training specialist, currently. **Orgs:** Founder & coordr, Black Women's Coalition, 1983; mentor, Develop Proj Magic, 1984-; consult, Jack Co Pub Housing Initiatives Training Prog, 1985; steering comt Mem, Ill Comn Black Concerns in Higher Educ, 1985-, vice chair, Southern Region, 1997, 1998; consult, Southern Ill Univ Carbondale Women's Studies Film Proj, 1986-; Am Asn Couns & Devel; Nat Coun Black Studies; exec dir, Star Human Serv Develop Corp Inc, 1987-; founder & convener, Assembly African Am Women, 1989; Kappa Delta Pi, 1987; fel Ill Comn Black Concerns Higher Educ, 1984; Am Asn Univ Women; Southern Il Univ Alumni Asn. **Honors/Awds:** Service Award, Eurma C Hayes Comp Child Care Servs PAC, 1977; Cert of Appreciation, Southern Ill Univ Carbondale Headstart, 1986; Iota Phi Theta Quintessence Award, 1984; Southern Ill Univ Carbondale BAC Acad Excellence Award, 1987, Paul Robeson Award; Faculty Staff Award, 1988; George S Counts Doctoral Award, 1990; Dedicated Service Award, ICBCHE, 1990; Alton Metropolitan Human Development Recognition Award, 1991; Southern Ill Univ Carbondale, Acad Excellence Award, Black Affairs Coun, 1991, Univ Woman of Distinction Award, Univ ADE Prof, 1998; Humanitarian Award, Southern Ill Univ Carbondale Black Affairs Coun, 1996. **Special Achievements:** Published 5 Poems in Literati, 1989; nominee, Outstanding Prof, Grad & Prof Educ, Southern Ill Univ Carbondale, 1994. **Business Addr:** Instructor, Southern Illinois University Carbondale, Ctr Basic Skills, Woody Hall Rm C7, Carbondale, IL 62901-4720.

STALLWORTH, ALMA G.
Government official. **Personal:** Born Nov 15, 1932, Little Rock, AR; married Thomas F Stallworth Jr; children: Thomas III & Keith. **Educ:** Highland Pk Jr Col, BA, Health Educ & Prom, 1949; Wayne State Univ, MA,Health Educ & Prom, 1951; Merrill Palmer Inst, attended 1965. **Career:** Parent Involvement Prog Head start Archdiocesan Detroit, cord, 1964-68; dir vol serv, 1968-69; St John's Day Care Ctr, dir, 1969-70; Oak Grove Day Care Ctr; ran for state Sen 7th Dist, 1974; Hist Dept City Detroit, dep dir, 1978; State Mich, rep, 1970-74, 1982-96, chair & rep, 1996-2005; vice chair, Telecommunications, State-Federal Assembly, NCSL, currently. **Orgs:** Oak Grove AME Ch; Demo Party; Natl Order Women Legislators; Mayor's Citizens Task Force; Natl Orgn Women Detroit Sect; State Training Sch Adv Coun; Natl Inst Women's Wrongs; Wayne Co Juvenile Justice Commn; exec comm, United Negro Col Fund, Natl Conf State Legis; hon, Alpha Kappa Alpha Sorority; brd dirs, Woman in gov; Heat & Warmth Fund, Wayne City Task Force on Infant Mortality; founder, pres emer, Black Child Develop Inst; founder, Black Caucus Found. **Honors/Awds:** Legislator Yr MI Assn Children's Alliance; Community Serv Award Lula Belle Stewart Ctr; Dedicated Serv & Support Award United Negro Col Fund, 1985; Outstanding Personal & Prof Commitment Award Planned Parenthood, 1985; Blue Cross Blue Shield Health & People PAC Award, 1986; Cert Achievement for Maternal & Child Health Progs Gov Blanchard & Dept Health; Spirit Detroit Award Gentlemen Wall St; Distinguished Serv Award MI Pub Health Assn; Susan B Anthony Award Detroit Chap Natl Org Women; Walter A Bergman Human Rights Award, Fed Teachers; Women's Hon in Pub Serv, Nurses Assn; Distinguished Serv Award, United Negro Col Fund; Phenomenal Women Award, Natl Assn Negro Bus & Prof Women; Leader in Women's Health, Natl Women's Lobby 1995; Dedicated Serv Award, Detroit East; Distinguished Serv to Detroit Comm, Detroit Pub Sch; Appreciation Award, Wayne Co Child Coordinating Coun; Legislator Yr, Arthritis Found; Vol Serv Award, United Negro Col Fund; You Make All Difference for Our World Award, Amitech. **Special Achievements:** Authored numerous policy papers and testified before Congress on economic,education and health issues affecting Black families and inner city communities; major legislative accomplishments are authorship of Michigan's Child Care Licensing Act, Michigan's Telecommunications Deregulation Statute & Michigan's Electricity and Natural Gas Restructuring Act.

STALLWORTH, ANN
Government official. **Personal:** Born May 15, 1932, DeKalb, TX; widowed; children: Charles, Patricia Banks, Lilye Chaffin, Rachel

Carr, Allen O Jr & EricDarrel. **Educ:** Langston Univ, bus admin; Delta Col, unit comput sci; Stockton Jr Col, grad, 1949. **Career:** Government official (retired); Pacific Tel, tel operator, supvr, asst operating mgr, 1963-68, personnel, employment, recruiting & coun, develop affirmative action plan, 1968-72, customer servs, educ & training, 1972-83, mkt adminr, sales, 1982-83; AT&T Info Systs, techn consult, mkt, 1983-85; trade SOURCES, chief exec officer, 1986-95. **Orgs:** Educ comt, Nat Asn Advan Colored People, 1970-94; credential comt, Dameron Hosp Bd Mem, 1970-; Bd Ed, Stockton Unified Sch Dist, 1973-90; Co-founder,first vpres, pres, chair bylaws, nominating comt, Calif Coalition Black Sch Bd, 1974-90; bd dir, usher bd, Christ Temple Church, 1975; treas scholar fund, 1978-86; pres, 1986-90, vpres, 1984-86; Stockton Chapt Links. **Honors/Awds:** Hon Life Mem James Monroe PTA, 1964; Commendation voc Ed Dr Wilson Riles Supt Pub Instr State CA, 1974; Black Woman Ed Stockton Comn, 1974; Nominee Soroptimist Woman of the Year Award, 1978; Women of Achievement Award, Nat Asn Advan Colored People, 1992; Girl Scout Role Model, 1994. **Home Phone:** (703)794-9101.

STALLWORTH, OSCAR B
Manager. **Personal:** Born Dec 5, 1944, Mobile, AL; married Elsie Thigpen; children: Oscar jr & Brett. **Educ:** BS, mech, 1966. **Career:** Castings & Brake Components Motor Wheel Corp, jr proj engr motor wheel, 1967-68; prod engr passenger car brakes & wheels, motor wheel, 1968-71, mgr, 1971. **Orgs:** Soc Automotive Engrs, 1967; Am Soc Metals, 1967; Am Foundryman's Soc, 1967; Boys Club Lansing; chmn, Voter Regis A Phillip Randolph Inst, 1972; vice chmn, Ingham Co Dem Party, 1970-72; adv, solicitor Jr Achievement, 1968; Alpha Phi Alpha Frat, 1964; mgr, Field Operations Political Campaigns, 1970; pres, Coland Inc.

STALLWORTH, YOLANDA
Administrator. **Personal:** Born Jan 16, 1959, Mobile, AL; daughter of Henry and Mattie Webb; married Alfred L Stallworth, Feb 15, 1982; children: Warren L & Sascha E. **Educ:** Tenn State Univ, BS, 1981; Xavier Univ, MA, 1997; Ohio Supt Leadership Develop class, grad, attended. **Career:** San Antonio State Sch, psych asst, 1986-90; Montgomery County Bd Mental Retardation & Develop Disabilities, asst dir, 1990-96; Hamilton County Bd Mental Retardation & Develop Disabilities, asst to supt, 1996-. **Orgs:** Zeta Phi Beta Sorority, 1st vpres, Pi Sigma Zeta, 1992-; adv bd mem, Wright State Univ, Biomed Rehab Eng; bd mem, Norcen Behavioral Health Systems. **Honors/Awds:** Ohio's MR/DD Superintendents Class, 1998; nominated for Applause Magazine/ Channel 12 Image Maker Award, 1998, 2000; Graduate of Urban Leagues Leadership Class, 1998; Surveyor of the Year, Comn Accreditation, 1996. **Special Achievements:** Honored by Commission on Rehab Facilities for Report Writing, 1996; spotlighted by African-American Success Guide, 1999-2000; performed vignettes on African-American Achievement for Channel 9 for month of Feb, 1996. **Business Addr:** Assistant to the Superintdent, Hamilton County Board of Mental Retardation & Developmental Disabilities, 1520 Madison Rd, Cincinnati, OH 45206, **Business Phone:** (513)794-3300.

STAMPER, HENRY J.
Executive. **Career:** First Federal Savings & Loan Asn Scotlandville, Baton Rouge, LA, chief exec; Henry J Stamper & Assoc, chief exec officer, currently. **Business Addr:** Cheif Executive Officer, Henry J Stamper & Assoc, 1287 Elysian Dr, Baton Rouge, LA 70810-2625.

STAMPLEY, GILBERT ELVIN
Lawyer. **Personal:** Born May 24, 1943, Baton Rouge, LA; married Ester J Francis. **Educ:** Grambling State Univ, BA, 1965; Tulane Univ Sch Law, JD, 1972. **Career:** Men's Affairs Jarvis Christian Col, dep dir, 1965-67; EEO Comn, case analyst, 1970-72; Smith & Stampley, atty, 1972-75; Harris Stampley Mckee Bernard & Broussard, atty; Am Bar Asn; Martinet Soc; La State Bar Asn; Nat Bar Asn; Nat Conf Black Lawyers Exec Comt; Nat Asn Advan Colored People; Palm-air Civil Improv Asn; Orleans Parish Prog Voters League, vpres; Young Dem Am; Urban League; atty, currently. **Orgs:** La State Dem Cent Com Dist, 1962; Earl Warren Fel, 1971-72; City Planning Comn New Orleans, 1976-81. **Military Serv:** AUS, E-5, 1968-70. **Home Addr:** 10201 Chevy Chase Dr, New Orleans, LA 70127. **Business Addr:** Lawyer, 1010 Common St Suite 700, New Orleans, LA 70112-2457, **Business Phone:** (504)566-1393.*

STAMPS, DELORES BOLDEN
School administrator, consultant. **Personal:** Born Mar 16, 1947, Monticello, MS; daughter of Balene Sutton and Peter James; married Alvin Stamps, Jun 22, 1985; children: Tiffany & Katrina; married James L Campbell (divorced); children: Keceya Campbell & Jason Campbell. **Educ:** Tougaloo Col, BA, 1968; Univ Southern Miss, MS, 1972, PhD, 1985; Harvard Univ, cert, 1974. **Career:** Jackson State Univ, asst prof educ, 1985-88, acad skills ctr, dir, 1976-88; Tougaloo Col, dir instnl res, 1988-89, vpres & instnl advan; Piney Woods Sch, Off Instnl Advan; D B Stamps Enerprises Inc, pres, currently. **Orgs:** Unit leader, League Women Voters, 1975-; chairperson, spec events comm, UNCF, 1985-; participant, Leadership Jackson, Jackson Chamber Comm, 1988; bd trustees, Miss Museum Art, 1989-. **Honors/Awds:** Benjamin E Mays Scholar, Ind Univ, 1986; Outstanding Women Leader in Jackson, Miss, Jackson Advocate newspaper, 1990. **Special Achievements:** Author of "Coping Abilities as a Predictor of Student Retention, Black Student Retention in Higher Education", 1988, "Self Concept of Ability, Self-Esteem, Locus of Control and Perception of the Opportunity Structure as Predictors of Coping Ability Among Selected Black College Students", Benjamin E Mays Academy Monograph Series, 1987, co-author of "From Whence They Come: An Assessment of Black College Experience at Historically Black Institutions". **Business Addr:** President, D B Stamps Enerprises Inc, 1210 Holbrook Cir, Jackson, MS 39206-2031, **Business Phone:** (601)362-6391.

STAMPS, JOE, JR.
School administrator. **Personal:** Born Dec 3, 1939, Houston, TX; married Mable Hubbard; children: Jo-Ellen, Bernadette & Joe III. **Educ:** Tex Southern Univ, 1959-62; Labor Studies, Linden-Hall Dawson, Pa, 1979 & 1982. **Career:** Pct 371 Harris Co, election judge, 1978-; pres, United Steelworkers Local 7682, 1979-82; Bd Educ, legis rep 1981-; bd mem, North Forest ISD, currently. **Orgs:** Philip Randolf Inst, 1963-; NABSE; vpres, Local 7682, 1993-97; NSBA Little Union Baptist Church, deacon, youth Sunday sch teacher; pres, N Forest ISD Bd Trustees; life mem, Tex, PTA; life mem, Texas Cong Parents Teacher Asn. **Honors/ Awds:** Outstanding Sch Bd Member, Region IV Tex. **Home Addr:** 8430 Gallahad St, Humble, TX 77078. **Business Addr:** School Board Member, North Forest ISD, 7201 Langley Rd, Houston, TX 77016, **Business Phone:** (713)633-1600.

STAMPS, LEON PREIST
Government official, auditor. **Personal:** Born Dec 29, 1953, Bronx, NY; married Barbara Logan. **Educ:** Boston Col, BS, Acct 1975; Northeastern Univ, MBA, Bus Policy, 1976. **Career:** Arthur Anderson & Co, acct, 1977-79; Roxbury Comm Col, acct prof, 1979; Xerox Corp, equip control mgr, 1979-81, ne reg control mgr, 1981-84; City Boston, city auditor controller (retired). **Orgs:** Bd dir, Boston Col Alumni Asn, 1975-; Acct Internship Continental Group Inc, 1976; consult dir public serv, Blue Cross & Blue Shield, 1976; mem large, Nat Asn Black Accountants, 1984-; Boston Black Media Coalition, 1985. **Honors/Awds:** The Young Alumni Achievers Award, Boston Col, 1985.

STAMPS, LYNMAN A., SR.
Clergy, army officer. **Personal:** Born May 31, 1940, Utica, MS; son of Milton and Emma Ross; married Margarett C Donaldson; children: Lynman A Stamps Jr. **Educ:** Lane Col Jackson, BA, 1968; Webster Univ, MAT, 1972; US Dept Justice, cert jail opers; Nat Inst Correct Admin Studies; Western Interstate Comn Higher Educ. **Career:** Ill State Sch Boys, cottage parent, 1960-62; Chicago Parent Soc Adj Sch Boys, family instr, 1962-63; AUS, MP, 1963-65; Trinity Temple CME Ch, 1964-66; Martin Tabernacle CME Ch, pastor, 1966-69; Parkers Chapel CME Ch, pastor, 1969-70; Clark Jr HS E St Louis, IL, civic teacher, 1968-71; Pilgrim Temple CME Ch, pastor, 1970-74; Radio Sta WESL E St Louis, mgr part owner, 1972-78; E St Louis, civil serv comnr, 1971-74; St Louis Correc Inst, supt, 1972-76; Coleman Temple CME Ch, pastor, 1974-83; Parrish Temple CME Church, pastor, 1983-84; First Christian Methodist Church, St Louis, pastor & founder, 1983-; Normandy Jr HS Normandy, MO, teacher, 1981-84; Marion Comn, managing partner; St Louis Bd Educ, military specialist, 1988-89; Pruitt Military Acad, St Louis, military specialist, 1988-03. **Orgs:** Life mem, Nat Asn Advan Colored People; Am Correct Asn; exec bd mem, E St Louis Madison St Clair Co Urban League, 1972-73; exec bd mem, E St Louis Model City Agency, 1972-73; vpres, Downtown Merchant Columbus, MS, 1985. **Honors/Awds:** Cert Hon, Utica Inst Jr Col, 1956; Award Plaque Offenders Chap AA, 1974; Man of thr Yr Award, Afro-Am Club Columbus, MS, 1985; Found/Pres, Trenton Civic League Trenton, TN; Cert Award, Outstanding Achievements Jobs Workshop Ex Offender Prog Human Dev Corp Prog Metro St Louis, 1976; Cert Appreciation, Gateway Jaycees & US Jaycees, 1976. **Military Serv:** AUS, spec 4th Class, 2 yrs; Good Conduct Medal, 1963-65. **Home Addr:** 12031 Mereview Dr, Saint Louis, MO 63146. *

STAMPS, SPURGEON MARTIN DAVID
Educator, school administrator. **Personal:** Born Jul 16, 1937, Nashville, TN; son of Spurgeon Martin David Sr and Nina Bessie Dobbins; married Miriam Cunningham Burney, Dec 28, 1961; children: Monique Yvonne & Spurgeon Martin David III. **Educ:** Tenn State Univ, BS, sociol, 1960; Wash State Univ, MA, sociol, 1965, PhD,sociol, 1974. **Career:** Cameron High Sch, teacher, counr, 1960-62; Wash State Univ, teaching asst, 1962-67; Norfolk State Univ, asst prof, 1967-77; Syracuse Univ, assoc procto prof, sociol, 1977-82; Univ S Fla, assoc dean & pro sociol, 1982-95, interim dean, Col Arts & Scis, 1995-96, dean, Col Arts & Scis, prof sociol, interim provost, 2000-01, provost & vpres for acad affairs, 2007. **Orgs:** Kappa Delta Pi, 1957-; Alpha Kappa Delta, 1965-; Southern Socioll Asn, 1982-; Manpower Utilization in Tidewater, Hampton Roads, VIR, 1969; established & served editor, Review ARO Issues & Culture, 1978-82; Participation High School Adolescents in Volunteer Activities, 1979; Black Elderly Presbyterians in NYC, 1982; Pi Gamma Mu, 1983-; Tampa-Hillsborough County Human Rights Coun, 1988-; Fla Ctr Children & Youth, exec com, 1990-; Literacy Volunteers Am, Fla, vip, 1990-; Golden Key Honor Soc, 1990-. **Honors/Awds:** Graduated with distinction, Tenn State Univ, 1960; Distinguished Service Award, Syracuse Univ, Office Minority Affairs, 1982; Phi Gamma Mu, Roll of Distinction, faculty advisor, 1985; Comparative Study of Blacks, White sand Hispanics in the Tampa Metropolitan Area, 1990. **Special Achievements:** Co-author, "If You Can Walk, You Can Dance. If You Can Talk, You Can Sing", 1995; Variations among Blacks in their reactions to criminal offenses, 1974; Salt City and its Black community. **Home Addr:** 6102 Soaring Ave, Temple Terrace, FL 33617, **Home Phone:** (813)988-8607.

STANCELL, DR. ARNOLD FRANCIS
Executive, educator. **Personal:** Born Nov 16, 1936, New York, NY; son of Francis and Maria Lucas; married Constance Newton, Apr 21, 1973; children: Christine. **Educ:** City Col NY, BS (magna cum laude), 1958; Mass Inst Technol, DSc,1962. **Career:** Mobil Oil Corp, Edison, NJ, scientist & res mgr, 1962-72, NY, planning mgr, 1972-76, vpres chemicals div, 1976-80, mgr corp planning, 1980-82, England, regional exe mkt & refining, 1982-84, NY, planning vpres, mkt & refining, 1985-86; vpres US oil & natural gas bus, 1987-88; VIR, vpres,Int Oil & Natural Gas Bus, 1989-93; GEO Tech, Ga Inst Technol, prof chem engr, prof emer chem engr, currently. **Orgs:** Am Inst Chem Eng, 1962-; Sigma Xi, 1965-; adv comt, Mass Inst Technol, 1976-; adv Comt, City Col, 1990-; adv comt, Carnegie-Mellon, 1999. **Honors/Awds:** Professional Achievement Award, NOBCCHE, 1975; Black Engineer of the Year,1992; Career Achievement, City Col NY, 1993; Nat Academic Engineer, 1997;Chemical Engineering Practice Award, AICHE, 1997; Outstanding Teacher Award, Ga Inst Technol, 1997. **Special Achievements:** Invited Visiting Prof, MIT, 1970-71, (offered tenure), 1998; patents for petro-chemical and polymer process and plasma processes at surfaces;Invited Speaker, Marshall Lecture, Univ Wis, Madison, 1991; honored educator. **Home Addr:** 15 Woodside Dr, Greenwich, CT 06830. **Business Phone:** (404)894-0316.

STANCELL, DR. DOLORES WILSON PEGRAM
Lawyer. **Personal:** Born Oct 26, 1936, New York, NY; married Vernon H; children: Timothy & Vernon. **Educ:** Rutgers Univ, BA, 1970; Rutgers Sch Law, JD, 1974; MI State Univ, Annual Regulatory Studies Prog, 1976. **Career:** Fordham Hosp, staff nurse, 1957-58; Beth Israel Hosp, staff nurse, 1958-62; Rutgers Urban Studies Ctr, rsch asst, 1968; Head Start MCEOC, nurse, 1967; Head Start, nurse, 1966; Middlesex County Legal Serv, legalintern, 1970; Jersey Shore Med Ctr, nurse, 1972; Rutgers Univ Rutgers J Comput & the Law, admin, 1973; Hon David D Furman Superior Ct Chan Div NJ, law secy, 1974-75; NJ Dept Pub Adv, Div Rate Counsel, asst dep pub adv. **Orgs:** Am Bar Asn, Sect Legal Educ & Admis Bar, 1977-78; Forum Comn Health Law,1977-78; Gen Pract, 1976-77; vpres, Women's Div, Nat Bar Asn, 1977-78; vpres, Civil Trial Advocacy Sect, 1977-78; Legislation & Uniform & State Laws Comn, 1977-78; Fed Bar Asn; Garden State Bar Asn; NJ State Bar Asn; Health League & Health Planning Serv Comt, 1976-78; Monmouth Bar Asn; Criminal Pract Comn, 1976-78; treas, Asn Black Women Lawyers, NJ, 1977-78; Rutgers Law Sch Alumni Asn; Rutgers Univ Alumni Asn; panelist, MRC-TV, NY Prog; Medical Costs, The Breath of Life 1977; Am Nurses Asn; NJ State Nurses Asn; vol, Ocean-Monmouth Legal Serv, 1972; vol, urban agent Rutgers Urban Studies Ctr, 1967-68; Pub Policy Forum Civil Disorders & Forum Future NJ Rutgers Univ, 1968; coord, Rutgers-Douglass Col Elem Sch Tutorial Prog, 1967-68; trustee, Unitarian Soc, 1970-72; Acad Adv Comt, 1977-78; bd mem, Parents Asn Rutgers Prep Sch, 1970-71; New Brunswick YWCA; Urban League; NAACP. **Honors/Awds:** Human Rels Award, Fordham Hosp, 1957. **Special Achievements:** First Vice-president of the Womens Division of the National Bar Association; articles Wilson, Computerization of Welfare Recipients, Implications for the Individual & The Right to Privacy for Rutgers Journal of Computers and The Law 163 (1974); Minority Workers 1 Womens Rights Law Reporter 71 (1972-73). **Business Addr:** 10 Commerce Ct, Newark, NJ 07102.

STANDIFER, BEN H.
Educator. **Personal:** Born Aug 24, 1934, Itasca, TX; son of Nathaniel C and Emma Jean; married Esther; children: Sonceria, Fawn, Ben jr & Corey. **Educ:** Prairie View A&M Col, BS, 1959, attended 1966; Carleton Col, attended 1965; Univ Tex, attended 1968; Ill Inst Tech, 1969; Cornell Univ, attended 1970; Tex Christian Univ, MA, 1972, cert supv, 1973; Tex Wesleyan Col, 1974; Northern Tex State Univ, cert admin, 1975. **Career:** Ft Worth Pub Sch, math teacher, 1959-73, math improvement specialist 1974-; FWISD, math instructional improv specialist, 1973-74; Dunbar Sr High Sch, Fort Worth Indep Sch Dist, prin, 1975-; Our Lady Victory Priv Sch Bd, pres. **Orgs:** Ft Worth Classroom Teacher Asn; Tex Classroom Teacher Asn; Nat Educ Asn; Tex Indust Educ Asn; Phi Delta Kappa Frat; Ft Worth Area Coun Teacher Math; Task Force Team Lay Acad United Meth Ch; bd mem, Ft Worth-tarrant Co Community Develop Fund Inc; steering com mem, Conf Advancement Math Teaching; organized Parent Stud Study Group Como High Community, 1960; pres, Home & Sch Asn; vpres, PTA, 1973. **Honors/Awds:** Received numerous awards; Outstanding Teacher & Teacher of the Year Award & Headliner in Education Award, Ft Worth Press Club. **Special Achievements:** Published books: "A Practical Guide to

Good Study Habits" 1969; created program at Western Hills HS in Audio Tutorial Instruction, 1970; organize ed tutorial program to help students in Wester Hills Eidglea Como Arlington Heights Communities, 1971; Published book of Audio Tutorial Instruction, 1972; Publication Improvement of Curricular/Instructional System, 1974. **Military Serv:** USAF 1954-58. **Business Addr:** Principal, Fort Worth Independent School District Public Schools, 3210 W Lancaster, Fort Worth, TX 76104.

STANISLAUS, REV. GREGORY K
Educator, clergy. **Personal:** Born Jun 9, 1957, New York, NY; son of Eula James Stanislaus and Gregory Talbert Stanislaus; married Ruth Y Dyer, Aug 20, 1988; children: Gregory St Jacques, Asia Malone & Kyla Paris. **Educ:** Univ Southern Calif, Los Angeles, CA, BS, Biol, 1981; Western State Univ Sch Law, Fullerton, CA, JD, 1985; New York Theol Sem, New York, Master Divinity, 1987. **Career:** McCutchen, Verleger & Shea, Los Angeles, Calif, legal researcher, 1981-86; Bd Educ, Brooklyn, New York, sci teacher, 1986-; Bethel Baptist Church, Brooklyn, New York, youth minister, 1988; St John Baptist Church, New York, pastor, currently. **Orgs:** Founder, Stanislaus Theatrical Group, 1985; staff, Brooklyn Ctr Urban Environ, 1987-; Nat Asn Advan Colored PeopleBrooklyn), 1989-91; Kings County Adv Bd, 1990-91; supt, Bethel Baptist Church Sunday Sch, 1990-; founder, Youth United Change World Int. **Honors/Awds:** Part Cover Story as Science Teacher, Black Enterprise, 1991; Honorary Award, Bethel Baptist Church, 1991. **Business Addr:** Pastor, St. John Baptist Church, 4 Henry St, Inwood, NY 11096, **Business Phone:** (516)239-1413.

STANLEY, CAROL JONES
Secretary (office). **Personal:** Born Mar 16, 1947, Durham, NC; daughter of Doctor Young and Willie Lyons; married Donald Andrew, Jul 21, 1990. **Educ:** NC Cent Univ, Durham, NC, BSc, 1969, School Law, 1974, MS, 1975; Univ NC, Greensboro, NC, 1990. **Career:** NC Cent Univ, Durham, NC, res asst, 1980-81; Fayetteville St Univ, Fayetteville, NC, adj instr, 1985-87; NC Cent Univ, Sch Bus, Durham, NC, adj instr, 1989; NC Cent Univ Sch Law, Durham, NC, admin secy, 1991-94, asst dir recruitment, 1994-, support staff fac serv. **Orgs:** NC Bus Ed Assoc, 1990-91; chairperson, Publicity Comt, N Cent Bus Educ Asn, 1990; tutor vietnamese, Immaculate Conception Church, 1990; Registered reader, Delta Sigma Theta Sorority; Asn Supv & Curriculum Develop; Nat Bus Educ Asn; Carolina Stud Info Syst. **Honors/Awds:** Delta Sigma Theta Scholarship, 1988-89; Law Office Mgt. **Home Addr:** 1611 Duke University Rd Apt 8F, Durham, NC 27701. *

STANLEY, MAJOR GEN. CLIFFORD L
Executive, military leader. **Personal:** Born Mar 31, 1947, Washington, DC; married Rosalyn Hill; children: Angela. **Educ:** SC State Univ, 1969; Johns Hopkins Univ, MS, 1977; Amphibious Warfare Sch, 1978; Naval War Col, 1983; USMC Command Staff Col, 1984; Nat War Col, 1988. **Career:** Marine Corps Air Ground Combat Ctr, commanding gen, 1998-2003, dep commanding gen, currently; Univ Pa, exec vpres, 2002-03. **Orgs:** Bd dir, White House Fel Asn; The McCormic Educ Found; life mem, Kappa Alpha Psi Fraternity; bd trustee, Spalding Univ; bd gov, Civil War & Underground Railroad Mus, Philadelphia; vice chmn, SC State Univ Found; pres, Philadelphia Alumni Chapter, SC State Univ Alumni Asn; pres, Scholar Am. **Honors/Awds:** Legion of Merit; Defense Meritorious Service Medal; Meritorious Service Medal with Gold Star; Navy Commendation Medal; Navy Achievement Medal. **Business Phone:** 800-279-2083.*

STANLEY, CRAIG A
State government official. **Personal:** Born Nov 20, 1955. **Educ:** Univ Hartford, BA, Polit Sci, 1998; Baruch Col, MPA, 1999. **Career:** Twenty Eigth Assembly Dist, assemblyman, 1996-; YMWCA Newark & Vicinity, dir corp progs, currently. **Business Addr:** Assemblyman, 28th Assembly District, State of New Jersey, 1200 Clinton Ave Suite 140, Irvington, NJ 07111, **Business Phone:** (973)399-1000.

STANLEY, DONNA JONES
Executive. **Personal:** Born Nov 19, 1955, Kentucky; daughter of Jane Dance; divorced; children (previous marriage): Stephanie Marie Reynolds; married Jerry; children: Stephanie. **Educ:** Murray State Univ, BS, social work, 1977; Univ Baltimore, MBA, 1986; Aspen Inst Humanistic Studies & Univ MDs Nonprofit Mgt Inst, cert, 1988; Harvard Univ, cert, 1996. **Career:** Westvaco Corp, Wickliffe, Ky, asst buyer, 1977-79; The Chimes Inc, asst dir adult training services, 1980-81; United Way Cent Md, dept dir, 1984-89; Assoc Black Charities, exec dir, 1989-2003; Urban League Greater Cincinnati, pres & chief exec officer, currently. **Orgs:** DST Sorority, 1976; br dir, Vol Action Ctr, Cent Md Inc, 1981-84; chair, Asn Baltimore Area Grantmakers; chair, MD State School-Based Health Ctr Initiative; Asn Black Found Exec; Nat Asn Black Found Exec. **Honors/Awds:** Outstanding Woman Award, Emmanuel Christian Community Church; Valued Hours Award, The Fullwood Found, 1993; Human & Civil Rights Award, Southern Christian Leadership Conf, 1993; Howard L Cornish Humanitarian Award, Omega Psi Phi Fraternity, 1994; Black Women in Sisterhood for Action, 1994; The Daily Record, Maryland's Top 100 Women, 1998, 2000; History Maker Award, Nat Asn Black Prof Womens Club, 1998; Service Award, Ecumenical Coun MD, 2000. **Business Phone:** (513)281-9955.

STANLEY, ELLIS M., SR.
Government official. **Personal:** Born Jun 13, 1951, Shallotte, NC; son of Lewis A and Mae Belle Bryant; married Iris M White, May 31, 1975; children: Ellis M Jr & Christopher J. **Educ:** Univ NC, Chapel Hill, BA, 1973. **Career:** Brunswick County Govt, Bolivia, NC, dir emergency mgt, 1975-82; Durham-Durham County Govt, Durham, NC, dir emergency mgt, 1982-87; Atlanta-Fulton County Govt, Atlanta, GA, dir emergency mgt, 1987-97; City Los Angeles, asst CAO, emergency prepardness div, 1997-2000, gen mgr, 2000-07; dir, Western Emergency Mgtt Servs, 2007; dir, DNC Planning for the City & County of Denver, 2009-. **Orgs:** Pres, Nat Forum Black Pub Admin, Atlanta Chap; pres, Nat Coord Coun Emergency Mgt, 1985, state rep, 1988-; Fulton Red Cross Adv Comt, 1987-; Red Cross Emergency Community Serv Comn, 1987-; Hazardous Mat Adv Coun, 1988-; Leadership Atlanta, class 1990; pres, Nat Defense Transp Asn, Atlanta Chap; NCCEM Cert Counselors; bd natural disasters, Nat Weather Svc; Modernization Transition Comt; Int Asn Emergency Managers; vpres, Bus & Indust Coun Emergency Planning & Preparedness; bd mem, Nat Inst Urban Search & Rescue; adj instr, Nat Terrorism Preparedness Inst; La Chap Am Red Cross, Disaster Preparedness Comn; comnr, Emergency Preparedness Comn Los Angeles; Bd Visitors Emergency Mgt Inst; Calif Forensic Sci Inst; Southern Calif Emergency Servs Asn; Los Angeles Transp Found. **Honors/Awds:** Presidential Citation, US Civil Defense Asn, 1983; testified several times before the US Congress on Emergency Mgmt, 1985-86; lead Delegation to China to study Emergency Mgt, 1988; presented at 1st Security Sem, Caribbean, 1988; adj instr, Nat Emergency Training Ctr; Certified Emergency Manager. **Business Addr:** Director, Office of Emergency Management, **Business Phone:** (303)458-7541.

STANLEY, DR. HILBERT DENNIS
Association executive, consultant. **Personal:** Born Feb 24, 1931, Cambridge, MD; widowed; children: Denise R & Guy Derek. **Educ:** Morgan State Univ, BS, biol, 1952, MS, 1972; Wayne State Univ, EdD, 1978. **Career:** Edmondson HS, prin, 1973-75; Rockefeller Found, fel, 1975-76; Lake Clifton HS, prin, 1979-81; Off Mayor Baltimore, educ liaison officer, 1981-84; Southwestern HS, prin, 1984-90; Morgan State Univ, instr; St Peter's Col, instr; Ner Israel Rabbinical Sch, instr; Training Inst Desegregated Educ, asst dir; Human Develop & Educ Liaison Officer, City Baltimore, dir; Nat Black Catholic Cong Inc, exec dir; Morgan State Univ Found, Bd Trustees, chair, currently. **Orgs:** Vice basileus, Pi Omega Chap, Omega Psi Phi Fraternity, 1978; pres, Baltimore Chap, Nat Alliance Black Sch Educrs, 1978-80; bd dirs, Arena Players, 1980-92; bd dirs, Afro Am Newspaper, 1981-83; chmn, Selective Serv Local Bd, 1982-85; treas, bd dirs, Nat Alliance Black Sch Educrs Found, 1988-96; immediate past pres, Morgan State Univ, Nat Alumni Asn, bd dirs, 1978-, nat treas, 1984-93, pres, 1993-98, bd dir, 1993-; Selective Servs Syst Bd; Md State, Dept Higher Educ Task Force Study Merger Morgan State Univ & Coppin State Col; exec dir, Nat Black Catholic Cong. **Honors/Awds:** Rockefeller Grant, 1975; Man of the Year, Omega Psi Phi Fraternity, 1980; Distinguished Alumni, Nat Asn Equal Opportunity Higher Educ, 1991; Honarary & Medal from His Holiness, Knight St Gregory Great, Pope John Paul II; Alumni Hall of Fame, Morgan State Univ; Hall of Fame, Nat Alliance Black Sch Educr. **Home Addr:** 413 George St, Baltimore, MD 21201. **Business Addr:** Chair of the Board of Trustees, Morgan State Univ Foundation, 1501 S 11th Ave, PO Box 172750, Bozeman, MT 59717-2750, **Business Phone:** (406)994-2053.

STANLEY, LANETT (LANETT STANLEY-TURNER)
State government official, consultant. **Educ:** Univ Tenn, Knoxville, BA, journ; Harvard Univ, John F Kennedy Sch Govt; Carver Bible Col. **Career:** Commun consult, currently; Ga State, House Rep, rep, 1987-, Dist 33, rep, Dist 53, rep, currently; House Democratic Caucus, secy, currently. **Honors/Awds:** One of 50 leaders of the future, Ebony Mag, 1992. **Special Achievements:** Only African American woman on the state Revenue Structure Commission; Youngest person elected to State General Assembly. **Business Addr:** Representative, Georgia House of Representatives, District 53, Coverdell Legis Off Bldg Suite 612, Atlanta, GA 30334, **Business Phone:** (404)656-0325.

STANLEY, THORNTON, SR.
Entrepreneur. **Personal:** Born Jan 1, 1937?; married; children: 4. **Educ:** Alabama A&M Univ, agr & landscape design, 1957. **Career:** Stanley Construct Co Inc, founder, 1961-; Stanley Construct Co Inc, pres, currently. **Orgs:** bd dirs, Top Ala Regional Coun Govt; pres, Top Ala Regional Coun Govt, currently. **Honors/Awds:** Small Business Person of the Year, US Small Bus Admin, 2001. **Special Achievements:** Awarded by Pres George W Bush, 2001. **Business Addr:** President, Stanley Construction Company Inc, 4410 Evangel Circle NW A, Huntsville, AL 35816, **Business Phone:** (256)837-6850.

STANLEY, WOODROW
Mayor. **Personal:** Born Jun 12, 1950, Schlater, MS; married Reta Venessa James; children: Heather Venessa & Jasmine Woodrina. **Educ:** Mott Community Col, attended 1969-71; Univ Mich, BA, polit sci, 1971-73; Univ Mich, Flint, MI, Candidate Master Pub Admin. **Career:** Whitney M Young St Acad, counr, 1974-77; Greater Flint OIC, asst serv coordr, 1977-79, case mgt coordr, 1979-83, job club coordr, 1983-91; Flint City Coun, councilman, 1983-91; Mayor, Flint, MI, 1991-2002; MI St rep, 2008-; Pub Sector Network Consult Group, consult, currently. **Orgs:** Flint Human Rels Comt, 1973-76; bd mem, McCree Theatre & Fine Arts Centre, 1975-90; bd mem, YMCA, 1976-77; bd mem, Valley Area Agency Aging, chair, 1982-91; bd mem, Econ Develop Corp, 1983-, chair, 1991; adv bd mem, Univ Mich Flint African-Afro Am Studies Prog, 1983-; steering comt, Coalition Greater Flint African Relief Fund 1984-85; Nat Black Caucus Local Elected Officials, 1987-; bd dirs, Mich Munic League, Legisl & Urban Affairs Comn, 1988-91; comt mem, Nat League Cities Human Develop Steering Comt, 1989-90; pres, MML, 1990; bd dirs, Nat League Cities, 1992-, adv coun, 1994-; bd dirs, 1992-94, pres, 1995, Mich Asn Mayors; convener, Tri-County Coun Mayors, 1992; Nat Asn Advan Colored People; vice chair, Mich Dem Party; Genesse County Bd Commissioners, comnr, currently; Ombudsman Adv Bd; bdmem, Foss Ave Christian Sch; alternate trustee, Flint Retirement Bd. **Honors/Awds:** Cert Achievement, Leadership Flint, 1975-76; Volunteer Service Award, Urban League Flint, 1981; Award of Recognition, Mott Adult High School, 1982; Distinguished Community Service Award, Foss Ave Baptist Church, 1983;Community Service Award, Eureka Lodge F&AM, 1986; Donald Riegle Community Service Award, Flint Jewish Fed, 1993; Mayor of the Year, Minority Women's Network Partners Community, 1994; Service Award, Black Caucus Found Mich, 1994; Booster of the Year, Sales & Mkt Execs Flint, 1995; African Am Man of Achievement Award, Dozier CME Church, 1996; Pioneer Award, Forum Mag, 1996. **Special Achievements:** Host of radio show "Words with Wood" on WOWE. **Business Addr:** Consultant, Public Sector Network Consulting Group.

STANLEY-TURNER, LANETT. See STANLEY, LANETT.

STANMORE, DR. ROGER DALE
Physician. **Personal:** Born Jan 20, 1957, Alanta, TX. **Educ:** Southwestern Union Col, BS, 1979; Meharry Medical Col, MD, 1984. **Career:** DC Gen Hosp, resident physician surg, 1984-85; Methodist Hosp, SUNY, resident physician, 1985-86; Dept Justice, chief med staff; Jacksonville Med Ctr, Jacksonville, AL, emergency room med dir, 1989-91; Parkway Med Ctr, med dir, emergency servs, 1991-96; Decatur Emergency Med Servs Inc, pres & CEO, 1996-; Gadsden-Etowah Emergency Med Servs, pres & CEO, 1998-; pvt pract, currently. **Orgs:** Am & Nat Med Asns, 1980-87; The Technol Transfer Soc, 1982-87; N Ala Emergency Med Serv, adv bd, 1991-95; Am Asn Physician Specialists, 1997-99. **Honors/Awds:** Am Col Surgeons Scholar, 1983; rep, Joint Comn Med Educ, 1983. **Home Addr:** 2 Asbury Rd, PO Box 18513, Huntsville, AL 35801, **Home Phone:** (904)755-8400. **Business Addr:** Physician, 7583 Wall Triana Highway, Madison, AL 35757, **Business Phone:** (256)547-6119.

STANSBURY, CLAYTON CRESVELL
Educator. **Personal:** Born Mar 20, 1932, Havre de Grace, MD; married Catherine Laverne Posey. **Educ:** Morgan State Univ, BS, 1955; Howard Univ, MS, 1962; Univ Md, PhD, 1972. **Career:** Howard Univ, instr psychol, 1962-63 & 1965-67; Univ Md, teaching asst psychol, 1963-65; Morgan State Univ, Baltimore, MD, asst dean freshman prog, 1970-73, Psychology Dept, chmn, 1973-75, actg dean stud affairs & dir, 1975-77, dir freshmen prog, 1975, prof psychol, 1975-96, vpres stud affairs, 1977-80, Stud Serv, vpres, 1978-96, dir honors prog, 1980-96, prof emer, 1996-. **Orgs:** Am Psychol Asn; Md Psychol Asn; Psi Chi Nat Honor Soc; Alpha Phi Alpha Fraternity; Urban League; life mem, Nat Asn Advan Colored People; bd dir, YMCA; Little League Baseball; Boy Scouts Am; United Meth Men; Proj Upward Bound; Morgan ROTC; hon mem PKT; Epworth United Methodist Church; Howard L. Cornish MSU Alumni Chap. **Honors/Awds:** Alumnus of the Year, Morgan State Univ; Distinguished Alumni Award, Nat Asn Equal Opportunity. **Special Achievements:** Author Portrait of a Colored Man. **Military Serv:** AUS 1955-57. **Business Addr:** Professor Emeritus, Morgan State University, Department of Psychology, 1700 E Cold Spring Lane, Baltimore, MD 21251, **Business Phone:** (443)885-3290.

STANSBURY, KEVIN BRADLEY
Educator. **Personal:** Born Aug 29, 1954, Morristown, NJ; son of Frederick Hartley and Muriel Hiller; married Renee Washington, May 17, 1996; children: Hartlei Imani. **Educ:** Brookdale Col, AA; Col St Elizabeth, BA, eng lit; NJ City Univ Grad Sch Educ. **Career:** Bell Commun Res, Admin Servs, mgr, 1982-93; AmiCorps, 1994-95; Red Bank Bd Educ, teacher, 1994-95; Long Branch Bd Educ, eng lit teacher, 1995-; Freshman Success Academy Plainfield High Sch, vice prin, currently. **Orgs:** Sigma Tau Delta, Int Eng Hon Soc, 1994-; Kappa Gamma Pi, Nat English Hon Soc, 1994-; Nat Educ Asn, 1995; Nat Asn Advan Colored People. **Honors/Awds:** NJ Black Achievers Award, 1992; Community Service Award, NJ Gen Assembly, 1994; US House Representatives, Community Serv Citation, 1994; Humanitarian Year, Asbury Park Ctr Love, 1994; Community Service Award, Negro Womens Bus Coun, 1995; Inspirational Leadership Award, Long Branch High Sch Hon Soc, 1998; cited as a role model &

community leader by PRS Clinton. **Special Achievements:** Created a Peer-Mentoring and Peer-Leadership Progtam at Long Beach High School called Visions; created a Mentoring Program at the Red Bank Middle School, 1988-90. **Business Addr:** Vice Principal, Freshman Success Academy, Plainfield High School, 950 Pk Ave, Long Branch, NJ 07060, **Business Phone:** (908)731-4390.

STANSBURY, MARKHUM L
School administrator. **Personal:** Born Apr 5, 1942, Memphis, TN; son of Willie (deceased) and Eliza Markhum (deceased); married Lucy Barber, Jun 4, 1966; children: Markhum Jr & Marlon B. **Educ:** Lincoln Univ, Jefferson City, Mo, 1960; Lane Col, Jackson, Tenn, BA, 1963; Memphis State Univ, Memphis, Tenn, 1965. **Career:** WDIA Radio, Memphis, Tenn, announcer, 1960-; Lane Col, Jackson, Tenn, pub relations dir, 1966-69; Holiday Inns Inc, Memphis, Tenn, pub relations mgr, 1969-83; Union Central Life Insurance Co, Memphis, Tenn, agent, 1983-84; Am United Insurance Co, Memphis, Tenn, agent, 1984-87; State Tenn, Nashville, Tenn, spec asst Gov, 1987-90; Memphis State Univ, Memphis, Tenn, asst to pres, 1990-. **Orgs:** Bd vchair, Emergency 911 Bd; bd vchair, trustee, St Andrew AME Church; bd mem, YMCA; bd mem, Goals Memphis; advisory bd mem, S Central Bell. **Honors/Awds:** 'Special Recognition Award', Rotary Club, 1988; 'Outstanding Service to Youth in Schools', Tenn Child Care Facilities, 1989; 'Award of Merit', Mayor, 1989; Delegate to General Conference, AME Church, 1988. **Home Phone:** (901)743-7042. **Business Addr:** Assistant to the President, Memphis State University, Office of the President, Administration Bldg Suite 203, Memphis, TN 38152, **Business Phone:** (901)678-5613.

STANSBURY, VERNON CARVER
Businessperson, chief executive officer. **Personal:** Born Jul 13, 1939, Lexington, MS; divorced; children: Nicole Elaine & Vernon III. **Educ:** Roosevelt Univ, BS, 1962; Kent Col Law, attended 1964; Harvard Bus Sch, MBA, 1973. **Career:** IBM, sr systs engr, 1962-67; Exxon Int, head fleet anal, 1967-71; Cummins Engine Co, gen mgr serv tools, 1973-78; Dept Com, dir export dept, 1978-81; Sci & Com Syst Corp, pres, 1981-, chief exec officer, currently. **Orgs:** Chmn, AASU-Harvard Bus Sch, 1972; chmn, William R Laws Found, 1974; chmn, ColumbusUnited Negro Col Fund, 1977; chmn, ERB-Sr Exec Serv, 1979; charter mem, Sr Exec Serv US, 1979; pres, DC Chap Harvard Black Alumni, 1980. **Honors/Awds:** Goldman Sachs Award, Harvard Bus Sch, 1974. **Special Achievements:** Outstanding Contributor White House Conference on Small Business, 1980. **Military Serv:** USAR, warrant officer, 1962-70. **Business Addr:** President, Chief Executive Officer, Scientific & Commercial Systems, 7600 Leesburg Pike E Bldg Suite 400, Falls Church, VA 22041, **Business Phone:** (703)917-9171.

STANTON, JANICE D
Counselor. **Personal:** Born Jun 26, 1928, Beaumont, TX; daughter of Joseph Dewey Splane and Myrtle Trimble Splane; married Rufus H Stanton Jr, Mar 7, 1944; children: Rufus H III, Deborah Stanton Burke & Robert T. **Educ:** Wiley Col, attended, 1944. **Career:** Counselor (retired); Galveston Col, bd regents, 1983-2004. **Orgs:** Pres bd trustees, Gulf Coast Regional Ment Health-Ment Retardation Ctr, 1980-82; bd counr, St Mary's Hosp, 1980-86; adv bd, Galveston Historical Found, 1984; vpres, United Way Galveston, 1985-87; Grievance Comt, District 5B, State Bar Texas, 1988-90; bd dirs, Lone Star Hist Drama Asn, 1989-92; pres, Texas Asn Community Col Bd Mems & Adminrs, 1990; adv bd, Children's Hosp, Univ Texas Med Br (UTMB) Galveston, 1992-. **Honors/Awds:** Image Award, Galveston Branch NAACP, 1983; Community Achievement Award, Zeta Phi Beta Sorority, 1983; Outstanding Citizen of the Year, Gamma Pi Lambda Chap, Alpha Phi Alpha, 1990; Steel Oleander award, 1997. **Home Addr:** 3615 Ave O, Galveston, TX 77550.

STANTON, ROBERT G
Government official, consultant, association executive. **Educ:** Huston-Tillotson Col, BS, Hon Doctorate Sci; Boston Univ, grad work; Unity Col, Hon Doctorate Environ Stewardship; Southern Univ, A&M Col, Hon Doctorate Pub Policy. **Career:** Grand Teton Nat Pk, pk ranger; Nat Parks-E, Wash, DC, VI Nat Pk, supt; Pk Serv, Atlanta, dep regional dir; Nat Pk Serv, dir, 1997; Yale Univ, Sch Forestry & Environ Studies, McCluskey Vis Fel Conser, res affiliate, currently; Nat Resources Coun Am, consult, currently; Howard Univ, Dept of Hist Pub Prog, vis prof, 2005, 2007. **Orgs:** Numerous memberships including Student Conserv Asn Inc; Nat Audubon Soc; Accokeek Found Piscataway Pk, Unity Col; Woods Hole Res Ctr; Eastern Nat & Guest Serv Inc; fel, Am Acad Pk & Recreation Admin. **Honors/Awds:** Numerous honors and awards including Outstanding Achievement Conservation Award, Accokeek Found, 2001; Fred M Packard International Parks Merit Award, IUCN's World Comn Protected Areas, 2001; The 2001 Chair Award, Nat Resources Coun Am, 2001; Carter G Woodson History Maker Award, Asn Study African Am Life & Hist, 2002; DHL, Tex A&M Univ; DSc, Hustson-Tillotson Univ; Doctor of Environ Agr & Mech Col. **Special Achievements:** First African American to head National Park Service. **Business Addr:** Consultant, Natural Resources Council of America, 1616 P St NW Suite 340, Washington, DC 20036, **Business Phone:** (202)232-6531.*

STANYARD, HERMINE P.
Teacher. **Personal:** Born May 7, 1928, Charleston, SC; daughter of Samuel Payne (deceased) and Mabel Comfort Washington (deceased); married George Dewey Stanyard Sr; children: Geormine Deweya, George Dewey Jr. **Educ:** SC State Col, BA, 1949; NY Univ, MA, 1952; Columbia Univ, Univ SC, adv guid, 1956, 1974, 1977; Citadel Col, attended 1967, 1980. **Career:** Teacher (retired); Barnes Elem Sch, Georgetown, teacher, 1949-50; Wilson High Sch, eng teacher, 1952-56; Laing High Sch, eng teacher, 1956-59, guid counr, 1959-67, eng & reading teacher/reading coordr, 1967-85. **Orgs:** Campaigner, Greater Chas YWCA, 1966-86; vol, Laubach Reading Teacher; chmn, SAT prog, 1976-82; pres, Charleston County Coun Int Reading Asn, 1977-79; chmn, Nominating Comt, SC State Reading Asn, 1979-81; chmn, Distinguished Teacher Mem, 1981-85; vol teacher, Morris St Baptist Church, Tutorial Prog, 1982-83, 1986; chmn, Elem & Mid Sch Tutoring, 1986-; co-chair, Poetry & Storytelling Ser Moja Arts Festival, 1991-96; Int Soc Poets, 1994-; chair, Sundown Poetry Ser Piccolo Spoleto, 1995, 1996; Delta Sigma Theta Sorority Inc. **Honors/Awds:** Cert of Appreciation & Mother of the Year, Morris St Bapt Church, 1979, 1984, 1985; Cer of Appreciation, Greater Chas YWCA,1983; Delta of the Year, Delta Sigma Theta Sorority Inc, 1983; Scroll of Honor, Omega Psi Phi Fraternity, 1984; Citation, Distinguished Woman of the 90's, Sigma Gamma Rho Sorority Inc, Delta Iota Sigma Chap, 1992; Spec Recognition, Lit Achievement, Phyllis Wheatley Lit Social Club, 1992; Serv Award, E Cooper Meals on Wheels, 1993; Cert of Appreciation Serv, Minnie Hughes Elem Sch, 1993, 1996; Community Serv Award, Arabian Ct 128, Daughters of Isis, 1994; Woman of the Year, Morris St Baptist Church, 1994; Cert of Appreciation Serv, Pan Hellenic Golden Voices Greeks, 1994; Cert of Appreciation Serv, Poetry Soc SC, 1994-95; Cert of Appreciation, Delta Sigma Theta Sorority Inc, 1994-96; Cert for Meritorious Serv, Avery Inst Afa His & Cult, 1995; Cert of Appreciation for Serv, Wilmot Fraser Elem Sch, 1996; Plaque of Appreciation, MOJA Festival Comn, 1997. **Special Achievements:** Publication: Book of Poetry, Lingering Thoughts, 1992; Verses for You and Me, 1995. **Home Addr:** 17 Charlotte St Apt A, Charleston, SC 29403. *

STAPLES, MAVIS
Singer. **Personal:** Born Jul 10, 1939, Chicago, IL; daughter of Roebuck and Oceala; divorced. **Career:** Staple Singers, R&B singer, 1951-; Albums: Mavis Staples, 1969; Only for the Lonely, 1970; A Piece of the Action, 1977; Oh What A Feeling, 1979; Mavis Staples, 1984; Time Waits for No One, 1989; Don't Change Me Now, 1990; The Voice, 1993; Mavis Staples & Lucky Peterson Spirituals & Gospel: Dedicated to Mahalia Jackson, 1996; Have A Little Faith, 2004; We'll Never Turn Back, 2007; Live: Hope at the Hideout, 2008. **Honors/Awds:** Rock & Roll Hall of Fame, inductee, 1999; Grammy Award for Lifetime Achievement, 2005; AMA "Spirit of Americana" Free Speech Award, First Amendment Ctr, 2007. **Special Achievements:** Ranked No 57 on VH1's 100 Greatest Women of Rock N Roll; Films: Graffiti Bridge, 1990; The Sacrifice of Victor, 1995; TV: "The Cosby Show", 1990; Blind Boys of Alabama: Go Tell It on the Mountain, 2004. **Business Phone:** (415)386-3456.*

STAPLES, ROBERT E.
Educator. **Personal:** Born Jun 28, 1942, Roanoke, VA; son of John Ambrose and Anna; divorced. **Educ:** La Valley Col, AA, 1960; Calif State Univ, Northridge, AB, 1963; San Jose Ste Univ, MA, 1965; Univ Minn, PhD, 1970. **Career:** St Paul Urban League, dir res, 1966-67; Bethune-Cookman Col, Daytona Beach, assoc prof sociol, 1967-68; Calif St Univ, asst prof sociol, 1968-70; Howard Univ, assoc prof sociol, 1970-73; Fisk Univ, vis prof, 1969-70, asst prof, sociol, 1970-71; Univ Md, adj prof, 1970-72; Univ Calif, San Francisco, prof sociol, prof emer, currenlty. **Orgs:** Ed, Western Jour Black Studies, 1978-; bd dir, Black World Found, 1980-; Am Acad Political & Social Sci; Nat Coun Family Rels, 1970-72; Am Asn Univ Prof; African Heritage Studies Asn. **Honors/Awds:** Distinguished Achievement, Howard Univ, 1979; Simon Bolivar Lecture, Univdel Zulia, Maracaibo, Venezeula, 1979; Distinguished Achievement, Nat Coun Family Rels, 1982; Visiting Fellow, Inst Family Studies, Australia, 1982; Marie Peters Award, Nat Council Family Rels, 1986; visiting Research Fellow, Centre Australia Indigenous Studies, Monash University, Melbourne, Australia. **Business Addr:** Professor Emeritus, University of California, Laurel Heights 455 3333 Calif St, PO Box 0612, San Francisco, CA 94143-0612, **Business Phone:** (415)476-2116.

STAPLETON, MARYLYN A
Government official, transportation consultant. **Personal:** Born Sep 25, 1936, St Thomas, Virgin Islands of the United States; daughter of Aletha C Callender John and Lambert George; married Frank (divorced 1983); children: Linda Elaine. **Educ:** Wash Bus Inst, New York, NY, AS, 1959; Hunter Col, NY. **Career:** Caribair Airline, St Thomas, VI, reservation agt, 1954-56; Macy's Dept Store, New York, NY, salesclerk, 1956-57; Gift Shop, New York, NY, salesclerk, 1957-63; Eastern Airlines Inc, NY, supvr, 1967-86; Caribbean Travel Agency, St Thomas, VI, travel agt, 1986-87; Gov VI, St Thomas, VI, dep comnr, 1987-91, asst comnr, 1991-95; Small Bus Environ Asst Prog, environ prog mgr, 1995-, coordr, currently; Internat Asn Plumbing Mech Officials, state exec dir, 1999; Dept Planning & Nat Resources, environ prog mgr, 20004-. **Orgs:** State-chair, Dem Party, 1986-99; Lioness Club, 1987-88; treas, Lioness Club, 1985-86; pub rels off, Nevis Benevolent Soc, 1966-85; mem chair, Lioness Club STT, 1988-89; pageant chair, Lioness Club STT, 1986-87. **Honors/Awds:** Melvin Jones Fellow, Lioness Club, 1989. **Home Addr:** PO Box 3739, St Thomas, Virgin Islands of the United States 00803. **Business Addr:** Environmental Program Manager, Coordinator, Small Business Environmental Assistance Program, Environmental Protection Division, Terminal Bldg 2nd Fl Cyril E King Airport, St Thomas, Virgin Islands of the United States 00802, **Business Phone:** (340)774-3320.

STARGELL, TONY
Football player. **Personal:** Born Aug 7, 1966, LaGrange, GA. **Educ:** Tenn State Univ, health & phys educ, 1990. **Career:** Football player (retired); New York Jets, defensive back, 1990-91; Indianapolis Colts, 1992-93; Tampa Bay Buccaneers, 1994-95;Indianapolis Colts, free agt, 1994-95; Kans City Chiefs, 1996; Chicago Bears, 1997; Kans City Chiefs, free agt, currently.

STARKEY, DR. FRANK DAVID
Labor relations manager. **Personal:** Born Aug 6, 1944, Indianapolis, IN; married Gunilla Emilia Ekstedt; children: Michael & Julia. **Educ:** Wabash Col Ind, AB 1966; Brown Univ, PhD, Chem, 1973. **Career:** IL Wesleyan Univ, prof, 1971-80; Gen Elec Co, mgr, 1980-82, mgr human resource prog, 1982. **Orgs:** Pres, Wabash Coun Racial Equality, 1965; chmn, Afro Am Soc, Brown Univ, 1967-71; mem state coun, Am Asn Univ Prof, 1972; mem grant rev panel NSF, 1980; GE Found Minority Eng Comt, 1980; comt mem, Am Chem Soc, 1983-85; bd mem, Selection Comt, Nat Assoc Biol Teachers, 1986. **Honors/Awds:** Alfred P Sloan Scholar, Wabash Col, 1962-66; NSF Traineeship, Brown Univ, 1966-70; Teacher of the Year, IL Wesleyan Univ, 1978; Outstanding Young Man of America, 1979; GE Honarary Black Achiever Indust Harlem, YMCA, 1986; Outstanding State Biology Teacher Award, Nat Asn Biol Teachers, 1986. **Home Phone:** (518)393-0043.

STARKS, DORIS NEARROR
Consultant. **Personal:** Born Jul 30, 1937, Conecuh County, AL; daughter of Cleveland H Jenkins and Virgie G; married Wilbert L Starks Sr, Dec 25, 1961; children: Wilbert L Jr & Garrick E. **Educ:** Tuskegee Univ, BSN, 1958; Cath Univ Am, MSN, 1965; Union Grad Sch, PhD, 1978. **Career:** County Col Baltimore, 1968-90; Dept Nursing, Pro Med Surg Nursing, 1968-80, asst chap, 1980-84, chap, 1984-86, Dept HTH Sci, chap, 1986-89, dir nursing & dir, prof, 1989-90; Coppin State Col, Div Nursing, asst dean, 1990-91, dean, 1991-98. **Orgs:** Chi Eta Phi, 1956-; Tuskegee Univ Alumni Asn, 1958-; Sigma Theta Tau Int Hon Soc Nurses, 1977-; Alpha Kappa Alpha, 1980-; Nat Asn Black Nursing Fac, 1990-; Nat Coalition 100 Black Women, 1991-; Epicureans, 1991-; Club Dejour, 1992-; Continental Soc Inc, Columbia, MD, Chap, vpres, 1992-; fel, Am Acad Nursing, 1997-. **Honors/Awds:** Outstanding Assistance to Minorities in HTH Careers, Balitmore Tuskegee Alumni Club, 1983; Contributions to Nursing Educ, County Col Baltimore Nursing Alumni, 1983; Outstanding Contribution to Nursing, Baltimore Chap Black Nurses Asn, 1984; Tuskegee Hall of Fame Inductee, Univ Sch Nursing, 1992; Leadership in Nursing, Md Found For Nursing, 1994. **Special Achievements:** Publ: "Mama Annie's Peanut Candy", Black Family Mag, 1981; "How to Prevent Cold Weather Illnesses", Black Family Mag, 1982; "Patchwork Reflection from a Nursing Instructor", Today's O.R. Nurse, 1984; Tuskegee: A Precious Memory, ABNF Jour, 1995; "Nursing Centers: A Resource for Underserved Communities", Jour Asn Black Nursing Fac, 1996; "Coppin State College Nursing Center: A Community Partnership", Jour Asn Black Nursing Fac, 1996; Holistic Retention: A Practical Approach, Success Stories: Retention of African American Nursing Students, Tucker Publ, 1999. **Military Serv:** Army Nurse Corps, 1st lt, 1959-62. **Home Addr:** 9068 Bellwart Way, Columbia, MD 21045, **Home Phone:** (410)997-8036.

STARKS, DUANE
Football player. **Personal:** Born May 23, 1974, Miami, FL. **Educ:** Univ Miami, lib arts. **Career:** Baltimore Ravens, corner back, 1998-2001; Ariz Cardinals, corner back, 2002-04; New Eng Patriots, corner back, 2005; Oakland Raiders, cornerback, 2006-07; Oakland Raiders, 2008; free agent, currently. **Orgs:** Pres, Starks Charitable Found. **Honors/Awds:** Super Bowl champion (XXXV); James Browm Award; 2007 Presidents Award.

STARKS, JOHN LEVELL
Basketball coach, basketball player. **Personal:** Born Aug 10, 1965, Tulsa, OK; son of Irene; married Jacqueline; children: John Jr & Chelsea. **Educ:** Okla State Univ, attended 1988. **Career:** Basketball player (retired) basketball coach; Golden State Warriors, guard, 1988-89, 1999-2000; NY Knicks, 1990-98; Chicago Bulls, 2000; Utah Jazz, guard, 2001-03; Westchester Wildfire, US Basketball League, head coach, 2003-04; MSG Networks home Knicks, pre and post game analyst. **Orgs:** Boys Brotherhood Repub; founder, John Starks Found, 1994-. **Honors/Awds:** NBA All-Defensive Second Team, 1993; NBA All-Star, 1994; NBA Sixth Man Award, 1996; Hank Iba Citizen Athlete Award, 1997; Good Guy Award, NY Press Photographers Asn, 1997. **Special Achievements:** Author: John Starks: My Life. **Business Addr:** Founder, John Starks Foundation, 1127 High Ridge Rd Suite 331, Stamford, CT 06905, **Business Phone:** (203)322-7788.

STARKS, RICK
Government official, vice president (organization). **Personal:** Born Apr 16, 1948, Scottsville, KY; son of Ruby and L C; married

Saundra Hardin, Nov 28, 1968; children: Derrick D & Shannon M. **Educ:** Western Ky Univ, BS, masters, pub serv, 1971, MPS, 1975; Univ Okla, Econ Develop Inst, 1986-88. **Career:** Bowling Green Parks & Rec Ctr, dir, 1971-72; Mammoth Cave Nat Park, tour guide, 1971; Barren River Area Develop Dist, recreation planner & proj supt, 1972-80; Tenn Valley Authority, Bowling Green, KY, econ develop, regional mgr, sr specialist, currently. **Orgs:** Vpres, Big Brothers/Big Sister, 1978-79; Bowling Green Human Rights Comn, 1978; vice polemarch, 1978-79, keeper recs, 1989-96, KAP Frat; chmn action comm, 1979-81, spec proj adv, 1988, Bowling Green Nat Asn Advan Colored People; developer, Nat Asn Advan Colored People Youth Improvement Grant, 1987; chmn, BRADD Econ Develop Comm, 1988; Ky Indust Develop Coun, 1989; bd dirs, UPPRE Inc, 1989-91; Bradd Pvt Indust Coun, 1989-; trustee bd, Taylor Chapel AME Church, 1996-98; Gov's Ky Infrastructure Authority, 1996-00; Gov's Comn Women, 1998-. **Honors/Awds:** Big Brother of the Year Award, Big Brothers Agency, 1979; Civitan Service Award, Bowling Green Noon Civitan, 1979; AWARE, Meritorious Service Award, 1980; Governor's Economic Development Leadership Award, James N. Gray Award, 2004.

STARKS, ROBERT TERRY
Educator. **Personal:** Born Jan 24, 1944, Grenada, MS; son of Lula Ella; married Judith Ann Minor; children: Kenya Mariama & Robert Willis. **Educ:** Loyola Univ, BS, 1968, MA, 1971. **Career:** Booz-Allen & Hamilton Inc, mgt & consult, 1968-69; Chicago Urban League, res specialist, 1969-70; Northern Ill Univ, dir black studies, 1970-72, assoc prof, 1972-, Kellogg Found, res fel, 1978-80, Harold Wash Inst Res & Policy Studies, founder; Horace H Rackham Sch Graduation Studies, Univ Mich, vis scholar, 1976; Mayor Harold Wash & City Chicago, issues consult, 1982-87; Goethe Inst, Berlin, Ger, Lang fel, 1986; N'Digo newspaper, Chicago, columnist & polit ed, 1992-; Urban Affairs Rev, ed bd, 1992-95; WRON Radio, Chicago, talk show host, 1995; Diversity Institutions & Corps, consult & lectr, 1987-; Robert T Starks & Assoc, founder & pres. **Orgs:** Coun, Nat Conf Black Polit Scientists, 1979-81; DuSable Museum Afro-Am Hist, 1980-; vpres, PUSH, Int Trade Bur, 1981-82; issues consult, Rev Jesse L Jackson Nat Rainbow Coalition & Oper, PUSH, 1981-; founder, chmn, Task Force Black Polit Empowerment, 1982-; founder, chmn, Free S Africa Movement Chicago, 1985-; fel, Leadership Greater Chicago, 1986-87; bd mem, Third World Conf Found, 1986-87; bd mem, Ill Chap, Am Civil Liberties Union, 1987-88; vice chmn, Nat Black United Fund, 1987, chair, 1988-; chmn bd, Ill Black United Fund, 1990-; Deutscher Akademischer Austausch Dienst, Interdisciplinary German Studies, Seminar, Phillips Univ, 1987; bd dirs, S Side Comt Art Ctr, Chicago, 1982-; bd dirs, African Am Family Comn Ill, 1995-. **Honors/Awds:** Nat Community Service Award, Nat Conf Black Polit Scientists, 1987; State Performance Award Community Service, Phi Theta Kappa-Lambda Rho, 1992; Distinguished Service Award, Non-Traditional Degree Prog, Northeastern Ill Univ, 1995. **Home Addr:** 1556 E Pk Shore E Ct, Chicago, IL 60637-2961. **Business Addr:** Associate professor political science & inner city studies, Northeastern Illinois University, Department of Education Leadership & Development, ICS 417 700 E Oakwood Blvd, Chicago, IL 60653, **Business Phone:** (773)268-7500 Ext 149.

STARR, FREDRO (FREDRO SCRUGGS)
Rap musician, actor. **Personal:** Born Apr 18, 1971, Queens, NY. **Career:** Actor & singer; Onyx, rap group mem, 1993-; Albums with ONYX: Bacdafucu, 1993; All We Got Iz Us, 1995; Shut 'Em Dow, 1998; Bacdafucup Part II, 2002; Triggernometry, 2003; Cold Case Files, 2008; Solo Albums: That B Them, 2000; Firestarr, 2001; Don't Get Mad, Get Money, 2003; Last Dayz, 2008; Films: Clockers, 1995; The Addiction, 1995; Sunset Park, 1996; Ride, 1998; Black & White, 1999; Light It Up, 1999; Save the Last Dance, 2001; Flossin, 2001; Vegas Vampires, 2003; Torque, 2004; Almost Gangsta, 2004; Forbidden Fruits, 2006; My Brother, 2006; A Day in the Life, 2007; Show Stoppers, 2008; Queen of Media, 2008; Darling Nikki: The Movie, 2008; The Next Hit, 2008; The Eddie Black Story, 2009; Busted, 2009; A Day in the Life, 2009; TV series: "Strapped", 1993; "Law & Order", 1994; "NewYork Undercover", 1995; "Moesha", 1996-2000; "Dangerous Minds", 1996; NYPD Blue", 1998-2002; "Promised Land", 1998; "In the House", 1998; "Commitments", 2001; "One Arrest", 2002; The Wire, 2002-03; "Justice", 2003; "Karen Sisco", 2003; "Dance 360", 2004; Title Racer, 2005; "Bloodlines", 2006; "Blade: The Series", 2006; "CSI: Miami", 2009. **Honors/Awds:** Best Supporting Actor, Cable ACE nomination. **Special Achievements:** Co-hosted Dance 360, Paramount Domestic Television's daily. **Business Phone:** (310)859-4000.*

STARR-WHITE, DEBI. See LIVINGSTON-WHITE, DR. DEBORAH J H.

STATEN, EVERETT R
Founder (Originator), executive, chief executive officer. **Personal:** Born Jun 17, 1951, Philadelphia, PA; son of Harris L and Juanita A; children: Kharee Harris Staten. **Educ:** Temple Univ, BA, 1980. **Career:** Bell Pa, sales consult, 1968-76; Metro Atlanta Black Pages, assoc pub, 1981-85; Black Enterprise Mag, sr account exec, 1986-88; Emerge Mag, co-founder & adv dir, 1988-91; Black Expo USA, vpres, 1991-96; Inner City Events, pres, 1991; The Staten Group, Inc, chief exec officer, 1991; The Mobil Nat African Am Cult Expo, Founder & ceo, currently. **Orgs:** Nat Asn Market Dev, 1980-; Nat Coalition Black Meeting Planners, 1994-; African-Am Chamber Congress Philadelphia, 1994-; Philadelphia Multicultural Affairs Congress, 1994-; Int Asn Exposition Mgt, 1995; Nat Asn Consumer Shows, 1996. **Honors/Awds:** Outstanding Service Award, Martin Luther King Ctr, Non-Violent Soc Change, 1986; Community Serv Award, Coors Brewing Co, 1986. **Business Phone:** (215)549-1600.

STATEN, MARK EUGENE
Banker. **Personal:** Born Jan 22, 1963, Stuttgart, Germany; son of Walter (deceased) and Janette; married Barbara Sandy, Jul 1, 1994; children: Marylynn Staten. **Educ:** Langston Univ, 1986. **Career:** Am State Bank, asst vpres, 1981-. **Orgs:** Kappa Alpha Psi; worshipful master, Masonic Lodge, Pyramid Lodge No 69; Nat Asn Advan Colored People. **Home Addr:** 1330 North Boston Ave, Tulsa, OK 74106, **Home Phone:** (918)587-4604. **Business Addr:** Assistant Vice President, American State Bank, 3816 N Peoria, Tulsa, OK 74106, **Business Phone:** (918)428-2211.

STATES, ROBERT ARTHUR
Executive, president (organization). **Personal:** Born Mar 19, 1932, Boston, MA; son of Earl H and Rosita A; married Eva D Smith, Feb 21, 1955 (died 1998); children: Lauren States Creary, Lisa Hamel & Robert Jr. **Educ:** Boston Univ, BS, 1953; Bentley Col, cert, 1957; Western New Eng Col, JD, 1968; NYK Univ Grad Law Sch, attended 1969-71. **Career:** US Veterans ADM, acct, 1961-62; US Internal Revenue Serv, IRS agt, 1962-69; Aetna Life & Casualty, income taxes & tax audits, dir, 1969-91; Triple Check Financial & Bus Servs, pres, currently. **Orgs:** Town East Hampton, Water & Sewer Authority, 1967-87, Econ Develop CMS, 1992-; Am Bar Asn, 1977-; Nat Soc Enrolled Agts, 1991-; Conn Soc Enrolled Agts, 1991-; Nat Asn Tax Practitioners, 1992-. **Military Serv:** USY, cpl, 1953-55. **Home Addr:** 49 Wangonk Trail, PO Box 238, East Hampton, CT 06424, **Home Phone:** (203)267-9408. **Business Addr:** President, Owner, Triple Check Financial & Business Services, 11 S Main St, Marlborough, CT 06447, **Business Phone:** (860)295-0729.

STATHAM, CARL
Executive. **Personal:** Born Dec 9, 1950, Macon, GA; son of Carl and Marie; married Gloria Marie Long; children: Stephanie & Christopher. **Educ:** Tuskegee Inst, BS, 1973. **Career:** Gen Motors, bus consult, 1973-77; Ford Motor Co, acct rep, 1977-80, mgr acct reps, 1980-83; Southside Ford Truck Sales, chief exec, acct gen mgr, 1983-84, pres, 1984-. **Orgs:** Co Ford Hwy Truck Dealer Coun, 1989. **Honors/Awds:** Top 100 Black Buss, Black Enterprise, 1984-88; Top 300 Dealers Parts & Service Volume, Ford Motor Co, 1984-88; Distinguished Service Award, Ford Motor Co, 1984-87. **Business Phone:** (773)247-8662.

STATON, CANDI. See STATON, CANZETTA MARIA.

STATON, CANZETTA MARIA (CANDI STATON)
Singer. **Personal:** Born Mar 13, 1943, Hanceville, AL; daughter of Ursie and Rosa; married Clarence Carter, Jan 1, 1970 (divorced 1973); children: Clarence Carter Jr; married Joe Williams, Jan 1, 1959 (divorced 1968); children: Marcus Williams, Marcel Williams, Terry Williams & Cassandra Hightower; married John Sussewell. **Career:** Capitol Records, recording artist, 1969-71; United Artists, recording artist, 1972-73; Wagner Brothres records, recording artist, 1974-80; Larecords, recording artist, 1981; Sugarhill Records, recording artist, 1982; Beracah Records, recording artist, 1983; Trinity Broadcasting Network, tv host, 1986; singer, currently; Albums: Young Hearts Run Free, 1976; Music Speaks Louder Than Words, 1977; House of Love, 1978; Chance, 1979; Candi Staton, 1980; Suspicious Minds, 1982; Make Me An Instrument, 1983; The Anointing, 1985; Sing A Song, 1986; Love Lifted Me, 1988; Night lites, 1989; Stand Up & Be A Witness, 1990; Standing On The Promises, 1991; I Give You Praise, 1993; It's Time, 1995; Cover Me, 1997; Outside In, 1999; Here's a Blessing, 2000; Christmas In My Heart, 2000; Glorify, 2001; Proverbs 31 Woman, 2002; His Hands, 2006; I Will Sing My Praise To You, 2008; Who's Hurting Now?, 2009. **Orgs:** Nat Acad Recording Arts & Sci, 1970. **Special Achievements:** Grammy nominations: 1971, 1973, 1984, 1987. **Business Addr:** Singer, Beracah Ministries, Cassandra Hightower, PO Box 870567, Stone Mountain, GA 30087, **Business Phone:** (770)266-0718.

STATON, DONNA HILL
Lawyer. **Personal:** Born Dec 5, 1957, Chester, PA; daughter of Donald B and Ethel B Hill; married Kerry D; children: 2. **Educ:** Princeton Univ, BA, Eng, 1979; George Wash Univ, Sch Law, JD, 1982. **Career:** Hon Joseph C Howard, US Dist Ct Dist Md, judicial law clerk, 1982-83; Piper & Marbury, litigation partner & assoc, 1983-95; Md, circuit ct judge, 1995; Md state dep atty gen, currently. **Orgs:** Bd dirs, Howard County Sexual Assault Ctr, 1982-86; Alpha Kappa Alpha Sorority Inc, 1983-; pres, Alliance Black Women Attys, 1987-88; bd govs, Md State Bar Asn, 1988-90; bd dirs, Peoples Pro Bono Action Ctr, 1990-92; comnr, Atty Grievance Comt MD, 1991-95; adv comt, US Dist Ct, Dist MD, 1991-95; bus adv bd, Col Notre Dame Md, 1993; bd dirs, Leadership Howard County, 1997-03; bd dirs, McDonnogh Sch; fel Md Bar Found. **Honors/Awds:** Honoree, AFRAM Expo Salute Black Women, 1992; Honoree, Alliance Black Women Atty, 1994; 100 Outstanding Black Women of Baltimore, Emmanuel Christian Comm Church; Black Marylanders of Distinction Award; MD Top 100 Women, 2000. **Special Achievements:** First African American circuit court judge in Howard County, MD; first African American woman deputy attorney general in MD. **Home Addr:** 13827 Lakeside Dr, Clarksville, MD 21029, **Home Phone:** (410)531-3914. **Business Addr:** Deputy Attorney General, Maryland State, 200 St Paul Pl, Baltimore, MD 21202-2021, **Business Phone:** (410)576-7051.

STATON, KERRY D
Lawyer. **Personal:** Born Aug 30, 1954, New Rochelle, NY; son of James and Marie; married Donna Hill, Aug 11, 1984; children: Brooke Avery & Lindsey Simone. **Educ:** Oberlin Col, BA, 1976; Univ Md Sch Law, JD, 1980. **Career:** Legal Aid Bur Inc, staff atty, 1980-82; Ellin & Baker, assoc, 1982-84; Schochor, Federico & Staton, partner, 1984-. **Orgs:** Phi Alpha Delta, 1979-; Am Bar Asn, 1980-; Md State Bar Asn, 1980-; Monument City Bar Asn, 1982-; Bar Asn Baltimore City, 1982-; Asn Trial Lawyers Am, 1984-; Am Judicature Soc, 1984-; Spec Comt Audit Procedures, 1985-86, Common Minorities Legal Prof, 1988-89; bd govs, Md Trial Lawyers Asn, 1988-95; Nat Bar Asn, 1990-; Comn Civilty, 1996; Fourth Circuit Judicial Conf; Trial Lawyers Pub Justice; Am Bd Trial Advocate; fel Md Bar Found; fel Howard County Bar Found; Reginald Heber Smith Law fel; Md State Deleg & Minority Caucus. **Honors/Awds:** Super Lawyer, Schochar, Federico & Staton, 2007. **Home Addr:** 13827 Lakeside Dr, Clarksville, MD 21029, **Home Phone:** (410)531-3914. **Business Addr:** Partner, Schochar, Federico & Staton, PA, 1211 St Paul St, Baltimore, MD 21202, **Business Phone:** (410)234-1000.

STATON, RHONDA BAILEY
Manager. **Career:** The Seattle Times Co, advert sales mgr, display sales mgr, metro, currently. **Business Addr:** Display Sales Manager, The Seattle Times, 1120 John St, PO Box 70, Seattle, WA 98109.*

STEANS, EDITH ELIZABETH
Executive. **Personal:** Born Sep 4, 1929, Anderson, IN; daughter of Ernest J Downing (deceased) and Mary L Adams Downing (deceased); divorced; children: Bruce, Judith, Carol, Stacy. **Educ:** Anderson Col, BA, 1976; Ball State Univ, MAS, 1978. **Career:** Madison Co Dept Pub Welfare, caseworker, 1969-72; Madison Co Superior Ct II, chief juv probation officer, 1973-79; State Ind, affirmative action dir, 1979-82; City Anderson, affirmative action & human rel dir, 1982-89; Univ Nebraska Med Ctr, affirmative action & equal employ opportunity dir, 1989-95. **Orgs:** Urban League, 1955-90; Nat Asn Advan Colored People, 1955-90; bd dir, Comm Justice Ctr, 1970-88; YWCA 1973-; Alpha Kappa Alpha Sor, 1978-; instr, Anderson Col, 1978-88; comnr, Mayor's Econ Develop, 1982-86; bd dir, St John's Hosp Chem Dependency, 1982-88; bd dir, Enterprize Zone Asn, 1984-87; St Mary's Church. **Honors/Awds:** Outstanding Citizen, NAACP, 1983. **Home Addr:** 1619 W 15th St, Anderson, IN 46016-3205, **Home Phone:** (765)642-3744.

STEARNS MILLER, CAMILLE LOUISE
Lawyer. **Personal:** Born Apr 25, 1956, Guthrie, OK; daughter of Lila Hobson Stearns and Hollis D Stearns; married Daryl Lee Miller, Nov 7, 1987; children: Kristen Danielle. **Educ:** Howard Univ, Wash, DC, BA (magna cum laude), 1978; Case Western Res Sch Law, Cleveland, Ohio, JD, 1981. **Career:** Ohio Atty Gen Off, Columbus, Ohio, asst atty gen, 1981-83; Ohio Dept Natural Resources, Div Oil & Gas, gen coun, 1983-85; Lewis & Munday PC, Detroit, Mich, assoc atty, 1985-91, partner, 1991-2000; Holland & Knight LLP, partner & atty, 2001-; San Antonio Chap, Links Inc, mem. **Orgs:** Alpha Kappa Alpha Sorority, 1981-; Nat Conf Black Lawyers, Columbus Chap, 1981-85; Am Bar Asn, 1981-; Detroit Bar Asn, 1985-; Detroit Pub Schs Role Model, 1985-91; Nat Coalition 100 Black Women, 1985-; bd mem, secy-treas, Wolverine Bar Asn, 1986-90, pres elect, 1990-91, pres, 1991-92; asst secy, Nat Bar Asn, 1991, bd mem, 1995-; Detroit Renaissance Links, 1990-; Detroit Chap, Jack & Jill Am, 1996-, San Antonio Chap, secy; bd mem, Alamo City Chamber Com; secy, San Antonio Youth Literacy Coun. **Honors/Awds:** Outstanding Service Award, Black Law Students Asn, Case Western Res Sch Law, 1981; Outstanding Contributions to Legal Community, Black Law Students Asn, Columbus, Ohio, 1984; Certificate of Appreciation, Detroit Pub Schs, 1986-88; President's Award for Outstanding Service, Nat Bar Asn, 1991-92; Resolution for Outstanding Service to the Community, US Cong House Rep, 1992; Resolution for Outstanding Service to the Legal Community & Community-at-large, Mich State Legis Senate, 1992; Resolution for Outstanding Service to the County, Mayor Detroit Coleman A Young, 1992; Resolution for Outstanding Service to the Legal County, Wayne County Exec Ed McNamara; Resolution for Outstanding Service to the County, Detroit Bd Educ. **Business Addr:** Partner, Attorney, Holland & Knight LLP, 112 E Pecan St Suite 112, San Antonio, TX 78205, **Business Phone:** 888-688-8500.

STEBBINS, DANA BREWINGTON
Government official. **Personal:** Born Nov 2, 1946, Baltimore, MD. **Educ:** Howard Univ Wash DC, BA, 1967; Howard Univ,

MSW, 1970; Howard Univ, JD, 1975. **Career:** Small Bus Admin, spl asst to the assoc adminr minority small us, 1980-; Nat Bar Asn, dir com law proj, 1978-80; Commodity Futures Trading Comn, atty/adv/spl asst, 1977-78; Super Ct, DC, Judicial clerk, 1975-77; Wilkes, Artis, Hedrick & Lane, parter; Pres, The Law Off Dana B. Stebbins Esq; Principal and CEO, The Cornelius Group, TCG, currently. **Orgs:** Am Bar Asn; Nat Asn Black Women Attys; Nat Bar Asn; Nat Asn Black Social Workers; Delta Theta Phi Legal Fraternity; Nat Asn Social Workers; Nat Conf Black Lawyers; pres, Dist Columbia Chamber Com, bd, Metropolitan YMCA; bd, Lab Sch. **Honors/Awds:** Hundred Most Powerful Women in Washington, Wash Mag.

STEED, JOEL EDWARD
Football player. **Personal:** Born Feb 17, 1969, Frankfurt, Germany; married D'Angela; children: Traicee Eileen. **Educ:** Univ Colo, BA, 1992. **Career:** Football player (retired); Pittsburgh Steelers, nose tackle, 1992-99; NFL, free agt, currently. **Honors/Awds:** Pro Bowl alternate, 1996.

STEED, TYRONE
Health services administrator, spokesperson. **Personal:** Born Aug 18, 1948, Norfolk, VA; married Irene; children: Kenyatta Uniquegu. **Educ:** Newark Sch Fine & Indust Art, Interior Design Dipl, 1972; Fashion Inst Techol, AAS Interior Design, 1973; Thomas Edison Col, BA, 1976; Kean Col NJ, MA, Org Develop, 1981. **Career:** New Horizons Inc, dist mgr, asst vpres, 1976-77; Girl Scouts Am, coun field rep, 1977-79; St Charles Kids Sch, teacher, 1979-80; Newark Office Aging, sr commun rel spec, 1980-; VA Med Ctr, Chief Crystal Grace, dir pub rel, spokesman, vol serv asst, currently. **Orgs:** Am Hosp Asn, 1981-; NJ Hosp Asn 1981-; pub rel dir, Am Hosp Asn Soc, 1982-; Seton Hall Univ Geront Adv Comt, 1982-; dir vol serv, NJ Asn, 1983. **Honors/ Awds:** 20 min film on Girl Scouts Girl Scout Council of Greater Essex Cty, 1977-79; 50 page thesis innovation & change in org Kean College of NJ, 1981-85. **Military Serv:** AUS, sp4 3 yrs; Expert 45 Pistol, 1965-68. **Business Addr:** Voluntary Service Assistant, Spokesman, VA Medical Center, East Orange Medical Center, Tremont Ave & S Ctr St, East Orange, NJ 07019, **Business Phone:** (201)676-1000 Ext 1771.

STEELE, BOBBIE L
Government official, educator. **Personal:** Born Oct 18, 1937, Cleveland, MS; daughter of Mary Rodges; married Robert P, Apr 10, 1956; children: Valerie, Joyce, Robert, Byron, Donna & Elisha. **Educ:** Ala AMA Col, attended 1956; Chicago's Teacher's Col, elem educ, 1966. **Career:** Educator, commissoner (retired); Chicago Bd Educ, sch teacher, 1966-86; Cook County Bd Commissioners, comnr, 1986-2006, interim pres, 2006. **Orgs:** Pres, Nat Asn Black County Officials; chair, Nat Asn County Officials Deferred Compensation Adv Comt; Nat Coun Negro Women; League Women Voters; Lake Shore Links Inc; United Missionary Baptist Church; Cook County Dem Women; bd mem, Oper Brotherhood; Alpha Kappa Alpha Sorority. **Honors/Awds:** Received over one hundred awards or citations for leadership & service; Chicago Women's Hall of Fame. **Special Achievements:** First African American woman to serve as Chairman of the Finance Commission of the Forest Preserve District of Cook County; First female Cook County President; Longest serving African American woman on the Cook County Board and the longest serving in the history of Cook County.

STEELE, CAROLYN ODOM
Executive, consultant. **Personal:** Born Aug 31, 1944, Augusta, GA; daughter of P C Odom and Marjorie Odom. **Educ:** Spelman Col, BA, 1966; Am Univ, MA, Comm, 1970. **Career:** Col Med & Dentistry NJ, mat developer, 1970; Minority Econ Develop Corp, admin asst educ, 1971; New York Addiction Serv Agency, dep dir pub rels & community info, 1972-76; Nat Health Coun, asst dir, commun coordr, 1976-77; Earl G Graves Ltd, dir pub affairs, 1977-83, corp commun, vpres, sr vpres; AT&T, corp affairs dir pub rels; mkt commun consult, currently. **Orgs:** Bd dirs, Nat Black Child Devel Inst; co-chair Corporate Women's Roundtable, Spelman Col; EDGES Group; Women Commun; bd mem, Nat Coalition 100 Black Women. **Honors/Awds:** Nat French Hon Soc Pi Delta Phi 1963; YWCA Acad Women Achievers, 1984; publications: "Talking with the Inner City", Public Relations Journal, 1969, "The Enigma of Drug Abuse", Journal of Practical Nursing, 1974. **Business Addr:** Consultant, 209-45 Bardwell Ave, Queens Village, NY 11429.

STEELE, DR. CLAUDE MASON
Educator. **Personal:** Born Jan 1, 1946, Chicago, IL; married Dorothy Munson; children: Jory Claire Claude & Benjamin. **Educ:** Hiram Col, Hiram, OH, BA, psychol, 1967; Ohio State Univ, MA, social psychol, 1969, PhD, social psychol, 1971. **Career:** Univ Utah, asst prof psychol, 1971-73; Univ Wash, asst prof psychol, 1973-77, assoc prof, 1977-85, prof psychol, 1985-87; Univ Mich, prof psychol, 1987-91, inst social res, res scientist, 1989-91; Stanford Univ, prof psychol, 1991-, chmn dept psychol, 1997-2000, Lucie Stern prof social sci, 1997-, co dir res inst comparative studies race & ethnicity, 1999-2002, dir ctr comparative studies race & ethnicity, 2002-, fac diversity coun, 2001-02, fac senate steering comm, 2002-02, fac senate, 2000-02. **Orgs:** Bd, Black Stud Psychol Asn, 1968-71; mem, Nat Inst Alcohol Abuse & Alcoholism, Psychosocial Res Study Sect, 1984-88; sec treas, 1987-88, Soc Exp Social Psychol, chmn, 1988-89; mem & bd dir, Am Psychol Soc, 1996-97; Am Psychol Asn Div 8 Exec Comm, 1988-91; fel, Ctr Adv Study Behavioral Sci, 1994-95; pres, Western Psychol Asn, 1996-97; Presidential Search Comm, 1999-2000; pres, Soc Personality & Social Psychol, 2002-03; bd, Trustees Develop Comm, Stanfort Univ, 2002-; pres, Soc Personality & Social Psychol, 2002-03. **Honors/Awds:** Dean's Teaching Award, Stanford University, 1995; Gordon Allport Prize in Social Psychology, Soc PsycholStudy Social Issues, 1997; Kurt Lewin Memorial Award, Soc Psychol Study Social Issues, 1998; Senior Award for Distinguished Contributions to Psychology in the Public Interest, Am Psychol Asn, 1998; Distinguished Scientific Contribution Award, Am Psychol Asn, 1998; Honorary Doctorate, Univ Chicago, 2000; William James Fellow Award for Distinguished Scientific Career Contribution, Am Psychol Soc, 2000; Donald Campbell Award, Soc Personality & Social Psychol, 2001; Honorary Doctorate, Yale Univ, 2002; Honorary Doctorate, Princeton Univ, 2003. **Special Achievements:** Associate editor of Personality and Social Psychology Bulletin in 1984-87. **Business Addr:** Professor, Department of Psychology, Stanford University, Rm 110 Bldg 420 Jordan Hall 450 Serra Mall, Stanford, CA 94305-2130, **Business Phone:** (650)725-9849.

STEELE, CLEOPHAS R., JR.
Judge. **Personal:** Born Jul 13, 1945, Dallas, TX; married Barbara; children: Sheri, Sharron, Cheronda. **Educ:** Univ Okla, BA & BS, 1967; Southern Methodist Univ, JD, 1970. **Career:** City Dallas, assoc judge, 1974-76; Dallas County, justice peace, currently. **Orgs:** Trustee & deacon, Goodstreet Baptist Church; Omega Psi Phi Fraternity, 1965-; bd mem, Dallas Alliance, 1978-84. **Home Addr:** 1531 Cove Dr, Dallas, TX 75216. **Business Addr:** Justice Of The Peace, Dallas County, 330 S R L Thornton Fwy Suite 112, Dallas, TX 75203.

STEELE, JOYCE YVONNE
Beautician. **Personal:** Born Dec 8, 1930, St Johns, Antigua-Barbuda; daughter of William Isaac and Agatha Isaac; married Richard Biddy (divorced 1965); children: Richard Biddy, Mark Biddy; married Edgar S Steele, Jul 13, 1979. **Educ:** Hopes Beauty Sch, London, Eng, dipl, 1961; Loriel Beauty Sch, Paris, France, dipl, 1968; Lee Col Sch Cosmetology, Baytown, TX, dipl, 1982. **Career:** Dame Yvonne Beauty Sch, Leister, Eng, owner, 1958-74; Am Caribbean Beauty Prod, Baytown, TX, owner, 1982-; Ultra Elegance Salon, Baytown, TX, owner, 1982-. **Business Phone:** (713)422-5100.

STEELE, LAWRENCE
Fashion designer. **Personal:** Born Jul 3, 1963, Hampton, VA; son of William Anderson and Winifred Delores. **Educ:** The Sch Art Inst Chicago, BFA, 1985. **Career:** Moshino, design asst, 1985-90; Prada, design asst, 1990-94; Lawrence Steele Design, designer, 1994-. **Special Achievements:** Participated in Florence Biennale, 1998; Designed wedding dress Jennifer Aniston, 2000; colaborated with artist Vanessa Beecroft for her performance, VB48, Genoa, Italy, 2001. **Business Addr:** Designer, Lawrence Steele Design, Via Seprio 2 20149, Milan, Italy.

STEELE, MICHAEL S.
Government official. **Personal:** Born Oct 19, 1958, Prince George's County, MD; son of William and Maebell; married Andrea Derrutt; children: Michael II, Drew. **Educ:** Johns Hopkins Univ, BA, 1981; Augustinian Friars Sem, Villanova Univ; Georgetown Univ Law Sch, JD, 1991. **Career:** Cleary, Gottlieb, Seen & Hamilton Law Offs, lawyer, 1991-97; Steele Group, founder & chief exec officer, 1998-; Md Republican Party, chair, 2000-02; Md lt gov, 2002-; Pope Benedict XVI, Vatican City, 2005-; CNN, "The Situation Room", polit pundit, currently. **Orgs:** Bd Trustees, Johns Hopkins Univ, 1981-85; assoc, Cleary, Gottlieb, Steen & Hamilton, 1991-97; Prince George's County Md Black Republican Coun, 1992; chair, Prince George's County Republican Cent Comt, 1994-00; chair, Md State Minority Outreach Task Force, 1995-97; delegate, Republican Party Nat Convention, 2000 & 2004; chair, Republican Party State Cent Comt, 2000-02; Nat Comn Fed Election Reform, 2001; bd visitors, US Naval Acad, 2002-05; Gov's Exec Coun, 2003-; chair, State House Trust, 2003-; chair, Gov's Comn Minority Bus Enterprise Reform, 2003; chair, Gov's Comn Qual Educ, 2004-05; State Planning Comt Higher Educ, 2004-; Gov's Subcabinet Int Affairs, 2005-. **Honors/Awds:** Man of the Year, Md State Republican, 1995; Vikki Buckley Political Leadership Award, Black Am's PAC, 2002. **Special Achievements:** First African American to serve in a Maryland state-wide office and the first Republican lieutenant governor in the state since the position was created in 1970; highest-ranking elected African American Republican in the United States. *

STEELE, RUBY L
Nurse, educator. **Personal:** Born in Marion, AL; daughter of Alexander Williams and Mamie Whitehead; married George, Mar 11, 1957; children: Jocelyn, Sonya, George & Christopher. **Educ:** Am River Col, Sacramento, Calif, AA, 1970; Metropolitan State Col, Denver, Colo, BS, 1974; Southern Ill Univ, Edwardsville, Ill, MS, 1979; St Louis Univ, St Louis, Mo, PhD, 1988. **Career:** Belleville Memorial Hosp, Belleville, Ill, nurse, 1975-78; Belleville Area Col, Belleville, Ill, instr, part-time, 1977-78; Southern Illi Univ, Edwardsville, Ill, instr, asst prof, 1979-87; Webster Univ, St Louis, MO, asst prof, 1987-90; Southeast Mo State Univ, Cape Girardeau, MO, assoc prof, 1990-94; Fort Valley State Col, pro & dir nursing prog, 1994; independent consulting, vol, currently. **Orgs:** Sigma Theta Tau, Nursing Honor Soc, 1980-; House Delegates, ANA, 1971-; steering committee, INA, 1975-; Asn Black Nursing Fac, 1987-; St Louis Univ Alumni, bd dirs; YWCA; Belleville News Democrat. **Honors/Awds:** NIMH Traineeship Graduate Study, 1977; Colorado Nurses Asn Grant BS Study, 1973; Am Cancer Soc Grant, Oncology Nurse Educators, 1981; Sacramento Med Soc Scholarship, 1969-71; fac fel, Purdue Univ, 1990.

STEELE, DR. SHELBY
Educator, writer, research scientist. **Personal:** Born Jan 1, 1946?, Chicago, IL; son of Shelby and Ruth. **Educ:** Coe Col, Cedar Rapids, Iowa, BA, polit sci; Southern Ill Univ, MA, sociol; Univ Utah, PhD, eng. **Career:** San Jose State Univ, prof eng, 1974-91; Hoover Inst, res fel, Robert J &Marion E Oster sr fel, currently; Harper's magazine, contributing ed, currently; writer; columist; The Content of Our Character: A New Vision of Race in America, 1991; A Dream Deferred: The Second Betrayal of Black Freedom in America, 1999; White Guilt: How Blacks & Whites Together Destroyed the Promise of the Civil Rights Era, 2006; A Bound Man: Why We Are Excited About Obama & Why He Can't Win, 2007. **Orgs:** Nat Asn Scholars; Am Acad Lib Educ; Univ Accreditation Asn; nat bd mem, Ctr New Am Community, Manhattan Inst. **Honors/Awds:** Nat Book Critics Circle Award, 1991; Emmy Award, 1990; Nat Humanities Medal, 2004; Bradley Prize, 2006; Writer's Guild Award; San Francisco Film Festival Award. **Special Achievements:** Host, PBS spec, Seven Days in Benson hurst. **Business Addr:** Senior Research Fellow, Hoover Institution, Stanford Univ, Stanford, CA 94305-6010, **Business Phone:** (650)723-1754.

STEELE, TOMMY
Writer, government official, clergy. **Personal:** Born Jul 26, 1950, Portsmouth, VA; son of Dr Thomas Melvin and Elizabeth Wood; children: Tommy Jr & Tiffany Gail; married Tonda. **Educ:** Norfolk State Univ, BA, history, 1977; Jameson Bible Inst, MDIV, 1978; Jameson Christiam Col, PhD, 1986; E NC Theological Inst, STB, 1995. **Career:** New Ahoskie Baptist Church, 1970-78; First Baptist Church, 1978-81; First Ledge Rock Baptist Church, sr pastor, 1981-83; Hardie Grove Baptist Church, sr pastor, 1981-83; Jerusalem Baptist Church, sr pastor, 1983; New Life Baptist Church, pastor, currently. **Orgs:** Home mission bd, Nat Baptist Convention; adv bd, Rider Univ; past chaplain, bd dir, Kappa Alpha Psi; chaplain, Trenton Police Dept; bd trustees, E NC Theological Institute; life mem, Elizabeth City State Univ Alumni Asn; life mem, NAACP; bd trustees, Apex Sch Theology; past bd dir, Kiwanis Club; Frontier Intl; Epsilon Delta Chi. **Honors/ Awds:** Numerous honorary degrees; more than 200 community, civic and religious awds. **Special Achievements:** First Afr Am Chaplain of the Trenton Police Dept. **Home Addr:** 218 Kensington Ave, Trenton, NJ 08618. **Business Addr:** Pastor, New Life Baptist Church, 1281 Biscayne Dr, Concord, NC 28027, **Business Phone:** (704)782-6215.

STEELE, WARREN BELL, II
Labor relations manager. **Personal:** Born Apr 14, 1923, Milledgeville, GA; married Victoria Kitchen; children: Holly Burns, Woody, William, Audrey Brown, Warren, Theresa Page, Frank. **Educ:** Paine Col, BA, 1947; The Am Univ, MA, 1965. **Career:** Cummins Engine Co Columbus IN, personnel adminr 1969-70; Cummins Engine Co Columbus IN, dir personnel & adminr, 1970-73; Frigiking Dallas, vice pres personnel 1973-75; Cummins Charleston Inc Charleston SC, personnel, div mgr, 1975-79; Cummins Charleston Urban League Columbus GA, exec loan, 1979-81; Signature Mfg Co Nashville TN, minority owner, 1981-83; Columbus Consolidated Govt Columbus GA, personnel officer 1983-84; Am Family Life Assurance Co Columbus, 1984-, sr vpres & asst dir mkt, 2000-. **Orgs:** Am Soc of Personnel Adminrs, 1976-; Tri-Co Personnel Asn, 1976-; chmn, Dorchester Co Sch Adv Bd, 1977-; bd mem, King's Grant Home Owners Asn, 1977-78; trustee, Voorhees Col Denmark SC; friend to Educ, Dorchester Cnty Tchrs Asn, 1979; bd Columbus GA C of C; Life Mgt Ins, fellow; past chair, Conf Bd's Nat Coun Mkg Exec; Harvard Sch scholarship Comt; bd mem, HCA'S Doctors Hosp, Columbus, ; bd mem, Methodist Home Children and Youth Found. **Honors/ Awds:** Bronza star; defense commen; Vietnam Def. **Military Serv:** AUS, lt col, 23 yrs. **Business Addr:** Senior Vice President, Assistant Director Marketing, Am Family Life Assurance Company Columbus, 1932 Wynnton Rd, Columbus, GA 31999, **Business Phone:** (706)323-3431.*

STEELE-ROBINSON, ALICE LOUISE
Educator. **Personal:** Born Mar 27, 1943, Concord, NC; daughter of Andrew A Steele and Neomia Pharr Steele; married Rev Harold O Robinson, Sep 21, 1991. **Educ:** Barber-Scotia Col, Concord, NC, BS, 1965; Appalachian State Univ, Boone, NC, MA, 1977; Univ NC-Charlotte, curric specialist, 1988. **Career:** Educator (retired): Moore County Schs, teacher, 1965-67; Concord City Schs, teacher, 1967-77, K-12 Reading & Lang Arts, coordr, 1977-

85, Head Start, dir, 1983-85; Cabarrus County Schs, Elem Educ Chap 1, ESEA, dir, 1986-95. **Orgs:** Delta Kappa Gamma Int Hon Soc Women Educ, 1979-; United Way Cabarrus County, Adv Panel, 1983-99; Rowan Community Col, Early Childhood Adv Bd, 1985-95; bd dirs, chair, Cabarrus County Red Cross, 1986-95; bd mem,chair, Cabarrus Victim Assistance Network, 1989-2000; Prince Hall Affiliate Order Eastern Star, 1989-2000; bd trustees, Rock Hill AME Zion Church, Concord, NC, 1989-2000; basileus, Zeta Phi Beta Sorority, Gamma Epsilon Zeta Chap, 1991-2000; precient chief judge, Cabarrus County Bd Elections, 1992-2000. Cabarrus County NAACP, past sec, ACT-SO, chair, 1992-98; exec secy, African Methodist Episcopal Zion Church, Woman's Home& Overseas Missionary Soc, 1995-2000; exec adminr, Woman's Home & Overseas Missionary, African Methodist Episcopal Zion Church Carol Werchan; Cabarrus County Sch Facilities Blue Ribbon Comt. **Honors/Awds:** First Place Religious Publ Award, AME Zion Church, NC, 1992; Presidential Award, Nat Asn Equal Opportunity Higher Educ, 1993; President's Plaque, Extraordinary Leadership, Barber-Scotia Col, 1993; Distinguished Service Award, Cabarrus County NAACP, 1993; Thirty Years of Exemplary Service-Leadership and Dedication Plaque, Cabarrus County Schs, 1995;North Carolina State Leadership Award, Nat Asn Fed Educ Prog Administrators, 1995; Encyclopedia African Am Educ, "Dr. Mable Parker McLean", 1996; Service Award, African Methodist Episcopal Zion Church, Woman's Home & Overseas Missionary Soc, 1999. **Special Achievements:** Published: Reading/Language Arts Curriculum Guide, (K-12), 1980; Concord District Heritage Journal; NC International Reading Asn, Reading TARHEEL Journal Editoral Board, 1991-93; Star of Zion, articles, 1995-2000. **Home Addr:** 3735 Rock Hill Ch Rd, Concord, NC 28027.

STEGER, C DON. See STEGER, DR. C DONALD.

STEGER, DR. C DONALD (C DON STEGER)
Government official. **Personal:** Born Aug 27, 1936, Huntsville, AL; son of Lula Cliff and Fred; married Elizabeth Sutton, Jun 1, 1966; children: Lisa Monique. **Educ:** Bethune Cookman Col, BA, 1964; Gammon Theol Sem, BD, 1968; Univ S Fla, PhD, 1972. **Career:** WOBS Radio Jacksonville, announcer, 1960-64; Tampa Inner City Progs, dir, 1968-71; McCabe Black Community Develop, dir, 1972-75; Pinellas County Fla Schs, adminr, 1975-77; City St Petersburg, Fla, dep city mgr, 1977-79; City Charlotte, asst city mgr, 1979-95; Pub Library Charlotte & Mecklenburg County, bd chair, currently. **Orgs:** Consult, US Civil Serv Comn, 1969-78; consult, Gen Electric Co, 1972-74; consult, Honeywell, 1975-77; bd dirs, Rotary Club Charlotte, 1975-; pres bd, Bethlehem Ctr Charlotte, 1985-86; chmn, Campaign Charlotte Mecklenburg United Way, 1986; dir, Found Carolinas, 1986-. **Honors/Awds:** Doctoral Dissertation, USAF, 1972. **Military Serv:** USAR, corpl, 1956-62. **Home Addr:** 6517 Hunter Pine lane, Charlotte, NC 28270. **Business Addr:** Board Chair, Public Library of Charlotte & Mecklenburg County, 310 N Tryon St, **Business Phone:** (704)336-2725.

STEIB, JAMES TERRY
Clergy, bishop, college teacher. **Personal:** Born May 17, 1940, Vacherie, LA; son of Vivian Jones and Rosemond. **Educ:** Divine Word Sem, theol deg, 1967; Xavier Univ, MA, guid & coun, 1973. **Career:** Priesthood, ordained, 1967; Divine Word Sem, asst dean stud, 1967-69, prov super, 1976-83; St Stanislaus High Sch, prof, 1967-76; Archdiocese St Louis, auxiliary bishop, 1984; Cath Diocese Memphis, bishop, 1993-; Titular Bishop Britonia. **Orgs:** Vpres, Conf Major Superiors Men, 1979-83; consult, African Am Cath Comt, Nat Conf Cath Bishops; bd dirs, Cath Exten Soc; bd dirs, Cath Univ Am; bd dirs, Cath Relief Serv. **Business Addr:** Bishop, The Catholic Diocese of Memphis, 5825 Shelby Oaks Dr, Memphis, TN 38134-7316, **Business Phone:** (901)373-1200.

STEINER, K LESLIE. See DELANY, SAMUEL RAY.

STENT, MADELON DELANY
Educator. **Personal:** Born Sep 22, 1933, Washington, DC; children: Michelle, Nicole & Evan. **Educ:** Sarah Lawrence Col, BA; Wellesley Col, MA; Columbia Univ, EdD, 1965; Teachers Col, grad. **Career:** City Univ New York, City Col, prof educ, 1963-, Div Interdepartmental Studies, dir, 1981-94; Fordham Univ Sch Educ, vis prof, 1969-71; Teachers Col, fac; Columbia Univ, fac; Queens Col, fac; Mills Col, fac; Random House-Knopf Mag, journalist & auth. **Orgs:** Educ con planner Voices Inc, 1966-; Nat Asn Black Sch Educrs, 1971-; Am Educ Res Asn, 1973-; nat chairperson, Higher Ed Comm Nat Alliance Black Sch Educrs; consult; HARYOU-ACT; Kappa Delta Pi Honor Educ Soc; US Off Educ; Univ Peurto Rico; Univ Calif. **Honors/Awds:** Student Ambassador Award in Spanish to Spain, 1952; Community Service Society Award, 1964; Ford Found Research Grantee, 1973; Ford Found Grantee, 1974; Rockefeller Scholar, Re Bellagio, Italy, 1975. **Special Achievements:** Author of Cultural Pluralism in American Higher Education, 1973, Minority Enrollment & Rep in Institute of Higher Education, Praeger Press, Special Studies International, 1974, Minorities in US Institutions of Higher Education, Praeger Press, Special Studies Internatio nal, 1976, Black Colleges: Internatioanal Perspectives, 1984, lecturer, Child Abuse & Maltreatment with International Partnership for Service Learning. **Home Addr:** 5700 Arlington Ave Suite 5B, Riverdale, NY 10471. **Business Phone:** (212)650-7000.

STENT, NICOLE M
Government official, health services administrator. **Personal:** Born Jul 22, 1960, New York, NY; daughter of Theodore R and Madelon Delany; married Mark A Graham, 1993; children: Imani Simone & Mark Anthony. **Educ:** Dartmouth Col, Hanover, NH, BA, 1982; Howard Univ Sch Law, Wash, DC, JD, 1985. **Career:** US House Rep, Cong Black Caucus, fel, 1983; Leftwich, Moore & Douglass, Wash, DC, legal intern, 1985; NYK Supreme Ct, law asst, 1986; NYC Financial Servs Corp, Sr proj mgr, 1987-88; City NYK, Mayor's Off African Am & Caribbean Affairs, dep dir, actg dir, 1988-90; NYC Offtrack Betting Corp, asst gen coun, 1991; NYC HTH & Hosps Corp, Affirmative Action & EEO, asst dir, 1992-97, exec asst, CRE Planning, Cot Health InterGovt Rels, 1998-; Paage Et Cie Ltd, bd mem, currently. **Orgs:** Dartmouth Lawyers Asn, 1985-; New York Urban League, 1990-. **Business Addr:** Board member, Paage Et Cie Ltd, 59 Beech Hill Rd, Scarsdale, NY 10583, **Business Phone:** (914)725-0343.

STEPHEN, JOYCE
Police chief. **Personal:** Born in Sumter, SC. **Educ:** John Jay Col Criminal Justice, BS, criminal justice, 1981. **Career:** Deputy Chief (retired); NY Police Dept, 1981, capt, dep inspector, dep chief. **Special Achievements:** First African American woman deputy chief of the New York police department.

STEPHENS, BOOKER T
Judge. **Personal:** Born Nov 3, 1944, Bluefield, WV; son of Robert L (deceased) and Estella (deceased); married Gloria M Davis; children: Ciara Midori & Booker Taliaferro. **Educ:** WV State Col, BA, 1966; Howard Univ, JD, 1972. **Career:** Asst prosecuting atty, 1977-78; WV House Deleg, 1979-82; State WV, Circuit Ct, Eighth Judicial Circuit, chief judge, currently. **Orgs:** Life mem, Nat Asn Advan Colored People, Earl Warren fel, legal defense fund, coop atty; Alpha Phi Alpha Fraternity; chmn, Standing Comt Polit Subdivisions, 1980; WV Judicial Asn; Am Bar Asn; WV State Bar Asn. **Honors/Awds:** Hall of Fame, WV State Col, 2002; Living the Dream Award, Gov, 2003. **Military Serv:** AUS, sp5, 1966-68. **Business Addr:** Chief Judge, Eighth Judicial Circuit, State of West Virginia Circuit Court, McDowell County Courthouse, County Courthouse, PO Box 310, Welch, WV 24801-0310, **Business Phone:** (304)436-8531.

STEPHENS, BRENDA WILSON
Librarian. **Personal:** Born Oct 22, 1952, Durham, NC; daughter of Leroy Wilson and Lucy Umstead; married Gregory, Mar 6, 1977; children: Seth & Sara. **Educ:** Vincennes Univ, Vincennes, Ind, 1971; Winston-19Salem State Univ, Winston-19Salem, NC, BS, 1974; NC Cent Univ, Durham, NC, MLS, 1981. **Career:** Orange County Pub Libr, Hillsboro, NC, libr asst, 1976-81, asst county librn, 1981-90, county librn, 1990-91, regional libr dir, 1991-. **Orgs:** NC Libr Asn, Pub Libr Sect, 1983-85; chair, adult serv, NCLA, Pub Libr Sect, 1987-93; pres, PTO-Cameron Pk Sch, 1988-89; pres, Kiwanis Club, 1990-; bd mem, United Way Greater Orange County, 1991-94; pres, Al Stanback Mid Sch, currently; bd educ, Orange County Sch, 1998-. **Honors/Awds:** Homecoming Queen, Vincennes Univ, 1970-71; Roadbuilders' Award, NC Library Asn Roundtable, 1997. **Military Serv:** AUS, sgt, 1974-76. **Home Addr:** 5807 Craig Rd, Durham, NC 27712. **Business Addr:** Regional Library Director, Orange County Public Library, 300 W Tryon St, Hillsborough, NC 27278.

STEPHENS, BROOKE MARILYN
Financial manager, writer. **Personal:** Born Jan 1, 1944, Atlanta, GA; daughter of Charles W Jr and Grace Anne. **Educ:** Fisk Univ, BA, 1963; Western Mich Univ, MLS, 1967; Harvard Bus Sch, attended 1972; Adelphi Univ, CFP, 1986. **Career:** Chase, W Africa, int trade offier; Citicorp Investment Servs, New York, sr investment consult; Financial writer & investment adv, pvt pract, currently; auth: Brooke Stephens Wealth Building Journal; Talking Dollars & Making Sense: A Wealth-Building Guide for African-Americans; It's Your Money:Everything You Need to Know to Be Your Own Financial Planner; Wealth Happens One Day At A Time 365 Days To A Brighter Financial Future; Men We Cherish: African American Women Praise The Men In Their Lives. **Orgs:** Financial Women's Asn New York; adv bd, chairs, econ literacy comt, Girls Inc; NY Soc Cert Financial Planners; Am Mgt Asn; Nat Asn Black Journalists. **Honors/Awds:** Listed in Who's Who in finance and industry, 1986. **Business Addr:** Financial Advisor, 314 W 231st St Suite 470, Bronx, NY 10463, **Business Phone:** (718)875-2575.

STEPHENS, CYNTHIA DIANE
Judge. **Personal:** Born Aug 27, 1951, Detroit, MI; daughter of Nathaniel Otis and Diane Shand; married Thomas Oliver Martin; children: Imani Diane. **Educ:** Univ Mich, BA, 1971; Atlanta Univ, postgrad, 1972; Emory Law Sch, JD, 1976. **Career:** Neighborhood Youth Corps Econ Opportunity, proj coordr, 1972-73; Nat Conf Black Lawyers, southern regional dir, 1976-77; Nat League Cities, coordr, 1977-78; Pan-African Orthodox Christian Church, gen coun, 1978-82; Mich Senate, assoc gen coun, 1979-82; Wayne Co Charter Comn, vice-chmn, 1980-81; Law Off Cynthia D Stephens, atty, 1981-82; 36th Dist Ct, judge, 1982-85; Wayne Co Community Col, fac, 1985-; Wayne Co Circuit Ct, judge, 1985-; Univ Detroit Mercy Law Sch, fac, 1986-90; Detroit Col Law, fac, 1990-95; Nat Judicial Col, fac, 1994; Third Circuit Ct, chief protempore judge, currently. **Orgs:** Nat Conf Black Lawyers, 1970-; Wolverine Bar Asn, 1979; bd mem, Wayne Co Neighborhood Legal Serv, 1980; New Detroit Inc, 1981-; Adv Comt, Am Corp Coun Pro-Bono, 1982-88; bd mem, Asn Black Judges Mich, 1982-89; Mich Dist Judges Asn, 1982-85; Greater Detroit Health Care Coun, 1983-85; Univ Mich Symposium Series Ctr African & Afro-Am Studies, 1984; Adv Bd, African Diaspora Proj Delta Inst, 1984-88; mem-at-large, City Wide Sch Comm Org, 1984-86; Delta Manor LDHA, 1984-, YMCA Downtown Detroit, 1984; Am Bar Asn Comm Judicial Eval, 1984-85; Delta Sigma Theta Detroit Alumni, 1984-85; Adv Bd, Mich Bar J, 1985-; bd comnrs, State Bar Mich, 1986-; Nat Asn Women Judges; Mich Judges Asn; Nat Bar Asn; State Bar Mich; Acad Adv Comt, Mich Judicial Inst. **Honors/Awds:** Outstanding Woman Award, Woodward Ave Presbyterian Church, 1982; Distinguished Service Award, Region 5 Detroit Pub Sch, 1983; Wolverine Bar member of the Year, 1984; Golden Heritage Award for Judicial Excellence, Little Rock Baptist Church, 1984; Outstanding Woman in Law, Hartford Mem Baptist Church, 1985; Distinguished Alumni Award, Cass Tech High Sch, 1987; Susan B Anthony Award, Nat Orgn Women, 1988; Anita Hill Award, Detroit Human Rights Comn, 1991; Fannie Lou Hammer Award, 1997. **Special Achievements:** published "Judicial Selection & Diversity," Michigan Bar Journal Vol 64 No 6 1985; contributor and Michigan Non-Standard Jury Instructor for West Group, 1999, 2001. **Business Addr:** Adjunct Professor, University of Detroit Mercy School of Law, 651 E Jefferson, Detroit, MI 48226, **Business Phone:** (313)596-0200.

STEPHENS, DAVID L.
Executive. **Educ:** Southern Univ, BS bus admin. **Career:** Ford Motor Co, sales mgt; Pavilion Lincoln Mercury, Austin, dealer cand; Falls Lincoln Mercury, dealer prin & pres; Stephens Automotive Group, pres & chief exec officer, plano, currently. **Orgs:** Jaguar N Am Dealer Opers Coun; Ford Motor Minority Dealers Asn; Tex Automobile Dealers' Asn; Legislative Comt; Nat Asn Minority Automobile Dealers; United Negro Col Fund; Am Cancer Soc; Crystal Charity Ball; Dallas Museum of Art; Tex Animal Control Asn; African Am Museum; Jesuit Found. **Honors/Awds:** Audi's first African-Am dealer; Bus Person of the Year, Wichita Falls Bur Com & Indust; First Fred Moses Minority Bus Develop Award, Plano Chamber Com. **Business Addr:** Chief Executive Officer, President, Stephens Automotive Group Inc, 4141 I-10 E, Baytown, TX 77521, **Business Phone:** (478)477-5123.*

STEPHENS, DOREEN Y
Marketing executive. **Personal:** Born Sep 10, 1963, Jamaica; daughter of Lolita. **Educ:** Univ Penn, BSE, chem engineering, 1985; Columbia Bus Sch, MBA, mkt, 1990. **Career:** Gen Foods, Battle Creek, MI, asst engineer, 1985-86, Cranbury, NJ, assoc engineer, 1986-88; White Plains, New York, asst prod mgr, 1990-95, sr brand mgr, 1995-97; Krafts Foods Int, coffee mkt mgr, 1997-98; Kraft Foods, Post Cereals, category bus dir, 1998-2002, vpres, post div & desserts div, 2002-03; vpres, strategy & new prods, post div, 2003; The League, vpres prog & mkt, currently. **Orgs:** National Black MBA Asn, 1990-; mentor, Black Scholars Mentor Prog, 1991-; alumni admis ambassador, Columbia Bus Sch, 1992; adv bd, Soaring Words; bd dir, In Roads Inc, Westchester, Fairfield County; bd dir, Girl Scouts Inc, Southwestern, CT. **Honors/Awds:** Dean's List, Columbia Business School, spring, 1990; Outstanding Women in Marketing & Communications, Ebony Mag, 2000. **Special Achievements:** US patent 317372, 1992. **Home Addr:** 26 Village Grn, Port Chester, NY 10573-2655. **Business Addr:** Vice President, The League, 35 James St, Newark, NJ 07102, **Business Phone:** (973)643-6373.

STEPHENS, E. DELORES B.
Educator. **Personal:** Born Nov 30, 1938, Danville, VA; daughter of Henrietta H Betts and G A Betts Sr; married Charles R, Nov 12, 1960; children: Chandra R & Charlita R. **Educ:** Spelman Col, BA, 1961; Atlanta Univ, MA, 1962; Emory Univ, PhD, 1976; Univ London, cert; Univ Exeter, Testamur. **Career:** Educator, author; Atlanta Sch Bus, instr, 1962-63; Norfolk State Univ, instr, 1963;Morehouse Col, prof, 1964-77, 1979-, Freshman Eng Prog, dir, 1984-94;Dillard Univ, assoc prof & dir, gov rel, 1977-79; USY, FORSCOM, edu spt,1980-83; St Leo Col, adj, 1987-95; Spelman Col, vis prof, 1991-94; Ind -Purdue Univ, Indianapolis, vis prof, 1994-95; Morehouse Col, Dept Eng, chair, prof, 1995-. Publications; "The Undergraduate English Major", co author; "A Tribute In Praise of Our Teachers"; "Evocations & Provocations : States of minds on Flags". **Orgs:** Col Lang Assn, 1975-; Int Eng Honor Soc, 1976-; Natl Coun Teachers Eng, 1984-; Upsilon Nu Chapter sponsor, 1985-; Natl Honors Coun, 1988-, teaching & learning comt, 1990-93, planning comt; Morehouse Brd Trustees; Links Inc,Magnolia Chapter, 1991-; S Atlantic Modern Lang Assn, 1994-; Assn Study Afro-Am Life & Hist, 1994-; Georgia Assn Women Educ, 1995-; Sigma Tau Delta; Assn Depts Eng. **Honors/Awds:** Educator of the Year, Alpha Psi Alpha, Alpha Rho, 1976; Mayoral Award,City of New Orleans, 1979; Service Award, Morehouse Prospective Studs Sem,1989; Service Award, Univ Ga Student Affairs, Parents Assn, 1989; Honorary mem, Gold Key

Soc, 1991; Phi Beta Kappa Soc, 1994. **Home Addr:** 1369 Cascade Falls Dr SW, Atlanta, GA 30311. **Business Addr:** Professor, Morehouse College, Department of English, 830 Westview Dr SW Brawley Hall 110, Atlanta, GA 30314, **Business Phone:** (404)681-2800.

STEPHENS, JAMAIN
Football player. **Personal:** Born Jan 9, 1974, Lumberton, NC. **Educ:** NC A&T Univ. **Career:** Football player (retired); Pittsburgh Steelers, tackle, 1997-98; Cincinnati Bengals, 1999-2002. *

STEPHENS, JOE. See STEPHENS, JOSEPH.

STEPHENS, JOSEPH (JOE STEPHENS)
Basketball player, real estate agent. **Personal:** Born Jan 28, 1973, Riverside, CA; son of Joseph and Cheryl. **Educ:** Univ Ark, Little Rock, attended. **Career:** Houston Rockets, forward, 1996-98; Vancouver Grizzlies, 1999-2000; B4 Development & Services LLC, prin, currently. **Business Phone:** (713)222-0080.

STEPHENS, REV. SHAHEERAH
Religious educator. **Career:** Transforming Love Community, founding pastor, currently. **Special Achievements:** Authored The Wealth Of a Spiritual Woman. **Business Addr:** Founding Pastor, Transforming Love Community, 15400 Plymouth Rd, Detroit, MI 48227-2006, **Business Phone:** (313)270-2325.

STEPHENS, TREMAYNE
Football player. **Personal:** Born Apr 16, 1976, Greenville, SC. **Educ:** NC State Univ. **Career:** Football player (retired); San Diego Chargers, running back, 1998-99;Indianapolis Colts, running back, 1999-2000.

STEPHENS, WILLIAM HAYNES
Judge. **Personal:** Born Mar 2, 1935, New Orleans, LA; son of William and Myrtle; children: Michael (deceased), Stuart, Patrick. **Educ:** San Jose State Univ, San Jose, CA, BA, 1956; Univ Calif, Hastings Col Law, JD, 1967. **Career:** Judge (retired); Nat Labor Rels Bd, atty, 1968; Contra & Costa County, dep pub defender, 1968-69; Bagley/Bianchi & Sheeks, assoc atty, 1969-72; Marin County Bar Asn, dir, 1970-73; law off, William H Stephens, atty law, 1972-79; Marin County Human Rights Comn, chmn, 1977-79; Marin County Dist, dist counsel, 1977-79; Marin County Superior Ct, arbitrator, 1977-79; Calif Agr Labor Rels Bd, admin law officer, 1978-79; Munic Ct County Marin, CA, judge, 1979; Supr Ct County Marin, CA, judge, 1988. **Orgs:** Amer Heart Asn, 1985-; Calif Judges Asn; Nat Bar Asn; Am Bar Asn. *

STEPHENSON, ALLAN ANTHONY
Government official. **Personal:** Born Oct 27, 1937, New York, NY; married Deloris; children: Diane & Allan Jr. **Educ:** Morgan St Col, BA, 1960; Ny City Univ, John Jay Sch, Crim Just, post grad. **Career:** Bus Educ Training, Intgerracial Coun Bus Opport, assoc dir, 1965-66; Urban League Westchester Co, dir econ develop & employ, 1966-67, assoc exec dir, 1967-68; Assist Negro Bus, exec dir, 1968-69; US Dept Com, Off Minor Bus Enterprise, acting dir & dep dir opers, br chief, 1970-73, reg dir,1973-77; US Small Bus Admin, Baltimore Dist Off, dist dir, currently. **Orgs:** Bd mem, exec comt, NY St Coun Urban Leagues, 1967-68; secy, bd dir, Asn Assist Negro Bus, 1967-70; bd dir, Oakland Mills Youth Conf, 1975-76; adv comt, Comp Statewide Plan Vocation Rehab Serv, 1967-69; bd dir, Sr Personnel Employ Comt, 1967-69; Statewide Manpower Panel Job Train Employ, 1967-69; US Dept Com, Incent Awards Comt, 1975-77; Judo & Karate Club Baltimore; Roots Assoc Adv Comt, Comp Statewide Plan Vocat Rehab Serv, 1965; chairperson, Maryland Awards Breakfast Prog, 2007. **Honors/Awds:** Outstanding Performance Award, US Dept Com, 1974-75; Presidential Citation, 1975. **Military Serv:** AUS, res, 1964-67; NYNG, 1961-64. **Business Addr:** District Director, US Small Business Administration, Baltimore District Office, 10 S Howard St Suite 6220, Baltimore, MD 21201.

STEPHENSON, CHARLES E, III
Executive. **Career:** Stepco SC Inc, Columbia, ceo, currently. **Business Addr:** Stepco of South Carolina Inc, Columbia, SC.*

STEPHENSON, DAMA F
Banker, executive. **Personal:** Born Oct 23, 1955, Kansas City, MO; daughter of Clarence R Stephenson Sr and Patricia M. **Educ:** Howard Univ, BA, 1977; George Wash Univ, MBA, 1981. **Career:** US Dept State, Agency for Int Develop, foreign affairs specialist, 1979-80; US Dept Com, Int Trade ADM, trade asst, 1980; CoreStates, Philadelphia Nat Bank, asst vpres, 1981-90; Com Bank Kans City NA, vpres, 1990; State Street Corp, vpres; Wachovia Corp, managing dir sales, 2005-. **Orgs:** Adv bd mem, Nat Black MBA Asn, 1990-; treas, Kans City 100 Most Influential Charitable Orgs, 1991-92; bd mem, Kans City Area March Dimes, 1992-; bd mem, Are You Committed Kansas City Inc, 1992-. **Honors/Awds:** Chapter Member of the Year, Nat Black MBA Asn, 1989; Outstanding Business & Professional Award, Dollars & Sense Mag, 1991. **Business Addr:** Vice President, Wachovia Corporation, 1 Wachovia Center, Charlotte, NC 28288, **Business Phone:** (704)374-6565.

STEPHENSON, DWIGHT EUGENE
Football player. **Personal:** Born Nov 20, 1957, Murfreesboro, NC; married Dinah; children: Dwight Jr. **Educ:** Univ Ala. **Career:** Football player (retired); Miami Dolphins, ctr, 1980-87. **Orgs:** Charity work, Baby House & Boy Scouts, S Fla. **Honors/Awds:** Man of the Year; Offensive Lineman of the Year, Natl Football League Players Assn, 1983-87; USA Today NFL Offensive Lineman of the Year; Silver Medal Valor, Miami-Dade Police Dept, 1984; Walter Payton Man of the Year Award; Walter Camp Man of the Year, 2005. **Special Achievements:** Inducted into the Virginia Sports Hall of fame, 1999.

STEPP, MARC
Association executive, vice president (organization). **Personal:** Born Jan 31, 1923, Versailles, KY; married Elanor. **Educ:** Wolverine Trade Sch, 1949; Lewis Bus Sch, 1951; Univ Detroit, BBA, 1963. **Career:** Association executive, vice president (retired); Chrysler, Highland Park, shop committeeman, chief steward, Chrysler-UAW Nat Negotiating Comt, vpres; Int Union, vpres; UAW Int, Region 1b, asst dir, UAW Region 1b, int rep, 1967-73, asst regional dir, 1973-74, int vpres, 1974-88; Common Pleas Ct, clerk; Community Health Asn, asst dir; Univ Detroit-Mercy, Inst Urban Community Affairs, exec dir. **Orgs:** UAW Int; exec bd dir, UAW Soc Tech Educ Prog; dir, Job Develop Training Prog; chmn, UAW SE MI Community Action Prog; Dexter Ave Baptist Church; NAACP; Trade Union Leadership Coun; Coalition Black Trade Unionists; Dem Black Caucus Steering Comt. **Honors/Awds:** Hon PhD, Lewis Col Bus, 1986, Saginaw St Univ, 1990, Univ Detroit, 1990. **Military Serv:** AUS, 1943-46.

STEPPE, CECIL H
Law enforcement officer. **Personal:** Born Jan 31, 1933, Versailles, KY; son of Esther and Grant; married Evelyn Lee Elliott; children: Gregory, Russell, Steven, Cecily & Annette. **Educ:** San Diego City Col, AA, sociol, 1961; Calif Western Univ, BA, sociol, 1964; Grossmont Col, Teaching Credential, 1972. **Career:** Law enforcement officer (retired); Grossmont Col, instr criminol dept, 1969-73; San Diego Co CA, supvr probation officer, 1968-73, dir juvenile intake, 1973-75, asst supt juvenile hall, 1975, finalization due-process syst adult inst, 1975-76; Camp W Fork, dir, 1976-77, dir adult inst, 1977-80, chief probation officer; San Diego Co, Dept Social Serv, dir, Comm Initiatives Health & Human Serv Agency, dir, Urban League, dir & chief exec officer. **Orgs:** Black Leadership Coun, 1980; co-covenor, Black Co Admin, 1980; vpres, Chief Probation Officers CA, 1983; Equal Opportunity San Diego Urban League, 1983; bd mem, Am Probation & Parole Asn, 1984; chmn, State Adv Bd, Victim/Witness Prog, 1984; bd mem, St Youth Prog; Mayors Crime Comn, Criminal Justice Coun; adv com, Interagency Youth; Nat Forum Black Pub Admin; Calif Black Correction Coalition; Am Probation & Parole Asn; Chief Probation & Parole Asn; Chief Probation Officers CA; San Diego Co Exec Asn; San Diego Rotary; Calif Welfare Dirs Asn; Am Pub Welfare Asn; Child Welfare League Am. **Honors/Awds:** Valuable Service, San Diego County Foster Parent Asn, 1984; National Probation Executive of the Year, 1989; Diegones Award, San Diego Chap Pub Rels Soc Am, 1993; Heart of San Diego, 1998. **Special Achievements:** Fred Lewis "Heart of San Diego" in August, 1998 - a cable show that regularly features prominent San Diegans, San Diego magazine's "Who's Who in 1994" as a San Diegan who would make a difference that year, San Diego Songs of My People: 100 African American Role Models. **Military Serv:** USAF, a 1/c, 1952-56.

STEPTO, ROBERT BURNS
Educator. **Personal:** Born Oct 28, 1945, Chicago, IL; son of Robert C and Anna Burns; married Michele A Leiss, Jun 21, 1967; children: Gabriel Burns & Rafael Hawkins. **Educ:** Trinity Col, Hartford Conn, BA (cum laude), eng, 1966; Stanford Univ, Calif, MA, 1968, PhD, 1974. **Career:** Williams Col, Williamstown, Mass, asst prof, 1971-74; Yale Univ, New Haven, Conn, dir undergrad studies, 1974-77, dir grad studies, 1978-81, 1985-89, Spring 1994, prof, 1984-, African American Studies, chair, 2005-08; Callaloo, assoc ed, 1984-88. **Orgs:** Chair, Comn Lits & Lang Am, Modern Lang Asn Am, 1977-78; Conn Humanities Coun, 1980-82; trustee, Trinity Col, 1982-92; Yale-New Haven Teachers Inst, advisor, 1985-; Anson Phelps Stokes Inst, advisor, 1985-; Am Lit bd eds, 1987-88; Southern Conn Lib Coun, advisor, 1987; Callaloo, 1988-; Am Studies Asn. **Honors/Awds:** Woodrow Wilson Found, Woodrow Wilson fel, 1966-67; Yale Univ, Morse fel, 1977-78; Nat Endowment Humanities, sr fel, 1981-82; Alumni Medal, Trinity Col, 1986; 175th Anniversary Alumni Award, Trinity Col, 1999. **Special Achievements:** 'From Behind the Veil: A Study of Afro-American Narrative', 1979; Edited with M Harper, 'Chant of Saints: Afro-Amer Literature, Art, Scholarship', 1979; Edited with D Fisher, 'Afro-Amer Literature: The Reconstruction of Instinction', 1979; 'The Selected Poems of Jay Wright', 1987; Contributor to the Columbia Literary History of the United States, 1987; Robert Frost, Bread Loaf School of English, 1995; Editor, 'American Literature', 'American Quarterly', 'Callaloo'; 'Blue As the Lake: A Personal Geography', 1998. **Home Phone:** (203)397-3566. **Business Addr:** Professor, African American Studies, English & American Studies, Yale University, 149 Elm St, PO Box 203388, New Haven, CT 06520-3388, **Business Phone:** (203)432-1170.

STEPTOE, JAVAKA
Artist, designer, illustrator. **Personal:** Born Apr 19, 1971, New York, NY; son of John and Stephanie Douglas. **Educ:** Cooper Union Advan Sci & Art, BA, fine arts, 1995. **Career:** Artist, currently; Book: Do You Know What I'll Do, 2000; A Pocket Full of Poems, 2001; Original Art Work Show, Soc Illustrators, 2001; Swan Lake Projects; Hot Day on Abbott Avenue, 2004; Scream; The Jones Family Express, 2003; My Sweet Baby, 2004; In Daddy's Arms I Am Talll; In Praise of Our Fathers & Mothers; designer, currently. **Orgs:** Am Libr Asn; Int Reading Asn; Reading Fundamental Inc. **Honors/Awds:** Coretta Scott King Award, Am Libr Asn, 1998; Image Award, Nat Asn Advan Colored People, 1998; Honor for "In Daddy's Arms I am Tall", Brooklyn Pub Libr, 1998; Excellence in Children's Books, Blue Bonnet, 1998. **Special Achievements:** Original Art Work show, Society of Illustrators, 1998, City Scape Mural, Helena Robinstein Literacy Center at Childrens Museum of Manhattan, 1989, Legends, Folklore and real Life Stories (group Art exhibit), Art Institute of Chicago, 2000, Children's book art from In Daddy's Arms I am Tall (exhibit), Memorial Art Gallery, 2000, Kuba Cloth design for Congo exhibit, Bronx Zoo. **Business Addr:** Artist, Designer, PO Box 330170, Brooklyn, NY 11233-0170.

STEPTOE, SONJA
Journalist. **Personal:** Born Jun 16, 1960, Lutcher, LA; daughter of Eldridge W Steptoe Jr and Rosa Jane Jordan. **Educ:** Univ Mo, Columbia, MO, BJ, 1982, AB, 1982; Duke Univ Law Sch, Durham, NC, JD, 1985. **Career:** Dow Jones & Co, New York, NY, staff reporter, Wall Street J, 1985-90; Time Inc, New York, NY, staff writer, Sports Illustrated, 1990-96, sr ed, 1996-97; National corresp, CNNSI, 1997; TIME Mag, sr corresp, 2002-07; O?Melveny & Myers LLP, client develop mgr, 2007-. **Orgs:** Bd dirs, Associated Black Charities, New York, 1989-94; Am Bar Asn, 1986-; Pennsylvania Bar Asn, 1986-; Nat Asn Black Journalists, 1987-; bd dirs, Univ Mo Arts & Sci Alumni Asn, 1986-97. **Honors/Awds:** Harry S Truman Scholar; Truman Scholar Found, 1980. **Business Addr:** Client Development Manager, O'Melveny & Myers LLP, 400 S Hope St, Los Angeles, CA 90071, **Business Phone:** (213)430-6384.

STERLING, H. DWIGHT, SR.
Newspaper executive. **Personal:** Born Jun 7, 1944, Waco, TX; son of Lawrence Sr and Susie Lucille; divorced; children: Sherilyn L Vaughn, H Dwight Jr, Keith Morris, Dana, Shantelle. **Educ:** Merritt Col, AA, 1969; CA State Univ, BA, 1972; Univ CA Berkeley, MA, 1973. **Career:** County Alameda, regional adminr, 1974-78; City Oakland, dist coordr, 1978-86; Oakland Cancer Control Prog, pub health educator, 1986-89; Nat Univ, Urban & Regional Planning, asst prof, 1990-91; Dwight Sterling Assoc, mgt consult, 1986-; Post Newspaper, exec asst, 1992-. **Orgs:** Chair, Pan African Chamber Com, Planning Comt, 1991-92; Alpha Phi Alpha Fraternity, Gamma Phi Lambda Chapter, 1984; Seventh Step Found, 1987-90, exec dir, 1991-92; Asn Black Health Educators, 1973-92; Bay Area Black Prof Health Network, 1974; Black Pub ADR Asn, 1979; Am Pub Health Asn, 1974; Bethel Missionary Baptist Church, 1962; West Coast Black Publishers Asn, 1992; div leader, Assault on Illiteracy Process, 1993. **Honors/Awds:** Superior Accomplishment, US Defense Dept, 1968; Scholarship, US Pub Health Serv, 1972; Certificate of Appreciation, Alameda County, for training 450 mgrs mgt objectives, 1975; City Oakland Mayor Dwight Sterling Day Proclamation, 1986. **Military Serv:** USY, e-4, 1963-66; Expert Rifle, 1963, US Defense Service Medal, 1966. **Business Addr:** Executive Assistant, Publisher, Post Newspaper Group, 630 20th St, Berkley Plaza Bldg, Oakland, CA 94612, **Business Phone:** (510)465-1927.*

STERLING, DR. JEFFREY EMERY
Physician. **Personal:** Born Jan 15, 1964, Chicago, IL; son of John Estes Sterling Sr and Ollie Mae Emerson. **Educ:** Northwestern Univ, Evanston, IL, BA, psychol, 1985; Harvard Univ Sch Pub Health, Boston, MA, MPH, 1991; Univ Ill, Col Med, Peoria, IL, MD, 1991. **Career:** Boston City Hosp Corp, Boston, MA, consult Comn, 1990; Cook County Hosp, Chicago, IL, resident physician-transitional/emergency med, 1991-; pvt pract, currently. **Orgs:** Chmn, bd dir, Stud Nat Med Asn Inc, 1988-91; project mgr, Wellness Coun Greater Boston Applied Res Forum, 1989-90; pres, One Step Before Premedical Or, 1982-84; vpres, Black Stud Alliance, Northwestern Univ, 1983-84; co-founder, pres, Jr Auxiliary Hyde Park Neighborhood Club, 1981-82. **Honors/Awds:** Jeffrey E Sterling, MD, MPH Gen Endowment Fund established Stud Nat Med Asn, 1991; Elected Chmn Emer, Stud Nat Med Asn, 1991; 'President's Certificate of Appreciation', Lincoln Univ, 1990; Ill Dept Pub Health, Scholarship, IDPH, 1986-91. **Business Addr:** Physician, 500 8th Ave, Fort Worth, TX 76104, **Business Phone:** (817)885-7701.

STERLING, JOHN
Chief executive officer. **Personal:** Married; children: 2. **Educ:** Jackson State Univ, comput sci. **Career:** Kraft Foods; Sears Logistics Syst; Synch-Solutions Inc, founder & ceo, 1998-. **Orgs:** Bd trustee, The Teachers Acad Math Sci; Boy Scouts Am; Woodlawn Orgn; Chicago Pub Schs; Union League Boys & Girls Club; ceo, Nat Urban League. **Business Addr:** President, Chief Executive Officer, Synch-Solutions Inc, 211 W Wacker Dr Suite 300, Chicago, IL 60606, **Business Phone:** (312)252-3700.

ST ETIENNE, GREGORY MICHAEL
Banker. **Personal:** Born Dec 24, 1957, New Orleans, LA; son of Emanuel and Geraldine. **Educ:** Loyola Univ, BBA, 1979, MBA,

1981; Grad Sch Banking S, cert, 1988. **Career:** Laporte, Sehrt, Romig & Hand, CPA's, sr auditor, 1981-85; Liberty Bank & Trust Co, exec vpres, 1985; First Independence Bank, Detroit, vice chmn & chief exec officer, currently. **Orgs:** St Thomas, Irish Channel Consortium, 1990-; Kingsley House, 1986; secy, Nat Bankers Asn, 1991-; pres, New Orleans Urban Bankers Asn, 1992; 100 Black Men, New Orleans Chap, 1992; secy, Inst Mental Hygiene, 1994-; dir, La State Mus Ound, 1996-. **Home Addr:** 7641 Crestmont Rd, New Orleans, LA 70126, **Home Phone:** (504)244-6184. **Business Phone:** (313)256-8400.

STETSON, JEFFREY P (JEFFREY PAUL STETSON)
Educator. **Personal:** Born Jun 5, 1948, New York, NY; son of Isabella and John; married Carmen Hayward, Jun 21, 1980. **Educ:** Framingham State Col, BA, 1973; Boston Univ, MEd, 1974, ABD, 1976. **Career:** Mass State Col System, dir affirmative action & alternatives individual develop, 1974-79; Boston Univ, Whitney Young Jr fel, 1975; Univ Lovell, dir affirmative action, 1979; Calif State Univ, dean fac & staff affairs, 1979-86; Calif State Univ, actg dir pub affairs, 1986-87; Calif State Univ, dir pub affairs, 1987-. **Orgs:** Pres & bd dirs, Black Alliance Scholar & Educ, 1981-84; pres & bd dirs, Concerned Helpers Inner Comn Endeavors, 1984-; Nat Asn Advan Colored People; Urban League; Am Asn Affirmative Action; Dramatists Guild, Los Angeles Black Playwrights; Los Angeles Actor's Theatre Playwrights Lab; Writers Guild Am West. **Honors/Awds:** CHOICE Community Serv Award, 1984; Louis B Mayer Award Outstanding Achievement Playwrighting, 1985; Nat Asn Advan Colored People Theatre Image Awards, 1987; Nat Playwrights Conf, 1988; Theodore Ward Theatre Award, 1989; Production Meeting, Am Playhouse, 1989. **Special Achievements:** 6 New York Audelco Theatre nominations. **Home Addr:** 14069 Marquesas Way Apt 310-D, Marina Del Rey, CA 90292-6051. **Business Addr:** Director of Public Affairs, California State University, 1250 Bellflower Blvd, Long Beach, CA 90802, **Business Phone:** (562)985-8432.

STETSON, JEFFREY PAUL. See STETSON, JEFFREY P.

STEVENS, ALTHEA WILLIAMS
Educator. **Personal:** Born Oct 23, 1931, Norfolk, VA. **Educ:** Calif State Univ, Los Angeles, BS, 1969; Rutgers Univ, MEd, 1974; Rutgers Univ, doc Can. **Career:** Los Angeles Co Probation Dept, stat coordr, 1966-68; Camden High Sch, instr data processing, 1970-75; Montclair State Col, instr bus educ & offsys adm, 1975-78; Bergen Co Comm Col, prof bus admin, 1977-78; Western Wyoming Col, div chmn, assoc prof. **Orgs:** Consult, comp Sweet water Co, WY Planning Bd, 1978-79; gen pub mem, WY Bd Cert Pub Accts, 1980-83; Asn Comput Mgt AVA, Nat Bus Educ Asn; Wood Buffalo Environ Asn. **Honors/Awds:** Omicron Tau Theta; Delta Pi Espilon.

STEVENS, BARRINGTON (BARRY STEVENS)
Manager. **Personal:** Born Nov 16, 1961, Miami, FL; son of Barrington and Bertha Stevens; married Catherine P Stevens, Sep 8, 1990; children: Barrington III, Isaiah. **Educ:** Johnson C Smith Univ, BS, 1983. **Career:** The Kroger Co, store mgr, 1983-90; Brown & Williamson Tobacco Corp, nat accts mgr, 1990. **Orgs:** Pres, Phi Beta Sigma, 1982-83. *

STEVENS, BARRY. See STEVENS, BARRINGTON.

STEVENS, EARL. See E-40, E.

STEVENS, GEORGE EDWARD
Educator. **Personal:** Born Mar 7, 1942, Philadelphia, PA; son of George Edward Stevens and Marstella Smalls Harvey; married Pamela Ann Giffhorn, May 30, 1977; children: Kwanza B & Charlie E. **Educ:** Delaware State Univ, Dover, DE, BS, 1971; Wash Univ, St Louis, MO, MBA, 1973; Thomas A Edison Col, Princeton, NJ, BA, social sci, 1976; Kent State Univ, Kent, OH, DBA, 1979. **Career:** Xerox Corp, Rochester, NY, financial analyst, 1972; Rohm & Haas Co, Philadelphia, PA, employee rels, 1973-75; Kent State Univ, Kent, OH, instr, 1978-79; Ariz State Univ, Tempe, AZ, from asst prof to assoc prof, 1979-83; Univ Cent Fla, Orlando, FL, assoc prof, prof interim dean, 1983-90; Oakland Univ, Rochester, MI, prof & dean, 1991-95; Kent State Univ, dean, prof, 1995-. **Orgs:** Acad Mgt; Decision Sci Inst; Rotary Club Kent, OH; bd mem, Soc Advan Mgt; pres & bd mem, Kent Regional Bus Alliance; bd mem, AARP Acad Adv Coun; US Small Bus Develop Coun; pres, Mid-Continent E AACSB Deans; ed bd mem, Advan Mgt J; peer review teams, AACSB; chair, adv, Pre-Candidacy Adv; Sigma Pi Phi Fraternity; Alpha Kappa Mu; Beta Gamma Sigma; Phi Kappa Phi; Pontiac Area Urban League; Soc Human Resource Mgt. **Honors/Awds:** College of Business Researcher of the Year, Univ Cent Fla, 1986, 1989; Scroll Club (Outstanding Research), Univ Cent Fla, 1988; Quill Club, Book Authors Group, Univ Cent Fla, 1991; AARP Andrus Fund Found Grant, 1989; NAFEO Distinguished Alumni Award, 1986; Golden Key Honor Soc, Delaware State Univ Alumni Hall of Fame, 1997; Special Citation, Am Cancer Soc, Dedicated Hard Work, Doctoral Students Asn. **Special Achievements:** Author, Cases and Exercises in Human Resource Management. Plaque for Outstanding Service, Leadership and Commitment, 1999; Outstanding Initiative, 1999. **Military Serv:** AUS, Specialist 4, 1964-66; Good Conduct Medal. **Business Addr:** Dean, Kent State University, College Business Administration, PO Box 5190, Kent, OH 44242-0001, **Business Phone:** (330)672-2772.

STEVENS, JOHN THEODORE, SR.
Manager. **Personal:** Born Feb 2, 1924, Detroit, MI; son of John Arthur (deceased) and Helen Valaria White (deceased); married Jimmie Rose Phillips, Jun 21, 1951 (died 1998); children: John T Jr & Sandra J. **Educ:** Wayne State Univ, Detroit MI, attended, 1950; Univ Detroit, Detroit MI, attended, 1956; Shorter Col, Little Rock AR, DHL, 1987. **Career:** Manager (retired); Anheuser-Busch Inc, Detroit MI, br salesman, 1954-63, spec rep, 1963-66, regional rep, 1963-71, Los Angeles CA, dist mgr, 1971-81, Woodland Hills CA, Western Region, mgr spec mkt, 1981-93. **Orgs:** Alpha Phi Alpha Fraternity, 1948-, Christ Good Shepherd Episcopal Church, 1971-, LA Chap, UNCF, 1973-; bd mem, Good Shepherd Manor, 1982-95; chmn, Los Angeles Co Fire Dept, 1983-87; bd mem, Golden State Minority Found, 1986-02; Los Angeles Co Fire Dept Adv Bd, 1988-90; Prince Hall Masons, 1989-; bd trustees, St Augustine's Col; Nat Asn Advan Colored People. **Honors/Awds:** Honorary Fire Chief, Fire Dept, Compton, CA, 1987. **Special Achievements:** Author: Black Leadership in Los Angeles, 1997. **Military Serv:** USN, machinist mate 3rd class, 1943-46. **Home Addr:** 3804 Lenawee Ave, Culver City, CA 90232.

STEVENS, DR. JOYCE WEST
Educator. **Personal:** Born Mar 15, 1936, Clayton, MO; daughter of John Lawrence West and Gertrude Mitchell; divorced; children: Janet Leslie & Melinda Stevens-Ademuyiwa. **Educ:** Loyola Univ Chicago, BS, 1960, MSW, 1964, PhD, 1993. **Career:** Cook County, Dept Pub Aid, social worker, 1960-66; YWCA Chicago, Head Start, dir, 1969-71; Michael Reese Hosp, res asst, 1971-72, social worker, 1974-91; Lake Bluff Homes Children, counr, 1972-73; Univ Ill Chicago, counr, 1973-74; Coun Social Work Educ, Minority fel, 1987-89; Loyola Univ Chicago, adj prof, 1990-92; Ill Consortium Educ Opportunity, fel, 1990-93; Smith Col Sch Social Work, Bertha Reynolds fel, 1991-92, instr, 1991-92; Boston Univ, asst prof, prof emer, currently; Child & Adolescent Social Work Jour, book rev ed, 1993-. **Orgs:** Nat Asn Social Workers, 1986-; Mass Acad Clin Social Workers, 1993-; Coun Social Work Educ, 1993-; DSS, Commonwealth Boston, prof adv comm, 1994-; IRB-Family Serv Boston & Latino Health Inst, 1998-; bd mem, Boston C Servs, 1998-; bd mem, Arts Progress, 1998-. **Honors/Awds:** Scholars Award, Child Welfare League Am, 1997. **Special Achievements:** The Role of Social Work in Practice, Research, and Professional Education, Case Western Univ, 1979; The Negotiation of Adulthood Status Among a Group of African American Lower Class Pregnant and Non-Pregnant Female Adolescents, dissertation, 1993; Adolescent Development and Adolescent Pregnancy Among Late Age African American Female Adolescents, Child and Adolescent Social Work Journal, 1994; A Critique of Theories, Affilia: Journal of Women and Social Work, 1996; Opportunity, Outlook and Coping in Poor Urban African American Females, 1997; African American Female Identity Development, 1997; Opportunity Outlook and Coping in Poor Urban African American Late Age Female Adolescent Contraceptors, Smith Studies, 1997; A Question of Values in SW Practice: Working With the Strengths of Black Adolescent Females, 1998; Early Coital Behavior & Substance Use Among African American Female Adolescence, 1998; Teen Parents & Welfare Reform: Findings from a Survey of Teen Parents Affected by Living Arrangements, 2000; Published Smart & Sassy: The Strengths of Inner City Black Girls, 2001; Child Bearing Among African American Female Adolescents: Crisis Intervention: Anticipatory Functioning Related to Family Infant Separation, Perinatology. **Business Addr:** Professor Emeritus, Graduate School of Arts & Sciences, Boston University, 705 Commonwealth Ave, Boston, MA 02215, **Business Phone:** (617)353-2696.

STEVENS, K KENDALL. See MATHEWS, DR. K KENDALL.

STEVENS, LISA MARIA
Zoo keeper, zoologist. **Personal:** Born Nov 20, 1955, Springfield, OH. **Educ:** Mich State Univ, BS, Zoology/Pre-Vet Med, 1977; AZA Sch Prof Mgt Develop Zoo & Aquarium Personnel. **Career:** Nat Zoological Park, animal keeper, 1978-81, asst cur, 1981-. **Orgs:** Potomac Valley Dressage Asn, 1981-; Am Zoo & Aquarium Asn, 1981-87, 1996-; Capital Dog Training Club, 1993-; Nat Capital Day Lilly Club, 1994-96. **Business Addr:** Associate Curator, Smithsonian, 3001 Connecticut Ave NW, Washington, DC 20008, **Business Phone:** (202)633-4800.

STEVENS, DR. MAXWELL MCDEW
Dean (Education), school administrator. **Personal:** Born Dec 3, 1942, Savannah, GA. **Educ:** St Augustine Col, BS, 1964; Atlanta Univ, MBA, 1970; Rutgers Univ, EdD, 1977. **Career:** Glenbrook Labs, chemist & group leader, 1964-68; Allied Chem Corp, mkt analyst, 1970-72; Somerset Co Col, asst dean instr; Raritan Valley Community Col, actg sr vpres acad affairs, interim sr vpres acad affairs, dean acad affairs & dir coop educ, currently. **Orgs:** Pres, Int Coop Ed Asn, 1974; pres, NJ Coop Ed Asn, 1974; adv bd, Ed Opportunity Fund Somerset County Col, 1980; pres, Am Mkt Asn; adv bd, Mid-Atlantic Training Ctr Coop Ed, Temple Univ; adv bd, Somerset Co Day Care Ctr; adv bd, Somerset County Col; serv learning adv, RVCC; NJ Coop Educ & Internship Asn. **Home Addr:** 15 Llewellyn Pl, New Brunswick, NJ 08901. **Business Addr:** Dean of Academic Affairs, Director of Cooperative Education, Raritan Valley Community College, Rte 28 & Lamington Rd, PO Box 3300, Somerville, NJ 08876, **Business Phone:** (908)526-1200 Ext 8804.

STEVENS, MICHELLE
Journalist. **Personal:** Born Feb 20, 1951, Chicago, IL; divorced. **Educ:** Northwestern Univ, BS, jour, 1973; John Marshall Law Sch, JD, 1982. **Career:** Chicago Sun-Times, asst home ed, dep ed, editorial pages, 1983-94, ed, editorial pages, 1995-97, night news ed, 1997-98, staff reporter, currently, Sunday Commentary ed. **Business Addr:** Staff Reporter, Chicago Sun-Times, 350 N Orleans, Chicago, IL 60654, **Business Phone:** (312)321-3000.

STEVENS, PATRICIA ANN
School administrator, government official, manager. **Personal:** Married Dwight; children: Kimberly & Kenneth. **Educ:** Monroe Community Col, AAS, liberal arts, 1968; State Univ NY Brockport, BS hist/psychol, 1970, MS, 1972, MS, admin, 1979; Nat Bd Certified Counselors Inc, cert, 1984; Univ Buffalo, PhD, 1994. **Career:** Monroe Community Col, counr, 1970-76, asst dir, 1976-81, dir, 1981-89; EOC State Univ NY, Brockport, exec dir, 1989-92; Monroe County Gov, cost reduction, proj mgr, 1992; Div Temporary & Disability Assistance, dep comnr; US Dept Housing & Urban Develop, Div Community Develop, mgr, currently. **Orgs:** Genesee Settlement House Inc, 1982-; vpres, United Neighborhood Ctrs Gr Rochester, 1982-; United Way, Bd, 1994; treasr, Joe Joe While Growth League, 1994. **Honors/Awds:** Outstanding Service & Dedication Grant, Rochester Area Spec Progs, 1983; Outstanding Administration, Standing Comm Blacks Higher Educ, 1984; Distinguished Service Award, Coun EOP Dirs, 1989; Leadership Award, Educ Opportunity Ctrs Dirs Coun, 1994. **Home Addr:** 476 Wellington Ave, Rochester, NY 14619. **Business Addr:** Manager, US Department of Housing & Urban Development, Division of Community Development, 50 W Main St 8100 City Pl, Rochester, NY 14614-1308, **Business Phone:** (585)428-5325.

STEVENS, REATHA J.
Association executive. **Personal:** Born Jun 21, 1931, Quitman, GA; divorced; children: Elinda, Ronald, Lavon. **Educ:** Savannah State Univ, BS; Univ GA. **Career:** executive (retired); Family Coun Ctr Savannah, community organizer social serv visitor, 1966-69; Dept Family & C Servs, caseworker 1969-70, casework supvr, 1970-72; Wesley & Community Ctrs Savannah, exec dir, 1972-96. **Orgs:** Social Planning Steering Bd United Way Chatham Ctny 1970-; GA Asn Young C, 1974-75; Armstrong-Savannah State Col Social Work Adv Coun, 1974-75; den mother, 1964-65; bd dirs, Frank Callen Boys Club, 1965-72; treas, 1970-71; consult, Savannah Asn Blind, 1968-69, bd dirs; Chatham Counc Human Relations, 1973-74; hon mem, Barons Goodwill Rehab Club; Savannah Fed Colored Women's Club, Inc. *

STEVENS, ROCHELLE
Track and field athlete, foundation executive. **Personal:** Born Sep 8, 1966, Memphis, TN; daughter of John Holloway and Beatrice Holloway. **Educ:** Morgan State Univ, BS, 1988. **Career:** Athlete (retired); Olympic silver medalist, 1992; Olympic gold Medalist, 1996. **Orgs:** Rochelle Stevens Scholarship Fund; Rochelle Stevens Invitational Track Meet; Rochelle Stevens Sports Clinic; Rochelle Stevens Fan Club. **Honors/Awds:** Three-time Female Athlete of the Yr, Morgan State Univ, 1985-88; received key to city of Memphis; honorary black belt in tae kwon do, 1992; Honorary Ambassador of MAR; Honorary Citizen of Parades; Eleven time NCAA All AMR; NCAA Division I 400 Meter Champion; Memphis Business Jnl Top 40 Under 40, 1997; Morgan State Univ "Varsity M" Club Hall of Fame, 1997. **Home Addr:** 3107 Belgrave Dr Suite 200, Memphis, TN 38119-9143, **Home Phone:** (901)753-0661. *

STEVENS, SHARON A
Journalist. **Personal:** Born Jun 14, 1949, Chicago, IL; daughter of Clarence B and Erma. **Educ:** Northern Ill Univ, BS, Journ, 1971; Columbia Univ, NYC, Fel, 1972. **Career:** WBBM Radio Chicago IL, reporter/anchor 1971-75; NBC Radio NYC, reporter/anchor 1975-78; WGBH-TV Boston MA, news reporter 1978-82; KTVI-TV St Louis MO, news reporter/anchorwoman, educ reporter; KSDK-TV, educ reporter, currently. **Orgs:** Alpha Kappa Alpha Sor Inc, 1968-, Am Fed Radio & TV Artists, 1971-; Greater St Louis Asn Black Journalists, 1985; vp-broadcast, Nat Asn Black Journalists, currently; bd dirs, Girls Inc, 1990-; bd dirs, St Louis Journalism Review, 1989-. **Honors/Awds:** Plexiglass Award, YMCA Black Achievers Award, 1974; Recognition Cert Outstanding Young Women Am Inc, 1977; Emmy Nomination, Nat Acad TV Arts & Sci, Boston Chap, 1979, 1980; Spec Recognition Boston Mag, 1979; Black Excellence Award, Best Series TV, 1987, Political Coverage TV, 1987; "Yes I Can", outstanding journalist, St Louis Metro Sentinel Newspaper, 1990; Emmy Nomination, NATAS, 1989. **Business Addr:** Education Reporter, KSDK-TV, 1000 Market St, Saint Louis, MO 63101, **Business Phone:** (314)421-5055.

STEVENS, THOMAS LORENZO, JR.
College administrator, executive director. **Personal:** Born Apr 9, 1933, Pine Bluff, AR; married Opal D Scott. **Educ:** Univ Ark, Pine

Bluff, BS, 1954; Univ Southern Calif, Los Angeles, MBA, 1975. **Career:** College Administrator (retired), Executive Director; Los Angeles Unified Sch Dist, acct & financial mgt supvr, 1961-67, asst retirement systems mgr, 1967-69, acct adminr, 1969; Los Angeles Community Col Dist, mgr retirement serv, 1969-73, dir budget, 1973-76; Los Angeles Trade-Tech College, pres, 1976; Fed Reserve Bank, bd dir, currently. **Orgs:** Com Asn, 1975-80; Asn MBA Exec, 1975-80; bd & vpres, Western Region Coun Black Am Affairs, 1977-80; comn finance, Calif Community & Jr Col Asn,1977-80; polit action comt, Asn Calif Community Col Adminr, 1977-80; bd governors & dirs, Goodwill Indust Inc, 1978-80. **Honors/Awds:** Community Service Award, Met Coun Responsive Admin, 1976; Citation of Appreciation for Community Service, Mayor Tom Bradley, 1976; Notable American Award, Am Biographical Inst, 1976-77; Community Service Award, Assembly women Gwen Moore, 1979. **Military Serv:** USN, storekeeper 3/c, 1955-57. **Home Addr:** 6220 Buckler Ave, Los Angeles, CA 90043. **Business Addr:** Board of Director, Federal Reserve Bank, 950 S Grand Ave, Los Angeles, CA 90015, **Business Phone:** (213)683-2300.*

STEVENS, TIMOTHY S
Association executive. **Educ:** Urban & Regional Planning; Polit Sci, BA. **Career:** Association executive (Retired); Humble Oil Co, Wash, DC, dealer sales trainee, 1967-68; Juvenile Ct, probation officer, 1968; Nat Asn Advan Colored People, youth dir, 1969; Pittsburgh Br Nat Asn Advan Colored People, exec dir 1970, pres; The Black Political Empowerment Proj, founder & chmn, currently. **Orgs:** Guest, Mike Douglas Show, 1972; ASCAP; AFTRA; AGVA; secy-treas, Stebro Enter; vpres, Arkel Publ Co & Stebro Rec; bd mem, Hill Hse Asn; bd mem, Hill Dist YMCA; host radio shows, WAMO, WWSW 14k radio; Manpower Adv Coun, Allegheny Co; Mayor's Art Comt; chmn, Black Polit Empowerment Project. **Honors/Awds:** Entertainment & Community Award, Black Community Pittsburgh Clubs United, 1970; He's a Black Man Award, 1973; Whitney Young Award, Poor People's Dinner, Pittsburgh, 1974. **Business Addr:** Founder, Chairman, The Black Political Empowerment Project, c/o Hill House Asn 1835 Ctr Ave, Pittsburgh, PA 15219, **Business Phone:** (412)758-7898.

STEVENS, WARREN SHERWOOD
Automotive executive. **Personal:** Born Jul 8, 1941, Urbana, OH; married Audrey Doreen Stevens, May 30, 1965; children: Warren D, Shanee A. **Educ:** Ohio State Univ, BS, bus admin, 1978. **Career:** USAF, admin clerk, 1960-64; Juvenile Diagnostic Ctr, mail clerk, 1964-65; Western Electric Co, cable former, 1965-68 & 1971-73, tester, 1968-71, Local IBEW union steward, 1970-71, chief union steward, 1971-73; Int Harvester, employee interviewer, 1973-74, indust engr, 1974-80; St Regis Co, staff indust engr, 1981-83; Urban Univ, dir admin; City Urbana, city councilman; Baumfolder Corp, time study & methods engr, 1984-85; Williams Hardware, salesman, clerk, cashier, 1986-; Executive Fundlife Insurance Co, ins agent, 1987-89; Hoffman Wood Products, working supvr, starting 1989; Honda Am, Assoc Rels, admin staff mem, 1989-. **Orgs:** MTM Asn, 1974; coach, Urbana City Baseball Prog, 1978; Champaign Co Am Cancer Soc Bd, 1980; pres, Champaign Co Am Cancer Soc Bd 1981, 1995-; Kiwanis Club 1982; coach Urbana City Baseball pony league, 1983; coach, Urbana Baseball Boosters, 1983; coach, Urbana City Baseball pony league, 1984; adv, Pub Educ Comm Am Cancer Soc Bd; former Urbana Local Outdoor Educ Bd; former sec, Urbana Men's Progressive Club; Democratic Champaign Co Central Comm & Exec Comm; ed, Urbana Lions Club Newsletter; Am Red Cross Champaign Unit bd; Am Cancer, trustee at-large, Ohio Div, bd trustees. **Honors/Awds:** Co-Chmn, 1981 Annual Crusade Am Cancer Soc Champaign Co 1981; Tape Line Project Standard Labor Cost System St Regis Co, 1981-83, Baumfolder, 1984-85; Standard Labor Cost Savings Baumfolder 1984-85; Am Red Cross Special Citation for Exceptional Volunteer Service. **Special Achievements:** First Black Trainee & Indus Engr Int Harvester, 1974; Held highest administrative position of any Black ever Urban University. **Military Serv:** USAF, a/2c, 4 yrs. **Business Addr:** Production Associate, East Liberty Plant, Honda of America, Marysville, OH 43040.

STEVENS, YVETTE MARIE. See KHAN, CHAKA.

STEVENSON, ALEXANDRA
Tennis player. **Personal:** Born Dec 15, 1980, La Jolla, CA; daughter of Julius Erving and Samantha. **Career:** Prof tennis player, currently; US Open, 1998-2004; Wimbledon, 1999-2001; French Open, 2000-03; Australian Open, 2000-04; Cincinnati Women's Open, 2006. **Honors/Awds:** Rolex Rookie of the Year, 1999; Bronze Medal, Pan Am Games, 2000. **Business Phone:** (713)978-6453.

STEVENSON, BRYAN A
Association executive, educator. **Personal:** Born Nov 14, 1959, Milton, DE; son of Howard Carlton and Alice Gertrude. **Educ:** Eastern Col, BA, 1981; Harvard Law Sch, JD, 1985; Harvard Univ, Kennedy Sch Gov, MPP, 1985. **Career:** Ala Capital Representation Resource Ctr, exec dir, 1989-95; Equal Justice Initiative Ala, founder & exec dir, 1995-; NY Univ Sch Law, from asst prof clin law to assoc prof clin law, 1998-2002; prof clion law, 2003-. **Honors/Awds:** Genius Award, MacArthur Found; Nat Medal of Liberty, ACLU; Wisdom Award for Public Service, Am Bar Asn; Public Interest Lawyer of the Year, Nat Asn Pub Interest Lawyers, 1996; received honorary degrees from Univ Pa, Georgetown Univ, Wash Univ & Eastern Univ. **Special Achievements:** published several books and articles including, "Deliberate Indifference: Judicial Tolerance of Racial Bias in Criminal Justice," Washington and Lee Law Review, 1994. **Business Addr:** Professor of Clinical Law, New York University School of Law, 245 Sullivan St Suite 628, New York, NY 10012, **Business Phone:** (212)998-6456.

STEVENSON, GEORGE
Executive director. **Career:** Detroit Mfg Training Ctr & Tigers game, exec dir, currently. **Business Phone:** (313)867-1666.

STEVENSON, JEROME PRITCHARD, SR.
Clergy, educator. **Personal:** Born Mar 28, 1941, Birmingham, AL; son of Jimmie and Dorothy; married Ida, Jun 20, 1981; children: Melissa, Jerome Jr & Julia P. **Educ:** Highland Park Col, AS, 1971; Wayne State Univ, BS, 1973, MS, 1986; William Tyndale Col, BRE, 1993; Ashland Theol Sem, MA, 1995, DMin, 1999. **Career:** Detroit Postal Serv, letter carrier, 1966-73; Detroit Pub Schs, sci teacher, 1975-77, lead teacher, 1980-; Ford Motor Co, mgt trainee, 1977-80; Renaissance Baptist Church, pastor, 1997-. **Orgs:** Nat Asn Advan Colored People, 1964-; Am Legion, 1995-; Am Asn Christian Counselors, 1995; Baptist Coun, 1995; Am Counseling Asn, 1996; Mich Progressive Conv, 1997; VFW, 1997; Am Baptist Conv, 1997. **Honors/Awds:** Junior Achievement, Distinguished Advisor Award, 1977-78; Distinguished Service Award, 1997; Vision Award, Life Choice, 1997; Distinguished Service Award, Nat Asn Advan Colored People, 1982. **Military Serv:** AUS, spec 4, 1959-61; Soldier of Cycle, 1959. **Home Addr:** 19952 Vaughan St, Detroit, MI 48219, **Home Phone:** (313)592-0252. **Business Addr:** Pastor, Renaissance Baptist Church, 1045 E Grand Blvd, Detroit, MI 48207, **Business Phone:** (313)922-7287.

STEVENSON, LILLIAN
Nurse. **Personal:** Born Nov 27, 1922, Indianapolis, IN; daughter of George and Jane; divorced; children: John Austin Anthony & Phillip Kelly. **Educ:** Indiana City Hosp, Sch Nursing, 1941-44; Mdme CJ Walker Col Cosmotol, 1958; Debbie's Sch Cosmetology. **Career:** Nursing Serv, City Ambulatory Health Ctr, Neighborhood Health Care Facility, charging nurse; supvr head nurse, staff nurse; foot care specialist, manicurist. **Orgs:** Pres, Black Nurse Asn Indianapolis, 1974-77; Ind Black Bicentennial Comn, 1976; Ind Conf Women, 1976; bd mem, St Vincent dePaul Soc, 1984; co-mem, Sisters of St Joseph-Trton IN, CSJ, 1986; Nat Black Nurse Asn; instr nurse, Marion Co Gen Hosp; surg supvr nurse, St Monica's Hosp; Ladies Aux Knights, St Peter Claver Ct; #97 Ind Christ Leadershp Conf; bd mem, Indianapolis Chap Oper PUSH; Nat Coun Negro Women; bd mem, Sub Area Coun Health Syst Agency; bd mem, NE Unit Am Cancer Asn; past bd mem, Model Cities Fed Cred Union; bd mem, Hillside Cult Ctr; bd, Catholic Charities; pres, Archdiocesan Black Catholics concerned. **Honors/Awds:** Certificate of Distinction, Ind Black Assembly, 1975; Gold medal winner, Nat Knights, St Peter, Claver, 1979; Drum Major Award, ICLC, 1983; Pro Ecclesia Et Pontifice Award, Long Serv Church, 1994. **Special Achievements:** Third black graduate nurse in Indianapolis, 1944. **Home Addr:** 1818 Sheldon St, Indianapolis, IN 46218.

STEVENSON, RUSSELL A.
Educator. **Personal:** Born Feb 17, 1923, Bronx, NY; married Dora L Anderson; children: Vanessa & Melanie. **Educ:** New Eng Conservatory Music, BM, 1948; Columbia Univ, MA, 1961; Univ Mich & NY Univ attended. **Career:** Educator (retired); Bny City Dept Parks, recreation leader, 1949-56; concert pianist & accompanist, 1949-96; Copiague Pub Sch, teacher & dir music, 1956-71; prof music, 1971-96; Suffolk Co Community Col, dept head,1976-96. **Orgs:** Bd dirs, Symphony New World, 1976-; charter mem, New York State Admin Music, 1963-; adjudicator, New York Sch Music Asn; charter mem, treas, Rolling Hills PTA, 1967-70; Alpha Phi Alpha; Phi Mu Alpha; NYSSMA; SCMEA-;MENC; NAJE; Rotary Intl. **Honors/Awds:** First Black Secondary School Music Teacher, Suffolk Co; Co Hist 238 QM WWII; Solo, Boston Pops, 1949; Solo Concert, Town Hall, 1956; Concert Tour, Univ Minn, 1950-51. **Special Achievements:** Concert tour to South Korea, 1982; soloist, Stony Brook Univ orchestra, 1991; concert tour to Vietnam, 1993. **Military Serv:** AUS, s & sgt, ETO, 1943-45. *

STEWARD, DAVID L.
Businessperson. **Personal:** Born Jul 2, 1951?, Chicago, IL; son of Harold and Dorothy; married Thelma; children: 2. **Educ:** Cent Mo Univ, BS, business administration, 1974. **Career:** Wagner Electric, prod mgr, 1974-75; Mo Pac RR, sales rep, 1975-79; Federal Express, sr acct exec, 1979-84; Transp Bus Specialists, owner, 1984-93; Transp Admin Servs, owner, 1987-90; World Wide Technol, founder & chmn, 1990-; Telcobuy.com, founder & chmn, 1997-; First Banks, dir, 2000-; Centene Corp, dir, 2003-; Campaign Chair, United Way of Greater St. Louis, 2005. **Orgs:** Bd more than a dozen charitable and civic organizations including exec comt & campaign chair, United Way Greater St Louis, Mo. **Honors/Awds:** Business Person of the Year for Missouri, Small Bus Admin, 1998; Technology Entrepreneur of the Year, Ernst & Young, 1998; Small Business Hall of Fame Inductee, SBA; Business Person of the Year, St Louis Sentinel; Entrepreneur of the Year, Nat Soc Black Engrs. **Special Achievements:** Named 100 Most Influential Black Americans by Ebony; Named America's 14th-Best Entrepreneur by Success Magazine; published a book - Doing Business by the Good Book, 2004. **Business Phone:** (314)569-7000.

STEWARD, ELAINE WEDDINGTON
Executive. **Personal:** Born 1963, Flushing, NY. **Educ:** St Vincent Col St John's, BS, athletic admin, 1984; St John's Univ SchLaw, JD, 1987. **Career:** Boston Red Sox, Boston, MA, assoc coun, 1988-90, asst gen mgr, 1990, vpres & club coun, currently. **Business Addr:** Vice President, Club Counsel, Boston Red Sox, 4 Yawkey Way, Boston, MA 02215-3496, **Business Phone:** (617)267-9440.

STEWARD, EMANUEL
Sports manager, boxer. **Personal:** Born Jul 7, 1944, Vivian, WV; son of Emanuel Steward Sr and Catherine; married Marie Estelle Steel, 1964; children: Sylvia Ann & Sylvette Marie. **Educ:** Henry Ford Community Col, attended 1970. **Career:** Prof boxer; Kronk Gym, part time head coach, 1971; Detroit Edison, master electrician, 1966-72; Securities & Life Ins, salesman, 1972-76; USA Boxing, nat dir coaching, 2002; Escot Boxing Enterprises Inc, pres, 1978-; Emanuel Steward's Pl, restauranteur; Kronk Boxing Intl Inc, pres; HBO, boxing commentator, currently; premier trainer/manager in boxing, currently. **Orgs:** Life mem, NAACP; franchise holder, Little Caesar's Pizza Chain; pres,Scholar Fund C; founder, Emanuel Steward Athletic Scholar. **Honors/Awds:** One Hundred and Nineteen lbs Champion, Natl Golden Gloves, 1963; Amateur Boxing Coach of theYear, US Amateur Boxing Coaches Asn, 1977; Manager & Trainer of the Year, Boxing Writers Asn, 1980; Manager & Trainer of the Year, World Boxing Coun, 1983; Life Enrichment Award, Focus Life, 1984; SCLC Youth Development Award, 1983; champions under tutelage, Thomas Hearns-WBC Super Welterweight Champion of the World; Milton McCrory-WBC Welterweight Champion of the World; Lightweight Champion of the World, Jimmy Paul-Intl Boxing Fedn; Duane Thomas WBC Super Welterweight Champion of the World;Tony Tucker IBF Heavyweight Champion of the World; Afro-American SportsHall of Fame, 1992; Inter Nat Boxing Hall Of Fame, 1996; World Boxing Hall of Fame. **Business Addr:** Boxing Commentator, HBO, 1100 Avenue of the Americas, New York, NV 10036.

STEWARD, LOWELL C.
Real estate appraiser. **Personal:** Born Feb 25, 1919, Los Angeles, CA; married Helen Jane Ford; children: Pamela, Lowell, Jr, Shelley. **Educ:** Santa Barbara State Col, BA, 1942; Univ Calif Los Angeles, attended 1952. **Career:** Lowell Steward Assoc, real estate appraiser. **Orgs:** Sr mem, Soc Real Estate Appraisers, 1970; pres & founder, Los Angeles Chap Tuskegee Airmen, 1974; past mem, bd dir, Consolidated Realty Bd; mem bd dir, Univ Calif, Santa Barbara Alumni Asn; past pres, Tuskegee Airmen Western Region; Kappa Alpha Psi; life mem, Nat Asn Advan Colored People; nat chmn, Tuskegee Airman Scholar Fund. **Honors/Awds:** Distinguished Flying Cross Air Medal, WWII; Lifetime Achievement Award, Univ Calif Santa Barbara Alumni Asn, 2004; Congressional Gold Medal, Continental Congress, 2007. **Military Serv:** Fighter pilot 332nd fighter group WWII major. *

STEWART, ALBERT C.
Educator, college teacher. **Personal:** Born Nov 25, 1919, Detroit, MI; son of Albert Q and Jeanne B Kaiser; married Colleen M Hyland. **Educ:** Univ Chicago, BS, 1942, MS, 1949; St Louis Univ, PhD, 1951. **Career:** Sherwin-Williams Paint Co, 1943-44; St Louis Univ, instr chem, 1949-51; Knoxville Col, prof chem & physics, 1953-56; John Carroll Univ, Cleveland, OH, lectr chem, 1956-63; Union Carbide Corp, int bus mgr, 1973-77, dir sales, 1977-79, nat sales mgr, 1979-82, dir univ rels, 1982-84; Western Conn State Univ, assoc dean, prof emer, currently. **Orgs:** Oak Ridge, Tenn Town Coun, 1953-57; pres & chmn, Urban League, Cleveland/NY, 1959-69; Rotary, Cleveland/NY, 1962-69; trustee, NY Philharmonic Soc, 1975-80. **Honors/Awds:** Alumni Merit Award, St Louis Univ, 1958; Cert Merit, Soc Chem Prof, Cleveland, 1962; Alumni Citation, Univ Chicago, 1966; Am Acad Arts & Sci; Am Chem Soc. **Military Serv:** USNR, lt (JG), 1944-56. **Home Addr:** 28 Hearthstone Dr, Brookfield Center, CT 06804. *

STEWART, ALISON
Journalist, television news anchorperson. **Personal:** Born Jul 4, 1966, Glen Ridge, NJ; daughter of Joseph T Jr and Carol; married Bill Wolff, Nov 4, 2006. **Educ:** Brown Univ, BA, Eng & Am lit, 1988. **Career:** Brown Univ radio station, deejay, prog dir, 1984-88; MTV, gofer, 1988-91, reporter, 1991; CBS News, corresp; ABC News, anchor; MSNBC, day time anchor, 2003-07 t . MSNBC, "The Most with Alison Stewart", host, 2006-07; NPR, "Bryant Park Project", host, 2007-08; NBC, "Weekend Today", newsreader; MSNBC, guest anchor, currently; NBC News, con-

tribr, currently. **Honors/Awds:** Peabody Award; Emmy Award. **Special Achievements:** First African American news reporter at MTV. **Business Addr:** Guest Anchor, MSNBC TV, 1 MSNBC Pl, Secaucus, NJ 07024, **Business Phone:** (201)583-5000.

STEWART, BERNARD
Television producer. **Personal:** Born Jul 3, 1950, Birmingham, AL; married Alice Faye Carr; children: Anthony. **Educ:** Ball State Univ, Muncie, IN, BS, 1974; S Conn State Univ, New Haven, CT, MS, Urban Studies, 1977, MS, media studies, 1979. **Career:** WBZ-TV, Boston, MA, exec news producer; WTNH-TV, New Haven, CT, producer; ESPN Int Inc, dir prog planning, 1987-91, vpres programming & prod, 1991-; ESPN Asia Pac, vpres & gen mgr, currently. **Honors/Awds:** Lapides Award, Ctr Urban Studies; Outstanding Young Man of America, US Jaycees. **Special Achievements:** Two Emmy Nominations, Nat TV Acad, 1978, 1979. **Military Serv:** USAF, sgt, 1971-75. **Business Addr:** Vice President, General Manager, ESPN Asia-Pacific, 935 Middle St ESPN Plz, Bristol, CT 06010.*

STEWART, DR. BESS
Educator. **Personal:** Born in Buffalo, NY; daughter of Curtis Boyd and Margaret Boyd; married Wilbert E, Nov 28, 1957; children: Kimberleyh. **Educ:** Incarnate Word Col, BSN, 1976; Univ Tex Health Sci Ctr, Sch Nursing, San Antonio, MSN, 1978; Univ Tex, Austin, PhD, 1986. **Career:** Baptist Hosp Sch Nursing, asst prof, 1976-78; Univ Tex Health Sci Ctr, San Antonio, Sch Nursing, assoc prof, 1979-; chair nursing educ, assoc dean stud, interim dean stud, 2003-05. **Orgs:** Vice chair, Am Nurses Coun Cult Diversity, 1982-87; Am Cancer Soc, 1988-; Am Nurses Credentialing Ctr, 1991-; fel, Am Acad Nursing, 1993; pres, Asn Black Nursing Fac, 1998-2000. **Honors/Awds:** W K Kellogg Leadership for Minority Women, 1982; ANA Clara Lockwood Award, 1982-84; ANA Minority Fellowship, 1984-86; Nurse of the Year, Am Nurses Dist 8, 1991; Excellence in Education Award, Univ Tex Health Sci Ctr San Antonio, 1991; Presidential Award for Excellence in Teaching, 1993; Johnella Banks Member Achievement Award, Asn Black Nursing Fac, 2004. **Special Achievements:** Publications: "A Staff Development Workshop," Journal of Staff Development, 1991, "Cultural Considerations," Psychiatric Nursing, 1991, "Cultural Diversity in Nursing, A Guide to Curriculum Development," 1986, "Role Strain, Anxiety & Depression in Black Matters," 1991, "Screening for Depression in African-American Elders," 1991. **Business Addr:** Associate Professor, University of Texas Health Science Center, School of Nursing, 4301 Broadway, San Antonio, TX 78209.

STEWART, BILL J. See STEWART, WILLIAM.

STEWART, BONITA COLEMAN
Marketing executive. **Educ:** Howard Univ, BA, jour; Harvard Bus Sch, MBA. **Career:** Nia Enterprises, co-founder, pres & chief operating officer; Chrysler Corp, dir; Dodge Car, Mkt Plans DaimlerChrysler, dir; IBM, exec mkt; DaimlerChrysler, Chrysler Brand Communs, mkt; Chrysler Group Interactive Communs, dir; Google Inc, vertical mkt dir automotive, 2006-. **Honors/Awds:** Outstanding Women in Marketing & Communications, Ebony, 2003. **Special Achievements:** Speaker, numerous mkt & interactive conf: iMedia, eTail, AD:TECH & Automotive CRM Roundtable; featured in various magazines including Automotive News, Brandweek, USA Today & Leaders Mag. **Business Addr:** Vertical Market Director, Automotive, Google Inc, 2000 Town Ctr Dr, Southfield, MI 48075, **Business Phone:** (248)351-6220.

STEWART, BRITTANICA
Business owner, beautician. **Personal:** Born Sep 16, 1950, Atlanta, GA; daughter of James and Bessie Gordon (deceased). **Educ:** Ophelia DeVore Sch Beauty & Charm, 1976; Int Mannequin Sch Models, 1978; Robert Fiance Sch Beauty, beauty salon hair stylist, 1983. **Career:** Ophelia DeVore School Beauty & Charm, teacher models, 1971-76; independent fashion model, 1975-82; Black Hair Is, asst mgr & fashion coordr, 1984-86; Brittanica & ASC, pres, 1986-; Bronner Bros Beauty & Brittanica Hair Studio, producer, summer fashion show, 1989-. **Orgs:** NY Ker Club, 1990. **Honors/Awds:** Award of Appreciation for Outstanding Achievement, Hal Jackson's Talented Teens, 1987, 1988; Award of Gratitude for Assistance, Arms Around Harlem Homeless, 1992; certificate of appreciation, Friends Sr Citizens Springfield Gardens & St Albans, 1991. **Special Achievements:** Advisor to Vogue Magazine for hair fashion, 1989-; guest speaker on WBLS Radio for hair fashion, 1988-; guest advisor on hair fashion, Essence Mag, 1989-. **Business Addr:** President, Brittanica Hair Studio, 864 Lexington Ave 2nd Fl, New York, NY 10021, **Business Phone:** (212)879-7030.*

STEWART, CARL E.
Judge. **Personal:** Born Jan 1, 1950?, Shreveport, LA; son of Richard and Corine. **Educ:** Dillard Univ, BA, 1971; Loyola Univ, JD, 1974. **Career:** Piper & Brown, atty, 1977-78; Off Atty Gen, State La, staff atty, 1978-79; Western Dist La, Dept Justice, asst US atty, 1979-83; La State Univ, adj instr, 1982-85; Stewart & Dixon, partner, 1983-85; Caddo Parish, State La, spec asst dist atty, 1983-85; City Shreveport, asst city prosecutor, 1983-85; La Dist Ct, First Judicial Dist, judge, 1985-91; La Ct Appeal, Second Circuit, judge, 1991-94; US Circuit, judge, 1994-. **Orgs:** Am Bar Asn; Black Lawyers Asn Shreveport-Bossier; Harry Booth Chapter Am Inn Ct; La Bar Asn; La Conf Ct Appeal Judges; Nat Bar Asn; Shreveport Bar Asn; Omega Psi Phi; Sigma Pi Phi. **Honors/Awds:** Distinguished Alumnus, Dillard Univ, 1998; Award of Excellence, Omega Psi Phi, 1998. **Special Achievements:** First African-American ever to serve on the Fifth Circuit. **Military Serv:** AUS, 1974-77. **Business Addr:** Judge, US 5th Circuit Ct Appeals, US Cthouse, 300 Fannin St Suite 2299, Shreveport, LA 71101, **Business Phone:** (318)676-3765.*

STEWART, CAROLYN HOUSE
Lawyer. **Personal:** Born Nov 11, 1952, Columbia, SC; daughter of Mary Green Myers; married Delano S Stewart; children: Delsha C Stewart. **Educ:** Univ S Fla, BA, 1974; Univ SC Law Ctr, JD, 1977. **Career:** Law Stud Civil Rights Res Coun, legal intern, 1975-76; Law Inc Legal Serv to Poor, legal intern, 1976; Univ SC Law Ctr, 1st black legal writing inst, 1976-77; Jim Walter Corp, assoc litigation coun, 1977-80; State Attorneys Off Hillsborough Co, asst state atty, 1980-81; Hillsborough County Atty, asst county atty, 1985-87; Butler & Burnette, atty, 1987-89; Travelers Ins Co, staff coun, 1989-94; MacFarlane Ferguson & McMullen, partner & shareholder firm, 1994-. **Orgs:** Kappa Alpha Sorority 1972-74, 1984-98; spec consult to pres, Nat Bar Asn; asst to pres, 1979, CLE, chmn, 1980, vpres, 1983-85, Fla Chap Nat Bar Asn; bd dirs, Tampa Orgn Black Affairs, 1980; bd dirs, Hillsborough County Ment Health Asn, 1980; bd dirs, Tampa Philharmonic Soc, 1980; Greater Tampa Chap, Jack & Jill Am, Inc, 1990-; legal adv, Gamma Theta Omega Chap; pres, Gamma Theta Omega Chap Alpha Kappa Alpha Sorority, 1992-95; chmn, Int Prog Comt, 1998-2002; life mem, Greater Tampa Urban League; Citizens Adv Comt to Pres, Univ S Fla; Tampa Heights Neighborhood Revitalization Alliance; secy, Educ Advances Found, 2002-; trustee, Hillsborough County Bar Found; vpres, Zeta Upsilon Chap; Alpha int secy, 2002-; Fla Bd Bar Examiners; Am Inst Parliamentarians; Hillsborough Asn Women Lawyers; Nat Asn Advan Colored People. **Honors/Awds:** Member of the Year, Fla Chap, Nat Bar Asn, 1983; Leadership Excellence Award, Tampa Chap, Epicureans Int, 1992; Sorority of the Year, Alpha Kappa Alpha Sorority Inc, 1995; Francisco A Rodriguez Award, Edgecomb Bar Asn, 2000. **Special Achievements:** Interviewed, Ebony Mag, 1997. **Business Addr:** Shareholder, Attorney, MacFarlane Ferguson & McMullen, 1 Tampa City Ctr 201 N Franklin St Suite 2000, PO Box 1531, Tampa, FL 33602-4997, **Business Phone:** (813)273-4246.

STEWART, CHARLES J
Government official, administrator. **Personal:** Born Nov 7, 1930, Montgomery, AL; son of Roy Clinton and Helen (deceased); married Annette Stokes, Jun 14, 1986; children: Malcolm Rogers, Valarie & Ellie Rose Stewart Williams. **Educ:** Richard J Daley Col, Chicago IL, AAS Fire Sci, 1976; Southern Ill Univ, Carbondale IL, BS, fire sci, 1978. **Career:** Chicago Fire Dept, Chicago IL, firefighter, 1962-67, Engr, 1967-78, lt, 1978-79, capt, 1979-88, dep dist chief, 1988-; consult, Citywide Detective Agency, 1987-. **Orgs:** Past master, King David Lodge #100 F&AM, PHA, IL, 1951; Oper PUSH, 1971, Chicago Urban League; Nat Asn Advan Colored People, 1987; Xi Lambda Chap, Alpha Phi Alpha Inc, 1988. **Honors/Awds:** Mason of the Year, MW Prince Hall Grand Lodge, Ill, 1965; Award Recognition, Ill Coun Delibration 33 degree, 1980; Cert Achievement, Chicago Fire Dept, 1981; Distinguished Serv Award, Oper PUSH, 1988; Afro-Am Symbol Excellence, Life Ctr Church, 1988. **Military Serv:** AUS, Tec 5, 1946-48, 1948-50, 1950-51. **Home Addr:** 1700 E 56th St Suite 901, Chicago, IL 60637-1970, **Home Phone:** (312)684-9347.

STEWART, DAVID KEITH
Baseball player, executive. **Personal:** Born Feb 19, 1957, Oakland, CA. **Career:** Baseball Player (retired), executive; Los Angeles Dodgers, 1978, 1981-83; Tex Rangers, 1983-85; Philadelphia Phillies, 1985-86; Oakland Athletics, 1986-92, 1995; Toronto Blue Jays, 1993-94; Milwaukee Brewers, pitching coach, 2002; NBX, MLB analyst, currently. **Honors/Awds:** World Series Champion, 1981, 1989 & 1993; Am League All-Star Team, 1989; Babe Ruth Award, 1989; World Series MVP, 1989; Roberto Clemente Award, 1990.

STEWART, DIANA BROWN
Association executive. **Educ:** BS, bus admin; Wayne State Univ, Masters Educ Coun Prog. **Career:** Jefferson E Bus Asn, exec dir. **Orgs:** Bd Detroit Eastside Community Collab; Bd Eastside Community Policing Partnership.

STEWART, DR. DONALD MITCHELL
Chief executive officer. **Personal:** Born Jul 8, 1938, Chicago, IL; son of Elmer Stewart and Ann Stewart; married Isabel Carter Johnston; children: Jay Ashton & Carter. **Educ:** Grinnell Col, BA, 1959; Yale Univ, MA, 1962; Grad Inst Int Studies,Geneva, Switz, studies int orgn & econ, 1962; Harvard Univ Kennedy Sch Govt, MPA, 1969, DPA 1975. **Career:** Ford Found, asst rep W Africa, 1962-64, prog asst, Mid E Africa Prog,1964-66, asst rep, Cairo, 1966-67, asst rep, N Africa, 1966-68, prog officer, Mid E Africa prog, 1968-69; The Univ Pa, exec asst pres, 1970-72, dir, comn leadership sem prog, 1973-75, assoc dean fac arts & sci, dir, col gen studies, counr provost, asst prof, res assoc, dir, continuing educ sch pub & urban policy, 1975-76; Spelman Col, pres, 1976-86, pres emer, currently; Col Bd, pres, 1987-99; Carnegie Corp, spec adv pres & sr prog officer, 1999-2000; Chicago Community Trust, emrita pres & CEO, 2005; Harris sch public Policy Studies, visit prof, currently. **Orgs:** Nat Acad Pub Admin; bd dir, Grinnell Col; bd dir, Prin Ins Co Iowa; Coun Foreign Rel; dir, New York Times Co; bd dir, Campbell Soup Co, 2005. **Honors/Awds:** Ford Found Study Award, 1972-73; DHL, Whittier Col, 1992; DHL, Miami Univ, 1993; DHL, Northern Kentucky Univ, 1993; Doctor Laws, Tuskegee Univ, 1994; Doctor Laws, Fairleigh Dickinson, 1994. **Special Achievements:** Publication "The Not So Steady State of Governance in Higher Education,"Aspen Inst Humanistic Studies position paper; Setting EducationalStandards in a Democracy, Vital Speeches of the Day 60, p 331-33, Mar 15,1994; Partnerships Have Never Seemed So Crucial to Reform, Education Week,Special Report, Apr 13, 1994; Building A Shared Future Preference,Educational Record 75, p 24-25, Spring, 1994; Improving Higher EducationOutcomes, A House of Many Doors, Trusteeship, Mar/Apr 1995; The PublicInterest Considered, Liberal Education, 1995. **Home Addr:** 5555 S Everett Ave Suite 113, Chicago, IL 60637. **Business Phone:** (773)702-8400.

STEWART, DOROTHY NELL
Government official. **Personal:** Born Sep 2, 1949, Centerville, TX; daughter of Murry B. Fortson Jr and Artince Houston-Fortson; children: Aretha R Ferrell, Craig-Murry III. **Educ:** Tarrant Co Jr Col; Amber Univ. **Career:** Fort Worth Police Dept, Fort Worth, pub safety dispatcher, 1973-80; City Fort Worth Action Ctr, admin aide, 1980-82, admin asst, 1982-84, coordr, off city mgr, 1984-. **Orgs:** Am Soc Pub Adminrs; prog chairperson, 1982-83, 1984-85, secy, 1983, N Tex Conf Minority Pub Admins; vice chairperson, 1985-86, co- chairperson, 1986-87, Urban Mgt Assts N Tex; chap pub rel officer, 1986-, Nat Forum Black Admins, coun pres, 1991; Tex City Mgt Asn; pres, Nat Forum Black Pub Admin, N Tex Chap, 1991; Forum Fort Worth; bd mem, Sickle Cell Dis Asn Am/Tex Chap; Minority Leaders & Citizen's Coun, bd mem, nominations comt chair. **Business Addr:** Manager, Fort Worth City Action Center, City Mgr Off, 1000 Throckmorton St, Fort Worth, TX 76102.*

STEWART, EDWARD L
Airline executive. **Personal:** Born Sep 17, 1957, Milwaukee, WI; son of Claud and Lena; married Carolyn, Oct 22, 1983; children: Cristin & Eric. **Educ:** Univ Wis, BA, jour, 1978. **Career:** Network Affiliates Milwaukee & Oklahoma, reporter; Southwestern Bell Telephone, mgr; Am Airlines, media spokesperson; Southwest Airlines, sr dir pub rels, 1990-06; Ticketmaster, vpres corp communications, 2006-07; Fleishman-Hillard, staff, 2007-. **Orgs:** Public Relations Soc Fame; Press Club of Dallas. **Business Addr:** Manager, Fleishman-Hillard Inc, 1999 Bryan St Suite 3400, Dallas, TX 75201, **Business Phone:** (214)665-1333.

STEWART, DR. ELIZABETH PIERCE
Educator. **Personal:** Born Apr 18, 1947, Laurel, MS; married Valentine. **Educ:** Stillman Col, BS, 1970; Univ Ala, MSW, 1972; Univ Pittsburgh, PhD, socialwork, 1986. **Career:** HEW Wash, DC, mgt analyst, 1971; Crawford Co Bd Assistance Meadville PA, housing specialist, 1973; Edinboro St Col, asst prof social work, 1973, prof. **Orgs:** Pres & treas, Penn Asn Under Grad Social Work Educ, 1978-80; bd mem, Community Health Serv, 1978-82; bd mem, United Fund Crawford Co, 1979-80; pres, Martin Luther King Scholar Found, 1980-82; pres, Penn Asn Undergrad Social Work Educrs; bd mem, Erie County Mental Health Mental Retardation Adv Bd. **Honors/Awds:** Outstanding Leadership in the Social Work Prof Local Chap NASW, 1978-80; JFK NATO Ctr Award, Erie PA, 1978.

STEWART, ELLA
Educator. **Personal:** Born in Vicksburg, MS; daughter of Lee Andrew and Mary Elizabeth Young. **Educ:** Los Angeles City Col, AA, 1980; Calif State Univ, BA, 1983, MA, 1989. **Career:** Los Angeles Trade Tech Col, adj speech prof, 1992-; Martin Luther King Dispute Resolution Ctr, Los Angeles, CA, comm mediator, 1996-97; Compton Col, asst prof of speech commun, 1996-. **Orgs:** Nat Commun Asn, 1987-; Am Asn Univ Women, 1996-; Los Angeles World Affairs Coun, 1996-; Black Women's Forum; KCET Community Serv TV, 2000-. **Honors/Awds:** Outstanding Scholarship, Nat Commun Asn, 1990; Certificate of Recognition, Compton Col. **Special Achievements:** Author, "Communication Between African Amer & Korean Amer: Before and After the Los Angeles Riots," in Los Angeles Struggles Toward Multiethnic Comm, Univ of Washington Press, 1993; co-author, textbook, Communication Competence: The Communication Handbook, 1998. **Business Addr:** Assistant Professor of Speech, Compton College, Department of Humanities Arts & Communication Studies, Rm Modular P2 1111 E Artesia Blvd, Compton, CA 90221, **Business Phone:** (310)900-1600 Ext 2238.

STEWART, DR. GREGORY
Counselor, school administrator. **Personal:** Born May 28, 1958, Cincinnati, OH; son of Margaret Marie Evans and Curtis. **Educ:** Univ Cincinnati, BSW, 1981; Miami Univ, OH, MS, 1982; Ohio Univ, PhD, 1993. **Career:** Denison Univ, asst dir admis, 1982-84,

asst to dean, 1984-85; Univ Cincinnati, admis officer, 1985-86; OH Univ, Col osteop Med, asst dir admis, 1986-88; Denison Univ, assoc dean studs, 1988-89; Northern Ky Univ, Highland Heights, KY, dir admis, 1989-94; Talbert House Drug & Family Counsel Ctr, therapist, 1990; Talbert House Drug & Family Counseling Ctr, therapist 1990; Univ Akron, dir admis, 1994-, fac mem, 1997-; Univ Akron, dir admis, 1994-, fac mem, 1997-; City Cincinnati, staff; Cent State Univ, vpres enrollment mgt & stud affairs, 2006-. **Orgs:** Nat Asn Col Admis Counr, 1982-; Human Serv Adv Comt. **Honors/Awds:** Youth Leadership Award, Cincinnati Community Chest & Coun, 1976; Outstanding Service Award, Northern Ky Univ Black Fac & Staff Asn, 1992; Bridge Builder Award, 2002; Outstanding Service Award, Ctr Access &Transition, 2006. **Business Phone:** (937)376-6011.

STEWART, BISHOP IMAGENE BIGHAM
Clergy. **Personal:** Born Jan 23, 1942, Dublin, GA; daughter of Rev Bigham. **Educ:** Univ Dis, AA, 1972. **Career:** Relig Coalition Reproductive Choice, chairwoman; The Greater Pearly Gates Baptist Church, pastor; African Am Women's Clergy Asn, nat chap, founder, chief exec officer & pres, currently. **Orgs:** Founder, House Imagene. **Honors/Awds:** Living the Dream Award, 1992; Women's Leadership Awards, DC Chamber Com, 2000. **Business Addr:** Founder, Chief Executive Officer, African-American Women's Clergy Association, 214 P St NW, Washington, DC 20001, **Business Phone:** (202)518-8488.

STEWART, JACQUELINE
College teacher, writer. **Educ:** PhD. **Career:** Univ Chicago, assoc prof; Northwestern Univ, assoc prof, currently;Author: Migrating to the Movies: The Making of Black Urban Film Culture,1893-1920. **Special Achievements:** Author Of "Migrating to the Movies: Cinema and Black Urban Modernity", 2005. **Business Addr:** Associate Professor, Northwestern University, The Graduate School, 633 Clark St, Evanston, IL 60208-1113.*

STEWART, JAMES A., III
Insurance executive. **Career:** Peoples Assured Family Life Ins Co, co exec, currently. **Business Addr:** Peoples Assured Family Life Insurance Co, 886 N Farish St, Jackson, MS 39202-2899.

STEWART, DR. JAMES BENJAMIN
Educator, school administrator. **Personal:** Born Jul 18, 1947, Cleveland, OH; son of Reuben Stewart and Clora Stewart; married Dr Caryl Sheffield, Sep 28, 2001; married Sharon (divorced 2001); children: Talibah, Lorin & Jaliya. **Educ:** Rose-Hulman Inst Technol, BS, 1969; Cleveland State Univ, MA, 1971; Univ Notre Dame, PhD, 1976. **Career:** Cleveland & Elec Illuminating Co, assoc tech studies engr, 1969-74; Dyke Col, part-time instr, 1972-73; Univ Notre Dame, asst prof econ & dir black studies prog; Pa State Univ, assoc prof econ, dir black studies prog, 1984-86, dir black studies prog, 1980-90, assoc prof labor & indust rels, 1989-; vice provost educ equity, 1990-98, prof labor studies & employment relations, 1998-; consult, diversity mgt & Africana Studies prog develop, 1985-; Review Black Polit Econ, ed, 1987-95. **Orgs:** Nat Coun Black Studies, 1975-, vice chair, 1981-85, pres, 1998-2002; Delta Tau Kappa, 1979-; Omicron Delta Kappa, 1982-; Phi Delta Kappa 1988-; Nat Econ Asn, 1984-, pres, 1994. **Honors/Awds:** Outstanding Volunteer Award, Rockview State Correctional Inst, 1987; Hon Outstanding Black Delawarean, Black Studies Prog & Student Government Asn, Delaware State Col, 1985; First Humanitarian Service Award, Forum on Black Affairs, 1985; Presidential Award, Nat Coun Black Studies, 1990; Award for Outstanding Contributions to Improving Equal Opportunity, Pa State Univ, 1992. **Home Addr:** 8101 Palomino Dr, Bridgeville, PA 15017, **Home Phone:** (412)221-2141. **Business Phone:** (412)675-9187.

STEWART, JAMES OTTIS, III
Football player. **Personal:** Born Dec 27, 1971, Morristown, TN. **Educ:** Univ Tenn. **Career:** Football player (retired); Jacksonville Jaguars, running back, 1995-99; Detroit Lions, running back, 2000-03.

STEWART, JARVIS CHRISTOPHER
Executive, lobbyist. **Personal:** Born Jun 24, 1968, Houston, TX; son of Rayfield and Autrey Stewart Dunlap. **Educ:** Prairie View A&M Univ, BA, 1991. **Career:** Off Secy, Alexis Herman, Dept Labor, spec asst, 1997-98; Off Rep Harold E Ford, Jr, chief staff, 1998-99; Capitol Coalitions, partner, 1999-2001; Stewart Barnes LLP, chmn & managing partner, currently. **Orgs:** Art & Drama Therapy Inst, 2000-01; adv bd, Ronald H Brown Found, 2001; Tavis Smiley Found, 2000-01; PAC trustee, DC Chamber Com, 2001; Democratic Nat Comt, African Am Leadership Coun, 2001; Wash Nat Baseball Club LLC; Cong Black Caucus Found Corp Adv Coun; Nat Conf & Caucus on the Black Aged, MenzFit; YMCA Nat Capital Area. **Business Addr:** Chairman, Managing partner, Stewart Partners LLC, 1333 H St NW W Tower 9th Fl, Washington, DC 20005, **Business Phone:** (202)833-9400.

STEWART, JOHN B., JR.
Firefighter. **Personal:** Born May 16, 1930, Hartford, CT; son of John Sr and Mattie Baker; married Gladys Strong Stewart, Jan 27, 1950; children: Wendy, William, Donald, John, Jeffrey, Holly. **Educ:** Univ Mass, Amherst, attended 1980; Univ Conn, Hartford, BA, 1991. **Career:** Firefighter (retired); City Hartford Fire Dept, CT, fire chief, 1952-92; City Hartford, CT, spec asst city mgr, 1971-76, actg dep city mgr, 1971-76; Stewart Assoc, prin; Hartford Ct Common Coun, majority leader, 1995-99; Collin Bennett Realty, broker, 1999. **Orgs:** founding chairperson, Int Asn Black Prof Firefighters, 1969-70; Consult, Int Asn Fire Chiefs, 1980-; chmn, Chief Officers Resource Comt, 1986-; chmn, Metrop Sect, IAFC, 1987-89; chmn, Conn Career Fire Chiefs, 1990-91. **Honors/Awds:** Outstanding Civic Employee Award, Greater Hartford Jaycees; American Society and Black Students Union Award, Barbados; Outstanding Community Service Award, Kiwanis; Connecticut Fire Marshal's Association Recognition Award; Roy Wilkins Award, Nat Asn Advan Colored People; Crispus Attucks Award. **Military Serv:** USN, seaman, 1947-56. **Business Addr:** Office Broker, Collin Bennett Realty, Hartford, CT 06112.*

STEWART, JOHN OGDEN
Lawyer. **Personal:** Born Dec 19, 1935, Springfield, IL; son of Arthur and Helen; married. **Educ:** Univ Calif, AB, 1959, Sch Law, JD, 1964. **Career:** US Atomic Energy Comn, contract adminr, 1965-66; Econ Opportunity Coun, gen coun, 1968-69; US Dept Housing & Urban Develop, Housing Opportunity Div, regional dir, 1969; San Francisco Legal Assistance Found, dir, 1970-74; Bechtel Corp, chief coun, corp atty, currently. **Orgs:** Comn Bar Examiners State Bar CA; Charles Hoston Law Club; bd dirs, San Francisco Gen Hosp; Comn Disadvantaged & Law State Bar CA; Calif State Bar Asn, 1966-; judiciary comn, San Francisco Bar Asn, 1970-73; treas, RENVC Ltd, currently. **Military Serv:** USY, sp/4, 1959-61. **Business Phone:** (415)768-1234.

STEWART, DR. JOHN OTHNEIL
Educator, writer. **Personal:** Born Jan 24, 1933; son of Ernest and Irene Holder; married Sandra McDonald; children: John Malcolm, Ernest Jabali & Ruth Laini. **Educ:** Calif State Univ, Los Angeles, Calif, BA, 1960; Stanford Univ, MA 1965; Univ Iowa, MFA, 1966; Univ Calif, La, PhD, 1973. **Career:** Univ Iowa, English instr; Calif State Univ, prof; Univ Ill, prof, anthrop & writer; Ohio State Univ, prof, 1984-91; UC Davis, prof African Studies, prof emer, currently. **Orgs:** Inst for Advanced Study Princeton, 1979-80. **Honors/Awds:** Amer Anthropol Assn; Winifred Holtby Prize for Novel Royal Soc Lit London, 1972. **Special Achievements:** Author: Coolie and Creole, 1973. **Business Addr:** Professor Emeritus, African American & African Studies, UC Davis, 2143 Hart Hall, Davis, CA 95616.

STEWART, JOSEPH M.
Executive, chief executive officer, founder (originator). **Personal:** Born Dec 23, 1942, Maringouin, LA; son of Willie Sr and Stella M (Patterson); married Clara J (St Amant), 1967; children: Erick J & Kendra L. **Educ:** Southern Univ, Baton Rouge, La, BA, foods & nutrit, 1965; Southern Univ, doctorate sci; Albion Col, doctorate pub serv. **Career:** Howard Univ, Wash, DC, dir food serv, 1969-71; Wash DC Pub Schs, Wash, DC, dir food serv & state dir child nutrit, 1971-80; Kellogg Co, Battle Creek, Mich, dir child feeding prog, 1980-81, dir corp commun, 1981-85, vpres pub affairs, 1985-88, chief ethics officer & sr vpres corp affairs, 1988-97; Stewart Industries LLC, co founder & chief exec off, currently. **Orgs:** Past bd dir, Am Sch Food Serv Asn, 1971-; IFMA, Int Gold & Silver Plate Soc, 1971-; bd dir, Battle Creek Area Urban League, 1983-88; bd mem, Battle Creek Area United Way, 1985-; bd dir, PRIDE Inc, 1986-88; bd governors, Pub Affairs Coun Am, 1987-; bd mem, Nat Agr-Users Adv, 1988-, State Mich Food & Nutrit Adv, 1988-; bd trustees, Battle Creek Health System, 1988-; chair bd, Battle Creek Health System, 1991; bd trustees, Grand Valley State Univ, 1991; regional bd dirs, Mich Nat Bank, 1990; bd trustees, Second Harvest Nat Network Food Banks, 1990; bd dirs, Med Educ SAfrican Blacks, 1990; Exec Leadership Coun, 1990; Sigma Pi Phi Frat, 1992. **Honors/Awds:** IFMA Silver Plate Award, 1974; Battle Creek Area Urban League Central Region Award, Nat Urban League, 1988; Whitney M Young Jr Community Service Award, 1989. **Special Achievements:** Author of several articles including: "American School Food ServicesJournal "; "Congressional Record," 1973, 1975 & 1976; "Jet Magazine,"1974; "School Food Service Journal," 1987. **Business Addr:** Chief Executive Officer, Stewart Industries LLC, 150 McQuiston Dr, Battle Creek, MI 49015-1076, **Business Phone:** (269)660-9290.

STEWART, KEBU
Basketball player. **Personal:** Born Dec 19, 1973. **Educ:** Calif State Univ, Bakersfield. **Career:** Philadelphia 76ers, forward, 1997-88; KK Vojvodina Novi Sad, 2003-05; Pallacanestro Cantu, 2005-06; SK Knights, South Korea, 2006-07; Red Star Belgrade, 2007; Riga Barons/LMT, Latvia, 2007-08; Real GM LLC, free agent,currently. **Honors/Awds:** NBA Draft, 1997; Big West Conference Men's Basketball Player of the Year, 1994. **Business Addr:** Free Agent, RealGM LLC, 109 N Russell St Suite 2, Marion, IL 62959, **Business Phone:** (618)993-7592.

STEWART, KENNETH C.
Clergy, missionary. **Personal:** Born Sep 28, 1939, Washington, DC. **Educ:** St Joseph's Col, BA, 1964; Capuchin Sem St Anthony, attended 1968. **Career:** Nat Orgn Bar Counsel Wash, DC, dir ch vocations, 1974-; Queen Angels Retreat Ctr Saginaw, retreat tm, 1973-74; St Boniface Parish, Milwaukee, pastor, 1970-73; Francis Comm Sch, Milwaukee, adminstr pub rels, 1969-70; St Francis, St Elizabeth, Milwaukee, parish assoc, 1968-69. **Orgs:** A solemnly professed friar, St Joseph Province of the Capuchin Order, 1963; Nat Black Cath Clergy Caucus; ordained priest, 1967. **Business Addr:** Provost of St Joseph-Capuchin, 1740 Mt Elliott, Detroit, MI 48207.

STEWART, KORDELL
Football player. **Personal:** Born Oct 16, 1972, Marrero, LA. **Educ:** Univ Colo. **Career:** Football player (retired); Pittsburgh Steelers, quarterback, 1995-2002; Chicago Bears, 2003; Baltimore Ravens, quarterback, 2004-05. **Honors/Awds:** Rookie of the Yr, Pittsburgh Steelers, 1995; Pro Bowl, alternate, 1996; All Madden Team, 1996-97; Louisiana's Most Valuable Player; New Orleans Player of the Year.

STEWART, LARRY
Basketball player. **Personal:** Born Sep 21, 1968, Philadelphia, PA. **Educ:** Coppin State Univ. **Career:** Wash Bullets, forward, 1992-95; Seattle Supersonics, 1997; Panellinious Greek League; Quimper, France, currently. **Honors/Awds:** NBA All-Rookie second team, 1992. **Business Phone:** (029)853-2580.

STEWART, LORETTA A
Secretary (Office). **Personal:** Born Jul 30, 1930, Muskogee, OK; daughter of James A Taylor and Agnes Taylor Berry; divorced; children: Arrilinda Delgoda, Darryl Delgoda, Calvin, Kevin & Shelia Jordan. **Educ:** Detroit Bus Inst, attended 1973-74; Henry Ford Community Col, attended 1975-76; Wayne State Univ, attended 1979-81. **Career:** Massey Ferguson, 1953-76; Wayne State Univ, 1975-79; Owens Corning Fiberglass, 1979-83; Stewart's Secretarial Serv, owner, 1981-82; Wendy's Franchise; Ford Elem Sch, 1984-87, ade secy; Southfield Sch Dist, substituting admin secy, currently. **Orgs:** MIC Cancer Found, bd mem; United Way; UNF; D'Accord Soc; Justice, Unity, Generosity, Serv. **Honors/Awds:** Heart of Gold Award, United Way, MIC Cancer Found, 1991; Citizen of the Week Award, WWJ News Radio 95, 1992. **Special Achievements:** Assists in fundraising for the fight against cancer. **Home Addr:** 29520 Sharon Lane, Southfield, MI 48076-5213. **Business Addr:** Substituting Administrative Secretary, Southfield School District, Southfield, MI 48034, **Business Phone:** (248)746-8588.*

STEWART, DR. MAC A.
Educator. **Personal:** Born Jul 7, 1942, Forsyth, GA; son of Zillia and Alonzo; married Ernestine Clemons; children: Bruce Kifle & Justin Che. **Educ:** Morehouse Col, BA, 1963; Atlanta Univ, MA, 1965; The Ohio State Univ, PhD, 1973. **Career:** Jasper County Training Sch, teacher/counr, 1963-64; Crispus Attucks HS, teacher, 1965-66; Morehouse Col, dir stud financial aid, 1966-70; The Ohio State Univ, asst dean, 1973-75, assoc dean, 1975-90, acting dean, 1990-91, dean, 1991-2000, vice provost, monority affairs, currently. **Orgs:** Consult, KY State Univ, 1978; mem bd dirs, Buckeye Boys Ranch, 1979-85; mem bd dirs, Bethune Ctr Unwed Mothers, 1980-83; consult, Wilberforce Univ, 1980; fac mem, Ohio Staters Inc, 1982-91; consult, The Ohio Bd Regents, 1986; consult, US Dept Educ, 1990; consult, Temple Univ, 1991; bd trustees, Columbus Acad, 1991-; consult, VA Common wealth Univ, 1992; Am Personnel Guid Asn; Am Col Personnel Asn; Nat Asn Stud Personnel Adminr; Mid-Western Asn Stud Fin Aid Adminr; Alpha Kappa Delta Nat Hon Sociol Soc; Phi Delta Kappa; Nat Hon Educ Fraternity; Phi Kappa Phi; Nat Honor Soc; Am Asn Higher Educ; bd mem, Human Subj Res Comt Children's Hosp. **Honors/Awds:** Distinguished Affirmative Action Award, The Ohio State Univ, 1984; Outstanding Alumni Award, Hubbard Sch, 1986; Distinguished Serv Award, Negro Educ Rev, 1992; Frederick D Patterson Award, United Negro Col Fund, 1992. **Home Addr:** 930 Notchbrook Dr, Delaware, OH 43015. **Business Addr:** Vice Provost, The Ohio State University, 203 Bricker Hall 190 N Oval Mall, Columbus, OH 43210, **Business Phone:** (614)292-5881.

STEWART, MAE E
City commissioner. **Personal:** Born Jun 4, 1926, Memphis, TN; daughter of John and Lilian (deceased); married Robert; children: Jacqueline, Robert Jr, Saundra & Ernest. **Career:** Cuyahan Metro Housing Aurhority, comnr, 1999-; Plain Talk Mae E Stewart, TV show, host; Government Official, Activist; E Cleveland City Comn, city comnr, pres. **Orgs:** Co-founder, Rozelle Superior Civic Asn, 1963; co-founder, E Cleveland Scholar Fund; Huron Road Hospital Asn; vpres, E Cleveland Second Ward Democrats Club; bd trustees, Ohio Munic League; exec bd, 21st Cong Dist; Nat League Cities, Human Resources Polit Comn; bd dir, E Cleveland Police Athletic League; Nat Asn Advan Colored People; Urban League; former dir, chair, Friends E Cleveland; House Com A M McGregor Retirement; NE OH Jazz Soc Inc; E Cleveland Comn Task Force; Regional Transit Authority, Redevelop Comn; Community Based Prosecution; citizens adv coun. **Honors/Awds:** East Cleveland Citizen of the Year, 1971. **Special Achievements:** First Black president, East Cleveland School District PTA, 1962; First Black woman elected to East Cleveland City Commission.

STEWART, MICHAEL (MICHAEL CURTIS YOGI STEWART)
Basketball player. **Personal:** Born Apr 24, 1975; son of Michael Stewart and Carolyn. **Educ:** Calif, attended 1997. **Career:**

Sacramento Kings, center, 1997-98; Toronto Raptors, center, 1998-02; Cleveland Cavaliers, center, 2002-04; Boston Celtics, center, 2003-04; Atlanta Hawks, 2004-05. **Honors/Awds:** Bronze medal-winning West team, 1994. *

STEWART, MICHAEL CURTIS YOGI. See STEWART, MICHAEL.

STEWART, PAUL ALLEN
Baseball player. **Personal:** Born Oct 22, 1978, Alexandria, VA. **Career:** Milwaukee Brewers, player, 1996-2002 & 2004; Red Sox, player, 2002-03; Tampa Bay Devil Rays, player, 2003-04; Pittsburgh Pirates, player, 2004.

STEWART, PAUL WILBUR
Curator, founder (originator). **Personal:** Born Dec 18, 1925, Clinton, IA; son of Eugene Joseph and Martha L Moore; married Johnnie Mae Davis, 1987; children: Mark, Tracy, Linda & Earl. **Educ:** Hampton Inst; Roosevelt Col; Moler Barber Col, cert, 1947. **Career:** Black Am W Found, curator; licensed barber, IL, WI, NY, CO; Black Am West Mus, founder, curator, currently. **Orgs:** Musician, Consult Co; Hist Rec Adv Bd Colo; established Afro-Am Bicentennial Corp Colo; Appointed Governor's Comn Highways, Bi-Ways Comt, 1989-. **Honors/Awds:** Interviewed by Denver TV & radio stations; featured in several magazines; Barney Ford Award, 1977; Black Educators United Award, 1977; George Washington Honor Medal Achievement, Valley Forge, 1985; Featured in Smithsonian Mag, (front cover), 1989. **Special Achievements:** Co-producer, documentary, "Blacks Here & Now", Educ TV, Ch 6, Denver, 1972. **Military Serv:** USN, seaman first class. **Business Addr:** Museum Founder, Curator, Black American West Museum, 3091 California St, Denver, CO 80205, **Business Phone:** (303)292-2566.

STEWART, PEARL
Journalist, educator. **Educ:** Howard Univ, BA; Am Univ, masters commun. **Career:** Oakland Tribune, ed, 1992-93; Howard Univ, ed stud newspaper, journalist-in-residence, 1994; Fla A&M Univ, jour instr; La State Univ, jour instr; Xavier Univ, jour instr; Tribune, San Francisco Chronicle, reporter; Harvard Univ Shorenstein Ctr Press, Polit & Pub Policy, fel, 1995; Univ Southern Miss, vis prof, 1995, adj prof, currently; Barry Bingham sr fel, 2006; media consult, currently. **Orgs:** Nat Asn Black Journalists; founder, chair, Black Col Commun Asn. **Honors/Awds:** Nat Achievement Award, Nat Asn Negro Bus & Prof Women, 1993. **Special Achievements:** First AFA woman editor of a US daily newspaper. Grants from the Freedom Forum to assist historically black college newspapers and journalism programs. **Business Addr:** Media Consultant, Visiting Professor, University of Southern Mississippi, School of Mass Communication and Journalism, Southern Hall 216 118 College Dr Suite 5121-0001, Hattiesburg, MS 39406-5121, **Business Phone:** (601)266-4258.

STEWART, RAYMOND C
Religious reformer. **Educ:** Cornell Univ, BS, econ & pub policy; Columbia Grad Sch Bus, MBA, 1980. **Career:** Salomon Brothers Inc, sec res analyst, 1979-83; Warren Marcus, co-mgr, 1983-; RASARA Strategies, founder & chief invest officer, 1992-. **Business Addr:** Founder, Chief Investment Officer, RASARA Strategies, 160 N State Rd, Briarcliff Manor, NY 10510-1403, **Business Phone:** (914)762-8777.

STEWART, RAYMOND C
President (Organization), executive, investment banker. **Educ:** Cornell Univ, BS, econ & pub policy; Columbia Grad Sch Bus, MBA, 1980. **Career:** Salomon Brothers Inc, sec res analyst, 1979-83; Warren Marcus, co-mgr, 1983-; RASARA Strategies, founder & chief invest officer, 1992-. **Business Addr:** Founder, Chief Investment Officer, RASARA Strategies, 160 N State Rd, Briarcliff Manor, NY 10510-1403, **Business Phone:** (914)762-8777.*

STEWART, RAYNA COTTRELL, II
Football player, football executive. **Personal:** Born Jun 18, 1973, Oklahoma City, OK; married Sonia, Dec 29, 1995; children: ShaRae, Tre, Mycah & Jadyn. **Educ:** Northern Ariz, BS, advert & bus admin, 1995; Tenn State Univ, MS, educ, admin & supvr, 2006. **Career:** Football player (retired), Football executive; Houston Oilers, defensive back, 1996; Tenn Oilers, 1997; Miami Dolphins, 1998; Jacksonville Jaguars, 1999-2000; Arena Football League, Austin Wranglers, 2003-04; Northwestern Univ, Dept Athletics, defensive grad asst, currently. **Business Phone:** (847)467-4455.

STEWART, RONALD PATRICK
Educator. **Personal:** Born Nov 14, 1942, Birmingham, AL. **Educ:** Drake Univ, BFA, 1966; OH Univ, MEd, 1968; Univ Cincinnati, MA, 1970. **Career:** Nat Teacher Corps, teacher, 1966-68; Hammond Sch City, 1968-69; Englewood Community Theatre, dir, 1969; Univ Cincinnati, instr, 1969-71; Univ Cincinnati, asst prof, 1971; Contemporary Arts Ctr, consult dir, 1974. **Orgs:** Bd & dir, Arts Coun OH River Valley; exec dir, Arts Consortium; co-convenor, Cultural Task Force Cincinnati; consult, Bicentennial Progs Queen City Met; adv comt, Beamon Hough Art Fund, Links Inc Steering Comt; Individual Artist, The Arts Coun OH River Valley; Nat Art Educ Asn; City Core Activity Comn; OH Art Educ Asn; Phi Delta Kappa. **Honors/Awds:** Numerous honors, prizes, awards, juried & invited art exhibitions.

STEWART, RUTH ANN
Manager. **Personal:** Born Apr 4, 1942, Chicago, IL; daughter of Ann M and Elmer A; married David L Lewis; children: Allegra, Jason, Allison & Eric. **Educ:** Univ Chicago, attended 1962; Wheaton Col Norton, Mass, BA, 1963; Columbia Univ, MS, 1965; Harvard Univ, attended 1974; John F Kennedy Sch Govt, attended 1987. **Career:** Philips Acad Lib, Andover, MA, 1963-64; Columbia Univ Libr, 1965-68; Macmillan Publishing Co, NYC, 1968-70; Schomburg Ctr Res Black Cult NY, 1970-80; New York Pub Libr, 1980-86; Nat Programs, Lib Cong, Wash, DC, 1986-89; Cong Res Serv, Wash, DC, 1989-95; Rutgers Univ Bloustein Sch Planning & Pub Policy, 1997-2003; New York Univ, Wagner Grad Sch Public Policy, 2003-. **Orgs:** Vis comt, Harvard Univ, 1976-88; trustee, Nat Park Found, 1978-84; Wheaton Col, 1979-99; Coun Foreign Rel, 1980-; Sch Libr & Info Sci, Univ Pittsburgh, 1988-94; Women's Foreign Policy Group, 1992-97; Lab Sch Wash, 1993-95; Studio in a School, 2000-; Berkeley Botanic Garden, 2000-; Smithsonian Inst Cooper- Hewitt Nat Design Mus, 2003-. **Home Addr:** 784 Columbus Ave Apt 10-O, New York, NY 10025.

STEWART, RYAN
Football player, radio host. **Personal:** Born Sep 30, 1973, Moncks Corner, SC. **Educ:** Ga Tech Univ. **Career:** Football Player (retired), Radio host; Detroit Lions, defensive back, 1996-2000; WQXI AM, Atlanta broadcasting studio, host, currently. **Business Phone:** (404)237-0079.

STEWART, SHANNON HAROLD
Baseball player. **Personal:** Born Feb 25, 1974, Cincinnati, OH. **Career:** Toronto Blue Jays, outfielder, 1995-2003; Minnesota Twins, 2003-06; Oakland Athletics, 2007; Toronto Blue Jays, 2008; free agent, currently. **Honors/Awds:** Playboy Playmate of the Month, 2000; Finished 4th in Am League Most Valuable Player voting, 2003.

STEWART, TYLITHA HELEN
Government official. **Personal:** Born Jul 9, 1981, Detroit, MI; daughter of Joe and Belvayona. **Educ:** Univ Mich, BA, polit sci, 2001, MBA 2006; Univ Mich Col Eng. **Career:** State Mich, policy anal, 2001-02; The Papyrus Group, ambassador emer, currently; City Detroit, Mayors Office-Strategic Mgt Ctr, proj mgr, 2002-04, strategy lead, 2005-, Tony Howard Basketball Camp, acad prog dir. **Orgs:** Detroit SNAP, 2002-; founder, Detroit Area Mentors Prog. **Honors/Awds:** Executive of the Month, City Detroit, 2002; named one of 2003 Young Leaders of the Future, Ebony, 2003. **Business Addr:** Strategy Lead, City of Detroit, Mayors Office, Mayors Office-Strategic Management Ctr, Detroit, MI 48226, **Business Phone:** (313)224-4589.

STEWART, W. DOUGLAS
Government official. **Personal:** Born Apr 8, 1938, Paterson, NJ; son of Irene Stewart; married Norma; children: Giselle. **Educ:** Fairleigh Dickinson Univ, BS, 1970. **Career:** Wend Realty, pres; NJ Bank NA, asst treas; City Paterson, dir div real estate & assessment; City Orange Township, tax assessor, dir finance dept; Atlantic City, tax assessor, currently. **Orgs:** Rotary; Jersey Ski; Int Asn Assessing Officers, NE Region Asn Assessing Officers; Soc Prof Assessors. **Honors/Awds:** Distinguished Service Award, Passaic Co Planned Parenthood, 1984; Past Officers Award, Passaic Co Child Care Coordr Agency, 1978. **Military Serv:** AUS 2 yrs. **Business Addr:** Tax Assessor, Atlantic City, 1301 Bacharach Blvd Room 606, Atlantic City, NJ 08401, **Business Phone:** (609)347-5380.

STEWART, DR. WARREN HAMPTON
Clergy. **Personal:** Born Dec 11, 1951, Independence, KS; son of Jesse Jared and Jessie Elizabeth Jenkins; married Serena Michele Wilson, Jun 18, 1977; children: Warren Hampton Jr, Matthew Christian, Jared Chamberlain, Justin Mitchell, Aaron Frederick Taylor & Jamila Imani. **Educ:** Coffeyville Community Jr Col, AA; Bishop Col, Dallas TX, BA, 1973; Union Theol Sem, New York, NY, MDiv, 1976, STM, 1977; Am Baptist Sem W, Berkeley, CA, DM, 1982; Ottawa Univ, DDiv, 1994. **Career:** Cornerstone Baptist Church, Brooklyn, NY, assoc minister, 1973-78; First Institutional Baptist Church, Phoenix, AZ, pastro, sr pastor, 1977-; Ottawa Univ, Phoenix Campus, adj prof; Fuller Theol Sem, Doctor Ministry Prog. **Orgs:** Life mem, Nat Advan Asn Colored People; evangelical bd, Nat Baptist Conv; Am Baptist Churches; Am Baptist Churches Ariz; bd mem, pres, Am Baptist Churches Pacific Southwest. **Honors/Awds:** Image Award, Nat Advan Asn Colored People; Award of Excellence in Black Church Studies, 1982; One of the ten most influential religious leaders in the Valley Phoenix, The Arizona Republic Newspaper, 1985; American Muslim Mission Award; Reverend William Hardison Memorial Award; Roy Wilkins Memorial Award, Nat Advan Asn Colored People, Maricopa County chapter; Humanitarian Award, Cent Dist Congress Christian Educ; Martin Luther King Jr Justice Award, First Int Baptist Church, 1988; Distinguished Service Award, United Nations Asn, Greater Phoenix chapter; Living Legend, Arizona Daily Star, 2002; honorary Doctor of Divinity, Ottawa Univ. **Special Achievements:** Led statewide campaign to win Martin Luther King Jr-Civil Rights Day, Arizona, 1992; Appointed Exec Sec of the Home Mission Bd of the Nat Baptist Convention, USA Inc. Auth: Interpreting God's Word in Black Preaching, Judson, 1984; established Samaritan House, emer shelter for homeless. Dr. Stewart served as the first General Chairperson for ARIZONANS FOR A MARTIN LUTHER KING, JR. STATE HOLIDAY. **Business Addr:** Senior Pastor, First Institutional Baptist Church, 1141 E Jefferson St, Phoenix, AZ 85034, **Business Phone:** (602)258-1998.

STEWART, WILLIAM (BILL J STEWART)
Executive. **Personal:** Born in Wilmington, TN. **Educ:** Tenn State Univ, BS, physics. **Career:** Apollo Programming Industries, pres & ceo, currently. **Orgs:** Glaucoma Res Found; Black Col & Universities (HBCU). **Business Addr:** President, chief executive officer, Apollo Programming Industries, 4546 El Camino Real Suite 215, Los Altos, CA 94022, **Business Phone:** (650)941-4030.

STEWART, DR. WILLIAM H.
Educator, clergy. **Personal:** Born Apr 18, 1935, Greensboro, NC; son of Harold W and Mildred Hancock; children: Candida. **Educ:** NC A&T State Univ, BS, 1960; Cent Mich Univ, MA, 1973; Blackstone Sch Law, JD, 1977; Western CO Univ, DB Adm, 1980. **Career:** Coop League USA, dir demonstration prog, 1966-69; General Elect Co Chic Blackstone Sch Law, JDago, training dir, 1969-70; City Ann Arbor, dir model cities prog, 1970-71; US Dept Housing Urban Dev, div dir, 1971-75; Exec Seminar Ctr US Civil Serv Comn, assoc dir, 1975-78; TN Valley Authority Div Energy, mgr, 1978-86; Mutual Housing Corp, exec dir, 1987-90; Knoxville Col, Div Bus & Social Sciences, dir, 1987-91; Mother Love Baptist Church, pastor, 1987-92; US Dept Energy, Southeastern Power Marketing Div, prog mgr, 1991-94; Macedonia Outreach Ministries, pres, 1994-96; Rochdale Institute, ceo, 1996-. **Orgs:** Alpha Phi Alpha Fraternity, 1959-; pres & bd dir, The Stewart-Candida Co, 1978-85; dean, Chattanooga Baptist Bible Col, 1981-84; pres & bd dir, Chattanooga Area Minority Investment Forum 1981-87; chmn & bd dir, Sun Belt Allied Industries, 1985-86; chmn, Seville-Benz Corp, 1986-93; pres, Operation PUSH, Chattanooga, TN, 1986-88. **Honors/Awds:** Youth & Commun Serv Frederick Douglass Chapter Hamilton Co 1981; Serv Award Lane Coll Jackson TN 1981; Distinguished Citizen City of Chattanooga TN 1981; Outstanding Mem Alpha Iota Alpha 1983; Distinguished Serv Sun Belt Assn Ind 1984; Humanitarian Award, Jas B Dudley High School Alumni Assn, 1988; Distinguished Service Award, Southeastern Power Admin, 1994; Doctorate of Divinity, Laurence Univ, 1968; Doctor of Laws, Buckner Univ, 1970. **Military Serv:** USY, sgt, 3 years. **Business Addr:** Pastor, New Monumental Baptist Church, 901 Woodmore Ln, Chattanooga, TN 37411-2312, **Business Phone:** (423)267-6106.

STEWART-COPES, MICHELE LYNN
Consultant, social worker. **Personal:** Born Feb 9, 1954, New Britain, CT; daughter of Charles Stewart and Bessie; married Aelix Copes, Jul 24, 1981; children: Tonya Wrice-Smith & Rashida. **Educ:** Cent Conn State Univ, BS, Eng, 1976, MS, guidance, 1980; State Conn, teacher cert, 1976; Univ Conn, MSW, 1988. **Career:** Urban League Greater Hartford, remedial teacher, 1976-78; YMCA, recruitment, placement specialist, 1978-80; Dept C & Families, social worker, 1980-83; Cath Family Servs, prog consult, 1983-87; St Francis Hosp, Teen Parent Prog, dir, 1987-94; SEET Consult, pres, 1992-; Conn State Dept Educ, educ consult, 1999-2000; Wraparound Pract Model, nat consult, currently; Vroon VanDenBerg LLP, skilled trainer, consult, therapist, currently. **Orgs:** Vpres, Coalition 100 Black Women, 1992-; Black Democratic Club, 1992-; Women League Voters, 1997-; chair, Nat Asn Advan Colored People, 1997-; bdmem, United Way, 1998-2000; bd mem, New Britain Found Pub Giving, 1999-2000. **Honors/Awds:** Outstanding Young Women of America, 1991; Women in Leadership Award, YWCA, 1995; Community Service Award, NAACP, 1995; Community Relations Award, US Dept Justice, 1995. **Special Achievements:** Congressional District 6 Advisory Council Permanent Commission on the Status of Women, 1996; Governor's Educational Improvement Panel Advisory Review Committee, 1997; Co-Author: Sexuality and Parenting Curriculum For Young Minority Fathers. **Military Serv:** First African American to be elected to the Board of Educ in New Britain, 1992-95. **Home Addr:** 281 Rocky Hill Ave, New Britain, CT 06051.

STICKNEY, JANICE L.
Consultant, pharmacologist, president (organization). **Personal:** Born Jul 21, 1941, Tallahassee, FL; daughter of William H (deceased) and Nerissa Lee (deceased). **Educ:** Oberlin Col, BA, 1962; Univ Mich, PhD, 1967. **Career:** UCSF, postdoctoral fel, 1967-68, instr, 1968-69, asst prof, 1969-72; Mich State Univ, asst prof, 1972-75, assoc prof, 1975-81, prof, 1981; GD Searle & Co, sr sci, 1981-83, assoc dir office sci affairs, 1983-87, dir dept med & scientific info, 1987-88; Brokenburr Stickney Assoc, pres, 1988-; J.L. Stickney, pres, currently. **Orgs:** Consult, FDA, 1971-80; adv coun, NIEHS, 1979-83; elected nominating comn, 1978, 1989, mem comn, 1981-84, counr 1984-87; Am Asn Advan Sci; Sigma Xi; Am Soc pharamacol & Exper therapeut; Am Heart Asn;

Int Soc cardiovasc Pharmacotherapy; Drug Info Asn; Am Med Writers Asn; AAAS; Asn Women Sci; Am Soc Clin Pharmacol & Therapeut; Drug Info Asn; Regulatory Affairs Profs Soc. **Special Achievements:** Author of many books.

STICKNEY, PHYLLIS YVONNE
Actor. **Personal:** Born in Little Rock, AR; daughter of Felix and Belle. **Educ:** Univ Calif Los Angeles, attended. **Career:** Streets of Fire, 1984; Beat Street, 1984; Frederick Douglass: An Am, 1986; House Party, 1990; Jungle Fever, 1991; Talkin ' Dirty After Dark, 1991; Malcolm X, 1992; What's Love Got to Do With It, 1993; The Inkwell, 1994; Die Hard: With A Vengeance, 1995; Tendrils, 1996; How Stella Got Her Groove Back, 1998; Big Ain't Bad, 2002; See Dick Run, 2008; TV series: "The Women of Brewster Place", 1989; "New Attitude", 1990; "Clippers",1991; "The Colored Museum", 1991; "A Different World"; "The Cosby Show"; "The Late Show"; "Show time at the Apollo"; "Daddy's Girl", 1996; "Linc's", 1999-2000; Stage credits include: Death & the King's Horseman; Striver's Row; The Contract, Know Your History, 2008. **Honors/Awds:** AUDEL CO Awards for Excellence in Black Theater. 1983, 1984. **Special Achievements:** One of the first comedians of color to perform at the Juste Pour Rire Comedy Festival in Montreal; writer/Creative Consultant on the ABC short lived series New Attitude a Castle Rock production. **Business Phone:** (212)307-1882.*

STICKNEY, WILLIAM HOMER
Writer. **Personal:** Born Apr 2, 1945, Nashville, TN; son of William Homer Sr and Nerissa Lee Brokenburr; divorced 1986; children: William Homer III. **Educ:** Prairie View A&M Univ, BS, 1968. **Career:** Baylor Col Med, Houston, lab tech, 1968-69; US Dept Agri, Houston, livestock inspector, 1969; Prairie View A&M Univ, Prairie View, lab technician, 1969-70; Houston Chronicle, Houston, sportswriter, 1970-. **Orgs:** US Basketball Writers Asn, 1978-; US Track & Field Writers Asn, 1989-; US Boxing Writers Asn, 1988-; Tex Sportswriters Asn, 1974-; Heisman Trophy Award, Selection Com, 1992-. **Honors/Awds:** Asod Press Managing Ed Asn Tex, Honorable Mention Spot Sports Reporting, 1994. **Home Addr:** 2916 Meadowgrass Lane, Houston, TX 77082.

STIELL, PHELICIA D
Lawyer, government official. **Personal:** Born Jul 21, 1959, Chancellor, AL; daughter of Elnor Sconyers Hornsby; divorced; children: Justin & Brooke. **Educ:** Ala A&M Univ, BS, 1981; Miss State Univ, 1983; Univ W Fla, MPA, 1985; Fla State Univ Col Law. **Career:** Thad Green Enterprises, career counr, 1981-82; Community Coun Serv, social worker, 1982-83; Air Force Systs Command, financial mgt specialist, 1985-91; Air Force Spec Operations Command, prog mgt analyst, 1991-; Steill law firm, atty & counr law, currently. **Orgs:** Alpha Kappa Mu, Nat Hon Soc, 1979; secy, Delta Sigma Theta Serv Sorority, 1980-; Am Soc Pub Adminr, 1984-86; Nat Coalition 100 Black Women, 1994-; conv chair, Dem Black Caucus Fla, 1994-; chair, Dem Black Caucus Fla Conv, 1994; DOD Exec Leadership Develop, 1995. **Honors/Awds:** Student Member Award, Inns Ct; Acad Scholar, Ala A&M Univ, 1977; Acad Fel, Miss State Univ, 1983; Management Intern Award, Off Personnel Mgt, 1985; Outstanding Business & Professional Award, Dollars & Sense Mag, 1992. **Business Addr:** Attorney, Counselor at Law, The Steill Law Firm, 1331 E Lafayette St Suite E, Tallahassee, FL 32301, **Business Phone:** (850)877-3529.

STILL, ART BARRY
Football player. **Personal:** Born Dec 5, 1955, Camden, NJ. **Educ:** Univ Ky, BA, 1978. **Career:** Football player (retired); Kans City Chiefs, defensive end, 1978-87; Buffalo Bills, defensive end, 1988-89. **Honors/Awds:** Most Valuable Player, 1980 & 1984; South eastern Conference Player of the Year, Univ Ky.

STILL, BRYAN ANDREI
Football player. **Personal:** Born Jun 3, 1974, Newport News, VA. **Educ:** Va Tech Univ, BS, commun. **Career:** Football player (retied); Gym coach; San Diego Chargers, wide receiver, 1996-99; Atlanta Falcons, 1999; Dallas Cowboys, 1999; coach, Gym class, Cosby High Sch, currently.

STILL, VALERIE
Basketball player, basketball coach, musician. **Personal:** Born May 14, 1961; married Robert Lock (divorced 2006); children: Aaron Still Lock. **Educ:** Univ Ky. **Career:** Basketball player, basketball coach (retired); Wash Mystics, Womens Nat Basketball Asn, player, asst coach; Prof caliber jazz, pop & concert pianist; Columbus Quest, forward, 1996; Orlando Miracle, asst coach. **Orgs:** Founder, Valerie Still Found; WNBA Player's Adv Coun; founder, Valerie Still Kids Improv Prog; charter mem, Am Basketball League Women. **Honors/Awds:** MVP ABL Championship Series; Ky Athletic Hall of Fame, 1996; UK Athletics Hall of Fame, 2005. **Special Achievements:** Experienced television actress and one of Italy's most visible sports &television stars; Host of her own television show in Italy-Still Basket.

STINSON, ANDREA
Basketball player. **Personal:** Born Nov 25, 1967, Cornelius, NC. **Educ:** NC State, 1991. **Career:** Basketball player (retired); Tarbes GB, france, 1992-94; Lavezzini Parma, Italy, 1994-95; Ahena Cesena, Italy, 1995-96; Thiene, Italy, 1996-97; Charlotte Sting, guard, 1997-04; Galatasaray Istanbul, Turkey, 1998-01; Botassport Adana, Turkey, 2001-02; Detroit shoch, guard, 2005; Central Cabarrus High Sch, Concord, North Carolina, coach, currently. **Honors/Awds:** Bronze Medal, Pan American Games, Havana, 1991. **Special Achievements:** She was selected as the female player of the year for the North Carolina High School Athletic Association in 1986-87. *

STINSON, CONSTANCE ROBINSON
Real estate agent. **Personal:** Born in Ontario;daughter of Theodore R Robinson and Eliza Smith Robinson; married Harold N Sr, Jun 14, 1949 (died 1984); children: Dr Harold N Stinson Jr. **Educ:** Barber Scotia Col, BS, 1949; Teachers Col, Columbia Univ, MA, 1962. **Career:** Burke County, Ga Sch Sys, teacher, 1940-67; Pearl High Sch, Nashville, TN, teacher, 1964-65; Eng Workshop, Southern Univ, Baton Rouge, LA, dir NDEA, 1966; Elon Miller Realty, Tuscaloosa, AL, realtor, 1971-94; Hamner Real Estate Inc, realtor, 1996-. **Orgs:** Ala Asn Realtors; Nat Asn Realtors; Womens Coun Realtors, 1972-; elder, Brown Mem Presbyt Church, Tuscaloosa, AL, 1972-; charter mem, life mem, Million Dollar Roundtable, Tuscaloosa, AL, 1979-; assembly mission bd, Presby Chrch 1982-85; mem bd dir, Presbyt Apts Northport, AL, 1982-85; Church Vocations Ministry Unit, Presby Church, 1985-92. **Honors/Awds:** Salesperson of the Year, Tuscaloosa Bd Realtors, 1979; Salesperson of the Year, Tuscaloosa Asn Realtors, 1996. **Special Achievements:** First Afro-American Realtor in Tuscaloosa. **Home Addr:** 1313 Wakefield Dr, Tuscaloosa, AL 35405. **Business Addr:** Realtor, Hamner Real Estate Inc, 1412 Univ Blvd, Tuscaloosa, AL 35401, **Business Phone:** (205)469-3236.

STINSON, DONALD R
Artist, vice president (organization). **Personal:** Born Jan 29, 1929, Detroit, MI; married Clara Key. **Educ:** E La Jr Col, 1949; Wayne Univ, 1951; Compton Jr Col, 1962. **Career:** Golden St Life Ins Co, field rep, 1956-71; Vetinary Hosp Long Beach, pract nurse, 1955-56; City Berkeley CA, rec dir, 1949-50; Nat Conf Artists, Nat Exec Bd, second vpres, currently. **Orgs:** Bd dir, Adv Med Diag Labs La; prog dir, bd mem, Willing Worker Mentally Retarded La; exec bd, Simon Rodias Towers Watts La; bd mem, Stewart Grant AME Ch La; Out Home Care Tech Adv Comt La; bd mem, Hub City Optimist Club Compton; Art W Asn Inc; Black Art Coun; CA Caretakers Org; owner, Billees Liquor; Nat Conf Artist; Watts Fest Art Show; CA Black Craftsman Show; Black Artisits Am. **Honors/Awds:** Master Enamelist Award, MaDonna Fest; Barnsdall all City Show La; won serval awards & hon while selling for Golden St Life Inst. **Military Serv:** USAF, A & 1c 1951-54. **Home Phone:** (323)757-6004. **Business Addr:** Vice president, National Conference of Artists, 361 W 125th St, New York, NY 10027, **Business Phone:** (212)410-7892.

STINSON, JOSEPH MCLESTER
Physician, educator. **Personal:** Born Jul 27, 1939, Hartwell, GA; married Elizabeth; children: Joseph Jr, Jeffrey & Julia. **Educ:** Paine Col, BS, 1960; Meharry Med Col, MD, 1964; Hubbard Hosp, intern, 1964-65. **Career:** Harvard Med Sch, res fel physiol, 1966-68; Meharry Med Col, assoc prof physiol, 1972-74; Vanderbilt Univ, fel pulmonary dis, 1974-76; Macy Faculty fel, 1974-77; Va hosp, consult pulmonary diseases, 1976-; Meharry Med Col, assoc prof & dir pulmonary dis, 1976-81; Meharry Med Col, Dept Physiol, chmn, 1981-84, assoc prof med & physiol, 1984-. **Orgs:** Bd dirs, Tenn Lung Asn, 1976-; Tenn Thoracic Soc, secy & treasurer, 1977-; pres, Tenn Thoracic Soc, 1985-87; bd dirs, Paine Col Nat Alumni Asn, 1985-; Am Physiol Soc; Thoracic Soc Sec, St Luke Geriatric Ctr; Tenn Heart Asn; Nashville Soc Internal Med. **Honors/Awds:** Pulmonary Academy Award, Nat Heart, Lung & Blood Inst, 1977-82; Alpha Omega Alpha; Memorial Award Excellence in Teaching, Meharry Medical College, 1999. **Special Achievements:** Numerous (24) Science Publications, 1969-76. **Military Serv:** USAF, maj, 1968-72. *

STINSON, LINDA
Librarian, librarian. **Personal:** Born Sep 1, 1965, Boston, MA; daughter of James and Frances Laverne Johnston. **Educ:** Emmanuel Col, BA, 1987; Simmons Col, MLS, 1989. **Career:** Emmanuel Col, lib asst, 1983-86; Boston Pub Libr, librarian, 1987-89; Rogers & Wells, New York, NY, ref librarian, 1989-90; Forbes Mag, New York, info specialist, ref librarian, 1991. **Orgs:** Black Librarians Asn, 1989; Spec Libraries Asn, 1989-. **Special Achievements:** Author: What Is This Sadness, American Poetry Anthology, 1987. **Business Addr:** Information Specialist, Reference Librarian, Forbes Magazine, Information Center, 60 5th Ave, New York, NY 10011.

STITH, ANTOINETTE FREEMAN
Marketing executive. **Personal:** Born Aug 10, 1958, Atlanta, GA; daughter of William Anthony Freeman and Eva Mae Cobb Freman; children: Larkin Antonio & Skeeter. **Educ:** Newport News Shipbuilding Apprentice Sch, Cert, 1981; Thomas Nelson Community Col, Hampton, VA, Indust Mgt Trainee Cert, 1982, AA, bus mgt, 1990. **Career:** Capitol Bankers Life, Norfolk, VA, mkt rep, 1990-; Reliance Standard Life, Norfolk, VA, mkt rep, 1990-; Financial Security Corp Am, Maitland, FL, mkt rep, 1991-; Newport News Shipbuilding, supvr. **Orgs:** Apprentice Alumni Asn, 1981-; pub rels officer, Coalition 100 Black Women, 1985-86; licensed real estate agent, 1985-; pub rels officer, charter mem, The Peninsula Chap Newport News, Hampton, VA. **Honors/Awds:** Real Estate Sales Assoc of the Month, 5-Star Real Estate, 1987; Outstanding Am Award, Outstanding Young Am.

STITH, BRYANT LAMONICA
Basketball player, executive. **Personal:** Born Dec 10, 1970, Emporia, VA; married Barbara; children: 2. **Educ:** Univ Va, attended 1992. **Career:** Basketball player (retired); Denver Nuggets, guard, 1992-2000; Boston Celtics, 2000-01; Cleveland Cavaliers, 2001-02; Los Angeles Clippers, guard, 2002; Nat Asn Stock Car Auto Racing, mgr, currently; SCORE, Inc, founder, currently. **Orgs:** SCORE, founder, exec dir; St. Paul Col, bd trustee. **Honors/Awds:** Most Valuable Player Award, 1992; Virginia Sports Hall of Fame, 2007. **Business Phone:** (434)848-9449.

STITH, CHARLES RICHARD
Clergy, ambassador. **Personal:** Born Aug 26, 1949, St Louis, MO; married Deborah; children: Percy, Mary. **Educ:** Baker Univ, BA, 1973; Interdenominational Theol Ctr, MDiv, 1975; Harvard Univ, ThM, 1977. **Career:** Wesley United Methodist Church, Boston, MA, minister, 1977-79; Harvard Div Sch, adjunct prof; Union United Methodist Church, sr pastor, 1979-94; Orgn New Equality, pres, 1985-98; ambassador to Tanzania, 1998-01; Boston Univ, African presial Archives & Res Ctr, dir, Visiting Prof, currently. **Orgs:** Incorporator Boston Bank Com, 1984; bd mem, WCVB-TV Editorial Bd; trustee, MLK Ctr Nonviolent Social Change; dir, United Way Mass Bay, 1986; People for the Am Way, 1994-98; adv bd, Fannie Mae, 1994-96; bd mem, Fleet Incity Bank, 1995-98; Intl Finance Corps Global Bus Sch Network, 2005; The United Nations Asn Greater Boston, 2005. **Honors/Awds:** Racial Harmony Award, Black Educators Alliance MA, 1984; Frederick Douglass Award, YMCA, 1985; Ingram Memorial Award, Boston Urban Bankers Forum, 1985. Paul Revere Bowl, City Boston, 1989; Honorary DD, Baker Univ, 1991; Morehouse Col, Inductee MLK Collegium Scholars, 2004; Doctor Humane Letters, Clark Atlanta Univ, 2006; Doctor Humane Letters, Univ South Carolina, 2006. **Special Achievements:** Author, Polical Religion, Abingdon Press, 1995. **Business Phone:** (617)353-5452.*

STITH, HANA L
Educator. **Personal:** Born Aug 25, 1928, Fort Wayne, IN; daughter of Miles Bryant and Viola; married Harold, Sep 3, 1948; children: Robin S. **Educ:** Wilberforce Univ, 1947; St Francis Col, BS, 1960, MS, 1965. **Career:** Fort Wayne Community Schs, teacher, 1960-96; African/African-Am Hist Soc, pres, 1999-; African/African-Am Hist Mus, cur, 2001-. **Orgs:** Secy, Ft Wayne Redevelopment Comn, 1974-86; Ft Wayne Metropolitan Human Rels, 1986-90; secy, Ft Wayne Bd Safety, 1990-96; chairperson, Afro-Am Entrepreneurs, 1990-98; Nat Asn Advan Colored People, 1998. **Honors/Awds:** Hope Award, 2001; Fort Wayne Women's Bur, 2001. **Special Achievements:** Frist female/longest tenure in history (12 yrs) on the Ft Wayne Redevelopment Comm. **Business Addr:** Curator, African/African-American Historical Museum, 436 E Douglas Ave, Fort Wayne, IN 46802, **Business Phone:** (260)420-0765.

STITH, DR. REP. MELVIN THOMAS
Educator, school administrator. **Personal:** Born Aug 11, 1946, Portsmouth, VA; married Patricia Lynch; children: Melvin Jr, Lori & William. **Educ:** Norfolk State Univ, BA, sociol, 1968; Syracuse Univ, Sch Martin J Whitman Mgt, MBA, 1973, PhD, mkt, 1978. **Career:** Syracuse Univ, dir, MBA prog, 1976-77, Martin J Whitman Sch Mgt, dean, currrently; Univ S Fla, asst dean/asst prof, 1977-82, assoc dean/assoc prof, 1982; Fla A&M Univ, assoc prof, 1982-85; Anheuser-Busch Inc, consult, 1982-83; Drackett Co, consult, 1984; Fla State Univ, dept chair mkt, 1985-91, Col Bus, dean, 1991-2004, Jim Moran prof bus admin; bd dirs, Esmor Corp, New York; Synovous Financial Corp; Fireman's Fund Ins Co, consut; Kent Publ Co, consut; JM Family Enterprises, consut; Univ Wis, lectr; Grad Mgt Admis Coun, chair; Am Hosp Supply, consut; Glembys, consut. **Orgs:** Polemarch, Syracuse Alumni Kappa Alpha Psi Fraternity, 1976-77; polemarch, Tampa Alumni Kappa Alpha Psi Fraternity, 1981; bd dirs, Tampa Branch Urban League, 1981; consult, Mgt Horizons, 1984, Am Hosp Supply, 1985; Fla Coun Educ Mgt, 1988-; social environ comm, 21st Century Coun, Tallahassee; bd dirs, Chamber Com, Tallahassee; Fla Black Bus Investment Bd; Tallahassee State Bank, Tallahassee; JM Enterprises Youth Automotive Prog, Deerfield Beach, FL; Sprint/United Tel Fla, Altamonte Springs, FL; Palmetto Hosp Trust Serv Ltd, Columbia, SC; Asn Advan Col Sch Bus; Beta Gamma Sigma; Sigma Rho Sigma Hon Soc; Phi Kappa Phi Honor Soc. **Honors/Awds:** Presidential Leadership Award, Fla Endowment Fund; Achievement Award, Kappa Alpha Psi Fraternity, 1988; Being There Award, Division of Student Affairs, Fla State Univ, 1989, Martin Luther King Jr Distinguished Scholar Award, 1990; Black Achiever, Tallahassee Branch, Nat Asn Advan Colored People, 1989; Academy of Distinguished Alumni, Inaugural mem, Norfolk State Univ, 2008. **Special Achievements:** Author, works include: Black Versus White Leaders: A Comparative Review of the Literature, w/Charles Evans and Kathryn Bartol, 1978; "Middle

Class Values in Black & White," Personal Values and Consumer Psychology, 1984; The Black Consumer and Value Systems; major program appearances include: discussant, "Off-Price Retailers Spin the Wheel of Retailing," Mid-Atlantic Marketing Assn, Orlando, FL, 1984; "The Importance of Values to the Black Consumer," 16th Afr Heritage Conference, Tampa, FL, 1984. **Military Serv:** AUS, Mil Intelligence, capt, 1968-71. **Home Addr:** 2588 Noble Dr, Tallahassee, FL 32312-2818.

ST JOHN, CHRISTOFF. See ST JOHN, KRISTOFF.

ST JOHN, KRISTOFF (CHRISTOFF ST JOHN)
Actor. **Personal:** Born Jul 15, 1966, New York, NY; son of Christopher and Maria; married Allana Nadal (divorced); children: Lola; married Mia (divorced); children: Julian & Paris. **Career:** Films: The Champ, 1979; Pandora's Box, 2002; Carpool Guy, 2005; Spiritual Warriors, 2007; "That's My Mama", 1975; "Happy Days", 1976; "Wonder Woman", 1977; "Roots: The Next Generations", 1979; "The Bad News Bears", 1979; "Beulah Land", 1980; "Foul Play", 1981; An Innocent Love, 1982; Sister, Sister, 1982; "CBS Afternoon Playhouse", 1982; "The Cosby Show",1984; "The Atlanta Child Murders", 1985; "ABC Afterschool Specials", 1985; "Charlie & Co.", 1985; "What's Happening Now!", 1987; "A Different World", 1988; Finish Line, 1989; "Generations", 1989; "Jake & the Fat man", 1991; "The Young & the Restless", 1991-2008; "Diagnosis Murder", 1994; "Hangin' with Mr. Cooper", 1994-95; "Martin", 1996; "The Jamie Foxx Show", 1997; "Living Single", 1997; "Pensacola: Wings of Gold", 1998; "Family Matters", 1998; "Suddenly Susan", 1998; "For Your Love", 1999; "Get Real", 1999; "Arli$$", 2002. **Honors/Awds:** Numerous honors & awards including 16 nominations, 2 Daytime Emmy Awards & 8 Image Awards. **Business Addr:** Actor, c/o William Morris Agency, 151 El Camino Dr, Beverly Hills, CA 90212, **Business Phone:** (310)859-4000.*

ST JOHN, PRIMUS
Educator. **Personal:** Born Jul 21, 1939, New York, NY; son of Marcus L St John and Pearle E; married Barbara Jean Doty; children: Joy Pearle & May Ginger. **Educ:** Univ Md; Lewis & Clark Col. **Career:** Mary Holmes Jr Col, West Point, MS, teacher; Univ Utah, teacher; Portland State Univ, Portland, OR, prof Eng, 1973-; Portland Arts Comn, mem, 1979-81; Portland State Univ, Dept Eng, prof Eng, currently; educ consult. **Orgs:** Fel Nat Endowment Arts, 1970, 1974, 1982; Bd dirs, Copper Canyon Press; bd dirs, Fishtrap Found; adv bd, Oreg Heritage Asn. **Honors/Awds:** Oregon Book Award, 1991; Western States Book Award. **Special Achievements:** Author: Skins on the Earth, 1976; Love Is Not a Consolation; It Is a Light, 1982; Dreamer, 1990; The Gift of Tongues, 1996; September 11: Coast Writers Approach Ground Zero, 2002; The Poet's Child, 2002; Poetry in Motion from Coast to Coast, 2002. Co-editor: Zero Makes Me Hungry, anthology, text, 1976; Dreamer, collection of poems, 1990; From Here We Speak, Oreg St Univ, 1993; Skins on the Earth, 1978; Communion: New & Selected Poems, Copper Canyon Press, 1999. **Home Addr:** 2064 Sunray Circle, West Linn, OR 97068-4802. **Business Addr:** Professor English, Portland State University, Department of English, 485 NH, PO Box 751, Portland, OR 97207, **Business Phone:** (503)725-3578.

ST JULIEN, MARLON
Jockey. **Personal:** Born Feb 13, 1972, Lafayette, LA; married Denise; children: Jasmin. **Career:** Evangeline Downs, 1989; Delta Downs, leading rider, 1993-94; Lone Star Park, leading rider, 1997-98; three-win day, Keeneland, leading rider, 1999; Kentucky Downs, leading rider, 1999-2000; Kentucky Derby, 2000. **Honors/Awds:** Numerous honors including Won his first stakes event, 1992; Won $100,000 stakes aboard Caro's Royalty in the Grand Prairie Gold Cup, Lone Star, 1997; Won his 1000th winner, 1998; 2000 has seen him capture five stakes; the Selene Stakes (Zoftig); the Grand Prairie Turf Challenge Stakes (Four On the Floor); the Lone Star Park Turf Spring (Caro's Royalty); the Pippin Stakes (Really Polish); & the Assault Stakes (Lightening Ball). **Special Achievements:** ABC Sports celebrated Black History Month with "Raising the Roof: Seven Athletes for the 21st Century," which aired Feb 5 2000, and featured St Julien, golfer Tiger Woods, & five other athletes; First African-American jockey since 1921 to ride in the Kentucky Derby in 2000. **Business Phone:** (502)366-7460.

ST MARY, JOSEPH JEROME
Labor activist, vice president (organization). **Personal:** Born Oct 27, 1941, Lake Charles, LA; married Elaine Guillovy; children: Jennifer Ann, Lisa Rene & Joseph J. **Educ:** Sowela Technol Inst, bus, 1968; Loyola Univ, labor course, 1984. **Career:** Plasterers & Cement Mason #487, recording sec, 1962-69, fin sec & bus mgr, 1970-; Calcasieu Parish Police Jury, vpres, 1979, 1980, 1993, pres, 1981-82. **Orgs:** Exec bd, Southwest Central Trades Coun, 1974-; vpres, Southwest La Bldg Trades Coun, 1974-; fin sec, A Phillip Randolph Inst, 1974-; vpres, La AFL-CIO, 1975-. **Honors/Awds:** Outstanding Leadership, Calcasieu Parish Police Jury, 1979-86; Calcasieu Private Ind Coun JobMatch, Outstanding Contribution, 1987-89; Faithful, Devoted, Unfailing Support for the City Wide Easter Egg Hunt, The Coalition for Community Progress, 1989; 10 Yrs Dedicated & Untiring Servs, Calcasieu Parish RSVP, 1990; Dedicated & Outstanding Servs, Cal Parish Police Jury, 1992; Recognition Servs Secy-Treas, Black Caucus, 1976-82; State La Police Jury Asn, 1988-92. **Home Addr:** 2828 Hwy 14, Lake Charles, LA 70601. **Business Addr:** Police Juror, Calcasieu Parish Police Jury, 1015 Pithon St, PO Box 3287, Lake Charles, LA 70601, **Business Phone:** (337)721-3687.

STOCKARD, BETSY
Government official. **Educ:** Ill State Univ, BS, Spec Educ, 1989; Richland Community Col, Assoc Degree,1986. **Career:** Decatur Area Tech Acad, Classroom instr; Decatur City Coun, councilwoman, currently. **Orgs:** Founder, Cent Ill first violence-gang prev Agency, 1993; bd mem Women Municipal Govt; Crime and Public Safety Comt Nat League Cities. **Honors/Awds:** Bronze Level Award for Leadership Training Skills, Nat League Cities;"Woman of Excellence (Leona Bowman) Government and Politics Award",YMCA-YWCA, 2002; Illinois Woman of Achievement Award", Lt. Governor Corrine Wood, 2002. **Special Achievements:** First African American woman to serve on council. **Business Phone:** (217)875-1936.

STOCKMAN, DR. IDA J
Educator. **Personal:** Born Sep 6, 1942, Sumner, MS; daughter of Samuel Jones and Angie Burton; married George Stockman, Oct 23, 1969; children: Demress Elise & Farah Nisa. **Educ:** Jackson State Univ, Jackson, MS, BS, 1962; Univ Iowa, Iowa City, IA, MA, 1965; Pa State Univ, State Col, PA, PhD, 1971. **Career:** Jackson State Univ, Jackson, MS, instr, 1965-66; Rehab Ctr, Binghamton, NY, speech & lang pathologist, 1966-67; Howard Univ, Washington, DC, from asst prof to assoc prof, 1971-79; Kantonsspital St Gallen, St Gallen, Switzerland, res assoc, 1972-76; Ctr Appl Ling, Washington, DC, res assoc, 1980-82; Mich State Univ, East Lansing, MI, assoc prof, 1982, Col Commun Arts & Sci, Dept Audiol & Speech Sci, prof, currently; J Ling & Educ, ed bd, 1988-; Howard J Commun, Howard Univ, Washington, DC, ed bd, 1988-. **Orgs:** Phi Delta Kappa Prof Hon Soc, 1981; bd dirs, Nat Asn Black Speech, Lang & Hearing, 1989-; bd dirs, Mich Asn-Deaf, Speech & Hearing Serv, 1989-; educ stand bd, Am Speech, Lang, Hearing Asn, 1990-. **Honors/Awds:** Information Exchange Scholar, World Rehab Fund Inc, 1985; Outstanding Woman Achiever, Mich State Univ, 1986; Distinguished Faculty Award, Mich State Univ; Distinguished Faculty Awards, State Mich Gov Bd Higher Educ; Scholar-Mentor & Bill Simpkins Service Award, NBASLH; Alumnus Award, Pa State Univ Col Health & Human Develop. **Special Achievements:** Editor and writer with more than 50 publication credits, written and co-authored works in a dozen journals, including some outside the field Science, Child Development, Language and Speech, language Learning, and Education, more than a dozen book chapters, and 150 referred and invited conference presentations. **Business Addr:** Professor, Michigan State University, College of Communication Arts and Sciences, Dept Audiol & Speech Sci, 203 Oyer Clin, East Lansing, MI 48824-1220, **Business Phone:** (517)353-6764.

STOCKMAN, SHAWN PATRICK
Singer. **Personal:** Born Sep 26, 1972, Philadelphia, PA; son of Thurman Sanders and JoAnn; married Sharonda Jones, Sep 1, 2003; children: 2. **Career:** Boys II Men, singer; Albums with Boys II Men: Cooley highharmony, 1991; II, 1994; Evolution, 1997; Full Cir, 2002; Throwback Vol1, 2004; The Remedy, 2007; Mo-Town, 2007; Love 2009; Soul Chem Proj, rec label, owner. **Business Addr:** Recording Artist, c/o J Records LLC, 745 5th Ave, New York, NY 10151, **Business Phone:** (646)840-5600.*

STOCKS, ELEANOR LOUISE
Association executive, chief executive officer. **Personal:** Born May 10, 1943, Taledigga, AL; daughter of Walter Locust and Cora Locust; married James A Stocks Jr; children: Kevin & Kim. **Educ:** Cent State Univ, BS, educ, 1965; Ohio Univ, MEd, 1971; Miami Univ, 1976-78. **Career:** Dayton Pub Sch, educr, 1966-69; Ohio Univ, adminr, 1970-72; Sinclair Comm Col, assoc prof, 1973-84; Ee & Jj Enterprises, pres, 1987-; DBA Cora's Inc, pres, 1987-; Govrs Minority Bus Coun, pres, ceo, currently. **Orgs:** Vpres, Dayton Chap Jack & Jill Am, 1984; bd mem, Human Serv Adv Bd, 1985-; pres, Ohio Coun Urban League Exec, 1986-; Nat Urban League Educ Initiative Comm, 1986; Nat Asn Advan Colored People, 1986-87; pres, charter mem Black Women Prof Develop; vpres, Nat Bus League, Dayton Chap, 1988-; pres, ceo, Springfield Urban League, 1985-. **Honors/Awds:** Jennings Scholar-Outstanding Educator, 1970; Service Award Twinning Prog NCNW Dayton, 1980; Producer Around Town with the Urban League, WIZE 1985. **Military Serv:** Publication: Education Materials, University Press Co 1978. **Business Addr:** President, Chief Executive Officer, Gr. Dayton African-Amerian Chamber Of Commerce, 184 Salem Ave, Dayton, OH 45406.

STOCKTON, CARLTON A
Executive. **Personal:** Born Oct 19, 1940, Martinsville, VA; son of Alonza and Willie Sue; married Margaret C Stockton, Jun 20, 1964; children: Khary Alonza. **Educ:** Saint Paul's Col, BS, 1962; Atlanta Univ, MA, 1969; Harvard Univ, MPA, 1977. **Career:** Executive (retired); City Highland Pk, Mich, dir model cities, 1969-72; Health Cares Financing Admin, Div Qual Control, dir, 1972-81; MCI Worldcom, vpres, 1982-98. **Orgs:** Chmn bd, Black Human Resource Network, 1991-92; chmn bd, Northern VA Urban League, 1992-95; Immanuel Church Hill, warden, 1996-98; chair develop comm, CLG William & Mary Endowment Asn, 1997-98; life mem, Omega Psi Phi fraternity; chair & bd trustees, St Paul's Col; pres & bd dir, Two Rivers Country Club; chair, Nominating W&M Muscarelle Museum Art. **Honors/Awds:** Outstanding Alumni, Saint Paul's Col Nat Alumni Asn, 1997. **Special Achievements:** Licensed lay minister, Episcopal Diocese of Southern Virginia, Vestry, Bruton Parish. **Home Addr:** 3201 Fowler, PO Box 5332, Williamsburg, VA 23185-7506.

STOCKTON, CLIFFORD
Manager, executive director. **Personal:** Born Sep 16, 1932, Memphis, TN; married Lois J Hampton; children: Angela, Clifford Jr & Brian. **Educ:** Tenn State Univ, 1954; Memphis State Univ; C C Inst; Univ Ga. **Career:** Memphis Pub Schs, teacher, 1956-68; Upward Bound Proj LeMoyne, Owen Col, teacher, 1967-68; NAB Training Prog Goldsmith's Dept Store, coordr, 1967-69; Human Resources C of C, assoc mgr, 1969-71, mgr, 1971-72; Bus Res Ctr, exec dir, 1972; Econ Dev Memphis Area C of C, assoc mgr; Memphis Regional Chamber, consult, sr adv logistics & pub policy & dir econ develop & mkt & res, currently. **Orgs:** Bd dirs, Boys Club Am; OIC; Memphis Vol Placement Prog. **Honors/Awds:** Booker T Wash Award, NBL, 1972; Outstanding Service Minority Bus. **Military Serv:** AUS, spec 3rd class, 1954-56. **Business Addr:** Senior Advisor of Logistics and Public Policy, Director of Research & Marketing, Memphis Regional Chamber, 22 N Front St Suite 200, PO Box 224, Memphis, TN 38101-0224, **Business Phone:** (901)543-3513.

STODGHILL, DR. RONALD
School administrator. **Personal:** Born Dec 21, 1939, White Plains, NY; son of Joseph and Marian; divorced; children: Kimberly Denise Minter & Ronald Stodghill III. **Educ:** Western Mich Univ, MA, Curric Develop & Coordr, 1961; Wayne State Univ, EdD, 1981. **Career:** City Detroit Dept Parks & Recreation, instr, 1961; Detroit Bd Educ, sci & eng teacher, 1963, biol teacher, 1963-65; Western Mich Univ Custer Job Corps, team leader, 1965-67; US Ind Custer Job Corp, maintenance sch adv adminr, 1967-68; MI-OH Regional Educ Lab, prog assoc, 1968-68; St Louis Pub Sch, assoc supt, 1976-79, dep supt, 1979-82, interim supt, 1982-83, dep supt instr, 1983-84. **Orgs:** Coordr comt, MI-OH Regional Educ Lab, 1968-69; dir educ, New Detroit Inc, 1973-76, assoc dir, 1970-73, bd dir, 1977-79, chmn, 1977, exec coun mem, 1979; Am Asn Sch Adminr; Asn Supv & Curric Develop; Int Reading Asn; Nat Alliance Black Sch Educrs. **Honors/Awds:** Special Achiever, 1979; Commission Recognition Award, Coca-Cola Bottling Co, 1982.

STODGHILL, WILLIAM
Labor activist. **Personal:** Born Oct 7, 1940, Mount Vernon, NY; son of Joseph and Marion (Wynn). **Educ:** Wayne State Univ, Detroit, MI, attended; Univ Detroit, Detroit, MI, attended. **Career:** Local 79 SEIU, Detroit, MI, oranizer, 1966-74; Local 50 SEIU, St Louis, MO, pres, 1978, pres emer, currently; Serv Employees Int Union, Wash, DC, vpres, 1979-. **Orgs:** Chmn, Local 50 Benefit Serv Trust & Pension, currently, Contract Cleaners Trust and Pension, currently; trustee, South African Freedom Fund, currently; Adv Comn on Civil Rights, currently; chmn, SEIU Health Care Div, currently; exec bd, A Philip Randolph Inst, currently; bd mem, United Way Greater St Louis, currently, St Louis Br NAACP, currently, Jewish labor Comn, currently; secy, treas, Central States Labor Coun, currently. **Honors/Awds:** Proclamation, Mayor St Louis, 1983; Isrel Solidarity Award, 1983; Martin Luther King Award, Martin Luther King Asn; Man of the Year, Minority Women, 1986; A Philip Randolph Award, A Philip Randolph Inst, 1986. **Military Serv:** AUS, sgt, 1962-64. **Home Addr:** 4060 Westminster Pl, Saint Louis, MO 63108, **Home Phone:** (314)531-4609. **Business Addr:** President Emeritus, Local 50, Service Employees International Union, AFL-CIO, CLC, 4108 Lindell Blvd, Saint Louis, MO 63108, **Business Phone:** (314)534-1710.

STOKES, BUNNY
Banker. **Career:** Banker (Retired); Citizen's Federal Savings Bank, Birmingham, AL, chief exec officer, 2003; Citizens Trust Bank, pres, 2004. **Orgs:** Birmingham Asn Realtors; Ala Asn Realtors; Nat Asn Realtors. **Special Achievements:** Bank listed at 19 on Black Enterprise's list of top African American-owned banks, 1998.

STOKES, CAROLYN ASHE
Educator. **Personal:** Born Nov 18, 1925, Philadelphia, PA; daughter of Charles Malcolm Ashe and Louisa Burrell; married Joseph H, Oct 29, 1947; children: Michael, Monica & Craig. **Educ:** Howard Univ, BA, 1947, Univ Calif, Berkeley, grad educ, 1970; John F Kennedy Univ, BA, lang & sociol, MA, consciousness & arts, 1983, leadership, 1987. **Career:** Scott Air Force Thrift Shop, WW II bookkeeper; Joseph H Stokes DDS, dental asst & off mgr; Citizen's Eisenhower Cong Comm, Wash, DC, dir pub rel res dept; Dept Com Immigration & Naturalization Serv/Office Price Admin Wash, officer; Media Group, script writer; Class Enterprises Art Consciousness & Well-Being Workshops, dir & founder; Conflict Resolution Panel, Contra Costa County, sr peer counr; Calif Sr Legis, org leadership consult, sr senator; CLAS

Choices-Hologramatic Planning Consult, dir & founder; Mentoring Partners Alliance, pres, dir & consult. **Orgs:** Pres, Annual meeting chair, Ment Health Asn Contra Costa Co; mem-at-large, planning chair, Adv Coun Aging; bd mem, Ctr New Am; pub rels comm, Family Serv East Bay; trustee, Health Career assistance comm Alta Bates Hosp Asn; bd mem, Howard Thurman Educ Trust; life mem, Nat Coun Negro Women; vol AAUW Diablo Int Resource Ctr; consult, Coun Civic Unity Orinda Lafayette Moraga; leadership comm, United Way Opportunity West; West Co Women's Forum, diversity chair, Am Asn Univ Women; Entrepreneurial Skills Ctr; mem, Inst Arts & Disabilities; bd mem, Helping Other People Evolve Inc; founder & dir, Diversity Dialogue Group, Mentoring Partners Alliance; Int Soc Poets; dir & founder, Bay Area Youth-On-The-Move. **Honors/Awds:** Distinguished Woman Award, AAUW; Outstanding Graduate, Howard Univ; Delta Sigma Theta Comm Service Award; United Way Vol Award; Am Christian Freedom Soc Award; Most Valuable Honored Person Award, Off Aging; Ctr New Ams; First Historical Award Black Family Asn Contra Costa Co; 5 Golden Poet Awards, World Poetry & Int Soc Poets Distinguished Poet Award; Administration Assistants Senior Award, Counr Christian Sr's Extension; 2 Awards, Contra Costa Co Supvr commendations; Congressman George Miller Award; Congressman Ron Dellums Award; State Assembly man Robert Campbell Award; City of Richmond Award; Contra Costa Co Great Am Family Award; Int Educators Hall of Fame inductee. **Special Achievements:** Is a published poet and a weekly columnist in Gibbs Magazine. **Home Addr:** 90 Estates Dr, Orinda, CA 94563. **Business Addr:** Director, Manager & Teacher, Family Management education/ Mentoring Partners Alliance, 90 Estates Dr, Orinda, CA 94563, **Business Phone:** (925)254-5191.

STOKES, CHRIS
Movie director, manager, chief executive officer. **Personal:** Son of Irene. **Career:** Franchise Boys, founder; The Ultimate Group, ceo, currently; mgr for various artists including IMX, B2k, Jhene, TG4, Gyrl, Tilt, Monteco, Sec N Sol, Quindon & Mq3; Films: House Party 4: Down to the Last Minute, 2001; Now That's What I Call Music, 2003; You Got Served, writer & dir, 2004; Somebody Help Me, producer, writer & dir, 2006. **Business Addr:** Owner, Chief Executive Officer, The Ultimate Group, 848 N La Cienega Blvd, West Hollywood, CA 90069.

STOKES, ERIC
Football player, scout. **Personal:** Born Dec 18, 1973, Hebron, NE; married Tisa; children: Erisa, Payton & Madison. **Educ:** Univ Nebr, sociol. **Career:** Football player (retired), Scout; Seattle Sea hawks, defensive back,1997-98, asst pro personnel, 2002-04, area scout, currently. **Orgs:** KAP; Fitz Pollard Alliance; Nat Football League Players Asn. **Business Addr:** Area Scout, Seattle Seahawks, 800 Occidental Ave S Suite 200, Renton, WA 98056.

STOKES, GERALD VIRGIL
Scientist, educator, research scientist. **Personal:** Born Mar 25, 1943, Chicago, IL; son of Henry and Louise Shelman; married Charlotte M Eubanks; children: Gordon K & Garrett K. **Educ:** Wilson Jr Col, AA, 1965; Southern Ill Univ, BA, 1967; Univ Chicago, PhD, 1973. **Career:** Univ Colo, 1973-76; Meharry Med Col, asst prof, 1976-78; George Wash Univ, asst prof, assoc prof, 1976-. **Orgs:** Asn Am Med Col, 1977-87; CSMM-chmn Am Soc Microbiol, 1984-; pres elect, Wash DC Br Am Soc Microbiol, 1986-87; rev comm, Minority Biomed Res Support, 1986-90; Am Soc Microbiol; bd scientific counsrs, Nat Ctr Infections Dis, CDC, Atlanta, 1993-96; Sigma Xi; mem, Health & safety comt. **Honors/ Awds:** ACS Fel, Univ Colo, 1973-75; NIH Post Doc Fel, Univ Colo, 1976; Sigma Xi George Wash Univ, 1978-; Am Acad Microbiol fel. **Business Addr:** Associate Professor, George Washington University, 2300 Eye St NW, Washington, DC 20037, **Business Phone:** (202)994-2850.

STOKES, HERB
Executive. **Personal:** Born in Newark, NJ; married Valeria. **Career:** Allied Van Lines, laborer, vpres qual mgt; Alliance Relocation Serv LLC, pres & chief exec officer, owner, currently. **Orgs:** Vice chair, Northwest Minority Bus Coun, 2002. **Business Phone:** 877-242-0455.

STOKES, JEREL JAMAL
Football player, talk show host, football executive. **Personal:** Born Oct 6, 1972, San Diego, CA; married Jill; children: Jayla. **Educ:** Univ Calif, Los Angeles, BS, sociol. **Career:** San Francisco 49ers, wide receiver, 1995-2002; Jacksonville Jaguars, 2003; New England Patriots, 2003-; Espn, "J.J., Josh and The Mouth"- cohost; NFL, free agent. *

STOKES, JOHNNIE MAE
Educator. **Personal:** Born Oct 15, 1941, Tuscaloosa, AL; married Julius; children: Salvatore & Zachary. **Educ:** Ohio State Univ, BS, educ, 1962; Portland State Univ, MS, educ, 1974. **Career:** Va Hosp Hines IL, clin dietn, 1963-65; Bronx VA Hosp, dietetic intrnshp, 1963; Chicago Bd of Health, mem & nutritionist, 1966-67; Va Hosp Vancouver WA, clin dietitian, 1967-69; Good Samrtn Hosp & Med Ctr, clinical dietitian, 1971-75; Mt Hood Community Col, coun instr. **Orgs:** Adv bd mem, E Multnomah Co Leag of Women Voters; Am & OR Dietetic Asn; Ore Asn Sch Couns; vpres, Portland Chap of Links Inc, 1979-81; Alpha Kappa Alpha Sor. **Honors/Awds:** Home ec hon Phi Upsilon Omericon; educ hon Phi Lambda Theta; Outstanding Young Women of Am, 1975.

STOKES, JULIE ELENA
Educator. **Educ:** Chaffey Community Col, AA, correctional sci, 1989; Calif State Univ, BA, psychol, 1991; Univ Calif, Riverside, MA, psychol, 1993, PhD, psychol, 1994. **Career:** Univ Calif, grad fel, 1991-92; San Bernardino, lectr, Life Span Develop, 1994, 1995; Calif State Univ, Long Beach, lectr African-Am Families Child Develop, 1994; Univ Calif, Riverside, lectr African-Am Families Child Develop, 1994, African-Am Family Res Coordr, site supvr, 1993-94, lectr, Study African Am Women, 1995; CA State Univ, Fullerton, from lectr to asst prof psychol, 1995-2003, assoc prof psychol, 2003-, Dept Afro-Ethnic studies, chair, currently; Orange County Dept Univ Calif, grad fel, 1991-92; San Bernardino, lectr, Life Span Develop, 1994, 1995; Calif State Univ, Long Beach, lectr African-Am Families Child Develop, 1994; Univ Calif, Riverside, lectr African-Am Families Child Develop, 1994, African-Am Family Res Coordr, site supvr, 1993-94, lectr, Study African Am Women, 1995; CA State Univ, Fullerton, from lectr to asst prof psychol, 1995-2003, assoc prof psychol, 2003-, Dept Afro-Ethnic studies, chair, currently; Orange County Dept Educ ACCESS Prog Safe Schs Evaluator, 2000-; Charles Drew Med Ctr OASIS Clin, Special Projs Nat Significance Proj Evaluator, 2000-03; Partnership Responsible Parenting Teen Preg Prog, proj dir, 1996-97, African An Family Res Proj, res dir, 1993-95; Social Sci Res Ctr, Fullerton, res assoc, 1997-; Bel Community Outreach & Human Develop, proj evaluator, 1997-; 100 Black Men, Passport to Future, proj evaluator, 1997-; San Bernardino County Ment Health, comnr, 1998-. **Orgs:** Western Psychol Asn, 1991-; Asn Black Psychologists, 1992-; Am Evaluators Asn; Am Psychol Asn, 1995-; Am Psychol Soc, 1995-; dir counseling, church adminr, exec comt mem, Eccelesia Christian Fellowship Church. **Honors/Awds:** University Honors, California State Univ, San Bernardino, 1991. **Special Achievements:** Publications: Co-author, "Cross's Stage Model Revisited: An Analysis of Theoretical Formulations and Empirical Evidence" Advances in Black Psychology, in press, 1995; co-author, "The Development of the Black Family Process Q-sort" The Handbook of Text and Measurement of Black Population, in press, 1995; co-author, "Assessing the Validity of the African Self-Consciousness Scale," Journal of Black Psychology; co-author, "The Home Environment as a Predicator of Achievement,", Journal of Negro Education. **Business Addr:** Associate Professor, Chair in the Department of Afro-Ethnic studies, University of California, Department of Psychology, H-324F 800 N State Col Blvd, PO Box 6846, Fullerton, CA 92834, **Business Phone:** (714)278-3845.

STOKES, DR. LILLIAN GATLIN
Educator, nurse. **Personal:** Born Feb 18, 1942, Greenville, NC; married Robert; children: Everett & Robyn. **Educ:** Kate Bitting Reynolds Sch Nursing, dipl, 1963; NC Cent Univ, BS, 1966; Ind Univ, MSc, 1969, PhD, educ psychol, 1997. **Career:** Norfolk Comm Hosp, staff nurse, 1963-64; Silver Cross Hosp, staff nurse, 1966-67; Purdue Univ, asst prof nursing, 1969-72; Nat Inst Health, peer review spec proj grants, 1977; Ind Univ, Sch Nursing, assoc prof, 1972-, dir diversity & enrichment, currently. **Orgs:** Am Nurs Asn; Ind St Nurse Asn; Nat Leag Nurs; chairperson, Aud Nurs Com Home Care Agency Gr Indianapolis, 1974-76; bd dir, Ind Univ Sch Nurs Alumni Asn, 1973-; Chi Eta Phi Sor; Sigma Theta Tau; Alpha Kappa Alpha Sor; Women's Aux Indianapolis Dist Dent Soc; Jack & Jill Am Inc, Coalition 100 Black Women; Links, Inc; exec coun, Ind Univ Alumni Assoc; bd dir, Girls Clubs Greater Indianapolis; fel, Am Acad Nursing, 2001; vpres, 2003-05, pres, Chi Eta Phi Sorority, 2005-; Ind Citizens League for Nurs; Midwest Nurs Res Soc. **Honors/Awds:** Lucille Petry Leone Award, Nat League Nurse, 1975; Special Achievement Award, Chi Eta Phi Sor, 1975; Lillian G Stokes Award, Ind Univ Sch Nursing Alumni Assoc, 1980; Outstanding Service Award, Jack & Jill Am Inc; Distinguished Service Award, Girls Clubs Greater Indianapolis Inc; Madame C J Walker Award, 1996; Distinguished Hoosier, Governor Ind, 1998; Mary Mahoney Award, Am Nurses Asn, 2000; Distinguished Alumni Award, NC State Univ, 2001; fel Am Acad Nurs, 2001; Joseph T Taylor Award for Excellence in Diversity, 2002; Distinguished Service Award, Annual Black Chamber of Commerce, 2006. **Special Achievements:** Co-author "Adult & Child Care a Client Approach to Nursing" CV Mosby Co, 1973, 2nd ed 1977; co-author "Medical-Surgical Nursing, Common Problems of Adults and Children Across the Life Span," 1983, second edition, 1987. **Business Addr:** Associate Professor, Director of Diversity & Enrichmen, Indiana University, School of Nursing, 1111 Middle Dr NU 122, Indianapolis, IN 46202-5107, **Business Phone:** (317)274-2806.

STOKES, LOUIS
Lawyer, congressperson (u.s. federal government). **Personal:** Born Feb 23, 1925, Cleveland, OH; son of Charles and Louise Stone; married Jeanette Frances Jay, Aug 21, 1960; children: Shelley, Louis C, Angela & Lorene. **Educ:** Case Western Res Univ, attended 1948; Cleveland Marshall Law Sch, JD, 1953. **Career:** Stokes, Character, Terry, Perry, Whitehead, Young & Davidson law firm, co-founder; US House of Rep, 11th Congressional Dist, Ohio, rep, 1968-98; House Appropriations Subcomt, VA-HUD-Independent Agencies; chmn, Appropriations Subcomt DC; mem, Subcomt Labor-Health & Human Serv Educ, mem, OH Congressional Del, dean; pvt pract, atty; Mandel Sch Applied Soc Sci, sr vis scholar; Case Western Univ, vis scholar, 1998; Squire, Sanders & Dempsey LLP, sr coun, currently. **Orgs:** Founding mem, Congressional Black Caucus; founder & chmn, Congressional Black Caucus Health Braintrust; Bd trustees, Martin Luther King Jr Ctr for Social Change, Forest City Hosp, Cleveland State Univ; bd dirs, Karamu House; vice chmn & trustee bd, St Paul AME Zion Church; fel, OH State Bar Asn; Cleveland Cuyahoga City, Am Bar Asn, Pythagoras Lodge No 9; exec comn, Cuyahoga City Dem Party; exec comn, OH State Dem Party; Urban League; Citizens League; John Harlan Law Club; Kappa Alpha Psi; Am Civil Liberties Union; Plus Club; Am Legion; African-Am Inst Intl Adv Coun; vpres, NAACP Cleveland Br, 1965-66; vice chmn, Cleveland Sub-Com US Comn on Civil Rights, 1966; guest lectr, Cleveland Br NAACP; vice chmn, PEW Environ Health Comn, Johns Hopkins Sch Pub Health; House Appropriations Comt; House Iran Contra Panel. **Honors/Awds:** Distinguished Serv Award; Cert Appreciation, US Comn on Civil Rights; William L Dawson Award, 1980; hon degrees: Wilberforce Univ, Shaw Univ, Livingstone Col, OH Col Podiatric Med, Oberlin Col, Morehouse Col, Meharry Med Col, Atlanta Univ, Howard Univ, Morehouse Sch Med, Cent State Univ, Xavier Univ. **Special Achievements:** first African Am mem of Congress, State OH; first African Am in the hist of the US Congress to retire having completed 30 yrs in off; named in hon, Howard Univ & NIH, have recognized Mr Stokes by naming certain bldg on their campuses after him. **Military Serv:** AUS, 1943-46. **Business Phone:** (202)626-6697.

STOKES, PATRICK
Association executive. **Career:** Verizon Communs, Retail Distribution Philadelphia Tri-State Region, dir; Verizon Wireless, vpres bus distribution, currently. **Business Addr:** Vice President National Distribution, Verizon Wireless, PO Box 3397, **Business Phone:** 800-555-8879.

STOKES, RUEBEN MARTINE
Executive. **Personal:** Born Mar 27, 1957, Los Angeles, CA; son of Bailey L Stokes (deceased) and Alma M; married Alana Maria Fullove, Mar 30, 1985; children: Rueben Martine II & Blair Elizabeth. **Educ:** Dartmouth Col, BA, 1979; Nat Univ, attended 1986-87. **Career:** Airborne Express, sales rep, 1981-82; N Am Van Lines Inc, territory sales mgr, 1982-85; Advan Traffic Serv Inc, mkt mgr, 1985-87; Mayflower Transit Inc, dist sales vpres, 1987-91; Allied Van Lines, nat sales dir, 1991-94; Ryder Move Management, nat sales dir, 1994; ADT Security Serv Inc, exec dir diversity & community affairs, currently. **Orgs:** Dartmouth Col Alumni Asn; Theta Delta Chi Frat Inc; bd dirs, NAHREP. **Honors/ Awds:** Letter of Commendation, Nat Merit Honor Soc, 1975; William J Tucker Fellowship Award, 1979; Ivy League Champion Football Team, 1978. **Special Achievements:** Author: Super Selling Secrets for the Real World, Fairway Press, 1994. **Business Addr:** Executive Director of Diversity and Community Affairs, ADT Security Services Inc., 5471 W Waters Ave Suite 788, Tampa, FL 60563, **Business Phone:** (813)806-7000.

STOKES, SHEREITTE CHARLES
School administrator. **Personal:** Born Apr 9, 1953, Philadelphia, PA; son of Eleanor Hasben and Shereitte C Stokes. **Educ:** Wilberforce Univ, BA, 1974. **Career:** Omega Psi Phi Fraternity, Inc, staff, 1971; AT&T, acct exec & indust consult, 1981-87; New Covenant Church of Philadelphia, dir stewardship, 1987-90; Macintyre Assoc, campaign dir, 1989-92; Philadelphia Opportunities Industrialization Ctr, develop dir, 1993-94; Univ Toledo, develop officer, 1995-96; Rutgers Univ, dir develop, 1996-99; Spelman Col, assoc vpres, 1999-. **Orgs:** Coun Advan & Support Educ, 1995-; bd trustees, NJ Ctr Outreach & Serv Autistic Community, 1997-99; NJ chap bd mem, Nat Soc Fund Raising Execs, 1998-99. **Honors/Awds:** Citizen of the Year, Omega Psi Phi Fraternity, 1996. **Business Addr:** Associate Vice President, Spelman College, 350 Spelman Lane SW, PO Box 1551, Atlanta, GA 30314-4399, **Business Phone:** (404)270-5855.

ST OMER, VINCENT V E
Educator, consultant. **Personal:** Born Nov 18, 1934, St Lucia, St. Lucia; married Margaret Muir; children: Ingrid, Denise, Jeffrey & Raymond. **Educ:** Ontario Vet Col, DVM, 1962; Univ Manitoba, MSc, 1965; Ontario Vet Col, Univ Guelph, PhD, pharmacol & toxicol, 1969. **Career:** Hamilton & Dist Cattle Breeders Assn, field veterinarian, 1962-63; Ontario Vet Col, Univ Guelph, lectr, 1965-67; Univ KS, Bureau Child Res, res assoc, 1968-71, adj prof, 1970-73; KS State Univ, Bureau Child Res, adj res assoc, 1972-74; Univ Med, Sch Med, asst prof, 1974; Univ MSR, Col Veterinary Med, Depart Veterinary Biomedical Scis, assoc prof, 1974-83, prof, dir graduate studies, 1976-79, dir, MNY High Sch Student Res Apprentice Prog, 1986-89; Univ W Indies, Sch Veterinary Med, special leave Univ MSR, prof & dir, 1989-91; Tuskegee Univ, Sch Veterinary Med, prof & assoc dean academic affairs, Depart Biomed Scis, prof pharmacol, currently. **Orgs:** Sigma Xi; Am Soc Vet Physiologists & Pharmacologists; Soc Neuroscience; MSR Vet Med Asn; CNF Res Workers Animal Dis, NYK ACA Scis; Behavioral Teratology Soc; Caribbean ACA Scis. **Honors/Awds:** Am ACA Vet Pharmacol & Therapeutics, fel.

Business Addr: Professor, Tuskegee University, Department of Biomedical Sciences, PO Box 1239, Tuskegee, AL 36088, **Business Phone:** (334)727-8473.

STONE, ANGIE (ANGELA LAVERNE BROWN)
Songwriter, singer, lyricist. **Personal:** Born 1961, Columbia, SC; married Lil' Rodney Cee; children: Michael. **Career:** Albums of Sequence: The Sequence, 1982; commercial rec artist, 1980s; released album as mem of Vertical Hold: Vertical Hold, 1992; songwriter, 1990s; solo album: Just A Pimp; Black Diamond, 1999; Mahogany Soul, 2001; Stone Love, 2004; Stone Hits: The Very Best Of Angie Stone, 2005; Films: The Hot Chick, 2002; The Fighting Temptations, 2003; TV: "Moesha", 2000; "Girlfriends", 2002; One on One, 2004; Ellen: The Ellen DeGeneres Show, 2007; Jimmy Kimmel Live, 2007; Later with Jools Holland, 2007; Writer: Bamboozled, 2000; Dr Dolittle 2, 2001; Blue Crush, 2002; Brown Sugar, 2002; The Fighting Temptations, 2003. **Honors/Awds:** Album of the Yr Award for Black Diamond, Billboard mag, 2000; Nominated for Grammy Awards, 2003, 2004; Dutch Edison Award, 2004. **Business Addr:** Singer, Arista Recs, 6 W 57th St, New York, NY 10019, **Business Phone:** (212)489-7400.

STONE, AUBRY L
President (Organization), chief executive officer. **Career:** Capitol Area Develop Authority, state comnr econ develop; Calif Black Chamber of Com, pres & chief exec officer, currently. **Orgs:** Nat Asn Advan Colored People; Black Chamber Com; Metro Chamber of Com; CalTrans Small Bus Roundtable; Mayors Econ Develop Coun; City Sacramentos Community Serv Comt; Dist Attorneys Citizen Cabinet. **Business Addr:** President, Chief Executitve Officer, California Black Chamber of Commerce, 2951 Sunrise Blvd Suite 175, Rancho Cordova, CA 95742, **Business Phone:** (916)463-0177.*

STONE, CHARLES SUMNER, JR. See STONE, CHUCK.

STONE, CHUCK (CHARLES SUMNER STONE, JR.)
Educator, journalist. **Personal:** Born Jul 21, 1924, St Louis, MO; son of Charles Stone and Madalence Stone; married Louise; children: Krishna, Allegra & Charles III. **Educ:** Wesleyan Univ, AB, 1948; Univ Chicago, MA, 1951. **Career:** CARE, overseas rep, 1956-57; New York Age, editor, 1958-60; Am Com Africa, assoc dir, 1960; WA Afro-Am Newspaper, White House corres/editor, 1960-63; Columbia Col, instr, journalist, 1963-64; Chicago Daily Defender, editor-in-chief, 1963-64; Rep Adam Clayton Powell Jr, special asst, 1965-67; Philadelphia Daily News, sr ed, columnist, 1972-91; Rep Robert NC Nix, editorial rsch specialist; Educ Testing Serv, dir minority affairs; Philadelphia Daily News, sr ed; Newspaper Enterprise Asn, syndicated columnist, 1989-; Univ Del, eng prof, 1991-2005; Univ NC, Walter Spearman prof journalism, Walter Spearman prof emer, 1991-2005; Montreal TV prog, panelist; WTVD TV 11, polit anal & ed, currently. **Orgs:** Chmn, Nat Conf Black Power; fel, founding mem, Black Acad Arts & Letters; Coun mem, Nat Conf Black Political Sci; founding mem & pres, Nat Asn Black Journalists. **Honors/Awds:** First prize, Best Column of Year, NNPA, 1960; Journalist of the Year, Capital Press Club, 1961; Annual Distinguished Citizen Award, CORE, 1964;Award of Merit for Journalist, Alpha Phi Alpha 1965; Politician-in-Residence, Morgan State Coll, 1969; Honorary LHD, Pembroke State University, NC; Honorary LHD, Wilberforce Univ, 1977; Honorary LittD, Rider Col, 1985; Outstanding Prof, Univ of Delaware Honor Soc, 1986; Honorary Federal Warden, US Bureau of Prisons, 1983; 1st Place, column, Pennsylvania Newspaper Publishers Assn; Laubach Excellence in Teaching Award, Univ of Delaware, 1989; Undergraduate Teaching Award, UNC-CH, 1992; Free Spirit Award, Freedom Forum, 1993; First Spearman professor of journalism, Univ NC; Missouri Honor Medal for Distinguished Service in Journalism, Univ Missouri, 1996; Thomas Jefferson Award, Univ NC, Chapel Hill, 2002; Trailblazer Award, North Carolina's Sit-In Movement Inc, Greensboro, 2005. **Special Achievements:** First president of the National Association of Black Journalists, 1875-77; First host of PBS's Black Perspectives On The News; Nominated twice for the Pulitzer Prize. **Military Serv:** USAF, navigator, 1943-45. **Business Addr:** Analyst & Editor, WTVD TV 11, 319 Fayetteville St Suite 107, Raleigh, NC 27601.

STONE, DOLORES JUNE
Labor activist. **Personal:** Born Jun 16, 1939, Mount Clemens, MI; daughter of Charles K and Annie R; married Kenneth Eugene Stone, May 23, 1955; children: Don Rico, Joyce Graham Adams, Denise D Neal & Kenneth Jr. **Educ:** Ford Motor, 240 Hrs Sewing, 1966; UAW, Black Lake Labor Class, 1971; MCCC, Speech, 1981. **Career:** The Fawns Temple, pdr, 1964; Local 400 UAW, joint coun, 1970, exec bd, 1971; Voice New Haven, p comm sec, 1980; Ford Motor, floor inspector; Order of the Eastern Star Supreme Lodge Intn; mem bd of dir, The New Haven Public Housing; The New Haven HS Citizens Adv Comm; Coldwell Banker McCulloch Judd Realty, Realtor, currently. **Orgs:** Trustee Village New Haven, 1982; sec, EI Ford Motor, 1983, leader, 1984; prec delegate New Haven Democrate, 1984; lioness sec, New Haven, 1984; historian, Village New Haven; bd dir, Downriver Med Facil, 1987; vpres, S E MCOGS City, Village Bloc, 1989; mem bd dir, New Haven Public Housing; New Haven HS Citizens Adv Community. **Home Addr:** 58580 Chennault Dr, New Haven, MI 48048. **Business Addr:** Realtor, Coldwell Banker McCulloch Judd Realty, 1690 McCulloch Blvd, Lake Havasu City, AZ 86403, **Business Phone:** (520)855-9195.

STONE, DWIGHT
Football player, police officer. **Personal:** Born Jan 28, 1964, Florala, AL; married Jennifer; children: Ciara, Cailin & Celena. **Educ:** Middle Tenn State Univ, BS, social work. **Career:** Football player (retired), Police officer; Pittsburgh Steelers, widereceiver, 1987-94; Carolina Panthers, 1995-98; New York Jets, 1999-2000; Charlotte Mecklenburg Police Dept, police officer, 2002-. **Honors/Awds:** John Madden All-Star Team Field Performance Award, 1991;Charlotte-Mecklenburg Police Fitness Award, 2002 & 2003; Police Officer Of the Year, 2008. **Business Addr:** Police Officer, Charlotte Mecklenburg Police Department, 3500 Latrobe Dr, Charlotte, NC 28211, **Business Phone:** (704)943-2400.

STONE, HAROLD ANTHONY
Marketing executive. **Personal:** Born Aug 9, 1949, New Bedford, MA; married Elizabeth G Bates. **Educ:** Univ Mass, Amherst, BB, 1969, BBA, 1973; Atlanta Univ, MBA, 1978. **Career:** Maxwell House Div & Gen Foods, sales rep, 1973-76; Coca-Cola USA Cincinnati, control & Mid east area spl mkt mgr, 1976. **Orgs:** Nat Asn Mkt Develop; NAACP; Oper PUSH Inc. **Military Serv:** USNR, 1971-77.

STONE, DR. JOHN S
Obstetrician, gynecologist. **Personal:** Born Jul 16, 1930, Tampa, FL; son of Edward W; married Gertrude Jane Holliday; children: Dr Faith Stone, Dr Enid Griner & John. **Educ:** Talladega Col, BS, 1951; Meharry Med Col, MD, 1956; Univ Tex St Joseph Hosp, 1972. **Career:** Houston Med Forum, pres, 1986-88; pvt pract, obstetrician/gynecologist. **Orgs:** Bd mem, Cent Life Ins Co Fla, 1973-87; founder, pres, St Elizabeth Hosp Houston Found, 1974-78; mem, United Fund Agency Operations Comm, 1975; mem, Am Med Asn, Tex Med Asn, Harris County Med Soc; bd mem, Catholic Charities, Central Life Ins Co Fla, 1978-87; pres med staff, Riverside Gen Hosp, 1981-82; bd mem, Catholic Charities, 1983-87; Houston Med Forum, 1986-87; mem, Am Med Asn, Lone State State Med Asn, Tex Med Asn, Houston Med Forum, Harris County Med Soc, Houston Acad med, Nu Boule. **Military Serv:** USAF, capt, 1957-59. **Home Addr:** 3402 Binz, Houston, TX 77004, **Home Phone:** (713)529-4281.

STONE, REESE J
Executive, executive director. **Personal:** Born Feb 26, 1945, Dublin, GA; son of Reese J Stone Sr and Mildred Andrews Stone; married Brenda Yearwood, Oct 25, 2000; children: Meris E. **Educ:** Tenn State Univ, Nashville TN, BS, 1966; Howard Univ, Wash, DC, MPA, 1973. **Career:** Howard Univ, assoc dir stud affairs, 1970-72; Nat Educ Asn, communs coord, 1972-79; Metropolitan Transit Authority, dir pub affairs, 1979-85; Planned Parenthood Fed Am, dir communs, 1985-87; Philip Morris Co Inc, mgr corp communs, 1987-91; Sandstone Assoc, 1991-; LLT Int Advertising, vpres bus develop; Nat Med Asn, dir external affairs, 1991-. **Orgs:** Vpres, prin, Com Real Estate-Sandstone Assoc Inc, Newark NJ, 1981-; mentor, Columbia Univ Mentor Prog, 1987-89; bd mem, Hisp Media Ctr, 1988-; Pub Affairs Coun, 1988-; Nat Press Club; Overseas Press Club; 100 Black Men. **Honors/Awds:** PRSA Big Apple Award, Pub Rels Soc Am, 1989; Ohio State Award, Am Bar Asn, 1990. **Special Achievements:** Hispanic 100, Hispanic Magazine, 1991. **Military Serv:** AUS, Alaskan Command, Fairbanks, 1968-70; Honorable Discharge. **Home Addr:** 57 Nishuane Rd, Montclair, NJ 07042. **Business Addr:** Director, National Medical Association, 1012 10th St NW, Washington, DC 20001, **Business Phone:** (202)347-1895.

STONE, RON. See STONE, RONALD CHRISTOPHER.

STONE, RONALD CHRISTOPHER (RON STONE)
Football player. **Personal:** Born Jul 20, 1971, Boston, MA; married Roxane; children: Ronnie & Ronna. **Educ:** Boston Col. **Career:** Dallas Cowboys, guard, 1993-95; New York Giants, 1996-2001; San Francisco 49ers, guard, 2002-03; Oakland Raiders, guard, 2004-05.

STONE, WILLIAM T
Lawyer, executive. **Personal:** Born Jan 8, 1931, Washington, DC; son of Thomas and Beulah; married Sara Cumber; children: William T Jr, Jacquelyn E, Michael R & Christopher D. **Educ:** Cent State Univ, BS 1953; New Eng Inst Anat, attended 1956; Am Univ, JD, 1961. **Career:** Law Pract, 1962-2000; Williamsburg City & James City Co Cts, substitute judge, 1968-2000; Whiting's Funeral Home, owner; Stone & Assocs, mgr & atty, 2000-. **Orgs:** Old Dominion, PA, Am, Williamsburg & Peninsula Bar Asns; VA Trial Lawyers Asn; Nat Funeral Dirs & Morticians Asn; VA Mortician's Asn; First Baptist Ch; Omega Psi Phi. **Military Serv:** Served 1953-55.

STOREY, BOB. See STOREY, ROBERT D.

STOREY, ROBERT D (BOB STOREY)
Lawyer. **Personal:** Born Mar 28, 1936, Tuskegee, AL; married Juanita Kendrick Cohen, May 9, 1959; children: Charles, Christopher & Rebecca. **Educ:** Harvard Univ, AB, 1958; Case Western Res Univ, JD, 1964; Tri-State Univ, LHD, 2000. **Career:** East Ohio Gas Co, atty, 1964-66; Legal Aid Soc Cleveland, asst dir, 1966-67; Burke Haber & Berick, partner, 1967-90; GTE Corp, dir, 1985-2000; McDonald, Hopkins Burke & Haber Co, partner, 1990-92; Thompson, Hine & Flory, partner, 1993; May Dept Stores Co, St Louis Mo, dir; Verizon New England Inc, dir, 2000-; Procter & Gamble, Cincinnati, Ohio, chmn, dir, 2000-06; Verizon Commun Inc, New York, NY, dir, currently. **Orgs:** City Planning Comn Cleveland, 1966-74; trustee, Phillips Exeter Acad, 1969-83-; trustee, Cleveland St Univ, 1971-80, chmn, 1979-80; trustee, Univ Sch, 1974-99; vpres, Asn Harvard Alumni, 1974-80; trustee, Great Lakes Sci Ctr; overseer, Harvard Univ, 1980-86; trustee, Univ Hosp Cleveland, 1982-90; trustee, Kresge Found, Troy Mich; trustee, George Gund Found, Cleveland Ohio; trustee, Spelman Col; trustee, Case Western Res Univ; Pub Policy Comt, Verizon New England Inc; Corp Governance & Policy Comt, Verizon Commun Inc, 2000-. **Honors/Awds:** Top 10 Young Men of the Year, Cleveland Jr COC, 1967; Chief Marshal, 25th Reunion, Harvard Class, 1958; Charles Flint Kellogg Award, ASN Episcopal Col, 1984. **Military Serv:** USMC, capt, 1958-61. **Home Addr:** 2385 Coventry Rd, Cleveland Heights, OH 44118, **Home Phone:** (216)321-3491. **Business Addr:** Director, Verizon Communications Inc, 140 W St Fl 29, New York, NY 10007, **Business Phone:** (212)395-1000.

STORY, CHARLES IRVIN
Executive. **Personal:** Born Aug 10, 1954, Richmond, VA; son of John R and Geraldine; married Deborah Ellis; children: Lachelle. **Educ:** Fisk Univ, BA, psychol, mgt, 1976; Univ Tenn, MPA, 1978. **Career:** Fisk Univ, personnel dir, 1977-78; INROADS, managing dir, 1978-81, reg dir, 1982, vpres, 1983, exec vpres, 1983-87, pres & chief exec officer, 1993-2005; Dept Econ & Community Develop, State TN, asst comnr, 1987-88; First Am Nat Bank, vpres opers, 1991-92; Exec Coaching Solutions Group Inc, pres, currently. **Orgs:** Alumni trustee, Fisk Univ, 1976-79; Leadership Nashville, 1981-82; bd mem, Sch Bus TN State Univ, 1982-83; bd mem, Rochelle Training & Rehab Ctr, 1982-83; chmn, Strategic Planning Comn Child Guid Ctr, 1984-; vice chmn, 1987; United Way Disabled Serv Panel, 1984-; Allocation Comn, Way Mid Tenn, 1989-93; bd mem, Nashville Bus Incubation Ctr, 1989-; bd mem, Goodwill Mid Tenn, 1989-, vice chmn, 1992; secy, bd mem, Ctr Non-Profit Mgt, 1990-; bd mem, Nashville Area Red Cross, 1990-; bd mem, Watkins Inst, 1990-; adv bd, AmSouth Bank, 1993-; bd dirs, Briggs & Stratton Corp, 1994-; adv bd, Hanigan Consult Group, 1996-; bd dirs, ChoicePoint Inc, 1997-. **Honors/Awds:** Ranked One, Col Grad Class, Fisk Univ, 1976; Outstanding Young Man of America, US Jaycees, 1978; Alumni Appreciation Award, INROADS, 1983; Distinguished Service Award, INROADS, 1984. **Home Addr:** 5505 Saddlewood Lane, Brentwood, TN 37027. **Business Addr:** President, Executive Coaching Solutions Group Inc, 5543 Edmondson Pike Suite 206, Nashville, TN 37211, **Business Phone:** (615)781-4278.

STORY, OTIS L
Executive director, hospital administrator. **Personal:** Born Nov 17, 1951, Anniston, AL; son of Tom Elbert and Martha Lou Wilson; married Ava D McNair, Jan 7, 1991; children: Otis L Story II, Jasmyn E, Avana Leigh & Prince James Elbert. **Educ:** Cornell Univ, Ithaca, NY, BA, 1976; Univ Chicago, Chicago, IL, MA, 1977; Univ Ala, Birmingham, Birmingham, AL, MAHH, 1981. **Career:** Ochsner Found Hosp, New Orleans, LA, admin asst dir, 1981-85; Univ Ala, Birmingham Hosp, admin asst admin, 1985-90; Univ Med & Dentistry NJ, adminr & chief operating officer, 1990-96; Health Alliance Greater Cincinnati, Cincinnati, Univ Hosp Inc, assoc exec officer, 1996-98; Quorum Health Resources, Mem Health Univ Med Ctr, Savannah, GA, exec vpres & chief operating officer, 1998-2001; Shands Jacksonville Med Ctr, chief operating officer, 2001, interim pres, chief exec officer; Huron Consulting Services LLC, exec dir, 2004; St. Vincent Catholic Med Ctr, St John's Queens Hosp, NY, exec dir, currently; Grady Health Syst, pres & chief exec officer, 2007-. **Orgs:** Nat Asn Health Care Exec, 1982-; Am Col Health Care Execs, 1982-; bd dir, N Jersey Blood Ctr; sr fel Nat Pub Health & Hosp Inst, 1995; Savannah On-Stage; Coastal Empire Coun; Boy Scouts Am; Univ Ala, Grad prog Health Admin, Alumni Asn. **Special Achievements:** 100 Black Men NJ. **Business Addr:** President, Chief Executive Officer, 80 Jesse Hill Jr Dr SE, Atlanta, GA 30303.

STORY, TIMOTHY KEVIN
Movie director, movie producer. **Personal:** Born Mar 13, 1970, Los Angeles, CA; married; children: 1. **Educ:** USC Sch Cinematic Arts. **Career:** Director, producer, editor & writer; Films: One of Us Tripped, dir & ed, 1997; The Firing Squad, dir, writer & co-ed, 1999; Urban Menace, writer, 1999; Barbershop, dir, 2002; Taxi, dir, 2004; Fantastic Four, dir, 2005; Fantastic Four: Rise of the Silver Surfer, dir, 2007; First Sunday, producer, 2008; TV Series: The 12th Man, exec producer, 2006; Standoff", 2006-07. **Honors/Awds:** Image Award, Nat Asn Advan Colored People, 2002. **Business Addr:** Director, William Morris Agency, 151 El Camino Dr, Beverly Hills, CA 90212, **Business Phone:** (310)274-7451.

STOTTS, VALMON D.
Clergy. **Personal:** Born Oct 24, 1925, Detroit, MI; married Ethel; children: Valmon Jr, Angela, Valarie. **Educ:** Detroit Bible Col, at-

tended 1957; Bible Sch Community Col, attended 1958; Wayne St Univ. **Career:** Unity Bapt Church, pastor, 1963-. **Orgs:** Counr Billy Graham Campaign, 1954; bd dir, Opportunity Ind Corp; Big Bros Am; pres Sherrill Sch PTA; chaplain Detroit Gen Hosp, 1969-70; 2nd vpres Coun Baptist Pastors; sec St Cong Evangelism; youth leader, inst Abouts. **Business Addr:** Unity Bapt Ch, 7500 Tireman Ave, Detroit, MI 48204.

STOUDEMIRE, AMARE CARSARES
Basketball player. **Personal:** Born Nov 16, 1982, Lake Wales, FL; son of Carrie Stoudemire. **Career:** Phoenix Suns, corner, 2002-. **Honors/Awds:** Rookie of the Year, 2002-03; Rookie of the Month, NBA Western Conf, 2002-03; winner, Wheel of Fortune's NBA Week, 2003; bronze medal, Olympics, Athens, 2004; All-NBA hons, 2004-05; Player of the Week, NBA Western Conf, 2004-05; Player of the Month, NBA Western Conf, 2005. **Special Achievements:** Featured on the cover of Sports Illustrated for Kids, 2003-04; Selected to play on the US Men's Olympic Team, 2004. **Business Addr:** Professional Basketball Player, Phoenix Suns, 201 E Jefferson St, Phoenix, AZ 85004, **Business Phone:** (602)379-7900.

STOUDMAIRE, DAMON
Basketball player. **Personal:** Born Sep 3, 1973, Portland, OR; son of Willie. **Educ:** Univ Ariz. **Career:** Basketball player (retired), coach; Toronto Raptors, guard, 1995-98; Portland Trail Blazers, 1998-05; Memphis Grizzlies, guard, 2005-8; San Antonio Spurs, 2008; asst coach, Memphis Grizzlies, currently. **Honors/Awds:** Oregon Player of the Year honor; NBA Rookie of the Year, 1996; Most Valuable Player, Schick Rookie Game, 1996. **Business Addr:** Assistant Coach, Memphis Grizzlies, 191 Beale St, Memphis, TN 38103, **Business Phone:** (901)888-4667.*

STOUT, LOUIS
Association executive. **Personal:** Born in Cynthiana, KY; son of John Stout (deceased) and Elizabeth; married Anna M, Aug 19, 1961; children: Juan RaMon. **Educ:** Regis Col, BA, 1959-63; Georgetown Col, Ky, attended 1973-75. **Career:** Lookout Mountain Sch Boys, Golden Colorado, counsr, 1963-65; Fayette Community Sch, Dunbar High Sch, teacher, coach, 1965-67, Tates Creek High Sch, teacher, coach, 1967-71; KHSAA, asst comnr, 1971-90, exec asst comn, 1990-94, comn, 1994-. **Orgs:** Sports chair, Ecquador, Lexington, 1978-85; bd adjustment, Lexington Urban Govn, 1990-; Kentucky Coun AIDS Prev, 1990-; nat chair, AAU, James E Sullivan Award, 1992-, nat exec comn, chair, 1992-; chair, AAU Zone B, 1992-; Hall of Fame Comn, Nat Fed High Sch, 1995-; Area Sports Authority Comm, Lexington, 1997-. **Honors/Awds:** Hall of Fame, 10th Region, Cent, 1989; Hall of Honor, KY ASA, 1993; Vision Award, Amateur Athletic Union, 1995; Hall of Fame, High Sch Baseball Coaches, 1997. **Business Addr:** Commissioner, Kentucky High School Athletic Association, 2280 Exec Dr, Lexington, KY 40511, **Business Phone:** (606)299-5472.

STOUT, STEVE
Executive. **Personal:** Born Jan 1, 1971?, New York, NY. **Educ:** Syracuse Univ. **Career:** Road mgr, 1990; Interscope Records, A&R exec, pres black music, 1998; Interscope Geffin A&M Records, exec vpres; PASS, founded, 2001-02, Translation, Consult & Brand Imaging, founder & ceo, 2005-. **Orgs:** Co-chmn, NY Fresh Air Fund. **Honors/Awds:** Humanitarian Award, 2004. **Business Addr:** Founder, Chief Executive Officer, Translation Consultation & Brand Imaging, 145 W 45th St Fl 12, New York, NY 10036, **Business Phone:** (212)299-5505.*

STOUTMIRE, OMAR
Football player. **Personal:** Born Jul 9, 1974, Pensacola, FL. **Educ:** Fresno State Univ, bus mkt. **Career:** Dallas Cowboys, defensive back, 1997-98; Cleveland Browns, 1999; New York Jets, defensive back, 1999; New York Giants, 2000-04; Wash Redskins, defensive back, 2005, 2007; New Orleans Saints, defensive back, 2006; Washington Redskins, 2007.

STOVALL, AUDREAN
Executive. **Personal:** Born Sep 18, 1933, Lexa, AR; daughter of John F Rice and Fredonia Little John Rice; married Williard; children: Darryl Byrd. **Educ:** Mercy Col Detroit, BS, 1984; Wayne State Univ, 1986. **Career:** MI Bell Tel Co, various positions, 1953-83; Electronic Data Syst, telecommunication specialist; US Sprint, acct consult; A B Stovall Consult, ITSI; MCI Customer Serv, supvr, 1985-86; Integrated Telecommunication Serv Inc, Detroit, Mich, entrepreneur, pres, owner, 1986-; AB Stovall Consult Inc, Detroit, Mich, owner, pres, 1987-. **Orgs:** Bus corp comn ABWA, 1963-; bus corp com, NBMBA, 1985-86; AFCEA; Am Bus Women's Asn; Urban League Guild; NAACP; Junior Achievement, Pioneers Am; Founders Soc Detroit Inst Arts; admis & fund comn; telethon comn United Negro Col Fund; Univ Detroit Mercy Alumna Planning Comn; Northwest Area Bus Asn, 1988-; Greater Detroit Chamber Com, 1988-; Nat Asn Female Exec, 1989-; Nat Black MBA Asn; bus & corp, Oakland County Bus Consortium, 1990; Mich Minority Bus Devt Corp. **Honors/Awds:** Project Business Volunteer Award, Jr Achievement; Detroit Guild Service Award, Urban League; Cert Recognition, Northwest Area Bus Asn, Comm Efforts; State Mich Spec Tribute Entrepreneur; US Sprint 100% Nat Acct Club; Honor Roll of Donors, Univ Detroit. **Home Addr:** 13131 Columbia, Redford, MI 48239-4600.

STOVALL, MELODY S. See Obituaries section.

STOVALL, STANLEY V.
Television news anchorperson, journalist. **Personal:** Born Feb 24, 1953, Rochester, NY. **Educ:** Ariz State Univ, BS, 1975. **Career:** KTVK-TV, anchorman, reporter & photographer, 1970-75; KTAR-TV, Phoenix, anchorman & reporter, 1975; KSDK-TV, St Louis, anchorman & reporter, 1975-78, anchorman, 1983-86; WBAL-TV, Baltimore, anchorman, 1978-83, co-anchor, 2003-; WCAV-TV, Philadelphia, news anchor & reporter, currently. **Orgs:** Greater & St Louis Asn Black Journalists, 1975-78; Asn Black Media Workers, Baltimore; Nat Asn Advan Colored People, Baltimore Br, 1980-83, St Louis Br, 1983-86. **Honors/Awds:** Mr Maryland Bodybuilding Champion, Baltimore, 1980; Mr South Atlantic Bodybuilding Champion, Baltimore, 1980; "Hard Hat" Award, Citizens Housing & Planning Asn, Baltimore, 1983; Baltimore City Council proclamation for Community Service, Baltimore, 1983; Journalist of the Year, Greater St Louis Asn Black Journalists, St Louis, 1986; Emmy Award for "Best News Anchor", St Louis, 1986. **Special Achievements:** First Black TV Anchorman in Phoenix; first African-American news reporter in the state of Arizona; at the age of 18, became the youngest news anchor in the United States. *

STOVALL-TAPLEY, MARY KATE
Mayor, funeral director. **Personal:** Born Dec 13, 1921, Uniontown, AL; daughter of Tim Sanders Sr and Estella Billingsley Sanders; married Turner Stovall, 1953 (deceased); children: Kathleen D Stovall Caldwell & Audrey Y Stovall Hayes. **Educ:** Ala State Univ, BS, 1949, Med, 1955; Atlanta Univ, MLS, 1969. **Career:** Perry County Bd Educ AL, teacher, 1943-51; Russell Co Bd Educ AL, teacher & librn, 1951-76; Town Hurtsboro, AL, counwomen, 1976-84, mayor, 1984-; Stovall Funeral Home, exec funeral dir & chief operating officer, currently. **Orgs:** State democratic exec comt, Democratic Party, 1991-; pres, E Ala Ment Health Bd Dirs; treas, E Ala Funeral Dirs Asn; chairwoman, Hurtsboro Ladies Aux. **Honors/Awds:** Martin Luther King Jr American Dream Award, Ala Dem Conf, 1984; Leadership in Government Award, 6th Annual Black Bus Sem, 1986; National Sojourner Truth Meritorious Service Award, Nat Asn Negro Bus, 1986. **Business Addr:** Executive Funeral Director, Chief Operating Officer, Stovall Funeral Home, 605 Main St, Hurtsboro, AL 36860, **Business Phone:** (334)667-7679.

ST PATRICK, MATTHEW
Actor. **Personal:** Born Mar 17, 1968, Philadelphia, PA; children: Tommy. **Career:** Films: Steel Sharks, 1996; Surface to Air, 1997; War, 2007; Sleepwalking, 2008; Ball Don't Lie, 2008; Alien Raiders, 2008; Sleepwalking, 2008. TV Series: "NYPD Blue", 1996-98; "General Hospital", 1997; "Mike Hammer, Private Eye", 1998; "All My Children", 1998-2000; "Six Feet Under", 2001-05; "Danny Phantom", 2004; "Reunion",2005; Tides of War, 2005; Policeman Hero, 2005-06; "Higglytown Heroes",2005-06; "Law & Order: Special Victims Unit", 2006; Backyards & Bullets, 2007; "Private Practice", 2009; "Saving Grace", 2009. Ruby's Tuesday, exec producer, 2005. **Honors/Awds:** Screen Actors Guild Award for Outstanding Performance by an Ensemble in a Drama Series, 2003, 2004. **Business Addr:** Actor, HBO Studio Productions, 120 E 23rd St Suite A, New York, NY 10010, **Business Phone:** (212)512-7800.*

ST PIERRE, DR. MAURICE
Educator. **Educ:** London Univ, BS; McGill Univ, MA; Univ WI, PhD. **Career:** Univ Guyana; Univ WI, Jamaica; Univ Md Baltimore County; Brit Guianas Civil Serv; Ministry Econ Develop; Morgan State Univ, prof, Dept Sociol & Anthrop, currently. **Special Achievements:** Author: Anatomy of Resistance: Anti-Colonialism in Guyana, 1823-1966, 1999; Giving Voice to the Poor: Poverty Alleviation in West Bengal and Bangladesh, 2002; Dr. Cheddi Jagan: The Making of a Movement Intellectual in Perry Mars and Alma Young, Caribbean Labor and Politics: Legacies of Cheddi Jagan and Michael Manley, 2004. **Business Addr:** Professor, Chair, Morgan State University, Department of Sociology and Anthropology, 1700 E Cold Spring Lane JB 439, Baltimore, MD 21251.

STRACHAN, LLOYD CALVIN, JR.
Electrical engineer. **Personal:** Born Apr 12, 1954, Greensboro, NC; son of Lloyd C Sr and Dorothy B Lane (deceased); married Carolyn Mintz, Oct 5, 1985; children: Camille. **Educ:** NC Agr & Tech State Univ, Greensboro, NC, BS, elec eng, 1976. **Career:** Carolina Power & Light Co, Telecom Construct Unit, from engr to sr engr, 1977-85, supt, 1985-89, Telecom Support Unit, mgr, 1989-92, Telecom Servs Sec, proj analyst, 1992-. **Orgs:** Am Asn Blacks Energy, 1989-; Inst Elec & Electronics Engrs; steering comt mem, Black Achievers, Raleigh Chap, 1991; registered mem, Prof Engr NC. **Military Serv:** Telecom Servs Sec, proj analyst, 1992-. **Business Addr:** Senior Analyst, Carolina Power & Light Company, Telecommunications Planning & Services Section, 411 Fayetteville St MS 7C3, Raleigh, NC 27602, **Business Phone:** (919)546-6523.

STRACHAN, DR. RICHARD JAMES
School administrator. **Personal:** Born Jan 21, 1928, Miami, FL; married Lorraine Farrington; children: Denia, Richard II, Reginald, Regina & Lori. **Educ:** Bethune-Cookman Col, BS, 1956; IN Univ, MS, 1966; Barry Univ, MS, 1972; Atlanta Univ, PhD Educ, 1978. **Career:** North Dade Jr Sr HS, teacher & athletic dir, 1960-66; Miami Central, dept head & band dir, 1966-72; Hialeah HS & Carol City & Norland, asst prin, 1972-81; COPE Sch North, prin. **Orgs:** Bd mem, NAACP; bd mem, YMCA; bd mem, Inner City Sch Dance; bd mem, Dade Co Admin Asn; bd mem, FL Alternative Admin Sch Educators; bd mem, Off Black Affairs, 1981-86; bd mem, Omega Psi Phi; bd mem, youth Adv Coun. **Honors/Awds:** Rockefeller Grant, 1975; Outstanding Bethune-Cookman Col Exelloc Club, 1975; Service Award, Sigma Gamma Rho DLSSA-NABSE-YMCA-NCAO Atlanta Univ, 1986. **Military Serv:** USAF, S & Sgt, 1946-49; Soldier of the Year, 1947-48.

STRAHAN, MICHAEL ANTHONY
Football player, manager. **Personal:** Born Nov 21, 1971, Houston, TX; son of Gene and Louise; married Wanda Hutchins; children: Tanita & Michael Jr; married Jean Muggli (divorced 2006). **Educ:** Tex Southern Univ, attended 1992. **Career:** Football player (retired), Manager; New York Giants, defensive end, 1993-2007; Michael Strahan Enterprises, owner. **Orgs:** Am Cancer Society, The Children Miracle Network, Housing Enterprises for the Less Privileged (H.E.L.P.), People for the Ethical Treatment of Animals (PETA), Starlight Children Found . **Honors/Awds:** Pro Bowl, 1997-99, 2001-05; Defensive Player of the Year, Nat Football League, 2001. **Special Achievements:** Worked for Fox network, 2001; playoffs and appeared on ABCs pregame show prior to Super Bowl XXXVII; FOXs Best Damn Sport Show during the 2004 and2005 post seasons. Strahan has also served as the Giants United Way Spokesman. One of the judge for December 7, 2004 contest Americas Craziest Sports Fan.

STRAIGHT, CATHY A
Journalist. **Personal:** Born Sep 20, 1963, Ocean Springs, MS; daughter of Turner Joseph Straight Sr and June Rose Spears. **Educ:** Univ Southern Miss, BS, journ, 1984. **Career:** The Hattiesburg Am, Hattiesburg, MI, reporter, copy ed, 1982-87; The Jackson Sun Jackson, TN, feature reporter, ed, 1987-89; The Brandenton Hearld, Brandenton, FL, features reporter on aging, 1989-90; The Tennessean, Nashville, TN, gen assignment, features, 1990; St Paul Pioneer Press, sr mgr & managing ed; USA Today, nat ed, currently. **Orgs:** Nat Asn Black Journalist, 1990-; Tenn Press Asn, 1990-; Miss Press Women Asn, 1985-87. **Home Addr:** 1199 Murfreesboro Rd, Nashville, TN 37217. **Business Addr:** National Editor, USA Today, 7950 Jones Branch Dr, McLean, VA 22108-0605.

STRAIT, GEORGE ALFRED, JR.
Journalist. **Personal:** Born Mar 24, 1945, Cambridge, MA; married Lisa Michelle McIver; children: Eric Mathew & Kevin Michael Angelo. **Educ:** Boston Univ, BA, 1967; Atlanta Univ, MS, biochem genetics, 1968-69. **Career:** CBS News, Wash corresp, 1976-77, gen assign corresp, 1977-81, White House corresp, 1979-81, med corresp, 1981; ABC News, medi & health reporter, 1983; Dr Spock Co, sr vpres, content & media, 2000-01; IssueSphere, Wash, DC, sr adv policy; Univ Calif, Berkeley, asst vchancellor pub affairs, 2003-. **Orgs:** Charter mem, Nat Asn Black Journalists; bd trustees, Kaiser Family Found; lay reader, Episcopal Church Am, 1984-. **Honors/Awds:** Asn Sci Writers Award, 1985; Harvard Univ Fel, 1986; Edward R. Murrow Award for Excellence, Overseas Press Club Am, 1986; Overseas Press Club Award, 1987; silver medal for reporting on minorities & HIV/AIDS, 1989; gold medal for reporting on sexism in health care system, 1995; Distinguished Alumni Award, Boston Univ, 1996; Columbia Univ Alfred I. DuPont awards. **Special Achievements:** First black sports anchor, WPVI, Philadelphia, 1972-74; wrote & produced "Black in White America," a critically acclaimed documentary on race; produced a documentary on the syphilis experiments on African American men in Tuskegee, Ala; produced stories that spotlighted race and gender discrimination in modern-day health care. **Business Addr:** Assistant Vice Chancellor For Public Affairs, Office of Public Affairs, 2200 Bancroft Way Suite 4204, Berkeley, CA 94720-4204, **Business Phone:** (510)643-6998.

STRATHER, VIVIAN CARPENTER. See CARPENTER, VIVIAN L.

STRAUGHTER, EDGAR, SR.
School administrator. **Personal:** Born Feb 8, 1929, Willis, TX; son of K J Straughter and Annie Lee; married Betty Harvey, Oct 22, 1954; children: Edgar, Lewis, Ernest, Johnnie, Sherman & Betty, Debra. **Educ:** Tex Southern Univ, 2 yrs. **Career:** Willis Independent Pub Sch Dist, pres; Quality Control supvr, La Pacific, presently; mayor, City Willis, Tex, 1989-93; mediator, Montomery Co. **Orgs:** Vpres, Montgomery Co Voters League; Willis Fire Dept, 1965-; drill instr 2yrs; Willis City Planning Comn; Willis Bd Educ, 9 yrs. **Honors/Awds:** AUS, corpl, 1950-52. **Special Achievements:** First black to serve as a President in Willis Independent Public School District. **Business Addr:** Quality Control Supervisor, Lousania Pacific of New Waverly Texas, New Waverly St, New Waverly, TX 77358, **Business Phone:** (713)592-1429.

STRAUTMANIS, MIKE
Government Official. **Personal:** Born Mar 24, 1969, Chicago, IL; married Damona. **Educ:** Univ of Illinois at Urbana-Champaign,

BS, 1991, Univ of Illinois College of Law, J.D., 1994. **Career:** Paralegal at Sidley Austin; Amer Assoc of Justice, 2001-05; Legislative Dir, Rep. Rod Blagojevich, 1999-01; General counsel, USAID, 1998-00; Chief counsel and Director of Public Laison and Intergovernmental Affairs on Obama's presidential team; Counsel to Barack Obama, 2005-08; Chief of Staff to Valerie Jarrett, 2008-. *

STRAWBERRY, DARRYL EUGENE
Baseball player. **Personal:** Born Mar 12, 1962, Los Angeles, CA; son of Henry and Ruby; married Lisa Watkins (divorced 1993); children: Darryl Jr; married Charisse Simons, Dec 1, 1993; children: Jewel Nicole, Jordan & Jade. **Career:** Baseball player (retired), association executive; NY Mets, outfielder,1980-90; Los Angeles Dodgers, outfielder, 1991-94; San Francisco Giants,1994-95; NY Yankees, 1995-99; analyst, Sports Net New York, currently. **Orgs:** Founder, The Darryl Strawberry Found, currently. **Honors/Awds:** John Murphy Award; Doubleday Award; Rookie of the Year, Nat League, 1983;Rookie Player of the Year, The Sporting News; All-Star Team, 1984-88,1990; Silver Slugger Award, 1988, 1990; Gotta Have Heart Award, 1999. **Special Achievements:** Guest apperance: "The Simpsons"; featured, "Chocolate Strawberry". **Business Addr:** Founder, The Darryl Strawberry Foundation, PO Box 400, St Peters, MO 63376, **Business Phone:** (636)634-1220.

STRAYHORN, EARL CARLTON
Surgeon. **Personal:** Born Aug 27, 1948, Bronx, NY; son of Rhudolphus Clemons Strayhorn and Lydia Strayhorn Blocker; married Louisa Sapp, Jun 1968 (divorced); children: Kharim & Jamal; married Valerie Moss, Apr 4, 2000. **Educ:** Harvard Univ, Cambridge MA, BA, 1971; Tufts Med Sch, Boston MA, MD, 1975. **Career:** Beth Israel Hosp, Boston MA, intern, 1975, resident, 1976-80, chief resident, 1980-81; MA Gen Hosp, fel vascular surg, 1982; Va Vascular Asn, Norfolk VA, vascular surgeon, transplant surgeon, 1983-96; Norfolk Community Hosp, Norfolk VA, chief vascular surgery, 1983-; Norfolk Gen Hosp, Norfolk VA, vice chmn surgery, 1988-, pres med staff, 1996-97; host community health radio prog WTJZ-Radio, 1988; Easter Va Med Sch, asst prof, clin surg; pvt pract physician, currently. **Orgs:** Am Med Asn, 1983-; Urban League; Nat Med Asn. **Honors/Awds:** National Science Foundation Grant, 1969-70; Ellis Memorial Award for Achievement in Surgery, Tufts Med Sch, 1975. **Special Achievements:** Author of articles for medical journal. **Business Addr:** Physician, 6160 Kempsville Rd Suite 317-B, Norfolk, VA 23502, **Business Phone:** (757)461-4278.

STRAYHORN, EARL E. **See Obituaries section.**

STRAYHORN, LLOYD
Writer. **Career:** Tree of Life Bookstore, teacher numerology, 1976-83; Big Red Newspaper, "Numbers and You", weekly columnist, 1978-; NY Amsterdam News, weekly column "Numbersand You", 1979-; Proj ENTER, teacher numerology, 1979-; Arts & Cult, teacher numerology, 1980-81; BMI Syndication, weekly columnist, "Astro/Numerology and You", 1980-; WLIB-AM, "Numbers and You"; Book: Numbers and You: A Numerology Guide for Everyday Living, 1980. **Special Achievements:** Appeared on national TV shows, such as "Oprah Winfrey", "Geraldo", Regis Philbin and Kathy Lee", "The Montel Williams Show" and "Tony Brown's Journal". **Business Addr:** Numerologist, Abby Hoffer Enterprises, 223 12 E 48th St, New York, NY 10017.

STREET, VIVIAN SUE
Administrator. **Personal:** Born Jun 21, 1954, Edgefield, SC; daughter of James Harry Bussey and Susie Bell Werts; married Ronnie Street, Sep 24, 1978 (divorced); children: Jermaine Toriano. **Educ:** State Univ NY Col, Brockport, BS, 1976; Col New Rochelle, MS, 1981. **Career:** Westchester Devel Ctr, Orangeburg, NY, spec educ teacher, 1971-76; Westchester Devel Serv, White Plains, NY, community residence supvr, 1977-78, placement coord, 1978-82; Letchworth Village Devel Serv, team leader, placement team, 1982-86; Black Caucus PS&T Workers PEF, vpres, 1983-; Westchester Devel Disabilities Serv, Tarrytown, NY, prog develop specialist, fiscal liaison, 1986-90, treatment team leader, 1990-92; Letchworth DDSO, develop disabilities prog specialist, 1992-95; Hudson Valley Develop Disabilities Serv Off, Develop Disabilities Prog, specialist, 1995-; PEF Div 276, steward. **Orgs:** Conv deleg, Pub Employees Fed, 1985-; steering comt, Black Tennis & Sports Found, 1986-; treasurer, NAACP Spring Valley NY, 1988-98, pres, 1999; Tops Tot s Nursery Sch, 1989-; CNL leader, Pub Employees Fed Div 336, 1992; United Way; bd trustees appointee, First Baptist Church; pres, Spring Valley Br, Nat Asn Adv Colored People. **Honors/Awds:** Humanitarium, Pub Employees Fed, 1987; Community Serv Award, United Negro Scholarship Fund, 1988; Community Serv Award, Black Tennis & Sports Found, 1988; Service Award, PEF Black Caucus, 1991. **Special Achievements:** 2001 Woman of Distinction. **Business Addr:** Developmental Disabilities Program Specialist, Hudson Valley Development Disabilities Services Office, PO Box 470, Thiells, NY 10984.*

STREETER, DEBRA BRISTER
Executive. **Personal:** Born May 23, 1956, Birmingham, AL; daughter of Edward Brister and Ella Scott Brister; married Otis Streeter Jr, Jul 29, 1984 (divorced 1990); children: Otis Brister & Sheeba L. **Educ:** Univ Ala, Birmingham, AL, cert acct, 1981; Booker T Wash Bus Col, Birmingham, AL, cert secretarial & sci, 1984. **Career:** Turning Point Prod, Birmingham, AL, admin secy, 1976-84, comptroller, 1988-; Zegarelli & Assoc, Birmingham, AL, secy, 1984-86; Beverly Health Care Ctr W, Fairfield, AL, secy & bookkeeper, 1986-87; Univ Ala, Birmingham, AL, secy, 1987-88. **Honors/Awds:** Accounting Honor Award, Booker T Washington Bus Col, 1975.

STREETER, DENISE WILLIAMS
Executive, chief financial officer. **Personal:** Born Apr 27, 1962, Washington, DC; daughter of Michael G and Patricia A Dorn; married Christipher M, Oct 5, 1985; children: Mikala P, C Christipher K & Ronald M. **Educ:** Howard Univ, Wash, DC, BBA, 1984. **Career:** Coopers & Ly brand, Wash, DC, staff acct, 1984-86; ICMA Retirement Corp, Wash, DC, mgr & trust acct, 1986-89; F S Taylor & Assts, Wash, DC, mgr, 1989-92; Nat 4-H Coun, proj dir, acct & financial admin, asst treas,1992-, sr vpres, proj dir & cfo, currently, asst treasurer, currently. **Orgs:** Chap pres, Int Fraternity Delta Sigma Pi, 1981-; chap pres, Nat Asn Black Accts, Inc, 1983-; Beta Gamma Sigma Nat Honor Soc, 1983-; Dist Columbia Inst CPAs, 1986-; Am Inst CPAs, 1986-; asst treas, Mt Pleasant Baptist Church, 1991-96; Am Soc Asn Execs, 1992-; Planning Comm, 1993; Eastern Region NABA Stud Conf, 1993-; officer, Ken moor Elem PTA, 1996-; leader, PG County 4-H Teen Coun, 1997; lead teacher, 10-12 Girls Cs Ministry, First Bapt Church Glenarden, 1997-. **Honors/Awds:** Outstanding New Member, 1985; The History of Black Accountancy: The First100 Black CPAs, 1990, Outstanding NABA Member, 1991, Nat Asn Black Accts. **Home Addr:** 2004 Parkside Dr, Mitchellville, MD 20721-4233, **Home Phone:** (301)218-6292. **Business Addr:** Project Director, Senior President & Chief Financial Officer, National 4-H Council, 7100 Connecticut Ave, Chevy Chase, MD 20815-4999, **Business Phone:** (301)961-2947.

STREETER, ELWOOD JAMES
Dentist. **Personal:** Born Jun 14, 1930, Greenville, NC; son of William and Hattie Forbes; married Martha; children: Agnes & Nicole. **Educ:** NC Col, BS, 1952; Howard Univ, DDS, 1956; Univ Calif, Los Angeles, cert, 1969. **Career:** Perez & Streeter Dental Corp, dentist, 1958-; La Co USC Med Ctr, dental attending staff; Hollywood Presbyterian Med Ctr, attending staff; pvt pract, currently. **Orgs:** Am Dental Asn; Calif Dental Asn; Sothern Calif Stomatognathic & Res Seminar; pres, Sothern Calif, Acad Gen Denist, 1978, past presidents advisory coun, 1979-; YMCA; NAACP; NC Col Alumni Asn; La Dental Soc Dental Care, mem, 1958-; Angel City Dental Soc, 1956-; partner, Amalgamated Devel Assoc; treas, Amada Enterprises Inc; treas, Allied Diversified Assoc; bd dir, Delta Dental Calif, 1994-. **Honors/Awds:** Fel Acad Gen Dent, 1972; Fel, Am Col Dentists, 1985; Fel, Intl Col Dentists, 1983; Fel, Pierre Fuchard Acad, 1988. **Military Serv:** USNR, capt, 1954-88. **Home Addr:** 665 E Mendocino, Altadena, CA 91001. **Business Addr:** Dentist, 3701 Stocker St, Los Angeles, CA 90008, **Business Phone:** (323)291-1024.

STREETS, FRAN A
Association executive, chief executive officer. **Career:** Bank San Francisco, from vpres to sr vpres, 1985-91; sr vpres mkt & investor rels, 1991-92; Wells Fargo Bank, City Dir Pvt Banking Div, vpres, 1992; Int Women's Forum, pres, 1997; Pac Bank, dir; San Francisco Ballet, co-chmn bd; Heald Col, chmn bd, 2001-, interim pres & chief exec officer, currently. **Orgs:** Adv bd, City Nat Corp; dir, Audit & Finance Comt, Loan Comt, Nominating & Compensation Comt, Pac Bank; comnr, City San Francisco's Libr Comn, chair, Finance Comt; Int Women's Forum, pres, bd dir, currently. **Special Achievements:** Numerous achievements in Bank of California including First African-American female on its Management Training Program, first female Corporate Lending Officer, first person of color to become a Branch Manager; First African American to be named president of the International Women's Forum. **Business Phone:** (415)808-3000.*

STREETS, TAI
Football player. **Personal:** Born Apr 20, 1977, Matteson, IL. **Educ:** Mich Univ. **Career:** Football player (retired); San Francisco 49ers, wide receiver, 1999-2003; Detroit Lions, wide receiver, 2004. **Honors/Awds:** Bo Schembechler Award; Athletic Academic Achievement Award.

STRICKLAND, DR. ARVARH E
Educator. **Personal:** Born Jul 6, 1930, Hattiesburg, MS; son of Clotiel Marshall and Eunice; married Willie Pearl Elmore Strickland, Jun 17, 1951; children: Duane Arvarh & Bruce Elmore. **Educ:** Tougaloo Col, Tougaloo, MS, BA, history, english, 1951; Univ Ill, Urbana, Ill, MA, educ, 1953, PhD, history, 1962. **Career:** Chicago State Col, asst prof, 1962-65, assoc prof, 1965-68, prof, 1968-69; Univ Mo, Columbia, prof, 1969-95, prof emeritus, 1995-, chmn dept history, 1980-83, interim dir black studies prog, 1986, 1994-95, Off vipres Academic Affairs, sr faculty assoc, 1987-88; interim assoc vpres, academic affairs, 1989, assoc vpres, academic affairs, 1989-91. **Orgs:** Am Asn Univ Prof; Missouri Advisory Commn Historic Preservation, 1976-80; Gen Bd Higher Educ & Ministry, The United Methodist Church, 1976-80, mem, exec comm; commr, Columbia Planning & Zoning Comm, 1977-80; Asn Study Afro-Am Life & History; Southern Historical asn; bd trustees, State Historical Soc Mo; co-chmn, Mayor's Steering Comm Commemorating the Contribution Black Columbians, Columbia, MO, 1980; mem, Fed Judicial Merit Selection Comm, Western Dist, Mo, 1982; Kiwanis Club, Columbia; Mo Historical Records Advisory Bd; commr, Peace Officers Standards & Training Commn, 1988-89. **Honors/Awds:** Kappa Delta Pi (education), 1953; Phi Alpha Theta (history), 1960; Kendric C Babcock Fel History, Univ Ill, 1961-62; Distinguished Serv Award, Illinois Historical Soc, 1967 Honor Soc Phi Kappa Phi, Univ Miss, 1973; Asn Danforth Found, 1973; Omicron Delta Kappa Nat Leadership Honor Soc, 1978; Martin Luther King Memorial Comm Award for Outstanding Community Serv, 1982; Faculty-Alumni Award, Alumni Assn Univ Mo, 1983; Serv Appreciation Award, Missouri Comm for the Humanities, 1984; Thomas Jefferson Award, Univ Mo, 1985; Off Equal Opportunity Award for Exemplary Serv in Enhancing the Status of Minorities, Univ Mo, 1985; Distinguished Alumni Award (Tougaloo Coll), Nat Assn for Equal Opportunity in Higher Educ, 1986; N Endowment for the Humanities, Travel to Collections Grant, 1986; Byler Distinguished Professor Award, Univ Mo, Columbia, 1994; St Louis American's Educator of the Year Award, 1994; publications: History of the Chicago Urban League, Univ of Illinois Press, 1966, Reprint, Univ of MO Press, 2001; Building the United States, author with Jerome Reich and Edward Biller, Harcourt, Brace Jovanovich Inc, 1971; The Black American Experience, co-author with Jerome Reich, Harcourt, Brace Jovanovich Inc, 1974; Vol I, From Slavery through Reconstruction to 1877; Vol 11, From Reconstruction to the Present Since 1877; Edited with an Introduction, Lorenzo J Greene, Working With Carter G Woodson, The Father of Black History: A Diary, 1928-30, Louisiana State Univ Press, 1989; Edited with an introduction, Lorenzo J Greene, Selling Black History for Carter G Woodson: A Diary, 1930-33, Univ of Missouri Press, 1996; co-editor, The African American Experience: An Historiographical & Bibliographical Guide, Greenwood Press, 2001. **Special Achievements:** A room has been named in Strickland's honor in the Memorial Student Union. establishment of the Strickland Endowed Professorship in African American History and Black Studies. **Military Serv:** AUS, sp-4, 1953-55; Hon discharge from reserves, 1961. **Business Addr:** Professor Emeritus, University of Missouri-Columbia College Arts & Science, Department of History, 112 Read Hall, Columbia, MO 65211, **Business Phone:** (573)882-6049.

STRICKLAND, CLINTON VERNAL, JR.
School administrator. **Personal:** Born Dec 19, 1950, Elmira, NY; son of Clinton V Sr and Grace Brooks; married Holly E Williams, Apr 21, 1973; children: Crystal V, Cicely V, Clinton III, Christopher V & Caitlyn V. **Educ:** Univ Rochester, BA, 1974, MA, 1975; State Univ New York, Brockport, cert study educ admin, 1977; State Univ New York, Buffalo, Doctoral Prog. **Career:** Rochester City Sch Dist, teacher, 1974-79, counr, 1979, dean stud,1980-82, jr high admin, 1982-84, project mgr Sch environ prog, 1984-85;Nathaniel Rochester Community Sch, vice prin; Adlai E. Stevenson Sch No.29, prin, currently. **Orgs:** Vol, Urban League Rochester NY Inc 1979-; bd dir, Off Black Ministries Catholic Diocese Rochester, 1982-83; chmn, Eureka Lodge 36 Educ &Charitable Trust; life mem, Theta Omicron Chap Omega Psi Phi Frat;trainer, facilitator, NYSCCT United Teachers; mem Phi Delta Kappa; pres &founder, Black Educ Asn Rochester. **Honors/Awds:** Gen Electric Fel, Boston Univ, General Electric Co, 1975; Outstanding Volunteer Award, Urban League, Rochester, 1982-84; Distinguish Service Award, Masons Eureka Lodge 36 Prince Hall Masons; Man of the Year, Nat Asn Negro Bus & Prof Women Rochester, 1987.

STRICKLAND, DEMERICK MONTAE. **See STRICKLAND, ERICK.**

STRICKLAND, DOROTHY S
Educator. **Personal:** Born Sep 29, 1933, Newark, NJ; daughter of Leroy Salley Sr and Evelyn Daniels; married Maurice R, Aug 27, 1955; children: Mark, M Randall & Michael. **Educ:** Kean Col, BS, 1955; NY Univ, MA, 1958, PhD, 1971. **Career:** Learning Disability Spec E Orange, teacher, reading consult, 1961-66; Jersey City State Col, Reading Dept, asst prof, 1966-70; Kean Col, from assoc prof to prof, 1970-80; NY Univ, adj prof; Teachers Col Columbia Univ, prof, 1980-85, Arthur I Gates prof Educ, 1985-90; Rutgers Univ, prof reading, 1990-2002, Samuel De Witt Proctor prof educ, 2002-. **Orgs:** Bd dir, Nat Coun Teachers Eng; Educ adv bd, Early Years Mag; chmn, Early Childhood Educ; jour reading instr, Websters New World Dictionary, comn Sprint Mag; pres, Int Reading Asn, 1978-79; Nat Comm Ed Migrant C; trustee, Res Found, Nat Coun Teachers Eng, 1983-86; Kappa Delta Pi; Pi Lamda Theta; Phi Delta Kappa; Am Educ Res Asn; Nat Asn Educ Young C. **Honors/Awds:** Woman of the Year, Zeta Phi Beta, 1980; Nat Research Award, Nat Coun Teachers Eng, 1972; Founders Day Recognition, NY Univ, 1971; Outstanding Teacher Educ Reading, Int Reading Asn, 1985; Award Outstanding Contribution Ed, Nat Asn Univ Women, 1987; emerging literacy, Int Reading asn, 1989; admin & supvr, reading prog, Teachers Col Press, 1989; Elected Reading Hall of Fame, Int Reading Asn, 1990; Distinguished Alumni Award, New York Univ, 1990; Outstanding Alumni

Award, Kean Col NJ, 1990; Bank Street Col Educ, DHL, 1991; Nat Council Teachers English Award Research; Rewey Bell Inglis Award, Nat Coun Teachers Eng, 1994; Recipient of the Jubilee Medal, Archdiocese of Newark, 1997; Outstanding Educator in the Language Arts, Nat Coun Teachers Eng, 1998; Recipient, Nat-Louis Univ Ferguson Award for Outstanding Contributions to the field of Early Childhood Education, 2005. **Special Achievements:** Author, editor, or co-editor, Language Arts: Learning and Teaching; Language Literacy and the Child, Process Reading and Writing; A Literature Based Approach, Emerging Literacy; Young Children Learn to Read and Write, The Administration and Supervision of Reading Programs, Educating Black Children; America's Challenge, Family Storybook Reading, Listen Children; An Anthology of Black Literature, Familie; An Anthology of Poetry for Young Children; Publications: Literacy Instruction in Half Day and Full Day Kindergartens, Newark, DE Intl Reading Asn, Morrow LM, Strickland, DS, & Woo, D, 1998. **Business Addr:** Samuel DeWitt Proctor Professor II, Rutgers University, Grad Sch Educ, 10 Seminary Pl Rm no 229, New Brunswick, NJ 08903, **Business Phone:** (732)932-7496.

STRICKLAND, ERICK (DEMERICK MONTAE STRICKLAND)
Basketball player. **Personal:** Born Nov 25, 1973, Opelika, AL. **Educ:** Univ Nebr. **Career:** Basketball player (retired); Dallas Mavericks, guard, 1996-2000; NY Knicks, 2000-01; Vancouver Grizzlies, 2000-01; Boston Celtics, 2001-02; Ind Pacers, 2002-03; Milwaukee Bucks, guard, 2004-05. **Honors/Awds:** All-Big Eight Defensive Hons, 1994-96; Most Valuable Player, 1996.

STRICKLAND, DR. FREDERICK WILLIAM, JR.
Physician. **Personal:** Born Aug 24, 1944, Kansas City, MO; son of Frederick William Sr and Ardene Graves; married Marina Karvounis, Jun 2, 1990 (divorced); married Gina Angove, May 4, 2002. **Educ:** Southwestern Col, BA, 1966; Drake Univ, MA, 1976; Col Osteopathic Med & Surg, DO, 1978. **Career:** Oklahoma City Pub Schs, sci teacher, 1967-69; Des Moines Pub Schs, sci teacher 1969-74; Des Moines Gen Hosp, intern/resident, 1978-80; UOMHS, prof family med, 1980-; COMS, clinic dir stud trainer, 1980-2001; Strickland Clinic for Family Practice, solo practitioner, 2001-. **Orgs:** AOA, 1978-; ACGP, 1980-; corp bd, Des Moines Gen Hosp, 1983-; Polk Co Democratic Central Comn, 1984-88; Des Moines Art Ctr, 1984-; adv comn, State Iowa DUR Comn, 1985-00; Plan & Zoning Comn, City Des Moines, 1985-95; DMGH Found Des Moines Gen Hosp, 1986-00; Asn Retarded Citizens, 1986-; Boys & Girls Club Des Moines Bd Dirs, 1988-; Bernie Lorenz Recovery House Bd Dirs, 1987-02; Central City Optimist Club, 1990-99; City Des Moines, Strategic Planning Comt; Asn Addiction Med; Polk County Bd Health. **Honors/Awds:** The Moundbuilder Award Southwestern Col, 1978; The DUR Award, Iowa Pharm Assoc, 1986-00; "Alcohol-Induced Rhabdomyolysis," Hawkeye Osteopath J, 1986; "Osteomyelitis of the Maxillary Antrum & Ethmoid Sinus in an Adolesent Male," Osteopath Med News, 1987. **Special Achievements:** Author, Don't Spoil the Broth, a paper on quality assurance, Am Osteopathic Hosp Asn Newsletter, 1989. **Military Serv:** AUS, Medical Corps maj, Iowa Army Nat Guard, 14 yrs; Flight Surgeon, Iowa Army Commendation Award, 1983-85. **Home Addr:** 4910 Country Club Blvd, Des Moines, IA 50312. **Business Addr:** Physician, Strickland Family Practice, 974 - 73rd St Suite 35, Des Moines, IA 50312, **Business Phone:** (515)440-2491.

STRICKLAND, FREDRICK WILLIAM, JR.
Football player. **Personal:** Born Aug 15, 1966, Ringwood, NJ; married Shay. **Educ:** Purdue Univ. **Career:** Football player (retired); Los Angeles Rams, linebacker, 1988-92; Minn Vikings, 1993; Green Bay Packers, 1994-95; Dallas Cowboys, 1996-98; Wash Redskins, 1999.

STRICKLAND, HERMAN WILLIAM, JR.
Banker. **Personal:** Born Sep 10, 1959, Blytheville, AR; son of Herman W Sr; married Rhonda, Mar 21, 1987; children: Ashlee & Aryn. **Educ:** Ark State Univ, BS, mgt, 1980; Univ Memphis, MBA, finance, 1991. **Career:** First Tenn Bank, mgt training prog, 1981-83, acct officer, 1983-84, vpres, Jr lender med serv, 1984-87, vpres, sr lender metro, 1987-93, vpres & sr credit officer, 1993-. **Orgs:** Jr Achievement, loaned exec, 1984-85; steering comn mem, Rozelle Elem Adopt-a-Sch, 1987-; bd mem, Synergy Found, 1992-; bd mem, Dixie Homes Boys Club, 1994-; Leadership Memphis, 1997. **Honors/Awds:** "Simply the Best" Award, Black Bus Dir, 1995. **Home Addr:** 9804 Woodland Run Lane, Cordova, TN 38018, **Home Phone:** (901)751-2887. **Business Addr:** vice President, First Tennessee Bank, 185 Madison Ave, Memphis, TN 38101, **Business Phone:** (901)523-4341.

STRICKLAND, MARK
Basketball player. **Personal:** Born Jul 14, 1970, Atlanta, GA. **Educ:** Temple Univ, attended 1992. **Career:** Ind Pacers, forward, 1994-95; Miami Heat, 1997-2000; NJ Nets, 2000-01; Denver Nuggets, 2000-01; Atlanta Hawks, 2001-02; Dallas Mavericks, 2003; Rockford Lightning, 2005-06; Deportivo San Jose Asuncion, 2007; Arena Amman, 2007-.

STRICKLAND, R. JAMES
Executive, business owner, president (organization). **Personal:** Born Feb 24, 1930, Kansas City, KS; son of Roosevelt Joseph and Mable Yvonne Roberts; married Deanna Cartman; children: James, Jay, Jeffrey, Deanna & Dori. **Educ:** Kans U, BS pharmacy, 1954. **Career:** Strickland Drugs Inc, pres & owner 1968-; Joslyn Clinic, mgr, 1954-68; boxing trainer, mgr. **Orgs:** Pres, Alpha Phi, Alpha Upsilon Chapter, 1953-54; housing chmn W Sub NAACP,1965; vpres, Nat Asn Advan Colored People West Sub Chap, 1966; vpres, MetImprov Asn, 1971; bd chmn, Met Improvement Ass, 1972-73; vpres, ChicagoConf Brother hood, 1977; bd chmn, Chatham Bus Asn, 1976-77; bd mem,Chicago Retail Druggist Asn, 1977; dir, Maywood Comt Spec Events, 1989-. **Honors/Awds:** Award Chicago Conf for Brother hood, 1974. **Home Addr:** 150 N Elmwood, Oak Park, IL 60302.

STRICKLAND, RODNEY
Basketball player, basketball executive. **Personal:** Born Jul 11, 1966, Bronx, NY. **Educ:** DePaul Univ, Chicago, IL, 1988. **Career:** New York Knicks, guard, 1988-90, San Antonio Spurs, 1990-92, Portland Trail Blazers, 1992-96, 2000-01; Wash Wizards, 1996-2001; Miami Heat, 2001-02; Minn Timberwolves, 2002-03; Orlando Magic, 2003-04; Toronto Raptors, 2004; Houston Rockets, 2005; Memphis Tigers, dir stud-athlete develop mgr, currently. **Honors/Awds:** NBA All-Rookie Second Team, 1989. **Special Achievements:** NBA Draft, First round pick, No 18, 1988. **Business Addr:** Director of Student-Athlete Development/ Manager, Memphis Tigers, University of Memphis, 570 Normal St, Memphis, TN 38111, **Business Phone:** (901)678-2331.

STRICKLAND-HILL, DR. MARVA YVONNE
Educator. **Personal:** Born Jun 18, 1952, Savannah, GA; daughter of W S Strickland; married Larry Hill, Aug 3, 1997. **Educ:** Clark Col, BA, 1974; Atlanta Univ, MA, 1976, PhD, 1988. **Career:** Clark Col, dean's list, 1973-74, cum laude graduate, 1974; Grambling State Univ, polit sci instr, 1979; Morehouse Col, polit sci instr, 1984; NC A&T St Univ, polit sci instr, 1985; Bethune-Cookman Col, asst prof, 1986; GA Southern Col, asst prof, 1988; DeKalb Col, asst prof, 1989-91; KY St Univ, polit sci asst prof, 1992-. **Orgs:** Zeta Phi Beta Sorority; Nat Conf Black Polit Scientists. **Honors/Awds:** Political Science Outstanding Achievement, 1974; fel Ford Found, 1974-76; Who's Among America's Teacher Distinguished Educator, 1995-98; Faculty Member of the Year, Phi Beta Sigma, 1997. **Special Achievements:** Invisible Giants of the Voting Rights Movement, co-author, Pearson, 1994. **Home Addr:** 215 Capital Ave Apt G-4, Frankfort, KY 40601, **Home Phone:** (502)875-1315. **Business Addr:** Assistant Professor, Kentucky State University, 400 E Main St Hathaway Hall, Frankfort, KY 40601, **Business Phone:** (502)227-6000.

STRICKLIN, JAMES
Cinematographer, photographer. **Personal:** Born Mar 27, 1934, Chicago, IL; son of Phillip and Harriet; married Manita-Joyce; children: Nicholas. **Educ:** Ill Inst Technol, BS, 1958; Art Inst Chicago, attended. **Career:** Univ Chicago, lectr film cinematography; Can Broadcasting Corp, cameraman, 1964-67; NBC-News, cinematographer & cameraman, 1967-75, videographer & tech dir, 1975-. **Orgs:** Ill Arts Coun, 1976-77; US Yacht Racing Union, 1982-; Int Penguin Class Dinghy Asn, 1985-; Jackson Pank Yacht Club, 1985-; race comt, Columbia Yacht Club, 1993; Nat Acad TV Art & Sci. **Honors/Awds:** Univ Ill photos exhibited Smithsonian Inst, 1962; co-auth, "With Grief Acquainted", 1963; Emmy Outstanding Cinematographer, 1971-72. **Special Achievements:** Numerous doc films. **Business Phone:** (312)836-5555.

STRINGER, C VIVIAN
Basketball coach. **Personal:** Born in Edenborn, PA; married William D (deceased) (deceased); children: David, Janine & Justin. **Educ:** Slippery Rock State Col, BA, 1970. **Career:** Cheyney State Univ, women's basketball coach, 1971-83; Univ IA, women's basketball coach, 1983-95; Rutgers State Univ, women's basketball head coach, 1995-. **Orgs:** Co-founder, Women's Basketball Coaches Asn; Voting Bd, Amateur Basketball Asn US; adv bd, Nike Coaches; ALL-AM Selection Comt, Kodak; adv bd, Women's Sports Found. **Honors/Awds:** Coach of the Year, Sports Illustrated, USA Today; Naismith Col Coach of the Year, Black Coaches Asn; Nat Coach of the Year, 1982, 1988, 1993; District V Coach of the Year, 1985, 1988, 1993; Communiplex Hall of Fame, 1987; Bronze Medal, Pan Am Games, coach, 1991; Big Ten Coach of the Year, 1991, 1993; Carol Eckman Award, 1993; Lifetime Achievement Award, Black Coaches Asn, 2004; Sports Hall of Fame, NJ, 2005. **Special Achievements:** NCAA Final Four, Cheyney State, 1982, Univ IA, 1993; World Championship Zone Qualification Tournament, coach, 1989; World University Games, coach, 1979, 1985; US Select Team, head coach, 1981; One of the youngest women's basketball coaches to reach 500 victories; one of the top five winningest active division I women's basketball coaches; First female African American coach to win 600 games in women's basketball. **Business Addr:** Head Coach Women, Rutgers University, Livingston Campus, Piscataway, NJ 08854.

STRINGER, THOMAS EDWARD
Circuit court judge. **Personal:** Born Jul 8, 1944, Peekskill, NY; son of Theodore and Fannie; married Lillian Jean Cooper; children: Thomas E Jr, Daryl Q, Rhonda E & Roderick E. **Educ:** New York Univ, Wash Sq Col, BA, math, 1967; Stetson Univ Col Law, JD, 1974. **Career:** Hillsborough Co State Atty's Off, staff atty, asst state atty, 1974-76; Rosello & Stringer, PA, staff atty, 1976-84; Hillsborough Co Ct, co judge, 1984-87; Hillsborough Co, admin judge, circuit judge, 1988-99; Second Dist Ct Appeals, judge, 1999-. **Orgs:** Nat Bar Asn, 1974-; Hillsborough Co Bar Asn, 1974-; bd dirs, Boys & Girls Clubs Greater Tampa Inc, 1976-; Omega Psi Phi Fraternity, 1980-; bd dirs, Bay Area Legal Serv, 1984-; bd overseers, Stetson Univ Col Law, 1986-; Bay Area Chamber Comn, 1986-. **Honors/Awds:** Citizen of the Year, Pi Iota Chap, Omega Psi Phi Frat, 1984; George E Edgecomb Award, Tampa Urban League, 1984. **Military Serv:** USAF, capt, 1967-71. **Business Addr:** Judge, Second District Court of Appeals, 801 E Twiggs St Suite 600, Tampa, FL 33602, **Business Phone:** (813)272-3430.

STRINGFELLOW, ERIC DEVAUGHN
Journalist, educator. **Personal:** Born Aug 31, 1960, Meridian, MS; son of Clintorice Sr and Delores Tartt; children: Courtney DeVon. **Educ:** Jackson State Univ, Jackson, MS, mass commun, 1982. **Career:** Com News, gen assignment reporter, 1982; The Clarion Ledger, reporter, 1982-86; Plain Dealer, reporter, 1986-91; Jackson Clarion Ledger, political ed, 1991-94; Jackson St Univ, adj prof, 1991-94, prof residence; Clarion Ledger, metro columnist, currently. **Orgs:** Pres, Jackson Asn Black Journalists, 1985-86, 1992-; parliamentarian, Cleveland Asn Black Journalists, 1987-89; pres, Cleveland Asn Black Journalists, 1989-91; pres, JSU Cleveland Alumni Chap, 1989-91; BlackMedia Workers, 1990-91; bd mem, Voice Calvary Ministries. **Honors/Awds:** John Hancock Award, John Hancock Co, 1985; Second Place Interpretive Reporting, Miss/La Asniated Press Contest, 1986. **Special Achievements:** Hundred Black Men of Jackson. **Home Addr:** 117 Kilkenny Blvd, Jackson, MS 39209. **Business Phone:** (601)961-7236.

STRIPLING, DR. LUTHER
Educator. **Personal:** Born Aug 25, 1935, Tingnall, GA; son of Luther and Catherine; married Myrtice Jones, Nov 7, 1957 (deceased); children: Cedric Ravel & Lloyd Byron. **Educ:** Clark Col, AB, 1957; Atlanta Univ, attended 1965; Univ Ky, MMus, 1968; Univ Colo, DMus, 1971. **Career:** Hamilton High Sch, teacher, 1957-66, chmn music dept, 1960-66; GA Interscholastic Assn, chmn vocal div, 1964-66; Univ Ky, instr, 1966-68; Univ Colo, 1970-71; Macalester Col, coordr vocal activities, 1971; S Ill Univ, Edwardsville, assoc prof, dir, opera workshop; Tarrant County Jr Col, NE Campus, 1984-95; Bel Canto Singles, prof, vocal music & dir, currently; Clark Atlanta Univ, Dept Music, prof, currently. **Orgs:** Nat Opera Asn Inc; Macalester Col Opera Workshop; Assoc Col Twin Cities Opera Workshop; Pilgrim Baptist Church; Nat Asn Teachers Singing, St Louis Dist Chap, 1980-82; numerous performances orchestral appearances directing papers in field; bd governors, NE Trinity Arts Coun, 1989-91. **Honors/Awds:** Contributor Burkhart Charles Anthology for Musical Analysis third Ed, NY Holt Rinehart & Winston 1978. **Home Phone:** (817)354-1502. **Business Phone:** (404)880-8000.

STRODE, VELMA MCEWEN
Executive. **Personal:** Born Oct 19, 1919, Jackson, MS; daughter of Rev McEwen and B T McEwen; married James W (deceased); children: James C. **Career:** Office Equal Employ Opportunity, US Dept Labor, dir, 1971-; Dept Justice, Community Rels Serv, sr community rels specialist; Community Ctr Utica NY, dir; The Velma McEwen Show, broadcaster. **Orgs:** Exec, Urban League, 1946-57; Acad Cert Social Workers; Alumni Asn Fed Exec Inst; Am Women Radio & TV; bd trustees, St Augustine's Col; United Way Bd DC; rep, Greater Metro United Way Bd; adv Capital Tower Proj Home Delinquent Young Women; Exec Women Gov Orgn; Nat Urban League; NAACP; Social Action Comn Delta Sigma Theta Sorority; Leadership Conf Civil Rights; adv bd, YWCA Tower. **Honors/Awds:** Recognition for outstanding performance of duties, US Dept of Labor 1973; activist award, Cleveland OH, 1974; outstanding service to humanity, St Augustine Col, 1975; the Chapel of Four Chaplains Philadelphia, 1975; the Conf Minority Public Admin Award, 1976; Am GI Forum Award, 1976; Equal Employment Opportunity Commn Award Dallas, 1976; EEO award, Fed Women's Prog, Texas Region, Equal Employment Opportunity Comn, 1976; hon citizen, Dallas TX, 1976; labor mgt award, Nat Black Women's Political Leadership Caucus, 1976.

STRONG, AMANDA L
Administrator, president (organization). **Personal:** Born Nov 22, 1935, Marvel, AR; daughter of Early Mae and Percy Watson; widowed; children: Cheryl Beard, Pamela Tender & Jerilyn S. **Educ:** St Vincents Hosp Sch Nursing, Dipl, 1954-57; Ind Univ, BSN, 1973; ANA, Cert, 1980; Ind Univ, MSN, 1983; Family Nurse Practitioner, cert. **Career:** Nurse Practitioner (retired); Ind Univ Med Ctr, asst head nurse, 1959-64; Vis Nurse Asn, supvr, 1964-72; Dept Corr, family nurse practr, 1974-80; Roudebush Vets Admin Med Ctr Home Based Primary Care Prog, nurse practr, 1980-, prog dir, HBPC, 1988-97; "Stuck on Wellness," Nikken Independent Distributor; Ind Sr Citizens' Ctr, audlt practrl NIKKEN health & wellness prod, distribr, currently. **Orgs:** Bd mem, Capitol Improv Bd, 1978-85; pres, Holy Angels Parish Coun, 1979-83; comm ch & bd mem, Coalition 100 Black Women, 1980-; black & minority health task force Ind State Bd Health;

stand comn Chronic Health Ind State Bd Health; bd mem, Ind State Bd Nurses & Nurse Practr Coun; pres, Ind Univ Sch Nursing, 1988-91; secy, Dist 5 Alumni Asn Bd Nursing, Ind State Nurses Asn, 1987-89; facilitator, Hosp Based Home Care Support Group, 1989-; vice chmn, Archdiocesan Pastoral Coun, Indianapolis, Ind; elected pres, Cath Found Bd, Archdiocese Indianapolis, Multi-Cultural Ministry Adv Comn; Frontline Vol, Indpls Mus Art; secy bd dir, Cath Community Found Archdiocese Indianapolis, currently. **Honors/Awds:** Those Special People Sigma Phi Communications Award; Cert Am Nurses Asn Adult Practr, 1995-2000; Martin Luther King Leadership Award, SCLC; Citizen of Day, WTLC Radio; chosen Hospital Based Home Care Nurse, 1985; Special Contribution Nursing Veterans Admin Nursing, 1989; Minority Nurse Role Model, Indianapolis Star, 1989; Sigma Theta Tau Nursing Hon Soc, 1989-; nominee, Federal Employee of the Year, Federal Government, 1991; Amvets, Distinguished Nurse Award; Vol Serv Award, Am Cancer Soc, 1995; Salute from WFMY Volunteerism. **Home Addr:** 402 E 46th St, Indianapolis, IN 46205, **Home Phone:** (317)283-2935.

STRONG, CRAIG STEPHEN
Judge. **Personal:** Born Sep 5, 1947, Detroit, MI. **Educ:** Howard Univ, BA, 1969; Detroit Col Law, JD, 1973. **Career:** Wayne Co Neighborhood Legal Serv, law intern & staff atty, 1970-73; Terry Ahmad & Bradfield, assoc atty, 1973; Elliard Crenshaw & Strong PC, partner, 1974-77; Recorder's Ct City Detroit Traffic & Ordinance Div, referee, 1978; City Detroit Recorder's Ct, Wayne Co 3rd Circuit Ct, judge, 1979-. **Orgs:** Past pres, Wolverine Bar Asn; regional dir, Nat Bar Asn; former recorder's ct com chmn, Detroit Bar Asn; vice chmn bd dir, Wayne Co Neighborhood Legal Serv; rep, assembly State Bar Mich; Prince Hall Masons 32nd Degree; bd dirs, Karmanos Cancer Inst; former pres, Asn Black Judges Mich; life mem, Nat Asn Advan Colored People; Alpha Phi Alpha Fraternity; 33 degree Masons; chair elect, Nat Bar Asn. **Honors/Awds:** Man of the Year Award, Detroit Urban Ctr, 1979; Howardite of the Year Award, Howard Univ Detroit Chap, 1979; Distinguished Service Award, Nat Coun Negro Women, 1980; Renaissance Award, 13th Dist Dem Party, 1982; Outstanding Museum Service Award, Afro-Am Mus Detroit, 1983; Humanitarian Award Excellence, Mother Waddles Perpetual Mission, 1983; Man Of The Year,North End youth Improv Coun, 1986; Award Of Appreciation, Boy Scouts Am Renaissance Dist, 1988; Civic & Community Contrib Award, Native Detroiter Mag, 1989; Legal Accomplishments Recognition, Wolverine Stud Bar Asn, 1990; Ron Brown Award Merit, Wolverine Stud Bar Asn, 1997; Spec Appreciation Award, SCLC, 1999; Charles H Wright Awar, 1999; Community Activism Award, Wolverine Bar Asn, 1999; Distinguished Service Award, Wolverine Bar Asn & Asn Black Judges, 2000. **Special Achievements:** Youngest president at age twenty-nine, Wolverine Bar Association. **Military Serv:** USNR-R, comdr, mil judge, 1988-93. **Business Addr:** Judge, Wayne Co 3rd Circuit Ct, Frank Murphy Hall of Justice, 1441 St Antoine, Detroit, MI 48226, **Business Phone:** (313)224-5260.

STRONG, DEREK LAMAR
Basketball player, race car driver. **Personal:** Born Feb 9, 1968, Los Angeles, CA. **Educ:** Xavier Univ, commun arts. **Career:** Basketball player (retired), race driver; Miami Tropics, 1991; Washington Bullets, 1992; Quad City Thunder, 1992-93; Milwaukee Bucks, 1993-94; Boston Celtics, 1994-95; Los Angeles Lakers, 1995-96; Orlando Magic, 1996; Los Angeles Clippers, 2000-01; ASA Late Model Series, race car driver, 2006-. **Honors/Awds:** Continental Basketball Assn, Most Valuable Player, 1993; Newcomer of the Year, 1993; All-Star first team, 1993; All-Defensive team, 1993. **Special Achievements:** First NBA player to successfully transition into stock car racing. **Business Addr:** Race Driver, ASA Late Model Series, 7360 Elm, Lexington, MI 48450, **Business Phone:** (810)650-6617.

STRONG, MACK (MACK CARLINGTON STRONG)
Football player, talk show host. **Personal:** Born Sep 11, 1971, Fort Benning, GA. **Educ:** Univ Ga. **Career:** Football player (retired); Seattle Seahawks, running back, 1994-2007; FoxSports Northwest, sportscaster, 2008-. **Honors/Awds:** NFL Pro Bowl, 2005; Assoc Press All-Pro, 2005; Pro-Bowl Twice, 2005, 2006; One Time First Team All Pro, 2005. **Business Addr:** Sportscaster, Fox Sports Northwest, 156th Ave SE Suite 3626, Bellevue, WA 98006, **Business Phone:** (425)641-0104.

STRONG, MACK CARLINGTON. **See STRONG, MACK.**

STRONG, MARILYN TERRY
Educator, teacher, basketball coach. **Personal:** Born Sep 10, 1929, Hartford, CT; daughter of George William Terry (deceased) and Odessa Callie Stewart (deceased); married Edward M (deceased). **Educ:** Univ Conn, BA, 1950, MA, 1965. **Career:** Teacher (retired); Hartford Bd Educ, elem phys educ teacher, 1950-60, sec phys educ teacher, 1960-84; Weaver High Sch, phys educ dept head, 1971-77, varsity basketball & softball coach, 1972-86, continuing educ teacher, 1984-89. **Orgs:** AAHPER, 1950-; vpres, CAHPERD, 1950-85; CEA & NEA, 1950-; golden life mem, pres, Hartford Alumnae Delta Sigma Theta Sor Inc, 1951-; leader chairperson, bd dirs, CT Valley Girl Scouts, 1951-; Order Eastern Star Stella Chap 16, 1957-; pres, treas, Hartford Jazz Soc, 1977-; CT Black Caucus, 1985-; treasurer, Links Inc, 1986-, 1990-92; Docent, Conn Hist Soc, 1989-; vol, Wadsworth Atheneum, 1989-; rec secy, Girl Friends Inc, 1994-98. **Honors/Awds:** Community Serv Award, Delta Sigma Theta, 1965; Outstanding Sec Educr, 1973, 1976; Maharishi Educ Award, 1977; Hartford Teacher of the Year, Hartford Bd Educ, 1981; Community Serv Award, Brass Key Inc, 1982; Community Serv Award, Nat Asn Negro Bus & Prof Women's Clubs Inc, Hartford Chap, 1986; Iota Phi Lambda, Beta Chap, Apple for the Teacher Award, 1988; Inspiration Award, Nat Asn Sports & Phys Educ, 1989; Marilyn T Strong Female Athlete Award, Weaver High Sch, 1990-. **Home Addr:** 42 Canterbury St, Hartford, CT 06112. *

STRONG, OTIS REGINALD
Executive, airline executive. **Personal:** Born Sep 26, 1954, Norfolk, VA; son of Mallie Swinson Smith and Otis; married Gloria W; children: Cayce J & Candace L. **Educ:** Elizabeth City State Univ, BS, 1976. **Career:** Delta Air Lines Inc, customer serv support agent, 1976-77, sr customer serv agent, 1978-83, sr passenger serv agent, 1983-84, consumer affairs rep, 1984-, systs baggage coordr, 1988-, elite services, currently. **Orgs:** Nat Asn Advan Colored People, 1976-, JOHER-AAHPR, 1976-; vpres, Uni-Time Inc 1984-; pres, Alumni Chap ECSU 1985-, Atlanta Alumni Chap ECSU, 1985-; coach/head, Fayette County Rec Asn, 1987-; coach, Fayette County AAU Basketball-GA, 1988-; Alpha Phi Alpha Frat, 1990-. **Honors/Awds:** Distinguished Alumni Award, 1986. **Home Addr:** 140 Neola Lane, Atlanta, GA 30349. **Business Addr:** Consumer Affairs Representative, Delta Air Lines Inc, Hartsfield International Airport, 1030 Delta Blvd, PO Box 20706, Atlanta, GA 30320, **Business Phone:** (404)715-2600.

STRONG- KIMBROUGH, DR. BLONDELL M
Management consultant, real estate agent. **Personal:** Born Jan 11, 1943, Fort Pierce, FL; daughter of Jeff McDonald (deceased) and Bertha McDonald; married Charles E; children: Stanford II & Jeff Bertram. **Educ:** Tenn State Univ, BS, 1964; Geo Peabody Col, Vanderbilt Univ, MLS, 1967; Univ Mich, PhD 1983; Univ Mich, Post-doctorate, 1985. **Career:** Lincoln Jr Col, librn & music instr, 1964-65; Indian River Jr Col, librn & asst cataloger, 1965-67; Meharry Med Col, libr dir, 1967-77; Fisk-Meharry Credit Union, gen mgr & treas, 1976-77; Univ Mich, post-doctorate fel, 1984-85, mgt consult; Bond Realty Inc, mgt exec, 1986-88; Bordeaux Realty Plus, pres & co-owner, currently. **Orgs:** Life mem, Nat Asn Advan Colored People, Nashville Br, 1991, treas, 1991, 1995-96; Alpha Kappa Alpha Sorority; Kappa Delta Pi Hon Soc; Beta Phi Mu Int Libr Sci Hon Soc. **Home Addr:** 3852 Augusta Dr, Nashville, TN 37201, **Home Phone:** (615)876-4863. **Business Addr:** President, Bordeaux Realty Plus, 3250 Dickerson Pke Suite 4, Nashville, TN 37207-2969, **Business Phone:** (615)227-3898.

STROTHER, GERMAINE D
Physician, educator. **Personal:** Born Oct 5, 1954, Enid, OK; daughter of Rev Earl L and Ruth B Strother; married Joseph Banks, Apr 12, 1980. **Educ:** OH State Univ Col Med, attended. **Career:** Pvt pract, currently; Univ Southern Calif, Sch Med, clin asst prof, currently. **Orgs:** Pres-elect, OH State Univ Col Med & Pub Health Med Alumni Bd Govs. **Honors/Awds:** Family med Fel Am Acad Family Physicians. **Business Addr:** Clinical Assistant Professor, University Southern California, School Medicine, Los Angeles, CA 92517-2358.

STROUD, HOWARD BURNETTE, SR. **See Obituaries section.**

STROUD, LOUIS WINSTON
Management consultant. **Personal:** Born Nov 21, 1946, Cincinnati, OH. **Educ:** Canisius Col, AB, hist, 1968; Harvard Grad Sch Bus Admin, MBA, fin, 1970; Univ San Francisco Sch Law, JD, 1976. **Career:** Mfrs Hanover Trust, corp planner, 1973, prod mgr disbursements 1974-76; Kaiser Aluminum & Chem Corp, merger acquisition specialist, 1976. **Orgs:** Harvard Bus Sch Club; Harvard Club.

STROZIER, YVONNE IGLEHART
State government official, educator. **Personal:** Born in Waco, TX; daughter of Bishop T D and Dessie Mae Truitt; married Arthur A, Oct 13, 1974; children: William Charles Wilborn, Thaddeus Iglehart Wilborn & Desi Artrice Iglehart Strozier. **Educ:** Bishop Col, Marshall Tex, BS, 1959; Prairie View A&M Univ, Prairie View Tex, MA, 1965; San Diego State Univ, Calif, 1968. **Career:** Conway Public Schs, Conway, Ariz, teacher, 1959-60; Waco Independent Sch Dist, Waco TX, teacher, 1961-65; El Dorado County Schs, Placerville, Calif, teacher, 1965-66; San Diego City Schs, San Diego, Calif, teacher, project dir, 1966-72; Calif Dept Educ, Sacramento, Calif, consult, 1972-. **Orgs:** Delta Sigma Theta Sorority, 1955-; Jack & Jill Inc, 1970-; co-founder, Calif Alliance Black Sch Educ, 1979-; exec bd, Nat Alliance Black Sch Educ, 1985-; corp bd mem, Calif Asn Compensatory Educ, 1985-; admin, Strozier Youth Ctr, 1986-; coord, The Speaker's Educ Breakfast Club, 1986-; Nat Alliance Black Sch Educ, 1986-; Coalition Black Meeting Planners, 1987-; bd mem, C H Mason Found-Church God Christ, 1988-; bd dir, Saints Acad & Col, Lexington, Miss. **Honors/Awds:** Outstanding Achievement, Calif Alliance Black Sch Educrs, 1980; Proclamation of Appreciation, Nat Asn Black Sch Educ, 1980; Outstanding Educator, Calif Dept Educ, 1983; Outstanding Achievement, Calif Asn Compensatory Educ, 1985, 1986; Proclamation of Appreciation, Inglewood Sch Dist, Inglewood, Calif, 1987. **Home Phone:** (916)424-9021. **Business Phone:** (916)657-2505.

STRUDWICK, LINDSEY H, SR.
Manager. **Personal:** Born Aug 8, 1946, Durham, NC; son of London L Sr and Christine Alston; married Gladys B, Nov 9, 1968; children: Lindsey Howard Jr & Casandra Michelle. **Educ:** Durham Bus Col, Durham NC, assoc degree sci & bus admin; Shaw Univ, Raleigh NC, BA; Southeastern Univ, Greenville SC, MBA. **Career:** Int Fertil Res, Chapel Hill NC, purchasing mgr, 1974-76; Northrop Corp, Res Triangle Pk NC, mgr purchasing & facil, 1976-78; Gen Tel Co, Durham NC, personnel asst, 1978-79; Northern Telecom Inc, Res Triangle Pk NC, group leader purchasing, 1979-81; Sci-Atlanta Inc, Atlanta GA, mgr purchasing & contracts, 1982-86; Coors Brewing Co, Golden CO, dir purchasing & materials, 1986-. **Orgs:** Nat Asn Advan Colored People, 1978-; Nat Asn Purchasing Mgt, 1978-; Am Prod & Inventory Control Soc, 1980-; Am Purchasing Soc, 1985-; bd dirs, Rocky Mountain Regional Minority Supplier Develop Coun, 1986-, chmn, 1986-88; bd dirs, Nat Minority Supplier Develop Coun, 1987-; bd dirs, Nat Minorities Bus Dirs, 1988-. **Honors/Awds:** Named Man of the Year, Nat Urban League, 1986; Corporate Citizenship Award, United Indian Develop Asn, 1988. **Military Serv:** AUS, first lt, 1966-69. **Home Addr:** 4908 Granby St, Denver, CO 80239, **Home Phone:** (303)373-5105. **Business Phone:** (303)277-5671.

STRUDWICK, DR. WARREN JAMES, SR.
Physician. **Personal:** Born Dec 23, 1923, Durham, NC; son of William Canady (deceased) and Mabel Christina Wormley (deceased); married Bette Catoe; children: Laura Strudwick-Turner, Warren J Jr & William J. **Educ:** Howard Univ, BS, 1948, MD, 1952. **Career:** Howard Univ, Wash, DC, instr surg, 1959-61, asst prof surg, 1961-; Greater Southeast Community Hosp, staff; Providence Hosp, vchair, surg dept, attending surgeon; Howard Univ Hosp, attending surgeon; Wash Hosp Ctr, staff; Children's Hosp, staff, pvt pract, currently. **Orgs:** Med Chirurgical Soc DC, bd governors, past mem; Zion Bapt Church; Kappa Alpha Psi; Produffers Golf Club; Am Bd Surgery, diplomate, 1960; Am Soc Abdominal Surgeons; Med Soc DC; Howard Univ, Med Alumni Asn, pres local chap; Am Cancer Soc; Am Med Asn; Nat Med Political Action Comn; NAACP; Urban League; Sigma Pi Phi. **Honors/Awds:** Am Col Surgeons, fel, 1962; Med Soc DC, Cert Meritorious Serv, 1997. **Special Achievements:** Published articles: "Biopsy in Modern Medical Practice," with Warren J Strudwick and Jack E White, JNMA, 1960; "Cancer of the Skin in Negroes," with Newton W Ricketts, Calvin Sampson, Warren J Strudwick and Jack E White, JNMA, 1961; "A Clinical Study of 5-Fluorouicil in a Variety of Far Advanced Human Malignancies," with Newton Ricketts, Warren J Strudwick and Jack E White, JNMA, 1962; "Carcinoma of the Stomach in American Negroes," Surg, Gynec, & Obstet, 1964. **Military Serv:** USMCR, 1943-46. **Home Addr:** 1748 Sycamore St NW, Washington, DC 20012.

STUART, IVAN I.
Military leader. **Personal:** Married Dorthey M; children: Ivan jr, Connie, Selwyn, JoAnn & Desire. **Career:** AUS. **Orgs:** Bd gov's, New River Comt Action & Prog; delegate, Dem Comt; Va Deacon Little River Bapt Ch Floyd; Masonic Lodge 146; Floyd Co Branch Nat Asn Advan Colred People, pres. **Military Serv:** AUS 1943-64; Letters of commendation.

STUART, REGINALD A
Journalist, writer. **Personal:** Born Nov 26, 1948, Nashville, TN; son of William and Maxie Allen; married Daryl Thomas. **Educ:** Tenn State Univ, BS, 1968; Columbia Univ, MJour, 1971. **Career:** Nashville Tennessean, reporter, 1968-69; WSIX-AM-FM-TV, 1969-70; John Hay Whitney Found, New York, NY, consult, 1972-74; New York Times, bus/fin news reporter, 1974-76, nat corresp, 1976-87; Philadelphia Daily News, 1987-90; Knight-Ridder Newspapers, Wash Bureau, asst ed, 1990-97, recruiter, currently; Emerge mag, contrib ed, 1995-2000. **Orgs:** NAACP; CME; Soc Prof Journalists. **Honors/Awds:** Carter G Woodson Nat Educ Asn Award, 1969; Nat Headliners Award, Best Team News Reporting, 1970; Service Award, NAACP, 1974; Wells Key, 1992; Ida B Wells Award, Nat Asn Black Journalists. **Home Addr:** 13102 Tamarack Rd, Silver Spring, MD 20904. **Business Addr:** Recruiter, Knight Ridder, 50 W San Fernando St Suite 1500, San Jose, CA 95113, **Business Phone:** (408)938-7700.

STUBBLEFIELD, DANA WILLIAM
Football player, football coach. **Personal:** Born Nov 14, 1970, Cleves, OH; children: Kayla. **Educ:** Univ Kans. **Career:** Football player (retired); San Francisco 49ers, defensive tackle, 1993-97; Wash Redskins, 1998-2000; San Francisco 49ers, 2001-02; Oakland Raiders, 2003; New England Patriots, 2004; Valley Christian High Sch, defensive line coach, cuurently . **Honors/Awds:** NFL Defensive Rookie of the Year, 1993; Pro Bowl appearances, 1994, 1995,1997; NFL Defensive Player of the Year, 1997. **Special Achievements:** Acted in Reindeer Games movie. **Busi-**

ness Addr: Defensive Line Coach, Valley Christian High School, 100 Skyway Dr, San Jose, CA 95111, **Business Phone:** (408)513-2455.

STUBBLEFIELD, JENNYE LEE WASHINGTON
Educator, nutritionist. **Personal:** Born Mar 6, 1925, Jacksonville, FL; daughter of Marion Washington and Ira Johnson Washington; married Charles, Jun 26, 1954. **Educ:** Tuskegee Inst, BS, 1946; Rutgers State Univ, MS, 1966. **Career:** Educator, nutritionist (Retired); William Jason High Sch, cafe mgr & voc foods teacher, 1950-56; St Francis Hosp Sch, nutrit, 1957-64; Helene Fuld Hosp Sch, 1964-70; Middlesex County NJ Head Start Prog, dir food serv, 1966-67; Home Econ Hamilton Township NJ, teacher, 1967-71; Dept Health Recreation & Welfare Trenton, dir, 1971-74; Aid-Low Income Alcoholics Trenton, dir, 1974-76; Trenton Public Sch Bd Educ, supvr home econ & family life educ progs, 1976-92; City Trenton, council woman 1976-90. **Orgs:** Am Dietetic Asn, 1964-; Am Home Econ Asn, 1967-89; Carver Youth & Family Ctr, 1983; Bilalian African Am Conf, 1983; Fairless Steel Black Caucus, 1984; Mercer Co NW Ward Dem Club, 1984; chmn, County Democratic Comm Mercer County, NJ 1984-85; LIFT, Comt Social Program, Trenton Asn Pub Schs, 1990; Nat Asn Advan Colored People. **Home Addr:** 21 Alden Ave, Trenton, NJ 08618.

STUBBLEFIELD, MICHAEL JEROME
Fashion designer, business owner. **Personal:** Born Feb 14, 1962, Detroit, MI; son of Wytche and Georgia; divorced. **Educ:** Univ Calif, Los Angeles, BA, 1986. **Career:** Michael J Stubblefield Collection, chief exec officer & designer, 1992-. **Special Achievements:** Black Enterprise Magazine, Rising Star Award Nominee, 1996. **Business Addr:** Chief Executive Officer, Designer, Stubblefield Collection, 1033 Basset St, Detroit, MI 48217, **Business Phone:** (313)843-3348.

STUBBLEFIELD, RAYMOND M.
Association executive. **Personal:** Born Aug 3, 1945, Abilene, TX; married Pat. **Educ:** NM Highland Col; Taft Col; San Diego State, BS, BA, 1969. **Career:** United Food & Com Workers Union, asst dir; Comm Rel Dept Retail Clks Int Asn, co-dir; Big Brothers, works correction officers. **Honors/Awds:** Commercial service award, San Diego Youth Leg, 1970. **Business Addr:** Assistant to Director, UFCW, 4552 Valley View Lane, Irving, TX 75038.

STUBBS, DR. GEORGE WINSTON
Physician. **Personal:** Born Sep 13, 1942, Brooklyn, NY; son of Cornelius A and Beryl Hinds; married Joyce Kennedy, Jun 22, 1968; children: George W II & C David L. **Educ:** Hunter Col, AB, 1964; Howard Univ, col med, MD, 1968. **Career:** Wills Eye Hosp, asst surgeon, 1977, assoc surgeon, 1993; Med Col Pa, asst prof surg, 1979; G Winston Stubbs MD Ltd, pres, 1982; Germantown Hosp, attending opthalmologist; Chestnut Hill Hosp, Attending Opthalmologist, Grad Hosp Country, Staff; pvt pract, currently. **Orgs:** Int Col Surg, fel, 1979; Pa Col Physicians, fel, 1980; Am Col Surgeon, fel, 1981; Am Acad Ophthalmol, 1977; Med Soc Pa, pres elect, 1993, pres, 1995; Heed opthalmic found, fel, currently. **Honors/Awds:** Physician Recognition Award, 1981, 1983, 1987. **Military Serv:** USPHS, lt cmdr. **Home Addr:** 530 E Mt Airy Ave, Philadelphia, PA 19119. **Business Addr:** Physician, 8121 1/2 Stenton Ave, Philadelphia, PA 19150, **Business Phone:** (215)248-2660.

STUBBS, LEVI. See Obituaries section.

STUBBS, TRAVIS, JR. See STUBBS, LEVI in the Obituaries section.

STUCKEY, SHEILA ARNETTA
Library administrator. **Personal:** Born Aug 12, 1964, Anderson, SC; daughter of Eugene J Stuckey Sr and Early D Stuckey. **Educ:** SC State Univ, BS, 1987; Univ Pittsburgh, MLS, 1989. **Career:** SC State Univ, coordr info retrieval serv/ref librn, 1989-94; KY State Univ, collection develop librn, 1994-96, acq unit head, 1996-2001, from asst dir to assoc, 2001-05, dir 2005-. **Orgs:** Am Libr Asn, 1988-; Black Caucus ALA, 1994-; KY Libr Asn, 1994-; cluster coordr, AKA Cent Region, 2001-02; pres, Alpha Kappa Alpha, Beta Upsilon Omega Chap, 2002-03. **Special Achievements:** Contributor, Noteable Black American Men, Gale, 1999, 2006; Contributor, Notable Black American Women, 2003; Contributor, Encyclopedia of African American Business, 2006. **Business Addr:** Director of Libraries, Kentucky State University, Paul G Blazer Library, 400 East Main St, Frankfort, KY 40601, **Business Phone:** (502)597-6852.

STUDDARD, CHRISTOPHER RUBEN. See STUDDARD, RUBEN.

STUDDARD, RUBEN (CHRISTOPHER RUBEN STUDDARD)
Singer, actor. **Personal:** Born Sep 12, 1978, Birmingham, AL; married Surata Zuri McCants, Jun 28, 2008. **Educ:** Ala A&M Univ, attended. **Career:** TV series: Christmas in Rockefeller Center, 2003; "8 Simple Rules for Dating My Teenage Daughter", 2005; "Life on a Stick", 2005; "All of Us", 2005; Eve, 2006; Albums: Flying Without Wings, 2003; Soulful, 2003; I Need an Angel, 2004; The Return, 2006; Love Is, 2009; Singles: "Flying Without Wings", 2003; "Superstar", 2003; "Sorry 2004", 2004; "What If", 2004; "I Need an Angel", 2004; "Change Me", 2006; "Make Ya Feel Beautiful", 2007; "Celebrate Me Home", 2008; J Records, singer, currently; "Together", 2009. **Orgs:** Owner, Ruben Studdard Found Advan Children Music Arts. **Honors/Awds:** Am Idol Winner, 2003; Teen Choice Award, 2003; Best New Artist Award, Nat Asn Advan Colored People, 2004; Soul Train Award; Two Billboard Music Awards; Billboard R&B/Hip Hop Award. **Home Addr:** PO Box 900, Beverly Hills, CA 90213-0900. **Business Addr:** Recording Artist, J Records, 745 5th Ave, New York, NY 10151, **Business Phone:** (646)840-5600.

STULL, DONALD L
Executive, architect. **Personal:** Born May 16, 1937, Springfield, OH; son of Robert Stull and Ruth Callahan Branson; married Patricia Ryder (divorced); children: Cydney Lynn, Robert Branson & Gia Virginia. **Educ:** Oh State Univ, B.Arch 1961; Harvard Grad Sch Design, March, 1962. **Career:** George Mason Clark, architect designer, 1958-62; Boston Fed Office Bldg Architects, designer, 1961-62; Samuel Glaser & Partners, proj dir, 1962-66; Stull Assoc Inc Architects, pres, 1966-83; Stull & Lee Inc Architects & Planners, pres, 1984-. **Orgs:** Boston Archit Ctr, 1972-; Resource Panel, Nat Endowment Arts, 1978-; adv bd mem, Mus Afro-Am Hist, Boston, 1979-; adv comn, Ohio State Univ, Sch Archit, 1980-; City Cambridge, Design Adv Group, 1980-90, 1994-; adv bd mem, Mus Nat Ctr Afro-Am Hist, 1982-; Boston Civic Design Community, 1987-98; vis comn, Harvard Grad Sch Design, 1988-94; adv comn, Suffolk Sch Bus Mgt, 1989-; Historic Boston, 1990-; trustee, Boston Found Archit, 1992-; vis design studio prof, Rice Univ Sch Archit, 1993; GSA's Public Bldg Serv, Nat Regist Peer Professionals, 1994-96; bd overseers, Inst Contemporary Art, 1996, 1997; Nat Accreditation Bd Col Sch Archit. **Honors/Awds:** Ten Outstanding Young Men Boston, 1970; Outstanding Young Men Am, 1970; Design Award, Jury Progressive Archit, 1972; Design Award Am Inst Arch; Design Award, HUD Housing, 1972; 100 Top Black Businesses, 1973; Presidential Design Award, Nat Endowment Arts, 1988; College of Fellows, Am Inst of Archit; Award of honor, Boston Society of Architects, 1997. **Business Addr:** President, Stull and Lee Inc, 38 Chauncy St Suite 1100, Boston, MA 02111, **Business Phone:** (617)426-0406.

STULL, EVERETT JAMES
Baseball player. **Personal:** Born Aug 24, 1971, Fort Riley, KS. **Educ:** Tenn State Univ. **Career:** Montreal Expos, relief pitcher, 1997; Atlanta Braves, 1999; Milwaukee Brewers, 2000-02; Minn Twins, pitcher, 2003; Reno Silver Sox, 2006; Laredo Broncos, 2006; The Grays, 2007. *

STULL, VIRGINIA ELIZABETH
Physician. **Personal:** Born May 7, 1939, Springfield, OH. **Educ:** Tex S Univ, BS, 1960; Am Univ, 1961; Univ Tex Med Sch, Galveston, MD, 1966; Capital Univ, 1972. **Career:** Physician pvt pract, 1967-; Bur Voc Rehab, field med consult, 1968-75; Columbus Bd Edn, sch phy, 1968-73; ER phy, 1967-71; Med Diagnostic Serv Inc, pres & owner, 1975-; Dept Physical Med & Rehab, Ohio State Univ Med Sch, clinical prof; St Anthony Hosp. **Orgs:** Am Med Women's Asn; Am Med Asn; Acad Med Columbus & Franklin County; Alpha Kappa Alpha Sor; Sigma Xi Am Sci Soc. **Honors/Awds:** Lambda Chi Outstanding Black Woman in Ohio, 1975; Flowers for Living Award, 1975; Award, Columbus Chap, Nat Epicureans Inc. **Business Addr:** Physician, Occupational Medicine Physical Medicine & Rehabilitation, 3100 Needmore Rd, Dayton, OH 45414.

STURDIVANT, COL. TADRIAL J
Police chief. **Career:** Mich State Police, dir, currently. **Business Addr:** Director, Michigan State Police, 51166 Plymouth Valley Dr, Plymouth, MI 48170, **Business Phone:** (734)455-1433.*

STYLES, FREDDIE L.
Artist. **Personal:** Born May 12, 1944, Madison, GA. **Educ:** Morris Brown Col, 1965; Atlanta Sch Art. **Career:** Clark Atlanta Univ, artist-in-residence; Clayton State Univ, artist-in-residence; Spelman Col, artist-in-residence; Morris Brown Col Drama Guild, costume set designer, 1963-65; Black Artist, Carnegie Inst, lectr, 1969; Expansion Arts Proj Black Artists, co-dir; Nat Urban League, organizer art exhib, 1975. **Orgs:** La Watercolor Soc, 1973-74; Cooperstown Art Asn, 1974-75; High Mus Art; Black Artists; Clarence White Contemp Art Gallery. **Honors/Awds:** King Baudouin Foundation Cultural Exchange Program grant, Community Found Greater Atlanta, 2001. **Special Achievements:** Work has been exhibited in numerous solo and group exhibitions including African American Abstraction at City Hall Gallery East in Atlanta, and Evolving, a solo show at the Airport Atrium Gallery at Atlanta Hartsfield-Jackson International Airport. **Business Addr:** Artist, The Museum of Contemporary Art of Georgia, 1447 Peachtree St, Atlanta, GA 30309.

STYLES, KATHLEEN ANN
School administrator. **Personal:** Born Aug 6, 1949, Baltimore, MD; daughter of Minnie V Brown Styles and Calvin P Styles. **Educ:** Coppin State Col, BS, elem educ, 1971, MS, spec educ, 1972; Univ Md, 1983. **Career:** CETA Prog, instr, 1971-72; Baltimore City Community Col, employ counr, 1974-76, col counr, 1976-79, actg dir stud act, 1979-80, prof develop specialist, 1981-, acting dir off campus & ext centers, asst exec dir enrollment mgt & registr, currently, Div Stud Affairs, exec dir, currently. **Orgs:** Housing adv, US Dept Housing & Urban Develop, 1972-73; Nat Task Force Career Educ, 1978-80; bd, SSD Inc, 1982-84; founder, Learning Intellectual Skills Advan, 1988-94; dir student affairs, harbor campus, 1994-. **Home Addr:** 5709 Gwynn Oak Ave, Baltimore, MD 21207. **Business Addr:** Executive Director, Assistant Executive Director, Baltimore City Community College, Division of Student Affairs, 2901 Liberty Heights Ave, Baltimore, MD 21215-7893, **Business Phone:** (410)462-8365.

STYLES, LORENZO
Football player. **Personal:** Born Jan 31, 1974, Columbus, OH. **Educ:** Ohio State Univ. **Career:** Football player (retired); Atlanta Falcons, linebacker, 1995-96; St Louis Rams, 1997-2000. **Orgs:** Founder, The Lorenzo Styles & Friends found.

STYLES, RICHARD WAYNE
Clergy. **Personal:** Born Jun 22, 1939, Waterbury, CT; son of James Lawrence Sr and Helene Marie Copeland; married Helen Penelope Horton; children: Richard Wayne Jr & Helene Rishae. **Educ:** Shaw Univ, BA, 1965; Southeastern Baptist Theol Sem, MDiv, 1969; Yale Divinity Sch. **Career:** Burlington Housing Authority, bd dirs, 1977-; Burlington Christ Acad, bd dir, 1980-83; Access, bd dir, 1980-84; Allied Church Alamance County, vice chmn bd dir, 1983-; Hospice Alamanee County, bd dir; Fair Housing Comt, bd dir; Ministerial Fellowship Alliance Alamanee County; First Baptist Church, sr pastor, currently; Shaw Univ Cape Fezr Ctr, prog bible, currently. **Orgs:** Recruiter, Crop Walk, 1977-; vol coun, Alamance County Court Syst, 1979-83; dean inst, United Bible Inst, 1980-; exec comn, N State Legal Aid, 1980-; chmn relig activities, Broadview Mid Sch, 1984-; exec dir, lamance County Headstart, 1984-; chair trustees bd, Gen Baptist Conv Inc, NC; bd dir, Homecare Providers; bd dir, Care Ministry; bd dir, United Way; bd dir, Family Abuse Services; bd dir, Christian Coun Serv; bd dir, Alamance Coalition Against Drug Abuse, Alamanee City Dept Social Servs. **Honors/Awds:** Good Shepherd Award, Boy Scouts Am, 1979; Volunteer Counselor Award, Gov James Hunt NC, 1983; Hon Doctorate, United Bible Inst. **Home Addr:** 612 Crestview Dr, Burlington, NC 27215. **Business Addr:** Senior Pastor, First Baptist Church, 508 Apple St, Burlington, NC 27217, **Business Phone:** (336)227-2542.*

SUBER, DIANNE BOARDLEY
College administrator. **Personal:** Children: Nichole Reshan Lewis, Raegan LaTrese Thomas & Nyjil Brevard. **Educ:** Hampton Univ, BS; Va Polytech Inst & State Univ, Blacksburg, VA, EdD; Univ Ill, Urbana/Champaign, MEd. **Career:** Greensboro, NC, first grade teacher; Newport News, VA, lead kindergarten teacher; Hampton Univ, dean admin servs, asst provost acad affairs, vpres admin; St Augustines Col, pres, 1999-. **Orgs:** Pres Bush's Bd Advisors to the White House Initiative on Historically Black Col & Univs; Am Coun Edu; bd dir, Central Region Wachovia Bank; United Negro Col Fund; Nat Asn Independent Cols and Univs; Bus & Technol Ctr; Triangle Family Servs; Asn Episcopal Cols; Consortium Doctors LTD; S E Raleigh Improvement Assembly; Livable Streets Comm. **Special Achievements:** First female to head St Augustines College. **Business Addr:** President, St. Augustines College, 1315 Oakwood Ave 110 Boyer Bldg, Raleigh, NC 27610, **Business Phone:** (919)516-4200.

SUBER, TORA
Basketball player. **Personal:** Born Nov 23, 1974, Coatesville, PA. **Educ:** Va Univ, attended 1997. **Career:** Charlotte Sting, guard, 1997-98; Orlando Miracle, 1999; Houston Comets,guard, 2004. *

SUBRYAN, CARMEN
Educator. **Personal:** Born Dec 30, 1944, Linden, Guyana; daughter of Lawrence and Sybil Allicock; divorced; children: Nicole & Natasha. **Educ:** Howard Univ, Wash, DC, BA, 1971, MA, 1973, PhD, Eng, 1983. **Career:** Univ DC, acad support, 1973-74; Howard Univ, Wash, DC, instr, prog co ordr, 1974, Ctr Acad Reinforcement, writing instr, currently. **Orgs:** Phi Beta Kappa, Howard Univ, 1971; Nat Coun Teachers Eng, 1980-84; Col Lang Asn, 1981-86; Nat Asn Develop Educ, 1985-87; GUYAID, 1985-. **Special Achievements:** Reprise, a book of poetry, 1984; "Walter Dean Myers", Article in Dictionary of Literary Biography, 1984; "A B Spellman", article in Dictionary of Literary Biography, 1985; Woman's Survival, booklet, 1989; Black-Water Women, a novel, 1997; Rachel's Tears, poetry, 2000. **Home Addr:** 11400 Pitsea Dr, Beltsville, MD 20705, **Home Phone:** (301)937-3428. **Business Addr:** Writing Instructor, Howard University, Center Academic Reinforcement, Acad Support Bldg B 2400 6th St NW Suite 102, Washington, DC 20059, **Business Phone:** (202)806-7787.

SUDARKASA, MICHAEL ERIC MABOGUNJE
Consultant, chief executive officer, founder (originator). **Personal:** Born Aug 5, 1964, New York, NY; son of Akin Mabogunje and Niara; married Joyce Ann Johnson, Nov 22, 1990; children: Jasmine Ayana Yetunde, Jonathan Michael Toure, Maya

Elizabeth Sade & Marielle Iman. **Educ:** Univ Mich, BA, high honors, history, 1985; Howard Univ, vis stud, 1983; Harvard Law Sch, JD, 1988; Unic San Diego, inst int and comparative law, Paris, France, 1990. **Career:** African Develop Bank, tech asst, pvt sector develop unit, 1988-89; Citibank-Abidjan, banking int, 1988-89; 21st Century Africa Inc, founder & consult, 1989-; Steel, Hector & Davis PC, Assoc, 1990; 21st Century Africa Inc, pres, 1990-97; Trade & Investment Prom Serv, dir, 1997-; Georgetown Univ, Grad Sch bus, adj lectr; Africa Bus Direct,co-founder & ceo, 2000-. **Orgs:** Overseas Develop Counc, Africa Roundtable; Am Bar Asn, chmn, Africa Law Comt; Calvert New World Fund, Soc Int Developt. **Honors/Awds:** "30 under Thirty" Entrant Award, Career Communs, Urban Profile Mag, 1992; Distinguished Young Alumni Award, first recipient, Harvard Black Law Stud Asn, 1992. **Special Achievements:** Author, publ, The African Bus Handbk, A Comprehensive Guide to bus Resources for US/Africa Trade and Investment, 1991-97; "Toward a Global Africa Econ Comt: A Billion People and a Trillion Dollar Mkt," working papers for issues forum at Cong Black Caucus, 1991;Africa News Service. **Home Addr:** 10919 Jarbol Ct, Silver Spring, MD 20901. **Business Phone:** (703)506-9600.

SUDARKASA, NIARA (GLORIA A MARSHALL)
School administrator, scholar. **Personal:** Born Aug 14, 1945, Ft Lauderdale, FL; married John L Clark; children: Michael Eric. **Educ:** Fisk Univ, attended 1956; Oberlin Col, AB, 1957; Columbia Univ, MA, 1959, PhD, anthrop, 1964. **Career:** School administrator (retired); Early Admis Col, Ford Found scholar, 1953-57; John Hay Whitney Oppty fel, 1959-60; Ford Found Foreign Area Training fel, 1960-63; Comn Comparative Study New Nations, Univ Chicago, fel, 1963-64; Carnegie Found Study New Nation fel, 1963-64; NY Univ, asst prof, 1964-67; Univ Mich, from asst prof to prof 1967-76, Ctr Afro-Am & African Studies, dir, 1981-84, assoc vpres acad affairs, 1986; Social Sci Res Coun fel, 1973-74; Sr Fulbright Res Schol, 1982-83; Lincoln Univ, pres, 1987-98; Fla Atlantic Univ, distinguished vis scholar; African-Am Res Libr & Cult Ctr, Ft Lauderdale, FA, scholar in residence, currently. **Orgs:** African Studies Asn, 1959-69, 1982-; fel Am Anthrop Asn, 1964-; fel Am Anthrop Asn Exec Bd, 1972-75; chmn, State Mich Comn Minorities Women & Handicappers Higher Educ, 1984-; bd dir, Ann Arbor Comn Ctr, 1983-; Am Asn Higher Educ, 1986; Coun Foreign Rels; Nat Asn Adv Colored People; Nat Coun Negro Women; Asn Black Anthropologists; Acad Educ Develop; USIA Trilateral Task Force N Am Edu; Peace Corps Nat Adv Coun; White House Comn Presidential Scholars. **Honors/Awds:** Achievement Award, Alpha Kappa Alpha; Achievement Award, Zeta Phi Beta; Achievement Award, Elks, City Ft Lauderdale. **Special Achievements:** Author The Strength of Our Mothers, Africa World Press, 1996; The first woman to serve as president of Lincoln University; Received 13 honorary degrees from U.S. and African universities; She is one of 75 women included in Brian Lanker's book, "I Dream a World: Portraits of Black Women Who Changed America". *

SUDBURY, LESLIE G.
Chemist. **Personal:** Born May 11, 1939, Meridan, MS; son of James and Mamie; married Audrey Faulkens; children: Leslie D, Pamela M, David G, Gloria M. **Educ:** Xavier Univ, BSc, chem, 1961; Notre Dame Grad Sch, chem. **Career:** Whitehall Labs, pharm control chemist, 1961-65; Miles Labs Inc, res chemist, 1966-73, supvr control chemist, 1973-78, mgr div control, 1978-82, mgr biological evaluation, 1982-85; IYHL Soccer, coach, 1980-82; ICN Immuno, oper mgr, 1985-89, dir lab opers, 1989-. **Orgs:** Am Chem Soc, 1966-; bd mem, NBLCC, 1976-85; bd dirs, treas, NOBC, 1977-85; secy & ed newsletter, Am Chem Soc, St Joseph Valley Sec, 1979-83; co-chmn, BAC Inter Community Comn, 1980-82; Am Soc Qual Control, 1982-86; Knights Peter Claver, 1984-85; Sec Council 251 KPC; St Augustine Parish, South Bend, IN. **Honors/Awds:** Outstanding Service, Am Chem Soc, St Joe Valley Sec, 1981; Outstanding Service, NBLCC Midwest Regional. **Military Serv:** AUS, 1962-64. *

SUDLER, PEGGY
Association executive, administrator. **Career:** Ministry Caring Inc, prog dir; City Wilmington, Del, resource ctr coordr, currently. **Business Addr:** Program Director, City of Wilmington Resource Center, 100 W 18th St Shortlidge Acad Rm 110, Wilmington, DE 19806-1497, **Business Phone:** (302)428-3620.

SUGGS, DR. ROBERT CHINELO
Educator, administrator. **Personal:** Born Dec 23, 1943, Newport, RI; son of Lewis and Beatrice; married Mary Louise Morrison; children: Lawrence, Sarah, Elizabeth & James. **Educ:** Barrington Col, BA, 1967; State Univ New York, Albany, MS 1971, EdD 1979. **Career:** Educator, Retired; State Univ New York, Albany, fel, 1971-73; State Univ NY, Dept Counr Educ, Brockport State Univ, asst prof, 1972-78; Community Bible Church, pastor, 1974-80; Ed Millersville Univ, Dept Counr, adj asst prof, 1982-85; Univ Md, Psycho physiol Clinic, clin asst prof, 1983-85; Crossroads Counseling Asns, therapist, 1983-; Christian Asn Psych Studies, newsletter ed, 1983-; Daystar Univ, Nairobi, Kenya, visiting prof, 1985-86; Messiah Col, assoc prof psycho, prof psychol, 1980-90, chair, 1984-85, dir personnel, 1990-92; Cornerstone Col, vpres acad affairs & dean, 1992-95; Malone Col, provost, 1995; Ashland Univ, provost, 2002-07. **Orgs:** Kappa Delta Pi, Rho Tau Chap; bd trustee, Judson Col, Elgin, IL, 1993-99; bd trustee, Pathway Inc, 1996-99; vpres, Canton Urban League, 1998-2001. **Honors/Awds:** Named to Top 500 High School Basketball Players in the US Dell Mag 1963; Outstanding Teacher Messiah Col, 1981.

SUGGS, TERRELL RAYMONN
Football player. **Personal:** Born Oct 11, 1982, Minneapolis, MN; son of Donald Sr and Lavern. **Educ:** Ariz State Univ. **Career:** Baltimore Ravens, Defensive End, 2003-. **Honors/Awds:** Parade All-Am, 2000; Gatorade Ariz Player of the Yr; Ariz Player of the Yr, USA Today; Nagurski Award, 2002; Defensive Rookie of the Yr, AP, 2003; Ted Hendricks Award, Lombardi Award, Bronko Nagurski Trophy, Bill Wills Award, 2002; Pro Bowler Selection Thrice, 2004, 2006, 2008. **Special Achievements:** Best player Ranking 60th in the nation, The Sporting News. **Business Addr:** Professional Football Player, Baltimore Ravens, 1 Winning Dr, Owings Mills, MD 21117, **Business Phone:** (410)701-4000.*

SUGGS, WILLIAM ALBERT
Educator, clergy. **Personal:** Born Jun 1, 1922, Capleville, TN; married Carnelia Tate. **Educ:** Tskg Inst, 1943; TN St Univ, 1949, MS, 1955. **Career:** educator, pastor (retired); Rchlnd Vocational Sch, teacher supvr, 1949-53; Hamilton HS, teacher dept chmn, 1955-; Friendship Bapt Church, pastor. **Orgs:** Memphis W TN TN Nat Educ Asns; Nat & Coun Soc Stds; pres Memphis & Shlby Co Alumini Asn, 1970; pres, Suggs Enterprises; Hamilton PTA. **Honors/Awds:** Certificate Merit Hamilton HS, 1974; num pub field. **Military Serv:** QMC, sgt, 1943-45. *

SUITE, DR. DEREK H
Physician. **Personal:** Born in Trinidad and Tobago; married Darcel Dillard. **Educ:** Columbia Univ, BS, MS; Hahnemann Med Univ, MD; Albert Einstein Col Med, post-grad study. **Career:** Emergency room doctor; Full Circle Health, co-founder, chief exec officer, 1999-; Full Circle Life, Marriage & Family Enrichment Ctr, chmn & Founder, currently. **Orgs:** Northeast & Mid-Atlantic Regional rep, Black Psychiatrists Am, currently; Acad Occupational & Orgn Psychiat; Intl Soc Sport Psychiatry. **Honors/Awds:** Lighthouse Humanitarian Award, 2004. **Business Addr:** Owner, Full Circle Health PLLC, 2105 Williamsbridge Rd, Bronx, NY 10461, **Business Phone:** (718)518-7600.

SULIEMAN, DR. JAMIL
Consultant. **Career:** Dallas Mavericks, team medical consultant, currently. **Business Addr:** Team Medical Consultant, Dallas Mavericks, 777 Sports St Reunion Arena, Dallas, TX 75207-4499, **Business Phone:** (214)988-0117.

SULLIVAN, DR. ALLEN R
School administrator, consultant. **Personal:** Born Jul 15, 1941, Cambridge, MA; son of Fernando Cortez and Dorothy E; married Deborah M Haywood; children: Raylene & Reginald. **Educ:** Northeastern Univ, BS, 1965; Syracuse Univ, MS, 1966, PhD, 1970. **Career:** New Eng Home Little Wanders, asst supvr res, 1962-65; Syracuse Pub Sch, spec educ teacher, 1966-68; Univ Minn, dir training teachers, 1971-75, assoc prof psychol educ studies, 1970-75; Dallas Independent Sch Dist, asst supt stud develop, exec dir stud develop & advocacy serv; Strategic Partnerships Inc, consult, currently. **Orgs:** Adv bd, Ft Worth State Sch, 1978-; bd dir, CT Gen N Am Cigna, 1984-; min adv comn coun, Except C, 1984-; bd chmn, Jr Black Acad Arts & Letters, 1984-; bd, Friends Art Dist, 1984-86; bd dirs, Dallas Co Ment Health & Ment Retardation; Omega Psi Phi Fraternity; bd dir, Dallas Challenge; bd dir, Dallas Youth Serv Corp; Coun Elders, Our Brothers Keeper. **Honors/Awds:** Outstanding Alumni Award, Northeastern Univ, 1982; 2nd Place color photography, State Fair Texas; Psychology Honorary, Psi Chi. **Business Addr:** Consultant, Strategic Partnerships Inc, 6034 W Courtyard Dr Suite 100, Austin, TX 78730-5066, **Business Phone:** (512)531-3900.

SULLIVAN, ANDREA D.
Writer, physician. **Educ:** Bastyr Univ, Seattle, WA, ND, 1986; Homeopathic Acad Naturopathic Physicians, diplomate; Univ Pa, PhD, sociol & criminol. **Career:** Am Univ, instr; Howard Univ, instr; Univ Md, instr; Nat Urban League, Admin Justice Dept, New York, asst dir, 1976-78; US Dept Housing & Urban Develop, Carter Admin, spec asst to the secy, 1978-80; Prevention Mag Health Books, contrib ed, currently; Essence, contrib ed, currently; Heart & Soul & Health Quest Mag, contrib ed, currently; Ctr Natural healing, naturopathic physicianm currently; Book: A Path to Healing: A Guide To Wellness For Body, Mind and Soul, 1998. **Orgs:** Founding mem, Am Asn Naturopathic Physicians; pres, DC Asn Naturopathic Physicians; Homeopathic Acad Naturopathic Physicians; Nat Ctr Homeopathy; chairperson, Naturopathic Med Bd, DC. **Honors/Awds:** Distinguished Alumni Award, Bastyr Univ. **Special Achievements:** Author of numerous articles for Prevention Magazine Health Books, "Essence," "Heart and Soul," "Health Quest," and more; was the first African American to receive a PhD from the University of Pennsylvania in sociology/criminology. **Business Addr:** Naturopathic Physician, Center for Natural Healing Inc, 4601 Conn Ave NW Suite 6, Washington, DC 20008, **Business Phone:** (202)244-4545.*

SULLIVAN, DR. EDWARD JAMES
Dentist. **Personal:** Born May 7, 1932, Cleveland, OH; son of Ann Lee Ervin; married Janet Grant; children: Kathi Ann, Steven & Alicia. **Educ:** Ohio State Univ, BS, 1956, DDS, 1969. **Career:** Univ Hosps Ohio State, pharmacist, 1957-64; Columbus Health Dept, dentist, 1969-73; dentist, pvt practice, 1969-; Columbus State Inst, dentist, 1973-79; Dept Pedodontics, OH State Univ, clinic instr, 1981-; Ohio State Univ, Columbus, OH, clin instr & pediat dent. **Orgs:** Bd mem, South State Health Ctr, 1975-77; bd dirs, Hilltop Health Ctr, 1977; delegate, Nat Asn Neighborhood Health Ctrs, 1977-80; mem bd, Columbus Area Community Health Ctr, 1978-81; vpres, Buckeye State Dent Asn; pres, Columbus Asn Physicians & Dentists; Columbus Dent Asn, pres, 1994-96. **Honors/Awds:** Certificate of Appreciation, Hilltop Health Ctr, 1977; Mayor's Voluntary Service Award, City Columbus, 1980. **Home Addr:** 2755 Mitzi St, Columbus, OH 43209. **Business Addr:** Clinical Instructor, Pediatric Dentistry, The Ohio State University, 342 McCampbell Hall 1581 Dodd Dr, Columbus, OH 43210, **Business Phone:** (614)292-3160.

SULLIVAN, EMMET G
Judge. **Personal:** Born in Washington, DC. **Educ:** Howard Univ, BA, polit sci, 1968, Sch Law, JD, 1971. **Career:** Neighborhood Legal Serv Prog Wash, 1972; Super Ct Judge James A Wash Jr, law clerk, 1973; Houston & Gardner, atty, 1973, partner; Houston, Sullivan & Gardner, partner, 1980; Howard Univ Sch Law, adj prof, prof, actg dean; DC Super Ct, 1984-91; DC Ct Appeals, assoc judge, 1991-94, US dist judge, Wash, DC, 1994-. **Orgs:** Nat Bar Asn; Wash Bar Asn; DC Bar Asn; Bar Ass DC. **Honors/Awds:** Reginald Heber Smith Fel; Thurgood Marshall Award Excellence, Howard Univ Alumni Asn; Ollie May Cooper Award, Wash Bar Asn. **Business Addr:** Judge, DC Ct Appeals, 333 Constitution Ave NW, Washington, DC 20001, **Business Phone:** (202)354-3260.

SULLIVAN, ERNEST LEE
Banker, executive. **Personal:** Born Dec 17, 1952, Columbus, OH; son of Robert Lee and Emma Jane. **Educ:** Capital Univ, BA, 1981; PHR Accreditation, 1983; Univ Va, Darden Sch, Exec Educ Prog, 1993. **Career:** Bank One Columbus, mgmt trainee, 1971-73, fraud investigator, 1973-76; prof recruiter, 1976-77, prof recruiter, 1977-79, employ mgr, 1979-81; Rockwell Int, prof staff mgr, 1981-82, employ mgr, 1982-85, mgr, staffing, employee rel, 1985-88; Bank One Ohio Chicago, IL, vpres, exec selection, 1988-91, nat staffing mgr, 1991-96, regional human Res mgr, 1996-97, sr vpres, mgr, exec recruiting & nat staffing, 1997-2003; Sullivan Staffing Strategies, pres & chief exec officer, 2003-. **Orgs:** Employ Mgr Asn, 1988-; personnel adv, Columbus Urban League, 1991-; adv bd, Cent State Univ, 1988-; bd mem, Westerville Chamber Com, 1992-; adv bd, Columbus Bd Educ, 1991-; pres, Jobs Columbus Prog, 1992-; bd pres, St Stephen's Community House, 1998-99; bd mem, Siemon Kenton Coun, Boy Scouts Am; appointed Gov Policy Bd, 1999-2000; bd mem, Leadership Columbus, 2000-; bd mem, Columbus Works, 2000-; bd mem, COTA; Personnel Soc Human Res Mgmt; Columbus Ohio Transit Authority Bd; Advisory Bd Capital Univ; chair Urban Advisory Bd Boy Scouts Am; vpres, Central State Advisory Bd; pres, Stephen's Community House Bd; chair, Youth Comm - Governor's Workforce Policy Bd. **Honors/Awds:** America's Best & Brightest, Dollars & Sense Mag, 1992; Hall of Fame, Columbus Metrop Housing, 1991; Pinnacle Award, 1993; Eagle Award, 1995; Lazarus Award, 1997; Rosevelt Thomas Award, 2000; Ohio State Univ Diversity Leaders Award, 2002; Silver Beaver Award, Boy Scouts Am, 2002; Honorary Distinguished Alumni Award, Cent State Univ, 2003. **Special Achievements:** He was selected by Dollars and Sense Magazine as One of America's Best and Brightest in 1992. **Home Addr:** 2258 Delavan Dr, Columbus, OH 43219. **Business Addr:** President, Chief Executive Officer, Sullivan Staffing Strategies, 1550 Lakeshore Dr, Columbus, OH 43204, **Business Phone:** (614)537-7506.

SULLIVAN, DR. J. CHRISTOPHER
Actor, entertainer. **Personal:** Born Sep 15, 1932, Greenville, TX; son of Jack and Veola; married Eloise Hicks (divorced); children: Jerome. **Educ:** Prairie View A&M Univ, BA, 1953; Univ Tex, MA, 1958, PhD 1964. **Career:** Abilene City Sch, teacher, 1955-58; Dallas Ind Sch, teacher, 1961-62; Prairie View A&M Univ, dir stud acts, 1962-63; Univ Tex, teacher, 1963-64; Screen Actors Guild, prof actor, currently; Films: DC Cab, 1983; Critters2: The Main Course, 1988; Arthur 2: On the Rocks, 1988; LA Bounty, 1989; Ghost, 1990; Caged in Paradise, 1990; Noises Off, 1992; TV series: "Starsky & Hutch", 1977; "Good Times", 1977; "Requiem for a Wino", 1977; "One Day at a Time", 1978; "Florence's Cousin", 1980; "The Jeffersons", 1980; "Murder, She Wrote", 1989; "Night of the Tarantula", 1989; "L.A.Law", 1991; "As God is my Co-Defendant", 1991. **Orgs:** Screen Actors Guild; Am Fedn TV & Radio Artists; Acad TV Arts & Scis; Los Angeles Olympics Org Comt; vpres, Beverly Hills/Hollywood Nat Assn Advan Colored People, 1984-87. **Honors/Awds:** Distinguished Alumni, Prairie View A&M Phi Beta Sigma Inc, 1980; Phi Beta Kappa; Merit of Achievement Drama, Univ Tex, 1984; Image Award/Best Actor Natl Assn Advan Colored People Beverly Hills, 1986. **Military Serv:** Infantry capt, 1953-57. *

SULLIVAN, JACK, JR.
Clergy. **Personal:** Born Jun 1, 1959, Cleveland, OH; son of Jack Sr and Gloria Mae Connor McCoy; married Gloria Jean Reeves, Jul 28, 1984; children: Nia. **Educ:** Ohio Univ, BS, commun, 1983; Lexington Theol Sem, MDiv, 1986; United Theol Sem, DMin,

1993. **Career:** Mid-Am Region, Christian Church, Disciples Christ, assoc regional minister, 1986-89; Second Christian Church, pastor, 1986-89; Homeland Ministries Christian Church, Disciples Christ, US & Canada, assoc, racial/ethnic & multicultural ministries, 1989-98; Christian Church Disciples Christ, NW regional minister, 1998-2006. **Orgs:** Nat Asn Advan Colored People, 1978-; Alpha Phi Alpha Fraternity Inc, 1984-; elder, youth dir, Faith United Christian Church, 1990-; big brother, Big Brothers, Indianapolis, 1990-; Asn Christian Church Educr, 1988-; Urban League Greater Indianapolis; vol, Am Heart Asn; Boy Scouts Am. **Honors/Awds:** George V Moore Award, Outstanding Field Ministry, Lexington Theological Seminary, 1986. *

SULLIVAN, JONATHON
Football player. **Personal:** Born Jan 21, 1981, Griffin, GA. **Educ:** Univ Ga; childhood and family develop. **Career:** New Orleans Saints, defensive tackle, 2003-05; New England Patriots, defensive tackle, 2006-. **Honors/Awds:** NFC All-Rookie, Pro Football, 2003. **Business Addr:** Professional Football Player, New England Patriots, 1 Patriot Pl, Foxboro, MA 02035, **Business Phone:** (508)543-8200.*

SULLIVAN, LENCOLA
Public speaker. **Personal:** Born in Morrilton, AR; married Roel Verseveldt. **Educ:** Univ Cent Ark, BS, speech & theatre arts. **Career:** KARK-TV, news reporter, weathercaster; KTTV-TV, Austin, TX, weathercaster; Lionel Hampton Orchestra, vocalist; Neth Am Community Trust, managing dir; int speaker. **Orgs:** Bd mem, NY Nat Speakers Asn; USO Inc; bd mem, Conextions Inc, currently. **Honors/Awds:** Inductee, Ark Black Hall of Fame. **Special Achievements:** Miss Arkansas, 1980; Miss Am, 4th runner-up, 1981; sang at the Inaugural Ball Celebrations for President Clinton in 1992 and 1996; First African-American woman to win preliminary awards in the pageant; guest appearances on the soap opera "All My Children," and many appearances in commercials and industrial films.

SULLIVAN, DR. LOUIS WADE
Physician, school administrator, educator. **Personal:** Born Nov 3, 1933, Atlanta, GA; son of Walter Wade and Lubirda Elizabeth Priester; married Eva Williamson, Sep 30, 1955; children: Paul, Shanta & Halsted. **Educ:** Morehouse Col, BS, biol, 1954; Boston Univ, Sch Med, MD, 1958. **Career:** NY Hosp-Cornell Med Ctr, internship; Harvard Med Sch, instr, 1963-64; NJ Col Med, asst prof, 1964-66; Boston Univ, asst prof, 1966-68, assoc prof,1968-74, prof med & physiol, 1974-75; Boston City Hosp, Boston, MA, dirhemat, 1973-75; US Dept Health & Human Servs, WA, DC, secy, 1989-93; Morehouse Col, prof biol & med, Med Educ Prog, dean, dir, 1975-81, Sch Med, dean, 1981-83, pres, 1987-89, 1993-2001; Boy Scouts Am, bd mem, currently. **Orgs:** Ad hoc panel blood diseases, Nat Heart Lung Blood Dis Bur, 1973; Sickle Cell Anemia Adv Comn, NIH, 1974-75; Nat Adv Res Coun, 1977; chmn, Med Educ S African Blacks, 1997-; Am Soc Hemat, Am Soc Clin Invest; Inst Med; Phi Beta Kappa; Alpha Omega Alpha; co-founder, Nat Asn Minority Med Educrs; founding pres, Asn Minority Health Professions. **Honors/Awds:** Trumpet Award, 1997; received dozens honorary degrees & has been honored by diverse orgns. **Special Achievements:** Published over 70 articles in med jour & mags, 1957-92; auth, The Educ of Black Health Prof, 1977; first dean, pres, Morehouse Col Sch Med, 1981; only African Am appointed cabinet position in the Bush Admin, 1989; hosted the public television show Frontiers of Medicine. **Business Addr:** Board Member, Boy Scouts of America, PO Box 152079, Irving, TX 75015-2079.

SULLIVAN, MARTHA ADAMS
Social worker, health services administrator, vice president (organization). **Personal:** Born Jun 13, 1952, Philadelphia, PA; daughter of Leon Henry Adams and Lillie Belle Foster; married James Pearly Sullivan; children: Mecca Jamilah, Malik Khalil. **Educ:** NY Univ, Wash Sq Col, BA, 1974; Hunter Col Sch Social Work, MSW, 1976; City Univ NY Grad Ctr, DSW, 1991. **Career:** Henry St Settlement Comt Consult Ctr, supv social worker/family therapist, 1976-83; pvt pract, psychotherapist, 1981-; Gouverneur Diag & Treat Ctr, Dept Behavioral Health, assoc dir, 1983-, asst dir psychiat, 1985, dir, 1998-, Ctr Older Adults & Their Families, dir, 1983, Inst Family & Community Care, consult; NY City Dept Health & Mental Hygiene, Bur Community Liaison & Training Div Mental Hygiene, dep comnr, 2001, dep comnr health prom & chem dependency, 2002; Minuchin Ctr Family, vis fac; Hunter Col Sch Social Work, adj fac; Lower Eastside Serv Ctr, NY City, exec vpres, currently. **Orgs:** Founding mem, Black Women Therapists Collective, 1978-91; Nat Asn Social Workers, 1985-; chairperson, Citywide Geriatrics Comn, 1988-98; Nat Caucus & Ctr Black Aged; Asn Women Psychol, 1990-99; Ctr Aging & Family, Ackerman Inst Family, 1996; chair, NY City Fedn Mental Health, Mental Retardation & Alcoholism Serv, 1998-00; founding mem, BPGNY & Assocs. **Honors/Awds:** Leadership Distinguished Cot Serv Award, St Augustine's Episcopal Church, NY City, 2001; Charles Walberg Award, 2002. **Special Achievements:** Co-author, "Women of Color and Feminist Practice," in Not for Women Only, 1986; auth: "The Homeless Older Women in Context: Alienation, Cutoff, and Reconnection," in J of Women & Aging, 1991; "Look Back and Wonder: Developing Family Oriented Mental Health Programs for the Elderly," newsletter of the American Family Therapy Assn, winter 1997; "May the Circle Be Unbroken," in A Cross-Cultural Look at Death, Dying and Religion. **Business Addr:** Executive Vice President, Lower Eastside Service Center, Pencer House, 630 East 6th St, New York, NY 10009.

SULLIVAN, ZOLA JILES
Educator. **Personal:** Born Nov 5, 1921, Tallahassee, FL; daughter of Willis James and Susie Baker; married William David, Apr 1, 1956; children: Yolanda Sullivan Shelton, William D II, Shirley & Dexter Shelton. **Educ:** Fla A&M Univ, BS, MS; Fisk Univ; Univ Mich, Ann Arbor; Univ Miami, FL, post masters work, 1961; Oxford Univ, English, 1965; Univ Ill Urban Champ, PhD, 1970; Consultant Ministry Educ, Nassau, BS, 1971. **Career:** Educator (retired); Broward Co Pub Sch Syst, Ft Lauderdale, teacher, 1942-43; Palm Beach Co Elem Sch, teacher, 1943-50; Fla A&M Univ, instructor 1950-53; Dade Co Pub Syst, prin elem teacher, 1953-71; Fla Int Univ Miami FL, asst prof educ, 1971-74, assoc prof educ, 1974-90; Fla Int Univ, founding prof, 1971; Fla Memorial Col, adj prof, 1990-91. **Orgs:** Chmn, Num Childhood Educ Comn; consult, Num Educ Asn; speaker lectr, Num Elem Schs; coodr, Num Educ Workshops; Num Educ Asn; speaker Num Ch Grps;Richmond Heights Women's Club FL; Alpha Phi Alpha Frat; Iota Pi Lambda Chap Miami; Fla Int Task Force Needs Assessment to Improve Educational Opportunities, Guinea; founding mem, Second Baptist Church, Miami, FL, 1963; adv bd, Black Heritage Mus Dade Count, 1989-; Primary Readers &Evaluators in First Editions of Eric Early Childhood. **Honors/Awds:** Recip num sch & career opport cert; pub num papers educ; NDEA Fel UnivIll, 1969-70; Fla Governor's Award, 1986; Outstanding Serv to African Educrs Political Leaders & Stud, recognized by FL Chap of the Natl Coun Int Visitor. **Special Achievements:** First Black Female to receive a PhD in Miami, Fl, Univ of IL, 1970. **Home Addr:** 11601 SW 141st St, Miami, FL 33176, **Home Phone:** (305)233-8515. *

SULTON, ANNE THOMAS
Lawyer, educator. **Personal:** Born Oct 24, 1952, Racine, WI; daughter of William Thomas and Esther Phillips; married James E Sulton Jr, Aug 11, 1981; children: James III, William & Patrice. **Educ:** Wash State Univ, Pullman, BS, 1973; State Univ NY, Albany, MA, 1975; Univ Md, College Park, PhD, 1984; Univ Wis, Madison, JD, 1985. **Career:** Spelman Col, criminol instr, 1976-78; Howard Univ, criminol instr, 1980-84; pvt pract atty, 1985-; Denver Nat Asn Advan Colored People, legal coun, 1993-99; NJ City Univ, assoc prof, currently. **Orgs:** Nat Asn Advan Colored People. **Special Achievements:** Awarded First Certified Black Female Pilot by Atlanta Negro Airmen Intl Flying Club Organization, in Atlanta, 1977; Edited book entitled "African American Perspectives on Crime", 1996; wrote book entitled "Inner City Crime Control", 1990. **Business Addr:** Associate Professor, New Jersey City University, Department of Criminal Justice, 2039 Kennedy Blvd P223, Jersey City, NJ 07305-1597, **Business Phone:** (201)200-3492.

SULTON, DR. JACQUELINE RHODA
Pediatrician, physician. **Personal:** Born Mar 27, 1957, Detroit, MI; daughter of Nathaniel O Holloway and Dorothy G Johnson; married Francis Arnold; children: Carmen Denease & Jonathan Francis. **Educ:** Spelman Col, BS, 1978; Meharry Medical Col, DM, 1982. **Career:** Tulane Univ, Sch Med, intern, residency, 1982-85; Robinson-Gouri Pediatric Group, New Orleans, pediatrician, 1984-85; Morehouse Sch Med, stud preceptor, 1992-; Oakhurst Community Health Ctr, staff pediatrician, 1985-88; pvt group practice, Pediatric & Adolescent Med, Lithonia, GA, 1989-; Emory Univ, Sch Nursing, stud preceptor, 1990-; DeKalb Med Ctr, Dept Pediatrics, chief, 1998-2000; Dekalb Medical Dept, co-chief, 2000-02; Sulton Pediatric Group PC, Lithonia, GA, currently. **Orgs:** Alpha Kappa Alpha Sor, Atlanta Med Asn Inc.; Am Acad Pediatrics, 1996. **Honors/Awds:** Atlanta Univ, Ctr Biol Honor Soc, 1976; Outstanding Acad Performance Biol, 1977; NAACP; Certificate of Merit, Stud Res, 1980; Am Acad Pediatrics, Board Certified, 1989, Fel, 1990, Recertified, 1997. **Home Phone:** (770)987-7423. **Business Addr:** Physician, Sulton Pediatric Group PC, 5910 Hillandale Dr Suite 355, Lithonia, GA 30058, **Business Phone:** (404)501-8300.*

SUMLER EDMOND, JANICE L.
Educator, lawyer. **Personal:** Born Aug 10, 1948, New York, NY; daughter of Lucille Jones (deceased) and Ernest (deceased). **Educ:** Univ Calif, Los Angeles, BA, 1970, MA, 1971; Georgetown Univ, Wash, PhD, 1978; Univ Calif Sch Law, Los Angeles, JD, 1985. **Career:** Spelman Col, Atlanta, Ga, vis prof, 1980-81; Lubic Memorial Law Scholar, 1983-84; Reginald Heber Smith Fel, legal aid Los Angeles, 1985-86; Clark Atlanta Univ, Atlanta, Ga, assoc prof, 1986-; Mack Haygood, McLean Attorneys, Atlanta, Ga, atty, 1989-95; pvt pract, Pine Lake, Ga, currently. **Orgs:** Nat vice dir, Asn Black Women Historians, 1986-88 & 1988-90; Ga Asn Black Women Attys, 1987-; recruiter, Georgetown Univ, 1988-. **Honors/Awds:** Southern Fel Fund Summer Research Award, 1988; Judicine Fel, US Supreme Court, Wash, 1991-92; Panel of Neutrals, Am Arbitration Asn. **Special Achievements:** The Forten-Purvis Women and the Antislavery Crusade," Journal of Negro History, 1981; "Personhood and Citizenship: Black Women Litigants, 1867-1890," Univ Mass Press, 1997. **Business Addr:** Janice L Sumler-Edmond, PO Box 1600, Pine Lake, GA 30072-1600, **Business Phone:** (404)297-9441.*

SUMMER, DONNA (LADONNA ANDREA GAINES)
Singer. **Personal:** Born Dec 31, 1948, Boston, MA; daughter of Andrew Gaines and Mary Gaines; married Helmut, Jan 1, 1971 (divorced 1974); children: Mimi; married Bruce Sudano, Jul 15, 1980; children: Brooklyn & Amanda Grace. **Career:** The Crow, band member; Theater: Hair, 1967; Porgy & Bess; Showboat; Godspell; The Me Nobody Knows; solo recording artist, 1975-; Albums: Star Collection, 1977; Greatest Hits, 1977; The Greatest Hits of Donna Summer, 1977; Star Gold, 1977; Lo Mejor De Donna Summer Vol-1, 1978; Lo Mejor De Donna Summer Vol-2, 1978; On the Radio: Greatest Hits Volumes 1 & 2, 1979; Wereldsuccessen, 1979; Walk Away: Collector's Edition, 1980; The Summer Collection: Greatest Hits, 1985; The Dance Collection: A Compilation of Twelve Inch Singles, 1987; 12 ers, 1990; The Best Of Donna Summer, 1990; The Complete Hits Collection, 1991; Donna Summer Best, 1991; The Dance Collection, 1991; The Donna Summer Anthology, 1993; This Time I Know It's For Real, 1993; Donna Summer Retrospective, 1994; The Complete Donna Summer, 1994; Endless Summer: Greatest Hits, 1994; Greatest Hits, 1995; Master Series, 1997; Millennium Edition, 1999; Greatest Hits, France, 2001; The Best Of/Millennium Collection, 2003; The Ultimate Collection, 2003; The Journey: The Very Best of Donna Summer, 2003; Gold, 2005; Chronicles, 2005; Millennium Collection, Best of Vol 2, 2006; Solo: "The Hostage", 1974; "Lady of the Night", 1974; "Love to Love You Baby", 1975; "Could It Be Magic", 1976; "Try Me, I Know We Can Make It", 1976; "Spring Affair", 1976; "Winter Melody", 1977; "I Feel Love", 1977; "Down Deep Inside", 1977; "I Remember Yesterday", 1977; "Love's Unkind", 1977; "I Love You", 1977; "Rumour Has It", 1978; "Once Upon a Time", 1978; "Back in Love Again", 1978; "Last Dance", 1978; "MacArthur Park", 1978; "MacArthur Park Suite", 1978; "Heaven Knows", 1979; "Hot Stuff", 1979; "Bad Girls", 1979; "Dim All the Lights", 1979; "No More Tears", 1979; "On the Radio", 1980; "Sunset People", 1980; "Walk Away", 1989; "The Wanderer", 1980; "Cold Love", 1980; "Who Do You Think You're Foolin", 1981; "Love Is in Control", 1982; "State of Independence", 1982; "I Feel Love", 1982; "The Woman in Me", 1982; "She Works Hard for the Money", 1983; "Unconditional Love", 1983; "Love Has a Mind of Its Own", 1983; "Stop, Look and Listen", 1984; "There Goes My Baby", 1984; "Supernatural Love", 1984; "Eyes", 1985; "Dinner with Gershwin", 1987; "Only the Fool Survives", 1987; "All Systems Go", 1988; "This Time I Know It's for Real", 1989; "I Don't Wanna Get Hurt", 1989; "Love's About to Change My Heart", 1989; "When Love Takes Over You", 1989; "In Another Place And Time", 1989; "State of Independence", 1990; "Breakaway", 1991; "When Love Cries", 1991; "Work That Magic", 1991; "Melody of Love", 1994; "I Feel Love", 1995; "Whenever There Is Love", 1996; "Does He Love You", 1996; "Carry On", 1997; "I Will Go with You", 1999; "Dream-A-Lot's Theme", 2004; "I Got Your Love", 2005; "I'm a Fire", 2008; "Stamp Your Feet", 2008; "Sand On My Feet", 2008; "Fame (The Game)", 2008. **Honors/Awds:** Top New Female Vocalist, 1975; Best Rhythm and Blues Female Vocalist, Nat Acad Recording Arts & Sci, 1978; Best Female Rock Vocalist, 1979; Favorite Female Pop Vocalist, Am Music Awards, 1979; Favorite Female Vocalist of Soul Music, 1979; Soul Artist of the Year, Rolling Stone Mag, 1979; Best Selling Album for Female Artist, 1980; Ampex Golden Reel Award for single and album "On the Radio", 1980; Best Rock Performance, Best of Las Vegas Jimmy Award, 1980; Grammy Award for Best Inspirational Performance, 1984; Hollywood Walk of Fame, Star, 1992; Grammy Award for Best Dance Recording, 1998. **Special Achievements:** Co-author, Ordinary Girl: The Journey, 2003.

SUMMEROUR-PERRY, LISA
Fashion model. **Personal:** Born Sep 5, 1962, Somers Point, NJ. **Educ:** Howard Univ, attended 1982. **Career:** Prudential Realty Group, legal secy, 1983-84; Sughrue Mion Zinn Macpeak & Seas, legal secy, 1984; Lenox China/Crystal, secy, 1985; Sands Hotel Casino, exec secy, 1985-86; TV series: "Mercury Rising", 1998; "Third Watch", 1999; "Law & Order: Special Victims Unit", 1999, 2001. **Orgs:** Nat Quill & Scroll. **Honors/Awds:** Southern Univ Academic Achievement Award; Miss Congeniality, Miss USA Pageant, 1986. **Home Addr:** 507 Grand St Apt 2D, Trenton, NJ 08611-2642. *

SUMMERS, DR. DAVID STEWART
Physician, educator. **Personal:** Born Feb 16, 1932, Canton, OH; son of William Edward Summers and Stewart Jordan Summers; married Ernestine Cumber, Nov 30, 1957; children: David S II & Timothy C. **Educ:** VA State Univ, BS, 1954; VA Union Univ (Electives only) 1955; Univ VA Sch Med, MD, 1959. **Career:** SUNY Upstate Med Ctr, Syracuse, intern resident & instr, 1959-63; Univ Rochester Sch Med & Strong Memorial Hosp Dept Neurol, instr asst prof dir EEG labs, 1967-72; McGuire VA Hosp, neurologist, 1967; Univ Utah Col MedDept Neurol, asst prof & electro encephalographer, 1972-76; Hill AFB Hosp& SLC VA Hosp, Neurol consult, 1972-76; DHEW, Natl coun serv & facilities dev disabled, 1974-77; State Utah, gov's black policy coun, 1975-77; Univ Utah, affirm action comt, 1975-77; St Vincent Health Ctr, neurologist & electro encephalographer, 1976-90; Headache Ctr, Neurol IST Western PEN,neurologist, 1991-93; Warren State Hosp, neurol dir, 1991-2000; Neurol consult, currently. **Orgs:** Am Acad Neurol, 1962-; E Assn Electro encephalographers 1971-; Am Epilepsy Soc 1971-; Epilepsy Found Am, 1972-; ber, Erie County & Pa Med Soc,1976-90; Natl Assn Advan

Colored People; Univ VA Alumni Assn, 1976-; Nat Med Assn, 1977-; Gateway Med Soc, 1994; Immanuel Lutheran Ch, 1980-86; ber, Natl Multiple Sclerosis Soc Northwest PA Br, 1986-90; Am Humanist Assn; People Am Way; AAAS; ACLU; NY Acad Sci; Menninger Soc; Natl Org Women; Planned Parenthood; Am United Separation Church & State; NOW; Pro-Choice Am; Planned Parenthood; NY Acad Sci; Natl Comt Sci Edu; Freedom Religion Found; Ctr Reproductive Law & Policy; neurology dept, Natl Afr Inst. **Honors/Awds:** Abby Aldrich Rockefeller Scholar, John D Rockefeller, 3rd 1951-54. **Military Serv:** AUS, Med Corps, capt, 3 yrs; Natl Def Serv Medal; Cert of Achievement Germany 1967. **Business Addr:** Neurologist, David Summers, 1520 Pasadena Dr, Erie, PA 16505-2727.

SUMMERS, LORETTA M
Consultant, president (organization). **Personal:** Born Oct 14, 1952, Cincinnati, OH; daughter of Stoughton and Lorena. **Educ:** Ind State Univ, BS, bus admin, 1974; Memphis State Univ, MBA, 1987; cert, sr prof human resources. **Career:** Dial Corp, employee rels mgr, 1985-86, human resources mgr, 1986-90; Sprint, from human resources mgr to dir human resources, 1990-93, exec asst, 1993-95, dir human resources, 1995-96, asst vpres human resources, 1996-99; Summers Adv Group, pres, 1999-; Baker Univ, adj fac; Johnson County Community Col, adj prof; Ottawa Univ, adj prof. **Orgs:** Asst chap rep, Gospel Music Workshop, 1997-; Soc HR Mgt; Nat BMBA; Youth Opportunities Unlimited; Nat Asn African Am HR; Inst Mgt Consults; Am Soc Training & Dev; Prof Woman Network Speakers Bur. **Honors/Awds:** Black Achiever in Business, Southern Christian Leadership Coun, 1997; Woman to Watch, KS City Star Newspaper, 1997; University Outstanding Faculty Member of the Year, 1998; Distinguished African American Women, Friends Yates Inc, 1999. **Special Achievements:** Hundred Most Influential African Am Kansas City, Globe Newspaper, 1998. **Business Addr:** President, The Summers Advisory Group Inc, PO Box 26523, Shawnee Mission, KS 66225-6523, **Business Phone:** (913)402-0400.

SUMMERS, RETHA
Consultant. **Personal:** Born May 4, 1953, Goldsboro, NC; daughter of Harvey (deceased) and Aletha. **Educ:** NC A&T State Univ, BS, bus admin, 1975; Campbell Univ, MEd, coun & guid. **Career:** Employ Security Comn, employ interviewer, 1976-77; Carolina Telephone, telephone co rep, engineering clerk; Bethesda Ministries, counr, currently. **Orgs:** Pres, Am Bus Women's Asn, 1984; Am Asn Coun & Develop, 1987; dir, Future Christian Leaders Am. **Honors/Awds:** Most Outstanding Business Student Award, N Lenoir High & Future Bus Leaders Am, 1971; Banner Award & Woman of the Year Award, Am Bus Women's Asn & Ram Neuse Chap, Kingston, NC, 1984. **Business Addr:** Counselor, Bethesda Ministries, PO Box 207, Tarboro, NC 27886, **Business Phone:** (252)937-4257.*

SUMMERS, DR. RODGER
School administrator. **Personal:** Born Jan 10, 1945, Philadelphia, PA; son of Viola Kemerlin and Bennie; married Dr Pamela F; children: Megan KF & Jordon F. **Educ:** Cheyney Univ, BS, educ, eng, 1968; Univ Vt, MA, eng, 1972; Ind Univ, EdD, higher educ, 1980. **Career:** Univ Vt, from asst dean stud to assoc dean stud, 1974-81; N Adams State Col, vpres stud affairs, 1981-84; W Chester Univ, vpres stud affairs, 1984; Binghamton Univ, vpres stud affairs, instr, currently. **Orgs:** Salvation Army Bd, 1981; bd dir, Nat Asn Stud Personnel Adminr, 1983; bd mem, YMCA, 1985. **Special Achievements:** Co-author, "Commuter Marriages", Vt Jour, 1981. **Business Addr:** Instructor of Student Affairs, Binghamton University, Division of Student Affairs, PO Box 6000, Binghamton, NY 13902, **Business Phone:** (607)777-4788.

SUMMERS, WILLIAM E., IV
Government official. **Personal:** Born Mar 11, 1943, Louisville, KY; son of William E III and Sallie Sellers; married Paulette Sweatt Summers, Jun 30, 1966; children: Kimberly, William, Anthony. **Educ:** Central State Univ, Wilberforce, OH, 1962; Univ Md, Far East Extension, 1965; Univ Louisville, Louisville, KY, 1971; Kentucky State Univ, Frankfort, KY, 1976. **Career:** City Louisville, Louisville, KY, admin asst to Mayor, 1968-74; State Ky, Frankfort, KY, civil rights compliance officer, 1974-76; City Louisville, Louisville, KY, Dept Sanitation, dir, 1976-79; Mr Klean's Janitor & Maintenance Serv, Louisville KY, vpres, 1979-82; Property Maintenance & Mgt Inc, Louisville KY, pres, 1982-86; City Louisville, Louisville, KY, Internal Opers, chief staff, 1986, deputy mayor opers, 2002-; Greater Louisville, Inc, exec vpres pub affairs, 2000-02. **Orgs:** Bd dirs, NAACP, Louisville Urban League, Big Brothers & Big Sisters, Kentuckiana Girl Scout Coun; bd overseers, Bellermine Col; Urban Affairs Asn, 1986, Soc Pub Admin, 1986, Conf Minority Pub Admin, 1987; bd dir, Humana Hosp Audubon, 1988, Nat Forum Black Pub Admin, 1989; Coun Higher Educ & Community on Equal Opportunities; bd dirs, Jefferson Community Col & Watterson Col, 1990. **Honors/Awds:** Leadership Louisville, Louisville Chamber Com, 1981; Leadership Kentucky, Kentucky Chamber Com, 1987; People to Watch, Louisville Mag; several training certificates. **Military Serv:** AUS, E-5, 1963-65. **Business Addr:** Deputy Mayor of Operations, Mayor's Office City of Louisville, 527 W Jefferson St, Louisville, KY 40202, **Business Phone:** (502)574-3061.*

SUMMERVILLE, WILLIE T
Educator. **Personal:** Born Aug 17, 1944, Sunshine, AR; son of Moses and Lenora; married Valerian A Summerville, Sep 9, 1966; children: Derrick, Shandra & William Moses. **Educ:** Ark AM&N Col, BS, 1966; Univ Ill, Champaign-Urbana, MS, 1967. **Career:** St Luke CME Church, choir dir, organist, 1966-; Champaign Unit Four Schs, elem music specialist, 1967-70; self-employed music consult, clinician, teacher, dir, 1970-; Urbana Sch District No 116, choral music teacher, 1970-; Canaan Baptist Church, minister music, 1977-. **Orgs:** Phi Beta Sigma Fraternity, 1963-; life mem, Music Educators Nat Conf; Nat Educ Asn; Univ Ill Alumni Asn, 1970-; Urbana Educ Asn, 1970-; bd mem, Canaan Found, 1995-; Rotary Int, Urbana Club, 1995-. **Honors/Awds:** Outstanding Young Educator, The Jaycees, 1974; Special Citation for Youth Work, Governor IL, 1976; Citizen of the Year, Phi Beta Sigma Fraternity, IL 1980; Urbana Rotary Vocational Achievement Award, 1994; Hometown Hero in Education, President Bill Clinton, 1998; ML King Outstanding Educator Award, Parkland Col, 2000. **Special Achievements:** Directed the Urbana High School Choir in a full Mass in the St Peter's Basilica, Rome, Italy, Mar 16, 1999; UHS choir in a special performance with Michael Bolton; UHS choir in a special performance with Barry Manilow; conducted seven gospel music workshops in England and Germany, US Air Force; conducted a special workshop, Reichold Center, St Thomas, US Virgin Islands. **Business Addr:** Choral Music Director, Urbana High School, 1002 S Race St, Urbana, IL 61801, **Business Phone:** (217)384-3505.

SUMMITT, GAZELLA ANN
School administrator. **Personal:** Born Feb 27, 1941, Wheatland, IN; daughter of John Ferrell Granger and Rhoda Gazella Howard Granger; married Paul O, Jul 11, 1964; children: Krista & Dana. **Educ:** Vincennes Univ, AS, 1964; St Mary-of-the-Woods Col, BS, 1983; Ball state,grad work; Ind State Univ, MS, 1993. **Career:** Vincennes Univ, secy pres, 1960-63, admin asst pres, 1963-80, asst pres admin & affirmative action officer, 1980-91, dir human resources & AAO,1991-2005, found rel asst, 2006-. **Orgs:** Dir & secy, Vincennes Univ Found, 1980-; state coord, Am Asn Women Community & Jr Cols, 1984-94; co-chairperson, Womens Div Knox County United Fund, 1985-91; secy Region V Am Assoc Affirmative Action, 1986-88;co-chair, Indiana Coalition Blacks Higher Educ, 1986; Hist Rev Bd City Vincennes, 1986; Steering Comt, March Dimes Walk Am, 1986-92; Steering Comt, Riley Childrens Hosp Campaign 1986-92; secy, Am Asn Affirmative Action, 1988-92, pres, 1992-94; bd dirs, 1988-96; Steering Comt, FCA,1991; Vincennes Housing Authority, counr, 1992-96, chair, 1993-95; chair, Am Asn Affirmative Action Found Bd, 1996-2000; Ind Comn Women, comnr,1997-2005, Vincennes Educ Found; First Church God, bylaws comt and Elder, 2005-; Soc Human Resources Mgrs; Col & Univ Personal Asn; Red Hat Soc, "Red Hot Poppies" chap, founding mem.; Red Skelton Gala committee, 2005-08. **Honors/Awds:** Women of the Year, ABWA, 1974; Stephen Bufton Memorial Grants, Am Bus Women's Asn, 1982, 1983; Blue & Gold Cord Award, Outstanding Prof Alumnus, Vincennes Univ, 1982; Greater Vincennes Area Church Women United Valiant Woman Award, 1983; Martin Luther King Support Award, 1988; Presidents Award, Am Asn Affirmative Action, 1990; Sagamore of the WABASH Award, Govt Ind, 1994; Distinguished Citizen Award, Governor IN, 2005; Outstanding Alumnus, Wheatland High School, 2005; Spirit of Community Award", IN Comnr Women, 2008. **Business Addr:** Foundation Relations Assistant, Vincennes University Foundation & Alumni, 1002 N 1st St, Vincennes, IN 47591, **Business Phone:** (812)888-5944.

SUMMITT, KRISTA E.
Executive. **Educ:** Vincennes Univ, attended 1985; Purdue Univ, attended 1987; George Wash Univ. **Career:** IBM, Res Triangle Park, Raleigh Durham, NC, sales rep, mkt commun planner, pc sales mgr, e-com proj mgr, currently. **Orgs:** Orange Grove Missionary Baptist Church, Durham. **Honors/Awds:** Golden Circle Award, IBM; Outstanding recent graduate award, Vincennes University. *

SUMNER, THOMAS ROBERT
Lawyer, circuit court judge. **Personal:** Born Dec 4, 1949, Louisville, KY; married Sherry Ann Beene; children: Nyshana, Rahman, Kamilah. **Educ:** Univ Ill, Chicago, BA, Sociol, 1971; John Marshall Law Sch, JD, 1977. **Career:** Cook County, Pub Defender Off, trial atty, 1978-82; Sumner & Smith, Partner, 1982-88; Univ Ill, Chicago, acad coun, 1971-77; Chicago Title Ins, title examiner, 1977; Cook State Ill, Circuit Ct, Cook County Judicial Circuit, assoc Judge, currently. **Orgs:** US Ct Appeals 7th Circuit, 1977; US Dist Ct Northern Dist Ill, 1977; pres, Cook Co Bar Asn, 1985-86; Am & Trial Lawyers Asn; Ill State Bar Asn, 1980; Am Bar Asn, 1980; bd mgr, Chicago Bar Asn, 1986-88; bd dir, Nat Bar Asn, 1986-87; Ill Judges Asn, 1988. **Business Addr:** Associate Judge, Circuit Court Cook County Judicial Circuit, Richard J Daley Ctr, 50 Wash St Rm 1001, Chicago, IL 60602, **Business Phone:** (773)869-7462.*

SUNDAY, DELENA
Executive, vice president (organization). **Career:** Nordstrom Inc, salesperson, Tacoma, WA, 1980, store mgr, dir diversity affairs, 1996-98, vpres, 1998-00, exec vpres, 2000-02, Human Resources and Diversity Affairs, exec vice pres, 2002-. **Business Addr:** Executive Vice President, Nordstrom, Inc, 1501 5th Ave, Seattle, WA 98101, **Business Phone:** (206)628-2111.*

SUNEJA, SIDNEY KUMAR
Radiologist. **Personal:** Born Jul 13, 1954, Chandigarh, India; married Kathleen. **Educ:** Howard Univ Col Medicine, MD, 1976; PhD, 1982. **Career:** Case Western Reserve Univ, intern, 1977; Howard Univ Hosp, Family Practice, resident, 1977-80, diagnostic radiol, 1980-83; Johns Hopkins Hosp, nuclear med fel, 1983-85; Charity Hosp, New Orleans, assoc dir nuclear med, 1985-87; LA State Univ Med Ctr, asst prof radiol, 1985-87; Howard Univ Hosp, asst prof radiol, 1987-97; Georgetown Univ Med Ctr, Viking radiol; Musculoskeletal MRI & imaging fel, 1998-99; Walter Reed Army Med Ctr, staff civilian radiologist, 1999; John Hopkins Med Inst, Breast Imaging fel, 2000-01; pvt pract, currently. **Orgs:** Asn Univ Radiologists; Am Ruentgen Roy Soc; Med Soc DC; Am Col Radiol; Soc Nuclear Med; Radiol Soc N Am; Am Med Asn; Southern Med Asn; bd mem, Am Bd Radiol, 1985; bd mem, Am Bd Nuclear Med, 1986; bd mem, Am Bd Family Pract, 1982; radiation safety comn, LA State Univ Med Ctr; NOLA; HUH; Am Bd certifications, Radiol & Nuclear Radiol; Am Bd Nuclear Med; Am Bd Family Practice. **Honors/Awds:** Physicians Recognition Award, Am Med Asn; Am Bd of Family Practice, Recertification, 1989. **Special Achievements:** Author of numerous peer-reviewed medical/scientific publications; lecturer: "Neuroreceptor Imaging with Positron Emission Tomography," "Nuclear Cardiology," New Orleans Fall Radiology CNF; "Nuclear Medicine, Breast Imaging, Magnetic Resorance Imaging," Annual Review Course, Howard Univ CME; AMA category 1 lectures; ABD in Medical Physiology, PRD curriculum, 1997-81. **Business Addr:** Dr Sidney Suneja, 8215 Osage Lane, Bethesda, MD 20817.*

SUPERNAW, KYWIN
Football player. **Personal:** Born Jun 2, 1975, Skiatook, OK. **Educ:** Univ Ind. **Career:** Football player (retired); Detroit Lions, defensive back, 1998-2001. *

SURE, AL B. (ALBERT JOSEPH BROWN, III)
Songwriter, singer, chief executive officer. **Personal:** Born Jun 4, 1968, Boston, MA; son of Cassandra and Al Brown; children: Quincy Brown, Albert IV & Devin. **Educ:** Manhattan Ctr Media Arts. **Career:** Albums: In Effect Mode, 1988; Private Times..& the Whole 9!, 1990; Sexy Versus, 1992; The Very Best of Al B. Sure!, 2003; The Hit, actor, 2007; Honey I'm Home, 2009; TV series: "The Fresh Prince of Bel-Air", 1990; "Private Times", composer, 1991; "David Bowie: Black Tie White Noise", 1993; "VH-1 Where Are They Now?", 2000; "Rock the Cradle", 2008; Singles: "Secret Garden"; "Nite & Day"; "Off On Your Own Girl"; "Rescue Me"; "If I'm Not Your Lover"; "No Matter What"; "Had Enuf"; "Right Now"; "Misunderstanding"; "Natalie"; "I'm Still In Love"; "Black Tie/White Noise"; ABS Entertainment.net Inc, ceo, currently. **Honors/Awds:** Received numerous awards including Grammy nominations, American Music Award, Soul Train Awards, New York Music Awards and over 30 ASCAP Awards. **Business Addr:** Recording Artist, c/o Warner Bros Records Inc, 3300 Warner Blvd, Burbank, CA 91505, **Business Phone:** (818)846-9090.*

SURTAIN, PATRICK FRANK
Football player. **Personal:** Born Jun 19, 1976, New Orleans, LA; son of Alced; married Michelle Weber, 2002; children: Patrick Jr & Paris. **Educ:** Univ Southern Miss, attended 1997. **Career:** Miami Dolphins, defensive back, 1998-2004; Kans City Chiefs, Cornerback, 2005-08; free agent, currently. **Orgs:** Founder, Patrick Surtain Found. **Honors/Awds:** Dolphins Community Service Award, 1999; Pro Bowl selection, 2002-04; All-Pro selection, 2002 & 2003. *

SUTHERLAND, FRANKIE
Educator. **Personal:** Born Apr 15, 1949, Greenville, MS; daughter of Mullen and Frankie; married Albert; children: Steven Craig. **Educ:** Tougaloo Col, BA, sociol, 1971; Chicago State Univ, MS, sch guid coun, 1991, MA, educ admin, 1996; Loyola Univ, doctoral candidate. **Career:** Chicago Pub Sch, Dist 299, teacher, 1984-92, Dist 147, counr, 1992-96, Dist 133, asst supt, prin, 1996-; Gen George Patton Sch Dist, Riverdale, Ill, interim supt, supt, 2004-. **Orgs:** Exec comm, Tougaloo Col Alumni, 1990; UNCF rep, Chicago Inter-Alumni Coun, 1996-; Ill Prins Asn, 1996; Asn Supvn & Curric Develop, 1997; Nat Asn Black Sch Educrs, 1997; Riverdale Redevelopment Corp, Ad Hoc Comm, 1998; gen chairperson, Ebony Fashion Fair, 1998-. **Special Achievements:** Paper: "Teacher's Perspective of School Climate", published, ERIC library resource, paper, Resources in Education, June 1995. **Home Addr:** 914 E 193rd Pl, Glenwood, IL 60425, **Home Phone:** (708)757-3146. **Business Addr:** Superintendent, General George Patton School District, 150 W 137th St, Riverdale, IL 60827, **Business Phone:** (708)841-2420.

SUTHERLAND, LYNNE
Dentist. **Educ:** DDS. **Career:** Pvt pract, dentist & periodontist, currently. **Business Addr:** Dentist, Periodontist, Private Practice, 2204 S Taylor Rd, Cleveland Heights, OH 44118-3007, **Business Phone:** (216)371-2510.*

SUTPHEN, MONA K.
Government Official. **Personal:** Born Nov 10, 1967; married Clyde Williams. **Educ:** Mount Holyoke College, BA, 1989;

received M.Sc from London School of Economics. **Career:** Managing dir Stonebridge, LLC; U.S. foreign Service Officer, 1991-00; Natl Security Council, 1998-00; US Mission to the United Nations; the office of the High Representative, in the State Dept of human rights bureau, US Embassy in Bangkok; White House Deputy Chief of Staff, 2009-. **Orgs:** Member of the Council on Foreign Relations. **Special Achievements:** Co-author of The Next American Century: How the US Can Thrive as Other Powers Rise (Simon & Schuster 2008). **Business Addr:** The White House, 1600 Pennsylvania Ave, NW, Washington, DC 20500, **Business Phone:** (202)456-1414.*

SUTTLE, RHONDA KIMBERLY
Association executive. **Career:** NAACP, national ACT-SO competition, chair, 2001, nat dir, currently. **Business Addr:** National ACT-SO Director, NAACP National Headquarters ACT SO, 4805 Mt Hope Drv, Baltimore, MD 21215-3297, **Business Phone:** (410)358-8900.*

SUTTON, CHARLES W.
Automotive executive. **Career:** McKinney Dodge Inc, owner, chief exec officer & gen mgr, 1998. *

SUTTON, CLYDE A., SR.
Journalist, executive, business owner. **Personal:** Born Oct 21, 1927, Atlanta, GA; married Evelyn Cook, Jun 14, 1953; children: Roswell, Cheryl, Francis, Clyde Jr & Terri Vinson. **Career:** Atlanta Newspaper Inc, 1962-; Sutton's Cascade Heights Hardware, owner, currently. **Orgs:** Am Numismatic Asn, 1956-. **Military Serv:** USC, 1st class seaman. **Business Phone:** (404)346-1552.*

SUTTON, DIANNE FLOYD
Management consultant, writer, educator. **Personal:** Born Dec 6, 1948, Houston, TX; daughter of Osborne English and Dorothy Woods; married Ronald N Sutton Jr, Sep 15, 1984 (deceased); children: Ronald Jr; married Thomas Jones Jr (divorced); children: Anthony Specer Jones. **Educ:** Harris Stowe State Col, BA, educ & sociol, 1970; Wash Univ, MA, educ,curric develop, 1974. **Career:** St Louis Pub Sch Syst, math instr, 1970-76; Wash Univ St Louis, MO,Experienced Teachers Grad fel, 1971; US Equal Employ Opportunity Comn, St Louis Dist Off, investr & conciliator, 1976-79, trainer & course design, 1979-85; Creations Dyan, design silk flowers & floral arrangements, 1979-87; independent mgt consult, 1982; US Dept Agr, employee develop specialist, 1985-87; Sutton Enterprises, pres, 1987-; Am Univ, adj prof, 1990-2002; Wash, DC, adv neighborhood comnr, 2002-. **Orgs:** Nat Asn Female Execs, 1976-; Training Officers Conf, 1980-; Nat RuralHealth Asn; exec bd mem, Training Officers Conf Wash DC, 1980-. **Honors/Awds:** Special Achievement Award, US Equal Employ Opportunity Comn, 1978, 1983;Distinguished Service Award, EEO Training Progs Trainers Officers Conf,1982; TOC Community Award, 1994; Outstanding Faculty Award, Grad Sch,USDA, 1997; TOC Distinguished Service Award, 2001. **Special Achievements:** Author of "Managing Your Starship: Multicultural Managing for the Twenty first Century," published in Cultural Diversity Sourcebook, 1996,testified at Senate hearing on small businesses for National Association for Self-Employed, 1996, elected to Policy Bd of Natl Rural Health Assn,2000-01, elected Advisory Neighborhood Commissioner for (4-A-06) in Washington, DC, 2002, 2004; Publication: Etiquette: A Guide to Thriving and Surviving in Today Workplace. **Business Addr:** President, Sutton Enterprises, 9847 Campbell Dr Suite 30, Kensington, MD 20895-3130, **Business Phone:** (301)585-1446.

SUTTON, GLORIA W.
Librarian. **Personal:** Born Feb 17, 1952, Kinston, NC; divorced; children: Dimitri. **Educ:** Lenoir Comm Col, AA 1972; E Carolina Univ, BS 1974; NC Cent Univ, MLS, 1987. **Career:** Retired; Lenoir Community Col, evening librn, 1974-75; Wayne Co Pub Libr, cataloguer, 1975-76; Sampson Tech Col, librn, 1976-81; Wake Technical Community Col, librn, 1981-2003. **Orgs:** NC Community Col Learning Resources Assoc; YMCA; youth minister Wake Baptist Grove Church; Shaw Div Sch Library; Wake Baptist Grove Church Library, 1985-86; Capital Area Library Asn 1985-86; Prof Develop Comm Wake Tech Col; YWCA; ReHI Consortium. **Honors/Awds:** Volunteer of the Year Garner Rd, YMCA, 1983; Gloria Sutton Scholarship Wake Tech Col 1984-; Youth Radio Ministry, WSES Radio, 1984-86; ; Wake Baptist Grove Church minister of Youth Services 1983; NC Community Col Leadership Sch, 1991; NCLA Leadership Institute, 1998. **Special Achievements:** Outstanding Young Women of Amer 1985. **Home Addr:** 206 Creek Channel Ct, Garner, NC 27529, **Home Phone:** (919)779-2943. **Business Addr:** Librarian, Wake Tech Comm Coll, 9101 Fayetteville Rd, Raleigh, NC 27603, **Business Phone:** (919)212-3837.*

SUTTON, JAMES CARTER
Purchasing agent. **Personal:** Born Jan 6, 1945, Lynville, TN; son of Felton Eugene and Nannie Readus (deceased); married Joyce Roach Sutton, Mar 20, 1989; children: Kyra. **Educ:** Wayne State Univ, BS, bus admin, 1975; Univ Detroit, MBA. **Career:** Eastman Kodak Co, supv buyer, 1984, admin asst to vpres, 1984-85, proj mgr bus ed, 1985-86, pub affairs planning dir, Worldwide Corp Sourcing, mgr & dir minority supplier progs, sr mgr, engine components purchasing; Chrysler Corp, purchasing agent. **Orgs:** Fredrick Douglas African Historical Mus Adv Comt; Bus Policy Rev Coun, 1988-; bd mem, Otetiana Coun Boy Scouts Am Inc, 1988-; chmn bd, Urban League Rochester, Nat Minority Supplier Develop Coun, 1990; Corp Dir Supplier Progs Kodak; bd mem, Inst Am Bus, 1992; secy, Chase Manhattan-Rochester Metro Adv Bd; Sigma Phi Pi. **Honors/Awds:** Citation for involvement with Big Brother Prog; Served as advisor to South African Black Bus Develop. **Military Serv:** USAF, e-5, 4 1/2 yrs. *

SUTTON, MARY A.
Software developer. **Personal:** Born Oct 12, 1945, Los Angeles, CA. **Educ:** Prairie View A&M Col, BS, 1966; Univ Santa Clara, MS, 1973. **Career:** Ford Aerospace & Commun, sr software engr; Martin-marietta, assoc engr, 1966-67; Lockheed, assoc engr, 1967-69; TRW Systs, proj mgr, 1969-76. **Orgs:** Past mem, Sunnyvale's TRW Affirmative Action Prog; pres, Sunnyvale Employees Asn TRW, 1973-74; Univ Santa Clara, Alumni Orgn, 1973-. **Honors/Awds:** First black, first woman mgr at TRW Sunnyvale. **Business Addr:** 1145 E Arques Ave, Sunnyvale, CA 94086.

SUTTON, REV. MOSES. **See Obituaries section.**

SUTTON, NATHANIEL K
Automotive executive. **Career:** Owens Corning Fiberglas, staff;IBM, staff; Olympia Fields Ford Sales Inc, chief exec officer; Sutton Ford, chief exec officer, 1989-. **Special Achievements:** Company ranked No 27 on Black Enterprise magazine's list of top 100 auto dealers, 1992. **Business Addr:** Chief Executive Officer, Sutton Ford, 21315 Cent Ave, Matteson, IL 60443, **Business Phone:** (708)720-8000.

SUTTON, NORMA J.
Lawyer. **Personal:** Born Jun 11, 1952, Chicago, IL; daughter of Harry Sams and Beatrice Ross; children: Edward. **Educ:** Loyola Univ, BA, 1974; Govs State Univ, MA, 1976; Loyola Univ Sch Law, JD, 1980. **Career:** Cemrel Inc, office mgr, 1975-77; N Am Co Inst, legal asst, 1977-80; Appellate Ct, judicial clerk, 1980-82; Soft Sheen Products, corp coun, 1982-85; Digital Equip Corp, managing atty, 1985; Cent Reg Law Group, mgr, currently. **Orgs:** Secy, 1986-87, vice chair, 1987-88, Ill State Bar Asn YLD; Am Bar As, Cook County Bar Asn; Digital Equip Corp Comn Relns Coun. **Honors/Awds:** Leadership & Serv, Loyola Univ Sch Law Chicago, 1980. *

SUTTON, DR. OZELL
Government official. **Personal:** Born Dec 13, 1925, Gould, AR; son of Charlie and Lula Belle Dowthard; married Joanna Freeman, May 9, 1947; children: Angela Martin, Alta Muhammad & Dietre Jo. **Educ:** Philander Smith Col, BA, 1950, HonD, 1971; Fisk Univ, Nashville, TN, attended 1961. **Career:** Government official (retired); Ark Dem, staff writer, 1950-57; Little Rock Housing Authority, relocations supvr, 1957-59; Winthrop Rockefeller, pub rels, 1959-61; Ark Coun Human Rels, exec dir, 1961-66; US Dept Justice, field rep CRS, 1966-68, Commun Rels Serv, state supvr, Ark state dir, 1969-72, reg dir SE region comn, 1972-03; Govt Winthrop Rockefeller Ark, special asst, 1968-69; dir Comm Rels, SE region, 1972-2003. **Orgs:** Relocation supvr, Litle Rock Housing Authority, 1959-61; dir, Ark Coun Human Rel, 1961-66; exec bd, Philander Smith Col, 1971; bd trustees, Friendship Baptist Church; exec bd, Atlanta Br Nat Advan Asn Colored People; gen pres, Alpha Phi Alpha Frat, 1980; exec bd, Leadership Conf Civil Rights; exec bd, Black Leadership Forum; chmn, Coun Pres Black Greek letter Orgn; pres, Voter Educ Project; chmn, Forum Comn Metro-Atlanta Crime Comn; co-chmn, Atlanta Black-Jewish Coalition; pres, Inter-Alumni Coun; chmn, Metro Atlanta Crime Comn; chmn, Voter Educ Project, 1986-; mem bd, Nat Advan Asn Colored People. **Honors/Awds:** Distinguished Serv Award, Nat Advan Asn Colored People, 1978; Distinguished Service Award, Alpha Phi Alpha Frat, 1979; Outstanding Performance Award, US Dept Justice, 1979-80; Distinguished Alumnus Award, Philander Smith Coll; more than 100 other awards from many orgn; Special Achievement Awards, US Dept Justice; US Attorney General Award; Distinguished Service Award, Nat Ctr Missing & Exploited C, 1994. **Special Achievements:** Book: The Black Experience in America, dramatic portrayal of black struggle; Watch Your Language, commentary on impact of racial & ethnicslurs; Cited as "100 Most Influential African American Leaders", EBONY Magazine. **Military Serv:** USMC, corpl, 1944-46. *

SUTTON, PERCY E.
Executive, lawyer, civil rights activist. **Personal:** Born Nov 24, 1920, San Antonio, TX; son of Samuel J. and Lillian Smith; married Leatrice O'Farrek, 1943; children: Pierre, Cheryl, Darryl. **Educ:** Prairie View age & mech Col; Tuskegee Inst; Hampton Inst; US Air Corps Cadet Training Sch, Tuskegee AL; US Air Corps Combat Intelligence Sch, Harrisburg, PA; Columbia Univ sch law; Brooklyn Law School, JD, 1950. **Career:** US Army Air Corps, cap, 1941-45; Air Force, Wash, DC, intelligence off & trial judge advocate, 1951-53, private practice, attny; Stud nonviolent coord Comt, civil-rights defense atty & consult; NY State govt, assemblyman, 1964-66; Borough Manhattan, pres, 1966-77; Inner-City Broadcasting Corp, chmn, bd dir, owner, 1972-91; Jesse Jackson presidential campaign, adv, 1984, 1988; ACTEL, co-founder; Synematics Inc, chmn & ceo. **Orgs:** Martin Luther King Dems; pres, NAACP, 1960-61; Am Mus Natural Hist, Mus City NY; nat dir, Urban League; Oper PUSH; Nat Caucus Black Elected & Appointed Officials. **Honors/Awds:** Golden Mike Award, Broadcasters Found, 2005; Boy Scouts Am, Distinguished Eagle Scout Award; Lamplighter Award, Nat Black Leadership Forum, 1987, 1997; Spingarn Medal, NAACP, 1986. **Military Serv:** USAF capt, combat intelligence officer, 1943-45, intelligence officer, judge advocate, 1950-53; Combat Stars for Serv in Italian & Mediterranean Theaters WWII. **Business Phone:** (845)255-0878.*

SUTTON, PIERRE MONTE
Executive, president (organization). **Personal:** Born Feb 1, 1947, New York, NY. **Educ:** Univ Toledo, BA, 1968; NY Univ; Harvard Univ Bus Sch, OPM Prog, grad. **Career:** NY Courier Newspaper, exec editor, 1971-72; Inner City Broadcasting Corp, Res & Analysis Corp, vpres, 1971, WLIB Radio, gen mgr, 1972-75, vpres, 1975-77, pres, 1977; Chmn & Chief Exec Officer, currently. **Orgs:** Bd mem, Minority Investment Fund, 1979-; first vpres, Nat Asn Black Owned Broadcasters, 1979-; chmn, Harlem Boy Scouts, 1975-; bd mem, exec, com New York City Marathon, 1979-; bd trustee, Alvin Ailey Dance Found, 1980-; bd mem, Better Bus Bur Harlem, 1972-77; bd mem, Hayden Planetarium, 1979-; Radio Advert Bureau. **Special Achievements:** Company ranked 40 on Black Enterprise's list of top 100 industrial & serv companies, 1998. **Military Serv:** USMC, E-4, 3yrs. **Business Phone:** (510)848-7713.*

SUTTON, DR. SHARON EGRETTA
Musician, artist, educator. **Personal:** Born Feb 18, 1941, Cincinnati, OH; daughter of Egretta Johnson and Booker Johnson. **Educ:** Univ Hartford, BMus, 1963; Columbia Univ, attended 1973; City Univ NY, MPhil, 1981, MA, psychol, 1982, PhD, psychol, 1982. **Career:** Orchestras: "Fiddler on the Roof," "Man of La Mancha," the Bolshoi, Moiseiyev & Leningrad Ballet Companies, 1963-68; Pratt Inst, vis asst prof, 1975-81; SE Sutton Architect, pvt pract, 1976-; Columbia Univ, adj asst prof, 1981-82; Univ Cincinnati, asst prof, 1982-84; Univ Mich, assoc prof, 1984-94, prof archit & urban planning, 1994-97; Univ Wash, prof archit urban design & planning, dir, CEEDS; Exhibitions: The Evans-Tibbs Collection in Wash, DC, fine artist, 1985; Your Heritage House in Detroit, MI, 1986, June Kelly Gallery in NYC, 1987, Univ Mich Mus Art 1988; Arts included in collections: The Libr Cong; The Mint Mus; The Baltimore Mus Art, Baltimore, MD; The Wadsworth Atheneum, Hartford, CT; Vanderbilt Univ, Fine Art Gallery, Miami-Dade Fla Pub Libr Syst. **Orgs:** Fel Am Inst Archit; Am Psychol Asn; Group VII Nat Fel, WK Kellogg Found, 1986-89; pres, Nat Archit Accrediting Bd, 1996-97; mayoral appointee, Seattle Design Comn, 2000-04; prin investr, "Constructing a Social Justice Framework Youth & Community Service, Ford Found, 2004; appointee, Seattle Design Review Bd, 2007-; founding dir, Urban Network: An Urban Design Program for Youth; dir, Ctr Environ Educ & Design Studies. **Honors/Awds:** Post Baccalaureat Award, Danforth Found, 1979-81; Design Research Recognition Award, Nat Endowment Arts, 1983; Education Award, Am Planning Asn, 1991; Life Achievement Award, Mich Women's Hall of Fame, 1997; Univ Mich Regent's Award for Distinguished Public Service; Distinguished Professional, Asn Col Schs Archit. **Special Achievements:** First Afro American woman to be named a full professor of architecture in the US, to serve as president of one of architecture's five collateral organization, the National Architectural Accrediting Board, and to receive the distinguished professor award from the Association of Collegiate Schools of Architecture; Second AFA Woman to be advanced to fellowship in the Am Inst of Architects; Author: Learning Through the Building Environment, 1985; Weaving a Tapestry of Resistance, 1996; articles in professional journals, registered architect in the states of New York and Washington, certified by the National Council of Architectural Registration Boards. **Home Addr:** 1017 Minor Ave The Gainsborough Apt 504, Seattle, WA 98104. **Business Addr:** Prof of Architecture & Urban Design, Adjunct Professor of Social Work, Director, CEEDS, University Washington, 208 P Gould Hall, PO Box 355720, Seattle, WA 98195-5720, **Business Phone:** (206)383-6052.

SUTTON, WILLIAM W., JR.
Journalist, editor. **Personal:** Born Jun 12, 1955, New Orleans, LA. **Educ:** Hampton Univ, BA, 1977; Rutgers Univ-Camden Law Sch. **Career:** Harvard Univ, Nieman fel, 1987-88;Post-Tribune, Gary, managing ed, 1991, newsroom mgr, 1992, ed & vpres, 1993; McClatchy Co Inc, News & Observer, asst managing ed, 1997, dep managing ed, 1997-; Times-Picayune, New Orleans, LA, reporter; Virginian Pilot, Norfolk, reporter; Gannett Co, Courier-Post, Cherry Hill, NJ; Philadelphia Inquirer, reporter. **Orgs:** pres & chief exec officer, Nat Asn Black Journalists, 1977, 1999-01; Omega Psi Phi Fraternity. **Honors/Awds:** Educ Diversity Award,

Maynard Ist Journ, 1996. **Business Addr:** Deputy Managing Editor, The News & Observer, 215 S McDowell St, PO Box 191, Raleigh, NC 27602.*

SUTTON, DR. WILLIAM WALLACE
School administrator. **Personal:** Born Dec 15, 1930, Monticello, MS; son of Talmon L and Bessie Lewis; married Leatrice Eva Hubbard; children: William W Jr, Averell H, Sheryl Smith, Alan D, Allison M & Gavin J. **Educ:** Dillard Univ, BA, 1953; Howard Univ, MS, 1959, PhD, 1965; Harvard Univ, IST Educ mgt, 1991. **Career:** School administrator (retired); DC Gen Hosp Wash, med Tech, 1955-59; Dillard Univ, instr prof biol, 1959-79, chmn div nat sci, 1969-79; Chicago State Univ, vpres & acad affairs & provost, 1979-85, prof biol sci, 1982-85; Kansas State Univ, vpres educ & student servs, prof biol, 1985-88; Mississippi Valley State Univ, pres, 1988-98. **Orgs:** Sigma Xi The Res Soc Am, 1955; bd dirs, Nat Conf Christians & Jews, 1968-79; bd dirs, Urban League New Orleans, 1970-78; bd trustees, WYES TV New Orleans, 1973-79; bd dirs, Methodist Hosp New Orleans, 1975-79; Am Coun Educ; past pres, Nat Inst Sci; Soc Sigma Xi; reg liaison off, Danforth Assoc Prog Danforth Found, 1975-79; consult, US Dept Educ, 1977-81, 1983-84; bd dirs, Am Heart Assoc LA, 1977-79; consult, Nat Res Coun Nat Acad Sci, 1980, 1982-83; consult, Inst Health Sci Consortium; deacon Chicago United, 1980-82; bd dirs, Greenwood-Leflore Chamber Com, 1989-91; Greenwood, MS Rotary Club; adv bd, Deposit Guaranty Nat Bank Greenwood, MS. **Honors/Awds:** Distinguish Award, Dillard Univ, 1982; Presidential Citation, Nat Asn Equal Opportunity, 1979, 1980; Distinguish Alumni Award, Dillard Univ, 1978; Silver Beaver Award, Boy Scouts Am, 1976; Man of the Middle South,Changing Middle S Mag, 1973; Beta Kappa Chi Scientific Honor Soc, 1955; Alpha Kappa Mu Honor Soc, 1990; Dillard Univ LLD, 1991. *

SUTTON, WILMA JEAN
Executive. **Personal:** Born Nov 11, 1933, Murphysboro, IL; married Clarence E. **Educ:** Univ IL, Urbana, cert mgt, 1969; Univ CT Storrs, cert, 1970; Univ IN, Bloomington, cert, 1976; Roosevelt Univ, Chicago, IL, BA, 1978, MA, 1979. **Career:** Chicago Title Ins Co Chicago IL, preliminary & examiner, 1951-64; Hyde Park Fed Savings & Loan Asn Chicago, exec vpres, 1964; Community Outreach Savages Am, VPres & Regional Supvr; Home Savings Am, vpres; Northeastern Il Univ, asst to Pres. **Orgs:** Bd of dirs Hyde Park Fed Savings & Loan Asn of Chicago; bd of dirs Hyde Park Nieghborhood Club; bd of dirs Loretto Adult Educ Ctr; mem Lambda Alpha Ely Chpt; mem UNICEF; mem US Savings & Loan League; mem Chicago Urban League; mem NAACP; mem IL Commn on the Status of Women; mem Museum of Sci & Industry; mem St Thaddeus Ch Appointment; mem Savings & Loan Adv Bd Gov Daniel Walker State of IL. **Honors/Awds:** Cert of recognition Nat Alliance of Businessmen; editorial reviews Ebony Mag/Jet Mag/Chicago Sun Times/Chicgo Tribune/Real Estate News; Eleanor Roosevelt Humanitarian Award, Roosevelt Univ. *

SWAIN, ALICE M. See Obituaries section.

SWAIN, HAMP, JR.
Consultant. **Personal:** Born Dec 3, 1929, Macon, GA; son of Hamp Sr (deceased) and Susie McIntosh; married Zenola Hardeman; children: Ronald Leo, Ouida Louise, Natalie Valencia & Jarvis Osmond. **Career:** Little Richard & The Hamptones, band leader, sax player 1949-56; WIBB, radio broadcaster, announcer, 1957-81; pioneer broadcaster, 1954-81; Huckabee Auto Co, sales consult, 1981-. **Orgs:** Nat Asn Advan Colored People; Wendell Mcintosh Bowl. **Honors/Awds:** Golden Voice Award, Jack Gibson Orgn, 1980. *

SWAIN, JAMES H
Lawyer. **Personal:** Born in Philadelphia, PA; married Sharon Matthews. **Educ:** Univ Bridgeport, BA, 1975; Temple Univ Sch Law, JD, 1978; Univ Pa Law Sch, LLM, 1986. **Career:** US Atty So Dist NY, summer intern, 1977; Third Circuit Ct Appeals, clerkship intern Hon A Leon Higginbotham, 1978; US Dept Labor, trial atty off reg solicitor, 1978-88; US Dept Justice, Eastern Pa, asst US atty, 1989-94; Asset Forfeiture Div US Atty, dep chief, 1994-2000, chief, 2000-03; Southern Dist Fla, US Atty's Off, exec asst US atty, 2003-. **Orgs:** Exec comt, Barristers Asn Philadelphia, 1979-80, 1986-89, legis rev com, 1978-82; bd dir, Community Legal Serv, 1988-94; bd dir, Wynnfield Residents Asn, 1988-94, exec vpres, 1992-93; Fed Bar Asn Philadelphia Chap, 1988-94; Philadelphia Bar Asn, 1989-94; Fed Bar Asn, Miami Chap, 1994-; Dade Co Black Lawyers Asn, 1994-; trustee, Mt Pleasant Baptist Church, Philadelphia, Pa; Fed Bar Asn, Miami Chap, 1996-; Inns Ct Univ Miami's Chap, 1996-; Nat Bar Asn, Fla State Chap, 1996-. **Honors/Awds:** Scholar of the Year Award, Rho Upsilon Chap, Omega Psi Phi Fraternity Inc, 1975-76; Distinguished Service Award, Black Am Law Stud Asn, 1977-78; Certificate of Appreciation, Barristers Asn Philadelphia, 1978-79, 1979-80; John Marshall Award, Omega Psi Phi Fraternity Inc, US Dept Justice, 1992. **Special Achievements:** Author: "Protecting Individual Employers: Is it Safe to Complain About Safety?," Univ Bridgeport Law Review, 1988; lectr, Asset Forfeiture, US Dept Justice & various Bar Asns, 1991-. **Business Addr:** Executive Assistant United States Attorney, Southern District of Florida, US Attorney Office, 99 NE 4th St, Miami Beach, FL 33132, **Business Phone:** (305)961-9000.

SWAIN, MICHAEL B.
Consultant, programmer analyst. **Personal:** Born Nov 5, 1965, Springfield, OH; son of Melvin and Charlene Freeman. **Educ:** Ohio Univ, BBA, 1987. **Career:** Data Image, comput programmer, analyst, 1987-89; SEMCO, comput programmer, analyst, trainer, 1989-90; Decision Systs Technologies Inc, proj mgr, 1994-98; Andersen Consult, LLP, consult, 1998. **Orgs:** Pres, Alpha Phi Omega Nat Serv Fraternity, 1986-87; treas, Springfield Metrop N Hill Housing Bd, 1988; bd chmn, develop chair, Springfield Urban League & Community Ctr, 1990-94; pres, Alpha Phi Alpha, 1991-96; educ chair, NAACP, 1991-93; gen chair, Ebony Fashion Fair, 1992-93. **Honors/Awds:** John Newton Templeton Award, Outstanding Sr Leader, Ohio Univ, 1987; Community Serv Vol of the Year, Wright-Patterson AFB, 1993. **Military Serv:** USAF, comput specialist, 1990-94. **Home Phone:** (404)373-9930.

SWAIN, DR. RONALD L
Educator, association executive. **Personal:** Born Oct 9, 1948, Macon, GA; son of Evelyn Denton and Hampton; married Chrystle A Bullock, Jun 9, 1973; children: Ronald. **Educ:** Duquesne Univ, Pittsburgh, Pa, BA, 1970, MEd, 1972; Shaw Divinity Sch Ral NC, MDiv, 1975; Univ NC, Chapel Hill, MEd 1983; George Washington Univ, DC, EdD, 1987; Harvard Univ, Grad Sch Educ, IEM, 1994. **Career:** Shaw Univ, dir coun, 1975-78, assoc dean stud, 1980-81, spec asst pres, 1981-84, dir develop, 1987-88, vpres instnl advan & planning 1988-94; Univ NC, Grad Stud Ctr, dir, 1978-80; Woodrow Wilson Nat fel, Princeton, NJ, 1981-84; United Negro Col Fund, fel doctoral study, 1985-87; United Negro Col Fund, nat develop dir, 1995-97; Wiley Col, pres, 1998-2000; Southwestern Univ, sr adv to pres strategic planning & assessment, 2000-. **Honors/Awds:** Century Club Distinguished Duquesne Alum, 2000. **Special Achievements:** Numerous publications. **Business Addr:** Senior Advisor to the President, Southwestern University, 1001 E Univ Ave, PO Box 770, Georgetown, TX 78626.

SWAIN-CADE MCCOULLUM, DR. VALARIE ENA
Vice president (organization). **Personal:** Born Sep 16, 1952, Philadelphia, PA; daughter of William Arch Swain and Ena Lindner Swain; married Henry W McCoullum Jr; children: Ena Marietta Cade & David Lloyd. **Educ:** Pa State Univ, BA, 1973; Temple Univ, MEd, 1977, DEd, 1978; Univ Pa, Philadelphia Child Guid Clin, Post-Doctoral Family Therapy, 1981; Wharton Sch Exec Educ Finance and Org Develop Prog, 1987; Harvard Univ, IEM, 1988. **Career:** Pa State Univ, tutor, 1971-72, peer counr, 1971-73; Sch Dist Philadelphia, teacher lang arts, 1972-74; Camden Schs, lang arts & reading teacher, 1974-76; Camden County Community Col Learning Skills Ctr, adminr & study skills specialist, 1976-77, counr, 1976-77; Dept Educ, field reader & curric consult, 1976-; Rutgers Univ, asst prof eng, 1976-78; Camden County Community Col, Learning & Study Skills specialist, 1976-77; Univ Pa, psychol educ specialist, 1978-80, asst prof/lectr 1978-82, fac master, WEB Du Bois Col House, 1978-80, asst vice provost undergrad studies, dir commonwealth prog, 1978-83, Grad Sch Educ, Sch Social Work, Sch Arts & Sci, adj fac, 1978-, asst assoc provost, 1983-85, exec asst provost, 1985-86, asst provost, 1986-88; mellon minority undergrad fel prog, prog coordr, 1989-, asst provost & asst pres, 1989-91, acting pres, 1991-92, 1994, chair, Commonwealth Ct Pennsylvania Sch Dist Phil Equity Team, assoc vpres, 1992-95, vice provost div univ life, 1995-. **Orgs:** Pa coord Tri-State Coun Equal Educ Opportunity, 1978-81; eastern regional rep ACT-101 Adv Comn, 1979-81; pres, Mid-Eastern Asn Educ Opportunity, 1983; pres, Pa Asn Educ Opportunity, 1981-83; bd mem & Mid-Atlantic Regional pres emer, Nat Coun Educ Opportunity; exec bd mem, Mid-Eastern Asn Educ Opportunity; League United Latin Am Citizens Adv Bd; Am Found Negro Affairs Med Steering Comt; Nat Asn Educ Opportunity, 1988; Cornell Univ Vis Comt, 1990; Philadelphia Urban League; chair, Commonwealth Ct Pa Educ Team Restructure Sch Dist Philadelphia, 1994-95; Philadelphia Open Studio Tours Planning Comm, 2006-; Ctr Emerging Visual Artists, 2007-. **Honors/Awds:** Nat Merit Scholar, 1969-73; NAACP Achievement Award, 1969; Dean's List State & Temple Univ, 1970-78; Temple Univ Doctoral Fel, 1976-77; Onyx Sr Honor Soc, Univ Pa, 1979; Pa Asn Educ Opportunity Outstanding Achievement Award, 1983; Temple Univ, Russell Conwell Center Award, 1983; Pa State Univ Achievement Award, 1983; IEM Fel, Harvard Univ, 1988; Woman of Color Distinguished Service Award, Univ Pa, 1991; Sphinx Sr Hon Soc, Univ Pa,1991; City Philadelphia City Coun Achievement Citation, 1992; Univ Pa Women Color Helen O Dickens, MD Lifetime Achievement Award, 2000; Pa Black Conference on Higher Education Dist Service Award, 2003, Penn State university College of Liberal Arts Centennial Fel, 2009. **Special Achievements:** Numerous publications including Retention: A Developmental Model, Cheyney University Press, 1992; A Philadelphia Primer: The School District of Philadelphia Educational Team Report, Commonwealth Court of Pennsylvania, 1994; Phildelphia Oppen Studio Tours, 2006, Center for Emerging Visual Artists; Chrysalis, 2008, Center for Emerging visual Artists; Birckyard Notebook, 2008, Northwest Artists Collevtice. **Business Addr:** Vice Provost, University of Pennsylvania, Division of University Life, 3611 Locust Walk, Philadelphia, PA 19104-6222, **Business Phone:** (215)898-5337.

SWAINSON, SHARON C.
Executive, baseball executive. **Personal:** Born in Powhatan, VA. **Educ:** George Mason Univ, BA, Eng, 1988; Drexel Univ, Exec MBA, 2001. **Career:** Independent sports producer, on-air talent, 1986-94; The Sharon PrattKelly Comt, mayoral campaign pres sec, 1994; Disney Sports Attractions, sports event mgr, 1994-95, sr sports opers mgr, events, 1995-97; sr prog mgr, TV events. 1997-98; Philadelphia Phillies, spec asst to pres,1998-2001, chief communs officer & spokesperson, 2001-. **Orgs:** Bd mem, Philadelphia Bus Leadership Group, 2002-; bd mem, Am Heart Asn,Eastern Region, 1999-; bd mem, Police Athletic League, Media Rels &Communs Comt, 1999; assoc dir, bd mem, Fla Citrus Sports & Citrus BowlsOrg, 1995-99; Beta Gama Sigma. **Business Addr:** Chief Communications Officer, Spokesperson, Philadelphia Phillies Baseball Club, 1100 S 2nd St, PO Box 7575, Philadelphia, PA 19101, **Business Phone:** (215)463-6000.

SWAN, DR. GEORGE W., III
Educator. **Personal:** Born Apr 4, 1957, Detroit, MI; son of George W Swan Jr and Henrene W Swan; married Deborah D Harris, Aug 16, 1980; children: George IV, Trevor Justin & Blake Aaron. **Educ:** Wayne State Univ, BA, speech commun & theatre, 1979, MEd, educ sociol, 1991, EdD, PhD, higher educ, 1999. **Career:** Lewis Co Bus, asst vipers, acad affairs, assoc dir, Upward Bound, 1981-82; Proj Job Club, dir, 1982, dir of col rel & title III, 1982-86; Wayne State Univ, exten ctr prog coordr, 1986-87; Wayne County Community Col, dir community rel, 1987-91, dir pub affairs, 1991-98, asst dean, Humanities & Social Sci, 1998-2001, regional dean, 2001-, pres, Eastern Campus, currently, Interim, vice chancellor, currently; WPXD-TV, Direct Impact Show, producer, host, 1996-99. **Orgs:** Bd mem, past pres, Lula Belle Stewart Ctr Inc, 1987-; Nat Coun Mktg & Pub Rel, 1989-98; bd mem, past chmn, Evergreen C's Serv, 1989-99; bd secy,DCC/Monroe County Pvt Indust Coun, 1990-96; bd mem, Child Welfare League A, 1993-; bd mem, Southern Wayne County Chamber Com, 1993-; vice chmn, Detroit Educ Cable Consortium, 1993-97; New Detroit Inc, youth & young adults comn, 1994-99; bd mem, Am Heart Asn, South Wayne, 1995-96; bd mem, Coun Accreditation Serv Families & C, 1997-; secy, Detroit Chap, Nat Coun Black Am Affairs; vice chmn, Mich Inst Nonviolence Educ, 1999-; bd mem, George Crockett Acad, 2000-; Detroit City Coun, Keep Detroit Beautiful Taskforce, 2000-. **Honors/Awds:** Outstanding Service Award, Downriver Coun Arts; Lobby Plaque for Outstanding & Dedicated Service, Evergreen C's Serv, 1992; Outstanding Community Involvement, WDTR 90.9 FM, 1993; Four Who Make A Difference, News Herald Newspaper, 1994; Outstanding Service Award, Lula Belle Stewart Ctr, 1994; Spirit of Detroit Awd, Detroit City Coun, 1999. **Home Addr:** 18690 Birchcrest Dr, Detroit, MI 48221. **Business Addr:** Interim, Vice Chancellor, Wayne County Community College District, Eastern Campus, 5901 Connor, Detroit, MI 48213, **Business Phone:** (313)496-2344.

SWAN, JOHN WILLIAM DAVID
Justice of the peace, executive, politician. **Personal:** Born Jul 3, 1935; son of John N (deceased) and Margaret E; married Jacqueline A D Roberts, 1965; children: 3. **Educ:** WVa Wesleyan Col, BA; Atlanyic Union Col, MA, 1991. **Career:** Rego Ltd, real estate salesman, 1960-62; John W Swan Ltd, founder, chmn, chief exec officer, 1962-; Bermuda Parliament, 1972, minister home affairs, 1978-82; Premier Bermuda, 1982-95; Swan Group Companies, chmn, 1995-. **Orgs:** Trustee, Bermuda Biol Sta Res; Young PRSs' Orgn, 1974-86; World Bus Coun, 1986; Chief Execs Orgn; Hamilton Rotary Club; sen, Jun Chamber Int, 1992. **Honors/Awds:** Poor Richard Club Philadelphia, 1987; International Medal of Excellence, 1987; Outstanding Learning Disabled Achiever Award, Lab Sch Wash, 1992. **Special Achievements:** Minister: Marine and Air Services; Labour and Immigration, 1977-78; Home Affairs, 1978-82. **Home Addr:** 11 Grape Bay Dr, Paget Parish PG 06, Bermuda, **Home Phone:** (809)236-1303. **Business Addr:** Chairman, Swan Group of Companies, 26 Victoria St, PO Box 2413, Hamilton HM 12, Bermuda, **Business Phone:** (441)295-1785.

SWAN, L. ALEX
Educator. **Personal:** Born Jan 17, 1938, Grand Turk, Turks and Caicos Islands; married Karla K. **Educ:** West Indies Col, AS, 1963; Leg Aspects Bus, assoc cert, 1964; Blackstone Law Sch, LLB, 1966; Oakwood Col, BS, 1967; Atlanta Univ, MA, 1969; Univ CA Berkeley, MS, PhD, 1972. **Career:** Fisk Univ, Dept Sociol, chmn; Univ CA Berkeley & Sonoma State Col, lectr; Miami-Dade Jr Col & Dinthill Tech HS, instr; Texas Southern Univ, Prof Sociol, currently. **Orgs:** Am Sociol Asn; Am Soc Criminology; Black World Found; NAACP, chmn, Leg Redress Comn, 1973-74; chair, faculty assembly/senate, Tex southern Univ. **Special Achievements:** Book: Cornelia's Struggle: A struggle for Truth, 2007. **Business Addr:** Professor Sociology, Texas Southern University, 3100 Cleburne St, Houston, TX 77004, **Business Phone:** (713)313-4287.

SWANIGAN, JESSE CALVIN
Auditor, educator. **Personal:** Born Nov 18, 1933, Widner, AR. **Educ:** Wash Univ St Louis, BS, 1966; St Louis Univ, MBA, 1977.

Career: EB Koonce Mortuary Inc, supvr trainee, 1961; Johnson Publ Co, staff rep, 1962; McDonnell Douglas Aircraft Corp, sr specialist auditing, 1963-97; Univ Mo, St Louis, adj prof & sr lectr finance, currently. **Orgs:** Ordained elder United Presby Church USA, 1976; life mem, Nat Asn Advan Colored People, 1976; consult, United Negro Col Fund Comn, 1979; Nat Asn Black Acct, 1977; Black Presby United, 1980; bd mem, Nat Black MBA Asn; treas, 100 Black Men Am Inc; bd mem, Carver House; founder, past pres, St Louis Black MBA Asn, 1988; pres, Nat Black Presby Caucus, 1993; vpres, 100 Black Men Metrop St Louis. **Honors/Awds:** Black Leader 1980 United Presby Church USA, 1979; Honor of Appreciation, Am Bus Women's Asn, 1989. **Home Addr:** 1519 Lyndale Ave, University City, MO 63130, **Home Phone:** (314)862-7158. **Business Addr:** Faculty, University of Missouri - St Louis, College of Business Administration, 1 Univ Blvd 1102 SSB Tower, St Louis, MO 63121, **Business Phone:** (314)516-5896.

SWANN, ERIC JERROD
Football player. **Personal:** Born Aug 16, 1970, Pinehurst, NC; married Celeste; children: Tevin, Austin & Eric Jr. **Educ:** NC State Univ. **Career:** Football player (retired); Phoenix Cardinals, defensive tackle, 1991-93; Ariz Cardinals, defensive tackle, 1994-99; Carolina Panthers, defensive tackle, 1999-2000; Electric co, currently. **Honors/Awds:** Two tiime All-Pro selection, 1995, 1996.

SWANN, EUGENE MERWYN
Lawyer. **Personal:** Born Aug 1, 1934, Philadelphia, PA; son of Earl and Doris; children: Liana, Michael & Elliott. **Educ:** Temple Univ, BS, 1957; Univ Mass, MA, Econs, 1959; Univ Calif, Berkeley, CA, LLB, 1962, JD. **Career:** Contra Costa Co, dep dist atty, 1963-67; Contra Costa Legal Servs, dir, 1967-77; Off Citizens Complaints, dir, 1983-84; SF Police Dept, 1984-85; Self Employed, lectr, atty, 1977-83; Univ Calif, Berkeley, pvt pract; Stanford Grad Sch Bus, pvt pract; Napa Valley Col, assoc, Econs & Bus Law, instr, currently. **Honors/Awds:** Outstanding Legal Service Attorney in Nation, 1974. **Home Addr:** 43 Donald Dr, Orinda, CA 94563. **Business Addr:** Instructor, Economics and Business Law, Napa Valley College, 2277 Napa Vallejo Hwy, Napa, CA 94558, **Business Phone:** (707)253-3000.

SWANN, LYNN CURTIS
Broadcaster, football player, politician. **Personal:** Born Mar 7, 1952, Alcoa, TN; married Charena; children: 2. **Educ:** Univ Southern Calif, BA, pub rels. **Career:** Pittsburgh Steelers, wide receiver, 1974-82; Ct TV, spec guest commentator, 2000; Pres Coun Phys Fitness & Sports, chmn, 2002-05; ABC Sports, sports announcer, sports analyst & broadcaster, 1976-2006; Hershey Entertainment & Resorts Co Bd, dir; H J Heinz Co, dir; Diamond Edge Capital Partners LLC, manging dir, currently; Swann Inc, pres, currently; Wyndham Int, bd dir. **Orgs:** Screen Actors Guild; Am Fedn TV & Radio Artists. **Honors/Awds:** MVP, Super Bowl X, 1975; Pro Bowl, 1977-79; Nat Football Found, Col Hall of Fame, inducted, 1993; Man of the Year, Walter Camp Football Found,1997; Pro-Football Hall of Fame, 2001. **Business Addr:** President, Swann Inc, 506 Hegner Way, Sewickley, PA 15143.

SWANSON, CHARLES
Lawyer. **Personal:** Born Aug 16, 1949, Camp Hill, AL; married Anne Elizabeth Fox; children: Tesfaye C, Tonya D, Tamara A & Charles Joseph. **Educ:** Univ Wis, Madison, BA, 1971; Univ Wis Law Sch, JD, 1973. **Career:** Univ Wis-Madison, teaching asst afro-am hist, 1970-73; Racine Co Pub Defenders Off, asst pub defender, 1974-75; Nat Asn Advan Colored People, legal redress, 1978-; pvt pract, atty, currently. **Orgs:** Racine Co, Am Bar Asn; Nat Asn Criminal Defense Lawyers; bd dirs, Racine Nat Asn Advan Colored People; Racine Optimist Club. **Honors/Awds:** Racine County Circuit Court Commissioner, 1980; Outstanding Young Man of America, 1984; Outstanding Director, Racine Jaycees. **Business Addr:** Attorney, 101 Atlantic Ave, New Orleans, LA 70114-1210, **Business Phone:** (504)561-8833.

SWANSON, EDITH MAYS. See Obituaries section.

SWANSON, DR. O'NEIL
Funeral director. **Career:** Swanson Funeral Home Inc, founder & pres, currently. **Orgs:** Fight For Freedom Fund Dinner, chair, 1994. **Honors/Awds:** Recipient Fight For Freedom Fund Dinner Freedom, 2006; recipient Justice Award, 2006. **Business Addr:** President, Swanson Funeral Homes Inc, 2210 ML King Ave, Flint, MI 48503-1030, **Business Phone:** (810)232-7469.

SWANSON, O'NEIL D.
Funeral director. **Personal:** Born in Birmingham, AL; children: O'Neil II, Linda E, Kimberly E. **Educ:** Cent State Univ, BS, 1953; Cincinnati Col Embalming, Mortuary Sci, 1956. **Career:** Swanson Funeral Home Inc, pres & chief exec officer, 2003-. **Orgs:** Exec bd dir & life mem, Nat Advan Asn Colored People; dir, First Independence Nat Bank Detroit, 1970-80; dir, Nat Alumni Assoc Cent State Univ, 1978, Nat Funeral Dirs & Morticians Assoc, 1979. **Honors/Awds:** Honorary Doctoral Degree, Shaw Col Detroit, 1974; Honorary Doctoral Degree, Cent State Univ, 1974. **Military Serv:** AUS, 1st Lt. **Business Addr:** President, Chief Executing Offiver, Swanson Funeral Home Inc, 2210 Martin Luther King Ave, Flint, MI 48503, **Business Phone:** (810)232-7469.*

SWAYNE, HARRY
Football player, athletic director. **Personal:** Born Feb 2, 1965, Philadelphia, PA; married Dawn; children: Tosca, Sher, Nina, Chris & Rod. **Educ:** Rutgers Univ, BS, sports mgt, 1990. **Career:** Football player (retired), athletic director; Tampa Bay Buccaneers, tackle, 1987-90; San Diego Chargers, 1991-96; Denver Broncos, 1997-98; Baltimore Ravens, 1999-2000; Miami Dolphins, tackle, 2001; chaplain, Chicago Bears, 2003-07; asst dir player prog, baltimore ravens, 2008- . **Honors/Awds:** Rutgers Football Hall of Fame, 2003; Won Super Bowl XXXV.

SWEAT, KEITH
Singer, songwriter, actor. **Personal:** Born Jul 22, 1961, Harlem, NY; son of Charles and Juanita; married; children (previous marriage): Keisha, Keia & Jordan; married Lisa Wu Hartwell (divorced); children: 2. **Educ:** City Col NY, BA, commun. **Career:** Singer, songwriter, actor, currently; Wall St, fl supvr; Jamilah, singer; New Jack City film soundtrack, contributor, 1991; Albums: Make It Last Forever, co-producer, 1988; I'll Give All My Love to You, 1990; Mississippi Masala, 1991; The Taking of Beverly Hills, 1991; Keep It Comin', 1991; New Jack City, 1991; Made in America, 1993; Get Up On It, 1994; Keith Sweat, 1996; Just a Touch, 1997; Still in the Game, 1998; Blue Streak, 1999; Didn't See Me Coming, 2000; Rebirth, 2002; Keith Sweat Live, 2003; The Best of Keith Sweat: Make You Sweat, 2004; Roll Bounce, 2005; Sweat Hotel Live, 2007; Just Me, 2008; The Magnificent, 2009; Films: Forbidden Fruits, 2006; Pastor Brown, 2009; TV: ''New Jack City'', 1991; "Rhapsody", 2000. **Honors/Awds:** Make It Last Forever, double-platinum album; Number one new male artist, Black Radio Exclusive, 1988; 16th Annual Trumpet Awards, 2008; BET Awards 2009. **Special Achievements:** Concert with Bell Biv Devoe, Johnny Gill, Ricky Harris. **Business Addr:** Singer, Atlantic Records, 1290 Avenue of the Americas, New York, NY 10104, **Business Phone:** (212)707-2000.

SWEAT, SHEILA DIANE
Financial manager. **Personal:** Born May 8, 1961, New York, NY. **Educ:** Hampton Inst, BS, 1983. **Career:** Moody's Investors Servs, credit analyst, 1984-86; Irving Trust Co, invest analyst, 1986-. **Orgs:** Hampton Alumni Asn, 1984-; Long Island Chap. **Business Addr:** Investment Analyst, Irving Trust Company, 1 Wall St, New York, NY 10015, **Business Phone:** (212)635-8740.

SWEATT, JAMES L, III
Surgeon. **Personal:** Born Jul 13, 1937, Ft Worth, TX; son of James L Jr and Jewell Juanita; married Mary Lois, 1962; children: James IV, William, Alisa & Mary Elizabeth. **Educ:** Middlebury Col, BS, Chem; Wash Univ Sch Med, St Louis, MD, 1958. **Career:** St Luke Presbyterian Church, church elder; St James L Sweatt III MD & Assocs, currently; Surgeon, pvt pract, currently. **Orgs:** Pres, Dallas County Med Soc, 1995, alternate delegate, Am med Asn, 1997; Tex Med Asn, Am col Surgeons; Soc Thoracic Surgeons; Am Med Asn; C V Roman Med Soc; Southwestern Med Fed, trustee; bd regents, Tex State Univ Syst; Grace Presbyterian Village. **Special Achievements:** Become first African American member appointed tothe board of directors of Parkland Memorial Hospital in Dallas, 1976; first African American president of the Dallas County Medical society, 1995. **Military Serv:** USAF, 1963-65. **Home Phone:** (214)331-8441. **Business Addr:** Thoracic Surgeon, James L Sweatt III MD & Associates, 2727 Bolton Boone Suite 102, DeSoto, TX 75115, **Business Phone:** (972)780-1851.

SWEET, CLIFFORD C
Lawyer. **Personal:** Born Aug 3, 1936, West Palm Beach, FL. **Educ:** San Jose State, BA 1959; Lincoln Univ, LLB, 1965. **Career:** Sweet & Sweet San Jose, pvt pract; Legal Aid Soc, staff atty, 1967; Legal Aid Soc Alameda Co, exec atty, 1971-98, exec dir, currently. **Orgs:** Fed & Inter-Am Bar Asns; State Bar CA; Urban League; Am Civil Liberties Union; Barrister's Club; Dem Lawyer's Club; legal couns Oakland Black Police Officer's Asns; Oakland Firefighter's Asn; Nat Org Women; Nat Asn Advan Colored People; COYOTE; Asian Law Caucus; Bananas Child Care; Disability Law Resources ctr; Legal Assistance Srs; Rubicon Battered Women. **Honors/Awds:** Award Appreciation Support Rendered, W Oakland Food Proj, 1984; Award Support Stands Excellence, Legal Serv Pac Reg, 1985; Cert Award Dedicated Services, West Berkeley Srs, 1991; Certificate of Award Assistance, Esperanza Resident Mgt Coun, 1991; Certificate of Award Dedication Provision Legal Servs Less Fortunate, Legal Servs Corp, 1992; Certificate of Appreciation Outstanding Litigation & Support Behalf Image Commission. **Home Addr:** 2717 Webster St, Berkeley, CA 94705, **Home Phone:** (510)843-3606. **Business Addr:** Executive Director, Legal Aid Society of Alameda County, 510 16th St Suite 560, Oakland, CA 94612, **Business Phone:** (510)451-9261.

SWEET, LOLITA
Business owner. **Educ:** Calif State Univ, bus mgt. **Career:** Corp Am, acct; Bay Limousines, owner, currently. **Orgs:** Brisbane Chamber Commerce. **Business Addr:** Owner, Bay Limousines, 114 Colby St, San Francisco, CA 94134, **Business Phone:** (415)334-4224.

SWEETS, ELLEN ADRIENNE
Editor, journalist, food writer. **Personal:** Born Feb 1, 1941, St Louis, MO; daughter of Nathaniel Allen and Melba Adrienne Ficklin; married Eric Dunning (divorced); children: Hannah Adrienne. **Educ:** Fairleigh Dickinson Univ, Madison, NJ; Wash Univ, St Louis, Mo; Antioch Col, Yellow Springs, OH. **Career:** The St Louis Post Dispatch, St Louis, Mo, reporter, 1969-77; The St Louis Civil Rights Enforcement Agency, St Louis, Mo, exec dir, 1977-81; AT&T, Short Hills, NJ, ed, 1981-89; The Dallas Morning News, Dallas, TX, food reporter, 1989-; Neiman Marcus Online, sr copywriter; The Dallas Morning News, ed; The Dallas Morning News, spec contributor. **Orgs:** Bd mem, Journalism & Women's Symposium; bd mem, Press Club of Dallas; The Writer's Garret. **Business Addr:** Special Contributor, The Dallas Morning News, PO Box 655237, Dallas, TX 75265, **Business Phone:** (214)977-8497.

SWIFT, KAREN A.
Labor relations manager. **Personal:** Born Mar 15, 1940, Kansas City, MO; daughter of William Reece Jr and Velma M Bass; married Leroy Swift (divorced 1985); children: Andrea R Ingram, Lisa J. Ingram; married Walter Ingram (divorced). **Educ:** Univ Miss Kansas City, BA, sec educ, Masters, coun guid, educ spec. **Career:** Westport High Sch, prin, 1980-88, eve sch prin, currently; KCMO Sch Dist, asst prin, Cent High Sch, 1986-87; Harrison Jr High Sch, prin, 1987-88; Hickman Mills Sch Dist, KCMO, dir personnel, 1988-95; Paseo Acad Visual Arts, vice prin. **Home Addr:** 7412 Larson Ave, Kansas City, MO 64133, **Home Phone:** (816)353-0431. **Business Addr:** Principal Evening School, Westport High School, Kansas City, MO 64138.

SWIFT, LINDA DENISE
Librarian. **Personal:** Born May 27, 1965, Detroit, MI; daughter of James (deceased) and Juliet Stanfield. **Educ:** Wayne State Univ, Detroit, Mich, BA, 1987, MSLS, 1990. **Career:** Mich Opera Theatre, Detroit, Mich, audience develop intern, 1987; WJBK-TV Channel 2, Southfield, Mich, pub serv intern, 1987; BAC & K Advertising, Birmingham, Mich, pub rels intern, 1987; Campbell Ewald Adv, Detroit, Mich, telemarketing mfg, 1988-89; Mich Bell, Detroit, Mich, res asst, 1989-90; Comerica Inc, Detroit, Mich, res librn, 1990-93; UAW Chrysler, librn; Gen Motors Corp, librn, currently. **Orgs:** Am Libr Asn, 1989-; vpres, Asn African Am Librarians, 1990-; Spec Libr Asn, 1990-. **Honors/Awds:** Achievement Award, Wayne State Univ, 1989-90. **Business Addr:** Librarian, General Motors Corp, 300 Renaissance Ctr, Detroit, MI 48265-3000, **Business Phone:** (313)556-5000.

SWIFT, MICHAEL AARON
Football player. **Personal:** Born Feb 28, 1974, Dyersburg, TN; married Jeanette; children: Janae & Michael Jr. **Educ:** Austin Peay St. **Career:** San Diego Chargers, 1997-98; Carolina Panthers, defensive back, 1999; Jacksonville Jaguars, corner back, 2000; Protein Technologies, analyst, 2000-01; Uniform People, sales rep, 2001-02.

SWIGGETT, ERNEST L
Administrator. **Educ:** Drew Univ; New York Univ; Penn State Univ, BS; Columbia Univ, MA; Emory Univ Candler Sch Theo, Cert UMCBA. **Career:** Unique New York Mag, comptroller, 1974-76; Harkless & Lyons Inc, prin, 1976-78; Salem United Methodist Church, bus admin, 1978-87; Salem Home Care Serv Inc, dir, 1980-87; New York Annual Conf United Methodist Church, treas & dir admin serv & finance, treas, currently. **Orgs:** Consult, workshops New York & Eastern Penn Conf New Eng; Central Tex United Methodist Church; Black Methodist Church Renewal Inc; Drew & New York Theol Seminaries, 1980-; United Methodist Asn Church Bus Admin; AUDELCO; Nat Asn Church Bus Admin; former dir, Gen Bd Global Ministries US Methodist Church; former nat chair, Black Methodists Church Renewal; Asn United Methodists Conf Treasurers; Strengthening The Black Church 21st Century; Gen & Jurisdictional Conferences United Methodist Church; 1988, 1992, 1996, 2000, 2004; Asn Pension Officers United Methodist Church; chair, Northeast Jurisdiction Comt Episcopacy; dir, United Methodist City Society. **Honors/Awds:** Publ: Unique New York Mag, Encore, Amsterdam News, New World Outlook, The Interpreter Mag; Pioneer Award, Salem Community Serv Coun Inc; Service Award, Bethany United Methodist Church, 1988; Service Award, Upper Madison United Methodist Church; Layman's Award, Janes UM Church; Man of the Year, Salem United Methodist Church; NY Conference Black Col Fund; William C Kirkwood Award, Brooklyn Methodist Home. **Home Addr:** 131 W 120th St, New York, NY 10027. **Business Addr:** Treasurer, Director of Administrative Services & Finance, New York Annual Conference of The United Methodist Church, 20 Soundview Ave, White Plains, NY 10605, **Business Phone:** (914)997-1570 Ext 212.

SWINDELL, DR. WARREN C.
Educator. **Personal:** Born Aug 22, 1934, Kansas City, MO; son of John Truman Jr and Estella Jaunita McKittrick; married Monica

Streetman, Jun 25, 1967; children: Warna Celia & Lillian Ann. **Educ:** Lincoln Univ MO, BS, Music Educ, 1956; The Univ MI Ann Arbor, MM, 1964; Univ IA, PhD, Music Educ, 1970. **Career:** Educator (retired); Central High Sch, Haiti, MO, band & chair dir,1956-57, dir musical act, 1959-60; Hubbard High Sch, dir music act, 1960-61; Flint MI Pub Schs, inst mus specialist, 1961-67; KY State Univ, chair & prof music, 1970-79, prof music, 1979-80; Ind State Univ, chair, dir & prof ctr, Dept African & African Am Studies, 1980-96, prof emer. **Orgs:** Evaluator, Nat Asn Sch Music Accred, 1977-78; screening panel, KY Arts Comn Proj, 1977-79; chaired State, Div & Nat MENC meetings, 1979-80; worshipful master, Prince Hall Lodge 16, 1991-92; pres, Region V, Nat Coun Black Studies, 1989-91; secy, IND Coalition BLKs Higher EDUC, 1992-93; first vpres, Indiana Coalition Blacks Higher Educ, 1994-95; pres, Indiana Coalition, 1996-99; Prince Hall Grand Lodge Jurisdiction Indiana, chmn masonic hist & educ; chair, Sch Instr, Prince Hall Masons, 1994-99; Terre Haute, Indiana Branch NAACP, first vpres, 1995-96, pres, 1997-99; elevated 33 Degree Grand Inspector Gen, United Supreme coun Ancient & Accepted Scottish Rite Free Masonry. **Honors/Awds:** Numerous Service Awards, NAACP, 1978-94; NEH Summer Seminar Col Teachers Grant, 1984; Faculty Res Grant Ind State Univ, 1985; IN State Univ Res Grant, 1987-88; Am Philos Soc Res Grant, 1988; Lilly Endowment Faculty Open Fel, 1993-94; Caleb Mills Distinguished Teaching Award, Univ Ind, 1996; Helm Fel Res Grant, The Lilly Librarian, Ind Univ, 1999. **Military Serv:** AUS, spl 4th class, 2 yrs. *

SWINER, DR. CONNIE, III
Physician. **Personal:** Born Sep 8, 1959, Washington, DC; son of Connie and Esther Wallace. **Educ:** Col William & Mary, BS, 1980; Howard Univ Col Med, MD, 1985. **Career:** Michael Reese Hosp, Chicago, IL, resident, 1987-90; Univ Ill, Col Med, Chicago, IL, asst prof, 1990-; Provident Hosp, physician; pvt pract, currently. **Orgs:** Am Med Asn, 1982-; Black Physicians Asn, Cook County Hosp, 1986-; Alpha Phi Alpha Frat Inc, 1978-; Howard Univ Med Alumni Asn, 1985-; Am Soc Anesthesiologists, 1987-. **Honors/Awds:** Alpha Omega Alpha Hon Med Soc, Howard Univ, 1985. **Home Addr:** 1501 "A" S Indiana, Chicago, IL 60605-2846. **Business Addr:** Physician, 500 E 51st St, Chicago, IL 60615, **Business Phone:** (773)572-2000.

SWINGER, HERSHEL KENDELL
School administrator, psychologist. **Personal:** Born Apr 16, 1939, Parsons, KS; married Sandra Marie Reese; children: Robbin D & Hershel K Jr. **Educ:** Calif State Univ Los Angeles, BA, psychol, 1966, MS, rehab coun, 1968; Univ Southern Calif, PhD, clin psychcol, 1978. **Career:** LA City Occup Health Srev, dir coun, 1970-74; Reg IX Ctr Child Abuse Neglect, dir, 1975-80; CA State Univ, Dept Coun Ed, assoc prof, 1979-; Reg IX Ctr C Youth & Families, dir, 1981-84; Southern CA Child Abuse Prev Training Ctr, dir, prof; Calif State Univ Los Angeles, prof coun educ, currently; Children's Insti Inc, sr vpres, clin serv, emer, currently. **Orgs:** Consult, Nat Ctr Child Abuse/Neglect, 1978-; Black Psychiat Asn, 1980-; vpres S Cent LA Reg Ctr, 1982-; exec mem, West Area Coun Alcoholism, 1983-; cons, psych El Centro Comm Ment Health Ctr, 1984-. **Honors/Awds:** Outstanding Service, LA City Supervising Soc Worker, 1982; Roy Wilkins Ed Award, Inglewood South Bay Nat Asn Advan Colored People, 1984; Outstanding Alumni, CA State Univ, 1984; Outstanding Community Service, Black Soc Workers of LA, 1984. **Military Serv:** AUS, specialist, 4, 1963-65. **Business Addr:** Senior Vice President Emeritus Clinical Services, Professor of Counselor Education, Children's Institute Inc, 711 S NH Ave, Los Angeles, CA 90005.

SWINGER, RASHOD ALEXANDER
Football player. **Personal:** Born Nov 27, 1974, Patterson, NJ. **Educ:** Rutgers Univ. **Career:** Football player (retired); Ariz Cardinals, defensive tackle, 1997-99.

SWINNEY, DR. T LEWIS
Physician. **Personal:** Born Jun 3, 1946, Nashville, TN. **Educ:** Benedict Col, BS, Hon, 1970; Meharry Med Col, MD, 1975. **Career:** Staten Island Hosp, internship, residency internal med, 1975-78; USN, chief pulmonary med, chief alcohol rehab unit, staff physician internal med, 1978-81; Pvt Pract, physician, currently. **Honors/Awds:** Physician of the Year, Queens-Corona, 1984. **Military Serv:** USN, lt comdr, 1978-81.

SWINTON, DR. DAVID HOLMES
Chief executive officer, executive, president (organization). **Personal:** Born Mar 18, 1943, New Haven, CT; son of Morris and Pearl; married Patricia Lewis; children: Olaniyan, Ayanna, Aisha, Malika, Omari & Akilah. **Educ:** NY Univ, BA, 1968; Harvard Univ, MA, 1971, PhD, econs, 1975. **Career:** Harvard Univ, teaching fel, 1970-71; City Col NY, lectr, 1971-72; Black Econ Res Ctr, asst dir res, 1971-73; WA Harriman Col Urban & Policy Sci, Undergrad Prog, assoc prof & dir, 1973-78; Urban Inst, dir, Minorities & Social Policy Prog, sr res assoc, 1973-78; Clark Col, Southern Ctr Studies Pub Policy Prog, dir, prof econ, 1981-87; Jackson State Univ Sch Bus, prof econ & dean, 1987-94; Benedict Col, pres & chief exec officer, currently. **Orgs:** Ed adv bd, Review Black Polit Econ, 1974-; econ adv, Nat Urban League, 1980-94; res coun mem, Econ Policy Inst, 1986-; bd trustees, Hinds City Econ Develop Dist, 1987-; adv bd, Jackson Enterprise Ctr, 1987-; Black Enterprise Bd Economist, 1990-; consult, Tenn Valley Authority, 1991-94; secy, SC Tuition Grants Higher Educ Comn, 1994-99; bd dir, SC Philharmonic; Capital City Club, 1994-; Rotary Club Columbia, 1994-; bd dir, Greater Columbia Chamber Comn, 1994-99; bd dir, Jr Achievement Greater Columbia Inc, 1994-; bd dir, United Way Midlands, 1995-2000; Columbia Econ Club; Cult Coun Richland & Lexington Cos; 100 Black Men SC Inc; Sigma Xi. **Honors/Awds:** Samuel Z Westerfield Award, Nat Economic Asn African Am Economist, 2005; Black Hall of Fame, South Carolina, 2007. **Special Achievements:** First African American chairman of Greater Columbia Chamber of Com Bd; Author: "Racial Inequality and Reparations, " The Wealth of Races, 1990," The Economic Status of Black Americans during the 1980's: A Decade of Limited Progress, " The Economic Status of Black America, 1990, "The Economic Status of African-Americans: Permanent Poverty and Inequality, "The State of Black America, 1991, "The Economic Status of African-Americans: Limited Ownership and Persistent Inequality," The State of Black America, 1992, writer of "The Economic Status of African-Americans during the Reagan-Bush Era, " The State of Black America, 1993. **Business Addr:** President, Chief Executive Officer, Benedict College, 1600 Harden St, Columbia, SC 29204, **Business Phone:** (803)253-5201.

SWITZER, LOU
Executive, founder (originator), chief executive officer. **Personal:** Born Oct 12, 1948, Orangeburg, SC; married; children: Gregory & Rhonda. **Educ:** Pratt Inst Brooklyn, NY, attended 1966-73. **Career:** Sherburne Assoc Inc NYC, draftsman & designer, 1966-70; Office Design Assoc Inc & NYC, draftsman & designer, 1970-71; WE Htton & Co NYC, asstdir facil, 1971-73; LCL Desing Assoc Inc NYC, partner, 1973-75; The Switzer Group Inc, pres, founder, 1975-, ceo, currently. **Orgs:** Young Pres's Orgn, 1989-; Peat Marwick Mid Market Adv Bd; New York Building Cong; Real Estate Bd NY. **Honors/Awds:** Entrepreneur of the Year, Nat Asn Acct, 1987; Interior Design Hall of Fame Award, 1993; Ellis Island Medal of Honor, Nat Ethnic Coalition Orgns NY, 1994; Man of the Year, 1995. **Business Addr:** Founder & Chairman, Chief Executive Officer, The Switzer Group Inc., 535 5th Ave Fl 11, New York, NY 10017-3610, **Business Phone:** (212)922-1313.

SWITZER, VERYL A.
Educator. **Personal:** Born Aug 6, 1932, Nicodemus, KS; married Fern N Stalnaker; children: Teresa, Veryl Jr & Calvin. **Educ:** Kans State Univ, 1954; Depaul Univ, grad work, 1969; KS State Univ, MS,1974. **Career:** Green Bay Packers, football player, 1954-55; Canadian, prof & football player, 1958-60; Chicago Pub Schs, teacher, 1959-69; Minority & Cultural Progs KS St Univ, dir, 1969-73; KS St Univ, dean minority affairs special progs, 1973-. **Orgs:** Faculty, Senate Univ Loan Comn; Univ Fair Practice & Housing Comn; Phi Delta Kappa; Nat Asn Student Personel Adminrs; bd Educ USD 383 Manhattan KS; chmn, KS Univ Athletic Coun. **Honors/Awds:** Recipient, Numerous awards including Kappa Alpha Psi Achievement Award; all-armed forces football team; all-am first team NFL 1953; all-am second team 1951-52; NEA & AP; K-State Sports Hall of Fame; Big Eight Sports writers Hall of Fame; KSHSAA Hall of Fame, 1995. **Military Serv:** USAF, 1st lt, 1956-58.

SWOOPES-JACKSON, SHERYL
Basketball player. **Personal:** Born Mar 25, 1971, Brownfield, TX; daughter of Louise Swoopes; married Eric, Jun 7, 1995 (divorced 1999); children: Jordan Eric. **Educ:** Tex Tech Univ. **Career:** Houston Comets, forward, 1997-2007; Seattle Storm, forward & out, currently; TV apppearances: "ESPNU Town-hall Meeting", 2005. **Honors/Awds:** NCAA Final Four Most Valuable Player, 1993; National Player of the Year,1993; US Oympic Women's Basketball Team, Gold Medal, 1996, 2000 & 2004; named the league Defensive Player of the Year in 2000, 2002 & 2003; Most Valuable Player, 2000, 2002 & 2005. **Special Achievements:** First woman to have a Nike basketball shoe named after her, the AirSwoopes. **Business Addr:** Professional Basketball Player, Seattle Storm, 1201 Third Ave Suite 1000, Seattle, WA 98101, **Business Phone:** (206)217-9622.

SWYGERT, H. PATRICK
School administrator. **Personal:** Born Mar 17, 1943, Philadelphia, PA; son of Leroy Huzzy and Gustina Huzzy; married Sonja E; children: Haywood Patrick Jr & Michael Branson. **Educ:** Howard Univ, BA, Hist, 1965, JD, 1968. **Career:** Temple Univ Sch Law, asst prof law, 1972-77; US Civil Serv Comn, gen coun,1977-79; Merit Systs Protection Bd, spec coun, 1979; Temple Univ Sch Law,coun, 1980, prof law, 1982, exec vpres admin; law clerk, Chap JudgeWilliam H Hastie, Fed Ct Appeals, 1968-69; admin asst, Cong Charles BRangel, 1971-72; Debevoise, Plimpton, New York, assoc, 1969-71; TempleUniv, exec vpres, 1987; State Univ NY, Albany, pres, 1990-95; US Dept Educ, Historically Black Cols & Univs Capital Financing Prog Adv Bd, chmn, 2002-06; Howard Univ, pres, 1995-2008. **Orgs:** Mem bd dir, Wynnefield Residents Asn, 1973-75; exec comt, Pub Interest Law Ctr Philadelphia, 1973-77, 1980-; exec comt, Legal Careers Proj Am Fed Negro Affairs 1974-77, Minority Affairs Asn Am Law Schs, 1974-77; vice chmn, Pub Serv Comm Philadelphia Bar Asn, 1975, l976; consult, Univ Wide Affirm Action, 1980; mem nominating comt, United Way SE PA, 1981; appointed by Gov Robert P Casey as state rep on Bd Southeastern PA Transportation Authority; bd dir, WHYY-TV WHYY-FM; vchmn, Philadelphia City Charter Revision Comn; Mid States Comn Higher Educ; chair, NY State Spec Comn Educ Struct, Policies & Practices, 1993-94; chair, Summer Games Organizing Comt, Spec Olympics, NY, 1995, bd dirs, Fannie Mae Found, 1999-; DC Emancipation Commemoration Comn, 2004-; Comn Presidential Debates; US Nat Comn UNESCO; hon mem, Golden Key NatHonorary Society. **Honors/Awds:** Commissioners Award for Distinguished Service, 1978; Certificate of Appreciation, HUD 1981; Black Law Students Award, Temple Univ Sch Law Chap1982; Presidential Citation, Nat Asn Equal Oppurtunity Higher Educ, 1984,Outstanding Alumnus, Howard Univ, Washington DC, l986; Jewish Nat FundTree of Life Award, 1994; DHL, Univ New Eng, 1997; Doctor of Laws, TempleUniv, 1999; Doctor of Laws, Tuskegee Univ, 2002; Medallion of theUniversity, State Univ NY, Albany, 2002; Special Friend Award, American Friends, 2003; Legend Award, Nat Urban League, 2005; Outstanding Educator Award, the New York State Black and Puerto Rican Legislative Caucus; Tree of Life Award, Jewish National Fund; Frederick Douglass Society Freedom Fighter Award; Distinguished Postgraduate Achievement Award, Law and Public Service, Howard Univ. **Special Achievements:** Appointed by President Clinton to chair one of six new branches ofBus-LINC. **Business Addr:** President, Howard University, 2400 6th St NW Suite 402, Washington, DC 20059, **Business Phone:** (202)806-2500.

SYKES, DR. ABEL B., JR.
School administrator, college president, dean (education). **Personal:** Born Jun 1, 1934, Kansas City, KS; married Sylvia; children: Dawn, Daphne & Leslie. **Educ:** Univ Mo Kans City, BA, hist, 1959; Univ Mo, MA, hist, 1960; Kans City Jr Col; San Diego State Col Univ Calif, grad studies, 1960-68; Univ Calif Los Angeles, Grad Sch Edn, 1971, Ed.D, 1971; Harvard Bus Sch, Inst Educ Mgt, cert, 1976. **Career:** O'Farrell Jr HS, instr, 1960-64; San Diego Evening Col, instr, 1962-64; Grossmont Col, instr, 1962-68; Compton Comm Col, dean instr, 1968-69, pres & supt, 1969-89; Kings River Comm Col, pres; Lansing Comm Col, Lansing, MI, pres, 1989-. **Orgs:** Chmn bd, Am Asn Comm Col, 1975-76; various leadership roles, Am Coun Educ; various leadership roles, Asn Governing Bds; Am Asn Univ Prof; Am Hist Asn; Chmn, numerous col accreditation teams; Sigma Pi Phi; Phi Delta Kappa. **Honors/Awds:** China Fulbright Award, 1986; Educator of the Year, Phi Delta Kappa, 1972. **Business Phone:** (517)483-1957.

SYKES, RAY A, III
Advertising executive, chief executive officer. **Personal:** Born in LeCompte, LA; divorced; children: Tracey, Raymonda & Ray Anthony. **Educ:** Santa Monica City Col. **Career:** Douglass Aircraft, machinist; Jack Box Restaurant, Los Angeles, owner; Superior Ford Minneapolis, pres/owner; Ray Sykes Buick Kingwood, Tex, pres & owner; Sykes Commun, pres, ceo, currently. **Orgs:** Civil serv comnr, City Houston; exec bd dirs, Boy Scouts Am; bd dir, UNCF; vpres, Houston Buick Dealers Asn; adv bd, Sch Bus Tex Southern Univ. **Honors/Awds:** Houston Area Urban League Small Business Award. **Military Serv:** AUS 1963-66; Purple Heart; Vietnam Veteran. **Business Phone:** (713)223-0333.*

SYKES, RICK. **See SYKES, WILLIAM RICHARD.**

SYKES, ROBERT A
Executive, vice president (organization). **Personal:** Born Dec 25, 1947, Gary, IN; son of Jasper and Mary; married. **Educ:** Fisk Univ, Nashville, Tenn, BA, philos, 1969. **Career:** Natural Gas Pipeline Co Am, Chicago, Ill, employ compliance adminr, 1970-75; Fermi Nat Accelerator Lab, Batavia, Ill, mgr eeo & community rels, 1975-78; Gen Mills, W Chicago, Ill, asst personnel mgr, 1978-79; Wash Gas Light Co, Springfield, Va, vpres human resources, 1979-. **Orgs:** Am Gas Asn; Am Asn Blacks Energy; vice chair, Melwood Horticultural Training Ctr; founder, Black Human Resources Network; Sr Human Resource Exec Forum. **Honors/Awds:** Elected to Phi Beta Kappa, 1969. **Business Addr:** Vice President, Human Resources, Washington Gas Light Co, 6801 Indust Rd, Springfield, VA 22151, **Business Phone:** (703)750-4440.

SYKES, VERNON LEE
Economist, state government official. **Personal:** Born Oct 2, 1951, Forrest City, AR; son of Walter Jr and Valley Louise Walker; married Barbara Ann, Dec 25, 1975; children: Stancy & Emilia. **Educ:** Ohio Univ Col Bus Admin, BBA, 1974; Wright State Univ, Dayton, MS, 1980; Kent State Univ, MPA, 1978; Harvard Univ, Cambridge, MPA, l986; Univ Akron, PhD, urban studies, 2001. **Career:** Akron Bd Ed, sub teacher, 1974-75; UNCI-Econ Develop Prog, sr mgt specialist, 1975-76; Summit City Criminal Justice Comn, planner res & eval, 1976-79; Akron City Coun, chmn, vice chmn, mem, 1980-83; Univ Akron, part time instr; Clarence Allen Realty, salesman; The Harvard Group; OH House Rep, 44th house dist, state rep, 1983-2000; Wayne Col, Dept Polit Sci, adj fac, 1981-98; Univ Akron, Community & Tech Col, Assoc Studies Dept, asst prof social Sci, 1998-2001; Kent State Univ, Polit Sci Dept, asst prof, 2001-; Kent State Univ, Columbus Prog ntergov-

ernmental Issues, dir, 2001-. **Orgs:** Interstate Coop, Energy & Environ, Ways & Means Reference, State Govt, Pay Equity Adv Comn, Travel & Tourism, High Speed Rail Task Force, Job Training Coord Coun; chmn, Audit Comt, Recycle Energy Comn, Health & Social Serv; vice chmn, Housing & Urban Develop, Downtown Redevelopment; mem, Parks & Recreation Comn, Finance Comn, Annexation Comn, Akron Summit/Medina Private Ind Coun, Summit Cty Human Serv Adv Comn, Mayor Roy Ray's Citizen's Financial Adv Comn, Western Econ Intl, Alpha Homes; vice pres, Alpha Libr Comn Inc, chmn Ed & Scholarship Comn Alpha Phi Alpha; dir, The Harvard Group 1987-. **Honors/Awds:** Emerging Leadership Award, Akron Frontiers Club Int, 1979; Outstanding Alumnus, Black Alumni, Ohio Univ, 1981; Councilman of the Year, Nat Asn Real Estate Brokers, Akron Chap, 1982; Community Service Award, Akron Summit Community Action Agency, 1984; Outstanding Alumni Award, Upward Bound Prog, Kent State Univ, 1985; Outstanding Service Award, Black Cult Ctr, Univ Akron, 1986; Legislator of the Year Award, Nat Asn Social Workers, Ohio Chap, 1987; Fair Housing Award, Ohio Fair Housing Cong, 1988; Fair Housing Award, US Dept Housing & Urban Develop, 1988; Outstanding Legislator, Ohio Caucus Black Sch Bd Members, 1990; Public Service Award, Fair Housing Contact Serv, Akron, Ohio, 1990; Resolution of Appreciation, Ohio Civil Rights Comn, 1992; State Independent Living Council Award, Ohio Rehab Serv Comn, 1992; Equal Opportunity/Affirmative Action Exemplary Practices Award, Am Soc Pub Admin, 1993; Special Achievement Award, US Dept Housing & Urban Develop, 1993; Legislator of the Year Award, Ohio Hunger Task Force, 1994; Legislator of the Year Award, Ohio Nurses Asn, 1995; Special Recognition, Ohio Asn Second Harvest Foodbanks, 1998; Community Service Award, Off Inst Diversity, Kent State Univ, 1999; Rising Star, Akron Summit Community Action Agency, 1999; Grateful Appreciation, Akron Community Health Resources Inc, 1999; Special Recognition, Ohio Legis Black Caucus, 2000; Hon & Recognition, Columbus City Coun, 2000; Jack Wolf Memorial Award, Secy State & Ohio Asn Election Officials, 2000. **Military Serv:** USMC, pvt 2 mos. **Home Addr:** 615 Diagonal Rd, Akron, OH 44320. **Business Addr:** Assistant Professor, Kent State University, The Department of Political Science, 302 Bowman Hall, Kent, OH 44240, **Business Phone:** (330)672-8948.

SYKES, WANDA (ADRIANA BEDOYA)
Comedian, actor. **Personal:** Born Mar 7, 1964, Portsmouth, VA; married David Hall, Jan 1, 1991 (divorced 1998); married Alex, Oct 25, 2008; children: Lucas Claude & Olivia Lou. **Educ:** Hampton Univ, BS, mkt, 1986. **Career:** Films: Tomorrow Night, 1998; Nutty Professor II: The Klumps, 2000; Down to Earth, 2001; Pootie Tang, 2001; Monster-in-Law, 2005; Clerks II, 2006; MySuper Ex-Girlfriend, 2006; Condom Nation, 2006; Evan Almighty, 2007; Licence to Wed, 2007; TV series: "The Chris Rock Show", 1997-2000; Best of the Chris Rock Show, 1999; "Curb Your Enthusiasm", 2000; "The Drew Carey Show", 2001; "Curb Your Enthusiasm", 2001-05; "Crank Yankers", 2002-03; "Wanda At Large", producer, 2003; "MTV: Reloaded", 2003; "Wanda Does It", exec producer, 2004; "Will & Grace", 2006; "Wanda Sykes: Sick & Tied", exec producer, 2006; "The New Adventures of Old Christine", 2006-09. **Orgs:** Alpha Kappa Alpha Sorority Inc. **Honors/Awds:** Primetime Emmy Award, 1999; American Comedy Award, Outstanding FemaleStand Up Comic, 2001; Emmy Awards, 2002, 2004 & 2005. **Special Achievements:** Ranks among Entertainment Weekly's 25 Funniest People in America. **Business Addr:** Actress, Endeavor Talent Agency, 9601 Wilshire Blvd Fl 3, Beverly Hills, CA 90210, **Business Phone:** (310)248-2000.*

SYKES, WILLIAM RICHARD (RICK SYKES)
Educator, television news anchorperson. **Personal:** Born Jan 22, 1948, Saginaw, MI; son of William Richard and Eleanor Wesley; married Marguerite Irene Cain, Sep 16, 1978; children: James William. **Educ:** Delta Community Col, Bay County, 1971; Cent Mich Univ Mt Pleasant, BS, 1973, MA, 1980. **Career:** WNEM-TV, Saginaw, prod cameraman, 1973-75, reporter anchor, 1975-81, news mgr, 1981-82; WDIV-TV, Detroit, sr assignment ed, 1982-90; Hermanoff & Assoc, Farmington Hills, vpres, 1990-; Cent Mich Univ, full prof, currently. **Orgs:** Adv bd mem, Horizons Upward Bound Cranbrook, 1990; adv trustee, Ronald McDonald Children's Charities, 1990; NAACP. **Honors/Awds:** Minority Achiever in Industry, YMCA of Metrop Detroit, 1984; Nat UPI Award, Spot News Coverage & Michigan UPI Award Spot News Coverage, United Press Int, 1981. **Special Achievements:** Presenter, Oxford Roundtable, Oxford Univ, Oxford, England, 2005. **Military Serv:** USY, cpt, 1968-69; Overseas Medals serv, Vietnam, 1969. **Business Addr:** Full Professor, Central Michigan University, Mount Pleasant, MI 48859, **Business Phone:** (989)774-4000.

SYLER, M RENE
Television news anchorperson, business owner, social worker. **Personal:** Born Feb 17, 1963, Belleville, IL; daughter of William Henry and F Anne McDonald; married Buff Parham; children: Casey & Cole. **Educ:** Am River Col, Sacramento, Calif, attended 1981-83; Azusa Pac Univ, Azusa, Calif, attended 1984-85; Calif State Univ, Sacramento, Calif, BA, psychol, 1987. **Career:** KTVN-TV, Reno, Nev, news reporter, 1987-89; KOLO-TV, Reno, Nev, news anchor, 1989-90; WVTM-TV, Birmingham, Ala, news anchor, 1990-92; WFAA-TV, Dallas, Tex, news anchor, 1992-97; KTVT-TV, Dallas, Tex, news anchor, 1997-02; "The Early Show", CBS News, news anchor, 2002-06; Susan G Komen Cure, ambassador, 2007; goodenoughmother.com, owner, currently; Circle Promise, co-chair, currently. **Orgs:** Nat Asn Advan Colored People, 1988-; Northern Nev Black Cult Awareness Soc, 1989-; Nat Black Journalists Asn, 1988-; publicity comt, jr bd, YWCA, 1990-; Life mem Nat Asn Black Journalists. **Honors/Awds:** TV Personality of the Year, Am Women Radio & TV, 1997; Gracie Allen Award, 2004. **Special Achievements:** Author of Good Enough Mother, 2007. **Home Addr:** 304-9 Beacon Crest Lane, Birmingham, AL 35209. **Business Phone:** (212)977-6990.

SYLVAS, DR. LIONEL B.
School administrator, college administrator. **Personal:** Born May 10, 1940, New Orleans, LA; son of Iona and Junius; married Kathrine; children: Angela & Antoine. **Educ:** Southern Univ, BS, 1963; Univ Detroit, MA, 1971; Nova Univ, EdD, 1975. **Career:** College Administrator (retired); Ford Motor Co, indust res anal, 1967-69, ed training spec, 1969-71; Miami Dade Community Col, assoc acad dean,1971-74, asst to pres, 1974-77; Southern Asn Col & Schs Eval Team, consult, 1974; Northern Va Comm Col, campus provost, 2001-04; Va Power Co, consult adv group, 1983-87. **Orgs:** Adv Bd Black Am Affairs, Nat Sch Vol Prog, 1974-78; pres, Southern Reg Couns, 1977-88; field reader, Titles III & IV Office of Educ, 1979; mem adv bd, Am Red Cross, 1982; panelist, Va Comn of the Arts; Const Bicentennial Comn Va. **Honors/Awds:** Outstanding Educr, Miami Dade Community Col, 1975. **Military Serv:** AUS, first lt, 1963-65. **Home Addr:** 6666 Old Blasksmith Dr, Burke, VA 22015.

SYLVESTER, MELVIN R
Educator. **Personal:** Born Mar 25, 1939, New Orleans, LA; son of John and Myrtle Howard; married Frances Modica; children: Lori Alaine & Kyle Eugene. **Educ:** Dillard Univ, BA, 1961; Long Island Univ, MSLS, 1966, MEd, 1973. **Career:** Dillard Univ, circulation lib, 1961-62; CW Post Lib, head circulation dept, 1962-64; Long Island Univ B Davis Schwartz Lib, head serials rec, 1964-, prof, prof emer, currently. **Orgs:** Fac & chap adv Tau Kappa Epsilon, 1965-; secy, Col & Univ Div Nassau Co Lib Asn, 1973-75; rep, CW Post Ctr Fac Coun, 1974-78; Martin Luther King Higher Educ Oppor Prog Adv Bd, 1974-78; Lib Fac Personnel Comn, 1974-78; Melvil Dui Marching & Chowder Asn, 1975-; adv bd, Friendship House Glen Core NY, 1975-78; Space Utilization Comn, CW Post Ctr, 1975-78; chmn, Space Utilization Comn, 1977-78; Comn Handicapped Glen Cove Sch, 1978-80; bd dir, Boy's Club Lincoln House Glen Cove NY, 1978-85; Day Care Head Start Ctr Glen Cove NY, 1979-89; stud affairs appeal comn CW Post Ctr, 1979-82; Greater NY Metro Area Chap ACRL, 1983-; 100 Black Men Nassau Sulk Inc, 1983-; Lions Int, 1983-; chairperson, Affirmative Action Task Force CW Post Ctr, 1984-86; Pre-Med Comn CW Post, 1984-; libr bd trust Glen Cove Pub Libr, 1984-93; Ala, NYLA, Nassau Co Lib Asn; chairperson, Instr Comt, CW Post, 1986-88; bd dir, Alliance Coun Ctr, 1986-89; Career Adv Group, CW Post, 1986-; N Am Serials Group Libraries, 1987-; Freshman Mentor Prog, CW Post, 1987-; bd trustees, Nassau Libr Syst, 1988-92; Campaign Comt & Youth & Family Serv Panel United Way Long Island, 1988-89; Legis Comt Long Island Resources Coun Inc, 1988-93; Univ Study Group V Long Island Univ LIU Plan, 1988; adv bd, Nassau County Dept Ment Health, 1988-92; LILRC Lobbyist Libr, 1990-92; GRASP-Comt CW Post, 1991-95; Univ Sect Comt Assoc Provost Enrollment Serv, 1996; Univ Outcomes Assessment Comn, 1997-; Univ Ad Hoc Libr Comn Serials, Periodicals Long Island Univ, chair. **Honors/Awds:** Contr screenings Lib J & Sch Lib J, 1971-78; printed publs, "Negro Periodicals in the US 1826-1960" an annotated bibliography; "A Library Handbook to Basic Source Materials in Guidance & Counseling" 1973; Faculty Recog Awd Alpha Phi Alpha 1979; Serv Awd Glen Cove Public Schools Comm on the Handicapped 1980; Public Serv Awd Malik Sigma Psi 1981; Twenty-Year Metal, Service and Recognition, LIU, 1984; Serv Awd African Student Convocation 1986; Student Govt Asn Awd for Serv to Students CW Post Campus 1986; Nassau Library System Award of Merit as Trustee, 1992; Nassau County Exec Citation as retired trustee, 1992; HEOP 25th Anniversary Service recognition Award, 1994; Newsmaker: Newsday, LI and Glencove Record Pilot, as curator of history exhibits from 1985-94, CW Post Campus. **Special Achievements:** Exhibits at www.cwpost/liunet.edu/cwis/cwp/library/libhome.2htm; lectr african Am hist, 1995-; author: Content Consultant and revisionist, book on Martin Luther King Jr, 2000. **Home Addr:** 50 Robinson Ave, Glen Cove, NY 11542. **Business Addr:** Professor Emeritus, Periodicals Department, Long Island University, CW Post Campus Northern Blvd, B Davis Schwartz Memorial Libr, Brookville, NY 11548-1300, **Business Phone:** (516)299-2000.

SYLVESTER, ODELL HOWARD, JR.
Law enforcement officer. **Personal:** Born Nov 3, 1924, Dallas, TX; son of Odell H Sr and Parthenia Wakefield; married Dorothy Lanning; children: Jennifer & Jon. **Educ:** Univ Calif, BDs, 1948; Univ Southern Calif, MPA, 1974; Harvard Univ, post grad. **Career:** Law enforcement officer (retired); Berkeley Calif, app chief police, 1977; Oakland Police Dept Bur Invest, commanding officer, 1971-77, dep chief, 1971, capt, 1963, lt, 1961, sgt, 1957, patrolman, 1949; Berkley chief police, 1981. **Orgs:** Oakland Police Dept New Careers Prog; Model Cities Intern Prog; dir, Bay Area Minor Recruit Proj; Am Soc Pub Admin; Calif Peace Officers Asn; Int Asn Chiefs Police; exec comt, Nat Orgn Black Law Enforcement Exec; pres, Oakland Boys & Girls Club, bd dir, advisor, currently; bd Gov, Goodwill Ind; Lake Merritt Breakfast Club; Lions Int Serv Club; Men Tomorrow; Kiwanis Int Serv Club; Oakland Cent YMCA; Family Serv Agy; Nat Conf Christ & Jews; NCP; Am Psychol Asn; Sigma Pi Phi; pres, Urban Mgt Asn, 1981-90. **Honors/Awds:** Awards Outstanding Service, Oakland Comn, 1968, 1969, 1971, 1976, 1981, 1985, 1987, 1989, 1990; Lifetime Achievement Award, Oakland Black Officers Asn, 1992. **Business Addr:** Advisor, Boys & Girls Clubs of Oakland Club Services Center, 3300 High St, PO Box 23203, Oakland, CA 94623, **Business Phone:** (510)444-8211.

SYLVESTER, DR. PATRICK JOSEPH
Educator. **Educ:** St Francis Xavier Univ, Canada, BA, 1960; Univ New Brunswick, Canada, MA, 1962; Univ PA, MA, 1967; Bryn Mawr Col, PhD, 1973. **Career:** West Chester Univ, assoc prof econ, 1968, prof econ & finance. **Business Addr:** Professor of Economics, Finance, West Chester University, Deptartment of Economics & Finance, 700 S High St, West Chester, PA 19380, **Business Phone:** (610)436-1000.

SYMONE, RAVEN (RAVEN-SYMONE CHRISTINA PEARMAN)
Entertainer, actor. **Personal:** Born Dec 10, 1985, Atlanta, GA; daughter of Christopher Barnard Pearman and Lydia Gaulden Pearman. **Career:** Actress, currently; Tv series include: "The Cosby Show", 1989-92; "Hangin With Mr Cooper", 1993-97; "Kim Possible", animated, 2002-; "That's So Raven", 2003-07; "The Dress Is Always Greener", 2006; "The Way They Were", 2007; guest-starred on A Different World", 1990; TV movies: Queen, 1993; The Cheetah Girls, 2003; guest appearance: Fresh Prince of Bel-Air; films: Dr Doolittle, 1998; Dr Doolittle 2, 2001; "That's So Raven", 2003-06; Dr Dolittle 3, 2006; Kim Possible, 2007; Col Rd Trip, 2008. **Orgs:** Am Fed TV & Radio Artists, 1989-; Screen Actors Guild, 1989-. **Honors/Awds:** Presenter at numerous award shows including: The Peoples Choice Awards, NAACP Image Awards, New York Music Awards, InterNat Emmy Awards; participant in various fundraising events including: Comic Relief 3, Night of 100 Stars 3, InterNat Earth Day Celebration, Pediatric AIDS Found; Youth in Film Award, Outstanding Young Actress, 1990-91; nominated, Peoples Choice Award, Outstanding Young TV Performer, 1991; nominated, NAACP Image Award, Outstanding Young Actress in a Series, 1991, 1992; SCLC, Junior Achievement Award for Excellence in TV Series; guest apppearances include: "Live with Regis & Kathie Lee," 1989-91; "The Oprah Winfrey Show", 1991; "The Arsenio Hall Show", 1990-91; "The Tonight Show," 1991; "The Today Show". **Special Achievements:** Signed solo artist rec contract with MCA Recs at the age of 5 years old.

SYPHAX, DR. BURKE
Physician. **Personal:** Born Dec 18, 1910, Washington, DC; son of William Custis and Nellie Smith; married Sarah Juanita Jamerson, Jul 1, 1939; children: Michael Burke, Gregory Custis & Stephen Wyatt. **Educ:** Howard Univ, BS, 1932; Howard Univ Med Sch, MD, 1936. **Career:** Physician (retired); Howard Univ, Col Med, officer, prof surg, chief div, gen surg, 1951-70, Dept Surg, chmn, 1957-70, from instr to assoc prof, 1940-58. **Orgs:** Kappa Pi Frat; Alpha Omega Alpha Hon Soc; Nat Med Asn; Soc Surg Alimentary Tract; Alpha Omega Alpha; Alpha Kappa Alpha; Alpha Phi Alpha; rockefeller fel, Strong Mem Hosp, Univ Rochester, 1941-42; fel, Am Col Surg, 1957. **Honors/Awds:** Outstanding Alumnus Award; New York Alumni Asn; Student Council Award; Distinguished Professor Award, 1974; DSc, Howard Univ, 1985; Certification in Surgery, Am Bd Surg, 1944. **Home Addr:** 1370 Hamilton St NW, Washington, DC 20011.

T

TABB, ROOSEVELT
Business owner. **Personal:** Born in Alabama. **Educ:** State Univ Col New York, Buffalo, BS, 1967, MBA, 1973. **Career:** Ford Motor Co, indust engr, 1967-69; Marine Midland Banks, loan officer, 1969-73; Fisher-Price Toys, mgr spec proj, 1973-78; Union Carbide Corp, acct mgr, 1976-90; Tabb & Assocs, pres, 1990-. **Orgs:** Past nat vpres, 1978, past pres, 1978-81, Nat Black MBA Asn; bd pres, Nat Minority Col Golf Scholarship Fund. **Business Addr:** President, Tabb & Associates, 665 E Dublin Granville Rd, PO Box 340888, Columbus, OH 43234, **Business Phone:** (614)880-0000.

TABOR, LILLIE MONTAGUE
Government official. **Personal:** Born May 13, 1933, Marianna, AR; married Norman. **Educ:** Univ Mich, MSW, 1961; Western Mich Univ, BA; Tuskegee Inst. **Career:** Detroit, nursery sch teacher, 1951-53; Bur Soc Aid, Detroit, social worker, 1954-57; Oak County C's Serv, child welfare worker, 1957-60; Mich,psyciat social worker, 1960-62; Dept Social Serv, admin, 1965-69;

MichCivil Serv Lansing, dir new careers, 1969-72; Social Serv Region 9 Wayne County, Consult Serv; State Mich, dep dir, 1963-65; Family Life Educ Merrill Palmer Inst, Detroit, assoc prof, 1968-71; Univ Mich, field instr soc, 1972-74. **Orgs:** Child Welfare League Am, 1964-68; bd mem, Neighborhood Serv Orgn, 1969-; adv comt, Vista Marie Sch, 1970-; NASW; Nat Asn Advan Colored People; Nat Coun Alcoholism Delegate, 1970, White House Conf C; Spec Review Successful Prog, 1970; Nat Inst New Careers Free press Frank Angelo Interesting Action People, 1971. **Business Addr:** Social Worker, Michigan State Plaza, 1200 6 St, Detroit, MI 48226.*

TABORN, DR. JOHN MARVIN
College teacher, president (organization). **Personal:** Born Nov 7, 1935, Carrier Mills, IL; married Marjorie Campbell; children: John Gregory & Craig Marvin. **Educ:** Southern Ill Univ, BS, 1956; Univ Ill, MA, 1958; Univ Minn, PhD, 1970; Harvard Bus Sch, Mgt Cert, 1971. **Career:** Minn Pub Sch, psychol, 1966-70; Univ Minn, youth develop consult, 1971-73, assoc prof, assoc prof emer, currently, Dept Afro-Am & African Studies, chair; J Taborn Assocs Inc, pres 1979-. **Orgs:** Nat Asn Black Psychologists, 1970-; prof mem, Am Psychol Asn, 1972-; consult, State Minn, 1973-82; bd dirs, Minneapolis Urban League, 1974-80; consult, Honeywell Inc, 1981-84; Sigma Pi Phi Frat 1983-; consult, Nat Asn Black Police 1984-; State Calif Educ, 1986-; vice chmn, Diversity Found Inc, currently. **Honors/Awds:** Monitor of the Year, Monitors Minneapolis, 1980; numerous scholarly publications. **Military Serv:** USNR, capt; National Defense, Armed Forces Reserve, Navy Expeditionary. **Business Addr:** President, J. Tabron Associates, 1219 Marquette Ave S Suite 80, Minneapolis, MN 55403, **Business Phone:** (612)338-9012.

TADEMY, LALITA
Writer. **Personal:** Born 1948, Berkeley, CA; daughter of Nathan Green Tademy Jr and Willie Dee Billes. **Educ:** Univ Calif, Los Angeles, BS, 1970, MBA, 1972. **Career:** Sun Microsystems, vp & gen mgr, 1992-95; author: Cane River, 2001, Red Rivers, 2007.

TALBERT, MELVIN GEORGE
Clergy, bishop. **Personal:** Born Jun 14, 1934, Clinton, LA; son of Nettles and Florence George; married Ethelou Douglas, Jun 3, 1961; children: Evangeline Violet. **Educ:** Southern Univ, Baton Rouge, LA, BA, 1959; Gammon Theol Sem, Atlanta GA, MD, 1962; Huston-Tillston Col, DDiv, 1972; Univ Pugent Sound, LLD,1987. **Career:** Clergy (Retired); Boyd Chapel, United Methodist Church, Jefferson TN, pastor, 1960-61; Wesley United Methodist Church, Los Angeles CA, assoc pastor, 1961-64; Hamilton United Methodist Church, Los Angeles CA, pastor, 1964-67; Southern Calif-Ariz Conf, Long Beach CA, district supt, 1968-73; Gen Bd Discipleship, Nashville TN, gen secy, 1973-80; United Methodist Church, Seattle WA, bishop, 1980-88; United Methodist Church, San Francisco CA, bishop, 1988. **Orgs:** Pres, Nat Coun Churches, 1966-99; Nat Asn Advan Colored People; adv comt, Seattle Mayor; bd mem, Seattle United Way; exec comt, central Comn, Finance Comn World Coun Churches. **Honors/Awds:** National Achievement Award, Nat Asn Black Women, 1965; Bible Translation & Utilization Awards, Nat Coun Churches, 2000.

TALBERT, TED
Television producer. **Career:** Journalist & historian; Univ Mo Sch Journ, lectr; Wayne State Univ, lectr; Wayne County Community Col, lectr; Co-founder & exec dir, Joe Louis Video Memorial Rm Cobo Ctr; WDIV-TV, Channel 4, producer, 1989-; Producer: "History of Detroit-area African Americans in the legal profession", 1991; "From Randolph to the Rouge: Black in the Union Movement," 1992; "Letterman of the Law". **Honors/Awds:** Detroit Emmy Award; Achievement of Merit Award, Ohio State Univ; Meritorious Achievement Award, Detroit Chap, Tuskegee Airmen. **Business Addr:** Producer, WDIV-TV Channel 4, 550 W Lafayette Blvd, Detroit, MI 48226, **Business Phone:** (313)222-0444.*

TALBOT, GERALD EDGERTON
State government official. **Personal:** Born Oct 28, 1931, Bangor, ME; son of W Edgerton and Arvella McIntyre; married Anita J Cummings, Jul 24, 1954; children: Sharon Renee Verloo, Regina L Phillips, Rachel Ross & Robin M. **Educ:** Dipl lessons in printing, 1970; ME State Apprenticeship Coun, cert apprenticeship for printing, 1972. **Career:** State government official (retired); Maine State Legis, 1972, 1974, 1976; Portland Savings Bank, corporator beginning 1975; Guy Gannett Publ Co, state rep. **Orgs:** Co-sponsor, Sexual or Affectional Preference Amendment, 1977; City Mgrs Policy Adv Comn, 1979; adv coun, State Maine, Dept Manpower Affairs, 1979; State Bd Educ, 1980; founder, Black Educ & Cultural Hist Inc, 1980; Nat Asn State Bds Educ (GAC), 1981; Educ Comn Task Force Sex Equality, 1982; Congressman McKernan's Task Force Children Youth &Families, 1983; Maine Congressional Citizens Educ Adv Comnn 1983; State Bd Educ, 1980, v chmn, 1981, chmn, 1983-84; corporator, ME Med Ctr, 1984; Gr Portland Federated Labor Coun, Portland Typographical Union Local 66; NAACP; Dem City Comn; Maine Asn Black Prog, ME Conf on Human Serv; Southern Maine Area Agency Aging, 1986; bd, trust Maine Vocational Tech Inst, 1986; bd dir, Portland United Way Inc, 1986; ME Project on Southern Africa, 1985; bd mem, US Selive Serv Syst, Maine, 1987; Veterans for Peace, 1988; Community Task Force Bias Crime, 1989; bd visitors, The Edmund SMuskie Inst Pub Policy, Univ Southern Maine, 1990; AARP, nat minority spokesperson, 1992; Nat Black Leadership Initiative Cancer, 1992; ALANA Conference Bd; US Comn Civil Rights, Maine; Tribute to Black Women Maine Awards Banquet, sponsor, 1992; Univ Southern Maine, African Am Archives Maine adv comt; Amistad Am, Maine Adv Coun. **Honors/Awds:** Golden Pin Award, 1967, Leadership Award, 1984, Twenty Years, 1964-84, NAACP, Portland Br; Hall of Fame Cert Laurel MS Nat Asn Advan Colored People, 1970-73; Outstanding Ser Comn & State Bangor, NAACP 1974; Viva Cert Recog & Appreciation, 1974; Cert of Appreciation, Nat Asn Human Rights Workers, 1979; Right-On Brother of Year Award; Certificate of Appreciation Maine Chap Multiple Sclerosis; Jefferson Award, Am Inst Pub Serv, WCSH-TV, 1980; Black History Maker of Maine Award, 1984; 'Maine State Board Education Award', 1984; Martin Luther King Award, Maine Martin Luther King Comn, 1988; first Place Certificate of Excellence, Maine Multicultural Festival 1987; Friendship Award, Portland West Neighborhood Planning Coun, 1989; Certificate of Achievement, People Regional Opportunity Program, 1990; Univ Southern Maine, DHL, 1995; Matlovich Award, 1990; Honorary Doctor of Humane Letters, Univ Southern Maine, 1995; John B Truslow, Md Area Agency on Aging Advocacy Award, 1995; Holocaust Human Rights Ctr, ME, 1995; Maine Channel Am Soc Pub Awards, 1995; Equity Inst Leadership Award, ME 1995; Larry Connolly Award, ME Lesbian/Gay Political Alliance, 1995; Ctr for Visions & Policy, 50 Years Improving the Lives of Black Ams, 1997. **Special Achievements:** First African American elected to the Maine State Legislature; Author, Visible Black History of Maine; Underground Railroad in Maine. **Military Serv:** USY, pfc, 1953-56. **Home Addr:** 132 Glenwood Ave, Portland, ME 04103, **Home Phone:** (207)772-6098. *

TALBOT, THEODORE A.
Educator, college teacher. **Personal:** Born Dec 22, 1923, Guyana; married Dorothy. **Educ:** Col Lib Arts, BA, 1949; Syracuse Univ, Sch Jour, MA, 1951; Baylor Univ;Tex A&M Univ. **Career:** Tex State Tech Inst, vpres, secy, bd regents; Paul Quinn Col, Div Humanities, chmn; Prairie View A & M Col, Dept Eng, assoc prof. **Orgs:** Bd dir, Am Tech Educ Asn; Nat Coun Teachers Eng; Conf Col Comn Community; S-control Mod Lang Asn; Coun Humanities Mod Lang Asn; Col Lang Asn; Edwards Chapel ANE Church; Alpha Phi Alpha Fraternity; Rotary Int; bd dirs, Minority Contractors Asn Waco; Heart Tex Coun Govt; Mclennan Co Human Serv Delivery Syst Prog Hon Consult State TX Coop Repub Guyana; bd mem, Rapoport Charter Sch.

TALIAFERRO, GEORGE
School administrator. **Personal:** Born Jan 8, 1927, Gates, TN; married Viola, Dec 1, 1950; children: Linda T, Renee, Donna & Terri. **Educ:** IN Univ Bloomington, BS, 1951; Howard Univ, Wash, DC, MSW, 1960. **Career:** Football player, school admin (retired); New York Yanks, player, 1950-51; Dallas Texans, 1952; Baltimore Colts, 1953-54; Philadelphia Eagles, 1955; Lafayette Square Community Ctr, Baltimore, dir, 1957-59; Prisoners Aid Asn, Shaw Residence, DC, caseworker,1959-66; United Planning Org DC, dir com action progs, 1966-68; Dico CorpMartin-Marietta Corp, Washington, DC, vpres & gen mgr, 1968-70; IN Univ, spec asst to pres, 1972; Morgan State Col, asst football coach, dean students, 1970-72; Couns Ctr & Drug Abuse Authority MD, exec dir, 1970; Big Ten Athletic Conf Spec Adv Comt, chmn, 1974. **Orgs:** Kappa Alpha Psi, 1948-; bd dirs, Baltimore Big Bros & Druid Hill YMCA, 1962-68; pres & found, Monroe Co Big Bros & Big Sisters, 1973-; chmn bd, Children's Organ Transplant Asn. **Honors/Awds:** Recipient All-Am All Big Ten & All State Awards Col Football Writers & Coaches, 1945-48; Football Hall of Fame; Ind Univ Hall of Fame, 1992; Volunteer of the Year Award, Children's Organ Transplant Asn, 2002. **Special Achievements:** First African-American to be drafted by an NFL team. **Military Serv:** AUS, corpl, 1946-47. *

TALIAFERRO, VIOLA J.
Judge. **Personal:** Born Sep 13, 1928, Evington, VA; daughter of Richard H Jones Sr and Mary Elizabeth Claiborne Jones; married George Taliaferro, Nov 24, 1950; children: Linda T Harvey, Renee A Buckner, Donna T Rutherford, Terri T Pendleton. **Educ:** Va State Col, BS, Bus Admin, 1947; Morgan State Univ, attended 1965; Johns Hopkins Univ, MLA, Polit Sci, 1969; Ind Univ, JD, 1977. **Career:** Baltimore Dept Welfare, social worker, 1957-63; Baltimore Pub Sch, teacher, dept head, 1965-72; Sr Citizens Ctr, dir; Reading & Study Skills Ctr, counr; Sch law, Ind Univ, Bloomingotn, IN, assoc instr; ICLEF Publ; pvt pratice, 1977-89; Monroe Circuit Ct, magistrate, 1989-95, judge, 1995-. **Orgs:** del, lawyer discipline cms; bylaws comn chap; Ind State Bar Asn; del, Am Bar Asn; Rotary Int; bd mem, Boy Scouts Am; comnr, Bloomington Pks & Recreation; chair, Ind State Bar Asn House Del, 1989-90; Ky Colonel, 1989; faculty, Ind Continuing Legal Educ Forum, 1992; Youth Serv Bureau; Community Serv Coun; Bloomington Symphony Orchestra; Camerata Chamber Orchestra; Vital Adv Bd Mem; bd mem, Youth Serv Asn; Community Found Bloomington & Monroe County; Salvation Army; Monroe County Bar Asn, 1977-; Am Bar Asn, 1977-; fellow, Ind Bar Found; fellow, Am Bar Found; Nat Coun Juvenile & Family Law Judges; Am Law Inst; former chair, Juvenile Justice Improvement Comt; Ind Human Resource Investment Coun. **Special Achievements:** Publ Delinquency: Detention, Waiver, Disposition, from IND Continuing Educ Forum, 1992. **Business Addr:** Judge, Monroe Circuit Court, 301 N Col Ave Rm 201, PO Box 547, Bloomington, IN 47404-3865, **Business Phone:** (812)349-2629.*

TALLEY, BEN. See TALLEY, BENJAMIN.

TALLEY, BENJAMIN (BEN TALLEY)
Football player. **Personal:** Born Jul 14, 1972, Griffin, GA. **Educ:** Tenn Univ. **Career:** Football player (retired); New York Giants, linebacker, 1995; Atlanta Falcons, 1998-99.

TALLEY, REV. CLARENCE
Educator, clergy. **Personal:** Born Jun 12, 1951, Pineville, LA; son of Albert Talley and Susie Edmond Newman; married Carolyn Westley, Nov 18, 1972; children: Clarence Jr & Crystal Ann. **Educ:** Southern Univ, Baton Rouge, BA, 1973; La State Univ, Baton Rouge, MFA, 1975; Houston Graduate Sch Theol, MA, 1991; Master's Grad Sch Divinity, Evansville, IN, DBS (theol), 2004. **Career:** Southern Univ, Baton Rouge, LA, instr, 1974; Prairie View Agr & Mech Univ, Prairie View, TX, prof art & archit, 1975-; Mt Corinth Missionary Baptist Church, minister. **Orgs:** Nat Conf Artist; Tex Sculpture Asn; Tex Soc Sculptors, Tex Asn Sch Arts. **Honors/Awds:** Second Place Acrylic, Southwest Arts Soc, Univ Tex Inst Tex Cult, 1985; Purchase Prize, 6th Annual Black Artist Exh First Louisville Bank, Kentucky, 1984; Honorable Mention, 1984 Regional Black Artist Ex George W Carver Museum, Austin, TX, 1984; second Runner Up, 1983 Regional Black Artist Ex George W Carver Mus, Austin, TX, 1983; Best of Show, Professional Division, Waller County Fair, 1985; Hays scholar to East Africa, 2000. **Special Achievements:** His artwork has been shown both nationally and internationally in numerous solo and group exhibitions; Publ: "A Call from God", 2000, "Lie After Lie After Lie,? 2008. **Home Addr:** 21119 Briarmeadow, Prairie View, TX 77446. **Business Addr:** Professor, Prairie View A&M University, School of Architecture, New School of Architecture & Art Bldg, PO Box 519, Prairie View, TX 77446-0519, **Business Phone:** (936)857-9807.

TALLEY, CURTISS J
Administrator. **Personal:** Born Jul 16, 1939, Holly Springs, MS; son of Curtis and Jessie Mae Rucker Draper; married Corene Davidson, Dec 21, 1968; children: Chrystal DaNise, Curtiss Carlos & Chemberly D. **Educ:** Kilroe Col Sacred Heart, Honesdale, PA, BA, 1964; Memphis State Univ, Memphis, TN, 1982; Loyola Univ, New Orleans, LA, MPS, 1988; Shelby State Community Col, Memphis, TN, 1990. **Career:** Administrator (retired); Cadet Sch, Holly Springs, MS, teacher & coach, 1966-72; Prudential Ins Co, Memphis, TN, dist agent, 1972-75; Thomas J Lipton Co Inc, Memphis, TN, sales rep, 1975-77; Wohl Shoe Co, Memphis, TN, supvr, 1977-78; St Joseph Church, Holly Springs, MS, christian social worker, 1978-81; Cath Diocese, Memphis, TN, dir multicultural ministries, 1981-2003; St Joseph Sch, teacher, 1985. **Orgs:** Fourth deg, Knights St Peter Claver, 1984-; vol, Prison Ministry, Shelby County Correctional Ctr, 1986-89; Serra Club, 1987-; Nat Black Cath Clergy Caucus, 1987; adv bd, Baptist Hosp, 1988; Nat Asn Black Cath Admin, 1990-; adv bd, Midtown Ment Health Asn, 1990; Aloysius Home Inc, AIDS Hospice, 1992; inter-religious affairs prof comt, St Peter Home C, 1992; vol chaplain, UT Med Ctr, 1992. **Special Achievements:** Ordained Deacon, Cath Diocese of Memphis, 1978. **Home Addr:** 1515 Waverly, Memphis, TN 38106.

TALLEY, DARRYL VICTOR
Football player, business owner. **Personal:** Born Jul 10, 1960, Cleveland, OH; married Janine; children: Alexandra & Gabrielle. **Educ:** W Va Univ, phys educ. **Career:** Football player (retired), Business owner; Buffalo Bills, linebacker, 1983-94; Atlanta Falcons, 1995; Minn Vikings, linebacker, 1996; Century Barricades Inc, owner, currenlty. **Honors/Awds:** Linebacker, Sporting News Col All-Am Team, 1982; played in AFC Championship Game, post-1988 season; Ralph C Wilson Jr Distinguished Serv Award, 2000. **Business Addr:** Owner, Century Barricades Inc, Lakeland, FL.

TALLEY, DIANNE W
Educator. **Personal:** Born Sep 14, 1955, Union, SC; daughter of Waddy and Lizzie Wright; married Michael F, May 24, 1980; children: Michanna & Michael F Jr. **Educ:** SC State Univ, BS; Univ SC, MEd; Clemson Univ, cert, supv, admin, 1997. **Career:** Jonesville Elementary, librn asst, 1977-79; Rutledge Col, adj instr, 1984-85; Greenville Tech Col, adjunct instr, 1984-87; Hillcrest High Sch, teacher, 1991-96; Bryson Middle Sch, admin asst, 1996-98; Green High Sch, asst prin, 1998-99; Berea High Sch, asst prin, 1999; Carolina High Sch & Acad, asst prin. **Orgs:** Asn Supervision & Curriculum, 1997-; Diversity Admin Leadership, 1999-; Nat Middle School Asn, 1996-; SC Alliance Black Educators, 1997-; SC Asn Sch Admin, 1997-; Greenville Children's Hosp, vol, 1995-; Greenville Literacy Asn, instr, 1996-; Jack & Jill Am Inc, 1999-; Prevent Child Abuse Carolina, 1995-.

TALLEY, JAMES EDWARD
Educator, mayor, radio host. **Personal:** Born Aug 22, 1940, Spartanburg, SC; married Barbara J Goins; children: James Carlton &

Deidra Sharee. **Educ:** Livingstone Col, BS, math & sci, 1963; Converse Col, 1968; SC State Univ,1972. **Career:** Educator (Retired), Mayor, Radio host; Bryson High Sch, teacher & coach, 1967-68; Carver High Sch, teacher & coach, 1968-70; WSPA-TV, TV show host, 1973-75; WKDY Spartanburg, radio show host, 1975-78; City Spartanburg, councilman, 1981-85; Wofford Col, football coach, 1981-94; Spartanburg, SC, mayor, 1993-; Spartanburg High Sch, teacher math. **Orgs:** LD Barksdale Sickle Cell Found, 1975-85; chmn, Bethlehem Ctr Trustees, 1978-81; chmn, Cammie F Clagget Scholar, 1979-85; basileus, Epsilon NuChap Omega, 1980-82; exec comt, Spartanburg Develop Coun; SC Munic Asn; Uptown Optimist Club; Comn Minority Affairs SC. **Honors/Awds:** Man of the Year, Mt Moriah Baptist Church, 1979; Omega Man of the Year, Epsilon Nu Chap Omega, 1980; Human Relation Award, Spartanburg City Educ Asn, 1983; Algernon Sydney Sullivan Award, Wofford Col; Nat Alumni Distinguished Citizen Award, Wofford College; Toast of the Town, Salvation Army; Neville Holcombe Citizen of the Year Award, Spartanburg Area Chamber Com; Kiwanis Club Citizen of the Year Award. **Military Serv:** USN, radioman; Man of the Year 1963-67; Honorable Discharge, 1967. **Business Addr:** Mayor, City of Spartanburg, 145 W Broad St, PO Box 1749, Spartanburg, SC 29306, **Business Phone:** (864)596-2000.

TALLEY, JOHN STEPHEN
Educator, college teacher. **Personal:** Born Dec 12, 1930, Sterlington, LA; married Furman; children: Kimberly & Stephen. **Educ:** Grambling Col, BS, 1954; Columbia Univ, MA, 1958; prof dipl, 1964. **Career:** Grambling Col, Nursery Sch, teacher, 1954-56, dir teacher, 1956-63, col teacher, 1964-66, coordr head start staff training progs, 1966; Queens Col, Early Childhood Educ Ctr Flushing, head teacher, supv teacher, 1963-64; State La, Off Econ Opportunity Grambling, regulations training officer, 1966-67; Grambling Col, teacher; Lincoln Parish, Kindergarten Progs, supvr; S Cent Regional Educ Lab Little Rock, consult; SW Region Off Child Develop Int. **Orgs:** La Educ Asn; Asn Childhood Educ; Int Asn C Under Six; Nat Asn Educ Young Children; Am Asn Univ Profs; Am Home Econs Asn; Day Care & Child Develop Coun Am; Alpha Kappa Alpha.

TALLEY, MICHAEL FRANK, SR.
Lawyer. **Personal:** Born Aug 14, 1945, Chesterfield, SC; son of Frank Sr (deceased) and Rosena A; married Dianne Wright, May 24, 1980; children: Michanna & Michael F Jr. **Educ:** SC State Col, BA, 1966; Howard Univ, MA, 1971, JD, 1976; Columbia Univ, graduate studies, 1973. **Career:** Wilson High Sch, SC, French teacher, 1966-69; Howard Univ, french lab instr, 1969-70 & 1973-76; SC State Col, French instr, 1970-71; Tenn State Univ, french instr, 1971-73; Pres Clemency Bd, White House, staff atty, 1975; Greenville Technical Col, bus law instr, 1984-90; NCP Legal Defense Fund, Earl Warren Legal fel, 1973-76; Pvt Pract, atty, 1977-. **Orgs:** Kappa Alpha Psi, 1965-92; SC State Col, Gamma Mu Honor Soc, 1966; Howard Univ Alumni Asn, 1971-2003; SC Bar Asn, 1976-01; SC Black Lawyers Asn, 1977-2001; mem bd dir, Legal Serv Western Carolina, 1978-82; US Ct Appeals, 4th Circuit; US Ct Appeals, 11th Circuit; Nat Bar Asn, 1985-2001. **Honors/Awds:** Certificate of Appreciation, SC Bar Pro Bono Prog, 1991; Plaque of Appreciation, Legal Serv Western Carolina, 1981. **Home Addr:** 208 Boling Rd, Greenville, SC 29611-7604. **Business Addr:** Attorney, 206 Green Ave, Greenville, SC 29601-3436, **Business Phone:** (864)233-6229.

TALLEY, SARAH
Public relations executive. **Career:** Metrop Detroit, Social Security Off, Pub Affairs Specialist, currently. **Orgs:** Inst Continuing Legal Educ. **Special Achievements:** featured in "Essence Magazine," serves as a columnist for the weekly "Michigan Chronicle" newspaper and has had a number of column features in the Detroit Free Press, including the "Money Report," "Financial Forum," and "Other Voices" sections. Ms. Talley has been a guest on several Detroit network and cable television programs, as well as on a number of local AM and FM radio stations.

TALLEY, WILLIAM B
Educator. **Personal:** Born Sep 22, 1955, Sumter, SC; son of Charles Winslow and Louise Bultmon Talley; married Tselate Betre, Jul 27, 1993; children: Massie Winslow. **Educ:** SC State, BA, psychol, 1976, MA, 1978; Southern Ill Univ, RhD, rehab, 1986. **Career:** State SC, counsr, trainee, 1976-78, vocational rehab counr, 1978-80, disability examiner, 1980-82; State La, LSU, educr, 1986-88; PSI Inc, counr, 1988-90; Univ MD, Eastern Shore, educr & chair, dir rehab servs, currently; Coppin State Col, asst prof. **Orgs:** Nat Rehab Asn, 1978-; Am Asn Coun & Devt, 1982-; NAACP, 1973-; vpres, Alpha Phi Alpha; Delta Omicron Lambda Chapter, 1994-; chair, Univ MD-Eastern Shore Fac Assembly, 1993-; chair & mem comt, MD Rehab Coun Asn, 1994-; Asn Black Psychologists, 1988-; Am Personnel & Guidance Asn, 1984-; Nat Asn Certified Hypnotherapists, 1988-; MD Rehab Asn, 1990-. **Special Achievements:** Certified Rehabilitation Counselor; Nationally Certified Counselor; License d Professional Counselor; Publications: The Predictors of Case Outcome for Clients in a Private Rehabilitation Program in Illinois, Dissertation Abstracts Int l, 1982; The Predictors of Case Outcome for Clients in Private Rehabilitation: An Illinois Study, The Journal of Private Sector Rehabilitation, 1988. **Business Addr:** Educator, Chair, University of Maryland Eastern Shore, Department of Rehabilitation Services, 934-5 Backbone Rd, Princess Anne, MD 21853-1299, **Business Phone:** (410)651-6261.

TAMIA (TAMIA WASHINGTON)
Singer. **Personal:** Born May 9, 1975, Ontario;married Grant Hill, Jul 24, 1999; children: Myla Grace & Lael Rose. **Educ:** Walkerville Col Inst. **Career:** Albums: Tamia, 1998; A Nu Day, 2000; Still, 2003; Officially Missing You, 2003; More, 2004; Between Friends, 2006, A Gift Between Friends, 2007; Hit Singles: "Stranger in the House," 2001; Honey, 2003; TV Series: "The Center," 2003; "Almost", 2007; Films: Speed 2: Cruise Control, 1997; Imagination, 1998; The Center, 2003; TV: Kenan & Kel; Beverly Hills 90210; Rock Me Baby; For Your Love. **Honors/Awds:** Grammy nominations, 1994, 1995, 1997, 2000; nominations for Juno Awards, 1999, 2001, 2005, 2007. **Business Addr:** Singer, Elecktra Entertainment, 75 Rockefeller Plz, New York, NY 10019, **Business Phone:** (212)275-4000.

TANDY, DR. MARY B
Publisher. **Personal:** Born Jan 13, Louise, MS; daughter of Florence Coleman (deceased); married O L (deceased); children: Bernice, Betty, Mary Ann, Alice M & Leroy Bryant. **Educ:** Ind Univ, 1966; Ivy Tech Col, AA, 1982. **Career:** Indiana Herald, owner & ed, publ, currenlty. **Orgs:** IDEA Ind Demo Eds, 1975; Spec prog chmn, Am Bus Women Asn, 1980-82; noble gov Household Ruth, 1980-82; Democratic precinct comn; publicity comn, Nat Asn Advan Colored People. **Home Addr:** 1914 Bellefontaine St, Indianapolis, IN 46202, **Home Phone:** (317)925-4184. **Business Addr:** Editor, Publisher, Indiana Herald, 2170 N Illinois St, Indianapolis, IN 46202, **Business Phone:** (317)923-8291.

TANKSLEY, ANN GRAVES
Artist, educator. **Personal:** Born Jan 1, 1934?, Homewood, PA; married John B; children: 2. **Educ:** Carnegie Mellon Univ, BFA, 1956; Art Stud League, Parsons Sch Design; New Sch Social Res. **Career:** Suffolk Co Community Col, adj art instr, 1973-75; artist, currently. **Honors/Awds:** Harlem Cultural Coun grant, 1981. **Special Achievements:** Book: The Six Fools, 2005. **Home Addr:** 18 Carlton Rd, Great Neck, NY 11021, **Home Phone:** (516)466-9639. **Business Addr:** Artist, 18 Carleton Rd, Great Neck, NY 10021, **Business Phone:** (516)466-9639.

TANN, DANIEL J
Lawyer. **Personal:** Born Nov 23, 1960, Philadelphia, PA; son of Gladys L and Fee Otis; married Kimberly A Smith, Jul 1988. **Educ:** La Salle Univ, BS, 1982; Drake Univ, JD, 1985. **Career:** Spear, Wilderman, Borish, Endy, Browning & Spear, Gen Pract Dept, managing atty, 1986-89; Gordon & Weinberg, PC, litigation atty, 1989-2001; Law Off Daniel J Tann, atty, currently. **Orgs:** NCP, 1980-; eastern Penn area dir, Nat Univ Sigma Chap, 1981-82, pres, 1988-90; bd dir, La Salle Univ Alumni, 1982-; Am Bar Asn, 1985-; Nat Bar Asn, 1985-; eastern regional legal coun, 1989-94, Phi Beta Sigma Fraternity Inc, eastern regional dir, 1997-; advisor & legal coun, Delta Theta Phi, Nu Sigma Youth Serv, 1990-; Pres Coun Assoc, 1991-2000; Philadelphia Bar Asn; Penn Bar Asn; Am Trial Lawyers Am; Com Law League Am; Lawyers Club Philadelphia; Barristers Asn Philadelphia. **Honors/Awds:** Joseph Drogan Scholarship, Drake Univ, 1982-85; Memorial Development Award, Phi Beta Sigma Fraternity, 1990; Appreciation Award, Boy Scouts Am, 1992; Warren E Smith Award, Outstanding Alumnus, LaSalle Univ, 1996. **Home Addr:** 1420 Walnut St Suite 1012, Philadelphia, PA 19102-4010, **Home Phone:** (215)670-0066. **Business Addr:** Attorney, Law Offices of Daniel J Tann, 420 Walnut St Suite 1012, Philadelphia, PA 19102, **Business Phone:** (215)670-0066.

TANNER, CRAIG
Executive, founder (originator), president (organization). **Personal:** Born Jan 1, 1962. **Career:** Urban Golf Gear, founder, chief erban officer & pres, 1997-. **Special Achievements:** Product line has been featured on various shows including: The Steve Harvey Show; The Hughley's; MTV Lyricist Lounge; The Bernie Mac Show; Malcolm & Eddy; Moesha; Soul Food; HBO The Wire; BET 106 & Park; Girlfriends; Products were also placed in the silver screen including: Two Can Play that Game; SWAT. **Business Addr:** Founder, President & Chief Erban Officer, Urban Golf Gear, Oakland China Town, 324 13 St, Oakland, CA 94612, **Business Phone:** (510)893-2499.*

TANNER, GLORIA TRAVIS
State government official. **Personal:** Born Jul 16, 1935, Atlanta, GA; daughter of Marcellus Travis and Blanche Arnold Travis; widowed; children: Terrance Ralph, Tanvis Renee & Tracey Lynne. **Educ:** Met State Col, BA, Polit Sci, 1974; Univ CO, MA, Urban Affairs, 1976. **Career:** Off Hearings & Appeals US Dept Interior, admin asst, 1967-72; Denver Weekly News, reporter, feature writer, 1972-76; 888 Real Estate Off, real estate salesperson, 1976; Lt Gov CO, exec asst, 1976-78; Sen Regis Groff Comt Off, exec dir, 1978, pub admin, 1978-; State Colo, state sen; Future Black Women Leaders Colo, natl exec dir (retired). **Orgs:** Pub chmn, Delta Sigma Theta, 1974; chair, Senatorial Dist 3 Dem Party, 1974-80; Am Soc Pub Admin, 1976; CO Black Women Polit Action CBWPA, 1976-80; exec bd, CO Comm on Women, 1976-79; Nat Assoc Real Estate Brokers. **Honors/Awds:** Outstanding Woman of the Year Award, Scott United Methodist Church, Denver, 1974; Denver Chamber Leadership Award, Denver Chamber Com, 1975; Outstanding Woman of the Year Award, Reginas Civic Club Denver, 1976; Outstanding Community Service Award, Barney Ford Community Service Award, Denver, 1977; Sen Groffs Community Service Award, Sen Groff, 1977. **Special Achievements:** First African American woman to serve as a Colorado state senator; second African American to be elected to a leadership position in the Colorado House of Representatives, where she was chair of the Minority Caucus. **Home Addr:** 2150 Monaco Pkwy, Denver, CO 80207, **Home Phone:** (303)355-7288. **Business Addr:** National Executive Director, Future Black Women Leaders of Colorado, 2150 Monaco Pkwy, PO Box 7217, Denver, CO 80207-1217, **Business Phone:** (303)355-7288.

TANNER, JAMES W., JR.
School administrator. **Personal:** Born Mar 18, 1936, Spartanburg, SC; married Priscilla; children: Tonya, Angela & James III. **Educ:** SC State Col, BSA, 1958; SC State Col, MEd, 1969; Univ SC, attended 1974. **Career:** School administrator(retired); Johnsonville Sch Dist No 5 Bd, teacher coordr dept head vo educ, 1973-74; Williamsburg Tech Col, dean stud servs. **Orgs:** Am Vocation Asn, 1962; SC Vo Agr Teacher Asn, 1962; Nat Vo Agr Teacher Asn, 1962; SC Vocational Asn, 1962; Nat Vacation Agr Teacher Asn, 1963; Nat Educ Asn, 1964; Boy Scout Master, 1970-74; pres, Florence Co Voters League, 1970-; Masonic Blue Lodge Master, 1970; dist rep, 1970, Florence Co Educ Asn, vpres, 1971, pres, 1973; bd educ Florence Co, 1973-74; treas,Cong Dist 6 Voters Educ Proj, 1973-74; bd dir, SC Educ Asn, 1974-; S eastern Regional Educ Bd, 1978-81; Florence Co Dept Social Serv Bd, 1989-93; SC Voc & Tech Coun, 1989-93; SC State Election Comt, 1993-96; trustee bd, SC State Univ, 1996-; bd dir, Tri-Co Health Clinic; Johnsonville-Hemingway Drug Community; recreation dir, Hickory Hill Comt; Johnsonville Devel Bd; Boy Scout post adv; chmn, Local Nat Asn Advan Colored People. **Honors/Awds:** Sears Roebuck Scholarship, Agr Ed, 1953; Recipient Distinguished Service Award, Agr Educ, 1969; Outstanding Secondary Educ Am, 1973; James W Tanner Jr Scholarship, named in honor, Williamsburg Tech Col. **Military Serv:** AUS, 1958-62. **Home Addr:** 263 AZALEA ST, PO Box 85, Johnsonville, SC 29555.

TANNER, TYRONE
School administrator, educator. **Personal:** Born Apr 14, 1971, Los Angeles, CA; son of Albert Watson and Lucy Mae; married Keisha W, Jun 28, 1998. **Educ:** Newberry Col, BA, history, 1994; Southern Univ, Masters, educ leadership, 1998; Univ Houston, attended, 1999. **Career:** New Orleans Marine Inst, GED coordr, 1995-96; JM Tate High Sch, Am hist teacher, 1997-98; Fontainebleau Jr High Sch, Am hist teacher, 1998-99; Houston Independent Sch Dist, human resource genist, 1999-2001, human resource recruiter, 2001; Fort Bend Independent Sch Dist, 6th grade prin, 2001; Tex Southern Univ, asst prof, Col Educ, currently. **Orgs:** Hundred Black Men Am, 1997-; NAACP, 1999-; Houston Area Alliance Black Sch Educr, 2000-; Nat Asn Sec Sch Principals, 2001-. **Honors/Awds:** National Collegiate Minority Leadership Award, 1992; Teacher of the Year, New Orleans Marine Inst, 1995; Teacher of the Year, Am Asn Sch Adminr, 1998; Outstanding Young Man of America, Outstanding Young Am, 1998. **Special Achievements:** Author: chap, "A German Experience", Lessons Learned: A Multicultural Perspective; Educational Leadership Challenges: What Principals say Concerns them about their Job, Int Jour Learning; created individual tutorial prog at Family Worship Acad; implemented "Zero Vacancies" prog, 36 schs. **Home Phone:** (281)416-0352. **Business Addr:** Assistant Professor, Texas Southern University, College of Education, 3100 Cleburne St, Houston, TX 77004, **Business Phone:** (713)313-7011.

TANTER, RAYMOND
Educator. **Personal:** Born Sep 19, 1938; married 1969. **Educ:** Roosevelt Univ, BA, 1961; Ind Univ, MA, PhD, polit sci, 1964. **Career:** Reagan-Bush admin, Secy Defense, personal rep; Gov Dept, vis res. Northwestern Univ, asst prof, 1964-67, assoc prof, 1967-72; Univ Mich, prof, 1972-; Hebrew Univ Jerusalem, vis prof intl rels, spring terms, 1973-78; Nat Security Coun & Nat Republican Comn; Georgetown Univ, vis prof & adj prof, currently. **Orgs:** Found & co-chmn, Iran Policy Comt; Wash Ins Near E Policy; Middle E Inst: Coun Foreign Rels. **Special Achievements:** Author: Modeling Intl Conflicts, 1974. Rational Decision Making, 1980. Who's at the Helm? Lessons of Lebanon, 1990; Rogue Regimes: Terrorism and Proliferation , "In a forest of world politics, the West slew a dying Soviet bear, and Washington sees additional beasts hiding in the woods'; Co-author , Balancing in the Balkans, 1999. **Business Addr:** Visiting Professor, Adjunct Professor, Georgetown University, 37 O St NW, Washington, DE 48109, **Business Phone:** (202)687-8217.

TAPPAN, DR. MAJOR WILLIAM
Dentist. **Personal:** Born Mar 18, 1924, Chester, PA; son of Pernie Smith Briggs; married Maria Arias, Dec 2, 1989; children: Eric Rowland, Ameedah Abdullah & Bobbi Jill. **Educ:** Howard Univ Lib Arts, 1944; Howard Univ Dent Sch, DDS, 1948; Columbia Univ, MPH, 1966. **Career:** Roselle, NJ, prv practr, 1948-67;

Denver Dept Health & Hosp, Community Dent Serv, dir, 1967-; Univ Colo Health Sci Ctr Dent Sch, assoc prof, 1970-; Dent Access Adminrs, chief exec officer, currently. **Orgs:** Consult, US Dept Labor Job Corps, 1973-; spec consult, Am Dent Asn, 1976; dir, Denticare CO Inc, 1983-; Nat Ctr Health Serv Res Study Sec, 1976-79; dir, Found for Urban & Neighborhood Develop Inc, 1984; CF Holmes Dent Soc Nat Dent Asn. **Honors/Awds:** Diplomate Am Bd Dent Pub Health. **Military Serv:** AUS, 1st lt, 1952-54. **Business Addr:** Chief Executive Officer, Dental Access Administrators Inc, 3216 High St, Denver, CO 80205, **Business Phone:** (303)394-0231.

TARPLEY, NATASHA ANASTASIA
Writer. **Personal:** Born Jan 6, 1971, Chicago, IL; daughter of Herman and Marlene. **Educ:** Howard UNV, visiting stud, 1991-92; Georgetown Univ Law Ctr, attended 1993-94; Harvard Univ, BA, 1993; Northwestern Univ, Sch Law, JD, 1996-98. **Career:** Beacon Press, author, currently. **Orgs:** Black Law Stud Asn, 1993-. **Honors/Awds:** Award for Poetry, Howard Univ, 1992; Award for Poetry, Wash, Cms Arts, Larry Neal, 1992, 1994; Award for Poetry, Radcliffe Col, Joan Gray Undermeyer, 1993; Fellowship for Poetry, Nat Endowment for the Arts, 1994-95; Fellowship for Poetry, Mass Cult Coun, 1994-95. **Special Achievements:** Testimony: Young AFA on Self-Discovery & Black Identity, Beacon Press, 1995; Girl in the Mirror & A Present Day Migration, for Minority from Beacon, 1997; I Love My Hair! - Childrens Book, Little Brook & CPN, 1998; Written articles for Essence Magazine, Cover Story on Black CLG Students, Oct 1993, Inventions Piece, Nov 1994; Book Reviews for the WAS Post, Los Angeles Times, The Quarterly Black Review and Chicago Tribune. **Business Addr:** Editor, Beacon Press, 25 Beacon St, Boston, MA 02108, **Business Phone:** (617)742-2110.

TARPLEY, ROY JAMES, JR.
Basketball player. **Personal:** Born Nov 28, 1964, New York, NY. **Educ:** Univ Mich, attended 1986. **Career:** Basketball player (retired), Dallas Mavericks, 1986-92; Aris Salonica, Greece, 1992; Olympiacos BC, 1993-94; Mich Mayhem,2006. **Honors/Awds:** NBA Sixth Man Award, 1988; NBA All-Rookie Team, 1987. **Home Addr:** 412 Goddard St, Panhandle, TX 79068, **Home Phone:** (806)537-3834. *

TARRY, ELLEN. See Obituaries section.

TARTER, JAMES H., III
Executive. **Personal:** Born Mar 6, 1927, New York, NY; married Marion; children: Krishna, Yasmin, Karim, James, Gamal. **Educ:** NY Univ; St Johns Univ; Inst Advan Mkt Studies; Advert Club NY, Honorary DD. **Career:** Tarter & Wetzel Co Inc, pres; NAACP Spl Contrib Fund, fund raising & pub rels nat dir develop, 1967-; Home Prods Corp, prod mgr; F&M Schaefer Co, adv supvr; Fuller Brush Co, br mgr; So Delicious Bakeries, pres, gen mgr; NAACP Nat Dept Tours, founder; NAACP Emergency Relief Fund, dir. **Orgs:** Nat Soc Fund Raisers; NY Soc Fund Raising Dirs; Advert Club NY; Knights Columbus. **Honors/Awds:** Recipient Honor City of New Orleans; Jeruselem Medal, Govt Israel; City Cr CTM. **Military Serv:** US Merchant Marine, 1944-49. **Business Addr:** 424 Madison Ave, New York, NY.

TARTER, ROGER POWELL
Educator, physician. **Personal:** Born Aug 27, 1930, New York, NY; son of James H and Elizabeth; married Ana Maria Hernandez, Oct 11, 1980; children: Roger Jr, Richard, Diana-Maria, Peter, Marcia-Elizabeth & Patricia. **Educ:** Iona Col, BS, 1953; Long Island Univ, MS, bio, 1959; Univ Bologna, Fac Med, MD, med & surgery,1964; Bernadean Univ Col Law, JD, 1994. **Career:** Educator(retired), Physician; Sloan Kettering Inst, Nat Inst Health, pre doctoral res fel, 1960; Westchester County, NY, asst pathologist-med examr, 1967-69; Montefiore Hosp & Med Ctr-MMTP, med dir, 1971-74; Spec Action Off Drug Abuse Prev, Mem US, expert, 1971-73; Albert Einstein Med Col, asst clin prof, Comm Health Social Med, 1972-76; Coney Island Hosp, Comprehensive Drug Abuse Treat Prog, prog dir, 1974-78; Maimonedes Hosp, Coney Island Hosp Affil, asst clin prof & attending pathol & med, 1974-78; NYC Bureau Prison Health Serv, Health Dept, med dir, 1978-81; private practice, 1981-90; Charles R Drew, Martin Luther King Jr Med Sch Found, sci & med adv, 1986-90; Mercy Col, Dept Psychol, Natural Sci & Criminal Justice, assoc prof; pvt pract, currently. **Orgs:** Alpha Phi Alpha Fraternity, ETA Chapter, New York City, 1951; Nat Asn Med Examr, 1969; Kiwanis Club, 1969; Nat Registry Specialist Microbiologist, Am Acad Microbiologists, 1970; Knights Columbus, 1970; adv bd trustees, Iona Col, 1972-; staff physician, New York State Athletic Comn, 1984; New York Acad Sci, 1985; Am Col Physician Exec, 1994; Am Col Med Adminr, 1994. **Honors/Awds:** Ochs Adler Scholarship, Post Grad Studies, Sloan Kettering Inst, 1956-58; Cancirco Snell Scholar, Cancer Res, Makerere Med Univ, Uganda, Africa, 1962; Honorary Police Surgeon, City Mount Vernon, New York, 1969; National Honor Soc in Psychology, Psi Chi; National Honor Soc in Criminal Justice, Alpha Phi Sigma; National Honor Soc in Biology, Beta Beta Beta; Brother Loftus Award, Outstanding Achievements in Med Arts, Iona Col, 1972. **Special Achievements:** Publications: JAMA, Vol 207, No 7, p 1347, Sudden Death Dueto (Coronary Atherosclerotic Heart Disease), 1969, JAMA, Vol 211, No 8, p 1331, Metaplasia of the Bronchial Epith, 1970, Journal of Addictions, Vol 10(1), pp 23-27, Ocular Absorption of Naloxone, 1975, fluent in Spanish and Italian. **Military Serv:** AUS, Med Serv Corp, private, 1953-55, Med Corp, major, 1963-90, Med Corp Reserves, 74th Field Hosp, chief prof serv, 1983-90; National Defense Medal; Good Conduct Medal; Combat Casualty Care Course Special Achievement, Army Service Ribbon; Army Component Reserve Medal. **Home Phone:** (914)376-2210.

TARVER, ELKING, JR.
Government official, manager. **Personal:** Born Nov 28, 1953, East Liverpool, OH; son of Elking Sr and Elsie Tarver-Byers. **Educ:** Gannon Univ, BS, Acct, 1976; Univ Md Grad Sch, MS, financial mgt, 1998. **Career:** US State Dept, acct, 1976-78; US Agr dept, asst regional inspector genl, 1978-93, dir, qual assurance, 1993-98; pvt pract certified pub acct, 1994-; US Dept Housing, audit mgr, currently. **Orgs:** Asn Black Accountants; Asn Govt Accountants, 1982-; Shiloh Baptist Church, 1983-; certified fraud examiner, Inst Certified Fraud Examiners, 1989; Certified Pub Acct, Am Inst Certified Pub Accountants, 1994. **Honors/Awds:** Certificates of Appreciation, 1998, 1999, 2000, 2001, 2002. **Home Addr:** PO Box 4554, Capitol Heights, MD 20791, **Home Phone:** (301)686-9292. **Business Addr:** Audit Manager, U.S. Department of Housing and Urban Development, Office of Public and Indian Housing, Real Estate Assessment Ctr 550 12th St SW Suite 100, Washington, DC 20410, **Business Phone:** (202)475-8814.

TARVER, GREGORY WILLIAMS
Politician. **Personal:** Born Mar 30, 1946, Shreveport, LA; married Velma Jean Kirksey; children: Gregory Jr, Ballestine, Lauren, Rebekah & Caroline. **Educ:** Grambling State Univ; Centenary Col. **Career:** JS Williams Fun Home, pres; Royal Life LA Ins Co, pres; lic fun dir; State Sen, currently; Charity Hosp, bd dir, 1973-75. **Orgs:** Shreveport Fun Dir Caddo Parish Police Juror; bd dir, LA Men Health Asn; Zion Baptist Church; chmn bd, Caddo Barber Col; pres, J S Williams Inc Co; Thirty Third Degree Mason; Universal Grand Lodge; Shriner; United Dem Campaign Com; Shreveport Jr C of C; Nat Asn Advan Colored People; Shreveport Negro C of C; Adv Coun YWCA. **Honors/Awds:** Outstanding Young Men of America, 1978; Black Leader of the Year, 1983-84. **Military Serv:** AUS, spec 5 E-5, 1967-69, state sen, 1984; Army Accom Medal. **Business Addr:** Senator, Louisiana Secretary of State, 1104 Pierre Ave, Shreveport, LA 71103, **Business Phone:** (318)676-7874.

TARVER, MARIE NERO
Government official, educator. **Personal:** Born Aug 29, 1925, New Orleans, LA; daughter of Charles L Nero Sr (deceased) and Daisy Lee Blackmore Nero; married Rupert J Jr; children: Rupert J, III, Charles LN, Stanley J, Gregory T, Bernard J & Cornelius A. **Educ:** Southern Univ Baton Rouge, BA, educ (cum laude), 1945; Univ Wis Madison Sch Jour, MA, 1947. **Career:** New Orleans Informer Newspaper, women's ed, 1945-46; Southern Univ Baton Rouge, eng instr, 1947-49; Galesburg High Sch, Galesburg, IL, eng teacher, 1954-56; Dutchess Comm Col Pough keepsie, eng instr, 1961-62; Marist Col Pough keepsie, eng instr, 1963-68; Model City Agency, asst dir planning, 1968-70, deputy dir, 1970-71, exec dir, 1971-77; City Pough keepsie, NY, dir social develop, 1977-90. **Orgs:** Nat Antapokritis Zeta Phi Beta Sorority Inc, 1948-52; Pres & bd educ, Poughkeepsie City Sch Dist, 1964-70; vpres, Nat Model Cities Comt Develop Asn, 1975-77; bd dirs, Dutchess Co NY, YMCA, 1970-74; chairperson bd dirs, United Way Dutchess Co NY Inc, 1979; chaiperson, United Way Campaign, 1982; comnr & chmn, Poughkeepsie Housing Authority; exec comm, Dutchess-Putnam Pvt Indust Coun; bd dir, Youth Resources Develop Corp; Mid-Hudson Reg Econ Develop Coun; Dutchess Co Arts Coun; trustee bd, Vassar Bros Hosp; New York St Asn Renewal & Housing Officials Inc; bd dirs, Dutchess County Child Develop Coun, Hudson River Housing Inc; Dutchess Dominica Partners Ams; Family Servs Inc; bd mem, C Home Poughkeepsie. **Honors/Awds:** First Recipient Sepia Award for Community Service, Alpha Phi Alpha Fraternity Inc Mid-Hudson Chap, 1976; Merit Award, Black Women's Caucus Polk, NY, 1979; Woman of the Year, Am Asn Univ Women, 1982; Alexis De Tocqueville Award, United Way Dutchess County, 1989; Gold Medal Humanitarian Award, St Cabrini, 1998; Women of Distinction, NY, 2005; President's Award, Marist Col. **Special Achievements:** First African-American member of the Poughkeepsie Board of Education; first African-American to gain city-wide election; first African-American Chairperson on the Board of Dutchess County United Way; first woman in 39 years to head the United Ways annual campaign. **Business Addr:** Board Member, The Childrens Home of Poughkeepsie, 10 Children Way, Poughkeepsie, NY 12601, **Business Phone:** (845)452-1420.

TARVER II, DR. LEON R
School administrator. **Personal:** Married Cynthia Loeb Tarver; children: 3. **Educ:** Southern Univ, BA, polit sci; Harvard Univ, John F Kennedy Sch Govt, MA, pub admin; Union Inst, PhD, pub admin. **Career:** Southern Univ Syst, Baton Rouge, LA, vice-chancellor admin, prof pub admin, prof pub policy & urban affairs, pres, 1997-2005, Nelson Mandela Sch Pub Policy & Urban Affairs, distinguished prof, currently. **Business Addr:** Distinguished Professor, Southern University, Nelson Mandela School of Public Policy & Urban Affairs, 410 Higgins Hall, Baton Rouge, LA 70813, **Business Phone:** (225)771-3092.

TASCO, MARIAN B.
Government official, city council member. **Personal:** Born in Greensboro, NC; daughter of Tom Benton and Alice; married Thomas Earle Williams (deceased); children: Charles Tasco, III. **Educ:** Bennett Col, attended 1958; Temple Univ, BS, bus educ, 1965. **Career:** City Philadelphia, city comnr, 1983-87, city coun woman, 1987-. **Orgs:** Deleg, Dem Conv, 1984, 1988, 1992; bd mem, Philadelphia Aiport Adv, 1988-; bd mem, Philadelphia Cult Fund; bd mem, Philadelphia Drama Guild, 1990-; Philadelphia Gas Comn; trustee, Bennett Col; nat pres, Women Munic Govt; hon chair & co-founder, Mayor's Telecommunications Policy & Adv Comn; bd mem, Elizabeth Blackwell Ctr; Dist Sorority; adv bd, Nat Polit Cong Black Women; Women's Way, Family Planning Coun Southeastern Pa; trainer, YWCA Leadership Inst; bd dirs, Nat League Cities; Recreation Fund; Mighty-Mighty 50th Ward Dem Exec Comt; chair, Philadelphia Gas Comn. **Honors/Awds:** Govt Award, Bright Hope Baptist Church, 1980; Winners Award, Women's Alliance Job Equity, 1985; Martin Luther King Jr Award, Salem Baptist Church, 1986; Achievement Award, United Negro Col Fund, 1986; Outstanding Serv & Committment Award, Philadelphia Affirmative Action Coalition. **Business Addr:** City Council Woman, City Philadelphia District 9, City Hall Rm 577, Philadelphia, PA 19107-3290, **Business Phone:** (215)686-3454.*

TASSIE, ROBERT V.
Marketing executive, business owner. **Personal:** Children: James & Jonathan. **Educ:** St John's Univ, attended; New Sch Social Res, attended; The Foreign Inst, Wash, DC, attended. **Career:** CBS TV Network, acct exec network sales, vpres sports sales; CBS Sports Div, vpres commun; Denver Nuggets, vpres mkt; Unity Media Inc, owner & pres, 1991-. **Orgs:** Int Soc TV Arts & Sci; bd mem, Ariz Sickle Cell Comn; Nat Minority Bus Coun. **Business Phone:** (212)687-3100.

TATE, ADOLPHUS
Insurance executive. **Personal:** Born Aug 18, 1942, Turrel, AR; son of Adolphus Tate Sr and Ruth Lee Johnson Tate; married Patricia Dawson; children: Adolphus III, Cherie Levelle & Faith Elizabeth Ann. **Educ:** La City Col, AZ, attended 1964. **Career:** Western & Southern Life Ins Co, assoc sales mgr, 1968-75, dist sales mgr, 1975-85, sales mgr, 1988. **Orgs:** Bowen Un Meth, 1969-; pres, Gardena Interest Neighbor, 1990-97, vpres,1971-73; vpres, Un Meth, 1976-86; Million Dollar Club Western & Southern Life Ins Co; Hollypary Comm Asn; co-chairperson, Bolden United Meth; 32nd-degree Prince Hall Mason; chairperson, Finance Comm Bowen Church,1983-85; secy, United Methodist Men 1987; chairperson, Trustee Bd Bowen UnMeth Church, 1989-93; Bowen United Methodist Church, chairperson, adv coun, 1994-97; pres, Knight West Club,1996; elected Worshipful Master, Western Knights 56, 1998. **Honors/Awds:** Policyholders Merit Award, 1971, 1976-79. **Special Achievements:** LUTCF, 1992. **Military Serv:** AUS, SP/4, 1964-66.

TATE, BRETT ANDRE
Executive. **Personal:** Born Apr 13, 1963, Seattle, WA; son of Margaret and Willis. **Educ:** Howard Univ, BA, bus mgt admin, 1986; Wash Univ, criminal law, 1988. **Career:** Congressman John Conyers, intern, 1986-88; Primerica Financial Serv, sr vpres, pres; Eastern Airlines, supvr & labor disputes mediator; B&G Building Maintenance Inc, founder, pres & chief exec officer, 1989-. **Orgs:** Usher bd, Metrop Baptist Church, 1991-92. **Honors/Awds:** Top Bus Orgn, 1990-91; Most Valuable Person, Primerica Financial Services, 1991; 40 UNDER 40 Achievement Award, The Network J, 2000; 'Outstanding American Award, Outstanding Young Am. **Business Phone:** (703)299-1781.

TATE, DAVID FITZGERALD
Football player. **Personal:** Born Nov 22, 1964, Denver, CO. **Educ:** Univ Colo. **Career:** Chicago Bears, defensive back, 1988-92; New York Giants, 1993; Indianapolis Colts, 1994-97.

TATE, DAVID KIRK
Lawyer. **Personal:** Born Apr 20, 1939, Detroit, MI; son of Andrew G and Izona Kirk; divorced; children: DeMarcus David Holland & Lisa Arlayne. **Educ:** Mich State Univ, East Lansing MI, BS, 1963; Univ Detroit Sch Law, Detroit MI, JD, 1973. **Career:** Patmon, Young & Kirk, Detroit MI, assoc, 1973-76; Detroit Edison Co, Detroit MI, staff atty, 1976-77; R J Reynolds Tobacco Co, Winston-Salem, NC, asst coun, 1977-82, coun corp & com, 1982-86, sr coun & asst secy, 1986-. **Orgs:** Am Bar Asn; NC Bar Asn; Wolverine Bar Asn. **Military Serv:** AUS, Infantry, capt, 1963-68; Bronze Star & Air Medal, 1968, combat infantrymans badge. **Home Addr:** 2736 Woodlore Trl, Winston-Salem, NC 27103-6546, **Home Phone:** (336)201-6836. **Business Addr:** Senior Counsel, Assistant Secretary, R J Reynolds Tobacco Company, 401 N Main St, Winston-Salem, NC 27104, **Business Phone:** (336)741-5000.

TATE, EARNEST L
Law enforcement officer. **Personal:** Married Norma Jean; children: Ricky & Terry. **Career:** City Selma, AL, asst polic chief, police chief. **Orgs:** Ala Peace Officers Asn. **Special Achievements:** First African Am chief of police for the city of Selma.

TATE, ELEANORA ELAINE
Journalist, writer. **Personal:** Born Apr 16, 1948, Canton, MO; daughter of Clifford Tate and Lillie Tate (raised by grandmother,

Corinne Johnson); married Zack E Hamlett III, Aug 19, 1972; children: Gretchen Tate. **Educ:** Drake Univ, Des Moines, IA, BA, jour, 1973. **Career:** Iowa Bystander, Des Moines, IA, news ed, 1966-68; Des Moines Regist & Tribune, reporter, 1969-76; Jackson Sun, Jackson, TN, staff writer, 1976-77; Memphis Tri-State Defender, free-lance writer, 1977; Kreative Koncepts Inc, Myrtle Beach, SC, writer, 1979-81; free-lance writer, 1982-; Positive Images Inc, Myrtle Beach, SC, pres & owner, 1983-93; Tate & Assocs media consult, 1993-; Author: "I'm Life," Children of Longing, Holt, Rinehart & Winston, 1970; "An Ounce of Sand, Impossible", Houghton-Mifflin, 1972; "Bobby Griffin," Off-Beat, Macmillan, 1974; Just an Overnight Guest, Dial Press, 1980; The Secret of Gumbo Grove, Franklin Watts, 1987; Thank You, Dr Martin Luther King, Jr!, Franklin Watts, 1990; "Ethel's Story," Storyworks Mag, 1992; Front Porch Stories at the One-Room Sch, Bantam Books, 1992; Retold African Myths, Perfection Learning Corp, 1992; "Secret of Gumbo Grove," play adaption, Scholastic Action Mag, 1993; "Hawkeye Hatty Rides Again," Am Girl Mag, 1993; A Blessing in Disguise, Delacorte, 1995; Don't Split the Pole: Tales of Down-home Folk Wisdom, Delacorte, 1997; "Momma's Kitchen Table," essay published in "In Praise of Our Fathers & Our Mothers," Just Us Books Publishers Inc, 1997; Just Overnight Guest, re-issued, Just Us Books Publs Inc, 1997; Recorded Books Inc, produced audio cassette tapes The Secret Gumbo Grove & Thank You, Dr Martin Luther King, Jr; "Tracing the Trilogy," pub African Am Rev, Spring 1998; "Novels With Deep Roots," pub Book Links mag, Jan 2000; Afr Amer Musicians, John Wiley & Sons, 2000; "Tell Me Who You Hang Out With & I'll Tell You What You Are," pub Lost & Found, 2000; The Minstrels Melody, Pleasant Co, 2001; "Raggedy Pants & the Dinosaur Wall," Scholastic Story Works, 2001; partic, Langston Hughes Libr Children's Book Roundtable, 2000, 2001; Also, article "With DiSsector-Eds, Even Children's Book, Authors Have to Take a Stand," pub, Obsidian III J, spring, 2001; "Don't Split the Pole," pub Big City Cool, 2002; co-author: Black Start of the Harlem Renaissance, 2002; "Langston Hughes, the Peoples Poet," pub Dream & Girl Mag, Nov-Dec, 2002; Abram's Way, 2003; "To Be Free, Steck-Vaughn", 2004. **Orgs:** Iowa Arts Coun Artists Schs & Community, 1970-89; SC Arts Comn Artists Educ, 1982-92; NAACP, Georgetown chap, Georgetown, SC, 1984-89; Concerned Citizens Operation Reach-Out Horry County, 1985-; bd govs, SC Acad Authors, 1986-90;, pres, secy, vpres, Horry Cult Arts Coun, 1986-92; Pee Dee Reading Coun, Myrtle Beach, SC, 1987-90; Arts Basic Currriculum Steering Comt, 1988-90; bd mem, Nat Asn Black Storytellers Inc, 1988-92, pres, 1991-92; NC Writers Network, 1993-; Twin Rivers Reading Coun IRA, 1993-99. **Honors/Awds:** Unity Award, Lincoln Univ, 1974; Community Lifestyle award, Tenn Press Asn, 1977; author of Just an Overnight Guest, Dial, 1980; fel children's fiction, Breadloaf Writers Conf, 1981; Parents Choice Award, 1987; The Secret of Gumbo Grove, F Watts, 1987; Presidential Award, Nat Asn Negro Bus & Prof Womens Clubs, Georgetown SC chap, 1988; author of Thank You, Dr Martin Luther King, Jr, F Watts, 1990; Grand Strand Press Asn Award, Social Responsibilities & Minority Affairs, 1988; Coastal Advert Fed, Addy Award, Positive Images Inc, 1988; Grace Brooks Memorial Humanitarian Award, SC Action Counc Cross-Cult Mental Health & Human Servs, 1991; Board of Director Award, Horry Cult Arts Coun, 1991; Distinguished Woman of the Year, Arts, Carteret County NC Coun Women, 1993; Excellent Communicator Award, Dept Pupil Servs, Horry County SC Sch Dist, 1990; Zora Neale Hurston Award, Nat Asn Black Storytellers, 1999; Dr Annette Lewis Phinazee Award, NC Cent Univ Sch Libr Info Sci, 2000; Parents Choice Recommended Award for African American Musicians, 2000; The Minstrels Melody named CBS & NCSS Noteable Children's Trade Book in Social Studies.

TATE, EULA BOOKER
Lobbyist. **Personal:** Born Nov 17, 1948, Ypsilanti, MI; daughter of Leslie Davis (deceased) and Genia Webster; married Ronnie G Tate; children: Ronald L, Donald D, Jennifer C, Stephen B. **Educ:** Univ MI, BS, 1977. **Career:** Chrysler Corp UAW Local 630, first vpres, 1967-80; Mich State Univ, labor educator; City Ypsilanti, MI, coun mem; United Auto Workers, legis rep. **Orgs:** Elks; Benevolent & Protective Order of Elks; Temple 1283; Nat Democratic Party; Nat Asn Advan Colored People; CBTU; Coalition Labor Union Women. **Honors/Awds:** Mich State Univ, Employee Recognition, 1983-84; Nominated Mich Chronicle's Churchwoman of the Yr ,1984; UAW Region 1-A, Distinguished Serv Award, 1989; Minority Women Network, Politician of the Yr, 1990; Minority Bus Owners Chamber of Commerce, Community Involvement Award, 1991; City of Ypsilanti Serv Award, 1991. **Business Addr:** Legislative Representative, UAW, Solidarity House, 8000 E Jefferson Ave, Detroit, MI 48214, **Business Phone:** (313)926-5000.*

TATE, GRADY BERNARD
Entertainer, college teacher. **Personal:** Born Jan 14, 1932, Durham, NC; married Vivian Tapp. **Educ:** NC Cent Univ, BA 1959; Am Acad Dramatic Arts, NY. **Career:** Positions include studio musician; NBC Tonight Show, musician; performed numerous night clubs prisons TV commercials; Johnny Carson's Tonight Show, drummer; singer: "I Got Six"; "Naughty Number Nine"; Howard Univ, jazz studies lectr, 1989-, teacher, mem, faculty. **Honors/Awds:** Special Award, Daytop Village Festival Music, New York, 1968; Record World All Star Band New Artist New York, 1968; Outstanding Achievement Award, Entertainment Hillside High Sch, Durham, NC, 1971; Humanitarian Award, NC Cent Univ, 1970-71; Overseas Jazz Club Award, 1971; Jazz Achievement Award, Jazz Home Club Am, 1971. **Military Serv:** USAF, 1951-55. **Business Addr:** Lecturer, Howard University, 525 Bryant St NW Suite 108 Room B36, Washington, DC 20059.*

TATE, GREG
Journalist. **Career:** Essayist and longtime staff writer for the Village Voice. **Orgs:** Founding member, Black Rock Coalition, 1985. **Special Achievements:** Conductor and music dir of Burnt Sugar; author, Flyboy in the Buttermilk: Essays on Contemporary Am, Simon & Schuster, 1992; author, Everything But the Burden: What White People Are Taking from Black Culture, Broadway Books, 2003; author, Midnight Lightning: Jimi Hendrix and the Black Experience, Lawrence Hill Books, 2003. **Business Addr:** PO Box 1054, Cooper Station, New York, NY 10276, **Business Phone:** (212)713-5097.*

TATE, HERBERT HOLMES
Lawyer. **Personal:** Born Feb 22, 1953, Karachi, Pakistan; son of Herbert H Sr (deceased) and Ethel Harris. **Educ:** Wesleyan Univ, BA cum laude, 1978; Rutgers Univ Sch Law, JD 1978. **Career:** Essex Co Prosecutor's Off Appellate Sect, law clerk, 1977-78; Hon Van Y Clinton, judicial clerk, 1978-79; Essex Co Prosecutor's Off, asst pros, 1979-83, trial sect dir juvenile trial sect, 1982-83; Carella Byrne Bain Gilfillan, assoc, 1983-85; pvt pract, atty, 1985-86; Urban Enterprise Zone Authority, pub mem, 1985-86; Bloomfield Col, adj prof, 1985; Essex Co Prosecutor's Off, prosecutor; State NJ Bd Public Utilities, pres, currently. **Orgs:** Kiwanis Int Newark Chap; NJ Bar, Fed Bar NJ Dist, Pa Bar; NJ State Bar Asn Criminal Law Comn, Exec Comn Criminal Law Sect; Essex Co Bar Asn; Nat Bar Asn; Nat Dist Atty Asn; Nat Black Prosecutors Asn; Nat Orgn Black Law Enforcement Execs; Int Narcotic Enforcement Officers Asn; State Youth Serv Comn, State NJ; Supreme Ct Task Force Minority Concerns; Co Prosecutors Asn; trustee, Boys & Girls Club Newark; trustee, Montclair Kimberley Acad. **Honors/Awds:** Commendation, City Newark Munic Coun; East Orange Optomist International Law Enforcement Award, 1987; Law Enforcement Award, Bronze Shields Inc, 1987; Law Enforcement Award, Nat Black Police Officers Asn, 1990. **Home Addr:** 169 Mt Pleasant Ave, West Orange, NJ 07052. **Business Addr:** President, State of New Jersey Board of Public Utilities, 2 Gateway Ctr, Newark, NJ 07102, **Business Phone:** (201)648-2013.

TATE, DR. JAMES A.
School administrator. **Personal:** Born Aug 7, 1927, Canton, MS; married Barbara; children: Lisa, Jayme & James Jr. **Educ:** Jackson State Col, BS, 1950; Mich State Univ, MA, 1970, PhD, 1975-. **Career:** Teacher (retired); Miss, elem teacher, asst prin, 1950-55; Detroit, elem teacher 1955-57; Mich elem teacher, 1959-70; sci teacher prin, elem schs,1968-70; Admis & Scholars Mich State Univ, asso dir, 1971-, dir, develop prog admis Off Admis, 1977. **Orgs:** Exec bd, Admin Prof Orgn, 1974-76; Career Planning & Placement Coun; Black Fac Adminr Asn; adv bd, Ypsilanti Area Comm Servs; Phi Beta Sigma; Am Personnel Guid Asn; Mich Counsrs Asn; Nat Cong Parents & Teachers; Nat &Mich Educ Asn; Mich Asn Sec Sch Prin; The Mich Asn Col Admission Counseling; MAAAO; Mich Asn Collegiate Registr & Admis Officers; Orgn Mich State Univ; YMCA; Urban League; Nat Asn Advan Colored People; Am Asn Collegiate Regist B Admis Officers; exec bd, Admin Prof Orgn, Mich Educ Asn; founder, Wood-Mere Neighborhood Org; trustee, Trinity AME Church, Disciplinary Adv Bd, Lansing Sch Dist. **Military Serv:** AUS, 1944.

TATE, LARENZ
Actor, movie producer. **Personal:** Born Sep 8, 1975, Chicago, IL; son of Larry and Peggy; married Tomasina Parrott; children: Miles Xavier. **Career:** Actor, Producer, Director; Film appearances: Menace II Soc, 1993; The Inkwell, 1994; Dead Press, 1995; Love Jones, 1997; The Postman, 1997; Why Do Fools Fall in Love, 1998; Love Come Down, 2000; Biker Boyz, 2003; A Man Apart, 2003; Crash, 2004; Ray, 2004; 187 Ride or Die, 2005, Waist Deep, 2006; TV series: The Royal Family, 1991; S Cent, 1994; Love Come Down, 2000; A Man Apart, 2003; "Love Monkey", 2006; Waist Deep, 2006, "Blue Blood", 2008; "Rescue Me", 2007-09; Director: The Hot Spot, 2005; Producer: Love Come Down, 2000. **Orgs:** Founder, The Tate Bros. **Honors/Awds:** Best Actor Award for Why Do Fools Fall in Love, Acapulco Black Film Festival, 1999; Screen Actors Guild Award, 2005; Black Reel Award, 2006; Screen Actors Guild Award, 2006. **Business Addr:** Actor, 1990 Bundy Dr, Los Angeles, CA 90025, **Business Phone:** (310)820-6666.

TATE, LENORE ARTIE
Consultant, psychologist. **Personal:** Born Apr 8, 1952, Los Angeles, CA; daughter of Earline Hopkins Tate and Wilbur B Tate. **Educ:** Mills Col, BA, 1974; Howard University, MS, 1977; Calif Sch Prof Psychol, PhD, 1980. **Career:** Prairie View A&M Univ, chp of psychology program, 1982-84; Ariz State Univ, asst Prof, 1984-86; Calif Legislature (Senate & Assembly), principal health policy consult; pvt pract, currently. **Orgs:** Asn Black Psychologists, 1992-; Alpha Kappa Alpha Sorority Inc, 1986-; bd mem, Am Soc on Aging, 1985-87; Minority Concerns Commity, 1984-87; Ariz's Govs Conf on Aging, 1984, co-chair, 1985; adv bd, County Sacramento Health Servs Cabinet, expert emeritus, 1992, Sacramento County, self-esteem task force, 1988-90, ment health adv bd, 1988-90, chr, 1989-92, vice chair, 1989; bd dir, Maricopa County NAACP, 1985-87. **Honors/Awds:** Nat Inst for Mental Health, Texas Research Inst for Mental Sciences, Geriatric Psychology Post-Doctoral Fellowship, 1980-82; Sacramento County, Outstanding County Service Award, 1991; Calif School of Professional Psychology-Fresno, Dean's Award, 1980; Auth: Adult Day Care. **Special Achievements:** Author, "Life Satisfaction and Death Anxiety in Aged Women," International Journal of Aging and Human Development, 1982; "Employment Opportunities for Geropsychologists," AMR Psychologist; "Adult Day Care: A Practical Guidebook and Manual," Activities, Adaptation and Aging, special issue, 1988; Calif Mental-Health System: The History of Neglect, Senate Office of Research, 1991. **Business Addr:** Psychologist, 648 Northfield Dr, Sacramento, CA 95833, **Business Phone:** (916)564-0400.

TATE, MATTHEW
School administrator, administrator. **Personal:** Born Sep 16, 1940, McComb, MS; married Rosemary Brymfield; children: Mathis Melone. **Educ:** Southern Univ, BS, 1963; Louisiana State Univ, attended 1964; Southern Univ, Med, admin, 1969; Southeastern Louisiana Univ, Education Specialist, 1974. **Career:** Principal (retired), Administrator; W S Young Constr Co, field coordr; Fed Summer Nutrit Prog, bookkeeper; La Asn Educr, rep, 1978-82; Wash Parish Police Juror, juror 1984, bd mem; Franklinton High Sch, asst prin to prin; Mother Hen's Nursery/Preschool, adminr, currently; Tate's Tax Serv, chief exec officer, currently; bd pres, Good Samaritan Living Ctr, currently. **Orgs:** Pres, Wash Parish Ed Asn, 1967; pres, Phi Delta Kappa, 1974; chair person, Supvry Comt Wash Parish Ed Fed Credit Union, 1980; sec, Franklinton Area Polit League; Comt Person Local Mental Health Asn; pres, Rural Franklinton Water Dist; bd mem, Rev Bd Capitol Region Planning Comn, La; Cong Contact Team LAE/NEA. **Honors/Awds:** Police Juror Washington Parrish Police Jury, Franklinton, LA. **Home Addr:** PO Box 368, Franklinton, LA 70438. **Business Addr:** Chief Executive Officer, Tate's Tax Service, 4500 Beech Rd, Temple Hills, MD 20748, **Business Phone:** (301)423-8249.

TATE, ROBERT (ROBERT LEE TATE)
Football player, football coach. **Personal:** Born Oct 19, 1973, Harrisburg, PA. **Educ:** Univ Cincinnati. **Career:** Football player (retired), coach; Minn Vikings, wide receiver, 1997-2001; Baltimore Ravens, wide receiver, 2002-03; Ariz Cardinals, wide receiver, 2004-06; ACES, behaviour coach.

TATE, ROBERT LEE. See TATE, ROBERT.

TATE, SHERMAN E
Executive. **Personal:** Born Oct 5, 1945, Marvell, AR; son of Rufus Tate Jr and Annie B Tucker; children: Amber Nicole DePries; married Marylene Williams. **Educ:** Philander Smith Col, Little Rock, AR, BA, 1970, DHL, Little Rock, AR, 1988. **Career:** City Little Rock, AR, consult, 1970; Ark State Personnel Div, Dept Finance & Admin, Little Rock, AR, personnel analyst, 1970-73; Ark Legis Coun, Little Rock, AR, personnel & budget specialist, 1973-75; Univ Ark Little Rock, dir personnel, 1975-77; Ark State Office Personnel Mgt, Little Rock, AR, admin, 1977-80; Ark La Gas Co, Little Rock, AR, asst vpres employee rels, 1980-83, vpres community & consumer rels, 1983-90, vpres, customer rels; Alltel Corp, vpres external affairs, 1998-; Fletcher-Tate Ford, co-owner; First Choice Chevrolet, GMC, Pontiac & Buick, co-owner. **Orgs:** Chmn, Greater Little Rock Chamber Com, 1989; treas, Am Asn Blacks Energy; Nat energy comt; NAACP; Nat adv coun; Nat Alliance Bus; bd dirs, One Nat Bank; chmn, Ark State Police Comn; bd dirs, Ctrs Youth & Families; bd trustees, Philander Smith Col; 100 Black Men Am; bd mem, Reynolds Inst Aging. **Honors/Awds:** Distinguished alumnus, Philander Smith Col. **Special Achievements:** First African-American elected chairman of the Greater Little Rock Chamber of Commerce. **Military Serv:** AUS, sgt; Natl Guard, major; received Bronze Star. **Home Addr:** 4008 Longview Rd, Little Rock, AR 72212-1925. **Business Addr:** Vice President External Affairs, Alltel Corp, PO Box 2177, Little Rock, AR 72203-2177, **Business Phone:** (501)374-2001.

TATE, SONJA
Basketball player. **Personal:** Born Sep 7, 1971. **Educ:** Ark State Univ, physical educ, 1993. **Career:** Columbus Quest, guard, 1996; Minnesota Lynx, guard, 1999-2000, guard, 2002-. **Business Phone:** (612)673-8400.*

TATE, SONSYREA
Journalist, educator, writer. **Personal:** Born Apr 22, 1966, Washington, DC; daughter of Joseph Tate and Meauvelle; divorced. **Educ:** Univ DC, BA, 1988. **Career:** Wash Post, ed aide, writer, 1986-89; Wash Times Newspaper, reporter, 1989-91; Va-Pilot Newspaper, reporter, 1991-93; US House Rep, off Eleanor Holmes Norton, asst; Sylvan Learning Syst, instr, 1997-; Wash Informer Newspaper, ed, currently; Author: Little X: Growing Up in the Nation of Islam. **Orgs:** Nat Asn Black Journalists, 1987-94. **Honors/Awds:** Echoes of Excellence Award, Hampton Roads Black Media Coalition, Nat Assn Black Journalist, 1993, Spot

News, 1994, Commentary & in-depth Series, 1992; Spot News Award, Va Press Asn, 1993; City Council Resolution for Community Service Journalism, Wash, DC, 1991; author "Little X: Growing Up in the Nation of Islam," Best Book for Young Adults, Best Book for Teen, Am Libr Asn, 1998. **Home Addr:** 339 17th St SE Apt 1, Washington, DC 20003, **Home Phone:** (202)396-7612. **Business Addr:** Editor, The Washington Informer Newspaper, 3117 Martin Luther King Jr Ave SE, Washington, DC 20032, **Business Phone:** (202)561-4100.

TATE, VALENCIA FAYE
Executive, vice president (organization). **Personal:** Born Sep 20, 1956, Petersburg, VA; daughter of Henry G (deceased) and Irene E; married Penfield W Tate III, Sep 26, 1981; children: Elleana Elizabeth Wilson. **Educ:** Antioch Sch Law, JD, 1981; James Madison Univ, BA, 1978. **Career:** Denver Juv Crt, clerk, 1982-84; Colo Nat Bank, acct adr, corp trust supvr, Mastercard & Visa, 1984-86; Denver Water, Mgr EEO & minority bus, supvr real estate contracts, supvr tap sales & records, 1986-95; CH2M Hill, vpres & dir, currently. **Orgs:** Past pres, Delta Sigma Theta, 1976-; Jr League Denver, 1987-; Leadership Denver Alumni Asn, 1992; Bd mem, Hist Paramount Theatre Found, 1992; Mile High Coun; Bd mem, Girl Scouts of Am. **Honors/Awds:** Leadership Denver Class, Denver Chamber Com, 1987; Nat Asn Negro Bus & Prof, Leadership 2000 Class, 1990. **Home Addr:** 2875 Albion St, Denver, CO 80207, **Home Phone:** (303)320-4665. **Business Addr:** Vice President, Director, Ch2m Hill, 6161 S Syracuse Way Suite 200, Greenwood Village, CO 80111, **Business Phone:** (303)706-0990.

TATEM, DR. PATRICIA ANN
Physical chemist. **Personal:** Born Aug 21, 1946, Wilmington, NC; daughter of Ozie T Faison Sr and Martha Louise Smith Faison; divorced; children: Paul Hadley. **Educ:** Bennett Col, BS, 1967; George Wash Univ, MS, 1970, PhD, 1984. **Career:** The Naval Res Lab, tech ed, 1967-72, res chemist, 1972-94, supervisory res chemist, 1994-. **Orgs:** Wash Chromatography Discussion Group; Am Chem Soc; The Combustion Inst; Sigma Xi. **Honors/Awds:** Summa Cum Laude Bennett Col, 1967; Co-recipient, National Research Lab, Research Publication Award for Applied Research, NRL, 1973; Recipient Edison Memorial Grad National Research Lab, 1978-81; Co-recipient National Research Lab Publication Award for Applied Research, National Research Lab, 1983; Black Engineer Award, Professional Achievement, Morgan State Univ/US Black Engr Mag, 1987; Council for Excellence in Government Fellow, 1994-95; Women of Color Technology Award. **Business Addr:** Research Chemist, Naval Research Laboratory, 4555 Overlook Ave SW Code 6180, Washington, DC 20375-5000, **Business Phone:** (202)767-6965.

TATUM, DR. BEVERLY DANIEL
Educator, school administrator, president (organization). **Personal:** Born Sep 27, 1954, Tallahassee, FL; daughter of Robert Alphonse and Catherine Faith Maxwell; married Travis James, Jul 28, 1979; children: Travis Jonathan & David Alexander. **Educ:** Wesleyan Univ, Middletown, CT, BA, psychol, 1975; Univ Mich, MA, clinic psychol, 1976, PhD, clinic psychol, 1984; Hartford Sem, MA, relig study, 2000. **Career:** Coun psychologist, 1979-83; Univ Calif, Santa Barbara, dissertation fel, 1980-81, lectr, dept black studies, 1982-83; Westfield State Col, asst prof psychol, 1983-86, assoc prof, 1986-89; pvt pract psycholgist, 1989; Mt Holyoke Col, assoc prof, 1989-96, prof, 1996-2002, psychol & educ dept chair, 1997-98, dean & vpres, stud affairs, 1998-2002, acting pres, 2002; Wesleyan Col, Stone Ctr, vis scholar, 1991-92; Spelman Col, pres, 2002-. **Orgs:** Bd dirs, Equity Inst, 1985-90, chair, 1988-90; bd trustees, Williston North hampton Sch, 1999-; Hartford Sem, bd incorporators, 2000-; Am Psycho lAsn; Am Educ Res Asn; Am Col Personnel Asn; Am Asn Univ Women; Nat Asn Multicultural Educ. **Honors/Awds:** Distinguished Service Award, Westfield State Col, 1986, 1987; Publication Award, Asn Women Psychol, 1994; five hon degrees; Brock International Prize, 2005. **Special Achievements:** Author: 'Assimilation Blues: Black Families in a White Community, 1987;Harvard Educ Review article, 1993; 'Why are all the Black kids sitting together in the Cafeteria', Basic Books, 1998. **Business Addr:** President, Spelman College, Office of the President, 350 Spelman Lane SW 1st Fl Rockefeller Hall, Atlanta, GA 30314, **Business Phone:** (404)270-5001.

TATUM, E R. See TATUM, ELINOR RUTH.

TATUM, ELINOR RUTH (E R TATUM)
Publisher. **Personal:** Born Jan 29, 1971, New York, NY; daughter of Wilbert and Susan. **Educ:** St Lawrence Univ, Canton, NY, BA, 1993; Stockholm Univ, attended 1994; New York Univ, Grad Sch Arts & Sci, MA, jour, 1998. **Career:** New York Amsterdam News, from asst publ to assoc publ, 1994-97, chief operating officer, 1996-97, publ, editor-in-chief, 1997-. **Orgs:** Wallenberg Comt US, 1994; NY Urban League, 1997-; chairwoman bd, Learning Tree Western Mass, 1997; US Comt UNIFEM 1997; Greater NY Chap Links Inc, 1998. **Honors/Awds:** Good Scout Award, Greater NY Coun Boy Scouts Am, 1997; Woman of the Year, NY Championship Block Rodeo, 1998. **Home Addr:** 41 2nd Ave, New York, NY 10001, **Home Phone:** (212)529-9902. **Business Addr:** Publisher, Editor-in-Chief, New York Amsterdam News, 2340 Frederick Douglass Blvd, New York, NY 10027, **Business Phone:** (212)932-7400.

TATUM, JAMES
Educator, lecturer, pianist. **Personal:** Born Jul 29, 1931, Mineola, TX; married Cleatrice. **Educ:** Prairie View A&M Univ, BA, 1951; Univ Mich, MMUS, 1953. **Career:** Butler Col, music dir, 1956; Murray Wright HS, fine arts dept head, 1957; The Contemporary Jazz Mass, composed, 1980; Spiritulotta Jazz Suite, recorded & published, composed, 1983; Oakl Univ, jazz piano instr, 1993; Wayne County Community Col, music instr, 1996, 1998. **Orgs:** Dir, Ceciliaville Cult Ctr, 1968; dir, Prog Alternative Creative Ed, 1975; music dir, Upward Bound Prog-Wayne State Univ, 1979; Act-So NAACP, 1982; pres, founder, James Tatum Found Arts, 1987; Int Asn Jazz Educrs; Nat Comt Black Jazz Caucus. **Honors/Awds:** One of the benefactors, 1994; Musician Year Award, Mich State Sen, 1998; Betty Gerisch Award, Lyric Chamber Ensemble, 1999; Living Dream Award, Amitech, 2001; Distinguished Service Award, Prairie View A&M Univ, Nat Alumni, 2001; Frederick Douglass Award, 2002. **Special Achievements:** Composed, Contemporary Jazz Mass, 1980, Lecturing & performing jazz concerts in schools, colleges & universities, 2000-03. **Military Serv:** AUS, PFC, 1983-55; Special Services Entertainment Award, 1955. **Business Addr:** Founder, President, James Tatum Foundation for the Arts, 20235 Alderton St, PO Box 32240, Detroit, MI 48232, **Business Phone:** (313)255-9015.

TATUM, KINNON RAY
Football player. **Personal:** Born Jul 19, 1975, Fayetteville, NC. **Educ:** Univ Notre Dame. **Career:** Carolina Panthers, linebacker, 1997-98; Tampa Bay Buccaneers, 2000.

TATUM, MILDRED CARTHAN
Government official, school administrator. **Personal:** Born Mar 26, 1940, Grady, AR; married Charles Leon Tatum Sr; children: Carl, Sharon, Charles, Jr, Gerald, Terrance & Edwin. **Educ:** Voca Sewing Class, 1959; Sharter Col, NLR, spec educ, 1979. **Career:** PTA, pres, 1969; Fed Prog, pres, 1980; Regional 6 Chap 1 Prog, treas,1981; State Dept PAC, treas, 1982; Pulaski Co Spec Sch Dist, bd pres, currently. **Orgs:** Owner 145 St Liquors, 1969; owner grocery store, 1981; bd dir for Metroplan, 1984; nat bd for AAS bd, 1984; Judge Wood appointee to internal board, 1985; owner rental houses. **Honors/Awds:** Nat Honor Soc, 1974; Key to City of La Chapter PAC, 1976; Outstanding Leader Sch Dist, 1983. **Special Achievements:** First Black President School Bd, 1984. **Business Addr:** Board President, Pulaski County Special School District, 925 E Dixon Rd, Little Rock, AR 72206, **Business Phone:** (501)490-2000.*

TATUM, WILBERT A. See Obituaries section.

TAULBERT, CLIFTON LEMOURE
Business owner, writer, marketing executive. **Personal:** Born Feb 19, 1945, Glen Allen, MS; son of Morgan and Mary; married Barbara Ann, Dec 22, 1973; children: Marshall Danzy & Anne Kathryn. **Educ:** Oral Roberts Univ, BS;1971; Southwest Grad Sch Banking, grad; South Meth Univ. **Career:** Bank Okla, Tulsa, OK, mkt vpres; Univ Village Inc, Tulsa, OK, adminr, beginning 1972; Spike USA Inc, pres & chief exec officer; Fremont Corp, Tulsa, OK, pres & owner, currently; The Bldg Community Inst, pres, currently, staff, Oral Roberts Univ. **Orgs:** Bd mem, Tulsa United Way; bd mem, Thomas Gilcrease Mus; bd mem, Tulsa Goodwill Indust; exec bd mem, Tulsa Metrop Chamber Com; bd mem, Bus Indust Develop Corp. **Honors/Awds:** National Volunteer, Natl Arthritis Fedn, 1985; Manager of the Year, Oklahoma Chapter Natl Mgt Assn, 1989. **Special Achievements:** Author, Once Upon a Time When We Were Colored, Coun Oak Publ Co, 1989; Watching the crops come in, 1996; Eight Habits of the Heart: The Timeless Qualities That Build Strong Communities, Within Our Homes and Our Lives, 1997. **Military Serv:** USAF, sgt, 1964-68. **Business Phone:** 888-388-6348.

TAYARI, KABILI
Manager. **Personal:** Born Jun 26, 1950, Wilson, NC. **Educ:** Jersey City State Col, BA, Media & Health Sci, 1974; Seton Hall Univ, grad study, 1976. **Career:** Hudson Co Welfare, analyst, 1974-78; Vornado Inc, mgr, 1974-79; Conrail Passenger Div, opers mgr, 1978-80; freelance lect, 1980-; Jersey City Bd Educ, chmn, 1996. **Orgs:** NAACP, 1968; African Heritage Studies Asn, 1970-; exec mem, NJ Asn Black Educ, 1972-; Am Federation State Co & Municipal Employs, 1974-76; coalition Black Trade Unionists, 1974-75; producer & critic Intl TV Asn, 1978-; Am Mgt Asn, 1978-; nat presiding officer Nat Black Independent Polit Party, 1980-; prog coordr & tutor, Title 20 Aftersch Recreation & Tutorial Prog Eastern Co YMCA, 1980-84; Nat Title I & Chap I Adv Coun; rep, Nat Black Leadership Roundtable; secy, Greenville Nat Little League; pres, Jersey City City Wide Parents Coun May, 1985-; NJ Black Issues Convention. **Honors/Awds:** Community Service Award, Black Asn Alumni Faculty Staff & Students Organ Jersey City State Col, 1981; Community Service Award, Title I & Chapter I Dist Wide Parents Adv Coun, 1985. *

TAYLOR, AARON MATTHEW
Football player, television game show host. **Personal:** Born Nov 14, 1972, San Francisco, CA. **Educ:** Univ Notre Dame, BA, sociol. **Career:** Football player (retired), Television game show host; Green Bay Packers, guard, 1995-97; San Diego Chargers, guard, 1998-99; ABC Sports, analyst; CBS Col Sports, analyst, 2003-. **Orgs:** Impact Endowment Fund. **Honors/Awds:** Lombardi Award, 1993; Notre Dame Lineman of the Year Award, Nat Football Found, 1993; Rookie of the Year, 1995.

TAYLOR, ALMINA
Musician, educator. **Personal:** Born Mar 24, 1933, Shelby, NC; daughter of Goald R and Willie Mae; married Charles H Taylor Jr, Aug 23, 1970; children: Angela T Bunch, Charles III, Barbara Spruill & Robert Owens III. **Educ:** Va State Univ, BS, vocal music educ, 1954, MS, music educ, 1971; Norfolk State Col, 1964 & 1967; Univ Richmond, 1980; Univ Va, 1977; Old Dominion Univ, 1981, 1986; Shenandoah Conservatory, 1983; Westchester Univ, 1985. **Career:** Person County High Sch, choral directress, 1954-55; Portsmouth Pub Schs, elem grades & music teacher, choral directress, 1955-62, jr high sch choral directress, 1962-79; Mt Pleasant Baptist Church, organist, choir directress, 1952-62; Norcom High Sch, music career teacher, choir directress, 1979-91; Fel United Church Christ, organist, choir directress, 1978. **Orgs:** Nat Educ Asn; Nat Music Educr Conf; Va Music Educr Asn; Portsmouth Educ Asn; Alpha Kappa Alpha Sorority; Portsmouth Chap Delicados Inc; Portsmouth Chap Pinochle Bugs; Portsmouth Alpha Wires. **Honors/Awds:** Choral Parents Norcom High Sch, VIP, 1983; 10 Year Service Award, Women's Fel, Fel United Church Christ, 1990; Portsmouth Chap Delicados Inc, Black Educators Award, 1993. **Home Addr:** 1409 Carson Crescent W, Portsmouth, VA 23701, **Home Phone:** (757)488-0381.

TAYLOR, ANDERSON
Real estate agent, teacher. **Personal:** Born in Autaugaville, AL; married Virginia Burgohoy. **Educ:** Tuskegee Inst AL, BS, 1956; Bradley Univ Peoria IL, MS, 1963; Atlanta Univ GA, attended 1965; GA Tech, attended 1968; Univ GA. **Career:** Real estate agent (retired); MS Voc Col Itta Bena MS, teacher, 1957-59; Douglass Sch, teacher, 1959-65; Carver Voc HS Atlanta, teacher, 1965-74; Walter F George HS, dct coord, teacher; self-employed, real estate. **Orgs:** Ed Lowndes City Christian Movement, 1966, Overseas Teacher Aid Prog Ethiopia NEA, 1967, Are Ind Arts Addis Tech TTI Univ, 1970; master Boy Scouts KeyW, 1962-64; deacon Bethel AME Ch, 1960-65; dir, Anti-Pov Prog Haynesville AL; faculty rep, Carver Voc Sch, 1971-74; chmn, Ind Arts Dept. **Honors/Awds:** Award, Spec Summer Prog Univ GA NEA, 1967; Teacher of the Year, 1974-75; Cert Ind Arts, Self-Study Career Ed Prog Univ GA. *

TAYLOR, ANDRE JEROME
Public utility executive. **Personal:** Born Sep 10, 1946, Mobile, AL; son of Doris Collins and Willie; married Vivian Buffis, Feb 14, 1982; children: Tara, Marla, Andre & Gordon. **Educ:** Tuskegee Inst, AL, attended 1967; Univ Ala, Tuscaloosa, AL, BA, 1972. **Career:** Public utility executive (retired); WBRC-TV, Birmingham, AL, public affairs dir, 1973-75; WACD Radio, Alexander City, AL, asst gen mgr, 1975; WBLX-FM, Mobile, AL, acct exec, 1975-77; Ala Ed TV Commis, Birmingham, AL, asst dir prog eval, 1977-79; Birmingham Cable Commun, Birmingham, AL, community rels dir, 1979-84; Ala Gas Corp, Birmingham, AL, asst vpres community affairs, vpres commun. **Orgs:** Exec comt, Jefferson Co Chap, Univ Ala Alumni Asn; prs cabinet, Univ Ala; exec comt, Birmingham Area Boy Scouts Coun; bd, Birmingham Chap, Am Red Cross; bd dirs, Nat Multiple Sclerosis Soc; Kappa Alpha Psi; AABE; Birmingham Asn Black Journalists; past chmn, Ala Veterans Leadership Prog; bd mem, Baptist Health Syst; pres, Ala Nat Alumni Asn, 2003-04; adv bd, Plank Ctr. **Honors/Awds:** Outstanding Alumni Public Relations, Univ Ala Sch Communs; Entrepreneur of the Year Award, Birmingham Black MBA Asn. **Special Achievements:** First black president of the Alabama's National Alumni Association. **Military Serv:** AUS, E-5, 1967-71; Purple Heart, Bronze Star.

TAYLOR, ANNA DIGGS (ANNA KATHERINE JOHNSTON)
Judge. **Personal:** Born Dec 9, 1932, Washington, DC; daughter of Hazel B Johnston and V D Johnston; married Charles C Diggs Jr, Jan 1, 1960 (divorced 1971); children: Douglass Johnston Diggs & Carla Cecilia Diggs; married Martin. **Educ:** Barnard Col, BA, 1954; Yale Univ, LLB, 1957. **Career:** Dept Labor, atty off solicitor, 1957-60; Wayne Co MI, asst prosecutor, 1961-62; Eastern Dist MI, asst US atty, 1966; Detroit off mgr, legis assist to US Rep Charles C Diggs Jr, 1967-70; Zwerdling, Maurer, Diggs &Papp, partner, 1970-75; City Detroit, asst corp coun, 1975-79; Wayne State Univ Sch Labor & Indust Rels, adj prof, 1972-75; City Detroit, Law Dept, supvr asst corp coun, 1975-79; Wayne State Univ Law Sch, adj prof, 1972-75; MI, Eastern Dist Detroit, US Dist Ct, judge, 1979-99, chief judge, 1996-98, sr judge, 1999-. **Orgs:** Trustee, Henry Ford Health System; Founders Soc, DIA; Community Found SEMI; Fed Bar Asn, State Bar MI, Wolverine Bar Asn, Women Lawyers Asn MI; trustee, Community Found S Eastern MI; yres, Yale Law Alumni asn; Fed Bar; Wolverine Bar; Black Judges Asn; Women Judges Asn; Nat Lawyer's Guild. **Honors/Awds:** NBA Women Lawyer's Division Award, 1981; Michigan SCLC Award, 1984; Calvary Church Bridge Bladders Award, 1984; Absalom Jones Award Michigan Black Episcopalians, 1986; Detroit-Wolverine Bar Asn Bench Bar

Award, 1990; Michigan Bell Living the Dream Award, 1991; Detroit Urban League Achievement Award, 1991; Histadrut Menorah Award, 1991; Women's Economic Club Dynamic Women Award, 1992; Steaker Bar Asn Trailblazers Award, 1995; Int Institute Hall of Fame, 1998; Marygrove Col, hon Doctor laws, 2000; Bleede Women Lawyers of MI Award, 2003. **Special Achievements:** First black woman judge to be appointed to the United States District Court for the Eastern District of Michigan & First black woman Chief Judge. **Business Addr:** Judge, United States District Court, Eastern District of Michigan, 231 W Lafayette Blvd Room 1031, Detroit, MI 48226, **Business Phone:** (313)234-5105.

TAYLOR, ARNOLD H.
Educator. **Personal:** Born Nov 29, 1929, Regina, VA. **Educ:** VA Union Univ, BA, 1951; Howard Univ, MA, 1952; The Cath Univ Am, PhD, 1963. **Career:** Social Univ, New Benedict Col, from instr to prof hist, 1955-64; Orleans,prof hist, chmn div soc sci, 1964-65; NC Centrol Univ, prof hist, 1965-70; Ford Found fel, 1969-70; Univ Conn, Sterrs, prof hist, 1970-72; auth:Travail & Triumph; Am Diplomacy & Narcotics Traffic, 1969; Black Life &Cult S Since the Civil War, 1976; Howard Univ, prof hist & dept chmn, 1972-2002, emer prof, 2002-. **Orgs:** Asn Study Afro Am Life & Hist; Social Hist Asn; Am Hist Asn; Orgn Am Historians; Am Hist Jadavpur Univ, Calcutta, India, 1967-68. **Honors/Awds:** Nat Endowment on the Humanities, 1968; Am Coun Learned Soc, 1969. **Military Serv:** AUS corpl, 1952-54. **Business Addr:** Emeritus Professor, Howard University, 2400 Sixth St, Washington, DC 20059.

TAYLOR, BENJAMIN GARLAND
Law enforcement officer. **Personal:** Born Feb 27, 1950, Detroit, MI; son of Douglas A Taylor (deceased) and Evelyn N; married Madonna Darlene; children: Angelena R. **Educ:** Wayne County Community Col, AS, 1976; Wayne State Univ, attended 1979. **Career:** Detroit Police Dept, eastern oper enforcement, 1975-82, criminal invest bur, gang squad, 1982-92, headquarters bur, clerical opers, 1992-, narcotics bur, 1997-, sgt, 1999-. **Orgs:** Wayne County Col Alumni Asn; Lieutenants & Sergeants Asn. **Honors/Awds:** Officer of the Year, Detroit Police Officers Asn, 1994; Award of Recognition, Detroit City Coun, 1986. **Special Achievements:** Lifesaving Citation, Detroit Police Dept, 1994, 1998; Detroit Police Dept, Chief of Police citation, 2001; 20 Citations and Commendations, Detroit Police Dept. **Military Serv:** US Marine Corps, corporal, 1968-74; Good Conduct Medal, Nat Defense Service Medal, FMF. **Home Addr:** 18645 Robson St, Detroit, MI 48235, **Home Phone:** (313)273-8209. **Business Phone:** (313)237-2555.*

TAYLOR, BILLY. See TAYLOR, WILLIAM EDWARD.

TAYLOR, BOBBY (ROBERT TAYLOR, III)
Football player. **Personal:** Born Dec 28, 1973, Houston, TX; son of Robert. **Educ:** Univ Notre Dame. **Career:** Football player (retired); Philadelphia Eagles, defensive back, 1995-2003; Seattle Seahawks, corner back, 2004.

TAYLOR, CARL
Chief executive officer, founder (originator). **Career:** First Impressions Group, chief exec officer, currently. **Business Addr:** Chief Executive Officer, First Impressions Group, 1249 Washington Blvd Suite 1210, Detroit, MI 48226, **Business Phone:** (313)963-9837.*

TAYLOR, CAROL
Association executive, journalist. **Personal:** Born Dec 27, 1931, Boston, MA; daughter of William and Ruth; married Rex Legall; children: Cindy & Harry. **Educ:** Elmira Col, 1951; NY Univ, 1956. **Career:** Mohawk Airlines, flight attend, 1958; Pearl & Edric Conners Theatrical Agency, mgr, 1961-63; Flamingo Magazine, London, England, journalist, 1962-63; exec secy, Barbados, 1964-68; private duty nurse, 1977-86; Inst Interracial Harmony Inc, pres, 1982-; freelance journalist; tv show presenter. **Orgs:** Institute for "Interracial" Harmony Inc, 1982-. **Honors/Awds:** Award for Committment, Black African Holocaust Coun, 1994; Honor Carol Taylor Day declared, Natl Action Network, 1996; Outstanding Woman of Culture Award, Natl Action Network, 1996; Achievement Award, Org Black Am Airline Pilots, 1998; Outstanding Dedication to Youth, Flatbush Boys & Girls Club, 2000. **Special Achievements:** First black flight attendant, Mohawk Airlines; founder & edi nursing jnl, Barbados, 1965; published numerous magazine & newspaper articles, 1960-; author, The Little Black Book, 1985. **Business Addr:** President, Inst Interracial Harmony Inc, 590 Flatbush Suite 11A, Brooklyn, NY 11225-4935, **Business Phone:** (718)856-1271.

TAYLOR, CAROL ANN
Lawyer. **Personal:** Born Jan 17, 1956, Toledo, OH; divorced; children: Stephanie Travis & Jeremy Travis. **Educ:** Carleton Col, BA, 1978; Univ Minnesota Law Sch, JD, 1981. **Career:** Western Life, contract analyst, 1982-85; Northwestern Nat Life, product develop analyst, 1985-87; Amerisure Life, claims/compliance mgr, 1987-88; Mich Mutual, assoc coun, 1988-89, coun, 1989-93, asst vpres, coun; Amerisure Mutual Ins Co, asst vpres, currently. **Orgs:** Minn Bar Asn, 1985-; Am Bar Asn, 1988-; Mich Bar Asn, 1988-; coun, Magnolia Neighborhood Bd, 1990-. **Honors/Awds:** Minority Achievers Award, YWCA, 1989; Parent Volunteer, Girls Scouts Am, 1992; Volunteer Tutor, Detroit Tutorial Ctr, 1993. **Home Addr:** 18155 Magnolia St, Southfield, MI 48075, **Home Phone:** (810)559-0858. **Business Addr:** Assistant Vice President, Amerisure Mutual Insurance Company, 26777 Halsted Rd, PO Box 2060, Farmington Hills, MI 48333-2060, **Business Phone:** (248)426-7938.

TAYLOR, CAROLE LILLIAN
Educator. **Personal:** Born in Pittsburgh, PA; children: Colette & Yvette. **Educ:** BS, 1971; MEd, 1972; PhD, 1973; spec dipl, 1975. **Career:** EPIC Inc, exec fdr; Akronite Mag, fashion ed, 1967-68; Tolatr Highland Park Prep Acad, exec dir, currently; EPIC Pitts Bd Educ, exec, 1973-77, teacher, 1972-77; Tolafr Acad Elem Sch, 1978; Univ Pitts, Am Asn Univ Profs, model instr. **Orgs:** Int Platform Asn; Doctorate Asn Univ Pitts; Am Asn Univ Profs. **Honors/Awds:** Outstanding accomplishments in letters, Delta Sigma Theta, 1976; Robert LVann Award, Pittsburgh Courier; Essence Woman Year, 1985, Essence Magazine, 1985; Those Eyes, album (jazz) 1986; Speak & Read, text (instructional manual reading prog) 1987. **Business Addr:** Executive Director, Tolatr Highland Park Preparatory Academy, 1112 N Negley Ave, Pittsburgh, PA 15206, **Business Phone:** (412)361-7733.

TAYLOR, CHARLES E.
Executive. **Personal:** Born Jun 5, 1944, Columbus, OH; son of Robert and Catherine; married Judy Marshall; children: Enid, Antjuan, Jerome. **Educ:** Ohio State Univ, Columbus OH, BA, 1967, MA, 1969, PhD, 1971. **Career:** S Side Settlement House, prog dir, 1967-68; Ohio State Univ, Columbus OH, teaching res assoc, 1968-69; Columbus Metrop Area Community Action Org, dir, 1969-70; VISTA, prog officer, 1969; Urban Resources, consult, 1970; Battelle Mem Inst, consult, 1970; Wash Internships Educ, intern, 1970-71; Inst Educ Leadership, staff assoc, 1971-72; Acad Contemp Problems, vpres opers, 1972-76; Wilberforce Univ, pres, 1976-84; Stand Oil Co, dir contrib & comm affairs, 1984-86; Stand Oil Co Marine Transport, gen mgr, 1986-89; Brand Implementation & Control, USA, mgr, 1989, mgr, Pub Affairs, 1991; Lamadie Amrop Int, partner, 1991-93, managing partner, 1993; Morris Brown Col, pres, 2003; The Hollins Group Inc, exec vpres, currently. **Orgs:** Steering community Develop Comn Greater Columbus, 1974-76; bd dir, chmn, Govt Rels Comm Berwick Civic Asn, 1974; bd dir, treas Columbus Area Leadership Prog, 1974-75; bd dir, CARE Regional Resources Bd, 1974-76; exec comt, Franklin County Dem Party, 1974-76; bd dir, chmn, personnel comm Neighborhood Develop Corp, 1974-76; Full Employment Action Coun; fel, adv bd, Joint Ctr Polit Studies; bd trustees, Franklin Univ, 1975-76; bd educ, Shaker Heights OH, 1985-89; bd dir, Ameritrust Develop Bank, 1988-; bd trustees, Univ Akron 1988-; fac, Inst Pract Polit; exec dir, Columbus Area Leadership Prog; dir, Ohio Educ Sem Am Educ Res Asn; Am Asn Sch Admin; Am Mgt Asn; Am Acad Polit & Social Sci; author producer Color Line WVKO radio; bd dir, chmn, prog com Columbus Urban League; bd dir Blacks Against Drugs Uhuru Drug Treatment Facility; chmn, Manpower Adv Coun for Columbus, Franklin Col. **Honors/Awds:** Community Service Award, Columbus Urban League; talents, style & lead award Columbus Area Lead Program; Award for Asst to Acad for Contemp Problems, Battelle Memorial Inst; Award for Inspiration to Help Humanity, Asn Black Sec. **Special Achievements:** Top 25 Black Managers, Black Enterprise; Professional of the Year, Black Prof Asn Cleveland. **Business Addr:** Executive Vice President, The Hollins Group Inc, 1720 Mars Hill Rd Suite 307, Acworth, GA 30101, **Business Phone:** (770)420-9506.

TAYLOR, DR. CHARLES E
College president, educator, businessperson. **Personal:** Born Jun 5, 1944, Columbus, OH; son of Robert and Catherine; married Judy; children: Enid, Antjuan & Jerome. **Educ:** Ohio State Univ, BA, 1967, MA, 1969, PhD (educ), 1971. **Career:** S Side Settlement House, prog dir, 1967-68; Ohio State Univ, Columbus OH, teaching res assoc, 1968-69; Columbus Metrop Area Community Action Org, dir, 1969-70; VISTA, prog officer, 1969; Urban Resources, consult, 1970; Battelle Mem Inst, consult, 1970; Wash Internships Educ, intern, 1970-71; Inst Educ Leadership, staff assoc, 1971-72; Acad Contemp Problems, vpres opers, 1972-76; Wilberforce Univ, pres, 1976-84; Stand Oil Co, dir contrib & comm affairs, 1984-86; Stand Oil Co Marine Transport, gen mgr, 1986-89; Brand Implementation & Control, USA, mgr, 1989, mgr, Pub Affairs, 1991; Lamadie Amrop Int, partner, 1991-93, managing partner, 1993; Morris Brown Col, pres, 2002-03; The Hollins Group Inc, exec vpres, currently. **Orgs:** Steering community Develop Comn Greater Columbus, 1974-76; bd dir, chmn, Govt Rels Comm Berwick Civic Asn, 1974; bd dir, treas Columbus Area Leadership Prog, 1974-75; bd dir, CARE Regional Resources Bd, 1974-76; exec comt, Franklin County Dem Party, 1974-76; bd dir, chmn, personnel comm Neighborhood Develop Corp, 1974-76; Full Employment Action Coun; fel, adv bd, Joint Ctr Polit Studies; bd trustees, Franklin Univ, 1975-76; bd educ, Shaker Heights OH, 1985-89; bd dir, Ameritrust Develop Bank, 1988-; bd trustees, Univ Akron 1988-; fac, Inst Pract Polit; exec dir, Columbus Area Leadership Prog; dir, Ohio Educ Sem Am Educ Res Asn; Am Asn Sch Admin; Am Mgt Asn; Am Acad Polit & Social Sci; author producer Color Line WVKO radio; bd dir, chmn, prog com Columbus Urban League; bd dir Blacks Against Drugs Uhuru Drug Treatment Facility; chmn, Manpower Adv Coun for Columbus, Franklin Col. **Honors/Awds:** Community Service Award, Columbus Urban League; talents, style & lead award Columbus Area Lead Program; Award for Asst to Acad for Contemp Problems, Battelle Memorial Inst; Award for Inspiration to Help Humanity, Asn Black Sec. **Special Achievements:** Top 25 Black Managers, Black Enterprise; Professional of the Year, Black Prof Asn Cleveland. **Business Addr:** Executive Vice President, The Hollins Group Inc, 1720 Mars Hill Rd Suite 307, Acworth, GA 30101, **Business Phone:** (770)420-9506.

TAYLOR, CHARLES EDWARD
Lawyer. **Personal:** Born Apr 19, 1931, Cincinnati, OH; son of I B and Lenora Braden; married Fern Godette. **Educ:** Brown Univ, Providence, AB, 1957; Harvard Grad Sch Bus, 1957-58; Georgetown Univ, JD, 1983. **Career:** IBM Corp, br mgr, sales, 1963-89, dir govt prog, 1978-89, prog mgr; Charles E Taylor Esq & Assoc, atty-at-law, currently. **Orgs:** Alpha Phi Alpha, 1963-; Nat Bar Asn, 1983-; Am Bar Asn, 1983-; DC Bar, 1983-; Africare, 1987-. **Military Serv:** AUS, lt, 1951-53. **Home Addr:** 9920 Hall Rd, Potomac, MD 20854, **Home Phone:** (301)299-4988. **Business Addr:** Attorney, Charles E Taylor Esquire & Associates, 1367 Conn Ave Suite 200, Washington, DC 20036, **Business Phone:** (202)728-9486.

TAYLOR, CHARLES ROBERT. See TAYLOR, CHARLEY R.

TAYLOR, CHARLEY R. (CHARLES ROBERT TAYLOR)
Football coach, consultant, football player. **Personal:** Born Sep 28, 1941, Prairie View, TX; son of James Stevenson and Myrtle; married Patricia Grant; children: Charley, Elizabeth Erin & Erica. **Educ:** Ariz State Univ. **Career:** Football Player(retired), Football coach (retired), consultant; Wash Redskins, prof football player, running back, receiver, halfback, split end, 1964-78, Front Office Dept, scout, 1978-81, receivers coach, 1981-94, consult, currently; Game & Inland Fisheries Community, Va, consult, 1983; Dept Conserv & Recreation, Va, 1999. **Orgs:** Northern Greater Love; Special Olympics, Mentally Retarded Bowls, 1963; appointed mem, Va Governor Charles Robb, Game & Inland Fisheries Community, 1983. **Honors/Awds:** Rookie of the Year, NFL, 1964; All Pro, 1967, 1974; Offensive Player of the Year, Wash Redskins, 1974; Pro Football Hall Fame, 1984; Tex Hall Fame, 1985; Redskins Ring Fame; Wash Touchdown Club Hall Fame, 1992. **Special Achievements:** NFL's 4th all-time leading receiver, 649 catches for 9130 yards; Washington Redskins, first round draft pick, 1964, all-time leader in touchdowns; Outstanding Citizen, City Grand Prairie, Tx, 1964; First rookie in 20 years to finish in the NFL's top 10 in both rushing (sixth with 755 yards) and receiving (eight with 53 catches for 814 yards). **Business Addr:** Consultant, Washington Redskins, Redskin Pk, PO Box 17247, Washington, DC 20041, **Business Phone:** (703)478-8900.

TAYLOR, DR. CHRISTOPHER LENARD
Dentist. **Personal:** Born Dec 21, 1923, Charlotte, NC; son of Russell B and Viola; children: Ballinger & Russell III. **Educ:** Johnson C Smith Univ, BS, 1945; Howard Univ Dental Sch, attended 1950; Jersey City Med Ctr, internship, 1951. **Career:** Self-employed dentist, Los Angeles, 1951-. **Orgs:** Coast Dir Johnson C Smith Univ Alumni Asn, 1954-; pres, Pac Town Club, 1960; pres, Los Angeles Chap Nat Asn Advan Colored People, 1962-64; gen chmn, Comn Police Brutality; Rally 2nd Bapt Ch, 1961; orgn gen chmn, Los Angeles Civil Rights Rally, 1963; chmn, United Civil Rights Comm; founder, chmn & life mem, Los Angeles Chap Nat Asn Advan Colored People; life mem, dinner, 1963-65; chmn bd, Chris T RB III Corp; chmn bd, T & T Dental Corp; Johnson C Smith Univ Charities; CORE; Howard Univ; United Way; Urban League; Johnson C Smith Alumni Asn; Omega Psi Phi Fraternity; Alpha Kappa Mu Fraternity; Pac Town Club; Am Dent Asn; Nat Dent Asn; Int Dental Soc; Angel City Dent Soc; life mem, Int Anesthesiol Soc; Westminster Neighbourhood Asn; Howard Univ Alumni Asn. **Honors/Awds:** Alumni Achievement Award, Howard Univ, 1966; Scroll for Civil Rights Achievement, Los Angeles City Coun, 1969; Award, Church of the Advent, 1970; ANC Mothers' Award, 1972. **Military Serv:** AUS, WWII, Korean War vet. **Business Addr:** Dentist, 8918 S Vermont Ave, Los Angeles, CA 90044.

TAYLOR, DR. CLEDIE COLLINS
Art museum director, educator. **Personal:** Born Mar 8, 1926, Bolivar, AR; daughter of Osie Gaines and Dallas; children: Paul Dallas (deceased). **Educ:** Wayne State Univ, BS, 1948, MA, 1957; L'Universita Per Stranieri, Cert etruscology, 1968; Wayne State Univ, SP cert humanities art & hist, 1970; Union Grad Sch, PhD, art hist, 1978. **Career:** Detroit Pub Sch, art teacher, 1979; Detroit Pub Sch, supvr art, 1980-; Wayne State Univ, instr fashion design, 1981; Pri Jewelry Design, practicing metal craftsperson; Children's Museum, asst dir, 1987-91; Arts Extended Gallery Inc, founder & dir, currently. **Orgs:** Chmn, Detroit Coun Arts, 1977-81; chmn, Minority Arts Adv Panel, Mich Coun Arts, 1982-; trustees, Haystack Mountain Sch Crafts, 1982-; Detroit Scarab Club, 1983-; adv & liason, Detroit Art Teachers Asn, 1983-; art adv, Nat Asn African Diaspora, 1980-; dir, Art Symposium Suri-

nam NAAD Conf, 1982; Berea Lutheran Church; Alpha Kappa Alpha Sorority; dir, Art Symposium Barbados; Mich Coun Arts, 1987-; bd, Michigan Arts Found, 1988-. **Honors/Awds:** Spirit of Detroit Award, City Detroit, 1983; Award, Spirit of Detroit, City Detroit Small Bus, 1988; Governor's Award for Contribution to Art Education, 1989. **Special Achievements:** Book published "Journey to Odiamola", 1978; "Words in a SketchBook", 1985; curator- "African Tales in Words And Wood", 1984; curator- "Tribute to Ernest Hardman" Exhibit Scarab Club, 1985; One Hundred Black Women for Art and Literature, 1989; First guest curator, Charles Wright Mus African History, Clearstory, 2000. **Business Addr:** Director, Arts Extended Gallery Incorporated, David Whitney Bldg 1553 Woodward Suite 2121, Detroit, MI 48226, **Business Phone:** (313)831-0321.

TAYLOR, CORA. See Obituaries section.

TAYLOR, DAISY CURRY
Government official. **Personal:** Born Jul 24, 1948, Fort Lauderdale, FL; married Theodore D; children: Tamila Annay & Tiffany Patrice. **Educ:** Bethune-Cookman, liberal arts, attended 1970; Nova Univ, MPA, 1975; Cong Prof Devel Cert Cong Asst, 1984. **Career:** Fla Mem Col, res analyst, 1970-71; City Ft Lauderdale, admin aide, 1971-74; City Oakland Pk, dir community affairs, 1974-84; Exquisito Serv Ft Lauderdale Mgt Consult Firm, chmn bd & pres; Congressman E Clay Shaw, cong aide, 1984-. **Orgs:** Bd dir, Area Agency Aging, 1974-; Early Childhood Develop, 1978-81; Community Action Agency, 1983-; Urban League; Nat Asn Advan Colored People; Task Force Black Aged Women Bus; Am Soc Pub Admin; The Forum Black Pub Admin; Urban League Guild; E Broward Med Asn Found; bd mem, Black Coalition Broward; bd mem, Coun African Am Econ Devel. **Honors/Awds:** Community Service, Area Agency on Aging, 1979; Outstanding Citizen Community Partnership, 1981; Outstanding Contribution, Broward City Mt Herman AME Church, 1985; Women in Business, 1986. **Business Addr:** Congressional Aide, E Clay Shaw, 299 E Broward Blvd, Fort Lauderdale, FL 33301.

TAYLOR, DR. DALE B
Educator, counselor. **Personal:** Born Jun 13, 1939, Topeka, KS; son of Wesley E and Cassie L Moten; married Marguerite Davis, Mar 14, 1981; children: Shannon Michelle Davis & Shawn Jeffery Taylor. **Educ:** Col Emporia, KS, 1959; Univ Kans, BMus Educ, 1963, Music Educ, 1971, PhD, 1984. **Career:** Milwaukee County Mental Health Ctr, music therapist, 1963; Mendota State Hosp, dir music ther, 1964-67; Univ Wis Eau Claire, dir music ther, 1969-, affirmative action adv & rev bd, 1994-, Dept Allied Health Prof, chair, prof & chair emer, currently; clin fac, Univ Kans, Dept AMEMT, 1979-80. **Orgs:** Co-founder, Wis Chap Music Ther, 1973; vis clinician, Univ Mo, Kans City, 1975; vis clinician, Mt Senario Col, 1975; assembly delegates & int relations comt, Nat Asn Music Ther Inc, 1976-83, 1985-97; pres, Great Lakes Region NAMT, 1976-78; vice commodore, Lake Wissota Yacht Club, 1978-80, commodore, 1985-87, racing chmn, 1981-83; grants review panelist, Wis Arts Bd, 1984-90; Eau Claire Affirmative Action Review Comt, 1984-90; bd dirs, Int Asn Music Handicapped Inc, 1986-91; adv comt, Univ Wis, Syst Inst Race & Ethnicity, 1988-90; planning comn, Univ Wis Syst Design Diversity Conf, 1989; conductor, accompanist, Eau Claire Gospel Choir, 1987-; Inst Arts Med Asn, 1990-; book & media rev ed, 1990-97, int advisory com 1990-, ed 1997-; vpres, Valley Gospel Choir; soloist, Valley Gospel Choir, 1992-. **Honors/Awds:** Spec ambassador, Europe People-to-People, 1962; US deleg, Int Symp Music Educ Handicapped, 1980, 1983, 1985; Pi Kappa Lambda Music Hon Soc; Hon Martin Luther King Memorial Libr Display, 1985; Biol Music Making Int Conf, 1987; US deleg, Int Soc Music Educ, Res Seminar Comn, Music Spec Educ, Music Thera & Music Med, Australia, 1988, Estonia, USSR, 1990, Korea, 1992, 1998; US deleg, Int Soc Music Educ, 1992; US deleg, First US Japan Int Arts Med Leadership Conf, 1993. **Special Achievements:** Author of "Biomedical Foundations of Music as Therapy"; author of 20 publication professional books & journals. **Business Addr:** Professor, Chair Emeritus, University Wisconsin-Eau Claire, Department Allied Health Professions, 105 Garfield Ave, PO Box 4004, Eau Claire, WI 54702-4004, **Business Phone:** (715)836-2628.

TAYLOR, DAVID RICHARD, III
Lawyer. **Personal:** Born Dec 17, 1949, Toledo, OH; son of David Richard Jr and Shirley L Swan; married Mary J Carrigan, Dec 12, 1987; children: Stacee L, Courtnee D, Davon R, Renesa Y, Evan K & Antoine L. **Educ:** Univ Toledo, BA, 1971, Col Law, JD, 1974. **Career:** Lucas County Juvenile Ct, referee, 1976-78; Lucas County Domestic Rels Ct, referee, 1978-80, chief referee, 1980-84; McConnell & Taylor Assocs, atty & partner, 1984-; State OH, atty gen, spec coun, 1989-90; Lucas County Ment Health Bd, atty & coun, 1990. **Orgs:** Life mem, pres, 1997-98, Nat Asn Advan Colored People, Toledo Br; life mem, Univ Toledo Alumni Asn; life mem, Kappa Alpha Psi Fraternity. **Honors/Awds:** Hall of Fame, Calvin M Woodward High Sch, 1999. **Special Achievements:** First African-American appointed attorney & referee, Lucas County Juvenile Domestic Relations Court, 1976; only African Ameriacn to serve as chief referee, 1980-84; publications: "After the Revelation: Show and Tell," The Christian Reporter, 2002; "The Danger of Being Blessed," The Full Gospel Baptist Times, 2002; "The Real Enemy of the Church," The Full Gospel Baptist Times, 2002; The Christian Reporter, 2002, "A Call to Greatness," The Full Gospel Baptist Times, 2002. **Home Addr:** 351 Sentry Hill Rd, Toledo, OH 43615, **Home Phone:** (419)531-5638. **Business Addr:** Attorney, Partner, McConnell & Taylor Associates, 316 N Mich St Suite 700, Toledo, OH 43624, **Business Phone:** (419)241-6282.

TAYLOR, DR. DAVID VASSAR
School administrator, educator. **Personal:** Born Jul 13, 1945, St Paul, MN; son of Eula Vassar Murphy and Clarence Taylor; married Josephine Reed, Mar 27, 1976; children: Tyrone & Kenneth. **Educ:** Univ Minn, BA, 1967; Univ Nebr, MA, 1971, PhD 1977; Harvard Univ, IEM Prog, 1985. **Career:** St Olaf Col, Northfield Minn, dir, Am minority studies prog, 1974-76; State Univ New York New Paltz Campus, chairperson, black studies dept, 1977-78; Hubert Humphrey Collection Minn Historical Soc, cur, 1978-79; Macalester Col, dir minority, spec serv prog, 1979-83; Col Charleston, dean undergrad studies, 1983-86; Minn State Univ Syst Office, assoc vice chancellor, acad affairs, 1986-89; Univ Minn, Gen Col, assoc prof, dean, 1989-2005; Morehouse Col, provost & sr vpres acad affairs, 2005-. **Orgs:** Bd dirs, Hallie Q Brown Comm Ctr, St Paul, 1978-79; Bd adv, Perrie Jones Libr Fund, St Paul, 1979-80; Minn Quality Life Study, 1979-80; vestry St Phillip's Episcopal Church 1978-81; bd trustees, Seabury Western Theol Sem, 1985-90; chair, bd, Penumbra Theatre Co; bd, Friends Saint Paul Pub Librs; treas, Jean Covington Fund; adv bd, Moore House Res Inst. **Honors/Awds:** Josie R Johnson Human Rights & Social Justice Award, Univ Minn, 1999. **Special Achievements:** Author bibliography & 3 articles. **Military Serv:** AUS, spec 5, 1969-70; Bronze Star & several commendations. **Business Addr:** Provost & Senior Vice President for Academic Affairs, Morehouse College, 830 Westview Dr SW, Atlanta, GA 30314.

TAYLOR, DR. DONALD FULTON, SR.
College administrator. **Personal:** Born Jul 10, 1932, Charles Town, WV; married Phyllis Shirley Jackson; children: Donald Jr, Keith C, Pamela Jackson, Mark J & Christy A Butts. **Educ:** Shepherd Col, AB, 1957; Johns Hopkins Univ, ScD, 1971; Va Union Univ, MDiv magna cum laude, 1982. **Career:** Darby Township High Sch, head, dept sci, 1958-65; Cheyney State Col, coordr, health sci, 1970-75; Norfolk State Univ, Sch Health Related Professions & Nat Sci, dean, 1975-95, dean emer, 1995-. **Orgs:** Pastor, Greater Mt Zion Baptist Church, 1985; chairperson, Eastern Va Health Educ Consort, 1985; bd dirs, Soc Aid of Sickle Cell Anemia, 1985; bd dirs, Nat Soc Allied Health, 1985; task force Med Aid, Orgn Transplant, 1985; bd dirs, Norfolk Area Health Educ Ctr, 1985; Prince Hall Masons, Norfolk Rotary Club; bd dir & treas, Norfolk Area Health Ed Ctr, 1985; Am Pub Health Asn, 1985; Va Asn Allied Health Prof, 1985; Va Pub Health Asn, 1985, Tidewater Metro Ministers Asn, 1985; bd dir, Chesapeake Hosp Authority, 1986-90; vpres, Norfolk Area Health Educ Ctr, 1986; adv bd, Juvenile Court Conf Comn, 1986-. **Honors/Awds:** Publication Allied Health Professions Admission Test, 1984; Carl Haven Young Award, Am Corrective Therapy Asn, 1984; Chapel of the Four Chaplins Award; Outstanding Educrs America-listing. **Military Serv:** AUS, pfc, 3-5 yrs; Silver Star, Bronze Star, 1948-51. **Home Addr:** 431 Ivy Cres, Chesapeake, VA 23325. *

TAYLOR, EARTHA LYNN
Lawyer. **Personal:** Born Oct 28, 1957, Gary, IN; daughter of Silas and Mirtha; divorced; children: Barrett Alexander Boone. **Educ:** Ind Univ, BS, 1979; Valparaiso Univ Sch Law, JD, 1985. **Career:** Steven Rolle & Madden, law clerk, 1986-87; Law Off Frank Hernandez, 1987-88; Law Offices Eartha Taylor, atty, 1988-. **Orgs:** J L Turner Legal Asn, 1988-; Dallas Asn Black Women Attys, 1987-; Dallas Bar Asn, 1989-; Nat Bar Asn, 1988-. **Honors/Awds:** Pro-Bono Award, Texas Legal Serv, 1991& 1992. **Business Phone:** (214)943-8801.

TAYLOR, EDGAR R
Marketing executive, executive director. **Personal:** Born Sep 7, 1953, Cheyenne, WY; son of Edgar N and Jeanette; married Cheryl, Jul 12, 1975; children: Carly, Scott & Allison. **Educ:** Adelphi Univ, BA, 1975; Imede Univ, Lausanne, Switzerland, exec develop, 1990. **Career:** Carnation Co, acct exec, 1978-80, dist mgr, 1980-82, region mgr, 1982-84, prom mgr, 1984-86, merchandising dir, 1986-90, category dir, 1990-91; Nestle USA, mkt dir, 1991-, Banking Div, dir. **Orgs:** Bd dir, Prom Mkt Asn Am, 1989-; bd dir, Los Angeles Regional Food Bank, 1990-. **Honors/Awds:** Reggie Award, Mkt Effectiveness, PMAA, 1989; Businessman of the Year, Dollars & Sense Magazine, 1994. **Business Phone:** (818)549-6000.

TAYLOR, EDWARD WALTER
Executive. **Personal:** Born Jul 17, 1926, Baltimore, MD; son of Elbert and Rebecca; married Alene Lassiter. **Educ:** Hampton Inst, 1950; Johns Hopkins Univ, Univ Maryland, 1974. **Career:** US Govt, chief drafting, 1950-59; Henry L Lives Balt, architect mgr, 1958-63; Westinghouse Electric, mech designer, 1960-73; Edward Q Rogers Balt, architect, 1964-67; Sultor Campbell Architects Balt, architect mgr, 1968-73; Atti Consult Ltd, owner, 1973-90; Morgan State univ, architect. **Orgs:** Nat Tech Assoc; Comt Develop Adv Comn; Howard Park Civic Assoc; AIA; NW Outer Urban Coaltion; Nat Asn Advan Colored People; tech adv Pan African Congress; dir, Model Cities Housing Corp; chmn, MD Comn Develop Comt, 1973; tech consult, E Baltimore Comt Corp; graphics adv, Voc Ed Baltimore Construct Specif IST; Construct Specif Inst; vice chairperson, EDUC COMT Concord Baptist Church; Concord Baptist Church, vice chair, Christian educ, 1991, church sch supt, 1992. **Honors/Awds:** Man of the Year Award; Samuel Cheevers Award; Tribute Award, Nat Tech Assoc; Service Award, Concord Baptist Church, 1987; Man of the Year, Dunbar High Sch Baltimore; Baptist Educational Awardee, 1988. **Military Serv:** USAF, 1944-46. *

TAYLOR, ELLIS CLARENCE, SR.
Engineer. **Personal:** Born Feb 4, 1931, New Hebron, MS; married Marva Manning Whitney, Aug 31, 1970 (divorced 1980). **Educ:** Universal TV & Electronics Systs, dipl, 1953; Cleveland Inst Electronics, dipl, 1956, dipl, 1988; Univ Kans, attended 1962; Cent Tech Inst, attended 1968; Univ Miss, Kansas City, video prod studies, 1982. **Career:** Engineer (retired); KPRS Radio, part-time engr, 1957-58; Taylor's TV Serv & Sales, 1957-63; AM-FM station KPRS, chief engr; Forte Record Co, founder, 1966-83; Freelance Music Producer & Contractor, 1967; KMBC TV, staff engr 1968-98. **Orgs:** Licensing exam bd mem, KC Radio & TV, 1961-84; IBEW Exec Coun, 1977-79; mem, Nat Asn Advan Colored People; founding bd mem, United Minority Media Asn Miss, 1974-77; mem, Black Music Asn, 1980; mem, Soc of Broadcast Engrs, 1980-; life mem, Univ Miss, Kansas City, Alumni Asn; mem, Audio Engineering Soc Inc, 1986-; mem, Nat Rep Sen Inner Circle, 1991-; Rec Indust Am, 1976-83; Heritage Found; President's Men Club, 2001-. **Honors/Awds:** Senatorial Medal of Freedom, 1994. **Military Serv:** US Navy, gunnery, SN 1st Class, 1948-50; China Service Medal. **Home Addr:** 1859 E 76th St, PO Box 320541, Kansas City, MO 64132-2150, **Home Phone:** (816)444-2399. *

TAYLOR, ERIC CHARLES
Lawyer. **Personal:** Born Jun 25, 1962, Sacramento, CA; son of John C Jr and Joan E. **Educ:** Dartmouth Col, BA, 1984; Univ Va Sch Law, JD, 1988. **Career:** Pettit & Martin, atty, assoc, 1988-90; Sonnenshein, Nat & Rosenthal, atty, assoc, 1990-92; County Coun, County Los Angeles, supv judge, dep county counr, currently. **Orgs:** Pres, Career Ambitions Inc, 1989-. **Honors/Awds:** Edwin Gould Scholar, Dartmouth Col, 1984. **Home Addr:** 8712-J Chessington Dr, Inglewood, CA 90305, **Home Phone:** (310)412-0390. **Business Addr:** Deputy County Counsel, Supervising Judge, County of Los Angeles, County Counsel, Rm 358 Kenneth Hahn Hall Admin 500 W Temple St, Los Angeles, CA 90012, **Business Phone:** (213)974-2101.

TAYLOR, DR. ESTELLE WORMLEY
College teacher. **Personal:** Born Jan 12, 1924, Washington, DC; daughter of Luther Charles and Wilhelmina Jordan; married Ivan Earle, Dec 26, 1953. **Educ:** Miner Teachers Col, BS, 1945; Howard Univ, MA, 1947; Catholic Univ, PhD, 1969. **Career:** Howard Univ, instr eng & humanities, 1947-52; Langley Junior High, eng teacher, 1952-55; Eastern Sr High, eng teacher, 1955-63; Dist Columbia Teachers Col, eng instr, prof, 1963-76; Federal City Col, assoc provost, 1974-75; Dist Columbia Teachers Col, acting acad dean, 1975-76; Howard Univ, eng prof, chmn dept, 1976-85, assoc dean Col Liberal Arts, 1985-86, dir, Grad Expository Writing, 1988-91, prof emer, currently. **Orgs:** Nat Coun Teachers Eng, 1955-80; Modern Lang Asn Am, 1963-; life mem, Col Lang Asn, 1963-; Shakespeare Asn Am, 1965, 1979-, vpres, 1979-81, corresponding sec, 1989-91, recording sect, 1991-92, Capital City Links Inc; vice chmn, 1983, Univ Dist Columbia bd trustees; exec mem comt, Folger Inst, 1982-91; public mem, US Dept State Foreign Serv Selection Bd, 1983; Comn Higher Educ, 1984-91; public mem, Sr Threshold Foreign Serv Appointments Selections Bd, Agency Int Develop, 1984; res bd advis, Am Bibliographical Inst Inc, 1985-; Women's Nat Democratic Club, 1987-90; Malone Soc, 1987-90; life mem, Nat Coun Negro Women; District of Columbia Urban League; life mem, NAACP; life mem, Asn Study Afro-Am Life & Hist; assoc ed, Jour Afro-Am & Geneal Soc, 1990-93; Delta Sigma Theta Sorority; bd adv, Col Arts & Scis, Howard Univ, 2002-. **Honors/Awds:** Rockefeller/Aspen Institute fellowship, 1978-79; Outstanding Teacher in College of Liberal Arts, Howard Univ, 1980; Outstanding Contribution to Higher Education award, Univ District Columbia, Col Human Ecol, 1988; Middle State Association Service Award, 1989; Outstanding Contributions to Historically Black Colleges Award, 1995; Alumni Award Distinguished Achievement, Howard Univ, 1997. **Special Achievements:** Author of Survival or Surrender: The Dilemma of Higher Education, 1975; author of The Ironic Equation in Shakespeare's Othello: Appearances Equal Reality, 1977; The Masking in Othello and the Unmasking of Othello Criticism, 1984. **Business Addr:** Professor Emerita, Howard University, 3221 20th St NE, Washington, DC 20018.

TAYLOR, FELICIA MICHELLE
Government official, educator. **Personal:** Born Feb 14, 1960, Concord, NC; daughter of Milton Lee and Shirley Alsbrooks. **Educ:** Cabarrus Community Col, pvt pilot ground sch, 1982; Univ

NC, Chapel Hill, BA, sociol, 1982, Charlotte, MS, criminal justice, 1984; Fla State Univ, PhD, criminol, 1987-. **Career:** Univ NC, Charlotte, admis counr, 1983-84; Barber-Scotia Col, asst financial planning & develop, 1984-85; Shaw Univ, Raleigh, prof, 1985-87, CAPE Ctr, Wilmington, adj prof, 1992; The Fla State Univ, instr, 1988-91, Acad Support Servs, tutor, 1989-91; Fla Agr & Mech Univ, adj prof, 1990-91; Fla Dept Health & Rehabilitative Servs, abuse registry counr, 1991; Univ NC, Wilmington, guest lectr, 1992; Fed Bur Prisons, res analyst, 1992-; Shaw Univ, Raleigh, NC, prof criminal justice, 1993-. **Orgs:** Sweet Carolines, 1980-82; Young Democrats, 1982-83, Cloud Cappers Ltd Asn, 1982-; Dist Inc 1984-; CVAN, Vol Asn Battered Women, 1985; intake counr, Probation & Parole, 1983-84; counr, Mecklenburg Co, Charlotte; chmn, UNICEF; Hall Rep, 1980-81; UNC-Ch sec dorm, 1981-82; co-chmn, Univ NC, Chapel Hill, first UNCF Tennis Tourn Cabarrus Co; adv, Soc Criminal Justice, 1985-87; Coop Col Task Force, 1986; Am Criminal Justice Soc,1987-; Criminol Asn, 1987-; Acad Criminal Justice Sci, 1989-90; Guardian Ad Litem, 1988-; Supreme Ct Hist Soc, 1994-; mediator, Durham County Mediation Servs, 1996-. **Honors/Awds:** Honor Court, Univ NC, Chapel Hill, 1980-82; Patricia Roberts Harris Fellowship, 1987. **Special Achievements:** Author, works presented: “Gender Bias Amongst State Institutional Drug Treatment Programs,” April 1990; “Effects of Pornography on Women,” April1988; Assn of Criminal Justice Professionals, “History of Women’s Prisons in the State of Florida”; Southern conf, “Role Play,” 1987. Univ NC, Charlotte, First graduate of Masters of Science Degree in Criminal Justice Management Program, 1984. **Home Addr:** PO Box 45, Landis, NC 28088.

TAYLOR, FRANK
Restaurateur, executive. **Career:** Troy Marriott, dir food & beverage; Sheraton Imperial Hotel, dir food & beverage; Marriott’s Parkway Grille, head develop & dir food & beverage; Sweet Georgia Brown, co-owner; Pittsburgh Fish Mkt; Seldom Blues Cafe; Detroit Lions, partner; Seldom Blues, pres & ceo, currently. **Honors/Awds:** Award of Excellence, Wine Spectator mag. **Business Addr:** President, Chief Executive Officer, Seldom Blues, 400 Renaissance Ctr, Detroit, MI 48243, **Business Phone:** (313)567-7301.

TAYLOR, FRANK ANTHONY
Manager. **Personal:** Born Jun 4, 1965, Galveston, TX; son of Essie L Taylor; married Carolyn A, Aug 10, 1996; children: Courtney L, Airielle V & James V. **Educ:** Alvin Sr Col, attended 1986; Am Hotel & Motel, 1988. **Career:** Marriott Brookhollow, food, beverage dir, 1990-92; Holiday Inn San Antonio, resident mgr, 1992-94; Seldom Blues Inc, vpres, 1994-96; Sheraton Hotel Imperial, dir food & beverage, 1996; Doubletree Hotel Corp, dir food & beverage; Marriott’s Parkway Grille Pontiac, head develop, dir food & beverage; Troy Marriott, dir food & beverage; Southern hospity Restaurant Group, pres & ceo, currently; Seldom Blues, pres & ceo, currently; Detroit’s Breakfast House & Grill Merchants Row, pres & ceo, currently. **Orgs:** Detroit Med Ctr; Detroit Econ Growth Corp; Mich Restaurant Asn. **Honors/Awds:** Cert Food & Beverage Exec, Am Hotel & Motel Asn, 1988. **Home Phone:** (412)635-0701. **Business Addr:** President, Chief Executive Officer, Southern Hospitality Restaurant Group LLC, 243 W Cong Suite 1060, Detroit, MI 48226, **Business Phone:** (313)963-1940.

TAYLOR, FRED (FREDERICK ANTWON TAYLOR)
Football player. **Personal:** Born Jan 27, 1976, Pahokee, FL; married Andrea; children: Nataajah & Inari. **Educ:** Univ Fla, sociol. **Career:** Jacksonville Jaguars, rightback, 1998-2008; New England Patriots, 2009-. **Orgs:** Spokesperson, Leukemia Soc Am & Lymphoma Soc Am; spokesman, Glades AsthmaProject. **Honors/Awds:** Pro Bowler, 2007. **Business Addr:** Football Player, Jacksonville Jaguars, 1 Stadium Pl, Jacksonville, FL 32202, **Business Phone:** (904)633-6000.

TAYLOR, FREDERICK ANTWON. See TAYLOR, FRED.

TAYLOR, REV. GARDNER CALVIN
Clergy. **Personal:** Born Jun 19, 1918, Baton Rouge, LA; son of Rev Washington Monroe and Selina; married Phillis Strong; children: Martha Taylor LaCroix. **Educ:** Leland Col, AB, 1937; Oberlin Grad Sch Theo, BD. **Career:** Harvard Divinity Sch; Yale Divinity Sch; The Concord Baptist Church Christ, 1948-90, sr pastor emer, currently; Bethany Baptist Church, Elyria, pastor; Beulah Baptist Church, pastor; Mount Zion Baptist Church, pastor . **Honors/Awds:** Presidential Medal, City Univ New York; Presidential Medal of Freedom, 2000. **Special Achievements:** Author: How Shall They Preach, 1976; The Scarlet Thread, 1981; Chariots Aflame, 1988; We Have This Ministry, 1996; Words of Gardner Taylor, 6 vols, 2002. **Business Addr:** Senior Pastor Emeritus, Concord Baptist Church of Christ, 833 Gardner C Taylor Blvd, Brooklyn, NY 11216, **Business Phone:** (718)622-1818.

TAYLOR, GAYLAND WAYNE
Civil engineer. **Personal:** Born Aug 12, 1958, Midland, TX; son of Samuel Lee and Ardis Faye Taylor-Padgitt. **Educ:** Prairie View A&M Univ, Prairie View, TX, BSCE, 1981. **Career:** EG & G Idaho Inc, Idaho Falls, ID, field inspector, material lab tech, 1977-78; Arco, Arp, TX, corrosion engr, 1979; Ariz Pub Serv Co, Phoenix, AZ, civil engr, 1982-90; FAA, civil engr, currently. **Orgs:** Nat sect, nat fundraiser, Nat Coun Black Engrs & Scientist, 1985-91; pub relations chair & editor, Ariz Coun Black Engrs & Scientists, 1982-86; bus owner, Minority Bus Enterprise City Phoenix, 1988; chmn, KPNX Minority Adv Bd, 1982-86; Phoenix City Club, Bus Owner Mem, 1989-91; auditor, Fair Housing, 1987; chair, Nat Black Coalition of Federal Aviation Employees (NBCFAE). **Honors/Awds:** Idealine, Ariz Pub Serv, 1990; Cert Achievement, Transmissions & Distribution Expo, 1982; Adult Develop Units, Univ Boy Scouting, 1982; Outstanding Leadership, Valley Christian Ctrs, 1983; Nominee Candidate Volunteer, The Ariz Democratic Party, 1988. **Military Serv:** NROTC, Midshipman 3rd class, 1978-80; Navy Blue Guard Drill Team. **Home Addr:** PO Box 610449, DFW Airport, TX 75261-0449. **Business Addr:** Civil Engineer, Federal Aviation Administration, 2601 Meacham Blvd ASW-45132F, Fort Worth, TX 76137-0451, **Business Phone:** (817)222-5344.

TAYLOR, GERREN
Fashion model, actor. **Personal:** Born Jan 1, 1990, Los Angeles, CA. **Career:** Actress & fashion model, currently; Films: America the Beautiful, 2007. **Business Addr:** Fashion Model, Elite Model Management, 345 N Maple Dr Suite 397, Los Angeles, CA 90210, **Business Phone:** (310)274-9395.*

TAYLOR, GILBERT LEON
Museum curator, consultant. **Personal:** Born May 5, 1937, Indianapolis, IN; son of Hugh Ross and Irene Crystal; children: 7. **Educ:** Univ Indianapolis, BS, 1958; Ind Univ, MS, 1969; Univ Mass, EdD. **Career:** Ind Pub Sch, teacher, 1959-63; Liberia Presbyterian Sch, ed teacher consult, 1963-66; Knoxville Col, adminr, 1966-68; Ind Univ, adminr,1968-70; Col Holy Cross, adminr, 1970-74; Univ Mass, Ford fel, 1974-76; pvt pract, consult, 1975-; C Mus, adminr, 1976-84; Butler Univ, admin,1984-86; Indianapolis Pub Sch, Crispus Attucks Ctr Mus, cur, 1991-. **Orgs:** Ed & Human Rights Ind Teachers Asn, 1983; co-host, Views & Visions TY ProgWTTV, 1983-; Long range Plan Comn, African-Am Mus Asn, 1983-85; Featured Personality United Press Int, 1983; coord, AFA Exec coun, 1984-; pres,Parent Centered Educ, 1984-85; long range plan comn, Madame Walker Urban Life Ctr, 1984-85; adv comn, Freetown Vill, 1984-85; adv comn, Training Inc, 1984-85; I V Tech Outreach Comt, 1989; trainer, OAR, 1991; fac,Witherspoon Performing Arts Ctr, 1991-; adv bd, 4 H Extension; bd mem, Etheridge Knight Festival; Indianapolis Progress Comn, Vision Indianapolis. **Honors/Awds:** Key to the City Tuskegee City, 1979; Recognition Award, Bahai Faith, 1983;Award for Appreciation, Concerned Males, 1989; Outstanding Leadership-,Career Beginnings, 1990; Certificate of Appreciation, Veteran’s Admin,1990; Certificate of Appreciation, African-Am Multicultural Ed, 1992; Certificate of Appreciation, IPS/IEA Multicultural Festival, 1992;Certificate of Appreciation, Indiana Watch Comn Award, 1992; Certificate of Appreciation, Annual 4H Ace Acad, 1993; Service Award, Martin L KingDay IPS Sch 20, 1994; Certificate of Appreciation, US Dept Housing & Devt, 1994; Open Window Award, Positive Change Network, 1995; Certificate of Volunteer Service, OAR, 1995; Indianapolis Indians Sch 26 Reunion Award, 1997; 100 Black Men, 1998; Jr Drum Mayor Award, Dr MLK, 2000. **Business Addr:** Curator, Crispus Attucks Center Museum, Indianapolis Public Schools, 1140 Martin Luther King Jr St, Indianapolis, IN 46202, **Business Phone:** (317)226-2432.

TAYLOR, HENRY F
Automotive executive. **Career:** Smokey Point Sales & Serv Inc, chief exec officer; Smokey Point Buick Pontiac GMC Inc, owner & chief exec officer, currently; Taylor Co, chief exec officer. **Business Addr:** Chief Executive Officer, Owner, Smokey Point Buick Pontiac GMC Inc, 16632 Smokey Point Blvd, PO Box 3008, Arlington, WA 98223, **Business Phone:** (360)659-0886.*

TAYLOR, DR. HENRY LOUIS, JR.
Educator. **Personal:** Born Sep 13, 1943, Nashville, TN; married Carol Dozier, Aug 28, 1987; children: Jean-Jacques, Keeanga & Chad-Cinque. **Educ:** Tenn State Univ, Nashville, Tenn, BS, 1965; Univ Tenn, Knoxville, Tenn,MA, 1966; State Univ New York Buffalo, Buffalo, NY, MA, 1973, PhD, urban hist, 1979. **Career:** Hampton Inst, Hampton, Va, assoc dir hearing clin, 1968-70; State Univ New York Buffalo, Buffalo, NY, coordr, independent study, learning ctr, 1972-74, assoc prof Am studies, founder, dir, Ctr Applied Pub Affairs Studies, 1987, prof, currently, dir, Ctr Urban Studies, currently; Univ Cincinnati, Cincinnati, Ohio, dir employee’s develop educ prog, 1974-76; Univ Cincinnati Med Sch, Cincinnati, Ohio, 1976-79; Ohio State Univ, Columbus, Ohio, asst prof, 1980-87. **Orgs:** Chair & chief consult, Buffalo Common Coun-Comn Urban Initiatives, 1988; Greater Buffalo Econ Develop Coordinating Comt, 1990-; Buffalo Pvt Indust Coun’s Econ Develop Coord Comt, 1990-; Greater Buffalo Develop Found’s Working Group Minority Econ, 1990; Urban League Adv Bd, 1991. **Honors/Awds:** Consult Smithsonian Inst, “Field To Factory: Afro-Am Migration, 1915-40”, An Exhibition at Nat Mus Am Hist, Wash, DC, 1986; Consult Nat Afro-Am Mus & Cult Ctr Proj, From Victory to Freedom: Afro-Am Life in 1950s, Columbus,1986; African Am & Rise Buffalo’s Post-Indust City, 1940-, Buffalo Urban League, 1990. **Special Achievements:** Editor, Hist Roots of the Urban Crisis: African Am in the Industrial City, 1900-50, Race & the City: Work, Community, & Protest in Cincinnati, 1820-1970, African Am & the Rise of Buffalo’s Post Industrial City, 1991. **Business Addr:** Director, Professor, State University of New York at Buffalo, Center for Urban Studies, 201G Hayes Hall, 3435 Main St, Buffalo, NY 14214-3087, **Business Phone:** (829)213-3212.

TAYLOR, HERBERT CHARLES
Executive. **Personal:** Born Feb 2, 1948, Red Jacket, WV; children: Herbert Jr & Holly. **Educ:** Detroit Col Bus, BA, 1977; Cent Mich Univ, MA, 1981. **Career:** Gen Motor Corp, purchasing mgr, 1966-84; Bing Steel Inc, exec vpres, 1984-85; Superb Mfg Inc, pres. **Orgs:** Nat Black MBA Asn, 1985-; bd mem, Nat Asn Black Auto Suppliers, 1986-. **Home Phone:** (313)933-6088. **Business Addr:** President, Superb Manufacturing Inc, 6100 15 Mile Rd, Sterling Heights, MI 48312, **Business Phone:** (313)268-2640.

TAYLOR, HOWARD FRANCIS
Educator. **Personal:** Born Jul 7, 1939, Cleveland, OH; married Patricia A Epps. **Educ:** Hiram Col, AB, 1961; Yale univ, MA, 1964; Yale univ, PhD, 1966. **Career:** IL Inst Tech, 1966-68; Nat Acad Sci, consult; Syracuse Univ, 1968-73; Princeton Univ, Chair African Am Studies Prog, prof, 1973-92, prof emer, currently. **Orgs:** NAAS; Am Sociol Asn; E Sociol Soc; Am Asn Univ Profs; Asn Black Sociol. **Honors/Awds:** Various grants; published two books; number articles. **Business Addr:** Professor Emeritus of Sociology, Princeton University, Department of Sociology, 147 Wallace Hall, Princeton, NJ 08544, **Business Phone:** (609)258-4547.

TAYLOR, HYCEL B.
Clergy. **Personal:** Born Apr 21, 1936, Columbus, OH; married Annie Bdallis; children: Chandra, Audreanna, Hycel, III. **Educ:** Fields Bible Inst, attended 1960; Kent State Univ, BFA, 1965; Vanderbilt Div Sch, MDiv, 1969, doctorate ministery, 1970; Oberlin Grad Sch Theol; Univ Chicago, Divinity Sch. **Career:** Northern Baptist Dist Asn, Union Grove Baptist Church, license preacher, 1956; Union Baptist Church, youth dir, 1959; Elizabeth Baptist Church, pastor, 1962-66; Howard Congregational Church, pastor, 1966-69; Fisk Univ, dean chapel, minister instr relig, 1969-70; Garret-Evangelical Theol Sem, assoc prof, 1970, prof emer; Martin Luther King Jr, consult, lectr, founder; Church & Black Experience, Garrett-Eangelical Theol Sem, Evanston, founder & developer; Second Baptist Church, Evanston, IL, sr pastor, currently; Vanderbilt Div Sch, scholar. **Orgs:** Artist sculpture, Martin Luther King Fund; Church & Ministry SE Conf United Church Christ; Life & Work Comt, Nashville Coun Churches; Nashville Urban & Ministers Cadre; Baptist Sem Develop Asn; bd trustees, Nashville OIC; Nashville Coun Human Rels. **Honors/Awds:** TW Graham Award, Homiletics Oberlin Col, 1966. **Military Serv:** USMC, res, 1953-59. **Business Addr:** Senior Pastor, Second Baptist Church, 1717 Benson Ave, Evanston, IL 60201.

TAYLOR, IRIS
Journalist. **Personal:** Born in Powhatan, VA; children: Tamarra & Christian. **Educ:** Rutgers Univ, Livingston Col, BA, jour, 1983; Columbia Univ, Sch Gen Studies, 1980. **Career:** Essence Mag, New York, NY, contributing writer, 1974-86; Johnson & Johnson, Chicopee Div, ed, Horizons Mag, 1980-83; The Star-Ledger, Newark, NJ, bus reporter, 1983-98; syndicated columnist, 1998-2000; Richmond Times Dispatch, Consumer columnist, 2000-. **Orgs:** Nat Asn Black Journalists, 1989-. **Honors/Awds:** Journalism Award, Lincoln Univ, 1979; Outstanding Journalism Award, White House Conf Small Bus, Minority Delegates Caucus, 1988; Small Bus Media Advocate of the Year, State NJ, US Small Bus Admin, 1989; Distinguished Service Award, NJ Press Women, 1989; Journalism Award, NJ Chap, Soc Prof Journalists, 1994; The Roses Scroll Woman of Achievement Award, NJ Asn Women Business Owners Inc, 1994; Salute to Women Leaders Award, NJ Asn of Women Business Owners, 1995. **Business Addr:** Consumer Columnist, Richmond Times-Dispatch, PO Box 85333, Richmond, VA 23293, **Business Phone:** (804)649-6349.

TAYLOR, DR. JACK ALVIN
Educator, school administrator. **Personal:** Born Jul 15, 1949, Pittsburgh, PA; son of Jean and Jack; married Janet Victoria Bivins; children: Marcus, Matthew & Jack III. **Educ:** Calif Univ Penn, BA, 1971, Med, 1975; Bowling Green State Univ, PhD, 1985. **Career:** Calif Univ Penn, dir coun & spec serv, 1972-75; Frostburg State Col, asst dir minority affairs, 1975-78; Bowling Green State Univ, stud develop & spec serv, 1978-85, asst vpres multicultural affairs, 1985-95; asst vpres student affairs, 1995-; interim asst dir Athletics Academic Advising, currently; mem, Carter Park Exec Bd. **Orgs:** PA Intercollegiate Athletic Asn Championship Team, 1970; Consultant Minority Affairs; Consultant Educ Develop Progs; Nat Asn Stud Personnel Adminr; Kappa Alpha Psi Fraternity Inc; Wood County Pub Defenders Comn. **Business Addr:** Interim Assistant Director, Bowling Green State University, 200A Memorial Hall, Bowling Green, OH 43403.

TAYLOR, JANICE A.
Lawyer, president (organization), judge. **Personal:** Born May 23, 1954, Brooklyn, NY; daughter of Walter Earl and Avis Griffin.

Educ: Col William & Mary, BA, 1975; State Univ NY, Buffalo Sch Law, JD, 1978. **Career:** NY City Transit Authority, atty, 1978-81, assoc atty, 1981-86; Dist Coun 37 AFSCME AFL-CIO, asst gen coun, 1986-87; Civil Ct City NY, small claims arbitrator, 1987; pvt pract, atty, 1987; Queens County, Civil Ct, judge, 1994-; Staten Island Rapid Transit Oper Authority, secy; St John's Univ Col Bus Admin, assoc prof law. **Orgs:** Legal coun, Concerned Citizens S Queens, 1981-87; parliamentarian, Delta Sigma Theta Inc, Queens Alumnae Chap, 1982; legal redress chairperson, Nat Asn Advan Colored People, Jamaica Br, 1983-85, 1987-88; regional coun mem, Nat Bar Asn, 1983-87; deaconette, Concord Baptist Church Christ, 1984-; bd mem, Black Women Transit, 1985-86; pres, Macon B Allen Black Bar Asn, 1985-88; secy, Network Bar Leaders, 1986-89; Guy R Brewer United Dem Club, 1989-94; United For Progress Dem Club, 1992-94; Queens County Women's Bar Asn, 1991-95; secy & bd mem, Jamaica Serv Prog Older Adults, 1990-94; officer, Black Law Stud Asn; vpres, Bd Asn Civil Ct Judges NY; anti-bias rep, Off Ct Admin. **Special Achievements:** Second African-American Female to be elected to the Civil Court in Queens County. **Home Addr:** 111 26 198th St, Jamaica, NY 11412. **Business Addr:** Judge, Queens County Civil Court, 88 11 Sutphin Blvd, Jamaica, NY 11435, **Business Phone:** (718)298-1000.

TAYLOR, JASON
Football player. **Personal:** Born Sep 1, 1974, Pittsburgh, PA; married Katina; children: Isaiah Paul , Mason Paul & Zoe Grace. **Educ:** Univ Akron. **Career:** Miami Dolphins, defensive end, 1997-07; Wash Redskins, defensive end,2008. Miami Dolphins, defensive end, 2009-. **Orgs:** Miami Proj Cure Paralysis; Cystic Fibrosis Found; Dan Marino Found;founder, Jason Taylor Found, 2004-. **Honors/Awds:** Miami Dolphin Newcomer of the Year; Pro Football All Rookie-Team; AFC Defensive Player of the Week, 2003; Dan Marino Most Valuable Player Award, 2004; Honorable mention All-American, 1996; Pro Bowl selection, 2000, 2002, 2004-07; Walter Payton Man of the Year Award, 2007. **Special Achievements:** Ten Sexiest Athletes, Sports Illustrated, 2001. **Business Addr:** Defensive End, Miami Dolphins, 7500 SW 30 St, Davie, FL 33314, **Business Phone:** (954)452-7100.

TAYLOR, JEFFERY CHARLES
Lawyer. **Personal:** Born Nov 15, 1957, Staten Island, NY; son of Robert D and Pauline D. **Educ:** Pace Univ, BS (cum laude), 1984; Hofstra Univ, Sch Law, JD, 1988. **Career:** Community Legal Servs Corp, intern, 1987-88; Paralegal Support Servs Inc, legal asst, 1988-89; Am Civil Liberties Union, law clerk, 1989-90; MD Legal Aid Bur Inc, staff, atty, 1990-. **Orgs:** Mar Prison Renewal Comt, 1991; Proj Raise Mar, 1991-; Proj 2000 Mar, 1992-93; fin dir, Renaissance Econ Develop Proj Pk Heights Inc, 1993. **Honors/Awds:** Mayors Citation for Outstanding Community Service, 1993. **Military Serv:** USF, a-1st class, 1976-79. **Home Addr:** 2912 W Coldspring Lane Suite C, Baltimore, MD 21215, **Home Phone:** (410)664-1563. **Business Phone:** (410)539-5340.

TAYLOR, JEROME
Educator. **Personal:** Born Jan 26, 1940, Waukegan, IL; son of George Washington and Willie Mae Taylor; married Tommie Nell; children: Kim, Lisa, Jacques & Zwehla. **Educ:** Univ Denver, BA, 1961; Ind Univ, PhD, 1965. **Career:** Menninger Found, fel, 1965-67; Ment Health Unit Topeka, dir, 1968-69; Univ Pittsburgh, Clin Psychol Ctr, dir, 1969-71, Psychol Educ, Sch Educ, & Africana Studies, assoc prof, currently, dir, Inst Black Family, currently; Ctr Family Excellence, exec dir, currently. **Orgs:** Am Psychol Soc; Asn Black Psychologists; Omicron Delta Kappa; Sigma Xi; Psi Chi; Nat Black Child Develop Inst; Nat Coun Family Rel. **Honors/Awds:** Chancellor's Distinguished Public Service Award, Univ Pittsburgh; Kujichaquilia Award, Sankofa Inst Pittsburgh. **Business Phone:** (412)648-7540.

TAYLOR, JOHN L.
Educator. **Personal:** Born May 7, 1947, Holly Springs, MS; son of Charlie E Sr and Cinderella Sims; married Naomi Ruth Thomas; children: Tony, Jonathan & Chere. **Educ:** Rust Col, BS, 1969. **Career:** Marshall County Dist 4, elected offical & election comnr; Independence High Sch, teacher, asst prin, currently. **Orgs:** Deacon & clerk, Baptist Church; mason, Waterford Lodge No 450; sunday sch eacher, Mt Moriah Baptist Church. **Honors/ Awds:** Teacher of the Day, Radio Sta, 1984; Acad Career Day, Univ Miss, 1985. **Home Addr:** 608 MULLINS RD rt 4, PO Box 107, Byhalia, MS 38611. **Business Phone:** (662)233-9966.

TAYLOR, JOHNNY
Basketball player. **Personal:** Born Jun 4, 1974. **Educ:** Univ Tenn-Chattanooga. **Career:** Orlando Magic, forward, 1997-98; Denver Nuggets, forward, 1998-2000; Toronto Raptors, forward, 2000; Chicago Bulls, forward, 2000-01; Portland Trail Blazers, forward, 2001; Philadelphia 76ers, forward, 2002; Roanoke Dazzle, forward, 2002-; Detroit Pistons, forward, 2003; Etosa Alicante, forward, 2005; Dexia Mons Hainaut (belgium), 2007. **Honors/ Awds:** Southern first Team Eurobasket.com, 1995, 1996; NCAA Sweet 16, 1996; All-FIBA Europe Cup, hon Mention, 2004; FIBA Europe Cup Conference N Champion, 2005. **Special Achievements:** FIBA Europe Cup Semifinals, 2004, 2005. *

TAYLOR, JOHNNY C
Lawyer. **Personal:** Born Jun 20, 1968, Ft Lauderdale, FL; son of Johnny C Sr and Deborah Mizell. **Educ:** Univ Miami, BSC, 1989; Drake Univ, MA, 1991; Drake Law Sch, JD, 1992. **Career:** Steel Hector & Davis, lawyer, 1992-93; Blockbuster Entertainment Corp, assoc gen coun, 1993-96, vp human resources, 1996-97; Alamo Rent-A-Car Inc, vp legal affairs, 1997-98; Compass Group USA, Charlotte, NC, Exec vpres, gen coun & secy; Paramont Parks/VIACOM, gen coun & sr vpres, human resources; McGuireWoods HR Strategies LLC, pres & sr consult, currently. **Orgs:** Amr Corp Coun Asn, 1994-; Drake Law Sch, bd counrs, 1994-99; Broward County Urban League, pres-elect, 1995-98; Univ Miami, president's coun, 1997-; Urban League Cent Carolinas, bd mem, 1998-99; Dell Curry Found, bd mem, 2000-; Soc Human Resource Mgt, bd dir, 2000-. **Honors/Awds:** Young Alumni Award, Orange Award, Univ Miami, 1994; Price Waterhouse, Up & Comers Award, 1996; Achiever Award, Am Family Asn, JM Family & Southest Toyota, 1998. **Home Addr:** 15600 Woodland Ridge Lane, Charlotte, NC 28278, **Home Phone:** (704)504-3773. **Business Addr:** President, McGuireWoods HR Strategies LLC, 100 N Tryon St Suite 2900, Charlotte, NC 20036-5317, **Business Phone:** (704)353-6216.

TAYLOR, JOSEPH
Athletic coach, educator. **Personal:** Born May 7, 1950, Richmond, VA; son of Choncie and Elnorma M; married Beverly, Mar 30, 1974; children: Aaron Joseph & Dennis Anthony. **Educ:** Western Ill Univ, BS, phys educ & health, 1972; Eastern Ill Univ, MS, educ admin, 1979. **Career:** HDC Sch, phys educ instr; H D Woodson High Sch, asst football coach, 1972-77; Eastern Ill Univ, asst football coach, 1978-80; Va Union Univ, offensive coordr, 1980-82, head football coach, 1984-91; Howard Univ, defensive coordr, 1982-83, head football coach, 1983-84; Hampton Univ, head football coach, 1992-, dir athletics, 2008. **Orgs:** Kappa Alpha Psi Fraternity, 1971-; bd trustees & vpres, Am Football Coaches Asn, 1978-; adv bd, Wilson Sporting Goods, 1994-; football exec bd, vpres, Div 1-AA, 1997-; Citizens Unity Comn, 1998-; Black Coaches Asn;adv bd, Am Football Quarterly, 1997-; pres, Am Football Coaches Asn. **Honors/Awds:** Coach of the Year, Sports Club Wash, DC, Richmond, VA, Norfolk, VA, Atlanta, Florida, 1986, 1988, 1992-94, 1997-98; SBN Coach of the Year, 1994, 1997; American Football Coach of the Year, 1986, 1992-94, 1997-98; CIAA Coach of the Year, 1986, 1992-94; MEAC Coach of the Year, 1997; HBCU Nat Champship, 1994, 1997; Eddie Robinson Coach of Distinction Award. **Special Achievements:** Published articles on professional dev in American Football Quarterly, 1994, AFCA summer manual, 1995; elected to Citizens Unity Commission, City of Hampton, 1998. **Home Addr:** 427 East Queen St, Hampton, VA 23669.

TAYLOR, JULIUS H
Educator. **Personal:** Born Feb 15, 1914, Cape May, NJ; married Patricia Spaulding; children: Dwight &Trena. **Educ:** Lincoln Univ, BA; Univ PA, MS, PhD. **Career:** WVa State Col, dept head, 1945; Morgan State Col, assoc prof, 1949, dept head & prof, 1951-78; Goddard Space Flight Ctr, NASA, contractor. **Orgs:** Chesapeake Am Asn Physics Teachers; Nat Com Physics Secondary Educ; presAAPT, 1962-63; rep, AAPT, 1964-65; Nat,Science Found; Travelers Aid Soc; Gov Science Adv Coun,; zone coun, Soc Physics Students Alumnus Yr Lincoln Univ, 1963. **Honors/ Awds:** Research award; Julius Rosenwald fel, Univ PA, 1943-44. **Home Addr:** 2319 Lyndhurst Ave, Baltimore, MD 21216, **Home Phone:** (410)367-3336.

TAYLOR, KARIN
Entrepreneur, fashion model. **Personal:** Born Nov 28, 1971, Kingston, Jamaica; married Bill Weinberg, 2001; children: 3. **Career:** Ford Modeling Agency, model; Miss June, Playboy, 1996; actress, appeared in Baywatch, Malcolm & Eddie & The Weird Al Show; host/spokesmodel, E! Gossip show & Playboy TV; Style House, Haverford, PA, owner, 2000-. **Orgs:** Spokeswoman, POWARS, Pet Owners with AIDS Resource Service; supporter, AIDS Projects, Los Angeles. **Special Achievements:** The first African-American actress to don the infamous red Baywatch. **Business Addr:** Owner, Style House, 20 Haverford Station Rd, Haverford, PA 19041-1507, **Business Phone:** (610)642-6828.

TAYLOR, DR. KENNETH DOYLE
Engineer, scientist. **Personal:** Born Nov 5, 1949, Hartford, CT; son of Adelaide P Tweedy Jordan and Frank K; married Mattie Jane Dolphy, Aug 25, 1972; children: Jerome Daniel. **Educ:** Univ CT, BS, 1971, MS, 1974, PhD, 1981; Rensselaer Polytech Inst, Hartford CT, MBA, 1988. **Career:** Picker Corp, design engr, 1973-74; St Francis Hosp & Med Ctr, mgr res lab, 1974-79; Univ CT, Dept Elec Engr, lectr, 1977-83; Hartford Grad Ctr, adj lect, 1982-; Nat Inst Health, asst dir, 1985-86; United Technol Res Ctr, sr proj engr, 1979-90; Pfizer Hosp Prods Group, dir, tech assessment, 1990-93; Valleylab, vpres res & develop, 1993-98; Medlogic Global Corp, vpres prod develop, 1998-99; CO Med Tech, pres, Colo Opers; Taylor Med Technol & Consult Inc, pres, currently. **Orgs:** Chmn & treas, Family Fed Credit Union, 1978-80, 1983-85; sr mem, Inst Elec & Electronics Engineering, 1983-; vpres Beta Sigma Lambda, Alpha Phi Alpha Frat, 1983-85; Sigma Pi Phi Fratm, 1984-; bd dirs, Conn Pre-Engineering Prog, 1989-91; bd dirs, Channel 3 Country Camp, 1989-91; treas, Hist Denver Inc, 1999-; treas, Beckworth Mountain Club, 1999; Am Col Clinical Engr, 1995-; Assoc Advan Med Instrumentation, 1993-. **Honors/Awds:** United Technologies Award, 1981; Distinguished Gradugate Award, Univ CT, 1982; AIAA Contribution to Society Award, 1985; President's Commn on Exec Exchange Class XVI, 1985-86; Registered Professional Engineer, State Connecticut, 1977. **Home Addr:** 375 Golden Eagle Dr, Broomfield, CO 80020-1272, **Home Phone:** (303)460-7416. **Business Addr:** President, Taylor Medical Technology & Consulting, Inc, 375 Golden Eagle Dr, Broomfield, CO 80020, **Business Phone:** (303)466-8718.

TAYLOR, KENNETH MATTHEW
Executive. **Personal:** Born in Jersey City, NJ. **Educ:** BS; MBA. **Career:** Witco Chem Corp NYC, sr auditor & financial analyst; Allied Chem Corp Morristown NJ, sr auditor; Colgate-Palmolive Corp NYC, sr accountant; Philip Morris Inc NYC, sr analyst & auditor; Bache & Co Inc NYC, sr brokerage acct; The Omega Psi Phi Fraternity Inc, dist auditor,currently. **Orgs:** Am Mgt Asn; Ins Internal Auditors; Nat Asn Black Acct; Nat Asn Acct NJ Chpt; Omega Psi Phi Frat; chmn, 2nd Dist Budget & Finance Com Newark, 1972-74; Nat Budget & Financo Com, 1973-74; keeper finance, Upsilon Phi Chap, 1970-74. **Honors/Awds:** Distinguished Award Chmn Finance Com, 1974. **Military Serv:** USAF. **Business Addr:** District Auditor, The Omega Psi Phi Fraternity Inc, 3951 Snapfinger Pkwy, Decatur, GA 30035, **Business Phone:** (404)284-5533.

TAYLOR, KIMBERLY HAYES
Journalist. **Personal:** Born Jul 9, 1962, Louisville, KY; daughter of James E Hayes and Loraine S Hayes; married Keith L Taylor, May 28, 1983. **Educ:** Morehead State Univ, Morehead, KY, BA, commun, 1984. **Career:** Courier-Journal, Louisville, KY, clerk/ writer, 1986-88; The Commercial-News, Danville, IL, police reporter, 1987-88; Observer-Dispatch, Utica, NY, ct criminal justice reporter, 1988; Peace On Our Minds, West Edmeston, NY, ed chief, 1990; The Hartford (CT) Courant, reporter; USA Today, reporter; Star Tribune, reporter, 1993-. **Orgs:** Nat Asn Black Journalists, 1986-; exec bd mem, Young & Teen Peacemakers Inc, 1990-; exec bd, Oneida Co Chap Nat Asn Advan Colored People, 1990-; dist comt, Boy Scouts Am, 1989-; Greater Utica Multiculturalism Coalition, 1990-. **Honors/Awds:** Top Well Done Award for "Street Under Siege" series, Gannett Inc, 1991. **Home Addr:** 15 Noyes St, Utica, NY 13502. **Business Addr:** Reporter, Star Tribune, 425 Portland Ave, Minneapolis, MN 55488.

TAYLOR, KOKO. See TAYLOR, CORA in the Obituaries section.

TAYLOR, LAWRENCE JULIUS
Actor, football player. **Personal:** Born Feb 4, 1959, Williamsburg, VA; son of Clarence and Iris; married Linda Cooley (divorced); children: 1; married Maritza Cruz; children: Lawrence Jr, Tanisha & Paula. **Educ:** Univ NC. **Career:** Football player (retired), actor; New York Giants, linebacker, 1981-93; Films: Water boy, 1998; Any Given Sunday, 1999; Shaft, 2000; Mercy Streets, 2000; Savage, 2003; The Comebacks, 2007. **Honors/Awds:** All-Am, NC; Atlantic Coast Conf Player of the Yr, 1980; played in East-West Shrine Game and Japan Bowl; unanimous All-NFL selection for 3yrs; top linebacker in NFL, NFL PA for 3 yrs; 2 time defensive MVP, Asniated Press; NFL Defensive Player of the Yr, Seagram's Computer Awards Prog; played in Pro Bowl; NFL Hall of Fame, inducted, 1999. **Special Achievements:** Author: Living on the Edge, 1987; Over the Edge, 2004.

TAYLOR, LINDA SUZANNA. See TAYLOR, MARIE DE PORRES.

TAYLOR, LORENZO JAMES, JR.
School administrator. **Personal:** Born Sep 1, 1925, Detroit, MI; son of Lorenzo Sr and Rosa Ephriam; widowed; children: James Richardson, Lamar Richardson, Ronnie Richardson, Amino Mohamed, Denise Richardson, Paul Dallas Taylor (deceased). **Educ:** Wayne State Univ, attended 1967. **Career:** School administrator (retired); Detroit Bd Educ, transp mgr-Regional; Mich Liquor Comn. **Orgs:** Dexter Ave Baptist Church; Metro Detroit Sr Dance Group; founding mem, Arts Extended Gallery Inc. **Special Achievements:** Collector of antique African and African American art. **Home Addr:** 2323 Waverly St, Detroit, MI 48238. *

TAYLOR, MARGARET. See BURROUGHS, DR. MARGARET TAYLOR.

TAYLOR, MARIE DE PORRES (LINDA SUZANNA TAYLOR)
Association executive, nun, government official. **Personal:** Born May 27, 1947, Los Angeles, CA; daughter of James and Isabel McCoy Clarke. **Educ:** Marylhurst Col, Marylhurst, OR, BA, 1970; Calif State Univ, San Francisco, CA, MA, 1976; Pacific Lutheran Sem, Berkeley, CA, 1982; Calif State Univ, Hayward, CA, 1986. **Career:** Holy Names High Sch, Oakland, CA, chair home econs dept, 1969-77; St Benedict Church, Oakland, CA, assoc pastor, 1977-82; Roman Cath Bishop, Oakland, CA, dir Black Catholics, 1982-89; Nat Black Sisters Conf, Oakland, CA, exec dir, 1982-; Oakland Pvt Indust Coun, Oakland, CA, prog coordr, 1989-91; City Oakland, asst mayor, job training & employ. **Orgs:** Chmn, bd dir, Bay Area Black United Fund; pres, bd dir, Oakland

Citizens Comt Urban Renewal; pres, United E Oakland Clergy; bd dir, Holy Names Col; vchmn, bd dir, Oakland Police Activity League; Mayor's Comt Homeless; bd mem, Patrons Arts & Humanities, 1991-, bd mem, 1990-, chmn, 1993-, Mary's Pence; Bd Voc Nursing & Psychiat Technician; bd mem, Alameda County; pres, Bd Vocational Nursing & Psychiat Technicians. **Honors/Awds:** Image Builders Award, Col Bounders Bay Area, 1981; Rose Casanave Service Award, Black Catholic Vicariate, Diocese, Oakland, CA, 1982; Outstanding Leadership in Bay Area Award, Links Inc, 1982; Martin Luther King Jr Award, United E Oakland Clergy, 1984; Woman of the Year, Oakland Young Women's Christian Asn, 1988; Ella Hill Hutch Award, Black Women Organized Polit Action, 1990. **Home Addr:** 5022 Camden St, Oakland, CA 94619.

TAYLOR, MARTHA
Police officer, clergy. **Personal:** Born Jul 26, 1941, Shreveport, LA; daughter of Henry and Viola Harris; married Royal Odell Taylor, Feb 14, 1975; children: Valerie L Thompson, Debra L Benton. **Educ:** Merritt Col, Oakland, CA, AA, 1977; Univ San Francisco, BA, 1979, MPA, 1981; Am Baptist Sem W, Berkeley, CA, MDiv; San Francisco Theol Sem, doctoral prog, attending. **Career:** Police officer (retired), clergy; Bay Area Rapid Transit Dist, Oakland, CA, police officer, 1973-77, police sergeant, 1977-81, police lt, 1981-83, support & analysis mgr, 1983-90, dept mgr, sta opers, 1990-92, asst chief transportation officerr, 1992-00; Bethel Missionary Baptist Church, bible instr, 1987-; ordained minister; Allen Temple Baptist Church, asst topastor; Allen Temple Leadership Training Inst, adj fac mem. **Orgs:** Pres, Black Managers & Professionals Asn, 1981-; Conf Minority Transit Officials, 1985-; past mem bd dir, E Oakland Youth Develop Ctr, CA, 1986-87; past vpres, Nat Forum Black Pub Adminr, Oakland chap, CA, 1986-88; mem exec bd, Black Women Organized Polit Action, 1986-; mem, Youth Mentor Prog, Oakland Pub Schs, CA, 1986-; chair comt training, Women Transit Am Pub Transit Asn, 1987-; Nat Negro Coun Women. **Honors/Awds:** Certificate of Recognition, Am Pub Transit Asn, Western Conf, 1985; Certificate for Outstanding Contributions, Am Pub Transit Asn, 1987; Meritorious Award, Nat Forum Black Public Adminr, 1991. **Special Achievements:** Author: The Challenge of Climbing the Organizational Ladder: A Matter Of Perspective, California Law Enforcement Association Police Recorder, 1988. **Home Addr:** 3828 Sequoyah Rd, Oakland, CA 94605. *

TAYLOR, MARY QUIVERS
School administrator. **Personal:** Born in Mobile, AL; daughter of Stephen Quivers and Elizabeth; widowed; children: Roderick Maurice & Pamela Bonita. **Educ:** Univ Ala, attended; Univ W Fla, BA, 1973; Univ S Ala, MEd, 1977. **Career:** Bishop State Community Col, coord & counr, 1985-92, admis counr, 1992-. **Orgs:** Vpres, Mobile Asn Black Social Workers, 1980-85, 1997-; Ala Couns Asn, 1993; Southern Asn Admis Counrs, 1995-; Nat Asn Black Social Workers, 1997-; Stone Street Baptist Church; City Mobile, Keep Mobile Beautiful Exec Bd, 1993. **Honors/Awds:** Keep Mobile Beautiful Award, City Mobile, 1993; Chancellor's Award (Outstanding Faculty), Ala Col Syst, 1996; Career Woman of the Year, Gayfers Career Club, 1997; Upcoming African Americans Award, The Leading Edge, 1998; Chancellor's Award, Ala Col System, 1999. **Home Addr:** 1452 Basil St, Mobile, AL 36603. **Business Addr:** Admission Counselor, Bishop State Community College, 414 Stanton St, Mobile, AL 36603, **Business Phone:** (334)473-8692.

TAYLOR, MAURICE DE SHAWN
Basketball player. **Personal:** Born Oct 30, 1976. **Educ:** Univ Mich, attended. **Career:** Los Angeles Clippers, forward, 1997-2000; Houston Rockets, 2001-05; New York Knicks, 2004-05; Sacramento Kings, 2006-07; Olimpia Milano, 2009-. **Honors/Awds:** Gold medal, U-22 Panamerican Championship, 1996; Schick All-Rookie Second Team, 1997, 1998. **Business Addr:** Professional Basketball Player, Olimpia Milano.

TAYLOR, MESHACH
Actor. **Personal:** Born Apr 11, 1947, Boston, MA; married Bianca, Jan 1, 1983; children: Yasmine, Esme & Tariq; (divorced 1970); children: Tamar. **Educ:** Fla A&M Univ. **Career:** Stage: Hair Nat Theatre Co; Organic Theatre Group; Goodman Theatre; Beauty & Beast, 1984; TV series: "Buffalo Bill", 1983; "Designing Women", 1986-93; "Dave's World", 1993-97; "Nothing Lasts Forever", 1995; "To Tell the Truth", 2000; "Static Shock", 2000; "Aftershock", 2000; "The Drew Carey Show", 2001; "What's Wrong with This Episode IV", 2001; "Ned's Declassified Sch Survival Guide", 2004-05; "Cheaters & Bullies", 2004; "Video Project & Sch Clubs", 2005; "All of Us", 2005; Liar, 2005; "The Unit", 2006; "Old Home Week", 2006; Films: Welcome to Oblivion; The Howling, 1981; One More Saturday Night, 1986; Mannequin, 1987; Mannequin II, 1991; Class Act, 1992; Jacks or Better, 2000; Friends & Family, 2001; Ned's Declassified Sch Survival Guide, 2004; All of Us, 2005; Tranced, 2006. **Honors/Awds:** Viewers for Quality Television Awards, 1988, 1989 & 1990; Best Ensemble Acting, River Run Int Film Festival, 2000. **Special Achievements:** Emmy Award nominated. **Business Addr:** Actor, 10100 Santa Monica Blvd 25th Fl, Los Angeles, CA 90067.

TAYLOR, MICHAEL
Management consultant, businessperson. **Personal:** Born Oct 13, 1958, New York, NY; son of Donald and Patricia; married Sandy Jones, Sep 5, 1987. **Educ:** Harvard Univ, BA, 1980; Stanford Univ, MBA, 1984. **Career:** Pacific Bell, syst analyst, 1980-82; Ducommon, asst mgr corp develop, 1983; Booz Allen & Hamilton, assoc, 1984-86; Infotech Planning Group, prin, 1986-90; Am Pop Video, corp pres, 1990-91; San Francisco Consult Group, vpres, 1991-94; Arthur D Little Inc, N Am Mgt Consult, managing dir IT media & electronics telecommunications, 1994-2003; Aurorex, co-founder & chief exec officer, 2003-. **Orgs:** Nat Black MBA Asn; charter mem, UJAMAA. **Home Addr:** 128-35 Skyline Blvd, Oakland, CA 94619. **Business Addr:** Co-Founder, Chief Executive Officer, Aurorex, Oakland, CA 94601, **Business Phone:** (510)482-8804.

TAYLOR, MICHAEL LOEB
Educator, arts administrator. **Personal:** Born Jan 11, 1947, Houston, TX; children: Christopher Kirrinkai Parrish & Jennifer Nichol Parrish. **Educ:** Univ Calif Los Angeles, BA, 1970, MA, 1972, MFA, 1974. **Career:** Univ Nairobi, Kenya, lectr, 1972-73, 1975-77; Western KY Univ, asst prof, 1977-81; Lewis & Clark Col, assoc prof, assoc prof emer, currently. **Orgs:** Design consult, African Heritage Ltd, Nairobi, Kenya, 1972-73, 1975-77; Mems Gallery, 1982-83; artist, Blackfish Gallery, Portland, OR, 1984; Comn Wash State Arts Comn, 1989. **Honors/Awds:** Fulbright Award (declined) Turkey, 1981. **Business Addr:** Associate Professor Emeritus of Art, Lewis & Clark College, 0615 SW Palatine Hill Rd, Portland, OR 97219, **Business Phone:** (503)768-7390.

TAYLOR, MILDRED D
Writer. **Personal:** Born Sep 13, 1943, Jackson, MS; daughter of Wilbert Lee and Deletha Marie; married Errol Zea-Daly, 1972 (divorced 1975). **Educ:** Univ Toledo, BA, attended; Univ Colo Sch Jour, MBA, attended. **Career:** Peace Corps, Ethiopia, taught Eng & hist, recruiter in the US; Univ Colo, organizer black studies prog & study skills coordr; Novels: Song of the Trees, Dial, 1975; Roll of Thunder, Hear My Cry, Dial, 1976; Let the Circle Be Unbroken, Dial, 1981; The Gold Cadillac, 1987; The Friendship, 1987; Mississippi Bridge, 1990; The Road to Memphis, 1990; The Well, 1995; The Land, 2001; Logan, 2004. **Orgs:** Univ Colo, Black Students Alumni Group. **Honors/Awds:** Award from the Council on Interracial Books for Children, 1975; New York Times Outstanding Book Award, 1975; Children's Book Showcase Award, 1976; Newbery Award, 1977; Horn Book Honor Award from Boston Globe; Coretta Scott King Award; Am Library Asn, honors, 1981; Coretta Scott King Award for Let the Circle Be Unbroken, 1982; Coretta Scott King Award for The Friendship, 1988; Christopher Award for The Gold Cadillac, 1988; Coretta Scott King Award for The Road to Memphis, 1990; Nat Coun Teachers Eng, ALAN Award for Significant Contribution to Young Adult Lit, 1997; Newbery Medal winner; Coretta Scott King Award for The Land, 2002. *

TAYLOR, MILDRED E. CROSBY
Labor relations manager. **Personal:** Born Dec 18, 1919, Centralia, IL; married David P. **Educ:** LaSalle Ext Univ, attended 1941; US Dept Agriculture Grad Sch, certificate; Exec Inst, exec develop training; US Dept Labor, leadership devel courses; Catholic Univ Wash DC. **Career:** Women's Bur US Dept Labor, conv planner ret social science advisor; Surgeon General's Off Dept Army, personnel asst; Surgeon Gen Off Dept Air Force, personnel specialist; keynote speaker panelist moderator meetings & seminars. **Orgs:** Women's Bur liaison black women's orngs employ; Secy Labors Vol Day Com; bd dir, Dept Labor Recreation Asn; charter mem, Toast masters Int; vpres, Air & Cruise Travel Adminr Wash DC; charter mem, DC Women's Comn Crime Prevention; charter mem, bd dir, Trinity AME Zion Ch Housing Corp; past pres, Century Club Nat Asn Negor Bus & Prof Women Inc; past loyal lady, ruler Order Golden Circle; past matron, Order Eastern Star; Urban League NAACP; past commandress, Mecca Ct Daughters; imperial conv directness Imperial Ct Daughters Isis; vol worker many charitable orgns. **Honors/Awds:** Recipient outstanding service award, Prentiss Inst Hon KY Col Gov Nunn, 1971; distinguished service award, Mecca Temple Ancient Egyptian Arabic Order Nobles Mystic Shrine; honorary dr of humanities deg Ministerial InstCol W Point MS, 1977.

TAYLOR, MILES EDWARD
Technician, engineer. **Personal:** Born Apr 25, 1964, Nyack, NY; son of Aubrey and Lillian Murray. **Educ:** C W Post Col, Long Island Univ, Brookville, NY, BA, 1986. **Career:** Fire Works Grucci, Brookhaven, NY, pyrotechnician, 1983-; Nyack High Sch, Nyack, NY, head cross country coach, 1987; Black Magic Video Prod, Nyack, NY, owner, 1987-; CNN New York, New York, NY, engr, 1987-. **Orgs:** Vpres, Nyack Fire Dept, Jackson Fire Eng Co No 3, 1980; Tau Kappa Epsilon, 1983-. **Business Addr:** Engineer, Control Room, CNN New York, 5 Penn Pl 22nd Fl, New York, NY 10001, **Business Phone:** (212)714-7858.

TAYLOR, NATALIE MANNS
Executive. **Personal:** Born Jul 14, 1959, Columbus, OH; daughter of Betty Manns Casey; married Timothy, Apr 6, 1985; children: Timothy Ryan. **Educ:** Radford Univ, Radford, VA, BS, bus mgt, 1982. **Career:** Food Lion, Inc, cashier, 1982-83, customer serv mgr, 1983-84, asst mgr, 1984-85, store mgr, 1985-86, mgt develop admin, 1986-88, front end training supvr, 1988-91, employee develop supvr, 1991-93, dir community affairs, employment develop, 1993-95, dir diversity planning, 1995-97, Diversity, vpres, 1997-2003; Capture Communications Resource Group, founder & pres, 2004-. **Orgs:** Bd dirs, Carolinas Minority Supplier Develop Coun, 1991; bd visitors, Livingstone Col Adv Bd, 1996-98; bd dirs, Metrolina Minority Supplier Develop Coun, 1996-; Co-chair & chair, Community Livingstone Col, 1996-98; Community Col Bus Admin Adv Bd, 1996-97; Nat Asn Female Exec, 1998-; bd dir, Winston-Salem Urban League, 1998-; Soc Human Resource Mgt, 1999-; chair, Equal Opportunity Day Gala Comm, 1999; Nat Asn Advan Colored People; United Negro Col Fund; Rowan Cabarrus. **Honors/Awds:** Positive Image Award, The Minority Recruiter, 1992; Community Service Award, VA NAACP, Area II Branches, Martin Luther King, Jr. 1998; Black Achiever, Winston Lake Family YMCA, 1999. **Special Achievements:** Under her leadership in the Diversity area, Food Lion, Inc. has received: Natl Assn for the Advancement of Colored People, Fair Share Award, 1995, 1997; NC NAACP, Corp Supporter Award, 1996; The Charlotte Post, Corp of the Yr Award, 1998; Carolinas Minority Supplier Develop Coun, Inc., Corp of the Yr Award, 1999. **Business Addr:** President, Founder, Capture Communications Resource Group, 2100 Fairfax Rd, Greensboro, NC 27407, **Business Phone:** (336)852-7500.

TAYLOR, NORMAN EUGENE
Government official. **Personal:** Born Nov 12, 1948, Newark, NJ; son of Edwin Alfred and Martha Small; married Theresa Singleton, Apr 26, 1980; children: Norman Assaf, Todd Farrell, Norman Amman, Joy Jamillah & Autier Dawn. **Educ:** Bethune-Cookman Col, Dayton Beach, FL, BA, 1970; Fla Atlantic Univ, Boca Raton, FL, MPA, 1976; Univ Miami Sch Law, 1991-92. **Career:** October Center Inc, Fort Lauderdale FL, dir, 1973-80; Norman E Taylor & Assoc, Inc, Miami FL, pres, 1980-83; Broward County Govt, Fort Lauderdale, FL, pub rel mgr, 1983-84, OEO dir, 1984-96, Off Econ Develop, dir, 1996-. **Orgs:** Omega Psi Phi Fraternity, 1967-; Broward Senior Exec, 1987-; Fla Asn Minority Bus Enterprise Officials, 1987-; chair, Metro-Broward Capital, 1987-; Airport Minority Advisory Coun, 1988-; Am Econ Develop Coun, 1996-; Urban Land IST, 1996-; Nat Forum Black Public Adminr; Coun Black Econ Develop. **Honors/Awds:** City & County Awards, Fort Lauderdale chapter Nat Asn Advan Colored People, 1978, 1980; Outstanding Service Award, October Center, Inc, 1980; Service of the Year, Urban League Broward County, 1990. **Military Serv:** AUS, E-4, 1971-73; Award for outstanding service in human relations, 1973. **Business Addr:** Director, Office of Economic Development, Broward County Board of County Commissioners, 115 S Andrews Ave A540, Fort Lauderdale, FL 33301-1802, **Business Phone:** (954)357-6155.

TAYLOR, ORLANDO L
College administrator. **Personal:** Born Aug 9, 1936, Chattanooga, TN; son of Leroy and Carrie Lee Sanders; married Loretta M, Jun 6, 1957; children: Orlando II & Ingrid Taylor-Boone. **Educ:** Hampton Inst, Hampton, VA, BS, 1957; Ind Univ, Bloomington, IN, MA, 1960; Univ Mich, Ann Arbor, MI, PhD, 1966. **Career:** Ind Univ, Bloomington IN, asst prof, 1964-69; Ctr Applied Ling, Wash DC, sr res fel, 1969-75; Univ DC, Wash DC, prof, 1970-73; Stanford Univ, vis prof; Univ Pitts, adj prof; Carnegie Found Advan Teaching, vis scholar; Howard Univ, Wash DC, prof, 1973-, dean comun, 1985-, vice provost res, currently. **Honors/Awds:** Distinguished scholar award, Howard Univ, 1984; Award of Appreciation, Am Speech-Language-Hearing Asn, 1990. **Special Achievements:** First African American president of the National Communication Association. **Business Addr:** Dean, Vice Provost, Professor, Howard University, 2400 6th St, Washington, DC 20059, **Business Phone:** (202)806-6800.

TAYLOR, DR. PATRICIA E.
Lawyer. **Personal:** Born Feb 17, 1942, New Haven, CT; married Howard F; children: Carla Y. **Educ:** Ill Inst Tech, BS, 1967; Yale Law Sch, JD, 1971. **Career:** Commun Prog Inc, commun worker, 1963-65; Onondaga Legal Serv, law clerk, 1971-73; Princeton Univ, vis lectr, 1974-. **Orgs:** Fel, Reginald Herber Smith, 1971-73; NJ Bar Asn; US Supreme Court Bar; assoc, Gen Coun Educ Testing Serv, Princeton, NJ; bd dir, ARC, 1972-73; bd dir, Allan Guttmacher Inst, 1986-89. **Honors/Awds:** Outstanding Young Woman of America, 1974. **Business Addr:** Manager, Education Testing Service, Rosedale Rd, Princeton, NJ 08541.

TAYLOR, PATRICIA TATE
Executive. **Personal:** Born Jan 13, 1954, Cleveland, OH; daughter of John Henry and Catherine Johnson. **Educ:** Case Western Res Univ, BA, 1977; Harvard Bus Sch, MBA, 1985; Fed Exec Inst, 1994; Capella Univ, PhD, Cand. **Career:** Standard Oil Co OH, acct, mkt human resources, 1977-83; Deloitte & Touche, info systs consult, 1984; Cresap McCormick & Paget, mgt consult, 1985-87; US Gen Acct Off, mgt expert, 1987-90, asst dir, Fed Mgt Issues, 1990-91, asst dir, Off Prog Planning, 1992-93, sr exec serv, Cand Develop Prog, 1993, dir, Acct & Info Mgt Div, 1994-97; Dept Defense, dir, Quality Mgt & Performance Measurement, 1997-99, dir, Training & Develop, 1999, assoc dir, Human Resource Servs, 1999-2002; Scholar-In-Residence, 2002-. **Orgs:** Exec Women Govt; indust adv bd, Cornell Univ, 1981-83; indust adv comt, Nat Asn Engineering Prog Adminr, 1981-83; Am Mgt Asn, 1985-; Harvard Alumni Asn, 1985-; Nat Asn Female Execs, 1985-; Black

MBA Asn, 1985-; acad fel, Harvard Univ Coun Opportunity Grad Mgt Educ, 1985; Govt Financial Mgrs Asn, 1990-; Sr Execs Asn, 2002-. **Honors/Awds:** Scholarship, Nat Achievement, 1972; Special Commendation Award, 1988; Top Bonus Recipient, 1989-02; Comptroller General's Award, 1992; Exceptional Civilian Service Award, 2001; Federal Women's Leadership Award, 2001. **Military Serv:** Army ROTC Cadet sgt Major 1973-75. **Home Addr:** 5602 Phelps Luck Dr, Columbia, MD 21045-2556, **Home Phone:** (301)596-0854. **Business Addr:** Scholar in Residence, Executive Women Government, 5602 Phelps Luck Dr, Columbia, MD 21045, **Business Phone:** (301)596-0854.

TAYLOR, PAUL
Executive director, government official. **Career:** State Mich, City Detroit, Inner City Sub Ctr, exec dir & proj coordr, currently. **Business Addr:** Project Coordinator, Executive Director, Inner City Sub Center, 8411 E Forest Ave, Detroit, MI 48214, **Business Phone:** (313)921-0200.

TAYLOR, PROF. PAUL DAVID
Health services administrator. **Personal:** Born May 1, 1937, Lexington, TN; son of Ray Otis (deceased) and Jessie Mae Williams (deceased); divorced; children: Paul David Jr & Bentley Christopher. **Educ:** Garden City Community Col, AS, 1957; Univ Kans, 1958. **Career:** Univ Colo Health Sci Ctr, biol lab tech, 1962-65, coordr organ transplant prog, 1962-92, res assoc, 1965-67, sr instr, 1969-92, prof emer, 1992-; Univ Pittsburgh, Presbyterian Univ Hosp, transplant admin, 1989-98; Veterans Admin Hosp, Pittsburgh, PA, health tech, 1990-97. **Orgs:** Task Force Minority Org Donation Western PA; Minority Affairs Comt, Nat Kidney Fed Western PA; ed bd, J Transplant Coord; Dept Health & Human Servs, Bur Health Resources Develop; master, Prince Hall Masons, Denver, 1967; chmn, jurisprudence, Grand Lodge Co & Jurisdiction, 1970-90; founding mem, N Am Transplant Coordrs Orgn, 1975-98; bd dirs, Colo Soc Prevent Blindness, 1977-80; treas, Am Soc Health & Transplant Profs, 1998-99. **Honors/Awds:** Citizenship Award, Prince Hall Masons Co & Jurisdiction, 1982; Citizenship Award, Hattie Anthony Resource Ctr, 1986; Man of Distinction, Lane Contempories Lane Col Alumni Asn, Denver Chap, 1989; Honoree, Cols Own African History Maker, 1993; BTAC, Denver, Black Transplantation Comt, 1993; bd dir, Howard Univ, Nat Mottep, 2000; Grandmaster's Award Master of the Year, MWPHGL Col, 2003; Paul W Stewart Volunteer of the Year Award, Black Am West Mus & Heritage Ctr, Denver, 2003. **Special Achievements:** Member of world's first human liver transplant team, Denver, CO, 1963; author or co-author of numerous scientific papers, 1965-; consultant & participant: Eurotransplant Coordinator organisation, Leiden Holland, 1983; Canadian Transplant Coord, Calgary, Alberta, 1983; 10th Annual Meeting of Japanese Transplantation & Artificial Organisation society, Sendai, Japan, 1985; Minister of Health & Welfare, Tokyo, Japan, 1985; Cardiovascular Transplantation Seminar, Osaka, Japan, 1985; 16th Annual Meeting North American Transplant Coordinators Organization, African Americans in transplantation lecture, Halifax, Nova Scotia, 1990; National Thoracic Organisation Transplant Nurses of Hospital Juan Canalejo, La Coruna, Spain, 1992; XIVth International Congress of the Transplantation Society, Paris, France, 1992; XVth International Congress of the Transplantation Society & International Transplant Coordinators Symposium, Kyoto, Japan, 1994; Inaugural Inductee, first national minority transplant, Hall of Fame, Pioneer Award, Mottep, Howard Univ, 1996. **Home Addr:** 507 S Magnolia Lane, Denver, CO 80224-1524, **Home Phone:** (303)333-2153. **Business Addr:** Professor Emeritus, University of Colorado Health Sciences Center, College of Nursing, 13120 E 19th Ave, PO Box C288, Aurora, CO 80045, **Business Phone:** (303)724-1812.

TAYLOR, DR. QUINTARD
Educator. **Personal:** Born Dec 11, 1948, Brownsville, TN; son of Quintard and Grace (Brown); married Carolyn Fain (divorced); children: Quintard, Jamila & William. **Educ:** St Augustine's Col, BA, 1969; Univ Minn, MA, 1971, PhD, 1977. **Career:** Univ of Minn, instr, 1969-71; Gustavus Adolphus Col, instr, 1971; Wa State Univ, asst prof, 1971-75; Calif Polytechnic State Univ, prof, hist, 1977-90; Univ Lagos, Akoka Nigeria, visiting Fulbright prof, 1987-88; Univ Ore, prof, 1990-96, adj prof, 1990-94, actg dir, 1992-93, dept head, 1997-99, Knight Distinguished Prof, 1998-99, Benjamin H & Louise L Carroll Vis Endowed Prof, 2006; Univ Wash, vis prof, 1995, Scott & Dorothy Bullitt prof, Amer hist, 1999-; Pepperdine Univ, vis prof, 1997, 2000. **Orgs:** Great Plains Black Museum, 1980-85; Afro-Am Cultural Arts Ctr, 1977-78; Nat Endowment for the Humanities, 1979-83; Martin Luther Fund, 1983-85, mem, 1979-; Endowment Comm "Journal Negro History" 1983-; Calif Black Faculty Staff asn, 1985-, Golden Key Nat Honor Soc, 1987-, Phi Beta Delta Society for InterNat Scholars, 1989-; Martin Luther King Vocational-Technical Col, Owerri Nigeria, 1989-, African-Amer Vocational Inst, Aba Nigeria, 1989-; Am Hist Asn; Asn Study Afro Am Life & History; Asn Asian Am Studies; Black Heritage Soc Wash State; Urban History Asn; Western History Asn. **Honors/Awds:** ASALH, Carter G Woodson Award, 1980; The Danforth Found, Kent Fel, 1974-77; Univ Minn, Bush Fel, 1971-77; NEH Travel & Collections Grant, Natl Endowment for the Humanities, 1988; The Emergence Afro-American Communities in the Pacific Northwest, 1865-1910; Carter G Woodson Award for best article published in the Journal of Negro History 1978-79; Meritorious Performance & Professional Promise Award, Calif Polytech State Univ,1986, Vivian A Paladin Award, Montana Historical Soc, 1996-97. **Special Achievements:** Written: In Search of the Racial Frontier: African Americans in the American West, 1528-1990; The Forging of A Black Community Seattle's Central District from 1870 Through the Civil Rights Era. **Business Addr:** Professor of American History, University of Washington, Department of History, PO Box 353560, Seattle, WA 98195, **Business Phone:** (206)543-5698.

TAYLOR, REGGIE
Baseball player. **Personal:** Born Jan 12, 1977, Newberry, SC. **Career:** Philadelphia Phillies, 2000-01; Cincinnati Reds, outfielder, 2002-03; Colo Rockies, outfielder, 2004; Tampa Bay Ray Devils, outfielder, 2005; Detroit Tigers, ctr field & left field, 2005; St. Louis Cardinals, 2005; Lancaster Barnstormers, 2006; Long Island Ducks, 2007; Atlanta Braves; Richmond Braves; Olmecas de Tabasco, 2008. Sioux Falls Canaries, currently. *

TAYLOR, DR. REGINA
Actor, playwright. **Personal:** Born Aug 22, 1960, Dallas, TX. **Educ:** Southern Methodist Univ, attended 1981. **Career:** Goodman Theater, distinguished artistic assoc, currently; Alliance Theatre, Atlanta, GA, writer-in-residence, currently; TV films: "Nurse",1980; "Crisis at Central High", 1981; "Concealed Enemies", 1984; "Lean on Me", 1989; "Howard Beach: Making a Case for Murder", 1989; "I'll FlyAway", 1991; "Law & Order: Mushrooms", 1991; "Jersey Girl", 1992; "I'llFly Away: Then and Now", 1993; "Law & Order: Virtue", 1994; "Children of the Dust", 1995; "Losing Isaiah", 1995; "Clockers", 1995; "The Keeper",1995; "Spirit Lost", 1996; "A Family Thing", 1996; "Courage Under Fire", 1996; "Feds", 1997; "Hostile Waters", 1997; "The Third Twin", 1997; "TheNegotiator", 1998; "Strange Justice", 1999; "Cora Unashamed", 2000; TV Series: "The Education of Max Bickford", 2001; "In From the Night", 2005;"The Unit", 2006;Stage: "Romeo & Juliet;, "As You like it"; "Macbeth"; "Machinal"; "A Map of The World"; "The Illusion"; "Jar the Floor"; "Tempest"; Playwright: "Oo-Bla-Dee, 2000; "Drowning Crow", 2003; "The Dreams of Sarah Breed love",2004; "A Night in Tunisia"; "Escape from Paradise"; "Watermelon Rinds"; "Inside the Belly of the Beast"; "Crowns", 2004; "Magnolia", 2009. **Honors/Awds:** Pea Body awd, Gracy Awd; L.A Dramalogue Awd; Q Award for Best Actress in a Quality Drama Series, 1992, 1993; Golden Globe Award for Best Performance by an Actress in a TV-Series, Drama,1993; Image Award for Outstanding Lead Actress in a Drama Series, 1995;New play Award, Am Critics Assn; NAACP Image Award For the Best actress in a Drama, 2008; Honorary Doc from DePaul univ. **Special Achievements:** Nominated twice for Emmy Award in Drama Series; first Black woman to play William Shakespeare's Juliet. **Business Addr:** Artistic Associate, Goodman Theatre, 170 North Dearborn Str, Chicago, IL 60601.*

TAYLOR, REGINALD REDALL, JR.
Educator, school administrator. **Personal:** Born Jun 30, 1939, Waycross, GA; son of Reginald R Taylor Sr and Ellen Butler; married Laurine Williams, Aug 11, 1963; children: Robyn Michelle. **Educ:** Fla A&M Univ, BS, 1961; Fort Valley State Col, MS, 1973; Valdosta State Col, Valdosta, Ga, 1990. **Career:** Pierce Co Bd Educ, Blackshear, Ga; Lee St High Sch, social studies teacher& band dir, 1961-69; Blackshear High Sch, social studies teacher & counr, 1969-72, Pierce Co High Sch, counr/asst prin, 1973-90, Ware Street Elem Sch, prin 1990-; City Blackshear, councilman, 1979-. **Orgs:** Composite Lodge #40, Fla A&M Univ, 1960; pres, Pierce Co Assoc Educrs, 1964, 1967, 1968; pres, Consolidated Mens Club Inc, 1973; bd dirs, Pierce Co Chamber Com, 1980-82; dir, Waycross Chorale Ensemble, 1988-90. **Honors/Awds:** Teacher of the Year, Pierce Co Teachers Asn Educr, 1965; Citizen of the Year, Pierce Co Chamber Com 1981; Father of the Year, Gaines Chapel AME Church, 1982. **Business Addr:** Principal, Ware Street Elementary School, 623 Sycamore St, Blackshear, GA 31516, **Business Phone:** (912)449-2078.

TAYLOR, RICHARD L. See Obituaries section.

TAYLOR, ROBERT, III. See TAYLOR, BOBBY.

TAYLOR, DR. ROBERT, III
Dentist, educator. **Personal:** Born Apr 12, 1946, Ashburn, GA; son of Susie Bell Hudson and Robert Jr; married JoAnne Davis; children: Robert IV, Quentin, Sonya & Bridget. **Educ:** Albany State Col, BS, 1966; Atlanta Univ, MS, 1970; Med Col GA, DMD, 1975; US Navy, Cert, 1976. **Career:** Telfair Co GA, chem instr, 1966-69; Henry Co GA, biol instr, 1969-70; US Navy, asst sr dent officer, 1975-78; Turner Job Corps GA, head dentist, 1978-82; gen dent, self-employed; dent terminoly instr; Taylor Dent Clins, dentist, currently. **Orgs:** Am Dent Asn; Nat Dent Asn; Am Acad Gen Dentists; Res Officers League; GA Acad Gen Dentists; Phi Bet Sigma Frat Inc; chmn bd, Nat Asn Advan Colored People; vpres, Cong Black Orgns; Jack & Jill Am; Albany State Col Found; Title Twenty Found; Prince Hall Mason Lodge 360; Knights of Columbus 4th Degree 3607; Post 512 Am Legion; VFW Post 7491; AL Ranken 142; Dougherty County Bd Health; Sowega Health Care Providers; Educ Project 2000. **Honors/Awds:** Certificates of Honor, Med Col GA, US Navy, Nat Asn Advan Colored People; Outstanding Young Men of America, 1980; HCOP Grant, Albany State Col, 1982. **Military Serv:** USN, lt comdr, 20 yrs. **Home Addr:** 512 S Monroe St, Albany, GA 31701, **Home Phone:** (229)435-4954. **Business Addr:** Dentist, Taylor Dental Clinics, 512 S Monroe St, Albany, GA 31701, **Business Phone:** (229)435-4954.

TAYLOR, ROBERT DEREK
Financial manager. **Personal:** Born Jul 2, 1961, Los Angeles, CA; son of Robert M Taylor and Geneva Williams; married Joy L Johnson, Jul 23, 1988. **Educ:** Calif State Univ, Northridge, BS, Eng, 1982; Stanford Law Sch, JD, 1986; Stanford Grad Sch Bus, MBA, 1986. **Career:** McKinsey & Co, prin, 1986-97; Blue Capital Mgt, managing dir, 1997-. **Orgs:** Chair bd dirs, Decorative Concepts Inc, chair; bd dirs, M2 Automotive Inc; bd dirs, Rebuild LA; bd trustee, Nat Urban League; bd trustee, LA Urban League; bd visitors, Stanford Law Sch; Frontier Airlines, bd dirs. **Business Addr:** Managing Director, Blue Capital Management LLC, 11111 Santa Monica Blvd Suite 1470, Los Angeles, CA 90025-3348, **Business Phone:** (310)914-9145.

TAYLOR, DR. RONALD LEWIS
College teacher, sociologist. **Personal:** Born Feb 27, 1942, St Petersburg, FL; son of David Taylor and Lillian Bell Miller; married Bernice Chavis, Dec 24, 1966; children: Kevin & Darryl. **Educ:** Bethune-Cookman Col, Daytona Beach, BA, 1963; Howard Univ, Wash, MA, 1965; Boston Univ, Boston, PhD, 1972. **Career:** US Dept Labor, res assoc & prog evaluator, 1963-64; Bethune-Cookman Col, dean men, 1964-65, dir, financial aid, 1965-67; Boston Univ, instr, lectr, 1967-72; Univ Conn, asst prof-full prof, 1972-, chair, sociol dept, 1981-86, Inst African-Am Studies, dir, 1993-99, vice provost Multicult & Int Affairs, 1999-. **Orgs:** Chair, DuBois-Johnson-Frazier Awards, Am Sociol Asn, 1987-90; exec comt, Am Asn Univ Profs, 1988-; ed bd, Am Jour Orthopsychiat, 1978-85; ed bd, Contemporary Sociology, 1980-84, 2000-02; Edial Bd, Univ Press New Eng, 1984-90; pres, Am Asn Univ Profs, Univ Conn Chap; ed bd, Jour Res Adolescence, 1994-; ed bd, Jour Men's Studies, 1992-; ed bd, Jour African-Am Male Studies, 1991-; ed bd, Race & Soc, 1997-02. **Honors/Awds:** Research fellow, Ford Found, 1970-72; Research fellow, Nat Endowment Humanities 1978-79; Distinguished Scholastic Achievement Award, Univ Mass, 1991. **Special Achievements:** Co-author: Black Male in Am, Nelson-Hall, 1977; Co-editor: Black Adolescence, GK Hall, 1990; Editor: African-American Youth, Praeger, 1995; Minority Families in US, Prentice-Hall, 1994, 1997, 2003. **Home Phone:** (860)872-0596. **Business Addr:** Professor of Sociology, Vice Provost for Multicultural & International Affairs, University of Connecticut, Department of Sociology, 241 Glenbrook Rd Unit 2215, Storrs, CT 06269-2215, **Business Phone:** (860)486-5848.

TAYLOR, RUTH SLOAN
Educator. **Personal:** Born Jun 8, 1918, Greenville, SC; widowed. **Educ:** EdD, 1962. **Career:** Summer HS Cairo, IL, eng teacher, 1946-48; Roosevelt HS Gary, IN, eng, 1948-66; Title I E SEA Gary, IN, sup, 1966-68; Ind Univ NW, asst chrmn div ed, 1969-. **Orgs:** Coop Ed Res Lab Prog Assoc, Northfield, IL, 1967; asst prof Ind Univ NW, 1969; assoc prof Ind Univ NW, 1972; pres, bd trustee, Gary Community Sch; consult, leec chmn Bi-Cen Comm, Ind Univ NW United Way Camp City Met Chmn, 1974; Nat Soc Act Comm Delta Sigma Theta Sorority, 1973; asst chmn, Div Ed Ind Univ NW, 1974-75; elected Nat Sec Delta Sigma Theta Sorority Inc. **Honors/Awds:** Auth of "Teaching in the Desegregated Classroom"; Outstanding cit award, Ed IU Dons Inc 1974. **Business Addr:** Indiana Univ NW, 3400 Broadway, Gary, IN 46408.

TAYLOR, S MARTIN
Executive. **Personal:** Born in Bangor, MI; married Anna Diggs. **Educ:** Western Mich Univ, BS, polit sci & econs, 1964; Detroit Col Law, JD, 1967; Marygrove Col, hon doctor laws degree. **Career:** New Detroit Inc, pres; Mich Dept Labor & Mich Employment Security Comn, dir; Detroit Edison, Detroit, MI, vpres govt rels, 1989, sr vpres, corp & pub affairs, DTE Energy Corp, Human Resources & Corp Affairs, exec vpres & sr vpres; Detroit Renaissance, interim pres. **Orgs:** Chair, Univ Mich, 1996, 2004-; chair, Arts League Mich; chair, Detroit Economic Growth Corp. **Business Phone:** (313)235-4000.

TAYLOR, DR. SANDRA ELAINE
Psychologist. **Personal:** Born Aug 8, 1946, New York, NY; daughter of Floyd Lee and Berthenia T; married Alvin Green, Apr 28, 1984 (divorced 1986); children: Kwam Taylor Green; married Walter C Bailey, Apr 17, 1970 (divorced 1977). **Educ:** Bronx Comm Col, Univ NY, AAS, 1965, AA 1969; City Col NY, BA, 1970; City Univ NY, PhD, 1976. **Career:** Bronx Psychiatric Ctr, head nurse, 1965-73; Albert Einstein Clinical Internship Prog Psychology, intern psychologist, 1973-74; City Col, City Univ, New York, adjunct lecturer, 1974-75; Bronx Psychiatric Ctr, staff psychologist, 1974-76; St Joseph's Col, adjunct asst prof, 1976-77; Marymount Col, adjunct asst prof, 1976-79, counseling psychologist, 1976-77; City Col/Harlem Hosp Ctr Physician Asst Prog, educational coord, 1977-80; Brooklyn Developmental Ctr, principal psychologist & exec Asst dir, 1980-81; Bronx Develop

Ctr, deputy dir treatment svcs, 1981-90; Kwam SET Publ Co Inc, pres, 1989. **Orgs:** Nat Asn Female Executives, 1983-. **Honors/Awds:** Numerous honors, awards, special achievements, publications such as "The New York Urban League Presents," WBLS radio station guest speaker, 1976; recipient of the First Pamela Galiber Memorial Scholarship Awd for Doctoral Dissertation Rsch in memory of NY State Senator Jos Galiber's late daughter The City Univ of NY, 1976; "The Meaning of Scholarship" New York Eastern Star Annual Scholarship Awd presentation principal speaker, 1976; "Ethnic Self-Hatred in Black Psychotics, A Preliminary Report" Journal of the Bronx State Hosp Vol 1 No 2 Spring, 1973; "Racism and Psychiatry" Bronx Psychiatric Ctr guest lecturer for visiting medical residents, 1973. **Home Addr:** PO Box 523, Bronx, NY 10451-0523.

TAYLOR, DR. SCOTT MORRIS
Physician. **Personal:** Born Oct 10, 1957, Berkeley, CA; son of Robert L Taylor. **Educ:** Morehouse Col, BS, 1980; Meharry Med Sch, MD, 1984. **Career:** Highland Hosp, surg resident, 1984-86; Martin Luther King Hosl, orthop resident, 1987-91; pvt pract, 1991-; C Hosp Med Ctr, Oakland, CA, staff, 1992-99; Healthsouth Industrial Clinic, Oakland, CA, consult, 1995-2001; Alta Bates Medical Group, physician, currently. **Home Phone:** (510)238-9600. **Business Addr:** Physician, 400-29th St Suite 400, Oakland, CA 94609-3549, **Business Phone:** (510)238-9600.

TAYLOR, SID E
Chief executive officer, president (organization). **Career:** Gen Motors, mgr, 1988; SET Steel Inc, founder, 1989; founder, Group of Co: SET Enterprises Inc, SBF Automotive & T & B Conveyor Products, currently; SET Enterprises Inc, pres & ceo, 2002-. **Orgs:** Founder, Intervale Cloverdale Lyndon Livernois Indust Park Asn, 1997; pres, Nat Asn Black Automotive Suppliers, 2003; Mich Minority Bus Develop Coun; NAACP; Econ Club of Detroit; Detroit Golf Club; adv bd mem, Jackson State Univ; bd mem, YMCA, Warren, MI. **Honors/Awds:** Ernst & Young Mich Entrepreneur of the Year, 2001. **Military Serv:** Served USMC, Vietnam. **Business Addr:** President, Chief Executive Officer, SET Enterprises Inc, 30500 Van Dyke Ave Suite 701, Warren, MI 48093, **Business Phone:** (586)573-3600.*

TAYLOR, SINTHY E
Executive. **Personal:** Born Aug 18, 1947, Dayton, OH; married Vivian Lorraine Lundy. **Educ:** Union Experimenting Cols & Univ Cincinnati, BS, 1977. **Career:** Dayton Model Cities Planning Coun, youth coordr, 1968-70; Dayton Youth Coalition, exec dir, 1970-75; Dayton Voter Registration Educ Inst, adminr, 1975-80; State Ohio Dept Admin Servs, job recruitment specialist, 1980-83; Taylor-Made Construct Co Inc, vpres bd dirs, 1980-; Commissioned Notary Pub, 1980-; Care-Free Property Mgt Co Inc, consult, 1986-; Midas Landscaping & Develop Co Inc, pres & ecol planner, 1986-; Dayton Democratic Progressive Clubs, pres, currently. **Orgs:** Chmn bd, Wesley Comm Ctr, 1975-76; Miami Consistory 26, 1981-; chaplin, Ancient Sq, 1981-; Royal Arch Masons, 1982-; Boone Commandery Knights Templar, 1982-; Solomon Johnson Coun 4 Royal & Select Masters, 1982-; Knights Mystic Shrine, 1982-; Order Easter Star 1983-; assoc pastor, St Paul AME Zion Church Dayton, 1983-; worthy patron, 1984; chmn ward & precinct, Democratic Voters League, 1985-86; chmn voter registration, Democratic Voters League, 1986-87; Heroines Jericho; Heroines Templars Crusade. **Honors/Awds:** Letter of Commendation President of the United States, 1976; Evangelist of the Year Award, AME Zion Church Connection, 1985. **Home Phone:** (937)277-2438. **Business Phone:** (937)235-1010.

TAYLOR, STACEY LORENZO
Military leader, marine corps officer. **Personal:** Born Sep 3, 1971, Sandersville, GA; son of Herbert and Annie; married Marsha, May 22, 1999; children: Nastacia D. **Educ:** Morris Brown Col, BS, acct, 1993; Fla State Univ, MBA. **Career:** US Marine Corps, air traffic controller, 1993-. **Orgs:** Kappa Alpha Psi Frat Inc, 1991-; Alpha Kappa Mu Honor Soc, 1992; Free & Accepted Mason, PHA, 1993-. **Honors/Awds:** Community Serv Award, City of New Orleans, LA, 1998. **Military Serv:** USMC, cap, 1993-. **Business Addr:** Air Traffic Controller, US Marine Corps, 2121 W Pensacola St Suite C, Tallahassee, FL 32304-3149, **Business Phone:** (850)574-4377.*

TAYLOR, STERLING R
Executive, consultant. **Personal:** Born Jan 5, 1942, Philadelphia, PA; son of Willie Ray and Ellanora K Bivens; married Sonia E Madden (divorced); children: Tiarzha M & Khara D. **Career:** Army & Air Force Exchange Serv, buyer, 1964-70; The Equitable Companies Inc, life underwriter, regist rep, 1970-; Seattle Br AXA Advisors LLC, financial consult, currently. **Orgs:** Past pres, Sothern Alaska Life Underwriters, 1974-75; past pres, Alaska State Asn Life Underwriters; life mem, exec comm, Nat Asn Advan Colored People Anchorage Br; founder, Alaska Black Caucus, past pres; comt chmn, Alaska Black Leadership Conf; ambassador, Life Underwriters Polit Action Comt; life mem, Alpha Phi Alpha, Nu Zeta Lambda Chap, past pres; past grand master, Prince Hall Masons, Alaska; bd chmn, Anchorage Community Health Ctr; chmn, Anchorage Transp Comn. **Honors/Awds:** Nat Sales Achievement Awards; Nat Quality Awards; Hall of Fame, The Equitable Companies Inc, 1982; Life Mem, Million Dollar Round Table, 1986; Nat Community Leadership Award, 1993. **Home Addr:** 200 W 34th Ave Suite 376, Anchorage, AK 99503-3969. **Business Addr:** Financial Consultant, 10500 NE 8th St Suite 1600, Bellevue, WA 98004, **Business Phone:** (206)728-2400.

TAYLOR, STUART A.
Educator, consultant. **Personal:** Born Jul 2, 1936, Providence, RI; married Ella Marie; children: Sandre, Stuart, Sabrina & Scott. **Educ:** Oakwood Col, BS, acct bus, 1960; Univ RI, MS, 1963; Ind Univ, PhD, indust mgt & psychol, 1967. **Career:** Harvard Bus Sch, assoc prof; mgt consult. **Orgs:** Acad Mgt; bd adv, Nat Urban League; founder, RI Com for Advan of Negro Ed; White House Fel Prog; Harvard Bus Sch African-Am Alumni Asn. **Honors/Awds:** US Dept of Urban Develop & Study Abroad. **Special Achievements:** First Black to become Licensed Public Accounting RI to Teach Full-time at Harvard Bus School.

TAYLOR, SUSAN CHARLENE
Dermatologist. **Personal:** Born Oct 7, 1957, Philadelphia, PA; daughter of Charles Taylor and Ethel Taylor; married Kemel W Dawkins, Mar 5, 1983; children: Morgan Elizabeth & Madison Lauren. **Educ:** Univ Pa, BA, biol, 1979; Harvard Med Sch, MD, 1983. **Career:** Columbia Presbyterian Med Ctr, resident dermat, 1986-89; Soc Hill Dermat, physician, 1989-; St Luke's Roosevelt Hosp Ctr, Skin Color Ctr, dir, 1999-. **Orgs:** AMA; Am Acad Dermat; Pa Med Soc; Med Soc Eastern Pa; Pa County Med Soc; Philadelphia Dermat Soc; trustee, Baldwin Sch; trustee, Univ Pa; Health Care Delivery Comt; Minority Student Mentors Prog; chair, Skin Color Soc; bd trustee, United Way Eastern Pa; Am Bd Internal Med. **Honors/Awds:** Alumni Award of Merit, Univ Pa. **Special Achievements:** Auth, Brown Skin Dr Susan Taylor's Prescription for Flawless Skin, Hair and Nails. **Business Addr:** Dermatologist, Society Hill Dermatology, 932 Pine St, Philadelphia, PA 19107, **Business Phone:** (215)829-6861.

TAYLOR, SUSAN L.
Publishing executive. **Personal:** Born Jan 23, 1946, New York, NY; daughter of Lawrence and Violet Weekes; married Khephra Burns; married William Bowles, Jan 3, 1967 (divorced 1971); children: Shana-Nequai. **Educ:** Fordham Univ, BA, social sci, 1991. **Career:** Negro Ensemble Com, former actress; licensed cosmetologist; Nequai Cosmetics, founder & pres, 1970-72; Essense mag, freelance writer, beautyed, 1970-71, fashion & beauty ed, 1971-81, ed-in-chief, 1981-2000, vpres, sr vpres, 1993, ed dir, ed-in-chief emer, currently; Essense Commun Inc, tv host, exec coordr, sr vpres, 1983; Nequai Cosmetics, founder; Nat CARES Mentoring Movement, founder & chief exec officer, currently. **Orgs:** Am Soc Mag Eds; Women Communs; Nat Asn Black Journalists; Black Women Publ; avid supporter, Comn Res Black Educ; adv bd Black Adminrs Child Welfare; founder, The Future PAC. **Honors/Awds:** Fifth Annual Kizzy Image & Achievement Award, 1981; Excellence in Media Award, Howard Univ, 1982; Women Communs Matirx Award, 1982; Nat Asn Negro Bus & Prof Womens Clubs, Bus Awards, 1983; inducted, Am Society Mag Eds (ASME) Hall of Fame, 2002; Henry Johnson Fisher Award; Honorary degree, Lincoln Univ; Honorary degree, Spelman Col; Honorary degree, Dillard Univ; Honorary degree, Bennett Col Women; Honorary degree, Univ Delaware; Honorary degree, Fordham Univ. **Special Achievements:** First African American woman to receive The Henry Johnson Fisher Award; Author: In the Spirit: The Inspirational Writings of Susan L Taylor, 1993; Lessons in Living, Anchor Books, 1995; Confirmation, coauthor, editor, 1997. **Business Addr:** Founder, Chief Executive Officer, National CARES Mentoring Movement, 230 Peachtree St Ste 530, Atlanta, GA 30303.

TAYLOR, T SHAWN
Journalist. **Personal:** Born Aug 23, 1966, Alton, IL; daughter of Robert Taylor and Armelia Jefferson. **Educ:** Univ Mo-Columbia, bachelor's degree, Jour, 1987. **Career:** Detroit Free Press, copy ed, 1988-89; Kans City Star, copy ed, 1989-90; Chicago Tribune, copy ed, 1990-96, reporter, freelance writer, currently. **Orgs:** Alpha Kappa Alpha Sorority Inc, 1986-; Nat Asn Black Journalists, 1987-. **Business Addr:** Freelance Writer, Chicago Tribune, 435 N Michigan Ave, Chicago, IL 60611.

TAYLOR, TAMARA
Actor. **Personal:** Born Sep 27, 1970, Ontario. **Career:** TV Series: "A Different World", 1991; "Freshman Dorm", 1992; "Party ofFive", 1997; Senseless, 1998; "Alternative Lifestyles", 1998; "Dawson's Creek", 1998; Graham's Diner, 1999; "Early Edition", 1999; Introducing Dorothy Dandridge, 1999; "Providence", 1999; "City of Angels", 2000; "OneSpecial Moment", 2001; "Hidden Hills", 2002; "Miracles", 2003; "Everwood", 2003; "Becker", 2003; "Without a Trace", 2003; "Six Feet Under", 2004;"CSI: Miami", 2004; "One on One", 2004; Diary of a Mad Black Woman, 2005;"SWAK", 2005; "Navy NCIS: Naval Criminal Investigative Service"; Serenity,2005; "Sex, Love & Secrets", 2005; "Special", 2005; "Lost", 2005; "Numb3rs", 2006; "Bones", 2006-07; Bones: Access All Areas, 2008; The Double Death of the Dearly Departed, 2009; The Girl in the Mask, 2009; The Beaver in the Otter, 2009; The Critic in the Cabernet, 2009; The End in the Beginning, 2009; Film: Senseless, 1998; Graham's Diner, 1999; Diary of a Mad Black Woman, 2005; Serenity, 2005; Gordon Glass, 2007. **Business Addr:** Actress, c/o NBC, 30 Rockefeller Plz, New York, NY 10112.*

TAYLOR, TENISHA NICOLE (TENISHA ABERNATHY)
Television producer. **Educ:** Clark Atlanta Univ. **Career:** CNN, Atlanta, news producer, currently, exec producer, currently. **Business Addr:** News Producer, Execurive producer, CNN, Saturday/Sunday Morning, 190 Marietta St NW, Atlanta, GA 30303, **Business Phone:** (404)827-5332.*

TAYLOR, DR. THEODORE D. See Obituaries section.

TAYLOR, TOMMIE W.
Public relations executive. **Personal:** Born Mar 4, 1929, Blytheville, AR; married Aubrey Taylor Sr; children: Aubrey Jr (deceased), Darryl E, Roderic K, Cabot O. **Educ:** Philander Smith Col, BA, 1955; Univ Ark, Little Rock. **Career:** Public relations executive (retired); licensed cosmetologist, 1948; Johnson Publ Co, stringer, 1954-65; Radio Sta KOKY-AM, prog asst, 1957-59; AR Baptist Col, registrar psych instr, 1959-61; Teletype Corp, civil rel assoc, 1962-75; AT&T Info Systs, pub rels rep, 1982-87. **Orgs:** Pres, Urban League Greater Little Rock, 1971-75; tammateous, 1984-85, 2nd anti basileus, 1985-86, 1st anti basileus, 1986-87, Sigma Gamma Rho Sor; dir, Young Peoples Bapt Training Union Dept NH Zion Baptist Church; bd trustee, Ark Baptist Col, 2001-. **Honors/Awds:** Outstanding Service Award, Urban League Greater Little Rock, 1973, 1975; Outstanding Volunteer Service Award, Urban League, 1975; Volunteer & Community Service Award, Urban League Guild, 1975; Appreciation Award, Youth Home Inc, 1979; Outstanding Service Award, Ark Bapt Col Camera Club, 1979; Appreciation Award, Nat Alumni Asn Ark Baptist Col, 1984; Distinguished Service Award, Philander Smith Col United Negro Col Fund, 1987; Active Participant Award, Nat Alumni Asn Ark Baptist Col, 1987; Honorary Drs Degree, Humane Letters, Ark Baptist Col, 1987; Outstanding Service Award, ABC Nat Alumni Asn, 1988; Nat Alumni Asn Award, Philander Smith Col, 1991; Certificate of Merit, State Ark, 1994; Award for 35 yrs of service, Sigma Gamma Rho, Theta Sigma chp, 1999; Presidential Award, Ark Baptist Col, Nat Alumni Asn, 2000; Recognition for Outstanding Contribution & Serv, Philander Smith Col, 2000. **Home Addr:** 806 S Miss St, Little Rock, AR 72205, **Home Phone:** (501)227-4565. *

TAYLOR, TYRONE CURTIS
Executive. **Personal:** Born Jul 20, 1953, Washington, DC; son of Arthur and Bernice; married Carolyn, Jun 2, 1979; children: Donovan & Briana. **Educ:** Wilmington Col, AB, 1975; Southeastern Univ, MBA, 1978. **Career:** NASA HQS, dir, Nat Serv, 1973-95; Fed Lab Conserv, Wash, DC rep, 1995-98; Unisphere Inc, exec vpres, 1998-2003; Capitol Advisors Technol, pres, 2003-; WVa High Technol Consortium Found, dir, Wash Rels, currently. **Orgs:** Minority Bus Technol Transfer Conserv, 1999-; NASA Minority Reserve Comt, 1999-2001; bd dir, Pediatric AIDS/HIV Care, 2002-; chair, small bus div, Nat Defense Industrial Assoc, 2002-; comt visitors, NSF, 2003-; Nat Res Steering Comt, 2003-. **Honors/Awds:** NASA Exceptional Service, 1992; Citations from US Congress, 1998. **Special Achievements:** Participation in Congressional Black Caucus Science & Technology Braintest. **Business Addr:** Director, West Virginia High Technology Consortium Foundation, 1000 Technol Dr Suite 1000, Fairmont, WV 26554, **Business Phone:** (304)366-2577.

TAYLOR, VALERIE CHARMAYNE
Advertising executive. **Personal:** Born Jan 19, 1962, Chattanooga, TN; daughter of Harvey E and Geneva Williams. **Educ:** Austin Peay State Univ, 1982; Mich State Univ, BA, telecommunications, 1985; Inst Educ Leadership, cert, 1987-88. **Career:** Mich Dept Nat Resources, community rels rep, 1983-85; Fed Social Security Dept, claims rep/asst spec emphasis coordr, 1985-86; Lansing Community Col, community rels mgr, 1986-88; State Bar Mich, commun mgr, 1988-89; Mich Travel Bur, mkt mgr, 1989-91; Jamestown-Yorktown Found, Commonwealth Va, dir pub affairs & mkt, 1991-94; Siddall Matus & Coushter, Advertising & Pub Rel, acct supvr, 1994-. **Orgs:** Nat pr chair, Delta Sigma Theta Sorority Inc, 1987-91; Nat Asn Mkt Developers; African-Am Pub Rels Soc; charter mem, Mich Black Media Asn, vpres, 1987-89; bd dir, Lansing Food Bank, 1987-90; secy, Lansing Martin Luther King Comn, 1989-90; co-chair citywide radiothon, Lansing Br Nat Asn Advan Colored People, 1988; bd dirs, Williamsburg Hotel/Motel Asn, 1991-; ad-hoc Econs Bd Pub Rels Soc Am; Asn Travel Mkt Exec, 1991-. **Honors/Awds:** Outstanding Serv Award, US Dept Health & Human Serv, 1986; Serv Appreciation Recognition, Delta Sigma Theta Sorority Inc, 1987; Serv Appreciation Cert, Lansing United Negro Col Fund, 1988. **Special Achievements:** Instituted museums first-time co-op ticket program, generating more than $200,000 in sales revenue & increasing visitation by 29% for record high levels; Implemented national media relations campaign for Virginia museums, resulting in first time feature coverage by CNN Headline News, Time Life Books, Americana Mag, Los Angeles Time & Walt Disney Prod, 1992; implemented Mich segmented marketing prog focusing on Chicago, increased visitation by 18% first year, 1991; developed Mich co-op travel marketing prog, increased travel

budget by $4.5 million - generated 190,000 additional travel inquires. **Business Phone:** (804)253-4138.

TAYLOR, VANESSA GAIL
Law enforcement officer, educator, basketball coach. **Personal:** Born Sep 15, 1960, Lafayette, LA; daughter of Dalton Belson Jr; married John F, Sep 15, 1979; children: Tiffany & Timothy. **Educ:** Univ Southwestern La, AS, 1982, BS, 1994; Acadiana Law Enforcement Training Acad, attended 1985; Drug Abuse Resistance Educ Training, 1991. **Career:** Law enforcement officer (retired), educator, basketball coach; Lafayette Parish Juvenile Detention Ctr, 1981-82; Lafayette Police Dept, clerk II, 1982-85, corporal, 1985-97; St Landry Parish Sch Brd, N Cent High Sch, spec educr & basketball coach, currently. **Orgs:** La Peace Officers Assn, 1987-; Munic Police Officers Assn, 1987-; Magnolia Peace Officers Assn, 1988-; Police Assn Lafayette, 1989-; Lafayette Youth Conf Comn, 1991-; Black Adoption & Foster Care Advocacy Brd, 1991-. **Honors/Awds:** Officer of the Month, Lafayette Police Dept, 1992; Officer of the Year,Nat Assn Blacks Criminal Justice, 1993; Officer of the Year, Crime Prev Adv Comn Nominee, 1993; Officer of the Year, Knights of Columbus 3202, 1992; Officer of the Year, Kiwanis Club, 1994; Trio Achievers Award, 1994; District Coach of the Year; Parish Coach of the Year; St Coach of the Year. **Special Achievements:** First female to become a motorcycle officer in the state of Louisiana. **Home Addr:** 191 Thelma Dr, Sunset, LA 70584, **Home Phone:** (337)662-5509. **Business Addr:** Basketball Coach, St Landry Parish School Board, North Central High School, Hwy 10, Lebeau, LA 71345, **Business Phone:** (337)623-4239.*

TAYLOR, VERNON ANTHONY
Army officer. **Personal:** Born Jul 31, 1946, Easton, MD; son of Wayman W Taylor Sr and Evelyn S Taylor; married Judith Woodson, Oct 27, 1973; children: Anne Marie. **Educ:** Morgan State Univ, BS, 1969; Del Law Sch, Widener Univ, JD, 1980. **Career:** Justices Peace Ct, magistrate, currently. **Orgs:** Rotary Int. **Military Serv:** USY Del Nat Guard, lt, March, 1970-96; Legion Merit; Meritorious Service Medal; Army Commendation Medal. **Home Phone:** (302)762-8488. **Business Addr:** Magistrate, Justice of the Peace Court System, 300 N Walnut St, Wilmington, DE 19801, **Business Phone:** (302)577-7234.

TAYLOR, VERONICA C.
School administrator. **Personal:** Born May 17, 1941, Pensacola, FL; married Raymond. **Educ:** Tenn State Univ, BS, 1962; Trenton State Col, MA, 1970. **Career:** Booker T Wash HS, instr, 1962-67; Trenton Pub Sch, speech therapist, 1967-88; Trenton State Col, co-adj fac, 1985; Jefferson Sch, fac; Robbins & Jefferson, asst prin, 1988-96; Grant Elem Sch, prin, 1998; DST, NJ State, coordr, 1997-99. **Orgs:** Bd dir, NJ Sickle Cell Soc, 1972-74; pres, Trenton Delta Sigma Theta, 1973-75; pres, TABS, 1974-77; vpres, Trenton Ed Assoc; NJ Ed Assoc Pol Action Fund, 1974-75; pres, vpres, Trenton Pan Hellenic Coun; bd dir, chmn, NJ EOF; pres, Womans Steering Comn, Shiloh Bapt Church, Nat Asn Advan Colored People; Nat Scholar Comn Delta Sigma Theta, 1983-88; Governor's Task Force Higher Educ; bd dirs, Merabash Mus; chairperson, NJ State Soc Action; nat exec bd, Delta Sigma Theta, 1988-92; Governor's Rev Comt Minorities Higher Educ; exec bd, Trenton Admins & Supvrs Asn; NJ Coordr Col Adv DST. **Honors/Awds:** Most All Around; Most Outstanding Female Graduate Wash, HS; Outstanding Commission Service Award, Trenton Delta Sigma Theta Inc; Outstanding Service Award, NJ Dept Higher Educ, 1982 & 1985, 1987; Outstanding Service Award, Shiloh Baptist Church; Outstanding Service Award, Tri State Social Action Comn DST; New Jersey Educational Opportunity Fund Leadership Award, Eastern Region DST; Pearl Certificate, Eastern Reg Conf, 1995; Outstanding Service Award-Students, Robbins Sch, 1996.

TAYLOR, VIVIAN A.
Government official. **Personal:** Born Oct 27, 1924, Maryland; married Lula M; children: Lavon E, Myron A. **Educ:** Stillman Col, attended 1943; Fisk Univ, attended 1948; State Univ NY, BA, 1973; Col Fredonia. **Career:** Jamestown Parks Dept, parks comnr, 1976-85; Black Awareness Studies, dir, 1984-85; TRW, bearings div; City Jamestown, city councilman. **Orgs:** Bd dirs, Jamestown Better Living; Environ Coun; original appointee Jamestown Human Rights Comm; bd dirs, Jamestown Family Serv; chmn bd trustees, Blackwell Chapel AME Zion Church; Boy Scout Comm; chmn, Jamestown Interacial Forum, 1962-65; City Charter Adv Comm, 1977; gov bd, Chautauqua Oppors Inc Anti-Poverty Agency, 1977-79; bd dirs, Crystal Ballroom Sr Citizens Ctr, 1981-84; United Auto Aerospace & Implement Workers Am, 1985; committeeman Chautauqua Co Democratic Comm, 1985; committeeman Jamestown City Democratic Comm, 1985. **Honors/Awds:** Cert Honor, AME Zion Church, 1978; Martin Luther King Jr Peace Award, Southern Tier Peace Ctr, 1982. **Military Serv:** Engrs demolition specialist, 3 yrs. **Home Addr:** 31 W 18th St, Jamestown, NY 14701. **Business Addr:** City Councilman, City of Jamestown, Municipal Bldg, 200 E Third St, Jamestown, NY 14701.

TAYLOR, DR. WELTON IVAN
Microbiologist, business owner. **Personal:** Born Nov 12, 1919, Birmingham, AL; son of Frederick Enslen and Cora Lee Brewer; married Jayne Rowena Kemp, Jan 1, 1945; children: Karyn & Shelley. **Educ:** Univ Ill, AB, 1941, MS, 1947, PhD, 1948. **Career:** Univ Ill, asst prof, 1948-54; Swift & Co, micro, 1954-59; Children's Memorial Hosp, micro-in-chief, 1959-64; consult, microbiologist, 1963-; Micro-Palettes Inc, pres, 1977-. **Orgs:** Founding chmn, Chicago Chap Episcopal Soc Cult & Racial Equality 1961; vpres, pres Chicago Med Mycol Soc, 1967-69; Am Soc Microbiol, 1947-, chair, 1966-75; Acad appointments, Assoc, Dept Pathol NW Med Sch, 1961-67; asst prof Univ Ill Sch Med 1965-69; assoc prof, Univ Ill Sch Med 1969-86; bd, Sci Adv, 1970-82; Am Bd Bioanalysis, 1973-82; bd dir, Am Asn Bioanalysts, 1970-82. **Honors/Awds:** James M Yard Brotherhood Award, Nat Conf Christians & Jews 1961; Diplomate Am Bd Med Microbiology, 1968; Fellow, Am Acad Microbiol, 1974; Editorial Bds Applied Microbiology/Am Soc Microbiol, 1968-70; Lab Med Amer Soc Clinical Pathology 1971-77; Test of Month Amer Asn Bioanalysts 1971-82; Journal of Clinical Micro Amer Soc Microbiol 1975-84; new species of bacterium "Enterobacter taylorae" named for him 1985; Special Research Fellowship, NIAID: Pasteur Inst, Lille, France, 1961; Central Public Health Laboratory, Colindale, London, England, 1962; Intl Dissemination of Salmonellae by Import/Export Foods; written more than 50 original scientific publications, book chapters and patents; formulated media/methods Salmonella/Shiqella detection used by FDA and Western Nations since, 1975; Invented, patented, manufactured and marketed microbiological diagnostic kits, founded Micro-Palettes Inc, 1977-89; Alumni Achievement Award, University of Illinois, Urbana, 1996; Pasteur Award, Illinois, Soc Microbiology, 1996; Scientific Achievement Award, Minority Microbiologists of Amer, Society for Microbiology, 2002; Hist Makers, 2003. **Special Achievements:** Expert Witness: food poisoning/infection, Hospital-acquired (nosocomial) infections, doctor-caused (iatrogenic) infections. **Military Serv:** AUS, 1st lt, liaison pilot, 1941-46; Ill Natl Guard, major, 1948-55.

TAYLOR, WILFORD, JR.
District court judge. **Personal:** Born Jan 15, 1950, Newport News, VA; son of Wilford Sr and Zenobia Miller; married Linda Holmes, Jul 3, 1976; children: Patrice D & Derek H. **Educ:** Hampton Univ, Hampton, Va, BS, bus mgt, 1972; Univ Richmond, Richmond, Va, MA, com, 1975; Marshall-Wythe Sch Law, Col William & Mary, Williamsburg, Va, JD, 1978. **Career:** Scott, Coles, Brown, Taylor & Melvin, PC, Newport News, Va, atty, 1979-82; City Hampton, Hampton, Va, dep city atty, 1983-85; Col William & Mary Sch Law, adj prof; Commonwealth Via, Hampton, Va, gen dist ct judge, 1985-95, circuit ct judge, currently. **Orgs:** Va State Bar Asn; Peninsula Bar Asn; Old Dominion Bar Asn; Asn District Ct Judges Va; Hampton Bar Asn; Nat Asn Advan Colored People, Hampton Chap; adv bd mem, Metrop YMCA; affirmative action comt mem, Marshall-Wythe Sch Law, Col William & Mary; Hampton Rotary Club; pres, Langley, PTA, 1990-; Am Judges Asn; Lawyers Helping Lawyers Comt. **Honors/Awds:** Man of the Year, Alpha Kappa Alpha Sorority, Hampton Chap, 1986; Man of the Year, Mega Psi Phi, Newport News Chap, 1990; St George Tucker Adjunct Professor Award, Col William & Mary Sch Law. **Military Serv:** AUS, lt; Army Commendation Medal, Meritorious Service Medal. **Home Addr:** 12 Sugarberry Run, Hampton, VA 23669, **Home Phone:** (804)850-3928. **Business Addr:** Circuit Court Judge, Hampton City Circuit Court, 101 King's Way Mall, PO Box 40, Hampton, VA 23669-0040, **Business Phone:** (757)727-6105.

TAYLOR, WILLIAM EDWARD (BILLY TAYLOR)
Jazz musician. **Personal:** Born Jul 24, 1921, Greenville, NC; married Theodora Castion; children: Duane & Kim. **Educ:** VA State, BS, music, 1942; Univ MA, EdD, 1975. **Career:** Pianist, composer, recording artist, arranger & conductor, actor, author, teacher & lectr. **Orgs:** Nat Coun Arts; Creative Artist Pub Serv; Newport Jazz Festival; NY Jazz Reperatory Co; secy, NY State Com Cult Resources; vpres, Nat Asn Rec Arts & Sci; pres, Jazz mobile. **Honors/Awds:** Cert of appreciation, City NY; numerous awards from Jazz Comm; hon Mus D VA State; Fairfield Univ & Clark Clg; Billy Taylor Collection Original Manuscripts; Col Fine Arts Howard Univ; Billy Taylor Lect Series Howard Univ; Peabody Award, 1981; Emmy Award, 1983; Nat Black Col Alumni Hall of Fame, 1991; Nat Medal of Art Award, President George Bush, 1992; National Medal of Arts, 1992; NEA Jazz Masters Award, 1998; Jazz Living Legend Award, Am Soc Composers, Authors and Publ, 2001; Grammy Award, 2004; Tiffany Award; Lifetime Achievement Award, Down Beat Mag; Hall of Fame for the International Association for Jazz Education. **Special Achievements:** In 1958, he was the Musical Director of NBC's The Subject Is Jazz, the first ever television series on the subject of jazz; Film: Sweet Dreams, 1985. **Home Addr:** 555 Kappock St, Bronx, NY 10463, **Home Phone:** (718)884-4613. **Business Addr:** Actor, 555 Kappock St, Bronx, NY 10463, **Business Phone:** (718)884-4613.*

TAYLOR, WILLIAM GLENN
Executive, banker. **Personal:** Born Oct 17, 1942, Loma Linda, CA; son of Lucille and W G; married Gwendolyn A Mayeaux. **Educ:** Riverside City Col, attended 1963; Univ San Francisco, BS, 1979. **Career:** Banker, Executive (retired); First Interstate Bank, bus serv supvr, 1965-72; Union Bank Calif, admin officer, 1972-76; Bank Calif, operations supvr, 1976-77; Home Savings Am, br mgr, 1977-83; Saving Admin Specialists, 1983-99; AT&T Broadband, regional dir, 1999-2002. **Orgs:** Pasadena Jr Chamber Com, 1965-67; Oakland Chamber Com, 1977-82; San Francisco Chamber Com, 1982-83; Optimist Int, 1982-83. **Home Addr:** 5967 Contra Costa Rd, Oakland, CA 94618.

TAYLOR, WILLIAM HENRY, SR.
Labor activist. **Personal:** Born Aug 28, 1931, Eathel, LA; married Thelma Watkins; children: Daryl, William Jr, Dawn, Diane. **Educ:** Univ IL Chicago, 1956; Roosevelt Univ, attended 1969. **Career:** Oil, Chem & Atomic Workers Union, Corp Coun, pres, 1971, Minority Affairs, chairperson, 1975-79, 1983;; Inter-Union Wet Corn Milling US & Can Coun, chairperson, 1979. **Orgs:** Adv coun Am Arbitration Assoc, 1971-75, 1982-84; pres, Bowen HS PTA, 1973-75; instr, Roosevelt Univ Labor Ed Prog, 1975; mem adv coun Comm Fund, 1975-79; pres, CEDA Southwest Develop Assocs, 1977-80, 1983; dir, Cook County CEDA Bd Dir, 1978-81; exec comn, Labor Coalition Pub Utility, 1981. **Honors/Awds:** Humanitarian Award, St Matthew AM Church, 1974; Special Citation Crusade Mercy, 1977. **Military Serv:** AUS, sgt E; UN Ribon, Good Conduct, 1952-54.

TAYLOR, WILLIAM L.
U.s. attorney, educator. **Personal:** Born Oct 4, 1931, Brooklyn, NY; married Harriett Rosen; children: Lauren R, Deborah L & David S. **Educ:** Brooklyn Col, BA, 1952; Yale Law Sch, LLB, 1954. **Career:** Nat Asn Adv Colored People, Legal Def & Educ Fund, atty, 1954-58; Am Dem Action, legis rep, 1959-61; US Comn Civil Rights, gen coun, 1963-65, staff dir, 1965-68; Yale Law Sch, sr fel, 1969-70; Nat Policy Rev, dir, 1970-86; Georgetown Law Sch, adj prof, 1986-; pvt pract atty, 1986-; Stanford Law Sch, prof law, 1996-97; Cath Univ Law Sch, adj prof. **Orgs:** Exec comt mem, Nat Bd Am Dem Action, 1971-; bd mem, Puerto Rican Legal Def Fund, 1976-; Meterop Wash Planning & Housing Asn, 1976-; Bars NY, DC; US Supreme Ct; chair, Citizens Comn Civil Rights. **Special Achievements:** Author: Hanging Together, Equality in an Urban Nation, 1971. **Military Serv:** AUS, 1956-58. **Business Addr:** Attorney-at-Law, Georgetown Law School, 600 New Jersey Ave, Washington, DC 20001, **Business Phone:** (202)662-9000.

TAYLOR-ARCHER, MORDEAN
Educator, school administrator. **Personal:** Born Jul 13, 1947, North Little Rock, AR; daughter of John L and Louella Henry; married Dwain E Archer, Sep 4, 1984. **Educ:** Univ Ozarks, BS, social sci, 1969; Univ Ark, MA, social, 1972; Brandeis Univ, MA, PhD, social policy, planning & admin, 1979; Harvard Univ, mgt develop prog, 1993. **Career:** Univ Ark, instr, 1970-74; National Res Coun, Ford Found fel, 1974-77; Boston Col, asst prof & coordr field work, 1975-78; Va Comonwealth Univ, asst dean & asst prof, 1978-90; Kans State Univ, asst provost, multicultural affairs, 1990-96, Diversity & Dual Career Develop, assoc provost, 1996-2001; Univ Louisville, Diversity & Equal Opportunity, vice provost, 2001-. **Orgs:** Nat Asn Black Social Workers, 1978-90; fel Human Rights, Herr Found, 1978; Nat Asn Social Workers, 1987-90; Nat Asn Stud Personnel Adminr, 1988-90; Asn Black Women Higher Educ, 1990; Am Asn Higher Educ, 1990; founder & mem, Kans Asn African Am Higher Educ, 1992-; Manhattan Retory Clubs, 1993-; League Women Voters, 1996-. **Honors/Awds:** Outstanding Faculty Award, Sch Social Work, Va Commonwealth Univ, 1981, 1984; Outstanding Administration Award, Multicultural Stud Coun & Blue Key Hon Soc, Kans State Univ, 1993; Appreciation Award, Founding Kans Asn African-Am Higher Educ, 1994; Barbara Jordan Outstanding Role Model Award, Big 12 Coun Black Student Govt, 1996; Martin Luther King Drum Major Award, Kans State Univ, 1997. **Business Addr:** Vice Provost for Diversity & Equal Opportunity, University of Louisville, 2310 S 3rd St, Louisville, KY 40292, **Business Phone:** (502)852-5719.

TAYLOR-THOMPSON, DR. BETTY E
School administrator, educator. **Personal:** Born Feb 6, 1943, Houston, TX; daughter of John Charles Taylor and Johnnie Mae Hart Brooks; married; married Oliver B Thompson Jr, Oct 20, 1985; children: Amnon James Ashe II & Ida Elizabeth Thompson. **Educ:** Fisk Univ, Nashville TN, BA, 1963; Atlanta Univ, Atlanta GA, MLS, 1964; Howard Univ, Wash, DC, MA, 1972, PhD, 1979. **Career:** Wash DC Pub Libr, technol librn, 1969-72; Tex Southern Univ, Houston TX, instr eng, 1974-75; Houston Independent Schs, Houston TX, eng teacher & librn, 1965-68, 1982-84; Tex Southern Univ, Houston, TX, assoc prof eng, 1984-89, Dept Eng & Foreign Lang, chair, 1989-91, assoc prof eng, 1991-98, prof, 1999-. **Orgs:** Col Lang Asn, co-chair, Black Studies Comt; Nat Coun Teachers Eng; pres, Southern Conf Afro-Am Studies, 1990-92; Conf Col Teachers Eng; Am Lit Asn; pres, Southern Conf Afro-Am Studies; Nat Col Teachers Eng; Am Asn Univ Women. **Honors/Awds:** Partic, Literature & Modern Experience Inst, Accra Ghana; Fulbright Award, Tanzania, Study & Res, 1997; Humanities Scholar, Univ Dar Es Saalam, Africa, Inst Arts Educ, 1997. **Special Achievements:** Publications: Oxford Campanion to African American Literature, 1997; Essays: Grant and Proposal Writing Hand Book, 1997; "The Martriarchal Tradition in Jubilee, by Margaret Walker," LSU Press, 1999; "Common Bonds From Africa to the US: Africanist Literary Theory," Jour of Black Studies, 2002. **Business Addr:** Professor of English, Texas Southern University, Department of English & Foreign Language, 3100 Cleburne St, Houston, TX 77004, **Business Phone:** (713)313-7616.

TEAGLE, TERRY MICHAEL
Basketball player. **Personal:** Born Apr 10, 1960, Broaddus, TX. **Educ:** Baylor Univ, BS, phys educ, 1982. **Career:** Basketball player (retired); Houston Rockets, 1982-84; Detroit Pistons, 1984-85; Golden State Warriors, 1984-90; Los Angeles Lakers, 1990-92; Houston Rockets, 1992-93. **Honors/Awds:** All-SWC; All-Am.

TEAGUE, GEORGE THEO
Football player, football coach. **Personal:** Born Feb 18, 1971, Lansing, MI; married Consuela; children: James II. **Educ:** Univ Ala. **Career:** Football player (retired), Football coach; Crimson tide Football team, starter, 1989-93; Green Bay Packers, def back, 1993-95; Dallas Cowboys, 1996, 1998-2001; Miami Dolphins, 1997; Harvest Christian Acad, athletic dir & head football coach, 2004-07; Carrollton Christian Acad, athletic dir, 2006-. **Orgs:** Pres, George Teague & Friends Found, 2002. **Business Addr:** Athletic Director, Carrollton Christian Academy, 2205 E Hebron Pkwy, Carrollton, TX 75010, **Business Phone:** (972)242-6688.

TEAGUE, GLADYS PETERS
Government official, executive. **Personal:** Born Sep 14, 1921, Muskogee, OK; married LD; children: Merron & Charles. **Educ:** Draughon's Bus Col, attended 1956-57; Corresp Course Postal Clerks, 1946. **Career:** Taft Post Off, postal clerk, 1946-63; First Baptist Church, asst church clerk, 1965-; Muskogee County, voter registr, 1984-; Town Taft, city clerk, 1984; Muskogee County, clerk, county clerk dep, 1981-. **Orgs:** Starlight Chap 11 OES, 1949-; beautician, Taft's Beauty Shop, 1951-53; notary, Muskogee County, 1962-; school bd, Dist I-17 Muskogee County, 1972; hon aux mem, Am Legion Post 84, 1973-; Muskogee County Fed Dem Women, 1981-. **Honors/Awds:** Superior Accomplishment Award, Post Off Dept, 1959.

TEAGUE, ROBERT
Executive. **Personal:** Born Oct 26, 1929, Durant, MS; married Tresa Marie Smith. **Educ:** Tougaloo Col, BA, 1955; Univ IL, MSW, 1961, Univ SC, 1966. **Career:** Ed Oakley Trng Sch, playground dir, 1958-59; IL Pub Aid Comt, 1959-60; Danville VA Neuropsychiatric Hosp, psychiatric team, 1960-61; Danville VA Neuropsychiatric Hosp, psychiatric team, 1960-61; Sepulveda VA Hosp, sr psychiatric soc worker, 1961-64; Pvt Marital Coun Clinic, assoc dir, 1962-64; CA Dept Mental Hygiene, pgm consult, 1965-67, sr psychiatric soc worker, 1964-65; Harbor View House, dir part owner, 1966-; Whitney M Young, Jr Psychiatric Hosp, dir owner prof placement serv pres exec dir, 1971-74; Psychiatric Pgms S Bay Mental Health Ctr, dir, 1974. **Orgs:** Chmn, Soc Work Res Comt VA Hosp Sepulveda, 1961-64; co fdr, Pvt Marital Guidance Clinic; bd dir, W Reg Conf Mental Health Pgm Mgt, 1974-76; Ad HocCom Mental Health Ctrs, 1974; consult, Westminister Neighbhourhood Assoc Mental Health Clinic, 1964-65; Greater LA Mental Health Assoc; bd dir, Nat Asn Soc Workers; LA Welfare Plng Coun; elder Westminister Presb Ch; pres, Col Alumni, 1965-67; bd dir, STEP Job Trng Proj; bd dir, S Cen Welfare Plng Coun, 1969-; nat Asn Soc Workers; CA Regis Soc Workers; Am Psy Asn; CA Welfare Conf; Acad Cert Soc Workers; Col Nursing Home Admin. **Honors/Awds:** LA men of tomorrow, YMCA; community service award, LA Sentinel, 1972; author of Var articles & resolutions. **Military Serv:** USAF, crypot oper, 1950-54.

TEAMER, DR. CHARLES C., SR.
School administrator. **Personal:** Born May 20, 1933, Shelby, NC; married Mary Alice Dixon, Aug 3, 1957; children: Charles Carl, Roderic F & Cheryl R. **Educ:** Clark Col, BA, 1954; Univ Omaha, post grad, 1962-63; Tulane Univ, post grad, 1965-66. **Career:** SC State Col Orangeburg, acct, 1955-56; Tenn State Univ Nashville, asst bus mgr, 1958-62; Wiley Col Marshall, Tex, bus mgr, 1962-65; Dillard Univ, New Orleans, vpres fiscal affairs, 1965-2002; World Trade Ctr, pres, New Orleans; chmn, Dryades Savings Bank, New Orleans, La, currently. **Orgs:** Dir, New Orleans Pub Serv Comn; bd dir, Common Fund; vpres, United Way New Orleans; past dir, pres, Nat Asn Col & Univ Bus Officers; vpres, bd dir, New Orleans Area Coun; treas, M & T Area Com Lafon Protestant Home; bd dir, Ochner Med Found Children's Hosp; New Orleans Chamber Commerce; Alpha Phi Alpha; life mem, Nat Comptroller Methodist Clubs; Masons; Shriners. **Honors/Awds:** Silver Beaver Award, Boy Scouts Am, 1968. **Special Achievements:** One of 10 Outstanding Citizens of New Orleans', 1979. **Military Serv:** AUS, 1956-58. **Business Addr:** Chairman, Dryades Savings Bank, 233 Carondelet St Suite 200, New Orleans, LA 70130, **Business Phone:** (504)598-7214.

TEASLEY, LARKIN
President (Organization), executive. **Personal:** Born Sep 23, 1936, Cleveland, OH; married Violet M Williams; children: Lisa, Erica & Laura. **Educ:** Fisk Univ, BA, 1957; Occidental Col, grad work actuarial sci, 1957-58; Univ Calif, Los Angeles, grad sch bus exec prog, 1971-72. **Career:** Golden State Mutual Life Ins Co, Los Angeles, asst actuary, 1958-63; NC Mutual Life Ins Co, actuary, 1963-69; Golden State Mutual Life Ins Co, pres & chief operating officer, 1980-90, dir, 1971-, chief exec officer, 1991-; chmn, 2001-. **Orgs:** Dir, Golden State Minority Found; dir, Broadway Fed Saving & Loan Asn; dir, Calif Chamber Com; dir, Los Angeles City Retirement Asn; fel, Soc Actuaries; Am Acad Actuaries; Nat Asn Bus Economists; Alpha Phi Alpha; Phi Beta Kappa; Beta Kappa Chi Sci Hon Soc. **Business Addr:** Chief Executive Officer, Chairman, Golden State Mutual Life Ins Co, 1999 W Adams Blvd, Los Angeles, CA 90018, **Business Phone:** (213)731-1131.*

TEASLEY, MARIE R.
Newspaper editor, president (organization). **Personal:** Born in Hannibal, MO; daughter of George A Wright (deceased) and Rose Trott Wright (deceased); married Ronald; children: Ronald Jr, Timothy, Lydia. **Educ:** Wayne State Univ; Univ Detroit. **Career:** Newspaper Editor (retired); Black Publications, writer, Aged 14; Fame Mag, writer; Pittsburgh Courier, writer; WSU campus paper; Philip Morris Co; NW Papers; Food & Music Radio, host; Regular TV Show Guest; MI Chronicle, club & soc writer, 1966, women's ed, 1991 (semi-retired), cruise rep, 1991-98, editor press assignment to Brazil, 1992, Los Angeles, Chicago & Dallas, 1993-94; Moscow, 1999. **Orgs:** Women Communications; adv bd, WXYZ; adv bd, Highland Park YWCA; Northwestern High School Alumni Asn; Detroit Chap Nat Asn Media Women; Cancer Soc; numerous Civic Orgs; chmn, founder, Detroit Sci Ctr Bus Fund, 1983; pres, Madonna Women on Action; Coalition of 100 Black Women; Urban League Guild; Nat Asn Travel Eds; Gamma Phi Delta Sorority, Delta Nu Chapter; life mem, Nat Asn Advan Colored People. **Honors/Awds:** Employee of the Year, MI Chronicle, 1972; SCLC Award, Top Communicator, 1973; Named Nat Media Woman of Year, 1974-75; Bridal Book edited Nat Asn Advan Colored People Award, 1974; Woman of Year, Catholic Archidose of Detroit, 1974; Detroit Chap Negro Bus & Prof Women Top Serv Award, 1974; Woman of Year, Detroit Chapter Media, 1974; NNAPA Best Women's Pages San Francisco, 1975; profiles in black CORE NY Publication, 1977; Top Jour Award, Bus & Prof Women, Nat Negro B&P Detroit Chap, 1977; Turner Broadcasting, Goodwill Ambassador to Moscow, 1986; Coalition of 100 Black Women; Outstanding Journ & Reporting, 1987; Community Serv Award, WC Exec William Lucas, 1986; NY Black Fashion Mus Reporting Award; Educ and Civics Awards, 1994-96; Serv Award, AA Sports Hall of Fame, 1996; Recog & Servs Award, Detroit City Coun. **Special Achievements:** named one of the 17 Women of Action, State of MI, 1999. **Home Addr:** 19317 Coyle St, Detroit, MI 48235. *

TEASLEY, NIKKI
Basketball player, basketball coach. **Personal:** Born Mar 22, 1979, Washington, DC; daughter of Ernestine. **Educ:** Univ NC, Chapel Hill, attended 2002. **Career:** Los Angeles Sparks, guard, 2002-05; Wash Mystics, guard, 2006-07; Atlanta Dream, 2008-09; Detroit Shock, currently. **Honors/Awds:** All-Star Game Most Valuable Player, 2003. **Business Addr:** Professional Basketball Player, Detroit Shock, 6 Championship Dr, Auburn Hills, MI 48326, **Business Phone:** (248)377-0100.

TEASLEY, RONALD
Educator, photographer, athletic coach. **Personal:** Born Jan 26, 1927, Detroit, MI; son of Ezra and Mattie; married Marie, Dec 18, 1948; children: Ronald Jr, Timothy & Lydia Vassal. **Educ:** Wayne State Univ, BS, 1955, MS educ, 1958. **Career:** Detroit Bd Educ, teacher, coach, suprv teacher, acting counsr, asst athletic dir; Mich Chronicle, photogr. **Orgs:** Kappa Alpha Psi Fraternity; Mich High Sch Baseball Coaches Asn; Afro-Am Sports Hall of Fame & Gallery; Negro League Baseball Players Asn; Yesterday's Negro League Found; Adv Bd, Masters Sr Sports Prog; dir, Sr Golf Prog; Negro League Baseball Players Museum; Meals On Wheels Golf Hall of Fame Comt. **Honors/Awds:** Basketball Coach of the Year, Detroit News, 1974, Baseball Coach of the Year, 1974; Outstanding Teacher of the Year, N Western Men's Club, 1975; Community Service Award, Committee For Student Rights, 1976; Communicator of the Year, Detroit Chap, Media Women, 1976; Wayne Univ Sports Hall of Fame, 1986; Mich High School Coaches Hall of Fame, 1989; Afro-American Sports Hall of Fame, 1994; Meals On Wheels Golf Hall of Fame, 1996; World Senior Games Awards; Michigan Senior Olympics Awards; Detroit Senior Olympics Awards. **Special Achievements:** Cited at Garfield and Spain Middle Schools for developing outstanding programs in intramural and inter school activities; coached evening and summer teams for Detroit Recreation Dept; coached NW Detroit Little League teams; first African American to captain high school basketball team;member of Saipan All-Stars, 1945; played with African American Travelling Teams in Detroit, 1940-45; eighth African American signed to the major leagues, played with Brooklyn Dodgers, Carman Cardinals; three time All-Star; amateur basketball: Ford All Stars, Great Lakes, Local 600,Local 49, Dee's Sporting goods, Heart of Detroit, Great Lakes Insurance,Highland Park Aces, Kappa Alpha Psi; travelled with wife to Soviet Union for MI Chronicle, 1986; made appearances on radio and TV; Wayne State Univ, One of Top Ten Athletes, 1947. **Military Serv:** USN, Sp A 3/c, 1946-47; Pac Ribbon. **Home Phone:** (313)863-0185.

TEEKAH, DR. GEORGE ANTHONY
Physician. **Personal:** Born Mar 29, 1948; son of George D and Lottie Wason; married Theresa Riley. **Educ:** Howard Univ, BS (hon), 1971, MD, 1975. **Career:** Greater SE Community Hosp, med dir ICU, respiratory therapy, 1980-83; Richmond Community Hosp, med dir, respiratory therapy, 1984-; pvt pract, currently. **Honors/Awds:** Beta Kappa Chi Scientific Hon Soc, 1972. **Home Addr:** 2721 Wicklow Lane, Richmond, VA 23236. **Business Addr:** Physician, 505 W Leigh St Suite 207, Richmond, VA 23220, **Business Phone:** (804)788-0556.

TEER, DEEN. See TEER, WARDEEN.

TEER, WARDEEN (DEEN TEER)
Government official, businessperson. **Personal:** Born Jul 8, 1945, Marvell, AR; daughter of Walter and Lillie M Townes; married Michael C Teer Sr, May 10, 1969; children: Michael Jr & Monte. **Educ:** Southern Ill Univ, BA, 1970. **Career:** Council member (retired), business executive; sr planner, City E St Louis, 1970-74; regional res dir, Nat Urban League, 1974-76; City Riverside, admin analyst, 1982-86, coun rels admin, 1986; Teer One Properties Inc, exec vpres, currently. **Orgs:** Bd mem, UCR Bot Gardens; Alpha Kappa Alpha Sorority; exec mgt prog, Univ Calif Riverside, 1992; comt chair, Orange Blossom Festival. **Honors/Awds:** Community Service Award, Nat Asn Advan Colored People, 2005; Presidents Award, Calif Asn Realtors, 2005. **Business Addr:** Executive Vice President, Teer One Properties Inc., 3978 Brockton Ave, Riverside, CA 92501, **Business Phone:** (951)784-1342.

TEEUWISSEN, PIETER
Lawyer. **Personal:** Born Sep 26, 1966, Ann Arbor, MI; son of John and Charlotte E; married Lisa M Teeuwissen. **Educ:** Princeton Univ, 1986; Tougaloo Col, BS, 1987; Univ Minn, JD, 1990. **Career:** Sloan Found fel, 1986; Mississippi Dept Human Servs, atty, special assignments, 1990-91; Cherry Given Lockett Peters & Diaz, assoc, 1992-93; Byrd & Assoc, sr assoc, 1993-97; Danks, Simon & Teeuwissen, managing partner, 1998-2004; Pieter Teeuwissen, Esq, PLLC, pvt pract, 2004-; Jackson, Miss, litigation & appellate cases, spec asst City Atty; Danks, Teeuwissen & Assoc, atty. **Orgs:** Vice-Chair, Miss Bd Bar Admissions; Am Bar Asn; Nat Bar Asn; Miss State Bar, minority involvement committee; Magnolia Bar Asn, special projects committee, mock trial competition; Omega Psi Phi. **Special Achievements:** Million Dollar Advocates Forum; Published in Mississippi College Law Journal, Numerous Community Awards; Frequent CLE Speaker. **Business Addr:** Attorney, 840 E River Pl Suite 607, Jackson, MS 39236, **Business Phone:** (601)420-1188.

TEI, DR. EBO
Educator. **Career:** Univ Ark, Planning Comn, mem, Psychol Prog, dir, Dept Social & Behav Sci, dept chair, prof, currently.

TEJADA, CHARLES
Judge. **Educ:** City Univ New York, City Col, BA, 1970; New York Univ Sch Law, JD, 1973. **Career:** Civil Ct City New York, judge, 1985-86; Family Ct, City New York, judge, 1986-90; Supreme Ct, New York County, justice, 1999-; Manhattan Supreme Ct, justice, 2002. **Business Addr:** Justice, New York State Supreme Court, 100 Centre St, New York, NY 10013, **Business Phone:** (212)374-4741.

TELFAIR, BRIAN KRAIG
Lawyer. **Personal:** Born Aug 11, 1961, Jacksonville, FL; son of Kenneth L and Roberta E. **Educ:** Va State Univ, BS, 1983; Univ Mass, Amherst, MEd, 1985, Col William & Mary, Marshall-Wythe Sch Law, JD, 1990. **Career:** Adult Career Devt Ctr, teacher, 1985-87; Sands Anderson Marks & Miller, legal intern, 1988-89; Commonwealth Va, Off Atty Gen, legal intern, 1989; The Dow Chem Co, atty, 1990-92; Miller, Canfield, Paddock & Stone, PLC, atty, 1992; Womble Carlyle Sandridge & Rice PLLC, atty, currently. **Orgs:** Omega Psi Phi Fraternity, 1987-; State Bar Mich, 1990-; Am Bar Asn, 1990-; Wolverine Bar Asn, 1992-; Va Asn Defense Atty; bd dir, William & Mary Law Sch Asn; bd dir, Greater Richmond Urban League, 1996-2001. **Honors/Awds:** The Order of Barristers, Col William & Mary, Marshall-Wythe Sch Law, 1990. **Business Phone:** (703)790-3310.

TEMPLE, DONALD MELVIN
Lawyer. **Personal:** Born May 27, 1953, Philadelphia, PA; son of Joseph and Ursula; married Vonterris Hagan; children: Caira Suki & Imani Korina. **Educ:** Howard Univ, BA, 1975; Univ Santa Clara Law Sch, JD, 1978; Georgetown Univ Law Ctr, LLM, 1982. **Career:** US Dept Housing, atty adv, 1978-80; US House Rep, sr staff coun, 1980-90; US House Rep, DC deleg, 1990; Donald M Temple PC, owner, 1991-. **Orgs:** Pres, Stud Bar Asn, Univ Santa Clara Sch Law, 1977-78; pres, Nat Conf Black Lawyers DC, 1980-81; Nat Bar Asn, 1980-97; pres, DC Chap, Concerned Black Men Inc, 1982-83; nat chmn, 21st Century PAC, 1983-87; Wash Bar Asn, 1984-97; Chmn, Charles Hamilton Houston Legal Educ Inst, 1984-97; Kappa Alpha Psi Fraternity, 1985-; Prince Hall Masonic Lodge, 1985-; chmn, Adam Clayton Powell Soc, 1987; chmn, DC Civilian Complaint Rev Bd, 1991-94; Pa Bar Asn. **Honors/Awds:** Role Model of Year, Legal Educ Nat Black Law Stud Asn, 1985; Best of Washington Hall of Fame, 1986; Harriet Tubman Award, Cong Black Asn, 1987; Outstanding Black Professional Business Exchange Network, 1987; Alumni of the Year, Geortown Law Ctr Black Stud Asn, 1988; Gertrude E Rush Award, Nat Bar Asn, 1990. **Business Addr:** Attorney at Law, Donald M Temple PC, 1200 G St NW Suite 370, Washington, DC 20005, **Business Phone:** (202)628-1101.

TEMPLE, EDWARD STANLEY
Educator, athletic coach. **Personal:** Born Sep 20, 1927, Harrisburg, PA; son of Christopher R and Ruth N Ficklin; married

Charlie B Law, Jul 22, 1950; children: Lloyd Bernard & Edwina R. **Educ:** Tenn State Univ, BS, 1950, MS, 1953; Pa State Univ, PhD, 1954. **Career:** Athletic coach, educator (retired); Tenn State Univ, head women's track coach, assoc prof sociol, 1950-94; US . Women's Track Team, track coach, 1958-94. **Orgs:** Kappa Delta Pi Educ Fraternity; Golden Key Honor Soc; Int Track & Field Comt; exec comt, Nashville Sports Coun; life mem, Tenn State Univ Alumni Assn; United States Olympic Comt, 1960, 1964, 1968, 1972, 1976, 1980, 1984;Nashville YMCA; Omega Psi Phi Fraternity; Clark Memorial United Methodist Church; Nat Col Athletic Assn; Track & Field Coaches Assn. **Honors/Awds:** National Track & Field Hall of Fame; Tennessee Sports Hall of Fame; Helms Hall of Fame; Tennessee State University Hall of Fame, Harrisburg, PA;Central Area Chapter Hall of Fame; Pennsylvania Sports Hall of Fame; Ohio Valley Conference Hall of Fame; Black Athletes Hall of Fame; Communiplex National Sports Hall of Fame. **Special Achievements:** Has Coached: 23 Olympic Medal Winners; 34 Nat Team Titles; 30 Pan-Am Games Medal Winners; 8 Nat Track and Field Hall of Fame Inductees; 40 Olympians(39 have 1 or more college degrees; He has published his biograpy "Only The Pure In The Heart Survive". **Home Addr:** 2628 Delk Ave, Nashville, TN 37208-1919, **Home Phone:** (615)244-5711. *

TEMPLE, HERBERT
Graphic artist. **Personal:** Born Jul 6, 1919, Gary, IN; married Athelstan. **Educ:** Art Inst Chicago, attended 1948. **Career:** Ebony Ebony Jr & Black World Mags, art dir; Supreme Beauty Prod Co, designs spec advert & promotional mat & packaging; Johnson Publ Co, art dir, 2002; Books: The Ebony Cook Book; Negro & Firsts in Sports; The Legend of Africana. **Special Achievements:** Chairman of Art Committee which Selected & Purchased $250,000 Worth of Paintings, Sculptures & Other Art Objects by Black Artists Around World for Perm Exhibition in Johnson Pub Co Bldg; judge for Numerous Art Shows. **Business Addr:** Art Director, Johnson Publishing Company, 820 S Mich Ave, Chicago, IL 60605.*

TEMPLE, JACKIE. See TEMPLE, DR. JACQUELINE B.

TEMPLE, DR. JACQUELINE B (JACKIE TEMPLE)
Educator. **Personal:** Born Nov 4, 1946, New Orleans, LA; daughter of David L Bartholomew Sr; divorced; children: Elisa Temple-Harvey & Elena M Temple. **Educ:** Spelman Col, BA, 1968; Univ New Orleans, MEd, 1985; Univ Wisc-Madison, PhD, 1997. **Career:** Real Estate Ctr New Orleans, sales & listing agent, 1979-82; Orleans Parish Sch Dist, Area II Spec Edu Off, spec educr, work adjust coord, 1977-89; Atlanta City Schs, spec educr, 1977-89; job developer, spec educr, 1990-93; Portland State Univ, assoc prof, currently. **Orgs:** Spelman Col Alumna Asn, 1968-; Coun Exceptional C, Asn Supv & Curric Develop, 1997-2003; Nat Asn Multicultural Educrs, 2002-03; Fulbright Scholars Alumna Asn, 2002. **Honors/Awds:** Academic Achievement Award, Atlanta City Schs, 1992; Honor Teaching Award for Distinguished Teaching, Atlanta Jour Const Newspaper, 1993; Minority Scholars Fellowship, Univ Wisc-Madison, 1993-97; J William Fulbright Lecture/Research Scholarship, Coun Int Exchange Scholars, 2001-02. **Special Achievements:** Univ Turku, Finland N Am Studies Org, Am Voices Sem, presenter, 2001; US Embassy, Copenhagen, Denmark, Black Hist Sem: Honored Guest/Speaker, 2002. **Business Addr:** Assistant Professor, Portland State University, Graduate School of Education, 615 SW Harrison St 608 D ED Education Bldg, PO Box 751, Portland, OR 97207-0751, **Business Phone:** (503)725-5858.

TEMPLE, ONEY D.
Executive, government official. **Educ:** Webster Col, Mo, BA, MA; Ohio State Univ, Emerging Leaders Inst, 2002. **Career:** McDonalds; IBM; Xerox; Univ Akron, adj fac; Off Governer, Akron reg liason; State & Local Govt Comn Ohio, mem bd, 1997-01; Ohio Dept Develop, Econ Develop Div, dep dir; Am Elec Power Energy Serv Inc, dir community serv, mgr energy mktg, pres; Cent State Univ Ohio, vice chair bd trustees, currently. **Orgs:** Ohio State Bar Asn; Ohio Hist Soc. **Special Achievements:** US Patent, 1978. **Business Addr:** Vice Chairperson of the Board of Trustees, Central State University, 1400 Brush Row Rd, PO Box 1004, Wilberforce, OH 45384.

TEMPLETON, GARRY LEWIS
Baseball player, baseball manager. **Personal:** Born Mar 24, 1956, Lockey, TX; son of Spiavia and Otella Williams; married Glenda Glenn, Dec 17, 1977; children: Garry II, Gerome & Genae Nicole. **Career:** Baseball player (retired), baseball manager; St Louis Cardinals, shortstop, 1976-81; San Diego Padres, infielder, 1982-91; NY Mets, 1991; Calif Angels Baseball Orgn, Cedar Rapid Kernals, A ball mgr, 1998, AA ball mgr, 1999; Salt Lake Stingers, mgr, 1998-2001; Gary IN Rail cats, mgr, 2003-04; Golden Baseball League's Fullerton Flyers, mgr, 2005-08. Palm Springs Chill. mgr. 2008. Long Beach Armada, mgr, 2009-. **Honors/Awds:** Baseball Digest & Topps Chewing Gum Rookie, All Star Team, 1977; MVP Award, 1985; All Star Team, 1977 & 1985. **Special Achievements:** Named to UPI & The Sporting News All-Star Teams; First Team Selection to AP & The Sporting News All-Star Squads; 34 Stolen Bases; 148 games more than any other shortstop in Natl League 1984; first player to get 100 hits batting left handed & right handed in a season. **Home Addr:** 13552 Del Poniente Rd, Poway, CA 92064. **Business Addr:** Team Manager of Long Beach Armada chill, Golden Baseball League, 2900 Orange Ave Suite 203, Signal Hill, CA 90755, **Business Phone:** (562)856-5551.

TENNANT, MELVIN, II
Manager. **Personal:** Born Jul 2, 1959, Bryan, TX; son of Melvin and Cora; children: Caroline, Brian, Matthew, Melanie. **Educ:** Rice Univ, BA, 1982. **Career:** Houston Convention & Visitors Bur, assoc dir, 1980-87; Corpus Christi Convention & Visitors Bur, convention div dir, 1987-88; Irving, TX, Convention & Visitors Bur, assoc dir, 1988-90; Okla Convention & Visitors Bur, pres & chief exec officer, 1990-92; Charlotte Convention & Visitors Bur, pres & chief exec officer, 1992-03; San Antonio Convention & Visitors Bur, exec dir, 2003-. **Orgs:** Houston Area Urban League 1984-, Nat Coalition Black Meeting Planners 1985-, Am Soc Asn Execs; bd mem, Patrons Humanities; bd mem, United Negro Col Fund, East Bay Chap; chair, Int Asn Convention & Visitors Bureaus; bd mem, Western Asn Convention & Visitors Bureaus; Nat Tour Asn. **Honors/Awds:** Certificate of Appreciation, Nat Tour Asn, 1984. **Business Phone:** (210)207-6700.*

TERBORG-PENN, DR. ROSALYN M
Educator, historian. **Personal:** Born Oct 22, 1941, Brooklyn, NY; daughter of Jacques Sr and Jeanne Van Horn; divorced; children: Jeanna C. **Educ:** City Univ New York, Queens Col, BA, 1963; George Washington Univ, MA, 1969; Howard Univ, PhD, 1978. **Career:** Morgan State Univ, prof hist, 1969-, coordr grad prog hist, 1977-95, PhD prog, dir, Grad Prog, grad coordr; Howard Community Col, adj fac, 1970-74; Ford Found, fel minorities, 1980-81. **Orgs:** Founder, Asn Black Women Historians, 1978; comnr, Howard Cty Md Comn Women, 1980-82; Hist ed Feminist Studies, 1984-89; Res & Pubations Comn, Md Hist Soc, 1989-96; chair, Am Hist Asn Comm Women Historians, 1991-93; Alpha Kappa Alpha Sorority Inc, Int Archives & Heritage Comn, 1994-96; comnr, Mary McLeod Bethune Coun House, Nat Hist Site, Fed Comn, 1996-. **Honors/Awds:** Grad History Essay Award, Rayford Logan, Howard Univ, 1973; Grad Fel Hist, Howard Univ, 1973-74; Vis Scholar Grant, Smithsonian Inst, 1982, 1994; Travel Colctions Grant, Nat Endowment Humanities, 1984; Letitia Woods Brown Award, 1987-88, Award for Best Anthology, 1995; Award for Best Book, Asn Black Women Historians, 1998; Anna Julia Cooper Award, Sage Women's Educ Press, 1995; Lorraine A Williams Leadership Award, 1998. **Special Achievements:** Author: Afro-American Woman-Struggles and Images, 1978, 1981, 1997; Women in Africa and the African Dispora, 1987, 1996; Black Women in America: An Historical Encyclo, 1993; Women in Africa & the African Diaspora: A Reader, 1996; African-American Women in the Struggle for the Vote, 1998. **Business Addr:** Graduate Coordinator, Professor of History, Morgan State University, History Department, Rm 326-B Holmes Hall 1700 E Cold Spring Lane, Baltimore, MD 21251, **Business Phone:** (443)885-3190.

TERO, LAWRENCE
Actor, social worker, wrestler. **Personal:** Born May 12, 1952, Chicago, IL; son of Nathaniel Tureaud Sr; married Phillys Clark (divorced); children: Lesa; children: Erika & T Jr. **Educ:** Prairie View A&M Univ, attended 1971. **Career:** Gym teacher; bouncer; wrestler; actor, currently; Illinois Army National Guard, 1975; Bodyguard Muhammed Ali, Leon Spinks, Donna Summer, Diana Ross, Rev Jesse Jackson, Michael Jackson; Films: Rocky III, 1982; Young Doctors in Love, 1982; The A Team, 1983-97; Mister T, animated, 1983; DC Cab, 1983; Straight Line, 1989; Freaked, 1993; The Magic of the Golden Bear: Goldy III, 1994; Spy Hard, 1996; Inspector Gadget, 1999; Not Another Teen Movie, 2001; Judgment, 2001; Undercover Brother, 2002; TV series: "The A-Team", 1983-87; "T. & T.", 1988-90; "Eek the Cat", animated, 1988-90; "Different Strokes", 1983; The Toughest Man in the World, 1984; "Eek! the Cat", 1992; "Blossom", 1994; "Martin", 1996; "Suddenly Susan", 1996; "Howard Stern", 1996-2002; "Sabrina the Animated Series", 1999; Malcolm & Eddie", 1999; Pecols, 2001; "WWF Raw Is War", 2001; "Praise the Lord", 2002; "Praise the Lord", 2002-04; "Teamo Supremo", 2002; "The Contender", 2005; "Late Night with Conan O'Brien", 2005-08; "The 100 Greatest TV Quotes & Catch phrases", 2006; "I Pity the Fool", 2006; Bring Back; The A-Team, 2006; Guys Choice, 2007; Taurus World Stunt Awards, 2007.Behind the Taurus, 2008; "Xpose", 2009. **Honors/Awds:** Football Scholarship. **Special Achievements:** Author: Mr. T: the Man with the Gold, 1984; Albums: Mr. T's Commandments,1984; Be Somebody or Be Somebody's Fool!, 1984. **Military Serv:** Military policeman. **Business Addr:** Actor, William Morris Agency, 1 William Morris Pl, Los Angeles, CA 90212, **Business Phone:** (310)859-4000.*

TERRELL, CATHERINE MILLIGAN
Educator. **Personal:** Born Oct 28, 1944, St Croix, Virgin Islands of the United States; daughter of Hugh and Exira; divorced; children: Natalie & Omar E. **Educ:** Temple Univ, Philadelphia, PA, BS, 1973; Antioch Univ, Yellow Springs, OH, MEd, 1974; Columbia Univ, New York, NY, PhD, 1991. **Career:** Sch Dist Philadelphia, Philadelphia, PA, asst prin, 1980-86; St Dunstan's Episcopal Sch, St Croix, VI, head, 1986-. **Orgs:** Phi Delta Kappa, 1987-. **Honors/Awds:** Educ articles, 1986, 1987; Pan African Nat Support Group, 1989; Bus & Prof Women's Club, 1990, Women of the Year, 1991. **Business Addr:** Headmaster, St. Dunstan, 21 Orange Grove Christiansted, St Croix, Virgin Islands of the United States 00820.

TERRELL, DONNA
Television news anchorperson. **Educ:** Cent Mich Univ, BA, broadcast & cinematic arts. **Career:** Kellogg Community Col, instr tv; WOTV, reporter & anchor; WKYC-TV, from med reporter, anchor & reporter; WKBD-TV, anchor; WWJ-TV, anchor; UPN Nightside News, anchor; KLRT Fox 16, co-anchor, 2004-. **Orgs:** Susan G Komen Breast Cancer Found; Make-A-Wish Found; Ctrs C & Family Serv; Achievement Ctrs for C; Nat Asn TV Arts & Sci; Nat Asn Black Journalists; Easter Seals Ark. **Honors/Awds:** 2 Emmy Awards; Asniate Press Award; Best of Detroit-2002, Detroit Free Press, 2002. **Special Achievements:** Cover several major events including Nelson Mandela's tour of the United States after his release from a South African prison. **Business Phone:** (501)225-0016.

TERRELL, DOROTHY
President (organization), computer executive, chief executive officer. **Personal:** Born Jun 12, 1945, Fort Lauderdale, FL; daughter of Charles W Sr and Pearl Weeks; married Albert H Brown; children: Dorian. **Educ:** Fla Agri & Mech Univ, BA, eng, 1966. **Career:** Digital Equip Corp, plant personnel mgr, 1978-80, group personnel mgr, 1980-84, plant mgr, 1984-87, group mgr, 1987; Sun Express, pres, 1991-97; Natural Microsystems, vpres corp opers, sr vpres, pres platform & servs group, 1998-2002; Initiative for a Competitive Inner City, pres & ceo; First Light Capital, partner, 2003-05; Competitive Inner City, sen vpres, 2005-07; Gen Mills Inc, dir, currently. **Orgs:** Delta Sigma Theta, 1965-; adv comt, OIC, 1984-87; comn mem, Boston C of C,1984-88; trustee, Social Policy Res, 1985-89; bd mem, Boston YWCA,1985-89; bd mem, Lera Park Community Develop, 1985-89; bd mem, BostonClub, 1986-89. **Honors/Awds:** Achievement Award, Snowden Assn, 1984; Film Choosing to Lead AMA, 1986;Achievement Award, YWCA, 1986; Black Achievers, YMCA, 1987; Hecht-ShawAward, 1987; Mus of Afro-Am Hist Award, 1988; Leadership Pioneer Award,1988; Edges Group Award, 1992: Women of Courage & Conviction Award,National Coun of Negro Women, 1993; Distinguished Alumni Award, FL A&MUniv, 1995; named one of 20 Women of Power & Influence in Corp Am, BlackEnterprise mag, 1997; Choice Leadership Award, Natl Women's Econ AllianceFound, 1997; named one of Top 50 Women Line Mgrs in Am, Exec Female mag. **Business Addr:** director, General Mills Inc, Nol General Mills Blvd, PO Box 1113, Minneapolis, MN 55426, **Business Phone:** (763)764-7600.*

TERRELL, DR. FRANCIS
Educator. **Personal:** Born Nov 25, 1944, Greensboro, GA; son of Carrie and Emery; married Sandra L; children: Ivanna Samal, Amani Shama & Elon Jadhal. **Educ:** Wilmington Col, BS, 1968; Univ Pittsburgh, MS, 1972; Univ Pittsburgh, PhD, 1975. **Career:** Univ Pittsburgh, post-doctoral fel, 1975-76; Tex Christian Univ, asst prof, 1976-80; N Tex State Univ, dir clin training, 1981-89; N Tex State Univ, assoc prof psychol; Univ N Tex, prof psychol currently. **Orgs:** Am Psychol Asn, 1976-80; Black Psychol Asn, 1976-80; Sigma Xi, 1976-80; regional ment health consult, US Labor Dept, 1978-; fel Am Psychol Asn, 1984; fel Soc Study Personality, 1984; fel Am Psychol Soc. **Special Achievements:** Published "Self Concept of Jnvls Who Commit Black on Blacks Crimes" Corrective & Social Psychiatry, 1980; "Effects of Race of Examiner & Type of Reinforcement on the Intelligence Test of Black Children" Psychology in the Schs, 1980; Over 40 Journals published. **Military Serv:** USN, 2nd class petty officer, 1978-84. **Business Addr:** Professor, University of North Texas, Psychology Dept, PO Box 311277, Denton, TX 76203, **Business Phone:** (940)565-2000.

TERRELL, FRANCIS D'ARCY
Lawyer. **Personal:** Born May 13, 1940, Caledonia, NY; married Mary Jane Hawthorne; children: Derek M, Randall D. **Educ:** Univ Toledo, BS, 1970; Columbia Law Sch, JD, 1973. **Career:** Shearman & Sterling, assoc atty, 1973-75; Pvt Pract, atty, 1975-77; Jones & Terrell, partner, 1977-82; Bronx Community Col, dep chmn & prof; City Col, Greenberg legal Studies Prog, Prof & Dir. **Orgs:** Am Bus Law Asn, 1984-. **Military Serv:** Lt col, 20 yrs; Bronze Star; Air Medal; Meritorious Service Medal; Commendation Medal; Combat Infantry Badge. *

TERRELL, FREDERICK O
Entrepreneur, banker, chief executive officer. **Personal:** Born in Hamtramck, MI. **Educ:** La Verne Col, BA; Occidental Col, MA; Yale Sch Mgt, MBA. **Career:** Coro Found, post-grad fel; Credit Suisse First Boston Corp, sr banker, managing dir & partner; Provender Capital Group LLC, co-founder, managing partner & ceo, 1997-. **Orgs:** Fin adv, US Dept Veterans Affairs; Bd NY Life Ins Co; Wellchoice Inc; Vanguarde Media Inc; chmn, Carver Bancorp Inc; Bd Adv Coro Found; partner, New York City Partnership. **Honors/Awds:** Deal of the Yr, 1985, 1993. **Special Achievements:** One of 25 "Hottest Blacks on Wall Street", Black Enterprise, 1992. **Business Addr:** Managing Partner, Chief

Executive Officer, Provender Capital Group LLC, 17 State St Suite 23, New York, NY 10004, **Business Phone:** (212)271-8888.

TERRELL, HENRY MATTHEW
Government official, lawyer. **Personal:** Born Dec 6, 1940, Caroline County, VA. **Educ:** VA State Col, BA, 1963; Howard Univ Sch Law, JD 1971. **Career:** Prudential Life Ins Co, mkt & salels rep, 1965-71; EGS Fin Mgt Cons, pres, 1971-; Aetna Ins Co, brokerage mgr, 1973-75; CT Hellmuth & Assoc, mgr, 1975-; Am Security & Trust Co, estate & pension admin, 1971-72; Henry M. Terrell & Assoc, currently. **Orgs:** Pres, VA State Col Alumni Assn, 1966-68; brd trustees, VA State Col Found,1974; regional dir, VA State Col Alumni Assn, 1974; Recorder Deeds, DC, 1990-2000; Brd Dirs, VA St Col Alumni Assn; past pres, Howard Univ Law Sch Alumni Assn; Alpha Phi Alpha; Delta Theta Phi Law Fraternity; bus mgr, Nubian Enterprises; dir, DC Chap Int Assn Fin Planners; Natl Patent Assn; mem, Dist Columbia Bar. **Military Serv:** AUS, capt, 1963-65, reserves, 1965-68. **Business Addr:** Attorneys, Henry M. Terrell Associates, 1625 Massachusetts Ave Suite 400, District of Columbia, WA 20036, **Business Phone:** (202)628-2727.

TERRELL, JOHN L
School administrator. **Personal:** Born May 19, 1930, Forest City, AR; son of Willie L and Velma Mclemore (deceased); married Betty R Phillips, Aug 16, 1950; children: Debra, Lanette, John & DeAnna. **Educ:** Muskegon Bus Col, Bus Admin, 1956. **Career:** School administrator (retired); Howmet Corp, x-ray tech, 1956-88; UAW Local 1243, sec-treas, 1958; Howmet Employee Credit Union, pres, 1962; Muskegon Heights Sch Bd, treas, 1969-79, vpres, 1979-85. **Orgs:** Pres, Muskegon Co Sch Bd Asn, 1987-91; pres, Muskegon Intermediate Sch Dist, 1989, 1991; VFW. **Military Serv:** AUS, pfc, 1952-54; Combat Medic Badge. **Home Addr:** 2336 Maffett St, Muskegon Heights, MI 49444.

TERRELL, MARY ANN
Judge. **Personal:** Born Jun 3, 1944, Jacksonville, FL; daughter of Quincy Gooden and Minnie Armstrong Gooden; married James Edward Terrell; children: Angela Rani, Mariessa Rebecca, James Stephen. **Educ:** Howard Univ, BA, 1966; Antioch Univ, MAT, 1969; Georgetown Univ Law Ctr, JD, 1980. **Career:** Peace Corps & India, volunteer, 1966-68; Antioch Col, dir admin asst prof hist, 1969-73; Dix St Acad, dir & founder, 1974-80; Mental Health Law Proj, lawyer, 1980-81; Dist Columbia City Coun, exec asst to council chmn, 1981-82; DC Dept Pub Works, hearing examiner, 1983-84; Antioch Sch Law, adjunct prof, 1987-; Off US Atty, asst US atty, 1984-89; Fed, Home Loan Bank Bd, Wa, DC, sr atty, 1989; FDIC & RTC, Wa, DC, coun litigation, 1989-90, coun, corp affairs, 1990-92; coun, Outside Coun Mgt Section, RTC, 1992-95; Dept Legal Progs, RTC, sr coun dir, 1993-95; FDIC, assoc dir, 1995; Superior Ct DC, judge, currently. **Orgs:** Treas, Nat Polit Congress Black Women, 1985-91; Nat Asn Black Women Attys, 1985-, Women's Div NBA, 1986-; Women's Bar Asn DC, 1987, Fed Bar Asn, 1987, The Wa Bar; bd dirs, Women Bar Asn, Wa, DC, 1990-92; co-chair, comt exec & judicial appts, GWAC-NBA, 1990-91; co-chair, person to person comt, THIS Meridan House Intl, 1990-; bd dirs, Fed Bar Asn, DC Chapter, 1988-; Dist Columbia Bar, 1983; Bar Asn Dist Columbia, comt chair, 1988-89; Fed Bar, DC Chapter, bd dirs; Wa Bar, NBA Conv Steering Comt, 1988, Law Day Dinner Comt, 1993; Nat Bar Asn, GWAC, judicial exec nomination community, 1990-91; Nat Asn Black Women Attys, Conf Steering Community, 1990; Women's Bar Asn, bd dirs; vice chair, Wa Lawyers Against Drugs; Black Asst US Atty Asn; Asst US Atty Asn; Exec Women Govt; adv comt mem, US Intl Cultural & Trade Ctr; vpres, Young People Communicating Inc; Temporary Panel Employees Appeal, appointed, 1992; Mayor's Citizen Budget Adv & Review Comt, appointed, 1992; Howard Univ Alumni Asn, Ad Hoc Exec; Comt Exec Bd; Voting Deleg, Dist Columbia Judicial Conf, 1985-87; DC Bar, secy, elected, 1994. **Honors/Awds:** Outstanding Community Service Award, Educ, 1980; appointed, Mayor's Intl Adv Coun, 1983-; selected, DC State Adv Comt for Hands Across Am, 1986; appointed, Legal Serv Bd Antioch Sch Law, 1986-; selected vice chair, Wa Lawyers Against Drugs Community, 1987; Appointed, Mem Temporary Panel Employees Appeal, 1991-93; Appointed, Mayor's Citizen's Budget Adv & Review Comt, 1992-94; Ebon Image Award, 2000. **Business Addr:** Judge, Superior Court District of Columbia, 500 Indiana Ave NW, JM 670, Washington, DC 20001, **Business Phone:** (202)879-1639.*

TERRELL, DR. MELVIN C
School administrator, educator. **Personal:** Born Oct 5, 1949, Chicago, IL; son of Cleveland and Ethel Lee McNeal. **Educ:** Chicago State Univ, BSEd, 1971; Loyola Univ, Chicago, MEd 1974; Southern Illinois Univ, Carbondale, PhD, 1978. **Career:** Kennedy-King Col, Chicago, stud devel specialist & coun instr, 1973-75; Eastern NMex Univ, coordr, counr black affairs & asst prof ethnic studies, 1977-78; Chicago State Univ, proj dir & asst prof educ, 1978-79; Univ Ark, Monticello, Learning Develop Center, dir, 1979-80; Univ Wis-Oshkosh, dir multicultural educ center, 1981-85; Univ Toledo, dir minority affairs & adj asst prof, 1985-88; Northeastern Ill Univ, prof counr educ, 1988-, vpres stud affairs, 1988-; Ill State Univ, vis prof, 1991; Florida State Univ, fel, 1993-94. **Orgs:** Vice chmn educ comt, NAACP Toledo Br, 1985-88; Educ Bd, Nat Asn Stud Personnel Admin J, 1986-89; Educ Bd, Leadership Educ, 1986-; chair educ comt, Alpha Phi Alpha, 1986-88; nat chmn, Ethnic Minority Network, Nat Asn Stud Personnel Asn, 1988-90; consult evaluator, N Cent Asn Cols & Univs, 1988-; vice chmn, Am Asn Higher Educ, 1989; chmn, Am Asn Higher Educ, Black Caucus Exec, 1991-93; life mem, Alpha Phi Alphi Fraternity Inc; eval team mem, Middle States Asn Cols & Univs; Nat Asn StudPersonnel Administrators; nat coordr, Minority Undergraduate Fel Prog, Nat Asn Stud Personnel Admin, 1994-98; chair, Exec Comt, Ill Comt Blacks Concerned Higher Ed (ICBCHE), 1995-; Am Col Personnel Asn. **Honors/Awds:** Outstanding Adminstrator, Univ Toledo, 1985 &, 1986; Administrator of the Year, Univ Toledo, 1986-88; Scott Goodnight Award, 1990; Ford Foundation Grant Cultural Diversity, 1992-94; Distinguished Service Award, IL Comt Black Concerns Higher Educ, 1999; Sadie M. Yancey Award, Nat Asn Student Affairs Professionals, 2002; Distinguished Service Award, Nat Asn Student Affairs Professionals, 2003; Research Award, 2004; Monarch Award, 2006; NASPA Region IV East Award, 2006. **Special Achievements:** Author, "From Isolation to Mainstream, An Institutional Committment" 1987; co-author, Model Field Based Program in Multicultural Educ for Non-Urban Univs 1981, "Multicultural Educ Centers in Acad Marketplace" 1987; author, Racism: Undermining Higher Education, 1988; editor, NAJournal Series on Cultural Pluralism, 1988; Scott Goodnight Award for Outstanding Performance of a Dean, 1990; co-editor, From Survival to Success: Promoting Minority Student Retention, 1988; Exemplary Leader in "Effective Leadership in Student Services," written by Linda M Clement & Scott T Rickard, Jossey-Bass, 1992; "Diversity, Disunity and Campus COT," NAT ASN of Student Personnel ADRs Monograph, 1992; Source of funding for minority student programming and its implications; Fund raising and development for student affairs; "Developing Student Government Leadership," New Directions for Student Services Monograph, Summer, 1994; editor, "Diversifying Student Affairs: Engaging, Retaining and Advancing AFA in the Profession," Ntl Assn of Students Affairs Professionals Journal, 2003; editor, "Retention of MNY Students," Ntl Assn of Student Affairs Professionals Journal, 2002; co-author, How MNY Students Experience College: The Implications for Planning and Policy, 2002; editor, Enhancing Student Learning: Setting the Campus Context, Amer Coll Personnel Asn. **Business Addr:** Vice President for Student Affairs, Professor of Counselor Education, Northeastern Illinois University, 5500 N St Louis Ave PE 1121, Chicago, IL 60625, **Business Phone:** (773)442-4608.

TERRELL, REGINALD V.
Lawyer. **Personal:** Born Mar 23, 1959, Vallejo, CA; son of Harold D and Codessa M. **Educ:** Saint Mary's Col, CA, BA, 1981; Univ Calif, JD, 1984. **Career:** Univ Calif, Davis, Law Review, staff, 1984; Burris Law Off, law clerk, lawyer; Terrell Law Group, owner, atty, currently. **Orgs:** Charles Houston Bar Asn, 1984-; Nat Bar Asn, 1984-; Calif State Bar, 1987-; Calif Consumer Atty's 1988-; bd mem, Saint Mary's Col, CA, 1992-97; trustee, Saint Mary's Col, CA, 1997-99; regent bd mem, Saint Mary's Col, CA, 1999-; Am Trial Lawyers Asn, 1999-. **Business Phone:** (510)237-3930.*

TERRELL, RICHARD WARREN
Executive. **Personal:** Born Nov 16, 1946, Fort Riley, KS; son of Warren and Mary; married Phyllis Eileen Hargrove; children: Wesley & Rodney. **Educ:** CA Polytech SLO, BSEL, 1968; San Jose State, MSEE, 1974. **Career:** Prairie View A&M, adj prof, 1976-77; IBM, engr, mgr, lsi packaging, 1968-90; Compaq Comput Corp, storage & printer systems staff, 1990; SE Lab Inc, sr vpres, gen mgr, currently. **Orgs:** Alpha Phi Alpha; Nat Asn Advan Colored People; Antioch Baptist Church; Jack & Jill Am. **Home Addr:** 4959 Massachusetts Dr, San Jose, CA 95136. **Business Addr:** General Manager, SE Laboratories Inc, 1065 Comstock St, Santa Clara, CA 95054, **Business Phone:** (408)727-3286.

TERRELL, ROBERT E.
Government official. **Personal:** Born Oct 4, 1943, Terry, MS; son of Rosie McNeil; married Karen K; children: Kelley L Carson. **Educ:** KS Univ, BS, 1966, MPA, 1975. **Career:** Retired; Turner House Inc, exec dir, 1971-74; City Ft Worth, budget analyst, 1974-77; Ft Worth Econ Develop Corp, exec dir, 1977-79; City Ft Worth, asst to city mgr, 1979-85; asst city mgr, 1985-92, city mgr, 1992-01. **Orgs:** Officer, Kappa Alpha Psi Frat, 1962-; fel, NASPAA, 1974-75; Nat Bd Conf Minority Pub Admin, 1979-81; Am Soc Pub Admin, 1979-; Asst Steering Com Intl City Mgt Asn, 1979-81; pres, Nat Forum Black Pub Adminrs, North Texas Chapter, 1987-89; life mem, NAACP, 1989- ; Task Force mgr, ICMA Coun, 1993-95; Pub Tech Inc, steering comt, 1992-; Tex City Mgt Asn. **Honors/Awds:** Adminstrator of the Year, N Tex ASPA Pub, 1988; Technology Leadership Award, Public Technol Inc, 1997. *

TERRELL, ROBERT L.
Educator, writer. **Personal:** Born Jul 19, 1943; married. **Educ:** Morehouse Col Atlanta, BA, sociol, 1969; Univ CA Berkeley, MA, jour, 1971; Univ CA Berkeley, PhD, educ, 1970. **Career:** Pub poems short stories books, 1967-; NY Post, reporter, 1967-68; So Reg Coun Atlanta, res writer, 1968-69; Newsweek Mag, stringer, 1968-69; Univ CA, teaching asst, 1969-70; Golden Gate Col, instr, 1969-71; San Francisco Chronicle, copy ed, 1970; CA Jour Teacher Ed, asst prof, 1971-76, ed, 1972-73; Off Res & Planning, coordr, 1974-75; St Mary's Col Morage CA, off experimental progs, 1975-76; Stanford Univ, asst prof, 1976; Univ MO, assoc prof jour, 1976-; Sch Jour Univ CA Berkeley, visiting prof, 1979; Beijing Review Mag, Beijing China, copy ed, 1981-82; NY Univ Dept Jour & Mass Commun, visiting prof, 1985-86; Univ Nairobi Sch Journ, Full bright prof, 1984-85; Univ Colorado, Assoc Prof, 1988-91; Univ Missouri; California St Univ, Interim Chair, Chair, prof, currently. **Orgs:** Am Asn Col Teacher Ed, Am Assoc Higher Ed, Am Ed Res Asn; bd dir, CA Coun Teacher Ed, Soc Col & Univ; managing ed CA Jour Teacher Ed, 1973; ed referee, CA Jour Teacher Ed, 1974-; adv, screening comt comn Coun Intl Exchange Scholars Fulbright Prog, 1980-83; Speech Commun Asn; Asn Educ Jour; Intl Commun Asn, 1992-96. **Honors/Awds:** Fellowship, CA State, 1969-72, Grad Minority, 1969-72, Fund Peace, 1970-71, NDEA, 1971-74; Deans Fellowship Univ CA, 1974-75; Professor of the Year, California State Univ; National Research Council Panelist, 2004; Kappa Tau Alpha; Outstanding Professor of the Year, California State Univ. **Business Phone:** (510)885-3292.

TERRELL, STANLEY E
Journalist. **Personal:** Born Feb 16, 1949, Newark, NJ; son of Millard E and Wilda M Johnson; children: Salimu Amini. **Educ:** Hampton Inst, 1966-68; Essex County Col, 1969-70. **Career:** The Star-Ledger, gen assignment news reporter, 1968-88, ed writer & columnist, 1988-. **Orgs:** Lectr, worked closely with NAACP; Urban League; Cong African People; Human Rights Comn; various tenant groups, juvenile progs, prison reform groups, drug rehab projects; founding mem, Black Heritage Day Parade Comn, 1979-. **Honors/Awds:** Merit Award, Newark Tenants Couns, 1974; Outstanding Achievement Award, Newark Human Rights Comn, 1974; 'Award from Newark Title I ESEA Prog for Outstanding Service to Newark Commission', 1975; Star-Ledger Bonus, 1971; New Jersey Black Achievers Award, 1989; Distinguished Service Award, Black Heritage Day Parade Comn, 1990. **Special Achievements:** Contributed articles to numerous magazines. **Home Addr:** 10 Hill St, Newark, NJ 07102. **Business Addr:** Columnist, The Star-Ledger, 1 Star Ledger Pl, Newark, NJ 07102, **Business Phone:** (973)297-5204.

TERRY, ADELINE HELEN
Lawyer. **Personal:** Born Apr 17, 1931, Wichita, KS; daughter of Clifford Johnson and Narcissus O; children: Catherine. **Educ:** Calif State Col, BA, Sociol, 1960; Southwestern Univ Law, LLB, 1969. **Career:** Lawyer (retired); La County Dist Atty, investr, 1960-62, dep dist atty; La County Supe Ct, domestic rel investr 1962-65; La County Probation Dept, 1965-69. **Orgs:** Asn Dept Dist Atty La; CA Dist Atty's Asn; Black Women's Lawyers LA; Langston Law Club; Women Lawyers LA; State Bar CA. **Home Addr:** 4620 Angeles Vista Blvd, Los Angeles, CA 90043, **Home Phone:** (213)294-0583.

TERRY, DR. ANGELA OWEN
School administrator. **Personal:** Born Feb 13, 1941, Memphis, TN; daughter of Addie Griffin Owen and William Franklin Owen, Sr; married Elbert A (deceased); children: Angela Daphne & Warren Marshall. **Educ:** Spelman Col, BA, 1962; Univ Vienna, cert, 1963; Fisk Univ, MA, 1964; Univ Conn, PhD, 1973; Harvard Univ, Cambridge, Mass, cert, 1987, Mgt Develop Prog Col & Univ Adminr Inst Educ Mgt. **Career:** School administrator (retired); Albany State Col, asst prof psychol, 1964-69; Prospect Psychol Serv Ctr, psychol serv worker, 1969-71; Harvard Univ, fel, 1969; Univ Conn, fel, 1971-73; Conn State Dept Educ, educ consult psychol serv, 1973-77; Univ Conn, asst dir, dept coun serv, 1978-83, asst vpres prog eval & res, 1983-89, asst vpres stud affairs, 1989-93, assoc vpres stud affairs, 1994-97; NASPA Jour, ed bd, 1988-91, 1993-96; NC Cent Univ, Durham, NC, vice chancellor stud affairs, 1993-94. **Orgs:** Am Asn Coun & Develop; Am Col Personnel Asn; Assoc Instnl Res; Dist Sorority Inc; Nat Asn Stud Personnel Adminr; Am Asn Higher Educ; Coalition 100 Black Women; hon mem, Golden Key Nat Honor Soc, 1990; Phi Delta Kappa; Nat Educ Honor Soc; Pi Lambda Theta Nat Educ Honor Soc; state coordr, Nat ID Prog Advan Women, 1992-93; adv bd, NASPA Region I, 1996-98; chair, Enrollment Mgmt Network, 1996-; Bd pres, Nasher Mus Art, Duke Univ, 2008-09. **Honors/Awds:** Scholar, Univ Vienna, 1963; Leadership, NC Central Univ, 1994; Service Award, African Cult Ctr, Univ Conn; Recognition Award, The Women's Ctr, Univ Conn; Outstanding Educator Award, Windham-Willimantic Chap, NCP. **Home Addr:** 36 Patriot Rd, Windham, CT 06280.

TERRY, CLARK
Musician. **Personal:** Born Dec 14, 1920, St Louis, MO; married Pauline Reddon (divorced); children: Gary (stepson); married Gwendolyn Paris. **Career:** Albums: Clark Terry, 1955; Duke With A Difference, 1957; Color Changes, 1960; Oscar Peterson Trio with Clark Terry, 1964; Yes, the Blues, 1981; To Duke & Basie, 1986; Portraits, 1988; The Clark Terry Spacemen, 1989; What a Wonderful World: For Louis, 1993; One on One, 2000; A Jazz Symphony, 2000; Herr Ober: Live at Birdland Neuburg, 2001; Live on QE2, 2001; Jazz Matinee, 2001; The Hymn, 2001; Clark Terry & His Orchestra Featuring Paul, 2002; Live in Concert, 2002; Flutin' & Fluglin, 2002; Friendship, 2002; Live! At Buddy's Place, 2003; Live at Montmarte June 1975, 2003; George

Gershwin's Porgy & Bess, 2004; Live at Marian's with the Terry's Young Titan's of Jazz, 2005; Pastel Music, pres; Etoile Music Prod Inc, pres; Clark Terry Big Bad Band; Itinerate Jazz. **Orgs:** Exec dir, Int Art Jazz. **Honors/Awds:** NEA Hall of Fame, 1991; Beacon in Jazz Award, New Sch Music, 1991; Down Beat Hall of Fame, 2000; Honorary Doctorates from Teikyo Westmar Univ, Berklee Sch Music & Univ New Hampshire; Grammy Award; two Grammy certificates; thirteen honorary doctorates; keys to cities; lifetime achievements & halls of fame awards. **Special Achievements:** Performed for seven U.S. Presidents, and was a Jazz Ambassador for State Department tours in the Middle East and Africa, author of Let's Talk Trumpet: From Legit to Jazz Interpretation of the Jazz Language, Clark Terry's System of Circular Breathing for Woodwind and Brass Instruments. **Military Serv:** USN. **Business Addr:** Musician, c/o Chesky Records, 355 W 52nd St 6th Fl, New York, NY 10019.

TERRY, FRANK W.
Government official. **Personal:** Born Jan 23, 1919, Los Angeles, CA; son of Woodford H and Jessie L; married Valdoras Hancock (died 1994); children: Charles Love, Susan Samples, Mike Terry; married Evelyn Ibanez, Sep 1998. **Educ:** Army Officers Candidate Sch, 1942; Los Angeles City Col, 1949. **Career:** Government official (retired); Freelance photographer reporter, 1946-50; Joseph V Baker Assoc, west coast rep, 1950-56; Douglas Aircraft Co, 1956-60; US Dept Labor Off Information, 1962-78; US Veterans Admin, 1978; Los Angeles Libr, comnr, 1978-93. **Orgs:** Chmn, Los Angeles Fed Exec Bd, 1975-76; bd mem, CA Governor's Comn for Employment Handicapped; bd mem, Col Fed Coun Southern CA, 1965-70; third vpres, LA Libr Asn; bd mem, Cultural Heritage Found; bd mem, Fed Black Hist & Arts; LA Urban League. **Honors/Awds:** Various publications, 1946-50; recipient, Certificate of Merit, LA Fed Exec Bd, 1967; Meritorious Achievement Award, US Dept Labor, 1970; Lula Fields Exec Award, Extraordinaire, 1972; Aztec Award, Mexican Am Opportunities Found, 1974. **Military Serv:** AUS, 1st lt, 1941-46. *

TERRY, GARLAND BENJAMIN
Dentist. **Personal:** Born Mar 27, 1927, Norfolk, VA; married Marie Walker; children: Michael Quentin. **Educ:** Ohio State Univ, BS, 1953; Col Dent Howard Univ, DDS, 1957. **Career:** Pvt pract, dentist, 1960-. **Orgs:** NJ Dent Asn; Am Dent Asn; Omega Psi Phi; Capital City Golf Club. **Military Serv:** AUS, 1946-49, Dental Corp, 1957-60. **Business Addr:** Dentist, 701 Rutherford Ave, Trenton, NJ 08618.*

TERRY, PATRICIA S
Educator, librarian. **Personal:** Born Aug 11, 1937, Brooklyn, NY; daughter of Philip Smith and Naomi McKeever Smith; married Namond, Sep 5, 2002; children: Naomi Brown, Mabel Mcleod, Derek Brown, Latrice Kendall, Arnold II & Edward Brown. **Educ:** Col New Rochelle, New Rochelle, NY, BA, liberal arts, 1979, MA, geront, 1988; Pratt Inst, Brooklyn, NY, MS, libr & info sci, 1980. **Career:** Brooklyn Pub Libr, Brooklyn, NY, supvr clerk/librn, 1969-81; Col New Rochelle, New Rochelle, NY, br librn, 1981-, adj fac, 1982-, coordr libr servs, 1992-, Gill Libr, ref librn, currently; NY Tech Col, Brooklyn, NY, adj fac, 1988-89; Intervention Asst Off, Calif Dept Educ, educ progs consult. **Orgs:** Pilgrim Church Brooklyn, NY, 1959-; Linden Plaza Polit Action Comt, 1979; pres, NY Black Librns Caucus Inc, tenure, 1984-86; exec bd mem, Am Libr Asn Black Caucus, 1985-87; Am Libr Asn; NY Lib Asn; NY Black Librns' Caucus; Black Women Higher Educ; Alumni Asn Col New Rochelle & Pratt Inst. **Honors/Awds:** Ten Years of Service Award, Brooklyn Pub Libr, 1979; Teacher of the Year, 1990; Service to the Col, Computerized Career Planning, 1991. **Business Addr:** Associate Professor & Coordinator of Library Services, Reference Librarian in Gill Library, College of New Rochelle, College of New Rochelle Library, 1368 Fulton St, Brooklyn, NY 11216.

TERRY, RICK
Football player. **Personal:** Born Apr 5, 1974, Lexington, NC; children: Jasmine. **Educ:** Univ NC. **Career:** Football player(retired), New York Jets, defensive tackle, 1997-98; Carolina Panthers, 1998-99.

TERRY, ROY
Executive, chief executive officer, president (organization). **Personal:** Born Dec 27, 1944, Dayton, OH; son of Velma G and Jesse A; married Willo; children: Corey & Cotina. **Educ:** Morehouse Coll, BA, 1966. **Career:** Terry Mfg Co Inc, pres & chief exec officer, 1972-. **Orgs:** Am Apparel Mfr Asn, 1969-; life mem, Nat Asn Advan Colored People, 1970-; founding mem, Many Bus Enterprise Legal Def & Educ Fund, 1980-; Ala Demc Conf, voting rights cordr, 1980-; Fed Res Bank, Birmingham Br, cbd, 1985-92; Oper PUSH, World Trade Coun, 1986-. **Honors/Awds:** Manufacturer of the Year, Black Enterprise Mag, 1974; AG Gaston Award, Ala Democratic Conf, 1980; Manufacturer of the Year, US Dept Commerce, 1989; Initial Shared Production Award, US Dept Defense, 1992; Bennie Award, Morehouse Col, 1993. **Special Achievements:** Author: Shared Production Concept, adopted as model, $3.5 billion Defense Agency, 1992; company ranked #59 on Black Enterprise's list of top 100 industrial/service companies, 1998. **Business Addr:** President, Chief Executive Officer, Terry Manufacturing Company Inc, PO Box 2926, Birmingham, AL 35202-3804.*

TERRY, SAUNDERS
Entertainer. **Personal:** Born Oct 24, 1911, Greensboro, GA; married Emma Taylor. **Career:** Buck & The Preacher, Finnians Rainbow, mus featured 1946; Cat on A Hot Tin Roof, 1955; Cisco Pike, 1972; Book of Numbers, 1973; Leadbelly, 1976; Crossroads, music sound track, 1985; The Color Purple, actor & music sound Track, 1985; Prof entertainer & harmonica player & singer. **Orgs:** SAG, 1985-; Teacher, Harmonica Playing; Comm Civic Asn; Am Fedn Musicians Local No 802; AFTRA. **Honors/Awds:** Cert, Preserv & Advan Harmonica, 1963. **Special Achievements:** Honored on U.S. Postage Stamp, 1998, numerous radio & TV music shows.

TERUEL, LAUREN
Fashion model, educator. **Personal:** Born in Chicago, IL; daughter of Joanne Scott and Hugo. **Educ:** Calif State Univ, Northridge, BA, Eng, 2000. **Career:** Calif State Univ Northridge, Nat Ctr Deafness, assoc proj coordr, currently. **Honors/Awds:** Miss Deaf American, 2000-02. **Special Achievements:** First African American crowned Miss Deaf Am. **Business Addr:** Associate Project Coordinator, California State University, National Center on Deafness, Chisholm Hall 18111 Nordhoff St, Northridge, CA 91330-8267, **Business Phone:** (818)677-2054.

TESSEMA, TESFAYE
Artist. **Personal:** Born May 5, 1951, Addis Ababa, Ethiopia. **Educ:** Fine Arts Sch, Addia Ababa, dipl, 1970; Howard Univ, MFA, 1976. **Career:** City Washington, muralist & prog coordr, 1976-77; The Harvest, graphics artist, 1976; Mus African Art, Washington, DC, designer & graphic artist, 1977-78; Arts DC, Washington, DC, mural prog coordr, 1978-80. **Special Achievements:** Arts competition, Addis Ababa, Ethiopia, 1967; mural, Howard Univ, Washington, DC, 1975; mural, Mus African Art, Washington, DC, 1978. **Business Addr:** Painter, Harlem Open Artsit Studio, 115 E 34th St, PO Box 810, New York, NY 10156, **Business Phone:** (212)795-7283.

THARPE, LARRY
Football player. **Personal:** Born Nov 19, 1970, Macon, GA. **Educ:** Tenn State Univ. **Career:** Football player (retired); Detroit Lions, tackle, 1992-94, 1997-98; Ariz Cardinals, 1995; New Eng Patriots, 1996; Pittsburgh Steelers, tackle, 2000.

THAXTON, JUNE E
Electrical engineer. **Personal:** Born May 28, 1961, Baltimore, MD; daughter of Fred (deceased) and Mildred; divorced. **Educ:** Howard Univ, BSEE, 1984. **Career:** Potomac Electric Power Co, engr elect syst, 1985-. **Orgs:** Am Asn Blacks Energy, 1991-; Inst Elec & Electronics Engineers, 1986. **Special Achievements:** Biographical article, US Black Engineer Magazine, 1986; Ebony Magazine, 1987. **Home Addr:** 1722 Lakeside Ave, Baltimore, MD 21218. **Business Addr:** Engineer of Electric System, Potomac Electric Power Company, 1900 Pa Ave NW, Washington, DC 20068, **Business Phone:** (202)872-2859.

THE ENTERTAINER, CEDRIC (CEDRIC ANTONIO KYLES)
Comedian, actor, writer. **Personal:** Born Apr 24, 1964, Jefferson City, MO; son of Rosetta Kyles; children (previous marriage): Croix Alexander & Lucky Rose Kyles; married Lorna Wells, Sep 3, 1999; children: Tiara, Croix & Rose. **Educ:** Southeastern Miss State Univ, BS, mass commun. **Career:** Films: Ride, 1998; Big Momma's House, 2000; The Smoker, 2000; The Original Kings of Comedy, writer, 2000; Kingdom Come, 2001; Dr Doolittle 2, 2001; Ice Age, voice, 2001; Barbershop, 2002; Serving Sara, 2002; Intolerable Cruelty, 2003; Barbershop 2, 2004; The Honeymooners, producer, 2005; Charlotte's Web, 2006; Code Name: The Cleaner, producer, 2007; Talk To Me, 2007; Welcome Home, Roscoe Jenkins, 2008; TV Series: "The Steve Harvey Show," 1996-2002; "Cedric the Entertainer Presents," 2002, "Invasion of the Katrinians", 2007; "The BoonDocks", 2007; TV Commercials: Bud Light advertisements, 2001; The Black Movie Awards, 2005; Champ Car World Series, CTE Racing-HVM, part owner, 2005-. **Orgs:** Kappa Alpha Psi Fraternity Inc. **Honors/Awds:** Richard Pryor Comic of the Year Award, BET, 1994; Image Award, 1999, 2000, 2001, 2002; NAACP Image Award for his voice work on "The Proud Family," 2003; St Louis Int Film Festival Award, 2005; Gotham Award, 2007. **Business Addr:** Actor, Universal Citywalk, 100 Universal City Plz, Universal City, CA 91608, **Business Phone:** (818)622-4455.

THELWELL, MICHAEL M EKWUEME (MIKE THELWELL)
Writer, educator. **Personal:** Children: Chinua & Mikiko. **Educ:** Howard Univ, BA, Eng lit, 1964; Univ Mass Amherst, MFA, 1968. **Career:** Jamaica Indust Develop, pub rels asst, 1958-59; Stud Nonviolent Coord Comn, dir wash office, 1963-64; Miss Freedom Dem Party, dir Wash office, 1964-65; Ed Chief, Howard Univ, Soc Humanities, Cornell Univ, 1968; Univ Mass, Amherst, W E B DuBois, Dept Afro-Am Studies, counr, 1969-75, assoc prof lit, 1972, prof, 1980-; Nat Endowment Arts, adv & consult, 1970; Nat Endowment Arts, Writers Fel, 1980-81; WGBH TV, PBS, sr adv, 1989. **Honors/Awds:** Inst Jamaica Centennial Medal, 1980. **Special Achievements:** Author: The Harder They Come, Novel, Pluto Press, London, 1980; Pleasures, Duties, and Conflicts, University of MA, 1987; Rage, Carroll & Gref, NY, 1992. **Business Addr:** Professor, University Massachusetts, Afro-American Studies 639 N Pleasant St, Amherst, MA 01003, **Business Phone:** (413)545-5169.

THELWELL, MIKE. **See THELWELL, MICHAEL M EKWUEME.**

THEODORE, YVONNE M.
School administrator. **Personal:** Born Mar 16, 1939, Prince Georges County, MD; divorced. **Educ:** Mt St Agnes Col, BA, 1961; Makerere Univ, Uganda, E Africa, MA, 1962; Johns Hopkins Univ, Cand M Lib Arts, 1976; Fisk Univ, Spec Courses Race Relig, 1964. **Career:** School administrator (retired); Mt St Mary's Namagunga, Uganda, E Africa, grad stud, teacher, 1961-64; Baltimore City Comm Religion Community, intergroup religion specialist, 1965-68; Provident Comp Neighborhood Health Ctr, from asst dir to dir, 1968-69; Johns Hopkins Univ, dir affirmative action, 1971-99, affirmative action officer, currenlty. **Orgs:** Nat Coun Negro Women; Col & Univ Personnel Asn; Kampala Singers, Interracial, Intercultural Classical Singing Group, Uganda, E Africa; Black Professionals Int Affairs; Am Asn Univ Women; Phi Delta Kappa Fraternity; Am Coun Alcoholism; Md Tech Asst Prog; programmer, In Good Taste, Manford Radio Reading Station; Am Asn Higher Educ, Black Caucus; Int Duke Ellington Soc; Md Asn Affirmative Action Officers; coordr, Nation's Capital Area Disabled Stud Serv; Baltimore Metro Area Job Serv Employer Community. **Honors/Awds:** Recipient Recognition for Youth Motivation, Nat Alliance Businessmen,1973-74; Academic Scholarship, Mt St Agnes Col; Recognition for Employee Recruitment, Am Indians. **Special Achievements:** Named illustrious Wmn Baltimore Afro-Am Newspaper, 1971. **Business Addr:** Affirmative Action Officer, Johns Hopkins University, Rm 205 Garland Hall 3400 N Charles St Suite 130, Baltimore, MD 21218-2696, **Business Phone:** (410)516-8075.

THERMILUS, JACQUE E (JACQUES EVENS THERMILUS)
Executive, chief executive officer. **Career:** Urban Constructors Inc, pres; Urban Orgn Inc, chief exec officer, owner, currently. **Business Phone:** (305)638-8100.

THERMILUS, JACQUES EVENS. **See THERMILUS, JACQUE E.**

THE ROCK. **See JOHNSON, DWAYNE DOUGLAS.**

THE ROSE. **See HINES, ROSETTA.**

THEUS, REGGIE WAYNE
Basketball player, basketball coach. **Personal:** Born Oct 13, 1957, Ingelwood, CA. **Educ:** Univ Las Vegas, NV, attended 1979. **Career:** Basketball player (retired), Basketball coach; Chicago Bulls, 1978-84; Kans City Kings, 1984-85; Sacramento Kings, 1985-88; Atlanta Hawks, 1988-89; Orlando Magic, 1989-90; NJ Nets, 1990-91; Ranger Varese, Italian League, 1991-92; TNT, TBS & Fox Sports, studio analyst; Univ Louisville, asst coach, 2003-05; NMex State Univ, head basketball coach, 2005-07; Sacramento Kings, head coach, 2007-09. **Orgs:** Little City Prog; Athletes For Better Educ, 1979; Nat Comm Against Child Abuse. **Honors/Awds:** Most Valuable Player, Univ Las Vegas, NV, 1979. **Special Achievements:** TV appearance: "Hang Time", NBC-TV; creative consult, "Like Mike". **Business Addr:** Head coach, Sacramento Kings, One Sports Pkwy, Sacramento, CA 95834, **Business Phone:** (916)928-0000.

THIBODEAUX, SYLVIA MARIE
Educator, clergy. **Personal:** Born Nov 26, 1937, Breaux Bridge, LA; widowed. **Educ:** BA, 1967; MA, 1973; DHL. **Career:** Cath Sch, Tulsa, elem teacher, 1960-62; Opelousa, teacher, 1962-63; Tulsa, teacher, 1963-65; Proj Commitment & Asn Urban Sisters, Boston, 1968-69; Witness Prog Educ Component, New Orleans, dir, 1967-68; St Joseph Community Sch, Boston, prin, 1970-74; Holy Family, New Orleans, unity leader & congregational leader, head of sisters, currently. **Orgs:** Bd mem, Campaign Human Develop, Nat Off Black Cath; Nat Black Sisters Conf; DESIGN; Minority Evaluators Ginn & Co; bd trustees, Educ Develop Ctr; consult, AFRAM Asn; Planning Comt, Black Educ Conf; Teacher Training Col & Relig Formation, Benin City, Nigeria, W Africa; SCLC Most Creative Educ Prog. **Honors/Awds:** NIA Award, Innovative Educ Prog; Outstanding Contrib Black Community Award, Roxbury Action Prog; Outstanding Educr Am Award.

THIERRY, JOHN FITZGERALD
Football player. **Personal:** Born Sep 4, 1971, Houston, TX. **Educ:** Alcorn State Univ. **Career:** Chicago Bears, defensive end, 1994-98; Cleveland Browns, 1999; Green Bay Packers, 2000-01; Atlanta Falcons, linebacker, 2002.

THIGPEN, DR. CALVIN HERRITAGE
Physician, lawyer. **Personal:** Born Jan 7, 1924, Greenville, NC; married Vera Belle Crawford; children: Calvin Jr & Karen. **Educ:** Va State Col, BS, 1953; Univ Va Health System, Sch med, MD,

1962, JD, 1974. **Career:** Hopewell, VA, teacher, 1953-58; Stuart Prod Co, cosmetics & chem plant mgr, 1957-58; Med Col Va, intern, 1962-63; Petersburg Gen Hosp, staff mem, 1963; pvt practice, 1963; Va State Col, assoc & physician, 1964-71; Petersburg Gen Hosp, vice chief, gen practice sect, 1969-70; Office Attorney Gen, VA, intern, 1972-73; Univ Va, res asst legal adv, 1973-74; Pvt Practice, atty, 1975-. **Orgs:** Sigma Pi Sigma Nat Physics Hon Soc; Beta Kappa Chi Nat Sci Hon Soc; Phi Delta Phi Legal Fraternity; Dem Com Hopewell, 1965-75; bd dir, Salvation Army; Hopewell Chamber Com; Old Dominion Med Soc; exec comt, Old Dominion Med Soc, 1965. **Honors/Awds:** pres, Nat Guardsmen Inc, 1967-70; Libr Human Resources, Am Bicentennial Res Inst, 1973; Fel Am Col Legal Med, 1976; Mem Bd Visitors, Va State Univ, 1978-82; Va Delegate to the White House Conf on Libr & Info Serv, 1979; Chief Staff Petersburg Gen Hosp, 1980; Diplomate Am Bd Legal Med, 1982. **Military Serv:** AUS, first Lt, 1944-49. **Home Addr:** 19801 Oakland Ave, Colonial Heights, VA 23834, **Home Phone:** (804)520-1883. **Business Addr:** Attorney, Physician, 734 S Sycamore St, Petersburg, VA 23803, **Business Phone:** (804)733-0111.

THIGPEN, DONALD A
Lawyer. **Personal:** Born Aug 22, 1946, Jersey City, NJ; son of Donald A and Dorothy E. **Educ:** Kent State Univ, BA, 1968; Howard Univ Sch Law, JD, 1974. **Career:** Kent State Univ, Human Rels Dept & Dept African-Am Studies, coordr Minority Affairs, 1968-71; Bureau Nat Affair, ed, Family Law reporter, 1974-79; DC Off Corp Coun, prosecutor, 1979-81, Civil Litigation, trial atty, 1981-85, DC Mental Health Systems Reorganization, coun, 1985-87, Govt Contracts, legislation atty, 1987-93, DC Redevelop Land Agency, gen coun, Land Use & Econ Develop, chief, 1993, sr counsel; pvt pract, currently; Int Coalition Economic Unity Inc, co-founder & gen counsel. **Orgs:** Co-founder & vpres, Waring-Mitchell Law Soc Howard County Md, 1992-93; co-founder & gen coun, Int Coalition Economic Unity Inc, 1992-99; asst treas, Nat Bar Asn, 1993-95, gen coun, 1995-96, 1996-99, exec comt, 1997-98, bd gov, regional dir, 1996-98;; assoc grand chief justice, Sigma Delta Tau Legal Fraternity, 1995-99; bd chair, vice pres, Wash Bar Asn, 1997-99, past pres; nat pres, Howard Univ Law Alumni Assoc, 1996-98 vpres, Locust Grove Homeowners Assoc, 1998-99; pres, Greater Wash Area Chap, Univ Law Alumni Asn; chair, Howard Law Alumni Comn; co-founder & vpres, Waring-Mitchell Law Soc, Howard County Md; assoc grand chief justice, Sigma Delta Tau Legal Fraternity; sr class pres & pres, Delta Theta Phi Law Fraternity; pres, Locust Grove Homeowners Asn; gen coun, Allen & Partners; charter mem, Charlotte E Ray Inn Am Inns Ct; mem, Retrospective Review Adv Comt, DC Ct Appeals; chief judge, Charles Hamilton Houston Inst, Moot Ct Competition; mem comt, DC Bar. **Honors/Awds:** Mayoral Commendation, Mayor DC, 1994; Dedicated Alumni Service, Howard Univ, Stud Bar Asn, 1994; Presidential Outstanding Service Award, Nat Bar Asn, 1996; Outstanding Achievement Award, Wash Bar Asn, 1997; Grande Award Community Serv, Prince Hall Masons & Evening Stars, 1998. **Special Achievements:** First African-American legal editor on the staff of the Family Law Reporter at the Bureau of National Affairs. **Home Addr:** 1820 Locust Grove Rd, Silver Spring, MD 20910-1379. **Business Addr:** Vice President, President, Washington Bar Association, PO Box 56551, Washington, DC 20002, **Business Phone:** (202)289-4247.

THIGPEN, EDMUND LEONARD
Musician, educator. **Personal:** Born Dec 28, 1930, Chicago, IL; son of Benjamin and Mary Berry; widowed; children: Denise Mary & Michel Edmund. **Educ:** Los Angeles City Col, attended 1949; Manhattan Sch Mus, attended 1955. **Career:** Performed Cootie Williams, 1951, Dinah Wash, 1954, Johnny Hodges & Bud Powell, 1955-56, Billy Taylor Trio, 1957-58, Oscar Peterson Trio, 1959-65; Ella Fitzgerald, 1968-72; free-lance musician Los Angeles, movies, jingles etc & working with Johnny Mathis, Pat Boone, Andy Williams, Peggy Lee,Oliver Nelson, Gerald Wilson; Ella Fitzgerald permanent mem trio, 1972; Copenhagen, freelance solo & guest artist & instr, Univ IL, Champaign &Urbana, vis prof Jazz Studies, 1994-95; Albums: Ed Thigpen Scantet #1, 2004; Ed Thigpen Rhythm Features, The Element of Swing; It's Entertainment; Mr. Taste; Easy Flight; drummer, currently. **Orgs:** Bd dirs, Percussion Arts Soc; co-nat chmn, Nat Asn Jazz Educr, 1991-94, dr-set & pecussion; co-chair dr-set, Int Asn Jazz Educr, 1991-93. **Honors/Awds:** Inductee, Percussive Arts Soc Hall of Fame; Humanitarian Award, Int Asn Jazz Educ, 2002; Danish Jazz Award, Int Fedn Phonagraph Indust, 2002. **Special Achievements:** The Sound of Brushes, 1999; Ryhthm Brought to Life: A Rhythmic Primer,2000. **Military Serv:** USY, 1952-54. **Home Addr:** Bagerstraede, DK-1617 Copenhagen, Denmark. **Business Addr:** Drummer, Ed Thigpen Productions, Bagerstraede 3 2nd Fl, DK-1617 Copenhagen V, Denmark, **Business Phone:** (453)324-4098.

THIGPEN, YANCEY DIRK
Football player. **Personal:** Born Aug 15, 1969, Tarboro, NC; married Maria Dunbar, 2003. **Educ:** Winston-Salem State Univ. **Career:** Football player (retired); San Diego Chargers, wide receiver, 1991;Pittsburgh Steelers, 1992-97; Tennessee Oilers, 1998; Tennessee Titans,1999-2000. **Honors/Awds:** Pro Bowl selection, 1995; 1997. *

THOMAS, ALTHEA SHANNON LAWSON
Educator. **Personal:** Born Jan 16, 1953, Ft Gaines, GA; daughter of Wilson Robert Lawson and Arra Lightner Lawson; married Eddie Walden Thomas; children: Shadrin Vandell & Jasil Conrad. **Educ:** Hampton Univ, BA, 1973; Univ Tenn, MS, 1975; Troy State Univ, attended 1984. **Career:** Wallace State Community Col, counr & instr, 1975-82; Wallace State Community Col, instr, 1982-2000; Wallace State Community Col, inst coordr, 2000; Wallace Community Col, coordr acad progs, currently, Acad Progs, Title III, activity dir, currently. **Orgs:** Ala Personnel & Guid Asn, 1975-82; pres, Young Women's Serv Club, 1977-79; chair, Henry County Bd Educ Bi-racial Comt, 1978-80; Nat Coun Negro Women, 1979-; secy, Wallace Col Educ Asn, 1986-88; pres, Delta Sigma Theta Sor Inc, Dothan Alumnae Chap, 1992-96; Delta Sigma Theta Sor Inc, vpres, 2002-. **Honors/Awds:** Dothan Jaycees Outstanding Young Person. **Business Addr:** Coordinator Academic Programs, Director, Wallace Community College, 1141 Wallace Dr Admin 116 E, Dothan, AL 36303, **Business Phone:** (334)556-2269.

THOMAS, ALVIN
Government official. **Personal:** Born Apr 11, 1951, New Orleans, LA. **Educ:** Southern Univ Agri & Mech Col, BA, Polit Sci, 1974; Union Baptist TheolSem, 1974; Universal Bible Inst. **Career:** Retired. Mt Bethel Baptist Church, secy, 1964-68; Mt Zion Baptist Church#1, asst pastor, 1967-69; USPHS Hosp, clerk, 1968-72; Iberville Parish Police Jury, police juror, 1972-76; La House Rep, page, 1972; Indust Plant Maintenance, supvr, 1972-74; Jerusalem Baptist Church St Gabriel, pastor, 1973-74; Bechtel Power Corp, off mgr, 1975; La, spec asst, 1976. **Orgs:** Lemoyne Comn Action Fin Comt, 1968-70; dir, Stud Govt Asn So Univ, 1970-71; vpres, E Iberville Improve Asn, 1971; Iberville Parish Indust Voters League, 1971; ward leader, Iberville Parish, 1971-73; Iberville Parish Housing Authority, 1972; La Police Jury Asn, 1972-76; Nat Asn Comn Elect Official, 1972-76; Iberville Parish Person Comt, 1972-76; Iberville Parish Finance Comn, 1972-76; Iberville Parish Gas Comn, 1972-76; Iberville Parish Law Enforce Comt, 1972-76; E Iberville Recreation Asn, 1972; Iberville Parish Ministerial Coun, 1972; Second Dist Baptist Asn,1972; Fourth Dist Baptist Asn, 1972; La Baptist Conv, 1972; Nat Bapt Conv USA Inc 1972; La Health Asn Comn, 1972-76; founder & pres, E Iberville Vol Fire Dept, 1972; Nat Foreign Miss Bd USA Inc, 1972; chmn, First Nat Black Polit Convent, 1972; Nat Dem Conv, 1972; vpres, Nat Asn Black Counties Officials, 1975-76; rep, Nat Legis Conf NACO, 1975; rep, Iberville Parish Police Jury. **Honors/Awds:** Outstanding Student, Govt Asn Worker, Southern Univ, 1970-71. **Home Addr:** PO Box 67, Carville, LA 70721.

THOMAS, ANTHONY J
Football player. **Personal:** Born Nov 7, 1977, Winnfield, LA. **Educ:** Univ Mich, sports mgt & commun. **Career:** Chicago Bears, running back, 2001-04; Dallas Cowboys, 2005; New Orleans Saints, running back, 2005-06; Buffalo Bills, running back, 2006-07. **Honors/Awds:** All-Big Ten, second & third-team All-Am hons; Football News Player of the Year, Semifinalist; Doak Walker Award; Breakout Player of the Year, Sporting News; NFL Rookie of the Year, Sports Illustrated, 2001; NFL Offensive Rookie of Year, 2002.

THOMAS, DR. ARTHUR E.
College president, executive. **Personal:** Son of Janie R Bradley; married Dawn. **Educ:** Cent State Univ, Wilberforce, OH, attended 1962; Miami Univ, MEd; Univ Mass, EdD. **Career:** Cent State Univ, Wilberforce, OH, vpres acad affairs, 1977-85, pres, 1985-95; pres emer, 1995-; Dayton Pub Sch Syst, fac; Wright State Univ, fac; Don King Productions Inc, dir community affairs. **Orgs:** Am Coun Educ; Nat Asn Equal Opportunity Higher Educ. **Special Achievements:** US Presidential Delegation to observe the first all-race election in South Africa. **Business Phone:** (937)376-6011.

THOMAS, ARTHUR LAFAYETTE, III
Video producer, editor. **Personal:** Born Jan 14, 1960, Trenton, NJ; son of Arthur and Hermione Smith; married Robin M Golden, Sep 5, 1992; children: Sydney Golden, Paige Leigh & Arthur IV. **Educ:** Rutgers Univ, BA, 1982; Am Univ, attended 1987. **Career:** Powell Bros Inc, tech servs mgr; Black Entertainment Television, videographer, currently. **Orgs:** Nat Asn Black Journalists; US Sen & House Rep News Galleries, 1987-. **Honors/Awds:** Cable Ace Award, nomination, 1998. **Special Achievements:** Attended President Clinton historical journey to Africa; One of the only two Black videographers chosen for the first sitting Presidents' visit to the African continent. **Home Addr:** 2913 Gracefield Rd, Silver Spring, MD 20904. **Business Addr:** Videographer, Black Entertainment Television, 1900 W Pl NE, Washington, DC 20018-1230.

THOMAS, ARTHUR R
President (Organization), executive. **Educ:** Southern Univ, Baton Rouge, BA, polit sci, 1973; Southern Univ Law Ctr, JD,1976. **Career:** La Dept Justice, staff atty; Renaissance Develop Corp, pres; Arthur R Thomas & Assocs LLC, pres, currently. **Orgs:** Int pres, Phi Beta Sigma Fraternity Inc. **Business Addr:** President, Arthur R Thomas & Associates LLC, 1755 Nicholson Dr, Baton Rouge, LA 70805, **Business Phone:** (225)344-7370.

THOMAS, DR. AUDRIA ACTY
Pediatrician, physician, physician. **Personal:** Born Jun 6, 1954, Washington, DC; married Robert A Leycock; children: Shaunta Lindsey & Shavon Thomas. **Educ:** Meharry Medical Col, MD, 1980; Fel, HUH, 1983-86. **Career:** Howard Univ Hosp, resident, 1980-83; St Thomas, St John Med Soc, chief allergy dept; Roy L Schneider Hosp, med staff, 1986; VI Dept Health, dir, currently. **Orgs:** Soloist VI Chriistian Ministries, 1959-86; Nat Med Asn, 1980-86; pediatric consult, 15-24 Free Clinic for Teenagers, 1980-86; consult, Virgin Island Lung Asn, 1986-; Am Acad Pediat; Am Acad Allergy & Immunol. **Honors/Awds:** Howard Univ Fel, Allergy Immunol, 1983-86. **Special Achievements:** Published paper, "Cystic Fibrosis in Black," Layman's Journal update in allergy, 1985. **Home Addr:** Charlotte Amalie, PO Box 595, St Thomas, VI 00804, **Home Phone:** (809)776-7782. **Business Addr:** Director, Virgin Islands Department of Health, 48 Sugar Estate, Charlotte Amalie, VI 00802, **Business Phone:** (340)774-0117.

THOMAS, BARBARA LOUISE
Association executive, president (organization), chief executive officer. **Personal:** Born Dec 5, 1947, Dublin, GA; daughter of Horace Sanders and Jerrie Lee Tart; children: 2. **Educ:** Bernard Baruch Col, BA, 1970; Columbia Univ, MBA, 1973. **Career:** CBS, Radio Div, clerk, 1973, TV Div, network cutins, dir finance & admin, sr vpres, 1989; Nat Black MBA Asn, vpres finance & admin, chief financial officer, 2001-03, pres & ceo, 2003-. **Orgs:** Life mem, Nat Black MBA Asn. **Special Achievements:** first Black woman to complete the CBS School of Management; first African American woman to serve as a senior vice-president in CBS. **Business Addr:** President, Chief Executive Officer, National Black MBA Association, 180 N Michigan Ave Suite 1400, Chicago, IL 60601, **Business Phone:** (312)236-2622.

THOMAS, BETTE
Association executive. **Career:** Dept Housing & Urban Develop; City N Chicago, mayor; Community Action Partnership Lake County, dir, currently. **Business Addr:** Board of Director, Community Action Partnership Of Lake County, PO Box 9059, Waukegan, IL 60079-9059, **Business Phone:** (847)249-4330.*

THOMAS, BLAIR
Football player, football coach. **Personal:** Born Oct 7, 1967, Philadelphia, PA; married Lisa; children: 3. **Educ:** Pa State Univ, BS, recreation & parks mgt, 1989. **Career:** Football player, coach (retired); New York Jets, running back, 1990-93; New England Patriots, running back, 1994; Dallas Cowboys, running back, 1994; Carolina Panthers, running back, 1995; Temple Univ, running back coach, 1998-2005; Football Univ, instr. **Honors/Awds:** Leading rookie rusher (326 yards), Am Football Conf, 1990.

THOMAS, BOBBY. **See THOMAS, ROBERT CHARLES.**

THOMAS, BRANDY
Chief executive officer. **Career:** Cyveillance Inc, founder, chmn & chief exec officer, 2000. **Business Addr:** Founder, Cyveillance Inc, 1555 Wilson Blvd Suite 404, Arlington, VA 22209-2405, **Business Phone:** (703)351-1000.*

THOMAS, BRODERICK
Football player. **Personal:** Born Feb 20, 1967, Houston, TX; married; children: Broderick Jr & Elijah. **Educ:** Univ NE. **Career:** Football player (retired); Tampa Bay Buccaneers, linebacker, 1989-93; Detroit Lions, 1994; Minn Vikings, 1995; Dallas Cowboys, linebacker, 1996-98. **Honors/Awds:** 36th Greatest Buccaneer Player of all-time, Bucpower.com, 2003.

THOMAS, CALVIN LEWIS
Football player. **Personal:** Born Jan 7, 1960, St Louis, MO; married Bernadine; children: Nikkita. **Educ:** Univ Ill, BA, 1984. **Career:** Football player (retired); Fullback; Chicago Bears, 1982-87; Denver Broncos, 1988. **Orgs:** Red Cloud Athletic Fund; Jr Variety Club; Big Brothers. *

THOMAS, CARL
Singer. **Personal:** Born Jun 15, 1970, Aurora, IL. **Career:** Albums: Emotional, 2000; Let's Talk About It, 2004; So Much Better, 2006; Singles: Summer Rain, 2000; I Wish, 2000; "Emotional", 2000; "She Is", 2004; Make It Alright, 2004; "My First Love", 2004; "Another You", 2006; 2 Pieces, 2007; Late Night Rendezvous, 2008. **Honors/Awds:** Nominee, Grammy Award, 2006. **Business Addr:** Recording Artist, c/o Bungalo Records, Universal Music Group, 1755 Broadway, New York, NY 10019, **Business Phone:** (212)841-8000.*

THOMAS, CARL ALAN
Educator, clergy. **Personal:** Born Mar 21, 1924, Jersey City, NJ; children: Edward, Algynan, Elaine & Stanley. **Educ:** Rutgers

Univ, BA, 1946; Union Sem, BD, 1949; NY Univ, MA, 1950; Univ KS, DD, 1970. **Career:** Fla A&M Univ, prof, 1960-64; Expert Int Living, dir, 1960; Wilberforce Univ, dean, 1964-66; Community Col Philadelphia, dir & dean; Lincoln Univ, PA, dean, 1968; African Methodist Episcopal Zion Church, pastor; Lincoln Univ Oxford, prof Black studies; Training Inst Lincoln Univ, teacher. **Orgs:** Alpha Psi Omega Frat; Kappa Alpha Psi Frat Swords & Shields Wilberforce, OH; Sons of Wilberforce OH.

THOMAS, CARL D. See Obituaries section.

THOMAS, CAROL M.
Government official. **Personal:** Born Dec 23, 1930, Washington, DC; married Laura Pedro; children: Kevin, Marla & Paul. **Educ:** Yale Univ, BA, 1953; John Hopkins Univ, MA, 1961. **Career:** Navy Dept, mgt intern, 1961; Navy Dept Wash, contract negotiator, 1961-64;Off Econ Opportunity Wash, br, 1964-65; Job Corps, proj mgr, 1965-67; Contracts Div Peace Corp Wash, dep dir, 1967-69; Peace Corps Sierraieone, dir, 1969-71; Off Civil Rights & Urban Affairs US Environ Protection Agency, dir, 1972-74; Am Soc Pub Adminrs, 1972-; Manasas Educ Found; Am Acad Polit & Social Scis, 1973-; Off Civil Rights US EPA Wash, 1974-77; Fed Trade Comn, secy, 1977-. **Orgs:** Reston Golf & Country Club, 1971-; exec, Comn Bd Dir, 1972-; Alpha Phi Alpha Frat; Fed City Club Wash, 1972-. **Military Serv:** USAF, 1954-59.

THOMAS, CHARLES COLUMBUS
Educator. **Personal:** Born Sep 10, 1940, McAlester, OK. **Educ:** Langston Univ, BA, 1962; Brooklyn Col, MFA, 1972; City Univ NY, attended 1977. **Career:** Afro-Am Folkloric Troupe, artistic dir, 1963-70; Leffert Jr High Sch, chmn, 1966-69; Egbe Omo Nago Folklorio Ensemble, dir, 1967-69; OEO Proj, dir, 1968; NY Community Col, asst prof, 1971-74; Afro-Am Inst Richmond Col, dir, 1972-73; Univ Ghana, vis prof, 1972; Ebony Success Libr, staff, 1972; Screen Actors Guild; Say Yes to Jesus, Gospel Musical, lead actor, 1992-99; "Life During War Time," Nuyorican Poets Cafe, NY, costume designer, 1993; Nat Black Theatre Festival, actor, 1999; KWANZAA Festival with Ossie Davis & Ruby Dee, dir, 2001; Opera, "Gethsemane Park," NY, lead actor, 2001; "Light in the Cellar," 2002; City Univ NY, Col Staten Island, asst prof; assoc prof performing & creative arts, 2003-; Staten & Island Repertory Ensemble, dir. **Orgs:** NY Coun Arts, 1968-70; Mayor's Coun Youth & Phys Fitness, 1969; African Heritage Studies Asn; Epsilon Chap Omega Psi Phi; Nat Acad Rec Arts & Sci; Nat Acad TV Arts & Sci. **Honors/Awds:** Research Award, City Univ NY, 1972; AUDELCO Theatre Award, 1991; Outstanding Alumni Award, Langston Univ, OK, 1995; President Citation, Nat Asn Equal Opportunity Higher Educ, Wash, 1995; Twentieth Century Achievement Award, Am Biog Inst, 1997; Xi Phi Chap Opportunity Achievement Award, 2000; Barber Scotia Col Achievement Award, 2001; Outstanding Faculty Award, Staten Island Col Stud Govt; Asn Black Educators of New York Award. **Special Achievements:** Contributing author of We Speak as Liberators, 1971, Rinds for Revolution 1971, Probes an introduction to & poetry 1973, Yarbird Reader 1977, vocalist with Roy Haynes Jazz Ensemble, Jimmy Owens Quartet, Bob Cunningham Trio, Marjorie Eliot's Jazz Parker Dwight Dickerson. **Business Addr:** Associate Professor, The City University of New York, College of Staten Island, Rm 224A Bldg 1P, Staten Island, NY 10314, **Business Phone:** (718)982-2525.

THOMAS, CHARLES RICHARD
Educator. **Personal:** Born Jun 6, 1933, Evanston, IL; widowed; children: Charles Jr & Markham. **Educ:** Univ Wis, BS, 1957; NW Univ, MA, 1966; NW Univ, attended 1970; Columbia Univ, Teachers Col, PhD, 1978. **Career:** Evanston HS, athletic coach, 1957-68, asst prin, 1964-67; Evanston Pub Sch, prin, 1968-71; Ill Off Educ, asst supt, 1971-73; N Chicago Sch Dist64, supt, 1973; Nat Louis Univ, asst prof educ, currently. **Orgs:** Ill Asn Sch Adminr; Am Asn Sch Adminr; Nat Alliance Black Sch Educr; Lake Co Asn Sch Adminr; Ill Asn Sch Bd Asn; Am Asn Sch Personnel Adminr; Asn Sup & Curric Develop; pres, Phi Delta Kappa, N Chicago Rotary Club; bd dir, Lake Co Urban Leg. **Honors/Awds:** Nat Asn Advan Colored People N Chicago Branch Award, Citizen Participation Sch Desegregation, Ill J Educ, 1972; Distinguished Serv Award, Am Asn Sch Adminr; Hall of Fame, Nat Alliance Black Sch Educr; Distinguished Alumni Award, Wis Alumni Asn. **Special Achievements:** Publ "Unique Problems Confronting the Black Sch Administrator,", Eric Doc Reprod Serv, 1972; "The Purpose & Value of HS Athletics.", Univ Mich, 1976; "Sch Desegregation what makes it work?", Ill sch bd j, 1977; Top 100 School Executives in North America, Executive Educator. **Military Serv:** USAR, capt, 1957-65. **Business Addr:** Assistant Professor of Education, National-Louis University, 122 S Michigan Ave, Chicago, IL 60603.

THOMAS, CHARLES W (CHUCK THOMAS)
Executive. **Personal:** Born Mar 9, 1940, Boston, MA; son of Charles Edward and Pauline Delores Walker; married Ellen V Bell; children: Kevin Charles & Tracey Ann. **Educ:** Northeastern Univ, Boston, AS, 1963, BS, 1967; Univ Redlands, Redlands, Calif, MA, 1983. **Career:** Raytheon Co, Bedford, Mass, draftsman, 1961-64, engr, 1964-67; RCA, Chelmsford, Mass, engineering mgr, 1967-70; Regional Transit, Sacramento, Calif, from asst gen mgr to gen mgr, 1970-81; SEPTA, Philadelphia, Pa, chief transp officer, 1981-85, from dep asst gen mgr opers to asst genl mgr opers, 1985-96, asst gen mgr, safety & risk mgt; Wash Metrop Area Transit Authority, Wash, DC, dep gen mgr operations, 1996-. **Orgs:** Alpha Phi Alpha Frat Inc. **Business Addr:** Deputy General Manager Operations, Washington Metropolitan Transportation Authority, 600 5th St NW, Washington, DC 20001, **Business Phone:** (202)637-7000.

THOMAS, CHERYL T
Association executive. **Personal:** Born Oct 31, 1946. **Educ:** Marquette Univ, BS, biol & BS, chem; Univ Ill, Chicago, MS, Physiol. **Career:** Dept Aviation, dir, mgt services, 1983-89; Dept Water, dir, personnel policy & utilization, 1989-92; Mayor Richard M Daley, City Chicago, dep chief staff, 1992-94; City of Chicago, Dept Bldgs, comnr, 1994-98; US Railroad Retirement Bd, City Chicago, chmn, 1998-2003.

THOMAS, CHRIS ERIC
Football player. **Personal:** Born Jul 16, 1971, Ventura, CA. **Educ:** Calif Poly-SLO, BA, eng. **Career:** San Diego Chargers 1993-94; San Francisco 49ers, wide receiver, 1995; Wash Redskins, 1997-99; St Louis Rams, 1999-2000; Kansas City Chiefs, 2001. **Honors/Awds:** California Polytechnic Hall of Fame, 2007.

THOMAS, CHUCK. See THOMAS, CHARLES W.

THOMAS, CLARENCE
Supreme court justice. **Personal:** Born Jun 23, 1948, Pin Point, GA; son of MC and Leola Anderson Williams; married Kathy Grace Ambush, Jan 1, 1971 (divorced 1984); children: Jamal Adeen; married Virginia Lamp, Jan 1, 1987 (divorced). **Educ:** Immaculate Conception Sem, attended 1968; Holy Cross Col, BA, 1971; Yale Univ Law Sch, JD, 1974. **Career:** Hill Jones & Farrington, legal aid, 1971-74; Atty Gen John Danforth, State Mo, staff mem, 1974-77; State Mo, asst atty gen, 1974-77; Monsanto Corp, legal coun, 1977-80; Senator John Danforth, leg asst, 1979-81; US Federal Govt, Dept Educ, asst secy civil rights, 1981-82; Equal Employment Opportunity Comn, chmn, 1982-89; US Ct Appeals Dist Columbia Circuit, appointed circuit judge, 1990-91; US Supreme Ct, assoc justice, 1991-. **Orgs:** Founder, Black Stud Union, Holy Cross Col, 1971; adv bd, Lincoln Review; Episcopal Church. **Special Achievements:** Second African American to serve on the nation's highest court; First black student to attend St John Vianneys Minor Seminary. **Home Addr:** 7542 Cross Gate Lane, Alexandria, VA 22310, **Home Phone:** (703)922-0148. **Business Addr:** Associate Justice, Supreme Court of the United States, One First St NE, Washington, DC 20543, **Business Phone:** (202)479-3415.

THOMAS, DAVE G.
Football player. **Personal:** Born Aug 25, 1968, Miami, FL; children: Zachary. **Educ:** Univ Tenn. **Career:** Football player (retired); Dallas Cowboys, defensive back, 1993-94; Jacksonville Jaguars, 1995-99; New York Giants, 2000-01.

THOMAS, DAVID
Executive. **Career:** Bishop State Community Col, dir SW campus, currently. *

THOMAS, DAVID ANTHONY
Educator, dean (education). **Personal:** Born Sep 26, 1956, Kansas, MO; son of Jewell Williams and Jesse; married Willetta Lewis, Aug 11, 1984; children: Sommer Iman, David Jr & Nelson Dubois. **Educ:** Yale Univ, BA, admin scis, 1978, MS, Phil, 1984, PhD, orga 1986; Columbia Univ, MA, orgn scis, 1981. **Career:** Columbia Univ, grad fel, 1980-81; Yale Univ, grad fel, 1981-85; Wharton Sch Univ Pa, asst prof, 1986-90; Harvard Bus Sch, from asst prof to assoc prof, 1990-99, tenured prof, 1998-, Exec Educ Prog, sr assoc dean & unit head org behav, currently, H Naylor Fitzhugh prof bus admin & dir facrecruiting, currently; J African Am Polit, Harvard Univ, ed bd, 1992. **Orgs:** Wharton School, Atlantic Richfield Found, 1986-90; bd mem, WGBH Community Adv, 1993-96; trustee, Shady Hill Sch, 1996-; bd mem, Partnership, 1997-. **Honors/Awds:** Victor Wilson Scholar, Yale Univ, 1974-78; Executive Roundtable Gislason Award, 1997; Best Symposium Award, Acad Mgt, 1997; George E. Terry Award for outstanding management book, 1999. **Special Achievements:** Book: Breaking Through: The Making of Minority Executives in America. **Business Addr:** H Naylor Fitzhugh Professor of Business Administration, Director of Faculty Recruiting & Senior Associate Dean, Harvard Bussiness School, Morgan Hall 340 Soldiers Field Rd, Boston, MA 02163, **Business Phone:** (617)495-6327.

THOMAS, DEBI (DEBRA JANINE THOMAS)
Figure skater, physician. **Personal:** Born Mar 25, 1967, Poughkeepsie, NY; married Brian Vanden Hogen, Jan 1, 1988 (divorced); married Chris Bequette, Jan 1, 1996; children: Christopher Jules Bequette II. **Educ:** Stanford Univ, BE, 1991; Northwestern Univ Feinberg Sch Med, 1997; Univ Arkansas Med Sci Hosp, surg residency; Martin Luther King Jr/Charles Drew Univ Med Ctr S Cent Los Angeles, orthopedic surg residency; Charles R Drew Univ, Los Angeles; Orthop Residency Prog, 2005. **Career:** Figure skater (retired), orthop surgeon, currently; skater; King-Drew Med Ctr, attending jr physician specialist, 2001-05; Centinela Hosp, Dorr Arthritis Inst, Ingle wood, CA, fel, 2006-07; Carle Clin Asn, Champaign-Urbana, IL, sub-specialist surg, 2007-. **Honors/Awds:** Gold Medal, Skate Am Int Minneapolis & St Ivel Int Great Britain; US Ladies Figure Skating Champion, 1986; US Championships, 1985, 1986, 1987, 1988; World Championship, 1986, 1987, 1988; World Figure Skating Championships, Bronze Medalist, 1988; US Nat title, 1988; Winter Olympics, 1988; San Jose Sports Hall of Fame, 1998; US Figure Skating Hall Fame, 2000. **Special Achievements:** First African American to win the US Figure Skating & World Figure Skating Championship Senior Titles, 1986; First African American to win an Olympic figure skating medal, 1988. **Business Addr:** Physician, Carle Clin, 602 W Univ Ave, Urbana, IL 61801, **Business Phone:** (217)326-1894.

THOMAS, DR. DENNIS
Athletic director, association executive, teacher. **Personal:** Born Sep 5, 1953, Heidelberg, MS; son of Russell and Marjorie. **Educ:** Alcorn State Univ, BS, 1974; Northeast La Univ, MEd, 1975; State Univ New York Buffalo, EdD, 1984. **Career:** Carroll High, Monroe, LA, teacher, 1976; Alcorn State Univ, instr, HPER, 1976-81; State Univ Buffalo, grad teaching asst, 1984; Alcorn State Univ, asst prof, HPER, 1984-86; Hampton Univ, tenured asst prof, 1989, chair, HPER, 1989-95, dir athletics, 1990-2003. **Orgs:** Am Alliance Health, Phys educ, Recreation & Dance; N Am Soc Sport Mgt; Nat Asn Collegiate Dirs Athletics; Va Asn Health, Phys Educ, Recreation & Dance; Nat Asn Supv & Curriculum Develop; comnr, Mid-Eastern Athletic Conf, currently. **Honors/Awds:** Athletics Director of the Year, Nat Asn Collegiate Dirs Athletics. **Home Addr:** 130 Pine Creek Dr, Hampton, VA 23669, **Home Phone:** (757)851-1683. **Business Addr:** Commissioner, Mid-Eastern Athletic Conference, 222 Cent Pk Ave Suite 1150, PO Box 62547, Virginia Beach, VA 23466-2547, **Business Phone:** (757)416-7100.

THOMAS, DEON
Basketball player. **Personal:** Born Feb 24, 1971, Chicago, IL; married Daphna. **Educ:** Univ Ill. **Career:** Dallas Mavericks, ctr, 1994; Univ Ill, ctr, 1990-94; Manresa, ctr, 1994-95; Girona, ctr, 1995-96; Unicaja, ctr, 1996-97; Sevilla, ctr, 1997-98; Maccabi RL, ctr, 1998-99; G. Canaria, ctr, 1999-2001; Caceres, ctr, 2001-03; T Telekom, ctr, 2002-03; Maccabi Tel Aviv, ctr; Bulgarian CSKA Sofia; Givat Shmuel; Maccabi Haifa BasketBall, ctr, currently. **Honors/Awds:** Maccabi Tel Aviv NBA Draft, 1994; Euroleague, 2003-04. **Business Addr:** Professional Basketball Player, Maccabi Heat Haifa, Habicorim 19, 31062 Haifa, Israel, **Business Phone:** (972)4836-3206.

THOMAS, DERMOND EDWIN
Lawyer. **Personal:** Married Kimberly Lynn Johnson. **Educ:** Wayne State Univ, grad. **Career:** Talented Youth Develop Inc, exec dir& founder; Fried, Frank, Harris, Shriver & Jackson, atty, currently. **Business Addr:** Attorney, Fried, Frank, Harris, Shriver & Jackson, One New York Plz, New York, NY 10004, **Business Phone:** (212)859-8193.*

THOMAS, DORIS
Executive. **Personal:** Married Henry; children: Chandra. **Career:** Executive (retired); Urban Financial Serv Coalition, vpres, 2004; Bank One Corp, vpres community develop & mkt officer. **Honors/Awds:** Career Alliance Amistad Award, Career Alliance Inc., 2004.

THOMAS, DUANE
Writer. **Educ:** Fashion Inst Technol, advert & commun. **Career:** Books: Body & Soul: The Black Male Book, 1998; Soul Style: Black Women Redefining the Color of Fashion, ed; More Body, More Soul, 2005. **Special Achievements:** Has contributed to Vogue, Elle, Harper's Bazaar, Talk, InStyle, Essence, O:The Oprah Magazine, and Esquire magazines. *

THOMAS, EARL
Executive, football player. **Educ:** Univ Houston, BS. **Career:** Chicago Bears, tight end, wide receiver, 1971; St Louis Cardinals, tight end, wide receiver; home building co, proj mgr; Oil Equipment co, sales trainee, 1980; Gold Line Supply, founder, 1980; Gold Line Refining Ltd, founder, pres & chief exec officer, managing gen partner, 1990-2001. **Special Achievements:** 28 Black Enterprises Top 100 list of Industrial/Service Companies, Rank 28, 1992. **Home Addr:** 11 Greenway Plz Suite 2602, Houston, TX 77046. *

THOMAS, EARLE FREDERICK
Executive. **Personal:** Born May 6, 1925, Preston, MD; married Bettie; children: Rodney & Sherri. **Educ:** Morgan State Col Univ, 1942; Hampton Inst; VA Bankers Sch, life underwriters. **Career:** Newport New Shipyard, machinist, 1951-59; Am Tobacco Co, state rep, 1959-68; John Hancock Mutual Life Ins Co, underwriter, 1966-68; Atlantic Nat Bank, pres, chief exec officer, dir sec, 1972-74, vpres dir sec, 1971-72, org, 1968-71; asst mgr, 1974-75; mkt officer, 1974; VA Nat Bank, mgr, 1975; loan exec, 1975. **Orgs:** Bd visitors Norfolk State Col, 1977; bd mem, Retail Merchants Asn, 1977-78; vpres, dir Tidewater Coun Boy Scouts; bd mem,

Tidewater Red Cross; dir, sec Tidewater Area Minority Contractors; bd mem, Sickel Cell Anemia; adv coun fourth Club; Sales Mkt & Exec Club; pres, Club; Norfolk CC; budget comn United Fund; treas, Norfolk State Col Found Martin Luther King Comn. **Honors/Awds:** Achievement award, 1975.

THOMAS, EDITH PEETE
Government official, nutritionist. **Personal:** Born Jul 30, 1940, Memphis, TN; daughter of James Walter and Carrie Bell; married Charles L, Aug 25, 1962; children: Stephanie Lynne & Charles Stephen. **Educ:** Fontbonne Col, BA, dietetics, 1960; St Louis Univ, MS, nutrition, 1966; Columbia Univ, EdM, nutrition educ, 1971; Indiana Univ, PhD, nutrition & adult educ, 1977; Univ Iowa, postdoctoral studies, pediatric nutrition, 1980. **Career:** Johns Hopkins Hosp, asst dir, dietetics & chief project nutritionist, 1966-68; Indiana Univ, lectr, adult educ, 1973-76; The Univ NC, Chapel Hill, Dept Nutrit, asst prof, 1977-78; Nutrit Consult Assocs, dir, 1978-80; US Dept Agr Extension Serv, nat prog leader, Expanded Food & Nutrition Educ Prog, 1980-86; George Mason Univ, visiting res prof, 1986-88; US Dept Agr Coop State Res, Educ & Extension Serv, nat prog leader org develop, 1988-. **Orgs:** Alpha Kappa Alpha Sorority, 1959-; Am Dietetic Asn, 1960-; Nat Hon & Prof Asn Educ, 1975; Am Educ Res Asn, 1978-; prog chairperson, DC Dietetic Asn, 1980-81, mem, 1980-; Am Home Econ Asn, prog planning comn, 1982-88; mem, DC Home Econ Asn, 1982-88, pres-elect, 1983-84, pres, 1984-85; mem, Am Eval Asn, Topical Interest Group, Minority Issues, 1989-, chair-elect, 1992. **Honors/Awds:** Nat Secy Sem Participant Cert, Army War Col, 1989; Cert of Merit, US Dept Agr Exten Serv, 1992. **Special Achievements:** March of Dimes Fel, 1984; Nat Training Labs, Org Develop Prog, postdoctoral prog, 1987-89. **Business Phone:** (202)690-4568.

THOMAS, EDWARD ARTHUR
Insurance executive. **Personal:** Born Dec 30, 1952, Georgetown, Guam; son of Andrew and Eunice; married Cecelia, Jun 12, 1976; children: Erklin, Arthur, Carla & Mahala. **Educ:** York Col CUNY, BA, 1977; Polytech Inst NY, MS, 1982; Univ Toledo, Col Law, JD, 1988. **Career:** Blue Cross, Blue Shield of Greater NY, internal auditor, 1977-80; Metropolitan Life Ins Co, sales rep, 1980-81; Ins Serv Off, actuarial asst, 1982-85; Blue Cross, Blue Shield Ohio, actuarial analyst, 1985-88; Penn Dept Ins, chief HMO/PPO, 1988-91; Keystone Health Plan East, vpres & gen coun rev div, 1991-92; Lomax Health Syst vpres managed care serv, 1992-94; New Century Consult Inc, pres & ceo, 1994-. **Orgs:** Penn Bar Asn, 1989-. **Business Addr:** President, Chief Executive Officer, New Century Consultants Inc, 900 E 8th Ave Suite 300, King of Prussia, PA 19406, **Business Phone:** (610)768-8078.

THOMAS, EDWARD S.
Hospital administrator. **Career:** Detroit Receiving Hosp, pres, currently. **Honors/Awds:** Meritorious Serv Key Award, Mich Hosp Asn, 1994. **Business Addr:** Senior Vice President, Detroit Receiving Hospital, 4201 St Antoine, Detroit, MI 48201, **Business Phone:** (313)745-3102.

THOMAS, ELEANOR M. See CLARK-THOMAS, ELEANOR M.

THOMAS, ERIC JASON
Football player. **Personal:** Born Sep 11, 1964, Tucson, AZ. **Educ:** Pasadena City Col; Tulane Univ. **Career:** Football player (retired); Cincinnati Bengals, cornerback, 1987-92; NY Jets, cornerback, 1993-94; Denver Broncos, cornerback, 1995. **Honors/Awds:** Post-season play, 1988: AFC Championship Game, NFL Championship Game, Pro Bowl.

THOMAS, ERMA LEE LYONS. See Obituaries section.

THOMAS, EULA WILEY
Educator. **Personal:** Born Apr 30, 1948, Arkadelphia, AR; daughter of Elmore Sr and Pernella Weaver; married Herman L; children: Traci A & Tiffani A. **Educ:** Ouachita Baptist Univ, BA, Speech & Drama, 1970; Henderson State Univ, MASAC Soc Agency Coun, 1976; Univ Colo Training Inst, attended 1980; Marquette Univ Training Inst Spec Prog, attended 1981; Wichita State Training Inst, attended 1984; Univ Ark, ABD. **Career:** AR Human Dev Ctr, recreation leader, 1970, speech pathologist, 1971-76; Henderson State Univ, coord handicapped serv, 1984-, counr, instr, 1976-, istr, 2006-; Thomas enterprises, owner, 2006-. **Orgs:** Clerk, secy, deaconess Greater Pleasant Hill Baptist Church; cosponsor Henderson State Univ Minority Stud Org, 1979-; pres, Arkadelphia Women's Develop Coun, 1980-; bd dir, Arkadelphia Chamber Com, 1983; chairperson Arkadelphia Christmas Parade, 1983, 1984-; Ark Coun Asn, Ark Asn Stud Asn Prog, NAACP; exec bd, Arkadelphia Housing Authority, 1989-; United Way Allocation Comt, 1991; Delta Sigma Theta Sorority Inc, trainer, 2003. **Honors/Awds:** WP Sturgis Found Grant Continuing Educ, 1966; Arkansas Handicapped Award for Special Educ 1971; Outstanding Advisor of the Year, Ark Black Stud Asn, 1991; Outstanding Community Service Award African Am, 2003. **Special Achievements:** Arkansas Black Students in Teacher Education. **Home Addr:** Friendship Dr Suite 4, Arkadelphia, AR 71923. **Business Addr:** Coordinator, Henderson State University, PO Box 7764, Arkadelphia, AR 71999-0001, **Business Phone:** (870)230-5104.

THOMAS, EUNICE S.
Association executive, government official. **Career:** US Dept Transp, Washington, DC; Family Support Admin, US Dept Health & Human Servs, actg asst secy, dir community servs. **Orgs:** Pres, Zeta Phi Beta Sorority Inc, 1986-92, nat exec bd mem, currently,grand basileus; Howard Univ, Washington, DC. **Business Addr:** National Executive Board Member, Zeta Phi Beta Sorority Inc, 1734 New Hampshire Ave NW, Washington, DC 20009, **Business Phone:** (202)387-3103.

THOMAS, FRANK EDWARD
Baseball player. **Personal:** Born May 27, 1968, Columbus, GA; son of Frank and Charlie Mae; married Elise Silver (divorced 1992); children: Sterling Edward, Sloan Alexandra & Sydney Blake. **Educ:** Auburn Univ, attended 1989. **Career:** Chicago White Sox, infielder, 1990-2005; Big Hurt Enterprises, founder, 1994-99; Oakland Athletics, infielder, 2006; Un-D-Nyable Rec, founder; Toronto Blue Jays, 2007-. **Orgs:** Pres, Frank Thomas Charitable Found, 1993. **Honors/Awds:** Players Choice Award, Major League Baseball Players Assn, 1993; Am League MVP, 1993, 1994; AL All Star Team, 1993-97; Alabama Batting Champion, 1997; Silver Slugger; AL Comeback Player of the Year Award, 2000. **Special Achievements:** First player in Major League history to win two silver slugger awards each at two different positions. **Business Addr:** Professional Baseball Player, Toronto Blue Jays, Skydome, 1 Blue Jays Way Suite 3200, Toronto, ON, Canada M5V1J1, **Business Phone:** (416)341-1000.

THOMAS, FRANKIE TAYLOR
Librarian. **Personal:** Born Oct 3, 1922, Samantha, AL; daughter of Nathan Taylor and Frankie Walker Taylor; married Ervin V Thomas, Jan 25, 1941 (deceased). **Educ:** Stillman Col, Tuscaloosa, AL, 1945; Ala State Univ, Montgomery, AL, BS, 1949; Univ Wisc, Madison, WI, MLS, 1960. **Career:** Librarian (retired); Fayette County Schs, Fayette, AL, teacher, 1946-48; Tuscaloosa Co Schs, Tuscaloosa, AL, teacher, 1949-58, librn, 1958-61; Ala A&M Univ, Normal, AL, head reference librn, 1961-67, head catalog librn, 1968-69; Stillman Col, Tuscaloosa, AL, asst librn cataloging, 1967-68; Univ Ala, Tuscaloosa, AL, reference librn head reference dept, dir staff develop, 1969-84. **Orgs:** Co-founder & mem, Mt Galilee Bapt Church, 1945; Am Libr Asn, 1960; Ala Libr Asn, 1961; Southeastern Libr Asn, 1962; League Women Voters Greater Tuscaloosa, 1969; Nat League Women Voters, 1969; Ala Asn Sch Bd, 1988; Nat Sch Bds Asn, 1988; Tuscaloosa County Bd Educ, 1988; Am Diabetes Asn; ADA Ala Tuscaloosa Co affiliate; Nat Asn Advan Colored People, Tuscaloosa County; life mem, Tombighbee Girl Scouts Coun; Friends Libr Tuscaloosa Pub; W Ala Chamber Com; All-State Sch Bd; Ala Asn Sch Bds, 1998. **Honors/Awds:** MegaSkills Award, Home & Schs, 1988; Northport Citizen of the Year, Chamber of Com, 1989; SAward, Stillman col, nat Alumni asn, 1994; Long Distance Runner Award, NAACP, 1995; Stillman Coll Distinguished Alumni, natl assn for Equal Opportunity in Higher educ, 1997; Mollie Allen Advocate for C Award, Tuscaloosa Co PTA Coun; Collins-Riverside Middle Sch dedicated its libr to Frankie Taylor Thomas, 2000; listed on Wall of Tolerance, Montgomery, AL, 2002; Leadership Award, Southern Christian Leadership Conf, 2003. **Special Achievements:** Library named on her honor as Frankie Thomas Library by Collins-Riverside Junior High School in Northport, Alabama. **Home Addr:** 1012 Mockingbird Ln, Northport, AL 35476. *

THOMAS, FRANKLIN A
Lawyer. **Personal:** Born May 27, 1934, Brooklyn, NY; son of James and Viola; children: Keith, Hillary, Kerrie & Kevin. **Educ:** Columbia Col, BA, 1956; Columbia Law Sch, LLB, 1963. **Career:** Southern Dist NY, asst US atty, 1964-65; NY Police Dept, dep police comnr charge legal matters, 1965-67; Bedford-Stuyvesant Restoration Corp, pres & chief exec officer, 1967-77; Citibank, dir, 1970-98; Pvt Pract, atty, 1977-79; PepsiCo Inc, dir; Citigroup, dir, pres; ALCOA, lead dir, 1977-; Ford Found, pres & chief exec officer, 1979-96; TFF Study Group, head, consult, 1996-2005, chmn, 2001-05; The Study Group, consult, 2005-. **Orgs:** Trustee, Columbia Univ, 1969-75; bd mem, Cummins Inc; adv comm, Sec State S Africa, 1985-87; bd mem, Lucent Technologies, 1996-; chmn, September 11th Fund, 2005; trustee, Friends Nelson Mandela Children's Fund USA; Friends Const Ct S Africa USA; trustee, Greentree Found; UN Fund Int Partnerships. **Honors/Awds:** LLD, Yale Univ, 1970; LLD, Fordham Univ, 1972; LLD, Pratt Inst, 1974; Award for Contribution to the Betterment of Urban Life, Lyndon B Johnson Found, 1974; Medal of Excellence, Columbia Univ, 1976; LLD, Pace Univ, 1977; LLD, Columbia Univ, 1979; Alexander Hamilton Award, Columbia Col, 1983. **Military Serv:** USAF, SAC, capt, navigator, 1956-60.

THOMAS, FRED
Law enforcement officer. **Career:** Police (retired); DC Police Dept, police off, 1985; Metrop Police Boys & Girls Club, head, 1985-92; Metrop Police Dept, DC, dep chief police, chief police, 1992-95. **Special Achievements:** Appointed Chief of Police by DC May Sharon Pratt Kelly, 1992.

THOMAS, FRED
Football player. **Personal:** Born Sep 11, 1973, Bruce, MS. **Educ:** Univ Tenn, Martin. **Career:** Seattle Seahawks, defensive back, 1996-99; New Orleans Saints, cornerback, 2000-07; free agent, currently.

THOMAS, GERALD EUSTIS
Military leader, government official. **Personal:** Born Jun 23, 1929, Natick, MA; son of Walter W and Leila L Jacobs; married Rhoda Holmes Henderson, Oct 3, 1954; children: Kenneth A, Steven E, Lisa D Jacobs. **Educ:** Harvard Univ, BS, 1951; George Wash Univ, MS, 1966; Yale Univ, PhD, 1973. **Career:** Military leader (retired), Government official; US Navy, comndg officer USS Impervious, 1962-63; Col Training Prog Bureau Naval Personnel, head, 1963-65; US Navy, comndg officer USS Bausell, 1966-68; Prairie View A & M Col, Naval ROTC Unit, prof naval sci & comndg officer, 1968-70; Yale Univ, lecturer, 1970-73; US Navy, comdr Destroyer Squadron Nine, 1973-75, rear admin, 1974-81; Comdr Cruiser Destroyer Group Five, 1974; US Dept Defense, acting dep asst secy defense int security affairs & dir Near E, S Asia, & Africa Region, 1976-78, Comtrapac, US Pac Fleet, 1978-81; State Dept, US ambassador Guyana, 1981-83, US ambassador Kenya, 1983-89. **Orgs:** Overseer, Bd Overseers, Harvard Univ, 1981-88; bd trustees, Univ San Diego, 1981-86; Orgn Am Historians; Alpha Phi Alpha; Greek-letter fraternity. *

THOMAS, GLORIA V.
Educator. **Personal:** Born in Brenham, TX; divorced; children: Dino, Paul & Edwin. **Educ:** Tex Southern Univ, BS, 1953, MS, 1965, admin cert, 1968; Sorbonne, France, cert French; Baylor Univ; Univ Southern Miss, Cert. **Career:** Phillis Wheatley High Sch Houston Independent Sch Dist, regist; Phyllis Wheatley Sr High Sch, chem teacher, 1959-72. **Orgs:** Big Bros of Houston, 1965; cancer found, 1970-74; Basileus Gamma Omega Zeta Zeta Phi Beta Sorority, 1971-72; Officer Houston Teachers Asn, 1971-72; vol Multi Schlerosis, 1972; sickle cell anemia, 1973-74; Civil Rights Comn, 1973-; United Fund Budget Panel, 1973; Human Rels Comn & Sexism Comn Huston Ind Sch Dist; Houston Teachers Asn; Tex State teachers Asn; Tex Classroom Teachers Asn; Nat Sci Teachers Asn; MacGregor Park Civic Club; E Bethel Bapt Chap; Tex Atomic Energy Comn; Black Caucus Nat Educ Asn. **Honors/Awds:** Scholar Sorbonne, 1954-56; 15 awards NSF, 1961-74; Nat Educ Award, 1968; res particip grant, 1961; Outstanding leadership Award, Zeta Phi Beta Sor, 1971; Tex Aec Univ Tex; Dr IGE Outcomes Achievement, 1974.

THOMAS, DR. HARRY LEE
Physician. **Personal:** Born Apr 5, 1919, Richmond, VA; married Betty; children: Harriet & Harry. **Educ:** Lincoln Univ, AB, 1939; Howard Univ, MD, 1946. **Career:** Howard Univ, intern, 1946-47, surg res, 1947-52, instr, 1952-53; USAF Hosp, chief surg, 1953-56; Va Outpatient Facility, consult, 1956-60; Mercy Douglass Hosp, sr attending surgeon; Med Col Pa, clinical prof surgery, currently. **Orgs:** Dir, Cancer Detection Proj, Mercy Douglass Hosp, 1958-63; bd dir, Am Cancer Soc, 1977. **Honors/Awds:** Distinguished Service Award, Med Col Pa; Golden Apple Teaching Award. **Military Serv:** USAF, capt, 1953-56. **Home Addr:** 7042 Lincoln Dr, Philadelphia, PA 19119. **Business Addr:** Clinical Professor, Surgery, Medical College of Pennsylvania, 5555 Wissahickon Ave, Philadelphia, PA 19144, **Business Phone:** (215)843-9050.

THOMAS, HENRY LEE
Football player. **Personal:** Born Jan 12, 1965, Houston, TX; married Eyvonne; children: Natasha & Sydney. **Educ:** La State Univ. **Career:** Football player (retired); Minn Vikings, defensive tackle, 1987-94; Detroit Lions, defensive tackle, 1995-96; New Eng Patriots, defensive line, 1997-2000. **Honors/Awds:** Pro Bowl, 1991, 1992.

THOMAS, DR. HERMAN EDWARD
Educator. **Personal:** Born Dec 12, 1941, Bryson City, NC; married Mary Knox; children: Terence, Maurice & Katrina. **Educ:** NC Agri & Tech State Univ, BS, cum laude, 1963; Duke Univ Divinity Sch, BD, 1966, ThM, hon, 1969; Hartford Sem Found, PhD, 1978. **Career:** Berkley High Sch, Aberdeen, NC, teacher, 1966-67; Morris Col, Stud Affairs, 1968-69; Springfield Col, Religion & Philos, instr, 1969-74, Black Studies, coordr, 1971-74; AAA Studies Univ NC Charlotte, asst dir, 1974-86; UTOP, dir, 1986-; Shaw Univ, vpres acad affairs, 2004-, prof emer civil rights activist & stud advocate, currrently. **Orgs:** Am Acad Religion, 1973-; chair, Steer Comt NC Coun Black Studies, 1975-76; assoc minister, Christian Educ, First Baptist Church-West; chmn emer, bdmem, bd dir, chair, Afro-Am Cult Ctr, 1979-84, 1999-2001; pres, Charlotte Chap, Southern Christian Leadership Conf, former bd mem, Charlotte-Mecklen burg Arts & Sci Coun; coordr, Humanist Afro-Am Hist Proj Charlotte, NC Humanities Comn, 1983-83. **Honors/Awds:** Mary Reynolds Bab cock Scholar, Duke Divinity Sch, 1963-66; Citizen of the Year, Pride Mag, 1999, Charlotte's 47 Most Influential African American Leaders, 2002; UNC Charlotte's Distinguished Service Award, 2005. **Special Achievements:** First African-American to earn Bachelor degree in divinity and master of theology degrees from the Duke University Divinity School. Auth: "ASummary and Critical Analysis of the Color of God: the Concept of God inAfro

American Thought", 1993; "Revisioning the American Dream: Individualism and Community in African American Perspective, " 1993;"J.W.C. Pennington: Abolitionist and Churchman", 1995. **Home Addr:** 5913 Craftsbury Dr, Charlotte, NC 28215. **Business Addr:** Vice President Academic Affairs, Emeritus professor, civil rights activist and student advocate, Shaw University, College of Arts & Sciences, 118 E S St, Raleigh, NC 27601, **Business Phone:** (919)546-8330.

THOMAS, HERMAN L.
School superintendent. **Career:** Arkadelphia Pub Schs, coordr, asst supt, currently. **Business Addr:** Assistant Superintendent, Arkadelphia Public Schools, 235 N 11th St, Arkadelphia, AR 71923, **Business Phone:** (870)246-5564.

THOMAS, HOLLIS
Football player. **Personal:** Born Jan 10, 1974, Abilene, TX; children: Hydeia. **Educ:** Northern Ill Univ. **Career:** Philadelphia Eagles, defensive tackle, 1996-2005; New Orleans Saints, defensive tackle, 2006-08; St Louis Rams, 2009-. **Orgs:** Partner, Asthma & Allergy Found Am, Southeast Penn Chap; Hollis ThomasFound. **Honors/Awds:** First-team All-Big West, 1995; NFL All-Rookie Team, 1996; Bert Bell Hero Award; Northern Illinois Athletic Hall of Fame, 2006. **Business Addr:** Defensive Tackle, New Orleans Saints, 5800 Airline Dr, Metairie, LA 70003, **Business Phone:** (504)733-0255.

THOMAS, IRMA
Singer. **Personal:** Born Feb 18, 1941, Ponchatoula, LA; married Emile Jackson, Jan 1, 1976; children: 4. **Career:** Albums: The New Rules, 1986; Down by Law, 1986; The Way I Feel, 1988; Simply the Best, 1991; True Believer, 1992; Walk Around Heaven: New Orleans Gospel Soul, 1994; The Story of My Life, 1997; Sing It!, 1998; My Heart's in Memphis: The Songs of Dan Penn, 2000; If You Want It, Come & Get It, 2001; Straight From The Soul, 2005; After the Rain, 2006; Wish Someone Would Care/Take a Look, 2006; A Woman's Viewpoint, 2006; Wish Someone Would Care/Take A Look, 2006. **Honors/Awds:** WC Handy Soul/Blues Female Vocalist of the Year Award, 1995, 1997; Pioneer Award, Rhythm & Blues Found; Gramy Award. **Special Achievements:** Appears annually at the New Orleans Jazz & Heritage Festival. **Business Addr:** Recording Artist, c/o Emile Jackson, PO Box 104, Gonzales, LA 70737, **Business Phone:** (225)647-8121.

THOMAS, ISAAC DANIEL, JR.
Executive. **Personal:** Born Jan 31, 1939, Birmingham, AL; married Mary E Ellison; children: Peter Neil & Isaac Daniel III. **Educ:** Eastern Mich Univ; Wayne State Univ, BA, 1960; LA City Col, attended 1966; Pasadena City Col, attended 1968. **Career:** Wayne City Boys Detention Home, boys group leader, 1960; All state Ins Co, casualty claims supv, 1966, div personnel mgr, 1969, western zone human resources mgr, 1971, urban affairs dir, 1976, asst vpres employee rels. **Orgs:** Bd mem, Oper Snowball Mental Health Assoc Greater Chicago; bd dir Southern Christian Leadership Coun; Du Sable Mus Chicago; SAFER Found Chicago; Kappa Alpha Psi. **Honors/Awds:** Motivator of Youth Award, YMCA Met Chicago Black & Hispanic Achievers Indust Recognition, 1978. **Military Serv:** AUS, sp 4, 1960-62. **Business Addr:** Assistant Vice President Employee Relations, Allstate Insurance Co, Allstate Plz, Northbrook, IL 60062.

THOMAS, ISIAH LORD
Sports manager, executive, basketball player. **Personal:** Born Apr 30, 1961, Chicago, IL; son of Mary; married Lynn Kendall, Jul 1985; children: Joshua & Lauren. **Educ:** Ind Univ, attended 1981, BA, 1987. **Career:** Basketball player (retired), coach, pres; Detroit Pistons, prof basketball player, 1981-94; Toronto Raptors, part-owner, exec vpres basketball opers, 1994-98; Am Speedy Printing Ctrs Inc, co-chmn, 1994-; Marquis Jet Partners Inc, adv bd mem; NBC, NBA analyst, 1999; Continental Basketball Asn, owner, 1999-2001; Ind Pacers, coach, 2000-03; Dale & Thomas Popcorn, partner, currently; Isiah Investments LLC, chmn & chief exec officer, currently; New York Knicks, pres basketball opers, 2003-, head coach, 2006-08; Fla Int Univ, head basketball coach, 2009-. **Orgs:** Founder, Isiah Thomas Found; bd mem, Chicago Stock Exchange; pres, NBA Players Asn, 1994-98; Am's Second Harvest; Easter Seals; Asn Help Retarded C; Isiah Thomas Scholar Fund, Ind Univ. **Honors/Awds:** Gold Medal, Pan-American Games, 1979; NCAA Champions, Men's Basketball, 1981; NBA All-Star Team, 1982-93; NBA All-Star Game Most Valuable Player, 1984 & 1986; Michiganian of the Year, 1985; NBA champion, 1989 & 1990; NBA Finals MVP, 1990; President's Cabinet Medal, Univ Detroit Mercy, 1992; Basketball Hall of Fame, 2000; Naismith Memorial Basketball Hall of Fame, 2000; Father of the Year, Nat Father's Day Comt, 2004. **Special Achievements:** Appeared as himself in films Hoop Dreams, 1994, Forget Paris, 1995; 100 Most Powerful People in Sports, Sporting News, 1999; 100 Most Influential Minorities in Sports, Sports Illustrated, 2003-04. **Business Phone:** (305)348-2000.

THOMAS, J. T.
Football player. **Personal:** Born Jul 11, 1971, San Bernardino, CA. **Educ:** Ariz State Univ. **Career:** Football player (retired); St Louis Rams, wide receiver, 1995-98.

THOMAS, JACQUELINE MARIE
Journalist. **Personal:** Born Aug 31, 1952, Nashville, TN; daughter of John James Thomas Jr and Dorothy Phillips. **Educ:** Briarcliff Col, AA, 1970, BA (Cum Laude), 1972; Columbia Univ, Sch Int Affairs, MA, 1974. **Career:** Chicago Sun Times, reporter, 1974-85; Courier J & Louisville Times, assoc ed, 1985-86; Detroit Free Press, assoc ed, 1986-92; Detroit News, news ed, 1992-94, Wash bureau chief, 1992-97; The Baltimore sun, ed page ed, 1997-. **Orgs:** Bd mem, Nat Press Found; Nat Asn Black Journalists; Am Soc Newspaper Eds; Nat Conf Ed Writers. **Honors/Awds:** Nieman Fel, Harvard Univ, 1983-84. **Business Addr:** Editorial Page Editor, Baltimore Sun, 501 N Calvert St, PO Box 1377, Baltimore, MD 21278, **Business Phone:** (410)332-6783.

THOMAS, JACQUELYN SMALL
School administrator, educator. **Personal:** Born Oct 25, 1938, Jacksonville, FL; daughter of James Purcell and Lillian Louise Graham; married Willie, Mar 30, 1970; children: Nicole Jacquelyn. **Educ:** Hampton Univ, Hampton, Va, BS, 1959; Columbia Univ, New York, NY, MA, 1963. **Career:** Richmond Pub Schs, Richmond, Va, teacher, 1959-65, guid counr, 1965-67, asst prin, 1967-72; J Sargeant Reynolds Community Col, Richmond, Va, adj teacher, 1979-82; C Ctr, Richmond, Va, dir, 1983; Etiquette & Protocol Sch LLC, owner & dir, currently. **Orgs:** Pres, Richmond Chap, Delta Sigma Theta Sorority, 1960-72; vpres, Old Dominion Vol League, 1979-80; pres, Richmond Chap, Jack & Jill Am, 1983-85; bd mem, Va Day Care Coun, Va Dept C, 1987-89; adv bd mem, Mayors Comn Young C, 1989-91; Coalition 100 Black Women, 1989-91; fin secy, James River Valley, Links Inc, 1991-93. **Honors/Awds:** Volunteer Service Award, Old Dominion Vol League, 1979; Jill Year, Richmond Chap, Jack & Jill Am, 1982. **Business Addr:** Owner, Director, The Etiquette and Protocol School LLC, 313 Burnwick Rd, Richmond, VA 23227, **Business Phone:** (804)264-8211.

THOMAS, JAMES ALBERT
School administrator. **Personal:** Born Mar 15, 1939, Des Moines, IA; married Deborah G, Dec 29, 2000; children: Michael A & Karin R Minter. **Educ:** Wesleyan Univ, BA, 1961; Yale Law Sch, JD, 1964. **Career:** US Dept Justice, Civil Rights Div, atty, 1964-66; Iowa Civil Rights Comn, exec dir, 1966-67; US Senate Subcomm Admin Pract & Procedures, gen atty, 1967-68; Yale Law Sch, assoc dean, lectr, Jack B Tate sr fel & Decanaladv, currently; Yale Univ, Master Saybrook Col, 1990-96. **Orgs:** Am Bar Asn, 1964-; Law Sch Admis Coun, 1969-90; Sigma Pi Phi, 1986-.

THOMAS, JAMES EDWARD. See THOMAS, JIM.

THOMAS, JAMES L
State government official. **Personal:** Born Jun 29, 1943, White Hall, AL; son of James McKinley and Rebecca Gregory; married Evelyn Juanita Hatcher, 1971; children: Angela Carter. **Educ:** AL State Univ, BS, 1965, MA, 1975. **Career:** Camden Acad High Sch, teacher, 1965-84; Wilcox Co High Sch, teacher, 1974-82, voc dir, 1982-89; State Ala, House Rep, state rep, 1982-; Wilcox Cent High Sch, prin dir, 1989-; Thomas Construct Co, owner, currently. **Orgs:** Treas, Nat Black Caucus State Legislators, 1990-94, vpres, pres; Nat Asn Sec Sch Prin; Wilcox Co Admins Asn; Nat Educ Asn; Ala Educ Asn; Wilcox Co Educ Asn; Ala Dem Conf; New S Coalition; First Missionary Baptist Church. **Honors/Awds:** Teacher of the Year, Western Catholic Educ Asn, 1972; Outstanding Leadership Award, CAPA, 1986. **Home Phone:** (334)872-6853. **Business Addr:** State Representative, Alabama House of Representatives, District 69, Rm 525-B 11 S Union St, Montgomery, AL 36130, **Business Phone:** (334)242-7701.

THOMAS, JAMES O.
Government official. **Personal:** Born Feb 12, 1930, Screven County, GA; married Jacqueline Seward; children: Toniae & James O III. **Educ:** Savannah State Col, BS, Chem, 1956; George Wash Law, 1957. **Career:** Government Official (retired); US Patent Off, primary examr, 1967; US Patent Off, supvr patent exr 1975; US Patent Off, group direction, 1979, Patent Process Servs, dep asst comnr. **Orgs:** Pres Assoc Investors Inc, 1957; pres, Savannah St Col Alumni, 1973; pres, Far NE-SE Cnon, 1974; chmn bd, Capitol View Develop Inc, 1978; vpres, HELP Inc, 1981; chmn, Savannah St Fedn, 1983; pres, 3847 Corp Inc, 1984. **Honors/Awds:** President's Club Savannah State Col, 1973-81; Cynus Wiley Savannah State Col, 1979; NAFEO Distinguished Alumni, Savannah State Col, 1981; Alumnus Of Year, Savannah State Col, 1982; Gold Medal US Patent Off, 1983; Medallion of Excellence, Savannah State Col, 1986; EEO Supervisory Achievement Award, Patent & Trademark Off, 1986. **Military Serv:** AUS, sgt, Korean Medal, Good Conduct, Defense Medal etc 1951. **Home Addr:** 4339 H St SE, Washington, DC 20019.

THOMAS, JAMES SAMUEL
Clergy, bishop. **Personal:** Born Apr 8, 1919, Orangeburg, SC; married Ruth Naomi Wilson; children: Claudie Williamson, Gloria Jean, Margaret Yvonne, Patricia Elaine. **Educ:** Clafin Col Orangeburg, AB, 1939; DD, 1953; Gammon Theol Sem Atlanta, BD, 1943; Drew Univ, MA, 1944; Cornell Univ, PhD, 1953; Bethune-Cookman Col, LLD, 1963; Simpson Col, 1965; Morningside Col, 1966; IA Wesleyan Col Coe Col, 1968; Cornell Col, LHD, 1965; OH Weslyan Univ, 1967. **Career:** Bishop (retired); Methodist Church, ordained to ministry 1942; Orangeburg Circuit, pastor 1942-43; York, SC, 1946-47; SC State Col, chaplain 1944-46; Gammon Theol Sem, prof 1947-53; Meth Bd Edn, asso dir 1953-64; IA Area Meth Ch, bishop beginning 1964; Meth Bd Edn, chmn dept educ insts; Meth Commn Christian Vocations, vice-chmn; Negro Colls Danforth Found, consult 1957-60; Perkins Sch Theol So Meth U, vis prof, 1958; Ohio East Episcopal Area of the United Methodist Church, resident bishop, 1976-88. **Orgs:** Tst Vbennett Simpson Claflin Clark Morningside Colls Gammon Theol Sem; Kappa Delta Pi; Phi Delta Kappa; Phi Kappa Phi. **Honors/Awds:** Youngest Methodist Bishop elected in 1964; The first black bishop of the North Central Jurisdiction of the Methodist Church.

THOMAS, JANE ROSCOE
College administrator, psychologist, dean (education). **Personal:** Born Dec 3, 1934, Brooklyn, NY; daughter of Herman Clinton Roscoe and Gladys Pelham; married Edward St Clair, Apr 8, 1961; children: Rebecca Pelham Thomas-Melbye. **Educ:** Univ Edinburgh, Scotland, 1954-55; Rockford Col, BA, 1956; Univ Mich, MA, 1957; Wayne State Univ, PhD, 1976. **Career:** Detroit Pub Schs, teacher, 1957-67; Wayne State Univ, Col Nursing, acad adv, 1968-73, Sch Med, Office Stud Affairs, counr, 1974-91; adjunct instr, 1977-86, adjunct asst prof, 1986-, Office Stud Affairs, dir Coun Servs, 1991-92, asst dean, stud affairs, 1992-, asst dean, spec progs, currently. **Orgs:** Co-Ette Club, 1957-; Detroit Study Club, 1958-; Detroit Inst Arts Founders Soc, 1961-; Wayne State Univ, Hilberry Theatre, The Understudies Women's Comn, 1970-; Am Asn Univ Profs, 1972-; Asn Am Med Cols; Am Red Cross; bd dir, United Way SE MI, 1981; exec comt, The Skillman Found, 1990-; Wayne County Med Soc, comn, Physician Health & Well Being, 1986-; bd dir, Mich Women's Found, 1991-; bd dir, MI's Children, 1992-, vchair, 1999-, chair, 2001-; bd trustees, St John Sr Community, 2000-. **Honors/Awds:** Grady B Murdock Humanitarian Award, Family Serv Am, 1983; Heart of Gold Award, United Found, 1984; Junior League of Detroit, Community Service Award, 1985; Woman of Acheivement Award, Anti-Defamation League, 1997; Women in the Workplace, Leadership Award, Mich Bus & Prof Asn, 2001. **Special Achievements:** Co-author, "Women Medical Students: A New Appraisal," Journal of the American Medical Women's Assn, November, 1978; co-author, "Expansion of Services for Medical Students," Journal of Medical Education, October, 1980; co-author, "Medical Student Impairment," MI Physician, September, 1985; author, "Forging a Band: The Minority Affairs Section and Project 3000 by 2000," The Newsletter of the Natl Network for the Health Science Professions, Spring, 1993; numerous presentations. **Business Addr:** Assistant Dean for Special Programs, Wayne State University, School of Medicine, 540 E Canfield 1369 Scott Hall, Detroit, MI 48201, **Business Phone:** (313)577-1463.

THOMAS, JANICE MORRELL
Educator. **Personal:** Born Oct 6, 1946, Elizabeth, NJ; married Aaron D. **Educ:** Rutgers Univ, AB, 1968, EdM, 1975. **Career:** Rutgers Univ, asst dir admis, 1969-71, assoc dir admis, 1971-72, acting dir admis, 1972-73, sr admis officer Newark Campus, 1985. **Orgs:** Am Asn Col Registr & Admis Officers; Middle States Asn Col Registr & Admis Officers; Nat Asn Col Admis Counrs; Am Col Personal Asn; Asn Non-White Counrs; Rutgers Univ Black Org Faculty; NJ Unit Nat Asn Negro Bus & Pro Womens Clubs; NAACP; Urban League Union Co; NJ Asn Col Admis Counrs; NJ Asn Black & Puerto Rican Admis Counrs; Am Personal & Guidance Asn.

THOMAS, DR. JEWEL M
Consultant, educator. **Educ:** Miles Col, BA, 1960; Univ Ala, EdS, 1976; CP Univ, EdD, 1984. **Career:** Lawson State Community Col, grad adv, sophomore class adv, 1980; Kappa Delta Epsilon, pres, 1981-84; Twentieth Century Club, pres, 1982; Lawson Community Col, prof; City Brighton, mayor; A&M Univ, part-time instr; Independent Mary Kay Consult, currently; Miles Col, assoc prof eng & speech, dir stud activities. **Orgs:** Nat Baptist Conv USA, 1980; Ala Women's Nat Conv, 1980; Ala Jr Col Asn, 1980; Ala Educ Asn, 1984; Ala League Municipalities Exec Comt, 6th Dist, 1990, 1992; Nat League Cities Comt & Adv Human Develop; bd dir, ARC, 1991; bd dirs & vpres, Jefferson Co Comt Econ Opportunity, 1991; Silver Haired Legislature, 1997. **Honors/Awds:** Sororority of the Year, Alpha Kappa Alpha, 1980; Outstanding Editor, Univ Ala Sch Educ, 1984; KDE Presidential Award, Univ Col, 1984; Advocate of the Poor Award, 1995, 1996. **Special Achievements:** First Lady Mayor in Brighton City, 1984; first black pres, Western Area Democratic Club, 1995. **Home Addr:** 4900 Letson St, Brighton, AL 35020-1049.

THOMAS, JIM (JAMES EDWARD THOMAS)
Basketball player, basketball coach. **Personal:** Born Oct 19, 1960, Lakeland, FL. **Educ:** Indiana Univ. **Career:** Basketball player (retired), basketball coach; US Nat Team, FIBA World Championship, 1982; Ind Pacers, 1984-85; Los Angeles Clippers, 1986; Minn Vikings, 1991; Timberwolves; World Basketball League, Calgary 88s; Nat Basketball League, Calgary Outlaws; CBA, Omaha Racers, player & asst coach; Evansville Thunder; Kansas City Sizzlers; Rapid City Thrillers; Spanish League, Murcia, pro player, 1993-94; Toronto Raptors, asst coach, 1994-2000, scout, 2000-01; Butch Carter, asst coach; Ind Univ, asst coach, currently. **Honors/Awds:** CBA Champions, Omaha Racers, 1993; CBA Championship, MVP, 1993. **Business Phone:** (812)855-2238.

THOMAS, JOAN MCHENRY BATES
Executive, government official. **Personal:** Born Jun 26, 1928, Atlanta, GA; daughter of Henry McHenry and Pearl Bonnett

McHenry; married Lee E (deceased); children: Edwin T Bates & Judith Z Stratton. **Educ:** Dept US Ag, 1960; Temple Business Sch, 1963. **Career:** Catering Bus, pres; Dept Human Resources, social worker; community service worker, currently. **Orgs:** Chair, US Military Widow, 1980; vpres, Ward 4 Democrats, treas, comt mem; N W Boundary Civic Asn, 1980-; pres, Am War Mothers, 1984-87; chair, Adv Neighborhood Comt, 1984; treas, DC Democratic Comn, 1988-92; nat carnation chmn, Nat Am War Mothers, 1989-92; chair, Adv Neighborhood Comn, 1989-90; DC conv chmn, Am War Mothers, 1989-. **Honors/Awds:** Outstanding Vol, Am Red Cross, 1974; Certificate of Apppreciation, President Ronald Reagan, 1980; Certificate of Apppreciation, Mayor Marion Barry, 1984; Outstanding Community Vol, 1984; Community Award, Rock Creek Church 1988; Outstanding Community Service Award, Sch Bd, 1992; Dedicated, Outstanding Northwest Boundary Civi Asn. **Home Addr:** 715 Varnum St NW, Washington, DC 20011. **Business Addr:** Committee Member, Ward 4 Democrats, Washington, DC.

THOMAS, JOE LEWIS
Singer. **Personal:** Born Jul 5, 1973, Columbus, GA. **Career:** Albums: Everything, 1993; All That I Am, 1997; My Name is Joe, 2000; Better Days, 2001; Love Joe, 2002; And Then, 2003; Joe Who?, 2006; Aint Nothin Like Me, 2007; New Man, 2008; Signature, 2009; "I'm In Love", 1993; "All Or Nothing", 1993; "The One For Me", 1993; "All the Things (Your Man Wont Do)", 1996; "Don't Wanna Be a Player", 1997; "The Love Scene", 1998; "Good Girls", 1998; "Still Not a Player", 1998; "Thank God I Found You", 1999; "I Wanna Know", 2000; "Treat Her Like a Lady", 2000; "Stutter", 2000; "Let's Stay Home Tonight", 2001; "It Won't End", 2001; "What If a Woman", 2002; More & More", 2003; "Ride Wit U", 2004; "Priceless", 2004; "I Wanna Get to Know Ya", 2004; Curious, 2005; "Where You At?", 2006; "If I Was Your Man", 2007; My Love", 2007; "We Are Family", 2008; "E.R. (Emergency Room)", 2008; "Why Just Be Friends", 2008. **Business Phone:** (212)727-0016.*

THOMAS, JOHN. See Obituaries section.

THOMAS, JOHN
Athlete, athletic coach, businessperson. **Personal:** Born Mar 3, 1941, Boston, MA. **Educ:** Boston Univ, BS Phys & Psych Rehab, 1963; Boston Conserv Music, Ballet, 1962-64; Boston Sch Bus, Acct, 1969; Am Red Cross, Basic Life Support Course CPR. **Career:** Athlete (retired), Coach, Businessman; Track & field athlete; Neighborhood Youth Corps, vocational counr; Hawthorne House Neighborhood Ctr, dir; Roxbury Ct, City Boston, probation officer; WCVB-TV Channel 5, acct exec; General Motors Truck Div, acct exec; New England Telephone, acct exec; AT&T Commun, acct exec; Boston Univ, track coach; businessman, currently. **Orgs:** Jr usher, bd Ebanzer Baptist Church; Cub Scouts, Boy Scouts, Eagle Rank, Silver Palms, Explorer Scouts-Apprentice Rank; chmn Explorer; bd mem Boys Clubs of Boston, Cooper Comm Ctr; bd mem Cambridge YMCA; mem Gov Counon Phys Fitness; mem pres Coun Phys Fitness; US Olympic Comt Spirit Team; intl dir Athlets United for Peace. **Honors/Awds:** Former World Record Holder, High Jump Broken, 1960; Bronze Medalist Rome Olympics, Co-Olympic Champ Tokyo Olumpics, Silver Medalist; Hall of Fame Inductee Helms Found, Boston Univ, US Track & Field. **Special Achievements:** World indoor record to 7'1-1/2" and broke the world outdoor record three times with a career best jump of 7'3-1/2" in 1960 while just 20 years old. **Home Addr:** 51 Mulberry St, Brockton, MA 02302, **Home Phone:** (508)584-7474.

THOMAS, JOHN
Basketball player. **Personal:** Born Sep 8, 1975, Minneapolis, MN. **Educ:** Univ Minn, attended 1997. **Career:** Minnesota Golden Gophers, cap, 1997; New York Knicks, 1997; Boston Celtics, forward, 1997-98; Toronto Raptors, 1998-2000; Minn Timberwolves, forward, 2004-05; Memphis Grizzlies, forward & ctr, 2005; Atlanta Hawks, ctr, 2005-06; New Jersey Nets, 2006. **Honors/Awds:** Gophers Most Valuable Player. *

THOMAS, JOHN CHARLES
Judge. **Educ:** Univ Va, BA, 1972; Univ Va Sch Law, JD, 1975. **Career:** Supreme Ct Va, judge; Hunton & Williams, partner, currently. **Orgs:** Mem bd trustees, Thomas Jefferson Found; Virginia Bar Asn; Richmond Bar Asn; Old Dominion Bar Asn; Nat Bar Asn; Am Bar Asn; Int Bar Asn; Am Arbitration Asn. **Honors/Awds:** Lifetime Image Award, Nat Asn Advan Colored People; Fellow, Am Acad Appellate Lawyers. **Business Addr:** Partner, Hunton & Williams LLP, 951 E Byrd St, Riverfront Plaza E Tower, Richmond, VA 23219-4074.*

THOMAS, JOHN HENDERSON, III
Psychologist. **Personal:** Born Sep 7, 1950, Washington, DC. **Educ:** Univ Detroit, AB, 1972; Univ Cincinnati, MA, 1976, DEd, 1982. **Career:** Mott Adults High Sch, consult, 1972; Univ Cincinnati, minority group coun ctr, 1973, Consult Serv, psychologist, 1975; Mott Adult High Sch, instr psych, soc, engr, 1973; Univ Cincinnati Walk-In-Clinic, psych; Ctr Develop Disorders, psych, 1976; Ct Domestic Rel Ct Common Prac, psychol, 1976, control clinic, 1976; Sonlight Lectr Inc, founder, pres. **Orgs:** Urban League; Nat Asn Advan Colored People; Black Stud; grad stud Psychol Asn, Kappa Alpha Psi. **Honors/Awds:** Voc Rehab Scholar, 1968-72; Achievement Ed Award, Urban League, 1968; Scholar Grad Studies Univ Cincinnati, 1973-76; Miss Black Am Leadership Award, 1973.

THOMAS, JOHN WESLEY
Psychiatrist. **Personal:** Born Feb 13, 1932, Birmingham, AL; son of James and Leila Berry Hatcher; divorced; children: Courtland W, Stephen M. **Educ:** Tenn State Univ, BA, 1953; Meharry Med Col, MD, 1959. **Career:** Rollman Inst Psychiat, Cincinnati, OH, psychiat residency, 1960-61; Western Psychiat Inst, psychiat residency, 1961-63; Gen Psychiat, Pittsburgh, PA, priv pract, 1963-; Various Hosp & Inst, Pittsburgh Area, psychiat consult & staff, 1963-; Univ Pittsburgh, Sch Med, clin instr psychiat, 1963-89. **Orgs:** Bd dir, Am Group Psychother Asn, 1980-83; fel Am Group Psychother Asn, 1985; Nat Med Asn; Am Group Psychother Asn; Am Psychiat Asn; Keystone State Med Soc; Tri-State Group Psychother Soc; Pittsburgh Psychiat Soc; Omicron Lambda Chap, Alpha Phi Alpha; Pi Chap, Chi Delta Mu; Am Med Asn; Psychiat Physicians Pa. **Honors/Awds:** George W Carver Award, Nat Achievement Club Inc, 1980. *

THOMAS, DR. JOHNNY
Sports manager. **Personal:** Born in Heidleberg, MS. **Educ:** Alcorn State Univ, 1978; Univ Tenn, Health and Physic Educ, 1979; Univ Mo, Columbia, Doctor of Educ Degree. **Career:** Univ Ark, asst head football coach, defensive special teams,recruiting coordinator, 1987-89; UAPB, asst prof health & physic educ; A lcorn State Univ, head Football coach. **Honors/Awds:** SWAC Announces 2007 Hall of Fame Inductees, 2007. *

THOMAS, JOHNNY B.
Government official. **Personal:** Born Nov 30, 1953, Glendora, MS; married Ella Rean Johnson; children: Leslie. **Educ:** Miss Valley State Univ, 1977 & 1978. **Career:** Tallahatchie City, constable, 1976-80; Town Glendora, alderman, 1981-82, mayor, 1984-88. **Orgs:** Chmn, Anti Crime Comn, 1976-80, Voters League, 1978-81; Criminal JusticePlanning Comn, 1980-85; Nat Asn Advan Colored People. **Honors/Awds:** Kirskey Found Equity & Justice. **Business Addr:** Mayor, Town of Glendora, 132 Main St, PO Box 90, Glendora, MS 38928.

THOMAS, DR. JOSEPH EDWARD, JR.
Law enforcement officer. **Personal:** Born Jun 22, 1950, Mattson, MS; son of Joseph E Sr and Clara R; married Carol Wynne Carmody, Oct 15, 1983; children: Shayla Y, Joseph III & Daniel Wesley. **Educ:** Alcorn State Univ, BS, math, 1972; Jackson community col, AS, law enforcement, 1984; Mich State Police Sch mgt, grad, 1985; AMR Mgt Asn, graduated, 1986; Mich Criminal Justice Inst, grad, 1989; FBI Nat Acad, attended 1989; Univ Va, addn studies, pub admis, 1989; Western Mich Univ, MS, pub admis, 1989; Nat Fire Acad, attended 1989, 1991-92; Mich State Sch Traffic Engr, attended 1990; US Secret Service Exe Sch, attended 1992; Oakland community col, addn studies, 1992; Eastern Mich Univ, edual leadership, doctorate, 2002. **Career:** Goodyear Tire & Rubber, supv, 1972-73; Montgomery Wards, salesperson, 1973-74; City Jackson, detective, lt, 1974-88; City Albion, dir, pub safety, 1988-91; Eastern Mich Univ, adj prof, currently; Oakland Community Col, adj prof, currently; Muskegon Community Col, adj prof, currently; City Southfield, chief, police dept, 1991-. **Orgs:** Nat Pub Safety Dir Asn, 1988-; Int Fire Chiefs Asn, 1988-; exec fire officer, Nat Fire Academy Asn, 1988-; Int Police Chiefs Asn, 1988-; bd dir, Mich Asn Chief Police, 1988-; FBI Nat Acad Asn, 1989-; Oakland County Sheriff Asn, 1991-; Police Exec Res Forum, 1991-; alt dist rep, Oakland County Police Chiefs Asn, 1991-; bd dir, Oakland County Narcotics Enforcement Team, 1991-; Kappa Alpha Psi Fraternity Inc; Nat Orgn Black Law Enforcemnet Exec; co chmn, Fight Crime, Invest Kids, currently. **Honors/Awds:** Section Representative, FBI Nat Acad, 1989; Silver Beaver-Bronze Big Horn Awards, Boy Scouts Am, 1987;Citizen of the Year, finalist; Jackson Citizen Pageant, 1988; Outstanding Service, State of Mich,Outstanding Professional Award, Int Police Mgt Asn, 1990; Distinguished Service Award, Mich Asn Chiefs Police, 1991; Senate Resolution, 1991; Southeastern Substance Abuse, CNL, Distinguished Service Award, 1992, 1996. **Home Addr:** 21275 Va St, Southfield, MI 48076. **Business Addr:** Chief of Police, Southfield Polic Department, 26000 Evergreen Rd, PO Box 2055, Southfield, MI 48076, **Business Phone:** (248)796-5300.

THOMAS, JOSEPHINE
Executive. **Career:** Thomas Foods Inc, vpres sales & mkt, currently. **Business Phone:** (732)968-0439.

THOMAS, JOYCE CAROL
Writer, educator. **Personal:** Born May 25, 1938, Ponca City, OK; daughter of Floyd Haynes and Leona Thompson Haynes; children: Monica Pecot, Gregory, Michael & Roy. **Educ:** Col San Mateo, AA, 1964; San Jose State Univ, BA, 1966; Stanford Univ, MA,1967. **Career:** Sec Sch teacher, 1967-69; San Jose State Col, asst prof, 1969-72; Contra Costa Col, teacher, 1973-75; St. Mary's Col, prof, 1975-77; San Jose State Col, reading prog dir, 1979-82; San Jose State Col, prof, 1982-83; Univ Tenn, Knoxville, Dept Eng, assoc prof, 1989-92, prof Eng, 1992-95; full-time writer, 1995-; Author: Bittersweet, 1973; Crystal Breezes, 1974; Blessing, 1975; Black Child, 1981; Inside the Rainbow, 1982; Marked by Fire, 1982; Bright Shadow, 1983; Water Girl, 1986; The Golden Pasture, 1986; Journey, 1988; A Gathering of Flowers: Stories about Being Young in America, 1990; When the Nightingale Sings, 1992; Brown Honey in Broom wheat Tea, 1993; Gingerbread Days, 1995; The Blacker the Berry, 1997; I Have Heard of a Land, 1998; Cherish Me, 1998; You Are My Perfect Baby, 1999; The Gospel Cinderella, 2000; The Bowlegged Rooster & Other Tales That Signify, 2000; Hush Songs: African American Lullabies, 2000; Joy!, 2001; Angel's Lullaby, 2001; A Mother's Heart, a Daughter's Love, 2001; House of Light, 2001; Abide with Me, 2001; Crowning Glory, 2002; Linda Brown, You Are Not Alone: The Brown v. Board of Education Decision, 2003. **Orgs:** Dramatist Guild; Author's Guild. **Honors/Awds:** Best Book, Young Adult Serv, Am Libr Asn, 1982; New York Times Outstanding Book of the Year, 1983; The Am Book Award & the Book Award, 1983; Outstanding Woman of the Twentieth Century, Sigma Gamma Rho, 1986; AK Governor's Award, State of Ark, 1987; Chancellor's Award for Res &Creativity, Univ Tenn, 1990; Citation, Oklahoma Senate, 1989; A Gathering of Flowers: Best Book Young Adults, Voice of Youth Advocates nominee,1991; Millionith Acquisition for the Univ Calif, Santa Cruz, Special Collections, 1991; Kentucky Blue Grass Award, 1995; Nat Conf Christians &Jews, 1994; Nat Coun of the Teachers of Eng, 1994; Am Lib Asn, 1994; YWCA, 1993; New York Pub Libr, 1993; Governor's Award, State Okla, 1998; Lifetime Achievement, Okla Ctr Book; Okla Book Award for HNSK Songs, 2000; Oklahoma Sequoia Book Award for I Have Heard of a Land, 2001; Coretta Scott King Honor Awards, 1983, 1984; Parents Choice Award; Poet Laureate Award; Parents' Choice Award, 2004; Oklahoma Book Award, 2005; Nat Book Award; American Book Award; 3 Coretta Scott King Honors; 2 Governor's Awards; 3 American Library Asn Awards; Inter Nat Reading Asn Award; ArrellGibson Lifetime Achievement Award; Arkansas Traveler Award; Poet Laureate Award: Center for Poets and Writers; Governor's Award, The Honorable Frank Keating, Governor of Oklahoma; Oklahoma life time achivement award; Coretta scott king/ALA book award; Cooperative book center's award. **Business Addr:** Author, Scovil Chichak Galen Literary Agency Inc, 381 Pk Ave S Suite 1020, New York, NY 10016.

THOMAS, JUANITA WARE (JUANITA GLEE WARE)
Educator, elementary school teacher. **Personal:** Born Oct 30, 1923, Little Rock, AR; married Morris E Thomas Sr; children: Roumania T Wiggins, Morris Jr, Veronica T Gray, Etelka & Pearl. **Educ:** Philadners Smith & Dunbar Jr Col, AA, elem ed, 1944; DC Teachers Col attended 1970; Howard Univ, attended 1974; N Va Community Col, attended 1984. **Career:** George W Carver Elem Sch, elem teacher, 1944; War Dept, typist, 1945; Hibbler & Hibbler Attorneys Law, law firm secy, notary, 1946; US Navy Dept, cong typist, 1948; US Navy Dept, examr, 1949-51; DC Public Schs,elem sub teacher, 1963-; Patterson Sch Admin Sch, elem teacher, 1974, 1980-81; Headstart Pre-School-United Planning Orgn, teacher, 1982-. **Orgs:** Elem secy, Nalle Elem Sch, 1956-63; pres, PTA Buchanan Elem Sch, 1957-65; secy, SE Civic Asn, 1963-65; chmn, SECA Beautification Prog, 1965-68; advcomt mem, Adv Neighbourhood Comn, 1975-85; W&V Womens Clubs-Nat Asn C W Clubs, 1985; red ribbon week chair, Calimesa Elem Sch; Parent Teacher Asn. **Honors/Awds:** Grass Roots Honoree, SE Civic Asn, 1965; Woman of the Year, NE Fedn Womens Clubs, 1976; Adv Neighborhoods Comn Outstanding Serv, 1981-84. **Special Achievements:** Celebrating 10 yrs "Home Rule in DC", 1975-. **Home Addr:** 1528 E St SE, Washington, DC 20003.

THOMAS, JUDITH
Executive director, chairperson. **Career:** Larry King Cardiac Found, co-chairperson, exec dir, 2004. *

THOMAS, KENDALL
Educator. **Personal:** Born Feb 22, 1957, East Chicago, IN. **Educ:** Yale Col, New Haven, Conn, BA, 1978; Yale Law Sch, New Haven, Conn, JD, 1982. **Career:** Columbia Univ City New York, New York, NY, from asst prof to assoc prof, 1984-92, prof, 1992-, Nash prof Law & co-dir Ctr Study Law & Culture, currently; Stanford Law Sch, vis prof; Priceton Univ, Am Studies & Afro-American Studies, vis prof. **Orgs:** Berlin Prize fel, Am Acad, Berlin, Ger; mem spl comt, Am Ctr, Paris; past chair, Jurisprudence & Law & Humanities sect, Asn Am Law Sch; founding mem, Majority Action Caucus AIDS Coalition, AIDS Prevention Action League. **Business Addr:** Nash Professor of law, Columbia University, School of Law, 435 W 116th St Rm, 608 Jerome Greene Hall, New York, NY 10027, **Business Phone:** (212)854-2288.

THOMAS, KIMBERLY L. See JOHNSON, KIMBERLY LYNN.

THOMAS, KURT VINCENT
Basketball player. **Personal:** Born Oct 4, 1972, Dallas, TX; son of John and Angela; married; children: Gabriella, Abigayl & Isabella. **Educ:** Tex Christian Univ, BS, psychol, attended. **Career:** Miami Heat, forward, 1995-97; Dallas Mavericks, 1996-98; New York

Knicks,1999-2005; Phoenix Suns, 2005-07; Seattle SuperSonics, 2007-08; San Antonio Spurs, 2008-09; Milwaukee Bucks, currently. *

THOMAS, LACY L
Executive. **Educ:** Chicago State Univ, BS, acct. **Career:** City Col Chicago, chief financial officer; United Microelectronics Corp, chief exec officer; John H Stroger Jr Hosp Cook Co, hosp dir; Univ Med Ctr, chief exec officer; Univ Nev, Off Protection Res Subj, fac, currently. **Orgs:** Metrop Chicago Healthcare Coun; Urban Chamber Com; Nev Hosp Asn; Univ Southern Nev Bd Dirs; Beta Alpha Psi; Las Vegas Urban Chamber Com; bd mem, Las Vegas-Clark Co Urban League; Alpha Phi Alpha Fraternities Inc. **Business Addr:** Faculty, University of Nevada, Office for the Protection of Research Subjects, 4505 Maryland Pkwy, PO Box 451047, Las Vegas, NV 89154-1047, **Business Phone:** (702)895-2794.*

THOMAS, REV. DR. LATTA ROOSEVELT, SR.
Clergy, educator. **Personal:** Born Oct 12, 1927, Union, SC; son of Pickett R (deceased) and Alsie Creshaw (deceased); married Bessie Lowery; children: Latta Jr & Ronald. **Educ:** Friendship Jr Col, Rock Hill, SC, AA, 1949; Benedict Col, BA, 1951; Colgate Rochester Divinity Sch, BD, 1955; Andover Newton Theol Sem, MS, sacred theol, 1966, DMin, 1973. **Career:** Monumental Baptist Church, pastor, 1952-63; Monumental Baptist Church, Elmira, NY, minister, 1955; Mt Olive Baptist Church, pastor, 1963-65; Benedict Col, chaplain, 1965-85, Dept Religion & Philos, from assoc prof to prof, 1968-95, acting dean stud affairs, 1974-75; Second Calvary Baptist Church, pastor, 1975-96; Morris Col, prof Religion, currently; Babcock Ctr, bd trustee, 1974-75. **Orgs:** Chmn, SC Acad Religion; SC Coun Holocaust, 1990-96; Am Asn Univ Prof, 1970-95; Kappa Alpha Psi; pres, Elmira Branch, Nat Asn Advan Colored People, 1957-62; fac rep, bd trustees, Benedict Col, 1973-75; exec bd, Friendship Ctr, 1978-82; Richland-Lexington Coun Aging, 1980-84; Progressive Nat Baptist Convention; Clin Pastoral Educ Adv Coun, 1984-90; Kiwanis; SC Democratic Party; exec bd, Greater Columbia Comm Relations Coun; Martin Luther King Jr Memorial Found Inc, 1984-96; Fighting Back Anti-Drug Abuse Coun, 1990-96. **Special Achievements:** Cited for civic service by Elmira Civic Improvement Club in 1960, Elmira Neighborhood House 1961, Elmira Br NAACP 1972, published numerous articles and two books Biblical Faith and the Black American in 1976 and the Biblical God and Human Suffering in 1987. **Business Addr:** Professor of Religion, Morris College, Division of Religion & Humanitus, 100 W College St, Sumter, SC 29150-3599, **Business Phone:** (803)934-3200.

THOMAS, LAURITA
Vice president (Organization), administrator. **Career:** Off Reg, dipl clerk; Univ Mich Health Syst, human resources, admin, allied health educ, dir, 1998-; Univ Mich Hosp & Health Ctr, staff; Off Allied Health Educ; Univ Mich, staff, 1972-, assoc vpres & chief human resource officer, 2004-; Bethel A M E Church, supt. **Orgs:** Med Ctr Employee Rels Asn; Soc Human Resources Mgt; Human Resources Planning Soc; Am Soc Healthcare Human Resources Admin; exec comt, Washtenaw County Workforce Develop Bd; dir emer, SOS Community Serv Bd; Delta Sigma Theta Sorority; Ann Arbor Chapter the Links. **Honors/Awds:** Laurita Thomas Diversity Champion Award, named in honor, 2005; Charles D Moody Award for Highest Achievement of Diversity and Excellence; Women of Distinction Award, Girl Scouts Huron Valley Coun; University Distinguished Service Award, Woman of the Year in Leadership, University of Michigan; ETCSG Leadership Award, Washtenaw County; Larry Warren Multicultural Health Achievement Award. **Special Achievements:** Publ: The Role of Human Resources, Aspatore Books. **Business Addr:** Associate Vice President, Chief Human Resource Officer, University of Michigan, 4021 Wolverine Towers, 3003 S State St, Ann Arbor, MI 48109-1281, **Business Phone:** (734)763-1284.*

THOMAS, LILLIE
Technologist. **Personal:** Born Oct 20, 1950, St Louis, MO. **Educ:** Forest Park Comm Col, AAS, 1970. **Career:** Peralta Hosp, spec procedure tech, 1975-79; MO Baptist Hosp, rad tech, 1970-74, spec procedure tech; SSM St. Joseph Health Ctr St Charles, dir oncology serv. **Orgs:** Am Registry Radiological Tech; Am Soc Radiological Tech; Bd, Christian Educ; asst financial secy, bd trustees, youth dir New Sunny Mount Bapt Ch. **Honors/Awds:** Excellence in health care award.

THOMAS, LINDA
Executive. **Educ:** Kent State Univ, bus admin. **Career:** Taco Bell Express, gen mgr northeast zone, currently. **Special Achievements:** First African American to be named general manager of the northeast zone. **Business Addr:** General Manager of Northeast Zone, Taco Bell Express, 11 Ves Dr Suite 170, Marlton, NJ 08053, **Business Phone:** (609)985-0500.

THOMAS, LIZ A.
Secretary (office). **Personal:** Born Apr 13, 1946, Portland, OR; daughter of Walter C Reynolds and Mildred E Squires Reynolds; married David A (divorced 1982); children: Ife-Airegin V E. **Educ:** Mills Col, Oakland, CA, BA, sociol & anthropol, 1968; Univ Calif, Berkeley, MSW, 1970; Univ Wash, Seattle, WA, health & social behavior, 1975, quantitative methods, 1979. **Career:** Emanuel Hosp, Portland, OR, emergency med staff, 1964-66; The Comm Act Prog, Portland, OR, community asst, 1966; Health Testing Serv, Berkeley, CA, med intake, 1967; People Pledged for Community Progress, Richmond, CA, planner & evaluator, 1968-69; Nat Comn Against Discrimination in Housing, San Francisco, CA, res asst, coordr, 1969; Berkeley Unified Sch Dist, Berkeley, CA, prog asst, 1969-70; Col San Mateo, CA, acad counr, 1970-73, instr, 1970-73; Univ Wash, Seattle, WA, asst dir career planning & placement off, 1973-85; Better Prepared, career consult, 1984-; King County Councilman, Seattle, WA, legis asst, 1985. **Orgs:** Vpres, Seattle Chapter, LINKS, 1989-91; vpres, bd dirs, Int Res Ctr, 1989-91; vpres, 1989-91, co-chair, 1990-91, Long Range Planning Comn, Seattle Children's Theatre; Nominating Comn, Seattle King Cuntyo Camp fire Coun. **Honors/Awds:** Leadership Tomorrow, 1985; Finalist, Fel in Cable Mgt, The Walter Kaitz Found, 1985; Commissioner at Large, The Goodwill Games, 1988-90; Leadership America, The Found for Women's Res, 1989; Participant, The ALKI Found, 1988; guest speaker, lectr, presenter. *

THOMAS, LORNA E
Movie producer. **Educ:** McGill Univ, BS, film & commun studies. **Career:** Swing Pictures, dir, producer & owner, currently; Black Entertainment Tv, supv prod, currently; TLC, dir & producer; MTV series, dir & producer. **Orgs:** Bd dir, Global Action Project. **Business Addr:** Director, Producer, Owner, Swing Pictures, 9 W 21st St Suite 503, New York, NY 10010, **Business Phone:** (212)807-0464.

THOMAS, DR. LUCILLE COLE
Librarian, educator. **Personal:** Born Oct 1, 1921, Dunn, NC; daughter of Minnie Lee Cole and Collie Cole; married George Browne (deceased); children: Ronald C & Beverly G Thomas. **Educ:** Bennett Col, BA, 1941; NY Univ, MA, 1955; Columbia Univ Sch, Lib Serv, MS, 1957; Bennett Col, Doctor Humane Letters, 1996. **Career:** Educator, Librarian (retired); Bibb Co Bd Educ, teacher, 1947-55; Brooklyn Pub Libr, librn, 1955-56; NY City Pub Sch, librn, 1956-68; NY City Bd Educ, supvr libr, 1968-77; NY City Bd Educ, dir elem sch libr, 1978-83; Weston Woods Inst, consult, 1983-86; New York City Bd Examrs, exam specialist, 1985-90; Grad Sch Libr & Info Studies Queens Col CUNY, vis prof, 1987-90. **Orgs:** Pres, NY Black Librns Caucus 1974-75; bd dirs, Am Reading Coun, 1976-89; pres, NY Libr Asn 1977-78; pres NY Libr Club 1977-78; coordr UNESCO/IASL Book Prog 1980-89; pres, Columbia Univ Schl Libr Serv Alumni Asn, 1980-81, sec, 1985-, chair, 1988-93; NYS Regents Adv Coun Learning Technol, 1982-89; Am Libr Asn, exec bd, 1985-91; St Johns Episcopal Church Brooklyn, Stewardship Comm, chmn, usher, vestry mem, 1986-88; Women's City Club, Educ Comm, chair, 1988-90, pres, int Asn Sch Librarianship, 1989-95, vpres, 1992; chair, educ comm, Women's City Club, 1989-92; vice chair, Nat Alumnae Leadership Comt, Bennett Col Capital Campaign; vpres Prog, 1990-92, vpres, Region II Trustees Div ALA, 1993-94; first vpres, pres, Alpha Kappa Alpha Sorority, 1991-94, 1992-98; AIA coun, 1992-2001; Brooklyn Pub Libr, trustee, New York City mayor, 1993-, secy bd trustees, 1997-99, vpres, bd trustees, 1999-2003; chair, Legis Comm Trustees Div ALA, 1994; ALA Legis Assembly, 1995-; honorary chair, Twenty-First Century Fund, Women's City Club NY, 1996-97; chair, Diversity Comn, 1999-2000; Int rels comm; Sch Librs Sect int Fed Libr Asns; Schomburg Corp & Schomburg Commn Preserv Black Cult; Centennial Comm Columbia Univ Sch Libr Serv; Pi Phi Omega Chap, parliamentarian; NY State Educ Comm, Eng lang arts assessment comm; Am Asn Schs Librn, int rels comm; Int Fed Libr Asn, rep UN & UNICEF; dir, US Bd Books Young People, 1995; co-coord Cluster III in AKA Sorority, N Atlantic Region; pres, bd trustees, St Mark's Day Sch; Am Libr Asn Honorary mem, 2003; pres, bd trustees, Brooklyn Pub Libr, 2003-. **Honors/Awds:** Medal of Excellence, NY State Bd 1984; Programs of Service Award, Eta Omega Omega Chap Alpha Kappa Alpha Sor; Grolier Award, Am Libr Asn, 1988; Service Award, ALA, Black Caucus, 1992; Distinguished Service Award, AASL, 1994; Humphrey Award, ALA, 1995; Trail Blazers Award, ALA Black Caucus, 1995; Silver Award, US Natl Comn Libr & Info Sci, 1996; Awarded Honorary Doctorate, Bennett Col, 1996; Outstanding Service Award, Pi Phi Omega; Outstanding Service Award, Alpha Kappa Alpha Basilei Coun, 1998; Phenomenal Woman Achievement, Bennett Col, 2000; Literacy Award, ALTA Am Libr Asn, 2001; Phenomenal Woman Award, Public Sch 241, NYC Bd Edu, 2002; selected hon mem, ALA, 2003; Oustanding Service Award, St Mark's Episcopal Church, 2003. **Special Achievements:** First African president of the New York City School Librarian's Association; First African-American elected president of the New York Library Club. **Home Addr:** 1184 Union St, Brooklyn, NY 11225, **Home Phone:** (718)778-1585.

THOMAS, DR. LYDIA WATERS
Executive. **Personal:** Born Oct 13, 1944, Norfolk, VA; daughter of William Emerson and Lillie Ruth Roberts; married James Carter (divorced 1970); children: Denee Marrielle. **Educ:** Howard Univ, Wash, DC, BS, zoology, 1965; Am Univ, Wash, DC, MS, microbiol, 1971; Howard Univ, Wash, DC, PhD, cytol, 1973. **Career:** Am Univ, Wash, DC, grad teaching asst, 1969-71; Howard Univ, Wash, DC, grad teaching asst, 1971-73; Mitre Corp, 1973-96; Mitretek Systs, pres & chief exec officer; Noblis Inc, pres & chief exec officer, currently. **Orgs:** VA Res Tech Adv Comn, 2001-; Northern Va Technol Coun, 2003-; Environ Adv Bd, US Corp Engrs; chmn, Chems Regulation Sub-Group USEA; Environ Res Develop Sci Adv Bd; Am Soc Toxicol; Nat Defense Indust Asn; Am Mgt Asn; trustee, George Washington Univ; Soc Macro Eng; dir, US Energy Asn; Supts Bus Indust Adv Coun Fairfax Co Pub Schs; assoc fel Am Inst Aeronaut & Astronaut; corp mem, Charles Stark Draper Lab Inc; Coun Foreign Rels; Superintendent's Bus/Indus Adv Coun, Fairfax Co Pub Sch; Int Women's Forum; Am Defense Preparedness Asn; Nat Defense Indust Asn; Teratology Soc. **Honors/Awds:** Tribute Women in the International Industry Award, YWCA, 1986; EBONE Image Award, Coalition of 100 Black Women, Northern, VA, 1990; Deans Award, Black Engr Yr Conf, 1991; Black Engineer of the Year Award, 2003; The Most Important Blacks in Technology, 2005; Lifetime Achievement Award, Women Technol, Sixth Ann Women Technol. **Special Achievements:** 50 Most Important Blacks in Research Science, 2004. **Business Addr:** President, Chief Executive Officer, Noblis Inc, 3150 Fairview Pk Dr, Falls Church, VA 22042, **Business Phone:** (703)610-2600.

THOMAS, MABLE
Government official. **Personal:** Born Nov 8, 1957, Atlanta, GA; daughter of Bernard and Madie Broughton. **Educ:** GA State Univ, BS, Pub Admin 1982, working on Masters in Pub Admin; Atlanta Sch Real Estate, Atlanta GA, Salesperson License, 1987. **Career:** GA Dept Natural Resources, personnel asst, 1978-79; City Atlanta Parks & Recreation, recreation super, 1980-81; GA State Univ Educ Talent Srch, res asst 1981-82; City Atlanta Comm Develop, worksite monitor 1983; Univ Black Life & Cult Comm, chairperson GA State 1982-83; GA Gen Assembly, senate intern 1984; Dist 31, state rep, served on house, educ, spec judiciary & indust rels standing comts, served on State GA housing needs study comn; Ga House Rep, 55th dist, rep, currently. **Orgs:** Vpres, GA State Univ Stud Govt Asn 1983-84; consult GA Democratic Party, 1984; adv coun Salvation Army Bellwood Boys & Girls Club, 1984-85; bd dirs, GA Legis Black Caucus, 1985; membership chair Black Women's Health Proj 1985; Hon mem chair NAACP Annual Membership Drive 1985; vol worker S Christian Leadership Conf 1981-; vol Martin Luther King Ctr for Nonviolent Social Change 1981-; vol United Way Metro Atlanta 1982-; Nat bd mem Nat Polit Congr Black Women 1985; bd mem West End Med Ctr; bd dirs Econ Opportunities Atlanta; bd mem, Ga Housing Coalition, 1988-89. **Honors/Awds:** GA State Univ Mortar Bd Leadership Award 1982; Salvation Army Bellwood Girls Club Comm Service Award 1983; GA State Univ Women Excellence Award 1983; Top Jesse Jackson Deleg to Democratic Nat Convention 1984; City Atlanta Cultural Affairs Bronze Jubilee Award 1984; Royal Ark Worshipful Masters Legion Hon Award for Social Justice 1985; Ebony Magazine 30 Leaders Future 1985; Outstanding Service Award Tony Garden Civic Asn, 1985; NAACP Civic Award, 1985; featured in Essence magazine August 1986 as Essence Women; Nat Asn Black Social Workers Human Service Award, 1986; Outstanding Freshman Legislator GA Legis Black Caucus 1986; featured in December 1986 Wash Post "New Black Women-Mold Breakers in MainStream"; voted one 20 Atlantans to Watch in 1987 by Atlanta Trib newspaper; featured, Essence Magazine Profile, 1988; front page coverage Fast Forward Magazine, 1989; featured, India's Nat newspaper, India Times, 1988; Outstanding Ga State Univ Alumni, GA State Univ, 1989. **Home Addr:** 765 Jones Ave NW, Atlanta, GA 30314.

THOMAS, MARLA RENEE. See Obituaries section.

THOMAS, DR. MARVETTE JERALDINE
School administrator. **Personal:** Born Jan 27, 1953, Montgomery, AL; daughter of Robert Marvin Thomas and Bernice Morgan Thomas; married Allen H Jackson; children: Janel Bernice Cobb. **Educ:** Austin Peay State Univ, BS, 1977; Murray State Univ, MS, 1980; George Peabody Col Vanderbilt Univ, EdD, 1984. **Career:** Northwest High Sch, spec educ teacher, chair spec educ spec needs counr, 1979-83; Vanderbilt Univ, teaching, grad asst, 1981; Nat Cert Counr, 1983; Women Non-traditional Careers WINC, dir proj 1986-; La State Univ Eunice, counr, 1984, acting dir spec serv & develop educ, dir spec serv, 1985-89, dir acad asst progs 1989-. **Orgs:** Nat Asn Univ Women; Am Asn Coun & Develop; Nat Coun Negro Women; Am Col Personnel Asn; La Asn Develop Educ; Southwest Asn Student Asst Prog; Opelousas Alumnae Chap Delta Sigma Theta Inc; past pres, Clarksville Tenn Alumnae Chapt Delta Sigma Theta; bd dir, Eunice C C; bd dir, Bayou Girl Scout Coun, 1987-; bd dir, Moosa Memorial Hosp, 1988-; pres, La Asn Student Assistance Prog, 1988-90; bd dir, Southwest Asn Student Assistance Prog, 1988-90; President's Coun, Nat Coun Educ Opportunity Asn, 1988; pres, Socialite Club Eunice, 1989-; pres, Socialite Soc & Civic Club; secy, 1990-; Delta Sigma Theta Sorority. **Honors/Awds:** Inductee Phi Delta Kappa, 1979; Chi Sigma Iota 1985; Outstanding Woman of Eunice, The Eunice News, 1987. **Business Addr:** Director of Academic Assistance Programs, Louisiana State University, PO Box 1129, Eunice, LA 70535.

THOMAS, MARY A.
Nurse. **Personal:** Born Jul 22, 1933, Gary, IN. **Educ:** Homer G Phillips Hosp Sch Nursing, St Louis, 1956; IN Univ, BS, 1968;

Valparaiso Univ, MLA, Sociol; Univ IL Med Ctr. **Career:** Retired: Cook Hosp Chicago, head nurse Obstetric, 1957-63; Chicago Osteop Hosp Chicago, head nurse Med Unit, 1963-64; Visiting Nurse Assoc E Chicago IN, staff nurse, 1964-68; Gary IN, sch nurse, 1968-71; Gary Health Dept, asst dir nurses, 1972-74; Gary Health Dept, dir nurses, 1974-95; Purdue Univ Calumet Hammond IN, asst prof nursing, 1995. **Orgs:** Consult Sr Cit Prog Gary IN, 1972-; counr, Sickle Anemia Proj, 1975; scholarship chmn Midtown Reg Nurses Club, 1971-; alumni IN Univ & Valparaiso Univ; bd mem, Fed Credit Union St Monica Ch, 1973; parish coun mem, 1974. *

THOMAS, HON. MARY MAXWELL
Circuit court judge. **Personal:** Born Mar 18, 1943, Waukegan, IL; daughter of Isaiah Williams Jr and Mary Etta Jordan; married James A Cooper, Nov 21, 1987 (divorced); children: Stacy L Thomas-Mosley & Owen L II. **Educ:** Mich State Univ, attended 1963; NMex State Univ, BA, 1966; Univ Chicago Law Sch, JD, 1973; Univ Nevada-Reno, judicial studies, 1996. **Career:** USN, comput programmer, 1967-70; Chicago Title Ins Co, atty title examr, 1973-74; City Evanston, Ill, asst city atty, 1974-77; US Attys Off, asst US atty, 1977-87; Sulzer & Shapiro Ltd, partner, 1987; Circuit Ct Cook Co, judge, 1987-. **Orgs:** Silver star mem, Alpha Kappa Alpha Sorority, 1962-; former bd mem, Cook Co Bar Asn, 1983-; Nat Bar Asn, 1983-; past chairperson, secy, bd mem, Ill Judicial Coun, 1987-; Womens Bar Asn Ill, 1987-; Nat Judicial Coun, 1987-; life mem, Nat Asn Advan Colored People, 1993-; Phi Kappa Phi Hon Soc, 1996; chairperson, Youth Outreach Comn, 2001. **Honors/Awds:** Honoree, Black Women Lawyers Chicago, 1991; Woman of Distinction, Ebony Man Mag, 1992, 1992; Chairperson's Award & Meritorious Service, Ill Judicial Coun, 1992-94; Kentucky Colonel Award Commonwealth KY, 1994; Pacesetter Award, Nat Coun Negro Women, 1994. **Business Addr:** Judge, Circuit of Cook County Illinois, 5600 Old Orchard Rd Suite 231-2, Skokie, IL 60077, **Business Phone:** (847)470-5961.

THOMAS, MATTHEW, JR. See THOMAS, MATTHEW MANJUSRI, JR.

THOMAS, MATTHEW MANJUSRI, JR. (MATTHEW THOMAS, JR.)
Artist, educator. **Personal:** Born Jun 12, 1943, San Antonio, TX; son of Matthew and Ella; married Bee, May 9, 1990; children: Illah & Hashim. **Educ:** San Fernando Valley Col, Van Nuys, Calif, 1961-63; Honolulu Acad Arts, Honolulu, Hawaii, 1963-64; Chouinard Sch Fine Arts, Los Angeles, Calif, 1965-67. **Career:** Visual artist, Ruth Bachofner Gallery, 1975-; Temecula Calif, artist-in-residence; Pyong, TAEK Int, Korea, artist-in-residence; Tacikawa Int, Japan, Taiwan, artist-in-residence. **Orgs:** Visual Artist & Chmn Visual Arts Dept., PS Arts Cross Roads, Conn; Founder & vpres, Arts Org, Los Angeles. **Honors/Awds:** Helen Londeberg L Feitelson, Art Fel Fund, Calif Arts Coun Grant, (Five Time Recipient), 1982-87. **Special Achievements:** First African Am in Art Collection Pyong, Tack Museum Art; First African Am in art collection of Pyong Taek Korea Museum of Art; First African Am in art collection at Kumho Museum of Art, Kwangiu, Korea. First African Am in art collection Nat Museum Contemporary Arts, Korea; First African Am art collection Taiwan Museum Art; had works of art exhibited in Spain, India, New Delhi, Korea, Japan, Taiwan, USA. **Home Addr:** 609 W 40th St, San Pedro, CA 90731-7107. **Business Addr:** Visual Artist, Ruth Bachofner Gallery, Bergamat Station, Bergamot Station Art Center, 2525 Mich Ave Suite G2, Santa Monica, CA 90404, **Business Phone:** (310)829-3300.*

THOMAS, MAUREEN A.
Law enforcement officer. **Career:** NY City Dept Invest, dep inspector gen. *

THOMAS, MAURICE MCKENZIE
Librarian. **Personal:** Born May 1, 1943, St Croix, VI; son of Maurice and Florence Bovell; married Monica Primas; children: Charles Randall & Onika Michelle. **Educ:** Long Island Univ, BA, Hist, 1973; Atlanta Univ, 1982; Ball State Univ, MLS, Libr & Info Sci, 1983. **Career:** Librarian (retired); Abraham & Strauss NY, sales person, 1969-73; Dept Educ The VI, social studies teacher, 1973-82, librn, info spec, coordr, social studies, 1987. **Orgs:** Courtyard Players Community Theatre, 1973-, Friends Petersen Pub Libr, 1983-, Sch Libr Asn, 1983-, Am Libr Asn, 1983-; bd mem, Theatre Dance Inc, 1983-84; Phi Delta Kappa. **Honors/Awds:** Libr Career Fel, US Dept Educ & Ball State, 1982-83; Territorial Scholar, VI Govt, 1982-83. **Special Achievements:** Joint author, Virgin Islands and Caribbean Communities. **Military Serv:** AUS, corpl sp4, 1962-65. **Home Addr:** PO Box 7475 Sunny Isle Christiansted, St Croix, VI 00820.

THOMAS, MAXINE SUZANNE
Educator. **Personal:** Born Jan 23, 1948, Junction City, KS; daughter of Morris Daniels; married Larry; children: Lauryn & Noel. **Educ:** Univ Wash, BA, 1970, JD, 1973. **Career:** WA, asst atty gen, 1973-76; Univ OR Sch Law, asst prof, 1976-89; Univ OR, asst dean, 1976-79; Kellogg Nat fel, 1985-1988; Fulbright, lectr, 1988; Univ Georgia, assoc dean & assoc prof, 1989-91. **Orgs:** Nat Asn Col & Univ Attys, 1974-76; standing com environ law Am Bar Asn, 1979-; hon mem, Phi Delta Phi, 1977-; OR Am Coun Educ Comn Promote Women Higher Educ Admin, 1978-; secy & gen coun, Kettering Found, Dayton, OH, currently. **Honors/Awds:** Nominated OR Outstanding Young Women, 1978. **Business Addr:** Secretary, General Counsel, Kettering Foundation, Dayton Ohio Office, 200 Commons Rd, Dayton, OH 45459, **Business Phone:** (937)434-7300.

THOMAS, DR. N CHARLES (NATHANIEL CHARLES THOMAS)
Clergy, administrator. **Personal:** Born Jun 24, 1929, Jonesboro, AR; son of Linnie and Willie James; married Juanita Fanny Jefferson (deceased); children: Gina Charlise, Nathaniel Charles & Keith Antony; married Mary Elizabeth, Jun 8, 1971. **Educ:** MS Indsl Col, BA, 1951; Lincoln Univ Theol Sem, BD, 1954; Lancaster Theol Sem, MDiv, 1974; Tex Col, DDiv, 1981. **Career:** CME Chs Waterford MS, pastor, 1949-51; Roanoke Va, 1954; Wrightsville Ark, 1954-57; Hot Springs Ark, 1957-60; Little Rock Ark, 1960-62; Memphis Tenn, 1966-67; CME Church, gen secy; pastor, Greenwood CME Church, 1980-81; Featherstone Temple, pastor, 1994; Christian Methodist Episcopal Church, dept personnel serv, gen secy. **Orgs:** Dir Christian educ, first Dist CME Ch, 1958-74, admin asst presiding bishop, 1954-74; admin Ministerial Salary, Supplement Prog CME Ch Gen Bd Pensions CME Ch, 1974-; secy Gen Conf CME Ch, 1970-; presiding elder S Memphis Dist, 1971-74; Gen Bd Christian Educ CME Ch, 1958-; secy Gen Correctional Bd CME Ch, 1971-; bd trustees, Smith-Keys Housing Proj, Texarkana Ark, 1969-; bd dir, Haygood-Neal Housing Proj Eldorado Ark, 1970-; bd dir, E Gate Vlge Union City Tenn, 1970-; bd trustees, Collins Chapel Hosp Memphis Tenn, 1974-; bd dir, Memphis OIC, 1972-; CME Ministers Alliance Memphis; Interdenom Ministers Alliance Memphis; gen secy, Gen Bd Personnel Serv, 1978; bd mem, Metrop Interfaith Asn, 1989-; Shelby County Interfaith Asn, 1990-; exec dir, New Day Coop, 1992. **Honors/Awds:** Dr Humanities, Tex Col Tyler, 1980; Golden Heritage Mem, Nat Asn Advan Colored People. **Home Addr:** PO Box 9, Tennessee, TN 38107.

THOMAS, NATHANIEL
College teacher, administrator, movie producer. **Personal:** Born May 22, 1957, Warren, OH; son of Ace and Rose. **Educ:** St Edwards Univ, BA, theatre arts, 1979; Univ Tex, Austin, grad study film, 1980; Univ SC, MFA, cinema prod, 1984. **Career:** Petrified Forest, stage prod actor, 1975; TV commercials, Coca-Cola & New York Life Ins, actor, 1978; Warner Brothers, USC Cinema fel, 1982; PBS film The Last of the One Night Stands, producer, 1982-83; Walt Disney Prods & Disney Channel, asst to prod exec, 1984; anti-alcohol pub serv announcement geared black women, The Zone, dir & producer, 1987; Under the Rainbow: Jesse Jackson '88 for Pres, dir & producer, 1988; featurette Universal Pictures Ghost Dad, dir & producer, 1989; Itchin' In My Heart, line producer; The Good Girls, music video; East of Hope St, writer, dir & producer, 1998; Nate Thomas & Assocs, film producer various proj; Stompin', producer & dir, 2007; Calif State Univ, Northridge, Dept Cinema & TV Arts, prof, Film Prod Option, head, currently. **Orgs:** Spec Youth Citation Urban League, 1975; pres, Jr Class St Edwards Univ, Austin, 1977-78; Screen Actors Guild, 1979-; AFTRA, 1979-. **Honors/Awds:** Scholar Morning Star, Grand Chap Order Eastern Star, 1976; Student Activities Award of Excellence, 1978-79, Dean's List, 1977-79, nominee Man of Year, 1979, St Edwards Univ, Austin, TX; Nat Dean's List, 1979; Scholarship, USC Ebonics Support Group, 1981; USC Tommy Award for Outstanding Achievement in Cinema TV, 1984; Cine Golden Eagle & Honors, San Francisco Int Film Festival, 1984; Award, Black Am Cinema Soc; Sony Innovator Award, Sony Corp, 1991; Honorable Mention, Wellington Film Festival, New Zealand, 1984; recognition & resolution, Warren, Ohio City Coun, 1992; inductee, Trumbull County Afro-American Hall of Fame, Warren, Ohio, 1992; Outstanding Teaching Award, Calif State Univ, Northridge, 1993; Inductee, Warren High Schs, Distinguished Alumni Hall of Fame, Warren, Ohio, 1994; Faculty Creativity Award, Calif State Univ, 1998; Jury Award, Hlwd Black Film Festival, 1999; First American in the Arts Award, 2000. **Special Achievements:** Director & producer of various 35 mm TV commercials, music videos, 1987-, feature film "East of Hope St," won Best Urban Drama at NY Intl Independent Film Festival 1998, Best Feature Film at New Orleans Urban Film Festival 1998, First Place, Cross Cultural at Black Filmmakers Hall of Fame Festival 1998, has been featured in a variety of newspaper articles including the L.A. Times and The L.A. Daily News, has also been featured on E! Entertainment Television, Starz Movie News & numerous other television entities nationally. **Business Addr:** Head of Film Production, Professor, California State University of Northridge, Department of Cinema & TV Arts, 18111 Nordhoff St, Northridge, CA 91330-8317.

THOMAS, NATHANIEL CHARLES. See THOMAS, DR. N CHARLES.

THOMAS, NINA M
Law enforcement officer, educator. **Personal:** Born in Bridgeport, CT; daughter of Eleanor McGarah and Livingston. **Educ:** John Jay Col Criminal Justice, BA, MA; Univ Conn, Storrs Conn, 1978; Univ New Haven, New Haven Conn; Housatonic Comm Col, 1997; Criminal Justice Command Inst, Farmington, Conn; Tunix Com-19Tech Col, 1997; Charter Oak State Col, 1997; Teikyo Post Univ, 1998. **Career:** Lieutenant (retired); Mechanics & Farmers Savings Bank, Bridgeport Conn, mortgage rep, 1978-83; Bridgeport Police Dept, Bridgeport Conn, police officer, lt, 1983; patrol & commun div, supvr, undercover detective; Monroe Col, Dept Criminal Justice, adj fac, currently; Conn Community Col, minority fel. **Orgs:** Nat Black Police Asn; Bridgeport Guardians Inc; First Baptist Stratford; Nat Black Women's Polit Cong; Nat Ctr Women Policing; Phi Theta Kappa; Waterbury Democratic Club; vol, Olympics, 1996; Swing Phi Swing; Social Fel Inc; bd mem, East Orange Police Athletic League. **Special Achievements:** First African-American female to hold both the rank of sergeant and lieutenant. **Home Addr:** 72 Hamden Ave, Waterbury, CT 06704, **Home Phone:** (860)260-5675. **Business Phone:** (914)632-5400.

THOMAS, ORLANDO
Football player. **Personal:** Born Oct 21, 1972, Crowley, LA; married Demetra, Feb 27, 1998; children: Alexis & Orlando Jr. **Educ:** Southwestern La Univ; La Lafayette Univ. **Career:** Football player (retired), asst coach; Minn Vikings, defensive back, 1995-2001; Comeaux High Sch, asst coach, currently. **Honors/Awds:** Rookie of the Year, 1995. **Business Addr:** Assistant Coach, Comeaux High School, 113 Chaplin Dr, Lafayette, LA 70508, **Business Phone:** (337)521-7000.*

THOMAS, DR. PAMELLA D
Physician, health services administrator. **Personal:** Born May 11, 1947, Westmoreland, Jamaica; daughter of Wellesley Johnston and Hyacinth Muir; married Earl A Thomas, Apr 9, 1977; children: Ramogi O & Monifa J. **Educ:** Univ West Indies, Jamaica, MD, 1974; Univ Wis, Med Col, MPH, 1989. **Career:** Brookdale Hosp, emergency room attending, 1979-83; NYC Transit, asst med dir, 1983-89; Lockheed Martin Aeronautical Systems Co, med dir, 1989-; Emory Univ, Rollins Sch Pub Health, asst adj prof, 1991, adj assoc prof, currently. **Orgs:** Am Col Occup & Environ Med, 1983-; Am Pub Health Asn, 1986-; Am Col Preventive Med, 1989-; Cobb County Med Soc, chair, public relations, 1989-95; Aerospace Med Asn, 1989-; Med Asn Ga, 1990-; AMA, 1990-; bd, Cancer Soc, N Cobb Unit, 1990-; fac adv bd, Sch Pub Health, Emory Univ, 1991-, Environ & Occup Health Div, acad adv coun, 1992. **Honors/Awds:** Physicians Recognition Award, Am Med Asn, 1990, 1995; Nominated Cobb County Woman of the Year, Wellstar Hosp Found, 1993; Women of Color Technology Award, 1998. **Special Achievements:** Listed in 'Who's Who in the World' & 'Who's Who in Health and Medical Services'. **Home Addr:** 4058 Sandy Lake Dr, Lithonia, GA 30058. **Business Addr:** Medical Director, Lockheed Martin Aeronautical Systems Co., 86 S Cobb Dr, Marietta, GA 30063-0328, **Business Phone:** (770)494-4131.

THOMAS, PATRICK ARNOLD
Executive, president (organization), business owner. **Personal:** Born Oct 6, 1956, Columbus, OH; son of Benjamin and Lucille W; married Shirley A Henry, Nov 25, 1979; children: Michelle, Kenneth & Nicholas. **Educ:** Kent State Univ, BA, bus admin, 1979; Nashville Tech Inst, AS, elec eng; ICS cert elect & electronic eng, 1980; Karras Seminar, cert effective negotiating skills, 1981. **Career:** Johnson & Johnson Permacel Tape Div, reg rep, 1979-80; Owens-Illinois Forest Prod Div, reg rep, 1980-82; Nat Search Firm, sr tech recruiter, 1983-85; Eng & Exec Search Inc, pres, owner, 1985-. **Orgs:** Kentuckiana Minority Supplier Develop Coun; Nat Asn Personnel Consult; First Int Personnel Consults; Inst Elec & Electronic Engrs; Louisville Chap, Urban League; Louisville Chap, Nat Asn Advan Colored People; Gerald Neal State senate Campaign, asst dir, speakers bur; Louisville PTA; Little League Basketball Coach Newburg Community CTR, div champion, 1989, runner-up 1990, 1991. **Business Addr:** President, Owner, Engineering & Executive Search Inc, 141 N Sherrin Ave Suite 221, Louisville, KY 40207, **Business Phone:** (502)895-3055.

THOMAS, PHILIP MICHAEL
Actor. **Personal:** Born May 26, 1949, Columbus, OH. **Educ:** Oakwood Col, Huntsville, AL, religion & philos; Univ Calif, Riverside; Univ Calif, Berkeley; DA, 1997. **Career:** Plays: Hair; No Place to Be Somebody, 1971; The Selling of the President, 1972; Reggae, 1980; Films: Sparkle, 1975; Mr Ricco, 1974; Book of Numbers,lead role, 1973; Wizard of Speed & Time, 1988; Miami Shakedown, 1993; River of Stone, 1994; Vampirates, 2001; Fate, 2003; Grand Theft Auto: Vice City Stories, 2006; TV appearances: "Medical Center"; "Police Woman"; "Toma," 1973; 'Good Times'; "Society's Child"; "Fight for Jennie," 1986; "False Witness," 1989; "Roots: The Next Generation; Miami Vice", 1984-89; "A Little Piece of Sunshine", 1990;"Extra large: Moving Target", 1990; "Perry Mason: The Case of the Ruthless Reporter", 1991; "Extralarge", 1991; Album: Living The Book of My Life; Singles: "Just the Way I Planned It", 1985; Videos: Grand Theft Auto: Vice City Stories, 2006. **Orgs:** Screen Actors Guild; Actors' Equity; Am Fed TV & Radio Artists. **Honors/Awds:** Golden Globe Nominee for Best Performance by an Actor in a TV-Series-Drama, 1986; Image Award, NAACP, 1987. **Special Achievements:** Promoted PMT women's clothing line, 1985.

THOMAS, PHILIP S.
Administrator. **Personal:** Born May 24, 1946, Accomac, VA; children: Terrance Seegers. **Educ:** Montclair State UNIV, BA

Theater, 1976. **Career:** Greater Paterson Arts Coun, exec dir, 1977-80; NJ State Coun Arts, arts develop coordr, 1980-82; Newark Symphony Hall, dir mkt, 1982-84; Newark Bd Educ, grants analyst, 1984-85; Carter G Woodson Found, artistic dir, 1985-92; New Jersey Performing Arts CTR, vpres arts edu, 1992-. **Orgs:** Bd dirs, Carter G Woodson Found, 1974-99; evaluator, Nat Endowment Arts, 1981-; bd dir, NJ Black Issues Convention, 1984-99; bd dirs, Educ Law Ctr, NJ, 1997-; Inst Sch Innovation, 1997-; Newark Boys Chorus Sch, 1993-99. **Honors/Awds:** Montclair State Col Speech & Theater Alumni Award, 1975; Fellowship Nat Endowment Arts, 1976; Freedom Fund Award, Paterson NJ NAACP, 1984; Scholarship-Martin Luther King Jr Community Nonviolent Training Program, 1982; Duke Ellington Award, Arts Paterson NJ, 1985. **Military Serv:** AUS, Spec 4, 1965-67. **Business Addr:** Vice President, NJ Performing Arts Ctr, Dept Arts Educ, 1 Center St, Newark, NJ 07102, **Business Phone:** (973)642-8989.*

THOMAS, DR. PRISCILLA D
County commissioner. **Personal:** Born Oct 26, 1934, Savannah, GA; daughter of Henry Robinson and Marie Edwards Baker; married Nathaniel Thomas, Sep 5, 1954; children: Deborah. **Educ:** Savannah State Col, Savannah, GA, BS, 1955; Bradley Univ, Peoria, IL, MS, 1960; Univ N Am, St Louis, MO, PhD, 1988. **Career:** County Commissioner (retired); Savannah Bd Pub Educ, Savannah, GA, elem teacher, 1956-67; Am Broadcasting Co, Savannah, GA, producer & hostess, TV pub serv programming, 1976-83, prin, 1968-86; Iota Phi Lambda Sorority Div, Savannah, GA, int pres, 1987-89; Thomas & Assocs, Savannah, GA, pres & chief exec officer, 1988; County Comn Chatham, Savannah, GA, county comnr, 1990-, vice chair, 1997; Conv & Visitors Bur, vpres mkt, 1995; Summer Bonanza Partnership, pres; State Bd Educ, 11th Congressional Dist, Atlanta, GA, rep; Savannah Ga Gen Assembly, sen. **Orgs:** Pub rel dir, Savannah Urban Dropout Collab, 1986-90; comnr, Citizens Crime Comn, 1986; nat liaison mem, Nat Legis Network, CBC, 1987; steering comt, Nat Coun Negro Women, 1989-91; local coordr, Nat Asn Counties Health & Human Serv, 1990; Coalition Black Meeting Planners; bd dir, vice chmn, Chatham Area Transist; founder, Chatham County Youth Comn. **Honors/Awds:** Mrs Black Heritage, Afro Am Life & Hist, 1976-77; On Air Personality Pioneer, Gospel Music Awards, 1983; Producer of the Year, Gospel Music Awards, 1983; 100 Top Black Business & Professional Woman, Dollars & Sense Mag, 1987; Kool Achiever Finalist, Kool Achievers, 1988; Woman Against the Odds, Polit Action Coun, 1988; Outstanding Woman of the Year, Savannah Bus & Prof Women Inc, 1991; Hometown Hero, WTOC-TV, 1994; Outstanding Citizen of the Year, Masons Int, Savannah Chap, 1994; MLK Day Celebration in Savannah, Parade Marshall; Hall of Fame, Dollars & Sense Mag, 1994; Nat Community Leader of the Year, Aunt Jemima Brands Quaker Oats Co, 1996. **Home Addr:** 1727 Chester St, Savannah, GA 31415.

THOMAS, RALPH ALBERT
Banker. **Personal:** Born Aug 5, 1954, Washington, DC; son of Joseph Samuel and Lucille Wade; married Valerie Thornton, Jun 9, 1990. **Educ:** Lehigh Univ, Bethlehem, BS, acct, 1976, MBA, finance, 1977. **Career:** Price Waterhouse & Co, Wash, intern, 1974, 1975, 1976, audit sr, 1976-80; Potomac Electric Power Co, Wash, proj syst acct, 1980-82; AT&T Info Syst, Murray Hill, NJ, mgr, cost & gov acct, 1982-84, mgr, corporate acct policy & res, Murray Hill, 1984-85, mgr, financial anal, large bus syst, Morristown, 1985-87; Citicorp, NA, New York, vpres, region audit head, 1987-. **Orgs:** DC Inst CPA's, 1982-; Am Inst CPA's, 1983-; Lehigh Univ Black Alumni Asn, 1983-; chmn, by-laws comt, Northern New Jersey Chapter Nat Asn Black Acct, 1985-; Urban Bankers Coalition, 1988-; exec coun, bd dir, 1980-, pres, 1990, Nat Asn Black Acct. **Honors/Awds:** Professional Achievement Award, Nat Asn Black Accts, Northern New Jersey Chapter, 1990; Outstanding Member Award, Nat Asn Black Accts, 1988; Alumni Award, Lehigh University Black Alumni Coun, 1989. **Home Addr:** 21 Ireland Brook Dr, North Brunswick, NJ 08902-4762. **Business Addr:** Vice President, Corporate Capital, Citicorp Securities Inc., 599 Lexington Ave 24th Fl Zone 9A, New York, NY 10043, **Business Phone:** (212)559-4375.

THOMAS, RALPH CHARLES
Lawyer. **Personal:** Born Apr 10, 1949, Roanoke, VA. **Educ:** US Int Univ, AA, 1973; Univ Calif, BA, 1975; Harvard Law Sch, JD, 1978. **Career:** Bergson, Borkland, Margolis, & Alder, atty assoc, 1978-80; George Wash Univ Nat Law Ctr, clin law inst, 1982-83; Law Off Ralph C Thomas III, chief coun, 1980-85; Nat Asn Minority Contractors, exec dir, 1985-92; NASA, asst adminr, assoc adminr, 1992-. **Orgs:** Nat Contract Mgt Asn; Sr Exec Asn. **Honors/Awds:** Federal Advocate Award, US Small Bus Admin, 1994; Advocate of the Year Award, Nat Asn Small Disadvantaged Bus, 1994; Exceptional Service Medal, NASA, 1994; Outstanding Leadership Award, Federal Small Bus Dir Interagency Coun, 1996; Federal Small Bus Advocate Award, Asian Am Bus Roundtable, 1996; Exceptional Achievement Medal, NASA, 1997; Ronald A Brown Award, Govt Excellence, Nat Coalition MNY Bus, 1999; Special Honor Award, World Asn Small & Medium Enterprises, 1999; Man of the Year, MNY Bus & Prof Network, 2000; Presidential Rank of Meritorious Exec, Exec Off Pres, 2000; Best of the Decade, MNY BUS News, 2000; Outstanding Leadership Medal, NASA, 2000; Pres Rank of Distinguished Executive, Exec Off Pres, 2001. **Special Achievements:** Author, African Americans in the Business of Space, Minorities in Business, vol III No 1, 1997. **Military Serv:** USAF, staff sgt, 1967-71; Air Force Commendation Medal, Vietnam, 1970. **Business Addr:** Associate Administrator for Small Disadvantaged Business Utilization, NASA, Rm 9F70 300 E St SW PO Box K, Washington, DC 20546-0001, **Business Phone:** (202)358-2088.

THOMAS, RAYMOND A
Artistic director. **Personal:** Born in St Louis, MO. **Educ:** Sch Art Inst Chicago, attended 1984. **Career:** Johnson Publ Co Inc, creative dir; Ebony Mag, creative art dir, currently. **Honors/Awds:** Best Short Film Award, Jamaican Int Film & Music Festival. **Business Addr:** Creative Art Director, Ebony Magazine, 800 S Mich Ave, Chicago, IL 60605.

THOMAS, REGINALD MAURICE
First lady, beautician, business owner. **Personal:** Born Jan 4, 1964, San Angelo, TX; son of Claude Leon Thomas Jr and Devada Roberts; married Lynn Regina Scott, Jun 15, 1985; children: Brittney Regina & Reginald III. **Educ:** Morehouse Col, Atlanta, Ga, attended 1982-83; Wayne State Univ, Detroit, Mich, attended 1983-84. **Career:** The GAP, Southfield, Mich, salesman, 1981-83; Metric Med Lab, Southfield, Mich, supvr, motor pool, 1983-87; City Detroit Parks & Rec, Detroit, Mich, landscaper, laborer, 1987-88, Detroit Fire Dept, Detroit, Mich, emergency med tech, 1988, fire fighter, currently; The Ultimate Barber Shop, owner, barber, currently. **Honors/Awds:** Lifesaver of the Year, E Detroit Med Authority, 1990. **Home Addr:** 18375 Grayfield St, Detroit, MI 48219, **Home Phone:** (313)535-1006. **Business Addr:** Owner, Ultimate Barber Shop, 19310 Grand River Ave, Detroit, MI 48223-1202, **Business Phone:** (313)387-0376.

THOMAS, ROBERT CHARLES (BOBBY THOMAS)
Composer, musician. **Personal:** Born Nov 14, 1932, Newark, NJ; son of Virginia Harris and Theophilus; married Nicole, Oct 22, 1966; children: Lorna & Marc. **Educ:** Juilliard Sch Music, BS, 1961. **Career:** Musician, composer (retired); Ballets USA, 1961-63; Sugar Boogie, music & lyrics, 1976; A Chorus Line, New York, NY, music coordr, 1975-90; Rutgers Univ's Mason Gross Sch Arts, assoc prof jazz percussion, 1993-96; Billy Taylor Prods, musician & composer; Billy Taylor Trio, drummer & lectr. **Orgs:** Consult, E Harlem Tutorial Prog, 1960-74; NY Jazz Repertory Co; Jazz Mobile; co-chairperson & percussion instr, "Jazz in July" workshops, Univ Massachusetts, Amherst. **Honors/Awds:** Shakespeare Key to City Cleveland; Theater World Award for "A Chorus Line", 1976; Best Musical Score Award for Score of "Notes in A Minor Key", Best Short Film, NY Univ Tisch Sch Arts, 1994. **Special Achievements:** Perfomed with Wes Montgomery, Herbie Mann, Carmen McRae, Burt Bacharach, Billy Taylor Orch (David Frost TV Show), co-produced, wrote theme BlackJour for WNET 1975, workshops & seminars Universities & Colleges. **Military Serv:** AUS, corpl, 1953-55. **Home Addr:** 777 De Lanoue Apt 504, Verdun, QC, Canada H3E 1V2.

THOMAS, ROBERT LEE, IV
Football player. **Personal:** Born Dec 1, 1974, Little Rock, AR. **Educ:** Henderson State Univ. **Career:** Dallas Cowboys, running back, 1998-2002; Kans City Brigade, 2004; Georgia Force, 2004-06; Colorado Crush, linebacker, 2007-. **Orgs:** Football coach, Fifth Annual Dallas Cowboys Let Us Play! Sports Camp, 2001. **Business Addr:** Linebacker, Colorado Crush, 6202 Dahlia St, Denver, CO 80022, **Business Phone:** (303)777-7717.

THOMAS, ROBERT LEWIS
Educator. **Personal:** Born Sep 25, 1944, Brewton, AL; son of Robert Lewis Sr and Earnestine Lane; married Wyvonnia Thompson, Jun 6, 1969; children: Michelle & Tiffani. **Educ:** Stillman Col, BA, 1967; Troy State Univ, MS, 1975. **Career:** Escambia Co Bd Educ, teacher, 1967-83; Brewton Police Dept, patrolman, 1969-; Faulkner State Jr Col, prof hist, 1983-; Faulkner State Community Col, Div Soc Sci, chairperson, currently. **Orgs:** Lifetime mem, Kappa Alpha Psi Fraternity, 1969-; Nat Asn Advan Colored People, 1983-; deleg, Conf Black Am Affairs, 1984-86; vpres, AEA Faulkner State, 1986-87, pres, 1987-88; deleg, AEA Conv, 1987-88; Ala Peace Officers Asn; Ala High Sch Athletic Asn; bd trustees, Zion Fountain AME Church; Ala Asn Historians, Nat Asn Advan Colored People. **Honors/Awds:** Achievement Award, Kappa Alpha Psi Fraternity, 1972; Achievement Award, Brewton Police Dept, 1980; Outstanding Police Officer, 1991. **Business Addr:** Chairperson, Faulkner State Community College, Social Science Division, 1900 Hwy 31 S, Bay Minette, AL 36507, **Business Phone:** (251)580-2131.

THOMAS, RODERICK
Consultant. **Personal:** Born Jan 12, 1939, Philadelphia, PA; son of Wiliam A and Virginia B Mosley; divorced; children: Jeffri Pierre, Roderick Jr & Shelley McGill. **Educ:** Temple Univ, BS, 1970; Drexel Univ, MBA, 1973. **Career:** DuPont CPN, org develop consult, 1973-78; Rod Thomas Assocs, prin, 1978-. **Orgs:** Dir, Fed Comt Encouragement. **Special Achievements:** Produced a video, Diversity: Making It Work for You, 1992.

THOMAS, RODNEY DEJUANE
Football player. **Personal:** Born Mar 30, 1973, Groveton, TX. **Educ:** Tex A&M Univ. **Career:** Football player (retired); Houston Oilers, running back, 1995-96; Tenn Oilers, 1997-00; AtlantaFalcons, 2001. **Honors/Awds:** Southwest Conference American Airlines Spirit Award; Aggie Heart Award, 1994.

THOMAS, RODNEY LAMAR
Football player. **Personal:** Born Dec 21, 1965, Los Angeles, CA. **Educ:** Brigham Young Univ. **Career:** Miami Dolphins, cornerback, 1988-90; Los Angeles Rams, 1991.

THOMAS, RODOLFO RUDY
Law enforcement officer. **Personal:** Born Feb 19, 1949, Highland Park, MI; son of Porter and Consuela; married Anna, Oct 3, 1990; children: Kimberly Stewart, Malia, Lattimer & Matthew Rodriguez. **Educ:** Highland Park Col, AA; Eastern Mich Univ, BS, police admin; Masters, interdisciplanary technol. **Career:** Detroit Police Dept, police officer, 1974-83; sgt, 1983-85; lt, 1985-87, inspector, 1987-89; commander/narcotics div, 1989-94; dep chief police, 1994-; Eastern Mich Univ, adj prof. **Orgs:** Optimist Club; Golden Key Honors Soc; Chamber Com Law Enforcement Consult; Drug Educ Adv; Community Policing Adv; City Heroin Task Force; Detroit Pub Sch Mentor. **Military Serv:** US Air Force, sgt, 1969-73. **Home Addr:** 8032 Third Ave, Detroit, MI 48202. **Business Phone:** (313)596-1870.

THOMAS, RON
Writer, educator. **Personal:** Born Sep 13, 1949, Buffalo, NY; son of Laughton F and Ormah Dennis; married Iris T Crossley, Aug 7, 1982; children: Kali C Thomas. **Educ:** Univ Rochester, BA, polit sci, 1971; Northwestern Univ, Masters, jour, 1973. **Career:** Rochester Times-Union, prep sports reporter, 1973-75; Chicago Daily News, col basketball, football reporter, 1975-78; San Francisco Chronicle, pro basketball reporter, 1978-82, sportswriter, 1984-93, news copy ed, 1994; USA Today, pro basketball ed/reporter, 1982-84; Home Box Office, doc researcher/feature producer, 1995; Marin Independent J, sportswriter, 1995-2000; San Francisco, examr, sports writer, 2000-03, freelance, currently; Author: "They Cleared the Lane: The NBA's BLK Pioneers," 2002; "Black Faces Still Rare in the Press Box"; "Sport in Society: Equal Opportunity or BUS as Usual?"; "Col of Marin Star Fought Beyond Basketball Court"; "The Black Coach Barrier"; "They Cleared the Lane"; Morehouse Col, Journ & Sports Prog, Dept Eng, dir, currently, fac, currently. **Orgs:** Nat Asn Black Journalists, 1978-; Bay Area Black Journalists Asn, 1980-; Pro Basketball Writers Asn, 1984-94; Pro Football Writers Asn, 1987-91; North Am Soc Sports History, 1992-. **Honors/Awds:** Best Sports Story Award, San Francisco Press Club, 1980; Best Sports Story Award, United Press Int, CAL & NEV, 1980; Honored for Excellence, Bay Area Black Journalists Asn, 1987; 3rd place, sportswriting, Nat Asn Black Journalists, 1997, 1st prize, sports column writing, 1999; Top 10 Features & Top 10 News stories for under 50,000 circulation, Asn Press Sports Eds, 1997; Second place for sportswriting, Asn Press News Exec Coun, CAL & NEV, 1997. **Home Addr:** 2726 Rawson St, Oakland, CA 94619-3259. **Business Addr:** Director Journalism and Sports Program, Faculty, Morehouse College, Department of English, Brawley Hall Rm 106 830 Westview Dr, SW Atlanta, GA 30314.

THOMAS, DR. RONALD F.
Educator. **Personal:** Born Jul 2, 1944, Wilmington, DE; married Marva Wyche, Dec 23, 1967; children: Ronald LeRoy & Olivia Necole. **Educ:** Delaware State Col, BS, 1967; Cent Mich Univ, Master, 1979, postgrad studies, 1987; Hamilton Univ, PhD, 2000. **Career:** Educator (retired); 7th grad math teacher, 1977; Capital Sch Dist, Dover DE, math instr, 1970-74, reading & math ctr, oper, Title VII, Title I; Telegraph Road Learning Ctr, comput lab supvr, math & sci teacher; Red Clay Sch Dist, Wilmington DE, math & sci teacher, 1988, math & reading lab, instr. **Orgs:** Groove Phi Groove Soc Fel, 1963, Va, 1967-; Del State Educ Asn, 1970-; Nat Educ Asn, 1970-; Capital Educ Asn, 1970-; Church Laymens Asn, 1970-; Human Rels Conf Represent Capital Sch Dist, 1972, 1973; Problems & Rels Comt, 1971-73, 32nd Degree Mason & Shriner, 1972-; lab del, assembly delegate, 1973, bldg rep, 1972-74, State Educ Asn; negotiation team for schs, 1974; chmn, nom comn, Del State Educ Assembly, 1974; pres, DE State Minority Ed Asn, 1974-76; Del Disadvantaged Found Inc, 1974-; VFW, 1974-, DOIC, GED, ABE Teacher, 1963; adv, Col Gospel Youth Group, 1974; vpres, De Front ierInt Club; Omega Psi Phi. **Honors/Awds:** State Civic Duty Award, 1962; Outstanding Sr Choir & Band, 1962; Outstanding Leaders In Elem & Sec Educ, 1976; Citizen of the Year Award for Dover, DE, 1985; Thirty-Third Degree, United Supreme Coun, 1988. **Special Achievements:** Recorded, "Love You So Bad Come Home Girl", "Your on Top Girl Slide On By"; first pl, All Army Talent Show, 1969. **Military Serv:** AUS, sgt, E-5, 1967-70; DE, NG, capt.

THOMAS, ROY L.
Manager, government official. **Personal:** Born Jul 27, 1938, Forest, MS; married Altemese Woods; children: Micheal, Sandra & Mark. **Educ:** Univ Md. **Career:** Hercules Inc, Glen Falls, prod foreman; Minority Bus Opportunities, enforcement officer; City Glen Falls, dir community develop. **Orgs:** Bd chmn, Local Housing Corp; Warren Co NY Sewer Dist 1; chmn, NY St Conf Nat Asn Advan Colored People, Prisons Affrs Comt; exec dir, Vol Housing Surv; bd & chmn, bd mem, E A dir ondack Econ Develop Auth;

bd mem, Warren Co Alcoholic Bev Con Bd; pres, Glen Falls Br Nat Asn Advan Colored People; Warren Co Rep Comn; NY Ancillary Manpower Planning Bd; Senate Lodge 456 F&AM Glens Falls. **Military Serv:** USAF, 4 Yrs. **Home Addr:** 11 Darwin Ave, Glens Falls, NY 12801, **Home Phone:** (518)793-1947. *

THOMAS, ROZONDA
Actor, singer. **Personal:** Born Feb 27, 1971, Atlanta, GA; daughter of Abdul Ali and Ava Thomas; married Dallas Austin; children: Tron. **Educ:** Ga Southern Univ, fashion design. **Career:** Albums: Ooooooohhh..On the TLC Tip, 1992; Crazy Sexy Cool, 1994; Fan mail, 1999; 3D, 2002; Now & Forever: The Hits, 2005; Singles: "Ain't 2 Proud 2 Beg", 1992; "What About Your Friends", 1992; "Baby-Baby-Baby", 1992; Sleigh Ride", 1992; "Hat 2 Da Back", 1993; "Get It Up", 1993; "Creep", 1994; "Red Light Special", 1995; "Switch", 1995; "Waterfalls", 1995; "Kick Your Game", 1995; "Diggin' On You", 1995; "This Is How It Works", 1995; "Silly Ho", 1998; "No Scrubs", 1999; "I'm Good At Being Bad", 1999; "Unpretty", 1999; "Dear Lie", 1999; "What It Ain't (Ghetto Enuff)", 2000; "Girl Talk", 2002; "Hands Up", 2002; "Damaged", 2003; "Turnbtable", 2003; "Come Get Some", 2004; "Bi-Polar", 2009; Films: House Party 3, 1994; Hav Plenty, 1997; Snow Day, 2000; Ticker, 2001; TV series: "Love Song", 2000; Snow Day, 2000; "A Diva's Christmas Carol", 2000; "That '70s Show", 2003; "The Parkers", 2004; "Strong Medicine", 2004. **Honors/Awds:** Four MTV Music Awards: Best R&B Video, Best Group Video, Best Video of the Year, Viewers Choice, "Waterfalls", 1995. **Business Addr:** Singer, Actress, c/o LaFace Records, One Capitol City Plz Suite 1500, Atlanta, GA 30326, **Business Phone:** (404)848-8050.*

THOMAS, SAMUEL
Executive. **Personal:** Born Aug 21, 1943, Malvern, AR; son of Robert and Altora Burks Boles; married Lura D Shannon, Mar 6, 1965; children: Samuel II & Jason Anthony. **Educ:** Monterey Peninsula Col, Monterey, CA, AA, 1974; Golden Gate Univ, San Francisco, CA, BA, 1977, MBA, 1984. **Career:** Pac Gas & Elec, pump test engr, 1977-78, mkt rep, 1978-80, local mgr, 1980-83, area mgr, 1983-86, employee participation adminr, 1986-90, continuing educ adminr, 1990; Am Protective Serv, acct mgr; Thomas & Assoc, pres, currently. **Orgs:** Pacifica Lions Club, 1980-91; Am Legion, 1982-91; Am Asn Blacks Energy, 1983-91; pres, Healdsburg Chamber Com, 1985-86; subscribing life mem, Nat Asn Advan Colored People, 1989-91; life mem, Nat Black MBA, 1989. **Honors/Awds:** Service Award, Am Legion, Pacifica Post, 1984; Service Award, Healdsburg Chamber Com, 1985; Community Service Award, Pac Gas & Elec, 1989; Dedicated Service Award, Math Engr & Sci Achievement, 1990. **Military Serv:** AUS, spec 4, 1962-65; Good Conduct Medal, 1965. **Business Addr:** President, Thomas & Associates, 10220 Singing View Ct, Las Vegas, NV 89129, **Business Phone:** (702)869-3379.

THOMAS, SAMUEL, III
Government official. **Career:** Mich State Legisl, state rep, 1997-, 4th Senate Dist-Detroit, state senator, currently. **Orgs:** Numerous memberships including Diabetes Asn Mich; Independent Policy Group; Matthew NcNeely Neighborhood Found; Plowshares Theater; bd dirs, 1000 Friends Metrop Detroit, 2003-. **Business Addr:** State Senator, 4th Senate District Detroit, 610 Farnum Bldg, PO Box 30036, Lansing, MI 48909-7514, **Business Phone:** (517)373-7918.*

THOMAS, SAMUEL HAYNES, JR.
Lawyer, real estate executive. **Personal:** Born Oct 2, 1941, Detroit, MI; son of Samuel Sr and Margaret; married Aug 1966 (divorced); children: Samuel Thomas III. **Educ:** Lafayette Col, AB, 1964; Harvard Law Sch, LLB, 1967. **Career:** Ford Motor Co, off gen coun, 1967-69; Jaffe, Snider, Raitt, Garratt & Heuer PC, 1970-77; Thomas & Pomeroy Inc, pres, 1977-80; Burlington Investments Inc, owner, 1980-; Thomas & Mancinelli Pizza Inc, pres, 1987-94; Detroit Inst Arts, trustee; Phoenix Mgt, vpres, 1994-. **Orgs:** Sigma Pi Phi Fraternity, 1993-95; State Bar Mich; Nat Bar Asn; Detroit Bar Asn; vchair, State Mich Building Authority; vchair, Metro Realty Corp. **Military Serv:** AUS, 1st lt, 1969. **Business Addr:** Vice President, Phoenix Management, 1900 W Liberty, Ann Arbor, MI 48103, **Business Phone:** (734)747-6666.*

THOMAS, SHERRI BOOKER
Geologist. **Personal:** Born in Richmond, VA; married Norman Thomas. **Educ:** VA State Univ, BS, 1980; Univ SC, MS, 1982. **Career:** Amoco, sr explor tech, 1978-79; Nat Assoc Black Geol & Geophysicists, secy, 1983-84; Conoco Inc, geol, 1982-93, sr adv, 1993. **Orgs:** Nat Assoc Black Geol & Geophys, 1982; secy, Ella Bouldin Missionary Soc 5 1983-; Am Assoc Petroleum Geol 1984, Geol Soc Am, 1985; Celestrial Choir Payne Chapel AME Church. **Special Achievements:** Article "Quartz Sand Province Changes" S Booker, R Ehrlich, 1981. **Business Addr:** Senior Advisor Human Resource, Conoco Inc, 600 N Dairy Ashford, PO Box 2197, Houston, TX 77252-2197, **Business Phone:** (281)293-1000.*

THOMAS, DR. SHERYL ANN BENNING
School administrator. **Personal:** Born in Columbus, GA; daughter of Calvin and Emma; married Lee M, Jun 10, 1970; children: Khalia M & Shaura A. **Educ:** Fisk Univ, BA; Tex Southern Univ, masters; Wayne State Univ, Ed Spec, PhD; LaSalle Univ. **Career:** Detroit Pub Schs, teacher, counr & adminr; Golightly Educ Ctr, prin & exec dir schs, currently. **Orgs:** Nat pres, Jack & Jill Am, 1996-98; Links Inc, Detroit chap; Delta Sigma Theta Sorority; Phi Delta Kappa. **Honors/Awds:** National Blue Ribbon School status, US Dept Educ, 1994; State Blue Ribbon School status, State Michigan Dept Educ; Educator of the Year, Phi Delta Kappa Wayne State, 1994. **Business Addr:** Executive Director of Schools, Detroit Public Schools, 8770 W Chicago, Detroit, MI 48204.

THOMAS, SIRR DANIEL
Construction manager. **Personal:** Born Jul 21, 1933, Huntsville, AL; married Barbara Williams; children: 5. **Educ:** Tuskegee Inst, plumbing & mech drawing; Knoxville Col, math. **Career:** Elmer A Thomas Plumbing Co, journeyman plumber, 1953-55, foreman, plumber, 1957-60; Howard & Howard Plumbing Co, Knoxville, journeyman plumber, 1960-63; Thomas & Thomas Inc, Chattanooga, owner, mgr, 1963; City Chattanooga, mayor, city councilman, 1990. **Orgs:** Nat Bus League; bd dir, Eastern Seabord Plumbing & Heating Asn; bd dir,Chattanooga Chap Nat Asn Advan Colored People; bd dir, Security Fed Savings & Loan Asn; bd dir, Peoples Bank; chmn, Minority Bus Comt. **Military Serv:** USY, 1955-56.

THOMAS, SPENCER
Physician. **Personal:** Born in Gadsden, AL; married Lela; children: Spencer Jr. **Educ:** Ala State Univ, BS, 1952; Howard Univ, MD, 1959. **Career:** Mercy Douglas Hosp Philadelphia, intern, house physician, 1959-61; Philadelphia Gen Hosp, urology spec training, 1972-76, asst attending physician, 1976-77; Holy Name of Jesus Hosp, now Riverview & Baptist Mem (now Gadsden Regional) Hosp, Gadsden, staff physician; pvt practice, Gadsden Ala, physician. **Orgs:** Indus Develop Bd Gadsden, 1968-72 & 1978-80; bd dir, Gadsden Progress Coun; sponsor, Project Headstart, 1964-72 & 1980-; pres, Community League for Advancement Social Socs Gadsden, 1969; founder & mem gov bd, Colley Child Care Ctr, Gadsden; med dir, Project Head Start, 1968-72; pres, Gadsden Alumni Asn Ala State Univ, 1979-; NAACP; Alpha Phi Alpha Fraternity Inc, Ala State Medical Asn, Nat Med Asn, AMA, SCLC, Howard Univ Med Alumni Asn; chmn, admin bd, trustee, Sweethome United Methodist Church, 1979-81; church lay leader, 1981-84; Gadsden City Bd Educ, 1980-90, vpres, 1984; bd trustees, Ala A&M Univ, 1980-87, chmn, 1982-84; pres, Gadsden-Etowah Ala Br, NAACP, 1982-94; pres, Ala State Alumni Asn, Gadsden Chap, 1979-; past mem, Chamber Cerce, Gadsden Ala. **Honors/Awds:** Recipient Service Award, Gadsden Progress Coun, 1972. **Special Achievements:** Gadsden Times Daily, weekly columnist. **Military Serv:** AUS, 1952-54. **Home Addr:** PO Box 835, Gadsden, AL 35902-0835. **Business Addr:** Physician, 1010 S 12th St, Gadsden, AL 35901-3811, **Business Phone:** (256)547-2293.

THOMAS, STEPHEN
Executive. **Educ:** Ohio State Univ, BS; Southern Ill Univ, Carbondale, PhD (community health). **Career:** Rollins Sch Pub Health, dir; Univ Md, fac; Minority Health Res Lab, cofounder; Emory Univ, assoc prof, 1992-2000; Univ Pittsburgh, Ctr Minority Health, dir, currently; Univ Pittsburgh, Philip Hallen Prof Community Health & Social Justice, currently. **Orgs:** Inst Med Comt, 1998; Nat Res Coun, consult, 1995. **Honors/Awds:** David Satcher Award, Health Promo & Educ. **Business Phone:** (412)624-5665.

THOMAS, TERENCE
Disc jockey, television producer, radio engineer. **Personal:** Born Nov 15, 1966, Brooklyn, NY; son of Tijuana G. **Educ:** Audio Rec Tech Inst, 1989. **Career:** TBTA, 1985-89; Master Lab Prod Studio, pres & ceo, currently; First Priority Music, E W Rec, currently; TV appearances: "The Arsenio HallShow," 1990; "Showtime at the Apollo," 1990; "In Living Color," 1992; "Soul Train," 1992; "NBA All-Star Game," 1992; "The Phil Donahue Show"; "The Geraldo Show"; "MTV"; "Yo MTV Raps"; "The Party Machine"; Films: Boomerang & Mo Money; Moesha; Joan Rivers; BET; Video Soul. **Orgs:** SAG; AFTRA. **Honors/Awds:** Nine gold records & six platinum records. **Business Phone:** (718)322-2258.

THOMAS, TERENCE A, SR.
Lawyer, law enforcement officer. **Educ:** Albion Col, BA, hist; Univ Wis Law Sch, JD. **Career:** Miller, Canfield, Paddock & Stone PLC, prin, atty; Raymond & Prokop PC, assoc; Mich Supreme Ct Justice Conrad L Mallet Jr, judicial clerk; St John Health (SJH), sr vpres advocacy & corp responsibility, 2003-. **Orgs:** Am Bar Asn; State Bar Mich; Wis Bar Asn; Detroit Metrop Bar Asn; Wolverine Bar Asn; Leadership Detroit Class XXI; Audit Comt, Detroit Econ Growth Corp; trustee, Music Hall Ctr; Detroit Regional Chamber Com. **Business Addr:** Senior Vice President of Advocacy & Corporate Responsibility, St John Health, St John Health Corp Serv Bldg 28000 Dequindre, Warren, MI 48092, **Business Phone:** (586)753-0465.*

THOMAS, THURMAN LEE
Football player, business owner. **Personal:** Born May 16, 1966, Houston, TX; married Patti; children: Olivia, Angelica & Annika Lee. **Educ:** Okla State Univ. **Career:** Football player (retired); Buffalo Bills, running back, 1988-99; Miami Dolphins, running back, 2000; Thurman Thomas Enterprises, Niagara Falls, NY, owner, 2002-. **Honors/Awds:** Pro Bowl, 1989, 1990, 1991, 1992, 1993; NFL MVP, 1992; Tex High Sch Hall of Fame, 1992; Buffalo Bills/Edge, Man of the Yr, 1993; Pro Football Hall of Fame, 2007. **Business Addr:** Thurman Thomas Enterprises, Niagara Falls, NY.

THOMAS, TIMOTHY MARK
Basketball player. **Personal:** Born Feb 26, 1977, Paterson, NJ. **Educ:** Villanova Univ, attended 1997. **Career:** Philadelphia 76ers, forward, 1997-99; Milwaukee Bucks, forward, 1999-2004; NY Knicks, forward, 2004-05, 2008-09; Chicago Bulls, 2005; Phoenix Suns, 2006; LosAngeles clippers, forward, 2006-08; Chicago Bulls, 2009; Dallas Mavericks, free agt, currently. **Honors/Awds:** The Sporting News Freshman of the Year, 1996-97; National Freshman of the Year, US Basketball Writers Assn, 1997; Schick, All-Rookie Second Team, 1997-98; Runner-up for the Sixth Man of the Year Award, 2000-01. **Business Addr:** Free Agent, Dallas Mavericks.*

THOMAS, TRA (WILLIAM THOMAS, III)
Football player. **Personal:** Born Nov 20, 1974, Deland, FL; son of William; married Rosa Chanea; children: 3. **Educ:** Fla State Univ, BS, criminol. **Career:** Philadelphia Eagles, tackle, 1998-2008; Jacksonville Jaguars, 2009-. **Honors/Awds:** NFC Pro Bowl, 2001, 2002, 2004; All pro Slection, Once, 2002. **Business Addr:** Offensive Tackle, Jacksonville Jaguars, 1 Stadium Place, Jacksonville, FL 32202, **Business Phone:** (904)633-2000.

THOMAS, HON. W. CURTIS
State government official, educator. **Personal:** Born Apr 11, 1948, Philadelphia, PA; son of Hattie M and Curtis; children: Salim & Kareem. **Educ:** Temple Univ, BS, educ, 1975, Ed Admin, 1977; Antioch Sch Law, JD, 1980. **Career:** Antioch Sch Law, Wash, DC, stud teacher, 1978-79; US Dept HEW, Wash, DC,law clerk, 1979-80; Commonwealth Pa, Harrisburg, Pa, law clerk, 1980-82; EP-NAC Inc, Philadelphia, exec dir, 1982-87; Pa House Representatives,181st Legis Dist, Philadelphia County, state rep, 1988-. **Orgs:** Chmn, Pa Legis Black Caucus; chmn, Health & Welfare Comt; State Gov &Labor Rels Comt; brd dir, Penn Higher Educ Assistance Agency; coun, State Government's Eastern Regional Conf Comt Health & Human Serv; founding mem, Democratic Study Group; bd mem, Philadelphia Commercial Develop Corp; Philadelphia Welfare Pride & Blacks Educating Blacks About Sexual Health Issues; co-founder; democratic chair, Children First; Senate Pub Health & Welfare Comn; Appropriations, Educ & Policy; Am Fed State Co & Munic Employees Union; Prince Hall Grand Lodge Free & Accepted Masons; Philadelphia Int Airport Adv Brd; Father's Day Rally Comn; trustee, Mt Carmel Baptist Church. **Honors/Awds:** E Luther Cunningham Service Award, E Luther Cunningham Community Ctr,1990; PUC Appreciation Award, Philadelphia Urban Coalition LeadershipComt, 1990; Self Help Initiative Award, Self Help Initiative Adv Comt,1990; MOC Voluntary Service Award, Mayors Off Community Serv, 1990. **Business Addr:** State Representative, Pennsylvania House of Representatives, 301 K Leroy Irvis, PO Box 202181, Harrisburg, PA 17120-2181, **Business Phone:** (717)787-9471.

THOMAS, REV. WALTER SCOTT
Clergy. **Personal:** Born Apr 2, 1950, Balto, MD; son of Calvin and Elizabeth; married Patricia G, May 15, 1976; children: Joi, Walter Jr & Joshua. **Educ:** Univ Maryland Col Park, BS, 1971; Howard Univ Divinity Sch, MDIV, 1976; St Mary's Univ & Seminary, DMIN, 1985. **Career:** New Psalmist Baptist Church, pastor, 1975-. **Orgs:** Pres, Baptist Minister's Conf Balto, 1986-88; pres, Millenium Pastor's Conf, 1998-2001; pres, Hampton Univ Minister's Conf, 1999-2002; bd dirs, Harbor Bank, 2000-; Sigma Pi Phi, 2001. **Honors/Awds:** Dean's Award, Howard Univ Divinity Sch, 2000. **Special Achievements:** Published: Spiritual Navigation for 21st Century, 2000; Good Men Makes Its Own Gravy, 2000; Edited: Outstanding Black Sermons Vol 4, 2001; Articles in: Afr Amer Pulpit. **Business Addr:** Pastor, New Psalmist Baptist Church, 4501 1/2 Old Frederick Rd, Balto, MD 21229, **Business Phone:** (410)945-3000.

THOMAS, WILBON
Business owner, farmer, government official. **Personal:** Born Mar 6, 1921, Midway, AL; son of Wilbon Thomas and Ada Brown; married Mary E Warren; children: 3. **Career:** Bullock County Schs, bus driver; farmer & serv sta operator, 1957-; Macon Co Racing Comn. **Orgs:** Vpres, 1954-56, pres, 1964-, NAACP; pres, Midway Improvement Club, 1956-64; First Baptist Church Bullock Co ESPO, Deacon; jury comm., Bullock City, Bullock City Dist Adv Coun Title I, BTU & Sunday Sch Teacher; state bd mem, ESPO; supt, Sunday Sch; pres, First Baptist Usher Bd; organizer, Sunday Sch Prog; Bullock Co Dem Exec Comm. **Honors/Awds:** Bullock City PTA Award; Service Award, ASCAARV; Ala NAACP; Youth Coun & Col; 2 Leadership Awards, Ala Baptist State Conv; Certificate, Personal & Family Survival; Proclamation of Achievement, Gov Guy Hunt 50th Wedding Anniversary March, 1991; Proclamation of Service, 43 Years Bus Driver Bullock Co Pub Sch Gov Hunt, 1991.

THOMAS, WILLIAM, III. See THOMAS, TRA.

THOMAS, DR. WILLIAM
School administrator. **Personal:** Born Jan 1, 1935, Cairo, IL; son of William H and Claudia Mae Campbell; married Majoice Lewis; children: Joyce D, Sharon S, William E & Anjanette, Marcus K. **Educ:** Southern Ill Univ, BS, 1967; Purdue Univ, MS, 1969, PhD, 1972. **Career:** City Gary Schs, head teacher, 1967-70; Purdue Univ, admin asst, 1970-72,David Ross fel, 1972, dir spec acad servcs & asst prof, 1973-75; Woodrow Wilson Found, Martin Luther King Jr fel, 1970-72; DePauw Univ, dir black studies & asst prof, 1972-73; Joliet Area Schs, educ consult, 1973-74;Office Educ Region V, 1974-75; Ind Dept Pub Instr, 1975-77; CIC Midwest Prog Minorities Engr, exec dir, 1975-77; Thomas Distrib, vpres, 1977-79;Cairo Sch Dist, from admin asst to supt, 1979-83; Carbondale Elem Sch,supt, 1983-87; New Orleans Pub Schs, LA, assoc supt, 1987-91; Greenville Pub Schs, MS, supt, 1991-94; Thomas Assocs, pres, 1994-; Philander Smith Col, dean instr, 1995-2000; educ consult, 2000-. **Orgs:** Vpres, secy & treas, Kiwanis Club Cairo, 1979-83; corp dir, Southern Med Ctr, 1980-84; Western Reg chmn, Egyptian Coun Boy Scouts Am, 1983-85; Carbondale Rotary Club, 1984-87; treas, Egyptian Coun Boy Scouts Am,1985-87; educ consult, Ill State Bd Educ, 1986-87; educ consult, James Nighswander Assocs, 1987-; educ consult, Nat Sch Servs 1988-; Partnership Educ Steering Comt, 1989. **Honors/ Awds:** Maintenance Man of the Month 13th Air Div, 1963; President's Award, Egyptian Council Boy Scouts Am, 1985. **Military Serv:** USAF Tech Sgt served 10 yrs; Natl Defense Serv Medal; Good Conduct Medal; Missile man's Badge.

THOMAS, WILLIAM HARRISON, JR.
Football player, football coach. **Personal:** Born Aug 13, 1968, Amarillo, TX; married Susan; children: Zion, Noah & Jonah. **Educ:** Tex A&M Univ. **Career:** Football player (retired), Football coach; Philadelphia Eagles,linebacker, 1991-99; Oakland Raiders, 2000-01; La Salle Univ, volunteer coach, currently. **Business Phone:** (215)951-1398.

THOMAS, WILLIAM L.
Executive. **Personal:** Born Apr 3, 1938, Cleveland; married Joyce; children: Menelik, Malaka. **Educ:** OH Univ; Univ Madrid; Ghetto Univ; Univ MD; OH Drug Studies Inst, 1974. **Career:** City Cleveland, engr inspector, 1968-69; Black Unity House Inc, fdr, exec dir. **Orgs:** exec com OH Black Polit Assembly 1974; Cleveland Black Polit Assembly, 1974; trustee, Community Action Against Addiction, 1971-75; African Liberation Support Com, 1969-75; Community Coalition Construction, 1971-75. **Military Serv:** USAF, a & 2c, 1960-65.

THOMAS-CARTER, JEAN COOPER
Educator, government official. **Personal:** Born Dec 16, 1924, Baltimore, MD; married Calvin Lavette; children: Jacques S Maultsby. **Educ:** Hampton Inst Hampton Va, BS, 1946; Howard Univ, Sch Soc Work, MSW, 1965; Univ Ala, Cert Mgmt, 1979. **Career:** Barrett Sch Girls, teacher, 1947-49; Baltimore City Dept Soc Servs, caseworker, 1949-57, casework suprv, 1957-66, dist suprv, 1966-71, dist supvr group day care, 1973-78, prog spec day care, 1978-79, chief & prog spec serv families, 1979-80, dist mgr, 1980-83, asst dir client serv oper, 1983-84, bureau chief adult & family servs; Logical Tech Serv Residential Drug Treatment Prog, dep dir, 1971-73. **Orgs:** Instr, Community Col Baltimore, 1970-; exec comt, Howard Univ Sch, Soc Work Alumni Assoc, Mayors Adv Coun Drug Abuse; co-chairperson, Conf Women State Servs; past v chairperson & bd dir, Xcell Drug Treatment Ctr; past bd dir, Baltimore Assoc Retarded Citizens; past, Md Conf Soc Concern; past budget allocations comt, United Fund; dir, Youth Ministry Our Lady Lourdes Parish, Baltimore MD, 1985-; bd mem, Campfire Coun Chesapeake, 1985-; volunteer panelist, Admin Review Bd Serv Families C, Baltimore Dept Social Serv, 1989-. **Honors/Awds:** Award of Recognition Chairperson, 1974. **Special Achievements:** Publ "Does Existing Social Policy, Service Programs, & Support Systems Help the Children of Women Involved in the Criminal Justice System?" Nat Inst of Health, 1979, "The Impact of PA Pmts & Social Policy on Family Functioning" Child Welfare League of Amer Eastern Reg Conf, 1980. **Home Addr:** 3855 Greenspring Ave, Baltimore, MD 21216. **Business Addr:** Assistant Director, Bureau Chief Adult & Fam Service, Baltimore City Social Service, 1510 Guilford Ave, Baltimore, MD 21202.

THOMAS-GRAHAM, PAMELA
Executive, writer. **Personal:** Born 1963, Detroit, MI; daughter of Albert and Marian; married Lawrence Otis Graham; children: Gordon. **Educ:** Harvard-Radcliffe Col, BA, econ; Harvard Bus Sch, MBA, 1988; Harvard Law Sch, JD, 1989. **Career:** Harvard Law Review, ed; McKinsey & Co, consult, partner, 1989-99; NBC, vpres, 1999-2001, pres, 2001; CNBC, pres & chief exec officer, 1999-2001, chief exec officer, currently; Author: A Darker Shade of Crimson; Blue Blood. **Orgs:** Phi Beta Kappa; bd dir, NY City Opera; bd dir, Am Red Cross Greater NY; bd dir, Girls Inc. **Honors/Awds:** Corporate Executive of the Year, Black Enterprise, 2001; Leadership Award, Nat Urban League, 2001; Matrix Award, NY Women Commun, 2001; Women of the Year, 2003; Captain Jonathan Fay Prize, Harvard-Radcliffe Col. **Special Achievements:** First Black Woman Partner, McKinsey & Co; 50 Most Powerful Black Executives. **Business Addr:** Chief Executive Officer, CNBC, 900 Sylvan Ave, Englewood Cliffs, NJ 07632, **Business Phone:** (201)735-2622.

THOMASON, MARSHA
Actor. **Personal:** Born Jan 19, 1976, United Kingdom. **Educ:** Manchester Metrop Univ, BA, Eng. **Career:** Oldham Theatre Workshop, actor, 1988; Plays: Our Day Out; Peace; BBC, "The8:15 from Manchester", 1990; BBC, "Pie in the Sky," 1994; TV Series: "Prime Suspect 5: Errors of Judgment," 1996; "Brazen Hussies," 1996; "Playing the Field", 1998; "Love in the 21st Century", 1999; "Table 12", 2001; Swallow, 2001; Burn It, 2003; Las Vegas", 2003-05; Cane, 2007; Messiah: The Rapture, 2008; "Lost", 2007-08; "Make It or Break It", 2009; "Easy Money", 2008-09; Films: Black Knight, 2001; Long Time Dead, 2002; Pure, 2002; The Haunted Mansion, 2003; My Baby's Daddy, 2004; The Nickel Children, 2005; The Package, 2006; Caffeine, 2006; The Fast One, 2006; The Tripper, 2006; Tug of War, 2006; LA Blues, 2007; Into the Blues 2- Reef, 2009. **Honors/Awds:** BFM Award, 2002. **Business Addr:** Actress, c/o Melanie Greene Management, 425 N Robertson Blvd, Los Angeles, CA 90048, **Business Phone:** (310)858-3200.*

THOMASON, WILLIAM, III
Entrepreneur. **Career:** Thomason Capital Mgt LLC, pres, chief investment officer & managing partner, 2000-. **Orgs:** Nat Asn Securities Profs. **Business Addr:** President, Chief Investment Officer, Thomason Capital Management LLC, 300 Frank H Ogawa Plz Suite 210, Oakland, CA 94612, **Business Phone:** (510)763-7300.*

THOMAS-RICHARDS, JOSE RODOLFO
Surgeon. **Personal:** Born Jul 28, 1944; married Lynette; children: Jose, Raoul. **Educ:** Andrews Univ, BA, 1966; Kans City Col Osteo Med, DO, 1970. **Career:** Orthop surgeon, self; Martin Luther King Hosp, dir emergency med, chmn, Dept Orthop & Hand Surg, dir rehab med; St Luke's Hosp, Truman Med Ctr-W, residency; Lakeview Orthop & Hand Ctr, orthop surgeon. **Orgs:** Kans City Med Soc, 1973; SW Clin Soc, 1974; Med Sec Cent State Conf Seventh Day Adventists; AMA, 1975; Mo State Med Asn, 1975; Jackson Co Med Soc, 1975; Col Emergency Med, 1975; NAACP, 1975; bd dir, Jackson Co Med Soc, 1977; Mo State Med Asn, 1977; Surg Hand, 1977-78; Golden Heritage NAACP; bd trustees, PUSH; Wyandotte Co Jail & Dept Sheriff Kans City; bd dir, Martin Luther King Hosp; Nat Med Asn; Fla Osteo Med Asn. **Honors/Awds:** Mead-Johnson Award, 1971. **Business Addr:** Orthopaedic Surgeon, Lakeview Orthopaedic and Hand Center, 3750 Emergency Lane Suite 1, Sebring, FL 33870.

THOMAS-RICHARDSON, DR. VALERIE JEAN
Consultant. **Personal:** Born Apr 21, 1947, Akron, OH; daughter of Rev Charles Jr and Mary Carson. **Educ:** Akron Sch Pratical Nursing, LPN, 1968-69; Thomas A Edison Col, BA soc sci, 1969-73; Univ Pittsburgh, MSW, 1974-76; Union Grad Sch, PhD, 1976-78; Medina Hosp, Cardiopulmonary Tech Training Prog; Int Apostolic Col Grace & Truth, doctorate christian educ, 1994. **Career:** NEOCROSS Inc, interim exec dir, 1978-79; The Gilliam Family Serv Ctr, exec dir, 1979-82; Cleveland Adult Tutorial Serv, exec dir, 1983-86; Georgian Allied Health Educ Serv, assoc dir; Int Apostolic Col Grace & Truth, Richmond, site coord, 1994; Greater Cleveland Tutorial Serv, exec dir, currently. **Orgs:** Zonta Club, 1969; bd mem, agency rep Ohio Legal Services Comns Consumer & Housing Task Force Comm Columbus, 1977-78; First aid & personal safety instr, cpr instr Am Red Cross, 1975-87; former med newsletter editor "Heartbeat" Am Heart Asn Pub, 1976; nat pres appointment exec comm Fed Coun Aging, Wash DC, 1978-; Am Asn Univ Women, 1984-86; Altrusa Greater Cleveland, 1985-86; bd mem Greater Cleveland Blood Pressure Coalition, 1985-87; Ohio Entrepreneur Women's Directory, 1986-87; hon mem research comn, Am Biog Inst; bd trustees, Int Apostolic Col Grace & Truth, Richmond, 1994; fel Int Bio Asn. **Honors/Awds:** National special cardiovascular tech testing site for credentialing examination admin, 1986; "Off-campus" site for Cuyahoga Community College's medical courses; Silver Medal of Honor, Am Bio Inst. **Home Addr:** 16000 Terrace Rd, East Cleveland, OH 44112, **Home Phone:** (216)249-2711. **Business Addr:** Executive Director, Greater Cleveland Tutorial & Training Services, 16000 Terrace Rd, East Cleveland, OH 44112, **Business Phone:** (216)249-2711.

THOMAS-SAMUEL, KALIN NORMOET
Television producer, television journalist. **Personal:** Born Nov 20, 1961, Baltimore, MD; daughter of Louis N Thomas and Katherine Foote Thomas. **Educ:** Howard Univ, Wash, DC, BA, Broadcast Jour, 1983. **Career:** Cable News Network, Atlanta, Ga; Cable News Network Travel Now Prog, corresp. **Orgs:** Vice chair, Atlanta Asn Black Journalists, 1991-93; Nat Asn Black Journalists, 1983-; Women Communs, 1980-83 & 1990-96; Sigma Delta Chi, Soc Prof Journalists, 1980-83, 1990-93; Alpha Kappa Alpha Sorority Inc, 1981-. **Honors/Awds:** Media Access Awards (2), Nat Easter Seals, 1989; Michigan Outdoor Writer's Award, Michigan Outdoor Writer's Association, 1990; Emory O Jackson Journalism Award, AK Sorority Inc, 1992; Nat Easter Seals EDI Award, 1993; Atlanta Asn Black Journalist Award, Feature Series, 1997; Md Off Tourism Develop Award, 1997. **Home Addr:** 829 Omaha Dr, Norcross, GA 30093. **Business Addr:** Correspondent, Cable Network News, 1 CNN Center, Atlanta, GA 30303, **Business Phone:** (404)827-2300.

THOMAS-WILLIAMS, ELAINE
Executive director. **Career:** Conn Minority Supplier Develop Coun, exec dir, 2002. **Orgs:** Nat Found Teaching Entrepreneurship. **Honors/Awds:** Woman of the Year, African Am Affairs Comn, 2001.

THOMAS-WILLIAMS, GLORIA M.
Association executive. **Personal:** Born Jul 5, 1938, New York, NY; married Evrard Williams; children: Michelle. **Educ:** NY Univ, Brooklyn Col. **Career:** Gloria Thomas Modeling Sch, prop; Schaefer Brewing Co, mgr pub rels; WCBS-TV, dir community affairs; Network Serv Inc, chief exec officer. **Orgs:** Prof Commentator; Mistress Ceremonies. **Honors/Awds:** Outstanding Achievement Award, Bottle & Cork Sales, 1970; Best Fashion Commentator, Cabaret Prods, 1971; Awards, Black Found Educ Sickle Cell, 1973; Woman of the Year, 1972; Community Service Award, 1973; Police File Commendation, 1974; Outstanding Performance of Community Service Strivers Award, The Guardians Asn, 1976; Community Service Award, Mt Calvary Methodist Ch, 1976; Alma John Community Service Award, 1984; Cert of Appreciation, Nat United Licensees Beverage Asn Inc, 1972; Certificate of Commendation, Nat Asn Visually Handicapped, 1979; Good Sportsmanship & Outstanding Service, WCBS-TV; Award of Merit, WCBS-TV, 1982; Mothers of Freedom Reward, 1984. *

THOMAS-WILLIAMS, JOVITA
Vice president (Organization). **Personal:** Born in Detroit, MI. **Educ:** Tuskegee Inst, BS; Cornell Univ, MBA & MILR. **Career:** AlliedSignal Automotive, dir corp human resource; Pepsi-Cola's Mich Bus Unit, dir human resource; Textron Automotive Co, vpres human resource; MGM Grand Detroit Casino, vpres human resource, 2003-. **Honors/Awds:** Secretary of Defense Employer Support Freedom Award, Under Secy Defense Personnel & Readiness, 2006. **Home Addr:** Detroit, MI. **Business Addr:** Vice President of Human Resources, MGM Grand Detroit Casino, 1300 John C Lodge, Detroit, MI 48226-2414.

THOMPAS, GEORGE HENRY, JR.
Law enforcement officer. **Personal:** Born Jun 26, 1941, Philadelphia, PA; son of George and Olliebea; married Sharon Patton (divorced); children: George III, Orlando, Rhonda, Troy, Derek, Tanay, Jason & Brandi. **Educ:** Fed Bur Law Enforcement Training Sch, cert, 1969; Philadelphia Police Acad, police officer, 1971; St Lukes & C Med Ctr, cert, 1973; Community Col Philadelphia, AA, 1978; Pa State Police Cert, spec instr; Munic Police Officers Educ & Training Comn, instrs cert. **Career:** Reading Railroad (Conrail), railroad policeman, 1968-71; City Philadelphia, police officer, 1971-85; Watterson Sch Bus & Technol, dir security training, 1985-; Philadelphia Housing Authority, police officer, 1986-; Dept Treas, policefield training officer. **Orgs:** Variety Club for Handicapped Children, 1968-; Guardian Civic League, 1971-; Fraternal Order Police, 1971-; Missing C Inc, 1986; brethren, Mount Olive Lodge No 27 F&AM, 1988. **Honors/Awds:** Public Service Safeway demonstrations for senior citizens groups and organizations, 1978-; Beneficial Suggestion Award, US Treas, 1998, Cash Award; Performance Award, 1998; Beneficial Suggestion Award; Special Award. **Military Serv:** AUS, PFC, 1963-66. **Home Addr:** 7943 Bayard St, Philadelphia, PA 19150, **Home Phone:** (215)549-7947. **Business Addr:** Police Officer, United States Mint, 151 N Independence Mall E, Philadelphia, PA 19106, **Business Phone:** (215)408-0114.

THOMPSON, AARON A
Government official. **Personal:** Born Jul 23, 1930, Philadelphia, PA; son of Alonzo A and Helen M Montier Blythe; divorced 1991; children: Aaron G, Brion R, Shelley L, Lillian E, Marsha L & Eugene. **Career:** Bell Telephone Penn, Philadelphia, PA, syst technician, 1986; City Camden, Camden, NJ, councilman, 1989-90, mayor, 1990-93. **Orgs:** Chmn, City Camden Parking Authority, 1988-89; bd mem, Cooper's Ferry Develop Asn; life mem, Telephone Pioneers; Camden Co NAACP; pres, Parkside Little League; pres, Parkside PTA.

THOMPSON, ALBERT N.
Chief executive officer, president (organization). **Career:** Vending Mach, owner, 1965; Pabst Blue Ribbon, wholesaler, 1975; Falstaff, wholesaler, 1975; Abelsons, retail beverage outlet owner; Pabst Blue Ribbon Prod, New York State, master wholesaler; Pabst Brewing Co, New York State Opers, dir, currently; Housing Authority Police Force, lt; Off Dist Atty, Invests Div, lt; Consol Beverage Corp, chief exec officer & pres, currently. **Orgs:** Founder, Bernice Riley Thompson Scholar Fund, 1985; Urban Resource Inst; Culinary Inst Am; Regional Plan Asn; NY City Partnership; NY Urban League; Harlem Dowling Soc; Serv Acad Review Bd Comn; Toys for Tots; Marine Corps Jr Cadets Scholar. **Honors/Awds:** Honor, Nat Chinese Women's Soc. **Military Serv:** USMC, master sgt, active & reserves, 30 yrs; Desert Storm. **Business Phone:** (212)926-5865.

THOMPSON, ALICIA
Basketball player. **Personal:** Born Jun 30, 1976, Big Lake, TX. **Educ:** Tex Tech, attended 1998. **Career:** Player (retired); New

York Liberty, forward, 1998; Indiana Fever, forward, 2000-02; NWBL,2002; Seattle Storm, forward, 2004-05. **Orgs:** Children's Miracle Network; ambassador, Stormin' the Sound off-season community program. **Honors/Awds:** Texas Tech Athletics Hall of Fame, 2008. *

THOMPSON, DR. ALVIN J
Physician. **Personal:** Born Apr 5, 1924, Washington, DC; son of Victor J Thompson Sr and Aurelia Pinchot Speller; married Faye; children: Michael, Donna, Kevin, Susan & Gail. **Educ:** Howard Univ, Col Liberal Arts, attended 1940-43, BS, 1981; Howard Univ Med Sch, MD, 1946; St Louis City Hosp, internship, 1946-47; St Louis Hosp, residency, 1947-51. **Career:** Pvt Practice, physician gastroenterology internal med, 1957-; Providence Hosp, gastroenterol lab founder, dir, 1963-77; Univ Wash, Sch med, clin prof; Providence Hosp, chief med, 1972-74; Veterans Admin Hosp, Univ Hosp, Harborview Med Ctr, attending physician; Providence Hosp, Swedish Hosp Med Ctr, attending staff; Veterans Admin Seattle, physician gastroenterologist, 1953-59. **Orgs:** Certified Am Bd Internal Med, 1953, recertified, 1974; alternate delegate, 1974-80 delegate, 1980-89; Inst Med, Univ Wash, 1955-; Am Med Asn; gov Am Col Physicians for Wash & Arkansas, 1974-78; Wash State Med Asn; Wash State Soc Internal Med; Puget Sound Health Planning Bd; Puget Sound Health Systems Agency; King Co Med Soc; King Co Comprehensive Health Planning Coun; King Co Blue Shield; Seattle Acad Internal Med; Providence Hosp; Am Col Physicians; Am Med Asn; Am Gastroenterologic Asn; Am Soc for Gastrointestinal Endoscopy; N Pacific Soc Internal Med; Am Soc Internal Med; Inst Med Nat Acad Scis; Nat Med Asn; pres, WSSIM, med staff Providence Hosp, KCMS, WSMA, Seattle Acad Med, State Asn Black Profs in health care, delte AMA, Pres, Wash State Asn for Biomedical Res; Seattle King County Bd Health. **Honors/Awds:** Kappa Cup for Superior Scholarship, Howard Univ, 1941; Robt H Williams Superior Leadership Award, Seattle Acad Internal Medicine, 1979; Inst med, Nat Acad Scis, 1978; Coun for Cooporate Responsibility Seattle Chamber Com, 1983; Nat Asn Med Minority Educrs for Outstanding Contrib in Health, 1983; Philanthropist of the Year, 1989; Wash Give's; Seattle Links Inc, Human Rights Day Award; Master, Am Col Physicians; Alpha Omega Alpha. **Special Achievements:** Publications: "Pernicious Anemia in the Negro," co-author, Journal of the Natl Med Assn, 1948; "Klebsiella Pneumoniae Meningitis," Archives of International Medicine, 1952, "Mesenteric Valvular Insufficiency," Northwest Medicine, 1962; numerous other editorials and articles. **Military Serv:** Appointed US Naval Acad, 1940; Howard Univ, ROTC, 1940-43, pfc, commanding officer, ASTP, 1943-46; AUS, first lt, 1946-48; US Air Force, capt, 1951-53; US Air Force Reserve, major, 1953-59. **Home Addr:** 8222 Avalon Dr, Mercer Island, WA 98040. **Business Addr:** Physician, 1600 E Jefferson No 620, Seattle, WA 98122, **Business Phone:** (206)325-3520.

THOMPSON, ANITA FAVORS
Government official. **Personal:** Born Feb 8, 1951, Kansas City, KS; daughter of Abraham and Barbara Franklin Neal; married Wayman Walter Favors, Sep 6, 1970; children: Jocelyn, Wayman Jr & Ahmad Khalil. **Educ:** Park Col, Parkville, MO, BA, 1977; Cent Mich Univ, MA, pub admin, 1981. **Career:** Area Agency on Aging, Kansas City, KS, 1973-82; City Kans City, asst city adminr, 1982-83; Kans State Dept Soc & Rehab Serv, Adult Serv, comnr, 1983; City Tallahassee, dep city mgr, 1990-95, sr asst city mgr, 1995-97, city mgr, 1997-. **Orgs:** NAACP; NFBPA; ASPA; Tallahassee Urban League; Alpha Kappa Alpha; ICMA; Nat Women Achievement Inc; PTI; NAPA; Tallahassee Chap Links Inc. **Honors/Awds:** Presidential Scholar, Park Col, 1977; Black Woman of Distinction, YWCA,Yates Branch, 1982; In Service to Kansas City Award, Panhellenic Coun, Kans City, 1983. **Special Achievements:** First African Am & first woman to become city manager in Tallahassee, FL. **Business Addr:** City Manager, City of Tallahassee, City Hall 300 S Adams St, Tallahassee, FL 32301, **Business Phone:** (850)891-2000.

THOMPSON, HON. ANNE ELISE
Judge. **Personal:** Born Jul 8, 1934, Philadelphia, PA; daughter of Leroy Henry and Mary Elise Jackson Jenkins; married William H, Jun 19, 1965; children: William H Jr & Sharon A. **Educ:** Howard Univ, Wash, Dist Columbia, BA, 1955; Temple Univ, Philadelphia, PA,MA, 1957; Howard Univ Sch Law, Wash, Dist Columbia, LLB, 1964. **Career:** Off of the Solicitor US Labor Dept Chicago, staff atty, 1964-65; Legal Aid Soc of Mercer Co, staff atty, 1966-67; Trenton, asst dep pub defender, 1967-70; Twp of Lawrence NJ, prosecutor, 1970-72; City of Trenton, muni ct judge, 1972-75; Mercer Co Trenton NJ, prosecutor, 1975-79; US Dist Ct, New Jersey, fed judge, 1979, sr dist judge, 2001-. **Orgs:** Am Bar Asn; NJ St Bar Asn; Fed Bar asn; Mercer County Bar Asn; Comt Munic Cts, 1972-75; deleg, Democratic Nat Conv, 1972; vice chmn, Mercer County Criminal Justice Planning Comt, 1972; NJ Supreme Ct, 1975-79;v pres, NJ County Prosecutors Asn, 1978-79; chmn juvenile justice comt, Nat Dist Atts Asn, 1978-79. **Honors/Awds:** Asn Black Women Lawyers Award, 1976; Distinguished Service Award, Nat Dist Atty Asn, 1979; Outstanding Leadership Award, NJ Co Prosecutors Asn, 1980;Gene Carte Memorial Award, Am Criminal Justice Asn, 1980; John Mercer Langston Outstanding Alumnus Award, Howard Univ Law Sch, 1981. **Special Achievements:** Notes ed, Howard Law Rev; first woman & first African-Am Co prosecutor, NJ; first African-Am to be appointed a judge of the US Dist Ct for the Dist NJ. **Business Addr:** Senior District Judge, United States District Court, Clarkson S Fisher Fed Bldg, 402 E State St Room 2020, Trenton, NJ 08608, **Business Phone:** (609)989-2123.

THOMPSON, ANTHONY
Entrepreneur. **Career:** Kwame Bldg Group Inc, pres & chief exec officer, currently. **Business Addr:** President, Chief Executive Officer, KWAME Building Group Inc, 1204 Wash Ave Suite 200, Saint Louis, MO 63103, **Business Phone:** (314)862-5344.*

THOMPSON, ART
Journalist. **Personal:** Born May 29, 1955, San Francisco, CA; son of Arthur Jr and Ocie Mae Matson; children: Arthur IV & Ania Rashida. **Educ:** W Los Angeles Col, Culver City, CA, AA, gen studies, 1976; Calif State Univ, Chicago, CA, BA, info & commun, 1978; Valley Electronics Sch, Van Nuys, CA, first class broadcasters license, 1980; Univ Ariz, Inst J Educ, Tucson, AZ, 1982. **Career:** Wave Newspapers, Los Angeles, CA, sports ed, 1978-81; Modesto Bee, Modesto, CA, sportswriter, 1981-84; St Louis Post-Dispatch, St Louis, MO, sportswriter, 1985-88; Orange Co Register, Santa Ana, CA, writer, 1988-. **Orgs:** Comt mem, Los Angeles Chap, Jack Yates Sr High Alumni; Baseball Writers Am Asn; Nat Asn Black Journalists; Pro Football Writers Am; Southern Calif Asn Black Journalists; US Basketball Writers Asn; Football Writers Asn Am; nat secy, NABJ Sports Task Force. **Honors/Awds:** Excellence Award, Greater St Louis Asn Black Journalists, 1988; Writing Award in News, Asn Press Sports Eds, 1990, 1992-; Writing Award, Asn Pub Serv Excellence, 1992; Orion Hall of Fame, 2007. **Business Addr:** Writer, Orange County Register, 625 N Grand Ave, Santa Ana, CA 92701, **Business Phone:** 877-469-7344.

THOMPSON, DR. BEATRICE R
Psychologist. **Personal:** Born May 5, 1934, Townville, SC; daughter of Elliott Rice and Canary Rice; married Harry S; children: Randy, Stephen & Darryl. **Educ:** SC State Univ, BA, attended; Atlanta Univ, MA, Eng, 1973; Univ GA, PhD, 1978. **Career:** Anderson, SC, High Sch Eng teacher, 1954-65, High Sch guid counselor, 1967-71,. sch psychologist, 1972; Tri-Co Tech Col, psychol instr, 1972-74; Westside Community Ctr, exec dir, 2006-. **Orgs:** Anderson United Way Bd; City Councilwoman, Anderson, SC, 1976-; SC Nat Bank Bd; Crippled C Bd; Family Counseling Bd; elected SC Dem Nat Com Woman, 1980; APGA; SCPGA; SC Pupil Personal Asn; SC Asn Sch Psychologists; NEA; Nat Coun Excep C; Nat Asn Black Psychologists; sec, Human Relations Coun; den mother; vol Cancer Soc; chmn, Sch Dist Five, Counselor Orgn; SC Pers & Guid Asn; pres, Zonta Int Bus & Prof Womens Club; Delta Sigma Theta Sor; Phi Kappa Phi Hon Soc; Phi Delta Kappa Hon Soc; sec-treas, SC AMEG; sec-treas, Anderson Family Counseling Ctr; pres, SC Municipal Asn, 1987-88. **Honors/Awds:** NDEA Guid & Counseling Fel; Gen Elec Guid Fel; South Carolina Headstart Association Award; The Omega Fraternity Citizen of the Year; South Carolina Party Service Award; The Beatrice Thompson Municipal Park. **Special Achievements:** First African-American elected to the Anderson City Council. **Home Phone:** (864)224-1990. **Business Addr:** Executive Director, Westside Community Center, 1100 W Franklin St, Anderson, SC 29622, **Business Phone:** (864)260-1093.

THOMPSON, BENJAMIN FRANKLIN
Administrator. **Personal:** Born Aug 29, 1947, Philadelphia, PA; married JoAnne Snow; children: Kaif. **Educ:** Boston State Col, 1974; Cambridge Col, MEd, 1979; Kennedy Sch Govt Harvard Univ, MPA, 1982. **Career:** MA Halfway Houses Inc, prog dir, 1975-78; MA Dept Corrections, dir prog, 1978-80; MA Dept Soc Servs, area dir, 1980-82; Dept Soc Servs, consult, 1983-84; Suffolk Cty Penal Dept, comnr, 1984-; Cty Boston, sr policy adv equal & humans rights, dep mayor, 1984; sch bus company, owner; Boston STRIVE, Exec Dir, currently. **Orgs:** Intl Halfway Houses Inc, 1976-84, Am Correctional Assoc, 1977-84; chmn Mayors Coordr Coun drug Abuse, 1984-85; candidate Boston Cty Coun, 1984. **Military Serv:** USAF, sgt, 4 yrs. **Business Addr:** Executive Director, Boston Strive, 434 Harrison Ave, Boston, MA 02118, **Business Phone:** (617)825-1800.

THOMPSON, BENNIE
Football player. **Personal:** Born Feb 10, 1963, New Orleans, LA. **Educ:** Grambling State Univ. **Career:** Winnipeg Blue Bombers, Canadian Football League, 1986-88; New Orleans Saints, defensive back, 1989-91; Kans City Chiefs, 1992-93; Cleveland Browns, 1994-95; Baltimore Ravens, 1996-99. **Honors/Awds:** CFL All-Star, 1988; Pro Bowls, 1991, 1998; Ed Block Courage Award, 1995; Unsung Hero Award, Playoff Corp, 1996.

THOMPSON, BENNIE G.
Government official, congressperson (u.s. federal government), politician. **Personal:** Born Jan 28, 1948, Bolton, MS; married London Johnson; children: BendaLonne. **Educ:** Tougaloo Col, BA, 1968; Jackson State Univ, MS, 1972. **Career:** Meadville, Miss, teacher, 1968-70; Tri-Co Community Ctr, proj dir, 1970-74; Town Bolton, alderman & mayor, 1973-79; Hinds Co, supvr, 1980-93; US House Reps, congressman, 1993-; Miss Second Dist, dem congressman, currently. **Orgs:** Asst dir, Teacher Corps, 1974-; chmn, bd, Farish St YMCA; Mt Beulah Develop Found; vchmn, bd, The Delta & Ministry; bd dir, S Regional Coun; Am Civil Libs Union; Asbury United Methodist Church; Kappa Alpha Psi Fraternity Inc. chmn, U.S. House Committee on Homeland Security, 2006. **Honors/Awds:** Outstanding Young Men of Miss Award, NAACP; Outstanding Personalities of South, 1971; Politician of the Year, Jackson State Col, 1973; 'Alumnus of the Year Award', Utica Jr Col, 1974; ranking mem, Homeland Security Comn, 2005. **Special Achievements:** The longest-serving African-Am elected official in the state of Mississippi; The first African American to chair the Homeland Security Committee in the House. **Home Addr:** PO Box 146, Bolton, MS 39041. **Business Addr:** Democratic Congressman, Mississippi Second District, 107 W Madison St, PO Box 610, Bolton, MS 39041, **Business Phone:** (601)866-9003.

THOMPSON, BETTE MAE
Librarian. **Personal:** Born Nov 12, 1939, Washington, DC; daughter of Louis Merritt and Dorothy Louise Hunter; married Jerry Ward O, May 3, 1963 (divorced 1980). **Educ:** Antioch Col, Yellow Springs, OH, BA, 1962; Univ Mich, Ann Arbor, MI, AMLS, 1968. **Career:** Librarian (retired): Perry Nursery Sch, Ann Arbor, MI, teacher, 1962-67; Detroit Pub Libr, Detroit, MI, children's librn, 1969; Ann Arbor Dist Libr, Ann Arbor, MI, ref libr, 1970-2004. **Orgs:** Am Libr Asn; Black Caucus Am Libr Asn; Pub Libr Asn; Mich Libr Asn; Asn African Am Librarians Mich. **Honors/Awds:** Beta Phi Mu. **Home Addr:** 648 Cloverdale St, Ann Arbor, MI 48105.

THOMPSON, REP. BETTY LOU
Government official, association executive. **Personal:** Born Dec 3, 1939, Helm, MS; daughter of William Sam Bolden and Lubirtha Lacy; married Jack Thompson, Jan 1, 1958; children: Anthony, Tyrone, Sonja & Kwame. **Educ:** Harris Teachers Col, BA, 1962; Hubbard Bus Col, cert, 1965; Wash Univ, cert, 1972. **Career:** Human Develop Corp, area coordr, 1964-90; Daniel Boone PTO Univ City, past pres, 1977-78; Women Munic Govt, past pres, 1983-84; St Louis Co Govt, spec asst, 1991-97; St Louis County, dist 72 rep, 1997-; MLK Mo Support Group, pres; K&M Delivery Serv, owner, currently; Mo House Rep, rep, currently. **Orgs:** Pres, Black Women Unity, 1975-79; Camp Fire Girls, 1982; pres, Dr MLK, 1988-89; Nat Asn Advan Colored People; Nat League Cities; Nat Asn Media Women; Better Family Life; pres, Dr Martin Luther King Jr St Louis Support Group. **Honors/Awds:** Community Service Award, Zeta Phi Beta Sorority, 1973; George Washington Carver Award, 1977; Employee of the Year, Human Develop Corp, 1978; Martin Luther King Leadership Award, 1985; Best Speaker of the Year Award, 1986-87; Dr MLK Award, 1987-88; Employee of the Year Award, 1989; Gwen Giles Award; Drum Major Peace Award; St Louis Caring Communities Humanitarian Award; Outstanding Legislative Mother of the Year Award; KMOX & Suburban Journal Women of Achievement Award; Ernest & DeVerne Lee Calloway Award. **Home Addr:** 8315 Seville Ave, St Louis, MO 63132. **Business Addr:** Representative, Missouri House of Representatives, Rm 134 201 W Capitol Ave, Jefferson City, MO 65101, **Business Phone:** (573)751-4265.

THOMPSON, BETTY TAYLOR
Educator. **Personal:** Born Feb 6, 1943, Houston, TX; daughter of John Charles Taylor and Johnnie Mae Hart Brooks; married Oliver B Thompson Jr, Oct 20, 1985; children: Amnon James Ashe II & Ida Elizabeth. **Educ:** Fisk Univ, BA; Atlanta Univ, MSLS; Howard Univ, MA, PhD. **Career:** Tex Southern Univ, prof, currently. **Business Phone:** (713)313-7616.

THOMPSON, BOBBIE FAY
Nurse. **Personal:** Born Dec 26, 1952, Moddy, TX; daughter of Leonard and Vera Henderson; married Chester Odell, May 25, 1986; children: Torey Ann Moore. **Career:** Tex Instruments, assembly worker, 1972-79; Am Dist Teleraph, dispatch oper, 1979-80; Leisure Lodge Nursing Home, CNA, 1981-82; Camlu-Care-Ctr, CNA, 1984-94; Heartland, CNA, 1994-97; Manor Care W, Certified Nurses Aide, 1997-2002. **Orgs:** Secy, Jeff Hamilton Homemaker Extension Club, 1996-00; vpres, Exclusive Golden Girls Club, 2001-02; pres, Eastside Neighborhood Watch Asn, 2000-02. **Honors/Awds:** Employee of the Month, Leisure Lodge Nursing Home, 1982; Employee of the Month, Camlu Care Center, 1992; Employee of the Month, Heartland, 1995; Humanitarian, Ebony Cultural Society, 2001; Employee of the Month, HCR Manor Care West, 2001. **Home Phone:** (254)773-3506.

THOMPSON, HON. BOBBY E.
Mayor. **Personal:** Born Aug 15, 1937, Florence, AL; son of William and Althea Thompson Lovelace; married Vera L Pride, Sep 3, 1960; children: Cheryl L & Karen E Thompson-Sprewer. **Career:** Mayor (retired); Uptown Meat Mkt, Waukegan, IL, owner, 1972-75; United Ins Co, Chicago IL, agent, 1977-83; City N Chicago, mayor, 1983-97. **Orgs:** Lake Co Econ Develop Comn, Community Action Bd; potentate, Prince Hall Shriners; 33rd Degree Mason, Rufus Mitchell Lodge No 107 Prince Hall; Nat Asn Advan Colored People, 1976-; blue ribbon comt mem, Nat Prince

Hall Shriners, 1988. **Honors/Awds:** Distinguished Service Award, We Do Care, 1981; Trend-Setter Award, LeMoyne-Owen Col Alumni Asn, 1989; Top Black Elected Off, Ill Black Elected Off, 1990.

THOMPSON, REV. CARL EUGENE
Insurance executive, clergy, real estate executive. **Personal:** Born Aug 9, 1953, Siler City, NC; son of Robert L and Minnie L; married Karen Mechelle McClain, May 3, 1981; children: Carla Michelle, Karen Nicole & Carl E Jr. **Educ:** NC Central Univ, BA, Philos, 1976; Univ Mass, Amherst, Masters Reg Planning, 1985, Duke Univ, attended 1992. **Career:** Town Pittsboro, patrolman, 1976-78; Home Security Life Ins Co, sales rep, 1978-80; N State Legal Servs, legal asst, 1980-83; licensed realtor, 1982-; Capital Development Inc, chief exec officer, 1982-; Charlotte Liberty Mutual Ins Co, sales rep, 1984-; Chatham Co, co comnr; Monumental Life Ins Co, sales rep, 1986-; Thompson Insu & Realty, owner, 1992-96; Beulah United Church of Christ, pastor, 1992-95; Thompson Insu & Realty, owner, currently; Central Carolina Community Col, workplace literacy coordr, Continuing Educ Pittsboro Campus, dir, currently, ABE instr, 1996-; Word of Life Christian Outreach Ctr, founder & co-pastor, currently. **Orgs:** Bd dirs, Capital Health Syst Agency, 1978; bd dirs, Joint Orange Chatham Comn Action 1980; bd dirs, Coun Aging Chatham Co, 1983; NC Woodcutters Asn, 1984-; Rural Econ Develop consult, 1984-; consult, Soc, Security 1984-; assoc minister, Wesley Chapel United Church Christ, 1986-; bd trustees, Central Caroline Tech Col, 1986-; chairs, County Minority Exec Comt. **Honors/Awds:** Nat Rural Fel, Nat Rural Fellows Inc NY, 1983-84. **Special Achievements:** In 1978, Mr. Thompson ran for the Chatham County Board of Commissioners and became the first African-American elected to the board. **Home Addr:** 67 Robert Thompson Rd, Bear Creek, NC 27207. **Business Addr:** Pastor, Word of Life Christian Outreach Center, PO Box 1068, Liberty, NC 27298, **Business Phone:** (919)837-2407.

THOMPSON, CAROL BELITA (CAROL THOMPSON COLE)
Government official. **Personal:** Born Aug 5, 1951, Washington, DC. **Educ:** Smith Col, BA, 1973; NY Univ, MPA, 1975. **Career:** Govt Dist Columbia, spec asst housing, 1979-81, dep mayor oper, act dir licenses, inv, 1981-83, dir consumer & reg affairs, 1983-86, mayor's chief staff, 1986-87, dep mayor econ develop, 1987-91; RJR Nabisco Inc, vpres govt & environ affairs; Pres Clinton, spec adv; Brookings Greater Wash Res Ctr, leadership coun mem; Curtex Group, adv; Venture Philanthropy Partners, pres & chief exec officer, currently. **Orgs:** Bd mem, Nat Conf Christians & Jews 1983-; bd mem, Ronald McDonald House, 1985-; bd pres, Asbury Dwellings Home Sr, 1985-; fel NASPFAA Urban Admin; co-chairperson, DC Downtown Partnership, 1987-; vpres proj planning, Fed City Coun; Lifetime Trustee, Urban Inst; trustee, Smith Col; bd dir, DC Agenda Support Corp. **Honors/Awds:** Martin Luther King Jr Fel; Outstanding Young Women in Am, 1982; Outstanding Prof Serv Award, Nat Asn of Negro & Professional Women, 1987; Outstanding Govt Serv Award, Nat Black MBA Asn, 1987. **Special Achievements:** First woman to be appointed City Administrator. *

THOMPSON, DR. CHARLES
Educator. **Personal:** Born Jan 15, 1954, Tachiakawa, Japan; son of Charles Thompson and Eiko Thompson; married Tita, Oct 28, 1975; children: Danielle, Lara & Charles. **Educ:** NYU, BE, 1976; Polytechnic Univ, MS, 1978; MIT, PhD, 1982. **Career:** Mass Inst Technol, teaching asst, 1978-81; Virginia Polytechnic Inst, asst prof, 1982-86; dir, Lab Comput Studies; Univ Mas, Lowell, dir, Lab Adv Comput; assoc prof, 1987-93, prof elec eng, 1993-, assoc dean, 1994-96; Center for Adv Comput & Telecommunications, co-dir, 1992-. **Orgs:** Acoustical Soc Am, fel, 1982-; Am Phys Soc, 1984-; NSBE, advisor, 1987-90, 1992-; Lucent Tech Bell Labs, fel bd, 1991-99; Soc Manufacturing Eng, sr mem & fac adv, 1996-99; Inst Elec & Electronic Engrs, sr mem, 1996-; AT&T Labs, fel bd, 1996-; SWE, advisor, 1995-97; fac adv, Soc Women Eng, 1995-96; Tau Beta Pi; fel Acoustical Soc Am. **Honors/Awds:** Outstanding Young Men in America Award, 1983; Analog Devices, Analog Devices Professor, 1987; Univ Mass, JE Blackwell Scholar, 1994; Tau Beta Pi, Eminent Engineers, 1995; President Award for Excellence in SME, 1997; AT&T Labs, Charles Thompson Mentor Award, 1998. **Special Achievements:** Proficient in: acoustics; telecommunications; computational engineering; fluid dynamics; linear/non linear systems. **Business Addr:** Professor, University of Massachusetts, Department of Electrical & Computer Engineering, 1 Univ Ave, Lowell, MA 01854, **Business Phone:** (978)934-3360.

THOMPSON, DR. CHARLES H.
Business owner, swimmer. **Personal:** Born May 24, 1945, Kimball, WV; son of Herbert and Ardella Richardson; married Harriet Jones, Jul 2, 1982; children: Charles Jr, Kellye, Eric & NaShawn. **Educ:** Fisk Univ, BS, 1967; Tenn State Univ, MA, 1968; LA State Univ, PhD, 1989. **Career:** Southern Univ, swimming coach, 1968-70; Dillard Univ, swimming coach, 1970-74; Tuskegee Univ, assoc prof, physical educ, 1975; Tuskegee Univ, head basketball coach 1975-88; Charlie Tees Screen Printing, owner, 1982-. **Orgs:** Kappa Alpha Psi, 1966; Aquatics dir, YMCA; Am Swmng Coaches Assoc; Am Alliance Health Phys Educ & Rec ARC; aquatics adv, Rec Dept 1973-74; Nat Assoc Basketball Coaches; pres, SIAC Basketball Coaches Assoc; info dir, SIAC, 1981-85. **Honors/Awds:** First Black Swimming Champion So AAU Coached, 1973; SIAC Coach of the Year, 1979; SIAC Championships, 1979, 1980, 1982. **Home Addr:** 1204 Johnson St, Tuskegee, AL 36088, **Home Phone:** (334)727-6957. **Business Addr:** Owner, The Great Tuskegee Trading Company, 1311 Old Montgomery Rd, Tuskegee, AL 36086, **Business Phone:** (334)724-0308.

THOMPSON, CLARISSA J.
Educator, school principal. **Personal:** Born Feb 24, 1930, Sugar Land, TX; divorced; children (previous marriage): Chanthini & Emmitt (divorced); children: Chanthini & Emmitt. **Educ:** Tex Southern Univ, BA, 1951, M.Ed, 1965. **Career:** Abraham Schwartz Firm, asst acct, 1951-52; WDSN High Sch, eng math teacher, 1952-55; Houston Independent Sch Dist, eng teacher, 1955-65, counr, 1965-71; Neighborhood Youth Corps, counr, 1970; Sharps town Jr High Sch, asst prin, 1971. **Orgs:** Harcourt Brace Invitational Conf, 1966; coun mem, Delta Sigma Theta Sorority, One Am Proj, 1970-72; TSTA Conv Dist IV, 1974; HPA Exec Bd, 1974-75; HPA Rep Consult Comt Opers, 1974-75; Asn Super & Curric Develop; TASCD; HASCD; Tex Asn Sec Sch Prins; Tex State Teachers Asn; Houston Prin Asn; Houston Coun Educ; Phi Delta Kaapa Fraternity; Blue Bonnet Garden Club; Macgregor Civic Club.Thompson.

THOMPSON, DR. CLEON FRANKLYN
School administrator. **Personal:** Born Nov 1, 1931, New York, NY; son of Cleon F Sr and Maggie Eady; married; children: Cleondra Thompson Jones. **Educ:** NC Cent Univ, BS, biol, 1954, MS, biol, 1956; Duke Univ, PhD, educ admin, 1977. **Career:** UNC-Chapel Hill Med Sch, sr research assistant; NC A&T State Univ, asst prof; Tuskegee Univ, asst prof & actg chmn, dept biol; Shaw Univ, vpres acad affairs, 1970, sr vpres, 1971-73; Univ NC, acting vpres, 1975-76, vpres stud serv & spec prog; Shaw Univ, Raleigh, interim vpres instnl advan, currently; Winston-Salem State Univ, chancellor emer, 1985-95. **Orgs:** Adv coun NC Comn Col Syst, 1978-81; bd dir, Shakespeare Festival, 1978-81; pres, Leadership Winston-Salem; bd dirs, Winston-Salem Bus. **Honors/Awds:** Man of the Year, Kappa Alpha Psi, 1970; ACE Fellowship Acad Admin Am Council on Educ, 1970-71. **Special Achievements:** Cleon F. Thompson Center named in honor. **Military Serv:** AUS, 2nd lt, 1953-55; Citation AUS Med Corps. **Business Addr:** Interim Vice President for Institutional Advancement, Shaw University, 118 E S St, Raleigh, NC 27601, **Business Phone:** (919)546-8260.

THOMPSON, DANIEL JOSEPH
Lawyer. **Educ:** Tuskegee Inst, attended 1948; Brown Univ, BA, 1970; Harvard Law Sch, JD,1973. **Career:** St Ala, asst atty gen, 1973-74; Auburn Univ, instr, 1974; Long Aldridge Honor Stevens & Summer, GA, atty, 1974-77; S Cent Bell Tel Co, atty, 1978-79; AT&T Co, Wash, DC, atty, 1979-. **Orgs:** Vpres, Ala Black Lawyers Asn, 1974; Am Bar Asn, 1975-80; bd dir, Atlanta Urban League, 1975-77; exec comt mem, Gate City Bar Asn, 1977; Atlanta Judicial Comn, 1977; Nat Bar Asn. **Business Addr:** Attorney, American Telephone & Telegraph Company, 1120 20th St NW 1000, Washington, DC 20036.

THOMPSON, DAVID (DAVID FARROD THOMPSON)
Football player. **Personal:** Born Jan 13, 1975, Okmulgee, OK. **Educ:** Okla State Univ, speech commun. **Career:** Football player (retired); St Louis Rams, running back, 1997-98; Nat football League Europe, Amsterdam Admirals, 1999. **Honors/Awds:** Carroll Rosen bloom Memorial Award, St Louis Rams, 1997.

THOMPSON, DAVID FARROD. **See THOMPSON, DAVID.**

THOMPSON, DAVID O'NEIL
Executive. **Personal:** Born Jul 13, 1954, Shelby, NC; son of Vellie and Ida; married Cathy; children: Erika & Brooke. **Educ:** NC State Univ attended 1975. **Career:** Basketball player (retired), motivational speaker; Denver Nuggets, guard, 1975-82; Seattle Supersonics, guard, 1982-85; Charlotte Hornets, youth progs coordr, 1988. **Orgs:** FCA; X NBA Players Asn; YMCA. **Honors/Awds:** Carolina's Athlete of the Year, 1973, 1974; named All Atlantic Coast Conf Player of the Year 1973, 1974, 1975; Three time First Team, All America, NAI Smith Award, 1975; Eastman Award Collegiate Basketball Player of the Year, 1974-75; Consensus College Player of the Year, 1975; Rookie of the Year, ABA, 1975-76; named CO Athlete of the Year 1975; All Star Game ABA, 1976; All Star NBA, 1977-79, 1983; Leading Vote Getter, All Star Game, 1977; Inducted into Scored 73 points in one game, 1978; Sports Magazine Performer of the Year, Pro Basketball, 1978; All NBA 1st Team, 1977, 1978; only player named MVP in both ABA & NBA All Star Game; Scored 10,000th point 1981; NC Sports Hall of Fame, 1982; Joe Mallamo Humanitarian Award, 1994; Carolina's Athlete of the Year, 1994; Named One of Five Best College Players in History, 1995; Naismith National Basketball Hall of Fame, 1996; Colorado Sports Hall of Fame, 1996.

THOMPSON, DR. DEBORAH MARIA
Physician. **Personal:** Born May 4, 1958, Philadelphia, PA; daughter of William C and Hazel Logan; married Omer Abadir, May 29, 1982; children: Adam Omer Abadir, Alia Marie Abadir & Amira A Abadir. **Educ:** Howard Univ, BS (Magna Cum Laude), 1980; Howard Univ, Col Med, MD, 1982; Univ Md, Post Grad, 1985. **Career:** Dept Family Med, Univ Md, chief resident, 1984-85; Community Health Ctr, med dir, 1985-89; Mid-Atlantic Permanente Med Group, Wash, DC, physician, 1989-. **Orgs:** Am Acad Family Physicians; Md Acad Family Physicians, 1989-. **Honors/Awds:** Alpha Omega Alpha Medical Honor Soc, 1982-; Dipl, Am Bd Family Practice, 1985-92, recertified, 1997-04; fel, Am Acad Family Physicians. **Business Addr:** Primary Care Lead Physician - Marlow Heights Medical Center, Mid-Atlantic Permanente Medical Group, 5100 Auth Way, Suitland, MD 20746.

THOMPSON, DEHAVEN LESLIE
Journalist. **Personal:** Born Aug 22, 1939, Philadelphia, PA; married Patricia Marlene Eberhardt; children: Shannon Leslie, Tara Neile. **Educ:** Geneva Col, BA, 1968. **Career:** Beaver Falls News Trib, 1st blk sports reporter 1959-64, 1st blk asst sports ed 1964-66; WTAE-TV & WTAE, RADIO AM Pittsburgh, ed-reporter 1966-70; Black Chronicle TV Show, 1968; WTAE-TV Pittsburgh, producer, assginment ed, 1970-75; WIIC-TV Pittsburgh, news & sports, reporter. **Orgs:** Pittsburgh Press Club; bd mem, Pittsburgh Pastoral Inst; Sigma Delta Chi; Pittsburgh Youth Motivation Task Force; Bob Moose Memorial Fund Comn. **Honors/Awds:** Penn Asso Press Award, Top Sports & News Story of Yr, 1973; Golden Quill Award Series, on Handicapped Athletics, 1977; Meritous Serv Award, Penn Hills NAACP, 1977. **Military Serv:** USNG, 6 yrs. *

THOMPSON, DERRICK
Music publisher. **Personal:** Born May 3, 1963, East St Louis, IL; son of John and Stevonne Gulley. **Educ:** Columbia Univ, BA, 1985. **Career:** EMI Music, dir sales, 1991-92; BMG Music Pub sr dir artist & repertoire,1993-97, vpres, artist & repertoire, 1998-2001, sr vpres, urban music,currently. **Honors/Awds:** Network Journal, 40 under 40 Award, 2000. **Business Addr:** Vice president, BMG Music Publishing, 1540 Broadway 28th Fl, New York, NY 10036, **Business Phone:** (212)930-3930.

THOMPSON, DR. EDWIN A.
College president. **Career:** Atlanta Metrop Col, GA, pres, pres emer, currently. **Business Phone:** (404)756-4044.

THOMPSON, ERIC R. **See Obituaries section.**

THOMPSON, FLOYD. **See Obituaries section.**

THOMPSON, FRANCESCA
School administrator, nun. **Personal:** Born Apr 29, 1932, Los Angeles, CA; daughter of Edward and Evelyn Preer. **Educ:** Marian Col, BA, 1960; Xavier Univ, MEd,1963; Univ Mich, PhD, 1972. **Career:** Marian Col, Indianapolis IN, chairperson theatre dept, 1966-82; Fordham Univ, asst dean & dir, currently, assoc prof African American studies, 1982-. **Orgs:** Fac, Martin Luther King Fellows 1973-; Broadway Tony Bd; Martin Luther King Jr Fel; adv bd, PUSH; Am Acad Theatre Fellows, 1998-. **Honors/Awds:** Key to the City, Clarksdale MS 1978, Cincinatti; Brotherhood Award, Nat Conf Christians & Jews; Jan 12 1981 declared by Mayor of Oakland CA to be Sister Francesca Thompson Day in appreciation for being "Scholar in Residence" for Oakland Public Sch System; Dr Martin Luther King Human Rights Award Indianapolis Educ Asn; NY State English Council Award Teacher Excellence Drama; Distinguish Alumnus Award Marian Col; Outstanding Teacher of the Year, Fordham Univ, 1986; Pierre Toussaint Award, Outstanding Service to the Black Catholic Community; Koob Award; NCEA Award, Outstanding Educator; Honorary Degrees: LeMoyne Col, Syracuse, NY, St Michael Col, Winooski, VT, Marian Col, Indianapolis, IN; Outstanding Alumnus Award, Dept of Theatre, Univ of MI, Ann Arbor, MI; American Theatre Asn Col of Distinguished Theatre Fellows; Appreciation for Research; Film Festival, 2001. **Special Achievements:** Sagamore of the Wabash Awd, IN gov; Commendation of Achievement, OH IN & TX senators. **Business Addr:** Assistant Dean, Director of Multicultural Affairs / Assistant Professor, Fordham University, McGinley Ctr Suite 211, 441 E Fordham Rd, Bronx, NY 10458, **Business Phone:** (718)817-4738.

THOMPSON, GAIL L.
Executive. **Personal:** Born in Brooklyn, NY. **Educ:** Pratt Inst; MBA. **Career:** NJ Performing Arts Ctr, vpres; Performing Arts Ctr Greater Miami, proj dir, 1999-04. *

THOMPSON, GARLAND LEE
Journalist, college teacher, executive director. **Personal:** Born May 2, 1943, Chester, PA; divorced; children: Consuella Alicia & Grace Lynn. **Educ:** Temple Univ, BA, journ, 1975, JD, 1983. **Career:** Bell Tel, PA, switchman, 1963-73; Philadelphia Community Col, instr GED preparation course, 1975-76; Philadelphia Inquirer, copy ed, 1975-78, ed writer, 1978-81, reporter, 1981-84; Philadelphia Tribune, exec ed; Sun, ed writer, 1992; Career Commun Group Inc, dir; Univ Baltimore Law Sch, prof; Hampton Univ, prof; US Black Engr & Info Technol & Hispanic Eng & Info Technol, ed dir. **Orgs:** Joint Comt Minority Editorialists, Broadcast Ed Asn, 1979-81; Nat Asn Black Journalists; Nat Conf

Ed Writers, 1979-81; fac ed, Inst Jorrn Ed-Editing Prog Minority Journalists, 1980, 1981, 1985; PA Bar Asn, 1984-. **Honors/Awds:** Barrister's Award, Temple Univ, 1982; Univ Kans, Freedom Forum Prof-In-Residence, 1992-93. **Special Achievements:** First African-American member, Inquirer Ed Bd, 1978-81; ed of nation's oldest African-American newspaper, Philadelphia Tribune; Put together largest single editorial in the Tribunes history, 100 pages, 1984. **Military Serv:** USN, electronics tech 2nd class, 1965-68; 2nd Honorman, 1966. **Home Addr:** Baltimore, MD 21278. *

THOMPSON, GAYLE ANN-SPENCER
School administrator. **Personal:** Born Aug 17, 1956, Detroit, MI; daughter of Edward Spencer Sr (deceased) and Annie R Spencer (deceased). **Educ:** Marygrove Col, BA, 1979, MA, 1989. **Career:** Marygrove Col, dir residence, 1978-79, coordr of stud servs, 1980-91, dir talent search, 1991-94; Marygrove Col, Job Placement & Developer, coordr, 1994-. **Orgs:** Marygrove Alumni Asn, pres-elect, 1990-, mem at large, 1989-90; Midwest Asn Stud Fin Aid ADM, 1992-; Because of Christ, tutor, 1992-; Marygrove Col Alumni Asn, president, 1993-. **Honors/Awds:** Marygrove Col, Iota Gamma Alpha, 1975-79; Southern Womens Athletic Conference, hon mention, 1977; Panelist Award, Mich Consolidated Gas Co, 1992; Martin Luther King, Chavez, Rosa Parks Col Day, presenter, 1992. **Business Addr:** Director, Renaissance Talent Search Project, Marygrove College, 8425 W McNichols Rd Rm 027, Detroit, MI 48221, **Business Phone:** (313)862-8000 Ext 225.

THOMPSON, GERALDINE
Nurse, consultant, educator. **Personal:** Born in Dunkirk, NY; daughter of George T and Hattie Dickey; married John W Thompson Sr, Nov 17, 1942; children: John Jr, Brian & Dennis. **Educ:** Jamestown Sch Practical Nursing, 1954; Jamestown Comn Col, 1968. **Career:** Jamestown Gen Hosp, staff nurse, 1954-75, psych nursing, 1975-85; Southern Chautaugua County, strategic planning consul, human serv agencies, currently. **Orgs:** Bd dirs, Ebony Task Force, 1984-; bd dirs, 1972-75, 1985-, bd pres, 1990-92, Jamestown YWCA; bd dirs, Jamestown Community Schs Coun, 1988-95;bd dirs, Chautauqua County Sch Bds Asn, 1987-90; Nat Caucus Black Sch Bd Mems; vice chair, Selective Service Bd, 1985-; vpres, Jamestown Democratic Women's Club, 1990-92; Jamestown Bd Pub Utilities, 1991-96; The Links Inc, Jamestown Chap, 1995-. **Honors/Awds:** Adv Comn Minority Issues New York State Sch Bds Assoc, 1987-90; Jamestown Woman of the Year, 1991; New York State's Governors Award for African American of Distinction, 1993. **Special Achievements:** First Woman Pres Jamestown Sch Bd, 1983-85; First black on Selective Serv Bd. **Home Addr:** 95 Liberty St, Jamestown, NY 14701, **Home Phone:** (716)664-5526.

THOMPSON, GLENDA M
Executive, marketing executive. **Personal:** Born Jun 20, 1954, Fort Worth, TX; daughter of Willie E Murray; married Tyron, Jun 23, 1984; children: Glenn Murray. **Educ:** Tex Christian Univ, BFA, commun, 1988. **Career:** WA Conv & Vistors Asn, conv sales exec, 1989-92; Aoni Shoreham Hotel, corp sales exec, 1992-94; Paul Quinn Col, dir alumni affairs, 1994-97; Gestures Mkt Commun, founder & pres, 2003-. **Orgs:** Bd mem, YMCA, E Br, 1996-; Pub Rels Soc Am, 1998-; bd mem, Ft Worth Metrop Black Chamber Comn, 1998-; Am Pub Transp Asn, 1998-; bd mem, Prevent Blindness, 1999-; vpres & secy, Neighborhood Link. **Honors/Awds:** Outstanding People in Tarrant County, Ft Worth Star Telegram, 1988; Outstanding Business Woman, Dollars & Sense Mag, 1990; Eagle Award, Ft Worth Black Chamber Com, 1999; Most Fascinating Blacks, Ft Worth Black News, 1999. **Home Addr:** 7413 Arbor Hill Dr, Fort Worth, TX 76120. **Business Addr:** Founder, President, Gestures Marketing Communications, PO Box 8702, Fort Worth, TX 76124, **Business Phone:** (817)907-5934.

THOMPSON, GLORIA CRAWFORD
Lobbyist, government official. **Personal:** Born Aug 12, 1942, Philadelphia, PA; divorced. **Educ:** Cheyney State Univ, PA, BS, Ed, 1968; St Joseph Col, PA, MBA, 1978; Temple Univ, PA, Pub Rels, 1962; Univ Pa, PA, Real Estate, 1973, Master, Govt Admin, 1990. **Career:** SmithKline Beckman Corp, adv & sales promo, 1968-72, news rels assoc, 1973-75; Opportunities Industrialization Ctr Am, ed, OIC Keynens, 1970-72; Nat Alliance Businessmen, dir, col rels, 1974-76; Smithkline Beckman Corp, adv & Sales prom, 1968-72, news rels asn, 1973-75, pub affairs asn, 1975-87, assoc mgr, Pa govt, 1987-; Ross Assocs, Philadelphia, PA, corp rels consult, 1989-. **Orgs:** Former nat secy, Nat Asn Mkt Developers (NAMD); Philadelphia Chap Pres (NAMD); Pub Affairs Comn PA, Chamber Com; State Govt Comn, Philadelphia Chamber Com; bd dir, Art Matters Inc; vchmn, bd dirs, Cheyney Univ Found, chmn, 1988-; Mayor's Office Community Serv, Adv Bd; Minority Retention Task Force, Hahnemann Hosp Univ. **Honors/Awds:** Pres Gerald Ford, 1975; dist award, Dr Charles Drew Awards Comn, 1980; recognition, Nat Alliance Businessmen, 1975; 'marketer of the Year', Nat Asn Mkt Developers, 1974; hon prof, Prairie View State Univ, 1975; Outstanding Young Women in Am, 1979-80. **Business Addr:** Public Affairs, Pennsylvania Federation of CDCs, 523 E Vernon Rd, Philadelphia, PA 19119, **Business Phone:** (215)848-9843.

THOMPSON, HERMAN G
Lawyer. **Personal:** Born in Cincinnati, OH; son of Roscoe and Thelma; married Roberta Brown; children: Collette Hill & Janice Marva. **Educ:** Ludwig Col Music, BME, 1952; Harris Teacher's Col, BA, 1957; Howard Univ, Sch Law, JD, 1968. **Career:** Charlotte, NC, asst dist atty, 1972; Pvt pract, atty, Wash, DC 1975-77, Southern Pines, NC, 1980-; US House Reps Post Off & Civil Serv Comn, atty, 1977-80. **Orgs:** Atty Com Dept, Off Minority Bus Enterprise, Wash, DC, 1972; pres, Moore County Chap, Nat Asn Advan Colored People, 1985-; chmn, Minority Affairs, Moore County Republican Party, 1985; NC State Bd Transportation, 1987-91; NC Asn Community Col Trustees. **Honors/Awds:** Community Service Award, NC Black Lawyers Asn, 1994; Freedom & Justice Award, Moore Co, NC, Nat Asn Advan Colored People, 1983. **Military Serv:** AUS, Pfc. **Home Addr:** 510 NW Broad St, PO Box 1181, Southern Pines, NC 28387-4805, **Home Phone:** (910)692-5500.

THOMPSON, IMOGENE A.
Educator. **Personal:** Born Aug 13, 1927, Stonewall, MS; married Rev Marcellous C; children: Marcellous C & Gail P. **Educ:** Jackson State Univ, BS, 1959; Univ Wis, MS, 1967. **Career:** Teacher (retired); Meridian Pub Sch, teacher, 43 Yrs. **Orgs:** Pres, Bapt Ministers' Wives Alliance, 1976-80; Lay Adv Com State Dept Ed, 1977-81; State Bd Mgrs Representing MS Congress Parents & Teachers, 1977-81; ed Com C of C 1979-81; pres, Asn Meridian Educrs, 1979-81. **Honors/Awds:** Outstanding Leadership Award, State Teachers Asn, 1976; Human Relationship Award, State Teachers Asn, 1976; 11th Edition Personalities of the State, Am Biographical Inst, 1980; MS Teacher of the Yr, State Dept Ed, 1980.

THOMPSON, JAMES W.
Dentist. **Personal:** Born Jan 8, 1943, Birmingham; married Charlie Mae; children: Scott Frederick. **Educ:** BS, 1970; DDS, 1974. **Career:** Wayne State Univ, tissue cult tech, 1961-65; Univ Tenn, 1965-67; Difco Labs, 1967-71; Wayne Co Community Col, 1971-74; Detroit Maternal & Infant Care Proj, dent, 1974-75; Jackson MI Pvt Prac, dent, 1975-. **Orgs:** Jackson Dist Dental Soc; Wolverine Dental Soc; Univ Detroit Black Dental Alumni Asn; career prog Detroit Pub Schs; Detroit Head Start Proj, Dental Svcs; Detroit Jaycees; C Hosp Christmas Party Com; Omega Psi Phi Frat; chmn Soc Act Com. **Honors/Awds:** Nat Health Prof Scholar; Robt Tindal Scholar.

THOMPSON, JEFFREY EARL
Certified public accountant, executive. **Personal:** Born Apr 13, 1955, Mandiville, Jamaica. **Educ:** Univ DC, BBA, 1980. **Career:** Nat Rifle Asn, asst comptroller, 1978-80; Mitchell/Titus & Co, sr acct, 1980-81; Leeny Redcross & Co, mgr, 1981-83; Thompson, Cobb, Bazilio & Assocs, PC, pres, 1983-, chief exec officer & founder, 1998-. **Orgs:** Am Inst Certified Pub Accountants, 1978-; Alumni Asn Col Bus & Pub Admin, Univ DC, 1980-; Nat Asn Black Accountants, 1980-; chair tax issues subcomt, DC Chamber Com, 1985-; bd dirs, Metrop Wash Airports Authority, 1998; treas, Lincoln Theater Found; finance chair, 100 Black Men Greater Wash; chair budget comt, 100 Black Men Am Inc. **Honors/Awds:** Most Outstanding Accounting Graduate, Univ DC, 1980; Most Outstanding Alumni, Univ DC, 1986; Honorary Doctor of Laws, 1997. **Home Addr:** 322 Peabody St NW, Washington, DC 20011. **Business Addr:** Founder President, Cheif Executive Officer, Thompson Cobb Bazilio & Associates PC, 1101 15th St NW Suite 400, Washington, DC 20005.*

THOMPSON, JESSE M.
School administrator. **Personal:** Born Nov 3, 1946, Oxford, MS; son of Irma Thompson and Jesse Thompson; children: Stacey L Thompson & Latoya S Taylor. **Educ:** Mott Community Col, AA, 1968; Eastern Mich Univ, BA, 1970; Univ Mich, MA, 1975; Central Mich Univ, MS, 1980. **Career:** Intake, Assessment & Referral Ctr, exec dir, 1973-88; Detroit Col Bus, mgt instr, 1976-; Mich St Univ, Sch Criminal Justice, staff specialist, 1980-85; CS Mott Community Col, treas, bd trustees 1980-87, dir human resources, 1990; City Flint, dir personnel & labor rels, 1988-90; Bunker Hill Community Col, exec vpres & chief financial officer, currently. **Orgs:** Chmn, Genessee County Criminal Justice Staff Adv, 1981-84; Flint Asn Black Adminr, 1981-84; Paul Harris Fel, Rotary Int, 1983-; Governor's Substance Abuse Adv Comn, 1989-91. **Honors/Awds:** Humanitarian of the Year, Flint Inner-City Lions Club, 1980; Social Worker of the Year, Mich Asn Black Social Workers, 1981. **Business Addr:** Executive Vice President, Cheif Financial Officer, Bunker Hill Community College, 250 New Rutherford Ave, Boston, MA 02129-2995, **Business Phone:** (617)228-2000.

THOMPSON, JOHN R
Executive. **Educ:** Mercy Col, BS, bus mgt. **Career:** Best Buy Co, Supply Chain & Bus Syst, sr vpres, 2001, BestBuy.com, sr vpres & gen mgr, currently; Gen Elec Co, mkt, finance & oper positions, Info Serv Div, mem; HP/Compaq, direct sales & ecommerce logistics position; DHL, Customer Logistics Solutions, mgr; Am Bus Develop Support & Prog Mgt Group, mgr; Goods Family Clothing Inc, chief info officer & exec vpres merchandise planning & logistics; Lee Apparel Co, vpres info syst & dist; Liz Claiborne Inc, chief info officer; Retail Syst Alert Group Inc, survr. **Orgs:** Nat Retail Fedn, Info Technol Coun; Voluntary Inter-Indust Commerce Stand; Best Buy C Found; Wendy's Int Inc; The Black Retail Action Group Inc. **Special Achievements:** Named one of the "75 Most Powerful Blacks in Corporate America" by Black Enterprise, 2005. **Business Addr:** Senior Vice President, General Manager, BestBuy.com, 7601 Penn Ave S, Richfield, MN 55423, **Business Phone:** (612)291-1000.*

THOMPSON, JOHN ROBERT
Basketball coach, basketball player. **Personal:** Born Sep 2, 1941, Washington, DC; son of Robert Thompson and Anna Thompson; married; children: John III, Ronald & Tiffany. **Educ:** Providence Coll, BA, econ, 1964, MA, guidance & counseling, UDC, 1971. **Career:** Basketball player, basketball coach (retired); Boston Celtics, 1964-66; St Anthony's High Sch, Wash, DC, head basketball coach, 1966-72; Georgetown Univ, Wash, DC, head basketball coach, 1972-99; US Olympic Basketball Team, asst basketball coach, 1976, head basketball coach, 1988; Commentator, TNT, Clear Channel Radio & Sports Talk 980, currently. **Orgs:** Past pres, bd of dir, Nat Asn Basketball Coaches, 1976-; trustee,Basketball Hall of Fame; Selection comt for several int & natcompetitions; Nike, bd of dirs, 1991-. **Honors/Awds:** NIT Championship Team, 1963; inducted into Providence College Hall of Fame, 1974; President's Award, Patrick Healy Award, Georgetown Univ, 1982; LHD Hon, St Peter's Coll, 1982; HHD, Wheeling Coll, 1982; US Basketball Writer's Assn Coach of the Year & The Sporting News, 1983-84, Natl Assn of Basketball Coaches, 1984-85; Big East Conference, 1979-80, 1986-87; Naismith Memorial Basketball Hall of Fame, 1999. **Home Addr:** 3767 Jay St NE, Washington, DC 20019. **Business Addr:** Board of Directors, Nike, One Bowerman Dr, Beaverton, OR 97005.

THOMPSON, JOHN W
Chief executive officer, executive, chairperson. **Personal:** Born Apr 24, 1949, Fort Dix, NJ; son of John H and Eunice; married Sandi; children: John E & Ayanna. **Educ:** Fla A&M, bus mgt, 1971; Mass Inst Technol, Sloan Sch Mgt, mgt sci, 1982. **Career:** IBM, sales rep, 1971-75, br off mgr, 1975-79, regional admin asst, regional mkt dir, 1980-84, asst to chief exec officer, 1984, dir midwest opers, 1990-93, head mkt US opers, 1993, gen mgr personal software prods, 1994-98; IBM Americas, gen mgr, 1997-99; Symantec Corp, chief exec officer & chmn bd dirs, 1999-; Nat Infrastructure Adv Comt, 2002; bd dir, Fortune Brands Inc; bd dirs, UPS; bd dirs, Seagate. **Orgs:** Bd dirs, Northern IN Pub Serv Co (NiSOURCE); bd dir, Teach for America; chair, Silicon Valley Blue Ribbon Task Force Aviation Security & Technol. **Business Addr:** Chairman of theBboard of Directors, Chief Executive Officer, Symantic Corp, 20300 Stevens Creek Blvd, Cupertino, CA 95014, **Business Phone:** (408)253-9600.

THOMPSON, JOHNNIE
Government official, army officer. **Personal:** Born Jan 10, 1930, Walterboro, SC; married Thelma; children: Anita, Glenn & Rochelle; married Thelma Clemmons, Jan 1, 1956; children: Anita, Glen Ronald & Rochelle. **Educ:** Palmer Col, AD, pub serv, criminal justice maj, 1976; Rice Bus Col, Charleston, SC. **Career:** Army Officer (retired), Council Member; Colleton County Polit Action, pres & founder, 1969; City Walterboro, Teledyne Inc, production supvr, 1971-83; Big-O Chrysler, new car salesman; City Walterboro, city councilman, coun mem, 1979-, mayor pro-tem, 1991-95, democrat, currently. **Orgs:** First exalted ruler, Colleton City Elk Lodge, 1975; 32nd Degree Mason; NAACP; Am Legion; Mt Olive Baptist Church; Tuskegee Airmen Inc; charter mem, TAI, Hiram E Mann, chap; Retired Enlisted Asn; SC Aviation Asn; George Wash Carver Consistory 162; Mystic Shrine Arabian Temple 139. **Honors/Awds:** Noble of the Mystic, Shrine Arabion Temple 139; Bronze Level of Professional Sales Chrysler, 1984; Salesman of the Year, Big-O Chrysler Plymouth Dodge; Recognition for COT Service, APA, Beta Kappa Lambda chap, 2001; Humanitarian Awd, Walterboro-Colleton Chamber of Comm, 2002. **Military Serv:** AUS, 1948-78; Armored Tank Platoon Sgt; Army Commendation; CIB; Bronze Star; Korean Pres Citation; Retired after 20 yrs hon serv served 11 mo combat in Korean War. **Home Addr:** 502 Padgett Loop, Walterboro, SC 29488. **Business Addr:** Democrat, Council Member, City of Walterboro, 242 Hampton St, Walterboro, SC 29488, **Business Phone:** (843)549-2545.

THOMPSON, DR. JOSEPH EARL, SR.
School administrator. **Personal:** Born in Columbia, SC; son of Hale B and Margaret Elizabeth Kennedy; married Shirley Williams, Nov 27, 1969; children: Shirley Elizabeth, Joseph Earl Jr & Amber Gale. **Educ:** Union Theol Sem, MDiv; New York Univ, MA, MEd, EdD. **Career:** School administrator (retired); Johnson C Smith Uni, Charlotte, NC, dir freshman sophomore studies, 1970-72; Southern Asn Cols & Sch, Atlanta, GA, assoc exec dir, 1972-84; Talladega Col, Talladega, AL, acad dean, 1984-88, interim pres, 1988-91; Atlanta Univ Ctr, Woodruff Library, exec dir. **Orgs:** Life mem, Nat Asn Advan Colored People; Kappa Delta Pi; Nat Asn Col & Univ Chaplains, 1960-72. **Honors/Awds:** DHL, Talladega Col, 1990.

THOMPSON, JOSEPH ISAAC
Postmaster general. **Personal:** Born Aug 21, 1922, Amelia County, VA; married Mabel K; children: Sina Joann. **Educ:** VA Union Univ, 1942. **Career:** US Post Serv, postmaster; pres, Postal

Worker's Union WI; Madison WI, alderman, 5 yrs. **Orgs:** Grand lect Prince Masonic Lodge; WI Dept Health & Soc Serv Oral Exam Bd; pres, City Madison Water Comn, 1970-75; Nat Asn Postmasters US. **Honors/Awds:** Sup Accomplish Award, Postal Serv, 1968. **Military Serv:** WW II vet.

THOMPSON, KAREN ANN
Financial manager. **Personal:** Born Jun 12, 1955, Fairborn, OH; daughter of Jack Long and Marlien Vaughn. **Educ:** Univ Mich, BS, 1977; Ind Univ, MBA, 1984. **Career:** Coopers & Lybrand, auditor, 1977-79; Cummins Engine Co, int collections mgr, 1979-82; Daimler Chrysler Corp, finance mgr; Automation Alley, mgr, Info Security, currently. **Orgs:** Alexis De Tocqueville, Univ Mich; dir, Am heart Asn Eastern Mich; treas, Port Huron Mus Arts & Sci; dir, Blue Water Area Am Heart Asn. bd dir, Nat Alumni Asn, Univ Dayton, 2001-. **Honors/Awds:** Certified Public Accountant State of IN 1980; Fellowship Consortium for Grad Study in Mgt, 1982-84. **Special Achievements:** Library Certificate, OH Hist Soc. **Home Addr:** 17576 Glenwood Blvd, Lathrup Village, MI 48076-2707. **Business Addr:** Manager, Information Security, Automation Alley, 2675 Bellingham, Troy, MI 48083, **Business Phone:** (248)457-3200.

THOMPSON, KEVIN LAMONT
Basketball player. **Personal:** Born Feb 7, 1971, Winston-Salem, NC. **Educ:** NC State Univ, attended. **Career:** Portland Trail Blazers, 1993-94; Illycaffe Trieste, Italy, 1994-95; Scavolini Pesaro, 1995-97; Viola Reggio Calabria, 1999-2000; Lineltexlmola, 2000-01; Polaris World Murcia, Spanish ACB; Plus Pujol Lleida, Spanish LEB, currently. **Business Addr:** Professional Basketball Player, Plus Pujol Lleida, Pavello Barris Nord, 25005 Lleida, BR, Spain.

THOMPSON, LANCELOT C. A.
Educator. **Personal:** Born Mar 3, 1925, Jamaica; son of Cyril Alfonso Thompson (deceased) and Vera Leolyn Reid Thompson (deceased); married Naomi E; children: Lancelot Jr, Carol Lynn & Angela Maria. **Educ:** Morgan State Univ, BS, phys inorganic chem, 1952; Wayne State Univ, PhD, 1955. **Career:** Wolmers Boys Sch, teacher, 1955-56; Penn State Univ, res fel, 1957; Univ Toledo, asst prof, 1958; asst dean, 1964; vpres, prof, 1966, dean of stud serv, 1966, vpres stud affairs, 1968-88, prof emer chem, 1988-. **Orgs:** Sigma Xi, 1956; Phi Kappa Phi, 1963; Blue Key 1964; chmn, local sect Am Chem Soc; NY Acad Sci; exec com, Nat Stud Personnel Adminrs, 1972; ed bd, NASPA Journ, 1972; pres, local group Torch Int, 1974; vice chmn, Toledo Red Cross, 1990-91; pres, Univ Toledo Retirees Asn, 1997-98; Ohio Coun Higher Educ Retirees, pres, 1998-99; Mayor's Com on Alcoholism; Toledo Develop Com; life mem, Nat Asn Advan Colored People. **Honors/Awds:** Key to Golden Door Award, Int Inst, 1973; Distinguished Bro Award, Midwestern Reg, Alpha Phi Alpha Frat, 1973; George F Hixton fel, 1999; Dr. Lancelot C.A. Thompson Academic Achievement Program, named in honor, Univ Toledo. **Special Achievements:** First Black Vice President of Student Affairs, Univ Toledo. **Business Addr:** Professor Emeritus, University of Toledo, 2801 W Bancroft, Toledo, OH 43606-3390, **Business Phone:** (419)530-2567.*

THOMPSON, LARRY D
Lawyer. **Personal:** Born Nov 15, 1945, Hannibal, MO; son of Ezra and Ruth Robinson Baker; married Brenda Taggart; children: Larry Jr & Gary. **Educ:** Culver-Stockton Col, Canton, MO, BA, 1967; Mich State Univ, MA, 1969; Univ Mich, Ann Arbor, JD, 1974. **Career:** Ford Motor Co, ind rels rep, 1969-71; Monsanto Corp, staff atty, 1974-77; King & Spalding, assoc, 1977-82, partner, 1986-2001; US Dept Justice, Northern Dist Ga, US atty, 1982-86; Dept Housing & Develop Investn, independent coun, 1995-99; US Dept Justice, dep atty gen, 2001-. **Orgs:** Am Bar Asn; Gate City Bar Asn; State Bar Ga; Mo Bar Asn; Nat Bar Asn; Ga Community Bicentennial US Const; bd dir, Atlanta Urban League; bd dirs, Woodward Acad, Col Park, GA; chmn, Ga Lawyers Bush, 1988; bd dirs, Ga Republican Found, 1989; chmn, Press Nat Security Coord Coun, 2001; Nat Asian Pac Am Bar Asn. **Honors/Awds:** District Alumni Award, Culver-Stockton Col, 1983; AT Walden Award, Gate City Bar Asn, 1984; Outstanding Achievement Award, Fed Bar Asn, 1992. **Home Addr:** 2015 Wallace Rd, Atlanta, GA 30331, **Home Phone:** (404)349-5297. **Business Addr:** Deputy Attorney General, US Department of Justice, 950 Pa Ave NW, Washington, DC 20530-0001, **Business Phone:** (202)353-1555.*

THOMPSON, LASALLE, III
Basketball player, business owner, basketball coach. **Personal:** Born Jun 23, 1961, Cincinnati, OH; married; children: Nickolas & Ruby. **Career:** Baskeball player (retired), basketball coach, business person; Kansas City Kings, 1983-85; Sacramento Kings, 1986-89; Ind Pacers, 1989-95, 1997; Denver Nuggets, 1996-97; San Diego Wildfire, gen mgr & head coach, 2000-01; Lasalle, strength and conditioning coach, currently; Prime Time Motors, Calif, co-owner. **Business Addr:** Co-Owner, Prime Time Motors, 2557 Albatross Way, Sacramento, CA 95815, **Business Phone:** (916)929-6651.

THOMPSON, LINDA JO
Association executive. **Personal:** Born Aug 29, 1953, Oklahoma City, OK; daughter of Moses E Paulden Jr (deceased) and Emma Lucille Jones Paulden; married French F Thompson Jr, Aug 6, 1977; children: Emerald Michelle & French F III. **Educ:** Lincoln Univ, Jefferson City, Mo, BA, 1975; Strayer Col, MS, bus admin. **Career:** Mid-Am TV, Jefferson City, Mo, off mgr, 1978-84; Zeta Phi Beta Sorority Inc, Wash, DC, exec dir, 1984-95; LJT & Assocs, Clinton, Md, consult, 1995-. **Orgs:** Nat Coalition Black Meeting Planners; bd mem, Nat Pan Hellenic Coun; bd mem, Black Women's Polit Action Forum; Am Soc Asn Exec, 1989-91; Int Soc Meeting Planners, 1990-91. **Honors/Awds:** Grantsman Training Prog, Grantsmanship Ctr, 1990. **Home Addr:** 9601 Hale Dr, Clinton, MD 20735. **Business Addr:** Consultant, LJT & Associates Inc, 9881 Broken Land Pkwy Suite 400, Columbia, MD 21046, **Business Phone:** (443)283-2500.

THOMPSON, DR. LITCHFIELD O
Educator, administrator. **Personal:** Born Apr 15, 1937; married Bernadette Pearl Francis; children: Gennet & Hailu. **Educ:** Univ London, London, UK, BS, sociol, 1969; Univ Oreg, Eugene, MA, sociol, 1972, PhD (sociol), 1975. **Career:** Barbados Advocate Barbados WI, advert clerk, 1955-59, advert layout spec, 1959-61; Ford Found fel, 1972-73; WV St Col, prof, sociol, 1974-, Dept Sociol & Phil, chair, currently. **Orgs:** Am Sociol Asn; N Cent Sociol Asn; Asn Black Sociologists, WV Sociol Asn. **Honors/Awds:** Radfan Medal Aden S Arabia, RAF 1966. **Special Achievements:** Published: "Black Nationalism & the Garvey Movement Toward an Understanding," Black Sociologist, 1978; How Cricket in West Indian Cricket? Caribbean Review, 1983; Franklyn Frazier: Mainstream or Black Sociologist? An Appraisal, Sociological Focus, 1982; "My Journey: From Barbados to the United States," publ in Foreign-Born African-Americans: Silent Voices in the Discourse on Race, Obiakor, 2002. **Military Serv:** RAF, 1961-66. **Business Addr:** Professor, Chair, West Virginia State College, Department of Sociology, 306 Hill Hall, PO Box 1000, Institute, WV 25112, **Business Phone:** (304)766-3145.

THOMPSON, LLOYD EARL
Physician. **Personal:** Born Apr 10, 1934, Kingston, Jamaica; married Mercedee Ball; children: Damon, Arie. **Educ:** Union Col Lincoln NE, BA, 1960; Howard Univ WA DC, MD, 1964. **Career:** Christian Welfare Hosp, chief of staff, 1977-79; Homer G Phillips Hosp, supt; Wash Univ Med Sch, clin instr; Pvt pract, physician; Provena St Marys Hosp, consult. **Orgs:** dipl, 1970, fel, 1972, Am Bd Otolarynology, 1970; pres, St Clair Med Soc, 1979; pres, Community Hosp Bd Dir, 1979; St Louis Ear Nose & Throat Club, Roman-Barnes Soc Ophthalmol & Otolaryngology; bd mem, So Ill Med Utilization Review Org. **Business Addr:** 7210 W Main St, Belleville, IL 62223.

THOMPSON, LOWELL DENNIS
Artist. **Personal:** Born Oct 8, 1947, Chicago, IL; children: Tanya Natasha. **Educ:** Art Inst Chicago, 1966. **Career:** Leo Burnett Co, art dir; J Walter Thompson Co, art dir, prod, & creative group head; McLann Erickson Adv, art dir, 1968-71; Young & Rubicam Adv, art dir, 1971-72; Greenwich Vlg NY, portrait art, 1971; Needham Harper & Steers Adv, art dir & producer, 1972-74; Am Assoc Adv Agencies, teacher, 1974. **Honors/Awds:** Two Awards Rep In Creativity 77 Show, Art Dir Mag; 1st Prize, Lk Meadows Art Fair, 1966. **Special Achievements:** Represented in Commun Arts Magazine, 1976; Honorable Mention Adv Club of NY, 1971; numerous Gold Keys & Scholarships in Scholastic Magazine Annual Art Competition. **Business Addr:** Prudential Bldg, Chicago, IL 60601.

THOMPSON, HON. M T, JR.
Judge. **Personal:** Born Apr 15, 1951, Saginaw, MI; son of M T Sr and Pecola Matsey; married Ivory C Triplet; children: Felica L & Monica R. **Educ:** Oakland Univ, BA, 1973; Northeastern Univ Sch Law, JD, 1977. **Career:** MI Supreme Ct, atty, 1977; Mich Bell Tel Co, mgr, 1973-74; Nat Labor Rels Bd, atty, 1977-79; Lewis White & Clay PC, atty, 1979-83; US Sixth Circuit Ct Appeals, atty, 1980; MT Thompson Jr PC, atty, 1983-97; Supreme Ct, atty, 1984; State Mich Dist Ct, 70th District Court, Saginaw, MI, judge, 1997-. **Honors/Awds:** Author "Institutional Employment Discrimination as a Legal Concept," 1981. **Home Addr:** 2207 Peale Dr, Saginaw, MI 48602, **Home Phone:** (517)790-8033. **Business Addr:** Judge, State of Michigan District Court, 70th District Court, 111 S Mich Ave, Saginaw, MI 48602, **Business Phone:** (517)790-5368.

THOMPSON, MARCUS AURELIUS
Musician, educator. **Personal:** Born May 4, 1946, Bronx, NY; son of H Louise Stewart and Wilmore. **Educ:** Juilliard Sch Lincoln Ctr NYC, BM, 1967, MS, 1968, DMA, 1970. **Career:** Juilliard Sch Lincoln Ctr, viola fac, 1969-70; Oakwood Col, Ala, asst prof music, 1970-71; Wesleyan Univ, Middletown CT, viola fac, 1971-73; Mt Holyoke Col, S Hadley MA, lectr, 1971-73; Mass Inst Technol, prof music, 1973-94, Robert R Taylor prof music, 1995-; New Eng Conserv, viola fac, 1983-; NEA Solo Recitalist fel; viola soloist, currently; MIT Chamber Music Society-a way, founder. **Orgs:** Viola d'Amore Society; Mem, Am Viola Society. **Honors/Awds:** Recip First Prize, Hudson Valley Philharmonic Young Artists Comp, 1967; Winner Young Concert Artist Inc, Auditions NY, 1967; Winner String Prize, Nat Black Colloquim Compet Kennedy Ctr Performing Arts, Wash DC, 1980. **Home Addr:** 11 Waverley Ave, Newton, MA 02458-2103, **Home Phone:** (617)969-4311. **Business Addr:** Robert R Taylor Professor of Music, Massachusetts Institute of Technology, 77 Mass Ave, Cambridge, MA 02139-4307, **Business Phone:** (617)253-1000.

THOMPSON, DR. MARK K
Neurosurgeon. **Personal:** Born Jul 29, 1961, West Islip, NY; son of Charles and Eiko. **Educ:** Harvard Univ, AB, 1983; Tufts Univ Med Sch, MD, 1990. **Career:** Temple Univ Hosp, Surg internship, 1990-91, Temple Univ Hosp Neurosurgery residency, 1991-96; Univ Toronto, Med Staff, NeuroSurg Spine fel, 1996-97; Brady Traumatic Brain Inst, neurosurg dir, 1997-99; Aitken Neuroscience Ctr, res consult, 1997-99; Jamaica Hosp, attend neurosurgeon, 1997-99; Lincoln Hosp, chief neurosurgeon, 2000-01; Columbia Univ, clin asst prof neurosurg, 2000-01; Kings County Hosp, spine dir, 2000-, chief neurosurgeon, 2000-; State Univ NY Downstate Med Ctr, asst prof, 2000-03, interim neurosurg prog dir, 2000-01, vice chmn, dept neurosurg, 2003-. **Orgs:** Am Asn Neurologic Surgeons, 1993-; Cong Neurologic Surgeons, 1993-; Harvard Club NY, 1986-. **Honors/Awds:** Outstanding Young Men of America, US Jaycees, 1984, 1987, 1998; Tufts Med Sch, Ruth Marguerite Easterling Community Service Award, 1990; Police Surgeon, New York Police Dept, 2003. **Special Achievements:** Public Health Dept Western Australia, Royal Flying Doctors of Australia, Aboriginal Health Liaison, 1990; Publ: Postenor Cervical Plate Fixation, 1996; Segmental Reconstruction of the Thoracic Spine with Pedicle Screw Fixation: A Safe and Effective Technique, 1996; Isolated Intramedillary Cervical Sarcoidosis: A Case Report and Review of the Literature, 1997; The Effects of Pentoxifylline on Spinal Cord Blood Flow After Experimental Spinal Cord Injury, 1999. **Business Addr:** Chief of Neurosurgery, Kings County Hospital, 450 Clarkson Ave, PO Box 1189, Brooklyn, NY 11203, **Business Phone:** (718)245-3131.

THOMPSON, DR. MAVIS SARAH (MAVIS BLAIZE)
Physician. **Personal:** Born Jun 22, 1927, Newark, NJ; daughter of Nathaniel Albert and Mavis Carolyn; married James Blaize, Apr 17, 1955; children: Clayton, Marcia Adele Callender, Sidney, Ronald & Kevin. **Educ:** Hunter Col, NYC, BA, 1947; Howard Univ Med Sch, MD, 1953. **Career:** Physician (retired); Kings County Hosp, internship, 1953-54; Kings County Hosp, resident internal med, 1954-57; Brooklyn, NY, pvt practice, 1957-76; Lyndon B Johnson Health Complex Inc, med dir, 1970-71, 1974-76; New York City Bd Educ, sch med instr, 1962-85; Medgar Evans Col, teacher, dept nursing, 1975-76; Kingsboro Med Group, family physician, 1976-95. **Orgs:** Bd dir, Camp Minisink New York City, 1973-; adv comn, Gerontological Serv Ad New Sch for Soc Res, 1983-; bd, Episcopal Health Servs; Am Pub Health Asn, Nat Med Asn, Am Gerontology Asn; den mother BSA; pres, Black Caucus Health Workers Am Pub Health Asn, 1976-77; lic lay St Georges Episcopal Church, Brooklyn. **Honors/Awds:** Community Service Award, St Mark's United Methodist Church, 1973; past pres, Award Black Caucus of Health Workers, 1977; Alberta T Kline Service Award, Camp Minisink 1980; lectr med, Care & Geriatrics, 1984-; Bishop's Cross, Episcopal Church, 1990. **Home Addr:** 2600 Netherland Ave, Bronx, NY 10463, **Home Phone:** (718)601-3652.

THOMPSON, MILT
Baseball player, athletic coach. **Personal:** Born Jan 5, 1959, Washington, DC; married Rhonda Scott, May 27, 1996; children: Torri, Jennifer Brooke, Courtney & Alyssa. **Career:** Baseball player (retired), athletic coach; Atlanta Braves, 1984-85; Philadelphia Phillies, player, 1986-88, 1993-94, coach, 1998-2000, outfield & base running coor dr, 2001-02, hitting coach, 2003-; St Louis Cardinals, outfielder, 1988-92; Houston Astros. 1994-95; Los Angeles Dodgers, 1996; Colorado Rockies, baseball player, 1996; Devil Rays, outfield & base running coor dr, 1997. **Business Addr:** Hitting Coach, Philadelphia Phillies, 1 Citizens Bank Way Citizens Bank Pk, PO Box 7575, Philadelphia, PA 19148, **Business Phone:** (215)463-6000.

THOMPSON, MOZELLE W
Federal government official. **Personal:** Born Dec 11, 1954; son of Charles and Eiko Suzaki. **Educ:** Columbia Univ, AB, 1976, JD, 1981; Princeton Univ, MPA, 1980. **Career:** US Dist Ct, clerk, 1981-82; Skadden, Arps, Slate, Meagher & Flom, assoc, 1982-90; Town of Babylon, NY, spec coun to supr, 1988-90; NY State Housing Financial Agency, NY State Med Care Facilities Financial Agency, NY State Affordable Housing Corp, NY State Municipal Bond Bank Agency, NY State Proj Financial Agency, coun, secy, 1990-93; Fordham Univ, Sch of Law, adj prof, 1992-93; State of NY Mortgage Agency, sr vpres, gen coun, 1993; US Treas Dept, dept asst sec, 1993-96, prin deputy asst secy, 1996-97; Fed Trade Comn, comnr, 1997-2006; Princeton Univ, visiting lectr, 1999; Stanford Law Sch, visiting scholar, 2001; Media Access Proj, bd dir, 2006-. **Orgs:** Vice chair, 1998-01, chair, 2000-, Consumer Policy Community; pres, Int Mkt Supv Network, 1999-00; vpres, Columbia Col Alumni Asn; Asn Black Princeton Alumni; exec bd, Practicing Atty Law Studs; Am Bar Asn; Nat Bar Asn; Asn Bar City NY; Columbia Law Sch Alumni Asn; Orgn Econ Develop & Cooper. **Honors/Awds:** Heritage Award, Columbia Col African-Am alumni, 1999; Mosaic Award, Am Advert Fed, 2003; Distinguished Service Award, Univ Calif, Berkeley Ctr Law & Technol & Boalt Hall Sch Law, 2004.

Special Achievements: Second African American to serve as a commissioner for the Federal Trade Commission; selected to give the annual Paul Robeson Keynote Address, 2002. **Business Addr:** Board Director, Media Access Project, 1625 K St NW Suite 1000, Washington, DC 20006, **Business Phone:** (202)232-4300.

THOMPSON, MYRON HERBERT
Judge. **Personal:** Born Jan 7, 1947, Tuskegee Institute, AL. **Educ:** Yale Univ, BA, 1969; Yale Law Sch, JD, 1972. **Career:** Ala Atty Gen Office, asst atty gen, AL, 1972-74; pvt pract law, 1974-80; Thompson & Faulk, partner, 1979; US Dist Ct, Mid Dist Ala, judge, 1980, chief judge, 1991-98, dist judge, currently. **Orgs:** Ala Bar Asn; State Bar Examrs, 1975-79; Am Bar Asn; Nat Bar Asn; Ala Lawyers Asn. **Special Achievements:** First African-American appointed to the US District Court, Mid District, AL; first African-American assistant attorney general of Alabama. **Business Addr:** District Judge, United States District Court, Middle Alabama, 1 Church St Suite B-100, PO Box 235, Montgomery, AL 36101-0711, **Business Phone:** (334)954-3650.

THOMPSON, PORTIA WILSON
Government official. **Personal:** Born Oct 23, 1944, Washington, DC; children: Lisa-Marie, Joseph M & Jared M. **Educ:** Howard Univ, BA, 1968. **Career:** Bd Governors Fed Res Syst, res asst, 1968-71, programmer 1971-74, econ syst analyst, 1974-80, asst equal employ opportunity dir, 1980-81, mgr equal employ opportunity, bd progs, 1982-84, equal employ opportunity progs officer, 1984-. **Orgs:** Consult, Soul Journey Enterprises, 1979-; life mem, Nat Asn Advan Colored People, 1980-; Am Asn Affirmative Action, 1980-; secy, Nat Black Hist Observance Comn, 1982-83; treas, Nat Black Heritage Observance Comt, 1983-; Friends Bethune Mus Archives Inc, 1984-; Nat Asn Banking Affirmative Action Dirs, 1985-; Friends Dusable Mus, 1985-; secy, Wash Metro Am Asn Affirmative Action, 1985-; Friends Armistad, 1986. **Special Achievements:** Outstanding contributions HD Woodson Sch Bus & Finance 1984-85. **Business Addr:** EEO Programs Officer, Board of Governors, Federal Reserve System, 20th & C Sts NW, Washington, DC 20551, **Business Phone:** (202)452-3693.

THOMPSON, REGINA
Nurse, educator. **Personal:** Born in Beckley, WV; daughter of Elder L and Gracie M Allen. **Educ:** Bluefield St Col, WV, BS; Lincoln Sch Nurses, NY, dipl; Columbia Univ, MA. **Career:** Sea View Hosp, Staten Island, NY, clin instr & actg asst educ dir; WalterReed Gen Hosp, Washington, staff nurse & actg head nurse; USPHS Hosp, NY, staff nurse; Wagner Col Sch Nursing, NY, instr & asst prof nursing; Clemson Univ, Col Nursing, SC, asst prof nursing, prof emer nursing, currently. **Orgs:** Nat Asn Black Nurses; Nat Asn Advan Colored People; Nat League Nursing; SC League Nursing; Am Nurses Asn; SC Nurses Asn; charter mem, Gamma Mu Chap Sigma Theta Int Honor Soc Nurses; SC League Nurses; bd dir, Oconee Chap, Am Red Cross; secy, SC Coun Human Rels; organizer, Oconee Co Chap MADD; SC Joint Pract Comn; chair, Publicity & Pub Rels Comt, Oconee Cancer Trust. **Honors/Awds:** New York Regents fel; Citizen of the Day, Local Radio Station; Woman of Achievement, Lambda Chap, Lambda Kappa Mu Sorority; Certificate of Appreciation, Oconne Co United Way Budget Review. **Special Achievements:** Research: E Colleaque, Hypertension, "Blood Pressure Patterns, Knowledge Level and Health Behaviors in Children and Adolescents," presented in Nairobi, Kenya and the University of South Alabama, 1989; Poetry: entries accepted for publication as follows: Great Poems of our times, National Library of Poetry, 1993, Library of Congress; Named an outstanding poet of 1994 by the National Library of Poetry, Library of Congress; Treasured Poems of America, any sparrow grass poetry, Forum Inc, Library of Congress. **Military Serv:** AUS, Nurse Corps, lt, 1957-60; USAF, Nurse Corps Res, capt. **Business Addr:** Professor Emerita of Nursing, Clemson University, College of Nursing, 714 Strode Tower, PO Box 72, Clemson, SC 29631.

THOMPSON, RHONDA DENISE
School administrator, athletic coach. **Personal:** Born Dec 21, 1969, Bartow, FL; daughter of Linda Thompson. **Educ:** Fla A&M Univ, BS, broadcast jour, 1993; Savannah State Univ, MPA, 2000; Nova Univ, PhD, currently. **Career:** Savannah St Univ, asst track coach, 1995, judicial affairs coordr, 2000-03; Cheyney Univ Penn, head coach, 2004-05, coordr athletic acad advising, 2004-07. **Orgs:** USA Track & Field Officials Asn & Coaches Asn, 1998-; Grad Asn Publ Admin,1999-; adv, Savannah State Univ Student Govt Asn, 1999-, judiciary adv,2000; Savannah State Univ Southern Asn Cols & Schs Intercol AthleticsSteering Comt, 2000; Nat Asn Student Affairs Profs, 2000. **Honors/Awds:** Junior Woman of Excellence, Savannah State Univ Ctr Coun, 1999. **Special Achievements:** Editor, Savannah State Univ Student Affairs Newsletter, 1999.

THOMPSON, RICHARD ELLIS
Educator. **Personal:** Born May 5, 1935, Gary, IN; son of Elija and Roberta May; children: Kevin. **Educ:** Beatty Memorial Hosp, psych-aide training cert, 1955; Ind Univ, Ala, 1956; Roosevelt Univ, BA, 1963, MA, 1966; DePaul Univ, EdM, 1973; Ill Admins Acad, cert, 1989. **Career:** Eduator (retired); Beatty Mem Hosp, psychiatric aide, 1955-56, 1957-58; Lake County C's Home, child care counr, 1958-63; Harlan HS, Chicago Bd Educ, hist teacher, 1963-70; Ill Dept Labor, employ counr, 1966-67; City Cols Chicago, teacher, registr & admin, 1966-70, 1973-79; Mayor's Summer Youth Prog Chicago, training spec, 1976, 1977, 1980-91; Harlan HS, asst prin, 1970-97; Chicago Pub Schs, consult, 1997-. **Orgs:** Chicago Asst Prin Asn, 1973-; Headstart Prog, first Church Love & Faith 1983-, trustee, 1982-; Phi Delta Kappa 1968-; notary pub, Notaries Asn Ill, 1979-; Nat Asn Sec Sch Princ, 1973-; consult, Curriculum Community Sch Educ, Chicago State Univ, 1984-. **Honors/Awds:** Achievement Award, Roosevelt High Sch, 1978; Outstanding Educator of AME, 1975; Outstanding Secondary Educator, AME 1975; Certificate of Apppreciation, Chicago Asst Prin Asn, 1978; Service Award, Div Educ Governors, State Univ Chicago, 1982; Distinguished Service Award, Chicago Asst Prin Asn, 1990. **Special Achievements:** 8 articles. **Military Serv:** USY, E-5, 1959-62; Good Conduct Award, 1961, Certificate of Achievement, 1962, Soldier of the Month, November 1960. **Home Addr:** 500 E 33rd St Apt 1601, Chicago, IL 60616, **Home Phone:** (312)225-5106.

THOMPSON, DR. ROBERT FARRIS
Educator, college teacher. **Personal:** Born Dec 30, 1932, El Paso, TX; married Nancy Gaylord; children: Alicia & Clark. **Educ:** Yale Univ, BA, 1955, MA, 1961, PhD, 1965. **Career:** Yale Univ, fac, 1961-, African & Afro-Am Art Hist, prof, 1964-, Col John Trumbull Prof, currently; Ford Found, res grant, 1962-64; Yale ConciliumInt & Area Studies grant, 1965; Univ Calif Mus Ethnic Arts, vis cur, 1970; Nat Gallery Art, vis cur, 1974; Nat Inst Med & Sci, 1975; Nat Inst MusZaire grant, 1976; Nat Gallery Art grant, 1977, 1979-80. **Orgs:** Am Coun Learned Socs, 1966-73; chmn, Humanities Comt African Studies Asn, 1966-70; African Studies Social Sci Res Coun Joint Comt. **Special Achievements:** Auth: African Influence on the Art of the United States, 1969; Black Gods& Kings, 1971; African Art in Motion, 1974; Four Moments of the Sun, 1981; Flash of the Spirit, 1983; organized exhibitions: The Four Moments of the Sun, 1981; The Face of the Gods: Shrines and Altars of the Black Atlantic World, 1985. **Business Addr:** Col John Trumbull Professor, Yale University, Department Historical Art, PO Box 208272, New Haven, CT 06520.

THOMPSON, RONALD ANTHONY
Basketball coach. **Personal:** Born Apr 7, 1969, Baltimore, MD; son of John and Gwendolyn; married Erica G, May 6, 2000. **Educ:** Georgetown Univ, BA, 1992. **Career:** Prudential, bond trader, 1992-93; Univ Ore, asst basketball coach, 1993-94; Loyola Col, asst basketball coach, 1994-96; Philadelphia 76ers, scout coordinator, 1996-98; Georgetown Univ, asst basketball coach, 1998; Ball St Univ, head basketball coach, 2006. **Orgs:** Black Coaches Asn. **Home Addr:** 6641 Wakefield Dr, Alexandria, VA 22307, **Home Phone:** (703)768-6224.

THOMPSON, ROSIE L
Educator. **Personal:** Born Aug 16, 1950, Macon, MS; daughter of Lula B Little and Willie Lee Little Sr; divorced; children: Cornelius Jr & Reginald Cornell. **Educ:** Jackson State Univ, BS, 1970, MS, 1976, PhD, 1997; Phillips Col, AS; Univ Ark, MEd, 1985. **Career:** Canton Pub Sch, sci teacher, 1970-71; Tougaloo Col, data operator, 1971, teacher, 1983; South Central Bell, data operator, 1972; Miss Sch Blind, teacher, 1972-79, orientation & mobility specialist, low vision clinician, 1985-92, asst prin, 1992-96, sec prin, 1996-98, supt, 1998-. **Orgs:** Bd mem, Asn Educ Blind; Asn Educ & Rehab Blind & Visually Impaired; bd mem, Miss Asn Educ & Rehab Blind & Visually Impaired; Black Women's Polit Action Forum; life mem, Zeta Phi Beta Sorority Inc, 1968-, past regional dir, 1994-96; state coord, Miss Black Women's Polit Action Forum, 1987-89; City Coun, Jackson, MS, 1999; Beta Club, Phi Beta Sigma Fraternity, 1999. **Honors/Awds:** Zeta of the Year, Zeta Phi Beta Sorority Inc, 1983, Outstanding Service Award, 1988, 1991; Outstanding Teacher's Award, Miss Sch Blind, 1988, 1990; Outstand Service Award, Black Women's Polit Action Forum, 1988, 1989; Outstanding Service Award, Miss Asn Educ & Rehab Blind & Visually Impaired, 1991; Community Service Award, 100 Black Women's Coalition, 1993. **Home Addr:** 1254 Eastover Dr, Jackson, MS 39211-6314, **Home Phone:** (601)982-7787. **Business Phone:** (601)984-8203.

THOMPSON, RYAN ORLANDO
Baseball player. **Personal:** Born Nov 4, 1967, Chestertown, MD; son of Earl and Arrie Lee; married Melody Blackstone, Feb 8, 1992; children: Ryan O Jr, Camren D & Taylor A. **Career:** Baseball player (retired); Toronto Blue Jays, prof baseball player, 1987-92; NY Mets, prof baseball player, 1992-95; Cleveland Indians, 1996; Houston Astros, 1999; NY Yankees, 2000; Fla Marlins, 2001; Milwaukee Brewers, 2002. **Orgs:** Md Prof Baseball Asn; Prof Baseball Asn. **Honors/Awds:** MVP, basketball, baseball & football, Kent County High Sch, 1986-87; Labatts Player of the Year, Toronto Blue Jays, 1989; Md Star Future, Md Prof Baseball Asn, 1993.

THOMPSON, SANDRA ANN
Superior court judge. **Personal:** Born in Hawkins, TX; daughter of L R Thompson and Maye. **Educ:** Univ Southern Calif, BA, 1969; Univ Mich Law Sch, JD, 1972. **Career:** Assembly Health Comt, State Calif, legis intern, 1972-73; Assembly Judiciary Comt, State Calif, analyst, 1973-75; Dept Consumer Affairs, State Calif, legis coordr, 1975-77; City Atty's Off, Inglewood, CA, depcity atty, 1977-81; Los Angeles County Dist Atty's Off, dep dist atty, 1981-83; S Bay Judicial Dist, comnr, 1983-84, judge, 1984-86, presiding judge, 1986-87, judge, 1987-; Los Angeles Super Ct, super ct judge, 2000-. **Orgs:** Calif Asn Black Lawyers; Calif Ct Comnrs Asn; Calif Judges Asn; life mem, Calif Women Lawyers; Langston & Minority Bar Asn; Nat Asn Women Judges; life mem, Nat Bar Asn; Phi Alpha Delta; Presiding Judges Asn; South Bay Bar Asn, South Bay Women Lawyers Asn; Torrance League Women Voters, 1985-; bd trustees, Casa Colina Found South Bay, 1987-; Am Asn Univ Women, Torrance Br, 1988-; bd dirs, Southern Calif Youth & Family Ctr, 1988-94; Los Angeles Urban League, Nat Am Advan Colored People Los Angeles Chap; chair, Los Angeles County Munic Court Judges Asn, 1991-93; chair, Munic Court Judges Asn,1991-92; bd dir, Nat Ctr State Courts. **Honors/Awds:** Woman of the Year, Torrance YWCA, 1992; Dr Martin Luther King Jr Human Dignity Award, 1994; Distinguished Service Award, Remraw Commanders Rite, 1995; Woman of the Year, Switzer Ctr, 2003; Joan Dempsey Klein Distinguished Jurist Award, Calif Women Lawyers, 2005. **Business Addr:** Superior Court Judge, Los Angeles Superior Court of California, 825 Maple Ave, Torrance, CA 90503, **Business Phone:** (310)222-6541.

THOMPSON, SHARON
Basketball player, basketball coach. **Personal:** Born Jan 21, 1976. **Educ:** Miss State Univ, psychology, 1998; Univ West Al, MA, Phys Educ. **Career:** Basketball player (retired), basketball coach: San Jose Lasers, forward, 1997; East miss Community Col, Scooba Campus, asst coach, Student Activities Dir, 2004. **Special Achievements:** SEC All-Time Great Basketball Player. *

THOMPSON, SID. **See THOMPSON, DR. SIDNEY A.**

THOMPSON, DR. SIDNEY A (SID THOMPSON)
School administrator. **Educ:** Calif State Univ, Los Angeles, MS, educ; Pepperdine Univ, LLD. **Career:** Los Angeles Unified Sch Dist, supt, 1997; Univ Calif Los Angeles, Educ Leadership Prog, sr fel, 1997-, prof. **Orgs:** PDK; bd dir, Nat Ctr Educ & Econ; Valley VOTE Inc; Los Angeles Maritime Inst; adv Bd, US Merchant Marine Acad. **Honors/Awds:** Superintendent of the Year, 1996. **Business Phone:** (310)206-1673.

THOMPSON, SYLVIA MOORE
Educator. **Personal:** Born Nov 4, 1937, Cincinnati, OH; daughter of Clinton Moore and Edna Moore; divorced; children: Yvette. **Educ:** Univ Cincinnati, BS, educ, 1960; Ohio State Univ, MA, educ, 1973; Ohio State Univ, post grad work. **Career:** Midwest Inst Equal Educ Oppors, consult, 1973; Off Minority Affairs, Ohio State Univ, consult, 1974; Columbus City Sch, prog coordr, 1975-77; Otterbein Col Reading Ctr, tutor, 1979-84; Chap I reading instr, 1991; Acad & Financial Assistance Serv, owner; Univ Cincinnati, adj prof; Coun Prof Recognition, field rep. **Orgs:** Pres, Columbus Alumnae Chap Delta Sigma Theta Inc, 1970-72; pres, Youth Serv Guild Inc, 1983-85, 1989-91; bus mgr, Columbus Girl choir, 1987-91; consult, Macedonia Baptist Church Educ Facil; treas, Bethune Serv Bd; bd dir, Learning Juncture. **Honors/Awds:** Outstanding Leadership Award, Delta Sigma Theta Inc, 1975-76; Meritorious Service Award, United Negro Col Fund, 1985-86; Dedicated Service Award, Univ Cincinnati, 2000. **Home Addr:** 1806 Andina Ave, Cincinnati, OH 45237, **Home Phone:** (513)641-5289.

THOMPSON, TAWANA SADIELA
Government official, editor. **Personal:** Born May 24, 1957, Tallahassee, FL. **Educ:** Fla A&M Univ, BS, jour/PR, 1976. **Career:** Fla A&M Univ Col Educ, ed The Educr, 1976-78; Ocala Star Banner, staff reporter, 1978-79; Capital Outlook Newspaper, ed in chief, 1979; Fla Occupational Info Coord Comn, clearinghouse coordr, 1979-80; Dade Co Partners Youth, admin officer, 1981-82; Metro Dade Co, pub info officer. **Orgs:** Exec bd mem, Dade Co Alumnae Delta Sigma Theta, 1983-; Nat Forum for Black Public Admin, 1984-85, 1987-88; consult, Fla Inst Educ & Precollegiate Prog, 1984-85; Urban League Greater Miami, 1984-; Coconut Grove Jaycees, 1984-; dep polit dir, Statewide Campaign, 1986; exec bd mem, Greater Miami Chap Nat Asn Media Women; consult, S Fla Bus League. **Business Addr:** Public Information Officer, Metro Dade County, 111 NW 1st St Suite 2510, Miami, FL 33128.

THOMPSON, DR. THEODIS
Executive. **Personal:** Born Aug 10, 1944, Palestine, AR; son of Percy and Grozellia M Weaver; married Patricia Holley; children: Gwendolyn L Ware, Theodis E II & Omari P Thompson. **Educ:** Tuskegee Inst, Ala, BS, 1968; Univ Mich, Ann Arbor, MPA, 1969, PhD, 1972; Harvard Univ, Cambridge, MA, PHSM, 1977. **Career:** Executive (retired); John T Stanley Co, New York, NY, sr chem tech, 1964-66; Inst Soc Res Univ Mich, Ann Arbor, MI, res assoc, 1969-71; Health Serv Adminr, Dept Howard Univ, Wash, DC, asst prof, chmn, 1973-77; Howard Univ Sch, Bus & Pub, Adminr, acting asst dean, 1977-78; Univ Southern Calif, Los Angeles, assoc prof, 1978-79; Memphis Health Ctr Inc, Memphis, TN, dir planning mkt res, 1979-85, chief admin officer, 1985-87,

pres & chief exec officer, 1987-88; Brooklyn Plaza Med Ctr Inc, Brooklyn, NY, chief exec officer, 1988-; Florence, SC, Portsmouth, VA, St Louis, MO, disc jockey & news reporter. **Orgs:** APHA, 1970-; Alpha Phi Alpha Fraternity Inc, 1962-; pres, Metro Wash Pub Health Asn, 1970-72; Black Caucus Health Workers, 1974-75; Nat Asn Community Health Ctrs, 1979-; Community Health Asn NY State Inc, 1989, bd dir, Community Assoc Develop Corp, 1989; host comt, Nat Asn People With AIDS; pres, MGNAA Inc. **Honors/Awds:** Pubilc Health Scholar, Univ Mich Sch Pub Health, 1970-72; Distinguished Service Award, NY Asn Black & Puerto Rican Legislators Inc, 1992; HRSA Adminstation Award, USDHHS, NY Field Off, 1997. **Home Addr:** 4038 Glenroy Dr, PO Box 751344, Memphis, TN 38125, **Home Phone:** (901)624-3369.

THOMPSON, TINA (TINA MARIE THOMPSON)
Basketball player. **Personal:** Born Feb 10, 1975, Los Angeles, CA. **Educ:** Univ Southern Calif, sociol, 1997. **Career:** Houston Comets, forward, 1997-2000; Rovereto Basket, Women's Nat Basketball League, 2001-02; Kumho Falcons, Women's Korea Basketball League, 2003; Houston Stealth, Women's Nat Basketball League, 2003; Spartak Moscow Region, Russia, 2006-07; Los Angeles Sparks, 2009-. **Honors/Awds:** All-WNBA First Team, 1997; Naismith Player of the Year, 1997; Player of the Week, WNBA, 2001; Most Valuable Player, NWBL Pro Cup, 2003; Olympic gold medal, 2004; Gold Medal, R William Jones Cup; named Opals World Challenge All-Tournament Team, 2006; WNBA All-Star Selection, 2009. *

THOMPSON, TINA MARIE. See THOMPSON, TINA.

THOMPSON, WARREN M
Executive, chairperson, president (organization). **Educ:** Hampden-Sydney Col, BA, managerial econ, 1981; Univ Va, Colgate Darden Grad Sch Bus Admin, MBA, 1983. **Career:** Roy Rogers, asst mgr, 1983, regional mgr; Thompson Hospity LP, founder, pres, chmn, 1992-. **Orgs:** Univ Va Bd Vis; Compass Group N Am; Pepsi-Cola African Am Adv Bd; Hilb Rogal & Hobbs; Nat Black MBA Asn. **Honors/Awds:** Outstanding Young Virginian, 1994; Entrepreneur of the Year, Nat Black MBA Asn, 1997; Annual Pioneer Award, Black Bus Stud Forum Darden, Grad Sch Bus Admin, 2000; Hon Doctorate Deg, Tex Col, 2002; Business Philanthropist of the Year; Abbot Award, Darden Sch Alumni Asn. **Business Addr:** President, Chairman, Thompson Hospitality LP, 505 Huntmar Pk Dr Suite 350, Herndon, VA 20170, **Business Phone:** (703)964-5500.

THOMPSON, WILLIAM C., JR.
Government official. **Personal:** Born in New York, NY; son of William Thompson Sr; married; children: one daughter. **Educ:** Tufts Univ. **Career:** Off Congressman Fred Richmond, aide, chief staff; Brooklyn, dep borough pres, 1983-94; George K Baum & Co, sr vpres, 1993-96; NY City Bd Educ, Brooklyn rep, 1994-96, pres, 1996-01; NY City, comptroller, 2001-; Tufts Univ, bd trustees. **Honors/Awds:** Hon doctorate, Long Island Univ; DHL, Mercy Col, 1998; Distinguished Service Award, Fedn African-American Civil Serv Orgns Inc, 2002; Brotherhood Award, 2002; DHL, Metrop Col New York, 2004; Legacy Award, Medgar Evers Col, City Univ New York; Pillar of Justice Award, Metrop Coun Jewish Poverty; Numerous awards foem various organizations such as Jewish National Fund, Jewish Community Relations Council of New York, etc. **Business Addr:** Comptroller, City New York, Municipal Bldg 1 Cte St, New York, NY 10007, **Business Phone:** (212)669-3500.*

THOMPSON, HON. WILLIAM COLERIDGE, SR.
Judge, lawyer. **Personal:** Born Oct 26, 1924, New York, NY; son of William W and Louise; married Barbara; children: William Jr & Gail. **Educ:** Brooklyn Col, BA, 1948; Brooklyn Law Sch, LLB, 1954. **Career:** Judge (retired), Attorney; City of NY, councilman, 1969-73; NY State, sen,1965-68; Supreme Ct of the State of NY, admin judge, 1974-76, assoc judge,1976-78; Supreme Ct Brooklyn & Staten Island, asst admin judge, 1978-80, appellate div, assoc justice, 1980-2001; Ross & Hill, atty pvt pract, 2001-. **Orgs:** Founder, Restoration Corp; dir, Bed-Stuy Youth Action; past reg dir, NAACP; dir, Bed-Stuy Restoration Corp; Am Bar Asn; Brooklyn Law Sch Alumni Asn; Metro Black Bar Asn; chmn, Blacks & Jews Conversation; treas, Judges& Lawyers Breast Cancer Alert; Comt Judicial Conduct; co-chair, Community Promote Pub Trust & Confidence In the Legal Syst. **Special Achievements:** First African American elected official to serve in the New York State Senate. **Military Serv:** AUS, sgt, 1943-46; Purple Heart; Combat Infantry Badge; Three Battle Stars. **Business Phone:** (718)855-2324.

THOMPSON, WILLIAM L
Lawyer, airplane pilot, executive. **Personal:** Born Jun 14, 1951, Orangeburg, SC; son of Willie J and Pearl Richburg; divorced; children: Taylor M & Sydney E. **Educ:** USAF, Acad, CO, BS, commandant's list, 1973; Calif State Univ, Sacramento, CA, MA, deans list, 1977; McGeorge Sch Law, UOP, Sacramento, CA, JD, 1980; Suffolk Univ Law Sch, Boston, MA, 1991-92, dean's list. **Career:** USAF, minority adv supt, 1973-74, Sacramento, CA, instr pilot, chief, life support, 1974-80; Delta Air Lines, Boston, MA, captain, 1980-; Summit Group Co, Boston, MA, pres, 1982-2000, chief exec officer, currently; Mass Aeronaut Comn, Boston, MA, comnr, 1983-2000; Regency Park Assoc, Boston, MA, managing partner, 1986-2000. **Orgs:** Comnr, Boy Scouts Am, 1982-89; chmn bd, Am Cancer Soc, 1983-; bd mem, Finance Comt, Northeast Health Systs, 1983-2000; bd mem, Security Nat Bank, 1984-86; bd mem, Bank New England, 1986-90; trustee, Bridgton Acad, 1994-96; bd mem, Eastern Bank & Trust Co, 1996-; pres, Boston Chap, Nat Asn Guardsmen, 1998-2000, Atlanta Chap, 2000-; found bd dir, Atlanta Tech Col, 2000-; 100 Black Men of Atlanta, 2001-; nat bd dirs, Am Cancer Soc. **Honors/Awds:** Outstanding Service, 1986; Distinguish Achievement, Boy Scouts Am, 1986; Volunteer of the Year, 1992; Distinguished Contributions, Mass Airport Mgrs Asn, 1995; Distinguished Service, Am Cancer Soc, 1996; Bell South, African Am Hist Calendar, 1998; Guardsman of the Year, Am Cancer Soc. **Military Serv:** USAF, capt, 1973-80; Air Force Commendation Medal, 1980, ATC Safety Award, 1978, Vietnam Service Medal 1972, Presidential Unit Citation, Longivity Medal. **Business Addr:** Chief Executive Officer, The Summit Group Companies LLC, 627 Belmont Crest Dr SE, Marietta, GA 30067, **Business Phone:** (770)952-1813.

THOMPSON, WILLIAM S
Judge. **Personal:** Born Nov 21, 1914, Mebane, NC; son of Samuel and Willie Mae Hughes; married Melvalee "Mickey" Mitchell, Apr 5, 1994; children: William Waller. **Educ:** Howard Univ, Washington, DC, BS, 1934; Robert H Terrell Law Sch, Washington, DC, LLB, 1939. **Career:** Judge (retired); Pvt Pract Law, Wash, DC, sr partner, 1944-69; DC Govt, Wash, DC, coun mem, 1966-69; DC Superior Ct, Wash, DC, assoc judge, 1973-74. **Orgs:** Pres, Nat Bar Asn, 1957-59; sec gen, World Peace Through Law Ctr, 1963-67, 1972-89; pres, Wash Urban League BD, 1966-69; adv bd, Jr Citizen Corps Inc, 1976-; chmn, Judicial Coun NBA, 1989-90; pres, Kiwanis Club Georgetown, DC, 1990-91. **Honors/Awds:** Whitney M Young Jr Memorial Award, Washington Urban League, 1974; LLD, Howard Univ, 1975; Distinguished Service Award, Nat Bar Asn, 1977; LLD, Lincoln Univ, 1981; LLD, St Augustine's, 1983; Charles H Houston Medallion of Merit, Washington Bar Asn, 1983. **Special Achievements:** The International Law Society Howard Univ School of Law renamed "The William S Thompson International Law Society," 1974. **Military Serv:** AUS, corporal, 1942-44, Good Conduct Medal, 1944.

THOMPSON, DR. WINSTON EDNA
School administrator, educator. **Personal:** Born Apr 9, 1933, Newark, NJ; daughter of Dorsey Nelson West and Cora Edna West; married Robert S, Sep 21, 1951 (divorced 1967); children: Darren Eric. **Educ:** Seton Hall Univ, BA, 1965; Columbia Univ, Teachers Col, MS, 1969; RutgersUniv, Ed.D, 1980. **Career:** Essex County Col, dir advising, counr, 1968-72; Rutgers Univ, Livingston Col, assoc dean students, 1972-75; Tomb rock Col, dean student dev,1975-76; Tomb rook Col, dean student develop, 1975-76; AT & T Bell Lab, consult, 1975-77; E Orange Bd Educ, adult educr, 1977-78; Salem State Col, vpres student servs, 1978-88; Conn State Univ, exec officer acad affairs & res, 1988-2003, trustee emer, 2003-. **Orgs:** Consult, Am Coun Educ, 1981-; adv bd mem, AAA New England, 1986-88; bd trustee; Morgan Memorial Goodwill Industries, 1986-88; adv bd mem & faculty, HERS Wellesley Col, 1982; bd mem, JJS Enterprise, 1979-; state educ coordr, Nat Coalition 100 Black Women, 1988-89. **Honors/Awds:** Salem State Col, recipient women's award, 1981; Univ MA Amherst, co-designer non-traditional doctoral prog, 1983; Northeastern Univ, Greater Boston Inter Univ Coun report, minority student retention, 1985; Distinguished Educator, Nat Coalition 100 Black Women, 1988; Meritorious Service Award, United Negro Col Fund Inc, 1989; Black Women & Black Men lecture & writing, 1989; Black Feminism, lecture & writing, 1989. **Home Phone:** (203)832-0072. **Business Addr:** Trustee Emeritus, Connecticut State University System, 39 Woodland St, Hartford, CT 06105, **Business Phone:** (860)493-0000.

THOMPSON-MOORE, ANN
Consultant. **Personal:** Born Oct 13, 1949, Edwards, MS; divorced; children: DeAnna. **Educ:** Jackson State Univ, BA, 1972, MS, Educ, 1974. **Career:** Jackson-Hinds County Youth Court, counr, 1972-74; MS Gulf Coast Jr Col, dir special serv prog, 1974-82; Northern IL Univ, counr, 1983-84; MS Governor's Off Fed & State Prog, special project officer IV, 1984-87; The Kelwynn Group, sr consult. **Orgs:** MS State Democratic Party, 1980; Phi Delta Kappa Frat E MS Chap, 1981; fundraising chair, Hinds County Democratic Exec Comn, 1984; pres, United Black Fund Miss, 1984; bd mem, Hospice Friends Inc, 1985; coordr, United Negro Col Fund, 1985-86, 1986-87; peer panelist, Miss Arts Comn, 1986; Farish St Bapt Ch; Delta Sigma Theta Sor Inc. **Honors/Awds:** Outstanding Young Woman in America, 1979. **Business Addr:** Senior Consultant, The Kelwynn Group, PO Box 1526, Jackson, MS 39215-1526.

THOMPSON-WRIGHT, DR. BRENDA SMITH
School administrator, lecturer. **Personal:** Born Jun 17, 1948, Richmond, VA; married Hugo Harrison Thompson; children: Rodney Harrison. **Educ:** Va Union Univ, BS, 1970; Va Commonwealth Univ, MS, 1977; Va Polytech Inst & State Univ, EdD, 1983. **Career:** Medical Col VA, lab specialist, 1970-75; J Sargeant Reynolds Community Col, instr, 1977-80; Doctoral Fellowship, State Coun Higher Educ Va, 1980, 81; State Coun Higher Educ VA, asst coordr, 1984-85; Va Union Univ, dir enrollment mgt, 1985; Fla A & M Univ, asst dean stud personnel servs, dir stud teaching, prof sec educ & found, asst dir, Collection Mgt, currently. **Orgs:** Pres, Nat Asn Univ Women Richmond Br, 1984-85; Richmond Prof Women's Network, VASFAA, SASFAA, NASFAA, VACRAO, SACRAO, NACDRAO; Nat Asn Advan Colored People; Alpha Kappa Alpha Sor. **Honors/Awds:** Distinguished Volunteer, Parent John B Gary Elem Sch, 1981, 83; Distinguished Alumni Award, Nat Asn Equal Oppor Higher Educ, 1986. **Home Addr:** 4004 Poplar Grove Rd, Midlothian, VA 23113.

THOMS, DONALD H
Television director. **Personal:** Born Feb 28, 1948, Baltimore, MD; son of McKinley and Henrietta Austin; married Mariana Davis, Jun 6, 1970; children: Tracie Nicole & Austin Curtis. **Educ:** Morgan State Univ, BA, sociol, 1971. **Career:** WBAL-TV, Baltimore, opers dir, 1967-73; Md Pub TV, Owings Mills, stage mgr, 1973-75, TV dir, 1975-80, producer, 1980-85, exec producer, 1985-90, sr exec producer, 1990-91, dir regional prods, 1991-93, dir prog mgt, 1993-96, vpres programming; Discovery Health Channel, interim gen mgr, vpres prod, currently. **Orgs:** Bd govs, Nat Capital & Chesapeake Bay Chap Nat Acad TV Arts & Sci; adv bd, CINE. **Honors/Awds:** Best Entertainment Program Television Director, 1988; NATPE InterNat-Iris Award Winner, Best Entertainment Prog, 1988; CPB Public Television Local Program Award-Silver Award, Corp pub TV, 1990; Bronze Award, Producer, Film & TV Festival New York, 1989; Emmy Awards; Emmy Award Exec Producer, 1992, 1993; Telly Award, 1993.

THOMSON, ALICE G
Chief executive officer, association executive. **Career:** Black Family Develop Inc (BFDI), chief exec officer, currently. **Business Addr:** Chief Executive Officer, Black Family Development Inc (BFDI), 2995 E Grand Blvd, Detroit, MI 48235, **Business Phone:** (313)758-0150.

THOMSON, CYNTHIA BRAMLETT
Executive. **Educ:** Univ Mich, BA; Mich State Univ, MA, nutrit; Wash Univ, St Louis, MA, bus admin. **Career:** Girl Scouts USA, nat pres, nat bd dir, chair, 2002-05; Midwest Stamping Inc, co-founder & vpres hr, 1993-. **Orgs:** Chair prog comt, bd mem & vpres corp planning, Girl Scout Coun Greater St Louis, 1989-93; bd dir, Girl Scout Nat, 1996; St Louis Sci Ctr; cur emer, Univ MO Syst; Women's Forum MO; Links Inc; Alpha Kappa Alpha Sorority; Girl Scout Seven Lakes Coun Inc. **Business Addr:** Vice President of Human Resources, Co-Founder, Midwest Stamping Inc, 3455 Briarfield Blvd Suite A, Maumee, OH 43537, **Business Phone:** (419)724-6970.

THOMSON, GERALD EDMUND
Educator, physician, college administrator. **Personal:** Born 1932, New York, NY; son of Lloyd Thomas and Sybil Gilbourne; married Carolyn Webber; children: Gregory & Karen. **Educ:** Howard Univ, MD, 1959. **Career:** Harlem Hosp Ctr, pres, 1976-78, dir med, 1971-85, dir nephrol, 1970-71;Columbia Col, assoc prof med, Phys & Surg, 1970-72; Columbia Univ, prof,1972-; Presbyterian Hosp, attending physician, 1970-; clin asst prof med,1968-70; Coney Island Hosp, assoc chief med, 1967-70; State Univ NY Med Brooklyn Hosp, attending physician, 1966-70; Univ NY, instr, 1963-68; clin dir, dialysis unit, 1965-67; NY Heart Asn, fel nephrol, 1965-65; chief resident, 1962-63; resident med, 1960-62; State Univ NY Kings Co Hosp Ctr,intern 1959-60, chief resident, 1962-63; Samuel Lambert, prof med, 1980-; Inwood Ambulatory Care Network, Wash Heights, pres, 1985-90; Columbia Presbyterian Med Ctr, exec vp, chief staff, 1985-91, Col Physicians & Surg, assoc dean, 1990-91, sr assoc dean emer, 1991-, Lambert & Sonneburn prof emer med, 1997-. **Orgs:** Presbyterian Med Bd, 1976-; Health Res Coun City, NY, 1972-81;hypertension adv comt, NY City Health Serv Admin, 1972-75; adv bd, NY Kidney Found, 1971-72; Health Res Coun City, NY, 1975-; NIH, 1973-74; advbd, Nat Asn Patient Hemodialysis & Transplantation, 1973-; Com Mild Hypertension Nat Heart & Lung Inst, 1976; clin trials rev com, 1980-85; bd dir, NY Heart Asn, 1973-81; clin & trials rev com, 1980-85; bd dir NY Heart Asn 1973-81; chmn, Com High Blood Press, 1976-81; chmn, Com Hypertension NY Met Reg Med Prog, 1974-76; AAAS, 1973-74; Am Fedn Clin Res Soc Urban Physicians, 1972-73; Am Soc Artificial Organs; NY Acad Med1974-; Alpha Omega Alpha; adv bd, Jour Urban Health, 1974-80; adv com Heart & Hypertension Inst NY State, 1984; NY Govs Health Adv Coun,1981-84; pub Health Coun, NY, 1983-95; Joint Nat Com High Blood Pressure, NIH, 1983-84, 1987-88; rev panel hypertension detection & monitoring bd study cardiovasc risk factors young, Nat Heart, Lung & Blood Inst., 1984-90; NY State Adv Com Hypertension, 1977-80; com non-pharm treatment hypertension, Inst Med Nat Acad Sci, 1980; adv bd, Nat Asn Patients Hemodialysis & Transplantation, 1973-83; adv bd, Sch Bio med Educ, CityUniv New York, 1979-83; Med News Network, 1993-95; Grad Med Educ Comn,State NY, 1984-86; Comm End-State Renal Disease, 1985, 1989-90; pres, WAHeights-Inwood Ambulatory Care Network Corp, 1986-91; bd dirs, Primary Care Develop Corp, 1993-; Med News Network, 1993-94; pres, WAHeights-Inwood

Ambulatory Care Network Corp, 1986-91; Mayor's Commn Health& Hosp Corp; dir, Harlem Ctr Health Promotion & Disease Prev; bd dirs, Primary Care Develop Corp; chair, Am Bd Internal Med, 1990-92;past pres, Am Col Physicians, 1995-96; pres, Asn Acad Minority Physicians, 1989-91;chmn, Federated Coun Internal Med, 1995-96; founder & past pres, New YorkSoc Nephrol; Am Bd Internal Med; fel Am Col Physicians; mem, Boards of Inst Profm in Med, Columbia; mem, Inst Med Nat Academies. **Honors/Awds:** Recipient Nat Medical Award, Nat Kidney Found, NY, 1984; Dean'sOutstanding Teaching Award, Col Physicians & Surgeons, Columbia Univ,1986; Outstanding Alumnus Award, Howard Univ, 1987; fel, Col Physicians SAfrica, 1996; Hon doctor sci, Morehouse Sch Med, 1997. **Special Achievements:** First African-American to become chairman of the American Board of Internal Medicine. **Business Addr:** Lambert & Sonneburn Professor Emeritus of Medicine, Senior Associate Dean, Columbia University, Department of Medicine, Rm 3-413 630 West 168th St, New York, NY 10032, **Business Phone:** (212)305-4158.

THOMSON, J PETER
Executive. **Educ:** Hampton Univ, BA; Wharton Sch Bus, MBA. **Career:** Bay Area Small Bus Develop Corp, dir; Black Adoption Placement & Res Ctr, dir; Nat Asn Investment Cos; Access 1 Commun, dir, currently; Bustos Media, dir, currently; Opportunity Capital Partners, managing partner, pres, currently. **Orgs:** Bay Area Small Bus Develop Corp; Black Adoption Placement & Res Ctr; Nat Asn Investment Cos; charter mem, Marathon Club. **Business Addr:** President, Opportunity Capital Partners, 2201 Walnut Ave Suite 210, Fremont, CA 94538, **Business Phone:** (510)795-7000.*

THOMSON, JOHN, III
Basketball player, basketball coach. **Personal:** Born Mar 12, 1966, Washington, DC; son of John Thompson. **Educ:** Princeton Univ, 1988. **Career:** Basketball player (retired), head coach; Gonzaga Col High Sch, player, 1984; Princeton Univ, asst coach, 1995-2000, head coach, 2000-04; Georgetown Univ, head coach, 2004-. **Honors/Awds:** Big East Tournament Championship, 2007; Big East Regular Season Championship, 2007, 2008. **Business Addr:** Head Basketball Coach, Georgetown University, Basketball Office 3700 O St NW, Washington, DC 20057, **Business Phone:** (202)687-2374.*

THOMSON, DR. THELMA B
College president. **Personal:** Born Jul 22, 1940, Jamaica, West Indies. **Educ:** Bethlehem Col, teachers dipl, 1960; London Univ, gen cert educ, 1965; Howard Univ, BA, 1970, MA, 1972, PhD, 1978. **Career:** May Day Primary Sch, teacher, 1960-65; Washington Post Newspaper, Part-time proofreader, 1966-72; Franklin Adult Educ Ctr, eng instr, 1966-72; Howard Univ, DC, grad asst eng, 1970-72; Upward Mobility Col, teacher, 1971-72; City Univ NY, Herbert H Lehman Col, lectr eng, 1974-82; Bowie State Col, asst prof & reading co-odr, 1974-76; Univ DC, Dept Eng, asst prof eng, 1976-79, dir freshman eng, 1979-81, asst chair, 1982-88, Grad Expository Writing Prog, dir, 1981-90, dir dept activities & teaching duties, 1984-86, Col lib & Fine Arts, assoc dean, 1988-90; Norfolk State Univ, Sch Arts & Letters, dean, 1990-98, vpres acad affairs, 1998-2002; Univ Md, Eastern Shore, pres, 2002-. **Orgs:** Comnr, Am Coun Educ (Women), 2003-; exec bd, Community Found, 2003-; Historian & Bd mem, Middle Atlantic Writers Asn, 1984-2000; Modern Language Asn; Nat Coun Teachers Eng; Phi Beta Kappa; African-Am Writers' Guild; nat pres, Col Lang Asn; co-founder, Caribbean Studies Asn. **Honors/Awds:** Outstanding Alumni, Bethlehem Col, 2001; Administrator of the Year, Norfolk State Univ, 2002; Md Govr & Legis Citations; 2002; Service Award, Southern Asn Cols & Schs, 2002-03. **Special Achievements:** Author, Seventeenth Century English Hymn: A Mode for Sacred and Secular Concerns, 1988. **Business Phone:** (410)651-6101.*

THORBURN, DR. CAROLYN COLES
Educator. **Personal:** Born Dec 20, 1941, Newark, NJ; daughter of Charles Edward and Dorothy Walker Coles. **Educ:** Douglass Col, BA, Span, 1962; Rutgers Univ, MA, Span, 1964, Phd, Span, 1972; Phd, nutrit, 1987. **Career:** Barringer HS, Span teacher, 1964-66; Rutgers Univ, teaching asst Span, 1966-67; Upsala Col, prof Span & coordr black studies, 1967-95; Union County Col, adj prof Span, 1992-98; Seton Hall Univ, E Orange Sch Dist, educ consult, 1995-, adj Span prof, currently. **Orgs:** Modern Lang Asn; Nat Coun Black Studies; Am Asn Univ Profs; Am Asn Teachers Span & Port. **Honors/Awds:** Romance Lang Honor Soc Phi Sigma Iota, 1972. **Special Achievements:** Author: Mastery of Conversational Spanish, 1992; Complete Mastery of Spanish, 1993; Complete Mastery of Spanish Workbook, 1994; Speak Spanish, 1-3 weeks at Learning Annex, NYC. **Business Addr:** Professor of Spanish, Seton Hall University, Educational Research Center Language School, 400 S Orange Ave, South Orange, NJ 07079, **Business Phone:** (973)761-9000.

THORNE, CECIL MICHAEL
Physician. **Personal:** Born May 13, 1929, Georgetown, Guyana; married Sandra; children: Timothy, Christine, Christopher, Jonathan & Victor. **Educ:** Queens Col; Lincoln Univ, AB, 1952; Mainz Univ, MD, 1957. **Career:** Springfield Hosp, intern res, 1958-62; W MA Hosp, demonstrator res, 1962-63; OH St Univ Patho, asst prof pathol, 1964-65; Newark PathologistsInc Licking Meml Hosp, pres. **Orgs:** Flw Am Col Patho; Am Soc Clinical Patho; clinical asn prof pathology OH St Univ, 1980; pres, elect OH Soc Pathologists; past pres, test OH Asn Blood Banks; past pres, Central OH Soc Patho; bd gov, OH Soc Pathol; lab com OH St Med Asn; AMA; OSMA; Licking Co Med Soc; Am Asn Blood Banks; Acad Clinical Lab Physicians & Sci; past chmn, bd dir Licking Co Chap Heart Asn; Licking Co ARG; past chmn, Central OH Blood Prog Com; chmn, Med Adv Com Central OH Blood Prog; past dir, Newark Area C C; chmn, Licking Co Metro Park Dist; Rotary Club.

THORNELL, PAUL NOLAN DIALLO
Secretary (Office). **Personal:** Born May 6, 1972, New York, NY; son of Richard Paul and Carolyn Atkinson. **Educ:** Univ PA, BA, 1994. **Career:** People for Am Way, sr legis rep, 1994-96; Sen Democratic Steering & Coordr Comt, assoc dir, 1998; VPres Al Gore, assoc dir legis affairs; Hill & Knowlton's, managing dir Pub Affairs; United Way Am, sr vpres, pub policy & field relationship; vpres Fed Govt Affairs Global Govt Affairs, Citigroup, currently. **Orgs:** Ctr Lobbying Pub Interest; DC Habitat for Humanity & Generations United. **Home Addr:** 1111 Noyes Dr, Silver Spring, MD 20910.

THORNELL, RICHARD PAUL
Educator. **Personal:** Born Oct 19, 1936, New York, NY; son of Joseph and Elizabeth; married Joan Talbert, 1964 (divorced 1969); children: David; married Carolyn O Atkinson, Sep 5, 1970; children: Paul Nolan Diallo & Douglass Vashon. **Educ:** Fisk Univ, magna cum laude, 1956; Pomona Col, 1955; Woodrow Wilson Sch, MPA, 1958; Yale Law Sch, JD, 1971. **Career:** Univ Faculty Senate, past chair; Rosenman Colin Freund Lewis & Cohen NY-C,assoc litigation dept 1975-76; US Comm Relations Serv Dept Justice, chief fed progms staff 1965-66; Africa Reg Officer US Peace Corps, chief program staff; US Dept State Agency for Intl Develop, econ & intl relofcr 1958-61; Howard Univ Sch Law, vpres & gen coun, 1984-88, prof law, currently. **Orgs:** Bars NY/DC/Fed Cts/US Supreme Ct; bd advs, Smithonian Environmental Res Ctr; bd dir, YMCA Wash DC, 1977-83; bd dir Africare, 1977-83; trustee, Phelps Stoke Fund, 1980-85; lay leader Int Comt, Nat Bd YMCA'S USA; exec com & gen coun, Fisk Univ Gen Alumni Asn, 1977-79; Phi Beta Kappa, Delta Chap, Fisk Univ, 1956-; elected coun, Foreign Relations; exec comt, Howard Univ Republic SA Project. **Honors/Awds:** Fisk Univ, Africare Distinguished Service Award; Fisk Univ Gen Alumni Assn, 1978; Grad Fellowship Princeton Univ; Fellowship Grant Yale Law Sch; Int Achievement Award Willilam S Thompson Int Law Soc dir com Nat Bd YMCA'S USA; exec com, 1980. **Military Serv:** USY, pfc, 1959-61. **Business Addr:** Professor of Law, Howard University, 2400 Sixth St NW, Washington, DC 20059, **Business Phone:** (202)806-6100.

THORNHILL, DR. HERBERT LOUIS
Physician. **Educ:** Univ Pittsburgh, BS, 1951; Howard Univ Col Med, Wash, DC, MD, 1955. **Career:** Montefiore Hosp & Med Ctr, asst attending, 1963-66, adj attending, 1966-67; Yeshiva Univ, Albert Einstein Col Med, instr, 1963-65, asst clinical prof rehab med, 1965-67; Harlem Hosp Ctr, asst dir rehab med, 1967-69, attending physician, 1969-, chief, amputee serv, 1969-, assoc dir, rehab med, 1969-78, acting dir rehab med, 1979-80, dir, rehab med, 1980-; Presbyterian Hosp, asst physician, 1968-84; Columbia Univ, Col Physicians & Surgeons, asst clinical prof rehab med, 1968-73, assoc prof clinical rehab med, 1973-85, prof clinical rehab med, 1985-. **Orgs:** Diplomate, Amer Bd Physical Med & Rehab 1964; Nat Med Asn, 1967-; Bronx Co Med Soc; Pub Comm 1970; Med Soc State NY; fel NY Soc Phys Med & Rehab, 1963-, prog chmn, 1970-71, vpres, 1971-72, pres elect, 1972-73, pres, 1973-74; Conference Rehab Med; NY Acad Med, 1968-; sec, Phys Med & Rehab, 1975-76, chair, 1976-77, adv coun, 1977-80; Am Acad Phys Med & Rehab, 1965-; Howard Univ Res & Training Ctr Access Rehab & Econ Opportunity, 1988-; surveyor, Comn Accreditation Rehab Facilities, 1982-89; mem, Med Adv Comn, Greater Harlem Nursing Home, 1974-87, chmn, 1981-82; Adv Comn Disab, Borough Manhattan, 1989-92; NY State Asn, Independent Living Ctrs, 1990-. **Honors/Awds:** New York City Independent Living Centers Award, 1991; Certificate of Appreciation, Harlem Hospital Auxiliary, 1994; Balm in Gilead Award, 1995; Legacy Award, Daughters Rizpah, 1998; Lifetime Achievement Award, Nat Med Asn, Manhattan Cent Med Soc, 1998. **Special Achievements:** Author of numerous publications and abstracts. **Military Serv:** USN, med officer, 1957-59; USNR, lt comdr. **Home Addr:** 2 Aberdeen Ave, Spring Valley, NY 10977. **Business Addr:** Director of Rehabilitation Medicine, Columbia University, Harlem Hospital Center, Rm 3125 506 Lenox Ave, New York, NY 10037-1802, **Business Phone:** (212)939-4401.

THORNS, ODAIL, JR.
Automotive executive. **Personal:** Born Jan 3, 1943, Pine Bluff, AK; married Mamie T; children: Michelle, Camille & Octavia. **Educ:** BS, chem, 1964; Kans State Univ, grad study 1964-65; Harvard Grad Sch Bus Admin, PMD, 1984. **Career:** Delco-remy Div GMC, asst supt mfg; chemist, process engr, res engr, mfg foreman, labor rel supvr, gen supvr mfg, plant supt, plant mgr, mfg mgr, oper mgr, dival dir personnel, dir; Qual Network & Synchronous Automotive Components Group, dir Engine Drive Bus Unit, Saginaw Div; Delphi Automotive Syst, Worldwide, gen dir mfg, global dir driveline, Aftermkt & Serv; saginaw, dir develop. **Orgs:** Indust Mgt Club; bd dir, St Manpower Training Comn; bd dirs, IN Forum & pres; chmn, Region III NAACP, 1974-75; chmn bd, United Way, 1979; Nat Bd NAACP, 1980-84; chmn bd, Comn Hosp, 1983-85; trustee, Peerless Lodge F & AM; dir, Madison Co Br NAACP; state adv, NAACP Women's Aux; pres emer, Ind State NAACP; chmn, Martin Luther King Memorial Comn; Golden Heritage mem, NCP; Saginaw Vision 2000. **Honors/Awds:** Man of Yr, Urban League Madison Co, 1972; B Harry Beckham Mem Award, NAACP, 1975; Loren Henry Award, NAACP, 1976; Distinguished Serv Award, United Way, 1979; Outstanding Achievement, Bus & Prof Leadership Develop Ctr, 1983; Distinguished Honoree, Urban League, 1983; Distinguished Serv Award, Comm Hosp, 1985; Professional Man of the Yr, Peerless Lodge F&AM, 1985; Life Membership, Hall Fame NAACP, 1985; Key Award, City of Anderson, Ind, 1991; Chancellors Club, UNV, 1997-. **Home Addr:** 3678 White Trillum Dr W, Saginaw, MI 48603-5804.

THORNTON, ANDRE
Baseball player. **Personal:** Born Aug 13, 1949, Tuskegee, AL; married Gertrude (deceased); children: Andre jr & Theresa (deceased); married Gail Jones; children: Jonathan & Dean. **Educ:** Cheyney State Col; Nyack Col. **Career:** Baseball player (retired); Chicago Cubs, infielder, 1973-76; Montreal Expos, infielder, 1976; Cleveland Indians, infielder, 1977-87; Global Procurement Management Co, owner. **Orgs:** Bd mem, Cleveland Coun World Affairs; Cleveland Zoological Soc; Cuyahoga Comm Col. **Honors/Awds:** Roberto Clemente Awd, 1979; Danny Thompson Meml Awd, Baseball Chapel; American League All-Star Team, 1982, 1984; Silver Slugger; Hall of Fame, Cleveland Indians, 2007; mem, Hall of Fame, Reading Phillies. **Special Achievements:** First baseman and designated hitter in Major League Baseball. *

THORNTON, CLIFFORD E. **See Obituaries section.**

THORNTON, CORA ANN BARRINGER
Executive. **Personal:** Born Jun 13, 1941, Washington, DC; daughter of George F Barringer and Pearl G; children: Johnnie R, Joseph T, Jerome F & Jenese E. **Educ:** DC Teachers Col, BS, 1964; Howard Univ, post grad, 1966; George Wash Univ, post grad, 1970; Trinity Col, MA, 1982. **Career:** Taft Junior High Sch, instr, math, 1964-73; St Mary's Sch, instr, math, 1976-79; Eastern High Sch, instr, math, 1979-85; Univ DIS, Dept Math, assoc prof, 1980-86; Barr-Thorn Enterprises, pres, ceo, 1981; Trinity col, Dept Math, assoc prof, 1984; Lady K Corp, pres & ceo, 1989-. **Orgs:** Nat coun Teacher Math; Delta Sigma Theta Sorority. **Honors/Awds:** Superintendent's Incentive Award, 1982. **Special Achievements:** Author: Learning Mathematics, LMASL, 1981; developer: Mathematics Games LMASL, 1981. **Business Phone:** (301)565-2395.

THORNTON, CORNELIUS
Executive, vice president (organization). **Educ:** Univ Iowa; Univ Chicago Grad Sch Bus, attended 1973. **Career:** Aetna Life & Casualty Ins Co, common stock analyst; Morgan Stanley, instnl equity res area; First Boston Corp, vpres, sr securities analyst; Goldman, Sachs & Co, vice pres, sr res analyst, 1992-. **Special Achievements:** Listed as one of 25 "Hottest Blacks on Wall Street," Black Enterprise, 1992; one of Wall Street's most outstanding brokerage analysts for 14 straight years, Institutional Investor, 1992. **Military Serv:** AUS, paratrooper. **Business Phone:** (212)902-1000.*

THORNTON, DOZIER W.
Educator. **Personal:** Born in Aliquippa, PA; son of Myrtle and Dozier; married Kazuko Otaki; children: Monica Thornton, Lisa Thornton & Hugh Heslep. **Educ:** Univ Pittsburgh, MS, PhD, 1966. **Career:** Mich State Univ, Dept Psychol, prof, 1965-2004, from assoc dean grad sch to asst dean grad sch, 1991-94, acting dean urban aff prog, 2004, prof emer, 2004-; psychtherapist. **Orgs:** Community Ment Health & Educ Consult; Am Psychol Assn; Mich Psychol Assn;The Listening Ear. **Honors/Awds:** Phi Kappa Phi. **Special Achievements:** Co author of the paper "Relationships between the Urban Built Environment, Social Capital and Human Health: Considerations for Future Research ". **Military Serv:** AUS, 1951-53. **Business Addr:** Professor Emeritus, Michigan State University, Department of Psychology, Kellogg Ctr Garden Level, East Lansing, MI 48824-1022, **Business Phone:** (517)353-8977.

THORNTON, IVAN TYRONE
Financial manager. **Personal:** Born Aug 8, 1961, Brooklyn, NY; son of Paul A and Esther; married Thomasina Toles, Apr 18, 1987; children: Ivana, Alyse & Lee-Joy. **Educ:** Howard Univ, Wash, BBA, finance, 1983; New York Univ, MBA. **Career:** Midas Investment Corp, Arlington, mgr, financial adminr, 1983-86; Merrill Lynch Pierce Fenner & Smith, New York, sr financial consult, 1986-89; Salomon Smith Barney, New York, vpres, regist investment adv, 1989-96; Credit Suisse First Boston, vpres, pvt equity sales, financial adv; Fiduciary Mgt Group LLC, managing partner,

currently. **Orgs:** Alpha Phi Alpha Fraternity, 1981-; pres, Howard Univ Alumni Asn, 1993-95; Am Mgt Asn, 1991; econ develop com, One Hundred Black Men Inc; Nat Asn Securities Profs; pub policy com, Black Exec Exchange Prog; Nat Urban League. **Honors/Awds:** Executives Club, Merrill Lynch Pierce Fenner & Smith, 1989; Division Leader, New Bus Develop, Salamon Smith Barney, 1990; Presidents Club, Salamon, Smith, Barney, 1993-96; chairmans coun, Credit Suisse First Boston. **Home Phone:** (973)275-5053. **Business Addr:** Managing Partner, Fiduciary Management Group LLC, 304 Pk Ave S 11th Fl, New York, NY 10010, **Business Phone:** (212)590-2360.

THORNTON, JACKIE C
Executive. **Personal:** Born Apr 26, 1960, Pine Bluff, AR; daughter of Laudell and Beatrice. **Educ:** Univ Ark Pine Bluff, BS, 1981; Univ Wis-Madison, MS, 1983. **Career:** Phillips Petrol, acct, 1981-82; IBM Corp, mkt sales asst, 1983; NCR Corp, educ analyst, 1984-88; Pitney Bowes, prod mkt mgr, 1988-91; United Am Healthcare Corp, New Prod Develop, 1992-94; Global Mkt & PR Inc, pres & owner, 1995-. **Orgs:** Dayton Chap Nat Black MBA Asn; Am Mkt Asn; Ga Minority Supplier Develop Coun. **Business Addr:** President, Owner, Global Marketing & PR Inc., 3330 Cumberland Blvd Suite 500, Atlanta, GA 30339, **Business Phone:** (678)638-6610.

THORNTON, DR. JOHN C
Executive. **Personal:** Born May 22, 1940, Louisville, KY; son of William and Alberta; married Rochelle A Ray; children: Ardell N & Timothy. **Educ:** Ky State Univ, BS, 1963; Northeastern Univ, MA, 1975; Union Grad Sch, PhD (criminal justice), 1976. **Career:** Chicago Bd Educ, teacher, 1963-66; City Chicago, comt organizer, res analyst, criminal justice, dir, 1966-81; Columbia Col, prof, 1977-84; McDonald's Franchise, owner, 1996. **Orgs:** Nat Black McDonald's Owners' Asn, 1981. **Honors/Awds:** Athletic Hall of Fame, KY State Univ, 1980. **Special Achievements:** Behavior Modification-The Road to Genocide, 1977. **Home Addr:** 10110 S Paxton, Chicago, IL 60617.

THORNTON, LESLIE
Lawyer, government official. **Personal:** Born May 2, 1958, Philadelphia, PA; daughter of Henry H and Ernestine L. **Educ:** Univ Pa, BA, 1980; Georgetown Univ Law Ctr, JD, 1983. **Career:** DC pub defender, 1983-87; Brand, Lowell & Ryan, assoc, 1987-89; Shea & Gardner, sr assoc, 1989-92; US Secy Educ, dep chief staff, 1993-96, chief staff, 1996; Dickstein Shapiro LLP, partner, 2004-; Career Educ Corp, bd dir, 2005-; Clinton Admin, sr exec. **Orgs:** DC Bar Asn; Greater Wash Area chap; Women's Law Div Outreach Community; Young Lawyers Div; Nat Bar Asn; Am Bar Asn. **Business Addr:** Partner, Dickstein Shapiro LLP, 1825 Eye St NW, Washington, DC 20006-5403, **Business Phone:** (202)420-2214.

THORNTON, DR. MAURICE
School administrator. **Personal:** Born Dec 31, 1930, Birmingham, AL; son of William Thornton and Alberta; married Elizabeth McDonald, Apr 15, 1961; children: Karen, Susan & Christopher. **Educ:** Alabama State Univ, BS 1952; Cleveland State Univ, MEd, 1975; Nova Southeastern Univ, EdD, 1981. **Career:** Cuyahoga Co Welfare Dept Cleveland, investigative caseworker & supvr titleV, 1958-67; Cuyahoga Co Welfare Dept Cleveland, coord neighborhood youth corps asst dir personnel dept, 1958-67; Cuyahoga Community Col Cleveland, eeo officer, minority recruiter & dir equal opportunity, 1967-82; State Univ New York Cent Admin, dir affirmative action compliance & affirmative action officer, 1982-90; State Univ New York Cent Admin, affirmative action progs dir, 1990-97; State Univ New York, Albany, adj prof, 1998, lectr, dept Africana Studies, currently. **Orgs:** Capital Dist Black & Puerto Rican Caucus, Am Asn Affirmative Action Officers; participant, Loaned Exec Prog; Leadership Develop Prog; consult training fund raising, Cleveland Found; chmn, Lee/Harvard Br, Nat Asn Advan Colored People Urban League; fund raiser, United Negro Col Fund; Omega Psi Phi Frat Inc; pres, Ala State Univ Alumni Asn; sire archon, Sigma Pi Phi Frat Beta Psi Chapt; treas, 369th Veterans Asn; deacon, United Presbyterian Church; vpres & pres-elect, Nova Univ Alumni Asn, New England, New York, 1989-90; secy bd, Camp Opportunity, Albany, NY, 1989-90; Am Math Asn; Am Mgt Asn; Capital Dist Human Rights Adv Comt, Adv Comt Restoration & Display New York States Mil Battle Flags; bd dirs, NCP; deacon, United Presbyterian Church. **Special Achievements:** ERIC Univ of CA; published dissertation "An Analysis of Cuyahoga Community College's Progress at Equal Opportunity Compliance"; addressed the Ohio General Assembly in Columbus OH; addressed the Assoc of Bds of Trustees of the Community Colls of the State Univ of New York (64 campuses, 30 are community colleges); Golden Diploma (Hon) Ala State Univ, 2002. **Military Serv:** AUS, corpl medical corpsman, 2 yrs; Good Conduct Medal, Letters of Commendation. **Home Addr:** 7 Keith Rd, Delmar, NY 12054. **Business Phone:** (518)442-4730.

THORNTON, OSIE M.
Association executive. **Personal:** Born Oct 6, 1939, Tuscaloosa, AL. **Educ:** Wayne St Univ, BA, 1961, MA, 1963. **Career:** Wayne Co Bur Soc Welfare; soc worker; CA Dept Rehab Nat Rehab Assoc, voc rehab counr; Am Personnel & Guidance Assoc; United High Blood Pressure Found; Nat Non-white Coun Assoc & Crenshaw Ctr Optimist Club; Big Bro Greater Los Angeles; licensed Child Family Marriage Counr. **Honors/Awds:** Man of Year Award, 1974, Optimist Club; citation for Community Achievement, LA Co Supvr James Hayes.

THORNTON, OTIS J.
Entrepreneur, car dealer. **Personal:** Born Jan 1, 1952?, Pocomoke City, MD; married Rosemary; children: 2. **Educ:** Lea Col, Minn, bus admin. **Career:** Gen Motors acceptance Corp, credit supvr, 1974; Joe Heidt Buick, Ramsey, NJ & Rea Buick Port Jervis, NY, sales consult & bus mgr, 1987-92; Coult Buick, Cherry Hill, NJ, owner, 1993; Ford dealership, 1995-96; E Brunswick, 1996; Chevrolet & Saturn franchises, Harlem Auto Mall, owner & operator; Gen Motors Acceptance Corp Platinum, dealer, currently; Gen Motors Cert Used Vehicle, dealer, currently; Gen motors Goodwrench Lifetime Serv Facility, dealer, currently; E Breunswick Buick-Pontiac-GMC, currently. **Orgs:** Gen Motors Minority Dealers Asn; Nat Asn Minority Dealers; Nat Asn Advan Colored People. **Special Achievements:** Black Enterprise Top 100 Auto Dealer, 1994, 2001, 2002; Entrepreneur of the Yr, Baptist Ministries Conf of Greater NY & Vicinity, 2001. **Business Phone:** (732)651-6200.

THORNTON, TRACEY
Government official. **Career:** White House, spec asst, pres legis affairs, dep asst, pres legis affairs & senate liaison, currently. **Orgs:** Electronic Frontier Found. **Business Addr:** Deputy Assistant to the President for Legislative Affairs & Senate Lia, The White House, 1st Fl E Wing Rm 107, 1600 Pennsylvania Ave NW, Washington, DC 20500, **Business Phone:** (202)456-6493.*

THORNTON, WAYNE T
Banker, chief executive officer. **Personal:** Born Aug 13, 1958, Harrisburg, PA. **Educ:** Morgan State Univ, BS, 1981. **Career:** Comptroller Currency, nat bank examr, 1979-85; Indust Bank Wash, asst vpres, 1985-87; Corvus Group Inc, chief exec officer, currently. **Orgs:** Realtor assoc, ERA Nyman Realty, 1985-; bd dirs, Univ Legal Serv, 1986-. **Honors/Awds:** Academic Merit Award. **Business Addr:** Chief Executive Officer, The Corvus Group Inc, 9701 Apollo Dr Suite 493, Largo, MD 20774, **Business Phone:** (301)322-8040.

THORNTON, WILLIE JAMES, JR.
Businessperson, president (organization), business owner. **Personal:** Born Jan 22, 1954, Nettleton, MS; son of Birdie and Willie; married L Kay Collins, Dec 10, 1977; children: Willie III, Timothy, Jessica & Monica. **Educ:** Univ NEB, BS, bus admin, 1976; MSP Col, MBA, 1983. **Career:** Travelers, supvr data processing, 1976-83; Xerox Corp, acct mgr mkt, 1983-86; Cleaning Solutions Inc, pres; Thornton's World Child Care, owner, 1998-; Summus Indust Inc, regional mgr, 2003. **Orgs:** Charter mem, Amberton Univ, 1983; Garland Chamber Com, 1986-; Dallas Fort Worth Minority Bus Develop Coun, 1986-; Independent Small Bus Asn, 1989-; Houston Bus Coun, 1990-; OKL Minority Supplier Develop Coun, 1990-; Ark Regional Minority Purchasing Coun, 1990-; Dallas Black Chamber Com, 1992; mentor, entrepreneur prog, Dallas Fort Worth Minority Bus Develop Coun, 1996. **Honors/Awds:** Xerox, Par Club, 1984; Cert Achievement, Basic Skill Sch, 1985; Cert Achievement, Acct Rep Sch, 1984; Acct Rep, 1985; Sales Rep of the Month, 1984; Cert Achievement, El Centro Col, Bldg Better Banking Relationships, 1989; Cert Achievement, Frito Lay, Bidding Techniques, 1989, Mkt Techniques, 1989; Cert Achievement, Xerox, Found Success, 1983; Honored for Service, Garland City Coun Econ Adv Group, 1990-93; Outstanding Service Award, Garland Chamber Com, Small Bus Coun, 1993, Awarded Committee Chair of the Year, 1993, Outstanding Serv Mem Bd Dir, 1993; Cert Completion course "Effective Personal Leadership," Garland Tex, 1993; Cert Completion "International Marketing," Garland Tex, 1993; Certificate of Apppreciation, Dallas-Fort Worth Minority Bus Develop Coun, Contributions made mem Vender Input Comt, 1994; Recognition of Achievement, 1996. **Home Addr:** 2221 Randi Rd, Rowlett, TX 75088, **Home Phone:** (972)412-2504. **Business Addr:** Owner, Thornton's World Child Care Center, 8421 W Villard Ave, Milwaukee, WI 53225, **Business Phone:** (414)393-0960.

THORPE, EARL HOWARD
Computer executive, chief executive officer. **Personal:** Born Oct 15, 1936, Raleigh, NC; son of Marvin W and Lucille B; married Michelle N; children: Eric E, Wendy M, Zoe F, Alexia M & Scarlett V. **Educ:** A&T State Univ, BS, 1958. **Career:** US Dept Labor, asst dir dept acct operations, 1972-79; Dis Off Employment Security, dir, off budget & finance, 1979-80; US Dept Labor, dir, offfinancial mgt serv, 1980-86; Thorpe Int Inc, chair, chief exec officer,1986-. **Orgs:** Alpha Phi Alpha Fraternity, 1956-. **Military Serv:** USY, spc 4, 1959-62. **Business Phone:** (202)857-7835.

THORPE, HERBERT CLIFTON
Aircraft pilot, engineer. **Personal:** Born Jan 9, 1923, New York, NY; married Jessie M Shorts; children: Jessica Thorpe & R Clifton. **Educ:** NYU, BEE. **Career:** Aircraft pilot, engineer (retired); Rome Air Develop Ctr, elec engr. Tuskegee airman. **Orgs:** Pres, Rome Br, NAACP; Mohawk Valley Frontiersmen; past pres, Cosmopolitan Ctr; Heritage Asn, Rome, NY. **Special Achievements:** June 7th is declared as Herbert C Thorpe Day in Rome, NY. **Military Serv:** Mil Serv, 2nd lt, 1943-46; 150 Distinguished Flying Crosses, one Silver Star, 14 Bronze Stars, 744 Air Medals. **Home Addr:** 6086 Shed Rd, Rome, NY 13440, **Home Phone:** (315)337-5018.

THORPE, JOSEPHINE HORSLEY
Lawyer. **Personal:** Born Jun 3, 1943, Elizabeth, NJ. **Educ:** Montclair St Col, BA, 1964; Seaton Hall Univ, Sch Law & Rutgers Sch Law, JD 1969. **Career:** Newark Legal Serv Proj, staff atty, 1969-70; Murphy Thorpe & Lewis, New York, law partner, 1970-73; gen pract law, Newark, NJ, 1973-74; Educ Law, atty, 1974-75; Gen Attys Orgn, Western Elec Co Inc, New York, atty, 1975. **Orgs:** Bar NJ; Bar NY; US Dist Ct, Dist NJ; vpres, Educ Law Ctr Inc, 1974-75; Garden St Bar Asn; Nat Bar Asn, 100 Women Integrity Govt. **Honors/Awds:** Recipient Regional Heber Smith Fellowship, 1969; first place in oral presentation of Appellants brief in Rutgers Moot Ct Competition, 1968. **Business Addr:** 195 Broadway, New York, NY.

THORPE, OTIS HENRY
Basketball player. **Personal:** Born Aug 5, 1962, Boynton Beach, FL. **Educ:** Providence Col, RI, 1984. **Career:** Basketball player (retired); Kans City Kings, forward, 1984-85; Sacramento Kings, forward, 1985-88; Houston Rockets, forward, 1988-95; Portland Trail Blazers, forward, 1995; Detroit Pistons, forward, 1995-97; Vancouver Grizzlies, forward, 1997-98; Wash Wizards, forward, 1998-99; Miami Heat, forward, 1999-2000; Charlotte Hornets, forward, 2001. **Honors/Awds:** NBA All-Rookie Second Team, 1985; NBA All-Star, 1992.

THORPE, WESLEY LEE, SR.
Executive director. **Personal:** Born Nov 20, 1926, Durham, NC; married Louise; children: Angela A, Wesley L Jr. **Educ:** A&T Univ Greensboro NC, grad, 1949. **Career:** Olin Matheson, scrap control mgr, 1952-56; Siskorsky Aircraft, inspector, 1956; Newhallville Cleaners, owner, 1965; Greaster New Haven Bus & Prof Mens Asn, exec dir; Delaney Cleaners Raleigh NC, asst mgr & tailor . **Orgs:** Widows Son Lodge 1 PH Mason NH; trustee, Immanuel Bapt Ch; sec Club 30 Inc; asst secy, Widows Son Lodge, 1955-56; bd dir, Community Progress Inc; bd Dir, BBB; bd Dir, JC New Haven. **Military Serv:** USN, 1945-46.

THRASH, JAMES
Football player. **Personal:** Born Apr 28, 1975, Denver, CO. **Educ:** Mo Southern State Univ, BS, criminal justice, 2001. **Career:** Wash Redskins, wide receiver, 1997-2000; Philadelphia Eagles, 2001-03; Wash Redskins, wide receiver, 2004-08. **Orgs:** Certified conditioning specialist, Nat Strength Prof Asn, 2003. **Honors/Awds:** Ed Block Courage Award, 2000; Unsung Hero Award, 2000; All-Am hons; First team All-Mid-Am Intercollegiate Athletics Asn hons; Special Teams Player of the Week, Nat Football League, 2004.

THREATT, ROBERT
Educator. **Personal:** Born Apr 4, 1928, Columbus, GA; married Helen Kilpatrick. **Educ:** Morris Brown Col, AB, 1949; Atlanta Univ, MA, 1958; Univ OK, edD, 1963. **Career:** Marshall Jr High, GA, teacher, 1953-58; GA St Dept Educ, 1958-61; Ft Valley St, chmn Dept Sec Educ, 1963-73; Morris Brown Col, pres, 1972-84. **Orgs:** NEA; Nat Asn Equal Opport Higher Educ; pres, GA Asn Educ; bd mem, Central Atlanta Progress; bd mem, Citizens Trust Bank. **Honors/Awds:** Teacher of Year, 1956; Alumnus Year, Morris Brown Col, 1971; Alumnus Year, Atlanta Univ, 1971. **Military Serv:** AUS, corpl, 1950-52.

THREATT, SEDALE EUGENE
Basketball player, basketball coach. **Personal:** Born Sep 10, 1961, Atlanta, GA. **Educ:** WVa Univ Inst Technol, attended 1983. **Career:** Basketball player (retired), basketball coach; Philadelphia 76er's, guard, 1983-87; Chicago Bulls, guard, 1987-88; Seattle Super Sonics, guard,1988-91; Los Angeles Lakers, guard, 1991-96; Houston Rockets, guard, 1996-97; Larissa, Greece, guard, 1997-98; Olympique Lausanne, guard, 2001-02; Australian SEABL Team, Nunawading Spectres, head coach, 2008-09. **Business Phone:** (610)39802-6711.

THROWER, JULIUS B.
Administrator. **Personal:** Born Mar 26, 1938, Mobile, AL; married Louise Green; children: Julian, Jason. **Educ:** AL State Col Mobile Ctr, 1962; AL State Univ, BS, 1964; Auburn Univ, MEd, 1971. **Career:** Mobile Co Pub Sch, high sch instr, 1964-66; SD Bishop State Jr Col, plant supvr, 1966-70; SD Bishop State Jr Col, coordr spec serv & develop, 1971-73; SD Bishop State Jr Col, dir veterans affairs, 1973-77; SD Bishop State Jr Col, dir admin, veterans coord. **Orgs:** Jr Col Leadership Conf Auburn Univ 1969; VCIP adv bd, US Dept HEW, 1975-76; former sr warden, F & AM Onyx Ldg 676, 1975-76; asst recorder, Shriner Palestine Temple, 1975-76; bd mgt, Metro YMCA Mobile Deaborn St Br; adv bd, Mobile Consortium CETA; past vice chmn, Am Asn Minority Prog Admin, 1977-78; comr Nat Comns Employ Policy, 1979.

Honors/Awds: SGA Award, student govt asn SD Bishop State Jr Col, 1976; Good Conduct Medal. **Military Serv:** USMC, col, 4 yrs.

THURMAN, ALFONZO
Educator. **Personal:** Born Oct 24, 1946, Mayfield, KY; son of Togo and Georgia May Jones; married Brazilian Burnette; children: Alfonzo II. **Educ:** Univ Wisc-LaCrosse, BS, eng, 1971; Univ Wisc-Madison, MA, educ policy studies, 1973, PhD, educ policy studies, 1979. **Career:** Univ Wisc-Whitewater, Minority Affairs, coordr, 1971-75; Univ Wisc-Oshkosh, Acad Develop Prog, dir, 1975-80; Northern Ill Univ, Spec Proj, dir, 1980-84, asst provost, 1984-87, Col Educ, prof, assoc dean, 1987-95, dean, 1996-; Univ Wisc-Milwaukee, Sch Educ, dean, 2001-. **Orgs:** Pres, Ill Asn Educ Opportunity Prog, 1983-84; chmn, DeKalb Human Rels Comn, 1983-86; parliamentarian, Mid-Am Asn Educ Opportunity Prog, 1989-90; bd dirs, Ill Asn Col Teacher Educ; pres, Holmes Partnership. **Honors/Awds:** Outstanding Leadership Award, ILAEOPP, 1985. **Special Achievements:** Author: Establishing Special Services on Campus; "Policy Making, Higher Education's Paradox", Thresholds 1986; Leadership of the Governing Bd & Cent Admin: Providing the Policy & Budgetary Framework for Incorporating Multicultural Elements into Coll & Univ Curric, co-authored with Carol Floyd, chapter, 1991; Trio Prog: A Proposal for Accrediting Programs Designed to Increase Underrepresented Groups in Higher Educ, chap, 1993. **Home Addr:** 527 Ridge Rd, DeKalb, IL 60115. **Business Addr:** Dean, University of Wisconsin-Milwaukee, School of Education, Enderis Hall 2200 E Kenwood Blvd, PO Box 413, Milwaukee, WI 53201-0413, **Business Phone:** (414)229-4721.

THURMAN, CEDRIC DOUGLAS
Banker, vice president (organization). **Personal:** Born May 5, 1964, Chicago, IL; son of Walter and Cleola Jr; married Michelle Speller, May 29, 1994. **Educ:** Univ Ill-Urbana, BS, finance, 1987; J L Kellogg Grad Sch Mgt, MBA, mgt strategy & mkt, 1996. **Career:** Harris Trust & Savings Bank, com banking trainee, 1987-89, int banking rep, Trade Finance, 1989-91, asst vpres community develop, 1991-93, vpres br mgt, 1993-, proj mgr, Personal Financial Serv Dept,1994-2000; Jones Lang LaSalle, chief diversity officer & sr vpres, currently. **Orgs:** Nat INROADS Alumni Asn, 1987-; Urban Bankers Forum Chicago, 1988-; bd mem, Univ Ill Com Alumni Asn, 1994-; area bd mem, Jr Achievement Chicago, 1995-. **Honors/Awds:** Religion Asst of the Year, 1982; INROADS Chicago Alumnus Year, 1988, 1993; Outstanding Mem, Urban Bankers Forum Chicago, 1990; Scholar, Nat Asn Urban Bankers, 1993, 1994; Alumnus of the Year Award, Kellogg Black Alumni Club, 2008. **Home Addr:** 2801 S King Dr, Chicago, IL 60616, **Home Phone:** (312)791-5675. **Business Phone:** (312)782-5800.

THURMAN, MARJORIE ELLEN
Educator. **Personal:** Born in Whiteville, NC. **Educ:** Fayetteville State Univ, BS, 1969; Seton Hall Univ, MA, 1977; Montclair State Univ, Thistle prog & admin cert, 1990. **Career:** Newark Bd Educ, teacher, 1969-; Essex Col Bus, instr, 1975-85; Sawyer Bus Sch, evening dean, 1979-80; Senator Wynona Lipman, part-time clerical, 1985-; SCS Bus & Tech Inst, part-time instr, 1986-; Malcolm X Shabazz High Sch, bus teacher. **Orgs:** YWCA, 1972-83; sunday sch teacher, St Paul's Church, 1978-80; adv, Sr Class MX Shabazz, 1985-87; Minority Bus Orgn, 1985-; Nat Bus Educ Asn; NJ Bus Educ Asn; Newark Teacher's Union; Alpha Kappa Alpha Sorority. **Honors/Awds:** Outstanding Teaching Plaque, Essex Col Bus, 1983; Teacher of the Month, SCS Bus & Tech Inst, 1987-88. **Special Achievements:** Created a successful program in Newark, NJ in 1981 called the "Newark Business Skills Olympics". **Business Addr:** Business Teacher, Malcolm X Shabazz High School, Newark, NJ 07108.

THURMOND, NATE (NATHANIEL THURMOND)
Sports manager, business owner, basketball player. **Personal:** Born Jul 25, 1941, Akron, OH. **Educ:** Bowling Green State Univ, BS, 1963. **Career:** Basketball player (retired), sports manager, business owner; San Francisco Warriors, player, 1963-71; Golden State Warriors, player, 1971-74, dir community rels; Chicago Bulls, player, 1974-75; Cleveland Cavaliers, player, 1976-77; Big Nate's BBQ Restaurant, San Francisco, owner, currently. **Orgs:** Bd mem, SCARE. **Honors/Awds:** Outstanding Play with Golden State, 1978; NBA Hall of Fame, 1985. **Special Achievements:** Named one of the 50 Greatest Players in NBA History. **Business Addr:** Owner, Big Nate's Barbeque Restaurant, 1665 Folsom St, San Francisco, CA 94103-3722.

THURMOND, NATHANIEL. **See THURMOND, NATE.**

THURSTON, CHARLES SPARKS
Dermatologist, physician. **Personal:** Born Mar 13, 1934, King and Queen, VA; married Marie; children: Renee, Cynthia, Patti, Carmen. **Educ:** Va State Col, BS, 1953; Meharry Med Col, MD, 1958. **Career:** Univ Mich Med Ctr, researcher, 1965-66; Howard Univ, asst clin prof, 1968-70; Georgetown Univ, 1968-70; G Wash Univ, 1968-70; Univ Tex, 1974-; Santa Rosa Hosp, chief dermatologist, 1978; Self employ, dermatologist. **Orgs:** Pres local chap, Alpha Omego Alpha, 1957-58; fel Am Acad Dermat, 1967-; AMA, 1968-; Mass Med Asn, 1968-; pres, Asn Mil Dermat, 1975; San Antonio Dermat Soc, 1975-; Am Col Physiol, 1975-; pres, CA Whittier Med Soc, 1977-78; vpres, Lone Star St Med Soc, 1977; chmn, Nat Dermat Sect, Nat Med Asn, 1977-79; Gamma Phi. **Honors/Awds:** R Braun Award, Outstanding Sr & Med Std Surg, 1958; cert, Achievement Surg Gen, 1970; V Marchbanks Award, Outstanding Air Force Physician, 1974. **Military Serv:** USAF, chief, aviation med, 1959-63, col, 1956-76; Wyo Beaumont Army Hosp, intern, 1959; Andrew AFB, 1966-68; USAF Surg Gen, consult, 1968-70, 1974-76; Weisbaden USAF Hosp, chief gen therapy serv, 1972-74, chief dermatologist, 1970-74; Wilford Hall USAF Hosp, training dir, chief, 1974-76; Meritorious Serv, Middle USAF. **Business Addr:** Dermatologist, 343 W Houston St Suite 909, San Antonio, TX 78205.*

THURSTON, DR. PAUL E.
Educator, college teacher. **Personal:** Born Jul 13, 1938, Williamsport, PA; son of Helen Louise. **Educ:** Lafayette Col, BS, 1960; Cornell Univ, PhD, 1964. **Career:** Tex Southern Univ, asst prof, 1966-73, assoc prof, 1974-81, prof, prof emer chem, currently. **Orgs:** Am Chem Soc; Am Asn Univ Prof; Phi Beta Kappa. **Honors/Awds:** Recipient of Dan forth fel & Woodrow Wilson fel. **Military Serv:** AUS, capt, 1960-64. **Business Addr:** Professor emeritus of chemistry, Texas Southern University, Department of Chemistry, 3100 Cleburne St, Houston, TX 77004, **Business Phone:** (713)313-1044.

THURSTON, WILLIAM A.
Clergy, architect, human rights activist. **Personal:** Born Jun 6, 1944, Chicago, IL; married Silvia M Petty; children: William A, Peter O, Omyia N, Pauline A. **Educ:** Graham Found Scholar, 1966; Univ IL, BA, 1967; Moody Bible Inst, 1979; Candler Sch Theol, 1980. **Career:** Oper PUSH, nat dir; Seymour S Goldstein Assoc Chicago, arch, 1965-67; Dubin Dubin Black & Moutoussamy Chicago, arch, 1967-69; Environment Seven Ltd Chicago, pntr dir planning, 1969-74. **Orgs:** Assoc minister Fellowship, Missionary Baptist Church; bd mem, Comprehensive Res & Develop Chicago Arch Assis Ctr; Nat Asn Housing Owners & Mgr.

TIBBS, HON. EDWARD A
Lawyer, government official. **Personal:** Born Apr 12, 1940, Pittsburgh, PA; son of Mayme Yager and Otis H; married Sheila Christian, May 10, 1988. **Educ:** Allegheny Community Col, assocs, 1976; Wilson Col, cert instr, 1980; Univ Pittsburgh, evening studies; Wilson Col, attended 1980-. **Career:** E Liberty-Garfield CAP, bd mem, 1968-74; Allegheny County, dem committeeman, 1970-81, paymaster, 1980-81; IBPOE W Elks, asst grand exalted ruler, 1982-; Allegheny County, dist magistrate, 1982-; Spec Ct Judges Allegheny County, first vpres, 1995; Lincoln, Larimer, Lemington, Belmar, Citizens Revitalization Develop Corp, exec dir, 1993-97; Commonwealth Pa, Dist Justice Ct Allegheny County, lawyer, currently. **Orgs:** Exec bd mem, Local 2596 CWA, 1973-80; chmn, Allegheny County Black Polit Assembly, 1976-77; exalted ruler, Greater Pittsburgh Elks, 1979-82; Comt Ethics Commun Workers Am, 1973-76; life mem, Nat Asn Advan Colored People; life mem, Sixth Mt Zion Baptist Church; vpres, Pittsburgh Job Corps, Community Rels Coun, 1992-. **Honors/Awds:** Community Service Award, Community Action Pittsburgh, 1975; Mr Elk, IBPOE W Pittsburgh, 1979; Meritorious Service Award, Pa Chaplains, Dept IBPOE W Pa, 1981; Distinguished Achievement Award, Steel City Coun 8 IBPOE W Pa, 1981; Leadership with Excellence Award, Faith Tabernacle Church, 1986; Hall of Fame, Westinghouse High Sch, 1996. **Military Serv:** AUS, specialist 4th class, 3 yrs; Missileman of the Month 1960. **Home Addr:** 6399 Olivant St, Pittsburgh, PA 15206. **Business Addr:** Lawyer, Commonwealth of Pennsylvania, District Justice Court Allegheny County, 1013 Lincoln Ave, Pittsburgh, PA 15206-2767, **Business Phone:** (412)661-8829.*

TIDWELL, ISAIAH
Banker. **Personal:** Born Feb 13, 1945, Charlotte, NC; son of William and Anna D; married Hellena O Huntley; children: William DeVane & Damion Lamar. **Educ:** NC Cent Univ, BS, 1967; Wake Forest Univ, MBA, 1980. **Career:** Banker (retired); NC Cent Univ, pres, 1965-67; Celanese Fibers Co, Charlotte, acct, 1967-70; Celanese Fibers Co, Rock Hill, cost acct, 1970-71, supvr, cost analysis, 1971-72; Wachovia Bank & Trust Co, regional vpres, pres, exec vpre & dir wealth mgt opers, 2001-05; Lincoln Nat Corp, bd dir; Lanc Inc, bd dir; Ruddick Corp, bd dir. **Orgs:** Comn Fin, NC Cent Univ Alumni Asn, life mem, 1967-76, pres, Charlotte Chap, 1974-76; Omega Psi Phi, 1969-76; Charlotte Chamber Com, 1973-76; chmn bd, Charlotte Bus Devel Orgn, 1974-76; bd mem, Charlotte Bus Resource Ctr, 1975-76; bd trustees, fin secy, Friendship Baptist Church-E Winston; pres, PTA Moore Alt Sch; life mem, Omega Psi Phi Fraternity Inc, Basileus; Statement Studies Comn Robert Morris Asn; Region IV Charlotte Adv Coun US Small Bus Admin; bd dir, chmn Bus II Div, Campaign United Way Forsyth Co, 1982; pres-bd dir, Winston-Salem Neighborhood Housing Serv; bd dir, Fin Comm YMCA-Metro Bd, City/Co Utility Comn Winston-Salem & Forsyth Co, 1984; W/S Chamber Com, W/S Rotary; Bachelor Benedict's Club; Sigma Pi Phi Fraternity; founder, Piedmont Club, 1985-; 100 Black Men Atlanta; Atlanta Rotary Club. **Honors/Awds:** Boss of the Year Award, Winston-Salem Chap, Am Bus Women's Asn, 1980; Omega Man of the Year Award, Winston Salem Chap, Omega Psi Phi Fraternity, 1983; Man Year, Winston-Salem Chronicle, 1988; Distinguished Service Award, Bachelor Benedict's Club, 1990. **Home Addr:** 1059 Hunters Brook Ct NE, Atlanta, GA 30319-4714, **Home Phone:** (404)760-9518.

TIDWELL, JOHN EDGAR
Educator. **Personal:** Born Dec 13, 1945, Independence, KS; son of Verlean and Harry Sr; children: Levert, Trudy & Tuere. **Educ:** Washburn Univ, BA, eng, 1969; Creighton Univ, MA, eng, 1971; Univ Minn, PhD, 1981. **Career:** Atchison Neighborhood Ctr, Atchison, KS, dir, 1969-70; Maur Hill Catholic Col Prep Sch, Atchison, KS, instr, 1968-70; Creighton Univ, Upward Bound Prog, instr, 1970 & 1971; Creighton Univ, New Careers Prog, instr, 1970-71; Univ Nebr, Omaha, instr, 1971-73; Univ Nebr, Omaha, Black Studies Dept, actg chmn, 1972-73; St Olaf Col, Am Minority Studies, dir, 1973-74; St Olaf Col, instr, 1973-75; Univ Minn, teaching assoc II, 1975-78; Am Lutheran Church Future Fac fel, 1975-77; Carleton Col, vis instr, 1977 & 1979; Univ Minn, Putnam Dana McMillan fel, 1979; Univ Ky, Eng Dept, asst prof, 1981-87; Yale Univ, vis fel, 1985-86; Nat Endowment Humanities fel independent study & res, 1985-86; Miami Univ, asst prof, 1987-92; Miami Univ, asst prof, 1987-92, assoc prof, 1993-99; Kan State Univ, vis scholar eng & ethnic minority studies, 1993; Univ Kans, Langston Hughes vis prof eng & african & am studies, 1994, assoc prof, 1999-. **Orgs:** Modern Lang Asn; Midwest Modern Lang Asn; Col Lang Asn; The Langston Hughes Soc. **Honors/Awds:** Nat Fellowships Fund Award, 1978-81; Jessamine Allen Dissertation Fund Award, Univ Minn, 1980; Grant for Research Graduate Assistant, Miami Univ, 1993-94. **Business Addr:** Associate Professor, University of Kansas, Department of English, 3027 Wescoe Hall, Lawrence, KS 66045-2115, **Business Phone:** (785)864-2583.

TIGGER, BIG (DARIAN MORGAN)
Radio host. **Personal:** Born Dec 22, 1972, The Bronx, NY. **Educ:** Univ Md. **Career:** FM92 Q, Baltimore, dj; Detroit FM98 WJLB, Miami's new 103.5 FM & New York City Power 105.1 FM, host; WPGC 95.5, Live in the Den, host, 2007-. **Orgs:** Street Corner found. **Special Achievements:** Six-year undefeated nighttime radio champion. **Business Addr:** Host, Live in the Den, 1270 Ave of the Americas 14th Fl, New York, NY 10020.

TILDON, CHARLES G., JR. **See Obituaries section.**

TILGHMAN, CYPRIAN O
Labor activist. **Personal:** Born May 19, 1913, Washington, DC; married Cecilia Cooke; children: 13; married Liz. **Career:** Former UCF Bd; HWC delegate; Md State & DC AFL-CIO, vpres; Hotel & Restaurant Local 25, advisor, consult, pres Emer, currently. **Orgs:** Former mem, MDTA; Skills Bank; Urban League; Old Dem Central Com; pres, JEB; Unit Here. **Honors/Awds:** Honored with 'a conference in my name', 2000. **Business Addr:** President Emeritus, Hotel & Rest Local #25, 1003 K St NW, Washington, DC 20001.

TILLERY, DWIGHT
Government official, president (organization). **Personal:** Born Mar 10, 1948, Cincinnati, OH; son of Wesley and Doris Mae. **Educ:** Univ Cincinnati, BA, 1970; Univ Mich, JD, 1972. **Career:** City Cincinnati, asst solicitor, 1973-74; Univ Cincinnati, vpres, 1974-77; adj asst prof law, 1975-77; Univ Cincinnati Law Sch, consult, 1977-78; Tillery & Assocs, partner, 1977-83; City Cincinnati, consult, 1980-82; State Ohio, Columbus, sr asst atty gen, 1983-85; Off Atty Gen, Columbus, consult, 1985; Miami Univ, asst prof bus law, 1985; incinnati, mayor, 1991; City Cincinnati, coun mem, 1997-98; Ctr Closing Health Gap Greater Cincinnati, pres & chief exec officer, currently. **Orgs:** Fel Am Nar Asn; Nat Bar Asn; Cincinnati Bar Asn; Asn Trial Lawyers Am; Black Lawyers Asn Cincinnati. **Business Phone:** (513)585-9872.

TILLEY, FRANK N.
Physician. **Personal:** Born Jul 17, 1933, New York, NY; married Frances A Payne. **Educ:** Columbia Col, BA, 1955; State Univ NY Sch Med Downstate Med Ctr, MD, 1959; Columbia Univ Sch Pub Health & Admin Med, MPH, 1964. **Career:** Jewish Hosp & Med Ctr Brooklyn Greenpoint Affiliation, emer serv attending physician, 1965-67, 1969-, asst dir EmerDept, 1971, coordr Ambulatory Care, 1971-73; United Mutual Life Ins Co, med dir, 1972-; Dept Environmental Med & Community Health State Univ NY Downstate Med Ctr, lectr, 1972-74; Dept Ambulatory Care Jewish Hosp & Med Ctr Brooklyn Greenpoint Affiliation, chief, 1973-; Dept Family Prac State Univ NY Downstate Med Ctr, clinical asst, 1974-; United Mutual Life Ins Co, bd dir, 1974-. **Orgs:** Fellow, Am Col Preventive Med; Am Col Emer Physicians; Med Soc State NY; Med Soc Co Kings; Provident Clinical Soc; Am Geriatrics Soc; Am Pub Health Asn; New York City Pub Health Asn; Am Soc Tropical Med & Hygiene; New York City Soc Topical Med; 100 Black Men. **Honors/Awds:** Commendation Medal, 1969; Certificate of Achievemnt, AUS, 1969. **Military Serv:** AUS, major, 1967-69.

TILLIS, DR. FREDERICK C.
Educator, composer, writer. **Personal:** Born Jan 5, 1930, Galveston, TX; son of General Gardner and Bernice Gardner; mar-

ried E Louise; children: Patricia & Pamela. **Educ:** Wiley Col, BA, 1949; Univ Iowa, MA, 1952, PhD, 1963. **Career:** Wiley Col, instr & dir, instrumental music, 1949-51, asst prof & chmn,dept of music, 1956-61, 1963-64; Grambling Col, prof music & head theory dept, 1964-67; Ky State Univ, prof & head music dept, 1967-69; Univ Mass, assoc prof, 1970-73, prof, music theory & composition & dir Afro Am music & jazz prog, 1973-97, dir U Mass jazz workshop, 1974-80, dir, fine arts ctr, 1978-97, assoc chancellor affirmative action & equal opportunity, 1990-97, Dept Music & Dance, prof emer, currently, Univ Fine Arts Ctr, diremer, 1998-; Poetry: In the Spirit & the Flesh, 1989; Images Mind & Heart, 1991; In Celebration, 1993; Of Moons, Moods, Myths, & the Muse, 1994; "Free as a Feather," Jazz Educators Journal, Dec 1994; Harlem Echoes, 1995; Children's Corner: From A to Z (poetry), 1998; Seasons, Symbols &Stones, 1999; Akiyoshidai Dairy, 2000; Shattered Ghosts & Southern Walls, 2002; Bittersweet Harvests, 2003; Albums: Freedom, 1970; Fantasy on a Theme by Julian Adderley, 1975; Music Frederick Tillis, Vol I, 1979; Quintet for Brass, 1980; Kcor Variations, 1980; Elegy, 1983; Swing Low, Deep River, 1984; Contrasts & Diversions: The Tillis-Holmes Jazz Duo, 1987; Voices Color, 1989; Crucificion, 1990; Paintings in Sound, 1990; The Second Time Around: The Tillis-Holmes Jazz Duo, 1991; Among Friends, The Billy Taylor Trio & Fred Tillis, 1992; Freedom: The Music Frederick Tillis, 1996; Festival Journey Concerto, 1998; Portraits from Gershwin's Porgy & Bess, 1999; A Tribute to Duke Ellington, 1999; prof emer, dept music & dance, Univ Fine Arts Ctr; Dir Jazz, Univ Massachusetts, Amherst, currently. **Orgs:** Music or DA bd dir, 1995; Chancellor's Exec Advisory Coun, 1994-; ALANA Honor Soc Bd, 1994-; Faculty Senate Coun Status Minorities, 1984-; Acad Am Poets; Am Composers Alliance; Am Fedn Musicians; Broadcast Music Industry; Ctr for Black Music Res; Int Assoc Jazz Educators; Music Educr Nat Conference; Trans Africa Forum; Am Music Ctr; Mass Music Educr Assoc; United Negro Col Fund; adv comm, Fac & Staff Capital Campaign, Univ Mass,1998-; chair, edu adv comm, Nat Music Found, 1998-; Mass Cultural Coun, 1997-; Musicorda bd of dir, 1995-. **Honors/Awds:** Recip United Negro Col Fund Fel, 1961-63; Rockefeller Fund Grant for Develop Compstn, 1978; Nat Endowment for the Arts, Composers Grant 1979; Chancellor, Univ Mass, Distinguished Lecturer, 1980; Mass Cultural Coun, Commonwealth Award org leadership, 1997; Distinguished Achievement Award Black Musicians CNF 1998; Recognition Award for 30 Years Serv Com for the Collegiate Edu Black and Other Minority Students (CCEBMS) 1998. **Military Serv:** US AirForce, 1952-56. **Business Addr:** Owner, P & P Publications, 55 Grantwood Dr, Amherst, MA 01002, **Business Phone:** (413)549-3632.*

TILLMAN, CEDRIC
Football player. **Personal:** Born Jul 22, 1970, Natchez, MS. **Educ:** Alcorn State Univ, attended. **Career:** Football player (retired); Denver Broncos, wide receiver, 1992-94; Jacksonville Jaguars, wide receiver, 1995; Ariz Rattlers, wide receiver, 1997-99. *

TILLMAN, CHRISTINE L.
Government official, social worker. **Personal:** Born Dec 14, 1952, Richmond, VA. **Educ:** Radford Col, BA, 1975; Va Commonwealth Univ, 1976; J Seargeant Reynolds Community Col, 1981, 1984. **Career:** Richmond Opport Indust Ctr, youth counr, 1975. **Orgs:** Basileus 1972-75; Alpha Kappa Alpha; mem bd dir, Dawn Progressive Assoc Inc, 1978-; Caroline Co Rec Adv Comn, 1984-, Caroline County Ext Serv Adv Coun, Va Politech Inst & State Univ, 1984-, Caroline County Bd supvrs, 1984-; v chmn, Caroline County Bd Supvrs, 1985, Caroline County Local Welfare Bd, 1985, Nat Asn Advan Colored People Caroline Chapt; bd mem, Tri-County Med Corp, 1985-; chmn, Caroline County Bd Supvrs 1987-. **Honors/Awds:** Honoree Negro Achievers Award, Caroline County Chap, Nat Asn Advan Colored People, 1984. **Special Achievements:** First Black Female Member in the Caroline County Board of Supervisors, 1987-. **Home Addr:** 30372 Sadie Lane Rd, Doswell, VA 23047. *

TILLMAN, GEORGE, JR.
Movie director, movie producer. **Personal:** Born Jan 26, 1969, Milwaukee, WI; married Marcia Wright; children: 1. **Educ:** Columbia Col, film & video, 1991. **Career:** Director, writer & producer; State Street Pictures, owner; Films: Paula, 1992; Scenes for the Soul, 1995; Soul Food, 1997; Men of Honor, 2000; Barbershop, producer, 2002; Barbershop 2: Back in Business, producer, 2004; Beauty Shop, producer, 2005; Roll Bounce, producer, 2005; TV series: Soul Food, exec producer, 2000; Barbershop, exec producer, 2005; The Brandon T. Jackson Show, exec producer, 2006. **Honors/Awds:** Midwestern Student Academy Award, 1990; Oscar Micheaux Excellence in Film Award, Nat Asn Black-Owned Broadcasters; Image Award, Nat Asn Advan Colored People. **Business Phone:** (310)369-5099.

TILLMAN, DR. JOSEPH NATHANIEL
Executive. **Personal:** Born Aug 1, 1926, Augusta, GA; son of Leroy and Canarie; married Areerat; children: Alice Tillman Thornton & Robert Bertram. **Educ:** Paine Col, BA, 1948; Northrop Univ, MS, 1975, MBA, 1976; Nova Univ, DBA, 1989. **Career:** Executive (retired); Rockwell Int, dir, 1958-84; Tillman Enterprises, staff, 1985. **Orgs:** Pres, Nat Asn Advan Colored People, San Gabriel Chap, 1984; pres, SocLogistics Engrs, Orange County Chap, 1985; chmn, Orgn Behav, Acad Mgt,1985; consult, Nat Univ, 1986. **Honors/Awds:** Presidential Citation, Nat Asn Equal Opportunity Higher Educ, 1986. **Special Achievements:** Numerous publications including "Computer Algorithm for OptimizingTestability" 1976; "Testability Optimizing at all Levels of Maintenance",1984; "An Evaluation of Middle Managers Coping Strategies in AerospaceIndustries as a Predictor of their Success", 1986; "Job Stressors andCoping Strategies of Aerospace Managers: Their Influence on Healthy LifeStyles and Job Performance", 1989. **Military Serv:** USAF, capt, 9 yrs, navigator bombardier, 1948-57.

TILLMAN, LILLIAN G.
School principal, elementary school teacher. **Personal:** Born Jan 27, 1934, Jamaica, NY; married; children: Kay Lynn & James Edward. **Educ:** Roosevelt Univ, BA, 1955; Hunter Col, attended 1952, 1961; NY Univ, attended 1954; Northwestern Univ, attended 1956; Queens Col, attended 1961; Russell Sage Col, attended 1973; State Univ NY, MS, 1975. **Career:** Educator (retired): Albany, teacher, 1955-57; Arbor Hill Sch, Albany, NY, teacher, 1956; Carousel Nursery Sch, teacher, 1960-61; Scudder Ave Sch, resource teacher,1962-66; Arbor Hill Elem Sch, Albany, NY, resource teacher, 1966-; NY State PTA, teacher fel, 1975; Street Acad, Clinton Ave Sch, prin, 1977-91. **Orgs:** Inst Study Educ Probs Occasioned Desegration State Univ NY, 1967-68; Nat Staff Develop Ctr, Sem Open Classroom, Denver, 1971; hon life mem, PTA, 1972; Continuous Progress Learning Inst, Albany, 1972; first pres, Urban League Guild Albany Area, 1973-76; Int Conf & Symp Trans-Cult Adaptation, Port-au-Prince, Haiti, 1973; consult, Conf Concern Absenteeism Schs, Chicago, 1974-75; pres, Albany Interracial Coun, 1978-80; City Club Albany; Phi Delta Kappa Fraternity; pres, vpres, chairperson, Spec Proj Comt, Albany Alumnae Chap, Delta Sigma Theta Sorority; vpres, chair person, Personnel Comt, Albany Interracial Coun; bd dir, Albany County, Div Youth; chairperson, Twin Proj, Albany Dist PTA; consult, Nat PTA; bd dir, Albany Urban League; Albany Pub Sch Teachers Asn; NY State United Teachers; NEA; Urban League Guild; Nat Asn Adv Colored People. **Special Achievements:** Cohostess, TV prog "Talking With the Tillmans" 1973-76.

TILLMAN, DR. MARY AT
Physician. **Personal:** Born Sep 4, 1935, Bristow, OK; daughter of Thomas Tuggle and Ruthie English Tuggle; married Daniel Thomas, Apr 20, 1957; children: Dana Tillman Chee & Daniel T Jr. **Educ:** Howard Univ, Wash, DC, BS, 1956, MD, 1960. **Career:** Self-employed, physician pediatrician, 1963-; City St Louis Dept Health & Hosps, physician-supvr, 1963-85. **Orgs:** Nat grammateus, Zeta Phi Beta Sorority, 1965-70; pres, Mound City Med Forum, 1980-82; comt adoptions, Am Acad Pediat, 1970-76; pres, Homer G Phillips Internes Alumni Asn, 1980-82; pres, bd dirs, Annie Malone C Home, 1991-94; Nat Med Asn; AMA. **Honors/ Awds:** Woman of Achievement in Medicine, St Louis Globe Democrat, 1982; Outstanding Alumni Award, Howard Univ Sch Med, 1985; YWCA, Leader Award, YWCA, 1987; Feature article, Making Mama's Dream Come True, Good Housekeeping Mag, 1986; Outstanding Nat Service Award, Zeta Phi Beta Sorority, 1986; Laymen's Award, Cote Brilliante Presby Church, 1988; Distinguished Service Award, Pediat Sect Nat Med Asn, 1991; 25 Years of Excellence Award, Barnes Hosp, 1994; Women in Medicine Award, Nat Med Asn, 2002. **Home Addr:** 26 Washington Terr, St Louis, MO 63112-1914, **Home Phone:** (314)361-1914. **Business Addr:** Pediatrician, 330 Northland Med Bu, St Louis, MO 63136-1412, **Business Phone:** (314)385-5522.

TILLMAN, PAULA SELLARS
Lawyer, government official, association executive. **Personal:** Born Jun 21, 1949, Chicago, IL; daughter of Herschel L (deceased) and Sylvia L Cookman (deceased); married James Tillman Sr, Jun 28, 1968; children: Lisa & James II. **Educ:** Loyola Univ, Chicago, BA, magna cum laude, 1974; DePaul Col Law, JD 1979. **Career:** Chicago Police Dept, youth officer, 1974-79, financial crimes invest, 1979-81, legal officer II, 1981-89, sergeant, 1988-; liaison mayor's comn women, 1984-, EEO officer, 1984-; Labor Rels Coun Cook County Pub Defender, currently; BT Express Trucking Inc, chief pres, currently. **Orgs:** Cook County Bar Asn, 1979-; comnr, Ill Atty Registration & Disciplinary Comn, 1981-; chairperson, personnel comn Chicago Coalition Against Abused Women, 1984-85; sec bd dirs, Providence St Mel High Sch, 1984-85; Leadership Greater Chicago, 1985-86; Campfire Inc, 1986-97; legis chairperson, Nat Hook-Up Black Women Chicago Chap, 1986-90; vpres, legis affairs, Sojourner's United Polit Action Comn, 1990-; pres & co-chair, Ill Women's Comn Elect Carol Moseley Brown; pres/bd dirs, Campfire Metropolitan Chicago, 1994; pres & co-founder, Women's Res Ctr, 1997-. **Business Phone:** (219)764-2100.

TILLMAN, DR. TALMADGE CALVIN, JR.
Accountant, educator, certified public accountant. **Personal:** Born Nov 26, 1925, Brunswick, GA; son of Talmadge and Lavonn; married Leola Bennings; children: Timothy & Philip. **Educ:** Ind Univ, BS, 1948; Syracuse Univ, MBA 1949; Univ Southern Calif, CA, CPA 1965, DBA, 1967; Univ Mass, postdoctoral study, 1972; Univ Colo, postdoctoral study, 1974; Univ Tex, postdoctoral study, 1988; Univ SC, postdoctoral study, 1989. **Career:** Tex Southern Univ, chmn acct, 1950-51; Sidney Spiegel CPA, auditor-acct; Joseph S Herbert & Co, acct; Gilbert Drummont CPA Dept, acct; E Los Angeles Col, assoc prof accountancy, 1962-68; Calif State Univ Long Beach, prof accountancy, 1968-91, prof emer accountancy, 1991-; Price Waterhouse, fac & fel, 1969. **Orgs:** Treas, Syracuse Univ Alumni Asn, 1953; pres, Ind Univ Alumni Asn, 1978-79; Basileus Omega Psi Phi, Lambda Omicron Chap, 1978-80; pres, Ind Univ Club, 1978-80; pres, Big Ten Club Southern Calif, 1990-91; pres, Syracuse Univ Club, 1992-93; Syracuse Univ Alumni Asn Southern Calif, 1992; pres, Univ Southern Calif Alumni Club, 1998. **Honors/Awds:** Van De Camp Award, Nat Asn Acct, 1968; National Achivement Award in Accounts Education, Nat Asn Black Acct, 1977; Omega Man of the Year, 1979; Number One Chapter in US during Presidency, Ind Alumni Asn; Citizen of the Year, 12th Dist Omega Psi Phi Fraternity. **Special Achievements:** First African American to earn MBA degree from Syracuse University. First African to receive doctorate from University of Southern California. First and only African to be president of Big ten club of Southern California. **Military Serv:** USN, storekeeper second class, 1944-46. **Business Addr:** Professor Emeritus of Accounting, California State University Long Beach, College of Business Administration, 1250 Bellflower Blvd, Long Beach, CA 90840, **Business Phone:** (562)985-4111.

TILLMON, JOEY
Law enforcement officer. **Personal:** Born Mar 1, 1953, Victoria, TX; son of Lawrence Eugene and Florence Ann; married Jill; children: Logan, Haven & Brandy. **Educ:** Clark City Comm Col, assoc deg criminal justice; Tex A&M Univ, BA. **Career:** Police officer (retired); N Las Vegas Police Dept, chief police. **Orgs:** Int Asn Chiefs Police; NOBLE; bd dir, Las Vegas "Vision 2003"; Southern NV Women's Prison Facil Community Rel bd; adv comn & Command Col Curric Comn & Strategic Planning, Community Col; Nat Orgn Black Law Enforcement Exec. **Honors/Awds:** Office of the Year, N Las Vegas Police, 1991; Governor's Award for Outstanding Community Program, 1994; honarary degelate, Clark Co Col Southern NV. **Special Achievements:** First African Am chief of police in Nevada's history. **Military Serv:** USAF, 1975-79; Good Conduct Medal.

TIMBALAND (TIMOTHY Z MOSLEY)
Music producer, rap musician. **Personal:** Born Mar 10, 1971, Norfolk, VA; married Monique Idlett; children: 1. **Career:** Albums: Welcome to Our World, 1997; Tim's Bio, 1998; Indecent Proposal, 2001; Under Construction Pt II, 2003; Cop That Shit, 2003; Interscope imprint label Beat Club, founder, 2000; "Steer" & "Put You on The Game", 2005; Music Composer: Doctor Dolittle, 1998; Can't Hardly Wait, 1998; Romeo Must Die, 2000; Nutty Professor II: The Klumps, 2000; G String Divas, 2000, 30 Years to Life, 2001; Lara Croft: Tomb Raider, 2001; Paid in Full, 2002; Hollywood Homicide, 2003; Timbaland Presents Shock Value, 2007; Wave of the Music, 2008. **Honors/Awds:** ASCAP Award for Most Performed Songs from Motion Pictures, 1999, 2001, 2002; Vibe Music Awards, 2007; Teen Choice Awards, 2007; MTV Video Music Awards; Belgium TMF Award, Best InterNat Urban, 2007; Grammy Awards, 2008. **Business Phone:** (212)333-8000.

TIMBERLAKE, DR. CONSTANCE HECTOR
Educator. **Personal:** Born in New Brunswick;married Charles; children: Christian & Curtis. **Educ:** Syracuse Univ, Doctorate Educ Admin, 1979; MS; BA, cum laude; NYS, cert. **Career:** Syracuse Univ, Col Human Develop, assoc prof, Chair Child Family Community Study, fac, currently; Syracuse Sch Dist, ABE prog, chief counr & admin; Neighborhood Ctr, exec dir; Syracuse Pub Sch Dist, comnr educ; Adolescent Pregnancy Prev Prog, proj dir, 1987-. **Orgs:** NY Sch Bd Asn; Prog Comn; mem planning comn, Cent NY Sch Bd Inst; AERA; AAUP; Syracuse Prof Women; HEW Task Force Social Justice Nat Literacy Vol Am; Human Rights Comn Syracuse & Onondaga Co; vpres, Syracuse NAACP; vice chmn, Coalition Qual Educ; vice chmn, Onondaga Urban League Guild; Nat Orgn Women; adv bd, Onondaga Community Col; adv coun, Neighborhood Health Ctr; Metr Ch Bd Human Serv Comn; Fair-Employ Rev Bd Onondaga Co; PEACE Head Start Self-Eval & Performance Stand Improv Plan; exec mem, Black Polit Caucus; numerous vol serv; trust Pi Lambda Theta Inc; pres, elect NYS Coun Family Rel Coun; SUNY Oswego Adv Coun Oswego NY; vice chmn, Syracuse Univ Black & Latino Fac Orgn, 1986-89; hon adv bd mem, For KidsSake, 1987; pres, NY Coun Family Rel, 1988-89; mem & prog dir, Syracuse-Boys Club Syracuse. **Honors/Awds:** Jefferson Award, WTVH-TV/Am Inst Pub Serv, 1989.

TIMBERLAKE, JOHN PAUL
Executive. **Personal:** Born Nov 12, 1950, Fackler, AL. **Educ:** Ala A&M Univ, BS, computer sci, 1975. **Career:** Chattanooga Bd Educ, sub teacher, 1975-77; TN Valley Auth, engr asst, 1976-77; Jackson Co NAACP, pres, 1977-; Dept Ind Relation, programmer & Analyst, 1977-. **Orgs:** Del, Jackson Co Voter's League; del, AL Dem Conf; Jackson Co NAACP; sr warden, Red Rose Lodge No 352; Jackson Co Chamber Com, 1980. **Honors/Awds:** Outstanding Achievement Award, Jackson Co NAACP, 1979; Harvester Award, 1979.

TIMMONS, BONITA TERRY
Physicist. **Personal:** Born May 6, 1963, Norfolk, VA; daughter of Earl Nathanial and Laura Mae Hines; married Disoungh Lee Tim-

mons, Sep 1, 1990. **Educ:** Purdue Univ, West Lafayette, IN, BS, 1986. **Career:** Nat Insts Health, Bethesda, MD, health physicist, 1987-89; Thomas Jefferson Univ, Philadelphia, PA, health physicist, 1990-. **Orgs:** Health Physics Soc, 1986-; Appalachian Compact Users Radioactive Isotopes, 1989-. **Honors/Awds:** Scholarship, Lions Club, 1981-82; Scholarship, Disabled Am Veterans, 1981-82. **Business Addr:** Assistant Health Physicist of Radiation Safety, Thomas Jefferson University, 19 Walnut St Nevil Bldg Suite 820, Philadelphia, PA 19107, **Business Phone:** (215)955-7813.

TIMMONS, OSBORNE LLEWELLYN. See TIMMONS, OZZIE.

TIMMONS, OZZIE (OSBORNE LLEWELLYN TIMMONS)
Baseball player. **Personal:** Born Sep 18, 1970, Tampa, FL. **Educ:** Univ Tampa. **Career:** Chicago Cubs, outfielder, 1995-96; Cincinnati Reds, 1997; Seattle Mariners, 1999; Tampa Bay Devil Rays, 2000; Chunichi Dragons, 2001; NY Mets, outfielder, 2004, Columbus Catfish, hitting coach, currently. *

TIMMONS, QUACY. See BARNES, QUACY.

TIMMONS-TONEY, REV. DEBORAH DENISE
Clergy, chaplain. **Personal:** Born Jan 8, 1961, Huntsville, AL; daughter of Emmett Timmons and Lela D Timmons; married Vincent Doyle Toney. **Educ:** J F Drake Tech Col, attended 1981; Ala Agr & Mech Univ, BS, 1987; Gammon Theol Sem, MDiv, 1990. **Career:** Redstone Arsenal, Facilities Engineering, procurement clerk, 1980-85, Prog Budget Analyst Br, budget asst, 1985-87; Gammon Theol Sem, admin asst, 1987-89; United Way, intern, 1990-91; Emory Univ Hosp, clin chaplain, 1990-91; Mt Mariah United Methodist Church, pastor, 1991-92; St Peter United Methodist Church, pastor, 1991-92; St Luke United Methodist Church, pastor, 1992-94; Asbury United Methodist Church, assoc pastor, 1994-96; Douglasville United Methodist Church, pastor, 1996-98; Lowe's UMC, pastor, 1998-2000; Spring Hill UMC, pastor, 2000-; Ala Agr & Mech Univ, Campus Ministry asn, chaplain, 1999-. **Orgs:** Secy, United Methodist Church, Bd Higher Educ; chairperson, nominations & personnel comt, Seminole Service Ctr Bd Dirs, 1992; Bd trustees, student rep, Gammon Theol Sem, 1988; Asn Clin Pastoral Educ Inc, 1990; Chaplain Asn, 1988; Nat Coun Negro Women Inc; affil mem, Nat Fedn Blind; correspondence secy, Greater Huntsville Ministerial Fel; Alpha Kappa Alpha Sorority Inc, Kappa Phi Omega Chap, 1993; Dixon Found Research & Develop, Women & Spirituality; founder, pres, Eagle Wing Ministries Int, 1999-. **Honors/Awds:** Outstanding Employee Award, Program Analyst Branch, 1986; Crusade Scholar, General Bd Global Ministries, 1988; Ministrial Scholarship, United Methodist Church Southeastern Jurisdiction, 1988; Outstanding Employee Award, Redstone Arsenal Engineering & Resources Management, 1988; Ford Foundation Fellow, Black Women in Church & Society, 1989. **Special Achievements:** First African-American woman ordained in the North Alabama Conference, UMC, 1992; first African-American woman to pastor in major denomination in Northwest Alabama; first female pastor, St Peter United Methodist Church, 1992, St Luke United Methodist Church, 1992, Asbury UMC, Douglasville UMC, Lowe's UMC; first African-American woman to be on radio program, "United Methodist Men's Hour," 1992; published numerous articles on Christian Literature; author, Stepping Out: Step Out of Your Comfort Zone, Step in Your Destiny, 2000; author, Be a Risk-Taker and Watch God Move, 2001. **Business Phone:** (256)461-7472.

TIMPSON, MICHAEL. See TIMPSON, MICHAEL DWAIN.

TIMPSON, MICHAEL DWAIN (MICHAEL TIMPSON)
Football player, television broadcaster, football coach. **Personal:** Born Jun 6, 1967, Baxley, GA; married Edwena; children: 2. **Educ:** Pa State Univ, BA, commun, 1990. **Career:** Football player (retired), Football coach; New England Patriots, wide receiver, 1989-94; Chicago Bears, 1995-96; Philadelphia Eagles, 1997; Miami Dolphins, 1999; FOX Sports Radio, sports analyst, 2000-07; Westminster Acad, head football coach. **Honors/Awds:** US Olympic Trials 200 meters, 1992; Timed 33.01 in the indoor 300 Meters, NCAA record.

TINGLE, LAWRENCE MAY
School administrator. **Personal:** Born Jul 26, 1947, Canton, MS; daughter of Peter L Smith and Mamie Lee Smith; married Robert Earl; children: Aubrey F, Shella A & Robert L. **Educ:** Alcorn State Univ, BS, 1968; Miss State Univ, chisanbop instr, 1979, M.Ed,1981; Miss State Univ Meridian, MS, M.Ed, AA, 1987. **Career:** Newton Co Improv Club, sec, 1976-79; Newton Pub Sch, classroom teacher, 1972-82; NAACP, secy, 1976-81; State MS Dept Math, lectr & writer, 1980; E Cent Jr Col, directress, 1982-; Jackson Pub Sch, health educ coordr, currently. **Orgs:** Deaconess Jerusalem MB Church, 1973-; secy, Newton Democratic Exec Comm1981-; Delta Sigma Theta; secy, Newton City Heroines Jericho; VBS instr, Jerusalem MB Church, 1982; eval chair, MS Asn Trio Prog Col, 1982-; 4-HClub, 1982-; vpres, Jerusalem MB Church Home Mission Soc, 1984-; sec, MSAsn Ed Opportunity Progs, l985, vpres, 1985; assoc matron, Order Eastern Star Calanthe; Friends Children MS, Inc, Jackson, MS Programs Adv Task Force; middle sch representative, Miss Biol Asn; Newton Political League;exec comt mem, Miss Democratic Party. **Honors/Awds:** Class Room Teacher MS Outstanding Educator, 1976; MS Asn Educ Oppurtunity Prog Personnel Service Award, 1985; Southeastern Asn Educ Opportunity Prog Personnel Certificate of Apppreciation, 1985. **Special Achievements:** First African-American Female SS Directress East Central Jr Coll Decatur MS. **Business Addr:** Health Education Coordinator, Kellogg Grant, Jackson Pub Sch, 101 Near St Enochs Complex, Jackson, MS 39203, **Business Phone:** (601)960-8965.

TINSLEY, DWANE L
Lawyer. **Personal:** Born Aug 12, 1953, Fayetteville, WV; son of Elizabeth. **Educ:** Howard Univ Sch Social Work, Davis & Elkins Col, BA, sociol, 1975, MA, social work, 1978; Brown W Bayne, fel, 1980; WVa Univ Col Law, JD, 1981; Harvard Law Sch, Nat Inst Trial Advocacy's, Teaching Advocacy Skills, 1995. **Career:** WVa Univ Col Law, Trial Advocacy Prog, instr, 1989-2001; pvt, partnership, assoc law pract & instr, 1979-91; US Atty's Off, asst US atty, 1987-91; WVa Ethics Comn, hearing examr, 1993-; WVa Bd Med, post-hearing adv, 1993-; Nationwide Ins Co, Trial Div, trial atty, 1992-95, spec prosecuting atty, 1995-96, admin trial atty, 1995-96, managing trail atty, 1996-97, spec invest unit officer, 1997; Nat Football League Contract Adviser, consult, 2000-; Hendrickson & Long PLLC, partner & atty, 2001-. **Orgs:** Treasurer, Fayette County, 1982-94; ethics comt, WVa State Bar Asn, 1988-94, minority lawyers comt, 1990-92; secy & treas, Finance Comt, Mountain State Bar Asn, 1987-92, pres, 1992-94; Am Bar Asn; Fayette Co Bar Asn; Int Asn Spec Invest Unit; Nat Bar Asn; Am Corp Coun Asn; Am Bd Trial Advocates; WVa Prosecuting Attys Asn. **Honors/Awds:** WVa Honor Scholar, 1971-75; Outstanding Black Attorney, Black Law Students Asn, 1987; Special Achievement Award, US Dept Justice, 1990. **Home Phone:** (304)343-1523. **Business Addr:** Attorney, Hendrickson & Long PLLC, 214 Capitol St, PO Box 11070, Charleston, WV 25339, **Business Phone:** (304)346-5500.

TINSLEY, FRED LELAND, JR.
Lawyer. **Personal:** Born Aug 30, 1944, Detroit, MI; married Ollie Brock. **Educ:** Southern Univ, BA, 1969, JD, 1972. **Career:** Reginald Heber Smith Fel Legal Serv, 1972; LA Const Conv, res asst, 1973; US Security & Exchange Comn, trial atty, 1973-75; Lone Star Gas Co, regulatory atty, 1975-77; Champman Tinsley & Reese, partner; Robinson & Hoskins LLP, atty, currently. **Orgs:** Bd dir, Ment Health Asn, Dallas, 1976-78; adv coun mem, Tex Employ Comn, 1977-79; assoc judge, Dallas Munic Ctr, 1978-; bd dir, Dallas Legal Serv Found Inc, 1979-; exec comt, Dallas County Dem Party, 1980-; bd dir, Jr Black Acad Arts & Letters Inc, 1980-. **Military Serv:** USMC, corp, 1963-67. **Business Addr:** Attorney, Robinson & Hoskins LLP, 400 S Zang Blvd Suite 920, Dallas, TX 75208.

TINSLEY-TALABI, ALBERTA
Government official. **Personal:** Born Aug 14, 1954; daughter of Willie Tinsley and Mary Louise Tinsley; married; married Bamidele A (divorced); children: Carla, David & Charles. **Educ:** Eastern Mich Univ, Ypsilanti, MI, BS, 1976; Wayne State Univ, Detroit. **Career:** Detroit Police Dept, Detroit, MI, rape counr, 1976-78; United Auto Workers, Detroit, MI, group worker, 1978-80; Comprehensive Youth Training & Community Involvement Prog, Detroit, MI, job develop counr, 1980-85; New Ctr Ment Health, Detroit, MI, stress mgt instr, 1985-87; Wayne County Comn, Detroit, MI, county comnr, 1987; Job Connection, proj specialist; Detroit City Coun, council woman, 1993-. **Orgs:** Nat Orgn Black County Officials; Nat Asn Counties; Women NACO; NAACP;Detroit Area Agency Aging; founder, Coalition Against Billboard Advertising of Alcohol and Tobacco (CABAAT); "Join Together Fellow" at Boston Univ; Founder, Mack Alive. **Honors/Awds:** Outstanding Service Award, Govt Admin Asn, 1988; Shirley Chisholm Award, Nat Polit Cong Black Women, 1988; Spirit of Detroit Award, City Detroit City Coun, 1988; Public Citizen of the Year, 1992; White House Special Service Award Recipient. **Business Addr:** Councilwoman, Detroit City Council, 1340 Coleman A Young Munic Ctr, 2 Woodward Ave, Detroit, MI 48226, **Business Phone:** (313)224-1645.

TIPPETT, ANDRE BERNARD
Sports manager, executive director, football player. **Personal:** Born Dec 27, 1959, Birmingham, AL; children: Janea Lynn, Asia, Madison & Coby. **Educ:** Ellsworth Community Col; Univ Iowa, BA, 1983. **Career:** Football player (retired), Executive Director, Sports Manager; New England Patriots, linebacker, 1982-93, dir of player resources, 1994-96, asst dir, pro-scouting, 1997-2003; dir, football develop & promotions, 2003, dir, pro-scouting, 2003-04, exec dir, currently. **Honors/Awds:** NFL Defensive Player of the Week, Pro Football Weekly & ESPN 1983; voted Best Linebacker/Defensive Back in AFC, 1984; Patriots' MVP, 1776 QB Club, 1984; AFC's Defensive Player of Week, Sports Illustrated & League Office, 1985; AFC Defensive Player of the Year Award; Defensive Player of the Year Award, New York Daily News; Big Brothers/Big Sisters-Tums Neutralizer of the Year Award; NFL Alumni Assn, Linbacker of the Year, 1987; NFL Player's Assn, Linbacker of the Year, 1985-87. **Business Addr:** Executive Director, New England Patriots, 1 Patriot Pl, Foxboro, MA 02035, **Business Phone:** (508)543-8200.

TIPTON, DR. DALE LEO
Physician. **Personal:** Born Jul 8, 1930, Parsons, KS; son of Dale and Ruby; children: Jill & Jan. **Educ:** Univ Calif, Berkeley, AB, Physiol, 1952; Univ Calif, San Francisco, MS, Pharmacology, 1959; Univ Calif, Sch Med, MD, 1959. **Career:** Kaiser Found Hosp, intern, 1959-60; Univ Calif, San Francisco, resident gen surg, 1960-62; Cancer Res Inst, Univ Calif, nat inst health fel, 1962-63; Univ Calif, San Francisco, resident otolaryngology, 1963-66; Univ Calif Sch Med, Dept Otolaryngology, clinical prof, 1976-; pvt Practice, physician. **Orgs:** Delegate, Calif Med Asn from San Francisco Medical Soc, 1968-69; bd dirs, San Francisco Med Soc, 1972-75; med adv, Calif Blue Shield, 1977-; chmn, Dept Ear Nose & Throat San Francisco Gen Hosp, 1970-76; chmn, Dept Ear Nose & Throat Franklin Hosp San Fran, 1968-; bd dirs, San Francisco Peer Review Org, 1983-86; chief med staff, Franklin Hosp, San Francisco, 1982-84. **Honors/Awds:** Diplomat Am Bd Otolaryngology, 1966; fel, Am Col Surgeons, 1970; Am Acad Otolaryngology, Head & Neck Surg, 1967-. **Special Achievements:** Published, "Changes in Golgi Apparatus of Islets of Langerhans in the Rat following Glucose & Insulin Admins" Endocrinology 1959; "Effects of Chlorpromazine on Blood Level of Alcohol in Rabbits" Amer Journal of Physiology 1961; "Duration of Bronchial Squamous Metaplasia Produced by Dogs by Cigarette Smoke Condensate" Journal of the Natl Cancer Inst 1964; "The Experimental Effects of Cigarette Smoke Condensate on Laryngeal Mucosa" published in proceedings of Int Congress of Otolaryngology 1965; "Osteochondroma of the tongue" Arch Path 1970; "Physiologic Assessment of Black People" Journal of Black Health 1975. **Military Serv:** USMC, first lt, 1953-55; USAR, lt col, 1984-. **Home Addr:** 458 Briarwood Dr, South San Francisco, CA 94080, **Home Phone:** (415)952-7509. **Business Addr:** Physician, 45 Castro St Suite 220, San Francisco, CA 94114, **Business Phone:** (415)621-6191.

TIPTON, DANELL
Athlete. **Personal:** Born Jul 22, 1973. **Career:** Int prof rodeo assoc, bull riding, 1995-; Event: Little Rock, 2003; Billing, 2003. **Honors/Awds:** Bull riding champion, 1995. *

TIPTON-MARTIN, TONI
Editor. **Personal:** Born Mar 6, 1959, Los Angeles, CA; daughter of Charles Hamilton and Beverly Dunbar; married Bruce Martin, 1992; children: Brandon, Jade, Christian. **Educ:** Univ Southern Calif, BA, 1981. **Career:** Waves Newspaper, Los Angeles, CA, food ed, 1980-91; Los Angeles Times, staff writer, 1983-91; Plain Dealer, Cleveland, food ed, 1991-. **Orgs:** Black Journalists Asn, 1980-91; Nat Food Ed & Writers Asn, 1991; pres, Southern Foodways Alliance. **Honors/Awds:** Media Award, Am Heart Asn, 1988; Nutrit Writing Award, Carnation County, 1988; Media Excellence Award, Am Heart Asn, 1989. **Special Achievements:** Coauthor of A Taste of Heritage: New African American Cuisine. **Business Addr:** Food Editor, The Plain Dealer, 1801 Superior Ave, Cleveland, OH 44114.*

TISDALE, PROF. CELES
Educator. **Personal:** Born Jul 31, 1941, Salters, SC; son of Norman and Rachel; married Ann Parker, Jun 25, 1966; children: Yvette, Colette & Eric. **Educ:** State Univ Col Buffalo, BS, 1963, MS, 1969, PhD, 1991. **Career:** PS 31 Buffalo, eng teacher, 1963-68; Woodlawn Jr High, eng dept chmn, 1968-69; WBEN TV, writer & producer, 1969; WBFO-FM Radio, writer & announcer, 1969-70; State Univ NY, Col Buffalo, eng instr, 1969-72; Buffalo Pub Sch Syst, eng instr; WKBW TV, talk show host, 1979-83; WKBW Radio, talk show host, 1984-86; Erie Community Col City, asst prof eng, currently. **Orgs:** Assoc dir, Buffalo Urban League, 1966-92; Young Audiences Inc, 1975-; bd dirs, Artpark, 1981-84; dir, Adolescent Voc Explor, 1985-88; Career Educr Buffalo Urban League, 1987-91; NY African Studies Asn. **Honors/Awds:** Chancellors Award for Teaching Excellence, State Univ NY, 1975; Man of theYear, Bus & Prof Women, 1977; Media Award, Sickle Cell Asn, 1978. **Business Addr:** Assistant Professor, Erie Community College, Department of English, 121 Ellicott St, Buffalo, NY 14203, **Business Phone:** (716)851-1322.

TISDALE, DR. HENRY NEHEMIAH
School administrator, college president. **Personal:** Born Jan 13, 1944, Kingstree, SC; son of Walter; married Alice Rose Carson; children: Danica Camille & Brandon Keith. **Educ:** Claflin Col, BS, 1965; Temple Univ, EdM, 1967; Dartmouth Col, MA, 1975, PhD, 1978. **Career:** Philadelphia Sch Dist, math instr, 1965-69; Del State Univ, prof math, 1969-85, instr & summer eng inst, 1978-85, asst dir inst res, 1978-85, asst acad dean, planning & Info mgt, 1986-87, sr vpres & chief acad officer, 1987-94; Univ Del, spec asst pres, 1985-86; Claflin Col, pres,1994-. **Orgs:** Bd mem, Holy Cross Sch System; State Del Task Force High Technol, 1986-87; United Negro Col Fund; Nat Asn Sch & Col United Methodist Church; Educ & Inst Ins Adminr; Am Coun Educ Comn Leadership Develop; Claflin Col Nat Alumni Asn; Conf Finance & Admin Adv Comt SC; Conf United Methodist Church; Leadership SC; chmn, SC Tuition & Grants Comn; Bd Dir, Edisto United

Way; bd gov, C Performing Arts Acad; Sigma Pi Phi Fraternity; Omega Psi Phi Fraternity; Trinity United Methodist Church. **Honors/Awds:** Southern Fellowship Fund Award, 1976-78; Man of the Year, Omega Psi Phi, 1981; Distinguished Alumni Award, Nat Asn Equal Opportunity Higher Educ; Educator of the Year Award, Nat Assoc Advan Colored People. **Special Achievements:** Listed in Who's Who Among Black Americans. **Business Addr:** President, Claflin College, 400 Magnolia St, Orangeburg, SC 29115-4476.

TISDALE, WAYMAN LAWRENCE
Basketball player, musician. **Personal:** Born Jun 9, 1964, Tulsa, OK; married Regina; children: 4. **Educ:** Univ Okla, attended 1985. **Career:** Basketball player (retired), musician; Ind Pacers, forward, 1985-89; Sacramento Kings, forward, 1989-94; Phoenix Suns, forward, 1994-97; Atlantic Rec, musician; Tisway Productions, owner, currently; Albums: Power Forward, 1995; In The Zone, 1996; Decisions, 1998; Face to Face, 2001; 21 Days, 2003; Hang Time, 2004; Way Up!, 2006. **Honors/Awds:** Three-time All-Am; Olympics US basketball, gold, 1984. **Business Addr:** Singer, Owner, Tisway Productions, Rendezvous Entertainment, 2211 Corinth Ave Suite 207, Los Angeles, CA 90064.

TITUS, LEROY ROBERT
Association executive. **Personal:** Born Dec 11, 1938, Pittsburgh, PA; married Anna Mary Adams; children: Shelley Meredyth, Sherre Mishel & Shelbi Melany. **Educ:** Lincoln Univ, AB, 1960. **Career:** Nat Insts Health, microbiologist, 1964-65; YMCA Pittsburgh, prog dir, 1965-69, Los Angeles, exec dir, chief exec officer; YMCA Fort Wayne/Allen Co, exec dir, 1969-72; Primerica Fin Servs, reg mgr, currently, reg vpres; Clothed Dignity, bus & prof training consult, currently, vpres bus & prof training, currently. **Orgs:** Dist vpres, Asn Prof Dirs; pres, Nat Black & Non White YMCA's; pres, YMCA's Serving Disadvantaged Communities; pres, PANDA Productions; Alpha Phi Alpha Fraternity; deleg nat coun, YMCA's USA, master trainer, 1981-. **Honors/Awds:** Human Serv Award, Asn Prof Direct, 1982; Outstanding Service Award, CITIES Inc, 1984; Dr Martin Luther King Human Dignity Award, La Metro YMCA, 1985; VPI Award, Nat Asn Advan Colored People, Los Angeles Chap, 1987. **Military Serv:** AUS, E-5. **Home Addr:** 13282 Briarwood St, Cerritos, CA 90703. **Business Addr:** Business & Professional Training Consultant, Vice President of Business and Professional Training, Clothed In Dignity, PO Box 14745, Long Beach, CA 90853, **Business Phone:** (562)961-9902.

TITUS, DR. MYER L.
College president. **Educ:** Philander Smith Col, attended 1954. **Career:** Col President (retired), State Bd Community Cols & Occup Educ, Denver, CO, assoc vpres, instrnl servs; Philander Smith Col, Little Rock, AR, pres, 1998. **Orgs:** Alpha Phi Alpha; Urban League, Comn on Arks' Future. **Honors/Awds:** Hon LLD, Univ Mo, 1991.

TITUS, ROBERT P
Accountant, businessperson. **Personal:** Born Jan 1, 1941?. **Educ:** Brooklyn Col. **Career:** Nemiroff, Cosmas, Titus & Colchamiro, partner; Mitchell & Titus & Co, managing partner, chief operating officer, 1973-, vice chmn, currently. **Orgs:** Pres, DC Chamber Com. **Special Achievements:** Co-founder of the largest minority-owned, certified public accounting firm in the United States. **Business Addr:** Managing Partner, Chief Operating Officer, Mitchell & Titus & Co, 2 Pk Ave, New York, NY 10016, **Business Phone:** (212)686-4777.

TITUS-DILLON, DR. PAULINE Y
Physician, educator. **Personal:** Born Jan 1, 1938, Jamaica; daughter of Ernest H Titus and Vera I Harvey; married Owen Christopher (deceased); children: Denyse & Paul. **Educ:** Howard Univ, BS, 1960; Howard Univ, Col Med, MD, 1964. **Career:** Howard Univ Hosp, post grad trainee internal med, 1964-68, from asst prof to prof, 1971-2003, from assoc dean to sr assoc dean acad affairs, 1980-2003, dean, 2003-, prof emer, 2003-; Georgetown Univ Hosp, Wash, DC, fel, endocrinology, 1968-69; Va Hosp Outpatient Clin Columbia SC, internist, 1969-71; DC Gen Hosp, chief, 1977. **Orgs:** DC Med Soc; fel Am Col Physicians; Prog Dirs Internal Med; Am Med Women's Asn Present; Alpha Omega Alpha Honor Med Soc Gamma Chap Present; Nat Med Assoc, NY Acad Sci, Am med Assoc. **Honors/Awds:** Daniel Hale Williams Award, Howard Univ, 1965, 1968; Excellence Award, Health Care Caribbean & Am Intercultural Org, 1996; Citation for Excellence, State Md, Delivery Health Care, 1996; diplomate, Am Bd Intn Med, Philadelphia, 1972; fel, NIH Bethesda, 1975-77; Inspirational Leadership Award, Student Coun, Howard Univ, Col Med, 1979; Superior Performance Award, Howard Univ, Dept Med, 1979. **Business Addr:** Professor Emeritus, Howard University College of Medicine, 520 W St NW Rm 527, Washington, DC 20059, **Business Phone:** (202)806-9494.

TOBIAS, RANDOLF A
Educator. **Personal:** Born Jan 16, 1940, Bronx, NY; married; children: Meredith, Maurice & Tonya. **Educ:** BA, 1961; MA, 1968; Columbia Univ, Teachers Col, EdD, 1976. **Career:** New York City Pub Schs, teacher, 1963-68; Mills Col Educ, instr, 1964-

71; Bedford Stuyvesant Talent Search, proj dir, 1968-69; Martin Luther King Jr Scholar Prog, Long Island Univ, 1969-; Long Island Univ, Brooklyn, Black Stud Cert Prog, dir, 1972-74; Shaw Univ, Raleigh, NC, Div Educ, dir, chairperson & assoc prof, 1975-77; Winston-Salem State Univ, Winston-Salem, NC, Div Educ, dir, chairperson & assoc prof, 1977-80; Queens Col, City Univ New York, Grad Dept Educ & Community Progs, assoc dean spec progs, 1980-87; chair, 1988-94, assoc prof sch admin, 1994, Dept Educ & Community Progs, assoc prof educ leadership, currently, prof, currently; Teacher Educ, Long Island Univ, asst prof; Mellon fel, 1983; Black Family Found Inc, Brooklyn, NY, dir, 1987-. **Orgs:** Trustee, Deer Park Bd Educ, Deer Park, NY; Va Union Univ Alumni Asn; Alpha Phi Alpha Fraternity; Am Asn Univ Prof; African Heritage Students Asn. **Honors/Awds:** Nat Fraternity of Student Musicians-Performance Awards, 1956 & 1957; Educational Honor Society Service Award, Kappa Delta Pi, 1996; Community Service Award, Suffolk County Black Caucus Democrats, 1997; Nnamdi Azikiwe Memorial Award for Youth Training, 1998. **Business Addr:** Associate Professor, Educational Leadership, Professor, Queens College, City University of New York, Department of Educational & Community Programs, Rm 033 Powdermaker Hall, Flushing, NY 11367, **Business Phone:** (718)997-5250.

TOBIN, LAUREN
Television broadcaster, chief executive officer. **Personal:** Daughter of Patricia (deceased); married; children: 1. **Educ:** Univ SC, broadcast jour. **Career:** CBS Entertainment, page, asst; Steven Bochco Productions, 1989; Fox Network, coordr & jr publicist; ABC TV Network, jr publicist & publicity dir, 1995-2006; Panther Pub Rels, founder & pres, 2006-; Tobin & Assocs, sr exec, 2008-. **Orgs:** Publicists Guild Am. **Honors/Awds:** Maxwell Weinberg Showmanship Award, Publicists Guild Am. **Business Addr:** Chief Executive Officer, Tobin & Associates Inc, 4929 Wilshire Blvd Suite 245, Los Angeles, CA 90010, **Business Phone:** (323)857-0869.*

TOBY, WILLIAM, JR.
Government official. **Personal:** Born Aug 12, 1934, Augusta, GA; son of William and Louise; married Diane Anderson; children: Michael & Kenneth. **Educ:** WVa State Col, BA, spanish studies, 1961; Adelphi Univ, MSW, 1963; Harvard Univ John F Kennedy Sch Govt, MPA, 1986. **Career:** Government Official (retired); HEW; Natl Urban League; New York Off Mayor, intergovernmental rels off, 1969-71; Health Edic Welfare Soc Rehab Serv, regional comnr, 1971-77; Health Care Fin Admin, reg admin, 1977-96. **Orgs:** Bd mem, Adelphi Univ; Natl Conf Social Welfare; brd overseers, New York Univ Grad Sch Pub Admin; act admin, US Dept Health & Human Serv. **Honors/Awds:** Exceptional Achievement, Sec Health Human Serv, 1982; Gubernatorial Citation, Gov NY, 1982; John W Davis Meritorious Award, W Va State Col,1984; Appreciation Award, Int Health Econ Mgt Inst, 1984; Meritorious Rank Award,1988. **Special Achievements:** First HCFA Leadership award in 1980. Honored by Adelphi Univ named Adelphi Alumni Of Distinction. **Military Serv:** USAF, corporal, 1951-55.

TODD, BEVERLY
Actor, television producer, administrator. **Personal:** Born Jul 11, 1946, Chicago, IL; married; children: Malik Smith. **Career:** Love of Life, 1951, 1968-70; "Deep Are the Roots", 1960; Roles in Poitier's: The Lost Man, 1969; They Call Me MISTER Tibbs!, 1970; Brother John, 1971; A Piece of the Action, 1977; Warner Bros, Los Angeles, CA,star: "Moving", 1988, "Clara's Heart", 1989, "Lean on Me", 1989; Paramount Pictures: "Sliver"; Syndicate-It Pro, Los Angeles, CA, co-producer: "A Laugh, A Tear", 1990-91; tv guest star: "Equal Justice", ABC-TV, 1991, "Falcon Crest", "Magnum P.I.", "The Redd Foxx Show", "Wise Guy", "A Different World", "Hill St Blues", "Roots"; HBO, Los Angeles, CA, co-producer: "The Don Jackson Story", 1991; dir: "I Need a Man", Embassey Theatre, LA. "The Bucket List", 2007. **Orgs:** Pres, Kwanza Found, 1991; Delta Sigma Theta. **Honors/Awds:** Ben, Friends of Black Oscar Nominees, 1990; Woman of the Yr, State of CA Legislature, 1990; 4 Time NAACP Image Award Nominee, 1978, 1984, 1988, 1989; Founder of the Malik Smith Scholar, 1989; Best Supporting Actress. **Special Achievements:** NAACP 4 Time Image Award Nominee, 1978, 1984, 1988, 1989; one of four women selected to write and produce "Tribute To The Black Woman" presented at the Shrine Auditorium in Los Angeles, California; A People's Choice Award.

TODD, CHARLES O
Educator, high school teacher. **Personal:** Born Nov 12, 1915, Lawrence, KS; son of Hazel Jr; married Geraldine Mann; children: Chrystal Todd Johnson & Karen Todd Lang. **Educ:** Emporia State Univ, BS, 1940; Kans Univ, MS, 1948; Univ Southern Calif, MFA, 1957. **Career:** Educator (retired); Douglas Sch, Mayview, Mo, teacher, 1940; Western Univ High Sch, Quindaro, Kans, teacher, 1941-42; Douglas Elem Sch, Manhattan, Kans, prin, 1943; Dunbar Jr High Sch, Tucson, Ariz, teacher, 1947-51; Manfield Jr High School, teacher, 1951-67; Tucson Sr High School, teacher, 1967-82. **Orgs:** Kans Teachers & Admin, 1943, Phi Delta Kappa, 1946; Alpha Phi Alpha 1950; treas, Tucson Fine Arts Asn, 1950; pres, Nat Asn Advan Colored People Tucson Credit Union, 1964; Tucson Civic Chorus, 1966-67; pres, bd dir, Tucson Civic Chorus,

1965; mentor, Tucson Big Brothers, 1966-67; treas, Tucson Br Nat Asn Advan Colored People, 1968-74; mentor, Acad Prep Excellence, 1987-89; Foster Care Rev Bd, 1988-96; pres, Eta Psi Lambda Chap, Alpha Phi Alpha, 1989; life mem, Dima Co Retired Teachers Asn. **Honors/Awds:** Service Award, Tucson Br Nat Asn Advan Colored People, 1975; Certificate of Recognition as a Connecting Link, Tucson Chap, 1994. **Military Serv:** US Air Corps, sgt, 1944-46; Air Campaign Medal. **Home Addr:** 848 E Grant Rd, Tucson, AZ 85719. *

TODD, CYNTHIA JEAN
Journalist. **Personal:** Born Jan 12, 1951, Peoria, IL; children: Wendy. **Educ:** Northern Ill Univ, DeKalb, BA, 1972. **Career:** Peoria J Star, reporter, 1969-73; WMBD-AM-FM TV Peoria, reporter, anchor, 1974-77; KSDK-TV St Louis, reporter, anchor, 1977-79; Harris Stowe State Coll, dir publ; St Louis Post-Dispatch St Louis, reporter, 1983-, dir, Newsroom Recruitment, currently. **Orgs:** Greater St Louis Black Journalist Asn, 1977-, AFTRA, 1977, Ill Newsbroadcasters Asn, 1975-77; adv comn, Univ City HS, Univ City MO, 1978; Alpha Kappa Alpha Sor; bd dirs, New City Sch, St Louis, 1980. **Honors/Awds:** Broadcast History Award, McLean County, Ill Hist Soc, 1976; Achiever in Industry Award, St Louis Metro Sentinel Newspaper, 1978; Nat Am Advan Colored People Media Roole Model Award, 1989; Missouri Asn Social Welfare Media Award, 1992. **Special Achievements:** Listed in Names & Faces Nat Publ, 1978. **Business Addr:** Reporter/Director of Newsroom Recruitment, St Louis Post-Dispatch, 900 N Tucker Blvd, Saint Louis, MO 63101, **Business Phone:** (314)340-8282.

TODD, MELVIN R.
Administrator. **Personal:** Born Apr 24, 1933, Oklahoma City, OK; married Menzola Anderson; children: Sharon, Myra, David. **Educ:** Langston Univ, BA, Hist, 1954; Univ Okla, MEd, sec, 1960; Univ OK, EdD, soc admin & gen admin, 1973. **Career:** Neb High Sch Okla City, asst prin, 1967-69, prin, 1969-71; Consultative Ctr Equal Educ Opport Univ Okla, field consult, 1971-73; Okla City Pub Sch, dir curriculum, 1973-75; Okla State Regents Higher Educ, spec asst chancellor & stud & officer, 1975-80; Okla State Regents Higher Educ, vice chancellor acad admin, 1975-91. **Orgs:** bd dir, E&C Trades Ltd, 1980; Okla Educ Asn; corp mem, Am Col Testing Prog Corp; Phi Delta Kappa; Urban League; NAACP. **Honors/Awds:** outstanding educr's award, Okla Educ Asn, 1975; distinguished alumnus award, Langston Univ, 1976; presidential citizen Nat Asn Equal Educ Opport Highter Educ, 1980. **Military Serv:** AUS, spec 3rd, 1954-56; Good conduct, AUS, 1954-56.

TODD, THOMAS N.
Lawyer. **Personal:** Born Sep 24, 1938, Demopolis, AL; son of Cleveland and Alberta; married Janis Roberts; children: Traci Neuborne, Tamarla Nicole. **Educ:** Baton Rouge, BA, polit sci, 1959, JD, 1963. **Career:** US Dept Labor, off solicitor, 1963-64; US Atty Chicago, officer, 1967-70; Comn Inquiry into Black Panthers & Law Enforcement NY, consult, 1970-72; Northwestern Univ, law prof, 1970-74; Chicago Capt Social CLC, pres, 1971; Oper PUSH, exec vpres, 1971-73; Midwest Task Force Comn Report "Search & Destroy," dir; Northwestern Univ Sch Law Chicago, asst prof law, asst dir ctr urban affairs; pvt pract, atty. **Orgs:** Supreme Court LA, 1963, US Court Mil Appeals, 1965, Supreme Court IL, 1967, US Court Appeals 7th Circuit, 1968, US Dist Court, No Dist IL, US Supreme Court, 1971, Chicago Community United Negro Col Fund; bd dir, Legal Opportunity Scholarship Prog; adv bd, IL Black Legislative Clearinghouse Chicago; adv bd, Afro-Am Patrolmans League Chicago. **Honors/Awds:** Ammer Jurisprudence Award; Law Week Award; JS Clark Memorial Award; Criminal Law Award, Soc Univ Sch Law; 1 of 10 Outstanding Young Men, Chicago Jaycees, 1970; Leadership Council, Met Open Comn, 1970; Certificate Achievement, Kappa Alpha Phi Northwestern Univ, 1971; Certificate Achievement, Afro-Am Policemens League, 1971; Lawndale Peoples Planning & Action Comn, 1971; SCLC Operation Breadbaskets Activist Award, 1971; IN Dem Org, 1971; Achievement Award, Mens Fed Soc Univ, 1972; Student Govt Award, Soc Univ, 1972; Power Inc Harambee Award, 1972; Listed One Thousand Success Stories, 1973; Biog pub Chicago Negro Almanac, 1973; Outstanding Achievement Award, The Nat Consumer Info Ctr, 1974; Black Excellence Award, Community Action PUSH Espo, 1974; National Education Award, Phi Beta Sigma, 1975; Meritorious Service Award, Nat Asn Black Political Sci, 1976; Appreciation Award, June tenth Comt, 1976; Appreciation Award, Nat Consumer Info Ctr host Tom Todd Show WLS Radio Chicago; "Voice Ebony" Radio Commercial Ebony Mag; honorary doctorate Laws, Grambling State Univ, 1987; honorary doctorate Laws, Syracuse Univ, 1990; honorary doctorate, Wilberforce Univ, 1993; honorary doctorate Talladega Col, 1998; honorary doctorate, Southern Univ A&M Col, 1999; honorary doctorate, Univ Maryland Eastern Shore, 2000; honorary degree, Bethuna-Cookman Col; History Maker, 2002. **Military Serv:** AUS; capt, judge advocate off, 1964-67. *

TODD, WILLIAM S
Airplane pilot. **Personal:** Born Mar 10, 1940, Portsmouth, VA; son of William S and Martha E Muckle; divorced; children: David M, Kelly Yvette & William S IV. **Educ:** Va Union Univ, BS, 1962.

Career: USAF, Commander C-135 Aircraft, lt col; USAF Acad, liaison officer, dep commander; Western Airlines, airline pilot Boeing 727, 1969-87, Boeing 737 capt, 1987-93; Delta 727 Airlines, 1993-96; Los Angeles, CA, Boeing 767, 757, captain, 1996-; City Bradbury, Bradbury, CA, chair planning comn, 1990-99; Delta Airlines, check pilot, instr pilot, 1991-; City Bradbury, CA, mayor, 2001-02. **Orgs:** Airline Pilots Asn, Alpha Phi Alpha Fraternity, US Jaycees; advert ed, mgr US Jaycees Publ, Accident Investr, Engineering & Air Safety Community Airline Pilots Asn; chmn, Comt Select City Slogan City Cerritos, CA; Youth Motivation Task Force, 1969-; Westside Fair Housing Coun, 1969-; campaign mgr, City Coun Candidate, 1974; owner, Spectral Illuminations; bd dirs, La County Sanitation Districts; bd dirs, Mid-San Gabriel Valley Consortium; bd dirs, League Calif cities. **Honors/Awds:** Awards, Youth Motivation Task Force, 1970, 1972; Jaycee Sound Citizen Award, 1974. **Military Serv:** USAF, capt, 1963-68; USAFR, Lt Col (retired); Air Medal w/2 Clusters, Small Arms Expert Marksman, Vietnam Expeditionary Medal, 1965, USAF, Meritorious Service Medal, 1984, USAF, Achievement Medal, 1988, Second Meritorious Service Medal, 1991-. **Business Addr:** Airline Pilot, Delta Airlines, Hartsfield Atlanta Airport, Atlanta, GA 30320.

TODMAN, JUREEN FRANCIS
School administrator. **Personal:** Born Jun 30, 1935, St Thomas, Virgin Islands of the United States; daughter of Sarah Steimbergen Joshua; divorced; children: Jens, Maurice & Monigue. **Educ:** Philander Smith Col, BA, BS, 1959; NY Univ; Col VI. **Career:** School administrator (retired); St Thomas Fedn Teachers, teacher secy, 1976-78, from vpres to pres, 1980-81, teacher, sec bd election; Govt Employees' Retirement Syst VI chap, bd trustees, 1990-92. **Orgs:** Alpha Kappa Alpha; pres, Women Aux Little League, 1972; treas, Cent Labor Coun, 1978-80; bd dir, chairperson fund raising, St Thomas E Lioness Methodist Church Choir, 1974-75 & 1984-85; secy, AAA Baseball League; bd dir, United Way; Govt Employee's Retirement Syst VI; secy, Bd Election, 1982-; chm, Joint Bd Election St Thomas, St John, St Croix, 1986-88; pres,St Thomas E Lioness Club, 1990-91. **Honors/Awds:** Athletic Scholarship, VI Educ Dept, 1954; Athletic Award Softball, Volleyball, Track; Hugo Dennis Award, Teachers Fedn, 1983; Outstanding Service, East Lioness Club District 60B, 1989. **Special Achievements:** Poetry published in local daily news.

TODMAN, TERENCE ALPHONSO
Consultant, executive, ambassador. **Personal:** Born Mar 13, 1926, St Thomas, VI; son of Alphonse and Rachel Callwood; married Doris Weston; children: Terence A Jr, Patricia Rhymer Todman, Kathryn Browne & Michael. **Educ:** Poly Inst Puerto Rico, BA, 1951; Syracuse Univ, MPA, 1953; Am Univ, post grad, 1954. **Career:** Officer (retired), executive; Dept St, intl rel officer, 1952-54, foreign affairs officer, 1955; UN Intern Prog, US nom, 1955; UN Trusteeship Coun Petit Com & Com, Rural Econ Develop, US rep, 1956-57; UN Gen Assembly, adv US del, 1956-57; Am Embassy New Delhi, India, polit officer, 1957-59; Am Embassy-Tunis, polit officer, 1961-64; Lome, Togo, DCM & charge d'affaires, 1965-68; Bur African Affairs Dept St, country dir for Kenya, Tanzania, Uganda & Seychelles 1968; US Ambassador to Chad, 1969-72; US Ambassador to Guinea, 1972-75; US Ambassador to Costa Rica, 1975-77; Asst Sec St for Latin Am Affairs, 1977-78; US Ambassador to Spain, 1978-83; US Ambassador to Denmark, 1983-89; US Ambassador to Argentina, 1989-93; Todman & Assocs Inc, pres, currently. **Orgs:** Am Foreign Serv Asn; fel Nat Acad Pub Admin; bd trustees, Univ VI; Coun on Foreign Rels; Am Acad Diplomacy; Atlantic Coun US; Constiuency Africa; Asn Black Am Ambassadors; Alpha Phi Alpha Fraternity; bd dir, Nat Endowment Democracy. **Honors/Awds:** Sup Honor Award, Dept State, 1966; Medal Honor Govt VI, 1977; Hall of Fame US Army Infantry Sch Ft, GA; Grand Cross Highest Order Isabela la Catolica, Spanish Govt, 1983; Grand Cross Order Dannebug by Govt Denmark, 1988; Distinguished Trustees Award, Col VI, 1985; Presidental Distinguished Service Award, 1985; Nat Pub Service Award, 1987; LLD, Colgate Univ, 1981, Syracuse Univ, 1986, Boston Univ, 1987; Hon Doctor Pub Service, Morgan State Univ, 1986; Equal Employment Opportunity Award, Foreign Affairs Agencies, 1987. **Special Achievements:** First African American to serve as US ambassador in Latin America. **Military Serv:** AUS, first lt, 1945-49. **Business Addr:** President, Todman & Associates Inc, PO Box 6334, St Thomas, VI 20004.

TOKLEY, JOANNA NUTTER
Social worker. **Personal:** Born in Nanticoke, MD; daughter of Clifton Nutter and Iolia Williams; married E James Tokley; children: Tyrone, Charles & Michael. **Educ:** Morgan State Univ, BS, 1962; Univ S Fla. **Career:** Hillsborough City Pub Sch, teacher, 1962-70, human rels spec, 1970-74; Tampa Urban Hillsborough League Inc, dep dir, econ develop, employ dir, 1974-82, exec dir, pres & chief exec officer, currently. **Orgs:** Alpha Kappa Alpha, 1958-, pres, 1966-69, 1975; Toastmasters Chap 1810, 1980-; Gov Constituency Against Child Abuse, 1984-; Tampa Chamber Comn, 1985; Leadership Tampa, 1989-; vpres, Nat Coalition 100 Black Women, 1989-; Comn 100, 1990-; Regional Workforce Develop Bd. **Honors/Awds:** S Atlantic Region Ruby J Gainer Human Relations Award, AKA, 1975; Outstanding Community Service, The Charmettes Inc, Mt Calvary Day Adventist Church, 1979, 1985; Eddie Mitchell Mem Community Service Award, City Tampa Off Comm Rels, 1980; Dist Dramatic Speech Toastmasters FL, 1981; Woman of the Year, The Orchid Club, 1983; Leadership Tampa, Greater Tampa Chamber Comn, 1988; Martin Luther King Jr Bust Award, Tampa Orgn Black Affairs; Nat Conf Medallion. **Business Addr:** President, Chief Executive Officer, Tampa Urban Hillsborough League Inc, 1405 Tampa Pk Plz, Tampa, FL 33605, **Business Phone:** (813)229-8117.

TOLAN-GAMBLE, JANET HELEN
Nurse, manager, consultant. **Personal:** Born May 5, 1915, Dallas, TX; daughter of Thomas E and Nellie Helen; married Toby (deceased). **Educ:** Biggers Bus Col; Oakland Merritt Bus Col; Univ Ark; Anchorage Br, DHL. **Career:** Manager, nurse, consultant (retired); Ark Dept Labor, minority specialist, 1965-80, supr, 1944-47; Oakland Naval Supply Depot, minority specialist; Alameda Community Outpatient Dept, minority specialist; Off Milo H Fritz MD, ophthal & otolaryngol. **Orgs:** Deaconess Shiloh Bapt Church, 1952-; pres, Anchorage Union & Missionary Soc, 1971; chmn bd dir, Opportunities Indust Ctr, 1974-76; deleg, WhiteHouse Conf Aging, 1995; bd chair, Anchorage Sr Ctr, 1999-2001; past vpres, Eye-Ear-Nose-Throat Found; Ark Nat Asn Advan Colored People; Ark Black Caucus; past pres, Ch Women United Int; dir founder, Minority Outreach Employment Serv; OES Order Eastern Star; Ark Coun Disabilities & Spec Educ; immediate past chmn, Older Alaskans Comn; Municipal Sr Adv Comn, Anchorage; past pres, North to Future Bd; parliamention, RPEA, Nat Pub Employees Asn; St Cardiovascular Team; Hon mem, Mothers Christian FelClub. **Honors/Awds:** Most Outstanding Religion, 1974, 1977; Meritorious Service Award, Univ Alaska Anchorage, 2000; P Worthy Matron Alpha Guide No 8; Grand Dep Worthy Matron Guiding Light United Grand Chap CA & AK; Volunteer of the Year Award, First Lady of Anchorage; Rosa Parks Award, WICS. **Special Achievements:** Founder of scholarship program, Shiloh Baptist Church; founder Janet Helen Tolan-Gamble and Toby Gamble Educational Trust Fund, board of directors, 1999. **Home Addr:** 3207 Westmar Cir, Anchorage, AK 99508-4336.

TOLBERT, DR. HERMAN ANDRE
Physician, psychiatrist. **Personal:** Born May 29, 1948, Birmingham, AL; son of John and Ruth. **Educ:** Stillman Col, BS, 1969; Univ Calif, San Diego, MD, 1973. **Career:** Ohio State Univ, res, 1973-77, child flw, 1977-78, asst prof, 1978-89; assoc prof, 1989-2001; prof, 2001-03, prof emeritus, 2003-; Insight Matters, editor, 1994-. **Orgs:** Minister flw, Am Psychiatric Asn, 1977; editor, Spectrm Newsletter, APA/NIMH Flws, 1981-83; Am Psychiatric Asn, 1978-, Am Acad Child Pschiatry, 1979-, Asn Acad Psychiatry, 1980-; secy, Psychiatric Soc Central Ohio, 1985-88; pres-elect, Psychiatric Soc Central Ohio, 1989-90, pres, 1990-91; dir, Div Child & Adolescent Psychiatry, Dept Psychiatry, Ohio State Univ. **Honors/Awds:** Fel Am Psychiatric Asn, 1977; dipl, Am Bd Psychiatry Neurol, 1980-82; bk chaps, Behavioral Problem Childhood & Adolescence; fel, Am Acad Child & Adolescent Psychiatry, 1982; fel, Am Psychiatric Asn, 1989. **Home Addr:** 8231 Windsong Ct, Columbus, OH 43235, **Home Phone:** (614)436-8201. **Business Addr:** Professor Emeritus, Ohio State University, 1670 Upham Dr, Columbus, OH 43210, **Business Phone:** (614)293-8234.

TOLBERT, JACQUELYN C.
School administrator. **Personal:** Born Dec 20, 1947, Kilgore, TX; married Melvin Eugene (divorced); children: Alexis N. **Educ:** Kilgore Col, AA, scholastic hon, 1968; Stephen F Austin State Univ, BA, 1970, MA, 1975, Mid-mgt adminr cert, 1980; East Tex State Univ. **Career:** Longview Independent Sch Dist, teacher, 1970-71; Kilgore Independent Sch Dist, teacher 1971-79, pub info coordr, 1979; Tidwell Elem Sch, asst supt; N Forest Independent Sch Dist, asst supt community relations. **Orgs:** Bd dirs, Longview Fine Arts Asn; Pub Relations Comn Jr Achievement E Tex; Delta Sigma Theta Sorority Longview Alumnae Chap, 1973-79; vpres, Tex Sch PR Asn, 1983-85; Nat Sch PR Asn Impact Comn, 1984-85; Nat Sch PR Asn J Coun, 1984-85; Tex Sch Admin Asn, 1984-; Prof Journalists Inc, 1985; Kilgore Kiwanis; bd dirs, Gregg County Am Heart Asn; bd dirs, Jr Achievement E Tex. **Honors/Awds:** Rookie of the Year, 1981; Bright Idea Award, Tex Sch Pub Relations Asn, 1982-83; Outstanding Woman Sigma Gamma Rho, 1985; Best of Contest, 1989, Professional Achievement, 1991, Tex Sch PR Assn, 1991; Auth: "How to Build a School Community Program", Tex Educ Agency, Tex Sch PR Asn, 1984. **Home Addr:** 2309 Pam St, Longview, TX 75602. **Business Addr:** Assistant Superintendent of Community Relations, North Forest Independent School District, 7201 Langley Rd 77016, PO Box 23278, Houston, TX 77228, **Business Phone:** (713)491-1035.

TOLBERT, ODIE HENDERSON, JR.
Educator, archivist. **Personal:** Born Aug 21, 1939, Memphis, TN; son of Odie H Sr and Rozina Tolbert; married Maganolia Smith; children: Alisa, Carla, Odie III. **Educ:** LeMoyne-Owen Col, BA, 1962; Northern IL Univ, MA, 1969; Fisk Univ, Adv Cert Black Studies Librarianship, 1973. **Career:** Educator (retired); Univ Memphis, catalog librn, assoc prof, 1969-02; assoc prof emeritus. **Orgs:** Univ Memphis Libr Asn, 1970-, TN Libr Asn, 1973-, Am Libr Asn & Black Caucus, 1973-; archivist Church God Christ, 1986-; disabled Am Veterans, 1965-; assoc mem, Ctr Black Music Res, 1988-; dir libr serv Pentecostal Temple COGIC, 1984-. **Honors/Awds:** Music Scholarship, Owen Jr Col, 1957-59; Internship Black Studies Librarianship Fisk Univ US Dept Educ, 1973; A Bibliography Dr Martin Luther King, Jr Collection Mississippi Valley Collection, Memphis State Univ Feb, 1983; The Church Libr Whole Truth newspaper, official paper Church God Christ April, 1988; Article: "Gospel Music in the Cogic Tradition," Rejoice Magazine, 1989; Poster Presentation: "Research on African American Gospel Music," ALA Annual Meeting, 1990; Religious Workers Guild Inc, COGIC, Special Achievement Award, November, 1993; Doctor Humanities, Trinity Hall Col Seminary April, 1994; Youth Move Cultural Heritage Preservation Educator's Hall of Fame, 1998; Gold & Blue Award, Manassas HS, 2000; article: "Astral Harmonies L'Histoire des Raymond Rasberry Singers," Soul Bag mag, 2000; State TN, proclamation, 1997; US CNG proclamation, 1998; Presidential Award, Univ Memphis, 2002. **Military Serv:** AUS, sp4, 1963-65. *

TOLBERT, TONY LEWIS
Football player. **Personal:** Born Dec 29, 1967, Tuskegee, AL; married Satasha; children: Anthony Lewis. **Educ:** Univ Tex-El Paso, BA, criminal justice, 1991. **Career:** Football player (retired); Dallas Cowboys, defensive end, 1989-97. **Honors/Awds:** All-Western Athletic Conf, 1988; Pro Bowl, 1996.

TOLENTINO, SHIRLEY A.
Judge. **Personal:** Born Feb 2, 1943, Jersey City, NJ; daughter of Jack Hayes and Mattie Theresa Kelly Tart; married Dr. Ernesto A. Tolentino; children: Ana Ramona, Candida. **Educ:** Col St Elizabeth, BA, 1965, LLD, 1980; Seton Hall Univ, Sch Law, JD, 1971; NY Univ, Grad Sch Law, LLM, 1981. **Career:** Henry Hudson Reg Sch, Highland NJ, teacher, Latin & Eng, 1965-67; Upward Bound Col St Elizabeth, asst proj dir, 1966-68, 1969-71; S High Sch Youngstown Ohio, teacher Latin & English, 1968-69; Va Newark, adjudicator 1971; State of NJ Div Law, dep atty gen, 1976; NJ City Mus Ct, judge, 1976-84; Super Ct NJ, judge, 1984-. **Orgs:** Hudson Cty Bar Asn; Garden State Bar Asn; Alumnae Bd Col St Elizabeth; NJ Alumnae Chap Delta Sigma Theta; NJ City Nat Asn Advan Colored People; Hudson City Urban League; pres, Nat Asn Women Judges; bd regents, St Peters Col. **Honors/Awds:** Rec Scholar to Coll of St Elizabeth; grad in top 20 rec hon in Philosophy. **Special Achievements:** Published "Stopping the Runaway Train: Jury Nullification," NBA Journal, Nov/Dec 1998; First full time female Mun Ct Judge in NJ; first black female judge in Jersey City & Hudson City; first black female judge in Superior Court of NJ. **Business Addr:** Judge, Superior Court 6th Vicinage, State of New Jersey, 595 Newark Ave, Hudson Co Admin Bldg, Jersey City, NJ 07306, **Business Phone:** (201)795-6668.*

TOLER, BURL ABRON
Educator. **Personal:** Born May 9, 1928, Memphis, TN; married Melvia Woolfolk; children: Valerie D, Burl Jr, Susan A, Gregory L, Martin L & Jennifer L. **Educ:** Univ San Francisco, BS, 1952; Univ San Fran, MA, 1966. **Career:** SF Unified Sch Dist, asst prin counr & teacher, 1955-74; Nat Football League, off, 1965-; SF, prin, 1965; SF Comm Col Dist, dir personnel, 1972-; Univ San Francisco, trustee, 1987-96, trustee emer, 1997-. **Orgs:** AFT; CTA; CASSA; SFASA; ERA; Asn Calif Community Col Adminrs; Kappa Alpha Psi; Nat Asn Advan Colored People; African Am Hist Soc; Grand Jury, 1961; Juvenile Just Com; bd dir, Booker T Washington Comm Cen; adv bd, YMCA; bd dir, Mt Zion Hosp, 1976; bd gov Univ SF; bd regents, St Ignatius Col Prep Sch; bd dir, SF Entertainment Cen Corp, 1976; Boys Cen, 1977; comr, San Francisco Police Dept, 1978-. **Honors/Awds:** Hall of Fame, Univ San Francisco; Isaac Hayes Achievements in sports Award, Vanguard Club, 1972; Hall of Fame, Africa Am Hist Soc, 1977. **Business Addr:** Trustees Emeriti, University of San Francisco, 2130 Fulton St, San Francisco, CA 94117, **Business Phone:** (415)422-6762.

TOLER, PENNY
Basketball player, sports manager. **Personal:** Born Mar 24, 1966, Virginia. **Educ:** Long Beach State Univ, attended. **Career:** Basketball player (retired), vice president, gen mgr; Montecchio, Italy, guard, 1989-91;Pescara, Italy, 1991-94; Sporting Flash, Greece, 1994-96; Ramat HaSharon, Israel, 1996-97; Los Angeles Sparks, 1997-99; Los Angeles Sparks, gen mgr, 2004-. **Honors/Awds:** Long Beach State Athletic Hall of Fame. **Business Addr:** General Manager, Vice President, Los Angeles Sparks, 555 N Nash St, El Segundo, CA 90245, **Business Phone:** (310)426-6000.

TOLES, JAMES LAFAYETTE, JR. **See Obituaries section.**

TOLIVER, GEORGE
Basketball executive. **Career:** NBAD League, supvr off; Nat Basketball Asn, referee, currently; Toliver Basketball Officiating Sch, guest clinician, currently. **Orgs:** Dir, Youth Basketball Camps, FIBA. **Honors/Awds:** Bronze Medal, 1994. **Home Phone:** (540)434-6037. **Business Addr:** Guest Clinician, Toliver Basketball Officiating School, PO Box 283, Harrisonburg, VA 22803.

TOLIVER, PAUL ALLEN
Executive. **Personal:** Born Sep 14, 1946, Baltimore, MD; son of Paul Arthur and Ruth Allen; married Jane D, Feb 15, 1969;

children: Jill Arlene & Paul Russell. **Educ:** Univ Cincinnati, BBA, 1968, MBA, 1973. **Career:** ATE Mgt & Serv Comp, sr vpres, 1973-84; San Francisco Municipal Railway, deputy gen mgr, 1984-88; Seattle Metro, dir transit, 1988-96; King County dept transp, dir, 1996-2002; Computer Intelligence Squared, vpres, transp, 2002-. **Orgs:** Former chair, bd dir, Norman Y Mineta Intl Inst Surface Trans Policy; Nat Urban League, bd dir, exec comm, 1994-97; Urban League Metro Seattle, chair bd dir, 1992-97; Am Public Transit asn, vpres, mgt & fin, 1992-94; Conf Minority Transp Officials, nat pres, 1986-88; African Am Agenda (Seattle), charter mem, 1993-; Transp Research Bd, 1988-; chair, Seattle Art Museum's African Arts Coun, 1993-; bd trustees, Seattle Art Museum, 1998-; bd dirs, Intelligent Transp Soc Am, 1999-2002; chair, Norman Y Mineta Intl Inst Surface Transp Policy Studies; chair, TCRP Project J-9. **Honors/Awds:** Am Public Transit Assn, Best (major city) Transit System, 1992; Conference of Minority Trans Officials, Sibling Leadership Award, 1988; King County, Dr Martin Luther King Jr Humanitarian Award, 1995; Jesse L Haugh Awd, Am Transit Assn, 1999. **Special Achievements:** Co-author of paper/presentation on IVHS Tech, 2nd Ann IVHS Conf, 1992; The Walls have Come Down, Passenger Transport, 1992; Management Basics, Passenger Transport, 1991; The Manager and the Computer, Passenger Transport, 1990; Technology and the Transit Manager, Presentation at APTA Annl, 1994; Technology Holds the key to Better Customer Svc, Passenger Transport, 1996; Why Its in the First Place, Passenger Transport, 1997; One of 25 Most Influential in bus Industry, Bus Ride Mag, 1998; "Govlink World Trade Organization Traffic Alert End King County Traffic Alert," Its Quarterly, Fall 2000. **Military Serv:** AUS, spec-5, 1969-71; Leadership (basic training), Good Conduct, 1971. **Business Addr:** Vice President, Computer Intelligence Squared, 701 5th Ave Suite 4200, Seattle, WA 98104, **Business Phone:** (206)262-8172.

TOLIVER, VIRGINIA F DOWSING
Library administrator. **Personal:** Born Nov 1, 1948, Tupelo, MS; daughter of Frank D Sr and Jessie Spearman; divorced; children: Wilmetta J Toliver-Diallo. **Educ:** Jackson State Univ, Jackson, Miss, BA, 1969; Univ Ill, Urbana, Ill, MSLS, 1973. **Career:** Alcorn State Univ, Lorman, Miss, serials librn, 1973-77, actg libr dir, 1974-77; Univ Southern Miss, Hattiesburg, Miss, coordr, info retrieval, 1977-81; Wash Univ, St Louis, Mo, dir, admin & planning, 1982-99, assoc dean admin, 1982-. **Orgs:** Am Libr Asn, 1982-87, 1989-; Ala Black Caucus, 1988-; Charmanine Chapman Soc, United Way, 1999-; Moderator, Presbytery Giddings Lovejoy, 2004; bd dir, Eden Theol Sem. **Honors/Awds:** Inst Info Retrieval, Lawrence Livermore Lab, 1977; Acad Libr Mgmt Intern, Coun Libr Resources, 1981-82. **Business Addr:** Associate Dean, Washington University Library, 1 Brookings Dr, Campus Box 1061, St Louis, MO 63130, **Business Phone:** (314)935-5400.

TOLLETT, DR. CHARLES ALBERT, SR.
Physician. **Personal:** Born in Muskogee, OK; son of Harrel E Tollett Sr and Hattie Mae Scruggs; married Katherine; children: Lynn, Charles Jr, Frank & Jeffery. **Educ:** Howard Univ, BS, 1950; Temple Univ Med Sch, MD, 1952; Temple, intern, 1953-56; Temple, surg resident, 1956-57; jr instr surg, 1956-57; sr surg resident, 1957; Temple Univ, DSc (surgery), 1957; Am Bd Surg, cert, 1958. **Career:** Semi-retired, gen surgeon, currently; St Anthony Hosp, chief surg, 1991-93; pvt pract, currently. **Orgs:** Phi Beta Kappa Med, AOA; Babcock Surg Soc; Howard Univ Alumni; Kappa Alpha Psi; Sigma Pi Phi; Philadelphia Co Med Soc; AMA; Oklahoma State Med Dental & Pharm Asn; OK Co & State Med Soc; OK Surg Asn; Am Col Surgeons; YMCA; Control Chap Oklahoma Howard Alumni Asn; bd, Oklahoma Am Ins Co; pres, Oklahoma Health Sci Ctr Faculty House, 1974; Areawide Health Planning Org; assoc clinical prof surg, Univ Oklahoma Health Sci Ctr; Nat Med Asn, Pan Pacific Surgical Asn; pres, bd, City County Health Dept, 1984-89; Governor's Comn on Oklahoma Health Care, 1992-93; Allen Chapel AME Church, trustee bd; NCP, life mem. **Honors/Awds:** Volunteer of the Year Award in Recognition of Outstanding Serv to the Eastside Br YMCA, 1984; Fel, Am Col Surgeons, 1960. **Special Achievements:** Contributing author, A Century of Black Surgeons: The USA Experience. **Military Serv:** AUS m/sgt, 1943-46. **Home Addr:** 214 E 17th St, Huntingburg, IN 47542. **Business Addr:** Physician, 214 E 17th St, PO Box 18936, Huntingburg, IN 47542, **Business Phone:** (812)683-6339.

TOLLIVER, CHARLES
Trumpet player, educator, music producer. **Personal:** Born Mar 6, 1942, Jacksonville, FL; son of Samuel and Ruth Lavatt; divorced; children: Charles Edward. **Educ:** Howard Univ, Col Pharm, 1960-63. **Career:** Strata-East Records, co-founder, pres, ceo, 1970-; New Sch Jazz & Contemp Music, adj prof, jazz orchestra, dir, 1992-. **Orgs:** Broadcast Music Inc, 1964-; Am Fed Musicians, 1964-. **Honors/Awds:** No1 Trumpetist, Downbeat Magazine, 1968; New England Conservatory of Music, 1975. **Special Achievements:** Composer, conductor, arranger of orchestral suite performed at Carnegie Hall, 1975. **Business Addr:** President, Chief Executive Officer, Strata-East Records, Grand Central Station, PO Box 36, New York, NY 10163.

TOLLIVER, REV. JOEL
Clergy, educator, administrator. **Personal:** Born Feb 26, 1946, Philadelphia, PA; married Sharon; children: Joel Jr & Paul. **Educ:** Lincoln Univ, BA, 1969; Yale Univ, MPH, 1971; Colgate Bexler Crozer Theol Sem, MDiv, 1985; State Univ NY, Buffalo, PhD, educ admin, 1995. **Career:** Univ Rochester, health educr, 1971; Radio Sta WAXI, talk show host, 1973-77; Empire State Col, asst prof, 1973; City Rochester, asst city mgr, 1974-82; Brockport State Col, consult, 1974, chaplain, admin & instr, 1987; Genessee Community Col, consult, 1974; Monroe Community Col, chaplain & adminr; DeVry Inst Technol, dean; Haven Rest Missionary Baptist Church, pastor, 2004-. **Orgs:** Bbd mem, United Church Ministry Inc, 1979; bd mem, Bridge Vol Inc, 1979; Urban League, 1979; Phi Delta Kappa Educ Soc, 1989; Alpha Phi Alpha Frat Inc; Alpha Phi Omega Nat Serv Frat; Benevolent Order Elks; Nat Sickle Cell Org; Martin Luther King Health Ctr. **Honors/Awds:** Young Man of American Commission Service, US Jaycees, 1977; Commission Service Award, Black Church & Comn, United Church Ministry Inc, 1978 & 79; Commission Service, Nat Asn Advan Colored People Elmira State Prison, 1980; Church & Community Service Award, United Church Ministry Inc, 1983; Editorial Excel Award, Black Stud Union Monroe Community Col, 1984; Outstanding Adult & Student Award, Rochester Area Col, 1985; Leadership Development Institute Award, State Univ NY, Brockport, 1986; Organization of Students of African Descent Award, Serv Afro-Am Stud, 1985-89; Award of Community Service, Nat Asn Negro Women, 1986; United Church Ministry Award, Serv Black Family & Community, 1986; Community Mediator, Hudson Valley Mohawk Asn, 1986; Certificate of Achievement, Martin Luther King Ctr Social Change, 1989-90; Conflict/Management Medicator, Ctr Dispute Settlement, 1990; New York State Assembly Award for Community Service, 1995; Phi Beta Delta Int Scholar, 1995. **Home Addr:** 1130 S Mich Ave Apt 2304, Chicago, IL 60605. **Business Addr:** Pastor, Haven Rest Missionary Baptist Church, 7901 S Stony Island Ave, Chicago, IL 60617-1016, **Business Phone:** (773)734-9055.

TOLLIVER, NED, JR.
Educator. **Personal:** Born May 2, 1943, Woodville, MS; son of Charlotte Bonney Tolliver and Ned Tolliver Sr; married Dorothy Bickham, Aug 23, 1969; children: Tony L & Daphne A. **Educ:** Miss Valley State Univ, BS, 1967; Western Mich Univ, cert, 1969; Jackson State Univ, cert, 1973; Delta State Univ, MA, 1983. **Career:** Negro Civic Club, corresp secy, 1973; E Side High Sch, team leader, Social Studies Dept, 1973-94; Summer Youth Prog, coordr, 1973-94; Cleveland Area Civic Club, vpres, 1978-; Selective Serv Bd, mem, Bolivar City, 1982-; Cleveland Bd Alderman, vpres, 1991; W Tallahatchie High Sch, prin, 1994-; Drew High Sch, prin, currently. **Orgs:** Cleveland Asn Educ, 1967-; Miss Asn Educr, 1967-; Nat Educ Asn, 1967-; sponsor, Citizenship Club, E Side High, 1968-; Dem Party Miss, 1977-; Notary Pub Bolivar Co MS, 1977-; bd trustee, United Baptist Church, 1980-; Nat Asn Advan Colored People, Cleveland Chap, 1982-; pres, Cleveland Area Civic Club, 1986; asst treas, Roar Found Inc, currently. **Honors/Awds:** Star Teacher, 1987-90, 1992-93. **Home Addr:** 1819 Cowan Dr, PO Box 814, Cleveland, MS 38732, **Home Phone:** (662)843-3176. **Business Addr:** Principal, Drew High School, 288 Green Ave, Drew, MS 38737, **Business Phone:** (662)745-8588.

TOLLIVER, DR. RICHARD LAMAR
Educator, clergy. **Personal:** Born Jun 26, 1945, Springfield, OH; married Ann Cecile Jackson (divorced 1987). **Educ:** Miami Univ, Oxford, OH, BA, relig, 1967; Boston Univ, Afro-Am studies, 1971, MA, polit sci, 1986; Episcopal Divinity Sch, Cambridge, MA, master divinity, 1971; Howard Univ, Wash, DC, PhD, polit sci, 1982. **Career:** St Cyprian's Church, Boston, MA, rector, 1972-77; St Timothy's Church, Wash, DC, rector, 1977-84; NSF fel, 1979-82; US Peace Corps, Kenya, assoc country dir, 1984-86; US Peace Corps, Mauritania, country dir, 1986-88; Howard Univ, Wash, DC, prof, 1988-89; St Edmund's Episcopal Church, Chicago, IL, rector, 1989-; St Edmund's Redevelop Corp, rector, 1990-. **Orgs:** Omega Psi Phi Fraternity, 1968-; Nat Conf Black Polit Scientists, 1982-; pres, St Edmund's Redevt Corp, 1989-; Beta Boule, Sigma Pi Phi Fraternity, 1991-; nat bd dir, Union Black Episcopalians; vip bd, St Edmund's Acad; bd trustees, Bennett Col. **Honors/Awds:** Distinguished Service Award, St Augustine's Col, 1983; Regional Finalist, White House Fel, 1983; Distinguished Achievement Medal, Miami Univ, 1996; Honorary Doctor of Divinity Degree, Honoris Causa, Seabury-Western Theol Sem, Evanston, IL, 1997. **Business Addr:** Rector, St Edmund's Episcopal Church, 1175 San Gabriel Blvd, Chicago, IL 60637, **Business Phone:** (626)793-9167.

TOLLIVER, STANLEY EUGENE, SR.
Lawyer. **Personal:** Born Oct 29, 1925, Cleveland, OH; son of Eugene and Edna; married Dorothy; children: Stephanie, Sherrie, Stanley Jr, Nathan. **Educ:** Baldwin-Wallace, Pre-Law, 1948; Cleveland Marshall Law Sch, LLB, 1951, LLD, 1968, JD, 1969. **Career:** Cleveland Assoc Realty Brokers, legal coun, 1954; Cong Racial Equality, legal coun, 1960-66; Rev Dr Martin L King Southern Leaders Christian Conf, legal advisor, 1965-68; CORE, atty, 1966; pvt pract, atty. **Orgs:** Pres, Nat Conf Black Lawyers, Cleveland Chap, 1975; class rep, Baldwin Wallace Col, 1980-82; reg dir, Nat Conf Black Lawyers, 1980; nat co-chmn, Nat Conf Black Lawyers, 1981; elected bd mem, Cleveland Sch Bd, 1981-; exec comt, Dem Party Cuyahoga Cty, 1981-; Cleveland Asn Black Educ, 1981-, Nat Black Sch Bd, 1984-; mem bd mgrs, Cleveland YMCA; marathon runner; elected pres Cleveland Bd of Educ 1987. **Honors/Awds:** Only elected public official from Ohio to be elected as a delegate to the National Democratic Convention for Rev. Jesse Jackson for President of the US; Hon Mention & Trophy Freedom Fighters, 1964; Hall of Fame, E Tech HS, 1978; Frank D Reeves Award, Nat Conf Black Lawyers, 1981; Business Award, WJMO Radio, Cleveland, 1983; Outstanding Alumnus, Baldwin Wallace Col, 1978; baritone soloist; NAACP (Cleveland Chapter) Freedom Award, 2000. **Military Serv:** AUS, pfc army counter intelligence, 1951-53; Passed Ohio Bar in the Army, 1953. **Business Addr:** Attorney, Private Practice, 1464 E 105th St Suite 404, Cleveland, OH 44106.

TOLLIVER, THOMAS C., JR.
Government official. **Personal:** Born Oct 16, 1950, Woodville, MS; son of Tom C and Sarah; married; children: Tommie C. **Educ:** Jackson State Univ, BS, 1972, MS, 1979; Univ Southern Miss, MS, 1978. **Career:** Wilkinson County High Sch, teacher, 1972-79; Wilkinson County, chancery clerk, 1979-. **Orgs:** Asst state dir, Alpha Phi Alpha Frat, 1970-75; bd dirs, Miss Chancery-Clerk's Asn, 1979-85; bd dir, chmn, Chatwell Club Inc, 1982-88; bd dir,Friends Armisted, 1984-; worshipful master, F&AM Prince Hall Masons, 1985;32nd degree mason, 33rd degree mason, Shriner. **Honors/Awds:** Man of the Year, Alpha Phi Alpha Frat, 1972-73. **Home Addr:** PO Box 1376, Woodville, MS 39669. **Business Addr:** Chancery Clerk, Wilkinson County 17th Chancery Court District, PO Box 516, Woodville, MS 39669, **Business Phone:** (601)888-4381.

TOMLIN, JOSEPHINE D
Banker. **Personal:** Born Jul 5, 1952, Pittsburgh, PA; daughter of Charles C and Hattie Holmes; married Mark Washington, Feb 22, 1990. **Educ:** Allegheny Col, BA, 1974; Univ Pgh, MEd, 1975. **Career:** Univ Pgh, prog coun, 1975-76; LaRoche Col, upward bound dir, 1976-81; Mellon Bank, Pittsburgh, corp demand despoit mgr, 1983-84, support serv sect mgr, 1984-85, retail systems mgr, 1985-88, loan services mgr, 1988-90, project consultant, vice pres, 1990-. **Orgs:** Bd dir Women's Ctr Pgh, 1978-80; bus & fin acad consut, Urban League, 1985-86; career oppor comm adv, Allegheny Col, 1987; Perry Traditional Acad Partnership Tutor Mellon Bank/Bd Educ, 1987; steering comm, Women's Forum, 1990-. **Honors/Awds:** Premier Achievement Award, Mellon Bank, 1985; Outstanding Trio Student, MAEOPP, 1986. **Home Addr:** 1205 Crucible St, Pittsburgh, PA 15220. **Business Phone:** (412)234-6744.

TOMLINSON, MEL ALEXANDER
Dancer, educator, clergy. **Personal:** Born Jan 3, 1954, Raleigh, NC; son of Tommy Willie Amos and Marjoriline Henry. **Educ:** NC Sch Arts, Winston-Salem NC, BFA, 1974. **Career:** Coach, teacher, speaker, choreographer & dancewear designer; Heritage Dance Theatre, Winston-Salem, dancer, 1972-74; Dance Theatre Harlem, dancer, 1974-77, 1978-81; Alvin Ailey Dance Theatre, NY, dancer, 1977-78; New York City Ballet, dancer, 1981-87; NC Dance Theatre, dir educ servs, 1988-89, dancer, 1988-; Boston Ballet, princ dancer, 1991-92, City Dance Outreach Prog, master teacher, 1991; Boston Conserv Music & the Harvard summer prog, prof dance ed, 1991-93; Univ NC, prof dance & theatre arts, 1993-96; Choreographer: "No Right on Red", 1987; "Carnival of the Animals", 1988; "Karenda", 1990; "Sonata 5", 1991; "Alas!", 1992; "In the Beginning", 1993; "Pedipieds", 1993; DTSW Studio, guest fac, currently; pastor, currently. **Orgs:** Independent Film & TV Alliance; Int Platform Asn; Am Fedn TV & Radio Artists; Am Guild Musical Artists. **Honors/Awds:** North Carolina Prize, NY Times, 1983; Elliot Award, 1993. **Special Achievements:** Filmed documentary, "With A Clear Voice," NBC-TV, 1993. **Business Addr:** Guest Faculty, DTSW Studio, 4200 Wyoming NE Suite B-2, Albuquerque, NM 87111, **Business Phone:** (505)296-9465.

TOMLINSON, RANDOLPH R.
Editor, newspaper publisher. **Personal:** Born Aug 28, 1920; son of Myrtle C Allen; married Algean; children: Randolph Jr, William, Marta, Edward, Levette. **Educ:** Escuela de Artes y Oficios, Panama City, attended 1936; Inst Nacional de Panama, attended 1940; Univ Panama, attended 1950; Northwest Univ, postgrad work, 1958. **Career:** Editor (retired); N Shore Examiner Newspaper, ed, publisher, 1995; La Nacion Panama City, ed page ed; Star & Herald Panama City, reporter; Panama Review, assoc ed. **Honors/Awds:** Outstanding Bus Award; Outstanding Citizen Award, Gamma Omicron Chap, Delta Sigma Theta Sorority; Journalistic Excellence Award, Media Women, Chicago Chap. **Special Achievements:** Candidate for Mayor of Evanston nominated by acclamation of black citizens of Evanston; served in a civilian capacity during WWII in the Canal Zone. *

TOMLINSON, DR. ROBERT
Educator, painter (artist), artist. **Personal:** Born Jun 26, 1938, Brooklyn, NY; son of Sydney and Julia Espeut. **Educ:** Pratt Inst, Brooklyn, BFA, 1961; Columbia Univ, Teachers Col, NY, 1963; CUNY Grad Ctr, NY, PhD, 1977. **Career:** This Week Mag, asst art dir, 1961-63; Ministere de l'Educ Nationale Paris, eng instr, 1963-68; HS Art & Design, NY, fr instr, 1968-72; Hunter Col NY, adj asst prof, 1972-78; Ford Found, Advanced Study fel, 1972-76; City Univ NY, fel, 1975-77; Emory Univ Atlanta, asst prof, 1978-84, assoc prof, 1984-93, int dir, 1990-91, prof, 1994-99, prof emer,

currently. **Orgs:** Am Soc Eighteenth Cent Stud Mod Lang Asn; chmn, Emory Univ Comn Status Minorities, 1980-81, 1984-85. **Honors/Awds:** Number 1 man exhibit of Painting Paris, London, NY, WA, 1968, 1971, 1979, 1984; Am Coun Learned Societies Grant, 1979. **Special Achievements:** Numerous exhibits including Contemporary Black Artists in America, Great Neck NY, 1997, 1999, 2000, 2002 (group), Viridian Artists Inc, New York, 2005 (solo), Farleigh Dickinson University, Hackensack, New Jersey, 2006 (solo) .

TONE-LOC (ANTHONY TERRELL SMITH)
Actor, rap musician. **Personal:** Born Mar 3, 1966, Los Angeles, CA; son of James Smith and Margaret. **Career:** Albums: Loc-ed After Dark, 1989; Cool Hand Loc, 1991; Wild Thing & Other Hits, 2003; Singles: "Wild Thing"; "Funky Cold Medina"; Films: The Adventures of Ford Fairlane, 1990; Fern Fully: The Last Rainforest, animated, 1992; Bebe's Kids, animated, 1992; Posse, 1993; Poetic Justice, 1993; Surf Ninjas, 1993; Ace Ventura Pet Detective, 1994; Blank Check, 1994; Heat, 1995; Spy Hard, 1996; Fakin' Da Funk, 1997; Freedom Strike, 1998; Titan AE, animated, 2000; Deadly Rhapsody, 2001; Storm Watch, 2002; TV series: "C-Bear & Jamal", 1996; "Thieves", 2001; "Static Shock", 2002; "The District", 2002; "Storm Watch", 2002; "The Night B4 Christmas", 2003; "The WB's Superstar USA", 2004; "Yes, Dear", 2005; "King of the Hill", 2005; "Totally Awesome", 2006; "Celebrity Rap Superstar", 2007. **Business Addr:** Actor, William Morris Agency, 1 William Morris Pl, Beverly Hills, CA 90212, **Business Phone:** (310)859-4000.

TONEY, ANTHONY
Football player, executive. **Personal:** Born Sep 23, 1962, Salinas, CA; married Mary Ann; children: Derrick. **Educ:** Hartnell Community Col; Tex A&M Univ. **Career:** Football player (retired), exec; Philadelphia Eagles, fullback, 1986-92; Boys & Girls Clubs Monterey County, sea side unit dir, 1994-. **Orgs:** Monterey County Safe Kids Coaliton.

TONGUE, REGINALD CLINTON
Football player. **Personal:** Born Apr 11, 1973, Baltimore, MD. **Educ:** Ore State univ. **Career:** Kans city chiefs, defensive back, 1996-99; Seattle Seahawks, defensive back, 2000-03; New York Jets, defensive back, 2004; Oakland Raiders, defensive back, 2005. **Honors/Awds:** Mack Lee Hill Award, 1996.

TOOMER, AMANI ASKARI
Football player. **Personal:** Born Sep 8, 1974, Berkeley, CA; son of Donald Sr; married Yola Dabrowski, Oct 19, 2002 (divorced 2007). **Educ:** Univ Mich. **Career:** New York Giants, wide receiver, 1996-2008; Kansas City Chiefs, 2009-. **Orgs:** Founder, Amani Toomer Found; Breast Cancer Res Found; Newark YMCA; Autism Coalition; Big BAM! Found. **Honors/Awds:** Man of the Year, 2003; Neighborhood Most Valuable Player, Ameriquest, 2004; United Way Hometown Hero, United Way New York, 2004. **Business Addr:** Wide Receiver, New York Giants, Giants Stadium, East Rutherford, NJ 07073, **Business Phone:** (201)935-8111.

TOOMER, CLARENCE
Librarian, administrator. **Personal:** Born Jun 12, 1952, Asbury Park, NJ; son of Hazel Markham and Willie. **Educ:** Livingstone Col, Salisbury, NC, BA, 1974; NC State Univ, Durham, NC, MLS, 1975, EdD. **Career:** NC A&T State Univ, Greensboro, NC, librn, 1975-77; Johnson C Smith Univ, Charlotte, NC, asst librn, 1977-80; Shaw Univ, Raleigh, NC, libr dir, 1980-88; Greensboro Col, Greensboro, NC, libr dir, 1988; Ala A&M Univ, J F Drake Learning Resources, libr dir, dean, currently. **Orgs:** NC Libr Asn, 1977-; Am Libr Asn, 1984-; Guildford Libr Club, 1988-; Asn Col & Res Libr, 1988-. **Business Addr:** Dean Libraries, Alabama A&M University, 4900 Meridian St, Normal, AL 35762, **Business Phone:** (256)372-4747.

TOON, ALBERT L.
Football player, executive. **Personal:** Born Apr 30, 1963, Newport News, VA; married Jane; children: Nick & 3 daughters. **Educ:** Univ Wis, BS, family resources. **Career:** Football player (retired), exec; NY Jets, wide receiver, 1985-92; Investor in residential & commercial real estate, owner & mgr; Burger King Franchise, Southern WI; Taco Bell franchisee, St Louis, dir & organizer; Capital Bank Corp, Madison, WI, vpres. **Honors/Awds:** First team All Big 10 NFL All-Rookie by Football Digest; MVP, NY Jets, 1986-88; Pro Bowl, 1986-88; Univ Wisc Hall of Fame, 1998.

TOO SHORT, A (TODD ANTHONY SHAW)
Rap musician. **Personal:** Born Apr 28, 1966, Los Angeles, CA. **Career:** Albums: Players, 1985; Don't Stop Rappin', 1988; Born to Mack, 1988; Life Is.Too Short, 1988; Short Dog's in the House, 1990; Shorty the Pimp, 1992; Get in Where You Fit In, 1993; Cocktails, 1995; Gettin' It, 1996; Can't Stay Away, 1999; You Nasty, 2000; Uncensored, 2000; Chase the Cat, 2001; What's My Favorite Word?, 2002; It's About Time, 2003; Married to the Game, 2003; Pimpin' Incorporated, 2006; Gangsters & Strippers, 2006; Blow the Whistle, 2006; Mack of the Century, Greatest Hits, 2006; Bible of a Pimp, 2007; I Love the Bay, 2007; Get Off the Stage, 2007; Dangerous Music Rec Label, founder; Up All Nite Recs, owner, currently. **Special Achievements:** Film Appearance: Get In Where You Fit In, 2003. **Business Addr:** Recording Artist, Jive Records, 137-139 W 25th St, New York, NY 10001, **Business Phone:** (212)727-0016.

TOOTE, GLORIA E. A.
Lawyer. **Personal:** Born Nov 8, 1931, New York, NY; daughter of Frederick A and Lillie. **Educ:** Howard Univ Sch Law, BA, 1952, JD, 1954; Columbia Univ Grad Sch Law, LLM, 1956. **Career:** Nat Affairs Section Time Magazine, former mem; New York City, prac law, 1954-71; Toote Town Publ Co & Town Recording Studios, pres, 1966-70; Action Agency Off Volunteer Action Liaison, asst dir, 1971-73; Dept Housing & Urban Develop, asst secy, 1973-75; author & lecturer; New York City, pvt practice, Trea Estates & Enterprices Inc, pres, currently. **Orgs:** Bd mem, Arbitrator Asn; Consumer Alert; Coun Econ Affairs Republic & Nat Black United Fund; Nat Bus League; Alpha Kappa Alpha Sorority; US Chamber Com; Nat Newspaper Publ Asn; Hoover Inst War; Revolution & Peace; bd dirs, Fannie Mae; mem bd governors, Nat Black United Fund; steering comt Citizens Republic. **Honors/Awds:** Newsmakers Award, Nat Assn Black Women Atty; YMCA World Service Award, Women's Nat Rep Club; Pol Leadership Award, Nat Newspaper Publ Asn; special achievement awards, Asn Black Women Attys. *

TORAIN, REV. TONY WILLIAM
Clergy, school administrator. **Personal:** Born Jun 27, 1954, Mebane, NC; son of William and Myrtle Juanita Woody; married Celestine Best, May 25, 1985; children: Tony William II (Nnamdi) & James Best (Jay). **Educ:** Univ NC, Chapel Hill, BA, 1975; Gordon-Conwell Theol Sem, MATS, 1978; Boston Univ, MA, 1980; Univ Md, Baltimore, MSW, JD, 1985. **Career:** Boston State Col, campus minister, 1978-80; Twelfth Baptist Church, assoc minister, 1978-80; dir elderly serv, Joint Orange-Chatham Comm Action, 1980-81; Off Atty Gen MD, clerk, 1982-83; Baltimore Asn Retarded Citizens, counr, 1983-85; Highway Church Christ, assoc minister, 1982-85; Highway Training Inst, dean, 1984-85; C H Mason Memorial COGIC, assoc minister, 1985-88; US Dept Health & Human Servs, employee coun serv asst, 1984-85, prog legal analyst, 1985-87; The Good Shepherd Church COGIC, Baltimore, MD, pastor & founder, 1989-; Univ Md, Sch Social Work, asst dean for Stud Sers & Minority Affairs, 1991-94, asst dean Stud Affairs, 1994-2000, assoc dean for Stud Affairs; Univ Baltimore, Sch Law, dean stud, currently. **Orgs:** Black & Jewish Forum Baltimore; dir, African-Am Cult Ctr, Towson State Univ; bd mem, Univ Md Sch Social Work, 1986-; Am Bar Asn, Comt Law Sch Admin; Comn Educ Church God Christ Inc. **Honors/Awds:** Scholarship, First Federal Scholar, 1973; Scholarship, Turrentine Scholar, 1975; Martin L King Jr Award for Ministry 1979. **Business Addr:** Dean of Students, University of Baltimore School of Law, 1415 Maryland Ave, Baltimore, MD 21201, **Business Phone:** (410)837-4468.

TORAN, KAY DEAN
Educator, president (organization). **Personal:** Born Nov 21, 1943, Birmingham, AL; married John Toran; children: Traci & John Dean. **Educ:** Univ Portland, BA, 1964; Portland State Univ, MSW, 1970. **Career:** Portland State Univ, asst prof coun, 1970-71, Grad Sch Soc Work, asst prof; Adult & Family Serv Publ Welfare, asst mgr field opers, 1976-79; Off Govt, dir affirm action, 1979-; Vol Am Ore Inc, pres & chief exec officer, 1999-. **Orgs:** Delta Sigma Theta Soc Serv Sor, 1964-; Girl Scouts Summer Camp, 1968; Girl Scouts, prog consult, 1969-70; Campfire Girls Inc, 1975-77; Met Fam Serv, 1976-82; Portland State Univ Found, 1980-; The Catlin Gable Sch, 1980-84. **Honors/Awds:** Res Grant Curric Devel Western Interstate Comm for Higher Education, 1973; Leader 80's Award NW Conf Black Publication Officials, 1979; Outstanding Young Woman America, 1980; Woman Excellence Delta Sigma Theta, 1982. **Special Achievements:** Published "Curriculum Devel" 1974. **Business Addr:** President, Chief Executive Officer, Volunteers of America Oregon Inc, 537 SE Alder St, Portland, OR 97214, **Business Phone:** (503)235-8655.

TORIAN, EDWARD TORRENCE
Executive. **Personal:** Born Dec 20, 1933, New Rochelle, NY; son of Edward (deceased) and Julia; married Pearl Cromartie; children: Curtis & Darlene. **Educ:** Westchester Bus Inst, cert acct, 1956; Iona Col, BBA, 1968, MBA Finance. **Career:** Perkin-Elmer Corp, sr contract acct, 1966-90; Hal-Tor Enterprises Co, partner & treas, 1970-; Danbury Common Coun, legislative leader, 1983, councilman-at-large, 1979-87; Hughes Danbury Optical Syst, sr admin, 1990; City of Danbury, Charter Rev Comn, mem, currently. **Orgs:** Nat Asn Acct, 1967-; Iona Col Alumni Asn, 1968-; NAACP 1980-; treas, Black Democratic Asn Danbury 1981-; sec Men's Coun, 1981-84, treas, 1990-, New Hope Baptist Church; bd trustees, bd, United Way Northern Fairfield County, CT. **Military Serv:** USN petty officer, 3rd class, 1951-54; Nat Defense Award. **Home Addr:** 18 Indian Head Rd, Danbury, CT 06811-2919, **Home Phone:** (203)746-4140.

TORRENCE, GWEN
Athlete, barber. **Personal:** Born Jun 12, 1965, Decatur, GA; married Manley Waller (divorced); children: Manley & E'mon. **Educ:** Univ Ga, attended 1987. **Career:** Athlete (retired), Hairdresser; US Olympic Team, track & field; hairdresser, currently. **Honors/Awds:** Gold Medal, World Univ Games, 1985, 1987; Bronze Medal, Nat Championships, 1986; Gold Medal, Pan Am Games, 1987; Gold Medal, Nat Championships, 1988; Gold Medal, Nat Indoor Championships, 1988, 1989, 1997; Silver medal, World Indoor Championships, 1989; Silver Medal, World Championships, Tokyo, Japan, 1991;Gold Medal, Summer Olympics, Barcelona, Spain, 1992; Gold Medal, Goodwill Games, 1994; Ga Sports Hall of Fame, 2000. **Business Addr:** Hairdresser, Atlanta, GA.

TORRENCE-THOMPSON, JUANITA LEE
Poet, writer, public relations executive. **Personal:** Born in Brockton, MA; daughter of James Lee Torrence and Dr Zylpha Mapp-Robinson (deceased); married Hugh, Dec 19, 1965; children: Derek Rush. **Educ:** New Sch, attended; State Univ New York Empire State Col, BS, bus commun, 1983; Fordham Univ, MA, commun, 1989; Fine Arts Work Ctr, Provincetown, MA, poetry fiction, 1998-00; Bank Street Col Educ, Writing Children, 2002. **Career:** UN Int Sch, Newsletter, ed, 1976-77; Nat Asn Theatre Owners, Pub Rel, ed asst, 1979-80; freelance writer, 1983-; State Univ New York, Empire State Col, newsletter, ed, 1985-87; Dorf & Stanton Comms, ed, 1987-88; Mutual New York, pr consult, 1988-90; Torrence-Thompson Pub Rels, prefabricateds, 1988-; poet/writer, 1995-; Col New Rochelle, adj prof, 1997; Torderwarz Publ Co, currently; Mobius, The Poetry Mag, owner, ed & publ, currently; Poems: Wings Span to Eternity, 1995; Spanning the Years, 1996; Black Enterprise artices; Celebrating a Tapestry of Life, 2003; Kantonsschule Rychenberg, Winterthur, Switzerland, 1998, Bahai, Singapore, 1995; The Pedestal Magazine online poem & essays on special 9/11 issue, 2001; An Eye for An Eye Makes the World Blind: Poets on 9/11 Anthology, 2002. **Orgs:** Nat Asn Black Journalists, 1989-; Poetry Soc Am, 1995-; Poets House, 1995-; Poets & Writers, 1996-; Am Asn Univ Women, 1992-; Fresh Meadows Poets, 2000-; Black Am Pub; Academy Am Poets; PRSA. **Honors/Awds:** Feature Article Award, Writer's Digest Mag, 1985; Meritorious Service Award United Negro Col Fund, 1994; Nashville Newsletter, 1994; First Prize, New York Pub Lib Poetry Contest, 1996; Robins Nest Mag, 1996; Outstanding Achievement Award, SUNY, Empire State Col, 1996; Margaret A Walker Short Story Award, 1999, 2000; Editor's Choice Poetry Awards; Children's Fiction Award, Writer's Digest, 2000; Paul Laurence Dunbar Poetry Award, 2000. **Business Addr:** Juanita Torrence-Thompson, Torderwarz Publishing Company, PO Box 671058, Flushing, NY 11367-1058.

TORRES, GINA
Actor. **Personal:** Born Apr 25, 1969, New York, NY; married Laurence Fishburne, Sep 20, 2002; children: Delilah. **Career:** Lincoln Ctr Theater Co; Films: Bed of Roses, 1996; The Substance of Fire, 1996; The Underworld, 1997; The Matrix Reloaded, 2003; The Matrix Revolutions, 2003; Hair Show, 2004; Fair Game, 2005; Serenity, 2005; Standoff, 2006; Five Fingers, 2006; Jam, 2006; I Think I Love My Wife, 2007; South of Pico, 2007; Standoff, 2007; Don't Let Me Drown, 2008; Criminal Minds, 2008; Pushing Daisies, 2009; Gossip Girl, 2009; TV appearances: One Life to Live, 1989-93; Unnatural Pursuits, 1991; "Law & Order", 1992-95; "MANTIS", 1994; "NYPD Blue", 1995; "Dark Angel", 1996; The Underworld, 1997; "Hercules: The Legendary Journeys", 1997-99; "Xena Warrior Princess", 1997; Profiler, 1997; La Femme Nikita, 1998; Encore!, Encore!, 1998; "Cleopatra 2525", 2000-01; "Alias", 2001-06; "Any Day Now", 2001-02; "Firefly", 2002-03; The Law & Mr. Lee, 2003; The Guardian, 2003; "The Agency", 2003; "The Henry Lee Project", 2003;"Angel", 2003; 24, 2004; Gramercy Park, 2004; "Justice League", 2004-06; "A Man of His Word", 2005; Soccer Moms, 2005; The Shield, 2006; Without a Trace, 2006; "Borderline", 2006; Standoff, 2006-07; "Dirty Sexy Money", 2007; "Boston Legal", 2008; Water & Power, 2009; "Pushing Daisies", 2009; Best Laid Plans, 2009; "The Unit", 2009; Applause for Miss E, 2009; Washington Field, 2009; Tailspin, 2009; "Eli Stone", 2009. **Honors/Awds:** ALMA Award for Outstanding Lead Actress in a Syndicated Drama Series, 2001; nominee, International Press Academy's Golden Satellite Award for Best Performance by an Actress in a Supporting Role, 2004. **Business Addr:** Actress, c/o Badgley Connor King Talent Agency, 9229 Sunset Blvd Suite 311, Los Angeles, CA 90069, **Business Phone:** (310)278-9313.*

TORRY, GUY
Actor, comedian. **Personal:** Born Jan 5, 1969, St Louis, MO; son of Robert and Rebecca; married Monica Renae Askew, 2002. **Educ:** Southeast Mo State Univ, BS. **Career:** Tv appearances: "Martin", 1995; "Sparks", 1996; "As Told By Ginger", 2000; "The X Files", 2000; "NYPD Blue", 2001; "The Shield", 2002; "One on One", 2002; "Blind Justice", 2005; Films: Sunset Park, 1996; Dont Be a Menace to South Cent While Drinking Your Juice in the Hood, 1996; The Good News, 1997; One Eight Seven, 1997; Back in Bus, 1997; Am History X, 1998; Ride, 1998; The Strip, 1999; Trippin', 1999; Life, 1999; The '70s, 2000; Pearl Harbor, 2001; The Animal, 2001; Don't Say a Word, 2001; Tara, 2001; With or Without You, 2003; The Runaway Jury, 2003; Jonah, 2003; Midnight Clear, 2005; Slow Burn, 2005; Funny Money, 2006; Flirt, 2006; The Last Stand, 2006; Dead & Deader, 2006; writer: Def Comedy Jam, HBO; Minor Adjustments; Moesha; "Blind Justice", 2005; Slow Burn, 2005; Funny Money, 2006. **Business Addr:** Comedian, Actor, William Morris Agency, 1325 Ave of the Ams Fl 15, New York, NY 10019, **Business Phone:** (212)586-5100.

TOSE, MAURICE B.
Chief executive officer. **Personal:** Born Jan 1, 1957, Fort Bragg, NC. **Educ:** US Naval Acad, BS, 1978. **Career:** Dept Defense Progs Techmatics Inc, Dir; Telecommun Systs Inc, chmn, chief exec officer & pres, currently. **Orgs:** Wireless Data Forum; AT&T's Diversity Roundtable; Intl Engg Consortium; Intelligent Network Forum; treas & vpres, U.S. Naval Acad Class, 1978; Annapolis Jaycees & Annapolis Kiwanis; treas, vpres, dir, Arundel Bay Homeowners Asn; Budget & Finance Coun, Antioch Apostolic Church; co-found, chmn bd, United Stated Naval Acad Samuel P. Massie Educ Endowment; Annapolis Neck Small Area Planning Comn; bd dirs, First Night Annapolis; bd dirs, Ginger Cove Retirement Community. **Honors/Awds:** Top Black Technology Entrepreneurs, Career Commun Group Inc. **Business Addr:** Chairman, Chief Executive Officer, Telecommunication Systems Inc, 275 W St, Annapolis, MD 21401, **Business Phone:** (410)263-7616.*

TOTTEN, BERNICE E. See Obituaries section.

TOTTEN, DR. HERMAN LAVON
Educator. **Personal:** Born Apr 10, 1938, Van Alstyne, TX; son of Derrall Scott and Dulvi Sims. **Educ:** Wiley Col, Marshall, TX, BA, 1961; Univ Okla, MLS, 1964, PhD, 1966. **Career:** Wiley Col, librn & dean, 1966-71; Univ Ky, assoc dean, 1971-74; Univ Ore, dean & prof 1974-77; Univ N Tex, prof & assoc dean, 1977-2001; fac exec asst to the pres, 2001-05; US Nat Comn Libr & Info Sci, comnr, 2005-. **Orgs:** Past pres, Tex Libr Asn; life mem, Am Libr Asn; trustee, Am Recs Mgt Asn. **Honors/Awds:** ACE Academic Internship Am Council Educ, 1970-71; CLR Fellow, Council Library Resources, 1977-78; Regents Professor, Univ North Tex, 1991; Association for Library & Information Science Education Award, 1991; Award of Merit for the Outstanding Alumnus, Alumni Assn Univ Okla, School Library & Information Studies, 1991; Black Caucus Award, Amer Library Asn, 1992; Outstanding Teacher Award, Asn for Library and Information Science Education, 1999; ALA Melvil Dewey Award, 2001. **Special Achievements:** Appointed trustee, ARMA International Educational Board of Trustees, 2001; Summer Commencement Speaker, UNT, 2001. **Home Addr:** 2100 Pembrooke Pl, Denton, TX 76205-8208, **Home Phone:** (940)383-1902. **Business Addr:** Commissioner, US National Commission on Libraries & Information Science, 1800 M St NW Suite 350 N Tower, Washington, DC 20036, **Business Phone:** (202)606-9200.

TOTTRESS, RICHARD EDWARD
Clergy, president (organization), chaplain. **Personal:** Born Nov 25, 1917, Newby Creek, OK; son of Rev M (deceased) and Louisa Headspoth (deceased); married Margarreau Fluorine Norton; children: 1 son (dec). **Educ:** Pacific Union Col, BA, 1943; Oakwood Col, BA, 1969; Langston Univ; Home Study Inst; Ministerial Internship Evangelism, TX, 1947; Univ Beverly Hills, MA & PhD, 1981. **Career:** Clergy (retired); Texaco Conf Texas SDA, minister, 1943; SW Region Conf, pastor & evangelist, 1947-52; S Atlanta Conf SDA, dist pastor & youth assoc, 1952-63; Oakwood Acad & Col, dean, 1963-66, Col pastor & chaplain, 1965-69, 1972-73; Oakwood Col Ch, co-pastor, 1973-79; Your Bible Speaks radio show, pres, producer & speaker, 1953; Westend SDA Church, assoc pastor, 1993. **Orgs:** Civilian chaplain, 1944; dir, Bibb County March of Dimes, 1961; Fel Int Biog Asn, 1970's & 1980's; coordr, Metro-Atlanta Area SDA Pastors, 1982-84; dir, Crusade for Voters Bibb County,GA, 1959-60; Book of Honor Am Biogr Instm 1979; broadcast progs, WEUP Radio, 1971-73. **Honors/Awds:** Special Plaques, Oakwood Col Fac & Stud Ch Bld, 1977; Spec Plaques, S Cent SDA, 1978; Plaque Notable Am Bicentennial Era, 1976; Cert Outstanding Sec Educr Am, 1975; Poet & Auth. **Military Serv:** ASR, chaplain, 1943-44. *

TOUSSAINT, LORRAINE
Actor. **Personal:** Born Apr 4, 1960, Trinidad, West Indies; daughter of Janet Beane (Deceased). **Educ:** Juilliard Sch, drama. **Career:** Films: Breaking In, 1989; Hudson Hawk, 1991; Point of No Return, 1993; Bleeding Hearts, 1994; Mother's Boys, 1994; Dangerous Minds, 1995; Jaded, 1996; Psalms from the Underground, 1996; The Spittin' Image, 1997; BlackDog, 1998; The Sky is Falling, 2000; The Soloist, 2009; TV series: The Face of Rage, 1983; ACase of Deadly Force, 1986; "One Life to Live", 1988; "A Man Called Hawk",1989; Common Ground, 1990; "Law & Order", 1990-2003; "227", 1990; Daddy,1991; "Tequila & Bonetti", 1992; Trial: The Price of Passion, 1992;"Bodies of Evidence", 1992; Red Dwarf, 1992; Class of '61, 1993; Love,Lies & Lullabies, 1993; "Where I Live", 1993; "Queen", 1993; "Where ILive", 1993; "The Sinbad Show", 1993; "Queen", 1993; A Time to Heal, 1994;"M.A.N.T.I.S.", 1994; "Amazing Grace", 1995; It Was Him or Us, 1995;"Murder One", 1995; "Bless This House", 1995; "Dark Skies", 1996;"Nightjohn", 1996; "Mr. & Mrs. Smith", 1996; If These Walls Could Talk,1996; Nightjohn, 1996; America's Dream?, 1996; "The Cherokee Kid", 1996;"Leaving L.A.", 1997; Promise Land, 1997; C-16:FBI, 1998; "BlackoutEffect", 1998; "Cracker", 1998; "Nothing Sacred", 1998; "Any Day Now",1998-2002; "Crossing Jordan", 2002-03; "Threat Matrix", 2003-04; Frasier,2004; Their Eyes Were Watching God, 2005; Judging Amy, 2005; The Closer,2005; "Numb3rs", 2005; "CSI: Crime Scene Investigation", 2006-07; UglyBetty, 2007; Saving Grace, 2007-09; ER, 2008; Believe the Unseen, 2008; "ER", 2008; Cover Me, 2009; Am I Going to Lose Her?, 2009; That Was No First Kiss, 2009; Popcorn, 2009; Looks Like a Lesbian Attack to Me, 2009; Am I Gonna Die Today?, 2009. **Business Addr:** Actress, c/o Warren Cowan & Associates, 8899 Beverly Blvd Suite 919, Los Angeles, CA 90048, **Business Phone:** (310)275-0777.*

TOUSSAINT, DR. ROSE-MARIE
Health services administrator, physician. **Personal:** Born Jun 15, 1956, Port-au-Prince, Haiti. **Educ:** Loyola Univ, BS, 1979; Howard Univ, MD, 1983. **Career:** NIH, res assoc; Howard Univ Hosp, gen surg residency, bd cert Gen Surg; Howard Univ Transplant Ctr, asst prof surg, assoc dir, 1971-77; Horus Corp, med dir, 1995-; holistic physician, 1995-. **Orgs:** Delta Sigma Theta Sor, 1978; vpres, All African Physicians N Am, 1984; chairperson. Liver Med Adv Comn; Wash Regional Transplant Consortium, 1993; Am Soc Transplant Surgeons; Transplant Soc; fel, Transplantation TE Starzl Transplantation Inst, Transplant Soc; vpres, Cheasepeake 1988; fel, Am Col Surgeon; S Eastern Oregon Procurement Org, 1996; bd trustees, Loyola Univ, Acad Achievement Comn, 1999; founding mem, Nat Transplant Found, 1999. **Honors/Awds:** Best Surgical Resident, DC Gen Hosp, 1985-86; Drew-Walker Surgical Resident Award; Ferebee Award in Medicine; Pioneers in Transplantation Award; Phenomenal Woman of the Yr, 1999; Sara Jones Award in Medicine, 2000. **Special Achievements:** Author; Never Question the Miracle-A Surgeons' Story, 1998. **Business Addr:** Holistic Physician, 777 E Atlantic Ave Suite 2306, Delray Beach, FL 33483, **Business Phone:** (301)891-9474.

TOVAR, STEVEN ERIC
Football player, athletic coach. **Personal:** Born Apr 25, 1970, Elyria, OH. **Educ:** Ohio State Univ. **Career:** Football player (retired), Football coach; Cincinnati Bengals, linebacker, 1993-97; San Diego Chargers, 1998, 2000; Carolina Panthers, 1999; Army Black Knights, linebackers coach, 2004-05; Miami Dolphins, football opers staff, asst coach, 2006; Univ Kansas, linebackers coach, currently. **Honors/Awds:** Special Teams Player of the Year, San Diego Chargers, 1998; Hall of Fame, Ohio State Univ Athletic, 2001; All-Big First Team, 2007.

TOWNES, CLARENCE LEE, JR.
Executive, activist. **Personal:** Born Jan 21, 1928, Richmond, VA; son of Clarence L Sr and Alice S; married Grace Elizabeth; children: Clarence III, Michael S, Lisa F & June E. **Educ:** VA Union Univ, BS, com, 1951. **Career:** Va Mutual Benefit Life Ins Co, dir training, 1948-66; Republican Nat Comm, asst to chmn, dir minority affairs, 1966-70; Joint Ctr Polit Studies, dir govt affairs, 1970-74; Metropolitan Coach Corp, pres, ceo, 1974-86; Richmond Renaissance Inc, dep dir, 1982-91, exec dir, currently. **Orgs:** Alternate deleg Republican Nat Conv, 1964; comm Rich Redev & Housing Auth, 1964-66; chmn Electoral Bd Richmond VA, 1979-84; bd dirs, VA Mutual Benefit Life Ins Co, 1985-88; Phi Beta Sigma Frat, 1945-; pres, coo, Jefferson Townhouse Corp, 1964-; bd dirs Consolidated Bank & Trust Co, 1970-; bd dirs Am Bus Asn, 1976-82; pres, Arts Coun Richmond, 1986-88, Richmond Pub Sch Bd, chair, 1992-. **Honors/Awds:** Citizenship Award, Astoria Benefical Club Richmond, 1968; Man of the Year, Iota Sigma Chap Phi Beta Sigma, 1969; Good Government Award, Richmond First Club, 1987; Brotherhood Citation Award, Richmond Chapter, Nat Conf of Christians Jews, 1987. **Military Serv:** AUS, 2nd lt 3 yrs. **Home Addr:** 3103 Hawthorne Ave, Richmond, VA 23222. **Business Addr:** Deputy Director, Richmond Renaissance Inc, 600 E Broad St Suite 960, Richmond, VA 23219.

TOWNES, JEFFREY ALLAN. See JEFF, DJ JAZZY.

TOWNES, HON. SANDRA L.
Judge. **Personal:** Born Jan 1, 1944?, Spartanburg, SC. **Educ:** Johnson C Smith Univ, BA, 1966; Syracuse Univ Col Law, JD, 1976. **Career:** Onondaga County Dist Atty Off, from asst dist atty to sr asst dist atty, 1977-86, chief asst dist atty, 1986-87; Syracuse Univ Col Law, adj prof, 1987-95; City Ct, Syracuse, NY, judge, 1988-99; Onondaga Community Col, adj prof, 1992-2001; Fifth Judicial Dist, NY State Supreme Ct, Justice, 2000-04; Appellate Div, Second Judicial Depart, NY State Supreme Ct, assoc justice, 2001-04; US Dist Ct, Eastern NY, dist judge, currently. **Orgs:** Mem NY Bar Asn; Mem NY Womens Bar Asn. **Business Addr:** District Judge, United States District Court, Eastern New York, 225 Cadman Plz E, Brooklyn, NY 11201-1818, **Business Phone:** (718)797-7425.

TOWNS, EDOLPHUS
Government official. **Personal:** Born Jul 21, 1934, Chadbourn, NC; son of Dolphus and Vergie; married Gwendolyn Forbes, Jan 1, 1960; children: Darryl & Deidra. **Educ:** NC A&T State Univ, Greensboro, BS, 1956; Adelphi Univ Garden City NY, MSW, 1973. **Career:** Medgar Evers Col, Brooklyn, New York City Pub Sch, teacher, dep hosp admin, 1965-71; Borough Brooklyn, dep pres, 1976-82; US House Reps, rep, 1983-. **Orgs:** Adv coun, Boy Scouts Am, Salvation Army, Phi Beta Sigma, Kiwanis; NAACP; Am Red Cross; Guardsmen; Boule; chmn, Cong Black Caucus, 1991-; Energy & Com Comt; Telecommunications & the Internet Subcomt. **Honors/Awds:** Hon degrees: DSC, NC A&T Univ, 1985, LLD, Shaw Univ, 1984, LLD, Aldelphi Univ, 1988, LLD, Va Sem Lynchburg, 1982; Recognized by the American Cancer Society; Recognized for "Efforts to Fight Mortality", Healthy Start; Named "Friend of the Nat Parks", Nat Parks & Conserv Asn; Legislator of the Year, Nat Coalition Poison Control Ctr; Legislator of the Year, Am Asn Community Health Ctrs; Legislator of the Year, Am Acad Physician Assts; Legislator of the Year, Am Acad Nurse Practitioners; Home Care Hero, Nat Asn Home Care; Education All-Star Team, Nat Educ Asn; Congressional Leadership Award, Am Col Nurse-Midwives. **Special Achievements:** First African American to serve as Deputy Brooklyn Borough President. **Military Serv:** AUS, 1956-58. **Business Addr:** Representative, US House of Representatives, 2232 Rayburn House Off Bldg, Washington, DC 20515, **Business Phone:** (202)225-5936.

TOWNS, MAXINE YVONNE
Clergy, educator. **Personal:** Born Jan 12, 1941, Chester, PA. **Educ:** Camden Co Comm Col Blackwood NJ, AA, 1975; Notre Dame Col Manchester NH, BA, 1978. **Career:** Wade Day Care Ctr Chester PA, day care asst, 1960-61; Diocese of Fresno CA, religion educ teacher, 1963-70; Boston MA, rec dir, 1970-72; Camden Co Jail, NJ, chaplain, 1972-77; Notre Dame Col, Manchester NH, dean studs, 1978-. **Orgs:** Secy bd, Southern NJ Prison Serv Comn, 1973-75; secy, Nat Balck Sisters' Conf, 1975-77; treas, NBSC, 1980-; enterd, Franciscan Sisters of the Atonement, 1961; planning comt, Annuan NBSC Meeting, 1977-79; planning com, NH Person & Guidance Asn, 1980; chairperson, NH Diocesan Vocation Comn, 1980-; pres, NH Col Person Asn, 1980-81. **Business Addr:** Notre Dame College, 2321 Elm St, Manchester, NH 03104.

TOWNS, DR. MYRON B, JR.
Physician. **Personal:** Born Dec 18, 1943, Greensboro, NC; son of Miriam Gould and Myron B Sr. **Educ:** Fisk Univ, BA, foreign langs, 1970; Meharry Med Col, MD, 1978; pathol residency, 1978-83; Vanderbuilt Univ Clinic, pharm fel, 1982. **Career:** The Tennesseean, copy editor, 1967-70; Waverly-Belmont Lab, co-organizer, 1972-74; Univ Ga, electron microscopist, 1974-75; Hebbronville Lab, owner, pathologist, 1984-86; Community Clinic, physician, 1985-86; Doctor's Clinic, 1986-87; Towns Clinic, primary & indigent care, 1987-93; JJ Clark Mkt, med dir, 1996-98; adolescent med generalist; pvt pract, currently. **Orgs:** Col Am Pathologists, former mem; Am Soc Clinical Path, former mem; Am Col Forensic Examiners; med IS; bds: Wildlife Rehab Ctr, 1987-92; ICS Sch Bd, 1990-92; certified foster parent; NAACP, life mem. **Honors/Awds:** Carter Woodson Award in jour, 1969; hons biochem & pathol res, Meharry Med Col, 1972-83; invited lectr drug abuse, tobacco & med ethics. **Home Addr:** 6324 Jackson St, Pittsburgh, PA 15206. **Business Addr:** Physician, 971 16th Ave N, Nashville, TN 37208, **Business Phone:** (615)973-2933.

TOWNS, ROSE MARY
Librarian. **Personal:** Born Jan 7, 1934, Houston, TX; married George Elbert. **Educ:** San Francisco State Col, BA, Social Sci 1955; Univ Calif, Berkeley, MLS, 1956. **Career:** Librarian (retired); Oakland Pub Lib Oakland CA, jr libr, 1956-60; Oakland Pub Lib Oakland CA, sr libr, 1960-62; Oakland Pub Lib, Oakland CA, supvr libr, 1962-66; Richmond Pub Lib Richmond CA, asst city libr, 1966-69; Richmond Pub Lib, Richmond CA, city libr, 1969-70; Ref Referral Proj N Bay Coop Lib Sys, coord, 1975-79; N Bay Coop Libr Syst, syst prog coord, 1979-82; Laney Col Libr, 1983-87; Bay Area Libr & Info Syst, proj coord, 1982-83; City Col San Francisco, librn & instr, 1987. **Orgs:** Intellectual Freedom Comt CA Lib Asn, 1966-69, 1980-; secy, Calif Libr Black Caucus N, 1972-73; secy, Calif Soc Libr; secy, Calif Libr Asn, 1979; Black Women Orgn for Polit Action; Calif Libr Black Caucus N; Long Range Planning Comt Calif Lib Asn; Am Libr Asn; Am Libr Asn Black Caucus; Calif Libr Asn. **Honors/Awds:** Delegate, Calif Govt Conf Lib & Info Serv, 1979.

TOWNS, SANNA NIMTZ
Educator. **Personal:** Born Oct 12, 1943, Hawthorne, NV; daughter of Margeurite Malarcher Nimtz and August H Nimtz Sr; divorced; children: Joseph IV & Jawad. **Educ:** Southern Univ, BA, 1964; Teachers Col Columbia Univ, MA, 1967; Univ Southern Miss, PhD, 1985. **Career:** Am Lang Prog Columbia Univ, Eng lang instr, 1969-71; Office Urban Affairs, State Univ NY, Buffalo, prog coord, 1973-75; Kuwait Univ, instr & admin, 1975-79; Eng Dept Univ New Orleans, lang coord & instr, 1980-82, 1985-86; Delgado Community Col, asst prof, asst chair, 1986-87, chair, commun div, 1987-92, assoc prof, Eng, 1992-. **Orgs:** Mem Nat Council of Teachers of English 1980-, LA Assoc Develop Educ, 1981-; Phi Delta Kappa 1984-; S Cent Modern Lang Assoc, 1986-; speaker, New Orleans Mus Art Speakers Bur, 1987; Delta Sigma Theta Sorority, 1962-; Conf Col Composition & Communs, 1980-. **Honors/Awds:** Graduate Fellowship, State of LA Bd Regents, 1982-85; Fulbright-Hays Seminars Aboard Participant, American University in Cairo, 1988; Fulbright Scholar Award, Comenius Univ, Bratislava, Slovakia, Jan-June 1994. **Business Addr:** Associate Professor English, Delgado Community College, Communication Division 615 City Pk Ave, New Orleans, LA 70119, **Business Phone:** (504)483-4093.

TOWNSEL, RONALD
Law enforcement officer. **Personal:** Born Nov 25, 1934, Chicago, IL; children: 3. **Educ:** George Williams Col, BS, 1957; Governors State Univ, MA, 1975. **Career:** Law enforcement officer (retired); Chicago Bd Educ, teacher, 1957-58; Chicago Fed Settlements, youth gang worker, 1958-60; IL Youth Comn, area parole supr juvenile parole agt, 1960-70; IL Dept Corrections, st supt adult parole, 1970. **Orgs:** ACA Compact St Governors; NICO; IPPCA. **Military Serv:** AUS, 1952-54.

TOWNSEND, ANDRE
Football player. **Personal:** Born Oct 8, 1962, Chicago, IL. **Educ:** Univ Miss. **Career:** Football player (retired); Denver Broncos, defensive end, nose tackle & defensive end, 1984-90. **Orgs:** Kappa Alpha Psi Fraternity Inc.

TOWNSEND, LEONARD
Judge. **Career:** State Mich, Wayne County, circuit judge, currently. **Business Addr:** Judge, State of Michigan, Recorder, 711 Coleman A Young Municipal Ctr Suite 1107, Detroit, MI 48226, **Business Phone:** (313)224-2437.

TOWNSEND, MURRAY LUKE, JR.
Government official. **Personal:** Born Jul 6, 1919, Indianapolis, IN; son of Murray L Sr (deceased) and Novella Foster; married Evelyn; children: Cheryl, Murray III & Frederick. **Educ:** Morehouse Col, BA, 1942; Boston Univ, LLB, 1949. **Career:** Government official (retired); PO, 1950-56; IRS, criminal investr, 1956-64; Boston & NY, dep equal employment policy officer, 1963-66; Small Bus Admin, sr compliance officer, 1967-81; Consult. **Orgs:** Omega Psi Phi Frat, 1939; deacon, Union Bapt Ch, 1955-62; Prince Hall Mason, 1963-; Middleboro Lakeville Ment Health Comn Coun, 1966; bd deacons, Cent Baptist Church, 1973-; Nat Asn Advan Colored People; 366th Infantry Vet Asn; adv comn, bd dir, New Eng Village Human Rights, 1979; Afro Am Vet US. 1980; elite lifetime mem, Morehouse Col Nat Alumni Asn. **Honors/Awds:** Citz Scholar Found Middleboro, 1968-70; Cits Scholar Found MA, 1970-72; Paul Revere Bowl Citz Scholar Found Am, 1976. **Military Serv:** Infantry, 1942-46, 1951-54; capt, 1951-54; Bronze Star w/2 Oak Leaf Clusters & V device, Silver Star Med, 1951, Infantryman's Badge w/Star; Purple Heart, 1951; Six Battle Stars. **Home Addr:** 95 Thomas St, Middleboro, MA 02346, **Home Phone:** (508)947-1584.

TOWNSEND, DR. NKECHIT FLORENCE
Association executive. **Career:** Prof psychol; The Asn Black Psychologists, mem comt chair, currently, regional rep, Midwestern Region, currently. **Business Addr:** Membership Committee Chair, The Association of Black Psychologists, PO Box 55999, Washington, DC 20040, **Business Phone:** (202)722-0808.

TOWNSEND, P A
Lawyer. **Personal:** Born Nov 29, 1914, Poplar Bluff, MO; son of Sol and Ava Porter; married Evelyn M; children: Prentice & Edward. **Educ:** Univ Kans, AB, 1934, LLB, 1937. **Career:** Lawyer (retired); Gen practice law, 1937-65; State Kans, spec asst atty gen, 1937-41; State Tax Comn, asst atty, 1947-52; State Corp Comn, asst atty, 1947-52; Missionary Bapt State Conv Kans, gen coun, 1948-62; Interstate Assoc Church God, gen coun, 1948-69; Prince Hall Grand Lodge Kans F&AM, grand atty, 1956-77, past grand master, 1979-81; Kans Conf, AME Church, atty; State Kans, pardon atty, 1965-67; State Corp Comn, asst gen coun, 1967-70; Dept Housing & Urban Develop, atty, reg coun, 1970-82; Municipal Court Topeka, judge pro-tem, 1983-90. **Orgs:** Del at large Rep Nat Conv, 1960; del Gen Conf, 1960, 1964, 1968, 1972, 1976, 1980, 1984, 1988; comn, Topeka Housing Auth, 1963-70; exec bd, Salvation Army, 1965; adv comn, Red Cross, 1966; Gen Conf Comn, 1964; pres, Judicial Coun, 1968-92; vchmn, Rep State Comn, two terms; vchmn, Shawnee Cty Central Comn; 33 Degree Mason. **Honors/Awds:** Shriner; Alpha Phi Alpha; Washburn Univ Centennial Fund Dr; Stormont-Vail Hosp Bond Dr; past comdr Jordan-Patterson Post #319, Amer Legion; former mem, Legal Redress Comn, NAACP; bd stewards, former mem, bd trustees, Douglass Hosp; pres, judicial coun, St John AME Church; Kansas Bar Asn, cert for 50 years meritorious service as an atty, 1987. **Military Serv:** Capt, WWII.

TOWNSEND, ROBERT
Television producer, administrator, actor. **Personal:** Born Feb 6, 1957, Chicago, IL; son of Robert and Shirley; married Cheri Jones, Jan 1, 1990 (divorced 2001); children: Sierra, Skylar & Isaiah. **Educ:** Ill State Univ; William Paterson Col, NJ; Hunter Col, NY; Beverly Hills Playhouse. **Career:** Experimental Black Actors Guild and Second City, Chicago, 1970; Ensemble Co, Off-Broadway productions & performed at local comedy clubs, 1970-80; Films: Cooley High, 1975; Streets of Fire, 1984; A Soldier's Story, 1984; American Flyers, 1985; Hollywood Shuffle, actor, dir & producer, 1987; Eddie Murphy Raw, dir, 1987; The Mighty Quinn, 1989; The Five Heartbeats, writer, dir & actor, 1991; The Meteor Man, 1993; The Taxman, 1999; Fraternity Boys, dir, 1999; Book of Love, 2000; Undercover Brother, 2002; Black Listed, 2003; TV Series: "Robert Townsend & His Partners in Crime", HBO, writer, actor, dir & producer, 1987-88; "The Parent Hood," Warner Bros, 1995; "Love Songs," dir, 1999; "Up Up & Away," dir, 2000; "Livin for Love: The Natalie Cole Story," 2000; "Holiday Heart," 2000; "Carmen: AHip Hopera," M TV, 2001; "10,000 Black Men Named George," 2002; "Spoken", 2005, 2006; "Gory Stories", 2005; "The World According to Kids", 2005; "Pilot Central", 2005; "Lisa Knight & the Round Table", 2005-07; "Souled Out", 2005; "Thousand Dollar Bee", 2005-07; "The B5 Christmas Special", 2006; "Rising", 2006; "Playhouse 22", 2006; "The Envy Life", 2006; "Pilot Central", 2006; "The Envy Life", 2007; "Of Boys & Men", actor & producer, 2007; "Partners in Crime", 2007; Townsend Entertainment Corp, owner & chief exec officer, currently; Black Family Channel, pres & chief exec officer, 2004-. **Honors/Awds:** Image Awards, Nat Asn Advan Colored People, 2001. **Business Phone:** (404)350-2509.

TOWNSEND, RONALD
Executive. **Personal:** Born Sep 23, 1941, Jacksonville, FL; married Dorothy; children: Michelle Townsend-Smith, Ronnie Jr & Gina. **Educ:** Baruch Col, NY, bus. **Career:** CBS-TV, staff, 1960-64, dir bus affairs & programming, 1964-69; C's TV Workshop, dir field serv, 1969; Pvt consult, 1997-; WTOP-TV, sta mgr, 1974-82; WTOP-TV, gen mgr; Gannett TV Group, pres, 1989, Nielsen Media Res Inc, bd dir, 1999; Rayonier Inc, dir, 2001-; ALLTEL Corp, dir, currently; Winn-Dixie Stores Inc, dir, currently. **Orgs:** Augusta Nat Golf Club; dir & trustee, Univ N Fla; Jacksonville Symphony Orchestra; Jacksonville Port Authority; United Way Northeast Fla; Freedom Forum Newseum; Nat Jewish Ctr Immunol & Respiratory Med. **Honors/Awds:** Honored by United Negro Col Fund, 1986; Trumpet Award, 1996. **Special Achievements:** First black member of the Augusta National Golf Club. **Business Addr:** Director, Rayonier Inc, 50 N Laura St Suite 19, Jacksonville, FL 32202, **Business Phone:** (904)357-9100.

TOWNSEND, WARDELL C
Government official. **Personal:** Born Oct 16, 1952, Baltimore, MD; son of Wardell Clinton Sr and Toyoko Yonamine; married Diane Martin, May 7, 1979; children: Sarah Sachiko, Claire Keiko, Jordan Hideto & Aaron Masao. **Educ:** Western Carolina Univ, BS, psychol, social welfare, 1975; WVa Univ, MSW, 1979. **Career:** Boys Club Asheville, group counr, 1975-76; Asn Sickle Cell Disease, health educr/outreach coordr, 1976-77; Human Resource Develop Found, planning & develop mgr, 1979-80; Henderson County, dir, Community Develop Dept, 1980-82; Cherokee Minority Bus Develop Ctr, bus develop mgr, 1982-83; US Rep, Jamie Clarke, proj dir, 1983; US Rep, Mike Espy, legis dir, assoc staff Budget Comt, admin asst/chief staff; US Rep, Doug Applegate, proj dir, 1985; Clinton Presial Transition Team, 1992-93; US Dept Agricul, asst secy admin, 1993; Exec Coach & Consult, assoc, currently; Townsend Dantai, pres, currently; Uman Res Assocs Inc, assoc, currently. **Orgs:** Nat Asn Social Workers, 1974-; Acad Cert Social Workers, 1982-; Diocesan Investment Comt, Episcopal Diocese Wash, 1991-; bd dirs, Admin Assts Asn, 1991-92, vpres, 1992; Coun African Admin Assts; Ascension Church; numerous past memberships; Japanese Am Citizens League, 1993-; House Admin Assts Alumni Asn, 1993-; Pres's Coun Mgt Improvement, 1993-; NC Democratic Club Wash, 1993-; Asian Am Govt Exec Network, 1996-. **Honors/Awds:** Membership Recruitment Award, US House Representatives, Admin Assts Asn, 1991; Special Recognition, Asian Pac Am Network Agr, 1993; Special Recognition, Western Carolina Univ Alumni Asn & Pi Gamma Mu Int Honor Soc, 1994; Hammer Award, VPres Al Gore, 1994; Special Recognition, Forum Blacks Agr, 1995; hon mem, Nat Fedn Fed Employees, 1995; African American Males Alumni Award, US Dept Agr, 1996; Special Recognition, Exec Potential Prog, 1996; Special Recognition, Defense Info Systs Agency, 1996. **Business Addr:** Consultant, Executive Coaching & Consulting Associates, 8908 Ellsworth Ct, Silver Spring, MD 20910, **Business Phone:** (301)585-4327.

TRAINER, JAMES E
Automotive executive. **Personal:** Born in Birmingham, AL; married Mattie; children: Eric, Marcus & Jameta. **Career:** Trainer Oldsmobile-Cadillac-Pontiac-GMC Truck Inc, chief exec officer. **Special Achievements:** Trainer was first African American salesman to work for Edwards Chevrolet in Birmingham, AL, the oldest Chevrolet dealership in the US, 1971; company led all US black-owned auto dealerships with sales of $254.6 million, 1992; Company is ranked No one on Black Enterprises list of Top 100 Auto Dealers, 1994.

TRAMIEL, KENNETH RAY, SR.
Counselor. **Personal:** Born May 31, 1946, Shreveport, LA; married Sandra Mackel; children: Kenneth Jr, Kendra & Kai. **Educ:** Univ Calif, Berkeley, BA, 1973; Calif State Univ, MS, 1976. **Career:** E Oakland Youth Develop, head counr, 1979-80; Fed Govt Vietnam Outreach prog, asst team leader, counr, 1980-82; Oakland Unified Sch Dist, head counr, col & scholar counr, 1982-, afrocentric curric & coun techniques, post traumatic stress disorder, currently; consult, currently. **Orgs:** Pres, Berkeley Youth Alternative, 1981-82; Oakland Personnel & Guidance Asn, 1982-; Calif Asn Gifted, 1984; vpres, Oakland Pub Sch Affirmative Action Comn, 1985-86; bd mem, Berkeley Juneteenth Asn Inc; bd mem, Racial & Ethnic Ministry Comt, The Presbyterian Church USA, Synod Northern Calif; pres, Calif Sch Counr Asn. **Military Serv:** AUS, personnel sp5, 2 yrs; Outstanding Section Leader, 1969. **Home Addr:** 2923 Jo Ann Dr, Richmond, CA 94806.

TRAMMEL, KIMBERLY ELISE
Actor. **Personal:** Born Apr 17, 1967, Minneapolis, MN; daughter of Marvin and Erna Jean; married Maurice Oldham, Jan 1, 1989 (divorced 2005); children: AjaBleu & Butterfly. **Educ:** Minneapolis Community Col; Univ Minnesota, BA, mass commun; Am Film Inst. **Career:** Films: Set It Off, 1996; Beloved, 1998; Bait, 2000; John Q, 2002; The Manchurian Candidate, 2004; Diary of a Mad Black Woman, 2005; Pride, 2007; The Great Debaters, 2007; TV movies:"The Ditchdigger's Daughters", 1997; "The Loretta Claiborne Story", 2000; "Bojangles", 2001; "The Twilight Zone", 2003; "Girlfriends", 2003; "Close to Home", 2005-07; "Private Practice", 2007; "Masters of Science Fiction", 2007; Gifted Hands: The Ben Carson Story, 2009; "Grey's Anatomy", 2009. **Orgs:** Northern Warehouse Artists' Coop. **Honors/Awds:** Cable Ace Award, Best Supporting Actress in Movie or Mini Series, 1997; CFCA Award for Most Promising Actress, 1999; Golden Satellite Award for Best Actress in a Supporting Role in a Motion Picture-Drama, 1999; Black Reel Award for Network/Cable-Best Supporting Actress, 2002; Black Reel Award, 2005 & 2006. **Business Addr:** Actress, Writers & Artists Group, 8383 Wilshire Blvd Suite 550, Beverly Hills, CA 90211, **Business Phone:** (212)391-1112.*

TRAMMELL, WILLIAM RIVERS
Insurance executive. **Personal:** Born Oct 19, 1926, Anniston, AL; son of Edward A Sr and Mattie Rivers; married Bertha Hicks. **Educ:** Clark Col Atlanta, AB, 1948; Columbia Univ NY, MA, 1961. **Career:** Calhoun Co Sch, jr high prin, 1948-65; Anniston Pub Sch, elem prin, 1965-75, interim sch supt, 1978-79, asst supt & dir finance, 1975-85; Protective Indust Ins Co Ala, dir 1989-. **Orgs:** Dir, Pilot State Kindergarten Prog, Anniston City Sch, 1973-77; secy, Anniston Airport Comn, 1980-86; Ala Gov's Comn Handicapped Employ, 1985-; treas, Calhoun Co Econ Develop Coun, chmn, 1986-; bd dir, Ala Easter Seal Soc, 1986-; bd dir, Omega Psi Phi Fraternity Theta Tau Chap, currently. **Honors/Awds:** Outstanding Service Award in Education, Alpha Kappa Alpha Sorority, 1984; Archon of the Year, Sigma Pi Phi Fraternity Beta Kappa Boule, 1986; Gold Award, Ala Easter Seal Soc, 1986. **Home Addr:** 2517 McKleroy Ave, Anniston, AL 36201, **Home Phone:** (205)236-4113. **Business Addr:** Chairman, Calhoun County Chamber of Commerce, Calhoun County's Economic Development Council, 1330 Quintard Ave, PO Box 1087, Anniston, AL 36202, **Business Phone:** (256)237-3536.

TRAMMER, MONTE IRVIN
Newspaper publisher. **Personal:** Born Nov 11, 1951, Birmingham, AL; son of Jimmie and Edwenia Wilson; married Hilda Hudson, May 20, 1972. **Educ:** Indiana Univ, Indianapolis, IN, 1975; Concord Law Sch Kaplan Univ, Exec JD. **Career:** Indianapolis Star, Indianapolis, IN, reporter, 1970-76; Baltimore Sun, Baltimore, MD, reporter, 1977-80; Detroit Free Press, Detroit, MI, bus writer, 1980-81, asst city ed, 1981-82; USA Today, Wash, DC, dep managing ed, 1982-86; Poughkeepsie Journal, Poughkeepsie, NY, asst to the publ, 1986; Saratogian, Saratoga Springs, NY, publ, 1986-98; Star-Gazette, Elmira NY, pres & publ, 1999-; The Ithaca Jour, publ, 2007-. **Orgs:** Chair, NY Newpapers Found; NY Newspaper Publ Asn; Chemung County NAACP; life mem, NAACP; Elmira Rotary; trustee, Empire State Col Found. **Military Serv:** Ind Army Nat Guard, 1971-76. **Business Addr:** President, Publisher, Star Gazette, PO Box 285, Elmira, NY 14902, **Business Phone:** (607)271-8210.

TRAPP, DONALD W.
Financial manager. **Personal:** Born Sep 28, 1946, Hampton, VA; son of Chester A Trapp and Ida Holt Trapp; married Shirley Ann Stokes; children: Rashaad, Brandon & Yvonne. **Educ:** Va State Univ, BS Bus Admin, 1968; Ind Univ, MBA, Finance, 1973. **Career:** Cummins Engine Co Inc, dir pricing, 1978-82, asst treas, 1977-78, finan spec, 1976-77; Irwin Mgt Co Inc, mgr treas reporting, 1973-76; Cummins Engine Co Inc, dir components strategy, 1982-83, dir int logistics,1983-84; Remote Equip Corp, pres, 1985-88; vpres & treas, UNC Ventures, Inc Boston, MA, 1988-90; Cummins Engine Co, Inc, dir strategic planning, 1991-92, dir bus develop, 1992-94, dir, electronics bus strategy, 1994-96,exec dir, electronics, 1996-97, vp & treas, 1997-2003, vp bus devel, 2003-, vpres, polit action comm. **Orgs:** C C, 1975; Kappa Alpha Psi Frat Inc, 1967-; bd dir, William R Laws Found,1975-84; bd dir, Columbus United Way Am, 1976-79; bd dirs, Accent Hair Salons, 1988-90; bd dirs, Xinix Corp, 1989-90; Nat Black Mba Asn. 1991-;bd, Columbus Enterprise Develop Corp, 1994-97; bd, Bartholomew County Big Brothers/Big Sisters, 1995-99; bd, Ind Univ Bus Sch Alumni Asn, 1996-99;bod, United Way Bartholomew County, 1996-2002, Columbus Regional Hosp Found, 2005-; bd dir, Community Educ Coalition. **Honors/Awds:** Achievement award, Wall St Jour, 1968; Distinguished Service Citation,United Negro Fund, 1977. **Military Serv:** AUS, first lt 1968-70; commendation med, 1968. **Home Addr:** 3241 Beechnut Ct, Columbus, IN 47203.

TRAPP, JAMES
Football coach, football player. **Personal:** Born Dec 28, 1969, Greenville, SC; married. **Educ:** Clemson Univ, CSUN, attending. **Career:** Football player (retired), Football coach; Los Angeles Raiders, 1993-94; Oakland Raiders, defensive back, 1994-98; Baltimore Ravens, 1999-2002; Jacksonville Jaguars, safety, 2003;

NFL Europe, Sea Devils, coaching staff, currently; D1 Sports Training, co-owner, currently. **Business Addr:** Coaching Staff, NFL Europe, Sea Devils, ArenA Blvd 73-75, 1101 DL Amsterdam, Netherlands, **Business Phone:** (003)1020465-0550.

TRAUGHBER, CHARLES M.
Government official. **Personal:** Born Feb 13, 1943. **Educ:** Tenn State Univ, BS, 1968, Grad Sch, 1970. **Career:** Tenn State Penitentiary, counr I, 1969, sr instnl counr, 1971; Adult Coun Serv Adult Inst State Tenn, dir, 1972; Tenn Paroles Bd, mem, 1972-, chmnbd, probation & parole, currently. **Orgs:** Am Correctional Asn; Nat Asn Advan Colored People; Tenn Correctional Asn; Am Paroling Asn. **Honors/Awds:** Outstanding Black Citizen Award; Chattanooga Civitan Club Award; Appreciation Award, Tenn Legis Black Caucus; Appreciation Award, Memphis Chap, Kappa Alpha Psi Fraternity, Appreciation Awards, Am Correctional Asn; Ben Baer Award, Asn Paroling Authorities Int, 1999. **Business Addr:** Chairman, Tennessee Board of Probation & Parole, 404 James Robertson Pkwy Suite 1300, Nashville, TN 37243-0850, **Business Phone:** (615)741-1673.*

TRAVIS, BENJAMIN
Lawyer. **Personal:** Born Apr 1, 1932, Brooklyn, NY; married Anne Fredd; children: Bennea, Benjamin Jr & Benjamin Frederick. **Educ:** Col Pugent Sound, 1951; San Francisco State Col, 1954; Univ Calif Hastings Col Law, JD, 1960. **Career:** Judge (retired); Atty pvt pract, 1961-66; Western Addition Law Off, opened first neighborhood legal serv off San Francisco chief coun, 1966-72; Community Educ Proj & Neighborhood Legal Newspaper, founder, 1968-; San Francisco State Col, lecturing prof, 1971; Emeryville Judicial Dist, Piedmont, Oakland, munic ct judge, 1976-81; Alameda Co, super ct judge. **Orgs:** Bd dir, Berkeley Neighborhood Legal Serv; bd dir, San Francisco Local Develop Corp; bd dir, Bay Area Social Planning Coun; vpres & bd dir, San Francisco Neighborhood Legal Asst Found; bd dir, Bayview Hunter's Point Community Health Ctr; bd dir, Tassili Sch; bd dir, Nat Legal Aid & Defender's Asn; consult, evaluator & tech asst, Volt Inc Civil Defenders Comn; bd dir, Nat Bar Asn; secy, Charles Houston Law Club, 1971; Task Force Comm Criminal Justice; bd dir, United Bay Area Crusade, 1972; Judicare Exp Prog, 1973; pres, Charles Houston Law Club, 1973-; League Women Voters Calif Educ Fund. **Honors/Awds:** Outstanding Contribution Award, Calif Black Correctional Coalition, 1978; The Honorable Judge Benjamin Travis Community Service Awards, named in honor, 1979; Distinguished Service Award, Judicial Coun, 1985; Honorary Citizen of Chicago Award, 1985; Outstanding Contribution, Nat Bar Asn, 1987; Distinguished Service Award, Calif Asn Black Lawyers, 1987, 1994; Inaugural Hall of Fame Award, Charles Houston Bar Asn, 1994. **Military Serv:** USAF, 1950-54.

TRAVIS, DEMPSEY J
Entrepreneur, consultant, real estate agent. **Personal:** Born Feb 25, 1920, Chicago, IL; son of Mittie Strickland and Louis; married Moselynne. **Educ:** Wilson Jr Col, AA, 1948; Roosevelt Univ, BA, 1949; Northwestern Univ Sch, Mortgage Banking, Cert, 1969; Olive Harvey Col, Hon Doctorate Econs, 1975; Daniel Hale Williams Univ, Hon Doctorate Bus Admin, 1976. **Career:** Sivart Mortgage Corp, pres, 1945-78; Travis Realty Co, founder & pres, 1949-; United Mortgage Bankers Am, founder & pres, 1960-73; Dempsey J Travis Securities & Investment Co, pres, 1960-76; Urban Research Press, pres; Travis Realty Co, entrepreneur, currently. **Orgs:** Trustee, Northwestern Mem Hosp, 1975-; dir, Uni Banc Trust, 1976-87; trustee, Chicago Hist Soc, 1985-; pres, Soc Midland Authors, 1988-90; Book Rev Critic, Chicago Sun-Times, 1991; bd trustees, Roosevelt Univ; Auditorium Theater; Black Music Ctr; Columbia Col; Garfield Pk Conserv; Nat Asn Advan Colored People. **Honors/Awds:** Numerous honors and awards including Hon Doctorate Arts Econ Sci, Olive-Harvey Col, 1974; Hon Doctorate Bus Admin, Daniel Hale Williams Univ, 1976; Honorary Doctorate of Humanities, 1982; Society of Midland Authors Award, 1982; Art Deco Award, 1985; Mary Herrick Award, 1990; Mary Herrick Award, 1990; Living African-American Heritage Award, 1992; Living African American Heritage Award, 1992; Ameritech Small Business Community Service Award, 1995; Ameritech Small Business Community Service Award, 1995; First America Award, Gustavus Myers Ctr Study Human Rights, 1996; Nat Literary Hall of Fame, 2000; Hon Doctorate Humanities, Governor's State Univ, 2001; Hon Doctorate Humanities, Governors State Univ, 2001; Harold Wash Col Black Women's Caucus Salute, 2001. **Special Achievements:** Author: Don't Stop Me Now, An Autobiography of Black Chicago, 1981; An Autobiography of Black Jazz, 1983; An Autobiography of Black Politics, 1987; Real Estate is the Gold in Your Future, 1988; Harold: The People's Mayor, 1989; Racism: American Style, A Corporate Gift, 1991; I Refuse to Learn to Fail, book, 1992; Views from the Back of the Bus, During WW II and Beyond, 1995; The Duke Ellington Primer, 1996; The Louis Armstrong Odyssey: From Jane Alley to America's Jazz Ambassador, 1997; Racism: Like a Merry Go 'Round, 'Round 'N 'Round It Goes, 1998; They Heard a Thousand Thunders, The Life and Times of Redd Foxx, 1999, The Victory Monument: The Beacon of Chicago's Bronzeville,1999; J Edgar Hoover's FBI Wired the Nation, 2000; The FBI Files on the Tainted and The Damned, 2001; An American Story in Red, White and Blue, Norman Granz: The White Moses of Black Jazz; Travis Realty Co, Urban Research Press Inc & DJ Travis Development Co., all three companies has been certified by the City of Chicago as an MBE (Minority Business Enterprises). **Military Serv:** AUS, Tech Sgt, 4 yrs. **Business Addr:** Entrepreneur, Travis Realty Co, 840 E 87th St, Chicago, IL 60619-6248, **Business Phone:** (773)994-7200.

TRAVIS, GERALDINE
Legislator. **Personal:** Born Sep 3, 1931, Albany, GA; daughter of Joseph T and Dorothy Marshall; married William Alexander Sr; children: William, Michael, Ann, Gerald & Gwendolyn. **Educ:** Xavier Univ, 1947-49. **Career:** Dem Nat Conv Miami, deleg,1972; Dem Mini-Conv Kans, deleg, 1974; Dem Nat Conv NY, deleg, 1976; State MT, legislator, 1975-77. **Orgs:** Co-chmn, Dem Party Minorities Comn, 1972-74; mem, Nat Steering Comn, 1973-74; State Coord Comn Int Womens Yr, 1977; Off Observer Nat Womens Conf, 1977; bd dir, YWCA Great Falls, 1979; co-chmn, Dem Women's Club; St Peter & Paul Cath Church; Nat Womens Polit Caucus; Nat Order Women Legislators; YWCA; Nat Coun Negro Women; Nat Asn Advan Colored People; Nat Urban League; Am Civil Liberties Union; Sierra Club; MT Womens Pol Caucus; MT Crime Control Bd, Human Resources Comn; Criminal Justice Info Comn; Precinct Comn Woman Precinct 42 Cascade City; MT Adv Comn US Comn Civil Rights; chmn, Cascade City Detoxification Adv Bd; Am Indian Action Coun; chmn, Sub-Comm Admin Justice; Ariz Precinct Comn Women; Democratic Dist No 12; Ariz Democratic State Comn. **Home Addr:** 7421 W Denton Lane, Glendale, AZ 85303-5753.

TRAVIS, JACK
Architect, interior designer. **Personal:** Born Mar 2, 1952, Newellton, LA; son of Sam L and Mary L Brown. **Educ:** Ariz State Arz, BA, 1977; Arz of Ill, Champaign Urbana, 1978. **Career:** Whisler-Patri, designer, archit, 1978; Pac Gas & Elec, draughtsman, archit, 1978-79; Eyes Group Design, designer, draughtsman, archit, 1979-80; Skidmore Owings & Merrill, designer, interior archit, 1980-82; Switzer Group Inc, designer, interior archit, 1982-84; Sydney Philip Gilbert Assoc, designer, interior archit, 1984; NBC Broadcasting Co, designer, interior archit, 1985; Fashion Inst Technol, adjunct prof; Pratt Ist Sch Interior Design, adjunct prof, currently; Parsons Sch Design, adjunct prof, currently; Jack Travis archit, prin, owner, 1985-. **Orgs:** Am Inst Archits, Nat AIA Task Force on Civil Rights & Cultural Diversity, 1992; NOMA; Nat Coun Archit Regist Bds; Nat Coun Interior Design Qualification; Harlem Comt Bd 10 mem, 2001. **Honors/Awds:** Forty Under Forty, Crain's NY bUS, 1992; Certif of Appreciation, Lanier High Sch, 2000; Certif of Appreciation, Jackie Robinson Middle Sch, 320, 2002. **Special Achievements:** Publications: "Afr Amer Architecture: From Idea to Published Design," JAE, 1993; "Cultural Differences & Their Manefestations," Blacklines, 2000; "Minor Architects: What You Don't Know," Natl Associates Committee Quarterly, 2003. **Business Addr:** Owner, Jack Travis Architect, 432 Austin Place Fl 2, Bronx, NY 10455-5006, **Business Phone:** (718)742-6791.

TRAVIS, TRACEY T.
Businessperson. **Personal:** Born 1962. **Educ:** Univ of Pittsburgh, BS, 1983 in Industrial Engineering; Columbia Univ, MBA, 1986. **Career:** Senior VP of Finance and CFO, 2005-; Senior VP, Finance of Limited Brands, Inc., 2002-04;CFO of Intimate Brands, Inc., 2001-02; CFO of the Beverage Can Americas group at American Natl Can, 1999-01; held finance and operations positions at Pepsi Bottling Group 1989-99. **Orgs:** Member of the board of directors of Jo-Ann Stores, Inc, the Lincoln Center Theater, the Executive Leadership Council Foundation, and the Ralph Lauren Center for Cancer Care and Prevention; Dir, Chairman of Audit Committee and Member of Corporate Governance Committee; Treasurer of the Ralph Lauren Foundation member of Financial Executives International, the Natl Assoc of Corp Dir, the New York Women's Forum. **Special Achievements:** Awarded a GM Fellowship to pursue her MBA; recognized by Treasury and Risk Management as on of the Top 25 Women in Finance, 2005; named one of the top 50 Women in Business by Black Enterprise magazine, 2006. **Business Addr:** Polo Ralph Lauren Corp, 650 Madison Ave., New York, NY 10022, **Business Phone:** (212)318-7000.*

TRAYLOR, PROF. ELEANOR W.
Educator. **Personal:** Born Dec 12, 1933, Thomasville, GA; daughter of Esther M G Williams Smith and Phillip Williams. **Educ:** Spelman Col, BA; Atlanta Univ, MA; Catholic Univ, PhD. **Career:** Dept Agri, Grad Sch, Eng Dept, chair, 1966-67; Howard Univ, Col Fine Arts,adj prof, drama, 1968-75; Hobart & William Smith Col, visiting humanist; Cornell Univ, visiting prof, lit, 1979-80; Tougaloo Col, visiting humanist, 1982; Montgomery Col, Eng, prof, 1965-90; Howard Univ, prof Eng,1990-, Humanities Dept, chair, 1990-93, Dept Eng, chair, 1993-. **Orgs:** Proj dir, Larry Neal Cultural Series, 1984; founder, Elders Advan Am LitPub Sch, 1984; Col Lang Asn; Modern Lang Asn; evaluator, African MuseumAsn; scriipt writer, Smithsonian Inst; script writer, Prog Black Am Cult; Nat CounTeachers Eng; panelist, Nat Endowment Humanities; lit. consultant, The NatBlacks Arts Festival (1994-); bd mem, The DC Reperatory Theater Company; bd mem, The Duke Ellington High School of the Performing Arts, The Assoc, of Am University Professors. **Honors/Awds:** Hazel Joan Bryant Recognition Award, Midwest African Theatre Alliance,1987; Black History Achievement Award for contributions to the advancement& preservation of African Literature, Peoples Congregational Church, 1989;Alumni Achievement Award, Catholic Univ, Lit criticism, 1989; LarryNeal-Georgia Douglas Johnson Award, The Marcus Garvey Mem Found, lit &community serv, 1989; The New Orleans Public School Advisory Board for African American Studies, 1993; Community Service Award, African Heritage Studies Association, 1993; The Amoco Foundation's Excellence in Teaching Award, 1993; The Howard University Academic Affairs' Departmental Leadership Award, 1994; The Howard University Undergraduate Student Assembly's Award for Achievement in Education and Literature, 1995; The National Hall of Fame for Writers of African Descent, 1999; Doctor of Humane Letters, Spelman College, 2002; The Washington DC Hall of Fame Award for Community Cultural Development, 2007. **Special Achievements:** Auth: College Reading Skills, Random House, 1966; The Dream Awake: A Multi-Media Production, 1968; The Humanities & Afro Literature Tradition,1988; Broad Sympathy: Howard Univ Oral Tradition Reader, Simon & Schuster,1996; numerous publications, dramatic scripts, multimedia productions, scholarly lectures and keynote addresses. **Business Addr:** Department Chair, English Department, Howard University, College of Arts and Sciences, Department English, PO Box 590492, Washington, DC 20059.

TRAYLOR, DR. HORACE JEROME
Association executive, educator. **Personal:** Born Mar 15, 1931, La Grange, GA; married Theola Dennis; children: Sheryl Lynn, Linda Gail, Yohanna Faye, Chequeta Renee & Tonya Yvonne. **Educ:** Zion Col, AB, 1953; Gammon Theolo Sem, BD, 1958; Univ Tenn, Chattanooga, MEd, 1965; Univ Miami, PhD, 1978. **Career:** Chattanooga City Col, pres, 1964-69; Univ Tenn, spec asst chancellor, 1969-71; Miami-Dade Comm Col, Open Col, dean, 1971-74, pres develop, 1974-79, vpres, inst advan, 1980-. **Orgs:** Treas, Leadership Inst Comm Develop Wash DC, 1969-73; founder & bd dir, United Bank Chattanooga, 1971-; adv bd, United Bank Chattanooga, 1971; treas, Coun Black Am Affairs-Am Asn Comm & Jr Col, 1974-; adv comm, Inst Study Educ Policy Howard Univ, 1967-; pres, Miami-Dade Comm Col Fund Inc, 1985-. **Honors/Awds:** VSmith-Taylor Award for Excellence in Journalism, 1958; Outstanding Young Man of Yr Award, Nat Jaycees, 1965; Ambassador Good Will, Human Relations Counc Chattanooga, 1969. **Business Addr:** Vice President, Institutional Advancement, Miami-Dade Comm College, MDC Kendall Campus 11011 SW 104 ST, Miami, FL 33176-3393, **Business Phone:** (305)237-2000.

TRAYLOR, KEITH
Football player. **Personal:** Born Sep 3, 1969, Little Rock, AR; married Krista; children: Brandon. **Educ:** Cent Okla Univ, indust safety, 1991. **Career:** Denver Broncos, defensive tackle, 1991-92, 1997-2000; Los Angeles Raiders, 1993; Green Bay Packers, 1993; Kans City Chiefs, 1993-96; Chicago Bears, 2001-03; New Eng Patriots, 2004; Miami Dolphins, 2005-07, free agent, currently. **Honors/Awds:** All-Lone Star Conference, 1990; All-Rookie, Pro Football Weekly & Football Digest, 1991; 3x Super Bowl champion XXXII, XXXIII, XXXIX.

TRAYLOR, ROBERT
Basketball player. **Personal:** Born Feb 1, 1977, Detroit, MI. **Educ:** Univ Mich, sports mgt & commun. **Career:** Milwaukee Bucks, forward-ctr, 1998-2000; Cleveland Cavaliers, 2001, 2004-05; Charlotte Hornets, 2002; New Orleans Hornets, 2003-04; Gestiberica Vigo, 2006; Santurce Crabbers, 2007.

TRAYNHAM, ROBERT LEE
Government official. **Personal:** Born Aug 9, 1974, Philadelphia, PA; son of Robert and Debra. **Educ:** Cheyney Univ, BA, polit sci; George Mason Univ, MA, polit comn. **Career:** Republican Nat Convention, intern, 1995-96; Black America's Polit Action Comt, Polit dir, 1996-97; America's Voice, Polit contributing panelist, 1996-; George Mason Univ, 1997-2001; US Sen Rick Santorum, dep saff dir, 1997, dep chief staff & dir comn; US Senate Leadership, dep chief staff; US Presidential Campaign, sr political adv; Comcast Network, CN8, bur chief & corresp, currently. **Orgs:** Nat Ctr Pub Policy Res, Proj 21; Republican Comns Asn; vice chair Republican Nat Comt, New Majority coun; Ctr Study Presidency; Nat Press Club; coun trustees, Cheyney Univ; pres, US Senate Press Secretaries Asn. **Business Addr:** Bureau Chief, Correspondent, CN8, The Comcast Network, 179 Amory Street, Brookline, MA 02446, **Business Phone:** (617)731-4160.

TREADWELL, DAVID MERRILL
Journalist. **Personal:** Born Feb 21, 1940, Dayton, OH; son of Euretta Moore Boyce and Timothy D Sr; divorced. **Educ:** Ohio State Univ, BA, Eng, 1964, MA, Jour, 1974. **Career:** US Bureau Land Mgt, pub rels spec, 1969-70; Ohio State Univ, asst dir intl progs, 1970-73; Assoc Press, reporter, 1974-80; LA Times, Wash correspondent, 1980-85, Atlanta bureau chief, 1985-89; NY Bureau correspondent, 1989-93; Kean Univ, asst prof, 1994-. **Orgs:** Kappa Alpha Psi; Nat Asn Black Journalists; Asn Educ Journ & Mass Communs; Nat Coun Teachers Eng; NJ Col Eng Asn. **Honors/Awds:** Sloan Found Fellowship, Econ Jour Princeton

Univ, 1979-80. **Military Serv:** USN, lt, 1964-69. **Business Addr:** Assistant Professor, Kean University, Department English, 1000 Morris Ave, E Campus 19, Union, NJ 07083, **Business Phone:** (908)737-3355.*

TREADWELL, FAY RENE LAVERN
Manager. **Personal:** Born May 9, 1935, Okolona, AR; daughter of James Johnson; widowed; children: Tina. **Educ:** AR Baptist Col, AA; LA St Col. **Career:** Drifters Inc, pres; Mark Lundquist Concert Promotions, mgr, currently. **Orgs:** Life mem, Nat Asn Advan Colored People; Personal Mgrs United Kingdom. **Business Addr:** Manager, Mark Lundquist Concert Promotions, 5 Tuckey Grove 130 Engle St, Ripley GU23 6JG, United Kingdom, **Business Phone:** (440)148322-4118.

TREADWELL, TINA MCKINLEY
Executive. **Personal:** Born Mar 21, 1958, New York, NY; daughter of George McKinley and Fayrene Johnson. **Educ:** Princeton Univ, BA, eng lit, 1980. **Career:** Merrill & Assoc, partner, casting dir, 1986-90; Treadwell & Assoc, pres, casting dir, 1990-96; Treadwell Prods, dir, producer, 1990-96; Blind Pig Prods, co-producer, 1996; Disney Channel, exec dir talent develop & music specialist, 1997, music specialist, vpres talent develop & alternative programming, currently; Treadwell Entertainment, pres, currently. **Orgs:** Bd mem, fundraising co-chair, Educating Young Minds, 1998-; Women in Film; Women in Cable; Namic. **Honors/Awds:** Image Award, Nat Asn Advan Colored People, 1996; California Critics Award, 1996; California Critics Ovation Award, 1996. **Special Achievements:** National Black Theatre Festival, producer, 1995. **Business Addr:** President, Treadwell Entertainment, 1321 Garden St, Glendale, CA 91201-2715, **Business Phone:** (818)243-2446.

TREE, SHADE. See JONES, MARVIN MAURICE.

TREES, CANDICE D.
Government official. **Personal:** Born Jul 18, 1953, Springfield, IL; daughter of Peggie D Neal Senor and Clarence L Senor; married John F Trees; children: Peggi, Jessi, Johanna. **Educ:** Sangamon State Univ, BA 1981. **Career:** Town & Co Bank, teller, 1976-77; State Ill Off Govt, exec corresp, 1977-79; City Springfield, city clerk, 1979-86; Circuit Ct Sangamon Co, clerk, 1986. **Orgs:** United Way Sangamon County; Jr League Springfield; prog vpres Springfield Area Arts Coun; treas Munic Clerks Ill; vpres Lincolnfest Inc; Springfield Area Labor Mgt Comm; admin vpres Springfield Area Arts Coun; Jr League Springfield; chmn bd, HAT Construct, 1986; bd dirs Kennerer Village C's Home; sec adv bd Salvation Army, 1987-; Greater Springfield Chamber Com, 1987-88; Ill Asn Ct Clerks; bd mem, Ment Health Ctr Cent Ill, 1987; Nat Asn Ct Mgrs; Asn Rec Mgr & Admin. **Honors/Awds:** Registered Munic Clerk, 1981; Plaque for Outstanding Service, Springfield Urban League 1985; Cert Munic Clerk, 1986; Cert Appreciation, USAF, 1986; State Co-chairing 50th Anniversary, March of Dimes, Cent Ill Chapter, 1988; Plaque for Service, Pres, Lincolnfest 1988. **Business Addr:** Clerk of the Circuit Court, County Bldg Rm 412, Springfield, IL 62701.*

TREMITIERE, CHANTEL
Basketball player, football player, basketball coach. **Personal:** Born Oct 20, 1969, Williamsport, PA; daughter of William and Barbara. **Educ:** Auburn, BA, public rels, 1991. **Career:** Basketball player (retired), basketball coach (retired), football player; Auburn Tigers, 1991; Auburn Univ, asst coach, 1991-92; Texas Univ, asst coach, 1992-93; Univ Mass, asst coach, 1993-96; Sacramento Monarchs, guard, 1997; Utah Starzz, 1998; Indiana Fever, 2000-01; YorkCity Noise, 2002; Independent Women's Football League, Shreveport Aftershock, quarterback. 2007. **Special Achievements:** Has appeared in the movie Double Teamed, 2002.

TRENT, DR. CALVIN R
Administrator, executive director. **Educ:** BA, psychol; MA, educ; PhD, clin psychol. **Career:** Dept Health & Wellness Promotion, City Detroit, MI, Bur Substance Abuse Prev, Treatment & Recovery, dir, Spec Population Health Serv Div, gen mgr, currently. **Orgs:** Co-chair, Partnership Drug Free Detroit & Recovery Community. **Special Achievements:** Written several articles for clinical and general public. **Business Addr:** General Manager, Director, Detroit Department of Health & Wellness Promotion, Special Population Health Services Division, Rm 317 B Wing 1151 Taylor Main Bldg, Detroit, MI 48202, **Business Phone:** (313)876-4566.

TRENT, GARY DAJAUN
Basketball player. **Personal:** Born Sep 22, 1974, Columbus, OH; children: Garyson Jr & Garyson. **Educ:** Ohio Univ. **Career:** Portland Trail Blazers, forward, 1995-98; Toronto Raptors, 1998; Dallas Mavericks, 1999-2001; Minn Timber wolves, 2001-04; Chicago Bulls, 2004; Panellinios, Greece, 2004-05, 2006-07; Lottomatica Roma, Rome, 2005-06. **Honors/Awds:** Mid-American Conference Player of the Year, 1993, 1994, 1995. **Business Addr:** Professional Basketball Player, Lottomatica Roma.*

TRENT, JAMES E.
Educational consultant. **Personal:** Born Jan 14, 1936, Uniontown, PA; married Rosalie Mahaley; children: Jamie, Kelly & Jill. **Educ:** Wayne State Univ, BS, Bus Admin, 1957; Univ Detroit, MBA, 1965. **Career:** Educator (retired); Chrysler Realty, vpres, community oper, 1970-79; City Detroit Mayor's Off, exec asst productivity, 1979-80; Chrysler Learning, vpres, govt training, 1980-86; Chrysler Motors, educ consult, 1986. **Orgs:** Pole march Kappa Alpha Psi Detroit Alumni, 1977-83; dir & secy, Metro Detroit Youth Found, 1978-95; pres, Detroit Asn Black Orgn, 1985-; pres, Detroit Black Inter-Greek Coun, 1985-88; dir, Univ Detroit Black Alumni, 1986-90; Metro Detroit NPHC Liason. **Honors/Awds:** Roy Wilkins Award, Detroit Asn Black Orgn, 1985. **Military Serv:** AUS, sgt e-5, 1959-60. **Home Addr:** 5366 W Briarcliff Knoll Dr, West Bloomfield, MI 48322, **Home Phone:** (248)538-9583.

TRENT, RICHARD DARRELL
School administrator, educator. **Personal:** Born Nov 23, 1925, Detroit, MI; married Cynthia Ganger; children: Giselle, Stephen & Bradley. **Educ:** Mich State Univ, E Lansing, AB, psychol, 1950; Teachers Col, Columbia Univ, NY, MA, develop psychol, 1951, EdD, social psychol, 1953. **Career:** Youth House New York, boys supvr, 1950-52; City Col, City Univ NY, lectr educ psychol, 1952-54; New York State Training Sch Boys, Warwick, NY, staff psychologist, 1954-57; Puerto Rico Inst Psychiatry Bayamon, Puerto Rico, dir res, 1957-61; National Inst Health & Med Res, Ghana Acad Sci, Accra Ghana, res officer, 1965-69; Brooklyn Col, City Univ New York, Dept Educ, assoc prof, 1965-69, prof emer, currently; Medgar Evers Col, City Univ New York, pres, 1970-84, pres emer, currently. **Orgs:** Educ Issues Southern Dist US Fed Ct, 1969; bd dir, New York Urban League,1969-71; mgr, ed Afro-Am Studies, 1969-74; Danforth Found Asn Prog,1969-70; external examiner, psychol, Univ Lagos, Lagos, Nigeria, 1973, 74,80; educ chmn, Brooklyn Bicentennial Comn, 1974; bd dir, Brooklyn Rotary Club, 1975; Nat Asn Equal Opportunity Higher Educ, Wash, DC, 1976; exec comt, Col Pub Agency Coun US Civil Serv Comn, 1977; Research Found Exec Comn, City Univ New York, 1978; bd dir, Counc Higher Educ Inst New York,1978; Comn Res & Liaison Am Asn St Col & Univ, 1979. **Honors/Awds:** Won numerous awards including: Man of Year, Brooklyn Club National Asn Bus & Prof Women's Club, 1972; Educational Award, Int Inc, Brooklyn, NY, 1973; Outstanding Services & Civic contributions, Pres Borough of Brooklyn, 1973; Award for Outstanding Contributions, National Conf Christ & Jews,1974; Published several articles. **Military Serv:** AUS, Lt, 1944-47. **Business Addr:** Professor Emeritus, Brooklyn College, School of Education, 2900 Bedford Ave, Brooklyn, NY 11210, **Business Phone:** (718)951-5000.

TRESCOTT, JACQUELINE ELAINE
Journalist. **Personal:** Born Jan 2, 1947, Jersey City, NJ; married Edward M Darden; children: Douglass. **Educ:** St Bonaventure Univ, BS, 1968. **Career:** The Washington Star, reporter, 1970-75; The Washington Post, reporter, 1975-, staff writer, currently. **Orgs:** Nat Asn Black Journalists; fac Summer Prog Minority Journalists, 1978-. **Business Addr:** Reporter, Washington Post, 1150 15th St NW, Washington, DC 20071.

TRESVANT, RALPH E.
Singer, actor. **Personal:** Born May 16, 1968, Boston, MA; son of Ralph Sr and Patricia; married Amber Serrano, Sep 18, 2004. **Career:** New Edition, musical group mem; singer & actor; Albums: Ralph Tresvant,1990; It's Goin' Down, 1993; Rizz-Wa-Faire, 2006; Singles: "Sensitivity",1990; "Stone Cold Gentleman", 1991; "Do What I Gotta Do", 1991; "Rated R", 1991; "Yo Baby Yo", 1991; "Money Can't Buy You Love", 1992; "Who's the Mack", 1993; "When I Need Somebody", 1994; "My Home girl", 2006; "Magic Underwear", 2008; "Never Noticed", 2008; Films: Motives 2, 2007; Paper Soldiers, 2002; Brown Sugar, 2002; Barbershop Blues, (voice), 2004; Triple Cross, (voice), 2005; Motives 2, 2007; TV series: "Krush Groove", 1985; "Knight Rider", 1985; "Top of the Pops", 1996; "New York Undercover", 1996; "Soul Train", 1994-04; "R U the Girl", 2005; owner, Rated R records. **Business Phone:** (510)895-9002.*

TRIBBETT, CHARLES A., III
Executive, chief executive officer. **Personal:** Born Oct 25, 1955, Louisiana; son of Charles Tribbett Jr and Dorris Morris; married Lisa; children: Jason, Charles & Jillian. **Educ:** Marquette Univ, BA, 1976; Univ Va Law Sch, JD, 1980. **Career:** Skadden, Arps, Slate, Meagher & Flom, Chicago, coop securities atty; Abraham & Sons, partner; Russell Reynolds Assocs Inc, managing dir, co-leader & chief exec officer bd serves pract, currently. **Orgs:** Dir, Northern Trust Corporation; Mem, Deans Advisory Bd NW Univ J. L. Kellogg School of Management; bd mem, Northern Trust Bank; mem, the Chicago Symphony Orchestra; mem, Chicago Coun Global Affairs; mem, Rush Univ Med Ctr. **Honors/Awds:** Phi Beta Kappa, 1976; Northern Trust Corp, Listed as one of 400 companies, Forbes 400 Best Big Companies, 2009. **Business Addr:** Co-Leader, Chief Executive Officer of Board Services Practice, Russell Reynolds Associates Inc, 200 S Wacker Dr Suite 2900, Chicago, IL 60606, **Business Phone:** (312)993-9696.

TRIBBLE, HUERTA CASSIUS
Government official. **Personal:** Born Sep 15, 1939, Terre Haute, IN; children: Huerta Lee, Steven Harold & Kevin Eugene. **Educ:** Ind State Univ, AB, 1961. **Career:** PR Mallory, pr ma eng, 1966-69; Ind Urban League Inc, proj dir asst dist, 1969-81; US Small Bus Admn, dir, 1983-. **Orgs:** Ind Minority Splr Dev Coun, 1983-85; coordr, Ind Minority Bus OppurtunityCoun, 1983-85; trust, Martin Ctr Col, 1984-85. *

TRIBBLE, KEITH
Athletic director. **Career:** Univ Nev, Las Vegas, assoc athletic dir, 1981-89; Sunshine festival football inc, exec dir, 1990-92; Univ central Fla, dir athletics,currently. **Orgs:** Orange Bowl comt, currently; managing dir, Blockbuster Bowl; chmn, football bowl Assn. **Special Achievements:** First african american executive director of a major bowl game (OrangeBowl), 1993. **Business Phone:** (407)823-2261.*

TRICE, JUNIPER YATES
Educator, clergy, mayor. **Personal:** Born Aug 10, 1921, Verona, MS; married Detris Delois Scales; children: Juniper Olyen & Harriman Robert. **Educ:** AB, 1942; BTh, 1950; DD, 1958; MEd, 1961; spl deg, admin, 1972. **Career:** Mayor (retired), Educator, Clergy; Hall's Chapel New, Albany, MS, pastor; City Rd Corinth, MS, pastor; Naylor Chapel, Pontotoc, MS, pastor; Aberdeen Dist, presided; Jennings Temple, Greenwood, MS, pastor; Greenwood Dist, presided; Booneville Sch, prin; Carter High Sch, Tishomingo, MS, staff; E High Sch, Fulton, MS, staff; W Bolivar High Sch, Rosedale, MS, staff; Rosedale Miss Sch, asst supt; City Rosedale, mayor, 2001; Bolivar County Coun Aging Inc, chmn, exec dir, currently. **Orgs:** Selective Serv Bd Bolivar County; City Coun; bd dir, S Delta Plng & Develop Dist Inc; exec bd, Delta Area Coun BSA; bd trust, MS Indus Col; presiding elder Christ Methodist Episcopal Church; Hwy Com Delta Coun; MS Teacher Asn; Nat Educ Asn; 32 degree Mason; secy, MS Educ Finance Comn; So Reglig Educ Bd; MS Adult Educ Asn; bd dir, First Nat Bank Rosedale; bd trustees, Bolivar County Hosp; MS Employment Security Coun. **Honors/Awds:** BSA Award for Outstanding Service 1970; Listed in Outstanding Person, 1971; Leader of America, Sec Educ, 1972; Silver Beaver Award for Oustanding Service, 1977. **Home Addr:** PO Box 819, Rosedale, MS 38769. **Business Phone:** (662)846-6161.

TRICE, TRENA
Basketball player, basketball coach. **Personal:** Born Aug 4, 1965, Norfolk, VA; married Derrick A Hill; children: Kiana. **Educ:** NC State Univ, BS, speech commun. **Career:** Basketball player (retired), basketball coach; New York Liberty, forward ctr, 1997; Fed Intl Basketball Assn; Hampton Univ, asst coach, 2002-04; NC State Univ, asst coach, 2004-. **Honors/Awds:** ACC Tournament Champion, 1985, 1987; ACC Season Champion, 1985; St & Smith hon mention All-Am, 1987. **Business Addr:** Assistant Coach, NC State University, Athletics Department, PO Box 8502, Raleigh, NC 27695-8501, **Business Phone:** (919)513-1808.

TRICE, WILLIAM B.
Dentist. **Personal:** Born Jan 28, 1924, Newton, GA; married Mildred Moore; children: Sheila T Bell, Angela M. **Educ:** Univ Pittsburgh, BS, 1951; DMD, 1953. **Career:** Pvt pract, dentist; Hamot Hosp, staff; Erie Univ Pittsburgh Sch Dentistry, coordr continuing educ; Univ Pittsburgh Sch Dental Med, lectr. **Orgs:** Am & Nat Dental Asns; Pierre Fauchard Acad; Fedn Dentaire Internationale; Intl Asn Dental Res; Am Asn Dental Res; Acad Gen Dentistry; Am Acad Dental Electrosurg; Alpha Phi Alpha; Rotary; pres, Am Heart Asn; Knights Columbus; trustee, Stoneleigh Burnham Sch Fellow Am Col Dentists; Intl Dental Asn. **Military Serv:** USN, 1946. **Business Addr:** Dentist, 1611 PEACH ST, STE 275, Erie, PA 16501.

TRICHE, ARTHUR
Public relations executive. **Personal:** Born Aug 16, 1961, Mound Bayou, MS; son of Arthur Sr and Beatrice Anderson; married Velma Slack Triche, Aug 16, 1986; children: Brandon Arthur. **Educ:** Tulane Univ, New Orleans, LA, BS, lib arts. **Career:** Tulane Univ, New Orleans, LA, asst sports info dir, 1983-86; La State Univ, Baton Rouge, LA, asst sports info dir, 1986-88; Detroit Lions, Pontiac, MI, asst dir, pub rels, 1988-89; Atlanta Hawks, Atlanta, GA, dir pub rels, 1989, vpres, media rels, currently; spokesman, currently. **Orgs:** NBA Pub Rels Dirs Asn, 1989-. **Special Achievements:** First black public relations director for an NBA team. **Business Addr:** Vice President of Media Relations, Atlanta Hawks Basketball, 1 CNN Ctr, Atlanta, GA 30303, **Business Phone:** (404)878-3821.

TRIM, JOHN H.
Educator. **Personal:** Born Apr 19, 1931, Ft Worth, TX; married Earnestine. **Educ:** Bishop Col, BA, Social Sci; Prairie View A&M Univ, cert vocational indust educ. **Career:** Neiman Marcus, 1957-64; Franklin D Roosevelt HS Dallas TX, cvae coordr instr master level, 1964-. **Orgs:** Prof Teacher Org; vpres Asn Adv Artists & Writers; Human Interest Colum Post Tribune News, 1970-; colum inst Porters & Quall Ecumenical News, 1975; deacon trust Morning Star Bapt Ch; Org orginal Dalworth Leadership Coun Grand Prairie TX; dir, community youth mural comt ctr. **Honors/Awds:** Wrote book poetry life; fine arts shows; Airman Mo, 1954; city Mo KNOX,1954; Service Award, 1969; Youth Award, 1973. **Military Serv:** USAF, 1953-57.

TRIMIAR, DR. J. SINCLAIR
Educator, physician. **Personal:** Born Dec 17, 1933, Lynchburg, VA; married Anna H; children: Stefanie & Jay. **Educ:** Howard

Univ, BS, 1960; Howard Univ, DDS, 1964; NY Univ, oral surg cert,1968. **Career:** Harlem Hosp Ctr, oral surg intern, 1964-65, anethesia res, 1965-67, oral surg res 1968-69, Dept Oral Surg, asst vis att; Harlem Hosp Ctr Respiratory Ther Serv, chief, 1969, dir, 1974; Ambulatory Anethesia Harlem Hosp Ctr, chief, 1970; Infections Com Harlem Hosp Ctr, co-chmn, 1971-74; Columbia Univ Col Physicians & Surgeons, asst prof clin anesthesiol; pvt pract, gen & family pract, currently. **Orgs:** Pres, Harlem Dental Soc Greater NY; pres, Harlem Hosp Soc Oral Surgeons;Am Dent Asn; Nat Dent Asn; First Dist Dent Soc; NY State Soc Oral Surgeons; Am Asn Respiratory Ther; Am Soc Oral Surgeons; Am Soc Dent Anesthesiol; One Hundred Black Men Inc; Omega Psi Phi Frat; Am Acad Pediat Dent. **Special Achievements:** First vice president of Black Caucus of Harlem Health Workers. **Military Serv:** USAF, 1952-56. **Home Addr:** 560 Riverside Dr, New York, NY 10027, **Home Phone:** (212)662-6516. **Business Addr:** Physician, Harlem Hospital Ctr, 506 Malcolm X Blvd, New York, NY 10037, **Business Phone:** (212)939-2890.

TRIPP, DR. LUCIUS CHARLES
Physician. **Personal:** Born Nov 10, 1942, Memphis, TN; son of Luke Samuel and Dorothy Watson; married Delores Whitus, Jul 23, 1963; children: Felicia. **Educ:** Univ Detroit, Detroit, MI, BS, 1964; Wayne State Univ, Med Sch, Detroit, MI, MD, 1968, neurosurg, 1974; Univ Mich, Ann Arbor, MI, MPH, 1983; Am Soc Addiction Med Inc, New York, NY, 1988. **Career:** Gen Motors, Detroit, MI, assoc med dir, 1974; Gen Motors, Livonia, MI, med dir, 1974-76; Gen Motors Proving Grounds, Milford, MI, div med dir, 1976-79; GMAD, Warren, MI, div med dir, 1979-84; Buick-Olds-Cadillac, Warren, MI, group med dir, 1984-; Gen Motors, Warren, MI, regional med dir, 1988; Wellness Group Inc, princ, head Occup & Environ Med Div, currently. **Orgs:** Executive bd mem, Boy Scouts Am, 1984-; vpres, internal affairs, Detroit Historical Soc, 1990; pres, Detroit Occup Physician Asn, 1990; state delegate, Mich Occup Med Asn, 1988-; pub health comt chmn, Wayne County Med Soc, 1990-; fel, Am Occupational Asn; Am Asn Automotive Med; Mich State Med Soc. **Honors/Awds:** Nathanial B. Rubinstein Humanitarian Award, Wayne State Univ, Med Sch, 1968; 'Award for Excellence in Community Service', Gen Motors, 1986; 'National Quality District Award', 1989, 'District Award of Merit', 1990, Boy Scouts of America; Boy Scouts, Silver Beaver Award, 1995; Honor Citation, Mich Div, Am Cancer Soc, 1989-90. **Special Achievements:** Published, 'the Clinical Practice Guideline for Acute Low Back Problems in Adults', 1995. **Military Serv:** AUS, Major, 1968-81; reserves, currently. **Home Addr:** 23060 Britner, Bingham Farms, MI 48025, **Home Phone:** (810)644-1337. **Business Phone:** (248)351-7890.

TRIPP, DR. LUKE SAMUEL
Educator. **Personal:** Born Feb 6, 1941, Atoka, TN; son of Luke Tripp Sr and Dorothy Tripp; married Hedy Bruyns; children: Ruth Sherman, Azania & Comrade. **Educ:** Wayne State Univ, BS, 1966; Univ Mich, MA, 1974, PhD, 1980. **Career:** Community Skills Ctr, math, sci teacher, 1972-73; Univ Mich, grad res dir, 1977-80; Univ Ill, asst prof, 1981-82; Southern Ill Univ, asst prof, 1982-89; St Cloud State Univ, asst prof, 1989-92, prof, 1992-, chair, Dept Community Studies, 2003. **Orgs:** Co-founder League Revolutionary Black Workers, 1969; dir, polit educ Nat Black Independent Polit Party, 1980-81; Nat Coun Black Studies, 1983; Ill Coun Black Studies 1983; Soc Ethnic & Spec Studies 1983; coord Southern Ill Anti-Apartheid Alliance, 1985-89; St Cloud State Univ, Minority Concerns Comte, 1989-; founder, Human Rights Coalition, 1990-. **Honors/Awds:** Fac Serv Award, Black Affairs Coun, 1983; Outst&ing Contribution, African Stud Asn, 1985, Cert Distinguished Serv, 1988, 1989; Outst&ing Fac Award, Black Affairs Coun, 1985; Outstanding Leadership, Carbondale Black Coalition 1986; plaque, "In Appreciation for Continuing the Struggle for Excellence", African-Am Student Asn 1989; plaque, Upliftment of the Human Spirit, Muslim Community Southern Ill, 1989; Distinguished Teacher Award, St Cloud State Univ; Mary B Craik Award Equality & Justice, 1990, Outstanding Faculty Award, Off Acad Affairs, 1991; Community Serv Award, VCC, African-Am Comt, 1989; Outstanding Work Rights Activist, 1992. **Special Achievements:** Author: "The Political Views of Black Students During the Reagan Era," The Black Scholar, vol 22, num 3, p 45-52, Summer 1992; "Race Consciousness Among African-American Students, 1980's," The Western Journal of Black Studies, vol 15, num 3, p 150-168, Fall 1991; Black Student Activists: Transition to Middle Class Professionals, Univ Press of America, 1987. **Business Addr:** Professor, Chair, St Cloud State University, Community Studies, 720 S 4th Ave Stewart Hall 392, St Cloud, MN 56301-4498, **Business Phone:** (320)255-3913.

TRIPPLETT, LARRY
Executive. **Educ:** Calif State Univ, Long Beach. **Career:** McDonalds; Nat Black McDonalds Operators Asn, pres, Western Div, vice chmn & pres, chmn & chief exec officer, currently. **Business Addr:** Chairman, Chief Executive Officer, National Black McDonald's Operators Association, PO Box 8204, Los Angeles, CA 90008, **Business Phone:** (323)296-5495.*

TROPEZ-SIMS, SUSANNE
Physician, educator. **Personal:** Born Apr 13, 1949, New Orleans, LA; daughter of Maxwell Sterling and Ethel Ross; married Michael Milroy Sims, Feb 19, 1995; children: Lisa L Arceneaux, Janifer S Tropez-Martin & James C White Jr. **Educ:** Bennett Col, BS, 1971; Univ NC, Chapel Hill, MD, 1975, MPH, 1981. **Career:** Univ NC, Chapel Hill, instr, 1979-82, asst prof, 1982-88; LSUMC, assoc prof, div chief, 1988-97; Meharry Med Col, prof & chairperson pediat, 1997-2005, Acad Support Servs, assoc dean clin affil & prof, 2005-, Clerkship dir, currently. **Orgs:** Am Pediat Asn, 1979-; Am Acad Pediat, 1979-; Am Acad Pediat Sch Health Comt, 1993-99; AMSPDC, 1997-2005; co-chair, Tenn Am Acad Pediat, Sch Health Comt, 1998-2000; Nat Med Asn. **Honors/Awds:** Martin Uskow Award, Am Acad Pediat, 1997. **Business Addr:** Associate Dean of Clinical Affiliation, Professor, Meharry Medical College, Department of Pediatrics, Old Hospital RM 2666, 1005 Dr D B Todd Blvd, Nashville, TN 37208, **Business Phone:** (615)327-6925.

TROTMAN, RICHARD EDWARD
Educator. **Personal:** Born Jun 22, 1942, East Orange, NJ; married Cordell Jones; children: Richard Jr & Raheem. **Educ:** Shaw Univ, BA, 1964; Kean Col, MA, 1971; Rutgers Univ, attended 1978; Waldon Univ, PhD, 1998. **Career:** Educator (retired); NJ Dept Educ, supvr, 1973-76; Kean Col NJ, assoc dir, 1976-79; Bergen Community Col, dir, 1979-82; Somerset County Col, Spec Educ Serv, dir, 1982; Raritan Valley Community Col, dir, 1982-2003, chief examr, dean col advan, 2002-03. **Orgs:** Passaic County Manpower Prog, Mayors Planning Coun, Paterson, NJ, 1971-73; NJ Educ Opportunity Funding Dirs, 1976-86; NJ Asn Black Educators, 1984-86; Nat Asn Advan Colored People, 1985-86; Nat Urban League, 1985-86; mem adv bd, Cent NJ Col, LD prog, 1989; Reach Prog Adv Bd, NJ Social Serv, 1989. **Special Achievements:** Workshops relating to multi-cultural aspects of learning styles, 1988-89.

TROTTER, ANDREW LEON
Government official. **Personal:** Born Sep 7, 1949, San Antonio, TX. **Educ:** NMex State Univ, BA, 1972. **Career:** Human Serv Dept, caseworker, 1972-79, supvr, 1979-. **Orgs:** Secy, Mt Olive Baptistist State Con Laymen Aux, 1974-; christian educ dir BSBC, 1983-; treas, New Hope Baptist Dist Laymen's Asn, 1985-; Dona Ana Branch Community Col, 1985-95; supt, church sch BSBC, 1990-; vpres, New Hope Dist Congress Christian Ed, 1997; treas, Human Serv Consortium; Am Pub Welfare Asn; musician, BSBC Mt Olive Baptist State Congress; El Paso Chap Gospel Music Workshop Am; Nat Asn Advan Colored People; treas, Asn Prof Supvr NM; coordr, Mt Olive State Music Workshop; Nat Baptist Conv USA Inc, Laymens Depart; bd mem, Adult Basic Educ; bd mem, RSVP Dona Ana City; mem, Mesilla Valley Civitan. **Honors/Awds:** Cert Achievement State NMex, 1982; Advanced Cert Nat Congress Christ Educ NBC, USA Inc, 1983. **Home Addr:** 1440 North Paxton, Las Cruces, NM 88001.

TROTTER, CORTEZ
Firefighter, commissioner. **Personal:** Born Jan 1, 1955. **Career:** Chicago Fire Dept, paramedic, 1976, Emergency Med Serv, paramedic-in-charge, area supvr, dep fire comnr, first dep fire comnr, 2000, Off Emergency Mgt & Commun, head, 2001-04, fire comnr, 2004-05, chief emergency officer, 2006-08; James Lee Witt Assocs, vpres & dir midwest region, currently. **Honors/Awds:** Fireslayer of the Year, 2005. **Special Achievements:** First Black fire commissioner of Chicago City. **Business Addr:** Vice President, Director of the Midwest Region, James Lee Witt Associates, 1501 M St NW, Washington, DC 20005, **Business Phone:** (202)585-0780.*

TROTTER, DONNE
Senator (U.S. federal government), state government official. **Personal:** Born Jan 30, 1950, Cairo, IL; son of James and Carita; married Rose Zuniga; children: 4. **Educ:** Chicago State Univ, BA, hist & polit sci, 1976; Loyola Univ Law Sch, MJ, health & policy jurisp. **Career:** Ill State House, mem, 1988-93; Ill State Senate, sen, leader Black Caucus, 1993-. **Orgs:** Chmn, Senate Appropriations I Comn; Com & Econ Develop. **Business Addr:** State Senator, Illinois State Senate, 17th District Senate Office, 8704 S Constance Suite 324, Chicago, IL 60617, **Business Phone:** (773)933-7715.

TROTTER, JAMES
Entrepreneur, executive. **Career:** ACME Muscle Scooters, pres, 1995-. **Business Addr:** President, ACME Muscle Scooters, 2821 N 4th St, Milwaukee, WI 53212.

TROTTER, JEREMIAH
Football player. **Personal:** Born Jan 20, 1977, Hooks, TX; married Tammi; children: TreMil & Jeremiah Jr. **Educ:** Stephen F Austin Univ, BS, bus mgt. **Career:** Philadelphia Eagles, linebacker, 1998-2001, 2004-06; Wash Redskins, 2002-03; Trott's Spot Car Wash, owner, 2003-; Tampa Bay Buccaneers, 2007; free agent currently. **Orgs:** Founder, Jeremiah Trotter Found. **Honors/Awds:** All Pro Bowl Selection Twice, 2000-01; Four Times Pro Bowler Selection, 2000, 2001, 2004, 2005.

TROTTER, LLOYD G
Executive. **Personal:** Married Teri; children: 3. **Educ:** Cleveland State Univ, BBA, 1972, PhD, Bus Admin, 2001. **Career:** GE Lighting, field serv engr, 1970; GE Electrical Distribution & Control, vpres & gen mgr, 1990-92, pres & chief exec officer, 1992-98; GE Industrial Systs, pres & chief exec officer, 1998-2003; GE Consumer & Indust, pres & chief exec officer, 2003-08; GenNx360, managing partner. **Orgs:** Bd dirs, Conn Pre-Engineering Prog; Americas Promise; chmn bd govs, Nat Elec Mfrs Asn; bd mem, Nat Asn Mfrs; bd, PepsiCo; bd dirs, Textron Inc, 2008-. **Honors/Awds:** Black Achievers in Industry Award, Harlem YMCA; Benjamin Mays Award. **Business Addr:** Director, Textron Inc., 40 Westminster St, Providence, RI 02903.

TROTTMAN, CHARLES HENRY
Educator, historian, scientist. **Personal:** Born Jul 29, 1934, Pine Bluff, AR; married Evelyn Marie Royal; children: Rodney, Jeniffer, Phyliss, Calliette & Charlette. **Educ:** Ark AM&N Col, BS, 1957; Tuskegee Inst, 1959; Syracuse Univ, MS, 1961; Univ NC, 1969; Univ Wis, PhD, 1972. **Career:** Coleman HS, instr, 1959; So Univ, asst prof chem, 1961-67; Ark AM&N Col, assoc prof chem, 1967-69; Univ Wis, res asst, 1969-72; Jackson St Univ, assoc prof chem, 1972-. **Orgs:** Fac, Sen Jackson St Univ 1974-76; consult, Argonne Nat Lab, 1974-76; dir, Nat Sci Found, 1977-78; Sigma Xi; Am Chem Soc; MS Acad Sci; Hist Sci Soc; MS Asn Educators; AAAS; Nat Asn Advan Colored People; AAUP; Omega Psi Phi Frat; Nat Orgn Prof Adv Black Chem & Chem Eng; Nat Inst Sci. **Honors/Awds:** Acad year fel Nat Sci Found, 1960-61; Ford Found fel, 1969-70; Southern Fel Grant, 1970-72; Nat Urban League Fel, 1974; Outstanding Eductors Am, 1974; Outstanding Chem & Chem Eng 1976. **Military Serv:** AUS, 1953-55.

TROUP, ELLIOTT VANBRUGH
Ophthalmologist, physician. **Personal:** Born Feb 28, 1938, Brunswick, GA; married Linda; children: Elliott Jr, Traci, Patrick. **Educ:** Fisk Univ, BA, 1959; Meharry Med Col, MD, 1963. **Career:** Univ Minn, residency ophthal, 1969; ophthalmologist, pvt pract. **Orgs:** Pres, St Paul Ophthal Soc, 1977-78; Acad Ophthal & Otolaryn; Nat Med Asn; AMA; Med Prod Div 3m Co; Alpha Phi Alpha Fraternity. **Honors/Awds:** Cert, Am Bd Ophthal, 1971. **Military Serv:** USAF, capt, 1964-66. **Business Addr:** Ophthalmologist, 1330 County Road B W, St Paul, MN 55113.

TROUPE, CHARLES QUINCY
State government official. **Personal:** Born May 12, 1936, St Louis, MO. **Educ:** Wash Tech Sch, attended; Denver Univ, attended. **Career:** Dem First Ward St Louis, committeeman; Amalgamated Transit Union, vpres; MO House Representatives, Dist 62, state rep, 1978-; elec contractor, currently. **Honors/Awds:** Mo State Employees Award for Exceptional Service, 1980; Optimist's Community Service Award, 1980; Community Service Award, Nat Alliance Postal & Fed Employees, 1981; Community Service Award, St Louis Ethical Police Asn, 1981; Child Care Award, Early Child Care Develop Corp, 1981;Community Service Award, Sigma Gamma Rho Inc, 1981; Humanitarian Award, 1982, Outstanding & Dedicated Service Award, 1983, Wellston Sch Dist; Outstanding Ded & Leadership Black Leadership Asn, 1983; Outstanding Service to the Community, Firefighters Inst Racial Equality, 1984; Community Service Award, Asn Black Collegians, 1984; Merit Award Dedicated Community Service, United Black Community Fund, 1984; Recognition Housing Rehab First Ward North side President Com Awards, 1985; Comm Involvement Award, Nat Black Child Develop Inst St Louis Affiliate19; Outstanding Leadership in the Interest of Missouri's Youth, Primary Care Coun Metro St.Louis, 1986; Missouri Perinatal Asn Award, 1986; Special Service Award for Efforts in Reducing Teenage Pregnancy, Mo Family Planning Asn, 1986. **Business Addr:** State Representative, MO House of Representatives, 201 W Capitol Ave Room 113, Jefferson City, MO 65101, **Business Phone:** (573)751-2851.

TROUPE, DR. MARILYN KAY
Educator. **Personal:** Born Sep 30, 1945, Tulsa, OK; daughter of Ernest Robinson and Lucille Andrew. **Educ:** Langston Univ, BA, 1967; Okla State Univ, MA, 1976, EdD, occupational & adult edu, 1993. **Career:** Tulsa Pub Sch, teacher, 1969-81, cosmetology, 1982-87; CETA City Tulsa, summer youth counr, 1980-; Okla State Univ, hist instr, 1981-82; Okla State Voc & Tech Educ, curric support, 1987-94; Lane Col, TCR Educ Prog, coordr, 1995-97, Div Liberal Studies & Educ, chair, 1995-97; Ky Dept Edu, Teacher Edu & Cert, dir, 1997-99; Ky State Univ, Educ Prof Standard Bd, div dir educator prep, 1999-. **Orgs:** Zeta Phi Beta Sor, 1985; bd dir, Stillwater Co, 1988-94; Nat Asn Minority Polit Women, 1988-89; bd mem, Cot Relations City Stillwater, 1991-94; bd mem, Park & Recreation City Stillwater, 1991-94; bd mem, Life Ctr Elderly, 1991-94; bd examiners, Nat Coun Accreditation Teacher Educ, 1997-; post secondary task force, KY Ctr Sch Safety, 2000-; Prof Development in Early Childhood Coun, 2000-; KY Lit Partnership, 2001; Cath Daughters Am Tulsa Ct; bd mem, Links Inc; Iota Lambda Sigma; Phi Delta Kappa; Theta Nu Sigma; Phi Alpha Theta; Langston Alumni, Nat Asn Advan Colored People; Nat State Local Bus & Prof Womens Club; Nat State Local Beauty Culturists League Inc; Am & Okla Voc Asn; Voc & Ideal Clubs Am; Am Voc Asn; charter mem, State & Nat Asn Advan Black Am Voc Educ; grad adv, Okla State Univ, Theta Beta Chapter; chair, Womens Adv Coun; vol, Frankfort Soup Kitchen; Okla Task Force, Goals Tomorrow, Adv Comt; Am Asn Univ

Women. **Honors/Awds:** Woman of the Year, North Tulsa Chap Bus & Prof Women, 1979; Leadership Stillwater, City Stillwater Co, 1990; Soror of the Year, AKA Sorority Inc, Local Chap, 1992-93. **Business Addr:** Director, Kentucky State University, Division of Educator Preparation, 1024 Capital Ct Dr Suite 225, Frankfort, KY 40601, **Business Phone:** (502)573-4606.

TROUPE, QUINCY THOMAS, JR.
Poet, educator. **Personal:** Born Jul 23, 1943, St Louis, MO; son of Quincy Sr and Dorothy Marshall Smith; married Margaret Porter; children: Antoinette, Tymme, Quincy, Porter. **Educ:** Grambling Col, BA, 1963; Los Angeles City Col, AA, 1967. **Career:** Watts Writers Movement, Los Angeles CA, creative writing teacher, 1966-68; Shrewd Mag, Los Angeles, assoc ed; Univ Calif, Los Angeles, instr creative writing & black lit, 1968; Ohio Univ, Athens, instr creative writing & third world lit, 1969-72; Richmond Col, Staten Island NY, instr third world lit; Columbia Univ, NY, fac grad writing Prog, 1985-; New York Found Arts fel, 1987; Styx River Mag, ed; Univ Calif, San Diego, prof, 1990-02; emer prof, currently; Books: Giant Talk: An Anthology of Third World Writing, 1972; The Inside Story of TV's Roots, 1978; Snake-Back Solos: Selected Poems 1969-77, 1979; James Baldwin: The Legacy, 1989; Miles: The Autobiography of Miles Davis, 1989; Weather Reports: New and Selected Poems, 1991; Take it to the hoop Magic Johnson, 2001; Little Stevie Wonder, 2005; The Architecture of Language, poems, 2006. **Orgs:** Poetry Soc Am. **Honors/Awds:** Int Inst Educ, travel grant, 1972; Nat Endowment Arts award, 1978; New York State Coun Arts grant, 1979; Am Book Award, Asn Am Publishers, 1980, Selected Poems, 1969-77, Reed Books, 1978; American Book Award, 1989. **Special Achievements:** California's first Poet Laureate, 2002. **Home Addr:** 1925 Seventh Ave Apt 7L, New York, NY 10026. **Business Addr:** Professor Emeritus, University of California, 9500 Gilman Dr, La Jolla, CA 92093.

TROUPE-FRYE, BETTY JEAN
Government official, nurse. **Personal:** Born Mar 8, 1935, St Louis, MO; daughter of Ruth Townsend Troupe and Phillip Jeffery Troupe; divorced; children: Armont, Mona Long Roberts & Evette Boykins. **Educ:** State Community Col, 1974; Tariko Col, BS, mgt, 1988; Webter Univ, MA, human resource develop, 1988-91. **Career:** Wellston Sch Bd, pres, 1981-84; Wellston City Coun, councilperson, 1982-84; Wellston First Ward, pres; Children's Home Soc, nurse, currently. **Orgs:** Nurse Olsten Health Serv; chmn, ANSCA, 1982-; Campaign Human Dignity,1984; St Louis Chap 46 OES Prince Hall Affiliate; ACORN; bd mem, BCDI, 2000-. **Honors/Awds:** Appreciation, Noble, 1982; Appreciation, Women Munic Govt, 1983; Appreciation, St Louis Head Start, 1983; Appreciation, Enforcers Amateur Athletic Asn. **Home Addr:** 1538 Ogden Ave, Saint Louis, MO 63133. **Business Addr:** Nurse, Children's Home Society, 9445 Litzsinger Rd, Saint Louis, MO 63144-2113, **Business Phone:** (314)968-2350.

TROUTMAN, DR. ADEWALE
Physician, administrator, educator. **Personal:** Born Mar 17, 1946, New York, NY; married Denise, Jul 29, 2000; children: Anasa & Nandi. **Educ:** Lehman Col, BA, 1969; State Univ New Yok, Albany, MA, 1972; NJ Med Sch, MD, 1979; Columbia Univ Sch Pub Health, MPH, 1993. **Career:** St Michaels Med Ctr, med dir, 1982-84; City Newark, med dir, 1987-90; United Hosp Med Ctr, dir emergency serv, 1985-97; Univ Med & Dent, asst clin prof, 1995-97; Fulton County, dir, Dept Health & Wellness, 1997; Univ Louisville Sch Pub Health, assoc prof, currently; Morehouse Sch Med, clin assoc prof, 2001-; Ft Valley State Univ, Dept Pub Health, adj fac, 2002-03; Emory Univ, adj fac, 2002-03; Louisville Metro Health Dept, dir, 2004-. **Orgs:** Am Soc Clin Hypnosis, 1982-; Nat Med Asn, 1990-; Am Pub Health Asn, 1994-; 100 Black Men Atlanta, 2000-; Black Centers of Health Workers, pres, 2000-; bd mem, Soc Advan African Am Pub Health Issues. **Honors/Awds:** Minority Health Institute Recognition, 1990; Barry Anderson Award, Devoted Serv Humanity, 1994; Friends of Labor Award, Fulton County, 1998; Pub Health Educ, 1999. **Special Achievements:** Published numerous articles in a variety of journals and magazines, is an internationally known speaker and consultant, a published poet, accomplished musician and dedicated father. **Home Phone:** (404)691-9608. **Business Addr:** Director, Louisville Metro Health Department, 400 E Gray St, Louisville, KY 40202, **Business Phone:** (502)574-6520.

TROUTMAN, PORTER LEE, JR.
Educator, association executive. **Personal:** Born Apr 4, 1943, Newellton, LA; married Bobbie Jean Martin; children: Gregory, Portia. **Educ:** Univ Nev, educ spec; S Univ Baton Rouge LA, BS; Northern Ariz Univ, MS, EdD, 1977. **Career:** Rec Center, dir, 1965-66; Clark Co Sch Dist, teacher, 1966-71; SELD Prog Title I, current spec, 1968; Clark Co Teacher Asn, staff rep, 1970-71; Univ Nev, Las Vegas, Dis Off Prof Studies, prof, 1974, Teacher Corps , lectr, assoc dir, 1971-74, dir, 1974-75; Nat Asn Multicult Educ, founder, 1990-. **Orgs:** CCSD Task Force; Actg Pring; Clark Co Teacher Asn; Clark Co Sch Dist Adv Facilities Com; chmn, Jo Mackey Elem Sch Adv Bd; Clark Co Teacher Asn; Human Rels Comn; Alternate Sen Jo Mackey Elem Sch; Nev State Ed Resolution Comt; Adv Stud Nat Ed Asn Univ; delegate, Nat Ed Asn Detroit delegate First Nat Cong Black Prof Higher Ed Univ Tex; Nat Educ Asn; Knights Columbus; Am Asn Sch Admin; Am Asn Col Teacher Ed, AACTE Comn Perf Based Educ; Kappa Delta Pi; Phi Delta Kappa Hon Soc. **Business Addr:** Founder, National Association for Multicultural Education, 5272 River Rd Suite 430, Bethesda, MD 20816, **Business Phone:** (301)951-0022.

TROUTT, HARRY
Executive. **Career:** Executive (retired); Homeowners Asn, pres; Seniors Inc, bd dirs; Comnr Human Rights Dist No 5 Santa Rosa. **Home Addr:** 1155 Adrienne Way, Santa Rosa, CA 95401. *

TROWELL-HARRIS, IRENE
Military leader, executive director. **Educ:** Columbia Hosp Sch Nursing, attended 1959; Squadron Officer Sch, by correspondence, 1968; Air Command & Staff Col, by correspondence, 1971; Jersey City State, NJ, BA, health educ, 1971; Yale Univ, MA, pub health, 1973; Nat Security Mgt Course, distinguished grad, 1981; Columbia Univ, doctorate health educ, 1983; Air War Col, by correspondence, 1990. **Career:** Military leader (retired), executive; Nat Guard Bur, first lt, 1963, capt, 1964, maj, 1973, lt col, 1980, col, 1988, brig gen, 1993, maj gen, 1998-2001; Dept Veterans Affairs, Ctr Women Veterans, dir, currently. **Orgs:** Aerospace Med Asn; ANA; APHA; NYSNA; Sigma Theta Tau; AMSUS. **Honors/Awds:** Distinguished Alumni Columbia Univ; Honorary DHL, Med Univ SC; Virginia Outstanding & Invaluable Service to the Community Award; Outstanding Performance Award. **Special Achievements:** First African American woman in the 357-year history of the National Guard to achieve the rank of brigadier general; First female, minority and nurse in the 349th year history of the National Guard to command a medical clinic. **Military Serv:** Nat Guard Bur, 1963-2001; Numerous award including Legion of Merit; Meritorious Service Medal; Air Force Outstanding Unit Award; Air Force Organizational Excellence Award with one oak leaf cluster; National Defense Service Medal with service star; Armed Forces Expeditionary Medal; Air Force Longevity Service Award Ribbon with seven oak leaf clusters; Armed Forces Reserve Medal with hourglass; Small Arms Expert Marksmanship Ribbon; Air Force Training Ribbon. **Business Addr:** Director, Department of Veterans Affairs, Center for Women Veterans, 810 Vermont Ave NW, Washington, DC 20420, **Business Phone:** (202)273-6193.

TROY, ADAM K.
Entrepreneur, chief executive officer. **Educ:** Morehouse Col, undergrad; Ohia State Univ. **Career:** Omni Mgt Group Ltd, managing partner & founder, 1996-; TROY, pres & chief exec officer, Currently. **Business Phone:** (614)509-0001.*

TROY, PATRICIA
Chief executive officer, administrator. **Career:** Advan Staffing Inc, pres & chief exec officer, currently. **Orgs:** co-chair, Nat Coalition 100 Black Women Signature Scholar. **Honors/Awds:** Small Business Person of the Year, SBA, 2001; Visionary Leadership Award, Nat Asn Advan Colored People, 2003; Lifetime Achievement Award, Urban Financial Serv Coalition, 2003; Strong, Smart, & Bold Award, Girls Inc, 2005. **Special Achievements:** Writes an employment column that is published in the local papers as well as on-line career web sites. **Business Phone:** (302)326-5400.*

TRUE, RACHEL INDIA
Actor. **Personal:** Born Nov 15, 1966, New York, NY; daughter of Richard true and Verona Barnes. **Career:** Films: CB4, 1993; Embrace of the Vampire, 1994; The Craft, 1996; Nowhere, 1997; Half Baked, 1998; With or Without You, 1998; The Big Split, 1999; The Auteur Theory, 1999; Groove, 2000; Who Is AB?, 2001; New Best Friend, 2002; The Pink eye, 2006; The Perfect Holiday, 2007; Killing of Wendy, 2009; Noah's Ark:The New Beginning, 2009; TV Series: "The Cosby Show", 1991-92; "Moment of Truth: Stalking Back", 1993; " A Girls' Guide to Sex", 1993; "Beverly Hills, 90210", 1993; "Dream On", 1994-95; "A Walton Wedding",1995; "The Drew Carey Show", 1997-98; "The Apartment Complex", 1999; "Once& Again", 1999-2000; "Love Song", 2000; "Half & Half", 2002-06; "Noah's Arc", 2006. **Business Addr:** Actress, c/o Lorrie Bartlett Gersh Agency, 232 North Canon Dr Beverly Hills CA 90210, Beverly Hills, CA 90210.*

TRUEBLOOD, VERA J
Engineer. **Personal:** Born Dec 10, 1962, Minneapolis, MN; daughter of Wiley Trueblood Jr and Maurine Alexander. **Educ:** Univ Minn, Minneapolis, MN, BS, mech engineering, 1985; Univ Mich, Ann Arbor, MI, currently. **Career:** Donaldson Mfg Co, Minneapolis, MN, product test engr, 1983-85; Chrysler Corp, Highland Pk, MI, product quality engr, 1985-. **Orgs:** Bd mem, scholar comt, Nat Alumni, Inroads/Metropolitan Detroit, Inroads, 1989-; bd dirs, Youth Develop Comt, Detroit Urban League, 1987-; community action comt, scholar comt, Black MBA Asn, 1989-; Explorer Scout Develop Community Develop, STRIVE, 1985-; Ind Ambassadors, Engineering Soc Detroit, 1986-; annual dinner chair, Single Minded Inc; bd mem, Detroit Urban League. **Honors/Awds:** Chairmans Award, Chrysler Corp, 1989; Directors Award, Chrysler Corp, 1988; Outstanding Young Woman of Year, 1987; Ebony Magazine, "10 Young Achievers," Johnson Publishing, August 1989. **Home Addr:** 8214 Santa Clara, Detroit, MI 48221, **Home Phone:** (313)563-1903. **Business Phone:** (313)589-5369.

TRUEHEART, WILLIAM E.
Association executive, president (organization). **Personal:** Born Jul 10, 1942, New York, NY; son of Louise Elnora Harris Trueheart and Junious Elton Trueheart; married Carol Ann Word, Jun 26, 1988. **Educ:** Univ Conn, Storrs, BA, 1966; Harvard Univ-Kennedy Sch Govt, Cambridge, Mass, MPA, 1973; Harvard Univ-Grad Sch Educ, Cambridge, Mass, EdD, 1979. **Career:** President, CEO(retired); Univ CT, Storrs, CT, asst to pres, 1969-70; Univ Conn-Col Lib Arts & Sci, Storrs, CT, asst to dean & dir acad adv ctr, 1970-72; Harvard Univ-John F Kennedy Sch Govt, Cambridge, MA, asst dean & dir master in pub admin prog, 1979-83; Harvard Univ-Off Governing Boards, Cambridge, MA, assoc sec to univ, 1983-86; Bryant Col, Smithfield, RI, exec vpres, 1986-89, pres, 1989-96; Harvard Univ, Grad Sch Educ, vis scholar, 1996-97; Reading Is Fundamental Inc, pres & chief exec officer; PNC Financial Corp, vpres; Nat Flag Found, founder & vpres; St. Clair Memorial Hosp, dir emer; Fleet Nat Bank, bd dirs; Fleet Nat Bank Southern New Eng Banking Group, bd dirs; Narragansett Elec Co, bd dirs; New Eng Educ Loan Mkt Corp, bd dirs; RI Pub Educ Fund, bd dirs; Nat Educ Fund Network, bd dirs; Woods Hole Oceanog Inst, bd dirs; RI Children's Crusade, bd dirs; Am Inst Cert Pub Accountants, bd dirs; Pittsburgh Found, pres & chief exec officer, 2001-07; Independent Sector, chmn emer, currently; Univ Pittsburgh, bd dirs; Allegheny Conf Community Develop, bd dirs, currently; Nellie Mae Educ Found, bd dirs, currently; Johnson & Wales Corp, bd dirs, currently; Highmark Blue Cross/ Blue Shield, bd dirs, currently; Common fund, bd trustees, currently. **Orgs:** Bd dir, Pub Educ Fund Network, 1990-; bd dir, Providence Chamber Com, 1990-; bd dir, Nellie Mae Inc, 1988-; bd dir, Fleet Nat Bank, 1990-; bd dir, Narragansett Electric, 1990-; Am Inst Cert Pub Accts; treas, Life span Inc; Narragansett Electric Co; New Eng Educ Loan Mkt Corp; chmn, RI Independent Higher Educ Asn; RI Pub Expenditure Coun; Woods Hole Oceanographic Inst. **Honors/Awds:** Littauer fel, Harvard Univ, 1973; Travelli fel, Charles I Travelli Found, 1973-79; Ford Found fel, Ford Found, 1974-79; ACE fel, Am Coun Educ, 1968-69; Black Alumni Asn Award Excellence, Univ CT, 1989; hon doctorate, Bryant Col, 1996, Johnson & Wales Univ, 1996; Man of the Year in Finance, Vectors/Pittsburgh, 2004; Distinguished Alumni Award. **Special Achievements:** First African American to head a four year, private college in New England; co-auth: Production Function Analysis in Higher Education: General Methodology & Applications to Four Year Black Colleges, Government Printing Office, 1977; auth: The Underside of Federal Involvement with Higher Education; The Federal Purse and the Rule of Law, Univ of Notre Dame, 1983. **Business Addr:** Trustee, Commonfund, 15 Old Danbury Rd, Wilton, CT 06897, **Business Phone:** (203)563-5000.

TRUESDALE, DR. CARLTON MAURICE
Scientist. **Personal:** Born May 25, 1954, High Point, NC; son of Emma and Gonzalee; married Linda, Aug 1, 1997; children: Wytheria, Tiffiany, Arthur, Carl & Emmanuel (deceased). **Educ:** Morehouse Col, BS, chem, 1976; Univ Calif, PhD, chem, 1983. **Career:** Corning Inc, sr scientist, 1983-86, sr res scientist, 1987-89, assoc, 1990-97, sr res assoc, 1998-2000, mgr, specialty fiber, applied res, 2001-02, res fel, 2005-. **Orgs:** NAACP, 1983-2008; Corning Chmn's Diversity Coun, 2001-03; Citizens Revitalizing Communities, 2003-04. **Honors/Awds:** Pioneer of the Year, NSBE, 1998; Corning Professional Women's Forum Diversity and Development Award, 2002; Distinguished Citizen Award, Economic Opportunity Program, 2005; Jefferson Award Community Serv, 2006. **Special Achievements:** 22 publications in referred journs, 1976-05; author, book chapter in Electro-Optics Handbook, 1993; author, award-winning packet for NSBE Exec Dir's Advancing Diversity, 2000; 22 patents granted, 7 additional filed; USBE & IT Mazagine's One of 100 most important Blacks in Technology, 2006-08. **Business Addr:** Research Fellow, Inorganic & Integration Technologies, Corning Inc, Sullivan Pk SPAR02-2, Corning, NY 14831, **Business Phone:** (607)974-3003.

TRUITT, KEVIN
Government official. **Personal:** Born Jan 2, 1953, Chicago, IL; son of Alfred Henry and Ethel Henry; married Karen, May 8, 1993; children: Marissa. **Educ:** Loyola Univ, BBA, 1975; DePaul Univ, MBA, 1977. **Career:** Arthur Young & Co, staff auditor, 1977-79; Baxter-Travenol, sr financial analyst, 1979-80; First Chicago, com banking officer, 1980-86; Harris Bank & Trust, asst vpres, 1988-89; Bank Hapoalim, asst vpres, 1987-88 & 1989-90; City Chicago Dept Revenue, dep dir revenue, 1991-; Mid Am Bank Fsb, exec, currently. **Honors/Awds:** Pullman Scholar, Pullman Educ Found, 1975; Outstanding Business & Professional Award, Dollar & Sense Mag, 1993. **Special Achievements:** The Money Yard Stick, Letter to the Editor, Financial World Mag, 1990. **Business Phone:** (773)481-4000.

TRUMBO, GEORGE WILLIAM
Judge. **Personal:** Born Sep 24, 1926, Newark, OH; son of George Frank and Beatrice; married Sara J Harper; children: Constance, James, Kimberlee, Karen & Adam. **Educ:** Ohio State Univ, BS; Case Western Res Law Sch, LLB. **Career:** Judge (retired); Sunday Sch teacher; Ct Common Pleas, referee, 1977-82; Cleveland Munic Ct, judge, 1982. **Orgs:** Dir, Jr Church Mt Olive Baptist Church; Nat Bar Asn; Greater Cleveland Bar Asn; Ohio Bar Asn; Cuyahoga Co Bar Asn; Elks Lodge IBPOE W; Kappa Alpha Psi; Nat Asn Advan Colored People; bd dir, Judicial Coun Nat Bar Asn; pres, Shaker Square Kiwanis Club; pres, trustee bd, Cleveland Pub Libr, 1984; chmn, Task Force House Corrections; pres, Northern Ohio Munic Judges Asn; El Hasa Temple No 28; United Supreme

Coun Ancient & Accepted Scottish Rite Freemasonry. **Honors/Awds:** Cuyahoga County Criminal Court Bar Association Award, 1973; Superior Judicial Service, 1982, 1984, 1985; Hall of Fame, Nat Bar Asn, 1993. **Military Serv:** USN, 1944-46.

TRUVILLION, VANESSA
Choreographer, executive. **Career:** Soul Food, choreographer, 1997; Joel Hall Dancers & Ctr, dancer, asst artistic dir, 2004. *

TRUVILLION, WENDY
Athletic coach. **Educ:** La State Univ, 1987; Ga State, sports admin. **Career:** Detroit Cheetah Track Club, co-founder; Georgia Tech Univ, asst track coach, 1988-93, head track coach, 1993; Penn State Univ, track coach; McEachern High Sch, varsity asst, track coach, currently. **Orgs:** USA Track & Field. **Business Phone:** (770)222-3710.

TSHOMBE, DAWN. See ROBINSON, DAWN.

TUBBS, WINFRED O'NEAL
Football player. **Personal:** Born Sep 24, 1970, Fairfield, TX. **Educ:** Univ Tex, psychol. **Career:** Football player (retired); New Orleans Saints, linebacker, 1994-97; San Francisco 49ers, 1998-2000. **Honors/Awds:** Pro Bowl, 1998; All-NFL (second team), 1997.

TUCKER, CHRISTOPHER
Comedian, actor. **Personal:** Born Aug 31, 1972, Atlanta, GA; son of Norris and Mary; children: Destin Christopher. **Career:** Actor, 1994-; Films: House Party 3, 1994; Friday, 1995; Panther, 1995; Dead Presidents, 1995; The Fifth Element, 1997; Money Talks, actor & exec producer, 1997; Jackie Brown, 1997; Rush Hour, 1998; Rush Hour 2, 2001; Rush Hour 3, 2007; TV series: "Hangin' with Mr Cooper", 1992; "Def Comedy Jam", 1994; Comedy Cafe, owner, currently. **Orgs:** Founder Chris Tucker Found. **Honors/Awds:** Blockbuster Entertainment Award, 1999; MTV Movie Award, 1999, 2008; Blimp Award, Kids' Choice Awards, 2002; Teen Choice Award, 2002. **Business Addr:** Actor, c/o Samantha Mast, Rogers & Cowan, 8687 Melrose Ave 7th Fl, Los Angeles, CA 90069, **Business Phone:** (310)854-8100.

TUCKER, CLARENCE T.
Manager, teacher, chairperson. **Personal:** Born Feb 22, 1940, Elba, AL; son of Samuel T. and Josephine; married Delores B Tucker, Nov 28, 1963; children: Reginald, Ryan. **Educ:** Ala A&M Univ, Huntsville, AL, BS; Atlanta Univ, GA, MS. **Career:** Chattanooga Pub Sch, Chattanooga, TN, teacher & dept chair, 1962-65, 1966-68; Clark Col, Atlanta GA, lab instr, 1968-69; Polaroid Corp, Waltam MA, process eng to prod mgr, 1969-, Small Bus Liaison Officer, currently. **Orgs:** Exec bd chmn, NOBCCUE. **Honors/Awds:** Outstanding Teacher Award, Chatanooga Science Fair Group, 1966; Outstanding Service Award, Atlanta Univ, 1984; Meritorious Service Award, NOBCCUE, 1985. **Home Addr:** 8 Longmeadow Rd, Westborough, MA 01581. **Business Addr:** Small Business Liaison Officer, Polaroid Corporation, 784 Memorial Dr, Cambridge, MA 02139.*

TUCKER, CYNTHIA ANNE
Journalist. **Personal:** Born Mar 13, 1955, Monroeville, AL; daughter of John Abney and Mary Louise Marshall; divorced. **Educ:** Auburn Univ, BA, 1976. **Career:** The Atlanta Jour, reporter, 1976-80, ed writer, columnist, 1983-86; The Philadelphia Inquirer, reporter, 1980-82; The Atlanta Constitution, assoc ed page ed, 1986-91, ed page ed, 1992-; Harvard Univ, Nieman fel, 1988-89. **Orgs:** Am Soc Newspaper Ed; bd dir, Int Media Women's Found; Nat Asn Black Journalists; Nat Asn Minority Media Execs; adv bd, Poynter Inst; African Am Planning Comn Inc. **Honors/Awds:** Exceptional Merit Media Award, Nat Women's Polit Caucus, 1993; Distinguished Writing Award for Commentary/Column Writing, Am Soc Newspaper Ed, 2000. **Special Achievements:** First black woman to edit the editorial page of a major daily newspaper, the Atlanta Constitution. **Business Addr:** Editorial Page Editor, The Atlanta Constitution, 75 Marietta St, Atlanta, GA 30303, **Business Phone:** (404)526-5084.

TUCKER, DR. DOROTHY M.
Psychologist, educator. **Personal:** Born Aug 22, 1942, Spartanburg, SC; daughter of James Anderson and Cleo Christine Fant. **Educ:** Bowling Green Univ, BS; Univ Toledo, MEd; Calif Sch Prof Psychol, PhD, 1976; Ohio State Univ, PhD, 1972. **Career:** Brentwood Public Schs & Ford Found, demonstration teacher & curric writer, 1963-65; Dept Defense, Spangdahlem, Germany, educr, 1965-67; Wright Inst Los Angeles, dir clinical teaching; Calif State Univ, Los Angeles, asst prof, 1968-69; Ohio State Univ, res assoc, 1969-71; Bureau Drug Abuse, Columbus, Ohio, consult psychol, 1971; Florida Int Univ, asst & assoc prof, 1971-74; Charles Drew Med Sch, assoc prof, 1977-78; fld dir, Cranston Senate Com, 1980; Office Speaker, Calif Assembly, Willie Brown Jr, special asst, 1981-84; Crenshaw Consortium, Los Angeles, Calif, pres, 1984-; Saybrook Inst, San Francisco, Calif, consult fac, 1989-; Los Angeles Police Dept, Calif Comn on Post, consult org psychol. **Orgs:** Western Psychol Asn; Am Psychol Asn; Asn Black Psychologists; S Calif Asn Black Psychologists; Asn of Soc & Behvrl Scientists; gov, Calif State Bar Bd Gov, 1990-; pres, Los Angeles Bldg & Safety Comn, 1990-; past chair, Calif Bd Psychol; treas, Asn Black Psychologist, Southern Calif; bd Gov, State Bar Calif; pres, Convenor Alliance AFA in Psychology; vpres Found State Bar Calif; judicial Coun, Access Fairness, Calif; Calif Psychological Asn, past chair, Public Interest Div, exec comt, pres-elect, 1998-99; AMR Psychol Asn, Urban Initiatives Comn, chair-elect, 1999. **Honors/Awds:** First chair, Fac Senate, FIU, 1972-74; First Chair, Fla State Univ Fac Senate, 1972-74; Pi Lambda Theta Educ Hon; Natl Women's Polit Caucus; Natl Orgn Women 1975; Black's Women's Forum, 1977; chmn exec com Forum 1979; commnr, CA Jud Nominees Evaluation Comn 1979; pres, United Negro Col Fund So CA Adv Bd 1980; cmmnr Inglewood Housing Comn 1980; nominee Sojourner Truth Awd 1974; Outstanding Woman, Calif Legislature, 1985; Women In Public Service Award, W side Women's Clinic, 1987; Calif Psychol Asn, Helen Mehr Public Interest Award, 1994; Silver Psy Award, 1995. **Business Addr:** Consulting Faculty, Saybrook Graduate School & Research Center, 747 Front St 3rd Fl, San Francisco, CA 94111-1920, **Business Phone:** 800-825-4480.

TUCKER, GERALDINE COLEMAN
Journalist. **Personal:** Born Mar 23, 1952, Cincinnati, OH; daughter of Robert A (deceased) and Marian Annamae Taylor; married Michael Anthony, Aug 31, 1980; children: Christopher Coleman Tucker. **Educ:** Kenyon Col, Gambier, OH, AB, 1970-74; Wayne State Univ, Detroit, MI, 1979; George Mason Univ, Fairfax, VA, 1985-86. **Career:** Beacon J, Akron, OH, reporter, 1975-79; Detroit Free Press, Detroit, MI, copy ed, 1979-82; USA Today, Arlington, VA, front page ed, spec sects ed, 1982-87, deputy managing ed, currently; Gannett News Serv, Arlington, VA, managing ed/Midwest, 1987-. **Orgs:** Wash Asn Black Journalists, 1982-; Nat Asn of Black Journalists, 1976-. **Honors/Awds:** Fel, Am Newspaper Publs Asn, 1987; Fel, Gannett Mgmt Seminar, 1989; Fel, US Dept Educ/African Studies, 1981. **Home Addr:** 8613 James Creek Dr, Springfield, VA 22152, **Home Phone:** (703)569-6471. **Business Phone:** (703)854-3400.

TUCKER, GERALDINE JENKINS
Lawyer. **Personal:** Born May 3, 1948, Newark, NJ; daughter of Richard Sr and Helen; married; children: Carmen Alicia. **Educ:** Fisk Univ, BA, eng, 1970; Howard Univ, MS, stud personnel admin, 1972; Univ Tex, JD, 1986. **Career:** Howard Univ, Wash DC, asst dir admis, 1970-73; Ford Found, Ford fel grad study, 1970; Calif Sch Prof Psychol, dean stud affairs, 1973-75; Hughes Aircraft Co La, sr personnel rep, 1975-77; ARA Food Servs LA, training mgr 15 states, 1977-78; Tex Rehab Comn Austin, civil rights specialist, 1978-80; NuScope Cons, pres, 1980-85; Lower Co River Authority, dir human resources, 1986-91; Austin Community Col, Off Human Resources, assoc vpres, currently. **Orgs:** Chair, Austin First Step Inc; Leadership Austin; Leadership Tex; secy, Austin Community Found; Top Ladies Distinction; Links Inc; Sinai Missionary Baptist Church; bd trustees, Fisk Univ, Nashville, 1970-74; columnist, Village Newspaper, Austin, 1970-; western bd adv, United Negro Col Fund, 1975-77; bd dir, Austin Women's Ctr, 1979-; Austin Area Urban League; Austin Nat Asn Advan Colored People; Austin C of C; Austin Children's Mus; pres, Howard Univ Alumni Asn, 1989; bd dirs, Austin Area Urban League, 1990; Jack & Jill, 1989; founder, Black Manager's Network, 1990. **Honors/Awds:** Alumni Leadership Award, Fisk Univ, 1970. **Home Addr:** 3202 Hyclimb Cir, Austin, TX 78723. **Business Addr:** Associate Vice President, Austin Community College, Office of Human Resources, 5930 Middle Fiskville Rd, Austin, TX 78752-4390, **Business Phone:** (512)223-7572.

TUCKER, JAMES F.
Educator. **Personal:** Born Nov 2, 1924, Brooklyn, NY; married Caroline Hamblin; children: Kenneth & Lauren. **Educ:** Howard Univ, AB, 1947, MA, 1948; Univ PA, PhD, 1957. **Career:** WV St Col, chmn dept bus, 1956-62; NC Cent Univ, chmn dept econs, 1962-65; US Dept Labor, dir oper, 1965-68; VA St Col, pres, 1968-70; VA Polytechnic Inst & State Univ, prof econ dept, 1970-74; Fed Res Bank Richmond, vpres. **Orgs:** Pres, bd dir Va Coun Econ Educ; Va St Adv Coun Vocat Educ; liason bd Nat Consumer Econs Proj; bd vis VA Polytechnic Inst & State Univ; bd trustees Howard Univ; adv bd dir, Richmond Mem Hosp. **Honors/Awds:** Auth Essentials Econ Prentice-Hall Inc, 1975; Current Econ Issues &Problems Rand McNally, 1976; Anathomy High-Earning Minor Banks, Am Bankers Asn, 1978; outstanding service award, Va Coun Econ Educ, 1978; various articles published. **Military Serv:** AUS, pvt, 1942-45.

TUCKER, KAREN
Editor. **Personal:** Born Jul 18, 1952, Washington, DC; daughter of Willie Jr and Marie Roberson. **Educ:** Trinity Col, Hartford, BA, 1974; Univ Hartford, Grad Study Cert, bus admin, 1979, Org Beh, 1979; Antioch Sch Law, Paralegal Cert, 1983, MA, 1984. **Career:** CT Gen, supvr admin, 1974-80; AT&T Long Lines, NJ, operations supvr, 1980-81; New York cost support/admin mgr, 1981-82; Pepper, Hamilton & Scheetz, legal ed, 1984-89; Steptoe & Johnson, legal ed, 1989-; Publications: Spec Task Force ABA Sect Int Law Pract, Report on the Proposed Rules of Procedure & Evidence, Int Tribunal Adjudicate War Crimes Comn, Former Yugoslavia, chief ed, 1995; articles: "Organizing Basics,", Wash Living, 1985; "Be Your Own Best Legal Editor,", The Docket, 1986; "Getting the Word Out," The Docket, 1988; "A Positive Life Step," Woman Engineer, spring 1992; Res & Writing, Practising Law Institute & Laurie Beth Zimet, Chapter 9; Basic Research & Writing for Legal Assistants; A Satellite Progr, 1994. **Orgs:** Affiliate mem, Nat Fedn Paralegal Asn Inc, 1990-; Trinity Club Wash; 2nd vpres & bd mem, Nat Capital Area Paralegal Asn, 1991-93; Nat Capital Area Paralegal Asn, 1993-; facilitator, Citechecking & Legal Res Sem, Univ Md, Alumni Paralegal Asn, 1993; fac mem, Legal Res & Writing Paralegals, Practising Law Inst, Nat Broadcast Simulcast, 1994; founding bd mem, vpres, Pub Rels, Nat Black Am Paralegal Asn; exec comt, Nat Black Am Paralegal Asn, 1994-96; ed, NBAPA Rev, 1994-96; speaker & facilitator, Latham & Watkins, 1996-2001. **Honors/Awds:** Class of 1916 Trophy, Trinity Col, 1984; Steptoe & Johnson Public Service Award, 1993; Publications: Jurisoft News, 1992. **Special Achievements:** Commentator, The Bluebook: A Uniform System of Citation, Harvard Law Rew Asn, 2000; NFPA PACE Registered Paralegal (RP), 2007-. **Business Addr:** Legal Editor, Steptoe & Johnson LLP, 1330 Connecticut Ave NW, Washington, DC 20036-1795, **Business Phone:** (202)429-3000.

TUCKER, LEOTA MARIE
Executive. **Personal:** Born Aug 1, 1944, New Haven, CT; daughter of Curtis Saulsbury and Viola Kittrell Goodman; married Robert Clifton, Jul 27, 1975; children: Ronald. **Educ:** Southern Conn State Col, BA, 1968; Univ New Haven, MA, 1975; Union Grad Sch, PhD, psychol, 1977. **Career:** Dixwell Crisis Prevnt Serv, proj dir, 1973; Yale & Univ Conn Mental Health Ctr, dir prevent & commun educ proj, 1975-78, mental health adminr, 1973-75; City of New Haven, dir welfare, 1978-80; Karonee Inc, Ctr Applied Behav Sci, pres, 1980-89; Tucker Assocs, New Haven, CT, sr assoc, 1989; Katherine Brennan Sch, Family Resource Ctr Initiative, dir, currently. **Orgs:** Bd dir, United Way Greater New Haven, 1978-; bd dir, ARC New Haven Chap, 1979-; bd dir, St Raphaels Hosp, 1980; Theta Epsilon Omega Chap; New Haven Chap Girl Friends Inc. **Honors/Awds:** Community Serv Award, Chi Omicron Chap Omega Psi Phi Frat, 1978; Outstanding Young Women Award, 1978; Community Service Award, Mt Zion SDA Church, 1978; Prof Award, New Haven Chap of the Black Bus Prof Club, 1979; Co-Winner, McGregor Award for Excellence, Applied Behav Sci, 1979.

TUCKER, DR. M BELINDA
Psychologist, educator. **Personal:** Born May 19, 1949, Washington, PA; daughter of Robert Benjamin and Margaret Louise Jones Tucker Chandler; married Russell L Stockard; children: Desmond Mosi & Daren Blake. **Educ:** Univ Chicago, AB, 1971; Univ Mich, MA, PhD, 1975. **Career:** Univ Mich, Inst Social Res, study dir, 1975-78; Univ Calif Los Angeles, Afro-Am Studies, asst dir, 1978-89, psychiat & Biobehavioral Sci Dept, asst res psychiat, 1983-, psychiat Dept, asst res psychiat, 1987, Afro-American Studies, actg dir, 1989, assoc prof psychiat, 1991, Family Res Consortium IV, dir, currently, prof psychiat & biobehavioral sci, currently, assoc dean grad div, currently. **Honors/Awds:** Res Scientist Develop Award; Independent Scientist Award. **Special Achievements:** Author, co-author, and editor of numerous books, monographs and journals, including The Decline of Marriage Among African Americans (Russell Sage, 1995); Family Relations (Whole Issue: Enduring Couples in Varying Sociocultural Contexts 2008); New Families, New Functions: Postmodern African American Families in Context. In V. C. McLoyd, N. E. Hill, Y K. A. Dodge (Eds.) Emerging issues in African American life: Context, adaptation, and policy (2005); Relative spousal earnings and marital happiness among African American and White women. Journal of Marriage and Family (2008); Diversity in African American families: Trends and projections. In M. J. Coleman and L. H Ganong (Eds.) Handbook of family diversity: Considering the past, contemplating the future (2004); Racial Ambiguity And Relationship Formation in the United States: Theoretical and Practical Considerations. Journal of Social and Personal Relationships, 20, 153-169 (2003). **Business Addr:** Professor of Psychiatry & Behavioral Sciences, Associate Dean, University of California Los Angeles, Semel Institute, 760 Westwood Plaza, SBG Box 62, Los Angeles, CA 90024-1759, **Business Phone:** (310)794-3669.

TUCKER, MARCUS O., JR.
Lawyer, judge. **Personal:** Born Nov 12, 1934, Santa Monica, CA; married Indira Hale; children: Angelique. **Educ:** Univ Southern Calif, BA, 1956; Howard Univ Sch Law, JD, 1960; Chapman Univ, MA, criminal justice, 1997; Regents Col, Univ State NY, BA, libarts, 1999. **Career:** Judge (retired); Santa Monica, pvt pract law, 1962-63, 1967-74; City Los Angeles, prosecutor, 1963-65; US Atty Off, asst US atty, 1965-67; Co Los Angeles, super ct comnr, 1974-76; Long Beach Munic Ct, judge, 1976-85; Los Angeles Super Ct, judge, 1985-, supv judge, 1991, 1992, presiding judge; Juvenile Ct, 1993-94, Div 245, judge. **Orgs:** Pres, John Langston Bar Asn, 1972-73, Legal Aid Found, 1977-78, Legal Aid Soc, 1972-73; bd dir, Boy Scouts Am Long Beach, 1978-93, Long Beach C C,1979-82; pres, Comn Rehab Inds Found; co-founder, Super Ct Irish Extern Prog, 1994-; master the bench, Exec Comn, Joseph Bell-Clarence Hunt Inn Ct, 1998-2000; Lions Club, Long Beach, 1999-. **Honors/Awds:** Judge of the Year, Juv Dept of Los Angeles Super Ct, 1986; Bernard Jefferson Jurist of the Yr, John Langston Bar Asn, 1990; Constitutional Rights Found, Law-Related Educ Award, 1992; Judge of the Yr, Long Beach Bar Asn,

1993; Jurist of the Yr, Juv Ct Bar Asn, 1997; First Ann Adoptions Conf, Judge of the Yr, 1997; Daniel O'Connell Award, Irish Am Bar Asn, 1999; John Langston Bar Asn's Hall of Fame, 2001; Nat Bar Asn Hall of Fame, 2002; 25-year Dedicated Serv Award, CA Judges Asn; Life Time Achievement Award, Nat Asn Advan Colored People. **Special Achievements:** First Santa Monica African American deputy city attorney; First African American to serve as presiding judge of the Long Beach Municipal Court. **Military Serv:** AUS, 1960-66.

TUCKER, MICHAEL ANTHONY
Baseball player. **Personal:** Born Jun 25, 1971, South Boston, VA; married Azurre; children: Aspen Chardanay. **Educ:** Longwood Col. **Career:** Kansas City Royals, outfielder, 1995-96 & 2002-03; Atlanta Braves, 1997-98; Cincinnati Reds, 1999-2001; Chicago Cubs, 2001; San Francisco Giants, 2004-05; Philadelphia Phillies, 2005; New York Mets, 2006; Wash Nationals, 2006; Boston Red Sox, 2007; Southern Maryland Blue Crabs, currently; Newark Bears of the Alantic League, 2009-.

TUCKER, MICHAEL KEVIN
Lawyer. **Personal:** Born Sep 16, 1957, Albany, NY; son of Carroll B and Norma G Foulkes; married Judith C Henry, May 15, 1989. **Educ:** Cornell Univ, BS, 1979; Boston Univ Sch Law, JD, 1983. **Career:** Int Bus Mach, Kingston, NY, recruiting specialist, 1979-80; Csaplar & Bok, Boston, MA, assoc, 1983-88; Bingham, Dana & Gould, Boston, MA, assoc, 1988-90; Ballard, Spahr, Andrews & Ingersoll, Philadelphia, PA, sr assoc, 1990; Gen Elec Capital Serv, Transp Int Pool & Modular Space, atty, currently. **Orgs:** Alpha Phi Alpha Fraternity, 1976-; Am Bar Asn, 1983-; Philadelphia Bar Asn, 1990-; Boston Bar Asn. **Business Addr:** Attorney, General Electric Capital Services, Transp Int Pool Modular Space, 3135 Easton Tpk, Fairfield, CT 06431.

TUCKER, NORMA JEAN
Educator. **Personal:** Born Jan 28, 1932, Muskogee, OK; divorced; children: Kumigawa & Keith. **Educ:** Langston Univ, OK, BS, 1953; Univ Okla, MEd 1966; Univ Calif, Berkeley attended; Calif State Univ attended. **Career:** Douglass High Sch, teacher, 1953-56; Oakland Tech High Sch, teacher,1962-68; Merritt Col, instr, 1968-72; N Peralta Col, coordr instr, 1972, acting dean instr, 1972, dean instr, 1973, dean col, 1974-75; Merritt Col,Oakland, Calif, dean instr, 1975, pres, 1982-88; Col Alameda, Alameda, CA, instr secretarial sci & bus, currently. **Orgs:** Sr vpres, bd dirs, United Way of the Bay Area; life mem, Alpha Kappa Alpha Sor; past pres, Alpha Nu Omega Chap Alpha Kappa Alpha Sor Inc; E Bay Area Club of Bus & Prof Women; vpres, bd dirs, Am Red Cross, Bay Area Chapter, 1994-95, 1996-98; chmn, Alameda County; Kappa Delta Pi; Coun on Black Am Affairs; former mem, Christian Educ Bd Park Blvd Pres Church; western areavice dir, The Links, Inc; life mem, Nat Asn Advan Colored People. **Honors/Awds:** Award Alpha Kappa Alpha Sor; Ida L Jackson Award, Alpha Kappa Alpha Sor; Outstanding Women of the E Bay, Allen Temple Bapt Ch; Honour Outstanding Women in an Unusual Prof, St Paul AME Church; featured February, 1986; Ebony magazine Black Women College Presidents, 1986; Charter Day speakerfor alma mater Langston Univ Langston, OK; several other hon & achievements. **Business Addr:** Instructor, College of Alameda, Secretarial Sci & Bus, 555 Atlantic Ave, Alameda, CA 94501, **Business Phone:** (510)522-7221.

TUCKER, PAUL, JR. See Obituaries section.

TUCKER, ROBERT L
Lawyer. **Personal:** Born Feb 14, 1929, Chattanooga, TN; married Shirley Cross; children: Terri E & Arnold. **Educ:** Tenn St Univ, BS, 1951; NW Univ Sch Law, JD, 1955. **Career:** Atty, pvt prac, 1955-68; Metro Inter-Ins Exchange, gen counr, 1963-65; McCoy Ming & Leighton Chicago, mem firm, 1963-65; NW Univ Sch Law, mem facil; US Dept Housing & Urban Develop, US asst reg adminr, 1968-71; McCarty Watson & Tucker, partner, 1971-73; Gen Couns, Metro Casualty Co Chicago, vpres, 1971-72; Tucker Watson Butler & Todd Attys Couns Law Chicago, partner, 1973-. **Orgs:** Gen couns & mem bd, People United Save Hum, 1971-; gen counr & trustee, MERIT Real Estate Invest Trust, 1972-; Am Bar Asn; Chicago Bar Asn; Cook Co Bar Asn; Comn Cand Chicago Bar Asn; Spec Com Civil Disorders; Phi Alpha Delta; Spl couns St Ill Comn Human Rel, 1974-; Alpha Phi Alpha; Am Judicature Soc; PUSH; Chicago Urban League; Nat Asn Advan Colored People; bd dir, Ill Div Am Civil Liberties Union; Roger Baldwin Found; Am Civil Liberties Union; Nat Asn Comn Legal Coun. **Honors/Awds:** Citation, Cook Co Bar Asn, 1969; Richard E Westbrook Memorial Award & Plaque Outstanding Contribution to Legal Profession, 1968; Hall of Fame, Nat Bar Asn, 1997. **Home Addr:** 6901 S Oglesby Ave, Chicago, IL 60649, **Home Phone:** (773)363-4691.

TUCKER, DR. SAMUEL JOSEPH
Psychologist. **Personal:** Born Nov 5, 1930, Birmingham, AL; son of Daniel and Lucille McGhee; married Arlene Kelly, Jul 12, 1958; children: Samuel Jr, Sabrina, Sharon & Sterling. **Educ:** Morehouse Col, Atlanta, BA, 1952; Columbia Univ NYC, MA, 1956; Atlanta Univ, PhD, 1969, Harvard Univ, Post Doctoral, 1973. **Career:** Psychologist (retired); Morehouse Col, dean studs, 1963-71; Univ Fla, Gainesville, asst prof, 1971-73; Edward Waters Col, Jacksonville, pres, 1973-76; Ala State Univ, Montgomery, dean & prof, 1976-78; Langston Univ, Okla, pres, 1978; Atlanta Human Develop Ctr, psychologist & pres, beginning 1978. **Orgs:** Consult Stanford Res Inst, Menlo Park, CA, 1965-70; consult, Princeton Univ, 1965-70; consult, Univ Mich, Ann Arbor, 1965-70; chap pres, Alpha Phi Alpha Frat Inc, 1971-73; Jacksonville Area Planning Bd, 1973-76; bd govs, Jacksonville Area C of C, 1973-76; Am Psychological Asn, 1958-; Nat Acad Neuropsychologists, 1988-. **Honors/Awds:** Travel Grant Ford Found, 1967; Res Grant Danforth Found, 1968; Res Grant, Univ Fla, 1972. **Special Achievements:** Publ: 'The Baby Boomers Survival Handbook For The 21st Century: Essential Strategies for Mental, Physical, Financial, Social, and Spiritual Success', 1999; 40 articles on mental health issues. **Military Serv:** AUS, Spec Serv, 1952-54. **Home Addr:** 735 Peyton Rd SW, Atlanta, GA 30311, **Home Phone:** (404)755-4244. *

TUCKER, SHERYL HILLIARD
Editor, journalist. **Personal:** Born Jul 13, 1956, Passaic, NJ; daughter of Arthur and Audrey; married Roger C Tucker III, Sep 15, 1985; children: Ara & Alexis. **Educ:** Cornell Univ, BA, 1978; Columbia Univ, Grad Sch Jour, MS, 1982. **Career:** CBS Special Interest Publications, ed, 1978-81; Tucker Hilliard Mkt Commun, exec vpres, 1987-90; Black Enterprise Magazine, ed-in-chief, 1982-95; Your Co Magazine, ed, 1995-97; Money Magazine, asst managing ed; Time Inc, exec ed, 2006-. **Orgs:** Am Soc Magazine Editors, bd mem, 1993-95; Nat Asn Black Journalist, 1982-, chair, Business Writers Task Force, 1994; March Dimes Nat Commun Coun, 1985-; Public Service Electric & Gas Co, Tech Adv, 1990-92; President's Coun Carnell Women, 1991-; vice chair, Carnell Mag, bd dir, 1992-99; St James Preparatory Sch, bd mem, 1992-. **Honors/Awds:** Unity Awards, Journalism; Glamour Magazine, Outstanding Young Working Women, 1986; YWCA Acad Women Achievers, 1985; Unity Awards, Jour; Magazine Week Editorial Excellence Award, 1992. **Home Addr:** 1 Ashley Rd, West Orange, NJ 07052, **Home Phone:** (201)731-5144. **Business Addr:** Executive Editor, Time Inc, 1271 Ave of the Americas, New York, NY 10020-1393, **Business Phone:** (212)522-1212.

TUCKER, WALTER RAYFORD
Government official, lawyer, clergy. **Personal:** Born May 28, 1957, Compton, CA; son of Walter R Jr and Martha; married Robin Marie; children: 2. **Educ:** Princeton Univ, attended 1976; Univ Southern Calif, BS, polit sci, 1978; Georgetown Univ Sch Law, JD, 1981. **Career:** Los Angeles Co, dep dist atty, 1984-86; City Compton, mayor, 1991-92; US Rep, 37th Cong Dist, CA, democrat, 1993-95; Heart Church Chicago, pastor, currently. **Orgs:** Nat Asn Advan Colored People; Kiwanis Club Compton; Los Angeles Co Bar Asn; S Cent Bar Asn; Langston Bar Asn. **Business Phone:** (708)387-1487.

TUCKER, DR. WILBUR CAREY
Physician. **Personal:** Born Apr 3, 1943, Philadelphia, PA; son of Wilbur and Rose; married Faye; children: Maria & Caren. **Educ:** Temple Univ, AB, 1965, MD, 1972; Howard Univ, MS, 1968. **Career:** Presbyterian Hosp, Dept Obstet & Gynec, Philadelphia, PA, acting chmn, 1990-91; Temple Univ, clinical instr, 1975-80; Univ Penn, Philadelphia, PA, clinical assoc prof, 1975-; Temple Univ Hosp, resident Obstet & Gynec, 1972-75; Office Naval Res, physiol, 1968; NASA, biochem, 1965-68; pvt pract, currently. **Orgs:** Phi Rho Sigma Med Frat; Omega Psi Phi Fraternity, 1966; Sigma Pi Phio Fraternity, 1991-. **Honors/Awds:** Fel, Am Coll Obstet & Gynec; diplomate, Am Bd Obstet & Gynec. **Home Addr:** 24 Hazelhurst Dr, Voorhees, NJ 08043, **Home Phone:** (609)435-0494. **Business Addr:** Physician, 3819 Chestnut St 51 N 39th St Suite 200, Philadelphia, PA 19104, **Business Phone:** (215)387-8776.

TUCKETT, LEROY E
Architect. **Personal:** Born May 21, 1932, New York, NY; son of Issac and Helen; divorced; children: Amy, Lori, Lee & Lise. **Educ:** Columbia Col, attended 1952; Pratt Inst, BArch, 1960. **Career:** LaPierre Litchfield & Partners, 1961-64; Charles Luckman & Assoc, proj architect, 1964-67; Petroff & Jones Architects, assoc partner, 1967-69; self-employed, LE Tuckett Architect PC, 1969-; State Univ NY, archit design instr, 1983-86; L E CADDD Corp, pres, 1986-. **Orgs:** Am Inst Architects, 1965-; charter mem, Nat Orgn Minority Architects, 1972-; vpres, NY Coalition Black Architects, 1973-; bd Higher Educ, review comt, CUNY, 1973-78; panelist, Am Arbitration Asn, 1978-; archit judge, mentor program, ACTSO, 1992; NCP; former chair, Durham Bus & Prof Chain, Econ Develop Comt; Durham Comn Affairs Black People; Durham Chamber Com. **Honors/Awds:** Charter Member Recognition, Nat Orgn Minority Architects, 1972; Founding Mem honor, NY Coalition Black Architects, 1992; Community Service recognition, First Calvary Baptist Church, 1998. **Military Serv:** USY, cpl, 1952-54. **Business Addr:** Owner, L.E. Tuckett Architect, NOMA, AIA, 2107 Stuart Dr, Durham, NC 27707-2263, **Business Phone:** (919)419-1715.*

TUCKSON, REED V
School administrator. **Educ:** Georgetown Univ Sch Med; Wharton Sch Bus, Health Care Admin & Policy. **Career:** DC, comnr pub health, 1986-90; Hosp Univ Pa, intern, resident, fel, Gen Internal Med; Prog March Dimes Birth Defects Found, sr vpres, 1990-91; Charles R Drew Univ Med & Sci, pres, 1991-97; UnitedHealth Group, Consumer Health & Med Care Advan, sr vpres, exec vice pres & chief med affairs, 2006-. **Orgs:** Sr vpres, Am Med Asn; Nat Patient Safety Found; Accreditation Coun Grad Med Educ; Accreditation Coun Continuing Med Educ. **Business Addr:** Executive Vice President, Chief of Medical Affairs, UnitedHealth Group, PO Box 1459, Minneapolis, MN 55440-1459, **Business Phone:** 800-328-5979.

TUFFIN, PAUL JONATHAN
Magistrate. **Personal:** Born Sep 9, 1927, Charleston, WV; son of Gerald D and Nellie Carter; married Virginia L Hamilton; children: Paula A, J Brian. **Educ:** Bluefield State Col, BS, 1951; Cleveland Marshall Law Sch, LLB, 1956, JD, 1968. **Career:** Magistrate (retired); US Post Off, clerk, 1952-55; Cleveland Bd Educ, sub teacher, 1952-54; IRS, revenue officer, 1955-59; US Veterans Admin, adjudicator section ch, 1959-84; Cleveland Municipal Court, referee 1984-95, magistrate, 1990-95. **Orgs:** Asst supt, Sunday sch & atty trustee bd St John AME Ch, 1957-; nat parliamentarian Bluefield State Col Nat Alumni Bd, 1986-87; Pi Omega Pi; NAACP, Kappa Alpha Psi. **Honors/Awds:** Meritorious & Conspicuous Service Military Order of the Purple Heart, 1984; Citation, Appreciation The Am Legion, 1984; Outstanding Service Award, Disabled Am Veterans, 1984; Disting Service Award, VFW Cleveland, 1984. **Military Serv:** AUS, corpl, 1 1/2 yrs. *

TUFON, CHRIS
Public utility executive, educator. **Personal:** Born Sep 18, 1959; son of Elias and Scolastica Ngong; married Bernadette Ahlijah, Jun 6, 1990. **Educ:** Brigham Young Univ, Provo, UT, BS, 1984, MS, 1986; Calif State Univ, Fresno, CA, MS, 1988. **Career:** Calif State Univ, Fresno, CA, lectr, 1988-89; Pac Gas & Elec Co, Hayward, CA, mkt assoc, 1989-. **Honors/Awds:** Student of the Year, Brigham Young Univ, 1985. **Business Phone:** (415)973-4212.

TUGGLE, DORIE C
Manager. **Personal:** Born Mar 31, 1944, Detroit, MI; daughter of Frank (deceased) and Pearl (deceased). **Educ:** Detroit Inst Com, AS, 1963; Univ Mich, attended 1965; Penn State Univ, attended 1978; UCLA, attended 1980. **Career:** IBM Corp, mkt mgr, 1977-79, equal opportunity prog mgr, 1979-80, regional personnel mgr, 1980-82, mgt develop mgr, 1982-85, employee rels mgr, 1985-87, div prog mgr, 1987-88; Lockheed, equal opportunity mgr, 1989-2000, sr mgr, Diversity & Equal Employment Opportunity, 2000-. **Orgs:** Vpres, bd, Atlanta Industry Liaison Group, 1989-; bd vice chair, secy, S Eastern Consortium Minorities Eng, 1989-; Alanta Merit Employment Asn, chp, 1990-; adv bd, Cobb County Urban League, 1991-; Girls Inc, com of 100, 1992-; NAACP, life mem; Tuskegee Airmen, Alanta cha, com chp, 1992-; Pres's Coun, Kennesaw State Col, 1992-. **Honors/Awds:** Hearts for Youth Award, City of Atlanta, 1991; AFA Woman Achievement Award, Dollars & Sense Magazine, 1992; US Dept of Labor, Affirmative Action Achievements, 1990; Gift of Time Volunteer, Cobb County Girls Inc, 1992; MNY Recruiter Newspaper Positive Image Award, Pee Dee Newspaper Group, 1992. **Special Achievements:** Guest columnist, MIC Chronicle, Detroit News, 1980, 1982; visiting lecturer, human resources mgt, labor relations, general mgt, 1980-; elected, Union Baptist Church BRD of Trustees, 1986; consultant, trainer, human resources; speaker, motivational techniques. **Business Addr:** Senior Manager Diversity & Equal Employment Opportunity, Lockheed Aeronautical Systems Company, 86 S Cobb Dr Dept 90-43, Marietta, GA 30063-0330, **Business Phone:** (404)494-5588.

TUGGLE, JESSIE LLOYD
Football player. **Personal:** Born Apr 4, 1965, Griffin, GA; son of Jesse Sr and Ada; married Dujuan; children: Justin & Jessica. **Educ:** Valdosta State Univ. **Career:** Football player (retired); Atlanta Falcons, linebacker, 1987-2000; Real Estate Bus, currently. **Honors/Awds:** Pro Bowl, 1992, 1994-95, 1997-98; Named to Sports Illustrated's All-Pro team in 1991; Awarded NFC Defensive Player, Month December, 1991; Man of the Year, Atlanta Falcons, 1993; Peach of an Athlete Award, 1996. **Special Achievements:** Most career tackles in Falcons' hist; at 5, NFL record for most touchdowns by recovery of opponents' fumbles; Jersey retired at Georgia Dome in Atlanta, 2003.

TUGGLE, REV. REGINALD
Publishing executive, clergy. **Personal:** Born Apr 9, 1947, Denver, CO; son of Mertis Jean Marie Hawkins and Otis Tuggle; married Evette Beckett; children: Karleenam, Regine Marie & Regine Perry; married Marie R Peoples (deceased). **Educ:** Cent Phillippine Univ, 1968; Bishop Col, BA, Philos & Psychol, 1969; Univ Ghana, Cert Econs, 1971; Union Theol Sem, MDiv, 1972; Yale Univ, Master Corp Ethics, 1975; Commonwealth Univ, Hon DD, 1985. **Career:** Memorial Presbyterian Church, pastor, 1973-; Urban League Long Island NY, exec dir, 1975-79; Town Hempstead Presiding Super, exec asst, 1979-81; Newsday Newspaper, community rels dir; Nassau Community Col, exec asst to pres, currently, dir col & community rels, currently. **Orgs:** Vchmn, Community Develop Corp; bd mem, Long Island United Way; trustee,

Dowling Col; chmn, Black Leadership Comn AIDS Nassau County; Chmn, Nassau County Health Systs Agency, 1979; chmn, Nassau County Dept Social Servs, 1980-81; vpres, Roosevelt Youth Bd 1983-; pres, Memorial Econ Develop Corp; moderator, Long Island, NY Presbytery; keynote speaker, N Atlantic Treaty Orgn. **Honors/Awds:** Community Service Award, Nassau County Press Club, 1975; Reginald Tuggle Day Award, Suffolk Co, 1979; Outstanding Professional Service Award, Roosevelt Inter-Agency Coun, 1979; Community Service Award, Hundred Black Men Nassau & Suffolk, 1982; Nassau County Martin Luther King Jr Humanitarian Award, 1987; Pastor of the Year, Nassau County African Am Historical Soc.

TUKUFU, DARRYL S
Association executive, educator. **Personal:** Born Jul 27, 1949, Cleveland, OH; married Myra C; children: Ricky & Khari Ture. **Educ:** Youngstown State Univ, AB, 1976; Univ Akron, MA, 1977, PhD, 1984. **Career:** Youngstown Urban League, deputy dir, 1971-75; Youngstown Hometown Plan, acting dir & EEO officer, 1975-76; Univ Akron, grad res asst, 1976-77; City Akron, EEO officer & labor standards enforcement officer, 1977-79; Akron-Summit Community Action Agency, mgr, 1979-80; Fair Housing Contact Serv, exec, 1980-82; Univ Akron, grad teaching asst, 1982-84; Kent State Univ, vis asst prof, 1984-85; Volunteer & Emp Project, project dir, 1985; Northeastern Univ, asst prof, 1985-86; Memphis State Univ, asst prof, 1986-90; LeMoyne-Owen Col, asst prof, 1990; Urban League Portland, pres & chief exec officer, 1990-93; Pub Servs Inst, exec dir; Corain Co Community Col, Pub Servs Div, div dir, 1993-96; Tukufu Group, pres, 1998-; Memphis Urban League, pres & chief exec officer; Crichton Col, Dept Liberal Arts & Humanities, assoc prof & vpres acad affairs, currently. **Orgs:** Comnr, Port Portland, 1991-93; exec comt mem, Leaders Roundtable, 1991-93; fel, Oregon Chap, Am Leadership Forum, 1991-; Minority Affairs Review Bd, NIKE Inc, 1991-93; Emanuel Med Ctr Found Bd, 1991-93; Northeast Econ Develop Alliance Bd, 1991-93; life mem, Nat Asn Advan Colored People; life mem, Kappa Alpha Psi Fraternity; Nat Speakers Asn; Miss Blvd Christian Church. **Honors/Awds:** Outstanding Contributions to the African American Community, LeMoyne-Owen Col, 1990; Appreciation, Educ Asn, 1991; Governor Roberts Oregon Transition Team Appreciation, 1991; Martin Luther King Day, Thank You, Beaverton High Sch, 1991; Appreciation Award, Youngstown, Ohio, Martin Luther King Day, 1992. **Special Achievements:** "Doctors of Love," Bev Johnson Show/WDIA, 1988-90; "Jesse Jackson & The Rainbow Coalition: Working Class Movement or Reform Politics", Humanity & Society, May 1990; "Tukufu's Rap," copyrighted motivational rap for students, 1992; A Guide Toward the Successful Development of African-American Males, 1997. **Business Phone:** (901)320-9700 Ext 1018.

TUNIE, TAMARA (TAMARA TUNIE BOUQUETT)
Actor, television director. **Personal:** Born Mar 14, 1959, McKeesport, PA; daughter of James W and Evelyn Hawkins; married Gregory Generet; married Greg Bouquett (divorced 1991). **Educ:** Carnegie Mellon Univ, BFA, 1981. **Career:** Films: Sweet Lorraine, 1987; Wall Street, 1987; Bloodhounds of Broadway,1989; Rising Sun, 1993; City Hall, 1996; The Money Shot, 1996; Spirit Lost, 1996; Quentin Carr, 1996; Rescuing Desire, 1996; Eve's Bayou, 1997; The Peacemaker, 1997; The Devil's Advocate, 1997; Snake Eyes, 1998; The Caveman's Valentine, 2001; Broadway: Lena Horne; Oh Kay; Sweet Lorraine; Dreamgirls, 2001; After-Life, 2007; TV series: "Spenser: For Hire", 1986;"As the World Turns", 1987-2007; "Tribeca", 1993; " Up On the Roof", 1994-97;"Good Time Charlie'; "New York Undercover", 1995-98; "Sea Quest DSV", 1995; "Bad Girls", 1995; "Dead Beat", 1996; "Caulkmanship", 1996; "Rebound: The Legend of Earl 'The Goat' Manigault", 1996; "Swift Justice". 1996; "Feds", 1997;"Chicago Hope", 1997; "Prince Street", 1997; "Taillight's Last Gleaming,",1997; "Missing Pieces", 1997; "Leggo My Ego,"1997; "I Love Lucy", 1997; "Sign o' the Times", 1998; "Sex & the City", 1999; "Law& Order: Special Victims Unit", 2000-08; "24", 2002; "Law & Order: Trialby Jury", 2005; "As the World Turns", 2006: Stage: "Loose Knit", 1993; "Troilus and Cressida", 1995; "Sheba", 1996; "Antony and Cleopatra", 2000; "Cat on a Hot Tin Roof"; "Lena Horne, Oh, Kay"; "Sweet Lorraine": Director: "The Science cool", currently. **Honors/Awds:** Antoinette Perry Award, co-producer, 2007. **Special Achievements:** She Sang "We Should Be Together For Christmas" for the A Soap Opera Christmas album. **Business Addr:** Actress, c/o William Morris Agency, 151 El Camino Dr, Beverly Hills, CA 90212, **Business Phone:** (310)859-4000.*

TUNLEY, NAOMI LOUISE
Nurse. **Personal:** Born Jan 10, 1936, Henryetta, OK; daughter of Alexander Tunley (deceased) and Ludia B Franklin (deceased). **Educ:** Dillard Univ, BS, Nurs educ, 1958; Univ Iowa, 1967; Univ MO, KC, MA, Sociol, 1974. **Career:** Nurse (retired); Va Hosp, staff nurse serv Ed; Okla City VA Hosp, assoc cheif nurs serv 1958-65; Iowa Luth Hosp, Des Moines, med & Surg instr, 1965-66; Mercy Hosp Iowa City, IA, emerg rm chrg nurs, 1966; Va Hosp, KC, assoc cheif nurs serv, charge Nurs, psychiatric unit, staff nurs, ins instr 1967-77, head nurs; patient care surgical coordr, 1977; Va Medical Ctr, Kansas City, MO, nurse mgr, 1977-94. **Orgs:** Trustee, Nat Coun Alcoholism & Drug Abuse, 1985; Nat Honor Soc Nurse; Am Red Cross; Am Sociol Asn; Big Sisters Org Am; Iowa Nurse Asn Instr Home Nurse; Am Red Cross; March Dimes; Muscular Dystrophy Asn; Mo Teacher Religious Ed, Faith Mission Chap. **Honors/Awds:** KC, Mo Nat Honor Soc, 1953-54; State Honor Soc, 1953-54; Scholar, EK Gaylor Philanthropist. **Special Achievements:** First Black to hold position as Associate Chief of Nurse Service, Oklahama City First Black to hold position as Medical-surgical Instr, Des Moines. **Home Addr:** 3120 Poplar Ave, Kansas City, MO 64128, **Home Phone:** (816)861-6545. *

TUNSIL, NECOLE
Basketball player. **Personal:** Born Aug 22, 1970. **Educ:** Univ Iowa, BCS, journalism & Commn. **Career:** Player (retired); Coach; Long Beach Stingrays, forward, 1997; Lakewood High Sch, coach. **Special Achievements:** U.S. Basketball Writers' all-Am Kodak Honorable Mention All-Am; Basketball Times Honorable Mention All-Am; first team all-Big Ten Conference selection; Three-time Big Ten Conference Player of the Week; Best Offensive Iowa Player. **Business Phone:** (727)893-2916.*

TUNSTALL, JUNE REBECCA
Physician. **Personal:** Born Jun 20, 1947, Baltimore, MD. **Educ:** Bennett Col, BS, 1969; Meharry Col, MD, 1974. **Career:** Worchester City Hosp, intern, 1974-75; Univ MA, fam phy & educ coordr fam prac dept, 1977, res, 1975-77; Surry Co HURA Proj, staff phys, 1978; Surry Co Fam Health Group Inc VA, staff phy, med dir, 1979-80; John Randolph Hosp Hopewell VA, staff phy, 1979-; Med Col VA Dept Fam Pract Richmond, instr, 1979-80. **Orgs:** Chair person, bd dir Surry Co Fam Health Group Inc, 1979-80; vpres, Surry Co Unit Am Heart Asn, 1979-80; pres, Surry Co Unit Am Heart Asn, 1980-81; VA Acad Fam Phys; Med Soc Southside VA; bd dir, So Chirstian Leadership Conf; Am Acad Fam Phys; MA Acad Fam Phys; New Eng Med Soc Bd; dir, Fam planning serv Gr Worcester; bd dir, United Way Ctrl MA. **Business Addr:** Physician, Po Box 354, Surry, VA 23883, **Business Phone:** (804)458-6396.

TUNSTALL, RICHARD CLAYTON
Executive. **Personal:** Born May 6, 1953, Warrenton, NC; son of Melvin D and Edna S; married Phyllis Fogg, Jul 2, 1977; children: Ashlyn Nikole & Richard Jr. **Educ:** NC State Univ, BS, indust engineering, 1975. **Career:** Corning Int, engineering, prod planning, prod mgt, 1973-87; Konica Mfg USA, prod control mgr, 1988-92, sr mgr planning & logistics, 1992; Konica Minolta Mfg USA Inc, vpres; ZINK Imaging Inc, sr mgr planning & logistics, currently. **Orgs:** Am Prod & Inventory Control Soc, 1992-; trustee, Mt Zion Baptist Church Inc, 1992-; NC World Trade Orgn, 1994-; bd mem, Greensboro Educ & Develop Coun, 1996-; Bennett Col Bus Adv Coun, 1999-. **Home Addr:** 6104 Westwind Dr, Greensboro, NC 27410, **Home Phone:** (336)299-6233. **Business Addr:** Senior Manager, ZINK Imaging Inc, 6900 Konica Dr, Whitsett, NC 27377, **Business Phone:** (336)449-8000.

TUNSTEL, EDWARD
Astronaut. **Educ:** Howard Univ, Wash, DC, mech eng, BS, ME, mech eng; Univ Nmex, PhD, elec & comput eng. **Career:** Robotic Intelligence Group, NASA, 1989, Nanorover Technol Task, cognizant engr, 1998-2000, MER Surface Mission Phase Team, Autonomous Navigation, flight systs engr, 2001-03; FIDO Rover, lead syst engr, 2000-02, Univ Robotics Software Study, task mgr, 2002-03, Task Field Integrated Design & Opers, lead systs engr, 2003, Mobility & Robotic Arm Subsyst: MER Spacecraft & Rover Eng Team, surface ops lead, 2003-; Distributed Spectrometer Mobility & Surv, task mgr, 2004-, group leader & sr robotics engr, currently. **Orgs:** Inst Elec & Electronics Engineers; Asn Advan Artificial Intelligence; Sigma Xi Sci Res Soc; NY Acad Sci; Am Soc Mech Engineers. **Honors/Awds:** NASA Group Achievement Award, Robotic Intelligence Team, 1991; JPL Minority fel, 1992; NASA Group Achievement Award, TOPEX S/C GDS Sci Data S/S, 1993; NASA/US Dept of Interior WT Pecora Group Award, TOPEX/Poseidon, 1998; JPL Notable Org Value Added Award, Improv & Innovation, 2001; NASA Group Achievement Award, Safe Rover Navigation Team, 2002; NASA Space Act Award, Cognitive Sensor Technol, 2003; NASA Group Achievement Award, MER Flt Syst Eng Team, 2004; NASA Group Achievement Award, MER Avionics Team, 2004; NASA Group Achievement Award, MER Project Opers Team, 2004; JPL SPOT Award, NASA SBIR Subtopic Mgt, 2005; NASA Group Achievement Award, MER 1st/2nd Ext Mission Teams, 2005. **Special Achievements:** Authored over 75 journal, book chapter & conference publications. **Business Addr:** Senior Robotics Engineer, NASA Jet Propulsion Laboratory, California Institute of Technology, 4800 Oak Grove Dr, PO Box 198-219, Pasadena, CA 91109.*

TUPPER, LEON E
Automotive executive, founder (originator). **Career:** Gilreath Mfg Inc, pres, owner & chief exec officer, 1990-2004; Arete Indust, founder & chmn, 2006-. **Orgs:** Trustee, Cleary Univ, 2006-. **Special Achievements:** Company is ranked No 76 on Black Enterprise mag Top 100 Black businesses. **Business Addr:** Chairman, Founder, Arete Industries Inc, 24400 Northwestern Hwy, Southfield, MI 48075-2413, **Business Phone:** (248)352-7205.

TURLEY, LOUIS EDWARD
Executive. **Personal:** Born Mar 11, 1952, South Bend, IN; son of Louis and Carrie Bell; married Phillis Mae, Jul 28, 1979; children: Michael Landon. **Educ:** Ball State Univ, BS, 1975; Ind Univ, MS, 1981. **Career:** S Bend Community Schs, instr & educr, 1978-86; ABJ Community Servs Inc, prog dir, 1990-98; Zeigler Habilitation Homes, asst admin, 1998-. **Orgs:** Nat Rehab Asn, 1990-94; Alpha Phi Omega; Nat Serv Fraternity; Kiwanis Club Am. **Honors/Awds:** Outstanding Young Man of America, 1986. **Special Achievements:** Study: 18 wks, Zimbabwe/Malawi Africa Comparison Education, 1986. **Business Addr:** Assistant Administrator, Zeigler Habilitation Homes Inc, PO Box 12526, Toledo, OH 43606, **Business Phone:** (419)382-9040.

TURMAN, GLYNN (GLYNN RUSSELL TURMAN)
Actor. **Personal:** Born Jan 31, 1946, New York, NY; married Aretha Franklin (divorced); children: Glynn Turman Jr (deceased); married Jo-Ann Allen; children: Delena Joy. **Career:** Films: Thomasine & Bushrod, 1974; Together Brothers, 1974; Cooley High, 1975; Minstreal Man; JD's Revenge, 1976; Penitentiary II, 1982; Secrets of a Married Man, 1984; Buffalo Soldiers, 1997; How Stella Got Her Groove Back, 1998; Light It Up, 1999; The Visit, 2000; Freedom Song, 2000; Men of Honor, 2000; The Seat Filler, 2004; Sahara, 2005; City Teacher, 2007; Kings of the Evening, 2008; Murder 101: New Age, 2008; TV series: "Peyton Place", writer, 1964; "The Parent Hood", dir, 1995; "The Wayans bros", dir, 1995; "Resurrection Blvd", 2000; "Big Apple", 2001; "The Wire", 2004-08; "Law & Order: Special Victims Unit", 2005; "The Bernie Mac Show", 2005; "All of Us", 2006; "Law & Order: Special Victims Unit", 2006; TV film: "Fire & Ice", 2001. **Honors/Awds:** Dramalogue Award; NAACP Image Award. **Business Addr:** Actor, Stone Manners Agency, 8436 W 3rd St Suite740, Los Angeles, CA 90048, **Business Phone:** (323)655-1313.

TURMAN, GLYNN RUSSELL. **See TURMAN, GLYNN.**

TURMAN, KEVIN
Clergy, president (organization). **Educ:** Harvard Univ, under grad; Yale Divinity Sch, MDiv; United Theol Sem, Dayton, OH, DMin. **Career:** Bethany Baptist Church, Brooklyn, assoc pastor; Ebenezer Baptist Church, Boston, pastor; Second Baptist Church Detroit, sr pastor, currently. **Orgs:** Pres, Mich Progressive Baptist Conv; pres, Metrop Organizing Strategy Enabling Strength. **Military Serv:** USNR, military chaplain, 26 yrs. **Business Addr:** Senior Pastor, Second Baptist Church, 441 Monroe St, Detroit, MI 48226, **Business Phone:** (313)961-0920.*

TURNBULL, DR. CHARLES WESLEY
Educator, governor. **Personal:** Born Feb 5, 1935, Charlotte Amalie, St Thomas, Virgin Islands of the United States; son of John Wesley and Ruth Ann Eliza Skelton. **Educ:** Hampton Univ, Hampton, VA, BS, 1958, MA, 1959; Univ Minn, Minneapolis, MN, PhD, 1976. **Career:** Virgin Island Dept Educ, St Thomas, VI, social studies teacher, 1959-61, asst prin, 1961-65, prin, 1965-67, asst comnr educ, 1967-79, comnr edu, 1979-87; Univ Virgin Islands, St Thomas, VI, prof hist, 1988-99; US Virgin Islands, gov, 1999-2007. **Orgs:** Alpha Phi Alpha Fraternity Inc, 1958-; Asn Caribbean Historians; Orgn Amn Historians; Coun Chief State Sch Offrs, 1979-87; bd trustees, Univ Virgin Islands, 1979-87; Virgin Islands Bd Elections, 1974-76; pres, Virgin Islands Hist Soc, 1976-; Virgin Islands Bd Educ, 1988-; Virgin Islands Humanities Coun, 1989-; Am Hist Asn; Nat Govs Asn; Southern Govs' Asn; Democratic Govs Asn. **Honors/Awds:** President Senior Class of 1958, Hampton Univ, 1958; Citation Contributions Virgin Islands History & Culture, Cult Educ Division Virgin Island Dept Educ, 1987; Citation for Excellence, Leadership & Serv Field Educ, Iota Phi Lambda Sorority, 1989; Citation Excellence Teaching, Charlotte Amalie High Sch Class of 1964, 1989; Citation Excellence Serv Humanity, Alpha Fraternity Inc, Theta Epsilon Lambda Chapter, 1992. **Home Addr:** Charlotte Amalie, PO Box 2265, St Thomas, Virgin Islands of the United States 00803, **Home Phone:** (809)774-7994.

TURNBULL, HORACE HOLLINS
Administrator. **Personal:** Born Mar 26, 1949, Greenville, MS; married Eunice Carter; children: LaChandrea, Tamari, Courtney. **Educ:** Tougaloo Col, BS, 1971; Columbia Univ, MA, 1975; Long Island Univ, MBA, 1978. **Career:** Abbott House Childrens Home, cons; Childrens Village, grp home parent; Leake & Watts Childrens Agency, soc worker, 1971-72; Planned Parenthood NYC, dir, coord, 1974-76; St Peters Sch, coord; St Mary's in-the-Field, res dir; Lakeside School, exec dir, 1983-86; The Equitable Financial Serv, registered rep. **Orgs:** vpres, Harlem Boys Choir Bd Dir; Interest Health & Human Serv Admin.

TURNBULL, RENALDO ANTONIO
Football player. **Personal:** Born Jan 5, 1966, St Thomas, Virgin Islands of the United States; son of George and Ellina; married Thea Lynn Winick, Mar 16, 1990; children: Royce Alexander. **Educ:** W Va Univ, BA, commun, 1990. **Career:** New Orleans Saints, linebacker, 1990-96; Carolina Panthers, 1997. **Honors/Awds:** Pro Bowl, 1993.

TURNER, ALLEN H.
Engineer. **Personal:** Born Oct 19, 1923, Detroit, MI; married Beverly K; children: Linda K. **Educ:** BS, elec eng, 1950. **Career:**

Engineer (retired); Tuskegee Inst, res asst, 1950-52; Ford Motor Co, Sci Lab, res engr, 1952-65, ICPD Div, supvr res & develop, 1965-72, Elec Syst Dept, supvr, 1972-82. **Orgs:** Electron Microscope Soc Am; Am Vacuum Soc; eng bd dir, Soc Am Family Serv. **Military Serv:** USAF, 2nd lt, WW II. *

TURNER, BAILEY W.
Consultant. **Personal:** Born Dec 18, 1932, Sadlersville, TN; married Ruby McClure; children: Carolyn & Gayle. **Educ:** Tenn State Univ, BS, 1956; PA State Univ, MEd, 1957; Union Grad Sch, PhD, 1977. **Career:** Lincoln Heights Pub Schs, teacher, 1960-61; Cincinnati Pub Schs, 1961-65; Comm Action Comn Cincinnati area, field rep comt organizer, 1965-67; Metropolitan Life, sales rep, 1967-72; Hamilton County Ct Common Pleas, bd libr trustees, 1984; Trustees Union Baptist Church, Bd chmn, 1987-99; Lit Network Gt Cincinnati, trustee, 1994-2000; Hamilton County Ct Common Pleas, pres bd, 2002; Hamilton County Ct Common Pleas, vpres, 2002-06; Polit Develop Nat Black Assembly, Little Rock, AR, instr; OH Black Polit Assembly, pres; Midland Nat Life, gen agent; Univ Cincinnati, adj asst prof; RST Pub Relations & Consult firm, sr assoc; Community Orgn, gen consult; Pendleton Heritage Ctr, consult; Coalition to Save Hillcrest Cemetery, pres; Black-White Employee Relations, consult, mgt training. **Orgs:** Pres, Avondale Community Coun, 1967-69; pres, Avondale Community Coun, 1967; United Black Community Orgns, 1969-70; chmn, Coalition Concerned Black Citizens, 1971-; pres, OH Black Political Assembly 1974; Coalition Concerned Black Citizens, Prince Hall FAM. **Honors/Awds:** Alumnus of the Year, Tenn State Univ, 1965; Outstandng New Jaycee, Cincinnati Jaycees, 1965; SCLC Cincinnati chap Distinguished Community Serv Award, 1969; PUSH Black Excellence Award, 1972; Trustee Emeritus. **Military Serv:** USAF, 1949-53.

TURNER, BENNIE L
Executive, senator (u.s. federal government). **Personal:** Born Aug 21, 1948, West Point, MS. **Educ:** Mary Holmes Col; Miss State Univ; Univ Miss, JD. **Career:** City prosecuting atty, 1976-69, county prosecuting atty, 1979-92; Turner & Assocs, partnet; T&W Commun, WACR-AM/FM, pres; Miss State Senate, vice chmn ins comt, sen, currently. **Orgs:** Pres, Nat Asn Black Owned Broadcasters Inc; Nat Asn Advan Colored People; Magnolia & Miss Bar Asn. **Business Addr:** Senator, Mississippi State Senate, Rm 404B - NC, PO Box 1018, Jackson, MS 39215, **Business Phone:** (601)359-3210.

TURNER, BILL
Automotive executive, chief executive officer. **Career:** Cumberland Chrysler-Plymouth Inc, chief exec officer, 1993-. **Special Achievements:** Co is ranked No 70 on Black Enterprise's list of top 100 auto dealers, 1994.

TURNER, CASTELLANO BLANCHET
Educator. **Personal:** Born Jun 14, 1938, Chicago, IL; son of James Julius Turner and Loretta Ganier Turner; married Barbara Formaniak, Apr 29, 1961; children: Adam Justin & Shomari Megan. **Educ:** DePaul Univ, BA, 1962, MA, 1963; Univ Chicago, PhD, 1966. **Career:** Chicago State Hosp, clin internship psychol, 1962-63, psychologist,1963; Univ Chicago, Exten Div, lectr psychol, 1965-68; Manteno State Hosp, Prog Psychologist, Woodlawn-Hyde Park-Kenwood Prog, 1966-68; Univ Chicago Med Sch, clin instr, 1966-68; Manteno State Hosp, Woodlawn-Hyde Park-Kenwood Proj, prog dir, 1967-68; Univ Chicago, Sch Social Serv Admin, sr res assoc; Univ Mass, Col Ed Black Stud, Coun & Tutoring Prog, dir, 1969-70; Univ Mass, Amherst, Boston, prof psychol, prof & dir clin psychol prog, 1989-96, inst actg dir, William Monroe Trotter Inst, interim dir, prof emer clin & community psychol, currently. **Orgs:** Am Psychol Asn; Asn Black Psychologists; Eastern Psychol Asn; Mass PsycholAsn. **Special Achievements:** Publication: co-author, Poverty, Resilience, and Academic Achievement among Latino College Students and High School Drop Outs, 1993. **Home Addr:** 95 Wood End Rd, Newton Highlands, MA 02461-1402. **Business Addr:** Professor Emeritus of clinical and community psychology, University of Massachusetts Boston, Department of Psychology, 100 Morrissey Blvd, Boston, MA 02125, **Business Phone:** (617)287-6341.

TURNER, DEBBYE
Broadcaster. **Personal:** Born in Honolulu, HI; daughter of Frederick Turner, Jr. **Educ:** Univ Missouri-Columbia, DVM 1991. **Honors/Awds:** Miss America 1990. *

TURNER, DIANE YOUNG
Library administrator, librarian. **Personal:** Born Jan 2, 1950, New Orleans, LA; daughter of William Young and Mary Montana Young; married John, Dec 26, 1976; children: Kyra Denita, Jayna Ymon & John Kenneth. **Educ:** Grambling Col, BA, 1972; State Univ New York, MA, 1974. **Career:** Renselaer Polytech Inst, Troy, NY, asst dir, admis; Roxbury Community Col, Roxbury, MA, dir, financial aid; Yale Univ, New Haven, CT, asst dir, financial aid, sr human resource specialist, dir, libr human resources, assoc univ librn human resource, training & security, currently. **Orgs:** Alpha Kappa Alpha Sorority, 1970-; Jr League Greater New Haven, 1985-89; bd mem, Greater New Haven Community Action Agency, 1988-99; pres, New Haven Chap Jack & Jill, 1989-94; pres, Hamden PTA Coun, 1989-91; bd mem, Greater New Haven Arts Coun, 1990-99; bd mem, YWCA Greater New Haven, 1990-92; pres, Hamden High Sch PTSA, 1993-96; vpres, Hamden Middle Sch PTA, 1998; New Haven Chap, Girlfriends, 1998-; vpres, 1999-2001, pres, 2001-, Hamden High Sch PTSO; pres-elect, Quota Int; bd dirs, Creative Arts Workshop, 2002-. **Honors/Awds:** Distinguished Mother Award, Jack & Jill, 1993; Elm Ivy Award, 1994; Hamden Notables Award, 1995; Secretary of State's Public Service Award, 2002; Hamden Black Notables Award, 2003. **Special Achievements:** Special Olympics World Games, dir of volunteers at Yale Univ; participated in Leadership Greater New Haven, Institution and Volunteer Action Agency, 1989-.

TURNER, DORIS (DORIS TURNER KEYS)
Association executive. **Personal:** Born Jun 30, 1930, Pensacola, FL; married Willie D Keys. **Career:** Dist 1199 Nat Union Hosp & Health Care Employees, exec vpres. **Orgs:** Sec Nat Union Hosp & Health Care Employees; union trustee Hosp League & Dist 1199 Trng & Upgrading; union trustee Nat Benefit & Pension Fund Hosp & Health Care Employees; Exec Comt Nat Benefit & Pension Funds; bd mem, Am Dem Action; bd mem, Martin L King Ctr Soc Change; State NY Comn Health Educ & Illness Prevention; Coalition Labor Union Women; appointed mem, NY State Hosp Review & Planning Coun, 1978-81. **Honors/Awds:** District services award, NY City Cent Labor Coun AFL CIO, 1969; award of merit, The Black Trade Unionist Leadership Comt NY Cent Labor Coun, 1974; Hispanic Labor Committee Award, 1978; Eugene V Debs & Norman Thomas Award, 1978; Bessie & Sarah Delaney Award.

TURNER, DR. DORIS J.
Educator. **Personal:** Born in St Louis, MO; daughter of Julius Adams Turner and Adeline Herndon. **Educ:** Stowe Col, St Louis, BA, 1953; Universidade da Bahia Salvador BahiaBrazil, attended 1963; St Louis Univ, PhD, 1967. **Career:** Ind Univ, vis scholar, 1987-88; Kent State Univ, assoc prof romance lang &lit, currently, Latin Am Studies, dir, currently. **Orgs:** Elected mem, chmn, Nat Off Steering & Comt, Consortium Latin Am StudiesProg, 1973-76; field reader, US Off Educ (HEW), 1976-77, 1979; DanforthAsn, 1976. **Honors/Awds:** Fulbright fel, Brazil, 1962-64; res grant, Brazil, Kent State Univ, 1976;NEH Summer fel, Brown Univ, 1979; Outstanding Teaching Award, Col Arts &Sci, Kent State Univ, 1986; Postdoctoral fel, Ford Found, 1987-88. **Business Addr:** Associate Professor of Romance Languages and Literatures, Director of Latin American Studies, Kent State University, 101 Satterfield Hall, Kent, OH 44242, **Business Phone:** (216)672-2150.

TURNER, DOUGLAS. **See WARD, DOUGLAS TURNER.**

TURNER, EDDIE WILLIAM
Police officer. **Personal:** Born Apr 21, 1931, Toledo, OH; married Jacquelyn H; children: Edward & Kimberly. **Educ:** Findlay Col, attended 1956; Univ Toledo, BS, 1977. **Career:** Toledo Police Dept, patrol officer, 1959-62, detective, 1962-68, community rels officer, 1968-78, crime prev officer, 1978. **Orgs:** Nat Asn Advan Colored People, Toledo Chap, 1976; adv bd, Vol Am; adv, Coun E Toledo Helping Hand; adv bd, E Ment Health Ctr; chaplin, Omega Fraternity, Xi Tau Chap; City Toledo Baseball & Softball Comn; pres, Med-City Football Adv Bd; 100 Mem Club. **Honors/Awds:** Crime Prevention Officer of the Year, Asn Crime Prev, 1979. **Military Serv:** AUS, corp, 1952-54. **Home Addr:** 2453 Greylyn Dr, Toledo, OH 43615, **Home Phone:** (419)537-1425.

TURNER, ELMYRA G.
Educator. **Personal:** Born Nov 27, 1928, Longview, TX; married James M; children: 3. **Educ:** BS, 1952; MEd, 1959; MEd, 1969; Tex southern Univ, admin cert, 1973. **Career:** Tex Southern Univ, secy, 1952; Crawford Elem Sch, 1953; Elmore High Sch, secy & teacher, 1954; Langston Elem Sch, teacher, 1959; Lockett Jr High, 1964; Lincoln Jr-Sr High, 1968; Sam Houston Sr High, counr, 1970; Deady Jr High, asst prin, 1970. **Orgs:** Houston Principals Asn, 1970-; Houston Coun Educ, 1972; supt com on Community Rels Area, 1972-74; Nat Coun Negro Women, 1973; Nat Asn Advan Colored People, 1973-74; Eval Panel Interviewrs-Area V PTA Deady Jr HighSch; vpres, Lockhart Elem Tex State Teachers Asn; Top Ladiel Distinction Inc; pres, Beta Pi Chap Iota Phi Lambda Sor Inc; organizer, Houston Chap Nat Tots & Teens Inc; Houston League Bus & prof Women; Home Improv & Protec Asn; chmn, Youth Comn; Delta Sigma Theta Sor Inc; Am Asn Univ Women. **Honors/Awds:** President's Award, 1971; Iota Phi Lambda Sor Inc; Outstanding Woman Yr, 1974-75; Iota Phi Lambda Sor Inc; Beta Pi Chap, Houston, TX; Human Rel Educ Award, outstanding achievement in human rels, 1977.

TURNER, ERIC SCOTT
Football player, politician. **Personal:** Born Feb 26, 1972, Richardson, TX; married Robin. **Educ:** Univ Ill, speech commun, MBA, human resource develop. **Career:** Football player (retired), Politician; Wash Redskins, defensive back, 1995-97; San Diego Chargers, 1998-2000; Denver Broncos, corner back, 2003; turner for congress, politician, currently; Morning star Christian Church, asst pastor, currently. **Special Achievements:** Involved with the national political process when he secured a position as an intern in California and Washington with Congressman Duncan Hunter, chairman of the House Armed Services Committee. **Business Addr:** Politician, Turner for congress, 11232 El camino real suite 150, San Diego, CA 92130, **Business Phone:** (858)350-9192.

TURNER, ERVIN (PETER TURNER)
Executive. **Personal:** Born Mar 20, 1948, Monroe, LA; married Kathleen Lindsey; children: Christopher Earl, Roanita. **Educ:** Ne LA Univ, 1972; Boys' Clubs Am, certification, 1974. **Career:** Ouachita Parish Police Jury, police juror; EPT Enterprise AAA LTD, pres & owner; Tri-District Boys' Club, exec dir, 1971-. **Orgs:** NAACP; NE LA Sickle Cell Anemia; NLU Booster Club Bus Action Assoc; Amer Entrepreneurs Asn; zoological Soc LA Purchase Gardens & Zoo; bd mem, Northeast LA Indus Develop Bd; bd mem, NE LA Indus Bd; bd mem, LA Minority Bus Develop Auth Bd; BCA Prof; coord, Volunteer Job Corps; secy, Luminous Civic Club; bd mem, Youth House Quachita; bd mem, Bus Action Asn; bd mem, Better Bus Bureau; exec secy, LA Area Coun BCA, 1974; vpres, N Delta Regional Planning. **Honors/Awds:** Man of the Year, St Philip Baptist Ch, 1975; Man of the Year, NAACP, 1978; Monroe's Outstanding Young Man, Monroe Jaycees, 1982. **Business Addr:** Executive Director, Tri-District Boys' Club, 2920 Louberta St, Monroe, LA 71201, **Business Phone:** (318)387-0903.

TURNER, EUGENE
Clergy. **Personal:** Born Apr 17, 1934, Macon, GA; married Sylvia Baskerville; children: Peter Eugene, Paul Eugene, Lennie Elis. **Educ:** Knoxville Col, BA; Pittsburgh Theol Sem, MDiv; Harvard Univ. **Career:** Clergy (retired); Pittsburgh, asst pastor; Patterson NJ, pastor; Philadelphia, organsing pastor; Presbeytery Philadelphia, asst leadership develop, coord Met Mission; Synod Golden Gate San Francisco, assoc exec; United Presby Church Syracuse NY, exec Synod Northeast; pres bd, Johnson C. Smith Theol Sem. **Orgs:** Bd mem, No CA Coun Church; bd mem, Nat Planned Parenthood 1964-66; bd mem, Coun Black Clergy; bd mem, Black Presby United; steering comt, Nat Black Conf, 1968; bd mem Model Cities Phila. **Military Serv:** AUS 1957-59. *

TURNER, FRANKLIN JAMES
Engineer. **Personal:** Born Aug 16, 1960, Birmingham, AL. **Educ:** Alabama A&M Univ, BS, 1983. **Career:** Rockwell Int, software engr, 1984-86; Northrop, software qual engr, 1986-. **Honors/Awds:** Pride Award for Engineering Outstanding Achievement, Rockwell Int, 1986. **Home Addr:** 19101 Pricetown Ave, Carson, CA 90746, **Home Phone:** (213)329-2896.

TURNER, GENEVA
Business owner, educator. **Personal:** Born Jul 6, 1949, Columbus, GA; daughter of George Robert (deceased) and Mollie Bell; married 1994; children: Gennyce Ashley Nelson. **Educ:** Columbus Col, AAN, 1971; GEO Southwestern, BSN, 1979; Univ ALA, MSN, 1982; Tex Woman's Univ, PhD, 1987. **Career:** Med Ctr, staff nurse, 1971, staff nurse, 1978-79; Talmadge Mem Hosp, staff nurse, 1971-73; RE Thomason Gen Hosp, charge nurse, 1973-74; Convalescent Ctr, charge nurse, 1974; USY Hosp, actg head nurse, 1975-77; Columbus Col, assoc prof nursing, 1979-93; Turner & ASC Consult, owner, 1989-; FamilyProjs Publs, owner, 1992-. **Orgs:** Am Nurses Asn, 1979-, scholar, 1986; Sigma Theta Tau, 1983-; Nat Coun Marriage & Family Rels, 1986-; deleg, Third Dist Nurses Asn, bd dirsl; secy, Res Officers Asn, scholar, 1986; Phi Kappa Phi, 1987-; Asn Military Surgeons US, 1988-; Asn Black Nursing Fac, 1989-93; Nat League Nursing Higher Educ, 1990-93; Nat Asn Nurses Bus, 1991-93; Publishers Mkt Asn, 1992-; Network Profs & Execs Inc, 1994-; Alliance Homelessness, 1994-. **Honors/Awds:** Outstanding Sophomore Teacher in Nursing, Columbus Col, 1981, Dr John Townsend Award for Outstanding Service to the Community in Medicine, 1983; Certificate of Appreciation, Combined Communities Southeast Columbus, 1989; Outstanding Service to the City of Columbus, Mayor's Off, 1990;Service Award, Greater Columbus Chap Alzheimer's Dis, 1991. **Special Achievements:** Disseminating Intravascular Coagulation, Nursing Interventions, 1991; Preceptorship Program: A Public Relations Tool, 1991; Dealing with Polychronic or Monochronic Individuals in the Work Place, 1992; Black Am Folk Medicine Health Care Beliefs: Implications for Nursing, 1992; "Theory of Homelessness Using Gibb's Paradigm", 1992; How to Plan a Spectacular Family Reunion, 1993; Fathers Cry, Too, 1995. **Military Serv:** USY Reserves, ltc, 1979-. **Home Addr:** 4815 Velpoe Dr, Columbus, GA 31907. **Business Addr:** Owner, Family Projects Publishers, 3009 Hamilton Rd, PO Box 6427, Columbus, GA 31907, **Business Phone:** (706)687-4296.

TURNER, GEORGE CORDELL, II
Executive, educator. **Personal:** Born Jun 3, 1937, McGehee, AR; son of George C Sr and Mary L; married Nancy C Turner, Aug 11, 1968; children: Melissa, George III. **Educ:** Univ Ark, Pine Bluff, hist & gov, attended 1959; Univ Ark, Univ Fla, Univ Ill. **Career:** Educator (retired); Helena-West Helena Pub Schs, instr, 1959-64; Conway Pub Schs, instr admin, 1964-69; Consumers Power, dir human resources, 1969. **Orgs:** Am Asn Blacks Energy, 1988-; Mich Chapter AABE, treas, 1991-; Charter Mem Jackson Serv

Club, held all offices, 1974-. **Honors/Awds:** Nat Alumni of the Year, Nat Asn for Equal Opp in Educ, 1994. *

TURNER, GEORGE R.
Podiatrist. **Personal:** Born Jun 14, 1944, Bryn Mawr, PA; married Betty; children: Gayle, Garrett & Avis. **Educ:** Lincoln Univ, AB, 1967; Temple Univ, EdM, 1969; Pa Col Podiatric Med, DPM, 1976. **Career:** Philadelphia Bd Educ, teacher, 1967-69; IBM, mkt rep, 1969-72; Pa Col Podiatric Med, 1972-76; Hardy's Orthop Appl Inc, consult; Lawndale Community Hosp, podiatrist. **Orgs:** Am Podiatry Asn; bd mem, Nat Podiatry Asn; Pa Podiatry Asn; Metro Podiatry Asn; Philadelphia County Podiatry Asn; Omega Psi Phi Fraternity. **Honors/Awds:** Morris prize, 1967; Outstanding Young Man in Am, 1976; Achievement Award, Metrop Podiatry Asn, 1976.

TURNER, GEORGE TIMOTHY
Automotive executive. **Career:** Plainfield Lincoln-Mercury-Merkur, Inc, Grand Rapids, MI, ceo, 1986-. **Business Addr:** Plainfield Lincoln-Mercury-Merkur Inc, 2424 28th St SE, PO Box 8705, Grand Rapids, MI 49518-8705, **Business Phone:** (616)363-5551.

TURNER, HARRY GLENN
Automotive executive. **Personal:** Born Jul 23, 1951, Chicago, IL; son of William and Ruby; divorced; children: John, Laura. **Educ:** UNIV IL, Sch Engineering, BME, 1976; Oakland UNIV, Graduate Sch Business ADMIN, MBA, 1979. **Career:** Chevrolet, engr, 1979-83, engineering mgr, 1983-85, exec engineering mgr, 1985-86, chief engr, export group, 1986, chief engr, body systs, 1987, large car prod planning, 1988-90, Corvette and Camaro prod planning, sporty car segment mgr, 1990-96; Gen Motors, motor sports strategic planning, 1996-, group mgr, currently. **Orgs:** BLK BOD Project. **Business Addr:** Group Manager, General Motors Corporation, GM Racing Division, P O Box 33170, Detroit, MI 48232-5170, **Business Phone:** (248)857-5000.*

TURNER, ISIAH
Government official. **Personal:** Born May 15, 1945, St Joseph, LA; son of Isiah and Leona Johnson; married Carmen Cayne, Jul 10, 1982; children: Damon Isiah & Terrie Lynn. **Educ:** Evergreen State Col, Olympia WA, 1986; Harvard Univ, 1987. **Career:** Government official (Retired); Seattle Opportunities Industrialization Ctr, Seattle WA, dir educ, 1971-79; Oper Improvement Found, Seattle WA, dir indust rels, 1980-83; Wash State Employ Security, Olympia WA, asst comnr, 1983-85, comnr, city mgr Richmond, 2004. **Orgs:** Nat Job Training Partnership; Nat Black Pub Adminr Forum; Blacks in Govt; Interstate Conf Employ Security Agencies; Northwest Conf Black Pub Offs; Wash State Economic Develop Bd. **Honors/Awds:** Adminr of the Year, Nat Job Serv Employer Comt, 1986; Job Training Prof of the Year, Nat Alliance Bus, 1988; Award of Merit, Int Asn Personnel Employ Security, 1989.

TURNER, JEAN TAYLOR
Educator. **Personal:** Born Nov 13, 1943, Philadelphia, PA; daughter of Clarence William (deceased) and Roberta Hargrove; children: Christopher Francis & Sean Michael. **Educ:** Univ Calif, Los Angeles, BSN, 1973, MN, 1975; Med Col Va, Va Commonwealth Univ, PhD, health servs orgn & res, 1987. **Career:** Fox Hills County Hosps, Los Angeles, staff develop dir, 1974-75; Va Commonwwealth Univ, Sch Nursing, Med Col Va, Dept Psychiatric Mental Health, intern, 1979-84, asst prof nursing admin, 1984-92; Nat Inst Mental Health, pre-doctoral fel, 1984-87; Univ Va, assoc prof nursing, 1992-98. **Orgs:** Am Nurses Asn, 1980-; Am Pub Health Asn, 1987-; Sigma Theta Tau Int Nursing Hon Soc, 1988-; Asn Black Nursing Fac Higher Educ, ed review bd, 1989-; Asn Health Servs Res, 1993-. **Honors/Awds:** Provost Award, Va Commonwealth Univ, 1990, Cert Recognition, Va Dept Mental Health, Mental Retardation & Substance Abuse Servs, 1991; Best Mentor Award, 1992; Johnella F Banks Award, Asn Black Nursing Fac Higher Educ, 1992. **Special Achievements:** Publs: "Participative Management: Determining Employee Readiness," Administration and Policy in Mental Health, 1991; "Measuring Adolescent Satisfaction with Nursing Care in an Ambulatory Setting," The ABNF Journal, 1991; "Recidivism and Mental Illness: The Role of Communities," Community Mental Health Journal, 1993.

TURNER, JESSE, JR.
Banker, financial manager. **Personal:** Born May 6, 1950, Memphis, TN; son of Allegra W. Turner and Jesse H. Turner; married Joyce Hays Turner; children: Jesse III, Michael, Christy, Brian. **Educ:** University of Chicago, BS, 1971; University of Chicago, MBA, 1973; Memphis School of Banking, 1979; ABA Stonier Graduate School of Banking, 1984. **Career:** Chairman of Tri-State Bank of Memphis, 1994. **Orgs:** NAACP, National Assistant Treasurer and National Board Member. **Honors/Awds:** Distinguished Service Award, NAACP Memphis Branch, 1993; Hall of Fame, Christian Brothers High School, 1995; Simply the Best CEO Award, 1996; Honorary Doctorate, Lemoyne-Owen College, 2004. *

TURNER, JESSE H
Banker, executive. **Career:** Tri-State Bank Memphis, TN, pres & chmn, currently. **Orgs:** Black Bus Asn. **Special Achievements:** Listed at #18 of 25 top financial companies, Black Enterprise, 1992, ranked #18, 1998. **Business Addr:** President, Chairman, Tri-State Bank of Memphis, 180 S Main St, Memphis, TN 38103, **Business Phone:** (901)525-0384.*

TURNER, JIM ALLEN
Football player. **Personal:** Born Nov 13, 1975, Jacksonville, FL. **Educ:** Syracuse Univ, psychol. **Career:** Football player (retired), Carolina Panthers, wide receiver, 1998-2001.

TURNER, JOHN B. See Obituaries section.

TURNER, JOHNNIE RODGERS
School administrator. **Personal:** Born Jun 23, 1940, Hughes, AR; daughter of Charlie Mae Watson Rodgers and Clayton Rodgers; married Larry; children: Larry R. **Educ:** LeMoyne-Owen Col, BS, 1962; Memphis State Univ, MEd, 1971. **Career:** Memphis City Schs, teacher, 1965-, supvr, dir, staff develop, 1986-90, co-dir, Prof Assessment Develop & Enhancement Ctr (PADEC), 1991-. **Orgs:** Pres, Memphis Br NAACP, 1977-78; pres, Memphis Alumnae Chap Delta Sigma Theta Sor,1978-80; Leadership Memphis, 1979-; ASCD, 1980-; Nat Staff Dev Coun, 1980-; MABSE, 1981-; Phi Delta Kappa, 1982-; Nat Alliance Black Sch Educrs, 1982-; bd mem, Health Educ & Housing Facility Bd Shelby County, Tenn, 1982-; pres, Memphis Alliance Black Sch Educrs (MABSE), 1988-90; exec comt mem, NAACP, currently. **Honors/Awds:** Merit Award for Outstanding Service Memphis Br, NAACP, 1975; co-ed "WhyDoesn't An Igloo Melt Inside?" handbook teachers gifted, 1978; Citizen ofthe Week, Gilliam Comt Station WLOK, 1978; Citizenship Award, MoolahTemple No 54 Shriner, 1979; Delta of the Year, 1983; Golden Apple Award,Nat Alliance Black Sch Educrs (NABSE), 1988. **Home Addr:** 752 W Levi Rd, Memphis, TN 38109, **Home Phone:** (901)785-6750. **Business Addr:** Executive Committee Member, NAACP, 588 Vance Ave, Memphis, TN 38126, **Business Phone:** (901)521-1343.

TURNER, JOSEPH ELLIS
Military leader, airplane pilot. **Personal:** Born Sep 2, 1939, Charleston, WV; son of Joseph (deceased) and Annetta Frances Malone (deceased); married Norma Jean Sims, Apr 25, 1959; children: Alan, Brian & Joseph Jr. **Educ:** WVa State Col, BS, math, 1961; Univ Southern Calif, aviation safety, 1968; Command & Gen Staff Col, grad; Indust Col Armed Forces, Air War Col; Senior Off Chem, CSE; Force Integration, CSE; Nat Orien, CSE; BG, Orien Conf. **Career:** U3a U6a 1963; CV2 1963; U8D, G, F, U21A 1968; First Officer L1011 Delta Air Lines, LAX, 1970-; USAR, maj gen, 1970-; Fixed wing OH58, 1975; UHIH, 1975; U3A 1976; rotary wing; Master Army Aviator; vice dir, dirate, Off Info Systems Command Control Commun & Computers. **Orgs:** NAI, 1969-; Airline Pilots Asn, 1970-; ROA, 1970-; Am Soc Miltary Comptrollers, 1984-; Orgn Black Airline Pilots, 1984-; Sr Army Res Commanders Asn, 1988; Armed Forces Commun Electronics Asn, 1988-; Signal Corp Regimential Asn, 1988-; Black Mil Hist Inst Am Inc, 1989-; Caribon Asn, Army Otter, currently. **Honors/Awds:** ROTC Hall of Fame, WVa State Col, 1984; General Officer Hall of Fame, Wva State UNiv, 1988; Distinguished Alumni Citation of the Year Award, NAFEO, 1989. **Military Serv:** AUS, col, 1961-70; USAR, maj gen, 1970-; Legion of Merit, 2 Bronze Stars, 3 Meritorious Service Medals, 3 Army Commendation Medals, 11 Air Medals, Army Achievement Medal, Presidential Unit Citation, Army Reserve Ribbon, Vietnam Service Medal with 8 Stars, Armed Forces Reserve Medal, Army Reserve Components Achievement Medal, Republic of Vietnam Campaign Ribbon, Master Army Aviator Badge, Republic Vietnam Gallantry Cross with Palm. **Home Addr:** 1630 Loch Lomond Trl SW, Atlanta, GA 30331.

TURNER, KIM SMITH
School administrator. **Personal:** Born Apr 11, 1959, New York, NY; daughter of Solomon Smith and Bernice Alford Smith; married Ray, Jan 19, 1980; children: Kory & Kortnie. **Educ:** Morgan State Univ, Baltimore, MD, 1977-79; State Univ Educ Opportunity Ctr, Albany, NY, Cert, 1980; Emory Univ, Atlanta, GA, 1989-. **Career:** State New York, Rochester Psychiat Ctr, Rochester, NY, 1981; US Gov Soc Security Admin, Atlanta Ga, secy, 1982-83; Am Rheumatism Asn, Atlanta, Ga, meetings coordr, 1983-86; Emory Univ Bus Sch, Atlanta, GA, dept oper coordr, 1986-90, bus mgr, 1990-94, actg assoc, dir exec progs, 1995, assoc dir fin & admin, 1995-99; dir HR, 1999-. **Orgs:** Pres, Emory Univ Employee Coun, 1987-88; Emory Univ pres's Comn Status Women, 1988-89; Nat Asn Advan Colored People, Atlanta Chap, 1988, 1990-; Emory Univ, EEOC Task Force, 1989; Emory Univ pres's Comn Status Minorities, 1989-92; co-founder, Emory's Black Educ Network, 1990; MEECA Chap Nat Coalition 100 Black Women; 1999, chair, Parking & Transp Comn, 2000-. **Honors/Awds:** Emory Profile, Emory Univ Campus Report, 1988; Promotion, People Sect, Jet Mag, 1990; Promotion Article, Chicago Tribune, 1990; Promotion Article, Atlanta Daily World, 1990; Community Service Award, Dr Martin Luther King, 2001. **Home Addr:** 2247 Jones Rd NW, Atlanta, GA 30318. **Business Addr:** Director of Human Resources, Emory University, Goizueta Business School, 1300 Clifton Rd, Atlanta, GA 30322, **Business Phone:** (404)727-6376.

TURNER, L ROBERT
President (Organization), chief executive officer. **Career:** Toyota Town, 1983-84; Butts Oldsmobile, 1984-89; Reliable Chevrolet, 1989-98; Showcase Chevrolet, 1998-2000; JK Chevrolet Isuzu, pres & chief exec officer, currently. **Honors/Awds:** Profit Enhancement Program Award, Gen Motors; Peak Performer Award, Gen Motors Minority Dealers Asn, 2006. **Special Achievements:** One of Black Enterprise Magazine's Top 100 Auto dealerships. **Business Addr:** President, Chief Executive Officer, JK Chevrolet Isuzu, 1451 Hwy 69, PO Box 1406, Nederland, TX 77627, **Business Phone:** (409)722-0443.*

TURNER, LANA
Real estate agent. **Personal:** Born Feb 8, 1950, New York, NY; daughter of Lee Arthur and Ida Ford; children: Eric M Fane. **Educ:** City Col NY, attended 1976; Sarah Lawrence Col, Bronxville, NY, attended 1989. **Career:** Men Who Cook, NY, pres, 1982; Denise Shaw Esq & Assocs, real estate agent, 1999-. **Orgs:** Adv bd, Manhattan Borough Historian Comn, 1986; chairperson, The Literary Soc, 1982; adv bd, Breast Exam Ctr, 1982. **Honors/Awds:** Author, Travelling Light, Pictures of Fathers, NY, Sarah Lawrence Col, 1988. **Home Addr:** 270 Convent Ave, New York, NY 10031. *

TURNER, LESLIE FORD
School principal. **Career:** Robert C Hatch High Sch, prin, currently. **Business Addr:** Principal, Robert C Hatch High School, PO Box 709, Uniontown, AL 36786, **Business Phone:** (334)628-4061.*

TURNER, LESLIE MARIE
Government official. **Personal:** Born Oct 2, 1957, Neptune, NJ; daughter of Robert and Jeanette. **Educ:** New York Univ, BS, 1980; George Town Univ Law Ctr, JD, 1985. **Career:** DC Ct Appeals, judicial law clerk, 1985-86; Akin Gump Strauss Hauer & Feld, sr assoc, 1986-93, counr, currently; US Dept Interior, asst secy territorial & int affairs, 1993-95, counr secy & dir off intergovenmental affairs, 1995-. **Orgs:** DC Coalition Environ Justice, 1995-; vice chair comn environ justice, Am Bar Asn, 1996-; comt pub understanding law, DC Bar, 1996-. **Home Addr:** 1333 New Hampshire Ave NW, Washington, DC 20036. **Business Phone:** (202)887-4000.

TURNER, LINDA DARNELL
Manager. **Personal:** Born Mar 29, 1947, River Rouge, MI; daughter of Beatreat and Alean Darnell; children: Akaia. **Educ:** Mercy Col Detroit, Detroit, MI, BA, 1981. **Career:** Independence Capital Formation, Detroit, MI, mgr, 1972-79; Detroit Econ Growth, Detroit MI, mgr, 1979-81; Barton Malow Corp, Southfield, MI, dir & vpres, 1998. **Orgs:** Bd mem, Major Corp Prog, NAMC, 1990-93; corp urban forum rep, Corp Urban Forum, 1983-; bd mem, Oakland Co Pvt Indust Coun, Oakland Co, 1989-; exec comt, Gen Bus Purchasing, MMBDC, 1987-; bd mem, Greater Detroit Alliance Bus, Detroit Chamber Com, 1988-, comt mem, EEO Comt, Assoc Gen Contractors, Detroit Br, 1990; exec bd, treas, ABBC, 1998-99. **Honors/Awds:** Bus Develop, Gov State Ga, 1989; Major Corp Achievement, NAMC, 1989; Minority Achiever, Detroit Young Women's Christian Asn, 1987; MBE Corp Role Model, Chrysler Corp, 1996; Cert Contract ADR, 1998; cert contract adminr, 1998. **Business Addr:** Director, Vice President, Barton Malow Corporation, 26500 American Dr, Southfield, MI 48034, **Business Phone:** (248)436-5000.*

TURNER, M ANNETTE
Administrator. **Personal:** Born Feb 17, 1953, Belhaven, NC; daughter of James W and Edna Mae Jones; married James Roderick Turner, Feb 14, 1971. **Educ:** Univ Louisville, Louisville, KY, BS, sociol, 1980, MS, 1987, BS, ed psychol, 1991. **Career:** St Denis Sch, Louisville, KY, teacher, 1975-84; Regional Youth Prog, Louisville, KY, coordr, 1984-89; Human Resource Plus, Louisville, KY, diversity consult, 1988-97; Archdiocese Louisville, Office African-Am Catholics, KY, exec dir, 1989-; Turner & Assocs, chief exec officer, 1992-. **Orgs:** Founder, Nat African Am Youth Ministry Network; chair, Nat Fedn Catholic Youth Ministry Ethnic Concern Comt, 1986-90; Grand lady, Knights Peter Claver Ladies Aux, 1989-90; exec bd mem, Nat Fed Catholic Youth Ministry, 1990-; Nat Coun Negro Women, 1990-; bd, One Church One Child, 1992-; bd trustees, Nat Black Catholic Cong, 1992; pres, Nat Asn Black Catholic Admins. **Honors/Awds:** Kujenga Vongoni, African Am Youth Leadership, 1985; Jr Horizon Youth Ministry Prog, Developed for African Am, 1988, 1991; Elizabeth Lange Award, Outstanding Leadership, Knights Peter Claver, 1989; Developed Community Rites Passage Process, 1990; Int & Nat Youth Ministry Award, Nat Fedn Catholic Youth Ministry, 1990. **Business Addr:** Executive Director, Archdiocese of Louisville, Office of Multicultural Affairs, 1200 S Shelby, PO Box 1073, Louisville, KY 40203, **Business Phone:** (502)636-0296.

TURNER, MARK ANTHONY
School administrator, accountant. **Personal:** Born Feb 23, 1951, Lynch, KY; son of William Earl and Naomi Miller Randolph; divorced; children: Andrea Kamille & Brittany E Nelson. **Educ:** Univ Ky Southeast Community Col, AA, 1972; Western KY Univ, BS, 1974. **Career:** Deloitte Haskins & Sells, sr asst, 1974-78; Bus Resource Ctr, sr consult, 1978-79; Ohio River Co, financial analyst, 1979-80; Arthur Young & Co, sr consult auditor, 1980;

Univ Col, Univ Cincinnati, asst dean, 1982-95; Mark A Turner & Assoc, sr partner, 1988-; Taxx Express, cpa, 1996-. **Orgs:** Treas, NABA Cincinnati Chap, 1980-84; founding mem, Cincinnati Chap Nat Asn Black Acct, 1980; treas, Bond Hill Community Coun, 1980-84; consult, Sickle Cell Awareness Group Greater Cincinnati, 1982-84; co treas, Cincinnatians Yates Coun, 1984-86; treas, Cent Community Ment Health Bd, 1990-91, bd trustees, 1989-91; Univ Col Minority Scholar Bd, 1988-91; pres, bd trustees, CCUB; founding treas, 4 Square Found. **Honors/Awds:** Ford Found Scholarship, 1973; Certificate of Appreciation, Junior Achievement, 1977-81; Certificate of Appreciation, Cincinnati Chamber Com Bus Resource Ctr, 1979-82; Certificate of Appreciation, The Union Experimenting Col, 1986; Distinguished Faculty-Administration, Delta Sigma Theta, 1990; Distinguished Faculty, Univ Cincinnati Evening Col, 1990; Prestigious Alumni Award, Lynch Colored Sch Lynch W Main Hist Asn. **Home Addr:** 5411 Carrahen Ct, Cincinnati, OH 45237. **Business Addr:** CPA, Taxx Express, 2248 Losantiville Ave, Cincinnati, OH 45213, **Business Phone:** (513)351-8299.

TURNER, MARVIN WENTZ
Chief financial officer, president (organization), founder (originator). **Personal:** Born Oct 17, 1959, Philadelphia, PA; son of Gilbert Jr and Frances B McAlister. **Educ:** Howard Univ, BBA, 1981; Temple Univ, attended 1986; George Wash Univ, MBA, 1988; Georgetown Univ Law Center, JD, 1998. **Career:** Prudential Ins, Fort Wash, PA, external rels adv, 1982-86; Mgt Enterprise, Philadelphia, PA, bus adv, 1984-86; CNA Ins, Wash, DC, policy analyst, 1986-88; Bell Atlantic-Network Sers Inc, Arlington, VA, mgr creative financial planning & analysis, 1988-93; Local Gov Insu Trust, chief oper officer, 1993-95; Hopkins Turner Wharton Inc, Bethesda, MD, managing dir, 1995-97; Am Intercontinental Univ, adj prof, 1998-2001; FinAssets Capital LLC, managing dir, 1995-2000; Univ Md Univ Col, adj prof, 1997-; Law Off Larson-Jackson, PC, atty, 1997-99; Baytree Investors Inc, managing dir, 1998-2000; NASD, securities arbitrator, 1999-2006; US Dept Housing & Urban Develop, field mgt officer, 1999-; Black Arrow Advisors Inc, founder & pres, 2006-. **Orgs:** Bus & Econ Develop Comn Nat Black MBA Asn, 1986-; treas, Nat Black MBA Asn, DC Chap, 1988-; Asn MBA Execs; Delta Sigma Pi Prof Bus Fraternity; Asn Individual Investors; Howard Univ Sch Bus & Public Admin Alumni Asn; Telecommunications Network Exchange; bd mem, United Way Nat Capital Area Mem & Allocations Bd; trustee, Nat Black MBA Asn Scholar Fund; life mem Wash Urban League; life mem Nat Asn Advan Colored People; bd dir, COT Hope; supvr comt mem, Wash Area Telephone Fed Credit Union; Wash Soc Investment Analysts; Financial Experts Inst; US Small Bus Admin. **Honors/Awds:** Scholarship Recipient, Nat Black MBA Asn, 1987; Elizabeth B Adams Memorial Award, 1988; Materials Management Cost Improvement Award, 1989; Scholarship Recipient, George Wash Univ. **Business Addr:** Founder, President, Black Arrow Advisors Inc, PO Box 3911, Capitol Heights, MD 20791.

TURNER, MELVIN E.
Law enforcement officer. **Personal:** Born Nov 5, 1947, Detroit, MI; son of M E and Martha; divorced; children: Naetta Williams, Tramale, Dorian. **Educ:** Madonna Col, assoc, 1976, BS, 1977; Univ Detroit, MA, 1979. **Career:** Wayne County, police officer, 1969, investr, 1973, sgt, 1976, lt, 1980, inspector, 1983, capt, 1987, police cmdr, 1988, exec dep chief, 1990, undersheriff/Chief Dep, 1991-99, expert witness law enforcement; FBI Nat Acad, 1986; BNDD Acad, 1973; Cities Hamtramck & Highland Park, Dir Pub Safety, 2000-; Sumpter Township Police, chief, 2004-07. **Orgs:** Nat Asn Chief Police; FBI Nat Acad Asn, 1986-; Int Narcotic Enforcement Officers Asn; Mich Sheriffs' Asn; bd dirs, Woodward Acad, bd pres, 2001. **Honors/Awds:** Citation for Valiant Service in the Line of Duty; Award of Special Honor; US Dept of Justice Commendation; Certificate of Award, 36th Dist Ct; Sheriff's Esteem Service Award; Distinguished Service Medal; Medal for bravery under fire. **Home Addr:** 4711 W Outer Dr, Detroit, MI 48235, **Home Phone:** (313)861-2359.

TURNER, MIKOEL
Association executive. **Personal:** Born Aug 22, 1950, New York, NY; son of Richard Turner and Enid Gordon; divorced; children: Mekell Mia. **Educ:** Cobleskill A&T Col, New York, AAS, 1971; Cornell Univ, Ithaca NY, BS, 1974; Univ Phoenix, masters degree, organizational mgt, 1999. **Career:** Marriott Corp, dept mgr, 1975-81, gen mgr, 1981-84; Fletcher Consult Serv, partner, 1982-; Bd Ed, NJ, supvr, 1984-88; Turner & Assoc, owner; New York Bd Educ, culinary arts coordr, 1990; Chelsea Catering, NJ, dept mgr, 1988; Guest Serv Healthcare Company, pres, 1994; NAT ASN Black Hospitality Prof, pres. **Orgs:** Bd mem, Union County Psychol Clinic; bd mem, Plainfield Econ Develop Corp. **Honors/Awds:** Food MGT Prof, certified; certified teacher; certified hospitality prof. *

TURNER, DR. MOSES
Educator. **Personal:** Born Mar 28, 1938, Athens, GA; son of Audly and Roberta; married Joan; children: Shaul, Lisa & Chris. **Educ:** Albany State Col, BA, 1962; Cent Wash State Col, MA, 1969; Wash State Univ, PhD, 1974; Harvard Univ, Inst Educ Mgt, 1982. **Career:** Pub sch teacher; Columbia Basin Community Col, chair & dir music prog, 1969-72; Wash State Univ, asst dean students, 1972-77; Tex Tech Univ, dean & dir stud life, 1977-79; Mich State Univ, vpres stud affairs, 1979-, prof educ admin; Peace Corps, South Africa, dir, currently. **Orgs:** Bd mem, Opera Co Mid-Michigan, Oakes Sports Prog, Boy Scouts Am; Governor's Prayer Breakfast Comn; Mich Black Caucus Found; bd mem, Himan Found Awarding Scholar Deserving High Sch Students; spokesperson, Youth Motivation Mich; bd mem, Lansing Symphony Bd Dirs; Subcomt Fed Stud Fin Assistance, Nat Asn State Univs & Land-Grant Cols; bd mem, Golden Key Nat Honor Soc; Lansing Asn Black Org; Lansing Chap Alpha Chi Boule; Ed Bd, Nat Asn Stud Personnel Administrators Inc; Nat Cong Black Fac. **Honors/Awds:** President's Award, Golden Key Nat Honor Soc, 1986. **Military Serv:** AUS, sgt. 1962-65. **Business Addr:** Professor of Educational Administration, Michigan State University, Department of Educational Administration, 426 Ericson Hall, East Lansing, MI 48824, **Business Phone:** (517)353-6676.

TURNER, PETER. See TURNER, ERVIN.

TURNER, REGINALD M
Lawyer. **Personal:** Born Feb 25, 1960, Detroit, MI; son of Reginald M Sr and Anne L; married Marcia Holland Turner, Jun 10, 1989. **Educ:** Wayne State Univ, BS, 1982; Univ Mich, Law Sch, JD, 1987. **Career:** Mich Supreme Ct, law clerk to Justice Dennis Archer, 1987-89; Sachs, Waldman, O'Hare, partner, 1989-2000; Detroit Mayors Dennis Archer & Kwame Kilpatrick, bd educ, 2002-03; Clark Hill PLC, partner, exec comt, 2000-; Comerica Inc, dir. **Orgs:** Mich Employment Adv Coun, Am Arbitration Asn; mem house del, Am Bar Asn; Labor & Employment Sect; life fel, Am Bar Found; bd dir, Am Soc Employers; Blue Ribbon Comn Mich Gaming; chmn, City Detroit Bd Ethics; City Detroit Brownfield Redevelopment Adv Comt; dir, Comerica Inc; Detroit Bd Educ; vchmn, Detroit Inst Arts; mem labor & employment sect, Detroit Metrop Bar Asn; vchmn, Detroit Police Found; Fed Mediation & Conciliation Serv; bd md, Hudson-Webber Found; chmn, United Way Southeastern Mich; secy, Wayne County Econ Develop Corp; Wayne County Aerotropolis Task Force; bd mem, Mich State Bd Educ; pres, Nat Bar Asn; mem Labor & Employment Sect; past pres, State Bar Mich; chmn, Mem Labor & Employment Sect United Way Southeastern Mich; State Bar Mich, comnr, 1995-, vpres, 2000-01, pres-elect, 2001-02, pres, 2002-03; bd govrs exec comm, Nat Bar Asn, 1995-, past gen coun, 1999-; past pres, Wolverine Bar Asn, 1987-; past pres, Barristers Detroit Metro Bar Asn, 1987-97; Detroit Bd Educ, 2000-; Governor John Engler's Blue Ribbon Comn Mich Gaming & City Detroit Brownfield Redevelopment Adv Comt; vichmn, Detroit Inst Arts; vchmn, Detroit Police Found. **Honors/Awds:** White House Fellow, 1996-97; Mich State Bar Found Fellow, 1995; Outstanding Young Lawyer, State Bar Mich, 1995; Am Bar Fed Fellow, 2002-; Best Lawyers of America, 2003-; Super Lawyer, 2005-; Lawyer of the Year, Michigan Lawyers Weekly, 2005. **Business Addr:** Attorney, Clark Hill PLC, 500 Woodward Ave Suite 3500, Detroit, MI 48226-3435, **Business Phone:** (313)965-8318.

TURNER, RICHARD M
School administrator, educator. **Personal:** Born in Charleston, SC; married Dolores Walker; children: 2. **Educ:** Fisk Univ, BA, 1956; Ind Univ-Bloomington, ME, 1961, DME, 1972. **Career:** South Cent Community Col, pres, 1979-85; Lane Community Col, pres, 1985-88; Nashville State Tech Inst, pres, 1988-91; Fisk Univ, assoc prof music, Dept Music, chmn, Fisk Jubilee Singers, dir; Wayne Co Community Col Northwest Campus, dean; Wayne Co Community Col, interim pres, 1994-95; Baltimore City Community Col, Dean Student Activities, 1971-74, Dean Fac & Provost, 1974-79, interim pres, 2004-06, prof emer, 2006-. **Orgs:** Am Asn Community Cols; Int Educ Comn Am Coun Educ; bd trustees, Nat Comn Coop Educ; bd mem, Nat Coun Black Am Affairs; United Way; Am Red Cross; Nat Conf Christians & Jews; Am Asn Univ Profs, 1963-, vpres, Ala conference, 1967-68; bd Trustees, Yale-New Haven Hosp, 1984-85; bd dirs, League Innovation Community Col, 1985-88; pres, Turner Assocs & Mentors Inc, 1996-2004; Am Coun Edu, 1979-2006. **Honors/Awds:** hon doc Humane Letters, Fisk Univ, 1980; Distinguished Alumnus Award, Fisk Univ, 1984. Spirit of Detroit Award, Detroit City Coun, 1995. **Military Serv:** AUS, 1957-63. **Business Addr:** Professor Emeritus, Baltimore City Community College, 2901 Liberty Heights Ave, Baltimore, MD 21215, **Business Phone:** (410)462-8325.

TURNER, ROBERT, JR.
Football coach. **Personal:** Born May 6, 1949, Midway, AL; son of Robert Turner Sr and Julia Ann; married Kimberly Jean; children: Nacole, Krishana & Kiaana. **Educ:** Ind State Univ, Terre Haute, IN, BS, 1972, MS, 1976. **Career:** Kokomo Haworth High Sch, Kokomo, IN, asst football/basketball coach, admin asst, 1972-75; Ind State Univ, spec team coordr & asst football coach, 1975-83; Fresno State Univ, asst football coach, 1983-89; Ohio State Univ, asst football coach, 1989-90; Purdue Univ, asst head football coach & offensive coordr, 1990-. **Orgs:** Am Football Coaches Asn; Black Coaches Asn; Nat Asn Advan Colored People; Ind State Univ Alumni Asn; Kappa Alpha Psi Fraternity; Fel Christian Athletes.

TURNER, ROBERT LLOYD
Legislator, state government official. **Personal:** Born Sep 14, 1947, Columbus, MS; son of Roosevelt and Beatrice; married Gloria Harrell; children: Robert, Roosevelt & Ryan. **Educ:** Univ Wisc, Parkside, BS. **Career:** Military personnel (rertired), Publ, personnel mgr, restaurant owner; Wisc State Assembly, state rep, 1991-. **Orgs:** Nat Asn Advan Colored People; Urban League; Democratic Party; Am Legion; South Gate Lodge 6 Prince Hall; alderman, Racine City Coun, 1976-2004; chmn, City Racine Finance Comt, 1987-2003; chmn, State Wisc Elections Bd, 1990; Community Develop Comt; chmn, Economic Develop Comt, City Racine; Assembly Comt Judiciary; Assembly Comt Criminal Justice & Homeland Security; Assembly Comt on Veterans Affairs; Assembly Comt on Rules; Assembly Comt on Orgn; State Wisc Bldg Comn, 1991-99; Gov Task Force on Fed Clean Air Act Implementation, 1993-94; Democratic Caucus, chmn, 2002, 2004. **Honors/Awds:** 33 Degree Mason, 1999. **Military Serv:** USAF, sgt, 1967-70; Commendation Medal for Meritorious Service Vietnam. **Home Addr:** 36 McKinley Ave, Racine, WI 53404. **Business Addr:** State Representative, Legislator, Wisconsin State Assembly, Rm 212 N State Capitol, PO Box 8953, Madison, WI 53708-8953, **Business Phone:** (608)266-0731.

TURNER, SHARON V
Government official. **Personal:** Born Jul 8, 1945, Kansas City, MO; daughter of O E Douglass and Eunice Weaver Douglass Shellner; divorced; children: Sheri Lynette Turner-Duff & Paul Eugene Jr. **Educ:** Park Col, Kans City, MO, BS, Soc AC psychol, 1993; Baker Univ, MS, mgt, Overland Park, KS, 1994. **Career:** Telecommunications mgr, 1966-93; Kans City Election Bd, MO, dir, 1994-. **Orgs:** Secy, Leon Jordan Scholar fund, 1984-95; trustee, Urban League, 1985-89; trustee, Rehab Loan Corp, 1987-89; chair, Scholar Comn, Southern Christian Leadership Conf, 1988-95; gen telethon chair, United Negro Col Fund, 1989; vpres, Black Achievers Soc, 1989-90; vpres, Black Chamber Com, 1989-90; pres, Urban League top Notch Team, 1991-93; bd dir, Kans City Visitors & Conv Bur, 1991-94; gala co-chair, Kans City Friends Alvin Ailey, 1992; first vpres, SCLC, 1992-95; fund develop chair, Jackson County Links, Inc, 1994-; The Elections Ctr, 1995-; Int Asn Clerks Recorders; Exec comt NCP, 2001-. **Honors/Awds:** Boss of the Year, Galaxy II Chapter ABWA, 1983; Black Achiever in Industry, 1983; Volunteer Service Award, YMCA, 1984; Star Panelist, UNCF, 1985; Special Recognition, Black Achiever in Industry, 1987; Outstanding Business Woman of the Year, Nat Asn Negro Bus & Prof Women, 1987; Presidents Award, Black Chamber Com, 1988; Juneteenth Women of Year, Black Archives, 1989; Difference Maker, Urban League, 1989; The Blunt Commission Election Reform, 2001. **Special Achievements:** Kansas City's 100 Most Influential Black Women, Kansas City Globe Newspaper, 1984; Kansas City Globe's 100 Most Influential, 1993. **Business Addr:** Director, Kansas City Election Board, 1828 Walnut Suite 300, Kansas City, MO 64108, **Business Phone:** (816)842-4820.

TURNER, SHIRLEY
Educator. **Personal:** Born Mar 22, 1936, South Bend, IN; divorced; children: Dawn, Kimberly & Steven. **Educ:** Western Mich Univ, BS, 1972, MA, 1977. **Career:** Fiskal Univ, dean studs, dir career planning & placement; Western Mich Univ, Placement Serv, asst dir; Western Mich Univ, Para Sch Learning Ctr. **Orgs:** Dir Educ, Urban Leg S Bend St Joseph County; Kalamazoo Pub Lib pub sch; bd dir, Planned Parenthood Asn; bd, Young Men's Christian Asn; Young Men's Christian Asn Community Outreach Adv; Youth Serv Syst Adv Bd; Cont Educ Young Women Adv Bd; consult, Upward Boun Univ Notre Dame; Planned Parenthood Teen Clinics; Delta Sigma Theta Serv Sorority; Dulcet Club Kalamazoo; Mich Asn N White Concerns; Kalamazoo Personnel Asn; Midwest Cool Placement Asn. **Honors/Awds:** Teach Award, Laubaugh Lit Inst; Award, Mich Nat All Bus Career Guid Inst; Award of Excellence, Western Mich Univ; Certificate of Academic Appreciation; Certificate of Career Exploration Excel. **Special Achievements:** Produced, directed video tape, demo prof interview tech. **Business Addr:** Director of Career Placement, Rider College, 2083 Lawrenceville, Lawrenceville, NJ 08648-3099.

TURNER, TERESA ANN
School administrator. **Personal:** Born Aug 17, 1971, Columbus, MS; daughter of William and Bernice. **Educ:** Jackson State Univ, BS, 1993, MST, 1995; Univ MS, Eds; Univ MS. **Career:** Jackson Pub Schs, teacher, 1993-96; Tupelo Pub Schs, asst princ, 1996-2003; Lawndale Elem Sch, princ, 2003-06. **Orgs:** MS Sci Teachers Asn, 1993-95; Nat Asn Secondary Sch Principals, 1998-; Lee County Big Brother Big Sister, 1998-; Phi Delta Kappa, 2000; Kappa Delta Pi; Delta Sigma Theta. **Honors/Awds:** graduated cum laude, Jackson State Univ, 1993, graduate magna cum laude, 1995; LD Hancock Award. **Special Achievements:** Wrote "Are Young Black Americans Becoming Too Complacent to Survive the 21st Century?" Legend Dec 1998; Consultant for Mississippi Sea Grant Program's Lab Manual, 1995; nominated Assistant Principal of the Year, NASSP, 1998-99. **Home Addr:** 1107 Nixon Dr, Tupelo, MS 38801, **Home Phone:** (601)842-3041.

TURNER, TINA
Singer. **Personal:** Born Nov 26, 1939, Nutbush, TN; daughter of Floyd Richard and Zelma; married Ike, Jan 1, 1962 (divorced 1978); children: Craig, Ike Jr, Michael & Ronald. **Career:** Ike & Tina Turner Revue, 1960-76; Solo Albums: Private Dancer, 1984,

Break Every Rule, 1986; Tina Live in Europe, 1988; Foreign Affair, 1989; Look Mein the Heart, 1990; What's Love Got to Do With It", 1993; Wildest Dreams, 1996; Good Hearted Woman, 1998; Twenty Four Seven, 1999; Back to Back, 2003; Country My Way, 2003; All the Best, 2004; Tina Turner Sings Country, 2005; Country in My Soul, 2005; All the Best: The Hits, 2005; Film appearances: Mad Max Beyond Thunder dome, 1985: Last Action Hero, 1993; Brother Bear, 2003; All the Invisible C, 2005; "80s", 2005; All the Invisible Children, 2005; Flushed Away, 2006; "Atrapats pel cap d'any", 2007; "Memories de la tele", 2008. **Honors/Awds:** Grammy Award for Record Of The Year, 1984; Grammy Award for Pop Female Vocal, 1984; Grammy Award for Rock Female Vocal, 1984; Grammy Award for Rock Female Vocal, 1985; Grammy Award for Rock Female Vocal, 1986; Grammy Award for Rock Female Vocal, 1988; 2 American Music Awards; Triple Platinum Album "Private Dancer"; Gold Single "What's Love Got To Do With It?"; Silver Disk Award "Let's Stay Together"; Honoree, ABAA Music Award, 1985; Honored with a star on the Hollywood Walk of Fame; MTV Video Award, 2005; Kennedy Center Honors, 2005. **Special Achievements:** Citation, Ms Magazine, 1984; author, I, Tina, My Life Story, 1986; Subject of the movie, What's Love Got to Do With It", 1993; Ranked 2 on VH1's Greatest Women of Rock N Roll; Ranked 6 on VH-1's 100 Sexiest Artists, 2002.

TURNER, TOM
Labor activist. **Personal:** Born Oct 31, 1926, River Rouge, MI. **Educ:** Tuskegee Inst; Montieth Col, Wayne State Univ, attended. **Career:** Wayne County AFL-CIO, admin asst to pres, 1964, vpres, 1967, pres, 1968; Metropolitan Detroit AFL-CIO, Pres, 1969-88; Detroit Nat Asn Advan Colored People, pres, 1970-72; Mich AFL-CIO, exec secy, secy & treas, currently; Great Lakes Steel, shipping checker; United Steelworkers Am, Great Lakes Steel, steward. **Orgs:** Pres, Detroit Nat Asn Advan Colored People, 1968-70; Boy Scouts & Boys, Girls Clubs Metropolitan Detroit; bd mem, Detroit Economic Growth Corp, currently. **Honors/Awds:** Walter Bergman Human Rights Award, 1989; Distinguished Warrior, Detroit Urban League, 2000; Michigan Distinguished Citizen Award; United Black Trade Unionist Citizen Award; Detroit Br Nat Asn Advan Colored People Freedom Fund Dinner Special Award; Boys Clubs Metropolitan Detroit Recognition Award. **Special Achievements:** First African American to head a labor council in the United States. **Military Serv:** AUS, World War II; Korean War; prisoner of war for six months; received the Purple Heart. **Business Phone:** (313)894-6348.*

TURNER, VIVIAN LOVE
Executive, manager, president (organization). **Personal:** Born May 25, 1947, Concord, NC; daughter of F Haywood Love and Othella Spears Love; married William H, Sep 6, 1969; children: Kisha, Jomo & Hodari. **Educ:** Livingstone Col, Salisbury, NC, BS, math, 1968; Univ Notre Dame, S Bend, IN, MA, educ, 1971. **Career:** Fisk Univ, Nashville, TN, programmer & analyst, 1971-73; Univ Md, Princess Anne, MD, lectr, 1974-77; Digital Equip Corp, Lanham, MD, sr educ specialist, 1977-79; Lexington Community Col, Lexington, KY, assoc prof, data processing tech, 1980-85; R J Reynolds Tobacco Co, Winston-Salem, NC, programmer & analyst II, 1985-90, mgr community prog dir contrib. & comm affairs, Currently. **Orgs:** Alpha Kappa Alpha Sorority, 1966-; Ky Acad Comput Users Group, 1980-85; stud chap sponsor, Data Processing Mgt Asn, 1981-85; dir Christian educ, Emmanuel Baptist Church, 1989-; Links, 1996-; bd mem, Winston Lake YMCA, 1990-91; bd mem, Forsyth County United Way, 1993-; bd, Winston-Salem State Univ, 1994-; life mem, Nat Asn Advan Colored People; pres, RJ Reynolds Found, 1998-. **Honors/Awds:** United Negro CollegeFund Scholarship, Livingstone Col, 1964-68; Alpha Kappa Mu Honor Society, 1967; Danforth Assoc, 1976-85; Volunteer of Year, Winston Lake YMCA, 1994; Winston-Salem Chronicle Woman of the Year, 1995; Distinguished Service Award, Seed Co 1997. **Business Addr:** Director Contributions and Community Affairs, RJ Reynolds Tobacco Co, PO Box 2959, Winston-Salem, NC 27102, **Business Phone:** (336)741-0049.

TURNER, W BURGHARDT
Educator. **Personal:** Born Jul 30, 1915, Jamaica, NY; son of Frank M Sr and Frosty Duncan; married Joyce Moore; children: Mitchell, Sylvia & Richard. **Educ:** Ky State Col, AB; Columbia Univ, MA. **Career:** New York City, Bay Shore, Patchogue, Long Island, teacher; Long Island Univ Southampton Col, assoc prof hist, 1965-68; State Univ New York, Stony Brook, asst prof hist, 1968-79, prof emer, 1979-. **Orgs:** Dir, Nat Ed Asn Proj Civil Rights, 1965; asst dir, Inst School Integration Southampton Col, 1966; pres, Nat Asn Advan Colored People; chmn, Suffolk County Human Rights Comm; vpres, United Fund; dir, Legal Aid Soc Suffolk County; chmn, Equal Opportunity Employment Comm SUNY Stony Brook; chmn, Curric Comm Continuing Ed; chmn & bd dirs, Econ Opportunity Coun Suffolk, 1986-87. **Honors/Awds:** Man of the Year, Men's Club Temple Beth-El, 1962; Man of the Year, Eastern Long Island Asn Negro Bus & Prof Women, 1963; Outstanding Service Award, Nat Conf Christian & Jews, 1972; W. Burghardt Turner Fellowship Prog, State Univ New York, Stony Brook. **Special Achievements:** Co-author of Caribbean Militant in Harlem, Univ of Indiana Press, Black American Writers, St Martins Press NY, introductions to The Name Negro: Its Origins and Evil Use, The Negro by WEB DuBois, Black Classic Press, Baltimore MA. **Military Serv:** AUS, 92nd Infantry Div, 1942-45. **Business Addr:** Professor Emeritus, State University of New York, PO Box 1554, Stony Brook, NY 11790, **Business Phone:** (631)420-1530.

TURNER, DR. WILLIAM H.
Educator. **Personal:** Born in Lynch, KY; married Vivian Love; children: Kisha, Jomo & Hodari. **Educ:** Univ Ky, BS, sociol, 1968, MS, sociol, 1971; Notre Dame Univ, PhD, sociol & anthropol, 1974. **Career:** Res Assoc to Alex Haley, 1971-91; Kentucky State Univ, Col Arts & Sci, fac, dean, 1983-84; Winston-Salem State Univ, fac, 1984-2002.; Berea Col, distinguished vis prof black & appalachian studies, 1988-89, interim pres, 2003-04; Brandeis Univ, vis res prof, 1990-91; freelance journalist/writer, currently; Fisk Univ, fac; Howard Univ, fac; Nat Endowment Humanities Chair, Appalachian Studies Berea Col, 2007-. **Orgs:** Trotter Group.

TURNER, DR. WILLIAM HOBERT
Educator, consultant. **Personal:** Born Jul 20, 1946, Lynch, KY; married Vivian Love; children: Kisha, William K & Hodari. **Educ:** Southeast Community Col, UK, grad, 1966; Univ Ky, BS, sociol, 1968; Univ Notre Dame, MS, sociol, 1971, PhD, sociol & anthrop, 1974. **Career:** Howard Univ, sr res fel, 1977-79; Univ Ky, asst prof sociol, 1979-83; Nat Res Coun, Ford Found fel, 1983; Ky State Univ, dean arts & sci, 1983-84, interim pres, 2003-04, vpres univ engagement & assoc provost multicultural & acad affairs, currently; Winston Salem State Univ, chmn social sci, 1985; Berea Col, distinguished vis prof Black & Appalachian studies, 1988-89; Brandeis Univ, vis res prof, 1990-91; B&C Int Inc, sr vpres; Turner & Assoc, pres, currently; Univ Pa, fel; George Washington Univ, fel; Duke Univ, fel. **Orgs:** Historian/archivist, Eastern Ky Social/Heritage Soc, 1977-; consult, USAID, 1986; comnr, Comn Relig Appalachia, 1986-; ed/publ, EKSC; Black Mountain Improvement Asn, 1988; Southern Regional Coun; Appalachian African Am Community Develop Ctr; Phi Beta Sigma Fraternity; trustee mem, Prince Hall Masons, Lees-McRae Col Bd; Trotter Group, Harvard Univ. **Honors/Awds:** Favorite Teacher Honor, Univ Md, Winston Salem State Univ & Berea Col; Mountain Spirit Award, 1994; Honored by numerous organizations for his leadership and public service. **Special Achievements:** Published essays and articles on subjects ranging from civil rights issues to the attitudes of college students. **Home Addr:** 5821 Brookway Dr, Winston-Salem, NC 27105, **Home Phone:** (336)744-5611. **Business Addr:** Vice president, Associate provost for Multicultural and Academic Affairs, University of Kentucky, University Engagement, 529 Patterson Off Tower, Lexington, KY 40506-0027, **Business Phone:** (859)257-3381.

TURNER, WILLIE
Educator. **Personal:** Born Feb 1, 1935; married Porter; children: Vincent, Austin, Nicole & Dina. **Educ:** MD St Col, BS, 1957; OH St Univ, MSc, 1959; PhD, virol, 1961. **Career:** MD State Col, lab asst, 1954-57; MD State Col, res asst, 1957; MD St Col, grad asst, 1957-59; OH St Univ, NIH, pre doctoral fel, 1959-61; Naval Med Res Inst, NIH postdoctoral fel, 1961-62; Meharry Med Col, instr microbial, 1962-63; TN St A&I Univ, lectr, 1962; Meharry Med Col, asst prof microbial, 1963-66; Nat Cancer Inst, NCI staff fel, 1966-69; Nat Cancer Inst, NCI sr staff fel, 1969-70, head microbial, 1970-71; Bowie State Col, 1969; Howard Univ, prof & chmn microbiol dept, 1971-. **Orgs:** Sigma Xi; Am Soc Microbiol; AAAS; NY Acad Sci; Am Asn Cancer Res; Tissue Culture asn; Soc Experimental Biol & Med; Am Asn Immunologists; chmn, Am Asn Med Sch; chmn, Am Asn Dent Sch. **Honors/Awds:** Recipient numerous NIH Research Grants; NIH ICC Exchange Fellow to Paris, 1971; NCI Cancer Center Core Grant, 1973. **Business Addr:** Professor, Howard University, College of Medicine, 520 W St NW, Washington, DC 20059, **Business Phone:** (202)806-6270.

TURNER, WINSTON E.
Educator. **Personal:** Born Aug 23, 1921, Washington, DC; son of Frederick Finley and Mary Montague; married Helen Smith; children: Lisa & Valerie. **Educ:** Miner Teachers Col, BS, 1947; NY Univ, MA, 1949; St Col Educ Plattsburgh, NY; DC Teachers Col; Georgetown Univ; Univ Bridgeport Ct. **Career:** Educator (retired); DC Pub Sch, teacher, 1947-54; Miner Teachers Col, monroe lab sch, 1954-57; DC Teachers Col, truesdell lab sch, asst prof educ, 1957-59; HD Cooke Elem Sch, Wash, DC, prin, 1959-69; River Terrace Elem Sch, Wash, DC, prin, 1976. **Orgs:** Life mem, Nat Educ Asn; Phi Delta Kappa; pres, Nat Asn Elem Sch Prins, 1974-75; DC Elem Sch Prin Asn; Asn Study Negro Life Hist; pres, vpres, treas; bd dirs SE Neighborhood House; bd Columbia Heights Boys Club; Queens Chapel Civic Asn; life mem, NAACP; Omega Psi Phi Frat; Pigskin Club Prins Asn, Wash, DC; exec comt coun officers, DC Pub Schs; Examining Panels Prin & Asst Prins, DC Pub Schs; Mt Horeb Bapt Ch. **Honors/Awds:** Guest lecture, Howard Univ, 1974; Outstanding Principal Award, DC Elem Sch Prin Asn, 1974; Outstanding Ret Teacher Award, Jr Citizens Corps 1978; Outstanding Public Service: Mayor Baltimore Md, Afro-Am Newspaper, Central Summerfield United Meth Church, 1980; Man of the year, New Bethel Baptist Church, 1981; publications: The Black Principal Bicentennial, Principal, 1976; Principals Pressure Cooker, Principal, 1977; Expanding Our Horizons through Global Educ, Principal, 1980. **Military Serv:** AUS, 1st sgt, 1942-46. *

TURNER, YVONNE WILLIAMS
Community activist, counselor. **Personal:** Born Apr 5, 1927, Birmingham, AL; daughter of John Harvey and Leitha W (deceased); married James L Turner Sr, Jun 9, 1945; children: Philandus C, Roderick G, Keith H, Leitha B, Stanley M. **Educ:** Booker T Washington Junior Col Bus, Birmingham, AL, dipl 1952; Rosetta Reifer's Sch Modeling, NY, cert, 1954; Anna Watson's Sch Millinery Designing, 1968; Dale Carnegie Sch, Birmingham, AL, cert, 1960; 100 or more workshops all descriptions. **Career:** Community activist (retired). Booker T Washington Insurance Co, Birmingham, AL, clerk, 1946-64; Clyde Kirby Insurance Agency, Birmingham, AL, secy, 1965-66; Dept Housing & Urban Devel, Birmingham, AL, clerk typist, 1966-77, comput technician, 1977-82, community resources specialist, 1982-86, prog asst single family div loan mgt, 1986-87; Birmingham Housing Authority, Birmingham, AL, housing counselor, 1987-90. **Orgs:** Ala Christian Movement Human Rights & Southern Christian Leadership Conf, 1956-; fund raiser, United Negro Col Fund, 1965-; Birmingham Design Review Comt, Birmingham, AL, 1979-85; mem, 1985-, Birmingham Arts Comn, Birmingham, AL; Jefferson-Blount-St Clair Ment Health/Ment Retardation Authority Bd, 1989-91; Birmingham's Image Comt, 1990-91; assoc mem, Ala State Univ Alumni, 1990-; Band Mother, Ala State Univ, 1979-; pres or bus mgr, Wilkerson Elem & A H Parker High Band Boosters, 1975-89; Red Cross Minority Involvement Comt, 1989-91; chartered mem, Magic City Chap Links Inc, 1993; served eight years as Ala Election Law Comnr; presently, Dep Registr. **Honors/Awds:** Cert recognition in field of bus, Booker T Washington Jr Col Bus Alumni Asn, 1978; plaque for 25 years of outstanding serv, Nat Southern Christian Leadership Conf, 1982; alumni merit award, Booker T Washington Jr Col Bus, 1984; named in House of Rep Resolution 125, 1988; HR & auth column "Socially Speaking," Birmingham Times, 1988-92; Honored by Gov Guy Hunt, Arts, 1989; Iota Phi Lambda Sorority, 1981; Alpha Phi Chi Sorority, 1985; Zeta Phi Beta Sorority, Women of the Year, 1990; Civil Rights Honoree during 1991 Martin Luther King Jr Birthday Celebration, Omisson Lambda Chpt; Alpha Phi Alpha Fraternity Inc; HUD's Faithful Serv US Government Award, 1987; Ladies of Distinction, Sixth Ave Bapt Church, 1992; SCLS Women, Spec Award, 1991; Channel 42, WBMG/TV Jefferson Award, Bronze Medal, Documentation on Civil Rights, 1992; United to Serve Am Diamond Award, 1992; WENN 107-WAGG 1320 and Anheuser's Citizen of the Week, 1991; 21st Century Human Rights Movement, Appreciation for Dedicated Services to Mankind, 1991; Cert Appreciation, Ala State Univ, Connection Day Comt, 1992; Curioso Club's Rose Award, 1992; Cert of Appreciation, Birmingham City Coun, Dist 4; Meritorious Serv Award, United Negro Col Fund Inc, 1993; Birmingham Comm Schs Appreciation, 1991-92; Honored for 14 years, Faithful and Dedicated Servs, Ala State Univ Marching Band of Montgomery AL, 1994; Community Serv Award, Birmingham Baptist Col, Black Catholic Ministries, Nat Islam; Invisible Giants of the Voting Rights Movement, Honored in Selma, Commendation of the Voting Rights March & Bloody Sunday, March 4, 1995; Plaque, Nat Asn Advan Colored People, Outstanding African Am, 1996; Acad Fine Arts Inc, Citizen Arts Award, 1996. **Special Achievements:** Lectured at the Birmingham Civil Rights Institute, "Yesterdays Voices of African-American Women of the Movement," 1996; Spoke at the Historic 16th Street Baptist Church where four little girls were killed, during Dr Martin Luther King's Birthday Celebration, 1997. **Home Addr:** 504 10th St, Birmingham, AL 35214. *

TURNER BROWN, SHADEY K
Advocate. **Career:** Judge Sheila Tillerson-Adams Circuit Ct, Prince George's Co, MD, judicial law clerk; Fannie Mae, Off Corp Justice, legal coun, currently. **Honors/Awds:** Young leaders of the Future Award, EBONY Mag, 2002-03. **Business Addr:** Legal Counsel, Fannie Mae, Office of Corporate Justice, 3900 Wis Ave NW, Washington, DC 20016, **Business Phone:** (202)752-7000.

TURNER-FORTE, DIANA
Educator, choreographer, dancer. **Personal:** Born Aug 24, 1951, Columbus, OH; daughter of Ethel S Turner and Everhart S Turner Sr; married Kenneth T, Aug 1993. **Educ:** Capital Univ, BA, 1985; Antioch Univ, MA, 1991. **Career:** Des Moines Ballet Co, dancer, soloist, 1980-81; Ohio Arts Coun, minority arts asst, 1981-83; Baltimore Sch Arts, fac, 1983-85; Ballet Met, fac, 1986-; Antioch Univ, adj fac, 1990-; Greater Columbus Arts Coun, founder & artistic dir, 1991-. **Orgs:** Dance advisory panelist, State Arts Coun, 1984-86; arts advisory panel chair, Franklin County Edu Coun, 1991; adv bd, Ohio Dance, 1991; fundraising comt, Third Ave Performing Space, 1992; bd trustees, WOSU Radio, 1992. **Business Addr:** Founder, Artistic Director, Greater Columbus Arts Council, 282 Gatewood Ave, Southern Pines, NC 28387-5908, **Business Phone:** (910)652-2787.

TURNER-GIVENS, ELLA MAE
Educator, consultant, organist. **Personal:** Born Jun 5, 1927, Los Angeles, CA; daughter of Ezekiel Moore and Ruth Dean; married Walter; children: Edward Samuel Turner. **Educ:** Univ Southern Calif, BMus, 1957; St Calif, Dept Educ, life diploma, spec second-

ary teaching credent music, 1965; Univ Calif, Los Angeles, Grad Sch, 1965, 1966, 1968; Calif Dept Educ, life diploma, stand secondary teaching credent Eng, 1968. **Career:** Foshay Jr High Sch, teacher, 1957-58; Markham Jr High Sch, teacher, 1958-66; Manual Arts High Sch, teacher summer, 1962; Markham Jr High SchSummer Opportunity Ctr Prog, teacher, 1965; Girls Social Adjust Sch, teacher, 1966-67; Los Angeles High Sch, teacher, 1967-71; Los Angeles Unified Sch Dist, teacher, 1971-. **Orgs:** Chmn Nat Adv Coun, Environ Educ; HEW; adv coun, HUD; Urban Studies Fel Prog, Textbook Adoption Comm Los Angeles Unified Sch Dist; adjudicator Southern Calif Vocal Asn; host, chmn Southern Calif Vocal Asn Choral Festivals; pres, Secondary Music Teacher Asn; chmn, bd dir, Do Re Me Child Develop Ctr; NEA, Calif Teacher Asn; Los Angeles Teacher Asn; Music Educ Nat Conf Life; Los Angeles County Music Educ Asn; Am Choral Dir Asn; Southern Calif Vocal Asn; Adv Health Coun; St Dept Health; Child Develop Adv Bd; Gen St Dept Health, consult; Calif St Dept Health,St Calif Personnel Bd, W Interstate Commn Higher Educ, Calif WorkIncentive Plan Prog, Neighborhood Adult Participation Proj, Delinquency Prev Ctr; Atty Gen, Vol Adv Coun, Neumeyer Found; rep St Control Comm; appointee Calif Gov Comm Employment Handicapped; St wide Planning Proj Vocat Rehab, Adv Comm Voc Rehab; sec adv Comm, Urban Affairs Inst; Dist Atty Adv Coun; dist Atty Legis Coun. **Honors/Awds:** Recipient 10th Dist PTA 4 year scholarship; Delta Sigma Theta Sor Scholar;E Star Scholarship Award, twice; Women's Polit Study Club Scholarship. **Special Achievements:** First black woman in US history to chair a National Advisory Council. **Home Addr:** 2158 W 82nd St, Los Angeles, CA 90047.

TURNIPSEED, CARL WENDELL
Banker. **Personal:** Born Dec 21, 1947, Baltimore, MD; son of Willis and Alice Poyner; married Joyce Hill, Jun 6, 1970; children: Danielle. **Educ:** Morgan State Col, BS, 1969; NY Univ Grad Sch Bus, MBA, 1974. **Career:** Fed Res Bank NY, acct, govt bonds, check proc, elect funds transfers, personnel, foreign rels, vp, pres, personnel function, Buffalo Branch, mgr, Bus Develop Office, head, 1969-; Fed Res Bank NY, exec vpres, financial serv, currently. **Orgs:** Union Baptist Church, 1980-; Nat Asn Advan Colored People, 1982-; Asn MBA Execs, 1982-; Urban Bankers Asn, 1983-; mem, Black MBA Asn 1983-; MBA Exec; 16th SEANZA Cent Banking Prog, 1986; Keeper Exchequer Brooklyn Long Island Alumni Kappa Alpha Psi Fraternity, 1988-; vis prof, Nat Urban League BEEP; Kappa Alpha Psi Fraternity; founding mem, Classroom Inc; bd chair, INROADS/Western NY; bd mem, United Way Buffalo & Erie County & Niagara Inst Trade Coun; Sigma Pi Phi Fraternity; Morgan State Univ Alumni Asn; Urban Bankers Coalition. **Honors/Awds:** Martin Luther King Jr Alumni Assoc NY Univ Award, 1978; President's Award, Excellence Fed Res Bank NY, 1987; Banker of the Year, Urban Bankers Coalition, 1992; Executive of the Year, Prof Secretaries Int, 1998. **Military Serv:** AUS, First lt 2 yrs. **Business Addr:** Executive Vice President, Federal Reserve Bank New York, 33 Liberty St, New York, NY 10045, **Business Phone:** (212)720-5000.

TURNLEY, RICHARD DICK, JR.
Banker, chief executive officer. **Personal:** Born Nov 15, 1933, Plaquemine, LA; son of Dorothy Banks; married Joyce Huntsberry; children: Tamera, Sharon & Richard. **Educ:** Southern Univ, BS, 1955, JD, 1972; Univ Wis, attended 1978. **Career:** State La, state rep, 1972-84; Southern Teachers & Parents Fed Credit Union, treas & mgr, chief exec officer, 1959-. **Orgs:** Free & Accepted Masons; Capitol City Golf Asn; Louis Sewell Boys Scouts; Southern Univ Alumni Asn; co-founder, La Legis Black Caucus; pres, Southern Univ Syst Found. **Honors/Awds:** Outstanding Contribution in Minority Bus Develop; Outstanding Service Award, La Justice Peace & Constables Asn; Pete Creer Lifetime Achievement Award, African Am Credit Union Coalition, 2008. **Military Serv:** AUS, 1955-61. **Business Addr:** Chief Executive Officer, Southern Teachers & Parents Fed Credit Union, 728 Harding Blvd, Baton Rouge, LA 70807, **Business Phone:** (225)775-8597.

TURNQUEST, SANDRA CLOSE
Executive. **Personal:** Born Jul 19, 1954, Bainbridge, GA; daughter of Frank and Daisy; divorced. **Educ:** Fla A&M Univ, Tallahassee, FL, BS, polit sci (magna cum laudae), 1975; Fla Atlantic Univ, Boca Raton, FL, MPA, 1977. **Career:** South Fla Water Mgmt Dist (SFWMD), dist admin off I-III, 1977-80, admin officer IV, 1980-84, asst to dir, 1984-87, exec asst, 1984-87, dir, admin serv, 1987, Dist W Palm Beach, dir human resources, 1987-94, Mgt Serv & Human Resources Dept, dir, 1999-2005, dep exec dir corp resources, 2005-. **Orgs:** Pres, Sickle Cell Found PB County, 1991-92; fin secy, Delta Sigma Theta Sorority, 1989-91; second vpres, Bus & Prof Women's Club, 1987-; Exec Women Palm Beaches; Vital Progs Leadership Palm Beach County, 1987; chairperson, fund-raising, Fla A&M Univ Alumni Asn; The Links Inc, West Palm Beach Chap, 1992-; pres, Delta Sigma Theta Sorority Inc, West Palm Beach Alumni Chap, 2003-; Soc Human Resources Mgt; Am Mgt Asn. **Honors/Awds:** 'Woman of the Year', Am Bus Women's Asn, 1981; Sickle Cell Found Palm Beach County, Outstanding Board Member, 1985; Eta Phi Beta Sorority, Community Service Award, 1985; J C Penney Golden Rule Award, Community Service, 1986; Tri County Business League Community Service Award, 1987; Black Awards, Woman of the Year, Palm Beach County, 1988; Up & Comers Award, 1992; Finalist in Govt Sec Pricewater, 1991; J Moran African-American Achiever Award in Gov, 1998; Women of Distinction Award, 2001; Finalist for the Chamber of Commerce Athena Award, 2006; Quiet Storm Award in Government from the Women Power Caucus/Broward County, 2007; One of South Florida's "25 Most Influential and Prominent Black Women, Success Magazine, 2007. **Business Addr:** Deputy Executive Director of Corporate Resources, South Florida Water Management District, 3301 Gun Club Rd, PO Box 24680, West Palm Beach, FL 33406, **Business Phone:** (561)686-8800.

TURPIN, MEL HARRISON
Basketball player. **Personal:** Born Dec 28, 1960, Lexington, KY. **Educ:** Univ Ky, attended 1979. **Career:** Basketball player (retired); Cleveland Cavaliers, 1985-87; Ut Jazz, 1988, Wash Bullets, 1990.

TUSAN, GAIL S
Judge, lawyer. **Personal:** Born Aug 3, 1956, Los Angeles, CA; daughter of Willie Tusan Jr and Lois Carrington Tusan; divorced; children: Ashley Lauren & Shannon Kyle. **Educ:** Univ Calif, Los Angeles, BA, 1978; George Wash Univ, JD, 1981. **Career:** US Dept Justice, intern, 1980-81; Kilpatrick & Cody, assoc, 1981-84; Asbill, Porter, assoc, 1984-86; City Ct Atlanta, admin law judge, 1984-89, judge, 1990-92; Joyner & Joyner, partner, 1986-90; Magistrate Ct Fulton, judge, 1986-90; Univ Nevada-Reno, Nat Judicial Col, fac, 1990-; State Ct Fulton Co, judge, 1992-95; Inst of Continuing Judicial Educ, fac mem; Ga State Univ Law Sch, fac mem; Super Ct of Fulton Co, judge, 1995-. **Orgs:** Ga State Bar, 1981-; Ga Asn Black Women Attys, pres, 1983, exec comm; Gate City Bar Asn; Atlanta Bar Asn; Judicial Procedure & Admin Adv Comn; Comn on Profism. **Honors/Awds:** Ebony, Thirty Leaders of the Future, 1985; Martin Luther King Jr Ctr for Nonviolence & Social Change Community Serv Peace & Justice Award, 1991; Justice Robert Benham, Law Related Supporter of the Yr Award, 1992; Cited by Ga Informer as one of Ga's 50 Most Influential Black Women, 1994; YWCA of Greater Atlanta's Acad of Women Achievers, Inductee, 1995. **Business Addr:** Judge, Superior Court of Fulton County, 185 Cent Ave SW Rm T8955, Ct Rm 8F, Atlanta, GA 30303, **Business Phone:** (404)302-8520.

TUTT, DR. WALTER CORNELIUS
Dentist. **Personal:** Born Jan 29, 1918, Birmingham, AL; son of Rev Walter Andrew Tutt and Corinne Flood Tutt; married Julia Smith (deceased); children: Lia. **Educ:** Livingstone Col, BS, 1939; Howard Univ, Grad Sch, 1942-43, DDS, 1957; Univ Florence, attended 1945. **Career:** Dentist (retired); NC Pub Sch, teacher 1941-42; VA Pub Sch, teacher, 1947-48; pvt pract, dent surgeon. **Orgs:** Robert T Freeman Dent Soc; Nat Dent Asn; Am Dent Asn; utilization rev sub-comm Home Care prog, DC Gen Hosp; past pres, Prince Williams County Teacher Asn, 1948; past pres, WA Grad Chap Chi Delta Mu Nat Med Fraterntiy; grand exec comm., Grand Chap Chi Delta Mu; Kappa Alpha Psi; past mem, adv comm, WA Alumni Chap Kappa Alpha Psi; bd dir, WA Alumni Chap Kappa Alpha Psi; Rock Creek E Neighborhood League, Pigskin Club WA; Howard Univ Gen & Dent Alumni Asn; treas, Hellians Inc. **Honors/Awds:** Conspicuous Service Award, Chi Delta Mu; Citation Distinguished Alumni of Historically Black, Col Nat Asn Equal Opportunity in Higher Ed. **Military Serv:** AUS, 1944-45; Combat Infantry Badge, 3 Battle Stars, 2 Campaign Ribbons, Good Conduct Medal.

TWIGG, DR. LEWIS HAROLD
Physician. **Personal:** Born Oct 5, 1937, Muskogee, OK; son of Lewis Twigg Sr and Ann R; married Myrna; children: Lewis III & Karen. **Educ:** Morehouse Col, BS, 1958; Atlanta Univ, MS, 1960; Meharry Med Col, Sch Med, MD, 1967. **Career:** Mich State Col, assoc clinical prof, dept obstet & gynec, reproductive biol human med; Hurley Med Ctr, vchmn, dept obstet & gynec, 1978-81; diplomate, Am Bd obstet & gynec; Fel, Col obstet & gynec; pvt pract physician, currently. **Orgs:** Flint Acad Surg; Alpha Phi Alpha Frat; diplomate Am Bd obstet & gynec; Fel Col obstet & gynec; Sigma Pi Phi Fraternity. **Honors/Awds:** Co-author, "Cutaneous Streptococcal Infections in Vietnam," Archives of Dermatology, Sept, 1971. **Military Serv:** AUS, capt, 1968-70; Bronze Star. **Home Addr:** 6242 Covered Wagon Tr, Flint, MI 48532. **Business Addr:** Physician, 4250 N Saginaw St, Flint, MI 48505, **Business Phone:** (810)787-2266.

TWIGGS, DR. LEO FRANKLIN
Artist, educator. **Personal:** Born Feb 13, 1934, St Stephen, SC; son of Bertha L Moultrie and Frank Twiggs; married Rosa Johnson, Jun 15, 1962; children: Kenneth, Darryl & Keith. **Educ:** Claflin Col, BA, 1956; NY Univ, Art Inst Chicago, MA, 1964; Univ Ga, EdD, 1970. **Career:** Lincoln High Sch, Sumter, SC, art teacher, 1958-64; SC State Univ, art prof, exec dir, Stanback Mus, 1964-98; prof emer, 2000-; Distinguished Artist Residence, Claflin Univ, 2000-. **Orgs:** Mus comt, State Mus 1972-; bd, vpres, SC Art Found, 1985-; African Am Mus Asn, chair, long range planning comt, 1985-; trustee, New Mount Zion Baptist Church, 1987-; Gov Sch Arts & Humanities, 1992; SC Hall Fame, 1992. **Honors/Awds:** Verner Award, Governor's Trophy in Arts, State of SC, 1981; Batik artist, over 60 one-man shows nationwide & Rome; Decca & Togoland; featured in Ebony, September, 1988; Hughie Lee-Smith: Exploring the Void Between Cynicign and Hope, 1997; Robert Reid; Poetic Journey, 1998. **Military Serv:** AUS Signal Corp, Sp/4, 1956-58. **Home Addr:** 420 Woodlawn Parlerdale Subdivision, Orangeburg, SC 29115, **Home Phone:** (803)534-9796. **Business Addr:** Distinguished Artist, Claflin University, 400 Magnolia St, Orangeburg, SC 29115, **Business Phone:** (803)535-5000.

TYLER, B J
Basketball player. **Personal:** Born Apr 30, 1971, Galveston, TX. **Educ:** DePaul Univ; Univ Tex. **Career:** Basketball player (retired); Philadelphia 76ers, point guard, 1994-95; Toronto Raptors, 1995-2000.

TYLER, CHERYL LYNNETT
Law enforcement officer. **Educ:** Spelman Col, sociol; Atlanta Univ, sociol. **Career:** Spec agent (retired); US Secret Serv, agent, spec agent. **Special Achievements:** Highest ranking African American female in the US Secret Service; has been personally responsible for the security of the President of the United States, past presidents and their families as well as visiting dignitaries.

TYLER, REV. GERALD DEFOREST
School administrator. **Personal:** Born Feb 28, 1946, Louisa County, VA; son of John and Annie; married; children: Michael Jerone & Jerome Duvall. **Educ:** Norfolk State Univ, BS, 1977, MA, 1983; Old Dominion Univ, PhD, 1983. **Career:** Dalmo Sales Co, salesman, 1964-66; USMC, adm orderly, 1966-69; Tidewater Regional Transit Syst, bus oper, 1969-77; Elizabeth City St Univ, spec asst to chancellor, 1977-84; Norfolk St Univ, dir univ rels, 1984-2000, mil prog coordr, 2000-, Reclamation Proj, st. **Orgs:** Nat Asn Advan Colored People, 1979-; adv, ECSU Student Chap Nat Asn Advan Colored People, 1980-84; NC St Employees Asn Inc, 1980-84; pres, Prof Bus Asn, 1980-81; alt deleg, Thirty Fifth Ann NCSEA Conv Comn, 1980-81; SHumanities Conf, 1980-82; chmn, NC St Employees Asn Inc, 1981-82; Greater Bibleway Temple 120 Club, 1981; vpres, Pasquotank Co Br, 1981-84; NC-SEA Inc Area 24 Exec Bd, 1981-84; adv, ECSU Sr Class, 1981-84; vice chmn, Pasquotank Co Voting Precinct 3B, 1981-82; NC-SEA Inc Bd Gov, 1981-82; chmn, NCSEA Inc Area 24, 1981-82; bd mem, Gov's FOTC Asn, 1982-84; bd mem, Albemarle Develop Auth, 1982-84; head adv, ECSU SrClass, 1982-84; NCSEA Inc State Organ Study Comt, 1982-83; Pasquotank CoVoting Precinct 3B, 1983-84; Pasquotank Co Improvement Asn, 1983-84; New-Towne Civic League, 1984-86; Tidewater Media Prof Asn, 1984-89; bd mem, New Towne Civic League, 1984-86; Va Social Sci Asn, 1984-94; Va Asn Printing, Publ & Pub Rels, 1986-; bd mem, Miss Black Va Pageant, 1986-88;bd dirs & adv, Pepper Bird Found, 1988; mem bd adv, Miss Col African Am Pageant, 1989-93; mem bd, Tidewater Charter, Am Red Cross, 1990-92; Hampton Roads Black Media Prof, 1990-; bd dirs & nominating comt mem, CounAdvan & Support Educ Dist III, 1993-95. **Honors/Awds:** Safe Driving Award, TRT, 1969-77; Certificate of Appreciation, UNCF, NY,1979; First Award Certificate as Assistant Head Coach, ECSU's Lady Vikings Softball Team, 1980-81; Employee of the Year Award, NCSEA Inc, 1981-82; Award for Outstanding Leadership, Unselfish & Dedicated Service Rendered Sr Class Adv, 1982-84; Outstanding Boxer Award, USMC. **Military Serv:** USMC, E-6/staff sgt, 6 yrs; Presidential Unit Citation; USN Commendation; Good Conduct Medal; Nat Def Medal.

TYLER, KATHRYN BRADFORD. **See PRIGMORE, KATHRYN TYLER.**

TYLER, LAUREN M
Businessperson. **Educ:** Yale Univ, BA; Harvard Bus Sch, MBA. **Career:** TSG Capital, partner; Allen & Co, dir & vpres; Quetzal/JP Morgan Partners, partner, 2000-05, managing mem, currently; JPMorgan Partners, partner, 2005-. **Orgs:** Fed Commun Comn, Fed Adv Comt; bd dirs, Archway Broadcasting Group; bd dirs, Col Sports TV; bd dirs, Radiovisa Corp; Investment Comt, Quetzal/JPMorgan Partners. **Business Addr:** Partner, JP Morgan Partners, 1221 Ave of the Americas, New York, NY 10020, **Business Phone:** (212)899-3400.*

TYLER, MICHAEL. **See TYLER, MYSTIKAL.**

TYLER, MYSTIKAL (MICHAEL TYLER)
Rap musician. **Personal:** Born Aug 22, 1970, New Orleans, LA; son of Marie Tyler. **Career:** Albums: Mystikal, 1995; Mind of Mystikal, 1996; Unpredictable, 1997; Ghetto Fabulous, 1998; Let's Get Ready, 2000; Tarantula, 2001, Price of the South, 2004; Chopped & Screwed, 2004. **Special Achievements:** Nominated for best rap album Grammy in 2003. **Military Serv:** AUS, combat engr.

TYLER, ROBERT JAMES, SR.
Real estate executive, government official, business owner. **Personal:** Born Dec 14, 1935, Darby, PA; son of Joseph and Katharine; married Phyllis E, Aug 30, 1958; children: Mary E & Robert J Jr. **Educ:** Univ Pa, ABA in Business 1978; William Pa Sch, Sch dir, 1998. **Career:** Philadelphia Svg Fund Soc, mortgage loan solicitor, 1967; Hope Develop Corp, mgt, 1971; First Pa Bank

NA, appraisal dept, 1973; Tyler Realty Co owner, 1978-; William Pa Sch, sch dir, 1998. **Orgs:** Numerous memships including trustee, First Baptist Church Darby, 1960-; Darby Bus Lianson, comt mem; Pa Notary Pub, pub safety, 1978-; Pa Real Estate Broker, 1978-; Nat Asn Advan Colored People, Darby Area Br, 1980-, exec comt, 1989-94, chair, housing comn, 1991-94; Darby Free Libr, bddirs, 1980-, treas, 1991-93; Co-chair, Equal Opportunities & Govt Agencies, Pa State Realtor, 1983-84; Wm Pa Sch Authority, 1983-; pres, Darby-Lansdowne Rotary, 1984-85; treas, Del County Bd Realtors, 1985; Equal Opportunity co-chair, Bd Realtors, 1985; Darby Salvation Army Adv Coun, 1985; dir, Del County Red Cross, 1985-88; Darby Bobo Coun, chair, 1987-88; pres, Del County Bd Realtors, 1988; bd dirs, Affordable Housing Opportunities Inc, 1990-; Grants, Recreation, Munic Serv, parking authority, Darby Boro Coun, chmn, 1991-95; Pa Certify Residential Appraiser, 1992-; Darby Bus Asn, 1992-; Del County Asn Realtors, co-chair, equal opportunity comn, 1993-; Darby Revitalization Task Force, 1994-; Del County Wm Pa Sch Dist, 1995; Task Force Sch Safety & Violence Prev; vice chmn, Delaware County Bd Assessment, 1995; Pa Asn Realtors, multiple listing comn, equal opportunity comn; DeL County Bd Assessment Appeals, 1996; County Action Agency Del County, 1998; Bd mem, William pa sch dist, currently. **Honors/Awds:** Civic Award, Chapel Four Chaplains 1970; Civic Award, Penguin Club Darby, 1972; Civic Award, First Baptist Church Darby, 1980; Community Service Award, Penguins Darby, 1988; Bd Mem Year, County Act Agency Del County, Pa, 2001. **Military Serv:** USMC, corpl, 12 yrs. **Business Addr:** Owner, Tyler Realty Co, 850 Main St, Darby, PA 19023, **Business Phone:** (610)461-2225.

TYLER, SHIRLEY NEIZER
School administrator. **Personal:** Born Jan 1, 1929, Philadelphia, PA; daughter of Frances Washington Neizer and Raymond F Neizer; divorced; children: Richard J Jr & Kathryn T Prigmore. **Educ:** Simmons Col, BS, MA; Univ Va. **Career:** School administrator (retired); NSA, exec secy, 1950-51; Nat Scholar Serv & Fund Negro Stud, staff assoc, 1953-54, assoc coun, prin; Arlington City Pub Sch Va, educr; Gilchrist Co, Boston, Va, personnel admin; US Nat Stud Asn, Madison, Wis, exec sec; Grace Episcopal Church, head sch. **Orgs:** Bd dir, Mid Atlantic Episcopal Sch Asn; Va Gov Ed Block Grant Comt; prin, Nat Asn Elem Sch, currently; Nat Asn Ed Young C, currently; chmn, vicechmn, Alexandria City Sch Bd, 1973-82; vice chmn, Alexandria Community Health Coun; INOVA Alexandria Hosp Corp; bd dir, Northern Va Family Serv; Nat Asn Advan Colored People; NOVA Urban League; Alexandria mem; Nat Coun Black Women; Alexandria City Community Partnerships Comt. **Honors/Awds:** Distinguished Service Citizens, Alexandria, Va; Outstanding Service in Education, Northern Va, Urban League; Outstanding Community Service, Nat Asn Advan Colored People, Alexandria Br; Community Activist, Hopkins HouseAsn; Alexandria Women's CMS; Alexandria Coun. **Home Addr:** 3703 Edison St, Alexandria, VA 22305.

TYNER, ALFRED MCCOY (MCCOY TYNER)
Jazz musician, music director. **Personal:** Born Dec 11, 1938, Philadelphia, PA; married Aisha; children: 1. **Educ:** W Philadelphia Music Sch; Granoff Sch Music. **Career:** Benny Golson/Art Farmer Jazztet, 1959; John Coltrane Quartet, 1960-65; solo performer, 1960-; Recordings: "Inception", 1962; "The Real McCoy", 1967; "Sahara", 1972; "Just Feelin'," 1985; "Soliloquy", 1992; "At the Warsaw Jamboree", 2000; "Live in Warsaw: Lady From Caracas", 2001; "Portau Blues", 2002; "Land of Giants", 2003; "Illuminations", 2004; Monk's Dream, 2004; Counterpoints: Live in Tokyo, 2004; "Quartet", 2006; Afro Blue, 2007; Guitars, 2008; Solo, 2009. **Honors/Awds:** Jazz Master, Nat Endowment Arts, 2002; "2003 Hero Award, 2003; GRAMMY award for Best Jazz Instrumental Album, 2004; honorary doctor of music degrees, Berklee College of Music, 2005; Presidential Merit Award from the Grammy Foundation, 2008. **Business Addr:** Jazz Pianist, Blue Note Management Group, 131 W 3rd St, New York, NY 10012.*

TYNER, CHARLES R.
Clergy, educator. **Personal:** Born Jun 23, 1950, Murfreesboro, NC; married. **Educ:** Shaw Univ, Raleigh, NC, 1972; Southeastern Bapt Sem Wake Forest, NC. **Career:** Mt Moriah Bapt Church, pastor, 1969; White Oak Bapt Church, pastor, 1972; Tarboro City Sch, admin asst supt . **Orgs:** W Roanoke Bapt Asn, exec com; Shaw Theol Alumni Asn; pres, Hertford Co Min Alliance; NC Asn Educ; Nat Asn Advan Colored People; Prince Hall Grand Lodge F & A Masons of NC; vpres, New Hope Bapt Asn. **Honors/Awds:** Merit Outstanding Leadership, Shaw Univ, 1969-72; Great Leadership, Comn Murfreesboro, NC, 1973; Outstanding Work Gen Bapt Conv NC, 1971-73.

TYNER, MCCOY. See TYNER, ALFRED MCCOY.

TYNER, REGINA LISA
Publishing executive. **Educ:** Univ Puget Sound, BS, Bus Admin, 1969, MA, Bus Admin, 1971; Harvard Univ, State & Local Exec Prog, 1980. **Career:** City Tacoma, minority emply spec civil serv coord, 1971-72; City Tacoma Tech Transfer Ctr, dir, 1972-77; Office Inter govt Affairs City Tacoma, dir, 1977; WA State Dept Retirement Systems, dep dir, 1977-79; City Seattle, dir, dept licenses & consumer affairs, 1979-86; Continental Tel NW, dir pub affairs, 1986-88; Am Commun Enterprises Inc, pres, 1988-; MWBE Digest, publ, currently. **Orgs:** Alpha Kappa Alpha Sorority Inc, 1975-; Vice chair found comn Int City Mgt Asn, 1975; rep, City Seattle Pub Tech Inc, 1982; bd dir, United Way King County, 1980-86; Am Soc Prof Admin, 1982; Leadership Tomorrow, 1983-87; instr, S Seattle Community Col, 1985; Ladies Auxiliary Veterans Foreign Wars, Post 2289, Seattle, WA, 1985-; bd dir, Wash Leadership Inst, 1988-, Munic League King County, 1988-, Medina C Servs, 1988-. **Honors/Awds:** Award of Excellence, Am Soc Pub Admin, 1986. **Business Phone:** (206)728-8911.

TYREE, OMAR (OMAR RASHAD TYREE)
Writer, journalist. **Personal:** Born Jan 1, 1969?, Philadelphia, PA; married Karintha; children: Ameer. **Educ:** Howard Univ, BA (with honors), print journalism, 1991. **Career:** The Capital Spotlight, reporter, asst ed, 1991; News Dimensions, chief reporter; Wash View Magazine, freelancer; MARS Productions, founder; Author, Colored, On White Campus (title later changed to Battlezone), 1992; participated in BET talk show pilot, For Black Men Only, 1992; Novels: Capital City, 1993; Flyy: Girl: Inside the Big City There's a Mad Obsession for Gold, Sex-n Money, 1993; Battlezone, 1994; A Do Right Man 1997; Single Mom, 1998; Sweet St. Louis, 1999; For the Love of Money, 2000; Just Say No!, 2001; Col Boy, 2002; Leslie, 2002; Diary of a Groupie, 2003; Cold Blooded, 2004; Boss Lady, 2005; What They Want, 2006; The Last Street Novel, 2007; Pecking Order, 2008. **Honors/Awds:** Entrepreneurial Spirit & Leadership Plaque, Multicultural Youth Inc, DC; NAACP Image Award, 2001; Phillis Wheatley Literary Award, 2006. **Business Addr:** Author, c/o Simon & Schuster, 1230 Ave of the Americas, New York, NY 10020, **Business Phone:** 800-223-2348.

TYREE, OMAR RASHAD. See TYREE, OMAR.

TYREE, PATRICIA GREY
Executive. **Personal:** Born Nov 8, 1942; married Winston E. **Educ:** Carlow Col, BS, 1966; Antioch Col, MA, 1973; Univ Pittsburgh, PhD, 1974. **Career:** Holy Family Sch, teacher, 1966-67; St Mary's Sch, teacher, 1967-68; Carlow Col, Proj Upward Bound Mt Mercy, moderator, 1968; Diocesan Off Econ & Oppurtunity, Compensatory Educ Prog, assoc dir, 1968-69; Nat Black Sisters' Conf, dir, 1969-72; Antioch Putnam Grad Sch Educ & Carlow Col, design training lab 1972-73; Design Progs Inc, 1972-74; Tyree Corp, corp vice pres & bus dir. **Orgs:** Bd dirs, Black Women's Community Develop Found. **Honors/Awds:** Religion in Action Award, Delta Sigma Theta.

TYREE-WALKER, IDA MAY
Real estate agent. **Personal:** Born Mar 16, 1941, Philadelphia, PA; daughter of Albert and Sophie; divorced; children: Dawn Walker-Anderson & Mark Gregory Walker. **Educ:** Philadelphia Col Textile & Sci, BS, bus admin, 1975; Bowie State Univ, MSA, admin mgt, 1992. **Career:** Philadelphia National Bank, sr financial analyst; Container Corp Am, controller, sales purchasing mgr; Bowie State Univ, asst internal auditor; Qual Care Dialysis Inc, opers mgr; Century 21 Real Estate LLC, prin, currently. **Orgs:** Nat Asn Women Bus Owners, 1995-97; mentor, BEGIN Prog, 1995-97; Nat Asn Health Servs Execs, 1995-97; chair, bd dir, Hosanna Ministries, 1996-98; bd dir, YMCA Black Achievers, 1996-97. **Honors/Awds:** Certificate of Excellence, Meridian Bank, 1995; Business Owner of the Year Nominee, NAWBO, 1996; Outstanding Leader, Phi Delta Kappa, 1996. **Military Serv:** USN Reserve, petty officer second class, 1979-81. **Business Addr:** Principal, Century 21 Real Estate LLC, 630 Germantown Pike, Philadelphia, PA 19444, **Business Phone:** (610)828-2700 Ext 239.

TYSON, ANDRE
Choreographer, dancer, educator. **Personal:** Born Jan 1, 1960?, Greenville, NC. **Educ:** Rutgers Univ, Newark, NJ, jour, 1978-80; Alliance Francaise, stud, 1992; Tenri Japanese Sch, stud, 1996; Power Pilates, New York, NY, cert, 1999, teacher educ, 2006; Power Pilates, Chicago, Ill, teacher educ, 2007. **Career:** Westport Dance Ctr, Westport, Conn, dance teacher, 1983; Alvin Ailey Am Dance Ctr, New York, NY, dance teacher, 1990-2004; Premiere Dance Theatre, Montclair, NJ, artistic dir, 1993; Laban Ctr Transitions Dance Co, London, Eng, rehearsal dir, 1993; Victoria Arts Collab, Victoria, Can, dance teacher, 1994; Associazione Italiana Danzatori Rome, Italy, dance teacher, 1995; Dance Point Osaka, Japan, dance teacher, 1995-96; Prof Dance Ctr, Tokyo, Japan, dance teacher, 1995-96; NC Sch Arts, Winston-Salem, NC, dance teacher, 1995-97; Hungarian Dance Acad, Winston-Salem, NC, dance teacher, 1995; Universidade Federal do Bahia Salvador, Brazil, dance teacher, 1996; Austin Contemp Ballet, Austin, Tex, dance teacher, 1996; Internationale Tanz Wochen Vienna, Austria, dance teacher, 1996; Arena 225, Zurich, Switz, dance teacher, 1996; Internationale Sommerakademie des Tanzes Koln, Ger, dance teacher, 1997 & 1999; Jacob's Pillow Lee, dance teacher, 1997; Smith Col, North Hampton, Mass, dance teacher, 1998; Univ SC, Columbia, SC, dance teacher, 1998; Univ Wis-Milwaukee, Peck Sch Arts, Dept Dance, assoc prof, 1998-2008; Anando Shankar Ctr Performing Arts, Calcutta, India, dance teacher, 1998; City Ballet Theatre, Milwaukee, Wis, dance teacher, 1998-2004; Milwaukee Ballet Sch, dance teacher, 1999 & 2000; City Ballet Theatre, Milwaukee, Wis, rehearsal dir, 1999-2000; TheaterSch Amsterdamse HogeSch voor de Kunsten, Netherlands, dance teacher, 2000; Ballet Tenn, Chattanooga, Tenn, dance teacher, 2001 & 2002; Ailey Camp Berkeley, artistic dir, 2001; Ko-Thi Dance Co, Milwaukee, Wis, artistic consult, 2001; Bucknell Univ, Lewisburg, Pa, dance teacher, 2002; Ballet Idaho, dance teacher, 2002; City Ballet Theatre, Milwaukee, Wis, artistic coordr, 2002; Lake Shore Dance Studio, Milwaukee, Wis, dance teacher, 2003-05 Calif Inst Arts, Dance Dept, asst dean & fac contemp technique, pilates & jazz, 2008-. **Orgs:** Compexions Dance Co, 1995-. **Home Addr:** 626 E State St Suite 1601, Milwaukee, WI 53202, **Home Phone:** (414)226-2374. **Business Addr:** Assistant Dean, Faculty, California Institute of Arts, School of Dance, 24700 McBean Pkwy, Valencia, CA 91355, **Business Phone:** (661)255-1050 Ext 2416.*

TYSON, ASHA
Writer, president (organization). **Personal:** Born Jan 1, 1970?, Detroit, MI. **Educ:** Suomi Col, assoc degree; Northern Mich Univ, BA, polit sci, MA, pub admin. **Career:** Northern Mich Univ, asst dean stud; Marygrove Col, dir personal finance; Asha Tyson Dynamics, pres, currently; ATD Publ, owner; motivational speaker; Author: How I Retired at 26!: A Step-by-Step Guide to Accessing Your Freedom & Wealth at Any Age, 2001. **Business Addr:** President, Asha Tyson Dynamics LLC, PO Box 442347, Detroit, MI 48244-2347, **Business Phone:** (313)393-5123.*

TYSON, BERTRAND OLIVER
Physician. **Personal:** Born Apr 3, 1931, Baton Rouge, LA; married Maureen; children: Lisa, Celeste, Bertrand Jr, Michelle, Kevin, Melissa, Amber. **Educ:** Howard Univ, BS, 1950; Meharry Med Col, MD, 1959. **Career:** Physician; Crown City Ob Gyn Med Grp Inc, pres; Bar Tram Ranch; Crown City Med Group Inc, 1973. **Orgs:** Alpha Phi Alpha Social Frat, 1947-; del Dem Nat Conv State LA, 1968; leader, Civil Rights Demon, 1963; Fellow, Am Col Ob Gyn; fellow, Intl Col Surgeons; Am Fertility Soc. **Military Serv:** AUS, corpl, 1952-54.

TYSON, EDWARD CHARLES
Manager. **Personal:** Born Jul 31, 1957, Brooklyn, NY; son of Dr Clarence and Cleo Tyson; married Diane K Tyson, Jun 27, 1992. **Educ:** Howard Univ, BA, 1979; Cent Univ, MBA, 1983. **Career:** Mfrs Nat Bank, asst br mgr, 1979-83; Life Va Ins Co, spec agent, 1983-85; COBO Conven Ctr, event mgr, 1985-90; Tampa Conven Ctr, mgr mkt & event serv, 1990-. **Orgs:** Omega Psi Phi Fraternity, 1977-; Nat Coalition for Black Meeting Planners, 1990-; Int Asn Assembly Mgrs, 1990-; Int Asn Exposition Mgrs, 1990-; Nat Forum for Black Public Admin, 1992-. **Honors/Awds:** Howardite of the Year, Howard Univ Alumni Asn, 1989. **Business Phone:** (813)274-8422.

TYSON, LANCE C
Lawyer. **Educ:** Lake Forest Col, BA; Univ Iowa Col Law, LLB. **Career:** Mayor's Off, chicago, IL, 1997; Kutak Rock LLP, assoc, atty; Govt Regulatory Law Pract Group, partner, currently; Freeborn & Peters LLP, partner, currently; Tyson Strong Hill LLC, atty, currently. **Orgs:** Chicago Bar Asn; 2016 Olympic Comt; Mt Sinai Hosp Bd; Loretto Hosp Adv Bd; Interfaith House Adv Bd; Nat Asn Bond Lawyers; Am Bar Asn. **Business Addr:** Partner, Freeborn & Peters LLP, 311 S Wacker Dr Suite 3000, Chicago, IL 60606, **Business Phone:** (312)360-6593.*

TYSON, LORENA E
Educator. **Personal:** Born Dec 1, 1933, Montclair, NJ; daughter of Alfred E and Clariee Love. **Educ:** Col St Elizabeth Convent Sta, BS, chem, 1956; Catholic Univ Am Wash DC, MS, chem, 1965; Seton Hall Univ, South Orange NJ, Math Cert, 1967; Rutgers Univ, attended 1975; NJ Inst Technol, attended 1978; Kean Col, NJ, Supvr, Cert, 1994. **Career:** Educator (retired); Sacred Heart Acad, Hoboken NJ, teacher, chemistry & math, 1956-59; St Joseph High Sch, Paterson, NJ, teacher, physics, chem & math, 1959-62; Catholic Univ Am, NSF Fellowship Chem, 1962-64; St Peter & Paul High St, Thomas VI, teacher, physics, chem & math, 1962-71; NSF Fel, Seton Hall, 1966-67; Essex County Col, Newark NJ, adj math, 1971-78; Kean Col NJ, adj math, 1971-83; Montclair High Sch, Montclair Bd Ed, chem teacher, 1971-97; Middlesex County Col, Edison, NJ, adj math teacher, 1989-93; Montclair High Sch, dept chair sci, 1994-97. **Orgs:** Nat Educ Asn; NJ Educ Asn; Montclair Educ Asn, 1971-95; Essex County Educ Asn, ACS Teacher Affil, 1974-98; League Women Voters Montclair, 1974-90; NJ Sci Teachers, 1975-98; NJEA Except Child Comn, 1975-90; EOF Adv Bd, Col St Elizabeth, 1976-83; Nat Coun Negro Women, 1978-82; NJ Math Teachers, 1979-83; Phi Delta Kappa, 1981-; treas, Phi Delta Kappa Montclair State Col, 1987-89; bd trustees, Montclair Vol Ambulance Unit, 1990-94; NJEA Human Rights Comn, 1997-; NJREA, 1997-; Prog Planning Comn, 1999- 2003; Centennial Comn, Col St Elizabeth, 1999-2000; Alumnae Asn bd dir, Col St Elizabeth, 1999-, secy, 2001- 2005. **Honors/Awds:** Human Relations Award, Essex County Educ Asn, West Orange, NJ 1980; Contribution to Education Award, Montclair Educ Asn, 1980; Resolution of Commendation, Montclair Bd Educ, 1980; NJ Governor's Teachers Recognition Program, 1987; Montclair Teacher of the Year, Montclair Bd

Educ, 1989; Eve Marchiony Outstanding Teacher Grant, Montclair Bd Educ, 1989; Edward J Merrill Award, Am Chem Soc, 1990; Middle Atlantic Regional Award, HS Chem Teaching, Am Chem Soc, 1992; Educator of the Year Award, Essex County Educ Asn, 1993; Princeton Distinguished Educator Award, 1994; Public School Teacher of the Year, 1995; Weston Award for Excellence, Knights Columbus Coun, 1996; Rev Edward M Farrell Distinguished Alumnus Award, Immaculate Conception HS, 1999; Honary Doctor of Law, Col St ELizabeth, 2000. **Home Addr:** 15 Montague Pl, Montclair, NJ 07042.

TYSON, MIKE (MICHAEL GERARD TYSON)
Boxer, actor. **Personal:** Born Jun 30, 1966, Brooklyn, NY; son of Jimmy Kirkpatrick and Lorna Smith; married Likha Spicer, Jun 9, 2009; children: 1; married Robin Givens, Feb 7, 1988 (divorced 1989); children: Michael D; married Monica Turner, Apr 1997 (divorced 2003); children: Reina & Amir. **Career:** Boxer (retired), Actor; professional boxer, 1985-2005; World Wrestling fed, special enforcer; Films: Crocodile Dundee in Los Angeles, 2001; Fool N Final, 2007; TV Series: "I Love 1980's", 2001; Den Lille og den store, 2001; "ESPN Sports Century", 2001; "Legendary Nights", 2003; "Beyond the Glory", 2003; "Driven", 2004; "Otro rollo con: Adal Ramones", 2004; "ESPN 25: Who's #1?", 2004; "Festival di Sanremo", 2005; "Jimmy Kimmel Live!", 2005; "Mad TV", 2005; "The Big Idea with Donny Deutsch", 2006; "Larry King Live", 2008; "Grand journal de Canal, Le", 2008; "High Chaparall", 2008. **Honors/Awds:** Heavy weight boxing champion, (WBC), 1986-90; heavyweight boxing champion, (WBA), 1987-90; heavyweight boxing champion, (IBF), 1987-90; heavyweight boxing champion, (WBC), 1996; heavyweight boxing champion, (WBA), 1996; boxer of the Year, WBC Quantas, US Boxing Writers & other organizations; triple crown winner; honorary doctor humane Letters, Central State Univ, 1988, WBC Quantas, US Boxing Writers and other organizations; featured athlete on fox sports net's beyond the Glory; Nominated for Teen Choice Award, 2009. **Special Achievements:** Youngest Heavyweight Champion in Boxing History; featured in Guinness Book of World Records; featured in Guinness Book of World Records; triple crown winner. acted in various films, alumbs & tv serials. special enforcer fora World Wrestling Entertainment match at Wrestle Mania XIV on March 29, 1998, in which he pretended to be a member of D-Generation X and ended uppunching out Shawn Michaels after making the 3 count for Stone Cold Steve Austin to win the WWE Championship from Michaels. *

TYSON, RON (RONALD TYSON PRESSON)
Singer, songwriter. **Personal:** Born Feb 8, 1948, Philadelphia, PA. **Educ:** Thomas Edison; Olney; Granoff Sch Music. **Career:** Singer/songwriter/producer: Albums: The Ethics Sing, 1967; Heaven Only Knows, 1973; The Magic of the Blue, 1974; Welcome Back, 1974; Thirteen Blue Magic Lane, 1975; Survival, 1975; The Very Best of South Shore Commission, 1975; Dance your troubles away, 1975; Love Committee, 1976; Locker Room, 1976; Break Away, 1980; All things happen in time, 1981; Hold your horses, 1983; Sal soul Classics Vol 1, 1990; Original Sal soul Classics: The 20th Anniversary, 1992; Love & Happiness, 1994; 25th Anniversary, 1994; This Is Where the Happy People Go: The Best of Trammps, 1994; Tightening it up, 1994; Give your body up, 1995; Passionate Breezes: The Best of the Dells 1975-91, 1995; Mazimim Classics Vol 2, 1995; Greatest Hits, 1996; People Get Ready: The Curtis May field Story, 1996; Best of Blue Magic: Soulful Spell, 1996; Smooth Grooves: A Sensual Collection Vol 6, 1996; Greatest Hits, 1996; Every body Dance, 1997; Super Rare Disco Vol 2, 1997; Keith Haring: A Retrospective The Music of His Era, 1997; Vol 1-Maximum Club Classics, 1997; Philly Sound: Kenny Gamble Leon Huff & the Story of Brotherly Love, 1997; Storm Warning: Philly Original Soul Classics Vol. 1, 1998; Maximum Club Classics Vol.2, 1998; Masters at work Masterworks: Essential Ken Lou House Mixes, 1998; Run away Best of Loleatta Holloway, 1999; Harris Machine/Here to Create Music, 1999; The best of Double Exposure, 1999; We Come In Peace/Take It To The Streets, 1999; Runaway Love: The Singles Anthology, 2000; Def com Vol. 2, 2001; Queen of the Night: The Ultimate Club Collection, 2001; Disco Heat, 2002; The Four Tops Anthology 50th anniversary, 2004; The Ethics, 1967-74; Love Committee; The Temptations, singer, master of ceremonies, currently. **Business Addr:** Singer, William Morris Agency, 1 William Morris Pl, Beverly Hills, CA 90212, **Business Phone:** (310)859-4000.*

TYUS, WYOMIA
Athlete, public relations executive. **Personal:** Born Aug 29, 1945, Griffin, GA; daughter of Willie Tyus and Marie; children: Simone. **Educ:** Tenn State Univ, BS, recreation, 1968. **Career:** Track athlete, 1962-75; Afro-Amer Ctr UCLA, research asst, 1969-70; Bret Harte Jr HS LA, phys edt chr, 1970-72; Beverly Hills HS, track coach, 1972-73; Intl Track Assn,pub rel staff, 1973-76; ABC coverage Olympic Games Montreal, commentator,1976; Councilman David Cunningham, community liason, 1978; US Dept Labors ponsored Sports Career Dev, instr, 1979-81; Coca-Cola USA, pub rels,1981-84; Olympic Committee; Black Studies Center, Univ Calif, LA; Los Angeles Unified Sch District. **Honors/Awds:** Gold Medal winner,Pan Amer Games, 1967; Winner three Gold Medals one Silver Medal, Olympic. **Special Achievements:** First athlete to win gold medals for a sprint in consecutive Olympics, 1964 & 1968; Appeared in US Talk Shows: The Merv Griffin Show, ABC Superstars,Challenge of the Sexes; Publications and film appearances, "Inside Jogging for Women" pub by Contemporary Books Chicago 1978; "Olympic Let Down-"Women's Sports Mag 1976; "Women in Sports" filmed by the Women's Sports Found 1979; "Women Gold Medal Winners" filmed by Bud Green span; TN Sports Hall of Fame Nashville 1972; US Track and Field Hall of Fame Angola, IN 1976; Black Athletes Hall of Fame New York 1978; Natl Track and Field Hall of Fame Charleston, WV 1980; Olympic Flag Carrier in the XXIII Olympic Games Los Angeles 1984; US Olympic Hall Of fame, 1985; Ten times AAU Natl Champ and All-Amer Athlete in both indoors and outdoors competition; Five times world record holder 50/60/70 and 100-yard dashes and 100 meters sprint; Represented the US in more than twenty international competitions winning most. *

U

UGGAMS, LESLIE (MARIAN UGGAMS)
Actor, singer. **Personal:** Born May 25, 1943, New York, NY; daughter of Harolde and Juanita; married Grahame Pratt, Oct 16, 1965; children: Danielle (Chambers) & Justice Pratt. **Educ:** NY Prof C's Sch; Juillard Sch Music, 1963. **Career:** Tv appearances: "Beulah", 1949; "Your Show of Shows", 1953; "The Milton Berle Show"; "Name That Tune"; "Sing Along With Mitch"; 1961-64; "Roots", 1979; "The Book of Lists", 1982; "Backstairs at the White House", 1982; "Christmas at Radio City, Fantasy"; Plays include: Hallelujah Baby, 1967, Her First Roman, 1968, Blues in the Night, 1982, Jerry's Girls, 1985, The Great Gershwin, 1987, Anything Goes, 1989; King Headley II, 2001; Films include: Black Girl, Skyjacked, 1972; Albums include: On My Way To You; numerous nightclub & musical variety show appearances; "A Different World", 1993; Sugar Hill, 1994; "All My Children", 1996. **Orgs:** Screen Actors Guild; Actor's Equity; Am Federation TV & Radio Artists; founder, BRAVO Chapter, City Hope; bd mem, Alvin Ailey Am Dance Theatre; bd mem, TADA; Delta Sigma Theta Sorority Inc. **Honors/Awds:** Best Singer on TV, 1962-63; Tony Award, Best Actress, Halleulajah Baby,1967; Emmy Award, Fantasy; Drama Critics Award, 1968; Critics Award, Best Supporting Actress, Roots, 1979; Emmy Nomination, Roots, 1979; Daytime Emmy Award, 1983; Anniversary Award, 2007. **Special Achievements:** Author of Leslie Uggams Beauty Book in 1962. **Business Addr:** Actress, William Morris Agency, 151 El Camino, Beverly Hills, CA 90212, **Business Phone:** (310)859-4000.

UGGAMS, MARIAN. See UGGAMS, LESLIE.

UKABAM, INNOCENT O.
Executive. **Personal:** Married Chidi; children: four. **Educ:** Univ Nigeria, BS; Univ Wis. **Career:** Protein Tech Int, area dir; DuPont Protein Technologies, St Louis, MO, mkt dir foodservice distrib, 2002. **Special Achievements:** First African American named area director of Central American & Caribbean divisions of Protein Tech Int. **Business Phone:** 800-325-7108.*

UKU, EUSTACE ORIS
Consultant, executive, lawyer. **Personal:** Born Jun 1, 1947, Ibadan, Oyo, Nigeria; son of Augustine and Mabel; married Jul 1, 1976 (divorced); children: Eustace Jr & Austin. **Educ:** Univ Lagos, Lagos, Nigeria, LLB, 1970; Nigerian Law Sch, Lagos, Nigeria, BL, 1971; Long Island Univ, Brooklyn, NY, MBA, 1974; Duquesne Univ, Pittsburgh, PA, Cert Law, 1981. **Career:** Lawrence & Co, Lagos, Nigeria, atty, 1971; Garrick & Co, Benin, Nigeria, atty, 1976-79; Delstacy Mgmt Serv, Benin, Nigeria, managing dir, 1976-79; Greater Pittsburgh Bus Develop Corp, Pittsburgh, PA, financial analyst, 1980-81; Equibank, Pittsburgh, PA, asst vpres, 1981-85; Exico Inc, Pittsburgh, PA, corp lawyer, pres & chief exec officer, 1985-. **Orgs:** Pennsylvania Bar Asn; dir, Functional Literacy Ministry; bd dirs, Umoja African Arts Co. **Business Addr:** President & Chief Executive Officer, Corporate lawyer, Exico Inc, 241 4th Ave, Pittsburgh, PA 15222-1709, **Business Phone:** (412)261-3073.

ULMER, KENNETH C.
Bishop, college teacher. **Personal:** Married Togetta; children: Kendan, RoShaun. **Educ:** Oxford Univ, Magdalene Col, Ecumenical Liturgy & Worship, 1994; Univ Ill, BA, broadcasting & music; United Theol Sem, doctorate ministry; Oxford Univ, Christ Church & Wadham Col. **Career:** Macedonia Bible Baptist Church, San Pedro, CA, founder, 1979; Faithful Cent Missionary Baptist Church, pastor, 1982; Biola Univ, adj prof; Pepperdine Univ, adj prof; Grace Theol Sem, Pastoral Ministry & Homiletics, instr; Fuller Theol Sem, instr; United Theol Sem, mentor; King's Col & Sem, adj prof, currently; Faithful Cent Bible Church, sr pastor, bishop, currently; Macedonia Int Bible Fel. **Orgs:** Calif Attorney Gen's Policy Coun Violence Prev; bd dirs, Rebuild Los Angeles Comn; bd dirs, Gospel Music Workshop Am; bd trustees, Biola Univ; Pastors Adv Coun, City Inglewood; bd trustees, Southern Calif Sch Ministry; founding bd mem, King's Col & Sem. **Special Achievements:** Author of four books: A New Thing, Spiritually Fit To Run The Race, The Anatomy Of God, In His Image. **Business Addr:** Bishop, Faithful Cent Bible Church, 333 W Florence Ave, Inglewood, CA 90301-1103, **Business Phone:** (310)330-8000.*

UMBAYEMAKE - HAYES, LINDA
Librarian. **Personal:** Born Feb 19, 1953, Cleveland, OH; daughter of C Morgan McDonald and Helen Loretta Ballard-McDonald; married Thomas Lee Hayes, Mar 27, 2004; children: Manu Rashad, Kumar Rashad, Bari Zaka, Mayi UmBayemake, Thurayya UmBayemake & Glenn Chinua Bayemake-Hurt. **Educ:** Cuyahoga Community Col, Cleveland, OH, AA, 1980; Kent State Univ, OH, BA, 1984; Tex Women's Univ, Denton, TX, MLS, 1989; Univ Ky, Lexington, MRC, 1998. **Career:** Denton City, Planning Dept, Denton, TX, planning asst, 1986-87; Tex Woman's Univ, Denton, TX, librn asst II, 1988-89; Univ N Tex, Denton, TX, librn asst II, 1988-89; Cuyahoga County Pub Libr, Warrensville Hts, OH, librn, 1989-90; Santa Fe Community Col, Grants, NM, librn, instr, 1990; Ga Dept Corrections, librn supvr, 1991-92; Ky State Univ, Frankfort, KY, reference librn, 1992-96; Owensboro Community Col, Owensboro, KY, asst librn, 1996; LUMBAY6 Intervention Journeys Inc, 1997-; Franklin City Pub Schs, substitute teacher, 1996-98; Ky Dept Ment Health, Offender Rehab Specist, 1998-2000; Book Wholesalers, Inc, Colction Develop, 1999-2000; The Univ Akron, STAR Coordr, 2001; E Cleveland Pub Libr, br mgr, Caledonia Br, 2001-; Fair Housing Servs, Akron, OH, tester, 2002-03. **Orgs:** Am Libr Asn, 1988-; Black Caucus Am Libr Asn; Ky Blacks Higher Educ, 1993-96; vice chair, ADA Network Adv Coun, 1998; Ky Citizens Foster Care Review bd, 1999-2000; Franklin County, Ky, Family Ct visitation, support comt, 1999-2000; bd dir, Kent City, OH Cable Comn, 2002-; Holden Parent Asn, 2000-04; secy, Roosevelt HS Parent-Teacher Org, Kent, OH, 2000-03; Longcoy Elem Parent Asn, 2004-; Kent State Univ Upward Bound Parent Adv Coun Secy, 2001-03. **Honors/Awds:** Hon Award of Service, Kent State Student Government, 1982-85; Hon Award of Service, COSO, 1982-85; Certificate of Service, Margaret Fain Elementary, 1990; Chi Sigma Iota, 1998; Elkhorn Middle School Site Base Council Award of Service, 1998; Foster Care review Committee Service Award, 2000, State KY, 2000. **Business Addr:** Branch Manager, East Cleveland Public Library Caledonia Br, 960 Caledonia Ave, Cleveland Heights, OH 44112, **Business Phone:** (216)268-6280.

UNAEZE, FELIX EME
Librarian, educator. **Personal:** Born Apr 12, 1952, Owerri, Imo State, Nigeria; son of James and Mary Mgbakwo Oguike; married Victoria Nwachukwu, Dec 22, 1984; children: Obi, Kenny & Laura. **Educ:** Lincoln Univ, BA, jour, 1980, MA, Polit Sci, 1981, MBA, mgt, 1983; UnivMo, Columbia, MALS, 1984. **Career:** Univ Lagos, Nigeria, libr asst three, 1971-73; Natl Libr Nigeria, Lagos, libr asst one, 1973-76; Lincoln Univ, Jefferson City, Mo, periodicals librn, adminr, ethnic studies, 1984-87; Northern Ill Univ, DeKalb, Ill, asst prof, bus econ librn, 1987-88; NMex State Univ, Las Cruces, NM, asst prof, bus ref librn, 1988-90; Ferris State Univ, Big Rapids, MI, head ref & instructional servs, 1990-2001; Chicago State Univ, Douglas Libr, dirLIS pub serv & assoc prof, 2002-, actg dir media & instr serv, 2003; Univ Wis-Superior, Jim Dan Hill Libr, dir, currently; assoc prof libr sci,currently. **Orgs:** Assn MBA Execs, 1984-88; Alpha Phi Alpha Fraternity, Inc, 1985; Black Caucus Am Libr Assn, 1986-; Am Libr Assn, 1988-; NMex Libr Assn, 1988-90; brd regents, Univ Wis Syst. **Business Addr:** Director, University of Wisconsin-Superior, Jim Dan Hill Library, Belknap & Catlin, PO Box 2000, Superior, WI 54880, **Business Phone:** (715)394-8346.

UNDERWOOD, ANTHONY
Automotive executive. **Personal:** Born Jan 23, 1957, Bessemer, AL; son of George Williams and Ruby; married Joyce Smith, Oct 3, 1976; children: Broderick Ryan & Roderick Bryan. **Educ:** Ford Dealer Training Prog, 1989. **Career:** Automotive Store, Talladega, owner, 1989; used car mgr; Dealers Trade Outlet, owner, 1995-2002; Anthony Underwood Automotive, pres & owner, currently. **Orgs:** Save The Youth; Am Red Cross. **Honors/Awds:** Nat Quality Dealer of the Year, Nat Independent Auto Dealer Asn, 2003. **Business Addr:** President, Owner, Anthony Underwood Automotive, 4006 Bessemer Hwy, Bessemer, AL 35020, **Business Phone:** (205)424-4033.*

UNDERWOOD, ARTHUR C.
Lawyer. **Educ:** Univ Wyo, BS, MBA; Univ Denver, JD. **Career:** Peat, Marwick, Mitchell & Co, CPA's, sr acct, 1973-75; Newman & Co, CPA's, independent consult, 1975; US Securities & Exchange Comn, legal intern, 1976, law clerk, 1977-78; Univ Wyo, acct, 1977; US State Dept officer, 1978; bus consult, 1979-80; Securities Clearing Colo Inc, atty, acct exec, 1982-84; Underwood & Assocs, owner, atty, 1981-. **Orgs:** Colo Soc Cert Pub Accts; Am Inst Cert Pub Accts; bd govs, Colo Bar Asn; Denver Bar Asn; Am Bar Asn; bd dir, Urban League Metrop Denver; treas, Urban League Metrop Denver; Joint Ctr Polit Studies. **Honors/Awds:** Fel Colo Bar Found. **Business Phone:** (303)755-2002.*

UNDERWOOD, BLAIR
Actor. **Personal:** Born Aug 25, 1964, Tacoma, WA; son of Frank and Marilyn; married Desiree, Jan 1, 1994; children: Paris, Brielle

Nicole & Blake Ellis. **Educ:** Carnegie-Mellon Univ. **Career:** Films: Krush Groove, 1985; The Second Coming, dir, 1992; Posse, 1993; Just Cause, 1995; Set It Off, 1996; Gattaca, 1997; Deep Impact; 1998; Asunder, 1998; The Wishing Tree, 1999; Rules of Engagement, 2000; Free to Dance, 2001; Final Breakdown, 2002; G, 2002; Full Frontal, 2002; Malibus Most Wanted, 2003; G; Hit Man; Straight Out of Compton 2; Something New, 2006; Madeas Family Reunion, 2006; The Hit, 2007; The Legend of Spyro: Dawn of the Dragon, voice, 2008, Weather Girl, 2009; The Bridge to Nowhere, dir, 2009, guest star on various TV shows: The Cosby Show, 1984; recurring role in One Life to Live, 1985-86; A Different World, 1987; Sex & the City. TV Series: ?LA Law?, 1987-94; ?High Incident?, 1996; ?City of Angels?, 2000; ?Fatherhood?, voice; LAX, 2005; ?Covert One: The Hades Factor?, 2006; ?Madeas Family Reunion?, 2006; TV episode: ?The Game?, 2007; ?The Wedding?, 2007; ?The Country House?, 2007; ?The Watch?, 2007; ?The Nutcracker?, 2007; ?Dirty Sexy Money?, 2007; ?The Real Thing?, 2007; ?Frasier?, 2007; ?The New Adventures of Old Christine?, 2007; ?Traffic?,2008; ?The Big Bang?, 2008; ?Beauty Is Only Spanx Deep?, 2008; ?In Treatment?, 2008; ?The Organ Donor?, 2008; ?The Convertible?, 2009; ?The Unexpected Arrival?, 2009; ?The Bad Guy?, 2009; ?The Facts?, 2009. **Orgs:** Phi Beta Sigma Fraternity Inc. **Honors/Awds:** Golden Globe Nominee, Best Performance by an Actor in a Supporting Role ina Series, Mini-Series or Motion Picture Made for TV, 1991; Humanitarian Award, Muscular Dystrophy Asn, 1993; Image Award, NAACP, 1994; Image Award Outstanding Lead Actor in a Television Movie or Mini-Series, 1999; Image Award for Outstanding Actor in a Drama Series, 2001; Artist of the Year, Harvard Univ, Harvard Found, 2002. **Special Achievements:** Voted one of People magazine's "50 Most Beautiful People" in 2000 and one of TV Guide's most influential faces of the 90s; author: Your Child's Soul, Simon & Schuster, 2005. **Business Addr:** Actor, William Morris Agency LLC, 151 El Camino Dr, Beverly Hills, CA 90212, **Business Phone:** (310)274-7451.

UNDERWOOD, FRANKYE HARPER
Educator, labor activist. **Personal:** Born Nov 19, 1953, Coal Valley, AL; daughter of Will and Sarah; married Harold Underwood, Dec 17, 1957; children: Angela, Harold Jr. **Educ:** Alabama State Univ, Montgomery AL, BS, 1957; Univ Alabama, Tuscaloosa AL, MA, 1968. **Career:** Anniston City Schs, Anniston AL, teacher, 1957-62; Walker County Bd Educ, Jasper AL, teacher, 1963-67; Alabama Educ Asn, Montgomery AL, vpres, 1987-88, pres, 1988-89; Jasper City Schs, Jasper AL, teacher, 1967-, sch bd, currently. **Orgs:** NEA; bd dir, Alabama Educ Asn; Alabama Comt Educational Excellence; trustee, Alabama State Univ. **Honors/Awds:** Teacher of Year Award, Jasper City Bd Educ, 1985. **Business Phone:** (205)384-6880.*

UNDERWOOD, JOSEPH M
Law enforcement officer. **Personal:** Born May 19, 1947, Dowagiac, MI; son of Joseph M Underwood Sr and Alma L; married Cindy L Glynn, Jul 22, 1989; children: Shannon & Sharon. **Educ:** Lake Mich Col, appl sci, attended 1978; Western Mich Univ, BS, criminal justice, 1982; FBI Nat Acad, grad, attended 1987. **Career:** Cass Co Sheriff's Dept, dep detective, 1973-79, Lt, 1979-82, Capt, 1982-85, undersheriff, 1985-88, sheriff, 1988, 1993-; Haggin-Wimberly Ford, asst bus mgr, fleet mgr, 1989-92. **Orgs:** Civitan Cass County; Westgate Ctr, bd mem, 1988-; trustee, House Prayer Community Church, 1987-93, Hospice 1998-; vpres, bd mem, Dowagiac Area Fed Credit Union; Vet Foreign Wars Post 10704; Dowagiac Rotary Club; Michigan Sheriff's Asn. **Honors/Awds:** Citizen of the Year Award, Sportsman Big 10 Club, 1992; Paul Harris Fel Award, Dowagiac Rotary, 2001. **Military Serv:** AUS, sgt, 1966-68; Purple Heart, Good Conduct. **Home Addr:** 26330 Beeson St, Cassopolis, MI 49031-9712. **Business Addr:** Sheriff, Sheriff Cass Company Sheriff, 321 M-62 N, Cassopolis, MI 49031, **Business Phone:** (269)445-8644.

UNDERWOOD, KING JAMES
Bishop. **Personal:** Born Apr 24, 1938, Panther Burn, MS; son of Judge and Sarah Parson; married Evelyn Miller, May 28, 1977; children: Jeff, James L Burnett, Greg, Theodore, Timothy Burnett, Angela R Patterson, Janet, Herbert D Burnett, Judy Grant, King James Jr. **Educ:** Industrial Training Institute, BA, BTH, MA, DM. **Career:** Gen Bishop, Gen Conf, Western Div, Free Will Baptist Inc, Ministers Conf, pres; Ken Annual Conf Western Div Free Will Baptist Inc, vice bishop, bishop, currently; Terre Haute Dist Ministers Conf, secy; St James Free Will Baptist Church, asst pastor; Emmanuel Free Will Baptist Church, pastor; New Free Will Baptist Church, pastor, general contractor, builder, currently. **Orgs:** Hiram Lodge No 10, Blue Lodge, chaplain; St James No 3 Grand Consistory, AASR, Grand Hosp; Champaign County, Nat Asn Advan Colored People; spiritual counr & advisor, Danville Correctional Ctr; Champaign County Jail Bd; Univ Ill; Eastern Ill Univ; Ind Univ; Boy Scouts; Urban league, Champaign County; ad bd, Rainbow Push Coalition, Champaign County; justice comt, Dr Martin Luther King Jr Advocacy. **Honors/Awds:** 2nd Place Award, State Il, Industrial Arts, 1960; Outstanding Teacher Award, Terre Haute District Conf Educ Department; Honorary Doctor of Divinity; Susan Freiburg Award. **Special Achievements:** Mayoral proclamation of "Bishop King James Underwood Day" in Urbana, Illinois. **Military Serv:** USN, seaman recruit, 1961. **Home Addr:** 1309 Tremont, Urbana, IL 61801, **Home Phone:** (217)367-8215. **Business Addr:** General Bishop, New Free Will Baptist Church, 601 East Grove St, Champaign, IL 61820, **Business Phone:** (217)355-2385.*

UNDERWOOD, MAUDE ESTHER
Executive. **Personal:** Born Jul 7, 1930, Cotton Valley, LA; married David C; children: Marcus, Sharon, Yvonne Holmes & James. **Educ:** Ruth Beauty Sch, dipl, 1958; Springhill HS, GED, 1979; Northwest LA Vo-Tech Sch, dipl, 1982. **Career:** State LA, LSU Ext agt, 1976; City Cullen, alderman, 1982,87; Black Comn Broadcast, prod, 1983-. **Orgs:** Organizer treas, Springhill-Cullen Improvement Asn, 1962; organizer treas, Cullen Ladies Club; chmn, Cystic Fibrosis; Order Eastern Star; orator, Clantha Pride LA; N Webster Chamber Com. **Honors/Awds:** Outstanding Service Award, Webster Parish Comn Action, 1978; Black Pride Award, Black Pride Comn, 1983; Bible Teachers Award, 13th N Calvary Dist, 1981. **Home Phone:** (318)994-2252.

UNDERWOOD, PAUL L, JR.
Cardiologist. **Personal:** Born Mar 23, 1960, Knoxville, TN. **Educ:** Morehouse Col, BS, biol; Mayo Med Sch, MD. **Career:** Henry Ford Hosp, residency, 1984-85; Mayo Grad Sch Med, residency, 1985-87; Cleveland Clin Educ Found, fel, 1990-93; Mercy Hosp, IA Heart Ctr, fel, 1993; N Phoenix Heart Ctr, cardiologist, currently; Advanced Cardiac Specialists, mgr, currently. **Orgs:** Sigma Pi Phi Fraternity; Black Bd Dirs Proj; Soc Cardiac Angiography & Intervention; Nat Med Asn; Am Heart Asn; Nat Bd Med Examrs; pres, 2004-06, bd dir, Asn Black Cardiologists Inc. **Honors/Awds:** Lincoln J Ragsdale Sr Outstanding Director Award, 2006. **Business Addr:** Manager, Advanced Cardiac Specialists, 201 W Guadalupe Rd Suite 209, Gilbert, AZ 85233, **Business Phone:** (480)892-2800.*

UNION, GABRIELLE M
Actor. **Personal:** Born Oct 29, 1972, Omaha, NE; daughter of Sylvester and Theresa; married Chris Howard. **Educ:** Univ NE; Cuesta Col; Univ Calif, Los Angeles, BA, sociol. **Career:** Fashion model; actress, currently; Film: She's All That, 1999; 10 Things I Hate About You, 1999; Love & Basketball, 2000; Bring It On, 2000; The Brothers, 2001; Two Can Play That Game, 2001; Abandon, 2002; Welcome to Collinwood, 2002; Deliver Us From Eva, 2003; Cradle to the Grave, 2003; Bad Boys II, 2003; The Breakup Handbook, 2003; Constellation, 2004; Breakin' All the Rules, 2004; The Honeymooners, 2005; Say Uncle, 2005; Running with Scissors, 2006; TV: "Moesha", 1996; "7th Heaven", 1996; "Star Trek: Deep Space Nine", 1997; "ER", 2000; "Friends", 2001; "Pepsi Smash", 2003; "The Sharon Osbourne Show", 2003; "Family Guy", 2005; "Timeless", 2006; "Into Night", 2006; "The Sea", 2006; "Daddy's Little Girls", 2007; "The Box", 2007; "The Perfect Holiday", 2007; "A Thousand Words by Friday", 2008; "Ugly Betty", 2008. **Honors/Awds:** Young Hollywood Award One to Watch, Female, 2001; Black Reel Award Theatrical, Best Supporting Actress, 2001; Am Black Film Festival Rising Star Award, 2003. **Special Achievements:** ranked No 52 in Maxims 100 Sexiest Women, 2002; ranked No 81 in Stuffs 103 Sexiest Women, 2003. **Business Addr:** Actress, Sutton Barth & Vennari Inc, 145 S Fairfax Ave Suite 310, Los Angeles, CA 90036, **Business Phone:** (323)938-6000.

UNSELD, WES
Sports manager, basketball player, basketball coach. **Personal:** Born Mar 14, 1946, Louisville, KY; married Connie; children: Kimberly & Westley. **Educ:** Univ Louisville, BA, 1968. **Career:** Basketball player (retired), basketball coach, basketball exec; Baltimore Bullets, 1968-73; Capital Bullets, 1973-74; Wash Bullets, 1974-81, vpres, 1981-96, asst coach, 1987, head coach, 1988-94, exec vpres & gen mgr, 1996-; Wash Wizards, exec vpres & gen mgr, 1996-2003. **Orgs:** Head, Capital Ctr Charities; vol, Kernan Hosp; bd trustees, Mt St Marys Col; Alpha Phi Alpha. **Honors/Awds:** Rookie of the Year, 1969; J Walter Kennedy Citzenship Award, 1975; Most Valuable Player, NBA Championship, 1978; Basketball Hall of Fame, 1988.

UPSHAW, REGAN CHARLES
Football player. **Personal:** Born Aug 12, 1975, Berrien Springs, MI. **Educ:** Univ Calif. **Career:** Football player (retired); Tampa Bay Buccaneers, defensive end, 1996-99; Jacksonville Jaguars, defensive end, 1999; Oakland Raiders, defensive end, 2000-02; Wash Redskins, defensive end, 2003; New York Giants, defensive end, 2004-05.

UPSHAW, SAM
Photojournalist. **Personal:** Born Jan 10, 1964, Louisville, KY; son of Samuel Upshaw Sr and Mary Lou Parmer. **Educ:** Western Ky Univ, Bowling Green, KY, photojournalism, 1987. **Career:** The Louisville Defender, Louisville, KY, intern, 1985; Tennessean, Nashville, TN, intern, 1986; Los Angeles Times, Los Angeles, CA, intern, 1987; Courier J, Louisville, KY, staff photogr, 1987-. **Orgs:** Nat Asn Black Journalists, 1986-; Nat Press Photogrs Asn, 1985-; Ky News Photogrs Asn, 1987-; co-founder & vpres, Western Ky Univ's Asn Black Communicators. **Honors/Awds:** Best of Gannett, Gannett Co Inc, 1988-89; Pulitzer Prize, Team (Staff) Coverage Gen News, 1989; Best of Show first Place Feature Picture Story, Third Place Sports and Honorable Mention Pictorial Kentucky News Photographers Asn Contest, 1989; Honorable Mention (Photojournalism), Nat Asn Black Journalists, 1990. **Home Addr:** 521 Baxter Ave, Louisville, KY 40204. **Business Addr:** Staff Photographer, The Courier Journal, 525 W Broadway, PO Box 740031, Louisville, KY 40201-7431, **Business Phone:** (502)582-4604.

UPSHAW, WILLIE CLAY
Baseball player. **Personal:** Born Apr 27, 1957, Blanco, TX; married Cindy; children: Brock Anthony, Courtney & Chad. **Career:** Baseball player (retired); Toronto Blue Jays, outfielder & infielder, 1978, 1980-87; Cleveland Indians, infielder, 1988; Bridgeport Bluefish, mgr, 1998-2001; Akron Aeros, mgr; San Francisco Giants, base coach; Mgr, Bridgeport Bluefish, currently. **Honors/Awds:** Manager of the year, Bridgeport Bluefish, 1998. **Special Achievements:** First Blue Jay to have 100 RBIs in a season, 1983.

URDY, DR. CHARLES E.
Educator. **Personal:** Born Dec 27, 1933, Georgetown, TX; son of William Braxton and Pearl Roberta Jackson; married Margaret Bright, Apr 7, 1962; children: Christopher Braxton Rodgers & Steven Eugene. **Educ:** Huston-Tillotson Col, BS, Chem, 1954; Univ Tex Austin, PhD, Phy Analytical Chem, 1962. **Career:** Huston-Tillotson Col, prof chem, 1961-62; NC Cent Univ, prof Chem,1962-63; Univ Tex Austin, post-doc Fel, 1962-63; Prairie View A&M Univ,prof chem, 1963-72; Dow Chem Co Freeport Tex, summer employee, 1970; MITLincoln Lab Boston, Nat Urban League Fel, 1972; Huston-Tillotson Col, profchem, 1972-93; Lower Colo River Authority, Environ Sci & Technol Develop-,mgr, 1993-; chmn, Austin Revitalization Authority. **Orgs:** Hon Soc Phi Lambda Upsion Alpha Kappa Mu; Nat Sci Found Fel, 1959; Univ Tex Fel, 1960; Procter & Gamble Fel, 1960; Alpha Phi Alpha Frat; Am Chem Soc; Am Crystallographic Asn; Sigma Xi; elected chmn, First Prairie View A & M Fac Coun, 1969; Fel Am Inst Chemists; numerous local civic orgn & comn; state sec-treas, Tex Asn Col Teachers, 1970; campaign mgr first Black Wilhelmina Delco elected Tex Legis Travis Co, 1974; Beta Kappa ChiHon Sci Soc; Cty Austin Charter Rev Comt; chmn, Black Voters Action ProjPol Com; elected coun mem, Austin City Coun, 1981-94. **Honors/Awds:** Recipient, Prairie View Alumni Award for Leadership, 1967; Huston Tillotson Alumni Award for Acad Achievement, 1967 Alpha Phi Alpha Frat Community Serv & Leadership Award, 1974; NAACP community service award,1975; City Austin community service award, 1976; Doctor Sci, Houston Tillotson Col, 1994; Whitney M Young Award, Austin Area Urban League,1994; Arthur B DeWitty Award for Human Rights, NAACP, 1977; Outstanding Texan, Legisl Black Caucus; Outstanding Educator of America. **Military Serv:** AUS, sp-3, 1954-57. **Business Addr:** Manager of Science & Technology, Lower Colorado River Authority, 3700 Lake Austin Blvd, PO Box 220, Austin, TX 78703.

USHER, U
Actor, singer. **Personal:** Born Oct 14, 1978, Dallas, TX; son of Usher III and Johnetta Patton; married Tameka, Aug 3, 2007; children: Usher V; married Rozonda Chilli Thomas (divorced). **Career:** Albums: Usher, 1994; My Way, 1997; All About U, 2000; 8701, 2001; Caught Up, 2005; Usher & Friends, 2005; TV guest appearances: "Moesha"; "The Parent Hood"; TV Movies: Geppeto, 2000; Films: The Fac, 1998; Light It Up, 1999; Tex Rangers, 2001; TV: "To Protect & Serve", 2002; "Attracting Opposites", 2003; "Episode" 29.18, 2004; "In the Mix", 2005; Usher: Evolution 8701: Live in Concert, 2002; In the Mix, 2005; One Night One Star: Usher Live, 2005; Rhythm City Volume One: Caught Up, 2005. **Honors/Awds:** Soul Train Award, Best R&B Album Male, for 8701, 2002; Top Artist, 2005; Usher Raymond Parkway, named in honor, 2005. **Special Achievements:** One of Teen People Magazine's "21 Hottest Stars Under 21," 1999; road named after him, the "Usher Raymond Parkway" in Chattanooga, Tennessee.

USSERY, TERDEMA LAMAR
President (Organization), basketball executive. **Personal:** Born Dec 4, 1958, Los Angeles, CA; son of Jean Hendrick and Terdema; married Debra Hubbard; children: Terdema L III & Elizabeth. **Educ:** Princeton Univ, Princeton, NJ, BA, dept honors, 1981; Harvard Univ, Cambridge, MA, MPA, honors, 1984; Univ Calif, Berkeley, CA, JD, 1987. **Career:** Morrison & Foerster, Los Angeles, CA, assoc, 1987-90; Continental Basketball Asn, dep comnr & gen legal coun, 1990-91, comnr, 1991; Univ Denver, grad sch bus, prof, 1991-; NIKE Sports Mgt, pres, 1994-96; California Law Review, exec ed; The Timberland Co, lead independent dir; TreeHouse Foods Inc, lead independent dir; Dallas Mavericks, pres & chief exec officer, 1996-; HDNet LLC, pres & chief exec officer, currently. **Orgs:** Grad mem, Ivy Club, 1981-; Denver Games Comm, Finance Comm; Los Angeles Young Black Profs, 1984; Denver Games Comm, 1990. **Business Phone:** (214)747-6287.

UTENDAHL, JOHN O
Investment banker. **Educ:** Long Island Univ; Columbia Bus Sch, MBA, 1982. **Career:** Salomon Bros, corp bond trader; Merrill Lynch Inc, vpres, mgr, sr bond trader; Utendahl Capital Partners LP, chmn, founder & ceo, currently. **Orgs:** Nat Bd Dirs, Securities

Indust Asn; Big Bros Big Sisters Org. **Honors/Awds:** Joseph Papp Racial Harmony Award, Found Ethnic Understanding. **Special Achievements:** Created the first minority-owned firm to specialize in taxable fixed-income securities; listed as one of 25 "Hottest Blacks on Wall Street", Black Enterprise Magazine, 1992; BE Top 100 Investment Banks List, ranked No 3, 2000; Featured in 'Fortune' as "the leading example of a new generation of black entrepreneurs on Wall Street"; Cited as one of the "The Top 25 Blacks on Wall Street", 'Black Enterprise'. **Business Addr:** Founder, Chief Executive Officer, Utendahl Capital Partners LP, 30 Broad St 21st Fl, New York, NY 10004, **Business Phone:** (212)797-2660.

UTLEY, RICHARD HENRY
Public relations executive. **Personal:** Born Jan 2, 1949, Pittsburgh, PA; married Audrey L Ross. **Educ:** Univ Pittsburgh, BA, 1972, Law Sch, 1972-73. **Career:** Penn Legal Serv, dir prog develop, 1980-82; City Harrisburg Dept Pub Safety, tech asst, 1982-83; Auditor Gen PA, asst dir, dep auditor general for admin, 2003-; Utley Assoc, pres, ceo; Pub Affairs Consult Inc, vpres; State Penn, The Bur Charitable Orgn, dir, currently. **Orgs:** Pres Utley Assoc; Nat Asn Advan Colored People; vice chair Harrisburg Housing Authority; sec of bd Center; bd dir. **Home Addr:** 122 Locust St, Harrisburg, PA 17104. **Business Addr:** Director, Bureau of Charitable Organizations, State of Pennsylvania, N Office Bldg Rm 308, Harrisburg, PA 17120, **Business Phone:** (717)783-1720.

UZOIGWE, DR. GODFREY N.
Educator, administrator. **Personal:** Born Sep 25, 1938; married Patricia Maria Cahill; children: Emeka Anthony, Amaechi Charles & Chinue Jaja. **Educ:** Univ Col Dublin, BA, Hons, 1963; Trinity Col, Dublin, Higher Dipl Educ, 1964; Christ Ch Oxford Univ, Eng, DPhil, History, 1967. **Career:** Makerere Univ, Kampala Uganda, hist lectr, 1967-70; Mich Univ, from asst prof hist to prof hist, 1970-84; Nig Nsukka Univ, visiting prof hist, 1976-77; Univ Calabar Nigeria, Dept Hist, prof & head, 1981-87, dean, facarts, 1984-87; Imo State Univ, Okigwe Nigeria, prof hist, 1987-91, dean,Col Humanities & Soc Sci, 1987-91, pioneer dir, Ctr Igbo Studies, 1988-91; Cornell Univ, visting sr fel, 1989; Abia State Univ, Uturu, dean, Col humanities & soc sci, 1991-92, pioneer dir, 1991-93, prof hist, 1991-95,dean, Col post grad studies, 1995-99; The Presidency, Abuja, Nigeria,visiting sr res prof hist, 1993-94; Lincoln Univ, PA, distinguished vis prof, 1997-98; Miss State Univ, Dept Hist, prof, head, 1999-. **Orgs:** Oxford Union Soc, Oxford, 1964-; Hist Asn, Ghana, 1967-; Royal African Soc, London, 1970-; Am Hist Asn, 1970-; African Studies Assn, USA, 1970-;Smithsonian Inst, 1974-; Intra Univ, Seminar Armed Forces & Society,1974-; Imo State Libr, Owerri, Nigeria, 1984-87; fel Hist Soc Nigeria,1987-; pres, Hist Soc Nigeria, 1988-92; The Oxford & Cambridge Club,Nigeria, 1985-; chair, Ahiajoku Lecure Planning Comn; Imo State, Nigeria,1991-95; chair brd, Esther Thompson Publishers, 1991-; Rhodes Scholar New Panel, Nigeria, 1991-; consult, Danchimach Nigeria Am Lab Sch, 1993-;group chair, Esther Thompson Consult, Owerri, Nigeria, 1995-; chair, Imo St Coun Arts & Cult, 1995; pres gen, Mbaitoli Cultural Union, Imo StateNigeria, 1996-; Bd mem, W African Res Assn, 2001-; Phi Alpha Theta; Phi Kappa Phi; Assn Third World Studies. **Honors/Awds:** Fel, The Research Club Mich Univ, 1978-; Hon Fel, Int Multi-Disciplinary Sci Inst, Col William & Mary, 1985-; Sports Certificate of Honor, Univ Calabar Nigeria, 1988; Hon Fel, The Inst Admin Mgt, Nigeria, 1992-; Chief Ugochinyere I, Ubomiri, 1996; Special Recognition Award, The Assn of Third World Studies, 2002; Golden Jubilee Award, Meritorious & distinguished service, 2005. **Special Achievements:** Publications: Revolution and Revolt in Bunyoro Kitara, London Long man,1970; Anatomy of an African Kingdom: A History of Bunyoro Kitara, New York Doubleday, 1973; Britain and the Conquest of Africa: The Age of Salisbury,Mich Univ, Press, 1974;Uganda: Dilemma of Nationhood, New York, Nok Publishers, 1982; A Short History of South Africa, Esther Thompson Publishers, 1988; Inter Ethnic & Religions in Nigeria, 1999; Foundations of Nigerian Federalism: The Colonial Period 1900-60, 1996; Troubled Journey: Nigeria Service the Civil War, Univ Press of America, 2003. **Business Addr:** Professor of History, Mississippi State University, 275 Allen Hall, Mississippi State, MS 39762.

V

V, BILLY. See VARGUS, BILL.

VALDES, PEDRO H
Executive, business owner. **Personal:** Born Jan 20, 1945, Havana, Cuba; son of Pedro H and Hesma; married Maria A Bermudez; children: Hesma, Pedro III & Xiomara. **Educ:** City Col NY, BA, 1969; Middlebury Col, MA, 1971; SUNY Stony Brook, attended 1973; NY Univ, attended 1975. **Career:** SEEK Prog, tutor, 1963-65; NY Philantropic League, rehabilitation counr, 1966-69; Alcur Tours Inc, tour guide & planner, 1968-72; Wm H Taft HS, Spanish Language teacher, 1969-72; State Univ NY Stony Brook, teaching asst dept hisp lang & lit, 1972-73; NY Col Podiatric Med, asst dean stud affairs, 1973-75, vpres stud affairs, 1975-77, exec vpres, 1977-80; Premo Pharmaceut Labs Inc, export sales mgr, 1980-81, exclusive export sales agent, int, 1981-82; Protecom Inc, pres, currently; Pedro's Wines, owner. **Orgs:** United Fedn Teachers, 1969-80; Am Asn Univ Prof, 1972-80; Am Asn Cols Podiatric Med, 1973-80; Am Pub Health Asn, 1973-; Nat League Nursing Policies & Procedures Comm 1977-; Nat Health Coun Inc, 1980-; Nat Ctr's Adv Coun Res Voc Educ, 1981-84. **Honors/Awds:** Outstanding Educator of America Award, 1974; Teaching Assistantship, State Univ NY Stony Brook, 1972-73. **Business Addr:** President, Owner, Protecom Inc, Pedro's Wines, Penns Dr, Winfield, PA 17889, **Business Phone:** (201)836-6312.

VALENTINE, DARNELL TERRELL
Basketball player, basketball executive. **Personal:** Born Feb 3, 1959, Chicago, IL. **Educ:** Univ Kans, BS, Pol Sci, 1981. **Career:** Portland Trail Blazers, 1981-86; Los Angeles Clippers, 1986-88; Cleveland Cavaliers, 1989-91; Nat Basketball Players Asn, Regional Rep, 1994-04; Trail Blazers, Dir Player Programs, 2004, exec, currently. **Business Phone:** (503)234-9291.*

VALENTINE, DIANN
Entrepreneur, designer. **Career:** DR Valentine & Assoc Inc, pres & founder, currently. **Special Achievements:** featured in the Los Angeles Times & Essence mag; Books include: Weddings Valentine Style, Atria, 2006; Valentine's creative journey: a publishing house. **Business Addr:** President, Founder, D R Valentine & Associates Inc, 1 South Fair Oaks Ave Suite 304, Pasadena, CA 91105, **Business Phone:** (626)395-0346.*

VALENTINE, HERMAN E
Executive. **Personal:** Born Jun 26, 1937, Norfolk, VA; son of Frank (deceased) and Alice (deceased); married Dorothy Jones; children: Herman Edward Jr & Bryce Thomas. **Educ:** Norfolk State Col, BS, 1967; Am Univ, attended 1968; Col William & Mary, attended 1972. **Career:** Grad Sch Dept Agr, exec officer, 1967-68; Syst Mgt Am Corp, founder, chmn & pres, 1970-; Norfolk State Col, Norfolk, VA, bus mgr, 1968-70. **Orgs:** Am Mgt Asn; Armed Forces Commun Electronics Asn; bd dirs exec comn, Greater Norfolk Corp; adv comm VA Chapter St Jude C Res Hosp; adv coun, Va Stage Co; Air Traffic Cent Asn; Tidewater Reg Minority Purchasing Coun; Soc Logistics Engs; bd dir, Operation Smile; bd dir, PUSH Int Trade Bur Inc; Old Dominion Univ; Hampton Roads Chamber Com; Downtown Norfolk Develop Corp; lifetime mem, Navy League United States. **Honors/Awds:** Presidential Citation, Nat Asn Equal Oppor in Higher Educ, 1981; Presidential Citation Entrepreneur of the Year, Dept Com Minority Bus Develop Agency, 1984; Delicados Inc Award Entrepreneurship, Blazing New Horizons, 1986; Citizen of the Yr Award, Outstanding Leadership & Serv to the Comm, 1986; Regonal Minority Manufacturing of Year Award, MBDA, 1988; Certificate of Recognition, lt govr, Commonwealth Va, 1987; Outstanding Businessperson of Year, State VA Award, black pres Roundtable Asn, 1987; Class III Supplier of the year Award, Nat Minority Supplier Develop Coun, 1987; Ambassador of the City of Norfolk, Ca, 1986; Black Diamond Award, Rev Jesse Jackson, Operation PUSH, 1989; Patriotic Service Award, US Savings Bond Campaign, US Treas Dept, 1989; Comm Service Award, Exemplary Blacks Bus, Inst Am Bus, 1989; Certificate of Recognition, African American Entreprener, New York City Police Dept, 1990; named one of 100 Most Influential Black Americans, Upscale mag, 1994; Black United Press Award, 2000. **Business Addr:** Owner, SMA MicroSystems LLC, 5 Koger Crt Suite 219, Norfolk, VA 23502-4107, **Business Phone:** (757)461-0559.

VALENTINE, J. T.
Lawyer. **Personal:** Born Sep 21, 1918, Suffolk, VA; son of Miles E and Annie; married Rosetta M Cason. **Educ:** Howard Univ, BS, 1948, LLB, 1951. **Career:** Lawyer (retired); Fed Aviation Admin, Wash Contracts Off, supvr procurement officer, 1966, chief contract serv, 1970, supvr contracts specialist, 1970, Small Bus, WA, officer, 1971, Law Div, indust rels officer. **Orgs:** Pres, Tuskegee Airmen, East Coast Chap; Israel Baptist Church; Nat Asn Advan Colored People; Nat Camping & Hiking Asn. **Military Serv:** USY, Tuskegee, airmen, 1943-46. **Home Addr:** 3608 Carpenter St SE, Washington, DC 20020. *

VALMON, ANDREW ORLANDO
Athletic coach, track and field athlete. **Personal:** Born Jan 1, 1965, Toms River, NJ; son of Oscar and Norma Haynes; married Meredith Rainey; children: Travis, Maya & Mallory. **Educ:** Seton Hall Univ, BA, mkt commun, 1987. **Career:** Georgetown Univ, Mens Track & Field, assoc head coach, 1995-2003; Univ Md, Terrapins, head coach, 2003-. **Orgs:** Phi Beta Sigma Fraternity Inc; founder, Ave Prog; spokesman, USOC. **Honors/Awds:** Inductee, NJ Sports Hall of Fame; Gold Medal, 4x400m relay, Olympic Games, 1988, 1992; NJ Athlete of the Year, 1990, 1992; Gold Medal, 4x400m relay, Goodwill Games, 1990, 1994; World Record Holder, 4X400m Relay; Athlete of the Year, Metrop Athletics Cong, 1990; Silver Medal, TAC Nat Championship, 1991; 2nd Place, IAAF Mobil Grand Prix, 1991; World Record & Gold Medalist, World Championships, 4X400m relay, Best Relay Ever & New World Record, 1993; Hall of Fame, Track and Field, Seton Hall Univ, 1997; President Award, USA Track & Field, 2002. **Business Addr:** Head Coach, Terrapins, University of Maryland, PO Box 295, College Park, MD 20742, **Business Phone:** (301)314-7070.

VAN AMSON, GEORGE LOUIS
Executive, banker, executive director. **Personal:** Born Jan 30, 1952, New York, NY; son of Adolph and Willie-Mae; married Wendy Alicia Tempro; children: Alexandra Case, Victoria Taylor & G A Schuyler Van. **Educ:** Columbia Col, AB, 1974; Harvard Bus Sch, MBA, 1982. **Career:** Revlon Inc, financial analyst, 1974-76; Citibank NA, asst controller, 1976-77; Goldman Sachs & Co, sr financial analyst, 1977-80, vpres, 1982-92; Morgan Stanley & Co Inc, vpres, Latin Am Trading, pres, 1992-94, prin, Intl Trading, co-head, 1995, prin, sr domestic trader, 1996, Inst Equities, managing dir, 2003-. **Orgs:** Dir, Alpha Phi Alpha Fraternity Inc, 1971-73; dir, Urban Leadership Forum, 1983-88; 21st Century PAC NY, 1984-87, Minisink Townhouse Inc, 1985-88; econ develop comt, 100 Black Men, 1985-; pres, HBS Black Alumni Asn, 1985-87; chmn, intl comt, Securities Traders Asn NY, 1987-89; trustee,Columbia Univ, 1994, trustee emer; trustee, Riverside Church, 1994. **Honors/Awds:** Curtis Gold Medal, Columbia Col, 1974; Leadership Award, Harvard Bus Sch, 1982; Distinguished Service Award, United Negro Col Fund, 1989; Global Leader for Tomorrow, World Econ Forum, 1992; John Jay Award, 2000, Alumni of Color Heritage Award, 2003, Community Impact Making a Difference Award, 2004, Alumni Medal, Columbia Univ, 2009. **Home Addr:** 210 W 90th St Suite 4B, New York, NY 10024-1241. **Business Addr:** Managing Director, Morgan Stanley Inc, Institutional Equity Division, 1585 Broadway, New York, NY 10036, **Business Phone:** (212)761-4000.

VANCE, COURTNEY B
Actor. **Personal:** Born Mar 12, 1960, Detroit, MI; married Angela Bassett, 1997. **Educ:** Harvard Univ, grad, 1978. **Career:** Stage: The Comedy of Errors, 1982; A Raisin in the Sun, 1983; Fences, Yale Repertory Theatre, 1985, Goodman Theatre, Chicago, 1986, Broadway, 1987; Romeo & Juliet, 1988; My C! My Africa!, 1989-90; Six Degrees of Separation, 1990-91; Film: Hamburger Hill, 1987; Hunt for Red October, 1990; The Adventures of Huckleberry Finn, 1993; Dangerous Minds, 1995; The Last Supper, 1995; Panther, 1995; The Preacher's Wife, 1996; Naked City, 1998; Cookie's Fortune, 1999; The Acting Class, 2000; Space Cowboys, 2000; D-Tox, 2002; HBO movie, Unchained Memories: Readings from the Slave Narratives; Whitewash: The Clarence Brandley Story, 2002; Tv Series: "Law & Order: Criminal Intent", 2001-06; "The American Experience", 2001-04; "State of Mind", 2007. **Honors/Awds:** Clarence Derwent Award, 1987; Theatre World, Citation, 1987; Obie Award, 1990; Tony Award, 1987, Best Lead Actor, 1991; Video Premiere Award, 2001. **Business Addr:** Actor, Endeavor Talent Agency, 9701 Wilshire Blvd, 10th Fl, Beverly Hills, CA 90210, **Business Phone:** (310)248-3000.

VANCE, ERIC DEVON
Football player. **Personal:** Born Jul 14, 1975, Tampa, FL. **Educ:** Vanderbilt Univ, BS, math & sec ed. **Career:** Football Player (Retired); Tampa Bay Buccaneers, defensive back, 1998-2001; Indianapolis Colts, safety, 2002. **Honors/Awds:** Rookie of the Year, 1998.

VANCE, DR. IRVIN E
Educator. **Personal:** Born Apr 8, 1928, Mexico, MO; son of Virgil Lee and Dorothy Ayers; married Dec 29, 1959; children: Barbara Ann Le Cesne, Velesha Ivy Vance & Katrina Iris Vance. **Educ:** Wayne State Univ, BS, 1957; Wash Univ, MA, 1959; Univ Mich, EdD, math, 1967. **Career:** Northeastern High Sch, math instr, 1957-59; Southeastern High Sch, math instr, 1959-62; Univ Mich, Math Dept, teaching fel, 1962-64, math instr, 1964-66; Mich State Univ, from asst prof to assoc prof math, 1966-71, prof math, 1989, Dept Math, prof emer, currently; NMex State Univ, dir black progs, 1971-72, from assoc prof math to prof math, 1971-89; Educ Develop Ctr, dir sch comt outreach proj one, 1973-75; Ley Col, lectr, 1974; Boston Univ, lectr, 1975. **Orgs:** Assoc dir, Grand Rapids Mich Middle Sch Math Lab Proj, 1967-68; Math Inst In-Serv Teachers, Mich State Univ, 1968, 1971; dir works oper, Col Teachers Math, Spelman Col, 1975; founder & dir, NMex State Univ Elem Teachers Math Proj, 1977-80; vpres, NMex Coun Teachers Math, 1978-81; reader advan placement exam math, Educ Testing Serv, 1979-84; pres, NMex Coun Teachers Math, 1984-85; prog chmn, Ann Conf NMex Coun Teachers Math, 1984-85; dir, Mich State Univ Math Proj Teachers Minority Youth, 1989-; bd dirs, Nat Coun Teachers Math, 1992-95; chair, Coord Comt Alliance Involve Minorities Math, 1992; pres, Benjamin Banneker Asn, 1993-95; chmn & mem, Math Educ Comt, Planning Grant Comt, Adv Comt, Promotion to Asn & Tenure Comt, Master Comt, Doctoral Comt, Comt Eval Ethnic Progs, NMex State Univ; External Affairs Comt & Nat Coun Teachers Math; chmn & bd dirs, Develop Res & Human Resources; Nat Coun Accreditation Teacher Educ; bd dir, Nat Asn Advan Colored People; judge, Black Hist Knowledge Bowl; Review Panel Minority Inst Sci Improvement Prog, NSF; dir, Mich State Univ Math Proj Mich Minority Youth; chair, Benjamin Banneker Asn Coord Comt; Math Asn Am. **Honors/Awds:** Glenn Gilbert Leadership Award, 2004. **Special Achievements:** Published numerous books and articles. **Military Serv:** AUS, 1950-52. **Business Addr:** Professor Emeritus, Department of Mathematics, Michiagn State University, PO Box 22115, East Lansing, MI 48824, **Business Phone:** (517)353-4693.

VANCE, LAWRENCE N.
Journalist. **Personal:** Born Dec 20, 1949, Chicago, IL; children: 2. **Educ:** Roosevelt Univ, BS, 1973; Chicago Kent Law Sch, JD,

1977. **Career:** Cook County Pub Defender, investgr, 1973-79, atty, 1977-79; Pvt Pract, atty. **Orgs:** Nat Bar Assocs, Cook Cty, IL, 1977-87. **Business Phone:** (312)236-5400.

VANCE, TOMMIE ROWAN
Manager. **Personal:** Born Apr 13, 1929, Frederick, OK; daughter of Alfred (deceased) and Victoria Mims (deceased); divorced; children: Michael, Nathan & Noretha. **Educ:** Golden Gate Univ, attended 1981. **Career:** Manager (retired); Gary's Grocery, cashier, 1955-59; Nevada Bell Telephone Co, mgr 1960-78; Pacific Telephone Co, mgr, 1978-90. **Orgs:** Washoe Co Demo Women's Club, 1968-72; chairperson, Reno Comn Status Women, 1972-74; Dem Ctr Comn, 1974-78; Nev State Dem Affirmative Action Comn, 1975-76; Int Women's Year Conf; 4th July Comt, Carson City, 1990; club secy, Reno-Sparks Negro Bus & Prof Women's Clubs, 1993-95. **Honors/Awds:** Speech Winner Pipe & Wire Toastmistress, 1968; Boss of the Year, Am Bus Women Sparks, 1971.

VANCE, VERA R
Educator. **Personal:** Born Jul 11, 1908, Waskom, TX; married; children: James R. **Educ:** BA, 1939; MEd, 1962; Grad Stud, 1971. **Career:** Velie Elem, teacher, 1924; Galilee Elementary Gilliam LA, teacher, 1929-31; Gainsville Elementary, prin teacher, 1931-45; Beaver Pond Elementary, prin teacher, 1945-47; Dixie Elementary, prin teacher, 1948-81; Mooretown Elementary Shreveport, teacher, 1951-56; Central Jr HS, teacher, 1959-61; JS Clarke Jr HS, teacher & counselor, 1961-72; Notre Dame High Sch, consult, 1973. **Orgs:** Secy, Inter Scholastic League; Tex & LA SS & BTU Congress, 1932-50; secy, Dist I SS Inst 1932-47; basileus of Sigma Gamma Rho; sec of chap, 1974; YWCA; Caddo Ed; ASS; Teachers Asn Am Personnel-Guid; LA Guid Asn; Breezy Hill Comm Club; treas, Trinity Bapt Chap. **Honors/Awds:** Award Sigma Gamma, RI, 1962; Award in bus Sigma Gamma RI, 1974.

VANCE, WILLIAM J., SR.
Clergy. **Personal:** Born Jan 14, 1923, Des Arc, AR; son of Ignatius D and Esther Butler; married Jacqueline G, Aug 24, 1947; children: Rene J Smith & William Jr (deceased). **Educ:** Roosevelt Univ, 1954; Moody Bible Inst, attended 1961; Gov State Univ, BA, 1974, MA, 1975; Parish Context Training, Pastoral Psysho-Ther, Inst, 1984. **Career:** Chicago Post Office, 1948-69; Older Boys & Girls Conf, bible teacher, counr, summer camp, 1958-74; Berean Baptist Church, pastor, 1969-91; pastor emer, 1991-; Ctr African Biblical Studies, Trinity United Church of Christ, bible teacher, 1980. **Orgs:** Chmn, bd dir, Douglass Tubman Christian Ctr, 1976-78; bd mem, Berean News, 1974, ed, 1969-75. **Honors/Awds:** Great Guy of Day, WVON, 1970; E Chicago Heights Comm Center Award, 1975; Great American Award, 1976. **Military Serv:** USAF, 1943-46. **Business Addr:** Pastor Emeritus, Berean Baptist Church, 5147 S Dearborn St, Chicago, IL 60609, **Business Phone:** (773)924-4349.

VANDERPOOL, ALEX. See MORRIS, NATHAN BARTHOLOMEW.

VAN DYKE, HENRY
Writer. **Personal:** Born Oct 3, 1928, Allegan, MI; son of Henry and Bessie. **Educ:** Univ MI, BA, 1953, MA, 1955. **Career:** Basic Books, ed, 1958-66; Kent State Univ, writer-in-residence, 1969-, prof emer, currently; Novels: Ladies of the Rachmaninoff Eyes, 1965, Blood of Strawberrs, 1969, Dead Piano, 1971, Lunacy & Caprice, 1987. **Honors/Awds:** Guggenheim, 1971; literary award, Acad Arts & Letters,1973; Distinguished Writing Award, Antioch Review, 2002. **Military Serv:** AUS corpl 1947-50. **Home Addr:** 40 Waterside Plz, New York, NY 10010. **Business Addr:** Professor Emeritus, Kent State University, Kent, OH 44242, **Business Phone:** (330)672-2727.

VANEMBRIQUES, ALEXANDRA
Basketball player. **Personal:** Born Apr 14, 1968. **Educ:** Univ Calif, Los Angeles. **Career:** Basketball player (retired); Holland, basketball player; Manresa, Spain, 1991-92; Texim Tonego, Holland, 1992-94; St Servais, Belgium, 1995-97; Bourges, France, 1997-98; Los Angeles Sparks, forward, 1998-99.

VAN EXEL, NICK
Basketball player. **Personal:** Born Nov 27, 1971, Kenosha, WI. **Career:** Basketball player (retired); Los Angeles Lakers, guard, 1993-98; Denver Nuggets, 1999-2001; Dallas Mavericks, 2001-03; Golden State Warriors, 2003-04; Portland Trail Blazers, 2004-05; San Antonio Spurs, guard, 2005-06. **Orgs:** Nat Benevolent Asn. **Honors/Awds:** All-Rookie second team, NBA, 1994; Chopper Travaglini Award; Victor Award; Comeback Player of the Year, 1998.

VAN HOOK, GEORGE ELLIS
Judge, lawyer. **Personal:** Born Aug 27, 1948; married Margaret Ann Kendrix Van Hook; children: Felecia Ann, Demetric, Alison Blossam & George Ellis III. **Educ:** Univ Ark, BSBA, mkt, 1970; Univ Ark Sch Law, JD, 1973. **Career:** Walker, Kaplan & Mays, legal intern, 1971; Eugene Hunt, law clerk, 1973; Hunt & Van Hook, atty, 1973-74; Ark State Hwy Dept, staff atty, 1974-76; gen pract, law, atty, 1976-77; pvt prac, atty, 1977-79; pvt pract, atty, 1979-; Union Co Child Support Enforcement Unit, contract atty, 1981-90; Union Co Munic Ct, magistrate, 1983-90; Union Co Dist Ct, judge, currently. **Orgs:** Bd advs, Union County Bar Asn; Salvation Army; bd dirs, Union County United Way; Progressive Gentlemen Inc; El Dorado Chamber Com; Union County Acad Found Inc; Boys & Girls Club El Dorado; Boy Scouts Union Dist; S Ark Arts Ctr; UALR Scholar Prog; Winthrop Rockefeller Scholarship Prog; Ark Cost Judiciary Study Comn, 1986; Ark Municipal Judges Coun; Ark Municipal League; Bd, Independent Living Ctrs; Harold Flowers Law Soc; Union County Community Found; State Ark Community Punishment Adv Bd. **Business Addr:** Union County Municipal Judge, Union County District Court, 3801 Oleta, PO Box 490, El Dorado, AR 71730, **Business Phone:** (870)863-5119.

VAN JOHNSON, RODNEY
Actor, business owner. **Personal:** Born Feb 20, 1961, Cincinnati, OH; children: Quincy. **Educ:** Univ Cincinnati, BS, educ. **Career:** Actor, business owner; Koya Skin Care, owner, currently; Film appearances: Dominic's Castle, 1994; Making the Rules, 1996; Tv guest appearances: Mad About You, 1992; Grace Under Fire, 1993; Jamie Foxx Show, 1996, 1997; Tv Episode: "Pensacola Wings of Gold", 1997; "The Young & the Restless", 1998; "Port Charles", 1999; "Passions", 1999-; "Girlfriends", 2000; "Hip-Ocracy", 2000; "The Eleventh Hour", 2002; Self: "The 28th Annual Daytime Emmy Awards", 2001; "Oh Drama!", 2002; "NBC's Funniest Outtakes", 2002; "SoapTalk", 2004; "Starting Over", 2005; "Passion for the Game", 2005. **Orgs:** Bd mem, Pancreatic Cancer. **Honors/Awds:** Hall of Fame, Univ Cincinnati Track & Field, 2002. **Business Addr:** Owner, Koya Skin Care, 13430 N Valleyheart Dr, Sherman Oaks, CA 91423-3122, **Business Phone:** (818)501-3371.

VAN LEE, REGINALD
Consultant, association executive. **Personal:** Born in Houston, TX. **Educ:** Mass Inst Technol, BS, civil engineering, MS, civil engineering; Harvard Bus Sch, MBA. **Career:** Booz Allen Hamilton, sr vpres, currently. **Orgs:** Exec Leadership Coun; MIT Nat Selection Comm; bd dirs, Thurgood Marshall Col Fund. **Honors/Awds:** C. Walter Nichols Community Service Award, NY Univ; Spirit of Cabrini Award, Cabrini Mission Found; Joseph Papp Racial Harmony Award, Found for Ethnic Understanding. **Special Achievements:** Co author of book - MEGACOMMUNITIES: How Leaders of Government, Business and Non-Profits Can Tackle Today's Global Challenges Together. Appeared numerous times on ABC's "World News This Morning" television program & CNBC speaking on the topics of CEO tenures, corporate values & enterprise resilience; One of the Top 25 Consultants in the world in "Consulting" magazine; One of NY's Finest Philanthropists; Black Engineer of the Year. **Business Phone:** (212)697-1900.

VAN LIEROP, ROBERT F
Lawyer, ambassador. **Personal:** Born Mar 17, 1939, New York, NY; son of Edward and Sylvia; married Toy; children: 1. **Educ:** Hofstra Univ, BA, Econ, 1964; NY Univ Sch Law, LLB, 1967. **Career:** NAACP, asst coun, 1967-68; Fleisher, Dornbush, Mensch, Mandelstam, assoc atty, 1968-71; Self-employed, film prod photojournalist, 1971-; Pvt Pract, atty, 1968-71; Van Lierop, Burns & Bassett law firm, partner & atty, 1978-81, 1994-; NY City Community Bd No 9 Manhattan, chmn, 1985-87; Repub Vanuatu, Ambassador to the United Nations, 1981-94; Films: A Luta Continua, producer; O Povo Organizado, producer; Cowan, DeBaets, Abrahams & Sheppard LLP, atty, currently. **Orgs:** Bd mem, Lawyers Comn for Human Rights; bd mem, Arthur Ashe Inst for Urban Health; bd dir, Black Econ Res Ctr; past mem exec comn, Am Comn on Africa; founding mem, Nat Conf Black Lawyers; former bd mem, Harlem Children's Theatre; past mem nat exec bd, Nat Lawyers Guild; past bd mem, NY Civil Liberties Union; bd dirs, Manhattan Borough Develop Corp, 1988-90; Am Bar Asn, African Law Comt; past chair; Asn the Bar the City New York, African Affairs Comt; chair, Coun Intl Affairs; NY State Bar Asn; Black Entertainment & Sports Lawyers Asn; life fel, Am Bar Found; Bar the District Columbia; Romare Bearden Found. **Honors/Awds:** George M Estabrook Distinguished Service Award, Hofstra Univ, 1991; Hofstra Univ Award, Alumni Achievement, 1993; Vanatu Independence Medal, Republic of Vanuatu, 1991; Grand Cross of the Order of the Infante Dom Henrique, Pres of Portugal, 1993; Doctor of Humane Letters, Donoris Causor, Hofstra Univ, 1994. **Military Serv:** USAF, 1956-60. **Business Addr:** Attorney, Cowan, DeBaets, Abrahams & Sheppard LLP, 41 Madison Ave 34th Fl, New York, NY 10010, **Business Phone:** (212)974-7474.

VANN, ALBERT
State government official. **Personal:** Born Nov 19, 1934, Brooklyn, NY; married Mildred E; children: Scott, Shannon, Fola & Binta. **Educ:** Univ Toledo, BBA, 1959; Yeshiva Univ, MS; Long Island Univ, MS. **Career:** New York State Assemblyman, Dist 56, 1974-2001; Vasar Col, Urban Ctr Black Studies, instr; New York City, Dist 36, coun mem, 2002-. **Orgs:** Dir, Talent Search Prog Dept HEW; NY State Assembly; founder & pres, African-Am Teachers Asn; bd dir, Bedford-Stuyvesant Restoration Corp; pres, Vannguard Civic Asn; chmn, NY State Blk & Puerto Rican Legis Caucus, 1977; bd mem, NAACP; mem, Blk Educs; Medgar Evers Col Comn Coun; mem, Alpha Phi Alpha Fraternity; chair, New York State Asn Black and Puerto Rican Legislators Inc, 1990-94; co-founder & first chair, Coalition for Comn Empowerment, 1982; chmn, Telecommunications & Energy Comn the Nat Black Caucus State Legislators, 1994; founder & exec mem, Vannguard Independent Democratic Assoc. **Honors/Awds:** Political Achievement Award, IDEA Inc; Community Service Award, Bus & Professional Negro Women Inc; Outstanding Educator Award, Bro & Sister Afro-Am Unity. **Military Serv:** USMC, sgt, 1952-55. **Business Addr:** Council Member, New York City Council, 250 Broadway 17th Fl, New York, NY 10007, **Business Phone:** (212)788-7354.

VANN, GREGORY ALVIN
President (Organization). **Personal:** Born Apr 17, 1954, Washington, DC; married Joan A Simpson. **Educ:** Howard Univ, BArch, 1977; Univ Fla, MConst Mgt, 1978; Drexel Univ, MBA, 1985. **Career:** Daniel Mann, Johnson & Mendenhall, draftsman, 1974-76, Bryant & Bryant Architects, designer, 1976-77; Whiting Turner Contracting Co, proj engr, 1977; Catalytic Inc, sr planning engr, 1978-81; Burns & Roe Inc, sr planning engr, 1981-84; Vann Orgn, pres, 1984-. **Orgs:** Am Asn Cost Engrs, 1980-; Am Inst Architects, 1986-87; Philadelphia Chap, Nat Black MBA Asn, 1986-; Cherry Hill Minority Civic Asn, 1986-. **Business Addr:** President, The Vann Organization, 11 Sayer Ave, Cherry Hill, NJ 08002, **Business Phone:** (856)486-4440.

VANNAMAN, MADI T
Executive director, manager. **Personal:** Born Jan 1, 1957, Aberdeen, MD; daughter of Charles Robert Thornton and Nobuko Otsuki Thornton; married Robbie L, Aug 8, 1987. **Educ:** Univ Kans, BS, bus, 1979, JD, 1983. **Career:** E&E Specialties, personnel dir, 1983-85; State Kans, personnel mgt specialist, 1985-86, mgt analyst, Depart Admin, 1986-89, acting benefits adminr, Depart Admin, 1989; Univ Kans, assist dir, Human Resources, 1990-. **Orgs:** Nat TIAA-CREF Adv Coun; Kans State Employees Health Care Comn. **Honors/Awds:** Employee of the month award, Univ Kans, 1999. **Business Addr:** Assistant Director, Human Resources & Equal Opportunity, University of Kansas, 1246 W Campus Rd Rm 103, Lawrence, KS 66045-7505, **Business Phone:** (785)864-4946.

VANOVER, TAMARICK
Football player, football coach. **Personal:** Born Feb 25, 1974, Tallahassee, FL; married Deidra; children: Tamarick Jr & Dedrick. **Educ:** Fla State Univ. **Career:** Football player (retired), Football coach; Las Vegas Posse, 1994; Kansas City Chiefs, wide receiver, 1995-99; San Diego Chargers, wide receiver, 2002; Lake City Christian Acad, head coach & athletic dir, 2006-. **Honors/Awds:** Mack Lee Hill Award, 1995. **Business Addr:** Head Coach, Athletic Director, Lake City Christian Academy, 3035 SW Pinemount Rd, PO Box 10521, Lake City, FL 32024, **Business Phone:** (386)758-0055.

VAN PEEBLES, MARIO
Movie director, actor, writer. **Personal:** Born Jan 15, 1957, Mexico City, Mexico; son of Melvin and Maria. **Educ:** Columbia Univ, BA, econ, 1980. **Career:** NY City Mayor's Off Mgt, analyst, 1979; Films: Sweet Sweetback's Baadasssss Song, 1971; South Bronx Heroes, 1985; Rappin', 1985; Heart break Ridge, 1986; Jaws: The Revenge, 1987; Identity Crisis, 1989; New Jack City, dir, 1991; Full Eclipse, 1992; Posse, 1993; Highlander III: The Final Dimension, 1994; Gunmen, 1994; Solo, 1996; Gang in Blue, 1997; Ali, 2001; The Hebrew Hammer, 2003; BAADASSSSS!, dir, 2003; Carlito's Way: Riseto Power, 2005; Hard Luck, dir, 2006; Killers in the House; Kerosene Cowboys, 2009; TV Series: "One Life to Live," 1982-83; "Sonny Spoon," 1988; "Rude Awakening, "2000-01; "44 Minutes," 2004; "LA Riots," 2004; "All My Children", 2008. **Orgs:** Screen Actors Guild; Actor's Equity; Am Fedn TV & Radio Artists; Dirs Guild Am. **Honors/Awds:** Emmy Award Nomination & Directors Guild Award, 1990; Bronze Halo Award; Pioneers of Excellence Award, World Inst Black Commun; Nat Asn Advan Colored People Image Award. **Business Phone:** (212)929-2525.

VAN PEEBLES, MELVIN
Actor, writer, composer. **Personal:** Born Aug 21, 1932, Chicago, IL; divorced; children: Mario, Megan & Melvin. **Educ:** Ohio Wesleyan Univ; Univ Amsterdam. **Career:** Dutch Nat Theatre; Mabon Nugent & Co, consult, 1984; Music video: Whodini's song "Funky Beat", dir; TV Writing Projects: "Just an Old Sweet Song", 1976; "Sophisticated Gents", 1981; "Amercian Stock Exchange", fl trader, 1984; Films: The Story of a Three Day Pass, writer & dir, 1967; Watermelon Man, actor, 1969; Slogan, writer, 1969; Don't Play Us Cheap, writer, 1973; Greased Lightning, writer, 1977; LA Law, actor, 1986; Jaws: The Revenge, actor, 1987; Vrooom Vroom Vrooom, writer, 1995; Gang in Blue, 1996; Love Kills, 1998; Time of Her Time, 1999; Smut, 1999; Antilles sur Seine, actor, 2000; Conte du ventreplein, Le, writer, producer, composer & dir, 2000; How to Get the Man's Foot Outta Your Ass, writer, 2003; Baltimore, 2003; The Hebrew Hammer, 2003; Hard Luck, 2006; Blackout, 2007; TV Progs: "Just an Old Sweet Song ", writer, 1976; "Living Single", 1996; "Calm at Sunset", 1996; "Homicide: Life on the Street", 1997; "The Shining", 1997; "Riot", 1997; "Classified X", writer, 1998; "Girlfriends", actor,

2005; "Unstoppable: Conversation with Melvin Van Peebles, Gordon Parks, & Ossie Davis", composer, 2005; "Girlfriends", 2005; "The 2006 Black Movie Awards", 2006; Plays: Ain't Supposed to Die A Natural Death, writer & producer, 1971; Don't Play Us Cheap, writer & producer, 1972; Author: Bold Money, A New Way to Play the Options Market, 1986; Bold Money: How to Get Rich in the Options Market, 1987; Director: Sunlight, 1957; Three Pickup Men for Herrick, 1957; Cinq cent balles, 1963; La permission, 1968; Sweet Sweetback's Baadasssss Song, 1971; Don't Play Us Cheap, 1973; Identity Crisis, 1989; Tales of Erotica, 1996; Gang in Blue, 1996; Le conte du ventre plein, 2000; The Real Deal, 2003; Confessionsofa Ex-Doofus-Itchy Footed Mutha, 2008. **Orgs:** Dirs Guild Am; French Directors Guild. **Honors/Awds:** First Prize from Belgian Festival for Don't Play Us Cheap; honorary doctorate, Hofstra Univ, 1995; Chevalier in the Legion D'Honneur, 2002. **Military Serv:** USAF, navigator-bombardier, 31/2 yrs. **Business Addr:** Actor, Simon & Schuster, 1230 Avenue of the Americas, New York, NY 10020, **Business Phone:** (212)698-7000.

VAN TRECE, JACKSON C.
Educator. **Personal:** Born Aug 31, 1928, Edwardsville, IL; married Dolores Wilson. **Educ:** Kans State Teacher Col, BS, 1952; Kans State Col, MS, 1960. **Career:** Educator (retired); NE Jr High Sch, teacher, 1952-56; NE Jr High Sch, counr, 1965-66; Sumner High Sch, Kansas City, KS, 1966-70; Univ Mo KC, asst vice chanchellor, stud affairs, 1980-85. **Orgs:** Boy Scouts Am Troop Leader, 1952-58; admin & dir, Black Motivation Training Ctr, Kans, 1970; NEA; Region VII Trio Proj Dir, Oreg; Trio Progs UMKC; Kappa Alpha Psi Frat; Area Youth Groups; exec bd, YMCA, 1973. **Special Achievements:** First African American academic dean of University of Missouri. **Military Serv:** AUS, 1946-48.

VANZANT, DR. REV. IYANLA
Association executive, writer, founder (originator). **Personal:** Born in Brooklyn, NY; divorced; children: Gemmia. **Educ:** Medger Evers Col, BS, summa cum laude, 1983; Queens Col, JD, 1988. **Career:** Auth, currently; Inner Visions Spiritual Life Maintenance Network, founder, exec dir, currently; Talk show, Iylanla, 2001. **Honors/Awds:** Alumni of the year, Nat Asn for Equal Opportunity Educ, 1994; Oni Award, Int Congress Black Women; 100 most Influential Women, Women's Day Mag, 2003; one of the country's most influential African Americans, Ebony Mag, 2004. **Special Achievements:** Author: One Day My Soul Just Opened Up; In the Meantime: Finding Yourself and the Love You Want; Tapping The Power Within; Acts of Faith; Faith in the Valley; The Spirit of a Man: A Vision of Transformation for Black Men and the Women Who Love Them; Yesterday I Cried: Celebrating the Lessons of Living and Loving. **Business Phone:** (301)419-8085.

VARGUS, BILL (BILLY V)
Television news anchorperson. **Personal:** Born Jun 21, 1956, Chicago, IL; son of Bill and Ione D; married Sue Serio, Dec 31, 1994. **Educ:** Temple Univ, BA, 1980. **Career:** WHYY TV, sports anchor, 1986-91; WWOR TV, sports anchor, 1992-93; WIVB TV, sports anchor, 1994-97; WTXF TV, sports anchor & reporter, currently. **Business Addr:** Sports Anchor, Reporter, WTXF-TV, Fox News Channel 29, 330 Mkt St, Philadelphia, PA 19106, **Business Phone:** (215)925-2929.

VARGUS, DR. IONE D.
Social worker. **Personal:** Born Jul 19, 1930, Medford, MA; daughter of Edward Dugger and Madeline Kountze Dugger-Kelley; married William H Adams (deceased); children: Suzanne Vargus Holloman & William D. **Educ:** Tufts Univ, AB, 1952; Univ Chicago, MA, 1954; Brandeis Univ, PhD, 1971. **Career:** Social Work Pract Family Serv, Child Welfare Pub Housing Home Mgt Informal Educ, 1954-71; Brandeis Univ, asst prof, 1969-71; Univ Ill, asst prof, 1971-74; Temple Univ, Sch Social Admin, assoc dean, dean, 1974-91, Family Reunion Inst, Sch Social Admin, chair, vol & founder, 1990-, actg vice provost undergrad educ, 1991-93, presidential fel, 1993-95, prof, prof emer, currently. **Orgs:** Trustee, Tufts Univ, 1981-91; bd mem, Tucker House II, 1990-96; bd mem, Multicultural Inst, 1990-; bd mem, Juv Law Ctr, 1991-99. **Honors/Awds:** Founders Award, Nat Asn Advan Colored People, 1991; Distinguished Service Award, Tufts Alumni Coun, 1993; Kwanzaa Holiday Expo Award, 1994: Academic Merit Award, 1997; Keeper of the Culture Award, 2002; History Maker's Education Maker, 2006. **Special Achievements:** Producer, radio doc on family reunions, WRTI; Author: Finding the Rest of Me: African American Family Reunions; published numerous articles; first African American & first female academic dean, Temple Univ. **Home Addr:** 16115 SHannondell Dr, Audubon, PA 19403. **Business Addr:** Founder, Professor Emeritus, Temple University, The Family Reunion Institute, School of Social Administration, 1301 Cecil B Moore Ave, Philadelphia, PA 19122, **Business Phone:** (215)204-6244.

VARNER, HAROLD R
Architect. **Educ:** Lawrence Technological Univ, BS, Archit; Gen Servs Admin, eng cert. **Career:** Howard Sims & Assocs, 1973, principal, 1976-2000; New Detroit Inc; Varner & Assocs, pres & chief exec officer, 2001-. **Orgs:** AIA Detroit, 1968; AIA Mich, 1968; Mich Bds Archit & Engrs; Detroit Pub Sch Voc & Tech Ctrs, task force. **Honors/Awds:** Hastings Award, 1996. **Special Achievements:** Formed MI requirements for Intern Development Program (IPP); Architect of the African American Museum, Detroit. **Business Addr:** President, Chief Executive Officer, Varner & Associatess, 615 Griswold St 320, Detroit, MI 48226, **Business Phone:** (313)964-9019.

VARNER, JAMES, SR.
Executive, educator. **Personal:** Born Nov 2, 1934, Jersey City, NJ; son of Charles and Mamie Dickerson; married Florence Johnson; children: 4. **Educ:** Univ Maine, BS, 1957; Rutgers Univ, MS, 1970, M City & Regional Planning, 1972. **Career:** Mt Sinai Hosp, chemist, 1957-58; Pub Sch, high sch teacher, 1960-66; Plainfield Comm Action, assoc dir, 1966; Morris Co Human Resources Agency, exec dir, 1966-82; Drew Univ, counr & lectr part-time, 1972-82; Black Enterprise Magazine, acct exec, 1982-85; Fallis Communs Inc, vpres, 1985-86; Info Mgt Resources Inc, vpres, 1970-; WMTR Radio, Morristown, NJ, host & producer, 1970-03; E Orange Bd Educ, E Orange, NJ, teacher, 1990-92; Univ Maine, asst dir admis minority recruitment, 1993-95; Univ Maine, adv, lectr & consult, 1995-; State Maine Human Right Comm, comnr. **Orgs:** Am Inst Planners; bd mem, Am Soc Planning Officials; Am Found Negro Affairs; Congress African Peoples; Rotary Club Morristown NJ; bd mem, Plainfield NJ Area YMCA; bd mem, Morris Co Nat Asn Advan Colored People; chmn emer, Nat Asn Planners, 1972; bd mem, Nat Asn Comm Develop; bd mem, Am Soc Planning Officials; pres, Greater Bangor Area Nat Asn Advan Colored People, 1994-; vice chmn, bd trustees, memphis univ sch, 2003. **Honors/Awds:** First place, NJ Jaycees Area Speak Up Finals, 1967; Community Service Award, Morris County Urban League Inc, 1989. **Special Achievements:** Host of radio program, Community Update. **Military Serv:** AUS, Capt. **Home Addr:** 531 S Brunswick St, Old Town, ME 04468.

VARNER, JEWELL C. See Obituaries section.

VARNER, DR. NELLIE M.
Financial manager, educator. **Personal:** Born Aug 27, 1935, Lake Cormorant, IL; daughter of Tommie and Essie Davis; married Louis S Williams (divorced 1964); children: Janniss LaTronia. **Educ:** Wayne State Univ, BS, 1958, MA, 1959; Univ MI, PhD, 1968. **Career:** Detroit Pub Sch, teacher, 1959-64; teaching fellowship, 1964; NDFL Fellowship, 1966-68; congressional internship, US Congress, 1966; Univ Mich, Coll Lit Sci & Arts, spec asst dean, 1968-70, CIC grant for Field Study in USSR, 1968; Ctr Russian & European Studies, fac assoc, 1968-78, asst prof polit sci, 1968-78; social Sci Res Coun Res Training Fellowship,1970-71; res grant Univ MI, 1970-71; recip res travel grant to study Black Political Elites Africa US & the Caribbean Carnegie Endowment for Int Peace, 1970-; Harvard Univ, res fel, 1970-71, res assoc, 1970-71; Univ Mich, Affirmative Action Progs, dir, 1972-75, Rackham Sch Grad Studies, assoc dean, 1976-79; Strather & Varner Inc Real Estate Invest Brokers, vpres, 1979-91; Primco Foods Inc, pres, 1988-93; N M Varner Co, pres, 1991-; At water Entertainment Assocs, vpres, 1994-98; Phoenix Entertainment LLC, chmn & chief exec officer, currently. **Orgs:** Am Coun Educ Comt Women Higher Educ, 1976-; Nat Sci Found Adv Com Minority Progs Sci Educ, 1977-; chair, Real Estate Adv Bd State MI, 1978-79; del,White House Conf Small Bus, 1980-; bd regents, 1980, regent emer, Univ MI;bd dir, Highland Pk YMCA, 1980-83; exec bd, Detroit Chap Nat Asn AdvanColored People, 1985-86; bd dir, Am Inst Bus, 1986-92; Southern Oakland CoBd Realtors, Detroit Bd Realtors; chair, Equal Opportunity Com Nat AsnState Univ & Land Grant Col; Econ Action Com New Detroit Inc; MI BdRealtors & Nat Bd Realtors; Equal Opportunity Task Force Am Coun Educ, Acad Affairs Fac Anal Proj Adv Com Univ MI, Senate Assem Adv Com Real Estate, state MI, exec bd, Wayne State Univ, Univ MI; Inst Gerontol; execcom, Ctr Afro-Am African Studies, Univ MI; HEW Title I State Adv Coun Bd Educ State MI; consult Nat Sci Found Panel Awards Minority Col & Univ,Proj Acad Affirm Action Training Int Assoc Official Human Rights Agency,Dept HUD US Govt; trustee, New Detroit Inc, 1987-91; dir, Inst Am Bus,1986-94; trustee, WTVS Channel 56, 1990-93; pres, The At water Found, 1995; bd dir, Detroit Entertainment LLC, 1996-99; bd dirs, Alumni Assoc, The Univ MI, 1998-; LSA Vis Comt, The Univ MI, 1997-2000; adv bd, Think Detroit Inc, 2000-. **Honors/Awds:** Florence Sweeney Scholarship, 1958; Detroit Women Principals ClubScholarship, 1959; Wilton Park Fellowship for Am participation Wilton ParkConf Steyning Sussex Eng, 1969; Distinguished Community Leadership AwardNat Asn Women Bus Owners, 1984; Delta Sigma Theta, Lillian Pierce BenbowAward, 1998. **Home Addr:** 1603 Balmoral Dr, Detroit, MI 48203. **Business Addr:** Chief Executive Officer, Phoenix Entertainment LLC, 660 Woodward Ave Suite 1110, Detroit, MI 48226, **Business Phone:** (313)962-5100.

VASSER, DELPHINE LYNETTA
Clergy. **Personal:** Born Dec 16, 1955, Flint, MI; daughter of Charles and Sister Ira L Williams; widowed. **Educ:** Emerson Col, BA, speech & commun, 1978; Suffork Univ, masters, pub admin, 1980; Oral Roberts univ, attending. **Career:** Greater Roxbury Corp, asst community rels dir, 1978-80; Mutual Omaha Insurance Co, SW Div Off, Off support, 1980-95; Bethel AME Church, pastor, 1988-90; Greater Johnson AME Church, pastor, 1991-; Tenth Dist AME Church, asst property mgr, travel adm, currently; Saint James African Methodist Episcopal Church, pastor, currently. **Orgs:** Founder, Gainesville Community Interdenominational Ministerial Alliance, 1989-90; bd mem & secy, African Am Pastors Coalition; pres, Tenth Dist Women Ministry; bd mem, Cong Nat Black Churches. **Honors/Awds:** Outstanding Leadership Award, Flint Central High, 1974; First Prize Oplehia Bonner Scholarship Award, Oplehia Bonner, 1974; Community Activist Award, Residence of Ferris. **Special Achievements:** Contributing writer, Sister to Sister Devotional. **Home Addr:** 5440 N Jim Miller Rd Apt 834, Dallas, TX 75227, **Home Phone:** (214)388-0601. **Business Addr:** Pastor, Saint James African Methodist Episcopal Church, 8401 Cedar Ave, Cleveland, OH 44103, **Business Phone:** (216)231-3562.

VAUGHAN, GERALD R.
Financial manager. **Personal:** Born Sep 9, 1957, Bronx, NY; son of Raymond and Juanita B Smith; married Ramona D Girtman. **Educ:** NC A&T State Univ, BS, 1980; Atlanta Univ, MBA, 1983; Adelphi Univ, CFP, 1985. **Career:** Liberty Mutual Ins Co, personal risk underwriter & indust regulator & tech analyst, 1976-80; Citizens & Southern Ga Corp, strategic planner & invest analyst, 1982-83; Entrepreneur, cert financial planner, 1985-; Grumman Corp, sr financial analyst, 1983-89; Ga Southern Univ, Asst Budget Dir, 2003-. **Orgs:** Asn MBA Execs, 1982-, Nat Black MBA Asn, 1982-; keeper finance, Omega Psi Phi Frat Inc, 1985-89. **Honors/Awds:** Fellowship Grants NC A&T St Univ & Atlanta Univ, 1975-83; Outstanding Young Americans, Int Biographical Inst, 1978-80. **Home Addr:** 3666 Cherry Ridge Blvd, Decatur, GA 30034. **Business Addr:** Assistant Budget Director, Georgia Southern University, PO Box 8033, Statesboro, GA 30460-8033, **Business Phone:** (912)681-5211.*

VAUGHAN, REV. JAMES EDWARD
Broadcaster. **Personal:** Born Mar 7, 1943, Herdford County, NC; son of John Henry and Jesse Mae Majette; married Renee J; children: Alvin, Patrinia & Meimii. **Educ:** NC Cent Univ, BA, art & eng, 1969; Southeastern Baptist Theol Sem, MDiv, seminarian, 1997-. **Career:** NY Courier Newspaper, managing ed, 1969; Capital Cities Comns Inc, promotions mgr, 1971-74; WYAH-TV, mgr promotion & producer, 1977-81; Christian TV Ministries Inc, founder, chmn & pres, 1980-; Small Bus Broadcasting Serv Co, founder, chmn & pres, 1982-; WJCB TV Tidewater Christian, founder, chmn & pres, 1983-; "Voices" TV Show, producer, 1998-; Christian Digital Media Ctr, founder, 1999; WTIK/WFTK Radio bd operator; Abundant Life Assembly Church, sr pastor. **Orgs:** Bd Chmn, Durham City/County Cable Adv Bd; pres, DCTV 8 Access Asn; PR chairperson, InterdenomiNat Ministerial Alliance Durham & Vicinity; bd dir, STOP Org; Am Mgt Assoc, InterdenomiNat Ministers Forum, AEHRO Broadcast Frat; vpres, Southern Christian Leadership Conf, VA; chmn, media Tidewater Jesus Assoc; chmn, black broadcast ownership Nat Relig Broadcasters; adv bd, Inner-City Ministers Prayer Breakfast, 1989-; bd dirs, Tidewater Chap Nat Conf Christians & Jews, 1991-; Portsmouth Area Ministerial Asn, 1986-. InterdenomiNat Ministerial Alliance, 1996-; Durham Ministers Asn, 1999. **Honors/Awds:** Citation of Merit, Nat Multiple Sclerosis Soc, 1984; Certificate of Service, Va State Adv Comm US Comn on Civil Rights, 1985; Oliver J Allen Award, WRAP Radio Gospel Music Awards, 1986; Excellence in Broadcast Pioneering, TCC Commun, 1986; Public Service Award, Portsmouth City Coun, 1987; Media Service Award, Athletes Better Am, 1990; Appreciation Award Inspirational Columnist, New Jour & Guide Newspaper, 1996. **Special Achievements:** Ex Umbra Radio/TV Broadcasts and weekly column 1977-. **Business Addr:** Founder, Chairman, Christian Television Ministries, PO Box 3195, Durham, NC 27715, **Business Phone:** (919)220-3226.

VAUGHANS, KIRKLAND CORNELL
Clinical psychologist, psychoanalyst. **Personal:** Born Jan 8, 1944, Chicago, IL; son of Charles Vaughans and Lillemae; married Renee Jones-Vaughans, Jun 6, 1987; children: Justine & David. **Educ:** Univ IL-Chicago, Chicago, IL, BA, 1972; Adelphi Univ, NY, Inst Advan Psychol Studies, MA, clin psychol, 1979, PhD, clin psychol, 1985; NY Univ, Postdoctoral Prog Psychotherapy & Psychoanalysis, cert specialization in clin psychotherapy & psychoanalysis, 1996; Adelphi Univ, Derner Inst, child & adolescent postdoctoral psychotherapy prog, 1998. **Career:** New Hope Guild, regional dir, 1992-; City Univ NY, Brooklyn Col, Grad Prog Sch Psycol, clin supvr, 1995-, City Col, Psychol Ctr, Dept Psychol child Prog, adj clin assoc, 1997-; Adelphi Univ, Derner Inst Advan Psychol Studies, asst clin prof, assoc clin prof, 1999-. **Orgs:** Am Psychol Asn, Div 29, 39, sect 20, 1989-; chmn, C Comt, Brooklyn Fedn Ment Health, 1987-89; NY Asn Black Psychologists; Int Soc Communicative Psychoanalysis & Psycholo-Ther; co-chair, NY State Psychol Asn, Comt Multicultural Concerns. **Honors/Awds:** Certificate of Appreciation, John F Kennedy Regular Dem club, 1989. **Special Achievements:** Editor, Journal of Infant, Childs & Adolescent Psycho-Therapy; published and presented numerous articles. **Military Serv:** AUS, specialist 4th class, 1962-65. **Business Addr:** Associate Clinical Professor, Adelphi University, 1 S Ave, PO Box 701, Garden City, NY 11530-0701, **Business Phone:** (516)877-3000.

VAUGHN, DR. ALVIN
Educator. **Personal:** Born Aug 30, 1939, Philadelphia, PA; son of Martha and Roger; married Eloise Stephens; children: Lois Jon-

neen & Edwards. **Educ:** Temple Univ, BS, 1963, MS, 1964; Int Grad Sch, EdD, 1984. **Career:** Educator(retired); Sch Dist Philadelphia, teacher, 1963-70; acting supvr, 1970-71, dept head, 1971-74, asst prin, 1974-2002, evening sch prin, 1976-2000. **Orgs:** Bd dir, Drew Comm Mental Health Ctr, 1975-85; counr/admin, Negro Trade Union Leadership Coun, 1978-84; bd sch dir, Chelten ham Township Pa, 1978-87; bd dir, Philadelphia PUSH, 1982-87; Chelten ham Art Ctr, 1982-86; Kappa Alpha Psi; Philadelphia Black Public Relations Soc. **Honors/Awds:** Achievement Award, Philadelphia Alumni Chap, Kappa Alpha Psi Fraternity Inc, 2002. **Home Addr:** 1376 Jasper Dr, Ambler, PA 19002, **Home Phone:** (215)628-3221.

VAUGHN, CLARENCE B
Scientist. **Personal:** Born Dec 14, 1928, Philadelphia, PA; son of Albert and Aretha Johnson; married Sarah Campbell, Sep 25, 1953; children: Steven, Annette, Carl & Ronald. **Educ:** Benedict Col, BS, 1947-51; Howard Univ, MS, 1951-53, 1955, MD, 1953-57; MD, 1957; DC Gen Hosp, Intern, 1957-58; Freedmans Hosp, Residency 1958-59; Wayne State Univ, PhD, 1965. **Career:** Res Physician, 1964-70; Milton A Darling Mem Ctr, clin dir, 1970-72; SW Oncolo Study Group, prin investor, 1978-94; Wayne State Univ, clin prof, 1988-; Providence Hosp, dir oncol, 1973-88; Southfield Oncol Inst Inc, dir oncol, pres, 1988-; Oakland Univ, clin prof. **Orgs:** Bd dir, Am Cancer Soc, Am Asn Univ Prof, AMA; nat chmn, Aerospace & Military Sect NMA, Am Soc Clin Oncol, Nat Med Asn, Wayne County Med Soc, Oakland County med Asn, Reserve Officers Asn, US Asn Military Surgeons, USAF Asn, Detroit Cancer Club, Detroit Physiol Soc; pres, Am Cancer Soc, Mich Div, 1986-; chmn adv comn, minority involvement field serv comn, Am Cancer Soc; educ review comn, Nat Cancer Inst; Nat Surgeon Reserve Officers Asn; Metropolitan Detroit Steering Comn for The Cancer Prevention Awareness; med dir, Oncol, Samaritan Health Ctr, 1986-; Southfield Oncol Inst. **Honors/Awds:** 'Outstanding Reserve Aerospace Medical Physician Award', 1974, 1979; 'Command Flight Surgeon of the Year', AFRES, 1974, 1979; Humanitarian of the Year, 1988. **Military Serv:** USAF, capt, 1959-61; USAF Reserves, col, 1978-87. **Home Addr:** 20051 Kelly Rd, Detroit, MI 48225, **Home Phone:** (313)372-7679. **Business Addr:** President, Director, Southfield Oncology Institute Inc./Southfield Oncology Associates, 21751 W 11 Mile Rd Suite 114, Southfield, MI 48076, **Business Phone:** (248)356-2828.

VAUGHN, COUNTESS DANIELLE
Actor. **Personal:** Born Aug 8, 1978, Idabel, OK; daughter of Leo and Sandra; married Joseph James, Jan 16, 2002; children: Jaylen. **Career:** Films: Trippin, 1999; Max Keeble's Big Move, actor & off admin asst, 2001; TV appearances: "227", 1985; "The Magical World of Disney", 1988; "Hangin' with Mr. Cooper", 1992; "Thea", 1993; "Roc", 1994; "Minor Adjustments", 1996; "Moesha", 1996; "Goode Behavior", 1997; "The Martin Short Show", 1999; "The Parkers", 1999-2004; "Star Search", 2003; "Mad TV", 2003; "I Love the '90s: Part Deux", 2005; "I Love the 80's 3-D", 2005; "The Tyra Banks Show", 2006; "Cuts", 2006; "Celebrity Rap Superstar", 2007; Thugaboo: Sneaker Madness, 2006; Thugaboo: A Miracle on D-Roc's Street, 2006. **Honors/Awds:** Image Award, Nat Asn Advan Colored People, 1998. **Business Addr:** Actress, c/o United Paramount Network, 11800 Wilshire Blvd, Los Angeles, CA 90025, **Business Phone:** (310)575-7000.*

VAUGHN, DAVID
Basketball player. **Personal:** Born Mar 23, 1973, Tulsa, OK. **Educ:** Memphis State Univ. **Career:** Basketball pleyer (retired); Orlando Magic, forward, 1995-97; Golden State Warriors, 1997-98; Chicago Bulls, 1997-98; New Jersey Nets, 1998-99; Ittihad, Syria, 2003.

VAUGHN, ED (MWALIMU EDWARD VAUGHN)
Business owner, state government official. **Personal:** Born Jul 30, 1934, Abbeville, AL. **Educ:** Fisk Univ. **Career:** Mich House Reps, state rep, 1998-2000; Detroit Pub Schs, teacher; Vaughn's Book Store, co-founder & proprietor, currently. **Orgs:** Nat Asn Advan Colored People; Elks; Omega Psi Phi. **Business Phone:** (313)557-3743.

VAUGHN, EUGENIA MARCHELLE WASHINGTON
Social worker. **Personal:** Born Oct 31, 1957, Columbus, OH; daughter of Eugene G and Lula Augusta Edwards; married Tannis Eugene, Jun 9, 1984; children: Shannon Eugene & Ieasha Michelle. **Educ:** Columbus Tech Inst, associate's deg, 1977; Ohio Dominican Col, BA, 1983; Ohio State Univ, MSW, 1985. **Career:** Franklin Co C Servs, caseworker I, 1977-83, child welfare caseworker II, 1984; Columbus Area Ment Health Ctr, contract worker, 1985; Franklin Co C Serv, child welfare caseworker II, III Foster Care, 1985-87, social worker III, 1987-89, treatment mgr, 1989-91, child welfare supvr II, 1991-. **Orgs:** Nat Asn Social Workers, Nat Asn Black Social Workers; LSW Status Nat Asn Social Workers, 1986; initiator Scholarship Alumni Asn; LISW, 1990. **Honors/Awds:** Minority Fellowship, 1983-84, Child Welfare Traineeship, 1984-85 OSU; Delta Epsilon Sigma Hon Soc, Alpha Delta Mu Social Work Honor Soc. **Home Addr:** 262 Eastcreek Dr, PO Box 534, Galloway, OH 43119. **Business Addr:** Child Welfare Supervisor II, Franklin Co Children Services, 1951 Gantz Rd, Grove City, OH 43123, **Business Phone:** (614)278-5843.

VAUGHN, GREGORY LAMONT
Baseball player. **Personal:** Born Jul 3, 1965, Sacramento, CA. **Educ:** Univ Miami. **Career:** Baseball player (retired); Milwaukee Brewers, outfielder, 1989-96; San Diego Padres, 1996-98; Cincinnati Reds, 1999; Tampa Bay Devils Rays, 2000-02; Colo Rockies, outfielder, 2003. **Honors/Awds:** Midwest Co-Most Valuable Player, 1987; Most Valuable Player, Am Assn, 1989; Four-time All-Star, 1993, 1996, 1998, 2001; NL Silver Slugger Award, 1998; NL Comeback Player of the Year, 1998.

VAUGHN, JACQUE
Basketball player. **Personal:** Born Feb 11, 1975, Los Angeles, CA. **Educ:** Kans Univ, attended 1997. **Career:** UT Jazz, guard, 1997-2001; Atlanta Hawks, guard, 2001-02, 2003-04; Orlando Magic,2002-03; NJ Nets, guard, 2004-06; San Antonio Spurs, guard, 2007-. **Honors/Awds:** Academic All-Am of the Yr, GTE, 1997; First Championship, Mem of Spurs, 2007. **Business Addr:** Professional Basketball Player, San Antonio Spurs, 1 AT T Center, San Antonio, TX 78219, **Business Phone:** (210)444-5000.*

VAUGHN, JANICE S
Health services administrator, educator. **Personal:** Born Jun 8, 1943, Augusta, GA; daughter of John Adam and Violet Allen Singleton; married Edward Vaughn III, May 28, 1966; children: Kellye Baugh, Hope Brown, Enyce Thompson & Janna Harper. **Educ:** Talladega Col, BA, 1964; Atlanta Univ, MSW, 1971; Univ Pittsburgh, MPH, 1978, PhD, 1979. **Career:** Atlanta Un Chatam County Dept Family & Children Servs, caseworker, 1968-71; Atlanta Univ, Sch Social Work, assoc prof & chmn, 1979-81, assoc dean, 1982-86, dir doctoral prog, 1983-87; Ga Dept Human Resources, Div Family & C Servs, dep dir, 1987-93; Ga Southern Univ, prof & asst vpres acad affairs, Master Social Work Prog, dir, 1993-95; Links Inc, Magnolia Chap, vpres, 1997-99; Morehouse Sch Med, Master Pub Health Prog, Dept Community Health & Prev, Family Health Track, track coord, 1998-, dir & prof, currently. **Orgs:** Nat Asn Black Social Workers, 1979-; comnr, Human Resources Res Rev, 1990; Jack & Jill Am, 1990-; chmn, Fulton County Bd Health, 1996-2000; chair, Fulton County Community Serv Bd Ment Health, 1996-2000; chairperson, Fulton County Health Dept, Community Serv Bd, 1997; Nat Adv Bd mem, Nat SIDS & Infant Death Prog, 1998; Self Study Steering Comt, Morehouse Sch Med, 1999; Am Pub Health Asn. **Honors/Awds:** Leadership, Ga Dept Human Resources, 1990; Service Award, Jack & Jill Am, 1990. **Special Achievements:** Led collaborations of "Granny Houses" facility for children of substance abusing mothers, replicated in 5 cities in GA. **Home Phone:** (912)898-1297. **Business Addr:** Director, Professor, Morehouse School Medical, Master of Public Health Program, 720 Westview Dr SW, Atlanta, GA 30310-1495, **Business Phone:** (404)752-1500.

VAUGHN, MARY KATHRYN
Government official. **Personal:** Born Sep 20, 1949, Kansas City, KS; daughter of Edward Parks and Kathryn Jones Parks; married Harvey L Vaughn Jr (died 1983). **Educ:** Col Wooster, Wooster, Ohio, BA, 1970; Rutgers Univ, NB, NJ, MSW, 1972; Harvard Univ Prog Sr Exec State & Local Govt, Cambridge, MA, 1985. **Career:** Jackson County Juv Court, Kans City, Mo, residential servs admin, 1973-78; Univ Kans, minority affairs outreach counr, 1978-79; City Kans, Mo, dept head, 1979; City Wichita Housing Serv, dir, 2004-. **Orgs:** Prog coordr, Mayor's Christmas Tree Asn, 1980-; Full Employ Coun, 1986-; Pres, US Conf City Human Servs Offs, 1990-; Pvt Indust Coun, 1990-; Ad Hoc Task Force Homelessness, 2006-. **Honors/Awds:** Grad, Centurions Leadership Prog, 1980; NEWS-Maker of the Year, NEWS House Shelter Battered Women, 1990; Grad, KC Tomorrow Leadership Prog, 1990. **Business Addr:** Director, City of Wichita Housing Services, City of Wichita, 455 N Main, Wichita, KS 67202, **Business Phone:** (316)462-3795.

VAUGHN, MO
Baseball player, business owner. **Personal:** Born Dec 15, 1967, Norwalk, CT. **Educ:** Trinity Pawling Sch, attended 1986. **Career:** Baseball player (retired), Business owner; Boston Red Sox, designated hitter, 1991-98; Anaheim Angels, 1999-2000; NY Mets, 2002-03; Mo Vaughn Hit Dog baseball clinic, Tufts Univ, owner & operator, currently; OMNI New York LLC, co-managing dir & co-founder, currently. **Honors/Awds:** Bart Giamatti Award, Baseball Assistance Team, 1995; Silver Slugger Award, 1995; American League Most Valuable Player, Baseball Writers' Asn Am, 1995; Trinity-Pawling's Hall of Fame, 2006.

VAUGHN, MWALIMU EDWARD. See VAUGHN, ED.

VAUGHN, DR. PERCY JOSEPH
College administrator, educator. **Personal:** Born Jan 11, 1932, New Orleans, LA; married Doris C (deceased); children: Percy Darrell, Rene, Denise & Tracy. **Educ:** Morris Brown Col, BS, 1957; Atlanta Univ, MBA, 1959; Tex Tech Univ, DBA, 1975; Harvard Univ, attended 1978. **Career:** Jackson Brewing Co, sales & pub relations rep, 1960; Southern Univ, asst prof, 1968; Tex Tech Univ, instr, 1972; Ala State Univ, dean, 1975-, prof, currently. **Orgs:** Fac coord, Nat Urban Leagues' Black Exec Exchange Prog, 1976; Nat Adv Counc Fac Coord Career Awareness Prog, 1976; proj dir, Small Bus Inst US Small Bus Admin, 1978; chmn bd, Ala Consortium Deans Col Bus Admin estab ASBCD, 1978; Active Corp Execs Nat SCORE & Am Coun Exercise Coun, 1978; pres, Ala Coun Deans Ala Asn Higher Educ Bus, 1979. **Special Achievements:** Co-author of : "Managing New Enterpises" 1976, "An Investigation of Small Bus Inven Policy" 1979; Article Free Enterprise in Focus 1978; The Approaching Eighties New Management Challenges 1979. **Military Serv:** AUS, 1948-52. **Business Addr:** Dean, Professor, Alabama State University, College of Business administration, 915 S Jackson St, PO Box 271, Montgomery, AL 36101-0271, **Business Phone:** (334)229-4124.

VAUGHT, LOY STEPHEN
Basketball player. **Personal:** Born Feb 27, 1968, Grand Rapids, MI; son of Loy Vaught Sr and Ozzie Friend Jager. **Educ:** Univ Mich, bus mgt, 1990. **Career:** Basketball player (retired); Los Angeles Clippers, forward-ctr, 1990-98; Detroit Pistons, 1999-2000; Wash Wizards, 2000-01; Dallas Mavericks, forward-ctr, 2000-01. **Honors/Awds:** NCAA Champions, Univ Mich Wolverines, 1989.

VAUGHTERS-JOHNSON, CECILIE A
Lawyer. **Personal:** Born Jul 29, 1953, Montclair, NJ; daughter of Vivian S and Alans H; married Robert W, Oct 12, 1985; children: Langston & Ciara. **Educ:** Ohio Univ, BBA, 1975; Georgetown Univ, Law Ctr, JD, 1978. **Career:** General Motors, Inland Div, comptroller's off intern, 1972-75; Clinton Chapman Law Off, assoc, 1978-82; Chapman, Norwind & Vaughters Law Firm, 1982-86; Cecilie Vaughters-Johnson, Esq, prof consult, 1987-; Nat Legal Adv, Jack & Jill Am, Inc, 2002-03; Legal Coun & Secy, Kidz & Co Inc, 2002-04; Pvt Pract, lawyer, currently. **Orgs:** Pres, Greater Wash Area Chap Women Lawyers Div, Nat Bar Asn, 1983-84; vpres, Wash Bar Asn, 1983-85; reg dir, Nat Bar Asn, 1984-85; Palo Alto Chap, vpres, Nat Asn Advan Colored People, 1987-89; Palo Alto Chap, bd dir, Red Cross, 1989-96; chief fin officer, Johnson Tri-Dom Found, 1990-; reg dir, Georgetown Black Law Alumni Asn, 1991-94; treas, PTA, Montclaire Sch, 1992-94; bd dir, Los Altos Parent Presch Asn, 1992-94; treas, Jack & Jill Am, San Jose Chap, 1996-98, pres, 2002-04; Cupertino Jr High Sch, PTA bd, 1998-2000. **Honors/Awds:** AFA Student Life Univ Calif, Santa Cruz, Humanitarian Award, 1997; Certificates Special Congressional Recognition, 1994; East Palo Alto City Coun, Certificate of Commendation, 1994; Nat Bar Assn, Women Lawyer's Div, President's Award, 1985; Black Am Law Students Assn, A J Cooper Award, 1978. **Business Addr:** Lawyer, 1635 Candace Way, Los Altos, CA, CA 94024-6243, **Business Phone:** (650)961-3312.

VEAL, HOWARD RICHARD
Executive. **Personal:** Born Oct 24, 1942, Jackson, MS; married Elizabeth; children: Howard Jr & Jason. **Educ:** Alcorn A&M Col, BS, 1966; Utcc Jr Col, attended 1964; Ind Univ, attended 1969. **Career:** Elkhrt Urban League, dir housing community serv, 1968-70, act exec dir, 1970-71; Springfield Urban League, pres & chief exec officer, 1972-. **Orgs:** Chmn, prog rev subcomt Gov Adv Coun Emp & Training, 1974; City Springfield Citz Adv Comn, 1974; pres, Ill Coun Urban League, 1975-; secy, Urban League Coun; Cent Reg Civic Serv; Bd Higher Educ Planning Comn, 1975; Omega Psi Phi Fraternity; adv plan comn, White Hs Conf Libr, 1977; First bd Zion Baptist Church. **Honors/Awds:** Outstanding Citizen Award, Nat Asn Advan Colored People, 1970, 1975; Outstanding Service Award, Springfield Urban League, 1976; NYNEX Scholarship Award, 1996. **Home Addr:** 2016 Randall Ct, Springfield, IL 62703, **Home Phone:** (217)528-5294. **Business Addr:** President, Chief Executive Officer, Springfield Urban League, 100 N 11th St, Springfield, IL 62703, **Business Phone:** (217)789-0830.

VEAL, DR. YVONNECRIS SMITH
Physician. **Personal:** Born Dec 24, 1936, Ahoskie, NC; daughter of Dempsey Porter and Zeora Ida Lewis; married Henry Veal Jr; children: Michael E. **Educ:** Hampton Univ, BS (magna cum laude), 1957; Med Col Va, Richmond, MD, 1962. **Career:** Jamaica Hosp, Sickle Cell Clinic, attending physician, 1967-69, Child Develop Clinic, pediatrician, 1967-69; Windham, Child Care, med staff physician, 1967-71; Pvt Practice Pediatrics, 1967-71; Carter Community Health Ctr, pediatrician, 1968-79; East NY Neighborhood Family Care Ctr, dir med affairs, 1975-81; Carter Community Health Ctr, med dir, 1981-84; US Postal Serv, contract physician, 1984-85, Long Island Div, field div med officer, 1985-93, NY Metro Area, sr med dir, 1993-. **Orgs:** Delta Sigma Theta Sorority Inc, 1955-, Gamma Iota Chap, 1955-57, pres, 1956-57, Queens Alumnae Chap, 1966-; NAACP; YWCA; Nat Coun Negro Women, 1965-67, 1980-, Am Med Asn, 1968-; Med Soc, State NY, 1968-; Queens County Med Soc, 1968-; Community Family Planning Coun, 1981-85; Nat Med Asn, 1966-, pres, 1995-96, chair bd trustees, 1989-91, numerous other positions, 1973-; Queens Pediatric Soc, 1973-84; Queens County Prof Standards Review Org, 1977-88; Health Systems Agency NYC, Queens Sub-Area Adv Comt, 1981-96; Dalton Sch PTA, 1970-81; Pre-Kindergarten Educ; ATLED, Inc Organizing Chair 1986-89, bd dirs, 1986-; Merrick Y Day Care; Comt for pres, 1980-84, Nat Nominating Comt, 1976-78, chair, Regional Nominating Comt, 1979-83, Am Col Occupational & Environ Med, 1992-; Am Heart Asn, 1992-; Nat Membership Servs Comt, 1991-95, Eastern Region Sci Lia-

sion, 2000-. **Honors/Awds:** New York State Senator Carol Berman, Community Service Certificate of Merit, 1979; East New York NFCC Community Bd Appreciation Award, 1981; United Negro Col Fund, Distinguished Leadership Award, 1984; Saint Albans Congregational Church, Special Award for Outstanding Contribution to Southeast Queens Community, 1984; Wives of Club 50, Special Award, 1988; Morris Brown Col, Cert of Appreciation, 1987-88; 'Special Achievement Award', US Postal Serv, 1989; Delta Sigma Theta, 'Certificate of Achievement', 1989; 'Appreciation Award', US Postal Serv, 1990; NY Chap, Morris Brown Alumni Asn, 'Associate Member of the Year Award', 1990; 'Pride in Performance Award', US Postal Serv, 1991; 'Susan Smith Mckinney Steward Medical Society Recognition Award', 1991; Morris Brown Col, 'Ivan Allen Jr Award for Excellence in Public Relations', 1993; Fel NY Acad Med, 1995-; "Yvonnecris Smith Veal", Achievement Ward, 1997; E NY Diagnostic & Treatment Ctr, 'US Postal Service National Medical Directors Award', 1997, Spot Award, 1998, Human Resources Process Recognition Award, 1998; numerous others. **Special Achievements:** The fifth African American student enrolled at the Medical College of Virginia in Richmond, 1960; The first woman to chair the Board of Trustees of the National Medical Association, 1989. **Home Addr:** 112-30 Farmers Blvd, Jamaica, NY 11412-2360, **Home Phone:** (718)740-9850. **Business Addr:** Senior Medical Director, US Postal Service, New York Metropolitan Area, 78-02 Liberty Ave, Ozone Park, NY 11417-9451.

VEALS, CRAIG ELLIOTT
Judge. **Personal:** Born Jan 21, 1955, Los Angeles, CA; son of Charles Edward and Rhoda Maida; married Barbara Martha O, Jul 23, 1977; children: Aaron Elliott & Philip Seth. **Educ:** Occidental Col, BS, 1977; Univ Calif, Los Angeles, Sch Law, JD, 1980. **Career:** Calif State Atty Gen, dep atty gen, 1981-83; Los Angeles Dist Atty, dep dist atty, 1983-94; Los Angeles Munic Ct, judge, 1994-97; State Calif, Los Angeles Super Ct, judge, 1997-. **Orgs:** La County Bar Asn, vice chair, Environ Law Air Qual Sub-Sect, 1992-93; Los Angeles County Bar Asn, exec comt mem, Criminal Law Sect, 1994-; Calif State Dep Dist Atty's Asn, 1986-94; Asn Dep Dist Atty's, 1986-94; Asn Dep Atty's Gen, 1981-83; Western Regionals Moot Ct Competition, judge, 1992; Los Angeles Municip Ct, temp judge, 1992; Phi Alpha Delta Law Fraternity, 1977-; Langston Bar Asn, 1994-; Constitutional Rights Found, 1989-; Calif Judges' Asn, mem, Criminal Law & Procedure Subcommittee, 1995-96; Municip Ct Judges' Asn, 1994-; Am Judges' Asn, 1994-; Atty Screening Comt, La Super Ct, 1994-; Constitutional Rights Found, mem, bd dirs, 1997-. **Honors/Awds:** Scholarship, Occidental Col, 1973-77; Calif State Scholarship, State Calif, 1973-77; law scholarship, Univ Calif Los Angeles Law Sch, 1977; Attorney of the Year, Los Angeles County Bar Asn & Const Rights Found, 1993; Commendation for Los Angeles Police Dept, 1996; Service Award, Asn Dep Dist Attys, 1994; Service Award, La Dist Atty's Off, Environ Crimes Div, 1994; Judge of the Year, Const Rights Found, 1997. **Special Achievements:** Competition judge for Constitutional Rights Found, Mock Trial Competition, 1989-. **Business Addr:** Judge, Los Angeles Superior Court, State of California, Clara Shortridge Foltz Criminal Justice Ctr, 111 N Hill St Ct Rm 122, Los Angeles, CA 90012, **Business Phone:** (213)974-5759.

VELAND, TONY
Football coach, football player. **Personal:** Born Mar 11, 1973, Omaha, NE; married Brooke; children: T J & Arianna. **Educ:** Nebr Univ. **Career:** Football player (retired), Football coach; Denver Broncos, defensive back, 1997; Carolina Panthers, 1998; Omaha Beef, Def Coordinator, 2002-. **Honors/Awds:** Super Bowl XXXII, 1997. **Business Addr:** Defensive Coordinator, Omaha Beef Football, 1804 Capitol Ave, Omaha, NE 68102, **Business Phone:** (402)346-2333.

VELEZ, LAUREN
Actor. **Personal:** Born Nov 2, 1964, San Juan, PR; married Mark Gordon. **Career:** Films: I Like It Like That, 1994; City Hall, 1996; I Think I Do, 1997; Buscando un sueno, 1997; The LaMastas, 1998; Taino, 1999; Prince of Central Park, 2000; Prison Song, 2001; Barely Buzzed, 2005; Dexter, 2006; Serial, 2007; TV appearances: "New York Undercover", 1995-98; "Oz", 1997-2003; "Thicker Than Blood", 1998; "St Michael's Crossing", 1999; "Love & Treason", 2001; "Dragnet", 2003; "Law & Order: Special Victims Unit", 2004; "Numb3rs", 2006-07; "Dexter", 2006-09; "Law & Order: Criminal Intent", 2008; "Ugly Betty", 2009. **Honors/Awds:** NCLR Bravo Award for Outstanding Actress in a Drama Series, 1996; ALMA Award for Outstanding Actress in a Television Series, 2001; Best Supporting Actress award, Long Island Film Expo Festival, 2006; Vision Award, Nat Asn Multi-Ethnicity Commun, 2007. **Business Addr:** Actress, c/o Home Box Office Inc.*

VELJOHNSON, REGINALD (REGGIE VEL JOHNSON)
Actor. **Personal:** Born Aug 16, 1952, New York, NY; son of Dan and Eve. **Educ:** Long Island Inst Music & Arts; NY Univ, BA, theater; studied under Lloyd Richards. **Career:** Films: But Never Jam Today, 1979; Wolfen, 1981; Inacent Black, 1981; The World of Ben Caldwell, 1982; Ghost Busters, 1984; Oh! Oh! Obesity!, 1984; Spell No 7, 1987-88; Film appearances: Wolfen, 1981; The Cotton Club,1984; Ghost busters, 1984; Remo Williams: The Adventure Begins, 1985; Crocodile Dundee, 1986; Armed & Dangerous, 1986; Die Hard, 1988; Plain Clothes, 1988; Turner & Hooch, 1989; Die Hard 2, 1990; A Fond Little Memory, 1991; Posse, 1993; Ground Zero, 2000; Like Mike, 2002; The King, 2002; Waitin' To Love, 2002; Death to the Super models, 2005; Hidden Secrets, 2006; Three Days to Vegas, 2007; Out at the Wedding, 2007; Steppin, 2008; Jelly, 2009; TV appearances: When Hell Freezes Over, I'll Skate, 1979; Kojak: The Belarus File, 1985; Doing Life, 1986; "Quiet Victory: The Charlie Wedemeyer Story", 1988; "The Bride in Black", 1990; "Jury Duty: The Comedy", 1990; "Perfect Strangers", 1988-89; "Family Matters", 1989; "The Joan Rivers Show", 1989; "Good Morning America", 1990; "The Byron Allen Show", 1991; "Regis & Kathy Lee", 1991; "The Arsenio Hall Show", 1991; "Grass Roots", 1992; "Yuletide in the 'hood(voice)", 1993; "One of Her Own", 1994; "Deadly Pursuits", 1996; "Ghost Whisperer", 2005; "Monk", 2006; Nerve Endings, 2007; On the Lot, 2007; Out at the Wedding, 2007 "Bones"; "Chuck" . 2008; Sunday Evening Haircut, producer, 2005. **Orgs:** Joseph Papp's Black/Hispanic Shakespeare Co; nat spokesman, Big Brothers Am, Pass It On Prog. **Home Addr:** c/o Jeralyn Bagdley, Bagdley Connor, Los Angeles, CA 90069. **Business Addr:** Actor, Lori DeWaal & Associates, 7080 Hollywood Blvd Suite 515, Los Angeles, CA 90028-6932, **Business Phone:** (323)462-4122.*

VENABLE, ABRAHAM S
Chairperson, executive. **Personal:** Born Apr 10, 1930, Washington, DC; married Anna Graham; children: Karen, Douglas & Stephen. **Educ:** Howard Univ, BA, 1951, MA, econ; Princeton Univ, Woodrow Wilson Sch Pub & Int Affairs, fel; Mass Inst Tech, sr exec prog. **Career:** Gen Motors Corp, exec dir urban affairs, 1971; US Dept Com, dir affirm action prog, 1966-68, dir minority bus enterprise, 1969-71; Motor Enterprise Inc, vpres, 1975-; New Ctr Develop Partnership, vpres, 1975-; Mass Inst Technol, sr exec prog. **Orgs:** Bd dirs, Nat Corp Housing Partnership Wash; chmn, BPRC; commr, Urban Affairs Com US C C; vice chmn, bd dir, Nat Bus League; bus adv, Com Cong Bulk Caucus; Nat Adv Coun SBA Govt; chmn, Inst Am Bus; vpres, Motor Enterprises Inc; vice chmn, Greater Detroit Foreign Trade Zone; bd dir, Detroit Br, Nat Asn Advan Colored People; hon mem, Beta Gamma Sigma.; Minority Bus Hall Fame & Mus Inc; chmn, Inst Am Bus, currently. **Honors/Awds:** Man of Year, Nat Bus League; OIC Humanitarian Award, Opportunities Industrialization Ctr Am; Outstanding Service Award, Nat Asn Advan Colored People; Outstanding Service Award, Nat Urban League; Minority Business Advocacy Award, School's Small Bus Develop Ctr, Howard Univ; Lifetime Achievement Award, US Dept Com; honorary degree, Shaw Col, Detroit; honorary degree, Grand Valley State Col, Mich. **Special Achievements:** Mr. Venable is the author of several articles dealing with black businessmen as well as a book, Building Black Business — An Analysis and a Plan . **Home Addr:** 300 Matherson Ct, Franklin, TN 37067. **Business Phone:** (202)408-5418.

VENABLE, ANDREW ALEXANDER, JR.
Library administrator, president (organization). **Personal:** Born Nov 11, 1944, Staunton, VA; married Maxine Cockrell; children: Angela, Andrew III. **Educ:** Va State Univ, Petersburg, BS, bus admin, 1967; Case Western Res Univ, Cleveland, MSLS, 1978. **Career:** Standard Oil Co Mkt Dept Ohio, capital budget planning controls analyst, 1968-70; Cleveland Pub Libr, asst dir personnel serv, 1970-71; dir finance admin serv, 1972-78, dep clerk treas, 1975-76, clerk treas, 1976-78, head comm serv, 1978, dep dir, 1999; dir & bd trustees, currently. **Orgs:** Pres, Pub Library Employees Credit Union, 1978-; libr tech adv comt, Cuyahoga Community Col, 1978-; Ohio Libr Asn; Am Libr Asn, 1978-; trustee, Urban League Greater Cleveland Inc, 1979-82; trustee, Consumer Protection Asn, 1979-; Cleveland City Club; trustee, Harvard Community Serv Ctr; allocations pnl United Way Serv, 1979-81; Beta Phi Mu Int Libr Sci Hon Soc, 1979. **Honors/Awds:** Andrew A Venable Scholar, Va State Univ Alumini Asn, 1973; Serv Appreciation Award, Alpha Phi Alpha Frat Inc, Cleveland Grad Chap, 1977; Outstanding Young Men of Am, 1978; Outstanding Greek of the Year, Greater Cleveland Pan Hellenic Coun, 1979. **Business Addr:** Library Dir, Cleveland Public Library, 325 Superior Ave NE, Cleveland, OH 44114, **Business Phone:** (216)623-2800.

VENABLE, MAX (WILLIAM MCKINLEY VENABLE, JR.)
Baseball player, athletic coach. **Personal:** Born Jun 6, 1957, Phoenix, AZ; married Molly; children: William Dion. **Career:** Baseball player (Retired); San Francisco Giants, outfielder, 1979-83; Montreal Expos, outfielder, 1984; Cincinnati Reds, outfielder, 1985-87; Calif Angels, outfielder, 1989-91; Chiba Lotte Marines, 1992-93; Dragons, hitting coach, 2004; Ft Wayne Wizards, hitting coach; Lake Elsinore Storm, hitting coach; Triple A Portland Beavers, Hitting Coach, currently. **Business Addr:** Hitting Coach, Triple A Portland Beavers, 1844 SW Morrison, PGE Pk, Portland, OR 97205, **Business Phone:** (503)553-5400.*

VENABLE, REV. ROBERT CHARLES
Clergy. **Personal:** Born Jan 26, 1950, Camden, NJ; married Cherly A Pitts; children: Tisa L, Lovell V, Marc R, Alvin, Labree, Justin, Steven & Eligah David. **Educ:** Shaw Univ, Bible Col. **Career:** New Wesley AME Zion Church, assoc pastor, 1975-82; Harris Temple AME Zion Church, pastor 1982-. **Orgs:** Bd educ, Camden City, 1982-96; dir educ, Camden Ministerial Alliance; chairperson, Affirmative Action; chairperson, BSIP; chairperson, Finance Educ Bd; Camden Ministerial Alliance; Penn Ministerial Alliance; Camden Dist Ministerial Alliance AME Zion Church; Nat Asn Advan Colored People; S Christian League Conf; Urban League; Asn Sch Bus Officials US & Canada; NJ Sch Bd Asn; PTA; Boy Scouts Am; Nat Black Caucus State Legislators; Nat Caucus Black Sch Bd Mem; Joint Ctr Political Studies; Nat Black Elected Officials; NJ Pan Methodist Comn Liaison; Penn Pan Methodist Celebration Finance; Camden Co Democratic Comn; Nat Parks & Conserv Wash, DC; Nat Trust Hist Preserv; Oriental Lodge No 1 F&AM-PHA. **Honors/Awds:** Youth Choir Christian Serv, New Wesley AME Zion Church, 1982; Christian Serv Award, Harris Temple AME Zion Church, 1983; Christian Serv Award, Elegant Charm Modeling Sch, 1985; Thirteenth Ward Whitman Park Little League, 1985-92; Community Serv Award, EL L Bonsall Sch, 1985; Community Serv Award, Camden County Coun Economic Opportunities, Inc, 1985; Christian Serv Award, Harris Temple AME Zion Church, 1986; Bishops EL Huff Community Serv Award, Union Am ME Church, 1990; Community Serv Award, Camden City Youth Asn, Inc, 1991; Community Serv Award, Prida Camden Lodge No 83, 1993; The Castle Award, Camden High School Outstanding Achievements, 1994. **Business Addr:** Pastor, Harris Temple AME Zion Church, 926 Florence St, Camden, NJ 08104, **Business Phone:** (856)541-6608.

VENABLE, WILLIAM MCKINLEY, JR. See VENABLE, MAX.

VENEY, MARGUERITE C
Insurance executive. **Personal:** Born Mar 8, 1949, Melfa, VA; daughter of George and Maggie Chandler; married. **Educ:** Va State Univ, BS, 1971; Northeastern Univ, MBA, 1995. **Career:** John Hancock Mutual Life Ins Co, contract Mgr, currently. **Honors/Awds:** Black Achievers Award, Boston YMCA, 1990. **Business Addr:** Contract Manager, John Hancock Mutual Life Insurance Co, 200 Berkley St B 9, PO Box 111, Boston, MA 02117.

VENSON, CLYDE R
Association executive. **Personal:** Born May 8, 1936, Alexandria, LA; son of Effie Kellum and Samuel S; married Annette Broussard, Dec 23, 1962; children: Jane A & Lisa A. **Educ:** Southern Univ, Baton Rouge, La, BS, sociol, 1960; FBI Nat Acad, Wash, DC, 1971. **Career:** Shelby Co Sheriff's Dept, Memphis, TN, dep sheriff, 1960-65; TN Dept Corrections, Memphis, TN, parole officer, 1965-85; TN Dist Atty Gen, Memphis, TN, asst chief criminal invests, 1985-88; Shelby Co Sheriff's Dept, Memphis, TN, dir traffic safety, 1988-91; Shelby Co Corrections, Memphis, TN, admin security, 1991-93; VCI & Assoc Inc, security consult, pres, 1993-2000; Memphis Housing Authority, dir security; Venson's Criminal Invests & Assocs, pres, 1991-; Nat United Law Enforcement Officers Asn, exec dir, currently. **Orgs:** Alpha Phi Alpha Fraternity, 1958-; exalted ruler, IBP Order Elks W, 1965-69; nat gen chmn, Memphis Kemet Jubilee Inc, 1985-; exec dir, Blacks Law Enforcement, 1986-; US/Japan Bilateral Session Legal Rels, Tokyo, Japan, 1988. **Honors/Awds:** Man of the Year, Nat United Law Enforcement Officers Asn, 1980; Memphian of the year, Moolah Shirine Temple 54, 2000-; Dr RQ Venson Pioneer Award, 2000. **Business Addr:** President, Executive director, National United Law Enforcement Officers Association Inc, 265 E McLemore Ave, Memphis, TN 38106-2833, **Business Phone:** (901)774-1118.

VERBAL, CLAUDE A
Engineer, executive. **Personal:** Born Nov 12, 1942, Durham, NC; son of Sidney Verbal Sr and Mary Gladys; married Dorothy Simmons. **Educ:** NC St Univ, BSME, 1964. **Career:** Buick Motor Div GMC, engr res develop, 1964-66, exp lab test engr, 1966-69, chassis design engr, 1969-73, staff proj engr supv experimental engr, 1974-75, asst supt qual control, 1976-77, supt qual control, 1977; Milford Proving Ground, engr supv, 1973-74; BOC Powertrain GMC, supt mfg, 1985-87; Serv Parts Oper GM, plant mgr, 1987-98; Wesley Indust, COO, 1999-. **Orgs:** Mid-Mi Gov Bd Soc Auto Engr, 1970-; Soc Mech Engr; Nat Soc Prof Engr Registered, 1971; Bsls Omcrn Rho Chap Omega Psi Phi Frat Inc, 1971-; bd dir, Hurley med Ctr, 1984-; nat bd dir, Soc Automotive Engr, 1988; pres bd dir, Hurley Med Ctr, 1989; Flint Airport Authority, 1991; pres, Pontiac Vis Nurses Asn, 1991; bd campaign chair, North Oakland United Way, 1992; pres, Soc Automotive Engrs, 1996; bd control, Mich Technol Univ, 1997-, chmn, 2000-01; bd dir, Flint Urban League; Pres, Flint Econ Develop Corp; Leadership Flint; FAM Masterr Mason Erk Lodge 32 Deg; Flnt Urban League Hrt City Adv Bd; first vpres, Flint Inner City Lion's Club; Water-ford Rotary Club. **Honors/Awds:** Young Engr of the Ur, Flint Chap Prof Engr, 1974; Omega Man of Yr, Omicron Rho Chap Omega Psi Phi, 1974; Nat Media Women Award, 1977; Distinguished Alumnus of North Carolina State Univ Award, 1997; Engineer of the Year Award, Flint chapter Nat Soc Prof Engr, 1997. **Home Addr:** 1800 Valley Lane, Flint, MI 48503. **Business Addr:** Chief Operating Officer, Wesley Industries Inc, 41000 N Woodward Ave Suite 395E, Bloomfield Hills, MI 48304.

VEREEN, BEN AUGUSTUS
Entertainer. **Personal:** Born Oct 10, 1946, Miami, FL; married Nancy Brunner; children: Benjamin, Malaika, Naja (deceased), Kabara & Karon. **Educ:** Pentacostal Theol Sem, New York, NY, attended. **Career:** Stage appearances: The Prodigal Son; Sweet Charity; Golden Boy; Hair; Jesus Christ Superstar; Pippin; Cabaret; Grind; TV appearances: "Roots", 1977; "Ben Vereen-His Roots", 1978; "Fosse", 2001; "Tenspeed & Brown Shoe"; "Webster"; "Great Performances: Dance in America", 2001; "Feast of All Saints", 2001; "Oz", 2006; "Law & Order: Criminal Intent", 2007; "Grey's Anatomy", 2007; "Grey's Anatomy", 2007; "Your Mama Don't Dance" 2008; Films: Sweet Charity; Funny Lady; Louis Armstrong-Chicago Style; All That Jazz; I'll Take You There, 1999; The Painting, actor, 2001; Idlewild, actor, 2006; Holiday in Bryant Park, 2007; & Then Came Love, 2007; Mama, I Want to Sing!, 2007; Tapioca, 2007. **Orgs:** Celebrity spokesperson, Big Brothers; nat celebrity spokesperson, A Drug-Free Am. **Honors/Awds:** Theatre World Award, Jesus Christ Superstar, 1972; Tony Award; Drama Desk Award; CLIO Pippin Humanitarian Award, Israel, 1975; George M Cohen Award, AGVA; Best Song & Dance Star; Best Rising Star; Entertainer of the Year, 1976; TV Critics Award, Roots, 1977; Image Award, Roots NAACP, 1977, 1978; 7 Emmy Awards for Ben Vereen-His Roots; Cultural Award Roots, Israel, 1978; Humanitarian Award, State of Israel, 1979; Eleanor Roosevelt Humanitarian Award, 1983; Helping Enforcement Reach Our Streets Award, City of Miami, 2002; TV Land Awards, 2007. **Business Phone:** (561)254-8335.

VEREEN, DIXIE DIANE
Editor. **Personal:** Born Nov 6, 1957, Colorado Springs, CO; daughter of Willie C and Dixie Lee Dorsey. **Educ:** Randolph Tech Col, Asheboro, NC, AAS photog, 1977. **Career:** Raleigh News & Observer, photogr, 1978-80; Newsday, photogr, 1980; Philadelphia Inquirer, photogr, 1981-82; USA Today, photogr & photo ed, 1982-85; USA Weekend, dir opers, 1986-90; Wilmington News J, asst managing ed, 1990; USA Today, design ed, 1991-. **Orgs:** Former Minority Affairs Comt Chairperson, Nat Press Photogr Asn, 1988; Nat Asn Black Journalists; White House Press Photogrs Asn. **Business Phone:** (703)854-8050.

VEREEN, MICHAEL L
Electrical engineer. **Personal:** Born Aug 15, 1965, Southport, NC; son of William B and Thelma L Hankins; married Erdyne L Yates. **Educ:** N Carolina State Univ, Raleigh, NC, BS, 1988. **Career:** Carolina Power & Light, Raleigh, NC, engr, 1985-89; GLAXO Smith Kline Inc, Zebulon, NC, engr, 1989-. **Orgs:** Bd dirs, Nat Soc Black Engrs, 1983-; Kappa Alpha Psi Fraternity Inc, 1987-; Rotary Club Wendell, NC; bd dirs, Eastern Wake Sr Citizen Ctr; steering comt, Wake County Communities In schs Prog; bd dir, Zebulon Chamber Com; bd dir, Vereen sch Dance Arts Inc; bd dirs, Eastern Wake Boys & Girls Club; bd dir, North Carolina Bus Comt Educ; pres, Rotary Club Wendell, 1996-97; Pleaseant Grove Baptist Church; supt, Wendell NC Sunday sch; pres, Rotary Club Wendell, 2000-01; NC Family Training & Conseling Ctr. **Special Achievements:** Copyright (Recloser Computer Program), Carolina Power & Light Co, 1989. **Home Addr:** 712 Moss Rd, PO Box 1194, Zebulon, NC 27597, **Home Phone:** (919)269-6197. **Business Addr:** Engineer, Glaxo Smith Kline Inc, 1011 N Arendell Ave, PO Box 1217, Zebulon, NC 27597, **Business Phone:** (919)269-1065.

VEREEN, NATHANIEL
Mayor. **Personal:** Born Mar 3, 1924, Forest City, FL; married Rosetta G; children: Mark, Roslyn, Nathaniel Jr, Gloria Ann & Valerie. **Educ:** Savannah State Col, BS, 1949; Bradely Univ, MA, 1952. **Career:** Eatonville Fl, councilman, 1958, part time mayor, 1963-72, mayor, 1973; Eatonville Diversified Inc, owner pres; Vrn Construct Co, owner & pres. **Orgs:** Org County Coun Legal Gov; Org County Dem Exec Com; adv bd, Vlnc Comm &Smnl Comm Cols; Tri-Co Gov Cities; secy, Fla Construct Lcns Bd; New Providence Bapt Ch; vpres, Central Fla Bass Club; Sportsman Asn Black Bass Anglers. **Military Serv:** AUS.

VEREEN-GORDON, DR. MARY ALICE
Educator, dean (education). **Personal:** Born Jul 9, 1950, Cerro Gordo, NC; married James Leon. **Educ:** NC A&T State Univ, BS, 1972; Atlanta Univ, MA, 1975; Univ WI, Madison, PhD, 1983. **Career:** Educator, Dean(retired); Winston-Salem State Univ, eng instr, 1975-76; Nakina High Sch, eng & french teacher, 1976-77; KY State Univ, eng instr, 1977-80; Morris Col, acad dean, 1984. **Orgs:** Phi Delta Kappa, 1981-; Am Educ Res Assoc, 1981-; Nat Asn Advan Colored People; Alpha Kappa Mu Nat Honor Soc. **Honors/Awds:** Advanced Oppor Fellowship, Adv Oppor Prog, 1980-82; Pre-Doctoral Scholarship for merit, WI Ctr Educ Res, 1982-83; Tribute to Women & Industry, YWCA, 1983; The Mary A Vereen-Gordon Memorial Scholarship, named in honor, 2006. **Special Achievements:** Co-author of A Noble Journey.

VERNON, ALEXANDER
Association executive. **Personal:** Married Nora. **Educ:** Masters degree, criminal justice. **Career:** Association executive (retired). Veterans Foreign Wars, Dept Tex, state comdr, 1996-97, Post 9191, comdr, All Am post comdr, All state post comdr, capt, state chief staff, state safety chair, Nat Security, co-chair, 1997-98, Dist 14, comdr, sr vice comdr; Killeen Police Dept, investr/detective. **Orgs:** Tex Veterans Comn; Jewish War Veterans, Tex rep, Nat Coun, 1998-2000. **Honors/Awds:** Brain Trust Award, Cong Black Caucus, 1999; Honorable Jesse Brown Leadership Award, Nat Coun, Houston, Tex, 2002. **Special Achievements:** First Black name as state commander in the department of Texas. **Military Serv:** AUS, Vietnam, two tours, 22 year veteran; Vietnam Service Medal with 1 silver and 2 bronze stars; Republic of Vietnam Campaign Medal; Bronze Star Medal with 1 Oak Leaf Cluster; Vietnamese Cross of Gallantry with Palm. **Home Addr:** 802 Haynes Dr, Killeen, TX 76543.

VERNON, EASTON D
Consultant, financial manager. **Personal:** Born Jan 14, 1934, Montego Bay, West Indies; son of Walter (deceased) and Serina (deceased); children: Theresa Howe, Steve, Michelle Medine, Lisa Fassari & David. **Career:** IDS Financial Serv, financial planner, 1973-85, dist mgr, 1985-87, div vpres, 1987-92, diversity consultant, financial planner, 1992-93; Vernon & Assocs, owner & consult, 1994-. **Orgs:** Vpres, Harlem Interfaith Counselling Service, 1977-; found bd, Westchester Community Col, 1991-. **Home Phone:** (914)674-6161. **Business Addr:** Owner, Consultant, Vernon and Associates, 130 Roundabout Trail, Camden-Wyoming, DE 19934, **Business Phone:** (302)698-5307.

VERNON, FRANCINE M.
Educator. **Personal:** Born Nov 14, 1939, New York, NY; married Bernard R; children: Richard, Carolyn-Michelle & Michael. **Educ:** Howard Univ, BS, 1961; Hunter Col, MS, 1973; Fordham Univ, dipl, 1976. **Career:** Dept HEW, claims rep, 1962-67; New York City Bd Educ, dir adult basic educ prog; Hunter Col, instr, 1973-75; Ossining Community Action Prog, exec dir, currently. **Orgs:** NY Asn outstanding Comm Educ; Nat Asn Pub Adult Educ; Kappa Delta Pi; Nat Asn Teachers Eng Speakers; pres, Ossng Nat Asn Advan Colored People; trustee, Afro-Am Found; pres, trust Ossng Bd of Educ; bd mem, Ossng Community Action Prog. **Honors/Awds:** Achievement award, Nat Asn Pub Continuing Adult Educ, 1975; recognisation award, Commrs Nat Conf on Career Educ, 1976; apprec Award Ossng Joycs, 1977. **Business Addr:** Executive Director, Ossining Community Action Program, 10 St Pauls Pl, PO Box 670, Ossining, NY 10562, **Business Phone:** (914)762-2369.

VERNON-CHESLEY, MICHELE JOANNE
Journalist. **Personal:** Born Aug 23, 1962, New York, NY; daughter of Hayden Arthur and Mae Sawyer; married Roger Thomas Chesley, Sep 19, 1987; children: Roger Thomas Jr, Christine & Maya. **Educ:** Long Island Univ, Brooklyn, NY, BA, jour, 1984. **Career:** Detroit Free Press, Detroit, MI, copy ed, 1984-86, asst news ed, 1986-88; page designer, 1988-90; reporter, 1991-93; coordr, high sch jour, 1993-94; dir, Jour Inst Minorities, 1994-97; The Virginian-Pilot, Health & Med Ed, features ed, currently. **Orgs:** Rep Assembly, The News Paper Guild, 1988-; Nat Asn Black Journalists, 1984-; Soc Newspaper Design, 1989-; Detroit E Area Residents Asn, 1990-; secy, Detroit Chap Nat Asn Black Journalists, 1985-86; chairwoman human rights comt, Newspaper Guild, 1990-. **Honors/Awds:** Design Award/Merit, Soc Newspaper Design, 1990; 'Intern of the Year', Detroit Free Press, 1984. **Home Addr:** 5224 Breezewood Arch, Virginia Beach, VA 23464-8472. **Business Addr:** Features Editor, The Virginian-Pilot, News Administration, 150 W Brambleton Ave, PO Box 449, Norfolk, VA 23501, **Business Phone:** (757)446-5562.

VERRETT, JOYCE M.
Educator, high school teacher, dean (education). **Personal:** Born May 26, 1932, New Orleans, LA; married Wilbert; children: Lester McKee, Jeannine, Stanley & Rory. **Educ:** Dillard Univ, BA, 1957; NY Univ, MS, 1963; Tulane Univ, PhD, 1971. **Career:** Educator(retired), Dean(retired); Orleans Parsih, LA, high sch teacher, 1958-63; Dillard Univ, Div Natural Sci, instr, prof biol, chmn; Gov State Univ, Col Arts & Sci, Chicago, dean. **Orgs:** Nat Asn Adv Colored People, 1960-; La Heart Asn, 1973-; Beta Kappa Chi Sci Hon Soc, Cancer Asn Greater ND, 1974; Alpha Kappa Mu Nat Hon Soc, 1956; Beta Kappa Chi Nat Sci Hon Soc, 1956; Reg 9 Sci Fair, 1958-; fel NSF Adv Study 1960-62; Ent Soc Am; Nat Inst Sci; Beta Bial & Hon Soc. **Honors/Awds:** Outstanding Educr Am, 1972. **Special Achievements:** First Black Women to receive PhD in Bio from Tulane Univ 1971.

VERRETT, SHANNON L.
Educator. **Career:** Early Col High Sch, principal. **Business Addr:** Principal, Early College High School, 2000 Lakeshore Dr, Education Bldg 244, New Orleans, LA 70148.*

VERTREACE, WALTER CHARLES
Lawyer, executive. **Personal:** Born Sep 17, 1947, Washington, DC; son of Walter C and Modena K; married Peggy A, May 14, 1977; children: Bryan (deceased), Kelly & Erin. **Educ:** Howard Univ, BA, 1968, MS, 1970; Temple Univ, Sch Law, JD, 1982. **Career:** USAF Human Resources Lab, res psychologist, 1970-72; Info Sci Inc, human resources consult, 1972-75; The Hertz Corp, mgr, EEO progs, 1975-76; INA Corp, mgr, eeo opers, 1976-80; Amerada Hess Corp, mgr & corp eeo, 1980-; NIMH fel; Howard Univ fel. **Orgs:** Bd dir, Equal Employment Adv Coun; past pres, United Way Central Jersey, 1990-92; Am Bar Asn; Nat Bar Asn; NJ State Bar Asn; past vchmn, Manhattan Affiliate NY Urban League; past vicechmn, Philadelphia Urban League; past pres, The EDGES Group Inc; Omega Psi Phi; past pres, NY State Adv Coun Employment Law; deacon, Grace Baptist Church, Germantown; chair, Tri-State Corp Campaign, UNCF; Lt Col, Chief Staff, PA Wing Civil Air Patrol. **Honors/Awds:** United Way Distinguished Volunteer, 1993; Civil Air Patrol Lamplighter Award, 1996; CAP Commander's Commendation; Meritorious Service Award; Chuck Yeager Aerospace Education Achievement Award; Gill Robb Wilson Award. **Special Achievements:** Author, 'Congratulations, You Received A Job Offer! Now What? - How to Evaluate a Job Offer'. **Military Serv:** USAF, first lt; Systems Command Certificate of Merit, 1972. **Business Addr:** Manager, Corporate EEO, Amerada Hess Corp, 1 Hess Pl, Woodbridge, NJ 07095-1229, **Business Phone:** (732)750-6408.

VERTREACE-DOODY, MARTHA MODENA
Educator, poet. **Personal:** Born Nov 24, 1945, Washington, DC; daughter of Walter Charles Vertreace and Modena Kendrick Vertreace; married Timothy John Doody, Dec 9, 2000. **Educ:** DIS Teachers Col, BA, 1967; Roosevelt Univ, MA, 1971, MPh, 1972; Mundelein Col, MS, 1981; Vermont Col, MFA, 1996. **Career:** Roosevelt High Sch, Eng instr, 1967-72; Rosary Col, assoc adj prof, 1981-82; Kennedy-King Col, poet-in-residence, 1976-95, distinguished prof, 1995-96, prof commun, currently. **Orgs:** Kappa Delta Pi Hon Soc, 1966-; Pi Lambda Theta Hon Soc, 1973-; Modern Language Asn, 1982-; Nat Coun Teachers Eng, 1982-; Midwest Modern Language Asn, 1982-; second vpres, Poets & Patrons, 1986-; Ill Asn Teachers Eng, 1986-; Soc Study Midwestern Lit, 1987-. **Honors/Awds:** Ford Found Fel, 1972; Excellence Writing, Ill Asn Teachers Eng, 1985; Lit awards, Ill Arts Coun, 1988, 1989, 1990; Gwendolyn Brooks Award for Significant Ill Poet, 1993. **Special Achievements:** Under a Cat's-Eye Moon, collection of poems, 1991; Second House from the Corner, collection of poems, 1986; Kelly in the Mirror, children's book, 1993; Oracle Bones, collection of poems, 1994; Light Caught Bending, collection of poems, 1995; Cinnabar, collection of poems, 1995; Maafa: When Night Becomes a Lion, collection of poems, 1996. Achievements: Second Mourning, collection of poetry, 1998; Smokeless Flame, collection of poems, 1998; Dragon Lady: Tsukimi, collection of poems, 1999; Glacier Fire, collection of poems, 2004. **Home Phone:** (773)363-0766. **Business Addr:** Professor of Communications, Kennedy-King College, 6301 South Halsted, Chicago, IL 60621, **Business Phone:** (773)602-5182.

VESEY, PAUL. See ALLEN, SAMUEL WASHINGTON.

VESSUP, DR. AARON ANTHONY
Educator, college teacher. **Personal:** Born Mar 28, 1947, Los Angeles, CA. **Educ:** North Eastern Wesleyan Univ, BS, 1970; Ill State Univ, MA, sci, 1972; Univ Pittsburgh, PhD, 1978; Univ Edinburgh, Scotland, media studies, 1984. **Career:** Ill State Univ, comt instr, 1971-72; City Bloomington, human rels coordr, 1972-75; Univ Pittsburgh, teaching fel, 1975-78; Rockwell Int, commun intern, 1977-78; Tex Southern Univ, asst prof commun, 1978-; Elgin Community Col, dir forensics, prof speech & drama, 1981-02, prof emer, 2002-; Univ Edinburgh, media studies fel; Inter cultural Commun, consult. **Orgs:** Ed, Interracial Comn Bloomington Press, 1977; dir, Grant Proj Tex Comn Humanities, 1979-80; Kellogg fel Speech-Commun; Soc Int Educ Asn; Tex Speech Comn Asn; US Tennis Asn; Int Comn Asn; Am Mgt Asn; Speech Commun Asn. **Honors/Awds:** Australian Peace Medallion; Silver Bowl, Int Platform Asn, Acad Poets. **Special Achievements:** Produced & hosted, Cultures in Focus; publ textbook in Urban Comm Winthrop Press, 1977; Co-author, Conflict Management Acad Mgmt Review, 1979; auth: Symbolic Communication, Understanding Racial Stereotypes Brethren Press, 1983; Beyond Cultural Anxieties: Ingredients of Fear, Tests of Character. **Business Addr:** Professor Emeritus, Elgin Community College, 1700 Spartan Dr, Elgin, IL 60123.

VEST, DONALD SEYMOUR
Business owner, executive. **Personal:** Born Apr 5, 1930, Ypsilanti, MI; son of Vida Carter and Eugene L; married Hilda Freeman, Jul 12, 1953; children: Karen, Donald Jr & Carl. **Educ:** Mich State Univ, East Lansing, BA, social serv, 1952. **Career:** Detroit Mutual Ins, Detroit, MI, agent, 1954-55; City Detroit, MI, play leader, 1955-56; State Mich, Detroit, MI, interviewer, 1956-57; City Detroit, MI, recreation instr, 1957-60; Boy Scouts Am, Detroit, MI, dist exec, 1960-62; Ford Motor Co, Dearborn, MI, mgr, 1962-87, personnel mgr,1987; Broadside Press, Detroit, MI, owner & bus mgr, currently. **Orgs:** Pres, Mus African-Am Hist, brd trustees, 1986-87, chair collections comn,1987-88; pres & brd dir, Brazeal Dennard Chorale, 1989. **Honors/Awds:** Community Service Award, Ford Motor Co, 1968-69; Special Service Award-,Detroit Brd Educ, 1977; Sankofa Award, Mus African-Am Hist, 1988; otstanding serv Awrd Admin, 2000. **Military Serv:** AUS, first lt, 1952-54. **Home Addr:** 4734 Sturtevant St, Detroit, MI 48204. **Business Addr:** Business Manager, Owner, Broadside Press, 1301 W Lafayette Blvd, Detroit, MI 48204, **Business Phone:** (313)963-8526.

VEST, HILDA FREEMAN
Publisher, editor. **Personal:** Born Jun 5, 1933, Griffin, GA; daughter of Pharr Cyral and Blanche Heard; married Donald Vest,

Jul 12, 1953; children: Karen, Donald Jr & Carl. **Educ:** Wayne State Univ, Detroit, MI, BS, educ, 1958. **Career:** Editor, Publisher (retired): Detroit Bd Educ, Detroit, MI, teacher, 1959-88; "Lyrics I", 1981; Broadside Press, Detroit, MI, publ, pres & editor, 1985-98; "Sorrows End", 1993. **Honors/Awds:** 'Southeastern Michigan Regional Scholastic Award', Detroit News, 1950; Writing Award for Poetry, Detroit Women Writers, 1982; featured in Broadside Poets' Theater, 1982; featured in Detroit Sings Series, Broadside Press, 1982. **Home Addr:** 4734 Sturtevant St, Detroit, MI 48204.

VESTER, DR. TERRY Y
Physician. **Personal:** Born Sep 9, 1955, Houston, TX; son of Willie T Busby; married Alphonza; children: Jennifer, Alexandria & Geoffrey. **Educ:** Univ San Francisco, BS, 1978; Howard Col Med, MD, 1982. **Career:** Montgomery Residency Prog family pract, 1982-85; Pvt Pract, physician, currently. **Orgs:** Amer Acad Family Physicians, 1982-87; Nat Med Asn, 1986-87; Southern Med Asn, 1986-87; Med Asn State Ala, 1986-87; Chambers Co Med Asn, 1986-87. **Home Addr:** 140 1st St SE, Lafayette, AL 36862, **Home Phone:** (334)864-7887. **Business Addr:** Physician, 140 1st St SE, Lafayette, AL 36862, **Business Phone:** (334)864-7887.

VIA, THOMAS HENRY
Engineer. **Personal:** Born Sep 12, 1959, Martinsville, VA; son of Henry and Margaret Dandridge. **Educ:** Solano Community Col, AS, welding technician, 1980, AS, machine tool technician, 1982; Community Col Air Force, AAS, metals technol, AAS, aircraft maintenance technol, 1982; Southern Ill Univ, BS, ind engineering technol, 1982; Golden Gate Univ, MBA, mgmt, 1984; Univ Calif, Berkeley Extenstion, cert voc educ & engineering, 1986. **Career:** Viking Steel, Anaheim, CA, ironworker, welder, 1983; Tegal Corp, Novato, CA, electro mech technician, 1984; Southern Ill Univ, Carbondale, IL, instr, mfg engr, 1985; Solano Community Col, Suisun, CA, part-time welding, machine tool, bus instr, 1982-; United Airlines, San Francisco, CA, jet mechanic, welder, 1985; Via Technols, Fairfield, CA, principal, mfg engr, 1985-. **Orgs:** D16 committee on robotics, C2 Thermal Spray Comm, Am Welding Soc, 1986-; Robotic Inds Asn, R15.06, safety standards comm, 1986-; tech forum, CASA/SME, 1986-; ASM Int thermal spray automation comt, 1988; A15.08 sensor interfaces comt, Automated Imaging Asn, 1986-; Robotics Intl Soc Mfg Engrs, bd advs, 1993-94. **Honors/Awds:** Challenges & Opportunities for Manufacturing Engrs, Soc Mfg Engrs, Nuts & Bolts, 1989; Editor, Curricula 2000 Workshop Proceeding, Soc Mfg Engrs, 1990; Soc Mfg Engrs, 'Outstanding Young Manufacturing Engineer Award', 1994; Solano Community Col, Distinguished Adjunct Faculty, 1997-98; Outstanding American Award. **Military Serv:** US AirForce, ssgt, 1977-81; USF, Reserve, until 1991. **Home Addr:** 2123 Madrone Dr, Fairfield, CA 94533, **Home Phone:** (707)425-8751. **Business Addr:** Manufacturing Engineer/Principal/Welding Instructor, Via Technologies, PO Box 2868, Fairfield, CA 94533-0286, **Business Phone:** (707)425-0365.

VICKERS, ERIC ERFAN
Lawyer. **Personal:** Born Feb 16, 1953, St Louis, MO; son of Robert and Claire; married Judy Gladney; children: Erica & Aaron. **Educ:** Wash Univ, BA, polit sci, 1975; Coro Found Fellowship Prog; Occidental Col, MA, 1976; Univ Va Sch Law, JD, 1981. **Career:** Bryan Cave, assoc atty; Vickers & Assocs, atty, currently. **Orgs:** Bd mem, Minority Bank; chmn bd, Islamic Ctr St Louis, 1983-85, bd mem, Am Muslim Alliance, 1995; founder, pres, N St Louis Econ Develop Inc, 2000; exec dir, Am Muslim Coun, currently. **Honors/Awds:** Outstanding MNY Effort, St Louis Chap Links, 1989; Legal Service Award, Mound City Bar Asn, 1989; Merit Award, St Louis Am, 1989; MNY Services Award, Mokan Construct Contractors, 1989; Malcolm X Distinguished Service Award, Universal African Peoples Orgn; Outstanding Achievement and Leadership in Activism, Law, Politics, and Economic Justice. **Special Achievements:** Recipient of numerous awards for his outstanding legal and activist services to the community; Making Hajj, 2002. **Home Addr:** 7436 Tulane Ave, Saint Louis, MO 63130-2937, **Home Phone:** (314)863-3251. **Business Addr:** Attorney, Vickers & Associates, 7436 Tulane Ave, Saint Louis, MO 63130-2937, **Business Phone:** (314)367-0120.

VICKERS, KIPP EMMANUEL
Football player. **Personal:** Born Aug 27, 1969, Holiday, FL; married Tracy; children: Treme, Trinity & Tajay. **Educ:** Miami Univ. **Career:** Indianapolis Colts, guard, 1995-97; Wash Redskins, guard, 1999, 2002; Baltimore Ravens, guard, 2000-01. **Honors/Awds:** Rookie of the Year, 1993.

VICK-WILLIAMS, DR. MARIAN LEE
Educator. **Personal:** Born in Newton Grove, NC; daughter of Reverend and Milford E; children: Linda Vick Davis & Charles Alphonso Vick. **Educ:** Fayetteville State Univ, BS, 1948; Univ Mich, MA, 1954; Syracuse Univ, CAGS, 1961; Duke Univ, EdD, 1968. **Career:** Educator (retired); NC Pub Sch, elem teacher, 1948-60; Bennett Col, dir reading ctr, 1961-62; Winston-Salem State Univ, asst prof reading, 1962-66; NC A & T State Univ, assoc prof reading educ, 1968-70; prof reading educ, 1970-77, Dept

Elem Educ, actg chmn, 1977-80, chmn, 1980-83, prof reading educ & grad adv reading majors, 1984-90. **Orgs:** Life mem, Nat Advan Asn Colored People; AKA, Beta Iota Omega Chap; Kappa Delta Pi; Phi Delta Kappa; NEA-NCAE; Int Reading Asn; St James Presbyterian Church; Fla State Univ Nat Alumni Asn; Nat Asn Equal Opportunity; Col Reading Asn; Am Educ Res Asn; Nat Reading Conf; Asn Supv & Curric Develop. **Honors/Awds:** Distinguished Alumni Award, Nat Asn Equal Opportunity, 1985; Alumni Achievement Award, Univ Nat Alumni Asn, Alumni Queen, 1993-94; Southern Education Fund Award. **Special Achievements:** Author of nine published articles in professional journals and books. **Home Phone:** (336)274-2319. *

VIEIRA, FRANKLIN
Association executive, chief executive officer, president (organization). **Career:** Caribbean Cargo & Package Serv, pres & chief exec officer, currently. **Business Addr:** Chief Executive Officer, President, Carribbean Cargo & Package Services Inc, JFK Intl Airport bldg 80 Cargo Area C, Jamaica, NY 11430, **Business Phone:** (718)995-2055.*

VILLAROSA, CLARA
Bookseller, entrepreneur. **Personal:** Children: Linda. **Educ:** Earned law degree. **Career:** Financier; psychologist; The Hue-Man Experience, Denver, Colo, owner & pres, 1984-2000; Hue-Man Books, Harlem, NY City, co-owner, 2002-. **Special Achievements:** One of the nation's most noted Black booksellers as a owner.

VILTZ, DR. STANLEY
Executive. **Personal:** Born Oct 4, 1944, Berkeley, CA; daughter of LB and Renee Benson; divorced; children: Raven & Wren. **Educ:** Univ Southern Calif, BA, 1965, MPA, 1974, Univ Calif, Los Angeles, EDD, 1998. **Career:** La Community Col Dist, coordr Community Serv, 1976-79, assist dean, voc educ, 1979-90, exec asst chancellor, 1991-92, dean, instr, 1992-95; Compton Community Col, vpres, stud & acad Affairs, 1995-2001, vpres voc & econ develop, spec proj, 2001-, vpres voc technol, extended studies, currently; BWLC, co-founder, currently. **Orgs:** Life Mem, Delta Sigma Theta; Charter Mem, Century City Chap, 1964-; exec bd, Asn Pan African Doctoral Scholars, 1996; sch Bd mem, West Angeles Church God in Christ, 2001-; Mgmt Develop Comn; Nat Public Serv Sorority; vpres prog Asn Pan African Doctoral Scholars. **Honors/Awds:** Am Coun Edu, Nat Leadership Indentification BWLC, 1994; Texaco, full scholarship for Leadership Am, AM Issues Forum, 2000. **Special Achievements:** Dissertion, Pathways to the Calif Community College Presidency for African American Women, 1998; author: "Role of Comm Colleges in Welfare to Work," Delta Research & Edu Foundation Monograph, 2000; "What Trustees Need to Know About Afr Amer Women Leaders," ACCT Quarterly, 2001. **Business Addr:** Vice President of Special Projects, Vice President of Vocational Technology, Compton Community College, 1111 E Artesia Blvd, Compton, CA 90221.

VINCENT, DANIEL PAUL
Executive. **Personal:** Born Jun 19, 1939, New Orleans, LA; son of Howard and Josephine; married Leatha; children: Dannette, Robin & Daryl. **Educ:** Southern Univ, BS; Loyola Univ, MBA; Univ No CO, MA; United Ecucators Credit Union, PhD, cand; Shrtr Col, Hon PhD. **Career:** Chrysler Corp, engr, 1966-68; Equity Funding Corp Am, rep, 1968-70; Total Community Action Inc, exec dir, 1969-; Mayor New Orleans, Mayor's Charter Rev Com, spec adv vice chmn, 1970-; EDU Inc, pres & chmn, 1975-; La State Univ Health Sci Ctr, consult lectr; TLN Univ, lectr; Xavier Univ, lectr; La Housing Assistance Corp, chmn; Human Serv Inst, founder; Archdiocese New Orleans, Off Black Catholic Ministries, Black Catholic Ministries Adv Bd, dir, currently. **Orgs:** Adv bd, NO Area Boy Scouts; pres, TCA Fed Credit Union; exec bd, Nat Asn Comn Develop; pres, LA Asn Comn Action Agencies; Nat Asn Housing & Redevelop; vice chmn, New Orleans Manpower Adv Planning Coun; bd dir, New Orleans Area Health Planning Coun; NY Stock Exchange; Additional Study Orleans Parish Sch Syst. **Honors/Awds:** Beta Gamma Sigma Honour Soc; Army Commander Medal John H Whitney & Fellowship. **Special Achievements:** Officials publications of Patterns of Poverty in New Orleans; manpower training needs for the City of New Orleans. **Military Serv:** AUS, capt, 1960-66. **Home Addr:** 6911 Lake Willow Dr, New Orleans, LA 70126-3105.

VINCENT, EDWARD
State government official. **Personal:** Born 1934, Steubenville, OH; married Marilyn; children: 2. **Educ:** Iowa State Univ, pub rels & advert; Calif State Univ, BA. **Career:** Inglewood Unified Sch Dist, bd trustee; Inglewood City Coun, 1979-83; Inglewood City, mayor, 1983-95; Calif State World Trade Comn, comnr; Calif Coastal Comn, alt comnr; Calif House Representatives, rep, 1996-2000, Dist 25, senator, 2000-. **Orgs:** AFL-CIO; Chair, California's Horse Racing Indust; California's Wine Indust; Col & Univ Admis & Outreach; Family Child & Youth Develop; Gov Oversight; US Conf Mayors; bd mem, Los Angeles County Bd Sanitation. **Honors/Awds:** All Big Ten and All-American honors in football; Cuactemoc Award, Cooperativa, 2000. **Special Achievements:** First African-American Mayor of the City of Inglewood. **Business

Addr: Senator, California State Senate, District 25, State Capitol Rm 5052, Sacramento, CA 95814, **Business Phone:** (916)651-4025.

VINCENT, IRVING H.
Administrator, educator, actor. **Personal:** Born Nov 28, 1934, St Louis, MO; married Delora Sherleen Sinclair; children: Terrel Lynn French, Mark, Paul & Samantha. **Educ:** St Louis Univ, BS, speech, 1957; HB Studios Lee Strasberg, prof actg, attended 1970; Brooklyn Col, 26 MFA credits, 1974; Third World Cinema, attended 1977. **Career:** Broadway, Off-Broadway, stage mgr, 1961-69; stage dir, 1966-; Downstate Med Ctr, personnel dir, 1966-69; Brooklyn Col, teacher, 1969-74; freelance video artist, 1977-81; DJR Inc, dir & producer, 1980; ABC-TV, unit mgr, 1981-2001; New York Univ, Opportunity Prog Video Lab, dir, 1994-. **Orgs:** Pres, Seminole Group, 1979-81; bd dir, Media Other Arts, 1981-. **Home Addr:** 155 Bank St, New York, NY 10014. **Business Addr:** Director, New York University, Opportunity Programs Video Lab, 8th Fl Greene St, New York, NY 10016.

VINCENT, MARJORIE JUDITH
Journalist, fashion model. **Personal:** Born Nov 21, 1964, Chicago, IL; daughter of Lucien and Florence Bredy. **Educ:** DePaul Univ, Chicago, IL, 1988; Duke Univ Law Sch, Durham, NC. **Career:** Brooks, Pierce, McLendon Humphries, Greensboro, NC, law intern, 1989; Mudge, Rose, Guthrie, Alexander & Ferdon, New York, NY, law intern, 1990; Miss Am, 1991; WGBC-TV, anchor & reporter, 1993-94; The Ohio News Network, anchor; news anchor, currently. **Orgs:** Alpha Kappa Alpha Sorority, 1987-. **Honors/Awds:** Hon chair, Coun Safe Families; Nat Ambassador, Childrens Miracle Network; Peace Begins at Home Award, Women Against Abuse; Law Scholar, Duke Univ Law Sch. **Special Achievements:** Miss Illinois, 1991; Miss America, 1991. **Business Phone:** (614)280-3600.

VINCENT, MARK SINCLAIR. See DIESEL, VIN.

VINCENT, TROY DARNELL
Football player. **Personal:** Born Jun 8, 1971, Trenton, NJ; married Tommi, Mar 19, 1994; children: Desire, Troy Jr & Taron. **Educ:** Univ Wis. **Career:** Miami Dolphins, defensive back, 1992-95; Philadelphia Eagles, 1996-2003; Buffalo Bills, 2004-06; Wash Redskins, 2006; NFL Players Asn, Bd Player Rep, vp, pres, 2004-08. **Orgs:** Founder, Love Thy Neighbor; Prof Bus Financial Network; Christian Athletes United Spiritual Empowerment; Christian Bus Network; All Pro Dad. **Honors/Awds:** Ed Block Courage Award, 1994, 2000-01; Pro Bowl, 1999-2003; All-Pro selection, 2000-02; Troy Vincent Day declared by NJ General Assembly, 2001; Walter Payton Man of Year, 2002. *

VINSON, ANTHONY CHO (TONY VINSON)
Football player. **Personal:** Born Mar 13, 1971, Frankfurt, Germany. **Educ:** Purdue Univ; Towson Univ. **Career:** Baltimore Ravens, running back, 1997-99.

VINSON, CHUCK. See VINSON, CHUCK RALLEN.

VINSON, CHUCK RALLEN (CHUCK VINSON)
Television director. **Personal:** Born Jul 14, 1956, Elkhart, IN; son of Ray Vinson and Charlotte Moxley; married Pamela, Jun 5, 1997; children: 2. **Educ:** Ball State, Muncie, Ind, attended 1975; Los Angeles Col, Los Angeles, Calif, attended 1977-80. **Career:** Director; Benson, stage mgr, 1980-84; Carsey/Werner Productions, "Cosby Show", stage mgr, 1984-87, dir, 1986-92; HBO Spec, Sinbad, Atlanta, GA, dir, 1990; Films: Latham Entertainment Presents, 2003; Tall, Dark, & Funny, 2005; America's Ready, 2005; Boyish Man, 2005; Looking for My Next Ex-Husband, 2005; TV series: "The Cosby Show", 1988-92; Sinbad & Friends: All the Way Live.. Almost!, 1991; "You Bet Your Life", 1992; Martin, 1992; "Clarissa Explains It All", 1991-93; "Thea", 1993; "The Fresh Prince of Bel-Air", 1992-95; "Sister, Sister", 1994-95; Sinbad: Son of a Preacher Man, 1996; 70's Soul Music Festival: Part 2, 1996; Twisted Puppet Theatre", 1996; "The Mystery Files of Shelby Woo", 1996-97; The Right Connections?, 1997; "Living Single", 1997; 29th NAACP Image Awards, 1998; "Sabrina, the Teenage Witch", 1997-98; Sinbad: Nuthin' But the Funk, 1998; Soul Music Festival: Part IV, 1998; "One World", 1998; 30th NAACP Image Awards, 1999; Soul Music Festival: Part 5, 1999; 31st NAACP Image Awards, 2000; Jamie Foxx: I Might Need Security, 2002; Big Time", 2003; "Last Comic Standing 2", 2004; Kims of Comedy, 2005; "Last Comic Standing 3", 2007. **Home Addr:** 4229 Fair Ave, Studio City, CA 91602. **Business Addr:** Director, c/o Latham Entertainment, 3200 Northline Ave Suite 132, Greensboro, NC 27408, **Business Phone:** (336)315-1440.

VINSON, NATHAN
Executive. **Career:** Motown First Fed Credit Union, bd pres & chmn, currently. **Honors/Awds:** Director of the Year, Nat Ctr Credit Unions. **Business Addr:** Board President, Chairman, Motown First Federal Credit Union, 2112 Holbrook St, Hamtramck, MI 48212, **Business Phone:** (313)872-1277.*

VINSON, ROSALIND ROWENA
Lawyer. **Personal:** Born Sep 25, 1962, Highland Park, MI; daughter of Roosevelt Massey and Mary S McGhee. **Educ:** Mich

State Univ, BA, 1983; Georgetown Univ, Law Ctr, JD, 1987. **Career:** Equal Employment Opportunity Comn, atty, 1989-. **Orgs:** Vice magister, Phi Delta Phi, 1986-87; vpres, H Carl Moultrie T Endowment, 1989-; secy, Black Law Alumni, Georgetown Univ Law Ctr, 1992-. **Honors/Awds:** Mary McCloud Bethune Award, Black Law Students Asn, 1987; First Year Pacesetter, 1986, Second Year Pacesetter, 1985. **Business Phone:** (202)663-4474.

VINSON, TONY. See VINSON, ANTHONY CHO.

VIOLENUS, AGNES A
Educator. **Personal:** Born May 17, 1931, New York, NY; daughter of Antonio and Constance. **Educ:** Hunter Col, BA, 1952; Columbia Univ Teachers Col, MA, 1958; Bank Street Col, prof cert comput educ, 1984; Nova Southeastern Univ, EdD, 1990. **Career:** NY State Educ Dept, head teacher day care ctr, 1952-53; NYC Bd Educ, teacher common br, 1953-66; City Col NY, adj adv, open educ prog, 1974-75, adj teacher mentor prog, 1990-91; York Col, Continuing Educ Div, adj instr comput, 1985-87; New York City, bd Educ, asst prin elem sch, 1966-91; City Col New York, supvr stud teachers, 1997-; Hunter Col, adj lectr, 1998-. **Orgs:** Asst secy, Bank St Alumni Coun, 1991-93;NY Affilate Nat Black Child Develop Inst, bd dirs, 1992-; NY Acad Sci, participant scientist sch prog, 1994-; pres, Schomburg Corp, 1995-98; treas sec, bd dirs, Hunter Col Alumni Asn, 1995-; vpres, treas, New York Pub Libr Volunteers, 1996-99; NY Club Nat Asn Negro Bus & Prof Women, co-chair scholar comn, 1991-99; bd of dirs, Hunter Col Scholar & Welfare Fund, 1997-; pres, Manhattan Psychiatric Ctr, bd visitors, 1999-. **Honors/Awds:** Kappa Delta Pi, 1958; Pi Lambda Theta, 1958; Phi Delta Kappa, 1981; Dedicated Service Award, Coun Supvr Adminrs, 1991; Appreciation Award, Aerospace Educ Asn, 1985; Ministry Seniors Certificate of Appreciation, Archdiocese NY Catholic Charities, 1996; Prof Achievement Award, New York Club, NANBPWC, 1997. **Home Addr:** 626 Riverside Dr Suite 24P, New York, NY 10031. **Business Addr:** Adjunct Lecturer, Certified Instructor, Hunter College, 695 Pk Ave 10th Fl NY, **Business Phone:** (212)650-3850.

VISHER, MARSHA WATTS. See WATTS, MARSHA.

VIVIAN, CORDY TINDELL
Clergy, executive director, president (organization). **Personal:** Born Jul 30, 1924, Howard County, MO; married W Octavia Geans; children: Jo Anna, Denise, Cordy Jr, Kira, Mark, Charisse, Albert. **Educ:** Western Ill Univ, BA, 1948; Am Baptist Theol Sem, BD, 1958; New Sch Social Res, doctorate, 1984; Western Ill Univ, doctorate, 1987. **Career:** Nat Baptist Conv, USA Inc, nat dir, 1955-61; 1st Community Church, pastor, 1956-61; Cosmo Community Church, pastor, 1961-63; SCLC, nat dir, 1962-67; Shaw Univ, minister, 1972-73, nat dir sem without walls, 1974-; Black Action Strategies & Info Ctr Inc, bd chmn, dir & pres, currently; Wartburg Theol Sem, vis prof. **Orgs:** Chmn, Nat Anti-Klan Network; Nat Black Leadership Roundtable; chmn, Southern Organizing Comn Educ Fund; bd mem, Inst Black World; bd mem, Int United Black Fund; co-dir, Southern Reg Twentieth Anniversary March Wash Jobs Peace & Freedom; bd mem, Southern Christian Leadership Conf, Southern Organizing Comn, Nat Coun Black Churchmen, African Inst Study Human Values; Racial Justice Working Group, Nat Coun Churches; Int Lect & Consult Tours Africa, Tokyo, Isreal, Holland, Manila, Japan. **Honors/Awds:** Author Black Power & The Amer Myth, Amer Joseph, Date & Fact Book of Black America; editor the Baptist, Layman Mag for Baptist Men; listed in 1000 Successful Blacks, The Ebony Success Library, Odyssey, A Journey Through Black Amer, From Montgomery to Memphis, Clergy in Action Training, Unearthing Seeds of Fire, The Idea of Highlander, The Trouble I've Seen. **Business Addr:** President, Director, Black Action Strategies & Information Center, 595 Parsons St, Atlanta, GA 30314.

VIVIANS, NATHANIEL ROOSEVELT
Engineer. **Personal:** Born Feb 6, 1937, Mobile, AL; son of Charlie Vivians and Ella Lett Sellers; married Dorothy C Willis; children: Venita Natalie & Mark Anthony. **Educ:** Tuskegee Inst, BSEE, 1961; Univ Dayton, MS Eng, 1973, MS mgt sci, 1977. **Career:** Engineer (retired); Aeronaut Systs Div, elec eng, 1964-71, prog mgr, 1971-80, tech advr, 1980-85, techn dir, 1985-87, co-dep, 1987; Univ Wilberforce, asst prof, 1980. **Orgs:** Basileus Omega Psi Phi Fraternity, 1957-; colonel & air force officer, AF Res, 1967-; EEO counr Aeronaut Systs Div, 1969-; trustee Holy Trinity Am Church 1975-; chap pres Nat Soc Prof Eng, 1970-; pres, WCPOVA, 1974-80; Sigma Pi Phi Fraternity. **Honors/Awds:** Outstanding Service, NSPE Greene Xenia, 1975; commendation, ASD/AE WPAFB, 1978; Man of the year, Omega Psi Phi Fraternity, 1980; Outstanding performance, Aeronaut Syst Div, 1983-84, 1986-90; Parent of the Year, Tuskegee Univ, 1988; 100 Men of Distinction. **Military Serv:** Air Defense Command, radar officer, 1961-64; USAF capt; USSAFRs col; Commendation 1967, 1974, 1980; Legion of Merit, 1995. **Home Addr:** 3479 Plantation Pl, Dayton, OH 45434.

VOGEL, DR. ROBERTA BURRAGE
Psychologist, educator. **Personal:** Born Jun 13, 1938, Georgetown, SC; daughter of Vivian Helen Bessellieu and Demosthenes Edwin Burrage, Sr; divorced; children: Duane Stephen & Shoshana Lynn. **Educ:** Temple Univ, Philadelphia, PA, BA, 1960, MA, 1962; Mich State Univ, E Lansing, MI, PhD, 1967; Ackerman Inst Family Ther, New York, NY, post-doctoral cert, 1981. **Career:** Mich State Univ, E Lansing, MI, instr, 1966-67, asst prof, 1967-68; Ctr Change, New York, NY, co-leader & staff mem, 1970-72; N Richmond Comm Ment Health, Staten Island, NY, staff psychologist, 1971-72; City Univ NY, Col Staten Island, NY, asst prof & counr, 1972-74, assoc prof, 1974-78, SEEK Prog, dep dir & coordr coun, 1978-, Off Spec Prog, 1981-88; RH Clark Assocs, consult & eval res, 1978-83; Steinway Family & Child Develop Ctr, consult & psychologist, 1984-88; Harlem-Dowling Child & Family Servs, consult & psychologist, 1989-. **Orgs:** Res fel, Nat Inst Health, 1964; dir clin serv, Black Psychol Inst, NY Asn Black Psychologists, 1978-81; adv bd mem, NY Urban League, Staten Island Br, 1980-; pres, NY Asn Black Psychologists, 1982-83; Staten Island Human Rights Adv Comm, 1986-; bd mem, Staten Island Ment Health Soc, 1987-; Staten Island Task Force AIDS, 1988-; comnr, NY Black Leadership Comn AIDS, 1988. **Home Phone:** (718)816-7272. **Business Addr:** Professor, Deputy Director & Coordinator of Counseling of SEEK Program, City University of New York, College of Staten Island, Rm 1A Bldg 112 2800 Victory Blvd, Staten Island, NY 10314, **Business Phone:** (718)982-2410.

VOLDASE, IVA SNEED
Aerospace engineer. **Personal:** Born Nov 9, 1934, Frankston, TX; daughter of Mr Bynus Sneed; divorced; children: Two sons. **Educ:** Prairie View A&M Univ, BA, math, 1954; El Camino Col, AA, math, 1977; Univ San Francisco, BS, 1983; CA State Univ, Dominguez Hills, comput sci, 1988. **Career:** Aerospace engineer (retired); N Am Aviation, math analyst, jr eng, 1954-59; STL, comput, math analyst, 1960-61; STL becomes TRW Inc, sr mem technical staff, 1961. **Orgs:** Carson Black Heritage Asn, pres, 1969-; Harriet Tubman Sch Unwed Mothers, original charter bd mem, 1970-90; Nat Coun Negro Women, pres, 1976-90; TRW SEA Bootstrap, pres, 1976-78; Int COCOMO Users group, affiliate, 1989-; Soc of Cost Est & Analysis, speaker, mem, 1989-; Int Soc Parametic Analysts, speaker, mem, 1990-; United Christian Women, ast gen coord, 1995-97. **Honors/Awds:** Women of Achievement Award, TRW DSSG Nat Women's Week, 1978; Community Serv Award, Vols of Am, 1983; Outstanding Software Parametic Tech Paper, Int Soc Parametic Analysts, 1997; Top Minority Women in Sci & Eng, Jour NTA, 1996; Black Engr of the Year, Community Serv, Coun Eng Deans of Historically Black Colleges and Career Communications Group, 1995. **Special Achievements:** Not All COCOMOs Are Alike, Technical Paper presented at a REVIC Conf, published, 1991; Parametic Modelling at TRW, SSCAG Symposium, published, 1997; The Use of Parametic Models for Historical Data, IConf, published 1997; Software Modelling Risk Management, technical class, class book, 1996; Minority Women in the Aerospace Labor Market, Career Conf for Women, 1978; speaks fluent Spanish; One among 25 black women in the US to enter into the Aerospace Engineering field in 1954 working on early US Satellites. *

VON MIKE MCGHEE, DAEDRA ANITA
Government official. **Personal:** Born Aug 29, 1944, Urbana, OH; daughter of Clarence and Charlotta; married Curtis Thomas McGhee II; children: Curtis Thomas McGhee III. **Educ:** Wayne State Univ, BA, 1999. **Career:** Detroit Medical Ctr, admin personnel generalist & employment reveiwer, 1968-77; City Nat Bank, personnel reviewer, 1977-79; Crocker Nat Bank, corp admin personnel rep, 1979-81; First Pacific Bank, corp exec asst Chief Exec Officer, 1981-83; Carter Hawley Hale Stores Inc, exec admin asst to exec vpres & div pres, 1983-84; NCCJ, volunteer, 1990-92, prog dir, 1992-99, assoc dir, 1999-; Sphinx Org, bd dir; Mich Gov's Off, dep dir govt & bus affairs, dir govt & bus affairs, currently. **Orgs:** Wayne County Juvenile Ct Citizen's Adv Comt; Women of Wayne Alumni Asn; life mem, NAACP; youth leadership fel, WK Kellogg Found; develop comn, Goodwill Indust Detroit Found; serv learning adv bd, Detroit Pub Sch; fel Eureka Communications; fel Ctr Creative Leadership; Alliance for a Safer Greater Detroit; Ctr Peace & Conflict Studies Alumni Asn, Wayne State Univ. **Honors/Awds:** 100 Outstanding Women, City of Detroit, 1993; Promising Programs Addressing Youth Violence Awd, Wayne State Univ, 1995; Alumni of the Yr, Wayne State Univ; Community Leader & Fel of the Yr, Eureka Communications, 2001; Building Bridges Award, Am Arab Anti-Defamation Comt. **Special Achievements:** Author: Crime Prevention Handbook-Is Your Business Safe?, 1995; Evaluation- An Imperative for Non Profit Organizations, 2000; Co-Author: Detroit Targets Elimination of Racial Profiling, 2001. **Business Addr:** Director Government and Business Affairs, State MI Gov Exec Off, Southeast MI Off Gov, 3022 W Grand Blvd Cadillac Pl Suite 14 150, Detroit, MI 48202, **Business Phone:** (313)456-0010.

VOOM, MAXI VOOM. See COLLINET, GEORGES ANDRE.

VOORHIES, LARK
Actor. **Personal:** Born Mar 25, 1974, Nashville, TN; married Miguel Coleman, Mar 9, 1996 (divorced 2004); married Andy Prince, May 8, 2007; children: 1. **Career:** Films: Saved by the Bell: Hawaiian Style, 1992; Saved by the Bell: Wedding in Las Vegas, 1994; The Last Don, 1997; How to Be a Player, 1997; Longshot, 2000; How High, 2001; Civil Brand, 2002; The Next Hit, 2008; TVseries: "Small Wonder", 1988; "Good Morning, Miss Bliss", 1988-89; "Savedby the Bell", 1989-93; "The Fresh Prince of Bel-Air", 1992; Saved by theBell: Hawaiian Style, 1992; "Martin", 1993; "Getting By", 1993; "Days ofOur Lives", 1993-94; "Saved by the Bell: The College Years", 1994; Savedby the Bell: Wedding in Las Vegas, 1994; "Me & the Boys", 1994; "Saved bythe Bell: The New Class", 1994; "In the House", 1997-99; "The Bold & TheBeautiful", 1995-96; "CBS School break Special", 1995; "Star Trek: Deep Space Nine", 1995; "Family Matters", 1995; "What About Your Friends",1995; "The Last Don", 1997; "Malcolm & Eddie", 1997; "In the House",1997-98; "The Love Boat: The Next Wave", 1998; "Mutiny", 1999; "The Parkers", 1999; "Grown Ups", 2000; Fire & Ice", 2001; "Widows", 2002; Boo Cocky, 2008; "Robot Chicken", 2008; "Black to the Future", 2009. **Honors/Awds:** Young Artist Award, 1990 & 1993. **Business Phone:** (818)972-4300.*

W

WADDELL, RUCHADINA LADESIREE
Lawyer. **Personal:** Born Feb 21, 1965, Wilmington, NC; daughter of Charles R and Ruth Weaver. **Educ:** Univ NC, Greensboro, BS, 1985; Univ Wisc, Sch Law, JD, 1989. **Career:** Dept Indust Labor & Human Rels, admin law judge, 1990-91; Dept Health Social Servs, asst legal coun, 1992; Grant Co, corp coun, 1992-94; Walworth Co, asst corp coun, 1994-97; Law Off Ruchadina L Waddell, lawyer, 1997-. **Orgs:** Wisconsin State Bar Asn; Grant County Bar Asn; Dane County Bar Asn; Phi Delta Phi; Delta Sigma Theta Sorority; AOF fel, Univ Wis, Law Sch, 1987-89. **Honors/Awds:** Outstanding Young Amerians Award. **Home Addr:** 321 N Front St, Wilmington, NC 28401. **Business Addr:** Lawyer, Law Office Ruchadina L Waddell, 321 N Front St, Wilmington, NC 28401.*

WADDELL, THEODORE R.
Electronics engineer. **Personal:** Born Mar 3, 1934, Wilmington, NC. **Educ:** Bethune-Cookman Col, attended 1954; NC A&T UNIV, BS, 1962; George Washington Univ, attended 1970. **Career:** Eng, various other positions; Common Carrier Bur, 1962-80; Fed Commun Comn, rep on campus recruitment of graduating studs at predominantly black Univ, 1965-; chief domestic, 1980-. **Honors/Awds:** Recipient Certificate Award, Fed Commun Comn, 1965, 1973, 1974. **Military Serv:** AUS, specialist 5, 1955-58. *

WADDY, JUDE (JUDE MICHAEL WADDY)
Football player, founder (originator). **Personal:** Born Sep 12, 1975, Washington, DC. **Educ:** William & Mary Col. **Career:** Football player (retired), owner; Green Bay Packers, linebacker, 1998-99; Berlin Thunder, 2002; San Diego Chargers, linebacker, 2003; Denver Broncos, 2002; Physipet, inventor.

WADDY, JUDE MICHAEL. See WADDY, JUDE.

WADE, ACHILLE MELVIN
School administrator. **Personal:** Born Nov 5, 1943, Clarksville, TN; son of Bennie Albert and Electra M Freeman; married Angela Nash; children: Chaka L. **Educ:** Okla State Univ, BA, 1966, MA, 1969. **Career:** Black Studies Ctr, Univ Calif Santa Barbara, acting dir, 1969-70; Black Studies Univ Omaha, Nebr, dir, 1970-71; Black Studies Vassar Col, dir,1971-73; Black Studies Univ Austin Tex, lectr, 1973-86; Moorhead State Univ Minn, Minority Stud Affairs, coordr, 1988-89; Yale Univ, asst dean studs, dir, Afro-Am Cultural Ctr, 1989-92; Upward Bound, Univ Bridgeport, Conn, dir, 1993; Univ RI, Multicultural Ctr, dir, 1994-. **Orgs:** Arts Comn City Austin, 1981-; bd mem, Laguna Gloria Art Museum, 1982-84; pres, Tex Asn Study Afro-Am Life & History Inc, 1985-88; bd mem, CTA fro-Am Historical Soc, 1990-; bd mem, New Haven Ethnic Hist Ctr, 1990-92; chair, RI Multicultural Dirs Group, 1998. **Honors/Awds:** Melvin Wade Day, Univ RI, 2002. **Business Phone:** (401)874-2851.

WADE, BERYL ELAINE
Lawyer. **Personal:** Born Jul 1, 1956, Wilmington, NC; daughter of Clarence W R and Geneva M S. **Educ:** Univ NC, Chapel Hill, BA, 1977; Univ Mich, Sch Law, JD, 1980. **Career:** Cumberland Co Dist Atty's Off, asst dist atty, 1980-82; NCA Senator Tony Rand, campaign coordr, 1982; NJ Justice Acad, legal instr, 1982-84; City Fayetteville, asst city atty/police atty, 1984-93; State NC, dep legis coun, Off Gov, 1993-95; Coun Gov James B Hunt Jr, 1996-. **Orgs:** Cumberland Co Bar Asn, 1980-93, Cumberland Co Bd HTH, 1988-94; NC State Bar, 1980-; comnr, ADM Rules Review CMS, 1985-90, 1992-; bd gov, NC Asn Black Lawyers, 1985-91, asst secy, 1991-; secy/treas, NCA Asn Police Atty's, 1987, pres, 1988; bd gov, United Way, 1988, chair, Nominating Comt, 1991, chair, Project Blueprint Comt, 1991-92, NCP, 1981-; trustee, Col Heights Presbyterian Church, 1990; bd visitors, UNC-CH, 1996-. **Honors/Awds:** Partial Award, 7th Dist Black Leadership Caucus, 1984. **Home Addr:** 303 S King Charles Rd, Raleigh, NC 27610, **Home Phone:** (919)250-0083. **Business Addr:** Counsel to the Governor, North Carolina State Government, Of-

fice of the Governor, 424 N Blount St, Raleigh, NC 27601-2817, **Business Phone:** (919)733-2698.

WADE, BRENT JAMES
Manager, writer. **Personal:** Born Sep 19, 1959, Baltimore, MD; son of James Bennett and Sylvia; married Yvette Jackson, Sep 29, 1979; children: Wesley Jackson & Claymore Dotson. **Educ:** Univ Md, BA, Eng, 1981. **Career:** Westinghouse Electric Corp, mkt rep, 1981-87; LSI Logic Corp, mkt mgr, 1987-89; AT&T, comput systs sr proj mgr, 1989-. **Special Achievements:** Author, Company Man, novel, 1992. **Business Addr:** Sales manager, AT&T, 175 E Houston, San Antonio, TX 78205, **Business Phone:** (210)821-4105.

WADE, CASEY, JR.
Government official, mayor. **Personal:** Born Oct 7, 1930, Pickens, MS; son of Casey Sr and Kate; married Doris Taylor Wade, Nov 12, 1967; children: Robert, Diane & Joycherie. **Career:** Ill Dept Ment Health, Kankakee, security Officer, 1966; Village of Sun River Terr, founder, mayor, currently. **Orgs:** Minister, Pleasant Grove Baptist Church, 1980-; mayor, Village Sun River Terrace, 1980-; Kankakee County Mayor's Asn, 1988; NAACP, 1982-; Teacher's Union, 1987-; Leadership Inst for Black Mayors Cert, 1990; Black Mayors Asn, 1990-. **Honors/Awds:** Governor's Hometown Award, State Ill plaque, 1987; Citizens United for Better Society Plaque, 1980; Certificate of Appreciation, Boy Scouts No 302, 1989, 1990; House Resolution No 2125, IL State house of Rep Certificate, 1990; mayor, Kankakee County Men of Progress Plaque, 1983; Nat Alliance Business, Nat Black Mayor Asn Certificate, 1990, 1991, 1992; Nat Alliance Leadership Nat Black Mayor Asn Certificate, 1990, 1991, 1992; Ill Clean & Beautiful Award, Ill Dept Com & Community Affairs Certificate, 1987. **Business Addr:** Mayor, Village of Sun River Terrace, 7267 E Chicago St, St Anne, IL 60964, **Business Phone:** (815)937-1200.

WADE, DAISY GRIFFIN HARRIS. See HARRIS, DAISY.

WADE, DR. EUGENE HENRY-PETER
Physician. **Personal:** Born Nov 20, 1954, Washington, DC; son of Samuel Wade and Dorothy Heyward Vallentine; married Portia Battle; children: Kim M, Eugene Henry-Peter II & Kara. **Educ:** Brown Univ, AB, ScB, 1978; Howard Univ, Col Med, MD, 1981; Univ Ala, Postgrad training. **Career:** Pvt Pract, family physician. **Orgs:** Co-chmn, NC Acad Family Physicians, Minority Affair Comm; Indigent Care Task Force NC Med Soc; NC Gen Assembly Indigent Health Care Study Commr; diplo, Acad Family Physicians. **Business Addr:** Physician, 1041 Kirkpatrick Rd, Burlington, NC 27215, **Business Phone:** (336)538-0565.

WADE, HAWATHA TERRELL. See WADE, TERRELL.

WADE, JAMES NATHANIEL
Executive. **Personal:** Born Oct 2, 1933, Patterson, NJ; children: Valarie, JaJa, Atiba. **Educ:** Voorhees Col, AA, 1954; St Augustines Col, BA, 1956; Howard Univ, MSW, 1967; Univ Pittsburgh, post grad, 1975. **Career:** Erie Community Action Comt, deputy opers, 1967-69; Erie Urban Coalition, exec dir, 1969-71; Dept Community Affairs & Commonwealth, deputy secy, 1971-73, gov spec asst, 1973-75, secy admin, 1975-79; Wade Communications, Inc, chairman bd. **Orgs:** chmn, First & Second Philadelphia United Negro Col Fund; vpres, The Basan Develop; exec comt, Crisis Intervention Network; bd mem, Philadelphia Dance Co; bd mem, Congreso De Latinos Unidos, Inc; life mem, NAACP; life mem, Kappa Alpha Psi; Nat Black MBA Association; Bay City Masonic Lodge. **Honors/Awds:** NAACP presidential award, 1975, humanitarian award, 1976; award of distinction, United Negro Col Fund, 1976; achievement & meritorium award, St Augustines Col; legion of honor award, Chapel of Four Chaplains; christian businessman of the year award, Am Union Church; president citation distinguished alumni award, Nat Assoc Equal Opp higher Educ; citizen of the year award, Omega Psi Psi. **Military Serv:** AUS, sp 4, 1956-58; Leadership Training Award, 1957.

WADE, DR. JOSEPH DOWNEY
School administrator. **Personal:** Born Jan 16, 1938, Beaumont, TX; son of Rufus and Lorene; married Judith Allen; children: Stacy & Joseph Jr. **Educ:** Ore State Univ, BS, 1959, MEd, 1961; Univ Ore, PhD, 1982. **Career:** Educator (retired); Compton Col, head football coach, 1969-71; Univ Ore, asst football coach, 1972-75, assoc dir admis, 1975-76, assoc dir, acad adv & stud serv, 1976-84, dir, acad adv & stud serv, adminr, dir, acad adv & stud serv. **Orgs:** Comnr, chair, Ore Comn Black Affairs; univ senate, Fac Adv Coun; exec coun, Nat Stud Exchange; bd trustee, Northwest Christian Col.

WADE, JOYCE K
Banker, vice president (organization). **Personal:** Born May 2, 1949, Chicago, IL; daughter of Ernest S Wade, Sr and Martha L Davis Wade. **Educ:** Northwestern Univ, Evanston IL, BS, educ, 1970; Univ Chicago, IL, MBA, 1977. **Career:** US Dept of Housing & Urban Development, Chicago IL housing rep, 1970-78; IL Housing Develop Authority, Chicago develop office rep, 1978-79; Community Bank Lawndale, chicago loan office rep, 1979-87, office chief exec officer, 1987-, mem Bd dir, 1988-; Habilitative Systs inc, vpres finance, currently. **Orgs:** Treas, Carole Robertson Ctr Learning, 1980-; mem bd control, treas & chair Loan Comn, Neighborhood Network & Housing Serv, Marshall Sq & Douglas Park, 1984-; Urban Renewal Bd City Chicago, 1987-; treas, Nat Asn Negro Bus & Prof Women, 1987-; dir, Am Civil Liberties Union IL, 1988-; Urban Bankers Forum Chicago, 1988-. **Honors/Awds:** Marilyn V Singleton Award, US Dept HUD, 1975; Bank Operation Outstanding Student Award, Asn Bank Oper Mgt, 1980; Positive Self Image Award, Westside Ctr Truth, 1988; Outstanding Service Award, Carole Robertson Ctr, 1989. **Special Achievements:** Top 100 Business & Professional Women, Dollars & Sense Magazine, 1988. **Business Addr:** Vice President Finance, Habilitative Systems Inc, 415 S Kilpatrick, Chicago, IL 60644, **Business Phone:** (773)854-8300.

WADE, KIM MACHE
Beautician, playwright. **Personal:** Born Sep 25, 1957, Manhattan, NY; daughter of Curtis L (deceased) and Rosa Jean; children: Rossi Jewel & Courtney Semaj. **Educ:** A&T State Univ, 1973; Univ NC, Greensboro, attended 1974; Shaw Univ, attended 1978; Sandhills Community Col, license cosmetology, 1986. **Career:** Moore County Arts Coun, playwright/producer, 1984; Innervision Theater Co, producer/playwright/dir, 1984-; Hometown News Mag, assoc ed, 1984-; Sandhills Community Col, instr; Mache Beauty Sta, owner. **Orgs:** Nat Asn Advan Colored People; Moore Co Chapter, 1975-; summer youth counr, Southern Pines Recreation Dept, 1984-85; missionary, Harrington Chapel Young Adult Missionary, 1986-; active coordr, Ebonette Cultural Club, 1986-. **Honors/Awds:** Young Black Achiever Award, Black History Month Observation, 1986. **Home Addr:** 240 S Stephens St, Southern Pines, NC 28387. **Business Addr:** Owner, Mache Beauty Sta, 388 N Stephens St, Southern Pines, NC 28387.*

WADE, LYNDON ANTHONY
Social worker, executive. **Personal:** Born Jun 30, 1934, Atlanta, GA; married Shirley M; children: Lisa, Nora, Jennifer & Stuart. **Educ:** Morehouse Col, AB, 1956; Atlanta Univ, MSW, 1958; Menninger Found Topeka Kans, adv cert psychol social work, 1963. **Career:** Social worker, executive (retired); Emory Univ, asst prof, 1963-68; Atlanta Urban League Inc, pres & chief exec officer, 1968. **Orgs:** Acad Cert Social Workers; Atlanta Action Forum; Nations Bank Com Reinvestment Comn; Jr League Adv Comt; Vision 20/20 Task Force; Atlanta Comt Pub Educ. **Honors/Awds:** Distinguished Community Service Award, Atlanta Morehouse Alumni Club, 1965; Distinguished Service Fulton City Medical Soc, 1971; Social Worker of the Year, N Ga Chap NASW, 1971; 10 Years Outstanding Service, Atlanta Urban League, 1978. **Military Serv:** USA Med Serv Corp, 1st lt, 1958-62.

WADE, MILDRED MONCRIEF
Nursing home administrator. **Personal:** Born Feb 5, 1926, Pittsburgh, PA; daughter of Lawrence Moncrief and Fannie Primus Moncrief; divorced; children: Judith L Johnson. **Educ:** Univ Pittsburgh, BA, 1947; Tuskegee Inst, EdM, 1951. **Career:** Nursing home administrator (retired); Selma AL Pub Schs, teacher, 1947-50;Tuskegee Inst, instr, 1951-52; YWCA, prog dir, 1953-55; Youth Develop Ctr, teacher, 1955-59; Home Aged, 1959-60; Dom Rel Ctr, counr, 1960-65; Pittsburgh Pub Sch, teacher, 1965-67; Louise Child Care Ctr, Pittsburgh, PA, asst exec dir, 1967-90; Lemington Home Aged, Pittsburgh, PA, administrative liaise, 1991. **Orgs:** Nat Conf Christians & Jews, Sickle Cell Soc Pittsburgh; Urban League Guild Pittsburgh; Nat Coun Negro Women Pittsburgh sec; Delta Sigma Theta Inc; Pittsburgh Alumnae chap; life NAACP; Wesley Ctr Am Zion Church, Pittsburgh, PA; African Heritage Rm Comn, Univ Pittsburgh, Pittsburgh, PA; Martin Luther King Jr, Outstanding Citizens Award, Hand in Hand Inc, 1986; bd mem, Urban League Pittsburgh, 1990-; bd mem, Lincoln, Larimer Revitalization Asn, 1989-. **Honors/Awds:** Outstanding Citizen Award, Pittsburgh City Coun, 1990; Council mans Cup Community Serv, City Coun Pittsburgh, 1990.

WADE, NORMA ADAMS
Journalist. **Educ:** Univ Texas, Austin, BJ, 1966. **Career:** Collins Radio Co Dallas, ed, proofer tech equip manuals, 1966-68; Bloom Advertising Agency, Dallas, advertising copywriter, prod asst, 1968-72; Post Tribune, Dallas, TX, staff writer & asst ed, 1972-74; Dallas Morning News, TX, staff writer & columnist, 1974-2002, writer, currently. **Orgs:** Dallas-Ft Worth Asn Black Communicators; Nat Asn Black Journalists. **Honors/Awds:** Juanita Craft Award, Nat Asn Advan Colored People, 1985; Bronze Heritage Award, 1989; Lifetime Achievement Award, Dallas & Ft Worth Asn Black Communicators, 1994; She Knows Where She's Going Award, Girls Inc Metropolitan Dalls, 1998. **Home Addr:** PO Box 655237, Dallas, TX 75265. **Business Addr:** Writer, The Dallas Morning News, 508 Young St, Dallas, TX 75202, **Business Phone:** (214)977-8222.

WADE, TERRELL (HAWATHA TERRELL WADE)
Baseball player. **Personal:** Born Jan 25, 1973, Rembert, SC. **Career:** Baseball Player (Retired); Atlanta Braves, pitcher, 1995-97; Tampa Bay Devil Rays, 1998; Cincinnati Reds, 1999; Houston Astros, pitcher, 2004; plumber, Atlanta area. *

WADE, UNAV OPAL
College administrator. **Personal:** Born Jan 1, 1930?; married Ernest (divorced); children: Gwendolyn, Gary, Aaron, Mike, Gregory, Margena & Ann. **Educ:** Morristown Normal Col; Col Alameda. **Career:** Charmetts Beauty Salon, owner, 1962-74; Beauty Salon, Jasper TX, owner, 1977-; Gen & Masonry Contractors, sec. **Orgs:** Secy, Alameda Br NAACP, 1966-67; treas, Alameda Br NAACP, 1968-69; pres, Alameda Br NAACP, 1970-75; chairwoman, Pvt Indust Coun, 1989-97; Jasper Beauticians Club, 1984-00; bd mem, Jasper Chamber Com, 1998; bd dir, Complete Health Serv; pres, Evergreen Baptist Church. **Honors/Awds:** Acheivement Award fund raising, NAACP, 1973; Recognition Award, Alameda Unified Sch Dist, 1976; Outstanding Award, Alameda Naval Air station, CA,1976; Outstanding Serv Award, Oakland Chap NAACP; Outstanding Serv Award, Alameda Sch Dist; Outstanding Serv Award, US Naval Air Station; Pres Award for outstanding comt Deep E Coun Govt; Sch Bd, Jasper Indep Sch District, 1998-00. **Special Achievements:** First African Am pres of Alameda Br of NAACP; First black woman to own and operate a business in downtown Alameda, CA, Jasper, TX, Newton, TX; author, "Little Tom the Slave Boy". **Business Addr:** 127 W Houston St, Jasper, TX 75951.

WADE, WILLIAM CARL
Manager, educator. **Personal:** Born Aug 24, 1934, Rocky Mount, VA; son of William Taft and Della Fox; married Mary Frances Prunty, May 14, 1955; children: Pamela Renee Stockard, Marcus Sidney & Carl Tracy. **Educ:** Franklin Univ, BS, 1968; Univ Dayton, MBA, 1972. **Career:** Ross Lab, financial reporting surv, 1966-72, credit mgr, 1976-77, customer serv & credit dir, 1977-90, fiscal serv dir, 1990-; Xerox Inc, acct analyst, 1972-74, credit mgr, 1974-76; Gen Motors, payroll acct, 1976; Franklin Univ, fac, currently. **Orgs:** Am Legion, 1965-; Franklin Univ Alumni Asn, 1968-; Univ Dayton Alumni Asn, 1972-; The Executive's Club, 1977-, pres, 1991-93; Cent Ohio Treas Mgt Asn, 1990-. **Honors/Awds:** Nat Asn Credit Mgrs, Certified Credit EXE, 1988, Credit Mgr Yr, 1989; Boy Scouts Am, Silver Beaver, 1979. **Military Serv:** USY, e-5, 1957-59. **Business Addr:** Faculty, Franklin University, 201 S Grant Ave, Columbus, OH 43215, **Business Phone:** (614)797-4700.*

WADE-GAYLES, DR. GLORIA JEAN
Educator, writer, editor. **Personal:** Born in Memphis, TN; daughter of Robert and Bertha Reese Willett; married Joseph Nathan, Aug 24, 1967; children: Jonathan & Monica. **Educ:** LeMoyne Coll, BA, 1959; Boston Univ, AM, 1962; George Washington Univ, attended 1967; Emory Univ, PhD, 1981. **Career:** Woodrow Wilson fel, 1959-62; Danforth Fel, 1974; Spelman Coll, instr English, 1963-64, from asst prof to prof, 1984-92, eminent scholar prof, currently; Howard Univ, instr English, 1965-67, DuBois fel; Morehouse Coll, asst prof, 1970-75; Emory Univ, graduate teaching fel, 1975-77, adj prof African Am studies; Talladega Col, asst prof, 1977-78; UNCF Mellon Res grant, 1987-88; George Washington Univ, adj fac mem; Dillard Univ, eminent scholar chair, prof. **Orgs:** Teacher COFO Freedom School & Valley View MS, 1964; WETV 30 -WABE-FM, bd dir, 1976-77; Guardians for Quality Educ, sec, 1976-78; editorial bd Callaloo, 1977-80; Coll Language asn, exec bd, 1977-80; NAACP, ASNLC, CORE; Alpha Kappa Alpha Sorority Inc; Jon-Mon Consultants Inc, partner; speech writer. **Honors/Awds:** Faculty Award of the Yr Morehouse Coll, 1975; Liaison with Natl Humanities Fac; Presidential Award for Scholar, Spelman Coll, 1991; CASE Natl Prof of the Year, 1991; Emory Medal, Asn of Emory Alumni, 1994; DHL, Meadville-Lombard Theol Sch, Univ Chicago; Master Teacher Of Nonfiction, Tn Williams Literary Fest; LeMoyne-Owen DuBois Scholar's Award; Malcolm X Award for Community Service, City of Atlanta. **Special Achievements:** Author: No Crystal Stair: Visions of Race & Sex in Black Women's Fiction, 1946-76, 1984; Anointed to Fly, 1991; Pushed Back to Strength, 1993; Moving in My Heart: African American Women's Spirituality, 1995; Rooted Against the Wind, 1996; Father Songs: Testimonies by African-American Sons and Daughters, 1997; Editor: My Soul Is a Witness: Afr-Amer Women's Spirituality, 1995; In Praise Our Teachers: A Multicultural Tribute to Those Who Inspired Us, 2003. **Business Addr:** Professor, Spelman College, Independant Study, 350 Spelman Lane SW, PO Box 338, Atlanta, GA 30314, **Business Phone:** (404)223-1433.

WADE-LEWIS, MARGARET
College teacher. **Educ:** NY Univ, PhD, linguistics. **Career:** State Univ NY, Col Lib Arts & Sci, chair Dept Black Studies & dir linguistics prog, assoc prof black studies, currently. **Honors/Awds:** Distinguished Teacher Award, State Univ NY, 2002. **Business Addr:** Associate Professor, State University of New York, 75 S Manheim Blvd Col Hall F 105, New Paltz, NY 12561, **Business Phone:** (845)257-2766.

WADE-MALTAIS, DR. JOYCE
Educator. **Personal:** Born Aug 4, 1930, Spanish Town, Jamaica; daughter of Ribton Montgomery and Lena Amanda Campbell; married Walter E, Dec 10, 1971 (divorced); children: Michelle Helene. **Educ:** Wilmington Col, attended 1954; Ohio State Univ, MA, 1956; Univ London, Eng, dipl audio-visual aids, 1964; Univ Calif, Riverside, PhD, 1981. **Career:** Col Desert, prof eng speech, 1966-99, adj prof, 1999-2003, 2004-05, prof emer Eng & Speech, currently; Joslyn Sr Ctr, creative writing/memoir writing instr, 2000; Chapmen Univ, adjunct prof, 2002. **Orgs:** Bd mem & chair

acad affairs, Palm Valley Sch, Palm Springs, 1984-90; consult, State Dept Educ, Eng La Familia High Sch, 1986-88; Rent Rev Comn, City Palm Desert, CA, 1987-; Calif Teachers Asn, 1990-2003; Delta Kappa Gamma Women Educr, 1990-; Martin Luther King Commemoration Comt, Palm Springs, 2000-; Delta Sigma Theta Sorority Inc, 2002-; vol, Va Waring Int Piano Competition; secy, Music Teachers Desert. Affirmative Action Comn & Equal Opportunity Coun, Riverside Co, CA; bd mem, Desert Chap ACLU-SC. **Honors/Awds:** Outstanding Teacher, Col Desert, 1992-98; Col Professor of the Year, Nat Asn Advan Colored People, 1992; Award for Education Excellence, Coochella Valley, 2000; Woman of Distinction, Col Desert. **Home Addr:** 73153 Shadow Mountain Dr, Palm Desert, CA 92260. **Business Addr:** Professor Emeritus, English and Speech, College of Desert, 43-500 Monterey Ave, Palm Desert, CA 92260, **Business Phone:** (760)346-8041.

WADEN, FLETCHER NATHANIEL, JR.
Executive. **Personal:** Born Jan 30, 1928, Greensboro, NC; son of Fletcher Sr and Rosa P; widowed; children: Betty. **Educ:** Am Bus Inst, 1948; Winston-Salem State Univ, 1974; NC A&T State Univ, 1975-76; Univ NC, 1987. **Career:** Ritz Loan, owner, gen mgr, 1951-57; Gnato's C Clothing Store, owner, 1960-70; Gnato's Construct cpn, pres, owner, 1979-; Nat Financial & Bus Consult Inc, pres; Waden Supply Co Inc, pres, currently. **Orgs:** DAV & VFW; Nat Suppliers Develop Coun Inc; NCP; Bus Enterprise Legal Defense & Educ Fund Inc; US Dept Defense, Defense Mfrs & Suppliers Asn; Pub Serv Comn SC. **Honors/Awds:** Honorary chair, bus Adv coun; National Leadership Award, Bus Adv coun, 2002; Republican Gold Medal, 2002. **Military Serv:** USY, 1948-51. **Business Addr:** President, Waden Supply Company Inc, 1110 Kendall Mill Rd, Thomasville, NC 27360, **Business Phone:** (919)472-4804.

WADSWORTH, ANDRE
Football player. **Personal:** Born Oct 19, 1974, St Croix, Virgin Islands of the United States. **Educ:** Fla State Univ. **Career:** Tampa Bay Buccaneers, defensive end, 1998; Ariz Cardinals, defensive end,1998-2000; New York Jets, 2007; free agent,currently. **Honors/Awds:** Best Defensive Lineman, NCAA, 1997; Rookie of the Year, Lombardi Award Finalist, 1997; elected into FSU Hall of Fame, 2004. **Special Achievements:** First African Am picked in 1998 NFL draft.

WAFER, DEBORAH
Physician. **Career:** UCLA Med Ctr, Nurse Practr; Agouron Pharmaceuticals Inc, mgr; Pfizer Inc, mkt mgr, currently. **Honors/Awds:** Corporate Award. **Business Addr:** Marketing Manager, Pfizer Inc, 235 E 42nd St, New York, NY 10017, **Business Phone:** (212)733-2323.*

WAGNER, ANNICE (ANNICE M WAGNER)
Judge, government official. **Personal:** Born Jan 1, 1937, Washington, DC; married. **Educ:** Wayne State Univ, BA, JD. **Career:** Government offical (retired), Judge; Nat Capital Housing Authority, gen coun, 1973-75; People's Counsel DC, staff, 1975-77; Super Ct DC, assoc judge, 1977-90; DC Ct Appeals, assoc judge, 1990; DC Supreme Ct, chief judge, 1994-; Harvard Univ, instr. **Honors/Awds:** Charlotte E Ray Award, Nat Bar Asn; Sixth Annual Trumpet Awards, 1988. **Special Achievements:** One of six African Americans to be appointed chief justice in the United Status. **Business Addr:** Chief Judge, Court of Appeals of the District of Columbia, 500 Ind Ave NW, Washington, DC 20001.

WAGNER, ANNICE M. **See WAGNER, ANNICE.**

WAGNER, DAVID H.
Lawyer. **Personal:** Born Jul 23, 1926, Davidson County, NC; married Mollie Craig; children: Brenda C, Davida S. **Educ:** A&T Univ, BS, 1948; A&T State Univ, MS, 1957; Wake Forest Univ, JD, 1968. **Career:** Pender Co, instr prin, 1954-58; Lexington NC, instr prin, 1958-66; Wachovia Bank, closing atty & housing spec, 1968-69; Atty, pvt pract, 1969-. **Orgs:** Gen couns Winston Mutual Life Ins, 1969-; pres, Urban Housing Inc 1970-; pres, Assoc Furniture Inc, 1970-; NBA; NC Black Bar Asn; Forsyth Co Bar Asn; NC Bar treas Goler Met AME Zion Church; vpres, life mem NAACP; bd mem & stockholder, Vanguard Invest Co; Forsyth Econ Develop Corp; life mem, Alpha Phi Alpha; life mem, NEA. **Military Serv:** AUS, 1st lt, 1948-53. **Business Addr:** Attorney, Private Practitioner, PO Box 12068, Winston-Salem, NC 27117-2068, **Business Phone:** (336)722-0272.

WAGONER, J ROBERT (TOM RIVERS)
Television producer, executive, writer. **Personal:** Born Mar 27, 1938, Concord, NC; son of Elijah James and Virginia L. **Educ:** Manhattan Sch Music, 1962-63; NC A&T State Univ, BS, eng drama, 1968; Univ NC, MA, film, tv & drama, 1974; Univ Southern Calif Grad Sch Cinema, attended 1983-84. **Career:** NC A&T State Univ, lectr, photography, 1964-67; Black Jour, writer, producer, dir, camera, 1968-71; Fayetteville State Univ, commun ctr designer, 1971-72; Black Fantasy, cinematographer, 1972; Cap Cities Community, promotions mgr, 1974-75; Transvue Films, writer, dir, 1975-79; Disco Godfather, writer & dir, 1980; Calif State Univ, Long Beach, assoc prof, 1980-83; Televersity, pres, chief exec officer, 1985-; Collegiate Cable Channel, chair bd, chief exec officer, currently. **Orgs:** Bushido Int, grand master, NC A&T Alumni Karate-do, 1967-; bd chmn, Greater African Am, All-Am Univ Marching Band, 1993-. **Honors/Awds:** Sci, Special Jefferson Broadcast Fel, Univ NC, 1968; Nat Acad TV Arts & Emmy, one of six producers, 1969; Movie Lab Fel, Int Film Seminars, 1969; White House Photographer's Asn Award, Univ F & V Prod Asn, 1972; WGBH Fel, WGBH Ed Found, 1992; CPB/SC Educl TV, delegate, Int TV Screen Conf, 1992. **Special Achievements:** City of Pasadena & The Ralph Parsons Co, special directing citation, 1978. **Military Serv:** USN, photo 2nd, 1956-60; USN Honorman (top photographer), Music Citation. **Business Addr:** President, Televersity, 179 E Franklin, Chapel Hill, NC 27514, **Business Phone:** (919)968-9836.

WAGSTAFF, JACQUELINE
City council member. **Career:** Northeast Cent Durham-Partners Against Crime; Durham City Council, mem, currently. **Orgs:** bd mem, Durham Pub Sch. *

WAIGUCHU, MURUKU
College teacher, educator. **Personal:** Born Nov 29, 1937, Kenya; son of Mugure and Waiguchu; divorced; children: 3. **Educ:** Cent Col, BA, polit sci, econ & bus admin, 1965; Queens Col, MA, pub admin, 1967; Temple Univ, PhD, pub admin, 1971. **Career:** St John's Univ, African Studies Ctr, instr, 1968-69; Rutgers Univ, Urban Univ, asst prof, 1969-70; William Paterson Col, NJ, assoc prof, chairperson, 1973-78, Pub Admin, prof, 1980, Sch Mgt, prof, Mkt & Mgt Sci, prof, currently; Univ Md, Col Park, Off Minority Stud Educ, dir, 1978-80; Columbia Univ, Teacher's Col, lectr. **Orgs:** AHSA; ASA; NCBPS; ABSW; NJABE; INCCA; Am Soc Pub Admin. **Special Achievements:** Edited a book: Management of Organizations in Africa. **Business Addr:** Professor, William Paterson University Christos M. Cotsakos College of Business, Department Marketing and Management Sciences, 300 Pompton Rd, Wayne, NJ 07470, **Business Phone:** (973)720-2000.

WAINWRIGHT, HON. DALE
Judge. **Personal:** Born in Nashville, TX; married Debbie. **Educ:** London Sch Econs, attended 1981; Howard Univ, summa cum laude, 1983; Univ Chicago Law Sch, law degree, 1988. **Career:** Haynes & Boone; Andrews & Kurth; Civil Dist Ct, 1999-2002; Temp Comn Supreme Ct, justice, 2001; Supreme Ct Tex, Republican justice, 2002, 2008-. **Orgs:** Am Law Inst; dir, Houston Bar Asn; dir, Houston Vol Lawyers Prog; dir, Tex Young Lawyers Asn; pres, Houston Young Lawyers Asn. **Honors/Awds:** Legal Excellence Award, Nat Asn Advan Colored People, 2000. **Business Phone:** (512)463-1332.

WAINWRIGHT, GLORIA BESSIE
Government official. **Personal:** Born Jul 13, 1950, Cleveland, OH; married Roy; children: Roy Jr & Jason. **Educ:** Case Western Reserve Univ, Cert, 1971; Jane Addams Sch Pract Nursing, Dipl, 1975; Cuyahoga Community Col, 1980. **Career:** Ward 5 Block Club, pres, 1980; New Bethel AME Church, steward bd, 1984-85; Bathsheba Order Eastern Star, chaplain, 1983; Oakwood Village City Coun, councilmem, 1984-. **Home Addr:** 7226 Wright Ave, Oakwood Village, OH 44146. **Business Addr:** Councilmember, Oakwood Village City Council, 24800 Broadway Ave, Oakwood Village, OH 44146.

WAINWRIGHT, DR. OLIVER O
Executive. **Personal:** Born May 6, 1936, Nanticoke, MD; son of Jesse and Victoria Nutter; married Dolores Moorman; children: Oliver Jr, Stephen C & Eric C. **Educ:** Hampton Inst, BS, 1959; William Paterson Col, MA, commun, 1972; Central Mich Univ, MA, indust mgt, 1974; US Army Command & Gen Staff Col, 1975; Nova Univ, MPA, 1980, DPA, 1981; Rutgers Univ, advan mgt, resident, 1985. **Career:** AUS, various positions to lt col, 1959-79; SCM Corp, mgr corp security, 1979-85; Mobil Corp, Stamford, Conn, corp security mgr, 1985-87; Am Int Group, New York, New York, asst vpres, dir corp security, 1987-; Hoffman-LaRoche Inc, dir corp security, currently. **Orgs:** Kappa Alpha Psi; mayoral appintment, Human Resources Coun Piscataway, 1980; trustee, N Stelton AME Church, 1980-81; Am Soc Indust Security, 1981-; Asn Polit Risk Analysts, 1982; bd dir, Acad Security Ed & Trainers, 1982-85; cert bd, Acad Security Ed & Trainers, 1983-85; assoc mem, Int Asn Chiefs; bd dir, Am Soc Indust Sec, 1985-87; Int Security Mgt Asn, 1985-; Alliance Concern Citizens, Piscataway, NJ; bd educ, Piscataway, NJ, 1987-90; Oversea Security Coun, US Dept State, 1988-90. **Honors/Awds:** Nat Training Award, Defense Intelligence Sch, Nat Training Officers Conf, 1977; Polit Risk Assessment Article, Risk Planning Group, 1980; Cert Protection, Prof Am Soc Indust Sec Int, 1981; Cert Security Trainer Acad Security Security Ed & Trainers, 1981; Black Achievers Indust Award, Harlem, YMCA, 1982; Mgt Future Article Security Mgt Mag, 1984; Certificate of Appreciation, bd dirs, Am Soc Ind Sec, 1987; Distinguished Service Award, L I University, Sch Pub Admin, 1985; Certificate of Appreciation, Community Service Award, Piscataway Sportsmen, 1989; Hon Cert, New York City Police Dept, 1990. **Military Serv:** AUS, Military Intelligence lt col, 1959-79; Bronze Star w/1 OLC; Air Medal w/2 OLC; Pres Unit Citation, Nat Defense Serv Medal, Defense Meritorious Serv. **Home Addr:** 63 Coventry Circle, Piscataway, NJ 08854. **Business Addr:** Director Corporate Security, Hoffman-LaRoche Inc, 340 Kingsland St, Nutley, NJ 07110, **Business Phone:** (973)235-2884.

WAITE, DR. NORMA LILLIA
Physician. **Personal:** Born in Kingston, Jamaica; married Ainsley Blair; children: Craig, Duane & Andre Blair. **Educ:** Howard Univ, BS, 1972; Howard Univ Med Sch, MD, 1977; Webster Univ, MA, health servs mgt, attended. **Career:** Brookdale Hosp, ob resident prog, 1977-81; Orlando Regional Hosp, Humana Hosp Lucerne, physician; Fla Hosp, physician, currently; pvt pract, physician, currently. **Orgs:** Fel, Am Col Obstetrics & Gynecol, 1982; fel, Am Bd Obstetrics & Gynecol; Cent FL Med Asn; Phi Beta Kappa Soc. **Business Addr:** Physician, Florida Hospital, 6000 Turkey Lake Rd Suite 112, Orlando, FL 32819, **Business Phone:** (407)363-9499.

WAITERS, DR. ANN GILLIS
Educator, school principal. **Personal:** Born Dec 5, 1939, Philadelphia, PA. **Educ:** Cheyney State Col, BS; Temple Univ, elem & urban educ. **Career:** William Penn Sch Dist, supt; Philadelphia Sch Dist, regional supt; Bodine High Sch Intl Affairs, prin; Univ Sch Rels Temple Univ, Philadelphia, fel; Temple Univ Col Educ, adj prof; Sch Dist Philadelphia, coordr int stud exchange prog, performance appraisal of admin & suprs; Temple Univ, reading teacher; Maritime Acad Charter Sch, prin, chief admin officer, chief exec officer, currently. **Orgs:** Rev Com Educ; Educ & Human Rel Com Asn Field Serv Teacher Edn; Black Educ Forum; Educ Equality League; Nat Coun Admin Women Educ; Penn Asn Supv & Curr Develop; PA Cong Sch Adminr; charter mem, Cong Sch Adminr. **Honors/Awds:** Principal of the Year, Educr Round Table; Phil Delta Kappa Service Award; Bicentennial Award, Nat Asn Univ Women; Appreciation Award, Linpark Civic Asn Trevose. **Business Addr:** Chief Executive Officer, Maritime Academy Charter School, 2275 Bridge St, Philadelphia, PA 19137, **Business Phone:** (215)535-4555 Ext 300.

WAITES-HOWARD, SHIRLEY JEAN
Public relations executive. **Personal:** Born Dec 29, 1948, Philadelphia, PA; daughter of James Harvey Waites (deceased) and Bessie E Hill Waites; married Alfred Howard Jr., Dec 31, 1989; children: Demarcus Reginald. **Educ:** Pa State Univ, BA, psychol, 1971; Bryn Mawr Grad Sch Social Work, MSS, 1977; Eastern Baptist Theol Seminary, Wynnewood, PA, currently. **Career:** Mental Health Consortium Inc, consult & educ specialist social worker therapist; W Philadelphia Community, consult & educ, 1971-77; Women's Network Consult, pub rels consult, 1974-; Baptist Childrens Serv, clinical dir, 1978-80; LaSalle Univ, coordr & instr, social work dept, 1980-83; Villanova Univ, instr, 1980-85; Haverford State Hosp, psychiat social worker, 1983-85; Lincoln Univ, instr, 1984; Priosn Proj, coordr; WDAS-AM Talk Show, prog asst, 1982-84; MaGee Rehab Hosp, staff social worker, 1987-. **Orgs:** Adv team mem, Triple Jeopardy Third World Women's Support Network; Nat Asn Black Psychologists; Nat Asn Black Social Workers; Nat Asn Social Workers. **Honors/Awds:** Achievement Award, Black Students LaSalle Univ, 1983; Achievement Award, MaGee Rehab Hosp, African Am Hist Month, February, 1989. **Home Addr:** 1708 N 55th St, Philadelphia, PA 19131. **Business Addr:** Staff Social Worker, MaGee Rehabilitation Hospital, Six Franklin Plaza, Philadelphia, PA 19102.*

WAITH, ELDRIDGE
Law enforcement officer. **Personal:** Born Jan 13, 1918, New York, NY; son of George and Montelle Russell; married Elsie Torres, Apr 12, 1971; children: Mariann C Ramos & Linda M Waith-Broadlick. **Educ:** John Jay Col Criminal Justice City Univ NY, BS, 1966. **Career:** Col Virgin Islands, instr, Police Sci, 1971; Virgin Islands Govt, comm pub safety, 1971-72; New York Bd Educ, chief adminr, Sch Safety, 1972-74; UBA Security Serv Inc, security cons, pres, 1974; Univ Virgin Islands, chief security, 1979-90; Virgin Islands Govt, dir narcotic strike force, 1990-92; New York Police Dept, asst chief inspector; NJ Civil Serv Comn Police Prom, consult; Police-Comm Rels Nat Conf Chris & Jews. **Orgs:** Nat Asn Advan Colored People; 100 Black Men; Guardians Asn Found NYCPD; VI Retired Police Orgn; Coun Retired Police, NYC; Noble. **Honors/Awds:** Received 17 Departmental awards for outstanding police work; numerous comm awards. **Home Addr:** PO Box 302413, Charlotte Amalie, Virgin Islands of the United States 00803.

WAITS, REV. VA LITA FRANCINE
Judge, lawyer, clergy. **Personal:** Born Jan 29, 1947, Tyler, TX; daughter of Melvin Jr and Sibbie Jones. **Educ:** Howard Univ, BA, 1969; Am Univ, MA, 1974; Tex Southern Univ, Thurgood Marshall Sch Law, JD, 1980. **Career:** WRC-TV & NBC, producer, 1971-74; Southwestern Bell Tel Co, mgr, 1975; Tex Southern Univ, instr, KTSU-FM, mgr, 1975-76; US Dept Energy, regional atty, 1980-81; Nat Labor Rels Bd, field atty, 1981-82; Law Off Va Lita Waits, prin, 1982-; City Tyler, alt munic judge, 1984-94; Jenkins Memorial Christian Methodist Episcopal Church, pastor, currently. **Orgs:** Smith County Bar Asn, 1982-; Supreme Ct, State Tex, Bar Admis Comt, 1983-87; Nat Bar Asn, 1984-; Leadership Tex, 1987-; founding pres, Tyler Metrop Chamber Com, 1989-92;

founding bd mem, Smith County Ct App Spec Advocates, 1989-; founder, Tyler Metro Chamber Com, 1990; pres, Delta Sigma Theta Sorority, Tyler Alumnae Chap, 1990-92; Nat Asn Black Women Lawyers, 1992-; secy, Tex Asn African Am Chambers Com, 1993-; founder, Ctr Non profit Develop, Houston, 1996; Leadership Tyler; asst prior, Order St Luke, Perkins Sch Theol chap; Exec Coun Hawk, Moore & Martin Halls, S Methodist Univ. **Honors/Awds:** Distinguished Graduate, Tyler Independent Sch Dist, 1983; Top Lady of the Year, Top Ladies Distinction, 1990; Leading African-Amercan, KLTV, Black Hist Portrait, 1991; Women of Distinction, Austin Metrop Bus Resource Ctr, 1992; Public Service Area Law, Omega Psi Phi, 1983; Service awards from numerous orgn including: Tyler Jaycess, Delta Sigma Theta Sorority, Rosebud Civitan Club, Longview Metrop Chamber Com, Texas Col, State Bar Tex Admis Comm, Bonner Elem Sch, DC Comn on Status Women, US Dept Justice, Bur Prisons; Dean's Hon Scholar, S Methodist Univ, Perkins Sch Theol; Hurley Found Scholar; Tadlock Scholar. **Special Achievements:** First African-American female attorney to hold judicial position in East Texas; assoc ed, Thurgood Marshall Law J, 1978-90; Coll of the State Bar of Tex, 1987-93. **Home Addr:** 3410 Dyer, PO Box 751395, Dallas, TX 75275-1395, **Home Phone:** (214)768-5973. **Business Addr:** Pastor, Jenkins Memorial Christian Methodist Episcopal Church, 604 N Van Buren St, Henderson, TX 75654, **Business Phone:** (903)657-6633.

WAKEFIELD, J. ALVIN
Consultant, president (organization). **Personal:** Born Jul 25, 1938, New York, NY; son of James Alvin and Dorothy Nickerson Bradshaw; divorced; children: Shawna Michelle & Adam Malik. **Educ:** Syracuse Univ, attended 1957; NY Univ, BA, eng lit, 1960; Pace Univ Grad Sch Bus, MBA, 1972. **Career:** Mobil Oil Corp, Boston, MA, employee rels asst, 1966-68; Celanese Corp, New York, NY, supvr personnel, 1968-70; Singer Co, New York, NY, recruiting mgr, 1970-73; Avon Products Inc, New York, NY, vpres admin, 1973-81; Korn/Ferry Int, New York, NY, vpres & partner, 1981-83; Wakefield Enterprises, Rutl, VT, pres, 1983-86; Gilbert Tweed Assocs, Pitts ford, VT, managing dir & partner, 1986-93; Wakefield Talabisco Int, pres, currently. **Orgs:** Chmn Coun Concerned Black Execs, 1970-73; bd mem, NY Urban League, 1980-83; exec comt, Vt Achievement Ctr, 1988-91; bd mem, Vt Bus Round table, 1988-; bd mem, New Eng Bd Higher Educ, 1990-91; Dem Party Exec Comt, 1993-95; Govs Coun Econ Advisors, 1994-; bd dirs, Trinity Col, 1994-2000; vice chmn, bd dir, Vermont Pub Radio, 1998-; pres, bd dir, Paramount Theatre. **Honors/Awds:** Academic Scholarship, Syracuse Univ, 1956; Outstanding Achievement Award, Black Retail Action Group, 1979; Partnership Award, Direct Selling Asn, 2000. **Special Achievements:** America's Top 100 Executive Recruiters, Career Makers, 1991; North Americas Top 150 Executive Recruiters, Career Makers, 1992, 1995. **Military Serv:** USAF, capt, 1961-66. **Business Addr:** President, Wakefield Talabisco International, Mendon Meadows Suite 8 13 US Rte 4, Mendon, VT 05701-9706, **Business Phone:** (802)747-5901.

WALBEY, THEODOSIA EMMA DRAHER (DODIE DRAHER)
Actor, singer, writer. **Personal:** Born Apr 13, 1950, Bangor, ME; married Daniel A Draher; children: Timothy W Wright, Stephen S Wright & Daniel Jr. **Educ:** Univ Md; Univ CO; Kinman Bus Univ. **Career:** Ritchie Family Album, co-writer; Films: Give Me A Break, 1980; Can't Stop the Music, 1980; La Borbichette; TV series: "The Ritchie Family", singer &actress, 1975; "Dinah Shore"; "Merv Griffin"; "Rock Concert"; "Midnight Special"; "Soul Train"; "Am Bandstand"; "Mike Douglas"; "Dance Fever-";"Soap Factory"; "Numerous countries around the world"; "Woman of Many Faces"; Can't Stop Prod, singer, dancer & actress. **Honors/Awds:** Gold & Platinum Records from around the world, 1976-77. **Home Addr:** 165 E 32nd St, New York, NY 10016.

WALBURG, JUDITH ANN
Financial manager, educator. **Personal:** Born Feb 19, 1948, New York, NY; daughter of Charles A and Florence Perry. **Educ:** Fisk Univ, Nashville TN, BA, 1969. **Career:** Olivetti Corp Am, NY, customer relations rep, 1970-72; United Negro Col Fund, NY, asst dir educ servs, 1972-75; Alumni Nat Org, dir, 1975-. **Orgs:** NY Alumni Asn, 1975-79; Nat Urban Affairs Coun, 1984-89; Corp Women's Network, 1986-89; bd mem, Coun Environ, 1987-89. **Honors/Awds:** Outstanding Young Woman of America, 1976 & 1978. **Home Addr:** 284 Convent Ave, New York, NY 10031. **Business Addr:** Director Alumni Groups National Organizations, United Negro College Fund, 120 Wall St Fl 10, New York, NY 10005-3902.*

WALCOTT, LOUIS EUGENE. See FARRAKHAN, LOUIS.

WALDEN, BARBARA
Executive, business owner, movie actor. **Personal:** Born Sep 3, 1936, Camden, NJ. **Educ:** Eccles Bus Col. **Career:** Films: The Private Lives of Adam & Eve, 1960; Car Wash, 1976; Freaky Friday, 1976; Frohes Fest, 1981; What A Way to Go; Global Affair; Bob Hope; Night of the Quarter Moon; TV Shows: "Disneyland", "Freaky Friday: Part 1", "Freaky Friday: Part 1", 1982;

Barbara Walden Cosmetics Inc, founder & pres, currently. **Orgs:** Bd mem, ACLU 1985-; United Way 1986-; bd mem, May Co So Calif Women's Adv Coun, 1986-; Comt 200, Coalition 100 Black Women; co-sponsor, Self- Image workshop sem; lecr at colleges, univs, women's groups, orgn, caucus, Los Angeles Unified Sch Dist yearly Career Day; keynote speaker New York's Dept States, Comn Econ Develop Prog, Syracuse, New york; guest lectr, Unic Calif Los Angeles, Women Mgt; guest lectr, Southern Calif, Bus Women's Caucus; bd dirs, Love Is Feeding Everyone. **Honors/Awds:** Women in Business Award; YWCA's Silver Achievement Award; Watts Summer Pageant Award; Special Merit Award, La Mayor Tom Bradley; The Baptist Business Women's Association Award; The Women's Network Conference Achievement Award; The Crenshaw La Tierra Business Women's Association Award; cited, Congressional Record; in depth interview in Entrepreneur Magazine entitled "Advice from Some of the Nation's Most Powerful Businesswomen"; Woman of the Year Award, State Calif Legis; First Annual Los Angeles Women Making History Award. **Special Achievements:** Author, Easy Glamour, Wm Morrow & Coy, 1983. **Business Addr:** Founder, President, Barbara Walden Cosmetics Inc., 5824 Uplander Way, Culver City, CA 90230, **Business Phone:** (310)823-4186.

WALDEN, DR. EMERSON COLEMAN
Physician. **Personal:** Born Oct 7, 1923, Cambridge, MD; son of Charles E and Lillian E; married Celonia; children: Emerson C Jr, Thomas E & Celonia. **Educ:** Howard Univ, MD, 1947. **Career:** Physician (retired); USAF Hosp Mitchell AFB, chief surg serv, 1951-53; Provident Hosp Baltimore, chief surg, 1964-68; Luther, Johns Hopkins, Provident, S Baltimore Gen Hosps, attending surg; Baltimore City Health Dept, part time sch physician; Pvt practice, physician. **Orgs:** Past pres, Nat Med Asn, pres, MD Med Asn; vpres, Monumental City Med Soc; bd regents, Univ Md; Baltimore City Med Soc; chmn, bd trustees, Nat Med Asn; dir, health serv, Providence Comprehensive Neighborhood Health Ctr; Alpha Chap. **Honors/Awds:** One of physicians who toured People's Rep of China, 1972. **Home Addr:** 301 St Paul Pl Suite 715, Baltimore, MD 21202, **Home Phone:** (410)528-1326.

WALDEN, NARADA MICHAEL
Singer, entertainer, musician. **Personal:** Born Apr 23, 1952, Kalamazoo, MI; married Anukampa. **Educ:** Western Mich Univ, 1970-72. **Career:** Music producer, drummer, singer & song writer; Warner Bros Recs, rec artist, writer & rec producer; songwriter Gratitude Sky, 1976-; various groups, drummer; various rec artists albums, pianist; Perfection Light Prod, pres, 1976-; Tarpan Studion Inc, owner, 1985-; Albums: Garden of Love Light, 1976; I Cry, I Smile, 1977; Awakening, 1979; The Dance of Life, 1979; Victory, 1980; Confidence, 1982; Looking At You, Looking At Me, 1983; The Nature of Things, 1985; Divine Emotions, 1988; Ricochet, 1991; Free Willy, 1993; Deliver Us from Eva, 2003; Zack and Miri Make a Porno, 2008.Singles:"Delightful", 1977; "Give Your Love a Chance", 1979; "I Don't Want Nobody Else", 1979; "I Shoulda Loved Ya", 1980; "Tonight I'm Alright", 1980; "The Real Thang", 1980; "Summer Lady", 1982; "Reach Out (I'll Be There)", 1983;"Gimme, Gimme, Gimme", 1985; "Divine Emotions", 1988; "Top of the Pops", 1988; "Soul Train", 1988; Whitney Houston: The True Story, 2002; Randy Jackson; 2005. **Honors/Awds:** Numerous honors & awards including Honorary Citizen Award, Atlanta, 1979;Honorary Citizen, New Orleans, 1980; Outstanding Black Contemporary ArtistAward, Bay Area Music Awards, San Francisco, 1982; Grammy Award, Best R&BSong "Freeway of Love" Aretha Franklin, 1986; Producer of the Year,Billboard Mag, 1986 & 1992. **Special Achievements:** Spokesperson for "The Peace Run", 1987. **Business Addr:** Owner, Tarpan Studios Inc, 1925 E Francisco Blvd Suite L, San Rafael, CA 94901, **Business Phone:** (415)485-1999.

WALDEN, DR. ROBERT EDISON
Educator. **Personal:** Born Apr 5, 1920, Boston, MA; son of Charles W Walden and Mary E James; married Ethel Lee Bazar, Jun 24, 1953; children: Kenneth E, Roberta E Miller, Robert E Jr, Mark E & Mary E Walden Mitchell. **Educ:** Lincoln Univ Chester County, PA, BA, 1942; Meharry Med Col, MD, 1945. **Career:** Lakin St Hosp Lakin, supt, 1962-65; Oakland County CMHS Bd, psychol dir, 1965-68; Med Col Ohio, assoc prof psychol, 1968-88; prof clinical psychol, 1988-90; prof emer, 1990-; pvt practr. **Orgs:** Med dir, Taft State Hosp, 1950-53; med dir, Cordelia Martin Health Ctr, 1969-72; Ohio Psychiatric Asn, 1969-94, pres, 1992-93; bd mem, Comn Planning Coun, 1969-72; Community Health Educ & Screen Prog 1972-76; pres, Northwest Ohio Psychiat Soc, 1972-73; psychol dir, Adult Psychol Hosp, 1977-88; chairperson, Ethics Comt Ohio Psychiat Asn, 1985-92; pres, Ohio Psychiatric Asn Educ & Res Found, 1990-92. **Honors/Awds:** Dipl, Am Bd Psychiat & Neurol, 1962-; life fel, Am Psychiatric Asn; Hon Distinguished Serv Award, Ohio Psychiat Asn, 1976, 1981, 1989. **Military Serv:** AUS, USAFR, USAR, col; Army Achievement; Good Conduct; Victory. **Business Addr:** Professor Emeritus, Medical College of Ohio, 3000 Arlington Ave, Toledo, OH 43614, **Business Phone:** (419)383-5695.

WALDON, HON. ALTON RONALD, JR.
Judge. **Personal:** Born Dec 21, 1936, Lakeland, FL; son of Alton R Sr and Rupert Juanita Wallace; married Barbara, Jun 3, 1961; children: Alton III, Dana & Ian. **Educ:** City Univ New York, John

Jay Col Criminal Justice, BS, 1968; NY Law Sch, JD, 1973. **Career:** New York City Housing Auth Police Dept, capt, 1962-75; NY State Div Human Rights, dep comnr, 1975-81; County Serv Group NYS OMRDD, coun, 1981-83; NY State Assembly, assemblyman 33rd dist, 1983-86; US House Rep, congressman,1986-87; NY State Invest Comn, comnr, 1987-90; New York State Senate, sen, 10th S D, 1991-2000; Ct Claims, NY, judge; NY Law Sch, Thurgood Marshall fel; NY State Crime Victims Bd, comnr, currently. **Orgs:** United Black Men Queens Inc; K C; Am Bar Asn; Alumni Asn NY Law Sch; Macon B Allen Bar Asn; bd dirs, USO Greater NY; Nat Asn Advan Colored People; F & M Prince Hall 33 degrees; Am Judges Asn; Alumni Asn; John Jay Col Criminal Justice; Asn Former Mems Cong Asn; Sigma Pi Phi Fraternity; Comus Club Brooklyn, NY; Nat Org Black Law Enforcement Execs; Housing Police Acad. **Special Achievements:** First African American Congressman elected from Queens, New York. **Military Serv:** AUS, specialist 4th class, 1956-59. **Home Addr:** 115103 222nd St, Cambria Heights, NY 11411, **Home Phone:** (718)723-6136. **Business Addr:** Commissioner, New York State Crime Victims Board, Rm 1000 55 Hanson Pl, Brooklyn, NY 11217.

WALKER, ADRIAN
Government official, columnist. **Career:** Boston Globe, columnist, currently. **Business Addr:** Columnist, Boston Globe, 135 Willim T Mrrssy Blvd, PO Box 55819, Boston, MA 02205-5819, **Business Phone:** (617)929-2011.

WALKER, ALBERTINA
Gospel singer. **Personal:** Born Aug 28, 1929, Chicago, IL; daughter of Camilla Colemon and Ruben; married Lesley Reynolds, Aug 20, 1967 (divorced); married Reco Brooks, 1991. **Career:** Gospel singer, currently; MGM film, Save the Children, performer, 1976;Songs: "I'm Still Here"; "Please Be Patient with Me"; "I Can Go to God in Prayer"; "I Got A Feeling (Everything Will Be Alright)"; "The Best is Yetto Come"; "Impossible Dream"; "Joy Will Come"; "God is Our Creator"; "Work on Me"; "In Shady Green Pastures"; "Don't Let Nobody Turn You Around-";"When God Dips His Pin of Love in My Heart"; "If I Perish"; "Ain't Got Tired Yet"; "Since I Met Jesus"; "Lord Keep Me Day by Day"; "Mary Don't You Weep"; "Remember Me"; "I Know the Lord Will Make a Way"; "I'm Willing"; "Show Some Sign"; "I Won't Be Back"; "Make It In". **Orgs:** Founder, World Famous Caravan Singers, 1952; bd mem, Oper PUSH, 1971-79;bd mem, Gospel Music Workshop Am, 1975-; governing bd, Rec Arts & Sci,Chicago Chap, 1985-; honorary mem, Eta Phi Beta, 1986-; life mem, Nat CounNegro Women. **Honors/Awds:** Four Gold records; Inter Nat Woman of the Year Award, PUSH, 1975; 9 Grammy Award nominations, 1981-87; Albertina Walker Scholarship, Cent State Univ, 1983; Albertina Walker Day, Mayor Harold Washington, 1986; Lifetime Achievement Award, 1986; Black Gospel Awards, London, England, 1986; honorary Doctor, Chicago Theological Seminary; Citizen Award, 1999; Chicago Senior Citizen Hall of Fame, 2001; CAGAG OF THE GMWA THE LIVING LEGEND AWARD, 2001; Gospel Music Hall of Fame, 2001; Stellar award, 2002. **Special Achievements:** Founded Albertina Walker Scholarship Fund in 1989, bench bearing her name placed in Grant Park, Chicago, 1994, street renamed Albertina Walker and the Caravans, numerous television appearances. **Home Addr:** 7740 S Essex Ave, Chicago, IL 60649.

WALKER, ALICE MALSENIOR
Writer. **Personal:** Born Feb 9, 1944, Eatonton, GA; daughter of Willie Lee and Minnie Tallulah Grant. **Educ:** Spelman Col, 1963; Sarah Lawrence Col, BA, 1965; Russell Sage Col, Phd, 1972. **Career:** Voter registration worker, GA; Head Start, MS, staff mem; NYC welfare dept, staff mem; writer-in-res & teacher black studies, Jackson State Col, 1968-69; Tougaloo Col, 1970-71; Wellesley Col & Univ MS-Boston, lectr lit, 1972-73; Univ CA-Berkeley, distinguished writer Afro-Am studies, 1982; Brandeis Univ, Fannie Hurst Prof Lit, 1982; Wild Trees Press, Navarro CA, co-founder & publ, 1984-; Author: Once, 1968; The Third Life of George Copeland, 1970; Five Poems, 1972; In Love & Trouble: Stories of Black Women, 1973; Langston Hughes: Am Poet, 1973; Revolutionary Petunias & Other Poems, 1973; Meridian, 1976; Diary of an African Nun, 1977; I Love Myself When I am Laughing, 1979; Good Night Willi Lee I'll See You In the Morning, 1979; You Can't Keep a Good Woman Down, 1981; The Color Purple, 1982; In Search of Our Mothers' Gardens, 1983; Horses Make a Landscape Look More Beautiful, 1984; The Color Purple, 1985; To Hell W Dying, 1988; Living by the Word, 1988; The Temple of my Familiar, 1989; Her Blue Body Everything We Know: Earthling Poems, 1965-90 Complete, 1991; Possessing the Secret of Joy, 1992; Film: Warrior Marks, producer; Warrior Marks, 1993; The Same River Twice: Honoring the Difficult; Anything We Love Can Be Saved, Random, 1997; A Poem Traveled down My Arm: Poem & Drawings, 2002; Absolute Trust in the Goodness of the Earth: New Poems, 2003; Everyday Use, 2003; Now is the Time to Open Your Heart, 2004. **Orgs:** Consult black hist, Friends C Miss, 1967; bd trustees, Sarah Lawrence Col, 1971-73. **Honors/Awds:** Merrill Writing fel, 1966; Mc Dowell Colony fel, 1967 & 1977-78; Nat Endowment Arts grant, 1969 & 1977; Radcliffe Inst fel, 1971-73; hon PhD, Russell Sage Univ, 1972; Lillian Smith Award, Southern Regional Coun, 1973; Nat Book Award nomination, 1973; Rosenthal Foundation Award, Am

Acad & Inst Arts & Letters, 1974; Guggenheim Award, 1977-78; Nat Endowment Arts fel, 1979; Nat Book Critics Circle Award nomination, 1982; Am Book Award, 1983; DHL, Univ Mass, 1983; Pulitzer Prize, 1983; O Henry Award, 1986; Sheila Award, Tubman African Am Mus, 1997; Literary Ambassador Award, University of Oklahoma Center for Poets and Writers, 1998. **Business Phone:** (212)782-9000.

WALKER, ALLENE MARSHA
Health services administrator. **Personal:** Born Mar 2, 1953, Chicago, IL; daughter of Major and Mabel H Thompson. **Educ:** Michael Reese Hosp Sch Med Tech, MT, 1973; Univ IL-Chicago, BS, 1974; Roosevelt Univ, MS, 1983. **Career:** Damon Clin Labs, lab supvr, 1974-85; Med Care HMO, provider rep, 1985-89; Jacqueline Inc, sec & treas, 1989; Med Care HMO, Maywood, IL, dir & prov serv, 1989-91, asst vp prov adm, 1991-92; HMO Ill, supvr Health Servs Progs, 1993-96. **Orgs:** Oper PUSH Inc, 1972-; HMO training coordr, Blue Cross & Blue Shield Ill, 1996, ed staff, currently. **Honors/Awds:** Bd Cert Am Soc Clin Pathologists, 1975. **Business Addr:** Editorial Staff, Blue Cross and Blue Shield of Illinois, 300 E Randolph St 25th fl, Chicago, IL 60601-5009, **Business Phone:** (312)653-4019.

WALKER, ANGELINA
Government official. **Career:** The White House, exec asst to coun vpres, currently. **Business Addr:** Executive Assistant to the Council for the Vice President, The White House, 1600 Pennsylvania Ave NW, Washington, DC 20500, **Business Phone:** (202)456-1414.

WALKER, ANNIE MAE
Educator. **Personal:** Born Jan 7, 1913, Daytona Beach, FL; married William H; children: Garland James. **Educ:** Bethune-Cookman Col, BS, Elem Educ, 1944; Bank St Col Educ, MS, 1946; Educ & Soc Adelphi Univ, MA, 1965; East Coast Univ, PhD, Anthropology, 1970; Yale Univ, Danforth Fellow, 1971. **Career:** New York Plainedge & Plainview Pub Schs, teacher & dir pre-sch progs; African Hist & Cult & Seminole Hist, prof lectr; State Univ NY, Stony Brook, prof educ. **Honors/Awds:** Outstanding Leadership Award, 1973; Martin L King Award, 1970; Black Studies Award, Danforth Found, 1970; Human Relations Award, Nat Conf Chris & Jews, 1969; Natioal Sojourner Truth Award, 1964; Most Promising Teacher Award, Bethune Cookman Col, 1944.

WALKER, ANTOINE DEVON
Basketball player. **Personal:** Born Aug 12, 1976, Chicago, IL; son of Diane; children: Crystal & Alana. **Educ:** Univ Ky. **Career:** Boston Celtics, forward, 1996-2003; Dallas Mavericks, 2003-04; Atlanta Hawks, 2004-05; Miami Heat, forward, 2005-07; Minn Timberwolves, 2007-. **Honors/Awds:** NBA, All Rookie Team, 1997; NBA Player of the Week, 2003. **Special Achievements:** First round pick, No 6, NBA Draft, 1996; NCAA-Div I, Championship, 1996. **Business Addr:** Professional Basketball Player, Minnesota Timberwolves, 600 1st Ave N, Minneapolis, MN 55403, **Business Phone:** (612)673-1600.

WALKER, ARMAN KENNIS
Banker. **Personal:** Born Oct 15, 1957, Minneapolis, MN; son of Simon W and Anna M Gallo; divorced. **Educ:** Univ Calif, Berkeley, BA, econ, 1979. **Career:** Wells Fargo Bank, com banking officer, 1979-83; Marine Midland Bank, asst vpres, 1983-85; Sanwa Bank Calif, vpres, sr mgr, 1985-92; Pine Cobble Partners, managing gen partner, 1990; OneUnited Bank, chief lending officer & calif regional pres. **Orgs:** Omicron Epislon Delta, 1979; co-chairperson, LA's Young Black Prof, 1989-; LA Urban Bankers Asn; bd dirs, Watts Heath Found, 1992-; bd trustees, treas, Church Christian, 1992-; co-chair, Banking & Finance Conf, 1992; co-chair, Calif Money Mgr Networking Forum, 1992; co-chair, African-Am Women Distinction Mixer, 1993. **Honors/Awds:** One of America's Best & Brightest, Dollars & Sense Mag, 1988; City Attorney, Los Angeles, Commendation, 1992. **Business Addr:** Chief Lending Officer, Regional President, OneUnited Bank, 3683 Crenshaw Blvd, Los Angeles, CA 90016, **Business Phone:** (323)290-4848.

WALKER, BETTY STEVENS
Lawyer. **Personal:** Born Feb 3, 1944, New York, NY; daughter of Anne Wood; married Paul T, Jun 17, 1965; children: Camarf, Tarik & Kumi. **Educ:** Spelman Col, Atlanta, BA, 1964; Harvard Law Sch, JD, 1967. **Career:** Harvard Bus Sch, res asst, 1966; Wake Opportunities Inc, Raleigh, coordr youth prog, 1968; Shaw Univ, curric consult, 1968, asst prof, polit sci, 1968-70; So Rwy Co Wash, DC, atty, 1974-77; Farmers Home Admin US Dept Agr, asst admin, 1977; Walker & Walker Assocs, atty, currently. **Orgs:** DC Ct Appeals; US Dist Ct DC; US Ct Appeals DC Dist; Supreme Ct US Am; DC Bar Asn; Wash Bar Asn; Nat Bar Asn; Spelman Col & Harvard Law Alumni Asn; fel John Hay Whitney, 1964; fel Aaron Norman, 1964; Bethel AME Church, Baltimore; steward, Bethel AME Church, 1989. **Honors/Awds:** Outstanding Leadership Award, Nat Asn Equal Opportunity, 1990. **Special Achievements:** First Black woman to Ames Competition 2 consecutive semesters at Harvard Law. **Home Addr:** 5033 Rushlight Path, Columbia, MD 21044, **Home Phone:** (301)596-6630. **Business Phone:** (202)842-4664.

WALKER, BRACEY WORDELL
Football player. **Personal:** Born Oct 28, 1970, Spring Lake, NC; married Levoda; children: Bracy Jr. **Educ:** Univ NC. **Career:** Football player(retired); Kans City Chiefs, defensive back, 1994, 1998-2001; Cincinnati Bengals, 1994-96; Miami Dolphins, 1997-98; Detroit Lions, 2002-05; free agent, NFL, currently. **Honors/Awds:** First-team All-America honors, Football Writers Asn, Second-team All-America pick, Sporting News; NFC Special Teams Player of the week Award, 2004. **Special Achievements:** Walker's 92-yard jaunt is the longest recorded blocked-field-goal return for a touchdown in NFL history; first non-Lions kick-returner to be given the NFC special teams award, since its inception.

WALKER, BRIAN
Football player. **Personal:** Born May 31, 1972, Colorado Springs, CO. **Educ:** Wash State Univ. **Career:** Wash Redskins, def back, 1996-97; Miami Dolphins, 1997-98, 2000-01; Seattle Sea hawks, 1999; Detroit Lions, 2002-04. **Orgs:** Prudential No Passing zone prog, 2000. **Honors/Awds:** NFLPA, Unsung Hero Award, 2000; AFC Def Player of the Week, 2000. *

WALKER, CAROLYN
Senator (u.s. federal government), state government official. **Personal:** Born in Yuma, AZ. **Career:** Ariz House Reps, Phoenix AZ, state rep, 1983-86; Ariz St, st sendist 23, 1986.

WALKER, CHARLES
Actor, educator. **Personal:** Born Jan 21, 1945, Chicago, IL; son of Charles and Robbie Edith Hutchinson; married Lillian Beatrice Lusk, Feb 7, 1976; children: Leah Cher & Chasen Lloyd; married Ilona Massey (divorced). **Educ:** Career Acad Sch Broadcasting, Milwaukee, WI, broadcasting degree, 1967; Wilson City Col, Chicago, IL, attended 1967; California State Univ, Los Angeles, CA, BA, 1980, MA, 1982. **Career:** WVOL-Radio, Nashville, TN, radio news reporter; WXYZ-TV, Detroit, MI, tv news rep, 1967-68; prof actor Los Angeles, CA, TV,film & commercials, 1968-; Los Angeles Unified Sch Dist, Los Angeles, CA, sub teach, 1980-; Calif State Univ, Los Angeles, CA, instr speech comm, 1980-81; City of Los Angeles, Los Angeles, CA, lectr work experience prog, 1981-83; Hollywood High Sch, Los Angeles, CA, teacher,1984; Los Angeles Southwest Col, Los Angeles, CA, instr pub speaking, 1984-; Calif State Univ, Dominguez Hills, CA, instr fund of speech, acting, & inter cultural comm, 1984-; Films: Gridiron Gang, 2006; Wake Up, Ron Burgundy: The Lost Movie, 2004; Anchorman: The Legend of Ron Burgundy, 2004; Soul Plane, 2004; First Watch, 2003; Rennie's Landing, 2001; Almost Famous, 2000; Nutty Professor II: The Klumps, 2000; TV Series: "Once & Again", 2000; "Dead Last", 2001;"Power Rangers Time Force", 2001; "NYPD Blue", 2001; "Just ShootMe!", 2003; "The Parkers", 2002; "The West Wing", 2002; "Navy NCIS: Naval Criminal Investigative Service", 2004;"Grey's Anatomy", 2005; "Blind Justice",2005;"Everybody Hates Chris", 2006; "Without a Trace", 2006; "What About Brian", 2006; "The Nine", 2007. **Orgs:** NAACP; Screen Actor's Guild; Am Federation TV & Radio Artists; Mt Zion Missionary Baptist Church. **Business Addr:** Professor, California State University Dominguez Hills, Speech/Theatre Department, 1000 EVictoria St, Carson, CA 90747, **Business Phone:** (213)516-3588.

WALKER, CHARLES E
Clergy. **Personal:** Born Jun 28, 1935, Chicago, IL; son of Charles and Mercedes Pierre; married Barbara Wicks, Sep 16, 1989; children: Pierre & Jason. **Educ:** DePaul Univ, BM, 1957, MM, 1959; Colgate Rochester Div Sch, BD, 1970. **Career:** Requiem Brother Martin, composer Jazz Mass & Dr Watts; Charles Walker Chorale, dir; 19th St Bapt Ch, pastor, minister, currently. **Orgs:** Liberian Symph Orchest, 1977; Am Asn Univ Profs; Am Symphony Orchestra League; Fedn Musicians; Theol Comn Nat Baptist Conv Scholar Comn; exec bd, Hampton Inst Ministers Conf; chmn, Foreign Mission Bd Nat Baptist Conv, Nat Baptist Conv, USA; nat vpres, E Reg Oper PUSH. **Business Addr:** Minister, 19th Street Baptist Church, 1253 S 19th St, Philadelphia, PA 19146, **Business Phone:** (215)389-2132.

WALKER, CHARLES EALY, JR.
Lawyer, educator. **Personal:** Born May 1, 1951, Anchorage, AK; son of Charles E Sr and Marguerite Lee; married Dorothy Sanders, Sep 17, 1983; children: Sydney & Courtney. **Educ:** Univ Calif, Santa Barbara, BA, magna cum laude, 1973; London Sch Econs, 1977; Boston Col Law Sch, JD, 1978. **Career:** Oxnard Union High Sch Dist, teacher, 1974-75; USDA Off Gen Coun, atty, 1978-79; Boston Super Ct, law clerk, 1979-80; Suffolk Univ Law Sch Coun Legal Educ Opportunity, teaching fel, 1980-82, 1987-89; Univ Mass, instr, 1980-82; Mass Ct Appeals, law clerk, 1980-81; Commonwealth Mass, asst atty gen, 1981-87; New Eng Sch Law, asst prof, 1987-; Boston Col, adj prof; Exec Elder affairs, gen coun; Mass Comn Against Discrimination, chair. **Orgs:** Pres & co-founder, Boston Col Law Sch Black Alumni Network, 1981-; chair, Mass Bar Asn Comt Bar Admin; pres, Roxbury Defenders Comt Inc, 1982-; Cambridge Econ Opportunity Comn, 1982-86; Nat Asn Advan Colored People Nat Urban League, 1985-; trustee bd & chmn, Good Shepherd Church God Christ, 1985-; ed bd, Mass Law Review, 1990-; pres, Mass Black Lawyers Asn Exec Bd, 1993-95; bd dirs, Wheelock Col Family Theatre; past chair, Mass Comn Against Discrimination; exec dir, Lawyers' Comt Civil Rights Under Law Boston Bar Asn, currently. **Honors/Awds:** Distinguished Serv Award, Proj Commitment Inc, 1988; Charles Hamilton Houston Distinguished Serv Award, New Eng Sch Law, 1990; William Kenneally Alumnus Year, Boston Col Law Sch, 1995; Top Ten Lawyers of the Year, Mass Lawyers Weekly, 1997; Excellence Legal Educ Citation, Govt Mass. **Special Achievements:** Author: Liquor Control Act: Alcoholic Beverages Control Commission, 1986; Violation of Injunctions: Criminal and Civil Contempt, MBA Restraining Orders and Injunctions, pages 1-15; Massachusetts Bar Association speaker, "Obedience is Better than Sacrifice," 1988; "The History and Impact of Black Lawyers in Massachusetts," Mass Supreme Judicial Work, Historical Law Soc Law Jour. **Home Addr:** 80 Maskwonicut St, Sharon, MA 02067-1216. **Business Addr:** Executive Director, Under Law of the Boston Bar Association, 294 Washington St Suite 443, Boston, MA 02108, **Business Phone:** (617)482-1145.

WALKER, CHARLES H
Lawyer. **Personal:** Born Nov 11, 1951, Columbus, OH; son of Watson H and Juanita Webb; married Amanda T Herndon; children: Katrina Della, Allison Lyles & Carlton Wesley. **Educ:** Tufts Univ, BA (magna cum laude), 1973; Emory Univ Sch Law, JD, 1976. **Career:** Lawyer (retired); Bricker & Eckler LLP, assoc, 1976-81, partner, 1982-, sr coun; I-670 Corridor Develop Corp, mem & pres, 1992-99; Thomas D Lambros Dispute Mgt Ctr LLC, exec dir, 1996-98. **Orgs:** Pres & mem, Columbus Acad Alumni Asn, 1979-83, 1993-95; Planned Parenthood Cent OH, 1984; chmn, Tufts Univ Alumni Admis Prog, Cent, OH; chairperson, Battelle Youth Scholars Prog, 1988-94; Prof & Legal Ethics Comn, 1988-96; City Columbus Sports Arena Comn, 1989; Ohio State Bar Asn; Columbus Light Opera, 1990-94; Columbus Neighborhood Housing Serv, 1990-94; mem, vpres & pres, Life Care Alliance. **Honors/Awds:** Service Award, Columbus Bar Asn, 1998. **Special Achievements:** Listed in Who's Who in American Law, Who's Who Among Black Americans, Who's Who in the Midwest, and Men of Achievement.

WALKER, CHARLES W
State government official. **Personal:** Born in Burke County, GA; married Shelia. **Educ:** Augusta Col, BA, bus admin. **Career:** Walker Group, founder & pres; BLs Restaurant & Dining; Ga Senate, senate majority leader. **Orgs:** Chmn, Ga Asn Human Rels Comn; Sickle Cell Adv Bd; founder & sponsor, CSRA Classic Football Game; Senate Budget Conf; State Comn Ment Health, Ment Restoration & Substance Abuse Serv Delivery; Govs Comn Health Care Reform; Southern Conf Legislators; Nat Conf State Legis; Alpha Phi Alpha Fraternity Inc; bd trustee, Mt Vernon Baptist Church; trustee, Morris Brown Col; trustee, Paine Col; trustee, Morehouse Sch Med. **Honors/Awds:** Public Service Award, Ment Health Asn, 1993; Legislator of the Year, Ga Pub Health Asn, 1993; Outstanding Legislator, Ga Coun Aging, 1993; Legislator of the Year, Ga Alliance Mentally Ill, 1993; Presidential Appreciation Award, 1993; Distinguished Service Award, Med Asn Ga. **Special Achievements:** First African American to be elected to the position of Majority Leader. **Military Serv:** USN.

WALKER, CHESTER (CHET WALKER)
Basketball player, movie producer. **Personal:** Born Feb 22, 1940, Benton Harbor, MI. **Educ:** Bradley Univ, Peoria, IL, attended 1960. **Career:** Basketball player (retired), film producer; Syracuse Nationals, forward, 1962-63, Philadelphia 76ers, 1963-69; Chicago Bulls, forward, 1970-75; independent film producer. **Honors/Awds:** NBA All-Rookie Team, 1963; NBA All-Star Team, 1964, 1966, 1967, 1970, 1971 & 1973; Greater Peoria Sports Hall of Fame. **Special Achievements:** Author of memoir entitled, "Long Time Coming: A Black Athlete's Coming-Of-Age in America", 1995.

WALKER, CHET. See WALKER, CHESTER.

WALKER, CURTIS. See BLOW, KURTIS.

WALKER, CYNTHIA BUSH
Educator. **Personal:** Born Dec 8, 1956, Fort Benning, GA; children: Christa S. **Educ:** Morehead State Univ, BA 1977, MHE, 1978. **Career:** Kent Metroversity, counr, 1978-80; Jefferson Comm Col, counr, 1980-, prof, currently. **Orgs:** Kent Asn Blacks Higher Educ; Col Student Personnel Asn Kent. **Business Addr:** Counselor, Jefferson Community & Technical College, 109 E Broadway, Louisville, KY 40202, **Business Phone:** (502)213-7238.

WALKER, DARNELL ROBERT
Football coach, football player. **Personal:** Born Jan 17, 1970, St Louis, MO; married D'Elbie; children: Darnell Robert Jr & Derra Lynn. **Educ:** Univ Okla. **Career:** Football player (retired), asst coach; Atlanta Falcons, defensive back,1993-96; San Francisco 49ers, 1997-99; Detroit Lions, 2000; Bacone Col,asst coach,2009; defensive backs coach, Southwest Baptist Univ, 2009-. **Business Addr:** Defensive Backs Coach, Southwest Baptist University, 1600 University Ave, Plaster Athletic Center Suite 209, Bolivar, MO 65613, **Business Phone:** (417)328-1764.

WALKER, DARRELL
Basketball coach. **Personal:** Born Mar 9, 1961, Chicago, IL; married Lisa; children: Darrell, Jerrell, Jarrett and Jarren & Felicia.

Educ: Univ Ark. **Career:** NY Knicks, 1983-86; Denver Nuggets, 1986-87; Wash Bullets, 1987-91; Detroit Pistons, 1991-93; Chicago Bulls, 1993; NBA Players Assn, field rep, 1993-95; Toronto Raptors, asst coach, 1995-96, head coach, beginning 1996; Wash Wizards, interim head coach, 1999-2000, dir player personnel, 2000-01; Wash Mystics, interim head coach; New Orleans Hornets, asst coach, currently. **Honors/Awds:** NBA Championship, 1993; inducted into the Arkansas Hall of Honor, 2008. **Special Achievements:** NBA Draft, First round pick, 1983. **Business Phone:** (405)208-4800.*

WALKER, DENARD ANTUAN
Football player. **Personal:** Born Aug 9, 1973, Dallas, TX. **Educ:** La State Univ. **Career:** Tenn Oilers, defensive back, 1997-98; Tenn Titans, 1999-2000; Denver Broncos, 2001-02; Minn Vikings, 2003; Oakland Raiders, 2004-05.

WALKER, DERRICK NORVAL
Football player. **Personal:** Born Jun 23, 1967, Glenwood, IL; married Rhonda. **Educ:** Univ Mich, educ. **Career:** Football player (retired); San Diego Chargers, tight end, 1990-93; Kansas City Chiefs, tight end, 1994-97; Oakland Raiders, tight end, 1999; Big Ten Network, commentator, currently. **Honors/Awds:** All-Am hon mention, Sporting News; all Big-Ten Conf first team.

WALKER, DOUGLAS F.
Editor. **Personal:** Born Dec 28, 1937, Detroit, MI; married Mattie Ruth. **Educ:** LaSalle Univ, BA; Wayne State Univ. **Career:** The Transition Newspaper, ed Model Neighborhood Health Prog; Libr Cong, Braille transcriber; Sound Off Newspaper, ed; author numerous articles various publ. **Orgs:** New Bethel Bapt Chap; Mayor's Com Human Resources. **Honors/Awds:** Achievement award Lion's, 1970; Citizen of Year Medal, 1971; Outstanding Newspaper Publ of Yr, 1973.

WALKER, DWAYNE M
Executive. **Personal:** Born Jul 11, 1961, Jena, LA; son of Arthur and Elnora. **Educ:** Calif State Univ, AA. **Career:** Hughes Aircraft, comput programmer; TRW, programmer & systs analyst; Ashton Tate, database products & software application develop mgr; DMR technol & mgt consult; Microsoft Corp, dir Windows NT & networking prod, 1987-94; Network Commerce Inc, chmn & chief exec officer, 1995-2002; Fidelity Nat Info Solutions, pres & coo; RealEC Technol, pres. **Orgs:** Chmn bd, US Connect, 1995-96; bd mem, Micro Gen Corp; bd mem, escrow.com; bd mem, Proznet; bd mem, Beyond Ventures, 1999-2001. **Special Achievements:** Co-author: Micro to Mainframe Creating and Integrated Environment, 1985.

WALKER, EDWIN L.
State government official. **Personal:** Born Aug 29, 1956, Richmond, VA; son of Thomas Job and Mary Ella Christopher; married Marcia Kay Alexander Walker, Jan 8, 1977; children: Jennifer Elaine. **Educ:** Hampton Univ, Hampton, VA, BA, mass media, 1978; Univ MO Columbia Sch Law, JD, 1983. **Career:** The Daily Press, Inc, Newport News, VA, dist mgr, 1978-80; MO Dept Social Serv, Jefferson City, MO, aging prog specialist, 1984-85, mgt analyst specialist, 1985-87, exec asst dir, 1987-88, prin asst dir, 1988, dir, div ageing, 1988; US Admin Ageing, dep asst secy, currently. **Orgs:** Columbia Human Rights Comn; MO Bd Nursing Home Adminr; exec adv comt mem, Nat Leadership Inst Ageing, 1990; adv comt mem, Nat Resource Ctr Minority Ageing Pop, 1990; nat adv comt mem, HealthWays Found, 1990. **Business Addr:** Deputy Assistant Secretary, US Admin Aging, 1 Mass Ave Suite 4100, Washington, DC 20201.*

WALKER, DR. ETHEL PITTS
Educator. **Personal:** Born Feb 4, 1943, Tulsa, OK; daughter of Wilhelmina Teresa Miller and Opie Donnell Pitts; married Phillip E, Aug 6, 1977; children: Travis Donnell. **Educ:** Lincoln Univ, BS, educ, 1964; Univ Colo, MA, speech & drama, 1965; Univ Mo, PhD, theatre, 1975. **Career:** Southern Univ, instr, 1965-68; Lincoln Univ, asst prof, 1968-77; Univ Ill,asst prof, 1977-79; Laney Col, instr, 1979-80; African Am Drama Co, exec dir, 1980; Univ Calif, asst prof, 1988; Wayne State Univ, vis asst prof, 1988-89; San Jose State Univ, Dept TV Radio, Film & Theatre, prof, 1989-. **Orgs:** Am Theatre Asn, 1984-85, chmn, 1985-; Nat Asn Dramatic & Speech Arts;Theta Alpha Phi Dramatic Fraternity; Speech Community Am; Zeta Phi Beta; chmn, bd, Christian Educ, Third Baptist Church; pres, Adv Coun, C'sPerformance Ctr; pres, Black Theatre Network, 1985-88; Asn Theatre Higher Educ; pres, Calif Educ Theatre Asn; pres, Legis Action Coalition Arts Educ. **Honors/Awds:** Ira Aldridge Scholar, 1963; Best Actress Award, Lincoln Univ Stagecrafters, 1963; Outstanding Editor, 1974; Outstanding Instructor, Sr Class Lincoln Univ, 1977; 'The Am Negro Theatre" Black Am Theatre; article "The Diction in Ed Bullins" In New Eng Winter, Encore, 1977; Krigwa Players: "A Theatre For, By & About Black People", Theatre J, 1989; Mother of the Year, Rep Teola Hunter, MI, 1989; dir, "To Be Young, Gifted And Black", 1991; "Incorporating African-American Theatre Into A Basic Theatre Course," Theatre Topic, 1992; life mem, Black Theatre Network; Inducted Consortium Doctors, 1993; Theatre in Excellence Award, ACTF region VIII,1998; inductee, Theatre Asn Hall of Fame, 2000; Living Legend Award, Nat Black Theatre Festival, 2001; Outstanding Professor Award, San Jose State Univ, 2006-07. **Special Achievements:** Directed "Medea," SJSU, 1996; ed, New/Lost Plays by Ed Bullins; co-ed,African-Am Scene book; directed, "Long Time Since Yesterday," 2000. **Business Addr:** Professor, San Jose State University, Department of Television, Radio, Film & Theatre, Hugh Gillis Hall 213 One Wash Sq, San Jose, CA 95192-0098, **Business Phone:** (408)924-4586.

WALKER, EUGENE KEVIN (GENE WALKER)
Executive, manager. **Personal:** Born Aug 12, 1951, St Louis, MO; son of Willie and Nadine; divorced; children: Kristen V. **Educ:** Cornell Univ, BS, 1975. **Career:** New York Hilton Hotel, conv serv mgr, 1975-76, acct exec, 1976-78, supt front serv, 1978-79; Hilton Hotel Philadelphia, exec asst mgr, 1979-81; Wash Hilton & Tower, exec asst mgr, 1981-85; Logan Airport Hilton, resident mgr, 1985-91; Greater Boston Conv & Visitors Bur, dir conv & customer serv; Greater Boston Conv & Visitors Bur, nat sales mgr. **Orgs:** Cornell Soc Hotelmen, 1975-; Cornell Club, 1975-; Coalition Black Meeting Planners, 1991-; chair internship comt, Acad Travel & Tourism, 1992-; chairman, Asn Conv Opers Mgrs; Prof Conv Mgt Asn, chair, currently. **Honors/Awds:** Certified Meeting Professional; Achiever Award, Privot Industry Council. **Home Phone:** (617)321-5696. **Business Addr:** Chair, The Professional Convention Management Association, 2301 S Lake Shore Dr Suite 1001, Chicago, IL 60616-1419, **Business Phone:** (312)423-7262.

WALKER, EUGENE P., SR.
Teacher, government official. **Personal:** Born in Thomaston, GA. **Educ:** Clark Col, BA, social studies, 1958; Johns Hopkins Univ, cert, 1968; Atlanta Univ, MA, hist, 1969; Duke Univ, PhD, hist, 1978. **Career:** Teacher, government official (retired); Drake High Sch, teacher; basketball & football teams, coach; Clark Col, teacher; DeKalb Col, vpres, Personnel & Community Rels; DeKalb Tech Inst, exec vpres; 43rd Ga Sen Dist, sen, 1984-92; Dept Juv Justice, comnr, 1995-99; Parole Bd, 1999-06. **Orgs:** Nat Asn Blacks Criminal Justice; Am Correctional Asn; Parole Asn Ga; chmn, bd dirs, DeKalb County Develop Authority; chmn, West Care-Ga Children's Ctr Bd Dirs; life mem, Nat Asn Advan Colored People; Greenforest Community Baptist Church.

WALKER, FELIX CARR, JR.
Advertising executive. **Personal:** Born Sep 1, 1949, Memphis, TN; son of Felix and Estelle. **Educ:** Memphis Col Arts, BFA, 1977. **Career:** Felix Way Advertising, pres/chief exec officer, currently. **Orgs:** Pres, Onyx. **Military Serv:** USN, BT2, 1969-73; Vietnam Service Award. **Home Addr:** 937 Peabody Ave, Memphis, TN 38104-6227. **Business Addr:** President/Chief Executive Officer, Felix Way Advertising, 937 Peabody Ave, Memphis, TN 38104-6227, **Business Phone:** (901)529-9987.

WALKER, FREEMAN, III
Executive. **Personal:** Born Jul 18, 1965, Roxboro, NC; son of Freeman Jr and Phyllis Umstead; married Kimberle Wathall, Jul 22, 1989. **Educ:** Univ Ga, BA, polit sci, 1987; NCA Central Univ, MPA, 1991. **Career:** Nations Bank, fin banking intern, 1984-87; Int Bus Mach, personnel intern, 1988; Orange Co dept Aging, asst dir, 1990; Durham Reg Hosp Corp, media specialist, 1991; Family Health Int, asst int crd, 1992; We-Saw Inc, dir. **Orgs:** Rotary Club N High Point, 1985; opp, 1988; Alpha Kappa Psi Prof Bus Fraternity, 1983-; Durham Companions, 1993-. **Home Addr:** 1800 Grande Oaks Rd, Durham, NC 27712-2046, **Home Phone:** (919)620-9488.

WALKER, GARY LAMAR
Football player. **Personal:** Born Feb 28, 1973, Royston, GA; children: Gary Jr. **Educ:** Auburn Univ. **Career:** Football player-(retired); Houston Oilers, defensive tackle, 1995-96; Tennessee Oilers, 1997-98; Jacksonville Jaguars, 1999-01; Houston Texans, 2002-05. **Honors/Awds:** Two time Pro Bowl selection, 2001, 2002; All-Pro selection, 2002.

WALKER, GENE. **See WALKER, EUGENE KEVIN.**

WALKER, GEORGE EDWARD
Artist. **Personal:** Born May 16, 1940, Memphis, TN; married Delores Prince; children: Genene. **Educ:** Memphis State Univ, BFA, MA. **Career:** Freelance designer & artist, 1969-71; artist, 1977-; Graphic Arts Memphis, owner & artist, 1978; Shelby State Comm Col, dir publ. **Orgs:** Alpha Phi Alpha, 1977. **Honors/Awds:** Pyramid Award, Advert Fedn Memphis, 1972 & 1977. **Special Achievements:** Designed & Published "Our Precious Baby" (1st complete black baby book) 1971. **Military Serv:** AUS, 1958-61. **Business Addr:** Artist, 1574 Pinecrest Dr, Memphis, TN 38111.

WALKER, GEORGE RAYMOND
Educator. **Personal:** Born Oct 13, 1936, Little Rock, AR. **Educ:** San Francisco State Univ, BA, 1959; Univ Southern Calif, MS, 1967, EdD, 1972. **Career:** San Francisco City Schs, teacher, 1959-62; US Dependent Schs Germany, teacher, 1962-67; US Dependent Schs Spain, dir curriculum, 1967-69; Compton Col, Compton CA, instr, 1970; Calif Comn Teacher Prep & Licensing, consult, 1971-72; Calif St Univ, Pomona, prof educ, 1972-76; Calif St Univ, Dominguez Hills, dean Sch Educ & prof grad educ, 1976-94. **Orgs:** Pres, CSUDH Chap Phi Delta Kappa, 1977-78; profs sec educ Nat Asn Sec Sch Prin, 1979-80; Alpha Phi Alpha Frat. **Honors/Awds:** Rosenwald Award, 1960; Ambassador's Award, German-Am Serv, 1964; American Studies Honor Award, Univ Notre Dame, 1968; Certificate of Appreciation, Res Utilization Bd State CA, 1977.

WALKER, DR. GEORGE T.
Composer, pianist, educator. **Personal:** Born Jun 27, 1922, Washington, DC; son of George T and Rosa King; children: Gregory & Ian. **Educ:** Oberlin Col, Mus B, 1941; Curtis Inst Music, artist diploma, 1945; Univ Rochester, DMA, 1956. **Career:** Dalcroze Sch Music, teacher, 1960-61; Smith Col, prof, 1961-68; Univ Colorado, vis prof, 1968-69; Rutgers Univ, 1969-92, prof emer, 1992-; Univ DE, prof, 1975-76; Peabody Inst Johns Hopkins Univ, prof, 1975-78. **Orgs:** New York City; mem ASCAP, Amer Symphony League. **Honors/Awds:** Fulbright fel, 1957; John Hay Whitney fel, 1958; Guggenheim fel 1969, 1988; Rockefeller fel, 1972, 1975; Am Acad & Inst Arts & Letters Award, 1981; Hon Dr Fine Arts, Lafayette Col, 1982; Hon Dr Music, Oberlin Col,1983; Koussevitsky Prize, 1988, 1998; Pulitzer Prize in Music, 1996; Hon Dr Letters, Montclair State Univ; Hon Dr Fine Arts, Bloomfield Col; Univ Scholar, Univ Rochester, 1996; Hon Dr Music, Curtis Inst Music, 1997; Letter Distinction, Am Music Ctr, 1998; Am ACA Arts & Letters, 1999; Am Classical Music Hall of Fame, 2000; Dorothy Maynor Outstanding Arts Citizen Award, Harlem Sch, Sch Arts, 2000; Hon Dr Music, Spelman Col, 2001, 2005; AI Dupont Award, 2001; First annual Classical Roots Award, Detroit Symphony, 2001; Annual Legacy Award, National Opera Association, 2007; Scarecrow Press released "Reminiscences of an American Composer and Pianist"-autobiography, 2009. **Special Achievements:** First Black Pianist to play with the Philadelphia Orchestra, first Black Pianist to play in Town Hall, NY, first black tenured faculty member, Smith College, first Black DMA recipient from the Eastman School of Music, first Black Composer to receive a John First Black Pianist to play with the Philadelphia Orchestra, First Black Pianist to Play in Town Hall, NY, First Black Composer to receive a John Hay Whitney Fellowship, First Black Graduate to receive a DMA from the Eastman School of Music, First Black to receive a John Hay Whitney Fellowship, first Black winner of the Pulitzer Prize In Music: Commissions from NY Philharmonic, Boston Symphony, Cleveland Orchestra, NJ Symphony, Kennedy Center Performing Arts, Las Vegas Philharmonic, National Endowment, Kindler Foundation, Fromm Foundation, NJ Youth Orchestra, Network for New Music: published over 90 works for orchestra, chamber orchestra, piano, strings, voice, organ, clarinet, guitar, brass, woodwinds & chorus. **Home Addr:** 323 Grove St, Montclair, NJ 07042. **Business Addr:** Professor Emeritus, Rutgers University, Newark, NJ 07102, **Business Phone:** (973)353-1731.

WALKER, DR. GREGORY T S
Musician, educator. **Personal:** Born Oct 19, 1961, Northampton, MA; son of George and Helen Hill; married Lori Wolf, Dec 30, 1995; children: Grayson Wolf. **Educ:** Ind Univ, BS, music, eng, 1983; Univ Calif San Diego, MA, comput music, 1985; Mills Col, MA, musical compos, 1987; Univ Colo, DMA, musical compos, 1992. **Career:** Boulder Philharmonic Orchestra, concert master, 1987; Univ Colo, Denver, assoc prof, 1991-; Dream N the Hood for Rapper and Orchestra, Colorado Sym, composer, 1994; Performances: Kaleidoscope: Music by African-American Women, Leonarda CD, with Helen Walker-Hill, 1995; Hsing-I, multimedia concert tour, 1998; George Walker Poem for Violin and Orchestra, Albany CD, Cleveland Chamber Symphony; Microphone for Amplified Orchestra, Detroit Symphony Orchestra, composer, 1998; Am Acad Arts & Letters, Charles Ives fel, 2000. **Honors/Awds:** Special Award, Am Soc Composers, Authors & Publ, 1997-00; UNISYS Competition winner, Detroit Symphony Orchestra, 1998. **Special Achievements:** First African American to win the Pulitzer Prize in Music during his lifetime, in 1996. **Business Addr:** Associate Professor, University of Colorado, Arts 288 Campus Box 162, PO Box 173364, Denver, CO 80217-3364, **Business Phone:** (303)556-4009.

WALKER, GROVER PULLIAM
Entrepreneur, lawyer, chief executive officer. **Personal:** Born Jan 14, 1941, Chicago, IL; son of Vernell Crawford and Rice; divorced; children: Jasmine. **Educ:** Univ Mont, AB, summa cum laude, 1963; Univ Calif Los Angeles, JD 1967; Harvard Bus Sch, MBA, 1971. **Career:** Calif State, atty gen, deputy atty gen, 1968-69; Rand Corp, consult, 1969; McKinsey & Co, int consult, 1970; Exxon Corp, corp atty, 1971-73; Johnson Prod Co, gen corp counsel, 1973-75; Los Angeles State Univ, asst prof law& bus admin, 1973; Chicago State Univ, asst prof law & bus, 1974; pvt law practice, financial planning, 1975-87; Calif Non-Ambulatory Med Servs Inc, pres, ceo, 1987-. **Orgs:** Calif Bar Assn, 1968; co chmn Afro Am Student Union Harvard Bus Sch, 1969; Ill Bar Assn, 1974; Florida Bar Assn, 1976; bd mem, New Wash Heights Community Develop Corp, 1976-77; Total Care Home Health Agency Fla, 1976-77; City Miami Florida Zoning Brd, 1977-79; Cook Co & Chicago Bar Assn; Harvard Bus Sch Century Club; Harvard Club Chicago; PAD Legal Frat; bd mem, Afro-Am Family Community Serv; exec dir, Black Agenda, 1982-84. **Honors/Awds:** Victor Wilson Scholar, Univ Mont, 1959-63; Harvard Leadership Award, 1970. **Business Addr:** President, Chief Executive Officer, California Non-Ambulatory Center, 2012 Rimpau Blvd, Los Angeles, CA 90016-1514, **Business Phone:** (323)936-0923.

WALKER, HERSCHEL
Football player, business owner. **Personal:** Born Mar 3, 1962, Wrightsville, GA; son of Willis and Christine; married Cindy; children: Christian. **Educ:** Univ Ga, BS, criminal justice, 1984. **Career:** Football player (retired), business owner; US Football League, NJ Gen,running back, 1983-85; Dallas Cowboys, 1986-89, 1996-97; Minn Vikings,1989-92; Philadelphia Eagles, 1992-95; NY Giants, 1995-96; H Walker Enterprises, chief exec officer & owner, currently; Renaissance Man FoodServ LLC, owner & chief exec officer, currently. **Orgs:** US Olympic Bobsled Team. **Honors/Awds:** Heisman Trophy, 1982; Maxwell Award, 1982; Walter Camp Award, 1982; 3 time All Am; USFL Outstanding Running Back, 1983, league leading rusher, 1983,1985, Most Valuable Player, 1985; Pro Bowl, 1987, 1988; Collegiate Football Hall of Fame, 2002; USFL All-Time Team. **Special Achievements:** Guest appearance, TV show, "The Hour of Power"; Fifth degree black belt inTae Kwon Do; performed with the Fort Worth Ballet. **Business Addr:** Owner, Chief Executive Officer, Renaissance Man Food Services LLC, 22 E Montgomery Crossroads, Savannah, GA 31406, **Business Phone:** (912)961-0002.

WALKER, HEZEKIAH (HEZEKIAH XAVIER WALKER)
Gospel singer, clergy. **Personal:** Born 1962, Brooklyn, NY; married Monique; children: KyAsia. **Career:** Gospel vocalist; Love Fellowship Tabernacle Church, pastor, currently; Albums: I'll Make It, 1989; Crusade Choir, 1990; Oh Lord We Praise You, 1991; Focus On Glory, 1992; Live In Toronto, 1993; Live in Atlanta At Morehouse Col, 1994; Live In New York By Any Means Necessary, 1995; Live In London, 1997; Presents The LFT Mass Choir, 1998; Family Affair, 1999; Hezekiah Walker Presents LFT Church Choir: Love Is Live, 2001; Family Affair, II: Live at Radio City Music Hall, 2002; 20/85 The Experience, 2005; Compilations: Gospel Greats, 1995; Hooked On The Hits, 2003; The Gospel Soundtrack, 2005; Essential Hezekiah Walker, 2007. **Honors/Awds:** Vision Award, 1994; Stellar Award, Best Music Video, 1994; Excellence Award, Gospel Music Workshop Am, 1994; Contemporary Choir of the Year, Gospel Music Workshop Am, 1994; Grammy nominee, Best Album by a Choir or Chorus, 1996, 1997, 1998; Best Gospel Album Award by a Choir or Chorus, 1995. **Business Addr:** Pastor, Gospel Vocalist, Love Fellowship Tabernacle Church, 464 Liberty Ave, Brooklyn, NY 11207, **Business Phone:** (718)235-2266.

WALKER, HEZEKIAH XAVIER. See WALKER, HEZEKIAH.

WALKER, DR. HOWARD KENT
Government official, educator. **Personal:** Born Dec 3, 1935, Newport News, VA; son of Jean K and William R Jr; married Terry B Taylor; children: Gregory & Wendy. **Educ:** Univ Mich, AB, high honors, 1957, MA, conley scholar govt, 1958; Boston Univ, PhD, 1968. **Career:** Boston Univ, African Studies fel, 1958-60; Boston Univ, teaching asst, 1960-62; George Washington Univ, from asst to assoc prof, 1966-70; Am Consulate Kaduna, consult, 1970-73; Dept State, desk officer, 1973-75; Am Embassy Amman, polit counr, 1975-77; Am Embassy Dares Salaam, dep chief mission, 1977-79; Am Embassy Pretoria, dep chief mission, 1979-81, charged affiaries, a/i; Am Embassy Lome, ambassador Togo, 1982-84; Foreign Serv IST, Foreign Affairs fel, 1984-85; Ctr Study Foreign Affairs Foreign Serv Inst, Foreign Affairs fel, 1984-85; Dept State, Off W Africa, dir, 1985-87; Off Inspector Gen, Dept State, sr inspector, 1987-89, Am Embassy Antananarivo, ambassador Madagascar, ambassado Islamic Repub Comoros, 1989-92; Nat Defense Univ, vpres; NATO Defense Col, Rome, dep commandant, 1993. **Military Serv:** USF, first lt, 1962-65.

WALKER, IAN ROBIN
Playwright. **Personal:** Born Feb 13, 1964, North Hampton, MA; son of George and Helen Walker-Hill; married Andrea C Trindle, Mar 16, 1997. **Educ:** Univ Colo, Boulder, BA, 1985. **Career:** Musician & playwright; Second Wind Prod Inc, co-founder, 1984-, playwright-in-residence, currently; Boulder Valley Sch Dist, theatre trainer, consult, 1989-91; E Bay Community Proj, Improv Theatre Proj. coordr, 1994-; Actor's Collective, co-founder, 1996-2000; Plays: Killing Time; Vigilance; Under Paradise (screenplay); Erin?s Hope; Ghost in the Light; The Stone Trilogy; A Beautiful Home for the Incurable; The Gravedigger?s Tango; The History of Stone. **Honors/Awds:** Numerous awards including DramaLogue Award, 1996; Best of San Francisco Fringe Festival (Acting), 1998; John Golden Prize, 2000; Best of San Francisco Fringe Festival (Direction), 2001; Best of San Francisco Fringe Festival (Light Design), 2003; Larry Corse International Playwriting Prize, 2006; Best Play: Bay One Act Festival (Playwriting), 2006. **Business Addr:** Playwright-in-Residence, Second Wind Productions Inc, 505 Faxon Ave Suite 6, San Francisco, CA 94112, **Business Phone:** (415)508-5614.

WALKER, JAMES, JR.
Executive. **Career:** Aptakisic Tripp Elem Sch Dist, asst supt, currently. **Orgs:** Adv coun, A Safe Place, Lake County Crisis Ctr. *

WALKER, JAMES CARTER. See WALKER, JIMMIE.

WALKER, JAMES ZELL, II
Editor, executive. **Personal:** Born Mar 23, 1932, Birmingham, AL; married Jeanette Adams; children: Jimmy Zelbulg, Debra Leartine, Ronnetta Marie, Freda Michetta, James, III. **Educ:** San Francisco Jr Col, 1955. **Career:** Clarion Defender Newspaper, ed; Knockout Indstrs Inc, pres; KGAR Radio, weekend disk jockey, 1968-76; KNEY Radio, talk show host, 1977; Organic & Bio Degradable Cleanser, mfr. **Orgs:** Trustee & chmn, Billy Webb IBPOE of W, 1962-70; co-founder, Miss Tan Am Pageant, 1965; bd mem, Portland Br Nat Asn Advan Colored People, 1967; Nat Bus Leg 1968; Nebr Portland YMCA; Freedom Black Fin, 1968; founder, Jimmy Bang Bang Youth Found, 1969; Portland City Club, 1970; charter Mem Albina Lions Club, 1970; sponsored, OR & WA, Black Am Contest, 1970-75; OR Black Caucus, 1972; mason Odd Fellws Pact Inc, 1972; C of C 69 Fed Title 1, 1973; pres, Jefferson PTA 1974-75, 1977-78; Nat Black Mfg 1977; Am Cancer Soc Neighborhood Chap, 1978-80; voting mem, Portland Local 8 & ILWU, 1980; sponser, Campfire Bonnie Blue Birds; co-chmn, Pub Sch Career Educ; Jefferson Cluster Study Com; adv bd, Beach Sch; adv comt, Jefferson High Portland Pub Sch Cold Card Mem Billy Webb Elks Bldg; Fisk Univ Boosters Club 9; Jesuit HS Parents Group. **Honors/Awds:** Diamond Belt, 1950; Golden Gloves, 1953-54; AAU Western Boxing Champ, 1954; San Francisco Pacif NW Pro Boxing Champ, 1958-63; Rose Fest Parade, 1968-71; Albina Women Leg Achievement Award, 1972; Spec Portland PMSC Award, 1973. **Special Achievements:** First Black nominated for major Political Party in OR Group, 1970. **Military Serv:** AUS, sgt, 1950-53; 3 Purple Hearts Bronze Star; 5 Battle Awards.

WALKER, JAY
Politician, business owner, president (organization). **Personal:** Born Jan 24, 1972, Los Angeles, CA; married Monique; children: 3. **Educ:** Howard Univ. **Career:** Football player (retired), Business owner, President; Barcelona Dragons,1995; Minn Vikings, quarterback, 1996-97; Sky Walker Flight Sch Football Camp, founder & chmn, 1998-; Walker Financial Serv, pres,currently; ESPN, sports analyst; Democrat, District 26, Prince George's County, 2007-; Mem, Legislative Black Caucus Maryland, currently. **Orgs:** Prince George's County Democratic Cent Comt, 2002-; Prince George's Black Chamber Com; Coalition Concerned Black Christian Men; House Del, 2007-;Legislative Black Caucus Md, 2007-; Task Force Establishment Vocational &Tech Educ High Sch Academies, Prince George's County, 2007-; Task Force Stud Phys Fitness, Md Pub Sch, 2008-; Task Force Study Thoroughbred Horse Racing, Rose croft Raceway, 2008-. **Honors/Awds:** Hall of Fame, Howard Univ Athletics, 2005. **Business Phone:** (301)749-5524.

WALKER, JERRY EUCLID. See Obituaries section.

WALKER, JIMMIE
Administrator. **Personal:** Born Nov 4, 1945, Mendenhall, MS; married Virginia Finley; children: Baron, Lorria & Erica. **Educ:** Prentiss Jr Col, Prentiss, AA, MS, 1967; LA Bapt Col, BA, 1969. **Career:** Sec Asn Prof Dir Cluster, 1974; bd mem, Youth Christ, 1975; bd mem, S Cent Rural Health Asn, 1979; bd mem, Farish St Historic Dist Revitalizatn Asn, 1980; Noon Optimist Club Jackson, 1980; bd mem, Voice Calvary Ministeries, 1980. **Orgs:** Sec Asn Prof Dir Cluster, 1974; bd mem, Farish St Historic Dist Revitalizatn Asn, 1980; Noon Optimist Club Jackson, 1980; bd mem, Youth Christ, 1975; bd mem, S Cent Rural Health Asn, 1979; bd mem, Voice Calvary Ministeries, 1980. **Honors/Awds:** Outstanding Basketball Player, Sports Writers Association Southern Califorina, 1969. Sports Ambassador S Pacific, 1970; inductee, Los Angeles Bapt Collab Hall of Fame, 1971.

WALKER, JIMMIE (JAMES CARTER WALKER)
Actor, comedian. **Personal:** Born Jun 25, 1947, Bronx, NY; married Jerelyn Fields, Feb 8, 1980. **Educ:** RCA Tech Inst, art announcing & trade radio eng. **Career:** WRBR, part time engr; WMCA radio, 1967; Films: Let's Do It Again, 1975; Rabbit Test, 1978; The Concorde-Airport 79, 1979; Airplane!, 1980; Stiffs, 1985; Doing Time, 1985; Kidnapped, 1986; My African Adventure, 1987; Water, 1985; Going Bananas, 1987; Guyver, 1991; Home Alone 2: Lost in New York, 1992; Monster Mash: The Movie, 1995; Open Season, 1995; Ripper, 1996; Plump Fiction, 1997; TV series: "Good Times", 1974-79; "The Love Boat", 1977-85; The Greatest Thing That Almost Happened, 1977; "B A D Cats", 1980; Murder Can Hurt You, 1980; "Today's F.B.I.", 1982; "Fantasy Island", 1980; "At Ease", 1983; "Cagney & Lacey", 1983; The Jerk, Too, 1984; The Fall Guy, 1984; "Bustin Loose", 1987; "Matchmaker host", 1987; "The Jerk, Too", 1984; "Murder Can Hurt You!", 1977; "Bustin' Loose", 1987; "An Evening of Comedy with Jimmie Walker & Friends", 1988; "Jimmie Walker & Friends II", 1989; "In the House", 1995; Deadly Games, 1995; Chienne de vie, 1996; "The John Larroquette Show", 1996; "Shriek If You Know What I Did Last Friday the Thirteenth", 2000; "Late Show with David Letterman", 1996-2007; "Hollywood Squares", 1999-2002; Son of the Beach, 2002; "George Lopez", 2003; A Very Elimidate Christmas, 2005; "Everybody Hates Chris", 2006-08; "The 100 Greatest TV Quotes & Catchphrases", 2006; The Real Match Game Story: Behind the Blanks, 2006; "Chelsea Lately", 2007; Back to the Grind, 2007; "TV Land Confidential", 2007; "Entertainment Tonight", 2008; Imps, 2009; Record album: Dyn-o-mite, Buddah Records; Video Games :Voice- Soap Betty, Ripper, 1996. **Honors/Awds:** Most Popular TV Performer, Family Circle Mag, 1975; Comedian of the Decade, Time Mag; various awards from civic groups in regard to role as JJ Evans. **Business Phone:** (310)550-4000.*

WALKER, JIMMY L
Automotive executive, business owner. **Career:** ULW Broadcasting, Inc, owner; Laurel Ford Lincoln-Mercury Inc, chief exec officer, owner, currently. **Special Achievements:** Co is ranked No 83 on Black Enterprise's list of top 100 auto dealers, 1994, ranked No 86, 1998. **Business Addr:** Owner, Laurel Ford Lincoln-Mercury Inc, 2018 Hwy 15 N, Laurel, MS 39440, **Business Phone:** (601)649-4511.

WALKER, JOHN LESLIE
Banker, vice president (organization). **Personal:** Born May 4, 1933, York, SC; son of Walter and Neely; married Mary Alberta Carlton; children: John L Jr & Karen F Walker-Spencer. **Educ:** Wilberforce Univ OH, BS, 1956; Stonier Grad Sch Banking Rutgers Univ, 1972; Harvard Exec Sem, 1978. **Career:** Cairo, Egypt Chem Bank, vpres, 1980-83; Paris, France Chem Bank, vpres, 1978-80; Repub Nat Bank New York, int pvt banking officer Mid E & Africa, 1988-91; US Dept Com, dept asst secy, 1994-96; Merrill Lynch, vpres, financial consult, 1996-. **Orgs:** Nat Bankers Asn, 1973-78; finance secy, United Black Men Queens Co NY, 1976-78; treas, Urban Bankers Coalition, 1977-78; African Develop Found, 1991-94; Kappa Alpha Psi Fraternity; Prince Hall Masons; NAACP; Urban League; chmn bd trustees, Wilberforce Univ; bd mem, Jamaica Serv Prog Older Adults. **Honors/Awds:** Serv Award United Black Men of Queens Co, 1978. **Military Serv:** AUS, sgt, 1956-58, Good conduct medal. **Business Addr:** Vice President, Merrill Lynch & Co, 4 World Financial Ctr 250 Vesey St, New York, NY 10080, **Business Phone:** (212)449-1000.

WALKER, JOSEPH M., III
Judge. **Career:** Suffolk Superior Ct, assoc justice, currently. **Business Addr:** Associate Justice, Suffolk Superior Court, McCormack PO & Cthouse, 90 Devonshire St Rm 1509, Boston, MA 02109, **Business Phone:** (617)788-8130.*

WALKER, KARA
Artist. **Personal:** Born Nov 26, 1969, Stockton, CA. **Educ:** Atlanta College of Art, BFA, 1991; Rhode Island School of Design, MFA, 1994. **Career:** Faculty member of the MFA program at Columbia Univ. **Honors/Awds:** John D. and Catherine T. MacArthur Foundation Achievement Award, 1997. **Special Achievements:** One of the youngest people to receive the MacArthur fellowship award, 1997;US representative to the 2002 Sao Paolo Bienal in Brazil; listed as "100 Most Influential People in the World", Artists and Entertainers, Time Magazine, 2007. **Business Addr:** Columbia University, Arts, School of the-visual Arts Division, 310 Dodge Hall, Mail Code: 1806, New York, NY 10027, **Business Phone:** (212)854-4065.*

WALKER, KAROL CORBIN
Lawyer, executive. **Educ:** New Jersey City Univ, BA, 1980; Seton Hall Univ Sch Law, JD, 1986. **Career:** Pitney Hardin Kipp & Szuch, 1987-89; Seiden Wayne LLC, parter, 1989-2007; LeClair-Ryan, partner, 2007-; US Dist Ct, Dist NJ, arbitrator & mediator; St John & Wayne Law Firm, partner, NJ. **Orgs:** NJ State Bar Asn, chair, 1998, pres, 2003-04; Garden State Bar Asn; trustee, Essex County Bar Asn; Morris County Bar Asn; Am Bar Asn; Nat Bar Asn; Nat Conf Bar Pres; trustee, Asn Fed Bar State NJ; fel Am Bar Found; New Jersey Inst Continuing Legal Educ. **Honors/Awds:** Professional Lawyer of the Year Award, NJ Commission, 2007. **Special Achievements:** first African American woman to attain Partner status at any major New Jersey law firm; One of New Jersey's Top 20 African American Business People, Bus News, 1999; One of New Jersey's top 25 Women of Influence, NJBIZ, 2003; co-author, How to Establish & Maintain a Professional Relationship, Garden State Woman Mag, 2003; co-author, Privileges Chapter of New Jersey Trial & Evidence Treatise, Inst Continuing Legal Educ, 2003; first African American President in the then 105-year history of the New Jersey State Bar Association; recognized her as one of New Jersey's "Super Lawyers" by New Jersey Monthly Magazine in 2005 & 2006. **Business Addr:** Partner, LeClairRyan, 2 Penn Plz E, Newark, NJ 07105, **Business Phone:** (973)491-3522.

WALKER, KENNETH R.
Journalist. **Personal:** Born Aug 17, 1951, Washington, DC; divorced. **Educ:** Catholic Univ Am. **Career:** Wash Star Newspaper, foreign corresp, nat affairs journalist & staff reporter, 1968-81; WJZ-TV Baltimore MD, prog moderator & asst producer, 1978-79; ABC News, polit corresp & news anchor, 1981-85; Nat Pub Radio, African bur chief; Independent TV producer, corresp; USA Today, Good Morning America, anchor: The Television Show, Night watch; Lion House Prod, pres, currently. **Orgs:** Exec vpres, Nat Media Syst Inc, 1970-74; mem bd dir, Townsend Reading CtrInc, 1976; bd dirs, Thurgood Marshall Meml Scholar Fund. **Honors/Awds:** Recipient, Washington Star Univ Scholarship, 1969; First Place, Washington-Baltimore Newspaper Guild Award, 1977; Emmy Award, Nat Acad TV Arts & Scientists, 1981; Dupont Gold Baton Award, Columbia Univ Sch Jour, 1981; Journalist of the Year Award, Nat Asn Black Journalists, 1985; Image Award, NAACP, 1985; Media Award for

Excellence, Africa Am Inst, 2001; Top award for radio journalism, Nat Asn Black Journalists, 2001. **Business Addr:** Owner, Lion House Publishing, 1119 Staples St NE, Washington, DC 20002, **Business Phone:** (202)388-5532.

WALKER, DR. KENNETH R.
Educator. **Personal:** Born Dec 19, 1930, East Providence, RI; son of Frank and Lillian; married Gail Beverly Smith; children: Kenneth Jr, Michele & Leanne. **Educ:** Providence Col, AB, 1957; RI Col, M.Ed, 1962; Boston Univ, Ed.D, 1977. **Career:** Educator (retired); East Providence RI Sch Dept, teacher, 1957-68, asst prin, 1968-70; RI Col, assoc prof, dir, Early Enrollment Prog; Johnson &Wales Univ, adj prof. **Orgs:** Consult HEW Title IV; mem Guidance & Personnel Assn; Intl Assn of Approved Basketball Officials; Collegiate Basketball Officials Assn; Assn Curriculum Devel Specialist; Amer Fedn Teachers; Rhode Island State Parole Bd; consult, Rhode Island State Dept Educ; Omega Psi Phi Fraternity; mem, Governor's Task Force, 1991; Report on Education Rhode Island; Big Brothers of RI; chairperson, State RI, Parole Bd Sex Offender Community Notification Unit. **Honors/Awds:** Exemplary Citizenship Award, 1974; IBA Man of Year Award, 1967; Recip Afro-Am Award EPHS, 1971; Serv to Youth Award No Kingston Jr HS 1969; RI Big Brother of Yr Award, 1963; Educ Award NAACP, 1980; Providence Col, HonSocD, 1983; East Providence High School Hall of Fame, 1987; Vincent O' Leary Award, 2004. **Military Serv:** AUS Sgt 1951-53. **Home Addr:** 399 Brown St, East Providence, RI 02914. *

WALKER, LANEUVILLE V
Insurance executive. **Personal:** Born Oct 13, 1947, Prospect, VA; daughter of Moses E Scott (deceased) and Sophia V; married Ernest L Walker II, Dec 1, 1964; children: Ernest L III & Steven S. **Educ:** Cortez Peters Bus Col, attended 1966; Univ Ala, attended 1968; Va Commonwealth Univ, BS, 1975. **Career:** Southern Aid Life Ins Co, ade asst, 1981-82, corp secy, 1982-88; Atlanta Life Ins Co, asst vpres, 1988-. **Orgs:** Asst secy, Friends Club Beulah Baptist Church, 1981-; mem prog comt, Delver Woman's Club, 1982-; trustee, bd mem, Third St Bethel AME Church, Missionary Soc, 1981, 1990; bd mem, Jackson Ward Bus Asn, 1990. **Honors/Awds:** Leadership Award, Third St Bethel AME Church, Women's Day Chap, 1992.

WALKER, LARRY MOORE
Artist, educator. **Personal:** Born Oct 22, 1935, Franklin, GA; son of Cassandra Walker and W B Walker; married Gwendolyn Elaine Howell; children: Dana, Larry & Kara. **Educ:** BS, 1958; Wayne State Univ, MA, 1963. **Career:** Col Pac, Univ Pac, prof & chmn, dept art, 1964-83; Detroit Pub Sch Syst, art instr, 1958-64; 30 one-man exhib; 60 group exhib; Ga State Univ, Dept Art, prof, chmn, 1983-85; Ga State Univ Sch Art & Design, prof, dir, 1985-96, chmn, prof emer, art & design, currently. **Orgs:** Stockton Arts Comn, 1976-77; Nat Asn Sch Art & Design, 1983-; Marta Arts Coun, 1983-; bd dir, Nat Coun Art Admin, secy, 1985, chmn, 1986, 1987; bd dir, Atlanta Arts Festival, 1986-89; adv coun, Binney & Smith Co, 1986-90; pres, Dekalb Coun Arts, 1987, 1989-90. **Honors/Awds:** Recipient, Pacific Family Award, 1968; Distinguished Faculty Award, 1975; Award for Leadership & Appreciation of Service to the Stockton Arts Commission, Ann Recognition Awards Prog, 1981; Plaque for Service to the Arts Community, Stockton City Coun, 1981; Certificate of Appreciation, Univ Pac, 1982; Founders Wall Plaque La Guardia HS of the Arts NYC: Certificare of Appreciation, Nat Coun Art Admin, 1988; Distinguished Alumni Award, Wayne State Univ, 2007. **Home Phone:** (404)498-7441. **Business Addr:** Professor Emeritus, Georgia State University, PO Box 3965, Atlanta, GA 30302-3965, **Business Phone:** (404)651-2000.

WALKER, DR. LARRY VAUGHN
School administrator. **Personal:** Born Aug 8, 1939, Meridian, MS; children: Derrick B & Terri L. **Educ:** Jackson State Col, BS, 1960; Fisk Univ, MA, 1964; Roosevelt Univ, MST, 1974; Northern Ill Univ, EdD, educ admin, 1983. **Career:** Sch administrator (retired); Wayne County Schs, teacher, 1961-63; Jackson Pub Schs, teacher, 1964-65; Proviso Twp High Sch, teacher, 1965-74, dean, asst prin, 1974-82; Oak Park & River Forest High Sch, assoc prin, asst supt, assoc supt, 1982-93. **Orgs:** Bd mem, Family Serv & Ment Health Oak Park, 1982-; presenter, Nat Assoc Sec Sch Principals, 1985; bd mem, Oak Park YMCA, 1985-. **Honors/Awds:** NSF grant, Summer Inst, Dillard Univ, 1963; NSF grant, Fisk Univ 1963-64.

WALKER, LEE H
Executive. **Personal:** Born Oct 6, 1938, Troy, AL; married Audrey Davis. **Educ:** Fordham Univ, New York, econ; Univ Chicago; Brooklyn Col, New York Univ; Ala State Univ. **Career:** Executive (retired); Am Prog New York, instr, 1960-61; Winston-Muss Corp New York, dir employee relation, 1961-70; Sears Roebuck & Co Chicago IL, grp dist mgr 1970-93; New Coalition Econ & Social Change, pres, currently. **Orgs:** Sears Roebuck & Co; Am Mgt Asn; Urban Problems Community, 1968-69; past mem, Local Draft Bd 1969-72; past pres, Political Club Rep; bd dirs, AIM, 1970, chmn 1970-72; Nat Urban League Guild NY; black rep, Westchester Co; past vpres, Nat Am Advan Colored People Brooklyn Br; Sigma Pi Phi, Delta Alpha Boule; dir, Coaliation, currently. **Honors/Awds:** Distinguish Service Award New Rochelle Br, Nat Am Advan Colored People, 1967; Black Achievers in Industry Award, Harlem Br YMCA 1972; Pioneer Award, Republican Nat Comt, 2001. **Business Addr:** President, The New Coalition for Economic and Social Change, 19 S LaSalle St Suite 903, Chicago, IL 60603, **Business Phone:** (312)377-4000.

WALKER, DR. LEROY TASHREAU
Educator, sports promoter. **Personal:** Born Jun 14, 1918, Atlanta, GA; son of Willie and Mary; widowed; children: LeRoy & Carolyn. **Educ:** Benedict Col, BA, 1940; Columbia Univ, MS, 1941; NY Univ, PhD, 1957. **Career:** Benedict Col Columbia SC, chmn phys educ, coach basketball, football, track & field 1941-42; Bishop Col Marshall TX, chmn phys dept, coach basketball, football, track & field 1942-43; Prairie View State Univ, 1943-45; NC Cent Univ Durham, chmn phys dept, coach basketball, football, track & field, head coach, 1945-73, vice chancellor univ rels, 1974-83, chancellor 1983-86, chancellor emer, 1986; US Olympic Comt, pres, ceo, 1992. **Orgs:** Educ spec, Cult Exchange Prog, Dept State, 1959, 1960, 1962; bd dirs, US Olympic Com author Manual Adapted Phys Educ, 1960; Phys Educ, Except Stud, 1964; dir prog planning, Peace Corps Africa 1966-68; Championship Tech Track & Field, 1969; chmn, Col Comnrs Asn, 1971-74; US Collegiate Sports Coun, 1972; chmn track & field, Com Athletic Union, 1973-75; bd dirs, USA China Relations Com; AAHPERD 1972; head coach, US Track & Field Team Olympic Games Montreal, 1976; US Olympic Comt, treas, 1988-92, pres, 1992-; chief mission, US Olympic Team, Barcelona, 1992; NEA; US Track Coaches Asn; Int Asn Athletic Fedns; Sigma Delta Psi; Alpha Phi Omega; Omega Psi Phi; pres, Nat Asn Intercollegiate Athletics; pres, Cent Collegiate Aetic Asn. **Honors/Awds:** Recipient James E Shepard Outstanding Teacher Award, Hamilton Watch Co, 1964; Achievement Award, Cent Intercollegiate Athletic Asn, 1967; Distinguished Alumnus Award, Benedict Col, 1968; Distinguished Service Award, Kiwanis Int, 1971; Gov's Ambassador Goodwill Award, 1974; O Max Gardner Award, 1976; HC Hall of Fame 1975; SC Hall of Fame, 1977; Nat Asn Sport & Phys Educ Hall of Fame, 1977; Robert Giegengack Award, The Athletics Congress Highest Award; Role Model Leader, NC State Univ, 1990; Achievement Life Award, Encyclopedia Britannica; Athletic Cong Hall of Fame; Helms Nat Hall of Fame; US Olympic Hall of Fame; Mid-Eastern Athletic Conf Hall of Fame. **Special Achievements:** Olympics consultant for the following national teams: Trinidad-Tobago Tokyo, 1964, Jamaica in Mexico City, 1968, Kenya in Munich, 1972. First African American president of the American Alliance for Health, Physical Education, Recreation, and Dance. **Business Phone:** (919)361-2355.

WALKER, DR. LEWIS
Educator. **Personal:** Born Oct 22, 1936, Selma, AL; son of Joseph Walker (deceased) and Thelma Watts Freeman; married Georgia Doles, Apr 18, 1964. **Educ:** BA, 1959; MA, 1961; Ohio State Univ, PhD, 1964. **Career:** Wilberforce Univ, stud instr, 1958-59; Ohio Higher Educ Asst Commn, admin specialist, 1962; Ohio State Univ, lectr, 1964; Ohio Hosp Asn, res specialist, 1964; W Mich Univ, from asst prof to assoc prof, 1964-71, prof, 1971, chmn, sociol, 1989, chair emer & prof emer, currently. **Orgs:** Douglass Comm Asn, 1965-69; Sr Citizens Inc, 1967; founder & dir, Kalamazoo Resources Develop Coun, 1967-68; consult & prog develop, Ford Motor Co, 1968-69, Police-Comm Relations Progs, 1968-70; ARC Bd, 1969-70; adv bd, Learning Village, 1970; Am Soc Asn, 1974-; Mich Soc Asn, 1974-; Miami Valley Soc Asn, 1974-; Kalamazoo Co Crime Comn, 1984-; bd, Goodwill Indus, 1986-, Differential Flow Systems Inc, 1986-; pres, Walker-Taylor Thermics Inc, 1984-, Spare Time Pursuits Inc 1986-. **Honors/Awds:** Distinguished Service Award, Jaycees, 1967; One of Five Outstanding Young Men of Michigan Jaycees, 1967; Award for Teaching Excellence, Western Mich Univ Alumni Asn, 1971; inventor, US patent on low pressure boiler heating system, 1984; invention, US patent on furnace system,1986; Distinguished Service Award, Western Mich Univ, 1989. **Military Serv:** Numerous in-service & human relations programs. Three US copyrights, registrations, on three separate game boards and texts. **Business Addr:** Professor Emeritus, Chair Emeritus, Western Michigan University, Department of sociology, 1903 W Michigan Ave, Kalamazoo, MI 49008, **Business Phone:** (269)387-2124.

WALKER, LINDA T.
District court judge. **Career:** Fulton Co, atty, 1998-99, Reg & Elections Off, dir, 1999; US Dist Ct Northern Dist Ga, magistrate judge, 2000-. **Business Phone:** (404)215-1370.*

WALKER, LISA
Executive director, manager. **Career:** Bridal registry, mgr; Macys, dir reg & coordr spec events, currently. **Business Addr:** Director of Regional Special Events, Macy's, 22 4Th St, San Francisco, CA 94103-3131, **Business Phone:** 800-723-2889.*

WALKER, LUCIUS, JR.
Clergy. **Personal:** Born Aug 3, 1930, Roselle, NJ; married Mary; children: Lucius, Donna, Gail, Richard, Edythe. **Educ:** Shaw Univ, AB; Andover Newton Theol Sem, MDiv; Univ Wisconsin, MA, 1963; Malcolm X Col, Hon LHD; Shaw Univ, Raleigh NC, LHD. **Career:** Interreligious Found Comt Orgn NY, exec dir, 1967-73; Nat Coun Churches Christ NY, assoc gen secy, 1973; Pastors for Peace, Exec Dir. **Orgs:** bd trustees, Shaw Univ; bd trustees, Andover Newton Theol Sch; Black Found Execs.

WALKER, LULA AQUILLIA
Government official. **Personal:** Born Mar 1, 1955, Derby, CT; children: William Zimmerman Jr, Tyron & Garrett. **Educ:** Shaw Col Detroit, Med Asst Cert, 1974; US Acad Health & Sci, Med Spec Cert, 1977. **Career:** Olson Dr Tenants Assoc, pres, 1979; Housing Authority City Ansonia, asst treas, 1980; City Ansonia, co chmn printing & signs, 1982, chmn, claims comn, 1984; Ansonia Bd Alderman, fourth ward alderman; St CT, menthealth worker II. **Orgs:** Adv bd, Valley legal Asst, 1980; asst recording secy, A Philip Randolph Lower Naaugatuck Valley Chap, 1982; bd Lower Naugatuck Valley Chap NAACP, 1983; seargent arms Lower Naugatuck Valley Chap Black Democratics, 1983;vice dgt, ruler Lily Valley Temple H406 IBPOE World, 1984-; chmn, ClaimsComn, 1986; serve olice Comn bd aldermen. **Honors/Awds:** Woman of the Month, Women's Ctr Ansonia, 1979; 3 Awards, Dedicated ServCommunity Friends Lulu Ansonia, 1984; Dedicated Service Plaque, Community Magicians AC, 1984. **Military Serv:** Army NG, sgt, 11 yrs; Army Nat Guard Achievement Medal, 1982.

WALKER, DR. M LUCIUS
Educator. **Personal:** Born Dec 16, 1936, Washington, DC; son of Inez and M Lucius; children: Mark & Monique. **Educ:** Morehouse Col, 1954; Howard Univ, BSME, 1957; Carnegie Inst Technol, MSME, 1958, PhD, 1966. **Career:** Howard Univ, Sch Engineering, asst dean, 1965-66, Dept Mech Engineering, from actg chmn to chmn, 1966-73, from assoc dean to dean, 1973-95, prof, prof emer, 1995; Engineering Coalition Schs Excellence Educ & Leadership, dir, 1990-97. **Orgs:** Biomed Cardiovascular Renal Res Team, 1966-73; consult, Ford Motor Co, 1971-; Engr Manpower Comt Engrs Coun Prof Develop, 1972-95; Biotech Resources Review Comt, Nat Inst Health, 1980-84; consult, Ctr Naval Anal, 1991-93; Am Soc Engineering Educ; Am Soc Mech Engrs; Tau Beta Pi; bd trustees, Carnegie Mellon Univ; Am Soc Mech Engrs; Ad Hoc Visitor Accreditation Bd Engineering & Technol; pres, Howard Univ Chap Sigma Xi. **Honors/Awds:** Nat Action Coun Minorities Engineering Lifetime Achievement; Black Educator of the Year Award for Higher Education. **Business Addr:** Professor Emeritus, Howard University, Department of Mechanical Engineering, 2300 6th St NW, Washington, DC 20059, **Business Phone:** (202)806-6600.

WALKER, DR. MANUEL LORENZO
Physician. **Personal:** Born Mar 22, 1930, Battle Creek, MI; son of Charles S and Manuella Beck; married Joan Lucille Carter Parks, May 8, 1980; children: Gregory Parks; married Romaine Yvonne Smith, Sep 26, 1951 (died 1978); children: Linda Lee & Lorenzo Giles. **Educ:** Howard Univ Col, BS, 1951; Howard Univ, Col Med, MD, 1955; Philadelphia Gen Hosp, Intern, 1955-56. **Career:** Mercy-Douglass Hosp, staff mem, 1958-73; pvt practice, 1958-; Mercy Catholic Med Ctr, staff mem, 1968-; Lankenau Hosp, staff mem, 1979-; St Joseph's Hosp, staff mem, 1987-95; St Ignatius Nursing Home, med dir, 1972-; Univ Pa Health System, staff mem, 1995-2006. **Orgs:** Am Med Asn; Nat Med Asn, Pa Med Soc & Philadelphia County Med Soc; vpres, Howard Univ, Med Alumni Asn, 1970-75; pres, Philadelphia Acad Family Physicians, 1982-84; Keystone State Med Soc, 1971-73; Med Soc Eastern Pa, 1968-70; Yeadon (PA) Bd Sch Dir, 1968-71; alumni pres, Class 1955-Howard Univ Med Asn; editor, MSEPulse Newsletter Med Soc Eastern Pa, 1969-. **Honors/Awds:** 'Practitioner of year', Philadelphia County Med Soc, 1979; alumni pres, Class of 1955 Howard Univ Med Sch, 1955-; legion, Honor Chapel of Four Chaplains, 1978-; med honor soc, Kappa Pi & Alpha Omega Alpha; 'Practitioner of the Year', Nat Med Asn, 1986; President's Award, N Philadelphia, NAACP, 1990; Mercy-Douglass Lectureship Award, Med Soc Eastern Pa, 1989. **Military Serv:** USNR, lt cmdr, 1956-66. **Home Addr:** 425 Jamaica Dr, Cherry Hill, NJ 08002. **Business Addr:** Family Physician, Medical Director, St Ignatius Nursing Home, 4401 Haverford Ave, Philadelphia, PA 19104, **Business Phone:** (215)349-8800.

WALKER, MAQUIS ROCHE. **See WALKER, MARQUIS.**

WALKER, MARGIE (MARGIE ROSE WALKER)
Educator, writer. **Personal:** Born Sep 23, 1952, Houston, TX; daughter of Elius and Lucy Rose; married Sherman Walker, Jan 1, 1975; children: Sherman Leo II & Shomari Lukata. **Educ:** Tex Southern Univ, BA, speech commun, MA, speech commun; Colo State Univ, post-grad studies. **Career:** Writer, 1988-; KTSU FM, prog & pub affairs dirs; KMJQ-Magic 102, Programming Dept; Houston Defender Newspaper, ed & reporter; Tex Southern Univ, Dept Commun, adj prof, currently; Books: Harvest the Fruits, Spirit of the Season, 1994; Sweet Refrain, 1994; Breathless, 1995; Indiscretions, 1996; Conspiracy, 1997; Public Affair, 1998; Season's Greetings, 1998; Kwanzaa Kupendi; Remember Me, 1999; Where There's a Will, 2004; Writers In The Schs, writer-in-residence. **Honors/Awds:** Alumnus of the Year, Tex Southern Univ, 1994; Lit Lion, Houston Chronicle Newspaper, 1996; Invited for Womens Studies Living Archive, Univ Houston, 1997; May Is Texas Writer's Month, Tex Monthly Mag, 1997. **Business Phone:** (713)313-7011.

WALKER, MARGIE ROSE. See WALKER, MARGIE.

WALKER, DR. MARIA LATANYA
Physician. **Personal:** Born Jul 3, 1957, Greenwood, SC; daughter of H W Walker Jr and Leola Grant; married Albert L Thompson, Jul 27, 1991; children: Albert IV & H Walker. **Educ:** Furman Univ, Greenville, SC, BS, 1978; Harvard Med Sch, Boston, MD, 1982; Grady Memorial Hosp, internship; Georgia Baptist Med Ctr, residency. **Career:** Emory Univ Sch Med, fac, clin physician; pvt pract, 1990-; Piedmont Minor Emergency Clin, clin physician, currently. **Orgs:** Delta Sigma Theta, 1976; Med Asn Ga; Peabody Acad Soc/Harvard Med Sch, Am Med Asn; Phi Beta Kappa Beta Chapter, Furman Univ, 1978. **Home Phone:** (404)264-0973. **Business Phone:** (404)237-1755.

WALKER, DR. MARK LAMONT
Educator, surgeon. **Personal:** Born Jan 5, 1952, Brooklyn, NY; son of Philip David and Ann Boston. **Educ:** City Col New York, BS, 1973; Meharry Med Col, MD, 1977. **Career:** Traumatology fel, Md Inst Emergency Med Serv Systs, 1982-83; Howard Univ Hosp, instr dept surg, 1983-85; Morehouse Sch Med, asst prof surg, 1985-90; assoc prof & chmn, 1990-94; Surg Residency, prog dir, 1990-96; Surg Health Collective, Surgeon, 1996-, med dir, currently. **Orgs:** Alpha Omega Alpha Honor Med Soc, 1976-; fel, Intl Col Surgeons, 1984; Asn Acad Surg, 1984; Atlanta Med Asn, 1985; Nat Med Asn, 1986; Cert Surg Critical Care, 1987; fel Am Col Surgeons, 1988. **Honors/Awds:** Daniel Hale Williams Award, Howard Univ, 1982; Award of Merit, Dept Surg, Howard Univ, 1985; Annual Awardee, Sci Skills Ctr, Brooklyn, NY, 1986. **Home Addr:** 4267 Palm Springs Dr, East Point, GA 30344, **Home Phone:** (404)768-1274. **Business Addr:** Surgeon & Medical Director, Surgical Health Collective, 777 Cleveland Ave SW Suite 305, Atlanta, GA 30315, **Business Phone:** (404)761-7482.

WALKER, MARQUIS (MAQUIS ROCHE WALKER)
Football player. **Personal:** Born Jul 6, 1972, St Louis, MO. **Educ:** Southeast Mo State Univ. **Career:** Football player (retired); Wash Redskins, defensive back, 1996; St Louis Rams, 1996-97; Oakland Raiders, 1998-99; Detroit Lions, 2000; free agent, St Louis Rams, 1996.

WALKER, MARY L
Television journalist. **Personal:** Born Nov 17, 1951, Shreveport, LA; daughter of Sam and Jennie V Johnson Wilson. **Educ:** La State Univ, Baton Rouge, LA, BA, 1973. **Career:** KJOY Radio, Stockton, Calif, advert rep, 1974; KTBS-TV, Shreveport, La, gen assignments reporter, 1974-76; KSAT-TV, San Antonio, TX, police beat reporter, 1976; Child Protective Serv, pub info dir & spokeswoman, currently. **Orgs:** Nat Asn Black Journalists, 1986-; Soc Prof Journalists, 1988-; comt mem, Martin Luther King Comt, City San Antonio, 1988-. **Honors/Awds:** Outstanding Achievement in News Media, Beta Omega Sigma, 1975; Nomination for Best Television Documentary, Nat Acad TV Arts & Scis, 1976; Media Award, Tex Pub Health Asn, 1977; Media Awards for Excellence in Reporting Concerns of Children, Best TV Documentary, Odyssey Inst, 1980; Communications Award, Iota Phi Lambda Soc, 1980; Best Television News Story: Film & Script, Sigma Delta Chi, 1980; Best Television News Documentary, Sigma Delta Chi, 1982; Best Documentary, Tex Associated Press, 1982; Best Public Affairs Documentary, Tex United Press Int, 1983, Civilian Service Award, TV Documentary, Dept Army, 1984; Best Spot News Story (Team Report), 1986. **Home Addr:** 3223 Howard Suite 57, San Antonio, TX 78212. **Business Addr:** Spokeswoman, Public Information Director, Child Protective Services, 3635 SE Military Dr, San Antonio, TX 78223, **Business Phone:** (210)333-2004.

WALKER, MAY
Law enforcement officer, police officer. **Personal:** Born Dec 18, 1943, New Orleans, LA; daughter of Thomas J Jackson and Beatrice Ball; married Thomas Walker Jr (divorced 1979); children: Jemal R. **Educ:** Tex Southern Univ, BA, 1969; Univ Houston, MA, 1975, JD; Tex A & M Univ, MIS, 1990; United Way Tex Gulf Coast, attended 1990. **Career:** Police officer (retired); Lockwood, Andrews & Newman Inc, Houston, TX, specif writer & librn, 1964-72; Houston Independent Sch Dist, instr, 1970-72; Light House Blind, Houston, TX, admin asst, 1972-74; Houston Police Dept, community liaison police officer, 1974. **Orgs:** AKA Sorority; NOBLE; Nat Coun Negro Women Inc; Nat Black Police Asn; Coalition 100 Black Women; League Women Voters & Women Community Serv. **Honors/Awds:** Outstanding Achievement, Afro Am Police Officer League; Outstanding Recognition, Black Police Asn; Outstanding Leadership Award, Over Hill Inc; Outstanding Leadership Award, Nat Coun Negro Women; Appreciation of Achievement Accomplished, Houston Police Dept, Black Police Selection; Outstanding Achievement Award, USN; Cert of Recognition, Sunnyside Neighborhood Ctr. **Home Addr:** 3810 Belgrade Dr, Houston, TX 77045. *

WALKER, DR. MELVIN E
Educator. **Personal:** Born Oct 23, 1946, Shivers, MS; son of Melvin E and Rosie; married Jeraldine Wooden; children: Daphne Melinda, Melvin Earl III & Melanie Latrice. **Educ:** Prentiss Jr Col, AS, 1967; Alcorn A&M Col, BS, 1969; Univ Ill, Urbana-Champaign, MS, 1971, PhD, 1973. **Career:** Ft Valley State Univ, Ft Valley, GA, from asst prof to assoc prof, 1973-84, coordr rural develop res, 1977-78, res dir, 1978-88, prof agri econ, 1984-, dean, 1987-88, 1990-98, actg pres, 1988-90. **Orgs:** Chair, Asn Res Dirs, 1982-86; chair, Asn 1890 Agri Adminrs, 1984-85; chmn, Asn Res Dirs, 1986-; vpres, Camp John Hope NFA Alumni Asn, 1986-; Am Agri Econ Asn; Camp John Hope NFA Asn; Optimist Club; bd dir & treas, Asn Social & Behav Sci; bd dir, GA Agr Econs Asn; Joint Coun Food & Agr Sci, USDA. **Honors/Awds:** Outstanding Service Award, USDA Honors Prog, 1982, US Dept Com Census Adv Bur, 1983; President's Outstanding Service Award, Ft Valley State Univ Agri Alumni Asn, 1984; Hon State Farmers Award, FFA, 1984. **Special Achievements:** author, Custom and Rental Rates Used on Illinois Farms, University of IL, 1973; author, "Poverty and Alienation: A Case Study," Journal of Social and Behavioral Sciences, 1978; author, "Effects of the Changing Structure of Agriculture on Nonwhite Farming in the US, the South, and Gerogia," Sociological Spectrum, 1984. **Home Addr:** 102 Duncan St, Ft Valley, GA 31030. **Business Addr:** Agricultural Economics Professor, Fort Valley State University, 1005 State Univ Dr 117 Tabor Agri Bldg, PO Box 5744, Ft Valley, GA 31030-3298, **Business Phone:** (478)825-6344.

WALKER, MOSES L
Health services administrator. **Personal:** Born Oct 21, 1940, Kalamazoo, MI; son of Arthur Walker Sr and Erie Smith; married Ruthie; children: Tari, Mark & Stacy. **Educ:** Western Mich Univ, BS, 1966, MBA, 1990; Wayne State Univ, MSW, 1968. **Career:** Douglass Comm Assn, outreach worker, 1966; Kalamazoo Co Comm Action Prog, team capt, 1966; Comm Serv Coun, adminr asst, 1966; Archdiocese Detroit, Comm Affairs Dept, 1967; Douglass Comm Assn, dir, assoc dir, 1968-78; Borgess Mental Health Ctr, exec dir, 1978-83; DeLano Clin Inc, pres, 1983-91; Borgess Med Ctr, Behav Med Serv, vpres; Borgess Health Alliance, Community Rels, exec dir; Family Health Ctr Inc, interim pres & chief exec officer, 2007-. **Orgs:** Chmn, Educ Advan Scholar Comn, 1973; chmn, United Negro Col Fund, 1973; dir, First Am Bank, MI, 1978-; pres, Asn Ment Health Adminr, MI Chap, 1987-89; chair, Mich Hosp Asn, 1988-; Kalamazoo City Comn; Northside Asn; Nat Asn Social Workers; steering comt, Nat Asn Black Social Workers. **Honors/Awds:** Outstanding Young Men of MI, Jaycees, MI Chap, 1969; Distinguished Service Award, Kalamazoo Chap, 1969; Outstanding Service Award, Northside Asn Educ Advan, 1972; Community Service Award, Southwestern MI Chap Nat Asn Social Workers, 1974; Distinguished Alumni Award, Wayne Stata Univ Sch Social Work, 1981. **Military Serv:** AUS, pfc, 1961-64. **Home Addr:** 1725 Cobb Ave, Kalamazoo, MI 49007. **Business Addr:** Interim President, Chief Executive Officer, Family Health Center Inc, 117 W Paterson St, Kalamazoo, MI 49007, **Business Phone:** (269)349-4257.

WALKER, PHILLIP E.
Artistic director. **Educ:** Loyola Univ Chicago, BA, theatre; Univ Ill-Urbana, MA, theatre hist; Univ Calif-Davis, MFA. **Career:** Am Conservatory Theatre; San Jose State Univ, Yuba Col; Santa Clara Univ; Lincoln Univ Miss; Univ Ill-Urbana; Oakland Ensemble Theatre, pres; African Am Drama Co, artistic dir, currently. **Orgs:** Touring arts Coordr, Calif Arts Coun; founding asst treas, Black Theatre Network. **Business Addr:** Artistic Director, African Am Drama Co, 30 E Julian Suite 218, San Francisco, CA 95112-4076.*

WALKER, RHONDA
Founder (Originator), television news anchorperson. **Personal:** Married Derrick. **Educ:** Mich State Univ, BA, commun. **Career:** WJBK Fox 2 News, Detroit, 1998-2002; spec prog: Thanksgiving Parade, Arts Beats& Eats, 35th Ryder Cup Matches, 2004, Major League Baseball's All-Star Game, 2005, Super Bowl XL, 2006 & North Am Int Auto Show Charity Preview Spec; WDIV-TV Local 4, news anchor, currently; Rhonda Walker Found, pres, currently. **Orgs:** Nat Asn Breast Cancer Orgns; Detroit Med Ctr; Mich Minority Bus Develop Coun; Nat Asn Black Auto Suppliers; Nat Asn Black Acctants; Hope United Methodist Church, Southfield, MI. **Honors/Awds:** "Winning Futures" Community Involvement Award; Mary Ball Advocacy Media Award; RARE Award, RARE found; Excellence in Mentoring award; Community Involvement Award; Mentor of the Year Award, Metro Detroit Mentor Collaboration; Salvation Army Distinguished Service Award; Detroit Fire Dept Community Service Award; Community Involvement Award, Nat Asn Black Women; Black Women Contracting Best Mentorship Award, Jack & Jill Am; Legacy & Philanthropy Award; Neal K Doc Fenkell Award, Sparky Anderson CATCH Found, 2007; Broadcast TV/Media Award, Mich Chapter Southern Christian Leadership Conf, 2008; Woman of Excellence Award, Mich Chronicle, 2008; Flame of Inspiration Award, Compuware 2008. **Business Addr:** Founder, Rhonda Walker Foundation, PO Box 251746, West Bloomfield, MI 48325, **Business Phone:** 800-652-2989.

WALKER, RONALD PLEZZ
School administrator. **Personal:** Born Oct 16, 1953, Boley, OK; married Glenda Gay; children: Terrance Scott. **Educ:** Langston Univ, BS, 1974; Cent State Univ, MEd, 1978; Okla State Univ. **Career:** Okla City Sch, sci teacher, 1973-76, bio-med prog dir, 1976-77, sci & eng ctr dir, 1977-80; Boley Pub Sch, supt, 1980; Geary County Sch, KS, supt, currently; Geary County Sch, bd dir, currently; Nat Asn Federally Impacted Sch, bd dir, currently. **Orgs:** Pres, Nat Young Adult Coun, CME Church; vpres, Langston Univ, Alumni Asn; vpres, Orgn Rural Okla Schs; pub relations dir, Zeta Gamma Lambda Chap Alpha Phi Alpha. **Honors/Awds:** Outstanding Young Man, Nat Jayceesm, 1980, 1984; Outstanding Service Award, Adams Day Care Ctr, 1983; Outstanding Service Award, Okla City Dist Young Adults, 1983. **Business Addr:** Superintendent, Geary County Schools, PO Box 370, Junction City, KS 66441-0370.

WALKER, ROSLYN ADELE
Museum director. **Educ:** Hampton Univ; Indiana Univ. **Career:** Museum director (retired); Univ Mus, Ill State Univ, dir; Nat Museum African Art, Smithsonian Inst, cur, sr cur, dir, 1997-2003. **Orgs:** African Studies Asn; Arts Coun African Studies Asn; Col Art Asn; Am Asn Museums, Art Table Inc; African Am Museums Asn. **Honors/Awds:** National Black Alumni Hall of Fame, 1997. **Special Achievements:** Co-author of African Art in the Cycle of Life.

WALKER, RUSSELL DEWITT
Safety engineer. **Personal:** Born Aug 30, 1946, New York, NY; son of Elizier Amos and Armstead; married Mary Ann Walker, Aug 30, 1968; children: Lisa, Danielle, Lael. **Educ:** Mt San Antonio Col, AA, 1967; Ventura Col, attended 1977; Calif State Univ, Northridge, attended 1979; Univ LaVerne, BS, 1980, MS, 1981. **Career:** Safety engineer (retired); Los Angeles County Dept Beaches, ocean lifeguard, 1965-72, sr ocean lifeguard, 1972-78, seasonal lt lifeguard, 1979-82, lt ocean lifeguard, 1982-92; Los Angeles County Fire Dept, capt lifeguards, 1992-98, asst chief lifeguard. **Orgs:** Pres, Sickle Cell Disease Servs Ventura County, 1976-96; Omega Psi Phi Fraternity, 1983-; int training officer, World Lifesaving Asn, 1985-; standards comt mem, So Calif Pub Pool Oper Asn, 1989-90; Asn Chiefs, 1994-; bd dir, pres, Aquatic Found Metro Los Angeles, 1994; bd dir, Pat McCormick Educ Found, 1996-. **Honors/Awds:** Letter of Commendation, Los Angeles County Sheriff, 1977; Letter of Appreciation, Romper Room Show, 1979; Service Award, Sickle Cell Anemia Disease Services of Ventura County, 1979; Certificate of Appreciation, Burke Aquatic Found, 1995; Certificate of Appreciation, Zenith Youth Homes, 1996. **Special Achievements:** Author of Emergency Medical Section of Ocean Lifeguard Manual, 1973; Designed & Developed Beach Lifeguard Training Program, 1977; Created, Developed & Planned Water Awareness Training Education, Recruitment Program, 1985; Initiated Planning & Implementation of Lifeguard 911 Emergency System, 1986; Established Emergency Response Guidelines Book for Central Section Ocean Lifeguards, 1993. **Military Serv:** US Navy, petty officer second class, 1967-72; National Defense Medal, 1967; Honor Student Medical Illustration School, 1969; Vietnam Service Medal, 1970, Good Conduct Medal, 1971; Marksman 45 Cal, 1971. **Home Addr:** 694 Pacific Cove Dr, Port Hueneme, CA 93041, **Home Phone:** (805)984-1221. *

WALKER, SAMAKI IJUMA
Basketball player, entrepreneur. **Personal:** Born Feb 25, 1976, Columbus, OH; children: Dabaji & Sakima. **Educ:** Univ Louisville, commun. **Career:** Dallas Mavericks, forward, 1996-99; San Antonio Spurs, 2000-01; Lady's & Gent's, owner, 2000-; Los Angeles Lakers, 2001-03; Miami Heat, 2003-04; wash Wizards, forward, 2004-05; Ind Pacers, forward, 2005-06; Unics Kazan, forward, 2006-07; Al Jalaa Aleppo, 2007-. **Special Achievements:** First round pick, No 9, NBA Draft, 1996. **Business Addr:** Professional Basketball Player, Al Jalaa Aleppo, Al Azeeziyyeh, Jabal an Nahr, Aleppo, Syrian Arab Republic.

WALKER, DR. SANDRA VENEZIA
Educator. **Personal:** Born Nov 1, 1949, Little Rock, AR; daughter of Otis L and Ardelia H Thomas; divorced; children: Brandon. **Educ:** Little Rock Univ, Little Rock, Ariz, 1966-68; Univ Mo, Kansas City, Mo, BA, 1970, MA, 1972; Wash Univ, St Louis, Mo, PhD, 1976. **Career:** Wash Univ, St Louis, Mo, adj asst prof, 1976-77; City Kansas City, Mo, dir pub serv & com support prog, dept housing & com develop, 1977-81; Univ Mo, Kansas City, Mo, dir affirmative action & acad personnel, 1981-85, asst dean, col arts & scis, 1985-. **Orgs:** Pres, Asn Black Sociologists, 1988-; sec & treas, Asn Black Sociologists, 1983-86; bd mem, Mo Sch Bds Asn, 1988-90; vpres, Kansas City, Mo Sch Bd, 1986-90. **Honors/Awds:** Achievement Recognition, Mo Legislative Black Caucus, 1985; Woman's Conscience, Panel Am Women, 1987; Image Award Education, Urban League, Greater Kansas City, 1990; Education Award, Black Archives Mid Am, 1990; Serv Award, Mo Sch Bds Asn, 1990. **Business Addr:** Assistant Dean, University of Missouri, Kansas City, College of Arts & Sciences, 4825 Troost Rm 215, Kansas City, MO 64110, **Business Phone:** (816)235-2736.

WALKER, DR. SHEILA SUZANNE
Writer, educator, anthropologist. **Personal:** Born Nov 5, 1944, Jersey City, NJ; daughter of Dr James O and Susan Robinson Walker Snell. **Educ:** Sorbonne & Inst d'Etudes Politiques, 1965; Bryn Mawr Col, BA, polit sci, 1966; Univ Chicago, MA, 1969, PhD (anthrop), 1976. **Career:** Elmhurst Col, lectr, 1969; Chicago

Model Cities Health Proj, res analyst, 1970; Chicago Urban League, res specialist, 1970; World Bank, Abidjan, Ivory Coast, translator, 1972; Harvard Univ Divinity Sch, res asst, 1972-73; Univ Calif Berkeley, from asst prof to assoc prof, 1973-86, Dept Afro-Am Studies, assoc prof, 1986-89; City Col, City Univ NY, vis assoc prof, 1987; Schomburg Ctr Res Black Cult, scholar-in-residence, 1987; Col William & Mary, prof anthrop, 1989-91; Tex Univ, Austin, Ctr African & African Am Studies, dir, 1991-2001, Col Liberal Arts, Dept Anthrop Annabel Irion Worsham Centennial prof, 1991-; Spelman Col, Atlanta, GA, William & Camille Cosby Endowed prof Humanities, 2002-04; fac, Social Servs, 2003-04, prof, currently; Auth: Ceremonial Spirit Possession in Africa & Afro-America, 1972; The Religious Revolution in the Ivory Coast: The Prophet Harris & the Harrist Church, 1983; African Roots/American Cultures; Africa in the Creation of the Americas, 2001; Documentary Video, Scattered Africa: Faces & Voices of the African Diaspora, 2002; Organizer- Inst conference on The African Diaspora & the Modern World, Feb 1996, Univ Texas; co-sponsored by the Univ Texas & UNESCO; co-editor, African Christianity: Patterns of Religious Continuity, 1979. **Orgs:** Int Exec Comt; Inst des Peuples Noirs, Ouagadougou, Burkina Faso, 1986-91; jury mem, Tenth Festival Panafricain de Cinema de; Ouagadougou, 1987-; Inst Scientific & Tech Comt, The Slave Route Proj, UNESCO, 1991-. **Business Addr:** Professor, Spelman College, 350 Spelman Lane SW, PO Box 308, Atlanta, GA 30314.

WALKER, SOLOMON W., II
Insurance executive. **Career:** Pilgrim Health & Life Insurance Co, Augusta, GA, chief exec, 1979-89.

WALKER, SONIA
Publicist, executive. **Personal:** Born Apr 10, 1937, Columbus, OH; married Walter; children: 3. **Educ:** Wilbur Force Univ, undergrad, 1956; Bennett Col, BA, 1958; Howard Univ Sch Soc Work, MSW, 1963. **Career:** elementary teacher, 1958-61; social work in priv & pub agency, 1963-74; Univ Chicago, Housing Staff, 1970-74; WHBQ-TV RKO-GEN, dir comn rel, 1975. **Orgs:** Memphis Asn Black Comt; bd dir, Memphis Orch Soc Memphis Urban Leag Nat Conf Christ & Jews Beale St Reprtory Co Memphis Art & Sci Comt; prog coordr, TN Womens Mtg; supt, adv coun Memphis Pub Sch; PUSH; NAACP. *

WALKER, STANLEY MICHAEL
Educator, lawyer. **Personal:** Born Jul 15, 1942, Chicago, IL; son of Georgia and Alfred; married Elizabeth Mary Pearson; children: Darryl & Edana. **Educ:** Harvard Col, AB, 1964; Yale Univ Law Sch, New Haven, CT, JD, 1967. **Career:** Judge A Leon Higginbotham US Dist Ct, law clerk, 1967-69; Dechert Price & Rhoads, assoc, 1969-70; Pepper, Hamilton & Scheetz, Assoc, 1970-71; Penn State Bd Law Exams, examiner, 1971-74; Comm Legal Serv, staff & mng atty, 1971-72; Greater Philadelphia Comm Develop Corp, exec vpres, 1972-73; The Rouse Co, sr atty, 1973-79; Univ Tex Sch Law, assoc prof, 1979-89; Exxon Co, USA, atty; Friendswood Develop Co, gen coun, 1995. **Orgs:** Am Bar Asn & Nat Bar Asn; Bars US Supreme Court, DA, PA, MD & TX; Austin Econ Develop Comm, 1985-89; alt mem, City Austin Bd Adjustment, 1985-86; Action Metropolitan Govt Comm, 1988-89.

WALKER, TANYA ROSETTA
Administrator. **Personal:** Born Apr 2, 1953, Philadelphia, PA; daughter of James and Lucille; divorced; children: Al Qadir R. **Educ:** Stenotype Inst New York, Cert, 1970; Rutgers State Univ, BA, 1974; Essex Col Bus, Cert Legal & Admin Asst, 1977. **Career:** Lofton & Lester Esqs, paralegal, 1979-83; Former Gov Brendan T Byrne, exec asst, 1983-85; Althear A Lester Esq, legal asst, 1985-92; Essex Cty Prosecutors Off, exec adv, 1992-. **Orgs:** Nat & Essex Cos Legal Secretaries & Paralegals Asn, 1979-89; Notary Pub NJ, 1982-; vol, Big Brothers & Big Sisters Am, 1983-88; bd mem, Boy Scouts Am, 1983-; bd dirs & vpres, Make-A-Wish Found NJ, 1983-86; Union County C C, 1986-87. **Honors/Awds:** Award of Excellence, Aunt Millie's Childrens Learning Ctr, 1984, 85; Achievement Award, Tri-City Sr Citizens Group, 1986; Black Heritage Award for Achievement, Teachers' Union, 1986; Recognition Award, Shearson Lehman Bros Inc, 1986. **Special Achievements:** First African American and First woman president Make-A-Wish, NJ. **Business Addr:** President, Make A Wish Foundation of NJ, 326 Morris Ave, Elizabeth, NJ 07208.

WALKER, TERRY
General, manager. **Career:** ABC TV, music supvr, 2004-; Tribe of Judah Christian Motorcycle Ministry, Brisbane, owner. **Business Addr:** Music Supervisor, ABC TV, 500 S Buena Vista St, Burbank, CA 91521-4551, **Business Phone:** (818)460-7477.*

WALKER, TRACY A
Manager. **Personal:** Born Jun 12, 1969, Detroit, MI; daughter of Charles N and Delma L. **Educ:** Univ Mich, Ann Arbor, BA, commun, eng, 1991; Wayne State Univ, MA, commun, 1997. **Career:** Univ Mich Ann Arbor, Housing Dept, minority peer adv, 1988-90, resident dir, 1990-91, spring, summer coord, 1991; Detroit Pistons, admin asst, 1991, county rels asst, 1992, educ prog coord, 1992, county rels supvr, 1992-95, asst dir community rels, 1995-97, dir community rels, 1997-. **Orgs:** DST Sorority Inc, 1989-, Detroit Alumnae Chap, 1993-; Blacks Advert, Radio & Television; NCP, lifetime mem; Univ Mich Alumni Asn; Nat Asn Female Exec; vpres admin, Women Community Detroit, 1996-97. **Honors/Awds:** Employee of the Year, Community Rels Dept, Detroit Pistons, 1991, 1992, 1994. **Business Addr:** Director of Community Relations, The Detroit Pistons, Palace Auburn Hills, 2 Championship Dr, Auburn Hills, MI 48326, **Business Phone:** (810)377-8244.

WALKER, VALAIDA SMITH
School administrator, educator. **Personal:** Born in Darby, PA; daughter of Samuel and Rosa Lee. **Educ:** Howard Univ, Wash, BS, 1954; Temple Univ, Philadelphia, MED, 1970, EdD, 1973. **Career:** Temple Univ, Philadelphia, prof, 1974-, chairperson, 1980-83, assoc dean, 1983-84, assoc vice provost, 1984-90, vice provost, 1987-90, vip studs affairs, 1990-02. **Orgs:** Pres's Comn Ment Retardation; pres, Am Asn Ment Retardation; PA Adv Bd Spl Educ; William Penn Adult Community Sch Adv Bd, 1976-; Knoll/Shaffer Bi-Partisan Comn, 1989-; exec advsr, Caribbean Asn Ment Retardation, Elwyn Inst bd Dirs. **Honors/Awds:** Chapel of the Four Chaplains Serv Award; Spl Educr of the Year, Sigma Pi Epsilon Delta, 1983.

WALKER, VERNON DAVID
Computer executive. **Personal:** Born Jun 16, 1950, New Rochelle, NY; son of Edward and Veronica; married Sabrina Highsmith, Jun 29, 1992; children: Aminah & Aliyah. **Educ:** Univ Md, BS, 1976. **Career:** Bendix Field Eng Corp, sr buyer, 1972-77; Satellite Bus Syst, sr procurement admin, 1977-82; MCI Telecommunication Corp, sr staff mem; Commun Networks Corp, vpres, currently. **Orgs:** One Hundred Black Men NY, 1993-; Nat Black MBA Asn, 1993-. **Honors/Awds:** Certified Purchasing Manager, Nat Asn Purchasing Mgrs, 1986; Certified Netware Engineer, Novell, 1995. **Home Addr:** 13 Hill St Suite 2, Norwalk, CT 06850-3007, **Home Phone:** (203)847-1471. **Business Addr:** Vice President, Communication Networks Corporation, 13 Hill St, Norwalk, CT 06850, **Business Phone:** (203)847-3000.

WALKER, W. VIRGINA
Entrepreneur. **Educ:** San Jose State Univ, BS, bus admin. **Career:** Enea Embedded Technol, gen mgr, Corp Strategy & Mkt, sr vpres, 2001-; CFO OSE Systs, exec vpres; CFO Sagent Technol, exec vpres. **Business Phone:** (480)753-9200.*

WALKER, WALTER LORENZO
School administrator, vice president (organization). **Personal:** Born Sep 4, 1935, Chicago, IL; married Sonia L Louden; children: Walter Noland, Aaron Jordan & Marcus Elliot. **Educ:** Univ Chicago, AB, 1955; Bryn Mawr Col, MSS, 1962; Brandeis Univ, PhD, 1969. **Career:** Howard Univ, staff assoc, 1963-66; Philadelphia Re development Asn, comm relations rep, 1962-63; Univ Chicago, vpres, 1969-74; Le Moyne Owen Col, pres, 1974, vice chancellor; Fed Res Bank St Louis, dir, 1978-80; Com Appl, clmnst, 1979. **Orgs:** Nat Asn Social Wrkrs; CORE; Nat Asn Advan Colored People; Urban League; Am Dem Actn; Coun Socila Work Educ, bd Dir 1st TN Nat Bnk 1980; bd mem, Am Cancer Soc; bd vpres, Memphis United Way, 1976; dir, Memphis Area Chamber of Com, 1977-79; Memphis Rotary Club; bd mem, Chicago C Care Soc. **Honors/Awds:** Golden Gavel, Chicago Caucus, 1974; Educator of Yr, Gr Memphis State, 1977; 100 Top Young Educrs, Change Mag, 1978; 10 Top Citizens in Memphis, Comm Appeal, 1980; Educator of Yr, Memphis, Phi Beta Sigma Tau Iota Sigma Chap, 1980. **Military Serv:** USAF, 1st lt, 1955-60. **Business Addr:** 807 Walker Ave, Memphis, TN 38126.

WALKER, WAYNE
Football player. **Personal:** Born Dec 27, 1966, Waco, TX. **Educ:** Tex Tech Univ. **Career:** Football player (retired); San Diego Chargers, wide receiver, 1989; San Antonio Riders, 1992; Ottawa Rough Riders, 1992-93; Shreveport Pirates, 1994-95; Saskatchewan Roughriders, 1996.

WALKER, WENDELL P
Administrator. **Personal:** Born Jun 6, 1930, Painesville, OH; son of Robert M and Evelyn Wieker; married Doris Thomas; children: Kevin, Andrea & Brian. **Educ:** John Carroll Univ, pre-med, 1948-49; Defiance col, BA, 1951; Univ kans, hemat, 1969-71; Western Reserv Univ, 1955-56; Lake Erie Col, teaching cert, 1972. **Career:** Administrator (retired); Poly Clinic Hosp, 1955-60; Northeastern Ohio Gen Hosp, Med Lab dir, 1960; City Painesville, Councilman; City Painesville, activist & leader; Painesville City Improv Corp, trustee & pres; Harvey High Sch, African-Am History Adult Educ Prog, teacher. **Orgs:** Nat bd Am Med Technol, 1976-81; pres, Oh State soc Am Med Technol, 1972-75; pres, Lake County health & Welfare coun, 1973-74; chmn, vchmn, Lake County Metropolitan Housing Authority, 1973-74; nat scientific comt, Am Med Technol, 1972, nominating comt, 1973, state bd, 1971-74, 1975-78; bd, United Way Lake County, 1974-76; vice chmn, Cent Br YMCA, 1973-74, chmn, 1975-76, bd, 1976; bd, Lake County YMCA, 1970; bd, pres, Free Clinic, 1975; NEO Hop, bd; cub pack chmn, Boy Scouts Am, Dan Beard Dist; bd pres, Catholic Serv Bur Lake County; bd pres, Lifeline Economically Disadvantaged Consumers; Lake Metro Housing; Coalition Homeless Task Force; Lake County Jail Comn; Soc Bank; Metropolitan Health Planning Corp Cleveland. **Honors/Awds:** AMT National Presidents Award, 1973; Journal Award, OSSAMT, 1973; Painesville Area Chamber Comm Outstanding Citizen, 1994; Defiance College Alumni Year, 1995. **Special Achievements:** Area Chamber of Commerce; fdr Free Clinic; Lake County Grand Jury Foreman, 1973; Painesville City council man, 1986-95, Last 4 years as council president; represented Painesville School Systems for State of ohio Consensus for education, KEDS Program; study for Lakeland col, need for education and vocation project projection for future; involved in first Project Testing for Sickle Cell Anemia (county-wide); social science inr for Painesville Night School; publication of numerous articles; Radio Personality-WBKC Radio, Fainesville, OH; First black student admitted to John Carroll University. **Military Serv:** AUS, Veteran Korean War.

WALKER, WESLEY DARCEL
High school teacher, football player. **Personal:** Born May 26, 1955, San Bernardino, CA; children: John, Taylor & Austin. **Educ:** Univ Calif; Mercy Col; Fordham Col, MEd. **Career:** Football player (retired); NY Jets, wide receiver, 1977-89; Sports Radio Show, commentator, currently; Park View Elem Sch, phys educ teacher, currently. **Honors/Awds:** Jets MVP, 1978; Two Pro Bowls, 1978 & 1982. **Home Addr:** PO Box 20438, Huntington Station, NY 11746-0857.

WALKER, WILBUR P.
Educator, teacher. **Personal:** Born May 6, 1936, Okmulgee, OK; son of Hugh and Mae Ella Hill; married Tomycine Lewis, Aug 30, 1958; children: Wilbur Jr & Natalie. **Educ:** Langston Univ, BA, 1958; Cent State Univ, MT, 1968; Univ Okla, EdD, 1974. **Career:** Educator (retired); Okla City Pub Schs, teacher, 1967-69; Urban League Okla City, dir comm org, 1969; Univ Okla, spec asst to pres, 1970-73; Okla Univ, dir special student prog, 1973-75; Benedict Col, dean acad affairs, 1975-78; Okla St Regents Higher Educ, dir student info serv, 1979-95. **Orgs:** Life mem, Phi Delta Kappa; Urban League Okla City, Black Inc; Nat Asn Stud Personnel Admin; Okla Col Personnel Asn. *

WALKER, WILLIAM B
Automotive executive. **Career:** New Castle Ford Lincoln-Mercury Inc, pres, owner, 1990-. **Special Achievements:** Company is ranked 96 on Black Enterprise magazine's 1997 list of Top 100 Black businesses. **Business Addr:** President, New Castle Ford Lincoln-Mercury Inc, 221 N Memorial Dr, PO Box 903, New Castle, IN 47362, **Business Phone:** (765)529-3673.

WALKER, WILLIAM PAUL, JR.
Executive. **Personal:** Born Jul 25, 1940, Denmark, SC; married Mamie Odena; children: Daryl Lamar. **Educ:** Howard Univ, BS, 1963, MD, 1967. **Career:** DC Gen Hosp, chf dept rdtn thrpy; Georgetown U, asst prof; Howard U, asst prof; Radiological Assocs, dept chmn. **Orgs:** DC Med Soc; Am Col Radiology; Med Chi DC; Mid Atlantic Soc Radctn Onclgst; Nat Med Assoc; Am Cancer Soc; Southern Medical Assoc; Randall Memorial United Methodist Ch. **Honors/Awds:** Upjohn Award, 1967; Alumni Award, Voorhees Coll, 1985.

WALKER, DR. WILLIAM SONNY
Government official. **Personal:** Born Dec 13, 1933, Pine Bluff, AR; son of James D and Mary V Coleman Bell; children: Cheryl D, James D II, Lesli W Williams & William L Jr. **Educ:** Univ Ariz Pine Bluff, BA, 1955; AZ State Univ, cert, 1962; Univ Oklahoma, cert, 1968; Fed Exec Inst, cert, 1979. **Career:** State AR & Governer Winthrop Rockefeller, agency dir & asst to governer, 1969-71; US Dept Housing & Urban Develop, div dir, 1971-72; US Off Econ Opportunity, regional dir, 1972-75; US Community Serv Admin, regional dir, 1975-81; Nat Alliance Bus, v pres; The Sonny Walker Group, founder & chief exec officer, currently. **Orgs:** Bd dirs, United Way Metro Atlanta, 1977-87; bd dirs, Martin Luther King Jr Ctr, Nonviolent Social Change, 1979-; bd dirs, Southern Christian Leadership Conf, 1980-87; bd dirs, Metro Atlanta Community Design Ctr, 1981-; bd dirs, Metro Atlanta Black & Jewish Coalition, 1981-87; vice chair, GA Asn Black Elected Officials & Corporate Round table, 1982-87; bd trustees, Metro Atlanta YWCA, 1982-89; pres, Re surgens Atlanta, 1984-85; chmn, Econ Develop Task Force Nat Conf Black Mayors, 1983-87; vice chair, bd trustees Metro Atlanta Crime Comn, 1983-; chmn, Collections Life &Heritage, 1984-87; bd dirs & chr, Pub Broadcasting Asn Atlanta, 1988-90; bd dirs, Consumer Credit CounAsn, 1984-; life mem, Kappa Alpha PsiFrat, NAACP; bd trustees chair, Bennett Col, 1991-; principal Ctr Excellence Government, 1988; pres, 100 Black Men Altanta, GA, 1991-; Metro Atlanta Rapid Transit Authority Bd Dirs, 1990-; chmn, Sustaining memship Enrollment Boy Scouts Am, 1990-92; GEO Partnership Excellence Educ, 1991-. **Honors/Awds:** Outstanding Public Service, State of GA House & Senate Resolutions, 1979; Achievement, Kappa Alpha Psi Frat, 1980; Community Service, Atlanta Bus League, 1984; Dr Laws, Shorter Col, Allen Univ, Edward Waters Col, Morris Booker Col; Distinguished Service Award, Atlanta Urban League, 1986; Roy Wilkins Award, Georgia NAACP, 1986; President's Award, Nat Conf Black Mayors Econ Develop Task Force, 1986; Leadership Award, Metro-Atlanta United Way, 1987; President's Award, Nat Alliance Bus, 1988. *

WALKER, WILLIE F
Association executive, president (organization). **Personal:** Born Feb 6, 1942, Vernon, AL; son of Naomi Ford and Willie B; mar-

ried Frizal Glasper, May 22, 1971; children: Shannon, Willie Jr, Alex & Teresa. **Educ:** Southern Ill Univ, BS, 1965; Univ Wis, MS, 1971. **Career:** Venice Sch System, teacher, 1965-69; Venice-Lincoln Educ Ctr, dir placement, 1971-73; Madison/St Clair County, dir manpower, 1973-76; Nat Urban League Regional Off, regional coordr, 1976-77; Madison County Urban League, exec dir, 1977-85; Dayton Urban League, Dayton, Ohio, pres & chief exec officer, 1985-. **Orgs:** Co-chair, Black Leadership Develop, 1986-; bd treas, Dayton Free Clin, 1987-; co-chair, Ohio Black Family Coalition, 1987-; bd mem, Ohio Elected Pub Officials, 1987-; bd secy, Ohio Coun Urban League, 1987-; Black Managers Asn, 1987-; pres, United Way Agency Exec, 1989; acct chair, United Way Campaign, 1989. **Honors/Awds:** Hon mem, Nat Bus League, 1985; Gold Award, United Way Greater Dayton, 1985-89; Community Service Award, Dayton Jobs Corps Ctr, 1987; Century Club award, YMCA, 1987; hon recognition, Black Leadership Develop, 1989; Black Agenda for the Year, Steering Comt, 1989 & 2000. **Business Addr:** President, Dayton Urban League, 907 W 5th St, Dayton, OH 45402.

WALKER, WILLIE LEROY
Government official. **Personal:** Born Dec 26, 1945, Detroit, MI; son of Stanley and Leila; married Edna Walker, Dec 17, 1966; children: Dwayne, Takesha. **Educ:** Wayne State Univ, BS, bus admin, 1971, MBA, mgt, 1974; Walsh Col, MBA, acct, 1990. **Career:** City Detroit, proj mgr, prod div, Mayor's off, 1975-78, div head, prog mgt Employ & Training, 1978-91, coordr, admin serv, Employ & Training, 1991-93, dep dir, Employ & Training, 1993, Detroit Employ & Training, 1994-. **Orgs:** Adv bd, Multi Media Partnership, 1995; adv bd, Mich Jobs Comn, 1994-, work-first, finance comt chair, 1994-; adv bd mem, Mich Dept Ed, 1984-; Booker T Wash Bus Asn, bd mem, 1995; audit comt mem, Ebenezer AME Credit Union, 1989-90, vice chair, 1991; Detroit Police Athletic League, mgr/asst coach, 1978-88; Mich Dept Ed, Mich Family Resource Coalition, 1995; Mercy Col, acct tutor acct club, 1987. **Honors/Awds:** Civic & Humanitarian Award, Arab Am & Chaldean Coun, 1994; Wayne State Univ, Beta Gamma Hon Soc, 1971; Appreciation Award, Highland Park Optimist Club, 1987; Jr Police Cadet Appreciation, Detroit Police Dept, 1985 & 1994; Dream Maker Award, Detroit Hispanic Develop Corp, 1999. **Special Achievements:** Pee Wee Hockey Travel Team, Nat Champions, 1984. **Military Serv:** USAF, sgt, 1964-68. **Business Addr:** Director, City Detroit, Detroit Employment & Training, 707 W Milwaukee 5th Fl, Detroit, MI 48202, **Business Phone:** (313)876-0674.*

WALKER, WILLIE M. **See Obituaries section.**

WALKER, WOODSON DUBOIS
Lawyer. **Personal:** Born Apr 6, 1950, Springfield, AR; married Hope Labarriteau King; children: Yedea H, Ajamu K, Fwatula, Ajani & Chike. **Educ:** Univ Ark Pine Bluff, BA, hist & philos, 1971; Univ Minn Sch Law, JD, 1974. **Career:** Walker Kaplan & Mays PA Little Rock, assov atty, 1976-77; Cent Minn Legl Serv Corp, Minneapolis, assoc atty, 1974-76; City Menifee Ark, city & atty, 1977; City Menifee Ark, city & atty, 1977; Cinula & Walker Pa, Little Rock, partner, 1978; City Allport Ark, legal consult, 1980; Walker & Dunklin, Little Rock, sr partner, currently. **Orgs:** Ark Bar Asn; Minn Bar Asn; Am Bar Asn; Nat Bar Asn, 1974; secy, Ebony Plz Corp, Little Rock Ark, 1976; Little Rock Wastewater Utility Comn, 1979; Ark St Bd Corrections, 1980; bd mem, Boatmen's Nat Bank; bd mem, AP&L Utility Co; Pulaski Bar Asn; W Harold Flowers Law Soc. **Honors/Awds:** Outstanding Student Leader, Zeta Phi Beta Sorority, Univ Ark Pine Bluff, 1971; Higher Achievements Award, Phi Beta Omega Fraternity Inc Chi Psi Rho Chap Pine Bluff Ark, 1971; Act of Kindness Service Award; Lawyer-Citizen Award, Pulaski County Bar Asn, 1981. **Home Addr:** 6805 Talmage, Little Rock, AR 72204. **Business Addr:** Senior Partner, Walker & Dunklin, 2020 Broadway St, Little Rock, AR 72201, **Business Phone:** (501)372-4623.

WALKER, REV. WYATT TEE
Clergy. **Personal:** Born Aug 16, 1929, Brockton, MA; son of John Wise and Maude; married Theresa Ann Edwards; children: Wyatt Tee jr, Ann Patrice, Robert Charles & Earl Maurice. **Educ:** Va Union Univ, BS, magna cum laude, 1950, MDiv, summa cum laude, 1953, LHD, 1967; Va Union Univ, LHD, 1967; Rochester Theol Ctr, Omin, 1975; Edward Waters Col, Hon DD, 1985; Gettysburg Col, LittD, 1988. **Career:** Clergy (Retired); Historic Gillfield Baptist Church, Petersburg, VA, minister, 1953-60; Dr Martin Luther King Jr, chief staff; SCLC, Atlanta, vpres, bd exec dir, 1960-64; Abyssinian Baptist Church, NYC, pulpit minister, 1965-66; Cannan Baptist Church of Christ NYC, minister, CEO, 1967-2004; Church Housing Development Fund Inc, president/CEO, 1975; Governor New York, special asst urban affairs. **Orgs:** World Peace Coun, 1971-; world comnr, Programme Combat Racism World Coun Churches; chair, Consortium Cent Harlem Develop; secy gen, pres, Religious Action Network Am Comt Africa,; chair bd dir, Nat Action Network. **Honors/Awds:** Received numerous human rights awards including Elks Human Rights Award, 1963; Nat Alpha Awards Civil Rights, 1965; Shriners Nat Civil Rights Award, 1974; Civil Rights Award, ADA, 1975. **Special Achievements:** Wyatt was the first African-American to meet with Chairman Yasir Arafat since the demilitarization of the Gaza Strip and Jericho, both occurrences underscoring his involvement as an antiapartheid activist and an advocate for Palestinian self-determination; Auth: Black Church Looks at the Bicentennial, Somebody's Calling My Name, Soul of Black Worship, Road to Damascus, The Harvard paper, Soweto Diary, Del World Conf on Religion and Peace, Japan, China Diary, Common Thieves, The Harvard Paper, Soweto Diary, Occasional Papers of a Revolutionary, Spirits that Dwell in Deep Woods; Top Fifteen Greatest African American Preacher In the US, Ebony Magazine, 1993; roles in "Mama, I Wanna Sing," & "Malcolm X".

WALKER-GIBBS, SHIRLEY ANN
Basketball coach. **Personal:** Born Nov 19, 1945, Bude, MS; daughter of Bruno Gibbs and Curlee; married Lonnie R Walker, Dec 24, 1968; children: Lonnie R Jr & Marino L. **Educ:** Alcorn State Univ, BS, health & phys rec, MS, athletic adm, health & phys educ-recr. **Career:** Los Angeles Sch Dist, HPER & Sci, teacher, coach, 1968-69; HISD, HPER & Sci, teacher, 1969-72; Alcorn State Univ, senior women's adminr, head women's basketball coach, 1977-2008. **Orgs:** NCAA Coun Comt, 1990-95; NCAA Women's Basketball, 1982-86; NCAA Basketball Officiating, 1992-94; NCAA Special Event, 1992-94; NCAA Minority Opportunity & Interest, 1990-95; NCAA Midwest Reg Advisory, 1990-93; NCAA Black Coaches Asn; Delta Sigma Theta Sorority, 1970-. **Honors/Awds:** Southwestern Conference, Coach of the Year, 1983-86, 1990-94; Alpha Phi Alpha, Outstanding Service Award, 1994.

WALKER-SLOCUM, FRANCES
Educator, pianist. **Personal:** Born Mar 6, 1924, Washington, DC; daughter of George Theophilus (deceased) and Rosa King (deceased); married H Chester Slocum (deceased); children: George Jeffrey Slocum. **Educ:** Dunbar High Sch, attended 1941; Oberlin Conserv, BMus, 1945; Curtis Inst, Philadelphia, 1945-46; Columbia Univ Teachers Col, MA, 1952, prof dipl, 1971. **Career:** Pianist (Retired), educator; Barber-Scotia Col, Concord, NC, 1947-48; Tougaloo Col, Miss, 1948-49; Third St Settlement Sch, New York, piano instr, 1957-64; Lincoln Univ, Pa, 1968-72; Univ DE, 1968-69; Rutgers Univ, New Brunswick, NJ, asst prof, 1972-76; Oberlin Conser Music, vis assoc prof piano forte, 1976-80, prof, 1981-85, chmn dept, 1986-91, prof emer, 1991-. **Orgs:** Pi Kappa Lambda, 1983-85; Spec Educ Opportunities Prog, 1985-88. **Honors/Awds:** Achievement Award, Nat Asn Negro Musicians, 1979, 1985; Lorain County Women of Achievement Award, Oberlin Col, 1985; Black Heritage Award, Langston Univ, 1986; Appreciation Award, Nat Bus & Prof Womens Club, 1995; Award of Distinction, Oberlin Col, 1998; Alumni Medal, Oberlin Col, 2004. **Special Achievements:** Completed 'Albums of music' by Samuel Coleridge Taylor, William Grant Still, Wendell Logan, and many lesser know minority composers; First African American tenured professor at the Oberlin Conservatory. **Business Addr:** Professor Emeritus, Oberlin Conservatory of Music, 39 W College St, Oberlin, OH 44074-1588, **Business Phone:** (440)775-8413.

WALKER-SMITH, REV. DR. ANGELIQUE KETURAH
Clergy. **Personal:** Born Aug 18, 1958, Cleveland, OH; daughter of Roosevelt V Walker and Geneva Willis; married R Drew, Aug 16, 1980. **Educ:** Kent State Univ, Kent, OH, BA, 1980; Yale Univ, Divinity Sch, New Haven, CT, MDiv, 1983; Princeton Theol Sem, Princeton, NJ, DMin, 1995. **Career:** WFSB-CBS TV, Hartford, CT, prod asst, 1982-83; Oper Crossroads Africa, New York, NY, develop dir, leader, 1983-85; Cent Baptist Church, Hartford, CT, assoc pastor, 1983-86; TEAM, Trenton, NJ, exec minister, dir, 1986-90; Lilly Endowment, Indianapolis, IN, consult, 1990-; The Church Fedn Greater Indianapolis, IN, project dir, 1991, interim exec dir, 1993-94, exec dir, 1995-; WKIV-Channel 6/AB, Faces Faith, TV host, 1992-; Keturah Productions, founder, ceo; Odyssey Big Screen, co-host, currently. **Orgs:** Off int affairs, Partners Ecumenism, Nat Coun Churches USA, 1986-88; secy, bd dirs, Nat Asn Ecumenical Staff, 1986-89; Ecumenical Liaison, Nat Baptist Conv, USA, Inc, 1989-94; pres, Global Exchange Study Assocs, 1990-; cent comt, World Coun Churches, 1991-. **Honors/Awds:** State of New Jersey Commendation Proclamation, New Jersey State Legislature, 1990; Mayoral Commendation Proclamation, Trenton, 1990; Valiant Christian Woman's Award, Church Women United, 1990. **Business Addr:** Executive Director, The Church Federation of Greater Indianapolis, 1100 W 42nd St Suite 345, Indianapolis, IN 46208, **Business Phone:** (317)926-5371.

WALKER-THOTH, DAPHNE LAVERA
Health services administrator. **Personal:** Born Sep 16, 1954, St Louis, MO; daughter of Zelma J McNeil Carson and Sidney J Carson Jr; married Mark Walker (divorced 1980); children: Aaron Walker; married Ismail, May 17, 1986; children: Candace Thoth. **Educ:** NE Mo State, Kirksville, Mo, BA, 1977; Univ Mo, MA, 1990. **Career:** Spectrum Emergency Care, Mo, commun asst, 1982-84; Boy Scouts Am, exploring exec, 1984-85; Voluntary Interdistrict Coord Coun, asst dir, 1985-90; Mkt Works, dir client serv, 1989-90; World Difference, community coordr, 1990-91; Progressive Youth Ctr, dir community partnership, 1991-98; Mo Inst Ment Health, project dir, 1998, proj, coordr, prin investr, currently; Mo Dept Ment Health, Div Alcohol & Drug Abuse, proj mgr. **Orgs:** Bd mem, Coun & Educ Support Serv Inc, 1993-. **Honors/Awds:** Community Partnership Service Award, 1994; Marietta Stepney Memorial Award, 1998; Volunteer of the Year, Committed Caring Faith Communities, 2004; Arkansas Traveler Award, 2004; Faith Works Award, Committed Caring Faith Communities, 2004; Excellence in Community Leadership Award, Faith Communities United & Catholic AIDS Ministry, 2006. **Special Achievements:** Series of articles on the plight of the elderly, Greater St Louis Association of Black Journalists, 1979; Series of articles on the plight of children, National Newspaper Publishers Association, 1980. **Business Addr:** Principal Investigator, Missouri Institute of Mental Health, 5400 Arsenal St C307 Dome Bldg, Saint Louis, MO 63139, **Business Phone:** (314)877-6440.

WALKER WILLIAMS, HOPE DENISE
School administrator. **Personal:** Born Dec 24, 1952, Chicago, IL; daughter of Welmon Walker and Maryann Walker; children: Albert Lee & Ebony Emani Denise. **Educ:** Harvard Univ Grad Sch Design, cert, 1981; St Ambrose Univ, BA, psychol, 1985. **Career:** African Am Drama Co, midwest regional coord, 1982-83; Dramatic Mkt Asn, opers mgr, 1983-84; Scott County Davenport IA, admin intern, 1985-86; Marycrest Col Davenport, campus counr, 1986-87, asst dean & dir acad adv, 1987-90; Northern Ill Univ, acad coordr; Augustana Col, asst dean stud servs, 1990-92, asst dean studs, 1991; Chicago Bears, intern, 1998; Univ Iowa, Hawkeye Football, asst dir & coordr, 2001-05; NC State Univ, bd dir, treas, currently; Univ New Orleans, dir student athletic support serv; Univ Colo, assoc dir acad servs, 2006-. **Orgs:** Treas, Quad Cities Career Womens Network, 1983; stud senator MBA Senate StAmbrose Col, 1985; Nat Asn Black MBAs, 1986; bd mem, HELP Legal Aid, 1986; panelist, United Way Allocations, 1987; bd mem, NACADA, 1988-; mem comt, nat treas, NAWE, 1993-95. **Honors/Awds:** Certificate of Appreciation, Conf Black Families, 1979 & 82; Certificate of Recognition, Church Women United, 1983; Yellow Belt Tae Kwon Do Karate, 1984; Junior Achievement, Recognition Personal Dedication, 1989-89, Hallof Fame Inductee, 1991; Award for New Professionals, ACAFAD, 1989; Award for New Professionals. **Home Addr:** 1217 Ripley St, Davenport, IA 52803. **Business Phone:** (303)492-1411.

WALL, TARA
Politician, association executive. **Educ:** Eastern Mich Univ, BS, telecommun & film. **Career:** Mich Gov John Engler Off, asst dir, 1999-2000; Repub Nat Comt, spokeswoman, press secy outreach, 2004-05, Minority Outreach Prog, sr adv, dir commun, 2005-07; Office Pub Affairs, dir, 2007-; WWJ & WKBD-TV, "Street Beat", creator, pub affairs dir, host & exec prod. **Orgs:** Vol team leader, Bush Cheney 2000 Campaign; Faith Intl Christian Ctr. **Business Addr:** Director of Public Affairs, Administration for Children and Families, 370 L'Enfant Promenade SW, Washington, DC 20201, **Business Phone:** (202)401-9215.*

WALLACE, ADRIAN L.
President (Organization). **Career:** Alpha Phi Alpha, gen pres, 1997-00; Wash, DC, Martin Luther King Jr. Nat Memorial Proj Found Inc, dir & pres. *

WALLACE, AL (ALONZO DWIGHT WALLACE)
Football player. **Personal:** Born Mar 25, 1974, Delray Beach, FL; son of Andrew; married Shelley. **Educ:** Univ Md, BS, health educ. **Career:** Jacksonville Jaguars, Off season/practice member, 1997; Philadelphia Eagles, defensive end, 1997-99; Chicago Bears, 2000; Miami Dolphins, practice/squad member, 2002; Carolina Panthers, defensive end, 2002-06; Buffalo Bills, defensive end, 2007; free agent, currently.

WALLACE, ARTHUR, JR.
School administrator, executive. **Personal:** Born Jun 12, 1939, Muskogee, OK; son of Arthur and Edna Collins; married Claudina Young, Oct 4, 1969; children: Dwayne, Jon & Charles. **Educ:** Langston Univ, Langston, OK, BS, 1960; Okla State Univ, Stillwater, OK, MS, 1962, PhD, 1964. **Career:** Gen Foods Corp, White Plains, NY, dir commodity res, 1964-67; Merrill Lynch, New York, NY, vpres & sr economist, 1967-71; Group IV Econ, New York, NY, sr partner, 1971-76; Int Paper, Purchase, NY, vpres & corp secy, 1976-; San Francisco State Univ, Sch Bus, dean, 1993-, prof mgt, currently. **Orgs:** Nat Adv Bd, US Dept Com, 1973-74; Adv Bd, Columbia Univ Workplace Ctr, 1985-89; Adv Bd, Scarsdale Day Care Ctr, 1985-88; trustee, Am Mgt Asn, 1982-84 & 1987-90; Am Econ Asn; Nat Asn Bus Economists; dir, San Franciso Convention & Vishes Bur; Romberg Tibron Res Ctr. **Home Addr:** 1085 Greenwich Suite 1, San Francisco, CA 94133. **Business Addr:** Dean, Professor of Management, San Francisco State University, Management Department, 1600 Holloway Ave, San Francisco, CA 94132-1722, **Business Phone:** (415)338-2138.

WALLACE, BEN
Basketball player. **Personal:** Born Sep 10, 1974, White Hall, AL; married Chanda Wallace, Jan 1, 2001; children: 2. **Educ:** Va Union Univ. **Career:** Wash Wizards, forward, 1996-99; Orlando Magic, 1999-2000; Detroit Pistons, 2000-06; Chicago Bulls, ctr, 2006-08; Cleveland Cavaliers, ctr, 2008-. **Honors/Awds:** NBA Defensive Player of the Year Award, 2001-02, 2002-03, 2004-05 & 2005-06. **Special Achievements:** Only player in NBA history to record 1,000 rebounds, 100 blocks, and 100 steals in 4 consecutive seasons (2001-04). **Business Addr:** Professional Basketball

Player, Cleveland Cavaliers, Quicken Loans Arena - The Q, 1 Ctr Ct, Cleveland, OH 44115, **Business Phone:** (216)420-2000.

WALLACE, C. EVERETT
Lawyer, government official, executive director. **Personal:** Born Aug 16, 1951, Chicago, IL. **Educ:** Northwestern Univ, BA, 1973, JD, taxation & corp law, 1976; Univ Chicago Sch Law, LLM. **Career:** Clausen Miller & Gorman Caffery & Witous Law Firm, res assoc, 1975-76; Memphis Light Gas & Water Div, Memphis, staff atty, 1976-77; Sen Howard Baker, US Sen, legal asst, 1977-80; Shelby County Black Rep Coun, legal coun & co-founder, 1977; Progressive Assembly Reps, gen coun & co-founder, 1979; US Senate, Budget Comn, sr anal & energy counr, 1980, sr legis asst, Dept Health & Human Serv, chief of staff; Dept Housing & Urban Develop, gen dep asst secy; Wallace Enterprise Int, pres; Nat Minority Franchising Inst, dir, currently. **Orgs:** Bar Tenn, 1977; vice chmn & co-founder, Black Rep Cong Staffer's Asn, 1979; coun secy, Republican Nat Conv; Nat Bar Asn; Am Bar Asn; pres, Alpha Mu Chap, Alpha Phi Alpha Frat Inc. **Honors/Awds:** Top Ten Debator, Northwestern Univ Ill State Contest; Nat Achievement Scholar, Thornton Township High Sch, Harvey, IL; Nat Merit Scholar; Ill State Scholar; Honors Grad, Northwestern Univ Sch Law. **Business Addr:** Director, National Minority Franchising Institute, Washington, DC.

WALLACE, CHARLES LESLIE
Real estate executive, chief financial officer, vice president (organization). **Personal:** Born Dec 26, 1945, Monmouth, IL; son of Harriet and Leslie; married Marie Elizabeth Lancaster, Jun 24, 1967; children: Allison & Bryan. **Educ:** Northern Ill Univ, BS, acct, 1967; Univ Chicago, MBA, finance, 1973; CPA, 1973. **Career:** Arthur Andersen & Co, auditor, 1967-74; Jos Schultz Brewing Co, financial analyst, 1974-76; Univ Foods Corp, treas, 1976-81; Pabst Brewing Co, treas, 1981-85; Norrell Corp, treas, 1985-87; N Milwaukee State Bank,pres, 1987-89; Ameritech Mobile Commun Inc, vpres finance & admin, 1989-94; Grucon Corp, vpres, chief financial officer, 1991-94; Steel tech Manufacturing Inc, chair & chief exec officer, 1994-2000; Baird & Warner, sr vpres & chief financial officer, 2001. **Orgs:** Finance Executives Inst, Chicago Chap; Am Inst of CPA's; Kappa Alpha Psi; Sigma Pi Phi. **Honors/Awds:** Black Excellence Award, The Milwaukee Times, 1989; Outstanding Accounting Alumnus, Northern Ill Univ, 1991; Outstanding College of Business Alumnus, Northern Ill Univ, 1995. **Military Serv:** USMC, First lt, 1967-72.

WALLACE, DERRICK D.
Executive, business owner, president (organization). **Personal:** Born Nov 4, 1953, Orlando, FL; son of Theressa Williams; married 2000; children: Daunte & Deja. **Educ:** Fla A&M Univ, BS, acct, 1975. **Career:** Price Waterhouse & Co, CPA, staff acct, 1975-77; Tuttle/White Constructors Inc, chief acct, 1977-79; Construct Two Group, owner, pres & chief exec officer, 1990-. **Orgs:** Bd mem, Cent State Asn Minority Contr; Greater Orlando Chamber Com, 1984; class mem, Leadership Orlando, 1988; bd mem, Greater Orlando Chamber Com, 1989; past chmn, Pvt Indust Coun Cent Fla; comnr, Mayor's Comn Arts; sub comt chair, Mayor's Youth Comn (bus involvement); Greater Fla Minority Purchasing Coun; partner, Partners Educ-Wash Shores Elem; partner, Partners Educ-Rock Lake Elem; sponsored minority (Black) Role Model Proj Orange County Schs, Pvt Indust Coun Chmn; bd mem, Orlando/Ore County Compact, 1990-91; bd mem, Additions, 1990-91; bd dirs, Econ Develo CMS Mid-Florida; Nat Asn Minority Contractors, past bd of dirs; founder, 100 Black Men of Orlando Inc; bd mem, Cent Fla Jobs Educ Partnership; bd dirs, Goodwill Industries; Cent Fla Fair, past bd of dirs; past chair, Mayor's Martin Luther King Comn; Minority/Women Bus Enterprise Alliance Inc; founding trustee, Bus Better Educ. **Honors/Awds:** Construction Firm of the Year, US Dept Com Minority Bus Develop Agency, 1984; Outstanding Young Man of America, 1986; Outstanding Achievement as Minority Business Entrepreneur, Cent Fla Minority Develop Coun Inc, 1988; Entrepreneur of the year GFMPL; Up Comer Award, Orlando Bus Jour & Price Water house, 1989; Walt Disney World Community Service Award Committee, 1991; Greater Orlando Chamber Comm "Top 25 Small Business" Award, 1997, 1998; "Florida 100" Award, Univ Fla, 1997 & 1998; Downtown Orlando Partnership "Mentorship" Award, 1995 & 1997; Drum Major Award for Business, Alpha Phi Alpha Frat Inc, 1993; African Am Chamber of Com, "Construction Co of the Year" Award, 1997; Inc Magazine Inc 500 list; Small Business Person of the Year, North Fla SBA Dist, 1998; Jim Moran Inst Entrepreneurial Excellence Award, Fla State Univ, 1998; Outstanding Performance Award, Black Bus Investment Fund, 1999; Distinguished Leadership Alumni Awd, Orlando Regional Coun, 2001; Regional Supplier of the Yr, Nat MNY Supplier Diversity Coun, 2001. **Business Addr:** Owner & President, Chief Executive Officer, Construct Two Group, 30 S Ivey Lane, Orlando, FL 32811-4222, **Business Phone:** (407)295-9812.

WALLACE, GEORGE E
Manager. **Career:** Hampton City, city mgr. **Business Addr:** City Manager, City of Hampton, 22 Lincoln St, City Hall 8th Fl, Hampton, VA 23669-3522, **Business Phone:** (757)727-6392.

WALLACE, HAROLD GENE
School administrator. **Personal:** Born Aug 13, 1945, Gaffney, SC; son of Charles T Wallace Sr (deceased) and Melinda Goudelock Wallace; married Carrie Lucinda Littlejohn, Jul 13, 1963; children: Toya Bonita, Shonda Lee, Harold Gene Jr & Charles Marion. **Educ:** Claflin Col, Orangeburg, SC, BS (summa cum laude), 1967; Duke Univ Div Sch, Durham, NC, MDiv, 1971. **Career:** School administrator (retired); Bethesda Presbyterian Church, Gaffney, SC, pastor & youth counr, 1968; Durham Comm House, counr, 1968-69; Duke Univ, Summer Transitional Prog, asst dir, 1969, asst dean undergrad educ, stud adv, 1969-72, assoc dir, 1970, co-dir, 1971, dir, 1972, asst provost, dean black stud affairs, interim dir comm & field work Afro-Am majors & sem instr Afro-Am studies, 1972-73; Univ NC, Chapel Hill, assoc dean stud affairs & dir dept spec progs, 1973-79, asst vice chancellor stud affairs, 1979-80, vice chancellor univ affairs, 1980-96, spec asst minority affairs, 1996-99. **Orgs:** Pres, Alpha Kappa Mu Nat & Honor Soc Claflin Col, 1966-67; Rockefeller fel, Duke Univ, 1967; group moderator, Regional Educ Bd Conf Black Stud & Univ, 1971; Nat Comn United Ministers Higher Educ, 1971-75; consult, Minority Stud Progs, Univ SC Furman & Wake Forest, 1971-78; secy & treas, Black Fac Staff Caucus, Univ NC Chapel Hill, 1974-80, chair person, 1987-90; bd dir, Wesley Found Campus Ministry, Univ NC, 1976-80; Inst Study Minority Issues, NC Cent Univ, 1977-; chairperson, Upward Bound Adv Bd, Univ NC, 1980-; chairperson, Black Culture Ctr Adv Bd Univ NC, 1990-; chair emer, Sonja Haynes Stone Black Culture Ctr, UNC-Chapel Hill. **Honors/Awds:** Faculty Awards, Black Stud Movement, Univ NC Chapel Hill, 1981, Univ NC Black Alumni Asn, 1982; Martin Luther King Jr Award, South Orange Black Caucus, Chapel Hill, NC, 1988; Award of Commitment to Justice and Equality, Butner NC Nat Asn Advan Colored People, 1989. **Special Achievements:** Published "Studies in Black" 1969, "Three Years of the Duke Summer Transitional Program" 1973.

WALLACE, HELEN WINFREE-PEYTON
School administrator, elementary school teacher. **Personal:** Born Dec 19, 1927, New York, NY; daughter of Hugh and Agnes; married Mr Walter (divorced); children: Walter S Peyton IV. **Educ:** Va Union Univ, BA, 1949, 1959; Northwestern Univ, MA, 1955; Univ Calif, Va State Univ, VCU, Univ Caltolica, Di Milano Italy, 1968. **Career:** School administrator (retired); Richmond Pub Sch, teacher, 1949-69, langarts consult, 1969-71, diag & prescriptive reading, coordr, 1971-75; Richmond Pub Sch, Chap I reading coordr, 1975. **Orgs:** Crusade for Voters, 1949; Nat Educ Asn, 1950; vpres, Richmond Educ Asn, 1950; consult, Comm Groups, 1975-83; pres, Elem Teachers Asn, 1967; vpres, Asn Classroom Teachers, 1973; Exec Bd Nat Asn Advan Colored People, IRA-RARC-VSRA; historian, Continental Soc, 1976-91; reading supvr, Chap I, 1979-93; pres, Richmond Chap, Continentals Inc, 2000-03. **Honors/Awds:** Teacher First Black to integrate Westhampton Sch, 1965-69; exec serv Chap I Reading Teacher, 1982; achievements Alliance for Black Social Welfare, 1983; co-sponsored Book Bowl. **Home Addr:** 8222 Whistler Rd, Richmond, VA 23227. *

WALLACE, DR. JEFFREY J.
School administrator. **Personal:** Born Apr 7, 1946, Mobile, AL; married Patricia A Henderson; children: Jeffrey, Jennifer, Justin & Jawaan. **Educ:** State Univ Col, Fredonia, BA, hist, 1968; State Univ NY, Buffalo, MEd, 1973, PhD, hist & philos educ, 1980. **Career:** State Univ NY, Fredonia, admin asst admis & rec, 1969-72, dir EOP, 1972-81, asst vpres acad affairs, 1977-81; State Univ Col, Buffalo, dir EOP, 1981-86, asst vpres acad affairs, 1986-. **Orgs:** State Univ NY Chancellors' Taskforce Minority Grad Opportunity, 1983; Nat Asn Acad Adv, 1984; bd chairperson, Buffalo Post-Secondary Consortium Special Progs, 1985; pres, Special Prog Personnel Asn, 1984-; evaluator/edconsult, PNJ Consult.

WALLACE, JOHN
Basketball player, television show host. **Personal:** Born Feb 9, 1974, Rochester, NY; married; children: John Jr & Joseph. **Educ:** Syracuse Univ, sociol. **Career:** Basketball player (retired); NY Knicks, forward, 1996-97; Toronto Raptors, 1997-99; NY Knicks, 1999-2000; Detroit Pistons, 2000-01; Phoenix Suns, 2001-02; Miami Heat, forward, 2003-04; Snaidero Udine, Italy, forward, 2005-06; Knicks C's Aid Soc Christmas, co-host. **Honors/Awds:** Sears Community Service Award, 1997-98. **Special Achievements:** NBA Draft, First round pick, No 18, 1996; appeared in the film He Got Game, 1998.

WALLACE, JOHN A.
Executive. **Educ:** Univ Pac, BA, pol sci, survey method & statistics. **Career:** Manugistics, vpres; Talus Solutions; Aeronomics, Inc; Axcicom, travel & hosp prac; Rainmaker Inc, vpres bus consulting, 2008-. *

WALLACE, JOHN M., JR.
Educator. **Educ:** Univ Chicago, BA, sociol; Univ Mich, MA, sociol, PhD, sociol. **Career:** Univ Pittsburgh, assoc prof, 2004-, Skillman Foundation grant, prininvestr, currently.

WALLACE, LINDA SKYE
Chief executive officer, executive. **Personal:** Born Nov 14, 1958, Akron, OH; daughter of William and Helen M Bell (deceased); divorced; children: Tamika Rachelle Dryden. **Educ:** Southern Ohio Col, assoc, 1985; Ohio Sch Broadcasting, dipl, 1987; Oglethorpe Univ. **Career:** Rick Angelo Commun, pres, 1989-98; Tamika Rachelle Life Enhancement Ctr Women, founder, 1997; Markara Lachelle Sch Performing Arts, founder, 1998. **Orgs:** Vol coord, Newbirth Inner City Life Ctr, 1999; Ohio Black Women Leadership Caucus, 1988. **Honors/Awds:** African American Women Excellent, YWCA, 1995; Governor Zell Miller Ga, Proclamation, 1998. **Special Achievements:** The Ultimate Payback, screenplay, 1997.

WALLACE, MILTON DE
School administrator, school principal. **Personal:** Born Jul 7, 1957, Tyler, TX; son of John and Thelma Jackson; married Gwendolyn, Apr 8, 1989. **Educ:** E Tex State Univ, BS, 1978, MEd, 1979; Univ N Tex, Denton, TX l988. **Career:** Com ISD, teacher, 1978-83, asst prin, 1983-84; Union Hill ISD, prin, 1984-87; Denton Independent Sch Dist, Denton, asst prin, 1987-90, head prin, 1990-2007; Longview High Sch, principal, 2007-. **Orgs:** Pres, RAWSCO Inc, 1983; vpres, Prof Mens Serv Club, 1983-84; Tex Asn Elem Sch Prins, 1983; owner M & L Educ Scholar Serv; Tex Asn Black Sch Educrs, 1989-; Tex Asn Secondary Sch Prin, 1984-95; Dir Summer Workshop, Tex Asn Stud Coun, 1989, 1990; Denton Adminrs Asn, 1987-95, vpres, 1991, 1993, pres, 1994-95; Nat Asn Secondary Sch Prin, 1991-95. **Honors/Awds:** Principal of Year, Tex Asn Secondary Sch Prin, 1990. **Home Addr:** PO Box 2843, Denton, TX 76202. **Business Addr:** Principal, Longview High School, 201 E Tomlinson Pkwy, Longview, TX 75605, **Business Phone:** (903)663-1301.

WALLACE, PAUL STARETT
Lawyer. **Personal:** Born Jan 22, 1941, Wilmington, NC; son of Paul and Mary Ligon; married Priscilla H Harris; children: Shaunia Patrese. **Educ:** NC Cent Univ, BS, 1962, JD, 1966. **Career:** US Copyright Off Libr Cong, copyright examr, 1966-71; Congional Res Serv, Libr Cong, former Sr legis atty, head Cong section, Am law div, 1984-86, coord multidis progs, 1986-96; Am Pub Law, Am Law Div, specialist 1996-; Libr Congress, Am Law Div, specialist 1996-. **Orgs:** Adv bd, Comn Action Human Serv Inc, 1983-; Fed Bar Asn News & Jour, 1980-81; secy, Coun Crct; vpres, Fed Bar Asn, 1981-82; pres, Capitol Hill Chap Fed Bar Asn, 1979-80; adv bd mem, Fed Bar News & Jour, 1980-82; nat vpres, DC Circuit Fed Bar Asn, 1981-82; chairperson, co-chair, Fed Bar Asn, Nat Mem Comt, 1982-83; Sect Admin Justice, 1984-89; Dist Columbia Bar Asn, US Supreme Court; continuing educ bd, Fed Bar Asn, 1985-; vice-chairperson, Libr Cong US Savings Bond Campaign, 1985; Omega Psi Phi, US Dist Ct for DC; US Court Appeals DC Circuit; ed, Fed Bar Asn News & Jour, 1984, 1986; US Dist Ct 8th Circuit, Phiha Delta Law Fraternity Int;, Nat & Am Bar Assoc; 33 Degree Mason; chairperson continuing educ bd, Fed Bar Asn, 1987-89; bd trustees, Peoples Congregational Church, 1985-90; church coun, Peoples Congregational Church, 1990-; bd dirs, Found Fed Bar Asn, 1991-; advisor, Found Fed Bar Asn, 1991; chmn, Diaconate Bd, Peoples Congregational Church, 1993-95; chmn, Church Coun, Peoples Congregational Church, 1996-2002; treasr, Found Fed Bar Asn, 1993-2002, dir emer, currently. **Honors/Awds:** Commendation Award Outstanding Qualities of Leadership & Dedicated Service, 1980; Distinguished Service Award, 1984; Federation Bar Asnation Longstanding & Dedicated Service Award, 1986; Scroll of Honor, Omega Psi Phi Fraternity, Alpha Omega Chap, 1991; Charter Life Fel, Found Fed Bar Asn, 2002. **Home Addr:** 3271 Van Hazen St NW, Washington, DC 20015. **Business Phone:** (202)707-7923.

WALLACE, PEGGY MASON
Government official. **Personal:** Born Sep 5, 1948, Salisbury, MD; daughter of Rayfield J Mason Sr (deceased) and Hattie A Mason (deceased); married Joseph R, Sep 15, 1979; children: Shawn. **Educ:** Morgan State Univ, BS, 1970; Univ Ill, MA, 1971. **Career:** Bell Lab, tech staff, 1972-75; Calculon Consult Firm, Syst analyst, trainer, 1975-81; Dept Navy, mgt info Systs, mgr, 1981-96, Mgt Info & Support Serv, head, 1996-. **Orgs:** Pres, Alpha Kappa Mu Hon Soc, 1967-70; charter mem, pres, Math Club, 1970; Fed Women's Prog, 1982-83; Dept Navy's Tutoring Prog, 1985-. **Honors/Awds:** Meritious Civilian Service Award, USN Strategic Syst Prog, 1990; four-year Scholar, Morgan State Univ, 1966; one-year Scholar, Univ Ill, 1971; numerous others. **Business Addr:** Manager, Management Information Systems & Support Services Branch, Strategic Systems Programs Department of Navy, 3801 Nebraska Ave NW, Washington, DC 20393-5446.

WALLACE, RASHEED ABDUL
Basketball player. **Personal:** Born Sep 17, 1974, Philadelphia, PA; son of Jackie and Sam Tabb; married Fatima; children: Ishmiel Shaeed, Malik, Nazir & Rashiyah. **Educ:** NC State Univ. **Career:** Washington Bullets, ctr-forward, 1995-96; Portland TrailBlazers,ctr-forward, 1996-2003; Atlanta Hawks, ctr-forward, 2003-04; Detroit Pistons, power forward, 2004-09; Boston Celtics, 2009-. **Orgs:** Founder, Stand Tall Sheed Found. **Special Achievements:** Launched record label, ULM (Urban Life Music), 2000. **Business Addr:** Professional Basketball Player, Boston Celtics, Fourth Fl 226 Causeway St, Boston, MA 02114.

WALLACE, DR. RENEE C
Psychologist, educator. **Personal:** Born in New Britain, CT; daughter of Elmo Sr and Chaudette J; widowed; children: Love &

Lovely. **Educ:** Cent Conn State Univ, BA, 1974; Univ IA, MA, 1975, PhD, 1977. **Career:** Univ Iowa, admin asst, 1974-77; Morgan State Univ, admin asst prof, 1977-79; Clayton Univ, adj fac, 1979-; James Madison Univ, coun psychologist, 1980-84; Wallace & Wallace Assocs, dir, 1980-; SUNY Potsdam, dir coun, 1984; Dept Corrections, adminr, 1986, prin, 1986-89; Cent Conn State Univ, New Britain, asst prof, 1989-; Fl A&M Univ, assoc prof, currently. **Orgs:** Secy, Phi Delta Kappa 1979; consult, Southern Asn Col & Sch, 1981, 1984; educ consult, Black Educ Res & Inf Ctr 1984; bd dirs, Nat Comm Educ Youth Energy. **Special Achievements:** Publications "prospective teachers' responses on an adjective checklist to descriptions of 3 students in 3 different socioeconomic classes," us govt, 1978; "black administrators & career stress," proceedings of the 8th nat conf on blacks in higher educ, 1983; "the ingredients of an idea: creativity in counseling," morgan bulletin, 1979; freshman guide & workbook morgan state univ, 1978; "developmental study skills program for student athletes," state dept educ vir, tech asst div, richmond vir, 1982; "the dynamic of career stress in black professional adms on white campuses," james madison univ review, harrisonburg, vir, 1982; "effects of teaching stress reducation coping techniques in the prevention of academic underachievement," proceedings of the 16th nat cnf of blacks in higher education, 1991; "biofeedback, biodots and stress: a technique for improving student academic performance," proceedings of the 16th nat conf black in higher edu, 1991, "mental skills training program for men's collegiate basketball players," research at central con state univ, 1992. **Home Addr:** 3308 Forest Redge Dr, Albany, GA 31707-1508. **Business Addr:** Associate Professor, Florida Agricultural And Mechanical University, College Of Education, 201 GEC B, Tallahassee, FL 32307, **Business Phone:** (850)599-3846.

WALLACE, RICHARD WARNER
Engineer. **Personal:** Born Nov 6, 1929, Gary, IN; son of Othello and Ruth; married Lillian Mozel. **Educ:** Purdue Univ, BS, 1951; George Washington Univ, Am Univ Wash DC, post grad studies. **Career:** Engineer (retired); USN Naval Sea Systs Command, designer devel & testing elec, electronic systs ships & submarines, 1951, mgt tech & logistics support navy's deep submergence vehicle progs, & nuclear powered submarine NR 1, 1951-85, TRW Systs Integration Group, asst proj mgr, 1985-94. **Orgs:** Life mem, Nat Soc Prof Engrs; bd dirs, Potomac Chap, Md Soc Prof Engrs; Am Soc Naval Engrs; Naval Submarine League; Marine Tech Soc; Amateur Radio; Astron; Photography; life mem, Alpha Phi Alpha; charter mem, Beta Mu Boule, Sigma Pi Phi; The Guardsmen, Wash DC Chap; registered prof engr, Wash DC, 1958-. **Honors/Awds:** Navy Meritorious Civilian Serv Award, 1974; Navy Group Achievment Award, 1972; Superior Civilian Serv Award, Dept Navy, 1985. **Military Serv:** AUS, sgnl corp, 1955-57. **Home Addr:** 30 Norwood Rd, Silver Spring, MD 20905. *

WALLACE, RICK. See WALLACE, RITCHIE RAY.

WALLACE, RITCHIE RAY (RICK WALLACE)
Executive. **Personal:** Born Mar 9, 1955, Hastings, NE; son of Andrew and Laura E; married Kenetta Brown; children: Joshua, Eboni & Ritchie II. **Educ:** Kearney State Col, BA, 1979. **Career:** Wallace Consulting Inc, pres, 1979-; Community Develop Resources, exec dir, currently. **Orgs:** Bd, Cot Bus Asn NEB, 1989-; life-time mem, NCP, 1989-; bd, Cornhusker Bank, 1991-94; Asn Gen Contractors, 1991-92; treas, Newman United Methodist Church, 1992; Newman United Methodist Church, Ethnic Local Church Comt, 1992-; econ develop consultant, City Lincoln Mayor's Off; pres, Lincoln Br Nat Am Advan Colored People, 1992-97; vpres, Nat Am Advan Colored People, 1994-. **Honors/Awds:** Business of the Year, Nebr Dept Roads, 1987; Business Recognition Award, City Lincoln, 1991. **Special Achievements:** Articles published in Omaha World Herald, May 5, 1990; Lincoln Journal, Jan 27, Feb 25, 1991. **Home Addr:** 3737 Mohawk St, Lincoln, NE 68510. **Business Addr:** Executive Director, Community Development Resources, 285 S 68th St Pl Suite 520, Lincoln, NE 68510, **Business Phone:** (402)436-2386.

WALLACE, RUBY ANN. See DEE, RUBY.

WALLACE, STEVE
Football player. **Personal:** Born Dec 27, 1964, Chamblee, GA; married; children: Steven. **Educ:** Auburn Univ. **Career:** Football player (retired); Birmingham Stallions, 1986; San Francisco49ers, tackle, 1986-96; Kans City Chiefs, 1997. **Honors/Awds:** Pro Bowl honours, 1992; Bobb Mckittrick Award, 1988.

WALLACE, THOMAS ALBERT
Counselor. **Personal:** Born Jan 31, 1954, Williamsburg, VA; son of William and Virginia Wallace; married Bettie L, Aug 8, 1991; children: Thomas Jr, Melissa & Christina. **Educ:** George Mason Univ, BS, 1980; Bowie State Univ, MA, 1991. **Career:** Lutheran Ministries GA, prog mgr, 1997-98; Savannah State Univ, stud affairs counr, 1998-. **Orgs:** Nat Orgn for Stud Affairs Profs, 1998; ACPA, 1998; Nat Orgn Am Disability Coordrs, 1998; GCPA, 1999. **Honors/Awds:** Emmy nominee: 1995, 1996, 1998. **Military Serv:** AUS, 1972-97; Meritorious Service Medal, 1997; Good Conduct Medal, 1997. **Home Addr:** 4 Watermill Ct, Savannah, GA 31419. **Business Addr:** Student Affairs Counselor, Savannah State University, 3219 College St King Frazier Stud Complex Rm 233, PO Box 20521, Savannah, GA 31404, **Business Phone:** (912)356-2202.

WALLACE-BENJAMIN, JOAN
Consultant, chief executive officer. **Educ:** Wellesley Col, BA, Psychol, 1975; Brandeis Univ, Heller Sch, PhD, Social Policy & Mgt, 1980; Univ Mass, Amherst, hon doctoral degree. **Career:** Boys & Girls Clubs of Boston, dir oper; ABCD Head Start, dep dir; ABT Assocs, res analyst; The Urban League of Mass, pres & chief exec officer, 1989-00; Whitehead Mann, consult. **Orgs:** Pres & chief exec officer, The Home Little Wanderers, 2003-. **Honors/Awds:** Lady Baden-Powel Good Scout Award, Boston Minuteman Coun, Boy Scouts Am, 2003; Lifetime Achievement Award, Rosie's Pl Boston, 2003; 100 Women of Power, Boston Mag, 2003; Academy of Women Achiever's Award, Boston YWCA, 2002; Humanitarian Award, Nat Conf Community & Justice; African American Achievement Award in Community Serv, Mayor Menino; 25th Anniversary Child Care Award, Family Day Care Prog Inc. **Business Addr:** President, Chief Execuitng Officer, The Home for Little Wanderers, 271 Huntington Ave, Boston, MA 02115, **Business Phone:** (617)267-3700.

WALLER, REV. DR. ALYN ERRICK
Clergy. **Personal:** Born Aug 8, 1964, Cleveland, OH; son of Alfred M and Belva J Walker; married Ellyn Jo, Jun 17, 1989; children: Ellynn Morgan & ErKya Lynn. **Educ:** Ohio Univ, BMus, 1987; Southern Baptist Theol Sem, MDiv, 1990; Eastern Theol Baptist Sem, PhD, 1998. **Career:** Army Nat Guard, chaplain asst, 1982-98; Simmons Bible Col, instr, psychol music, 1989-90; Canaan Missionary Baptist Church, music minister; First Baptist Church, pastor, 1990-94; Enon Tabernacle Baptist Church, pastor, 1994, sr pastro, currently; Christian Urban Theological, seminary teacher, 1999; Alyn Waller Ministries. **Orgs:** Penn Conv, 1987-; Nat Baptist Conv USA Inc, 1987-; Lott Carey Foreign Mission Conv, 1987-; Allegheny Union Baptist Asn, 1987-90; Pittsburgh Minister's Conf, 1987-90; vpres, Monongahela Balley Nat Asn Advan Colored People, 1988-90; Monoghela Valley Drug & Alcohol Task Force, 1988-90; bd dir, Philadelphia Baptist Asn, 1999-. **Honors/Awds:** Men of the Year, Penn State Baptist Conv, 1996; Outstanding Young Men of America, 1988; Distinguished Leadership Award, Men Making a Difference, 2000; GEGI Music Award, 2000. **Military Serv:** Army Nat Guard, 1982-88. **Business Addr:** Senior Pastor, Enon Tabernacle Baptist Church, 230 W Coulter St, Philadelphia, PA 19144, **Business Phone:** (215)276-7200.

WALLER, EUNICE MCLEAN
Educator. **Personal:** Born Jun 29, 1921, Lillington, NC; daughter of Absalom and Mary Tucker; married William DeHomer, Aug 9, 1958; children: Deborah & Kenneth. **Educ:** Fayetteville State Univ, BS (highest honors), 1942; Univ Pa, MS, 1952; NC Central Univ, psychol attended 1954; Univ Vt, math attended 1963. **Career:** Educator (retired); Harnett HS, teacher, 1942-46; Shawtown HS, teacher, 1947-55; Fayetteville Univ, teacher, 1955-56; Sarah Nance Elem Sch, teacher, 1956-58; Eiton Elem Sch, teacher, 1958-60; Connecticut Col, instr, 1965-71; Clark Lane Jr High, teacher, 1961-93. **Orgs:** Pres, NCNW, New London section; AAUW, Delta Kappa Gamma; trustee, Waterford Country Sch; pres, Waterford Educ Asn, 1965-66, treas, 1969-75; pres, Dr Martin Luther King Trust Fund, 1969-84; pres bd dirs, Child Guidance Clinic, 1976-78; NEA; dir, Connecticut Educ Asn, 1979-82; corporator, Lawrence Memorial Hosp, 1975-92; trustee, Mitchell Col, 1975-; trustee, Connecticut Col, 1988-89; mayor, City New London, 1988-89; city counr, City New London, 1987-89; trustee, Southern CON Easter Seals Rehabilitation Ctr; chairperson, NCP, New London Chapter, polit action; pres, New England Asn Black Ed; Shiloh Baptist Church; trustee, Dr. Martin Luther King Memorial Scholar Trust Fund; bd dirs, New London Develop Corp. **Honors/Awds:** Dr. EE Smith Memorial Award, Fayetteville Univ, 1942; Nat Sc Fel, Univ Vermont, 1963; Human Relations Award, Connecticut Educ Asn, 1980; OIC Comm Serv Award, New London, 1982; NAACP McNair Award for Political Involvement, 1984. **Home Addr:** 337 Vauxhall St, New London, CT 06320-3837, **Home Phone:** (860)443-1012.

WALLER, LARRY
Entrepreneur, contractor. **Personal:** Born Jun 9, 1947, Chicago, IL; son of Willis and Hulena Hubbard; married Ruby L. Waller, Dec 24, 1969; children: Kelly D. Waller. **Educ:** Malcolm X Col, Chicago, IL, AA 1974; Gov State Univ, Park Forest S, IL, BS, 1978, MBA, 1979. **Career:** Assoc with Fullerton Mech Contractors, Elk Grove Village, IL, 1969-76; Dyd Construction, Phoenix, IL, supt, 1977-79; Pyramid Industs Inc, Riverdale, IL, pres, 1979-. **Orgs:** Dir, Black Contractors United, 1979-; Nat Asn Independent Bus, 1979-, Asn Energy Engrs, 1984-, Builders Asn Chicago, 1984-; founder & dir, Black Mech Contractors Asn, 1983-; original founding comn, Ben Wilson Found, 1985-; comt mem, Black Musicians Hall of Fame, 1986-87, Little Ciy Found, 1986-. **Honors/Awds:** Copyright on seminar material, "Wisdom," 1989. **Special Achievements:** Became first black company to install elevators in the US, 1987. **Military Serv:** USAF, E-4, 1965-69, honorable discharge. *

WALLER, LOUIS E. See Obituaries section.

WALLER SHOCKLEY, LINDA
Administrator. **Educ:** Univ Bridgeport, BA, journ. **Career:** Gannett Co, reporter, news ed, bur chief & city ed; Lawnside Historical Soc Inc, pres, currently; Dow Jones Newspaper Fund, dep dir, 1988-. **Orgs:** Trustee, Lawnside Historical Soc Inc; bd mem, Dow Jones & Co Inc; chair, Minority Affairs Comt, Gannett Co. **Honors/Awds:** 'Community Service Award', Nat Asn Black Journalists, 2007. **Business Addr:** Deputy Director, Dow Jones Newspaper Fund, PO Box 300, Princeton, NJ 08543-0300, **Business Phone:** (609)520-5929.

WALLICK, ERNEST HERRON
State government official. **Personal:** Born Jan 15, 1928, Huntingdon, TN; married Jean Ellen Allen; children: Claudia Marie Barkley & John Herron. **Educ:** Tenn A&I State Univ, BS, 1950; Mich State Univ, MS, 1955. **Career:** Carroll County Bd Educ, high sch voc educ instr, 1950-51; Mich Wayne County, Dept Soc Servs, pub welfare worker, 1955-58, spec investr, 1958-64, asst supv personnel, 1964-65, supv off mgt, 1965-66, supv mgt planning, 1966-67; Mich Dept Civil Servs, dir spec progs, 1967-72, dir spec & regional serv div, 1972-75, dir bur selection, 1975-82, chief dep dir, 1982-96. **Orgs:** Lansing Community Col Social Work Curric Adv Comt, 1970-75; State Voc Rehab Adv Coun, 1973-80; Gov's Mich Equal Employ Opportunity Coun, 1975-82; Trinity AME Bd Trustees, 1978-; mem & treas, Alpha Chi Boule Sigma Pi Phi Frat 1982-; Mich Correctional Officer's Training Coun, 1982-, Gov's Mich Equal Employ & Bus Opportunity Coun, 1983-; bd trustees, Alpha Phi Alpha Frat, 1985-; pres, Nat Inst Employ Equity, 1985-; Nat Urban League; Nat Asn Advan Colored People; Phi Beta Kappa Honor Soc. **Honors/Awds:** Outstanding Public Serv & Achievements, Mich Civil Serv Selection Syst, Mich Senate Concurrent Resolution, 1979; Mayor's Proclamation Outstanding Public Serv EEO & Personnel Admin Detroit MI 1979. **Military Serv:** AUS, staff sgt, 1951-53. **Home Addr:** 1400 Wellington Rd, Lansing, MI 48910.

WALLS, FREDRIC T
Clergy. **Personal:** Born Oct 28, 1935, Denver, CO; married Delorez Louise; children: Fredric T, II, Agu Odinga-Ivan & Malaika Annina-Emma Delorez Louisa. **Educ:** Los Angeles City Col, AA, 1957; Knoxville Col, BA, 1963; Princeton Theol Sem, MDiv, 1963; Union Grad Sch, PhD, 1979; Urban Training Inst, Chicago, cert Univ Tenn. **Career:** Clergy (Retired); Westminister Neighborhood Asn, organiser, 1960; Good Shepherd-Faith, Broadway & Sound View Presby Church, stud asst pastor, 1960-63; Bel-Vue Presby Church, LA, supply asst pastor, 1964-65; Knoxville Col, assoc dean students, 1965-68, dir Upward Bound, 1967-68; Univ Presby Church, minister, 1968-69; Houston Urban Univ, pastor, 1969-80; Univ Houston, chmn dept religious activities, 1974-; Danforth-Underwood fel, 1976-77; Self-Development People Presby Church, USA, dir. **Orgs:** Pres sr class, JCFremont Sr High Sch, 1953-54; pres sr class, Knoxville Col, 1959-60; treas sr class, Princeton Theol Sem, 1962-63; Gulf Coast Presby Com, 1969-; bd dir, Cit Good Sch, 1969; Presby Housing Comn, 1969-74; Human Rels Training Houston Police Cadets, 1970-72; bd dir, Ministries Blacks Higher Educ; bd dir, Houston Met Ministries, vice pres, 1971-74, pres, 1975-76; SW Steering Com, United Presby HEW, 1971-74; Nat Comun Comt, United Ministries Higher Educ, 1972-75; exec comt, Tex United Campus Christian Life Comn, 1973-75; Houston Jail Chaplaincy Exec Comt, 1973-75; Bi-Racial Com HISD, 1973-75; policy bd, United Ministries Higher Educ; exec dir, Fund for the Self-Develop People United Presby Church. **Honors/Awds:** Outstanding Young Men Am, 1966.

WALLS, GEN. GEORGE HILTON, JR.
School administrator, military leader. **Personal:** Born Nov 30, 1942, Coatesville, PA; son of Philip Robert and Elizabeth Gibson; married Portia D Hall, Jun 12, 1977; children: George III, Steven & Kevin. **Educ:** West Chester State Univ, West Chester, PA, BS, educ, 1964; NC Cent Univ, Durham, NC, MA, educ, 1975; Nat War Col, Wash, DC, 1982-83. **Career:** US Marine Corps, brigadier gen, 1965-93; NC Cent Univ, spec asst chancellor; State NC, chief dep auditor; State Auditor, chief dep NC off; Lincoln Elec Holdings Inc, bd mem, currently. **Orgs:** Marine Corps League, 1991; Montford Point Marine Asn, 1991; Sigma Pi Phi; Rotary Int; Carolina Sem; bd mem, Thomas Industries Inc; bd mem, PNC; bd mem, The PNC Fin Services Group Inc. **Honors/Awds:** Inductee, Chapel Four Chaplains, Valley Forge, PA, 1986; Honorary Doctor of Humane Letters, Va Union Univ, 1993; Roy Williams Meritorious Service Award, NAACP, 1993; Humanitarian Service Award, Chapel Four Chaplains, 1993. **Military Serv:** USM, brigadier gen, 1965-; Navy Commendation Medal, 1967; Navy Achievement Medal, 1970; Meritorious Service Medal, 1982; Legion Merit, 1987; Defense Superior Service Medal, 1992; Distinguished Service Medal, 1993. **Home Addr:** 100 Canberra Ct, Cary, NC 27513. **Business Addr:** Board Member, Lincoln Electric Holdings Inc, 22801 Saint Clair Ave, Cleveland, OH 44117, **Business Phone:** (216)481-8100.

WALLS, MELVIN
Educator, government official, football coach. **Personal:** Born Nov 9, 1948, St Louis, MO; married Veronica Estella Robinson;

children: Farrell L & Delvin L. **Educ:** St Louis Community Col, Florissant Valley, AA, 1973; Harris Teachers Col, BA, 1976. **Career:** St Louis City Sch, wrestling coach, 1977-83, tennis coach, 1979-80, baseball coach, 1981, football coach, phys educ teacher; City Northwoods, city collector; Gateway Tech Jaguars, football head coach. **Orgs:** Treas, Boy Scouts Am, 1981-; coord, Normandy Baseball, 1981-. **Honors/Awds:** All Conf Player, St Louis City Sch, 1965-67; All Star Player, St Louis City Sch, 1965-67; Proj MEE Award, 1983; NMC Human Serv Award, 1987. **Business Addr:** Football Coach, Gateway Tech Jaguars, 5101 McRee Ave, St Louis, MO 63110-2082.

WALSH, EVERALD J.
Health services administrator. **Personal:** Born May 6, 1938, New York, NY; children: Evette Michelle & Eric Michael. **Educ:** City Col NY, BA, 1963; Adel phi Univ, MSW, 1970, CSW, 1980. **Career:** Catholic Youth Org, group worker 1963-66; Little Flower C Serv, group Supr, Soc Worker, 1966-71; Fed Addiction Agency, exec dir, 1971-74; Manhattan C Psychiatric Ctr, team leader, 1974-77; Colony S Brooklyn Houses, dir mental retardation staff training prog, 1978-; Brooklyn Develop Ctr. **Orgs:** Nat Fed Concerned Drug Abuse Workers, 1972.

WALTER, DR. JOHN C.
Educator. **Personal:** Born May 5, 1933. **Educ:** Ark AM&N Col, BS, Mech Engineering, Hist; Univ Bridgeport, MA, Am Hist;Univ ME Orono, PhD, Afro-Am & US Hist. 1972. **Career:** Purdue Univ, instr hist, 1970-72, asst prof hist, 1972-73; IN Univ Kokomo,vstg asst prof black politics, 1971-73; John Jay Col Criminal Justice CUNY, assoc prof hist, chmn black studies, 1973-76; Bowdoin Col, dir, asst prof hist Afro-Am Studies Prog, 1976-80; Smith Col, assoc prof Afro-Am Studies; Univ Washington, Dept Am Ethnic Studies, prof. **Orgs:** Dir, Afro-Am Studies Prog Bowdoin Col, 1976-80; org, 1st chmn, 1976-80; exec bd mem, 1978-; New England Conf Nat Coun Black Studies; exec comt Five Coll Black Studies, 1982-; bridge comt & instr Smith Col, 1980-; develop & org Bridges Pluralism 1983-; contrib ed Jour Afro-Am in NY Life & History State Univ Col NY, 1976-; UMOJA A Scholarly Jour Afro-Am Affairs Univ CO,1976-; Review Afro-Am Issues & Culture Syracuse Univ, 1976-; New England Jour Black Studies Hampshire Col, 1981-; Am Historical Asn, Assoc Caribbean Historians, Asn Study African-Am Life & Hist, Caribbean Studies Asn, Col Lang Asn, New England Historical Asn, Nat Asn Interdisciplinary Ethnic Studies, Org am Historians, Soc Historical Asn; consultnison Univ, 1979; Wesleyan Univ, 1978; reader Nat Endowment Humanities, Univ Press Am. **Honors/Awds:** Num res, book reviews & pub incl, Passion Equality, 1977; Politics & Africanity West Indian Soc Brown Univ, 1983; The Black Immigrant & Political Radicalism Harlem Renaissance 61st Annual Conf Asn Study Afro-Am Life & Hist, 1976; Franklin D Roosevelt & Arms Limitation, 1932-41; Hofstra Univ Conf 1982, Politics & Africanity West Indian Soc Brown Univ 1983, The Transformation Afro-Am Politics, The Contribs West Indian Immigrant Colby Col, 1983; Women & Identity Caribbean Smith Col Women's Studies Cluster Comn Sem, 1983; Enterprise Zones, Conservative Ideology Free-Floating Political Fantasy Simon's Rock Bard Col Bulletin, 1984.

WALTER, MILDRED PITTS
Writer. **Personal:** Born Sep 9, 1922, Sweetville, LA; daughter of Paul Pitts and Mary Ward; married Earl Lloyd, 1947 (died 1965); children: Earl Lloyd & Craig Allen. **Educ:** Southern Univ, Scotlandville, BA, 1944; Calif State Univ, elementary teaching cert, 1954; Antioch Col, MEd. **Career:** Los Angeles City Schs District, teacher, 1955-70; Western Interstate Higher Educ, consult, 1970-73; Houghton Mifflin Co, writer, 1969-; Fiction: Lillie of Watts: A Birthday Surprise, 1969; Lillie of Watts Takes a Giant Step, 1971; The Liquid Trap, 1975; Ty's One-Man Band,1980; The Girl on the Outside, 1982; Because We Are, 1983; My Mama Needs Me, 1983; Brother to the Wind, 1985; Trouble's Child, 1985; Justin & the Best Biscuits in the World, 1986; Mariah Loves Rock, 1988; Have a Happy, 1989; Two & Too Much, 1990; Mariah Keeps Cool, 1990; Tiger Ride, Macmillan, 1994; Darkness, 1995; Second Daughter, 1996; Suitcase, 1999; Ray & the Best Family Reunion Ever, 2001; Non Fiction: The Mississippi Challenge, 1992; Kawanzaa: A Family Affair, 1995. **Orgs:** Soc Children's Book Writers & Illustrators; Author's Guild. **Honors/Awds:** Irma Simonton, Black Honor Book, 1981; Public TV, Reading Rainbow, 1983, 1985; Christian Sci Monitor, Best Book: Writing, 1982; Parent's Choice Award, Literature, 1983-85; ALA Social Resp Round Table, Coretta Scott King Honorable Mmention, 1984, Corretta Scott King Award, 1987. **Business Addr:** Author, Houghton Mifflin Co, 222 Berkeley St, Boston, MA 02116, **Business Phone:** (617)351-5000.

WALTERS, ARTHUR M.
Social worker. **Personal:** Born Nov 6, 1918, Magnolia, KY; married NoraLee Bryant; children: Reginald G, Artye M, Michele B. **Educ:** Colo Col, BA; Univ Louisville, MEd; Engr Sch, assoc adv eng. **Career:** Louisville Urban League, soc serv admin, exec dir, 1946-70; Econ Develop & Employ, Educ & Youth Incentives, dir; Prospect/Harrods Creek Neighborhood Asn Inc, incorporator & dir. **Orgs:** Alpha Phi Alpha Fraternity; bd dir, Boys Haven; bd dir, KY Educ TV; bd dir, Louisville C Bus Resource Ctr; Louisville & Jefferson Co Human Rels Comn Employ Comt; Louisville Labor Mgt Comt; NAACP; Retired Officers Asn; Soc Am Mil Engrs; Downtown Rotary Club; adv counc, KY Min Bus Enterprise; Pres Comt Employ Handicapped. **Honors/Awds:** AFL-CIO Gr Louisville Cent Labor Counc Comn Serv Award, 1970; Cited Bd Educ, Louisville Pub Sch, 1971; Merit Comm Serv Medallion, Louisville & Jefferson Co Human Rels Comn, 1972; Outstanding Kentuckian, Int Asn Personnel Employ Security, 1974; citation, State KY, 1975; Merit Award, Alpha Kappa Alpha Sorority, 1975; Whitney M Young Jr Award, Lincoln Found, 1976; Distinguished Serv Citation, United Negro Col Fund; cert achievement, Nat Urban League Exec Devel Prog; hon alumnus, UNCF; Good Neighbor Award, LOU; Black Students Award, Univ Louisville. **Special Achievements:** Listed in 1000 Successful Blacks, Ebony Success Library, 1973; appearance on KY Educ TV, "Bicent Profile of Outst Kentuckians", 1976; Young Gifted & Black Hon Roll, Plymouth Settlement House; Ambassador Goodwill, City Louisville. **Military Serv:** AUS, lt col ret, 1962; Decorations Commend Medal; Bronze Star; Soldiers Medal; Am Campaign Medal; European-african-middle Eastern Campaign Medal W/4 Bronze Serv Stars; WW II Victory Medal; Army Occup Medal; Nat Defense Serv Medal; Korea Serv Medal w/1 Silver Serv Star; Armed Forces Res Medal.

WALTERS, CURLA SYBIL
Educator. **Personal:** Born Jun 3, 1929. **Educ:** Andrews Univ, BA, 1961; Howard Univ, MS, 1964; Georgetown Univ, PhD, Cellular immunol, 1969; Karolinska Inst, Post Doc, 1970. **Career:** Howard Univ, res, asso, 1964-65; Co Univ, instr, asst prof, 1971-74; Howard Univ, Dept Med, adjunt asso prof, currently. **Orgs:** Am Asn Immunologist, 1972-. **Honors/Awds:** AAS Parker Fel Award, 1963; fel, Am Asn Univ Women, 1969; NIH, grant Award, 1974-77; Biomed Res Support grant, 1975-76; Nat Inst Ageing grant, 1977; Infection & Immunol Proc Soc Exp Bio & Med & Fedn Proc. **Business Addr:** Adjunct Associate Professor, Howard University, College of Medicine, Department Microbiology, 2400 6th St, Washington, DC 20059, **Business Phone:** (202)806-6100.

WALTERS, FRANK E.
Athletic trainer. **Personal:** Born Aug 26, 1954, Munich, Germany; son of Ulysses and Alma; married Anne Marie, Aug 14, 1976; children: Jason & Tiffany. **Educ:** Brooklyn Col, BS, 1976; Ind State Univ, MS, 1977; Tex A&M Univ, PhD, 1988. **Career:** Pharr San Juan, Alamo HS, Pharr, Tex, teacher & athletic trainer, 1977-78; MB Smiley HS, Houston, Tex, teacher & athletic trainer, 1978-81; Prairie View A&M Univ, hd athletic trainer, 1981-83; Tex A&M Univ, asst prof, 1983-90; DC Pub Schs, Athletic Health Care Serv, coordr, asst dir athletics, currently. **Orgs:** Ed bd, J Nat Athletic Trainers Asn, 1990-96; ed bd, Athletic Training Sports Health care Perspectives, 1991-96; Nat Athletic Trainers Asn; chmn, Ethnic Minority Adv Coun, 1991-94; Univ Wash; guest fac, Nat Leadership Inst, 1991-92, 1994-95; Res Awards Comt, Mid Atlantic, 1992-95; Educ Task Force, Nat Athletic Trainers Asn, 1995-96; sports med adv com, Nat Fed State High Sch Asn, 1996-97; Educ Coun Exec Comt, 1997-. **Honors/Awds:** Certificate of Merit, Univ Tex Dent Sch, Continuing Educ, 1983; Sports Medicine Alumnus Award, Dept Phys Educ, Brooklyn Col, 1986; First Outstanding Alumnus Award, Athletic Training Dept, Ind State Univ, 1994; Outstanding Service Award, Nat Athletic Trainers Asn, Ethnic Minority Adv Coun, 1995, Outstanding Service Award, Educ Task Force, 1997; Most Distinguished Athletic Trainer, Nat Athletic Trainers Asn, 2003. **Special Achievements:** Published Microfilm Your Student Emergency Cards, The Physician & Sports Medicine, 1981; JC Sterling & MC Meyers, Tennis Elbow A Brief Review of Treatment, 1988; Quarterback Mouth guards & Speech Intelligability, The Physician & Sports Medicine, with RM Morrow, WA Kuebker, M Golde, 1984, 1988. **Business Addr:** Assistant Director of Athletics, District of Columbia Public Schools, Department of Athletics, 825 N Capitol St, Nebraska, Washington, DC 20002, **Business Phone:** (202)442-5885.

WALTERS, GEORGE W
Insurance agent. **Personal:** Born Sep 3, 1950, Bridgeport, CT; married Elizabeth Kramer-Walters, Nov 16, 1996. **Educ:** S Cent Community Col; Huebner Sch Col Studies, Am Col. **Career:** GW Walters Ins, pres & owner, currently; gen agent, broker, currently; Life Underwriters Training Coun, fel. **Orgs:** Million Dollar Round Table; Life Underwriters Polit Action Comn; Provident Mutual Leader's Asn; Nat Asn Ins & Financial Advs; Conn AFA Hist Soc; First Blk Stud Union, New Haven, CT; Greater New Haven Asn Afr Am; Universal Life Church, ordained minister, doctor motivation; NCP. **Honors/Awds:** Nat Quality Award; Nat Sales Achievement; Cert Life Pres's Club; Wall Fame; Grand Award; Balance Performance Award, Provident Mutual; Milestone Club; Scholar, Urban League Greater New Haven; Premier Gen Agt, Bankers Life NY. **Business Addr:** Owner, GW Walters Insurance Agency, 200 Hilton Ave Suite 53, Hempstead, NY 11550, **Business Phone:** (516)489-4422.

WALTERS, HUBERT EVERETT
Educator. **Personal:** Born Apr 27, 1933, Greenville, NC; divorced; children: Sonya Yvette, Hubert Sharif, Narda Rebecca & Julian Herman. **Educ:** NC Cent Univ, BA, 1955; Va State Univ, 1959; E Carolina Univ, MM, 1965; Boston Univ, Sch Theol, pursing MDiv. **Career:** Tex Col Tyler, Tex, chmn dept Music, 1965-66; Shaw Univ Raleigh, NC, asst prof Music, 1966-69; Harvard Univ, lectr Black Music, 1970-74; Goddard Col VT, lectr Black Music, 1971-73, instr; Boston St Col, asst proj Music, 1971-82; Boston Col, lectr Black Music, 1982-, prof, currently; UnivMass-Boston, asst prof Music 1982, prof. **Orgs:** Vpres, NC State Music Teachers, 1963; Music Educr Nat Conf; Am Choral Dir Asn; Omega Psi Phi Frat; deacon, Emmanuel Bapt Church; minister, Worship Peoples Baptist Church, Boston Mass; charter mem, Black Studies Dept Harvard Univ. **Honors/Awds:** LO Kelly Award for Excellence in Music, NC Cent Univ, 1955; Nat Music Honor Soc; Martin Luther King Jr fel Award, Woodrow Wilson Found, 1969; Arts Council Award, Arts Boston Col; Outstanding Alumni Award, E Carolina Univ, 2007. **Special Achievements:** First African-Americans to obtain a degree from East Carolina and the first from the School of Music. **Military Serv:** AUS, sp 3. **Business Addr:** Professor, Boston College, 301 Lyons Hall 140 Commonwealth Ave, Chestnut Hill, MA 02167, **Business Phone:** (617)552-3238.

WALTERS, MARC ANTON
Educator. **Personal:** Born Jul 18, 1952, New York, NY. **Educ:** City Col New York, BS, 1976; Princeton Univ, PhD, 1981. **Career:** Mass Inst Technol, NIH fel, 1982-84; New York Univ, assoc prof, 1985-; Exxon fel, 1991. **Orgs:** Am Chem Soc; AAAS; NAACP; Nat Orgn Prof Advancement Black Chemists & Chem Eng; New York Acad Sci. **Honors/Awds:** Sciences Skills Center Award, 1992. **Special Achievements:** Proficient in French. **Business Phone:** (212)998-8477.

WALTERS, MARY DAWSON
Library administrator, librarian. **Personal:** Born Oct 6, 1923, Mitchell County, GA; married William Lamar Gantt; children: Marjorie M Smith & Robert H McCoy. **Educ:** Savannah State Col Savannah, Ga, BS; Atlanta Univ Atlanta, Ga, MSLS, 1957; OH State Univ Col, OH, russian courses, 1963; OH Historical Soc Col, OH, oral hist cert, 1966; Miami Univ OH, libr mgt cert, 1973. **Career:** Library administrator (retired); Ga Pub Sch, pub sch teacher, 1943-52; Carver Jr High Sch, sch librn, 1952-56; Albany State Col, libr dir, 1956-61; Ohio State Univ Col, G&E lbrn, 1961-63, Processsing Div, head, 1963-71; Calif State Univ, La, Acquistions Dept, head, 1974-78, collection develop officer, 1978-84, asst univ librn, 1980, mgr collection develop prog, 1984-88. **Orgs:** Counr, Am Libr Asn, 1982-86; comm status women libr, 1984-86; Black Caucus Ala, 1974-.

WALTERS, RONALD
Educator, executive director. **Personal:** Born Jul 20, 1938, Wichita, KS; married Patricia Ann. **Educ:** Fisk Univ, BA, hist, 1963; Am Univ, MA, 1966, PhD, 1971. **Career:** Georgetown & Syracuse Univ, instr; Brandeis Univ African & Afro-Am Studies, chmn, 1969-71; Howard Univ, chmn polit sci, 1971-74, prof polit sci; Univ Md, prof govt polit, currently, African-Am Leadership Inst, dir, currently. **Orgs:** Pres, African Heritage Studies Asn; mem bd, Nat Black Election Study, Inst Social Res, Univ Mich; mem adv bd, Southern Christian Leadership Conf; founder, Nat Black Independent Polit Party; secy & founding mem, Nat Black Leadership Roundtable; founder & mem bd, TransAfrica; consult, UN Spec Comn Against Apartheid Security Coun; consult, W K Kellogg Found; Am Polit Sci Asn; bd dir, Ralph Bunch Inst. **Honors/Awds:** Distinguished Community Service Award, Howard Univ, 1982; Distinguished Scholar/Activists Award, Black Scholar Mag, 1984; The Ida B Wells Barnett Award, Nat Alliance Black Sch Educrs, 1985; Congressional Black Asniates Award, 1986; Fannie Lou Hammer Award, Nat Conf Black Polit Scientist, 1996; Ida B Wells W E B DuBois Award, Distinguished Scholarship, Nat Coun Black Studies, 2000; Alumnus of the Year, Sch Int Serv Am Univ, 2000. **Special Achievements:** Speaks & writes on US Foreign Policies toward Africa & Black American Politics, over 100 articles in several scholarly journals, eight books in press. **Business Addr:** Director, Professor in Government and Politics, University of Maryland, African American Leadership Institute, Lefrak Hall Suite 2169, College Park, MD 20742, **Business Phone:** (301)405-1787.

WALTERS, RONALD L., JR.
Music producer. **Personal:** Born Sep 16, 1970, Chicago, IL; son of Ronald and Sandra. **Educ:** Columbia Col, BA, music, 1995. **Career:** Elias Music, composer & producer; Steve Ford Music, composer & producer; Slang Music, composer & producer; Music On The Move, music teacher; Am Idol, guest music dir, 2004. TV : Barry Manilow: Songs from the Seventies, 2007. **Orgs:** BMI; Am Fedn Musicians; All Nations Mission Church; pres, Anointed Ones. **Honors/Awds:** Jazz Student of the Year, Chicago State Univ, 1993; Teacher of the Year, St. John de La Salle, 1996. **Special Achievements:** Producer of three commercially released recordings, 1994, 1995, 1996. **Business Addr:** Principal, Ronald Walters & Associates PC, 53 W Jackson Blvd Suite 1250, Chicago, IL 60604, **Business Phone:** (312)341-0801.

WALTON, ANTHONY SCOTT
Writer. **Personal:** Born Mar 8, 1965, South Bend, IN; son of Cullen Walton Jr and Judith Elaine Tidwell Walton. **Educ:** Vanderbilt Univ, Nashville, TN, BA, 1987. **Career:** Detroit Free Press, Detroit, MI, sports writer, 1987-. **Orgs:** Alpha Phi Alpha Fraternity Inc, 1984-; mentor, Project Male Responsibility, 1988-. **Honors/Awds:** Honorable Mention, Best Enterprise Story, Associ-

ated Press, 1991. **Home Phone:** (313)579-1202. **Business Addr:** Sports Writer, Detroit Free Press, 321 W Lafayette, Detroit, MI 48231, **Business Phone:** (313)222-6661.

WALTON, CAROL ANN (KARA WALTON)
Social scientist, educator. **Personal:** Born Mar 17, 1935, Niagara Falls, NY; daughter of Wilker and Carol Smitherman Dozier; married Ortiz Montaigne, Jun 29, 1957; children: Omar Kwame. **Educ:** NY State Univ Col, Buffalo, BS, 1957; Suffolk Univ, MA, 1963; Univ Calif, Berkeley, Urban educ fel, 1970; Univ Calif, Berkeley, PhD, 1975; Howard Univ, PhD, 1977. **Career:** Berkeley Unified Sch Dist, sr res assoc, 1972-73; West Lab, dir admin servs, 1974; Univ Calif, Berkeley, prog analyst & eval consult, 1975-76; Multi Ethnic Inst Res & Eval, vpres, 1975-; Howard Univ, post-doctoral fel NIE, 1977; Archidiocese NY Head Start, eval dir, 1986-92. **Orgs:** Alpha Kappa Alpha, 1955-60; adv mem, Berkeley Unified Sch Dis, supt desegregation comt, 1967-68; Am Edu Res Asn, 1969-86; Pi Lambda Theta, 1971-83; Kappa Delta Pi, Gamma Mu chap, 1975-84; vpres, E Bay Ment Health, 1978-82; Community Coun W Harlem, 1988-89, 1998-2000. **Honors/Awds:** Research Award, Nat Inst Alcohol Abuse & Alcoholism, 1977-80. **Special Achievements:** Co-author, Black Papers on Black Edu, Other Ways Publications, 1968; developed survey of part-time edu; developed surveys & studies of experimental schools, 1972-73; co-principal grant investigator, Natl Institute on Alcohol Abuse & Alcoholism, 1978-80. **Home Addr:** 1129 Bancroft Way, Berkeley, CA 94702-1849, **Home Phone:** (510)649-0504. **Business Addr:** Vice President, Multi Ethnic Institute for Research and Education, 1129 Bancroft Way, Berkeley, CA 94702, **Business Phone:** (510)649-0504.

WALTON, DR. EDWARD D.
Educator. **Personal:** Born in Montgomery, AL. **Educ:** Howard Univ, Wash, BS, 1969; Univ Md, College Park, PhD (chem), 1979. **Career:** US Naval Acad, Md, fac; Lawrence Hall Sci, Univ Calif, prog coordr, 1985-86; Calif State Poly tech Univ, Pomona, Dept Chem, fac, 1987-, prof, 1997-, co-dir, currently. **Orgs:** Past pres, Nat Orgn Prof Advan Black Chemists & Chem Eng; rev comt, Nat Assessment Educ Progress Sci; Educ Testing Serv's Comt SAT II Chem Exam;Nat Acad Sci. **Honors/Awds:** Distinguished Teaching Award, Calif State Poly tech Univ. **Military Serv:** USN, comdr. **Home Addr:** PO Box 517, Mt Baldy, CA 91759. **Business Addr:** Professor of Chemistry, California State Polytechnic University, 3801 W Temple Ave, Pomona, CA 91768-2557, **Business Phone:** (909)869-3661.

WALTON, ELBERT ARTHUR, JR.
Government official, lawyer. **Personal:** Born Feb 21, 1942, St Louis, MO; son of Elbert A Sr and Luretta Ray Hawkins; married Juanita Alberta Head; children: Rochelle, Rhonda, Angela, Elbert III & Johnathan. **Educ:** Harris Jr Col, AA, 1963; Univ Mo, St Louis, BA, bus, 1968; Wash Univ, MBA, 1970; St Louis Univ, JD, 1974. **Career:** Continental Oil Corp, fin analyst, 1969; Univ Mo, St Louis, instr, bus law & acct, 1971-78; atty, 1974; St Louis Munic Ct, judge, 1977-78; Mo House Rep, state rep 61st dist, 1979-93; Metro Law Corp PC, owner & atty, currently. **Orgs:** Beta Alpha Psi Hon Acct Fraternity, 1971; Phi Delta Phi Int Legal Frat, 1973; nat vpres, Nat Asn Black Act, 1976-77; parliamentarian, Mound City Bar Asn, 1979; parliamentarian, Mo Legis Black Caucus, 1979-85; grand counr, Omega Psi Phi Frat 1980-83. **Honors/Awds:** Omega Man of the Year, Omega Psi Phi Fraternity, St Louis, MO, 1964; Outstanding Achievement Award, Nat Asn Black Acct, 1976; Citizen of the Year, Omega Psi Phi Fraternity, St Louis, MO, 1978. **Military Serv:** USNR, E-4, 1959-61. **Business Addr:** Attorney, Metro Law Corp PC, 8776 N Broadway, St Louis, MO 63147-2225, **Business Phone:** (314)388-3400.

WALTON, HANES
College teacher. **Personal:** Born Sep 25, 1942, Augusta, GA; son of Estelle Brown Walton and Hanes Thomas Walton; married Alice Williams, Apr 10, 1974; children: Brandon & Brent. **Educ:** Morehouse Col, Atlanta, Ga, BA, 1963; Atlanta Univ, Atlanta, Ga, MA, 1964;Howard Univ, Wash, DC, PhD, 1967. **Career:** Guggenheim fel; Rockefeller fel; Savannah State Col, Savannah, Ga, prof,1967; Univ Mich, Dept Polit Studies, prof, currently, Ctr Polit Studies, sr res scientist, currently, Ctr Afro american & African Studies, fac, currently. **Orgs:** Nat Conf Black Polit Scientists, 1971-; Am Polit Sci Asn, 1967-; SouthernPolit Sci Asn, 1967-; Asn Study Afro-Am Life & Hist, 1967-; Phi BetaKappa; Alpha Kappa Mu; Pi Sigma Alpha. **Honors/Awds:** Distinguished PhD Alumni Award, Howard Univ, 1993; Faculty Cornerstone Award, 2007. **Special Achievements:** Co- authored Civic Participation in American Cities and also Authored Many Articles and Research papers. **Business Phone:** (734)936-1768.

WALTON, DR. HARRIETT J.
Educator. **Personal:** Born Sep 19, 1933, Claxton, GA; daughter of Mable Rose Myrick Jr and Ester James Jr; divorced; children: Renee Yvonne, Anthony Alex, Jennifer Denise & Cyrus Bernard. **Educ:** Clark Col, AB, math, 1952; Howard Univ, MS, math, 1954; Syracuse Univ, MA, math, 1957; GA State Univ, PhD, 1979; Atlanta Univ, MS, Computer Sci, 1989. **Career:** Educator (retired); Hampton Inst, instr math, 1954-55, asst prof mathm, 1957-58; Morehouse Col, instr math, asst prof math, assoc prof math, prof math, 1958-2000. **Orgs:** Clerk Providence Baptist Church, 1968-84; secy & treas, Nat Asn Math, 1982-; treas, Phi Delta Kappa, 1984-85; deacon, Providence Baptist Church, 1984-; mem, adv bd, Benjamin E Mays Acad; Beta Kappa Chi; treas & pres, Delta Sigma Theta; YWCA; Nat Asn Advan Colored People; consult, Atlanta Pub Sch; Math Asn Am; Nat Coun Teachers Math; mem, Pi Mu Epsilon; mem, Phi Beta Kappa. **Honors/Awds:** UNCF Fac Fel, 1964-65, 1975-77; NSF Sci Fac, 1965-66; Proj Dir Control for Math Educ, 1981-84; Proj Dir, Math Middle Sch Teachers, 1981-82; Bronze Woman of the Year, Iota Phi Lambda Sorority, 1984; Phi Beta Kappa Delta, GA Morehouse Col, 1984. **Home Addr:** 860 Venetta PL NW, Atlanta, GA 30318.

WALTON, JAMES DONALD
Executive. **Personal:** Born Jan 31, 1952, Albany, NY; son of Zymora Louise Burrell Walton (deceased) and Allen Walton (deceased); married Nadine Renee, Aug 23, 1991; children: Darius James & Talib Justice. **Educ:** Univ Vermont, BS, 1975. **Career:** Xerox Corp, sales rep, 1976-79; Abbott Lab, chem syst specialist, 1979-82, nat acct mgr, 1982-83, dist mgr, 1984-87, sr recruitment mgr, nat sales mgr, vpres worldwide mkt, vpres US sales, 2005; regional mkt mgr, 1987-90, regional mgr, 1990-94, hemat syst, nat sales mgr, diagnostics div, div vpres, worldwide mkt, 1995-2002; Thermo Electron, vpres glqbal sales; Allen & Burrell Consult, vpres, us sales. ceo & pres; Black Bus, owner, currently; Global Recruiters Oak Park, founder, pres, managing partner, currently. **Orgs:** Bd dir, Calra Abbott Found. **Honors/Awds:** First Black Dist Mgr, 1983; First Black Regional Mkt Mgr, 1987; Regional Mkt Mgr of the Year, 1988; First Black Regional Mgr, 1990; First Black Nat Sales Mgr, 1995; First Black Vpres Mkt & Sales. **Home Addr:** 949 Fairoaks Ave, Oak Park, IL 60302. **Business Addr:** President, Managing Partner, Global Recruiters of Oak Park, 8700 W Bryn Mawr Presidents Plaza II Suite 800 S, Chicago, IL 60631, **Business Phone:** (773)714-5053.

WALTON, JERRY
Executive. **Career:** BMW Hudson Valley, staff, employ dept, gen mgr, currently. **Orgs:** Bd mem, Miles Hope Breast Cancer Found. **Business Addr:** General Manager, BMW Hudson Valley, Department Employ, 2068 S Rd Rte 9, Poughkeepsie, NY 12601, **Business Phone:** (845)462-1030 Ext 1010.

WALTON, KARA. See WALTON, CAROL ANN.

WALTON, DR. MILDRED LEE
School administrator. **Personal:** Born Dec 8, 1926, Atlanta, GA; daughter of James Forrest and Pauline Dickerson; married Borah W; children: Berle Burse, Denise Fernandez & Charna Burse. **Educ:** Spelman Col, BA, 1947; Atlanta Univ, MA, 1962; Nova Univ, EdD, 1976; Harvard Univ, Summer fel, 1984. **Career:** DeKalb County Sch System, teacher, 1947-56; Turner High Sch, teacher, 1956-69; Harwell Elem Sch, prin, 1969-73; Atlanta Univ, asst prof, 1970; Miles Elem Sch, princ, 1973-87; Georgia Assoc Elem Sch Prins, exec dir, 1987-. **Orgs:** SE zone dir, Nat Assoc Elem Sch Prin, 1980-83; adv bd, Rockefellar Fund for Art Educ, 1981-85; found bd, Am Assoc Univ Women, 1982-85, Phi Delta Kappa, 1984-85; St Paul's Vestry St Paul's Episcopal Church, 1984-87; pres, Nat Assoc Elem Sch Prins, 1985-86; Delta Kappa Gamma Hon Soc, 1986-; pres, Nat Alumnae Asn Spelman Col. **Honors/Awds:** Boss of the Year, Nat Business Women's Assoc, 1983; Bronze Woman in Educ Black Heritage Assoc, 1984; Georgia Educ Excellence State Bd Educ, 1984; Nat Distinguished Prin, US Dept Educ, 1986. **Home Phone:** (404)696-0001. **Business Addr:** Executive Director, Georgia Association of Elementary School Principals, 1176 Oakcrest Dr, Atlanta, GA 30311.

WALTON, DR. ORTIZ MONTAIGNE (ORTIZ MONTAIGNE)
Musician, sociologist. **Personal:** Born in Chicago, IL; son of Peter Leon and Gladys Matilda Porche; married Carol Dozier, Jun 21, 1957; children: Omar Kwame. **Educ:** Roosevelt Univ, BS, 1967; Univ Calif, Berkeley, CA, MA, 1970, PhD, 1973. **Career:** Musician Hartford New Haven, Springfield, Bridgeport Sym Orchestras, 1951-54; Buffalo Philharmonic Orchestra, 1954-57; Boston Sym Orchestra, 1957-63; Chicago Asn Retarded Children, prog coordr, 1964-66; Cairo (Egypt) Sym, musician, 1963-64; Chicago Fedn Settlement, dir, 1964-68; Univ Calif, Berkeley, Prof social, 1969-74; Dept African-Am Studies, Univ Calif, Berkeley, instr, 1974-76; Wright IST Berkeley, grad sch instr, 1974-75; Univ Calif Santa Cruz, mem bd studies social, 1975; Sample Survey Alcohol & Drug Use Among Adolescents & Young Adults, Nat Inst Alcohol Abuse & Alcoholism, prin investigator, 1978-81; contrabass soloist, author & composer; Multi-Ethnic Inst Res & Educ, pres, 1978-;Athanor Recs, pres, currently. **Orgs:** Univ Calif, Santa Cruz, 1975; Wright Inst Berkeley, 1974-75; double assist, Boston Sym Orchestra, 1957-63; NY Debut Recital, Mekin Concert Hall, NYC, 1989; Am Sociol Asn; Int Soc Bassists; Chamber Music Am. **Special Achievements:** Composed Night Letter for unaccompanied contrabass dedicated to Edward Kennedy Ellington 1968, recorded solo contrabass works of WA Mozart & recorded premiere of The Walton Statement by Arthur Cunningham 1986, author of work on the sociology of Amer music "Music, Black White & Blue"published by William Morrow, "Toward a Non-Racial, Non Ethnic America" Multi America, ed. Ishmael Reed Pub. Vicking Press, 1997, The Art of the Boss Viel, Live in Paris, Music of the Baroque Era, 1992.

WALTON, R KEITH
College administrator. **Personal:** Born in Birmingham, AL; married Aubria D Corbitt; children: Rachel, Alexander & Gabrielle. **Educ:** Yale Col, BA,1986; Harvard Law Sch, JD,1990. **Career:** US District Ct, Northern District of AL, law clerk, 1990-91; US Dept Treas, chief staff, enforcement, 1993-96; King & Spalding, assoc, 1991-93; White House Security Rev, dep dir, 1994-95; Columbia Univ, univ secy, 1996-2007, sr mem, 2007-. **Orgs:** NY advisory bd, Enterprise Found, 1996-; Coun Foreign Rel NY, 1996-, co-chair, 2000-; dir, Apollo Theatre found; dir, Orchestra St Luke's; Asn for a Better NYK, 2001-; Alpha Phi Alpha; Century Asn; Am Law inst; Coun US & Italy; trustee, Sanctuary Families. **Business Addr:** Senior Member, Columbia University, 535 W 116 St 211 L 211 Low Memorial Lib, New York, NY 10027.

WALTON, REGGIE BARNETT
Government official, judge. **Personal:** Born Feb 8, 1949, Donora, PA; son of Theodore and Ruth; married; children: 1. **Educ:** WVa State Col, BA, 1971; Am Univ Wash Col Law, JD, 1974. **Career:** Defender Asn PA, staff atty, 1974-76; US Atty Off DC, asst US atty, 1976-80, exec asst, 1980-81; Super Ct DC, assoc judge, 1981-89, dep presiding judge, 1986-89; Off Nat Drug Control Policy, assoc dir; US Dist Ct, DC, judge, 2001-; United States Foreign Intelligence Surveillance Court, Judge, 2007; Harvard Univ Law Sch Advocacy Workshop, instructor. **Orgs:** Am Bar Asn; Wash Bar Asn; Dist Columbia Bar Asn; Judicial Conf DC, 1980-; Nat Inst Trial Advocacy Advocates Asn, 1985-; Big Bros Am, 1987-; bd dirs, Nat Ctr Missing & Exploited C, 1990-; Big Brothers Big Sisters of Am; Alpha Phi Alpha Fraternity; Chairperson, Nat-Prison Rape Reduction Commission, 2004; federal judiciary's Criminal Law Committee, 2005; faculty mem, Nat Judicial Col Reno, Nevada. **Honors/Awds:** Distinguished Serv Award, Bar Asn DC Young Lawyer's Sect, 1989; Community Service Award, Alpha Phi Alpha Inc, Iota Upsilon Lambda Chap, 1990; President's Image Award, Madison County Indiana Urban League, 1990; The Distinguished Serv Award, NJ State Assn of Chiefs of Police, 1990; James R Waddy Meritorious Serv Award, The W Va State Col Nat Alumni Asn, 1990; one of 14 judges profiled in a 1994 book entitled Black Judges On Justice: Perspectives From The Bench. **Business Phone:** (202)354-3290.*

WALTON, DR. TRACY MATTHEW
Radiologist. **Personal:** Born Nov 12, 1930, Columbia, SC; married Mae Yvonne Squires, Jan 1, 1955; children: Adrienne, Tracy III, Terri & Brien. **Educ:** Morgan State Col, BS 1953; Howard Univ Col Med, attended 1961. **Career:** Freedman's Hosp, asst radiol, 1965-66; Howard Univ, asst radiol, 1965-66; Georgetown Univ Sch Med, clin instr, 1968; DC Gen Hosp, med officer, 1967-71, actg chief med officer, 1971, chief med officer, 1971-80; Univ DC, med dir, med radiography prog, dept health sci, 1994-. **Orgs:** Nat Medical Asn, 1961-, treasurer, Region II; Rgnl radiotherapy comt, Met Wash Regnl Med Prog, 1968-; Cancer Aid Plan Com DC Chap ACS, 1968-81; chmn, Am Cancer Soc, 1968-, pres, DC div, 1984; adv bd, United Nat Bank Wash, 1974-; licensure, SC Bd Med Examr, 1981; vpres, DC Div Am Cancer Soc, 1983-; bd trustees, chmn, 1990-91, pres, 1994-95, Nat chmn, Radiol Sect Nat Med Asn, 1983-; Med Soc DC, provisional speaker house delegs, 1992; Nat Med Asn; Am Col Radiol; So Med Asn; licensure, Md Bd Med Exam; DC Bd Med Exam; Medico Chirurgical Soc DC, Morgan State Col. **Honors/Awds:** Pres, Medico-Chirurgical Soc DC, 1975-78. **Home Addr:** 7506 9th St NW, Washington, DC 20012-5038. **Business Addr:** Radiologist, General Practitioner, 4118 Grant St NE, Washington, DC 20019-3550, **Business Phone:** (202)396-8600.

WAMBLE, CARL DEELLIS
Administrator, naval officer, real estate agent. **Personal:** Born Apr 11, 1952, Kansas City, KS; son of Amos Sylvester Sr (deceased) and Geraldine Phillips (deceased); married Naomi Jean Cannon, Apr 17, 1976; children: Christopher DeEllis & Christina Rochelle. **Educ:** Philander Smith Col, BS, biol, 1975; Webster Univ, MA, health serv mgt, 1983. **Career:** Navy Official (retired), real estate agent; Vr Med Clin, Fallon, operating room technician, 1977-78; USS McKean, DD784, commun officer, electronic platerial officer, 1979-81; USS NJS, BB62, weapons, 2nd battery officer, 1981-84; Orgal Effectiveness Ctr, Yokosuka, OE consult, 1984-86; Naval Hosp, Yokosuka, Japan, operations mgt officer, 1986-87; Naval Sch Health Sci, master training specialist, 1987-90; Br Med Clin, Treasure Island, officer-in-charge, 1990-93; NATO Allied Forces Southern Europe, Naples, Italy, 1993-96; Uniform Services Univ Med Sch, co comdr, asst commandant, 1997; real estate agent. **Orgs:** APA Frat, 1971-; Alpha Phi Omega Frat, 1971-; Nat Naval Officers Asn, 1982-; Surface Warfare Officers Asn, 1990-; Am Acad Medical Adminr, 1991; Am Military Evangelizing Nations. **Honors/Awds:** Meritorious Service Medal; Joint Defense Service Medal; Orgal Effectiveness Ctr, Yokosuka, Orgal Effectiveness Consult, 1984; Navy Commendation Medal, 1984 & 1990; Navy Achievemant Medal, 1986. **Military Serv:** USN, Lt Comdr, 1975-.

WAMBU, MUTHONI
Administrator, political consultant. **Educ:** Howard Univ, BS, jour, 1997. **Career:** Am Fedn Labor Congress Indust Orgns, Comt Polit

Educ Polit Contrib Comt, coordr; Baker Wambu & Assocs, partner & owner, 2000-. **Orgs:** Delta Sigma Theta Sorority. **Business Phone:** (202)463-9633.*

WANSEL, DEXTER GILMAN
Composer, singer. **Personal:** Born Aug 22, 1950, Bryn Mawr, PA; married Lorna Millicent Hall (divorced). **Career:** Philadelphia Int Rec, dir artist, repertoire, musician & rec artist, 1980; Wansel Enterprises, independent rec producer, 1973-75; Various Rec Co, musician, arranger, orchestral dir, synthesizer & programmer, 1973-75; Albums: Life on Mars, 1976; What the World Is Coming To, 1977; Voyager, 1978; Time is Slipping Away, 1979; Captured, 1986; Digital Groove World, 2004; Voyager And Time Is Slipping Away, 2005; Jazz In The City, 2007; Disco, 2008. **Orgs:** Wissahickan Civic Asn, 1978. **Honors/Awds:** Twenty Eight Gold & Platinum Records; Grammy Award, Am Asn Rec Artists, 1978. **Military Serv:** AUS, e-5, 3 yrs. **Business Addr:** Singer, Philadelphia International Records, 309 S Broad St, Philadelphia, PA 19107, **Business Phone:** (215)985-0900.

WANSLEY, LISA PAYNE
Publicist. **Personal:** Born Apr 2, 1962, Bronx, NY; daughter of Harold Sr and Florence Grant; married Terrance A Wansley, Mar 24, 2001. **Educ:** Univ Dayton, Dayton, Ohio, BA, 1984; Fordham Univ, Bronx, NY, MA, 1989. **Career:** Girls Club NY, Bronx, NY, dir youth employ servs, 1984-86; Monroe Bus Col, Bronx, NY, community liaison, 1986-87; Union Theol Sem, New York, NY, dir housing, 1987-89; Bronx Mus Arts, Bronx, NY, dir pub affairs, 1989-92; Gov Mario Cuomo, regional rep, 1992-95; Off Bronx Dist Atty, dir community affairs, admin chief, currently. **Orgs:** Network dir, Nat Asn Female Execs, 1983-; founder, network dir, NIA: A Minority Women's Prof Network Inc, 1984-; 100 Blacks in Law Enforcement Who Care; pres & founder, Bronx Asn African Am Profs; bd trustees, Bronx Mus Arts, 1994-95; bd dirs, Edenwald Community Ctr. **Honors/Awds:** Humanitarian Award, NIA: A Minority Women's Prof Network, 1988; Woman Year, All Saints Roman Cath Church Harlem, 1990; COT Serv Award, Bronx Ctr Progressive Servs, 1992; Outstanding Serv, Bronx Democratic Party, 1994; Achievement Award, Nat Coun Negro Women, 1995; COT Serv, East Laconia Asn, 1997; Women of the-Year, Bronx YMCA, 1998. **Business Addr:** Administrative Chief, Office of the Bronx District Attorney, 198 E 161st St, Bronx, NY 10451, **Business Phone:** (718)590-2405.

WANTON, EVA C.
Educator. **Personal:** Born Jan 1, 1935?, Tunderbolt, GA; married Albert E Wanton; children: Jacquelyne G Maxey, Debra P Mitchell, Michelle V Jones, Dwanna Di Shon. **Educ:** Savannah State Univ, BS, 1961; Interamerican Univ, MA, 1964, PhD, 1970; Fla State Univ, PhD, 1980. **Career:** Fla A&M Univ, dir summer session, 1971-75, asst dean, 1975-79, dir gen educ, 1977-79, dean, 1982-. **Orgs:** Chamettes Inc, 1971-; bd mem, Jack & Jill Found, 1986, nat pres, 1989-; bd dirs, Mothers In Crisis. **Honors/Awds:** Dean of the Year, Fla A&M Univ, 1986. **Home Addr:** 3736 Sulton Ct, Tallahassee, FL 32312. **Business Addr:** Dean, Florida A&M University, Martin Luther King Blvd, Tallahassee, FL 32307.

WARD, ALBERT A. See Obituaries section.

WARD, ANNA ELIZABETH
Government official, consultant. **Personal:** Born Dec 20, 1952, Miami, FL; married Sterling Andrew; children: Johnathan Travis & Rochelle Marie. **Educ:** Miami Dade Com Col, AA, 1978; Fla Int Univ, BS, crim justice, 1980, MPA, 1980. **Career:** Fla Int Univ, 1971-80; Village El Portal, mayor; Sangamon State Univ, circulation dept admin, 1980-81; City Dallas, asst to asst city mgr,1981-83; Miami Dade Col, 15 yrs; Dallas Cty Com Col Dist, asst internal auditor, 1984-85; City Emporia, VA, asst to city mgr; Martin Luther King Econ Develop Corp, pres & chief exec officer; Metro Miami Action Plan Found, exec dir, currently. **Orgs:** Pres, N Cent Tex COMPA, 1982-83; prog moderator, Int City Mgt Asn, 1982;mediator, Dispute Mediation Dallas Inc 1982-85; Better Bus Bureau Dallas,1982-85; teen counr, Women Community Serv, 1983; co-chairperson, prog comUrban Mgt Asst N Tex, 1983; bd mem, N Cent Tex ASPA, 1983-85. **Honors/Awds:** Nominee Outstanding Young Am, 1981; Serv Award, N Tex Conf Minority Pub Admin, 1983. **Special Achievements:** Author: Public Management ICMA, 1982-84. **Military Serv:** AUS, Pvt 7 mo's; Defense Award, Cert Achievement, 1974-75. **Home Addr:** 5737 Valley Mills Dr, Garland, TX 75043.

WARD, ARNETTE S.
School administrator, educator. **Personal:** Born Dec 2, 1937, Jacksonville, FL; daughter of Isiah and Albertha E; married John W; children: Elra Douglas. **Educ:** Edward Jr Col, AA; Fla A&M Univ, BS, 1962; Ariz State Univ, MA, 1972. **Career:** Lincoln High Sch, teacher, 1963; Fla A & M Univ, asst prof, 1964; Fall Recreation Dept, dir recruitment, 1964; Roosevelt Sch Dist, elem sch teacher, 1968; Mesa Comm Col, counr, 1971; dean of stud serv, 1979; Chandler-Gilbert Community Col, Chandler, Ariz, provost, 1985-92, pres, 1992-2002, pres emer, 2002-. **Orgs:** Comn on Trail Court Appt, 1985; nominating comn, Ariz Cactus Pine Girl Scout; Black Women in High Educ, 1986; Am Assoc Comm & Jr County, 1986; Nat Coun Black Am; Affairs Coun AACJS; Am Assoc of Women in Jr Col, 1986; pres, Delta Sigma Theta, 1986; Nat Coun Instructional Admin, AACJC. **Honors/Awds:** Music Scholar, Edward Water Jr Col, 1957; hon mention as singer, Alex Haley "Author of Roots," 1974; Outstanding Participation, Tempe Sch Dist, Black Culture Week, 1976; Women of the Year, Mesa Soroptomist & Delta Sigma Theta, 1977 & 1984; Merit Award, Black Youth Recognition Conf, 1982. **Home Phone:** (602)961-4195. **Business Addr:** President Emeritus, Chandler-Gilbert Community College, 2626 E Pecos Rd, Chandler, AZ 85225-2499, **Business Phone:** (602)732-7000.

WARD, BILL
Association executive. **Career:** Habitat Humanity Int, midwest regional dir, currently. **Business Addr:** Midwest Regional Director, Habitat for Humanity International, 1920 S Laflin St, Chicago, IL 60608, **Business Phone:** 800-643-7845.

WARD, CALVIN
Banker. **Personal:** Born Dec 10, 1955, Chicago, IL; son of Thomas (deceased) and Annie M (deceased). **Educ:** Ill State Univ, BS, 1977; DePaul Univ, Grad Sch Bus, MBA, 1989. **Career:** OSCO Drugs Inc, asst gen mgr, 1977-83; Northern Trust Co, vpres, currently. **Orgs:** Nat Black MBA Asn, Chicago Chap, pres, 1985; Urban Bankers Forum Chicago, 1986; Nat Asn Urban Bankers, 1986; United Negro Col Fund, telethon, 1987. **Honors/Awds:** Certificate of Recognition, 1990; Brother of the Year, Alpha Phi Alpha Fraternity Inc, 1992; Member of the Year, Chicago Chap, Nat Black MBA Asn, 1991. **Home Addr:** 2821 W Seipp, Chicago, IL 60652, **Home Phone:** (773)471-6461. **Business Addr:** Vice President, The Northern Trust Co, 50 S LaSalle St, Chicago, IL 60675, **Business Phone:** (312)444-2388.

WARD, CALVIN EDOUARD
Educator. **Personal:** Born Apr 19, 1925, Atlanta, GA; son of Jefferson Sigman and Effie Elizabeth Crawford; married Adriana Wilhelmina deGraaf-Ward, Oct 11, 1962 (divorced 1976). **Educ:** Northwestern Univ, Evanston, IL, bachelor music, 1949, master music, 1950; Staats Akademie fuer Musik, Vienna, Austria; Univ Vienna, Austria, PhD, 1955. **Career:** Educator (retired); Fla A&M Univ, Tallahassee, Fla, inr, music, Univ organist, 1950-51; Southern Univ, Baton Rouge, LA, assoc prof, music, Univ organist, 1957-59; SCA State Col, Orangeburg, SC, prof, chair, Dept Music & Fine Arts, 1959-61; Kingsborough Cot Col, City Univ NY, 1964-66; Tuskegee Univ, Tuskegee Inst, AL, assoc prof, chm, Dept Music, conductor, Tuskegee Concert Choir, 1968-72; Johns Hopkins Univ, Peabody Inst, Baltimore, MD, fac, theory, Afa classical music, 1972-73, appl music, organ, 1973-77; Univ Md, Baltimore County, MD, fac, AFA studies, 1976-77; Coppin State Col, Baltimore, MD, prof, music, 1973-83; Trenton Pub Schs, Trenton, NJ, music spt; prof music edr & spt, Afa classical music; free lance consult, choralonductor & elem sch resource person; Calvin Edouard Ward Educ Fund Minority Studs, chief adv. **Orgs:** Am Choral Dirs Asn; Am Guild Organists; Am Humanities Forum; African Am Music Opportunities Asn; Nat Educ Asn; NJ Educ Asn; Trenton Educ Asn; Phi Mu Alpha Sinfonia. **Honors/Awds:** Pi Kappa Lambda, Nat Music Fraternity for Excellence in Scholar & Performance; Fulbright Fellowship Award, 1951; Fulbright-Hays Faculty Research Aboard Award, 1977; Fulbright Senior Visiting Lecturer Award, 1986; African Am Exchange of Scholars Award, 1978-79; Caribbean-Am Exchange of Scholars Award, 1980; selected for taping, Oral History Dept's Files, Md Historical Soc; NJ Govs Tcr Recognition Program Award, 1990-91. **Special Achievements:** Visiting proships and guest lectureships: Cuttington Univ Col, Monrovia, Liberia, W Africa, Kenyatta Univ Col, Univ Nairobi, Kenya, E Africa, St Petersburg State Conservatoire, St Petersburg, Russia, St John's Theol Col, Morpeth, New S Wales, Australia; First participant in Fulbright Prog Vis Prof to the USSR to both lecture & perform; First visiting prof to State Conservatory of Music, Vilnius, Lithuanian SSR, USSR; First Am to make known the classical tradition of African Music in the USSR; First Am guest lectr at the State Conservatory of Music, Riga, Lativian SSR, USSR; First Am organist to perform upon the world-renowned pipe organ in the Dome Cathedr Riga, Lativian SSR, USSR. **Military Serv:** US Infantry, Sgt, Chaplain's Asst, NCO Entertainment Specialist, 1946-48. *

WARD, CARLA MOSBY. See MOSBY, CARLA MANE.

WARD, CHARLIE
Basketball player, basketball coach, football coach. **Personal:** Born Oct 12, 1970, Thomasville, GA; married Tonja, Aug 26, 1995; children: 2. **Educ:** Tallahassee Community Col; Fla State Univ, therapeut recreation. **Career:** Basketball player (retired), basketball coach, football coach; Milwaukee Brewers, pitcher, 1993; NY Knicks, guard, 1994-2004; San Antonio Spurs, 2003-04; Houston Rockets, 2004-05, asst coach; Westbury Christian Sch, Houston, TX, asst coach, 2007-08, head football coach, 2008-. **Honors/Awds:** Heisman Trophy, 1993; Johnny Unitas Award, 1993; James E. Sullivan Award, 1993; Walter Camp Award, 1993; Maxwell Award, 1993; Davey O'Brien Award, 1993; Col Football Hall of Fame, 2006. **Business Addr:** Head Football Coach, Westbury Christian School, 10420 Hillcroft, Houston, TX 77096-9946.

WARD, CHRISTOPHER EVAN
Lawyer. **Personal:** Born Jul 8, 1971, Atlanta, GA; son of Leila Bates and Evan Jr; married Meka Brumfield Ward, Jun 6, 1998. **Educ:** Morehouse Col, BA, 1993; Univ Miami, Sch Law, JD, 1997; Univ Ga. **Career:** Fulton County Pub Defender, staff atty, 1998-00; Fulton County Dist Atty, sr asst dist atty, 2000; Dekalb county, atty; Vaughan & Evans LLC, atty, currently. **Orgs:** Ga Asn Criminal Defense Lawyers, 1998-00; Gate City Bar Asn, 2000; State Bar Ga. **Home Addr:** 2985 Dodson Dr, Atlanta, GA 30344, **Home Phone:** (404)349-5069. *

WARD, DANIEL
School administrator, school superintendent. **Personal:** Born Mar 15, 1934, Memphis, TN; son of Gus; married Margie Marie Brittmon; children: Muriel Dawn, Maria Diane & Marcus Daniel. **Educ:** Tenn State Univ, BS, Music Educ, 1956; USAF, Multi-Engine Pilot Training Sch, Cert, 1957; USAF Radar Controller Training, Cert, 1958; USAF Air Force Instr Course, Cert, 1960; TN State Univ, MS, Sec Sch Instr, 1960; USAF Air Command & Staff Sch, Cert, 1976; Drug & Alcohol Abuse Workshop, Cert, 1975; 36 post-grad hours. **Career:** School administrator (retired); USAF, pilot and radar contr, 1956-59; Douglass HS, prog coordr, 1962-65; Hyde Park Elem Sch, asst prin, 1965-67; Grant Elem Sch, prin, 1967-68; Porter Jr HS, prin, 1968-70; Douglass HS, teacher vocal music, 1960-62; Vance Jr HS, prin, 1970-81; Fairley HS, prin, 1981-83; Memphis City Schls, dist IV supt, 1983, asst supt, sec dept, 1987-94. **Orgs:** Asn Supv & Curric Devel; Omega Psi Phi Frat; AASA; TN State Univ Alumni Asn; Nat Guard Asn TN; bd trustees, Metropolitan Baptist Ch; vchmn emer, pres, Memphis-Shelby County Airport Authority, 1967-99; Nat Asn Advan Colored People. **Honors/Awds:** Four-year scholarships to: TN State Univ, AR State Univ, Howard Univ, LeMoyne Coll, Stillman Coll; Omega Man of the Year, Epsilon Phi Chap, 1976, nominated 1980; Omega Citizen of the Year, 1992; Awarded Meritorious Service Medal by Pres of the US, 1981; First Oak Leaf Cluster, 1984; Minute-Man Award for Outstanding Service to the TN Air Natl Guard; Danforth Admin Fellow, 1983-84. **Military Serv:** USAF, lt col, 28 years. **Home Addr:** 6746 Briarmeadows Dr, Memphis, TN 38120. *

WARD, REV. DARYL
College president, clergy. **Personal:** Born Sep 12, 1957, Cincinnati, OH; son of Maudie and Lester; married Vanessa Oliver Ward, Mar 27, 1982; children: Joshua, Rachel & Bethany. **Educ:** Col Wooster, BA, 1979; Georgetown Univ, Law Ctr, JD, 1985; Colgate Rochester Divinity Sch, MDiv, 1986. **Career:** Fed Energy Regulatory Comn, legal intern, 1982; Rochester Soc Prevention Cruelty to C, legal intern, 1984-85; United Theol Seminary, dir of admis, 1986-89, dean African Am ministries, 1986-96; Omega Baptist Church, pastor, 1988-; United Theol Sem, Dayton, Ohio, exec vpres & COO, 1989-93, pres & COO, 1993-96, pres emeritus, currently. **Orgs:** Benjamin E Mays Fel, Fund for Theol Educ, 1984, 1985; bd trustees, Good Samaritan Hosp, 1989-98; Tony Hall's Congressional Adv Council, Dayton, 1991-; Ohio State Bar Asn; Victoria Theatre Bd, 1993-; Hospice of Dayton, 1993-96; pres, Urban Outreach Found, 1997-99; pres emer, United Theol Sem. **Honors/Awds:** Parity 2000 Award, Dayton's Ten Top African American Males, 1994; Society Bank's Community Recognition Award, 1993; Inducted into Morehouse College Martin Luther King Jr Board of Preachers, 1993; Dayton Volunteers Community Service Award, Certificate of Merit, 1991; Up & Comers Award, 1990; Rochester Area College Outstanding Adult Student, 1986. **Special Achievements:** Keynote Speaker: Central State University, Wilberforce University, College of Wooster, Mississippi Valley State, Florida Memorial State, Bishop College, University of Dayton, Wittenberg University, Mount Union College, Wright State University, Ohio Northern University Law School; Keynote Speaker: National Afro-American History Museum, "The Church and the Civil Rights Movement;" Author of Papers: Church Renewal and Recruitment for Ministry," Networking for Globalization: Creating Intercultural Partnerships in Predominantly White Settings". **Business Addr:** Pastor, Omega Baptist Church, 1821 Emerson Ave, Dayton, OH 45406-5803, **Business Phone:** (937)278-1006.

WARD, DEDRIC LAMAR
Football player, football coach. **Personal:** Born Sep 29, 1974, Cedar Rapids, IA. **Educ:** Northern Iowa Univ, BA, psychol. **Career:** Football player (retired), Football coach; New York Jets, wide receiver,1997-2000; Miami Dolphins, 2001-02; Baltimore Ravens, 2003; New England Patriots, 2003; Dallas Cowboys, 2004; Mo State Univ, coach, 2006; Ariz Cardinals, offensive quality control, 2007-08; Kansas City Chiefs, coaching staff, 2009-. **Honors/Awds:** Super Bowl champion XXXVIII. **Business Addr:** Coaching Staff, Kansas City Chiefs, 1 Arrowhead Dr, Kansas City, MO 64129, **Business Phone:** (816)920-9300.

WARD, DR. DORIS
County government official. **Career:** County government official (retired); San Francisco Community Col Dist, trustee, Bd Supvrs, pres, 1990; County San Francisco, supvr, 1980, assessor. *

WARD, DORIS MARGARET
Government official, commissioner. **Personal:** Born Jan 27, 1932, Chicago, IL; daughter of Robbie Floyd and Jesse Keys. **Educ:** Ind Univ, BA, 1953, MS, 1964; San Francisco State Univ, MA, 1974; Univ Calif, PhD. **Career:** Government official, Commissioner

(retired); Indianapolis Pub Sch, teacher, 1959-67; Ind State Teacher Corps, team leader, 1967-68; San Francisco State Univ, adj lectr, 1969-70, 1972; Mateo County Off Educ, coordr; San Francisco Bd Supervisors, pres; San Francisco, City & County, assessor, 1995-2006. **Orgs:** Betty J Olive Memorial Found; vpres, San Francisco Black Leadership Forum; Black Women Orgn Action; consult, Waterloo Iowa Sch, Sioux City, Milwaukee, MN; Dayton Police Dept Conflict & Violence; vpres, bd dir, San Francisco Community Col Dist, 1972-; Minority Affairs Assembly Asn Community Col; exec coun, Asn Study Afro-Am Life & Hist; nat bd, western reg bd coun, Black Am Affairs Asn Am Community & Jr Col; Nat Asn Advan Colored People; SF Div Nat Women's Polit Caucus; Alpha Kappa Alpha; comnr, Asian Art Mus, San Francisco, 2005-. **Honors/Awds:** NDEA grant, 1966, Lilly Found grant, 1967, Ind State Univ; NDEA, Univ Calif, 1968; Special Merit Award, Sup Reporter, 1973; Rockefeller Found Grant, 1974; Community Service Award, Kappa Alpha Psi, 1975; Living Legend Award, Black Women Orgn Action, 1975; Distinguished Women Award, Girls' Club, Med-Peninsula & Lockheed Missilies & Space Co Inc, 1975; Bicentennial Award, Trinity Baptist Church, 1976; Recognition Exemplary Community Leadership Award, Black Student Psychol Asn, 1976; Govt Honorary, Pi Sigma Alpha; Education Honorary, Pi Lambda Theta; publ "Indianapolis Comm Ctr Proj", 1968-69. **Business Addr:** Commissioner, Asian Art Museum, 200 Larkin St, San Francisco, CA 94102, **Business Phone:** (415)581-3500.

WARD, DOUGLAS TURNER (DOUGLAS TURNER)
Actor, playwright. **Personal:** Born May 5, 1930, Burnside, LA; son of Roosevelt and Dorothy Short; married Diana Hoyt Powell; children: 2. **Educ:** Wilberforce Univ; Univ Mich; Paul Mann's Actors Workshop, actor training. **Career:** Theater appearances include: Lost in the Stars, 1958; A Raisin in the Sun, 1959; The Blacks, 1961-62; One Flew Over the Cuckoo's Nest, 1963; Day of Absence, actor & writer, 1965; Kongi's Harvest, 1968; The Reckoning, actor & writer, 1969; Perry's Mission, dir, 1971; Frederick Douglass Through His Own Words, 1972; The River Niger, actor/writer, 1972; The First Breeze of Summer, 1975; The Offering, 1977; Old Phantoms, 1979; Ride a Black Horse, director, 1971; A Ballet Behind the Bridge, dir, 1972; Waiting for Mongo, dir, 1975; Livin' Fat, dir, 1976; Home, dir, 1979; A Season to Unravel, dir, 1979; A Soldier's Play, dir, 1981; Ceremonies in Dark Old Men, 1984; Negro Ensemble Co, co-founder & artistic dir, 1967-; Films: Man & Boy, 1972; TV series: "East Side/West Side", 1963; Ceremonies in Dark Old Men, 1975; Go Tell It on the Mountain, 1985; The Women of Brewster Place, 1989;"Law & Order", 1993; "Cosby", 2000; "For Love of Olivia", 2001. **Honors/Awds:** Obie Award, Happy Ending, 1966; Creative Arts Award, Happy Ending, Brandeis Univ, 1969; Vernon Rice Drama Desk Award, Best Play, Day Absence, Happy Ending, 1966; Obie Award, The River Niger, 1973; Tony Award nomination, Best Supporting Actor, 1974; Boston Theatre Critics Circle Award, 1986. **Home Addr:** 222 East 11th St, New York, NY 10003. *

WARD, EVERETT BLAIR
Administrator, association executive. **Personal:** Born Nov 6, 1958, Raleigh, NC; son of William H and Dorothy Williams; married Cassandra Lloyd Ward, Jun 12, 1982. **Educ:** St Augustine's Col, BA, 1982; NC State Univ, MA. **Career:** Westinghouse Elec Corp, Raleigh, mkt asst, 1980-82; NC Dem Party, Raleigh, NC, polit dir, 1983-89, exec dir, 1989-93; NC Dept Transp, adminr local & community affairs, Prog Minority Serving Inst, dir, Hist Black Col Univ Prog, dir, currently. **Orgs:** Life mem, Alpha Phi Alpha Fraternity Inc, Phi Lambda Chap; Raleigh Hist Properties; comn chmn, elder, Davie St Presbyterian Church USA; NC Black Leadership Caucus; Raleigh-Wake Citizens Asn; adv bd, Mechanics & Farmers Bank; Dem Nat Comn; Wake Co Dem Men; NC Literary & Hist Asn. **Honors/Awds:** Martin Luther King, Jr Service Award, NC Asn Educr, 1986; Distinguished Alumni Award, Nat Asn Equal Opportunities Higher Educ, 1990; NAACP Humanitarian Award, Wendell-Wake Chap, 1993. **Business Addr:** Director, North Carolina Department of Transportation, 1500 Mail Service Ctr, Raleigh, NC 27699-1500.

WARD, FRANCES MARIE (FRANCES WARD-JOHNSON)
Journalist. **Personal:** Born Mar 23, 1964, Goldsboro, NC; daughter of Joe and Occie Whitfield. **Educ:** NC Agr & Tech State Univ, Greensboro, NC, BA, Eng, 1986, MA, attended; Univ NC, Phd, attended. **Career:** Assoc Press, Raliegh, NC, bur news reporter broadcast writer, 1986; Wilson Daily Times, Wilson NC, feature writer, 1988-89; Greensboro News & Record, Greensboro, NC, feature writer, 1989; A&T, public rels; Elon Univ, adj prof, 1995-99; Ctr Creative Leadership, commun mgr, 1995-99; Elon Univ, Sch Commun, assoc prof, 2003-. **Orgs:** Triad Black Media Profs, Greensboro, NC, 1990-; Nat Asn Advan Colored People, Reidsville, NC, 1991; Nat Asn Black Journalists, 1990-; NC Press Women's Asn, 1990-; Saint's Delight Church, Goldsboro, NC, 1981-; Sigma Tau Delta, Nat Hon Soc Eng Majrs, 1983-. **Honors/Awds:** 2nd Place Award Winner For Profiles, NC Press Women's Asn, 1990; Most Promising Journalism Student Award, NC A&T State Univ, 1985; English Dept Award, NC A&T State Univ, 1986. **Business Addr:** Associate Professor, Elon University, School of Communications, McEwen 010-B 2850 Campus Box, Elon, NC 27244, **Business Phone:** (336)278-5738.

WARD, GARY LAMELL
Baseball player. **Personal:** Born Dec 6, 1953, Los Angeles, CA; children: Daryle. **Career:** Baseball player (retired); Minnesota Twins, outfielder, 1979-83; Texas Rangers, outfielder, 1984-86; New York Yankees, outfielder & infielder, 1987-89; Detroit Tigers, outfielder, 1989-90; International League, Charlotte Knights, hitting coach, 1999-2001; Chicago White Sox, hitting coach, 2008; Charlotte Knights, Batting coach, currently. **Honors/Awds:** American League Rookie of the Year, Baseball Digest, 1979-81; AmericanLeague All-Star Team, 1983 & 1985.

WARD, HASKEL SEARS. See WARD, HASKELL G.

WARD, HASKELL G (HASKEL SEARS WARD)
Consultant, administrator. **Personal:** Born Mar 13, 1940, Griffin, GA; son of George Ward and Margaret Poe Dumas; married Kathryn Lecube Ward, Jun 14, 1980; children: Alexandra & Michelle. **Educ:** Clark Col, BA, 1963; Univ Calif Los Angeles, MA, 1967. **Career:** Ford Found, staff; City New York, dep mayor, 1979; Health & hosps Corp, New York, chmn bd, 1979-; Community Develop Agency, comnr; State Dept, Africa adv & policy plng staff; Ward Assocs, consult, currently; Global Alumina Corp, sr vpres gov rel, currently. **Orgs:** Bd dir, Am Coun Ger; Mid-Atlantic Club; bd dirs, The New York Partnership; bd dirs, African Med Res Found; bd dirs, Am Coun Ger. **Honors/Awds:** Woodrow Wilson Hon Fel; John Hay Whitney Fel; several awards for citizenship, community service and achievement. **Special Achievements:** First African American on the policy planning staff of the State Department during the Carter Administration. **Business Phone:** (212)351-0000.

WARD, HORACE T.
Judge. **Personal:** Born Jul 29, 1927, La Grange, GA; married Ruth LeFlore, Jun 9, 1956 (died 1976); children: Theodore J (deceased). **Educ:** Morehouse Col, Atlanta, GA, BA, 1949; Atlanta Univ, Atlanta, GA, MA, 1950; Nwestern Univ Sch Law, Chicago, IL, JD, 1959. **Career:** Hollowell, Ward, Moore & Alexander, Atlanta, GA, atty-at-law, 1960-68; State Ga, Atlanta, GA, state senator, 1965-74; City Atlanta, Atlanta, GA, dep city atty, 1968-69; Fulton County, Atlanta, GA, asst county atty, 1970-74, civil court judge, 1974-77; State Ga, Atlanta, GA, superior court judge, 1977-79; US Dist Court, judge; US Dist Ct, Northern Dist Ga, sr judge, currently. **Orgs:** Alpha Phi Alpha Fraternity Inc, 1948-; Phi Beta Kappa, Delta Ga; Am Bar Asn; Nat Bar Asn. **Honors/Awds:** Distinguished Alumni Award, Atlanta University; Bennie Service Award, Morehouse Col; Merit Award, Nwestern University, Hall of Fame, National Bar Asn, The Gate City Bar Association; A Heroes, Saints and, Legends Award, The Wesley Woods Foundation, 1976; Hon Doctor Laws, Morehouse Col, La Grange Col; Trumpet Award Civil Rights Advocate, Turner Broadcasting System, 2004. **Special Achievements:** First African American to challenge the racially discriminatory practices at Horace Ward the University of Georgia; Atlanta Magazine listed him as one of 200 people who shaped Atlanta. **Military Serv:** AUS, Corporal, 1953-55. **Home Addr:** 215 Piedmont Ave NE, Atlanta, GA 30303. **Business Addr:** Senior Judge, United States District Court Northern Georgia, 1252 Richard B Russell Fed Bldg & US Courthouse, 75 Spring St SW, Atlanta, GA 30303-3309, **Business Phone:** (404)215-1330.

WARD, DR. JAMES DALE
Educator. **Personal:** Born Feb 3, 1959, Nettleton, MS; son of J L Ward and Alice Harper Marion. **Educ:** Univ Miss, BA, jour & sociol, 1980; Univ Cincinnati, MPA, pub affairs, 1983, PhD, polit sci, 1988. **Career:** Knoxville News-Sentinel, staff writer, 1980; WCBI-TV Columbus, TV reporter, 1980-86; Univ New Orleans, asst prof, 1990-94; Univ NMex, vis asst prof, 1995-98; NMex State Univ, assoc prof, 1998-2005; Miss Univ Women, Col Arts & Sci, Dept Hist, Polit Sci, Geog & Paralegal Studies, assoc prof polit sci, 2005-. **Orgs:** Am Soc Pub Admin; Am Polit Sci Asn; Conf Minority Pub Add. **Special Achievements:** Publications: Privatization Review; Public Administration Quarterly; Public Productivity Management Review; Public Administartion Review; International Journal of Public Administration; Presial Studies Quarterly; International Encyclopedia of Public Policy Administration. **Business Addr:** Associate Professor of Political Science, Mississippi University for Women, College of Arts & Science, Dept Hist Polit Sci Geog & Paralegal Studies, PO Box 1634 W, Columbus, MS 39701, **Business Phone:** (662)329-7386.

WARD, DR. JERRY WASHINGTON
Educator. **Personal:** Born Jul 31, 1943, Washington, DC; son of Jerry Washington and Mary Theriot. **Educ:** Tougaloo Col, Tougaloo, MS, BS, 1964; Ill Inst Technol, Chicago, IL, MS, 1966; Univ Va, Charlottesville, VA, PhD, 1978. **Career:** Ill Inst Technol, teaching asst, 1965-66; State Univ NY, Albany, NY, teaching fel, 1966-68; Upward Bound Prog, coordr Eng, 1970-71; Tougaloo Col, Tougaloo, MS, from asst prof to prof Eng, 1970-2002, chmn dept Eng, 1979-86, 2001-02, Lawrence Durgin prof Lit, 1988-2002; United Negro Col Fund fac grant, 1974-75; Univ Va, instr transition prog, 1974; Kent fel, 1975-76, 1976-77; Univ Va, fac, 1976-77; NEH Inst Southern Black Cult, fac, 1981; Spelman Col, fac, 1982; Miss Comm Humanities, fac, 1983; NEH Summer Seminar Col Teachers, Tougaloo Col, dir, 1984; Nat Endowment Humanities, Wash, DC, prog officer, 1984; Univ Miss, Eng Dept, vis prof, 1987; UNCF Scholar-in-Residence, Talladega Col, 1987-88; Commonwealth Ctr, Univ Va, Charlottesville, VA, prog dir/prof, 1990-91; Fac Resource Network Seminar, NY Univ, 1993; Univ Memphis, Moss chair excellence Eng, 1996; Nat Humanities Ctr, fel, 1999-2000; Dillard Univ, distinguished prof Eng & African World Studies, 2002-. **Orgs:** Alpha Phi Alpha Fraternity Inc, 1961-; exec comt, Col Lang Asn, 1974-76, black studies comt, 1977-91; chair, Div Black Am Lit, Modern Lang Asn, 1986-87; Miss Adv Comt, US Civil Rights Comn, 1988-98; The Authors Guild, 1988-; adv bd, George Moses Horton Soc, Study African Am Poetry, 1997-; exec coun, Soc Study Southern Lit, 1997-99; African Am Lit & Cult Soc; Am Lit Asn. **Honors/Awds:** Outstanding Teaching Award, Tougaloo Col, 1978-80, 1992; UNCF Distinguished Scholar Award, 1981-82; Humanities Teacher Award, 1995; Public Humanities Scholar Award, 1997; Darwin T Turner Award Excellence, African Am Lit & Cult Soc, 2000; InterNat Literary Hall of Fame for Writers of African Descent, Chicago State University, 2001. **Special Achievements:** Teacher of the Year, Tougaloo College, 1993. **Military Serv:** AUS, Spec-5, 1968-70. **Business Addr:** Professor of English & African World Studies, Dillard University, Department of English, 2601 Gentilly Blvd, New Orleans, LA 70122, **Business Phone:** (504)816-4502.

WARD, KEITH LAMONT
Lawyer. **Personal:** Born Nov 12, 1955, Bridgeport, CT; son of Willie and Vera S; married Jacqueline; children: Alexandra. **Educ:** Southern Univ, BA, 1978; Southern Univ Law Ctr, JD, 1982. **Career:** Keith L Ward PLC, atty, currently. **Business Addr:** Lawyer, President, Keith L Ward PLC, 185 Devon Dr, Mandeville, LA 70448, **Business Phone:** (985)869-0612.

WARD, LENWOOD E
Executive. **Educ:** NC Central Univ, Durham, BS, 1963. **Career:** Arco, CA, org & co adv, 1973-74, sr employee rels adv, 1974-78, employee rels mgr, 1978-, org & co mgr, 1978-80, corp employee rels mgr, 1980-89, human resources servs mgr, 1989-. **Business Addr:** Manager of Human Resources Services, ARCO, 515 S Flower St AP 4265, Los Angeles, CA 90071, **Business Phone:** (213)486-1670.

WARD, LLOYD DAVID
Executive. **Personal:** Born Jan 22, 1949, Detroit, MI; married Estralita, Jun 27, 1970; children: Lloyd II & Lance. **Educ:** Mich State Univ, BS, eng, 1970; Xavier Univ, MBA, 1984. **Career:** Procter & Gamble, mgr, 1970-85, Div Mfg, mgr, 1985-86, adv mgr, pkg soap & det, 1986-87, vpres & gen mgr, dishcare, 1987-88; Ford Motor, mgr, 1977-78; Pepsi Co Inc, Pepsi-Cola E, vpres opers, 1988-91, W Div Frito-Lay, pres, 1991-92, Cent Div Frito-Lay, pres, 1992-96; Maytag Corp, Maytag Appliances, exec vpres & pres, 1996-98, pres & ceo, 1998-2001; iMotors, chmn, ceo; US Olympic Comt, secy gen, ceo, 2001-03; BodyBlocks Worldwide LLC, chmn, currently; Belo Corp, bd dir; JP Morgan Chase Co, bd dir; Cent & Southwest Corp, bd dir. **Orgs:** Exec Leadership Coun; bd dir, President's Coun Phys Fitness & Sports; bd dir, Ronald McDonald House; bd dir, Dallas YMCA; bd dir, Paul Quinn Col; bd dir, Jimmy Johnson Found; bd dir, Inroads Southwest Ohio. **Honors/Awds:** American Best & Brightest Business & Professional Men and Women, Dollars & Sense Mag, 1995; Executive of the Year, Black Enterprises Mag, 1995; Jack Breslin Life Time Achievement Award, Mich State Univ, 1996; Alumni of the Year Award, Mich State Univ; Marketer of the Year, BrandWeek Mag; Outstanding Leadership Award, Ctr Creative Leadership. **Special Achievements:** Black Belt, Karate; First African American CEO of US Olympic Comm. **Business Addr:** Chairman, BodyBlocks Worldwide LLC, 3340 Peachtree Rd NE Suite 1800, Atlanta, GA 30326, **Business Phone:** (404)364-1997.

WARD, MELISSA
Airplane pilot, airplane pilot. **Educ:** Univ Southern Calif, BS, bus admin, 1986. **Career:** Tex Air Force, flight instr, 1988-91, aircraft comdr, co-pilot, capt, beginning, 1997; Tenn Air Nat Guard, capt; United Airlines, flight officer, beginning 1992, capt, currently. **Honors/Awds:** Women's Basketball NCAA Champions, 1983, 1984. **Special Achievements:** First female African American capt for commercial airline; First female African-American stud in pilot training, fighter pilot rating & instr pilot, Tex Air Force. **Business Addr:** Captain, United Airlines, 1200 E Algonquin Rd, Elk Grove Township, IL 60007, **Business Phone:** (847)700-4000.

WARD, REV. MELVIN FITZGERALD, SR.
Clergy. **Personal:** Born Jul 2, 1918, New Bern, NC; son of Dolphin and Nancy Forbes; married Lessie Pratt, Sep 12, 1940; children: Dorothy Buckner, Mary Francis Martin, Nancy Bullet & Melvin F Jr. **Educ:** National Bible Inst, DD, 1944; Lawson Bible Inst, BTh, 1945; Teamers Bible Inst, DD, 1972; Union Christian Bible Inst, DD, 1974; Livingston Col, Salesbury, NC, Doctor of Divinity, 1976; Clinton Jr Col, Rork Hill, SC, Doctor of Divinity, 1975; Union Christian Bible Inst, Master Divinity, 1984-. **Career:** African Methodist Episcopal Zion Church, minister 1943-, pastor, 1940-91; TWIU, pres, 1950-68; Tobacco Works Int Union, rep, 1977; Bakery Confectionery & Tobacco Workers, Union AFL-CIO-CLC, Kensington, MD, rep. **Orgs:** Bd mem, home mission bd, AME Zion Ch; bd trustee, Christian Bible Inst; dir, Pub Rel VI

& South Am Conf; Human Rel Comn, 1960-65. **Honors/Awds:** Award Pres of Local 256 TWIU 25 yrs; Appreciation Award for Dedicated Service & Unselfish Service, Hood Theological Seminary, 1989. **Military Serv:** Rifleman, Good Conduct Medal, 1943; Quarter Master, tech sargent, 1944. **Business Addr:** Pastor, African Methodist Episcopal Zion Church, PO Box 1634, Wilson, NC 27893.

WARD, NOLAN F
Lawyer. **Personal:** Born Jan 14, 1945, Columbus, OH; son of Clifforn Loudin and Ethel Shaffer (deceased); married Hazel Williams, Sep 6, 1966; children: Penelope Kaye. **Educ:** Prairie View A&M Univ, BA, MA, 1968; Univ NE, 1967; S Univ, 1969; Univ Tex, JD, 1973. **Career:** State Tex, chmn exec dir, Tex Employment Comn; Gov Dolph Briscoe, legal staff, 1976-; Pvt Pract, 1975; Co Judge Bill Elliott, clerk, 1975; St Rep Anthony Hall, admin aid, 1973-74; EEOC, case analyst, 1970-73; Waller ISD, instr, 1967-69; Job Corps, advr, 1966-67; atty gen, Austin, TX, 1983-. **Orgs:** Nat Asn Advan Colored People; Tex Bar Asn; Omega Psi Phi; Omicron Kappa Delta; Delta Theta Phi; Thurgood Marshall Legislative Sec; Dist & Co Atty Asn, Urban League. **Home Addr:** 12900 Trailwood Rd, Austin, TX 78757. **Business Addr:** Attorney, Attorney General, 6421 Camp Bowie Blvd Suite 312, Fort Worth, TX 76116, **Business Phone:** (512)239-5803.

WARD, DR. PERRY W.
College president. **Educ:** Miles Col, BS; Univ Ala, MSW, PhD. **Career:** Miles Col, instr, adult educ prog, 1969-71, assoc dir emergency sch asst prog, 1972-73, dir emergency sch aid act prog, 1973-75; Univ Ala, Grad Sch Social Work, adj prof, 1977-82; Birmingham Pub Schs, dir fed progs admin,1975-79; Univ Ala, dir basic educ, 1979-87; Lawson State Community Col, Birmingham, AL, pres, 1987-. **Orgs:** Pres, Ala Col Asn; vpres, Cent Ala Athletic Asn; Mercedes Benz Pride Comn; nat bd mem, Am Asn Community Cols; bd mem, Compass Bank; bd mem, Univ Ala Health Servs Found; pres, Birmingham Urban League. **Honors/Awds:** Outstanding Service Award; Boy Scouts of America Appreciation Award, Nat Asn Advan Colored People; Academy of Fellows Distinguished Educators Award, I-D-E-A; Kermit Mathison Outstanding Community Col Administrator Award. **Business Addr:** President, Lawson State Community College, 3060 Wilson Rd, Birmingham, AL 35221, **Business Phone:** (205)925-2515.

WARD, RONALD R
Lawyer. **Personal:** Born Jun 12, 1947, Sacramento, CA; son of Robert L and Audrey; married Willetta L, Aug 26, 1978; children: Sara A. **Educ:** Calif State Univ, BA, 1973; Univ Calif, Hastings Col Law, JD, 1976. **Career:** State Wash, Off Atty Gen, state asst atty gen, 1979-82; Levinson, Friedman Law Firm, atty law, partner, 1982-; Jones & Ward PLLC, partner & atty, currently. **Orgs:** Loren Miller Bar Asn, 1979-; bd gov, Wash State Trial Lawyers Asn, 1989-95; pres-elect, Wash State Bar Asn, 2003-04, pres, 2004-05; King Co Bar Asn; Nat Bar Asn; Am Bar Asn House Deleg; Am Bd Trial Advocates. **Honors/Awds:** Special President's Recognition Award, Wash State Trial Lawyers Asn, 1995; Super Lawyer, Wash Law & Polit Mag, 2003; Ron R Ward President's Award, named in honor, 2006; Outstanding Plaintiff Trial Lawyer Award, Wash Defense Trial Lawyers, 2006; Distinguished Service Award, Anheuser-Busch Co, Nat Bar Asn; Washington State Trial Lawyers President's Award, 2006. **Special Achievements:** First African-American to serve as president of the Washington State Bar Association. **Military Serv:** AUS, 1967-69. **Business Phone:** (206)957-1272.

WARD, RONNIE (RODNEY GLEN)
Football player. **Personal:** Born Feb 11, 1974, St Louis, MO. **Educ:** Univ Kans. **Career:** Miami Dolphins, linebacker, 1997. *

WARD, SANDRA L
Executive. **Personal:** Born May 23, 1963, Atlanta, GA; daughter of Aston Roy and Betty Jean. **Educ:** Howard Univ, BA, 1985; John Marshall Law Sch, attended 1995. **Career:** EPIC Radio Network, sr acct exec; Supreme Ct Ga, Off Comn & Progs, dir. **Orgs:** Black Entertainment & Sports Lawyers Asn; Nat Urban League; Nat Asn Media Women; Howard Univ Alumni Asn. **Honors/Awds:** America's Top Business & Professional Women Award, 1991; Chief Justices's Award for Excellence in Public Service, 2000. **Special Achievements:** "Tribute to Business and Professional Men & Women," Dollars and Sense, July 1991. **Home Addr:** 275 Dix-Lee On Dr, Fairburn, GA 30213.

WARD, VELMA LEWIS
Scientist. **Personal:** Born in Columbus, OH; daughter of John F and Anna C; divorced; children: Broderick Lewis. **Educ:** Univ Mich, attended 1949; Wayne State Univ, BS, MT, 1953, Col Med, MS, biochem, 1961, Inst Geront, grad cert, 1986, PhD, 1996. **Career:** Lafayette Clinic, Detroit, MI, res assoc, Clin Lab, asst dir, biochem, 1956-84; Drake Inst Sci Consult, 1971-73; Detroit Area Pre-Col Engineering Prog, asst dir, 1985-91; Philadelphia Geriatric Ctr, res prof mgr, 1992-94; Wayne State Univ, vis asst prof, 1996-98, adj prof, 1998-. **Orgs:** New York Acad Scis; Asn for Women in Sci, AWIS-DAC, exec bd, vp; The Geront Soc Am; Am Anthrop Asn; Asn for Anthropol & Geront; Am Asn Univ Women; Res Review Bd, Southfield Oncol Inst; Mich US Navy Scholar Info Team, NAVSIT, Detroit; US Navy Official Educrs Visiting Team, Pensacola, FL; Alpha Delta Theta, Med Tech; Alpha Kappa Alpha Sorority; Navy League US; Reg Am Soc Clin Path; Am Chem Soc. **Honors/Awds:** Distinguished Alumna Award, Northville High Sch, 1992; Am Inst Chemists, Fellow; Sigma Xi, Fel; Royal Soc Chem, 1996; 'Top Fifty Minority Women Scientists', Nat Tech Asn Scientists & Engrs, NTA, 1996; Minority Graduate Research Training Award, Nat Inst Aging, 1992. **Special Achievements:** Has authored several papers and has presented papers widely. **Home Addr:** 16500 N Pk Dr Apt 1210, Southfield, MI 48075. **Business Addr:** Adjunct Faculty, Wayne State University, Department of Anthropology, 137 Manoogian Hall, Detroit, MI 48202, **Business Phone:** (313)577-2935.

WARD, WALTER L., JR.
State government official. **Personal:** Born Oct 28, 1943, Camp Forest, TN; son of Walter and Kathryn; divorced; children: Dionne & Walter L III. **Educ:** UW-Milwaukee, BS, 1969; Univ Wis Law Sch; Milwaukee Area Tech Col; Marquette Univ, grad work. **Career:** State Wis, Dist 17, state rep, 1972-. **Orgs:** Coun work; chmn, bd mem, OIC Indust Adv Bd; Martin Luther King Orgn; chmn,Jr Chamber Com; vice chmn, Opportunities Industrialization Ctr Greater Milwaukee Indust Adv Bd; bd dir, Milw Girls Club; Biennial comt assignments, 1979-. **Home Addr:** 3124 N 13th St, Milwaukee, WI 53206. **Business Addr:** 325 W State Capitol, Madison, WI 53702, **Business Phone:** (608)266-0960.

WARDEN, GEORGE W
Insurance agent. **Personal:** Born May 18, 1944, Richmond, VA; son of George Sr and Hilda Y; married Sylvia Washington, Apr 9, 1966; children: Monica, Nicholas & Cecilia. **Educ:** Va Union Univ, BS, 1966. **Career:** State Farm Ins Co, ins agt, currently. **Orgs:** Vpres, Rosa Park Scholar Found; Nat Asn Life Underwriters; Oakland Co Life Underwriters; Detroit Property & Casualty Agents Asn, Kiwanis Club. **Honors/Awds:** National Achievement Sales Award, Nat Asn Life Underwriters, 1992-98; Legion of Honor, 1998-02; Life Honor Agent; Leading Health Producer, 2001. **Business Addr:** Agent, State Farm Insurance Company, 24361 Greenfield Suite 201, Southfield, MI 48075-3165, **Business Phone:** (248)569-8555.

WARDER, JOHN MORGAN
Banker, businessperson, president (organization). **Personal:** Born Jan 7, 1927, Ellsworth, KS; son of Beulah and Warner; married Margie (died 1989); children: Linda, Kent & David; married Benola Foster, 1992. **Educ:** Univ Kans, BA, 1952. **Career:** Businessperson (retired); Litho Supply Depot Inc, Minneapolis, Minn, off mgr, 1952-62, vpres, 1962-68; Plymouth Nat Bank, pres, 1969-82; First Plymouth Nat Bank, cbd, 1982-84; First Bank Minneapolis, vpres urban develop, 1984-86; First Bank Syst Inc, vpres urban develop, 1987-88; Relax Back Store Franchise, pres, owner, 1992-. **Orgs:** Chmn, Zion Baptist Church Bldg Coun, 1962-64; trustee, Macalester Col, 1970-81; bd mem, Minneapolis Found, 1972-81; Helen Harrington Trust, 1972-; Bush Found Panel Judge, 1973-; treas, Minneapolis UNCF Campaign, 1975-; Alpha Phi Alpha Frat; co-chmn, Alpha Phi Alpha, 1978; Nat Conf Com; Minneapolis Club; Prince Hall Masons; Dunkers Club; vice chmn, 1980-85, bd mem, 1985-, Nat Med Flwsps Inc; treas, Delta Dent Minn, 1984; trustee, Univ Minn Med Found, 1985-; bd mem, Minn News Coun; treas, W Harry Davis Found, 1986-;bd mem, Minn Bus League, 1985-; Nat Asn Advan Colored People; Minneapolis Urban League; Zion Bapt Ch Cty Mpls. **Honors/Awds:** Disting Serv Award, 1964; Outstanding Serv Award, Afro Am Edu Asn, 1968; Gtr Mpls C C Award, 1973; Miss Black Minn Outstanding Achievement Award, 1975; Minneapolis Urban League's Cecil E Newman Humantarian Award, 1976; Man of the Year Award, Insight Publ, 1977; Outstanding Service Award, Alpha Phi Alpha, 1978; Man of the Year Award, Alpha Phi Alpha, 1979; Outstanding Service Award, Minn Black Chemical Abuse, 1982; Minn Urban League Volunteer Service Award, 1986; Nat Conf Christian & Jews Brotherhood & Sisterhood Humanataria, 1991. **Military Serv:** USY, 1946-47; USAF, corpl, 1947-48. **Home Addr:** 1201 Yale Pl Suite 1210, Minneapolis, MN 55403-1958. **Business Addr:** President, Owner, Relax The Back Store, 7533 France Ave S, Edina, MN 55435, **Business Phone:** (612)831-3205.

WARD-JOHNSON, FRANCES. **See WARD, FRANCES MARIE.**

WARDLAW, ALVIN HOLMES
Educator. **Personal:** Born Jan 3, 1925, Atlanta, GA; married Virginia Cage; children: Alvia W Shore & Joy Elaine. **Educ:** Morehouse Col, BS, 1948; Atlanta Univ, MS, 1950; Univ Mich, attended 1954; Univ Wis, attended 1966. **Career:** Tenn State Univ, asst prof, 1950-65, actg dept head, 1969-72; Tex Southern Univ, Coop Ctr Minn Math & Sci Teaching Proj, dir, 1963-64; Upward Bound Proj, dir, 1970-73; EPDA Inst Tenn State Univ, assoc dir, 1970-73; Tex Southern Univ, asst vpres acad affairs; Tex Tech Univ, dir fin reporting. **Orgs:** Rockefeller Found Fel, 1952-54; NSF Fac Fel, 1959-60; consult, Adminr Conf Houston Indep Sch Dist, 1960; Carnegie Found Fel, 1965-66; Nat Sic Inst Southern Univ; fac rep, Athletics Tenn State Univ, 1969-72; NAIA Dist eligibility com, 1971-73; pres, Tex Asn Stud Assist Progs, 1973; Athletic Adv Coun, 1974-75. **Military Serv:** AUS, 1944-46.

WARDLAW, MCKINLEY, JR.
Educator. **Personal:** Born Jul 24, 1927, Columbus, GA; son of McKinley and Rosa P Robinson; married Thelma Sears, Aug 3, 1951; children: Pamela Lynch, Vanessa D Morrison & Marcus K. **Educ:** Univ Dover, MD. **Career:** Kent Cty Vo-Tech, Woodside, DE, dir guidance, 1970-79; Dept Pub Instr, Dover, DE, state supvr, 1979-89; Delaware State Univ, Dover, DE, assoc prof, 1989. **Orgs:** Kappa Alpha Psi Frat, 1949-; professional mem, AMS, 1960-; DASA, 1979-, DSBA 1982-, ROA, 1982-; vpres, Capitol Sch Dist Sch Bd, 1982; com pilot; Gov's Coun Long-Term Care, 1992-. **Honors/Awds:** Kappa Man of the Year, Dover Alumni Chapter, 1983; Certificate of Appreciation, Del State Bd Educ, 1989; Certificate of Appreciation, Capital Bd Educ, 1989; Certificate of Appreciation, Kappa Alpha Psi Fraternity, 1989. **Military Serv:** US Air Force, maj, 1951-70. **Home Addr:** 617 Buckson Dr, Dover, DE 19901.

WARE, ALBERT M
Automotive executive. **Personal:** Born Oct 13, 1952, Detroit, MI; son of Albert and Bessie; married Wendy R, Jun 26, 1982; children: Christina M & Albert B. **Educ:** Wayne State Univ, BSME, 1977. **Career:** Ford Motor Co, suspension systems engr, 1977-81; Gen Motors, chassis syst engr, 1981-91, supervisor, chassis syst, 1991-92, vehicle syst integration mgr, 1993-94; Gen Motor, vehicle syst integration, mgr, 1994-95, truck plant integration eng, dir, 1996-98, plant support team eng, dir, 1998. **Orgs:** Dir, Pre Eng Educ Prog, Detroit Sec, SAE, 1987-; Chmn bd, finance & development committee, Detroit Area Pre Col Eng Prog, 1992-; bd trustees, SAE fed, 1996. **Honors/Awds:** US Black Eng Mag & Several Corp Sponsors, 1988-89; Spec Recognition Award, SAE, 1989; Black Engineer of the Year President's Award, Eng Deans Historically Black Col & Univ, 1994. **Special Achievements:** Sixth Annual Alumi Asn, Design & Fabrication Seminar Award, for developing a new innovative forged aluminum design for use in a high volume automotive application, 1985. *

WARE, ANDRE
Radio host, football player. **Personal:** Born Jul 31, 1968, Galveston, TX; son of Robert and Joyce. **Educ:** Alvin Community Coll, Univ Houston; BS, Marketing. **Career:** Football player (retired), Radio host; Detroit Lions, 1990-93; Minn Vikings, 1994; Los Angeles Raiders, 1994; Jacksonville Jaguars, 1995;Canadian Football League: Ottawa Rough Riders, 1995; British Columbia Lions, 1996; Toronto Argonauts, 1997; European NFL: Berlin Thunder, 1999; Houston Cougar Radio Network, color commentator; CBS, sports commentator; Houston Texans Radio Network, game anal; ESPN SEC Network, Analyst, currenlt. **Honors/ Awds:** Heisman Trophy, 1989; Davey O'Brien Award, 1989; College Football Hall of Fame, 2004; Named UPI National Player of the Year; Chevrolet Offensive Player of the Year; Southwest Conference Player of the Year. **Business Addr:** Game Analyst, ESPN Regional, 11001 Rushmore Dr, Charlotte, NC 28277, **Business Phone:** (704)973-5000.

WARE, BARBARA ANN. **See SCOTT-WARE, BARBARA ANN.**

WARE, CARL H.
Executive, executive director. **Personal:** Born Sep 30, 1943?, Newnan, GA; son of U B and Lois Wimberly; married Mary Clark, Jan 1, 1966; children: Timothy Alexander. **Educ:** Clark Col, BA, 1965; Carnegie Mellon Univ, postgrad, 1966; Univ Pittsburgh, MPA, 1968; Harvard Bus Sch, intl sr mgt prog, 1991. **Career:** Atlanta Housing Authority, dir, 1970-73; City of Atlanta, pres city coun,1974-79; Coca-Cola Co, Atlanta, GA, urban & govt affairs specialist, 1974-79, USA spec markets vpres, 1979-82, sr vpres, 1986-91; Northeast Europe & Africa, dep pres, 1991-93; Africa Group, pres, 1991-2000; Global Pub Affairs & Admin Div, exec vpres, 2000-03; sr advisor to chmn, 2003-05; Chevron Corp, dir, 2001-. **Orgs:** Policy Com Nat League Cities; GA Munic Asn; Comn Develop Comt; bd dirs, Metro Atlanta Coun Alcohol & Drugs; elected to Atlanta City Coun, 1973; bddirs, US Civil Rights Comn, 1983; Nat Coun Black Agencies, 1983-; United Way Metro Atlanta, 1983-; trustee, Clark Col; mem, Gammon Theol Sem; GA State Univ Found; Sigma Pi Phi; bd trustees, Clark Atlanta Univ; bd dirs, Georgia Power Co; bd dirs, PGA TOUR Golf Course Properties Inc; bd dirs, Southern Africa Enterprise Develop Fund; bd dirs, Med Educ South African Blacks; bd dirs, The Africa-Am Inst; Coun Foreign Relations. **Honors/Awds:** Numerous Civic Awards. **Business Phone:** (925)842-1000.

WARE, CHARLES JEROME
Association executive, lawyer. **Personal:** Born Apr 22, 1948, Anniston, AL; son of John Edward and Vonnie Marie; married Lucinda Frances Hubbard; children: Lucinda-Marie. **Educ:** Univ Fla Gainesville, fel med & sci, 1969, 1971; Univ Ala Sch Med, attended 1971; Talladega Col AL, BA 1970; Howard Univ Law Sch, JD, 1975; Boston Univ Sch Bus MA, MBA fel 1976. **Career:** Inst for Study Educ Policy, legal legis & econ asst 1974-75; Boston Col Law Sch, atty writer & consult, 1975-76; Boston Univ Martin Luther King Ctr, atty, 1976; Middlesex Co MA Dist Attys Off, asst dist atty, 1976-77; Arent Fox Kintner Plotkin & Kahn, anti-trust atty, 1977; Criminal Div US Dept Justice, trl atty, appellate atty, 1977-79; US Dept Justice, anti-trust atty, 1979-82; US Immigration, judge, 1980-81; US Fed Trade Comn, first asst to dir bur

competition, 1982-83, spec coun chmn 1983-86; St Paul's Col Lawrenceville VA, exec vpres & genl coun, 1986-87; Charles Jerome Ware, PA, atty, counr, 1988-. **Orgs:** Life Mem NAACP 1966-, SCLC 1966-; dir & ed Am Bar Asn; Asn Trl Lawyers Am; Nat Bar Asn; DC Bar Asn, PA Bar Asn 1975-, MD Bar Assoc, VA Bar Assoc; founder & pres, William Monroe Trotter Polit Res Inst 1978-; Nat legal advisor Nat Tots & Teens Inc 1986-; Gen Counsel, Md State Conf NAACP. **Honors/Awds:** Finalist White House Fellowship Prog 1978; Outstanding Young Columbian Columbia MD Jaycees, 1979; Outstanding Young Man of America, Am Jaycees Montgomery AL 1980. **Special Achievements:** Youngest immigration judge to ever be appointed in the history of the U.S. (1981); auth, Winning In Small Claims Court, 1990; auth, Fifty-Two(52) Secrets of Successful Cross-Examination, 1997; auth, Understanding the Law: A Primer, 2008. **Home Addr:** 5032 Rushlight Path, Columbia, MD 21044. **Business Addr:** Attorney, Charles Jerome Ware Attorney & Counselor, 10630 Little Patuxent Pkwy Suite 113, 1000 Century Plaza Bldg, Columbia, MD 21044-3273, **Business Phone:** (410)730-5016.

WARE, DYAHANNE
Lawyer. **Personal:** Born Jul 26, 1958, Chicago, IL; daughter of Freddie Mae and Clinton; children: Sherry Goldman & Tracey Love. **Educ:** Univ IL, BA, 1980; The John Marshall Law Sch, JD, 1984; Univ Chicago, Grad Sch Bus, MBA, 1990. **Career:** Encyclopedia Britannica USA, atty, FTC compliance audit staff, 1984-85, staff atty 1985-86, atty general counsel/dir legal compliance staff; spec foreign asst, Guadeloupe, FWI; Lexis-Nexis, corp counsel consult, 1994-95; Com Clearing House, int sr attorney, 1995-96, assoc gen coun; pvt pract atty, currently. **Orgs:** League Black Women; Chicago Bar Asn, 1985-; Am Bar Asn; Chicago Vol Legal Servs; nat bd realtors, Urban League, Nat Conf Black Lawyers; Cook County Bar Asn, 1990; Nat Black MBA Asn, 1989-90. **Honors/Awds:** Honoree YWCA Leadership Award, 1985; Honoree YMCA Black & Hispanic Leaders of Indust, 1987. **Business Addr:** Associate General Counsel, PO Box 18125, Chicago, IL 60015-3867, **Business Phone:** (312)213-2436.

WARE, DR. GILBERT
Educator. **Personal:** Born Jul 21, 1933, Elkton, VA; divorced. **Educ:** Morgan State Univ, BA, 1955; Princeton Univ, MD, PhD, 1962. **Career:** State MD, prog exec, 1967-68; Wash Tech Inst, exec asst to pres, 1968-69;The Urban Inst, sr res staff mem, 1969-70; Drexel Univ, assoc prof & prof polit sci, 1970. **Orgs:** Life mem, Nat Asn Advan Colored People; exec dir, Judicial Coun Nat Bar Asn, 1971-81; bd dirs, Hist Soc US Dist Ct Eastern PA, 1986-. **Honors/Awds:** Fel Ford Found; fel Am Coun Learned Soc; fel Am Philosophical Soc; fel Metropolitan Appl Res Ctr; Presidential Award, Nat Bar Asn, 1977. **Special Achievements:** Publ: "From the Black Bar, Voices for Equal Justice," Putnam 1976;"William Hastie, Grace Under Pressure," Oxford Univ Press 1984. **Military Serv:** AUS, 1st lt, 4 yrs.

WARE, HENRY A, JR.
Chief executive officer. **Career:** Southaven Pontiac Buick GMC Inc, owner & chief exec officer, currently. **Orgs:** Gen Motors Minority Dealers Asn. **Honors/Awds:** GM Mark Excellence Award; GM Leaders Distinction Award. **Business Addr:** Owner, Chief Exec Officer, Southaven Pontiac Buick GMC Inc, 78 Goodman, Southaven, MS 38671, **Business Phone:** (662)349-5600.*

WARE, IRENE JOHNSON
Radio broadcaster. **Personal:** Born Apr 24, 1935, Blackshear, AL; married Fred E; children: Darryl, Ronald. **Educ:** Allen Inst, 1953; Besteda's Sch Cosmetology, 1961. **Career:** Gospel Serv ABC & Dunhill Records, dir; WGOK Radio, announcer & gen mgr, 1962-; Record World Mag NYC, gospel ed, 1967-. **Orgs:** NATRA; BAMA; GMWA; exec dir, Nat Asn Gospel Announcers & Affiliates; gospel editor, Black Radio Exclusive Magazine; vpres, bd dir Gospel Music Asn, 1980; bd dir, OIC Mobile Area; Operation PUSH Chicago; elected pres, Nat Black Programmers Coalition. **Honors/Awds:** Named 1 Top 10 Gospel Announcers, Open Mike Mag, 1965; Humanitarian Award, NATRA, 1971; Woman of the Yr, Black Radio Conf, 1977; Gospel Announcer of Year, Gospel-Music Workshop of Am, 1979; Black Gospel Announcer of Year Award, SESAC, 1978; Outstanding Citizen of the Year, Stewart Memorial CME Ch, 1980; Jack Walker Award for Excellence in Broadcasting, NATRA, 1973; Excellence in Broadcasting, Utterbach Concert Choir Carnegie Hall, 1969; Gospel Announcer of The Year Award, NBPC. *

WARE, JANIS L
Newspaper publisher. **Personal:** Daughter of J Lowell. **Educ:** Univ Ga, BS, bus admin. **Career:** The Atlanta Voice, Black Press USA Network, publ, 1991-; Voice News Network, pres. **Orgs:** Exec dir, Summech Community Develop Corp, 1989-; chair, Southside Med Ctr; City Atlanta, Beltway Steering Comt; Atlanta Zoning Task Force; chair, vice chair, Atlanta Housing Authority; Habitat Humanity; Empire Real Estate Bd; Atlanta Bus League. **Honors/Awds:** One of the 100 Most Influential Women in Atlanta, Atlanta Bus League; Who's Who of Black Atlanta; Women Making the Mark Award recipients, Atlanta Mag. **Business Addr:** Publisher, The Atlanta Voice Newspaper/Voices News Network Inc, 633 Pryor St SW, Atlanta, GA 30312, **Business Phone:** (404)524-6426.

WARE, JEWEL C
Government official. **Personal:** Daughter of Mattie. **Career:** Wayne County Comn, comnr, 1995-, chair, 2003; Wayne County, commissioner, currently. **Orgs:** Chair, Wayne County Comn, 2003-; vice chair, Comt Audit; vice chair, Subcomt Sr Citizen Affairs; Health & Human Serv Comt; Pub Safety & Judiciary Comt; Legis Res comt; Genesis Lutheran Church; Nat Black Caucus Aging Coalition Labor Union; Mack Alive; Pittman Memorial Housing Develop. **Business Addr:** Commissioner, Chair, Wayne County Commission, Wayne County Bldg 600 Randolph Suite 449, Detroit, MI 48226, **Business Phone:** (313)224-0900.

WARE, JOHN
Government official, city manager. **Educ:** Ouachita Baptist Univ, BA; Syracuse Univ, MPA. **Career:** City Dallas, city mgr, 1993-98; 21st Century Group, pres & chief exec officer, 1996-; City Newport News, asst city mgr; City Austin, Texas, asst city mgr. **Business Addr:** President, Chief Executive Officer, 21st Century Group LLC, 200 Crescent Ct Suite 1600, Dallas, TX 75201, **Business Phone:** (214)965-7999.

WARE, JOHN E.
College teacher. **Educ:** Mich State Univ, DMA. **Career:** Xavier Univ, dept music, prof & chair, currently. *

WARE, JUANITA GLEE. **See THOMAS, JUANITA WARE.**

WARE, OMEGO JOHN CLINTON
Consultant. **Personal:** Born Mar 13, 1928, Washington, DC; son of Omego J C Sr and Bertha Shipp; married Elinor Gwen Smith; children: Karl R, Keith R & Karlene R. **Educ:** Georgetown Univ, BS foreign commerce, 1960; US Army War Col, Grad 1969. **Career:** CIA, SIS Off dir, Ombudsman, Dir Ctr Study Intelligence, 1955-82; Univ Calif, Lawrence Livermore Nat Lab, adminr, Counter Terror Specialist; US Dept Energy, Wash, IIntelligence consult, adv, 1982-83; Ware Assoc Int, pres, currently. **Orgs:** BSA; SCIP. **Honors/Awds:** CIA Awards, charter mem, Senior Intelligence Serv; First "Trailblazer" Award, Cent Intelligence Agency, 1991; 50th Anniversary Trailblazer Award, CIA, 1997; Special DOE awards. **Military Serv:** RA mil intelligence & Counter Intelligence, 1946-55. **Home Addr:** 3244 Pope St SE, Washington, DC 20020. **Business Addr:** President, Ware Associates International, 3244 Pope St, Washington, DC 20020-2318, **Business Phone:** (202)584-9683.

WARE, R DAVID
Lawyer. **Personal:** Born May 20, 1954, Franklin, GA; son of Roosevelt Sr and Lorine Kelly; married Sharon Ward, Sep 2, 1978; children: Jerris, Candace & Breana. **Educ:** W Ga Col, BA, eng, 1976; Univ Ga Sch Law, JD, 1979. **Career:** Coun Legal Educ Opportunities, teaching asst, 1977; Small Bus Develop Ctr, grad staff consult, 1978-79; PRO Larry E Blount, res asst; Kilpatrick & Cody, assoc, 1979-82; Vaughn, Phears & Murphy, assoc, 1982-83; Law Off R David Ware, pres, 1983-; Floyd, Jones & Ware, partner, 1985-89; Thomas, Kennedy, Sampson, Edwards & Patterson, partner; State Ct, magistrate judge; Supreme Ct, magistrate judge; Ware & Assocs, pres; CSMG Sports Inc, Exec vpres sports, 2003; Fulton County Dist Attorney's Off, Pub Safety Div, staff atty, sr atty, 2004-. **Orgs:** State Bar Ga; Gate City Bar Asn, exec comt, 1984, vpres, 1985, pres, 1987-88; Atlanta Bar Asn; Nat Bar Asn; Am Bar Asn; Atlanta Vol Lawyers Found; Fulton County Bd Ethics, 1989-. **Honors/Awds:** Alumnus of the Year, Univ GA Sch Law, 1981-82; numerous college & law school honors. **Special Achievements:** "How to Select a Sports Agent," 1983; "Why Are There So Few Black Sports Agents?" Sports, Inc, 1988; The Effects of Gender and Race on the Practice of Law, State Bar of Ga, 1992. **Business Phone:** (404)730-4000.

WARE, WILLIAM
Insurance executive. **Personal:** Married Carole M Wiggins. **Educ:** Goddard Col, BA, MA, environ risk mgt & ins. **Career:** William J Ware & Assoc, pres & chief exec officer, currently. **Orgs:** Chmn & exec dir, Ga Asn Ins Prof; chmn, Atlanta Exchange Found Inc; coordr, Prof Bus Proj, Role Models, Career Day Prog Stud; life mem, Disabled Am Veterans; Leadership COBB Class 1994-95; COBB COC; numerous others. **Honors/Awds:** Certificate of Appreciation, Atlanta Olympic force; Certificate of Appreciation, Atlanta Asn Ins Prof. **Business Addr:** President, Chief Executive Officer, William J. Ware & Associates Inc & Success Guide, 3655 Cherokee St Suite 21, Kennesaw, GA 30144-2026, **Business Phone:** (770)420-8555.

WARE, DR. WILLIAM LEVI
Educator. **Personal:** Born May 15, 1934, Greenwood, MS; son of Leslie Ware (deceased) and Katherine Bowden; married Lottie Herger, Apr 18, 1958; children: Felicia Joyner, Trevor Ware & Melvinia Abdullah. **Educ:** Miss Valley State Univ, Itta Bena, BS, MS, 1957; Calif State Univ, Los Angeles, CA, MA, 1969; Univ Southern Calif, Los Angeles, CA, PhD, 1978. **Career:** Educator (retired); Greenwood Pub Sch, health educ & coach, 1957-63; Bellflower Pub Sch, phys educ & coach, 1963-72; Calif State Univ, Northridge, CA, asst prof, 1964-78; Miss State Univ, Miss State, MS, assoc prof, 1979-90; Miss Valley State Univ, prof, educ dept chair, 1990; Mississippi Valley State Univ, asst to pres, 1995-98; comt outreach specialist, exec dir serv learning, 1998. **Orgs:** Dir, United Way Oktibbeha City, 1982-85; Boy Scouts Am, Pushmatha Coun, 1983-85; Volunteers Youth, 1985; pres, Kiwanis Club, Starkville, 1986-87. **Honors/Awds:** Service Award, Calif Congress Parents & Teachers Inc, 1969; Leadership Starkville, Starkville Chamber Com, 1985; Kiwanian of the Year, 1985; Distinguished Educ Award, IDEA, 1987; Outstanding Service Award, Phi Delta Kappa, 1989; Pres Citation; Nat Asn Equal Opportunity Higher Educ, 1989; Fac Fel & Found Mid-South, 1994. **Home Addr:** 75 Choctaw Rd, Starkville, MS 39759.

WAREHAM, ALTON L.
Dentist, educator. **Personal:** Born Jul 1, 1920, New York, NY; son of Samuel and Esther; married Helene; children: Roger, Lynn Howell. **Educ:** Lincoln Univ, PA, AB, 1942; Howard Univ Col Dent, DDS, 1948. **Career:** Dentist (retired); Medicaid Comn NY City, chmn, 1968; Dent Care Serv 125th St, asst dir, 1968-69; Headstraight Prog NY, chmn, 1970-72; Blue Shield Blue Cross Dent Care Prog NY City, consult, 1972; Greater Harlem Nursing Home, dent consult, 1977; Harlem Hosp, Oral Surg Dept, dentist & educator. **Orgs:** fel Acad Gen Dent, 1982; fel Suppl Continuing Educ Acad Gen Dent, 1984; fel Am Col Dent, 1992; NAACP; PA Urban League; 1st Dist Dent Soc; ADA; NY State Dept Correctional Serv, Regional Div Dentists. **Honors/Awds:** Appreciation Award, Harlem Hosp & Oral Surg Clin, 1984. **Military Serv:** AUS, capt, 1952-54; Bronze Star; Unit Award; Combat Med Badgem, 1953. **Home Addr:** 2235 Fifth Ave, New York, NY 10037. *

WAREHAM, ROGER
Lawyer. **Educ:** Harvard Univ, BA, 1972; Columbia Univ Law Sch, JD, 1976. **Career:** John Jay Col Criminal Justice, fac; Col New Rochelle, Sch New Resources, fac; Thomas, Wareham & Richards LLP, Brooklyn, NY, atty, currently. **Orgs:** Int Secy-Gen, Int Asn Against Torture; Nat Conf Black Lawyers; Bur US Non-Govt Orgn Comt Human Rights. **Business Phone:** (718)941-6407.

WARFIELD, ERIC ANDREW
Football player. **Personal:** Born Mar 3, 1976, Vicksburg, MS. **Educ:** Univ Nebr. **Career:** Kans City Chiefs, defensive back, 1998-06; New England Patriots, pract squad mem, 2006; community mentor, currently. **Orgs:** Love Fund for Children.

WARFIELD, MARSHA
Comedian, actor. **Personal:** Born Mar 5, 1954, Chicago, IL. **Career:** Actress, 1974-; stand-up comic & comedienne in clubs throughout US & Canada, 1976-; Films: D C Cab, 1983; Mask, 1985; Gidget Goes to Harlem, Caddyshack II, 1988; TV: "The Richard Pryor Show", 1977; "Riptide", 1983; "The Marva Collins Story", 1981; "Night Court", 1986-92; "Teddy Pendergrass in Concert" comic, 1982; "Harry Anderson's Sideshow" comic, 1987; "Comic Relief" 1987; "Just for Laughs" 1987; "On Location", comic, 1987; "The Thirteenth Annual Circus of the Stars", 1988; "Marsha", hostess, 1990; "The Marsha Warfield Show", 1990-91; "Living Single", 1997; "Clueless", 1998; "The Joint", 1998; "The Love Boat: The Next Wave", 1999; guest appearance, "Veronica's Closet", 1999; Writer: "The Richard Pryor Show", 1977; "Uptown Comedy Express", 1987. **Honors/Awds:** Winner, San Francisco Nat Stand-up Comedy Competition, 1979.

WARFIELD, ROBERT N
Financial manager, executive. **Personal:** Born Nov 29, 1948, Guthrie, KY; married Gloria Jean. **Educ:** Eastern Ky Univ, BA, 1970; Columbia Univ Grad Sch Jour, attended 1971; Stanford Univ, Grad Sch Bus & Wharton Bus Sch. **Career:** Orion Broadcasting, news reporter & photogr, 1971-72, prom & advert mgr, 1972-73; WAVE-TV, Louisville, KY, producer, 1973-75; WTNH-TV, New Haven, CT, prod mgr; WDIV-TV, Detroit, MI, from asst news dir to news dir, 1979-84, vpres news, 1984-89, sta mgr, 1989-91; Alpha Capital Mgt Inc, Detroit, MI, cofounder & partner, 1991; Alpha Partners LLC, chair investment rev comt, pres & chief exec officer, currently. **Orgs:** Co-founder, Alpha-Munder Found, 1991. **Business Phone:** (313)963-4911.

WARFIELD-COPPOCK, NSENGA
Psychologist. **Personal:** Born Oct 28, 1949, Minneapolis, MN; daughter of Walter and Grace; married Bertram Atiba, Jan 17, 1970; children: Khary Coppock, Akua Coppock & Safiya Warfield. **Educ:** The Am Univ, BA, Psychol, 1971, MEd Spec, Educ, 1972; The Fielding Inst, PhD organizational psychol, 1985. **Career:** Asn Black Psychol, nat admin, 1971-81, orgn psych; Baobab Assoc, Inc, pres, founder, speaker, writer, Wash DC, currently. **Orgs:** Consult, The Gray Panthers, 1980-; consult AMTRAK, 1982; hist bd dir, Asn Black Psychol, 1982-87; Asn Black Psychol, 1971-; fel, HEW Wash, DC 1972; fel, Nat Sci Found, 1979-82; Various Child, Aging & Women's Orgn; Office Substance Abuse Prev. **Special Achievements:** article "Liberation & Struggle" in Reflctns in Black Psychol, 1977; numerous papers, presentations & workshops; books: Teen Pregnancy Prevention: A Rites of Passage Resource Manual 1989; Transformation: A Rites of Passage Manual for African American Girls 1988; Afro centric Theory & Applications, Vol 1: The Adolescent Rites of Passage, 1990; Afro centric Theory and Applications, Vol 2, 1992; African Sisterhood: Rite of Passage, 1994. **Business Addr:** President,

Organizational Psychologist, Baobab Associates Inc, 7614 16th St NW, Washington, DC 20012-1406, **Business Phone:** (202)726-0560.

WARMACK, GREGORY
Artist, sculptor. **Personal:** Born Jan 1, 1948?. **Career:** Artist, sculptor, mixed media artist, jewelry designer; Self-employed, artist, 1978-; DuSable Mus Afro-Am Art, vis artist, 1986; Expressway's Children's Mus, Chicago, vis artist, 1986; Boston Col Art, vis artist, 1987; Ill State Mus, Lockport, vis artist, 1988, Univ Chicago, vis artist, 1989; Dallas Mus Art, vis artist, 1990; Field Mus, Chicago, vis artist, 1991; Sibell-Wolle Fine Arts, Univ Colo, vis artist, 1992; Wabash Col, Crawfordsville, Ind, artist-in-residence, 1994; TASA Conf, Univ Tex, Tyler, vis artist, 1995; Mus Int Folk Art, Sante Fe, NMex, vis artist, 1996. **Honors/Awds:** Children's Defense Fund Award, 1995; Artist of the Year Award, Folk Art Soc Am, 1997. **Special Achievements:** 11 foot Coca-Cola bottlecap sculpture for the 1996 Olympics in Atlanta. **Business Addr:** Artist, c/o Judy A Saslow Gallery, 300 W Superior, Chicago, IL 60610, **Business Phone:** (312)943-0530.

WARMACK, KEVIN LAVON
Executive. **Personal:** Born Dec 20, 1956, Chicago, IL; son of Kenneth and Jacqueline Elliott; married Delma LaSane; children: Delma, Kevin II, Nadia & Marcus. **Educ:** Ripon Col, BA, 1979; Keller Grad Sch Mgt. **Career:** Lawyer's Word Processing Ltd, mgr, 1979-81; Mayer Brown & Platt, asst super, 1981-83; Arnstein Gluck Lehr, legal asst, 1983-85; Hisaw & Schultz, legal asst, 1985-86; McSherry & Gray Ltd, legal asst, 1986-87, law resources, 1987-88; Nat Asn Securities Dealers, sr compliance examr, 1988-95; Rodman & Renshaw, Assoc, Regulatory Acct, 1995-96; Warmack Consulting, Ltd, pres, curently; Melvin Securities Corp, mgr, currently; Broker Dealer Appliance Consulting; SBK-Brooks Investment Corp, chief compliance officer, currently. **Orgs:** Nat Black MBA Asn, 1989-; bd mem, Harvard Sch; Woodgate Fathers; Church St John The Evangelist Episcopal Church; Nat Asn Black Accts; Securities Indust Asn; Nat Asn Securities Profs; pres, Chicago Chapter. **Home Phone:** (773)933-0480. **Business Addr:** President, Warmack Consulting Ltd, 7632 S Shore Dr Unit 1D, Chicago, IL 60649, **Business Phone:** (773)933-0480.

WARMLY, LEON
Manager. **Personal:** Born Apr 28, 1941, Shreveport, LA; son of Joe Williams and Gertrude Williams. **Educ:** Bill Wade Sch Modern Radio, Cert, 1966; San Diego City Col, AA, 1973; San Diego State Univ, San Diego, CA, BA, 1982, CA, comm col instr credentials, 1990. **Career:** Manager (retired); KDIG-FM Radio, San Diego, CA, announcer, 1966-67; KFMB Radio, San Diego, CA, new reporter, 1973-75; Toastmaster's Int, Dist 5, San Diego, CA, publicity dir, 1974-75; Monford Pt Marine Asn, San Diego, CA, publicity dir, 1975-79; DECA Commissary, Imperial Beach, CA, store mgr, 1991-96. **Orgs:** Toastmasters Int Dist 5; San Diego Club Bi Centennial 2675, 1969-74; chmn bd dir, Bay Vista Methodist Heights Apts HUD, 2001. **Honors/Awds:** KFMB Radio News Scholarship, 1973. **Military Serv:** USMC, Corporal E 4, 1962-66; Armed Forces Expeditionary Medal, 1963. *

WARNER, EDWARD L.
Clergy. **Personal:** Born Oct 20, 1939, Franklin Township, NJ. **Educ:** Rutgers Univ, AB, 1961; Mdiv, 1964. **Career:** St Albans, vicar, 1964-67; St Augustine's Episcopal Church, rector. **Orgs:** Diocesan Coun & Steering Comt Coun; Standing Comt; chmn, Mayor's Comn Human Rights New Brunswick NJ; past pres, InterdenomiNatMinisterial Alliance; bd educ & chmn, Community Rel Comn Presby. **Honors/Awds:** Interracial Award, 1969; Omega Si Phi Citizenship Award, 1973; Citizenship Award, Kansas City C C, 1974.

WARNER, ISIAH MANUEL
Scientist, educator. **Personal:** Born Jul 20, 1946, Bunkie, LA; son of Humphrey and Irma Warner; married Della Blount, Jun 1, 1968; children: Isiah M Jr, Chideha Charles & Edward. **Educ:** Southern Agr & Mech Univ, BS, chem, 1968; Univ WV, PhD, anal chem, 1977. **Career:** Battelle Northwest, Richland, WA, res chemist, 1968-73; Univ Wash, Chem Dept, teaching asst, 1973-75, res asst, 1975-77; Tex Agr & Mech, asst prof, 1977-82; Emory Univ, Dept Chem, assoc prof, 1982-86, prof, 1986, Samuel Chandler Dobbs prof, 1987-92; NSF, prog officer anal & surface chem, 1988-89; La St Univ, Philip W West Prof anal chem, 1992-, chair, dept chem, 1994-97, Boyd prof, 2000-, Off Strat Initiatives, vice chancellor, 2001-, Howard Hughes med inst prof, 2002-. **Orgs:** RCMI External Adv Comt, 1992-; NY Acad Scis, 1995-; Am Chem Soc, Minority Taskforce, 1996-98; Nat Acad Sci, Chem Sci Roundtable, 1997-98; rep, Coun Undergrad Res, 1998; adv coun bd, Nat Inst Gen Med Sci, NIH, 1999-2002; Nat Orgn Black Chemists & Chem Engrs; Soc Appl Spectroscopy; Sigma Xi; NAm Chap Int Chemometrics Soc; Soc Fluorescence. **Honors/Awds:** Presidential Award for Excellence in Science, Mathematics, & Engineering Mentoring, 1997; Lifetime Mentor Award, AAAS, 2000; Distinguished Faculty Award, La State Univ, 2000; Louisiana Professor of the Year, CarnegieFound CASE, 2000. **Special Achievements:** Author of numerous articles, book chapters and books. **Home Addr:** 13020 Springview Ave, Baton Rouge, LA 70810, **Home Phone:** (225)769-3017. **Business Addr:** Boyd Professor, Louisiana State University, Department of Analytical & Environmental Chemistry, 232 Chpoin Hall Suite 436, Baton Rouge, LA 70803-1804, **Business Phone:** (225)578-2829.

WARNER, MALCOLM-JAMAL
Singer, actor. **Personal:** Born Aug 18, 1970, Jersey City, NJ; son of Robert Warner and Pamela. **Career:** Actor, 1984-; dir, 1989-; musician, 1990; TV series: The Cosby Show, 1984-92; Here & Now, 1992-93; The Magic Sch Bus, animated, 1994-98; Malcolm & Eddie, 1996-2000; Jeremiah, 2002-04; Listen Up, 2005; Dexter, 2006; Films: The Father Clements Story, 1987; Drop Zone, 1994; Tyson, 1995; The Tuskegee Airmen, 1995; Restaurant, 1998; A Fare to Remember, 1998; author of Theo & Me, Growing Up Okay, Dutton, 1988; Reflections: A Story of Redemption, 2004; I am Perfect, 2005; Contradictions of the Heart, 2006; Fools Gold, 2008; Malcolm Jamal Warners Miles Long, owner, currently. **Orgs:** Chair, Nat PTA; nat chmn, Miracle Network Telethon; co-chair, Black Family Reunion Celebration. **Honors/Awds:** NAACP Image Award, Best Performance by an Actor in a Comedy, for "The Cosby Show"; NAACP Key of Life Image Award; winner, "Celebrity Poker Showdown," 2003. **Special Achievements:** Nominee, Emmy Award, 1986; ranked 32 in VH1 list of the "100 Greatest Kid Stars"; nominee, BET Comedy Award, 2005. **Business Addr:** Actor, Singer, Warner Management, 13547 Ventura Blvd, New York, NY 10010, **Business Phone:** (818)385-1641.

WARNER, DR. NEARI FRANCOIS
College administrator. **Personal:** Born Jul 20, 1945, New Orleans, LA; daughter of Enell (Brimmer) Francois and Cornelius; divorced; children: Jimmie D Warner Jr. **Educ:** Grambling State Univ, BS, 1967; Atlanta Univ, MA, 1968; La State Univ-Baton Rouge, PhD, curric & instr, 1992. **Career:** Southern Univ New Orleans, assoc prof Eng, 1968-75, dir, Upward Bound, 1976-88, dean, jr division, 1989-94; Grambling State Univ, asst vpres acad affairs, 1994-96, vp develop, 1997-98, provost & vpres acad affairs, 1998-2000, acting pres, 2001-04, pres, currently. **Orgs:** La Asn Stud Assistance Progs, pres, vp, sec, 1974-88; Alpha Kappa Alpha Sorority, grad adv, regional committee, 1975-2002; Southwest Asn Stud Assistance Progs, bd mem, 1987-89; Gov's Task Force Tech Prep, bd mem, 1991-93; The Links Inc, treasurer, facet chair, 1997-2002; La Endowment the Humanities, exec bd sec, 1998-; Conference La Cols & Univs, sec, 1999-2000; La Women in Higher Educ, pres-elect, 2002-; Golden Key, Pi Gamma Mu & Alpha Gamma Delta Soc, Austerlitz Street Baptist Church, New Orleans; New Rocky Valley Baptist Church, Grambling. **Honors/Awds:** Southern Univ-New Orleans, Outstanding Teacher for Division of Freshman Studies, 1973, 1974; Omega Psi Phi Fraternity/Links Inc, Unsung Hero, 19901993; Nat Resource Ctr for Freshman Year Experience, Nat Freshman Advocate, 1992; YWCA, New Orleans Role Model, 1992; Nat Asn for Equal Opportunity, Distinguished Alumnae, 1996; Mary B Singleton Award, Delta Sigma chap of Alpha Phi Alpha Fraternity Inc. **Special Achievements:** Author: handbook, Handbook for Upward Bound Participants, 1980; monograph, Pre-College Compensatory Programs: Science in Upward Bound, 1989; preface, An Interdisciplinary Approach to Issues and Practices in Teacher Education, 1998; book chapter, Developing a Perspective for an Assessment Model for Developmental Education Programs, 1999; book chapter, Enhancing Academic Achievement Through a Continuum of Literacy activities, 2001; From a pool of 188 international nominees, Warner was selected as one of twelve for Outstanding National Freshman Advocate by the National Resource Center for the Freshman Year Experience; The first acting woman President of Grambling State University. **Business Addr:** President, Grambling State University, 100 Founders St Long-Jones Hall, PO Box 607, Grambling, LA 71245, **Business Phone:** (318)274-6117.

WARREN, ANNIKA LAURIN
Clergy. **Personal:** Born Dec 8, 1959, Hartford, CT; daughter of Hubbard H I and Annie McLaurin; married Mozallen McFadden, Jul 11, 1987; children: Shomari McFadden & Catherine Alannie McFadden. **Educ:** St Augustine's Col, BA, urban affairs, 1981; Va Theol Sem, MDiv, 1984. **Career:** Greater Hartford Chamber Com, Weaver High Sch, drop-out prev counr, 1983-91; Christ Church Cathedral, staff priest, 1984-88; St Monica's Episcopal Church, rector, 1991-. **Orgs:** Alpha Kappa Alpha, 1977-; Alpha Kappa Mu Honor Soc, 1981-; bd dir, Greater Hartford Urban League, 1989-90; Coalition of 100 Black Women, 1990-; bd dir, Greater Hartford United Way, 1992-; bd dir, Hartford Action Plan Infant Health, 1992-. **Honors/Awds:** Harriett Tubman Book Award, 1983. **Special Achievements:** First African to be ordained to the Episcopal Priesthood in the Diocese, 1985. **Home Addr:** 197 Ridgefield St, Hartford, CT 06112-1837, **Home Phone:** (203)293-1076. **Business Addr:** Rector, Christ Church Cathedral, 45 Church St, Hartford, CT 06120, **Business Phone:** (860)527-7231.

WARREN, BETH I (BETH IMOGENE WARREN)
Executive. **Personal:** Born Oct 3, 1938, Atlanta, GA; daughter of Gladstone L Chandler; married Theodore J, Aug 29, 1964; children: Beth Angela. **Educ:** Wheaton Col, Norton, MA, BA, 1959; Simmon Col Sch Social Work, MSW, 1963. **Career:** Roxbury Children's Service, exec dir, 1971-75; Dept of Public Welfare, asst commissioner, 1975-76; Univ of Southern Maine, dir of eeo, 1978-82, assoc vp of hr, 1982-92, assoc prof, 1985-92; Cornell Univ, assoc vp for hr, 1992-95, visiting fellow, 1995-98; Workworld's Human Resource Corp, pres/CEO, 1996-. **Orgs:** Alpha Kappa Alpha Sorority, 1958-; Soc Human Resource Mgt, 1985-; Am Soc Training Develop, 1985-; nat bd, Col & Univ Personnel Asn, 1991-95; Soc Human Resource Planning, 1995-; bd,Oxfam Am, 1995-; diocesan bd, Episcopal Church Women, 1997-; Am Mgt Asn, 1998-. **Honors/Awds:** Creativity Award, 1987; Diedrich K Willars Award, Col & Univ Personnel Asn, 1988; Award for Excellence, ME Comn Women, 1990. **Special Achievements:** Co-author, College & University Disability Management, 1996; Certified Seminar Human Resource Professional, 1998-; Certified Human Patterns International Administrator, 1997-. **Business Addr:** President, Chief Executive Officer, WorkWorlds, PO Box 92487, Atlanta, GA 30311-4304, **Business Phone:** (404)755-0988.

WARREN, BETH IMOGENE. **See WARREN, BETH I.**

WARREN, CLARENCE F
Car dealer. **Personal:** Born Feb 15, 1941, Detroit, MI; son of Clarence R and Opal C; married Geraldine, Sep 5, 1964; children: Uvanuka. **Educ:** Wayne State Univ, BA, 1963; Univ Ga, advan studies. **Career:** Kroger Co, corp dir, labor rels, 1958-86; PS I Love Yogurt, chair, chief exec officer, 1986-89; Network Video, pres, chief exec officer, 1986-89; 32 Ford Mercury Inc, pres & chief exec officer, 1989-. **Orgs:** Dir, Nat Asn Minority Auto Dealer, 1990-; NCP; Urban League; Wayne State Univ Alumni; Ford Lincoln Mercury Minority Dealer Asn, 1994. **Honors/Awds:** Minority Supplier of the Year, Cincinnati Minority Supplier Develop Coun, 1992; Top Profit DD Dealer in US, Ford Motor Co, 1992; Top Profit Dealer Award, Ford Motor Co, 1994. **Special Achievements:** Opened New Store, Sidney Ford Lincoln Mercury, Sidney, Ohio; Company ranked 10 on Black Enterprise's list of top 100 auto dealerships, 1998. **Business Addr:** President, Chief Executive Officer, 32 Ford Mercury Inc, 610 W Main St, Batavia, OH 45103, **Business Phone:** (513)732-2124.

WARREN, GERTRUDE FRANCOIS
Educator. **Personal:** Born Jul 4, 1929, Detroit, MI; daughter of John Henry and Lela Long; married Minor, Sep 20, 1979; children: Lela Valsine Battle & Herbert W Francois Jr. **Educ:** Eastern Mich Univ, Ypsilanti, Mich, BS, 1949, MS, spec educ, PhD. **Career:** Meisners, Detroit, Mich, personnel mgr, 1950-55; Ypsilanti Bd Educ, Ypsilanti, Mich, teacher; Detroit Bd Educ, Detroit, Mich, teacher eng, dept head. **Orgs:** Pres, Palm Leaf Club, 1955-; comnr, Pub Housing, 1965-70; comnr, Mental Health, Wash Co, 1970-79; parliamentarian, Alpha Kappa Alpha Sorority, 1970-74; mem chair, Dorcas Soc, 1971-; comnr, Low Cost Housing, 1971-; Nat Asn Advan Colored People, 1981-; secy, Kings Daughters, 1985; Steering Comt, REACT, 1987-; budget chair, New Era Study Club, 1987-; pres, Mich State Asn Colored Women's Clubs, 1987; advisor, Metro Women's Civic Club, 1988-. **Special Achievements:** Founded First Scholar for Blacks, Mich State Asn, 1988. **Home Addr:** 26842 Hopkins St, Inkster, MI 48141, **Home Phone:** (313)561-4694.

WARREN, HERMAN LECIL
Educator. **Personal:** Born Nov 13, 1933, Tyler, TX; son of Cicero and Leola Mosley; married Mary K, Oct 12, 1963; children: Michael J, Christopher L & Mark H. **Educ:** Prairie View A&M, BS, 1953; Michigan State Univ, MS, 1962; Univ Minn, PhD, 1969. **Career:** Olin Chem Corp, New Haven CT, res scientist, 1962-67; USDA, Beltsville, MD, plant pathologist, 1969-71; USDA, Purdue Univ, W Lafayette, IN, from asst to assoc prof & plant pathologist, 1971-89; Va Polytech Inst & St Univ, prof, plant pathol, 1989-2003, prof emer, 2003-. **Orgs:** Am Phytopathological Soc; New York Acad Sci. **Honors/Awds:** African Scientific Inst, fel, 1993; Commonwealth Vis Prof Va. **Special Achievements:** Publ, Translation alterations in maize leaves responding to pathogen infection, paraquat treatment, or heat shock, 1988; Nuclear RNA polymer ase II in maize leaves infected with Bipolaris maydis, 1991; Interrelationship of nitrogen nutrition with maize (Zea mays) grain yield, nitrogen use efficiency and grain quality, 1992; Expansion of lesions induced by races 1, 2 and 3 of Bipolaris zeicola, 1993; Inheritance of resistance to Exserohilum turcicum, 1993; Fungal invasion of kernels and grain mold damage assessment in diverse sorghum germ plasm, 1996; Diallel analysis of Diplodia ear rot resistance in maize, 1998. **Military Serv:** AUS, first lt, 1953-56. **Business Addr:** Professor Emeritus, Virginia Polytechnic Institute and State University, Department of Plant Pathology, Physiology, and Weed Science, 413 Price Hall Va Tech, Blacksburg, VA 24061-0331, **Business Phone:** (540)231-7486.

WARREN, JAMES KENNETH
Manager. **Personal:** Born Jan 1, 1947, Detroit, MI; son of Amos and Ocie Chapman; married Diedre Peterson (divorced 1978); children: Jacqueline Carmila Plair. **Educ:** Howard Univ, Wash, BA, 1970. **Career:** BASF Corp, Dearborn, mgr planning, 1976-79, area sales mgr, 1979-88, spec prog developer, 1988-91, tech training mgr, currently. **Orgs:** Howard Univ Alumni Asn, 1970-91; Automotive Serv Indust Asn, 1974-91; Automotive Training

Mgr Coun, 1991. **Home Phone:** (313)862-9244. **Business Addr:** Technical Training Manager, US Automotive Refinish, BASF Corporation, 1609 Biddle Ave, Wyandotte, MI 48192, **Business Phone:** (734)324-6000.

WARREN, DR. JOSEPH DAVID
Educator. **Personal:** Born Apr 2, 1938, New York, NY; son of Harold H Sr and Geroldine McDaniel; divorced; children (previous marriage): Makeda, Settt & Kara; married Martha L. **Educ:** NC A&T Univ, Greensboro NC, BS, econ, 1969; Brandeis Univ, Waltham Massachusetts, MA, social research, 1973, PhD, social work, 1983. **Career:** United Planning Orgn, Wash DC, dir comt orgn, 1965-67; Policy Mgt Syst, New York, NY, nat VISTA training coordr, 1967-69; Brandeis Univ, Waltham Massachusetts, exec dir Upward Bound, 1970-75; Boston Univ, Sch Social Work, asst prof planning & applied res, 1972-758; Commonwealth Massachusetts, Boston, Massachusetts, asst secy educ affairs, 1975-79; Newton Community Sch, Newton, chmn, 1976-79; Afro-Am Inst, assoc prof african am studies, 1978; Northeastern Univ, Boston, Massachusetts, urban asst pres, 1979-82, dir community affairs, 1982-90, assoc prof African-Am Studies, 1990-; Northeastern's Community Outreach Center, dir & prin investr, currently. **Orgs:** Pres, Develop & Training Assoc; chmn, Indust Sites Develop Asn, Boston Mayor's Minority Bus Adv Coun, Massachusetts Human Resource Ctr; United Way Greater Boston, Roxbury Multi-Serv Ctr; trustee, Emmanual Col; Michael S Dukakis Community Develop Coordinating Coun, 1982-89. **Honors/Awds:** Massachusetts Black Achievers Award; Phi Kappa Phi Society Award; First Annual Massachusetts Affirmative Action Award; Award For Minority Business, Gov Massachusetts; Award for Youth Service, Mayor Boston. **Military Serv:** USAF & USNAFR, comdr, 1956-94. **Home Addr:** 102 Beaumont Ave, Newton, MA 02460, **Home Phone:** (617)969-5007. **Business Phone:** (617)373-2351.

WARREN, DR. JOSEPH W
Businessperson, educator. **Personal:** Born Jul 2, 1949, Rocky Mount, NC; son of James W Jr and Marjorie Johnson; married Cynthia Taylor, Jul 2, 1972; children: Camille, Joseph II & Jerrick. **Educ:** Oakwood Col, BA, 1971; Ohio State Univ, MA, 1973, PhD, 1982. **Career:** United Negro Col Fund fel, 1971; Ohio State Univ, grad asst, 1973-76; Lake Mich Col, adj prof, 1978-80; Andrews Univ, assoc prof eng, prof eng, currently; Highland Inst, Benton Harbor, family life dir. **Orgs:** Founder, Mid-Am Network Marketing Inc, 1984-; co-founder, Scholastic Study Lab, Andrews Univ, 1984; Inst Christian Educ & Youth Develop, 1985-; founder & owner, Mid-Am Premiere Brokerage, 1986-; founder & dir, Ctr Bldg Self-Esteem African-Am Youth, 1990-. **Honors/Awds:** Research Grant, Andrews Univ, 1984 & 1992. **Home Addr:** 508 N Bluff, Berrien Springs, MI 49103. **Business Addr:** Professor of English, Andrews University, Nethery Hall 112 100 Old US 31, Berrien Springs, MI 49104, **Business Phone:** (269)471-3168.

WARREN, JOYCE WILLIAMS
Judge. **Personal:** Born Oct 25, 1949, Pine Bluff, AR; daughter of Albert Lewis Williams and Marian Williams Johnson; married James Medrick Warren, Feb 26, 1972; children: Jonathan, Jamie & Justin. **Educ:** Univ Ark, Little Rock, Ark, BA, 1971, JD, 1976; Nat Coun Juv & Family Ct Judges & Nat Col, 1983-. **Career:** Gov Bill Clinton, Little Rock, Ark, admin asst, 1979-81; pvt law pract, Little Rock, Ark, atty-at-law, 1981-82; Cent Ark Legal Servs, Little Rock, Ark, staff atty, 1982; Pulaski Co, Ark, Little Rock, Ark, juv judge, 1983-87, paternity judge, 1987-89; State Ark, Little Rock, Ark, circuit judge, 1989-. **Orgs:** Sigma Gamma Rho Sorority Inc, 1968-; Am Nat Ark & Pulaski Co Bar asn, 1971-; Nat Coun Juv & Family Ct Judges, 1983-; Ark Judicial Coun, 1989-; Ark State Bd Law Examr, 1986-93. **Honors/Awds:** Very Spec Ark Women, Ark Sesquicentennial Off Event, 1986; Gold Medal for Excellence in Law, Sigma Gamma Rho Sorority Inc, 1986; Ark Prof Women of Distinction, Worthen Bank Women's Adv Bd, 1988; Resolution for Outstanding Servs, Pulaski Co Quorum Ct, 1988; Top 100 Women in Ark, 1995, 1996, 1997; Ark Coalition for Juv Justice, Juvenile Judge of the Year, 2000. **Business Addr:** Circuit Judge, State of Arkansas, Circuit Court, 6th Judicial Circuit, Pulaski County Courthouse, 3001 W Roosevelt, Little Rock, AR 72204, **Business Phone:** (501)340-6725.

WARREN, MICHAEL
Actor, television producer. **Personal:** Born Mar 5, 1946, South Bend, IN; married Susie W (divorced); children: Koa, Cash, Grayson & Makayla. **Educ:** Univ Calif, Los Angeles, BA, theatre arts. **Career:** TV series: "Hill St Blues", actor, 1981-87; "City of Angels", actor, 2000; "The District", actor, 2001; "The District", actor, 2001; "Girlfriends", actor, 2001; Normal Again, actor, 2002; "Buffy the Vampire Slayer", actor, 2002; "Soul Food", actor, 2002; Secret Agent Man, actor, 2003; "JAG", actor, 2003; "Lost & Found", actor, 2004; "The Division", actor, 2004; "American Dreams", actor, 2004; Kevin Hill, actor, 2005; "Night Stalker", actor, 2005; "Kevin Hill", actor, 2005; "Night Stalker", actor, 2006; "Lincoln Heights", actor, 2007; "Girlfriends", actor, 2007; Films: Fast Break, actor, 1979; Norman. Is That You", actor, 1976; Drive, He Said, actor, 1971; Dreamaniac, actor, 1987; TV movies: The Child Saver, actor, 1989; The Kid Who Loved Christmas, actor, 1990; Buffalo Soldiers, actor, 1997; The Wedding, actor, 1998; Family Matters, producer; Step By Step, producer; Hangin' With Mr Cooper, producer; TV pilot, Home Free, actor, producer, 1988. **Honors/Awds:** All-Am Basketball Player, Univ Calif, Los Angeles,; Acad All Am NCAA, 1966; Emmy Award nomination (Hill Street Blues).

WARREN, NAGUEYALTI
School administrator, educator. **Personal:** Born Oct 1, 1947, Atlanta, GA; daughter of Frances Herrin; married Rueben C; children: Alkamessa, Asha & Ali. **Educ:** Fisk Univ, BA, 1972; Simmons Col, MA, 1974; Boston Univ, MA, 1974; Univ Miss, PhD, 1984; Goddard Col, MFA, 2005. **Career:** Northeastern Univ, instr, 1977-78; Univ Calabar, lectr, 1979; Fisk Univ, asst prof & chairperson, Dept Eng, 1984-88; Emory Univ, asst dean, assoc prof, 1988-97, assoc dean Arts & Sci, 1997-, sr lectr & dir undergrad studies, currently. **Orgs:** Col Lang Asn; Mod Lang Asn; Southern Conf Afro-Am Studies; adv bd mem, W E B Du Bois Found. **Honors/Awds:** Golden Poet Award, World Poetry Asn, 1985. **Special Achievements:** Book: Lodestar and Other Night Lights, New York, Mellen, 1992; Southern Mothers: Fact and Fiction in Southern Women's Writing, LSU Press, 1999; Poetry published in the following The American Poetry Anthology, Mississippi Earthworks, Janus, Riders of the Rainbow, Earthshine; The Atlanta Review. **Home Addr:** 7469 Asbury Dr, Lithonia, GA 30058. **Business Addr:** Senior Lecturer, Director Undergraduate Studies, Emory University, Department African American Studies, 550 Asbury Cir 207 Candler Library, Atlanta, GA 30322, **Business Phone:** (404)727-6847.

WARREN, OTIS, JR.
Real estate executive. **Personal:** Born Aug 25, 1942, Baltimore, MD; son of Otis Sr and Rose; married Sharon, Nov 22; children: Otis Warren III. **Educ:** Community Col Baltimore, AA, bus. **Career:** Otis Warren & Co, pres & owner, 1970-. **Orgs:** Pres, Greater Baltimore Bd of Realtors, 1983; Med Mutual, 1988; Nations Bank, 1989-; Nat Asn Realtors, 1989-91; Higher Edu Comn, 1990; Fannie Mae Adv Bd, 1990-91; NCP; Baltimore City Chamber Com, 1992. **Honors/Awds:** Realtor of the Year, Greater Baltimore Bd Realtors, 1976, Realtor Fair Housing Service Award, 1990; Distinguished Service Award, Morgan State Univ, 1990. **Special Achievements:** Obtained largest minority contract with the govt for the devt of an office bldg in downtown Baltimore, 1990; Business Opportunity Fair Honoree, MDDC, 1991; MAR Asn Realtors, Equal Opportunity Housing, 1991. **Business Addr:** President, Chief Executive Officer, Otis Warren & Company, 10 S Howard St Suite 110, Baltimore, MD 21201, **Business Phone:** (410)539-1010.

WARREN, RICKY
Businessperson. **Career:** Artco Syst Inc, co-owner, currently. **Business Addr:** Co-owner, Artco Syst Inc, 1810 Forest Lakes Ave SE, Atlanta, GA 30317, **Business Phone:** (404)635-9001.*

WARREN, ROLAND C
Executive, president (organization). **Personal:** Born in Toledo, OH; married Yvette Lopez-Warren; children: Jamin & Justin. **Educ:** Princeton Univ, pschol; Univ Pa, Wharton Sch, MBA. **Career:** PepsiCo; IBM; Princeton Univ, assoc dir develop; Goldman Sachs & Co, financial consult; Nat Fatherhood Inititative, pres, currently. **Orgs:** Bd, Southern Home Serv; Urban Family Coun. **Business Phone:** (301)948-0599.

WARREN, DR. RUEBEN CLIFTON
Health services administrator, government official. **Personal:** Born Aug 16, 1945, San Antonio, TX; son of Bobbye Owens; married Nagueyalti; children: Alkamessa Dalton, Asha & Ali. **Educ:** San Francisco State Univ, BA, 1968; Meharry Med Col, DDS, 1972; Harvard Sch Dent Med, residency dental pub health, 1975; Harvard Sch Pub Health, MPH, 1973, Dr PH, 1975. **Career:** Univ Lagos, Nigeria, West Africa, 1975-76; Harvard Sch Dent Med, instr, 1976-77; Univ Conn Health Ctr, asst prof, 1977-80; State Miss, dent dir, 1981-83, Med Ctr, clinic assoc prof, 1982-83; Meharry Med Col, assoc prof & dean, 1983-88, Sch Dentistry, adj prof, 1998-; Ctr Disease Control & Prevention, Atlanta, GA, assoc dir minority health, 1988-97; Morehouse Sch Med, Dept Preventive Med & Community Health, clinic prof, 1989-; Emory Univ, Rollins Sch Pub Health, Dept Behavioral Sci & Health Educ, adj prof, 1996-; Agency for Toxic Substances & Disease Registry, assoc adm, 1997-. **Orgs:** Meharry Alumni Asn; Nat Dent Asn; Nat Asn Advan Colored People; Am Pub Health Asn; Am Asn Pub Health Dentistry; chairperson, Caucus on Pub Health & Faith Communities PHA, 1997; chap, Nat Dent Asn Del CNF Africa, 1982; UN C's Fund. **Honors/Awds:** Student of the Year, Meharry Med Col, 1970; 2nd Place Award, Table Clinics, 1971; Omega Man of the Year, Delta Chap, 1971-72; Intermediate-Undergrad Omega Man of the Year, 5th Dist, 1971-72; Award for Outstanding Achievement, Dental Col Int Col Dentists, 1972; Community Service Award, Roxbury Med Tech Inst, 1973; President's Award, Nat Dent Asn, 1978; Distinguished Alumni Award, Harvard Sch Dent Med, 1990; Honorary Doctor of Medical Science, Meharry Med Col. **Special Achievements:** Author, 80 publications including: "Implementing School-Based Dental Services, The MSP Model," 1984, "Community Diagnosis: A Comprehensive Needs Assessment Approach for Minority and Underserved Communities," 1996, and "Health and Well Being; A Clearer Vision," 1996; 115 presentations including: "A National Management Model to Facilitate Health Service for Head Start Children," presented at National Head Start Association 9th Annual Training CNF, 1982, "Your Cup is Half Full: Not Half Empty," at Conf Black History Makers, 1996, "HIV/AIDS in the US," at Black History Showdown, 1995, and "Higher Ground," at NC Dept of Environment, 1995. **Home Addr:** 7469 Ashbury Dr, Lithonia, GA 30058. **Business Addr:** Administrator for Urban Affairs, Agency for Toxic Substances and Disease Registry, Centers for Disease Control and Prevention, Rm Bldg 37 E-28 1600 Clifton Rd NE, Atlanta, GA 30333, **Business Phone:** (404)639-5060.

WARREN, DR. STANLEY
Educator. **Personal:** Born Dec 18, 1932, Indianapolis, IN; son of Stanley Johnson and Rachel. **Educ:** Ind Cent Col, BS, 1959; Ind Univ, MAT, 1964, EdS, 1971, EdD, 1973. **Career:** Ind-Purdue Univ, acad counr, 1969-71; DePauw Univ, dir, 1973-79, prof educ & dean acad affairs, 1985, prof & dean emer, currently; Purdue Univ, human rels consult, 1992-95; Marion Co Dept Pub Welfare, case worker; Indiana polis Pub Sch, teacher admin; Indiana Comn Humanities, assoc. **Orgs:** Asn Study Negro Life & Hist; Urban League; Am Asn Teacher Educr; Ind Coalition Blacks in Higher Educ; Afro-Am Hist & Geneal Soc; Head Start Policy Coun; Univ Indianapolis Alumni Asn; Great Lakes Col Asn; Ind Hist Soc; Historic Landmarks Found Ind. **Military Serv:** AUS. **Business Addr:** Professor & Dean Emeritus, DePauw University, PO Box 37, Greencastle, IN 46135-0037, **Business Phone:** (765)658-4800.

WARRICK, ALAN EVERETT
Lawyer. **Personal:** Born Jun 18, 1953, Hampton, VA; son of John H (deceased) and Geri; married; children: Alan Everett II, Whitney Blair & Everett Alan. **Educ:** Howard Univ, BA, (magna cum laude), 1975; Ind Univ Sch Law, Indianapolis, JD, 1978. **Career:** Joint Ctr Polit Studies, res asst, 1972-74; Ind Civil Rights Comn, civil rights specialist, 1975; US Senator R Vance Hartke, campaign aide, 1976; Marion Co Prosecutors Off, intern, 1977-78; Ind Law Rev, assoc ed, 1977-78; Branton & Mendelsohn Inc, atty, 1978-1982; City San Antonio, Judge, munic ct; Law Off Alan E Warrick, atty, 1989-. **Orgs:** Sec, San Antonio Trial Lawyers Asn, 1979-80, vpres, 1980-81, bd dirs, 1981-82; bd mem, San Antonio Festival Inc, 1982-, exec comt, 1992-; selection panel, Golden Rule Award JC Penney, 1984; exec bd govs, United Way San Antonio, 1985-; Am Bar Asn; bd govs, Nat Bar Asn, 1990-; Asn Trial Lawyers Am; TX Young Lawyers Asn; TX Trial Lawyers Asn; San Antonio Bar Asn; San Antonio Young Lawyers Asn; pres, San Antonio Black Lawyers Asn, 1990-; bd dirs, State Bar Tex, 1991-93; Ancient Free & Accepted Masons; Omega Psi Phi Fraternity, Van Courtland Social Club; chair, AFA Lawyers Sect, 1993-94. **Honors/Awds:** First Place Award Winner, Am Bar Asn Regional Moot Ct Competition, 1978; Scroll Honor for Outstanding Achievement Field Law, Psi Alpha Chap Omega Psi Phi Fraternity, 1982; Achievements Recognition, Van Courtlandt Social Club, 1982; Man of the Year, Elks Mission Lodge 499; Citizen the Year, Psi Alpha Chap Omega Psi Phi Fraternity, 1982; Appreciation Award, Alamo Br YMCA, 1983; Outstanding Leadership Award, Alpha Tau Omega Chap, Alpha Kappa Alpha Sorority, 1984; Recognition Award, Smart Set Social Club, 1984; Phi Beta Kappa, Howard Univ; Pi Sigma Alpha Political Science, Honor Soc; Iota Phi Lambda Honoree Law Enforcement, 1985; Outstanding Service Award, Judicial Coun, Nat Bar Asn, 1989. **Business Addr:** Attorney, Law Offices of Alan E Warrick, 3423 River N Dr, San Antonio, TN 78230, **Business Phone:** (210)696-1695.

WARRICK, BRYAN ANTHONY
Basketball player. **Personal:** Born Jul 22, 1959, Moses Lake, WA. **Educ:** St Josephs Univ, attended 1982. **Career:** Basketball player (Retired), coach; Washington Bullets, 1982-84; Los Angeles Clippers, 1985; Milwaukee Bucks, 1986; Indiana Pacers, 1986; Rancocas Valley Regional High Sch, coach. **Honors/Awds:** All-Am, AP & The Sporting News.

WARRICK, DELIA MAE. See WARWICK, DEE DEE in the Obituaries section.

WARRICK, MARIE DIONNE. See WARWICK, DIONNE.

WARWICK, DEE DEE. See Obituaries section.

WARWICK, DIONNE (MARIE DIONNE WARRICK)
Singer. **Personal:** Born Dec 12, 1940, East Orange, NJ; daughter of Lee Drinkard and Mansel; married Bill Elliott, 1967 (divorced 1975); children: David & Damion. **Educ:** Ed Hartt Col Music, Hartford, CT. **Career:** Gospel singer & organist with the Gospel aires & Drinkard Singers, 1955-60; solo performer, 1960-; Dionne Warwick Design Group Inc, co-founder, 2002; Singles: "Don't Make Me Over", 1963; "This Empty Place", 1963; "Anyone Who Had a Heart", 1963; "Make the Music Play", 1963; "Walk On By", 1964; "A House is Not a Home", 1964; "You'll Never Get to Heaven (If You Break My Heart)", 1964; "Reach Out For Me", 1964; "Who Can I Turn To", 1965; "You Can Have Him", 1965; "Here I Am", 1965; "Looking With My Eyes", 1965; "Are You There (with Another Girl)", 1966; "Message to Michael", 1966; "Trains Boats & Planes", 1966; "Another Night", 1966; "I Just

Don't Know What to Do with Myself", 1966; "Alfie", 1967; "The Windows of the World", 1967; "I Say a Little Prayer", 1967; "(Theme from) Valley of the Dolls", 1967; "The April Fools", 1968; "Do You Know the Way to San Jose", 1968; "Always Something There to Remind Me", 1968; "Promises, Promises", 1968; "This Girl's in Love with You", 1969; "You've Lost That Lovin' Feelin'", 1969;"I'll Never Fall in Love Again", 1970; "Make it Easy on Yourself", 1970;"Paper Mache", 1970; "Let Me Go to Him", 1970; "Who Gets the Guy", 1971; "Then Came You", 1974; "Take it From Me", 1975; "Once You Hit the Road", 1975; "I'll Never Love This Way Again", 1978; "Deja Vu", 1979; "After You", 1980; "No Night So Long", 1980; "Some Changes Are For Good", 1981; "Friends in Love", 1982; "Heart breaker", 1982; "All the Love in the World", 1983; "How Many Times Can We Say Goodbye", 1983; "Take the Short Way Home", 1984; "Finder of Lost Loves", 1985; "Run to Me", 1985; "That's What Friends Are For", 1985; "Love Power", 1987; "Reservations for Two",1987; "Another Chance to Love", 1988; Albums: Presenting Dionne Warwick, 1964; Anyone Who Had a Heart, 1964; Make Way for Dionne Warwick, 1964; The Sensitive Sound of Dionne Warwick, 1965; Here I Am, 1965; Dionne Warwick in Paris, 1966; Here Where There Is Love, 1967; On Stage & in the Movies, 1967; Windows of the World, 1967; The Magic of Believing, 1967; Valley of the Dolls & Others, 1968; Soulful, 1969; Greatest Motion Picture Hits, 1969; Dionne Warwick's Golden Hits, Vol 1, 1969; Dionne Warwick's Golden Hits, Vol 2, 1970; I'll Never Fall in Love Again, 1970; Very Dionne, 1971; Promises, Promises, 1971; From Within, Vol 1, 1972; Dionne, 1973; Just Being Myself, 1973; Then Came You, 1975; Track of the Cat, 1975; Love at First Sight, 1977; Dionne, 1979; No Night So Long, 1980; Hot! Live & Otherwise, 1981; Heart breaker, 1983; Finder of Lost Loves, 1985; Dionne & Friends, 1986; Anthology, 1962-71, 1986; Then Came You, 1986; Masterpieces, 1986; Reservations for Two, 1987; Sings Cole Porter, 1990; Friends Can Be Lovers, 1993; Celebration in Vienna, 1994; Aquarela Do Brazil, 1995; Dionne Sings Dionne, 1998; The Definitive Collection, 1999; Soulful Plus, 2004; Love Songs, 2005; My Favorite Time of the Year, 2004;Say a Little Prayer, 2004; Me & My Friends, 2006; Gospel Album "Why We Sing?", 2008; Carr/Torr/Warwick Productions Inc, co founder; Warwick Design Group, co founder, currently. **Orgs:** Owner, BRAVO (Blood Revolves Around Victorious Optimism); spokeswoman, Am Sudden Infant Death Syndrome Inst; participant USA Africa song "We Are the World" & performed at Live Aid Concert; proceeds from sale album "Friends"to the Am Found AIDS Res; established Warwick Found help fight AIDS; hon mem, Zeta Phi Beta Sorority Inc. **Honors/Awds:** Grammy Award for Pop/Rock/Contemporary-Other, 1968; Grammy Award forPop/Rock/Contemp-Other, 1970; Grammy Award for Pop Female Vocal, 1979; R & B Female Vocal, 1979; Whitney M Young Jr Award, Los Angeles Urban League; Star on Hollywood Walk of Fame, 1985; Entertainer of the Year, 1987; Chairman's Award For Sustained Creative Achievement, 1998; Heroes Award, Natl Acad Rec Arts & Sci NY chp, 2003; lifetime achievement award, R & B Found, 2003. **Special Achievements:** Ranked No 42 on VH1's Greatest Women of Rock N Roll; Author of "My Points Of View", 2003. **Business Addr:** Singer, c/o Red Entertainment Group, 16 Penn Plz Suite 824, New York, NY 10001, **Business Phone:** (212)563-7575.

WASH, DAVID K.
Physician. **Educ:** Wayne State Univ; Am Bd Med Sci, Bd Family Med, cert. **Career:** Va Park Med Ctr, physician; Barbara Ann Ctr Family Med, physician, currently; Sinai/Grace Hosp, physician, currently; St John Macomb Hosp, physician, currently. **Business Phone:** (248)905-5470.

WASH, DAVID KEANE
Physician. **Personal:** Married Ursula Kelley, Aug 27, 2004. **Educ:** Wayne State Univ Sch Med, MD, 1999. **Career:** St. Elizabeth Family Practice, physician; Thea Bowman Health Ctr, physician, currently. **Business Addr:** Physician, Thea Bowman Health Center, 20548 Fenkell, Detroit, MI 48223, **Business Phone:** (313)255-3333.*

WASH, GLENN EDWARD
Construction manager. **Personal:** Born Feb 26, 1931, Grand Rapids, MI; son of George and Ethel; children: Glennda Marie. **Educ:** Highland Park Col; Univ Detroit; Builders Exchange (CAM), Urban Land Inst. **Career:** AJ Etkin Construct Co, Oak Park, MI, construct supt, 1957-61; Leonard Jarosz Construct Co, Oak Pk, MI, construct supt, 1954-57; construct supt, Practical Homes Builders, Oak Pk, MI, 1961-65; construct supt, HL Vokes Co, Cleveland, OH, 1965-67; Glenn E Wash & Assoc Inc, pres, 1977-. **Orgs:** Asn Gen Contracts Am, Detroit Chap, 1977-01; Eng Soc Detroit, 1977-01; Better Bus Bur, 1979-2001; secy & chmn, Mich Minority Bus Develop Coun, 1979-85; bd trustees, New Detroit Inc, 1980-01; Minority Input Comt, Wayne State Univ, 1984-85; Comt Soc Econ Policy, Am Concrete Inst, 1984-85; chmn, Governors Construct Safety Stand Comn, 1986-; Coun Better Bus Bur. **Military Serv:** USN, builder. **Home Addr:** 9000 E Jefferson, Detroit, MI 48214. **Business Addr:** President, Glenn E Wash & Assoc Inc, 14541 Schaefer Hwy, Detroit, MI 48227, **Business Phone:** (313)838-0800.

WASHINGTON, ADA CATHERINE
Educator, songwriter, composer. **Personal:** Born Sep 19, 1950, Shreveport, LA; daughter of Willie J Miller Sr and Elizabeth J; married Valdemar L, Aug 11, 1984; children: Valdemar L II & Christopher J. **Educ:** Grambling Col, BS, music educ, 1972; Eastern Mich Univ, med, 1982. **Career:** Flint Bd Educ, teacher, 1973-85; Citizens Com Savings bank, dir, 1993; Mott Community Col, consult, 1995; Album: Aunty K N'Em in Pigsburgh, 2006. **Orgs:** Bd mem, Cedar St Childrens Ctr, 1986-87; Delta Sigme Theta Sorority, 1984-; Jr League Flint, 1986-88; pres, Pierians Inc, Flint Chapter, 1990-93; nat law day chairperson, Am Lawyers Auxiliary, 1994; state law day chairperson, Mich Lawyers Auxiliary, 1993; pres, Genesee Bar Auxiliary, 1989-90; bd mem, McLaren Regional Med Ctr Found, 1995-. **Honors/Awds:** Ike Award, Distinguished Service, Eisenhower Comt Sch, 1980; African American Women of Achievement Award, Dozier Mem CME Church, 1995. **Home Addr:** 1505 Arrow Lane, Flint, MI 48507-1882, **Home Phone:** (810)742-2441.

WASHINGTON, ADRIENNE TERRELL
Columnist. **Personal:** Born Mar 28, 1950, Washington, DC; daughter of Earl Anthony Randall and Gwendolyn W Johnson; married Milton Robert, Mar 26, 1969 (divorced); children: Misti E & Mario E. **Educ:** Hampton Univ, 1969; Northern Va Comm Col, 1976; Howard Univ, 1982; Am Univ, 1986. **Career:** The Alexandria Gazette, reporter, 1972-73; Folger Shakespeare Libr, ed & admin asst, 1973-75; The Washington Star, reporter & ed asst, 1975-81; WRC TV, metro ed, futures ed, 1982-87; The Washington Times, deputy metro ed, asst metro ed & dist bur chief, 1987-91, columnist, 1991-. **Orgs:** Washington Asn Black Journalists, 1975-86; Nat Asn Black Journalists, 1979-; Leadership Washington, 1993-; Sasha Brice Youthworks Anti-Violence Campaign, 1993-95; Capital Press Club, 1993-; Women of Washington, 1994-; Monroe E Trotter Group, 1994-; Nat Soc Newspaper Columnists, 1994-; Md/DC/Del Press Asn, 1996. **Honors/Awds:** The Washington Baltimore Newspaper Guild, 1979; Soc Prof Journalist, 1993, 1994, 1997; Nat Soc Newspaper Columist, 1994; Am Asn Univ Women, 1994. **Home Phone:** (703)379-5253. **Business Addr:** Columnist, The Washington Times, 3600 New York Ave NE, Washington, DC 20002-1947, **Business Phone:** (202)636-3182.

WASHINGTON, ALONZO LAVERT. See WASHINGTON, ALONZO LAVERT.

WASHINGTON, ALONZO LAVERT (ALONZO LAVERT WASHINGTON)
Publisher, writer, activist. **Personal:** Born Jun 1, 1967, Kansas City, KS; son of Millie C; married Dana D, Mar 24, 1993; children: Antonio S Davis, Akeem Alonzo, Kamaal Malik, Malcolm, Khalid & Alona. **Educ:** Kansas City Comm Col; Pioneer Comm Col; KC Media Proj Commun. **Career:** AD HOC Group Against Crime, gang & youth counr & intervention specialist, 1990-92; Swope Parkway Health Ctr, outreach specialist & counr, 1992-94; Omega 7 Comics Inc, pres, publ, writer & designer, 1992-. **Orgs:** Pres, Black Nat Cong, 1990-; hon mem, Black United Front, 1990-; AD HOC Group Against Crime, 1990-; New Democracy Movement, 1993-; pres, Asn African Am Comic Book Publ, 1994-. **Honors/Awds:** Numerous honors & awards including Certification of Appreciation, Mayor Emanuel Cleaver II, 1993; Malcolm X Leadership Award, Black United Front, Kans City Chap, 1991; Publisher of the Year, UB & UBS Commun Systs, 1992; Distinguished Community Service Award, United Minority Media Asn, 1993; Golden Eagle Community Service Award, Kans City Masterminds Alliance, 1994. **Special Achievements:** Creator of the first African American comic book to deal with social issues, 1992; Owner of the first African American-owned comic book company to manufacture an action figure. **Home Addr:** 1155 E 75th Ter, Kansas City, MO 64131, **Home Phone:** (816)444-4204. **Business Addr:** Owner, President, Omega 7 Comics Inc, PO Box 171046, Kansas City, KS 66117, **Business Phone:** (913)321-6764.

WASHINGTON, ALTON J.
Government official. **Educ:** Ariz State Univ, BS, polit sci, MS, pub admin. **Career:** Phoenix City Hall, dep pub work dir, dir human resource servs, dep city mgr, 1998-02, spec asst city mgr, 2002-. **Orgs:** Am Soc Pub Admin; Acad Polit Sci; bd dir, Valley Sun United Way; Blue Cross Blue Shield Ariz; chair, Deferred Compensation Plan Bd; Ariz Hispanic Chamber Com. *

WASHINGTON, ANTHONY
Athlete. **Personal:** Born Jan 16, 1966, Glasgow, MT; married Lesley; children: Colemen & Turner. **Educ:** Univ Syracuse. **Career:** USA Track & Field Inc, track & field athlete. **Honors/Awds:** Pan Am Games champion, 1991; USA Champion, 1991, 1993, 1999; Olympic Trials champion, 1992-96; World Champion, 1999, 2000; gold medal, discus event, 1999; 3rd IAAF World Championships in Athletics, 1991; 7th IAAF World Championships in Athletics, 1999.

WASHINGTON, ARNIC J.
Government official. **Personal:** Born Nov 19, 1934, Ladson, SC; married Rosalee Williams; children: Myra & Raymond. **Educ:** Nielson Computer Col Charleston SC. **Career:** Lincolnville Sc, vice mayor, 1967-. **Orgs:** Chmn, St Dept; Health Dept; Pub Bldg Dept; SC Municipal Asn, SC; Small Towns Asn, SC; Black Mayors Asn; Southern E Conf Black Elected Officials; Southern E Regional Coun Inc Nat League Cities; Berkeley Co Chap Nat Asn Advan Colored People; W Master Saxon Lodge #249 FAM Midland Park, SC; chmn trustee bd, Wesley Meth Ch Ladson SC; pres, Willing Workers; Admin Bd; Coun Ministries; Adult Class Teacher; vpres, Carnation Gospel Singers. **Honors/Awds:** Certificate of Recognition, SC Legis House Rep Outstanding Contributions in Field of Com & Pub Affairs; For Civic & Polit Leadership & Accomplishments in Country Charleston; Outstanding Performance as Councilman, Historic Town of Lincolnville, SC. **Military Serv:** USAF, airman first class, 1954-57. **Business Addr:** PO Box 536, Summerville, SC 29483.*

WASHINGTON, ARTHUR, JR.
Social worker. **Personal:** Born Oct 22, 1922, St Louis, MO; son of Arthur Sr and Frankey Riley; married Toni; children: Steven Elliott, Marjory Anita, Tiffany Elizabeth, Nancy Wooten. **Educ:** Univ Louisville, BA; Kent Sch Social Work Univ Louisville, MSW. **Career:** Retired: IL Dept soc Servs, caseworker, 1954-55; Fam Serv Ctr Kalamazoo, marriage counr, 1955-65; Kalamazoo Dept Social Servs, child welfare supvr, 1956; Kalamazoo City, comnr, 1959-67; Kalamazoo Col Social Work, instr, 1963-65; Calhoun Coun Dept Social Servs, deputy dir, 1965-72; MI Dept Social Servs, dir admin, asst payments, 1972-76; Bureau Field Op, admin consult, asst payments; Kalamazoo City Dept Social Servs, deputy dir; Kalamazoo Coun Dept Social Servs, admin asst, 1979-89. **Orgs:** Pres, Kalamazoo Chapter NAACP, 1957-60; County Bd Comnr, 1959-65; chmn, Kalamazoo Recreation Comt, 1959-65; bd mem, Kalamazoo Human Rels Comn, 1959-60; org leader, Kalamazoo Bombardiers Drum & Bugle Corp, 1960-71; Al Zabir Tpl Shriners, 1966-67, 1980-; advisory comt Kalamazoo Valley Jr Col; Northside COT ASN, vip, 1992; Douglas COT CTR, bd mem, 1992; Family IST, vip, 1992; Mayor's Task Force, 1992; Kalamazoo DPT Social Serv, bd mem, 1992; Pride Place, bd mem, 1992; Safe House, bd mem, 1992. **Honors/Awds:** Outstanding Masonic Award, Plaque Outstanding Achievement Northside Assoc; Certificate & Plaque Outstanding Citizenship NAACP; other civic awards; Irvins Gilmore Lifetime Achievement Award, 1989; Community Service Award, Kalamazoo NAACP, 1989. **Military Serv:** AUS, corpl, 1943-46; reserves, 1946-48. *

WASHINGTON, DR. ARTHUR CLOVER
Educator. **Personal:** Born Aug 19, 1939, Tallulah, LA; married Almrta Hargest; children: Arthur, Angela & Anthony. **Educ:** Tex Col, BS, 1961; Tuskegee Inst, MS, 1963; Ill Inst Tech, PhD, 1971. **Career:** Talladega Col, instr, 1965-67; City Col Chicago, assoc prof, 1967-71;Langston Univ, prof, 1972-74; Prairie View A&M Univ, dean grad sch, prof,1974-91; Tenn State Univ, vpres, Acad Affairs, 1991-93, prof, 1993-97; Fla A & M Univ, prof biol sci, dean, Col Arts & Sci, 1997-. **Orgs:** Extramural assoc, NIH, 1979; pres, Woodedge Civic Asn, 1981; nat exec sec,Nat Inst Sci, 1983-. **Honors/Awds:** American Men & Women Science, 1982. **Special Achievements:** Published several scientific articles, 1974-87. **Business Addr:** Dean, Professor, Florida A & M University, Col Arts & Sci, 208 Tucker Hall Bldg 19, Tallahassee, FL 32307, **Business Phone:** (850)412-7767.

WASHINGTON, BEN JAMES, JR.
Executive. **Personal:** Born Feb 10, 1946, Chicago, IL; son of Frances and Bennie; divorced; children: Stephanie & Bennie III. **Educ:** Wright Col, 1976; Harold Wash Col, cert, 1988. **Career:** Aldens Catalog Inc, exec mgr, 1968-76; Penn-Corp Financial Inc, mgr, 1977-81; Health Tech Indust Inc, pres & ceo, 1985; Whitestar Sportsgear Inc, pres & ceo, currently. **Orgs:** Pres, Am Animal Asn Inc, 1977-86; pres, ed, Am Pet Asn Inc, 1981-86. **Honors/Awds:** Outstanding Achievement, Penn-Corp Financial, 1981; Outstanding Entrepreneur, MNY Bus Enterprise, 1987; inducted Hall of Fame, 1995. **Military Serv:** USN, e-3, 1963-67. **Business Addr:** President, Chief Executive Officer, Whitestar Sportsgear Inc, 2755 Bernice Rd, Lansing, IL 60438.

WASHINGTON, BETTY LOIS
Executive, lawyer. **Personal:** Born Apr 16, 1948, New Orleans, LA. **Educ:** Southern Univ New Orleans, BA, 1970; Mich State Univ, MA, 1971; Tulane Univ Sch Law. **Career:** Southern Univ New Orleans, counr, 1972-73; N Urban League, prog dir, 1973-75; Desire Area Comm Coun, exec dir, 1975-79; Southern Univ Syst, bd supvr, 1978-80; Teach A Brother, exec dir, 1979-80; Ward Design Team, team chief, 1985; Images Corp, sec, 1985; Mgt Assoc, pres; Mgt Assoc New Orleans, pres, 1985; pvt pract atty, currently. **Orgs:** Phi Alpha Theta Hist Honor Soc; Zeta Phi Beta Sor; credit com, Southern Univ Alumni Asn. **Honors/Awds:** Outstanding Volunteer Award, Lansing MI Juvenile Ct Syst, 1971; Outstanding Women in America, Nat Affil, 1978. **Business Addr:** Attorney, 8500 Fordham Ct, New Orleans, LA 70127-2006, **Business Phone:** (504)945-4683.

WASHINGTON, BILL. See WASHINGTON, WILLIAM MONTELL.

WASHINGTON, CARL
Association executive. **Career:** Urban Mkt Corp Am, co-founder & pres, 1999-. **Business Addr:** Co-Founder, President, Urban Marketing Corporation of America, 1450 S Fairfax Ave, Los Angeles, CA 90019, **Business Phone:** (323)934-8622.

WASHINGTON, CARL DOUGLAS
Executive. **Personal:** Born Aug 11, 1943, Tuscaloosa, AL; son of Sam and Estella; married Charlene; children: Carl, Micheal,

Chimiere & Jason. **Educ:** Long Beach State Univ, BA, Pol Sci, Speech, 1967. **Career:** Freedom Invest Corp, pres, 1977; Teleport Oil Co, pres; Kong TV Inc, pres, chmn; Washington Bros Dist Co, pres. **Orgs:** Comn Improv League, 1965; Big Brother Prog, 1966; comt mem, Optimist Club, 1966; Kappa Alpha Psi; Hunter Point Boys Club; Soc of 100 Men; San Francisco Police Athlectic League; bd, San Francisco Black Chamber Com; Bd, Brown Boys Home; org mem, San Francisco Pvt Ind Coun. **Honors/Awds:** Top 100 Black Bus Am, 1982-86; Athlete of Year, Long Beach Poly High Sch; Outstanding Black Business, SF Black Chamber; Col Dean's List.

WASHINGTON, CONSUELA M
Lawyer. **Personal:** Born Sep 30, 1948, Chicago, IL; daughter of Hilliard L and Conzoella Emanuelita Brulee. **Educ:** Upper Iowa Univ, Fayette, IA, BA, cum laude, Polit Sci, 1970; Harvard Univ, Cambridge, MA, JD, 1973. **Career:** Kirkland & Ellis, Chicago, assoc, 1973-74; Allis-Chalmers Corp, Corp Law Dept, atty, 1975-76; Securities & Exchange Comn, off chief coun, div corp finance, atty advr, 1976-79, spec coun, 1979; US House Reps, Comn Energy & Com, coun, 1979-94; minority coun, 1995-2000, sr minority coun, 2001, sr minority coun, currently. **Orgs:** Ill Bar Asn; Harvard Law Sch Asn; Harvard Club Wash; Scholastic Hon Soc, Upper IA Univ, Hon Leadership Soc 1968-70; Harvard Bd Overseers, 1987-93; Med Educ SAfrican Blacks, US Bd dir, 1995-. **Honors/Awds:** Bradley Invit Speech Tourn Award, Excellence 1969; Notable Am 1978-79; Equal Employ Opportunity Award, SEC 1978; Alumni Achievement Award, Upper IA Univ 1977. **Special Achievements:** Dean's List, 1967-70. **Business Addr:** Senior Counsel, Committee on Energy & Commerce, 320 23rd St S Apt 201, Arlington, VA 22202.

WASHINGTON, COQUESE
Basketball player, basketball coach. **Personal:** Born Jan 17, 1971, Flint, MI; married Raynell Brown; children: Quenton & Rhaiyan Kamille. **Educ:** Univ Notre Dame, BA, 1992. **Career:** Basketball player (retired), basketball coach; Flint Northwestern High Sch, teacher; Hoosier All-Stars; New Eng All-Stars; Portland Power, guard,1997-98; NY Liberty, 1998-99; Womens Nat Baseball Players Asn, founding pres, 1999-01, exec vpres, 2001-03; Houston Comets, guard, 2000-02; Ind Fever, guard, 2001-03; Notre Dame women's basketball, asst coach, 2004, assoc head coach, 2005; Penn State women's basketball, head coach, currently. **Honors/Awds:** Frances Pomeroy Naismith Award, 2001. **Business Phone:** (610)892-1200.*

WASHINGTON, CRAIG ANTHONY
Lawyer, congressperson (u.s. federal government). **Personal:** Born Oct 12, 1941, Gregg County, TX; son of Roy and Azalia; children: Craig II, Chival, Alexander, Cydney & Christoper. **Educ:** Prairie View A&M Univ, BS, 1966; Tex Southern Univ Law Sch, JD, 1969. **Career:** Tex Southern Univ Law Sch, asst dean, 1969-70; self-employed atty;Tex House Rep, 1973-83; Tex Senate sen, 1983-89; US House Rep, mem (D-TX), 1989-95; Craig Wash Law Firm, Houston, Tex, atty, currently. **Orgs:** Nat Bar Asn; Tex Bar Asn; past pres, Houston Lawyers Asn; Houston Bar Asn; Harris Co Criminal Lawyers Asn; Tex Criminal Defense Lawyers Asn; Tex Trial Lawyers Asn; Galveston Co Criminal Lawyers Asn; Houston Chap Am Civil Liberties Union; Houston Bill Rights Found; Nat Conf Crime & Delinquincy; Nat Asn Advan Colored People; adv bd mem, Focus Mag; chmn, Houston Lawyers Asn Legis Comt; Houston Bar Asn Planning Comt; Martin Luther King Jr Community Ctr; Southern Regional Coun, Atlanta, Ga; St James Episcopal Church, Houston, Tex. **Honors/Awds:** Landmark case Award, Nat Asn Advan Colored People, Houston, 1980; William F Pollard Award, A Phillip Randolph Inst, 1982; Outstanding Criminal Defense Lawyer of the Year, State Bar Tex, 1985.

WASHINGTON, DANTE DENEEN
Soccer player, television broadcaster. **Personal:** Born Nov 21, 1970, Baltimore, MD; son of Yolanda Robinson and Don Washington. **Educ:** Radford Univ, BA, hist &pol sci, 1992. **Career:** Soccer Player (retired), Television Broadcaster; Howard Co Libr, libr page, 1987; John Elicker, architect apprentice, 1987-88; Joe Wyzkoski, resident mgr, 1990-92; Columbia Day Soccer Camp, coach, 1988-95; World Cup Org Comm, admin asst, 1993-94; NBC Olympics, logistics coordr, 1995-96;Columbus Crew, soccer player, 1996, 2000-03, 2005; Dallas Burn, soccer player; VA Beach Mariners, soccer player, 2003-04; Real Salt Lake, forward, 2005; Baltimore Blast, MISL, 2005; Columbus Crew's TV broadcasts, color commentator; Major League Soccer, ambassador, 2007. **Orgs:** Keeper, records & exchequer, Kappa Alpha Psi Fraternity, 1990-92. **Honors/Awds:** Soccer All-Am, NSCAA, NCAA Div I, 1991;State Of Virginias Player of the Year, 1991; Acad All-Am, 1992; Alumni Minority Scholar, Radford Univ, 1991-92; MLS Player of the Month, 2000; MLS Player of the Week, 1997, 2000, 2001. **Special Achievements:** Met Pres Clinton as part of his work as the league's anti-drug spokesperson, 1998; First Afro American to score a goal for the US Natl Team. **Home Addr:** 90 Southwind Dr, Gahanna, OH 43230, **Home Phone:** (614)471-7140.

WASHINGTON, DARRYL MCKENZIE
Manager. **Personal:** Born Jan 29, 1948, New York, NY; son of McKenzie T and Leslie Taylor; married Barbara Gore, Aug 22, 1970; children: Monika, Matthew & Morgan. **Educ:** NC A&T State Univ, Greensboro, NC, BSEE, 1974. **Career:** RJR Archer Inc, Winston-Salem, NC, engr, 1974-78; Miller Brewing, Eden, NC, tech servs mgr, 1978-; The Wash Group, Principle Inspector, currently. **Orgs:** Inst Elec & Electronics Engrs, 1967-; Soc Mechanical Engr, 1989-; Nat Food Processors Asn, 1989-; Am Inst Plant Engrs, 1989-; Soc Prof Real Estate Inspectors; NC Lic Home Inspectors Asn. **Military Serv:** AUS, 1st Lt, 1970-72. **Business Addr:** Principle Inspector, The Washington Group, PO Box 1661, Reidsville, NC 27323, **Business Phone:** (336)280-0507.

WASHINGTON, DAVID WARREN
Administrator. **Personal:** Born Jan 13, 1949, Mound Bayou, MS; married Clotee Woodruff; children: Rynetta Rochelle, Vernekia Bradley, Monique Caldwell, Rodney Brown & Vietta Leflore. **Educ:** Coahoma Jr Col, AA, 1970; Delta State Univ, BS, 1972, addn grad study, guidance & coun, 1972-74; Ford Found Leadership Develop Prog, Leadership Deg, 1975. **Career:** Ford Found Leadership Develop Prog, 1974-75; Bolivar Co Community Action Agency, equal opportunity officer, 1977-79; serving third term as vice-mayor, Town Pace, Miss; Bolivar Co Headstart Personnel & Training, dir human resources, currently; Delta Health Ctr, Mound Boyon, consult, currently. **Orgs:** Former mem, Bolivar Co Democratic exec comn, 1984-86; sch bd chmn, Bolivar Co Sch Dist I; election comnr, Bolivar County Dist I, 1984-88; Spangle Banner MB Church; chmn, Bolivar Co Election Comnr, 1988-92; chmn by-laws comn, Bolivar Co Asn Black Officials, 1989-92; chmn bd, election Comn, 1984; dir, Bolivar Co Summer Food Serv Prog; former pres, Pace Voters League; chmn, Bolivar Co Election Comn; committee chair, Delta Health Ctr; human resource & training dir, Co Head Start, currently. **Honors/Awds:** In Appreciation Outstanding Serv, Bolivar County Community Action Agency Bd Dir, 1980; Outstanding Serv, Miss Pace Community Asn, 1980; Concern & Dedication Shown, Staff Bolivar County Headstart Training Ctr, 1982; Appreciation for Faithful Serv, St James Missionary Baptist Church, 1983; Most Outstanding Citizen Award, Pace Community Asn, 1983; Dedicated Serv Award, Parents Bolivar County Headstart Training Ctr, 1984. **Home Addr:** PO Box 245, Pace, MS 38764, **Home Phone:** (601)723-6742. **Business Addr:** Director, Human Resources, Bolivar County Headstart program, 810 E Sunflower Rd Eastgate Ctr Suite 120, PO Box 1329, Cleveland, MS 38732, **Business Phone:** (662)846-1491.

WASHINGTON, DR. DENZEL
Actor, video producer. **Personal:** Born Dec 28, 1954, Mount Vernon, NY; son of Denzel Washington; married Pauletta Pearson, Jun 25, 1983; children: John David, Katia, Malcolm & Olivia. **Educ:** Fordham Univ, BA, jour; Am Conserv Theatre, actg; Wynn Handman, actg. **Career:** Theater appearances: Coriolanus, 1979; One Tiger to a Hill, 1980; When the Chickens Come Home to Roost, 1981; A Soldier's Play, 1981-83; Every Goodbye Ain't Gone, 1984; Checkmates, 1988; Richard III, 1990; tv movies:"Wilma", 1977; "Flesh & Blood", 1979; "In Harm's Way" video for BeBe-Winans, dir, 1997; "Half Past Autumn: The Life & Works of Gordon Parks", 2000; tv series: "St Elsewhere", 1982-88; films: Carbon Copy, 1981; A Soldier's Story, 1984; Power, 1986; Cry Freedom, 1987; For Queen & Country, 1989; Heart Condition, 1990; The Mighty Quinn, 1989; Glory, 1989;Mo' Better Blues, 1990; Ricochet, 1991; Mississippi Masala, 1992; MalcolmX, 1992; Much Ado about Nothing, 1993; Philadelphia, 1993; Crimson Tide, 1995; Virtuosity, 1995; Devil In A Blue Dress, 1995; The Preacher's Wife,1996; Courage Under Fire, 1996; Fallen, 1997; He Got Game, 1998; The Siege, 1998; The Hurricane, 1999; Remember the Titans, 2000; Training Day, 2001; John Q, 2002; Antwone Fisher, dir & producer, 2002; Out of Time,2003; Man on Fire, 2004; The Manchurian Candidate, 2004; Inside Man, 2006;Deja Vu, 2006; American Gangster, 2007; The Great Debaters, dir, 2007; The Taking of Pelham 1 2 3, actor, 2009. **Orgs:** The Boys & Girls Clubs Am, Nat spokesperson. **Honors/Awds:** Obie Award, 1982; Image Award, NAACP, 1988; Best Performance by a Supporting Actor, 1990; Golden Globe Award, 1989; Academy Award, 1990;American Black Achievement Awards; Ebony Career Achievement Award, 1994; Audelco Award, When the Chickens Come Home to Roost; Best Actor Award,NAACP, 1998; New York Film Critic's Circle Award; Critic's Award, Boston Society of Film; Dallas/Ft Worth Film Critic's Asnn Award; Chicago Film Critic's Award; Golden Globe Award; Academy Award, 2001; Critics Asn Awards for Best Actor, Los Angeles Film, 2001; Black Entertainment Awards for Best Actor, 2001; Black Reel Award for Theatrical Best Actor, 2001;Boston Society of Film Critics Awards for Best Actor, 2001; Image Award for Outstanding Actor in a Motion Picture, 2001; AFI Film Award, Actor of the Year, 2002; MTV Movie Award for Best Villain, 2002; Oscar Award for Best Actor in a Leading Role, 2002; Black Reel Award for Theatrical, Best Actor, 2002; Image Award for Outstanding Actor in a Motion Picture, 2002;Kansas City Film Critics Circle Awards for Best Actor, 2002; Black Reel Awards for Theatrical, 2003; Image Award for Outstanding Actor in a Motion Picture, 2003; Image Award for Outstanding Supporting Actor in a Motion Picture, 2003; Stanley Kramer Award, 2003; Tree of Life Award, 2003. **Special Achievements:** Golden Globe Nominee for Best Performance by an Actor in a Motion Picture Drama, 2002; Honorary doctorate humanities degree, Morehouse College. **Business Addr:** Actor, c/o ICM, 8942 Wilshire Blvd, Beverly Hills, CA 90211.

WASHINGTON, DEWAYNE NERON
Football player, manager. **Personal:** Born Dec 27, 1972, Durham, NC; married Adama; children: Dj, Demi & Delaney. **Educ:** NC State Univ, BA, mult disciplinary studies; Univ Pa, Wharton Bus Sch, NFL Bus Mgt & Entrepreneurial Prog, 2005. **Career:** Football player (retired), Manager; Minn Vikings, defensive back, 1994-97; Pittsburgh Steelers, corner back, 1998-2003; Jacksonville Jaguars,corner back, 2004; Kansas City Chiefs, corner back, 2005; Green fire Devel, bus develop mgr, 2007-. **Orgs:** Pres, Dewayne Wash Found,1995-2004; brd trustees, Union Baptist Church; Durham YMCA Brd; NC St Alumni Brd. **Honors/Awds:** Twice Pittsburg Steeler Man of the Year Award. **Special Achievements:** Co-hosted a weekly radio show in Pittsburgh on ESPN Radio 1250. Serves asa national spokesman for Spina Bifida. Served as the Steelers spokesmanfor the United Way. **Business Phone:** (919)667-9770.*

WASHINGTON, DR. EARL MELVIN
Educator. **Personal:** Born Jun 22, 1939, Chicago, IL; son of Hester L and Henry W; married Dianne Elizabeth Taylor; children: Jason Todd & Tiffany Anne. **Educ:** Western MI Univ, BA, 1963, MA, 1968; Univ MI, 1971; Western MI Univ, EdD. **Career:** Cleveland Pub Schs, teacher, 1963-68; Kalamazoo Valley CC, instr, 1968-70; Western MI Univ, asst prof communs, 1975-82, assoc prof communs, dir black fac devel prog, 1982-2001, asst dean, 1984-2001, assoc prof, communs, trustee, assoc prof emer, currently; The IST Study Race Ethnic Rels, dir, consult & workshop presenter. **Orgs:** Vpres, Kalamazoo PTA; press & publ dir, Kalamazoo Metro Branch NAACP, 1984-84; vpres, 100 men Kalamazoo, 1983-85; papers presented including Nat Asn Equal Opportunity; Phi Kappa Phi. **Special Achievements:** Several papers presented; co-author of The First Two Years; various articles published in communication, educ & communication quartery and black issues in higher education 1980. **Business Addr:** Associate Professor Emeritus, Western Michigan University, 1903 W Michigan Ave, Kalamazoo, MI 49008, **Business Phone:** (269)387-1000.

WASHINGTON, EARL S.
Executive, chairperson, executive director. **Personal:** Born in Los Angeles, CA. **Educ:** Calif State Univ, LA, BS, bus. **Career:** Rockwell Int, Anaheim, CA, mkt analyst, vpres bus develop, vpres strategic mgt & int, Autonetics Marine Systs Div, vpres & gen mgr, Rockwell corp Off, vpres advert & pub rels, sr vpres mkt & communs; Financial Partners Credit Union, chmn & dir, currently. **Orgs:** Executive Leadership Coun; bd trustee, Harvey Mudd Col. **Special Achievements:** First African-American vice president at Rockwell International. **Business Addr:** Chairman, Director, Financial Partners Credit Union, PO Box 7005, Downey, CA 90241-7005, **Business Phone:** (562)923-0311.

WASHINGTON, EARLENE
Manager, statistician. **Personal:** Born Nov 15, 1951, Brookhaven, MS; daughter of Lonnie McLaurin and Geraldine Gaston McLaurin; married Ralph Campbell, Jun 16, 1973; children: Latonya, Kimberly & Jasmine. **Educ:** Alcorn State Univ, Lorman, MS, BS, 1973; Jackson State Univ, Jackson, MS, 1973; Miss Col, Clinton, MS, MBA, 1975. **Career:** Utica Jr Col, Utica, MS, accts payable/inventory mgr, 1973-79; Miss Power & Light, Jackson, MS, statistician, 1979-86, contract adminr, procurement spt, 1986-. **Honors/Awds:** Dean's List, Alcorn State Univ, 1969-73, National Honor, 1969-73, President Scholar, 1971-73. **Home Addr:** 6009 Woodlea Rd, Jackson, MS 39206-2144. **Business Addr:** Procurement Specialist, Purchasing/Material Management, Mississippi Power & Light Company, 308 E Pearl St, Jackson, MS 39201, **Business Phone:** (601)949-9247.*

WASHINGTON, DR. EDITH MAY FAULKNER
Counselor, consultant, president (organization). **Personal:** Born Jul 28, 1933, Queens, NY; daughter of Edalia Magdalene O and Henry Ozman Faulkner; married George Clarence; children: Desiree Elaine Singletary, James Henry & Edalia Magdalene Kelley. **Educ:** NY State Univ Col, Buffalo, BS, H, Ec, Ed, 1968, MS, H, Ec, Ed,1971; Ind Univ, Gas City, Ind, DHR, Human Relations Psych, 1973; Elmira Col, MS, Ed, Behav Sci, 1981. **Career:** SEEK Disadvantaged Students, coordr, 1969-71; New York State Univ, Buffalo, instr, Afro-Amer studies, 1969-71; PEACE Inc, consult, 1971; New York State Off Drug Abuse Serv Masten Pk Community Rehab Ctr, inst teacher, 1971-76; New York State Off Drug Abuse Serv, Manhattan Rehab Ctr, inst teacher, 1976-77; Church God Christ, Cent Am W Indies, mission worker/teacher, 1980-; New York State Dept Correction Serv, acad classification analyst, correction counr, retired 1991; WFHW Channel 58, cohost with spouse of weekly TV show; Applied Christianity Inc, consult, counr, currently. **Orgs:** Co-founder, Afro-Am Cult Ctr, Buffalo, New York, 1960; past state pres,Bus & Prof Women, Church God Christ; bd mem, Church God Christ Dept Missions; mem & workshop leader, Corrective Educ Asn, 1971; past prod/dir, Benefits Missions Church God Christ Inc, Missions Benefit Breakfast; execdir, Anegada House Cult Inst; bd mem, Nat Asn

Advan Colored People Elmira Corning Ctr, 1977; bd mem, Adv Coun Citizens Adv Coun Comnr Social Serv, 1978; Southern Tier Regional Planning Bd, 1976; Chemung Co Planning Bd, 1976, Applied Christianity Church God Christ, 1980-; ordained Evange list Independent Holiness Assembly Church Inc, 1986; vol nutritionist/coordr, Applied Christianity Inc, Food Pantry; admin, Applied Christianity Church God Christ. **Honors/Awds:** Ford Co Town Crier Award, Ford Motor Co; Outstanding Community Service Award, 1969; Outstanding Community Service Award, ACCEP Buffalo, New York, Frontier Citizens & Agng Comn, Cult Educ Prog Ctr, 1970; Outstanding Academic Achievement Award, Pentecostal Temple Church God Christ, 1971; Outstanding Community Servicve Award, Chemung Co, 1979; Humanitarian Award, Nat Asn Blacks Criminal Justice, 1985; Mt Nebo Ministries MLK Drum Major for Freedom Award, co-recipient w/spouse, Rev G C Washington, 1986; hon mem, Sigma Gamma Rho, 1988. **Home Addr:** 1341 S Ave, Niagara Falls, NY 14305, **Home Phone:** (716)285-0513. **Business Addr:** Consultant, Counselor, Applied Christianity Inc, 410-414 W Gray St, Elmira, NY 14901, **Business Phone:** (607)732-1142.

WASHINGTON, EDITH STUBBLEFIELD
Executive, consultant. **Personal:** Born Jan 1, 1948?, Almo, KY. **Career:** SSOE Inc, Toledo, OH, chief specif coordr; Unive Toledo Col Engineering, instr; Construct Specifications Inst, pres; Stubblefield Group Inc, pres, 1994-. **Special Achievements:** The Construction Specifications Institute first female president of the Toledo Chapter; First Afro-American woman to be elevated to Fellowship, 1997. **Business Phone:** (419)535-0888.

WASHINGTON, EDWARD. See Obituaries section.

WASHINGTON, EDWARD, JR.
Manager. **Personal:** Born Nov 25, 1931, Logan County, KY; married Ruth Shorton; children: James, Phillip, Terry, Bobby, Francine Wynn, Cherri & Nancy. **Career:** Auburn Hosiery Mill, foreman; fireman; emer worker; ambulance svc. **Orgs:** Barroh River Health System; Adairville City Coun; S Hogan Cham Comn; Mason. **Special Achievements:** Ky's first African American councilman, 1970.

WASHINGTON, ELMER L.
Educator. **Personal:** Born Oct 18, 1935; married Anna Ross; children: Lisa & Lee. **Educ:** Tex Southern Univ, BS, 1957, MS, 1958; Ill Inst Tech, PhD, 1965. **Career:** Univ Chicago, res asst, 1958-61; Pratt & Whitney Div United Aircraft, asst proj engr & res assoc, 1965-69; Chicago St Univ, dean natural sci & math, 1972-74, Univ, vpres Res & Develop, actg vpres stud affairs, dean Col Arts & Scis, dean Natural Scis & Math, prof emer; Univ Prof Ill, chief contract negotiator, 1992-2000. **Orgs:** AAAS; Am Chem Soc; Electro chem Soc; Am Asn Univ Prof; Am Asn Univ Adminsr; Alpha Kappa Mu Honor Soc, 1956. **Honors/Awds:** Welch Found Scholarship, 1957; Petroleum Research Fellowship, 1961-65; Phi Lambda Upsilon Scientific Honor Soc, 1964.

WASHINGTON, EMERY, SR.
Clergy. **Personal:** Born Feb 27, 1935, Palestine, AR; son of Booker Taliferro and Fannie Mae Norrington; married Alice Marie Bogard, Oct 1, 1965; children: Ekila Denese, Marie Antoinette & Emery Jr. **Educ:** Philander Smith Col, BA, 1957; Va Theol Sem, MDiv, 1961; Christ Church Col, Canterbury Eng, grad study, 1988. **Career:** Clergy (Retired); St Andrew's Episcopal Church, 1961-65; Christ Church Episcopal, 1961-71; Episcopal Diocese Ark, 1971-76; St Michael's Episcopal Church, 1973-76; Emmanuel Episcopal Church, 1976-83; All Saints' Episcopal Church, 1983-2001. **Orgs:** Pres, Alpha Phi Alpha, 1954-; dep, Gen Conv Dep, 1969, 1970, 1973, 1991, 1994; pres, Union Black Episcopalians, 1975-; chair, Racism Comn, 1985-86, 1991-93, Leadership, St Louis, 1988-89, diversity facilitator, 1997-99; develop chair, St Louis Clergy Coalition, 1985; Leadership St Louis Inc, 1988-89; Focus St Louis Inc, Valuing Our Diversity, 1989-; St Louis Black Leadership Roundtable, 1991-; dep gen conv, Cong Allied Community Improvement, 2000, vpres, 2000-01, pres, 2002; Faith Beyond Walls, 2000-; Nat Comn Nat Concerns, 2000-. **Honors/Awds:** Clergy of the Year, Diocese Arkansas, 1970; Literacy Promoter, Alpha Kappa Alpha, 1990; John D Buckner Award, 1990; Excellence in Religion, 1992; William M. Alexander Service Award, Alpha Phi Alpha, 1999; Unsung Hero Award, Univ Montana / Columbia & Black Expo, 1999; Bishop's Award, 2001; Human Develop Corp of Metro STL, 2001; Hond DD, Eden Theological Seminary, 2002. **Special Achievements:** Designed the "Shield of All Saints," 1987; Author, copyright, 1987; Designed two stained glass windows: Baptism and Communion, 1988-;guest speaker 80th Celebration of First African American Bishop E T Demby. **Home Phone:** (314)567-5308.

WASHINGTON, ENRICO ALICENO. See WASHINGTON, RICO.

WASHINGTON, ERIC (ERIC MAURICE WASHINGTON)
Basketball player. **Personal:** Born Mar 23, 1974, Pearl, MS. **Educ:** Univ Ala, attended 1997. **Career:** Idaho S, USA D League; Zhejiang C, China; Jerusalem, Israel; Denver Nuggets, guard, 1997-99; guard forward, 2003; Tampereen Pyrinto, finland, Shooting Guard, Small Forward, currently. **Business Phone:** (033)146-7683.*

WASHINGTON, ERIC MAURICE. See WASHINGTON, ERIC.

WASHINGTON, FRANK
Executive, consultant, president (organization). **Personal:** Born Apr 4, 1921, Philadelphia, PA; married Barbara Merriweather, Aug 15, 1995; children: Frank, Kevin (deceased) & Michele (deceased). **Educ:** William Paterson Sch Bus; Dale Carnegie Training Inst; Pepsi Cola Col Mkt. **Career:** Executive (retired), consultant; Harlem Globetrotters, basketball player, 1945-60; Pepsi Cola Bottling, community rels Mgr, 1960-90, consult, 1990-94; Coca Cola Bottling, consult, 1998-. **Orgs:** Founding mem, Nat Asn market Developers, 1970s-; founding mem, Nat Negro Golf Asn, Philadelphia, 1970-, vpres, 1990-92; Nat Asn Advan Colored People; founder, pres, Frank Wash Scholar Fund, Inc, 1995-. **Honors/Awds:** Marketeer Year Award, Nat Asn Market Devel, Living Legend Award, 1997; Salesman Year, Christian Street YMCA; Sportsman Year, Norristown Men's Club; Coun Spanish Speaking Organ, Community Awareness Award; Am Found Negro Affairs (AFNA), Distinguished America Award; PUSH, Jesse Jackson Award; OIC Am Award; Outstanding Achievement Award, Black Legends Prof Basketball, 1998. **Military Serv:** USN, boatswain mate sps, 1942-45. **Home Addr:** 514 Greenhill Lane, Philadelphia, PA 19128.

WASHINGTON, GLADYS J. (GLADYS J CURRY)
Educator, president (organization). **Personal:** Born Mar 4, 1931, Houston, TX; daughter of Eddie Joseph and Anita Joseph. **Educ:** BA, attended 1952; MA, attended 1955; Univ So CA & Tulane Univ, addl study; Univ London, England, summer, 1981. **Career:** Educator, President (Organization) (retired); So Univ Baton Rouge, Eng instr; So Univ New Orleans, assoc prof Eng; TX So Univ, assoc prof Eng. **Orgs:** Col Lang Asn, S Cent Modern Langs Asn; Nat Coun Teachers Eng; Tex Asn Col Teachers, Women in Action; Church Women United; secy, S Cent Lang Asn (Women of Color Section), 1988-89; Modern Lang Asn & Southern Conf Afro-Am Studies, 1988-; pres, Churches Interested Premature Parentage, 1989; artistic dir, Cyrenian Prods (Drama Group) 1985; pres, Arts Collective Houston, currently. **Honors/Awds:** Alpha Kappa Mu Nat Honor Soc; Lambda Iota Tau Lit Honor Soc; has done extensive work with school & little theatre groups in New Orleans & Houston; pub "View points From Black Amer" 1970; ed "Cultural Arts Review"; A World Made Cunningly, A Closer Look at the Petry's Short Fiction, CLA Jour, 1986; Teacher of the Year, Tex Southern Univ, 1988; auth, A Core Curriculum Approach to College Writing, Littleton, MA, Copley Publ Group, 1987. **Special Achievements:** Ann Petry, "The Narrows"; James Weldon Johnson, "Autobiography of an Ex-Coloured Man"; Lorraine Hansberry, "A Raisin in the Sun" in Master plots II: African-American Literature, 1993; Alice Childress, The African-American Encyclopedia, Supplement, 1996; Ann Petry "In Darkness and Confusion" and "Solo on the Drums" in Master plots II, Short Story, Supplement, 1996; "The Chambered Nautilus", Oliver Wendell Holmes, in Master plots II, Poetry Supplement, 1998; Paule Marshall in Critical Survey of Long Fiction, 2nd Revised Edition, 1999. *

WASHINGTON, GWENDOLYN
Physician. **Career:** Pvt Pract, med doctor, currently. **Business Addr:** Medical Doctor, Private Practice, Northwestern Medical Plz, 29255 Northwestern Hwy, Southfield, MI 48034, **Business Phone:** (248)350-8890.*

WASHINGTON, REV. HENRY L
Clergy. **Personal:** Born Nov 15, 1922, Earlington, KY; married Azlea; children: Argene, Lamar, Henry & Clyone. **Educ:** Ashland Theol Sem, OT-NT, 1976; Dyke Coll, cert realtor, 1978. **Career:** Metro Ins Co, sales rep, 1969-76; Alpha & Omega COGIC, pastor, 1970-85; Mansfield City, OH, councilman, 1983. **Orgs:** Pres, Concerned Black Citizens, 1976-78; Real Estate Mgrs Asn, 1978-85; community, chmn, NAACP, 1982-84; Richland Transit Bd, 1983-84, Affirmative Scholarship Delaware State Univ, 1984-85. **Honors/Awds:** House of Rep State of OH, 1979; Mayors Awd City of Mansfield OH, 1982. **Military Serv:** AUS, pfc, 18 months; Purple Heart, European Theater Ribbons, 1943-44. **Home Addr:** 312 Second Ave, Mansfield, OH 44905. **Business Addr:** Pastor, Alpha & Omega Church Of God In Christ, 530 Pearl St, Mansfield, OH 44905, **Business Phone:** (419)526-6353.

WASHINGTON, HERBERT L
President (Organization). **Career:** Syracuse Minority TV Inc, owner; McDonald's Restaurants, owner & oper, currently; HLW Fast Track Inc, pres, currently; M&T Bank, dir, currently. **Orgs:** Community Reinvestment Act Comt; bd dirs, Youngstown Chamber Com. **Business Addr:** President, HLW Fast Track Inc, 4900 Market St, Youngstown, OH 44503, **Business Phone:** (330)783-5659.*

WASHINGTON, HERMAN A, JR.
Educator. **Personal:** Born Jul 12, 1935, Norfolk, VA; son of Herman A and Naomi Hucles; married Daryl E Jordan, Aug 11, 1990; children: Keith, Lori, Michael, David, Tunja & Gina. **Educ:** Manhattan Col, BEE, 1958; NY Univ, MBA, 1973. **Career:** Western Electric, engr, 1958-59; G C Dewey CRP, consult, 1959-61; IBM, prog mgr & sys analyst, 1961-69; Systs Discipline Inc, vpres, sr proj mgr, 1969-71; City NY Addiction Servs Agency, dir, 1971-72; LaGuardia Community Col, prof, 1972-2006, prof emer, 2006-; GMLC Associates Ltd, founder, 1982-; Model Cities prog, vpres. **Orgs:** Pres, Brookhaven Lab Community Adv Coun; 100 Black Men Long Island, 1974-; Suny Col Optometry, Col Coun, 1978-2000; Family & Children's Asn, 1988-; bd, United Way Long Island, 1990-96; bd, Cath Charities, 1991-00; trustee, S County Pub Libr, 1999-02, pres, PTA; pres, Nat Asn Advan Colored People; pres, Civic Asn of the Setaukets, 1982-; mem, Stony Brook Univ Community Adv Counc, 1997, chmn, 2005-. **Honors/Awds:** Man of the Year, 100 Black Men Long Island, 1989; United Caring Award, United Way Long Island, 1991; Every Day Hero, Newsday, 2000; Public service Award, NYS Optometric Asn, 2000; Humanitarian of the Year, Family & Children's Asn, 2001. **Home Addr:** 261 Durkee Lane, East Patchogue, NY 11772-5820, **Home Phone:** (631)289-5828. **Business Addr:** Professor Emeritus, LaGuardia Community College, Comput Info Systems Department, 31-10 Thomson Ave, Long Island City, NY 11101, **Business Phone:** (718)482-7200.

WASHINGTON, ISAIAH, IV
Actor. **Personal:** Born Aug 3, 1963, Houston, TX. **Educ:** Howard Univ. **Career:** Films: The Color of Love, 1991; Land Where My Fathers Died, 1991; Strictly Business, 1991; Crooklyn, 1994; Alma's Rainbow, 1994; Clockers, 1995; Dead Presidents, 1995; Stonewall, 1995; Girl 6, 1996; Get on the Bus, 1996; Love Jones, 1997; Bulworth, 1998; Rituals, 1998; Mixing Nia, 1998; Out of Sight, 1998; True Crime, 1999; A Texas Funeral, 1999; Kin, 2000; Dancing in September, 2000; Veil, 2000; Romeo Must Die, 2000; Sacred Is the Flesh, 2001; Exit Wounds, 2001; Welcome to Collinwood, 2002; Ghost Ship, 2002; This Girl's Life, 2003; From the Outside Looking In, 2003; Hollywood Homicide, 2003; Trois 3: The Escort, 2004; Dead Birds, 2004; Wild Things 2 (voice), 2004; The Moguls, 2005; TV series: Law & Order, 1991; "Strapped", 1993; "Lifestories: Families in Crisis", 1994; "Homicide: Life on the Street", 1994; "NYPD Blue", 1995; "New York Undercover", 1996; "Mr & MrsLoving", 1996; "Soul of the Game", 1996; "Living Single", 1996; Joe Torre:Curveballs Along the Way, 1997; "High Incident", 1997; "Ally McBeal",1998; "Always Outnumbered", 1998; "Soul Food", 2000; "All My Children",2001; "Touched by an Angel", 2001; "Grey's Anatomy", 2005-07; "Bionic Woman", 2007; The Cleaner, 2008. **Orgs:** Pan African Film Festival. **Honors/Awds:** Image Award, 2006 & 2007; Screen Actors Guild Award, 2007, 2008, Nominated. **Military Serv:** USAF. **Business Phone:** (310)656-0400.*

WASHINGTON, JACQUELIN EDWARDS
Association executive. **Personal:** Born May 20, 1931, St Augustine, FL; daughter of Clarence Edwards and Grace Benson Albert; married Kenneth B; children: Saundra, Byron, Kristin. **Educ:** Fisk Univ, BA, 1951; Wayne State Univ, MSW, 1965. **Career:** Detroit Dept Pub Welfare, case worker & supvr, 1957-63; Detroit Pub Schs, sch social worker, 1965-75; New Options Personnel Inc, pres, 1975-80; Bendix Corp, Southfield, MI, mgr, human resources, 1980-85; Vixen Motor Co, Pontiac, MI, dir, human resources, 1985-88; Pontiac Area Urban League, Pontiac, MI, pres, ceo; Planned Parenthood SE MI, pres, chief exec officer, 1999; Wayne State Univ, chmn bd gov, currently. **Orgs:** Nat Asn Soc Workers; State MI Employ Agency Coun, 1978-80; trustee, Detroit Inst Arts, 1975-81; pres, Detroit Club Nat Asn Negro Bus & Prof Women, 1978-80; vpres, Girl Scouts Metro Detroit, 1979-80; NOW Legal Defense & Educ Fund, 1979-91; bd mem, MI Abortion Rights Action League, 1990-91; bd mem, St Joseph Mercy Hosp, Pontiac, MI; exec, MI Coun Urban League; exec dir, Planned Parenthood SE MI; exec vpres, ACLU Fund MI; Chmn, Central UM Ch Community Develop Corp; treas, planned parenthood Affiliates MI; Alpha Kappa Alpha Found Detroit; chmn, Adminr Coun, Central United Methodist Ch; Founders Soc; Sojourner Found. **Honors/Awds:** Spirit of Detroit Award, Detroit Common Coun, 1978; Female Pioneer Award, Women Lawyer Asn, 1978; Feminist of the Year Award, Detroit Chap Nat Orgn Women, 1978; Sojournor Truth Award, Nat Asn Negro Bus & Prof Women. **Business Addr:** chairman Board of Governors, Wayne State University, 4743 Cass Ave, Detroit, MI 48202-1201, **Business Phone:** (313)577-2972.*

WASHINGTON, JACQUELINE ANN
Executive. **Personal:** Born May 2, 1968, Highland Park, MI; daughter of William and Cora Johnson; married Kenneth B. Washington, Jun 5, 1993. **Educ:** Eastern Mich Univ, BS, 1990; Central Mich Univ, MA, 1995. **Career:** City Ypsilanti, personnel asst, 1990-91; Wellness Plan, human resources rep, 1992-93; Huron Valley Ambulance, human resources coordr, 1993-. **Orgs:** Treas & vpres, Alpha Kappa Alpha, 1989-; Human Resources Asn Greater Detroit, 1993-; Ann Arbor Area Personnel Asn, 1994-. **Honors/Awds:** Hardest Worker Award, Alpha Kappa Alpha Sorority Inc, 1990.

WASHINGTON, JAMES A
Newspaper publisher, newspaper editor. **Personal:** Born Apr 26, 1950, Chicago, IL; son of Frank S and Cecelia Burns Jones; mar-

ried Victoria Meek, May 9, 1980; children: Patrick James & Elena Cecele. **Educ:** Southern Univ, Baton Rouge, La, BA, 1971; Univ Wis, Madison, Wis, MA, 1973. **Career:** Tenn State Univ, Nashville, Tenn, worked Develop Off; Am Heart Asn, pub rels specialist; Dallas Ballet, pub rels mgr; Focus Commun Group, Dallas, Tex, founder & pres, 1980; Dallas Weekly, Dallas, Tex, owner & publ, 1985-; Ad-Mast Publishing Co, Dallas, Tex, chmn, currently. **Orgs:** Bd dirs, Cotton Bowl; I Have a Dream Found; Sci Pl; Dallas Zool Soc; Family Guid Ctr; adv coun small bus & agr; Fed Res Bank Dallas; chmn, minority bus adv comt, Dallas Independent Sch Dist; Dallas Together; exec comt & bd, Dallas Chamber Com; Am Heart Asn; Greater Dallas Planning Coun; Jr Achievement; admis comt, United Way, 1983; chmn pub rels comt; Nat Newspaper Publishers Asn. **Honors/Awds:** Danforth Fel, Univ Wis-Madison; Woodrow Wilson Fel. **Business Addr:** Publisher, The Dallas Weekly Newspaper, 3101 Martin Luther King Blvd, PO Box 151789-179, Dallas, TX 75215, **Business Phone:** (214)428-8958.

WASHINGTON, DR. JAMES EDWARD
Optometrist. **Personal:** Born Jun 19, 1927, Beaufort, NC; son of John Cole and Nancy Parker Sandlin; married Ethelyn Marie Irby Pigott, Jun 2, 1984; children: Jeffrey, Shelly & John. **Educ:** Fayetteville State Univ, attended; New York Univ, Wash Square Col, attended; N Ill Col Optometry, BS, 1953; N Ill Col Optometry, OD, 1954; Rutgers Univ, Grad Sch Newark, MPA, 1983. **Career:** Nat Optometric Asn, reg dir, 1972-79; Essex County Optometric Soc, pres, 1974; Nat Optometric Asn, pres, 1974-75; Diversified Vision Servs, exec dir; Pvt practice, solo practitioner; pvt practice, optometrist, currently. **Orgs:** Chmn, bd dir, NOA, 1975-76; preceptor, Pa Col Optometry; fel, Col Optometrists Vision Devel; vis lectr, New England Col Optometry; Am Optometric Asn, Nat Optometric Found, New Jersey Optometric Asn, Essex County Optometric Soc, Optometric Extension Prog Found, Nat Optometric Asn, NJ Eye Care Coun; health adv bdn E Orange Head Start; adv bd, Montclair State Col Health Careers; Am Pub Health Asn; NJ Pub Health Asn. **Honors/Awds:** 'Optometrists of the Year', Essex County Optometric Asn, 1972; Optometrist of the Year Nat Optometric Asn, 1973; Tomb & Key Honor Optometric Frat; Black Heritage Award, City E Orange, 1987; Distinguished Service Award, New Jersey Optometric Asn, 1987, Dr EC Nurock Award, 1993; Ill Col Optometry, 'Presidential Medal of Honor', 1999; NJ Soc Optometric Physicians Award, 2000, hon by Hist Soc E Orange; local NAACP chap, President's Award, 2002; US Senate Recognition, 2002. **Military Serv:** AUS, 1946-49. **Business Addr:** Optometrist, 104 S Munn Ave, East Orange, NJ 07018, **Business Phone:** (973)675-5392.

WASHINGTON, JAMES LEE, SR.
Mayor. **Personal:** Born Jun 14, 1948, Glendora, MS; son of Jessie James Washington and Ella Wee Billingsley Johnson; married Zenolia Hayes, Dec 22, 1974; children: James Jr & Jessica Nicole. **Educ:** Coahoma Community Col, Clarksdale, MS, AA, 1970; Campbellsville Col, Campbellsville, KY, BS, 1972; Delta State Univ, Cleveland, MS, 1986. **Career:** Coahoma Agr HS, head basketball coach; Coahoma Jr Col, head men's basketball coach; Friars Point NC, mayor; Coahoma Community Col, teacher & head men basketball coach, currently. **Orgs:** Nat Conf Black Mayors; Nat Conf Coaches. **Honors/Awds:** Outstanding Serv Award, N Atlantic Conf Boys Track, 1976; Class A State Championship Coahoma Agricultural HS (basketball), 1984; Coach of the Year, 1984-85; Won St Championship, Jr Col, 1986-87. **Home Addr:** 601 Broad St, Crenshaw, MS 38621, **Home Phone:** (662)383-2310.

WASHINGTON, JESSE
Editor. **Personal:** Born Jun 3, 1969, New York, NY; son of Judith Washington and McCleary. **Educ:** Yale Univ, BA, 1992. **Career:** Assoc Press, reporter, 1992-93, nat ed, 1993-95; New York, asst bur chief, 1995-96; Vibe Mag, chief & managing ed, 1996; The Associated Press, entertainment ed, currently. **Orgs:** Kappa Alpha Psi Fraternity Inc, 1987-. **Business Addr:** Entertainment Editior, The Associated Press, 450 W 33rd St, New York, NY 10001, **Business Phone:** (212)621-1500.

WASHINGTON, JOHN CALVIN, III
Government official, vice president (organization). **Personal:** Born Dec 12, 1950, Coatesville, PA; son of Mildred and John II; children: Nathaniel, John IV & Tamara. **Educ:** Coatesville Sr HS, diploma, 1968; Coll Prep. **Career:** City S Coatesville, coun mem; South Coatesville Borough, vpres, currently. **Orgs:** Elk Mt Vernon Lodge 151, 1975; NAACP, 1975; vol, Va Med Ctr, 1978; Chester County Recreation Coun, 1981; master mason, Lily Valley 59, 1981; dir, S Coatesville Recreation, 1981; FOP, 1981; Hypertension Ctr, 1981; chmn, Grievance Comt Handicapped S Coatesville, 1984; chmn, Property Comn, 1984; Chester County Planning Comn Bd. **Business Addr:** Vice President, South Coatesville Borough, 136 Modena Rd, South Coatesville, PA 19320, **Business Phone:** (610)384-1700.

WASHINGTON, JOHNNIE M.
Clergy, secretary (organization), president (organization). **Personal:** Born Sep 23, 1936, Paris, TX; married Naaman C; children: Mary M Jones, Leontyne. **Educ:** Southern Evang Asn, LVN, 1970, DD, 1974; Roosevelt Univ, BS, 1979. **Career:** McGraw Concern, Munich, Ger, secy financial, 1964-68; Hotel Dieu Hosp, endoscopy supr, 1970-; Nat Gastroenterol Tech, cert gi technician, 1973-80; NY Univ, Albany, ungrad nurse, 1977-80; El Paso Nat Asn Adv Colored People, pres, 1979-; Full Gospel Temple, rev, 1985; Church God Christ, Off Gen Secy, regional dir. **Orgs:** Secy, El Paso Black Caucus, 1977-. **Honors/Awds:** Cert of Appreciation, Black Hist Week, 1975; Outstanding Black Citizen, White Sands Missile Range, 1978; Cert of Appreciation, YMCA, El Paso, 1979; Outstanding Civil Rights Award, Nat Asn Adv Colored People, 6 Region Conf, 1980. **Business Addr:** President, National Association of Advanced Colored People, 4631 Atlas Ave, Memphis, TX 79904.*

WASHINGTON, JOSEPH R., JR.
Educator. **Personal:** Born Oct 30, 1930, Iowa City, IA; married Sophia Holland; children: Bryan Reed & David Eugene. **Educ:** Iron Cross Univ, WI, BA, 1952; Andover Newton Theol Sch, BD, 1957; Boston Univ, ThD, 1961. **Career:** Dillard Univ, dean of chapel asst prof philos religion, 1961-63; Dickinson Col, religion, chaplain asst prof, 1963-66; Albion Col, religion, dean chapel assoc prof, 1966-69; Beloit Col, religion, dean chapel prof, 1969-70; Univ Va, Religious Studies, prof & chmn, Afro-Amer Studies, 1970-75; Univ Calif, Riverside, Religious Studies, prof, Black Studies, chmn. **Orgs:** Am Soc Chris Etheics; Am Acad Religion. **Honors/Awds:** Books publ, Black Religion, 1964; Politics of God, 1967; Black & White Power Subreption, 1969; Marriage in Black & White, 1970; Black Sects & Cult, 1972. **Military Serv:** AUS, lt military police, 1952-54.

WASHINGTON, JOSIE B.
Educator. **Personal:** Born Mar 13, 1943, Leona, TX; daughter of Josephine Brooks and J B Brooks; married Eugene J; children: Eugenia J & Giovonna J. **Educ:** AA, BA, MS. **Career:** San Juan Sch Dist, 1968; Sacramento Co Welfare Dept Bur Invest, 1972; State Dept Rehab, 1974; Sacramento City Unified Sch Dist; Sacramento Urban League, site admin, head counr & chief examiner, currently. **Orgs:** Sacramento Urban League; Youth Develop Delinq Proj Bd; Neighborhood Counc; adv, Youth Outreach; Vista Neuva Adv Comn; N Area Citizen Better Govt; NatRehab Asn; Calif Sch Bd Asn; San Juan Unified Sch Dist; adv comt, Bus Skills Handicapped; trustee, clerk, Grant High Sch Dist Bd Educ; Sacramento Area Regional Adult & Vocational Educ; Coun rep, Sacramento County Sch Bd; Sacramento County Central Democratic Comn; Sen SI Hayakawa CA Constituency Coun; Comt elect Mayor Tom Bradley Govt Calif; Comt elec tv pres Mondale Pres; Comt elect Pres Jimmy Carter; NAACP. **Honors/Awds:** Written contributions Resource Directory Black Bus Sacramento area; first Black woman elected Grant Bd Educ; invited hite House President Jimmy Carter, 1980. **Business Addr:** Head Counselor, Chief Examiner, Sacramento Urban League, 2420 N St, Sacramento, CA 95816.

WASHINGTON, KEITH
Singer. **Personal:** Born in Detroit, MI; married Stephanie Grimes. **Career:** Back-up singer; Albums: Make Time for Love, 1991; You Make It Easy, 1993; tv guest appearance, Martin, 1992; General Hospital; Poetic Justice, 1993; The Meteor Man, 1993; KW, 1998; "Bring it On", 1998; The Good Life 1979-86, 2001. **Honors/Awds:** Make Time for Love, nominated, Grammy Award, 1992. **Special Achievements:** Has worked with the Jacksons, George Clinton, Miki Howard, and Stevie Wonder. **Business Phone:** (310)865-4500.*

WASHINGTON, KERRY
Actor. **Personal:** Born Jan 31, 1977, Bronx, NY. **Educ:** The George Washington Univ, theater prog, 1998; Michael Howard Studios, attended. **Career:** Films: Magical Make-Over, 1994; Our Song, 2000; 3D, 2000; Save the Last Dance, 2001; Lift, 2001; Take the A Train, 2002; Bad Company, 2002; The United States of Leland, 2003; The Human Stain, 2003; Sin, 2003; Against the Ropes, 2004; She Hate Me, 2004; Ray, 2004; Strip search, 2004; Sexual Life, 2005; Mr & Mrs Smith, 2005; Fantastic Four, 2005; Wait, 2005; Little Man, 2006; The Last King of Scotland, 2006; The Dead Girl, 2006; Fantastic Four: Rise of the Silver Surfer, 2007; I Think I Love My Wife, 2007; Woman in Burka, 2008; Lake view Terrace, 2008; Miracle at St Anna, 2008; Life Is Hot in Cracktown, 2009; A Thousand Words, 2009; Night Catches Us, 2009; Mother and Child,2009; TV Series: "ABC After school Specials", 1994; "Standard Deviants", 1996; "NYPD Blue", 2001; "Law & Order", 2001; "100Centre Street", 2001; "The Guardian", 2002; "Boston Legal", 2005-06; "Psych", 2008: L'Oreal Group, Spokesperson, currently. **Honors/Awds:** Teen Choice Award, 2001; Future of Film Award, Urbanworld Film Festival MECCA, 2002; Image Award, Nat Asn Advan Colored People, 2005; Best Outstanding actress In a Motion Picture awd, 2005. **Business Addr:** Actress, c/o Abrams Artists Agency, 9200 Sunset Blvd Suite 1130, Hollywood, CA 90069, **Business Phone:** (310)859-0178.*

WASHINGTON, LEANNA M
Government official. **Personal:** Born Jul 28, 1945, Philadelphia, PA; daughter of LeAnna M Brown; divorced; children: Tony, Edward & Tracey. **Educ:** Lincoln Univ, MS, 1989. **Career:** Philadelphia Parking Authority Employee Assistance Prog, mgr; Pa State rep, 1993-; Pa state senate dist 4, senator. **Orgs:** Bd trustees, Lincoln Univ; Nat Org for Women Legislators; bd mem, Pa Hospice Network; Women Legislator's Lobby; Teenshop Inc; exec comt, Nat Black Caucus, State Legislators; Nat Asn Advan Colored People; Alpha Kappa Alpha; Flemming Fellows Leadership Inst; NW Action Polit Alliance; Women in Govt; Lincoln Univ Alumni Asn; Pi Gamma Mu, Alpha lambda Chp; Wadsworth Area Bus Asn; Women in Transition; Gaudenzia Eastern Region Adv Bd. **Honors/Awds:** Chairperson's Award, Teenshop, Grace chap, 1994; Civic Award, Young Legends, 1998-00; Appreciation Award, Pa State Conf NAACP brs,1998; InterNat Human Rights Award, CCHR, 2000; Exceptional Meritorious Service to the Citizens of Philadelphia, House Democratic Caucus, 2002; Founder's Award, Berean Institute, 2002; Women of Distinction, Soroptimist InterNat, 2002; Spirit of the Constitution, Delta Sigma Theta Sorority, 2002; Service & Leadership, Gaudenzia Inc, 2004; Distinguished Leadership Award, Community Col of Philadelphia, 2004; Pacesetter Award, Women Legislators? Lobby, 2005; Women of Distinction, Philadelphia Business Journal, 2005; Profiles in Excellence, GIANT Stores, 2005; Drum Major for Social Justice, Office of Lieutenant Governor, 2005. **Business Addr:** State Senator, Pennsylvania House of Representatives, Irvis Office Bldg Rm 126, Senate Box 203004, Harrisburg, PA 17120, **Business Phone:** (717)783-2175.

WASHINGTON, LEONARD
Law enforcement officer. **Personal:** Born Nov 3, 1945, Pittsburgh, PA; son of Leonard Washington Sr and Anniebelle; married Celestine (Mickie) Washington, Nov 2, 1968; children: Leonard III, Maurice & Alonzo. **Educ:** Mercyhurst Col, Erie, PA, AA, 1978; Calif Univ Penn, BA, 1980. **Career:** N Am Rockwell, draftsman, 1968-73; PA State Police, trooper, 1973-78, corporal, 1978-80, sgt, 1980-82, lt, 1982-88, capt, 1988-98, maj, 1998, Bur Emergency & Spec Opers, dir, 2001. **Orgs:** Nat Asn Advan Colored People, 1987-; PA Chiefs Police Asn, 1988-; Nat Orgn Black Law Enforcement Exec, 1998-. **Honors/Awds:** Commissioners Commendation, PA State Police, 1982. **Military Serv:** Army Airborne, sgt, 1964-67.

WASHINGTON, LEROY
Educator, artist. **Personal:** Born May 1, 1925, Greenville, FL; married Edith; children: 4. **Educ:** FL A&M Univ, BA, 1950; Univ Miami, attended 1972. **Career:** Artist, educator (retired); Charlotte Jr Col, drama coach; Dade Pub Sch Miami, drama coach; Booker T Washington High Sch; Miami Sr High Sch; Miami Jackson Sr High Sch, drama coach & teacher; SW Miami Sr High Sch; sabbatical; Miami Northwestern Sr High Sch, teacher. **Orgs:** Past pres NC High Sch Drama Asn; Fla State Interscholastic Speech & Drama Asn; Dade County Speech Teacher Asn; UTD Prof Sect; Screen Actors Guild; Nat TV & Radio Broadcasters Union; Youth Emphasis Club Sponsor; NW Br YMCA; Model Cities; dir, vpres, CL Williams Memorial Scholarship Fnd Inc; sponsor, Creative Dance & Interpretative Reading Training Classes; Comm Sch Vol WorkCongregational Church Open Door. **Honors/Awds:** Man of Year, 1975; Zeta Phi Beta Sorority; Miami Chap; Outstanding Citizen & Civic Leader, Charles L Williams Memorial Scholar Found; TV Personality of the Month, BTW Alumni Asn; coached drama grp Booker T Washington HS; invited as one of top eight drama grps throughout cty to perform at Univ of IN; 2nd place Rowe Peterson's annual drama photo contest; 2nd place Natl Thespian Soc annual printed prog contest. **Military Serv:** USAF, corpl, WWII; first lt Korena Conflict. *

WASHINGTON, LESTER RENEZ
Government official. **Personal:** Born Feb 3, 1954, Kansas City, KS; son of Willie and Mable Watson; married Roberta Martin (divorced 1979); children: Jennifer, Lesley, Lester Jr, Travis & Corey; married Luberta Brown, Oct 4, 1980. **Educ:** Univ Iowa, BBA, 1977; Univ Mo, attended 1980-. **Career:** Lunam Corp, Kans City, MO, mgr, 1979-81; Southland Corp, Kans City, MO, mgr, 1981-85; City Kans City, Kans City, MO, mgr MBE/WBE prog, 1985-. **Orgs:** Bd dirs, East Attucks Community Housing, 1990-; Ad Hoc Group Against Crime, 1986-; Nat Asn Advan Colored People, 1980-; Prince Hall Mason Lodge No 77; bd dirs, Minority Network Asn, 1990-; White House Deleg Minority Bus, 1989-. **Honors/Awds:** Member of Year, Alpha Phi Alpha, 1976; Advocate of Year, Minority Contractors Asn, 1988. **Business Addr:** Manager, MBE/WBE/Contract Compliance Division, City of Kansas City, Missouri, 414 E 12th St 4th Fl, Kansas City, MO 64106, **Business Phone:** (816)274-1432.

WASHINGTON, DR. LINDA PHAIRE
Scientist. **Personal:** Born Aug 11, 1948, New York, NY; married Joey Washington; children: Kamau & Imani. **Educ:** Boston Univ, BS, biol, 1970; Mt Sinai Med Ctr City Univ NY, PhD, 1975. **Career:** Laguardia Col, lectr, 1973-75; Rockefeller Univ, res fel, 1975-77; City Univ, asst prof, 1976-77; Howard Univ Col Med, asst prof, 1977-79; Tuskegee Inst, Dept Biol, prof, 1981-; Cell Culture Sci Ctr, dir, 1981-, prof immunol & cell biol, Nat Sci Res Div, dir, 1984-; Int Progs Tuskegee Inst Liberia Linkage, consult, 1982-83; Ctr Adv Training Cell & Molecular Biol, adv res training, 1983; Argonne Nat Lab, bioscientist & prog admin, Div Educ Prog, sr prog leader, 1995-. **Orgs:** GRSRC Subcommittee Nat Inst

Health DRR, 1983-87; Gen Res Support Review Comt, NIH DRR, 1983-87; proposal reviewer, Nat Sci Found, 1985; panel reviewer, NIH DRR, 1986-87. **Honors/Awds:** Murray J Steele Award, NY Heart Asn, 1975; Nominee Recognition Award, Am Asn Univ Women Educ Prog, 1980; Outstanding Fac Award, Tuskegee Inst, 1981; UNCF Distinguished Scholars Award, United Negro Col Fund, 1984-85. **Business Addr:** Senior Program Leader, Argonne National Laboratory, 9700 S Cass Ave DEP 223, Argonne, IL 36088.

WASHINGTON, LIONEL
Football player, football coach. **Personal:** Born Oct 21, 1960, New Orleans, LA; children: Deron. **Educ:** Tulane Univ, sports admin. **Career:** Football player (retired), football coach; St Louis Cardinals, cornerback, 1983-86; Los Angeles Raiders, cornerback, 1987-94, 1997; Denver Broncos, 1995-96; Oakland Raiders, cornerback, 1997; Green Bay Packers, asst defensive backs coach, 1999-2004, defensive nickel package & cornerbacks coach, 2005-. **Business Phone:** (920)569-7500.

WASHINGTON, LORENZA BENARD
Executive. **Personal:** Born Oct 16, 1972, Marshall, TX; son of Benard Washington Sr and Lorenza. **Educ:** Univ N Tex, bachelor arts & sci, 1996. **Career:** Consolidated Freightways, sales exec, currently. **Orgs:** Big Brothers Big Sisters, 1991-94. **Honors/Awds:** Consolidated Freightways, Most Valuable Employee, 1997. **Home Addr:** 4127 Polaris Dr Suite 2021, Irving, TX 75038. **Business Addr:** Sales Executive, Consolidated Freightways, 8505 N Freeport Pkwy Suite 500, Irving, TX 75063, **Business Phone:** (972)929-1202.

WASHINGTON, MALIVAI
Tennis player, president (organization). **Personal:** Born Jun 20, 1969, Glen Cove, NY; son of William and Christine. **Educ:** Univ Mich, attended 1989. **Career:** Professional tennis player (retired), pres; tennis player, 1989-99; MaliVai Washington Kids Found, founder & pres, 1994-. **Honors/Awds:** Col Tennis Player of the Year, Univ Mich, 1989; Rookie of the Year, Tennis Mag, 1990; won 2 NCAA titles, Univ Mich; Fed Express Int tennis tournament, winner, 1992; Winner, US Mens Clay Ct Championships, 1992. **Special Achievements:** US Davis Cup Team, 1993-94, 1996-97; US Olympic Team, 1996; first African Am male to reach a Wimbledon final since 1975. **Business Phone:** (904)301-3786.

WASHINGTON, MARIAN
Basketball coach. **Personal:** Married; children: Josie. **Educ:** West Chester State Col, BA, physics, 1970. **Career:** Basketball coach (retired): Univ Kan, grad asst health phys educ & recreation, 1972, Women's athletics dir, 1974-79, Women's Basketball Team, head coach, 1973-2004. **Orgs:** Vpres, Black Coaches Asn, 1991, pres, 1992. **Honors/Awds:** Coach of the Year, Black Coaches Asn; Lifetime Achievement Award, Black Coaches Asn, 2003; Women's Basketball Hall of Fame; Carol Eckman Award. **Special Achievements:** The first African-American to coach on an Olympic women's basketball staff serving as an assistant on the 1996 U.S. Olympic gold medal winning team; The first African-American woman to serve as head coach for a U.S.international team guiding the 1982 U.S. Select team to a silver medal in Taiwan; First female to be elected president of the BCA; First person to serve consecutive terms as president of the Black Coaches Association; Been inducted into the West Chester Stare Hall of Fame; Been inducted into the Kansas University Hall of Fame. *

WASHINGTON, MARVIN ANDREW
Football player. **Personal:** Born Oct 22, 1965, Denver, CO; children: Evan. **Educ:** Univ Idaho, criminal justice. **Career:** New York Jets, defensive end, 1989-96; San Francisco 49ers, 1997, 1999; Denver Broncos, 1998.

WASHINGTON, MARY HELEN
College teacher. **Personal:** Born Jan 21, 1941, Cleveland, OH; daughter of David C and Mary Catherine Dalton. **Educ:** Notre Dame Col, BA, 1962; Univ Detroit, MA, 1966, PhD, 1976. **Career:** Ohio Pub Schs, High sch teacher Eng, 1962-64; St John Col, Cleveland, instr Eng, 1966-68; Univ Detroit, Detroit, MI, asst prof Eng, 1972-75, dir Ctr Black Studies, 1975; Boston Harbor Col, Univ Mass, Boston, assoc prof Eng; Univ Md, Dept Eng Lang & Lit, prof, 1990-. **Orgs:** Nat Coun Teachers Eng; Col Lang Asn; Mich Black Studies Asn; Am Studies Asn. **Honors/Awds:** Richard Wright Award for Literary Criticism, Black World, 1974; Women of Color Award, Pres's Comn Women's Issues, 2005; Lyndhurst Prize; has been awarded five honorary doctorates and earned six fellowships, including a Ford Foundation Fellowship and a Wellesley Center for Research on Women Fellowship. **Special Achievements:** Anthologist, Memory of Kin: Stories About Family by Black Writers; her work on Anna Cooper, Dorothy Sterling, Zora Neale Hurston, Alice Walker and others has been highlighted in her 27 articles and essays, 18 reviews and 36 lectures over the past 26 years. In addition she has published four books and is currently collaborating on a fifth. **Business Addr:** Professor, University of Maryland, Department of English Language and Literature, College Park, MD 20742.

WASHINGTON, MARY PARKS
Artist, educator. **Personal:** Born in Atlanta, GA; daughter of Walter Parks; married Samuel; children: Eric & Jan. **Educ:** Spelman Col, BA, 1946; Univ Mexico, attended 1947; San Jose State Univ, San Jose, CA, MA, Fine Arts 1978; San Jose State Univ, painting grad. **Career:** Howard Univ, 1948-51; Dartmouth Jr HS, teacher, 1961-80; Union Sch Dist, teacher. **Orgs:** Rosenwood Scholar Black Mt Col, 1947; bd mem, Nat Asn Advan Colored People; chmn, 1958-; San Jose Art League, 1960, 1977; Human Relations chmn, Union Sch Dist Teachers Asn, 1968-72; bd mem, Info Referral Santa Clara Co, 1974-75; Calif Teachers Asn; Nat Cong Artists; Nat Art Asn; coun mem, Calif Art Educ Asn; coun dir, Tutoring Prog Minority Stud; charter mem, San Jose Chapter AKA Sorority; San Jose Chapter Jack & Jill; Collector's Choice chmn fund raising, San Jose Art League; Am Cancer Soc. **Honors/Awds:** Artist of Year, Links Inc. **Special Achievements:** Published: Black Artist on Art Vol 1; A Soul A Mirror by Sarah Webster Fabia; The Spelman Story; Black Soul, Ebony Mag; num one woman shows; Johnson Publishes Art College.

WASHINGTON, DR. MICHAEL HARLAN
Educator. **Personal:** Born Sep 25, 1950, Cincinnati, OH; son of Herbert and Willa; children: Michael Jr, Milo Robeson & Chi. **Educ:** Raymond Walters Col, AA, 1971; Univ Cincinnati, BS, 1973, MEd, 1974, Educ Founds Dept, EdD, 1984; Am Univ, Cairo, Egypt, Arab hist, cult, polit & relig, 1991. **Career:** Univ Cincinnati, learning skills specialist, 1974-79; Northern Ky Univ, learning skills specialist, 1979-80, assoc prof hist, 1980-95, Afro-Am Studies prog, dir, 1986-, full prof hist, 1995-; Tokyo Christian Women's Univ, Fulbright lectr; Kyoritsu Women's Univ, Tokyo, Japan, lectr, 2001. **Orgs:** Northern Ky Univ, Consults Off In-Service Educ, 1980; Univ Cincinnati, United Christian Ministeries & Black Campus Ministries, 1980-81; Univ Cincinnati, Med Ctr, 1980; Northern Ky Univ, Div Continuing Educ, 1980-81; Ky Asn Teachers Hist, 1981; Inservice Teacher Training, SW Bus Col, 1982; Black Hist Archives Community, 1985-; Phi Alpha Theta, 1985-; Minority Students Retention Scholar, Northern Ky Univ, founder, 1986; Afro-Am Studies Prog, Northern Ky Univ, founder, 1986. **Honors/Awds:** Outstanding Professor of the Year, Northern Ky Univ, 1996; Distinguished Alumni Award, Raymond Walters Col 1996. **Special Achievements:** Author: "On Time," publ Am Poetry Anthology, 1986; "Academic Success and the College Minority Student", 1986; Co-author, "Undoing Racism", 1997; Numerous publications consisting of several monographs and dozens of articles which appear in a number of anthologies, encyclopedias and journals. **Business Addr:** Professor of History, Director, Afro American Studies Program, Northern Kentucky University, 415 Landrum Acad Ctr, Highland Heights, KY 41099, **Business Phone:** (859)572-6483.

WASHINGTON, MICKEY LYNN
Lawyer, football player. **Personal:** Born Jul 8, 1968, Galveston, TX. **Educ:** Tex A&M Univ, BS, sociol, 1990. **Career:** Football player (retired), Lawyer; New Eng Patriots, defensive back, 1990-91; Washington Redskins, 1992; Buffalo Bills, 1993-94; Jackson ville Jaguars, 1995-96; New Orleans Saints, 1997; Fort Bend Dist Attorneys Office, clerk; Taylor & Ernster Law Firm, union rep; PC & Assoc, atty, 2002; Southern Dist Fed Ct, lawyer; Miss Cts, Fifth Circuit, lawyer; Tex State Ct, lawyer; Wash & Ernster LLC, atty, currently. **Orgs:** Union rep, Nat Football Players Asn; State Bar Col; Nat Employment Lawyers Asn. **Honors/Awds:** Texas Rising Stars, 2007. **Business Phone:** (713)821-9433.

WASHINGTON, NANCY ANN
Certified public accountant, auditor. **Personal:** Born Nov 30, 1938, Kansas City, KS; daughter of E B Owens and Essie Mae Williams Owens; widowed; children: Georgetta Grigsby, Bertram Grigsby & Charles Washington III. **Educ:** KCK Community Col, Kansas City KS, AA, 1977; St Mary Col, BSBA, 1979; Univ Mo Kansas City KS, MBA, 1989. **Career:** Internal Revenue Serv, Kansas City MO, agent, 1979-80; Wash Acct Serv, Kansas City KS, owner, 1980-83; Kansas Corp Comt, Topeka KS, sr utility regulatory auditor, 1983-88; Bd Public Utilities, Kansas City KS, internal auditor, 1988-. **Orgs:** League Women Voters 1985-, AICPA 1987-, KS Cert Public Accountants Soc, 1988-, Inst Internal Auditors, 1988-; treas, Am Asn Black Energy; owner, Untouchable Concepts Beauty Salon, Kansas City, KS. **Honors/Awds:** Candlelight Service Award, KCK Community Col, 1976. **Home Addr:** 809 N 57th St, Kansas City, KS 66102, **Home Phone:** (913)287-8324. **Business Addr:** Internal Auditor, Board of Public Utilities, 700 Minnesota Ave, Kansas City, KS 66101, **Business Phone:** (913)573-9123.

WASHINGTON, OSCAR D
Educator, musician, poet. **Personal:** Born Feb 18, 1912, Tulsa, OK; married Doretha Lumbard; children: Cynthia & Alisa. **Educ:** Creighton Univ, BS, 1935; Univ Mich, MS, 1948; St Louis Univ, PhD, 1973. **Career:** St Louis Bd Educ, teacher; poet; writer; musician; scientist; Soli Music Publishers Ballad Record Co, pres & organizer; songwriter; US Govt, chemist, 1943; St Louis Argus, newspaper columnist, 1974. **Orgs:** Broadcast Music Inc; organizer, Prof Teachers Orgn, Bristow, OK, 1945; Bristow Civic Improvement Orgn; Bristow Chamber Com, 1946. **Honors/Awds:** Quiz Kids Best Teacher, 1948; Star Award, Nat Sci Teachers Asn, 1956. **Military Serv:** World War II, govt chemist.

WASHINGTON, PATRICE CLARKE
Airplane pilot. **Personal:** Born Sep 11, 1961, Nassau, Bahamas; daughter of Peggy Ann and Nathaniel Clarke; married Ray, 1994. **Educ:** Embry-Riddle Aeronautical Univ Daytona Beach; BS, aeronaut science, 1982. **Career:** Trans Island Airways, pilot, 1982-84; UPS Airlines, flight engr, 1988-90, first officer, 1990-94, captain, 1994-. **Orgs:** Organization of Black Airline Pilots. **Special Achievements:** First African American female to obtain rank of captain for a major airline; first female to fly for Trans Island Airways and Bahamasair; first Afr American female pilot UPS. **Business Addr:** Captain, United Parcel Service, 1400 N Hurstbourne Pkwy, Louisville, KY 40223, **Business Phone:** (502)329-3000.

WASHINGTON, REGYNALD G.
Executive. **Educ:** Fla Int Univ, BS, Int Hotel & Restaurant Admin; Grad, Exec Tech Chicago. **Career:** Magic Pan Restaurant, gen mgr; Air Terminal Servs Inc, gen mgr Food & Beverage; Concessions Int Inc, corp sr vpres, corp exec vpres, W coast reg vpres & gen mgr; Walt Disney World Co, dir Resort Food & Beverage Opers, gen mgr, food & beverage; Disney Regional Entertainment, vpres & gen mgr, 2004. **Orgs:** Educ Inst Am Hotel & Motel Asn; Educ Found Nat Restaurant Asn; Ga Hospitality & Travel Asn; Adv Bd Mem, Sch Hotel & Restaurant Admin, Ga State Univ; Adv Bd Mem, Sch Hospitality Mgt, Univ Delaware; past pres, Ga Restaurant Asn; past bd dir, Atlanta Symphony Orchestra; bd dir, Fla Restaurant Asn; Bd Trustees Educ Found, Nat Restaurant Asn; Treas, Nat Restaurant Asn, 2001-02, vchmn bd, 2001-02, chmn bd, 2003-. **Honors/Awds:** Industry Leader of the Year Award, Ga Hospitality & Travel Asn, 1994. **Special Achievements:** Keynote Speaker for the MultiCultural Foodservice & Hospitality Alliance and the Southern California Restaurant Association conference August 27, 2001 in Los Angeles, CA ; Moderated Salute to Excellence Forum for the Educational Foundation of the National Restaurant Association, May 2001; Delivered Commencement address for the Chattanooga State Community College, May 12, 2001, Chattanooga, TN; Speaker for the Educational Foundation of the National Restaurant Association during the Chain Operators Exchange (COEX) conference February 29, 2000 in Las Vegas, NV ; Delivered keynote address for the National Restaurant Association Education Foundation's Salute to Excellence for May, 1992, May, 1995 and May 1998; Named one of The NRN 50 The New Taste Makers, Nation's Restaurant News, Vol. 33, No. 4, January 1999; Lifetime Penn State Conti Professor for the School of Hospitality Management for Pennsylvania State University, 1999. *

WASHINGTON, RICO (ENRICO ALICENO WASHINGTON)
Baseball player. **Personal:** Born May 30, 1978, Milledgeville, GA. **Career:** Pittsburgh Pirates, 1999-2002; San Diego Padres, 2002-04; Tampa Bay DevilRays, 2004; Minor League, Montgomery Biscuits, 2005; Springfield Cardinals, 2006; Minor League, Memphis Redbirds, 2006-09; Uni-Pres 7-Eleven Lions, Chinese Prof Baseball League, 2009-. **Honors/Awds:** S Atlantic League All-Star C, 2005; All-Star 3B, Southern League, 2005;Player of the Week, 2006. **Business Addr:** Professional Baseball Player, Uni-Pres 7-Eleven Lions, Uni-President Enterprises Corp., 301 Chung Cheng Rd, Yungkang 710, Taiwan.

WASHINGTON, ROBERT BENJAMIN, JR.
Lawyer. **Personal:** Born Oct 11, 1942, Blakeley, GA; married Nola Wallette, Dec 27, 1969; children: Todd & Kyle W. **Educ:** St Peters Col, BS, econ & polit sci, 1967; Howard Law Sch, JD, 1970; Harvard Univ Law Sch, LLM, 1972. **Career:** Howard Law Sch, cobb fel, 1969, teaching fels, 1970-72; US Senate Com Dist Columbia, atty, 1971-72; Howard Univ Law Sch, assoc prof law & dir commun skills, 1972-73; Christopher Columbus Col Law, lectr, 1972-73; US House Reps Com Dist Columbia, atty, 1973-75; George Washington Univ Law Ctr, lectr, 1975, assoc prof law, 1978; Danzansky, Dickey, Tydings, Quint & Gordon, sr partner, 1975-81; Georgetown Law Ctr, assoc prof, 1978-82; Finley, Kumble, Wagner, sr partner & mem Nat Mgt Comt, 1981-87, managing partner, Wash office, 1986-88; Finley, Kumble, Wagner, Heine, Underberg, Manley, Myerson & Casey, Wash, DC, co-managing partner, 1986-88; Laxalt, Wash, Perito, & Dubuc, managing partner, 1988-91; Wash & Christian, managing partner, 1997-99; Wash Strategic Consult Group Inc, chmn & chief exec officer, currently; Caribbean Cage LLC, chmn & chief exec officer, 2004-; Las Vegas Gaming Inc, dir, 2006-07. **Orgs:** Dist Columbia Bar Asn; Am Bar Asn; Nat Bar Asn; Wash Bar Asn; Fed Bar Asn; Am Judicature Soc; Supreme Ct Hist Soc; Phi Alpha Delta Legal Fraternity; bd mem, Nat Bank Wash, 1981-89; bd mem, Medlantic Healthcare Group; bd mem, Medlantic Mgt Corp; bd mem, Healthcare Partners; bd mem, AVW Electronic Systs Inc; bd mem, Home Group (AmBase); bd trustees, Corcoran Gallery Art; bd mem, Nat Symphony Orchestra Asn; Metrop AME Church. **Home Addr:** 4555 Dexter St NW, Washington, DC 20007, **Home Phone:** (202)338-0971. **Business Addr:** Chairman, Chief Executive Officer, Caribbean Cage LLC, Citibank Towers Fl 16 252 Ponce de Leon Ave, San Juan, PR 00918, **Business Phone:** (787)758-8609.

WASHINGTON, ROBERTA
Executive. **Educ:** Howard Univ, Wash, DC, BArch; Columbia Univ, NY, MS, archit. **Career:** Mozambique, head, provincial design office, 1977-81; Roberta Washington Architects PC, prin & owner, 1983-; Univ sch archit, juror & lectr. **Orgs:** Nat Coun Ar-

chit Registration Bds; LEED Accredited Prof; Am Inst Architects; past pres, Nat Org Minority Architects; past pres, NY State Bd Archit. **Business Phone:** (212)749-9807.

WASHINGTON, ROBIN
Journalist, editor. **Personal:** Born Dec 29, 1956, Chicago, IL; son of Atlee David and Jean Birkenstein; married Lynn Goldberg, 1977 (divorced 1996); children: Erin Jenica. **Educ:** Ill Inst Tech, engineering sci, attended 1977. **Career:** Loyola Univ Medical Ctr, ed, 1977-78; Save Buying Guide, ed, 1978-83; MinnEngineer, founder, publisher, 1983-86; Lake County, MN, News-Chronicle, publisher, ed, 1986-87; WGBH-TV, producer, reporter, 1987-89; BET News, corresp, 1989-92; Northeastern Univ, adj prof, 1991; Fel Reconciliation, communications dir, 1991-92; Bay State Banner, managing ed, 1993-96; Emerson Col, adj prof, 1994; Wombat Media, pres, 1996-; Boston Herald, sports copy ed, 1996-98, columnist, 1996-2004; Duluth News Tribune, ed, currently. **Orgs:** Bd mem, Two Harbors, Minn Chamber Com, 1986; pres, Boston Asn Black Journalists, 1990, 1999-; bd mem, Univ Mass, Boston, Summer Jour Prog, 1991-; Nat Endowment Arts, Radio Grants panelist, 1994; chair, co-founder, Alliance Black Jews, 1995; parliamentarian, exec bd mem, Nat Asn Black Journalists NABJ, 1997-2001; bd mem, New Eng Press Asn, 1997-99. **Honors/Awds:** Freedom of Information Award, Minn Newspaper Asn, Lake County News-Chronicle, 1986; fellow, WGBH Educational Foundation, Science Broadcast Journalism, 1987; NY Radio Festival, Gold Award, Grand Award, Best of Show, for Vietnam: Radio First Termer, Interlock Media/Nat Public Radio, 1988; NABJ Radio News Award for Orange Line Farewell, NPR Crossroads, 1988; New England Emmy for Vermont: The Whitest State in the Union, WGBH_TV, 1989; Asniated Church Press Most Improved Publication Award, Fellowship magazine, 1992; American Bar Assn, Silver Gavel Award for You Don't Have to Ride Jim Crow!, 1996. **Special Achievements:** The Boston Globe, Los Angeles Times, op-ed contributor, 1995; Black & Jewish Like Jesus & Me, "Multi-America", essayist, Ishmael Reed, Viking, 1997.

WASHINGTON, DR. ROMANUEL, JR.
Administrator. **Career:** Chiropractic Arts & Sci Clin, owner, currently. **Business Addr:** Owner, Chiropractic Arts & Sci Clin, 3300 Crawford St, Houston, TX 77004-2927, **Business Phone:** (713)522-3878.*

WASHINGTON, ROOSEVELT, JR.
Educator. **Personal:** Born Feb 8, 1932, Swan Lake, MS; married; children: LuWanna, Ronald, Kenneth & Pamela. **Educ:** Roosevelt Univ, BA, 1960, MA, 1962; Marquette Univ; Chicago State Univ; DePaul Univ, adv study; No Il Univ, EdD. **Career:** Ctr St Sch & Fulton Jr HS, teacher & counr, 1960-61; Manley Upper Grade Ctr, teacher & dept chmn, 1961-68; McDade Elem Sch, asst prin, 1968-69; Noll Univ, 1969-71; Marquette Univ, asst prof, 1971-74; Harambee Independent Comn Sch Inc, chief admin, 1973-74; Univ N Tex, Denton Tex, prof teacher educ & admin, 1974-. **Orgs:** Nat Asn Sec Sch Prins; Am Educ Res Asn; Asn Supervision & Curric Devel; Phi Delta Kappa; Am Asn Sch Admin; Nat Orgn Legal Problems Educ. **Special Achievements:** Published numerous articles. **Military Serv:** USN, HM3, 1950-54. **Home Addr:** 2125 Woodbrook, Denton, TX 76205. **Business Addr:** Professor, University of North Texas, College of Education, Kendall Hall 149, Denton, TX 76203, **Business Phone:** (817)565-2947.

WASHINGTON, ROSE WILBURN
Association executive. **Personal:** Born Sep 4, 1940, Daphne, AL; daughter of Emory William and Emma L Chancley; married Regis G McDonald, Oct 22, 1983; children: Gerald, Carlos, Werhner Von & Tanya Monica. **Educ:** State Univ, Oneonta, BS, 1975; Marywood Col, MS Ed, 1979; City Col, NY, 1988-. **Career:** Charles Loring Brace Youth Camp, dir, 1978-80; Tryon Sch Boys, dir, 1980-83; Spofford Juvenile Detention Ctr, NYC, exec dir, 1983-85; Dept Juvenile Justice, NYC, asst comnr, 1985-90, comnr, 1990-94; Dallas Co Juvenile Dept, dir/chief probation officer, 1994-95; Berkshire Farm Ctr & Serv Youth, exec dir, exec dir emer, currently. **Orgs:** Presidential appointee, Nat Juv Justice Coord Coun, 1994-; bd gov, Am Correctional Asn; chair, Juvenile Detention Comm; auditor, Comn Accreditation; Nat Asn Juv Correctional Agencies; New York State Detention Asn; Nat Black Child Develop Inst; Westchester Co Black Women's Polit Caucus. **Honors/Awds:** Carter G Woodson Acad, Leadership & Support, 1988; Nelson Rohlilahla Mandela, NY Asn Black Psychologists, 1993; Outstanding Leadership, Det Juv Justice, New York, 1994; Devotion & Leadership, Spofford Juv Ctr, 1994. **Special Achievements:** "Black Identity, Where We've Been Where We Are," 1981; Presented paper at Thistletown Regional Cte, Ontario, Canada, "Casemanagement as a Crisis Intervention In a Secure Setting," 1987; presented paper at the Chapel Hill Workshop, "Accountability: Is There Light at the End of Tunnel?" 1989; featured in PBS Documentary, "In Search of Excellence," 1989; Kennedy Sch Govt Case Study, "Taking Charge: Rose Wash & Spofford Juvenile Detention Ctr," Harvard Univ, 1989. **Business Addr:** Executive Director Emeritus, Berkshire Farm Center Services for Youth, 13650 Rte 22, Canaan, NY 12029-3500, **Business Phone:** (518)718-4567.

WASHINGTON, RUDY
Association executive, basketball coach. **Personal:** Born Jul 14, 1951, Los Angeles, CA; married Gail Terry; children: Crystal Wilks, Corey Wilks, Raymond Washington & Rudy Jr. **Educ:** Univ Redlands, grad. **Career:** Locke High Sch, junior varsity basketball coach; Verbum Dei High Sch, basketball coach, 1976-77; Univ Southern Calif, asst basketball coach, 1977; Los Angeles Lakers, asst coach, 1982-83; Compton Jr col, head basketball coach, 1983-84; Clemson Univ, head basketball coach, 1984-85; Univ IA, coaching staff, 1986-90; Drake Univ, head basketball coach, 1990-95; Southwestern Athletic Conf, comnr, 2001-. **Orgs:** Eexc dir & founder, Black Coaches Asn; Nat Asn Basketball Coaches; Women's Basketball Coaches Asn; 100 Black Men of Los Angeles. **Honors/Awds:** Coach of the Year, 1993; Nat Asn Basketball Coaches, Coach of the Year 1993; "Thirty Most Valuable Professionals in the Business of Sports, Black Enterprise mag; 100 Most Powerful People in Sports,The Sporting News. **Special Achievements:** Author of two books on rebounding. *

WASHINGTON, SAMUEL, JR.
Educator. **Personal:** Born Aug 28, 1933, Jacksonville, FL; son of Alphonso Kelly and Bernice Kelly; married Bessyee G, Jul 8, 1955; children: Rommell E Renee E. **Educ:** Fla Agr & Mech Univ, BS, 1955, MEd, 1972; Fla State Univ, 1979-81. **Career:** AUS, officer, 1955-77; Fla Agr & Mech Univ, dir admis, 1977-83, univ registr, 1983-92, assoc vpres, 1992. **Orgs:** Phi Delta Kappa, 1972-; Nat Asn Col Deans, registr, admis, treas, 1978-; Am Asn Col Deans, registr, admis officer, 1983-; bd dirs, Tallahassee Urban League, 1993-. **Honors/Awds:** Man of the Year, Phi Delta Kappa, 1973; Leadership Award, Alpha Phi Alpha Fraternity, 1983. **Military Serv:** AUS, lt coll, 1955-77; Bronze Star, Meritorious Serv Medal, Commendation Medal. **Home Addr:** 2512 Lindsey Ct, Tallahassee, FL 32310.

WASHINGTON, DR. SANDRA BEATRICE
Educator, counselor. **Personal:** Born Mar 1, 1946, Nashville, TN; daughter of Henry F Tucker and Sadie Lewis; divorced; children: Howard LaMont. **Educ:** Loyola Univ, BA, 1968; Univ Nebr, MS, 1977; Vanderbilt Univ, EdD, 1990. **Career:** Sacred Heart Grade Sch, teacher, 1968-71; Omaha OIC, instr, 1972-73; Greater Omaha Community Action, counsr/supvr, 1972-75; PCC/Head Start, pi/soc serv coordr, 1976-78; Metro-Tech Community Col, counsr/career develop, 1978-81; Computer Inst Youth, educ coordr, 1984-85; Nashville Pub Sch, counr, 1986-99, chairperson, Guid Dept, 1994-; Univ Tenn, Stokley fel, 1992; Mid Tenn State Univ, psych dept, adj prof, 2000-01; Cohn Adult High Sch, Guid Counr, currently. **Orgs:** Career consult Girl's Club Omaha, 1978-81; counsr-on-call, Planned Parenthood Nashville, 1985-; ed newsletter, Chi Sigma Iota, Coun/Acad & Prof Hon Soc Int, 1991; ed bd, Elem Sch Guid & Coun, 1991-94. **Honors/Awds:** Outstanding Young Women of America, 1978-79; Nat bd Cert Counrs, TN, State Cert Counr; Excellence in Counseling Award, UT Knoxville, 1997; Teacher Award, Frist Fund, 1999; Technical Preparation Consortium Grant Award, 2001-02. **Special Achievements:** International Foundation for Education and Self-Help, counselor/volunteer, Nairobi, Kenya, East Africa, 1995-96; selected for Middle Tennesses State University sponsored Japan Field Study tour of Educational and Economic Organizations, 1999. **Business Addr:** Guidance Counselor, Cohn Adult High School, 4805 Pk Ave, Nashville, TN 37209, **Business Phone:** (615)298-8053.

WASHINGTON, DR. SARAH M
Educator. **Personal:** Born Aug 10, 1942, Holly Hill, SC; daughter of David Harry (deceased) and Sarah Harmon; married Jun 4, 1967 (divorced); children: Walter Dawit Washington. **Educ:** Tuskegee Inst, Tuskegee, AL, BS, 1964; Univ Ill, Urbana, IL, MS, 1970, PhD, 1980. **Career:** Spartanburg Dist, Inman, SC, eng teacher, 1964-65; Anderson Pub Schs, Anderson, SC, eng teacher, 1965-67; Sumter Schs, Sumter, SC, social studies teacher, 1967-68; Ala State Univ, Montgomery, AL, eng instr, 1971-74; Univ Ill, Urbana, IL, teaching asst, 1974-80; SC State Col, Orangeburg, SC, assoc prof eng & modern lang, 1979-. **Orgs:** Pres, Orangeburg Branch, Asn Study Afro-Am Life & Hist, 1980-85; pres elect, 1991, chaplain, 1982-89, Phi Delta Kappa; SC State Dept Writing Adv Bd, 1983-89; Am Asn Univ Women; reader, Nat Teachers Exam, 1989; Nat Coun Teachers Eng; Nat Black Child Develop Inst; field coordr, Assessment Performance Teaching, 1988-90. **Honors/Awds:** Sigma Tau Delta Natl Eng Honor Soc, 1981. **Special Achievements:** Author of literary biog of Frank Horne, 1985, Scholar of Let's Talk About It, a national reading program. **Business Addr:** Associate Professor of English and Modern languages, South Carolina State University, PO Box 7534, Orangeburg, SC 29117, **Business Phone:** (803)536-8849.

WASHINGTON, SHAUNISE A
Executive. **Personal:** Born Feb 29, 1964, Columbia, SC; daughter of Walter and Elizabeth Hammond; married Donald T Washington, May 24, 1997; children: Michael & Chad. **Educ:** Univ SC, BS, 1985. **Career:** Township Auditorium, SC, staff; Lt Gov off, staff; Phillip Morris USA, 1987-93, sr acct mgr, sales, 1993-94, dist mgr, sales, 1994-95, dir, trade mkt, 1995-96, dir, trade & bus rel, 1996-98, dist dir, state govt affairs, 1998-99, dir, Was relations, 1999-2000; Altra Corp Serv, vpres, external affairs, 2000-02, vpres, govt affairs policy & outreach, 2002-. **Orgs:** Nat Black Arts Festival, 1998-; bd co-resource comt, Delta Research & Educ Found, 2001-; Nat Coalition on Black Civic Participation, 2001-; Executive Leadership Coun, 2002-; The Future PAC, 2002-; Congressional Black Caucus Found, 2002-; DC Chamber Com. **Honors/Awds:** Certificate of Appreciation, US House of Representatives, 1999; Wash Metropolitan, Top 40 Under 40, 2000; Network Journal, Top 25 Influential Black Women, 2001; NY YWCA, Woman of Achievement, 2002; Nat Coalition on Black Civic Participation, Spirit of Democracy, 2002; Donald H McGannon Award, Nat Urban League, 2003. **Special Achievements:** Authored Time Management Workshop, 1994; Authored Planning/Organization Skills Workshop, 1994; Represented Philip Morris USA in sales recruitment ads, 1996, 1997, 1998. **Business Addr:** Vice President, Government Affairs Policy & Outreach, Altria Corp Services Inc, 101 Constitution Ave NW Suite 400 W, Washington, DC 20001, **Business Phone:** (202)354-1548.

WASHINGTON, SHERRY ANN
Administrator, painter (artist). **Personal:** Born Oct 28, 1956, Detroit, MI; daughter of William and Virginia Hall; married Floyd Haywood (divorced 1984); children: Khalid R Haywood. **Educ:** Univ Mich, BA, Gen Studies, 1977. **Career:** Govt adminr, 1981-88; Sherry Washington Gallery, owner, 1989-; BWW Group, founder; Wayne County Coun Arts, arts consult, 1989-93. **Orgs:** Delta Sigma Theta Sorority, 1974-; Nat Asn Advan Colored People, 1984-; bd mem, Detroit Inst Arts, Friends African Art, 1988-; bd mem, Detroit Cult Affairs Comt; bd mem, Metrop Growth & Develop Corp; Black Women Contracting Asn. **Honors/Awds:** Alumni of the Year, Am Ctr Int Leadership, 1987; Distinguished Woman of the Year, Coalition 100 Black Women, 1992; Outstanding Community Service Award, Mich Black Caucus, 1993; Community Service Award, Links Inc, 1995; Salute to Excellence, Top Ladies Distinction, 1997; Leadership Arts Award, Women's Justice Ctr, 1999; Distinguished Community Award, SBC, 2002. **Home Addr:** 1300 E Lafayette, Detroit, MI 48226, **Home Phone:** (313)222-1523. **Business Addr:** Owner, Sherry Washington Gallery, 1274 Libr St, Detroit, MI 48226, **Business Phone:** (313)961-4500.

WASHINGTON, STAN
Vice president (Organization). **Career:** Am Express, Com Card, Western Region, vpres & gen mgr; Znetix, bd dir; chmn, Los Angeles Convention & Visitors Bur, 2006-. **Orgs:** Los Angeles Sports & Entertainment Comn; Los Angeles Metro YMCA; Bowers Mus; Mus African Am Art. *

WASHINGTON, TAMIA. See TAMIA.

WASHINGTON, TED. See WASHINGTON, THEODORE, JR.

WASHINGTON, TERI
Basketball executive. **Career:** Denver, spokeswoman; Nat Basketball Asn Commun, sr dir community rels, currently. **Orgs:** Nat Basketball Asn marijuana rehab prog, spokeswoman. **Business Phone:** (212)407-8000.*

WASHINGTON, THEODORE, JR. (TED WASHINGTON)
Football player. **Personal:** Born Apr 13, 1968, Tampa, FL; son of Ted Sr; married Verlisa; children: Ashley, Allison, Adrianne, Teddy & Thadeous. **Educ:** Univ Louisville. **Career:** San Francisco 49ers, defensive tackle, 1991-93; Denver Broncos, defensive tackle, 1994; Buffalo Bills, defensive tackle, 1995-2000; Chicago Bears, defensive tackle, 2001-02; New England Patriots, defensive tackle, 2003; Oakland Raiders, defensive tackle, 2004-05; Cleveland Browns, defensive tackle, 2006-07; free agent, currently.

WASHINGTON, DR. THOMAS
Educator. **Personal:** Born Dec 8, 1937, Rock Island, IL. **Educ:** Univ Ill, BA, 1961, MA, 1964; Univ Minn, PhD, 1982. **Career:** Champaign Centennial HS, teacher Eng, Span, 1968-70; Hamline Univ Minn, instr Span, 1970-73; Women's Self Defense Empowering Women, lectr, instr, 1972-; Univ Minn, instr Span, 1974-78, 1980-81. **Orgs:** Women's Self Defense seminars & workshops 1982; The Nodarse Lang Learning Method, 1978-; Sigma Delta Pi; Phi Kappa Phi Nat Hon Soc.

WASHINGTON, TODD PAGE
Football player, football coach. **Personal:** Born Jul 19, 1976, Nassawadox, VA; married Shannon; children: Cameron, Ava & Zane. **Educ:** Va Tech, BS, phys educ, 1998. **Career:** Tampa Bay Buccaneers, ctr, 1998-2003; Houston Texans, ctr, 2003-05; SanDiego Univ, asst coach, offensive coord, currently. **Business Addr:** Assistant Coach/ Offensive Coordinator, San Diego University, 5998 Alcala Pk, San Diego, CA 92110, **Business Phone:** (619)260-4600.

WASHINGTON, TOM
Sports manager. **Personal:** Born Dec 25, 1957, Ft Smith, AR. **Educ:** Norfolk State Univ, cum laude, 1978. **Career:** Nat Basketball Asn, staff mem, referee, currently. **Orgs:** Amachi Big Brothers Prog; Sharon Baptist Men's fel; C's Choice Adoption Agency; Mt Zion Baptist Youth Orgn; PGA Juniors Prog. **Business Addr:** Referee, National Basketball Association, 645 5th Ave 15th Fl, New York, NY 10022, **Business Phone:** (212)826-7000.

WASHINGTON, UKEE (ULYSSES SAMUEL WASHINGTON, III)
Television news anchorperson, actor. **Personal:** Born Aug 20, 1958, Philadelphia, PA. **Educ:** Dover High Sch; Univ Richmond.

Career: WBBH-TV, anchor; KYW-TV Sta, news anchor; CBS Broadcasting Inc, CBS 3,news anchor, currently; Tv: "Death of Innocence", 2002, "Brothers in Arms", 2003, "Out of the Ashes", 2003. **Orgs:** Philadelphia Boys Choir's "elite". **Business Addr:** TV News Anchor, CBS Broadcasting Inc, CBS 3, 1555 Hamilton St, Philadelphia, PA 19130, **Business Phone:** (215)977-5300.

WASHINGTON, ULYSSES SAMUEL, III. See WASHINGTON, UKEE.

WASHINGTON, VAL L. See WASHINGTON, VALDEMAR LUTHER.

WASHINGTON, VALDEMAR LUTHER (VAL L WASHINGTON)
Lawyer, circuit court judge. **Personal:** Born Jun 21, 1952, Baltimore, MD; son of Vivian E and G Luther; married Ada C Miller, Aug 11, 1984; children: Valdemar L II & Christopher James. **Educ:** Baltimore Polytech Inst, BA, 1970; Mich State Univ, BA, 1974; Univ Mich Law Sch, JD, 1976. **Career:** Baker Law Firm Bay City, assoc lawyer, 1977, 1981-86; Acct Aid Soc Flint, dir, 1978; Pvt Pract, atty, 1978-80; Robinson Washington Smith & Stanfield, partner, 1981; Circuit Ct Judge Genesee County, judge 1986-96, chief ct circuit judge, 1990-91; Univ Mich, adj lecttr, 1989; Wayne State Sch Law, adj lectr, 1995; SETTLEmate Inc, pres, chief facilitator, currently. **Orgs:** Mich State Bar Asn; Big Sisters Bd Dirs; Flint Community Found, Mensa, 1980-; pres, Theatre Adv Bd, 1982-83; Legal Redress Comn, Nat Asn Advan Colored People, 1984-86; Am Judges Asn, 1986-87; Mich Trial Lawyers Asn, 1986-; Am Trial Lawyers Asn, 1986-; Am Col Civil Trail Mediators; life mem, MENSA; pres, Genesee County Bar Asn. **Honors/Awds:** University Rhodes Scholar, Mich State Univ, 1974; Argus Award, Genesee County Consortium Child Abuse & Neglect, 1989. **Business Phone:** (810)743-0101.

WASHINGTON, DR. VON HUGO
Educator, actor. **Personal:** Born Mar 9, 1943, Albion, MI; son of Alice Coleman and Hugh; married Frances Mosee, Mar 6, 1974; children: Von Jr & Alicia Rene. **Educ:** Western Mich Univ, Kalamazoo, MI, BA, sociol, 1974, MA, theatre, 1975; Wayne State Univ, Detroit, MI, PhD, speech commns & J, 1979. **Career:** Univ Mich, Ann Arbor, MI, dir, black theatre, 1975-77; Wayne State Univ, Detroit, MI, dir, black theatre, 1979-88; Western Mich Univ, Kalamazoo, Mi, dir, multi-cult theatre, 1989-, prof, Theatre, Currently. **Orgs:** Artistic dir/co-founder; Afro-Am Studio Theatre, Detroit, 1983-86; Black Theatre Network, 1986-96; pres & cofounder, WAS Prod Inc, 1992-. **Honors/Awds:** Career Development Chair, Wayne State Univ, 1983; Achievement Award, Mich Found Arts, 1984; Carter G Woodson Education Award, Wayne State Univ, 1984; Alumni Faculty Service Award, Wayne State Univ, 1988; Best Actor, Detroit News, 1990. **Military Serv:** USAAF, TSGT, 1961-72, Commendation Medal, 1965, Bronze Star, 1967,Meritorious Service Awards, 1967, 1972. **Business Addr:** Professor, Director, Western Michigan University, Department of Theatre, 1903 W Michigan Ave, Kalamazoo, MI 49008-5360, **Business Phone:** (269)387-3220.

WASHINGTON, DR. WARREN MORTON
Scientist. **Personal:** Born Aug 28, 1936, Portland, OR; son of Edwin Sr and Dorothy Morton; married Mary C; married LaRae Kemp, Oct 30, 1959 (divorced 1975); children: Teri Lyn Ciocco, Kim Ann Pierce & Tracy LaRae Cannon-Smith; married Joan A Washington, Jul 24, 1978 (died 1984); children: Jocelyn Montgomery, Michelle Meney & Quentin Hunt. **Educ:** Oregon State Univ, Corvallis, OR, BS, physics, 1958, MS, meteorol, 1960; Penn State Univ, PhD, meteorol, 1964. **Career:** Stanford Res Inst, mathematician, 1959; Penn State Univ, res assoc, 1960-63; Nat Ctr Atmospheric Res, Boulder, CO, res scientist, 1963-, prog scientist, 1972-73, proj leader, 1973-74, sr scientist, 1974-87, dir, climate & global dynamics div, 1987-95, Climate Change Res Sect, sect head, sr scientist, 1995-; Univ Mich, adj assoc prof meteorol, 1968-71. **Orgs:** Fel Am Meteorol Soc, 1980, pres, 1994, hon mem, 2006; fel AAAS, 1981; fel The Alumni Fel Prog, Penn State Univ, 1989; fel The Alumni Fel Prog, Ore State Univ, 1990; Am Geophysical Union; Nat Sci Bd, 1994-2006, chair, 2002-04; Nat Acd Eng, 2002; Am Philos Soc, 2003. **Honors/Awds:** Distinguished Alumni Award, Penn State Univ, 1991; Distinguished Alumni Award, Ore State Univ, 1996; Exceptional Service Award, Dept Energy Biologican & Envir Research Program, 1997; Sigma Xi Distinguished Lectr, 1998-99; Nat Weather Service Modernization Award, 1999; Dr Charles Anderson Award, Am Meteorol Soc, 2000; Celebrating 20th Century Pioneers Atmospheric Science Award, 2000, Howard Univ; Bonfils-Stanton Found Award, 2000; Reed Col Vollum Award, Distinguished Accomplishment in Sci & Technol, 2004; Science Spectrum Trailblazer, Sci Spectrum Mag, 2006; Honorary DSc, Oregon State Univ, 2006; Charles Franklin Brooks Award, Am Meteorol Soc, 2007; Honoray DSc, Bates Col, 2008. **Special Achievements:** One of 16 scientists featured in the Chicago Museum of Science and Industry "Black Achievers in Science" Exhibit. **Home Addr:** 8633 E Iliff Dr, Denver, CO 80231. **Business Addr:** Senior Scientist, Section Head, Climate Change Research Section, National Center for Atmospheric Research, Climate & Global Dynamics Division, PO Box 3000, Boulder, CO 80307-3000, **Business Phone:** (303)497-1321.

WASHINGTON, WENDY
Executive. **Educ:** Vassar Col, BA, hist. **Career:** Arista Recs, mgr publicity, 1994; Universal Motown Recs, sr vpres media rels; Zomba Label Group, sr vpres media rels, 2007-.

WASHINGTON, WILLIAM
Banker. **Personal:** Born in Chicago, IL; son of Susie M. **Educ:** Illinois Inst Technol, BS, sociol, bus econs, MS, mgt, finance. **Career:** LaSalle Home Mortgage Corp, mortgage collections, mortgage originations, home improvement loan coordr, sec mortgage mkt coordr, mortgage loan underwriting mgr, vpres, currently. **Orgs:** Christian educ dir, New Friendship Baptist Church Robbins, Ill; Teen Living Prog Chicago; Soc Mortgage Profs; NFBC Homeless Servs. **Honors/Awds:** Fed Housing Admin, Direct Endorsement Residential Underwriter; Accredited Residential Underwriter, Mortgage Bankers Asn Am; Black Achiever in Industry Awards, Young Men's Christian Asn. **Military Serv:** AUS, spc-4. **Business Addr:** Vice President, LaSalle Home Mortgage Corp., 4242 N Harlem Ave, Norridge, IL 60634-1283, **Business Phone:** (708)456-0400.

WASHINGTON, WILLIAM MONTELL (BILL WASHINGTON)
Executive. **Personal:** Born Apr 2, 1939, Columbia, MO; son of William Washington and Narcissia Washington. **Educ:** Lincoln Univ Mo, BS, Educ & Math, 1962; Univ Mo Kans City, MA, Educ, 1970. **Career:** KC Mo Sch Dist, high sch teacher & coach, 1963-67; Urban League Kans City, assoc dir econ develop, 1967-71; United Telecommunications Inc, affirmative action officer, 1971; Sprint, dir, cre rel, 1990; Swope Community Enterprises, secy bd dir, currently; Kans City Parks & Recreation Comn, comnr, currently. **Orgs:** Omega Psi Phi, 1959; bd dir, Metro YMCA, 1973; adv bd, United Negro Col Fund, 1976; chmn bd, Urban League Kans City, 1978; chmn, Black COT Fund; KC Harmony, 1996; HTH Midwest; INROADS Kans City; Bruce R Watkins Cult Heritage Ctr; Urban League, Kans City; YMCA Kans City; Compensation Comt. **Honors/Awds:** Outstanding Leadership Award, Minority Bus Awareness Prog, Black Econ Union, 1977. **Home Addr:** 7509 E 74th St, Kansas City, MO 64133. **Business Addr:** Commissioner, Kansas City Parks & Recreation Commission, 4600 E 63rd St Trfwy, Kansas City, MO 64130, **Business Phone:** (816)513-7500.

WASOW, OMAR
Executive. **Educ:** Stanford Univ, BA, 1992; Harvard Univ, MA, 2008-. **Career:** Stuyvesant Student Union, Stuyvesant High Sch, New York, pres, 1987-88; Congressman William Gray III, House Rep, Majority Whip, DC, intern, 1990; Strictly Bus, Citizens Comt NYC, assoc dir, 1992-93; Stanford Univ, CA, teacher, 1992; New York Online, Diaspora Inc, Brooklyn, NY, pres & founder, 1993-99; MSNBC, Secaucus, NJ, technol analyst, 1996-; BlackPlanet.com, Community Connect Inc, exec dir, 1999-2005. **Orgs:** Brooklyn Excelsior Charter Sch, Brooklyn, NY, 2000; Am Soc Mag Editors, 2002-05; Stanford Sch Edu, 2004; YMCA, New York, 2005-06. **Honors/Awds:** Catalyst Award, Nat Asn Minority Media Executives, 2005. **Business Addr:** Technology Analyst, MSNBC, 1 Msnbc Plz, Secaucus, NJ 07094, **Business Phone:** (201)583-5000.

WATERMAN, JEFFREY TREVOR
Consultant. **Personal:** Born Sep 25, 1971, Rocky Mount, NC; son of Connie Walston Jr and Carolyn Walston. **Educ:** St Augustine Col, BA, 1993; Univ Akron, MA, 1996. **Career:** Innovex Inc, pharmaceut consult; Eisa, sales rep, 2006-. **Orgs:** APA Fraternity Inc, 1991-. **Special Achievements:** Carnegie Hall performance, 1988; thesis: A Cluster Analysis of Martin Luther King's "I've Been to the Mountaintop". **Home Addr:** 1614A Treetop Trail, Akron, OH 44313.

WATERS, BRENDA JOYCE
Journalist, television news anchorperson. **Personal:** Born Jan 29, 1950, Goldsboro, NC; daughter of Dilliah and Levi. **Educ:** Univ MD, BS, 1973; Am Univ, MS, 1975. **Career:** WTVR-TV-6, reporter & anchor, 1975-76; WLOS-TV-13, reporter & anchor, 1977-79; WPXI-TV-11, reporter, 1979-85; KDKA-TV-2, weekend anchor & reporter, 1985-. **Orgs:** NAACP 1981-. **Honors/Awds:** Cert of Recognition Jimmy Carter Fed Disaster Assist Admin 1977; 1st Place Assoc Press Award, 1982, 1984; Cecile B Springer Womenpower Award; 100 outstanding women in the community, Ebenezer Baptist Church. **Business Addr:** Weekend Anchor, Reporter, KDKA-TV-2, 1 Gateway Ctr, Pittsburgh, PA 15222, **Business Phone:** (412)575-2245.*

WATERS, CRYSTAL
Singer, songwriter. **Personal:** Born Oct 10, 1964, Philadelphia, PA; married Lamont Reese; children: Morgan & Lindsay. **Educ:** Howard Univ, Comput Sci. **Career:** Albums: Surprise, 1991; Storyteller, 1994; Crystal Waters, 1997; The Best Of, 1998; Gypsy Woman - The Collection, 2001; 20th Century Masters - The Millennium Collection: The Best of Crystal Waters, 2001; Singles: "Megamix", 1992; "You Turn Me On", 1993; "In De Ghetto", 1996; "Come On Down", 2001; "Enough", 2001; "Night in Egypt", 2001; "My Time", 2003; "Destination Unknown", 2004; "Lies", 2001; "Destination Calabria", 2007; "Dancefloor", 2008; Never Enough, 2009. **Honors/Awds:** Billboard Music Award, 1994. **Business Phone:** (925)736-1991.*

WATERS, DIANNE E
Entrepreneur. **Personal:** Born Apr 28, 1954, Austin, TX; daughter of Billie Bacon Richards; married Clifton, Nov 19, 1983; children: Jamil. **Educ:** N Tex State Univ, BS, 1979. **Career:** Barretts Product Co, regional dir, 1980-85; Concessions Unique Inc, pres, 1986-. **Orgs:** Alpha Kappa Alpha, 1974; founding mem, Airport Minority Adv Coun, 1988; Jack & Jill Am, 2001. **Honors/Awds:** Quest For Success, Dallas Black Chamber, 1992; Parent Teacher Asn Award, 1994. **Business Addr:** President, Concessions Unique Inc, 501 Wynnewood Village Suite 102B, Dallas, TX 75224, **Business Phone:** (214)946-1444.

WATERS, GARY STEVEN. See Obituaries section.

WATERS, JOHN W
Executive, educator, clergy. **Personal:** Born Feb 5, 1936, Atlanta, GA; son of Henry (deceased) and Mary Annie Randall (deceased). **Educ:** Fisk Univ, BA, 1957; Atlanta Univ Summer Sch, 1958; Univ Geneva Switzerland, Cert, 1962; GA State Univ, 1964, 1984; Boston Univ, STB, 1967, PhD, 1970; Univ Detroit, 1975. **Career:** Educator (retired); Army Ed Ctr Ulm Western Germany, admin, 1960-63; Atlanta Bd Ed, instr, 1957-60, 1963-64; Myrtle Baptist Church W Newton MA, minister, 1969; Ctr Black Studies Univ Detroit, dir, assoc prof, 1970-76; Interdenom Theol Ctr, prof, 1976-86; Gr Solid Rock Baptist Church Riverdale, minister, 1981; sr vpres, 1984; Primerica Financial Serv, Col Park, sr vpres, 1984-2001; Greater Solid Rock Baptist Church, sr minister, 1980-2005. **Orgs:** Am Acad Relig, 1969; Soc Biblical Lit, 1969; bd trustees Interdenom Theol Ctr, 1980-84; bd dir, Habitat Humanity Atlanta, 1983; vpres, Col Park Ministers fel; chair S Atlanta Joint Urban Ministry, 1984-94; Prison Ministries Women, 1988-96; pres, Coun Overseers, New Era Baptist Conv Ctr, 1996-01; pres, Clayton County Ministers Conf, 2000. **Honors/Awds:** First Faculty Lecturer, Interdenominational Theol Ctr, 1979; Religion Leader of the Year, Concerned Black Clergy Metropolitan Atlanta, 2000. **Military Serv:** AUS, sp, 1960-63. **Home Addr:** 1516 Niskey Lake Trl SW, PO Box 310416, Atlanta, GA 30331-0416, **Home Phone:** (404)344-8104.

WATERS, KATHRYN
Vice president (Government), executive. **Educ:** Univ MD, BA, MCP. **Career:** MD State Railroad Admin, freight rail planner, 1981-82, sta develop coordr, 1982-83, Commuter Rail Mkt, mgr, 1983-84; MD State Railroad Admin, mgr planning, 1984-92; MARC Train Serv, asst dir, 1992-94; MD Transit Admin, chief oper & budget planning, 1994-95; MD Transit Admin, MARC Train Serv, chief operating Offr, 1995-2002; Dallas Transit Syst, Trinity Railway Express, vpres commuter rail, 2002-; MD Commuter Rail Syst, MARC Train Serv, actg mgr, mgr. **Orgs:** Past chair, Commuter Rail Comm; Am Pub Transit Asn; MD Chap; Conf Minority Transp Offs; adv bd, Eno Transp Found; Rail Safety Adv Community; Fed Railroad Admin. **Special Achievements:** First African Am & woman in MD to manage a commuter railway service. **Business Addr:** Vice President, Trinity Railway Express, Commuter Rails 1401 Pacific Ave, Dallas, TX 75202, **Business Phone:** (214)979-1111.

WATERS, MARY D
Human services worker, government official. **Personal:** Born Aug 27, 1955, Greenville, AL; daughter of William and Willie M. **Educ:** Detroit Bus Inst, 1975; Univ Mich, BA, lib studies, 1988. **Career:** McDonalds, 1973-75; Nat Bank Detroit, 1975-76; Blue Cross Blue Shield, benefit specialist; Mich House Rep, state rep, currently. **Orgs:** Facilitator, Metropolitan Detroit Youth Found, 1988-89; Collections Pract Bd; bd mem, d Direction, 1990-92; vice chair, Detroit Charter Rev Comn; Mgt asn, Blue Cross/ Blue Shield; Int Asn Bus Communs; Univ Mich Alumni; NAACP. **Honors/Awds:** Blue Cross/Blue Shield, Pride in Excecllence; Employee Suggestion Program. **Special Achievements:** On Detroit Column, Detroit News. **Business Addr:** State Representative, Michigan House of Representatives, PO Box 30014, Lansing, MI 48909-7514.

WATERS, MAXINE
Congressperson (u.s. federal government), congressional representative (u.s. federal government). **Personal:** Born Aug 15, 1938, St Louis, MO; daughter of Remus Moore and Velma Moore Carr; married Sidney Williams, Jul 23, 1977; married Edward (divorced 1972); children: Edward & Karen. **Educ:** Calif State Univ, Los Angeles, BA, sociol. **Career:** Head Start, asst teacher; Los Angeles City Councilman David Cunningham, dep; State Calif, assembly woman; Dem Party, chief dep whip; US House Rep, 35 Dist Columbia, rep, 1990, congresswomen, currently. **Orgs:** Dem Nat Comt; del alternate, Dem Conventions; Comn Status Women, Nat Women's Polit Caucus Adv Comt; Comt Black PACS; nat bd dir, Trans Africa; chief co-founder & pres, Black Women's Forum; House Comt Banking, Finance & Urban Affairs; Veterans Sub committee Educ, Employment, Training & Housing; Banking Sub committee Housing & Community Opportunities; co-chair, Cong Urban Caucus; nat co-chair, Clinton Pres Campaign; Cong Black Caucus; Cong Progressive Caucus; founding mem & chair, Out Iraq Cong Caucus. **Honors/Awds:** Freedom & Justice Award, Detroit Nat Asn Advan Colored People, 2001; Hon doctorates, Spelman Col & NC Agri & Tech State Univ. **Special Achievements:** First woman to be ranked 4 on the leadership team; First African American female mem of Rules Comm; First non lawyer on the Judiciary Comm; One of the outstanding

leaders at the Intl Women's Year Conf in Houston; sponsored legislation concerning tenant protection, small bus protection, the limiting of police strip-and-search authority. **Business Addr:** Congresswoman, United States House of Representatives, 2344 Rayburn House Off Bldg, Washington, DC 20515, **Business Phone:** (202)225-2201.

WATERS, NEVILLE R
Business owner, radio director. **Personal:** Born Feb 22, 1957, Washington, DC. **Educ:** Springfield Col, BS, 1978, MA, 1980; Georgetown Univ, MBA. **Career:** WMAS Radio, announcer, 1980-81; A&M Records, prom, merchandising, 1982-83; WQXQ Radio, traffic dir & music dir, 1983; WOL Radio, prog dir; Metro-Talk, producer & dir; DC Today, producer; The Waters Group, founder & owner, currently. **Honors/Awds:** Walter Kaitz Found Award; Achievement in Radio Award; Addy Award; Effie Award; Adrian Award, Hospitality Sales & Mkt Asn; Jack the Rapper's Radio Prog Dir of the Year; Graduate Fellowship Award, Nat Broadcasting Co. **Special Achievements:** Gold and platinum albums from artists as varied as LL Cool J, Anita Baker and Gregory Abbott. **Business Addr:** Founder, The Waters Group, 222 Longfellow St NW, Washington, DC 20011.

WATERS, PAUL EUGENE, JR.
Executive. **Personal:** Born Sep 9, 1959, Harrisburg, PA; son of Paul E Sr and Sylvia Byers; married Sonja Powell Waters, May 24, 1987; children: Paul E, III, Meredith Colleen. **Educ:** Lincoln Univ, attended 1980; Temple Univ, Philadelphia, PA, BA, 1984. **Career:** NY Times Cable TV, Cherry Hill, NJ, acct exec, 1984-86; WHTM TV, Harrisburg, PA, acct exec, 1986-88; United Artists, Baltimore, MD, gen sales mgr, 1988-91; CNBC, Fort Lee, NJ, dir local advert. **Orgs:** Nat Asn Advan Colored People, 1972-; Omega Psi Phi Fraternity, 1978-.

WATERS, SYLVIA ANN
Journalist. **Personal:** Born Sep 29, 1949, Corsicana, TX. **Educ:** E Texas State Univ, BA, 1971. **Career:** Corsicana Daily Sun Newspaper, reporter, 1972-, prog dir Boys & Girls Clubs. **Orgs:** Publicity chairwoman Navarro Co United Fund, 1975-; Nat Fedr Press Women, Tex Press Women, 1982-; pres, Jackson Ex-Students Asn, 1983-; Nat Asn Advan Colored People, 1986; Nat Asn Black Journalists, 1986-; Am Bus Women Asn Golden Horizons Chap, 1986-; chairwoman Navarro Co Coalition Black Demo, 1986-. **Honors/Awds:** James Collins Scholarship 1968; Tex Press Women third place award in photography, 1987. **Home Addr:** 601 E 14th Ave, Corsicana, TX 75110. **Business Addr:** Reporter, Program Director, Corsicana Daily Sun Newspaper, 405 E Collin, Corsicana, TX 75110.

WATERS, WILLIAM DAVID
Government official. **Personal:** Born Sep 14, 1924, Camden, NJ; son of William A and Rebecca Jones; married Viva Edwards. **Educ:** Temple Univ Philadelphia, BS, acct, 1947, MBA, acct, 1948. **Career:** Government Official (retired); IRS, Mid-Atlantic Region Philadelphia, fiscal mgt & officer, 1964-66; Albany, asst dist dir, 1966-67; Baltimore, asst dist dir, 1970-73, dist dir, 1973-74; Mid-Atlantic Region, regional comnr, 1974-85; NJ Casino Control Comn, comnr, 1986-91. **Orgs:** Vpres & dir, YMCA Camden County, 1980-; St John's United Methodist Church Columbia; Housing Task Force Columbia, MD. **Military Serv:** AUS, 1st lt (USAR), 1943-52. **Home Addr:** 1011 Rymill Run, Cherry Hill, NJ 08003.

WATERS, WILLIAM L.
Executive. **Personal:** Born Sep 23, 1941, Philadelphia, PA. **Educ:** BS, 1966. **Career:** Consolidated Edison, NY, design engr, 1966-68, cost engr, 1968-71; proj construct engr, 1971-73; William L Waters Inc, pres, currently. **Orgs:** Mech Contractors Asn Am; Nat Asn Minority Contractors; Coun Construct & Prof NY; 100 Black Men NY. **Honors/Awds:** Recipt Black Achievers Award, 1972. **Business Addr:** President, William L Waters Inc, 24 Main St, Mysersville, MD 21773, **Business Phone:** (301)293-2585.

WATERS, WILLIE ANTHONY
Conductor (music). **Personal:** Born Oct 11, 1951, Goulds, FL; son of Lee Andrew and Valuda Hooks. **Educ:** Univ Miami, BMus, 1973; Memphis State Univ, MMus, 1975. **Career:** Memphis Opera Theatre, asst conductor, 1973-75; San Francisco Opera, artistic adminr, 1975-79; Greater Miami Opera, music dir, 1982-85, artistic dir, 1985-92, prin conductor, 1992-95; New World Sch Arts, actg dean, 1992-93; Conn Opera Co, music dir, 1996-99, gen & artistic dir, conductor, 1999-, artistic dir, 2007-. **Orgs:** Alpha Phi Alpha, 1972-73; Phi Mu Alpha, 1973-75. **Honors/Awds:** Distinguished Alumni, Univ Miami; Martell, Prix De Martell, 1991, Hon Doctorate, Univ Hartford, 2005. **Special Achievements:** First Black Artistic Director of Major American Opera Co, 1985; Conducted First Production of Porgy & Bess in South Africa, 1996. **Business Addr:** Artistic Director, Conductor, Connecticut Opera, 226 Farmington Ave, Hartford, CT 06105, **Business Phone:** (860)527-0713.

WATFORD-MCKINNEY, YVONNE V (YVONNE VICTORIA WATFORD-MCKINNEY)
Lawyer, government official. **Personal:** Born Jan 1, 1948?, Brooklyn, NY. **Educ:** Mount Holyoke Col, BA, S Hadley, 1970; Wayne State Univ Law Sch, JD, 1980. **Career:** US Dept Justice, asst US atty, 1983-. **Orgs:** Wake County Am Heart Asn, 1995-; State Bar Mich; State Bar NY; Fed Bar Asn; State Bar NC. **Business Addr:** Assistant US Attorney, US Attorneys Office, 310 New Bern Ave Suite 800 Fed Bldg, Raleigh, NC 27601-1461, **Business Phone:** (919)856-4530.

WATFORD-MCKINNEY, YVONNE VICTORIA. See WATFORD-MCKINNEY, YVONNE V.

WATKINS, ANTHONY E
Cardiologist. **Educ:** Howard Univ Col Med, MD, 1966. **Career:** Johns Hopkins Univ Sch Pub Health, internship, 1967; Wash Hosp Ctr, residency, 1973, fel, 1974, vpres, Med Staff Develop, currently; fel, Veterans Admin Med Ctr, 1976; Pvt Pract, cardiologist, currently.

WATKINS, ARETHA LA ANNA
Journalist. **Personal:** Born Aug 23, 1930, Blairsville, PA; daughter of Clifford Fox Sr and Carrie Thompson; married Angelo Watkins Sr, Apr 14, 1967; children: Angelo Watkins, Jr. **Educ:** Wayne State Univ, attended 1950; Wayne State Univ, Col Lifelong Learning; Marygrove Col. **Career:** Detroit Courier, staff writer, 1963-64, asst to ed, 1964-66; MI Chronical, staff wirter, columnist, 1966; MI Chronicle Publ Co, asst managing ed, 1968-81; managing ed, 1981-. **Orgs:** Sigma Delta Chi Prof Journ Soc Prog Comt Asn, 1968; adv bd mem, Sigma Delta Chi Prof Journ Soc; NAACP. **Honors/Awds:** Best Ed Award, Nat Newspapers Publ Asn, 1972; Black Communicator Award, MI SCLC, 1972; Dist Comn Serv Award, Lafayette Allen Sr, 1974; Community Serv Award, Aopha Theta Chap Gamma Phi Delta, 1981; Corp Serv Award, African Am Mus Detroit, 1984; Sojourner Truth Award, Bus Woman of the Year, Detroit Chap Nat Asn Negro Bus & Prof Women's Clubs Inc, 1984; MI SCLC Martin Luther King Jr Award, 1986. **Business Addr:** Managing Editor, Michigan Chronicle, 479 Ledyard, Detroit, MI 48201.*

WATKINS, DR. CHARLES B
Educator, school administrator. **Personal:** Born Nov 20, 1942, Petersburg, VA; son of Charles B Sr and Haseltine Thurston Clements. **Educ:** Howard Univ, BSME, 1964; Univ New Mexico, MS, 1966, PhD, 1970. **Career:** Sandia Nat Labs, staff mem, 1964-71; Howard Univ, asst prof, 1971-73, dept chmn & assoc prof, 1973-78, prof & chmn, 1978-84, 1985-86; Nat Gov Asn, sr fel, 1984-85; City Col NY, dean, sch eng, 1986-2000, Herbert G Kayser prof mech eng, 2000-, Ctr Mesoscopic Modeling & Simulation, dir, currently. **Orgs:** Consult, USN, 1975-82; Nat Sci Found, 1976-78; AUS, 1979; nat chair, dept heads comn, 1986-87, mem bd, engrg educ, 1986-88, vice chair, engrg & pub policy dir, 1987-88, assoc fel, Am Inst Aeronaut & Astronaut, 1993; Am Soc Engrg Educ; bd dirs, Parsons Brinkerhoff Inc, 1994-98. **Honors/Awds:** Elected Tau Beta Pi, 1963; elected Sigma Xi, 1978; Ralph R Teeter Award, Soc Automotive Engrs, 1980; Fel, Am Soc Mech Engrs, 1990; fel, AAAS, 2005. **Business Addr:** Herbert G Kayser Professor, Director, The City College of New York, Department of Mechanical Engineering, Steinman Hall 237 160 Convent Ave, New York, NY 10031, **Business Phone:** (212)650-5439.

WATKINS, CHERYL L (CHERYL L WATKINS-SNEAD)
Executive. **Educ:** Univ Mass, mech eng; Purdue Univ, MBA. **Career:** Gen Elec Corp; Banneker Indust Inc, pres & ceo, currently. **Special Achievements:** First African American female to earn a mechanical engineering degree from the Univ of Mass, 1981; the only black student in her MBA class at Purdue Univ; One of only a few of the country's female entrepreneurial mechanical engineers of any race; Small Business Leader of the Year. **Business Addr:** President, Chief Executive Officer, Banneker Industries Inc, 582 Great Rd Suite 101, North Smithfield, RI 02896, **Business Phone:** (401)534-0027.

WATKINS, CRAIG
Lawyer. **Personal:** Born Nov 16, 1967. **Educ:** Prairie View A&M Univ, BA, polit sci; Tex Wesleyan Univ Sch Law, JD. **Career:** Pvt Pract, defense atty, currently. **Orgs:** Am Bar Asn; Nat Asn Criminal Defense Lawyers; Texas Criminal Defense Lawyers Asn; Dallas Criminal Defense Lawyers Asn; Friendship-West Baptist Church, Kappa Alpha Psi Fraternity, Prairie View A&M Univ Alumni Asn, Nat Asn Advan Colored People Dallas Br. **Honors/Awds:** Received numerous awards and recognitions; Dallas Urban League Torch Award. **Special Achievements:** First African American District Attorney elected in Texas. **Business Addr:** 2531 Martin Luther King Jr Blvd, Dallas, TX 75215, **Business Phone:** (214)428-7799.*

WATKINS, DONALD
Executive. **Personal:** Born Sep 8, 1948, Parsons, KS; son of Levi and Lillian; married DeAndra Johnson (divorced); children: Donald Jr, Drew, Derry & Dustin; married; children: Claudia Rose. **Educ:** S Ill Univ, attended 1970; Univ Ala, law, 1973. **Career:** Law off Fred B Gray; own law off, Birmingham, Ala, 1979; Birmingham City Coun, 1979-83; spec coun mayor Birmingham, 1985-99; Masada Oxynol, owner, currently; Voter News Network, founder, 2006-; Donald V. Watkins, P.C. Fund, pres, currently. **Orgs:** Trustee, Ala State Univ, 1994-01; founder, chmn bd, AlAm Bank, 1999-; life mem, Alpha Phi Alpha Fraternity Inc. **Business Addr:** Chairman of the Board, Founder, Alamerica Bank, 2170 Highland Ave Suite 150, Birmingham, AL 35205, **Business Phone:** (205)558-4600.

WATKINS, DURAND
Basketball coach. **Career:** Mich Mayhem Roster, asst coach, currently. *

WATKINS, HANNAH BOWMAN
Educator. **Personal:** Born Dec 23, 1924, Chicago, IL; widowed; children: Robert A, Melinda Geddes & Melanie E. **Educ:** Fisk Univ, Nashville, TN, BA, 1947; Univ Chicago, attended 1949; Jane Addams Sch Soc Work, grad courses, 1969; Ill Dept Pub Health st, cert audiometrist, 1978. **Career:** Univ Chicago, clin res assoc, 1947-60; Ill Dept Pub Aid, med soc worker, 1960-73; Ill Dept Pub Health, pub health training consult & supvr, 1973-, grants mgt consult; Clinic in Altgeld Chicago, consult, 1975-. **Orgs:** Exec comt mem, Chicago Hearing Conserv Comn, 1975-; secy, alumni commn, Fisk Univ 1976-; Nat Assoc Univ Women, 1978-; vpres, midwest region Fisk Univ Gen Alumni Asn, 1979-81; Health Systs Agency Coun City Chicago Health Systs Agencies, 1980-; exec Coun mem, Ill Pub Health Asn,1980-82; Lincoln Congregational United Chap of Christ; bd trustees, Hull House Asn; bd dirs, Parkway Comm House; Black Caucus Pub Health Workers; Am Pub Health Asn; comm IL Pub Health Asn. **Honors/Awds:** Special Commendation, Health Coord Patricia Hunt Chief Family Health, IDPH, 1977-80; Special Commendation, Walter J Leonard Pres, Fisk Univ, 1979. **Special Achievements:** Publishings: "Effect ACTH on Rheumatoid Arthritis" Jour Am Chem Soc, "Lipoprotein & Phospholipoid in Animals" Journal Am Chem Soc, "Early Identification Pregnant Adolescents & Delivery of WIC Serv," Am Jour Pub Health, 1985.

WATKINS, HAROLD D, SR.
Firefighter. **Personal:** Born Feb 19, 1933, Detroit, MI; son of Clara B McClenic and Jesse; married Edna Jean Ridgeley, Dec 22, 1954; children: Harold D Jr, Kevin Duane & Keith Arnette. **Educ:** Macomb Community Col, Mt Clemens, MI, AA, 1976. **Career:** Firefighter (retired); City Detroit, fire fighter, 1955-76, sgt, 1976-78, lt, 1978-84, capt, 1984-88, battalion chief, 1988, chief fire operations, 1988-93, exec fire comnr, 1994-98. **Orgs:** Llife mem, Nat Asn Advan Colored People; 47-4900 Spokane Block Club, 1959-; Pres, Lay Ministers, CME Church, 1965-; bd dir, 1986-, pres, Manhood Orgn, 1988-; Int Bd Fire Chiefs; Int Asn Black Firefighters Phoenix; Black Prof Fire Fighters Asn. **Military Serv:** USAF, s/sgt, 1950-54. *

WATKINS, IRA DONNELL
Educator. **Personal:** Born Feb 12, 1941, Waco, TX; son of Artist Watkins and Lois; children: Sina. **Career:** Family First Art Prog, art teacher; Tenderloin Self Help Ctr; Hosp House Art Prog, art teacher; Nat Inst Art & Disabilities, interim dir & instr, currently. **Orgs:** Pro Art, artist; artist, AMES Art Gallery; artist, John Natsoulas Art Gallery; artist, SF Rental Gallery. **Honors/Awds:** Tenderloin Times Art Contest, 1991; Art Transit Project SF, 1995. **Home Phone:** (510)420-1413. **Business Addr:** Interim Director, Instructor, National Institute of Art & Disabilities, 551 23rd St, Richmond, CA 94804, **Business Phone:** (510)620-0290.

WATKINS, JAMES DARNELL
Dentist, vice president (organization). **Personal:** Born Aug 29, 1949, Reidsville, NC; son of James Granderson and Sadie Lamberth; married Hardenia; children: Daryl Granderson, Deveda Camille. **Educ:** VA Polytech Inst, State Univ Blacksburg VA, BS, biology, 1971; Med Col Va, Sch Dent Richmond, DDS, 1975. **Career:** Pvt pract, dentist, 1977-. **Orgs:** Am Dent Asn & Acad Gen Dent, 1975-; sec, Old Dominion Dent Soc, 1978-; vpres, Century Investment Club, 1979-; Nat Asn Advan Colored People; Grad Chap Groove Phi Groove Soc Fel Inc; Beau Brummels Social & Civic Club; fel Acad Gen Dent; pres, bd dir, Citizens Boys Club Hampton VA; Penninsula Dent Soc, VA Dent Asn; pres, VA Bd Dent, 1993-; Am Dent Asn's Coun Dent Educ & Comn Dent Accreditation, 1995-98; Int Col Dentists; fel Am Col Dentists; ADA rep to Dent Asst Nat Bd. **Honors/Awds:** President's Award, Old Dominion Dent Soc, 1986; Dentist of the Year, Old Dominion Dent Soc, 1987, 1990; gov appointee, State Bd Dent, 1989; Laymen of the Year, Boys Club Bd Dirs, 1995. **Special Achievements:** Elected first Black president of the Virginia State Dental Board; US Naval Reserve Dental Unit, Little Creek Amphibious Base, appointed first Black commanding officer, promoted to rank of captain in US Navy Reserve, 1991. **Military Serv:** USN, dental corps, lt, 1975-77; USNR, dental corps, capt, 1977-. **Business Addr:** Dentist, 3921 Kecoughtan Rd, Hampton, VA 23669-4532.*

WATKINS, JOSEPH PHILIP
Journalist. **Personal:** Born Aug 24, 1953, New York, NY; married Stephanie Taylor; children: Tiffany Ann, Courtney Andrea. **Educ:** Univ PA, BA, hist, 1975; Princeton Theol Sem, MA Christian Educ, 1979. **Career:** Talladega Col, chaplain religion instr, 1978-79; Ind Purdue Univ Ft Wayne, campus minister, 1979-81; US Sen Dan Quayle, asst state dir, 1981-84; US Cong, Republican nominee for 10th dist, 1984; Merchants Nat Bank, commercial ac-

cts rep, 1984; Saturday Evening Post, vpres & dir missions, 1984-. **Orgs:** Bd dir, Big Brothers Greater Indianapolis; bd dir, Arthritis Found Indianapolis; bd dir, Poison Control Ctr Ind; Nat Asn Advan Colored People; bd dir, Salvation Army of Indianapolis; bd dir, Penrod Soc; bd dir, C's Bur; adv bd Training Inc; bd dir, Humane Soc; bd dir, Jameson Camp; life mem, Nat Asn Advan Colored People. **Honors/Awds:** Winner IN Jaycees Speak-Up Competition, 1983; winner US Jaycees Speak-Up Competition, 1983. **Special Achievements:** Selected as one of the Outstanding Young Men of Amer 1983; selected as one of 50 Young Leaders of the Future by Ebony Magazine 1983; selected as one of the 10 Outstanding Young Hoosiers by the IN Jaycees 1984. **Business Addr:** Vice President, Director of Missions, Saturday Evening Post, 1100 Waterway Blvd, Indianapolis, IN 46202.

WATKINS, KENNETH
Executive. **Career:** Urban Solutions Inc, vpres, currently. *

WATKINS, LENICE JACKIE
Publisher, executive. **Personal:** Born Dec 17, 1933, Palestine, TX; son of Will and Ruby; married Ethel L Sims; children: Geraldine, Deborah, Ricky, Sabrina & Lenice. **Educ:** Univ Denver, BA, 1960. **Career:** Afro Am Newspaper Wash DC, gen assignment reporter, 1960-61; Cleveland Call & Post, gen assignment reporter, 1961-63; Jet Mag, copy educr, 1963-73; Town of Sunset, mayor, 1976-82; Ethelynn Publ Co, owner; Evening Times, reporter, photographer, 1985-99; Ethelynn Publ Co, freelance writer, 1991. **Orgs:** Pres, Marion-West Memphis Lions Club; comdr, James Green VFW Post 9934; Earle & Sunset, Ark; bd, past pres, E Ark Regional Mental Helath Ctr. **Special Achievements:** Author: Die as Fools, 1991; The Damned Black Press Writing for It, 1995. **Military Serv:** USAF, 1952-56. **Business Addr:** President, Marion-West Memphis Evening Lions Club, 176 Watkins Cove, West Memphis, AR 72301, **Business Phone:** (870)739-3997.

WATKINS, DR. LEVI, JR.
Educator, surgeon. **Personal:** Born Jun 13, 1944, Montgomery, AL; son of Lillian and Levi. **Educ:** Tenn State Univ, BS, bio, 1966; Vanderbilt Univ, Sch Med, MD, 1970. **Career:** Johns Hopkins Hosp, surgical intern, 1970-77, cardiac Surgeon, 1978-; Am Col Surgeons, fel; Johns Hopkins Univ, prof cardiac surgery & assoc dean, 1991-. **Orgs:** NYAS; Soc Thoracic Surgeons; Soc Black Acad Surgeons; Asn Thoracic Surgery; Am Col Chest Physicians; SE Surgical Cong; North Am Soc Pacing & Electrophysiol; Asn Acad Minority Physicians; Physicians Human Rights; Baltimore City Med Soc; Soc Univ Surgeons; Asn Acad Surgery; Hypertension Task Force, Health Systs Agency Md; Bd dir, Am Heart Asn Md; diplomate, Nat Bd Med Examiners; nat bd, Robert Wood Johnson Minority Fac Develop Prog; Alpha Phi Alpha fraternity; Alpha Kappa Mu honor Soc; Beta Kappa Chi honor Soc; Alpha Omega Alpha medical honor Soc. **Honors/Awds:** Highest Honors, Pres, Student Body, Student of the Year, Tenn State Univ, 1965-66; Nat Med Fellowship Awardee, 1966-70; Baltimore's Best, Mayor William Donald Schaffer, 1986; Alpha Omega Alpha; Doctor of Humane Letters, Sojourner-Douglass Col, 1988, Meharry Med Col, 1989, Spelman Col, 1996, Morgan State Univ, 1997; ohns Hopkins Univ Alumni Asn Heritage Award, 1999; Vanderbilt Medal Honor outstanding alumni, 2002. **Special Achievements:** The first African American to achieve the positions of Associate Dean of the Johns Hopkins University of School of Medicine and full Professor of Cardiac Surgery, the first black ever admitted and the first black to graduate from Vanderbilt institution, the first black chief resident in cardiac surgery at Johns Hopkins Hospital, professionally, he performed the world's first human implantation of the automatic implantable defibrillator in February of 1980 and subsequently developed several different techniques for the implantation of this device.Over fifty associations now exist throughout America, For this, he was featured in the September 1999 issue of Science, the official publication for the American Association for the Advancement of Science. published two books recently, African-American Medical Pioneers by Charles H. Epps, Jr. and Noteworthy Publications by African-American Surgeons by Claude H. Organ, Jr., M.D., featuring his achievements, in April of 1993 his life and work were featured on national television on PBS' New Explorers program entitled "A Dream Fulfilled," in 1996 his life was featured again on Maryland Public TV. **Business Addr:** Professor of Cardiac Surgery, Associate Dean of Postdoctoral Programs, Johns Hopkins University, 600 N Wolfe St, Baltimore, MD 21287-4618, **Business Phone:** (410)955-8502.

WATKINS, LOTTIE HEYWOOD
Executive, chief executive officer. **Personal:** Born in Atlanta, GA; widowed; children: Joyce Bacote & Judy Yvonne Barnett. **Educ:** Booker T Wash High Schs, 1935; Reids Sch Bus. **Career:** Clerk, chief executive officer (retired); Alexander-Calloway Realty Co Atlanta, sec 1945-54; Mutual Fed S&L Asn, teller-clerk, 1954-60; LottieWatkins Enterprises, pres, ceo, 1960. **Orgs:** Sec So Christian Leadership Conf 1967; vice chmn Fulton Co Dem Party 1968; Fulton Co Jury Comnr, 1972-; Gov's Comm Voluntarism, 1972; Fulton Co Bd Registration & Elections 1973-; Citizens Exchange Brazil, 1973; participant White House Conf Civil Rights; GA Residential Finance Auth, 1974; chmn, Am Cancer Soc; chmn, Comm Chest; exec comm bd dir, Nat Asn Advan Colored People; League of Women Voters, Atlanta Women's C of C; active mem, innumerable civic & prof organs. **Honors/Awds:** Recipient of various leadership citations including: citations from Pres John F Kennedy, Pres LB Johnson, vice pres Hubert Humphrey; 10 Leading Ladies Atlanta Channel 11 Commission Service Award. **Special Achievements:** First African American female real estate broker in the Atlanta market.

WATKINS, MELVIN
Basketball player, basketball coach. **Personal:** Born Nov 15, 1954, Reidsville, SC; married Burrell Bryant; children: Keia, Marcus & Manuale. **Educ:** Univ NC, Charlotte, BA, econ, 1977. **Career:** Basketball player (retired), basketball coach: NBA, Buffalo Baves, 1977-78; Univ NC, Charlotte, asst coach, 1978-87, assoc head coach, 1987-96, head basketball coach, 1996-98; Tex A&M Univ, head basketball coach, 1998-04; Univ Mo, assoc head coach, 2004-. **Orgs:** Co-chair, Battered Women's Shelterl; 100 Black Men of Charlotte. **Honors/Awds:** Ray Meyer Coach of the Year Award, Conference USA, 1997; title, Sun Belt Conference, 1977. **Special Achievements:** Fianl Four, UNCC, 1977; C-USA White Division title, UNCC, 1997; C-USA AmDiv, second place, UNCC, 1998; first person in UNCC hist to be involved as player or coach in all eight post-season appearances. **Business Addr:** Associate Head Basketball Coach, University Missouri, Intercollegiate Athletics, 395 Hearnes Ctr, Columbia, MO 65211, **Business Phone:** (573)882-6501.*

WATKINS, DR. MICHAEL THOMAS
Surgeon. **Personal:** Born Nov 17, 1954, Washington, DC; son of Harding Thomas and Muriel Knowles; married Paula Pinkston, May 25, 1985; children: Steven Thomas & Adrienne Elise. **Educ:** NY Univ, New York, NY, AB, 1976; Harvard Med Sch, Boston, MA, MD, 1980. **Career:** Johns Hopkins Hosp, Dept Surg, Baltimore, MD, intern, 1980-81, asst resident, 1981-82; Uniformed Servs Univ Health Scis Sch Med, Bethesda, MD, res fellow, 1982-84, res instr, 1983-84; Strong Memorial Hosp, Dept Surg, Rochester, NY, Sr resident, 1984-85, chief resident, 1985-86; Univ Rochester Sch Med, instr surg, 1985-86; Harvard Med Sch, Boston, MA, clinal fellow in surg, 1986-87; Mass Gen Hosp, Boston, MA, Vascular Surg Dept, chief resident, 1986-87, Vascular Surgeon Res, MA, dir, currently; Boston Univ Sch Med, Dept Surg, Boston, MA, res fellow, 1987-88, asst prof Surg & pathology, 1988-; Boston City Hosp, Mallory Inst Pathol, Boston, MA, res assoc. **Orgs:** Nat Med Asn; Am Heart Asn, Thrombosis Coun; fel Am Col Surgeons; Nat Bd Med Examrs; Am Bd Surg; Soc Univ Surgeons; Soc Black Acad Surgeons; Soc Vascular Surg. **Honors/Awds:** Resident Teaching Award, Dept Surg, Univ Rochester, Rochester Gen Hosp, 1986; Minority Med Fac Develop Award for In Vitro Response Vascular Endothelium to Hypoxia & Reoxygenation, Robert Wood Johnson Found, 1987-91; Grant-in-Aid for Phospholipid & Free Fatty Acids in Hypoxic Vascular Cells, Am Heart Asn, 1990-93; author with C.C. Haudenschild, H. Albadawi, "Synergistic Effect Hypoxia & Stasis on Endothelial Cell Lactate Production, Journal Cellular Biol, 1990; R29 Res Award, Endothelial Cell Responses to Acute Hypoxia & Reoxygenation, NIH, 1993-97; VA Merit Review Res Award, Signal Transduction in Hypoxic Vascular Cells, 1994-97. **Special Achievements:** Author with M.R. Graff, C.C. Haudenschild, F. Velasques, R.W. Hobson, "Effect Hypoxia & Reoxgenation Perfused Bovine Aortic Endothelial Cells, Journal Cellular Biol, 1989; author numerous other articles & presentations. **Military Serv:** AUS Med Corps, capt, 1982-89; Army Commendation Medal, 1984. **Business Addr:** Director, Massachusetts General Hospital, Division Vascular Surgeory, 15 Parkman St, Wang Ambulatory care 458, Boston, MA 02114, **Business Phone:** (617)726-0908.

WATKINS, MOZELLE ELLIS
Government official, commissioner. **Personal:** Born May 18, 1924, Crockett, TX; daughter of Leroy (deceased) and Sallie Elizabeth Fleeks (deceased); married Charles Philip Watkins, Mar 20, 1948 (deceased); children: Phyllis Caselia Watkins Jones, Eunice Juaquina Watkins Cothran. **Educ:** Hughes Bus Col, dipl, 1945; Extended Sch Law, attended 1960; Famous Writers Sch, Hartford, cert, 1970; Cath Univ, cert pub speaking, 1970; Georgetown Univ, Sch Law, attended 1977; Montgomery Col, span cert, 1978. **Career:** Government official (retired); Fed Govt, statist clerk & secy, 1945-69; Anacostia Citizens & Merchants Asn, admin asst, 1969-70; Montgomery County Govt Human Rel Comn, investr, 1971-93; DC Adv Neighborhood, comnr, 1976-96. **Orgs:** 19th St Baptist Church, 1946-; comt mem, DC Gov ANC-5A Single Dist 14, 1976-92; Brookland Comn Corp, 1978-89; chairperson, ANC 5A, 1978, 1979, 1985; 12th St Neighborhood Corps, 1979-89; pres, Jarvis Mem Club, 1983-; bd dir, Christian Educ, 1985-89; deleg, DC Dem State Conv, 1986; Northeast News Publ, 1986; 19th St Baptist Church, deaconess, 1987-; Ward V Unity County Comn, 1988; vice chairperson, DC Adv Neighborhood Comn 5A, 1989; bd dir, Nat Found Deaf, 1989-96; Montgomery County, Comn Employ People Disabilities, 1989-93; Adv Neighborhood Comn 5A, 1989; Woodridge Orange Hat Team, 1992-; elected comt mem, ANC 5A Single Dist 11, 1992-96; vpres & pres, Chinese-Am Lions Club, 1994-96, 2002-03; Nat Asn Advan Colored People; Woodridge Civic Asn; Gateway Community Asn; TASSL Block Club; Upper Northeast Family Day Comn; Citizens Adv Comt Dist Bar; Anacostia Citizens & Merchants Asn; DC Coun; Dept Defense, Bur Supplies & Accounts; coun mem, Ward V William R Spaulding; DC Chap Howard Univ, Moorland-Spingarn Res Ctr. **Honors/Awds:** Outstanding Serv & Dedication, State Tex, 1991; Cert of Recognition, Am Soc, 1992-93; Cert of Election, 1993-95; Cert of Recognition, Fifth Dist DC Metrop Police Dept & Citizens Adv Coun, 1996; ANC-5A Resolution Dedicated Commitment & Serv to the Community, 1999; Cert of Appreciation, Am Red Cross. **Special Achievements:** Author "Two Zodiac Calendars," 1975 & 1977; author proposal entitled "Resolution for the Conservation of a Section of the Nation's Capital as a Tribute to ARO" published in the DC Register, 1977. **Home Addr:** 3225 Walnut St NE, Washington, DC 20018. *

WATKINS, PRICE I.
Government official. **Personal:** Born Dec 27, 1925, Abbott, MS; son of Wooster and Alice Brown; married Elliott Mae Williams (divorced 1971); children: Dorrance, Bruce, Kenneth; married Pearl Carrol Poyser, 1972; children: Andre Raphael. **Educ:** San Diego City Col, AA, 1966; San Diego State Univ, BA, 1970; Pepperdine Univ, Los Angeles, CA, MPA, 1977; Calif Coast Univ, PhD, 1985; Univ Pheonix, MBA, 1995. **Career:** Government official (retired); US Marine Corps, Okinawa, JP, comn chief, 1958-62; US Marine Corps, San Diego, CA, training officer, 1962-69; US Marine Corps, Vietnam, tel officer, 1967-69; US Marine Corps, CA, maint officer, 1971-76; Wells Fargo Gd Serv, Los Angeles, CA, oper mgr, 1978-83; Internal Revenue Serv, Elmonte, CA, taxpayer serv rep, 1986-87. **Orgs:** 1st Marine Div Asn, 1953-; Am Polit Sci Asn, 1970-; Am Legion, 1974-; Repub Nat Comt, 1977-; Relig Sci Practitioners Asn, 1986-91; Church Jesus Christ Latter-Day Saints, 1989. **Honors/Awds:** Valley Forge Hon Cert, Freedoms Found, Valley Forge, 1972, 1975. **Military Serv:** US Marine Corps, capt, 1944-76; 5 awards, 1944-62; Navy Commendation Medal, 1968; Cert of Commendation, 1976; Good Conduct Medal. **Home Addr:** 119 S Alta Vista Ave, Monrovia, CA 91016, **Home Phone:** (626)358-0437. *

WATKINS, ROLANDA ROWE
Entrepreneur. **Personal:** Born Feb 22, 1956, Detroit, MI; daughter of Carlos Rowe and Doris Louie Rowe; married James Abel, Aug 30, 1986. **Educ:** Wayne State Univ, Detroit, MI, exec secy, stenographer, certi, 1973; Detroit Bus Inst, Detroit, MI, exec secy, cert, 1976; Detroit Col Bus, Dearborn, MI, assoc, bus admin, 1981, bachelor bus admin, 1988, masters, bus admin, 1998. **Career:** Provident Mutual Life Ins, Southfield, MI, secy, 1980; Chevrolet Central Off, Warren, MI, secy, 1981; Midwestern Assocs, Detroit, MI, secy, 1982-; Downtown Fish & Seafood, Detroit, MI, owner, 1987-97; Academy of Oak Park, bus educ teacher, 1999-; Carring Kids, founder, currently. **Orgs:** Founder, coordr, Caring Kids Youth Ministry, 1983-; Washington Blvd Merchants Asn, 1987-. **Honors/Awds:** Go 4 It Award, WDIV-TV 4, 1985; Devoted & Invaluable Service to the Youth, 14th Precinct, Detroit Police Dept, 1985; Senator Carl Levin, 1985, 1986; Governor James Blanchard, 1986, Mayor Coleman Young, 1986-93; Devoted & Invaluable Service to the Commendations, 1987;Youth, 2nd Precinct, Detroit Police Dept, 1987; Dedicated Service to Community, New Detroit, Inc, 1989; Spirit of Detroit Award, 1989; Outstanding Entrepreneurial Achievements, 1989; Black Women in Business Award, Nat Asn Negro Bus & Prof Women's Club, Inc, 1989; Nat Sojourner Truth Award, Nat Asn Negro Bus & Prof Women's Club, Inc, 1990; Living the Dream Award, Blacks Govt, 1992-93; Key to the City of Detroit, Mayor Coleman Young, 1993; Jefferson Award, 1995; WDIV and Hardee's Hometown Heros Award, 1993; Jefferson Award Winner, 1995; Community Service Award, 1997. **Special Achievements:** Serving free Thanksgiving Dinner to over 9000 homeless people, 1986. **Business Addr:** Founder, Caring Kids, PO Box 23161, Detroit, MI 48223, **Business Phone:** (313)614-8675.

WATKINS, ROSYLN
Law enforcement officer. **Personal:** Born Dec 20, 1956, Omaha, NE. **Career:** Zor Productions, owner, 1998-; Alameda County Sheriff's Off, dep sheriff investr, currently. **Orgs:** Vice chmn, Nat Black Police Asn, 1989-; officer, Drug Abuse Resistance Educ, 1996-; Crime Prev Officer, 1996-; secy, dir, Lovelife Found, 1998-. **Business Addr:** Deputy Sheriff Investigator, Alameda County Sheriff's Office, 1401 Lakeside Dr Fl 12, Oakland, CA 94612, **Business Phone:** (510)272-6878.

WATKINS, SHIRLEY R
Government official, consultant. **Personal:** Born Jan 7, 1938, Hope, AR; daughter of Robert Robinson; married George R; children: Robert T & Miriam Cecelia. **Educ:** Univ Ark Bluff, BS, 1960; Univ Memphis, MEd, 1970, post graduate, 1991; Johnson & Wales Univ, hon doctorate, 2000. **Career:** Univ Ark Exten Serv, asst negro home demonstration agent, 1960-62; Memphis City Schs, fourth grade teacher, 1962-63, home econs teacher, 1963-69, food serv supvr, 1969-75, dir nutrit serv, 1975-93; US Dept Agr, dep asst secy, FCS, 1993-94, dep undersecy, FNCS, 1994-95, dep asst secy mkt & regional progs, 1995-97, under secy FNCS, 1997-; Pa State Univ, continued prof; SR Watkins & Assocs LLC, pres & founder, currently. **Orgs:** Alpha Kappa Alpha, 1958-; life mem subscribing golden heritage, Nat Asn Advan Colored People, 1970-; pres, ASFSA, vpres, sect chair, legisl comt, 1982-90; pres, Les Casuale, vpres, treas, hospitality, 1982-93; chmn, IFMA Int Gold & Silver Plate Soc, secy, treas,1982-92; ed, MOLES, 1990-93; pres, Phi Delta Kappa, vpres progs, 1991-93; fin secy, Soc Inc,

1992-95; ASBO; TASBO. **Honors/Awds:** Silver Plate, Int Food Manufacturers Asn, 1988; Hon Doctorate Food Serv, 1988; Outstanding Achievement Award, Tennessee Gov, 1989; Outstanding Alumni Award, UAPE, 1993; Iris Award, Tenn ADA, 1993; Outstanding Achievement Award, Memphis Bd Educ, 1993; Outstanding Contributions Community Award, Memphis City Coun, 1994; AKA Prominent Black Woman Award, 1998; Hon Mem Award, Am Dietetic Asn, 1999; NC NW Mary McLeod Bethune Award, 1999; Women in Government Award, Good Housekeeping Mag, 2000; Diplomate Award, Nat Restaurant Asn, 2000. **Business Addr:** President, SR Watkins & Associates, 16612 Sea Island Ct, Silver Spring, MD 20905, **Business Phone:** (301)476-7533.

WATKINS, TED
Executive. **Personal:** Born Sep 3, 1923, Meridian, MS; married Bernice Stollmach; children: Ted Jr, Tamlin, Timothy, Tom, Teryl, Lyssa. **Career:** Watts Labor Comm Action Comt, founder, 1966-; UAW, int rep, 1966-. **Orgs:** Mayors Bicentennial Comt; Jr Achievement Exec Bd; vpres, Martin Luther King, Gen Hosp Auth Comn; United Civil Rights Cong; Watts-willowbrook -Compton Improv Asn; STEP; LA Citizens Adv Comn; Watts Citizens Adv Comt; Watts Sta Comt; Police Adv Coun; adv comt, Upward Bound, Univ CA; Watts Comn Devlop; LA County Delinquency & Crime Comn; Watts-willowbrook Dist Hosp Med Prog; mem Citizens Resource Comn bd Educ; LA Urban Coalition; SE Col Adv Comt; Black Heritage Subcomt. **Honors/Awds:** Asn Elem Sch Administrs, 1968; Cath Labor Inst, 1968; Benedict Canyon Asn 1969; Awards Baha'i Human Rights, 1970; City LA Human Rels Comn, 1971; Interracial Coun Bus Opportunity, 1971; Urban League, 1971; County LA, 1972; Am Soc Pub Adminstrs, 1972; Coun Comn Clubs, 1973; DA County LA, 1973; Outstanding Comt Service Award, Watts NAACP, 1977; Outstanding Comn Service Award; Help Pub Serv Found, 1978; Participation in Black Econ Develop Award, Black Businessmen's Asn, LA, 1978; Recog & Apprec Outstanding Contributions Comn, Oscar Joel Bryant Asn 1978; Outstanding Service Award, Training & Res Found Head Start, 1979; Award, The Senate-cA Legis, 1980; Outstanding Contributions & Devotion, City Compton, 1980; Recog Humanitarian Concepts, Black Caucus CA Dem Party, 1980; Award, Assembly womMaxine Waters, 1980; Cert Spec Cong Recog, 1980; Honor Award, Serv Employees Joint Coun SEIU AFL-CIO, 1980. **Military Serv:** AUS, 1942-44. **Business Addr:** Founder, The Watts Labor Community Action Committee, 10950 S Central Ave, Los Angeles, CA 90059, **Business Phone:** (323)563-5639.

WATKINS, TIONNE
Singer, actor. **Personal:** Born Apr 26, 1970, Des Moines, IA; married Dedrick Rolison (divorced 2004); children: Chase Rolison. **Career:** Singer & actress; TLC, group mem; Albums: Ooooooohhh.. On the TLC Tip,1992; Crazy Sexy Cool, 1994; Fan Mail, 1999; 3D, 2002; Singles: "Touch Myself", 1996; "Ghetto Love", 1996; "My Getaway", 2000; "Tight To Def",2000; "Someday", 2009; Films: House Party 3, 1994; Belly, 1998; TV series: "CBS School break Special", 1992; Living Single, 1997; "One World Music Beat", 1998; "TLC:Sold Out", 2000; "Class of 3000", 2006; The Apprentice, 2009. **Orgs:** Spokesperson, Sickle Cell Disease Asn Am. **Special Achievements:** Book: "Thoughts", 1999; Named one of the 50 most beautiful people of theworld by People Magazine twice for the year 1994 & 2000. **Business Addr:** Singer, Actress, c/o Sony BMG Music Entertainment, 550 Madison Ave, New York, NY 10022, **Business Phone:** (212)833-8000.*

WATKINS, DR. WALTER J.
School superintendent. **Educ:** PhD. **Career:** Sch City Hammond, supt, currently. **Business Addr:** Superintendent, School City of Hammond, 41 William St, Hammond, IN 46320-1948, **Business Phone:** (219)933-2400.*

WATKINS, WILLIAM, JR.
Executive. **Personal:** Born Aug 12, 1932, Jersey City, NJ; son of William J Watkins and Willie Ree Blount; married Sylvia I Mulzac; children: Cheryl, Rene M, Linda M. **Educ:** Pace Univ, BBA, 1954; NY Univ, MBA, 1962. **Career:** Executive (retired); Consol Edison Co NY Inc, staff asst, 1957-65; Volkswagen Am Inc, syst mgr, 1965-71; Volkswagen NE, Wilmington, MA, exec, 1971-72; New England Elect Sys Westborough, MA, exec, 1972-82; Naragansett Electric Co, vpres, 1982-86, exec vpres, 1992-98; New England Power Serv Co, vpres, 1986-92. **Orgs:** bd dirs, Bank Boston RI, 1987-99; Leadership RI, 1992-97; INROADS Central New England, 1993-97; Nat Conf Christians & Jews, 1993-97; chmn, RI Indust Competitiveness Alliance, 1994-97; RI Hosp, 1994-97; Lifespan, 1997-00;chair & bd trustees, RI Sch Design, 1998-00. **Honors/Awds:** Human Relations Award, Urban League Bergen City, 1963; Urban League RI Community Service Award, 1986 & 1996; John Hope Settlement House Award, 1987; SBA Minority Advocate of the Year Award, 1994; Developer of the Year, Am Econ Develop Coun, 1996. **Military Serv:** AUS, sp4, 1955-57. **Home Addr:** 5114 87th Ct E, Bradenton, FL 34211, **Home Phone:** (941)752-6376. *

WATKINS, WYNFRED C
Manager, association executive. **Personal:** Born Apr 15, 1946, Toledo, OH; son of Clifford G and Marie B Marr (deceased); married Brenda J Sparks, Mar 18, 1967; children: Suzan Marie & Tara Edwina. **Educ:** Bowling Green State Univ, Bowling Green, OH, 1966. **Career:** JC Penney Co Inc, Saginaw, MI, dist mgr, 1990-93, Dallas, TX, dir geog mkts, vpres & dir investor rels, 1998-2000, sr vpres & dir commun & public affairs, 2000-05, sr vpres & dir diversity, 2005-. **Orgs:** Chmn, JC Penney Northeastern Regional Affirmative Action Comt Southwest, Cleveland, OH, 1989, 1990; bd mem, Adv Bd Parma Gen Hosp, Cleveland, OH, 1989; spiritual aim chmn, Kiwanis Club Saginaw Westshields, currently; Zion Baptist Missionary Church, Saginaw, currently; life mem, Nat Asn Advan Colored People; bd dirs, Dallas Black Dance Theatre; trustee bd dires, Jarvis Christian Col; chmn bd dirs, Junior Achievement Metrop Dallas. **Honors/Awds:** Store Manager of the Year Award, JC Penney, Cleveland District, 1989; various company awards for beating sales/profit objectives. **Business Addr:** Chairman, JCPenney Afterschool Fund, PO Box 10001, Dallas, TX 75301-4317, **Business Phone:** (972)749-2430.

WATKINS SNEAD, CHERYL
President (Organization), administrator. **Educ:** Univ Mass, mech eng; Purdue Univ, MBA. **Career:** Gen Elec, mgt; Peerless Precision, Lincoln, owner; Banneker Indust Inc, pres, chief exec officer & owner, currently. **Orgs:** Amica Ins Co; state deleg, US Small Bus Admin Nat Adv Coun; Textron Chamber Sch. **Honors/Awds:** New England Minority Entrepreneur of the Yr, 2000; Labor & Enterprise Award, RI Black Heritage Soc, 2003; Woman of Courage Emerging Bus Award, Nat Fed Black Women Bus Owners; Have received numerous awards, both for business accomplishments and ongoing civic work. **Business Addr:** President, Chief Executive Officer, Banneker Industries Inc, 678 Wash Hwy, Lincoln, RI 02865, **Business Phone:** (401)333-4487.*

WATKINS-SNEAD, CHERYL L. **See WATKINS, CHERYL L.**

WATLEY, JODY
Singer. **Personal:** Born Jan 30, 1959, Chicago, IL; married Andre Cymone (divorced); children: Lauren & Arie. **Career:** Solo singer; songwriter; producer; model; Avitone Recordings, chief exe cofficer, currently; Dancer, Soul Train; vocalist, Shalamar, 1977-84; SoloAlbums: "Affairs of the Heart", 1992. "Intimacy", 1993; "Affection", 1995; "Flower", 1998; "Midnight Lounge", 2001; "Ocl Looking For a New Love Oco Remix EP", 2005; "Borderline", 2006; "Live with Regis & Kathie Lee", 2006; "Unsung", 2009. **Honors/Awds:** Grammy, Best New Artist, 1988; nomination: Soul Train Music Award, Album of the Year, 1988, MTV Video Music Award, "Some Kind of Lover", 1988, MTV Video Music Award, "Real Love", 1989; six top ten singles from album Larger than Life, 1989; Billboard Lifetime Achievement Award, 2007. **Special Achievements:** Appearance at the White House, 1992; ranks at the 144 most successful R&B artist of all time according to Billboard Magazine; First African-American woman to portray Betty Rizzo in the Broadway revival of "Grease"; One of MTV Video Music Award's most nominated artist ever, with ten nominations. **Business Phone:** (973)579-7763.

WATLEY, MARGARET SEAY
Educator. **Personal:** Born Oct 19, 1925, Nashville, TN; widowed. **Educ:** Tenn A&I State Univ, BS, 1947; HM Nailor, Cleveland, MS, 1957; Columbia Univ, MA, 1965. **Career:** Educator (retired); Jasper Co, GA, teacher, 1950-53; Winchester Comm Sch, 1958; New Haven Pub Sch, teacher. **Orgs:** Life mem, Nat Educ Asn; life mem, NANB BWC Inc; pres, New Haven Club; Nat Asn Negro Bus Prof Women's Clubs Inc, 1971-72; New Haven Educ Asn, 1972-76; CT Educ Asn; CT Del NEA Rep Assembly, 1972; NE Dist Org Nat Asn Negro Bus & Prof Women's Clubs Inc, 1976; founder & organizer, Elm City Sr Club & Elm City Youth Club, 1976; Elm City Young Adult Club, 1977; reappointed organizer, NE Dist Gov NANBPW Inc, 1979; pres, Elm City Sr Club New Haven & Vicinity, 1977-81; Christian Tabernacle Baptist Church; bd dir, League Women Voters New Haven, dir voters serv, New Haven Scholar Fund; bd dir, New Haven Colony Hist Soc, 1995-01; Edgerton Garden Conservancy Bd; Libr Bd city New Haven; treas, African-Am Women's Agenda, 1992-01; Friends Grove St Cemetery; bd dir, New Heaven Free Pub Libr. **Honors/Awds:** Outstanding Elementary Teachers of America, 1972; Outstanding Participation Award, NANB & PW Clubs Inc 1976 & 1977; Leadership Development Award, Conn Educ Asn; Nat So journer Truth Meritorious Service Award, Elm City Sr Club, 1978; Mary B. Ives Award, New Haven Pub Libr; vol Extra ordinare Award, Greater New Haven Asn vol Administrators. **Business Addr:** Board of Directors, New Haven Free Public Library, 133 Elm St, New Haven, CT 06510, **Business Phone:** (203)946-8130.

WATLINGTON, JANET BERECIA
Government official. **Personal:** Born Dec 21, 1938, St Thomas, Virgin Islands of the United States; married Michael F MacLeod; children: Gregory & Kafi. **Educ:** Pace Univ NY, 1957; George Washington Univ, WA DC, 1977. **Career:** ACTION Wash DC, asst dir cong affairs, 1979-; Hon Ron deLugo US House ofReps, WA DC, admin asst, 1968-78; Legis VI St Thomas, exec secy, 1965-68. **Orgs:** Co-chmn, Dem Nat Conv Rules Comn, 1976; appointee, Dem Party ComnPresidential Nomination & Party Struc, 1976; dem nominee cong, VI, 1978;vchairperson, Dem Nat Comn, Eastern Region, 1972; steering com, Dem NatCom Black Caucus, 1974; exec com, Dem Party Chtr Comn, 1974; Cong BlackCaucus, 1974; charter mem, Sr Exec Serv Fed Govt, 1979; dir, VI Fed ProgsOff. **Business Addr:** 806 Connecticut Ave NW, Washington, DC 20525.

WATSON, AARON
School administrator, lawyer, consultant. **Personal:** Children: Jennifer, Andrew & Jana. **Educ:** Univ Notre Dame, BS(Accounting); Duke Univ, JD. **Career:** Atlanta Sch Bd, pres, 1994-2001; pvt pract atty & bus consul, currently; A-AB2, pres; Greenberg Traurig, atty; MeritSpan Holdings Inc, pres; Deloitte & Touche, acct. **Orgs:** Bd Comnr, Atlanta Housing Authority. **Business Addr:** Attorney & Business Consultant, Atlanta, GA 30307.

WATSON, ANNE
Financial manager. **Personal:** Born Feb 19, 1945, Belzoni, MS; married John. **Educ:** Western Mich Univ, BA 1970; Univ MI, attended 1976. **Career:** Western Mich Univ, tutor counr & asst dorm dir, 1967-70; Shaw Col Detroit, financial aid dir, 1971-76; Univ Detroit, financial aid dir; Wayne St Univ, financial aid counselor, 1974-75; Dept HEW, consult, 1976, discussion leader, 1977-; MI Financial Aid Asn, presentor & panelist, 1980. **Orgs:** Nat Asn Fin Aid Adminstr, 1975-80; chairperson, Comn Physically & Mentally Handicap 1978-79; bd dir, Black United Fund, 1979-80. **Honors/Awds:** Cert, Moton Consortium Dept HEW, 1974-75; Cert Moton Consortium, Dept HEW,1975, MSFAA Distinguished Service Award, 1999.

WATSON, ANNIE MAE
Association executive. **Career:** Nat Assoc Advan Colored People, exec comt mem, currently. **Business Addr:** Executive Committee Member, National Association for the Advancement of Colored People, 1104 Broadway Ave Suite F, PO Box 782, Seaside, CA 93955.*

WATSON, BARBARA
Business owner. **Career:** La Tienda Inn & Duran House, owner, 1994-. **Business Addr:** Owner, La Tienda Inn & Duran House, 445-447 & 511 W San Francisco St, Santa Fe, NM 87501, **Business Phone:** (505)989-8259.

WATSON, BEN
Television journalist. **Personal:** Born Jan 28, 1955, Muskegon Heights, MI; son of Bennie Sr and Lionel Matthews; divorced. **Educ:** Cent Mich Univ, Mount Pleasant, MI, BA, 1978. **Career:** WZZM TV, Grand Rapids, MI, tv camera operator, 1978-79; WEYI TV, Flint, MI, tv reporter, 1979-80; WOTV, Grand Rapids, MI, tv reporter, 1980-83; WLMT TV, Grand Rapids, MI, tv reporter, 1983-86; Grand Rapids Press, Grand Rapids, MI, newspaper weekend reporter, 1983,84; WMC TV, Memphis TN, tv reporter, 1986-. **Orgs:** NAACP 1986-; Nat Asn Black Journalists, 1987-; Omega Psi Phi, 1975-; Manna Outreach, 1990-; Profiles Recent Develop. **Honors/Awds:** Communicator Award, Am Cancer Soc, 1983; Journalism Award, Flint Urban League, 1979; Achievement Award, Interpreting Serv Deaf, 1989; Volunteer Award, Miss Blvd Chap Church, 1990; Gabriel Award, 1999; Nat Asn Black Journalist Award; The Hal Walton Journalism Award, Am Cancer Soc. **Business Addr:** TV Reporter, Anchor, WMC-TV, News Department, 1960 Union Ave, Memphis, TN 38104, **Business Phone:** (901)726-0416.

WATSON, DR. BERNARD C.
Educator. **Personal:** Born Mar 4, 1928, Gary, IN; son of Homer Bismarck Watson and Fannie Mae Browne Watson; married Lois Lathan, Jul 1, 1961; children: Barbra D & Bernard C Jr. **Educ:** Ind Univ, BS, 1951; Univ Ill, MEd, 1955; Univ Chicago, PhD, 1967; Harvard Univ, Cambridge, MA, postdoctoral advan admin, 1968. **Career:** Gary Pub Sch, Gary, Ind, teacher, counr, prin, 1955-65; Univ Chicago,Chicago, Ill, staff assoc, 1965-67; Philadelphia Sch Dist, 1967-70; Temple Univ, chmn, dept urban educ, 1970-75, vpres, acad admin, 1976-81; William Penn Found, pres & chief exec officer, 1982-93; HMA Found, chmn, 1994-97; Temple Univ, presidential scholar, 1994, urban Educ, endowed chair & anchor, currently. **Orgs:** Bd dir, AAA Mid-Atlantic; vice chmn, Nat Adv Coun Educ Professions Develop, 1967-70; mem vis comt, Harvard Univ Grad Sch Educ, 1981-87; steering comt & exec comt, Nat Urban Coalition, 1973-89; mem vis comt, Harvard Col, Dept Afro-Am Studies, 1974-78; Nat Coun Educ Res, 1980-82; Pennsylvania fed judiciary nominating comn, 1981-89; sr vice chmn & bd dir, Nat Urban League, 1983-96; vice chmn & bd dir, Pennsylvania Conv Ctr Authority, 1986-; vice chmn, Pennsylvania Coun on Arts, 1986-93; William TGrant Fedn Comn on Work, Family & Citizenship, 1987-88; secy bd, New Jersey State Aquarium, 1988-93; chmn, Ave Arts, Inc, 1992-97; Judicial Conduct Bd, Supreme Ct Pennsylvania, 1993-97; trustee, Thomas Jefferson Univ, 1993-94; Nat Adv Coun Historically Black Col & Univ, 1994-97; Am Philos Soc; Am Acad Polit & Social Sci; Phi Delta Kappa; Kappa Delta Pi;Adv Comn, Patterson Res Inst CLG Rund/UNCF, 1996-; pres, bd trustees, Barnes Fund, 1999-. **Honors/Awds:** More than 100 major awards, including 22 honorary degrees; author, In Spite of the System: The Individual & Educ Reform, 1974; Plain Talk About Educ: Conversations with Myself, 1987; Testing: Its Origin, Use and Misuse, 1996; Colored, Negro, Black: Chasing the American Dream, 1997; 13 monographs;

chapters in 28 books; 100 career folios; 35 articles in professional journals; Dr Bernard C Watson Grad Sem Room and Award presented for best social sci dissertation in Temple Univ, Col of Educ. **Special Achievements:** First endowed chair in honor of an African American in Temple University's history. **Military Serv:** USAF, first Lt, 1951-54. **Business Phone:** (215)204-2523.

WATSON, BOB. See WATSON, ROBERT JOSE.

WATSON, CAROLE M.
Social worker, chief financial officer. **Personal:** Born Aug 3, 1944, New Orleans, LA; daughter of Herman and Frances; divorced; children: Dionne T. **Educ:** Western Mich Univ, BS, 1965; Wayne State Univ, MSW, 1970. **Career:** Milwaukee Area Tech Col, instr, 1972-73; Tenn State Univ, Dept Social Welfare, instr, curric cord, 1973-77; Univ Tenn, Sch Social Work, asst prof, 1977-79; WZTV Channel 17 Black Pulse, hostess, 1981-85; Nashville Urban League, exec dir, 1979-85; Bay Area Urban League, Oakland, CA, vpres, pres, chief exec officer, 1985-90; United Way, San Francisco, CA,sr vpres, chief investment officer, 1990-. **Orgs:** Delta Sigma Theta Nashville Alumnae, 1963-; Acad Cert Social Workers,1975-; adv coun, Brd Cert Master Soc Workers, 1980-81; dir, Tenn Chap Nat Assn Social Workers, 1980; first vpres, natl coun execs, Nat Urban League; consumer adv comn, S Cent Bell; brd dir, Tenn Opp Prog Legal Serv Middle, TN, NAACP, Bay Area Assn Black Social Workers, 1986-. **Honors/Awds:** Appreciation Award, Alpha Delta Mu, Nat Soc Worker Hon Soc Iota Chap, Tenn St Univ, 1978; Congressional Record Award, Bill Booner 5th Congresional Dist State Tenn, 1985; 'Wall of Distinction', Western Mich Univ, 1986;employee of the Year, Bay Area Urban League, 1987; Appreciation Award,Calif Asn Black Social Worker, 1989. **Special Achievements:** Citizen of the Year, Riverside Seventh-day Adventist Church. **Business Addr:** Chief Investment Officer, United Way of the Bay Area, 1212 Broadway Suite 530, Oakland, CA 94612, **Business Phone:** (510)451-3132.

WATSON, CHESTER N.
Auditor, vice president (organization). **Educ:** Rochester Inst Technol, BS, acct, 1974. **Career:** Bell Atlantic Corp, exec officer & vpres internal auditing; Lucent Technol Inc, vpres corp audit & security; Gen Motor Corp, gen auditor, currently. **Orgs:** Bd Trustees, Rochester Inst Technol, currently. *

WATSON, CLYNIECE LOIS
Physician. **Personal:** Born Jan 27, 1948, Chicago, IL; married Sloan Timothy Letman III; children: Sloan Timothy Letman IV. **Educ:** Loyola Univ, BS, 1969; Meharry Med Col, MD, 1973; Univ Ill, MPH, 1977. **Career:** Cook Co Hosp, Dept Pediat, resident, 1973-75; Provident Hosp, assoc med dir, 1977; pvt pract, pediatrician, currently. **Orgs:** Am Med Womens Asn; Am Pub Health Asn; Black Caucus Health Workers; Am Col Preventive Med; Am Med Asn; St Med Soc; Med Soc Ill; Pub Health Asn; Am Asn Univ Women; Nat Med Asn; bd dir, Komed Health Ctr; Phi Delta Kappa Hon Educ Fraternity; Womens Fel Congregation Church; bd, Religions Educ, Congregational Church; Meharry Alumni Asn; Univ Ill Alumni Asn; Asn Physicians Cook Co, 1971-73; Lambda Alpha Omega Chap, Alpha Kappa Alpha Sorority Inc. **Honors/Awds:** Merit Award, Womens Fel Congregational Church; Outstanding Young Citizen Chicago Jaycees, 1980; fel Martin Luther King Jr. **Home Addr:** 500 E 51st St, Chicago, IL 60615, **Home Phone:** (312)572-2696.

WATSON, CONSTANCE A.
Public relations executive. **Personal:** Born Aug 17, 1951, Nashville, TN; children: Shannon. **Educ:** TN State Univ, MSSW, 1978. **Career:** Dede Wallace Mental Health Ctr, psychiatric social worker, 1973-82; Neuville Indust, dir ocean pac div, 1982-86; W W & Associates Pub Rels, pres & founder, 1985-. **Orgs:** Chairperson, Nat Hook Up Black Women, 1980-82; Exec Comt, Nat Asn Advancement Colored People, 1984-86; vpres, Nat Asn Advancement Colored People, 1986-; bd dir, Found Educ, 1984-. **Honors/Awds:** Achievement Award, Golden W Mag, 1987. **Special Achievements:** Public relations consultant for major Hollywood and Los Angeles celebrities and events, ie 19th NAACP Image Awdstelevised on NBC. **Business Phone:** (213)752-4770.

WATSON, DANIEL
Business owner, investment banker, consultant. **Personal:** Born Apr 11, 1938, Hallettsville, TX; married Susan Smallwood; children: Pamela, Bradley, Stanley, Jodney & Narlan. **Educ:** Univ Wash, BS 1959, MS 1965. **Career:** Wash Nat Inst, agent, 1966-68, mgr, 1968-71, gen agent, 1971; Daniel Watson Agency, owner & founder, currently. **Orgs:** Seattle Planning Redevel Coun, 1967-71; Nat Gen Agents & Mgrs Asn, 1971-; Chicago Asn Life Underwriters, 1979. **Honors/Awds:** Agency Builder Award Wash Nat, 1970-75, 1977. **Special Achievements:** Article published Psychological Reports, 1965. **Business Addr:** Founder, Owner, Daniel Watson Agency Inc, 2607 W 22nd St Suite 46, Oak Brook, IL 60523.

WATSON, DENNIS RAHIIM
Lecturer, writer, educator. **Personal:** Born May 14, 1953, Hamilton, Bermuda; son of Eula Watson-Stewart and Arthur Daniels. **Educ:** Harlem Preparatory Sch, Fordham Univ, NY, attended 1976; Pace Univ, attended 1978; NY Univ, attended. **Career:** Theater of Everyday Life, exec dir, 1980-83; New York City Coun, exec asst, 1983-84; Natl Black Youth Leadership Coun, founder, pres & chief exec officer, 1984-. **Orgs:** UNCF, 1980-86; NY Urban League, 1980-86; volunteer Bay view Correctional Facility for Women, NY, 1980-86; Nat Alliance Black Sch Educators, 1984-86; Coun Concerned Black Execs, 1980-86; NAACP, 1984-86; Black Leadership Round table, 1984-86. **Honors/Awds:** Performing Arts Award, Sigma Gamma Rho, 1984; Nat Black Leadership Round table Award, 1984; US Dept of Justice Drug Enforcement Admin Volunteer Award, 1984; Mayors Ethnic New Yorker Award, 1985; Presidential White House Citation, 1985; Pvt Sector Initiative Award, 1986; Bayview Correctional Facility for Women Male Performer of the Yr, 1986; OIC Appreciation Award, 1988; Leadership Appreciation Award, Univ Calif Los Angeles, 1989; The Black Women Task Force Award, 1989; Nat Black Grad Student Award, Miss State Univ, 1990; Black Student Alliance Award, Univ Va; City of New York, Human Res Admin Spec Award; Apple P, Delta Sigma Theta Youth Award; Western Mich Univ Student Leadership Conf Award, 1991; Fla Int Univ Black Family Award; Youth Award, Aspira, Family Christian Asn Am; Black Historian Month Award, Burlington County Col. **Special Achievements:** Americas Best & Brightest Young Business & Professional Man, 1987; One of America's most powerful motivational speakers.

WATSON, PROF. DENTON L
Writer, public relations executive, journalist. **Personal:** Born Dec 19, 1935, Kingston, Jamaica; son of Ivy L Watson and Audley G Watson; married Rosa Balfour, Sep 1, 1963; children: Victor C & Dawn M. **Educ:** Univ Hartford, BA, 1964; Columbia Univ, Grad Sch Jour, MS, 1965; Cath Univ Chile, Inter Am Press Asn scholar, 1967. **Career:** Hartford Courant, reporter, 1965-67; Time Magazine, writer; Ncp Dept Pub Rels, asst dir, 1971; The Baltimore Sun, ed writer; author; State Univ NY, Col Old Westbury, Am Studies, assoc prof, 1992-; proj dir & ed, The Papers of Clarence Mitchell, Jr. **Orgs:** The Am Hist Asn; Nat Asn Balck-Journalists; The Authors Guild Inc. **Special Achievements:** Author: Lion in the Lobby, Clarence Mitchell Jr's Struggle for the Passage of Civil Rights Laws; The Papers of Clarence Mitchell, Jr., Volumes I & II, III. **Military Serv:** USN, ae-3, 1957-59. **Home Addr:** 137 W Seaman Ave, Freeport, NY 11520, **Home Phone:** (516)546-3754. **Business Addr:** Associate Professor, State University of New York, College Old Westbury, PO Box 210, Old Westbury, NY 11568-0210, **Business Phone:** (516)876-2889.

WATSON, DR. DIANE EDITH
Congressperson (u.s. federal government). **Personal:** Born Nov 12, 1933, Los Angeles, CA; daughter of William Allen Louis and Dorothy Elizabeth O. **Educ:** Los Angeles City Col, AA; Univ Calif, Los Angeles, BA, 1956; Calif State Los Angeles, MS, 1967; Claremont Col, PhD, educ admin, 1986. **Career:** Los Angeles Unified Sch Dist, teacher, 1956-60, asst prin & teacher, 1963-68; AUS Okinawa & France, teacher, 1960-63; Los Angeles Unified Sch Dist Child Welfare & Attendance, asst supr, 1968-69; Dept Guidance Los Angeles Unified Sch Dist, sch psychologist, 1969-70; Calif State La Dept Guidance, assoc prof, 1969-70; Univ Calif Sec Schs Allied Health Proj, depdir, 1969-71; Health Occup Los Angeles Unified Sch Dist, specialist, 1971-73; Los Angeles Unified Sch Dist, sch psychologist, 1973-75; Bd Educ, mem, 1975-78; Calif State Senate, Dist 26, senator, 1978-98, Health & Human Servs Comt, chairperson, 1981-; United States Ambassador Micronesia, 1999-2000; US House Rep, congresswoman, 2001-. **Orgs:** Dem Nat Comt; founder & pres, Nat Orgn Black Elected Legis Women; Calif Elected Women's Asn Educ & Res; Nat Adv Panel mem, Univ Calif Ctr Study Eval; Med Policy Comn; author & adv com mem, McGraw Hill/Gregg Div; consult, Calif Comn Status Women; Nat Sch Bds Asn; Calif Sch Bds Asn; mem, Calif Asn Sch Psychologists & Psychometrists; LA Elem Coun & Guid Asn; United Teachers LA; Calif Teachers Asn; hon life mem, PTA; mem exec bd, Coun Great Cities Schs; bd mem, Stevens House; Friends Golden State Minority Found; Nat Black Womens Polit Caucus; Coun Black Admins; Calif Dem Cent Com Educ Comn; Nat Asn Advan Colored People; Media Women; Alpha Kappa Alpha Nat Sorority. **Honors/Awds:** Alumnus of the Year Award, Calif State Univ La, 1980; La Comn Col Alumnus of the Year Award, 1980; Outstanding Rep Award, Sacramento Asn Black Attorneys, 1981; Alumnus of the Year Award, Univ Calif, 1982; Com Col Senator of the Year Award, 1983; Legislator of the Year, State Coun Develop Disabilities, 1987; Black Woman of Achievement Award, Nat Am Advan Colored People Legal Defense Fund, 1988; Ca State Psychol Asn Humanitarian Award; Bank of Am Award; Outstanding Comn Serv Award, YWCA; Mary Ch Terrell Award. **Special Achievements:** First African-American woman to be elected to the Los Angeles Unified School District Board of Education; Author: Health Occupations Instructional Units-Secondary Schools, 1975;Planning Guide for Health Occupations, 1975; co-author, Introduction to Health Care, 1976. **Business Addr:** Congresswoman, US House of Representative, 125 Cannon HOB, Washington, DC 20515-0533, **Business Phone:** (202)225-7084.

WATSON, DR. ELIZABETH DARBY
Educator. **Personal:** Born Nov 18, 1945, Harlem, NY; daughter of Samuel Darby and Jayne Doswell Darby; divorced; children: Leslie Watson Bray, L Roger Watson III & Ercell I Watson II. **Educ:** Columbia Union Col, BS, 1967; Howard Univ, MSW, 1969; Andrews Univ, PhD, 2001. **Career:** Tenn Christian Med Ctr, dir social servs, 1981-87; Rebound CHI Facilities, prog coordr coun, 1987-89, community developer, 1989-90; Cumberland Hall, psychiatric social worker, 1991; Orchard Grove, consult, 1991-98; Andrews Univ, assoc prof, 1991-, dir Genesis Single Parent Prog, 1991-97, Ctr Intercultural Relations, assoc dir, 1993-95, dir admis, 1997-, BSW prog dir, 2003-. **Orgs:** Nat Asn Social Workers, 1981-; Coun Social Work Educ, 1991-; bd mem, Mich League Human Serv, 1991-2000; Lake Union Women's Ministries Comt, 1993-97; Lake Region Women's Comt, 1993-; vpres bd, United Way Berrien Co, 2002-; chair, Black Hist Celebration Comt, 2002-. **Honors/Awds:** Excellence Award, Operation Reach Back, 1995; Notable Adventist Women of Today, SDA Church, 1995; BSCF Courage Award, Andrews Univ, 1998. **Special Achievements:** Author, children's stories, 1981; seminars & workshops, 1981; srmons & motivational presentations, 199-; author, women's devotional stories, 1995. **Home Addr:** 1652 Broadway, Niles, MI 49120. **Business Phone:** (616)471-3156.

WATSON, GARY
Lawyer. **Career:** Pvt Pract, lawyer, currently. *

WATSON, GENEVIEVE
Educator, college administrator. **Personal:** Born Apr 2, 1950, Gilbert, LA; daughter of Joe Thomas Jr and Laura Gilbert Thomas; married Alvin Watson Jr, Jun 16, 1972; children: Alvin L, Gene L & Thomas L. **Educ:** Grambling Col, Grambling, BA, 1972; Drake Univ, Des Moines, MAT, 1978. **Career:** Drake Univ, Des Moines, spec servs coordr, 1974-81; asst dir, financialaid, 1981-85; assoc dir financial aid, 1985-86; Univ Ariz, Tucson, asst dir financial aid, 1986-88, actg assoc dean studs, 1989-90, assoc dir, financial aid, 1988-95; Phoenix Col, dir, financial aid, 1995-, secy, currently. **Orgs:** Minority concerns comt, exec coun, Mid-West Asn Stud Fin Aid Admn,1983-86; pres, Iowa Asn Stud Fin Aid Admn, 1986; Scholar serv governance Comn, Col Bd, 1984-86; comn mem, IA Gov's Task Force on Ed, 1985-86; exec coun, rep at large minority concerns chair, Western Asn Stud Fin Aid Admn, 1990-92; past pres, pres, pres-elect, exec coun, Ariz Asn Stud Fin Aid Adminrs, 1990-93; Tucson United Way, Fund Distribution Steering Com, 1995;Col bd, Western Regional Planning Com; bd dir, Nat Asn Stud Financial Aid Adminrs; co-chair, Fund Develop Com, Western Asn Stud Fin Aid Admin,1997-98; vpres mem, Nat Coun on Black Am Affairs, 2009. **Honors/Awds:** Nominated for UA Award for Excellence, Univ Ariz, 1990. **Special Achievements:** Presenter: "The Tax Reform Act & Stud Fin Aid," NASFAA, 1988; "SuccessfulStrategies for Ethnic Individuals," "Critical Issues in Grad & Prof SchFinancial Aid," WASFAA, 1992; First Black female president AASFAA(1991-92) & IASFAA (1986). **Business Addr:** Director, Financial Aid, Secretary, Phoenix College, 1202 W Thomas Rd, Phoenix, AZ 85013.

WATSON, GEORGETTE. See Obituaries section.

WATSON, HON. J. WARREN
Judge. **Personal:** Born Feb 20, 1923, Pittsburgh, PA; son of James Warren and Eula Henderson; married Carole A Whedbee; children: James Guy, Meredith Gay Young, Wrenna Leigh, Robert Craig, Sheila Tyler & Kevin McDowell. **Educ:** Duquesne Univ, BA, polit sci, Econ, 1949, LLB, 1953. **Career:** Judge (retired); Pvt pract, atty, 1954-66; City Pittsburgh, city solicitor, 1960-66; Commonwealth PA, judge; Ct Common Pleas Allegheny Co, Fifth Judicial Dist Pa, sr judge. **Orgs:** Bd mem, Judicial Inquiry & Review Bd, 1981-85; chmn, Media Rel Comt Bd Judges, 1984; bd mem, Estate Planning Comt St Trial Judges Conf, 1984; pres, coun Carlow Col; bd dir, Comt Action Pittsburgh; trustee, Community Serv PA. **Honors/Awds:** Man of the Year, Disabled Am Veterans, 1969; Hon Mem Chiefs Police; Certificate of Merit, Nat Asn Negro Bus Prof Civic & Cult & Polit Endeavor, 1972. **Military Serv:** USN, 3 yrs.

WATSON, JACKIE
Police officer, president (organization). **Personal:** Born Oct 29, 1968, Jackson, MS; daughter of Jerry and Laura. **Educ:** BS, Criminal Justice, 1994; GWP & Counseling, MSEd, 1998. **Career:** Jackson Police Dept, police woman, 1992-; Eve's Fruit Inc, owner, pres, currently. **Orgs:** Nat Asn Advan Colored People; Police Union Asn. **Home Phone:** (601)957-5884. **Business Addr:** Police Officer, Jackson Police Department, 327 E Pascagoula St, Jackson, MS 39201.

WATSON, DR. JANICE
Executive. **Educ:** Andrews Univ, BA, MA; Univ Minnesota, PhD. **Career:** Andrews Univ, assoc prof commun, prof commun, currently. **Business Addr:** Professor of Communications, Andrews University, 8743 Univ Blvd, Berrien Springs, MI 49103-0640, **Business Phone:** (269)471-3405.*

WATSON, JOANN NICHOLS
Civil rights activist. **Personal:** Born Apr 19, 1951, Detroit, MI; daughter of Rev Lestine Kent Nichols Franklin and Jefferson Nichols Sr; divorced; children: Damon Gerard, Celeste Nicole, Stephen Bernard & Maya Kristi. **Educ:** Univ Mich-Ann Arbor,

BA, jour, 1972; Mich State Univ, attended 1975; New York Univ, Inst Educ Leadership, Educ Policy Fel Prog, 1987; Lewis Col Bus, Hon Doctorate, DHL, 1996. **Career:** Community Parents Child Care Ctr, exec dir, 1973-75; Lake Mich Col, instr, racism & sexism, 1975-76; Coalition Peaceful Integration, ed, social worker, 1976-77; Focus Hope, resource coordr, 1978; YWCA Metro Detroit, br exec dir, 1976-87; YWCA USA, asst exec dir, 1987-90; NAACP, Detroit br, exec dir, 1990-97; Daily Urban Announcer Talk Show Host, WGPR "Wake Up Detroit, Joann Watson Show," 1996-; Editorial columnist Michigan Citizen 50,000 subscribers, 1996-; JoAnn Watson System Inc, chief exec officer & pres; Equality Compliance Inc, chief exec officer & pres; Detroit City Coun, coun mem, 2003-. **Orgs:** Nat Coun Negro Women 1979-; Women's Conf Concerns, 1979-; Wayne State Univ, Upward Bound Alumni Asn, 1980-; Mich Women's Hall Fame Rev Panel, 1982-; vpres, Mich NAACP, 1982-87; Racial Justice Working Group Nat Coun Churches, 1987-; Asn Black Women Higher Educ 1987-; Black Child Develop Inst, 1987-; exec bd, Nat Proj Equality EEO, 1988-; pres, New York Alumni New York Inst Educ Leadership, 1988-; Nat Interreligious Civil Rights Comn, 1988-; co-founder, vice chair nat bd, Ctr Study Harassment African-Am, 1991-; bd mem & exec comt, United Way Community Serv, 1991-; bd mem, Nat Coun Alcoholism & Other Dependencies, 1991-; Pay Equity Network, Coalition Labor Union Women, mem, 1991-; bd dirs, Am Red Cross, 1992; YWCA, Detroit; Ctr Dem Renewal; bd dirs, Am Civil Liberties Union, 1992-; hon trustee, Cranbrook Peace Found, 1992-; nat bd mem, Nat Alliance Against Racist & Polit repression, 1992-; adv bd mem, Nat Lawyers Guild, 1993-; Women Bd, Coalition Women Corp Bds, Am Jewish Comt, founder & co-chair, 1994-; bd mem, Self Help Addiction Rehab, 1994-; bd dir, Detroit Women's Forum, 1995; Nat Asn Blacks Radio, 1995-; bd dirs, New Detroit Inc, 1996-. **Honors/Awds:** Thalheimer Awards, Newsletter Ed, Mich Mobilizer, NAACP, 1978-88; State Mich Govr & Legis Proclamation, 1987; City Detroit "Spirit of Detroit" Award, 1987; Life Achievement Award, Womens Equality Day, City Detroit, 1987; Hall of Fame Award, YWCA Detroit, 1987-88; organizer & co-sponsor, Martin Luther King first Ann Youth Conf, 1988; vice chair, 25th Commemorative March Wash, 1988; Minority Womens Network, "Civil Rights Activist of the Year," 1990; Special Recognition Award, Nat Anti-Klan Network, 1996; Distinguished Alumnus of the Year &Leonard Sain Award, The African-American Alumni Univ Mich, 1996; Ameritech Black Advocacy Panel, Humanitarian of the Year Award, 1996; Detroit Col of Law, Humanitarian Awd, 1996; Nigerian Foundation of Michigan, Special Recognition Awd, 1996; Michigan Civil Rights Commission, Distinguished Svc Commemoration Award, 1995; East Side Slate, Outstanding Comm Svc Award, 1996; Malcolm X Academy, Ancestors Day Awd, 1996; Natl Council of Negro Women, Outstanding Comm Leader Awd, Detroit Section, 1994; Detroit Urban League, Distinguished Comm Svc Awd, 1995; US Dept of Labor, Working Women Count Leadership Awd, 1996; WXYZ-TV - Channel 7, Outstanding Women Awd, 1995; Natl Lawyers Guild, Detroit Chap, Anniversary Awd, 1994; Natl Council of Negro Women, Natl Tribute to Women Awd, 1994; Alternatives for Girls, Annual Awd, 1994; Bennett Coll, Greensboro, NC, Distinguished Achievement Awd, 1994; Senate Star of MI, Tribute Awd, 1994; City Council Resolution, Tribute Awd, 1994; Wayne County Comm, Tribute Awd, 1994; City of Detroit, Mayoral Proclamation, Tribute Awd, 1994; United Comm Svcs, Tribute Awd, 1994; Natl Political Congress of Black Women, Distinguished Svc Awd, 1994; Wayne County Clerk, Tribute Awd, 1994; Detroit City Clerk, Tribute Awd, 1994; Inner City Sub Center, Distinguished Svc Awd, 1994; Annual Malcolm X Comm Ctr, African Heritage Awd, 1993; Mich Civil Rights Commission, Distinguished Achievement Awd, 1994; Woman of the Year Awd, Zeta Phi Beta Sorority Inc, 1994. **Special Achievements:** First woman to serve as Executive Director of the Detroit Branch NAACP. **Home Phone:** (313)934-1557. **Business Phone:** (313)224-4535.

WATSON, JOE
Chief executive officer. **Career:** Virginia Governor Mark Warner's Transition Team, Dir Personnel, 2001; Strategic Hire, Without Excuses, pres & chief exec officer, currently. **Orgs:** cofounder, Af Am Chief Exec Officer Coun; Chmn, Virginia High Tech Partnership; Chmn, Greater Reston Chamber Com. **Business Addr:** President, Chief Executive Officer, Strategic Hire, 1851 Alexander Bell Dr Suite 301, Reston, VA 20191, **Business Phone:** (703)467-9093.*

WATSON, JOHN CLIFTON
Journalist, college teacher. **Personal:** Born Jan 22, 1954, Jersey City, NJ; son of John and Clementine; married Laura St Martin, Nov 13, 1994. **Educ:** Rutgers Col, BA, 1975; Rutgers Univ, Sch Law, JD, 1980. **Career:** Jersey City State Col, writing instr, 1992-94; Rutgers Col Newark, Jour instr, 1992-; Jersey Jour, news ed, reporter, 1975; Am Univ, Sch Commun, asst prof, currently. **Orgs:** Garden State Asn Black Journalists, 1992-. **Honors/Awds:** First Place Spot News Reporting Award, N Jersey Press Asn, 1983; First Place Spot News Reporting Award, NJ Press Asn, 1983; Sports Writing Award, Hudson County Newspaper Guild, 1983. **Business Addr:** Assistant Professor, American University, Department Communication, 4400 Massachusetts Ave NW, Washington, DC 20016-8017, **Business Phone:** (202)885-2060.

WATSON, JOSEPH W
Educator, college teacher, chemist. **Personal:** Born Apr 16, 1940, New York, NY; married Mary Slater; children: Ruth, Jerome, Jennifer & Elizabeth. **Educ:** City Col New York, BS, 1961; Univ Calif Los Angeles, PhD, 1966. **Career:** Univ Calif San Diego, from assoc prof to prof, 1966-2007, provost, 1970, vice chancellor student affairs, prof emer chem, 2007-. **Orgs:** Am Chem Soc; Nat Orgn Prof & Advan Black Chems & Chem Engrs; Calif Black Col Fac & Staff Asn Inc; Calif Student Aid Comn, 1987-, chair, 1990-92; Nat Asn Advan Colored People; life mem, Urban League. **Honors/Awds:** Anniversary Medal, City Col NY, 1973; Outstanding Young Man, San Diego, 1975. **Business Addr:** Professor Emeritus, University of Califonia, Department of Chemistry & Biochemistry, 9500 Gilman Dr, La Jolla, CA 92093.

WATSON, JUSTIN SEAN
Football player. **Personal:** Born Jan 7, 1975, Bronx, NY. **Educ:** San Diego State Univ, BA, criminal justice. **Career:** Football player (retired); St Louis Rams, running back, 1999-2001.

WATSON, KAREN ELIZABETH
Executive. **Personal:** Born Sep 11, 1957, New York, NY; daughter of James L and D Jaris E Hinton; married; children: Erika Faith Allen, James Austin Allen. **Educ:** Bard Col, BA, Am studies, 1979. **Career:** Mondale - Ferraro presial Campaign, pres advance, 1984; Select Comn Narcotics Abuse & Ctrl, US House Rep, pres secy, 1983-85; Capitol J, Wash, DC, reporter, res, 1985; Pub Broadcasting Serv, Alexandria, VA, assoc dir, news & pub affairs, 1985-92; Southern Ctr Intl Studies, Atlanta GA, tv & educ consult, 1993-94; WGBH Educ Found, Boston, MA, deputy proj dir, Africans Am, 1992-94; Echostar Commun Corp, govt affairs dir, currently. **Orgs:** Radio & TV News Dirs Asn. **Honors/Awds:** WGBH Appreciation Award, WGBH Educ Found, 1991-93; Judge Robert F Kennedy Awards; Judge Corp Public Broadcasting Local programming Awards, 1985-93. **Special Achievements:** Outstanding Coverage of the Disadvantaged, 1990. **Business Addr:** Government Affairs Director, Echostar Communication Corporation, 1233 20th St NW Suite 701, Washington, DC 20036-2482, **Business Phone:** (202)293-0981.

WATSON, LEIGHTON
Media executive, business owner. **Career:** La Tienda Inn, innkeeper; La Tienda Inn, owner, 1994-. **Business Addr:** Owner, La Tienda Inn, 445 447 W San Francisco St, Santa Fe, NM 87501.*

WATSON, MARY ELAINE
Educator. **Personal:** Born Aug 24, 1942, Springfield, OH; daughter of Ferdinand Benjamin and Lillie Belle Quisenberry Clarke; widowed; children: Monyca Lynn Gordon & Aaron Marshall. **Educ:** Miami Univ, Oxford, OH, BS, educ, 1964. **Career:** Middletown Monroe City Sch, teacher, 1964-99; J&W Fashions & Designs, co-owner, currently; Mary Elaine Watson Arts, pres, currently. **Orgs:** Alpha Kappa Alpha Sorority, 1962; Girl Scouts Am, leader, 1969-95, bd dir, 1986-88; counr, OH 4-H, 1978-87, 1998-99; Nat Asn Advan Colored People; adv asst, Girls Assembly & Sojourner Truth No 13, 1985-99; deaconess, Mt Zion Missionary Baptist Church, Middletown, OH, 1994-; Nat Sorority Phi Delta Kappa Inc, 1995; Order Eastern Star, Chap 55, 1995. **Honors/Awds:** Image Award, Nat Asn Advan Colored People, 1998. **Home Addr:** 6194 Hamilton Middletown Rd, Middletown, OH 45044. **Business Addr:** President, Mary Elaine Watson Arts, 6194 Hamilton Middletown Rd, Middletown, OH 45044, **Business Phone:** (513)539-8955.

WATSON, MICHAEL A.
Executive. **Personal:** Born in Mobile, AL. **Educ:** Duke Univ, BA; Columbia Univ, BL. **Career:** NY off Hunton & Williams & Milbank, Tweed, assoc; NY Life Ins Co, from asst gen counsel to named vpres & dep gen counsel, 1996-. **Orgs:** Congressional Black Caucus Found. **Special Achievements:** First vice president in the Office of General Counsel at New York Life Insurance Co. **Business Addr:** Vice President, Deputy General Counsel, New York Life Insurance Company, 51 Madison Ave Suite 3200, New York, NY 10010, **Business Phone:** (212)576-7000.*

WATSON, MILTON H
Executive, vice president (organization). **Personal:** Born Mar 12, 1927, Detroit, MI; son of Elzie L Watson and Fannie M Watson; married Mary Kathryn; children: Milton P & Kathryn M. **Educ:** Wayne State Univ, BA, 1949; Univ Mich, MSW, 1962. **Career:** Executive (retired); OMNI Care Health Plan, corp secy, bd trustees, 1971; Health Coun Inc, exec dir; Millar Agency Equitable Life Assurance Soc, asst agency mgr; State Mich, supvr c div dept soc serv; Harvard Univ JF Kennedy Sch Govt, lectr, 1971; Univ Mich Sch Pub Health, lectr, 1971; Cottillion Club, fin secy, 1971-84; Nat Healthcare Scholars Found, vpres, vice chmn, currently. **Orgs:** Am Pub Health Asn; Nat Asn Social Workers. **Military Serv:** USMC. **Business Addr:** Vice Chairman, Vice President, National Healthcare Scholars Foundation, 300 River Place Suite 4950, Detroit, MI 48207, **Business Phone:** (313)393-4549.

WATSON, PERRY
Basketball coach. **Personal:** Born May 1, 1950, Detroit, MI; married Deborah; children: Paris. **Educ:** Eastern Mich Univ, BA, 1972, MA, 1976. **Career:** Head Basketball Coach(Retired); Southwestern High Sch, Detroit, boy's basketball coach, counselor, 1979-91; Nike all-star camp, dir; Univ Mich, asst men's basketball coach, 1991-93; Univ Detroit-Mercy, Detroit Titans, head basketball coach, 1993-2008. **Honors/Awds:** Horizon League Tournament Championship, 1994, 1999; Horizon League Regular Season Championship, 1998-99; Horizon League Coach of the Yr, 1998. **Business Addr:** Head Basketball Coach, University Detroit-Mercy, Detroit Titans, 4001 W McNichols Rd, PO Box 19900, Detroit, MI 48221-3038, **Business Phone:** (313)993-1731.*

WATSON, PERRY, III
Automotive executive. **Personal:** Born Apr 16, 1951, Muskegon Heights, MI; son of Perry Jr and Roberta; married Ida Janice Reynolds, Aug 4, 1979; children: Perry, Robert, Anthony & Maya. **Educ:** Western Mich Univ, BBA, 1973, MBA, 1976. **Career:** Keene CRP, Purchasing agent, 1974; County Muskegon, contract specialist, 1975; Xerox Corp, acct rep, 1977-83, mkt mgr, 1980-83, sales operations mgr, 1983-85, dist syst mgr, 1985-90; Brookdale Dodge, pres, 1993-. **Orgs:** Omega Psi Phi Fraternity; Jack & Jill Am; Exec Black Forum; Boy Scouts Am; Black Men Rise; Chrysler MNY Dealers Asn. **Business Addr:** President, Brookdale Dodge Inc, 6800 Brooklyn Blvd, Brooklyn Center, MN 55429, **Business Phone:** (612)560-8000.

WATSON, ROBERT JOSE (BOB WATSON)
Baseball player, vice president (organization), manager. **Personal:** Born Apr 10, 1946, Los Angeles, CA; married Carol, Oct 5, 1968; children: Keith & Kelley. **Educ:** LA Harbor Col; Empire State Col, BS, Bus, Mgt & Econ. **Career:** Baseball player (retired); Vice President; Houston Astros, baseball player, 1966-79, outfielder, gen mgr, 1993; Boston Red Sox, player, 1979; New York Yankees, prof baseball player, 1980-82, gen mgr, 1995-98; Atlanta Braves, 1982-84; Oakland A's, full-time batting coach; Major League Baseball's, vpres, currently. **Orgs:** Bd mem, YMCA & Metro, Houston, 1988-; honorary bd mem, UNCF, Houston, 1989-. **Honors/Awds:** Nat League All Star, 1973-75; Hall of Fame, Houston Astros, 1989. **Special Achievements:** The first ever African Am to serve as a gen mgr in the major leagues, 1993. **Military Serv:** US Marine Corps, sgt, 1966-71. **Business Addr:** Vice President, Major League Baseball, 350 Pk Ave, New York, NY 10022, **Business Phone:** (212)339-7800.

WATSON, SOLOMON B
Lawyer. **Personal:** Born Apr 14, 1944, Salem, NJ; son of Denise A Jones and S Brown Watson Jr; married Brenda J Hendricks, Apr 28, 1984; children: Katitti M & Kira P. **Educ:** Howard Univ, Wash, DC, BA, english, 1966; Harvard Law Sch, Cambridge, Mass, JD, 1971. **Career:** Bingham, Dana & Gould, Boston, Mass, assoc, 1971-74; New York Times Co, New York, atty, 1974-76, asst secy, 1976-79, secy, 1979-89, gen coun, 1989, asst gen coun, 1984, gen coun, 1989-2005, vpres, 1990, sr vpres & chief legal officer, 2006-. **Orgs:** New York & Mass Bars; Am Bar Asn; Asn Bar City NY; Legal Affairs Comm Newspaper Asn Am; 100 Black Men Inc; dir, Am Corp Coun Asn; Nat Bar Asn; adv bd, Agent Orange Settlement Fund; Angler's Club NY. **Honors/Awds:** Nat Equal Justice Award, 2002; Pioneer of the Profession Award, Minority Corp Counsel Assn, 1998; Distinguished Service Award, ACCA, Greater NY Chap, 1999; Nat Equal Justice Award, Nat Asn Advan Colored People, Legal Defense & Educ Fund Inc, 2002. **Special Achievements:** Black Enterprise magazine's list of America's Top Black Lawyers, 2003. **Military Serv:** AUS, First Lt, 1966-68; Two Bronze Stars;Two Army Commendation Medals. **Business Addr:** Senior Vice President, Chief Legal Officer, The New York Times, 229 W 43rd St, New York, NY 10036, **Business Phone:** (212)556-7531.

WATSON, THERESA GRACE LAWHORN. **See WATSON, THERESA LAWHORN.**

WATSON, THERESA LAWHORN (THERESA GRACE LAWHORN WATSON)
Executive, lawyer. **Personal:** Born Jun 15, 1945, Washington, DC; daughter of Julius Carlos and Dorothy Mae; married Jerry B Watson Jr (divorced 1973); children: Carole Johanna. **Educ:** Howard Univ Wash DC, BA, cum laude, 1969; George Wash Univ, National Law Cen DC, JD, 1973; Indiana Univ Grad Sch of Savings & Loan, cert, 1982. **Career:** Office of Gen coun, dept Housing & Urban Develop, atty-adv, 1973-77; Senate Subcom on Housing & Urban Affairs, asst minority coun, 1977-79; Dechert Price & Rhoads, assoc atty, 1979-80; Am Savings & Loan League Inc, exec vpres, 1980-88; pvt pract atty, 1988-. **Orgs:** Am Nat Fed Bar Asn, 1973-; DC Bar, 1973; US Dist Ct, 1974; Women in Housing & Fin; US Supreme Ct, 1976; treas, MA Black Lawyers Asn, 1976-77; exec comt, Black Senate Legis Staffers, 1977-78; treas, Women's Bar Asn DC 1979-80; Bd Appeals & Review DC, 1979-80; chmn, bd dir, DC Housing Fin Agency, 1982-85; bd dir, Women in Housing & Fin 1980; 1986-90; trustee, chmn, 1988-90; DC Retirement bd. **Business Addr:** Attorney, 717 D St NW Suite 210, Washington, DC 20004, **Business Phone:** (202)332-1969.

WATSON, TIMOTHY S
Auditor, entrepreneur. **Educ:** Fla A&M Univ, BS, acct. **Career:** KPMG Peat Marwick LLP, supv sr auditor; Ernst & Young LLP,

supv sr auditor; Wash, Pittman & McKeever, LLC, staff auditor; Deloitte & Touche LLP, staff auditor; Watson Rice LLP, staff auditor; Ameritech Corp, Dept Internal Audit; Aon Corp, Dept Internal Audit; Ill Tool Works Inc, Dept Internal Audit; Benford Brown & Assoc LLC, managing partner, currently. **Orgs:** State Ill, lic CPA; Am Inst Cert Pub Acct; Ill CPA Soc; treas, Chicago chap, Nat Asn Black Accts; instr, Nonprofit Financial Ctr; adv bd, GA Doty Health Educ Fund. **Business Addr:** Managing Partner, Benford Brown & Associates LLC, 8135 S Stony Island Ave, Chicago, IL 60617-1749, **Business Phone:** (773)731-1300 Ext 103.

WATSON, TONY J.
Military leader, president (organization). **Personal:** Born May 18, 1949, Chicago, IL; son of John and Virginia; married Sharon, Jul 21, 1984; children: Erica & Lindsay. **Educ:** US Naval Acad, BS, 1970; Golden Gate Univ, MBA, 1989. **Career:** Potomac Electric Power Co, opers coordr, 1981-83; USS Birmingham, SSN 695, weapons officer, 1983-84; USS Hammerhead, SSN 663, exec officer, 1984-86; USS Jacksonville, SSN 699, comndg officer, 1987-89; US Naval Acad, dept commandant, 1989-93; Submarine Squadron 7, comdr, 1992-93; Ops, Nat Military Command Ctr, dep dir, 1993, rear adm, 1997; Ctr Mil & Pvt Sector Initiatives, chief exec officer, 1997; US Alliance Group, founder & chief exec officer, 2000-; QualxServ Govt Solutions, chief exec officer; Alliance Leadership Group, chief exec officer; TCE Global Energy Corp, chmn & chief exec officer, currently. **Orgs:** US Naval Inst, 1987-; Naval Submarine League, 1993-; past chap pres, Nat Naval Officers Asn; co-chmn, Black Engr Year Alumni Asn, currently; bd dir, Serv Disabled Veteran Enterprises Inc. **Honors/Awds:** Most Outstanding Officer, Navy League US, 1976; Black Engineer of Year, Coun Deans of Eng HBCU's, Govt, 1988; Am Heritage & Freedom Award, 3rd Baptist Church, 1990; Roy Wilkins Leadership Award, NAACP, 1991; Order of Lincoln Award, State of IL, 1994. **Special Achievements:** Nuclear Submarine & Submarine Squadron, 13 subs, comdr, 1987, 1992; Recipient of Rear Admiral Kauffman Sword, as person most likely to become future supt of US Naval Acad; He was the first African-American in the Navy's submarine force history to be promoted to the rank of Rear Admiral.He was the first African-American to achieve the rank of Brigade Commander as a third year midshipman. **Military Serv:** USN, rear admiral, 1970-97; Legion of Merit Medal, 1993; 4 Meritorious Service Medals, 1987-92; 3 Navy Commendation Medals, 1976, 1983, 1985; 1Navy Achievement Medal, 1974. **Business Phone:** (770)240-5303.

WATT, GARLAND WEDDERICK
Judge. **Personal:** Born Feb 10, 1932, Elizabeth City, NC; married Gwendolyn LaNita Canada. **Educ:** Lab Sch, Prep Ed; Elizabeth City St Univ; NC Cent Univ, AB, 1952; (magna cum laude); Harvard Univ, DePaul Univ, JD 1961. **Career:** Circuit Ct Cook Co, judge, 1975-79; gen pract, atty, 1961-75; DePaul Law Rev, assoc ed, 1960-61; Turner, Cousins, Gavin & Watt, partner, 1961: Indecorp, Inc, Sonicraft, Inc, Inner City Industries, Inc, dir & gen couns; Watt W Garland & Assoc LLC, atty, currently. **Orgs:** Bd mem, Independence Bank, Chicago; adv bd, Supreme Life Ins Co Am; Union League Club, Chicago; Econ Club, Chicago; Nat Asn Advan Colored People, Chicago; vice chmn, Legal Redress Com, chmn, 1964-70; bd mem, Joint Negro Appeal; City Club Chicago, 1971-73; Chicago Hearing Soc, 1972-74; comn, Cook County, Chicago, IL State Bar Asn; Am Bar Asn; bd mem, Am Red Cross, 1973; Supreme Ct IL Hearing Bd, Atty Regist & Disciplinary Comn, 1973-75; mem comn, Character & Fitness, Ill Supreme Ct (1st District); Chicago Mortgage Attys Asn; Nat Asn Bond Lawyers & Govt Finance Officers Asn; Nat Asn Securities Prof; bd mem, Mus AFA History Inc; Ada S McKinley Community Serv Inc; S E Chicago Comn; Sigma Pi Phi; Beta Boule; Omega Psi Phi; Alpha Kappa Mu Honor Soc; Prince Hall Masons 33; Union League Club Chicago; Econ Club Chicago; Royal Coterie Snakes; Chicago Assembly. **Honors/Awds:** Richard E Westbrooks Award, Cook County Bar Asn, 1972; Judical Award, Cook County Bar Asn 1975; PUSH Found Award, 1977; Judge of the Year Award, Cook County Bar Asn, 1979. **Home Addr:** 5201 S Cornell Ave 10B, Chicago, IL 60615. **Business Addr:** Attorney, Watt W Garland & Associates LLC, 53 W Jackson Blvd Suite 504, Chicago, IL 60604-3701, **Business Phone:** (312)663-1440.

WATT, MELVIN L
Congressperson (U.S. federal government). **Personal:** Born Aug 26, 1945, Mecklenburg County, NC; married Eulada Paysour Watt; children: Brian & Jason. **Educ:** Univ NC, Chapel Hill, BS, 1967; Yale Univ, JD, 1970. **Career:** Chambers, Stein, Ferguson & Becton, atty, 1971-72; Ferguson, Stein, Watt, Wallas & Atkins Law Firm, atty, partner, 1972-92; NC State Senate, 1985-87; US House Rep, congressman, 1992-. **Orgs:** Life mem, NAACP; Mt Olive Presby Church; Mecklenburg County Bar; chmn, Congressional Black Caucus, 2005-06. **Honors/Awds:** Hon degrees from NC Agr & Tech State Univ, Johnson C Smith Univ, Bennett Col & Fisk Univ. **Special Achievements:** One of the first two African-Americans elected to Congress from North Carolina in the Twentieth Century. **Business Addr:** Congressman, US House Representative, 1230 W Morehead St Suite 306, Charlotte, NC 28208-5214, **Business Phone:** (704)344-9950.

WATTERS, LINDA A
Commissioner. **Personal:** Born Aug 7, 1953, Dayton, OH; daughter of Arthur Davis and Arlessie Cooper Davis; married Ronald Edd, May 25, 1985. **Educ:** Bowling Green State Univ, BA, bus admin, econ, 1975; Univ Dayton, MBA, 1979. **Career:** Gen Motors Corp, Finance Staff, analyst; Comerica Bank, loan analyst, corp banking officer, asst vpres, vpres, 1988-96; Mich Nat Bank, vpres & relationship mgr; Stand Fed, vpres & relationship mgr; Detroit Com Bank, pres & ceo; Conf State Bank Supvrs, Dist 2, bd dirs & chairs, currently; Office Financial & Ins Serv, comnr, 2003-07; KPMG LLP, managing dir ins, currently. **Orgs:** Detroit Chap, Nat Black MBA Asn; volunteer, Bd-MI Opera Theatre; Urban Bankers Forum; Delta Sigma Theta Sorority; bd dir, Detroit Regional Chamber Com; bd dir, Detroit Downtown Develop Authority; bd dir, Metro Growth & Develop Corp; bd dir, United Am Healthcare Corp; exec adv coun & bd visitors, Wayne State Univ, Sch Bus Admin; dir, United Am Healthcare Corp; chair, United Am Healthcare Corp, Finance Comm; dir, Metropolitan Growth & Develop Corp; bd trustees, Hutzel Women Hosp; dir, Detroit Regional Chamber Com, exec comm; Urban Fin Servs Coalition; Nat Black MBA Asn; bd visitors, Wayne State Univ, Sch Bus Admin; dir, Detroit Downtown Develop Authority. **Honors/Awds:** Top 100 Black Bus & Prof Women, Dollars & Sense mag, 1986. **Business Addr:** Managing Director Insurance, KPMG LLP, 303 EWacker Dr, Chicago, IL 60601-5212, **Business Phone:** (312)665-1000.

WATTERS, RICHARD JAMES. See WATTERS, RICKY.

WATTERS, RICKY (RICHARD JAMES WATTERS)
Football player, entrepreneur. **Personal:** Born Apr 7, 1969, Harrisburg, PA. **Educ:** Notre Dame, BA, graphic design. **Career:** Football player (retired), chief exec officer; San Francisco 49ers, running back, 1991-94; Philadelphia Eagles, 1995-97; Seattle Seahawks, 1998-2002; Tigero Entertainment, chief exec officer, currently; Albums: "Any Given Sunday". **Honors/Awds:** Humanitarian of the Year, Am Cancer Soc, 1994; Five Times Pro Bowl Selection, 1992-96; All Pro Selection Thrice, 1994-96; Super Bowl XXIX Champion. **Special Achievements:** Pnly player in NFL history to rush for 1,000 yards with three different franchises; appeared on The Tonight Show with Jay Leno & NFL Blast, which featured many stars in the NFL, LL Cool J's show, "In The House", which appeared on the UPN Network; Author: For Who For What, a Warrior's Journey.

WATTLETON, ALYCE FAYE (FAYE WATTLETON)
Television show host, president (organization), executive. **Personal:** Born Jul 8, 1943, St Louis, MO; daughter of George and Ozie; married Franklin Gordon (divorced). **Educ:** Ohio State Univ, BS, nursing, 1964; Columbia Univ, MS, nursing, midwifery, maternal & infant health, 1967. **Career:** Miami-Dade Hosp, instr; Miami Valley Sch Nursing, Dayton, OH, instr, 1964-66; Dayton Pub Health Nursing Asn, asst dir nursing, 1967-70; Dayton-Miami Valley chap Planned Parenthood, Dayton, OH, exec dir, 1970-78; Planned Parenthood Federation Am Inc, pres, 1978-92; Ctr Advan Women, pres, 1995; Tribune Entertainment, tv show hostess, currently. **Orgs:** Chairperson, Young Presidents Orgn, Metro Chapter; bd dirs, Ecofund, 1992; bd dirs, Nat Comt Responsible Philanthropy; adv coun, Woodrow Wilson Sch Pub & Int Affairs, Princeton Univ; adv comt, The Nature Conservancy; nat adv bd, Inst Prof Excellence; adv coun mem, Young Sisters & Brothers Mag, BET; Women's Forum; Am Pub Health Asn; bd trustees, Calif Wellness Found; bd trustees, Henry J Kaiser Family Found; pres, Ctr Advan Women, currently. **Honors/Awds:** Spirit of Achievement Award, Albert Einstein Col Med, Yeshiva Univ, 1991; GALA 10 Honoree, Birmingham Southern Col, 1991; 20th Anniversary Advocacy Award, Nat Family Planning & Reproductive Health Asn, 1991; Commencement Address, Antioch Univ, 1991; Women of Achievement Award, Women's Projs & Prod, 1991; Claude Pepper Humanities Award, Int Platform Asn, 1990; Pioneer of Civil Rights & Human Rights Award, Nat Conf Black Lawyers, 1990; Florina Lasker Award, NY Civil Liberties Union Found, 1990; Whitney M Young Jr Service Award, Boy Scouts Am, 1990; Ministry of Women Award, Unitarian Universalist Women's Feation, 1990; Margaret Sanger Award, 1992; Jefferson Public Service Award, 1992; Dean's Distinguished Service Award, Columbia Sch Pub Health, 1992; Nat Women's Hall of Fame, 1993 & 1996; Honorary degree: Hon doctorate, St. Pauls Col, 1985; Hon doctorate, Spellman Col, 1986; Hon doctorater, Northeastern Univ Law Sch, 1990; DHL, Long Island Univ, 1990; DHL, Univ Pa, 1990; LLD, N eastern Univ Law Sch, 1990; LHD, Bard Col, 1991; DHum, Oberlin Col, 1991; LLD, Wesleyan Univ, 1991; Hon doctorate, Bard Col, 1991; Hon doctorate, Wesleyan Univ, 1991; Hon doctorate, Oberlin Col, 1991; Hon doctorate, Wesleyan Univ, 1991; Hon doctorate, Univ Chicago, 1992; Hon doctorate, Haverford Col, 1992; Hon doctorate, Hofstra Univ, 1992; Hon doctorate, Simmons Col, 1993; Hon doctorate, Bates Col, 1994; Hon doctorate, Claremont Grad Univ, 2007. **Special Achievements:** First woman to serve as president of the Planned Parenthood Federation of America; first African American woman honored by the Congressional Black Caucus; published memoir, Life on the Line. **Business Phone:** (212)391-7718.

WATTLETON, FAYE. See WATTLETON, ALYCE FAYE.

WATTLEY, THOMAS JEFFERSON
Entrepreneur. **Personal:** Born Aug 28, 1953, Dallas, TX; son of Thomas Jefferson and Johnnie Scott; married Cheryl Elizabeth Brown; children: Marissa, Scott, Elizabeth & Andrew. **Educ:** Amherst Col, BA, 1975; Yale Sch Org & Mgt, MPPM, 1980. **Career:** LTV Corp, corporate planner, 1980-82; Grant Thornton, sr mgt proj dir, 1982-86; Stewart-Wattley Mat Handling Equip Co, pres & chief exec officer, 1987; TJW Enterprises Inc, pres, chief exec officer, 1991-. **Orgs:** Chmn bd dirs, Creative Learning Ctr, 1981-86; bd dir, Dallas Black C C, 1983-; Dallas Assembly 1984-; Mayor's Task Force Housing & Econ Develop Southern Dallas, 1985; mem bd dirs, Child Care Partnership Inc, 1986-; Chief Exec Round Table, 1988; Dallas Planning & Zoning Comn, 1990; bd trustees, Paul Quinn Col, 1991; bd mem, Dallas Citizens Coun, 1991; bd mem, St Paul Med Ctr Found; bd mem, Soc Int Bus Fel. **Honors/Awds:** America's Best & Brightest Young Business Professional, Dollars & Sense Mag, 1986; Quest for Success Award, 1989. **Home Addr:** 1620 Kent St, Dallas, TX 75203. **Business Addr:** Chief Executive Officer, TJW Enterprises Inc, 6060 N Cent Expwy Suite 560, Dallas, TX 75219, **Business Phone:** (214)520-7545.

WATTS, ANDRE
Pianist. **Personal:** Born Jun 20, 1946, Nuremberg, Germany; son of Herman and Maria Alexandra Gusmits. **Educ:** Philadelphia Acad Music, 1963; Peabody Inst, BM, 1972. **Career:** Philadelphia Orchestra Children's Concert, pianist; NY Philharmonic Orchestra, pianist, 1963; Los Angeles Philharmonic, pianist; Philadelphia Orchestra; Chicago Symphony, pianist; Boston Symphony, pianist; Cleveland Orchestra, pianist; London Symphony, pianist, 1966; Lincoln Ctr, pianist, 1976, 1985; United Nations Day performance with Eugene Ormandy & the Philadelphia Orchestra, pianist; BBC presentations London Symphony,pianist; PBS telecasts with Seiji Ozawa & the Boston Symphony in performances of the Liszt A Major & the Saint Saens G minor concertos;Lincoln Ctr New York Philharmonic & Zubin Mehta, pianist, 1987-88; Casals Festival, pianist; recordings, The Chopin Recital, The Schubert Recital;Univ Md, artist in residence, 2000-; Ind Univ, Sch Music, prof, currently. **Orgs:** Classical Action: Performing Arts Against AIDS. **Honors/Awds:** Lincoln Center Medallion, 1974; Gold Medal of Merit Award, Nat Soc Arts & Letters, 1982; Distinguished Alumni Award, Peabody Conserv Johns Hopkins Univ, 1984; Avery Fisher Prize, 1988; honorary doctorates: Yale Univ,Albright Col, Univ PA, Miami Univ OH, Trinity Col, Julliard Sch Music; honrary degree, Brandeis University, 2009. **Special Achievements:** Soloist for US State Dept; toured Soviet Union with San Francisco Symphony, 1973; Copland's "A Lincoln Portrait" at Ford's Theatre, 1975; ten years on series "Great Performers," Lincoln Ctr; performed first full-length piano recital in the history of television, 1976; performed the first full-length recital to be aired nationally in prime time, 1985; First Black concert pianist to achieve international super stardom. **Business Addr:** Professor, Indiana University, School of Music, Merrill Hall 003 1201 E 3rd St, Bloomington, IN 47405-2200, **Business Phone:** (812)855-5105.

WATTS, DR. ANNE WIMBUSH
Educator, school administrator. **Personal:** Born Jan 1, 1943, Grambling, LA; daughter of V E Wimbush and R P Wimbush; married William, Mar 25, 1967 (deceased); children: Michael Kevin & Christopher Nolan. **Educ:** Grambling State Univ, BS, 1962; Univ Wis, MA, 1964; Atlanta Univ, MA, 1966; Georgia State Univ, PhD, 1982. **Career:** Grambling State Univ, instr, 1964-65; Jackson State Univ, instr, 1965-66;Atlanta Univ, instr, 1966-67; Spelman Col, vis prof, 1991; Morehouse Col, class dean, prof, dir, summer acad, 1991-, vice provost, assoc vpres acad affairs, currently. **Orgs:** Consult, Natl Black Polit Action Forum, 1987-89; Natl Cancer Inst Adv Com, chairperson curric comt, 1988-90; intl pub ed, 100 Women Atlanta,1988-; Natl Coun Negro Women, 1990-; intl consult, AKA Sorority Inc, 1991-; Atlanta Job Corps Ctr, adv comt, 1992-. **Honors/Awds:** Hon mem, Phi Beta Kappa Honor Soc, 1992; Hall of Fame, Grambling St Univ, inducted mem, 1991; Golden Key Nat Honor Soc, 1992; NAFEO Disting Alumni Award, GSU, 1990. **Special Achievements:** The Litteratus, founder and editor, 1984-;Articles: Three Voices, 1988; MJ: Modern Job, 1991-. **Home Addr:** 5245 Orange Dr, Atlanta, GA 30331, **Home Phone:** (404)349-4646. **Business Addr:** Associate Vice President, Director, Morehouse College, 830 Westview Dr, Atlanta, GA 30314, **Business Phone:** (404)572-3660.

WATTS, BEVERLY L.
State government official. **Personal:** Born Feb 4, 1948, Nashville, TN; daughter of William E Lindsley and Evelyn L Lindsley; divorced; children: Lauren. **Educ:** Tenn State Univ, BS, sociol, 1969; Southern Ill Univ, MS, 1973. **Career:** Chicago Model Cities Prog, activ coordr, 1972-74; US Dept Health, Educ &Welfare, equal opportunity specialist, 1974-78; US Dept Agr, Civil Rights/EEO, regional dir, 1978-87, 1989-91; Ill Minority Female Bus, execdir, 1987-89; RGMA Inc, sr consult, 1991-92; Ky Commn Human Rights, exec dir, 1992-2004; US Dept Housing & Urban Develop, Nat Fair Housing Training Acad, exec dir, currently. **Orgs:** Nat bd mem, Nat Urban Affairs Coun, 1981-93; bd dirs, former pres,Affirmative Action Asn, 1982-92; IAOHRA, 1993; bd mem, Kentuckian Minority Purchasing Coun, 1993; Ky Coun Postsecondary Educ Equal Opportunity Comt,1993; bd mem, Nat Asn Human Rights Workers; March Dimes Bd; agencies bd,Int Asn Human Rights; Leadership Louisville Bd; pres, Int Asn OfficialHuman Rights Agencies, 2000-; bd dirs, Metro United Way;

bd dirs, KyWomen's Leadership Network; bd dirs, ACLU; leadership adv comt, StennisCtr S Women Pub Serv; bd dirs, 1997-2000, chair, 2001-, Women Execs StateGovt; pres, Int Asn Official Human Rights Agencies, 2001-03; fel WomenExecs State Govt. **Honors/Awds:** OAE Partnership Award, US Dept Agr, 1990; Outstanding Contributor Award, RGMA, 1991; nominee, Bus & Prof Women River City Woman Achievement, 1998;Individual Human Rights Award, Nat Asn Human Rights Workers, 1998; Kentucky Charles W Anderson Laureate Award, 1999; Pacesetter Award, Stennis Ctr S Women Pub Serv; Kentucky Hall of Fame, Kentucky Commission on Human Rights, 2005. **Special Achievements:** Graduate of Leadership Louisville; Leadership Kentucky; Kentucky Women'sLeadership Network; selected to attend as an observer the UN Fourth WorldConference for Women, Beijing, China; second term President of theInternational Association of Official Human Rights Agencies, 1999;recipient of Business and Professional Women River City "Women ofAchievement" Award; accorded an Anderson Laureate; attended UN World ConfAgainst Racism, Racial Discrim, Zenophobia & Related Intolerance, Durban,S Africa, 2001. **Business Addr:** Executive Director, US Department of Housing and Urban Development, National Fair Housing Training Academy, 451 7th St SW, Washington, DC 20410, **Business Phone:** (202)708-1112.

WATTS, DAMON SHANEL
Football player. **Personal:** Born Apr 8, 1972, Indianapolis, IN; married Veronica; children: Alisha. **Educ:** Ind Univ, sports commun. **Career:** Football player (retired); Indianapolis Colts, defensive back, 1994-97.

WATTS, J. C., JR. (JULIUS CAESAR WATTS)
Congressperson (u.s. federal government), football player, executive. **Personal:** Born Nov 18, 1957, Eufaula, OK; son of JC Watts Sr and Helen; married Frankie Jones; children: LaKesha, Jerrell, Jennifer, Julia & JC Watts III. **Educ:** Univ Okla, Norman, OK, BA, Jour, 1981. **Career:** Football player (retired), political contributor, business owner; Canadian Football League, Ottawa, Canada, quarterback, Ottawa Roughriders, 1981-85, Toronto Argonauts, 1986; Watts Energy Corp, Norman, OK, pres, owner, 1987-89, Sunnylane Baptist Church, Del City, OK, youth dir, 1987-94, assoc pastor, 1994-; Okla State Corp comn, comnr, 1990-94; US House Reps, Okla, congressman, 1994-2002; House Repub Leadership, conf chmn, 1998-2004; CNN, Analyst; JC Watts Companies, founder & chmn, currently. **Orgs:** Bd mem, Fel Christian Athletes, OK, 1981-; Nat Drinking Water Adv Coun; OK Special Olympics; JC and Frankie Watts Found; co-founder, Coalition for AIDS Relief in Africa; bd mem, Africare; bd mem, Boy Scouts of Am; bd mem, U.S. Military Academy, West Point; bd mem, Restoring the Am Dream. **Honors/Awds:** Most Valuable Player, Orange Bowl, 1980-81; Most Valuable Player, Grey Cup Game, CFL, 1981; Black Achievement Award, Univ Okla, 1981; Orange Bowl Hall of Honor, 1992. **Special Achievements:** First black Republican elected in a Southern state to a federal office in120 years; co-founder, American Community Renewal and New Markets Act, 2000; author, Community Solutions Act of 2001. **Business Addr:** Chairman, Founder, JC Watts Companies, 600 13th St NW Suite 790, Washington, DC 20005, **Business Phone:** (202)207-2854.

WATTS, JOHN E.
Executive director, clergy. **Personal:** Born Oct 19, 1936, Atlanta, GA; married. **Educ:** AL St Univ, BS, 1958; Intl Theol Ctr, MDiv, 1961; Pepperdine Univ, MA, 1972. **Career:** 3 Chs, pastor, adminr, 1959-69; prog coordr, writer, 1966-68; City Vallejo, asst city mgr com rels, 1968-70; Intergovernmental Mgt, prog mgr, lt gov officer, 1970-73; Model Cities Agency, exec dir officer mayor; Kyles Temple AME Zion Church, pastor, currently. **Orgs:** Omega Psi Phi; NAHRO; Am Soc Urban Planners; life mem, Nat Hum Rights Dir; Intl Human Rights Org. **Honors/Awds:** 1st Black City Administrator City Vallejo; Most Outstanding Young Clergyman, AME Zion Ch. **Business Addr:** Pastor, Kyles Temple AME Zion Church, 101 Temple Way, Vallejo, CA 94591, **Business Phone:** (707)643-4343.

WATTS, JULIUS CAESAR. See WATTS, J. C., JR.

WATTS, LUCILE A
Judge. **Personal:** Born in Alliance, OH; daughter of George Bailey and Doris Bailey; married James. **Educ:** Detroit Col Law, LLB, JD, 1962. **Career:** Judge (retired); Twp Royal Oak, gen coun; House Labor Comn, legal coun; Lucile A Watts PC, pres; City Detroit Common Pleas Ct, judge; Third Judicial Circuit Ct, judge, 1992; FACES Inc, bd dir, legal adv, 2004. **Orgs:** Am Bar Asn; Mich Bar Asn; Detroit Bar Asn; Women Lawyers Mich; Wolverine Bar Asn; pres, Womens Div Nat Bar Asn; pres, Metro Soc Crippled Child & Adults; chmn, bd dir, Focus Hope; YWCA; Detroit Golf Course Prop Own Asn; Delta Sigma Theta; Cath Inter-Racial Coun; Womens Econ Club; life mem, Nat Asn Advan Colored People; pres, Asn Black Judges Mich; reg dir, Nat Asn Women Judges; bd trustees, Cent Mich Univ. **Honors/Awds:** Award for Outstanding Service, Nat Bar Asn. **Special Achievements:** First African American woman in Michigan to be elected to the Circuit Court. **Home Addr:** 1180 W McNichols Rd, Detroit, MI 48203, **Home Phone:** (313)861-0119.

WATTS, MARSHA (MARSHA WATTS VISHER)
Association executive. **Career:** Urban League Greater Cincinnati, exec vpres, sr vpres, Youth, Health & Leadership currently. **Orgs:** Cincinnati USA Regional Chamber; Connect Execs & Bus Leaders; bd mem, Everybody Rides Metro; adv bd mem, ACF Enterprises; Pi Sigma Zeta Chapter, OH. **Business Addr:** Executive Vice President, Urban League Greater Cincinnati, 3458 Reading Rd, Cincinnati, OH 45229-3128, **Business Phone:** (513)281-9955.

WATTS, PATRICIA L
Executive, consultant. **Personal:** Born Apr 26, 1949, Los Angeles, CA; daughter of James C and Marjorie A; children: Marshan L & Mondel E. **Educ:** Univ La Verne; Calif State Univ, Dominguez. **Career:** Southern Calif Edison, clerk trainee, 1974-75, counter cashier, 1975-76, customer serv bookkeeper, 1978-79, supvr's coordr, 1979-80, energy servs rep, 1980-87, area mgr, 1987-93; Community Renewal, proj mgr; FCI Mgt Consults, pres & chief exec officer, 1998-. **Orgs:** Vpres, Am Blacks Energy, 1991-; pres, Soroptimist Inglewood/Hawthorne, 1991-93; bd dir, Black Women Achievement; Inglewood YMCA, 1991-; bd dirs, Inglewood Chamber Com, 1991-; Nat Forum Black Pub Adminrs, 1991-; Black Women's Forum, 1991-93; bd dirs, Hawthorne Chamber Com, 1991-93; bd dir, Community Build; bd dirs, Calif Black Chamber Com. **Honors/Awds:** YWCA Leader Luncheon XIV, Honoree, 1989; Black Women of Achievement Award, 1991; Woman of the Year, Calif State Legislature 50th Assembly Dist; Team Kenyon Award, 1992; Fremont HS Hall of Fame, Inductee, 1992. **Home Addr:** 2032 W 109th St, Los Angeles, CA 90047. **Business Addr:** President, Chief Executive Officer, FCI Management Consultants, 5900 S Eastern Ave Suite 152, Commerce, CA 90040, **Business Phone:** (323)726-9566.

WATTS, DR. ROBERTA OGLETREE
School administrator. **Personal:** Born May 12, 1939, Lawrenceville, GA; daughter of Walter and Jennie; married Roger William Sr; children: Roger Jr & Roderick Dewayne. **Educ:** Tuskegee Inst, BSN, 1961; Emory Univ, MN, 1969; Univ Ala, EdD, 1982. **Career:** Va Hosp, staff nurse, 1961-62; Etowah County Health Dept, staff nurse, 1969; Jacksonville State Univ, asst prof, 1969; Jacksonville State Univ, dean & prof, 1983, dean emer; Excel Inst, headmistress. **Orgs:** Chairperson, Etowah Quality Life Inc, 1978-85, Colley Child Care Ctr Inc, 1970-, Deans Bacc & Higher Degree Prog, 1984, Human Rel Coun; Alpha Kappa Alpha, 1975, Wisteria Club, 1964; Kappa Delta Pi; Gadsden Bd Educ, 1994-99. **Honors/Awds:** Achievement Award, Nat Asn Advan Colored People, 1982; Service Award, Alpha Kappa Alpha, 1983, Am Asn Univ Women, 1982; Etowah Quality Life. **Special Achievements:** First African-American faculty member in Jacksonville State University. **Business Phone:** (256)782-5425.

WATTS, ROLANDA
Television talk show host, actor, chief executive officer. **Personal:** Born Jul 12, 1959, Winston-Salem, NC; daughter of Roland and Velma Gibson. **Educ:** Spelman Col, Atlanta, Ga, BS & BA, 1980; Columbia Univ Grad Sch Jour, New York, MS, jour, 1981; Howard Fine Actg Workshop, Los Angeles, Calif, actg; Aaron Speiser Actg Workshop, Los Angeles, Calif, comedy. **Career:** Talk show host, journalist, actor, writer, producer, chief exec officer; WFMY-TV, Greensboro, NC, gen assignment reporter; NBC weekend anchor; WABC-TV, news anchor & reporter; Lifetime Television, Attitudes, host, 1987-88; Inside Edition, news mag, sr corresp, weekend anchor & producer, 1988; PAX-TV, Lie Detector, host, 2005; Watts Works Productions, ceo & pres, currently; Films: Girl 6, 1996; The Stupids, 1996; Shackles, 2005; PAX-TV, Lie Detector, host; Green Stone Media, radio host, 2006-07; PBS Kids animated program Curious George, voice; TV series: "Life Stories: Families in Crisis", 1992; "Sister, Sister", 1997-98; "Smart Guy", 1998; "The Jamie Foxx Show", 1999; "The Steve Harvey Show", 2000; "The West Wing", 2000; "The Division", 2001;"7th Heaven", 2001; "Days of Our Lives", 2001-08; "The District", 2001;"For Your Love", 2002; "One on One", 2003; Maniac Magee, 2003; "Boston Public", 2003; "The Bold & the Beautiful", 2003; "The Proud Family", 2003; "Yes, Dear", 2004; "Ned's Declassified School Survival Guide", 2004; "My Wife & Kids", 2004; "JAG", 2004; "Complete Savages", 2005; "Temptation", 2007; "Can You Teach My Alligator Manners?", 2008. **Orgs:** Bd dirs, Literacy Vols New York; bd adv, New York Univ Dent Sch; bd adv, Rahway State Prison Lifers Group; spokesperson, UNCF; vol tutor, Hollywood Educ & Literacy Proj. **Honors/Awds:** DHL, Winston-Salem State Univ, Winston-Salem, NC, 1997; "Broadcast Legend", McDonald's Corp, 2008; "Rolonda Day", named in honor, New York. **Business Phone:** (323)465-5100.

WATTS, WILSONYA RICHARDSON. See Obituaries section.

WATTS DAVIS, BEVERLY
Executive, administrator. **Educ:** Trinity Univ, San Antonio, BA; Webster Univ, Jeffersonville, MA. **Career:** San Antonio Fighting Back, exec dir; San Antonio United Way, sr vp; US Dept Health & Human Serv Nat Ctr Advan Prev, consul; Ctr Substance Abuse Prev, Substance Abuse & Mental Health Serv Admin, US Dept Health & Human Serv, dir, 2003-. **Orgs:** Bd Trustees, chair, vice-chair, secy, Austin Reg Community Col; chair, Multi-Cultural Affairs Comt Tex Com Alcohol & Drug Abuse; bd dirs, NOWS Crime Prevention Coalitions Americaschair; Tex Task Force local drug control. **Honors/Awds:** Governor of Texas' Volunteer Award; FBI Director's Award for Community Leadership; Commander's Award for Outstanding Leadership, Dept Defense; Gould Wysinger Award, US Dept Justice; US Volunteer of the Year Award, 1997; San Antonio Women's Hall of Fame, 1998; Faith-based & Community Leadership Award, SAMHSA, 2001; Pecemaker Award, San Antonio Bar Found, 2002. **Business Addr:** Director, Center for Substance Abuse Prevention (CSAP), Substance Abuse & Mental Health Services Admin, 1 Choke Cherry Rd Rm 4-1056, Rockville, MD 20857, **Business Phone:** (240)276-2420.

WAUGH, JUDITH RITCHIE
Broadcaster. **Personal:** Born Jun 5, 1939, Indianapolis, IN. **Educ:** Ind Univ, BA, 1961, MA, 1969. **Career:** Indianapolis Pub Schs, teacher eng & humanities, 1961-73; McGraw Hill Broadcasting WRTV 6, dir human resources, pub affairs dir. **Orgs:** Nat Asn Advan Colored People; pres, Indianapolis Chap Links, 1989-91; Cathedral Arts; Crossroads Rehab Ctr; Dance Kaleidoscope; Walker Theatre Ctr. **Honors/Awds:** John Hay Fellowship, Northwestern Univ, 1964-65; NDEA Grant, Purdue Univ, 1966. **Home Addr:** 3965 N Meridian St, Indianapolis, IN 46208, **Home Phone:** (317)924-3022.

WAULS, INEZ LA MAR
Commissioner. **Personal:** Born Feb 11, 1924, Williamson, WV; divorced; children: Agatha Kenner, Rita, Luther J Jr & Ronald. **Educ:** Howard Univ, Wash, DC, BA, 1951. **Career:** Foster Care Serv LA City, Dept Soc Svc, soc work consult, 1955-; Allpha Kappa Alpha Sor Theta Alpha Omega Chapt, gramma, 1976-; Howard Univ Alumni Assoc, west reg rep; LA Cty Symphony League, pres, 1977-79; Bel Vue UN Presbyterian Church, presiding elder, 1977-80, 1980-81; Nat Comn Women, nat dir, 1978-80; Compton Comm on the Stat of Women, comnr. **Orgs:** Minority womens task force Calif, State Comm Stat of Women 1984-; re-elected to far west reg rep, Howard Univ, 1984-86. **Honors/Awds:** Consistent Serv Award, Howard Univ Alumni Asn S Calif, 1962; Jill of the Year, Jack & Jill of American Inc, S La, 1976; Sor of the Year, 1979; Exemplary Citizenship, 20 yrs of Civic & Cult Serv Mayor & City Coun, Compton, CA, 1979.

WAY, CHARLES CHRISTOPHER
Football player, executive director. **Personal:** Born Dec 27, 1972, Philadelphia, PA; son of Cleveland Way and Jacqueline Way; married Tahesha; children: 3. **Educ:** Univ Va. **Career:** Football player (retired); New York Giants, fullback, 1995-99, dir player develop, currently. **Business Addr:** Director of Player Development, New York Giants, Giants Stadium, East Rutherford, NJ 07073, **Business Phone:** (201)935-8111.

WAY, DR. CURTIS J.
Publishing executive, chief executive officer. **Personal:** Born Jun 19, 1935, Columbia, SC. **Educ:** Benedict Col, BA, 1962; NU Univ, MPA 1970; Fordham Univ, New Sch Soc Res, Grad Stud; Nova Univ, DPA, 1977. **Career:** Philadelphia County Juvenile County, prob off; Newark Title Proj dir, training & job develop; Newark City Neighborhood Youth Corps, dep dir, summer exec dir, 1965-67; Nat Asn Advan Colored People & Multi-Purpose Ctr, dir, chmn bd; Newark Inst Urban Prog, ceo; Sickle Cell Anemia Assoc, ceo, currently; Spoon Book Publ, ceo, currently. **Orgs:** Consult, Nat Alliance Bus; dir, City of Passaic NJ; proj housing consult, Neighborhood Youth Corp, 1967-69; planner & prog develop, Early Childhood Ed; planner & prog develop, NJUP Theater Arts Newark NJ, Sickle Cell Anemia Proj; fund raiser & alumni org Am Inst Planners; Am Soc Planning Official; Am Soc Publ Admin, Am Acad Pol & Soc Sci; past trustee Benedict Col; past mem Reg Health Planning Coun, Newark Urban Coalition, Minority Econ Devel Corp; past pres, NJ Chap Benedict Alumni; life mem, Nat Asn Advan Colored People; founder, Hillcreek Commun Ctr Philadelphia, NAACP Multi-Purpose Ctr & Cult Ctr; panelist Am Arbitration Assoc; 32Degree Mason. **Honors/Awds:** Outstanding Service Award, Benedict Col, 1970; Outstanding Service Award, Dept HUD 1971; Excellent Citation Service Award, L Miller Civic Assoc, 1972; Better Comm Newark Br NAACP, 1973; Outstanding Comm Service Newark, 1973,79; Outstanding Leadership Award, NAACP MPC, 1974. **Military Serv:** AUS, sgt, 1953-57; Appreciation Award USN, 1971; Outstanding Service Award USN Recruiting, 1972. **Business Addr:** Chief Executive Officer, Spoon Book Publishing, 870 Langford Rd, Blythewood, SC 29016, **Business Phone:** (803)691-0146.

WAY, GARY DARRYL
Lawyer. **Personal:** Born Feb 25, 1958, Newark, NJ; son of Robert and Pearl Rosser Childs; married Jill Green, Nov 28, 1987. **Educ:** Rutgers Col, New Brunswick, BA, 1980; NY Univ Sch Law, NY City, JD, 1983. **Career:** Haight, Gardner, Poor & Havens, New York City, assoc, 1983-86; Nat Basketball Asn, New York City, staff atty, 1986-88; NBA Properties Inc, New York City, asst gen coun, 1988; Nike Inc, sr asst coun, sr sports mkt coun, managing partner & head, currently. **Orgs:** Org State Bar Asn. **Special Achievements:** Author of "Japanese Employers and Title VII," 1983. **Military Serv:** AUS, capt, 1980-; Distinguished Military Grad, Rutgers Army ROTC, 1980; Army Achievement Award with

Oak Leaf Cluster. **Business Addr:** Managing Attorney & Head, Senior sports marketing counsel, NIKE Inc, Sports Law Practice Group, Rm DF-4 1 Bowerman Dr, Beaverton, OR 97005-6453, **Business Phone:** (503)671-2583.

WAYANS, DAMON
Comedian, screenwriter, actor. **Personal:** Born Sep 4, 1960, New York, NY; son of Howell and Elvira; married Lisa Thorner, Apr 24, 1984; children: Damon Jr, Michael, Cara Mia & Kyla. **Career:** Actor, currently; Films: Beverly Hills Cop, 1984; Hollywood Shuffle, 1987; Roxanne, 1987; Colors, 1988; I'm Gonna Git You Sucka, 1988; Punchline, 1988; Earth Girls Are Easy, 1989; Look Who's Talking Too (voichief exec officerver); The Last Boy Scout, 1991; Mo' Money, 1992; Blankman, 1994; Major Payne, 1995; Celtic Pride, 1996; The Great White Hype, 1996; Bulletproof, 1996; Harlem Aria, 1999; Goosed, 1999; Bamboozled, 2000; Marci X, 2003; Behind the Smile, writer, actor, producer, dir, 2004; Farce of the Penguins, 2006; TV: "In Living Color", writer, actor, 1990-92; "413 Hope Street", creator, producer, 1997; "Pilot", 2001; "My Wife & Kids", writer, actor, producer, 2001-05; "Failure to Communicate', 2002; "Calvin Goes to Work", 2004; "The Underground", writer, actor, producer, dir, 2006. **Honors/Awds:** BET Comedy Award, Outstanding Lead Actor in a Comedy Series, for My Wife & Kids, 2004; People's Choice Award, Favorite Male Performer In a New TV Series, for My Wife & Kids, 2002. **Special Achievements:** Nominated for awards like Emmy Awards, 1990 1991 1992, MTV Movie Awards, 1992, Image Awards, 2002, 2003, 2004, 2005, Golden Satellite Awards, 2003, 2005, BET Comedy Award, 2005. **Business Addr:** Actor, Comedian, Wife N Kids Productions, c/o Columbia Pictures Entertainment Inc, 10202 Wash Blvd, Culver City, CA 90232-3195, **Business Phone:** (310)280-8000.

WAYANS, KEENEN IVORY
Actor, comedian, talk show host. **Personal:** Born Aug 6, 1958, New York, NY; son of Howell and Elvira; married Daphne, Jan 1, 2001 (divorced 2004); children: Jolie, Nala, Keenen Jr, Bella & Daphne Ivory. **Educ:** Tuskegee Univ, Alabama. **Career:** Actor, currently; Films: Star 80, 1983; I'm Gonna Git You Sucka, 1989; ALow Down Dirty Shame, 1994; The Glimmer Man, dir, 1996, Most Wanted, 1997;The Keenen Ivory Wayans Show, producer, 1997; Scary Movie, dir, 2000; My Wife & Kids, 2001; Scary Movie, writer, 2000; Scary Movie 2, dir, 2001; White Chicks, dir, 2004; Little Man, dir, 2006; Thugaboo: A Miracle on D-Roc's Street, writer, 2006; The Life & Times of Marcus Felony Brown, producer & writer, 2008; TV: "CHiPs", 1977; "Cheers", 1982; "For Love &Honor", 1983; "In Living Color", exec producer & head writer & actor, until 1993; "The Keenan Ivory Wayans Show", talk show host; "My Wife & Kids", 2001; Dance Flick, 2009. **Orgs:** Alpha Phi Alpha Fraternity Inc. **Honors/Awds:** Emmy Awards, 1990; PGA Awards, 1992; BET Comedy Awards, 2004. **Special Achievements:** Nominated for Emmy Awards, 1992, Emmy Awards, 1990 & 91, Razzie Awards, 2005 & 2007. **Business Phone:** (818)560-1000.

WAYANS, MARLON (MARLON L WAYANS)
Actor. **Personal:** Born Jul 23, 1972, New York City, NY; son of Howell and Elvira; married Angelica Zackary; children: Shawn Howell & Arnai Zackary. **Educ:** Howard Univ, Sch Performing Arts, NY, grad. **Career:** Films: I'm Gonna Git You Sucka, 1988; Mo' Money, 1992; Above the Rim, 1994; Don't Be a Menace to South Central While Drinking Your Juice in the Hood, 1996; The Sixth Man, 1997; Senseless, 1998; Requiem for a Dream, 2000; Scary Movie, 2000; Dungeons & Dragons 2000; The Tangerine Bea, 2000; Scary Movie 2, 2001; The Lady killers, 2004; Behind the Smile, 2004; White Chicks, 2004; Little Man, 2006; Norbit, 2007; Dance Flick, 2009; G.I. Joe: The Rise of Cobra, 2009; TV series: "In Living Color", 1990; The Best of Robert Townsend & His Partners in Crime, 1991; "In Living Color", 1992-93; "The Wayans Bros", 1995-99; "Wayne head", 1996-97; "Happily Ever After: Fairy Tales for Every Child", 1999; "Dream girl", 1999; "Summer Music Mania", 2001; "Six Degrees", 2006; "Thugaboo: Sneaker Madness", 2006; Thugaboo: A Miracle on D-Roc's Street, 2006. **Honors/Awds:** BET Comedy Award, 2004. **Business Addr:** Actor, c/o United Talent Agency, 9560 Wilshire Blvd Suite 500, Beverly Hills, CA 90212-2401, **Business Phone:** (310)273-6700.*

WAYANS, MARLON L. See WAYANS, MARLON.

WAYANS, SHAWN
Actor, movie producer, movie director. **Personal:** Born Jan 19, 1971, New York City, NY; son of Howell and Elvira; married Ursula; children: Laila, Illia & Marlon. **Career:** Actor, producer, director & writer; Films: I'm Gonna Git You Sucka, 1988; Don't Be a Menace to South Central While Drinking Your Juice in the Hood, co-exec producer, actor & writer, 1996; New Blood, 1999; Scary Movie, producer, actor & writer, 2000; Open Mic, 2000; Scary Movie 2, co-exec producer & actor, 2001; Scary Movie 3, writer, 2003; White Chicks, producer, actor, screenplay & stoty, 2004; Little Man, writer & producer, 2006; Scary Movie 4, writer, 2006; Dance Flick, 2009; TV series: "In Living Color", 1990-94; The Best of Robert Townsend & His Partners in Crime?, 1991; "MacGyver", 1991; "Hangin' with Mr. Cooper", 1993; "The Wayans Bros", 1995-99; "Waynehead", 1996-97; "Happily Ever After: Fairy Tales for Every Child", 1999; Thugaboo: Sneaker Madness, dir, exec producer & writer, 2006; Thugaboo: A Miracle on D-Roc's Street, dir, exec producer & writer, 2006; The Life & Times of Marcus Felony Brown, exec producer & writer, 2008. **Honors/Awds:** Won BET Comedy Award, 2004; Won Razzie Award, 2007; Nominated for Blockbuster Entertainment Award, 2001. **Business Addr:** Actor, c/o Montgomery Glick & Co, 5951 Variel Ave, Woodland Hills, CA 91367, **Business Phone:** (818)999-6967.*

WAYNE, GEORGE HOWARD, SR.
School administrator. **Personal:** Born Mar 10, 1938, Meridian, MS; son of Jerry; married Juanita R Robinson; children: Lisa Monet, George Howard Jr & Kimberly Ann. **Educ:** Univ Nebr, MA, 1967; Univ Colo, MPA, 1971; Univ Denver, MA, EdD, 1979. **Career:** Asst prof hist 1972-76, intelligence officer, 1967-71; Univ Colo, asst prof 1974; USAF Acad; Colo Dept Educ; Calif St Univ, vpres stud affairs, fac emer, currently. **Orgs:** Pres, Kappa Alpha Psi Fratenity, 1978, bd dirs, 1980; pres, Aspen Educ Consulting; Phi Alpha Theta; NAACP; Am Soc Pub Admin. **Honors/Awds:** Race Relations a time phase III Air Univ Rev, 1972; Industrial Use Disadvantaged Am, Air Univ Rev 1974; Black Migration Colo Journal of the Week, 1976; Black Alcoholism: Myth vs Res, 1978. Outstanding Kappa AlphaPsi Frat, 1979. **Military Serv:** USAF; Bronze Star, Meritorious Service Medal, Commendation Medal. **Home Phone:** (303)215-1266. **Business Addr:** Faculty Emertius, California State University, 6000 J St, Sacramento, CA 95819, **Business Phone:** (916)278-6060.

WAYNE, NATE (NATHANIEL WAYNE, JR.)
Football player. **Personal:** Born Jan 12, 1975, Chicago, IL; married Tamiko; children: Nata, Tamia & Nalen. **Educ:** Univ Miss, BS, criminal justice. **Career:** Football player (retired); Denver Broncos, linebacker, 1998-99; Barcelona Dragons, 1999; Green Bay Packers, 2000-02; Philadelphia Eagles, 2003-04; Detroit Lions, 2005. **Honors/Awds:** Defensive Most Valuable Player Award, Rebel Club of Jackson, 1996; Super Bowl champion XXXIII.

WAYNE, NATHANIEL, JR. See WAYNE, NATE.

WAYNER, RICHARD
Chief executive officer. **Career:** TRACE TV, Alliance TRACE Media, chmn, chief exec officer, currently. **Business Phone:** (212)902-1000.

WAYNEWOOD, DR. FREEMAN LEE
Dentist. **Personal:** Born Jun 30, 1942, Anson, TX; married Beverly; children: Tertia & Dorian. **Educ:** Univ Tex, attended; Univ Wash, BAED, 1970, DDS, 1974. **Career:** Real Estate, salesman, 1968-71; Weyhauser, 1970-71; Richardson's Assoc, constr res, 1971-73; Pvt pract, dentist; FL Waynewood & Associates, PA, pres, currently. **Orgs:** Am Dent Asn; Minn Dent Asn; St Paul Dist Dent Soc; Am Soc Prev Dent; Am Soc Dent C; staff mem, United Hosp St Paul; bd mem, Model Cities Hallie Q Brown Comm Ctr; Alpha Phi Alpha; Flight Unlimited; bd mem, Webster Sch; St Paul Opera Workshop. **Military Serv:** USN, comdr, Vietnam Campaign Ribbon Nat Def, 1964-68. **Home Addr:** 1148 Grand Ave, St Paul, MN 55105, **Home Phone:** (651)224-0001. **Business Addr:** President, Waynewood & Associates PA, 393 Dunlap St N Suite 310, St Paul, MN 55103, **Business Phone:** (651)647-9697.

WEAD, DR. RODNEY SAM
Administrator. **Personal:** Born Jun 28, 1935, Omaha, NE; son of Sampson Lester and Daisy Shanks; divorced; children: Denise Michelle Wead Rawles, Owen Eugene, Ann Lineve Wead Kimbrough & Melissa Cheryl Wead Rivas (divorced). **Educ:** Dana Col, Blair, NE, BS, educ, 1957; Roosevelt Univ, Chicago, IL, MA, urban studies, 1976; The Union Inst, Cincinnati, OH, PhD, sociol, 1981. **Career:** Creighton Univ, prof, 1986-; United Methodist Community Centers Inc, Omaha, NE, exec dir, 1983-; Community Renewal Soc, Chicago, IL, assoc exec dir, 1973-83; Grace Hill Settlement House, Inc, pres & chief exec officer (retired), dir, currently. **Orgs:** Kappa Alpha Psi Fraternity Inc, 1955-; Clair United Methodist Church, Omaha, NE, 1955-; life mem, NAACP, 1967-; mem, Nat Asn Black Social Workers, 1981-; comnrn Metrop Area Transit, Omahan NE, 1985-; bd dirs, N Side Villa, Omaha NE, 1986-; adv comt, Old N Neighborhood Partnership, Univ Miss Lincoln Univ. **Honors/Awds:** Econ Democracy Low Income Neighborhoods, res publ, 1982; Outstanding Volunteer, Urban League Nebraska-Omaha, 1987; Dr Rodney S Wead Scholar, Dana Coll, Blair NE, 1989; The African-Am Family in Nebraska, res publ, 1989. **Business Addr:** Director, Grace Hill Settlement House, 2600 Hadley, Saint Louis, MT 63106, **Business Phone:** (314)539-9500.

WEARING, MELVIN H
Law enforcement officer. **Educ:** Univ New Haven, AS, 1981, BS, 1984. **Career:** Police (retired); New Haven Police Dept, police officer, 1968-73, detective, 1973-84, sergeant, 1984-88, lt, 1988-91, chief detectives, 1991-93, asst chief police, 1993-97, chief police, 1997-2003. **Orgs:** Nat Orgn Black Law Enforcement Execs; Police Exec Res Forum; New Haven City Silver Shields; New Haven City Detectives Asn; Conn State Police Asn; Nat Asn Advan Colored People; bd dirs, Child Develop Inst Conn Inc; Int Asn Chiefs Police. **Honors/Awds:** Youth Service Award, New Haven Bd Young Adult Police Comnrs; Outstanding Public Service Achievement Award, New Haven City Silver Shields; Special Recognition Freedom Award, Nat Asn Advan Colored People, 1994; Citizen of the Year, Omega Psi Phi, 1995; Man of the Year, Nat Asn Negro Bus & Prof Women's Clubs Inc, New Haven Chap, 1996; Community Leadership Award, FBI Dirs, 1999; Community Policing Award, IACP, 1999. **Special Achievements:** First African Am in New Haven police dept to hold following positions: chief of detectives, asst chief of police, chief of police; co-author: The Police-Mental Health Partnership: A Community-Based Response to Urban Violence, Yale Univ Press, 1995.

WEARY, REV. DOLPHUS
Clergy. **Personal:** Born Aug 7, 1946, Sandy Hook, MS; son of Albert Weary and Lucille Granderson; married Rosie Marie Camper, Aug 15, 1970; children: Danita R, Reginald & Ryan D. **Educ:** Piney Woods Jr Col, AA, 1967; Los Angeles Baptist Col, BA, 1969; Los Angeles Baptist Theol Sem, M Rel Ed, 1971; Univ So Miss, MEd, 1978. **Career:** Voice Calvary Ministries, dir summer leadership, 1968-71, dir, 1971-75; Los Angeles Baptist Col, coach freshmen team, 1969-71; Piney Woods Sch, coorde christian educ, 1975-84; Mendenhall Ministries Inc, pres, 1986. **Orgs:** Pres, Mission Miss, 1998-; bd dir, Voice Calvary Health Ctr; So Cent MS Rural Health Asn; Koinonia Farms Americus GA; Voice Hope Dallas TX; Nat Alumni Asn, Piney Woods Sch; Mendenhall Ministries bd; Nat Black Evangelical Assoc bd; nat bd, Faith Work; bd dir, mem, Miss Religious Leadership Conf, MRLC; bd dir, mem, Miss Children's Home Soc; Mendenhall Chamber Com; Nat Black Evangelical Asn; Nat Asn Evangelicals; Evangelical Coun Fin Accountability; Belhaven Col. **Honors/Awds:** Alumnus of the Year, Los Angeles Baptist Col, 1979; Mississippi Religious Leadership Award, 1985; Humanitarian Award, Central Mississippi Legal Serv, 1985; Outstanding Citizen of the Year, Civic Circle Club Simpson County. **Special Achievements:** In 1967, Dolphus Weary became the first African-American to earn a scholarship to Los Angeles Baptist College; author, I Ain't Comin' Back, 1990; While President of Mendenhall Ministries, this organization was honored by former President George Bush in receiving the 541st Daily Point of Light Award; Renowned speaker for many organizations, including teams in the National Football League. **Business Addr:** President, Mission Mississippi, PO Box 22655, Jackson, MS 39225-2655, **Business Phone:** (601)353-6477.

WEATHER, DR. LEONARD, JR.
Surgeon, gynecologist. **Personal:** Born Jul 6, 1944, Albany, GA; son of Leonard and Lucille; married Bettye Jean Roberts, Apr 13, 1970; children: Marcus & Kirstin. **Educ:** Howard Univ, Col Pharm, BS, 1967; Rush Medical Col, MD, 1974. **Career:** Johns Hopkins Univ, intern, resident, 1978; Tulane Univ, instructor 1978-86; Xavier Univ, assoc prof, 1984-; Omni Fertility Inst, dir 1985; pvt pract, currently. **Orgs:** Dir & vpres Bayou Federal Svgs & Loan, 1983-; dir, YMCA, 1984-; host radio talk show Doctor's Corner, WYLD AM 940, 1985-; mem, Omega Psi Phi Frat, 1985; pres, Black Leadership Awareness Coun, 1985; nat pres, Chi Delta Mu Medical Frat, 1986; bd trustees, economic develop chair, Nat Med Assoc, 2003-. **Honors/Awds:** Book "Why We Can't Have a Baby," 1985; article "Carbon Dioxide Laser Myomectomy" Journal Natl Medical Assoc, 1986; "CO2 Laser Laproscopy-Treatment of Disorders of Pelvic Pain & Infertility" 1986. **Military Serv:** AUS. **Home Addr:** 6831 Lake Willow Dr, New Orleans, LA 70126, **Home Phone:** (504)242-1317. **Business Addr:** Physician, Private Prctice, 2120 Bert Kouns Loop, Shreveport, LA 71118, **Business Phone:** (318)671-5320.

WEATHERS, ANDRE
Football player, football coach. **Personal:** Born Aug 6, 1976, Flint, MI. **Educ:** Univ Mich. **Career:** Football player (retired), Football coach; New York Giants, defensive back, 1999-2000; Univ Michi, head coach defensive coordr, 2007; Genesee County Patriots, head coach; coach, Flint Central High Sch, currently. **Honors/Awds:** All Big Ten as a Corner.

WEATHERS, CARL
Actor. **Personal:** Born Jan 14, 1948, New Orleans, LA; married Mary Ann Castle, Feb 17, 1973 (divorced); children: Matthew & Jason; married Rhona Unsell, Feb 20, 1984 (divorced); married Jennifer Peterson, Apr 14, 2007. **Educ:** San Diego State, theater arts. **Career:** Oakland Raiders, professional football player(retired); B.C. Lions Canadian Football League, 1971 to 1973; stage appearance: Nevis Mountain Dew, 1981; tv appearances: "The Hostage Heart", 1977; "The Bermuda Depths", 1978; "Braker", 1985; "Fortune Dane", 1986; "The Defiant Ones", 1986; "Fortune Dane", 1986; "Tour of Duty", 1987; "In the Heat of the Night", 1988; "Dangerous Passion", 1990; "Street Justice", 1991; "OP Center", 1995; "Assault on Devil's Island", 1997; "Shadow Warriors II:Hunt for the Death Merchant", 1999; "Sheena", dir, 2000; "The Shield", 2002-; "For the People", dir, 2002; "Partners", 2003; "Arrested Development", 2004; "Allien Blood", 2005; "Spawn: The Animation", 2006; films: Friday Foster, 1975; Bucktown, 1975; Rocky, 1976; Close Encounters of the Third Kind, 1977; Semi-Tough, 1977; Force 10 from Navarone, 1978; Rocky

II, 1979; Death Hunt, 1981; Rocky III, 1982; Rocky IV, 1985; Predator, 1987; Action Jackson, 1988; Hurricane Smith, 1992; Happy Gilmore, 1996; Little Nicky, 2000; Eight Crazy Nights, voice, 2002; Balto III: Wings of Change, voice, 2004; Mercenaries, voice, 2005; The Sasquatch Dumpling Gang, 2006; "The Comebacks", 2007; "Spawn:The Animation", 2007; "Phoo Action", 2008; "ER", 2008; "Brothers", 2009; Stormy Weathers Prods, founder. **Honors/Awds:** Football Hall-of-Fame coach, Don "Air" Coryell. **Business Phone:** (818)906-0322.

WEATHERS, DIANE
Executive. **Career:** Black Enterprise Mag; Newsweek Mag; Consumer Reports Mag; Redbook mag, sr ed, news features; ESSENCE mag, ed-in-chief, 2001-05. **Orgs:** Nat Pub Radio. *

WEATHERS, J. LEROY
Clergy, army officer. **Personal:** Born May 21, 1936, Georgetown County, SC; married. **Educ:** Allen Univ, AB, 1964; Dickerson Theol Sem, SC, BD, 1965; Urban Training Ctr for Christian Mission, Chicago, IL, attended 1970; Univ Miami Drug Ed, 1973; Air Force Chaplain Sch, 1974. **Career:** Young Chapel AME Church Irmo SC, pastor, 1960; Mt Olive AME Church Myrtle Beach SC, pastor, 1961-; Myrtle Beach AFB SC, civilian aux chaplain, 1975. **Orgs:** Del Gen Conf AME Church, 1968; civilian adv, Religious Adv Comt Myrtle AFB SC, 1969; pres, Myrtle Beach Ministerial Asn, 1973-74, secy, 1975-76; Mil Chaplains Asn; SC Comn on Pastoral Care Alcohol & Drug Abuse, 1975-76; Masonic Lodge 423; life mem Nat Asn Advan Colored People; fed, pres , Myrtle Beach Nat Asn Advan Colored People; chmn, Mayor's Bi-racial Comn, 1964; Horry-Georgetown Ec Opport Bd, 1965-; trustee, Allen Univ; asst treas, SC Nat Asn Advan Colored People, 1969-73; Myrtle Beach C of C, 1970; vchmn, Dem Party Myrtle Beach, 1970-72; chaplain, Myrtle Beach Jaycees, 1970-74, dir, 1971-72; Horry Co Ambulance Serv Comn; Fed Prog Adv Coun, Horry Co Dept of Ed 1971; secy, Kiwanis Club of Myrtle Beach, 1971; numerous others com. **Honors/Awds:** Recipient Outstanding Leadership Award, Mt Olive AME Ch, 1967; cert of Merit SC, Nat Asn Advan Colored People, 1967; cert of Appreciation, Ec Opport Comn Act, 1971; Spkr-of-the-Month Award, US Jaycees, 1971-72; Jaycee-of-the-Month, Myrtle Beach Jaycees, 1972; Key Man Award, Myrtle Beach Jaycees, 1972; Kiwanian-of-theYr, 1972; Outstanding Young Man Award, Jaycees, 1972; Outstanding Young Man With Distinguished Serv Award, SC Jaycees, 1972; educ bldg at Mt Olive AME Ch named the JL Weathers Religious Ed Bldg, 1973; Hm Coming Award, Singleton AME Ch SC, 1973; Cit of Yr, Beta Tau Chap of Omega Psi Phi Frat; Distinguished Unit Pres & Unit Citation; AF Outstanding Unit Award. **Military Serv:** AUS, 1953-55, Army Good Conduct Medal, Nat Def Serv Medal.

WEATHERS, MARGARET A.
Association executive. **Personal:** Born Feb 9, 1922, Forest City, AR; daughter of Lillie Allman and Oscar Allman; married Ernest A Weathers; children: Margaret Kathryn. **Educ:** Lincoln Univ; Western Reserve Univ; MS, Indust Col; Tulane Univ, Cert Inner City Training Prog, 1971; Capital Univ, BA. **Career:** Association executive (retired); MO, teacher, 1940-50; GM Chevrolet Plant Cleveland, worker, 1951-55; Child Welfare Dept Cleveland, operated nursery, 1955-60; Head Start Comt Act Youth & Coun Churches, teacher, 1964-66; Cleveland Div Rec, 1966-70; Weathers Unique Cleaners, co-mgr; EA Weathers Realty; Weathers Travel Agency; Mags Kustard, co-owner; Multi-Serv Center, past pres corp bd; Lk Erie Girl Scout Coun, field dir, 1985, mem specialist, 1993. **Orgs:** Past mem, Health Planning & Develop Comn, Welfare Fed; past bd mem, Hough Area Develop Corp & Coun; pres, Church Women United Greater Cleveland, 1996-98. **Honors/Awds:** Plaques Hough Multi-Serv Ctr Bd, 1973; Parkwood CME Church, 1973; Cert Merit, Hough Comn Coun, 1973; plaque One Who Served with Dedication, The Hough Multi-Serv Ctr Bd Trustees; Cong Achievement Award; City Cleveland Congratulatory Award, 1977; Denominational Rep Church Women United for the CME Church; assoc dir scouting Ministries, Girl Scouts USA, CME Church. **Home Addr:** 1610 Ansel Rd, Cleveland, OH 44106, **Home Phone:** (216)795-7526. *

WEATHERSBEE, TONYAA JEANINE
Writer. **Personal:** Born Jun 7, 1959, Jacksonville, FL; daughter of William and Wallace. **Educ:** Univ Fla, BS, jour, 1981. **Career:** Pensacola News Jour, reporter, 1981-85; Fla Times-Union, reporter, 1985-92, copy ed, 1992, reporter, 1993, interim Ga ed, 1994, zone ed, 1994-95, columnist, 1996-. **Orgs:** Jacksonville Asn Black Communicators, 1986-95; Nat Asn Black Journalists, 1986-; Nat Trust Hist Preserv, 1994-99; bd mem, Bridge Northeast Fla, 1996-2001; Leadership Jacksonville, 1994-95; First Coast Black Communicators Alliance, 1995-2001; William Monroe Trotter Group, 1997-; Jacksonville Asn Black Journalists, 2002-; Nat Press Club, 2003-; Soc Prof Journalists, 2003-; Investigative Reporters & Eds, 2002-; Univ Fla Alumni Asn, 2003-. **Honors/Awds:** Third Place for Columns, Fla Soc Newspaper Ed, 1999; First Place, Opinion Writing, Fla Press Club, 2000; Honorable Mention for Columns, Fla Soc Newspaper Ed, 2000; First Place Commentary Salute to Excellence, NABJ, 2000; Third Place, Commentary, S Fla Chap Soc Prof Journalists Sunshine State Awards, 2002; Second Place, Commentary, Fla Press Club, 2002; Sunshine State Awards, Honorable Mention, Commentary, 2003. **Special Achievements:** Scriptwriter for Mayo Clinic Video Alzheimer's Disease: What Every African-American Needs to Know, 1998, managing editor and writer on Home Away from Home: Africans in the Americas, commentaries have also been published in the Houston Chronicle, Baltimore Sun and Kansas City Star. **Business Addr:** Columnist, The Florida Times-Union, 1 Riverside Ave, Jacksonville, FL 32206, **Business Phone:** (904)359-4251.

WEATHERSBY, JOSEPH BREWSTER
Clergy. **Personal:** Born Nov 23, 1929, Cincinnati, OH; son of Albert and Gertrude; married Louberta, Oct 28, 1950 (divorced). **Educ:** Berkeley, Divine Sch, STM, 1960; Salmon P Chase Col, BBA. **Career:** St Mary Episcopal Church, rector, 1960-68; Saginaw Urban Ministry, ombudsman, 1969-72; St Clement Episcopal Church, rector, 1972-74; Saginaw Off, Civil Rights Dept, exec, 1975-83; Mental Health Dept, civil rights exec, 1986-. **Orgs:** Alpha Phi Alpha Fraternity, 1979-. **Military Serv:** UMCR, Corp. **Home Phone:** (313)699-9094.

WEATHERSPOON, CLARENCE
Basketball player. **Personal:** Born Sep 8, 1970, Crawford, MS; married Hazel. **Educ:** Univ Southern Miss. **Career:** Philadelphia 76ers, forward, 1992-97; Golden State Warriors, 1997-98; Miami Heat, 1999-2000; Cleveland Cavaliers, 2000-01; New York Knicks, 2001-04; Houston Rockets, 2003-05; Boston Celtics, 2005; free agent, currently. **Honors/Awds:** Southern Mississippi Hall of Fame.

WEATHERSPOON, JIMMY LEE
Government official. **Personal:** Born Mar 10, 1947, Ft Lauderdale, FL; married Marian Wilson; children: Joy LaWest, Kendra LaVett. **Educ:** Automation Sch, cert, 1968; Fla Atlantic Univ. **Career:** IBM, asst systs analyst, 1980-; Carver Cmmty Middle Schl PTA, adv bd, 1981-82, vpres, 1982-83; Delray Beach Voters League, vpres, 1982-84. **Orgs:** Chmn, Community Primitive Bapt Church Trustees, 1982-; rep, Dist 69 Palm Beach County Democratic Exec Comm, 1984; Delray Beach Democratic Club, 1984; Naciremas Club Inc, 1984. **Special Achievements:** Vice mayor polled highest vote in 1984 Delray Beach, first black so honored. **Business Addr:** Associate Systems Analyst, IBM, PO Box 1328, Boca Raton, FL 33432.*

WEATHERSPOON, TERESA GAYE
Basketball player, basketball coach. **Personal:** Born Dec 8, 1965, Pineland, TX; daughter of Charles Sr and Rowena. **Educ:** La Tech, phys educ, 1988. **Career:** Basketball player (retired); basketball coach; NY Liberty, guard, 1997-03; Los Angeles Sparks, guard, 2004; Westchester Phantoms, head coach, 2007; Louisiana Tech, coaching staff, 2008; interim head coach, 2009; coach, 2009-. **Orgs:** Women's Sports Found. **Honors/Awds:** Gold Medal, 1986; Gold Medal, Goodwill Games; Gold Medal, World Univ Games, 1987; La State Player of the Yr, 1988; Gold Medal, US Olympic Basketball Team, 1988; Wade Trophy, 1988; Bronze Medal, US Olympic Basketball Team, 1992; All-WNBA 2nd Team, 1997; WNBA Defensive Player ofthe Yr, 1997, 1998; The Best of NY Award, NY Mag; All-Star games, 1999-2003. **Special Achievements:** Author: "Teresa Witherspoon's Basketball for Girls", 1999. *

WEAVER, A. M. (AISSATOU MIJIZA WEAVER)
Artist, curator, arts administrator. **Personal:** Born Jul 31, 1954, Philadelphia, PA; daughter of Sallye A Warr; divorced. **Educ:** Univ Arts, BFA, painting; Md Inst Col Art, MFA, painting. **Career:** Baltimore Sch Arts, instr, art hist & painting, 1983-84; Neighborhood Reinvestment Corp, field serv officer, 1985-87; Asian Am Art Ctr, develop coordr, 1988; The Printmaking Workshop, asst dir, 1989-90; St George Acad, art instr, 1990-91; The Painted Bride Art Ctr, dir visual & media arts, 1992-98; Samuel S Fleisher Art Memorial, fac, 1992-. **Orgs:** City of Philadelphia Off Arts & Cult, 1992-96; bd mem, Jane D Kent, St Nicholas Day Care Ctr, 1993-94; Prog comt, Contemporary Mus, 1995-; bd mem, Nat Asn Arts Orgn, 1995-98; women's comt, Col Arts Asn, 1997-98. **Honors/Awds:** Baltimore Best Award for Radio Programming, City of Baltimore, 1984; Best Gallery Award for the Best Gallery in Philadelphia, 1994. **Home Addr:** 5320 Haverford Ave, Philadelphia, PA 19139, **Home Phone:** (215)747-7953. **Business Addr:** Faculty, Samuel S Fleisher Art Memorial, 719 Catharine St, Philadelphia, PA 19147-2811.

WEAVER, AFAA MICHAEL
Educator. **Personal:** Born Nov 26, 1951, Baltimore, MD; son of Otis and Elsie; married Ronetta I Barbee, Apr 1, 1978 (divorced 1985); married Eleanora Maddox, Dec 1, 1970 (divorced 1976); married Aissatou Mijiza, Sep 27, 1986; children: Kala Oboi. **Educ:** Univ Md, attended 1970; Regents Col, BA, 1986; Brown Univ, MFA, 1987. **Career:** Essex County Col, lectr, 1987-88; Seton Hall Law Sch, writing specialist, 1988-90; City Univ New York, lectr, 1988-90; New York Univ, adj asst prof eng, 1988-90; Rutgers Univ, assoc prof eng, 1990-98; PEN Arts Concil fel, 1994; Simmons Col, alumnae prof eng, 1998-; Nat Taiwan Univ, fulbright fel, 2002. **Orgs:** Poetry Soc Am; Dramatists Guild; Acad Am Poets; Nat Writers Union; exec bd, Pen New England, 2001. **Honors/Awds:** Nat Endownment for the Arts Fellowship, 1985; Penn Fel Arts, 1998. **Special Achievements:** Published poetry books: Water Song, 1985; Some Day It's A Slow Walk to Evening, 1989; My Father's Geography, 1992; Stations In A Dream, 1993; Timber and Prayer, 1995; Talisman, 1998; Sandy Paint, 2000; The Ten Lights of God, 2000; Multitudes: Poems Selected and New, 2000; Plays: Rosa; The Last Congregation; The Hammer; Berea. **Military Serv:** AUS, E-4, 1970-73. **Business Addr:** Alumnae Professor of English, Simmons College, Department of English, 300 The Penway, Boston, MA 02115, **Business Phone:** (617)521-2175.

WEAVER, AISSATOU MIJIZA. See WEAVER, A. M.

WEAVER, FRANK CORNELL
Marketing executive. **Personal:** Born Nov 15, 1951, Tarboro, NC; son of Frank B and Queen Lewis; married Kathryn Ann Hammond, Oct 11, 1980; children: Christina. **Educ:** Howard Univ, BSEE, 1972; Univ NC Chapel Hill, MBA, mkt, 1976. **Career:** Westinghouse, asst sales engr, 1972-73; NC Central Univ, asst prof, 1975; Mellon Bank, credit analyst, 1976-77; RCA Astro-Space Div, mgr commun satellites, 1977-88; Gen Dynamics Commun Launch Serv, dir, Wash off, 1988-90; UNET Commun Inc, Fort Wash, Md, pres & chief exec officer, 1990-93; FAA, Assoc Admin Off Com Space Transp, appointed Pres Clinton, 1993-97; The Boeing Co, dir, telecommunications policy, 1998-. **Orgs:** Bd dir, Direct Broadcast Satellite Asn, 1990-91; vis prof, Nat Urban League BEEP, 1978-; panelist, Cong Black Caucus Comm Braintrust, 1983; RCA Minorities Engineering Prog; chmn emer, Wash Space Bus Roundtable; Soc Satellite Prof; financial secy, Nat Space Club; Tau Beta Pi Engr Hon Soc; bd dirs, U.S. Telecommunications Training Inst; bd, KIN Found. **Honors/Awds:** Hon Doctor Science, St Augustine's Col, Raleigh, NC; Honoray Doctor Humane Letters, Shaw Divinity School, Raleigh, NC; Distinguished Author, RCA, 1984, 1985; arlem YMCA Black Achiever Indust, 1986; McGraw Hill Yearbook Sci & Technol; Black Engineer of the Year Deans Award, 2003. **Special Achievements:** "D-Sign Graphics", "UDI Supermkt" Case Studies Minority Venture Mgt, 1975; "Intro to Commun Satellites", RCA Engr, 1983; "RCA's Series 4000 Commun Satellites", Satellite Comm, 1984; "DBS Satellite Tech", IEEE Electro, 1985; "Atlas Family of Launch Vehicles," 1991; Via Satellite Mag, "Satellite 100" Top Exec, "A Communication Satellite Dedicated To Delivery of Educational Programming", 29th Space Cong Proceedings, 1992. **Home Addr:** 6311 Battlement Way, Alexandria, VA 22312. **Business Addr:** Director of Telecommunications Policy, The Boeing Company, 1200 Wilson Blvd, Arlington, VA 22209, **Business Phone:** (703)465-3448.

WEAVER, DR. GARLAND RAPHEAL, JR.
Dentist. **Personal:** Born Jun 8, 1932, Baltimore, MD; married Barbara C Gee; children: Garland III & Edward. **Educ:** Howard Univy, BS, 1958, DDS, 1966. **Career:** Pvt pract, dentist, currently. **Orgs:** Med Dental Soc; mem, Kappa Alpha Psi Fraternity. **Home Addr:** 5441 Pk Heights Ave, Baltimore, MD 21215, **Home Phone:** (410)542-1225. **Business Addr:** Dentist, 5441 Pk Heights Ave, Baltimore, MD 21215, **Business Phone:** (410)542-1225.

WEAVER, GARY W.
Real estate executive. **Personal:** Born Sep 3, 1952, Washington, DC; married BV Goodrich. **Educ:** VA Commonwealth Univ, BS bus admin, 1974. **Career:** Trifam Sys Inc, owner, 1977-; Va Hsg Dev Auth Richmond, proj mgr, 1975-77; City of Richmond, zoning officer, insp dept, 1974-75; Asn Fed Appraisers, appraiser, 1978-; Soc Real Estate Appraisers, assoc, 1978-; N VA Bd Rltrs, rltr, 1978-; Merit Properties, prin & broker. **Orgs:** Adv bd, Horizon Bank Va. **Business Addr:** Owner, Trifam Systems Inc., PO Box 3490, McLean, VA 22180, **Business Phone:** (703)281-4186.

WEAVER, GEORGE LEON-PAUL
Consultant. **Personal:** Born Jun 18, 1912, Pittsburgh, PA; son of George and Josephine; married Mary. **Educ:** Roosevelt Univ, attended 1940-42; Howard Univ Law Sch, attended 1942-43; Howard Univ, attended 1962. **Career:** CIO Civil Rights Comt, dir, 1943-55; AFL-CIO Civil Rights Dept, exec dir, 1955; Int Confederation Free Trade Unions, 1955-57; Int Labor Org Geneva Switzerland, spec asst dir gen, 1969; World ORT Union, consult, 1975. **Orgs:** CIO War & Relief Comm, 1941-42; asst to sec treas CIO, 1942-55; exec sec, AFL-CIO 1955-58; spec asst, Sec Labor, 1961; asst sec, Labor Int Affairs, 1969; mem bd, United Negro Col Fund; chmn, Atlanta Univ Ctr. **Special Achievements:** Published material related to his career in the international labor movement and to his interest in fair employment practices and African-American education.

WEAVER, HERBERT C
Civil engineer. **Personal:** Born in Pittsburgh, PA; son of Joseph G and Lucy Gardner; married Rayma Heywood; children: Carol & Jonathan. **Educ:** Univ Pittsburgh, BS, 1961. **Career:** Commonwealth Pa, bridge designer, hydraulic engr; Rust Engineering Co, civil engr; Pullman Swindell Co, proj engr, civil engr; Allegheny County Dept Engineering & Construction, project mgr; Herbert C Weaver Assoc Inc, pres, founder; Allegheny County Sanitary Authority, project mgr, currently. **Orgs:** ASCE, PSPE,

NSPE; appt to panel arbitrators Am Arbitration Asn, 1970; reg prof engr; reg land surveyor; trustee, Grace Presbyterian Church, 1963-; vpres, Booster Club Wilkinsburg Christian Sch, 1971-72; E Hills Pitt Club, 1974-; asst track coach, Churchill Area Track Club, 1980-85; cert official, USA-Track & Field, 1980. **Military Serv:** AUS. **Home Addr:** 2104 Swissvale Ave, Pittsburgh, PA 15221-1569, **Home Phone:** (412)243-6881. **Business Addr:** Project Manager, Alcosan-Allegheny County, Sanitary Authority, 3300 Preble Ave, Pittsburgh, PA 15233-1092.

WEAVER, DR. JOHN ARTHUR
Physician. **Personal:** Born Nov 23, 1940, Hemingway, SC; son of Arthur C and Winnie Mae Williams; married Yvonne Jackson; children: Jennifer & Jessica. **Educ:** Virginia Union Univ, BS, 1964; Howard Univ, MS, 1968, PhD, 1970, MD, 1978. **Career:** NC State Univ, assoc prof, chem, Greensboro, NC, 1970-74, summer, 1975; Howard Univ, intern, 1978-79, resident, 1979-81; The Johns Hopkins Insts, fel, nuclear med, 1981-83; Weaver Med Assocs, PC, pres, 1983-; Howard Univ Hosp, asst prof, radiol, 1991-93; Va Med Ctr, 2001-; pvt pract, currently. **Orgs:** AMA; NMA; RSNA; SNM; Richmond Med Soc, past pres; ASNC. **Honors/Awds:** NSF grantee, 1972; NIH grantee, 1972; Piedmont grantee, 1973. **Business Addr:** Physician, PO Box 26448, Richmond, VA 23227, **Business Phone:** (804)266-5069.

WEAVER, MARISSA
Executive director. **Career:** Americas Black Holocaust Mus Inc, exec dir. **Orgs:** Chairwoman, Milwaukee Mus bd. *

WEAVER, REGINALD LEE
Association executive, educator. **Personal:** Born Aug 13, 1939, Danville, IL; son of Carl and Mary Alice; married Betty Jo Moppin; children: Reginald Von & Rowan Anton. **Educ:** Ill State Univ, BA, 1961; Roosevelt Univ, MA, 1973. **Career:** Gen Electric; Sch Dist 152, teacher, 1961-; Budget Comt, 1971-81; Ill Educ Asn, vpres, 1977-81, pres, 1981-87; PACE Comt Ill, vice chmn, 1977-81; Staff & Retirement Comt, chmn, 1979-81; Nat Educ Asn, vpres, 1996-2002; Nat Educ Asn, pres, 2002-. **Orgs:** Teacher Cert Bd Ill Off Ed, 1972-83; delegate, World Confederation Orgns Teaching Prof, 1976-80; Masons, 1965-; pres, Harvey Educ Asn, 1967-68; Harvey Educ Asn, Negotiatong Team, vice pres, 1970; Nat Educ Asn, Int Rels Comt, 1975-81; Nat Educ Asn, Exec Comt, 1989; Nat Bd Prof Teaching Standards, 1989; Dept Ed, Hall Fame, Ill State Univ; Nat Asn Advan Colored People; Nat Coun La Raza. **Honors/Awds:** Human Relations Award, Ill Educ Asn, 1974; Spirit of Liberty Award, People Am Way, 2005; George Meany Latino Leadership Award, US Hispanic Leadership Inst, 2006; DHL, NC Shaw Univ, 2006; Doctor of Public, SC State Univ, 2007; Lincoln Univ, Honorary Doctor; Leadership Award,US Action Progressive; President's Award, Nat Conf Black Mayors; Influential Black Educators Award, Ebony; Human Relations Award, Ill Educ Asn. **Special Achievements:** Outstanding Young Men of America, 1972; Numerous Speaking Engagements, 1977-. **Business Addr:** President, National Education Association, 1201 16th St NW, Washington, DC 20036-3290, **Business Phone:** (202)822-7944.

WEAVER, WILLIAM COURTSWORTHY, II
Clergy, high school principal. **Personal:** Born Jul 11, 1929, Edgefield, SC; son of Allen and Minnie Simpkins; married Virginia Nadine Dawkins, Jun 28, 1969; children: William III, James Allen. **Educ:** Allen Univ, BA, 1955; Philadelphia Divinity Sch, BS, Theol, 1960; Episcopal Divinity Sch, MDiv, 1972. **Career:** Clergy (retired), High school principal; Cent High Sch, asst prin, 1955-57; Saint Paul's Church, rector, 1960-68; Saint Matthias Parish, rector, 1968-72; Church Redeemer, rector, 1972-79; Saint Andrew's Church, rector, 1979-83; Shaw Univ, adjunct prof, 1980-85; Epiphany Church, rector, 1992; Hospice Health Serv, chaplain; Odyssey Health care, spiritual care coord. **Orgs:** Comnr, Charleston Housing Authority, 1992; Comnr, Charleston Naval Shipyard legislative, 1991; bd trustees, Hanahan Acad, 1983-86; Comn Ministry, 1979-83; bd trustees, Voorhees Col, 1960-64; Orangeburg Housing Authority, 1960-64; Orangeburg Civil Rights Movement, 1960-64; Sumter Civil Rights Movement, 1960-64. **Honors/Awds:** Volunteer Service Award, Charleston County Sch, 1992; Cities in Schools Award, Cities Schs, 1992; Certificate of Appreciation Award, City Charleston, 1992; Pastor's Appreciation Award, Epiphany Church, 1992; Appreciation Award, Clark Corp Acad, 1992. **Special Achievements:** Book: Father Divine: The Genius of the Man from Georgia, 1960; The Winds of Change, 1960; Who is the Man?, 1975; The Celebrated Imposter, 1981; Celebrating Time, 1991. **Military Serv:** USY, pvt first class, 1951-53; Good Conduct, 1952; European Occupation, 1953. *

WEBB, GEORGIA HOUSTON
School administrator. **Personal:** Born May 16, 1951, Moorseville, AL; daughter of George Houston and Annie Thatch Harris; married Harold Webb, Jan 6, 1984; children: Ayinde Pendleton Webb. **Educ:** Univ Iowa, Iowa City, Iowa, BA, philos, 1973; Univ Wis, Whitewater, Wis, MS, coun, 1974. **Career:** Univ Wis, Eau Claire, Wis, career counr, 1974-76; Cornell Univ, Ithaca, New York, asst dir minority affairs, 1976-80; Mount San Antonio Col, Walnut, Calif, instr, 1984-88; Scripps Col, Claremont, Calif, sr asst dir admissions, 1988-90; The WEBB Connection, co-fed, pres, 1990-; Univ Calif, Berkley, dir, southern area outreach, currently. **Orgs:** Pomona Valley-Nicaragua Friendship Proj, 1988-; delegate, State Central Comt, Calif Democratic Party, 1988-; bd mem, Community Friends Int Studs-Claremont Col, 1989-; Claremont League Women Voters, 1989-; Calif Rainbow Coalition; Los Angeles Democratic Party; Upland Bus & Prof Women's Club; League Conserv Voters; nominee, Nat Asn Advan Colored People. **Business Addr:** Director of Undergraduate Admissions, University of California at Berkeley, Office of Undergraduate Admissions, 110 Sproul Hall No 5800, Berkeley, CA 94720-5800, **Business Phone:** (510)642-6000.

WEBB, HAROLD H.
Government official. **Personal:** Born Apr 30, 1925, Greensboro, NC; son of Vina Wadlington Webb and Haywood Eugene Webb Sr; married Lucille Holcomb, Jan 15, 1949; children: Kaye. **Educ:** A&T State Univ, Greensboro, NC, BS, biol, 1949; MS, educ administration, 1952. **Career:** Hillsborough, teacher, 1948-54, prin, 1954-62; State Sci Consult, Raleigh, 1962-66; Nat Def Educ Act, asst dir, 1966-69; Hum Rel, asst dir, 1969-70; Tit I ESEA, dir, 1970-73; Comp Educ, dep asst supt, 1973-77; Off State Personnel NC, state personnel dir, 1977-86; NC Gen Assembly, legis agt; Wake County, bd comnr, 2003-; New Millennium, LLC, consult; Charlotte Hawkins Brown Historical Found, Inc, exec dir. **Orgs:** Pub Welfare Outstanding Adminr Orgn Co Schs, 1960; deleg, Nat Conf Educ Poor Chicago, 1973; chmn, Wake County NC Planning Bd, l988-; Univ NC Bd Govs, l989-; NEA; NSTA; vice chmn NC Asn Adminr Comp Educ; Nat Comp Educ Mgt Proj; truste, Wake Tech Inst; bd dir, Raleigh Little Theatre; bd dir, New Bern Ave Day Care Cent; bd dir, Raleigh Coun Aging; exec comt, Raleigh Citizens Asn; bd trustee, Shaw Univ. **Honors/Awds:** Hon Degree Doctor of Humanities, NC A&T State Univ, l978; Tarheel of the Week, Raleigh News & Observer, l980; Distinguished Service Award, St.Augustine's Col & Shaw Univ; Nat Alumni Achievement Award, NC A&T State Univ; Cong Gold Medal, Tuskegee Airmen, 2007. **Military Serv:** AUS, 1943-46. **Home Addr:** 1509 Tierney Circle, Raleigh, NC 27610. **Business Addr:** Commissioners, Wake County, 1509 Tierney Circle, Raleigh, NC 27610, **Business Phone:** (919)856-5573.

WEBB, DR. HARVEY
Dentist. **Personal:** Born Jul 31, 1929, Washington, DC; married Z Ozella; children: Tomai, Harvey III & Hoyt. **Educ:** Howard Univ, BS, 1956, DDS,1960; Howard Univ, MS, 1962; Johns Hopkins Univ, MPH, 1967. **Career:** USAR, major (retired), dentist; Howard Univ, intern, 1960, instr, 1962-63; pvt pract, 1960-77; Grp Health Asn Am, 1962-63; Johns Hopkins Univ, 1969-71; Constant Care Com Heallth Ctr, exec dir, 1971-87; Univ Md Sch Nur, 1976-77. **Orgs:** Bd mem, MD Heart Asn, 1969-74;trustee, 1978-85, bd mem, 1979-82, Howard County Gen Hosp, 1978-85; pres, Health Resources Inc, 1978-80; Cent MD Health Sys Agen, 1980-81; Alpha Phi Alpha; Am Dental Asn; Nat Dental Asn; Robert T Freeman Dent Soc; AAAS; Int Asn Dental Res; DC Dental Soc; Maimonides Dental Soc; DC Pub Health Asn; DC Health & Welfare Coun; Am Pub Health Asn; Polit Action Com RT Freeman Dent Soc; Am Asn Pub Health Dentists; MD State Pub Health Asn; coord Comm Vol Dental Serv; Dental Coord, Provident Hosp; Balt City Dental Soc; life mem, NAACP; Howard Univ Alumni; Neighbors Inc; Brightwood Civic Asn; WA Urban League; bd dir, WA, DC Home Rule Comm; Sarasota County review bd, 1994-97; bd mem, S W Hospice, 1995-97; bd mem, N Port Area Chamber Com, 1995-97; Tiger Bay Club, 1994-; Asolo Theatre, Angel, 1995-; Venice Found grant review comt, 1995-97; bd mem, North County Ed, 1994-; chair, Sarasota County democratic exec, 1992-, issues, 1994-95; pres, Holistic Healthworks, Inc, 1995-97; bd mem, N Port Kiwanis, 1996-97; pres, N Port Utility Adv Comt, 1994-; Unity Church Sarasota; bd mem, N Port Democratic Club, 1992; Friends Selby libr, 1994-; Venice Hosp Community Health Assessment Comm, 1992-95; bd mem, Hispanic Am Alliance, Inc, 1996-; Fla Acad African Am Cult, 1995-; Sigma Pi Phi-Boule, 1997; coord, Black Hist Month, N Port, FL, 2002; Asn Study African Am Life & Hist, 2002; sec, Manasota Basin bd, SW FL Water Mgmt Dist, 1997-2004; Manasota Basin Bd, 1999-2002. **Honors/Awds:** Outstanding Men of Decade, 1979; Com Serv Award, Pi Eta Chi, 1979; NM Carroll Meth Home Award, 1980; numerous publs & presentations. **Military Serv:** AUS, 2nd lt, 1948-52; USAR, major, 1953-70 (retired). **Home Addr:** 6601 Ruff St, North Port, FL 34286.

WEBB, HORACE S
Executive, president (organization). **Career:** Entergy Corp, sr vpres external affairs, 1999-, Entergy Charitable Found, pres & chief exec officer, currently. **Orgs:** Chmn, Cong Black Caucus Found, currently. **Business Addr:** President, Chief Executive Officer, Entergy Corporation, Entergy Charitable Foundation, PO Box 61000, New Orleans, LA 70161, **Business Phone:** (504)576-4360.

WEBB, JAMES EUGENE
Executive. **Personal:** Born Aug 31, 1956, Cleveland, OH; children: Brian James, Richard Anthony, Khalam James-Kirsten, Elijah Kharmonee, Larry & Brandon. **Educ:** Cleveland Inst Banking, 1976; Cuyahoga Community Col, 1978. **Career:** Warrensville Ctr Mentally Retarded, caseworker, 1975-78; Rep Steel, mill wright, 1978-82; Culligan Water Int, sales mgr, res sales Fla & Ill, 1985-89; Webb Manufacturing/Webb World Inc, pres, 1982-. **Orgs:** Consult, Career Progs, Cleveland Pub Schs, 1985; vpres, Cleveland Bus League, 1985-86; speaker for several groups; parent adv comn, Canterbury Sch. **Honors/Awds:** Business of the Year for City of Cleveland (Webb Mfg), 1984; Entrepreneur of the Year City of Cleveland, 1984; Man of the Year, Cleveland Sr Coun, 1985. **Business Addr:** President, Webb World Inc, 9200 Folsom Ave, Cleveland, OH 44104, **Business Phone:** (216)491-0103.

WEBB, JAMES O
Administrator, president (organization). **Personal:** Born Nov 25, 1931, Cleveland, OH; son of Bessie R and James O Sr; married Frankie L Lowe; children: Lisa S & Paula R Webb Dixon. **Educ:** Morehouse Col, BA, 1953; Univ Mich, MBA, actuarial sci, 1957. **Career:** Mutual NY, actuarial asst 1957-62; Supreme Life Ins co, vpres actuary, 1962-66; Blue Cross-Blue Shield Ill, sr vpres, 1966-84; Dent Network Am, pres & ceo, 1984-94, chm, bd dir, 1990-94; James O Webb & Assoc, pres & ceo, currently; pres, Managed Dent Care Canada, 1986-94; Baker-Eubanks, LLC, managing prin, 1995-; Village Glencoe, pres, 1993-2001. **Orgs:** Dir, South Shore Bank, 1975-89; dir, treas, exec comn Am Acad Actuaries, 1975-78; Planning Exec Inst, Midwest Planning Asn; founder & convenor, Bus Develop Inst Blue Cross-Blue Shield, 1983-88; pres, Glencoe Sch Bd, 1971-77; exec comt, vpres No Cook Cty Pvt Indust Coun, 1983-86; founder & chmn, dir Home Investments Fund, 1968; Chicago Metro Housing & Planning Coun, 1980-85; gov comm Health Asst Prog, 1979-83; Security Sol Inc, chmn, 1995-; Harris Trust & Savings Bank, dir; Harris Bank Corps, Harris Bankmont; Harris Bank, Glencoe, Northbrook, dir; Ill Facilitates Fund, dir, 1996-00; Evanston-Northwestern Healthcare, dir, 1999; Chicago Bot Garden, 1999-; bd trustees, NC Arts Coun, 2006. **Honors/Awds:** Outstanding Businessmen's Award, Young Blacks Polit, 1984. **Military Serv:** AUS, corpl E-4, 1953-55.

WEBB, JOE
Clergy, executive. **Personal:** Born Aug 18, 1935, San Antonio, TX; married Frances (deceased); children: Joe Jr, Linda Ray, Vincent & Daniel; married Barbara (divorced 1999). **Educ:** San Antonio Col, Assocs; St Marys Univ, Pre-Law Courses; HEB Mgt Sch, Cert; Guadalupe Theol Sem, Assoc Minister. **Career:** YMCA, pub rels dir, 1957-69; HEB Supermarket, store dir, 1969-80; Neighborhood Grocery Store, independent grocer, 1980-; Webb Way Supermarket, pres & owner 1983-; City of San Antonio, city councilman, 1977-91; Handy Stop Convenience Store, secy, treas, owner, 1980-; Pleasant Zion Baptist Church, pastor 1986-; independent grocer, 1980-93; Webway Supermarket, 1983-85; Webbs Eastlawn Food Ctr, currently. **Orgs:** Black Congressional Caucus, 1977-; state grand sr warden Masonic Lodge, 1981-; assoc minister, Zion Star Baptist Church 1982-; steering comt mem, Nat League Cities 1983-85; chmn, Jesse Jackson Campaign, 1984; chmn, bd dirs, AAOMMS of North & South Am Imperial Grand Coun NBC/LEO; treas, Reg Dir XVII, 1987-89; Alamo City Chamber Com; State Tex MW St Joseph Grand Lodge, grand master, 1996, grand sr warden, 1981-96. **Honors/Awds:** Father of the Year 20th Century Club; Man of the Year Elks; Patterson Award United Negro College Fund; Honorary Doctors, Guadalupe Theol Seminary, 1985. **Business Addr:** Owner, Webbs Eastlawn Food Center, 2226 Burnet, San Antonio, TX 78202.

WEBB, JOSEPH
Executive. **Career:** The Stump LLC, owner, 1999-; Motorola Inc, head corp staffing & relocations; MGM Mirage Inc, staff. **Business Addr:** Owner, The Stump LLC, 205 W Randolph St Suite 1630, Chicago, IL 60606, **Business Phone:** (312)372-8255.

WEBB, JOSEPH G
Police officer, lawyer. **Personal:** Born Dec 3, 1950, Chicago, IL; son of Wellington M and Mardina G Williams; married Marilyn L Bell, Oct 23, 1978; children: Alishea R, Ami R & Ciara M. **Educ:** Univ Colo, Boulder CO, AA, 1971; Metropolitan State Col, Denver CO, BA, 1987; Univ Denver Col Law, Denver, CO, JD, 1991. **Career:** Denver Gen Hosp, ment health worker, 1972-77; Denver Police Dept, sgt, 1977; Ireland, Stapleton, Pryor & Pascoe, PC, gen coun, currently. **Orgs:** Nat Black Police Asn, 1983-; Colo Bus League, 1985-86; Colo Black Roundtable, 1985-; consult, Oasis Proj, 1986-87, NE Denver Task Force Drug Abuse, 1988-89. **Honors/Awds:** Citizens Appreciate Police Award; SCAT Appreciation Award; Peer Support Recognition Award; Black Officer of the Year; Officer of the Month; Optimist International Law Enforcement Recognition; Intelligence Bureau Appreciation Award; National Black Police Association Leadership Award. **Business Addr:** Counsel, Ireland Stapleton Pryor & Pascoe PC, 1675 Broadway Suite 2600, Denver, CO 80202, **Business Phone:** (303)623-2700.

WEBB, LINNETTE
Hospital administrator. **Personal:** Born in Charleston, SC; daughter of Carl and Naomi (Deceased). **Educ:** Lehman Col, attended; Baruch Col, MPA. **Career:** Renaissance Diag & Treat Ctr, staff; Harlem Hosp Ctr, exec dir; Health & Hosps Corp, New York, sr vpres & exec dir. **Orgs:** Chairperson, Greater Harlem Nursing Home, Bd Dirs. **Honors/Awds:** Fel mem, The New York Acad Med, New York.

WEBB, MELVIN RICHARD
Educator. **Personal:** Born Feb 9, 1940, Cuthbert, GA; married Brenda Janet Burton. **Educ:** Albany State Col, BS, 1992; Atlanta Univ, MS, 1968; OH State Univ, PhD, 1977. **Career:** Lee Co Bd Educ, sci teacher, 1962-63; Dougherty Co Bd Educ, biol & chem, 1963-66; Atlanta Bd Educ, biol teacher, 1967-69; Clark Col, prof biol & sci educ, 1972-, Resource Ctr Sci & Engineering, asst dir, prof biol, 1978-. **Orgs:** Nat Sci Teachers Asn; GA Sci Teachers Asn; Phi Delta Kappa; NAACP; Soc Christian Leadership Conf. **Honors/Awds:** Science Department Citation, Albany State, 1962; STAR Teacher, GA State CC, 1969; Academy Year Grants, Atlanta Univ & OH State Univ; Nat Sci Found, 1966-67 1969-70; Presidential Award for Excellence in Science, Mathematics and Engineering Mentoring, 2001; Aldridge/ McMillan Excellence in Teaching Award, 2001. **Business Addr:** Professor, Clark Atlanta University, 223 James P Brawley Dr Room 3005A RCST, Atlanta, GA 30314, **Business Phone:** (404)880-6978.

WEBB, REGINALD (REGGIE WEBB)
President (Organization), chairperson. **Personal:** Born Mar 25, 1948, South Bend, IN. **Educ:** Calif State Univ, Los Angeles, polit sci. **Career:** US Coast Guard, 1966-69, Nat Black McDonald's Operators Asn, chmn & chief exec officer, 1994-97; Nat Black McDonald's Operators Asn, pres, currently. **Orgs:** Chmn, Nat Leadership Coun McDonald's. **Honors/Awds:** 365Black Award, McDonald's, 2004. **Business Phone:** (630)623-6988.*

WEBB, RICHMOND JEWEL, JR.
Football player. **Personal:** Born Jan 11, 1967, Dallas, TX. **Educ:** Tex A&M, BS, indust distrib, 1993. **Career:** Football player (retired); Miami Dolphins, tackle, 1990-2000; Cincinnati Bengals, tackle, 2001-02. **Honors/Awds:** Earned Many post season hons in 1990 included: NFL Rookie of the Yr; ProBowl appearances; Rookie of the Yr, United Press Intl AFC; SportsIllustrated Rookie of the Yr, 1990; Sporting News Rookie of the Yr; 2ndteam All-Pro from Col & Pro Football Newsweekly, 2nd team All-AFC, UnitedPress Intl, 1990, 1993; All-Rookie teams; United Press Intl; Outstanding Offensive Lineman, Miami Dolphins, 1990-94; Rookie of the Yr, S Fla Media; Tommy Fitzgerald Award; first-team All-AFC hon, The Football News, 1992; first-team All-AFC hon, United Press, 1992; Outstanding Offensive Lineman, S Fla Media, 1990-95. **Special Achievements:** First tackle in Dolphins hist to be selected to the Pro Bowl as a starter; the first Dolphins offensive lineman to win the hon since Dwight Stephenson in 1987.

WEBB, SCHUYLER CLEVELAND
Psychologist, military leader. **Personal:** Born Jun 28, 1951, Springfield, MA; son of Cleveland and Bettye Wright; children: Kayla Monique. **Educ:** Morehouse Col, BA, cum laude, 1974; Am Inst Foreign Study, cert, 1975; Univ Mass, MS, 1978; Nat Univ, MBA, 1986; Pacific Grad Sch Psychol, PhD cand, currently. **Career:** Univ Mass, asst trainer & alcoholism counr, 1974-77; Inst Studying Educ Policy Howard Univ, res asst, 1978; Lawrence Johnson & Assoc Inc, tech staff cont, 1978-81; Howard Univ, Ctr Sickle Cell Disease, Wash, DC, ed comm mem/consult, 1979-81; Higher Horizons Day Care Ctr, Crossroads, VA, consult 1980-81; USN Med Serv Corps, res psychologist & hosp corpsman, 1981; Naval Health Research Ctr, San Diego, res psychologist, 1983-86; Diving & Salvage Sch, Panama Beach, Fla, instr & res psychologist, 1986-87; Naval Biodynamics Lab, New Orleans, res psychologist, admin & equal opportunity officer, 1987-91; Defense Equal Opportunity Mgt Inst, Patrick AFB, res intern, 1991; Naval Bur Personnel, dep dir res psychologist, 1994; Navy Inspector Gen Off, tech consult, 1994. **Orgs:** Asn Military Surgeons; Human Factors Soc; Sleep Rsch Soc; Asn Black Psychologists; Am Psychol Asn; pub rels & scholar comn, Nat Naval Officer Asn, San Diego Chap, 1983-; co-chair, Cult Heritage & Black Hist Comn, San Diego, USN, 1984-86; advan open water diver, Prof Asn Diving Instructors, 1986-; NAACP, Alpha Phi Alpha, Urban League; equal opportunity officer, combined fed campaign officer Morehouse Alumni Asn; vpres membership, nat Naval officers Asn, 1988-89; econd Harvest Food Bank 1987-; Asn for the Study Classical African Civilizations, 1990-. **Special Achievements:** Certificate of Achievement in Community & Counseling Psychology, 1974; Horace Barr Fellowship, 1974-77; Collegiate Commission for the Education of Black Students Fellowship, 1974-75; Our Crowd Scholarship; Springfield Teachers Club Scholarship; Community Service Award, Springfield Col; Academic Scholarship 4 year tuition scholarship, Morehouse College, 1970-74; Psychology Department honors, Morehouse College, 1974; National University leadership Scholarship, Nat Univ, 1984; "Jet Lag in Military Operations", Naval Health Res Ctr, San Diego, CA 1986; publ:"Comparative Analysis of Decompression Sickness", Jour Hyperbaric Med, 2:55-62, 1987; Duty Under Instruction Scholar, USN, 1991-94. **Military Serv:** USN comdr; Leadership Award, Pistol Sharpshooter, Physical Fitness Award, Commendation Letter; Rifle Expert, 1988; Defense Equal Opportunity Mgt Inst Internship, 1991.

WEBB, SHELIA J
Health services administrator. **Educ:** PhD. **Career:** City New Orleans, dir health dept; Ctr Empowered Decision Making, dir, currently.

WEBB, SPUD
Television show host, basketball player, businessperson. **Personal:** Born Jul 13, 1963, Dallas, TX. **Educ:** Midland Col, Midland, TX, attended 1983; NC State Univ, Raleigh, NC, attended 1985. **Career:** Basketball player (retired), television show host, businessperson; Atlanta Hawks, guard, 1985-91, 1995-96; Sacramento Kings, guard, 1991-95; Minn Timberwolves, guard, 1996; Scaligera Verona, Italy, 1996-97; Orlando Magic, guard, 1998; Dallas Mavericks, host, pre-game & post-game shows; Spud Webb Enterprises, owner, currently; delivering keynote addresses, currently. **Honors/Awds:** NBA Slam Dunk Contest, 1986. **Business Phone:** 888-883-7783.

WEBB, STANFORD
Executive. **Career:** R Stanford Webb Agency, pres & founder, 1925-. **Business Addr:** Founder, President, R Stanford Webb Agency, 216 Asheland Ave, PO Box 3320, Asheville, NC 28802, **Business Phone:** (828)258-2663.

WEBB, UMEKI
Basketball player. **Personal:** Born Jun 26, 1975. **Educ:** NC State, 1997. **Career:** Phoenix Mercury, guard, forward, beginning, 1997; Lubbock Hawks. *

WEBB, VERONICA LYNN
Fashion model, journalist, actor. **Personal:** Born Feb 23, 1965, Detroit, MI; daughter of Doug and Marion. **Educ:** Parson's Sch Design; New Sch Social Res. **Career:** Ford Model Mgt, freelance model; Interview, Andy Warhol, contributing ed, 1990; Spike Lee's Jungle Fever, supporting role, 1991; Revlon Consumer Products Corp, colorstyle spokesperson, 1992; Films: Malcolm X, 1992; Damon, 1998; 54, as VIP Patron, 1998; Holy Man, 1998; Big Tease, 1999; In Too Deep, 2000; Becker, 2001. **Orgs:** Steering comt head, Black Girls Coalition, 1989-; sustaining mem, Planned Parenthood, 1992-; 21st Century Party, 1992-. **Honors/Awds:** Model of the Year, New York Mag, 1994. **Special Achievements:** First African-Am woman in the hist of the fashion indust to be awarded a multi-million dollar contract by Revlon Inc, 1992; columnist, Paper Mag, New York, 1990; auth: Veronica Webb-Sight: Adventures in the Big City, 1998. **Business Phone:** (212)688-1636.

WEBB, WELLINGTON E.
Mayor, executive. **Personal:** Born Feb 17, 1941, Chicago, IL; married Wilma J; children: Keith, Tony, Allen & Stephanie. **Educ:** Colo St Col, BA, sociol, 1964; Univ N Colo, Greeley, MA, sociol, 1972. **Career:** Denver pub schs, teacher; Colo St Univ Manpower Lab, dir, 1969-74; Colo House Rep, St rep, 1972-77; Colo Carter/ Mondale Campaign, 1976; US Dept Health & Human Serv, regional dir, 1977-80; Dept Regulatory Agencies, exec dir, 1981-86; City Denver, auditor, 1987-90, mayor, 1991-2003; Nat Conf Black Mayors, pres; US Conf Mayors, pres; Harvard Univ's Kennedy Sch Govt, guest lectr; Nat Conf Dem Mayors, pres; Webb Group International, founder, 2003-; Maximus Corp, bd dir. **Orgs:** Chmn, Dem Caucus CO House Rep, 1975-; chmn, Health Welfare & Inst Com, 1975-76; del, Dem Nat Conv, 1976, 1992; trustee bd, Denver C's Hosp, 1975-; bd dir, Denver Operation PUSH, 1975-; bd dir, Denver Urban Coalition, 1975; chmn, United Negro Col Fund, 1973-75; vpres, pres, Nat Conf Black Mayors. **Honors/Awds:** Barney Ford Award for Political Action, 1976; Leadership of Year Award, Thomas Jefferson HS, 1976; Nat Wildlife Federation's 1999 Achievement Award; The Wellington E Webb Municipal Office Building, named in honor, 2002; Distinguished Public Service award, 2003; US Conference of Mayors highest honor; Outstanding Achievement in Public Policy award; Hon doctorate, Univ Colo, Denver; Hon doctorate, Metrop State Col. **Special Achievements:** First African American Mayor of Denver; Only African-American candidate for the DNC chairmanship. **Home Addr:** 2329 Gaylord St, Denver, CO 80205.

WEBB, REV. WILLIAM
Disciples of Christ clergy. **Personal:** Married Violene C; children: Yolanda & Lafayette. **Educ:** Philander Smith Col, attended 1956; Va Union Univ, MDiv, 1959. **Career:** Second Baptist Church, pastor, currently. **Business Phone:** (775)786-1017.

WEBB, WILMA J.
Labor activist. **Personal:** Born May 17, 1943, Denver, CO; daughter of Frank Wendell Gerdine (deceased) and Faye Elizabeth Wyatt Gerdine; married Wellington, 1971; children: Keith, Anthony, Stephanie, Allen. **Educ:** Univ Colo, Denver; Harvard Univ; John F Kennedy Sch Govt. **Career:** Mobil Corp, admin assoc; Bank Denver, admin assoc; City Denver, legislator; Colo House Rep, state rep; US Labor Dept, Region 8, secretary's rep, 1997-. **Orgs:** Denver Children's Home; chair, Martin Luther King Jr Colo Holiday Comn; founder, chair, Mayor's Comn on Art Culture & Film; Colo Joint Budget Comm; Zion Baptist Church; Delta Sigma Theta sorority. **Honors/Awds:** Martin Luther King Jr Humanitarian Award; hon doctorate, Colo Institute of Art; Carter G. Woodson Award, Nat Educ Asn; Legislator of the Year Award, Asn Retarded Citizens; Political Award, Colo Banking Asn. **Special Achievements:** First African American to serve Region 8; first woman to serve Region 8; first minority female mem of Colorado Joint Budget Comm. **Business Phone:** (720)264-3000.*

WEBBER, BILL. See WEBBER, WILLIAM STUART.

WEBBER, CHRIS
Basketball player. **Personal:** Born Mar 1, 1973, Detroit, MI; son of Doris and Mayce. **Educ:** Univ Mich, psychol. **Career:** Golden State Warriors, forward, 1993-94, 2008-; Wash Wizards, 1994-98; Sacramento Kings, 1998-2005; Philadelphia 76ers, forward, 2005-07; Detroit Pistons, 2007. **Orgs:** Founder, Timeout Found. **Honors/Awds:** Schick NBA Rookie of the Year Award, 1994; Most Valuable Player, 2000-01; Western Conference Player of the Week, 2001-02; Western Conference Player of the Month, 2002-03; Sacramento Kings/Oscar Robertson Triple Double Award; NBA Community Assist Award, 2003; Wish Maker of the Year, 2003. **Special Achievements:** Ranked No. 64 in SLAM Magazine's Top 75 NBA Players of all time in 2003. **Business Addr:** Professional Basketball Player, Golden State Warriors, 1011 Broadway, Oakland, CA 94607, **Business Phone:** (510)986-2200.

WEBBER, PAUL R., III
Judge. **Personal:** Born Jan 24, 1934, Gadsden, SC; son of Paul Jr and Clemmie; married Fay DeShields; children: Paul IV, Stephen, Nikki. **Educ:** BA, 1955; South Carolina State Univ, JD, 1957. **Career:** Neighborhood Legal Serv Prog, Dist Columbia, managing atty, 1967-69; Antitrust Div US Dept Just, trial atty, 1964-67; Golden State Mutual Life Ins Co LA, assoc coun, 1960-64; UCLA, asst law lib, 1959-60; Allen Univ, Columbia, SC, pvt pract & lect, 1958-59; Dolphin Branton Stafford & Webber, atty, 1969-77; Howard Univ, lectr; George Washington Univ Law Sch, adjunct prof, summer, 1973; DC Super Ct, sr judge, 1988-98. **Orgs:** Am, Nat, Dist Columbia, California & South Carolina Bar Asns; Alpha Phi Alpha; gen coun, Sigma Pi Phi; The Guardsmen; past chmn, Civil Pract & Family Law Sec Nat Bar Asn; Judicial Coun Washington Bar Asn; Nat Asn Parliamentarians, 2001. **Honors/Awds:** Trial Judge of the Year, unanimous vote Trial Lawyers Asn Metro Washington DC, 1985-86. *

WEBBER, WILLIAM STUART (BILL WEBBER)
Government official, commissioner. **Personal:** Born Oct 17, 1942, Hartshorne, OK; children: Natalie Jewell, Stuart Franklin & Timpi Armelia. **Educ:** Eastern Okla A&M Univ, attended 1960-62. **Career:** Rancher Santa Gertrudis Breeder, 1958-; Rockwell Int, electronic technician, 1964-83; Pittsburg County, county comnr, 1983-99. **Orgs:** Mason AF&M, Pittsburg County Cattleman's Asn, 1967-; real estate developer; prof coon hunter, Prof Coon Hunters Asn, 1981-85; Church God Christ; Am Cattle Breeder's Asn. **Honors/Awds:** Hall of Fame, Am Cattle Breeder's Asn. **Military Serv:** Okla Nat Guard, ES, 8 years. **Home Addr:** Rt 1 Box 240, Hartshorne, OK 74547.

WEBER, CARL
Writer, publisher. **Educ:** Va State Univ, attended; Va State Univ, MBA, attended. **Career:** Urban Books, founder, publisher & ed dir, currently; Author: Baby Momma Drama, Married Men, Lookin' for Luv, 2000, Married Men, 2001, Baby Momma Drama, 2003, Player Haters, 2004, The Preacher's Son, 2005, So You Call Yourself a Man, 2005, The First Lady, 2006. *

WEBER, DANIEL
Lawyer, government official. **Personal:** Born Sep 25, 1942, New Orleans, LA; married Shirley Ann Nash; children: Akilah F, Akil K. **Educ:** Los Angeles City Col, hist, 1963; Calif State Col, La, BA, Sociol, 1968; Univ Calif, Los Angles, School Law, JD, 1971. **Career:** Los Angeles City Atty Off, law clerk, 1972-73; Calif State Atty Gen, grad legal asst, 1973-74; Grossmont Col, teacher, 1974-75; Legal Aid Soc of San Diego, atty, 1975; Employ Develop Dept State of Calif, legal coun, 1975; Mira Mesa Jr Col, teacher bus law, 1979-82; Soc Sec Admin Office, govt lawyer, 1976-83; Pvt Pract of Law, self employed, 1983. **Orgs:** Bd dir, Nat Asn Advan Colored People, 1973-, 1976-80, chmn, 1976-80, treas 1978-79, 1979-80, court comm pres, 1981-82, 1984-85; San Diego Munic Ct Appt Atty List, 1976; bd of gov, 1977, chmn, 1977-80, judicial sel pres-elect, 1979-80, pres, 1980-81; Calif Asn Black Lawyers; San Diego bd of zoning Appeals, 1978-82; bd dir, State Fed & Appellate Defenders Inc, 1979-80; Indigents Defense Bd, 1979-80; Aequus Dist Comt, BSA, 1980-; bd dir & chmn, Bay Area Perinatal AIDS Ctr, 1981-; bd gov, San Diego Bar Asn; Am Bar Asn; Nat Bar Asn 1981-82; Phi Alpha Delta; rep, mem bar rels comn Stud Bar Asn; rep, stud rep, acad senate sub-comt equal opportunity; comnr of housing, Grad Student Asn; org mem, Black Law Students Asn; chmn, BLSA Defense Comm, co-chmn BLSA Recruitment Comn; org mem, Univ Calif Los Angles; clerk, Law Journ; pres, Earl B Gilliam Bar Asn. **Honors/Awds:** Cert of Appreciation, 1979-80; Outstanding Pres Award, 1980-81; Calif Asn Black Lawyers; Outstanding Pres Award, 1981-82; Earl B Gilliam Bar Assoc of San Diego Cty; Cert of Appreciation for Serv on Bd of Zoning Appeals City of San Diego; Spec Commendation 1983; City Coun San Diego; Resolution for Outstanding Serv Legal Prof; Calif State Assemblyman Pete Chacon 79th Assembly Dist; Cert Appreciation for Outstanding Contribs to the Delivery of Vol Legal Serv Calif, 1983; The State Bar of Calif Bd of Gov; Outstanding Serv Award 1985; San Diego Volunteer Prog.

WEBER, DR. SHIRLEY NASH
School administrator. **Personal:** Born Sep 20, 1948, Hope, AR; daughter of Mildred (deceased) and David Nash; married Daniel; children: Akilah Faizah & Akil Khalfani. **Educ:** Univ Calif, LA, BA, speech commun, 1970, MA, speech commun, 1971, PhD, speech commun, 1975. **Career:** Episcopal City Mission Soc, LA,

caseworker, 1969-72; Calif State Col, LA, instr, 1972; San Diego State Univ, prof, 1972-, prof & chairperson, currently; San Diego City Schs, San Diego, CA, pres bd educ, 1990-91. **Orgs:** Bd mem, Calif Black Fac & Staff, 1976-80; regional ed, Western Jour Speech, 1979-; pres, Black Caucus Speech Comm Asn, 1980-82; adv bd, Battered Women's Serv YWCA, 1981-; pres, Nat Comm Asn, 1983-85; Coun 21 Southwestern Christian Col, 1983-; vpres, Nat Sorority Phi Delta Kappa Delta Upsilon Chapter; trustee, Bd Educ, San Diego Unified Sch Dist, 1988-96; dir, Acad Effectively Teaching African Am Stud; dir, Nat Asn Advan Colored People. **Honors/Awds:** Outstanding Young Woman in America, 1976, 1981; Outstanding Faculty Award, 1981, 1988, 1990; Black Achievement Action Enterprise Development, 1981; Women of Distinction Women Inc, 1984; National Citation Award, Nat Sorority Phi Delta Kappa, Inc, 1989; Citizen of the Year, Omega Psi Phi Fraternity, 1989; Carter G Woodson Education Award, NAACP, San Diego, 1989. **Special Achievements:** Became one of seventeen Woodrow Wilson fellows out of a class of over 6,000 from UCLA in 1970, also hosted her own talk show. **Business Addr:** Professor of African Studies, Chairperson of Black Studies Department, San Diego State University, AL 371 5500 Campanile Dr, San Diego, CA 92182, **Business Phone:** (619)594-6550.

WEBSTER, CHARLES
Dentist, army officer. **Personal:** Born Dec 15, 1936, LeCompte, LA; son of Charles Webster Sr and Carrie Hills. **Educ:** Southern Univ, BS, 1959; Howard Univ, MS, 1971, Col Dent, DDS, 1977; St. Elizabeth Hosp, residency training. **Career:** GA Ave Kiwanis Club, bus mgr, 1984-85; Dept Human Servs, dent officer; pvt pract, dentist, currently. **Orgs:** Kappa Alpha Psi, 1957-; dent intern St Elizabeth Hosp WA DC, 1977-78; dent dir, Montgomery Co Detention Ctr, 1978; Am Soc Dent C, 1978; Am Dent Soc, 1981; Asn Military Surgeons, 1981, Anethesiol Training Uniform Serv Med Sch, 1982-84; Robert T. Freeman Dent Soc; Nat Dent Asn; Eta Chi Sigma Hon Biological Soc; Beta Beta Beta Hon Biol Soc. **Honors/Awds:** Cert, Am Cancer Soc, 1977. **Military Serv:** AUS, lt col, Army Nat Guard, 1981-97 (retired). **Business Addr:** Dentists, 7723 Alaska Ave NW, Washington, DC 20012.*

WEBSTER, JOHN W, III
Software developer. **Personal:** Born Oct 19, 1961, Highland Park, MI; son of Melceina L Blackwell and John W Jr; married Michele S Peters, Feb 19. **Educ:** Mass Inst Technol, Cambridge, Mass, BSCS, 1983, MSCS, 1987. **Career:** Int Bus Mach Corp, Cambridge, Mass, scientific staff mem, 1983-87, scientific proj mgr, 1987-88; Int Bus Mach Corp, Res Triangle Park, NC, commun & system mgt designer, 1988-89, develop mgr, 1989; Permitsnow Inc, chief exec officer; Softcomp Inc, vice chmn & pres, chief exec officer, currently. **Honors/Awds:** Outstanding Technical Achievement Award, Int Bus Mach, 1986; Invention Achievement Award, Int Bus Mach, 1989. **Business Phone:** (301)840-3855.

WEBSTER, KAREN ELAINE
Government official. **Personal:** Born Jan 7, 1960, Atlanta, GA; daughter of Donald and Isabell Gates. **Educ:** Univ Va, BA, 1982; Ga State Univ, MA, 1991. **Career:** Grocery Manufacturers Am, state legislative aide, 1983; Fulton County Govt, law clerk, judge, 1984, law clerk, solicitor general, 1984-88, dir, victim & witness prog, 1988-91, exec asst county mgr, 1991-92, exec dir, intergovt affairs, 1992-94, chief staff chmn; Fulton County Dist 2, comnr, 1999-01; Beers Skanska Inc, sr vpres, 1999-02; Atlanta Downtown Improvement Dist Bd, 2002-. **Orgs:** Bd mem, Regional Leadership Inst; chair, nominating comt, YWCA, Greater Atlanta; southern area secy, Links Inc, 1993-; vpres, selection comt, Outstanding Atlantans, 1994; dist adv, Atlanta Junior League, 1994-; Bd dir, Regional Leadership found, 1994; bd mem, The Southern Inst, 1994-. **Honors/Awds:** Regional Leadership Institute, 1993; Leadership America, 1994. **Special Achievements:** First female to hold a countywide position on the Fulton County Board of Commissioners. *

WEBSTER, LARRY MELVIN, JR.
Football player. **Personal:** Born Jan 18, 1969, Elkton, MD. **Educ:** Univ Md. **Career:** Football player (retired); Miami Dolphins, defensive tackle, 1992-94; Cleveland Browns, 1995; Baltimore Ravens, 1997-2001; New York Jets, 2002. **Honors/Awds:** Baltimore Ravens Super Bowl XXXV Champions.

WEBSTER, LENNY
Baseball player. **Personal:** Born Feb 10, 1965, New Orleans, LA. **Career:** Baseball player (retired); Minn Twins, catcher, 1989-93; Montreal Expos, 1994, 1996, 2000; Philadelphia Phillies, 1995; Baltimore Orioles, 1997-99; Boston Red Sox, 1999.

WEBSTER, LESLEY DOUGLASS
Lawyer. **Personal:** Born Jun 9, 1949, New York, NY; son of Bernard; married Jules A Webster; children: Jules S Webster. **Educ:** Northeastern Univ Boston, BA, 1972; Georgetown Univ Law Ctr, JD, 1975; Wharton Col; Rutgers Univ. **Career:** Cambridge Redevel Authority Mass, comt organiser, 1970-72; Criminal Justice Clin, Georgetown Univ Law Ctr, prosecution coord, 1974-75; US Dept Energy, Region II, NY, atty, adv, 1975-77; Col Staten Island, NY, adj prof, 1977-78; US Dept Energy, Reg II, NY, dep regional coun, 1977-79; Northville Ind Corp, compliance coun, 1979-84; NY Dept Com, dep comnr, coun; City New York Parks & Recreation Dept, atty, currently. **Orgs:** Chairwoman bd, Asn Energy Prof, 1980-84. **Honors/Awds:** Superior Serv Award, US Dept Energy, 1976. **Business Addr:** Attorney, City of New York parks and Recreation Department, Arsenal Central Park, New York, NY 10021.

WEBSTER, MARVIN NATHANIEL. **See Obituaries section.**

WEBSTER, NIAMBI DYANNE
Educator. **Personal:** Children: K Tyronne Colemon. **Educ:** Drake Univ, BA, eng, 1973; Mankato State Col, MS, curriculum & instr, 1975; Univ Iowa, PhD, curriculum & instr, 1991; Jacksonville Theol Soc,ThD. **Career:** Des Moines Pub Schs, instr, 1975-78; Iowa Bystander, free lance writer, assoc ed, 1976-80; Univ Iowa, coordr minority prog, 1978-83; Iowa Arts Coun, touring music & theatre folk artist, 1978-; Univ Iowa, grad asst instr, 1980-83; Coe Col, instr dir special servs; Skidmore Col, dir multicultural & int stud affairs, 1989-91; Sonoma State Univ, Am Multicultural Studies Dept, asst prof, currently; Wooddale High Sch,instr, currently. **Orgs:** Outreach counselor YMCA Des Moines, 1974-78; instr Gateway Oppor Pageant, 1975-78; press & publicity chair NAACP Des Moines Chap, 1976-78; founder/dir Langston Hughes Co of Players, 1976-82; co-chair Polk CoRape/Sexual Assault Bd, 1977-80; artist-in-the schools IA Arts Coun, 1978-; 6th Judicial Dist Correctional Serv CSP & News Editor Volunteer, 1984-; chairperson Mid-Amer Assoc of Ed Opportunity Prog Personnel Cultural Enrichment Comm, 1984-; mem Delta Sigma Theta Sor, Berkeley Alumnae; Iowa City Comm Schools Equity Comm mem, 1985-87. **Honors/Awds:** Comm Service in the Fine Arts NAACP Presidential, 1978; Black Leadership Awd Univ of IA, 1979; Social Action Awd Phi Beta Sigma Frat, 1980; Outstanding Young Woman in the Arts NAACP Natl Women Cong, 1981; Women Equality & Dedication Comm on the Status of Women, 1981; Trio Achievers Awd Natl Cncl of Educ Oppor Assoc, 1985; Outstanding Woman of the Year Awd Linn Co Comm, 1986. **Home Addr:** 10 Meridian Circle, Rohnert Park, CA 94928. **Business Addr:** Instructor, Wooddale High School, 5151 Scottsdale Ave, Memphis, TN 38118, **Business Phone:** (901)416-2440.

WEBSTER, THEODORE E.
Executive. **Personal:** Married; married. **Educ:** MBA. **Career:** Webster Eng Co Inc, Dorchester, Mass, pres & chief exec officer, 1977-. **Orgs:** pres, Mass Chap Nat Assn Minority Contractors; chmn, Mass Alliance Small Contractors; Burroughs Group; Veterans Benefits Clearing house; US Dept Labor. **Honors/Awds:** 20th Century Boston Exhibit, Boston Pub Lib. **Business Addr:** President, Chief Executive Officer, Webster Engineering Company Inc, 2300 Crown Colony Dr Suite 101, Quincy, MA 02169, **Business Phone:** (617)265-5500.

WEBSTER, WILLIAM H
Lawyer. **Personal:** Born Oct 26, 1946, New York, NY; son of Eugene Burnett and Verna May Bailey; married Joan Leslie; children: Sydney. **Educ:** New York Univ, BA (cum laude), 1972; Univ Calif, Berkeley, Sch Law, JD, 1975. **Career:** Black Law J, Univ Calif, Berkeley, res assoc, 1973; Nat Econ Develop & Law Proj, post-grad, 1974-76; Nat Econ Develop & Law Ctr, Berkeley, CA, atty, 1976-82; Hunter & Anderson, partner, 1983-; Webster & Anderson, managing partner, atty, 1993-; Martin Luther King fel. **Orgs:** Nat Training Inst Com Econ Develop, Artisans Coop Inc; Mayors Housing Task Force Berkeley; State Bar Calif; US Dist Ct No Dist Calif; US Tax Ct; Nat Asn Bond Lawyers; Nat Bar Asn; Charles Houston Bar Asn; City Berkeley Citizens Com Responsible Invests; Kappa Alpha Psi. **Honors/Awds:** NY State Regents Incentive Awards; Howard Mem Fund Scholar; Alpha Phi Alpha Scholar; pub, "Housing, Structuring Housing Develop," Econ Develop Law Ctr Report, 1978, "Tax Savings through Intercorporate Billing," Econ Develop Law Ctr Report, 1980;various other publications. **Business Addr:** Attorney, Managing partner, Webster & Anderson Law Office, 469 9th St Suite 240, Oakland, CA 94607-4047, **Business Phone:** (510)839-3245.

WEBSTER, WINSTON ROOSEVELT
Lawyer. **Personal:** Born Apr 22, 1943, Nashville, TN. **Educ:** Fisk Univ, AB, 1965; Harvard Univ, LLB, 1968. **Career:** Neighborhood Legal Serv Prog, staff atty, 1968-69; Urban Inst, think tank researcher, 1969-70; Off Legal Servs WA, supervisory gen atty, 1970-72; Practicing Atty, 1971-; Cable TV Info Ctr, regional dir, 1972-74; Tex Southern Univ, law prof, 1974-77; Tex Southern Univ, mem bd regents, 1979-. **Orgs:** US Dist Ct DC & TC; Superior Ct DC; Supreme Ct TX; DC Bar Asn; TX Bar Asn; Am Asn Trial Lawyers; Nat Conf Black Lawyers; bd dir, Nat Paralegal Inst, 1972-75; legal adv comt, TX Asn Col Teachers, 1976-77; bd gov, WA Athletic Club, 1974. **Honors/Awds:** Hon Citizen New Orleans, 1971; Duke of Paducah, 1972; KY Col, 1973; Professor of Yr, Thurgood Marshall Sch of Law, 1976-77; Outstanding Young Men of Am, 1977; Num Articles.

WEDDERBURN, DR. RAYMOND
Hospital administrator, surgeon. **Personal:** Born May 1, 1961, Kingston, Jamaica. **Educ:** Brown Univ; Cornel Univ Med Col, 1986; Univ Miami, Jackson Mem Hosp-19Surgical Critical Care Fel, 1993. **Career:** St Luke's-Roosevelt Hosp Ctr, resident, surg, 1987-91, Dept Surg, Chief-Trauma & Critical Care. **Honors/Awds:** Resident' Award for Excellence in Teaching, St Luke's-Roosevelt Hosp Ctr, Dept Surg, 1993-94, 1996-97, 1999-00. **Special Achievements:** Publ: Management of Paroxysmal Atrioventricular Nodal Reentrant Tachycardia in the Critically Ill Surgical Patient. Kirton OC, Windson J, Civetta, JM, Cudson-Civetta J, Wedderurn R, Gomez DV, Shatz J, Hudson-Civetta S, Komanduri S. Critical Care Medicine: 25 (5):May 1997;761-6; Failure of Splanchnic Resuscitation in the Acutely Injured Trauma Patient Correlates with Multiple Organ system Failure and Length of Stay in the ICU. Iirton O, Windsor HJ,Wedderburn R, Hudson-Civetta J, Shatz, D, Mataragas N, Civetta J. Chest:113(4): April 1998, 1064-9. **Business Phone:** (212)523-2211.

WEDDINGTON, BILL
Educator. **Educ:** Calif State Univ, Chico, BA, MA; Univ San Francisco, EdD. **Career:** Napa Valley Col, prof psychol, coun, currently. **Orgs:** Counr, Acad Stand & Practices Comt, Napa Valley Col. **Business Addr:** Professor of Psychology, Napa Valley College, 2277 Napa-Vallejo Hwy, Napa, CA 94558.

WEDDINGTON, DR. RACHEL THOMAS
Educator. **Personal:** Born Mar 9, 1917, Atlantic City, NJ; daughter of Ralph Thornton (deceased) and Laura Frances (deceased). **Educ:** Howard Univ, Wash DC, AB, 1938, AM, 1940; Univ Chicago, PhD, 1958. **Career:** Rosenwald Found, fel, 1946-48; Atlantic City New Jersey, 1941-45; Howard Univ, instr, 1948-57; Merrill-Palmer Inst Detroit, res assoc, 1957-61; Queens Coll NY, asst, assoc prof, 1961-75; CUNY, univ dean teacher educ, 1975-79, prof, 1975-85, prof emer. **Orgs:** Pi Lambda Theta Univ Chicago, 1947; Kappa Delta Pi Howard Univ, 1954. **Home Addr:** 575 Main St, New York, NY 10044.

WEDDINGTON, DR. WAYNE P, JR.
Otolaryngologist. **Personal:** Born Dec 24, 1936, McGehee, AR; son of Wayne Pennoyer L and Amanda Tyler; married Dolores Johnson, Dec 2, 1957. **Educ:** Univ Arkansas, AM&Normal Col, BS, 1958; Howard Univ, Col Med, Wash, DC, MD, 1963; Andrews Air Force Base, Camp Springs, MD, intern, 1964. **Career:** Temple Univ Health & Sci Ctr, Philadelphia, PA, resident; ORL Germantown Hosp & Med Ctr, Dept Otolaryngology, Philadelphia, PA, chmn, 1974-; Neuman Med Ctr, Philadelphia, PA, staff physician; St Christopher's Hosp, staff physician; Weddington Ent Assocs MC, Philadelphia, PA, owner & CEO, 1981-; Episcopal Hosp, Dept Otolaryngology, sect chief, 1992; pvt pract, currently. **Orgs:** Fel, Am Acad Otolaryngology; 1972-; Fel, Col Physicians Philadelphia, 1990-; Nat Med Asn; Pennsylvania Acad Otolaryngology, 1972-; fel, African Sci Inst. **Home Addr:** 901 Laburnum Lane, Wyncote, PA 19095. **Business Addr:** Founder, Weddington Ent Assoc Inc, 827 E Upsal St, Philadelphia, PA 19119, **Business Phone:** (215)438-3898.

WEDDINGTON, DR. WILBURN HAROLD, SR.
Physician, educator. **Personal:** Born Sep 21, 1924, Hiram, GA; son of Charlie Earl and Annie Mae Moore; married Rose Carline Howard, Mar 15, 1979; children: Wilburn H Jr, Cynthia D, Kimberly K, Marisia D & Wilburn C. **Educ:** Morehouse Col, Atlanta, Ga, BS, 1944; Howard Univ, Wash, DC, MD, 1948; Univ Buffalo, Buffalo, NY, Radiol; Harvard Univ, Electrocardiography, 1962; Univ Mexico, course obstet & pediat; Howard Univ, family med rev. **Career:** Mercy Hosp, staff physician, 1957-70; Grant Hosp, staff physician, 1957-; St Anthony Hosp, staff physician, 1958-; Ohio State Univ, Col Med, Columbus, Ohio, staff physician, 1970-88, clin assoc prof, 1980-85, prof clin family med, assoc dean med, prof emer clin family med, currently. **Orgs:** Am Med Asn, 1952-; Nat Med Asn, 1954-; Ohio State Med Asn, 1958-; Columbus & Franklin Co Acad Med, 1958-; Am Soc Hypnosis, 1963; Ohio Acad Family Physicians, 1968-; Cent Ohio Acad Family Physicians, 1968-; mem, 1968-, Am Acad Family Physicians, fel 1974-; co-founder, Columbus Asn Physicians & Dentistry, 1973-; Omega Psi Phi; Sigma Pi Phi. **Honors/Awds:** Citizen of the Year, Mu Iota Chap, Omega Psi Phi, 1985; Regional IV Award, Nat Med Asn, 1985; Citation Tremendous Record of Professional Achievement, Gen Assembly Ohio Senate, 1987; Recognition of Dedicated Service in the Field of Medicine, Ohio House Reps, 1987; Special Recognition for Dedicated Service as a member of the Governor's Task Force on BLK & MNY health, Gov Ohio, 1987; Recognition for Outstanding Performance & Service in Columbus BLK COT, Columbus Urban League, 1987; Dedication Award for Outstanding Service to Ohio State University, World Week, 1988; Citation for Dedicated Leadership as Chair of the Com health Affairs, Am Acad Family Physicians, 1988; 7th Annual Distinguished Affirmative Action Award, State Univ, 1989; Educator of the Year Award, Ohio Acad Family Physicians, 1991; Distinguished Service Award, Ohio State Univ, 1999. **Special Achievements:** Co-author, "Surgery Practice and Perceived Training Needs of Selected Ohio Family Physicians," Journal of Family Practice, Sep 1986; "Review of Literature Concerning Racial Effects on Medical Treatment and Outcome," Jour Am Bd Family Practice, 1990; numerous editorials. **Business Addr:** Professor Emeritus, Ohio State University, Department of Family Medicine, 2231 N High St, Columbus, OH 43201, **Business Phone:** (614)293-2653.

WEDGEWORTH, ROBERT W, JR.
Librarian, school administrator. **Personal:** Born Jul 31, 1937, Ennis, TX; son of Robert Sr and Jimmie Johnson; married Chung Kyun. **Educ:** Wabash Col, BA, 1959; Univ Ill, MS, libr sci, 1961. **Career:** KC Publ Libr, cataloger, 1961-62; Seattle Worlds Fair Libr 21, staff mem, 1962; Park Col, asst librn, 1962-63, head librn, 1963-64; Meramec Community Col Kirkwood, head librn, 1964-66; Brown Univ Libr, asst chief order librn, 1966-69; Libr Resources & Tech Serv off, ALA Jour, ed; Rutgers Univ, asst prof; Univ Chicago, lectr; Columbia Univ, Sch Libr Serv, dean, 1985-92; Univ Ill, Urbana-Champaign, interim librn, 1992, univ librn & prof libr admin, 1993-2001; Laubach Literacy Int, pres; ProLiteracy Worldwide, pres & ceo, 2002-07. **Orgs:** NAACP; Pub Serv Satellite Consortium Bd; adv coun mem, Am Libr Asn; trustees, Newberry Libr; Adv Comt, US Book & Libr; vpres, Wabash Col Alumni Bd; mem adv, Coun WBEZ Chicago; Am Antiquarian Soc; exec bd mem, 1985-91, pres, 1997-97, Intl Fed Libr Assoc & Institutions; SYRACUSE 20/20's Educ Task Force; chair, Comt Accreditation, ALA, 2003-05. **Honors/Awds:** DHL, Syracuse Univ, 2008. **Special Achievements:** editor of two major reference works, ALA Yearbook, 1976-85 and the World Encyclopedia of Library and Information Services, 3d edition, 1993; co-author of Starvation of Young Black Minds: The Effects of the Book Boycotts in South Africa, 1989. *

WEEKS, DEBORAH REDD
Lawyer. **Personal:** Born Dec 23, 1947, Brooklyn, NY; daughter of Warren Ellington Redd and Edna Loretta Mayo Redd; divorced; children: Monteil Dior & Kristienne Dior. **Educ:** Fisk Univ, Nashville, Tenn, BA, 1970; Univ Ky, Lexington, Ky, JD, 1978. **Career:** Ky State Govt, Frankfort, Ky, dir contract compliance state Ky, 1980-83; Urban League, Lexington, Ky, dir adoption, 1983-85; WLEX-TV, Lexington, Ky, Talk Show Host, 1984-86; State Univ NY, Brockport, NY, dir, AA/EEO, 1986-89; Monroe Co, Rochester, NY, coun dir AA/EEO, 1989-90; Health & Hosp Corp, New York, NY, assoc legal, 1991; Dept Bus Serv, New York, NY, comnr, currently. **Orgs:** Coalition of 100 Black Women, 1984-; Links, 1988-; chmn, EEO Comt, Harlem Bus Alliance, 1989-; RACOL Ctr Bd, 1990-; Negro Bus & Prof Women, 1990-. **Honors/Awds:** Kentucky Colonel, State Ky, 1986; Multiculturism, New York Asn Col Personnel Admin, summer, 1987. **Home Phone:** (718)789-4794. **Business Addr:** Commissioner, Department of Business Services, 110 William St, New York, NY 10038, **Business Phone:** (212)513-6300.

WEEKS, RENEE JONES
Judge. **Personal:** Born Dec 28, 1948, Washington, DC. **Educ:** Ursuline Col, BA, 1970; Rutgers Law Sch, JD, 1973. **Career:** Judge (retired); State NJ, dep attorney gen, 1973-75; Prudential Ins Co Am, staff, 1975-89; Super Ct NJ, judge, 1989-2009. **Orgs:** Past pres, Women's Div, Nat Bar Asn; Am Bar Asn; past pres, Asn Black Women Lawyers NJ, 1975-77; Asn Black Women Lawyers NJ, 1977-; past assttreas, Nat Asn Black Women Attys; Nat Asn Women Judges, 1986-; Alpha Kappa Alpha; Minority Interchange; former vpres, Nat Bar Asn, 1979-81; formerchair judicial coun, Nat Bar Asn, 1995-97; former trustee, Essex Co Bar Asn; past sec, Garden State Bar Asn; Nat Coun Juvenile & Family Ct Judges; former mem, New Jersey Family Prac Comt & Domestic Violence Working Group; former mem, NJ Supreme Ct, Minority Concerns Comt; former sec, Judicial Coun, Nat Bar; Nat Bar Judicial Coun; Alpha Kappa Alpha Sorority; Rho Sorority. **Honors/Awds:** Young Lawyers Division Section Award, NJ State Bar, 1980; President's Award, Nat Bar Asn, 1984; Garden State Bar Award, 1998; Mem Distinction Award, Essex County, 2001; Rho Gamma Omega Chapter, 2002. **Special Achievements:** First African-American woman to preside New Jersey's general equity and probate court. First African-American woman appointed in Essex Co Court; first African-American woman assistant general counsel at Prudential Insurance.

WEEMS, LUTHER B. **See AKBAR, DR. NA.**

WEEMS, VERNON EUGENE, JR.
Lawyer. **Personal:** Born Apr 27, 1948, Waterloo, IA; son of Eugene and Anna Marie Hickey. **Educ:** Univ IA, BA, 1970; Univ Miami Sch Law, JD, 1974. **Career:** US Small Bus Admin, atty & advisor, 1977-81; Weems Law Off, atty, 1978-; Nation United Inc, pres, chief exec officer & chmn bd, 1982-85; Weems Prod & Enterprises, chief exec officer & consult, 1987-. **Orgs:** Am Bar Asn, 1977-82, Iowa State Bar Asn, 1977-82; affil, St Johns Lodge Prince Hall, 1977-86, Fed Bar Asn, 1979-82; bd dirs, Black Hawk County Iowa Br, Nat Asn Advan Colored People. **Honors/Awds:** Publication "Tax Amnesty Blueprint for Economic Development", 1981; Leadership Award OIC/Iowa, 1982; Service Appreciation Award Job Service of Iowa, 1985; Recognition of Excellence 1986. **Business Addr:** Attorney, Weems Productions & Enterprises, PO Box 72, Waterloo, IA 50704-0072, **Business Phone:** (319)233-6058.

WEISS, ED, JR.
Automotive executive. **Career:** Allegan Ford-Mercury Sales Inc, Allegan, Mich, chief exec, 1984-. **Business Phone:** (616)673-5591.

WEISS, JOYCE LACEY
Educator. **Personal:** Born Jun 8, 1941, Chicago, IL; daughter of Lois Lacey Carter; divorced. **Educ:** Bennett Col, BA, 1963; Troy State Univ, MS, 1971; Univ MI, EdD, 1988. **Career:** Coweta County GA, elem class teacher, 1963-64; Montgomery AL, elem class teacher, 1964-69; Montgomery AL, elem sch principal, 1969-75; Troy State Univ, instr & supvr student teachers, 1975-, asst prof & dept chmn, elem educ; Huntingdon Col, assoc prof educ, currently. **Orgs:** Delta Sigma Theta; Montgomery AL Chap Nat Asn Advan Colored People; Links Inc; Nat Educ Asn, 1963-; Zeta Gamma Chapter Kappa Delta Pi, 1973-; Asn Teacher Educrs, 1975-; Troy Univ Chap Phi Delta Kappa, 1980-; Int Reading Asn; Ala Reading Asn; Am Educ Res Asn; Ala Educ Asn. **Honors/Awds:** Nat Merit Scholar Bennett Col, 1959; Sch Educ Fel Univ MI, 1984-85; Rackham Grad Fel, 1985; MI Minority Fel, 1985-87; Sch Educ, Dean's Merit Fel, 1988; Rackham Sch Grad Studies, dissertation/thesis grant, Univ MI, 1987; Mich Minority Merit Fel, 1985-87, Sch Educ Fel, 1985-86; Dearborn Diversity Grants, Univ MI, 2001. **Business Addr:** Associate Professor, Huntingdon College, Cloverdale 121B 1500 E Fairview Ave, Montgomery, AL 36106, **Business Phone:** (334)833-4444.

WEISS, LEVEN C.
Manager. **Career:** DaimlerChrysler Corp, dir community rels, civic & community rels sr mgr, currently. **Business Addr:** Senior Manager of Civic and Community Relations, DaimlerChrysler Corporation, 1000 Chrysler Dr, Auburn Hills, MI 48326-2766, **Business Phone:** (248)512-2950.*

WEISSINGER, THOMAS
Librarian. **Personal:** Born Jul 29, 1951, Silver Creek, NY; son of Tom and Hattie Bryant; married Maryann Hunter, Jun 2, 1973; children: Thomas Jr, Sandra & Eric. **Educ:** State Univ NY, Sch Arts & Sci, Buffalo, NY, BA, 1973; Univ Pittsburgh, Sch Arts Sci, Pittsburgh, PA, MA, 1978; Univ Pittsburgh, Sch Libr & Info Studies, Pittsburgh, PA, MLS, 1980. **Career:** Newark Pub Libr, NJ, city hall librn, 1980-82; Rutgers Univ, New Brunswick, NJ, bibliog instr coordr, 1982-85; Cornell Univ Libr, Ithaca, NY, head, John Henrik Clarke Africana Libr, dir, 1985-2001; African Ctr Develop & Strat Studies Ijebu-Ode, Nigeria, consult, 1994-; Arthur R Ashe Jr Foreign Policy Libr, consult, 1996-; African & African Am Serials Periodical Contents Index, consult, 1997-; Univ Ill Libr, Urbana-Champaign, Urbana, IL, Afro-Am bibliographer & assoc prof libr admin, 2001-, assoc prof African Am studies, 2003-, head Afro-Am Libr Unit, currently. **Orgs:** Am Libr Asn, 1980-; chair, Black Caucus Am Libr Asn Pub Comt, 1984-87; African Studies Asn, 1991-; exec comt mem, Africana Librarians Coun, 1992-94; secy, Coop Africana Microfilming Proj, 1993-95. **Honors/Awds:** Co-compiler, Black Labor Am: A Selected Annotated Bibliog, Westport, CT, Greenwood Press, 1986; compiler, Current Bibliog, Black Am Lit Forum, 1988; asst ed, Black Caucus of Am Libr AsN Newsletter, 1984-88; Author: "African American Reference Books & the Reviewing Media" The Reference Librn, No 45/46, 137-51,"Defining Black Studies on the World Wide Web," Journ of Academic Librianship, 25 July 1999, 288-93; Libr Consult, African Ctr Develop & Strategic Studies, Ijebu-ode, Nigeria, 1994; Libr Consult, TransAfrica Forum, Wash, DC, 1996. **Business Addr:** Associate Professor of Library Administration, Associate Professor of African American Studies, Univerity of Illinois, Afro-Americana Library, 1408 W Gregory Dr, 328 Library, Urbana, IL 61801, **Business Phone:** (217)333-3006.

WELBORN, EDWARD, JR.
Executive director. **Career:** Gen Motors Corp, GM Design Studio, exec dir, currently. **Business Addr:** Executive Director, General Motors Corp, GM Design Studio, 300 Renaissance Ctr, PO Box 300 MC 482-C27-B22, Detroit, MI 48265-3000, **Business Phone:** (313)556-5000.

WELBURN, CRAIG
Executive, chief executive officer. **Personal:** Son of Craig T and Diane; married Eugenia. **Educ:** James Madison Univ, BA, 1996. **Career:** McDonald's Corp, National Black McDonald's Operators Asn, pres philadelphia region, NE Div, pres, restaurant owner, head, chmn & chief exec officer, 1998-01, 2004-. **Orgs:** bd dirs, Ronald McDonald House; bd dirs, Del Valley Friends Sch. **Business Phone:** (323)296-5495.*

WELBURN, EDWARD THOMAS, JR.
Automotive executive. **Personal:** Born Dec 14, 1950, West Chester, PA; son of Edward Welburn Sr and Evelyn Thornton Welburn; married Rhonda Doby; children: Adrienne & Brian. **Educ:** Howard Univ, BFA, 1972. **Career:** GM Design Staff, creative designer, 1972-75, sr creative designer, 1976-81, asst chief designer, 1981-89, Oldsmobile studio, chief designer; Chevrolet, vehicle chief designer, currently; General Motors, exec dir, 2002-03, chief designer, 2003-. **Orgs:** Cabinet, 1983-; Founders Soc Detroit Inst Art. **Honors/Awds:** Alumni of the Year, Howard University Student Asn, 1989. **Special Achievements:** First African American to rise to what is considered one of the most prestigious jobs in the automotive industry. **Business Addr:** Chief Designer, General Motors Design Center, PO Box 33170, Detroit, MI 48232-5170, **Business Phone:** (817)608-2346.

WELBURN, RON. **See WELBURN, RONALD GARFIELD.**

WELBURN, RONALD GARFIELD (RON WELBURN)
Writer, educator. **Personal:** Born Apr 30, 1944, Berwyn, PA; son of Howard Watson and Jessie W; married Cheryl Donahue, 1988; children: Loren Beatty, Justin Beatty & Elliott Welburn. **Educ:** Lincoln Univ, PA, BA, 1968; Univ Ariz, MA, 1970; NY Univ, PhD, 1983. **Career:** Syracuse Univ, Syracuse, NY, asst prof Afro-Am studies, 1970-75; Rutgers Univ, New Brunswick, NJ, Inst Jazz Studies, asst prof Eng, 1983; Western Connecticut State Univ, Danbury, CT, asst prof english; Univ Mass, Dept Eng, prof, currently. **Orgs:** Bd mem, Eagle Wing Press, 1989-. **Honors/Awds:** Silvera Award for poetry, Lincoln Univ, 1967 & 1968; fel Smithsonian Inst & Music Critics Asn, 1975; Langston Hughes Legacy Certificate, Lincoln Univ, 1981; Wordcraft Circle of the Americans Writer of the year, 2002 Award for Creative Prose. **Special Achievements:** Author: Peripheries: Selected Poems, 1966-1968, Greenfield Review Press, 1972; Heartland: Selected Poems, Lotus Press, 1981; Council Decisions: Poems, American Native Press Archives, 1991; "Roanoke and Wampum"; "A Most Secret Identity: Native American Assimilation and Identity Resistance in African America". **Home Addr:** PO Box 420, Hadley, MA 01035-0420, **Home Phone:** (413)549-4518. **Business Phone:** (413)545-5518.

WELCH, ASHTON WESLEY
Educator. **Personal:** Born Jun 17, 1947; son of J W and Ina I; married Helen M Wanken, May 29, 1976. **Educ:** Univ Hull, UK, 1966-67; Wilberforce Univ, BA, 1968; Univ Wis, Madison, cert, 1971, MA, 1971; Univ Birmingham, UK, PhD, 1979. **Career:** Richmond Col, UK, 1987-88; Creighton Univ, coordr black studies, 1975-, hist chmn, 1986-93, assoc prof, 1975-, dir, Hons prog, 1998-, William M Barry prof, 2001-. **Orgs:** African Studies Asn, 1971-; Asn Study Afro-Am Life & Cult, 1973-; bd dirs, Great Plains Black Mus, 1975-88; Nat Coun Black Studies, 1976-; bd dirs, Nat Asn Ethnic Studies, 1977-; bd dirs, Creighton Fed Credit Union, 1986-; African Lit Asn, 2001. **Honors/Awds:** Robert F Kennedy Award for Excellence in Teaching, Creighton Univ, 1992; Dean's Award, for Excellence in Advising, Creighton Univ, Col Arts & Scis, 1993; Distinguished Faculty Award, Creighton Univ, 1996; Outstanding Volunteer of the Yr, Creighton Fed Credit Union, 1996; Dean's Award for Excellence In Teaching, Creighton Univ, Col Arts & Sci, 1999; Dedicated Service Award, 100 BLK Men, Omaha chap, 2001; Award for Excellence in Prof Service, Creighton Univ, Col Arts & Sci, 2002; Charles C Irby Award, Nat Asn Ethic Studies, 2002. **Special Achievements:** Author: Omaha: Positve Planning for Peaceful Integration, 1980; National Archives Ivory Coast, 1982; Ethnic Definitions as Reflections Pub Policy, 1983; BLK or AFA: What's in a Name?-A Critique, 1990; Jihad, Just War: Thru Views, 1991; Civil Rights Act 1968, 1992; Making an African-Am Population: Omaha, 1993; Emancipation in United States, 1993. **Business Addr:** Associate Professor of History, Creighton University, 2500 California Plaza 341 Administration, Omaha, NE 68178, **Business Phone:** (402)280-2884.

WELCH, HARVEY
School administrator. **Personal:** Born Jun 5, 1932, Centralia, IL; married Patricia Kay; children: Harvey, Gordon, Karen & Brian. **Educ:** Southern Ill Univ, Carbondale, BS, 1955, MS, educ, 1958. **Career:** Southern Ill Univ, actg vpres stud affairs, dean & vice chancellor stud affairs, 1985-99, vice chancellor emer, 1999-. **Orgs:** Nat Asn Advan Colored People; Carbondale Planning Comn, 1976-78; Ill Guid & Personel Asn; Adv Bd Ill State Scholar Comt; Mid-West Equal Educ Opportunity; Southern Ill Univ, Am Asn Coun & Develop Asn; Nat Asn Stud Personal Admin; Nat Asn Stud Financial Aid Admin; Nat Asn Women Deans; Rotary Int; Southern Ill Regional Social Serv; chair, Epiphany Lutheran Church All Saints; Joint Service Comt, 1973. **Honors/Awds:** Distinguished Military Student, 1954; Hon Mention, Little All Am Basketball, 1954; Asn Honorary, Sco High Sch fel, Southern Ill Univ, Carbondale, 1958; Metetorious Service Medal, 1975; Service to Southern Illinois Award, Jackson Co Chap, Southern Ill Univ Alumni Asn, 2000; Pillars of the Profession Award, Nat Asn Stud Personnel Adminr, 2001. **Military Serv:** USAF, cornel, 1955-75. **Home Phone:** (618)529-1661. **Business Addr:** Vice Chancellor Emeritus, Southern Illinois University, 1900 N Illinois Ave, Carbondale, IL 62901-6899, **Business Phone:** (618)453-2121.

WELCH, JESSE ROY
Executive director, educator. **Personal:** Born May 29, 1949, Jonesville, LA; married Vickie Ragsdale (divorced); children: Symia. **Educ:** Wash State Univ, BA, 1971, ED, 1977. **Career:** Big Brother-Big Sister Prog Benicia CA, dir, head counr, 1967-68; Pullman YMCA, program adv, 1968-70; Wash State Univ, fin aid counr, 1970-71, assoc dir admissions, transfer articulation specialist; The Col Success Found (formerly Wash Educ Found), dir col prog, 2005. **Orgs:** Participant Johnson Found Wingspread Conf on Minority Groups in Col Student-Personnel Prog, 1971; Am Assoc Col Registrars & Admissions Officers, 1971-, WA State Univ Affirmative Action Coun, 1972-74; comt min affairs WA Coun HS Col Rel, 1973-; consult, Spokane Nursing Sch Minority Affairs Comt Spokane, 1973-74, WICHE Fac Devel Meet Minority Group Needs, 1973-74; adv bd, 1974-, co-chmn, 1974-76 YMCA Pullman WA. **Honors/Awds:** Numerous publications & papers. **Business Addr:** Director of College Programs, The College Success

Foundation, 1605 NW Sammamish Rd Suite 100, Issaquah, WA 98027, **Business Phone:** (425)416-2000.

WELCH, LOLITA
Health services administrator. **Personal:** Born in Detroit, MI. **Educ:** Univ Detroit, BBA, 1989. **Career:** State MI, minority bus specialist, 1990-95, acct mgr, 1995-97; Detroit Med Ctr, mgr, 1997; MGM Grand Detroit Casino, dir purchasing currently. **Orgs:** Coun Supplier Diversity Prof, Officer, 2001. **Honors/Awds:** Corporate One, 1999, 2000. **Business Addr:** Director Purchasing, MGM Grand Detroit Casino and Deb, 1300 John C Lodge, Detroit, MI 48226, **Business Phone:** (887)888-2121.

WELCH, DR. OLGA MICHELE
Educator, school administrator, dean (education). **Personal:** Born Dec 30, 1948, Salisbury, NC; daughter of S E Barnes; married George E; children: Taja Michele & Stephani Amber. **Educ:** Howard Univ, BA, salutatorian, hist, eng, educ 1971; Univ Tenn, MS, deaf educ, 1972, EdD, educ admin & super, 1977. **Career:** Model Sec Sch Deaf, instr, 1972-73, Tenn Sch Deaf, instr, 1973-75, sup vprin, 1977-78; Univ Tenn, Dept Spec Educ & Rehab, asst prof, 1977-82, assoc prof & dir, 1982-93, dir deaf educ prog, Rehab & Deafness Unit, prof; Duquesne Univ, Sch Educ, prof & dean, currently. **Orgs:** Interdenomi nat Concert Choir, 1975-; chmn, Girl Scout neighborhood, 1977-; Coun Except C; Alexander Graham Bell Asn; Conv Am Instr Deaf; Nat Educ Asn; Asn Supr & Curric Develop; vpres, Knoxville Chap Nat Black Women's Hook-Up, 1980-81; Project HELP tutorial prog disadvantaged students, 1983; Am Educ Res Asn; co-dir, Project Excel. **Honors/Awds:** Phi Beta Kappa; Phi Delta Kappa; Phi Kappa Phi; Phi Alpha Theta; appointed National Educ Adv Bd, 1983; E C Merrill Distinguished Research Award, 1990, 1992; Dept Award, "Most Creative Dissertation Topic", Chancellor's Award, Univ Tenn, 1998. **Special Achievements:** Olga Welch is the first black woman to serve as a dean of Duquesne University's School of Education. **Business Addr:** Professor, Dean School of Education, Duquesne University, 600 Forbes Ave, Pittsburgh, PA 15282, **Business Phone:** (412)396-6000.

WELDON, RAMON N.
Law enforcement officer. **Personal:** Born Jul 26, 1932, Keokuk, IA; son of Clarence and Virginia; married Betty Jean Watkins, Jul 24, 1955; children: Ramon N Jr. **Educ:** Keokuk Sr High Sch, dipl, 1951. **Career:** Law enforcement officer (retired); Keokuk Police Dept, patrolman, 1962-74, detective, 1974-80; capt, 1980-82; chief police, 1982-87. **Orgs:** Lee County Juvenile Restitution Bd, 1982; Keokuk Humane Soc, 1982; trustee, Keokuk Library Bd 2nd six year term; active mem, Iowa Chief's Assoc Nat Chief's Asn Int Chief's Asn, 1982-; chmn, United Way Bd; Hoerner Y Ctr Bd; chmn, Tri-State Coalition Against Family Violence; Lee County Compensation Bd, chmn. **Military Serv:** AUS, Corp, 2 yrs; Soilder of the Month, 1953. **Home Addr:** 2510 Decatur St, Keokuk, IA 52632.

WELLS, BARBARA JONES
Manager. **Personal:** Born Apr 18, 1939, Waterproof, LA; daughter of Willie Ray and Ruth Lee Johnson; married Washington, Jun 1, 1968. **Educ:** Grambling State Univ, BS, biol, educ, 1962; Southern Univ, Baton Rouge, LA, MS, biol, educ, 1968; Univ Iowa, further study, 1972; Univ New Orleans, 1978. **Career:** Tensas Parish Sch, St Joseph, LA, bio/chem teacher, 1962-68; Rapides Parish Schs, Alexandria, LA, chem teacher, 1968-70; New Orleans Pub Sch Syst, bio/chem teacher, 1970-80; Xavier Univ, New Orleans, LA, chem teacher, 1980-81, summer, 1979, 1980; New Orleans Pub Sch, New Orleans, LA, sci supvr, 1981-86; La Power & Light Co, New Orleans PSI, LA, communs rep, 1986-91, cot rels mgr, 1991-. **Orgs:** Fin & corres secy, DST Sorority, New Orleans Alumnae Chap, 1981-83, 1989; pres, Am Asn Blacks Energy, La Chap, 1988-90; treas/founder, DST Found, New Orleans Chap, 1988-; bd, NCW, YWCA Greater New Orleans, Vol Am; adv bd, New Orleans Pub Schs, COT Educ, Sci & Eng Fair Greater New Orleans, Carver Health Clin; vpres, La Literacy Found, New Orleans Alumnae Chap, 1991, bd, 1992; Xavier Univ Youth Motivation Task Force, 1990; proj dir, Metrop Area Guild; Nat Asn Advan Colored People. **Honors/Awds:** Unsung Hero Award, Links, Cresent City Chap, 1990; Outstanding Service in Science; Recipient Award, Pres Ronald Reagan, 1986; Recipient Award, Gov La, 1986; Recipient Award, Mayor New Orleans, 1986 & 1988; Recipient Award, State Sen, 1990. **Home Addr:** 11309 Waverly Dr, New Orleans, LA 70128. **Business Addr:** Community Relations Manager, Louisiana Power & Light Company, 639 Loyola Ave, New Orleans, LA 70112, **Business Phone:** (504)569-4000.

WELLS, BILLY GENE
Mayor, executive, business owner. **Personal:** Born in Bluff City, TN; son of Harley Boyd Wells and Grace Isbella Black; married Irene Elizabeth Coleman, Dec 31, 1962; children: Cynthia Anita & Rebecca Jean. **Career:** Tenn Eastman Co, Kingsport, TN, printer, 1964-; B&I Offset Printing, Bluff City, TN, owner, 1971-; City Bluff City, TN, mayor, 1985. **Orgs:** Bd mem, Sr Citizens, United Way & Teen World, all 1985-; Martin Luther King Jr State Holiday Community, 1986-. **Honors/Awds:** First black mayor elected in Tennessee; first mayor elected 3 times in a row in Bluff City.

WELLS, BONZI (GAWEN DEANGELO WELLS)
Basketball player. **Personal:** Born Sep 20, 1976; son of Gawen Wells and Christine Scaife Coleman; married; children: Duane, Gawen & Christian. **Educ:** Ball State Univ. **Career:** Detroit Pistons, 1998; Portland Trail Blazers, 1998-2004; Memphis Grizzlies, 2004-05; Sacramento Kings, guard & forward, 2005-06; Houston Rockets, 2006-08; New Orleans Hornets, 2008-. **Honors/Awds:** All-Am Hons. **Business Addr:** Professional Basketball Player, New Orleans Hornets, 1250 Poydras St Fl 19, New Orleans, LA 70113, **Business Phone:** (504)593-4700.

WELLS, DR. ELMER EUGENE
School administrator. **Personal:** Born Oct 6, 1939, Mt Pleasant, IA; married Georgia Lee Gehringer; children: Monte, Debra, Christian & Kori. **Educ:** Univ Alaska, MA 1970; Univ NM, PhD 1974. **Career:** Low Mt Boarding Sch Bur Indian Affairs Ariz, 1962-64; Mobil Oil Co SantaFe Springs CA, explor worker, 1964-65; Off Econ Opportunity, teen postdir, 1965-66; Bur Indian Affairs Pt Barrow AK, teacher/asst prin/prin,1966-71; Albuquerque Pub Sch, teacher, 1973-74; Univ Southern Colo,Teacher Corps Cycle 9 & 11 Pueblo, educ spec, 1974-78; Int Student Serv Univ Southern Colo, dir, 1978. **Orgs:** Pres/founder, Albuquerque Ethnic Communities Inc, 1973-74; pres/founder,CO Ethnic Communities Inc, 1975-80; exec bd, Pueblo Chap Nat Asn Advan Colored People, 1979-80; "Destroying a Racial Myth" The Social Studies Vol69 No 5, 1978; TV Debate Grand Wizard KKK Colo Springs Involvement Prog Channel 11, 1979. **Honors/Awds:** Speaker Annual Freedom Fund Banquet Colo Springs Chap, Nat Asn Advan Colored People, 1980. **Special Achievements:** Publ "The Mythical Negative Black Self Concept" R & E Res Asn, 1978. **Business Addr:** 2200 Bonforte Blvd, Pueblo, CO 81001.

WELLS, GAWEN DEANGELO. See WELLS, BONZI.

WELLS, IRA J. K., JR.
Lawyer. **Personal:** Born Oct 26, 1934, New York, NY; married; children: Joseph, Anita, JoAnne. **Educ:** Lincoln Univ, BA 1957; Temple Law Sch, LLD. **Career:** US Ct App 3rd Cir Phila, law clerk & ct crier 1964-66; US Dist Ct Eastern Dist PA, law clerk 1966-68; US Dept Housing & Urban Develop Philadelphia, atty, 1968; Pvt Pract, atty, currently. **Orgs:** Bd dir Zion Invest Asn Inc; Zion Non-Profit Char Trust; Opport Ind Cent Inc; OIC Int Inc 1968-; Ejay Trav Inc, 1970; Nat & Am PA & Philadelphia Bar Asn; treas, Philadelphia Int Prog, 1974-75; Barristers Club of Phila; Lawyers Club Phila; bd dir, Mental Health Asn Penn; treas & bd dir, Mental Health Asn, 1977-78; leg coun, East Man Group Homes Inc; E Mt Airy Neighborhood Inc. **Military Serv:** AUS, sp/4, 1957-59. **Business Addr:** Attorney, Private Practice, 351 E Gowen Ave, Philadelphia, PA 19119, **Business Phone:** (215)247-7042.*

WELLS, JAMES A.
Executive. **Personal:** Born Aug 13, 1933, Atlanta, GA; married Mary E; children: James A, Jr, John F. **Educ:** BSEE, 1965; MSAT, 1976. **Career:** Process Equipment Design IBM-Endicott, eng, 1965-67; Aerospace & Avionic Comput Syst Final Test IBM-Owego, 1967-74; Systs Test Mgr, IBM-Owego, proj engr, 1974. **Orgs:** Assoc mem, Inst Elec Electronics Engrs Asn; vpres, Jaycees; den leader, WEBELOS; mem Amvets; AOPA. **Military Serv:** USAF, sgt, 1952-57.

WELLS, PATRICK ROLAND
Clergy, educator. **Personal:** Born Apr 1, 1931, Liberty, TX; son of Luther T Sr and Stella Wickliff. **Educ:** TX Southern Univ, BS, 1957; Univ NE Lincoln, MS, 1959, PhD, 1961; Sacred Heart Sch Theol, MDiv, 1993. **Career:** Educator, Clergy (retired); Fordham Univ, asst prof pharamacol, 1961-63; Univ NE, asst prof pharamacol, 1963-65, assoc prof & dept chmn, 1965-70; Col Pharm, TX Southern Univ, dean & prof, 1970-90; St Francis Assisi Cath Church, pastor, 1993; Diocese Galveston Houston, ordained Roman Cath Priest, 1993; Episcopal Vicar, Central Vicariate, 2000. **Orgs:** TX Pharmaceutical Asn, Am Pharmaceutical Asn, Nat Pharmaceutical Asn, Sigma Xi Sci Hon, Rho Chi Pharmacy Hon; St Philip Neri Parish; St Philip Neri Coun 222 Knights Peter Claver; host, Radio Show "Lifeline" KTSU-FM, 1976-90; lay oblate Order St Benedict; Asn Minority Health Prof Schs; Am Asn Cols Pharm; Grand regent Kappa Psi Pharmaceutical, 1983-87; editor, Journ Nat Pharmaceutical, Asn, 1987-90; Nat Black Catholic Clergy Caucus; bd dirs, Sacred Heart Sch Theol. **Honors/Awds:** Outstanding Educator, Texas Pharm Asn, 1990; Dean Emeritus, Tex Southern Univ, 1990; Dehon Distinguished Ministry Award, 1999; prelate honor, "Reverend Monsignor," granted Pope John Paul II, 2000. **Military Serv:** USAF, s & sgt, 1951-55. *

WELLS, PAYTON R.
President (organization), business owner. **Personal:** Born Jun 24, 1933, Indianapolis, IN. **Educ:** Butler Univ Indianapolis IN, 1955-57. **Career:** Payton Wells Ford Inc, pres; GM & Ford Motor Co Automotive Sch; Payton Wells Chrysler, Dodge Jeep Eagle, pres; Payton Wells Automotive Group,2005; Payton Wells Chevrolet, Owner. **Orgs:** Bd mem, Jr Achievement; Nat Assn Advan Colored People; Urban League; vpres, Flanner House Inc; bd mem, Anderson Symphony Orchestra. **Honors/Awds:** Junior Achievement of Central Indiana Business Hall of Fame, 2002. **Military Serv:** AUS, pfc, 1953-55. **Business Addr:** President, Payton Wells Automotive Group, 1510 N Meridian St, Indianapolis, IN 46202, **Business Phone:** (317)638-4838.

WELLS, ROBERT BENJAMIN, JR.
Administrator. **Personal:** Born May 21, 1947, Cleveland, OH; married Phillis Sharlette McCray; children: Michelle Renne. **Educ:** Miami Dade Comn Col, AA, 1974; FL A&M Univ, BS, 1976; NC Central Univ, Law Student, 1985. **Career:** Gen Tel Southeast, serv cost admin, 19878-80, gen acct suprv, 1980-81, gentax suprv, 1981-. **Orgs:** Consult, Youth Motivation Task Force, 1979-82; pres, Employees Club, 1980-81; dept rep, United Way Campaign, 1982-84; chmn, Econ Develop Comn, NC Assoc Black Lawyers Land Loss Prev Proj; vpres mkt, Nat Assoc Accts; chmn, Nat Alliance Bus Youth Motivation Task Force; pres, Durham Area Chap, Nat Assoc Accts, 1986-88; GTE Loaned Exec, United Way Campaign, 1986; chmn, Greater Durham United Way Loaned Exec Alumni Comn, 1987. **Honors/Awds:** Distinguished Service Award, Miles Col Birmingham AL, 1982; Distinguished Service, Plaque Edward Waters Col, Jacksonville, FL, 1984; Distinguished Service, Plaque Fla A & M Univ, Tallahassee, 1986. **Military Serv:** USAF, sgt, 4 yrs; Distinguished Service Medal, Bronze Medal, 1966, 1968. **Business Addr:** General Tax Supervisor, General Telephone of the Southeast, 3632 Roxboro Rd, PO Box 1412, Durham, NC 27702.

WELLS, RODERICK ARTHUR
Municipal government official, president (organization). **Personal:** Born Feb 10, 1952, New Orleans, LA; son of Thomas L Jr and Maggie L; married Betty Lewis, Dec 18, 1976; children: Rashaad Aneisha & Roderick Lewis. **Educ:** Southern Univ BR, BS, 1975, MEd, 1981. **Career:** Kaiser Aluminum, production foreman, 1982-83, environ tech, 1980-81; City BR, Human Servs Division, prog planner, 1983-84; EBR Mosquito Abatement, asst dir, 1986-, biologist, 1984-86, pres, currently. **Orgs:** Naval Reserve Asn, 1982-; SU Fed Comm Officers, 1985-; LA Pesticide Applicators, 1988-; Am Mosquito Control Asn, 1988-; Naval Memorial Asn, 1989-; BR High Sch Football Offs, 1990-; bd dirs, LA Mosquito Control Asn, 1991-, pres, 1994; chair, Recruiting Assist Coun, 1994-. **Honors/Awds:** Coaches Award, Brec Football Coach, Baby Jags, 1990-91; Fathers & Sons Award,Cub Scouts Pack 47, 1992; Presidential Award, LMCA, 1994. **Military Serv:** USN, cap, 1975-80, active reserve, 1982-98; comd officer, 197880; Surface Warfare Officer, Sharp Shooter Pistol, Nat Defense, Navy Achievement, Sea Serv, Expert Rifle, Navy Commendation. **Home Addr:** 10717 Foster Rd, Baton Rouge, LA 70811, **Home Phone:** (225)775-1232. **Business Addr:** Assistant Director, President, East Baton Rouge Mosquito Abatement, 2829 Lt Gen Ben Davis Ave Metro Airport, Baton Rouge, LA 70807, **Business Phone:** (225)356-3297.

WELLS, THEODORE V, JR.
Lawyer. **Educ:** Col Holy Cross, BA, 1972; Harvard Bus Sch, MBA, 1976; Harvard Law Sch, JD, 1976. **Career:** Paul, Weiss, Rifkind, Wharton & Garrison LLP, atty & litigation partner, currently. **Orgs:** Co-chair, White-Collar Criminal Sect, Nat Asn Criminal Defense Lawyers; Am Col Trial Lawyers; Practising Law Inst Trial Advocacy Prog; teaching team mem, Harvard Law Sch Trial Advocacy Workshop; nat treas, Democrat Bill Bradley's Presidential Campaign; bd dirs, CIT Corp; trustee, NJ Performing Arts Ctr; trustee, Holy Cross Col; trustee, Nat Asn Advan Colored People Legal Defense Fund. **Honors/Awds:** Lawyer of the Year, Nat Law J, 2006. **Special Achievements:** One of America's best white-collar defense attorneys, Nat Law Jour. **Business Phone:** (212)373-3089.*

WELLS, TINA
Entrepreneur. **Educ:** Hood Col, BA commun arts, 2002; Univ Pa Wharton Sch Bus mkt mgt post-baccalaureate prog. **Career:** Buzz Mkt Group, chief exec officer, currently. **Orgs:** Adv bd, Christopher Reeve Found; Viral & Buzz Mkt Asn; adv bd, inducted the Friends Orphans Proj, FRIENDS; Kids for Kids Advisory Bd. **Honors/Awds:** Black Voices Black Female Entrepreneurs Award, AOL; the Essence 40 Under 40 Award; Billboard's 30 Under 30 Award. **Special Achievements:** The Voices Black Women Business Leaders Top Ten List.

WELLS, VERNON
Baseball player. **Personal:** Born Dec 8, 1978, Shreveport, LA. **Career:** Toronto Blue Jays, 1999-. **Orgs:** Honorary Commissioner, Toronto Rookie League. **Honors/Awds:** AL co-player of the week, 2003 & 2006; Gold Glove Award, 2004 & 2005. **Business Addr:** Professional Baseball Player, Toronto Blue Jays, 1 Blue Jays Way Suite 3200, Rogers Centre, Toronto, ON, Canada 65815, **Business Phone:** (416)341-1000.*

WELLS-DAVIS, DR. MARGIE ELAINE
Manager. **Personal:** Born Apr 27, 1944, Marshalltown, IA; daughter of Ida and Gladstone; married Allan C; children: Allana. **Educ:** Simpson Col, AB, 1966; Syracuse Univ, MA, 1968; Univ Cincinnati, PhD, 1979. **Career:** St Louis Syracuse, NY, teacher, 1966-68; Univ Cincinnati, asst dean students, 1968-70; Syracuse Univ, actg dir, 1971; Cent Comn Health Bd, coordr consult educ,

1972; US Pub Health Serv DHEW, sociologist 1973; EHarlem Ext Serv Jewish Hosp, consult, 1973-76; Cincinnati Health Dept, dir staff & org develop, 1974-77; Procter & Gamble, affirmative action coordr, 1977-; Procter & Gamble, human resources mgr, currently. **Orgs:** Am Soc Training & Develop, 1977-80; Original Develop Network, 1978-80; bd mem, New Life Girls, 1977-80; treasr & bd mem, Cincinnati Human Relations Comn, 1978-80; bd mem, Cincinnati Womens City Club, 1979-80; bd mem, Gen Protestant Orphan Home; Grassroots Leadership Acad. **Honors/Awds:** Resolution for Outstanding Service, City Cincinnati Bd Health, 1976; Hon Soc Epsilon Sigma, Gold Key Hon Soc, 1966; Alumni Achievement Award, Simpson Col, 1990. *

WELLS-MERRICK, LORRAINE ROBERTA
Educator. **Personal:** Born Jan 5, 1938, Syracuse, NY; daughter of Robert Wells and Dorothy Copes Wells; married James A Merrick Jr (divorced). **Educ:** Cheyney State Univ, Cheyney, Pa, BS, 1959; Syracuse Univ, Syracuse, New York, MS, 1973, doctoral candidate, currently. **Career:** City Sch Dist, Syracuse, New York, teacher, 1959-69, prin/adminr, 1970-79, dep supt, 1979-88; New York State Educ Dept, Albany, New York, asst comnr, 1988-. **Orgs:** Syracuse chap, Links Inc, 1976-; NCNW, 1960-; Syracuse Alumnae, Delta Sigma Theta Sorority Inc, 1973-; Nat Grand Basileus, Lambda Kappa Mu Sorority, 1985-90. **Honors/Awds:** Outstanding Educr, Grade Teacher Mag, 1973; Outstanding Soror, Lambda Kappa Mu Sorority, 1974; Woman Achievement Educ, Delta Sigma Theta Inc, 1975; Post-Stand Woman Achievement, Syracuse Newspapers, 1980. **Home Addr:** 404 Kimber Rd, Syracuse, NY 13224. **Business Addr:** Assistant Commissioner, New York State Education Department, General and Occupational Education, Washington Ave 979 EBA, Albany, NY 12234, **Business Phone:** (518)473-7155.

WELMON, VERNIS M
School administrator, educator. **Personal:** Born Mar 13, 1951, Philadelphia, PA; son of Vernis B and Sara H; married Pamela Blake, Oct 10, 1987; children: Ain. **Educ:** Temple Univ, BA, 1980; Columbia Univ, MA, 1982; Pa State Univ. **Career:** US State Dept, Bur Human Rights & Humanitarian Affairs, intern, 1980; Multinational MGT EDU, intern, 1981; Pa State Univ, Smeal Col Bus Admin, reser, 1981, PhD & MS progs coordr, 1983-85, instr, 1983-, asst dean minority affairs, 1985, Dean Diversity Enhancement, currently, asst prof bus admin, currently; Univ West Indies, guest lectr, 1991. **Orgs:** Phi Chi Theta, 1991-; Acad Polit Sci; Am Acad Polit & Social Sci; Nat Coun Black Studies; Pa Conf Higher Educ; Black Resources CTR; TransAfrica; numerous other civic groups. **Honors/Awds:** Marcus Garvey Scholastic Award, 1978; Pres's Scholar, 1979; Rosenthal Fel, US State Dept, 1980; Temple Univ; Phi Beta Kappa, 1980; Pa State Univ, Spicher Serv Award, 1986. **Special Achievements:** Author: "Import - Export: International Challenge for Black BUS," NAT BUS, Dec 1988; "Africa in Perspective: Myths & Realities," Review Black Polit Economy, 1989; "New Economic Challenges for Africa & Caribbean," Ember Magazine, 1991. **Business Addr:** Assistant Dean for Diversity Enhancement, Assistant Professor of Business Administration, Pennsylvania State University, Smeal College of Business Administration, 210J Bus Bldg, University Park, PA 16802, **Business Phone:** (814)863-0474.

WELSING, FRANCES CRESS
Psychiatrist. **Personal:** Born Mar 18, 1935, Chicago, IL; daughter of Henry N and Ida Mae. **Educ:** Antioch Col, BS, 1957; Howard Univ, Sch Med, MD, 1962. **Career:** Cook Co Hosp, intern, 1962-63; St Elizabeth Hosp, res gen psychiatry, 1963-66; Children's Hosp, fel, child psychiatry, 1966-68; Howard Univ, Col Med, asst prof pediatrics, 1968-75; Hillcrest Children's Ctr, clinic dir, 1975-76; Pvt Pract, currently. **Orgs:** Nat Med Asn; Am Med Asn; Am Psychiatric Asn. **Special Achievements:** Author, "The Cress Theory of Color Confrontation & Racism", "The Isis Papers". **Business Addr:** Physician, 7603 Georgia Ave NW Suite 402, Washington, DC 20012, **Business Phone:** (202)829-0430.

WERTZ, ANDREW WALTER, SR.
School administrator, executive. **Personal:** Born Dec 18, 1928, Hamlet, NC; son of Johnnie B Hodges Cooks and Andrew J Wertz; married Bernice Spires; children: Alonzo W, Janis M, Brian L, Andy Jr, Ray J. **Educ:** Lincoln Univ, Pa, BA, 1949; USAF Command & Staff Col, 1965; Syracuse Univ, MS, 1980. **Career:** School administrator (retired), executive; Detective Serv Inc, pvt investr, 1950; USAF, navigator & admin, 1950-70; Hamilton Col, dir, Bristol Campus Ctr & dir stud activities, 1970-88; freelance consult & admin; host dir, Region 2 conf Asn Col Unions Int, 1978; Mohawk Valley Club Frontiers Int, pres, 1975-77; A Better Chance Inc, bd mem, 1977-80, pres, 1988-; Frontiers Int Found Inc, bd dirs, pres & chief exec officer, 1987-93. **Orgs:** Bd mem, OIC Utica, 1972-74; bd mem, ARC Utica Chap, 1973-79; bd mem, Coun Churches, Mohawk Valley Area, 1974-78; Nat Conf Asn Col Unions Int, 1976; coordr minority progs Asn Col Unions Int, 1979; Nat Asn Advan Colored People; Kappa Alpha Psi. **Honors/Awds:** Pentagon Soc, Hamilton Col, 1975; Internal Service Award, Frontiers Int, 1978; Outstanding Service Award, First Dist Frontiers Int, 1990. **Special Achievements:** First African American Cashier at Pennsylvania Fruit Company Inc, 1949. **Military Serv:** USAF, lt col, 1950-70; Distinguished Service Award, 1968.

WESCOTT, ABRAHAM
Government official. **Career:** City Akron, Dept Planning & Urban Develop Land Mkt, Develop Serv Div, relocation officer, currently.

WESLEY, BARBARA ANN
School administrator. **Personal:** Born Jun 7, 1930, Wichita, KS; widowed; children: Ronald Frank & John Edgar. **Educ:** Univ Puget Sound, BA, 1963; Univ Puget Sound Tacoma, MEd, 1972; Univ Mass, EdD, 1977. **Career:** Clover Pk Sch Dist, elem teacher, 1960-64; Tacoma Pub Sch, classroom teacher, 1964-74; Westfield St Col, proj dir, 1974-75; Alternative Prog Tacoma Pub Sch, educ specialist, 1975-78; Ariz State Univ, Delta Kappa Gamma fel, 1978; Foss High Sch Tacoma Public Sch, high sch admin, 1978-79; Wilson High Sch, Tacoma Pub Sch, admin, 1979-82; Magnet Prog, dist admin, 1982-. **Orgs:** Inst Elem Teachers Denver Univ, 1969; Adult Educ Inst Univ WI; NY State Univ Albany, 1972-73; NSF, 1972-73; bd trustees, Tacoma Comm Col, 1977-82;Delta Sigma Theta; brd dirs, YWCA Tacoma, 1977-78; brd dirs, Campfire Tacoma, 1979-83; State Voc Coun Voc Educ, 1982-; Wash Women Employ & Educ Brd Dirs, 1982-; Phi Delta Kappa, Delta Kappa Gamma. **Business Addr:** District Administrator, Magnet Prog Tacoma Public School, Central Admin Bldg, PO Box 1357, Tacoma, WA 98401.

WESLEY, CLARENCE E.
Executive. **Personal:** Born Sep 24, 1940, Coffeyville, KS; married Peggy L; children: Keira, Marquel. **Educ:** Pittsburgh State Univ, BS, 1962; Wichita State Univ, MA, 1968. **Career:** teacher & admin asst, 1962-70; Wichita State, KS State, Sterling Col, lectr, 1968-75; Upward Bound Wichita State, asst dir, 1969-70; Wichita Area C C, mgr comm develop; Wichita Pub Sch System. **Orgs:** Pres, Wes & Berry Int; pres, Ctrl System Develop Corp; bd dir, KS C Minority Bus;Nat Adv Coun Small Bus Admin; pres, Wichita Urban League; chmn & trustee coun, Black Heritage Park, KS; trustee & dir, Wichita Coun Ch; CETA Manpower Bd; bd dir, Vet Adv Coun. **Honors/Awds:** cert merit, Nat Alliance of Bus & Wichita Pub Sch Sys, 1972; Wichita's Distinguished Service Award, 1973; Recipient Outstanding Young Man, KS; KS Outstanding Citation, 1974; KS Public City of Year, 1975; NCCJ State Brotherhood Award, 1975. **Business Addr:** 350 W Douglas, Wichita, KS 67202.

WESLEY, CLEMON HERBERT, JR.
Executive, military engineer. **Personal:** Born Feb 24, 1936, Daingerfield, TX; son of Zannie Benson (deceased) and Clemon Herbert (deceased); married Modestine Delores Truvillion, Sep 27, 1958; children: Yolanda Wesley Harper, Deborah Wesley Hall & Eric. **Educ:** Prairie View A & M Univ, BS, 1957; Army War Col & Armed Forces Staff Col, attended; Shippensburg State Col, MS, 1970; LaSalle Univ, LLB, 1972. **Career:** TEXCOM, Inc, Landover, MD, founder, pres & chief exec officer, 1981-. **Orgs:** Pres, Nat Bus League Southern Md; bd mem, Coalition Concerned Black Christian Men; Phi Beta Sigma Educ Found; Nat Urban League Black Exec Exchange Prog; Prince George's County Chamber Com; Minority Bus Enterprise Legal Defense & Educ Fund; Mt Zion United Methodist Church; Prairie View A & M Alumni Asn; AUS War Col Alumni Asn. **Honors/Awds:** Business Achievement Award, Nat Bus League Southern Md, 1986; Service Industry Award, US Dept Com, 1987; Nat Minority Small Bus Person of the Year & Minority Small Business Firm of the Year for region III, US Small Bus Admin, 1988; Advocate of the Year, Small & Minority Business, 1990; Outstanding Business Leader Award, Black Accts Inc; African American Leadership Award, Kunta Kinte Celebrations Inc; Governors Award for Market Expansion, State MD. **Special Achievements:** The Nations Largest Black Businesses, Black Enterprise 100's; Prince Georgian of ther Year, Prince George County; Black Engineer of the Year, Coun Deans Historically Black Cols & Univ Mobile Corp & US Black Engr Mag. **Military Serv:** AUS, Signal Corps, 2nd Lt, 1957, retired col, 1981; served Dept Army Headquarters, 1975-79; received Vietnam Service Medal, Bronze Star, and Legion of Merit. **Business Addr:** President, Founder, Chief Executive Officer, TEXCOM Inc, 600 Washington St, Portsmouth, VA 23704, **Business Phone:** (410)956-6775.

WESLEY, DAVID BARAKAU
Basketball player. **Personal:** Born Nov 14, 1970, San Antonio, TX. **Educ:** Baylor Univ, phys educ. **Career:** Continental Basketball Asn, Wichita Falls Texans, 1992-93; NJ Nets, 1993-94; Boston Celtics, 1994-97; Charlotte Hornets, guard, 1997-02; New Orleans Hornets, 2002-04; Houston Rockets, guard, 2004-06; Cleveland Cavaliers, guard, 2006-07; Baylor Bears men's basketball team, student manager, currently. **Honors/Awds:** Continental Basketball Asn, All-Rookie First Team, 1992-93; Southwest Conference's Most Valuable Player; NBA Eastern Conference Champions, 2007. *

WESLEY, HERMAN EUGENE, III
Evangelist, publisher. **Personal:** Born Oct 17, 1961, Newark, NJ; son of Herman E Jr and Anne M; married Sonja McDade, Jun 22, 1985; children: Brandon JeMarcus. **Educ:** Southwestern Christian Col, AS, 1981; OKL Christian Univ, BS, 1983, Nat Acad Christian Studies, MA, biblical studies & church growth, 2002. **Career:** Church Christ, evangelist, 1986-; Revivalist Mag, publ, 1989-; Ebony News Jour Tex, publ, 1992-; Christian Square Co Tex, ceo, 1992-; Southside Church Christ, minister; Wash Douglas Tribune, ed-in-chief, currently. **Orgs:** Comnr, Denton Housing Authority, 1989-92; exe bd, NCP, Denton Branch, 1990-; chair, Multicultural Adv CMS, 1989-92; chmn bd, Martin Luther King Jr Ctr Adv Bd, 1989-92; chair, Black Leadership Coordinating CNL, 1991-; founding chmn, Denton Black Chamber Com. **Honors/Awds:** President's Award, NCP, Denton County Chap, 1990; Alumni of the Year, Southwestern Christian Col, 1992; Civic Service Award, City Denton, 1992. **Business Phone:** (334)263-6098.

WESLEY, JOSEPH
Football player. **Personal:** Born Nov 10, 1976, Jackson, MS. **Educ:** La State Univ. **Career:** Football player (retired), San Francisco 49ers, linebacker, 1999-2000; Jacksonville Jaguars,linebacker, 2001. **Honors/Awds:** Rookie of the Yr, 1999.

WESLEY, NATHANIEL, JR.
Executive. **Personal:** Born Jan 13, 1943, Jacksonville, FL; married Ruby L Williams; children: Nataniel Wesley III. **Educ:** FL A&M Univ, BS, 1965; Univ MI, MHA, 1971. **Career:** Albert Einstein Col Med, adminr & consult, 1971-72; NY City Health & Hosp Corp, spl asst to vpres, 1972-73; SW Community Hosp, dept dir, 1973-75; Sidney A Sumby Memorial Hosp, exec dir, 1975-76; Meharry Med Col, asst prof, 1977-79; DC Hosp Asn, asst exec dir; Ins Pub Health Col Pharm Pharmaceutical Sci, dir; Division Health Care Mgt, Sch Allied Health Sci, Fl A&M Univ, dir, 2002-. **Orgs:** Secy & exec, Nat Asn of Health Serv, 1974-78; pres, Detroit & Nashville Chapters NAASE, 1975-79; pres, NRW Assoc Inc; BCHW Alpha; Am Pub Health Asn. **Honors/Awds:** Nominee, Am Col Hosp Adminrs; WK Kellogg Fellow ACEHSA Wash, DC; Service Award, BSO Univ MI Ann Arbor, 1977; Community Service Award, Peoples Community Serv Detroit, 1978; Teacher of the Year, Meharry Med Col, 1979-. **Business Addr:** Director Health Care Management Division, Florida A&M University, Health Care Management Division, School of Allied Health Sciences, Tallahassee, FL 32307, **Business Phone:** (850)561-2020.

WESLEY, VALERIE WILSON
Writer. **Personal:** Born Nov 22, 1947; children: Jamal. **Educ:** Howard Univ, BA, philosophy, 1970; Banks Street Col Educ, MS, early childhood educ; Columbia Univ, MS, jour. **Career:** Scholastic News, assistant ed; Essence Magazine, executive ed; freelance writer; Ramapo Col, adj, curerntly; Tamara Hayle Series: When Death Comes Stealing, 1994; Devil's Gonna Get Him, 1995; Where Evil Sleeps, 1996; No Hiding Place, 1997; Easier to Kill, 1998; The Devil Riding, 2000; Dying in the Dark, 2004; Of Blood & Sorrow, 2008; Willimena Rules Series: How to Loose Your Cookie Money, 2004; How to Almost Ruin Your Class Play, 2005; 23 Ways to Mess Up Valentine's Day, 2006; How to Face Up to the Class Bully, 2007; How to Have the Best Kwanzaa Ever, 2007; Willimena & the Cookie Money 2001; Novels: Where Do I Go from Here?, 1993; Freedom's Gifts, 1997; Ain't Nobody's Business If I Do, 1999; Always True to You in My Fashion, 2002; No Way of Dying, 2004; Playing My Mother's Blues, 2005; Chapbooks: How to Lose Your Class Pet, 2003; Tales of Willimena, 2004; How to Fish for Trouble, 2004; Non fiction:Afro-Bets Book of Black Heroes from A to Z: An Introduction to Important Black Achievers for Young Readers, 1988. **Honors/Awds:** Griot Award, Nat Asn Black Jour, 1993; Excellence in Adult Fiction award, Am Lib Asn, 2000. **Business Addr:** Writer, c/o Author Mail, 10 E 53rd St 7th Fl, New York, NY 10022.

WESSON, CLEO
Government official. **Personal:** Born Aug 27, 1924, Ozan, AR; married Julia (deceased); children: Helayne. **Educ:** Gary Col. **Career:** City Gary Common Coun, councilman. **Orgs:** John Will Anderson Boys Club; Lake City Lodge 182; King Solomon Lodge 57;Magic City Consistory 62; Mohomet Temple 134; Rebecca Chap 39; Sallie Wyatt Stewart Guild; Urban League Northwest Indiana Inc; life mem, NAACP; Israel CME Church; bd dir, March Dimes. **Honors/Awds:** Recipient, Certification of Merit, Gary Branch NAACP, 1965; Service Award,3rd Episcopal Dist, CME Church, 1965;Distinguished Service & Outstanding Leadership, pres, Common Coun, City Gary, 1966; J Claude Allen, Presiding-Bishop Seepa, 1967. **Military Serv:** USAF, 1943-45. *

WESSON, HERB J. See WESSON, HERMAN JASON, JR.

WESSON, HERMAN JASON, JR. (HERB J WESSON)
Government official. **Personal:** Born Nov 11, 1951, Cleveland, OH; son of Herman Sr (deceased) and Gladys Wesson-Strickland; married Fabian, Jun 11, 1981; children: Douglas, Ralph, Herb III & Justin. **Educ:** Lincoln Univ, BA, hist, 1999. **Career:** Councilman Nate Holden, chief of staff, 1987-92; Supvr Yvonne B Burke, chief of staff, 1992-98; State Calif, assembly representative, 1998-; Tenth Dist, Los Angeles, councilman, currently. **Orgs:** Mid-City Chamber Com, 1992-; Culver City Chamber Come, 1992-; bd dirs, Martin Luther King Hosp Found, 1992-02; bd mem, Second Dist Educ Found, 1996-; advisory bd, African Community Resource Ctr, 1997-02; ex-officio trustee, Calif State Univ, 2002-; ex-officio regent, Univ Calif, 2002-. **Honors/Awds:** Agape Found, Combating Domestic Violence, 2001; Public Service Award, Greater Los Angeles Chamber Com, 2001; Political

Achievement Awd, New Frontier Dem Club, 2002; Legislator of the Year, Calif Asn Black Trial Lawyers, 2002; Blue Water Network, Global Warming Leadership, 2002. **Business Addr:** Council Member, City Council, 1819 S Wern Ave, Los Angeles, CA 90056, **Business Phone:** (323)733-8233.

WEST, BRUCE ALAN
Sales manager. **Personal:** Born Mar 31, 1957, Los Angeles, CA; son of Lenon and Betty; married Cathy, Jul 22, 1982; children: Chastin & Cheldon. **Educ:** Miss State Univ, BA, 1978. **Career:** Thrifty Drug Stores, asst mgr, 1980-85; Lindsey Prod Co, sales rep, 1985-86; Brown & Williamson Tobacco Corp, sect mgr trade mkt. **Orgs:** Univ Human Rels Comn, 1975-76; Phi Beta Sigma Fraternity, 1976-; Theta Iota Chap, 1976-. **Home Phone:** (805)523-3345.

WEST, CHERYL L
Playwright. **Personal:** Born Jan 1, 1965?, Chicago, IL. **Educ:** Univ Ill Champaign-Urbana. **Career:** Social worker; teacher; playwright, currently; Plays: Holiday Heart; Puddin 'n Pete; Play On!; Birdie Blue; Jar the Floor; Before It Hits Home; Librettist; Film: Glitter, story writer, 2001; TV series: "Holiday Heart", producer, 2000. **Honors/Awds:** Susan Smith Blackburn Prize, co-winner, 1990; AUDELCO Award, 1991; Helen Hayes Charles McArthur Award, 1992; National Endowment for the Arts Playwrighting Award, 1995-96; Best Play Award, Beverly Hills/ Hollywood Nat Asn Advan Colored People, 1995; Jeff Award for Best Musical. **Business Addr:** Playwright, c/o The Gersh Agency, 41 Madison Ave 33rd Fl, New York, NY 10010, **Business Phone:** (212)997-1818.

WEST, CORNEL
School administrator, educator. **Personal:** Born Jun 2, 1953, Tulsa, OK; married Elleni (divorced); children: Clifton; married Elleni. **Educ:** Harvard Univ, BA, eastern lang & lit; Princeton Univ, PhD. **Career:** Yale Univ Divinty Sch, prof, 1984; Le Monde Diplomatique, Am corresp; Yale Divinity Sch, educr; Univ Paris, educr; Harvard Univ, African Am studies fac; Harvard Univ, Du Bois fel; Princeton Univ, Dept Religion, prof, currently, Dept Afro-Am Studies, dir. **Orgs:** Alpha Phi Alpha; World Policy Coun; Modern Lang Asn. **Honors/Awds:** William Sanders Scarborough Prize, Modern Lang Asn. **Special Achievements:** Author: Race Matters, Beacon Press, 1993; co-author with bell hooks, Breaking Bread: Insurgent Black Intellectual Life, South End Press, 1992; Prophesy Deliverance! An Afro-American Revolutionary Christianity, Westminster/John Knox Press; The American Evasion of Philosophy: A Genealogy of Pragamatism, Univ Wis Press; The Cornel West Reader; Democracy Matters; appeared as Councillor West in the science fiction films Matrix Reloaded and Matrix Revolutions and recorded commentaries on philosophy for all three films in the Matrix trilogy for their DVD release, along with integral theorist, Ken Wilber. **Business Addr:** Professor, Princeton University, Department of Religion, 1 Palmer Sq Suite 315, Princeton, NJ 08544, **Business Phone:** (609)258-0021.

WEST, DENISE JOYNER
Marketing executive. **Personal:** Born in New Jersey; daughter of Carver and Olivia; married Alfred L; children: A Justin J. **Educ:** Douglass Col, BA; Rutger Grad Sch Mgt, MBA. **Career:** Nabisco, assoc prod mgr, 1980-85; Revlon, mkt mgr, 1985-88; Advanced Mkt, mkt coordr, 1988-90; Eastman Kodak, mkt develop mgr, 1990-92; Lorillard Tobacco Co, sr brand mgr, 1992-97; Essence Commun, dir corp mkt, 1997-2000; Bus Develop officer, 2000; Wychwood Profs, prin, owner, 2002-. **Orgs:** Nat Black MBA Asn; fund raising co-chair, NY Chapt, 1985-86; Westfield YMCA Black Achievers, 1998-2001. **Business Phone:** (908)789-0431.

WEST, DOUG (JEFFERY DOUGLAS WEST)
Basketball player, basketball coach. **Personal:** Born May 27, 1967, Altoona, PA; married Wuela; children: Tyson & Braedyn. **Educ:** Villanova Univ, Villanova, PA, BA, commun, 1989. **Career:** Basketball player (retired), coach; Minn Timberwolves, guard & forward, 1989-98; Vancouver Grizzlies, guard, 1998-2001; Canon-McMillan High Sch, boys' varsity & jr varsity asst coach, 2001-03; Win by 2 LLC, founder & owner, currently; Duquesne Univ, basketball asst coach, 2006; Villanova Wildcats, asst coach, currently. **Orgs:** Philadelphia Big Five; Retired Nat Basketball Players Asn. **Honors/Awds:** Blair County Sports Halls of Fame; Big Five Hall of Fame. **Business Phone:** (610)519-6000.

WEST, ED. See WEST, EDWARD LEE, III.

WEST, EDWARD LEE, III (ED WEST)
Football player. **Personal:** Born Aug 2, 1961, Colbert County, AL; married Kecia; children: Jennifer, Edward Lee IV & Whitley. **Educ:** Auburn Univ. **Career:** Football player (retired); Green Bay Packers, tight end, 1984-94; Philadelphia Eagles, 1995-96; Atlanta Falcons, 1997.

WEST, GEORGE FERDINAND, JR.
Lawyer. **Personal:** Born Oct 25, 1940, Adams Co, MS; son of George Ferdinand Sr (deceased) and Artimese M; married Billie Guy; children: George III, Heath & Jarrod. **Educ:** Tougaloo Col, BA, 1962; S Univ, Sch Law, JD, 1966; Univ Miss, JD, 1968. **Career:** Natchez Adams Co Sch Bd, appt, co-atty, 1967-95; State Adv Bd Voc Educ, appt, 1968; Natchez-Adams Co C of C, appt, dir, 1974; Jeff Co Sch Sys, atty, 1974; Miss Sch Bd Asn, dir, atty; Radio Prog, "FACT-FINDING", moderator; Copiah-Lincoln Jr Col Natchez Br, bus law prof; Natchez News Leader, managing ed; Pvt Pract, Natchez, MS, currently. **Orgs:** Miss Bar Asn, 1968; res, procter, Miss State Univ, 1973; Nat Asn Advan Colored People; Natchez Bus & Civic League; vpres, Gov Com Hire Handicap; trust, sunday sch teacher, Zion Chap AME Church; contributing ed, Bluff City Post, 1978-; chmn, Natchez-Adams Sch Bd, 1988-. **Honors/Awds:** Outstanding Young Men in America, 1967-; Community Leader of America, 1972; Lifetime Rosco Pound fel, 1972; Most Distinguished Black Attorney Travelers Coalition, 1988; Doctor of Humane Letters, Natchez Col, 1989; Man of the Year, Natchez, MS, Nat Asn Advan Colored People, 1990; Man of the Year, Natchez Bus & Civic League, 1991; Most Outstanding Atty, Nat Asn Advan Colored People, 1992; Outstanding Attorney for the African Methodist Episcopal Southern Dist & Man of the Year, Zion Chapel AME Church, 1995; Pioneer and Leadership Award, 1997-98. **Special Achievements:** Radio Prog, "FACT-FINDING"; Recorded first music album entitled, "Ole Time Way", 1993. **Business Addr:** Attorney, 10 St Catherine St, PO Box 1202, Natchez, MS 39121-1202, **Business Phone:** (601)442-3324.

WEST, DR. GERALD IVAN
Psychologist, dean (education). **Personal:** Born Jun 3, 1937, St Louis, MO; son of Frank and Effie; married Blondel B McKinnie, Aug 20, 1960; children: Gerald I West Jr. **Educ:** Univ Denver, BA, 1958; Southern Ill Univ, MS, 1963; Purdue Univ, PhD, 1967. **Career:** San Francisco State Univ, Dept Coun, chair, Col Ethnic Studies, interim dean, Univ Dean Fac, Col Health & Human Serv, prof emer, currently. **Orgs:** Past pres, Western Asn Counr Educrs & Supvrs; Am Psychological Asn; SigmaPi Phi; Kappa Alpha Psi. **Honors/Awds:** Annual Memorial Award, Asn Black Psychologist, 1980; Annual Award, Pub Advocates, 1983; Certificate of Honor, City County, San Francisco, 1983; Professional Development Award, Am Asn Coun & Develop, Multicultural Coun, 1985; Award of Merit, San Francisco State Univ, 1985; Admin Fellow, Calif State Univ, 1987; H B McDaniel Award, Stanford Univ, 1992. **Special Achievements:** Elected as first Human Rights Comnr, Calif Personnel & Guid Asn, 1973;lead case of Larry P vs State of California, first successfully litigated case disproving the theory of racial genetic intellectual inferiority according to IQ tests, which led to federal law prohibiting the use of IQ tests to place African American children in classes for the retarded in California. **Military Serv:** USAR Med Servs Corps, lt, 1966; 374th Gen Hosp, biochemist. **Business Addr:** Professor Emeritus, San Francisco State University, San Francisco, CA 94132.

WEST, DR. HERBERT LEE, JR.
Educator. **Personal:** Born May 4, 1947, Warrenton, NC; son of Wilhemenia Jones West and Herbert Lee West Sr; married Mary Bentley; children: Tamekah Denise & Marcus Delaney-Bentley. **Educ:** NC Cent Univ, BA 1969; Univ Minn, MA, 1972, PhD, 1974. **Career:** Univ Minn, Teacher asst, 1972; Univ Md, Baltimore County, asst prof, 1974-80; Howard Univ, asst prof, 1980-85; fac intern, House Urban Develop, 1980; adv, Summer Work Prog-Prince Georges County, Md; educr/admin, Howard County Bd Educ, 1985-; Villa Julie Col, assoc prof, 1993. **Orgs:** Nat Asn Advan Colored People; Triangle Geographers; Nat Coun Black Studies; Assoc Study Afro-Am Life; Black Stud Achievement Prog, Howard County, Md. **Honors/Awds:** Comga Grad Fel, Univ Minn, l969; Ford Found Fel, 1971; NEH Fel, Atlanta Univ, 1978; Outstanding Teacher, Univ Md, Baltimore County, 1978 & 1979; NEH Fel, Univ NC, 1983; Summer Fel, UMTA/Atlanta Univ, 1984; Smithsonian Fel, Smithsonian Inst, 1985; Univ Ind guest lectr, 1988; NEH Fel, Columbia Univ, l989; moderator, broadway show sarifina, Kennedy Ctr, 1990; voted Outstanding educr, MD, 1998. **Home Addr:** 6316 Loring Dr, Columbia, MD 21045. **Business Addr:** Educator, Howard County Board of Education, 10910 Rte 108, Ellicott City, MD 21043, **Business Phone:** (410)992-0500.

WEST, JEFFERY DOUGLAS. See WEST, DOUG.

WEST, JOHN ANDREW
Lawyer. **Personal:** Born Sep 15, 1942, Cincinnati, OH; married Miriam Evonne Kennedy; children: Melissa Evonne. **Educ:** Univ Cincinnati, BA, BS, 1966; Salmon P Chase Law Sch, JD, 1971. **Career:** Pitzer West Cutcher & Gilday, atty; GE Co Large Jet Engine Div, buyer & contract admin, 1968-71; Hamilton Co Courthouse, judge, currently. **Orgs:** Nat Am & Ohio Bar Asn, 1972-; chmn, Hamilton Co Pub Defender Comn, 1976. **Home Addr:** 4508 Spring Meadow Dr, Cincinnati, OH 45229. **Business Addr:** Judge, Hamilton County Courthouse, 595 Hamilton County Courthouse 1000 Main St, Cincinnati, OH 45202, **Business Phone:** (513)946-5785.

WEST, DR. JOHN RAYMOND
College administrator, educator. **Personal:** Born Apr 9, 1931, Birmingham, AL; son of John H and Mignonette Mason; married Suzanne Marie Lancaster; children: Ronald, John Jr, Gerald, Reginald, Teresa, Semara, Tia & Joshua. **Educ:** Calif State Univ, Fullerton, BA, Anthrop, 1969, MA, Anthrop, 1970; Nova Univ Fla, EdD, Admin, 1975. **Career:** S Counties Gas Co, sr scheduler, 1961-69; State Calif, employment serv officer, 1969-70; Santa Ana Col, anthrop, sociol, prof, 1970-; Nova Univ, cluster coordr, 1975-90; Saddleback Col Mission Viejo, instr, 1976-; Afro Ethnic Studies Calif State Univ Fullerton, lectr; Santa Ana Col, dir, assoc dean, dean stud serv, 1973-86; Santiago Canyon Col, Humanities & Sci, div chair, currently, Dept Anthropol & Sociol, prof. **Orgs:** Founding pres, Orange County Chap Sickle Cell Disease Res Found, 1972; 100 Black Men Orange County; bd dirs, vpres, Legislative Affairs Western Region Counc on Black Am Affairs; bd dir Assoc Calif Comn Col Admin, 1972; bd dir, Calif Comn Col Extended Oppty Prog & Serv, 1977-79. **Honors/Awds:** Five publications: Clearinghouse Clearing UCLA, 1974-75. **Military Serv:** USMC, gunnery sgt, 1950-61; presidential Unit Citation & United Nations Serv, 1950. **Business Addr:** Chair, Professor, Santiago Canyon College, School of Social Sciences, 8045 E Chapman Ave, Orange, CA 92869, **Business Phone:** (714)628-4870.

WEST, JOSEPH KING
Judge. **Personal:** Born Sep 11, 1929, Yonkers, NY; son of Ralph West and Nellie Brown West; married Shirley Arvene Gray; children: Rebecca & Joseph Jr. **Educ:** Howard Univ, BS 1952; Brooklyn Law Sch, JD, 1961. **Career:** City of Yonkers, asst corp coun, 1964-65, city ct judge, 1983-84; County Westchester, dep dist atty, 1965-82; Elected County Ct Judge, 1984, re-elected, 1994; St of New York, 9th Judicial Dist, supv judge,criminal ct, 1991-98; NY Supreme Ct judge; Co Ct, judge, currently. **Orgs:** Alpha Phi Alpha Frat, 1948-; bd dirs, Yonkers Big Brother-Big Sisters, 1982-, St Joseph's Hosp, 1983-; life mem, Alpha Phi Alpha Fraternity; life mem, NAACP. **Honors/Awds:** Achievement Award Asn of Black Lawyers of Westchester Co, 1981; Comn Serv Westchester Rockland Guardians Asn, 1984; Comn Serv Award Yonkers Coun Churches, 1985; Civic Award Frederick D Patterson Alpha Phi Alpha, 1987. **Military Serv:** AUS, 1st lt, 1952-56. **Business Addr:** Judge, Westchester Co, 111 Grove St, White Plains, NY 10601, **Business Phone:** (914)285-4305.

WEST, LENA L
Executive. **Personal:** Born in White Plains, NY. **Career:** Freelance technology consult, 1994-97; xynoMedia Technol, founder & chief exec officer, currently. **Orgs:** Tech dir & bd mem, Sister to Sister Int, 1996-2002; Kindness Strangers, 2001-03; bd mem & secty, redIbis, 2003-04; CBLit, Technol Dir, 2003-04; Women in Power, 2003-04; Women Presidents? Org; Ctr Women's Bus Res Advisory Bd; BlogHer Bus Advisory Bd; Women's Congress Nat Advisory Bd. **Honors/Awds:** Top 25 Women in Silicon Alley, Alley Cat News, 2000. **Special Achievements:** Writer: REGINE magazine, Black Tech mag, The Network Journal, The KIP Bus Report; Jan 2002 cover of Black Enterprise; quoted in Inc Magazine, Entrepreneur Magazine, Cisco iQ Magazine, and Fortune Small Bus. **Business Addr:** Founder, Chief Executive Officer, XynoMedia Technology, 1 Saw Mill River Rd Suite 190, Yonkers, NY 10701, **Business Phone:** (914)377-0600.

WEST, MARCELLA POLITE
Educator. **Personal:** Born in Savannah, GA; daughter of James H (deceased) and Mary Smith (deceased); divorced; children: Maralyn Craddock & Rodney Cecil. **Educ:** St Philip Sch Nursing Med Col Va, 1946-48; Montclair State Col, MA, 1973; Upsala Col, 1969; Newark State Col, 1971. **Career:** Cornelius E Gallagher 13th Congressional Dist NJ, cong staff, 1957-66; NJ Comn Action & Training Inst Trenton, NJ, training officer, 1966-67; Bergen Co Comn Action Prog, Hackensack, NY, training dir, 1967-69; Montclair State Col, admin to vice provost, 1969-71; Urban Educ Corps Montclair State Col, dir, 1971-73; Montclair State Col Div Student Personnel Svc, educ adv counr, 1973-; Rutger's Univ Intern Prog, 1966-67; Inner City Broadcasting Corp WLIB, bd dir; WLIB/ WBLS AM/FM, exec com, 1972-; Human Devel Consulting Serv Inc, consult & facilitator, 1975; Montclair State Col, coord & adv, currently. **Orgs:** Am Mgmt Asn, 1967-71; Am Soc Training & Devel, 1967-73; officer,Local/State/Regional & Nat Participation of NAACP 1956-67; Delta Sigma Theta Sorority; Phi Delta Kappa Educ Fraternity; Hudson Co Dem & Com Woman 1959, 1964, 1975; del, Nat Dem Women, 1963-64; del, Pres Nat Com Civil Rights 1962-; del, Educ Conf Harvard Univ Black Congressional Caucus, 1972; guest journalist, Jersey Journal covering civil rights/events, including 1962; Nat Youth Adv Bd, 1961; NJ State Conf NAACP Branch, 1963; Spanish Teacher Corps, 1970; corp sec, Inner City Broadcasting Corp, NY, 1978-90; bd trustees, Sr Care & Activities Ctr, Montclair, NJ, 1989. **Honors/Awds:** NAACP Serv Award Jersey City Branch, 1965; Am Mgmt Asn Sup Cert, 1966; Serv, Govt of NJ Affirmative Action Awareness Program, 1986-87; Certificate of Appreciation, State of NJ, Dept of Civil Serv: The Next Phase, 1987; Merit Award Program, Montclair State Col, Upper Montclair, NJ, 1989; Certificate of Appreciation, Minority Student Mentor Prog, Montclair State, 1991.

WEST, MARILYN H.
Chief executive officer, business owner. **Educ:** Waynesburg Col, PA, Math; Univ Pittsburgh, Grad Sch Pub Health. **Career:** Allegheny Health Dept, Pittsburgh, statistician, asst dir planning; Continuing Educ Proj Mental Health, dir; Va Commonwealth

Univ, dir Planning, Mental Retardation & Substance Abuse Serv; Va Cert Pub Need Prog, dir; M H West & Co Inc, owner, chmn & chief exec officer, currently. **Orgs:** Parent delg, White House Conf Educ, 1992; cong appointee, White House Conf Small Bus, 1995; Delta Sigma Theta Sorority; The Links Inc; Jack & Jill of Am; Coalition of 100 Black Women & Continental Societies; St Philips Episcopal Church; vestry; chmn, Bon Secours Joint Hospitals Bd; exec comt, Richmond Renaissance; adv bd, Metropolitan Bus League; exec comt, C Home Soc; exec comt, Atlantic Rural Exposition; chair, Richmond & Capital Area Workforce Invest Bds; exec comt, Richmond City Police Found, the Am Red Cross; former chair, Leadership Metro Richmond; serverd on the bd numerous orgns & bus. **Honors/Awds:** 100 power players, Greater Richmond Region, Richmond Mag, 1998; The annual Leadership Award, 2000; Nat Asn Women Bus Owners Award & Community Serv Award, Omega Psi Phi Fraternity, 2000. **Business Addr:** Chairman & Chief Executive Officer, Owner, M H West & Company Inc, 700 E Main St Suite 904, Richmond, VA 23218, **Business Phone:** (804)782-1938.

WEST, MARK ANDRE
Basketball player, sports manager, vice president (organization). **Personal:** Born Nov 5, 1960, Petersburg, VA; married Elaina; children: Marcus. **Educ:** Old Dominion Univ, BS, finance. **Career:** Basketball player (retired), vpres; Dallas Mavericks, ctr, 1983-84; Milwaukee Bucks, 1984; Cleveland Cavaliers, 1984-88; Phoenix Suns, 1988-94; Detroit Pistons, 1994-96; Cleveland Cavaliers, 1996-97; Indiana Pacers, 1997-98; Atlanta Hawks, 1998-99; Phoenix Suns, 1999-2000; Phoenix Suns, asst gen mgr, 2001; Native Am Basketball Invitational, co-founder; Phoenix Suns, vpres player prog, currently. **Honors/Awds:** All-Am, The Sporting News, 1981; Silver Medal, FIBA World Championship, 1982. **Special Achievements:** Featured in the July 19, 1999 Fortune Magazine about being a licensed broker since 1992. **Business Addr:** Vice President of Player Programs, Phoenix Suns, 201 E Jefferson St, Phoenix, AZ 85004, **Business Phone:** (602)379-7900.

WEST, PHEORIS
Educator, artist. **Personal:** Born Aug 17, 1950, Albany, NY; son of James and Mary Wilson McDowell; married Michele Barbette Hoff, May 5, 1979; children: Jahlani, Adwin, Pheannah & Adji West. **Educ:** State Univ NY Col Brockport, 1970; PA Acad Fine Arts, 4 yr prof cert, 1974; Yale Univ, MFA, painting, 1976. **Career:** Ohio State Univ, asst prof, assoc prof art, currently; Hillhouse HS New Haven, Ct, artist-in-residence 1976; Educ Ctr Arts, dir & artist-in-residence, 1976. **Orgs:** Nat Conf Artists, 1970; Artist Equity, 1978-; bd mem, CMACAO Cultural Arts Ctr, 1979-; Bahia Bridge 1988-; bd mem, Columbus Art League, 1988-; Nat Endowment Arts Expansion Arts Panel; Ohio Arts Coun. **Honors/Awds:** Cresson Award Travelling Fellowship to Europe PA Acad of Fine Arts, 1973; J Scheidt Award Travelling Fellowshio to Ghana, 1974; Special Recognition, Ohio House Rep, 1988; Individual Artists Grant, Ohio Arts Coun, 1988. **Business Addr:** Associate Professor, Ohio State University, Department of Art, 128 N Oval Mall, Columbus, OH 43210, **Business Phone:** (614)292-0929.

WEST, PHILLIP CURTIS
Mayor. **Personal:** Born Nov 30, 1946, Natchez, MS; son of Sam and Elodie; married Carolyn Mosby; children: Dana, Danessa, Kareem & Samuel. **Educ:** Alcorn State Univ. **Career:** Adams County, supvr, 1980-97; Adams, Jefferson & Franklin Counties, Dist 94, state rep; City Natchez, mayor, 2004-. **Orgs:** Chmn, Miss Legis Black Caucus; pres, Boys & Girls Club Miss-Lou; chmn emer, Sadie V Thompson Era Reunion; chmn, Miss Asn Supvrs Minority Caucus; pres, Natchez High PTA; chmn, Adams County Dem Party; little league coach, TM Jennings Baseball League; pres, Natchez Br, Nat Asn Advan Colored People; vpres, Miss State NAACP; Rose Hill Missionary Baptist Church; Mason & Eastern Star Lodges; Omega Psi Phi Fraternity; Alcorn State Univ Alumni Asn. **Honors/Awds:** Alcorn State University Sports Hall of Fame, 2004. **Special Achievements:** Phillip West was selected to be inducted into the Alcorn State University Sports Hall of Fame, 2004; first African-American president of the Adams County Board of Supervisors. **Business Addr:** Mayor, City of Natchez, 124 S Pearl St, PO Box 1185, Natchez, MS 39120, **Business Phone:** (601)445-7555.*

WEST, ROYCE BARRY
Lawyer, politician. **Personal:** Born Sep 26, 1952, Annapolis, MD; son of Willis and Gloria Morris Ashford; married Carol Richard West, Jul 25, 1987; children: Steve, Tara, Royce, Remarcus, Rolando, Roddrick & Brandon. **Educ:** Univ Tex, Arlington, BA, 1975, MA, 1979; Univ Houston, JD, 1979. **Career:** Harris County Dist Attorneys Off, Houston, TX, asst dist atty, 1979-80; Dallas County Dist Attorneys Off, Dallas, TX, asst dist atty, 1979-84; Royce West & Assocs, Dallas, TX, lawyer, 1984-88; Brown, Robinson, & West, Dallas, TX, lawyer, 1988-91; Robinson, West & Gooden, partner & atty, 1992-; Tex state senator, 1993-. **Orgs:** Bd dirs, Tex Turnpike Authority, 1983-90; deacon, Good Street Baptist Church, 1984-; bd secy, Dallas County Dental Health, 1989-; co-chmn, United Negro Col Fund, 1990; pres, JL Turner Legal Asn, 1990-91; circle ten exec comt, Boy Scouts Am; Dallas County Democratic Party Finance Coun; life mem, NAACP; Nat Bar Asn. **Honors/Awds:** Won several awards including: Distinguished Service Award, Dallas Black Chamber Com, 1988; LLD, Paul Quinn Col, 1997; LLD, Huston-Tillotson Col, 2000; Dr. Martin Luther King Justice Award; Shining Star Black Lawmaker, African Am News & Issues, 2001; Tex Hosp Advocacy Tribute, Tex Hosp Asn, 2005; Heart of Honor Award, Am Heart Asn, 2005; Tex Fedn of Human Socs Appreciation Award, 2005; Dallas Pan-Hellenic Coun State of Urban Dallas Educ Forum, 2005; Friend of Educ Tex Classroom Teachers Asn, 2006. **Business Addr:** The Honorable Royce West, Texas State Senator, Capitol Sta, PO Box 12068, Austin, TX 78711, **Business Phone:** (512)463-0123.

WEST, DR. TOGO DENNIS, JR.
President (organization), lawyer, chief executive officer. **Personal:** Born Jun 21, 1942, Winston-Salem, NC; son of Togo Dennis and Evelyn Carter; married Gail Estelle Berry, Jun 18, 1966; children: Tiffany Berry & Hilary Carter. **Educ:** Howard Univ, BSEE, 1965, JD, 1968; Winston-Salem Univ, DLaw, 1996; Gannon Univ, D Law, 1968. **Career:** Duquesne Light & Power Co, elec engr, 1965; Sughrue Rothwell Mion Zinn & McPeak, patent researcher, 1966-67; US Equal Employ Opportunity Comn-,legal intern, 1967; Covington & Burling, law clerk, 1967-68, summer assoc,1968, assoc, 1973-75, 1976-77; Hon Harold R Tyler Judge, US Dist Ct,Southern Dist, NY, law clerk, 1968-69; Howard Law J, managing ed, 1968;Dept Justice, assoc dep atty gen, 1975-76; Dept Navy, gen coun, 1977-79; Dept Defense, spec asst sec & dep sec, 1979-80, gen coun, 1980-81; Patterson Belknap Webb & Tyler, partner, 1981-90; Northrop Corp Inc, sr vpres, govt rels, 1990-93; Veterans Affairs secy, 1998-2000; Joint Ctr Polit & Econ Studies, pres & chief exec officer, currently; Nat Capital Area Coun, Pres, currently. **Orgs:** Dist Bar, 1968; NY Bar, 1969; US Mil Appeals, 1969; dir, Wash Coun Lawyers, 1973-75; US Supreme Ct, 1978; US Ct Claims, 1981; comnr & chair,Dist Law Rev CMS, 1982-89; trustee, Aerospace Corp, 1983-90; Nat Coun Friends Kennedy Ctr, 1984-91; bd dirs, DC Law Stud Ct Prog, 1986-92;trustee, Ctr Strategic & Int Studies, 1987-90; chair, Legis Bur, 1987-89;bd dirs, Greater Wash Bd Trade, 1987-93; chair, DC Comn Pub Educ, 1988-93;trustee, Inst Defense Anal, 1989-90; financial comt mem, Episcopal Diocese Wash, 1989-; Protestant Episcopal Cathedral Foun, 1989-; DC Ct Appeals Comn Admis, 1990-93; trustee, Shakespeare Theatre Folger, 1990-93;trustee, NC Sch Arts, 1990-; bd consult, Riggs Nat Bank, 1990-93; chair,Kennedy Ctr & Friends Bd, 1991-; Am Bar Asn; NBA; Eagle Scout Bronze Palm;St John's Church, Lafayette Square, Vestry; Alpha Phi Omega Fraternity; Phi Alpha Delta Fraternity; Sigma Pi Phi Fraternity. **Honors/Awds:** Eagle Scout Award with Bronze Palm, Boy Scouts Am, 1957; Howard Univ, ServAward, 1965; Distinguished Pub Serv Medal, Dept Defense, 1981, 1998;Distinguished Eagle Scout Award, 1995; Distinguished Civilian Serv, Dept Amry; Distinguished Pub Serv, Dept Navy, 1998; Except Civilian Serv, Dept Air Force, 1998; Silver Buffalo Award. **Military Serv:** USY, served to capt judge, adv gen corps, 1969-73; decorated Legion of Merit; Meritorious Service Medal; AUS, secy, 1993-98. **Business Addr:** Chief Executive Officer, President, Joint Center for Political and Economic Studies, 1090 Vermont Ave NW Suite 1100, Washington, DC 20005-4928.*

WEST, VALERIE Y
Educator. **Personal:** Born Jul 8, 1965, Newport News, VA; daughter of Woodrow W Sr and Lula A. **Educ:** Hampton Univ, BA, 1987; VA Commonwealth Univ, MFA, 1992. **Career:** Lindsay Middle Sch, 8th grade Eng teacher, 1989-90; VA Commonwealth Univ, adj instr, 1990-92; VA Union Univ, asst prof theatre, 1992-, chair, dept fine arts, 2000-. **Orgs:** Nat Conf African Am Theatre, 1992-; Black Theatre Network, 1992-94; VA Speech Commun Asn, 1994-; Am Alliance Theatre Educ, 2000-. **Honors/Awds:** Aspen Inst, Wye Fellowship, 1995. **Special Achievements:** Blue Blood, dir, 1993, Joe Turner's Come & Gone, asst dir, 1993, VA Union Univ, Ain't Misbehavin, make-up artist, 1994, "A Look at the Academic Significance of Educational Theatre," 1994, Livin' Fat, dir, 1994, The Amen Corner, dir, 1994, "Vinnette Carroll: A Portrait of a Director," 1995; MLK Gala, The Carpenter Ctr, Richmond VA, stage mgr, 1995. **Business Addr:** Assistant Professor Speech & Drama, Chair of Fine Arts, Virginia Union University, 1500 N Lombardy St, Belgian Friendship Bldg 1st fl, Richmond, VA 23220, **Business Phone:** (804)342-3916.

WEST, WILLIAM LIONEL
Pharmacologist, college teacher. **Personal:** Born Nov 30, 1923, Charlotte, NC; son of Lionel Beresford and Cornelia T Hairston; married Edythe Kearns, Apr 27, 1972; children: William II & Edythe P. **Educ:** Johnson C Smith Univ, BS, 1947; State Univ Iowa, PhD, 1955. **Career:** St Univ Iowa, res asst zool, 1949-54; Radiation Res, Dept Col Med St Univ Iowa, res assoc, 1954-56; Col Med Howard Univ, assoc prof pharmacol, asst prof pharmacol, instr pharmacol, 1956-69; Col Med Howard Univ, prof dept pharmacol, 1969-72; Howard Univ, prof, chmn dept pharmacol, 1972-92, prof, dept radiol, 1971-92. **Orgs:** Am Soc Pharmacol & Exp Therapeut; Int Soc Biochem; Am Nuclear Soc; Am Asn Clin Chem; Am Soc Zoologist; Soc Experimental Biol & Med; Am Physiol Soc;Am Inst Chemist; Asn Cancer Res; fel, Am Inst Chem; Int Acad Law & Sci; Sigma Xi Sci Soc; NY Acad Sci; fel, AAAS. **Honors/Awds:** Outstanding Scholar, Howard Univ, Ctr Health & Sci, 1986. Published numerous articles. **Military Serv:** Army Air Corp, T/5, 1943-46; Asiatic Pacific Service Good Conduct Medal, 2 Bronze Service Stars, World War II Victory Medal. **Home Addr:** 10287 Paige Rd Ivy Hill Farm, Woodford, VA 22580-2625. **Business Addr:** Professor Emeritus, Howard University College of Medicine, Department of Pharmacology, Washington, DC 20059, **Business Phone:** (202)806-6311.

WESTBROOK, BRYANT
Football player. **Personal:** Born Dec 19, 1974, Charlotte, NC. **Educ:** Univ Tex. **Career:** Football player (retired); Detroit Lions, defensive back, 1997-2001; Dallas Cowboys, 2002; Green Bay Packers, 2002-03. **Honors/Awds:** Chuck Hughes Most Improved Player Award, 2000. **Special Achievements:** First round pick, No 5, NFL Draft, 1997. *

WESTBROOK, JOSEPH W., III
Educator, school superintendent. **Personal:** Born Jul 13, 1919, Shelby County, TN; son of Joseph W Westbrook II and Clara Nelson; married Dorothy Greene, Jul 13, 1939; children: 4 (1 deceased). **Educ:** AB, attended 1943; MA, attended 1961; PhD, attended 1970. **Career:** Educator, School superintendent (retired); Devel Plan of Decentralization, dir; Supvr Sec Instr, 8 Yrs; Sr HS, asst prin, 3 Yrs; Class rm Teacher Athletic Coach, 15 Yrs; area supt, Memphis City Schs, Memphis, TN, 1971-81. **Orgs:** Sigma Pi Phi Fraternity; Nat Educ Asn; Asn Supv & Curric Devel; Phi Delta Kappa Ed Frat; Nat Sci Supvrs Asn; pres, Tenn Educ Asn; Memphis Educ Asn; Nat Sci Teachers Asn; Am Asn Sch Adminrs; Nat Asn Sec Sch Prins; Exec Comt Nat Coun Teachers Retirement; bd dirs, Memphis Urban League; bd dirs, Dixie Homes Goodwill Boys Club; Glenview YMCA; Frontiers Club Int; Memphis Reg Sickle Cell Coun; pres, Alpha Phi Alpha Frat; Local Chap; Exec Comt United Way Memphis; Exec Comt LeBonheur Hosp; bd dir, Nat Urban League l978-82; bd dir, Nat Asn Sickle Cell Dis, l979-83; bd dir, Nat Educ Asn, l984-90; pres, Nat Educ Asn, l984-90. **Honors/Awds:** Acad professional devel award, Nat Acad Sch Execs; Outstanding Alumnus LeMoyne-Owen Col, l973; Greek of Year, Alpha Phi Alpha Fraternity Memphis Chap, l973; Melrose Schlorship fund, 2002. **Home Addr:** 1711 Glenview Ave, Memphis, TN 38106. *

WESTBROOK, MICHAEL
Football player, wrestler. **Personal:** Born Jul 7, 1972, Detroit, MI; son of Bobby Sledge and Mercy. **Educ:** Univ Colo. **Career:** Football player (retired), Wrestler; Wash Redskins, wide receiver, 1995-2001; Cincinnati Bengals, wide receiver, 2002; cage fighter, currently.

WESTBROOK, PETER JONATHAN
Executive. **Personal:** Born Apr 16, 1952, St Louis, MO; son of Moriko Westbrook; married Susan Miles, Jan 1, 1996; children: Dorian. **Educ:** New York Univ, NY, BS, 1975. **Career:** Peter Westbrook Found, pres, founder & exec dir, 1991-. **Orgs:** Bd dir, United States Olympic Comn, 1992-; Abyssinian Bapt Church, 1992-; trustee, Arthur Ashe Athletic Asn, 1996-; bd mem, New York City Sports Comn, 1996-. **Honors/Awds:** Olympic Bronze Medalist, 1984; UNESCO Award; Japanese American of The Biennium Award, 1998. **Special Achievements:** Author: "Harnessing Anger"; six-time Olympian; flag-bearer for 1992 Olympics; first African Am bronze medalist for fencing, 1984; 13-time US Nat fencing champion; Guiness Book of World Records, record holder; featured on 60 Minutes II, 2003. **Business Addr:** Founder, Executive Director, President, Peter Westbrook Foundation, 119 W 25th St, PO Box 7554, New York, NY 10116, **Business Phone:** (212)459-4538.

WESTBROOKS, LOGAN H.
Executive, consultant, president (organization). **Personal:** Born Aug 28, 1937, Memphis, TN; married Geraldine Douthet; children: Babette. **Educ:** Lincoln Univ, BA, bus admin, 1975, MA, Biblical coun. **Career:** Source Record Co Inc, founder, pres, 1977-; Calif State Univ LA PAS Dept, part-time prof, 1977-; Int Mkt CBS Records, vpres, 1977; Spec Mkts CBS Records Int, dir, 1971-76; Spec Mkt Col Records US, dir, 1970-71; R&B Mercury Rec, dir Nat promotion, 1970; Mkt Capitol Records Inc, from admin asst to vpres, 1969-70; R&B Capitol Rec, mid-west prom mgr 1965-67; RCA Vic Dist Corp, from mgt trainee asst to mkt mgr; Ambassador Africa, Annual African Music Festival, 1997; Recording co, exec, 2008-. **Orgs:** Co-founder, Cont Inst of Tech, 1971; mem Omega Psi Phi; PUSH Chicago; FORENY; bd trust Merit Rl Est Invst Trust Chicago, 1973; consultant, Nat Med Asn, 1971; pres, West brooks Artist management; vp of mktg, Soul Train Productions & Record Co. **Honors/Awds:** Recognition Commission Certificate, LA City Coun, 1970; Certificate of Merit, LA Urban League, 1970; Merit citation proj, 1975; Boston 1973; spec pres, Mrs Martin Luther King, Atlanta, 1974; Distinguished Alumni, Lincoln Univ, 1983. **Military Serv:** AUS, 1961-63. **Business Addr:** 280 S Bev Dr Suite 206, Beverly Hills, CA 90212.

WESTBROOKS, PHIL (PHILLIP WESTBROOKS)
Mayor. **Personal:** Born in Chandler, AZ. **Educ:** Chandler-Gilbert Community Col, attended 1991; Mesa Community Col, AA; Ariz State Univ, BA, pub & urban recreation, MA, pub admin. **Career:** City Chandler, councilman, 1998, vice mayor, 2004-06. **Orgs:** Fel, Ariz State Univ Community; exec adv, Improving Chandler Area

Neighborhoods; advocacy chair, Am Heart Asn, Oper Heartbeat; YMCA; Chandler Boys & Girls Club; Maricopa Asn Govt Human Serv Comt; Harry Mitchell Cong; Ariz Asn Retarded Citizens; Desert Cancer Found Ariz; charter mem, Optimist Club Chandler; dir educ, Chandler Regional Hosp. **Honors/Awds:** African American Achievement Award, 100 Black Men, 2004.

WESTBROOKS, PHILLIP. **See WESTBROOKS, PHIL.**

WESTER, RICHARD CLARK
Firefighter, city council member. **Personal:** Born Sep 24, 1945, West Palm Beach, FL; son of Walter and Hazel Fisher; married LaDarn Hudson Wester (divorced 1986); children: Anita Michelle Wester, Angela Monique Wester. **Educ:** Fla State Fire Col, Ocala; Valencia Community Col, Orlando, FL, attended 1988. **Career:** Firefighter (retired); City Riviera Beach Fire Dept, Riviera Beach, FL, chief, 1969. **Orgs:** Nat Forum Black Pub Adminr, 1981-; treas, Fire Chiefs Asn Palm Beach County, FL, 1990-; Training Officers Asn Palm Beach County, FL. **Honors/Awds:** Ricky Award, JFK High School Class of '65, 1990. **Special Achievements:** First Black Firefighter, Palm Beach County, FL; First Black Lieutenant of Fire, Palm Beach County, FL; First Black Captain of Fire, Palm Beach County, FL; First Black Fire Chief, Palm Beach County, FL; First Black Chief in the State of Florida of a major municipality. **Military Serv:** AUS, specialist 4th class, 1965-67; Expert Rifle Hon Discharge. *

WESTFIELD-AVENT, LISA
Executive. **Career:** Twentieth Century Fox, licensing; Mattel Toys; Sony Signatures, dir domestic sales; Nelvana Commun, vpres, domestic licensing; MGM Consumer Prods, vpres, domestic licensing, 1999-2002; MGM Prods, vpres worldwide licensing & retail develop, 2002-. *

WESTMORELAND, SAMUEL DOUGLAS
College teacher, educator. **Personal:** Born May 29, 1944, West Chester, PA; son of Nip T Sr and Ella Dee Ingram; married Mary E Hampton; children: Lesia A, Samara E & Diana Haskins. **Educ:** Kutztown State Col, BS, 1966, MEd, 1971; Lehigh Univ, MA. **Career:** World Cultures, teacher, 1967-71; Kutztown Univ, assoc prof social & anthrop, 1971-. **Orgs:** Consult, Black Cult Orgn, Kutztown State Col, 1970-71; Black Conf Higher Educ, 1972-74; Nat Asn Advan Colored People, 1972; Black Conf Basic Educ, 1972-73; lectr, Educ & The Black Child, Downington Br, Nat Asn Advan Colored People, 1972; Nat Conf Black Family, 1976-87; chairperson, Pa Sociol Asn Conf, 1983-84; exec bd, Asn Sci & Behav Sci, 1984-87; chair, Nat Conf Black Family, 1989-92; chair, life mem comt, ASBS, 1990-97; Asn Black Sociologists; Eastern Sociol Soc; Pa Sociol Soc; Lehigh Valley Black Admin; pres, Asn Social & Behav Scientist Inc. **Business Addr:** Associate Professor, Kutztown University of Pennsylvania, Department of Anthropology & Sociology, PO Box 730, Kutztown, PA 19530, **Business Phone:** (610)683-4740.

WESTON, LARRY CARLTON
Lawyer. **Personal:** Born Jul 6, 1948, Sumter, SC. **Educ:** SC State Col, BA, 1970; Univ SC, JD, 1975. **Career:** BF Goodrich Footwear Co, asst personal mgr, 1970-72; Gray & Weston Attys Law, atty, 1976-. **Orgs:** Adv bd, YWCA, 1977-78; Dist coun SC Conf Br NAACP, 1978-; bd dir, vice chmn, Sumter Co Pub Defender Corp, 1979-; Sumter Co Comn Higher Ed, 1979-; Sumter Co Election Comn, 1980-. **Business Addr:** General Practice Lawyer, Weston & Taylor, 201 N Main St, Sumter, SC 29150-4958.*

WESTON, MARTIN V
Journalist. **Personal:** Born Mar 14, 1947, Philadelphia, PA; son of Rubin and Cozetta Walker; married Brenda Catlin, May 23. **Career:** Philadelphia Bulletin, Philadelphia, PA, ed writer, 1979-82; Channel 6-TV, Philadelphia, PA, producer vision, 1982-83; W Wilson Goode, Mayor, Philadelphia, PA, spec aide, 1983; Newsday, Melville, NY, ed writer, 1984-. **Orgs:** Nat Asn Black Journalists. **Special Achievements:** Author, "Prized Banister Found in One Quick Step". **Business Phone:** (516)454-2911.

WESTON, SHARON (SHARON WESTON BROOME)
Government official. **Personal:** Born Oct 1, 1956, Chicago, IL; daughter of Lucille and Willie; married Marvin Alonzo Broome; children: 3. **Educ:** Univ Wis, LaCrosse, BA, 1978; Regent Univ, Va Beach, MA, 1984. **Career:** Arts & Humanities Coun Greater Baton Rouge, regional develop officer, 1985; Discover Mag, sales mgr, 1985; Finesse & Assocs, Baton Rouge, LA, exec dir, 1985-; Baton Rouge Opera, mkt & promotions asst, 1986; Nathan Group, dir commun, 1987-; WKG-TV, pub affairs dir, cohost, "IMPACT", Baton Rouge, 1987; Metrop Dist 7, City Baton Rouge, councilwoman, 1989, state rep, 1991; La State Senate, senator dist 15, currently. **Orgs:** Adv, Love Outreach Faith Fel, 1985-; La Ctr Women Govt; Capital Area United Way; bd dirs, Real Life Educ Found, 1989; Am Heart Asn; comt mem, La Elected Women Officials; bd mem, finance & exec comt, Ctr Women & Govt, 1991. **Honors/Awds:** Cert Human Resource Consult, Performax Systems Int, 1985; Certificate of Appreciation, S Baton Rouge Kiwanis Club, 1985; Certificate of Appreciation, Zeta Phi Beta Sorority Workshop Consult, 1989; Achievement Award for Accomplishments, Greens Chapel AME Church, 1989; Outstanding Talent & Spiritual Leadership to the Community Award, Mayor & Gov, 1990. **Special Achievements:** "Top 25 Most Influential Women - Leading The Way In The Capital City". **Business Addr:** Senator, Louisiana State Senate, District 15, PO Box 52783, Baton Rouge, LA 70804-4183, **Business Phone:** (225)359-9352.

WESTRAY, REV. KENNETH MAURICE
Clergy. **Personal:** Born Jun 15, 1952, Washington, DC; son of Kenneth Maurice Sr and Jean Virginia Hughes. **Educ:** US Merchant Marine Acad, Kings Point, NY, BS, 1974; Mt St Mary's Semi, Emmitsburg, MD, 1978; St Patrick's Sem, Menlo Park, CA, MDiv, 1979; Grad Theol Union, Berkeley, CA, attended 1986. **Career:** Am Export Isbrandsten Lines, New York, NY, third mate, 1974-76; Nativity Grammar Sch, Wash, DC, teacher, 1979; Sacred Heart Parish, San Francisco, CA, deacon, seminarian, 1980-83; St Elizabeth Parish, San Francisco, assoc pastor, 1983-85; Sacred Heart Parish, San Francisco, pastor, 1985-2000; St Sebastian Parish, Greenbrae, CA, pastor, 2000-. **Orgs:** Bd mem & past pres, Archdiocese San Francisco Black Cath Apostolate Affairs, 1979-; mem & former bd mem, Nat Black Cath Clergy Caucus, 1980-; counr, Archdiocese San Francisco Priests Coun, 1985-88; regent, Saint Ignatius High Sch, 1986-89; bd mem, Nat Fedn Priests Coun, 1988-; bd mem, Cath Charities San Francisco, 1988-92. **Special Achievements:** Rep to Int Federation of Priests Council, Ghana, 1988. **Military Serv:** Naval Reserves, Lt, 1974-91. **Business Addr:** Pastor, St Sebastian Parish, 373 Bon Air Rd, Greenbrae, CA 94904, **Business Phone:** (415)461-0704.

WETHERS, DR. DORIS LOUISE
Physician. **Personal:** Born Dec 14, 1927, Passaic, NJ; daughter of William A and Lilian Wilkinson; married Garvall H Booker, Dec 25, 1953 (deceased); children: Garvall H Booker III, Clifford Wethers Booker & David Boyd Booker. **Educ:** Queens Col, NY, BS (magna cum laude), 1948; Yale Univ, Sch Med, MD, 1952. **Career:** New York Presbyterian Med Ctr, attending pediatrician, 1956-2000; St Luke's-Roosevelt Hosp Ctr, dir pediatrics, 1973-79, attending pediatrician, 1973, founder & dir comprehensive Sickle Cell prog, 1978-2000; Columbia Univ Col Physicians & Surgeons, prof clinic pediatrics, 1987-2000, spec lectr, currently. **Orgs:** Am Pediatric Soc; fel Am Acad Pediatrics; NY County & State Med Socs; Susan Smith McKinney Steward Med Soc; Am Soc Pediatric Hemat/Oncol; chair, NIH Consensus Develop Conf, Screening Sickle Cell Dis, 1987; adv coun, Nat Heart, Lung, & Blood Inst, 1991-94; med adv bd, Sickle Cell disease Asn Am, 1999-. **Honors/Awds:** Preceptor of the Year, NYC Health Res Training Prog, 1991; Recognition Award, Southern Regional Sickle Cell Asn, 1993; Community Service Award, St Luke's-Roosevelt Hosp Ctr, 1993; Recognition Award, Hearbeats Jamaica Inc, 1995; Lifetime Achievement Award, Manhattan Cent Med Soc, 1999; Honorary Doctor of Science Degree, Queens Col, 1999. **Special Achievements:** Introduction to the Sickle Cell Trait Conference, 11th Nat Neonatal Screening Symposium, Corpus Christi TX, 1995; Newborn Screening for Sickle Cell Disease, 2nd International African Symposium on Sickle Cell Disease, 1995; Missed Diagnosis of S Korle-bu in Prenatal Diagnosis and Newborn Screening, 16th Annual Mtg of the Nat Sickle Cell Disease Prog in Mobile, Alabama, 1991; numerous other publications in professional journals and contributions to medical texts. **Home Addr:** 1201 Cabrini Blvd Apt 57, New York, NY 10033, **Home Phone:** (212)928-2600. **Business Addr:** Director, Columbia University College of Physicians and Surgeons, 630 W 168th St P&S 3-401, New York, NY 10032, **Business Phone:** (212)305-3806.

WHACK, RITA COBURN
Novelist, television producer. **Personal:** Born Jun 13, 1958, Harvey, IL; daughter of Charles G and Willie E; married Harold Lee Whack, Jun 25, 1983; children: Christine & Harold Jr. **Educ:** Ill State Univ, attended 1976; Columbra Col, Chicago, IL, attended 1977; Northwestern Univ, BA, 1980. **Career:** WBBM & WTTW, Chicago, doc producer, 1995-2001; WYCC, Chicago, producer, currently; Chicago Pub Radio, WBEZ-FM, contribr; auth: Meant to Be, 2002. **Orgs:** Founding mem prayer ministry, New Faith Baptist Church, 1998-2002, youth ministry adult leader, 2000-03; Nat Asn Black Journalists, 2002-03. **Honors/Awds:** Emmy Award, African Soil, Afr Am Agr, 1995-96; Emmy Award, 2000-01. **Home Addr:** 1413 Heather Hill Crescent, PO Box 607, Flossmoor, IL 60422, **Home Phone:** (708)957-4806. **Business Addr:** Contributor, Chicago Public Radio, 848 E Grand Ave, Chicago, IL 60611, **Business Phone:** (312)948-4600.

WHALEY, CHARLES H
Executive. **Personal:** Born Jan 15, 1958, Elmhurst, NY; son of Charles III and Edna; married Jeanette Smith, Sep 26, 1987. **Educ:** Queensborough Community Col, AAS, 1979. **Career:** Gen Tel & Electronics, test engr, 1979-81; Gen Dynamics Communs Co, opers engr, 1981-83; United Technols Communs Co, project mgr, 1983-86; Telex Comput Products, project mgr, 1986; Pertel Communs Corp, pres, 1986-91; Pertel Commun NE Inc, pres, 1990-. **Orgs:** Minority bus roundtable, Hartford Chamber Com, 1990-91; bd dirs, New York High Sch Telecommunications, 1991-; Minority Input Comt, Connecticut Minority Supplier Develop Coun. **Honors/Awds:** SBA Award for Excellence, 1993; Shinning Star Award, Minority Supplier Develop Coun, 1998. **Business Addr:** President, Pertel Communications of New England Inc, 750 Main St Suite 506, Hartford, CT 06103, **Business Phone:** (860)249-5800.

WHALEY, EDWARD I
College administrator. **Educ:** SUNY Col Oneonta, BS. **Career:** State Univ NY, SUNY Col Oneonta, alumni prog coordr, counr, currently. **Business Addr:** Counselor, SUNY College at Oneonta, State University of New York, Ravine Pkwy, Oneonta, NY 13820, **Business Phone:** (607)436-3500.

WHALEY, DR. JOSEPH S
Physician. **Personal:** Born Nov 29, 1933, Yuma, AZ; son of Sexter and Elizabeth; married Doris Naomi Pettie, Jun 7, 1957; children: Craig T & Dawna T. **Educ:** Univ Ariz, BA, 1954; Hahnemann Univ Hosp, Sch Med, MD, 1958. **Career:** USAF, physician flight surg, 1959-63; Private Practice Tucson, AZ, 1963-; Secy-Treas, Pima County Med Soc, Tucson. **Orgs:** St pres Ariz Chap, Am Acad Family Physicians, 1972; Am Med Asn, 1980-; bd dir, Ariz Physicians IPA, 1983-; Masonic Lodge; Archon Sigma Pi Phi Boule Frat; Kappa Alpha Psi. **Honors/Awds:** Phi Beta Kappa Univ Ariz, 1954; Dist Military Grad Univ Ariz, 1954; High Hon Grad Univ Ariz, 1954. **Military Serv:** Air Force Capt, 1959-63. **Home Addr:** 4710 N Camino Luz, Tucson, AZ 85718. **Business Phone:** (520)792-0309.

WHALEY, MARY H.
School administrator. **Personal:** Born Jan 1, 1937?, Clarksville, TN; daughter of Sadie Beatrice Allen Harrison and Adolphus David Harrison; divorced; children: Brian Cedric & Kevin Allen. **Educ:** Fisk Univ, AB, 1959; Univ Tenn, Sch Social Work, MSW, 1968, doctoral student, 1978-, Univ Tenn, Knoxville, Tenn, EdD, 1990. **Career:** Tenn Dept Human Serv, caseworker, 1961-63, casework supvr, 1966-72, staff consult E Tenn, 1972-74; Knoxville Col, vis instr, 1971-73, assoc dean students, 1974-78; Univ Tenn, professional asst, 1978-; Knoxville Col, Morristown, Tenn, assoc acad dean, 1989-90; Knoxville Col, Knoxville, Tenn, head, Div Bus & Social Sci, asst acad dean, assoc prof, 1990-; Dynamic Connections Inc, Chief Exec Officer, currently. **Orgs:** Chmn, Various community Nat Asn Social Workers, 1968; chmn, various community Asn Black Social Workers, 1972; bd dir, Phyllis Wheatley, 1972-74; Community Improv Found Bd, 1972-74; bd dirs, Planned Parenthood, 1973-77; UTSSW com Minority Admis & Retention, 1974-76; League Women Voters, 1976; bd dir, Helen Ross McNabb 1977; bd dir, Tenn NASW Chap, 1985; Friends Black C, 1985-; Community Youth Mentoring, 1989-; Friends Black C State Adv comt & local affiliate; Social Serv Panel, Tenn Black Legis Caucus; adv comt Child & Family Serv; bd mem, Nat Resource Ctr Family Based Serv, Univ Iowa; Bijou Lime lighters; nominating community Girl Scout Coun; RAM House Bd; chairperson panel, United Way Greater Knoxville, 1990-; Dynamic Connections, 1999-. **Honors/Awds:** Appreciation of Service, Helen Ross McNabb Ctr, 1983; Moderator Women's Asn First United Presbyterian Church, 1986-, deacon, 1987-90, elder, 1990-; Appreciation of Service to Girl Scouting, 1990; Dept Human Serv Work C, 1990; CAC Leadership Class, 1990; Plaque of Appreciation for Support & Wisdom, Knoxville Col, 1993; Boys & Girls Club, Laura Counr Br Bd, 1991-, prog chair, 1992-93; Zeta Phi Beta Sorority; Charter Mem, Knoxville Chap Jack & Jill; Comnr-Presbytery E Tenn, 1993-. **Special Achievements:** Edited, What Next? Child Welfare Service for the 80's, 1982; project director & co-author, Parmanency Planning, The Black Experience, 1983; contributed "Ethnic Competent Family Centered Services", Basic Family Centered Curriculum for Family Service Workers & Parent Aides.

WHALEY, WAYNE EDWARD
Educator. **Personal:** Born Oct 23, 1949, Lincoln, DE; married Janice Evans; children: Sean & Dane. **Educ:** Del State Col, BS, 1971; Univ Del, MA, 1977. **Career:** Red Clay Sch Dist, asst prin, 1978-86; Smyrna Sch Dist, teacher, 1971-75, asst prin, 1978-86, teacher, 1986-. **Orgs:** YMCA & Del Special Olympics; Del Exceptional C Coun, 1985; bd pres, Centennial United Methodist Church, 1985; Nat Assoc Equal Opportunity Higher Educ, 1986; bd mem, Wilmington Lions Club, 1986; Nat Sch Curriculum Asn, 1986. **Honors/Awds:** Man of the Year, Epsilon Chap Omega Psi Phi, 1982. **Special Achievements:** Special Mbr Governor's Task Force Educ, 1976. **Business Addr:** Instructor, Smyrna School District, Main St, Smyrna, DE 19977.

WHALUM, REV. KENNETH TWIGG
Clergy. **Personal:** Born Mar 23, 1934, Memphis, TN; son of Hudie David and Thelma Miller Twigg; children: Kenneth Twigg Jr, Kirk Wendell & Kevin Henry. **Educ:** LeMoyne Col, attended, 1957; Tenn Baptist Sch Relig, DD, 1975; Univ Mich; Univ Tex, Austin; Memphis State Univ; Harvard Univ, 1981. **Career:** Clergy (Retired); US Postal Serv, mem, dir personnel, 1968-71, mid-south asst dist mgr, 1971-77, south reg gen mgr employee rels div, 1977-79, dist mgr, Mich dist, 1979-81; Olivet Baptist Church, sr pastor. **Orgs:** Vpres, Tenn Baptist M&E Conv, 1977-81, pres, 1981-85; vpres, Nat Baptist Conv USA Inc, 1981-85, mem bd dirs, 1981-; bd dirs, Morehouse Sch Relig, 1981-; bd trustees, LeMoyne-Owen Col, 1983-; vice chmn, LeMoyne-Owen Col, bd trustees, 1985-86; bd dirs, Goals Memphis, 1986-; chmn, labor in-

dust comn, Nat Asn Advan Colored People, 1987-; city councilman, Dist 4, Memphis City, 1988. **Honors/Awds:** Jerry D Williams Award, Community Serv Agency, 1977; Man of the Year Award, ACT Memphis, 1979; CW Washburn Achievement Award, Booker T Washington High Sch, 1982; Man of the Year Award, Shelby Co Dist Asn, 1985; Life & Golden Heritage Nat Asn Advan Colored People, 1985; Golden Gallery Distinguished Alumni Award, Lemoyne-Owen Coll, Memphis, TN, 1987. **Military Serv:** USN, personnel man second class, 1951-55; Nat Defense Medal, Korean Serv Medal, Good Conduct Medal, 1951-55.

WHALUM, KIRK
Musician. **Personal:** Born Jul 11, 1958, Memphis, TN; married Ruby styne; children: 4. **Educ:** Tex Southern Univ, saxophone. **Career:** Saxophonist, 1985-; Film: The Prince of Tides, actor, 1991; TV: "Jean Michel Jarre Rendezvous Houston: A City in Concert", 1986; Albums: Floppy Disk, 1985; And You Know That!, 1988; The Promise, 1989; Cache, 1993; In This Life, 1995; Joined at the Hip, 1996; Colors, 1997; Gospel According to Jazz? Chapter 1, 1998; For You, 1998; Joy, 1999; Unconditional, 2001; Hymns In The Garden, 2000; The Christmas Message, 2001; BWB - Groovin', 2002; The Best of Kirk Whalum, 2002; Gospel According to Jazz: Chapter 2, 2002; Into My Soul, 2003; Kirk Whalum Performs the Baby face Songbook, 2005; Ultimate Kirk Whalum, 2007; Round trip, 2007, The Gospel According To Jazz Chapter III, 2008. **Orgs:** Boys & Girls Club; Houston Leukemia/Lymphoma Soc. **Honors/Awds:** Eight Grammy Nominations & 2 Stellar Awards. **Business Addr:** Saxophonist, c/o Variety Artists International, 793 Higuera St Suite 6, San Luis Obispo, CA 93401, **Business Phone:** (805)545-5550.

WHARTON, A. C., JR.
Educator, lawyer, mayor. **Personal:** Born Aug 17, 1944, Lebanon, TN; married Ruby; children: A C III, Andre Courtney & Alexander Conrad. **Educ:** TSU, BA, polit sci, 1966; Univ MS, JD, 1971. **Career:** EEOC, decision drafter, 1967-68; trial attorney, 1971-73; Lawyers Comt Civil Rights Under Law, proj dir, 1973; Univ MS, adj prof; Shelby County TN, pub defender, 1980; Pvt Pract, Wharton & Wharton; Equal Employ Opportunity Comn, investr; Shelby County, mayor, currently. **Orgs:** Past exec dir, Memphis Area Leagul Serv Inc; Am Bar Asn; Nat Legal Aid & Defender Asn; Nat Bar Asn; TN Bar Asn; NAACP; pres, Leadership Memphis Alumni Asn, 1979; Oper PUSH; Urban League. **Honors/Awds:** US, Attorney General Honor Law Graduate Program, 1971. **Business Addr:** Mayor, Shelby County, 160 N Main Suite 625, Memphis, TN 38103, **Business Phone:** (901)545-4311.

WHARTON, DR. CLIFTON REGINALD, JR.
Association executive, executive. **Personal:** Born Sep 13, 1926, Boston, MA; son of Clifton R Wharton Sr and Harriette Banks; married Dolores Duncan; children: Clifton III (deceased) & Bruce. **Educ:** Harvard Univ, BA, 1947; Johns Hopkins Univ, MA, 1948; Univ Chicago, MA, 1956, PhD, 1958. **Career:** Am Int Asn Econ & Social Develop, head reports & anal dept, 1948-53; Univ Chicago, res assoc, 1953-57; Agr Develop Coun Inc, 1957-69; Agr Develop Coun Assoc, Southeast Asia, 1958-64; Agr Develop Coun Am Univ Res Prog, dir, 1964-66, actg dir coun, 1966-67, vpres, 1967-69; Mich State Univ, pres, 1970-78; State Univ New York (System), chancellor, 1978-87; TeachersIns & Annuity Asn & Col Retirement Equities Fund, chmn & chief exec officer, 1987-93; Dept State, Dep Sec State, 1993; Knight Found Comn, vice chairman, 2005; Knight Found Comn, co-chmn, 2006-; dir, Burroughs Corp;dir, Equitable Life Assurance Soc; dir, Fed Res Bank of New York; dir, Federated Dept Stores; dir, Ford Motor Co; dir, Harcourt General; dir, NY Stock Exchange; Agr Develop Coun, economist & vpres; dir, Gannett Co Inc; dir, Kellogg Co; dir, Phillips Petroleum Co; dir, Nat Pub Radio; dir, COMSAT; dir, Mich Bell; dir, NY Telephone Co; dir, Capital Bank & Trust Co. **Orgs:** Bd overseers, Teachers Ins & Annuity Asn; Tenneco; Time Inc; trustee, Ctr Strategic & Int Studies; trustee, Glimmer glass Opera; trustee, City Ctr. **Honors/Awds:** Awarded sixty one honorary degrees from various universities in US; Man of Year, Boston Latin Sch, 1970; Amistad Award, Am Missionary Asn, 1970; Joseph E Wilson Award, 1977; Alumni Medal, Univ Chicago, 1980; Samuel Z Wester field Award, Nat Econ Asn, 1985; Benjamin E Mays Award, Boston Black Achievers, YMCA, 1986; Black History Makers Award, New York Asniated Black Charities, 1987; Frederick Douglass Award, NY Urban League, 1989; Rockefeller Public Service Award, 1993; Africare Legacy Award, 2005. **Special Achievements:** First Black Chairman & CEO of Fortune 500 company, TIAA-CREF, 1987; Named first Black chancellor of the State Univ of New York; First Black chairman Rockefeller Found; First Black admitted Johns Hopkins Univ Sch Adv Int Studies; First African American president of Michigan State University.

WHARTON, DOLORES D
Association executive. **Personal:** Born Jul 3, 1927, New York, NY; daughter of V Kenneth Duncan and Josephine Bradford Owens; married Clifton R Wharton Jr; children: Clifton III & Bruce. **Educ:** Chicago State Univ, BA. **Career:** Phillips Petroleum Co; Kellogg Co, dir; Gannett Co, dir; Fund Corp Initiatives Inc, founder, chmn, corp dir. **Orgs:** Nat Coun Arts Nat Endowment Arts, 1974-80; trustee, Mus Modern Art, 1977-87; dir, Albany Inst Hist & Art, 1977-87; Asia Soc, 1982-87; trustee, Mass Inst Tech, 1987-94; Albany Law Sch; bd mem, Nat Pub Radio; bd mem, Mich Bell Telephone Co; bd dir, New York Telephone Co; bd dir, Mich Nat Bank; bd dir, Key Bank, Albany; bd dir, Bank & Trust Co, Albany; trustee emer, Ctr Strategic & Int Studies. **Honors/Awds:** Received hon degree from various univ. **Special Achievements:** Mrs. Wharton was elected the first woman and first black to the board of the Phillips Petroleum Company; auth, Contemporary Artists of Malaysia: A Biographic Survey. **Business Addr:** Trustee Emeritus, Center for Strategic and International Studies, 1800 K St NW, Washington DC, WA 20006, **Business Phone:** (202)887-0200.

WHARTON, MILTON S
Judge. **Personal:** Born Sep 20, 1946, St Louis, MO. **Educ:** Southern Ill Univ, Edwardsville, BS, 1969; DePaul Univ, Sch Law, JD, 1974. **Career:** St Clair Co Pub Defender, chief judge, atty; Ill Judiciary, judge, 1976; pvt pract atty, currently. **Orgs:** Vice chmn, Ill St Bar Asn, Standing Comt Juvenile Justice; vice chmn, St Louis Bi-state Chap, Am Red Cross; bd mem, YMCA S Ill; bd mem, St Marys Hosp, E St Louis; bd mem, Higher Educ Ctr St Louis; life mem, St Clair Co Bar Asn, pres, 2002-03. **Honors/Awds:** Alumnus of the Year, Southern Ill Univ, Edwardsville, 1977; Man of Year, Nat Coun Negro Women, E St Louis, 1982; Man Of Year, S Dist Ill Asn Club Women, 1982; District Service Award, Belleville Jaycees, 1983; Civic Service Award, Phi Beta Sigma-Zeta Phi Beta, 1985; Citizen of the Year Award, Omega Psi Phi Fraternity Inc, 2003; North Central Province Humanitarian Award, St Clair Co Bar Asn, 2003. **Business Addr:** Attorney, 23 Hilltop Pl, E St Louis, IL 62203, **Business Phone:** (618)398-0612.

WHARTON BOYD, LINDA F.
Government official, consultant, educator. **Personal:** Born Apr 21, 1961, Baltimore, MD; daughter of Rev Frank Wharton and Thelma L Kirby Wharton; children: Milton Boyd. **Educ:** Univ Pittsburgh, BA, 1972, MA, 1975, PhD, 1979; George Wash Univ, CPM, 1998. **Career:** Howard Univ, asst grad prof, 1979-85; Wash DC Off Mayor, commun consult,1984-86; DC Dept Admin Serv, dir pub affairs, 1986-88; DC Dept Recreation,dir commun, 1988-92; Alcohol & Drug Abuse ServAdmin, chief criminal justice, 1992-95; DC Dept Human Serv, sr asst, dirpolicy & commun, 1996-97; Off Cable TV & Telecommunications, interim dir,1997-98; Exec Off Mayor, dir commun, 1997-2000; DC Dept Health, Off Commun& Community Rels, dir, 1997; Off Commun, DC Dept Human Serv, 2000,Community Human Serv, dir, dep off mayor, 2000; DC Pub Schs, chief commun officer, Off Commun & Pub Info, dir; Univ Pittsburgh, Affinity council dir, 2009; Wharton Group, pres, 1990-. **Orgs:** Delta Sigma Theta Sorority, 1970-; Nat Speech Commun Asn Black Caucus,1975-79; bd mem, Nat Arts Prog Nat Coun Negro Women, 1979-; Pub Rels Soc Am, 1997-; consult, Nat Asn Advan Colored People Labor & Indust Sub-Comn Commun; chairperson, Joint Chap Event, Nat Coalition 100 Black Women Inc; first vpres, Black Pub Rel Soc; bd mem, Edward C Mazique Child Parent Ctr; mem, Asbestos Abatement Community Outreach Campaign. **Honors/Awds:** Outstanding Black Women's Award, Commun Arts Creative Enterprises, 1974;Doctoral Hon Sem Prog, Howard Univ Speech Commun, 1977; Nat Public Radio Documentary Award, 1985; Bethune Legacy Award, Nat Coun Negro Women, 1986;Communicator of the Year Award, 1999. **Special Achievements:** Author: "Black Dance, It's Origin and Continuity", Minority Voices, 1977; advisor: "Stuff," children's program, NBC-TV, Washington, DC. **Business Addr:** Director, Wharton Group Inc, 7215 16th St, Washington DC, WA 20011, **Business Phone:** (202)291-6435.

WHATLEY, ENNIS
Clergy, basketball player. **Personal:** Born Aug 11, 1962, Birmingham, AL; married Ritza. **Educ:** Univ Ala, attended 1983. **Career:** Basketball player (retired), clergy; Chicago Bulls, 1983-85; Cleveland Cavaliers, 1986; Wash Bullets, 1986, 1987; San Antonio Spurs, 1986; Atlanta Hawks, 1988; Los Angeles Clippers, 1989; Wichita Falls Texans CBA, 1990; Portland Trail Blazers, 1991-92 & 1996-97; Israel DVAT, 1992-93; Atlanta Hawks, 1994-95; Kids in His Christian Daycare, minister, 1996-97; Lithuania Kalgiris Team, 1997-98; pastor, currently. **Orgs:** Pres & co-founder, Christian Outreach Orgn; Sapphire Ministries; founder, Ennis Whatley Enterprises. **Business Addr:** Founder, Ennis Whatley Enterprises, 9705 Wash Blvd N, Laurel, MD 20723, **Business Phone:** (301)604-9293.

WHEAT, ALAN
Government official, consultant. **Personal:** Born Oct 16, 1951, San Antonio, TX; son of James and Jean; married Yolanda Townsend, Aug 11, 1990; children: Alynda, Christopher & Nicholas. **Educ:** Grinnell Col, BA, 1972. **Career:** HUD Kans City, Mo, economist, 1972-73; Mid-Am Reg Coun, Kans City, econ, 1973-75; Co Exec Off KC, aide, 1975-76; Miss House Reps Jefferson City,rep, 1977-82; Cong 5th Dist, Mo, congressman, 1983-94; CARE Found, vpres pub policy & govt rels, 1995-97, bd dirs, 2006; Wheat Govt Rels Inc, pres, 1998-. **Orgs:** Rules Comt, Select Comn Children Youth & Families; chmn, Sub comt Govt Opers & Metro Affairs Comn Dist Columbia; Select Comt Hunger, US House Reps, beginning 1990; comnr, Martin Luther King Jr, Fed Holiday Comn, beginning 1989; pres, Cong Black Caucus Found, beginning 1990. **Honors/Awds:** Third freshman Congressman hist to be appointed to the Rules Comt; Best Freshman Legislator, St La Mag, 1977-78; 1 of 10 Best Legislators Jefferson City News Tribune, Mo Times Newspaper, 1979-80. **Business Addr:** President, Wheat Government Relations Inc, 1201 S Eads St Suite 2, Arlington, VA 22202, **Business Phone:** (703)271-8770.

WHEAT, DEJUAN SHONTEZ
Basketball player. **Personal:** Born Oct 14, 1973, Louisville, KY. **Educ:** Univ Louisville, sociol. **Career:** Minnesota Timber wolves, guard, 1997-98; Vancouver Grizzlies, 1999. mexico, Soles de Mexicali, currentlly. **Business Addr:** Player, Soles de Mexicali.

WHEAT, JAMES WELDON, JR.
Executive. **Personal:** Born Mar 16, 1948, Tuskegee, AL; son of James Weldon and Emogene Dupree; married Panchit Charanachit, Dec 19, 1975; children: Saranya J & Annalai B. **Educ:** Grinnell Col, Grinnell, Iowa, BA, 1969; Cornell Univ, Ithaca, NY, MBA, 1971; Univ Chicago, cert, advan mgt, 1982. **Career:** Bankers Trust Co, New York, NY, vpres, 1973-84; Corning Inc, asst treas; Corning Int Corp, treas, cfo. **Orgs:** Soc Black Professionals, 1986-. **Military Serv:** USAF, First Lt, 1971-73.

WHEATLEY, TYRONE
Football player, football coach. **Personal:** Born Jan 19, 1972, Inkster, MI; married Kimberly; children: 2. **Educ:** Univ Mich, sports mgt, 2005. **Career:** Football player (retired), Football coach; New York Giants, running back,1995-98; Miami Dolphins, 1998-99; Oakland Raiders, running back,1999-2004; Tampa Bay Buccaneers, coaching intern, 2005; Univ Mich, Mich Wolverines, track coach, 2005-06; Dearborn Heights Robichaud High Sch, head football & track coach, 2006-07; John Fontes, asst coach, 2008; coach, Ohio Northern Univ, 2008; asst coach, Eastern Michigan Univ, 2009. **Orgs:** Minority Fel Internship Prog, Nat Footbll League. **Honors/Awds:** Most Valuable Player, 1993; Big Ten high hurdle champion. **Special Achievements:** First round, 17th overall NFL draft pick, 1995. **Business Addr:** Assistant Football Coach, Eastern Michigan University.

WHEATON, FRANK KAHLIL
Movie producer, lawyer. **Personal:** Born Sep 27, 1951, Los Angeles, CA; son of James Lorenzo and Helen Ruth Alford; married Jean Carn, Sep 23, 1975 (divorced); children: Jean, Joseph, Maryam, Marissko & Summer; married Robin Louise Green, Aug 6, 1988. **Educ:** Willamette Univ, 1971; CA State Univ, Northridge, BA, 1973; Univ West Los Angeles Sch Law, JD, 1986. **Career:** WHUR-FM, broadcast announcer, eng, producer, 1973-74; NBC, broadcast eng, 1975-78; Freelance TV, actor & producer, 1975-; 300 TV Coms Nat Employers Coun, legal rep, 1984; Mgt Group, chmn, 1984-; Creator & Exec Producer, Michael Jordan & UNCF Celebrity Golf Classic, 1988-89; Law Offices Bickerstaff & McNair, Off Coun, 1993-; Off Spokesperson, City Compton, 1999-; Creator & Exec Producer, James Worthy All-Star Basketball Clinic, 1991-; Milton Berle Celebrity Golf Classic, Producer, 1990-91; Producer, "World's Fastest Athlete," ABC, 1990-91; "Sports Greats: One On One with David Hartman," ESPN, 1994; Scolinos, Sheldon & Nevell, coun mem, currently. **Orgs:** Bd mem, Black Entertainment & Sports Lawyers Asn, (BESLA), 1993-; bd mem, Big Brothers Greater Los Angeles, 1994-; bd mem, 28th Street & Crenshaw YMCA, 1994-; bd mem, Markham Theatre Proj, 1994-; Sports Lawyers Asn; Am Bar Asn; Nat Basketball Players Asn; Screen Actors Guild. **Honors/Awds:** City of Compton, CA, Mayoral Resolution, 1986, Mayoral Proclamation, 1992. **Business Addr:** Counsel Member, Scolinos, Sheldon & Nevell, 225 S Lake Ave 14th Fl, Pasadena, CA 91101, **Business Phone:** (626)793-3900.

WHEATON, KENNETH TYRON. See WHEATON, KENNY.

WHEATON, KENNY (KENNETH TYRON WHEATON)
Football player. **Personal:** Born Mar 8, 1975, Phoenix, AZ; married Franchell; children: Kendall. **Educ:** Univ Ore. **Career:** Dallas Cowboys, defensive back, 1997-99; Detroit Fury, 2002; Toronto Argonauts, defensive back, 2003-09; free agent, currently. **Honors/Awds:** CFL All-Star, 2007.

WHEATON, WENDY E
Chief executive officer, radio host. **Personal:** Born May 5, 1965, Boston, MA; daughter of Ronald and Ruth Wheaton. **Educ:** Emerson Col, BA, 1988; Univ Calif, Los Angeles, grad cert, 1999. **Career:** News anchor, 1989; Investigative Group Int, mkt dir; Extra, television producer; commentator, various nat television shows; Wheaton Entertainment Inc, chief exec officer, currently; Independent Public Relations, Marketing, TV development, 2008. **Orgs:** Nat Asn Television Prog Exec; Nat Asn Women Bus Owners. **Special Achievements:** Black Enterprise Magazine, 2003; Nationally Syndicated 2000-07; Finalist, The Hollywood Black Film Festival, 2007; Producer,"Testimonies of Faith". **Business Addr:** Chief Executive Officer, Wheaton Entertainment Inc, PO Box 101, Burbank, CA 91503.

WHEELAN, BELLE SMITH
School administrator, educator. **Personal:** Born Oct 10, 1951, Chicago, IL; daughter of Frank (deceased) and Adelia (deceased);

divorced; children: Reginald. **Educ:** Trinity Univ, BA, 1972; La State Univ, MA, 1974; Univ Tex, PhD, 1984. **Career:** San Antonio Col, assoc prof psychol, 1974-84, dir develop educ, 1984-86, dir acad support serv, 1986-87; Thomas Nelson Community Col, dean stud serv, 1987-89; Tidewater Community Col, Portsmouth Campus, 1989-91; Community Col, Portsmouth Campus, 1989-91; Cent VA Community Col, pres, 1992-; Central VA Community Col, pres, 1992-98; Northern Va Community Col, pres, 1998-2001; Va Gov, secy, 2001-05; Comn Cols, pres, Currently. **Orgs:** Aka Sorority Inc, 1969-; Am Asn Women Comm & Jr Cols, 1983-91; pres, Tex Asn Develop Educr, 1987; Portsmouth Sch Bd, 1991; Portsmouth Col, 1990-91; Ideal Develop Authority Lynchburg, 1992-; Lynchburg Chamber Com Bd, 1993-97; Cent Health Bd, 1993-95; Nat Conf Christians & Jews, 1993-95; YWCA Lynchburg, 1993-95, pres, 1994-95; Lynchburg Rotary Club, 1992-, pres elect, 1995, pres, 1996. **Honors/Awds:** Distinguished Graduate Award, Univ Tex Col Educ, 1992; Blue Ridge Chapter of Girl Scouts, Woman Distinction, 1994-. **Special Achievements:** First African American & the first woman to serve in the Commission on Colleges of the Southern Association of Colleges and Schools. **Business Addr:** President, Commission on Colleges, 1866 Southern Lane, Decatur, GA 30033, **Business Phone:** (404)679-4500.

WHEELER, BETTY MCNEAL
Educator. **Personal:** Born Oct 10, 1932, St Louis, MO; daughter of Theodore D McNeal and Claudia Smith Ambrose; married Samuel (deceased); children: Gayle. **Educ:** St Louis Univ, BS, 1953; Univ MO, St Louis, MEd, 1970. **Career:** Educator (retired); Metro St Louis Pub High Sch, prin, 1971, work study cord, 1969-71, instr cord, 1967-69, reading specialist, 1966-67, elec teacher, 1963-66; Metro Acad & Class High Sch found, prin, 1972-98. **Orgs:** Natl Assn Sec Sch Prins; Assn Supv & Curr Dev; St Louis White House Conf Ed; Urban League Ed Com; brd dirs, Urban League, 1973-; brd dirs, Metro YMCA; NCP; AKA Sor; installed mem, Delta Kappa Gamma Soc; Hon Soc Women Educ, 1975; Danforth Found Sec Sch Admin Fel Prog; Inst Educ Leadership Fel Prog. **Honors/Awds:** Salute to Excellence Award for School Administrators, St Louis AmNewspaper, 1989; Shero Award for Service in Education, Coalition of 100Black Women, Metro St. Louis Chapter, 1998. **Special Achievements:** St Louis Brd of Education dedicated Metro Academic and Classical High Sch Auditorium, the Wheeler Auditorium.

WHEELER, BEVERLY
College administrator. **Personal:** Born in Palestine, TX; daughter of Ruth Henry. **Educ:** Univ Tex, BA, social work; SW Tex State Univ, MA. adult & developmental educ. **Career:** Southwestern Univ, admis counr, assoc dir admis, 1996. **Orgs:** Pres, Tex Asn Admis Coun. **Business Addr:** Associate Director of Admission, Southwestern University, 1001 E Univ Ave, Georgetown, TX 78626, **Business Phone:** (512)863-6511.*

WHEELER, CHESTER A
Executive director. **Career:** City Macon, Dept Econ & Community Develop, dir, proj mgr, currently. **Business Addr:** Director of Economic & Community Development, City of Macon, Economic & Community Development Department, 439 Cotton Ave, Macon, GA 31201, **Business Phone:** (478)751-7190.

WHEELER, HEASTER
Executive director. **Educ:** Clark Atlanta Univ; Wayne County Community Col; Wayne State Univ. **Career:** City Detroit Fire Dept, firefighter; State Rep Carolyn Kilpatrick, legis asst; State Govt Affairs Ameritech, mgr; Detroit Pub Schs, Off Govt Rels; Mich House Reps, Curtis Hertel, dep dir commun; NAACP, Detroit Br, exec dir, 1999-. **Orgs:** Dept Community Rels Speakers Bur; pres, Phoenix; co-convener, Mich Legis Black Caucus Summit; All Kids First, 2000; Fel Chapel Church; Univ Dist Community Asn; Booker T Washington Bus Asn; Advocates & Leaders Police & Community Trust; Citizens Alliance Prisons & Pub Safety; Mich Land Use Leadership Coun; Nat Asn Advan Colored People. **Business Addr:** Executive Director, Detroit Branch NAACP, 2990 E Grand Blvd, Detroit, MI 48202, **Business Phone:** (313)871-2087 Ext 2422.

WHEELER, LEONARD TYRONE
Football player, president (organization). **Personal:** Born Jan 15, 1969, Taccoa, GA; married Chandra; children: Lindsey. **Educ:** Troy State Univ, BS, bus admin. **Career:** Football player (retired), President; Cincinnati Bengals, defensive back,1992-96; Minnesota Vikings, 1997; Carolina Panthers, 1998; Athletes Health Inc, founder. Wheeler Enterprises Inc. **Orgs:** Christian Athletes United Spiritual Empowerment. **Business Addr:** Founder, president, Wheeler Enterprises Inc, 10300 Otterdale Court, Charlotte, NC 28277.

WHEELER, MARK ANTHONY
Football player. **Personal:** Born Apr 1, 1970, San Marcos, TX; son of Peggy Burleson; married Diona; children: Devin. **Educ:** Tex A&M Univ. **Career:** Football player(retired); Tampa Bay Buccaneers, defensive tackle, 1992-95; New England Patriots, 1996-98; Philadelphia Eagles, 1999. **Honors/Awds:** Athletics Hall of Fame, 1993.

WHEELER, DR. MAURICE B.
Librarian. **Educ:** Shorter Col, BMus, 1980; Univ Mich, MMus, 1982, MILS, 1987; Univ Pittsburgh, PhD, libr sci, 1994. **Career:** Detroit Pub Libr, cur, 1987-90; Univ Mich Libr, staff develop & recruitment officer, 1990-93, asst dean, 1993-95; Detroit Pub Libr, dep dir, 1995-96, dir; Univ N Tex, Sch Libr & Info Sci, assoc prof, currently. **Orgs:** Am Libr Asn; bd dir, exec search comt, Friends Detroit Pub Libr; vchmn, bd dir, Detroit Area Libr Network; group facilitator & mentor, Snowbird Leadership Inst, 1998, 2000; Humanities Ctr, steering comt, Wayne State Univ; ed bd, J Bibliog Instr Electronic Resources; bd dir, human resources comn, Literacy Volunteers Am; adv bd, Urban Libr J. **Special Achievements:** Numerous publ. **Business Addr:** Associate Professor, University of North Texas, School of Library and Information Sciences, PO Box 311068, Denton, TX 76203-1068, **Business Phone:** (940)565-2445.*

WHEELER, PRIMUS
Hospital administrator. **Personal:** Born Mar 3, 1950, Webb, MS; married Earlene Jordan; children: Primus III & Niki. **Educ:** Tougaloo Col, BS, biol, 1972; Hinds Jr Col, AD, applied sci, 1977; Jackson State Univ, MST, educ, 1982. **Career:** Univ Miss, Med Ctr, respiratory therapy tech, 1975-77, respiratory therapist, 1977-78, instr respiratory ther, 1978-80, instr & clin coordr, respiratory ther, 1980-81, chmn, asst prof, respiratory ther, 1981-86; Apria Health Care, region vp, 1986-96; UMC, dir ambulatory servs, 1997-; Jackson Med Mall Found, pres, exec dir, 2001-. **Orgs:** Miss Soc for Respiratory Therapists, 1978-; Am Asn for Respiratory Ther, 1978-; advr, UMC Med Explorers Post 306, 1983-; Nat Soc for Allied Health, 1984-; bd dirs, Northwest Jackson YMCA, 1984-; Miss Hosp Asn. **Honors/Awds:** Scholastic Honor, Phi Kappa Phi Nat Honor Soc, JSU, 1982; One of 30 Outstanding Mississippians; Leadership MS Delegate, 1985. **Military Serv:** USAF, Honorable Discharge, 1973. **Home Addr:** 132 Azalea Circle, Jackson, MS 39206. **Business Addr:** Executive Director, Jackson Medical Mall, 350 W Woodrow Wilson Ave Suite 107, Jackson, MS 39213, **Business Phone:** (601)982-8467.

WHEELER, ROBYN ELAINE
Presidential aide. **Personal:** Born Dec 7, 1963, Brooklyn, NY; daughter of Raleigh and Muriel. **Educ:** Hunter Col, BA, media studies, 1988. **Career:** CNN-NY, field producer/assignment ed, 1988-95; NBC-Chicago, assignment ed, 1995-98; US Rep Bobby L Rush, communs dir, 1998-. **Orgs:** Black Rels Soc Chicago; Coun Advan & Support Educ; Chicago Asn Black Journalists, 1995-; vpres of mem, Black Pub Rels Soc Am, 2001-. **Honors/ Awds:** Features Award, New York Association of Black Journalists, 1993; Unity Award, Univ Missouri, 1994; Outstanding Spot News Coverage, Chicago/Midwest Emmy Award, 1996. **Home Addr:** 1617 E 50th Pl 14B, Chicago, IL 60615, **Home Phone:** (773)955-8675. **Business Addr:** Director of University Relations, Chicago State University, 95th St King Dr, Chicago, IL 60628, **Business Phone:** (773)995-2388.

WHEELER, SHIRLEY Y.
Nurse, educator. **Personal:** Born Feb 14, 1935, Pittsburgh, PA; married Bennie Jr; children: Teresa Marie & Bryan Joseph. **Educ:** Univ Pittsburgh, BSN, 1957, MNEd, 1965, Post Master's Ed, 1967-68. **Career:** Magee Woman's Hosp Pittsburgh, staff nurse, 1957-58; Montefiore Hosp Pittsburgh, staff nurse, 1958-59; Lillian S Kaufmann Sch Nursing, instr & maternity nursing, 1959-60; Univ Pittsburgh Sch Nursing, instr maternity nursing, 1963-67, asst prof maternity nursing, 1967-72; Duquesne Univ Sch Nursing, assoc prof 1972-. **Orgs:** Org Childbirth Ed, 1967; test writer, Maternity Nurse Certification Exam; Master's Degree Rep Nursing Aluminee Assoc; Univ Pittsburgh; moderator, Nurses Assoc, Am Col Obstetricians & Gynecologists Conf, 1974; Clinical Specailist Maternity & Infant Care, 1963; Sigma Theta Tau Prof Nurses Hon Soc; Univ Pittsburgh Sch Nursing; Dept Maternity Nursing, Univ Pittsburgh Sch Nursing; Black Stud Nurses Univ Pittsburg; vpres, Univ Pittsburgh Nurses Alumni Asn, 1976, pres, 1977; Resolutions Com PA Nurses Asn; Minority Recruitment, Univ Pittsburgh Sch Nursing; nurse, Am Youth Chorus Eurpoean Tour, 1977; chmn, Duquesne Univ, curriculum develop, 1986-88; Nurse Recruitment Coalition, 1988-91; vchmn, African Am Alumnae, Univ Pittsburgh, 1989-90; chmn, African Am Alumna, Univ Pittsburgh, 1990-91. **Honors/Awds:** Achievement Award for Teaching Friends of Braddock, 1990. **Home Addr:** 129 Mayberry Dr, Monroeville, PA 15146.

WHEELER, DR. SUSIE WEEMS
Educator. **Personal:** Born Feb 24, 1917, Bartow County, GA; daughter of Percy and Cora Smith Canty; married Daniel Webster Sr, Jun 7, 1941; children: Daniel Jr. **Educ:** Ft Valley State Col, BS, 1945; Atlanta Univ, MEd, 1947, EdD, 1978; Univ Ky, sixth year cert, 1960, 1977; Univ Ga, educ specialist, 1976. **Career:** Educator (retired); Bartow County & Cartersville, classroom teacher, 1938-46; Bartow Cartersville Calhoun Systems, jeanes supvr, 1947-63; Atlanta Univ, teacher summers, 1962-64; Bartow County Sch Syst, curric dir, 1963-79; Daily Tribune News, columnist, 1978-83; Ga Stud Finance Comn, 1985-89. **Orgs:** State rep Assoc Supvr & Curric, 1962-64; pres, Ga Jeanes Assoc, 1968-70; pres, Ga Asn Supvr & Curric, 1970-72; writing comm, The Jeanes Story, 1979; vpres, Bartow Cartersville Chamber Commerce, 1980-82; ed rep Am Asn Univ Women, 1980-82; Nat nominating comm Delta Sigma Theta, 1985; restoration chair, Rosenwald Sch, Noble Hill-Wheeler Mem Heritage Ctr, 1985, coordr, currently; world traveler Friendship Force, 1980-92; Helen A Whiting Soc; Chair, Int Relations, Am Asn Univ Women, 1987-89; Nat Planning & Develop Comm, Delta Sigma Theta, 1989-92; Ga Stud Finance Comn, State GA, 1985-89, 1989-93; chair, Int Delta Kappa Gamma, 1978-91; Minority Hist Preserv Comm, 1989-91; Georgia Trust Hist Heritage Educ Comm, 1990-91; mem adv bd, kennesaw State Univ, currently. **Honors/Awds:** Johnnye V Cox Distinguished Award, Ga Asn Supvr & Curric, 1975; Bartow County Woman of the Year, Prof & Bus Women, 1977; Oscar W Canty Community Service Award, 1991; Award for Appreciation, New Frontiers Inc, 1997. **Home Addr:** 105 Fite St, Cartersville, GA 30120. **Business Addr:** Noble, Noble Hill-Wheeler Memorial, 2361 Joe Frank Harris Pkwy NW, Cartersville, GA 30120, **Business Phone:** (770)382-3392.

WHEELER, THEODORE STANLEY
Athletic coach. **Personal:** Born Jan 30, 1931, Chattanooga, TN; divorced; children: Theodore, Mary Frances & James. **Educ:** Univ Iowa, BS, 1957. **Career:** Athletic coach (retired); Univ Iowa, asst track coach, 1972, head track coach, 1978-96. **Honors/Awds:** Four Times Big Ten Champion; Melbourne Australia Drake Hall of Fame, 1962; Athletics Hall of Fame, Univ Iowa, 2000. **Military Serv:** AUS, 1953-55. *

WHIGHAM, LARRY JEROME
Football player, football coach. **Personal:** Born Jun 23, 1972, Hattiesburg, MS. **Educ:** Northeast La Univ, criminal justice. **Career:** Football player (retired), Football coach; New Eng Patriots, defensive back, 1994-2000; Chicago Bears, defensive back, 2001-02; Pearl River Community Col, defensive back coach & special teams defensive coach, 2003-08. **Honors/Awds:** Mackey Award, 1996; AFC Special Teams Player of the Week, 1997.

WHIPPER, HON. LUCILLE SIMMONS
State government official, educator. **Personal:** Born Jun 6, 1928, Charleston, SC; daughter of Joseph Simmons and Sarah Marie Washington Simmons Stroud; married Rev Benjamin J Whipper Sr (deceased); children: Benjamin J Jr, Ogretta W Hawkins, Rosmond W Black, J Seth, Stanford Edley (deceased) & Cheryl D Hamilton. **Educ:** Talladega Col, BA, Econ Soc, 1948; Univ Chicago, MA, Pol Sci, 1955; SC State Col, coun cert, 1961. **Career:** State Rep (retired); Charleston Co Sch, teacher & counr, 1949-65; Burke HS, counr & chmn dept, 1965-73; Charleston Co Off Econ Opportunity, admin & prog dir, 1966-68; Charleston Co Sch, dir proj, ESAA, 1975-77; Coll Charleston, asst to the pres & dir human rels, 1973-75, 1977-81; SC House Rep, state rep, 1986-96. **Orgs:** Mental Health Comt, 1969-71; Mayor's Adv Comn Human Rels, 1971; pres, Gamma Xi Omega, Chap, Alpha Kappa Alpha, 1978-80; Comn Minimal Competency SC Gen Assembly, 1977-78; SC Adv Tech Educ, 1979-; SC Adv Coun Voc & Tech Educ, 1979-; Charleston Constituent Bd Twenty, 1980-84; Col Entrance Exam Bd; past pres, Avery Inst Afro-Am Hist & Cult, 1980-84, 1987-89; past pres, Charleston, SC Chap Links Inc, 1984-86. **Honors/Awds:** Fel grant grad study, Univ Chicago, 1954-55; Community Service Award, Charleston Chap Omega Psi Phi, 1968; DHL, Morris Col, 1989; DHL, Univ Charleston, 1992; SC Black Hall of Fame, 1995; The Order of The Palmetto, 1996; SC African Am Hist calendar, Bellsouth, 2003.

WHISENTON, ANDRE C.
Government official. **Personal:** Born Feb 4, 1944, Durham, NC; son of Andrew C and Margret Y; married Vera Norman; children: Andre Christopher & Courtney Yvonne. **Educ:** Morehouse Col, BPS, 1965; Atlanta Univ, MLS, 1966. **Career:** Naval Sea Sys Command, lib dir, 1973-76; US Dept Labor, exec develop prog, 1979, lib dir, 1980-82, chief, dir, Equal Employ Opportunity Complaints Off, 1987-. **Orgs:** Bd mem, Nat Asn Blacks Within Govt, 1985; Nat Asn Advan Colored People, 1988; Alpha Phi Alpha, 1988; Montgomery Co MLK Jr Commem Comn, 1988-89, bd mem, 1990-91. **Honors/Awds:** DOL ECO Award, 1978; Fed Womens Impact Award, 1979; Secy of Labor Rec Award, 1982; Board Service Award, 1986. **Home Addr:** 1204 Canyon Rd, Silver Spring, MD 20904. **Business Addr:** Director, US Department of Labor, Equal Employment Opportunity Complaints Office, 200 Const Ave NW, Washington, DC 20210, **Business Phone:** (202)693-6000.

WHITAKER, FOREST
Actor, movie director, administrator. **Personal:** Born Jul 15, 1961, Longview, TX; son of Forest Whitaker Jr and Laura Francis Smith; married Keisha, May 4, 1996; children: 2. **Educ:** Calif State Poly tech Univ; Univ Southern Calif. **Career:** Films: Fast Times at Ridge mont High, 1982; The Color of Money, 1986; Platoon, 1986; Good Morning Vietnam, 1986; Stakeout, 1987; Bird, 1988; Downtown, 1989; Johnny Handsome, 1989; A Rage in Harlem, 1991; Hit man,1992; Article 99, 1992; Dr Giggles, 1992; Conscenting Adults, 1992; The Crying Game, 1992; Body Snatchers, 1993; Blown Away, 1994; Species, 1995; Phenomenon, 1996; Hope Floats, dir, 1998; Ghost Dog: The Way of the Samuri, 1999; Light It Up, 1999; Battlefield Earth, 2000; Four Dogs Playing Poker, 2000; Green Dragon, 2001; The Follow, 2001; The Fourth Angel, 2001; Feast of All Saints, dir, 2001; Panic Room, 2002; Phone Booth, 2002; Deacons for Defense, actor & dir, 2003; First Daughter, dir,2004; Amercian Gun, 2005; Mary, 2005; A Little Trip to Heaven, 2005; The Last King of Scotland, 2006; The

Shield, 2006; The Air I Breathe, 2007,Ripple Effect, 2007; The Great Debaters, 2007; Vantage Point, 2008; Street Kings, 2008; Powder Blue, 2009; Hurricane Season, 2009; Winged Creatures, 2009; TV prog: "Criminal Justice", 1991; "Body Snatchers", 1997;"Heart of the Matter", 2006; "Jigsaw", 2006; "Tell Me No Secrets", 2006;"Smoked", 2006; "Of Mice & Lem", 2006; "Postpartum", 2006; "A House Divided", 2007; "Murmurs of the Heart", 2007; "On the Jones", 2007; "Back to One", 2007; "Meter Made", 2007; "American Dad!", 2007-09. **Honors/Awds:** Received several awards including: Best Actor, Cannes Film Festival, 1988; Blockbuster Entertainment Award, 1997; Emmy Award, 2003; Black Reel Award, 2003, 2004, 2007; Actor of the Year, The Magazine, 2006; BSFC Award, 2006; British Independent Film Award, 2006; Hollywood Film Award, 2006; FFCC Award, 2006; DFWFCA Award, 2006; CFCA Award, 2006; Oscar Award, 2007; BAFTA Film Award, 2007; BET Award, 2007; Image Award, 2007; Critics Choice Award, 2007; Golden Globe, 2007; New York Film Critics Circle; Best Actor Award, Los Angeles Film Critics Asn; Best Actor Award, Nat Bd Review; nominated for Best Actor, Broadcast Film Critics Asn & Screen Actors Guild. **Special Achievements:** Golden Globe Award-nominated and BAFTA - nominated.

WHITAKER, LOUIS RODMAN
Baseball player, baseball manager. **Personal:** Born May 12, 1957, New York, NY; son of Louis Rodman Sr and M R Williams; married Crystal McCreary; children: Asia & Sarah. **Career:** Baseball player (retired), baseball coach; Detroit Tigers, second baseman, 1977-95; spec coach, 2003-. **Honors/Awds:** American League Rookie of the Year Award, 1978; Am League Silver Slugger team, The Sporting News, 1983-85; Gold Glove Award, 1983-85; Am League All-Star Team, 1983-87.

WHITAKER, MICAL ROZIER
Theatrical director, educator. **Personal:** Born Feb 10, 1941, Metter, GA; son of Ellis and Alma Mical; married Georgenia; children: Mical Anthony. **Educ:** Howard Univ, attended 1961; Am Acad Dramatic Arts, New York City, attended 1962; Circle-in-the-Square, New York City, attended 1966; NCA & T State Univ, BFA, 1989. **Career:** East River Players, founder, artistic dir, 1964-76; Union Settlement's Dept Perf Arts, founder, dir, 1972-76; Ossie Davis & Ruby Dee Story Hour, producer, dir, 1977-78; Richard Allen Ctr Cult & Art, artistic dir, 1978-81; Ga Southern Univ, theatre dir, Dept Communication Arts, asst prof, prof emer. **Orgs:** Co-founder & coord, Lincoln Ctr St Theatre Fest, 1970-81; dir, Black Theatre Fest USA Lincoln Ctr, 1979; dir, Int Black Theatre Fest Lincoln Ctr, 1980. **Honors/Awds:** AUDELCO Award, Dir Musical, 1979; Paul Robeson Theatre Award, NC A&T State Univ, 1989. **Special Achievements:** CEBA radio sta production "The Beauty of Things Black" 1978; Emmy Production & Set Design "Cellar George" Seattle Chap, 1979. **Home Addr:** 515 Wash St, Metter, GA 30439.

WHITAKER, PERNELL
Boxer, athletic trainer. **Personal:** Born Jan 2, 1964, Norfolk, VA; married Rovanda (divorced); children: Dominique, Pernell Jr & Dantavious and Devon. **Career:** Boxer (retired); prof boxer, 1984-2005; trainer, currently. **Orgs:** Retired boxers found. **Honors/Awds:** World Boxing Council, Welterweight Title Holder; World Championships, Lightweight, Silver Medal, 1982; Olympics, Lightweight, gold medal, 1984; IBF Lightweight Champion, 1989-92; WBC Lightweight Champion, 1989-92; WBA Lightweight Champion, 1990-92; IBF light Welterweight Boxing Champion, 1992-93; WBC Welterweight Champion, 1993-97; WBA Light Middleweight Boxing Champion, 1995-95.

WHITAKER, VON FRANCES
Nurse, educator, psychologist. **Personal:** Born in New Bern, NC; daughter of Cleveland W Best and Lillie Best (deceased); married Roy Whitaker Jr; children: Roy III. **Educ:** Columbia Union Col, BS; Univ Mar, Baltimore City Campus, MS; Univ NC Chapel Hill, PhD. **Career:** Wash Adventist Hosp, staff nurse; Prince Georges County Mar Health Dept, pub health nurse; Howard Univ, instr nursing; Coppin State Col, instr nursing; Univ NC Chapel Hill, visiting lectr nursing; Univ MSR-Columbia, asst prof; Boston Col, asst prof; Univ Tex Heath Sci Ct, San Antonio, asst prof; Ga Southern Univ, assoc prof; Memorial Med Ctr Hosp, Savannah GA, res coordr, currently. **Orgs:** Chair res comt, Am Soc Opthalmic Registered Nurses, 1988-; grant rev panel, Nat Ist Health, 1991-94; chair nominations comt, Am Pub Health Asn, Pub Health Nursing Section, 1992-93; Tex Nurses Asn, Membership Comt D No 8, 1992-94; Planned Parenthood San Antonio & S Tex, 1993-95; Eye Bank San Antonio, 1992-94; C A Whittier Med Auxilary, chairperson nursing Scholar, 1993. **Honors/Awds:** Fellow, Univ NC Chapel Hill, 1977-78; Sigma Theta Tau Inc, Nat Hon Soc Nursing, 1979; Bush Inst Child & Family Policy, Fel, 1979-81; co-winner, Southeastern Psychol Asn, Comt on Equality Prof Opportunity Stud Res Competition, 1988. fellow Am Acad Nursing; Certificate of Apppreciation, Agency for Health Care Policy & Res, 1992. **Special Achievements:** Numerous presentations & workshops national & internationaly, 1984-93; Whitaker & Aldrich, a breast self exam prog for adolescent spec educ studs, 1993; Sexual Dysfunction, Nursing Diagnosis In Clinal Pract, 1992; Violence Risk, Nursing Diagnosis In Clinal Pract, 1992, Whitaker & Morris ORG, Key for a Successful Presentation, numerous other articles, 1992. **Home Addr:** 5308 Bayberry Lane, Greensboro, NC 24755-1139. **Business Addr:** Research Coordinator, Memorial Medical Center Hospital, Dept Res, Savannah, GA 31411, **Business Phone:** (912)351-3000.

WHITAKER, WILLIAM THOMAS
Television journalist. **Personal:** Born Aug 26, 1951, Philadelphia, PA; son of William T and Marie Best Whitaker; married Teresita Conley Whitaker, Feb 12, 1982; children: William Thomas Jr & Lesley Rakiah. **Educ:** Hobart Col, BA, Am hist, 1973; Boston Univ, Mass, African Am studies, 1974; Univ Calif, Berkeley, Sch Jour, grad study. **Career:** KQED, San Francisco, researcher/writer, 1977-78, news producer, 1979-81; WBTV, Charlotte NC, reporter, 1981-84; CBS News, correspondent, Atlanta, 1984-89, Tokyo, 1989-92, Los Angeles, 1992-; Hobart & William Smith Col, CBS News, correspondent, currently. **Orgs:** Nat Asn Black Journalists, 1985-89; Los Angeles Asn Black Journalists, 1993-; CBS Black Employees Asn, 1993-; Nat Asn Advan Colored People, 1993-; Ctr Early Educ. **Honors/Awds:** Emmy Award, Acad TV Arts & Sci, 1998; Doctorate Human Letters, Hobart & William Smith Col, 1997; Striving for Excellence Award, Minorities Broadcasting, 2000. **Business Addr:** Correspondent, Los Angeles Bureau, Hobart & William Smith College, CBS News, Rm 23 7800 Beverly Blvd, Los Angeles, CA 90036, **Business Phone:** (213)852-2202.

WHITAKER, YOLANDA. See YO, YO.

WHITAKER-BRAXTON, BEVERLY
School administrator, executive. **Career:** Richmond Pub Schs, prin, 1978-84, exec dir Support Serv, currently. **Business Addr:** Executive Director, Richmond Public Schools, 301 N 9th St 13th Floor, Richmond, VA 23219.*

WHITBY, DR. LINDA
Physician. **Career:** Pvt Pract, physician, currently. **Business Addr:** Physician, Private Practice, PO Box 999, Edgewater, MD 21037, **Business Phone:** (301)868-3212.*

WHITE, ALAN SCOTT
Executive, association executive. **Career:** Colliers Int, staff. **Orgs:** Pres, Jefferson E Bus Asn; Detroit/Wayne County Inc. **Business Phone:** (248)540-1000.

WHITE, ALVIN, JR.
Clergy, executive, chief executive officer. **Personal:** Born in Houston, TX; son of Alvin Sr (deceased) and Louis Renee; married Carolyn Joyce Smith; children: Alvin III, Daniel Lynn & Paul Christopher. **Educ:** Univ Tex, Austin, BBA, 1976, MBA, 1986. **Career:** Johnson & Johnson, mgr, personnel, 1968-71; Pepsi Co, Inc, dir personnel admin, 1971-79; ABC Inc, dir, compensation, 1979-81; United Gas Pipeline, vpres, human resources, 1981-90; Ivex, vpres, human resources, 1990-91; Pizza Hut Int, vpres, human resources, 1991-95; Frito-Lay, group vpres, human resources, 1995-98; AEA Service Solutions, founder, owner; Vistana Inc, sr vpres, 1998-2000; Green Leaf Development System Inc, chairman & ceo, currently; Shiloh Baptist Church, sr pastor, 2001-. **Orgs:** Alpha Phi Alpha Fraternity, 1970-; Mt Pleasant MBC, Windemere FL; adv bd, KSU Sch Bus, 1992. **Honors/Awds:** Legend Award, Univ Tex. **Military Serv:** USY, sargent, 1968-72. **Home Addr:** 3401 Lilas Ct, Windermere, FL 34786-7612. **Business Addr:** Chairman, Chief Executive Officer, Green Leaf Development System, Inc, 8516 Old Wintergarden Rd Suite 101, Orlando, FL 32835, **Business Phone:** (407)822-9224.

WHITE, ANTHONY CHARLES GUNN. See KAMAU, MOSI.

WHITE, ARTHUR W, JR.
Executive. **Personal:** Born Oct 25, 1943, St Louis, MO; married Virginia A Green; children: Arthur W III. **Educ:** Lincoln Univ, BS, 1965; 1967; USAF Mgt Anal Sch, cert grad (Distinguished Military Grad), 1967. **Career:** Equitable Life Assurance; Soc US, admin trainee, 1965-66, group sales rep, 1971-74, div group sales mgr, 1974-76, dir sales, 1976-77, vpres, 1977; United Mutual Life Insurance, pres & ceo, 1985; NYC Summer Jobs '90 Prog exd; Texas Health Choice LC, dir commercial sales, 1999-. **Orgs:** Vpres, NAACP 1961-62; Alpha Phi Alpha, 1962; chmn, social performance comm Equitable Life Assurance Soc, 1984; adv bd, Bronx Lebanon Hosp, 1986; NJ State Investment Adv Coun, 1989; adv bd The Salvation Army Greater NY, 1986; Leadership Dallas, Class 2000; Dallas 2012 Olympic Bid Comn. **Honors/Awds:** Outstanding Performance Award, Equitable Life Assurance Soc Group Oper, 1969; Man of the Year Award, Alpha Phi Alpha; Outstanding Achiever, Econ Develop New Era Demo Club 1985; TOR Special Inspiration Award, Theatre Renewal, 1986; Notable Americans. **Military Serv:** USAF, capt, 1966-71. **Home Addr:** 1105 Greenbrair Dr, Garland, TX 75115-3248. **Business Addr:** Director, Texas Health Choice L C, 9330 Amberton Pkwy, Dallas, TX 75243.

WHITE, ARTIS ANDRE
Dentist. **Personal:** Born Sep 13, 1926, Middletown, OH. **Educ:** Morehouse Col, BS, 1951; Howard Univ, DDS, 1955; UCLA, Post Doctoral Cert, 1970. **Career:** UCLA, lectr, 1969-72; Drew Postgrad Med Sch LA, lectr; Martin Luther King Hosp, Maxillofacial Prosthetic Div, LA, dir, 1972-; Univ Guadalajara Mex, lectr, 1975-; pvt pract, maxillofacial prosthetics, dentist, 1972. **Orgs:** Fellow, Royal Soc Health Engr; fellow, Acad Dentistry Intl; Am Prosthdontic Soc, Am Cleft Palate Assoc, Am Dental Assoc, Nat Dental Assoc; fellow, Acad Dentistry Handicapped, Am Assoc Hosp Dentists; Acad Maxillofacial Dentistry.

WHITE, DR. AUGUSTUS A., III (ELLIOTT WHITE)
Surgeon, educator. **Personal:** Born Jun 4, 1936, Memphis, TN; son of Augustus A and Vivian Dandridge; married Anita Ottemo; children: Alissa Alexandra, Atina Andrea & Annica Akila. **Educ:** Brown Univ, BA, 1957; Stanford Univ, MD, 1961; Karolinska Inst Sweden, PhD, 1969; Univ Hosp, rotating intern, 1962; Presbyterian Med Ctr, asst residential surgeon, 1963; Yale-19 New Haven Hosp, asst residential orthopedic surgeon, 1965, chief resident 1965; Newington C Hosp, resident 1965; Va Hosp New Haven, Conn, chief resident 1966; Nat Inst Health, orthopedic trainee, 1969; Harvard Bus Sch, Advan Mgt Prog, 1984. **Career:** Va Hosp W Haven, Conn, consult orthopaedic surgeon, 1969-78; Hill Health Ctr, consult orthopaedic surgeon, 1969-78; Yale Univ Sch Med, orthopaedic surgery, assoc prof 1972-76, prof 1976-78; Conn Health Care Plan, chief orthopaedics, 1976-78; Harvard Univ Sch Med, prof orthopaedic surgery; Massachusetts Gen Hosp, visiting orthopaedic surgeon; C Hosp Med Ctr, sr assoc orthopaedic surgery; Peter Bent Brigham Hosp, assoc orthopaedic surgery, 1979-80; Sidney Farber Cancer Inst, consult div surgeon; Brigham & Woman's Hosp; Beth Israel Deaconess Med Ctr Boston, orthopaedic surgeon chief, 1978-90; Orthopaedic Surgeon Chief, emer, currently; Harvard Med Sch, Oliver Wendell Holmes Soc, master, currenty; Ortho Logic Corp Phoenix, Ari, chmn scientific adv bd, 1990-91; Am Shared Hosp Servs, San Francisco, Calif, bd officers, 1990-91; Harvard Med Sch, Ellen & Melvin Gordon prof med educ, 2001, orthopaedic surgeon, currently. **Orgs:** Brown Univ Community Dept Orthopaedic Surgeons, Yale Univ Sch Med, 1972-73; Brown Univ Community Med Educ; Med Conf Community Beth Israel Hosp; Faculty Coun, Community Harvard Medical Sch; area concent adv, Musculoskeletal Harvard-MIT Div Health Sci & Tech; sub-Comm prof, Harvard Med Sch, 1982; ed bd SPINE, reviewer, Harper & Row, 1976-82; ed bd, Annals Sports Med, 1983; reviewer, New England J Med; New Haven Chapter Nat Advan Asn Colored People; Sigma Pi Phi Fraternity, 1979; visitng prof over 11 col & univs; visiting comn, minority Life & Educ Brown Univ, 1985, 1986; pres, Cervical Spine Res Soc, 1988-89; chair, Diversity Comn Am Academy Orthopedic Surgeon; founding pres, J Robert Gladden Orthopaedic Soc, 1990-2000; Health Policy Coun, Am Acad Orthopaedic Surgeons; Coun Academic Affairs, Am Acad Orthopaedic Surgeons, 2001; nat adv Coun, Nat Ctr Minority Health & Health Disparities, 2002. **Honors/Awds:** Ebony Magazine Black Achievement Awards, 1980; Eastern Orthopaedic Association Award, Spine Res, 1980; Distinguished Service Award, Northfield Mt Hermon Alumni Asn, 1983; William Rogers Award, Alumni Brown Univ & Delta Upsilon Fraternity, 1984; Delta Upsilon Frat Award Outstanding Achievement, 1986; Honorary, DHL Univ New Haven, 1987; Honorary Doctor Med Sci, Brown Univ, 1997; Honorary Doctor Sci, Southern Conn State Univ, 2000; Nix Ethics Award, Clinical Orthopaedic Soc, 2002; Brown Bear Award, Brown Alumni Asn, 2002; Athletic Hall of Fame, Northfield Mount Hermon, 1990; Outstanding Orthopaedic Scholar, Nat Med Asn, 1994. **Special Achievements:** Clinical Biomechanics of the Cervical Spine, 2nd ed, Lippincott, co-author, 1990; Author, "Your Aching Back", Revised Edition, Simon & Schuster, translated and published in Germany, 1990; co-Author Biomechanics in the Musculoskeletan System, Churchill Livingstone, 2001; Published over 150 Clinical & Scientific Articles. **Military Serv:** AUS, Capt Med Corps, 139th Med Detachment KB Vietnam, 1966-68; BronzeStar, 1967. **Business Addr:** Orthopaedic Surgeon, Harvard Medical School, 25 Shattuck St, Boston, MA 02115-0962, **Business Phone:** (617)432-1000.

WHITE, DR. BARBARA WILLIAMS
School administrator, social worker. **Personal:** Born Feb 26, 1943, Macon, GA; daughter of Ernestine Austin; married; married Julian E; children: Tonja & Phaedra. **Educ:** Fla A&M Univ, BS, 1964, BS, 1974, MSW, 1975, PhD, 1986. **Career:** Lake County Pub Sch, teacher, 1964-65; Duval County Pub Sch, teacher, 1965-73; Leon County 4-C Coun, dir, 1975-77; Fla A&M Univ, from asst prof, 1977-79 to assoc dean, 1979-92; Univ Tex, Austin, Sch Social Work, dean, 1993-, Ctr African American Studies, prof, currently. **Orgs:** Acad Certified Social Workers, 1978-; nat vpres, Nat Asn Social Workers, 1983-85; comnr on accreditation, Coun Social Work Educ, 1984-87; Links Inc, Tallahassee Chapter, Alpha Kappa Alpha Sor; vpres, United Way Leon County, 1988-91; pres, Nat Asn Social Workers, 1991-93; Int Asn Sch Social Work; mem, Class Leadership Texas. **Honors/Awds:** Social Worker of the Year, NASW Fla Chapter, 1982; Fla Bd Regents Grant Grad Study, 1982-83, 1983-84; Teacher of the Year, Fla State Univ, 1986; Professor of the Year, Sch Social Work, Fla State Univ, 1988-89; International Rhoda G. Sarnat Award, Nat Asn Social Workers. **Special Achievements:** Editor of book "Color in a White Society," Published by NASW, 1985; Published author in professional journals & books-general theme, Black American. **Business Addr:** Dean, Centennial Professor, University of Texas, Rm 2 202B 1 Univ Sta D3500, Austin, TX 78712, **Business Phone:** (512)471-1937.

WHITE, BEVERLY ANITA
Television journalist, television news anchorperson. **Personal:** Born Aug 4, 1960, Frankfurt, Germany; daughter of Modesta Brown and Freeman. **Educ:** Univ Tex, Austin, TX, Jour, 1981. **Career:** KMOL-TV (NBC), San Antonio, TX, news intern, 1980; KCEN-TV (NBC), Waco, TX, reporter, 1981-84; KENS-TV (CBS), San Antonio, TX, reporter & anchor, 1984-85; WKRC-TV (ABC), Cincinnati, OH, reporter & anchor, 1985-89; WTVJ-TV (NBC), Miami, FL, reporter/anchor, 1989-92; Univ Southern Calif, adj prof; KNBC-TV, NBC4, reporter & co-anchor, 1992-, gen assignment reporter, currently; Univ Southern Calif, adj prof. **Orgs:** Nat Asn Black Journalists, 1985-; pres, Black Journalists Asn Southern Calif, pres, 1995-96. **Honors/Awds:** Peabody Award, WTVJ-TV/NBC Miami, 1992; Best Local News Reporter, LA's New Times mag, 1997; Scholar Residence, Citrus Col. **Business Addr:** Reporter, Co-anchor, NBC4, 3000 W Alameda Ave, Burbank, CA 91523, **Business Phone:** (818)840-4444.

WHITE, BILL
Baseball executive, baseball player. **Personal:** Born Jan 28, 1934, Lakewood, FL; divorced; children: 5. **Educ:** Hiram Col, attended 1953. **Career:** Baseball player (retired), baseball executive; New York Giants, infielder, 1956, San Francisco Giants, infielder, 1958, St Louis Cardinals, infielder, 1959-65, 1969; Philadelphia Phillies, infielder, 1966-68; WPVI-Radio, Philadelphia, PA, sportscaster, 1967-68; WPIX-TV, New York, NY, broadcaster/baseball analyst, 1970-88; Nat League Prof Baseball Clubs, New York, NY, pres, 1989-94. **Orgs:** Comt baseball veterans, Nat Baseball Hall Fame, 1994-, bd dirs, 2000-. **Honors/Awds:** Nat League All-Star Team, 1959-61, 1963-64; World Series champion, 1964; Gold Glove Award, 1960-66. **Special Achievements:** First African-American president of National League; second black player to ever play for a Carolina League team.

WHITE, BILLY RAY
Government official, mayor. **Personal:** Born Jun 29, 1936, Center, TX; married Zerlene Victor; children: Elbert Ray, William Douglas, Jeanetta Marie, Johnetta Marie, CharlesVernon & Billy Ester. **Educ:** Prairie View A&M Univ Tex, attended 1955-57. **Career:** Meth Hosp Lubbock Tex, clerk, 1957-64; Varian Assoc Calif, mechanic, 1964-77; Ray Chem Corp Calif, buyer, 1977; Menlo Park, mayor. **Orgs:** Consult, gr Menlo-Atherton Bd Raltors; plan bd State Calif E Palo Alto, 1971-72; chmn, plan comm City Menlo Park, 1974-78; chmn, HCD bd Coof San Mateo, 1978-; bd dir, Ctr Independence Disabled Inc. **Honors/Awds:** First Black elected to Council City Menlo Park; Tulip L Jones Women's Club Inc, 1978; Man of Yr, Belle Haven Home Asn, 1980. **Special Achievements:** First black mayor of Menlo Park. **Home Addr:** 1131 Menlo Oaks Dr, Menlo Park, CA 94025. **Business Addr:** Buyer, Ray Chemical Corp, 300 Constitution Dr, Menlo Park, CA 94025.

WHITE, BRYAN
Automotive executive. **Career:** Mission Blvd Lincoln-Mercury Inc, pres, currently. **Orgs:** Nat Auto Sport Asn. **Special Achievements:** Company is ranked #36 on Black Enterprise magazine's 1997 list of Top 100 Black businesses. **Business Addr:** President, Mission Blvd Lincoln Mercury Inc, 24644 Mission Blvd, Hayward, CA 94544, **Business Phone:** (510)886-5052.

WHITE, CAROLYN
Educator. **Educ:** Wayne State Univ, BA, MA. **Career:** Highland Pk Community Sch, dir spec educ, currently. **Orgs:** Secy & treas, Greater Northeast Optimist Club. **Honors/Awds:** Golden Apple Award; Jerry White Memorial Award; Award of Excellence, Leadership & Community Collaboration VSA Arts Mich, 2004. **Business Addr:** Director Special Education, Highland Park Community Schools, 15900 Woodward, Highland Park, MI 48203, **Business Phone:** (313)957-3002.*

WHITE, CHARLES E.
Executive. **Educ:** Univ Detroit, BA, Bus Admin. **Career:** Executive (retired); Ford Motor Co; Borg Warner; Lear Corp, mgr, supplier develop, dir, supplier diversity & develop, vpres, supplier diversity & develop, 2000. **Orgs:** Am Soc Quality Control; Soc Mfr Engrs. *

WHITE, CHARLES R.
Civil engineer. **Personal:** Born Nov 25, 1937, New York, NY; son of Clarence R and Elise; married Dolores; children: Darryl, Sherryl. **Educ:** Howard Univ, BS, 1959; Univ S Calif, MS, 1963. **Career:** Civil engineer (retired); Civil engr planner, registered prof engr, CA, 1965; State Calif, LA Dept Water Resources Southern Dist, prog mgr geothermal resources; chief planning br, chief, southern dist. **Orgs:** Omega Psi Phi Frat, 1956; Am Soc Civil Engrs, 1957; Tau Beta Pi Town Hall of CA, 1970; Toastmasters Int, 1970. **Honors/Awds:** Principal author Planned Utilization of Ground Water Basins San Gabriel Valley, 1969; Meeting Water Demands Chino-Riverside Area, 1971; Meeting Water Demands San Juan Area, 1972; co-author, Water & Power from Geothermal Resources CA-An Overview, 1974; publ paper on Lake Elsinore Flood Disaster of March, 1980; Nat Acad Press, 1982; author, San Bernardino-San Gorgonio Water Resources Mgt Invest, 1986. **Home Addr:** 30433 Calle La Resolana, Rancho Palos Verdes, CA 90275, **Home Phone:** (310)377-2062. *

WHITE, CHRISTINE LARKIN
Nurse, chief executive officer. **Personal:** Born Mar 12, 1946, Birmingham, AL; daughter of Robert and Catherine Mills; married Roger, Dec 24, 1969; children: Eugena & Karen. **Educ:** Tuskegee Inst, Tuskegee, AL, BSN, 1968; Univ Ala, MSN, 1976. **Career:** Univ Hosp, Birmingham, AL, staff nurse, 1968-70, 1974-77, staff develop,1977-80, dir psychiat nursing, 1980-; Manpower Training & Develop, Akron,OH, instr, 1970; Planned Parenthood, Akron, OH, clin nurse, 1971-73; Teges Corp, pres & ceo, currently. **Orgs:** Epsilon Beta Chap Chi Eta Phi, 1966; Omicron Omega Chap, Alpha Kappa Alpha, 1979; Quality Assurance Community Med & Dental Staff, Univ Ala Hosp, 1985-88; Nursing Res Community Univ Hosp, 1986-87. **Home Addr:** 212 4th Ave S, Birmingham, AL 35205, **Home Phone:** (205)252-8519. **Business Addr:** President, Chief Executive Officer, Teges Corporation, 3191 Coral Way Suite 504, Miami, FL 33145, **Business Phone:** (305)461-6700.

WHITE, CLARENCE DEAN
Financial manager, artist. **Personal:** Born Nov 27, 1946, Ellaville, GA; son of Charlie George and Tymy Hartage. **Educ:** Univ Paris, attended 1968; Morehouse Col, BA (cum laude), 1969; Northwestern Univ, MBA, 1972. **Career:** First Nat Bank, Chicago, trust officer, 1969-82; Artist & Art Critic, freelance basis; Clarence White Contemp Art, art dealer, 1974-95. **Orgs:** Mens Coun Museum Contemp Art, Chicago; dir, Film Symp, 1976-85; pres, Belmont HillsHomeowners Assoc, currently. **Business Phone:** (404)753-8144.

WHITE, CLAUDE ESLEY
Lawyer. **Personal:** Born Jan 2, 1949, Bridgeton, NJ; son of John (deceased) and Viola; married J Denise Rice; children: Claude Jr, Stephanie, Christopher & Alicia. **Educ:** Rutgers Col, BA, polit sci, 1971; Rutgers Law Sch, JD, 1974. **Career:** Pitney Hardin & Kipp, assoc atty, 1974-76; Grand Met USA, atty, 1976-85; Quality Care Inc, vpres & gen coun, 1985-87; Staff Builders Inc, vpres & gen coun, 1988-89; Burns Int Security Serv, div coun, 1989-91; Paragon Enterprises Int, pres & chief exec officer, currently; Integramed Am Inc, gen coun, 1995, asst secy, 1998, vpres, 2002-. **Orgs:** Chmn, Rutgers Col Econ Opportunities Prog Adv Comt; Nat Study Register, 1971; bd dir, Inmate-Self Help Com Inc, 1974-76; chmn, bd trustees, treas, St Paul Bapt Ch; Am Asn Bar City New York; adv bd, Sigma Delta; bd dir, Nat Assoc Home Care, 1986-89; chmn, Home Health & Staffing Serv Assoc, 1987-88; secy, Comt Nat Security Co, 1991-; 100 Black Men S Metro Atlanta, 1992-; Ben Hill United Methodist Church. **Business Addr:** Vice President, IntegraMed America Inc, 2 Manhattanville Rd 3rd Fl, New York, NY 10577-2113, **Business Phone:** (914)253-8000.

WHITE, CLAYTON CECIL
Educator, special education teacher, founder (originator). **Personal:** Born Nov 4, 1942, New York, NY; married Le Tretta Jones; children: Shannon. **Educ:** Temple Univ Col Music, MusB, 1964, MusM, 1969. **Career:** Sch Dist Philadelphia, music teacher, dept head, 1964-69; Community Col Philadelphia, Music Dept, assoc prof, 1970-; Nat Opera Ebony, choral dirs, chorus master & conductor, 1976-; Clayton White Singers, music & dir/founder, 1978-. **Orgs:** Dir, Cult & Educ Ctr, Heritage House, 1962-69; Minister Music Canaan Baptist Church, 1980.

WHITE, CONSTANCE C. R.
Journalist. **Personal:** Born in London, England; daughter of Randall White and Hazel; married Denrick Cooper; children: Nefatari Cooper, Kimathi Cooper. **Educ:** NY Univ, BA, jour. **Career:** NY Mag, Writer; MS Mag, Numerous underground publs, assist ed, 1985-86; Freelance; Women's Wear Daily, assoc sportswear ed, 1988-93; Elle Mag, exec fashion ed, 1993-95; NY Times, fashion writer & reporter, 1995-; Ebay Inc, style dir, currently. **Orgs:** Pres & founder, Fashion Outreach, 1992-; Fashion Group, 1993-95; bd mem, Women In Need, 1994-. **Special Achievements:** Interviewed the world's top designers including: Calvin Klein, Donna Karan, Ken Lagerfeld, etc; author, Style Noir: The First How-to Guide to Fashion Written With Black Women in Mind, Perigree, 1998. **Business Phone:** (408)376-7400.*

WHITE, COUNCILL, JR. See WHITE, JOSEPH COUNCILL.

WHITE, D. RICHARD
Lawyer. **Personal:** Born Aug 5, 1947, Richmond, VA; children: Maleeka Renee. **Educ:** NY City Community Col, AAS, 1968; Bernard Baruch Col, BBA, 1974; Kans Univ, JD, 1983. **Career:** Reliance Ins Co, claims adj; Liberty Mutual Ins Co, claims exam, 1972-83; Nationwide Inter-Co Arbitration, arbitrator, 1977. **Orgs:** Omega Psi Phi, Dem Club of NY; founder, Coop Adventure, 1977; Nat Free Lance Photographers Asn, 1977; Com for a Better NY. **Honors/Awds:** Bedford-Stuyvesant Civic Award, 1974; Achievement Scroll, Omega Psi Phi, 1974; Bernard Baruch Act Collgian Award, 1974; Recognition of Achievement Reliance Ins Co, 1976.

WHITE, DEBRA Y
Government official. **Personal:** Born Sep 4, 1966, Portsmouth, VA; daughter of Preston Diggs and Mary; married Alan F White, Aug 27, 1988; children: Tiffani V & Alexis D. **Educ:** Old Dominion Univ, bus admin. **Career:** City Portsmouth, sr dep city clerk, 1991-96; City Portsmouht, chief dep city clerk, 1996-97, city clerk, 1997-. **Orgs:** Va Munic Clerks Asn, 1991-; Int Inst Munic Clerks, 1991-; co-leader, Girl Scout Colonial Coast Coun, 1997-. **Honors/Awds:** City Employee of the Year, Merriamac Kiwanis Club, 1994; Clerk of the Year, Va Munic Clerks Asn, 1998. **Special Achievements:** First African-American to officially serve as the city clerk in Portsmouth and the youngest person appointed to the post. **Business Addr:** City Clerk, City of Portsmouth, 6th Fl 801 Crawford St, Portsmouth, VA 23704, **Business Phone:** (757)393-8639.

WHITE, DEIDRE R
Journalist. **Personal:** Born Jun 8, 1958, Chicago, IL; daughter of Thomas and Vivian. **Educ:** Univ Ill, Chicago, IL, BA, 1979. **Career:** CBS/WBBM-AM, Chicago, IL, desk asst, 1979-83, news writer, 1983-87, afternoon producer, 1987-89, managing ed, 1980-90, asst news dir/exec ed, 1990-. **Orgs:** Nat Asn Black Journalists; Radio Television News Dirs Asn; Writers Guild Am; bd dirs, Univ Ill, Alumni Asn; CBS Mentor vols, 2007. **Honors/Awds:** Kizzy Award, Kizzy Found, 1990; 100 Women to Watch in 1991, Today's Chicago Woman, 1991. **Business Addr:** Assistant News Director, Executive Editor, WBBM-AM/CBS News, 630 N McClurg Ct, Chicago, IL 60611, **Business Phone:** (312)944-6000.

WHITE, DEVON MARKES
Baseball player, baseball executive. **Personal:** Born Dec 29, 1962, Kingston, Jamaica; married Colleen; children: Thaddeus, Davellyn Rae & Anaya Jade. **Career:** Baseball player (retired), baseball executive; Calif Angels, outfielder, 1985-90; Toronto Blue Jays, outfielder, 1991-95; Fla Marlins, outfielder, 1996-97; Ariz Diamondbacks, outfielder, 1998; Los Angeles Dodgers, outfielder, 1999-2000; Milwaukee Brewers, outfielder, 2001; Wash Nationals, outfield coordr, 2007-08, spec asst, Player Dev, 2008-. **Honors/Awds:** Am League All-Star Team, 1989; Gold Glove Award, 1988-89, 1991-95.

WHITE, DR. DEZRA
Physician. **Personal:** Born Dec 11, 1941, Beaumont, TX; married Geraldine; children: Dezra Jr, Nicole & Darren. **Educ:** Morehouse Col, BS, 1963; Univ Tex, MD, 1968. **Career:** Houston Med Forum, asst secty; Univ Tex, Med Sch, clinical assoc; Dept Obstet & Gynec, St Elizabeth Hosp, chmn, 1980-84, 1984-85; Mid-Town Obstet-Gynec Assocs, physician, pvt prac, currently. **Orgs:** Am Asn GYN LSP, Harris Co Med Soc; Houston Obstet & Gynec Soc, Nat Med Asn; pres, Houston Morehouse Alumni Asn; Alpha Phi Alpha, Tots & Teens; fel, Am Col Obstet & Gynec; certified Am Bd Obstet & Gynec. **Home Addr:** 2105 Jackson St Suite 100, Houston, TX 77003. **Business Phone:** (713)659-5010.

WHITE, DR. DON LEE
Educator. **Personal:** Born in Los Angeles, CA; son of Willie Rose Benson Brown and Kenneth White. **Educ:** Los Angeles City Col, AA, 1949; Calif State Col, BA, 1952; Univ S Calif, MM, 1959; Stanford Univ, study toward Dr Musical Arts, 1969; Univ Southern Calif, study toward Dr Musical Arts, 1972. **Career:** Educator (retired); Prairie View A &M Col, organist, 1955-61; Los Angeles City Col, instr music, 1961-62; Jefferson High Adult Sch, instr, 1961-63;Trade Tech Col, instr, 1962-63; Calif State Col LA, lectr, 1962-64; Calif State Univ LA, assoc prof, 1964, prof music. **Orgs:** Bd mem, Nat Assn Negro Musicians; D/w Community Chorale, 1998-; dir, Music So CA Conf AME Church; dir, Music Fifth Dist AME Church; adv brd, Calif State Univ. **Honors/Awds:** Afro-Amer Hymnal, 1978; lect, "The Black Experience in Art, Aestetic meaning of Black Religious Music", Calif State Polytech Univ, 1983;Honorary doctorate, Univ Monrovia, 1984; an Annotated Biography Negro Composers State LA Found Grant. **Special Achievements:** First Vice Pres of the National Association Negro Musicians Inc, 1983. **Military Serv:** USN, 1945-47. **Home Addr:** 4144 W 62nd St, Los Angeles, CA 90043.

WHITE, DONALD R.
Government official. **Personal:** Born Oct 14, 1949, Oakland, CA; son of Louis R and Barbara A Morton; married Lillian P Green, Feb 14, 1982; children: 3. **Educ:** Calif State Univ, Hayward, CA, BS, bus admin. **Career:** Arthur Young & Co, San Francisco, CA, auditor, 1971-75; Agams, Grant,White & Co, Oakland, CA, auditor, 1975-85; County Alameda, Oakland, CA,treas-tax collector, currently. **Orgs:** Nat Asn Black Accountants, 1972-; ex-officio mem, Alameda County Employees Retirement Asn Bd Trustees; chairperson, Ad Hoc Audit; chairperson, GASB Community Investment Comt; Ad Hoc Eval Comt; E Oakland Youth Develop Ctr Found; City Oaklands Budget Adv Comn; Nat Asn Advan Colored People; Am Inst Cert Pub Accountants; Calif Soc Cert Pub Accountants. **Special Achievements:** First African American elected as County Treasurer-Tax Collector of Alameda County. **Business Addr:** Treasurer-Tax Collector, Alameda County, 1221 Oak St Room 131, Oakland, CA 94612.

WHITE, EDWARD CLARENCE
Financial manager. **Personal:** Born Oct 9, 1956, Newark, NJ; son of Edward C White Sr and Viola L Williams White. **Educ:** Princeton Univ, BA Econ 1977; New York Univ, MS Quantitative Anal, 1981. **Career:** Merrill Lynch Pierce Fenner & Smith, indust anal, 1977-79; LF Rothschild Unterberg Towbin, vpres, 1979-83; E F Hutton & Co vpres, 1983-86, first vpres, 1986-87; Tucker Anthony

(John Hancock Financial Serv), New York, NY first vpres, 1988; Technol LBO Partners, LP, managing gen partner, 1988-90; Lehman Brothers, vpres, 1990-92, sr vpres, 1992-95, managing dir, 1995-; sr semiconductor equipment anal. **Orgs:** NY Soc Securities Anals 1978-. **Honors/Awds:** CFA Designation, Asn Invest Mgt & Res, 1984; Ranked among top anal worldwide Euro Money Mag Global Res Surv, 1985; ranked runner up Inst Invstr Mag Anal Surv, 1986; Lehman Brothers Ten Uncommon Values Award, 1993, 1995 & 1999; Ranked 2 out of 633 anal Bloomberg Bus News, 1995; Surv US Stock Recommendations; Ranked 3 Inst Investor Mag, Anal Surv, 1995; Ranked Runner Up, Investor Mag, Anal Surv, 1996, 1998; Ranked Reuters Surv, 1997-99; Cited Instnl Investor, Mag Home Run Hitter, 1995, 1996; Wall St Journ All-Star Surv, 1999.

WHITE, ELLIOTT. See WHITE, DR. AUGUSTUS A., III.

(CABRERA) WHITE, ELOISE J.
Educator. **Personal:** Born Dec 9, 1932, Evinston, FL; daughter of Zebbie Johnson (deceased) and Maude S Johnson (deceased); married Marion C Cabrera (deceased); children: Yolanda Alicia Cabrera-Liggins; married Charles J. **Educ:** Fla A&M Univ, BS, educ, 1954; Indiana Univ, MS, educ, 1963; Nova Univ,Educ Leadership, EdD, 1985; Mich State Univ, community educ; Univ South Fla, adult educ. **Career:** Teacher (retired); Broward County Sch Syst, elem teacher, 1954-56; Elem Dept Sch, US Dependent Sch Baum holder, Ger, teacher, 1956-57; Howard WBlack, High Sch teacher, 1958-63, counr, 1963-66; Neighborhood Youth Corp,Fed Prog, counr, 1966-77, asst proj dir, 1966-69; Hills City Pub Sch, supvr comm educ prog, 1969-77, Williams Elem, prin, 1977. **Orgs:** Nat Community Educ Asn; Am Asn Univ Women; Fla Asn Community Educ; Tampa Urban League; Fla Adult Educ Asn; Nat Asn Advan Colored People, Nat Coun Negro Women; Tampa Alumnae Chap Delta Sigma Theta Sorority, May Week &Awards Day, Golden Life chair, Corr Sec; Orgn Concerned Parents; Eastern Seal Adv Bd; bd dirs, Girl Scouts; bd dirs, Hillsborough Community ColFound; St Peter Claver Cath Church; Hillsborough County Asn Sch Adminr. **Honors/Awds:** Numerous honors & awards including Rising to the Top Award, Am Univ Women Asn, 1990; Outstanding Principal, All Star Educ Gala, 1991; Parishioner of the month of July, St Peter Claver Church, 1992; Distinguished Educator Award, 1993; Plaque Distinguished Service, FACE; Boy Scouts Award;Certificate for Outstanding Contribution, Hillsborough Community Col Adv Comt; Outstanding Educator Award, Golden SABLE Inc; Boss of the Year, ABWA; Outstanding Leadership Award, Delta Sigma Theta; Outstanding Leadership Award, Community Educ, Fla Atlantic Univ. **Home Addr:** 613 N Gomez Ave, Tampa, FL 33609-1631. *

WHITE, ERNEST G
Business owner. **Personal:** Born Dec 12, 1946, Dayton, OH; son of George W and Fannie C; married Mae Charlotte Lampkins; children: Yvette M White Ransan, Letika & Charika. **Educ:** Cent State Univ, BA, 1968; Gen Motors Dealer Devel Acad; Univ Detroit, attended 1975. **Career:** George White Oldsmobile, vpres, gen mgr, 1974-80; Ernest White Ford-Lincoln-Mercury, chief exec. **Orgs:** Minority Dealer Oper; Kiwanis Delaware, OH Chap; Frontier Int; Operation PUSH; C C; bd dir, Black Ford-Lincoln-Mercury; nat bd dir, Black Ford-Lincoln & Mercury Dealer Asn, Great Lake Region. **Honors/Awds:** Outstanding, New & Used Car Minority Oper, 1980; Recognition, Gov State Ohio, 1980-85; Truck Leadership Award, 1982; Outstanding Business Award, 1983; Dealer with Direction Award; Ford Motor Co, 1984; Black Consumer Goods of the Year, 1984; Lincoln & Mercury Central Region Linchpin Award, Breakthrough Soc, 1984. **Special Achievements:** Top 100 Businessmen in Nation, Black Enterprise Mag, 1984; First and only second generation Black new car dealer in America.

WHITE, EVELYN M
Government official. **Personal:** Born in Kansas City, MO. **Educ:** Cent Mo Univ. **Career:** US Dept Agr, dep dir personnel, dir personnel; US Dept Health & Human Servs, dep asst secy human resources, 1997, Off Secy, prin dep asst secy admin & mgt, 2001-, acting dir, prog support ctr, 2003-, sr exec serv, currently. **Honors/Awds:** Unsung Hero Award, US Dept Agri, 1993; Distinguished Service Award, Secy Agr; Vice President Award, 1993, 1996; George Washington Carver Hall of Fame, 1996; Presidential Rank Award, 1999; Distinguished Service, 2003. **Special Achievements:** First African & first female to hold the position of director of personnel for the USDA. **Business Addr:** Senior Executive Service, United States Department Health & Human Service, Rm 309F Health & Human Serv Bldg 200 Independence Ave, Washington, DC 20201, **Business Phone:** (202)690-7431.

WHITE, FRANKIE WALTON
Lawyer. **Personal:** Born Sep 8, 1945, Yazoo City, MS; daughter of Serena Brown and William Howard; children: Carlyle Creswell. **Educ:** Wellesley Col, 1964-65; Tougaloo Col, BA (magna cum laude), 1966; Univ Calif, Los Angeles, MA, 1967; Syracuse Univ, Syracuse, NY, 1972-73; Univ MS, JD, 1975. **Career:** Fisk Univ, instr eng, 1967-69; Wellesley Col, lectr eng, 1969-70; Tougaloo Col, asst prof eng, 1970-71; Syracuse Univ, asst dir financial aid, 1971-72; Cent Miss Legal Serv, staff atty, 1975-77; State Miss, spec asst atty gen, 1977, asst atty gen; Tex Southern Univ, stud legal counr, 1977-79; Univ NC Greensboro, SERVE Ctr, MS Dept Educ, sr policy res analyst, currently. **Orgs:** Alpha Kappa Alpha Sor Inc, 1964-; Magnolia, Miss Bar Asn, 1975-; Links Inc, 1977-; Comn Col Southern Asn Col & Sch, 1982-; bd trustees, Southern Asn Col & Sch, 1988-91; Leadership Jackson, 1989-; chmn, Coun State Educ Atty, 1990-91; bd dirs, Nat Asn State Bd Educ, 1991. **Honors/Awds:** Woodrow Wilson fel; Reginald Heber Smith Comm Lawyer fel; Women Achievement Award in Law & Govt Women for Progress of Mississippi Inc, 1981; Distinguished Alumni Citation, Nat Asn Equal Opportunity Higher Educ, 1986. **Special Achievements:** First african american female to be appointed special asst atty gen, 1977, & asst atty gen, 1986. **Home Addr:** 931 Rutherford Dr, Jackson, MS 39206-2033. **Business Addr:** Senior Policy Research Analyst, University of North Carolina at Greensboro, SERVE Center, Cent High Bldg 359 NW St, PO Box 771, Jackson, MS 39201, **Business Phone:** (601)359-3501.*

WHITE, FREDERIC PAUL, JR.
Educator. **Personal:** Born Feb 12, 1948, Cleveland, OH; son of Frederic Paul and Ella Johnson; married; children: Alfred Davis & Michael Lewis. **Educ:** Columbia Col New York, BA, 1970, JD, 1973. **Career:** Educator(retired); Squire Sanders & Dempsey, assoc atty, 1973-78; Cleveland State Univ, from asst prof to assoc prof, 1978-86, prof emer, 1986-, assoc dean, 1994-. **Orgs:** Bd trustees, Cleveland Legal Aid Soc, 1981-84; Trinity Cathedral Comm Develop Fund, 1981-89; pres, Norman S Minor Bar Asn, 1984; actg judge & referee, Shaker Heights Municipal Ct, 1984-90; Omega Psi Phi Fraternity Inc; Zeta Omega Chapter; host, CSU City Focus radio show, 1981-85; bd advrs, African-Am Mus, 1986-90; charter mem, 100 Black Men of Cleveland Inc, 1998-. **Special Achievements:** Books written are "Ohio Landlord Tenant Law," West Publishing, Co, 1984, 2nd ed, 1990, annually; 2 law review articles, Cleveland Housing Ct, Ohio Open Meeting Law; Contrib Author Antieau's Local Govt Law; co-author chapts "Criminal Procedure Rules for Cleveland Housing Ct"; Frequent guest on local TV/radio landlord-tenant law subjects; contributing editor, Powell on Real Property; Thompson on Real Property. **Business Addr:** Associate Dean, Professor Emeritus, Cleveland State University, 1801 Euclid Ave, Cleveland, OH 44115, **Business Phone:** (216)687-2000.

WHITE, GARY
Executive. **Career:** Savers Inc, chief exec officer; Gymboree Corp, chief exec officer; Target Inc, exec vpres, Operations Mervyn's Stores & vpres west coast stores; Wet Seal Inc, chief operating officer, 2006-08; United Retail Group Inc, chief exec officer, 2008-. **Business Addr:** Chief Executive Officer, United Retail Group Inc, 365 W Passaic St, Rochelle Park, NM 07662, **Business Phone:** (201)845-0880.

WHITE, GARY LEON
Executive. **Personal:** Born Dec 17, 1932, Ontario;son of George W and Anna Louella Talbot; married Inge Topper; children: Karen, Janet, Gary, Christopher & Steffanie. **Educ:** Univ Md; Wayne State Univ; Carnegie Mellen Univ, Pittsburgh Grad Sch Indust Admin, 1980. **Career:** Cobo Hall, conv, 1960-64; Jam Handy Org, assoc prod, 1964-64; Tom Thomas Orgn, exec vpres & gen mgr, 1965-70; White Assoc Inc, pres, 1970-75; Ford Motor Co, mgr, 1977-87; City Detroit, dir pub info, 1975-77; Jones Transfer Co, chmn, chief exec officer; Automotive Logistics Productivity Improve Syst, pres & chief exec officer. **Orgs:** Bd dir, Metro Affairs Corp; bd dir, United Way; bd dir, Monroe MI; bd dir, Monroe High Sch Scholar Fund; Nat Minority Enterprise Legal Defense Fund; Greater Detroit Interfaith Round Table Nat Conf Christians & Jews, Boysville, Mich; Nat Asn Black Automotive Suppliers; Nat Asn Advan Colored People; adv bd, Liberty Mutual Ins Co; African Develop Found; regional adv coun, Small Bus Admin; bd gov, Mich Trucking Asn; Jobs & Econ Develop Task Force; Detroit Strategic Planning Proj; Commun Comn; Am Trucking Asn; vice chmn, Booker T Wash Asn, 1991-. **Honors/Awds:** Testimonial Resolution, Detroit City Coun; Outstanding Service, Corp Coordr, NMSDC; Concurrent Resolution, Mich Legis, 1987; Certificate of Special Tribute, Gov, State Mich, 1987; Letter of Commendation, Pres Ronald Reagan, 1987; Black Enterprise Magazine Top 100, 1988. **Military Serv:** USAF NCO, 1952-57. **Business Phone:** (810)353-0242.

WHITE, DR. GEORGE. See Obituaries section.

WHITE, GEORGE GREGORY
Journalist. **Personal:** Born Dec 3, 1953, Detroit, MI; son of George Bernard and Edna; divorced. **Educ:** Mich State Univ, E Lansing, MI, BA, Hist & Jour, 1975, MA, African Hist, 1981. **Career:** Minneapolis Tribune, Minneapolis, MN, reporter, 1975-79; US News & World Report, Detroit Bur, correspondent, 1982-84; Detroit Free Press, Detroit, MI, reporter & columnist, 1984-87; Los Angeles Times, Los Angeles, CA, reporter, 1988-99; Univ Calif, Ctr Communs & Community, Los Angeles, asst dir & ed, currently. **Orgs:** Dir, bd mem, La Chap Nat Asn Black Journalists, 1990-; constitutional affairs comt mem, Nat Asn Black Journalists, 1990-; World Affairs Coun, LA, currently; bd adv, Youth Radio; bd dir, Los Angeles Press Club; vpres, Black Journalists Asn Southern Calif. **Honors/Awds:** Honors Col, Mich State Univ, 1971-75;Lilly Endowment Fel, 1979-81; Los Angeles Press Club Award for Outstanding Dedication, 1992; Pulitzer Prize, Los Angeles Times Riot Coverage Team; Los Angeles Times Team Awarded, 1994; Asniated Press Award, 1995. **Business Phone:** (310)206-3117.

WHITE, GEORGE W.
Judge. **Personal:** Born Jan 1, 1931, Duquesne, PA. **Educ:** Baldwin-Wallace Col, attended 1951; Cleveland-Marshall Col Law, JD, 1955. **Career:** Judge (retired); pvt pract, atty, Cleveland, OH, 1956-68; Ct Common Pleas, Ohio, judge, 1968-80; US Dist Ct, Northern OH Dist, judge, 1980-99. **Orgs:** Am Bar Asn, Federal Bar Asn; Nat Adv Coun, Cleveland-Marshall Col Law, Cleveland State Univ. **Honors/Awds:** Leadership & Justice Award, Thurgood Marshall Scholar Fund, 2005. **Special Achievements:** First African American to serve as Chief Judge of the United States District Court for the Northern District of Ohio. **Business Phone:** (216)687-2344.

WHITE, HOWARD A (HOWARD ALBERICK WHITE)
Lawyer, educator. **Personal:** Born Oct 6, 1927, New York, NY; son of John Alberick and Maud Lyn; married Evelyn, Jan 26, 1931. **Educ:** City Col (CCNY), BEE, 1949; St Johns Univ, JD, 1954; New York Univ, MPA, 1959. **Career:** Powsner, Katz & Powsner, assoc, 1954-62; Fed Communs Com, gen atty, (pub utilities), 1962-63, Mobile Radion Br, chief, 1963-64, Domestic Radio Div, asst chief, 1964-65, Common Carrier Bur, asst chief, 1965-66; Communs Satellite Corp, gen atty, 1966-68; ITT World Commun Inc, NY, regulatory coun, 1968-70, vpres gen coun, 1970-73; ITT Commun & Info Serv, Secaucus, NJ, exec vpres, gen coun, 1973-87; St Johns Univ Sch Law, prof law, 1988-. **Orgs:** Fed Communs Bar Asn; Am Bar Asn; NY State Bar Asn; 100 Black Men. **Special Achievements:** "Five Tuning The Federal Govt Role in Public Broadcasting," 46 Fed Comm LJ 491, 1994. **Military Serv:** AUS, PFC, 1946-47. **Business Addr:** Professor, St. Johns University, School of Law, 8000 Utopia Pkwy, Jamaica, NY 11439, **Business Phone:** (718)990-6013.

WHITE, HOWARD ALBERICK. See WHITE, HOWARD A.

WHITE, IDA MARGARET (IDA KILPATRICK JONES)
Government official, manager. **Personal:** Born Aug 1, 1924, Atlanta, GA; married Luther Randolph (deceased); children: Victor A Jones & Russell C Jones. **Educ:** Spelman Col Atlanta, AB (Summa Cum Laude), 1945; Atlanta Univ, MA, Sociol, 1946; Fed Exec Inst, attended 1973; Brookings Inst, attended 1979. **Career:** Government official, Manager (retired); NY Dept Welfare, case work supvr, 1958-61; Dept HUD, NY, Regional Office, dir relocation, 1966-70; Dept HUD, NY, Area Office, dir housing mgmt, 1970-74; Cleveland Dept Community Develop, dep dir, 1974-77; Cleveland City Coun, exec asst to pres, 1977-78; Dept HUD, Richmond Office, mgr; HUD, Washington, DC, mgr, until1989; independent consult, housing, community develop, beginning 1990. **Orgs:** Guest lectr, Practicing Law Inst, 1970; lectr, NYU, 1971; lectr, Cleveland State Univ, 1976; lectr, Case Western Reserve & Kent State Univ, 1977; lectr, Builders Inst, VPI; Am Soc Pub Admin; past mem, bd, Eliza Bryant Home for the Aged Kathryn Tyler Neighborhood Ctr; Real Property Inventory; Neighborhood Housing Servs. **Honors/Awds:** First Black Woman NY Area Office Dept HUD, 1970-74; Award Salute to Black Clevelanders The Greater Cleveland Inter church Coun & Cleveland Call &Post 1979. **Home Addr:** 6016 26th St, Arlington, VA 22207. **Business Addr:** Manager, Washington Field Office, Department of Housing Urban Development, 451 7th St SW, Washington, DC 20410.

WHITE, JACK E
Journalist. **Personal:** Born Jun 30, 1946; married Cassandra Clayton; children: Kristen. **Career:** Wash Post, reporter, 1966-68; Race Rels Info Ctr, Nashville, TN, staff writer, 1968-72; Time Mag, staff writer, 1972-79, Nairobi Bur, chief, 1979-82, New York, corresp, 1982-84, Chicago Bur, chief, 1985-88, dep chief corresp, 1987-88, sr ed, Nat ed, 1988-92; ABC-TV World News Tonight, sr producer, 1992-93; Time Mag, Nat corresp. **Orgs:** Nat Asn Black Journalists. **Honors/Awds:** Harvard University, Neiman Fellow, 1976-77. **Special Achievements:** Co-author, Roberts vs Texaco: A True Story of Race and Corporate America, Avon Bks, 1998.

WHITE, DR. JACOB E
Physician. **Educ:** MD. **Career:** Pvt Pract, physician, currently. **Business Addr:** Physician, 3741 Mcdougall St, Detroit, MI 48207, **Business Phone:** (313)921-8866.

WHITE, JAHIDI
Basketball player, actor. **Personal:** Born Feb 19, 1976, Saint Louis, MO. **Educ:** Univ Georgetown, attended 1998. **Career:** Basketball player(retired); Washington Wizards, forward, 1998-04; Phoenix Suns, 2003-04; Charlotte Bobcats, guard, 2004-05; Cleveland Cavaliers, 2006-07; Film Appearances: Showdown at Area 51, 2007. **Orgs:** Jahidi White Charitable Found. *

WHITE, JALEEL AHMED
Actor. **Personal:** Born Nov 27, 1976, Pasadena, CA; son of Michael and Gail. **Educ:** Univ Calif Los Angeles, attended 2001.

Career: TV series: "Charlie & Company", 1985-86; "Kids Don't Tell", 1985; "The Leftovers", 1986; "Family Matters", 1989-98; "Camp Cucamonga", 1990; "The Adventures of Sonic the Hedgehog", 1993-96; "Sonic the Hedgehog", 1993-95;"The Fresh Prince of Bel-Air", 1995; "Sonic Christmas Blast", 1996; "Grown Ups", 1999-2000; "Sonic Underground", 1999; "The Jeffersons", 1984; "Step By Step", 1991-97; "Full House", 1991; "Fresh Prince of Bel Air", 1995; "111 Gramercy Park", 2003; "Inspector Gadget's Last Case", 2003; "Half & Half", 2005; "Boston Legal", 2007; "The Game", 2007; Films: Big Fat Liar, 2002; "Diagnosis Murder", 1997; The Howard Stern Show, 1994; Meego, 1997; Puff, Puff, Pass, 2006; Who Made the Potatoe Salad?, 2006; Kissing Cousins, 2007; Dreamgirls, 2006; Green Flash, 2008; The Call of the Wild, 2008; Road to the Altar, 2009. **Honors/Awds:** Image Award, Best Child Actor TV Comedy, Nat Asn Advan Colored People, 1992, 1993; Sammy Davis Jr Award; Youth Achievement Award, 1993; Image Award, Best Male Actor TV Comedy, Nat Asn Advan Colored People, 1997; Won Image Award, 1994, 1995. **Home Addr:** c/o Gail White, PO Box 580, Agoura Hills, CA 91376, **Home Phone:** (818)324-4074. **Business Addr:** Actor, Shuman Company, 3815 Hughes Ave 4th Fl, Culver City, CA 90232, **Business Phone:** (310)841-4344.

WHITE, JAMES LOUIS, JR.
Executive. **Personal:** Born Jul 14, 1949, Charlottesville, VA; son of James Louis White and Myrtle Virginia Garland White; married Cynthia Phina Austin, Jun 29, 1973; children: James Louis III, Charles Marquas & Matthew David. **Educ:** St Paul's Col, Lawrenceville VA, BS 1973; Univ Kans, Lawrence KS, cert, 1982; Univ Pa, Philadelphia PA, cert, 1982; Fla State Univ, Tallahassee FL, attended. **Career:** Centel Tel, div & dist eng Charlottesville VA, 1973-74, dist mgr & personnel mgr Des Plaines IL, 1974-75, asst staff mgr Chicago IL, 1975-77, asst customer serv mgr Fla state oper, 1977-79, gen customer staff mgr Chicago, 1979-84, gen customer serv mgr Fla state oper, 1984-88; Centel Cellular, FL, regional vpres, beginning 1988-; 360 Degree Commun, regional pres, 1995-97; 360 Degree Long Distance, pres, 1997; Alltel Communs, vpres, currently. **Orgs:** Chamber Com & Econ Club, 1985-89; pres, Big Ben Independent Tele Pioneer Asn, 1988; mem bd dir, Dick Howser Ctr Cerebral Palsy & Fla Spec Olympics, 1989. **Special Achievements:** Author of article "Centel Puts Prewiring Costs Where They Belong," Team magazine, August 15, 1980. **Business Addr:** Vice President External Affairs, Alltell Communication, 601 Riverside Ave, Jacksonville, FL 32204, **Business Phone:** (904)854-5996.

WHITE, JAMES MATTHEW, JR.
Educator. **Personal:** Born Mar 13, 1958, Salisbury, MD; son of James and Irene White; married Shelly, Aug 9, 1980; children: Hope & Michel. **Educ:** Univ Md Eastern Shore, BA, 1982; Wilmington Col, MA, 1990, EdD, 2000. **Career:** Univ Md Eastern Shore, residence counselor, 1982-91, dir stud activities, 1991-2001, asst to vpres stud affairs, 2001-. **Orgs:** Pres, Princess Anne Town Comnr, 1996-98, vpres, 1998-; life mem, APA Fraternity Inc, 1978-; founder, Princess Anne Youth Orgn, 1999-; Asn Col Unions Int, 1991-. **Honors/Awds:** Brother of the Year, 1986, 1997; Award for Service and Leadership Fund. **Business Addr:** Assistant to the Vice President for Student Affairs, University of Maryland Eastern Shore, Student Services, College Backbone Rd, Princess Anne, MD 21853-1299, **Business Phone:** (410)651-2200.

WHITE, JANICE G
School administrator. **Personal:** Born Aug 21, 1938, Cincinnati, OH; daughter of Murray C Gray and Odessa Parker Grey; married Amos J White Jr, Sep 1, 1962; children: Janine, Amos III & David. **Educ:** Western Reserve Univ, BA, 1963; Capital Univ Law Sch, JD, 1977. **Career:** Legal Aid Soc Columbus, Reginald Heber Smith Community, Law fel, 1977-79; Franklin Co Pub Defender, juvenile unit, pub defender, 1979-80; Ohio State Legal Servs Asn, legis coun, 1980-84; State Employment Rels Bd, labor rels specialist, 1984, administrative law judge, 1984-88; Capital Univ Law & Grad Ctr, alumni rels & multi-cult affairs dir, 1988-. **Orgs:** Am Bar Asn; Ohio Bar Asn; Cent Community House; Links Inc; Nat Conf Black Lawyers; Women Lawyers Franklin Co Inc; Columbus Comn Community Rels; Delta Sigma Theta Sorority Inc; United Negro Col Fund. **Honors/Awds:** Outstanding Woman, United Church Christ, Ohio Conf, 1985; Outstanding Delta, Columbus Alumnae Chapter, 1986; Meritorious Service Award, United Negro Col Fund Inc, 1989. **Special Achievements:** Reginald Heber Smith, Community Law Fel, 1977-79; Assisted in the negotiations for release of hostages from Teheran, 1980. **Home Addr:** 2429 Dale Ave, Columbus, OH 43209, **Home Phone:** (614)237-0819. **Business Addr:** Director, Alumni Rels & Minority Affairs, Capital Univ Law & Grad Ctr, 303 E Broad St, Columbus, OH 43215-3200, **Business Phone:** (614)445-8836.

WHITE, JESSE C.
Government official. **Personal:** Born Jun 23, 1934, Alton, IL; divorced. **Educ:** Ala State Col, BS, 1957; N Tex State Univ, grad work, 1966. **Career:** Isham Memorial YMCA, phys educ dir, 1955-74; Jenner Sch, teacher, 1959-63; Schiller Elem Sch, teacher, 1963-90; Ill Gen Assembly, state rep, 1975-77, 1979-92, Chicago Bd Ed Phy Ed, prog coordr, 1990-92; Cook County, recorder deeds, 1992-99; State Ill, secy state, 1998-99, 2002-;re-elected again in 2006; Democratic committeeman. **Orgs:** Founder, Coach Jesse White Tumbling Team, 1959-; Chicago Cubs orgn, 1959-66; scoutmaster, Boy Scouts Am, 1967-. **Honors/Awds:** Most Dedicated Teacher Award, Citizen's Sch Comt, 1969; Excellence in Education, Supt Pub Instr, 1974; Partner in Building Better Communities, Gov James R Thompson, 1985; Legislator of the Year, Child Care Asn Cycle, Community Service Award, 1987; Excellence in Public Service, Ill Hosp Asn, 1987; Southwestern Athletic Conf Hall of Fame, 1995; Chicago Public League Basketball Coaches Hall of Fame, 1995; Alabama State Univ Sports Hall of Fame, 1999. **Special Achievements:** First African-American to serve as Illinois Secretary of State. **Military Serv:** AUS, 101st Airborne, 1957-59; Ill Army Nat Guard, 44th Support Ctr, clerk& typist, 1973-74. **Home Addr:** 300 W Hill St, Chicago, IL 60610, **Home Phone:** (312)944-0949. **Business Addr:** Secretary, State of Illinois, 213 Statehouse, Springfield, IL 62706, **Business Phone:** (217)782-2201.

WHITE, JO JO (JOSEPH HENRY WHITE)
Athletic director, basketball player. **Personal:** Born Nov 16, 1946, St Louis, MO; children: Brian J. **Educ:** Univ Kans, attended 1969. **Career:** Basketball Player (retired); Boston Celtics, guard, 1969-79, dir spec proj, community rels rep, 2000-; Golden State Warriors, guard, 1979-80; Kans City Kings, guard, 1981; CBA, guard, 1987-88. **Honors/Awds:** Player All Star Team, 1970-77; US Gold Medal Olympic Basketball Team, 1968; 2 NBA World Champ Teams; MVP Playoffs, 1976; 13th All-Time NBA Scorer (13546 pts). **Business Addr:** Director of Special Projects & Community Relations, Boston Celtics, 151 Merrimac St, Boston, MA 02114-4714, **Business Phone:** (617)854-8000.

WHITE, JOHN CLINTON
Journalist. **Personal:** Born May 5, 1942, Baltimore, MD; married Elaine B; children: Anthony C, David E. **Educ:** Morgan State Univ, BS, 1970. **Career:** WJZ-TV, news producer & Writer, 1968-69; The Balt Afro-Am, reporter, 1969; The Evening Sun, reptr, 1969-72; The WA Star, staff writer. **Orgs:** Managed ed, The Spokesman Morgan State Univ, 1969-70; treas, Asn Black Media Workers, 1975-77; Nat Asn Advan Colored People. **Honors/Awds:** Group W Award, completion of Westinghouse Broadcasting Int prog, 1968. **Military Serv:** USAF, 1961-64.

WHITE, JOHN H
Photojournalist. **Personal:** Born Mar 18, 1945, Lexington, NC; son of Reid Ross and Ruby Mae; children: Deborah, Angela, Ruby & John Henry. **Educ:** Central Piedmont Community Col, AAS, 1966. **Career:** Chicago Daily News, photogr, 1969-78; Chicago Sun-Times, photojournalist, 1978-; Columbia Col, Chicago, artist-in-residence, instr, 1978-, head photojournalism dept, 1988-. **Orgs:** Pres, Chicago Press Photographers Asn, 1977-78. **Honors/Awds:** Pulitzer Prize, Feature Photography, 1982; Nat Press Photogrs Asn, 'Joseph A Sprague Memorial Award', 1989; Chicago Jour Hall of Fame, Inductee, 1993; Nat Press Photogr's Asn, 'Award of Excellence in General News Photography', 1994; Nat Headliner Award, 1991; Robert F Kennedy Journalism Award, 1979; Associated Press Award, 1991; World Press Photo Competition Award, 1979; Illinois United Press International Awards, 1982; Chicago Asn, 'Black Journalists Award', Outstanding Journalist, 1984; Nat Press Award, Mandela Release, 1991; Illinois Press Photographer's Asn, Photographer of the Year Award, 1971, 1979, 1982; Chicago Medal of Merit, 1999; Studs Rekel Award, 1999. **Special Achievements:** Photo exhibits: "My People: A Portrait of AFA Culture," Rockefeller Ctr, New York, 1991; "The Soul of Photojournalism," Comenius Univ, Slovakia, 1993; "John H White: Portrait of Black Chicago," Natl Archives Exhibit, 1997; contributed to the book and exhibit: "Songs of My People;" published books: This Man Bernardin, 1996; The Final Journey of Joseph Cardinal Bernardin, 1997. **Business Addr:** Photo Editor/ Staff Photographer, Chicago Sun-Times, 401 N Wabash Ave, Chicago, IL 60611, **Business Phone:** (312)321-3000.*

WHITE, JOSEPH COUNCILL (COUNCILL WHITE, JR.)
Executive. **Personal:** Born May 12, 1942, Mobile, AL; son of Council and Estelle White; married Theresa Lorraine Carraway, Jun 4, 1966; children: Shawn Lenard & Derrick Gerrard. **Educ:** Ala State Univ, BS, 1965; Atlanta Univ, MS, 1967; Washington State Univ, PhD, 1970. **Career:** Chevron Chem Co, tech coordr, regist, 1985-88; Abbott Labs, dir regulatory affairs, 1988-92, qual assurance & regulatory affairs, div vpres, 1992-99; Cardinal Health Inc, vpres qual mfg, 1999-2000, sr vpres qual, 2000-. **Orgs:** Vice chmn, Abbott Labs Employee Credit Union, 1989-99; pres, Big Brother/Big Sister Lake Co, 1991-99; adv coun, Nat Inst Environment Health Sci, 1996-99; Parental Drug Asn; Kappa Alpha; Fla A&M Univ Sch Pharmaco Bd Visitors. **Home Addr:** 13 Georgetown Ct, Basking Ridge, NJ 07920, **Home Phone:** (908)781-1551. **Business Addr:** Senior Vice President of Quality, Cardinal Health Inc, 7000 Cardinal Pl, Dublin, OH 43017, **Business Phone:** (614)757-5000.

WHITE, JOSEPH HENRY. **See WHITE, JO JO.**

WHITE, LT. GEN. JUNE JOYCE
Police officer. **Personal:** Born Feb 25, 1949, Flushing, NY; daughter of Jean Dolores DeVega Hampton and Marion Luther Hampton; married James R, Dec 1, 1984; children: Wenty Morris III, Ellie Morris, Mario St John, Lena, James, Clifton, Roxanne, Jasmine & Chamara. **Educ:** Queens Col, Flushing NY, 1969-71; NYC Health & Hosp, New York NY, respiratory ther cert, 1973; NMex Corrections Acad, Santa Fe NM, cert officer, 1983. **Career:** Police officer (retired); New York City Hosp Police, police officer, 1973-74; Jamaica Hosp, Jamaica NY, respiratory therapist, 1975-76; Brunswick Hosp, Amityville, NY, respiratory therapist, 1978-83; NMex State Corrections, Cent NM Corrections Facil, Los Lunas NM, officer, 1983, lt, 1984-88. **Orgs:** Nat Asn Advan Colored People, 1969-, chair, Educ Comm, 1988; NM Correctional Workers Asn, 1983-88; consult, NM Multi Investors, 1983-91; pres, Black Officers Asn NM, 1983-91; NM Spec Needs C, 1984-91; NM deleg, Nat Black Police Asn, 1985-; pres, Rio Rancho Human Rights Comn, 1988-90; host chair, Nat Black Police Southern Region Conf, 1988; Comn Defense Human Rights Workplace, 1988-91; Am Correctional Asn. **Honors/Awds:** Joseph "Tree Top" Turner Achievement Award, Nat Black Police Asn, 1987; Guardian of the Treasury, Govs Off, 1988; Award of Excellence, Black Officers Asn NM, 1989; Award of Excellence, Black Officers Asn New Mexico, 1990. **Special Achievements:** Ed, NM Law Enforcement Journal, 1983-91; panelist, "Women Officers, Rewards & Regrets," Natl Black Police, 1986; founder, Outstanding Service Black Officers of NM, 1986; TV special "Blacks in Law Enforcement: Racism & Sexism," 1988; 4th culture TV special "History of Black Officers Asn NM," 1988. **Home Phone:** (505)891-8022.

WHITE, KARYN
Singer. **Personal:** Born Oct 14, 1965, Los Angeles, CA; daughter of Vivian and Clarence; married Terry Lewis, Mar 31, 1991; children: Tremain, Chloe, Brandon & Ashley Nicole. **Career:** Flyte Time Prod, Minneapolis, vocalist; Warner Bros Rec, vocalist; Albums: Karyn White, 1988; Ritual of Love, 1991; Make Him Do Right, 1994; Sweet & Sensual, 1995; Rhino Hi-Five: Karyn White-EP, 2005; Sista Sista, 2006; Superwoman: The Best, 2007; Songs: "Facts Of Love", 1986. **Honors/Awds:** Billboard Music Award, 1989. **Special Achievements:** Debut album sold 2 million copies producing three Top 10 singles & four No 1 rhythm & blues hits, 1988; Grammy Award nomination, 1989; American Music Award, 1989. **Business Addr:** Singer, c/o Warner Bros Recording, 3300 Warner Blvd, Burbank, CA 91505, **Business Phone:** (818)846-9090.

WHITE, KATIE KINNARD
Educator. **Personal:** Born Feb 28, 1932, Franklin, TN; daughter of Arthur and Era Smith; married Joseph White, Jun 29, 1963; children: Joletta, Angela. **Educ:** Tenn State Univ, Nashville, BS, 1952, MS, 1959; Eastern Michigan Univ, Ypsilanti, attended 1961; George Peabody Col, Nashville TN, attended 1965; Walden Univ, Naples FL, PhD 1976. **Career:** Educator (retired); Bedford County Schs, Shelbyville TN, teacher, 1952-53; Shelbyville City Schs, Shelbyville TN, teacher 1953-59; Nashville City Schs, Nashville TN, teacher, 1959-62; Tenn State Univ, Nashville TN, prof sci educ, 1962-70, prof biophys sci & coordr teacher educ biol, 1970-97. **Orgs:** Imperial Club; Carondelet Civic Asn; Nat Asn Biol Teachers; Nat Coun Negro Women; Nat Asn Advan Colored People; Alumni Asn Tenn State Univ; Tenn Acad Sci; hon adv bd mem, Am Biog Inst, 1982-89; pub educ co-chair, Assault Illiteracy Prog, 1988; nat pres (Grand Basileus), Sigma Gamma Rho, 1988-92; bd dir, Sigma Gamma Rho; fund fel, Nat Educ Fund, Sigma Gamma Rho. **Honors/Awds:** Outstanding Service Award, Sigma Gamma Rho, 1964 & 1976; citation, Outstanding Young Women Am, 1965; Teacher of the Year, Tenn State Univ, 1975; listed in "Salute to Business & Professional Women," Dollars & Sense, 1989; author of articles "The Maturation of Biology as a Science" 1965, and "The Place of Biology in Family of Human Knowledge" 1971, both in Tenn State Univ Faculty Journal; co-author of books Learning About Living Things for the Elementary School, and Learning About Our Physical World for the Elementary School, both 1966, and A Laboratory Manual for the Biophys Sci, 1981; co-author The Legacy Continues, 1994; co-author From Whence We Came, 1999. **Special Achievements:** Listed among 100 Most Influential Blacks, Ebony, 1989, 1990, 1991, 1992. **Home Addr:** 9007 Oden Ct, Brentwood, TN 37027. *

WHITE, DR. KEITH L.
College administrator. **Personal:** Born Jul 30, 1948, Boston, MA; married Cheryl C, Aug 2, 1981. **Educ:** Morehouse Col, BA, 1972; Wayne State Univ, MEd, 1992, EdS, 1997, EdD, 1999. **Career:** Archdiocese Detroit, teacher & adminr, 1974-84; Thirty sixth Dist Court, probation officer, 1985-87; Detroit Bd Educ, teacher, 1987-90; Wayne State Univ, admin, adj prof, 1991-, Wayne County, dir, currently. **Orgs:** APA Fraternity Inc, 1967-; chair, Doctors Inc Network & Support Group, 1996-; adv bd, Proj Soaring Retention Prog, 1999-; Asn Continuing Higher Educ, 1999-; chair, Wayne County Child Foster Care Review Bd, 2000-03; UAW, Community Caring Scholarship, 2000-; YMCA Minority Achievers, 2001-. **Honors/Awds:** Certificate of Service, President's Commission on the Status of Women, Wayne State Univ, 2000; Certificate, Outstanding Dissertation Submission, Phi Delta Kappa, 2000; Outstanding Leadership in the Community, Wayne State Univ, 2001; Minority Achiever, YMCA, 2001. **Special Achievements:** Author: "Disserting A Dilemma: The Black Male Crisis in Higher

Education,"Black Issues in Higher Education, 1994; Presentation: "Entering the Pipeline: Considering Doctoral Study," Minority Male Teacher Cert Program-WSU, 2000; "Our Community: Building a Strong Foundation through Community Service," YMCA Minority Achievers, 2002; "You Are What We See: Building Character," YMCA Minority Achievers, 2002. **Business Addr:** Director, Wayne State University, 7800 W Outer Dr Suite 300, Detroit, MI 48235, **Business Phone:** (313)577-0613.

WHITE, KENNETH EUGENE, SR.
Military leader, business owner. **Personal:** Born Mar 9, 1953, Columbus, OH; son of David and Helen; divorced; children: Kenneth E II & Malcolm J. **Educ:** Ohio State Univ, BS, 1977. **Career:** Military leader, Business owner (retired); Investor Real Estate Services, broker, 1977-; USAR, recruiter, 1987; 4 Life Enterprises, owner, 1991-. **Orgs:** St Mark 76A Masons; past pres, Central Ohio Young Republican, 1979; I Know I Can, vol, 1988-; Toastmaster, 1990-; 100 Black Men Cent Ohio; adv, Knights 100 Mentoring Prog. **Honors/Awds:** Recruiter Ring, AUS, 1993; Mentor of the Year Award, Columbus Army Recruiting Baltalion, 1997; Blue Ribbon, Photography, OH State Fair, 1998. **Military Serv:** USAR, sargent first class; Gold Badge Recruiter Ring; Member Glen E Morrell order Recruiting Excellence. **Home Phone:** (614)252-4845. **Business Addr:** Owner, Your Favorite Photographer, 2127 Leeonard Ave, Columbus, OH 43219, **Business Phone:** (614)252-4845.

WHITE, LEO, JR.
Military leader. **Personal:** Born Nov 3, 1957, California; son of Leo and Winifred; married Jacqueline Murray, Aug 1991. **Educ:** Cumberland Col, BS, 1980. **Career:** USY, Transp, capt, 1980-. **Orgs:** Bd dirs, USS Olympic Comt, 1992-96, athlete adv coun, 1992-96; Va Peninsula Chamber Congress. **Honors/Awds:** Olympia Award, 1983. **Special Achievements:** USS Olympic Team, Judo Athlete, 1984, 1992; Military Athlete of the Year, Timmie Award, 1983; Black Belt Hall of Fame, 1983. **Military Serv:** Meritorious Service Medals.

WHITE, LUTHER J
Automotive executive. **Personal:** Born Feb 10, 1936, Gary, IN; son of Luther White and Viarda; married Archousa Bobbie; children: Keith, Kelli, Eric, Alan & Scott. **Educ:** Drake Univ. **Career:** Westfield Ford Inc, Westfield, MA, owner, ceo. **Business Phone:** (413)568-1951.

WHITE, MABEL MESHACH
Real estate agent. **Personal:** Born in Bastrop County, TX; daughter of Benjamin Meshach and Mary; married William E. **Educ:** Bus Col; Bishop Col. **Career:** William E White's Real Estate Co, real estate broker, currently. **Orgs:** Pres, Good St Missionary Soc; finance secy, Dallas Asn Real Estate Brokers; treas, Zeta Amicare Kappa Zeta Chap of Zeta Phi Beta; past pres, Bus & Prof Women's Club; chmn, Pub Educ Am Cancer Soc; bd dir, Day Care Asn Metro Dallas; Skyline Voc Sch; finance secy, LK Williams Inst Bishop Col; bd dir, Holmes Street Found; life mem, YWCA; NCW; Nat Asn Negro Bus & Prof Women; Woman's Aux, Nat Bapt Conv; Nat Asn Advan Colored People; Integrated Citizens Group; chair, bd mem, MAR Cancer Soc; bd mem, United Way; vpres, Dallas Civic Garden Ctr. **Honors/Awds:** Woman of Year, 1965; Willow Award, Dallas Black Chamber of Commerce, 1988; Yellow Rose of Texas, State Texas, 1992; Christian Service Award, Good St Baptist Church; Nat Sojourner Truth Award; Bishop College Inst Award; Am Cancer Award; Foley's Savvy Award; KOOL Achievers Award, Nat Bus & Prof Clubs Inc. **Business Addr:** Real Estate Broker, Blair White Real Estate, 2509 Martin Luther King Jr Blvd, Dallas, TX 75215, **Business Phone:** (214)428-2847.

WHITE, MARGARETTE PAULYNE MORGAN
Journalist. **Personal:** Born Sep 11, 1934, Tattnall County, GA; daughter of Mr and Mrs Riley Morgan; married Frank White; children: Lairalaine. **Educ:** Reids Bus Col, dipl, 1952; Morris Brown Col, BA, 1957; Univ Toledo; Univ Tenn; Ga State Univ, cert. **Career:** Teacher, 1957-66; communications specialist, 1967-69; Morris Brown Col, dir Public relations & dir special events proj; Atlanta Enquirer, assoc ed & columnist, 1988-; Atlanta Housing Authority; Mgt & Training Corp, community & pub rel specialist, currently. **Orgs:** Nat PR dir Bus & Prof Women's Asn, 1973; PR chmn Delta Sigma Theta; Guys & Dolls Inc; Am Bus Women; Atlanta Club Bus & Prof Women; founder & pres, Sparklers Inc; founder, Atlanta Jr Club; pres, Gay G Club; Atlanta League Women Voters; Leadership Atlanta; Nat Urban League; 100 Women Int; life mem, Award Journal Educ Asn; nat treas, Nat Asn Media Women. **Honors/Awds:** Newspaper Fund Fel; Wall St Jour fel; Leading Lady Atlanta, Assoc Ed, Atlanta Inquirer 1977; Delta Women Breaking New Ground Award; Appreciation Award Journ Educ Asn; Best Youth Page Award, NRPA; Nat Media Woman of the Year; Alumna of the Year, Morris Brown Col; The President's Award, Founder's Cup, Media Women Inc; Black Women Achievers, Southern Bell, 1990; Bronze Woman of the Year, 1992. *

WHITE, MARILYN ELAINE
Educator. **Personal:** Born Jul 30, 1954, Gary, IN; daughter of Herschel and Martha Williams; divorced; children: Chris, Kyle & Kory. **Educ:** Univ Mich, BA, 1976; Oakland Univ, MAT, 1992, PhD, 1998. **Career:** Detroit Public Sch, reading specialist, 1976-; Marygrove Col, prof educ, 1998-. **Orgs:** Nat Coun Teachers Eng, 1985-; Mich Reading Asn, 1990-; Friends African & African Am Art, exec bd, 1993-; Metro Detroit Reading Coun, 1994-; Mich Asn Comput-related Users Educ, 1994-; Nat Alliance Black Sch Educ, 1995-; head educ agenda, Women's Leadership Inst, 2001; Int Reading Asn; adv bd, Nat Healthcare Scholars Found. **Honors/Awds:** Martha Luther King, Caesar Chavez, Rosa Prks Future Faculty Fellowship, 1990; Area F All-Star Teacher, DPS, 1995. **Special Achievements:** Dissertation, The Effect of Distant Audiences on Students' Writing, 1998; presentation, "Supporting Literacy In A Secondary Reading/Computer Lab," Addescent Literacy Forum, 2000. **Home Addr:** 5229 Bishop, Detroit, MI 48224, **Home Phone:** (313)300-9354.

WHITE, MAURICE
Songwriter, television producer, singer. **Personal:** Born Dec 19, 1941, Memphis, TN. **Educ:** Chicago Conservatory Music. **Career:** Singer; producer; composer; bandleader; Chess Rec, studio drummer, 1962-67; Earth, Wind & Fire, founder & mem, 1971-; albums: Kalimba Prod, 1983; Undercover - Paul Taylor, 2000; Gratitude 5.1 Surround Sound, 2001; "Get Over It", composer, 2001; The Essential Earth, Wind & Fire, 2002; "Austin Powers in Goldmember", composer, 2002; That's The Way Of The World Live In '75, 2002; Live In Rio, 2002; The Promise, 2003; "Get Up!", composer, 2003; "Be Cool", composer, 2005. **Honors/Awds:** Rock and Roll Hall of Fame, 2000; Grammy Awards; American Music Awards; Star On Hollywood Walk of Fame; Bet Lifetime Achievement Award; Ascap Rhythm & Soul Heritage Award; Nat Asn Advan Colored People Image Awards. **Business Addr:** Singer, Magnet Vision Inc, 1358 Fifth St, Santa Monica, CA 90401, **Business Phone:** (310)576-6140.

WHITE, MICHAEL JAI
Actor. **Personal:** Born Nov 10, 1967, Brooklyn, NY; married Courtenay Chatman, Aug 6, 2005. **Career:** Films: The Toxic Avenger, Part II, 1989; The Toxic Avenger Part III: The Last Temptation of Toxie, 1989; Teenage Mutant Ninja Turtles II: The Secret of the Ooze, 1991; Ring of Fire, 1991; True Identity, 1991; Universal Soldier, 1992; Spawn, starring role, 1997; City of Industry, 1997; Ringmaster, 1998; The Bus Stop, 1998; Thick as Thieves, 1999; Breakfast of Champions, 1999; Universal Soldier: The Return, 1999; Exit Wounds, 2001; Pandora's Box, 2002; Honor Among Thieves, 2002; Justice, 2003; Kill Bill Vol 2, 2004; Getting Played, 2005; Undisputed II: Last Man Standing, 2006; Why Did I Get Married?, 2007; The Dark Knight, 2008; The Slammin' Salmon, 2009; Black Dynamite, 2009; Blood and Bone, 2009; Three Bullets, 2009; TV series: "Tyson", 1995; "Mutiny", 1999; "Freedom Song", 2000; "Wonderland",2000; "Chapter Eighteen", 2001; "Hotel", 2003; "Chin Music", 2004; "The Doomsday Sanction", 2005; "Spawn: The Animation", 2006; "The Legend of Bruce Lee", 2008. **Honors/Awds:** Nominee, Best Male New comer for the Blockbuster Entertainment Awards, 1997. **Special Achievements:** Is an accomplished martial artist, holding seven legitimate black belts indifferent martial arts styles with a specific focus in Kyokushin karate(although his style incorporates aspects of many different martial arts forms). **Business Phone:** (323)866-0900.*

WHITE, MICHAEL REED
Mayor. **Personal:** Born Aug 13, 1951, Cleveland, OH; married Tamera. **Educ:** Ohio State, BA, educ, 1973, MA, pub admin, 1974. **Career:** Cleveland City Coun, asst, 1976-77; City Cleveland, councilman, 1978-84; Burks Elec Co, sales mgr, 1982-85; Beehive & Doan Partnership, partner, 1983-84; Burks Develop Corp, assoc, 1984-85; OH Senate, 21st Dist, OH,senator; State Ohio, Columbus, OH, state senator, 1984-89; City Cleveland, OH, mayor, 1990-2002. **Orgs:** Bd mem, Glenville Housing Found, 1978-; bd mem, Glenville Develop Corp,1978-; bd mem, Cleveland Scholar Prog, 1981-85; Glenville Festival Found;United Black Fund; Greater Cleveland Dome Corp; Royal Ridge-Pierce Found;Waterfront Devel Corp; Am Constitution Freedom, Univ Circle Inc. **Honors/Awds:** Outstanding Young Leader, Cleveland Jaycees, 1979; Service Award, East Side Jaycees, 1979; Outstanding Service Award, Nat Asn Black Vet Cleveland Chap, 1985; Community Service Award, East Side Jaycees.

WHITE, NAN E.
Consultant. **Personal:** Born Mar 15, 1931, Jacksonville, IL; daughter of Mitchell Cook and Grace L; married Wilmer M, Apr 29, 1950; children: Michael Anthony. **Educ:** Bradley Univ, BS, 1952; George Warren Brown Sch Social Work, Wash Univ, MSW, 1955; Chicago Univ Sch Continuing Educ Summer Inst, 1964. **Career:** Consultant (retired); Family & C Serv Greater St Louis, work-study stud, caseworker III, stud supvr, 1954-67; Lincoln HS, East St Louis, IL, sch social worker, 1967-68; Annie Malone Children's Home, social work dir, therapist, 1968-69; satellite Group Home Girls, dir, 1971-73, Annie Malone Children's Home, exec dir, 1970-78; independent child welfare, consult, 1979-84. **Orgs:** Allocations panel, United Way, 1978-88, admissions comn, 1989-94, priorities comn, 1992-94; St Louis Div Family Serv, permanency planning review teams, 1982-85; School System including Counpregnant teenagers, 1985-87; St Louis Pub Sch Syst, 1985-89; Southern Poverty Law Ctr, 1993-; Am Cancer Soc & St Louis Pub Y Read Tutoring Prog, 1996-97; vol Servs, Storytime, Buena Park Libr Dist, 1999-; Ladies Auxilary VFW, 2001-; Long Beach, CA, Veterans Hosp; NCP. **Honors/Awds:** Zeta Phi Beta Sorority, Award for Civic Service, 1976; Federal Award, Annie Malone Children's Home, 1991; Volunteer Recognition Award, Library, 2001; George Washington Carver Award for Service to Youth, Sigma Gamma Rho Sorority. **Home Addr:** 4902 St Andrews Cir, Buena Park, CA 90621.

WHITE, NATHANIEL B. See Obituaries section.

WHITE, PAUL CHRISTOPHER
Health services administrator. **Personal:** Born Mar 23, 1947, Oklahoma City, OK; son of Edward and Minnie Clara Butler Colbert; married Sheila Antoinette Riggins, Jun 9, 1966; children: Paul C II, Simone Crystal, LaShelly Minnie, Corrine Jepahl Rashad, Brandon Thomas Edward & Bryson Chester Matthew. **Educ:** Fresno City Col, Fresno, Calif, AA, 1968; Fresno State Col, Fresno, Calif, BA, 1969; Calif State Univ, Fresno, Calif, MPA, 1986. **Career:** St Agnes Med Ctr, Fresno, Calif, asst adminr, 1975-78, dir personnel, 1978-80; Fresno Co Health Dept, Fresno, Calif, asst hosp adminr, 1980-83, sr staff analyst, 1983-87, ment health syst dir, 1987-88, asst dir health, 1988-93, assoc hosp adminr, chief exec officer, 1993-. **Orgs:** Nat Asn Advan Colored People, 1966-; vice chmn, Fresno Co Econ Opportunity Comn, 1987-94, asst exec dir, currently; United Black Men, 1989-; Calif Black Infant Health Leadership, 1990-; Martin Luther King Unity Comt, 1990-; Fresno Co Econ Opportunities Comn. **Honors/Awds:** African American Museum Appreciation, African Am Mus Comt, 1987; Certificate of Appreciation, Nat Asn Advan Colored People, 1988; Image Award, Nat Asn Advan Colored People, 1989; Certificate of Appreciation, City Fresno, 1989. **Home Addr:** 5476 W Bedford Ave, Fresno, CA 93722, **Home Phone:** (559)277-8033. **Business Addr:** Chief Executive Officer, Fresno County Health Department, 1900 Mariposa Mall Suite 208, PO Box 11867, Fresno, CA 93721-2525, **Business Phone:** (209)263-1563.*

WHITE, PAUL EDWARD
Government official. **Personal:** Born Aug 19, 1941, Brazil, IN; son of William Clarance and Lillian Olivia Brackette; married Somphon, Apr 10, 1969. **Educ:** Valparaiso Univ, BA, 1964; Univ Hawaii, attended 1966; Stanford Univ, attended 1980. **Career:** Government Official (retired); Foreign Serv Officer; Int Training & Develop Alliance Bldg Expert; US Agency Int Develop, minister counr for develop coop & mission dir. **Orgs:** Numerous memberships including Int Hon Soc; past pres, Toastmasters Int; Soc Am Magicians Int Brotherhood Magicians; Lions; Rotary Int; bd dirs, Aid Artisans Inc, currently. **Honors/Awds:** Govt Laos, Order of 3 Million Elephants, 1970; US Presidential Award, 1990 & 2001; Distinguished Career Award, USAID, 1999; numerous US Government Merit Awards. **Special Achievements:** Speaks fluently: Lao, Thai, Khmer, Korean, Japanese, Spanish and Russian; photography exhibited; painting exhibited; performed magic internationally. **Business Addr:** Board Director, Aid to Artisans Inc., 331 Wethersfield Ave, Hartford, CT 06114, **Business Phone:** (860)947-3344.

WHITE, PERSIA
Actor, singer. **Personal:** Born Oct 25, 1972, Miami, FL; married Saul Williams; children: Mecca. **Career:** Actress, musician, activist; Black in White, band mem, currently; XEO3,band mem, currently;"Problem Child", 2009; Films: Blue Chips, 1994; Frankie D, 1996; Blood dolls,1999; Red Letters, 2000; Stalled, 2000; Earthlings, producer, 2003; The Fall of Night, 2007; Everyday Joe, actress & co-producer, 2007; Spoken Word, 2009. TV series: "Another World", 1964; "Goode Behavior", 1996; Saved by the Bell: The New Class", 1996; "Malibu Shores", 1996; "Suddenly", 1996; "NYPD Blue", 1996;"Breaker High", 1997; "Buffy the Vampire Slayer", 1997-2004;"Another World", 1999; "Clueless", 1999; Operation Sandman, 2000; "Girlfriends",2000-07; "Operation Sandman", 2000; "Angel", 2001; "Unscripted", 2005. **Orgs:** Humane Soc US; Global Green; Farm Sanctuary; Citizens Comn Human Rights;People Ethical Treatment Animals; Sea Shepherd Conserv Soc; brd dir, Sea Shepherd Conservation soc. **Honors/Awds:** Humanitarian of the Year, PETA, 2005. **Business Addr:** Board of Director, PO Box 2616, Friday Harbor, WV 98250, **Business Phone:** (360)370-5650.*

WHITE, RALPH
Real estate agent, association executive. **Career:** White Ralph Bail Bonds, owner, currently; Real estate agent; Comn Status African Am Males, comn mem; Stockton City Coun, mem. **Orgs:** Pres, Stockton Nat Asn Advan Colored People; founder, Stockton Youth Found. **Special Achievements:** First African American to be elected vice-mayor of the city of Stockton, 1972. **Business Addr:** Owner, White Ralph Bail Bonds, 2230 S Airport Way, Stockton, CA 95206, **Business Phone:** (209)464-8371.

WHITE, RALPH L.
Executive, businessperson. **Personal:** Born Mar 13, 1930, Decatur, AL; son of Edmond and Bertha M; married Chrysanthemum Robinson, May 6, 1955; children: Rodney M, Lorrie C & Kimberly L. **Educ:** Ala A&M Col, Huntsville, BS, 1951; Tex

Christian Univ, Ft Worth, MS, 1965;Webster Univ, St Louis MO, MBA, 1983. **Career:** Herf Indust Inc, Little Rock, AR, pres & founder, 1972-75; Southwestern Bell Tel Co, AR, worked eng planning, switching syst eng, outside plant construct, dist personnel mgr, regional mgr external rels; MDI Inc, pres & chief exec officer, currently. **Orgs:** Nat Biol Hon Soc, 1964; consult, AR Bus Coun, 1988; trustee, Hendrix Col, 1988-; Govs Task Force Sch Dropouts, 1988-89; Little Rock Chamber Com Educ Comn, 1988-; bd dir, AR Pvt Indust Counil, 1988-; AR Advocates C &families, 1989, Legis Planning Group C. **Special Achievements:** Author of Effect of Capacitor Discharge on Microorganisms, 1965. **Military Serv:** USAF, lt col, 1952-72; Air Force Inst Tech, honor grad, 1958; comdr of best electronics squadron in 2nd Air Force, 1967-68; Air Force Commendation Medal, 1971; Air Force Meritorious Service Award. **Home Addr:** 913 S Hughes St, Little Rock, AR 72204, **Home Phone:** (501)661-9333. **Business Addr:** President, Chief Executive Officer, MDI Inc, 913 S Hughes St, Little Rock, AR 72203, **Business Phone:** (501)661-9332.

WHITE, RANDY
Basketball player. **Personal:** Born Nov 4, 1967, Shreveport, LA. **Educ:** LA Tech Univ, Ruston, LA, 1989. **Career:** Basketball Player (retired); Dallas Mavericks, forward, 1990-94; Peristeri Athens, 1994; Pfizer Reggio Calabria, 1994?95; Joventut Badalona, 1995?96; Maccabi Tel Aviv, 1996?98; CSKA Moscow, 1998?99; Aris Thessaloniki, 1999; Near East BC, 1999.

WHITE, RAYMOND RODNEY
Government official. **Personal:** Born Feb 15, 1953, Newark, NJ; son of Henry W, Sr and Lucille M Jackson Sr; married Linnie B Adams; children: Raymond Rodney Jr. **Educ:** Rutgers Univ, BA, 1975; Ga Inst Tech, Master Planning, 1977; Carl Vinson Inst Gov, cert, 1988; Ga Tech Col Architecture, PhD-. **Career:** Fulton Co Planning Dept, planner II; Plainfield City, sr planner, 1977-78; Williams Russell & Johnson Inc, sr planner, 1981-82; Harrington George & Dunn PC, sr planner, 1982; Oglethorpe Power Corp, land use analyst, 1982-83; econ develop mgr, prin planner, 1983-; Dekalb County Planning Dept, dir, 1992-94. **Orgs:** Am Planning Asn 1979-; planning task force chmn, Col Park Neighborhood Voters League, 1980-; DeKalb County Chamber Com, 1983-; bd mem, Foxhead Develop Corp, 1983-; vol, Habitat Humanity Atlanta, 1984-; pres, Develop Alliance Unlimited Inc, 1984-; Ga Indust Developers Asn, 1984-; Nat Forum Black Pub Admin, 1984-; Metro Atlanta Chamber Com; Corp Mkt Task Force, South Side Develop Task Force; local exhibit comt chmn, Am Planning Asn, 1988-89; co-chair, UNCF Bus Community, 1989-91; Am Inst Certified Planners, 1990; secy, 1990, director, 1991, 1992, Ga Planning Asn; Decatur-Dekalb YMCA Bd, 1990, 1991, 1992; bd dir, Ga Indust Developers Asn; Dekalb comt mem, County Dist Boy Scouts Am, 1992; vice chair econ develop comt, 100 Black Men Am, Inc, Dekalb County Chap; Comn mem, Governor's Int Adv Coun, 1992-; Atlanta Regional Comn Alumni, 1992; historian, Male Acad, 1994-96; dev comt chair, Soccer Streets, Inc, 1995-96. **Honors/Awds:** Deptal Distinction Academic Excellence, Rutgers Univ, 1975; Certificate of Award Distinguished Community Serv, Col Park Civic & Educ Club, 1984; Certificate of Appreciation, Georgia Planning Asn, 1986; Meritorious Service Award, United Negro Col Fund, 1986; Leadership DeKalb Palque, 1988, DeKalb County Chamber Commerce, GA, 1988; Youth Leadership DeKalb Program Org Plaque YLD Progrm DeKalb County, GA, 1989; Outstanding Service Award, 100 Black Men of Am Inc, DeKalb County Chap, 1993, 1994; President's Achievement Award, 1996; Key Leadership Award, Boy Scouts Atlanta Area Coun, 1994; Excellence in Service Award, Ninety-Nine Cents Breakfast Club, 1995. **Home Addr:** 3972 Cheru Dr, Decatur, GA 30034.

WHITE, RICHARD C.
Manager. **Personal:** Born Feb 22, 1941, New York, NY. **Educ:** NY Univ, BS, 1962; Howard Univ, JD, 1967. **Career:** Boston Symphony Orch, asst mgr; pvt consult & artist mgr. **Orgs:** NAACP; ACLU; Phi Alpha Delta Legal Frat.

WHITE, RICHARD H
School administrator. **Personal:** Born Jun 1, 1950, Chicago, IL; son of Herman and Luvenia; married Valencia Peters, Sep 4, 1982. **Educ:** Catholic Univ, Washington, DC, BA, 1973; Howard Univ, Washington, DC, MA, 1979. **Career:** Am Red Cross, Atlanta, Ga, dir develop, 1980-85; Civitan Int, Birmingham, Ala, dir develop, 1985-88; Riverside Community Col, Riverside, Calif, chief develop officer, 1988-90; Morris Brown Col, Atlanta, Ga, vpres develop, 1990-92; Emory Univ, Robert W Woodruff Lib, 1992-97; Clark Atlanta Univ, vpres, 1998-. **Orgs:** Ga Joint Bd Family Pract, Gov & State Ga, 1984; Child Abuse Prev Bd, Gov & State Ala, 1986; sr exec, Serv Rank Rev Bd, 1996; bd mem, Nat Soc Fund Raising Execs. **Honors/Awds:** Outstanding Young People Atlanta, 1983; Leadership Atlanta, 1984; Young Man Amerian, 1985. **Business Addr:** Vice President, Clark Atlanta University, 223 James P Brawley Dr, Atlanta, GA 30314, **Business Phone:** (404)880-8000.

WHITE, RICHARD THOMAS
Lawyer. **Personal:** Born Jan 10, 1945, Detroit, MI; son of Raymond Wendell and Joyce Loraine Thomas; married Tanya; children: Richard T Jr, Devin A & Andrew S. **Educ:** Morehouse Col, BA, hon, 1967; Harvard Univ Law Sch, Cambridge, MA, JD, 1970. **Career:** Dykema Gossett, assoc, 1970; Patmon, Young & Kirk, PC, assoc, 1971-72; Lewis, White & Clay, PC, founder & pres; Auto Club Group, sr vpres, secy, gen atty, currently. **Orgs:** City Detroit Human Rights CMS, 1964-65; Am Bar Asn, Corp & Health Law Sect, 1970-; Nat Health Lawyers Asn, 1975-; finance com, bd, Detroit-Macomb Hosp; compensation com, bd dirs, United Am Health Care Corp, 1983-; bd dir audit comt, Detroit Med Ctr, 1990-95; bd dir, Am Basic Indust Inc, 1991-; vice chair, MIC Transportation CMS, 1991-; comnr, Foreign Claims Settlement Comn, 1995-; numerous others. **Business Addr:** Senior Vice President & secretary, General counsel, The Auto Club Group, 1 Auto Club Dr, Dearborn, MI 48126, **Business Phone:** (313)336-1284.

WHITE, ROBERT C
Police chief. **Personal:** Born May 6, 1952, Richmond, VA. **Educ:** Univ DC, BA, pub admin, 1993; Johns Hopkins Univ, MS, appl behav sci, 1996. **Career:** Wash Metrop Police Dept, officer, sgt, lt, capt, inspector, comdr; Dept Emergency Response Team, 1987-92; Planning & Res Div, 1992-94; Fourth Police Dist, Wash, DC, 1994-95; Metrop Police Dept, asst chief police, 1997; DC Housing Authority, dir pub safety; Greensboro Police Dept, chief police, 1998-2001; Louisville Metro Police Dept, chief police, 2003-. **Special Achievements:** first Metro Louisville's Chief of Police. **Business Addr:** Chief of Police, Louisville Metro Police Department, 768 Barret Ave, Louisville, KY 40204, **Business Phone:** (502)574-2111.

WHITE, ROBERT L.
Association executive. **Personal:** Born Mar 22, 1916, Jackson, MS; married Helen Harper; children: Helen Oladipo, Roberta Battle, Robert H, Ramon, William, Elizabeth, Dorothy, Mark, Mary, Stephen, Christopher. **Educ:** Howard Univ. **Career:** exec (retired); US Post Office, employee; NAPFE, pres, 1982-89. **Orgs:** Nat pres, Nat Alliance Postal Fed Employ; pres, WA Local 1953-70; past bd dir, NAACP; past mem, bd dir WA Urban League; past bd mem, Christ Child Settlement House; assoc mem, Dem Nat Com. **Honors/Awds:** One of the 100 Most Influential Black Americans Ebony Mag, 1971-74; Civil Rights Award, DC Civic Assoc, 1972; National Leadership Award, Nat Urban Coalition's Distinguished, 1984; Hon DL Howard Univ, 1984.

WHITE, RONDELL BERNARD
Baseball player. **Personal:** Born Feb 23, 1972, Milledgeville, GA; married Zanovia; children: Zaiya. **Educ:** Jones High Sch, attended 1990. **Career:** Montreal Expos, 1993-2000; Chicago Cubs, 2000-01; NY Yankees, 2002; San Diego Padres, 2003; Kans City Royals, 2003; Detroit Tigers, 2004-05; Minn Twins, 2006-07, free agent, currently. **Honors/Awds:** Player of the Year, Atlanta Journal-Constitutions, 1990; All-Star selection, 2003. **Home Addr:** 11111 Pine Lodge Trail, Davie, FL 33328. **Business Phone:** (612)375-1366.*

WHITE, RORY WILBUR
Basketball coach, basketball player. **Personal:** Born Aug 16, 1959, Tuskegee, AL; married Julie; children: Rory Jr, Josh & Jenna. **Educ:** Univ S Ala, phys educ, 1982. **Career:** Basketball player (retired), basketball coach; Phoenix Suns, 1982-84; Milwaukee Bucks, 1984; San Diego Clippers, 1984; Los Angeles Clippers, 1985-87; CBA, 1989-90; ID Stampede, asst coach, 1998-2000, head coach, 2000, 2002-03; Fargo-Moor head Beez, head coach, 2001; Los Angeles Clippers, Head coach, currently. **Honors/ Awds:** Sun Belt Player of Year, Univ S Ala, 1979; All-Conf honors; Coach of the Month. **Business Phone:** (701)258-2255.

WHITE, DR. SANDRA LAVELLE
School administrator, educator. **Personal:** Born Aug 30, 1941, Columbia, SC; daughter of Christopher O and Rosena E Benson; married Dr Kenneth Olden, May 19, 1984; children: Heather Alexis. **Educ:** Hampton Inst, BA, boil, 1963; Univ Mich, MS, microbiol, 1971, PhD, microbiol, 1974. **Career:** Sloan Kettering Inst Cancer Res, res asst 1963-69; AT&T, res asst, 1969; Univ Mich Dept Microbiol, teaching asst, 1969-71, Med Sch, asst lectr microbial, 1970, guest lectr immunol, 1973; Howard Univ Col Med, asst prof Microbiol, 1974-76, assoc prof microbiol & oncol, mem Cancer Ctr, 1979-92, Cancer Ctr, adj fac; Nat Inst Health, staff fel, 1976-79; Duke Univ Med Ctr, assoc res prof, 1993-98; NC Cent Univ, Dept Biol, prof & chair, Ctr Math, Sci & Technol Educ, dir, currently. **Orgs:** Nat Sci Found Traineeship, 1970-71; Pathol B Study Sect Nat Insts Health, 1980-84; Bd Scientific Counselors, Div Cancer Biol & Diag, Nat Cancer Inst, NIH, 1985-89; Nat Bd Med Examrs, Microbiol Test Comt, 1989-93; bd dir, GLYCO Design Inc; bd dir, NC Mus Life & Sci; Am Soc Microbiologists; Am Asn Women Cancer Res; Delta Sigma Theta Sorority Inc; Am Soc Cell Biol; Am Asn Cancer Res, 1990-; Am Asn Immunol, 1991-; bd dirs, NC Mus Life & Scis; bd dir, Women Action Prev Violence & Its Causes; Links Inc; Jack & Jill AME Inc; Smaty Set Inc. **Honors/Awds:** Ford Found Fellowship, 1970-74; Kaiser Permanente Award, Excellence in Teaching 1982. **Business Addr:** Director, North Carolina Central University, Center for Math, Science & Technology Education, 206 Lee Biol Bldg, Durham, NC 27707.

WHITE, SELMA STEWART
Music director. **Career:** Retired Teachers Asn Chicago, music dir & exec dir, currently. **Business Addr:** Music Director, Executive Director, Retired Teacher Association of Chicago, 6736 S Oglesby Ave, 220 S State St Room 210, Chicago, IL 60604-2180, **Business Phone:** (312)939-3327.

WHITE, SHARON BROWN
School administrator. **Personal:** Born Sep 29, 1963, Pineville, LA; daughter of Eva M Brown; married Wilbur James. **Educ:** Grambling State Univ, Grambling, BS, 1985; Alcorn State Univ, Lorman, MS, 1988. **Career:** Alcorn State Univ, Lorman, sec, 1985-88, admin asst, 1988; Fisk Univ, Nashville, sec, 1989, dir, career planning & placement, 1989-. **Business Addr:** Director, Fisk University, 1000 17th Ave N Basic Col Bldg Rm No 202, PO Box 4, Nashville, TN 37208-3051, **Business Phone:** (615)329-8631.

WHITE, STEPHEN GREGORY (STEVE WHITE)
Football player. **Personal:** Born Oct 25, 1973, Memphis, TN. **Educ:** Univ Tenn, BA, psychol. **Career:** Tampa Bay Buccaneers, defensive end, 1996-2001; New York Jets, 2002.

WHITE, STEVE. See WHITE, STEPHEN GREGORY.

WHITE, SYLVIA KAY
Fashion consultant. **Personal:** Born Dec 5, 1955, Washington, DC; daughter of James Odessa and George D Sr (deceased). **Educ:** Fashion Inst Tech, AA, 1975; State Univ NY, fashion buying. **Career:** Alexander Inc, buyer, men's, 1975-83; Montgomery Ward Inc, buyer, boys, 1983-87; Nordstroms, McClean, sales men's merchandise, 1988-. **Orgs:** Trustee, 1985-, First Union Baptist, Budget & Finance Comn, chair, 1986-88. **Honors/Awds:** Outstanding Young Women of America, 1985. **Home Addr:** 7912 Grant Dr, Lanham, MD 20706. **Business Addr:** Sales men, Nordstroms, 8075 Tysons Corner Ctr, Mc Lean, VA 22102, **Business Phone:** (703)761-1121.

WHITE, DR. TOMMIE LEE
Psychologist, counselor, college teacher. **Personal:** Born May 20, 1944, Dublin, GA; son of Mack F Sr and Daisy. **Educ:** Yankton, BA, 1966; Univ SD, MA, 1967; Univ Southern Calif, PhD, 1974, PhD 1982; Bd Cert Dipl Pscyhopharmacol, Prescribing Psychol, Regist (FPPR). **Career:** Horace Mann Jr H LA, teacher hist & phys educ, 1967-70; Univ SD, grad asst 1966-67, asst res dir, 1967; US Olympic Team, Psychologist; Calif State Univ Northridge, Dept Kinesiol, fac, 1970-2005, chair & prof, prof emer, 2005-; clin, coun psychologist, pvt practice; Samra Univ, Doctoral Adv Comt, bd mem. **Orgs:** Am Psychol Asn; Asn Black Psychologists; Calif Faculty Asn; Calif Psychol Asn; Am Fedn Teachers; clin, coun Sport Psychologist, US Olympic Comm & USATF; AAASP; Phi Delta Kappa, Alpha Phi Alpha Fraternity Inc, APA-Exercise & Sport Psychol. **Honors/Awds:** SD Col Track Athlete of Decade 1960-69; Alumni of Year, 1976; All-Am Track Hon 1965; SDak Athlete of Year Award, 1965; Hall of Fame, Howard Wood, 1978; dean's list hon stud Yankton Col, 1965-66; Track & Field News All-Am Award, 1971; World's best record 60 meter high hurdles 74 sec Moscow, 1972; prof high hurdles, 13.4 Sec 1973; Nat Amateur Athlete Rep to AAU 1975-. **Special Achievements:** Published: "Seven Keys to Hurdling Excellence" Coach and athletic dir, 2002; "the relationship between physical educ admin values & their attitudes toward education Innovations," 1974, "The Relationship Between Cognitive Style and Locus of Reinforcement" 1978, "Essentials of Hurdling" Athletic Journ 1980, "Hurdling-Running Between The Hurdles" Athletic Journal 1980; Publications: "Reparenting Schizophrenic Youth in a Hospital Setting", 1985; Presentations: "African-Amican Athletes: Distorted Visions and Shattered Dreams," "Standing Alone: The Spinal Injured," 1992; "Diversity in Sports: Are We Doing Enough"," 1993.

WHITE, TYTRAL T
Basketball coach. **Business Addr:** Basketball Coach, Petersburg High School, 207 Jefferson Ave, Petersburg, VA 26847.

WHITE, WENDELL F
Executive. **Personal:** Born Aug 20, 1939, Atlanta, GA. **Educ:** Morehouse Col, BA, 1962; Atlanta Univ, MBA, 1967; Univ Calif La, addn studies. **Career:** Williamson & Co Real Estate, 1961-65; Johnson Publ Co; Gen Motors Corp, 1965; Coca-Cola Co, mkt exec, 1965-70; US Dept Com, dir off minority bus enterprise, 1970-74; Empire Investment Enterprises Inc, pres; Empire Realty, pres. **Orgs:** Former pres, Empire Real Estate Bd; Atlanta Bus League; former mem, Citizens Trust Bank Adv Bd; former mem, Nat Asn Market Developers; former mem, bd dir, Travelers Aid Soc; SCLC; Nat Asn Advan Colored People; Urban League, Butler St YMCA. **Honors/Awds:** Leadership Award, Butler St YMCA; Letter of Commendation from Pres of US; Cert Merit, Nat Asn Advan Colored People. **Military Serv:** AUS, 1963-65. **Business Addr:** President, Empire Realty, 569 Joseph Lowery Blvd St SW, Atlanta, GA 30310, **Business Phone:** (404)758-1462.

WHITE, WILLIAM E.
Media executive. **Personal:** Born Jun 28, 1934, St Louis, MO; son of Ephriam and Laura; married Virginia M McDade; children: Diana, William Jr, Arnold. **Educ:** Lincoln Univ. **Career:** Kansas City Monarch, Memphis Red Sox, Kansas City Athletics Org Chicago White Sox, prof baseball player; Kirby Co, franchise factory dis-

tribr; WETU Montgomery, owner; KIRL Radio, chmn & gen mgr. **Orgs:** deacon, Newstead Ave Baptist Church; O'Neal Twins & Interfaith Choir, bus mgr; bd mem, Nat Gospel Workshop Am, Nat Gospel Evangelist Musicians & Choral Orgn; Nat Asn Advan Colored People; Manpower Planning & Training Coun St Louis County, States Comt Citizens Adv Comn Mal-Practice; Women Self Help Bd, Salvation Army Bd, Pace Bd, St Charles County Bd of Realtors, Employers Support Nat Guard & Reserve. **Honors/Awds:** Business Man of the Year, Elks Lodge. **Military Serv:** Armed Forces, Pres's personal hon guard; Hon Discharge. **Business Addr:** Chairman, General Manager, KIRL-AM, 3713 Hwy 94 N, St Charles, MO 63301.*

WHITE, WILLIAM J
Manager. **Personal:** Born Mar 3, 1935, Bouard, PA; son of Ira and Katie; married Idella M Hatter; children: Sheryl, Karen & Sandra. **Educ:** Westminster Col, BA, 1957; Alex Hamilton Bus Inst; Youngstown State Univ, mgt training prog metallur courses. **Career:** Manager (retired); Weirton Steel corp, logistics admin; Sharon Steel Corp, trainee, 1957-59, qual control anal, 1960, qual control anal, 1960, stock foreman, 1960-62, heat balance cal, 1962-65, sr melter, 1965-68, gen foreman degassing, 1968-69, support trans labor & mat control; support mat control, 1969, mgr primary rolling & plant support serv, 1985. **Orgs:** Jr Chamber, 1959; Ys Men, 1962; shenango Valley Urban League, 1968-75; Shenango Valley United Fund, 1969-72; pres, Westminster Col Alumni Asn, 1974; adv bd, McDowell Nat Bank; dir, George Jr Rep; dir, Nat Asn Advan Colored People; dir, Boy Scouts of Am, 1974; pres, Kiwanis, 1979; trustee, Westminster Col, New Wilmington, PA, 1991. **Honors/Awds:** Recip Little All Am Football AP, 1955-56; first black foreman gen foreman supt Sharon Steel Corp hist; Indiana County Hall of Fame, 1990. **Military Serv:** AUS, sgt, 1957-63.

WHITE, WILLIAM JOSEPH
Electrical engineer. **Personal:** Born Aug 6, 1926, Philadelphia, PA; son of James Earle and Mary Valentine; married Althea de Freitas; children: Karen, William Jr. **Educ:** A&T Col, attended 1943; Syracuse Univ, attended 1950; NY City Univ, BS, 1960; US Army Command & Gen Staff Col, attended 1966. **Career:** Electrical Engineer (retired); Andrea Radio & TV, tech writer, 1955; NY Transit Authority, elec engr, 1958; Fed Aviation Admin, elec engr, 1961-87, Systs & Equip Br, mgr; Cong Church Hempstead Monthly, ed, 1989-; Hempstead, ed; Hempstead Little League, monthly newsletter ed. **Orgs:** chmn bd trustee, United Cong Church, 1970-72; pub rels, Hempstead Little League, 1970-78; Pres, Local 2791 Am Fed Govt Employ, 1972-80; pres, SE Civic Asn, 1972-; pres, Hempstead Bd Ed, 1973-78; Authors Guild, 1974-; Nat Writers Club, 1975-, Hempstead Planning Bd. **Honors/Awds:** Man of the Year, Hempstead Little League, 1972; Outstanding Community Serv, CRUSH, 1988; Martin L King Jr Mem Award, United Black Christians, 1990; Humanitarian Award, Hempstead NAACP, 1991. **Special Achievements:** Listed in, Community Leaders & Noteworthy Americans, Contemporary Authors vols 97-100, Men of Achievement; Free Lance Writer, Frequent Flyer, Newsday/Nat Rifleman Christian Herald. **Military Serv:** AUS, major, 1945-46, 1950-53; US Navy Appl Sci Lab; elec engr, 1959; CIB; Purple Heart 2; Bronze Star; Assorted Minor Awards; USAR, major. **Home Addr:** 174 Lawson St, Hempstead, NY 11550. *

WHITE, WILLIAM T., III
Executive. **Personal:** Born Nov 12, 1947, Jacksonville, FL; married Patricia E; children: William Thomas IV. **Educ:** Bethune-Cookman Col, 1966; TN State Univ, BS Polit Sci, 1969; Emory Univ, MA Metropolitan Govt, 1972. **Career:** Office Mayor, Model Cities Atlanta GA, res eval spec, 1973-75; Inst School Res, res assoc, 1975-78; Grassroots Inc, exec dir, 1978-80; DeKalb County Planning Dept, human serv facilities coordr, 1980; Lurie Investments Inc, exec vpres. **Orgs:** Worshipful Master Royal Ark Masonic Lodge F & AA York Rite Masons, 1978; past Grand Jr Warden Smooth Ashlar Grand Masonic Lodge, 1978-82; bd Community Rel Comn DeKalb Cty, 1979-82; CEO, Kirkwood & Edgewood Eastlake Econ Develop Corp, 1982; Nat Forum Black Pub Admin, 1983; SE Atlanta Intown Businessmen Asn 1985; DeKalb-Atlanta Voter's Coun, 1982; bd mem, SE Atlanta YMCA. **Honors/Awds:** Grad Fellowship Emory Univ, 1970; Illus Inspector Gen Nat Supreme Coun Scottish Rite 33rd degree Mason, 1978; Outstanding Young men Am, 1979; Lt Col Aid de Camp Office Govt State GA, 1983; Spec Deputy Sheriff DeKalb Cty; Worshipful Master of the Year Masons, 1980-81.

WHITE, WINIFRED VIARIA
Executive. **Personal:** Born Mar 23, 1953, Indianapolis, IN; daughter of Walter H and Winifred Parker; married Kenneth Neisser, May 28, 1989; children: Alexis. **Educ:** Harvard Radcliffe Col, BA, 1974; Lesley Col, MA, Educ. **Career:** NBC, mgr, proj peacock, 1981-82, c progs, 1982-84, dir, c progs, 1984-85, vpres, family progs, 1985-89, dir, motion pictures TV, 1989-. **Orgs:** Bd dirs, Harvard-Radcliffe Club, 1983-; bd govrs, TV Acad, 1986-; bd dirs, Planned Parenthood, 1986-; bd dirs, Women In Film, 1990-. **Business Phone:** (818)840-3538.

WHITE, WOODIE W
Clergy. **Educ:** Paine Col, BA; Boston Univ Sch Theol, MDiv. **Career:** United Methodist Church, southern & cent Ill conf, bishop, head, 1984-92; Ind State United Methodist Church, bishop, head, 1992-2006; Emory Univ, Candler Sch Theol, bishop residence, currently. **Orgs:** Pres, Bishop Coun, 1996-97. **Honors/Awds:** Distinguished Alumni Award, Boston Univ, Sch Theol, 1970; Distinguished Service Award, United Comm Negro Hist, 1974; Hon Degrees: Univ Evansville, Adrian Col, Rust Col, McKendree Col, Ill Wesleyan Coll, MacMurray Col, Paine Coll, Univ Indianapolis, Martin Univ. **Special Achievements:** First African-Am named to lead the United Methodist Church in Ind, 1992. **Business Addr:** Bishop-in-Residence, Emory University, Candler School of Theology, Bishops Hall 500 S Kilgo Circle, Atlanta, GA 30322, **Business Phone:** (404)727-0734.

WHITE, YOLANDA SIMMONS
Educator. **Personal:** Born Apr 6, 1955, Baltimore, MD; daughter of Carlton and Edna Eva Johnson; married Edward Clarence, Jul 15, 1978. **Educ:** Princeton Univ, Princeton, NJ, BA (Hons), 1977; Yale Univ, New Haven, CT, MA, 1978, MA, philos, 1980, PhD, 1982. **Career:** World Without War Coun, NY, proj dir, 1980-81; Y S White & Co, pres, 1982-84; Queensborough Community Col, asst to dean, 1985-88; St Francis Col, assoc dean, 1988-91; Audrey Cohen Co; Wagner Col, Hofstra Univ, Currently. **Orgs:** Bd dirs, Asn Black Women Higher Educ, 1989; Bd dirs, UNA-New York, 1989-91; head mem, CMTE. **Honors/Awds:** NYNEX, $11,400 Study Grant, population of Afro-Am Credit Mgrs.

WHITEHEAD, ANDRE
Executive, business owner. **Personal:** Born Feb 22, 1967, Portsmouth, VA; son of Richard and Bessie; children: Lake. **Educ:** Norfolk State Univ; Liberty Univ, BA, 1988. **Career:** Whitehead Media Ventures, owner & ceo, currently. **Orgs:** Bd mem, Roanoke Community Rels Comn; bd mem, New Vistas Sch, 1999; exec bd mem, Nat Asn Advan Colored People, 1999, youth coun chairperson, Lynchburg, VA, 2001; chairperson, Omega Psi Phi, Gamma Omega, 2000. **Honors/Awds:** D-Day Memorial Award, D-Day Nat Mem, 1999; Award of Participation, 4th Regional Conf Community Rels, 2000; Image Award in Television Media, Nat Asn Advan Colored People, Roanoke, 2001. **Business Addr:** Chief Executive Officer, Owner, Whitehead Media Ventures, 306 Blue Ridge St, PO Box 41, Lynchburg, VA 24505, **Business Phone:** (434)528-9828.

WHITEHEAD, ARCH COLSON CHIPP. See WHITEHEAD, COLSON.

WHITEHEAD, ARCH S. See WHITEHEAD, ARCH SYLVESTER.

WHITEHEAD, ARCH SYLVESTER (ARCH S WHITEHEAD)
Consultant. **Personal:** Born Feb 24, 1936, New York, NY; son of Archie Sulvester Jr and Lorenza Selina Clarke; married Mary Ann Woody-Whitehead, Nov 19, 1960; children: Ann Irma Whitehead-Moore, Lynn Lorraine Whitehead-Goode, Arch Colson Chipp Whitehead & Colson Arch Clarke-Whitehead. **Educ:** DARtmouth Coll, BA, 1958; Columbia Univ Graduate Sch Business, 1970. **Career:** Witty Polon Mgt Consultants, res assoc, 1959; Arch S Whitehead Assocs, consult, managing partner, 1959-. **Orgs:** Pi Lambda Phi Frat, 1955-; chair, bd trustees, LeCole Francaise, 1982-83; Nat Asn Exec Recruiters, Exec Comt, 1984-85; bd trustees, Assoc Black Charities, 1986-88; 100 Black Men, 1986-88; Black Alumni Dartmouth Asn, 1990-; Grand Boule Sigma Pi Phi Frat, 1993-; Cornerstone InterNat Group, Eastern Region Adv, 1998-; African Am Studies & Librarianship. **Honors/Awds:** Excellence In Enterprise Award, Monroe Col, 1999; Certificate of Appreciation, Consortium Info & Telecommunications Execs, 2000. **Special Achievements:** Guest expert on 60 Minutes, 1995; author of 3 best selling novelettes; author, "Career Management In Corporate America", 1999. **Business Addr:** Managing Partner, Arch S Whitehead Associates Inc, 51 Terry Dr, PO Box 1424, Sag Harbor, NY 11963, **Business Phone:** (516)725-4226.

WHITEHEAD, COLSON (ARCH COLSON CHIPP WHITEHEAD)
Writer. **Personal:** Born Jan 1, 1969?, New York, NY; son of Arch and Mary Ann; married Natasha Stovall. **Educ:** Harvard Col, attended 1991. **Career:** Writer, currently; Village Voice, New York, NY, television critic; Books: The Intuitionist, 1999; John Henry Days, 2001; The Colossus of New York: A City in Thirteen Parts, 2003; Apex Hides the Hurt, 2006. **Honors/Awds:** New Voices Award, Qual Paperback Book Club, 1999; Whiting Writers' Award, 2000; Editors' Choice, NY Times, 2001; Young Lions Fiction Award, NY Pub Lib, 2002. **Business Addr:** Author, c/o Random House Inc, 1745 Broadway, New York, NY 10036, **Business Phone:** (212)782-9000.

WHITEHEAD, DAVID WILLIAM
Executive, vice president (organization). **Personal:** Born Sep 7, 1946, Cleveland, OH; son of Mack Thomas and Leila Wall; married Ruvene Proa, Oct 19, 1968; children: Lisa & Lora. **Educ:** Cleveland State Univ, Cleveland, OH, BA, 1968, JD, 1973. **Career:** Executive (retired); Cleveland Bd Educ, Cleveland, OH, teacher, 1968-73; Howard, Watson & Whitehead, Cleveland, OH, self-employed atty, 1973-79; Cleveland Elec Illum Co, Cleveland, OH, atty, 1979; First Energy Corp, region vip, 2001-, Chief Ethics Off, vpres & corporate secy. **Orgs:** Bd dir, United Way Serv; pres emer, Neighborhood Ctr Asn; vpres, bd comnr, Cleveland Metroparks; bd trustees, Cleveland Scholarship Prog Inc; bd dir, Cleveland State Univ Found; bd dir, First Tee. **Honors/Awds:** Distinguished Alumnus Award, Cleveland State Univ Asn Black Faculty & Staff, 1990; Civic Service Award, Citizens League Greater Cleveland, 1996; Excellence Award, William O Walker Salute to Ct, 2000; Black Professional of the Year, 2005; The African American Male Achiever, 2006. **Special Achievements:** Hundred Black Men of Greater Cleveland Organization.

WHITEHEAD, JAMES T, JR.
Pilot, flight engineer. **Personal:** Born Dec 10, 1934, Jersey City, NJ; divorced; children: Brent, Janet, Kenneth, Joel & Marie. **Educ:** Univ Ill, BS, 1957. **Career:** Pilot, flight engineer (retired); USAF, Univ Ill, commd 2nd lt, 1957-AFROTC; USAF, pilot training, 1958; KC-135, co-pilot, 1959-63; KC-135, aircraft commander, 1963-65; Vietnam combat, 1965; U-2 Reconnaissance, aircraft commander, 1966-67; TWA, flight engr, 1967, first officer, Boeing 707, 1968, flight engr/instr/check airman B-747. **Orgs:** Airlines Pilot Asn, 1967; ALPA activities; TWA co-chmn Hazardous Materials Comn, 1974-; TWA Master Exec Counc Fleet Security Comn, 1975; pres, Kiwanis Madison Township, NJ, 1968; Jaycees Madison Township, 1973-; served as squadron commander 103rd Tactical Air Support Squardon, 1977-83; appointed as Headquarters, PA Air Nat Guard dir opers, 1983-, promoted to Colonel, 1983; Kappa Alpha Psi Frat; chmn, 111th Tactical Air Support Group Minority Recruit com, 1972-74. **Honors/Awds:** Outstanding Asn Mem, Madison Township Jaycees 1974; Pres, Old Bridge Township Bd Educ, elected 3 years, 1975. **Special Achievements:** First black U2 pilot. **Military Serv:** USAF, 1957-67, col.

WHITE-HUNT, DEBRA JEAN
Executive, educator. **Personal:** Born Jul 21, 1951, Detroit, MI; daughter of Sylvester White and Jean; married Bruce James Hunt, Oct 19, 1985; children: Alise Frances. **Educ:** Mich State Univ, BA, 1972; Wayne State Univ, MEd, 1975. **Career:** Detroit Pub Sch, dance & health teacher, 1973-95; Detroit-Windsor Dance Acad & Co, artristic dir & owner, 1984-; Martin Luther King Jr Sr High Sch, teacher, currently. **Orgs:** Golden life mem, Delta Sigma Theta Sorority Inc, 1970-; Detroit Inst Arts Founders Soc, 1994; NAACP. **Honors/Awds:** John F Kennedy Artist Fel, Kennedy Ctr Performing Arts, 1987; Dance Teacher of the Year, Mich Dance Asn, 1988; National Educator Award, Milken Found, 1990; Michiganian of the Year, Detroit News, 1990; Leadership America, 1995. **Home Addr:** 19541 Cranbrook Dr, Detroit, MI 48221, **Home Phone:** (313)861-8188. **Business Addr:** Teacher, Martin Luther King Jr Senior High School, 3200 E Lafayette, Detroit, MI 48207, **Business Phone:** (313)494-7373.

WHITEHURST, CHARLES BERNARD, SR.
Government official. **Personal:** Born Jun 4, 1938, Portsmouth, VA; son of John E Sr (deceased) and Bernice N (deceased); children: Lisa W Pretlow & Charles Jr. **Educ:** Norfolk State Univ, BS, Magna Cum Laude, 1978; Univ Colo, Boulder, Grad Degreem, Bank Mkt, 1982. **Career:** USMC, major, 1955-76 (retired); Cent Fidelity Bank, asst vpres & loan officer, 1977-85; Portsmouth City, treas, 1986-93, city coun, 1998, 2002; Century Capital, dir, coo & cfo; Century Capital Holdings Inc, coo; Century Capital Mortgage Inc, vice chmn & mktg dir. **Orgs:** Portsmouth Sch Bd, 1977-81; pres, Portsmouth Chamber Com, 1982; chmn, Portsmouth Seawall Festival, 1984-85; bd dir, Old Dominion Univ, 1984-88; Maryview Hosp, 1985-88; pres, Downtown Portsmouth Asn, 1987-89; pres, Retired Officers Asn, Portsmouth Area Chap, 1989; pres, Eureka Club Inc, 1991-93, 1996-97; golden heritage, life mem, NAACP; Optimist Club; pres, Virginia Games, Inc; pres, Sports Mgt & Promotions, Inc; vpres, Port City Publishing, Inc; staff writer, Port Cities Concerns; founder, past pres, African Am Hist Soc, Portsmouth, VA; chmn, Urban Sec, VA; exec comt, Municipal League, VML, 2003; chmn, Southeast Pub Serv Authority, 2002-03; dist chmn, Merrimal Dist, BSA, 2002; chmn, Portsmouth Schools found; chmn, Elected Mems Comt, Solid Waste Asn N Am, 2003. **Honors/Awds:** Alpha Kappa Mu Honor, Soc Norfolk State Univ, 1978; Distinguished Alumni, NAFEO Wash DC, 1984; Eurekan of the Year, Eureka Club Portsmouth, 1984; Citizen of the Year, 1985; Treasurer of the Year, Treas Asn Va, 1992; Sigma Gamma Rho, Alpha Sigma Chapter, 1992; LHD, Va Bible Inst; LHD, Providence Bible Col & Theol Seminary, 2003. **Special Achievements:** First African citizen of Portsmouth; poet: The Other Side of a Gemina, anthology, 1986. **Military Serv:** USM, major, 21 yrs; Good Conduct, three stars; Navy Achievements; Navy Commendation w/Combat V; Staff Serv Honor Medal; Repub S Vietnam. **Business Addr:** President, Diverse Financial Services, PO Box 1363, Portsmouth, VA 23705, **Business Phone:** (757)393-0598.*

WHITEHURST, STEVEN LAROY
Writer, business owner, school administrator. **Personal:** Born Mar 3, 1967, Chicago, IL; son of Steven Fondren and Oneda Fondren-Whitehurst; married Noreen Halbert, Jun 27, 1992. **Educ:** Thornton Community Col, AA, hist, 1987, AS, geog, 1988; Chicago State Univ, BA, hist, minor polit sci, 1990. **Career:** South Suburban Col, grad ambassador, 1988-90; Equal Employ Op-

portunity Comn, investr, 1990-91; South Suburban Col, acad skills, transition adv, 1991-94, dir stud develop, 1994-97; Steven Whitehurst Homepage, owner, 1998-. **Orgs:** Thornton Community Col Affirm Action Adv Comt, 1988; Phi Theta Kappa, Psi Pi Chap, 1989-; Cook County Bd Elections, elections judge & registr, 1990; Am Black Book Writers Asn, 1991-; Equal Employ Opportunity Comt, 1991; ILAEOPP, 1991-92; MAEOPP, 1991-92; Multicultural Publ Exchange, 1992-94; Proj Vision, head proj & task force, 1994-97; Phi Alpha Theta, 1997-. **Honors/Awds:** Creative Excellence Award, New Scriblerus Soc, 1988; Outstanding Service Award, 1992, Role Model of the Year, 1993, South Suburban Col; Black Lit Achieve Award, Black Booksellers Trade Asn, 1993; Your Black Book Guide Bestseller Award for Words From An Unchained Mind, Rodney King & La Rebellion; Malcolm X Award For Self-Actualization, AFRIQUE Commun, 1994; Hero Award, 1995; ETS Award, South Suburban Col, Educ Talent Search, 1996; New Scriblerus Society Creative Excellence Award. **Special Achievements:** Contributor, Rodney King & The La Rebellion, 1992; Moderator, City of Harvey, Mayoral Debate, 1995; Panelist, African Amercian History Month Round Table Discussion: The State of Black Amercian, sponsored by The Times Newspaper, 1995. **Home Addr:** 240 Yates Ave Apt 1 South, Calumet City, IL 60409, **Home Phone:** (708)862-2950.

WHITELY, DONALD HARRISON
Counselor, educator. **Personal:** Born Mar 4, 1955, Tarrytown, NJ; son of Henry Harrison Whitely and Helen Elizabeth Cardwell Whitely; married Angela Smith, Jan 2, 1980; children: Asha Elizabeth & Maya Nicole. **Educ:** State Univ New York, Albany, New York, BA, 1977; John Jay Col Criminal Justice, New York, MPA, 1982. **Career:** IBM, Harrison, New York, inventory control asst, 1980-82; Jewish Child Care Agency, Pleasantville, New York, diag unit counr, 1983-88; Malcolm-King Col, Harlem, New York, from asst dir HEOP to dir HEOP, 1988-89; Westchester Community Col, Valhalla, New York, admis counr/instr, 1989, asst prof/counr, assoc prof/counr, currently. **Orgs:** Higher Educ Opportunity Prog Professional Orgn, 1988-89; Westchester Educ Coalition, 1989-; Admis Adv Comt, West Chester Community Col, 1989-; fac adv, African Cult Club, West Chester Community Col, 1990-; Mid States Asn Col Registr & Officers Admis, 1989-; State Univ New York, Multicultural Community. **Honors/Awds:** Distinguished Community Service Award, Tarrytown Community Opportunity Ctr, 1992; Community Service Award, NAACP, 1995; Adult Recognition Award for Community Service, Westchester City Youth Bd & Bur, 1998. **Special Achievements:** First African American elected, Bd Trustees, Village Tarrytown, 1992, Relected to 3rd term, 1996; Coordr, Open Views Youth Group Tarrytowns; asst hd coach, Tarrytown Pop Warner Football; Village Tarrytown Liaison; Tarrytown Sch Bd Munic Housing Authority. **Home Addr:** 16 Mechanics Ave, Tarrytown, NY 10591. **Business Addr:** Associate Professor, Admissions Counselor, Westchester Community College, State University of New York, 75 Grasslands Rd Administration Bldg Rm 210, Valhalla, NY 10595, **Business Phone:** (914)785-6741.

WHITEN, MARK ANTHONY
Baseball player. **Personal:** Born Nov 25, 1966, Pensacola, FL. **Career:** Baseball player (retired), athletic coach; Toronto Blue Jays, outfielder, 1990-91; Cleveland Indians, outfielder, 1991-92, 1998-2000; St Louis Cardinals, outfielder, 1993-94; Boston Red Sox, outfielder, 1995; Philadelphia Phillies, outfielder, 1995-96; Atlanta Braves, outfielder, 1996; Seattle Mariners, 1996; NY Yankees, outfielder, 1997; Tex Rangers, hitting coach, 2005, Rangers Rookie League club, hitting coach 2006.

WHITE-PARSON, WILLAR F
Educator, nurse. **Personal:** Born Nov 11, 1945, Norfolk, VA; daughter of Joseph S White and Willar M White; married Wayman L, Aug 5, 1985; children: Davida Josette White. **Educ:** Hampton Univ, BSN, 1974, MA, guidance & counseling, 1976, MSN, 1979; Old Dominion Univ, PhD, urban service curriculum development, 1984. **Career:** Norfolk State Univ, assoc prof nursing, 1974, Dept Nursing, prof & chair, currently; Norfolk Psychiat Ctr, nursing supvr, 1990-92; Sentara Norfolk Gen Hosp, psychiat nurse consult, 1991-; Pvt Pract, nurse psychotherapist, 1991-. **Orgs:** Am Asn Univ Professors, 1976-; Nat League Nursing, 1989-; Va League Nursing, 1989-; Asn Black Nursing Fac Higher Educ, 1990-; Am Nurses Asn, 1990-; VIR Nurses Asn, 1990-; Tidewater Acad Clin Nurse Specist, 1991-; Va Coun Clin Nurse Specist, 1991-. **Honors/Awds:** Kappa Delta Pi Hon Soc, 1976; Sigma Theta Tau Hon Soc, 1979; Minority Fel, Old Dominion Univ, 1984; Res Award, Asn Black Nursing Fac Higher Educ, 1992; Am Acad Nursing, fellow, 1994. **Special Achievements:** LPN to ADN, BSN: An Accelerated Curriculum Track, $550,000 grant, 1988-92; "A Comparison of Parenting Profiles of Adolescent Mothers," dissertation, 1984; "Parenting Profiles of Battered Women," 1980. **Home Addr:** 5008 Kemps Farm Pl, Virginia Beach, VA 23464, **Home Phone:** (804)495-6115. **Business Addr:** Professor and Chair of Department of Nursing, Norfolk State University, Department of Nursing, 700 Pk Ave, Norfolk, VA 23504, **Business Phone:** (757)823-8600.

WHITE-PERKINS, DENISE M
Health services administrator, physician. **Educ:** Univ Mich Med Sch; MetroHealth Med Ctr, OH; Univ Mich, MD, PhD. **Career:** Henry Ford Health Syst, family pract, currently. **Orgs:** Dir, Inst Multicultural Health. **Business Addr:** Director of the Institute of Multicultural Health, Henry Ford Health System, Family Practice 4401 Connor, Detroit, MI 48215, **Business Phone:** (313)823-9800.*

WHITESIDE, ERNESTYNE E.
Educator. **Personal:** Born in Pine Bluff, AR. **Educ:** Mech & Normal Col, Pine Bluff, BA, agri; NY Univ, MA; Europe, post grad;Ouachita Univ, Arkadelphia; Okla Univ; Univ Ariz. **Career:** Dollarway Pub Sch Dist, eng instr. **Orgs:** Pres, Jeferson Co Reading Coun; Ariz Educ Asn; Asn Classrooms Teachers;Nat Ariz Coun Teachers Eng; Nat Reading Coun; Nat Asn Univ Women; Gov'sCoun Aerospace Educ; St Orgn Minority Evolvement; Nat Alumni Asn A M & NCol; Eastern Star; Delta Sigma Theta; Am Woodman Asn. **Honors/Awds:** Hon Citizen, Negro Youth Orgn; Outstanding Teacher Mo, Townsend Park HighSch; Outstanding Service, Youth Jack & Jill, 1974. **Special Achievements:** Listed in Dict of International Biog Vol 12.

WHITE-WARE, GRACE ELIZABETH
Educator. **Personal:** Born Oct 5, 1921, St Louis, MO; daughter of Dr James Eathel White Sr and Madree Penn White; married Aug 17, 1947 (widowed); children: Oloye Adeyemon (James Otis Ware II). **Educ:** Harriet Beecher Stowe Teacher's Col, BA, 1943; Columbia Univ, NY, attended1945; Scott Fores man Inst summer, attended 1951; Wayne State Univ, attended 1966; St John Col, John Carroll Univ, attended 1975; Kent State Univ, attended 1976; Ohio Univ, attended 1978. **Career:** Educator (retired); St Louis, Chicago, NY, Cleveland, teacher, 1946-82;Cleveland Pub Sch, teacher elem & adult educ, 1954-82; Delta Sigma Theta Sor Inc, mem founder, Tutoring & Nutrition Proj, prog adminr, 1983-88. **Orgs:** Greater Cleveland Neighborhood Ctr Asn; Food First Prog; Black Econ Union; Youth Understanding Teenage Prog; Cleveland Coun Human Rels; Cong Racial Equality; Tots & Teens; Jr Women's Civic League; Afro-Am Cult Hist Soc;Talbert Clin & Day Care Ctr; Langston Hughes Lib; Women's Allied Arts Asn; Nat Asn Advan Colored People; Phyllis Wheatley Asn; Nat Coun Negro Women;Nat Sor Phi Delta Kappa; Top Ladies of Distinction Inc; Smithsonian Inst; Phi Delta Kappa Fraternal Group, 1979-; regional & nat treas, Eta Phi Beta Sor Inc, 1980-88; Delta Kappa Gamma Soc Int, The Nat Mus Women in Arts; Kiwanis Int, 1987; treas, Nat Asn Univ Women, 1987-. **Honors/Awds:** Outstanding Volunteer of the Year, NY, 1949; Outstanding Teacher Award,1973; Certificate of Appreciation, Cleveland, 1973; Master Teacher Award-Martha Jennings, 1973; Pan-Hellenic Outstanding Greek Award, 1979,1984; Educ Serv Award Urban League of Greater Cleveland, 1986; Humanitarian Award Top Ladies of Distinction Inc, 1986. *

WHITFIELD, ALPHONSO
Banker. **Educ:** Union Col, MA; Carnegie-Mellon Univ, MS. **Career:** Vpres, Prudential Ins, 1972-85; Nat Minority Supplier Develop Coun, pres, 1985-88; Fed Home Loan Bank New York, pres, 1988-94; Mutual Fed Savings bank Atlanta, pres & chief exec officer, 1994-98; Vital Inc, chmn, currently. **Orgs:** Regional Lender Consortia, co-founder; pres, Nat Minority Supplier Develop coun; vpres, Social Investments Prudential Ins Am; vpres, Com Group Progress Investment Asn. **Business Phone:** (404)523-3435.

WHITFIELD, DONDRE T.
Actor. **Personal:** Born May 27, 1969, Brooklyn, NY; married Salli Richardson, Sep 8, 2002; children: Parker Richardson & Dre Terrell. **Career:** Films: Bright Lights, Big City, 1988; Homeboy, 1988; Home boyz II: Crack City, 1989; White Man's Burden, 1995; Happy Birthday, 2001; Two Can Play That Game, 2001; Biker Boyz, 2003; Mr. 3000, 2004; The Salon, 2005; Pastor Brown, 2009; TV series: "The Cosby Show", 1985-87; "Diff'rent Strokes", 1986; "Another World", 1989-90; "ABC After school Specials", 1990; "All My Children", 1991-94; "The Crew", 1995; "The Jamie Foxx Show", 1996; "Martin", 1997; "Between Brothers", 1997; "Living in Captivity", 1998; Secret Agent Man, 2000; Alien Fury: Countdown to Invasion, 2000; "The X Files", 2000; "Nash Bridges", 2000; "NYPD Blue", 2001; On the Edge, 2001; "Girlfriends", 2001-02; "Inside Schwartz", 2001; "Hidden Hills", 2002; "The Partners",2003; "Strong Medicine", 2004; "Second Time Around", 2004; "Half & Half", 2004; "Less Than Perfect", 2004; "Briar & Graves", 2005; "Jake in Progress", 2005; "Ghost Whisperer", 2005-06; Our Thirties, 2006; "CSI: Miami", 2006; Cold Case, 2008; "Samantha Who?", 2009. **Business Addr:** Actor, c/o Writers & Artists Agency Inc, 8383 Wilshire Blvd Suite 550, Beverly Hills, CA 90211, **Business Phone:** (323)866-0900.*

WHITFIELD, JENENNE
Executive. **Personal:** Born Aug 29, 1961, Pontiac, MI; daughter of Dan and Delores; married Tyree Guyton, Oct 5, 2001; children: Chloe D Whitfield-Butler. **Educ:** Wayne State Univ, attending. **Career:** Self-employed agent, 1994-; Heidelberg Proj, bd mem, 1994-, exec dir, currently. **Orgs:** Hon bd mem, Mona Mus, 2000-. **Special Achievements:** Author "Thoughts on the Heidelberg Project," Southern Quarterly, Spring 2001. **Business Addr:** Executive Director, The Heidelberg Project, 3360 Charlevoix, Detroit, MI 48219.

WHITFIELD, KENNARD O
Cartographer, mayor. **Personal:** Born May 28, 1933, St Louis, MO; son of Ossie and Nettie Whitfield; married Ettie Jean, Apr 1, 1967; children: Stacy Marie Ruff & Lorna Jean Whitfield. **Educ:** Xavier Univ, attended; St Louis Univ, BS, 1958, MPA, 1963; Yale Univ, attended. **Career:** Ccartorapher (retired), Mayor (retired); Defense Mapping Agency, cartographer/div chief, 1958-93; City of Rock Hill, mayor. **Orgs:** United Way, loan exec, 1971-73; St Lousi County Munic League, 1973-, pres, 1987-88; MO Munic League, 1973-, pres 1990-91; Metro Sewer Dist Civil Srvice Comm, 1973-94; Community Adv Bd KSDK-TV, 1986-; Nat Conf Black Mayors, pres MO Chap; Nat League Cities, 1994-; MO Seismic Safety Comn, 1994-. **Honors/Awds:** East/West Gateway Coordinating Council, Government Achievement Award, 1998; MO Municipal League, Distinguished Service Award, 1999. **Military Serv:** AUS, 1953-55. **Home Addr:** 507 Hinsdale Ct, Rock Hill, MO 63119, **Home Phone:** (314)961-3910.

WHITFIELD, LYNN C.
Actor. **Personal:** Born May 6, 1953, Baton Rouge, LA; daughter of Valerian Smith; married Van (divorced); married Brian Gibson, Jul 4, 1990 (divorced 1992); children: Grace. **Educ:** Howard Univ, BA. **Career:** TV: Heartbeat, 1988; The Women of Brewster Place, 1989; Stomp in at the Savoy; The George McKenna Story; The Johnnie Mae Gibson Story; Cosby Mysteries, 1994; The Josephine Baker Story; The Wedding, 1998; The Color of Courage, 1999; Deep in My Heart, 1999; A Girl Thing, 2001; The Cheetah Girls, 2003; Redemption: The Stan Tookie Williams Story, 2004; Strong Medicine, 2004; The Cheetah Girls 2, 2006; Shark: Pilot, 2006; films include: Dr Detroit, 1983; Silverado, 1985; Sluggers Wife, 1985; A Thin Line Between Love & Hate, 1996; Eves Bayou, 1997; Stepmom, 1998; A Time for Dancing, 2000; Head of State, 2003; Madeas Family Reunion, 2006; Confessions, 2006; The Cheetah Girls 2, 2006; Shark, 2006; Kings of the Evening, 2008; The Women, 2008; Mama, I Want to Sing, The Rebound, 2009. **Orgs:** Alpha Kappa Alpha Sorority Inc; Links Inc. **Honors/Awds:** Emmy Award, The Josephine Baker Story, 1991; Alumni Achievement Award, Howard Univ, 1992; Image Award, TV Drama Supporting Actress, NAACP, 1998; Image Award for Outstanding Performance in a Youth or C's Series/Spec, 2000. **Business Addr:** Actress, William Morris Agency, 151 El Camino Dr, Beverly Hills, CA 90212.

WHITFIELD, ROBERT
Chief executive officer, football player. **Personal:** Born Oct 18, 1971, Carson, CA; children: Laniece & Kodi. **Educ:** Stanford Univ. **Career:** Football player (retired), chief executive officer; Atlanta Falcons, tackle, 1992-2003; Jacksonville Jaguars, 2004; New York Giants, 2005-06; pre game analyst, Sky Sports; Patch werk Recordings, chief exec officer. **Honors/Awds:** All-Pro selection 1996; Pro Bowl, 1998. **Business Phone:** (404)874-9880.

WHITFIELD, VAN
Novelist. **Personal:** Born Jan 1, 1960, Baltimore, MD. **Career:** Employed at Lorton Prison, Wash, DC; worked in Mayor's Youth Initiative Office, Wash, DC, 1995; Whitfield Entertainment LLc, owner. **Orgs:** Founder, Education Works. **Honors/Awds:** Nominated for six Ben Franklin awards for Beeperless Remote, 1997; featured in a wide range of periodicals including Ebony, Essence, Publisher's Weekly, Black Issues Book Review, BET Weekend, Jane, MODE, The Washington Post, The Baltimore Sun, The LA Times, The NY Daily News, The Miami Herald and a host of other publications around the world; California Book award, 2000; "Book Oscar", 2002; received six Ben Franklin Award nominations. **Special Achievements:** 'Beeperless Remote', publ, 1997; 'There's Something Wrong with Your Scale!', 1999; wrote scripts for UPN TV series, Grown Ups, 2000; Guys in Suits, publ, 2001; Dad Interrupted, 2004. **Business Phone:** (212)939-9725.

WHITING, ALBERT NATHANIEL
School administrator, educator. **Personal:** Born Jul 3, 1917, Jersey City, NJ; son of Hezekiah O and Hilda; married Lottie Luck; children: Brooke E Whiting. **Educ:** Amherst Col, AB, 1938; Fisk Univ, MA, 1941; The Am Univ, PhD, 1948, 1952. **Career:** Educator (retired); Bennett Col, instr sociol, 1941-43, 1946-47; Atlanta Univ, asst prof sociol, 1948-53; Morris Brown Col, dean Col, 1953-57; Morgan State Col, dean Col, 1957-67; NC Central Univ, pres chancellor, 1967-83, chancellor emeritus. **Orgs:** MD Comn New York World's Fair; comn acad affairs, Am Coun Educ, 1968-70; mem bd dirs, Am Coun Educ, 1970-73 1974-75; mem bd trustees, Educ Testing Serv, 1968-72; policies & purposes comn, bd dirs pres, Am Asn State Cols & Univs; Col Entrance Examination Bd; mem bd dirs, Nat League Nursing Inc, 1970-71,; vpres, 1971-74, 1975-78, treas, 1978-84; Intl Asn Univ Presidents; mem bd dirs, NC Mem Hosp, 1974-77; Joint Panel Grad Record Examinations Bd & Coun Grad Sch US; bd govs exec comt bd Res Triangle Inst Res Triange Park NC; mem bd dirs, Greater Durham Chamber Com; US Civil Serv Comn Southern Region; mem bd dirs, Gen Telephone Co Southeast; mem bd dirs, Rose'sres, Inc 1981-88; mem bd regents, Univ MD Syst, 1988-92. **Honors/Awds:** National Urban League Fellowship, Univ Pittsburgh; Teaching & Research Fellow, Fisk Univ; Alpha Kappa Delta Honor Sociological Fraternity; numerous books reviews & contributions professional journals; Six Hon Degrees LLD's & LHD's. **Military Serv:** AUS, 1st Lt, 1943-46. *

WHITING, BARBARA E
Lawyer. **Personal:** Born Jul 28, 1936, Tabb, VA; widowed. **Educ:** Hampton Inst Hampton Va, BS, 1963; Howard Univ Sch Law, JD,

1963. **Career:** Lawyer (retired); US Customs Serv Wash, customs law specialist, 1964-96; Howard Univ Dept Med, med secy, 1957-63; Howard Univ, librn, 1964. **Orgs:** Pres, Howard Law Alumni Asn, 1974-78; Nat Bar Asn, Greater Wash chap, Women Lawyers Div, 1974-; vol, Oper Sue, 1974. **Honors/Awds:** First Black female appointed Customs Law Specialist, US Customs Service. **Home Addr:** 2831 Hillcrest Dr SE, Washington, DC 20020.

WHITING, BRANDON RENEE
Football player. **Personal:** Born Jul 30, 1976, Santa Rosa, CA; son of Thomas. **Educ:** Univ Calif. **Career:** Football player (retired); Philadelphia Eagles, defensive tackle, 1998-2003; San Francisco 49ers, 2003-04. **Honors/Awds:** Pro Football Weekly, All-Rookie Team, 1998.

WHITING, LEROY
Government official, executive director. **Personal:** Born May 17, 1938, Rodney, MS; son of Johnnie and Gertrude Jackson; married Annette Mattie Watkins, Aug 24, 1959; children: Oran. **Educ:** Alcorn A&M Col, BS, 1959; Mich State Univ, MAT, 1965; Univ Ill, Chicago, attended 1980. **Career:** Government official (retired); Meridian Bd Educ, MS, sci teacher, 1959-60; Chicago Bd Educ, IL, sci teacher, 1960-68; City Chicago, IL, dir external affairs, asst to mayor, 1968, spec asst to planning & develop comnr, 1993, Intergovernmental Comn, exec dir, 2001. **Orgs:** Alpha Phi Alpha, 1957-; bd trustees, Francis Parker Sch, 1968-75; chair, User Requirement Pub Tech Inc, 1980; GAP Community Orgn, 1983-; Nat Forum Black Pub Admins, 1986-89; Dent Assisting Nat Bd, 1988-; chair church coun, Hartzell Memorial United Methodist Church, Chicago, 2003; Alpha Kappa Mu Hon Soc. **Military Serv:** AUS, res spec 2, 1958-61. **Home Addr:** 3344 S Calumet Ave, Chicago, IL 60616. *

WHITING, VAL
Basketball player. **Personal:** Born Apr 9, 1972. **Educ:** Stanford Univ, attended 1993. **Career:** San Jose Lasers, 1996-97; Seattle Reign, center, 1997-99; Detroit Shock,center, 1999; Minn Lynx, ctr, 2001-02; Game shape Inc, founder. *

WHITING, WILLIE
Judge. **Personal:** Born in Chicago, IL; daughter of James and Elise Jones Harkness; divorced. **Educ:** John Marshall Law Sch, LLB, JD, 1950. **Career:** Judge (retired); GJ Harkness Law Firm, law clerk, atty, 1950-55; Cook Co Dept Pub Welfare, caseworker, resource consult, 1955-56; Nat Asn Advan Colored People, Chicago, exec sec, 1957-59; City Chicago, asst corp coun, 1959-61; Circuit Ct, magistrate; Cook Co, asst state atty, 1961-65, asst US atty, 1965-66, assoc judge circuit ct, 1970-78, circuit judge, 1978. **Orgs:** Ill Bar Asn, 1951; Am Asn Univ Women; hon mem, Delta Kappa Gamma Educ Soc; Nat Bar Asn; Am Bar Asn; US Dist Ct & US Supreme Ct, 1964-; adv coun, Cook Co Temp Juv Detention Ctr, Hm Ec Related Occup; Cook Co Nat Women's Bar Asn; adv bd, Midwest Comn Coun; Am Vets Comn; mem bd, Chicago, Nat Asn Advan Colored People; pres, Prof Women's Club; life mem, Zeta Phi Beta Sorority Inc; adv coun, Urban Health Comn, Univ Ill, Chicago, 1984-; Ill Judges Asn; Ill Judicial Coun; Nat Bar Asn; comn adv coun, Urban Health Prog. **Honors/Awds:** Certificate of Appreciation Award, Young Lawyers Sect, Chicago Bar Asn, 1985-88. **Military Serv:** AUS, pfc, 1944-46. **Home Addr:** 680 N Lake Shore Dr Suite 720, Chicago, IL 60611, **Home Phone:** (312)280-8018.

WHITLEY, WILLIAM N.
Executive, architect. **Personal:** Born Apr 29, 1934, Rochester, NY; married Kaysonia Forney; children: Kyle, Kym, Scott. **Educ:** Kent St Univ, BS, 1957. **Career:** Whitley-Whitley Inc, vice pres arch; Registered in OH, IL, IN. **Orgs:** Am Inst Archs; Archs Soc OH; Cleveland Eng Soc; Soc Arch Design, 1974; OH Prestressed Concert Assoc Design, 1973; Women's Allied Arts Assoc, 1974. **Honors/Awds:** United Torch Progressive Architect Design Award, 1972; AIA Am Soc Arch 1st Hon Design, 1969. **Military Serv:** USAF, capt, 1958-60.

WHITLOW, BARBARA WHEELER
Executive. **Personal:** Born Jul 20, 1939, Sale City, GA; daughter of Benjamin Wheeler Sr and Luecilla Donaldson Wheeler; married Charles E, Dec 27, 1964; children: Charlene Gena & Darlene Denise. **Educ:** Albany State Col, 1961; Atlanta Jr Col, 1981. **Career:** Fed Bur Invest, res analyst, 1964-67; Defense Contract Admin, qual control specialist, 1967-85; Lows Enterprise, Inc, pres & chief exec officer, 1985-. **Orgs:** Secy, Region IV 8a Contractors Asn, 1991-. **Honors/Awds:** Show Stoppers Award, Ga Minority Purchasing Coun, 1992; Salute to Black Business Owners, Atlanta Tribune, 1992; Salute to Small Business Suppliers, Lockheed Aeronaut Systs Co, 1992; Administrator's Award for Excellence, US Small Bus Adminr, 1996. **Special Achievements:** Founder of Lows Enterprises, Inc, Minority Female-Owned Electronic Mfg Firm, 1985. **Home Phone:** (404)344-8795. **Business Addr:** President, Chief Executive Oficer, Lows Enterprises Inc, 3966 Shirley Dr, PO Box 310032, Atlanta, GA 30336, **Business Phone:** (404)699-0582.

WHITLOW, DR. WOODROW, JR.
Research scientist. **Personal:** Born Dec 13, 1952, Inkster, MI; son of Woodrow and Willie Mae O; married Michele C Wimberly, Jan 6, 1971; children: Mary Annessa & Natalie Michele. **Educ:** Mass Inst Technol, Cambridge, MA, SB, 1974, SM, 1975, PhD, 1979. **Career:** NASA Langley Res Ctr, Hampton, VA, res scientist, 1979-86, res scientist/group leader, 1986-88, sr res scientist, 1988-89; NASA, Wash, DC, prog mgr, astrophysics, 1990, prog mgr, structures & dynamics, asst head, aero serv elasticity br, 1990-91, head, aero dynamics br, 1991-94, dep dir, Aeronautics Progs, 1995-97; chief, Structures Div, 1997-98, dir, Critical Technols Div, 1994; NASA Glenn Res Ctr, Cleveland, Ohio, dir, Res & Technol, 1998, deputy dir, 2003-05, dir, 2005-; adjunct prof, Old Dominion Univ, 1987-; lectr, Cairo Univ Aeronaut Seminar Series, 1988. **Orgs:** Am Inst Aeronaut & Astronaut; coach, Phillips Athletic Asn Girls Softball, 1981-84; pres, Hampton Univ Lab Sch Adv Bd, 1982-83; MIT Aeronaut & Astronaut Vis Comt, 1987-93; MIT Educ Coun, 1987-; Women in Aerospace, 1991-; Nat Tech Asn, 1983-. **Honors/Awds:** First place, Student Research Competition, AAIA New England Section, 1974; James Means Memorial Prize, MIT Aeronautics and Astronautics, 1974; special achievement awards, NASA Langley Research Center, 1982, 1986, 1989; Black Engineer of the Year in Government, Career Communications Group, 1989; Outstanding Performance Award, NASA Langley, 1990; NTA Engineer of the Year, 1996; MIT Martin Luther King Alumni Award, 2000. **Home Addr:** 17141 Amber Dr, Cleveland, OH 44111-2901. **Business Addr:** Director, John H Glenn Research Center, 21000 Brookpark Rd Mail Stop 3 - 5, Cleveland, OH 44135, **Business Phone:** (216)433-3193.

WHITMAL, NATHANIEL. **See Obituaries section.**

WHITMORE, CHARLES
Government official, conservationist. **Personal:** Born Jan 25, 1945, Mason, TN; son of Morris Whitmore and Katherine; married Cynthia M Huff, Jul 19, 1969; children: Lashawn, Charles Marcus & Corey Demond. **Educ:** Tenn State Univ, BS, agron, 1969, MS, plant sci, 1970. **Career:** Natural Resources Conserv Serv, Midwest Region, Madison, WI, soil conservationist, 1970, dist conservationist, 1973-76, state res specialist, 1976-79, state res specialist, 1976-79, area conservationist, 1979-85; dep state conservationist, 1985-87, state conservationist, Maine, 1987-91, state conservationist Ill, 1991-94, Conserv Planning Div, dir, 1994, regional conservationist, Conservation Opers Div, actg dir, currently; USDA, SCS, state conservationist, currently. **Orgs:** Asn Ill Soil & Water Conserv; Am Soc Agronomy; Prof Soc Black SCS Employees; Prince Hall Masonic Lodge; Bangor Lodge 22; Ill Gov, land & water task force. **Honors/Awds:** USDA Superior Service Award, 1976; Special achievement awards, 1976, 1984, 1991; Outstanding Performance Awards, 1980, 1981, 1990; Alumnus of the Year Award, Tenn State Univ, 1992. **Business Phone:** (217)398-5267.

WHITMORE, DARRELL
Baseball player. **Personal:** Born Nov 18, 1968, Front Royal, VA. **Career:** W Va Mountaineers, right field, 1989-90; Fla Marlins, 1993-95.

WHITNER, DONNA K
Librarian. **Personal:** Born Jan 24, 1951, Champaign, IL; daughter of Lawrence and Gladys McMullen. **Educ:** Western Col, Oxford, OH, BA, 1973; Univ Ill, Urbana, IL, MLS, 1977; Univ Mo-Kans City, Kans City, MO, MBA, 1995. **Career:** Western Col, Oxford, OH, work grant stud, 1969-73; Urbana Sch Dist No 16, Urbana, IL, asst to dir librs, 1973-76; Univ Ill, Champaign, IL, grad asst, 1976-77; Women's Employment Couns Ctr, Champaign, IL, researcher, 1977-78; Univ Ill, Champaign, IL, residence halls librn, 1978-86; Kans City Pub Libr, Kans City, MO, Tech Serv, dir, 1986-; grad, Centurions, Leadership Develop Prog, Greater Kans City Chamber Com. **Orgs:** Am Libr Asn, 1980-; Pub Libr Asn, 1986-; Mo Libr Asn, 1986-; vchair, Tech Servs Coun, Mo Libr Asn, 1990-91. **Honors/Awds:** Woman of the Year, Western Col, Am Asn Univ Women, 1972-73. **Home Addr:** 2510 Grand Ave Suite 801, Kansas City, MO 64108. **Business Addr:** Director Technical Services, Kansas City Public Library, Department of Finance, 311 E 12th St, Kansas City, MO 64106, **Business Phone:** (816)701-3480.

WHITNEY, CHRISTOPHER ANTOINE
Basketball player. **Personal:** Born Oct 5, 1971, Hopkinsville, KY. **Educ:** Lincoln Trail, attended; Clemson Univ, attended. **Career:** San Antonio Spurs, guard, 1993-95; Rapid City Thrillers, CBA, 1995; Fla Beachdogs, CBA, 1995-96; Wash Bullets, 1996-97; Wash Wizards, 1996-2002, 2004; Denver Nuggets, 2003; Orlando Magic, guard, 2003; Scavolini Pesaro, 2003-04.

WHITNEY, ROSALYN L
School administrator. **Personal:** Born Jan 12, 1950, Detroit, MI; daughter of Robert L Smith and Esther L DeCuir Hocker; children: Gina Michelle Lee. **Educ:** Oakland Univ, Meadowbrook, Mich, Sch Music, attended 1966; Eastern Mich Univ, Ypsilanti, Mich, BA, 1971. **Career:** Probe Inc, Detroit, Mich, vp mkt, 1973-78; CBS Inc, Records Division S Detroit, Mich, acct exec, 1978-82; Barden Communs, Detroit, Mich, dir mkt, 1984; New Detroit Inc, Detroit, Mich, dir media relations, 1984-91; Detroit Pub Schs, asst supt communs, 1991-. **Orgs:** Bd mem, Non Profit Pub Rels Network, 1991-92, vchair bd, Creative Arts Collection, 1982-; bd mem, Detroit Wayne County Family Servs, 1992; bd mem, Int Visitors Coun Metro Detroit, 1985-92; St Dunstans Guild Cranbrook, 1989-92; Detroit Press Club, 1984-; Automotive Press Asn; Nat Sch Pub Rels; Nat Asn Television Arts & Scis; NAB; Detroit Producers Asn; Am Soc Composers, Authors & Publs. **Honors/Awds:** Spirit Detroit, City Detroit, City Coun, 1979; CBS Detroit Branch of the Year, CBS Inc, 1980. **Business Addr:** Assistant Superintendent Communications, Detroit Public Schools, 5057 Woodward Ave Rm 218, Detroit, MI 48202, **Business Phone:** (313)494-2244.

WHITNEY, DR. W MONTY
Educator, administrator. **Personal:** Born Sep 7, 1945, Philadelphia, PA; son of Wilbur M and Bessie M; married Bettye Roberts; children: Erica & Michelle. **Educ:** Lycoming Col, BA, 1967; Howard Univ, MS, psychol, 1969; Mich State Univ, PhD, psychol, 1974. **Career:** Southern Univ, instr, 1969-71; Univ Cincinnati, asst prof, 1974-76; Seven Hills Neighborhood Houses Inc, assoc dir; Morehouse Col, Dept Psychol, asst prof, prof psychol, currently, interim chair, currently. **Orgs:** Pres, Social Tech Systs, 1978-; nat pres, Asn Black Psychol, 1984-85; TransAfrica, Nat Asn Advan Colored People. **Special Achievements:** Author-;"Black Social Scientist and Innovative Action Research", The Journal of Black Psychology, 1975. Co author, Research Strategies for Social Change, Minority Issues in Mental Health, Reflections of Black Psychology. **Home Addr:** 2825 Spain Dr, Atlanta, GA 30344. **Business Addr:** Professor of Psychology, Morehouse College, Department of Psychology, Rm 231 Dansby Hall 830 Westview Dr SW, Atlanta, GA 30314, **Business Phone:** (404)681-2800 Ext 2626.

WHITNEY, WILLIAM B
Executive, chief executive officer. **Educ:** Benedict Col, BS, biol, 1962; Univ SC, chem, 1966-68; Univ Calif, vis scholar, 1970; Harvard Univ, JFK Sch Bus, exec mgt prog, 1981. **Career:** Ford Found Fel, 1970-71; Greenville Urban League Inc, exec dir, 1973-79, pres/chief exec officer, 1991-; State SC Div Employ & Training, exec asst gov, 1979-86; State Bd Tech & Comprehensive Educ, spec asst employ & community affairs, 1986-91; Whitney Corp Columbia, pres,1990-; Whitney Pl, chief exec officer, 1990-; Whitney & Whitney Develop Corp, pres, broker incharge, 1990-92. **Orgs:** Bd dirs, Cities & Schs; Nat Asn Advan Colored People; bd dirs, Greenville Area Nations Bank; bd chmn, SC Comn Poverty & Deprivation; bd dirs, Greenville YMCA; bd dirs, Clemson Univ Bd Visitors; Greenville Rotary Club; bd dirs, Palmetto Project. **Military Serv:** AUS, 1962-65. **Business Addr:** President, Chief Executive Officer, The Urban League of the Upstate, 15 Regency Hill Dr, Greenville, SC 29607, **Business Phone:** (864)244-3862.

WHITSETT, JAMES A, JR.
Executive. **Personal:** Born Feb 27, 1952, Greenfield, MA; son of James A Sr and Myrtle Whitsett. **Educ:** Syracuse Univ, BS, 1974. **Career:** Freelance TV, producer; CT Pub Broadcasting Inc, CT Public TV, vpres local programming, sr vpres local programming, currently. **Orgs:** Big Brothers; Nat Acad TV Arts & Sci. **Honors/Awds:** One to One Media Award; Excellence Award, Sigma Delta Chi; Communication to a Black Audience Award; 7 Regional Emmy Awards. **Business Addr:** Senior Vice President of Local Programming, Connecticut Public Broadcasting Inc., Connecticut Public Television & Radio, 1049 Asylum Ave, Hartford, CT 06106, **Business Phone:** (860)278-5310.

WHITT, DWIGHT REGINALD
Clergy, priest, president (organization). **Personal:** Born Jul 17, 1949, Baltimore, MD. **Educ:** Loyola Col, AB, 1970; Pontif Fac Immaculate Conception, STB, 1974, STL. **Career:** Ordained Roman Cath priest, 1976; Order Friars Preachers, mem; Spalding Col, chaplain; Dominican House Studies, pres, currently. **Orgs:** Nat Black Cath Clergy Caucus. **Business Addr:** President, Dominican House of Studies, 487 Michigan Avenue NE, Washington, DC 20017.

WHITTAKER, SHARON ELAINE
College administrator. **Personal:** Born Sep 6, 1952, Gary, IN; daughter of Robert and Edith Elizabeth. **Educ:** Howard Univ, BA, 1974, MEd, 1976; Ill State Univ, PhD, 1983; Havard Inst Educ Mgt, grad, 2000. **Career:** McKinley Tech High Sch, teacher, 1974-75; Cromwell Acad, teacher, counr, 1975-77; Howard Univ, residence hall counr, 1976-79; Ill State Univ, dir, 1979-84; Paine Col, dean students, 1984-90; Mary Holmes Col, vpres acad affairs, 1990-95; Stillman Col, vpres stud affairs, 1995-. **Orgs:** Nat Asn Stud Personnel Adminr; Nat Asn Stud Affairs, prof & pres, 1993; Phi Beta Kappa; Am Asn Univ Women; Bus Prof Women Inc; Alpha Kappa Alpha Sorority Inc. **Honors/Awds:** Phi Beta Kappa George N Leighton Award, Howard Univ, 1974; Human Relations Award, Ill State, 1983. **Home Addr:** 241 Meadow Ridge Dr, Tuscaloosa, AL 35405, **Home Phone:** (205)758-6149. **Business Addr:** Vice President for Student Affairs, Stillman College, 3600 Stillman Blvd, PO Box 1430, Tuscaloosa, AL 35403, **Business Phone:** (205)366-8838.

WHITTAKER, TERRY MCKINLEY
School administrator. **Personal:** Born Mar 14, 1950, Newport News, VA; son of Blanche Sutton and Julius; divorced; married

Beverly. **Educ:** Univ Wis-Madison, BA, 1972; Univ Minn, MA, 1974; MA, educ psychol, 1981; Univ Del, EdD, admin & Policy. **Career:** Youth Coun Bur Brooklyn NY, juvenile delinquent officer, 1973; Univ Minn, pre-major advisor, 1974-76, bus sch coordr stud affairs, 1976-79; INROADS, dir, 1979-83; Univ Delaware, Resources Insure Successful Engrs Prog, dir, 1983-87, dir undergrad advisement & stud serv, 1987-92, Fortune dir, 1991-92, Lerner Col Bus & Econ, asst dean, 1992-2003, asst provost stud diversity & success, 2003-. **Orgs:** Kappa Alpha Psi, 1969-; Am Soc Training & Develop, 1980-; Brandywine Prof Assoc, 1984-; Nat Acad Advising Asn, 1985-; chmn, Region A Nat Assoc Minority Eng Prog Adminrs, 1986-; Del Soc Prof Engrs; Nat Engrs Week Festivities Comn, 1986; Nat Assoc Acad Affairs Admins, 1986; bd dirs, Forum Advan Minorities Eng, 1992-; chair, United Negro Col Fund Sch Campaign, 1995; chair, Educ Div Del United Way Campaign, 1996-2001; MBNA Educ Found, 1997-2006; bd dir, Metropolitan Wilmington Urban League Founding, 2000-; bd dir, Aberdeen Civic Asn, 2001-; trustee mem, Christiana Care Health Syst, 2002-; bd dir, United Way Del, 2003-; Nat Asn Stud Personnel Adminrs; Nat Asn Diversity Officers Higher Educ; Univ's Pillard Soc, Univ Del. **Honors/Awds:** Ivan Williamson Award, Univ Wis, 1972; Twin City Student Assembly Outstanding Contribution Award, Univ Minn, 1979; Commission Service Award, Kappa Alpha Psi, 1982; Minnesota Guidance Associate Award, 1983; Black Alumni Achievement Award, Univ Minn, 1983; Educator of the Year, INROADS Philadelphia Inc, 1985; Faculty Senate Excellence in Undergraduate Advising Award, Univ Del, 2000; Leon and Margaret Slocomb Professional Excellence Award; Outstanding Achiever in Education Award, Brandywine Prof Asn; Outstanding Community Service Award, Aberdeen Civic Asn. **Home Phone:** (302)368-7909. **Business Addr:** Assistant Provost for Student Diversity and Success, University of Delaware, Alfred Lerner College of Business and Economics, 303 Alfred Lerner Hall, Newark, DE 19716, **Business Phone:** (302)831-2551.

WHITTED, EARL, JR.
Lawyer. **Personal:** Born Mar 26, 1931, Goldsboro, NC; married Ruby Weaver; children: Lynn, Stephen, Kenneth. **Educ:** NC Cent Univ, BA, LLB, JD, 1955. **Career:** Pvt Prac, atty, 1970-; Criminal Law Legal Cons Fed Housing Prog, atty. **Orgs:** Goldsboro Bd Aldermen. 1964-; Nat Asn Advan Colored People; Alpha Phi Alpha. **Honors/Awds:** Man of the Yr award, Alpha Phi Alpha, 1970. **Military Serv:** AUS, 1956-58. **Business Addr:** Attorney at Law, 105 S John St, Goldsboro, NC 27533.

WHITTEN, BENJAMIN C.
Educator. **Personal:** Born Jul 25, 1923, Wilmington, DE; married Lucretia Bibbins; children: Benjamin Jr. **Educ:** BS, indl educ; Pa State Col, MS, indl arts educ, 1948; Pa State Univ, EdD, indl educ, 1961; Rutgers Univ; Univ MD. **Career:** Va, training specialist, 1946-67; Carver Voc Tech High Sch, asst prin, 1958-63, indust arts teacher, 1958; Edmondson High Sch, asst prin, 1963-64; Granville Woods Gen Voc Sch, prin, 1964-66; Cherry Hill Jr High Sch, Baltimore, prin, 1966-68; Baltimore City Pub Sch, asst supvr voc educ; Gen Voc Sch, Baltimore, MD, prin. **Orgs:** Bd dir, MD Voc Asn; chmn, Voc Educ Com Coun of Great Cities Sch; chmn, Am Voc Asn Task Force on Voc Educ in Urban Area, 1972-; pres, Nat Asn Large City Dir Voc Educ, 1974-; Gov Man power Adv Comt; Nat Adv Comt; Nat Ctr for Voc Tech Educ Ohio State Univ; Kappa Phi Kappa; Iota Lambda Sigma; Phi Delta Kappa; Pi Omega Chap of Omega Psi Phi. **Military Serv:** AUS, m/sgt, 1943-46.

WHITTEN, DR. CHARLES F. See Obituaries section.

WHITTEN, ELOISE CULMER
Executive. **Personal:** Born Apr 23, 1929, Philadelphia, PA; married Charles F; children: Lisa A & Wanda J Whitten-Shurney. **Educ:** Temple Univ, BA, Polit Sci, 1950; Univ Pa, MA, Polit, Sci, Pub Admin, 1951; Wayne State Univ, Univ Mich. **Career:** Univ Pa Inst State & Local Govt, res asst, 1951-52; Detroit Urban League, dep dir housing dept, 1963-64, dep dir community affairs dept, 1970-71; Wayne State Univ, exec secy, 1966-67; Wayne County Community Cole, instr, 1980; Shaw Col, instr, 1980. **Orgs:** Delta Sigma Theta, 1949-; Planned Parenthood League Detroit, 1959-; Mich County Social Serv Asn, 1963-; Detroit-Wayne County Community Ment Health Bd, 1973-; Wayne County Social Serv Bd, 1974-; bd dir, First Independence Nat Bank, 1983-97; Greater Wayne County Links, 1983-; Mich Dept Ment Health, mem multicultural adv comt, 1985-; Int Planned Parenthood Fed, mem western hemisphere region bd, 1990-; Family Preservation Commun Comt, 1990-; United Community Serv, 1990-; Am Pub Welfare Asn; Nat Conf Social Welfare; Wayne State Univ, mem adv comt sch social work, 1993-; Mich Asn Black Social Workers; Detroit Asn Black Human Serv Adminr. **Honors/Awds:** Sojourner Truth Award, Nat Orgn Black Bus & Prof Women, Detroit Chap, 1980; Mich's Outstanding Black Women, Detroit Hist Soc, 1984; National Business and Professional Women's Award for Social Activism, Dollars & Sense Mag, 1986; Michigan Youth Conference & Youth Advocacy Award, 1993; Partners in Community Services Award, Black Caucus Found Mich, 1993; Michiganian of the Year, 2002. **Special Achievements:** Organized the first area-wide conference on the problems of unwed pregnancy and single parents; helped found Homes for Black Children and changed adoption agency requirements to ease adoption of black children, 1967; developed the Lula Belle Stewart Center, one of the first centers in the country established to provide services for single, African American, low-income women, 1969. **Home Addr:** 14540 Vassar Dr, Detroit, MI 48235, **Home Phone:** (313)864-0991.

WHITTEN, THOMAS P
Administrator. **Personal:** Born Sep 26, 1937, South Carolina; son of Benjamin J and Hattie Brown; married Ruthann DeAtley, Jul 26, 1964; children: Karen, Alexander & Bryan. **Educ:** Lincoln Univ, Jefferson City, MO, BA, 1963; Case Western Reserve Univ, Cleveland, OH, 1964. **Career:** Inner City Protestant Parish, Cleveland, OH, group unit leader, 1962; Chicago Renewal Soc, camp dir, 1963; League Park Ctr, Cleveland, OH, dir youth employ, 1963-64, dir spec interest groups, 1963-65; Int House RI, exec dir, 1965-67; Providence Human Rel Comn, field investr, 1966-67, exec dir, 1970-73; Harriet Tubman House, Boston, MA, 1967-68; Hall Neighborhood House, Bridgeport, CT, assoc exec dir, 1973-77; John Hope Settlement House, Providence, RI, exec dir, 1977-. **Orgs:** City Providence Affirmative Action Comn, 1975; Lippitt Hill Tutorial, Wiggin Village Housing, 1979; Providence Branch Nat Asn Advan Colored People, West End Community Ctr, 1980; Minority Adv Comn; Congresswoman Claudine Schneider; corp mem, Citizens Bank, Vol Action, Deputy Reg State RI, First Unitarian Church Providence, RI; RI Comn Judicial Tenure & Discipline; bd dirs, Decisions Inc, New Haven, CT; Mount Hope Neighborhood Assoc; United Neighborhood Ctrs Am; adv comt, Central High Sch, Hope High Sch, WPRI-TV. **Honors/Awds:** Citizenship Award, City Providence, 1984; Agency Exec Year, Opportunities Industrialization Ctr, 1985; Joseph G LeCount Medal, Providence Branch, Nat Asn Advan Colored People, 1987; Nat Conf Community & Justice, Humanitarian Award, 1998. **Military Serv:** AUS, Lt, 1956-59; Good Conduct Medal, Sharp Shooter, Unit Citation, 1958. **Business Addr:** Executive Dir, John Hope Settlement House, 7 Burgess St, Providence, RI 02903, **Business Phone:** (401)421-6993.

WHITTINGTON, BERNARD M.
Football player. **Personal:** Born Aug 20, 1971, St Louis, MO; married Dana, Feb 14, 1997. **Educ:** Ind Univ, sports mgt. **Career:** Football player(retired). Indianapolis Colts, defensive tackle, 1994-2000; Cincinnati Bengals,defensive tackle, 2001-02. **Honors/Awds:** Rookie of the Year, 1994.

WHITTINGTON, DR. HARRISON DEWAYNE
Educator, college teacher. **Personal:** Born Jun 9, 1931, Crisfield, MD; son of Maryland; married Louise Holden. **Educ:** Morgan State Col, BS, 1952; Pa State Univ, MEd, 1961; Nova Univ, EdD, 1980. **Career:** CG Woodson Sch Crisfield, teacher, 1954-62, prin, 1962-68; Somerset Co Bd Educ, coordr, 1968-70, dir field progs, 1968-70, sch supt, 1988-92; Md State Dept Educ, coordr human rels, from asst supt to supt, 1974-81; Univ Md, Eastern Shore, fac, dir field experiences. **Orgs:** Nat Educ Asn, 1968-70; chmn, Nat Hard Crab Derby Parade, 1971-73; Teacher's Asn, Somerset Co; Md State Teacher's Asn; Md Asn Supvr & Curric Develop; Md Coun Admis Compensatory Educ; Asn Sch Bus Off; Phi Delta Kappa; Am Asn Supvr & Admin; Md Asn Publicly Supported Con Educ; Somerset Co Admin Asn; Omega Psi Phi; Md Adv Coun; Comm Coord Child Care; Md County Family Rels, Mason; bd dir, Somerset Co Head Start; chmn, bd dir, Somerset Co Soc Servs Agency; bd dir, ARC; McCready Mem Hosp; Somerset Co Heart Asn; Rec Comn; pres, Int Asn Basketball Off; Phys Fitness Comn; Com Org Prog; Morgan State Univ Nat Alumni Asn; Athletic Cert Prog, Self-Study Steering Comt, Univ Md, Eastern Shore; Shore up, chmn, 2007; vis bd, Univ Md Eastern Shore; chair, somerset bd educ, 2009-13. **Honors/Awds:** Community Leader of America Award, 1969; Omega City of Year, 1971; Outstanding Education in America, 1973-74; Outstanding Black Community Leader, 1974, 1976; Chancellors Award, UNES, 1978; Omega Man of the Year, 1978; Afro-American of the Year, 1982; Outstanding Citizen; Community Achievement Award, 1985. **Special Achievements:** In 1988 H DeWayne Whittington was made first black superintendent of schools of Somerset County. **Military Serv:** US Infantry, capt, 1952-54.

WHITTLER, DR. THOMAS (TOMMY E WHITTLER)
Educator. **Personal:** Born Sep 27, 1955, Chicago Heights, IL; son of Thomas and Pearl; divorced. **Educ:** Bradley Univ, BA, 1977, MA, 1979; Purdue Univ, PhD, 1985. **Career:** Univ Kent, asst prof, 1985-91, assoc prof, 1991-2001; DePaul Univ, assoc prof mkt, 2001-. **Orgs:** Am Mkt Asn, 1985-; Asn Consumer Res, 1986-; Soc Consumer Psychol. **Honors/Awds:** Great Teacher Award, Univ Kent, 1995. **Special Achievements:** Co-author: Viewer's Reaction to Racial Cues in Advertising, 1991; Model's Race: A Peripheral Cue in Advertising, 2002; author: Viewer's Processing of Actor's Race & Message Claims, 1989; The Effects of Actor's Race Message Claims in Advertising, 1991. **Business Addr:** Associate Professor of Marketing, DePaul University, 1 E Jackson Blvd DePaul Ctr 7521, Chicago, IL 60604, **Business Phone:** (312)362-5418.

WHITTLER, TOMMY E. See WHITTLER, DR. THOMAS.

WHITWORTH, CLAUDIA ALEXANDER
Editor, publisher. **Personal:** Born Nov 7, 1927, Fayetteville, WV; married Clifton B Whitworth Jr (deceased); children: Robyn A Hale, Stanley R Hale, Eva J Crump, B Clifton Whitworth. **Educ:** Bluefield State Col; Nat Bus Col. **Career:** Roanoke Tribune, linotype operator, 1945; Roanoke Tribune, ed, publisher, owner, 1971-; Norfolk State Univ, pres rountable & bd visitors, 1989-95; NY City, Cleveland, Fayetteville Newspapers, linotype operator. **Orgs:** Bd mem, WBRA-TV; Am Red Cross; Roanoke Fine Arts Mus; Mill Mountain Playhouse; bd dir, Roanoke Voc Ed Found, Roanoke Pub Schs; adv bd, Salvation Army; Roanoke Col Constance J Hamlar Mem Fund Comt; League Older Am; Meals on Wheels; Baha'i Faith, Spiritual Assembly; NAACP; YWCA; chair, Employee Rels Comt; Welfare reform Comn; Agency Aging; Bradley Free Clin; Batterer Womens Shelter. **Honors/Awds:** Woman of the Year, Omega Zeta Chap, Zeta Phi Beta, 1982; Nat Coun Criminal Justice BrotherhoodSisterhood Award, 1993; A Tribune to Women of Colour, US Postal Workers, 1997; Roanoke's Citizen of the Year, 2004. **Special Achievements:** Selected Leaders Pictorial Review Yesterday & Today, 1976; Outstanding Serv News Media, 1 of 20 Civic Leaders selected from throughout the State of VA to accompany Gov Linwood Holton to Strategic Air Comm Hdq Offutt NE Roanoke Valley Bus League & Ladies Aux VFW #1444. **Business Addr:** Editor, Publisher, Roanoke Tribune, 2318 Melrose Ave NW, Roanoke, VA 24017.

WHITWORTH, DR. E LEO, JR.
Dentist. **Personal:** Born in Kingston, Jamaica; son of Eabert and Violet; married Jennifer Ann Brown; children: Bianca, Lennox Valencia & Isaac. **Educ:** Northeastern Univ, BA, 1971; Howard Univ, DDS, 1976; Northeastern Univ, MBA, 1994. **Career:** St Anns Bay Hosp, dent surgeon, 1976-77; Comprehensive Clinic Kingston Jamaica, dent surgeon, 1976-77; Pvt Practice, dent, 1977-; Mattapan Health Clinic, dent dir, 1977-79; Harvard Univ, clinic instr operative dentistry, 1981; Whitworth Dent Assocs, dentist, currently. **Orgs:** Am & Nat Dent Asns, 1977-, Metrop Dist Dent Soc, 1977-, Mass Dent Soc, 1977-; pres, William B Price Unit Am Cancer Soc, 1978-80; Commonwealth Study Club, 1979-, Acad Gen Dentistry, 1979-; chairperson, Mass Div Am Socs Conf, "Meeting the Challenge of Cancer in Black Ams", 1980-81; completed post grad course, Mid-Amer Orthodontic Soc, 1983; Int Orthodontic Org, 1986; bd dirs, William B Price Unit Am Cancer Soc; Congressional Adv Bd; life mem, NAACP; Northeastern Univ, corp bd, 1994; bd dirs, Mattapan Community Develop Corp, 1996. **Honors/Awds:** Martin Luther King Community Award, 1994. **Home Addr:** 3 Loew Cir, Milton, MA 02186. **Business Addr:** Dentist, Whitworth Dental Associates, 542 River St, Mattapan, MA 02126, **Business Phone:** (617)298-8200.

WHYTE, AMELIOUS N.
College administrator. **Personal:** Born Mar 15, 1968, Brooklyn, NY; son of Amelious N Whyte Sr and Dorothy. **Educ:** Univ Southern Calif, BS, 1990; Univ Minn, MA, 1997. **Career:** Univ Minn, Stud Develop, assoc to assoc vpres, 1993-2000; Boynton Health Serv, Chem Health Prog coordr, 1995-2000; Bd Regents, asst to exec dir, 2000, asst to chief student affairs officer, currently, chief of staff, Office of Student Affairs, currently; Stud Today Leaders Forever, bd chair. **Orgs:** HOBY, counr, alumni adv, 1995-; Phi Gamma Delta, academic advisr, bd mem, 1998-; Out Front Minnesota, bd mem, 2000-; bd dir, Stud Today Leaders Forever, currently. **Honors/Awds:** Volunteer of Year, HOBY, 1999. **Business Addr:** Chief of Staff, University of Minnesota, Office for Student Affairs, 109 Appleby Hall 128 Pleasant St SE, Minneapolis, MN 55455, **Business Phone:** (612)624-2678.

WHYTE, GARRETT
Educator, artist. **Personal:** Born Sep 5, 1915, Mt Sterling, KY; married Horrezelle E. **Educ:** NC A&T State Univ, BS, art Ed, 1939; Sch Art Inst, Chicago, IL, grad study, 1951. **Career:** Educator (retired); Chicago Defender, artist, 1947-51; Chicago Agency, art dir, 1951-56; Chicago Dunbar Voc HS, art teacher, 1956-72; Chicago City Col System, art prof, 1972-80. **Orgs:** Bd mem, Southside Comm Art Ctr, 1962-85, Nat Conf Artists, DuSable Mus Afri-Am Hist. **Honors/Awds:** Winner of Grand Award, Reg Vocational Exhibit, 1970-72. **Special Achievements:** Creator of cartoon comic "Mr Jim Crow" Chicago Defender, one of the first civil rights graphic satires 1946-51, 2 page color reprod of painting Midwest Mag Chicago Sun-Times in 1965, American Federation of Teachers Magazine Chang Ed "Children of the Ghetto" in 1967, art gallery magazine work reprod in 1968, Black Power in the Arts 1970, Black Dimension in Contemp Amer Art 1971, art work reprod Chicago Sun-Times Magazine "Mid-West", Glory Forever 1974, cover story Chicago Defender Magazine "Accent" 1974, slides and lecture on paintings at Art Institute of Chicago "The Art of Garrett Whyte" in 1975, art exhibitition in Felician College in 1975, painting Wolfson Collection NY Life Institute in 1974. **Military Serv:** AUS, sgt, 1942-45. **Home Addr:** 8648 Kenwood, Chicago, IL 60619.

WICKER, DR. HENRY SINDOS
Physician. **Personal:** Born Aug 8, 1928, New Orleans, LA; married Geralyn; children: Henry Jr & Stephen. **Educ:** Xavier Univ, BS, 1948; Howard Univ, MD, 1953. **Career:** St Elizabeth's Hosp, chief, dept ophthalgy; Am Bd Ophthalgy, dipl; Am Acad Ophthalgy, fel; Howard Univ, asst prof; George Washington Univ, asst prof; pvt prac, currently. **Orgs:** Medico-chirurgical Soc; Med Soc

DC; Nat Med Asn; Am Med Asn; bd dir, Nat Conference Christians & Jews, 1971-75; bd regents, Ascension Acad, 1970-74; bd dir, Mater Dei Sch, 1970-74; Alpha Phi Alpha frat; Sigma Pi Phi Frat. **Military Serv:** USAF, capt, 1957-60; USAFR, maj, 1960-75. **Home Addr:** 4239 Blagden Ave NW, Washington, DC 20011-4253. **Business Addr:** Physician, 5505 5th St NW Suite 303, Washington, DC 20011-6587, **Business Phone:** (202)829-6281.

WICKER, LISA J LINDSAY
Executive. **Personal:** Born in Greenville, MS; married; children: 2. **Educ:** Mich State Univ, BS; Cent Mich Univ, MA. **Career:** LinWick & Assocs, pres & sr consult, currently; 101 Best Companies to Work For in Metropolitan Detroit, founder & chmn, currently; Gen Motors Corp, mgr employee enthusiasm strategies; Wayne State Univ Sch Bus Admin, adj prof; MGM Grand Detroit Casino, vpres human resources. **Orgs:** Historically Black Cols & Univs; Alpha Kappa Alpha Sorority, Inc. **Honors/Awds:** Career Communications Group National Women of Color Professional Achievement Award. **Special Achievements:** First african female to become the vice president of Human Resources at MGM Grand Detroit; one of the most successful business women in Detroit, Detroit News; Auth: The Winning Spirit: Building Employee Enthusiasm. **Business Addr:** Founder & Chairman, 01 Best Companies to Work For in Metropolitan Detroit, c/o Teri Lindsay Fobbs, PO Box 80145, Rochester, MI 48308, **Business Phone:** (248)895-1088.

WICKHAM, DEWAYNE
Journalist. **Personal:** Born Jul 22, 1946, Baltimore, MD; son of John T and DeSylvia Chase; married Wanda Nadine Persons, Jun 1987; children: Vanessa Baker, Zenita & Mikella Nicole. **Educ:** Community Col Baltimore, 1970-72; Univ Md, BSJ, 1974, Cert Afro-Am Studies, 1974; Univ Baltimore, MPA, 1982. **Career:** Baltimore Evening Sun, MD, reporter intern, 1972-73; Richmond Times-Dispatch, VA, copy editing intern, 1973; US News & World Report, Wash, DC, Capitol Hill corresp, 1974-75; Baltimore Sun, MD, reporter, 1975-78; WBAL-TV, Baltimore, MD, talk show host, 1976-89; Gannett News Serv, Arlington, VA, columnist, 1985-; USA Today, columnist, 1988-; Del State Univ, distinguished prof jour, 2001-; Inst Advan Journ Studies, dir, 2001-. **Orgs:** Life mem, NAACP; adv bd, Multicultural Mgt Prog Univ MO Jour Sch, 1986-92; pres, Nat Asn Black Journalists, 1987-89; Alumni Asn Bd, Univ Baltimore, 1989-90; bd visitors & chairperson, Howard Univ Sch Jour, 1992-94. **Special Achievements:** Screenwriter of Judge Not, United Image Entertainment, 1992, author of Woodholme, Farrar, Straus & Giroux, 1995, Fire at Will, published by USA Today Books, 1989, editor of Thinking Black, Crown Books, 1996, author of Bill Clinton and Black American, Ballontine Books, 2002. **Military Serv:** US Air Force, sgt, 1964-68; Vietnam Service Medal; Good Conduct Medal. **Business Addr:** Columnist, Gannett News Service/USA Today, 7950 Jones Br dr 10th Fl, McLean, VA 22107, **Business Phone:** (703)276-5800.

WICKLIFF, ALOYSIUS M., SR.
Lawyer. **Personal:** Born Oct 11, 1921, Liberty, TX; married Mary E Prilliman; children: 4. **Educ:** Am Univ, BS; Catholic Univ Am, LLB, 1949. **Career:** Lawyer (retired); Tex Southern Univ, assoc prof, 1995-58; Fulbright & Jaworski, atty, 1975, partner, 1982; pvt pract, atty, currently; Mc Gowan Wickliff & Asn, atty. **Orgs:** Knights Peter Claver; Eliza Johnson Home Aged Negros; Tex Soc Finance Corp; Tex Finance & Invest Co; Community Chapel Funeral Home; Community Chapel Funeral Benefit Asn; MES-BIC pres Harris Co Coun Orgn, 1975, 76; Bus & Prof Men's Club, 1973; Houston Lawyers Asn. **Honors/Awds:** Community Service Award, 1967; campaign manager, Barbara Jordan US Congress. **Military Serv:** AUS, 372nd infantry, WW II. *

WICKWARE, DAMON
President (organization), automotive executive. **Career:** Bayview Ford Lincoln-Mercury LLC, chief exec officer & pres, currently. **Orgs:** Nat Asn Minority Automobiles Dealers; Mobile Area Chamber; Eastern Shore Chamber Com; Mobile Chamber Com. **Business Addr:** Chief executive officer, President, Bayview Ford Lincoln-Mercury LLC, 27180 Hwy 98, Daphne, AL 36526, **Business Phone:** (251)626-7777.

WIDEMAN, JAMILA
Basketball player. **Personal:** Born Oct 16, 1975, Amherst, MA; daughter of John Edgar. **Educ:** Stanford Univ, BA, political sci, African-Am studies, 1997; NY Univ Sch Law. **Career:** Los Angeles Sparks, basketball player, 1997-98; Cleveland Rockers, 1999; Portland Fire, point guard, 2000; Elitzur Ramla, Israel, 1999-2000. **Honors/Awds:** Named Most Caring Athlete of the Year, 1998. **Special Achievements:** AP All-America, honorable mention, 1996. *

WIDEMAN, JOHN EDGAR
Writer, educator. **Personal:** Born Jun 14, 1941, Washington, DC; married Judith Ann Goldman (divorced 2000); children: Daniel, Jacob & Jamila Ann. **Educ:** Univ Pa, BA, 1963; Oxford Univ, B Phil, 1966. **Career:** Writer, 1966-; Howard Univ, instr, 1965; Univ Pa, instr, 1966-74, Afro-Am Studies Prog, dir, 1971-73, asst basketball coach, 1968-72; Univ Wyo, Laramie, WY, profeng, 1975-86; Univ Mass, Amherst Campus, Amherst, MA, prof eng, 1986; Author: A Glance Away, 1967; Hurry Home, 1970; The Lynchers, 1973; Hiding Place, 1981; Brothers & Keepers, 1984; Reuben, 1987; Sent For You Yesterday, 1983; Brothers and Keepers, 1984; The Homewood Trilogy, 1985; Reuben, 1987, Fever, 1989; Short Stories: Philadelphia Fire, novel,1990; The Stories of John Edgar Wideman, stories, 1992; The HomewoodBooks, 1992; Fatheralong: A Meditation on Fathers & Sons, Race & Society,1994; Two Cities, 1998; Fanon, 2008; writer, currently. **Orgs:** Tour-Europe Near E, 1976; Phi Beta Kappa, 1976; Am Acad Arts & Scis, 1992; bd dir, Am Asn Rhodes Scholars; state & nat selection comt, Rhodes Competition; Nat Humanities Fac; Agenda for Black Power. **Honors/Awds:** Rhodes Scholar, Oxford England, 1963-66; Philadelphia Big Five Basketball Hall of Fame, 1974; PEN/Faulkner Award for Fiction, 1984, 1991; American Book Award, 1990; Benjamin Franklin Scholar Award, Univ Pa. **Special Achievements:** The only writer to have been awarded the PEN/Faulkner Award for Fiction twice; first African American in more than a half-century to earn the important academic award; second African-American to win a Rhodes Scholarship. **Business Addr:** Writer, Houghton Mifflin Co, 222 Berkeley St, Boston, MA 02116, **Business Phone:** (617)351-5000.

WIDENER, WARREN HAMILTON
Government official. **Personal:** Born Mar 25, 1938, Oroville, CA; son of Arnold and Ruby Lee Epperson Brewer; married Mary Lee Thomas; children: Warren Jr, Michael & Stephen. **Educ:** Univ Calif, Berkeley, AB, 1960; Boalt Hall, Univ Calif, JSD, 1967. **Career:** Real Estate Safeway Stores, atty, 1968-70; Berkeley, CA, councilman, 1969-71; Housing & Econ Develop Law Proj, Univ Calif, atty, 1970-72; Berkeley, CA, mayor, 1971-79; CA NHS Found, pres 1977; Urban Housing Inst, pres, 1979; Alameda Co Supvr, 1989-92. **Orgs:** Bd dir, Golden West Fin Corp, 1980-94; bd dir, World Savings & Loan Asn, 1980-94; pres, Nat Black Caucus Local Elected Officials, 1975; bd dir, The Col Prep Sch, 1984; bd dir, Berkeley Repertory Theatre, 1984; bd dir, E Oakland Youth Dev Ctr, 1984. **Honors/Awds:** Dist Citizen Bay Area Urban League, 1975; Chmn, Mayors Del Hungary, 1978. **Military Serv:** USAF, capt, 4 yrs. **Home Addr:** 307 Deer Hollow Dr, Napa, CA 94558, **Home Phone:** (707)258-9770.

WIGFALL, SAMUEL E.
Financial manager. **Personal:** Born May 4, 1946, Jacksonville, NC; married Mildred Z Jones; children: Tara & Darian. **Educ:** NC A&T State Univ, BS Acct, 1969; Univ Louisville, Cost Acct Sys, 1973; Governor's State Univ IL, MBA work, 1978; NY Univ, Capital Inv Acq Sem,1982. **Career:** Brown & Williamson Tobacco Co, financial acct, 1969-73; Johnson & Johnson Corp, sr cost acct, 1973-77; Brunswick Corp, sr financial analy, 1977-79; Sherwood Medical Co, Div Fin Plng & Budget Mgr, 1979-83, nat dealer comn mgr, 1983-. **Orgs:** Scout master Broadway Temple Scout Troop, 1971-72; dir, B&W Employee's Credit Union 1972; advisor Jr Achievement KY, 1972; pres, sr choir Broadway Temple AME Zion Church 1972, 1973; vpres, Richmond Park ILJaycees, 1975; dir, Brunswick Employees Credit Union, 1976. **Honors/Awds:** Varsity football scholarship NC A&T State Univ, 1965-69; parts control procedure manual, Johnson & Johnson Corp, 1972; youth motivation prog, Chicago Asn Com & Ind, 1973-74; pub annual budget manual Brunswick Corp, 1978; Speaking of People, Ebony Magazine, 1984. **Business Addr:** National Dealer Commission Manager, Tyco health Care/Sherwood Medical Company, 1831 Olive St, Saint Louis, MO 63103.

WIGGINS, DR. CHARLES A
Physician. **Personal:** Born Aug 17, 1943, Pennington Gap, VA; son of Rebecca McCarrol and Charlie. **Educ:** Morristown Col, AA, 1963; Fisk Univ, BA, 1965; Meharry Medical Col, MD, 1969. **Career:** Charles A Wiggins MD, med dir; Crestview Nursing Home, med dir; Nashville Manor, med dir; Meharry/Hubbard Hosp, Skilled Nursing Facility, med dir, pvt pract, currently. **Orgs:** Nat Med Asn, RF Boyd Med Scis, Southern Med Asn, NY Acad Sci, Am Geriatrics Soc, Tenn Long Term Physician Soc. **Military Serv:** AUS, Med Corp maj, 2 yrs. **Home Addr:** 3512 Colony Pt W, Nashville, TN 37217, **Home Phone:** (615)361-5304. **Business Phone:** (931)728-7677.

WIGGINS, CHARLIE RAY. See SAADIQ, RAPHAEL.

WIGGINS, DAPHNE CORDELIA
Clergy. **Personal:** Born Oct 21, 1960, Newark, NJ; daughter of Arthur Lee Sr and Thelma G. **Educ:** Eastern Col, BA, 1982; Eastern Baptist Theol Sem, MDiv, 1985. **Career:** Eastern Col, resident asst, 1981-82; Second Baptist Church, Wayne, PA, assoc minister, 1981-84; Yeadon Presby Church, pastoral asst, 1983; Saints Memorial Baptist Church, Bryn Mawr, PA, dir youth ministries, 1984-85; Union Baptist Church, Pawtucket, RI, assoc minister, interim pastor, 1989-90, assoc pastor, currently; Brown Univ, assoc chaplain, 1985-. **Orgs:** Nat Asn Campus & Univ Chaplains, 1985-; univ rep, Soc Organized Against Racism, 1985-; bd mem, Dorcas Place, 1986-88; bd adv, One Church One Child Adoption Prog, I987-; vpres, Soc Organized Against Racism New Eng, 1989-91; vpres, 1987-88, Ministers Alliance RI, treas 1990-; exec bd, Interfaith Call Racial Justice, 1990-; exec bd, Black United Methodists & Related Ministries Higher Educ, 1990-; bd mem, African-Am Ministers Leadership Coun. **Honors/Awds:** Ordination Second Baptist Church Wayne PA, 1983; Recognition of Ordination American Baptist Churches RI, 1987. **Home Addr:** 212 Cottage St Apt 1, Pawtucket, RI 02860. **Business Addr:** Associate Pastor, Union Baptist Church, 904 N Roxboro St, Durham, NC 27701, **Business Phone:** (919)688-1304.

WIGGINS, EDITH MAYFIELD
College administrator. **Personal:** Born Mar 18, 1942, Greensboro, NC; children: Balaam & David. **Educ:** Univ NC, Greensboro, BA, 1962, MSW, 1964. **Career:** College administrator (retired); NC Memorial Hosp, pediatric Clin social worker, 1964-67; Dept Defense Middle Sch, Clark AFB, Phillipines, guidance counr, 1970-71; Int Church Coun Social Serv, social worker,1971-72; Univ NC, dir campus, 1972-, asst vice chancellor & assoc dean stud affairs, 1981-96, interim vice chancellor. **Orgs:** Nat Asn Social Workers; past mem, Chapel Hill Human Rel Comm Order Valkyries Univ NC, 1976; Order Golden Fleece, Univ NC, 1976; Acad Cert Social Workers; Nat Asn Social Workers, 1977-; bd educ mem, Chapel Hill, Carrboro, 1979; mem bd visitors, Univ NC, 2007-, chmn, Local Relations.

WIGGINS, JOSEPH L.
Educator, administrator. **Personal:** Born Feb 13, 1944, Norfolk, VA. **Educ:** State Col, BA, 1966; Old Dominion Univ, MS, 1970, cert adv study educ leadership serv & res; Univ NC, attended 1967. **Career:** Shelton Park Elem Sch, Va Beach, prin, 1974-; Portsmouth City Sch Bd, asst elem sch prin, 1972-74, Admin Coordr Stand Qual & Prog, admin asst to supt, currently; Norfolk City Pub Schs, teacher; Norfolk State Col, asst instr govt. **Orgs:** Sigma Rho Sigma; life mem, Kappa Alpha Psi Fraternity; life mem, Nat Educ Asn; Va Asn Sch Execs; Va Educ Asn; trustee, St Thomas AME Zion Church Norfolk. **Honors/Awds:** Acad Achievement Award, Epsilon Zeta Chap, Kappa Alpha Psi, 1965; Active Chap, Achievement Award, Eastern Prov Coun, Kappa Alpha Psi, 1965; Alumni Serv Fraternity Award, Eastern Prov Coun, Kappa Alpha Psi, 1969; Citation, Leaders Am Elem Educ, 1971; Achievement Educ Award, Eastern Prov Coun, Kappa Alpha Psi, 1973; Outstanding Young Men of Am, 1974, 1975; Achievement Award, Norfolk Alumni Chap, Kappa Alpha Psi, 1974. **Business Addr:** Administration Assistant, Portsmouth City School Board, 2512 George Mason Dr, Virginia Beach, VA 23456.

WIGGINS, LILLIAN COOPER
Business owner, government official, journalist. **Personal:** Born Jun 26, 1932, Cincinnati, OH; daughter of Ben Cooper (deceased) and Fannie Girdy Cooper; married Adolphus (died 1989); children: Karen & Michael. **Educ:** Cortex Peters Bus Sch, attended 1953; Howard Univ, Berlitz Sch Lang Foreign Serv Inst & In Serv Training Sch; USMC Puerto Rico Univ, attended 1957. **Career:** USMC, property & supply off, 1950; Wash DC, Ghana Embassy, 1960-65; Ghana Govt, press & info officer; Wash Afro-Am Newspaper, journalist, past ed; Lil & Face Place, co-owner; Adv Neighborhood Comn, comnr, currently. **Orgs:** Past pres, DC Tots & Teens; pub relations dir, Nat Tots & Teens; talk show hostess "From the Desk of Lil" sta WHUR; former memship chmn, Capitol Press Club; former mem, State Dept Corres Asn; Women Jour; Media Women; appointed DC comn Women Status; roving chair, Orgn Black Activist Women; vpres, Cornelius Wiggins Int Black Owned Bus; appointed, polit action chairperson, DC Br, Nat Asn Advan Colored People; founder, DC Survival Conf; Eagles, Black Entrepreneurs; bd mem, United Black Fund; Sigma Delta Chi; vice chair, DC Charitable Games Control Bd; charter bd mem, DC Lottery, 1981-83; chmn, Indian Acres, currently. **Honors/Awds:** Journalist of the Year, 1965; First Prize National Publishers Convention, 1974. **Military Serv:** USMCR 1957. **Business Phone:** (540)582-6314.

WIGGINS, MITCHELL LEE
Basketball player, basketball coach. **Personal:** Born Sep 28, 1959, LaGrange, NC. **Educ:** Clemson Univ; FL State Univ. **Career:** Basketball player (retired), basketball coach; Chicago Bulls, 1983-84; Houston Rockets, 1984-90; Philadelphia 76ers Rosters, 19991-92; CBA, 1988; Spearfish XBA, head coach, 2002; European Football League, Milon Nea Smirni basketball club; European Football League, Sporting Athens. **Honors/Awds:** US team, World Games in Columbia, 1982. *

WIGGINS, PAUL R
Banker, vice president (organization), president (organization). **Personal:** Born May 19, 1955, Sarasota, FL; son of Paul and Adele; married Cassandra F Robinson, Jul 21, 1984; children: Paula R & Chelsea R. **Educ:** Fla Memorial Col, BS, bus adm, acct, 1981. **Career:** SunBank Tampa Bay, vpres & credit dept mgr, currently. **Orgs:** Omega Psi Phi, 1979-; bd mem, Tampa Bay Urban Bankers ASN, 1986-; Leadership Tampa Alumni, 1988-; Tampa Bay Male Club, chair, 1989-; bd trustees, finance comt, Fla Memorial Col, 1992-; pres, Nat Asn Urban Bankers, 1993-94. **Military Serv:** USY, E-4 specialist, 1973-76; Grad, Non-Comn Officers Acad. **Business Phone:** (813)224-2616.

WIGGINS, WILLIAM H., JR.
Educator. **Personal:** Born May 30, 1934, Port Allen, LA; married Janice Louise Slaughter; children: Wesley Howard & Mary Ellyn.

Educ: Ohio Wesleyan Univ, BA, 1956; Phillips' Sch Theol, BD, 1961; Louisville Prebyn Theol Sem, MTh, 1965; IN Univ, PhD, 1974. **Career:** Lane Col, prof, 1961-62; Freeman Chapel CME Church, pastor, 1962-65; TX Col, dir rel life, 1965-69; IN Univ, grad teaching asst & lectr, 1969-73, asst prof, 1974-79, assoc prof, prof emer, 1980-. **Orgs:** Fel, Folklore Inst IN Univ; found, dir Afro-Am Folk Archive IN Univ; soc reg dir IN Chap Asn Study Afro-Am Life & Hist; Smithsonian Inst African Diaspora Adv Gr Comt; exec bd, Hoosier Folklore Soc; ed bd Jour Folklore Inst; pres, Am Folk life Fest, 1975-76; field work Smithsonian Inst, 1975-76; pres, Asn African Am Folklorists Minister Christian Meth Epis Ch; Am Folklore Soc; Nat Coun Blk Studies; Asn Study Afro-Am Life & Hist; Asn African & African-Am Folklorists; Hoosier Folklore Soc; Pop Cult Asn; Num Grants. **Honors/Awds:** Number grants & fellowships; num pub; doc film "In the Rapture" anthologized weeks appear num publ & jour. **Business Addr:** Professor Emeritus, Indiana University at Bloomington, Department of Folklore, 107 S Indiana Ave, Bloomington, IN 47405-7000, **Business Phone:** (812)856-1172.

WIGGS, JONATHAN LOUIS
Photographer. **Personal:** Born Sep 20, 1952, New Haven, CT; son of Alma Varella and Louis. **Educ:** State Univ New York, Oswego, BA, 1980; Tsukuba Univ, Imbaraki, Japan, attended 1978. **Career:** Raleigh News & observer, staff photogr, 1983-87; St Petersburg Times, lab technician, staff photogr, 1987-90; Boston Globe, staff photogr, 1989-. **Orgs:** Nat Press Photogrs asn, 1980-; Boston Press Photogrs asn, 1982. **Military Serv:** USN, Petty Officer, 3rd Class, 1971-74; Naval Hosp Corpsman, Nat Defense Medal. **Business Addr:** News Photographer, Boston Globe, 135 Morrissey Blvd, PO Box 2378, Boston, MA 02107, **Business Phone:** (617)929-3173.

WILBER, IDA BELINDA
Administrator. **Personal:** Born Feb 8, 1956, Jonesborough, LA; daughter of Clayton Johnson and Rosie B Johnson. **Educ:** Northern Ariz Univ, BS, polit sci, 1978, MA, educ & coun, 1991; Univ Ariz, Col Law, 1978-79. **Career:** Ariz Dept Corrections, New Down Ctr Girls, chief security, 1985-86, New Down Juvenile Inst, prog mgr, 1986-88, Desert Valley, program adv, 1988-90; Ariz Dept Juvenile Corrections, transition adv, 1990, training mgr community serv, 1990-91; Catalina Juvenile Inst, supt, 1991-92; Ariz State Dept Youth Treatment & Rehab, asst chief child care, 1992-; pvt pract, lawyer, currently. **Orgs:** Nat Asn Blacks Criminal Justice, conf chair, 1987, pres, 1989-91, publicity chair, 1991-, nat chair, 1992; United Way, impact spending comn, 1991; bd dirs, Ariz Black Town Hall, res & reports; Am Correctional Asn; bd dirs, Planned Parenthood Southern Ariz; audience participation chair, UNF; state publicity chair & grad adv, ZPB, Omicron Zeta Zeta Chap. **Honors/Awds:** Outstanding Senior Woman, 1978, President's Award, 1978, Mortar Board, 1977-78, Dept Juvenile Corrections, Professionalism Award, 1990, Northern Ariz Univ. **Special Achievements:** Author: Black Adolescents & the Juvenile Justice System in Arizona, 1990; Profile & Status of Black Males in Arizona, 1991; Final Report of Arizona Black Town Hall, Profile & Challenges of Black Policy Makers in Arizona, 1992. **Business Addr:** Lawyer, 7777 E Golf Links Rd, Tucson, AZ 85730.

WILBER, MARGIE ROBINSON
Government official, association executive. **Personal:** Born in Florence, SC. **Educ:** SC State Univ, AB, 1942; Am Univ, grad study, 1955; George Wash Univ, attended 1958; Dept Agr Grad Sch, attended 1966. **Career:** Marion, SC, teacher, 1942-44; Wash State Dept, 1945-83, supvry ed publ div, 1962-83; Neighbourhood Adv Comn, elec comnr, 1976; Crime Stoppers Club Inc, founder & exec dir, currently. **Orgs:** Bd dirs, DC Women's Comn Crime Prev; bd dirs, Woman's Nat Dem Club, 2003; Wash Urban League; Nat Asn Advan Colored People; DC Fedn Bus Prof Women's Club; Delta Sigma Theta Sorority. **Honors/Awds:** Community Service Award, Boy's Club Greater Wash, 1968; Senate Citation, Cong Rec, 1969; US Presidential Citation, 1970; Community Service Award, Sigma Gamma Rho Sorority, 1971; composer, DC-TRIBUTE Nat Capital, 1971; Future Am; Safe C, 1972; Action Fed Employee Distinguished Vol, 1973; Community Service Award, Iota Chi Lambda, 1973; Community Service Award, United Nation's Day, 1973; Outstanding Citizen Award, Capitol Hill Restoration Soc, 1974; Wash Vol Act Award, 1977; Children kinder to each other, 1980; Hon PRS Reagan, Rose Garden, 1985; "Margie Wilber Day", Mayor, DC, 1987; Dedicated Community Service, DC Metrop Police Deptt, 1988; Community Leader of the Year, Kiwanis Club, 1996; Woman of the Year, Shiloh Baptist Church, Wash, DC, 1997; Let's Get Together, Etiquette Zone 2003; "From Whence We Came" Award, Allstate Insurance Co. **Special Achievements:** Appeared as contestant in the National television program "To Tell the Truth," "The Real Margie Wilber," 1968; testimony before the Select CCOM on Crime, House of Representatives, 1970. **Home Addr:** 1366 S Carolina Ave SE, Washington, DC 20003. **Business Addr:** Founder, Executive Director, Crime Stoppers Club Inc, 1366 SC Ave SE, Washington, DC 20003-2371, **Business Phone:** (202)547-7867.

WILBON, JOAN MARIE
Lawyer. **Personal:** Born Aug 21, 1949, Washington, DC; daughter of Louise and Addison; married; children: 2. **Educ:** New York Univ, BA (honors), 1971; George Washington Univ Law Sch, Wash, DC, JD, 1974. **Career:** Dept Labor Off Solicitor, law clerk, 1974; Equal Employment Opportunity Comm, trial atty, 1974-76; Howard Univ Sch Law, supv atty, 1976; Nat Bar Asn, EEO Div, dep dir, 1976-78; Dept Justice, trial atty, 1978-82; Joan M Wilbon & Assocs, atty, 1981-. **Orgs:** Am DC Womens Wash Bar Asns; PA Bar Asn; bd dirs, Intergenerational Theater Co; bd dirs, Coun Court Excellence; trustee, DC Bar Client Security Fund. **Honors/Awds:** Presidential Scholar, Adelphi Univ, 1967; Martin Luther King Scholar, NY Univ, 1969-71; Federal Employee Litigation, Nat Bar Law Jour, 1978. **Business Addr:** Attorney, Joan M Wilbon & Associates, 1120 Connecticut Ave NW Suite 1020, Washington, DC 20036, **Business Phone:** (202)737-7458.

WILBURN, VICTOR H.
Architect. **Personal:** Born Jan 23, 1931, Omaha, NE; son of Katherine and Victor; married Sally (divorced); children: Kim, Diane, Susan, Leslie, Victor, Jeff. **Educ:** Univ Chicago, attended 1954; Harvard Univ, attended 1959. **Career:** Victor Wilburn Assoc Architects & Mgrs, owner, 1962-; Urban Devel Group Inc, pres, 1970-; Univ Va & Howard Univ, prof. **Orgs:** Am Inst Architect; Am Inst Planners. *

WILCHER, SHIRLEY J
Government official. **Personal:** Born Jul 28, 1951, Erie, PA; daughter of James S Wilcher and Jeanne (Evans) Cheatham. **Educ:** Mount Holyoke Col, AB, cum laude, 1973; New Sch Soc Research, MA, 1976; Harvard Law Sch, 1979. **Career:** Proskauer Rose Goetz & Mendelsohn, assoc, 1979-80; Nat Women's Law Ctr, staff atty, 1980-85; US House Representatives Committee Educ & Labor, assoc coun, 1985-90; Nat Assn Independent Cols & Universities, gen coun & dir, state relations, 1990-94; Off Fed Contract Compliance Progs, dep asst secy, 1994, asst secy, 2000. **Orgs:** ABA; Nat Bar asn; Nat Conf Black Lawyers; Interim Exec Dir, Am Asn Affirmative Action, currently. **Honors/Awds:** Special Projects ed, Harvard Civil Rights, Civil Liberties Law, Harvard Law Sch, 1979. **Special Achievements:** Certificate Pratique de Langue Francaise, Paris, 1972. **Business Phone:** (202)349-9855.

WILCOX, JANICE HORDE
School administrator. **Personal:** Born Nov 2, 1940, Baltimore, MD; daughter of Robert Harrison and Gertrude Baker; married Marvin Marlowe, Oct 14, 1972 (divorced); children: Kia Miguel Smith; married Robert Augustus Smith, Feb 8, 1958 (divorced 1968). **Educ:** Coppin State Col, Baltimore, MD, BS, 1965; Pepperdine Univ, Los Angeles, CA, MS, 1976. **Career:** St Croix Pub Schs, VI, teacher, 1965-66; Wash DC Pub Schs, teacher, 1966-68; Los Angeles City Schs, teacher, 1968-73, reading coordr, 1973-75, early childhood educ coordr, 1975-77; CAL Comm Teacher Prep & Licensing, consult, 1977-78; US Dept Educ, prog analyst, 1978-81, educ prog supt, 1983-88, spec asst higher educ progs, 1988-95, chief staff, higher educ progs, 1995-. **Orgs:** Nat Coun Negro Women, 1965-; Nat Asn Advan Colored People, 1968; Nat Urban League, 1970-; Alpha Kappa Alpha, 1974-; League Women Voters, 1978-; Nat Coalition 100 Black Women, 1988-90; founder, Patuxent Women's Coalition, 1987-95, pres, 1990-; Am Asn Univ Women, 1985-; Asn Black Women Higher Educ, 1988-90; La Coterie, 1997-; Links, Inc. **Honors/Awds:** Outstanding Fundraiser, Wilshire Heritage Group, 1973, 1976; Woman of the Year, Calif Women's Asn, 1974; Distinguished Citizen, Jefferson Coalition, 1976; Outstanding Achievement Awards, US Dept Educ, 1984, 1985, 1986, 1989, 1990, 1992, 1993, 1994, 1995, 1997, 1998 & 1999. **Home Addr:** 1001 Spring St Suite 905, Silver Spring, MD 20910. **Business Addr:** Chief of Staff, US Department of Education, Higher Education Programs, Portals Bldg Rm C-80 SW, Washington, DC 20202, **Business Phone:** (202)260-3207.

WILCOX, THADDEUS
Banker, president (organization). **Career:** Southeast Bank; Peoples Nat Bank Com, pres & chief exec officer, 1999.

WILDER, CORA WHITE
Educator, lecturer. **Personal:** Born Jul 31, 1936, Columbia, SC; married Kenneth; children: Michelle, Maxine, Marilynn & Marlene. **Educ:** Howard Univ, attended 1956; Howard Univ Sch Social Work, attended 1958. **Career:** Dept Pub Welfare, WA, DC, child welfare worker, 1958-61; VA Clin, Brooklyn, clin social worker, 1961-63; VA Neuro-Psychiat Hosp, Montrose, NY, 1963-64; Rockland & Co Ment Health Clin, Monsey, NY, psychiat social worker, 1964-67; St Agatha Home C, supvr; Fordham Univ, field work instr, 1967-69; Rockland Community Col Human Serv Dept, asst prof & coord offield instr, 1969; Rockland Comm Col, assoc prof social sci dept, 1984, prof pluralism & diversity, currently. **Orgs:** Secy, Am Fedn Teachers, 1973; dir, Comp Child Welfare Sem Scandinavia; Delta Sigma Theta Sorority; life mem, Nat Asn Advan Colored People; Rockland Negro Scholarship Fund; Day Care & Child Devel Coun Rockland Co; co-hosted radio prog, 1972-75; Rockland Co Cit adv comm, affirmative action comm; United Way, 1972-74, bd dir, 1974-; Rockland Co Bicentennial Comt, 1975; comy person, Rockland Co Dem Comt; gov's appointee bdvisitors, Letchworth Vlg Devel Ctr; co-partner Kenco Art Assoc Art Dist & Cons; consult, Staff Devel & Programming in Day Care & Child Welfare; Nat Conf on Artists; bd dir, Asn Community-Based Artists of Westchester. **Honors/Awds:** Outstanding Leadership Award, Spring Valley Nat Asn Advan Colored People,1972. **Business Addr:** Professor Pluralism & Diversity Department, Rockland Community College, 145 College Rd, Suffern, NY 10901.

WILDER, JASON BARNARD
Interior designer, accountant. **Educ:** Fla A&M Univ; Harrington Col Interior Design. **Career:** Joffrey Ballet Chicago, staff acct; Graystone Home Chicago, interior designer, currently. **Business Addr:** Interior Designer, Graystone Home of Chicago, 2937 N Clerk St, Chicago, IL 60657, **Business Phone:** (773)388-9992.*

WILDER, KURT (KURTIS T WILDER)
Judge. **Personal:** Married Cindy; children: Alycia & Klif. **Educ:** Univ Mich, AB, polit sci, 1981; Univ Mich, Law Sch, JD, 1984; Gen Jurisdiction, 1993; Financial Statements Courtroom, 1993. **Career:** City Cleveland Prosecutor's Off, litigation intern, 1983; First Dist Ct Appeals; Circuit Ct, judge & chief judge; Foster, Swift, Collins & Smith, PC, litigation atty, 1984-89; Butzel Long, PC, litigation atty, 1989-92; Washtenaw Co, 22nd Judicial Circuit Ct, circuit judge, 1992-; State Mich, 1st Dist Ct Appeals, judge, currently. **Orgs:** Exec bd, Legis Comn, Mich Judges Asn; Am Judges Asn; State Bar Mich; fel Mich State Bar Found; Wolverine Bar Asn; Vanzetti Hamilton Bar Asn; Am Bar Asn; chmn, Mich Asn Community Corrections Adv Bds; Am Red Cross, Washtenaw Co Chap, Strategic Planning Comn, bd dirs, Fin Develop Comn, co-chair; bd trustees, Nat Kidney Found Mich; adv bd, Washtenaw Coun Arts; Nat Asn Advan Colored People; secy, Black Child & Family Inst, bd dirs, 1986-89; bd dirs, Ingham Co Bar Asn, 1989-91; human res coun, Ann Arbor Area Chamber Com, 1990-92; vice chair, Corrections Comn, State Mich, 1991; Ann Arbor Citizens Qual Serv Comn, 1992-93; Washtenaw County Bar Asn. **Special Achievements:** First African-Am judge appointed to Washtenaw Co's Circuit Ct, 1992. **Business Addr:** Circuit Judge, State of Michigan, First District Court of Appeals, 3022 W Grand Blvd Cadillac Pl Suite 14-150, Detroit, MI 48202, **Business Phone:** (313)456-0010.*

WILDER, KURTIS T. **See WILDER, KURT.**

WILDER, LAWRENCE DOUGLAS
Government official, educator. **Personal:** Born Jan 17, 1931, Richmond, VA; son of Robert and Beulah; married Eunice (divorced 1978); children: Lynn, Loren & Lawrence Jr. **Educ:** VA Union Univ, BS, chem, 1951; Howard Univ Sch Law, JD, 1959. **Career:** Wilder, Gregory & Assoc, founder atty firm; State of Va: Richmond, state sen, 1969-85; lt gov, 1986-90; Common wealth of VA, gov, 1990-94; Richmond,mayor, 2005-; VA Common wealth Univ, distinguished prof, currently. **Orgs:** Am Bar Asn; Am Trial Lawyers Asn; Va Bar Asn; Am Judicature Soc; Old Dominion Bar Asn; Richmond Trial Lawyers Asn; Richmond Chamber Com; Richmond Urban League; Red Shield Boys Club; Crusade for Voters, NAACP; vpres, Va Human Relations Coun; vice chmn, United Negro Col Fund; past mem, Nat Conf Lt Governors; co-chaired, Wilder-Bliley Charter Comn, 2002; chmn, Gov Mark Warner's Comn on Efficiency & Effectiveness, 2002. **Honors/Awds:** Certificate of Merit, Va State Col, 1974; Hon Doctor of Laws, 1979; Distinguished Alumni Award, VA Union Univ, 1979; Man of the Year Award, Omega Psi Phi; Astoria Benefit Asn Award, Delver Women's Club; Citizenship Award, 4th African Baptist Church; Alumnus of the Year, 1970; Certificate of Merit, 1974; Howard Univ Law Sch, 1970; Civic Award, Omega Psi Phi Third Dist; Civitan Award, Red Shields Boys Club; Three dozen Hon degrees; Nat Asn Advan Colored People Spingarn Medal; Anna Eleanor Roosevelt Medallion of Hon; SCLC Drum Major for Justice Award; B'Nai B'rith's Gt American Traditions Award; Thurgood Marshall Award of Excellence. **Special Achievements:** First black state senator, Va, 1969; Wilder became the first mayor of the city of Richmond, Virginia; first African-American to be elected governor in the US. **Military Serv:** AUS; Bronze Star for Heroism during Korean War, 1952. **Business Phone:** (804)646-7970.

WILDERBRATHWAITE, GLORIA
Physician, Administrator. **Educ:** Howard univ, BS; Georgetown, MD, 1993; George Washington Univ, MPH, 1998. **Career:** Dir, Mobile Health Programs, Children's National Medical Center. *

WILDERSON, DR. FRANK B., JR.
Psychologist, educator. **Personal:** Born Jan 17, 1931, Lutcher, LA; son of Frank Wilderson and Valentean; married Ida Lorraine Jules; children: Frank III, Fawn, Amy, Wayne & Jules. **Educ:** Xavier Univ, BA, 1953; Univ Mich, MS, 1957, PhD, 1962. **Career:** Educator (retired); Orleans Parish Pub Schs, teacher, 1953-57; Univ Mich Child Psychiatric Hosp Sch, teacher, 1957-58; Reading Clin Univ Mich, dir, 1958-61; Out Patient Educ Prog, dir, 1961-62; Univ Mich Sch Educ, lectr, 1960-62; Univ Minn, asst prof to prof asst dean 1962-74, vpres, stud affairs, 1975-90, prof psychol, 1990, prof emer, currently. **Orgs:** Classroom Mgt Withdrawn C, 1963; Minn Psychol Asn; Am Psychol Asn; Coun-Execept C; Coun C Behav Dis; nat adv com Handicapped C; adv com, US Pub Health Serv; nat adv com, Handicapped Childrens Early Ed; chmn, HEW/BEH Panel; Minn Asn Group

Psychotherapy; Minn Asn Brain-Damaged C; Asn Black Psychologist; pub comn, Coun Except C; dir, Bush Found; trustee Breck Col Prep Sch; Phi Delta Kappa; Black Coalition; chmn, Univ Com Develop BA Prog Area Afro-am Studies Pub. **Special Achievements:** Books published like: A Concept of an Ideal Teacheral-Pupil Relationship in Classes for Emotionally Disturbed Children, 1967; An Exploratory Study of Reading Skill Deficiencies & Psychiatric Symptoms in Emotally Disturbed Children 1967. **Business Addr:** Professor Emeritus, University of Minnesota, Educational Psychology, 56 E River Rd 250 Educ Sci Bldg, Minneapolis, MN 55455-0364, **Business Phone:** (612)626-0367.

WILDERSON, THAD
School administrator, psychologist. **Personal:** Born Nov 13, 1935, New Orleans, LA; married Beverly; children: Troy, Dina, Lori & Marc. **Educ:** Southern Univ, BS, 1960, MA, 1968; Tulane Univ, addn psychol courses; Univ Minn, Doctoral candidate. **Career:** Tulane Univ, interviewer/analyst, 1959-69; St James Parish Sch, teacher 1960-65; Orleans Parish Sch, teacher/counr, 1965-69; Juvenile Diagnostic Ctr, counr, 1966; Upward Bound, counr, 1968; Macalester Col, assoc dean students/dir Minority Prog Psychologist, 1969, coordr community rels; psychologist pvt pract, 1970-; Carleton Col, counr/consult, 1971-75; Minn State Dept Educ, consult, 1973-; Thad Wilderson & Assoc, psychologist, currently. **Orgs:** Am Personnel & Guid Asn; Minn Personnel & Guid Asn; Am Psychol Asn; Midwest Psychol Asn; Minn Psychol Asn. **Honors/Awds:** Outstanding Community Service Award, Minn Urban League. **Special Achievements:** Published numerous articles including, "Housing Discrimination in New Orleans", Tulane Univ, 1970; "Impact of Model City Educ Progs upon the Model City Area", 1973; "Techniques for Assessing Minority Students", 1974; "Guidance Under the Knife A Case Study" 1974; "Factors Assoc with Drop Outs of Negro HS Students in Orleans" 1974. **Business Addr:** Psychologist, Thad Wilderson & Associates, 475 Univ Ave W Suite 103, St Paul, MN 55103, **Business Phone:** (651)225-8997.

WILDS, CONSTANCE T.
Educator. **Personal:** Born Jul 22, 1941, Stamford, CT; married Willie E; children: William Ernst. **Educ:** Fairfield Univ, MA, 1972; Wilberforce Univ, BA, 1969. **Career:** Western Conn State Col, Student Affairs Off, dean stud affairs counr com, coordr, 1971-73; Neighborhood Youth Corps, dir manpower; CTE Inc, actg dir, admn asst. **Orgs:** Conn Sch Counr Asn; Am Pub Gardens Asn; Am Personnel & Guid Asn; Asn Black Personal Higher Educ; vpres, Minority Higher Educ; Master Plan Higher Ed; Urban League; Mental Health Asn; Afro-Am Dem Club. **Honors/Awds:** Cert, Am Forum Int Study.

WILDS, JETIE BOSTON, JR.
Government official. **Personal:** Born Jan 10, 1940, Tampa, FL; son of Jetie Wilds Sr and Minnie Lee; married Ozepher Virginia Harris; children: Jemelle, Jeria. **Educ:** Morehouse Col, BA, maths, 1962; Portland State Univ, MS, admin, 1972. **Career:** Government official (retired); USDA Forest Serv, job corps official, 1966-69, personnel mgt specialist, 1970-75, dir civil rights, 1975-86, dir mgt planning, 1986-l989, spl asst agency chief, 1992-94; US Off Personnel Mgt, quality exec, 1989-92; USDA Forest Serv, spl asst to agency chief, 1992-94; USDA Off Secy, deputy dir civil rights enforcement, 1994-96, dir Mgt Serv, 1997; WTMP, "Citizen's Report," host, 1997. **Orgs:** Am Mgt Asn; Am Forestry Asn; Am Soc Pub Admin; Nat Asn Advan Colored People; Omega Psi Phi Frat; Nat Forum Black Pub Adminrs. **Honors/Awds:** Distinguished Alumni Award, Nat Asn Equal Opportunity in Higher Educ, 1986; Outstanding Employee of the Year; Jaycees Man of the Year; Am Bus Women Boss of the Yr. **Special Achievements:** Articles published in National Association of Personnel Workers, Washington State Ed Journal. **Home Addr:** 10405 Green Hedges Dr, Tampa, FL 33626. *

WILES, LEON E.
Educator. **Personal:** Born May 28, 1947, Cincinnati, OH; married Maliaka Johnson; children: Tanzania & Saleda. **Educ:** Baldwin-Wallace Col, cert; Harvard Univ, cert; Yale Univ, cert; Philander Smith Col, BA (cum laude), psychol, 1970; Univ Pittsburg, MEd, 1972; Univ SC-Columbia, PhD, educ admin. **Career:** Slippery Rock St Col, chairperson, 1974-78; Penn State Univ, dir fresh am studies, 1978-82; Univ SC, dean stud, 1982, assoc chancellor stud affairs, vice chancellor stud & diversity affairs; Clemson Univ, chief diversity officer, 2008-. **Orgs:** Phi Delta Kappa; YMCA Black Achievers, Adv Comn; Personnel Asn Bd, SC Col; Progressive Men's Club Spartanburg. **Honors/Awds:** Davis Cup, 1994-95; Progressive Men's Outstanding Achievement Award, 1995; Omega Outstanding Educator, 1996; Piedmont Assembly Outstanding Citizen; Nat Asn Stud Personnel Admin; Spartanburg Repertory Theater Adv Comn; Upstate Diversity Leadership Award, Riley Inst, Furman Univ & Greenville Chamber Com, 2007. **Home Addr:** 201 Powell Mill Rd, Spartanburg, SC 29301. **Business Addr:** Chief Diversity Officer, Clemson University, 109 Daniel Dr, Clemson, SC 29634, **Business Phone:** (864)656-3311.

WILEY, AARON L
U.S. attorney. **Educ:** Univ Calif, Los Angeles; Univ Mich Law Sch, JD. **Career:** Northern Dist Tex, asst US atty, currently. **Business Addr:** Assistant US Attorney, Norther District of Texas, 1100 Commerce St, Dallas, TX 75242-1027, **Business Phone:** (214)659-8600.*

WILEY, CHUCK
Football player. **Personal:** Born Mar 6, 1975, Baton Rouge, LA. **Educ:** La State Univ, BS, pre-phys ther. **Career:** Football player (retired); Carolina Panthers, defensive end, 1998-99; Atlanta Falcons, 2000-01; Minn Vikings, 2002-03; New York Giants, 2004. **Orgs:** Twin Cities community; United Way; Epilepsy Found, Minn; ARC Hennepin-Carver. **Honors/Awds:** Defensive Most Valuable Player. **Special Achievements:** Film Appearance: Hood Rats, 2001.

WILEY, EDWARD, III
Journalist. **Personal:** Born Dec 23, 1959, Baltimore, MD; son of Edward Wiley Jr and B Maye Robinson. **Educ:** Calif State Univ, Fresno, CA, BA, journ, 1984. **Career:** Fresno Bee, CA, staff writer, 1982-86; Rep Tony Coelho, CA, spec asst, 1986-87; Educ Daily, Alexandria, VA, writer, ed, 1987-88; Black Issues Higher Educ, Fairfax, VA, asst managing ed, 1988-93; Children's Defense Fund, ed, 1992-98, managing ed, 1994-97; Nat Wildlife Fedn, 1997-98; US District Ct, deputy monitor, 1998-2002; BET.com, staff writer & managing ed, currently. **Orgs:** Nat Asn Black Journalists, 1988-; Educ Writers Asn, 1990-; life mem, Pi Eta Chi, 1983-; Sigma Delta Chi, 1982-. **Honors/Awds:** Educ Press Asn, Distinguished Achievement Award, series, 1989, feature writing, 1989; Young, Gifted & Black Award, Calif State Univ, 1990; Rosa Parks Meritorious Achievement Award, 1983. **Home Addr:** 3611 Cherryvale Dr, Beltsville, MD 20705-3841. **Business Addr:** Staff Writer, BET.Com, 1235 W St NE, Washington, DC 20018-1211, **Business Phone:** (202)608-2000.

WILEY, FLETCHER HOUSTON
Lawyer. **Personal:** Born Nov 29, 1942, Chicago, IL; son of Fletcher and Mildred Berg; married Benaree Drew Pratt; children: Pratt Norton & Benaree Mildred. **Educ:** USAF Acad, BS, 1965; Univ Paris, L Inst Des Etudes Politiques, attended 1966; Georgetown Univ, MS, Am hist, 1968; Harvard Law Sch, JD, 1974; John F Kennedy Sch Govt, MPP, pub policy, 1974. **Career:** ABT Assocs Inc, consult, 1972-75; Goldstein & Manello PC, sr partner; Fine & Ambrogne, atty, 1975-78; Budd, Wiley & Richlin, PC, atty & managing partner, 1979-89; Wiley & Richlin, PC, atty & pres, 1989-91, dir econ develop & indust corp, 1980-93; PRWT Servs Inc, staff; Fitch, Wiley, Richlin & Tourse, PC, pres, 1991-; PRWT Holdings, pres & chief operating officer; Bingham McCutchen LLP, of coun, currently; TJX Companies Inc, dir, currently. **Orgs:** Assoc comt mem, Mass Alcoholic Beverage Control Comn, 1977-81, 1983-84; bd mem, Dana-farber Cancer Inst, 1978-86; Boston Chamber Com, 1980-; Econ Devel & Indus Corp, 1981-; co-invstr, Unity Bank & Trust Co, 1982; New England Aquarium, 1982-86; chmn, Govt commr, Minority Bus Develop, 1985-; nat pres, Black Entertainment & Sports Lawyers Asn, 1986-; Coolidge Bank & Trust Co. **Honors/Awds:** Recipient of numerous civic and professional awards. **Special Achievements:** Ten Outstanding Young Leaders, Boston Jaycees, 1978. **Military Serv:** USAF, capt, 4 yrs. **Business Phone:** (617)951-8978.

WILEY, FORREST PARKS
Executive. **Personal:** Born Nov 1, 1937, Weldon, NC; married Gloria; children: Joseph, John & Linda. **Educ:** Tuskegee Isnt, BS, 1966. **Career:** Executive (retired); WR Grace, res asst bio chem, 1967-70; New Ventures Inc, dir res, 1970-73; Letterflex Systems WR Grace, syst engr, 1970-73, reg mgr, 1973-75; Harris Corp Dilitho Syst, mgr sls mgr serv mgr. **Orgs:** Pres, Tuskegee Alumni Housing Found, 1977-; bd dir, WA Tuskegee Housing Found; Nat Geog Soc; Bot Soc Am; Am Soc Plant Physiologists; Am Inst Biol Sci; Tuskegee Alumni Asn; pres, Wa-tuskegee Clb; Int Platform Asn.

WILEY, GERALD EDWARD
Executive. **Personal:** Born Jun 20, 1948, Belleville, IL; son of George and Mary; married Marquita Trenier; children: Raymond & Johanna. **Educ:** St Louis Univ, BS, sociol, 1970, MA, urban affairs, 1974. **Career:** Container Corp Am, personnel mgr, 1974-75; Gen Dynamics, employee rels dir, 1975-78; Wiley, Ette & Assoc, vpres, 1978-79; Monsanto Co, dir human resources, 1979-. **Orgs:** Chmn, Howard Univ Cluster Exec Coun, Fla A&M; exec comt, St Louis Univ Billiken Club; bd dirs, Franklin Neighborhood Asn; St Clair County Planning Comn. **Honors/Awds:** Illinois Basketball Hall of Fame, 1977; Metro Area Hall of Fame, 1987; St Louis University Hall of Fame, 1993. **Home Addr:** 13 Towne Hall Estates, Belleville, IL 62223. **Business Addr:** Director, Monsanto Co, 800 N Lindberg Blvd, Saint Louis, MO 63167, **Business Phone:** (314)694-1000.

WILEY, HERLEY WESLEY
Clergy, consultant. **Personal:** Born Dec 16, 1914, Caswell County, NC; married Doris White; children: Howard Wesley & Dennis Wayne. **Educ:** BTh, 1944. **Career:** Clergy (retired); 1st Baptist Church, pastor, 1943-47; Friendship Baptist Church, 1947-53; Forsyth County, mission dir, 1953-55; Zion Baptist Church, 1955, 1964-68; pastor, 1985; Baptist churches, Wash, DC, consult; Covenant Baptist Church, pastor. **Orgs:** Dir coop ministries, Southern Baptist Home Mission Bd, Southern Baptist Conv, 1968-; Budget Comn, Progressive Nat Baptist Conv; exec bd, Lott Carey Foreign Missionary Conv; Coun Chairs Greater Wash; Inter-Faith Comn.

WILEY, JOHN D., JR.
Educator. **Personal:** Born Sep 24, 1938, Fodice, TX; married Clara. **Educ:** BS, 1959; MS, 1960; Univ Houston. **Career:** Dillard Univ, instr, 1960-63; Inst Serv Educ & Advan Study, consult, 1967-70; Tex Southern Univ, asst prof, 1970-79, assoc prof, 1980-, Dept Math, 1989-. **Business Addr:** Professor, Texas Southern University, Department of Mathematics, 3100 Cleburne Ave, Houston, TX 77004, **Business Phone:** (713)527-7580.

WILEY, DR. KENNETH LEMOYNE
Physician. **Personal:** Born Jan 10, 1947, San Antonio, TX; son of Elmer and Dolores Shields (deceased); married Linda Diane Nixon, Jun 29, 1974 (deceased); children: Kenneth Jr & Brian. **Educ:** Trinity Univ, BS, 1968; OK State Univ, MS, 1970; Meharry Med Col, MD, 1977. **Career:** Pvt pract, internal med, 1980-. **Orgs:** Alpha Phi Alpha; Alpha Omega Alpha; Soc Sigma Xi. **Military Serv:** AUS, capt; Bronze Star, Tech Serv Medal. **Home Addr:** 6150 Eastover Dr, New Orleans, LA 70128, **Home Phone:** (504)283-4182. **Business Addr:** Physician, 105 St Rose Ave, St Rose, LA 70087, **Business Phone:** (504)466-6028.

WILEY, LEROY SHERMAN
Government official. **Personal:** Born Oct 30, 1936, Sparta, GA. **Educ:** Ft Valley St Col, BS, 1960; Clark Col, 1968; Univ GA, 1966-69; GA Col, MS 1975-77. **Career:** Ft Valley St Col, supv maintenance dept, 1958-60; Hancock Cent HS, instr dept chmn, 1960-61; Boddie HS, instr, 1963-64; Hancock Cent HS, instr, chmn sci dept, 1964-70; Hancock County, clerk Super Ct, 1970-; Upward Bound Study Ctr, dir, 1973; Learning Ctr, couns asst field rep, 1975; Hancock County Emergency Mgt Agency, dir, coordr, 1984-. **Orgs:** Post comdr Am Legion #530, 1984-85; Mem Kappa Alpha Psi; CB Radio Club Inc; Masonic Orders; Hancock County Dem Club; Hancock County Br Nat Asn Advan Colored People; GA Asn Black Elected Officials; Veterans Asn GA ColMilledgeville; GA Ed Assoc; GA Farm Bur Assoc; Nat Assoc Retarded C; County Officials Assoc GA; comt chmn, BSA; mem, trustee bd St Mark AME Church. **Honors/Awds:** Outstanding Contrib Civil Rights Movement Hancock City, 1982. **Special Achievements:** First black since reconstr & only black serving as clerk of Superior Court. **Military Serv:** Army GA, Nat Guard, 2yrs. **Home Addr:** PO Box 642, Sparta, GA 31087-0642, **Home Phone:** (404)444-7434.

WILEY, MARCELLUS VERNON
Football player, business owner. **Personal:** Born Nov 30, 1974, Compton, CA; children: Morocca Alise. **Educ:** Columbia Univ, sociol. **Career:** Buffalo Bills, defensive end, 1997-2000; San Diego Chargers, defensive end, 2001-03; Dallas Cowboys, defensive end, 2004; Jacksonville Jaguars, 2005-06; Dat Dude Entertainment, owner. **Honors/Awds:** National Defensive Player of Week, Sports Illustrated, 1994; Walter Payton Man of the Year Award, Nat Football League, 2002. **Special Achievements:** Invited to judge the Miss Universe Pageant in Panama, 2003.

WILEY, MARGARET Z. RICHARDSON
Executive. **Personal:** Born Jun 27, 1934, Jackson, NC; married Sampson; children: Brian, Judith. **Educ:** City Col NY, 1956; Scott's Col, Cosmetology, 1965; IN Univ, 1969. **Career:** Summit Labs Indianapolis, educ & mkt dir, 1965-72; Americana Salon, owner; Nat Develop Coun, exec dir, 1972-78; Devco Local Develop Corp, pres, 1973-78; Nat Minority Supplier Develop Coun, exec dir & chief oper officer, 1978-97. **Orgs:** Adv bd Enterprising Women; Revenue Planning Bd Montclair NJ, 1978; NAACP, 1980. **Honors/Awds:** Recipient Outstanding Sales & Outstanding Management & Sales Awards, Summit Labs Indianapolis, 1969-70; Distinguished Achievment Service Award, The Links Inc Seattle, 1976; Mayor Citation, City Baltimore, 1979; recipient Woman's Outstanding Award, Bus NAACP NY, 1980; recipient Woman of the Year Award, Serv & Develop Minority Bus Nat Asn Black Manufactors Wash DC, 1980.

WILEY, MAURICE
Secretary (office). **Personal:** Born Jan 13, 1941, Pine Bluff, AR; son of Hosie Wiley. **Educ:** Univ Ark-Pine Bluff, BS, 1963; Calif State Univ Los Angeles, MA, 1972. **Career:** Pasadena Unified Sch Dist, math teacher, 1966-69; Inglewood Unified Sch Dist, math teacher, 1969-72, guidance counr, 1972-82, coordinated col prep prog, 1982-88, admin asst supt, l989-; Inglewood Unified Sch Dist, career& col adv, currently. **Orgs:** Phi Delta Kappa Educ Frat, 1974-; pres, Inglewood Coun & Psychol Asn,1986; partic, NAFEO Conf Nations Black Col, 1986; partic, UCLA Counr Inst Univ Calif, 1986; Inglewood Mgt Asn, Inglewood Centinela Valley Youth Coun Adv Comn; Inglewood Educ Found, currently; Consult Col Prep Prog & H SCoun; Inglewood Chamber Com Educ Comn. **Honors/Awds:** Outstanding Young Men, Am Pasadena Chamber Com, 1970; Most Eligible Bachelor, Ebony Mag, 1971; Counr & Teacher of the Yr, Inglewood High Sch,1980; Award of Excellence, Inglewood Sch Dist, 1984; Comm Unity Commendation, City Inglewood Calif, 1986; Inglewood Chamber

Com Commendation, 1989; Calif Lottery Millionaires Club, 1989-; Young Black Scholars Role Model of the Yr, 1992; California Lottery's Hero in Education award, 2003. **Military Serv:** AUS, staff sgt, 1963-65; Outstanding Achievement Award, 1965. **Home Addr:** 3823 Lorado Way, Los Angeles, CA 90043. **Business Addr:** College Advisor, Inglewood Educational Foundation, 401 S Inglewood Ave, Inglewood, CA 90301, **Business Phone:** (310)680-5150.

WILEY, MORLON DAVID
Basketball player, basketball coach. **Personal:** Born Sep 24, 1966, New Orleans, LA; married Stacey; children: Jeremiah. **Educ:** Calif State Univ, Long Beach, CA, attended 1988. **Career:** Basketball player (retired), basketball coach; Dallas Mavericks, 1988-89, 1992-93, 1994-95, player develop staff, 2000-04; Orlando Magic, 1989-92, asst coach, 2004-; San Antonio Spurs, 1991; Atlanta Hawks, 1991-93, 1995; Miami Heat, 1994. **Business Addr:** Assistant Coach, Orlando Magic, 8701 Maitland Summit Blvd, Orlando, FL 32810, **Business Phone:** (407)916-2400.

WILEY-PICKETT, GLORIA
Government official. **Personal:** Born Jul 5, 1937, Detroit, MI; daughter of Elmer and Fannie Smith; divorced; children: Michele Joy. **Educ:** Detroit Inst Tech, attended 1956; Wayne State Univ, attended 1982. **Career:** Government official (retired); US Dept Defense, acct tech, fed women prog coordr, 1971-73, supvr procurement asst, 1973-75; US Dept Labor & ESA/OFCCP, equal opportunity specialist, 1975-81, supvr equal opportunity specialist, asst dist dir, 1995. **Orgs:** Sub comn, SE Mich March Dimes Fashion Extravaganza, 1971; Nat Asn Human Rights Workers, 1981; Nat Asn Female Execs Inc, 1983-; treas, DGL Inc, 1984-86; bd dirs, Mich Chap NAHRW, 1989; chairperson, Prog Comt, Am Bus Womens Asn, Spirit Detroit Chap, 1985; Founders Soc, Detroit Inst Arts; Nat Asn Human Rights Workers; Nat Asn Female Execs Inc; Nat Asn Advan Colored People. **Honors/Awds:** Letter Commendation Performance DOD DLA DCASR; Special Achievement Award, Outstanding Contributions EEO Prog, Dept Defense DLA DCASR. **Home Phone:** (248)353-0269.

WILFONG, HENRY T
Association executive, president (organization), accountant. **Personal:** Born Feb 22, 1933, Mount Olive, AR; son of Henry T Wilfong Sr and Geraldine; married Aline Jane Guidry; children: Bernetta & Brian. **Educ:** Univ Calif Los Angeles, BA, 1958, MBA, 1960. **Career:** Nat Asn Minority CPA Firms, pres, 1971; CA city councilman, 1973; Wilfong & Co, sr partner; Minority Small Bus/Capital Ownership Develop, Small Bus Admin, assoc admin; Nat Asn Small Disadvantaged Bus, pres, currently. **Orgs:** Calif Coun Criminal Justice, 1974; bd dir, Nat Bus League; bd dir, Calif Soc CPA'S; Bush-Cheney Transition Team-SBA Adv Group; Dept Energy, Small Bus Adv Comt; Nat Coun Policy Review-Black Capitalism; Presidential Task Force Int Pvt Enterprise; NASA Adv Coun; chair, NASA Minority Bus Resource Adv Comt. **Honors/Awds:** 10 Top Minority Bus Year Award, 1972; Fred D Patterson Award, 1974; Lifetime Achievement Award, Asian-Am Bus Roundtable, 2004. **Special Achievements:** 91st African American CPA in United States; first African American to receive MBA form UCLA-1960. **Military Serv:** AUS, S/sgt, 1954-56. **Business Addr:** President, National Association of Small Disadvantaged Businesses, 5520 Waters Dr, Savannah, GA 31406.

WILFORD, GLORIA GANTT
Research scientist. **Personal:** Born May 23, 1945, Charleston, SC; married. **Educ:** Hampton Inst, VA, BA, biol, 1965, Med Univ SC, Charleston, MS, 1972. **Career:** US Naval Res Lab, WA, DC, tech librn, 1965-69; Burke High Sch, Charleston, teacher, 1969-70; Dept Med & Dept of Basic Clinical Immunol & Microbiol, res scientist, 1974-78; Med Univ SC, Dept Neurochem Med, Charleston, res scientist, 1978. **Orgs:** Am Soc Microbiol; Choraliers Music Club, Charleston; Hampton Alumni Asn, Charleston; YWCA; Morris St Baptist Church, Charleston; Alpha Kappa Alpha, 1963-. **Honors/Awds:** Pub sci paper on Immunologic Responses Assoc with Thoracic Duct Lymphocytes. *

WILFORK, ANDREW LOUIS
Government official. **Personal:** Born Apr 27, 1947, Quitman, GA; children: Jermaine. **Educ:** Fla Int Univ, BS, social work, 1974. **Career:** Metro-Dade County Waste Dept, serv rep, 1971-72, enforcement officer to coordr, 1972-74, area supvr, 1974-78; Miami Dade County Pub Works Dept, transfer sta, 1978-80, supvr transfer sta admin, 1980-86, supt, 1986-, Dept Solid Waste Mgt, dir, currently. **Honors/Awds:** Certificate of Recognition, Peabody Solid Waste Mgt, 1979; Certificate for Valuable and Distinguished Service to the State of Florida. **Military Serv:** AUS, sgt, 3 yrs. **Business Addr:** Director, Miami Dade County, Department of Solid Waste Management, 8675 NW 53rd St Suite 201, Miami, FL 33166-4598, **Business Phone:** (305)594-1520.

WILHOIT, CARL H.
Engineer. **Personal:** Born Aug 15, 1935, Vandalia, MO; married Daisy Glascoe; children: Raquel, Marcus. **Educ:** Lincoln Univ, 1960; Howard Univ, BS, 1962; Catholic Univ, 1973. **Career:** New Town Devel DC Dept Housing & Community Develop, engr coordr; DC Dept Highways & Traffic, civil engr, 1962-67; Dept Civil Engg Fed City & Col Washington DC, lectr, 1975-76. **Orgs:** ASCE; Nat Asn Housing & Redevelop Officials, 1971; Nat Soc Prof Engrs, 1977. **Military Serv:** USAF, a & 1c, 1955-58.

WILKENS, LEONARD RANDOLPH (LENNY WILKENS)
Basketball coach, basketball player. **Personal:** Born Oct 28, 1937, Brooklyn, NY; son of Henrietta Cross Wilkens and Leonard R Wilkens; married Marilyn J Reed, Jul 28, 1962; children: Leesha, Randy & Jamee. **Educ:** Providence Coll, BA, econ, 1960. **Career:** Basketball player (retired), basketball coach; St Louis Hawks, 1960-68; Seattle Super Sonics, player & coach, 1968-72; Cleveland Cavaliers, 1972-74; Portland Trail Blazers, player, 1974-75, coach, 1975-76; Seattle Super Sonics, head coach, 1977-85, gen mgr, 1985-86, vchmn, 2006, pres basketball opers, 2007; Cleveland Cavaliers, head coach, 1986-93; Atlanta Hawks, head coach, 1993-2000; Toronto Raptors, head coach, 2000-03; NY Knicks, head coach, 2004-05. **Orgs:** Hon chmn, Mary mount-Cavs RP Golf Classic, 1987-; chair, Make-a-Wish Golf Tournament, 1988; Boys & Girls Clubs, Greater Cleveland; Catholic Diocese, Cleveland; Rainbow Babies; Children's Hospital; Kidney Found; NBA Players Asn, vp, 1961-69; NBA Coaches Asn, pres. **Honors/Awds:** National Invitation Tournament, Most Valuable Player, 1960; Rhode Island Heritage Hall of Fame, 1961; NBA All-Star Game, Most Valuable Player,1971, representative, 1973; coached Seattle Super Sonics to NBA Championship, 1979; City of Hope Sportsman of the Year, Congressional Black Caucus Coach of the Year, CBS Coach of the Year, Black Publisher of America Coach of the Year, 1979; hon doctor of humanities, Providence Col, 1980; Urban League-Witney Young Outstanding Citizen Award, 1980; Golden Shoe Award, Shoes for Kids, 1988; Digital NBA Coach of the Month, December, 1988; enshrined in the Naismith Memorial Basketball Hall of Fame, 1990; All-Star; Baset ball Weekly, Coach of the Year; City of Hope/Sport Magazine, Victor Award, 1994; IBM/NBA Coach of the Year, 1994; Most Outstanding Player in the New England Area, 1960, 1961; NIT-NIKE Hall of Fame; NYC Basketball Hall of Fame; Brooklyn Hall of Fame; US Olympic Basketball Team, Atlanta, head coach, 1996; Basketball Hall of Fame, coach, 1998; hon doctorates: Providence Univ, 1988; Seattle Univ, 1995. **Special Achievements:** United States Olympic Men's Basketball Team, asst, 1992, coach, 1996; Winningest coach in NBA history; participated in more games as player and/or head coach than anyone else in league history; winningest coach in Cleveland history, 1992-93; autobiography, Unguarded: My Forty Years Surviving in the NBA; One of the 50 Greatest Players in NBA History 1996. **Military Serv:** AUS, Qm Corps, second Lt, 1961-62.

WILKERSON, BRUCE ALAN
Football player. **Personal:** Born Jul 28, 1964, Loudon, TN; married Antionette; children: Starkicia & Jeremy. **Educ:** Univ Tenn. **Career:** Los Angeles Raiders, tackle, 1987-94; Jacksonville Jaguars, 1995; GreenBay Packers, 1996-97; Oakland Raiders, 1998; Aluminum Co Am, staff.

WILKERSON, DANA
Basketball player, actor. **Personal:** Born Feb 27, 1969. **Educ:** Long Beach State Univ. **Career:** Long Beach Stingrays, guard, 1997-98. Film: Slam City with Scottie pippen, 1994. *

WILKERSON, HON. DIANNE
State government official, senator (u.s. federal government). **Personal:** Born in Arkansas. **Educ:** Am Int Col, BS, Public Admin, 1978; Boston Col Law Sch, JD, 1981. **Career:** State Mass, state sen, 1993-2008. **Orgs:** Convener, Annual Twenty First Century Black Mass Conf; co-chair, Hynes Conv Ctr; Boston Common Parking Garage Legis Comn; Steering Comm for Lawyers Comm for Civil Rights under Law; bd mem, Action for Boston Community Develop; Delta Sigma Theta Sorority Inc; Morning Star Baptist Church; Comn to Eliminate Racial & Ethnic Health Disparities; chair, State Admin & Regulatory Oversight; vice chair, Joint Comm Financial Servs; Senate common Ways & Means; Bonding, Capital Expenditures & State Assets Educ; Ment Health & Substance Abuse; adv bd mem, Asian Am Civic Assoc; ex-officio mem, Boston State Hosp Citizens Adv Committe; Caucus of Women Legis, NE Univ Community Task Force; Roxbury Strategic Master Plan Oversight Committee. **Special Achievements:** First African-Am female to hold senate seat for Mass; First African American female to obtain a partnership in a major Boston law firm; Highest-ranking Black elected official in the Commonwealth of Massachusetts; Attended Nat meetings & appeared on local news affiliates of CBS, NBC and ABC News, Urban Update, New England Cable News, Crossfire, The Group and BET.

WILKERSON, PROF. MARGARET BUFORD
Educator. **Personal:** Born Apr 3, 1938, Los Angeles, CA; daughter of George and Gladys; married Stanley; children: Darren, Cullen & Gladys-Mari. **Educ:** Univ Redlands, BA, hist (magna cum laude), 1959; Univ Calif Los Angeles, Teachers Cred, 1961; Univ Calif, Berkeley, MA, dramatic art, 1967, PhD, dramatic art, 1972. **Career:** YWCA, Youngstown Ohio, adult prog, dir, 1959-60; YWCA, Los Angeles, dir, 1960-62; Jordan High Sch, Los Angeles, Calif, drama & eng teacher, 1962-66; Eng Dept Dramatic Art Dept, lectr, 1968-74; Univ Calif, Berkeley, Dept Afro-Am Studies, lectr, 1976-83, Ctr Study Educ & Adv Women, dir, 1975-83; Am Coun Educ, Kellogg lectr, 1980; Univ Calif, Berkeley, African Am Studies Dept, prof & chair, 1988-94, Dramatic Art Dept, Ctr Theater Arts, chair & dir, 1995-98, prof emer, currently; Ford Found, dir media arts & prog officer, 1998. **Orgs:** Ford fel, Dissertation Ford Found, 1970, Nat Res Coun, 1983-84; Berkeley Black Alumni Club, Univ Calif, 1976; Am Theatre Asn, Black Theatre Prog, 1979-85; Bus & Prof Womens Found, 1983; Am Coun Educ, Nat Identification Prog Women Admins, 1980; Nat Res Coun humanities, Doct Comm, 1983; Calif Arts Coun, 1984; Nat Coun Negro Women; Black Alumni Club, Univ Calif, Berkeley; Nat Asn Advan Colored People; Kumoja Players, 1971-75; San Francisco Theological Seminary, 1987-97; Asn Theatre Higher Educ, chair, Awards Comn, 1996-98. **Honors/Awds:** DHL, Univ Redlands, 1980; Rockefeller Found, 1982-83; Honoree, Equal Rights Advocates, 1989; Award for Exemplary Educational Leadersip / BlackCaucus Am Asn Higher Educ, 1990; Profile Excellence, KGO-TV, San Francisco, 1990; Career Achievement Award for Outstanding Educator, Am Theatre Asn, 1996; Black Theatre Network Lifetime Memorial Award. **Special Achievements:** Co-author: Black Scholar theatre issue & other publs; author of "9 Playsby Black Women" New American Library 1986. **Home Phone:** (510)215-0609. **Business Addr:** Professor Emeritus, University of California, Department of African American Studies, 660 Barrows Hall Suite 2572, Berkeley, CA 94720, **Business Phone:** (510)642-7084.

WILKES, JAMAAL
Consultant, basketball player. **Personal:** Born May 2, 1953, Berkeley, CA. **Educ:** Univ Calif, LA, 1974. **Career:** Basketball player(Retired), Broker: Golden State Warriors, 1975-77, Los Angeles Lakers, 1978-85, Los Angeles Clippers, 1985-86; Prof Designation, Investment Real Estate; CAL Real Estate Broker; CAL Ins Agent & Broker. **Orgs:** Los Angeles Urban League bd dirs; bd dirs, Western Region United Way; bd trustees, UCLA Found; bd governors, LA Athletic Club. **Honors/Awds:** All Star Team, 1976, 1981, 1983; 4 time NBA World Champion; 2 time NCAA Basketball & Scholastic All-Am; UCLA Athletic Hall of Fame; GTE Academic Hall of Fame, inductee, 1990; Boys & Girls Club America, Natl Hall Fame,Inducted; Award General BUS Studies. **Special Achievements:** Series 7 & 63 Securities Licenses. *

WILKES, REGGIE WAYMAN
Football player, entrepreneur. **Personal:** Born May 27, 1956, Pine Bluff, AR. **Educ:** GA Tech Univ, BS, biol, 1978; Morehouse Sch Med. **Career:** Football player (retired), exec; Philadelphia Eagles, Linebacker, 1978-85; Atlanta Falcons, 1986-87; GS Capital LP, founder, currently; Pro-Cap LLC, pres, 1999-.

WILKES, DR. SHELBY R
Ophthalmologist. **Personal:** Born Jun 30, 1950, Crystal Springs, MS; married Jettie M Burnett; children: Martin & Andrew. **Educ:** Alcorn State Univ, BS (Summa Cum Laude), 1971; Johns Hopkins Univ, Sch Med, MD, 1975. **Career:** Univ Rochester, Sch med, Dept Surg, intern-resident, 1975-76; Mayo Clinic, resident, 1977-79; MA Eye & Ear Infirmary, fel retina serv, 1980-81; Univ Ill, Eye & Ear Infirmary, res fel, 1976; Harvard Univ, Sch Med, clinic asst ophthalmology, 1982-83; Emory Univ, Sch Med, asst prof ophthalmology; Morehouse Sch Med, Atlanta, GA, asst clinic prof, dept surg; vitreoretinal surgeon, ophthalmologist; Atlanta Eye Consults, pres, currently. **Orgs:** Alpha Phi Alpha, NAACP, Atlanta Med Asn, Ga State Med Asn, Asn for Res in Vision & Ophthalmology 1978-, Am Med Asn, 1978-; fel, Am Acad Ophthalmology 1981-; Nat Med Asn, 1981-; bd dir, Am Diabetes Asn, Ga Affiliate Inc, 1985. **Honors/Awds:** Hons Soc, Alcorn State Univ, 1970-71; Ophthalmic Alumni Award, Mayo Clinic, 1980; Distinguished Alumni Citation, Nat Asn Equal Opportunity Higher Educ, 1985. **Special Achievements:** Wrote papers: with E S Gragoudas, "Regression patterns of uveal melanomas after proton beam irradiation" Ophthalmology, 1982 89,7 p840; with M Beard, D M Robertson & L Kurland "Incidence of retinal detachment" Rochester MN Amer Journal of Ophthalmology, 1982. **Home Addr:** 3215 Cascade Rd SW, Atlanta, GA 30311. **Business Phone:** (404)881-6417.

WILKIE, EARL AUGUSTUS T
School administrator, counselor. **Personal:** Born Mar 15, 1930, Philadelphia, PA; son of Roland and Evelyn. **Educ:** Cheyney Univ, BS, educ, 1961; Temple Univ, educ media, 1975; Univ Pa, MFA, 1978; Philadelphia Col Arts, sculpture workshop, 1979; Fleisher Mem, ceramics, 1982; Westminster Theol Sem, relig study, 1985. **Career:** Elwyn Inc, dir voc training, 1962-65, dir adult educ progs, 1965-69, Jr & Sr High Sch Work Study Prog, 1964-75, Progs & Residential Serv, coordr, 1977-80, Am Inst, exec dir, 1981-84; Horizon House, dir voc rehab, 1985; United Rehab Serv, dir oper, 1986, Out-Patient Dept, Child Guid Dept, dir, 1987; Child Stabilization Ctr, dir, 1990;, Jerusalem Elwyn Inst, Millie Shiam Ctr, Swedish Village, Jerusalem, Israel, consult, 1991; Pa Inst Tech, counr & admin; Vineland Training Sch, exec dir; consult, currently. **Orgs:** Exec comt mem, Nat Conf Artists, 1982; sponsor, Philadelphia Coun Arts, City Philadelphia, 1988-89; exec dir, Allens Lane Art Ctr Visual & Performing Arts, 1989. **Honors/Awds:** First Prize, Afro-Am Mus, Philadelphia, 1980; Certificate

of Appreciation, Exchange Club, Vineland, NJ, 1982; Appreciation award, United Rehab Serv, 1985; Fulbright Fellowship Grant. **Special Achievements:** Publications: Guidelines for Developing Individual Habilitation Plan, designer, "Something Is Wrong", Trends Jour Resources, United Presby, 1970. **Military Serv:** USAF, 1951-55. **Business Addr:** Consultant, 2734 Island Ave, Philadelphia, PA 19153, **Business Phone:** (215)724-3036.

WILKINS, ALLEN HENRY
Educator, consultant, landscape architect. **Personal:** Born May 23, 1934, Elberton, GA; son of William and Mattie Lue Allen; married Jean E (divorced). **Educ:** Tuskegee Inst, BS, 1957; Catholic Univ, MS, 1973. **Career:** Educator (retired); Wash DC Govt, Dept Highways, horticulture inspector, 1961-69; Navy Facilities Engrs, landscape architect, gen engr, 1969-73; Univ Dist Columbia, prof horticulture & landscape design. **Orgs:** Licensed landscape architect State MD; Amer Soc Landscape Architects; vpres, Wash DC Nat Educ Asn, 1982-84; AmHorticulture Scientists, 1986; Alpha Psi Alpha; chmn, deacon bd, choir mem, Wash DC Plymouth Congregational Church; Tuskgee Airmen. **Honors/Awds:** Public Service Award, Wash DC Govt, 1960; Citation for Pub Serv, Mayor City Greenbelt, MD, 1985. **Special Achievements:** First Black horticultural inspector for Washington DC Govt. *

WILKINS, BETTY
Journalist, editor. **Personal:** Born Mar 31, 1922, Braddock, PA; married; children: Gloria, Raymond, Robert Jr, Donald, Margaret, Patricia. **Educ:** Denver Opportunity Sch Jour, attended 1957. **Career:** KFML Radio, 2 hr gospel show; KC Call, Denver ed; KDKO Radio, soc columnist with Honey Bee's show; Negro Weekly, assoc ed & soc ed; Denver Weekly News, ed. **Orgs:** Pres, Sophisticates & Soc & Civ Club; vpres, Astro Jets; secy, Pond Lily; Jane Jefferson Dem Club; Mayors coun human relations; Bronze Dau Am; State Asn Colored Womens Clubs; Coun Negro Women; CO Spress Womens Club; black del Geo McGovern from Denver to Miami 1972; comt woman, E Denver, 20 yrs; res, Delta Mothers Club; Zion Circle Seven; The Denver Beauty Guild; life mem & pub rel chmn, Nat Asn Advan Colored People. **Honors/Awds:** Syl Morgan Smith Comt Award Trophy, 1976; Pub Relation Award, Astro Jets, 1977; Originator of "Ten Best Dressed Black Women" Denver; Miss Bronze Dau Award, 1958; Robert L Vaden Award, 1972; Harriet Tubman Dist Serv Award, 1973; Women of the Year, 1972; Comt Award, Metro Club, 1979; Hall of Fame Award, May D & F, 1980.

WILKINS, CHARLES O
Management consultant. **Personal:** Born Jun 18, 1938, Louisville, KY; married Diane Blodgett, Jun 19, 1975; children: Nicole & Jennifer. **Educ:** Central State Univ, Wilberforce, OH, BA, 1961; Univ Calif, Grad Sch, Los Angeles, CA, 1963. **Career:** Johnson & Johnson, Raritan, NJ, supvr, employment, 1965-72; The Singer Co, New York, NY, mgr, world headquarters personnel, 1972-80; NYS Urban Develop Corp, New York, NY, vpres, human resources, 1980-84; Performance Plus Mgmt Consulting, E Brunswick, NJ, pres, 1984-; vpres, human resources, YMCA, Greater New York, 1991-. **Orgs:** Alpha Phi Alpha, 1958-; Sigma Pi Phi (Boule), 1987-; Am Soc Personnel Admin, 1991-; Urban League BEEP; bd mem, Health Watch; NJ Philharmonic Orchestra. **Military Serv:** USY, first Lt, 1963-65. **Business Addr:** Vice President of Human Resources, YMCA of Greater New York, 333 7th Ave 15th Fl, New York, NY 10001, **Business Phone:** (212)630-9615.

WILKINS, DAVID BRIAN
College teacher, educator. **Educ:** Harvard Col, BA, 1977; Harvard Law Sch, JD, 1980. **Career:** US Ct appeals Second Circuit Law, clerk to hon chief judge, 1980-81; US Supreme Ct, law clerk to hon Thurgood Marshall, 1981-82; Nussbaum, Owen & Webster, assoc specializing Civil Litigation, 1982-86; Harvard Univ, fel, 1989-90; Ctr Ethics & the Prof, fac assoc, 1990-; Prog Legal Prof, dir, 1991-; Univ Chicago Law Sch, vis prof, 1995; Thurgood Marshall Lectr; Pope & John Lectr; Frankel Lectr; Wythe Lectr; Martin Luther King Day Lectr; Van Arsdell Lectr; Allen Siegel Lectr; Arthur W Fiske Lectr; Iredell Lectr; WM Keck Lectr; Tanner Lectr; The Robert D & Leslie Kay Raven Lectr; Stuart Rome Lectr; Lynn J Gould Mem Lectr; Francis X Reilly Lectr; Prog Lawyers & Prof Serv Indust, dir, 2004-; Harvard Law Sch, Kirkland & Ellis Prof Law, 1996; Lester Kissel Prof of Law, 2008. **Orgs:** Judicial Conf US Ct Appeals DC Circuit, 1984; Judicial Conf US Ct Appeals Second Circuit, 1988; Am Asn Law Sch, 1991-93; bd dir, Law & Soc Asn, 1994-97; vis resr, Am Bar Found, 1995; sr resr, Am Bar Found, 1997-; Am Bar Asn; Open Soc Inst, 1998-2000; bar mem, Dist Columbia; US Dist Ct DC. **Honors/Awds:** Albert M Sacks-Paul A Freund Award, Teaching Excellence, 1998; Iredell Lect, Univ Eng, 2000; Arthur W Fiske Lect, Case Western Reserve Sch Law, 2001; Wythe Lect, William & Mary Sch Law, 2002; Martin Luther King Day Lect, Seattle Bar Asn, 2002; Van Arsdell Lect, Univ Ill Sch Law, 2002; Allen Siegel Lect, Duke Law Sch, 2002; Frankel Lect, Univ Houston Law Ctr, 2003; Thurgood Marshall Lect, Roger Williams Sch Law, 2004; Pope & John Lect, N western Law Sch, 2004. **Special Achievements:** Six African-American tenured professor at Harvard Univ; Published: The Black Bar: The Legacy of Brown v Board of Education and the Future of Race & the American Legal Profession; Problems in Professional Responsibility for a Changing Profession; Published numerous articles & books. **Business Addr:** Professor, Harvard School of Law, 1563 Mass Ave, Hauser 312, Cambridge, MA 02138, **Business Phone:** (617)495-0958.

WILKINS, GERALD BERNARD
Basketball player. **Personal:** Born Sep 11, 1963, Atlanta, GA; married Vita; children: Jasmine Alexandria & Holli Dai. **Educ:** Moberly Area Jr Col, Moberly, MO, 1982; Univ Tenn-Chattanooga, Chattanooga, TN, 1985. **Career:** Basketball player (retired); New York Knicks, guard, 1985-92, Cleveland Cavaliers, 1992-95; Vancouver Grizzlies, 1995-96; Orlando Magic, 1996-99.

WILKINS, HERBERT PRIESTLY
Executive. **Personal:** Born Jan 9, 1942, Boston, MA; son of William Wilkins and Katherine; married Sheran R Morris; children: Herbert Jr, Monique & Michelle. **Educ:** Boston Univ, BS, 1965; Harvard Univ, Grad Sch Bus Admin, MBA, 1970. **Career:** Lucas, Tucker & Co, prin, 1969-73; Urban Nat Corp, sr vpres, 1973-75; Wilkins & Co, consult, 1975-77; Syndicated Communs Inc, Wash, DC, pres, 1977-89; Syncom Mgt Co Inc, pres, 1977-89, chmn & shareholder, currently; Synsom Group Venture Capital Funds, Wash, DC, managing gen partner, 1990-; Ariz Radio Inc, pres, owner; KMIK Fm Phoenix, AZ, owner; Allur Kansas Inc, pres; KNRX-FM Kans City, KS, owner; Lyn Commun Corp, pres; K QA Citronelle, AL, owner. **Orgs:** Mem, bd overseers, Harvard Community Health Plan Boston, 1973-83; former chmn bd, Nat Asn Investment Co, 1979-83; pres, Stellar Commun Corp, 1981-89; dir, Nat Asn Minorities Cable TV, 1983-90; mem, mgt, bd mem, Dist Cablevision, L P, 1983-99; pres, OFC Inc, 1984-89; dir, Black Entertainment Tv, 1984-; dir, Chicago Cable Tv, 1985-; dir, Freedom Nat Bank, 1987-90; BET Holdings Inc, TCI Great Lakes; bd mem, Cowles Media Co, 1994-98, bd chair, majority share holder, 1993; bd mem, Urban Commun Transp Corp; bd mem, B2E Markets Inc; founding chmn, Bd Entrepreneurial Growth & Investment Inst; chmn, Nat Asn Investment Cos. **Honors/Awds:** Service Award, Nat Cable TV Asn, 1983; Service Award, Federal Commun Adv Comt Minority Ownership, 1984; Service Award, Nat Asn Investment Co; Service Award, Nat Cable Tv Asn. **Business Addr:** Chairman, Shareholder, Syncom Funds, 8401 Colesville Rd Suite 300, Silver Spring, MD 20910, **Business Phone:** (301)608-3203.

WILKINS, JACQUES DOMINIQUE
Basketball player, basketball executive. **Personal:** Born Jan 12, 1960, Paris, France; married Nicole Berry, Sep 26, 1992. **Educ:** Univ Ga, attended 1983. **Career:** Basketball player (retired), basket ball exec; Atlanta Hawks, prof basketball player, 1983-94, spec asst exec vpres, 2001-04, vpres basketball, 2004-; Los Angeles Clippers, 1994; Boston Celtics, 1994-95; Panathinaikos Athens, 1995-96; San Antonio Spurs, 1996-97; Team-System Bologna, 1997-98; Orlando Magic, 1999. **Orgs:** United Negro Col Fund. **Honors/Awds:** MVP, SEC Tournament, 1981; NBA All-Rookie Team, 1982-83; NBA Player of theWeek Award; NBA Scoring Title, 1985-86; NBA Slam Dunk title, 1985 & 1990; NBA Player of the Month, January, 1986; All-NBA first team, 1986; All-NBA second team, 1987-88, 1991 & 1993; All-NBA third team, 1989 & 1994; Ga Sports Hall of Fame, 2004; Atlanta Sports Hall of Fame, 2005; Naismith Mem Basketball Hall of Fame, 2006. **Special Achievements:** NBA Draft, First round pick, #3, 1982; NBA, All-Star game, 1986-94. **Business Addr:** Vice President of Basketball, Atlanta Hawks, Centennial Tower, 101 Marietta St NW Suite 1900, Atlanta, GA 30303, **Business Phone:** (404)878-3800.

WILKINS, JANICE F
Executive. **Educ:** Xavier Univ, New Orleans, 1967; Golden Gate Univ, MBA, acct, 1987. **Career:** Intel Corp, finance controller, 1980, dir internal audit & vpres finance & enterprise servs, currently. **Orgs:** The Inst Internal Auditors. **Business Addr:** Vice President of Finance & Enterprise Services, Director of Internal Audit, Intel Corporation, 2200 Mission Col Blvd, Santa Clara, CA 95052, **Business Phone:** (408)765-8080.

WILKINS, JOSETTA EDWARDS
Educator. **Personal:** Born Jul 17, 1932, Little Rock, AR; daughter of James Wesley Edwards and Laura Bridgette Freeman Edwards; married Henry Wilkins III, Oct 30, 1954 (deceased); children: Calvin Tyrone, Henry IV, Cassandra Felecia, Mark Reginald & Angela Juanita. **Educ:** AM&N Col, BSE, 1961; Univ Ark, MEd, 1967; Okla State Univ, EdD, 1987. **Career:** Educator (retired); Ark Coun & Farmer Workers, dep dir, man-power training, 1967-73; Univ Ark, Pine Bluff, asst dir & coordr, coop educ, 1973-76, dir, coop educ, 1977-87, dir univ relations & develop, 1987-88, prof, trustee; Breast Cancer Res, chair; Pine Bluff State, rep. **Orgs:** Jefferson Co Juvenile Detention Comn; United Methodist Church; Episcopacy Comt; chair polit activities comt, Martin Luther King Jr, Holiday Comn; Am Asn Coun & Develop; Am Asn Adult & Continuing Educ; Ark Personnel & Guidance Asn; Lit Coun Adv Bd; Joint Educ Comm. **Honors/Awds:** Outstanding Service Award, Phi Beta Sigma, 1992; Recognition Award, Ark Democratic Black Caucus, 1992; Outstanding Service Award, Blacks in Govt, Cent Ark Chapter, 1992; Appreciation Award, Phi Beta Lambda, 1992; Outstanding Service Award, Coop Educ Prog, 1992; Josetta Wilkins Awards, named in honor. **Special Achievements:** Delivered a graceful and moving speech to the gathering of academic and scientific leaders at UAMS & members of her family; Dr. Josetta E. Wilkins Chair was established on August 20, 2003 at UAMS - First African-American to receive this honor at UAMS. **Home Addr:** 303 N Maple, Pine Bluff, AR 71601, **Home Phone:** (501)534-5852.

WILKINS, KENNETH C
County government official, vice president (government). **Personal:** Born Sep 20, 1952, New York, NY; son of June I (Whitehead) and James A. **Educ:** Shaw Univ, Raleigh, NC, BA, 1974; Bowling Green State Univ, Bowling Green, OH, MA, 1975; Univ Ky, Lexington, JD, 1978. **Career:** NC Dept Correction, Raleigh, legal staff, 1978-79; Shaw Univ, Raleigh, NC, asst exec vpres, 1979-83; Wake County, Raleigh, NC, register deeds, 1983; NC Dept State Treas, southern regional vpres, currently. **Orgs:** Mediation Serv Wake County, 1982-; exec comm, NC Leadership Forum, 1985-; bd mem, Haven House, 1986-; bd mem, Garner Road Family YMCA, 1986-; chair, United Negro Col Fund Campaign, Raleigh, 1988-; Nat Asn of Counties; NC Asn of Registers of Deeds. **Honors/Awds:** Distinguished Alumni Public Service Award, Shaw Univ, 1984; Heart & Soul Award, WAUG-AM, 1988; plaque, Garner Road YMCA, 1988; fellow, NC Inst Polit, 1989. **Business Addr:** Southern Regional Vice President, North Carolina Department of State Treasurer, 325 N Salisbury St, Raleigh, NC 27603-1385, **Business Phone:** (919)508-5176.

WILKINS, DR. LEONA B. See Obituaries section.

WILKINS, RAYFORD, JR.
Executive. **Personal:** Born Aug 9, 1951, Waco, TX; son of Rayford and Loyce; married Lorena, Jul 1, 1978; children: Donovan Campbell. **Educ:** Univ Tex, BA, 1974; Univ Pittsburgh, Mgt Prog, Exec, 1987. **Career:** Southwestern Bell Telephone, com asst, 1974; Pac Bell Bus Communs Servs, pres, sales; Bus Commun Servs, pres, 1997-99; Southwestern Bell telephone, pres & ceo, 1999-2000; SBC Pac Bell & SBC Nevada Bell, pres & ceo, 2000-05. group pres, 2005-. **Orgs:** Bd dir, Carver Avademy, 1999-2000; bd dir, H&R Block, 2000-; bd trustees, San Francisco Mus Modern Art, 2001-; bd mem, San Francisco Comn Jobs, 2001-; bd mem, YMCA San Francisco, chmn bd, Cingular Wireless. **Honors/Awds:** CEO of the Year, Minority Supplier Coun, 1997; Eagle Award, Nat Eagle Leadership Inst, 1997; Distinguished Alumnus, Waco Independent Sch Dist, 2000; Distinguished Alumnus. **Special Achievements:** Black Enterprise Mag, Top 50 African Am, 1999; The 100 Most Important Blacks in Technology, U.S. Black Engr & Info Technol mag; The Top 100 Blacks in Corporate America, Black Prof mag, 2005, The 75 Most Powerful African Americans in Corporate America, Black Enterprise mag; The 50 Most Important African Americans in Technology, eAccess Corp, 2005. **Business Addr:** Group President International Operations, SBC Pacific Bell & SBC Nevada Bell, 2600 Camino Ramon Rm 4cS100, San Ramon, CA 94583, **Business Phone:** (925)866-2600.

WILKINS, RILLASTINE ROBERTA
Systems analyst, mayor. **Personal:** Born Jul 24, 1932, Taft, OK; daughter of Canzaty and Willie; married Clarence E (deceased); children: Nathlyn Barksdale & Clarence Henry. **Educ:** Muskegon Community Col; Muskegon Bus Col; Technol Instr Inst; Univ Wis, Eau Claire. **Career:** Mayor, System Analyst (retired): Gen Telephone Co, MI, telephone oper, 1957-62, serv rep, 1962-67, div community instr, 1967-71, contact records supvr bus accts, 1973-79, phone mart mgr, 1979-81, customer serv mgr, 1981-83, analyst customer rels, 1983-88; mayor Muskegon Heights, MI, 1999-2007. **Orgs:** Chairperson, Human Resources Comn, Muskegon County; chairperson, Community Develop Comn, bd mem, Econ Develop Comn, City Muskegon Heights; bd mem, Muskegon Area Transcript Syst, Muskegon County; chairperson, Zoning Bd Appeals City Muskegon Heights; chairperson, Community Serv Comn, Muskegon County; past pres, Urban League Bd dir; NAACP; past pres, Every Woman's Place; past pres, Tri-City Woman's Club; past pres, Urban League Guild Greater Muskegon; bd mem, Heritage Hosp; bd mem, Greater Muskegon Chamber Com; bd mem, Black Women's Polit Caucus Greater Muskegon; St Bd Podiatric Med; pres, Women in Municip Govt, State Mich, 1979; co-chairperson, Allocations & Review Comt, United Way, 1980-81; bd mem, secy, Greater Musk Seaway Fest, 1980-82; vpres, Mondale Task Force Youth Employment, 1980; vchmn, Reg Planning Comn, Muskegon County, 1981; chairperson, Community Emer Clrghs, 1983; reg convenor, Nat Urban League, 1983-84; Jr Achievement Advr, 1972; pres, NBC/LEO, Nat Black Caucus, 1988-90. **Honors/Awds:** Jr Achievement Adv, 1972; Speakers Bur, Gen Telephone, MI, 1973; Citizens Award, Residents Muskegon & Muskegon Heights, 1974; 'Certificate of Commendation', Muskegon Community Col, 1979; Boss of the Day WZZR, Grand Rapids, MI, 1980; 'Certificate of Merit', St Josephs Christian Community Ctr, 1980; Pace Award, Muskegon Community Col, 1980; Plaque of Congratulations, Black Women's Polit Caucus, 1980; Chosen Woman of the Year, Black Women's Polit Caucus, 1983; named Ambassador, Lagos Univ, Nigeria, 2002; named Woman of Accomplishment/Courage, 2003; Mich Women's Found, Woman of Accomplishment, Muskegon Community Col, 2001. **Special Achievements:** First Woman Post Advisor for Explorers Career Development, 1973; Muskegon

Heights' first female city council member. **Home Addr:** 2305 5th St, Muskegon Heights, MI 49444.

WILKINS, DR. ROGER L
Scientist, business owner. **Personal:** Born Dec 14, 1928, Newport News, VA; married Nasira Ledbetter (deceased); children: Yvonne Diane & Roger (deceased). **Educ:** Hampton Inst, BS, 1951; Howard Univ, MS, 1952; Univ So CA, PhD (chem physics), 1967. **Career:** Scientist (Retired), Business Owner; Lewis Flight Propulsion Lab, aeronaut res scientist, 1952-55; Rocketdyne, sr tech specialist, 1955-60; Aerospace Corp, sr staff scientist, 1960-91, advan study grant, 1965-66; Roger Wilkins Gifts, owner, currently. **Orgs:** Combustion Inst; Am Inst Aeronauts & Astronauts; Gen Alumni Asn Univ So CA; pres, 1972-92; So CA Nat Hampton Alumni Asn treas, 1974-75; Hon Chemical Soc. **Honors/Awds:** Urban League Vocation Award, 1965; Service Award Nat, Sor Phi Delta Kappa Beta 1969.

WILKINS, ROGER WOOD
Educator. **Personal:** Born Mar 25, 1932, Kansas City, MO; son of Earl W and Helen Natalie Jackson Clayton; married Patricia A King, Feb 21, 1981; children: Amy T, David E & Elizabeth W C. **Educ:** Univ Mich, AB, 1953, JD & LLB, 1956; Cent Mich Univ, LLD (hon), 1975. **Career:** NY Atty, 1956-62; State Dept, foreign aid dir, spec asst, 1962-66; US Dept Justice, Wash DC, asst atty gen US, 1966-69; Ford Found, New York NY, prog dir, asst pres, 1969-72; Wash Post, Wash DC, ed bd, 1972-74; New York Times, New York NY, ed bd & columnist, 1974-79; Wash Star, Wash DC, assoc ed, 1980-81; Inst Policy Studies, Washington DC, sr fel, 1982-; CBS, NY, radio commentator, 1982-85; Mutual Broadcasting, Alexandria, Va, radio commentator, 1985-87; George Mason Univ, Fairfax, Va, Clarence J Robinson Prof Hist & Am Cult, 1987-; Princeton Univ, Woodrow Wilson Sch lectr, 1987; Nat Pub Radio, Wash, DC, radio commentator, 1990-. **Orgs:** Bd mem, Nat Asn Advan Colored People, Legal Defense Fund, 1970-, Pulitzer Prize Bd, 1980-89, Fund Investigative Jour, 1980-, Villers Found, 1987-, Nat Const Ctr, 1988-, PEN/Faulkner Found, 1989-, Univ DC, 1989-; vice chair bd, African-Am Inst, 1982-; Comn Racial Justice Policy, Joint Ctr Pol Studies, 1982-; mem comn overseers, Harvard Univ Afro-Am Studies, 1984-; Steering Comn, Free S Africa Movement, 1984-; chmn, Pulitzer Prize Bd, 1987-88. **Honors/Awds:** Shared Pulitzer Prize for reports on Watergate, 1972; Roger Baldwin Civil Liberties Award, New York Civil Liberties Union, 1987; Coordinated Nelson Mendela's Visit US, 1990. **Special Achievements:** He has written for the New York Times, the Washington Post and the Washington Star. Author of numerous articles in scholarly journals and of a highly acclaimed autobiography, A Man's Life,1982; and with former U.S. Senator Fred R. Harris he edited Quiet Riots: Race and Poverty in the United States. **Business Addr:** Professor, Clarence J Robinson Professor of History and American Culture, George Mason University, Department of History and Art History, 214 E Bldg 4400 Univ Dr, Fairfax, VA 22030-4444.

WILKINS, THOMAS A.
Government official, consultant. **Personal:** Born Feb 1, 1930, Lawrenceville, VA; married A Delores Bohannon; children: Lisa Delores, Thomas Alan & Mark Anderson. **Educ:** St Pauls Col, BS, 1951; NY Univ, MA, 1957; N Va Univ, DPA, 1976, MPA, 1975. **Career:** Dept Corrections, New York, prin instr, 1955-57; Voc Serv Dept Corrections, New York, asst dir, 1957-59; Voc Rehab Serv Glenn Dale Hosp, DC Dept Pub Health, chief, 1959-65; US Dept Labor, Man power admin, 1965-72; DC Dept Man power, dir, 1972; US Dept Labor, Off Oper Planning, Implementation & Rev, dep dir; Fla Inst Technol, Grad Sch Bus Admin, adj prof; mgt consult, currently. **Orgs:** Am Soc Pub Admin; bd dir, Inter state Conf Employment Sec Agency Inc; Fed Bus Asn; Am Personnel & Guid Asn; Nat Voc Guid Asn; charter mem, Nat Rehab Coun Asn; Nat Rehab Asn; Mayor's Cabinet DC; Mayor's Adv Com Narcotics Addiction DC; Metro Wash DC Bd Trade; DC Bicentennial Comn; Fed Adv Bd DC Sch Syst; Fed Rev Team, Coord Comn Child Care DC; Omega Psi Phi; DAV & mem Reston Home owners Asn; Hunters Woods Village Coun, Reston, Va; bd trustees, St Paul's Col; bd mem, Fair Housing Inc; Mayor's Overall Econ Devel Com; bd trustees, Davis Mem Goodwill Indust. **Honors/Awds:** Outstanding Performance Award, Man power Admin, 1969; Distinguished Trustee Award, St Pauls Col, 1972; Sustained Superior Perf Award, US Dept Labor, 1974. **Business Phone:** (703)709-8466.

WILKINSON, BRENDA
Poet, writer. **Personal:** Born Jan 1, 1946, Moultrie, GA; daughter of Malcolm Scott and Ethel Anderson Scott; married; children: Kim, Lori. **Educ:** Hunter Col, City Univ New York. **Career:** United Methodist Church, Bd Global Ministries, Wilkinson, staff writer; Books: African American Women Writers; The Civil Rights Movement; Jesse Jackson: Still Fighting for the Dream. **Orgs:** Authors Guild; Authors League Am. **Special Achievements:** National Book Award nominee in 1976 for Ludell; Ludell and Willie was named one of the outstanding children's books of the year by New York Times and a best book for young adults by American Library Association, both in 1977.

WILKINSON, DAN
Football player. **Personal:** Born Mar 13, 1973, Dayton, OH; married; children: Brooklyn, Daniel Jr, Taylor, Sydne & Kennedy. **Educ:** Ohio State Univ. **Career:** Cincinnati Bengals, defensive end, 1994-97; Wash Redskins, 1998-2003; Detroit Lions, defensive tackle, 2003-05; Miami Dolphins, defensive tackle, 2006-07. **Honors/Awds:** Defensive Game Ball, 1997; All-Pro Team, Sports Illustrated, 2003. **Special Achievements:** Selected by Cincinnati Bengals as first pick overall in first round of NFL draft, 1994.

WILKINSON, DONALD CHARLES
Educator. **Personal:** Born Feb 12, 1936, Madison, FL; divorced; children: Donald Clark. **Educ:** Wilbur Wright Tech, 1964; Detroit Inst Tech, 1965; Univ Mich, BA 1968; Sonoma State Col, MA 1972. **Career:** Detroit Water Dept, engr, 1956-61; Detroit Courier, staff writer & repoter, 1961-62; WJ Maxey Boys Training Sch, boys supr 1965-69; Educ Develop Ctr, Newton, MA, 1970-71; sculptr in wood, 1970; Sonoma State Col, asst prof & counr Physiology, prof psychol, 1971-92. **Orgs:** Alpha Phi Alpha; Freelance Civil Rights Activist, 1960-68; consult, Black Tutorial Proj, 1965; adv, Morgan Communty Sch, 1970-71; Ford Found Grantin Early Childhood Educ; res & teaching British Infant Sch Syst, Sherard Infant Sch Eng.

WILKINSON, DR. DORIS
Educator, college teacher, sociologist. **Personal:** Born Jun 13, 1936, Lexington, KY; daughter of Howard Thomas and Regina L Wilkinson. **Educ:** Univ Ky, BA, 1958; Case Western Univ, MA, 1960, PhD, 1968; Johns Hopkins Univ, MPH, 1985; Harvard Univ, postdoctoral study, 1990, 1991. **Career:** Macalester Col, assoc & full, prof, 1970-77; Am Soc Asn, exec assoc, 1977-80; Howard Univ, prof, 1980-84; Univ Va, Charlottesville, VA, vis prof, 1984-85; Harvard Univ, Cambridge, MA, vis scholar, 1989-90, vis prof, summers, 1992, 1993, 1994, 1997; Univ Ky, Lexington, KY, prof sociol, currently, African Am Heritage, dir, currently. **Orgs:** Pres, DC Sociol Society, 1982-83; bd overseers, Case Western Res Univ, 1982-85; pub educ, Com Am Cancer Society, 1982-85; exec officer, budget comn, Am Sociol Asn, 1985-88; pres, Society Study Soc Prob, 1987-88; vpres, Am Sociol Asn, 1991-92; Ky Comn Women, 1993-96; pres, Eastern Sociol Society, 1993; Ky AFA Comn, 1994-; ASA coun, 1995-97. **Honors/Awds:** Woodrow Wilson Fel, 1959-61; NIH Fel, 1963-66; NIE Grant, 1978-80; Omicron Delta Kappa Nat Leadership Hon, 1987; NCI, res contract, 1985-88; Dubois-Johnson-Frazier Award, Am Sociol Asn, 1988; Grant Ky Humanities Council Award proj Afro-Am physicians, 1988-89; Ford Fel, Harvard Univ, 1989-90; Hall of Distinguished Alumni, Univ of Ky, 1989; Public Humanities Award, Ky Humanities Coun, 1990; Women's History Month Award, Midway Col, 1991; Great Teacher Award, 1992; Distinguished Professorship, 1992; Distinguished Scholar, Asn Black Sociologists, 1993; Lydia Rappaport Distingushed Scholar, Smith, 1995; Social Work Hall of Fame, Univ Ky, 1999; Ky Humanities Grant, 2000; Presidents Inaugural Diversity Award, Univ Ky, 2003; Coretta Scott King Award, Alpha Kappa Alpha sorority, 2007. **Special Achievements:** First African-American female appointed to a full time position at Univeristy of Kentucky in 1967. First African-American elected to the Hall of Distinguished Alumni. **Business Addr:** Professor, Director, Heritage Project, University of Kentucky, Department of Sociology, 1561 Patterson Off Tower, Lexington, KY 40506, **Business Phone:** (859)257-4415.

WILKINSON, MARIE L
Executive. **Personal:** Born May 6, 1910, New Orleans, LA; daughter of Charles and Maude La Beau; married Charles; children: Donald & Sheila Scott. **Educ:** New Orleans Univ, Bus, 1921; Straight Col. **Career:** P & W Truck Parts & Equip Inc, owner, pres; Aura Human Rel Comn, pres; Marie Wilkinson Child Develop Ctr, pres; Aurora Feed Hungry Inc, pres. **Orgs:** Founding pres emer, Aurora Urban League, 1978. **Honors/Awds:** Cath Woman of Year, Diocese Rockford, 1956; Citizenshp Citation Award, No Ill Dist Optmist, 1968; Beautiful People Award, Chicago Urban League, 1970; Key to the City, Aurora, Ill, 1988; Hon Doctor Laws, Honoris Causal, Aurora Univ, 1990. **Home Addr:** 648 N View St, Aurora, IL 60506. **Business Addr:** Owner, P&W Truck Parts & Equipments Inc, 648 N View St, Aurora, IL 60506.

WILKINSON, RAYMOND M
Automotive executive. **Personal:** Born Oct 28, 1943, St Louis, MO; son of Raymond M Sr and Elizabeth; married Betty J Taylor, Nov 6, 1965; children: William, Ray III & Heather. **Educ:** Gen Motors Inst, Flint, MI, dealer-operator degree, 1981. **Career:** US Postal Serv, St Louis, MO, carrier, 1961-75; Don Darr Pontiac, St Louis, MO, salesperson, 1975-80, mgr, 1981-83; Ray Wilkinson Buick-Cadillac Inc, pres; Poughkeepsie Chevrolet Cadillac Inc, owner & pres, currently. **Orgs:** Nat Asn Advan Colored People-Racine, 1984-, UNCF-Racine, 1985-; bd mem, Racine Wed Optimists, 1984-, West Racine Businessmen, 1985-, Racine Sickle Cell, 1986-; 100 Black Men Milwaukee, 2002. **Honors/Awds:** Best Buick Dealer in Class, Buick Motor, 1986-88, 1990, 1992-94; MNY Small Business Award, Racine NCP, 1989; B E's 100, Black Enterprise Mag, 1992, 1994, 1995, 1996, 1997, 1999, 2000, ranked number 11, 1998; number 9, 2000, number 4, 2001; Racine Youth Leadership Acad, 1994-98. **Special Achievements:** Black Enterprise's list of Top 100 Auto Dealers, ranked 4th, 2001. **Business Addr:** Owner, President, Poughkeepsie Chevrolet Cadillac Inc., 1960 S Rd, Poughkeepsie, NY 12601, **Business Phone:** (866)230-8630.

WILKINSON, RAYMOND M
Executive. **Personal:** Born May 22, 1966, St Louis, MO; son of Raymond Jr and Betty J; married Jeanette Heredia, Jun 28, 1996; children: Wiliam, Wesley, Raymond IV & Jordan. **Educ:** Univ Pa, Wharton Sch Bus, 1988; Nat Automotive Dealer Asn Acad 1995. **Career:** Gen Motors, Pontiac Div, 1988-91; Ray Wilkinson, Buick Cadillac, gen sales mgr, 1991-95; Poughkeepsie Chevrolet-Olds-Cadillac, pres & owner, 1997-. **Orgs:** Gen Motors Minority Dealers Asn, 1997-2003; bd mem, Poug Area Chamber Com, 1998-2003; bd mem, Rehab Progs Inc, 1998-2003; bd mem, United Way Dutchess County, 1999-2003; bd mem, Am Heart Asn, 2000-03; bd mem, Helen Hayes Hosp Found, 2001-03. **Honors/Awds:** Black Enterprise, Top 100 Auto Dealer Listing, 1997-02; Miller Brewing Co, 2nd Generation Business Recognition, 1999; Honors Award for Courage, Helen Hayes Hosp, 2000. **Business Addr:** President, Owner, Poughkeepsie Chevrolet-Cadillac Inc, 1960 South Rd, Poughkeepsie, NY 12601, **Business Phone:** (845)298-1193.

WILKINSON, DR. ROBERT SHAW, JR.
Physician. **Personal:** Born Jul 11, 1928, Brooklyn, NY; son of Robert Shaw (deceased) and Melissa Ruth Royster (deceased); married Carolyn Elizabeth Cobb, Jun 24, 1951; children: Amy Elizabeth, Karin Lynn & Robert Montague. **Educ:** Dartmouth Col, BA, 1950; NY Univ, MD, 1955. **Career:** George Wash Univ, clinic prof med; Am Bd Int Med, dipl; Group Health Asn Inc, staff physician, 1962-68; George Wash Univ Hosp, attending physician, 1962-; pvt practice, physician, 1968-96; med adv, Inter-Am Develop Bank 1976-; Georgetown Univ Med Ctr Community Practice Network, 1996-2002; Georgetown Univ, Div Gen Med, asst prof med, 1996-98, assoc prof med, 1998-2002; Georgetown Univ Hosp, attending physician, 1996-; pvt practice, 1968-96, 2002-; Sibly Mem Hosp, attending physician, 2002-. **Orgs:** Med Soc DC, AMA, fel, Am Col Physicians; SPP Fraternity, Espilon Boule, 1971-; Acad Med Wash, DC, 1975-, pres, 1998-00. **Honors/Awds:** The Dartmouth Alumni Award, Dartmouth Col, 1987; Distinguished Achievement Award, Am Heart Asn, nation's capitol affiliate, 1986; Am Col Physicians, Wash DC Chap Laureate Award, 1999. **Military Serv:** AUS, MC capt, 1956-58. **Home Phone:** (202)723-5956. **Business Addr:** Physician, 730 24th St NW Suite 7, Washington, DC 20037, **Business Phone:** (202)338-5050.

WILKS, GERTRUDE
School administrator. **Personal:** Born Mar 9, 1927, Duboc, LA; married Otis; children: Otis Jr, Danny & Patricia. **Career:** Mothers for Equal Educ, dir, 1965; Nairobi Day & High Sch, founder & dir, 1966-80; East Palo Alto Munic Coun, mayor; Gertrude Wilks Acad, founder & dir, 1981-. **Orgs:** Founder, MEE, 1955; founder, Res Corp, 1965; founder, Sat Tutorial Day Sch, 1966; org, Annette Latorre Nursery & Sch, 1967; founder, Mothers Home mkng Ind, 1968; org, Black & White Conf; org, MEE Educ Day Care, 1970; org, MEE Extended Day Care, 1976; consult, HEW; consult, Ravens wood Elem Dist; consult, Stanford Teacher Training; consult, San Jose Sch Dist; consult, Palo Alto Sch Dist; consult, Col San Mateo; consult, Foothill Col; consult, Wright Inst Coun; EPA Munic coun; mayor, 1976; United Way Plng; chmn bd trustees, Great Friendship Bapt Ch; commr & vice chmn Redevel E Palo Alto; charter mem, Nairobi Col Bd, 1963-72; comm coun, Ravens wood Elem Dist; bd dir, EPA Neigh Health Ctr; comnr, San Mateo Co Econ Opportunity Comn; ex-of mem, Comt Action Coun; pres, Missionary Bapt Soc; dir & founder, Mothers Equal Educ. **Honors/Awds:** Outstanding community service, OICW, 1966; Black Child Development Institutional Award, 1973; Phoebe Hearst Award, 1974; Citizen Award, Kiwanis Club, 1976; Bicen Award, Trinity Baptist Church, 1976; Service Mankind Award, Los Altos Sertoma Club, 1977. **Home Addr:** 1194 Saratoga Ave, East Palo Alto, CA 94303. **Business Addr:** Founder, Director, Gertrude Wilks Academy, 1194 Saratoga Ave, East Palo Alto, CA 94303.

WILKS, JAMES LEE
Association executive. **Personal:** Born Feb 5, 1951, Chester, SC; son of James A and Ivry; married LaVon Wilks, May 10, 1991; children: Lega, Louia, Jordan. **Educ:** Bernard M Barnett, BBA, 1973. **Career:** Am Express, asst dir internal servs, 1980-85; Agency Child Develop & Head Start, fiscal coordr, 1985-95, vpres finance, 1995-. **Orgs:** pres, Father's Rights Metro, 1990-. **Honors/Awds:** Father of the Year, Fathers Rights Metro, 1994. **Home Addr:** 384 Greene Ave, Brooklyn, NY 11216-1108. *

WILLACY, HAZEL M
Lawyer. **Personal:** Born Apr 20, 1946, Mississippi; daughter of Willie Barnes Martin and Julious Martin; married Aubrey B; children: Austin Keith & Louis Samuel. **Educ:** Smith Col, BA, 1967; Case Western Reserve Univ, JD, 1976. **Career:** Bureau Labor Stats, libr economist, 1967-72; Baker Hostetler, atty, 1976-80; Sherwin Williams, labor rel atty, 1980-82, asst dir, labor rels, 1983-87, dir, Labor Rels, 1987-93, Empl Policies & Labor Rels, dir, 1993-2002, vpres empl Policies & Labor Rels, chair, 2002-. **Orgs:** Am Bar Asn; OH State Bar Asn; Northeast Chap, Indust Rels Res Asn; bd trustees, Meridia Physician Network, 1995-; bd trustees, Boy Scouts Am, Greater Cleveland Chap; Labor & Employment Rels Asn Oh Chap; vis comt, Case Western Reserve Univ. **Honors/Awds:** Order of Coif, 1976. **Special Achieve-**

ments: Articles published 1970, 76, 80. **Home Addr:** 3337 Brainard Rd, Cleveland, OH 44124. **Business Addr:** Vice President, Chair, Sherwin Williams Company, Employ Policies & Labor Rels, 101 Prospect Ave NW Midland Bldg, Cleveland, OH 44115, **Business Phone:** (216)566-2000.

WILLIAM, THOMPSON E.
Government official. **Personal:** Born Dec 26, 1924, New York, NY; married Elaine Allen; children: 2. **Educ:** Brooklyn Col, BA; LLB. **Career:** NY State Senate, mem, 1964-66; NY City Coun, mem; Bd pres, Brooklyn rep. **Orgs:** Am Bar Asn; Bedford Stuyvesant Lawyers Asn; exec bd regional dir chmn legal redress com Brooklyn Br. **Honors/Awds:** Dem Recipient Purple Heart Combat Infantrymen's Badge. **Military Serv:** AUS, WW II. **Business Addr:** Board President, Brooklyn representative, 768 Putnam Ave, Brooklyn, NY 11221.

WILLIAMS, REV. A CECIL
Clergy. **Personal:** Born Sep 22, 1929, San Angelo, TX; married Janice Mirikitani; children: Kim & Albert. **Educ:** Houston-Tillotson Col, BA, 1952; Perkins Sch Theol, BD, 1955; Pacific Sch Religon, Grad Work. **Career:** St Paul Methodist Church, asst minister, 1954; Methodist Church, minister, 1955; Houston-Tillotson Col, chaplain & teacher, 1956-59; St James Methodist Church, minister, 1961-64; Glide Mem United Methodist Church, minister, 1964-2000, ceo, currently. **Orgs:** Christian Soc Crisis; bd mem, Martin Luther King Ctr Soc Change; host, KPIX-TV Vibrations New People. **Honors/Awds:** Man of the Year, Sun Reporter, 1967; Emmy Award, San Francisco National Acad TV Arts & Sci 1972; featured in PBS-TV special hosted by Maya Angelou, 1992. **Special Achievements:** A Cecil Williams was one of the first five African American graduates of the Perkins School of Theology at Southern Methodist University in 1955; Pub in many magazines. created Glide Celebrations. **Business Addr:** CEO, Minister, Glide Memorial United Methodist Church, 330 Ellis St, San Francisco, CA 94102, **Business Phone:** (415)674-6000.

WILLIAMS, AARON
Basketball player. **Personal:** Born Oct 2, 1971; married Heather, 1997; children: Danyelle, Cameron & Aaron Jr. **Educ:** Xavier Univ, criminal justice. **Career:** Utah Jazz, forward, 1993-94; Milwaukee Bucks, 1994-95; Denver Nuggets, 1996-97; Vancouver Grizzlies, 1996-97; Seattle Supersonics, 1997-99; Wash Wizards, 1999-2000; NJ Nets, 2000-05; Toronto Raptors, 2004-06; New Orleans Hornets, ctr & forward, 2005-06; Los Angeles Clippers, ctr forward, 2006-. **Honors/Awds:** MCC Defensive Player of the Year. **Business Addr:** Professional Basketball Player, Los Angeles Clippers, 1111 S Figueroa St Suite 1100, Los Angeles, CA 90015, **Business Phone:** (213)742-7500.

WILLIAMS, ADA L.
School administrator. **Personal:** Born Aug 22, 1933, Waxahachie, TX; daughter of Henry Lee and Lueada Gregory Lewis; married Clyde L, Jun 8, 1957; children: Adrian Dwight. **Educ:** Huston-Tillotson Col, BA, 1955; North Tex State Univ, MA, 1968. **Career:** School Administrator (retired); Dallas Independent Sch Dist, dir, counr, emp rels, 1979-2002. **Orgs:** Life mem, NEA; TEA evaluation team, 1975; NE Univ Eval Team, 1975; Tex Asn Parlimentarians, Nat Asn Parlimentarians; pres, Classroom Teachers Dallas, 1975-79; mem coord bd, Nat Counc Accreditation Teacher Educ; St Paul AME Church; Nat Asn Advan Colored People; chair, Dallas Teachers Credit Union Bd, 1976-; Delta Sigma Theta Sor Inc; pres, Epsilon; Delta Kappa Gamma Soc Inc; Oak Cliff B & PW Club Inc; Nat Coun Accreditation Teacher Educ; vis team, Univ N Fla, Eastern New Mexico Univ & Okla Christian Univ; parliamentarian, Tex PTA, 1984-86; appeals bd, NEA/NCATE 1985-; pres, Nat Asn Prof & Exec Women, currently. **Honors/Awds:** Teacher of the Year, 1969-71; Obudswoman Award, S Dallas B&PW Club, 1984; Outstanding Educator Tex Legislation, 1983-85; Achievement Award, Nat Women Achievement Orgs, 1987; Honored Tex PTA Honorary Life Membership, 1987; Achievement Award, Delta Kappa Gamma Soc, 1981-89; Trailblazer Award, S Dallas B&PW Club Inc, 1976; many educ, civic, religious, and club Awards; Honored by the Dallas Independent Sch Dist Bd Educ, 1997. **Business Addr:** President, National Association of Professional and Executive Women, 3280 Sunrise Hwy Suite 209, Wantagh, NY 11793, **Business Phone:** (516)933-4830.

WILLIAMS, AENEAS DEMETRIUS
Football player. **Personal:** Born Jan 29, 1968, New Orleans, LA; married Tracy; children: Saenea, Tirzah, Cheyenne & Lazarus. **Educ:** Southern Univ, acct. **Career:** Football player (retired); Phoenix Cardinals, defensive back, 1991-93; Ariz Cardinals, defensive back, 1994-2000; St Louis Rams, defensive back, 2001-04; Spirit of the Lord Family, clayton, MO, church minister, currently. **Orgs:** Kappa Alpha Psi Fraternity Inc. **Honors/Awds:** NFC Defensive Rookie of the Year, NFL Players Asn; Hall of Fame San Francisco 49ers; Pro Bowl, 1994-2003. **Special Achievements:** Came in on a cornerback blitz from Youngs blindside, and came up with a clean hit. This occurred on national television, a Monday Night Football game.

WILLIAMS, ALEXANDER, JR.
Judge, lawyer. **Personal:** Born May 8, 1948, Washington, DC. **Educ:** Howard Univ, BA, govt, 1970; Howard Univ Sch Law, JD, 1973, Sch Divinity, MA, religious studies & ethics, 1991. **Career:** Seventh Judicial Circuit, Md, law clerk, 1973; Pvt Pract, atty, 1974-86; Fairmount Heights, munic atty, 1975-87; Prince George's County Pub Defender's Off, asst pub defender, 1977-78; Howard Univ Sch Law, prof, 1978-89; Glenarden, munic atty, 1980-87; Prince George's County, atty, 1987-94; US Dist Ct, Dist Md, fed judge, 1994-. **Orgs:** Md Bar Asn, 1973; DC Bar Asn, 1974; founder, J Franklyn Bourne Bar Asn; Nat Prince George's County Bar Asns; Comn Med Discipline, 1980-85; Wash Suburban Sanit Comn, 1983-87; States Attys Coord Coun, 1987-89; Ct Appeals Standing Comt Rules Pract & Procedure, 1984-86; Handgun Roster Bd, 1992-94; Walker Mem Baptist Church, Wash, DC; honorary doctorate, Southeastern Univ, 1995. **Business Addr:** Federal Judge, US District Court, 6500 Cherrywood Lane, Greenbelt, MD 20770, **Business Phone:** (301)344-0660.*

WILLIAMS, ALFRED HAMILTON
Football player, radio host. **Personal:** Born Nov 6, 1968, Houston, TX; married Lena; children: Dominique, Justin & Christopher Alfred. **Educ:** Univ Colo. **Career:** Football player (retired), radio show host; Cincinnati Bengals, defensive end, 1991-94; San Francisco 49ers, 1995; Denver Broncos, 1996-99; Sports radio 950 The FAN Studios, radio host, currently. **Honors/Awds:** Butkus Award, 1990; Pro Bowl, 1996; All-Pro selection, 1996. **Business Phone:** (303)321-0950.

WILLIAMS, ALVIN LEON
Basketball player. **Personal:** Born Aug 6, 1974, Philadelphia, PA; son of Alvin Williams Sr. **Educ:** Villanova Univ, BA, 1997. **Career:** Player (retired); Coach: Portland Trail Blazers, guard, 1997-98; Toronto Raptors, guard, 1998-06; Los Angeles clippers, guard, 2007; Toronto Raptors, asst coach, currently. **Honors/Awds:** All-Metro Philly; All Am, 1998. *

WILLIAMS, ALYSON
Entertainer, actor, singer. **Personal:** Born May 11, 1961, New York, NY; daughter of Robert Lee Booker and Shirley M. **Educ:** City Col NY; Marymount Manhattan Col. **Career:** Singer & actress; Albums: Raw, 1989; Alyson Williams, 1991; " Livin' Large! ", 1991; It's About Time, 2004; Singles: "Yes We Can Can", 1987; "Less Than Zero", 1987; "Make You Mine Tonight", 1987; "Sleep Talk", 1989; "My Love is So Raw", 1989; "Just Call My Name", 1989; "I Need Your Lovin", 1990; "Not on the Outside", 1990; "Can't Have My Man", 1992; "Just My Luck", 1992; "Everybody Knew But Me", 1992; Plays: Wicked Way, I Need A Man. **Special Achievements:** First guest vocalist to perform with Branford Marsalis & the Tonight Show Band, 1992. **Business Addr:** Actress, Singer, Def Jam Recordings, 825 Eighth Ave, New York, NY 10019, **Business Phone:** (212)491-4914.

WILLIAMS, DR. ANITA SPENCER
Educator. **Personal:** Born in Philadelphia, PA; daughter of Thomas and Julia Walker; married Willie G, Jun 7, 1958; children: Diane, Stephen & Karen. **Educ:** Cheyney Univ, Cheyney, PA, BS, 1967; Temple Univ, Philadelphia, PA, EdM, 1971, EdD, 1988. **Career:** Sch Dist Philadelphia, PA, teacher, 1967-71, reading specialist, 1971-85, auxiliary vice prin, 1985-86, teacher trainer, 1986-87, admin asst, 1987-96; Gratz Cluster, cluster leader, 1996; Philadelphia Sch Fund, project mgr, currently. **Orgs:** Alpha Phi Sigma Nat Honor Soc, 1966-; Int Reading Asn, 1972-; consult, Progress Educ Prog, 1977-80; Black Women's Educ Alliance, 1980-82; educ dir, Waters Community Ctr, 1980-88; Phi Delta Kappa Educational Fraternity, 1985-; Alleghany W Found. **Honors/Awds:** First Scholar of the Year, Cheyney Univ, 1966. **Business Addr:** Project Director, The Philadelphia Education Fund, Benjamin Franklin Pkwy Suite 700, Philadelphia, PA 19103.

WILLIAMS, ANN CLAIRE
Judge. **Personal:** Born Aug 16, 1949, Detroit, MI; daughter of Joshua Williams and Dorothy Williams; married David J Stewart, Aug 25, 1979; children: one son, one daughter. **Educ:** Wayne State Univ, Detroit MI, BS, 1970; Univ Michigan, MA, 1972; Univ Notre Dame Law Sch, Ind, JD, 1975. **Career:** Judge Robert A Sprecher, law clerk, 1975-76; US Attys Off, Ill, asst atty, 1976-85; Northwestern Univ Law Sch, adj prof & lectr, 1979-; John Marshall Law Sch, adj prof & lectr, 1979-; Criminal Receiving & Appellate Div, dep chief, 1980-83; US Attys Off, Organized Crime Drug Enforcement Task Force North Cent Region, chief, 1983-85; Judicial Conf US, Chair Ct, 1993-97, comt mem, 1990-93; Nat Inst Trial Advocacy, bd trustees, fac, 1979-; US District Ct, judge, 1985-99, 2001. **Orgs:** Bd trustees, Univ Chicago Lab Sch, 1988-; bd trustees, Univ Notre Dame, 1988-; bd trustees, Mus Sci & Indust, 1991-97; pres, Fed Judges Asn, 1999-01; chair, Just the Beginning Found. **Honors/Awds:** Edith S Sampson Memorial Award, Illinois Judicial Coun, 1986; Thurgood Marshall Award, Chicago Kent College Law, 1986; Headliner Award, Women of Wayne State Univ Alumni, 1987; Honorary JD, Lake Forest College, 1987; Honorary Doctor of Public Service, Univ Portland, 1993; Honorary JD, Univ of Notre Dame, 1997; Earl Dickerson Award, Chicago Bar Asn, 1997; Women with Vision Award, Women Bar Asn Ill, 1998. **Business Addr:** Judge, US District Ct Appeals 7th Circuit, Room 2612 Dirksen Fed Bldg, 219 S Dearborn St, Chicago, IL 60604.*

WILLIAMS, DR. ANN E A
School administrator. **Personal:** Born Sep 21, 1946, Jacksonville, FL; divorced. **Educ:** Fla A&M Univ, BS, 1968. **Career:** Duval Co Juvenile Ct, coun, 1969; A Philliph Randoph Inst, exec coun; FL Jr Col Jax FL Adult Educ, instr; Minority Affairs Com Duval Teachers United; Duval Co Bd Pub Instr, instr, asst prin; Sisters Connection Int Network Inc, exec dir & founder, currently. **Orgs:** Jacksonville Jaycees; HOPE Chapel Christian Assembly Inc, Cub Scout Den Leader; pres, Dem Women's Fla Inc; Dem Exec Com; Nat Coun Negro Women Inc; exec com, Nat Asn Advan Colored People League Women Voters; vpres, Duval Teachers United; mem comt, YWCA; United Meth Women; vol, Jacksonville Inc, NABSE. **Home Addr:** 6479 San Juan Ave, Jacksonville, FL 32210, **Home Phone:** (904)695-2126. **Business Addr:** Founder, Executive Director, Sisters Connection International Network Inc, 6479 San Juan Ave Suite 1, Jacksonville, FL 32210, **Business Phone:** (904)695-2126.

WILLIAMS, ANNALISA STUBBS
Executive, judge. **Personal:** Born Sep 23, 1956, Youngstown, OH; daughter of Eula Grace Harris Stubbs and Julius Saffold Stubbs; married Michael D, Sep 7, 1985; children: Michael James (dec), Alexandria Katherine-Grace Williams & James Robert II. **Educ:** Kent State Univ, BA 1977; Univ Akron, MA, 1979; Univ Akron Law Sch, JD, 1984. **Career:** Kent State Univ, pre-law adv, 1976-77, orientation instr 1976-77, resident staff adv, 1976-77; Ohio Civil Rights Comn, investr/intake spec, 1977-79; Metro Regional Transit Auth, personnel equal employment minor bus dir, 1979-84, employ rels officer, 1984-85; City Akron, asst law dir, 1985-89; Roadway Services Inc, Akron, Ohio, mgr, 1989-; Akron Munic Ct, Judge, 2003-. **Orgs:** Delta Sigma Theta, 1980-; Urban Leagues Youth Comt; bd dirs, Info Line; bd trustees, Prep Ohio; Delta Sigma Theta Sor Inc; Akron Barristers Club; Akron Bar Asn; Akron Urban League; West Side Neighbors; treas, Comn Re-elect Councilman Michael D Williams; trustee, Ohio Ballet, 1988-. **Honors/Awds:** Superior Scholar, Alpha Lambda Delta, Kent State, 1977; Distinguished Scholar, Pi Sigma Alpha, Kent State, 1977; Outstanding Black Student, Black United Students, Kent State 1977; First place, Akron Law Sch Client Coun Competition, 1983. **Home Addr:** 584 Avalon Ave, Akron, OH 44320. **Business Addr:** Judge, Akron Municipal Court, 217 S High St, Akron, OH 44308, **Business Phone:** (330)375-2570.

WILLIAMS, ANNIE
School administrator. **Personal:** Born Jun 2, 1970, Springfield, IL; daughter of Rachel Brooks; children: Ashley Walton & Fletcher Williams Jr. **Educ:** Lincoln Land Community Col, AS, bus admin; Univ Ill, Springfield, BA, mgt, 2002, MS, pub admin, 2004. **Career:** Touchette Reg Hosp, acct asst, 1996-97; Med Transp Mgt, commercial acct coordr, 1998; Mary Bell Transp, co owner, 1998; Ill Community Col Bd, acct asst, 1999-2002, asst dir adult educ & family lit & prog compliance, 2002-04. **Orgs:** Funding task force, Ill Community Col Bd, 2002-, adv coun, 2002-. **Honors/Awds:** Eminent Scholar, Ill Community Col Bd, 2000, 2002. **Business Addr:** Assistant Director for Adult Education & Family Literacy Program Compl, Illinois Community College Board, 401 E Capitol Ave, Springfield, IL 62701, **Business Phone:** (217)785-0213.

WILLIAMS, ANTHONY A
Mayor, executive. **Personal:** Born Jul 28, 1951, Los Angeles, CA; son of Lewis III and Virginia; married Diane Simmons; children: Asantewa Foster. **Educ:** Yale Col, BA, polit sci; Harvard Univ, Kennedy Sch Govt, MS; Harvard Law Sch, JD. **Career:** Boston Redevelop Authority, head neighborhood housing & develop, 1988-90; St. Louis's Community Develop Agency, exec dir, 1990-91; State Conn, dep controller, 1991-93; US Dept Agr, chief financial officer, 1993-95; State DC, chief financial officer, 1995-98; Govt DC, mayor, 1999-2007; Friedman Billings Ramsey Group Inc, partner, currently. **Military Serv:** USAF. **Business Addr:** Partner, Friedman Billings Ramsey Group Inc, 1001 19th St N, Arlington, VA 22209, **Business Phone:** (703)312-9500.

WILLIAMS, ARMON ABDULE
Football player, television broadcaster. **Personal:** Born Aug 13, 1973, Tempe, AZ. **Educ:** Univ Ariz. **Career:** Football player (retired),broadcaster, health & fitness trainer; Houston Oilers, 1997; Minnesota Vikings; New Orleans Saints; Barcelona Dragons, 1998; health & fitness dir; health & fitness personal trainer, currently; COX A7 Sports, announcer, currently. **Business Phone:** (480)225-4357.

WILLIAMS, ARMSTRONG
Public relations executive, columnist, talk show host. **Personal:** Born Feb 5, 1959, Marion, SC; son of James and Thelma. **Educ:** SC State Col, BA, polit sci & Eng, 1981. **Career:** Television host, radio host, columnist & media executive; B&C Associations, vpres govt & int affairs; US Equal Employment Opportunity Comn, Confidential asst to chmn; US Dept Agr, presidential appointee; US Rep Carrol Campbell, legis asst; Legis aide, US Sen Strom Thurmond; WOL Radio 1450 AM, Wash. DC, host, 1991; Syndicated shows, Talk America Radio Network, host, 1995; Salem Radio Network, host, 1998, TV One, "On Point", host, 2002-05; guest commentator, CNN, MSNBC, NPR; Crisis mag, columnist; The Right Side Production Inc, founder & chief exec officer, currently; Graham Williams Group, founder & chief exec officer, currently. **Orgs:** Adv bd, Child-Help USA, 1982; Phi Beta

Sigma; bd, The Wash Afro-Am Newspaper; bd, Carson Scholars Fund; Pres Comm White House Fellows; bd mem, Youth Leadership Found; bd dir, Independence Federal Bank. **Honors/Awds:** Bicentennial Public Speaking Award, 1976; ROTC Sojourner Award, 1978; Youth of the Year, Cong Black Caucus, 1982-83; Falcons Public Service Award, The Falcons, 1983-84; Public Service Award, Phi Beta Sigma,1982-83; Lib Arts Howard Univ Sch Lib Arts, 1983-84; One of 30 most influential young Blacks in Am, Ebony Mag, 1985; appeared on Phil Donahue Show Feb 25, Am Top Black Conservatives; Beyond Blame, 1995; Vanity Fair Hall of Fame, 1996. **Special Achievements:** Authored : Beyond Blame-How We Can Succeed by Breaking the Dependency Barrier. **Business Addr:** Chief Executive Officer, The Graham Williams Group, 201 Massachusetts Ave NE Suite C3, PO Box 75134, Washington, DC 20002-4957, **Business Phone:** (202)546-5400.

WILLIAMS, ARNETTE L.
Educator. **Personal:** Born in Logan, WV; married Clarence L; children: Cheryl & Reginald. **Educ:** BS, 1943. **Career:** Marion County WVa, former teacher. **Orgs:** Former vol work Girl Scouts Boy Scouts Little League PTA Grey Lady ARC Military Hosps Overseas; chairwoman, bd co-founder Reston Sect Nat Coun Negro Women, 1973; Reston Planned Parenthood Comm Established Community Clin, 1974; Planned Parenthood Coun No, Va; Wolf Trap Asn Performing Arts; FISH; United Fund; Int Womens Org, 1975; Social Club "Sagarities" Serv Oriented; Lions Aux.

WILLIAMS, DR. ARTHUR LOVE
Physician. **Personal:** Born Jun 4, 1940, Priscilla, MS; married Patricia; children: Terri, Toni & Tara. **Educ:** Jackson State Col, BS, 1962; Meharry Med Col, MD, 1966; Hubbard Hosp, Intern, 1966-67; Hubbard Hosp, resident, 1970-73. **Career:** Med Prog Baylor Col Med, teacher comt, 1974-; Hubbard Hosp, Dept Internal Med, instr, asst prof, chief resident, 1972-74; Univ Tex, Med Educ Prog, teaching staff, 1976-; St Elizabeth Hosp, chief staff, pres med, 1977-; Pvt Prac, physician, currently. **Orgs:** Houston Med Forum; Harris Co Med Soc; Nat Med Asn; AMA; bd mem, CCEMS 1976-77; secy, Houston Med Forum 1977; chmn, Educ Com, 1975-77; ann, GPA-Forde Mem Lectur & Banq, 1975-77; bd cert, Internal Med, 1973; chmn, PPO Bd, St Joseph Hosp, 1994-95, gov bd, 1994-96, chmn, Dept Med, 1992-94. **Honors/Awds:** Air Medal Commendation, 1969-70; Flight Surgeon, 1967-70. **Military Serv:** USAF, capt, 1966-70. **Home Addr:** 10715 Fawnview Dr, Houston, TX 77070, **Home Phone:** (281)469-8754. **Business Addr:** Physician, Mullins & Williams, 4315 Lockwood Dr, Houston, TX 77026, **Business Phone:** (713)675-2651.

WILLIAMS, AUBIN BERNARD
Executive, construction engineer. **Personal:** Born Mar 27, 1964, Detroit, MI; son of Eddie C Sr and Sadie J Francis. **Educ:** Wayne State Univ, Detroit, Mich, BS, 1987. **Career:** Williams & Gilliard, Detroit, Mich, field supt, 1978-82; A & S Construct, Detroit, Mich, mkt rep, 1982-85; Williams & Richardson Co Inc, Detroit, Mich, pres; Williams Corp, chmn, currently. **Orgs:** Mkt comt, Assoc Gen Contracts Am, 1988-; Detroit Econ Club, 1988-; secy, Asn Black Gen Contractors, 1989-; Nat Asn African Am Bus, 1991-. **Honors/Awds:** Construction Company of the Year, Dept Com, 1989; Company of the Year, Nat Asn Black MBA's, 1989. **Home Addr:** 8200 E Jefferson Suite 1410, Detroit, MI 48214. **Business Addr:** Chairman, Williams Corp, 1201 E Grand Blvd, Detroit, MI 48211, **Business Phone:** (313)961-5755.

WILLIAMS, AUDREAN
Entrepreneur. **Educ:** Wayne State Univ, BA, MA. **Career:** Precious Memories Wedding Chapel, owner, currently; Lula Belle Stewart Ctr, pres, currently; Detroit Pub Sch, teacher; Inst Design & Technol, col instr; Wayne Co Community Col, col instr; Blue Cross Blue Shield, Mich, trainer & curric developer. **Orgs:** Prog dir, Youth Develop Comn. **Business Addr:** Owner, Precious Memories Wedding Chapel, 19174 Livernois Ave, Detroit, MI 48221-1716, **Business Phone:** (313)864-9333.

WILLIAMS, DR. AUDREY (AUDREY WILLIAMS MEYERS)
Educator. **Personal:** Born Apr 11, 1939, Brooklyn, NY; daughter of Louis Hayworth and Gwendolyn Ashby; married Louis, Apr 6, 1974; children: Alyson Kemba. **Educ:** City Univ NY, Queens Col, BA, 1959; CCNY, MA, 1965; Univ CT, PhD, 1973. **Career:** NYC Bd Ed, teacher trainer, reading specialist, classroom teacher, 1959-70; Morgan State Univ, prog developer, Univ Without Walls, 1972-73; CUNY, Baruch Col, prof, chair, prog dir, actg dean, 1973-2001, prof emer, currently. **Orgs:** NY African Am Techs Asn, 1966-74; Col Reading Asn, 1974-95; Am Col Personnel Asn, 1978-88; Intl Reading Asn, 1980-91; Nat Asn Black Sch Educ, 1981-86; Asn Black Women Higher Educ, 1985-91; CUNY SEEK Dirs Coun. **Honors/Awds:** Univ CT, EPDA fel, 1970-72, Day of Priole honoree, 1977; Ford Found fel, 1971-72; Fulbright Award, 1989, 1991-92; Service Award, Col Reading Asn, 1992; CUNY Res Found grants & NY State Education grants. **Special Achievements:** Author of numerous articles in professional journals & book chapters. **Business Addr:** Professor Emeritus, Baruch College, City University of New York, Academic Advisement Center, One Baruch Way, New York, NY 10010.

WILLIAMS, BARBARA ANN
Air traffic controller. **Personal:** Born Jun 12, 1945, Cleveland, OH; daughter of Edward Jordan and Beatrice Williams Hill (deceased); married Howard Louis Williams, Jan 6, 1973; children: Nicole Yvonne. **Educ:** Cuyahoga Community Col, Cleveland, OH, 1965; Fed Aviation Admin, air traffic controller, mgt training progs; Embry-Riddle Aeronaut Univ, Daytona Beach, FL. **Career:** Fed Aviation Admin, Cleveland, OH, journeyman air traffic controller, 1970-77, training specialist, 1977-84, area supvr, 1984-88, sr mgr/area mgr, 1988-; Fed Aviation Admin, Des Plaines, IL, qual assurance specialist, 1984. **Orgs:** Nat treas, Prof Women Controllers, 1978-81; pres, Negro Bus & Prof Women, Cleveland Club, 1985-89; Cleveland Chapter, Jack & Jill Am, 1986-; gen chair, Ebony Fashion Fair, Negro Bus & Prof Women, Cleveland Club, 1986; Fed Mgrs Asn, 1986-; Links, Inc, 1988-. **Honors/Awds:** Federal Woman of Achievement Award, Cleveland Fed Exec Bd, 1984, 1986; Tribute, Congressman Louis Stokes, 1986; Professional of the Year, Negro Business & Professional Women, 1987; Admin Award of Excellence, Federal Aviation Admin, 1988; Professional Award, 1988. **Home Addr:** 25510 S Woodland Rd, Beachwood, OH 44122. **Business Addr:** Area Manager Air Traffic, Federal Aviation Administration-Cleveland ARTCC, 326 E Lorain St, Oberlin, OH 44074.*

WILLIAMS, BARRY LAWSON
Executive. **Personal:** Born Jul 21, 1944, Manhattan, NY; son of Otis and Ilza; married Adrienne Maria Foster, May 24, 1977; children: Barry, Jaime & Andrew. **Educ:** Harvard Col, BA, 1966; Harvard Bus Sch, MB, 1971; Harvard Law Sch, JD, 1971. **Career:** Mckinsey & Co, sr consult, 1971-78; Bechtel Group, mgr prin, 1978-87; Pac Gas & Electric Co, dir, 1990-96; CH2M Hill Co Ltd, dir; Am Mgt Asn, pres & chief exec officer, 2000-01; Williams Pac Ventures Inc, pres, 1987-; Corning fel. **Orgs:** Dir, Northwestern Mutual Life, 1986-; dir, PG & E Corp, 1992; dir, Simpson Mfg, 1994-95; pres, Harvard Alumni Asn, 1994-95; dir, CompUSA, 1995-2000; SLM dir, USA Group, 1995; dir, RH Donnelly & Co, 1998-; dir, CH2M Hill, 1995-; Newhall Land & Farming, 1996-2003; Kaiser Health, 1999-2003. **Honors/Awds:** Silver Spur Award; Allston Burr Award; Harvard Medal. **Home Addr:** 1737 Alhambra Lane, Oakland, CA 94611, **Home Phone:** (510)339-6364. **Business Addr:** President, Williams Pacific Ventures Inc, 4 Embarcadero Ctr Suite 3700, San Francisco, CA 94111, **Business Phone:** (415)896-2311.

WILLIAMS, BART H
Lawyer. **Educ:** Yale Univ, BA, 1984; Yale Law Sch, JD, 1987. **Career:** Cent Dist Calif, asst US atty, 1991-94; Munger, Tolles & Olson LLP, co-managing partner, African-Am partner, litigation assoc, 1987-91, atty, currently, Walt Disney Co, pres; lead trial coun, Sr Hyundai Motor Am exec. **Orgs:** Am Bar Asn Litigation Sect; LA County Bar Asn Task Force; bd dirs, Alliance Childrens Rights; bd trustees, Charles R Drew Univ Med & Sci. **Honors/Awds:** 45 Under Forty-Five " The Rising Stars of the Private Bar. **Business Addr:** Attorney, Munger, Tolles & Olsen LLP, 355 S Grand Ave Suite 3500 35th Fl, Los Angeles, CA 90071, **Business Phone:** (213)683-9295.*

WILLIAMS, BENJAMIN VERNON
Journalist. **Personal:** Born Jan 25, 1927, St Louis, MO; married Vivian Hickman; children: Benjamin Jr, Gregory & Alan. **Educ:** San Francisco State Univ, BA, 1961. **Career:** Journalist (retired); San Francisco Sun-Reporter, news reporter 1963-66; San Francisco Examiner, newspaper reporter, 1963-66; San Francisco State Univ, lectr 1968-79; KPIX-TV Ch 5, news reporter, 1966-91; tutor. **Orgs:** Oakland Athletic Club, 1975-; bd dirs, Am Red Cross Oakland Br; Am Heart Asn Alameda Chap. **Honors/Awds:** Jane Harrah Award in Journalism, San Francisco Lawyers Club, 1965; San Francisco Press Club Award (2), San Francisco Press Club (tv & radio news), 1966 & 1971; McQuade Award Distinguished Programming, Asn Catholic Newsmen, 1974; Broadcast Media Award for Single Accomplishment & Highest Standards in TV-News, San Francisco State Univ, 1976; 2 Emmy Awdars for TV News No CA Emmy, 1976-77. **Military Serv:** AUS, sgt, 1945-47. **Home Addr:** 7818 Hansom Dr, Oakland, CA 94605.

WILLIAMS, BERNABE FIGUEROA. **See WILLIAMS, BERNIE.**

WILLIAMS, BERNIE (BERNABE FIGUEROA WILLIAMS)
Baseball player, musician. **Personal:** Born Sep 13, 1968, San Juan, PR; married Waleska, Feb 23, 1990; children: Bernie Jr, Beatriz & and Bianca. **Educ:** Univ Puerto Rico. **Career:** NY Yankees, outfielder, 1991-92, ctr fielder, 1993-2006; musician, currently. **Honors/Awds:** AL LCS MVP, 1996; Five-time All-Star, 1997-2001; Four AL Gold Glove-CF, 1997-2000; AL All Star Team, 1997-99; AL Batting Champion, 1998; Four-time World Series Champion, 1996-2000; Silver Slugger Award winner, 2002. **Special Achievements:** Album: The Journey Within, musician, 2003; "La Salsa En Mi", "Desvelado; "Just Because";"Para Don Berna"; "Samba Novo", "La Salsa En Mi", 2003. *

WILLIAMS, DR. BERTHA A.
Educator, psychologist. **Personal:** Born Jul 10, 1927, Brighton, TN; divorced; children: Kenneth M. **Educ:** Ariz State Univ, BA, 1964; Ariz State Univ, MA, 1966, PhD, 1973; Mercy Ctr Spiritual Dir Inst, cert. **Career:** Luke Elem Sch Luke AFB, teacher, 1963-67, consult, 1967-71; Ariz State Univ Tempe, consult, 1971-73; Univ Tenn, Knoxville, asst prof & psychologist, 1973-76; Univ Calif Los Angeles, consult psychologist, 1976-; Univ Calif Berkeley, fac; San Damiano Retreat Ctr, counr & guide. **Orgs:** Bd dirs, Desert Sch Fed Credit Union, 1968-71; consult, Sch Bd Louisville KY, 1975; bd mgt, YWCA, 1977-80; vpres bd mgt, YWCA, 1980-. **Honors/Awds:** Outstanding Achievement in Educ Univ Tenn, 1974; "Trust & Self-Disclosure Among Black Coll Students" Jour Counsel Psychol, 1974; "Black Women, Assertiveness vs Aggressiveness" Jour Afro-Am Issues, 1974; "Assertion Training" The Orientation Review 1978.

WILLIAMS, DR. BETTY SMITH
Nurse, educator. **Personal:** Born Jul 22, 1929, South Bend, IN; daughter of John Wesley and Nellie Mae Lindsay; married Harold Louis, Jul 10, 1954. **Educ:** Howard Univ, BS; Western Res Univ, MN; Univ Calif, Sch Nursing, Los Angeles, MS; Sch Pub Health Univ Calif Los Angeles, Dr PH. **Career:** Vis Nurse Asn, Cleveland, staff nurse, 1954-55; Los Angeles City Health Dept, staff nurse, 1955-66; Mt St Mary's Col, Los Angeles, asst prof,1956-69; Charles Drew Post Grad Med Sch, Los Angeles, pub health nurse consult, 1970-71; Univ Calif, Los Angeles, Sch Nursing, asst prof, 1969-,asst dean student affairs, 1974-75, asst dean acad affairs, 1975-76; Sch Nursing, Colo Health Sci Ctr, Denver, dean & prof, 1979-84; Calif State Univ, Long Beach, prof, 1988-96, prof emer, currently; Kaiser Permanente, consult; Delta Sigma Theta Ctr, Life Develop, exec dir. **Orgs:** Fel Am Pub Health Asn, 1969; founder & pres, Coun Black Nurses Inc, 1969-74; nat treas, DST Telecomm Inc, 1971-73, pres, 1975-79; bd dir, Blue Cross Southern Calif, 1976-80; dir, bd dir, Blue Cross Calif, 1986-95;founding charter mem, bd dirs, exec comt, pres, Nat Black Nurses Asn,Wash, DC, 1995-99; nat hon mem, Iota Phi Lamda Sorority, 1997-; pres, Nat Coalition Ethnic Minority Nurse asn, 1998-; Delta Sigma Theta Inc PublicServ Org; Op Womanpower Inc; Watts Towers Art Ctr; Com Simon Rodia's Towers In Watts; Charles Drew Post-Grad Med Sch Continuing Educ Nurses Task Force; pres, Los Angeles Alumnae Chap, Delta Sigma Theta Inc; lifemem, Nat Asn Advan Colored People; mem, Nat Caucus Black Health WorkersAPHA; affirmative action task force, Am Nurses Asn; mem, Calif Nurses Asn; fel Am Acad Nursing; hon mem, Chi Eta Phi. **Honors/Awds:** Nat Sojourner Truth Award, Nat Bus & Profl Womens Clubs Inc, 1972; Distinguished Alumna Award, Case Western Res Univ, Sch Nursing, 1998; Unsung Hero Award, Congressional Black Caucus Spouses, 1999; inducted in African American History Calender, 2003. **Business Addr:** Professor Emeritus, California State University, Department of Nursing, 1250 N Bellflower Blvd, Long Beach, CA 90840, **Business Phone:** (562)985-4111.

WILLIAMS, BEVERLY
Basketball player. **Personal:** Born Nov 9, 1965. **Educ:** Univ Tex, BA, kinesiology, 1991. **Career:** Texas longhorns, guard, 1984-88; Long Beach Stingrays, guard, 1997; Ind Fever, 2000; Sacramento Monarchs, guard, 2002. **Honors/Awds:** Women's Hall of Honor, 2009. **Special Achievements:** All-American guard, Kodak, 1988; Two-time All-SWC selection. *

WILLIAMS, BIG CAT. **See WILLIAMS, JAMES OTIS.**

WILLIAMS, BILLY DEE (WILLIAM DECEMBER WILLIAMS, JR.)
Actor. **Personal:** Born Apr 6, 1937, New York, NY; married Teruko Nakagami; children: Corey, Miyako & Hanako. **Educ:** Nat Acad Fine Arts & Design. **Career:** Films: The Last Angry Man, 1959; The Cool World; A Taste of Honey; Hallelujah Baby; Firebrand of Florence; Lady Sings the Blues, 1972; Mahogany, 1975; Scott Joplin, 1977; The Empire Strikes Back, 1980; Night-Hawks, 1981; The Return of the Jedi, 1983; Marvin & Tige, 1983; Fear City, 1984; Deadly Illusion, 1987, Batman, 1989; Secret Agent OO Soul, 1990; Driving Me Crazy, 1991; Alien Intruder, 1993; The Prince, 1996; Steel Sharks, 1996; Moving Target, 1996; Mask of Death, 1996; The Contract, 1998; The Visit, 2000; The Ladies Man, 2000; The Last Place on Earth, 2000; Very Heavy Love, 2001; Good Neighbor, 2001; Undercover Brother, 2002; Constellation, 2005; Hood of Horror, 2006; Fanboys, 2008; TV films: Carter's Army, Brian's Song, The Glass House, The Hostage Tower, Children of Divorce, Shooting Stars, Chiefs, Christmas Lilies of the Field, Scott Joplin, Time Bomb, The Impostor, The Right People, Oceans of Fire, Courage, The Return of Desperado, Dangerous Passion, The Jacksons: An American Dream, Marked for Murder, Percy & Thunder, Message from Nam, Falling for You, Triplecross, Hard Time; Epoch: Evolution, 2003; Television Appearances: The Jeffersons; The Interns; The FBI; Mission Impossible; Mod Squad; Police Woman; Dynasty; Promised Land; The Hughleys, 1998; Gideon's Crossing, 2000; 18 Wheels of Justice, 2000; The Big Breakfast, 1992; Broadway & off-Broadway appearances: Hallelujah Baby; Ceremonies in Dark Old Men; Fences. **Orgs:** Actors Workshop in Harlem. **Honors/Awds:** Emmy nomination for Brian's Song. **Business Phone:** (310)277-7779.

WILLIAMS, BILLY LEO
Baseball player, athletic coach. **Personal:** Born Jun 15, 1938, Whistler, AL; married Shirley; children: Valarie, Nina, Julia &

Sandra. **Career:** Baseball player, outfielder (retired), coach; Chicago Cubs, outfielder, 1959-74, minor league hitting instr, 1978-79, hitting instr, 1980-82, coach, 1986-87, 1992-, spec asst pres; Oakland Athletics, outfielder, 1975-76, coach, 1983-85; Cleveland Indians, coaching asst. **Honors/Awds:** Rookie of the Year, Baseball Writers Asn Am, 1961; Player of the Year, Nat League, 1972; Major League Player of the Year, The Sporting News, 1972; All Star Game six times; Holds the Nat League rec most consecutive games played (1117); Tied major league recs, 1968; hit 3 home runs one game,1968; tied major league rec most consecutive doubles one game, 1969; Chicago Sports Hall of Fame, 1982; Baseball Hall of Fame, 1987; had jersey No 26 retired by the Chicago Cubs, 1987.

WILLIAMS, BILLY MYLES
Manager. **Personal:** Born Sep 6, 1950, Kings Mountain, NC; son of Willis Frank and Mattie Ashley; married Rosemarie Delores Wesson. **Educ:** Univ NC, Chapel Hill, BS, 1972; Central Mich Univ, MS, 1980. **Career:** Martin Marietta Chem, 1972-74; Dow Chem Co, 1974-, lab dir, res & develop dir; Nat Acad Scis, sr prog officer, currently. **Orgs:** Mem Sigma Xi, 1982-; Sigma Iota Epsilon, 1984-; AAAS, 1985-; Big Brothers; chmn, Midland Sect Am Chem Soc, 1988-89. **Business Addr:** Senior Program Officer, National Academy of Sciences, Naval Studies Board, 500 Fifth St N W, Washington, DC 20001.

WILLIAMS, BOBBY
Football coach. **Personal:** Born Nov 21, 1958, St louis, MO; married Sheila; children: Nataly & Nicholas. **Educ:** Purdue Univ, BS, general mgt, 1982. **Career:** Ball State, running backs coach, defensive backs coach, 1983-84; Eastern Michigan, offensive backfield coach, 1985-89; Kansas, receivers coach, 1990; Michigan State, running backs coach, 1990-99; Michigan State Univ, head football coach, 1999-02; Detroit Lions, coach, 2003; LSU Athletic Dept, wide receivers, 2003, assoc head coach, 2004; miami Dolphins, running back coach, 2005-06; Tight Ends Coach & Special Teams Coordinator, Ala, 2008-. **Orgs:** Omega Psi Phi Fraternity, Inc. *

WILLIAMS, BRAINARD
Automotive executive. **Career:** Hayward Pontiac-Buick-GMC Truck, pres, currently. **Business Phone:** (510)582-4436.

WILLIAMS, BRANDON
Basketball player. **Personal:** Born Feb 27, 1975, Collinston, LA. **Educ:** Davidson. **Career:** LE Haure, France, prof basketball player, 1996-97; CBA, La Crosse Bobcats, 1997-98; Golden State Warriors, guard, 1998; San Antonio Spurs, forward,1999; Detroit Pistons, 2002; Milwaukee Bucks, forward, 2004-05; Sioux Falls Sky force, Guard, 2005; MACU, guard, 2007-. **Honors/Awds:** All-District honors; Honorable mention, all NBDL, 2002-03. *

WILLIAMS, BRIAN CARSON. **See DELE, BISON.**

WILLIAMS, BRIAN MARCEE
Football player. **Personal:** Born Dec 17, 1972, Dallas, TX. **Educ:** Univ SC, public admin, 1996. **Career:** Football player (retired); Green Bay Packers, linebacker, 1995-2000; New Orleans Saints, 2001; Detroit Lions, 2001-03. *

WILLIAMS, BRIAN O'NEAL
Entrepreneur, baseball player. **Personal:** Born Feb 15, 1969, Lancaster, SC. **Educ:** Univ SC. **Career:** Baseball player (Retired), entrepreneur; Houston Astros, pitcher, 1991-94; San Diego Padres, 1995; Detroit Tigers, 1996; Baltimore Orioles, 1997; Houston Astro, 1999; Chicago Cubs, 2000, reliever & baseball opers asst; Cleveland Indians, 2000; Columbus Clippers, 2001; Body Works LLC, owner, currently. **Honors/Awds:** NL Rookie of the Year, 1992.

WILLIAMS, BRUCE E.
Executive. **Personal:** Born Sep 2, 1931, St Paul, MN; married Wilma Allen; children: Deborah Lynn, Lisa Marie. **Educ:** Mankato State Col, BS, 1956; MS, 1970; Union Grad Sch, PhD, 1977. **Career:** Juv Detention Group, supvr, 1960-61; Registered Basketball & Football, official; Summer Staff Develop Prog Minneapolis Pub Schs, dir, 1966; Minneapolis Schs, teacher, 1962-68; Minneapolis Schs, prin, 1968-71; Minneapolis Schs, asst supt, 1971-72; Rockefeller Found, asst dir. **Orgs:** Am Asn Sch Adminr; Asn Supervision & Curriculum Develop Nat Alliance Black Sch Educ; Mankato State Col Alumni Asn; YMCA; vpres Afro-Am Educ Asn; Hall fame Mankato State Univ; Rockefeller Found Fellow; trustee, Macalester Col St Paul; pres, gen educ bd NY Sch Bd Syst; NY State Human Rights Adv Coun; Educ Adv Comt Nat Urban League; NY Gov's Adv Comt Black Affairs. **Military Serv:** AUS, sp, 4th class, 1957-59.

WILLIAMS, BUCK (CHARLES WILLIAMS)
Basketball coach, basketball player. **Personal:** Born Mar 8, 1960, Rocky Mount, NC; married Mimi; children: Julien & Malek. **Educ:** Univ Md, College Park. **Career:** Basketball player (retired), basketball coach; US Olympic Team, 1980; NJ Nets, forward, 1981-89, Portland Trail Blazers, 1989-96; NY Knicks, 1996-99; Md Madness, coach, 2006-. **Orgs:** Pres, NBA Players Asn, 1994-97; hon chmn, March Dimes; Emanuel Hosp's Children's Gala. **Honors/Awds:** ACC Rookie of the Year, 1979; NBA Rookie of the Year, 1982; Rocky Mount Twin County Hall of Fame, 2006. **Business Addr:** Basketball Coach, Maryland Madness Inc, 15110 Springfield Rd, Darnestown, MD 20874, **Business Phone:** (301)424-9478.

WILLIAMS, CALVIN JOHN, JR.
Football player. **Personal:** Born Mar 3, 1967, Baltimore, MD. **Educ:** Purdue Univ, hotel & restaurant mgt,attended. **Career:** Football player (retired); Philadelphia Eagles, wide receiver, 1990-96; Baltimore Ravens, 1996. *

WILLIAMS, CAMILLA ELLA
Opera singer, educator. **Personal:** Born Oct 18, 1919, Danville, VA; married Charles T Beavers (deceased). **Educ:** VA State Univ, BS, 1941. **Career:** Created role Madame Butterfly First black contract singer New York City Ctr, 1946; First Aida at New York City Ctr, 1948; First NY perf Mozart's "Idomeneo" w/Little Orch Soc, 1950; First tour Alaska, 1950; First European tour, 1954; First Viennese perf Menotti's "Saint of Bleecker St", 1955; Am Fest Belgium, 1955; First African tour for US State Dept, 1958-59; First tour Israel, 1959; guest Pres Eisenhower-concert for Crown Prince of Japan, 1960; tours Europe, Asia & Australia, 1962; NY perf Handel's "Orlando"; First tour Poland, 1974; Bronx Col, prof voice, 1970; Brooklyn Col, prof voice, 1970-73; Queens Col, prof voice, 1974-; IN Univ, black prof voice, 1977, emer prof music, currently. **Orgs:** Nat Soc Arts & Letters, 1981. **Honors/Awds:** Honored Govt VA Linwood Holton Distinguished Virginian, 1971; listed Danville VA Museum of Fine Arts & History Hall of Fame, 1974; Camilla Williams Park designatd in Danville VA, 1974; honored by IN Univ Sch Music Black Music Students Orgn Outstanding Achievements in the field of music, 1979; honored by Gov Julian M Carroll of KY as a "Kentucky Colonel", 1979; Hon mem Sigma Alpha Iota, 1980; honored guest NY Philharmonic 10000th Concert Celebration, 1982; honored by Philadelphia Pro Arte Soc, 1982; Disting Award Ctr Leadership & Develop, 1983; included first ed Most Important Women Twentieth Century, new Grove's Dictionary Music & Musicians, 1984; Taylor-Williams student residence hall named at VA State Univ honor Billy Taylor & Camilla Williams; Honorary Doctor of Music, Va St Univ, Petersburg, 1985; Arts & Humanities Award, Va State Univ, 1989. **Special Achievements:** First African American to sing with the New York City Opera; first black prof of voice to teach at Central Conservatory of Music Beijing People's Republic of China 1983. **Home Addr:** 2610 E 2nd St, Bloomington, IN 47401, **Home Phone:** (812)336-3099. **Business Addr:** Emerita Professor of Music, Indiana University, School of Music, 2805 E Tenth St, Bloomington, IN 47408-2601, **Business Phone:** (812)855-8547.

WILLIAMS, CARL. **See KANI, KARL.**

WILLIAMS, CARLETTA CELESTE
Nurse. **Personal:** Born Mar 5, 1956, Steubenville, OH; daughter of Franklin T Platt Sr and Catherine B Scruggs Platt; married Calvin C Williams Jr; children: Charles, PJ & Cecilia. **Educ:** WV Northern Community Col, AD, Nursing, 1977; W Liberty State Col, BS, Nursing, 1986; Duquesne Univ, MSN, nursing admin, 1992. **Career:** OH Valley Hosp, dietary aide, 1972-77; Weirton Med Ctr, Weirton, WV, reg nurse, 1977-79, CCU, 1980-, hd nurse, critical care unit, 1986, dir critical care, 1992, cardiopulmonary adminr, 2001-; Johns-Hopkins Hosp, reg nurse CCU, 1979-80. **Orgs:** AACN 1986-; BPW 1986-; church nurse Second Baptist Church, 1987; mem, Golden Star Chorus, Second Baptist Church, 1988. **Honors/Awds:** CCRN, 1983-01; Woman of the Year in Health Care, Cameo-The Womens Ctr, Steubenville, OH, 1990; Sigma Theta Tau, 1992; Shero Award, Ohio Comn Minority Health, 2006. **Home Addr:** 522 Maxwell Ave, Steubenville, OH 43952. **Business Addr:** Administrator, Weirton Medical Center, 601 Colliers Way, Weirton, WV 26062, **Business Phone:** (304)797-6000.

WILLIAMS, CAROL H
President (Organization), chief executive officer, chief financial officer. **Educ:** Northwestern Univ, attended. **Career:** Leo Burnett Co, Chicago, vpres; Foote, Cone & Belding, San Francisco, sr vpres & creative dir; Carol H Williams Advertising, pres, chief exec officer & chief creative officer, currently. **Orgs:** Cong Black Caucus; Nat Asn Advan Colored People. **Honors/Awds:** Missouri Honor Medal for Distinguished Serv in Jour. **Special Achievements:** The first African-American female creative director and vice president of the Leo Burnett Co. **Business Addr:** President, Chief Executive Officer, Chief Creative Officer, Carol H Williams Advertising, 555 12th St Suite 1700, Oakland, CA 94607, **Business Phone:** (510)763-5200.

WILLIAMS, CAROLYN G
School administrator. **Educ:** Wayne State Univ, PhD, Higher Educ. **Career:** Highland Park Community Col, dean stud affair; Los Angeles Southwest Col, pres; Wayne County Community Col, vice provost, acad & stud affairs; Bronx Community Col, pres, currently. **Orgs:** Chair, Am Asn Community Col; bd mem, Asn Am Col & Univs; bd mem, Nat Articulation & Transfer Network; chair, Community Col; bd mem, Res Found, City Univ NY. **Business Addr:** President, Bronx Community College, W 181st & Univ Ave, Bronx, NY 10453, **Business Phone:** (718)289-5100.

WILLIAMS, HON. CAROLYN H
Judge. **Personal:** Born Jan 1, 1943?, Washington, DC. **Educ:** George Wash Univ Nat Law Ctr, BA, Polit Sci, 1964, JD, 1968. **Career:** MI Circuit Ct, Family Div, presiding judge, currently; Kalamazoo Co Bar Asn, Kalamazoo Co Circuit Ct, judge probate, 1994-. **Orgs:** Pres, Mich Probate Judges Asn; Am Bar Asn; Mich Bar Asn; Kalamazoo Co Bar Asns; Delta Sigma Theta; Women Lawyers SW Mich; State Mich Child Support Coordinating Coun, 1997-; State Bar Mich, Open Justice Comn, 1998-. **Honors/Awds:** Women Aware Award, YWCA, 1987; William H Hastie Award for Significant Contributions in Law, Omega Psi Phi, Upsilon Pi Chap, 1987; Glass Ceiling Award, Kalamazoo Network, 1997; Red Rose Citation, Kalamazoo Rotary, 1997; Women of Achievement, Kalamazoo YWCA, 1998. **Home Addr:** 2237 Lorraine, Kalamazoo, MI 49008. **Business Addr:** Probate Judge, Kalamazoo County Bar Association, Kalamazoo County Circuit Court, 1400 Gull Rd, Kalamazoo, MI 49048, **Business Phone:** (616)385-6001.

WILLIAMS, DR. CAROLYN RUTH ARMSTRONG
Educator, scholar, consultant. **Personal:** Born Feb 17, 1944, Birmingham, AL; daughter of Lois Adel America Merriweather and Lonnie; married James Alvin Williams Jr, Mar 16, 1968. **Educ:** Tenn State Univ, BS, 1966; HI Univ, cert Asian Studies, 1970; Northwestern Univ, MA, 1972; Cornell Univ, MA, 1978, PhD, 1978. **Career:** Barringer HS, hist teacher, 1967-69; Thomas Jefferson HS, hist teacher, 1969-70; Union Col, instr dept hist, 1970-73; Tompkins County Comm Col, adj prof, 1973-76; SUNY Cortland, lectr & instr, dept hist, 1973-76; Cornell Univ Career Ctr, assoc dir, 1976-82; Harvard Univ, head proctor, 1983; US Senator Paul Tsongas, spec proj asst, 1983; NC Cent Univ, from asst to vice chancellor univ relations, 1983-87; Vanderbilt Univ, Minority Affairs & Women Engineering Prog, asst dean & assoc prof, 1987-97; biomed coordr, 1993-; Tenn State Univ, adj prof hist; NASA sec Navy Summer Res Residential Prog, consult, 1997; St Cloud State Univ, Col Social Sci, assoc dean, 1999-. **Orgs:** Exec bd mem admin, counrs NAWDAC, 1980-82; Comm Blacks Higher Ed & Black Col & Univ, 1980-81; ed consult, LeMoyne Col Higher Ed Preparation Prog, 1981-; ed consult & co-founder, Youth Data Inc, 1981-; exec bd mem, Phi Delta Kappa, Nat Asn Women Deans; Delta Sigma Theta Inc; counsrs jour bd, Nat Asn Women Admin, 1986-88; exec regional bd, Nat Soc Black Engineers, 1987-; proposal reader US Dept Educ, 1989-; Rotary Int; tech coordr Nat Soc Women Engineers, 1989-91; nat secy, Women Sci, 1992-94; bd chair, 1992-94, exec bd dirs, 1992-, NAMEPA Region; nat adv comm, NIH, biomed res support, 1993-; Comm Nat Inst Environ, adv bd, 1993-; NSF Site Reviewer Gateway Coalition, 1994-; treas, NAMEPA Region B, 1996-98; founding officer, sec MIN chapter, Black Women Higher Educ; Concerned Citizens Group; ed bd, St Cloud Times Newspaper; bd dir, YMCA, St Cloud, MN; Leadership Prog, St Cloud Chamber Comm. **Honors/Awds:** Woodrow Wilson Admin Fellow, 1983-86; Thycydidean Honor Soc Awd, YWCA Women Achievement Award; Phi Delta Kappa, Sigma Rho Sigma Honor Soc Awd Phi Alpha Theta Awd; Doctoral Dissertation Funded by Rockefeller Found, Fellowship/Scholarship Cornell Univ, Northwestern Univ; YMCA Women Achievement Awd, 1984-85 & 86-87; Burton Lecturer for Harvard Univ Ed School Colloquaim Bd, 1983; Nat Society Black Engineers Community Leadership Award, 1987; National Society of Black Engineers Charles E Tunstall Award for Best MNY ENG Program in US, 1990-91; NAMPERA Ryn B Award, 1992; Vanderbilt Univ, Affirmative Action Award, September, 1989-90; NAMEPA Region B Award, 1993-96; NAMEPA Region B Chain Awd, 1996; NAT Appreciation Award, NAT Society of Black ENRs, 1997; United Negro College Fund Speaker, Award Recipient, 1998; Appreciation Awd, Assoc Women In Science Bd. **Special Achievements:** First Black Dean in engineering School; First woman dean in engineering school. **Business Addr:** Associate Dean, St. Cloud State University, College of Social Sciences, 101 Whitney House 720 Forth Ave S, St Cloud, MN 56301-4498, **Business Phone:** (320)308-0121.

WILLIAMS, DR. CARROLL BURNS, JR.
Educator, scientist. **Personal:** Born Sep 24, 1929, St Louis, MO; son of Carroll and Maxine Henderson; children: Robyn Claire, Margaret & Carroll Blake. **Educ:** Univ Mich, BS, 1955, MS, 1957, PhD, 1963. **Career:** US Forest Service, res forester, 1961-65, res entomologist, 1965-68, proj leader, 1968-72; Yale Sch Forestry, lectr, 1969-72; US Forest Servc, forest insect ecologist, 1972-75, pioneer sci, 1975-84; proj leader, 1984-88; Univ Calif, Berkeley, adj prof, 1988-. **Orgs:** Consult, Ecology & Ecosystems NSF, 1971-74; tech consult, USFS Insecticide Field Tests, 1973-; Entomol Soc Am; Soc Am Foresters; dir, Berkeley Sch Bd Berkeley Unified Sch Dist, 1977-84; vis prof, Black Exchange Prog, Nat Urban League, 1975-84; bd dirs, Berkeley-Albany YMCA, 1979-; bd dirs, Berkeley Rotary, 1990-94; bd trustees, New Perspectives Inc, Alcohol & Drug Coun, 1985-87; dir, E Bay Regional Park Dist, Ward 1, 1991-92; bd, Berkeley Pub Educ Found, 1993-95. **Military Serv:** USM, staff sgt, 1950-53. **Home Addr:** 89 Arden Rd, Berkeley, CA 94704, **Home Phone:** (510)841-0612. **Business Addr:** Adjunct Professor, University of

California, Department of Forestry, 108 Mulford Hall, Berkeley, CA 94720, **Business Phone:** (510)642-8092.

WILLIAMS, CASSANDRA FAYE
Paleontologist. **Personal:** Born Aug 16, 1948, Sherrill, AR; daughter of Lewis and Millye L Dickerson-Beatty; children: Kyra Erica. **Educ:** Northeastern Ill State Univ, 1967; Univ Ark, Pine Bluff, AR, BS, 1970; Ky State Univ, S Dakota Sch Mines, 1978; Tulane Univ, New Orleans, LA, MS,1979. **Career:** Univ Chicago Hosps & Clinics, Chicago, IL, clinic biochemist, 1970-71; Orleans Parish Sch Bd, New Orleans, LA, biol teacher, 1971-72; Chevron USA, New Orleans, LA, exploration palaeontologist, 1972-. **Orgs:** Am Asn Stratigraphic Palynologists; Gulf Coast sect, Soc Econ Palaeontologists & Mineralogists; Int Comn Palynology; Am Asn BlacksEnergy; Tau Iota Mu; pres, New Orleans club, 1985-86, nat conventionco-chair, 1986, Nat Asn Negro Bus & Prof Women's Clubs; Delta Sigma Theta. **Honors/Awds:** Voluntary service awards, NAACP, 1984, Chevron USA, 1984; outstanding-achievement awards, Nat Asn Negro Bus & Prof Women's Clubs, 1984, 1986;outstanding serv award, New Orleans chap, Nat Bus League, 1987; WorldService Award, & Volunteer Service Award, Girl Scouts Am, 1988. **Home Addr:** 7601 Briarwood Dr, New Orleans, LA 70128. **Business Addr:** Plaeontologist, Chevron USA, 935 Gravier St Room 748, New Orleans, LA 70112, **Business Phone:** (504)592-6325.

WILLIAMS, CATHERINE G.
Government official, executive. **Personal:** Born Nov 21, 1914, Des Moines, IA; married Richard Jr. **Educ:** Cortez Bus Col, grad, 1948; Univ Iowa, MA, soc work, 1965; Drake Univ, soc & psychol; Simpson Col, LHD, 1981. **Career:** Prof dancer; typist; Div of Comm Serv IA Dept Soc Serv, dir, 1973-75; Iowa Dept of Social Serv, dep commr, 1975-81; Bur Family & Adult Serv Iowa Dept Assocs, dir; Bur Family & Adult Serv ID of Soc Serv, assoc Dir; IA Dept of Social Serv, child welfare staff dev; Polk Co Iowa Dept of Social Serv Com, child welfare supr; Johnson & Williams Assocs, consult, 1981. **Orgs:** Nat Asn Advan Colored People Scholar; commr Planning & Zoning Commn Des Moines 1980-; bd mem, Willkie Hosue Inc; Health Facilities Coun; City of Des Moines Planning & Zoning Comt; Proj Helper Bd; Coun Human Serv; Simpson Col Task Force Minority Stud Concerns, United Way; Model Cities Allocation Comt; Community Rels Task Force; Nat Asn Advan Colored People; Jewish Fed. **Honors/Awds:** Social Worker of the Yr, Nat Asn Soc Workers, Iowa Chap, 1980; Iowa Women's Hall of Fame, 1980; Black Women of Achievement Cult Develop Com, 1980; MarkHall Lectr, Univ of Iowa, Sch of Social Work, 1980; Volunteer Award, State of Iowa, 1984; YWCA/Mary Louise Smith Racial Justice Award, 1990; Sch Social Work Distinguished Alumnae Award, The Univ Iowa, 1990; Iowa African-Americans Hall of Fame, 1999; PACE, 1999; Nat Black Child Develop Inst Award, 2000. **Special Achievements:** Became the highest-ranking African-American female in state government and one of the highest ranking in social services nationally.

WILLIAMS, CHARLENE J.
Journalist. **Personal:** Born Jul 13, 1949, Atlantic City, NJ. **Educ:** Boston Univ, BS, 1971; Columbia Univ, MS, 1972. **Career:** Columbia Univ, adminr asst, 1971-72; WTOP Radio Post Newsweek Stas Inc, Wash DC, radio news ed, 1972-; Westinghouse Broadcasting Co NY, part-time rewriter; WBUR Boston Univ FM Radio Sta, disc-jockey, ed writer, prod dir; Boston Univ, Year Book Hub, gen assignment ed; WCRB Waltham Am Fed TV & Radio Artists. **Orgs:** Commun Asn; Sigma Delta Chi; Adams Morgan Orgn; vol, Heart Fund; ARC; DC Black Repetory; CRI Inst; pres, Stud Body Boston Univ, 1970-71; pres, Stud Body Columbia Univ, 1971-72. **Honors/Awds:** Nat Honor Soc Atlantic City High Sch, 1967; Scarlet Key Honor Soc Boston Univ, 1971.

WILLIAMS, CHARLES. See WILLIAMS, BUCK.

WILLIAMS, CHARLES C
Real estate developer, government official, commissioner. **Personal:** Born Oct 10, 1939, Pontiac, MI; children: Charles C III, Cassandra & Veronica. **Educ:** Fla Agr & Mech Univ, Polit Sci, 1962; NC Central Univ Law Sch, 1963. **Career:** Atlanta Reg Comn, dir commun, 1974-78; Ga Power Co, manpower resources coordr, 1978-80; Amertelco Inc, exec vpres, 1980-84; Air Atlanta, spec consult chair bd, 1984-; Fulton City, Bd Comn, comnr, currently. **Orgs:** Bd mem, W End Med Ctr, 1980-83; bd managers, Asn City Commisioners Ga, 1978-; vpres, Nat Asn Counties, 1985-88; exec comt mem, Nat Dem City Officials, 1985-; dist mem, large Boy Scouts Am, 1985-86; bd mem, Neighborhood Justice Ctr, 1985-86; Mem Coalition 100 Black Men; GABEO; Nat Asn Advan Colored People; Kappa Alpha Phi; Nat Asn Black County Officials; W End Neighborhood Develop, Inc. **Honors/Awds:** Plaque YMCA Butler St Century Club, 1973; Community Service Award, Atlanta Southside Community Heallth Center; Certificate of Appreciation, W End Med Ctr; plaque from Atlanta Medical Asn 1980; Atlanta Business League Torch Bearer Award, 1985; plaque Concerned Citizens Atlanta; plaque Jomandi Prod, 1986; United Negro Col fund; Neighborhood Arts Center; Metro Atlanta SCLC Community Service Award; Hearts & Hands Fdn Hanicapped, Inc. **Business Addr:** Commissioner, Fulton County Commissioners, 165 Central Ave, Atlanta, GA 30303, **Business Phone:** (404)572-2458.

WILLIAMS, CHARLES E
Lawyer. **Personal:** Born May 10, 1946, New York City, NY. **Educ:** Franklin & Marshall Col, AB, 1966; Columbia Univ Sch Law, JD, 1969. **Career:** Marshall Bratter Greene Allison & Tucker NYC, assoc, 1970-72; Nat Asn Advan Colored People Legal Defense & Ed Fund Inc, asst counsel; Bur Labor Serv City NY, dir, 1978-79; Dep Sec State NY State Dept, gen counsel, 1979-82; State NY, acting secy state, 1982; NY City Housing Authority, gen counsel, 1983-86; NY City Sch Construction Authority, vpres & gen counsel, 1989-93; Peckar & Abramson, Partner & lawyer, currently. **Orgs:** NY City Bar Asn; Nat Basketball Asn; Nat Conf Black Lawyers; bd dir, Upper Manhatten Empowerment Zone; bd trustees, Saint Frances Col; Am Bar Asn. **Military Serv:** USAR, spl 4/c, 1969. **Business Addr:** Partner, Lawer, Peckar & Abramson, 546 5 th Ave, New York, NY 10036, **Business Phone:** (212)382-0909.

WILLIAMS, CHARLES EARL
Government official, firefighter. **Personal:** Born Jul 29, 1955, Memphis, TN; son of Perry and Ardelia. **Educ:** Univ Mich, Fire Acad, beginning & advan fire fighting; Tustin Mich Sch Arson Investigators. **Career:** River Rouge Fire Dept, sgt, 1987, lt engineer & line lt, 1991, capt engr, 1994, fire marshal, 1994-. **Orgs:** Downriver Mutual Aid Fire investigators, 1994-; Int Asn Fire Investigators, 1994-; pres, Union Local 517, River Rouge Firefighters Asn, 1994-; Demolition Comt & Renovation, City River Rouge, 1994-. **Special Achievements:** First African-American Fire Marshal for City of River Rouge, MI; City-wide Education in Fire Prevention. **Business Addr:** Fire Marshal, River Rouge Fire Department, 10600 W Jefferson Ave, River Rouge, MI 48218, **Business Phone:** (313)842-2929.

WILLIAMS, CHARLES J., SR.
Clergy, bishop. **Personal:** Born Apr 1, 1942, Wayne County, NC; married Linda Oates; children: Valerie, Charles, Jr, Antraun. **Educ:** Christian Inst, attended 1966; Shaw Univ, AB, 1973; M Div, 1975; Ibis, DMin, 1975. **Career:** Cherry Hosp, Clin I Chaplain, ment health teacher, 1960-74; Western Assembly Disciples of Christ Churches, bishop. **Orgs:** Chmn, Western Disciples Chs of Christ Coun Bd, 1969-72; pastor, White Oak Disciples Church, 1968-; chmn, Evangelism Com of Wester Assy NC Asn of Chaplains, 1972-74; Disciples Churchs of Christ Coun; bd mem, Afro-ministers Alliance; Masons Founder, Western Assembly Disciples of Christ Ushers Conv, 1970; Bishop, 1977; Alpha phi Alpha Fraternity; Free & Accepted Masons; CS Brown Masonic Lodge 782; Nat Asn Advan Colored People. **Honors/Awds:** Shepherd of Distinction, Christian Church Disciples of Christ; Jerusalem Pilgrims Award. **Business Addr:** Council Member, Mayor Pro-Tem, 1406 S Slocumb St, Goldsboro, NC 27530.*

WILLIAMS, CHARLES MASON, JR.
School administrator. **Personal:** Born Nov 25, 1960, Newark, NJ; son of Charlie and Genetta; married Maritza Farnum-Sharp, Aug 6, 1988 (divorced); children: Aleida Mercedes. **Educ:** Rider Col, BA, 1984; Rutgers Univ, MPA, 1989. **Career:** Essex County Col, EOF officer, 1984-86; Rider Col, asst dir, admissions, 1986-87; Trenton State Col, EOF acad advisor, 1989-2002; The Col New Jersey, Dir, Equal Opportunity & Affirmative Action, currently. **Orgs:** NJS Educ Opportunity Fund Prof Asn, 1984-, corresponding secy, 1984-86, sector representative, 1993; Committe on Undergraduate Progs, Practices & Standards, 1992-; Rider Col Inter-Cultural Alumni Asn, 1990-. **Honors/Awds:** NJEOFPA, Service Award, 1986; Outstanding Staff Award, Trenton State Col, Col Union Bd, 1990. **Business Addr:** Director, The College of New Jersey, PO Box 7718, Ewing, NJ 08628-0718, **Business Phone:** (609)771-1855.

WILLIAMS, DR. CHARLES THOMAS
Executive, executive director. **Personal:** Born May 4, 1941, Charleston, MO; son of Melvin and Mary; married Janet E McLaughlin; children: Robin, Tracey, Justin, Drew & Douglass. **Educ:** Lake Mich Col, AA, 1962; Western Mich Univ, BS, 1965; Univ Mich, MA, 1970, PhD, 1971. **Career:** Detroit Sch, teacher, 1965-69; Mich Educ Asn, educ consult, 1971-73, educ adminr, assoc exec dir, 1973-84; Nat Educ Asn, assoc dir human & civil rights, 1984-. **Orgs:** Nat Alliance Black Sch Educrs, Am Soc Curric Develop, Phi Delta Kappa, Black Roundtable, Martin Luther King Jr Ctr Nonviolent Social Change; bd mem, Ctr Democratic Renewal. **Business Addr:** Associate Director Human, Civil Rights, National Education Association Building, 1201 16th St NW, Washington, DC 20036, **Business Phone:** (202)822-7700.

WILLIAMS, CHARLIE
Football player. **Personal:** Born Feb 2, 1972, Detroit, MI. **Educ:** Bowling Green State Univ, BS, sociol. **Career:** Football player (retired); Dallas Cowboys, defensive back, 1995-2000.

WILLIAMS, CHARLIE J
Association executive, u.s. attorney. **Personal:** Born Jun 22, 1947, Camphill, AL; son of Jimmy D and Cora M; divorced; children: Renell & Darnella. **Educ:** Wayne State Univ, BS, recreation leadership, 1970, MPA, 1975; WSU Sch Law, JD, 1980; Walsh Inst Taxation Prog masters, 1982. **Career:** City Detroit, deputy dir, Pub Works Dept, 1978-79; dir housing, 1979-80, exec asst mayor, 1980-82, dir, personnel, 1982-83, chief exec asst & chief staff, Mayors Office, 1992-93, dir, Water & Sewerage Dept, 1993-94; New Detroit Inc, pres, 1994-96; Wayne Countys Airport Authority Bd, bd mem, 2006-; MPS group, bd mem, 1990-07, pres & chief exec officer, 2007-. **Orgs:** State Bar MI, 1981-; bd mem, Comprehensive Health Serv Detroit, 1982-; pres, Howard Baker Found, 1993-; Private Industry Coun, 1994-; bd mem, MI Cancer Found, 1994-; bd mem, Jr League, 1994-; Wolverine Bar Asn, 1994-; Booker T Wash Bus Asn, 1994-. **Honors/Awds:** Michigan Horseman of the Year, Mich United Thoroughbred Breeders & Owners Asn, 1991; President's Volunteer Action Award, Pres US, 1994. **Business Addr:** Chief Executive Officer, MPS Group, 2920 Scotten St, Detroit, MI 48210, **Business Phone:** (313)841-7588.

WILLIAMS, CHARLOTTE LEOLA
Health services administrator. **Personal:** Born May 28, 1928, Flint, MI; married Charles Clifford Williams Sr; children: Charlita Walker, Charles C Williams Jr, Cathryn Sanders. **Educ:** Flint Sch Practical Nursing, Cert, 1961. **Career:** Health Services Administrator (retired); St Joseph Hosp, Flint, recovery rm nurse, 1961-65; Flint Bd Educ, counr, 1965-68; Genesee Co Govt, elected off, 1965-84; Flint Osteo Hosp, asst to pres, 1980-83; Beecher Ballenger Health Syst, asst to pres, 1983-90; City Flint, equal opp contract compliance officer, 1990. **Orgs:** Co comn, Genesee Co Bd Comn 1st Female Elected, 1965-80; chair, Genesee Co Bd Health, Genesee Co Health Dept, 1968-85; pres, Nat Asn Counties 1st Black Female, 1979-80; bd mem, YWCA Greater Flint, 1980-; aging comt, MI Off Serv Aging, 1983-; bd mem, United Way Genesee & Lapeer Counties, 1985; officer, Quinn Chapel AME Church. **Honors/Awds:** Downtown Merchants Award, Flint Downtown Merchants, 1976; Polit Achievement, Negro Bus & Prof Womens Club, 1975; Pub Serv Award, Nat Asn Counties, 1980; AME Church Missionary Award, African Methodist Episcopal Church Missionary Women, 1983; Law Day Award, Genesee Co Bar Asn, 1984. **Home Addr:** 2030 Barks St, Flint, MI 48503. *

WILLIAMS, CHERYL L
Executive. **Personal:** Born Dec 31, 1954, San Diego, CA; daughter of Joseph and Edna Payne; married Peavy, Dec 18, 1976; children: Derryl Jr & Cheryl. **Educ:** San Jose State Univ, BS, psychol, 1977; San Diego State Univ, summer prog, 1978; Univ Calif-San Diego, PPS, credential prog, 1981. **Career:** San Diego City Sch, hearing & placement officer, 1978-83; Nat Circuits, mkt dir, 1983-84; San Diego Circuit Bd Serv, pres, 1984-. **Orgs:** Webster Community Coun, 1986-; Delta Sigma Theta Sorority, 1976-. **Honors/Awds:** Minority Small Business Person of the Year, US Small Bus, 1989. **Business Addr:** President, San Diego Circuit Board Services Inc, 4645 Ruffner St Suite 204, San Diego, CA 92111, **Business Phone:** (858)279-6518.

WILLIAMS, CHRISTOPHER J
Executive, chief executive officer. **Career:** Harrah's Entertainment, bd dir; Wal-Mart Stores, Inc, bd dirs, 2004-; The Williams Capital Group, chmn & ceo, currently. **Business Addr:** Chairman, Chief Executive Officer, The Williams Capital Group, LP, 650 5th Ave 11th Fl, New York, NY 10019, **Business Phone:** (212)830-4500.

WILLIAMS, CLARENCE
Consultant. **Personal:** Born Oct 1, 1945, Shreveport, LA; son of Leonard Sr and Hearlean Willis; children: Kevin M, Makala O & Maleah R. **Educ:** Southern Univ; Seattle Community Col. **Career:** Seattle Black Fire Fighter Asn, pres, 1970; Int Assocs Black Prof Fire Fighters, nw region dir, 1975, exec vpres & a/a officer, 1980; Seattle Fire Dept, lt, 1981; Barden Cablevision Seattle, dir operations, 1982; IABPFF, pres, 1984-88; Pryor, McClendon & Counts Investment Bankers, consultant, 1993; New Beginnings Christian Fellowship, deacon & dep chief, Discipleship Ministry, dir, asst chief opers, currently. **Orgs:** Pres & bd dir, CACC, 1975; bd mem, NW Conf Black Public Officials, 1980; co-chmn, Sea Urban League Scholarship Fund Raising, 1981; trustee, Mt Zion Baptist Church, 1981; chmn publicity, Girls Club of Puget Sound, 1984; bd mem, Seattle Urban League; rep, Nat Black Leadership Roundtable; mem, WA State MLK Jr Commission; Alumni Leadership Tomorrow Prog/Seattle Chamber of Comm; mem, Southern Univ Alumni of Seattle WA; registered lobbyist, State of WA, 1993; pres, Int Asn Black Fire Fighters; pres & treas, Central Area Motivation Prog. **Honors/Awds:** Hon Fire Fighter, Shreveport, La Fire Dept, 1976; Most Outstanding Young Man of America, US JayCees, 1978 & 1981; Furthering the Cause of Human Rights, United Nations Asn, 1979; Affirmative Action Award, Seattle Urban League, 1982; Community Service Award, Black Law Enforcement Officers Asn, 1984; Men of Achievement, 1996; Strathmores Whos Who in America, 1998. **Military Serv:** Wash State NG, spec 4th class. **Home Addr:** 10723 53 Ave S, Seattle, WA 98178-2104.

WILLIAMS, CLARENCE
Photographer, photojournalist. **Personal:** Born Jan 1, 1968, Philadelphia, PA. **Educ:** Temple Univ, BA, mass commun, 1992. **Career:** Philadelphia Tribune, intern; York Daily Rec, intern; Times Community Newspapers, intern, staff; Los Angeles Times,

staff photogr, 1995-2003; photographer, currently. **Honors/Awds:** Picture of the Year Contest, 1996; Pulitzer Prize for feature photog, 1997; Robert F Kennedy Journalism Award, 1997; Journalist of the Year, Nat Asn Black Journalists.

WILLIAMS, CLARENCE
Football player. **Personal:** Born Jan 20, 1975, Crescent City, FL. **Educ:** Fla State Univ. **Career:** Buffalo Bills, running back, 1998.

WILLIAMS, REV. DR. CLARENCE EARL
Clergy. **Personal:** Born May 10, 1950, Tuscaloosa, AL. **Educ:** St Joseph Col, Rensselaer IN, BA, sociol & french, 1973; Cath Theol Union Chicago, MDiv, MA, 1980; Union Inst, PhD, educ & commun, 1998. **Career:** Nat Black Seminarians Asn, bd chmn, 1970; Acad Afro-World Comm, founder & pres, 1977; St Anthony RC Ch, pastor, 1978; The Black Cath Televangelization Network, pres, 1986; Black Cath Ministries Archdiocese Detroit, dir, currently; Inst Recovery Racisms, founder & dir, 1990-. **Orgs:** Exec dir, This Far by Faith; bd trustee, Madonna Univ, 1997-; Missionaries the Precious Blood a Roman Cath. **Honors/Awds:** The Fr Clarence Williams Award, Nat Black Catholic Seminarians Asn, 1984; Keep the Dream Alive Award, 1997; Dr Martin Luther King award, 1998; The Archbishop Jame Lyke Award, Global Ministry, 1999; Dr King Unity & Peace Award, 1999. **Special Achievements:** Books: Recovery from Everyday Racisms, 1999; Racial Sobriety: A journey from hurts to healing, 2002; Spanish workbook, 2004; Portuguese workbook, 2005; The Black Cath Chapel Air nat radio evangel prog; created in 1983 the "Come & Go" evangelization training prog cassettes & filmstrips; participant int "Mass for Shut-Ins" TV prog from Detroit 1982-; producer of documentary series on TV "Search for a Black Christian Heritage"; producer & host of syndicated TV series "Black & Catholic" 1986; First producer & dir of Black vocations filmstrips 1978; First black priest ordained in Diocese of Cleveland 1978.

WILLIAMS, DR. CLARENCE G.
Educator. **Personal:** Born Dec 23, 1938, Goldsboro, NC; married Mildred Cogdell; children: Clarence Jr & Alton. **Educ:** NC Cent Univ, BS, 1961; Hampton Univ, MS, 1967; Univ Conn, PhD, 1972; Cornell Univ, grad study, 1965; Harvard Univ, post doctoral study, 1975. **Career:** Williamsburg Pub Schs Va, teacher, 1961-64; Hampton Univ, asst dean men, instr, 1964-68; Univ Conn, prof counsr, 1968-72; Mass Inst Technol, asst dean grad sch, 1972-74, spec asst to pres, Off Minority Educ, actg dir, 1980-82, asst equal opportunity officer, 1984-94, adj prof urban studies & planning, adj prof urban studies & planning emer, currently; consult, BankNew Eng, 1986-92; Recipient Hampton Inst Summer Study fel; Ford Found fel Admin. **Orgs:** Phi Delta Kappan; NC CU Alumni Asn; Univ Conn Alumni Asn; Alpha Phi Alpha; Founder, co-chmn, Black Admin Conf Issues Facing Black Admin Predominantly White Inst, 1982-84; consult, founder, Greater Boston Inter Univ Coun, 1984-; bd dir, Buckingham Browne & Nichols Sch, 1985-91; bd dir, Freedom House, 1986-92; founder, bd dir, Concerned Black Men Mass, 1989; bd dir, New Repertory Theater. **Honors/Awds:** Reflections of the Dream, 1975-94; certificate, Harvard Univ Inst Educ Mgt, 1975; YMCA Black Achievers, 1979; Freedom House Award, 1986; 100Listing Black Influentials, Boston, 1987-91; Excellence in Leadership, Minority Educ, Mass Inst Technol, 1990; Muchas Gracias Award, Hispanic Community, Mass Inst Technol, 1990; Platinum Service Award, 1999; Latino Cot Award, 2000. **Special Achievements:** Publications are: "Proceedings First National Conference on Issues Facing Black Admin at Predominantly White Colleges & Univs", "Black Students on White Campuses During a Period of Retrenchment", "Role Models and Mentors for Blacks at Predominantly White Campuses", Intuitively Obvious, 1993; Tech & the Dream: The Back Experience, Mass Inst Technol, 1999, 2001. **Business Addr:** Adjunct Professor of Urban Studies and Planning Emeritus, Massachusetts Institute of Technology, 77 Massachusetts Ave, Cambridge, MA 02139-4307.

WILLIAMS, CLYDE
Lawyer. **Personal:** Born Feb 23, 1939, South Carolina; married; children: 2. **Educ:** JD, BA, 1965. **Career:** Williams, DeLaney & Simkin, former atty. **Orgs:** Gen Coun Off Staff, Fed Housing Admin DC; Wayne Township Bd Richmond; elected pub official mem, Rep Party of IN; vpres, Hoosier State Bar Asn; ABA Asn; Nat Bar Asn. **Business Addr:** 48 S 7 St, Richmond, IN 47375-0068.*

WILLIAMS, CODY
Government official. **Personal:** Married Jeri; children: Alanna, Alan Travis & Cody Jerard. **Educ:** Univ Okla, BA; Ariz State Univ, MBA; Harvard Univ, John F Kennedy Sch Gov, grad. **Career:** Minority & Women-owned bus prog, former coordr; Intel, diverse workforce specist & affirmative action counr; Security Pacific Bank, vpres & affirmative action Officer; Phoenix City Coun, councilman, mayor, 1994-; Alms & Hosanna Consul, pres, currently; Univ Phoenix, Ariz State Univ, instr, currently; Greater Phoenix Black Chamber Com, pres, chief exec officer, currently. **Orgs:** Nat League Cities, 1994-; Nat Black Caucus Local Elected Offs, 1995-; comm adv bd, Adult Probation Dept; Nat Asn Advan Colored People. **Honors/Awds:** Rev Williams Hardison Memorial

Service Award; Community Excellence Proj, Partner for Excellence Award; Maricopa County Adult Probation Dept & Garfield Organization Award; Man of the Year Make a Difference Found; Hall of Fame, 2003. **Special Achievements:** Only the third African American ever elected to the Phoenix City Council. **Business Addr:** President, Chief Executive Officer, Greater Phoenix Black Chamber of Commerce, 201 E Wash St Suite 350, Phoenix, AZ 85003, **Business Phone:** (602)307-5200.

WILLIAMS, CURTIS CORTEZ
Clergy, funeral director. **Personal:** Born Dec 15, 1957, Detroit, MI; married Joyce; children: Jaclyn Denee, Curtis Cortez II, Janel Denise. **Educ:** Extension Sem Southern Baptist, 1978; Metro Jail Ministry Sem, 1980; AR Baptist Col, 1980; Detroit Col Bus, BA, 1987; Marygrove Col, MA, Pastoral Ministry, 1996. **Career:** Gen Motors, 1978-87; Trinity Chapel Funeral Home, admin & owner, 1989-; Aijalon Baptist Church, pastor, 1989-; Saturn Corp, 1990-92. **Orgs:** Fisher YMCA, instr, 1977-79; Detroit Recieving Hosp, chaplain, 1979-; alumnus, Marygrove Col. **Honors/Awds:** honorary doctor of divinity; TN Sch Religion; Certificate Appreciation, Mayor Coleman Young, 1989; Spirit Detroit Award, Detroit City Coun, 1984-85, 1989; Distinguished Service Award, Wayne County, 1989; Commeration, MI State House Rep, 1992. **Business Phone:** (313)532-8182.*

WILLIAMS, CYNDA (CYNTHIA WILLIAMS)
Actor. **Personal:** Born Jan 1, 1966?, Chicago, IL; married Roderick Plummer; children: 1; married Arthur Louis Fuller (divorced 1998); married Billy Bob Thornton (divorced 1992). **Educ:** Ball State Univ. **Career:** Films: Mo Better Blues, 1990; One False Move, 1992; Grey Knight, 1993; Wet, 1995; The Tie That Binds, 1995; Condition Red, 1995; Gang in Blue, 1996; Tales of Erotica, 1996; Spirit Lost, 1996; The Sweeper, 1996; Black Rose of Harlem, 1996; The Last Call, 1998; Relax. It's Just Sex, 1998; Caught Up, 1998; The Courage to Love, 2000, Hidden Blessings, 2000; MacArthur Park, 2001; March, 2001; With or Without You, 2003; Shooter, 2004; When Do We Eat?, 2005; Frankie D, 2007; Divine Intervention, 2007; Beautiful Loser, 2008, Tru Loved, 2008; TV appearances: Tales of the City,1993; "New York Undercover", 1997; "The Wedding", 1998; "Introducing Dorothy Dand ridge", 1999; "Hidden Blessings", 2000; "The Courage to Love", 2000; "Violation", 2003; "Our House", 2006. **Special Achievements:** Nominee for Independent Spirit Award. **Business Phone:** (310)553-5200.*

WILLIAMS, DANIEL
Football player. **Personal:** Born Dec 15, 1969, Ypsilanti, MI. **Educ:** Univ Toledo. **Career:** Denver Broncos, defensive end, 1993-96; Kansas City Chiefs, 1997-2000.

WILLIAMS, DR. DANIEL EDWIN
Clinical psychologist. **Personal:** Born Nov 24, 1933, Mobile, AL; son of Robert and Demaris Lewis Brown; married Mildred E Olney, Jun 15, 1957; children: Denise, Michele & Melanie. **Educ:** Seton Hall US, Orange, NJ, BA, 1962; St Johns Univ, New York, MS, 1963, PhD, 1968. **Career:** Mt Carmel Guild, Newark, NJ, psychologist, 1963-65; E Orange, NJ, Pub Schs, sch psychologist, 1965-68; Daniel E Williams, PhD, PA, clin psychologist, 1974-; Montclair State Univ, assoc prof, psychol, prof emer, currently. **Orgs:** Pres, Nat Asn Black Psychologists, 1980-81; pres, New Jersey chap, Asn Black Psychologists, 1973-75 & 1981-83; bd mem, Psychological Examiners, State New Jersey, 1973-75; bd educrs, Plainfield, NJ, 1972-74. **Honors/Awds:** ABPP dipl, clin psychol, Am Bd Prof Psychol, Am Psychological Asn, 1977. **Military Serv:** USAF, staff/sargent, 1951-55. **Home Addr:** 1837 Rangewood Ct, Plainfield, NJ 07060. **Business Addr:** Professor Emeritus, Montclair State University, Dickson Hall 401 One Normal Ave, Montclair, NJ 07043, **Business Phone:** (973)655-4228.

WILLIAMS, DANIEL LOUIS
Contractor. **Personal:** Born Aug 15, 1926, Hardeeville, SC; son of Adbell Williams Sr and Mattie Freeman; married Pauline Cave; children: Sharon, Daniel Jr, Brenda, Derrick, Devon & Dewitt. **Educ:** Savannah State Col, 1946-48. **Career:** Masons (Prince Hall), sr warden, 1950; Shriners, Ill potentate, 1968-70; St Phillips Baptist Church, decon, 1968; Beaufort-Jasper Career Educ Ctr, vchmn, 1974; Career Educ Ctr, chmn, 1986; Jasper County; sch bd mem. **Military Serv:** USN, stm first class, Victory award, 1944-45. **Home Addr:** Williams Ave, PO Box 417, Hardeeville, SC 29927, **Home Phone:** (843)784-5925.

WILLIAMS, PROF. DANIEL SALU
Educator. **Personal:** Born Feb 14, 1942, Brooklyn, NY; son of David D and Loriene H; married Sheila; children: Peter & Megan. **Educ:** Brooklyn Col, BA, Art, 1965; Univ Ore, MA, Jour, 1969. **Career:** Ohio Univ, assoc prof, art, 1969-88, Photography, 1980-81, 1989-91, asst provost, 1987, prof, 1988, dir, Minority Grad Stud Recruitment, 1994; photography dept, 1995, asst vpres, minority grad affairs, 1997. **Orgs:** Nat Conf Artists 1972; Soc Photographic Ed, 1970; Images Gallery,Cincinnati, Ohio, 1987-91. **Honors/Awds:** OH Univ Res Grant, 1982, 1984; Univ Oreg, 1967-69; Langston Hughes Vis prof & African Am Studies, Univ Kans, 1992; Individual Artist Fel, Ohio Arts coun, 1983-85, 1988,

1990; The nat African Am Museum & Cultural ctr, Wilberforce, Ohio; Ohio Univ Res Grant, 1997. **Special Achievements:** Photomontage wall murals (12 panels), 22' high x 25' wide each and three simultaneous slide show projections depicting life 1950's era, "African Am Life from WW II to the Civil Rights Act of 1965," completed 1988; Art work in Permanent Collections: Studio Museum in Harlem, NY; Museum Modern Art, NY; Natl Museum Am Art, Smithsonian Institution, Wash DC; Univ Kans; Princeton Univ; Haver ford Col, Haver ford, Pa. **Home Addr:** 2 Orchard Lane, Athens, OH 45701-1343. *

WILLIAMS, DARRYL EDWIN
Football player. **Personal:** Born Jan 8, 1970, Miami, FL; married Marlina; children: Darryl Jr. **Educ:** Miami Univ. **Career:** Football player (retired); Cincinnati Bengals, defensive back, 1992-95; Seattle Seahawks, 1996-99; Cincinnati Bengals, 2000-01.

WILLIAMS, DR. DAVID GEORGE
Physician. **Personal:** Born Jan 5, 1939, Chicago, IL; married Judith; children: Sheryl, John & Jacqueline. **Educ:** Provident Hosp Chicago, RN, 1961; Trenton State Col, BA, 1972; HahneMann medical Col Philadelphia, MD, 1976. **Career:** Physician, pvt pract, cons, prison furlough bd. **Orgs:** Vpres, Med Class, 1972; resident Univ, PA, 1976-79; dir med, NJ Prison Syst, 1977; pres, Bell-Williams & Med Asn, PA, 1979; Am Med Asn. **Honors/Awds:** Hon soc, Trenton State Col, 1972. **Military Serv:** AUS, 1960; AUS, Capt, 1963-68; Nat Defense Serv Medal; Vietnam Serv Medal, 1965; Rep Vietnam Campaign Medal.

WILLIAMS, DEBORAH ANN
School administrator. **Personal:** Born Nov 28, 1951, Washington, DC; daughter of Harold and Marguerite Stewart Hamilton. **Educ:** Ripon Col, AB, 1973. **Career:** Overlook Elem & Prince George's MD, teacher; C&P Telephone Co, serv rep; US Dept Educ, sr educ prog specialist. **Orgs:** PRS Voices Corinthian (VCC) Baptist Church; Northern Va Choral Guild. **Honors/Awds:** Director's Superior Service Award, Nat Inst Educ, 1979. **Business Addr:** Senior Education Program Specialist, US Department of Education, OERI, 400 Maryland Ave SW, FB6 Room 3W241, Washington, DC 20202-6200, **Business Phone:** (202)219-2204.

WILLIAMS, DEBORAH BROWN
Clergy. **Personal:** Born Dec 15, 1957, Detroit, MI; daughter of Ellis Brown and Gloria Cole; married Gregory, Jun 11, 1983; children: Gregory C II & Gianna Charise. **Educ:** Wayne State Univ, Detroit, MI, BS, Educ, 1980; Garrett-Evangelical Theol Sem, Evanston, IL, Masters, Divinity, 1983. **Career:** Ebenezer AME Church, Detroit, MI, staff minister, 1977-80; Trinity AME Church, Waukegan, IL, stud minister, 1982; Emmanuel Temple AME Church, Chicago, IL, supply pastor, 1983; St Paul AME Church, Glencoe, IL, senior pastor, 1983-. **Orgs:** Chicago Ministerial Alliance, 1983-; fourth dist coordr, African Methodist Episcopal Connectional Women Ministry, 1988-92; bd dir, chmn, minority task force, Ill Prairie Girl Scout Coun, 1989-; secy, Chicago Annual Conference, 1989-; nat minority recruiter, twelfth Nat Workshop Christians & Jews, 1989. **Honors/Awds:** Mediation Moments African Methodist, contribr, AME Publ, 1986. **Business Phone:** (847)835-4421.

WILLIAMS, DEBRA D
Computer executive. **Personal:** Born Aug 20, 1959, Philadelphia, PA; daughter of John Luther and Dorothy Gertrude. **Educ:** Pa State Univ, BA, social welfare, 1979; Am Univ, MS, telecommunications mgt, 1985; Univ Md, MS, telecommunications mgt, 1995. **Career:** Bur Census, computer sys programmer, 1980-87, analyst, 1987-90, computer specialist, 1990-96, computer services div chief, 1996; Coop State Res Educ & Exten Serv, Info Systs & Technol Mgt, opers dir, currently. **Orgs:** Delta Sigma Theta Sor. **Honors/Awds:** Women of Color Technology Award for Government Leadership, 1998. **Special Achievements:** First female computer services division chief at the Census Bureau. **Business Addr:** Operations Director, Cooperative State Research Education & Extention Services, Information Systems & Technology Management, 4132 Waterfront Ctr, Washington, DC 20250, **Business Phone:** (202)720-4241.

WILLIAMS, DENIECE
Songwriter, singer. **Personal:** Born Jun 3, 1951, Gary, IN; married Ken Williams (divorced); children: 2; married Christipher Joy, Jan 1, 1981 (divorced 1982); children: Kenderick & Kevin; married Brad Westering, Jan 1, 1986 (divorced); children: Forrest. **Educ:** Purdue Univ, nursing. **Career:** Gospel &soul singer, Actress; Former mem, Wonderlove, back-up singer, Stevie Wonder & Earth Wind & Fire; albums: "Too Much, Too Little, Too Late," duet with Johnny Mathis, 1978; This Is Niecy, 1976; My Melody, 1981; Niecy, 1982; I'm So Proud, 1983; Hot On the Trail; My Melody; Special Love; Let's Hear It for the Boy, 1984; So Glad I Know, 1986; Water Under the Bridge, 1987; I Can't Wait, 1988; As Good As It Gets, 1989; This Is My Song; This Is Niecy, bonus track, 2005; Christian Prod Co, founder; TV: "The Goodwill Industries Telethon", 1981; "Family Ties", 1982; "Noises Off", 1992; "VH-1 Where Are They Now?", 2000-02; "Oh Drama", 2002; "Celebrity Duets", 2006; "This is David Gest", 2007. **Honors/Awds:** "It's Gonna Take a Miracle," Grammy Award nomination, 1983; So

Glad I Know, Grammy Award, 1986. **Special Achievements:** presented her own BBC radio show in the UK, showcasing the best in new gospel and inspirational music. **Business Addr:** Singer, c/o Agency for Preferred Artists, 1141 Seabright, Los Angeles, CA 90069.

WILLIAMS, DICK ANTHONY
Actor. **Personal:** Born Aug 9, 1938, Chicago, IL; married Gloria Edwards (died 1988); children: 2. **Educ:** Malcolm X Col; Kennedy King Col. **Career:** New Federal Theatre, co-founder; Film appearances include: Uptight, 1968;The Last Man, 1969; Who Killed Mary What's 'Er Name', 1971; The Anderson Tapes, 1971; The Mack, 1973; Five on the Black Hand Side, 1973;Slaughter's Big Rip-Off, 1973; Dog Day Afternoon, 1975; The Long Night,1976; Deadly Hero, 1976; The Deep, 1977; An Almost Perfect Affair, 1979;The Jerk, 1979; The Star Chamber, 1983; Summer Rental, 1985; Mo' BetterBlues, 1990; Edward Scissorhands, 1990; The Rapture, 1991; The Gifted,1993; The Players Club, 1998; A Room Without Doors, 1998; Hot Boyz, 1999;Black Listed, 2003; Jonah, 2003; Virgin Again, 2004; The Stolen Moments of September, 2007; Steam, 2007; Blood & Bone, 2009; TV Series: "Something So Right", 1982; "Keeping On", 1984;"Cagney & Lacey", 1984; For Us the Living: "The Medgar Evers Story", 1984;"Trauma Center", 1984; "Hart to Hart", 1984; "Trapper John MD", 1984;"Stingray", 1986; "Theeting", 1989; "Home front", 1991; "Percy & Thunder", 1993; "The Mutant Watch", 2000; "Banister Head", 2001; "Cupid & Psycho",2002; "Two Days of Blood", 2002; "The Shield", 2002. **Honors/Awds:** Drama Desk Award, Tony nomination, AUDELCO Theatre Award, all for What Winesellers Buy, 1974; Tor Award & Tony nomination, both for Black Picture Show, 1975; AUDELCO Award Black Theatre Recognition Award, 1975. **Special Achievements:** Playwright of numerous pieces including: One, Black & Beautiful, A Big of Black, directed & produced numerous plays. **Business Addr:** Actor, International Creative Management, 8942 Wilshire Blvd, Beverly Hills, CA 90211, **Business Phone:** (310)550-4000.*

WILLIAMS, DONALD
Executive, president (organization). **Personal:** Son of Elmer and Jean. **Career:** Williams Graphics Inc, chief exec officer, pres, currently. **Business Phone:** (412)321-9250.

WILLIAMS, DONALD EUGENE
Executive, clergy. **Personal:** Born Jan 4, 1929, DeLand, FL; son of John Kenner and Willie Bertha Kenner; married Leah Keturah Pollard, Sep 11, 1955; children: Donald jr, Celeste & Michele A. **Educ:** Kane Bus Sch, attended 1952; Shelton Col, attended 1954; Wayne Col, attended 1972. **Career:** Church God, pastor, 1962-76; Church God World Serv, dir minority, 1976-81, assoc dir, 1987-; Church God Missionary Bd, assoc exec secy, 1981-87. **Orgs:** Pres, Ministerial Asn, 1964-69; vpres, Literacy Coun, 1964-69; city jail chaplain, Wayne Cty Mich, 1972-76; police chaplain, Detroit Police Dept, 1972-76; Comn Human Rights, 1983-89; dir, Rotary Int, 1983-; Ind St Police Chaplain, 1990-97; life mem, Nat Asn Advan Colored People. **Honors/Awds:** Dedicated Service, Girls Clubs Am, 1969; Dedicated Service, Boys Clubs Metrop Detroit, 1975; Dedicated Service, Detroit Police Dept, 1976; Outstanding Service Award, Church God Missionary Bd, 1987. **Home Addr:** 652 Goodrich Dr, Deltona, FL 32725, **Home Phone:** (386)532-0695. **Business Addr:** Associate Executive Secretary, Church of God Missionary Board, 1303 E 5th St, Anderson, IN 46018, **Business Phone:** (765)642-0256.

WILLIAMS, DONALD H.
Educator. **Personal:** Born Oct 29, 1936, Chicago, IL; son of Theresa P and Herbert G; married Sharon Rebecca Hobbs, Jun 18, 1983; children: David, Jonathan & Rebecca. **Educ:** Univ Ill, BA, 1957, MD, 1962; Univ IL Res & Educ Hosp, internship, 1962-63, residency, 1964-67. **Career:** Univ Chicago, instr, asst prof, 1967-71; Conn Mental Health Ctr, chief inpatient serv, 1971-73, Med Eval Unit, head, 1973-78, chief comm supp serv, 1973-79, asst chief clin aff, 1979-84; Yale Univ, asst prof, 1971-77, assoc prof psych, 1977-84; Mich State Univ, prof & chairperson psychiat, 1984-89, emer prof psychiat, 1990-; Thurgood Marshall Inst, dir, 1998-. **Orgs:** Am Publ Health Asn, 1968; Am Ortho psychiatric Asn, 1968; consult, Nat Inst Mental Health, 1971-81; consult, W Haven Veterans Admin Hosp, 1971-80;fel, Am Psychiat Asn, 1974; treas, Black Psychiatrists Am, 1978-80; Nat Med Asn, 1968-; sec, Black Psychiatrists Am, 1996-98, vpres, 1998-; Soc Psychiat. **Honors/Awds:** IL Psychiatric Soc Research Award Referee, 1968. **Special Achievements:** Written 17 articles & numerous professional presentations. **Military Serv:** AUS, Res Psychiat 801 Gen Hosp, 1968-69; Cpt Med Corps, IL Nat Guard,1963-68. **Business Addr:** Emeritus Professor of Psychiatry, Michigan State University, A222 E Fee Hall, East Lansing, MI 48824-1316, **Business Phone:** (517)353-3888.

WILLIAMS, DOROTHY DANIEL
Educator. **Personal:** Born Aug 22, 1938, Kinston, NC; daughter of Willie Mae Wingate (deceased) and Fonie (deceased); divorced; children: William Daniel. **Educ:** Hampton Inst, BSN, 1960; New York Univ, grad courses, 1965; E Carolina Univ, MS, HEC, 1977, MSN, 1980. **Career:** New York City & Los Angeles, CA, staff nurse, 1960-66; Einstein Hosp, Bronx, NY, head nurse, 1966-69; Baltimore City Sch, Voc Div, teacher, 1969-73; Lenoir Mem Hosp, Sch Nursing, instr, 1973-74; E Carolina Univ, Sch Nursing, asst prof maternal-child nursing, asst prof emer, currently. **Orgs:** Nat Nurse Honor Soc, Beta Chap, Sigma Theta Tau, 1978; law comn mem, NCNurse Asn, 1983-85; secy, conv deleg Dist 32, NCNA, 1983-85; vpres, DeltaRho Zeta Chap, Zeta Phi Beta Sor Inc, 1983-85; lectr, State Bd Nursing RevCourses, AHEC; mem, Sch Nursing Curric Comn, 1980-, chmn, 1981-82, 1985,1997-; developer, Leadership Sem; adv, ECU Lambda Mu Chap Zeta Phi Beta,1983-; ECU Greek Affairs Advisor Comn, 1984; panelist, consult, developer,Adolescent Pregnancy/Parenting Sem; laws comn, Asn Black Nursing FacHigher Educ, 1986-; res bd advisors, Am Biog Inst Inc, 1987; bd rev, ABNFJ, 1991-; chairperson, nominating Comn, ABNF, 1999; mem task force, InfantMortality & AIDS, Comn Task Force Comn Rels; ECU Pre Med, Pre Dental Adv Coun, 1992-; bd mem, Comn Health Ctr; Golden Lamp Soc, 2008. **Honors/Awds:** HERA, for Outstanding Sorority Advisor, Panhellenic Coun ECU, 1986; Zeta of the Year, Delta Rho Zeta Chap, Zeta Phi Beta Sorority, 1988, 1993. **Special Achievements:** Selected to participate in the minority health leadership workshop, ChapelHill, NC in 1985. **Business Addr:** Assistant Professor Emerita, East Carolina University, School of Nursing, 600 Moye Blvd, Greenville, NC 27834, **Business Phone:** (252)744-6433.

WILLIAMS, DOROTHY P.
School administrator. **Personal:** Born Nov 24, 1938, Tallahassee, FL; divorced; children: Gerald Herbert & Debra Michelle. **Educ:** Fla A&M Univ, BS, 1960; Syracuse Univ, MSLS, 1967; Univ N Fla, attended 1975. **Career:** Lincoln Mem HS, librn, 1960-61; JW Johnson Jr HS, head librn, 1962-68; Raines HS, head librn, 1968-71; Univ N Fla, asst dir libs, 1971-82; Fla A&M Univ, dir publ, 1983, vpres univ relations, 1999, asst corp sec, bd trustees, currently, exec dir. **Orgs:** EEO/AA coord, Univ N Fla, 1976-82; staff coord, State Bd Educ Adv Comn Educ Blacks Fla, 1984-; bd mem, Jacksonville Comm Economic Dev Coun, 1981-83; pres, Jacksonville Nat Coun Negro Women, 1978-81; pres, Jacksonville Chapter Links Inc, 1985-87; pres, Friends FAMU Black Archives, 1985-88; bd dirs, FAMU Found, exec dir, 1993-. **Honors/Awds:** Teacher of the Year, James Weldon Johnson Jr HS, 1966; Service Award, Alpha Kappa Alpha Sorority, 1978; Community Service Award, Grant Mem AME Church, 1979, 1988, 1990; Rattler Pride Award; Gallery Distinction, Fla A&M Univ, 1987; Distinguished Alumni Award, 1993. **Home Addr:** 748 E 9th Ave, Tallahassee, FL 32303. **Business Addr:** Assistant Corporate Secretary, Florida A & M University, 1500 S Martin L King Jr Blvd, Tallahassee, FL 32307, **Business Phone:** (850)599-3376.

WILLIAMS, DOUG
Singer, administrator. **Career:** Albums: Heartsongs, 1995; Duets, 2001; When Mercy Found Me, 2003; Blackberry Rec, pres & ceo, currently. **Business Addr:** President, Chief Executive Officer, Blackberry Rec, PO Box 818, Summit, MS 39666.*

WILLIAMS, DOUG LEE
Football coach, executive, football player. **Personal:** Born Aug 9, 1955, Zachary, LA; son of Robert and Laura; married La Taunya, 2002; children: Ashley, Adrian, Douglas Jr & Jasmine. **Educ:** Grambling State Univ, BS, educ, 1978. **Career:** Football player (retired), football coach, executive; Tampa Bay Buccaneers, quarterback, 1978-82, personnel exec, currently; Oklahoma Outlaws, quarterback, 1984; Ariz Wranglers, quarterback, 1985; Wash Redskins, quarterback, 1986-89; Pointe Coupee Cent, athletic dir & head coach, 1991; Northeast High Sch, head coach, 1993; Jacksonville Jaguars, col scout, 1995; Morehouse Col, head coach, 1997; Grambling State Univ, head coach, 1998-2003. **Honors/Awds:** Col Football Hall of Fame, 2001; Joseph J Tomlin Award, Pop Warner, 2004. **Special Achievements:** First team All-Am; Most Valuable Player of Super Bowl XXII, 1988. **Business Addr:** Personnel Executive, Tampa Bay Buccaneers, 1 Buccaneer Pl, Tampa, FL 33607, **Business Phone:** (813)870-2700.

WILLIAMS, DR. DWIGHT
Nuclear engineer, educator. **Personal:** Married Sonja. **Educ:** NC State Univ, BS, nuclear eng, MS, nuclear eng; Univ Md, PhD, nuclear eng. **Career:** US Dept Energy, asst prog mgr, 1994-95; Waste Policy Inst, assoc engr, 1995-96; Prototype Int Data Ctr, nuclear scientist, 1996-2000; US Dept Defense, sr nuclear engr, 2000-04, chief engr & prin nuclear physicist, 2004-05, prin nuclear physicist, 2005-; Mass Inst Technol, Martin Luther King Vis Prof, 2006-. **Orgs:** Am Nuclear Soc, 1997-; Nat Soc Prof Engrs, 1997-; Soc Eng Educ, 1998-; Am Phys Soc, 2002-; prog evaluator, Accreditation Bd Eng Technol, 2003-; bd dir, Houston Acad, 2006-; bd dir, Mathcount, 2006-; vpres, Md Soc Prof Engrs, 2006-. **Honors/Awds:** Southern Regional Education Board Doctoral Scholars Award, 1998-2001; Young Engineer of the Year, Md Soc Prof Engrs, 2003-04; National Young Engineer of the Year, 2005-06; AEDC Humanitarian of the Year, Nat Soc Blach Engrs, 2006; Dominion Energy Excellence in Leadership Award, 2007. **Special Achievements:** First African American to be named National Young Engineer of the Year by the National Society of Professional Engineers. **Business Addr:** Martin Luther King Visiting Professor, Massachusetts Institute of Technology, Department of Nuclear Science and Engineering, 77 Mass Ave NW14-2323, Cambridge, MA 02139-4307, **Business Phone:** (617)253-4244.*

WILLIAMS, DR. E FAYE
Business owner, state government official, radio host. **Personal:** Born Dec 20, 1941, Melrose, LA; daughter of Frances Lacour and Vernon. **Educ:** Grambling State Univ, BS, (magna cum laude), 1962; Univ Southern Calif, MPA, pub admin, 1971; George Wash Univ, DC, educ policy fel, 1981; Howard Univ Sch Law, JD, (cum laude), 1985; City Univ Los Angeles, PhD, 1993. **Career:** Professor/Teacher, Radio Talk Show Host, Business Woman, Peace & Human Rights Activist, Attorney, Former Congressional Candidate, Minister; Los Angeles City Schs, teacher/dept chairperson, 1964-71; Nat Educ Asn, dir Atlanta assoc educ, 1971-73, dir overseas ed assoc, 1973-75; Mich Educ Asn/NEA, dir orgn & pub rels, 1975-81, dir prof develop & human rights, 1981-82; DC Comt, Cong fel judiciary & ed; Off Gen Coun Nat Football League Players Asn Sports Law, intern; Larvadain & Scott Law Offices, atty-at-law; Southern Univ Law Ctr, Baton Rouge, La, prof law; Natural Health Options, pres & chief exec officer, currently. **Orgs:** Numerous memberships including Alpha Kappa Mu Nat Hon Soc, 1959-; life mem, Delta Sigma Theta, 1959-; nat pres, Grambling State Univ Alumni Asn, 1981-90; bd dirs, Partners Peace; bd dirs, Coun Nat Interest; Women Mutual Security; bd dir, Grambling Univ Athletic Found; treas, Straight Talk Econ Roundtable; chairperson, Nat Black Fair; candidate, US Cong won 49.3% vote after winning Dem Nom; US House Representatives, Wash, DC, staff coun, 1990-; counr, Nat Cong Black Women; teacher, Col Kids. **Honors/Awds:** Numerous honors and awards including Outstanding Alumnus Award, Historically Black Col NAFEO, 1981; Joan of Arc Award, La Women Polit; Hall of Fame, Black Women Attorneys, 1986; Martin Luther King Jr Commemorative Award, 1988; They Dare to Speak Out Peace Award, 1993; Delta Legacy Award, 1994; Blessed Are the Peacemakers Award, 1995; Community Service Award, Asian Benevolent Soc, 1999; Iota Phi Lamda Sorority's (a Nat organization of business and professional women) Woman of the Year award; Star Performer Award, Asian Benevolent Soc; African Hebrew Israelites, Humanitarian Award; Woman Entrepreneur of the Year award, Indiana Black Expo; Distributor of the Year Award, Unither Pharma, 2003. **Special Achievements:** Numerous articles and books published.; She is one of Ebony Magazine's "100 Most Influential Black Americans? "and Ebony's Power 150". **Home Phone:** (202)554-0159. **Business Addr:** President, Chief Executive Officer, Natural Health Options Inc, 1251 4th St SW, Washington, DC 20024, **Business Phone:** (202)554-0159.

WILLIAMS, E THOMAS
Banker. **Personal:** Born Oct 14, 1937, New York, NY; son of Edgar T "Ned" and Elnora Bing; married Auldlyn Higgins; children: Brooke Higgins Bing Williams & Eden Bradford Bing Williams. **Educ:** Brooklyn Coll, BA, econs, 1960. **Career:** Banker (retired); Chase Manhattan Bank, vpres & sr loan officer for int pvt banking, 1972-83; Fordham Hill Owners Corp, pres, 1983-89, chmn, 1990-92; Elnora Inc, pres & chief exec officer, 1993-98. **Orgs:** Trustee, Boys Harbor Inc; trustee, Cent Park Conservancy Bd, Long Island Chap-East- Nature Conservancy; trustee, Atlanta Univ Ctr; bd mem, Nat Am Asn Colored People Legal Defense Fund; Sigma Pi Phi; 100 Black Men Inc; Thomas Franklin Bing Trust; Nehemiah Housing Trust; dir chair audit comt, Fiduciary Trust Co Int; trustee, Vestry Trinity Church Wall St, Church Heavenly Rest Calvary/st. Georges Church; trustee, Cadral Church St John Divine Treas; Schomburg Ctr Res Black Cult; chmn, Schomberg Soc; trustee, Grace Mansion Conservancy; trustee, Brooklyn Mus; trustee, Mus Modern Art, Aquisition Comt Studio Mus Harlem,Art Study Group, Naples, Fla; Univ Club, NY; River Club, NY; Knickerbocker Club, NY; Revielle Club, NY; Comus Club, Brooklyn; Omega Psi Phi. **Honors/Awds:** Patron of the Arts Award, Studio Museum, Harlem, 1987. **Special Achievements:** First black elected officer of a commercial bank in Baltimore, MD, Maryland National Bank; Sponsor of the largest coop eviction tenant sponsored conversion in the history of New York city, Fordham Hill Owners Corp, 1982. Black Enterprise cover story, April, 1986; New York Magazine cover story, January 19, 1987. **Military Serv:** Peace Corps, Ethiopia I 1962-63. **Home Addr:** 145 E 74 St, New York, NY 10021, **Home Phone:** (212)472-3111.

WILLIAMS, EARL
Musician, educator. **Personal:** Born Oct 8, 1938, Detroit, MI; son of Paul and Evelyn Webb; married Ronda G Snowden MD, Dec 21, 1985; children: Earl Jr, Kevin, Damon, Lauren & Brandon. **Educ:** Detroit Conserv Music, attended 1951; Detroit Inst Musical Arts, attended 1953; Borough Manhattan Comm Col, attended 1975; Empire State Col, New York, NY, BA, 1988. **Career:** Paul Williams Orchestra, musician, drummer, 1957-59; Eddie Heywood Trio, musician, 1959-61; Rec & TV & Radio, studio drummer, 1961-73; Sam "The Man" Taylor Japan Tour, drummer, 1964-65, 1972; Music Matrix Publ Co, musician & pres; State Univ Old West bury, Old Westbury, NY, adj instr, 1991-92; Five Towns Col, Dix Hills, NY, adj instr, 1991-94; Long Island Univ, CW Post Campus, Brookville, NY, adj instr, 1994-, percussion fac, currently; Valerie Capers Trio, staff. **Orgs:** Broadcast Music Inc BMI, 1960; Nat Acad Recording Artists Arts & Sci, 1979. **Special Achievements:** Drummer with, Diahann Carroll-Cannes Film Festival 1965, WNET-TV "Soul Show" 1968-69; NBC-TV "Someone New Show" 1969-72, ABC-TV "Jack Parr Show", 1973-74, Lena Horne, 1973-74, A Chorus Line (Broadway), 1975-

79, Alvin Ailey Dance Co 1979, Jean-Pierre Rampal 1980-81, JVC Jazz Festival, Nice, France, 1989, North Sea Jazz Festival, The Hague, The Netherland, 1993, Mary Lou Williams, Women in Jazz Festival Kennedy Center, 1997, Nassau County Jazz Legends in the African-American Community, 2001. **Business Addr:** Percussion Faculty, Long Island University, Department of Music, 720 Northern Blvd, Brookville, NY 11548, **Business Phone:** (516)299-2474.

WILLIAMS, DR. EARL, JR.
Clergy, school administrator, government official. **Personal:** Born Mar 27, 1935, Thomasville, GA; son of Flossie Adams and Earl Williams Sr; married Faye Harris, Dec 10, 1958; children: Earl III, Jennifer, Angela, Thomas & Jeffrey. **Educ:** Fort Valley State Col, Fort Valley, GA, BA, 1963; Valdosta State Col, Valdosta, GA, MA, 1975. **Career:** Prof baseball, 1956, 1957, 1962; City Thomasville, GA, mayor, 1985-89, city coun mem, 1980-91; Thomas Co Bd Educ, Thomasville, GA, prin, 1963-91, trustee, currently; Presbyterian Church, Thomasville, GA, pastor, 1980-. **Honors/Awds:** Elected to the Hall of Fame, Fort Valley State Col, 1985; Doctor of Law, Faith Col Birmingham, AL, 1986. **Special Achievements:** First Black City Council Person in Thomasville, GA, 1981-; first Black Mayor City of Thomasville, GA, 1985-89. **Military Serv:** USMC, E-4, 1958-61; Most Valuable Player, USMC, 1959-61; All Marine Team 1959, 1960, 1961. **Home Phone:** (229)226-6207. **Business Addr:** Trustee, Central Middle School, Thomas County Board of Educations, 200 N Pinetree Blvd, Thomasville, GA 31792, **Business Phone:** (229)225-4380.

WILLIAMS, EARL WEST
Government official, executive director. **Personal:** Born Jul 20, 1928, Montgomery, AL; married Frances Jenkins; children: Earl Jr, Reginald & Eric. **Educ:** Morehouse Col, attended 1947; Alabama State Univ, BS, 1950; Cleveland State Univ, attended 1973. **Career:** Cleveland Bd Educ, teacher, 1953-55; Beneficial Finance Co, asst mgr 1956-62; Cleveland City Community Develop, citizen participation adv 1962-64, proj dir 1964-70; Community Rels Bd, exec dir. **Orgs:** Pres, 1986-87, Nat Asn Human Rights Workers; trustee, Greater Cleveland Interchurch Coun, Off Sch Monitoring & Community Rels, St James AME Church; Leadership Cleveland, Omega Psi Phi Frat Inc, Beta Rho Boule-Sigma Psi Phi Frat. **Honors/Awds:** US Congressional Certificate of Achievement, US Congress, 1982; Distinguish Award, Cleveland, Community Rels Bd, 1986; Outstanding Citizen, Omega Psi Phi Frat, 1986; President's Certificate of Appreciation, Nat Assoc Human Rights Workers 1986. **Military Serv:** AUS t/sgt 2 yrs.

WILLIAMS, EDDIE NATHAN
Research scientist. **Personal:** Born Aug 18, 1932, Memphis, TN; son of Ed and Georgia Lee Barr; married Jearline F Reddick, Jul 18, 1981; children: Traci (Halima) Frink, Edward L Williams & Terence Reddick. **Educ:** Univ Ill, Urbana, BS, 1954; Atlanta Univ, grad study, 1957; Howard Univ, grad study, 1958. **Career:** Atlanta Univ, Atlanta, postgrad study, 1957; Atlanta Daily World Newspaper, Atlanta, reporter, 1957-58; Howard Univ, Wash DC, postgrad study, 1958; US Senate Comt Foreign Rels, Wash, DC, staff asst, 1959-60; US Dept State, Wash, DC, foreign serv res officer, 1961-68; Univ Chicago, dir ctr policy study, vpres, 1968-72; Joint Ctr Polit & Econ Studies, Wash, pres, 1972-2004, pres emer, 2004-. **Orgs:** Nat Coalition Black IVIC Participation, Riggs Nat Corp; vice chair, Black Leadership Forum; Coun Foreign Rels, Omega Psi Phi; Sigma Pi Phi; Resource Develop Bd, Univ Ill; Campaign Comm, Ernest N Morial Asthma & Respiratory Disease Ctr; AAAS; Nat Acad Pub Adminrs. **Honors/Awds:** Adam Clayton Powell Award, Cong Black Caucus, 1982; Keynote Address Award, Nat Conf Black Polit Scientists, 1988; Achievement Award, Black Alumni Asn, Univ IL, 1988; Prize Fellows Award, MacArthur Found, 1988; Washingtonian of the Year Award, Washingtonian Mag, 1991; National Builder Award, Nat Black Caucus State Legislators, 1992; Alumni Hall of Fame, Memphis City Sch, 2000; Lamplighter Award Leadership, BLF, 2001; 100 Most Influential Organization Leaders, Ebony Mag, 2002. **Special Achievements:** Author of numerous newspaper, magazine, journal, and book articles. **Military Serv:** AUS, first lt, 1955-57. **Business Addr:** President Emeritus, Joint Center for Political and Economic Studies, 1090 Vt Ave NW Suite 1100, Washington, DC 20005, **Business Phone:** (202)789-3500.

WILLIAMS, DR. EDDIE R
School administrator, educator. **Personal:** Born Jan 6, 1945, Chicago, IL; son of E R and Anna Maude Jones; married Shirley King Williams, May 31, 1969; children: Karen Lynn, Craig DeWitt & Evan Jonathan. **Educ:** Ottawa Univ, Ottawa, BA, math, 1966; Columbia Univ, PhD, math, 1971. **Career:** Northern Ill Univ, assoc prof math, 1970-91, assoc dir, operating budgets, 1978-83, budget & planning, dep dir, 1983, dir, 1983-85, asst vpres acad affairs, Div Finance & Planning, vpres, 1985-96, sr vpres, finance & facil, 1996-2000, exec vpres, Bus & Finance, chief oper, 2000-, assoc prof, currently. **Orgs:** Asst pastor, dir, youth activities, S Pk Baptist Church, 1970-, sr pastor, 1997-; Univ Affirmative Action Comt, 1974-; Univ Resource Adv Comn; Presidential CMS Status Minorities; Am Math Soc. **Honors/Awds:** Illinois State Certification of Recognition, Sen Margaret Smith, 2000. **Military Serv:** USN, res capt, 1981-; Navy Commendation Medal, 1990; Campus Liaison Officer of the Year, 1991. **Home Addr:** 175 Buena Vista, DeKalb, IL 60115. **Business Addr:** Associate Professor, Northern Illinois University, Complex Variables & Mathematics Education, 1425 W Lincoln Hwy, DeKalb, IL 60115-2825, **Business Phone:** (815)753-1000.

WILLIAMS, PROF. EDNA C.
Educator, musician. **Personal:** Born Oct 22, 1933, Chicago, IL. **Educ:** Roosevelt Univ, BM, 1957, MM, 1959. **Career:** Professor (retired); John Hay Whitney fel, 1959; Joliet Conservatory Mus, instr, 1962-64; Northern Ill Univ, prof music, accompanist, currently. **Orgs:** Ill Asn Supv & Curric Develop, 1974; Nat Asn Teachers Singing, 1965; bd mem, Nat Asn Negro Musicians, 1976; minister music, Monumental Baptist Church, 1995-. **Honors/Awds:** Sue Cowan Hintz Voice Award, 1955; Kenwood Male Chorus Award, 1959. **Business Addr:** Accompanist, Northern Illinois University, Department of Music, DeKalb, IL 60115.

WILLIAMS, EDWARD ELLIS
Executive, vice president (organization), pharmacist. **Personal:** Born Jun 23, 1938, Hazelhurst, MS; married Sarah Robertson; children: Karen & Edward Jr. **Educ:** Univ Ill, Col Pharm, 1963. **Career:** Walgreen, asst mgr, 1964-65, store mgr, 1965-68, dist mgr, 1968-79, dist mgr, 1979-91, regional vpres, 1991-. **Orgs:** Chicago South End Jaycees, 1966; Chicago Pharmacist Asn, 1967; dir events Miss State Traveling Club, 1976. **Honors/Awds:** Outstanding Young Man of the Year, Chicago S End Jaycees, 1966; Special Achiever Chicago, YMCA 1978; Humanitarian Award, Miss State Traveling Club, 1979. **Business Addr:** Regional Vice President, Walgreen Co, 200 Wilmot Rd, Deerfield, IL 60015, **Business Phone:** (847)914-2500.

WILLIAMS, EDWARD JOSEPH
Banker. **Personal:** Born May 5, 1942, Chicago, IL; son of Joseph and Lillian; married Ana Ortiz; children: Elaine & Paul. **Educ:** Roosevelt Univ, BBA, 1973. **Career:** Mut Home Delivery, Chicago, owner, 1961-63; Harris Trust & Savings Bank, Chicago, exec vice pres, 1964-. **Orgs:** Consumer Adv Coun, Wash, 1986-; chmn, Provident Med Ctr, 1986; dir, Chicago Capital Fund; dir, Chapin-May Found, 1988-; dir, Low Income Housing Trust Fund, 1989-; pres, Neighborhood Housing Serv, 1990-; trustee, treas, Adler Planetarium; adv comm chair, Art Inst Chicago; dir, Chicago Botanic Garden; dir, Chicago Coun Urban Affairs, vice chair; dir, Leadership Coun, Metro Open Communities; dir, Neighborhood Housing Servs Chicago, former pres; trustee, Provident Med Ctr, former chmn; trustee, Roosevelt Univ; Nat Bankers Asn; Urban Bankers Forum, The Economic Club Chicago. **Honors/Awds:** Distinguished Alumni Award, Clark Col, Atlanta, 1985; Pioneer Award, Urban Bankers Forum, 1986. **Home Addr:** 1336 S Plymouth 4W, Chicago, IL 60605. **Business Addr:** Executive Vice President, Harris Bank, 111 W Monroe 4W, Chicago, IL 60603, **Business Phone:** (312)461-2121.

WILLIAMS, DR. EDWARD M
Oral surgeon. **Personal:** Born Dec 10, 1933, Augusta, GA; married Davide Bradley (divorced); children: Brent, Kurt & Scott. **Educ:** Morehouse Col, BS, 1954; Atlanta Univ, MS, 1963; Howard Univ, DDS, 1968, cert oral surg, 1971. **Career:** Atlanta Pub Sch Sys, teacher, 1958-63; Pvt Pract, oral surgeon, currently. **Orgs:** Am Dent Asn, Ga Dent Asn; Am Soc Oral Surg; Ga Soc Oral Surg; Internal Asn Oral Surg; Fel Am Dent Soc Anethesiology; NAACP; Am Cancer Soc; YMCA; Alpha Phi Alpha; Beta Kappa Chi. **Honors/Awds:** Award in Anesthesiology, Award in Periodontics, Howard Univ, 1968. **Military Serv:** AUS, 1956-58. **Home Addr:** 3377 Ardley Rd SW, Atlanta, GA 30311. **Business Addr:** Oral Surgeon, 75 Piedmont Ave NE Suite 440, Atlanta, GA 30303, **Business Phone:** (404)659-3166.

WILLIAMS, ELDREDGE M
Insurance executive. **Career:** Universal Life Ins Co, exec vpres & chief operating officer, currently. **Home Addr:** 5134 Dycus Cove, Memphis, TN 38116, **Home Phone:** (901)396-2623. **Business Phone:** (901)525-3641.

WILLIAMS, DR. ELLA O.
Educator. **Personal:** Born Jun 21, 1931, Skippers, VA; daughter of Thomas and Mary Owens; married Charlie, Apr 19, 1958; children: Kalimah Matthews & Karl. **Educ:** St Paul's Col, BS, 1952; NY Univ, MA, 1957; Walden Univ, EdD, 1978; Clark Atlanta Univ, DA, 1987. **Career:** Pierce Col, instructor, 1972-95; Wallace Community Coll, instructor, 1995-96; Univ W Fla, coor, student teacher, 1996-99; Pensacola Junior Col, instructor, communications, 1999-2000; Okaloosa Walton Comm Coll, instructor, 2001-. **Orgs:** Delta Sigma Theta Sorority, 1952-; Phi Beta Kappa, 1972-; Wash Hist Soc, 1985-89; AARP, 1985-89; Inst Africa, Hamlin Univ, 1986-87; Links Inc,1986-. **Honors/Awds:** Certificate, NEH, 1982; Woman of the Year, Zeta Phi Beta, 1986; Certification, Washington Commission for the Humanities, 1988; Certification, Nat Coun Teachers Eng, 1989. **Special Achievements:** Dissertations: "Ethnic Studies in Community College," "The Harlem Renaissance;" exhibit: "Profiles in African American History;" film: The Life and Times of Malcolm X, King, The Man of Love; poetry: "African America History;" books: Designs for Liberations, Strength to Carry On; Author : The Effects of Ethnic Studies on the Attitudes and Concepts of Community-College Students.

WILLIAMS, REV. ELLIS
Clergy. **Personal:** Born Oct 27, 1931, Raymond, MS; son of Currie and Elise Morrison McDowell; married Priscilla Norman, Jan 9, 1954; children: Debra Lucas, Rita Singleton, Claude, Lathan, Glenn & Zelia. **Educ:** Loyola Univ, BA, 1972, MEd, 1974, MCJ, 1981. **Career:** New Orleans Police Dept, police officer, 1965, fingerprint tech, 1968, polygraphist, 1974, police comdr; Jefferson Voc & Tech Sch, lectr, 1981; Historic Second Baptist Church, New Orleans, LA, assoc minister, currently. **Orgs:** Historian Kappa Delta Pi, 1973-74; vchmn, La Polygraph Bd, 1981-82; La & Int Asn Ident; Freedmens Missionary Baptist Asn La; Nat Baptist Training Union; Sunday Sch Congress; Nat Orgn Black Law Enforcement Exec; Imperial Coun, Prince Hall Affiliation; Eureka Consistory #7 Prince Hall Affiliation; United Supreme Coun, Prince Hall Affiliation. **Special Achievements:** Author: From the Dust to Paradise. **Business Addr:** Associate Minister, Historic Second Baptist Church, 2505 Marengo St, New Orleans, LA 70115.

WILLIAMS, ELVIRA FELTON
Health services administrator. **Personal:** Born May 13, 1937, Washington, DC; daughter of Rev Edward P and Ocia A Felton; married Irving C, Jun 8, 1963; children: Andrea E, Donna R, Irving C II & Michael V. **Educ:** Howard Univ, BS, 1959; Univ Wis-Madison, MS, 1960; Southeastern Univ, MBPA, 1979. **Career:** Howard Univ, instr, 1960-64; Univ Wis-Milwaukee, instr, 1964-67; METCO, Mass State Dept Educ, coordr, 1971-74; Nyakohoja Pri Sch, educ specialist, 1974-77; Mont Co Pub sch, teacher specialist, 1979-83; Md State Dept Educ, proj specialist, 1983-85, dean studs, 1985-87; Adventures Health, Educ & Agr Develop Inc, exec dir, 1987-. **Orgs:** Gr Boston YWCA Comt Admin, 1969-73; US Comt Civil Rights, New England Chap, 1972-74; Exec Comt, Radcliff Col Prog Health Care, 1973-74; Co Exec Spec Proj Task Force, 1977-79; Am Friends Serv Comt, Mid Atlanta, 1979-81; vpres, Exec Comt, Mont Co, Nat Asn Advan Colored People, 1981-85; WETA-CH 26 Community Adv Coun, 1983-85; Community Adv Comt, Holy Cross Hosp, 1985-87. **Honors/Awds:** Distinguished Service, Md State Bd Educ, 1984; Outstanding International Service, AKA Sorority & Group Health Asn, 1992 & 1994; Women of Distinction, Col Women Stud Leaders, 1995; College Distinguished Service in International Community, H U Med, 1997. **Special Achievements:** Kwanzaa Celebration, Smithsonian Learning Series, 1978-82; County Exec Committee on Committees publication, 1979; Sixth Grade African Curriculum, MCPS, 1983; High School Project publications (4), MSDE, 1984-85; 2000 Notable American Women, Int Links, 1992. **Home Addr:** 6324 Windermere Circle, Rockville, MD 20852, **Home Phone:** (301)530-8155. **Business Addr:** Executive Director, Adventures in Health, Education and Agricultural Development, 6324 Windermere Cir, PO Box 2049, Rockville, MD 20852, **Business Phone:** (301)530-3697.

WILLIAMS, ELYNOR A
Executive, president (organization). **Personal:** Born Oct 27, 1946, Baton Rouge, LA; daughter of Lillian Henry Davis and Henry Davis. **Educ:** Spelman Col, BS, Home Econs,1966; Cornell Univ, MPS Communication Arts, 1973. **Career:** Eugene Butler Jr-Sr High sch, home econs teacher, 1966-68; Genl Foods Corp, publicist package editor copy editor, 1968-71; Cornell Univ, COSEP tutor, 1972-73; NC Agricultural Extension Svc, comm specialist, 1973-77; Western Elec, sr pub rels specialist, 1977-83; Hanes Group Winston-Salem, dir corp affairs, 1983-86; Sara Lee Corp, dir pub affairs, 1986-90, vpres, pub responsibility, 1990; Chestnut Pearson & Assocs, pres & managing dir, currently. **Orgs:** Bd dirs, Univ NC Greensboro, 1981-91; bd dirs, YWCA, 1984-86; adv bd, NC Women's Network, 1985; Nat Tech Adv Comm OICs Am Inc, 1985-92; exec, Comm Nat Women's Econ Alliance, 1985; vpres, publ affairs & comm bd dirs Gr Winston-Salem Chamber Com, 1985-86; Bus Policy Review Coun, 1988-; Women's Inst, 1988-; bd dirs, Cosmopolitan Chamber Com, Chicago, IL, 1988-91; bd, Nat Coalition Hundred Black Women, 1991-; Nat Hisp Corp Coun; Nat corp adv bd Nat Orgn Women; corp adv bd, Nat Women's Polit Caucus; League Women Voters; Int Asn Bus Comm; Pub Rels Soc Am; Nat Asn Female Execs; bd dirs, Exec Leadership Coun. **Honors/Awds:** District Alumnae of the Year, Nat Asn Equal Opportunity Higher Educ, 1983; Bus & Entrepreneurship Award, Nat Alumnae Asn Spelman Col, 1984; Honorable Doctor of Humane Letters, Clincon Jr Col SC, 1984; Academy of Achievers, YWCA NY 1984; Boss of the Year, Winston-Salem Chap Prof Secretaries Int, 1984-85; Outstanding Contribution in Business Winston-Salem Chap, Nat Coun Negro Women, 1985; Kizzy Award, Black Women's Hall of Fame, 1987; Outstanding Service Award, Nat Coun Negro Women, Midwest chapter, 1988; Black & Hisp Achievers Indust Award, YMCA, 1988; Vanguard Award, Women Communs Inc, 1988; Spectra Award of Excellence, Int Asn Bus Communicators, Chicago, IL, 1988; Racial Justice Award, YWCA, 1988; Trio award, Univ Ill, 1989; Silver Trumpet, Pub Club Chicago, 1990; Southern Christian Leadership Conference's Drum Major for Justice Award. **Special Achievements:** Selected as one of 100 "Best and Brightest Black Women in Corporate America"; Leadership America Participant, Ebony 1990. **Business Addr:** President, Managing

Director, Chestnut Pearson & Associates, 222 E Chestnut St, Chicago, IL 60611, **Business Phone:** (312)587-3247.

WILLIAMS, ENOCH H.
Government official. **Personal:** Born Jun 21, 1927, Wilmington, NC; son of Pauline and Howell; married Elizabeth Peterson (divorced); children: Kamau Kokoyi & Charrise Williams Adamson; married Marian Johnson. **Educ:** NY Sch Social Res, attended 1958; New York Univ, Real Estate Inst, attended 1967; Long Island Univ, BS, 1967. **Career:** Government official (Retired); Stuyvord Action Coun, founder & former vpres, 1964-66; Sch Dist No 11, Bronx, admin officer, 1967;Youth-in-Action Inc, community orgn specialist, 1967-69; Brooklyn Local Econ Develop Corp, pres, 1967-73; Enoch Williams & Assocs Inc, pres,1967-77; Commerce Labor Indust corp Kings, vice chmn, bd dirs, 1968-77;Housing Develop Corp Coun Churches, exec dir, 1969-78; Columbia Univ, Fed Annual Housing Specialist Prog, lectr, 1970-72; Housing Develop & Mgt Training Seminars, dir, coordr & lectr, 1970-76; New York City Coun, city councilman, 1978-97. **Orgs:** Vpres, Unity Dem Club, 1961-73; chmn, Businessmen Adv Bd, 1966-67;Seminole County Dem Exec Comn, 2003; Urban League; Nat Asn Advan Colored People; Interfaith Housing Strategy Comn New York; Citizens Housing &Planning Coun; duty training officer, New York City Selective Serv; youth serv comt chmn, New York State; committeeman, 55th AD; former state dir, New York City Selective Serv; former mem, Am Inst Housing Consultants;Community Serv Soc. **Honors/Awds:** Several military & civic awards. **Special Achievements:** Delegate of National Democratic Convention, 1968, 1972 & 1992; Elected to New York City Council, 1977, 1982, 1985, 1989 & 1991; Elected District Leader, 55th Assembly District, 1986, 1988, 1990 & 1992. **Military Serv:** New York Army National Guard, brigadier general, retired, appointed rank of major general, 1990. **Home Addr:** 1471 Clearwater Ct, Heathrow, FL 32746.

WILLIAMS, ERIC C.
Basketball player. **Personal:** Born Jul 17, 1972, Newark, NJ; son of Clarence Williams (deceased) and Patricia; children: Raquiesh. **Educ:** Providence Col, attended. **Career:** Boston Celtics, forward, 1995-97; Denver Nuggets, 1997-98; Boston Celtics, 2000-04; Cleveland Cavaliers, 2004; New Jersey Nets, 2004; Toronto Raptors, 2004-06; San Antonio Spurs, 2006-07; Charlotte Bobcats, 2007. **Orgs:** Believe in Me The Eric Williams Found, 2003. *

WILLIAMS, ERIK GEORGE
Football player, football coach. **Personal:** Born Sep 7, 1968, Philadelphia, PA; children: Shay & Cassius. **Educ:** Cent State Univ, OH. **Career:** Football player (retired), Football Coach; Dallas Cowboys, tackle, 1991-2000; Baltimore Ravens, 2001; Dallas Cowboys, asst offensive line coach. **Honors/Awds:** Four Pro Bowls, 1993, 1996-97, 1999.

WILLIAMS, ETHEL LANGLEY
Librarian. **Personal:** Born in Baltimore, MD; daughter of William H and Carrie A; married Louis J Williams (deceased); children: Carole J Jones. **Educ:** Howard Univ, AB, 1930; Columbia Univ NYC, BS, 1933; Howard Univ, MA, 1950. **Career:** Retired: Bd Pub Welfare Wash DC, caseworker, 1933-35; Libr Congress, process filer & order searcher, 1936-40; Moorland Spingarn Collection, supvr project, 271 & 328, works progress admin, 1939; Howard Univ, reference librarian cataloger, 1941-47; Howard Univ Sch Religion Libr, librarian 1946-75; Writings, A Catalogue Books Moorland Found 1939, Af-Am Newspaper, 1945-46, Negro History Bulletin 110-16, 1945, Journal Negro Educ, 1945-46, Handbook Instr Use Sch Rel Libr, 1955, Revised, 1968; Biographical Dir Negro Ministers, Editor, 1965, 1970, 1975. **Orgs:** Co editor, Af-Am Rel Studies A Comprehensive Bibliography Locations Am Libraries, 1970, Howard Univ Bibliography & Af & Af-Am Religious Studies, 1977. *

WILLIAMS, EUGENE
Football player. **Personal:** Born Oct 14, 1968, Blair, NE; married Melissa; children: Maya. **Educ:** Iowa State Univ. **Career:** Miami Dolphins, guard, 1991-92; Cleveland Browns, 1993-94; Atlanta Falcons, 1995-99. **Orgs:** Big Brothers & Big Sisters. **Honors/Awds:** Doug Dieken Humanitarian Award, Cleveland Browns Touchdown Club, 1994.

WILLIAMS, DR. EUGENE, SR.
Consultant, writer, educator. **Personal:** Born Nov 23, 1941, Orange, VA; son of Victor V Sr and Bertha M; married Mary H Johnson; married Helen M Barbary, Jun 8, 1985 (divorced); children: Eugene Jr. **Educ:** St Paul's Col, BS, 1964; Univ Va, MEd, 1967; Univ Miami, EdD, 1972. **Career:** Jackson P Burley High Sch, Charlottesville, VA, eng teacher, 1964-72; Howard Univ, coordr sec educ, 1972-78; Lawrence Johnson & Assoc Inc, sr res scientist & curric designer, 1978-80; DC Pub Sch Systs, supvr, dir, test imrpove; Soujourner Douglass Col, dean, 1981-82; Dunbar High Sch,Wash, DC, asst prin, 1983-89; Annapolis Road Acad Sch, eng teacher, currently; Acad Resources Unlimited Inc, founder, currently; AUTHOR:Getting the Job You Want with the Audiovisual Portfolio: A Practical Guide for Job Hunters & Career Changers, 1981; Keys to Quick Writing Skills:Sentence Combining & Text Reconstruction, 1982; Blueprint for Educational Change: Improving Reasoning, Literacies, & Science Achievement with Cooperative Learning, 1992; It's A Reading Thing: Help Your Child Understand: A Parent's Guide to Improving Students' Verbal Performance on Standardized Examinations Like the PSAT & SAT, 1992; Grounded In The Word: A Guide to Mastering Standardized Test Vocabulary & Biblical Comprehension, 1997; The Secret: His Word Impacting Our Lives, 2007. **Orgs:** Nat Alliance Black Sch Educr; mem, Alpha Phi Alpha. **Honors/Awds:** Compatriot in Education Award, Kappa Delta Pi, 1976.

WILLIAMS, DR. EUPHEMIA GOODLOW
Educator. **Personal:** Born Oct 17, 1938, Bagwell, TX; daughter of Blanche M Pouge Goodlow and Otis J Goodlow; married James A (divorced 1987); children: Caren, Christopher, Curt & Catherine. **Educ:** Univ Okla, Norman, Okla, BS, 1961; Univ Colo, Boulder, Colo, MS, 1973, PhD, 1981. **Career:** Okla City-Co Health, Okla City, Okla, pub health nurse, 1966-70; Univ Colo, Boulder, Colo, campus nurse, 1973-74; Univ Colo, Denver, Colo, asst prof, instr, 1974-81; Cameron Univ, Lawton, Okla, assoc prof & chair, nursing, 1981-82; Metrop St Col, Denver, Colo, dept chair & prof, assoc prof-nursing, 1982-88; Southwest Mo St Univ, Springfield, Mo, prof & dept head, nursing, 1988-; Colo State Univ, prof emer, currently. **Orgs:** Am Nurses Asn; Am Pub Health Asn; fac counr, Alpha Kappa Chap, Sigma Theta Tau, Int Hon Soc Nursing, 1976-78; Human Rights Comn, Colo Nurses Asn, 1984-88; chairperson, Coun Deans & Dirs Nursing Progs Colo, 1886-87. **Honors/Awds:** Leadership Springfield, Springfield Chamber Com, 1989-90; Nurse Educator of the Year, SW MO Nursing Educ Consort, 1990. **Business Phone:** (719)549-2100.

WILLIAMS, DR. EVERETT BELVIN
Association executive. **Personal:** Born Oct 26, 1932, Hennessey, OK; married Marianne Hansson; children: Karin Cecelia & Barbro Susanne. **Educ:** Denver Univ, BA, 1955; Columbia Univ, MA, 1957, PhD, 1962, MS, 1970. **Career:** Various NY & NJ VA Hosps, trainee, 1957-60; Hunter Col, lectr, counsr, 1960-62; Columbia Univ, Teachers Col, res assoc, 1961-62, counsr, 1963-64, dir, 1964-71; assoc prof, 1970-71, assoc dean, 1970-71, adj prof, 1971-75, vpres operations, 1972-75, vpres col bd prog, 1975-77; Barnard Col, lectr, 1962-63; Educ Testing Serv, sr vpres prog areas, 1982; Williams & Weisbrodt, partner/private consult; Turrell Fund, exec dir, 1989-. **Orgs:** Certified Psychologist, NY, 1964; res fel Conf Learning & Educ Process, 1965; bd dir, Lisle Fellowship, 1964-67; bd trustees, Dalton Schs, 1967-74; NY State Comn C, 1971-74; Harvard Bd Overseers, 1973-74; dir, Index Fund Am Inc, 1974; Am Psychol Asn, AAAS, NY State Psychol Asn, Philosophy Sci Asn, Am Acad Polit & Soc Sci, Asn Educ Data Sys, Asn Computing Machinery, Asn Symbolic Logic, Phi Delta Kappa, Kappa Delta Pi; adv com, Response NYSPA Social Issues; Inst Elec & Electronic Engrs; sr consult, Belmar Comput Serv Inc; chmn Asn Black Psychol; field assessment officer, field selection officer, Peace Corps; field selection officer, Teachers Corps; consult, psychol, SEEK Prog; consult, Metro Ment Health Clinic; consult, Fresh Air Fund; consult, Nat Ur League; chmn, Review Com Testing Minorities; Intercoll Knights; Nat Sci Found; Omicron Delta Kappa, Psi Chi, Phi Beta Kappa, Danforth Fellowship, Danforth Teaching; fel Sigma Xi. **Special Achievements:** Author: Introduction to Psychology, 1963, Deductive Reasoning in Schizophrenia, 1964, Asn Between Smoking & Accidents, 1966, Driving & Connotative Meanings 1970. **Business Phone:** (201)325-5108.

WILLIAMS, DR. FELTON CARL
School administrator. **Personal:** Born Mar 30, 1946, Los Angeles, CA; son of Abraham and Lula M; married Mary Etta Baldwin; children: Sonia Yvette & Felton Jr. **Educ:** Los Angeles Harbor Community Col, AA, 1970; Calif State Univ, Long Beach, BA, bus admin, 1972, MBA, bus admin, 1975; Claremont Grad Sch, PhD, educ admin, 1985. **Career:** Calif State Univ, Long Beach, jr staff analyst, 1972-73, admin asst, 1972-73, supvr, 1974-79; Learning Ctr Long Beach State, mgr; Calif State Univ, Dominguez Hills, affirmative action officer, asst to pres, 1985-86, assoc dir; Drew Physicians prog USC, consult; Learning Assistance Ctr, dir student progs, 1991-; Scaramento City Col, dean counsel serv, 1993-96; Long Beach City Col, dean, Sch Bus Trade & Indust, 1997-98, Sch Bus & Social Sci, dean, 1997-. **Orgs:** Pres, San Pedtro-Wilmington Nat Asn Advan Colored People, 1976-; pres, Region I Nat Asn Advan Colored People, 1979-80; bd mem, Selective Serv Syst, Region IV, 1981, Employee Readiness Support Ctr, 1986-87; CSULB Alumni Bd, 1991; Alpha Kappa Alpha Sorority Inc, 2001. **Honors/Awds:** Outstanding Alumnus, Los Angeles Harbor Col, 1989; Education Service Award, Greater Compton, YMCA, 1989; Pearl Award, Outstanding Work & Service in Education, 2001. **Military Serv:** AUS, specialist, 5 E-5, 2 yrs. **Business Phone:** (562)938-4302.

WILLIAMS, FITZROY E
Computer executive, president (organization). **Personal:** Born Nov 6, 1953, St James, Jamaica; son of Lester and Lurena; married Yvonne, Aug 20, 1977; children: Jhamel & Joshua. **Educ:** Col Arts Sci & Technol, asst electronic eng, 1977. **Career:** Jamaica Int Telecommunication, sr tech, 1972-81; Sci Atlanta, sr engr, 1982-95; Dem Nat Conv, dir technol, 1995-96; Tri-Millennium Technologies, pres, 1996-. **Business Addr:** President, Tri-Millennium Technologies Inc, 225 W Washington St Suite 2200, Chicago, IL 60606.

WILLIAMS, FRANK J
Real estate agent. **Personal:** Born Aug 29, 1938, Arkansas; son of Ada Frye Jones and Seldon; married Joanne; children: Michael, Craig, Renee & Jannie. **Educ:** Bogan Jr Col; Kennedy-King Col; Real Est Inst Cent YMCA Community Col. **Career:** US Post Off, mail carrier, 1961-66; Midwest Realty, salesman, 1966-68, sales mgr, 1968-70; EW Realty Co, prof, 1970-71; Lic Real Estate Broker, 1969-; F J Williams Realty Co, founder, pres, 1971-; Realtors Real Estate Sch, instr, currently. **Orgs:** Pres, Nat Asn Real Estate Brokers; Lic Real Estate License Law Off Liaison Comn; Nat Asn Realtors-Area Prop; Mgmt Broker Va Admin; instr, Real Est Sales & Brokerage Real Est Inst Cent YMCA Community Col; instr, Real Est Trans Course Chicago Real Est Bd Hall Inst Univ Chicago; chmn, Housing Comn, Nat Asn Advan Colored People, pres, Chicago Southside Br, 1978-85; asst chmn, Adv Comn Utilization Subsidies Increase Black Adoptions; chmn, SE Sect Luth Athletic Asn; Urban Homestead Coalition; Chicago Real Est Bd Admis Comn; Timothy Luth Church; Community Develop Adv Comt; chmn, Chicago Real Est Bd's Equal Opportunity Comn; chmn, New Horizons Task Force Gov James R Thompson; Recreanal Task Force Gov James R Thompson; adv bd, Black Black Love; bd mem, Black Hist Chicago Dusable Fort Dearborn Historical Comn Inc; Cancer Prevention Soc; secy, Chicago Bd Realtors, 1987; bd mem, Community Investment Corp, 1988; bd mem, Ada S McKinley Serv, 1989; bd mem, Neighborhood Housing Serv, 1989; pres elect, Chicago Bd Realtor, 1989-90. **Honors/Awds:** Education Development Award, Dearborn Real Estate Bd; Education Certificate of Appreciation, Phi Beta Lambda; Award of Achievement, Calif Asn Real Estate Brokers Inc; Black Businessman of the Month Award, Chicago South End Jaycees; Award of Recoginition, Chicago Real Est Bd, 1973; Elmore Baker Award, Dearborn Real Est Bd; Appreciation Award, Realtors Real Estate Sch; Outstanding Service Award, Nat Caucus & Ctr Black Aged Inc; Cert Real Estate Brokerage Mgr-CRB; Certificate Residential Specialist-CRS. **Home Addr:** 9428 S Damen Ave, Chicago, IL 60620. **Business Addr:** Real Estate Broker-Appraiser, F J Williams Realty, 7825 S Wern Ave, Chicago, IL 60620, **Business Phone:** (773)737-5600.

WILLIAMS, FRANK JAMES
Artist, educator. **Personal:** Born Feb 17, 1959, Chicago, IL; son of Arthur Green and Barbara J; married Rebecca P Rubalcava, Apr 15, 1991; children: Rachel Elizabeth & Sarah Jean. **Educ:** St Edward's Univ, painting & design, 1978-80; Univ Okla, BFA, painting & drawing, printmaking & design, 1984; Univ Calif, MFA, painting & drawing, 1988; Skowhegan Sch Art, 1989. **Career:** Univ Calif Los Angeles, teaching assoc, 1987-88; Daniel Weinberg Gallery, preparator, 1988-89; St Monica Col, art instr, 1990-91; Los Angeles Co Mus Arts, preparator, 1992; Bishop Mora Salesian High Sch, art chairperson, art teacher, 1992-94; Calif Afro-Am Mus, artist-in-residence, 1995; Barnsdall Art Ctr, art instr, 1997; Univ Calif Los Angeles Exten, art instr, 1998; Riverside Community Col, instr; Los Angeles Trade Tech, instr. **Honors/Awds:** Graduate Opportunity Fellowship, 1985; Hortense Fishbaugh Memorial Scholarship, Univ Calif, Los Angeles, 1988; Sydney A Temple Scholarship, 1988; Skowhegan Art Fellowship, Skowhegan Sch Painting & Sculpt, 1989. **Home Addr:** 1709 Monte Vista St, Pasadena, CA 91106.

WILLIAMS, FRED
Basketball coach, mayor. **Personal:** Born in Lumberton, MS. **Career:** USCU, asst coach, 1983-90, head coach, 1995-97; Utah Starzz, head coach, 1999-2001; San Diego Siege, head coach; City of Kountze, mayor; Atlanta Dream, asst coach, currently. **Honors/Awds:** NWBL Coach of the Year, 2006. **Business Addr:** Assistant Coach, Atlanta Dream, 83 Walton St NW Suite 500, Atlanta, GA 30303, **Business Phone:** (404)604-2626.*

WILLIAMS, GARY C.
Educator. **Personal:** Born Jan 7, 1952, Santa Monica, CA; son of James Williams and Eva Williams; married Melanie Reeves, Jun 28, 1980; children: Jennifer & Sara. **Educ:** Univ Calif Los Angeles, BA, 1973; Stanford Law Sch, JD, 1976. **Career:** Calif Agr Labor Rel Brd, staff coun, 1976-79, staff atty; Am Civil Liberties Union Found Southern Calif, staff atty, 1979-85, asst legal dir,1985-87; Loyola Univ Sch Law, prof, 1987-. **Orgs:** Southern Christian Leadership Conf Los Angeles, bd dir; ACLU Southern Calif, brd dir; Mt Hebron Baptist Church, chmn; Stanford Law Sch Brd Vis;pres, Brd Dir Am Civil Liberties Union Southern Calif; prog dir, Natl Inst Trial Advocacy. **Special Achievements:** Hastings Const Law Quart, "The Wrong Side of the Track" Southwestern Univ Law Rev; "Can Government Limit Tenant Blacklisting?"; publisher of scholarship articles: "Drum Major for Justice: Leading the March Toward Social Justice" and "California's Constitutional Right to Privacy: Can It Protect Private Figures from the Unauthorized Publication of Confidential Medical Information?" . **Business Addr:** Professor of Law, Loyola University School of Law, 919 Albany St, Los Angeles, CA 90015-1211, **Business Phone:** (213)736-1090.

WILLIAMS, GAYLE TERESE TAYLOR
Journalist. **Personal:** Born Apr 5, 1964, Bronx, NY; daughter of Mararuth and Arthur James; married Terry Desmond, Apr 15, 1989. **Educ:** Fordham Univ, Bronx, NY, BA, 1984; Columbia Univ, New York, NY, MSJ, 1986. **Career:** Newsday, Long Island,

NY, reporter intern, 1984; New York Newsday, New York, NY, ed asst, 1984-85; New Haven Regist, New Haven, CT, reporter, intern, 1985; Worcester Telegram & Gazette, Worcester, MA, reporter, 1986-89; New Haven Regist, New Haven, CT, reporter, 1990-91; Gannett Suburban Newspapers, reporter, 1991-94, reader services ed, 1994-96; United Way Westchester & Putnam, vice pres commun, 1996-99; Jl News, asst ed, 1999-2003, asst Life & Style ed, 2003-. **Orgs:** Nat Asn Black Journalists, 1986-; bd mem, Conn Asn Black Journalists, 1990-91; Westchester Black Journalists Asn, pres, 1991; Westchester Black Journalists Asn, vice pres, 1992-96; YWCA White Plains, 1996-. **Honors/Awds:** Volunteer Award, Bentley Gardens Nursing Home, 1990; Reporting Award, "Best of Gannett," 1992; Gannett Employee Merit, 1996; several "Mighty Pen" Awards, Gannett Suburban Newspapers, 1994-96; volunteer awards, YWCA White Plains, 1997-03. **Home Addr:** 333 Hillside Ave, White Plains, NY 10603-2807, **Home Phone:** (914)686-5224. **Business Addr:** Assistant Life & Style Editor, The Journal News, 1 Gannett Dr, White Plains, NY 10604, **Business Phone:** (914)694-5011.

WILLIAMS, GENEVA J.
Association executive, executive. **Personal:** Married Otha; children: Monique, Otha, Devon. **Educ:** Morgan State Univ; Bryn Mawr Col, BS, Social Sci. **Career:** United Way Community Serv, co-founder, exec vpres & chief oper officer; City Connect Detroit, pres & chief exec officer, 2001-. **Orgs:** Greater Detroit Volunteer Leadership Coalition, mbr; chair, United Way Am C & Families Nat Roundtable; Annie Casey-Harvard Fel Prog; chair, Detroit Compact Stakeholders Coun, 1987-95; Nat Asn Black Social Workers; co-founder & pres, Black Family Develop; chair & vice-chair, Western Mich Bd Trustees. **Honors/Awds:** Heritage Award, Ford Motor Co; Dynamic Women Award, Woman's Econ Club; Women Achievement Award, Anti-Defamation League; Community Serv Award, Mich Bus & Prof Asn; "From Whence We Came" Award, Allstate Insurance Co; "People Helping People" Award, Traveler's Aid Soc; Silver Cup Award, Mich First Lady Michelle Engler; "Winning Ways" Award, Wayne County; Award Excellence, United Way Am. **Special Achievements:** One of Detroit's 100 Most Influential Women; Michigan chronicle as one of the Most Influential Black Women in Metropolitan Detroit. **Business Addr:** President, Chief Executive Officer, City Connect Detroit, 163 Madison St 3rd Fl, Detroit, MI 48226, **Business Phone:** (313)963-9814.*

WILLIAMS, GEORGE
Athletic coach. **Career:** World Outdoor Championships, Seville, Spain, 1992-93; St Augustine's Col, mens head coach, 1999-; US Mens Olympic team, Athens, Greece, track & field coach, 2004, athletic dir, currently. **Honors/Awds:** CIAA indoor track and field coach of the year, 2005-06; CIAA Men's Cross Country Coach of the Year Award, 2006. **Business Addr:** Athletic Director, St Augustine College, 1315 Oakwood Ave, Raleigh, NC 27611, **Business Phone:** (919)516-4236.

WILLIAMS, GEORGE L., SR.
School principal. **Personal:** Born Aug 6, 1929, Florence, SC; married Jean McKiever; children: Sandra, George Jr, Karen & Charles. **Educ:** SC State Col, AB Pre-Law Major, 1953, Masters Educ & Public Sch Admin,1961; Catholic Univ. **Career:** School principal (retired); Pilgrim Ins, dist mgr, 1953-55; Chestnut High Sch, govt & econ teacher, 1956; Whittemore High Sch, govt & econ teacher,1960; Conway High Sch, hist & geog teacher, 1968, asst prin, 1969; Coastal Carolina Col, evening prof, 1969-74; N Myrtle Beach High Sch, prin, 1974-86. **Orgs:** Nat Asn Sec Sch Principals; State Asn Sec Sch Principals; Horry County Asn Sch Admin, Omega Fraternity Inc; adv delegate, Nat Stud Coun Convention,1965; pres, Horry County Asn Sch Admin, 1974; delegate, Nat Educ Convention, 1974 & 1975; pres, Horry County Educ Asn, 1975; chmn, Conway Housing Authority, 1979; discussion chmn, Nat Asn Sec Sch Principals,1982; appointed by Pres Ronald Reagan to Local Selective Serv Bd; chmn of bd, McKiever's Funeral Home Inc; bd of trustees, First Citizen Bank; bd of trustees, Conway Hosp Inc. **Honors/Awds:** Omega Man of the Year', Beta Tau Chap, 1975; chmn bd of trustees, Horry Georgetown Technical Col, 1977-84. **Business Addr:** Retired Principal, North Myrtle Beach High School, 3750 Sea Mountain Hwy, Little River, SC 29582, **Business Phone:** (843)399-6171.

WILLIAMS, GEORGE R
Association executive, executive. **Personal:** Born Apr 13, 1962, Fort Riley, KS; son of John and Yuson; married Trudy, Jun 15, 1985; children: Timothy, Jeremy, Geordy & Sydney. **Educ:** Kans State Univ, AS, 1983, BS, 1984; Friends Univ, MS, family ther, 2001. **Career:** Boeing Co, sr specialist info syst, 1986-98; Urban Youth Leadership, pres, 2000-01; Nat Ctr Fathering, exec dir, 1998-2001. **Orgs:** Bd mem, Victory Temple Christian Life Ctr, 1998-2002; Am Asn Marriage & Family Ther, 1999-2002; Watch Dogs Across Am, 2001; Psi Chi, 2001. **Special Achievements:** Author: Quenching The Father-Thirst Curriculum, 2000; READ (Reconnecting Education and Dads) to Kids Curriculum, 2001; Developing A Dad Curriculum, 2002. **Business Addr:** Executive Director, Urban Fathering Partnership, National Center for Fathering, 2700 E18th Suite 258, Kansas City, MO 64127, **Business Phone:** (913)378-1055.*

WILLIAMS, GEORGE ROGER, III
Football player. **Personal:** Born Dec 8, 1975, Roseboro, NC. **Educ:** NC State Univ. **Career:** Football player (retired); New York Giants, defensive tackle, 1998-2000.

WILLIAMS, GEORGE W., III
Educator. **Personal:** Born Dec 27, 1946, Chattanooga, TN; married A Virginia Davis; children: Darius. **Educ:** Lane Col Jackson TN, BS, 1968. **Career:** Wis Educ Asn Coun, organizer, 1973-; Beloit Mem High Sch Beloit WI, math teacher, 1968-73; vpres, 1971; Beloit Educ Asn, pres, 1973; Rock Valley United Teachers, bd dirs, 1972-73. **Orgs:** Wis Coun Math Teachers, 1968-73; Wis Educ Asn, 1968-74; Official Black Caucus, 1971-73; Greater Beloit Kiwanis Club; Alpha Phi Alpha; bd dirs,Black Resource Personnel; del to rep assembly Wis Educ Asn, 1969-73; del Nat Educ Asn Conv, 1971-73; del & chmn, Resolutions Comt, 1971-73; bd dirs, Beloit Teen Ctr, 1971-73; chmn, Martin Luther King Scholarship Fund. **Honors/Awds:** Beloit Corp Scholarship Award, 1972; Outstanding Teacher of Beloit, 1972. **Business Addr:** WI Educ Assn, 10201 W Lincoln Ave, Milwaukee, WI 53201.

WILLIAMS, GEORGIANNA M
Educator. **Personal:** Born Sep 23, 1938, Kansas City, KS; daughter of Walter George Carter Sr and Marguerite Buford Carter; married Wilbert B Sr; children: Candace R Cheatem & W Ben, II. **Educ:** Univ Mo, Kans City, BA, 1972, MPA, 1973; Ford Fel Prog, MPA, 1973; Drake Univ, educ admin, 1986; Iowa State Univ, Danforth Prog, 1992. **Career:** Kans City, Mo Sch Dist, lang develop specialist, 1972-77; Des Moines Sch Dist, 20th century reading lab specialist, 1977-81, reading teacher, 1981-86, gifted/talented consult, 1986-; Univ Iowa Gifted Educ, Connie Belin fel, 1982; Drake Univ, Des Moines, IA, instr, 1987-89. **Orgs:** Bd dirs, Young Women's Resource Ctr, 1985-; Young Women's Resource, 1985-90; Int Reading Asn; Iowa Women Educ Leadership, 1987-; Alpha Kappa Alpha; Drake Univ Grad Adv Coun; Asn Supv & Curric Develop, Iowa Women Educ Leadership, Nat Asn Gifted Children, Iowa Talented & Gifted Asn, Des Moines Talented & Gifted Coun, Des Moines Pub Schs Staff Develop Adv Coun, Prof Growth Adv Comn, Nat Alliance Black Sch Educrs; Houghton Mifflin Teacher Adv Coun, 1989-; Phi Delta Kappa, 1989-; State Hist Soc Iowa, 1990-; bd dirs, Edco Credit Union, 1992-; Delta Kappa Gamma Soc Int, 1992-; Nat Middle Sch Asn, 1991-; Phi Lambda Theta Hon Fraternity; Phi Theta Kappa Honor Fraternity. **Honors/Awds:** Ford Fellowship Grant, 1973; Thatcher Award, Nat Daughters Am Revolution, 1986. **Home Addr:** 4809 80th Pl, Des Moines, IA 50322-7344. **Business Addr:** Consultant, Des Moines Independent School District, 1800 Grand Ave, Des Moines, IA 50307.

WILLIAMS, GERALD
Football player, educator. **Personal:** Born Sep 8, 1963, Waycross, GA. **Educ:** Auburn Univ, attended; Duquesne Univ, elem educ. **Career:** Football player (retired); teacher; Pittsburgh Steelers, nose tackle, 1986-92; Carolina Panthers, 1995-97; Green Bay Packers, defensive end, 1997; First Assembly Christian Sch, hist teacher. **Honors/Awds:** Chief Award, 1991.

WILLIAMS, GERALD FLOYD
Baseball player. **Personal:** Born Aug 10, 1966, New Orleans, LA. **Educ:** Grambling State. **Career:** Baseball player (retired); New York Yankees, outfielder, 1992-96 & 2001-02; Milwaukee Brewers, 1996-97; Atlanta Braves, 1998-99; Tampa Bay Devil Rays, 2000-01; Fla Marlins, 2003; New York Mets, 2004-05. **Honors/Awds:** AAA All-Star Team, Nat Asn.

WILLIAMS, GEROME
Football player. **Personal:** Born Jul 9, 1973, Houston, TX. **Educ:** Univ Houston. **Career:** San Diego Chargers, defensive back, 1997-98.

WILLIAMS, GREGORY HOWARD
Educator, school administrator. **Personal:** Born Nov 12, 1943, Muncie, IN; son of James A Williams and Mary; married Sara Catherine, Aug 29, 1969; children: Natalia, Zachary, Carlos & Anthony. **Educ:** Ball State Univ, BA, 1966; Univ MD, MA, 1969; George Wash Univ, JD, 1971, MPhil, 1977, PhD, 1982. **Career:** Delaware Co, In, dep sheriff, 1963-66; US Senate, legal aide, 1971-73; GW Wash Proj Wash, DC, coord, 1973-77; Univ Ia, assoc dean law prof, 1977-87, prof law, 1987-93; Ohio State Univ, Col Law, dean, Carter C Kissell prof law, 1993-2001; City Col NY, pres, currently. **Orgs:** Consult, Foreign Lawyer Training Prog, Wash DC, 1975-77; consult, Nat Inst (Minority Mental Health Prog), 1975; Iowa Adv Comm US Civil Rights Commn, 1978-88; Iowa Law Enforcement Acad Coun, 1979-85; pres, Asn Am Law Sch, 1999. **Honors/Awds:** Certificate of Appreciation, Univ Iowa Black Law Students Asn, 1984; Distinguished Alumni Award, George Washington Univ Nat Law Ctr, 1994; LosAngeles Times Book Prize, 1995; A. Leon Higginbotham Award, Nat Bar Asn, 1999; Dean of the Year, Nat Asn Pub Interest Law, 1999. **Special Achievements:** Book, Law & Politics of Police Discretion, 1984; Written article are:"Police Rulemaking Revisited" Jour Laws & Cont Problems, 1984; "Police Discretion" IA Law Review, 1983; book The Iowa Guide to Search & Seizure, 1986; Author of: Life on the Color Line, The True Story of a White Boy Who Discovered He Was Black, 1995. **Business Phone:** (212)650-7000.

WILLIAMS, GREGORY M
Automotive executive. **Career:** Sentry Buick Inc, Omaha, NB, chief executive, 1988; Pontiac-GMC Truck Inc, Tustin, CA, chief exec, 1989. **Business Addr:** Chief Executive, Pontiac-GMC Truck Inc, PO Box 5016, Thousand Oaks, CA 91359-5016.

WILLIAMS, GUS
Basketball player. **Personal:** Born Oct 10, 1953, Mount Vernon, NY; son of Rosanna Williams. **Educ:** Univ Southern Calif, commun, 1975. **Career:** Basketball player (retired); Golden State Warriors, guard, 1975-77, Seattle Super Sonics, guard, 1978-84; Wash Bullets, guard, 1985-86; Atlanta Hawks, guard, 1987. **Orgs:** Mentor, Boys & Girls' Club. **Honors/Awds:** NBA All-Rookie team, 1976; League's Comeback Player of the Year, 1982; All Am Hons. All Star, 1982; USC Hall Of Fame.

WILLIAMS, HAL
Actor, business owner. **Personal:** Born Dec 14, 1938, Columbus, OH; son of Kenneth M Hairston; children: Halroy Jr & Terri. **Educ:** Theatre 40; Theatre West; Ralph Nichols Workshops; Ohio State Univ, Columbus, OH; Columbus Sch Art & Design, Columbus, OH. **Career:** TV: "On the Rocks"; "Sanford & Son"; "Sanford"; "That Girl"; "227"; "Private Benjamin"; "The Waltons", "Harry O", "The Sinbad Show", "Moesha"; "Knots Landing", "The White Shadow", "Nobody's Perfect", "Off the Wall", "The Jeffersons", "Caribe", "SWAT", "Gunsmoke", "Kung-Fu", "Good Times", "Police Woman", "The Magician", "Cannon", "Grandpa Roosevelt"; "The 10 Commandments", "The Young Landlords", "All the Money in the World", "Police Story", "Skin Game", "Roots II-The Next Generation", "The Celebrity & the Arcade Kid"; "Cherokee Kid"; "Westside Waltz"; "Moonlight", 2007; "Generation Gap", 2008; "Snow 2: Brain Freeze", 2008; Films: Private Benjamin; Hard Core; On the Nickel; Cool Breeze; Escape Artist; The Rookie; Theater appearances: Spring Raining;Crossroads Hollywood Theatre; 1970; Right on Brother; Oxford Theatre, 1970; The Man Nobody Saw, 1970-74; Bakers Dream; LA Actors; Theatre, 1973; Midnight Moon at the Greasy Spoon; LA Actors Theatre, 1976; To Find A Man; Harman Art Theatre, 1988; 227; Marla Gibbs Cross roads Theatre, 1983-84; Amen Corner, Cambridge Players, 1988; I Remember, Kennedy Ctr, 1993; Help Somebody, Baptist Temple, 1997; Guess Who, 2005; Halmarter Enterprises Inc, Los Angeles, CA, owner, currently. **Orgs:** Bd mem, LA Actors Theatre, 1976-; Watts Health Found, Nat Brotherhood Skiers Western Region Orgn; Nat Brotherhood Skiers; United States Ski Asn, Four Seasons W; bd mem, Challengers Boys/Girls Club, Los Angeles, CA, 1975-; Screen Actors Guild; Actors Equity; Am Fedn TV & Radio Artists, 1971-. **Honors/Awds:** Image Award, Nat Asn Advan Colored People, 1986; Drum Major Award, Southern Christian Leadership Conf, 1987. **Business Addr:** Owner, Halmarter Enterprises Inc, 3870 Crenshaw Blvd, Los Angeles, CA 90008, **Business Phone:** (323)298-1013.

WILLIAMS, HARDY
Lawyer, state government official. **Personal:** Born Apr 14, 1931, Philadelphia, PA; married Carole; children: Lisa, Anthony Hardy, Clifford Kelly & Lanna Amia. **Educ:** Pa State Univ, grad; Univ Pa, LLD. **Career:** Community Legal Servs, bd mem, practicing atty; Pa Gen Assembly, rep, 1970-82, state senator, 1983-; Black Family Servs Inc; Blacks Networking Progress Inc; African Am Delaware Valley Port Corp. **Orgs:** Delaware Valley Ecumenical Coun. **Honors/Awds:** Hardy Williams Award for Excellence, first recipient, Black Law Sch Asn, Univ Pa; Big Brother's Recognition Award; Outstanding Citizen Award, Brotherhood Jaycees; Senator of the Year, Chiropractic fel Pa, 1990; Buffalo Soldiers Award. **Business Addr:** State Senator, Pennsylvania General Assembly, 6630 Lindbergh Blvd, Philadelphia, PA 19142, **Business Phone:** (215)492-2980.

WILLIAMS, HAROLD, JR. See PERRINEAU, HAROLD, JR.

WILLIAMS, HAROLD DAVID
Executive. **Personal:** Born Jun 3, 1944, Fayetteville, NC; son of Willie Raymond and Willie Ann; married Sharon A, Dec 19, 1974; children: Markeith, Carmen & DeNai. **Educ:** Coppin State Col, MS, 1978; The Johns Hopkins Univ, MAS, 1987; State Univ NJ, mgt cert, 1994. **Career:** Amtrak, buyer, 1980-82; Baltimore Gas & Elec, buyer, 1982-87, procurement admin, 1987-89, dir procurement opportunity program; Md Pub Serv Comn, comnr, 2002-. **Orgs:** Minority Bus Develop Edison Electric Inst, 1993-96; Am Asn Blacks Energy, 1994-; chair, Md DC Minority Supplier Develop Coun, 1995-96, vice-chair, 1996-; Dept Energy Natural Gas Minority Bus Develop Roundtable, 1996-; bd dirs, Jim Rouse Entrepreneurial Fund, 1997; bd dirs, Alliance, Inc, 1997; Purchasing Mgt Asn Md; Omega Psi Phi Fraternity. **Honors/Awds:** Parren J Mitchell Award, 1993; Eagle Award, National Eagle Leader-

ship Inst, 1994; Black Achievers Award, 1994; Distinguished Creative Award, US Dept Com & Small Bus Admin, 1994; J William Parker Award, Maryland Minority Contractors Asn, 1996; Governor's Citation & Mayors Citation, 1996; Distinguished Alumni Award, Nat Asn Equal Opportunity Higher Educ, 1997; Paul Harris Fellow Award, Rotary Found, 1997. **Special Achievements:** Recognized by Sen Paul Sarbanes & the Fullwood Found for Outstanding service, 1997;. **Business Addr:** Commissioner, Maryland Public Service Commission, 6 St Paul St 12th Fl, Baltimore, MD 21202, **Business Phone:** (410)767-8116.

WILLIAMS, HAROLD L, JR.
Consumer advocate. **Personal:** Born Jul 19, 1958, Louisville, KY; son of Harold and Frances; children: Harold III. **Educ:** Univ Louisville, BS, acct, 1981. **Career:** Brown & Williamson Tobacco Corp, consumer res analyst, currently. **Orgs:** Am Inst CPA's; Ky Soc CPA's. **Home Addr:** 1111 S Western Pkwy, Louisville, KY 40211, **Home Phone:** (502)774-4322. **Business Addr:** Consumer Research Analyst, Brown & Williamson Tobacco Corp, 401 S 4th St Suite 200, PO Box 35090, Louisville, KY 40202-3404, **Business Phone:** (502)568-7000.

WILLIAMS, HAROLD LOUIS
Architect. **Personal:** Born Aug 4, 1924, Cincinnati, OH; son of Geneva C Timberlake and Leonard H; married Betty L Smith. **Educ:** Wilberforce Univ Acad, grad, 1943; Talladega Col, 1946-47; Miami Univ, OH BArch 1952; Univ Southern Calif, 1976. **Career:** Harold L Williams Assoc Archt & Urban Planners, owner, 1960-; Paul R Williams FAIA, proj arch, 1955-60; Fulton Krinsky & DelaMonte, arch draftsman, 1952-55. **Orgs:** AIA; founding mem, Nat Org Minority Arch; vpres, NOMA, 1976-77; Soc Am Registered Arch; Constr Specs Inst; Nat Pres NOMA, 1982; pres, NOMA Found, 1995-; fdg 1st pres MNY Arch & Planners; Univ Southern Calif Arch Guild; LA C of C; LA Gen Plan Task Force, 1977; LA Town Hall Forum; chmn, Comm Simon Rodia's Towers Watts 1966-70; vpres bd dir Avalon Carver Comm Ctr, 1964; Western Reg Urban League; life mem, NAACP. **Honors/Awds:** Achievement Award Comm Simon Rodia's Towers in Watts 1970; Award for Design Excell Compton City Hall; Award Design Excel LA Child Dev Ctr; Society Am Reg Arch 1973; Onyx Award NOMA 1975; Design Excellence, State Office Building, Van Nuys, CA, NOMA, 1985; Design Excellance, Compton Civic Center, NOMA, 1984; Advancement to Membership NOMA Counsel, 1993; Advancement to Col Fellows, AIA, 1994. **Military Serv:** USNR, radioman 1st class, 1943-46. **Home Addr:** 5630 Arch Crest Dr, Los Angeles, CA 90043, **Home Phone:** (323)294-4676.

WILLIAMS, DR. HARRIETTE F.
School administrator. **Personal:** Born Jul 18, 1930, Los Angeles, CA; daughter of Orlando Flowers and Virginia C Flowers; married Irvin F; children: Lorin & Lori. **Educ:** Univ Calif Los Angeles, BA, 1952; Calif State Univ, LA, M Sec Admin, 1956, Gen Pupil Personnel Serv Credentials; Univ Calif Los Angeles, Gen Admin Credential, Community Col Admin Credentials, Gen Elem Teaching Credential, 1973, PhD, Urban Educ Policy & Planning, 1973. **Career:** Sch administrator (retired); Dana JH; Mann JH, teacher & counr; Ramona High Sch, head counr & acting prin, 1960-63; Drew Jr High Sch, head counr, 1963-66; Div Sec Educ, proj coordr & asst admin coordr, 1966-68; Hollen beck Jr HS, vice prin, 1968; Bethune Jr HS, vice prin, 1968-70; Univ Calif Los Angeles, fel & asst dir, 1970-73; Pepper dine Univ, asst prof, 1975-80; Palisades High Sch, asst prin, 1973-76; Foshay Jr High Sch, prin, 1976-80; Manual Arts High Sch, prin, 1980-82; Sr High Sch Div, dir instr, 1982-85, admin opers, 1985-91; educ consult; Univ La Verne, adj prof. **Orgs:** Pi Lambda Theta, 1952; Delta Sigma Theta Inc; Kappa Delta Pi, 1972; Delta Kappa Gamma, 1977; Nat Asn Second Sch Prin; adv bd, Honor Socs; Jr High Vice Prin Exec Comt; Sr High Asst Prin Exec Comt; Women Educ Leadership; Statewide Asn Calif Sch Adminr; state chairperson, Urban Affairs; Region16; pres, Asn Calif Sch Adminr Region XVI, 1989-90; resource person, Liaison Citizen Prog; chmn, Accreditation Teams Western Asn Schs & Cols; citywide chmn, Girls Week; sponsor, Student Week, 1984-91; sponsor, GirlsWeek, 1981-84; exec bd mem, Univ Calif Los Angeles Doctoral Alumni Asn;vpres, exec bd, 1982-84, Coun Black Adminr; bd dirs, 1982-84, vpres, 1992-94, 2000-; Ralph Bunche Scholar Comt; bd dirs, Univ Calif Los Angeles Gold Shield, pres, Gold Shield, 1998-2000; Univ Calif Los Angeles Educ Asn; Calif State Univ, Los Angeles Educ Support Group; treas, Ingle woodPac Chap, Links Inc, 1987-89; pres, Lullaby Guild, 1987-89; mem, 1970-,pres, 1994-97, treas, 2000-03, Wilfandel Club; mem, Los Angeles County Comnrs, C & Families, 1996-, chmn, 2003, UCLA Alumni Asn, the NAACP, NatCoun of Negro Women. **Honors/Awds:** Los Angeles Mayor's Golden Apple Award, 1980; Hon Life Membership, PTA, 1975, 1981, 1990; Sojourner Truth Award, Los Angeles Chap Nat Asn Bus &Prof Women's Clubs; Minerva Award; Sentinel Community Award; Affiliated Teachers of Los Angeles Service Award; Univ Calif Los Angeles Award of Excellence, Black Alumni Univ Calif Los Angeles; Arthur Ashe Award. **Home Addr:** 6003 Wrightcrest Dr, Culver City, CA 90232. **Business Addr:** Member, Commission for Children, Youth & their Families, 22nd Fl 200 N Spring St, Los Angeles, CA 90012, **Business Phone:** (213)978-1840.

WILLIAMS, HARVEY
Entertainer, teacher, school administrator. **Educ:** UAPB, Bs; Univ Ariz, MS, educ, PhD, educ admin. **Career:** Teacher; Work Study Coordinator; School Administrator; Entertainer; Promotor/ Manager in the Music Industry. **Orgs:** NAACP; Nat Musician Union; Imperial Mystic Shrine; United Supreme Coun; 100 Black Men of Am. Princ Haal Masons; ELKS/VFW; UAPB Alumni; IAM Youth. **Honors/Awds:** Urban League Man of the Year; Coach of the Year (Football and Track); Educator of the Year; Jefferson Award. **Special Achievements:** Started the Black College Tour for the State of Arizona. **Military Serv:** US Army 1969-71. Earned Silver Star, Bronze Star, and Purple Heart. **Home Addr:** 007500. *

WILLIAMS, DR. HARVEY JOSEPH
Dentist. **Personal:** Born Sep 4, 1941, Houston, TX; married Beverly; children: Nichole, Natasha, Nitalya & Steven. **Educ:** San Fernando Valley State Col, BA, 1964; Univ Calif, Los Angeles, 1964-65; Howard Univ Col Dent, DDS, 1969; Howard Univ Col Dent, Cert Ortho, 1969-71. **Career:** Gen pract, 1969-71; Nat Med Asn, asst regional dir, proj 75, 1971-74; Univ Calif, clin prof, 1972-84; Martin Luther King Jr County Hosp, staff orthodontist, 1972-80; pvt pract, orthodontist, 1972-; Pvt Dent Pract, expanded, 1983, renamed The Tooth Spa Group Pract; Records & Angel City Productions, CEO & owner; Williams Enterprises, CEO & owner; County Los Angeles, Contraction For Pvt Dent Servs; H Claude Hudson Comprehensive Health Ctr, 1989-92; Hubert H Humphrey Comprehensive Health Ctr, 1990-; Edward R Royal Comprehensive Health Ctr, 1995-. **Orgs:** Western Dent Soc; Nat Dent Soc; Am Asn Ortho; Pac Coast Soc Ortho; Am Dent Asn; Angel City Dent Soc; Channels mayor City LA; comm Ind & Com San Fernando Valley; comm econ develop NE San Fernando Valley; bd trustees, Western Dent Soc; adv bd, LA Mission Col. **Honors/Awds:** Certificate of Appreciation, Pac Coast Soc Ortho; Commendation, City Inglewood, Los Angeles County. **Home Phone:** (818)776-9001. **Business Addr:** Dentist, 8615 Crenshaw Blvd, Inglewood, CA 90305, **Business Phone:** (310)677-1152.

WILLIAMS, HAYWARD J
Dentist. **Personal:** Born Jun 27, 1944, Port Arthur, TX; married Haslett J; children: Hoyt & Jason. **Educ:** La Southwest Col, predental major, 1967; Univ So Calif, DDS, 1976. **Career:** Dentist (retired); Dublin Ga, dentist pvt pract, 1976; Ga Correctional Dept, dentist. **Orgs:** Bd dir, NAACP, 1980; vpres, Optimist Club Laurens Dublin, 1980; Laurens County Bd HTH. **Honors/Awds:** AFDH Scholar, 1976; Most Inspiring Minority Student, Univ So Calif, 1976.

WILLIAMS, HEATHER ANDREA
Educator, writer. **Educ:** Yale Univ, MA, PhD; Harvard Univ, JD. **Career:** Author: Self-Taught: African American Education in Slavery & Freedom, 2005; Univ NC, Chapel Hill asst prof hist, assoc prof, currently. **Business Phone:** (919)962-2381.*

WILLIAMS, DR. HELEN ELIZABETH
Educator. **Personal:** Born Dec 13, 1933, Timmonsville, SC; daughter of Eugene Weldon and Hattie Pearl Sanders Baker; children: Broderick Kevin & Terrence Meredith. **Educ:** Morris Col, BA, 1954; Phoenix Col, cert, 1959; Atlanta Univ, MSLS, 1960; Queens Col, cert, 1966; Univ Ill-Urbana, CAS, 1969; Univ WI-Madison, PhD,1983. **Career:** Williams Mem High Sch, St George, SC, teacher & librarian, 1955-57; Carver High Sch, Spindale, NC, teacher & librarian, 1957-58; Percy Julian Elem Sch, librarian, 1959-60; Brooklyn Pub Libr, librarian, 1960-62; Mt Vernon Pub Libr, librarian, 1963-64; Jenkins Hill High Sch, librarian & teacher, 1964-66; Westchester Co Library Syst, librarian, 1966; White Plains City Pub Schs, librarian, 1966-68, 1969-73; Bro-Dart Inc, libr consult, 1976-81; Univ Md, Col Park, MD, lectr, 1981-83, prof; Univ South Pac, Suva, Fulbright prof, 1988-89. **Orgs:** Beta Phi Mu Int Libr Sci Hon Fraternity, 1960-; fel Higher Educ Act, 1966; fel Nat Defense Educ Act, 1967-68; fel Comn Instnl Coop, 1973-76; Libr Admin & Managerial Asn, 1977-80; Black Caucus Am Libr Asn, 1977-; Md Educ Media Org, 1981-; Am Libr Asn, 1977-; Am Asn Sch Librarians; Young Adults Serv Div; Asn Libr Serv C; Nat Coun Negro Women, Inc 1990-. **Honors/Awds:** Distinguished Alumnus Award, Morris Col, 1985; Distinguished Alumni of the Year Citation, Nat Asn Equal Opportunity Higher Educ, 1986. **Special Achievements:** Editor of "The High/Low Consensus," Bro-Dart Publishing Co, 1980, editor of "Independent Reading, K-3" Bro-Dart Publishing Co, 1980, Book Reviewer School Library Journal, 1981-, editor Books By African American Authrosand Illustrators for Children and Young Adults, American Library Asn.

WILLIAMS, DR. HENRY P
Educator. **Personal:** Born Sep 3, 1941, Birmingham, AL; son of Carrie Clanton and Charles Williams; married Joyce, Sep 28, 1968; children: Gavin Charles & Courtney Joy. **Educ:** State Univ NC, Fayetteville, NC, BS, 1967; State Univ New York Col, Brockport, EdM, 1973; State Univ New York, Buffalo, New York, EdD, 1983. **Career:** Wilson Magnet Schl, Rochester, New York, prin, 1980-85; Va Polytech Inst, Dept Educ Admin, lecr, 1985-86; Roanoke City Pub Schs, Roanoke, Va, dept supt, 1986-88; State Univ New York, Oswego, New York, lectr, vis prof, 1989-90; Syracuse Univ, Syracuse, New York, lecr, 1989-90; Syracuse City Sch Dist, Syracuse, New York, supt, 1989; Sch Dist, Little Rock, Ark, Supt; Sch Dist, Kans City, Mo, supt, currently. **Orgs:** Bd dirs, United Way Cent New York, 1989-; bd dirs, Onondaga Savings Bank, 1989-; comt mem, congressman James Walsh's Human Adv Community, 1989-; exec bd, Hiawatha Coun Boy Scouts Am, 1989-; adv bd, Syracuse Area Salvation Army, 1990-; Black Educators Asn. **Honors/Awds:** Educator of the Year, Phi Delta Kappa, 1983; Educational Leadership Award, Magnet Schs, Rochester, New York, 1985; Dedicated Educator Award, Eta Rho Lambda, Alpha Phi Alpha, 1985; Distinguished Alumni Award, State Univ NC, Fayetteville, 1988; Prism Award, 1990; United Negro College Fund Meritorious Service Award, 1994 & 1995. **Business Phone:** (816)418-7641.

WILLIAMS, HENRY R
Oral surgeon, dentist. **Personal:** Born Nov 3, 1937, Birmingham, AL; married Juanita; children: Leslie Alison, Mark & Matthew. **Educ:** Univ Cincinnati, BS, 1959; Meharry Med Col, DDS, 1967; Univ MD, resident oral surg, 1970. **Career:** Albert B Sabin, res asst, 1959-61; Leon H Schmidt, res asst, 1961-63; Christ Hosp, Inst Med Res, staff, 1963-67; Provident Hosp, intern, 1968-70; Univ Md, resident oral surg; Pvt pract, dentist & oral surgeon, currently. **Orgs:** Nat Dental Asn; treas, MC Dental Soc; bd, Oral Surg; Middle Atlantic Soc & Baltimore Soc Oral Surgseons. **Honors/Awds:** Winner Nat Elks oratorical contest, 1954. **Special Achievements:** First Black Oral Surgery Resident in UNiversity of Maryland. **Business Addr:** Dentist, 308 Kerneway, Baltimore, MD 21212.

WILLIAMS, DR. HENRY S
Physician. **Personal:** Born Aug 26, 1929, New York City, NY; son of Hiram and Margaret; married Frances S; children: Mark, Paul & Bart. **Educ:** NY City Col, BS, 1950; Howard Univ, MD, 1955; Brooke Army Hosp, intern, 1956; Letterman Army Hosp, resident, 1957-60. **Career:** La Co Sheriff's Dept, radiologist; Charles R Drew Med Sch La, clinical assoc prof, radiology, interim pres, med & sci, 1989-91; pvt practice, radiologist, currently. **Orgs:** Calif Bd Med Quality Assurance; diplomate, Nat Bd Med Examiners; diplomate, Am Bd Radiol; fel, Am Col Radiol; fel, Am Col Angiology; La Radiological Soc; Calif Radiological Soc; Nat Med Asn, Golden State Med Asn; emer trustee, Charles R Drew Univ Med & Sci, 20003-; Am Med Asn; Calif Med Asn; La County Med Asn; past mem, Calif Physicians Serv; past mem, The Harvard Sch; past mem, Joint Comn Accreditation Hosps; past chmn, Urban Health Comt Calif Med Asn; past counr, Calif Med Asn. **Military Serv:** AUS, Med Corps maj. **Home Addr:** 1061 Loma Vista Dr, Beverly Hills, CA 90210. **Business Phone:** (213)295-7778.

WILLIAMS, HERB E.
Basketball coach, basketball player. **Personal:** Born Jun 26, 1946, Chicago, IL; son of Austin Williams and Mary Poole; married Marilyn O, Jul 22, 1965; children: Allen, Mikki, Douglas & Mary. **Educ:** Univ Evansville, Evansville, IN, BA, 1968; Chicago State Univ, Chicago, IL, MA, 1982. **Career:** Basketball player (retired); basketball coach; Centralia High Sch, Centralia, IL, asst basketball coach, 1970-72; Rich SHigh Sch, Richton Pk, IL, head track & asst basketball coach, 1972-74;Hillcrest High Sch, Country Club Hill, IL, head basketball coach, 1974-75;Evanston High Sch, Evanston, IL, head basketball coach, 1975-84; Mich State Univ, East Lansing, MI, asst basketball coach, 1984-90; Idaho State Univ, Pocatello, ID, head basketball coach, 1990. **Orgs:** Nat Asn Basketball Coaches, 1983-; Rotary Club, 1990-; secy, Chessman Club, 1980-84; IL Basketball Coaches Asn, 1970-86; Idaho Coaches Asn, 1990. **Honors/Awds:** IL Basketball Hall of Fame, 1974; Evansville University Hall of Fame, 1980; Centralia IL Sports Hall of Fame, 1990; IL Basketball Northern Dist Coach of the Year, 1984, Kiwanis Club Man of the Year, Evanston, IL, 1984; Big Sky Conference, coach of year, 1994.

WILLIAMS, HERB L.
Basketball player, basketball coach. **Personal:** Born Feb 16, 1958, Columbus, OH; married Deborah; children: Erica & Jabriele. **Educ:** Ohio State, attended 1981. **Career:** Basketball player (retired), basketball coach; Ind Pacers, forward-ctr,1982-89; Dallas Mavericks, 1989-92; New York Knicks, 1992-95, asst coach, 2001-05, 2006-; interim head coach, 2005-06; Toronto Raptors, 1995; new York Knicks, asst coach, currently. **Honors/Awds:** All-Am selection; Ohio's Class AAA Player of Year.

WILLIAMS, DR. HERBERT LEE
Physician. **Personal:** Born Dec 23, 1932, Citronelle, AL; divorced; children: Lezli & Candace. **Educ:** Talladega Col, BA, 1952; Atlanta Univ, MS, 1954; Meharry Med Col, MD, 1958. **Career:** Surgeon, pvt prac, 1965-. **Orgs:** Pres, Herbert Williams MD Inc; Alpha Omega Alpha Hon Med Soc; dipl, Am Bd Surg; fel, Am Col Surgeons; Int Col Surgeons; Am Soc Abdominal Surgeons, Chf surg serv, Williams AFB Hosp, 1963-65. **Military Serv:** USAF, maj. **Home Addr:** 4508 Don Rodolfo Pl, Los

Angeles, CA 90008. **Business Addr:** Physician, 323 N Prairie Ave Suite 425, Inglewood, CA 90301.

WILLIAMS, HERMAN
Government official. **Personal:** Born Dec 7, 1943, Washington, DC; children: Herman III, Daniel & James. **Educ:** Acad Health Scis, 1973; Baylor Univ, 1975; Montgomery Col, 1980. **Career:** Upper Maple Ave Citizens Asn, liaison, 1980; Comn Landlord Tenant Affairs, comnr, 1980-82; Metrop Wash Planning & Housing Asn, bd mem, 1980-82; Metrop Coun Govts, comn mem, 1983; City Takoma Pk, City Councilman,1980-87. **Orgs:** Bd dirs, United Planning Asn, 1964-65; founder, Winchester Tenants Asn, 1978; vpres, Parkview Towers Tenant Asn, 1980; city-Counman, liaison, Upper Maple Ave Citizens Asn, 1981; organizer, Takoma Parks Ceremony, honor Martin Luther King Jr, 1982-; instrumental redistricting, Takoma Park voting policy, 1982; establishing, Dept Housing, 1983; organized Takoma Park Youth Day. **Honors/Awds:** Elizabeth Skou Achievement Award, Winchester Tenants Asn, 1978; second Black elected official in Takoma Park, MD, 1890-; selected for Honorary Dinner Comn, Nat Asn Advan Colored People, 1984-85. **Special Achievements:** Only Black elected official in Montgomery County, MD. **Military Serv:** AUS, specialist 5, 1974-77; Expert Field Med Badge, 1976; Letter of Commend Good Conduct, Nat Defense, 1974-77.

WILLIAMS, HERMAN, JR.
Commander in chief. **Educ:** Univ Md Sch Eng, Nat Fire Serv Staff, cert Fire Serv Instr & Motor Fleet Supvr; Catonsville Community Col, Fire Mgt; Univ Baltimore, Mgt & Personnel Admin. **Career:** Commander in chief (Retired); Baltimore City fire dept, fire fighter, 1954, commnr transp, 1988, Baltimore City Fire Dept, chief, 1992-2001, pump operator, Lt & fire acad, capt & fire safety Officer, & Battalion Chief fire prev bur; Dept Pub Works, chief admin servs, 1984, exec asst dir pub works. **Orgs:** Phi Bets Sigma Fraternity Inc; Vulcan Blazer Inc; Int Asn Fire Chiefs; chmn bd dirs, Munic Employees Credit Union Baltimore City; bd mem, Munic Golf Corp. **Honors/Awds:** LOE Award, 2004.

WILLIAMS, HILDA YVONNE
Executive. **Personal:** Born Aug 17, 1946, Washington, NC; daughter of Willie Joseph and Martha Jane Blount. **Educ:** Hunter Col, New York, NY, 1978-80. **Career:** Teachers Col, exec sec, 1964-67; Bus Careers, exec, 1967-69; Esquire Mag, admin asst, 1969-73; RCA Corp, admin asst, 1973-75, regional prom mgr, 1975-87; Polygram Records, regional prom, 1987-89; Capitol Records, New York, NY, regional prom, 1989-90; Warner Bros Records, New York, NY, co-nat dir, black music promoter, 1990-98; Virgin Records, staff, 1998-, sr nat dir, currently. **Orgs:** NAACP, 1976; Black Music Asn, New York Chapter; bd dir, Nat Black Music Asn, 1986-88. **Honors/Awds:** Black Achiever in Industry, YMCA of Greater New York, 1982; Jack the Rapper Black Music Award, 1990. **Home Phone:** (201)445-1259. **Business Addr:** Co-National Director, Black Music Promotion, 75 Rockefeller Plz, New York, NY 10019, **Business Phone:** (212)484-6775.

WILLIAMS, HOMER LAVAUGHAN
Physician. **Personal:** Born Dec 10, 1925, Kalamazoo, MI; married Ruth; children: Aaron, Valerie, Andre. **Educ:** OH Col Chiropody, DSC, 1954; Western MI Univ, BS, 1962; Howard Univ Sch Med, MD, 1966. **Career:** Akron Gen Hosp, Dr ortho surg, 1971; Orthopaedist, self. **Orgs:** Charles Drew Soc; LA Co Med Asn; AMA; Nat Med Asn Chmn orthopaedic & bd Morningside Hosp. **Honors/Awds:** W Adams Hosp Pub "Intraosseous Vertebral Venography in Comparison with Myelograph in Diagnosing Dis" 1969. **Military Serv:** AUS, capt, 1944-46. **Business Addr:** 336 E Hillcrest Blvd, Inglewood, CA 90301.

WILLIAMS, HOWARD COPELAND
Economist, educator, executive director. **Personal:** Born May 29, 1921, Quitman, GA; son of Edward and Janie; married Blanche; children: Stephanie, Howard. **Educ:** BS, MS; PhD, 1953. **Career:** Executive director, Educator & Economist (retired); A&T State Univ, assoc prof, 1947-51; OH State Univ, assoc prof, 1953-61; NC State Univ, post doc fel, 1956; Soc Sci Coun, travel Grant, 1964; Mershon Nat Security Prog, grant; Nommensen Univ, Medan, Indonesia, vis prof, 1961-63; Africa Reg Study Big Ten Univ's evaluate AID Univ Contracts Worldwide, home campus liaison, 1965-67; OH State Univ, prof, 1964-71; Off Spec Trade, Rep Exec Off Pres, sr agr adv, 1973-75; ASCS Off Admin, dir analysis staff, 1976-81; ASCS, dir commodity analysis div, 1981-87. **Honors/Awds:** Social Sci Res Coun. **Military Serv:** AUS, pfc, 1942-46. **Home Addr:** 12621 Prestwick Dr, Fort Washington, MD 20744. *

WILLIAMS, DR. HUBERT
Police officer. **Personal:** Born Aug 19, 1939, Savannah, GA; married Annette; children: Alexis, Susan & Hubert Carl. **Educ:** Elec Engr Tech, cert, 1962; John Jay Col Criminal Justice, AS, 1968, BS,1970; Harvard Law Sch, fel, 1971; Rutgers Univ Sch Law, JD, 1974; Fed Bur Invest Acad Nat Exec Inst, 1977. **Career:** Newark High-impact Anti-crime Prog, exec dir, 1973-74; Newark Police Dept,police officer, 1962-73; Rutgers Sch Criminal Justice, adjunct prof; Newark City Police Dept, police dir, 1974-85; Police Found, pres, currently. **Orgs:** Int Asn Chiefs Police; Am Soc Criminology; adv com Nat Inst; pres Nat Orgn Black Law Enforcement Officers; adv bd, Police Found Exec Training Sem,1976; selection com mem, City Stanford CT Pol Ice Chief, 1977; Fed BurInvest Acad Nat Exec Inst, 1977; New Scotland Yard Eng, 1977; selection com mem, City LA Police Chief, 1978; pres, Nat Asn Police Com Relations Officers, 1971-73; Mayors Educ Task Force, 1971-76; bd dirs, Nat Asn Urban Criminal Justice Planners, 1972-74; Intl Asn Chiefs Police, 1973-; trustee, Two Hundred Club, 1973-; bd dir, Police Exec & Res Forum, 1975-; camp mgmt com, UMCA, 1975-78; Am Bar Asn, 1976-; founding pres, Nat Orgn Black Law Enforcement Exec, 1976-79; NJ Bar Asn, 1976-; Fed Bar Asn, 1977-; St & Com Educ Task Force, 1977-; adv bd, Esex Co Col Criminal Justice Prog, 1978-; consult to pub safety com, Nat League Cities, 1978-; edit adv bd mem, John Jay Col Jour Am Acad Prof Law Enforcement, 1978-; 74th Dist Rotary Intl. **Honors/Awds:** Res fel, Harvard Law Sch for Criminal Justice; Bronze Shields & Merit Awards, 1965; honored Com for Incentive for Human Achievement, 1967;Humanitarian Award, Newark Businessmens Asn, 1968; Appreciation Award, SWard Little League, 1970; Leadership Award, Nat Asn of Police Comn Rels Officer, 1973; Achievement Award Police Acad Asn, 1974; Man of Year Award,4H, 1974; Appreciation Award Spcl Police Assn 1975; Achvmt Award Bronze Shields Orgn 1975; Comm Serv Award Speedy Olympics, 1975; Recog Excel Award, Dr King Comn Ctr, 1976; spec Crime Recog Award, NJ Voice Newspaper,1977; spec Narcotic Enforcement Award Drug Enforcement Admin, 1977; Appreciation Award Newark Intl Airports 50th Anniv, 1978; publ articles various magazines, 1978-79. **Special Achievements:** Youngest Chief Executive Officers of a Major Police Department in the US. **Business Addr:** President, Police Foundation, 1201 Conn Ave NW, Washington, DC 20036-2636, **Business Phone:** (202)833-1460.

WILLIAMS, DR. HUGH HERMES
Educator, physician. **Personal:** Born Nov 11, 1945, Port-of-Spain, Trinidad and Tobago; son of Hugh Lionel and Norma D Balcon Baird; married Leandra M, Jul 8, 1977; children: Kelly Victoria & Janelle Victoria. **Educ:** Univ West Indies, Kingston, Jamaica, attended 1972, Howard Univ, Wash, DC, 1976, McMaster Univ, Hamilton, Ontario, Canada, attended 1978, Cleveland Clinic Found, Cleveland, Ohio, attended 1980. **Career:** Univ Tenn, Memphis, instr, 1980-81, asst prof, medicine, 1981-90, assoc prof, 1990-91, clinical assoc prof, 1991, pvt practice, currently. **Orgs:** Am Soc Nephrology; Nat Kidney Found; Int Soc Nephrology; Am Soc Internal Med; Am Heart Asn; fel, Am Col Physicians. **Special Achievements:** Author: "Reversible Nephrotic Range Proteinuria and Renal Failure in Athero Embolic Renal Disease," 1989, "Altered Sensitivity of Osmotically Stimulated Vasopressin Release in Quadriplegic Subjects," 1989. **Business Addr:** Physician, 220 S Claybrook St Suite 206 Shelby, Memphis, TN 38104, **Business Phone:** (901)276-6277.

WILLIAMS, DR. IRA JOSEPH
Clergy. **Personal:** Born Aug 5, 1926, Elizabeth City, NC; son of Moses; married Elsie Moore; children: Pamela, Anthony & Angela. **Educ:** Kingsley Sch Rel, BTh, 1952, BD, 1954; Am Bible Col, DD; Union Chris Bible Inst, BA, 1972; Univ NC; Pacific Col, 1974; Va Bible Univ, PhD, 2001; Howard Univ, attended; Shaw Univ, Cert Social Studies & Baptist Doctrine. **Career:** Antioch Baptist Church, Norfolk VA, minister, currently. **Orgs:** Civil Rights Coord Team, Nashville; exec bd mem, Old Eastern Baptist Asn, NC; nat Pres, United Chris Front Brotherhood; moderator, Old Dominion Missionary Baptist Asn; exec bd of Va, Baptist State Conv; Mayors Adv Comt; adv bd, Atlantic Nat Bank; exec bd, Norfolk Com Improvement Educ; life mem, NAACP; mem, Hampton Ministers Conf; Prelight Nat Interfaith Holy Convocation. **Honors/Awds:** Citation of Honor, Womens Aux of Norfolk Community Hosp; Community Leaders & Noteworthy American, 1976-77; Humanitarian Plaque, SE Tidewater Oppor Proj; Man of the Year, WRAP Radio Station Tidewater, VA, 1979; Mason 32Deg; author of several pamphlets; Excellence Award, NAACP, 1990; City of Norfolk, VA, 1990. **Military Serv:** USN WWII, Korean War. **Business Addr:** Pastor, Antioch Baptist Church, 3763 Brennan Ave, Norfolk, VA 23502.

WILLIAMS, IVORY D.
Storyteller. **Personal:** Born Sep 12, 1949, Detroit, MI; children: Ivory D. Williams III. **Career:** Storyteller, present; Sales Mgr., ATT, 1971-1994. **Home Addr:** PO Box 312802, Detroit, MI 48231.

WILLIAMS, J BYRD. **See WILLIAMS, JUDITH BYRD.**

WILLIAMS, JAMAL
Football player. **Personal:** Born Apr 28, 1976, Washington, DC; son of Harriet; married Surel; children: Joy D & Jasmine D. **Educ:** Okla State Univ, sociol, 1997. **Career:** San Diego Chargers, defensive tackle, 1998-. **Honors/Awds:** Ed Block Courage Award, 2002; Defensive Player of Year, San Diego Chargers, 2004; Lineman of Year, San Diego Chargers, 2004; Chargers Alumni Player of Week, 2004, 2005. **Special Achievements:** Named a first-alternate to the Pro Bowl, 2004. **Business Addr:** Defensive Tackle, San Diego Chargers, 4020 Murphy Canyon Rd, San Diego, CA 92123, **Business Phone:** (858)874-4500.

WILLIAMS, JAMEL
Football player. **Personal:** Born Dec 22, 1973, Gary, IN; married Sarah; children: Kaden, Jackson & Bryson. **Educ:** Univ Nebr, BS, commun. **Career:** Football player; Wash Redskins, defensive back, 1997-99; Green Bay Packers, safety, 1999-2000; sales repr, Fed-Ex Kinkos, 2007.

WILLIAMS, JAMES
Public utility executive. **Personal:** Born Dec 15, 1934, Huntsville, AL; son of William Clemons and Ovenia Smith; divorced; children: James E Jr, Gwendolyn A Iley & Regina L. **Educ:** Franklin Univ, assoc deg, bus admin, 1978; Southern Ill Univ, BS, occup educ, 1978; Mich State Univ, MBA prog, 1983. **Career:** Pub Utilities Comn Ohio, utilities examr II, 1975-83, utilities examr III, 1983-85, supvr, 1985-86, pub utilities adminr, 1986-. **Orgs:** Veteran's comt chmn, Nat Asn Advan Colored People, Columbus Br, 1988-92; nat grand secy, York Rite Masons, 1990-; co-chairperson adv bd, Am Cancer Soc, 1993-. **Honors/Awds:** Spec recognition, CALP Grad, Ohio House of Rep, 1986; Outstanding Serv Award, Am Cancer Soc, 1991-92; Community Serv Award, Columbus Dispatch, 1992. **Military Serv:** USAF, tech sgt, 1954-75; Outstanding Noncomission Officer, 1969; Commendation Medal, 1975. **Business Addr:** Public Utilities Administrator, Public Utilities Commission of Ohio, 180 E Broad St 6th Fl, Columbus, OH 43215-3793, **Business Phone:** (614)466-4687.

WILLIAMS, JAMES ARTHUR
Educator. **Personal:** Born May 9, 1939, Columbia, SC; married; children: Angela, Melody & James II. **Educ:** Allen Univ, BA, music ed, 1960; Univ Ill, MS, 1964. **Career:** Calif Johnson High Sch, educator, 1960-69; Morris Col, 1965 & 68; Stillman Col, Dept Music, chmn; Univ Ill, fac; Allen Univ, Columbia, fac; SC Pub Sch, staff; Sidney Park CME Church SC, choir dir; Bethlehem Baptist Church SC, staff. **Orgs:** Bd dir, Columbia SC Choral Soc, 1967-69; adjudicator, Univ Ala, 1972; Tuscaloosa Co Jr Miss Pageant, 1972; Guest Cond All City High Sch Chorus SC; Columbia SC All City HS Chorus; Univ Ala, Tuscaloosa, AL; Tuscaloosa Comt Singers, AL; pres, Palmetto St Music Teachers Asn; Am Choral Dir Asn; Music Educators Nat Conf; Alpha Phi Alpha Frat Inc; Steering Comt Mus Arts Dr; bd dir, Tuscaloosa Comt Singers; Music Com Tuscaloosa Arts & Humanities Coun.

WILLIAMS, JAMES E., JR. **See Obituaries section.**

WILLIAMS, JAMES EDWARD
Executive. **Personal:** Born Apr 29, 1943, Berkeley, CA; son of J Oscar Williams Sr and Ruth E Williams; divorced; children: Erin & Landin. **Educ:** San Francisco State Univ, BA, 1969; Golden Gate Univ, MBA, 1974. **Career:** ITEL Corp, int chief financial officer, 1971-81; Tektronix Corp, controller, 1982-84; Syntex Corp, treas & vpres, 1984-86; Masstor Syst, chief financial officer, 1987-89; Tegal Corp, chief financial officer 1990-92; LePro Corp, pres, 1992-. **Orgs:** Bd, Nat Asn Cre Tres, 1985-; Fin Officers Northern Calif; Treas Club San Francisco; bd mem, Hubert Hoover Boys & Girls Club Menlo Park. **Special Achievements:** Int Finance Sem, Portland State Univ, 1983; Guest speaker: Euromency Conf Treas Mgt, London, 1986; Santa Clara & San Jose State Univers, 1989.

WILLIAMS, DR. JAMES H., JR.
Educator. **Personal:** Born Apr 4, 1941, Newport News, VA; son of James H and Margaret L Mitchell; children: James H III & Mariella L. **Educ:** Newport News Shipyard Apprentice Sch, mech designer, 1965; Mass Inst Tech, SB, 1967, SM, 1968; Trinity Col, Cambridge Univ, PhD, 1970. **Career:** Newport News Shipbuilding & Dry Dock Co, apprentice-sr design engr, 1960-70; Int consult, 1970-; Mass Inst Technol, prof mech eng & writing & humanistic studies, 1970, prof of teaching excellence, 1991, prof emer, currently. **Orgs:** NTA, 1975, ASME, 1978, ASNT, 1978; Diag Eng, 1983; Nat Sci Found, 1985-87. **Honors/Awds:** Charles F Bailey Bronze, Silver & Gold Medals, 1961-63; Ferguson Scholar, Mass Inst Technol, 1963-67; So Fel Fund Fel, Cambridge Univ, 1968-70; Ralph Teetor Award, SAE, 1974; Everett Moore Baker Award, Outstanding Undergrad Tech MIT, 1973; Grant NSF Faculty Partic, 1974; DuPont professorship; Edgerton professorship; Den Hartog Distinguished Ed Award 1981; Charles F Hopewell Faculty fel. **Business Addr:** Professor Emeritus, Massachusetts Institute of Technology, Department Mechanical Engineering, Rm 3-360 77, Massachusetts Ave, Cambridge, MA 02139, **Business Phone:** (617)253-2221.

WILLIAMS, DR. JAMES HIAWATHA
Chancellor (education), president (organization). **Personal:** Born Sep 10, 1945, Montgomery, AL; son of James Hiawatha and Johnnie Mae Robinson-Strother; married Jann A Fleming, Feb 13, 1994; children: James M, John V (deceased), Kasha G & Jameelah I. **Educ:** Los Angeles City Col, AA, 1967; Calif State Univ, Los Angeles, BA, 1973; Pepperdine Univ, Los Angeles, MS, 1974; Wash State Univ, Pullman, WA, PhD, 1983. **Career:** Chancellor (retired); Calif State Polytechnic Univ, Pomona, asst prof,1977-81, assoc dean & assoc prof, 1980-85, dean col arts & prof; Spokane Community Col, pres, 1995-99; Arapahoe Community Col, pres; Yosemite Community Col Dist, chancellor, 2004-06. **Orgs:** Phi Delta Kappa, 1977-; pres, Pomona Valley Nat Asn Advan Colored People,1984-86; Phi Beta Delta, 1988-; exec bd mem,

Nat Asn Ethnic Studies,1988-95, pres, 1992-; Phi Kappa Phi, 1989-; pres-elect, Coun Cols Arts & Scis, 1994; Littleton Rotary Club. **Honors/Awds:** Prism of Excellence Award, Jerry Voorhis Claremont Dem Club, 1986; Martin Luther King Jr Humanitarian Award, Pomona Valley Nat Asn Advan Colored People, 1987; Services to Youth, Claremont Area Chapter Links Inc, 1988; Distinguished Alumnus Award, Calif State Univ, Los Angeles, 1994.

WILLIAMS, JAMES OTIS (BIG CAT WILLIAMS)
Football player, football coach. **Personal:** Born Mar 29, 1968, Pittsburgh, PA. **Educ:** Cheyney State Univ Pa. **Career:** Football player (retired), Football Coach,Radio Colo Analyst; Chicago Bears, tackle, 1991-2002; Chicago Rush, rad color analyst; Concordia univ, off line coach, currently. **Honors/Awds:** Bears Assn, Brian Piccolo Award, 2001.

WILLIAMS, JAMES R
Lawyer, judge. **Personal:** Born Sep 16, 1933, Lowndes County, MS; married Catherine; children: Michael & Jacqueline. **Educ:** Univ Akron, BA, 1960, JD, 1965. **Career:** Judge, Lawyer (retired); Northern Dist Ohio, US atty, 1978-82; Parms Purnell, Stubbs & Williams, partner 1969-78; Guren, Merritt, Feibel, Sogg, & Cohen, pvt pract; Akron Munic Ct, judge; City Akron, councilman-at-large, 1970-78; Summit Co Common Pleas Ct, admin judge, presiding judge, judge. **Orgs:** Treas, Akron Bar Asn; pres, Summit Co Legal Aid Soc; nat pres, Alpha Phi Alpha Fraternity Inc; Ohio Bar Asn; Am Bar Asn; pres, Common Pleas Judges Asn, Ohio. **Honors/Awds:** Outstanding Achievement Award, Alpha Phi Alpha, 1973; Liberian Humane Order of African Redemption Citation, Dr William R Tolbert Jr, Pres Rep Liberian, 1973; Top Hat Award, Pittsburgh Courier, 1977; Ebony's 100 Most Influential Black Ams, 1980; NationalA Award of Merit, Alpha Phi Alpha Fraternity's. **Military Serv:** AUS, 1953-55. **Home Addr:** 1733 Brookwood Dr, Akron, OH 44313, **Home Phone:** (330)867-7536.

WILLIAMS, DR. JAMES THOMAS
Educator, physician. **Personal:** Born Nov 10, 1933, Martinsville, VA; son of Ruth E Thomas and Harry P; married Jacqueline, Apr 21, 1962; children: Lawrence & Laurie. **Educ:** Howard Univ, BS, 1954, MD, 1958; Am Bd Internal Med, dipl, 1967-,recertified, 1974, 1980; Am Bd Endocrinol & Metabolism, dipl, 1972. **Career:** Philadelphia Gen Hosp, intern, 1958-59; DC Gen & Freedmens Hosp, resd,1959-62, 1964-65; Howard Univ Col Med, fel endocrinol, 1965-67; DC GenHosp, physician, 1967-2000; Howard Univ Hosp, physician, 1967-; HowardUniv, Col Med, asst prof, 1967-74, assoc prof, 1974-85, prof, 1985-. **Orgs:** Am Diabetes Asn; med officer, Home Care Prog, DC Govt, 1968-89;Medico-Chirurgical Soc DC; Nat Med Asn; Med Soc DC; Endocrine Soc; fel AmCol Physicians; Alpha Omega Alpha Honor Med Soc; Sigma Pi Phi Fraternity;fel Am Col Endocrinol. **Military Serv:** AUS, MC capt, 1962-64. **Home Addr:** 13414 Tamarack Rd, Silver Spring, MD 20904, **Home Phone:** (301)384-8495. **Business Addr:** Professor of Medicine, Howard University, College of Medicine, 520 W St NW, Washington, DC 20059, **Business Phone:** (202)806-6270.

WILLIAMS, DR. JAMYE COLEMAN
Editor. **Personal:** Born Dec 15, 1918, Louisville, KY; daughter of Jamye Harris Coleman and Frederick Douglass Coleman Sr; married McDonald Williams, Dec 28, 1943; children: Donna Williams. **Educ:** Wilberforce Univ, BA, 1938; Fisk Univ, MA, 1939; Ohio State Univ, PhD, 1959. **Career:** Educator (retired); Edward Waters Col, Jacksonville FL, educr, 1939-40; Shorter Col Little Rock, 1940-42; Wilberforce Univ OH, 1942-56; Morris Brown Col, 1956-58; Tennessee State Univ, 1959-87, dept head Communs, 1973-87; AME Church Review, ed, 1984-92. **Orgs:** Exec comm., Nashville Br NAACP, 1960-; Registry Election Finance TN, 1990-96; Nat Conf Community & Justice (NCCJ), 1988-; World Methodist Coun, 1981-91; bd mem, Nashville Community Found, 1991-; bd Govs, Nat Coun Church, 1976-; Theta Alpha Phi; Pi Kappa Delta; Kappa Delta Pi; bd dir, John W Work III Found; Links Inc; Delta Sigma Theta; Nat Asn Adavan Colored People; trustee, Community Found. **Honors/Awds:** Teacher of the Year, Tenn State Univ, 1968; Outstanding Teacher Award, 1976; Woman of the Year, Nashville Davidson & Co Bus & Prof Women's Club, 1978; Citizen of the Year, Nashville Alumnae Chap Delta Sigma Theta, 1979; co-editor "The Negro Speaks: The Rhetoric of Contemporary Black Leaders"; Salute to Black Women Award, Howard Univ, 1986; Distinguished Service Award, Tenn State Univ, 1988; Lifetime Achievement Award, Kappa Alpha Psi Fraternity, 1990; Recipient with McDonald Williams, Human Relations Award, The Nat Conf Christians & Jews, 1992; inductee, Acad Women of Achievement, 1996; recipient with McDnoald Williams, Joe Kraft Humanitarian Award, 2002; Honorary Degrees, The InterdenomiNat Theol Ctr; Morris Brown Col; Payne Theol Sem. **Home Addr:** 125 Wynfield Way SW, Atlanta, GA 30331.

WILLIAMS, JAN
Financial manager. **Educ:** NC A&T State Univ, BS, Finance & Eng; Pepperdine Univ, MBA, Finance; Naval Post Grad Sch, MS. **Career:** Marine Corps, officer; W End Med Ctr Bd Dir, treas; NASD, mem; AXA Adv LLC, financial adv, retirement planning specialist, 1997-. **Orgs:** Alliance Bersteins Elite Adv Team; AXA & Black Enterprise Ski Challenges; 100 Black Mens Pres Coun; Ga Dent Asn; Morehouse Sch Med Alumni Asn; The Links Nat Assembly; instr, Good Choice Inc; 100 Black Men Am. **Special Achievements:** Bicycles in 500 mile events annually to raise money for AIDS vaccine research.

WILLIAMS, JANICE L.
Manager. **Personal:** Born Aug 23, 1938, Allentown, PA; daughter of William E Merritt and Cora L Merritt; children: Lisa & Jerome. **Educ:** Muhlenberg Col, BA, 1970; Lehigh Univ, MEd, 1974. **Career:** Muhlenberg Col, asst dir admis, 1970-74; Pa Power & Light Co, mgrplacement & EEO prog, 1974-. **Orgs:** Bd mem, YWCA, 1975-77; pres, Negro Cult Ctr, 1975-77; bd mem, Head Start Lehigh Valley, 1975-77; Muhlenberg Col, Coun Continuing Educ, 1976; Educ Comn, Pa Chamber Com, 1976-77; bd mem, Allentown Police Civil Serv, 1979-, United Way Lehigh City, 1981-88; bd mem, Friends Comn, Muhlenerg Col Corp, 1987-89; dir, Allentown Sch Bd Educ, 1987-; Muhlenberg Col Bd Assocs, 1987-89; pres, Lehigh Valley Personnel Asn, 1989-90. **Honors/ Awds:** Woman of the Year, Allentown Nat Asn Advan Colored People, 1987.

WILLIAMS, JARVIS ERIC
Football player. **Personal:** Born May 16, 1965, Palatka, FL; married; children: Jarvis Jr. **Educ:** Univ Fla, attended. **Career:** Football player (retired); Miami Dolphins, safety, 1988-93; NY Giants, defensive back, 1993-94. **Special Achievements:** Recorded 14 interceptions, including one for a touchdown.

WILLIAMS, JASON HAROLD
Government official. **Personal:** Born Nov 11, 1944, Baltimore, MD; son of James Edward and Mary Boyd. **Educ:** Univ Md, Col Park, MD, BS, 1966; Univ Calif, Los Angeles, CA, 1973. **Career:** Building Servs, Los Angeles, CA, exec asst, 1971-73, dep dir, 1973-75, chief dep dir, 1975-82, dir, 1982-85; Facilities Mgmt, Los Angeles, CA, asst dir, 1985-87; Los Angeles County, Dept Health Servs, Los Angeles, CA, sr asst, hosps admin, 1987-. **Orgs:** Mem allocations comt, United Way Los Angeles, 1975-; United Way Bd, United Way Los Angeles, 1983-85; chmn, spec task force, United Way Los Angeles, 1988-; treas, Southern Calif Chap, Nat Forum Black Public Adminrs, 1990-91; fin chair, Forum '91 Planning Comt, 1990-91. **Honors/Awds:** Silver & Gold Leadership, United Way, 1979-82, 1984-89; Outstanding Leadership, Brotherhood Crusade, 1980-82, 1985-87; Award of Appreciation, Los Angeles Olympic Org Comt, 1984; Award of Recognition, Los Angeles Olympic Org Comt, 1984; Distinguished Leadership, United Negro Col Fund, 1986; Award of Appreciation, USC Black Alumni Asn, Ebonics Support Group, 1990. **Military Serv:** USAFR, second Lt, 1962-66. **Business Phone:** (213)240-8372.

WILLIAMS, JAY OMAR
Football player, businessperson. **Personal:** Born Oct 13, 1971, Washington, DC; married Erica; children: Jamye, Jai & Roman. **Educ:** Wake Forest Univ. **Career:** Football player (retired), Consultant; St Louis Rams, defensive end, 1995-99; Carolina Panthers, 2000-01; Miami Dolphins, 2002-04; gun consult, currently.

WILLIAMS, JAYSON
Television broadcaster, basketball player, business owner. **Personal:** Born Feb 22, 1968, Ritter, SC; son of Elijah Joshua and Barbara; married Tanya; children: Monique & Ejay. **Educ:** St John's Univ, attended. **Career:** Basketball player (retired), analyst, business owner; Philadelphia 76ers, forward, 1990-92, NJ Nets, forward (retired), 1992-99; NBC TV, analyst; T.R.Y. J's, co-owner, currently. **Honors/Awds:** Player of the Week, NBA, 1998. **Special Achievements:** Hosted own live Internet broadcast, "Jayson's Boardroom"; Staged charity softball games for Tomorrow's C Inst; auth, Loose Balls, 2000; Guest actor on television sitcoms, including Spin City and Cosby; Guest actor, New Jersey Turnpike. **Business Addr:** Owner, T.R.Y. J's, 29 S Warren St, Downtown Trenton, NJ 08608, **Business Phone:** (609)392-4370.

WILLIAMS, JEAN CAROLYN
Educator. **Personal:** Born Aug 30, 1956, Mullins, SC; daughter of Remel Graves Gause and Fred Gause Jr; married Vaugn McDonald Williams Jr, Jul 21, 1979. **Educ:** Spelman Col, Atlanta, GA, BA, Spanish, 1978; Univ Iberoamericana, Mexico City, Mexico, MAT, Spanish lit & Spanish cult, cert, 1983; Univ GA, Athens, cert, 1987; Ga State Univ, Atlanta, MAT, educ & Spanish, 1983, EdS, educ & Spanish, EdD, educ & Spanish; Nova Southeastern Univ, Ft Lauderdale, Fla, EdS, educ leadership & Sch improv, EdD, educ leadership & Sch improv. **Career:** Douglas Co Schs Syst, Douglasville, GA, Spanish teacher, 1978, teacher eng second lang, 1982-86, 1990-92, arts & lang dept, prin; Beulah Elem Sch, prin, currently; Ga Dept Educ, ambassador, speaker, consult, 1988; Gov's Task Force Teacher's Pay Performance, 1991. **Orgs:** Mem steering comt, Acad Alliances, 1986-; mem staff devel, Coun, Douglas Co Schs, 1986-; head, Instrnl & Prof Devel Comt, Douglas Co Asn Educrs, 1987-88 & 1989-90; chair challenge, Douglas Co High Sch, 1989-92; Foreign Lang Asn Ga; nat pres elect, Am Asn Teacher Spanish & Portuguese, 1992-95; Ga Athletic Coaches Asn; adv bd, Southern Conf Lang Teaching, Am Asn Ga; Phi Delta Kappa; Alpha Kappa Alpha; Delta Kappa Gamma; Nat Educrs Asn's Cong Contact Team; Prof Negotiation Task Force; Prof League Schs, Leadership Team; Performance Learning Syst Inc, instr. **Honors/Awds:** Douglas County Teacher of the Year, Douglas Co Schs, 1987-88; Georgia Spanish Teacher of the Year, 1987; Georgia Teacher of the Year, Ga Chap, Am Asn Teachers Spanish & Portuguese, 1987-88; Georgia Teacher of the Year Award, Encyclopaedia Brittanica, Good Housekeeping, & Coun Chief State Sch Officers, 1987-88; Certificate of Excellence, Foreign Lang Asn Ga, 1988; Excellence in Education Award, Nat Asn Sec Sch Prin, 1988; Burger King Award for Excellence in Education, 1988; Excellence in Education Award, Coun Chief State Sch Officers, 1988; Milken Family Foundation National Educator, 1990; Director of the Year, Foreign Lang Asn Ga, 1994; Director of the Year, Foreign Lang Elem Sch, 1994; Principal's Award, Ga Leadership Inst Sch Improv, 2004. **Home Addr:** 6703 Sutton Pl, Douglasville, GA 30135. **Business Addr:** Principal, Beulah Elementary School, 1150 Burnt Hickory Rd, Douglasville, GA 30134, **Business Phone:** (770)651-3311.

WILLIAMS, JEAN PERKINS
Labor relations manager. **Personal:** Born Sep 21, 1951, Mt Olive, NC; daughter of Willie R; divorced; children: Sonja. **Educ:** Cornell Univ Sch Indust Rels, cert eeo spec, 1976; Pace Univ White, Plains, NY, BS, liberal studies, 1981; NC Agri & Tech State Univ, Greensboro, NC, MA, adult educ, 1989. **Career:** Ciba-Geigy Corp, New York, corp eeo coordr, 1975-76, sr personnel admin, 1976-78; Am Cyanamid Lederle Labs, equal opportunity affairs mgr, 1978-80; Am Home Products Corp, personnel mgr, 1980-83; Goodyear Tire & Rubber Co, employ mgr; Guilford Tech Community Col, dir personnel, 1990. **Orgs:** Task force mem, Equal Employ Opportunity Comn, WA 1975-76; bd dir, Union Child Day Care Ctr, White Plains, NY, 1976-77; Corp Womens Network, 1976-80; Nat Asn Advan Colored People, 1977-79; bd mem, Cent NC Sch Deaf, 1980-83; Am Bus Womens Asn, 1982-; search comt mem exec dir, YWCA-Greensboro, 1986; Personnel Mgrs Asn, Greensboro, NC.

WILLIAMS, JEANETTE MARIE
School administrator. **Personal:** Born Jul 11, 1942, Shaw, MS; daughter of Lonnie and Mary; married Jan 1, 1960 (widowed); children: Renee L Burwell, Howard S Jr, Karen A & Sharon A Gober. **Educ:** Wilson Jr Col, 1968; Chicago State Univ, BS, Biol, 1969; Chicago State Univ, MS, Biol, 1977; Northern Ill Univ, EdS, 1995. **Career:** Haven Middle Sch, teacher, 1971-72; Chicago Pub Schs, teacher, 1972-74; Malcolm X Col, curriculum spec, 1974-77; Kennedy-King Col, asst prof biol, Title III, dir, 1983-86, asst dean stud servs, distinguished prof, 1998-99, prof biol sci, currently. **Orgs:** Nat Asn Biol Teachers, 1978-; Asn for Supvr & Curric Develop, 1980; pres, Asn Study African Am Life & Hist, 1982-; consult, Educ Mgt Asn, 1982-83; advisor, Phi Theta Kappa, 1982-, pres Chicago Br; bd dir, Black Women's Hall of Fame, 1983-; bd of dir, Kennedy-King Col, Nat Youth Sports Prog, 1987-; Am Asn of Univ Women, 1989-; Am Asn of Women in Conn & Junior Cols; NCW Inc; AKA INT Sorority, Xi Nu Omega Chap. **Honors/Awds:** Scholar Chicago Chemical Co, 1971; Advisor's Hall of Honor Illinois, PhiTheta Kappa, 1984; Distinguished Teacher Award Local 1600, Kennedy King Chap, 1984; Advisor's Hall of Honor Ill Phi Theta Kappa, 1985; Ill Phi Theta Kappa Most Disting Advisor 1985; Outstanding Ill Advisor, Phi Theta Kappa, 1989; Illinois Advisors Hall of Honor, Phi Theta Kappa, 1989, 1991; Women on the Move in the City Col, City Cols Chicago, 1990. **Business Addr:** Professor of Biology, Chicago City Coll, Kennedy-King College, 6301 S Halsted St, Chicago, IL 60621, **Business Phone:** (773)602-5000.

WILLIAMS, JEFFREY LEM
Journalist. **Personal:** Born Sep 21, 1959, Delhi, NY; son of Diane and Odell Williams Sr; children: Alia. **Educ:** State Univ New York, New Paltz, BA, 1981; Univ Md, MA, 1985. **Career:** Frederick News-Post, copy ed, 1986; Lexington Herald-Leader, copy ed, 1987-88; Hartford Courant, copy ed, 1988-91; The Chicago Tribune, asst metro copy ed, metro copy ed, asst suburban ed, currently, SW Bur Chief. **Orgs:** Nat Asn Black Journalists, 1987-. **Honors/Awds:** Chancellor's Award, State Univ New York, 1981; Recruitment Award, State Univ New York, 1981, Dean's List Award, 1980-81. **Business Addr:** Assistant Suburban News Editor, The Chicago Tribune, 435 N Michigan Ave 4th Fl, Chicago, IL 60611, **Business Phone:** (312)222-3232.

WILLIAMS, JENNIFER SCOTT. **See SCOTT, JENNIFER J.**

WILLIAMS, JEROME
Basketball player, basketball executive. **Personal:** Born May 10, 1973, Washington, DC. **Educ:** Montgomery Col, attended; Georgetown Univ, BA, sociol. **Career:** Basketball player (retired), executive; Detroit Pistons, forward, 1996-2001; Toronto Raptors, 2001-04, community rep, 2006-; Chicago Bulls, 2003-04; NY Knicks, forward & ctr, 2004-05. **Orgs:** Phoebe Found; MADD; Optimist Club Southfield; founder, Jerome Williams Rookie Camp & Mentor Prog. **Honors/Awds:** J Walter Kennedy Citizenship Award, 2000; Nat Award, Fannie Mae Home Team Partnership,

2000; Good Guys in Sports, Sporting News, 2002. **Special Achievements:** Film Appearances: Harold; Kumar. **Business Addr:** Community Representative, Toronto Raptors, 40 Bay St Suite 400, Toronto, ON, Canada M5J 2X2, **Business Phone:** (416)815-5600.

WILLIAMS, JEROME D.
Educator. **Personal:** Born Jan 11, 1947, Philadelphia, PA; son of Jerome and Gloria; married Lillian Harrison, Jun 21, 1969; children: Denean, Derek, Daniel, Dante & Dachia. **Educ:** Univ Pa, Philadelphia, PA, BA, 1969; Union Col, Schenectady, NY, MS, 1975; Univ Colo, Boulder, CO, PhD, 1986. **Career:** Gen Electric Co, Schenectady, NY, sr publicist, 1969-78; Solar Energy Res Inst, Golden CO, mgr, pub info, 1978-81; Pa State Univ, Univ Park, PA, assoc prof, 1987; Univ Tex, Austin, Ctr African & African-Am Studies, prof, 2003-; F J Heyne Centennial prof commun, currently. **Orgs:** Am Mkt Asn, 1980-; Asn Consumer Res, 1982-; Acad Mkt Sci, 1984-; Am Psychol Asn, 1986-; exec bd, Soc Consumer Psychol, 1989-. **Honors/Awds:** Received teaching awards from almost every institution where he has taught full-time or been a visiting professor, including the Chinese University of Hong Kong, Howard University, the National University of Singapore, Penn State University and The University of Texas at Austin. **Special Achievements:** One of the first professors in the country to teach courses in multicultural marketing and advertising. **Business Addr:** Professor, University of Texas at Austin, College of Communication, 1 Univ Station A0900, Austin, TX 78712, **Business Phone:** (512)471-7302.

WILLIAMS, JEWEL L
Social worker, executive. **Personal:** Born Feb 11, 1937, Canton, MS; married Frank (divorced); children: Anthony, Frank, Kerry, Debra Whitehead & Darcy Donaldson. **Educ:** Mary Holmes Jr Col, Bus; Jackson State Univ, Soc, 1971. **Career:** Government official (retired); Head Start, community organizer, 1966-73; Canton Pub Schs, social worker, 1974-84; Universal Life Ins Co, sales rep, 1984-86; City Canton, alderman, 1979-94; WMGO Radio Sta, dir pub affairs. **Orgs:** Asst secy, Woman Progress; secy, bd dir, MYL Family Health Ctr, 1973-79; bd mem, Cent Miss Legal Serv, 1976-83; bd mem, Nat Asn Advan Colored People, 1979-; pres, Madison County Women Progress, 1980-82; exec comt, MS Democ Party; pres, Lucy C Jefferson Federated Club Inc; bd dirs, Rainbow Literacy; bd dirs, Canton Chambers Com; bd dirs, Save C Madison County; Madison County Hist Soc. **Honors/Awds:** Outstanding Service, Project Unity Inc, 1979; Outstanding in Community Women for Progress, 1983; Outstanding Sales Service, Universal Life Ins Co, 1985; Outstanding Award, Jackson Links Inc. **Home Addr:** 513 Cauthen St, Canton, MS 39046, **Home Phone:** (601)859-9278.

WILLIAMS, JOANNE LOUISE
Journalist. **Personal:** Born Apr 10, 1949, Milwaukee, WI; daughter of John J Williams and Vida Eugenia Smith Williams; divorced; children: John Brooks Nicholson & Christopher Nicholson. **Educ:** Northwestern Univ, Evanston, IL, BS, 1971. **Career:** WTMJ-TV & Radio, Milwaukee, WI, anchor, reporter, producer, 1971-76; WGN-TV & Radio, Chicago, IL, reporter, producer, writer, 1976-79; WITI-TV, Milwaukee, WI, anchor, former medical reporter, educ reporter, 1979; MyFox Milwaukee, anchor, reporter, currently. **Orgs:** Pres, Milwaukee Press Club, 1982; Milwaukee Forum, 1982-87; Future Milwaukee Grad, 1982; pres, NAB, 1983-99; pres, WIS Black Media Asn; bd dir, Wis Tennis Asn; bd, Milwaukee Tennis Educ Found. **Honors/Awds:** Woman of Color Award, Milwaukee Black Women's Network, 1983, 1999; First Television Fellowship, Case Western Res Sch Med, 1987. **Business Addr:** Anchors, Reporter, MyFox Milwaukee, 1999 Bundy Dr, Los Angeles, CA 90025, **Business Phone:** (310)584-2000.

WILLIAMS, JOE H.
Government official, business owner. **Personal:** Born Oct 7, 1937, Tuskegee, AL; married Marilyn Bryant Hainesworth; children: Melani & Mario. **Educ:** Republic Indus Educ Inst, Elect Maint, 1970-78. **Career:** General Motors Corp, electrician 1965-; Williams Electric Co, owner 1973-; Seventh Ward Warren OH, councilman 1977-; Precinct D Warren OH, prec inct comm head 1984-; Warren 7th Ward, councilman, pres; Joe Williams Elec Co Inc, owner, currently. **Orgs:** Bd mem, Nat Asn Advan Colored People, 1968-; pres, W Warren Improv Coun, 1968-; King Solomon Lodge 87; bd mem, Warren Electrician Bd, 1980-; elected pres, Warren City Coun, 1990-2000; mem, Nat Steering Committee of Clinton/Gore 1996 Campaign. **Honors/Awds:** Hon Mayor, Tuskegee, Ala, 1977; General Motors Award for Excellence, Gen-Motors, Lordstown, 1984; Outstanding Community Service Award, NAACP, 1984;Distinguished Service Award, Black Elected Official City Warren, Nat AsnNegro Bus & Prof Women's Club, OH, 1985; Joe H Williams Day April 14,named in hon, 1985; Outstanding Community Service Award, Mayor Daniel JSferra Warren, OH; Governor's Special Recognition, Richard Celeste, 1985;Hon Auditor of State, Thomas E Ferguson, 1985; City Coun Citation, JerryCrispino; New York Assembly Citation, Larry Seebrook, 1991. **Home Addr:** 2855 Peerless Ave SW, Warren, OH 44485. **Business Addr:** Owner, Joe Williams Electric Co Inc, 2855 Peerless Ave SW, Warren, OH 44485, **Business Phone:** (330)898-4477.

WILLIAMS, JOHN
Basketball player. **Personal:** Born Aug 9, 1962, Sorrento, LA; married Karen; children: John Jr, Johnfrancis, Johnpaul & Johnna. **Educ:** Tulane Univ, 1985. **Career:** Basketball Player (retired); Cleveland Cavaliers, forward-ctr, 1986-95; Phoenix Suns, 1995-98; Dallas Mavericks, forward & ctr, 1998-99. **Orgs:** Alpha Phi Alpha. **Honors/Awds:** Player of the Week, NBA, 1986; NBA All-Rookie Team, 1987; Metro Conf Player of the Year.

WILLIAMS, JOHN ALFRED
Writer, educator, actor. **Personal:** Born Dec 5, 1925, Jackson, MS; son of John Henry and Ola Mae Jones; married Carolyn Clopton, 1947 (divorced); children: Gregory D & Dennis A; married Lorrain Isaac, 1965; children: Adam J. **Educ:** Syracuse Univ, BA, eng & j, 1950, DLitt, 1995; Grad Sch, 1950-51; Hon Doctor Lit, Southeastern Mass Univ, 1978; State Univ New York, DLitt, 2001; Univ Rochester, DLitt, 2003. **Career:** Educator (Retired), Writer, Actor; Work foundry & supermarket, 1951;Onondaga County Welfare Dept, caseworker, 1952; Gold State Mutual, CBS,NBC-TV, 1954; Comet Books Press, publicity dir, 1955; Abelard-Schuman, asst pub, 1957-58; Amer Comm Africa, dir info, 1957; spec events WOV NY, 1957; contributed Herald-Tribune Book Week 1963-65; Holiday Mag Europe, 1965-66; Teaching: Col Virgin Islands, lectr black lit, 1968; CUNY, lectr, creative writing, 1968-69; Macalester Col, visiting prof, 1970; Audience Mag, ed bd. 1970-72; Amer J, 1972-74; Univ Calif Santa Barbara, regent slectr 1973; LaGuardia Comm Col, visting prof, 1973-78; Univ Hawaii, visiting prof, 1974; Boston Uni, visiting prof, 1978-79; Rutgers Univ, prof, 1979-94; New York Univ, visiting prof, 1986-87; WNET-TV writer, bd of dir Coord Coun Lit Mags, 1983-85; Paul Robeson Prof of Eng, 1990-93; Bard Col, visiting prof, 1994-95; Univ Houston, visiting prof, 1994; Bard Col, fel, 1994-95; Novels & Poems: The Angry Ones, 1960; Night Song, 1961; Sissie, 1963; Beyond the Angry Black, 1966; The Man Who Cried I Am, 1967; Sons of Darkness, Sons of Light: A Novel of Some Probability, 1969; Captain Blackman, 1972; Mothersill & the Foxes, 1975; Junior Bachelor Soc, 1975; Click Song, 1982; The Berhama Account, 1985; Jacob's Ladder, 1987; Safari West: Poems, 1998; Clifford's Blues, 1999; Africa, Her History, Lands & People, 1963; This is My Country, Too, 1965; The King God Didn't Save: Martin Luther King, Jr, 1970; The Most Native of Sons: Richard Wright, 1970; Amistad 1, 1970, Amistad 2, 1971; Flashbacks: A 20-Year Diary of Article Writing, 1973; Minorities in the City, 1975; The McGraw-Hill Intro to Lit, 1st ed, 1984, 2nd ed, 1994; If I Stop I'll Die: The Comedy & Tragedy of Richard Pryor (with Dennis A. Williams), 1991; Drama: Last Flight from Ambo Ber, 1981; August Forty-Five, 1991: Vanqui (libretto), 1999; Safari West, 1998; Transform, 2003. **Honors/Awds:** National Inst Arts & Letters, 1962; Centenial Medal, Outstanding Achievement, Syracuse Univ, 1970; J Richard Wright Jacques Romain Award,1973; National Endowment, 1977; American Book Award, 1983, 1998; US Observer, 23rd Premio Casa Award, 1985, Distinguish Writer Award, Middle Atlantic Writers, 1987; Michael Award, NJ Literature Hall of Fame, 1987; Carter G. Woodson Award Mercy Col, 1989; Lind back Award Distinguished Teaching, Rutgers Univ, 1993; Black Writers Hall of Fame, 1998; name sake of the John A. Williams Lecture Series, Rutgers Univ, 1999; President's Award, Hartwick Coll, 2001; ohn Oliver Killens Award for Fiction, 2002; QBR Phyllis Wheatley Award, 2002. **Special Achievements:** February 2 proclaimed John Williams Day in the City of Syracuse, NY, 1988. **Military Serv:** USNR, Pharm Mate 3/c, 1943-46. **Home Addr:** 693 Forest Ave, Teaneck, NJ 07666. **Business Addr:** Actor, Barbara Hogenson Agency, 165 W End Ave, New York, NY 10024.

WILLIAMS, REV. JOHN HENRY
Clergy. **Personal:** Born Feb 24, 1948, Venice, IL; married Emma Jean Johnson; children: Reginold, Dean, John Jr, Shelonda, Nicole & Milton. **Educ:** Southern Ill Univ, Edwardville, attended 1978; State Comm Col, E St Louis, attended 1981. **Career:** Venice Independent Baseball League, pres, 1970-81; Nat Asn Advan Colored People, Madison Br, pres, 1976-80; Venice Citizen Community Develop, chmn, 1977-78; People Org Benefit C Venice, pres, 1981-83; New Salem MB Church, pastor 1982-;Venice Local Utilities Bd, vice chmn, 1983-; Venice Neighborhood Crime Watch Prog, mem, 1984; Venice City, IL, alderman, 1989-. **Orgs:** Int Union Operating Engrs 1971-; Free & Accepted Ancient York Rite Mason, 1972-; former pres, Venice Park Bd Comn, 1982-83; River Bluff Girl Scouts Coun, 1992. **Honors/Awds:** Two Local Awards, Madison Branch Nat Asn Advan Colored People, 1980; Citation for Community Serv Tri-Cities Area United Way, 1982; Pastor of the Year Award, Spot Light Review, 1983; Community Serv Award, Madison Progressive Women Orgn, 1984; Arkansas Travel Cert Award, Arkansas State Governor Bill Clinton, 1986; Achievement Award, Bethel AME Church, 1986; Project Cleanup Drugs & Alcohol Cot Award, 1990; Kool Achiever Awards, Nominee, 1992; Martin Luther King Jr Cot Award, Venice Public Sch, Junior Beta Club, 1992. **Business Addr:** Pastor, New Salem MB Church, 1349 Klein St, Venice, IL 62090, **Business Phone:** (618)452-3157.

WILLIAMS, JOHN L
Football player. **Personal:** Born Nov 23, 1964, Palatka, FL. **Educ:** Univ Fla. **Career:** Football player (retired); Seattle Seahawks, fullback, 1986-93; Pittsburgh Steelers, 1994-95. **Honors/Awds:** Pro Bowl, 1990-91.

WILLIAMS, DR. JOHN L
Dentist, clergy, executive. **Personal:** Born Dec 31, 1937, Lubbock, TX; son of Rev Nathaniel Williams and Mary Williams; married Annie L Emmanuel; children: LeCretria, Stephanie, John John, Nandilyn, John Mark, LaShunda, Samuel John & John Luther Jr. **Educ:** Tex Southern Univ, BChem, 1960; Howard Dent Sch, DDS, 1965. **Career:** Faith Tabernacle COGIC, gen practr & pastor, currently; A Williams & Sons Funeral Home, owner, dir, currently; DDS, currently. **Orgs:** Charles H George Dent Soc, 1965; Acad Gen Dent; Am Chem Soc; supt So Houston Dist, 1983; Tex Dent Asn; Houston Dist Dent Soc, 1989; Am Dent Asn. **Honors/Awds:** Sal Dunbar Sr Hi Lubbock, Tex, 1956; Alpha Phi Alpha Frat, 1960; Acad Gen Dent, 1976. **Home Addr:** 4436 So MacGregor Way, Houston, TX 77021. **Business Addr:** Director, Owner, A Williams & Sons Funeral Home, 7811Cullen Blvd, Houston, TX 77051, **Business Phone:** (713)738-2234.

WILLIAMS, JOHN R.
Optometrist. **Personal:** Born Mar 14, 1937, Richmond; married Sandra; children: 3 Sons. **Educ:** Va Union Univ, BS 1959; Ill Col Optometry, OD, 1963. **Career:** Optometrist, Pearl Vision Ctr, Va, currently. **Orgs:** Am Optometric Asn, 1960-; Nat Optometric Asn, 1968-; Metro Dev Corp, 1972-; Asn Investors, 1972-73; mem Capitala Reg Park Auth, 1968-71; bd mem, Salvation Army Boys Club, 1965-74; bd mem, Friends Asn; bd mem, Big Bro Am, 1968-74; bd mem & vice chmn, Church Hill Multi-serv Ctr. **Business Addr:** Optometrist, Pearle Vision Center, 107 Junction Dr, Ste D, Ashland, VA 23005-2200.

WILLIAMS, DR. JOHNNY WAYNE
School administrator. **Personal:** Born Dec 18, 1946, Lewisburg, TN; son of James A and Essie M; married Coralee Henry, Jun 23, 1968; children: Kimberly M. **Educ:** Tenn State Univ, BS, 1968; Univ Northern Colo, MA, 1974; Troy State Univ, EdS, 1981; Univ Sarasota, EdD, 1993. **Career:** USAF, officer positions, 1968-88; NC A & T State Univ, chair, Dept Aerospace Studies, 1985-88; Columbia State Community Col, exec dir job training progs, 1988-90, dean stud servs, 1990-94, vpres stud servs, 1994-98; Tenn Technol Ctr, Nashville, dir, 1998-. **Orgs:** Maury County Fed Credit Union, dir, 1991-; Maury County Voc Prog, 1991-; Job Trainings Pvt Indust Coun, 1992-; Maury County Lit Coun, 1993-. **Special Achievements:** Dissertation, Air Force ROTC, Cadet Attitudes Toward Field Training, 1981; Dissertation, Swinging Door, Dropout Characteristics at a Small Rural Community Col, 1993. **Military Serv:** USAF, lt col, 1968-88; Commendation Medal; 3rd Oak Leaf Cluster; Meritorious Service Medal, 2nd Oak Leaf Cluster. **Home Addr:** 324 Alden Cove Dr, Smyrna, TN 37167. **Business Addr:** Director, Tennessee Technology Center, 100 White Bridge Rd, Nashville, TN 37207.

WILLIAMS, JOSEPH BARBOUR
Insurance executive, president (organization). **Personal:** Born Aug 20, 1945, New York, NY; son of Joseph Pins Barbour Jr and Mary Alice Porter; married Felicia Ann Thomas, Jun 7, 1972; children: Christie Dawn. **Educ:** Talladega Col, Talladega, AL, BA, 1967. **Career:** Cent Life Ins Fla, Tampa FL, pres, ceo, 1972; Cent Life Employees Credit Union, Tampa, FL, pres, 1987-. **Orgs:** Asst treas, Greater Tampa Urban League, 1984-; Hillsborough Bd Consumer Affairs, 1986-90; Nat Asn Advan Colored People, Tampa Chap, 1990-. **Honors/Awds:** Blount Trophy For Agency Offices, Exceptional Performance, National Ins Asn, 1985; Certificate of Merit, Outstanding performance ins bur, National Ins Asn, 1982, 1976; Service Award, Adv For Omega Psi Phi Fraternity, Univ S Fla, 1974. **Military Serv:** USN, Lt, 1968-72; National Defense Serv Medal, 1968.

WILLIAMS, JOSEPH E
Executive, president (organization), chief executive officer. **Educ:** Boston Univ Sch Mgt, BA, finance; Wharton Sch, Univ Pa, MBA, multinational enterprise & finance. **Career:** Salomon Brothers; First Nat Bank Chicago; BankBoston Global Capital Mkt, dir investor sales; Hibernia Southcoast Capital Inc, 1998, pres & ceo, 2003-04; Beacon St Financial Group, pres, currently. **Orgs:** Front runner, New Orleans Redevelop Authority; Urban League Greater New Orleans. **Business Addr:** President, Beacon Street Financial Group LLC, 4 Grand Cypress Ct, New Orleans, LA 70131.

WILLIAMS, DR. JOSEPH HENRY
Physician. **Personal:** Born Jun 15, 1931, Columbia, SC; son of Carter Edmund and Ruby Catherine Winthrop; married C Patricia; children: Joseph Jr. **Educ:** Howard Univ, BS, 1950, MD, 1954; New York Univ, dipl, 1960. **Career:** Park City Hosp, attending surgeon, 1962-. **Orgs:** Am Bd Surg, 1967; Fairfield County Med Soc; Conn St Med Soc; Am Bd Psychiatry & Neurol Inc, 2004-. **Honors/Awds:** fel, Am Soc Abdominal Surgeons, 1963; Fel, Am Col Surgeons, 1982. **Military Serv:** AUS, 1956-58. **Home Addr:** 6901 Old York Rd, Philadelphia, PA 19126-2234.

WILLIAMS, JOSEPH LEE
Executive. **Personal:** Born Mar 25, 1945, Madison, WV; son of Joseph Lee Sr and Loretta M Lawson; married Shirley Ann Johnson, Jan 24, 1965; children: Yvette, Yvonne, Mary & Joseph. **Educ:** Marshall Univ, BBA, Fin, 1978; Mayors' Leadership Inst, 1984. **Career:** Ebony Golf Classic, founder, dir, 1971-87; City

Huntington, mem city coun, 1981, asst mayor, 1983-84, mayor, 1984-85; Basic Supply Co, chmn, pres, chief exec officer, 1977-; Abigail Adams Nat Bancorp, Wash, DC, dir, 1988-; Unlimited Future Inc, dir, 1991-96; First Sentry Bank, dir, 1996-; Consolidated Bank & Trust Co, chmn, pres, chief exec officer, 2005-; Energy Serv Acquisition Corp, independent dir, mem audit comt, 2006-. **Orgs:** Community Huntington Urban Renewal Authority, 1983-85; Huntington Rotary Club, 1983-92; bd dirs, Huntington Area Chamber Com, 1984-85; bd trustees, Cabell-Huntington Hosp, 1984-85; Cabell-Huntington Hosp Found Bd, 2002-; bd dirs, United Way River Cities, 1984-90; City Huntington Interim Loan Comn, 1985-87; Nat Asn Advan Colored People; Huntington Area Chamber Com, WVa Partnership Progress Coun, 1989-93; bd dirs, Huntington Ind Corp; past exec bd mem, United Way River Cities Found; Marshall Univ, Col Bus, adv bd, 1994-2004; US SBA Nat Adv Coun, 1997-2000; bd govs, Marshall Univ, 2001-05; WVa Workforce Investment bd, 2001-. **Honors/Awds:** Outstanding Black Alumni, Marshall Univ, 1984; Outstanding Citizen Award, Huntington, WVa Negro Bus & Prof Women's Clubs, 1985; Subcontractor of The Year, WVa SBA, 1987; Minority Bus Person of the Year, WVa SBA, 1988; featured in Union-Carbide Corp's Nat News mag, 1989; featured in E I du-Pont de Nemours & Co's TEMPO Nat Newsletter, 1989; Huntington, VA, Med Ctr's Black Hist Month Award, 1990; Ernst & Young Inc, Merrill Lynch Entrepreneur of the Year, regional finalist, 1991; one of 50 most influential in Huntington Tri-State area, Huntington Herald, 1999; WVa Minority Bus Develop Ctr's Innovator Award, 2003. **Business Addr:** President, Chief Executive Officer, Basic Supply Co Inc, 628 8th Ave, PO Box 936, Huntington, WV 25712-0936, **Business Phone:** (304)523-1587.

WILLIAMS, JUAN
Radio host, writer, journalist. **Personal:** Born Apr 10, 1954, Colon, Panama; son of Rogelio L and Alma Geraldine; married Susan Delise, Jul 1, 1978; children: Antonio Mason & Regan Almina. **Educ:** Haverford Col, BA, philos, 1976. **Career:** Wash Post, reporter & columnist, 1976-99; America's Black Forum, host, 1996-; Fox News, anchor, 1997-, Fox News Sunday, panelist, currently; Nat Pub Radio, Talk of the Nation, radio show host, 2000-01, sr corresp, currently; Books: Eyes on the Prize: America's Civil Rights Years, 1954-1965, 1987; Thurgood Marshall: American Revolutionary, 1998; (with Q Dixie) This Far by Faith: Stories from the African-American Religious Experience, 2003; My Soul Looks Back in Wonder: Voices of the Civil Rights Experience, 2004; (with D Ashley & S Rhea) I'll Find a Way or Make One: A Tribute to Historically Black Colleges, 2004; Enough: The Phony Leaders, Dead-end Movements, & Culture of Failure That Are Undermining Black America—& What We Can Do about It, 2006; (Author of essays) Black Farmers in America, 2006. **Orgs:** Number of bds including bd trustees, Haverford Col; Aspen Inst Commun & Soc Prog; Wash Jour Ctr; NY Civil Rights Coalition. **Honors/Awds:** Numerous honors & awards including Front Page Award, Wash-Baltimore Newspaper Guild, 1979; Education Writers of America Award, 1979; Columnist of the Year, Washingtonian, 1982; DuSable Museum Award, 1985; Emmy Award for documentary writing, 1989; Bill Pryor Award for investigative reporting; Outstanding Book Award, Myers Ctr Study Human Rights US; Best National Book Award, Time mag; honorary doctorates, Haverford Col & State Univ NY. **Business Addr:** Senior Correspondent, National Public Radio, 635 Massachusetts Ave NW, Washington, DC 20001, **Business Phone:** (202)513-2300.

WILLIAMS, JUDITH BYRD (J BYRD WILLIAMS)
Artist, chief executive officer. **Personal:** Born Jul 5, 1952, Philadelphia, PA; daughter of Henry and Frances. **Educ:** Cushing Col, AS, 1973; Cheyney State Col, BA, 1975; ITT Tech Inst, Info Technol Multimedia, 2005. **Career:** Media Court House, intake worker; Del County Intermediate Unit, TA, artist, 1982-2003; J Byrds Prods, chief exec officer, 2001-. **Orgs:** Pottstown Art Guild, 1995-98; J Byrds Gospel Review, 2002-03; Black History Chair, YWCA Pottstown, 2003; founder & chief exec officer, Frances Bell Williams Scholar. **Honors/Awds:** Most Honorable Artist of the Year, 1995; Women Excel Award, Young Women Christian Award Pottstown, 1998. **Special Achievements:** Author of Art Between Curriculum, 1999, song "You Know I Love", 2004, Multimedia Valedictorian, ITT Technical Institute, 2005.

WILLIAMS, JUNIUS W.
Lawyer. **Personal:** Born Dec 23, 1943, Suffolk, VA; son of Bernyce White and Maurice Lanxton; children: Camille, Junea. **Educ:** Amherst Col, BA, 1965; Yale Law Sch, JD, 1968. **Career:** Newark Community Develop Admin & Model Cities Prog, dir, 1970-73; Pvt Pract, atty, 1973-83, 1985-; City Newark, cand for mayor, 1982; Essex Newark Legal Serv, exec dir, 1983-85; Return to the Source, NJ, bus mgr, vocalist, instrumentalist, 1985-; real estate developer, Newark, NJ, 1987-; Irvington, NJ, legis counr, 1990-94, atty, 1994-. **Orgs:** Founder & dir, Newark Area Planning Asn, 1967-70; co-chmn, Comn Negotiating Team, NJ Col Med & Dent Controversey, 1967; fel MARC, 1967-68, 1973; pres, Nat Bar Asn, 1978-79; Equal Opportunities Fund Bd, 1980; Essex County Ethics Comn, 1980; founder & pres, Leadership Develop Group, 1980-; bd trustees, Essex County Col, 1980-84; fel Inst Pol Kennedy Sch, Gov Harvard Univ, 1980; pres, Yale Law Sch Asn, NJ, 1981-82; founder & chmn, Ad Hoc Comn, Univ Heights, 1984-86; consult & developer, Univ Heights Neighborhood Develent Corp, 1986-93; guest speaker & lectr, Yale Univ, Harvard Law Sch, Rutgers Univ, Cornell Univ, Univ NC; bd dirs, Agr Missions Inc; Essex County Bar Asn; Critical Minorities Probs Comn; Nat Asn Housing & Redevel Officials; consult, Coun Higher Educ Newark; mem & secy, Newark Collaboration Group. **Honors/Awds:** Distinguished Serv Award, Newark Jaycees, 1974; Concerned Citizens Award, Bd Concerned Citizens, Col Med & Dent, NJ. **Special Achievements:** Youngest person to be elected president of the National Bar Association. **Business Addr:** Attorney, Town Irvington, Munic Bldg, Irvington, NJ 07111, **Business Phone:** (973)399-8111.*

WILLIAMS, KAREN ELAINE
Airline executive. **Personal:** Born Apr 5, 1956, Louisa, VA; daughter of Marion Buckner and Curtis Jasper; married; children: Cossia & Yvette. **Educ:** Renton Vocational Inst, cert, 1976; Lake Wash Vocational Tech, cert, 1977; Griffin Bus Col, BA, 1980. **Career:** Ideal Realty Co, secy/receptionist, 1984-86; Deloitte Haskins & Sells, admin support, 1986-87; Boeing Co, data base controller, 1987-88, scheduler & planner, 1988-92, employee dev specialist, 1992-96; Eastern Star; cert training adv, 1996-. **Orgs:** Electronettes Drill Team, tres; AIO Charter asn. **Honors/Awds:** Cert Training Proficiency, 1988; Cert Training Scheduler Briefing, 1989; Pride Excellence Award, 1987, 1990.

WILLIAMS, KAREN HASTIE
Lawyer. **Personal:** Born Sep 30, 1944, Washington, DC; daughter of William H and Beryl Lockhart; married Wesley S Williams Jr; children: Amanda Pedersen, Wesley Hastie & Bailey Lockhart. **Educ:** Univ Neuchatel Switz, Cert, 1965; Bates Col, BA, 1966; Fletcher Sch Law & Diplcy Tufts Univ, MA, 1967; Columbus Law Sch Cath Univ Am, JD, 1973. **Career:** Supreme Ct, clerk: Fried Frank Harris Shriver & Kampelman, asn atty, 1975-77; US Senate Comn Budget, chief coun, 1977-80; Off Fed Procurement Policy Off Mgt & Budget, adminr, 1980-81; Crowell & Moring, coun, 1982, sr partner, currently; ABA Sect Public Contract Law, chair, 1992-93; Chubb Corp, bd dir; Continental Airlines, Inc, bd dir; Gannett Co, Inc, bd dir; Wash Gas Holdings Co, bd dir. **Orgs:** Past chmn, Am Bar Asn Pub Contract Law Sect; bd dir, Sun Trust Bank; Lawyers Comn Civil Rights Under Law; bd dirs, Wash Gas Light Co; chair, Black Stud Fund; bd dir, NAACP Legal Defense Fund; former mem, Trilateral Comn; bd dirs, Continental Airlines Inc; bd dirs, Chubb Corp; Nat Contract Mgt Asn; Black Women Lawyers Asn; Nat Bar Asn; bd dir, SunTrust Bank; bd dir, Federal Nat Mortgage Asn Found. **Honors/Awds:** Director's Choice Award, 1993; Nat Women's Econ Alliance; Breast Cancer Awareness Award, Columbia Hosp Women, 1994; Judge Learned Hand Award, Am Jewish Comt, 1995. **Home Addr:** 1001 Pa Ave NW, Washington, DC 20004, **Home Phone:** (202)624-2680. **Business Addr:** Partner, Crowell & Moring, 1001 PA Ave NW, Washington, DC 20004-2595, **Business Phone:** (202)624-2680.

WILLIAMS, DR. KAREN RENEE
Physician. **Personal:** Born Jan 27, 1954, Baton Rouge, LA; daughter of Alvin C and Eva Castain; married Cornelius A Lewis, Jul 30, 1983; children: Geoffrey P Lewis & Brittany E Lewis. **Educ:** Xavier Univ, BS 1975; Howard Univ Col Med, MD 1978; Tulane Univ, Pediat Residency Prog, 1978-81. **Career:** LA State Univ Sch Med & Earl K Long Hosp, instr & dir pediat emergency room, 1981-87, asst prof pediats, 1987-99, head pediat infectious diss, pediat dept, 1985-, assoc prof clinical pediats, 1999-; pvt pract, currently. **Orgs:** East Baton Rouge Parish Med Assoc, 1981-87, East Baton Rouge Parish Med Soc, 1985-87; Alpha Omega Alpha Med Honor Soc. **Home Addr:** 5990 Stratford Ave, Baton Rouge, LA 70808, **Home Phone:** (225)248-8084. **Business Addr:** Physician, 5825 Airline Hwy, Baton Rouge, LA 70808, **Business Phone:** (225)358-1095.

WILLIAMS, KARL DANELL
Football player. **Personal:** Born Apr 10, 1971, Albion, MI. **Educ:** Tex A&M, Kingsville. **Career:** Football player (retired); Tampa Bay Buccaneers, wide receiver, 1996-2003; Ariz Cardinals, wide receiver, 2004.

WILLIAMS, KATHERINE
Artist, educational consultant. **Personal:** Born Sep 7, 1941; daughter of Hugh L and Norma D Baird; divorced; children: Garvin J. **Educ:** Harvard Univ, MEduc, 1984, EdD, 1987. **Career:** Workers Bank Trinidad & Tobago, opers officer & actg chief acct, 1971-75; Matouk Int, import officer, 1976; Caribbean segment Festival Am Folklife Smithsonian Inst, coordr, 1979-80; Festivals Mag, ed & publ, 1979-83; Smithsonian Inst, Res Inst Immigration & Ethnic Studies, consult, 1979-83; Dept State Wash DC, consult, writer & software evaluator, 1985-86; NY Dept Social Serv, prog mgr, 1987-90; Instrnl Systs, Inc, Hackensack, NJ, dir prog planning & implementation, consult, 1990-94; educ planning consult,1994-; US Dept State, Foreign Serv Promotions Bds, 1999, 2003; US Dept Educ, reader, proposals, 2003. **Orgs:** Harvard Club Wash, DC; mem, 1999-, secy, 2003-04, Pub Mem Asn Foreign Serv (USA). **Honors/Awds:** Women of Achievement, Montgomery Co, 1977; Fellowship grant, DC Comm Arts& Humanities, 1981. **Special Achievements:** Author of Computers, Our Road to the Future, used as text Washington DC Public Sch System 1982-, author of Where Else But America?; Fitting Them Together; A 2-CD set of paintings and poems, photographic exhibit Museum of Modern Art of Latin America OAS Washington, DC 1981; Solo shows of water colours acrylics and oils: Sumner Museum & Archives, Washington DC, 1998, Touchstone Gallery, Washington DC 1998; Gutman Library, Harvard Univ, Cambridge, MA 1998, 1999, 2000, National Center Gallery, US Geological Survey 1999, Space Telescope, Johns Hopkins Univ, Baltimore, MD, 1999, NASA, Goddard Space Flight Center, Greenbelt, MD 2001, work shown incorporate offices and three embassies for in-house and public display, Group shows in Washington, DC, New York City, NY, Flint, MI, Stockholm,Sweden, University of Maryland, MD, Univ New England, ME, Tuscon Museum,AZ, and, Mobile Museum of Art, AL.

WILLIAMS, KATHLEEN (KATHY WILLIAMS)
Business owner. **Personal:** Married Bob; children: 4. **Educ:** Southern Nazarene Univ, BS, org leader, Oklahoma City Univ, Fin Planner Designation. **Career:** Regist Broker & Dealer; Regist Invest Adv; FSC Securities Corp, financial adv; Williams Financial Servs Group Inc, owner & pres, currently; Jack and Jill of America, Inc, 2008-. **Orgs:** NASD; SIPC; bd Dirs, Oklahoma Coun Econc Educ; Co founder, bd dir, Shawna Nicole Williams Scholarship Memorial, Inc. **Honors/Awds:** Leadership award, Leadership Oklahoma City; Outstanding Community Service award, Alpha Kappa Alpha Sorority, Inc. **Special Achievements:** Featured in such publications as Journal Record, Daily Oklahoman, and Black Enterprise Magazine. **Business Phone:** (405)843-6855.

WILLIAMS, KATHRYN
Museum director, educator. **Personal:** Born Dec 25, 1949, Blytheville, AR; daughter of Clifton R and Eddie Bell Hunter-Yearby; divorced; children: Allan Wicker, Tonya LaNette & Toya Marie Wicker. **Educ:** Univ MI-Flint, 1986; Mott Comm Col, 1988. **Career:** Gen Motors-Buick, quality control, 1972-96; Foliage Decorations Kate, 1974-; Comm DoJo Martial Arts Sch Self-defense, founder & teacher, 1980-82; Museum Afrikan Am Hist, founder & pres, curator & researcher, currently; Agiza Histia Habari Newsletter, publ & ed, 1992-; Satora's Afrikan Dance & Drum Sch, founder, 1998-; Museum Black Am Hist Flint, founder & curator. **Orgs:** Asn Museums African Am Hist; Nat Coun Negro Women; Mich Underground Railroad Network; MI Coalition Human Rights & Free South Africa; Greater Flint Arts Coun; Soc African Am Storytellers; Nat Asn Advan Colored People; Nat Million Women's March. **Honors/Awds:** Certificate of appreciation, Genesee County Democratic Party; Dorothy McNeal Award, Flint Asn Black Social Workers; Woman of the Year, HER Mag, 1999; Outstanding Volunteer Service, Comm Leadership Volunteer Recognition Task Force, 2000. **Special Achievements:** First African American woman to hold the position of Floor Check in Quality Control at General Motors-Buick, author of The Stop: The Underground Railroad in Flint, Michigan. **Business Addr:** Curator, Researcher, Museum of African American History, PO Box 660, Flint, MI 48501, **Business Phone:** (810)789-7324.

WILLIAMS, KATHY. See WILLIAMS, KATHLEEN.

WILLIAMS, KEITH DAVID. See DAVID, KEITH.

WILLIAMS, KELVIN EDWIN
Educator. **Personal:** Born Aug 16, 1964, Detroit, MI; son of Mary; married Latrese Williams, Nov 17, 1990; children: Kyrah. **Educ:** Fla Mem Col, BS. **Career:** Miami Dade Pub Sch, learning disabilities teacher, 1987-; Inst Black Family Life Inc, prog dir, exec dir & educr, 1993-; Nat Fed Interscholastic Off Asn, referee, 1994-. **Orgs:** Kappa Alpha Psi Fraternity, 1983-; Miami-Dade Law Enforcement Task Force & Intergroup Rels, 1993; Miami Alliance Black Sch Educr, 1994-; 500 Role Model Excellence Prog, 1995-; vol, Off Comnr Barbara Carey, 1996-; environ cbo adv bd, Miami-Dade Sports, 1997; bd mem, Arabian Nights Found, 1997-. **Honors/Awds:** Black Role Model, Mount Olive Primitive Baptist Church, 1994-95; Role Model Award, 500 Role Model Excellence Program, 1995; Honorary Juvenile Justice Deputy, Dept Juvenile Justice, 1995. **Home Addr:** 5001 SW 150th Terr, Miramar, FL 33027. **Business Addr:** Executive Director, Educator, Institute of Black Family Life Inc, 16405 NW 25th Ave, Miami, FL 33054, **Business Phone:** (305)628-4354.

WILLIAMS, KEN
Baseball player, baseball executive. **Personal:** Born Apr 6, 1964, Berkeley, CA; married Jessica; children: Temeka, Dedrick, Ken Jr, Kyle & Tyler. **Career:** Baseball player (retired), baseball executive; Chicago White Sox, player, 1986-89, dir minor league opers & spec asst to chmn, 1995-96, vpres player develop, 1997-2001, sr vpres & gen mgr, 2000-; Detroit Tigers, 1989-90; Toronto Blue Jays, 1990-91; Montreal Expos, prof baseball player, 1991; SportsChannel, studio analyst, 1995. **Special Achievements:** First African-American general manager in Chicago sports history and the third in major-league history. **Business Addr:** Senior Vice President, General Manager, Chicago White Sox, 333 W 35th St, Chicago, IL 60616, **Business Phone:** (312)674-1000.

WILLIAMS, KENNETH HERBERT
Lawyer, government official. **Personal:** Born Feb 15, 1945, Orange, NJ; married Susan Marie Griffin; children: Kenneth H &

Meryl E. **Educ:** Howard Univ Liberal Arts, BA, 1967; Howard Univ, Sch Law, JD, 1970. **Career:** US Capitol Police, patrolman, 1969-70; Newark Urban Coalition, asst to dir, 1970; City E Orange, judge munic, 1977-82, asst city coun, 1972-75; Ernst & Ernst CPA Firm, tax atty, 1970-71; City E Orange, city councilman, 1984-85; Nat Redevelopment, LLC, co-owner & partner, currently. **Orgs:** NAACP, 1970-, Am Bar Asn, 1971; counsel E Orange Jaycees, 1972; chmn, City E Orange Juvenile Conf Comt, 1973-75; Nat Bar Asn; Judicial Comn, 1977-82, Am Judges Asn, 1978; Am Bar Asn; Garden State Bar Asn. **Honors/Awds:** 'Outstanding Black Attorney', Black Women Lawyers NJ, 1979; White House Fellow Nomination, 1981; Outstanding Citizenship, NJ Fed Colored Women's Clubs Inc, 1984; Certificate of Appreciation, Seton Hall Univ, 1985. **Military Serv:** ROTC, 1963-65. **Business Addr:** Owner, Partner, National Redevelopment LLC, 550 Broad St 2nd Fl, Newark, NJ 07102, **Business Phone:** (973)286-0050.

WILLIAMS, KENNY RAY
Basketball player. **Personal:** Born Jun 9, 1969, Elizabeth City, NC. **Educ:** Barton County Community Col; Elizabeth City State. **Career:** Ind Pacers, forward, 1990-94; Lyon, 1995-96; Forli, 1996-97; Hapoel Jerusalem, 1997-98, 1998-99, 2000-01; Boston Celtics, 2000-01; Troy Pilsener Izmir, 2000; Rocky Mountain Summer League, Denver Nuggets, 2001-02; Bnei Herzeliya, 2001-04; Maccabi Ironi Ramat Gan, 2004-05; Maccabi Givat Shmuel, 2005-06.

WILLIAMS, KEVIN L.
Football player. **Personal:** Born Aug 4, 1975, Pine Bluff, AR. **Educ:** Okla State Univ. **Career:** Football player (Retired); New York Jets, defensive back, 1998-2000; Miami Dolphins, 2000; Houston Texans, 2002. *

WILLIAMS, KEVIN RAY
Football player. **Personal:** Born Jan 25, 1971, Dallas, TX. **Educ:** Miami Univ, Fl. **Career:** Dallas Cowboys, wide receiver, 1993-96; Ariz Cardinals, 1997; Buffalo Bills, 1998-99; San Francisco 49ers, wide receiver, 2000.

WILLIAMS, KIM
Basketball player. **Personal:** Born Oct 14, 1974. **Educ:** W Ark Community Col, 1995; DePaul Univ. **Career:** Utah Starzz, guard, 1997-98; Minnesota Lynx, guard, 1999; Chicago Blaze, guard; Maxpreps, 2008-. **Honors/Awds:** Conference USA Player of the Year, 1997. *

WILLIAMS, DR. LAFAYETTE W
Dentist. **Personal:** Born Dec 17, 1937. **Educ:** Morehouse Col, BS, 1960; Meharry Med Col, DDS, 1968. **Career:** Central St Hosp, Milledgeville, GA, mem staff, 1968-69; Pvt Practice, Valdosta, dentistry 1969-; Valdosta Nursing Home, Int Nursing Care Ctr, mem staff. **Orgs:** Valdosta Black Comm Action Group; Beta Kappa Chi; Alpha Phi Alpha; Mason Shriner, 32 Deg; Elk mem; Fedn Dentaire Internatiolnale; trustee, Lowndes Co Prog Voters League; Nat Asn Realtors; Am Prof Practice Asn; Puritan Int Dent Soc; Am Soc for Preventive Dentirstry; Chicago Soc; Acad Gen Dentistry; Nat Dent Asn; Am Dent Asn; GA; SW Ldist Dental Socs; owner Reasonable Rentals Valdosta-lowndes Co; C of C; NAACP. **Business Addr:** Dentist, Valdosta Nursing Home, International Nursing Care Centre, 415 S Ashley St, Valdosta, GA 31601, **Business Phone:** (229)242-3102.

WILLIAMS, LARRY
Educator. **Personal:** Born Nov 27, 1965, Washington, DC; son of Sallie E Williams and Eddie N Williams; divorced. **Educ:** Pa State Univ, attended music, 1985; Peabody Conservatory Music, BM, music, 1988, grad performance dipl, 1990. **Career:** New World Symphony Orchestra, 1990-92; Fla Int Univ, brass dept, chair, prof horn, 1990-92; Miami Brass Consort, hornist, 1992-94; Univ Md, Baltimore County; Johns Hopkins Univ, Peabody Inst, Preparatory, Brass/Wind Dept, chair, horn instr, 1994-, Centennial High Sch, coordr, Adult & Continuing Educ Prog, dir, currently; Univ Mich, distinguished vis prof. **Orgs:** Adv, Arts Talented Youth Prog, 1994-97; dir, Herald Brass Prog, 1994-; chair, Brass & Winds Dept, Peabody Prep, 1994-; Lyric Brass Quintet, 1998; Morpheus Trio, 1998; Int Horn Soc. **Honors/Awds:** Second Prize, Concerto Competition, Yale Gordon Trust, 1990; Peabody Conservatory, Soloist, Graduation Ceremony, 1990; Career Development Grant, Peabody Inst, 1996-98. **Special Achievements:** Peabody News, "Heralding A New Program," 1994; Tours: Japan, Europe, US, 1994-; Ebony Magazine, "Fifty Leaders of Tomorrow," 1995; CD-The Morpheus Trio, 1998. **Home Addr:** 1101 N Calvert St Apt 709, Baltimore, MD 21202. **Business Addr:** Chair, Director, Peabody Institute of the Johns Hopkins University, Preparatory Brass & Winds Department, 1 E Mt Vernon Pl, Baltimore, MD 21202, **Business Phone:** (410)659-8100 Ext 1129.

WILLIAMS, LARRY C.
Lawyer. **Personal:** Born May 17, 1931, Seneca, SC; married Theresa; children: Margo, Larry Jr, Edward, John, David Lauren, Joseph. **Educ:** Howard Univ, BA, 1954, LLB, 1959. **Career:** Houston, Waddy, Bryant & Gardner; Variable Annuity Life Ins Corp; Corp Coun Off DC, asst corp coun; Larry C Wiliams & Asn, atty, currently. **Orgs:** Regional Coun US & Brewers Asn; gen coun Nat Bus League; Nat Funeral Dir & Morticians Asn; United Way Nat Capitol Area; past pres, DC C C; Metro WA Bd Trade; bd Metro YMCA; bd mem, Nat Coun Christians & Jews; life mem, Alpha Phi Alpha Frat Inc; 32nd Degree Mason; Shriner; Mecca Temple 10; Transition Comn Develop Orgn First City Coun under Home Rule. **Business Addr:** Attorney, Owner, Larry C Williams & Associates, 666 11th St NW Suite 1050, Washington, DC 20001, **Business Phone:** (202)842-2222.*

WILLIAMS, LASHINA BRIGETTE
Administrator. **Personal:** Born Oct 22, 1957, Houston, TX; daughter of Chauncey K Morrow Jr and Myrtle Morrow; divorced. **Educ:** Prairie View A&M Univ, BS, 1980; Atlanta Univ, MBA, 1984. **Career:** Phillips Petrol, mech engr, 1980-82; Digital Equip, intern, 1983; IBM, Gaithersburg, Md, prod planning & prog mgt, 1985-. **Orgs:** Nat Black MBA Asn, 1983-; Delta Sigma Theta Sorority. **Honors/Awds:** IBM Appreciation Award, 1992, 1994. **Home Addr:** 3819 Ridgeview, Missouri City, TX 77489. **Business Addr:** Production Planning & Program Management, IBM Corp, 800 N Frederick Ave, Gaithersburg, MD 20879, **Business Phone:** (301)240-0111.

WILLIAMS, DR. LEA E
Association executive, educator. **Personal:** Born Dec 21, 1947, Paducah, KY; daughter of Nathanial H and Mae Frances Terrell. **Educ:** Ky State Univ, Frankfort, KY, BA (with distinction), elem educ, 1969; Univ Wis, Milwaukee, WI, MS, curric & instr, 1973, Teachers Col, Columbia Univ, New York, NY, MA, 1977, EdD, 1978. **Career:** Milwaukee Pub Sch, WI, sixth grade teacher, 1969-73; Milwaukee Area Tech Col, WI, ABE instr, 1973-74; United Negro Col Fund, New York, NY, prog evaluator, 1978-80, proposal writer, 1980-81, CAI res dir, 1981-82, Educ Serv, asst dir, 1982-86, Educ Serv, dir, 1982-86, Educ Serv, vpres, 1988-89; Nat Action Coun Minorities Engineering, exec vpres, 1989-2004; Nat African-Am Women's Leadership Inst Inc, exec dir, currently; NC A&T State Univ, interim assoc vice chancellor acad affairs univ planning & assessment, currently, interim dir, 2007-. **Orgs:** Alpha Kappa Mu Hon Soc, 1969; Phi Delta Kappa, 1975; ed bd, Thrust employ jour, 1980-85; panelist, Nat Endowment Humanities, 1983-85; Nat Leadership Forum, Am Coun Educ, 1986; Am Educ Res Asn, 1986-; consult ed, NY Gov's Adv Comm Black Affairs, 1987-88; pres, Asn Black Women Higher Educ, 1987-89; adv comm, Asn Am Col, 1988; comnr, Nat Asn Independent Cols & Univs, 1988-91; exec bd, Am Asn Higher Educ, 1989-91; div chairperson, Nat Asn Women Educ, 1989-91, ed bd, Initiatives, 1989-; bd govs, Am Asn Engineering Socs, 1989-95; bd dir, Triangle Coalition Sci & Technol Educ, 1991-95, vpres & bd dir, 1993-95; bd trustees, Family Dynamics Inc, 1993-; adv coun, Harlem Br YWCA, 1995-. **Honors/Awds:** Unity Award, Lincoln Univ, MO, 1990; Paducah Black Historian Achievement Award in Education, 1991; Distinguished Service Award, Ky State Univ, 1994. **Special Achievements:** Author of "The United Negro College Fund in Retrospect" 1980, "The Plight of Jr Fac at Black Private Colls" 1985, "Missing, Presumed Lost: Minority Teachers in the Nation's Classroom" 1989. **Business Addr:** Interim Associate Vice Chancellor, North Carolina Agricultural & Technical State University, 1601 E Market St, Greensboro, NC 27411, **Business Phone:** (336)334-7006.

WILLIAMS, DR. LEON LAWSON
Government official. **Personal:** Born Jul 21, 1922, Weeletka, OK; son of Lloyd R and Elvira E Lott; children: Karen E, Leon L Jr, Susan P Rogers, Penny, Jeffery & Alisa O. **Educ:** San Diego State Univ, BA, 1950; Univ San Diego Sch Law, attended 1961; Nat Univ, Doctorate, 1985. **Career:** Government official (Retired); San Diego County Sheriff Dept, admin officer, 1957-66; Neighborhood Youth Corps, dir, 1966-70; San Diego Urban League, exec dir, 1968; City San Diego, councilman, 1969-82; Fed Mart Corp, consult, 1972-76; County San Diego, supv, 1983-95; San Diego Metrop Transit Develop Bd, chmn. **Orgs:** Alpha Pi Boule Sigma Pi Phi Frat, 1976-91; chair, bd supervisors, County San Diego, 1985 & 1990; dir, San Diego Col Retailing, 1986; life mem, Nat Asn Advan Colored People; dir, Metro Transit Develop Bd, Nat Asn Counties; pres, Calif State Asn Counties; dir, San Diego Region Water Reclamation Bd; chmn, Serv Authority Freeway Emergencies. **Honors/Awds:** Outstanding Contribution Award, Nat Asn Advan Colored People, 1978; Black Achievement Award, 1981; Freedom Award, 1981; Distinguished Service Award, Nat Asn Advan Colored People, 1985; Distinguished Serv Community Black Fedn San Diego County, Greater San Diego Bus Asn, Metro Transit Develop Bd, Nat Cult Found. **Special Achievements:** First Black Chairman of the Board of Supervisors, County of San Diego Black Leadership Council, 1985; Recognition for being First Black Chairman, Bd Supervisors, County San Diego, Black Leadership Coun, 1985.

WILLIAMS, DR. LEONA CLARICE
Administrator, school superintendent. **Personal:** Born Dec 26, 1936, Los Angeles, CA; married Jarrod B Williams; children: Jarrod Barrett II & Courtni Clarice. **Educ:** Calif State Univ, Los Angeles, BA, 1966; Calif State Polytech Univ, MA, 1974; Univ Nebr, Lincoln, PhD, 1978. **Career:** Los Angeles Unified Sch Dist, teacher, 1965-66; Ontario-Montclair Sch Dist Ontario, CA, teacher, 1966-72; Fr Flanagan's Boys Town Sch Syst NE, reading specialist, reading coordr, asst prin, curric coordr, 1972-79; Riverside Unified Sch Dist, prin Monroe Elem, prin Cent Middle Sch, dist dir spec educ, 1979-82; Lucerne Valley Union Sch Dist CA, dist supt, 1982; One Schwide Charter Sch Technol Inc, bd pres & chief exec officer, currently. **Orgs:** Phi Delta Kappa; Asn Calif Sch Adminr; Asn Supv & Curric Develop, Lucerne Valley Chamber Com. **Honors/Awds:** US Congressional Award, 1984. **Business Addr:** Board President, Chief Executive Officer, One Schoolwide Charter School of Technology Inc, 1790 Washington St, PO Box 52255, Riverside, CA 92506, **Business Phone:** (909)780-2590.

WILLIAMS, LEONARD
Manager, executive. **Personal:** Born Sep 7, 1945, Youngstown, OH; son of Willie and Arvella Church; married Diane L Williams; children: Lucy A Sams. **Educ:** Youngstown State Univ, Youngstown, OH, AAS, 1973, BS, 1975, MS, 1979. **Career:** Executive (retired); Com Shearing, Youngstown, OH, draftsman, 1969-70; Youngstown Police Dept, OH, patrolman, 1970-77, sergeant, 1977-81, lt, 1981-85; Youngstown Bd Educ, part-time security officer, 1973-85; Eastern Ohio Forensic Lab, part-time polygraph examr, 1976-78; Tri-State Lab, part-time polygraph examr, 1978-85; E Cleveland, OH, Civil Serv Comn, consult; Cuyahoga County Jail, Cleveland, OH, adminr, 1985-87; Univ Akron, OH, prof, 1987-92; Ohio Dept Rehab & Correction, Bur Adult Detention, jail inspector, 1992-96; Mahoning County Justice Ctr, dir corrections, 1997-98, dep sheriff, 2000. **Orgs:** Bd mem, Nat Black Police Asn, 1981-90; co-founder & bd mem, United Humanitarian Fund, 1982-; chair, Eastern Region NBPA, 1983-87; chair, Nat Black Police Asn, 1986-88; Ohio Ct Claims Pub Awareness Adv Coun, 1988-89. **Honors/Awds:** Police Officer of the Year, Bd Realtors, 1970; Member of the Year, Black Knight Police Asn, 1976; Man of the Year, Nat Asn Negro Bus & Prof Women, 1983; Mem of the Year, Eastern Region NBPA, 1984; Renault Robinson Award, NBPA, 1987; Chairman Award, Nat Black Police Asn Eastern Region, 2000; Master Mason of the Year, Benevolent Grand Lodge, OH, 2000. **Special Achievements:** Author: Peace Keeping and the Community: A Minority Perspective, 1988; Use of Excessive Force in the Minority Community, 1989. **Military Serv:** USAAF, E-3, 1963-67. **Home Addr:** 530 Plum St, PO Box 761, Youngstown, OH 44501.

WILLIAMS, LEROY JOSEPH
Auditor. **Personal:** Born Apr 13, 1937, New Orleans, LA; married Verna M Lewis; children: Linda M Thomes, Gregory C Lewis & Sandra Lewis. **Educ:** Olympic Col, AA, 1969; Univ WA, BA, 1972; Univ Puget Sound, attended 1974. **Career:** City Seattle, city coun legis auditor; USN Exchange Bremerton, buyer 1960-61; The Boeing Co, cost acct, 1972-73, mat controller, 1961-72; Seattle Model City Prg, fiscal consult, 1972-73; Municipality Metrop Seattle, audit mgr, 1972-. **Orgs:** Sch supt, 1965-70, mem trustee bd, 1965-, Sinclair Baptist Church, 1960-; Hamma Hamma #35 Masonic Lodge Prince Hall Grand Lodge Wash Jurisdiction, 1965-; Cascadian Consistory PHA AASR, 1970-; Bremerton Sch Bd, 1971-77; Williams Pvt Tax Consult, 1972-; charter mem, Cr Union Audit Comt, 1972-73; Olympic Col Asn Higher Educ, 1973-; Wash State Ferry Adv Comt, 1973-77; Wash State Educ TV Comn, 1974-77; legis rep, Wash State Sch Dir, 1974-; Aldephil Inst, 1975-; supreme Coun, 33 Deg Mason, 1977; Worshipful Master Hamma Hamma Lodge #35; African Am Affairs Comn, app by Gov Mike Lowery, 1995; Asn Govt Accountants. **Military Serv:** USN, 3rd class yoeman, 1955-59. **Business Addr:** Audit manager, Municipality Metropolitan Seattle, 600 4th Ave Municipal Bldg, Seattle, WA 98104.

WILLIAMS, LESLIE J.
Health services administrator, army officer. **Personal:** Born Aug 18, 1947, New Orleans, LA; children: Kimberly, Kevin. **Educ:** Southern Univ BR, BS Pre Med, 1967; Southern Univ NO, BS Bus Admin, 1975, AA Real Estate, 1978. **Career:** VD & Tuberculosis Clinic New Orleans Health Dept, admin dir, 1979-83; City Health Dept, fiscal Officer; La Army Nat Guard, Command Chief Warrant Officer, currently. **Orgs:** Urban League Greater New Orleans; Nat Asn Real Estate Brokers; Am Public Health Asn; 32 Degree Mason Ancient & Accepted Scotch Rite Free Masonry, 1980-85; instr Southern Univ New Orleans, 1983-85. **Honors/Awds:** Licensed Real Estate Salesperson LA; Licensed Sanitarian State LA; Cert Participation Am Med Asn, 1981. **Military Serv:** AUS commissioned warrant officer, 2-11 yrs; Army Achievement Medal; Nat Defense Ribbon. **Business Addr:** Command Chief Warrant Officer, Louisiana Army National Guard, 5445 Point Clair Rd, Carville, LA 70721, **Business Phone:** (225)319-4880.*

WILLIAMS, DR. LISA R.
Educator, management consultant. **Personal:** Born Feb 11, 1964, Toledo, OH. **Educ:** Wright State Univ, BS, bus, 1986, MBA, 1988; OH State Univ, MA, 1992, PhD, 1992. **Career:** Dayton Power & Light, mkt analyst, 1984-87; Gen Motors, mkt analyst, 1987;Cent State Univ, asst prof bus, 1988-89; Penn State Univ, asst prof bus logistics; William Res Inc, founder, pres & chief exec officer, currently. **Orgs:** Alpha Kappa Alpha Sorority, 1990-; Coun Logistics Mgt, 1990-; Am Soc Transp & Logistics, 1992-; African Am Women Investment Group, treas, 1993-. **Honors/Awds:** Four

Year Academic Scholarship, Wright State Univ, 1982-86; Wright St Univ, Dean's List, 1983-84; Univ Grad Fel, OH State Univ, 1989-90; Logistics Fel, Coun Logistics Mgt, 1991; Penn St Univ, Fac Res Grant, 1992-94; Teaching Excellence Award, Penn State Univ, 1997; Outstanding Contributor to the Marketing Profession Award, Mkt PhD Proj, 2000; TrailBlazer & Pioneer in Marketing Award, Sam M Walton Col Bus, 2000. **Special Achievements:** First African-American Woman to Graduate with PhD in Bussiness from Ohio St, 1992; Book: Evolution Status & Future of the Corp Transportation Function, 1991; Understanding Distribution Channels: Inter organizational Study of EDI, 1994; Moving Toward LIS Theory Dev: A Framework of Adoption,1995; Shipper, Carrier & Consultant Perspectives of EDI, 1995; advice sought by the Clinton Administration's President's Commission on Critical Infrastructure Protection; First to hold a multi million dollar chair in her field; Author;"Leading Beyond Excellence", "Stop struggling; Get Rich, Stay Rich". **Business Addr:** President, Cheif Executive Officer, Williams Research Inc, 3525 Del Mar Heights Rd, San Diego, CA 92130, **Business Phone:** (619)671-9997.

WILLIAMS, LLOYD
President (organization). **Career:** Greater Harlem Chamber Com, pres & chief exec officer, currently. **Special Achievements:** Author: reate a memory, Stanley's Famous. **Business Addr:** President, Chief Executive Officer, Greater Harlem Chamber of Commerce, 200A W 136th St, New York, NY 10030, **Business Phone:** (212)427-7200.

WILLIAMS, LLOYD L
Legislator. **Personal:** Born Jul 26, 1944, St Thomas, Virgin Islands of the United States; married Irene Creque; children: Lisa Marie & Taya Ayanna. **Educ:** Moravian Col, BA, 1966; NY Univ, MA, cert orthodics & presthetics; VA Commonwealth Univ, MA; Am Univ Wash, MA, polit sci. **Career:** Youth Club Action, adv tutor; Wayhne Aspinall JHS, teacher, Dept Social Welfare, voc rehab counsr; VI Legis, from spec asst to legislator, 1972; VI 10th, 11th, 12th & 13th Legis, majority leader, 1976-78; Legis Virgin Islands, VI 14th Legis, sen, currently; Pub Safety Comn, chair. **Orgs:** Task Force Criminal Code Rev Proj; Bd Tri-Island Eco Devel Coun; Bd VI Montessori Sch Deleg Const Conv. **Home Addr:** 2 Estate Raphune Charlotte Amalie, PO Box 7458, St Thomas, Virgin Islands of the United States 00801. **Business Phone:** (340)693-3701.

WILLIAMS, LOIS STOVALL
College administrator, chief executive officer. **Personal:** Married Anderson J Jr; children: 8. **Educ:** Morgan State Univ, BS, natural sci; Loyola Col, MS, psychol; Univ Conn, PhD, higher educ admin; Harvard Univ, Inst Educ Mgt, cert. **Career:** Norfolk State Univ, prof psychol; Hampton Univ, Ctr Teaching Excellence, dir; Am Testing Serv, sr vpres admin; Passaic Co Community Col, dean instr; Knoxville Col, pres, 1995; Va Beach City Pub Schs; Wiltex Inc, founder & chief exec officer, 1999-. **Special Achievements:** First female president of Knoxville College, 1995. **Business Phone:** (757)961-3734.

WILLIAMS, LONDELL
Government official. **Personal:** Born Apr 23, 1939, Texarkana, AR; married Mary; children: Londell GeoAna John & Marian Londelon. **Educ:** Univ Ark, 1955; Los Angeles St Col, BA, 1958; Los Angeles Bible Inst, dD, 1960. **Career:** AUS Corps Engr, contract specl, 1955-58; US Treas Dept Bur Customs, acct tech, 1958-59; AUS, personnel specl, 1964-68; Ave Bapt Ch, pastor, 1969-; Dept HEW Soc Security Admn, claims Develr, 1969-; Park Ave Bapt Church, pastor-tcr, 1969-; City Texarkana, Tex, ward three, asst mayor, 1977-2006; city councilman. **Orgs:** Texarkana Ministerial Alliance, 1971-77; grand master, Master Mason AF & AM Bronzeville Lodge 83, 1974-77; jury comnr Miller, Hempstead, Lafayette, Howard, 1975-76; Texarkana Ark & Texarkana Tex C C, 1976-; City Bd Dir Texarkana Ark, 1977-; bd mem, Texarkana Human Develop Ctr, 1977. **Honors/Awds:** Bert Lambert Award, 1974-75; Outstanding Integrity & Character Displayed in City, 1973; high quality Increase Award, HEW, 1976; Dr Martin Luther King Award, 1995; Earl Holmes Award, Outstanding Leadership & Excellence Serv Rendered All Texarkanians, 1996; Leadership Award, 2008; Wilbur Award Nominee; Sharp Shooter Award; Good Conduct Medal. **Special Achievements:** First ever elected Black City Councilman in Texarkana, Arkansas or Tex,1976; First Black Mayor ever elected, 1992-95. **Military Serv:** One Hundred & One Airborne Div AUS, AUS Lambert Awd, 1974-75; Otsdng Integrity & Character Displayed in City, 1959-61. **Home Addr:** 6 Preston Cir, Texarkana, AR 71854-5839.

WILLIAMS, DR. LONNIE RAY
School administrator. **Personal:** Born Jan 21, 1954, Stephens, AR; son of Rosie M and Lonnie. **Educ:** Univ Ark, Fayetteville, BSBA, 1977, MEd, 1983, EdS, 1991, EdD, 2001. **Career:** Univ Ark-Fayetteville, police patrolman, 1976-78, night mgr, stud union, 1978-84, dir minority engineering, 1983-86, asst dean students, 1986-91, asst vice chancellor stud serv, 1991-2003; Ark State Univ, assoc vice chancellor stud affairs, 2003-. **Orgs:** Adv bd mem, Region V, Nat Soc Black Engineers, 1984-87; Region B, chairperson elect, NAMEPA, 1985-86; chairperson, Ark Asn Multicultural Coun, 1986-87; Ark Asn Coun Guid & Develop, 1986-; bd mem, Wash County Equal Opportunity Agency, 1988-91; bd dirs, N Ark Girl Scouts Am; pres-elect, 1993-95, Ark Asn Multicultural Coun & Develop, pres, 1995-97; exec bd mem, Ark Col Personnel Asn, 1992-96; Ark Coun Asn, Am Coun Asn, 1995-; Am Col Personnel Asn, 1995-; bd mem, Asn Black Cult Ctr, 1996-; Nat Asn Stud Personnel Adminr, 1997; Daisy Gatson Bates Holiday Comt State Ark; Ark State Rep, Omega Psi Phi, 1999-; bd dir, onesboro Church Health Ctr, 2004-; bd trustee, Ark Baptist Col, 2005. **Honors/Awds:** Outstanding Service Award, Univ Ark Chap, NSBE, 1983-86; Outstanding Faculty/Staff Mem Black Stud Asn, 1987; Employee of the Year, Prof Non-fac, Univ Ark, 1991; Advisor of the Year, Ark Black Students Asn, 1993; Special Recognition Award,Univ Ark Black Alumni Soc,1990, 1993, 1995, 2000, 2003; Andrew J Lucas Serv Award, Ark Alumni Asn, 2000; Dr Martin L King, Jr, Achievement Award, Northwest Ark Dr MLK Planning Comt, 2001; Lonnie R. Williams Bridging Excellence Award, Univ Ark Black Students Asn, 2001, Living Legacy Award, 2004; Friend of Diversity Award, Ark State Univ, 2005; Distinguished Performance Award for Execellence, Ark State Univ, 2006; Mossie J. Richmond, Jr. Outstanding Leadership Award, Ark Col Personnel Asn, 2006;Unsung Heroes Award, Ark Asn Multicultural Coun & develop, 2007; Thomas E Patterson Educ Award, Ark Democratic Black Caucus, 2008. **Home Addr:** 204 E Lawson Rd, Jonesboro, AR 72404. **Business Addr:** Associate Vice Chancellor for Student Services, Arkansas State University, PO Box 106, Jonesboro, AR 72467-0106, **Business Phone:** (870)972-2048.

WILLIAMS, LORECE P.
Educator. **Personal:** Born Jan 22, 1927, Luling, TX; married Nathan H; children: Nicholas & Natalie. **Educ:** Huston Tillotson Col, BS, 1947; Our Lady Lake Col, MSW, 1962. **Career:** ARC Brooke Army Med Ctr, dir, 1969-; Our Lady Lake Col, prof social work, 1965-69; Incarnate Word Col, San Antonio, diagnostician, 1969; San Antonio Jr League, Incarnate Word Clergy, lectr & group leader; Our Lady Lake Univ, prof emer social work, currently. **Orgs:** Fac Welfare Coun; Alpha Kappa Alpha Sorority; Race & Rel Comn; Gov Comn Crime & Prev; Cath Family & Child; Child Serv Bur; Nat Asn Social Workers; Coun Social Work Educ; Theta Sigma Phi. **Honors/Awds:** Excellence in Writing Awards, Theta Sigma Phi. **Special Achievements:** Co-author Bi-entennial Book, Folklore Texas Cultures. **Business Addr:** Professor Emeritus, Our Lady of the Lake University, 411 SW 24 St, San Antonio, TX 78207, **Business Phone:** (210)434-6711.

WILLIAMS, LORENZO
Basketball player. **Personal:** Born Jul 15, 1969, Ocala, FL. **Educ:** Polk Community Col; Stetson Univ. **Career:** Charlotte Hornets, ctr, 1992, 1993-94; Orlando Magic, 1992; Boston Celtics, 1992-93; Orlando Magic, 1993-94; Dallas Mavericks, 1994-96; Wash Bullets, free agent, 1996; Wash Wizards, forward, 1997-2000; Five Star Basketball Camp, Univ Cent Fla, coach, currently.

WILLIAMS, HON. LOUISE BERNICE
Association executive, government official. **Personal:** Born May 30, 1937, Abinton, PA; daughter of Richard S Duncan and Mary Grasty Duncan; divorced; children: Cynthia Whitfield, Robert Whetts, Brian Whetts & Kimberly Williams. **Educ:** Lancaster Sch Bus, attended 1964; Lincoln Univ; Shippenburg State Col, Cert Dist Justices, 1973. **Career:** Dist Justice Off, admin clerk, 1970-73; City Lancaster 3rd & 7th Ward, dist justice, 1973-85; Girls Serv Lancaster Inc, pres, 1975-81; Consolidated Dist Justice Off, City Lancaster, admin dist justice, 1983-85; Pa Bd Pardons, 2000-; Community Cult Diversity, Millersville Univ; City Lancaster, Community Develop & Planning Personnel, pub safety chair, currently, pres, currently. **Orgs:** Planned Parenthood Lancaster, 1978-81; Urban League Lancaster, 1979-84; Nat Asn Advan Colored People, 1980-82; Lancaster County Dist Justice Asn; bd mem, Planned Parenthood Lancaster County, 1988-; bd pardons, Commonwealth Pa; Lancaster Independent Trash Haulers Asn. **Honors/Awds:** Boss of the Year, Am Bus Women's Asn, 1976; Outstanding Citizen, City Lancaster, 1981; Past President Award, Girls Serv Lancaster Inc, 1981. **Home Addr:** 331 S Franklin St, Lancaster, PA 17602. **Business Addr:** Chair Public Safety, President, City of Lancaster, Community Development & Planning, 331 S Franklin St, PO Box 1599, Lancaster, PA 17602, **Business Phone:** (717)291-1374.

WILLIAMS, LUCRETIA MURPHY
School administrator. **Personal:** Born Aug 16, 1941, Springfield, OH; daughter of Wilbur Otho and Lenore Dorsey Smith; children: David Walter Bentley & Robin Lenore Goodwin. **Educ:** Cent State Univ, BS, Elem Educ, 1965, MEd, Guidance & Coun, 1969; Ohio State Dept Educ, gen aptitude test battery training, vocational guidance training cert, 1974; Xavier Univ, admin cert elem & sec, 1976. **Career:** School administrator (retired); Onondago Co Welfare, social worker, 1966-67; AT&T Technols, personnel counr, summer, 1970; Columbus Pub Schs, guidance counr, 1969-77, asst prin, 1977-78; Neptune Township Pub Schs, princl, 1978-79; Columbus Pub Schs, admin, 1979-99; asst supt, stud servs,1994-98, Interim Acceleration & Extra Help coordr, currently. **Orgs:** Life mem, Nat Alliance Black Sch Employees; Nat Asn Sec Sch Prins; Ohio Alliance Black Sch Educ; Columbus Alliance Black Sch Educ; Columbus Admin Asn; Columbus Central Office Admin Asn; Delta Sigma Theta; Mayor's Coun on Youth. **Honors/Awds:** Columbus Area Leadership Prog, 1989; Commendation Ohio House Reps, 1988,1992; Commendation Ohio Senate, 1992. **Special Achievements:** A Comparative Study of Faculty Knowledge of Guidance Serv in the High Schools of Springfield, Ohio', Master Thesis, Central State Univ, 1969;Author, "Columbus Schools, Police Unite for Zero Tolerance," School Safety Update, Nov 1996. **Business Addr:** Interim Acceleration, Extra Help Chief Operating Officerrdinator, Columbus Public Schools, 270 E State St, Columbus, OH 43215, **Business Phone:** (614)365-5000.

WILLIAMS, REV. DR. MACEO MERTON
Clergy, school administrator. **Personal:** Born Oct 27, 1939, Baltimore, MD; married Margaret D Moon. **Educ:** Morgan State Univ, AB, 1966; Univ Baltimore, MPA prog, 1976; Wesley Theol Sem, MDiv Prog, 1985; Howard Univ, MDiv, 1986; Howard Univ Divinity Sch, DMin, 1991. **Career:** State MD, probation agent, 1965-66; Dept Housing, area coordr, 1966-71; US Dept Labor, Concentrated Employ Prog, coordr, 1971-74; Bay Col, MD, dean students, 1974-79; MD Parole Comn, 1983-88; Centreville-Cordova Charge United Methodist Church, pastor, 1986-90; Simpson United Methodist Church, pastor, 1991-95; Martin Luther King Jr Memorial United Methodist Church, pastor, 1995-. **Orgs:** Bd mem, Dept Housing & Comn Develop UMC, 1970-; bd trustees, Keswick Nursing Home, 1973-76; pres, Five in Five Dem Club, 1974; Charter Revision Comn, 1974-76; Prince Hall Grand Lodge F&AM, MD Zion Lodge No. 4; Nat Asn Student Servs; Nat Asn Col Coun; Morgan State Univ Alumni; Howard Univ Alumni; life mem, Black Methodists Church Renewal; life mem, Nat Asn Advan Colored People; Pi Omega Chap; bd trustees, Baltimore City Col, 2001-. **Honors/Awds:** Hall of Fame, Baltimore City Col, 1997; Outstanding Alumni, Booker T. Washington Jr. High School, 2007. **Special Achievements:** Longest serving commissioner in state history. **Business Addr:** Pastor, Martin Luther King Jr Memorial United Methodist Church, 5114 Windsor Mill Rd, Baltimore, MD 21207.

WILLIAMS, MALINDA
Actor. **Personal:** Born Dec 3, 1975, Elizabeth, NJ; married Mekhi Phifer (divorced 2003); children: Omikaye. **Educ:** Actor's Conserv, New York. **Career:** Films: High School High, 1996; Sunset Park, 1996; A Thin Line Between Love & Hate, 1997; Damn Whitey, 1997; An Invited Guest, 1999; The Wood, 1999; Dancing in September, 2000; Half & Half, 2003; The District, 2004; Exposure, 2005, Idlewild, 2006; A Day in the Life, 2007; Daddy's Little Girls, 2007; First Sunday, 2008; A Day in the life, 2009; TV series: Captain Planet & the Planeteers", 1990; Laurel Avenue, 1993; "Sister, Sister", 1994-95; "Moesha", 1996; "Outreach", 1999; "Soul Food", 2000-04; "The Big Much 'IDo' About Nothing Episode", 2003; The District, 2004; "Fear Eats the Soul", 2004; "The Getaway", 2006; Windfall, 2006. **Honors/Awds:** Nominee, NAACP Image Award for Outstanding Actress, Drama Series SoulFood, 2003, 2004, 2005. Nominee, Black Reel Award, 2000. **Business Addr:** Actress, c/o West Entertainment, 6255 W Sunset Blvd Suite 923, Los Angeles, CA 90028, **Business Phone:** (323)468-9470.*

WILLIAMS, DR. MALVIN A, SR.
Educator. **Personal:** Born Apr 20, 1942, Mayersville, MS; son of Oscar and Catherine; married Delores G; children: Angela, Katrina, Tiffany & Malvin Jr. **Educ:** Alcorn State Univ, BS, math, 1962; AZ State Univ, MNS, 1966; Univ Southwestern LA, PhD, 1971-75. **Career:** Greenville Pub Schs, educr, 1962-65; Alcorn State Univ, instr maths, 1966-71, comput programmer & analyst, registrar & asst dean acad affairs, 1975-76, assoc prof stats & vpres acad affairs, 1976-2005, interim pres, 2006-. **Orgs:** Bd dirs, Watson Chapel AME Church, 1975-; mem planning & steering comt, Mgmt Info System Jackson MS, 1979-; bd dirs, Claiborne Co Chamber Comt, 1982-; chmn, Coun Chief Acad Officers, 1984-86; Am Statistical Asn; Am Maths Soc; Am Asn Higher Educ; Am Asn Acad Deans & VPres; Phi Delta Kappa; Miss Acad Scis; Nat Asn Cols, Deans, Registrs & Admis Officers; SACS Peer Evaluator. **Honors/Awds:** Sci Faculty Fellowship Award, NSF, 1971-72; ASU Ed Off Personnel Assoc Boss of the Year, 1982. **Business Addr:** Interim President, Alcorn State University, 1000 ASU Dr, Alcorn State, MS 39096-7500, **Business Phone:** (601)877-6143.

WILLIAMS, MARCUS DOYLE
Judge, lecturer. **Personal:** Born Oct 24, 1952, Nashville, TN; son of John F and Pansy D; married Carmen Myrie Williams MD; children: Aaron Doyle, Adam Myrie. **Educ:** Fisk Univ, BA, 1973; Catholic Univ Am, Sch Law, JD, 1977. **Career:** Off Commonwealth Atty, asst commonwealth atty, 1978-80; George Mason Univ, lectr bus legal studies, 1980-95; Off Co Atty, asst co atty, 1980-87; Gen Dist Ct, judge, 1987-90; Circuit Ct, judge, 1990-; Nat Judicial Col, fac, 1992. **Orgs:** Bd mem, Fairfax-Falls Church, Criminal Justice Adv Bd, 1980-81; freelance writer & reviewer, 1981-; Am Bus Law Asn, 1984-; bd assocs, St Paul's Col, 1986-87; vice chmn, Continuing Legal Educ Community, Fairfax Bar Asn, 1986-87; Virginia deleg, Nat Conf Spec Ct Judges, 1990; Omega Psi Phi Fraternity, 1971; bd visitors, The Catholic Univ Am Sch Law, 1998-; chmn, Victims Crime Community, Nat Conf Trial Judges, Am Bar Asn, 1996-; Circuit Ct Jury Mgt Comt;

Legislative & Bd Supvr Rels Comt; Circuit Ct Rep Coun Govts. **Honors/Awds:** Beta Kappa Chi, Scientific Honor Soc, Fisk Univ Chapter, 1973; Distinguished Youth Award, Off Army, Judge Advocate Gen, 1976; Thomas J Watson Fel, 1977-78; Service Commendation, Fairfax Co Bd Supvr, 1987; Service Appreciation Award, Burke Fairfax Jack & Jill, 1989; articles: "Arbitration of Intl Com Contracts: Securities and Antitrust Claims," Virginia Lawyer, 1989, "European Antitrust Law Application Am Corp," Whittier Law Review, 1987, "Judicial Review: The Guardian Civil Liberties & Civil Rights," George Mason Univ Civil Rights Law Jour, 1991, "Lawyer, Judge, Solicitor, Gen Educ: A Tribute to Wade H McCree, Jr," Nat Black Law Jour, 1990; Am Participant Prog Lectures, Liberia, Zambia, Botswana, sponsored USIA, 1990; Service Appreciation Award, Black Law Students Asn Catholic Univ, 1990; Otis Smith Alumnus Award, 1997. **Business Addr:** Judge, Circuit Court, Fairfaxcounty, 4110 Chain Bridge Rd, Fairfax, VA 22030.

WILLIAMS, MARGARET ANN
Government official. **Personal:** Born Dec 25, 1954, Kansas City, MO. **Educ:** Trinity Col, attended; The Annenberg Sch Commun, Univ PA, attended. **Career:** Ctr Budget & Policy Priorities, dep dir, 1989-85; Children's Defense Fund, dir commun, 1985-90; The White House, Office of Hilary Clinton, asst to the pres & chief of staff to the first lady, 1993-97; Fenton Communications, pres, 2000-01; Griffin Williams, partner, 2005-; John F Kennedy Sch Govt, Cambridge, MA, fel, currently. **Orgs:** Phi Beta Kappa Soc; bd dir, Delat Financial Corp; Clinton Global Initiative; Dem Nat Comt.

WILLIAMS, MARGO E
Journalist. **Personal:** Born Dec 30, 1947, St Louis, MS; daughter of James R and Bertha. **Educ:** Harris Teachers Col, BA, 1970; St Louis Univ, MA, 1972; Southern Ill Univ, BA, 1975; St Louis Univ, Post Grad. **Career:** St Louis Bd Educ, teacher & counr, 1970-75; KMOX-TV, CBS, St Louis, TV teacher, 1973-75; Southern Ill Univ, acad advisor, 1975-76; WMAR-TV, Baltimore, MD, host & producer, 1976-77; WKBN-TV, CBS, Youngstown, OH, minority affairs dir, 1977-82; TV & radio producer & host, 1982-88; WKBD TV, Detroit, MI, News reporter/writer, producer/host "For The Record"; society freelance writer, Black History segments, Detroit News, Detroit, MI; Barden Cablevision, sr producer, 1989-92; Margo E Williams & Assocs Inc, Public Relations Firm, Detroit, MI, pres & chief exec officer, 1990-; The Crisis, Black Enterprise, freelance writer. **Orgs:** Alpha Kappa Alpha; Nat Asn Advan Colored People; Urban League; Soc Prof Journalists; vpres, Am Bus Women's Assoc, 1983-87; Altrusa Club Int; media-workshop coord, vpres, pres, Nat Asn Black Journalist, 1983-84; chmn, Ways & Means Comt, 1984; coord, Women's Career Workshops; Jim Dandy Ski Club; hosted, United Negro Col Telethon, ABC, Youngstown, OH; co-coord, Afro-Am Festival, Youngstown, OH; pres, Consumer Credit Adv Bd, Youngstown, OH; Your Heritage House Writers; Women's Econ Club; Nat Asn Women Bus Owners; bd mem, Booker T Washington Bus Asn; bd mem, Family Serv Detroit & Wayne County, 1995-. **Honors/Awds:** Received 15 Community Service Awards, 1977-84; Outstanding Black Woman in the Media; Ohio Media Award, Honored for Community Service with a special resolution & plaque, Youngstown City Coun; Appeared in Glamour Magazine Career Section; Woman of the Year Award, 1982; Appeared in Ebony Magazine, Broadcasting Magazine, Millimeter Magazine & RCA Today Magazine; Guest Speaker, Special Programs, Black History Month, Youngstown State Univ; Motivational Speaker, Women's Conf of Concerns, Detroit, MI, 1989; Black Professionals In Film and Video Award, 1991; Outstanding Business Women of the Year Award, Am Bus Women's Asn, 2001. **Home Addr:** 615 Griswold Suite 820, Detroit, MI 48226. **Business Phone:** (313)961-6622.

WILLIAMS, MARTHA S.
Educator. **Personal:** Born Nov 30, 1921, Philadelphia, PA; divorced. **Educ:** State Col, BS, 1949; Wayne State Univ, MSLS, 1971. **Career:** Phil Tribune, newspaper exper, 1942-44; nursery sch, teacher, owner,1949-64; Detroit Sch, librn, 1964-74; Gary Neigh House, dir nursery prog; Foch Sch, arts teacher, 1974-; Bristol England, exchange teacher, 1977. **Orgs:** Am Lib Asn; Asso Sch Libr; Mich Asn Media Educ; Rep Party; prec del GaryInd; vc hmn, Gary City Rep Comm; del, State Conv; del Rep, Nat Conv, 1976; Mich Rep State Comm Nat Black Rep Counc; Pct Police Community Coun; Greater Christ Bapt Ch; Sch Community Coun Nat Comn Libr & Inform Serv, 1977; Delta Sigma Theta Sor.

WILLIAMS, DR. MATTHEW ALBERT
Physician. **Personal:** Born Jun 24, 1929, Atlanta, GA; son of Charles R and Alberta Hendricks; married Vira E Kennedy; children: Linda M Lucas, Nanci J Newell & Pamela L Steele. **Educ:** Morehouse Col, Atlanta, Ga, BS, 1950; Howard Univ Wash, DC, MD, 1955; Harbor Gen Hosp Torrance, CA, int med, 1961. **Career:** Paradise Vallley Med Staff, pres, 1975-77; pvt pract, currently. **Orgs:** Am Clg Physicians; Am Soc Int Med; Alpha Pi Boule; Alpha Omega Alpha; Hon Med Soc; mem exec comt, Paradise Valley Hosp; past mem coun, San Diego Med Soc, 1977; past mem coun, San Diego Soc Int Med, 1977; mem Bd Overseers Univ Calif, San Diego, 1984; Alpha Phi Alpha Frat; Alpha Pi Boule. **Honors/Awds:** Elder United Pres Church. **Military Serv:** USNR, lt comm med, 1955-66. **Home Addr:** 5740 Daffodil Lane, San Diego, CA 92120. **Business Phone:** (619)267-8300.

WILLIAMS, MAXINE BROYLES
Social worker. **Personal:** Born in Pittsburgh, PA; widowed. **Educ:** Wilberforce Univ, BS; Univ Md, Advan Social Admn; WSU, Leadership Training & Publ; WCSW, In-Training Prog, Cert Ed Soc Serv. **Career:** Wane Co Probate Ct Med Div, 1940-45; Wayne Co Dept Soc Welfare, 1949-66; Wayne Co Ment & Estates Div, 1966-73. **Orgs:** Dir, Publicity & Pub Rel Commun Comn; St Matthew's & St Joseph's Epis Church; exec bd mem, African Art Gallery Comn, vestry-woman St Matthew's & St Joseph's Epis Church; pub rel AAGC; founder, Soc Detroit Inst Arts; consult, Santa Rosa Community Group; Women's Com United Negro Col Fund; Cathedral Church St Paul Chap; coord Coun Human Rels; Church Women United; League Women Voters; Detroit Asn Women's Clubs; Detroit Hist Soc; Int Inst; Metro YWCA; NW Voters Regist Group; Alpha Kappa Alpha Sorority; Alpha Rho Omega Detroit; NAACP; Detroit Friends Pub Libr Inc; Detroit Urban League; Soc Workers Club Detroit; exec bd mem, Women's Coun United Negro Col fund; chmn, Annual Banquet UNGF; exec bd, Am Asn Univ Women; pres, Parish Coun St Matthew's & St Jos Episcopal Church. **Honors/Awds:** Gen Chairperson & Coord, Anniversary Celebrations, St Mattew's St Jospeh's Ecopal Church; 1941-86; 30 Yr Serv Medallion, Alpha Kappa Alpha Sor, 1946-77; Humanitarian Award, Wo-He-Lo Literary Soc; 15 yr Serv Pin Detroit Urban League, 1953-68; numerous awards for Vol Work & Community Participation; Spirit Detroit Award in Recognition of Exceptional Achievement Outstanding Leadership and Dedication to Improving the Quality of Life; Award of Merit of many years of serv to Friends of African ArtFounders Soc Detroit Inst of Arts; Community Award, Vol Work Detroit Receiving Hosp; Nation-Wide Net Work Participant, Boston, MA, Conv, Amer Asn Univ Women; Citation Detroit Church Woman United; Induction Prestigious Quarter Century Club, Nat Urban league; Annual meeting Los Angeles Ca Detroit Citation AAUW 25 Yr Serv Pin Detroit Urban League.

WILLIAMS, DR. MCDONALD
Educator. **Personal:** Born Nov 13, 1917, Pittsburgh, PA; son of Alexander and Margaret Bailey; married Jamye Harris Coleman, Dec 28, 1943; children: Donna. **Educ:** Univ Pittsburgh, BA, 1939, LittM, 1942; Ohio State Univ, PhD, 1954. **Career:** Educator (retired); Wilberforce Univ Ohio, educr, 1942-56; Tuskegee Inst, vis prof eng, 1955; Morris Brown Col, GA, educr, 1956-58; Atlanta Univ, 1957; Tenn State Univ, educr, hons prog dir, 1958-88; AME Church Review, Nashville, TN, assoc ed, 1984-92. **Orgs:** Modern Lang Asn; NW Nashville Civitan Club; exec comt, Northwest YMCA Ctr; exec comt, Nashville Br, NAACP, 1968-; Alpha Phi Alpha, Sigma Pi Phi, Golden Key; vice chair, State Bd Prof Responsibility, 1998-2003. **Honors/Awds:** Teacher of the Year, Tenn State Univ, 1979; Corp sec, NW Nashville Civitan Club; Outstanding Service Award, Tenn State Univ, 1988. **Special Achievements:** Wellness Ctr, Northwest YMCA renamed 'McDonald Williams Wellness Center'; Honors Ctr, Tenn State Univ renamed 'McDonald Williams Honors Center', 1995; co-editor, "The Negro Speaks: The Rhetoric of Contempory Black Leaders". **Home Addr:** 125 Wynfield Way SW, Atlanta, GA 30331.

WILLIAMS, MCGHEE (MCGHEE WILLIAMS OSSE)
Executive. **Personal:** Born in Columbus, GA. **Educ:** Univ SC, advert. **Career:** Sears, copywriter & layout artist; KFC, mkt mgr; Gen Mills Restaurant Group, mkt mgr; TRM Inc, mkt dir; Burrell Commun Group, managing dir mkt innovations; Burrell Commun Group, co-chief exec officer, 2007-. **Orgs:** Am Advert Fedn Mosaic Coun; Metrop Chicago Bd Children's Home & Aid Soc Ill; Nat Adv Bd Strive Media; Adv Bd, Ctr Brand Res, Univ Tex, Austin; bd dirs, Am Asn Advert Agencies; Ad Coun Bd Dir; Bd Advisors Strive Media. **Honors/Awds:** Multiethnic Ad Campaign of the Year, Am Advert Fedn; Chicago Minorities in Business Leadership Award, Clear Channel Radio-Chicago, 2007. **Business Addr:** Co-Chief Executive Officer, Burrell Communications Group, 233 N Mich Ave, Chicago, IL 60601, **Business Phone:** (312)297-9600.*

WILLIAMS, MELVIN
Singer, guitarist. **Personal:** Born Feb 21, 1953, Smithdale, MS. **Career:** Albums: Back to the Cross, 1988; Never Seen Your Face, 1998; The William Brothers, lead guitarist; Blackberry Rec, secy, treas & rec artist, currently. **Honors/Awds:** Traditional Male Vocalist of the Year, 1998. **Special Achievements:** Was nominated in three categories at the 1998 Stellar Awards Ceremony for his album "Never Seen Your Face". **Business Addr:** Secretary, Treasurer, c/o Blackberry Records, PO Box 818, Summit, MS 39666.*

WILLIAMS, DR. MELVIN D
Educator, school administrator. **Personal:** Born Feb 3, 1933, Pittsburgh, PA; son of Aaron and Gladys; married Faye W Strawder; children: Aaron E, Steven R & Craig H. **Educ:** Univ Pittsburgh, AB, econ (Hons), 1955, MA, anthrop, 1969, PhD Anthrop, 1973; Carlow Col, Nat Cert Sec Educ, 1973. **Career:** Wholesale periodical Distribution Co, owner & operator, 1955-66; Johnson Publ Co, field rep, 1958-61; NDEA Title IV, fel anthrop, 1966-69; Carlow Col, fac instr, asst prof, dept sociol & anthrop, 1969-75; Colgate Univ, Olive B O'Connor, chair, 1976-77; Univ Pittsburgh, fac, assoc prof, anthrop, 1976-79, Int Jour Cult & Social Anthrop, assoc ed ethnology, 1976-79, adj res prof, anthrop, 1979-82; Purdue Univ, fac, prof anthrop, dept sociol & anthrop, 1979-83; Univ Md Col Pk, affiliated prof, urban studies, 1984-88, fac, prof anthrop, 1983-88; Univ Michigan, prof anthrop, 1988-, fac assoc, Comprehensive Studies Prog, 1988-91; Univ Mich, Ctr Afro-Am & African Studies, fac assoc, 1992-; vis lectr, Am Anthropological Asn. **Orgs:** Twenty Four Acad committee including chmn minority affairs comt, Colgate Univ, affirm action comm; deans grad rev bd, Fac Arts & Sci, rep fac assembly, Univ Pittsburgh; Univ senate, Purdue Univ; chancellors commn ethnic minority issues, campus senate represent anthrop & Afro-Am studies, pres, Black Fac Staff assoc, Univ Md; Ombudsman, 1991-93, senate assembly, 1993-96, Univ Mich; 24 memberships including fel, vis lectr Am Anthrop Assoc, Am Assoc Univ Prof, Anthrop Soc Wash, Phi Delta Kappa, pres, orgn NAACP, Sigma XI, Soc Ethnic & Spec Studies, NY Acad Sci, fel, Soc Appl Anthrop, Deans Coun, Univ Michigan.African Studies Asn; fel Am Anthropological Asn; AAAS;Am Asn Univ Adminr; Am Asn Univ Prof; Am Ethnol Soc; Am Sociol Asn; Anthrop Soc Wash; Asn Sociol Religion; Asn Study Afro-Am Life & History; Asn Sociol Religion; Coun Anthropol & Educ; District Columbia Sociol Soc; Ethnic Planning Comt Pittsburgh Coun on Higher Educ; Nat Coun Black Studies; Northeastern Anthrop Asn; Phi Delta Kappa; A Prof Educ Fraternity; Nat Asn Advan Colored People; Religious Res Asn; Sigma Xi: The Scientific Res Soci N Am; Univ Mich Chapter; Soc Med Anthrop; Soc for Psychol Anthrop; Soc Ethnic & Special Studies; The Economic Club Pittsburgh, Inc. Soc Study Social Problems; Soc Sci Study Religion. **Honors/Awds:** Fifty One honors & awards including Black Achiever Award, Talk Mag; Hon Reception Recognition Scholarly Achievements, Dept Anthrop, Univ Pittsburgh, 1975; MC, The Presidents Dinner Graduating Seniors, Carlow Col, 1975; Bishops Service Award, Catholic Diocese Pittsburgh, 1975; Hadley Cantril Memorial Award, 1976; received highest teaching evaluations in the history of the univ, 1976; keynote speaker, Afro-Amer Family Conf, Purdue Univ; invited speaker, Martin Luther King Program. **Special Achievements:** Fifty three publications including, "Observations in Pittsburgh Ghetto Schools", Anthrop Educ Quarterly, 1981; "On the St Where I Lived", Holt Rinehart & Winston, 1981; "Notes from a Black Ghetto in Pittsburgh)", Critical Perspective Third World Am Race Class Cult Am, 1983; "Community in a Black Pentecostal Church"; Author, Community in a Black Pentacostal Church; On the Street Where I Lived; The Human Dilemma; Race for Theory. **Military Serv:** AUS, Pa Nat Guard. **Business Addr:** Professor, University of Michigan, Department of Anthropology, 222B W Hall, Ann Arbor, MI 48109.

WILLIAMS, DR. MELVIN WALKER
Physician. **Personal:** Born Jan 28, 1939, New York, NY; son of Shirley C and Wilhelmina Curtis; married Marilyann Thomas; children: Jennifer & Martin. **Educ:** Fordham Univ, BS, 1960; Howard Univ, Col Med, MD, 1967; Harvard Univ, Sch Pub Health, MPH, 1973. **Career:** US Pub Health Serv Hosp, internship, 1967-68; US Public Health Serv, command officer, 1967-77, 1980-2000; St Elizabeth's Hosp, 1968-70; Mass Gen Hosp Boston, residency, 1970-73; NIMH-Staff Col, assoc dir, 1973-77; Job Corp Health Office, US Dept Labor, consult, 1973-; NIMH, teacher, 1973-77; pvt practice, psychiat, 1973-; Howard Univ, teacher, dept psychiat, 1974-75; Am Bd Psychiat & Neurol, certified, 1976; Howard Univ, asst clinical prof, dept psychiat, 1976-93; Am Bd Psychiat & Neurol, examiner, 1977-; Dist Columbia, interim commissioner Mental Health, 1992-93. **Orgs:** Black Psychiatrists Am; Nat Med Asn; Alliance for Psychiat Prog; Am Psychiat Asn; Am Med Asn; Command Officers Asn US Pub Health Serv; WA Psychiat Soc Chi Delta Mu Frat; Kappa Alpha Psi Frat; assoc, NIMH Mental Health Career Develop Prog, 1970-75; fel, Harvard Med Sch Dept Psychiat, 1970-73; Customised Officers Asn US Pub Health Serv, 1967-. **Special Achievements:** Co-author, Black Parent's Handbook, 1975. **Military Serv:** SUU Pub Health Serv, capt, 1967-77, 1980-00. **Home Addr:** 9016 Alton Pkwy, Silver Spring, MD 20910. **Business Addr:** Physician, 1616 18th St NW Suite 101, Washington, DC 20009, **Business Phone:** (202)265-8708.

WILLIAMS, MICHAEL D. (MIKE WILLIAMS)
Football player. **Personal:** Born Jan 11, 1980, Dallas, TX; married Enisha. **Educ:** Univ Tex, Youth and comm studies. **Career:** Buffalo Bills, offensive tackle, 2002-05; Jacksonville Jaguars, offensive tackle & guard, 2006; Washington Redskins, 2009-. **Business Addr:** Football Player, Washington RedSkins, 21300 Redskin Park Dr, Ashburn, VA 20147, **Business Phone:** (703)726-7000.*

WILLIAMS, MICHAEL DOUGLAS
Basketball player. **Personal:** Born Jul 23, 1966, Dallas, TX. **Educ:** Baylor Univ. **Career:** Basketball palyer (retired); Detroit Pistons, guard, 1988-89; Phoenix Suns, 1989-90, Charlotte Hornets, 1989-90; Ind Pacers, point guard, 1990-92; Minn Timberwolves, guard, 1992-98; Toronto Raptors, 1998-99. **Orgs:** Founder, Assist-for-Life Found, 1992; developer, In The Paint Classic, Urban League. **Honors/Awds:** NBA Champions, Detroit Pistons, 1989; NBA, All-Defensive Second Team, 1991-92.

WILLIAMS, MICHAEL MICHELE
Actor. **Personal:** Born Aug 30, 1966, Evansville, IN; daughter of Jerry Thomas and Theresa Williams. **Career:** Films: New Jack City, actress, 1991; The Sixth Man, actress, 1997; Ali, actress, 2001; Dark Blue, actress, 2003; How to Lose a Guy in Ten Days, actress, 2003; TV series: "New York Undercover", actress, 1994; "Homicide: Life on the Street", actress, 1998-99; "ER", actress, 1999-; TV movies: "The Substitute 2: Sch's Out", actress, 1998; "Homicide: The Movie", actress, 2000; TV mini-series: "Trade Winds", actress, 1993; "Peter Benchley's Creature", actress, 1998; "Kevin Hill", actress, 2004; The Hunt for the BTK Killer, actress, 2005; Company Town, actress, 2006; Judy's Got a Gun, actress, 2007; Law & Order: Special Victims Unit, actress, 2007; House M.D., actress, 2007. **Business Addr:** Actress, The Gersh Agency, 232 N Canon Dr, Beverly Hills, CA 90210, **Business Phone:** (310)274-6611.

WILLIAMS, MICHELLE (TENETRIA MICHELLE WILLIAMS)
Singer. **Personal:** Born Jul 23, 1980, Rockford, IL; daughter of Dennis and Anita. **Educ:** Ill State Univ, criminal justice. **Career:** R&B group, Destiny's Child, 2000-; Albums: Survivor, 2001; Eight Days of Christmas, 2001; Solo Albums: Heart To Yours, 2002; Do You Know, 2004; Broadway: Aida, 2003-04; Unexpected, 2008. **Honors/Awds:** Grammy Award; Best New Artist, MOBO Awards, 2002; Lead Female Actress, 18th Annual NAACP Theatre Awards, 2008; Best R&B Vocal Performance By a Female Artist, New Now Next Awards, 2008. **Business Phone:** (212)833-8000.*

WILLIAMS, MIKE. See WILLIAMS, MICHAEL D.

WILLIAMS, MILTON. See EL-KATI, MAHMOUD.

WILLIAMS, HON. MILTON LAWRENCE
Judge. **Personal:** Born Nov 14, 1932, Augusta, GA; son of William Richard and Helen Reilly; married Rose King Williams, Oct 22, 1960; children: Milton Jr & Darrie T. **Educ:** NY Univ, BS, 1960; NY Law Sch, LLB, 1963. **Career:** Allstate Ins Co, staff atty; Small Bus Admin, regional coun; Hunts Point Legal Serv, gen coun & dir; Knapp Comn, assoc gen coun; McKay Comn Attica, exec dir; NYC Civil Serv Comn, spec prosecutor; Criminal Ct City NY, judge, 1977-78; NY County Criminal Ct, supv judge, actg justice supreme ct, 1978-83; NY Supreme Ct, admin judge first judicial dist, 1983-85; NY State Supreme Ct, justice, dep chief admin judge, 1985-93, Appellate Div, First Dept, assoc justice, 1994-2001, 2003-, Appellate Div, presiding justice, 2002. **Orgs:** Asn Bar City NY; bd trustees, NY Law Sch; bd trustees, St John's Univ; Am Asn Sovereign Mil Order Malta; bd trustees, St Patrick's Cathedral; bd trustees, Inner-City Scholar Fund; Pres Comn White House Fel; Sigma Pi Phi Fraternity; Zeta Boule. **Honors/Awds:** Charles Carroll Award, The Guild Catholic Lawyers; Harlan Fiske Stone Award, NY State Trial Lawyers Asn; Humanitarian Award, NY County Lawyers Asn; Outstanding Achievement Award, Bronx Black Bar Asn; Judge Capozolli Award, NY County Lawyers Asn; Golda Meir Award, Jewish Lawyers Guild; Metrop Black Bar Asn Award; Gold & Silver Award, Guardians Asn. **Military Serv:** USN, 2nd class petty officer, 1951-55. **Home Addr:** 511 E 20th St, New York, NY 10010, **Home Phone:** (212)475-5617. **Business Addr:** Associate Justice, Appellate Division First Department, 27 Madison Ave, New York, NY 10010, **Business Phone:** (212)340-0400.

WILLIAMS, MOE (MAURECE JABARI WILLIAMSX)
Football player, horse trainer. **Personal:** Born Jul 26, 1974, Columbus, GA; son of Marethia. **Educ:** Univ Ky, social work. **Career:** Football player(retired); Minn Vikings, running back, 1996-2000, 2002-05; Baltimore Ravens, running back, 2001; St Louis Rams, running back, 2006, horse race trainer, currently. **Orgs:** Twin Cities Community. **Honors/Awds:** All-Am hons, 1995; Doak Walker Award, 1995; Second Team All-Sec hons. **Special Achievements:** Won his first horse race as a trainer at the Calder Race Course in Miami, Florida.

WILLIAMS, MONTEL
Talk show host, executive. **Personal:** Born Jul 3, 1956, Baltimore, MD; married Grace; children: 4. **Educ:** Naval Acad Prep Sch, 1975; US Naval Acad, BS, 1980; Defense Language Inst, BA, russian, 1983. **Career:** Motivational speaker; Montel Williams Show, host & exec producer, 1991-; CBS, Matt Waters, actor, 1996; Film: Am Dreams, 2003; Am Candidate, 2004; Second Time Around, 2004. **Orgs:** Adminr nonprofit Asn. **Honors/Awds:** Spec Serv Award, US Chamber Com, 1988; Man of the Year, Esquire Mag, 1988; Award for Meritous Work With Youth, Omaha Pub Sch, Omaha Pub Sch, 1991; NATAS Emmy Award, 1995-96; Silver Satellite Award, 1996; Silver Satellite Award, Am Women in Radio & Tv, 1996; Crystal Apple Award, 1996; Man of Courage Award, Tommy Hilfiger Annual Race to Erase MS gala, 2001; Vanguard Award, Outstanding Man of the Year, Asn Black Harvard Women, 2003. **Special Achievements:** First African-Am male talk-show host on daytime tv; filmed introduction to motion picture Glory; first African Am enlisted marine selected to attend the Naval Acad Prep Sch; hosted a community affairs prog in Denver entitled "The Fourth R: Kids Rap About Racism," for which he won a local Emmy; Auth: Mountain Get Out of My Way, 1996; numerous others. **Military Serv:** US Marine Corps, officer, 1974; Armed Forces Expeditionary Medal; Humanitarian Serv Medal; two Navy Expeditionary Medals; Navy Achievement Medal; two Navy Commendation Medals; two Meritorious Serv Awards. **Business Addr:** Host, Executive Producer, Montel Williams The Show, 433 W 53rd St, New York, NY 10019, **Business Phone:** (212)830-0300.

WILLIAMS, MONTY
Basketball player, basketball coach. **Personal:** Born Oct 8, 1971, Fredericksburg, VA; married Ingrid, Jul 21, 1995; children: 3. **Educ:** Univ Notre Dame, commun & theatre, 1994. **Career:** Basketball player (retired), basketball coach; New York Knicks, forward, 1994-96; San Antonio Spurs, 1996-98; Denver Nuggets, 1999; Orlando Magic, 2000-02; Philadelphia 76ers, forward, 2003; Portland Trail Blazers, asst coach, 2005-. **Orgs:** Fel Christian Athletes; vol, Youth Ministry Prog, San Antonio.

WILLIAMS, MORRIS
Executive, accountant. **Personal:** Born in Texarkana, AR; son of Edward and Izora; married Geraldine Copeland; children: Shawn Copeland. **Educ:** Wayne State Univ, BS, BA, 1940; Univ Detroit, grad studies. **Career:** Detroit Housing Comn, jr acct, 1941-47; Morris O Williams & Co, owner, pres, 1948-. **Orgs:** Nat Soc Pub Acct; past treasr, Ind Acct Asn Mich; bd dirs, YMCA, Fisher Br; Omega Psi Phi Fraternity; African Methodist Episcopal Church; life mem, Nat Asn Advan Colored People; Detroit Idlewilders Inc; Nat Supreme Coun, A & ASR Masons; Nat Asn Enrolled Agts; Nat Soc Accts; Nat Rifle Asn. **Special Achievements:** Founded the under graduate chapter, Nu Sigma of the Omega Psi Phi Fraternity, Wayne State University. First African in Michigan State to Qualify as an enrolled agent for the US Treasury dept. **Military Serv:** Infantry vol officer cand, 1943. **Business Addr:** President, Morris O Williams & Co, 2101 W Grand Blvd, Detroit, MI 48208-1105, **Business Phone:** (313)894-3900.

WILLIAMS, MOSES, SR.
Police officer. **Personal:** Born Aug 15, 1932, Franklin Parish, LA; married Matra; children: Rhonda, Matra, Lula, Otha, Brenda, James, Jessie, Moses Jr, Robert, Allen, Betty. **Career:** Police officer (retired); Tallulah Police Dept, 23 years. **Orgs:** Pres, Steering Comn, 1967-77; vpres, Madison Vote League Inc, 1964-84; pres, Delta Comn Action Colo Gov Treen Staff, 1979-83; bd dir, Develop Block Grant Wash DC; elected to state, HH Way from the 5th Regional, 1980-; pres, vpres bd dirs, Delta Comn Action, 1965-76; pres, Madison Parish Bd Econ Develop Loan Bd, 1971-77; Madison Parish Police Jury, vpres, 1972-77, serving 5th term, currently; HEW Police Jury Asn; Municipal Police Off Asn; 5th Dist Black Caucus Comn; comnr, Madison Parish Port; adv coun bd, Title IV Sch Bd; Nat Asn Advan Colored People; RDA Rural Develop Asn; Magnolia St Peace Off Asn; BSA; McCall Sr High PTA; Marquis Who's Who Publ Bd, 1976-77; 5th Dist LA Educ Asn, 1972; Evening Star Lodge No 113 1972; La Police Officer Asn; City Tallulah, auxiliary police officer; Criminal & Juvenile Justice Comt; Appointed to NACO Steering Comt, Justice & Public Safety Steering Comt, WA DC; Appointed to Drainage Public Works & Water Resources Comt; Elected pres, 5th Region Dist Police Jury Asn, LA; Elected, finance chmn, Madison Parish Police Jury; Elected, chmn, All Black Election officerial Madison Parish. **Honors/Awds:** Colone Gov Staff, 1973, 1979-83; Reg VII Drug Training & Resource Ctr. **Special Achievements:** Only Black in the state of LA who was a Police officer & an Elected Police Juror at the same time. **Home Addr:** 601 W Green St, Tallulah, LA 71282. *

WILLIAMS, NAOMI B
Educator, school administrator. **Personal:** Born Dec 4, 1942, New Smyrna, FL; married Mac James Williams Sr; children: Pam, Mac Jr, Essie, Brenda Yolanda, Roderick & Wendell. **Educ:** Bethune-Cookman Col, BS, 1963; Fla A&M Univ, Med, 1973; Stetson Univ, Cert Coun, 1974; Rollins Col, Specialist Educ 1976; Nova Univ, EdD, 1980; Int Bible Inst & Sem Asn Relig Educ, ministers Dipl. **Career:** Volusia County Pub Schs, teacher, 1963-67, dean girls & counsr, 1967-73, asst high sch prin, 1973-74; Daytona Beach Jr Col, dir admis & recruiting, 1974-78; St Petersburg Jr Col, col registr, 1978-, campus registr & dir admis, 1986; Volusia County Pub Sch, math & sci teacher, recruiter. **Orgs:** Am Asn Col Registr & Admis Officers; Fla Asn Col Registr & Admis Officers; Fla Asn Community Cols; Southern Asn Col Registr & Admis Officers; past bd dirs, United Way; Bethune-Cookman Col Alumni Asn; past bd dirs, Spirit; educ dir, Mt Carmel Baptist Church; Sunday sch teacher, Mt Carmel Baptist Church; Grad Chap Kappa Delta Pi; Grad Chap Delta Sigma Theta Sorority; Urban League; adult adv, Clearwater Youth Coun NAACP; dir adult sunday sch dept, Mt Carmel Baptist Church; Top of the World Kiwanis Club. **Honors/Awds:** Graduation Speaker, Trinity Arts & Tech Acad, The Philippines; Teacher of the Year Award, Campbell Sr High Sch, Daytona Beach; Mother of the Year, Ben & Mary's Kindergarten, Daytona Beach; founders day speaker Delta Sigma Theta Sorority, Clearwater Branch; Gulfcoast Bus Womens Asn; COT Volunteer Certificate; St Petersburg Jr Col; Certificate, Women on the Way Challenge; Counselor of the Year Award, Mainland Sr High Sch. **Special Achievements:** First Black Female Assistant Principal in a Sr High School Volusia County Schs Daytona Beach Fl; First Black Dir of Admissions Daytona Beach Comm Coll Daytona Beach FL; First Black Registrar St Petersburg Jr College. **Home Addr:** 1300 Ridge Ave, Clearwater, FL 33755-3659, **Home Phone:** (813)461-5827. **Business Addr:** Registar, St. Petersburg Junior College, 2465 Drew St, Clearwater, FL 33765-2898, **Business Phone:** (727)341-3170.

WILLIAMS, NAPOLEON
Executive, government official, president (organization). **Personal:** Born Nov 24, 1919, Vienna, GA; married Joyce Henry; children: Gail L & Sonya. **Educ:** Ft Valley State Col, BS, soc studies, natural Sci; Atlanta Univ, MA, admin; Atlanta Sch Mortuary Sci. **Career:** Vienna High & Indust Sch, prin, 1952-70; Vienna High Sch, prin, 1970-76; Ga Southwestern Col, instr, 1977-78; JW Williams Funeral Home, pres, currently. **Orgs:** Pres, GMA Third Dist, 1984-85; Dooly Co Bi-Racial Comm; 32 Degree Mason; Noble Mystic Shrine Am; chmn, Dooly Co Bd Health; Nat Asn Advan Colored People; bd of dir, W Cent GA Comt Action Coun. **Honors/Awds:** Int Personnel Res Creativity Award, Creative & Successful Personalities, 1972; Distinguished Serv Award, Recipient City Vienna, 1976; Distinguished Serv Award, Recipient Ft Valley State Col, 1981; Gtea Meritorious Service to the Cause of Education. **Military Serv:** WWII Vet; WWII Vict Medal; Am Serv Medal; Europ/African/Middle E Serv Medal; Good Cond Medal; AR 600-68 Philippine Liber Serv Ribbon. **Business Addr:** President, JW Williams Funeral Home, 407 W 17th Ave, PO Box 516, Cordele, GA 31010-0516, **Business Phone:** (229)273-2683.

WILLIAMS, NATALIE
Basketball player, business owner. **Personal:** Born Nov 30, 1970, Long Beach, CA; daughter of Robyn Barker and Nate. **Educ:** Univ Calif, Los Angeles, BSW, 1994. **Career:** Basketball player (retired); Am Basketball League, Portland Power, ctr, 1996-99; Utah Starzz, 1999-02; Ind Fever, forward, 2003-05; Natalie's Restaurant, owner. **Honors/Awds:** All-Am, 1993-94; Pac-10 Athlete of the Decade, 1996; Utah's Woman Athlete of the Century, 1996; All-ABL First Team, 1997-98; All-ABL & All-Star Team, 1997-98; led in rebounding, scoring, 1997-98; Most Valuable Player, Am Basketball League, 1998; Olympic Gold Medal, World Champion US Women's Basketball Team, 2000; named to All-WNBA First Team, 2001; Gold Medal, 2000 Summer Olympics, Sydney, Australia, 2000. **Special Achievements:** She carried the Olympic Torch, Salt Lake City, 2002 Winter Olympics. She also was named to the United StateShe carried the Olympic Torch, Salt Lake City, 2002 Winter Olympics. She also was named to the United States 2002 World Championship Games team. s 2002 World Championship Games team. *

WILLIAMS, NORMAN J
Chief executive officer, chairperson. **Career:** Ill Serv Fed S&L Asn, chief exec officer & chair, currently. **Orgs:** Chmn. Ill League Fin Insts, 2007-08. **Business Addr:** Chief Executive officer, Board of Chairman, Illinois Service Federal S&L Association, 4619 S King Dr, Chicago, IL 60653, **Business Phone:** (773)624-2000.*

WILLIAMS, NORRIS GERALD
School administrator. **Personal:** Born May 12, 1948, Oklahoma City, OK; son of Mattye and Norris; married Carolyn Ann Moch, Aug 28, 1970; children: Diarra Koro, Ayanna Kai, Jawanza Jamaal & Norris Emanuel. **Educ:** Wiley Col, Tex, BS (hons), 1970; Cent State Univ Okla, MS, 1977. **Career:** Douglass High Sch, Okla City, all conf pitcher, 1966; Okla City Pub Schs, coach, 1970-75, teacher 1970-77; Park & Rec Dept Okla City, mgr, 1970-82; Images KFGL & KAEZ, radio talk show host, 1977-78; Univ Okla, black stud serv, coordr 1977-, minority stud serv, dir, 1988-, Henderson Scholar Prog, dir, currently; Black Dispatch Pub Co, sports ed, 1979-82; R&B Prod, Jam Prod, Feyline Prod, C&F Prod, promotional consult, 1979-82. **Orgs:** Secy, treas, Kappa Alpha Psi, 1968-70; pres, KAZI Community Serv, 1972-73; pres, Images Community Serv, 1976-78; pres, Assoc Black Personnel, Univ Okla, 1979-80; pres, Assoc Black personnel 1982-83; OKABSE, 1984-85; comn Okla Black Hist Soc 1984-85; Alpha Chi Chap Kappa Alpha Psi; polemarch Norman Alumni Chap, Kappa Alpha Psi 1986-88. **Honors/Awds:** Outstanding Student, Kappa Alpha Psi Alpha Chi Wiley Col, 1969; Baseball Coach of the Year, Capitol Conf, OKla City, 1975; Staff Person of the Year, Black Peoples Union, Univ Okla, 1977-79; Community Service Award, 1983; Outstanding Achievement Award, Univ Okla, 1984; Comnr Higher Educ, Okla Assoc Black Sch Educr, 1985; The City of Norman Human Rights Award, 2001. **Business Addr:** Director, University of Oklahoma, Henderson Scholarship Program, Rm E-130 Couch Tower 1524 Asp Ave., Norman, OK 73072, **Business Phone:** (405)325-0850.

WILLIAMS, NOVELLA STEWART
Association executive. **Personal:** Born Jul 13, 1927, Johnston County, NC; daughter of Charlie and Cassie; married Thomas Williams, Oct 5, 1944; children: Charles, Frank, Willis, Thomas, Kim, Michelle, Pam. **Educ:** Rutgers Univ, attended 1971; Univ Pa Wharton Sch, 1974. **Career:** Citizens Prog, founder & pres, 1974-. **Orgs:** Chmn, bd dir W Philadelphia Comt Free Sch, 1969-; Harcourt-Brace-World-Measurement & Conf, 1969; dir, Philadelphia Anti Poverty Comn, 1970-; vice chmn, YMCA, 1970; coordr, 513 Women's Comt Carter-Mondale Camp; White House

Conf Hunger, 1970; Red Book, 1970; pres, House Foreign AffSubcomCongressnal Rec, 1970; Seven Sch, 1971; prin, Nat Ed Assoc, 1972; Peoples Health Serv, 1973-; partner & consult Ed Mgt Assoc, 1973-; consult US Consumer Prod Safety Comn, 1975-76; secy, bd dir Health Sys Agency SE PA, 1976-; bd dir, RCHPC; bd dir, SE PA Am Red Cross, 1976; By Laws; person & consumer aff Comt Philadelphia Health Mgt Corp, 1976-; del Dem Nat Conv, 1976; dem Crdntl Comt 1976; Dem Rules Com, 1976; Dem Del Whip, 1976; bd dir, Philadelphia Urban Coalitiion, 1977; oard trustees, Lincoln Univ, 1977; trustee, United Way, 1981, co-chairperson, The Philadelphia Urban Coalition, 1989-. **Honors/Awds:** Human Rights Award, Philadelphia Comn Human Rels, 1968; Community Organization Award, OIC, 1970; Outstanding Service Award, White House Conf Small Bus, 1980. **Business Addr:** Founder, President, Citizens Progress, Inc, 5236 Market St, Philadelphia, PA 19139, **Business Phone:** (215)474-8633.*

WILLIAMS, DR. OLIVER J
Educator, college administrator. **Educ:** Western Mich Univ, MSW, 1980; Univ Pittsburgh, MPH, 1984, PhD, 1985. **Career:** Women's advocate; batterer intervention counr; trainer; Univ Minn, Inst Domestic Violence African Am Community, exec dir, dir, currently; Univ Minn Sch Social Work, prof, currently. **Orgs:** Family Violence Prevention Fund; Nat Coun Juvenile & Family Court Judges. **Special Achievements:** Contributed few publications. **Business Phone:** (612)624-9217.*

WILLIAMS, DR. ORA
Educator. **Personal:** Born Feb 18, 1926, Lakewood, NJ; daughter of Charles Williams and Ida Bolles Roach Williams. **Educ:** Va Union Univ, Richmond, Va, AB, 1950; Howard Univ, Wash, DC, MA, 1953; Univ Calif, Irvine, Calif, PhD, 1974. **Career:** Educator (retired); Southern Univ, Baton Rouge, La, instr, 1953-55; Tuskegee Inst, Tuskegee, Ala, instr, 1955-57; Morgan State Univ, Baltimore, Md, instr, 1957-65; Camp Fire Girls, Inc, New York, NY, prog adv, 1965-68; Calif State Univ, Long Beach, Calif, prof, 1968-88, prof emer, 1988; Va Union Univ, vis prof, 1990-91. **Orgs:** Col Lang Asn; BEEM-Black Experience Expressed Music, bd, 1982; NAACP; Afro-Am Youth Asn, 1984; Dist Sorority. **Honors/Awds:** co-auth: "Johnny Doesn't/Didn't Hear", J Negro Hist, 1964; auth: American Black Women in the Arts and Social Sciences: A Bibliographical Survey, Scarecrow Press, 1973, 1978, 1994; auth: Just Like Meteor: A Bio-Bibliography of the Life and Works of Charles William Williams; Second Annual Achievement Award, Humanities & Performing Arts Res, Va Union Univ Alumni Asn Southern Calif, 1983; Pillar of the COT Award, Long Beach COT Improv League, 1988; Outstanding Service Award, Mayor Long Beach, 1988; Consortium of Doctors, Savannah, Ga, 1993. **Home Addr:** 305 Baldwin Rd, Glassboro, NJ 08028. **Business Addr:** Long Beach, CA 90840.

WILLIAMS, PAT
Football player. **Personal:** Born Oct 24, 1972, Monroe, LA; married Valarie; children: Crystal, Alesha & Pat. **Educ:** Tex A&M Univ. **Career:** Buffalo Bills, defensive tackle, 1997- 2004; Minnesota Vikings, defensive tackle, 2005-. **Honors/Awds:** Ed Block Courage Award, 2003; Three Pro Bowls, 2006-08. **Business Addr:** Defensive Tackle, Minnesota Vikings, 9520 Viking Dr, Eden Prairie, MN 55344, **Business Phone:** (952)828-6500.

WILLIAMS, PATRICIA ANNE
Judge. **Personal:** Born Dec 16, 1943, New York, NY; daughter of David Charles Jr and Kathleen Valerie Carrington. **Educ:** Cornell Univ, BA, 1965; Cert African Inst Columbia Univ, MA, 1967; Yale Univ Law Sch, JD, 1972. **Career:** SDNY, asst US atty, 1977-86; Willkie Farr & Gallagher, assoc atty, 1972-76; New Haven Legal Asst Assoc, legal clerk, 1971-72; New York City Crim Justice Co-ord Coun, law clerk summer, 1970; Phelps-Stokes Fund NYC, sec admin asst, 1967-69; Supreme Ct New York, County Bronx, Criminal Div, actg justice, currently; NY Law Sch, adj fac, currently. **Orgs:** Asn Bar City New York; Fed Bar Coun; Am Judges Asn; Judicial Friends; NY County Lawyers Asn. **Honors/Awds:** Recognition Award, Criminal Justice Sect New York County Lawyers, 1996; fellowship, Aspen Inst Law & Soc Seminar, 1997. **Business Addr:** Acting Justice of Criminal Division, Supreme Court of New York, County of the Bronx, 851 Grand Concourse, Bronx, NY 10451, **Business Phone:** (718)590-3722.

WILLIAMS, DR. PATRICIA HILL
School administrator, consultant. **Personal:** Born May 3, 1939, Richmond, VA; daughter of Marshall and Virginia; divorced; children: Tory Therese. **Educ:** State Univ NY, Old Westbury, BA, 1976; NY Inst Tech, MA, Commun Art, 1981; State Univ NY, Stony Brook, MA, lib studies, 1991; Harvard Grad Sch Educ, Grad Cert, mgt develop, 1992; Calif Coast Univ, EdD, 1996. **Career:** Sch Administator (retired), Consult; Babylon Beacon Newspaper, assoc editor, 1971-79; NY Amsterdam News, columnist, 1972-84; Am Cancer Soc, pub info officer, 1977-80; Kellogg fel Int Develop, 1984-86; State Univ NY, Farmingdale, fac, from asst to pres, vpres, 1999-2000, vpres external affairs, 2000-05; Suffolk County Human Rights Comnr, 1990-; Pres Bush's Bd Adv Hist Black Col & Univ, 1991; Partners the Am, Int Am exec bd, 1992-94, Int Bd Dir, chair; African Develop Found Bd Adv, 1993; Inter-Am Found, vice chair bd dir; develop consult pvt pract, currently. **Orgs:** State Univ Confederation Alumni Asn, 1983-; State Univ NY, Coun Univ Advan, 1985; former comnr, Babylon Historic Comm; Pres Reagan's appointee, Nat Adv Coun Women's Educ Prog, 1987-90; northeast region chairperson Nat Black Republic Coun; Life mem, NAACP, NCNW; founding bd, Episcopal Charities Long Island, 1992; Pres Clinton's appointee to the Inter-Am Foundation, 1995-2000; Links Int, Eastern Shore Chp; exec dir, Appointed by Pres George W Bush Rep to UN/DPI/NGO, exec comt, currently; Alpha Kappa Alpha Theta Iota Omega, charter; past pres, Long Island Chap 100 Black Women; Nat chair, Pub Policy, Nat Coalition 100 Black Women, 1998-2002; pres, 100 Black Women Long Island Found, 1998; vpres, Long Island Women's Agenda, 1998. **Honors/Awds:** Woman of the Year Media Award, Bethel AME Church, 1980; PR Award of Excellence, LI Flower Show, 1983; Woman of the Year, New York State Council of Black Republicans, 1986, 1987, 1988; Outstanding Alumna of the Year, State Univ NY Col of Old Westbury, 1988; Newsday Community Service Award, 1990; Honoree in Edu, Li Ctr for Bus & Professional Women, 1992; Woman of the Year, Zonta of Suffolk; Victims Info Bur Domestic Violence, Jr League of LI, 1996; Alumna Award, State Univ of NY, 1999; NY State Senate Woman of Distinction, 1999; June Teacher Award/Education, Hecksher Museum, 2001; Top 50 Women on Long Island, Long Island Bus News, 2002; State Univ of NY, Cuad Hall of Fame, inducted, 2003.

WILLIAMS, PAUL
Federal government official. **Personal:** Born Aug 6, 1929, Jacksonville, IL; son of Russell and Bernice Wheeler; married Ora Mosby; children: Reva. **Educ:** Ill Col, BA, 1956; Fed Exec Inst, 1971; Brookings Inst, 1975; Harvard Univ, Kennedy Sch Govt, 1980; Am Univ, cert, Exec Develop Sem, 1984; Pac Inst, cert, Facilitator Investment Excellence, 1988. **Career:** Government Official (retired); City Chicago, dir finance, 1956-63; Dept State, int admin officer, 1963-68; United Planning Orgn, assoc dir finance & admin, 1964; HUD, dir, Off Mgt Housing, FHA comnr, dir, 1968-90, Fair Housing, gen dep asst & secy, 1993-94, dep asst & secy, Mgt & Opportunity Fair Housing, 1994-96. **Orgs:** Treas, Housing & Urban Develop Chap Sr Exec Asn, 1989, pres, 1991-93. **Honors/Awds:** Citation for Outstanding Government Service, Md Govs, 1963-96; commendation, US Comn Pac, 1967; Nominee, Presidential Award for Outstanding Civilian Service, 1973; Certificate of Merit, 1974; Superior Service Award, Housing & Urban Develop, 1975; citation recipient, US Secy State; Distinguished Citizens Award, 1976, honorary degree, Ill Col, 1979; Outstanding Performance Rating 1982, 1983; Senior Executive Service Performance Award, 1983; Certificate of Special Achievement, Comm Fraud Waste & Mismanagement, 1984; Certificate of Special Achievement, 1984; Outstanding Performance Rating, 1993-96; Distinguished Service Award, Housing & Urban Develop Sec, 1996; ALFA. **Military Serv:** USY, 1948-52.

WILLIAMS, PAUL S
Lawyer, executive. **Personal:** Born Oct 9, 1959, San Francisco, CA; son of Dr Henry S and Frances S; married Laura Coleman Williams, Sep 15, 1984; children: Scott C & Ryan S. **Educ:** Harvard Col, AB, 1981; Yale Law Sch, JD, 1984. **Career:** Gibson, Dunn & Crutcher, assoc, 1984-87; Vorys, Sater, Sermour & Pease, assoc, 1987-90; Borden Inc, coun, 1990-94; Information Dimensions Inc, vpres, gen coun, 1994-95; Cardinal Health Inc, dep gen coun, 1995-97, vpres, deputy gen coun, 1997-99, sr vpres, dep gen coun, 1999-2001, exec vpres, chief legal officer & secy, 2001-. **Orgs:** OH Bar asn, 1987-; Columbus Bar asn, 1987-; Calif Bar asn, 1984-; Am Corp Counsel asn, 1996-; pres, bd trustees, The Columbus Acad, 2001-; dir, State Auto Financial Corp, 2003-; Leukemia and Lymphoma Soc; Cent Ohio Chapter Am Corp Counsel Asn; Aman Bar Asn Minority In house Counsel Group; Salesian Boys & Girls Club Columbus; Buckeye Ranch; Arthritis Found Cent Ohio. **Business Addr:** Executive vice president, chief legal officer & secretary for Cardinal, Cardinal Health Inc, 7000 Cardinal Pl, Dublin, OH 43017, **Business Phone:** (614)757-5000.

WILLIAMS, PAUL T
Lawyer. **Personal:** Born Mar 14, 1952, Trenton, NJ; son of Eloise and Paul D; married Ammie Felder, Feb 6, 1986; children: Marlowe, Paul III & Alexandra. **Educ:** Yale Univ, BA, 1974; Columbia Univ, Sch Law, JD, 1977. **Career:** Walker & Bailey, assoc, 1977-82; NY State Assembly, Banking Comt, coun, 1982-84; Barnes, Wood, Williams & Rafalsky, partner, 1984-86; Wood, Williams, Rafalsky & Harris, partner, 1986-95; One Hundred Black Men Inc, asst coun, secy, 1986-2000, pres, 2000; Williams & Harris, partner, 1995-98; Bryan Cave LLP, partner, 1998-2006; Toussaint Capital Partners LLC, pres, 2006-. **Orgs:** Metrop Black Bar Asn, 1986-; Sigma Pi Phi Fraternity, 1996-; Riverside Church, 1998-; Am Bar Asn, 1998-; Judiciary Comn, Asn Bar City NY, 1998-; interim bd mem, Hale House, 2000-; bd mem, City Park Dept Bd. **Honors/Awds:** Ford Foundation Trustee's Scholar to the American University in Cairo, 1972. **Special Achievements:** America's Top Black Lawyers in Black Enterprise Magazine, 2003. **Business Addr:** President, Bryan Cave LLP, 110 Wall St 2nd Fl, New York, NY 10005, **Business Phone:** (212)328-1800.

WILLIAMS, PAULETTE. See SHANGE, NTOZAKE.

WILLIAMS, PELHAM C
Executive. **Personal:** Married Mary Ellen; children: Tyrone C, Pelham L III & Pamela L. **Career:** Williams-Russell & Johnson Inc, chmn & chief exec officer, currently. **Orgs:** Metro Atlanta Chamber Com; Metro Atlanta Regional Leadership Found. **Special Achievements:** Listed as No 95 of 100 top industrial service companies, Black Enterprise, 1992. **Business Addr:** Chairman, Chief Executive Officer, Williams-Russell and Johnson Inc, 771 Spring St NW, Atlanta, GA 30308, **Business Phone:** (404)853-6800.*

WILLIAMS, PEYTON
School administrator. **Personal:** Born Apr 10, 1942, Cochran, GA; son of Peyton Williams and Georgia Reddick; married Sandra E Pryor; children: Rachelle Lenore & Tara Alyce. **Educ:** Ft Valley State Col, BS, 1964; Tuskegee Inst, MEd, 1968; Univ Ga, EDS, 1977; Ga State Univ, PhD, 1982. **Career:** Principal (retired); Central High Sch, Sylvania, GA, asst Prin, 1964-68, prin, 1968-69; State Schs & Spec Activities, Ga Dept Educ, assoc state supt, 1977-87; Cen Middle Sch, prin, 1970-77; Ga Dept Educ, staff, 1977-2002, assoc state supt, 1987-95, Georgia P-16 Initiative, co-facilitator, 1995. **Orgs:** Chmn, First Dist Prof Develop Comn; Ga Teacher Educ Coun, 1974-77; Ga Asn Educrs, Gov Task Force; secy, Ga Middle Sch Prins Asn, 1973; Adv Com Gov Conf Educ, 1977; bd dir, Screen-Jenkins Regional Libr, 1973-77; bd dir, Screven Co, Dept Family & Children Svcs; Citizens Adv Coun, Area 24 Mental Health, Mental Retardation; bd dir, CSRA Office Econ Opportunity, 1971-77; Bd dir, Screven Co C C, 1974; Screven-Sylvania Arts Coun; adv bd, Screven Co Asn for Retarded Children; Omega Psi Phi Fraternity; Selective Serv Local Bd 128; Policy Com CSRA OEO; scoutmaster, Boy Scout Troop 348; organist choir dir, St Paul Bapt Church; Nat Dropout Prevention Network, chmn exec bd, 1992-; pres, Asn Supervision & Curric Develop, 2002-03; Sigma Pi Phi Fraternity, Grand Grammateus, Exec Secy; pres & consult, Asn Supv & Curriculum Develop Int, 2002-. **Honors/Awds:** Educator of the Year, Screven-Sylvania Optimist Club, 1976; Distinguished Service Award, Screven Co, Bd Educ; Most Valuable Mem Trophy, Ga Coun Deliberation 32 Degree Masons PHA; Outstanding Service Award, Screven Co Chap, NAACP; Plaque Appreciation, Screven Co, Chap Am Cancer Soc; Meritorious Service Award, St Paul Bapt Ch; 'Administrator of the Year Award', Phi Delt Kappa, 1980; Governor's Award for outstanding service in state government, State Ga; Distinguished Service Award, Southern Asn Col & Sch. **Special Achievements:** Published the monograph, What It Means To Be A Professional Educator in 2001. **Business Addr:** Grand Grammateus/Executive Secretary, Sigma Pi Phi Fraternity of the Grand Boule, Philadelphia, PA.

WILLIAMS, PHILIP B.
Lawyer. **Personal:** Born Dec 30, 1922, Gonzales, TX; married Frances A. **Educ:** Roosevelt Univ, BSC, 1952; DePaul Univ, LLB, 1963, JD, 1969. **Career:** Chicago, clerk, 1947-52; IRS, collection officer & revenue agent, 1952-64; Serv Fed Savings & Loan Assocs, mgr, 1964-66; Self Employed Atty, 1966-. **Orgs:** Bd coun mem, Park Grove Real Estate Inc, 1967-; bd coun mem, Crestway Maint Corp, 1970-; mem, Cook County, Ill State & Am Bar Asn; Tech Asst Adv Bd; United Builders Asn Chicago; Comt Adv Coun; Chicago Baptist Inst. **Military Serv:** AUS, sgt, 1943-45. **Business Addr:** Lawyer, Private Practice, 445 E 87th St, Chicago, IL 60619-6003.

WILLIAMS, DR. PRESTON N
Educator, minister (clergy). **Personal:** Born May 23, 1926, Alcolu, SC; son of Anderson James and Bertha Bell McRae; married Constance Marie Willard; children: Mark Gordon & David Bruce. **Educ:** Washington & Jefferson Col, AB, 1947, MA, 1948; Johnson C Smith Univ, BD, 1950; Yale Univ Divinity Sch, STM, 1954; Harvard Univ, PhD, 1967. **Career:** Pa State Univ, asst chaplain, 1956-61; Boston Univ Sch Theol, prof, 1970-71; Christian Century Mag, ed at large, 1972-; Harvard Divinity Sch, acting dean, 1974-75, Harvard's WEB Du Bois Inst, acting dir, 1975-77; Summer Leadership Inst, dir, 1998-; Nagoya Univ Japan, guest prof & speaker, 1996; Houghton, prof theol & contemporary change, 1971-2002. **Orgs:** WEB DuBois Inst, 1975-77; Am Acad Relig, 1975-; Am Soc Christian Ethics, 1974-75; Phi Beta Kappa. **Honors/Awds:** Harvard Foundation Medal, 1994; W E B Du Bois Medal, 2000; Harvard University established the Preston N Williams Black Alumni/ae Award in his honor. **Special Achievements:** Author: "An African American Perspective on the Nature and Criteria of Theological Scholarship." Theological Education, Vol. 32 (Autumn 1995): 71-78. **Business Addr:** Houghton Research Professor of Theology & Contemporary Change, Harvard Divinity School, 45 Francis Ave, Cambridge, MA 02138, **Business Phone:** (617)495-5766.

WILLIAMS, RALEIGH R.
Real estate agent, football coach. **Personal:** Married Vernell Johnson; children: Rudolph, Karen, Kevin & Kenneth. **Educ:**

Univ Omaha, econ. **Career:** Real Estate Agent (retired); R R W Reality Construct & Income Tax Serv, rebroker, income tax consult, gen contractor & mgt consult. **Orgs:** Pres, Dulleton Ctr NAACP; Boy Scout Master; Am Inst Indust Eng; pres, Young Men Bus Assoc; tres, OEO; NCO Qtr. **Honors/Awds:** Spec Recognition, NAACP Chap. **Special Achievements:** Baseball Champion, Colo Springs, 1965; mgr, Little League Baseball; coach, Little League Football. **Military Serv:** USAF 1952-72; Perrin AFB, 1967. *

WILLIAMS, RALPH O
Executive, chief executive officer, chairperson. **Career:** ROW Sci Inc, founder, chmn & chief exec officer, 1992-98. **Honors/Awds:** Minority Contractor of the Year Award, 1994.

WILLIAMS, RANDOLPH
Lawyer. **Personal:** Born Mar 29, 1944, Montgomery, AL; children: Randall. **Educ:** Bowie State Col, BA, 1969; Georgetown Univ Law Sch, JD, 1973. **Career:** City Philadelphia, Dist Atty's Off, asst dist atty, 1977-. **Orgs:** Nat Conf Black Laywers, Nat Bar Asn, Am Bar Asn, Nat Dist Atty Asn; PA Bar Asn; Dist Columbia Bar Asn. **Military Serv:** USAF, airman, 1st class, 1962-65. **Business Addr:** Assistant District Attorney, City Philadelphia, District Attorney's Office, Library 5th Fl 1421 Arch St, Philadelphia, PA 19102-1507, **Business Phone:** (215)686-8000.*

WILLIAMS, RASHEDA
Public relations executive. **Career:** Kumon North America Inc, Midwest Public Relations Coordr, currently. **Business Addr:** Midwest Public Relations Coordinator, Kumon North America Inc, 300 Frank W Burr Blvd 5th Fl, Teaneck, NJ 07666, **Business Phone:** (248)290-0450 ext 233.

WILLIAMS, REGGIE
Basketball player, basketball executive. **Personal:** Born Mar 5, 1964, Baltimore, MD; married Kathy; children: 5. **Educ:** Georgetown Univ, Wash, DC, attended 1997. **Career:** Basketball player (retired), basketball executive; Los Angeles Clippers, forward, 1987-90; Cleveland Cavaliers, forward, 1989-90; San Antonio Spurs, forward, 1990-91; Denver Nuggets, forward, 1991-96; Ind Pacers, forward, 1996; NJ Nets, forward, 1996; Jericho Christian Acad, boys basketball prog, head coach, currently. **Orgs:** Nat Basketball Asn. **Special Achievements:** NBA Draft, 1987.

WILLIAMS, REGINA VLOYN-KINCHEN
Government official. **Personal:** Born Nov 15, 1947, Detroit, MI; daughter of Nathaniel Kinchen (both deceased) and Mary Lee; married Drew B; children: Traci A, Kristin L & Drew Michael. **Educ:** Eastern Mich Univ, BS 1971; Virginia Commonwealth Univ, MPA 1987. **Career:** City Ypsilanti, dir personnel & labor rels, 1972-79; City Richmond, dir personnel, 1979-82; Commonwealth VA, state dir personnel & training,1982-85; J Sargeant Reynolds Comm Col, adj prof, 1982-; City Richmond, VA,asst city mgr, 1985-89; Nat Fire Training Acad, adj fac, 1989-; City SanJose, San Jose, CA, asst city Mgr, 1989-94, city mgr, 1994-99; San Jose State Univ, San Jose, CA, adj fac, 1991; City Norfolk, city mgr, 1999-. **Orgs:** Former pres, Nat Forum for Black Pub Adminrs; former vpres, Int City Mgt Asn; co-founder, Nat Acad Pub Admin; past pres, Richmond Chap Conf Minority Pub Adminrs; workshop leader, guest lectr, Nat prof confs; Alpha Kappa Alpha Sor Inc; founding mem & vpres South Bay Chap 100 Black Women. **Honors/Awds:** Contributor to Virginia Govt textbook "By the Good People of Virginia", byC Fleming; Serwa Award, Virginia Chap, Nat Coalition of 100 Black Women,1989; Public Service Award, Mercury Newspaper & Women's Fund, 1994. **Special Achievements:** First African American to hold San Joses city manager. **Business Addr:** City Manager, City of Norfolk, 810 Union St 1101 City Hall Bldg, Norfolk, VA 23510, **Business Phone:** (757)664-4242.

WILLIAMS, REGINALD CLARK
Government official, clergy. **Personal:** Born Aug 22, 1950, DeLand, FL; son of Geraldine L Merrick; married Ella Mae Ashford; children: Deirdre LaFay, Andre Terrell. **Educ:** Seminole Jr Col, AA Gen Studies, 1977; Univ Cent Fl, BS, Bus Admin, 1980. **Career:** East Central FL Reg Planning Co, res analyst, 1971-77; Volusia County, Volusia Planning Dept, program coordr, 1977-80, community develop admin asst, 1980-81, acting dir, 1985-86, community develop, dir, 1981-86, community serv dir, 1986-. **Orgs:** Coach West Volusia Pop Warner Football Asn, 1976-84; Nat Assoc Housing & Redevelop Off, 1977-; sponsor Electrifying Gents, 1982-84; bd mem, FL Community Develop Asn, 1983-, chair, 1987, Community Housing Res Bd, 1984-88; nat Forum Black Pub Adminr, chmn, West Volusia Martin Luther King Planning Comt; bd mem, chair Alcohol, Drug Mental Health Planning Coun, 1992; Stewart Treatment Ctr Adv Bd; deacon, Mt Calvary Free Will Baptist Church, 1988-92, minister, 1992-. **Honors/Awds:** Certificate Recognition, West Volusia YMCA, 1981; Certificate Appreciation, Youth St Annis Prim Baptist Church, 1982; Certificate Appreciation, Electra Lytes Charity Club, 1983; Coach of Year, West Volusia Pop Warner Parents Asn, 1983; Certificate Recognition, Electra Lyles Charity Club, 1985; Recognition, Volusia County Constituency Children, 1988, Certificate Appreciation. United Way, 1990, Certificate Appreciation, Cocaine Babies Junior Service League, 1989, Community Service Award, Stewart Treatment Ctr, 1990. **Business Addr:** Director, Volusia County, Department Community Service, 123 W Indiana Ave, DeLand, FL 32720-4611, **Business Phone:** (904)736-5955.*

WILLIAMS, REGINALD T.
Executive, president (organization), chief executive officer. **Personal:** Born May 14, 1945, Newark, NJ; married Dorothy; children: Remington & Sunshine. **Educ:** Essex City Col, AAS, 1970; Rutgers Univ, NB, BA, 1972; Temple Univ Philadelphia, MA, 1975. **Career:** Essex City Urban League, dir econ develop & employ, 1969-72; City Newark, NJ, dir consumer affairs, 1970-72; Bucks County Community Action Agency,asst exec dir, 1973-74; Various Corps & US Govt, consult minority affairs, various corps, 1973-; United Way Cent, MD, dir affirmative action, 1976-79; Urban League Lancaster City, PA, exec dir; Procurement Resources Inc, chief exec officer & pres, currently. **Orgs:** Secy, Eastern Reg Coun Urban League; dept host, Eve Mag WJZ-TV Baltimore. **Honors/Awds:** Consumer Protection Award, US Fed Trade Comm, 1971; Human Relations Award, Howard County, MD, 1976; Outstanding Young Columbian Award, Columbia Jaycees, 1979. **Special Achievements:** Author: 2nd Tier Minority Purchasing: Effective Strategies in Supplier Diversity; A Buyers Guide To Doing Business With Minority Vendors; appearson natl TV; quoted in the media as an acknowledged expert in the discipline. **Business Phone:** (678)423-0447.

WILLIAMS, RICHARD LEE
Public relations executive. **Personal:** Born Sep 11, 1959, Edenton, NC; son of Luther L Williams, Sr and Annie M. **Educ:** NC A&T State Univ, BS, 1984; Wake Forest Univ, MBA, 1998. **Career:** Raleigh Times, reporter, 1984-87; Gannett Suburban Newspapers, asst city ed, 1987-92; Winston-Salem Chronicle, exec ed, 1993-94; RJ Reynolds Tobacco Co, pub rels rep, 1994-. **Orgs:** Steering comm chmn, 1996, vice chmn, 1996-, chmn, 1998-01, Winston-Salem Urban League, 1996-, vice chmn, Best Choice Ctr, mkt & pub rels comm chmn, 1996-; Piedmont Opera, former bd mem, 1993; Piedmont Jazz Festival, chmn, 2000-. **Honors/Awds:** Merit Award, Nat Newspapers Publ Asn, 1994. **Home Addr:** 1676 Quillmark Rd, Winston-Salem, NC 27127. **Business Addr:** Public Relations Representative, RJ Reynolds Tobacco Co., 3872 Reynolds Rd, Winston-Salem, NC 27106, **Business Phone:** (336)741-0672.

WILLIAMS, DR. RICHARD LENWOOD
Dentist. **Personal:** Born Mar 11, 1931, Schenectady, NY; married Martha E; children: Brian Lenwood, Kevin Allyn, Darren Wayne & Lori Elaine. **Educ:** Fisk Univ, BA, 1953; Howard Univ, DDS, 1957. **Career:** Queens Gen Hosp, 1958-73; Self Employed Dent, 1977. **Orgs:** Clinical Soc Queens; Alpha Phi Alpha; Les Amis of Queens. **Business Addr:** Dentist, 12027 Guy R Brewer Blvd, Jamaica, NY 11434, **Business Phone:** (718)276-4644.*

WILLIAMS, RICKY, JR.
Football player. **Personal:** Born May 21, 1977, San Diego, CA; son of Sandy; married; children: Marley, Asha & Prince. **Educ:** Univ Tex, attended 1999. **Career:** New Orleans Saints, running back, 1999-2001; Miami Dolphins, running back, 2002-03 & 2005-. **Honors/Awds:** Doak Walker Award, 1997-98; Heisman Trophy, 1998; Maxwell Award, 1998; Walter Camp Award, 1998; Player of the Year Award, Walter Camp Found; National Player of the Year Award, Assoc Press; Offensive Player of the Year, Football News; Player of the Year Award, The Sporting News; Pro Bowls, 2002. **Business Addr:** Running Back, Miami Dolphins, 2269 Dan Marino Blvd, Miami Gardens, FL 33314, **Business Phone:** (305)626-7323.

WILLIAMS, RITA
Basketball player. **Personal:** Born Jan 14, 1976. **Educ:** Univ Conn, attented, 1998. **Career:** Wash Mystics, guard, 1998-99, 2007-; Ind Fever, guard, 2000-02; Houston Comets, 2002; Seattle Storm, guard, 2003-04; Charlotte Sting, guard, 2004;Chicago Sky, guard. **Honors/Awds:** Big E Championship, Most Outstanding Player, 1998. *

WILLIAMS, ROBERT B.
Lawyer. **Personal:** Born Aug 10, 1943, Washington, DC; married. **Educ:** Univ Md, BA, 1966, Sch Law, JD, 1972. **Career:** Self-employed, pvt pract, atty, currently. **Orgs:** Howard City Bar Asn; Am Bar Asn; pres, Ellicott City Rotary Club MD; Sigma Phi Epsilon; Baltimore Rubgy Football Club. **Honors/Awds:** Dean's list, Univ Md. **Military Serv:** USY, spec 4, 1967-69; Army Commendation Medal. **Business Addr:** Attorney, 8386 Court Ave, Ellicott City, MD 21043-4595.*

WILLIAMS, ROBERT H.
Physician, educator. **Personal:** Born Dec 1, 1938, Washington, DC; married Judy R. **Educ:** Howard Univ, BS, 1959, MS, 1960; Howard Univ Col Med, MD, 1964; Am Bd Family Pract, cert. **Career:** Howard Univ Col Med, Family Pract, asst prof; Comm Group Health Found Inc, med dir; Walter Reed Army Hosp & Med Officer, intern & resident, 1965-67; DeWitt Army & Hosp, chief med clinics, 1968-69, 15th inf div vietnam, med officer, 1967-68; Howard Univ Hosp, resident, 1969-73, physician, currently; Harvard Col med, fel, 1970-71; physician pvt pract, currently. **Orgs:** Nat Med Asn; Med Soc of DC; chmn, Family Pract Scientific Prog; Nat Med Asn, 1971. **Honors/Awds:** Milton K Francis Scholar Award, 1961; bronze star Army Commendation Medal, 1968; combat medic badge, 1968. **Military Serv:** AUSMC, capt/major, 1964-69.

WILLIAMS, ROBERT L
Government official. **Educ:** Jackson State Univ. **Career:** Jackson Metrop Crime Comn, community coordr; Jackson, MS, councilman; Jackson City, asst mayor, currently. **Special Achievements:** Youngest councilmember ever elected in Jackson, MS. **Business Phone:** (601)960-1084.*

WILLIAMS, DR. ROBERT L
Educator. **Personal:** Born Feb 20, 1930, Biscoe, AR; married Ava L; children: Robbie, Julius, Yvonne, Larry, Reva, Dorothy & Robert A Michael. **Educ:** Philadner Smith Col, BA, 1953; Wayne State Univ, Med, 1955; Wash Univ, PhD, 1961. **Career:** Ariz State Hosp, asst psychologist, 1955-57; Va Hosp, psychol trainee, 1957-61, St Louis asst chief psychol serv, 1961-66; Spokane WA, exec dir hosp improve, 1966-68; NIMH, 9th region ment health consult psychol, 1968-69; Va Hosp, chief psychol serv, 1969-70; Wash Univ, assoc prof psychol, 1969-70, prof psychol, dir black studies prog, 1970-74; Robert L Williams Assoc Inc, founder, pres, 1973-; Wash Univ, prof psychol, prof emer, psychol, currently. **Orgs:** Bds & comms, NIMH, 1970-72; nat chmn, Assoc Black Psychologists; Am Personel & Guidance Asn; chmn bd dir, Inst Black Studies Inc Cognitive Styles Black People, Identity Issues, Personality Develop Black People; dir, Comprehensive Treatment Unit & Psychol Consult, Lindell Hosp, St Louis, MO. **Honors/Awds:** Citizen of the Year, 8th Dist Meeting KC, Mo, 1983; Yes I Can Award, 1984. **Special Achievements:** Author: The Collective Black Mind: Toward An Afro-Centric Theory of Black Personality. **Business Addr:** Professor Emeritus, Washington University, Department of Psychology, PO Box 1125, St Louis, MO 63130-4899, **Business Phone:** (314)935-0000.

WILLIAMS, ROBERT LEE
School administrator. **Personal:** Born Jul 19, 1933, Lorman, MS; married Wilma McGee; children: Schelia, Robert, Philvester, Dennis & Meshell. **Career:** Sch adminr (retired). Bd Educ, Jefferson County Public Sch, Fayette, Miss, 1966-90. **Honors/Awds:** NAACP Award, 1969; hon citizen Kenner, La, 1969; Miss State Conv, NAACP, 1969. **Home Addr:** Rodney Rd Rt 2, PO Box 132, Lorman, MS 39096. *

WILLIAMS, ROBERT LEE
School administrator, educator. **Personal:** Born Jun 3, 1936, Shreveport, KY; son of M C and Thelma; married Dorothy Young; children: Janis, Jennifer, Ginetta & Tara. **Educ:** Grambling State Univ, BS, 1959; Xavier Univ, 1960; LA Tech Ruston, 1970; Southern Univ Baton Rouge, MS, 1970. **Career:** Pvt Employment Agency, owner, 1964; Southern Univ Shreveport, teacher, 1967-, dir, 1978, chmn speech dept, 1979, dir evening div, assoc prof eng, currently; Prod Co, staff, 1968. **Orgs:** Dixie Janitorial Serv, 1970-85; Restaurant, 1972; bd mem, Caddo Par School Bd, 1975-84; bd dir, Caddo Community Action Agency, 1975-84. **Honors/Awds:** Grant in cont ed Southern Univ New Orleans, 1972; Received approx 50 awards. **Home Addr:** 1538 Martha Ave, Shreveport, LA 71101. **Business Addr:** Associate Professor of English, Southern University, Rm A-60 L C Barnes Admin Bldg 3050 Martin Luther King Jr Dr, Shreveport, LA 71107, **Business Phone:** (318)674-3363.

WILLIAMS, ROBY S
President (Organization), association executive. **Career:** Black Bus Asn Memphis, Tenn, pres & ceo, currently. **Business Addr:** President, Chief Executive Officer, Black Bus Asn Memphis, 555 Beale St, Memphis, TN 38103, **Business Phone:** (901)526-9300.

WILLIAMS, RODNEY ELLIOTT
Police chief, government official. **Personal:** Born Nov 14, 1928, San Francisco, CA; son of Nelson and Ruby; married Joyce Gray; children: Rodney II, Brian & Vivian. **Educ:** San Francisco City Col, AA, 1956; San Francisco State Univ, BA, 1972; Golden Gate Univ, MA, 1973. **Career:** Police chief (retired); San Francisco Police Dept, dir, 1969-77; City & County San Francisco, insp police, 1983; Peralta Community Col Dist, chief police, 1983-88; 9th Circuit United States Ct Appeals, special dep US marshal. **Orgs:** Bd dir, Westside Ment Health, 1971-75; Reality House W, 1972-76; bd dir, Comn Streetwork Ctr, 1972-76; guest lecturer, Golden Gate Univ, 1973; Life teaching credential State Calif Comm Col Dist Pub Admin. **Honors/Awds:** Cert Hon, Bd Supvr 1968; Liberty Bell Award, SF Bar Asn, 1974; commendation, Calif State Assembly, 1983; commendation, Calif State Senate, 1983. **Military Serv:** AUS, 1951-53. *

WILLIAMS, ROGER L
Automotive executive. **Career:** Southwest Ford Sales Inc, chief exec officer. **Special Achievements:** Co is ranked No 68 on Black Enterprise's list of top 100 auto dealers, 1994.

WILLIAMS, ROLAND LAMAR
Football player. **Personal:** Born Apr 27, 1975, Rochester, NY. **Educ:** Syracuse Univ, BS, speech commun. **Career:** Football

player(retired); St Louis Rams, tight end, 1998-2000; Oakland Raiders, 2001-02; Tampa Bay Buccaneers, 2003; Oakland Raiders, 2004; Atlanta Falcons, 2005; Studio Analyst, Col Football Versus, currently. **Orgs:** Founder, Roland Williams Youth Lifeline Found. **Honors/Awds:** Offensive Rookie of the Year, St Louis Rams, 1998; Walter Payton NFL Man of the Year Award; Oakland Raiders Man of the Year Award. **Business Addr:** Founder, Youth Lifeline Foundation, 6 McBride & Sons Dr Suite 103, Chesterfield, MO 63005, **Business Phone:** (636)536-7770.

WILLIAMS, RONALD
Mayor. **Career:** Tuskegee Inst High Sch, prin; former aide; City Tuskegee, mayor. **Orgs:** Greenwood Bapt Church; Nat Bus League; Elks, Optimist Int; Masons; Shriners; Alpha Phi Alpha Fraternity; Bd Trustees, Tuskegee Univ, 1996-2002. **Honors/Awds:** InterNat Service Award, Optimist Club; Service Award, Tiger Cubs Pack 170; Distinguished Serv Award, Tuskegee Inst Middle Sch.

WILLIAMS, RONALD CHARLES
Lawyer. **Personal:** Born Jun 19, 1948, Corsicana, TX; divorced; children: Steven & Anita. **Educ:** Colo Sch Mines, BS, 1971; Univ Utah, MBA, 1978; Univ Colo, JD, 1979. **Career:** US Dept Interior, patent coun, 1979-82; Storage Tech Corp, corp & patent coun, 1982-85; Williams Mgt Group Inc, pvt pract, atty, currently. **Orgs:** Pres, Tapestry Films Inc; bd dirs, Cadric Drug Rehab Orgn. **Military Serv:** AUS, capt, 4 1/2 yrs. **Business Phone:** (303)295-0521.

WILLIAMS, RONALD LEE
Government official. **Personal:** Born Aug 31, 1949, Washington, DC; married Fern M; children: Ron Williams II, Nateshia & Natiia M. **Educ:** Univ DC, attended 1977. **Career:** Shaw UM Food & Clothing Bank, vice chmn, 1981-; SE Vicarate Cluster Churches, chmn bd, 1984-85; Adv Neighborhood Comn, chairperson, 1984-; Camp Simms Citizen Adv Task Force, chmn, 1984-; Christian Social Concerns, dir. **Orgs:** Mil personnel tech secy, Army Discharge Review Bd, 1973-; bd mem, Concerned Citizens Alcohol/Drug Abuse, 1982-, Comt Action Involvement, 1983-; United Way, 1983; UBF, 1983-; chairperson, Hands Across Community, United Methodist Church, 1990-93; coordr, Summer Tent Ministry, 1990-92; exec dir, Black Community Developer Prog Inc. **Honors/Awds:** Letters of Appreciation, Commendations & Plaques, Community Orgn, Mayor, City Coun, 1980. **Military Serv:** AUS, 124th Signal Battalion, 3 yrs. **Business Addr:** Director, Church & Soc Christians for Social Concerns, 2525 12th Pl SE, Washington, DC 20020.

WILLIAMS, RONALD WESLEY
Computer executive, manager. **Personal:** Born Nov 16, 1946, Chicago, IL; son of Richard G and Odessa Shelton; divorced; children: Donna & Michele. **Educ:** Chapman Col, BA, 1974. **Career:** United Airlines, asst vpres, 1976-79, passenger serv mgr, 1979-80, city mgr, 1980-83, customer serv mgr, 1983-84, gen mgr customer serv; Hewlett-Packard Co, dist mgr, Software Support mgr, currently. **Orgs:** Treas N Merced Calif Rotary Club, 1974; Skal Club, 1976; vpres, Lions Club, 1979; Toledo Sales & Mkt, 1980; bd mem, WGTE TV Comm Adv Bd, 1980; comt mem, Bowling Green Univ, Aerotech Adv Comm, 1980; vol, United Way Corp Rep, 1981; Madison, WI, Pub Safety Review Bd, 1989-; bd dir, Wexford Village Home Owners Asn, 1989-. **Honors/Awds:** Award of Merit, United Airlines, 1988. **Special Achievements:** private pilot, 1976-. **Military Serv:** Ill Army Nat Guard, 1966-67.

WILLIAMS, ROSA B.
Public relations executive, association executive. **Personal:** Born Sep 29, 1933, Starke, FL. **Educ:** Santa Fe Community Col, AA, 1976. **Career:** Community Action Agency, super Outreach workers, 1965-70; Bell Nursery, supervising cook, 1965-70; Community Action Agency, super, 1971-72; Alachua Co Coordr Child Care, eligibility worker, 1972; Sunland Ctr Dept of HRS, activities coordr, 1983; Rosa B Williams Community Ctr, owner. **Orgs:** chmn, Concerned Citizen Juvenile Justice; League Women Voters; chmn, Alachua Co Democratic Club; Alachua Co Democratic Exec Comt; chmn, Debonaire Social Club; bd dirs, Shands Hosp; chmn bd dirs, United Gainesville Community Develop Corp; Comn Status Women; Sickle Cell Orgn Alachua Co; Alachua Co Girls Club Am; NW 5th Ave Neighborhood Crime Prev Prog; adv coun Displaced Homemaker Prog; 1st vice chmn Alachua Co NAACP; dir United Way; Alachua Co Coordr Child Care; Alachua Co Econ Develop; Community Policy Adv Comt; chairperson, Black on Black Task Force. **Honors/Awds:** Recognition Contribution Cult Arts Coalition; Gainesville Sun's 6th Most Influential Citizen Recognition; Community Serv Award, NAACP, 1968; Very Important Citizen Recognition, City Gainesville, 1974; Leadership & Achievement Award, Alpha Phi Alpha Frat, 1974; dir, United Way, 1968-71, 1975-80; Outstanding Serv to Community Award, Gainesville Rev Issues & Trends, 1978; Community Serv Award, Alpha Phi Alpha, 1979; Distinguished Serv to the Comm in Field of Educ Lodge 1218 IBPOE Elks, 1983; Distinguished Serv Award, Alachua Co Educ Asn, 1983; Citizen Against Criminal Environ Gainesville Police Dept, 1984; Springhill Baptist Church contribution to Black Community, 1984. **Business Addr:** Owner, Rosa B Williams Community Center, 524 NW 1st St, Gainesville, FL 32602, **Business Phone:** (352)334-2193.

WILLIAMS, ROY LEVY
Public relations executive. **Personal:** Married Patricia Ryder Williams, 1961; children: Marc, Lauren. **Educ:** Wayne State University, Master of Urban Planning. **Career:** Daimler-Chrysler, Manager of Community Relations, 1984;. **Orgs:** President and CEO, Detroit Urban League; Chairman, Michigan State Housing Development Authority; Board Member, Detroit City Planning Commission; Member, Steering Committee of Detroit Neighborhood Housing Services; National Board Member, NAACP; VP, Highland Park Chamber of Commerce; EVP, HR Devco. **Honors/Awds:** National Jewish Labor Committee's Human Rights Award, 1995; WWJ Radio Station's Citizen of the Week. *

WILLIAMS, RUBY MAI
Association executive. **Personal:** Born Aug 30, 1904, Topeka, KS; married Melvin. **Educ:** Kans State Teachers Col, teaching credential, 1931. **Career:** Real estate sales; Calif State Employ, coun & placement, 1932-36; Golden State Life Ins Co, cashier & clerk, 1936-43; Nat Youth Work Comt, 1962-69; Pasadena NAACP, 1966. **Orgs:** Pres, Pasadena Dem Womens Club, 1967-68; pres, Interracial Womens Club, 1969-70; org & pres, NW Citizens of Pasadena, 1978; chmn, Pasadena Recreation Comn, 1971-72; adv Comt, Citizens Urban Renewal, Pasadena 1977; mayors comt, Pasadena City, 1979-; adv comt, Kid Space Mus C, 1979-. **Honors/Awds:** Citizen of Year, Pasadena Human Rels, 1975; listed in Pasadena 100 Yrs of History 1975; Woman of Year, Knights Pythians, Los Angeles, CA, 1976; Citizens Award, PTA, 1977; YWCA Woman of Year, Pasadena YWCA, 1977; Youth Work Award, Nat Youth Work Com NY 1977. **Special Achievements:** First Black Kindergarten Teacher Topeka.

WILLIAMS, RUDY V.
School administrator, vice president (organization). **Personal:** Born in Waxahachie, TX; married Ora Ruth Pitts; children: Keith W, Derwin B, Cedric L & Risha V. **Educ:** Huston-Tillotson Col Austin Tex, Bus Admin; Univ AZ Tucson, MEd, 1964; Fla Atlantic Univ, Boca Raton FL, edS, 1975. **Career:** Miami-Dade Community Col, assoc dean, 1970-, admin asst, 1969-70; Comm Action Agency EOPI Miami FL, prog admin, 1966-69; Sears Roebuck & Co, salesman, 1967-69; Tucson Pub Sch, teacher, 1963-66; Bur Indian Affairs, prin teacher, 1956-63; Southern Asn Col & Sch, consult, 1972-; Fla Int Univ Miami, adj prof, 1975-. **Orgs:** Phi Beta Sigma Frat, 1952-; vpres, St Albans Day Nursery, 1970-; Phi Delta Kappa, 1972-. **Honors/Awds:** Unemployment Waste Away, FL, Voc Jour, 1978; "FL Comm Col Occupational Deans & Dir Competencies" un pub, 1979; "Viable Guidance for the Minority Student" Minority Educ, 1979. **Military Serv:** AUS, sgt, 1954-56.

WILLIAMS, RUSSELL, II
Television producer, music producer. **Personal:** Born Oct 14, 1952, Washington, DC; children (previous marriage): Myles Candace & Khemet Ellison; married Rosalind. **Educ:** The Am Univ, BA, film prod & lit, 1974; Univ Sound Arts, electronics cert,1979. **Career:** WRC/NBC-TV, audio engr, 1973-75, 1977-78; WMAL-TV, audio engr, 1975-76; Sound Is Ready, motion picture sound rec owner; Intersound Studios, studioengr, 1981; Univ Calif, Sch Radio, TV, Film, assoc prof, 1990; Am Univ, Columbia Univ, Howard Univ, UCLA & others, masters class lectr, 1990-; Univ Southern Calif, assoc prof, 1995; Am Univ, artist-in-residence, 2002; sound & sound mixer, currently; Films: Valley Girl, boom operator, 1983; Making the Grade, 1984; Doctor Duck's Super Secret All-Purpose Sauce,1986; Good to Go, 1986; Invaders from Mars, 1986; Number One with a Bullet, 1987; In the Mood, 1987; The In Crowd, 1988; Field of Dreams,1989; Glory, 1989; A Gnome Named Gnorm, 1990; Dances with Wolves, 1990; True Identity, 1991; Jungle Fever, 1991; Boomerang, 1992; Mo' Money, 1992; The Distinguished Gentleman, 1992; Drop Zone, 1994; It's Pat, 1994; The Brady Bunch Movie, 1995; How to Make an American Quilt, 1995; Waiting to Exhale, 1995; B.A.P.S, 1997; The Dinner, 1997; The Players Club, 1998; The Negotiator, 1998; Life, 1999; Rules of Engagement, 2000; Training Day, 2001; Kingdom Come, 2001; Golden Dreams, 2001; The Sum of All Fears, 2002; Martin Lawrence Live: Run teldat, 2002; Deliver Us from Eva, 2003; Incident at Loch Ness, 2004; Funeral for a Friend, 2007; Festivale, 2007; TV series: Television Parts Home Companion, 1985; "Sledge Hammer!", 1986;Billionaire Boys Club, 1987; Terrorist on Trial: The United States vs.Salim Ajami, 1988; Inherit the Wind, 1988; The Women of Brewster Place,1989; Heat Wave, 1990; Percy & Thunder, 1993; "The Parent 'Hood", 1995; "Moesha", 1996; Run for the Dream: The Gail Devers Story, 1996; 12 Angry Men, 1997; The Temptations, 1998; Little Richard, 2000; Rules of Engagement, 2000; The American Experience, 2006. **Orgs:** Acad Motion Picture Arts & Sci Sound Br; Acad TV Arts & Sci Sound Br; Alliance Black Entertainment Technicians; Int Alliance Theatrical Stage Employes, Local 695. **Honors/Awds:** Two Emmy Awards, 1988; Oscar Award, 1990 & 1991. **Business Addr:** Sound Recordist, c/o William Morris Agency LLC, 1 William Morris Pl, Beverly Hills, CA 90212, **Business Phone:** (310)859-4000.

WILLIAMS, S. ROBERT
Football player. **Personal:** Born May 29, 1977, Shelby, NC. **Educ:** NC Univ. **Career:** Football player (retired); Kansas City Chiefs, defensive back, 1998; Seattle Seahawks, defensive back, 1999.

WILLIAMS, SAMM-ART (SAMUEL ARTHUR WILLIAMS)
Playwright, actor, administrator. **Personal:** Born Jan 20, 1946, Burgaw, NC; son of Samuel and Valdosia. **Educ:** Morgan State Col, BA, polit sci & psychol, 1968. **Career:** Plarwright; Freedom Theatre, co mem, 1968-73; Negro Ensemble Co, 1973-78; Theater appearances: Nowhere to Run, Nowhere to Hide, 1974; Liberty Call, 1975; Waiting for Mongo, 1975; The First Breeze of Summer, 1975; Mark's Playhouse, 1975; Eden, 1976; The Brownsville Raid, 1976-77; Night Shift, 1977; Black Body Blues, 1978; Nevis Mountain Dew, 1978-79; Old Phantoms, 1979; Home, 1982-83; Films: The Wanderers, 1979; Dressed to Kill, 1980; Night of the Juggler, 1980; The Color of Friendship, 1981; Blood Simple, 1984; Hot Resort, 1985; A Rage in Harlem, 1991; TV appearances: "227", 1987; "Frank's Place," story ed &actor, 1987; "A Rage in Harlem", 1991; "All My Children"; "Search for Tomorrow"; "Mike Hammer"; writings: "Welcome to Black River," 1975; "The Coming," 1976; "Do Unto Ots," 1976; "A Love Play," 1976; "The Last Caravan", 1977; "Brass Birds Don't Sing", 1978; "Home", 1979-80;"Sophisticated Ladies", contribr, 1981; "Friends", 1983; "Eyes of the American", 1985; "Cork", 1986; "Fresh Prince of Bel-Air", writer &producer, 1990; "Marting", 1997; "The Good News", 1997; Writings Stage: Welcome to Black River, Season-Within-a-Season,1975; The Coming and Do Unto Others, 1976; The Last Caravan, 1977; Brass Birds Don't Sing, 1978; Home, 1979; The Sixteenth Round, 1980; Friends, 1983; Eyes of the American, 1985; "Eve of the Trial" in Orchards, 1986; Cork, 1986. **Orgs:** Omega Psi Phi Frat, 1967-; Screen Actors Guild; Writers Guild Am; Dramatists Guild. **Honors/Awds:** John Gassner Playwriting Award, Home, Outer Critics Circle, 1980; AudelcoRecognition Award, Home, 1980; North Carolina Governor's Award, 1981;Outstanding Writing in a Variety or Music Program, 1985. **Special Achievements:** Antoinette Perry Award, nomination, Best Play, Home, 1980; Tony Awardnomination, Home, 1980. **Business Phone:** (212)586-5100.*

WILLIAMS, SAMUEL ARTHUR. **See WILLIAMS, SAMM-ART.**

WILLIAMS, SANDRA K.
Lawyer. **Personal:** Born Mar 17, 1954, Houston, TX; daughter of Joe and Claretha Bradley; children: Katherine A. **Educ:** Smith Col, Northampton, MA, AB, 1975; Univ Mich, Ann Arbor, MI, JD, 1978. **Career:** Nat Labor Rels Bd, Wash, DC, staff atty, 1978-81, Los Angeles, CA, field atty, 1981-82; CBS Broadcasting Inc, Los Angeles, CA, labor atty, 1982-89, broadcast coun, 1989-90, dep w coast coun, 1990-95, asst gen coun, 1995-99, vpres sr corp coun, 1999-. **Orgs:** Tex State Bar Asn, 1974-; Wash State Bar Asn; DC State Bar Asn; Calif State Bar Asn; La County Bar Asn, 1983-; Black Women Lawyers Asn Los Angeles, 1985-; Calif Asn Black Lawyers, 1986-. **Business Addr:** Vice President, Senior Corporate Counsel, CBS Broadcasting Inc, CBS Television City, 51 W 52nd St, New York, NY 10019.*

WILLIAMS, SANDRA ROBERTS
Educator. **Personal:** Born Nov 2, 1940, Houston, TX; daughter of Brownie and Thelma; children: David & Michele. **Educ:** Texas Southern Univ, Houston, BM, Educ, 1961; Univ New Mexico, Albuquerque, MA, 1980. **Career:** Houston Independent Sch, music & classroom teacher, 1962-64; Albuquerque Public Schs, classroom teacher, 1964-70; Univ New Mexico, acad adv & counr, 1973-81; Univ Texas, Med Br, prog coord, 1982-, dir recruitment, currently. **Orgs:** Consult, Saturday Biomed Sci Forum; Nat Asn Med Minority Educ; Sci Inc; Sch Health Progs, adv Comt; Delta Sigma Theta Inc; Galveston Alumni; Nat Tech Asn. **Special Achievements:** Publications: "Medical School Familiarization Program, Health Careers Network," Vol III, No 2, November, 1983; "Academic Support Services presents, Learning Strategies Workshop, Featuring Test Taking and Reading Skills," w/JE Spurlin, UTMB Publication, March, 1983. **Business Addr:** Director of Recruitment, Coordinator, University of Texas Medical Branch, One Univ Sta, Austin, TX 78712-0390, **Business Phone:** (512)471-3821.

WILLIAMS, SAUL
Poet, musician, actor. **Personal:** Born Feb 29, 1972, Newburgh, NY; children: Saturn. **Educ:** Morehouse Col, BA; Tisch Sch Arts, New York Univ, MFA. **Career:** Since 1995 has performed poetry readings; published books of poetry include: Sorcery of Self, 2001; She, 1999; The Seventh Octave, 1998; film work includes: K-Pax, 2001; voice-over for lead character, Origin of Cotton, 2000; Kings of LA, 2000; star & co-author, Slam, 1998; recordings include: "Penny For A Thought & Purple Pigeons", 2000; Amethyst Rock Star, 2001; TV: "Street Time", 2002; "Snoop, There It Is", 2003; "Not in My Name", 2003; "Saul Williams",

2004; "Lackawanna Blues", 2005; "The Inevitable Rise & Liberation of NiggyTardust!", 2007. **Honors/Awds:** "Breakout Performance" Award, New York Independent Film Project, for Slam; Grand Slam Champion, Nu-yorican Poet Cafe, 1996.

WILLIAMS, SCOTT CHRISTOPHER
Basketball player, television broadcaster. **Personal:** Born Mar 21, 1968, Hacienda Heights, CA; married Lisa; children: Benjamin Sinclair. **Educ:** Univ North Carolina. **Career:** Basketball player (retired), TV analyst; Chicago Bulls, ctr forward, 1990-94; Philadelphia 76ers, 1994-98; Milwaukee Bucks, 1999-2001; Denver Nuggets, 2001-02; Phoenix Suns, 2002-04; Dallas Mavericks, 2003-04; Cleveland Cavaliers, 2004-05; tv color commentator, 2005-06; FSN Ohio, color analyst, 2006-. **Honors/Awds:** NBA Champions, Chicago Bulls, 1991, 1992, 1993. **Special Achievements:** One of only eight players in NBA history to have won championships in each of his first three years in the league. **Business Addr:** Television Color Analyst, FSN Ohio, 9200 S Hills Blvd Suite 200, Broadview Heights, OH 44147.

WILLIAMS, DR. SCOTT W.
Educator. **Personal:** Born Apr 22, 1943, Staten Island, NY; son of Roger K and Beryl E. **Educ:** Morgan State Col, BS, math, 1964; Lehigh Univ, MS, Math, 1967, PhD, Math Topology, 1969; George Ivanovich Gurdjieff. **Career:** Int Bus Machines, 1964; Pa State Univ, Allentown Ctr, instr, 1968-69;Morgan State Col, instr, 1969; Pa State Univ, Univ Pk, res assoc, 1969-71; State Univ NY, Buffalo, asst prof, assc prof math, 1977-; Inst Med & Math; Charles Univ, Prague; Rochester Folk Art Guild, instr; Am Math Soc Notices, ed; Topology Atlas, regular columnist, 1997-01. **Orgs:** Am Math Soc; Rochester Folk Art Guild; chmn, Balck Uhuru Soc, 1967-69; consult, Nat Sci Found; Ford Found; Nat Res Coun; Nat Security Agency; Nat Pub Radio; Circle Brotherhood asn; bd mem coun, Afro Am Res. **Honors/Awds:** Chancellor of SUNY Award, 1981; Outstanding Father of the Year, 1997. **Special Achievements:** Paint in acrylics, 1983-96; comput graphics, 1996-; Played saxophone, piano & congas professionally, 1959-69, Selected to be one of the 50 Most Important Blacks in Research Science by Science Spectrum Magazine and Career Communications Group.

WILLIAMS, SERENA (SERENA JAMEKA WILLIAMS)
Tennis player, actor, fashion designer. **Personal:** Born Sep 26, 1981, Saginaw, MI; daughter of Richard and Oracene. **Educ:** Art Inst Fl, attended. **Career:** Prof tennis player, 1995-; Aneres, owner & fashion designer, 2004-; TVSeries: "My Wife & Kids", 2002; "Street Time", 2003; "Law & Order: Special Victims Unit", 2004; "The Division", 2004; "Higglytown Heroes", 2005;"ER", 2005; "Loonatics Unleashed", 2007; "Avatar: The Last Airbender", 2007. **Orgs:** Women's Sports Found. **Honors/Awds:** Champion Singles, Grand Slam Cup, 1999; Champion singles, Los Angeles, 1999; Champion singles, Indian Wells, 1999; Champion singles, Paris Indoors, 1999; Champion doubles, French Open, 1999, 2002; Champion singles & doubles, US Open, 1999, 2002; Champion doubles, Olympics, 2000; Championdoubles, Wimbledon, 2000, 2003; Champion, Australian Open, 2001, 2003, 2005; Champion singles, Indian Wells, 2001; Sanex Championship, singles, 2001; Champion, State Farm Tennis Classic, 2002; Champion, Nasdaq-100 Open, 2002, 2004; Champion, Italian Open, 2002; Champion singles & doubles, Wimbledon, 2002; Champion, Princess Cup, 2002; Champion, Sparkassen Cup, 2002; Female Athlete of the Year, Assoc Press, 2003; Sportswoman of the Year, Laureus World Sports Acad; Female Athlete of the Year, ESPY; Female Tennis Player of the Year, 2003; Celebrity Role Model, 2003; Champion, China Open, 2004. **Special Achievements:** First sisters (Serena & Venus) to win the Olympic doubles event in 2000; Became the first ranked player in the world on July 8, 2002; first African American to win the US Open since 1958; By winning the 2003 Australian Open achieved an historic Serena Slam-winning all four Grand Slam tournaments in a row; ranks 7 female tennis player in the world. **Business Addr:** Owner, Fashion Designer, Aneres, 4199 Maya Cay, Jupiter, FL 33458, **Business Phone:** (561)630-9400.*

WILLIAMS, SERENA JAMEKA. See WILLIAMS, SERENA.

WILLIAMS, SERET SCOTT. See SCOTT, SERET.

WILLIAMS, SHAUN LEJON
Football player. **Personal:** Born Oct 10, 1976, Oakland, CA; son of Kenneth and Sheliah; children: Tyson, Jordan & Cameron. **Educ:** Univ Calif, Los Angeles, pre-psychol. **Career:** NY Giants, safety, 1998-2005; Carolina Panthers, 2006. **Honors/Awds:** All-American honors from Blue Chip. **Special Achievements:** Featured in Prep Football Report & Super Prep magazines; named to the Super Prep All-Far West team & Long Beach Press-Telegram's "Best of the West" squad.

WILLIAMS, SHERMAN
Editor. **Personal:** Born Jan 1, 1961, Fort Benning, GA; son of Thomas and Addie. **Educ:** Ohio State Univ, Columbus, OH, BA, 1983. **Career:** Pub Opinion, Chambersburg, PA, staff photogr, 1984-85; Standard-Examiner, Ogden, UT, staff photogr, 1985-87; The Hartford Courant, Hartford, CT, staff photogr, 1987-, picture ed, 1990-91; The Philadelphia Inquirer, picture ed, 1991-; Milwaukee Jour Sentinel, sr ed Visuals, 2000-. guest fac, Am Press Inst. **Orgs:** Nat Press Photographer Asn, 1985-; Nat Asn Black Journalists, 1986-; vpres, Conn Asn Black Communicators, 1987-; Historians Double Diamonds Ski Club, 1989-90; student clip contest chair, Nat Press Photographers Asn, 1990-91; co-prog dir, bd dir, Greater Hartford Minority Jour Prog, 1990-91; AssocPress Photo Mgr, pres 2004; dir, Nat Asn Black Journalists Visual Task Force. **Honors/Awds:** Photographer of the Year, 1988; Honorable Mention, Nat Asn of Black Journalists Photo Contest, 1989; 1st & 3rd Place Photo Awards, Conn News Photogs, 1991; 4th Region 1, NPPA Contest, 1988; First Place News Photo, Northern Short Course.

WILLIAMS, DR. SHIRLEY YVONNE
Physician. **Personal:** Born in Washington, DC. **Educ:** Howard Univ, 1955, 1959; New York, Med Ctr, resident, 1962. **Career:** New York Med Ctr, neurol, 1962; Henry Ford Hosp, 1965; Outpatient Ambulatory Serv, dir. **Orgs:** St Bd Mental Health; St Coun Alcohol & Drugs; chmn, Asn Conn Out patient Clinics; Asn Nervous & Mental Disease; Am Psychol Asn; Am Acad Sci; Nat Med Asn; AMA; Fair field Co Asn; life mem, NAACP; chmn, Keystone House; mem bd, Carver Found Father Looney, 1977; bd mem, Norwalk Hosp; bd mem, Med Examiners for the St Conn. **Honors/Awds:** Fel, Am Psychiatric Asn. **Home Addr:** 5208 Colorado Ave NW, Washington, DC 20011.

WILLIAMS, SIDNEY B., JR.
Lawyer. **Personal:** Born Dec 31, 1935, Little Rock, AR; son of Sidney B Sr and Eloise Gay Cole; married Carolyn. **Educ:** Univ Wis, BS, 1961; George Wash Univ, Law Sch, JD, 1967. **Career:** Upjohn Co, patent atty; US Patent Office, patent examiner; Gen Am Transp Corp, res develop engr; Montreal Alouettes, prof football player; Flynn Thiel Boutell & Tanis PC, atty, currently. **Orgs:** Mich DC Bar Asn; Kalamazoo County Mich Am Nat Patent Law Asn; bd trustees, Borgess Hosp; regional bd dir, Comerica Bank; bd dir, Douglas Community Asn; All Am Football Team Chem & Eng News, 1957-58; Iron Cross Hon Soc, 1958. **Military Serv:** USMCR. **Business Addr:** Attorney, Flynn Thiel Boutell & Tanis PC, 2026 Rambling Rd, Kalamazoo, MI 49008.*

WILLIAMS, SIMBI KALI. See KHALI, SIMBI.

WILLIAMS, STANLEY KING
Government official. **Personal:** Born Jan 25, 1948, Columbus, GA; son of Robert and Lucille Willis; married Judy Chichester, Apr 5, 1986; children: Lanita L & Malik K. **Educ:** Shaw Univ, Raleigh, NC, BA, 1970. **Career:** Shaw Univ, stud counr, 1967-70; COPE Newark, youth job develop specialist, 1968-69; NC Dept Corrections, classification specialist, 1970; AUS Ger, neuropsychiatric tech drug coun, 1970-72; Prog Gales Maternity Clin, coordr, 1972-74; Dept Manpower, job develop specialist, 1972; Veterans Employment DC Dept Labor Veterans Admin Regional Off, supvr & coordr, 1976-86; DC Dept Employment Serv, supvr, 1986-89, opers mgr, NE Employment Ctr, 1989-94; S Capital Employment Ctr, opers mgr, 1994-95; US Dept Labor, dir veterans employment & training, 1995-. **Orgs:** Chmn, Mt Pleasant Adv Neighborhood Comn, 1976-80; consult sex educ prog, Dept HR, 1973; adv, DC Govt ANC Citizens Neighborhood Coun Coord Comnr, 1975; pres, King Enterprises Inc; Am Legion WA Alliance Neighborhood Govts; del, DC Black Assembly; Shaw Univ Alumni Asn; Sch Without Walls PTA; Econ & Polit Trends; SAfrican Self-determination; Smithsonian Fel, Smithsonian Inst; coordin & supvr, Veterans Employment Ctr VA Regional Off, 1976; pres, King Enterprises, 1976; vice chmn, Shiloh Baptist Church, Wash DC, 2001; Am Legion, Carter G Woodson Chap, Asn Study African Am Life & Hist; first vice chmn, Brotherhood Shiloh Men, Shiloh Baptist Church, 1996; AMVETS; bd dirs, Shiloh Family Life Ctr Found; bd dirs, DC Private Indust Coun, 1997; Bachelor Benedict Inc, 2000. **Honors/Awds:** Appreciation Award, ANC 70, 1977; Congressional Appreciation Award, Congressman Fountroy, 1978; Outstanding Service Award, Mt Pleasant Adv Neighborhood Comn, 1978; Meritorious & Distinguished Service Award, VFW, 1978; Commend Award, Vietnam Veteran Civic Coun, 1978; Community Service Award, Nat Black Veteran Orgn, 1979; promoter & sponsor, promoted largest gospel convention given in Washington, DC, 1983; Community Service Award, DC City Coun, 1982; Man of the Year Award, Shiloh Baptist Church, 1998. **Military Serv:** AUS, sgt E-5, 1970-72. **Home Addr:** 1806 Lawrence St NE, Washington, DC 20018, **Home Phone:** (202)526-8521. **Business Addr:** Director Veterans Employment, Training, US Department of Labor, 609 H St NE Suite 539, Washington, DC 20001, **Business Phone:** (202)671-2143.

WILLIAMS, DR. STERLING B., JR.
Physician, educator. **Personal:** Born Apr 3, 1941, Little Rock, AR; divorced; children: Angela, Spencer & Sterling III. **Educ:** Univ Ill, BS, 1963; Northern Ill Univ, MS, 1966; Univ Ariz, Med Ctr, MD, 1973, PhD. **Career:** Ill Technol Res Inst, res asst, 1963; Sch Nursing, Univ Ariz, Med Ctr, instr, 1971; Pvt practice, physician, 1976-; Univ Kans, Med Ctr, assoc prof, 1979-; Columbia Univ Col Physicians & Surgeons, prof, 1987; Harlem Hosp Ctr; dir dept Obstet & Gynec, 1987; Am Col Obstetricians & Gynecologists, vpres, currently. **Orgs:** Nat Coalition Health; gen coun, KC Union Presbyterian; coordr, Minority Stud Admissions Adv Comt; Univ Kans, Med Ctr, KC Civic Chorus, Alpha Phi Alpha Soc Frat, Sigma Xi Res Hon soc, NIH Predoctoral Fel, Univ Ariz, 1966-69; solo singing pref, KC Symphony Orchestra; vice chmn, Presbyterian Coun Theol & Culture; Kaw Valley Med Soc, Sigma Pi Phi Frat. **Honors/Awds:** Phi Eta Sigma Scholastic Hon. **Home Addr:** 11101 Luttrell Lane, Silver Spring, MD 20902-3556. **Business Addr:** Vice President, American College of Obstetricians and Gynecologists, 409 12Th St SW, Washington, DC 20090-6290, **Business Phone:** (202)638-5577.

WILLIAMS, SYLVIA J.
Educator. **Personal:** Born Jul 11, 1939, Washington, DC; daughter of Wallace Burnett and Mary Coghill Burnett; children: Deborah Bushrod & Rodney. **Educ:** Bowie State Col, BS, 1964, MA, 1970; Univ Md, attended. **Career:** Prince Georges Co, Bd Educ, teacher, 27 yrs. **Orgs:** Past secy, King George Citizens Asn, 1973-74; nat co-chairperson Region 7, Nat Asn Advan Colored People, 1987-, vpres, 1991; redistricting comt mem, King George Co, VA, 1991; chmn, Educ Comn Local Branch; past coun & testing coord, Sickle Cell Asn; secy, Vikingettes Social Club; Dial aRide; coord, Local Rainbow Coalition, Wilder Lt Gov, Host & Hostesses Mayor Marion Barry's Inagural Reception; coord, Health & Soc Serv Nat Capitol Baptist Conv; bd mem, Rappohonack Asn; mem exec bd, Citizens Adv Comt DC; vpres, Project Shares. **Honors/Awds:** Charlotte B Hunter Citizenship Award, 1962; Mayors Youth Council Award,1963; Sickle Cell Association Award, 1971-83; American Citizenery Award, 1983; Instructor of the Year, Mt Bethel Baptist Asn, 1983; Out standing Service Award by Life Membership Division, Nat Off Nat Asn Advan Colored People, 1983; Rainbow Coalition Award of Merit, 1984; American Humanitarian Award, 1984; Presidential Award, Wash DC, Nat Asn Advan Colored People, 1990; Keeper of the Flame Award, NCP, 1992; Unsung Heroine Award, Nat Asn Advan Colored People; Merit Award, Nat Women Nat Asn Advan Colored People. **Special Achievements:** Citizen of the Year, Omega Psi Phi, 1974; Volunteer of the Year, AT &T Bell Labs.

WILLIAMS, T. JOYCE
Educator. **Personal:** Born Jan 24, 1930, Muskogee, OK; married Paul Jr; children: Cheryl Elizabeth Jackson, Jacquelyn Elaine Miller & Starla P Potts. **Educ:** Wichita State Univ, BA, 1965, EdM, 1974. **Career:** Educator (retired); Bd Educ, USD, 259, teacher, 1965-85. **Orgs:** Leadership Acad, trainer local bldg dir, KNEA, 1975-76; Ethnic Minority Caucus NEA Wichita, 1975-76; Pub Affairs TV Prog, NEA Wichita 1975; PR & R Com NEA Wichita, 1979; Local State Nat Rep Assemblies NEA, 1974, 1975,1979, 1980; Sigma Gamma Rho Sorority; Nat Asn Advan Colored People; Political Action Com, 1979; Holy Savior Cath Ch Wichita; Vol God's Food Pantry-Holy Savior Church, 1986-88; Elected Human Resources Bd, City Wis,1989; Elected four years term CPO, NE Wichita, 1994-; Nominated Int soci Poets, 1996-97; eucharist adorer, St Paul Newman Ctr, 2001; eucharist minister, Holy Savior, 2002-03. **Honors/Awds:** Wichita's Teacher of the Year, 1975; Letter of Appreciation from CPO Coordinator, 1995; Poetry.com Award for outstanding Achievment in Poetry, 2000; Best Poems & Poets Millenium Award. **Special Achievements:** Speaker-rep address House Reps, Topeka, Kans, 1995; Poem, Entry "Through the Hourglass My Vision," Mama Joyce Williams, nat lib poetry, 1996-; poems published in "Best Poems of 1997," and "Best Poems of 1998;" exhibiton the WWW at http://www.poets.com; book of poetry, Pearls of Life, 2000; poem entry, Amer at the Millenium; Entry, Best Poems and Poets, 2001, 2002; Honored, coun elders, 2003; tutor students, USO-259. **Home Addr:** 4025 Christy St, Wichita, KS 67220.

WILLIAMS, TARA
Basketball player. **Personal:** Born Jul 23, 1974, newport news, VA; daughter of Thomas Nelson and Ethel Williams. **Educ:** Auburn Univ. **Career:** Phoenix Mercury, forward, 1997; Detroit Shock, 1998-; Portland Fire,guard, 2001; eagles, guard, 2003-06; 2008-09. *

WILLIAMS, TED. See WILLIAMS, THEODORE.

WILLIAMS, TENETRIA MICHELLE. See WILLIAMS, MICHELLE.

WILLIAMS, TERRI L.
School administrator. **Personal:** Born May 18, 1958, Bridgeton, NJ. **Educ:** Howard Univ, BS, 1981, MEd, 1984. **Career:** Wash Alcohol Coun Ctr, admin asst, 1980-82; Howard Stud Spec Servs, educ specialist, 1984-85; Howard Upward Bound, sr counr, 1985-86; St Lawrence Univ, asst dir admis, 1986-. **Orgs:** Delta Sigma Theta Inc, 1978-; pub rels coordr, BOF Howard Univ Alumnae, 1983-; volunteer, DC Mayor's Re-election Comn, 1986; exhibitors coordr, Mid-Eastern Asn Educ Opport Prog Personnel, 1986. **Honors/Awds:** Outstanding Young Women of America, 1982, 1985; MEAEOPP Conference Service Award, 1986; Mayor's Summer Youth Employment Program Contribution Award. **Home Addr:** RD 2 Russell Rd, PO Box 166, Canton, NY 13617.

WILLIAMS, TERRIE MICHELLE
Consultant, executive. **Personal:** Born May 12, 1954, Mt Vernon, NY; daughter of Charles and Marie; children: Rocky (adopted).

Educ: Brandeis Univ, BA, psychol & sociol, 1975; Columbia Univ NY, MA, social work, 1977. **Career:** New York Hosp, med social worker 1977-80; Black Filmmaker Found, prog admin, 1980-81; Black Owned Comn Alliance, exec dir, 1981-82; World Inst Black Commun, exec dir, 1982; Essence Commun Inc, vp/dir corp commun, 1982-87; Terrie Williams Agency, pres, 1988-. **Orgs:** Founder, Stay Strong Found, 2001-; Brandeis Univ Alumni Asn; Nat Corp Adv Bd; communs community Am Heart Asn; Women Communs. **Honors/Awds:** D Parke Gibson Award, Pub Rels Soc Am, 1981; Building Brick Award, New York Urban League, 1987; Matrix Award in Public Relations, Women Communs, 1991; Phillip Dorf Mentoring Award, NY Chap, Pub Rels Soc Am; Marietta Tree Award, Citizen's Comt NY. **Special Achievements:** Co-author: The Personal Touch, Warner Books, 1994; author: Stay Strong: Simple Life Lessons for Teens, 2001; A Plentiful Harvest: Creating Balance and Harmony Through the Seven Living Virtues, 2003. **Business Addr:** President, The Terrie Williams Agency, 382 Cent Pk W Suite 7R, New York, NY 10025, **Business Phone:** (212)316-0305.*

WILLIAMS, THEARTRICE T
Consultant. **Personal:** Born May 16, 1934, Indianola, MS; son of Fred Mack and Ollie Gray; married Mary Louise Sales, May 19, 1962; children: Christopher, Jeffrey & Laurie. **Educ:** Univ Ill, BA, 1956; Univ Pa, MSW, 1962; Northwestern Univ, attended 1971. **Career:** Phyllis Wheatley Comm Ctr Mpls, exec dir, 1965-72; State Minn, ombudsman corrections, 1972-83; Minneapolis Comm Develop Agency, dir pub housing, 1983-85; Humphrey Inst Pub Affairs Univ Minn, sr fel, 1985-91; Rainbow Res, sr proj assoc; Minneapolis Pub Sch, Bd Educ, dir & treasurer, currently. **Orgs:** Chmn, Minority Scholarship & Grants Prog Am Luth Ch, 1970-87; Trustee Minneapolis Fdn, 1974-83; dir, The Citizens League, 1980-83; pres bd, Oper De Novo; comnr Minn Sentencing Guidelines Comn, 1986-. **Honors/Awds:** Leadership flow Bush Federaion, Mn, 1970; dist Serv NASW Mn Chapter, 1977, Nat Chapter, 1983; outstanding achievement Nat Asn Blacks in Criminal Justice, 1978; Polemarch, St Paul-Minneapolis Alumni Chapter, Kappa Alpha Psi Fraternity, 1988-; Achievement Award North Central Province, Kappa Alpha Psi Fraternity; Venture Capital Job Develop Strategies for The Black Community, Special Report; Humphrey Inst of Public Affairs, 1987; The Church as Partner in Community Economic Develop, special report; Humphrey Inst Pub Affairs, 1990. **Special Achievements:** First vpres Nat Assn of Social Workers 1981-83. **Military Serv:** AUS, sp4, 1958-60. **Business Addr:** Director, Treasurer, Minneapolis Public Schools, John B Davis Educational Services Center, 807 NE Broadway St, Minneapolis, MN 55413.

WILLIAMS, THEODORE (TED WILLIAMS)
Automotive executive. **Personal:** Born Jul 6, 1951, Chicago, IL; son of Theodore Williams Sr and Shirley; married Olivia, Jun 12, 1976; children: Theodore III & Brandon N. **Educ:** Trinadad State Col, attended 1973. **Career:** Bob Neal Pontiac, Toyota, sales mgr, 1972-84; Jarrell Pontiac, Toyota, sales mgr, 1984-85; Bonnie Brook Ford, Ford Motor Co, 1985-88; Shamrock Lincoln-Mercury Inc, pres & chief exec officer, 1988-. **Orgs:** Rotary Club S Bend, 1989-; Crime Stoppers, 1989-92; NAACP, 1992-; Nissan Dealer, adv coun, 1992-; Minority Bus Dev Coun, 1992-; St Joseph Chamber Com, 1992-; Michiana Community Hosp, 1992-; Lincoln-Mercury Dealer Asn, 1993-. **Honors/Awds:** Entrepreneur of the Year, Minority Bus Develop Coun, 1993. **Special Achievements:** Company ranked No 73 on Black Enterprise's list of top 100 automobile dealerships, 1998. **Business Addr:** President, Chief Executive Officer, Shamrock Lincoln-Mercury Inc, 120 W McKinley Ave, Mishawaka, IN 46545, **Business Phone:** (219)256-0211.

WILLIAMS, THEODORE R.
Educator. **Personal:** Born Jan 17, 1931, Palestine, TX; married Louise M Pogue; children: Wayne R, Darrell R, Brian K, Marica L, Thea Elaine. **Educ:** Tex Southern Univ, BS, 1952, MS, 1954; Ore State Univ; St Lawrence Univ; Univ Wash; Ariz State Univ; Univ Iowa, PhD, 1972. **Career:** St Philip's Col, chmn biol dept, 1954-75, asst, assoc dean, 1972-82, acting pres, 1982, vpres acad affairs emer, 1986. **Orgs:** Phi Beta Sigma Fraternity, 1951; bd trustees, San Antonio Museum Assoc, 1973-82; adv bd mem, United Col San Antonio, 1973-; dir, Bexar Co Anemia Assoc, 1978-80; appraisal rev bd mem, Bexar Appraisal Dist, 1985-; dir, Guardianship Adv Bd, 1985-; mem, Sigma Pi Phi Fraternity, 1988; prog officer, Tex Higher Edu Coord Bd, 1991-. **Honors/Awds:** National Med Fel Grant, 1959-60; Summer Grant, National Sci Found, 1959, 1961, 1963, 1967; Fel, Southern Fel Found, 1969-71; Beta Kappa Chi Scientific Hon Soc; vpres , Academic Affairs Emeritus St Philip's Col, 1986. **Military Serv:** AUS, pfc, 2 yrs. **Home Addr:** 1315 Virginia Blvd, San Antonio, TX 78203.

WILLIAMS, TONY
Football player. **Personal:** Born Jul 9, 1975, Germantown, TN; married Cherilyn; children: Tony Christopher. **Educ:** Memphis Univ, BS, educ. **Career:** Football player(retired); Minn Vikings, defensive tackle, 1997-2000; Cincinnati Bengals, defensive tackle, 2001-04; Jacksonville Jaguars, defensive tackle, 2006. **Honors/Awds:** Defensive Lineman of the Yearr, Memphis Univ.

WILLIAMS, TONYA LEE
Actor. **Personal:** Born Jul 12, 1958, London, England; married Robert Simpson (divorced 1991). **Educ:** Ryerson Col, Toronto. **Career:** Films: Skull duggery, 1983; Spaced Invaders, 1990; The Borrower, 1991; Seventeen Again, 2000; Maple, exec producer, 2001; Poor Boy's Game, 2007; Finding Fathers Toe, 2007; TV series: "Polka Dot Door", 1971; Check It Out, 1985-86; As Is, 1986; Captain Power & the Soldiers of the Future", 1987; "Falcon Crest", 1987; "Hill Street Blues", 1987; "Street Legal", 1987; The Liberators, 1987; "What's Happening Now!", 1987; A Very Brady Christmas, 1988; "Matlock", 1989; Nasty Boys, 1989; A Peaceable Kingdom, 1989; Generations, 1989; "A Very Brady Christmas", 1988; "The Young & the Restless", 1990-2007; Piece of Cake, 1990; "Getting By", 1993; Counterstrike", 1993; "Silk Stalkings", 1994; "PSI Factor: Chronicles of the Paranormal", 1998; "Tonya Lee Williams: Gospel Jubilee", 2004; Kink in My Hair, exec producer & dir, 2004; "A Perfect Note", 2005. **Orgs:** Founder, ReelWorld Film Festival; hon mem, Sigma Gamma Rho Sorority. **Honors/Awds:** Crowned Miss Black Ontario, 1977; Image Award, Nat Asn Advan Colored People, 2000 & 2002; Dr Bird Award; TV Cases, Ribbon of Hope Award; Nominated for Image Award, 2009. **Business Addr:** Actress, c/o William Morris Agency, 151 El Camino Dr, Beverly Hills, CA 90212, **Business Phone:** (310)859-4000.*

WILLIAMS, DR. TRINA RACHAEL (TRINA R SHANKS)
Research scientist, college teacher, activist. **Personal:** Born Nov 6, 1970, New Orleans, LA; daughter of Dwight Nichols and Sheila A. **Educ:** Wash Univ, St Louis, MO, BS, bus admin, 1992, MSW, 2000, PHD, 2003; Oxford Univ, MPhil, comparative social res, 1996. **Career:** Fun Ctr, Inc, found & dir, 1990-92; Nat Community Educ Asn, intern, 1991; Minority Youth Entrepreneurship Prog, dir, 1992; US Peace Corps, small bus consult, 1992-94; Milwaukee Village Sch, consult, 1995-96; Stand Children, Wash, DC, consult, 1996-97; Christian Community Serv, Inc, Nashville, TN, exec dir, 1997-98; Chancellor's Fellowship, 1998; Univ Mich, asst prof social work, currently; co investr, SEED Impact Assessment study, currently. **Orgs:** Coun Social Work Educ, 1999-2003; Asn Am Rhodes Scholars, 1995-2003; volunteer, Centennial Olympic Games, 1996; Volunteer & Staff, US Olympic Festival, St Louis, 1994; volunteer & informal counr, Coalition for Homeless, Wash, DC, 1991; volunteer, Pan-Am Games, Indpolis, IN, 1987; North Am Asn Christians in Social Work, 1999-2003; exec dir, Christian Community Serv. **Honors/Awds:** Shepley Award, Wash Univ, 1992, Rhodes Scholarship, Rhodes Trust, 1993; Young American Award, Boy Scouts Am, Nat Coun, 1992; All-USA Col Academic First Team, USA Today, 1992. **Special Achievements:** Peace Corps Certificate of Learning Proficiency in Spanish (rating, 3), 1994. **Business Addr:** Assistant Professor Social Work, University of Michigan, School of Social Work, Rm 3726 SSWB 1080 S Univ, Ann Arbor, MI 48109, **Business Phone:** (734)764-7411.

WILLIAMS, TYRONE M., JR.
Football player. **Personal:** Born Oct 22, 1972, Philadelphia, PA; married Amy; children: Deshon, Amandre, Teryn & Tayvian. **Educ:** Univ Wyo. **Career:** Chicago Bears, defensive end, 1997; Philadelphia Eagles, 1999-2000; Kansas City Chiefs, 2000-01; Wash Redskins, 2001; British Columbia Lions, defensive tackle, 2002-08; Winnipeg Blue Bombers, 2009. **Honors/Awds:** CFL All-Stars, 2006, 2007. **Business Phone:** (604)661-3626.

WILLIAMS, ULYSSES JEAN
Educator, counselor. **Personal:** Born Sep 15, 1947, Memphis, TN; daughter of Ann Moton Warren and Ulysses Warren; married Foster Williams Sr; children: Tasha A, Foster, LaQuentin D, AnQuentin T. **Educ:** Philander Smith Col, 1967; Univ Central Ark, BSE, 1969, MSE, 1973; Ark State Univ, Cert Behavior Disorders, 1980, Gifted & Talented Cert, 1985; AR State Univ, Elem Principalship Cert, 1987, Counr Cert, 1992. **Career:** Cotton Plant Elem Sch, secy, 1969-70; Helena-West Helena Pub Schs, 1970-78, 1988-89; East Ark Regional Mental Health Ctr, educ specialist, 1978-81; Lucilia Wood Elem Sch, educr, 1982-88; Holly Grove Pub Schs, 1989-; MSE, counr educ, 1993; direct instr coordr; asst elem prin. **Orgs:** Ark Educ Asn, 1970-; Nat Educ Asn, 1970-; PTA, 1970-; Arkansas Counr Asn, 1989-; Ark Multicultural Asn, 1989-; Ark Voc Asn, 1989-; pres, Theta Gamma Zeta; Theta Gamma Zeta, founding pres, 4 years; adv to Amicae; regional & state coordr S Cent Region; chmn Oper, Big Vote; NAACP; Second Baptist Church; chmn Christian Bd Ed; secy, Matrons; dir, church choir; Gifted & Talented, adv comt; Helena-West Helena Bd Educ, 1980-86; state dir, AR Zeta Phi Beta Sor Inc, 1987-92; Elaine Six Yr Plan Comn; comt mem, Gov's Rural Develop Action Prog, 1987-88; Laubach Bd Mem, tutor, 1988-. **Honors/Awds:** Outstanding Elementary Teacher of America, 1975; developed Educ Component Adolescent Residential Facility, 1978-81; Outstanding Service,Educ Specialist, 1980; Dedicated Service, Therapeutic Foster Parents, 1981-84; Zeta Year, 1982; Outstanding Service, Community & Church, 1983; AR Zeta year Award, 1985; Outstanding Service, South Cent Region Zeta Phi Beta Sor Inc; Zeta Phi Beta, Outstanding Service, State Dir, Educ Bd Appointee. **Special Achievements:** Organizer: Archonette, teenage girl orgn; Theta Gamma Zeta Branch of Zeta Phi Beta Sorority Inc; Young Adult Choir and Church Scholar Fund; Parenting Univ, conduct parenting class & other workshops of interest; African-Am Male Mentor Group, part of the Holly Grove Schs; designed report card and daily independent worksheet for emotionally disturbed youth.

WILLIAMS, VANESSA A.
Actor, parking enforcement agent. **Personal:** Born May 12, 1963, Brooklyn, NY; married Andre Wiseman; children: Omar Tafari. **Educ:** Marymount Manhattan Col, BA. **Career:** Films: New Jack City, 1991; Fatal Bond, 1992; Candyman, 1992; Drop Squad, 1994; Mother, 1996; Boogie Nights, 1997; Breakdown, 1997; Punks, 2000; Our America, 2002; Like Mike, 2002; Baby of the Family, 2002; Like Mike, 2002; Black Listed, 2003; Santa, Baby!, 2003; Gift for the Living, 2005; Hummingbird, 2008; Contradictions of the Heart, 2009; Imagine That, 2009; TV series: "Melrose Place", 1992-93; "Murder One", 1995-96; A Woman of Color, 1997; "Incognito", 1999; "Playing With Fire", 2000; Our America, 2002; "Soul Food", 2000-04; "Heavy Gear", animated, 2001; Allergic to Nuts, exec producer, 2003; "Dense", exec producer, 2004; Driving Fish, co-exec producer, 2004; Ice Spiders, 2007; Cold Case, 2007; "Lincoln Heights", 2008; "Knight Rider", 2009; "Everybody Hates Chris", 2009. **Honors/Awds:** Three NAACP Image Award nominations; Image Award for Outstanding Actress in a Drama Series, 2003. **Business Addr:** Actress, c/o Showtime Networks Inc, 1633 E Broadway, New York, NY 10019, **Business Phone:** (212)708-1600.*

WILLIAMS, VANESSA LYNNE
Actor, singer. **Personal:** Born Mar 18, 1963, Tarrytown, NY; daughter of Milton and Helen; married Ramon Hervey II, Jan 2, 1987 (divorced 1997); children: Melanie, Jillian & Devin; married Rick Fox, Sep 26, 1999; children: Sasha Gabriella & Kyle (stepson). **Educ:** Syracuse Univ, BFA, musical theater. **Career:** Actress, singer, fashion model; Former Miss Am; Albums: The Right Stuff, 1988; The Comfort Zone, 1991; The Sweetest Days, 1994; Star Bright, 1996; Next, 1997; Greatest Hits - the first ten years, 1998; Silver & Gold, 2004; Everlasting Love, 2005; Singles: The Right Stuff, 1988; Dreamin,1988; (He's got) The Look, 1988; Darlin I, 1988; The Comfort Zone, 1991; Runnning back to you, 1991; Save the Best for Last, 1991; Just fortnight, 1991; Work to do, 1991; For all the children, 1994; Betcha Never, 1994; You can't run, 1994; The Way that you love?, 1994; The Sweetest Days, 1994; Hostess, Showtime At The Apollo; Soul Train, Live!, Dick Clark Presents, Club MTV, BET's Video Soul, & Live at the Improv; Readings from the Slave Narratives; TV series: Full Exposure: The Sex Tapes Scandal, 1989; The Kid Who Loved Christmas, 1990; Stompin' at the Savoy, 1992; The Jacksons: An American Dream, 1992; "Kiss of the Spider Woman", 1994; Bye Bye Birdie, 1995; Nothing Lasts Forever, 1995; The Odyssey, 1997;Future sport, 1998; L.A. Doctors, 1999; Don Quixote, 2000; "The Courage to Love", 2000; "A Diva's Christmas Carol", 2000; WW3, 2001; "Ally McBeal",2002; Keep the Faith, Baby, 2002; "Boomtown", 2003; Beck & Call, 2004;"South Beach", 2006; "Ugly Betty", 2006-08; The Beautiful World of Ugly Betty, 2007; Films: The Pick Up Artist, 1987; Under the Gun, 1988; Eraser,1996; Hoodlum, 1997; Soul Food, 1997; Dance With Me; 1998; Another You,1991; Light It Up, 1999; The Adventures of Elmo in Grouchland, 1999; Shaft, 2000; Johnson Family Vacation, 2004; My Brother, 2006; And Then Came Love, 2007. **Honors/Awds:** Numerous awards and honors including Miss America, 1983; Billboard Music Award, 1993; Theatre World Award, 1994; Academy Award, 1995; Soul Train Awards, 1996; MTV Video Music Award, 5 New York Music Awards, Image Awards, Mother Hale Award, Golden Satellite Award, 2002 & 2008, Humanitarian Award; NAACP Image Award, 1997, 2007 & 2008; Hollywood Walk of Fame, 2007, Jacobi Children's Arts Award, 2007; Teen Choice Awards, 2007. **Special Achievements:** First black contestant in the hot seat on "Who Wants to Be a Millionaire", 1999; Ranked #56 on VH1's 100 Sexiest Artists; First black woman to be crowned "Miss America"; Grammy, Emmy, and Tony Award nominee. **Business Addr:** Actress, William Morris Agency, 1 William Morris Pl, Beverly Hills, CA 90212, **Business Phone:** (310)859-4000.*

WILLIAMS, VENUS. **See WILLIAMS, VENUS EBONE STARR.**

WILLIAMS, VENUS EBONE STARR (VENUS WILLIAMS)
Tennis player, business owner. **Personal:** Born Jun 17, 1980, Lynwood, CA; daughter of Richard and Oracene. **Educ:** Art Inst, Ft Lauderdale, 2007. **Career:** V Starr Interiors, owner, 2003-; prof tennis player, currently. **Honors/Awds:** Grand Slam Cup, singles, Champion, 1998; Miami, singles, Champion, 1998; Okla City, singles & doubles, Champion, 1998; Zurich, singles, Champion, 1999; New Haven, singles, Champion, 1999; Italian Open, singles, Champion, 1999; Hamburg, singles, Champion, 1999; Miami, singles, Champion, 1999; Okla City,singles, Champion, 1999; US Open, doubles, Champion, 1999; French Open, doubles, Champion, 1999; Olympics, singles & doubles, Champion, 2000; US Open, singles, Champion, 2000; Wimbledon, singles & doubles, Champion, 2000; Australian Open, doubles, Champion, 2001; Ericsson Open, singles, Champion, 2001; Wimbledon, singles, Champion, 2001; US Open, singles, Champion, 2001; Thalgo Australian Womens Hardcourts, singles, Champion, 2002; Gaz De France, singles, Champion, 2002; Proximus Diamond Games singles, Champion, 2002; Bausch & Lomb,singles, Champion, 2002; Wimbledon, doubles, Champion, 2002; Australian Open, doubles, Champion, 2003; Family Circle Cup, singles, Champion, 2004; J & S Cup, singles, Champion, 2004; Istanbul Cup, singles, Champion, 2005; Wimbledon, singles,

Champion, 2005. **Special Achievements:** Venus became the first African American woman to reach the 1 ranking on the WTA Tour; By winning the 1999 French Open doubles title with Serena, the duo became the first sisters to win a Grand Slam crown together in the 20th century; Currently attends fashion design school; She has also designed a collection of leather apparel that is sold exclusively at Wilson's Leather; started her own interior design business, V Starr Interiors; Won the gold medal in doubles at the 2000 Olympics with her sister Venus, becoming the first sisters to win the Olympic doubles event. **Business Addr:** Professional Tennis Player, US Tennis Association, 70 W Red Oak Lane, White Plains, NY 10604-3602, **Business Phone:** (914)696-7000.

WILLIAMS, VERNICE LOUISE
Manager. **Personal:** Born Aug 13, 1934, Indianapolis, IN; daughter of Herman S Whitelaw Sr and Laura Chubbs Guthrie; married Andrew I, Aug 26, 1950; children: Crystal B Thomas, Andrea J, Marlon I, Sherman A, Dewayne M & Karen R. **Educ:** Indiana Univ-Purdue Univ Indianapolis, attended 1970-72. **Career:** Manager (Retired); Army Finance C&R, Ft Benjamin, Harrison IN, auditor, 1952-67; Ind Bell, Indianapolis IN, mgr, 1974-92. **Orgs:** Bd mem & vice chair, Ind Black Expo, 1974-; mem steering comt, United Negro Col Fund, 1982-; bd mem, Dialogue Today, 1985-; bd mem, Police Chief Adv Coun, 1987-; chair, IBE Youth Corp, 1988-. **Honors/Awds:** Minorities Engineering, Indiana Bell, 1984; Leadership Award, Chamber Com, 1986; Outstanding Volunteerism, United Way, 1988; Mt Summitt award, Ind Bell, 1989; Presidents Club award, Ind Bell, 1989; prog coord, 100 Black Men of Indianapolis Inc. **Special Achievements:** 200 Most Influential Blacks In Indiana, Outstanding Women In Indiana. **Home Addr:** 6136 N Meridian W Dr, Indianapolis, IN 46208.

WILLIAMS, VERNON ALVIN
Government official, lawyer. **Personal:** Born Aug 1, 1947, Washington, DC; son of Charles Brown and Lois; married Joanne; children: Tisha Johnson. **Educ:** Marietta Coll, BA, 1969; George Washington Univ Law Ctr, JD, 1972. **Career:** Interstate Commerce Commission, attorney, 1972-84; Self employed, attorney, 1984-96; Interstate Commerce Commission, sec, 1993-96; Surface Transportation Board, sec, 1996-. **Orgs:** DC Bar asn, 1972-. **Honors/Awds:** Outstanding Diversity Award, Dept of Transportation, 1997; Comm Service Award, 1999, 2000. **Business Addr:** Secretary, Surface Transportation Bd, 1925 K St NW Suite 711, Washington, DC 20423, **Business Phone:** (202)565-1650.

WILLIAMS, VERNON R
Automotive executive. **Career:** Greenville Ford Lincoln-Mercury Inc, pres & chief exec officer, currently. **Business Addr:** President, Chief Executive Officer, Greenville Ford Lincoln-Mercury Inc, 4001 State St Hwy 30, PO Box 1927, Greenville, TX 75403, **Business Phone:** (903)455-7222.

WILLIAMS, VESTA
Actor, singer. **Personal:** Born Jan 1, 1963?, Coshocton, OH. **Career:** Wild Honey Band, singer; Albums: Vesta, 1986; Vesta 4U, 1988; Mississippi Burning, 1988; Special, 1991; Everything-n-More, 1993; Relationships, 1998; Singles: "Once Bitten Twice Shy", 1986; "Congratulations", 1988; "Sweet Sweet Love", 1988; "Special", 1990; "Person to Person", 1990; Film:Posse, 1993; TV Episode: "Sister, Sister", actress, 1998-99; "Greek to Me", actress, 1998; singer, currently. **Special Achievements:** TV appearance: "Jack and Jill". **Business Phone:** (818)777-4000.

WILLIAMS, W BILL
Executive. **Personal:** Born Aug 19, 1939, Chicago, IL; son of William Sr and Ellen Brassfield; married Syleste Tillman, Aug 29, 1965; children: Karen, Kevin & Keyth. **Educ:** Chicago State Univ, Chicago, IL, BS, bus mgt; Loading Supr's Course, London, England, British Airways Corp. **Career:** United Airlines, Chicago, IL, cert meeting prof & operation supr, 1960-63; Butler Aviation, Chicago, IL, oper supr, 1963-70; Sullair Corp, Michigan City, IN, sales engr, 1970-75; Chicago Conv & Tourism Bur, Chicago, IL, dir sales, 1975-89, asst vpres, vpres, 1989-; K & J Shine Parlors, Chicago, IL, owner, 1985-. **Orgs:** Mkt dir, IBPOEW, 1985-; int vip & conv chmn, Rat Pack Int, 1985-; sovereign grand inspector gen, United Sup Coun, PHA, 1987-; life mem, Kappa Alpha Psi Fraternity, 1982-; bd mem, Nat Coalition Black Meeting Planners, 1985-89; vpres, Soc Gov Meeting Planners. **Honors/Awds:** Outstanding Achievement Award, Urban Progs W, YMCA, 1985-; Man of the Year, Norman La Harry Scholar Found, 1985; Black Innovator Award, 1982; Outstanding Service Award, Chicago State Univ, 1979. **Military Serv:** USMC, cpl, 1957-60, Good conduct medal. **Business Addr:** Vice President of Sales Diversity, Chicago Convention & Tourism Bureau, 2301 S Lake Shore Dr, Chicago, IL 60616.

WILLIAMS, W. CLYDE
School administrator, clergy. **Personal:** Born in Cordele, GA; married Elaine; children: Joyce, Clyde, John, Gregory. **Educ:** Holsey Cobb Inst 1951; Paine Col, BA 1955; Howard Univ, BD, 1959; Interdenom Theol Ctr, MRE, 1961; Atlanta Univ, MA, 1969; Paine Col, DD, 1972; Univ AL, PhD, 1976. **Career:** NY St Coun Church, chaplain, 1957-58; Howard Univ, asst dir stud act, 1959-; Bethlehem Ctr, Augusta, Ga, dir boys work, 1954-56; Christ Meth Epis Church, exec secy, dir youth work & adult educ, 1960-63; Interdenom Theol Ctr, registr & dir admin, 1967-69, dir, 1963-67; Asn Christ Train & Serv, staff assoc, 1969; assoc gen secy consult, Church Union, 1969-71; Miles Col, pres, 1971-86; Coun Trenholm State Tech Col, Montgomery, inter pres; W. Clyde William Neighborhood Networks Ctr, founder. **Orgs:** Adv comt, US Dept State; mem stud fin aid coun, US Dept HEW; res adv panel, US Off Educ Sch Monitor & Consum Prot Proj; Sickle Cell Dis adv com, NIH; co-chmn Comt Aff Com Oper New Birmingham; vice chmn, Ala Comt Human & Pub Policy; bd dir, Unit Negro Col Fund; bd dir, Birmingham Cable Comn; bd dir, Birmingham Urban League; bd dir, Nat Comn Black Chmn; bd dir, Am Nat Red Cross; bd trustee, Birmingham Symphony Asn; exec bd, BSA; exec comt, Jefferson County Child Develop Coun; City Adv Coun, Jefferson County; Birmingham Manpower Area Plan Coun; Lay Adv Coun, St Vincent's Hosp; NAACP; YMCA; Alpha Phi Alpha Frat Educ; Hon Soc Kappa Delta Pi, 1975. **Honors/Awds:** Man of Year, Omega Psi Phi Frat; Alumni Achievment Award, Paine Col, 1971; Outstanding Educ Soc Beauty Cong, 1972; Outstanding Educ Fed Soc Coop, 1975; City of Birmingham Mayor's Cit, 1974. **Business Addr:** Miles Coll, P O Box 3800, Birmingham, AL 35208.

WILLIAMS, WALLACE C
Executive. **Personal:** Born in North Carolina; divorced; children: Wallace Jr & Joyce. **Educ:** Boro-Hall Acad NY, 1946; Pace Col NY, attended 1948; Columbia Univ, attended 1950; Detroit Inst Tech, BS, 1958; Wayne State Univ, bus tech, 1970; Univ Detroit. **Career:** NY State Employ Serv, interviewer, 1947-53; US Bur Prisons, correctional aid prison fiscal officer, 1953-58; Mich Employment Securities Comn, interviewer, 1958-65, employment sec exec, 1965-69; Mich Dept Com, econ develop exec, 1969-; CCAC-ICBIF, dir, 1979; Mich Dept Labor, coord Manpower Prog; J L Dumas Construction Co, bus develop mgr, consult; State Mich, Off Minority Bus Enterprises, dir; Detroit Econ Growth Corp, dir City Detroit; METCO Eng Servs Inc, vpres bus develop; Royal Oak Township Planning Comn, chmn; Univ Mich, Sch Bus, dir, 1986-96. **Orgs:** Trustee, Exec Coun Trade Union Ldrshp Coun; past pres, Booker T Washington Bus Asn; exec bd, Inner City Bus Improvement Forum; chmn, Minority Bus Oppor Com; ed & publ, Minority Bus Newsletter; bd mem, HOPE Inc; New Detroit Minority Adv Com; Wayne Co Bd Comnr Minority Adv Co; serv officer, VFW TF Burns Post 5793; bd mem, Lewis Bus Col; bd dir, People's Comm Civic League; Bus Adv Com Detroit Chamber Com; Tr Bd Orchestra Hall Found; golden heritage, Nat Asn Advan Colored People; coord, Christian Prison fellowship Prog; asst reg vpres, Nat Bus League; vice chmn, Highland Pk YMCA; Adv Planning Coun Wayne Co; dir, Minority Bus Serv, Univ Mich, Ann Arbor. **Honors/Awds:** Community Service Award, Booker T Washington Business Asn; Businessman of the Year Awards, Wayne County Bd Comnrs & Gamma Phi Delta, 1984; Outstanding Public Service Award, Mich Lupus Found; Outstanding Service Award, State Mich; Spirit of Detroit Award, City Detroit; Appreciation Award, US Dept Com; City Flint, Mich Proclamations from Mayor Woodrow Stanley; City Coun, Mayor Coleman Young, City Detroit; Appreciation Award, City Coun, Royal Oak Township; Bethel AME Church Missionary Soc. **Military Serv:** AUS, sgt, 1942-46. **Business Addr:** Director, University of Michigan Business School, 506 E Liberty St, Ann Arbor, MI 48104.

WILLIAMS, WALLY JAMES, JR.
Football player. **Personal:** Born Feb 20, 1971, Tallahassee, FL; children: Bronson. **Educ:** Fla A&M Univ. **Career:** Football player (retired); Cleveland Browns, center, 1993-95; Baltimore Ravens, 1996-98; New Orleans Saints, 1999-2003. **Honors/Awds:** Ed Block Courage Award, 1997.

WILLIAMS, HON. WALTER
Lawyer, judge, educator. **Personal:** Born Jun 13, 1939, Yazoo City, MS; son of Walter Sr and Mary Lee Knight; married Helen M Hudson, Jul 4, 1964; children: Toni Marshea. **Educ:** Univ Wis, Cert, 1961; John Marshall Law Sch, JSD, 1970; Jackson State Univ Jackson MS, 1962. **Career:** Williams Slaughter & Williams, partner; Malcolm X Col, teacher; Circuit Ct Cook County, assoc judge, 1999-2003, supervising judge, currently. **Orgs:** Am Bar Asn; Chicago Bar Asn; pres, Cook County Bar Asn; Ill State Bar Asn; Nat Bar Asn; Alpha Phi Alpha Frat; Jackson State Univ Alumni Asn; John Marshall Law Sch Alumni; Ill Judicial Coun; Ill Judges Asn; Am Judges Asn. **Honors/Awds:** Leadership Award, Cook County Bar Asn, 1964; Jr Coun Award, Cook County Bar Asn, 1975; Outstanding Yazoo Citizen Award, 1975; Outstanding Achievement Award, Yazoo Brothers Club, 1987; Appreciation Award, Jackson State Univ, 1993; Kenneth E Wilson Award, Cook County Bar Asn, 1993; Distinguished Service Award, Ill Coun Juvenile & Family Ct Judges, 1994; Certificate of Recognition, Chicago Police Dept, Second Dist, 1996; Leadership & Service Award, Cook County Bar Asn, 1997; Chairperson's Special Award, Ill Judicial Coun, 1998. **Military Serv:** DOS, spec e-5, 1966. **Home Addr:** 5555 S Everett, Chicago, IL 60637. **Business Addr:** Supervising Judge, Circuit Court of Cook County, Richard J Daley Ctr 50 W Wash St, Chicago, IL 60602, **Business Phone:** (312)603-2600.

WILLIAMS, WALTER ANDER
Basketball player. **Personal:** Born Apr 16, 1970, Washington, DC; married April; children: Ty. **Educ:** Univ Md, BA, mgt & consumer studies, 1992. **Career:** Basketball player (retired); Sacramento Kings, guard-forward, 1992-96; Miami Heat, 1996; Toronto Raptors, 1996-98; Portland TrailBlazers, 1998-99; Houston Rockets, 1999-2002; Dallas Mavericks, 2002-03. **Special Achievements:** Film appearance: Eddie, 1996; Appeared in the music video for number one song "Only Wanna To Be With You" by Hootie and the Blowfish; Established a $125,000 scholarship fund at Maryland which benefits minority students in honor of his late father, Walter Sr.

WILLIAMS, WAYNE ALLAN
Research scientist. **Personal:** Born Oct 8, 1964, Brooklyn, NY; son of Isreal and Rose; married. **Educ:** Davidson Col, BA, classical studies, 1989; Boston Col, MEd, statist anal & measurement, 1991; Harvard Univ, technol & human develop. **Career:** Philadelphia Pub Schs Testing Reform, statist consult, 1990-91; Boston Col, Develop Off, res asst, 1990-91; Educ Develop Ctr, res intern, 1991; Boston Col, Career Ctr, statist consult, 1991-94; Boston Col, Ctr Study Testing, Eval & Educ Policy, fac res asst, 1991-93; Basic Plus Math Proj Eval, co-eval, 1992-93; Lesley Col, Algebra Proj Eval, statist consult, 1993-95; Grad Sch Educ Career Ctr, statist consult, 1993-95; Harvard Univ Divinity Sch, statist res assoc; Mass Inst Technol, Reflective Community Prac fel, 2001-03; Empowering Technol Inc, chief exec officer, currently. **Orgs:** Am Educ Res Asn, 1991-; Phi Delta Kappa, 1992-; Baker fel, Harvard Univ, 1993-95; co-founder, Benjamin Banneker Charter Sch, initial bd trustees, 1994-96; Black Data Processing Asn; Asn Comput Mach. **Honors/Awds:** Cumberland County Med Soc Award, 1983; Fayetteville Chap Links Honoree, 1983; Eumenean Literary Soc Cert, Davidson Col, 1987; AME Zion Church, North Charlotte Dist Outstanding Service Award, 1987; Academic Awareness Certificate for Academic Achievement, Davidson Col, 1989; Nat Hon Soc, 1992. **Special Achievements:** Author: "Developing a Multi-tiered Database for Measuring Systemic School R eform," 1995. **Home Addr:** 22 Peabody Terr, Cambridge, MA 02138.

WILLIAMS, WESLEY S
Lawyer. **Personal:** Born Nov 13, 1942, Philadelphia, PA; married Karen Roberta Hastie, Jan 1, 1968; children: Amanda, Bo & Bailey. **Educ:** Harvard Univ, magna cum laude, BA, 1963, JD, 1967; Woodrow Wilosn Fel Fletcher Sch Law, dipl, MA, 1964; Columbia Univ, LLM, 1969, JSD, 1969; Harvard Law Sch, SJD, 1997. **Career:** DC Council, legal counsel, 1967-69; Columbia Univ, assoc-in-law, 1968-69; US Sen Com DC, counr, legal counsel, 1969-70; Georgetown Univ law Ctr, adj prof law, 1971-73; Covington & Burling, partner, 1975-, assoc, 1970-75; DC City Coun, counr, 1967-69; Lockhart Co Inc, pres, chief exec officer, co chmn, 1978-; Blackstar Commun Inc, bd dir, 1987-; Broadcast Capital Inc, chmn & bd dir, 1989-92; Fed Res Bank Richmond, bd dir, 1997-; Salomon Inc, bd dir, 1997-. **Orgs:** Circuit Judicial Conf, 1971-; Exec Ecom Wash Lawyers' Com Civil Rights Under Law, 1972-; bd dir, Nat Symphony Orch Asn, 1972-; Com Legis Bar, 1973-; pres, Bd Trustees, Family & Child Serv Wash, 1974-; US Circuit Judge Nominating Comn, 1977-; counsel, DC Bar, 1979-81; pres, bd trustees, Nat Child Res Ctr, 1980-; life mem, Wash Urban League; sr trustee, mem, Exec Comt, bd trustees, Penn Mutual Life Ins Co, Philadelphia, Pa, currently; exec comt, Wash Lawyers Comt Civil Rights Under Law; Am Law Inst; life fel, Am Bar Found; coun past pres, Harvard Law Sch Asn, 1992-94; Alpha Phi Alpha & Sigma Pi Phi Fraternities; St Thomas Yacht Club; City Club Wash; Metrop Club Wash; Waltz Group Wash. **Home Addr:** 2500 Virginia Ave NW, Washington, DC 20037-1901. **Business Addr:** President, Chief Executive Officer, Lockhart Companies Incorporated, 44 Estate Thomas, PO Box 7020, St Thomas, Virgin Islands of the United States 00802, **Business Phone:** (340)776-1900.

WILLIAMS, WILBERT. **See Obituaries section.**

WILLIAMS, WILBERT EDD
Software developer. **Personal:** Born Sep 13, 1948, Fayetteville, NC; son of Edd and Mary Moore; married Yolanda Faye DeBerry; children: Danica Michelle & Donata Merie. **Educ:** Fayetteville State Univ, BS, 1977; Univ MI-Ann Arbor, MS, 1978; Duke Univ, MBA, 1986. **Career:** USN, digital display tech, 1967-74; Bell Labs, mem tech staff, 1977-79; ABB T&D Co, syst & software engr, 1979-86, mgr prod software, 1986. **Orgs:** Am Soc Naval Engrs, 1978-; Jack & Jill Am, 1982-; corp minority spokesperson, Westinghouse, 1983-; comm ambassador, Westinghouse Electric, 1983-; St Matthew Budget & Finance Comt 1984-; vpres, St Matthew Scholar Comt, 1986-87. **Honors/Awds:** Fel, Univ MI Bell Labs, 1977-78; Distinguished Corporate Alumni, NAFEO, 1983; Tuition Support for Duke MBA Westinghouse Electric, 1984-86; Corporate Community Service, Westinghouse Electric, 1988. **Military Serv:** USNR lt comdr, 23 yrs; Armed Forces Reserve Medal, 1986.

WILLIAMS, REV. WILBERT LEE
Educator, clergy, bishop. **Personal:** Born Aug 25, 1938, Corsicana, TX; son of Calvin Sr and Mamie; married Catherine L

Lemons, Dec 30, 1961; children: Sheila, Stuart & Cynthia. **Educ:** Prairie View A&M Col, BS, 1960; Howard Univ Sch Law, JD, 1971; Inst New Govt Attorneys, 1971; Howard Univ Sch Divinity, MDiv, 1990. **Career:** US Dept Agr, farm mgt supvr, 1965-68; United Planning Org, Wash DC, exec officer, 1968-71; US Dept Agr Off Gen Coun, Wash DC, atty, 1971-84; US Dept Agr, equal opportunity officer; The First New Horizon Baptist Church, founder, pastor, bishop, currently. **Orgs:** Past vpres & founding mem, CHASE Inc; DC Neighborhood Reinvestment Comn; bd dir, Neighborhood Legal Serv Prog, Wash DC; bd trustee, United Planning Org, Wash DC; pres & founder, The First New Horizon Comt Develop Ctr. **Honors/Awds:** First Annual Achievement Award, OEO Nat Adv Comt, Legal Serv Prog, 1968; Asst Secy Agr Award for Excellence, 1980; DHL, Faith Christian Univ & Schs, 2001. **Military Serv:** AUS, 1961-64. **Home Addr:** 7908 Old Branch Ave, Clinton, MD 20735, **Home Phone:** (301)856-9177. **Business Addr:** Bishop, The First New Horizon Baptist Church, 9511 Piscataway Rd, PO Box 176, Clinton, MD 20735, **Business Phone:** (301)856-9177.

WILLIAMS, WILLIAM DECEMBER, JR. See WILLIAMS, BILLY DEE.

WILLIAMS, PROF. WILLIAM THOMAS
Educator. **Personal:** Born Jul 17, 1942, Cross Creek, NC; son of Hazel Davis and William T; married Patricia A DeWeese; children: Nila & Aaron. **Educ:** New York City Community Col, AAS, 1962; Pratt Inst, BFA 1966; Skowhegan Sch Painting & Sculpture, 1965; Yale Univ, MFA, 1968. **Career:** Pratt Inst, painting fac, 1970; Sch Visual Arts, painting fac, 1970; City Univ New York, Brooklyn Col, prof art, 1971-; Skowhegan Sch Painting & Sculpture, res painting fac, 1971, 1974, 1978; Va Commonwealth Univ, distinguished vis commonwealth prof art, 1984; John Simon Guggenheim fel, John Simon Guggenheim Memorial Found, 1987; Mid-Atlantic Found fel, 1994. **Orgs:** Govenor Skowhegan Sch Painting & Sculpture, 1972-90; artistic bd, Cinque Gallery 1978-90; bd trustees, Grace Church Sch, 1984-87. **Honors/Awds:** Individual Artist Award, Painting Nat Endowment Arts & Humanities, 1965, 1970; Faculty Research Award, City Univ New York, 1973, 1984, 1987; Annual Award for Lifetime Achievement, Studio Mus, Harlem, 1992. **Business Addr:** Professor of Art, City University of New York, Brooklyn College, 5122 Boylan Hall, Brooklyn, NY 11210, **Business Phone:** (718)951-5181.

WILLIAMS, WILLIE, JR.
Executive. **Personal:** Married Nellie Redmond. **Educ:** Benedict Col, BA; Rutgers Univ, grad study; MI State Univ; SC St Col; Univ SC. **Career:** Willie Williams Real Estate Inc, pres & Founder; Richland Co, inst pubschs; Upward Bound Univ SC, couns; Midland Tech Ctr; Benedict Col, placement dir; SC Chap NAREB, pres; Palmetto Home Counseling Inc & Success Investment Co, chmn bd. **Orgs:** Columbia Bd Realtors; St Manufacturings Housing Comn; Richland Co Planning Comn; Bd Dir Columbia Urban League; adv bd, Columbia Opportunities Industrialization Ctr SC; bd trustees, Benedict Col; Friendship Jr Col; life mem, Nat Asn Advan Colored People; Omicron Phi Chap Omega Psi Phi; city chmn, 1974 UNCF Campaign. **Business Addr:** President, Willie Williams Real Est Inc, 6023 Two Notch Rd, Columbia, SC 29223.

WILLIAMS, DR. WILLIE, JR.
Educator. **Personal:** Born Mar 24, 1947, Independence, LA; son of Willie Williams Sr and Leanner Booker; married Deborah A Broady; children: Willie III. **Educ:** Southern Univ, BS, 1970; Iowa State Univ, MS, 1972, PhD, 1974. **Career:** Lincoln Univ, chmn Sci Math div, prof & chmn physics, 1978-80; Lincoln Univ, assoc prof, 1979-84, Dept Defense, phys scientist, 1980-82, prof, physics, 1984-; Lincoln Adv Sci & Eng Reinforcement Prog (LASER), 1981-96; Lincoln Univ LU-AAUP, pres. **Orgs:** Consult, Mobil Oil Co, 1977; phys scientist, Nat Bureau Stands, 1979; NASA Fel NASA 1979; ONR Fellow Naval Res Lab, 1980; chmn Cheyney Lincoln Temple Cluster, 1978-80; PRIME Bd Dir, 1977-, AAUP NY Acad Sci, Sigma Xi; dir, Lincoln Adv Sci & Eng Reinforcement Prog, 1981-96; Oxford Rotary, 1986-89; Am Phys Soc; Math Asn Am; Am Asn Physics Teachers; AAAS; NYK Acad Sci; Sigma Pi Sigma; Philadelphia based LASER Prog, pre-col effort. **Honors/Awds:** Lindback Award, Lincoln Univ, 1976; CLT Award, Cheyney Lincoln Temple Cluster, 1974-78; Excellence in Science & Technology; White House Initiative on HBCU's, 1988; Participaton in Science Symposium, Physics Dept, Southern Univ, 1991; Participation in African-American History Month. **Special Achievements:** US Navy, Int Logistics Control Office, 1991. **Business Addr:** Professor, Lincoln University, Department of Physics, 125 Wright Hall 1570 Baltimore Pike, Lincoln University, PA 19352, **Business Phone:** (484)365-7474.

WILLIAMS, DR. WILLIE ELBERT
Educator, mathematician. **Personal:** Born Jun 6, 1927, Jacksonville, TX; married Doris Lee Matlock; children: Lois E, Willys E, Donald A, Linda W & Dorwyl L. **Educ:** Huston Tillotson Col Austin, Tex, BS, Math (cum laude), 1952; Tex S Univ Houston, MS, Math, 1953; Mich State Univ, PhD, Math, 1972. **Career:** Educator, Mathematician (Retired); Lufkin Independent School Dist, teacher, 1953-59; Cleveland Bd Educ, 1960-73; Case-Western Reserve Univ, 1964-68; Deep Accelerated Math Prog, 1973-78; Florida Intl Univ, assoc prof. **Orgs:** Consult Nat Follow Through Prog, 1974-75; Second Bapt Ch, 1975-80; Omega Psi Phi Frat State Fla, 1979-80; Concerned Black Educ in Higher Educn Fla, 1980-81; evaluator Col Title III Progs; vpres, chair anti crime comm PULSE; Black Faculty Fla Intl Univ; lectr BAM; recruiter Black Faculty & Black Students. **Honors/Awds:** Univ Colo, Outstanding Teacher Award, 1954; Martha Holden Jennings Found, Master Teacher Award, 1973. **Military Serv:** AUS, corpl, 1945-49; Occupation Good Conduct Medal. **Home Addr:** 9781 SW 148 St, Miami, FL 33176, **Home Phone:** (305)251-7998.

WILLIAMS, WILLIE J.
Educator. **Personal:** Born Jan 8, 1949, Chester County, SC; married Louvenia Brooks. **Educ:** Voorhees Col, BS. **Career:** Indust Educ Develop Corp, proj dir Jobs 70 prog, 1970-73; Custom Packagers & Processors Inc, Atlanta, GA, personnel dir, 1973-74; Colquitt County Bd Educ, Moultries GA, teacher, 1974-. **Orgs:** Honor Soc Finley Sr High Sch, 1964-66; Omega Psi Phi Frat, 1968-; Free Accepted Masons, 1973-; Colquitt County Civil Defense Rescue Team, 1973-; Nat St & Local Educ Asn, 1974-75; Steering Comt Quarter Sys Colquitt County Sch, 1974-75; Amateur Softball Asn Umpires, 1975-; registered Emer Med Tech St Ga; St Ga Dept Defense Rescue Workers. **Honors/Awds:** Dale Carnegie Certificate of Appreciation, 1973.

WILLIAMS, WILLIE JAMES
Athletic coach, educator. **Personal:** Born Sep 12, 1931, Gary, IN; son of Orrie (deceased) and Elnora; married Barbara, Dec 31, 1955; children: Darla & Margot. **Educ:** Univ Ill, BS, 1955; Ind Univ, MS, 1971. **Career:** Sch City Gary Ind, teacher-coach, 1958-82; Univ Ill, assoc head men's track coach, sprint coach, 1982-2000; sprint & hurdles consult, currently. **Orgs:** NCAA Track & Field Asn, 1982-. **Honors/Awds:** Gold medal, 4 X 100 relay, Pan Am Games, Mex City, 1955; World's Fastest Man, 1956; Inducted into Indiana High School Coaches Track & Field Hall of Fame, 1980. **Special Achievements:** Set world record in 100 meter dash, Int Track & Field Fed, 1956, alsoracked up nine individual Big Ten Championships during his career, winningthe 60 yard dash twice, the 70 yard hurdles twice, two titles in the 100yard dash, and three more in the 220 yard dash, published Track Article on-Sprinting, The Coaching Clinic, Prentice Hall, February 1980. **Military Serv:** AUS, spec-1, 1955-57; Int Military Sports, sprint champion, 100 meterdash, 1956. **Home Addr:** 1607 Trails Dr, Urbana, IL 61801, **Home Phone:** (217)337-6616.

WILLIAMS, WILLIE JAMES, JR.
Football player. **Personal:** Born Dec 26, 1970, Columbia, SC; married Melissa; children: Dominique. **Educ:** Western Carolina Univ. **Career:** Football (retired), 2006: Pittsburgh Steelers, defensive back, 1993-96 & 2004-06; Seattle Sea hawks,1997-2003.

WILLIAMS, WILLIE L
Law enforcement officer. **Personal:** Born Oct 1, 1943, Philadelphia, PA; son of Willie L Williams Sr and Helen S; married Oct 22, 1966; children: Lisa, Willie L Jr & Eric. **Educ:** Northwestern Univ, cert, police admin, 1978; Philadelphia Col Textiles & Sci, ABA, 1982; Pub Safety Media Inst, 1986; Ctr Creative Leadership, Eckerd Col, sr leadership, 1986; Harvard Univ, Police Exec Research Forum, cert, 1987; FBI Nat Exec Inst, 1989; St Joseph Univ, MS, 1991. **Career:** Law enforcement officer (retired); Fairmont Park Guards, police officer, 1964-72; City Philadelphia, police detective, 1972-74, police sgt, 1974-76, Juvenile Aid Div, police lt, 1976-84, 22nd & 23rd Police Dist, police capt, comdr, 1984-86, Training Bur, Civil Affairs Div, N Police Div, police inspector, head, 1986, dep comnr admin, 1988, police comnr, 1988-92; City Los Angeles, Police Dept, chief police, 1992-97; Hartsfield Atlanta International Airport, fed security dir. **Orgs:** Nat Orgn Black Law Enforcement Executives; Int Asn Chiefs Police; Alpha Signian Lambda Nat Honors Soc; Pa Juvenile Officers Asn; Southeastern Pa Chiefs Police; Los Angeles County Chiefs Asn; Janes Memorial Methodist Church, West Oak Lane Youth Asn; Boy Scouts Am. **Honors/Awds:** William French Smith Award; recipient of ten police Dept commendations & numerous civic awards. **Special Achievements:** First African-American police commissioner of both the Philadelphia Police Department and the Los Angeles Police Department.

WILLIAMS, WILLIE LAVERN
Educator. **Personal:** Born Dec 24, 1940, Little Rock, AR; married Margaret Jean Lee; children: Gregory, Kristy, Karen & Stephen. **Educ:** San Jose State Col, BA, 1962; Calif State Univ, Long Beach, teaching cert, 1963; Univ Ariz, MEd, 1977. **Career:** Calif State Univ, Long Beach, coach, 1963-64; Compton High Sch, educ & coach, 1964-69; Univ Ariz, adj assoc prof & coach, 1969-. **Orgs:** Nat Asn Advan Colored People; Nat Urban League, 1972-; regional chmn, Athletics Cong, 1974-; reg VII rep, US Track Coaches Asn, 1976-80; chmn, US Olympic Comt, 1977-; regional dir, Track & Field USA, 1978. **Honors/Awds:** Coach of the Year, Calif Inter scholastic Fed, 1969; NCAA Region VII Coach of Year, Nat Col Athletic Asn, 1972.

WILLIAMS, WILLIE S
Psychologist. **Personal:** Born May 8, 1932, Prattville, AL; married Marva R Flowers; children: Kevin, Keith & Karla. **Educ:** Wichita State Univ, AB, Chem & Math, 1958; Xavier OH, MEd, Admin & Personnel Serv, 1960; Mich State Univ, PhD, Counsel Psychol, 1970. **Career:** Case Western Res Univ Sch Med, assoc dean stud affairs; NIMH Min Ctr, asst chief Psychol Res & Training Prog; Univ Cincinnati, sr counselor & asst prof psychol, Cincinnati Police Dept, psychol counselor; Willie S Williams PhD Inc, pres, currently. **Orgs:** Pres, Phi Delta Kappa ANWC; Am Personnel & Guild Asn; treas, Asn Black Psychologists; Am Psychol Asn; Kappa Alpha Psi. **Military Serv:** AUS, 1953-55. **Home Phone:** (216)831-8009. **Business Addr:** President, Willie S Williams PhD Inc, 20310 Chagrin Blvd, PO Box 22257, Shaker Heights, OH 44122, **Business Phone:** (216)491-9405.

WILLIAMS, YARBOROUGH, JR.
Government official, teacher. **Personal:** Born Mar 24, 1950, Warrenton, NC; married Carolyn M; children: Consherto V, Yarborough & Juroid C. **Educ:** NC State Univ, voc; Vance Granvillco Col, drafting. **Career:** Franklinton City Schs, teacher, 17 yrs; Warren County Pub Sch Dist, sch bdmem. **Orgs:** Nat Asn Advan Colored People; pres, Warren County Polit Action Coun; pres-,Boys Club; Warren County Bd Election; Warren County Dem Party; NC Sch BdAsn. **Honors/Awds:** Teacher of the Year, Asn Gen Contractors Am, 1986. **Home Addr:** 571 Shocco Spring Rd, Warrenton, NC 27589.

WILLIAMS, PROF. YVONNE CARTER
Educator. **Personal:** Born Feb 12, 1932, Philadelphia, PA; daughter of Patterson H (deceased) and Evelyn Lightner (deceased); married Theodore, Jul 3, 1954; children: Lynora A, Alison P, Meredith J & Lesley Y. **Educ:** Pa State Univ, BA (cum laude), 1953; Harvard Law Sch, attended 1954; Univ Conn, MA (honors), 1955; Case Western Reserve Univ, PhD, 1981. **Career:** Univ Conn, Dept Educ, admin asst; Ashland Wayne Community Action Commission, dir res, 1964-66; Wayne County Head start, social worker,1967-68; Wooster Pub Schs, visiting teacher, 1968-69; Ohio State Univ, lecturer, 1971-72; Lilly Endowment, consult & evaluator; NEH, Middle States & N Central Assocs; Col Wooster, asst to dean, asst prof pol sci, Dept Black Studies, dir, 1973-74, assoc prof, Dept Pol Sci & Black Studies, prof, dir, 1983, dean faculty, 1989-95, prof, emer, 2000-. **Orgs:** Wayne County Bd Mental Health & Retardation, 1969-76; Wooster City Charter Commission, 1971-72; League Women Voters delegate to Nat Convention, 1972; Head Start Parents' Adv Coun, 1970-73; Mayor's Alternate to NEFCO, 1974-75; Col Hills Retirement Village 1973; Wooster City Charter Review Commission, 1980; City Wooster Human Relations Coun, 1978; Wooster Community Hosp, 1981; Health Trustee Inst, 1986-88; Advisory Bd, Wayne County Adult Basic Educ, 1987-89; Ohio Humanities coun, 1989-96. **Honors/Awds:** John Hay Whitney Fel; Case Western Reserve Univ; Alumni, AHS Fel; Jessie Smith Noyes Found Scholarship; Faculty Develop Grant, Col Wooster, Morris Fund. **Special Achievements:** Inducted in Ohio Women's Hall of Fame, 2003. **Home Addr:** 659 College Ave, Wooster, OH 44691. **Business Addr:** Professor Emerita, College of Wooster, Department of Black Studies and Political Science, 1189 Beall Ave, Wooster, OH 44691, **Business Phone:** (330)263-2000.

WILLIAMS, YVONNE LAVERNE
Lawyer. **Personal:** Born Jan 7, 1938, Washington, DC; daughter of Verna L Rapley and Smallwood E. **Educ:** Barnard Col, BA, 1959; Boston Univ, MA, 1961; Georgetown Univ, JD, 1977. **Career:** US Info Agency, foreign serv Officer, 1961-65; African-Am Inst NY, dir womens Africa comn, 1966-68; Benedict Col, Columbia, SC, assc prof African Am studies, 1968-70; US Cong Wash, DC, press sec Hon Walter Fauntroy, 1970-72; African-Am Scholars Coun Wash, DC, dir 1972-73; Leva Hawes Symington Martin, Wash, DC, assoc atty, 1977-79; Brimmer & Co Wash, DC, asst vpres, 1980-82; Tuskegee Univ, vpres Fed & Int Rel & Legal Coun 1983-96; Acad Educ Develop Pub Policy & Int Affairs Fel Prog, vpres & nat dir, 1996-. **Orgs:** Oper Crossroads Africa, 1960-, Barnard-in-Wash, 1960-; Am Bar Assoc, 1980-, Nat Bar Asn, 1980-, Dist Columbia Bar, 1980-; alumnae trustee, Barnard Col, 1988-92; bd dir, Golden Rule Apartments, Inc, 1986-. **Honors/Awds:** Boston Univ, Africa Res & Studies Prog Fel, 1959-60. **Special Achievements:** Author, "William Monroe Trotter, (1872-1934)"; in Reid "The Black Prism," New York, 1969. **Business Phone:** (202)884-8000.

WILLIAMS BOYD, SHEILA ANNE
Manager. **Personal:** Born Apr 11, 1951, Chicago, IL; daughter of Kathryn Naomi Walker; divorced; children: Christine Williams, Kelly, Jamie & Michael Blakley. **Educ:** Olive Harvey Jr Col, Chicago, IL, assoc arts, acct high hon, 1975; Roosevelt Univ, Chicago, IL, BS & BA, acct with hon, 1977; Univ Chicago, Chicago, IL, exec MBA prog, 1992. **Career:** Ernst & Young, Chicago, IL, sr auditor, 1977-79; Amoco Corp, Chicago, IL, mgr, prof audit pract, 1979-92, mgr, banking coord & develop, 1993, mgr, credit coord, 1994-. **Orgs:** Bd govrs, Chicago Chap, Inst Internal Auditors, 1989-92; treas, Nat Black MBA Asn, Chicago, 1990; bd mem, Univ Chicago Exec Prog Club, 1993-. **Honors/Awds:** CPA, IL, 1979; Certified Internal Auditor, 1983; Member of the Year, 1990; Outstanding Business & Professional Award, Dollars & Sense Mag, 1991. **Special Achievements:** 100 of the Most Promising Black Women in Corporate America, Ebony Mag, 1991. **Business Phone:** (312)856-3200.

WILLIAMS-BRIDGERS, JACQUELYN L
Government official. **Personal:** Born Feb 27, 1956, Washington; married Daniel Bridgers; children: 2. **Educ:** Syracuse Univ, BA, 1977; Maxwell Sch Pub Affairs & Citzenship, MPA, 1978. **Career:** Gen Acct Off, assoc dir for housing & community develop, mgt analyst; US State Dept, inspector gen, 1995-2001; Int Affairs & Trade Gen Acct Off, managing dir, currently. **Orgs:** Chair, Bd External Auditors, Orgn Am States; adv bd, Maxwell Sch Pub Affairs & Citizenship. **Honors/Awds:** Arthur S Flemming Award; Meritorious Serv Award, GAO, 1992; DHL, Southeastern Univ, 1996. **Special Achievements:** First African American and first woman inspector general US State Department, 1995. **Business Addr:** Managing Director, International Affairs and Trade Office, General Accounting, Rm 4T55A 441 G St NW, Washington, DC 20548.

WILLIAMS DAVIS, EDITH G
Geophysicist. **Personal:** Born Apr 8, 1958, Passaic, NJ; daughter of Ester Jean Rudolph and James E; married Warren C Davis Jr, May 25, 1984. **Educ:** Univ Miami, BS, geol, 1981, geological expedition Guatemala C Am, 1978; Stanford Univ, MS, geophys, 1982, geophysical field expedition Nevada, 1982; Univ Tex, Austin, MBA, 1991. **Career:** Oxygen Isotopic Lab, coord, 1977, Dr Cesare Emiliani, 1977-78; US Geol Survey, geol field asst, 1980; Marathon Oil Co, geophysical asst, 1981; US Geol Survey, exploration geophysicist, 1981-82; Mobil Oil Inc, exploration geophysicist, 1983-86; Continental Airlines, Houston, TX, gen sales reservation, 1987; Univ Tex, Grad Sch Bus, Dean off, Austin, minority student affairs coordr, 1987-89; 3M Headquarters, St Paul, MN, marketing intern, 1988; Prime Network, Houston, Tex busdevelop, 1990; The Household of Faith, Tex Reservists Trust Fund, Houston, TX, admin of trust fund, 1991; ABBA Mktg Exchange; co-founder; Texas Natural Resource Conservation Commn, prog admin. **Orgs:** Miami Geological Soc, 1976-78; pres, United Black Students Organ, 1978-79; sci coord, Upward Bound Prog, 1979; Delta Sigma Theta Sor, 1979; AGU, 1981-82; AAPG, 1982-84; Amer Asn of Exploration Geophysics, 1982-84; vice pres, MBA Women's Asn; Nat Blank Men Asn, recording Sec, 1987-. **Honors/Awds:** John F Kennedy/Martin Luther King Scholarship Grant, 1977-80; President's List, 1978; United Black Students President's Award 1978; Univ Miami Honors Scholarship, 1978; Shell Oil Scholarship Grant, 1978-80; Amer Geologic Union Award, 1981-82; US Geol Survey Fel, 1981-82; Am Geol Inst Fel, 1981-82; Natl Black MBA Fel, 1987; Consortium for Graduate Study in Management Fel, 1988. **Home Addr:** PO Box 141753, Austin, TX 78714, **Home Phone:** (512)239-1345. *

WILLIAMS-DOTSON, DARYL
Architect. **Personal:** Born Dec 14, 1958, Daytona Beach, FL; daughter of Ernest J and Arnita Green; divorced; children: Michael S Burrows, Chloe W Dotson & Lyle W Dotson. **Educ:** Southern Univ & A&M Col, B Arch, 1984. **Career:** Varney Sexton Lunsford Aye Architects, 1985-89; Clark Tribble Harris Li Architects, 1989-90; Clyde E Woods & Assoc Inc, assoc, 1991-98; Williams-Dotson Assoc Inc, 1995; WDI Archit Inc, owner, currently. **Orgs:** Nat Coun Architects Regist Bd; Prof Am Inst Architects; Nat Asn Women Bus Owners; Nat Orgn Minority Architects; Alpha Chi Nat Honor Scholar Soc. **Home Addr:** 5774 Grandiose Dr, Indianapolis, IN 46228, **Home Phone:** (317)253-3142. **Business Addr:** Owner, WDI Architecture Inc, 15 W 28th St, Indianapolis, IN 46208, **Business Phone:** (317)251-6172.

WILLIAMS-DOVI, JOANNA
School administrator. **Personal:** Born Apr 16, 1953, Harrisburg, PA; daughter of Thomas Edison Williams Sr and Bertha Manervia Brown Williams; married Sewar M (divorced 1983). **Educ:** Cheyney Univ, Cheyney, PA, BA, 1977; Penn State Univ, Middletown, PA, MEd, 1997. **Career:** Penn State Univ, Middletown, PA, admin asst, EET Prog, 1984-88, Off Multicultural Recruitment & Community Affairs, asst dir admis, 1988-. **Orgs:** Leader, Girl Scouts Coun Am, 1979-83; Penn Asn Col Admis Counr, 1987-; Am Asn Collegiate Registrars & Admin Off, 1987-; Nat Asn Col Admin Counr, 1987-; Delta Sigma Theta Sorority Inc, 1990-; Penn Col Personnel Asn, 1990-. **Business Addr:** Assistant Director of Admissions, Pennsylvania State University, Office of the Multicultural Recruitment and Community Affairs, Swatara Bldg, Middletown, PA 17057-4898.

WILLIAMS-GARNER, DEBRA
Writer, consultant, association executive. **Personal:** Born Feb 9, 1957, Washington, DC; daughter of Ernest E Sr and Sadie Lark; married David Garner, Oct 2, 1982; children: Brooke N Garner & Evan D Garner. **Educ:** Univ Bridgeport, Bridgeport, CT, BA, 1979; Am Univ, MA, 1999. **Career:** Wash Star Newspaper, Wash, DC, freelance writer, 1979-81; Libr Cong, Wash, DC, ed & writer, 1981-85; Environ Defense Fund, Wash, DC, media specialist, 1985-89; Providence Hosp, Wash, DC, pub rels specialist, 1987-89; Am Heart Asn, Wash, DC, dr communs, 1989-92; freelance writer & prom consult, 1993-; Wash Hosp Ctr, Media rels specialist, 1993-95; MD Asn HMOs, dir Commun, 1996-98; MD Teachers Asn, pub rels specialist, 1998-; Books: Pipedreams, 1988; Sister Spirit, 1999; Poems: "Poet on Fire for Jesus"; "Words on the Wall". **Orgs:** Delta Sigma Theta, Fort Washington Alumnae Chap, 1990-92; Delta Sigma Theta, Fort Wash Alumnae Chap, 1990-92; AFA Writers Guild, 1989-; Am Acad Poets, 1994-; Something Inspirational Prods, vp & co-founder; Poetic Voices, publicity coord. **Honors/Awds:** Isiah Robinson Media Award, Univ Bridgeport, 1979; 2nd Place Winner, Poetry Contest, PA Writers Conf, 1994. **Home Addr:** 6606 Lansdale St, District Heights, MD 20747.

WILLIAMS-GREEN, JOYCE F.
School administrator, educator. **Personal:** Born Sep 6, 1948, Sanford, NC; daughter of Joseph A Williams; married Edward W, Sep 1, 1984. **Educ:** NC Cent Univ, BS, 1970; Herbert H Lehman Col, MS, 1976; Va Polytech Inst & State Univ, EdD, 1984. **Career:** New York Pub Sch, teacher, 1971-76; Livingstone Col, dir learning ctr, 1976-80; Va Polytech Inst & State Univ, Cunningham res fel, 1983, dir & asst provost, 1987-. **Orgs:** Citizen rep, Blacksburg in the 80's, 1984-86; consult, Janus Learning Ctr, 1986, NC A&T, 1986; co-chair, Phi Kappa Phi, 1986-87; mem res comn, NACADA, 1986; bd mem, Warm Hearth Fdn, 1986-; bd mem, New River Community Sentencing Inc; Govs Monitoring Comt, 1990-. **Honors/Awds:** Nat Cert Merit, NACADA, 1986. **Special Achievements:** Publ: "The Effect of the Computer on Nat Educ", Computing Conf proceedings, 1983. **Business Phone:** (703)231-5812.

WILLIAMS-HARRIS, DIANE BEATRICE
School administrator. **Personal:** Born Feb 1, 1949, Newark, NJ; divorced; children: Karl & Elayne. **Educ:** Boston Univ, BA, 1971; Rutgers Univ, Grad Sch Educ, MEd, 1977. **Career:** Prudential Ins Co, pension admin, 1971-73; Rutgers Univ Office Undergrad Admissions, asst to the dir, 1973-76, asst dir, 1976-78, dir, 1978-82, assoc dir, 1982-. **Orgs:** Nat Assoc Col Admissions Counrs, Delta Sigma Theta, 100 Black Women. **Honors/Awds:** Sponsored participant in Women in Higher Educ, 1977; Rutgers Univ Merit Awd, 1986, 1993. **Business Addr:** Associate Director of Undergraduate Admissions, Rutgers University- New Brunswick Campus, PO Box 2101, New Brunswick, NJ 08901-1281, **Business Phone:** (732)932-4636.

WILLIAMS-HAYES, THEA
Educator. **Personal:** Born Jun 19, 1974, Gulfport, MS; daughter of Rev Rosemary and Rev Theodore. **Educ:** Tougaloo Col, BA, 1997; William Carey Col, Gifted cert, 1999, MEd, 1999; Univ Southern Miss, PhD, 2003. **Career:** Pass Christian Pub Schs, third grade teacher, 1997-98, gifted educ teacher, 1998-2000, 2002-03; Univ Southern Miss, grad asst, 2000-02; Nicholls State Univ, asst prof educ, 2003-. **Orgs:** Alpha Kappa Alpha Sorority Inc, 1993-; Kappa Delta Pi, 1996; Int Reading Asn, 2000-; Col Reading Asn, 2000-; Phi Kappa Phi, 2001-; Nat Coun Teachers Eng, 2002-. **Honors/Awds:** Outstanding Elementary Educator Award, Tougaloo Col, 1997; Student Achievement Award, USM Afro-Amer Student Org, 2001, 2002. **Special Achievements:** Nat Coun Teachers Eng Conf, presenter, 2002; Col Reading Asn Conf, presenter, 2002, 2003; Int Reading Asn, presenter, 2003. **Business Addr:** Assistant Professor of Education, Nicholls State University, 233 Polk Hall, PO Box 2035, Thibodaux, LA 70310, **Business Phone:** (985)448-4335.

WILLIAMS MEYERS, AUDREY. **See WILLIAMS, DR. AUDREY.**

WILLIAMS-MYERS, ALBERT J
Educator, writer. **Personal:** Born Mar 10, 1939, Edison, GA; son of Bessie Irene and C Kilmer; married Janice Diane Redmond, Oct 11, 1962; children: M Maluwa & Plaisimwana Renee. **Educ:** Wagner Col, BA, 1962; UCLA, life-time teaching cert, 1969, MA, 1971, PhD, hist, 1978. **Career:** Mobilization Youth, work group leader, 1962-63; All Saints Parish Sch, teacher 8th through 11th grade, 1963-64; Col Virgin Islands, head resident & dir activ, 1964-65; Ford Found, res Africa & middle E grad fel, 1973-74; Carleton Col, prof, 1976-79; SUNY Albany African Am Inst, exec dir, 1990-91; SUNY Col New Paltz, prof, currently. **Orgs:** St club worker, NYC Youth Bd, 1965-66; volunteer, US Peace Corps, Malawi, Africa, 1966-68; African Studies Asn, 1971-80; pres, NY African Studies Asn, 1985-88; NCP, Ellenville, Chapter, 1985-. **Honors/Awds:** Distinguished African American Researcher Award, Hist Hudson Valley, 1992. **Special Achievements:** Writer of "A Portrait of Eve: History of Black Women in Hudson Valley," 1987, Making The Invisible Visible: AFAs in New York History, 1994, "Slavery, Rebellion and Revolution in The AMEs: A Historiographical Scenario on the Theses of Genovese and Others," Journal of Black Studies 26, 4 March 1996, Journal of Afro-Americans in New York Life and History, July 1997, NY City, African Americans and Selected Memory: An Historiographical Assessment of a Black Presence Before 1877, books published include "Long Hammering: Essays on the forging of an African American Presence in the Hudson River Valley to the Early Twentieth Century," Africa World Press, 1994, "Destructive Impulses: An Examination of An American Secret in Race Relations: White Violence," University Press of America, 1995, On the Morning Tide: Afr Amers, History & Methodolgy In the Historical Ebb & Flow of Hudson River Society, 2003, African Dreams: To Tell Their Story of Old New York. **Home Phone:** (914)255-8257. **Business Addr:** Professor, State University of New York, College at New Paltz, College Hall F-106, New Paltz, NY 12561, **Business Phone:** (845)257-2760.

WILLIAMSON, CARL VANCE
Government official. **Personal:** Born Oct 3, 1955, Portsmouth, VA; son of Carolyn and Shelton. **Educ:** Va Commonwealth Univ, BS, 1977; Univ S Fla, MBA, 1984. **Career:** Group W Cable Inc, financial analyst, 1983-85; MCI Telecommunications, supvr-acct & analysis, 1985-86; Hampton Redevelopment/Housing Authority, housing mgt supvr, 1986-; Newport News Redevelopment & Housing Authority, dir pub housing. **Orgs:** Omega Psi Phi Frat Inc, 1974-; Am Asn MBA Execs, 1984-; Nat Black MBA Asn, 1985-; NAACP. **Home Addr:** 475 Water St Apt 206, Portsmouth, VA 23704.

WILLIAMSON, CARLTON
Football player, executive. **Personal:** Born Jun 12, 1958, Atlanta, GA; married Donna; children: Kevin & Joshua. **Educ:** Univ Pittsburgh, BS, 1981. **Career:** Football player (retired), Executive; San Francisco 49ers, safety, 1981-87; Waffle House Inc, sr vpres, currently; Univ Pittsburgh, safety. **Honors/Awds:** All Rookie, 1981. **Business Phone:** (404)355-5562.

WILLIAMSON, CLARENCE
Manager. **Personal:** Born Oct 15, 1949, Fort Benning, GA; son of Clarence Williamson, Sr and Edda R Farmer; widowed; children: Tannis Jenine & Clarence Todd. **Educ:** Morris Brown Col, BA, 1971; Emory Univ, mgt cert, 1979; Clark Atlanta Univ, MPA, 1993; Georgia Tech, Ec. Dev. Cert, 2000. **Career:** Citizens & Southern Nat Bank, vpres, 1971-83; Com-Med Corp, vpres, 1983-94; Sweet Auburn Improvement Asn, mgt specialist, 1995; Morris Brown Col, alumni affairs dir, 1996-98; Morehouse Sch Med, adminr, 1998; Atlanta Technical Col, edu prog spec, 1998-2002, vpres, currently; W Ray Wallace & Assoc, proj mgr. **Orgs:** Alpha Phi Alpha Fraternity, 1968-; Morris Brown Nat Alumni Asn, 1980-; NABEO Corp Roundtable, 1980-85; 100 Black Men Atlanta, 1992-; bd mem, S Fulton Chamber Com, 1999-; steering comt, Red Oak Network Ctr, 1999-; bd mem, S Fulton Dollars Scholars, 1999-; bd mem, United Way Fulton County, 2002. **Honors/Awds:** Certified Economic Developer, GA Dept Tech & Adult Educ, 2000; Achievement Award, South Fulton Chamber Com, 2001. **Special Achievements:** Author: C & S Commercial Credit Documentation Manual, 1975; Morris Brown Nat Alumni Asn Handbook, 1997. **Business Addr:** Vice President Economic Development, Atlanta Technical College, 1560 Metropolitan Pkwy Sw, Atlanta, GA 30310, **Business Phone:** (404)225-4511.

WILLIAMSON, CORLISS MONDARI
Basketball player, basketball coach. **Personal:** Born Dec 4, 1973, Russellville, AR; son of Jerry Williamson and Bettye; children: 3. **Career:** Basketball player (retired), basketball coach; Sacramento Kings, forward, 1995-2000; Toronto Rapters, 2000-01; Detroit Pistons, 2001-04; Philadelphia 76ers, 2004-05; Sacramento Kings, 2005-07; Ark Baptist Col, asst coach, currently. **Honors/Awds:** Gatorade National Player of the Year, 1992; Most Valuable Player of the Final Four, NCAA; SECs Mens Basketball Player of the Year, 1994, 1995; NBAs sixth Man of the Year Award, 2002; NBA champion, 2003-04. **Business Addr:** Assistant Coach, Arkansas Baptist College, 1621 Dr Martin Luther King Dr, Little Rock, AR 72202, **Business Phone:** (501)517-3185.*

WILLIAMSON, ETHEL W
Educator, museum director. **Personal:** Born Nov 28, 1947, Hallandale, FL; daughter of Harvey and Essie L; married Daniel A, Jun 20, 1970; children: Jason D. **Educ:** Cent State Univ, BS, eng, 1969; Teachers Col, Columbia Univ, MA, MEd, guidance, 1973; Rutgers-The State Univ, NJ, mus studies cert, 1992. **Career:** Huntington Nat Bank, training asst, 1969-71; NJ Inst Technol, asst dir, 1973-79, dir, Educ Opportunity Prog, 1978-79; Douglass Col, Rutgers Univ, asst dean stud, 1979-81; Union County Col, counsr generalist, 1986-90; Cooper-Hewitt, Nat Mus Design, Smithsonian Inst, proj coord, AFA design archive, 1991-. **Orgs:** Delta Sigma Theta Sorority, 1968-; historian, North Jersey Chapter Jack & Jill AME, 1985-91; historian, Union County Cult & Hist Comn, City Plainfield, 1986-89; AFA Mus Asn, 1991-; Sisters United NJS, 1992-; prog comt chair, NJS Chapter Cent State Univ Alumni Asn, 1992-. **Honors/Awds:** Minority Graduate fellowship, Teachers Col, Columbia Univ, 1971, 1972; Academic Internship Award, Smithsonian Inst, Off Mus Prog, 1991. **Special Achievements:** Co-curator of first individual exhibition by an AFA designer, Cooper-Hewitt Museum; Established a Nat AFA design archive, Cooper-Hewitt; "Engineering Opportunity Program: A Concept and a Commitment," National Technical Association Journal, 1976. **Home Addr:** 901 Grant Ave, Plainfield, NJ 07060, **Home Phone:** (908)561-4088. **Business Addr:** Project Coordinator, Cooper-Hewitt National Museum Design, Smithsonian Institution, Department of Decorative Arts, 2 E 91st St, New York, NY 10128, **Business Phone:** (212)849-8400.

WILLIAMSON, DR. HANDY, JR.
School administrator, consultant. **Personal:** Born Oct 24, 1945, Louin, MS; son of Handy Williamson Sr and Lilla M Nobles; married Barbara Jean Herndon, Dec 28, 1968; children: Lilla-Marie Juliana. **Educ:** Pineywood Jr Col, Pineywood, MS, AA, 1965; Alcorn State Univ, Lorman, MS, BS, 1967; Tenn State Univ, Nashville, TN, MS, 1969; Univ Miss, Columbia MO, MS, 1971, PhD, 1974. **Career:** Tenn State Univ, Nashville, TN, res asst, 1967-69, res dir, 1977-85; Univ Miss, Columbia, Mo, grad res asst, 1969-74; Tuskegee Univ, Tuskegee, AL, assoc dir res, 1974-77; USAID, Wash DC, dir, 1985-88; Univ Tennessee, Knoxville.

TN, dept head & prof, 1988-; Tuskegee Univ Prof Agr workers conf, lectr, 2000; Miss Univ, vice provost, 2001-, prof agr econ, currently. **Orgs:** Gamma Sigma Delta, 1971; bd mem, 1972-73, sec chair, comm chair, Univ Mo, 1974-; Black Culture Ctr, Univ Mo; AAEA; Title V Comt Rural Develop, 1975-77; pres, Phi Beta Sigma, Tuskegee chap, 1975-77; charter mem, Optimist Club Tuskegee, 1975-77; Task Force Energy, 1976-77; Southern Region's Small Farm Functional Network, 1976-77; United Methodist Men, 1977; Am Agr Econs Asn; Soc Agr Econs Asn; secy-treas, Asn Res Dirs, 1977-85; chmn, Tenn Coun Agri Deans, 1977-85; consult, Tenn Valley Authority, 1979-80; consult, Bd Intl Food & Agric Develop, 1981-85; mem, legisl subcomn, ESCOP, 1981-84; Paster Parish Comn, Clark UMC Church, 1981-85; US Joint Coun Food & Agri, 1982-83; bd dirs, Asn Int Dirs, 1982-87; bd mem, Asn Int Prog Dirs, 1984-88; bd dirs, Asn State Univ Dirs Int Agri Develop prog, 1984-88; chmn, Tenn Coun Agr Deans, 1984; NASULGC; White House Comm liaison, USAID, 1985-88; dir, Va Bus Develop Ctr, 1987-; SAEA Hon Life Membership Comt, 1990-93; chmn, AAEA Comt Status Blacks, 1991-93; vice chmn, Southern Agr Econ Dept Heads Asn, 1991-92; vpres, Knoxville chap, Kiwanis Club, 1993, bd dir; BOD United Methodist Found, 1994-; mentor, Black Achievers Ass, Knoxville TN, 1995-; charter mem, pres-elect, Sigma Pi Phi, 1996; Tenn State Univ Agribusiness Coun, 1996-; nominations comm, Univ Mo, 1996-; Tenn Asn Col Teachers Agri; Urban League; treas, Soc Dept Heads Asn. **Honors/Awds:** Gamma Sigma Delta, 1971; Outstanding Young Man of America, 1973, Univ MO; co-auth: small farms in Tennessee, 1985; Presidential Plaques, Tenn State Univ, 1985 & 1987; Outstanding Service, USAID/Wash DC, 1986; Distinguished Alumni, Alcorn State Univ, 1987; mem Pres Club, Univ Tenn, 1988; Institute Leadership Effectiveness, Univ Tenn, 1989; Outstanding Black Agricultural Economist, Am Agri Econ Asn, 1990; Men of Achievement, 1992; American Men & Women of Science, 1993; Presidential Award, Tenn State Univ, 1993; Distinguished Alumni Award, Univ Miss, Columbia, 1993; Black Achiever's Award, YMCA, Univ Tenn, 1995; Professional Recognition Award, Univ Ga, Collaborative Res Support Prog, 1996; Leadership Development Training Award, Univ PR-Mayaguez, 1996; Professional Recognition Award, Univ Tenn, Ronald McNair Postbaccalurate Achievement Program, 1996; ACE Executive Fellow Award, Univ Calif, 1997-98; Alumni Hall of Fame, Tenn State Univ, 2000; Leadership Award, Asn Res Dir, 2000; Leader, People's Ambassador Delegation Cuba, 2000. **Home Phone:** (423)675-4565. **Business Addr:** Vice Provost for International Programs, Professor, University of Missouri-Columbia, 211 Jesse Hall, Columbia, MT 65211, **Business Phone:** (573)882-9060.

WILLIAMSON, HENRY M
Association executive, clergy. **Personal:** Born in Arkansas. **Educ:** Purdue Univ Calumet Campus, BA, Sociol; Garrett-Evangelical Theol Sem, Evanston, Ill, Master Divinity, advan work Clin Pastoral Educ. **Career:** Israel CME Church, assoc minister, 1967-69; St. Paul CME Church, assoc pastor, 1972-73; Oper PUSH, nat pres, ceo, 1991-92; Carter Temple, Rev. **Orgs:** Founder & ceo, One Church One Sch Community Partnership Prog; trustee, Phillips Sch Theol ITC, Atlanta, Ga; chmn, Social Justice & Human Concerns Comn CME Church. **Honors/Awds:** Hon Doctor Divinity deg, United Theol Sem Monroe, La. **Special Achievements:** 52nd Bishop of the Christian Methodist Episcopal Church. *

WILLIAMSON, KEITH
Executive, lawyer. **Personal:** Born May 16, 1952, St Louis, MO; son of Irving A Williamson; married Addie; children: 1. **Educ:** Brown Univ, BA, econs & sociol, 1974; Harvard Univ, JD & MBA, 1978; New York Univ Law Sch, LLM, taxation. **Career:** Covington & Burling, tax lawyer, 1978-81; Revis & McGrath/Fulbright Jaworski, dir tax, 1981-88; Pitney Bowes Capital Corp, Capital Serv Div, dir, 1988-99, pres, 1999-2002, Global Credit Serv Div, leader, 2002-04, chief exec officer, currently; Centene Corp, sr vpres, gen coun & co secy, 2006-. **Orgs:** Exec Leadership Coun; Delta Nu Boule; bd mem, Stamford Mus. **Honors/Awds:** Fortune Magazine list of 50 most powerful blacks in corporate America. **Business Addr:** President, Chief Executive Officer, Pitney Bowes Inc, Capital Service Division, 1 Elmcroft Rd, Shelton, CT 06926-0700, **Business Phone:** (203)356-5000.

WILLIAMSON, DR. LIONEL
Educator, administrator. **Personal:** Born Aug 6, 1943, Louin, MS; son of Handy and Lilla N; married Mae I, Jun 6, 1968; children: Keschler S Love & Lionel LeMarc Williamson. **Educ:** Alcorn State Univ, BS, agr educ, 1967; Univ Mo, MS, agr econs, 1975, PhD (agr econs), 1977. **Career:** Voc agr educ teacher, 1967-72; Univ Mo, grad res asst, 1972-77; Ky State Univ, exten & res admin, 1977-85; Univ Ky, Dept Agr Econ, ext prof, 1985-, asst dean diversity, 2004-. **Orgs:** Southern Agr Econs Asn, 1977-; Am Agr Econs Asn, 1977-; Asn Coop Educ, 1985-; Nat Asn Cols & Teachers Agr, 1986-; Nat Econs Asn, 1989-90; Gamma Sigma Delta; Asn Ky Exten Specialists; Coun Agr Sci & Tech (CAST). **Honors/Awds:** Outstanding Extension Program Award, Asn Ky Exten Specialists, 1991. **Special Achievements:** One of 15 Outstanding Black Agricultural Economists, American Agricultural Economics Association, 1990. **Business Addr:** Assistant Dean for Diversity, Extension Professor, University of Kentucky, 306 Charles E Barnhart Bldg, Lexington, KY 40546-0276, **Business Phone:** (859)257-1637.

WILLIAMSON, MICHAEL T. See WILLIAMSON, MYKELTI.

WILLIAMSON, MYKELTI (MICHAEL T WILLIAMSON)
Actor. **Personal:** Born Mar 4, 1957, St Louis, MO; son of Elaine; married Olivia Brown, Jul 2, 1983 (divorced 1985); married Cheryl Chisholm (divorced 1994); children: Phoenix; married Sondra Spriggs, Apr 26, 1997; children: Nicole & Maya. **Career:** Films: Streets of Fire, 1984; Wildcats, 1986; You Talkin' to Me?, 1987; Number One with a Bullet, 1987; Miracle Mile, 1988; The First Power, 1990; Free Willy, 1993; Forrest Gump, 1994; Waiting to Exhale, 1995; Heat, 1995; How to Make an American Quilt, 1995; Free Willy 2: The Adventure Home, 1995; Con Air, 1997; Truth or Consequences, N.M., 1997; Double Tap, 1997; Species II, 1998; Primary Colors, 1998; Gideon, 1999; Three Kings, 1999; Ali, 2001; The Assassination of Richard Nixon, 2004; After the Sunset, 2004; Get Rich or Die Tryin', 2005; Lucky Number Slevin, 2006; Fatwa, 2006; ATL, 2006; Spinning Into Butter, 2007; August Rush, 2007; Vice, 2008; Ball Don't Lie, 2008; Black Dynamite, 2009; TV series: "Starsky & Hutch", 1978; "The White Shadow", 1979-80; "The Righteous Apples", 1981; "The White Shadow", 1981; "Father Murphy", 1981; "The Righteous Apples", 1981; "Desperate Lives", 1982; "Alice", 1983; "Hill Street Blues", 1983-86; "Bay City Blues", 1983; "Miami Vice", 1984-85; "Cover Up", 1984-85; "Gimme a Break!", 1984; "MiamiVice", 1985; "The Bronx Zoo", 1987; "JJ Starbuck", 1987; "The Bronx Zoo",1988; "Police Story: Monster Manor", 1988; "Psywars", 1989; "China Beach", 1989; "Midnight Caller", 1988-91; "A Killer Among Us", 1990; "The New WKRPin Cincinnati", 1991-93; "Other Women's Children", 1993; "Forrest Gump", 1994; "Time Trax", 1994; "The Outer Limits", 1995; "Soul of the Game", 1996; Buffalo Soldiers, 1997; 12 Angry Men, 1997; Soul of the Game, 1996; Having Our Say: The Delany Sisters' First 100 Years, 1999; "The Hoop Life", 1999; Holiday Heart, 2000; "The Fugitive", 2000-01; Our America, 2002; "Touched by an Angel", 2002; "Boomtown", 2002-03; The Secret Service, 2004; Monk, 2004; "Third Watch", 2005; Justice, 2006; Kidnapped", 2006-07; "CSI: NY", 2007; Raines, 2007. **Honors/Awds:** Nominated for Humanities Prize, Image Award, 2003, MTV Movie Award, 1995. **Business Addr:** Actor, c/o William Morris Agency Inc, 1325 Avenue of the Americas, New York, NY 10019, **Business Phone:** (212)586-5100.*

WILLIAMSON, SAMUEL P
Government official. **Personal:** Born Mar 5, 1949, Somerville, TN; son of Julius Williamson Jr and Izoula Smith; married Brenda Joyce Lee, Sep 15, 1970; children: Keith Ramon W & Yulanda Marie W. **Educ:** Tennessee State Univ, BS, Math & meteorology, 1971; NC State Univ, BS, Meteorology, 1972; Webster Univ, St Louis, MO, MA, Mgt, 1976, Am Univ, attended post grad studies engineering technol mgt. **Career:** Atomic Energy Comn, Oak Ridge, TN, res stud, 1969; Dept Com, NOAA, Nat Weather Serv, Silver Spring, MD, dir, NEXRAD, 1977-, fed coordr meteorology, currently. **Orgs:** Am Meteorological Soc, 1980-; Nat Guard Asn, 1980-; officer, bd trustees & finance, Mt Calvary Baptist Church, 1986-; Sr Execs Serv Asn, 1988-; Am Mgt Asn, 1989-; Int Elec/Electronics Engrs Soc, 1989-. **Honors/Awds:** Superior Performance Achievement Award, 1978-90. **Military Serv:** USAF, Lt Col, 1971-91; Charleston AFB, SC, weather detactment comdr, 1972-77; Air Force Commendation Medal, DCANG, Air Force Achievement Medal, DCANG. **Home Addr:** 19121 Barksdale Ct, Germantown, MD 20874. **Business Addr:** Federal Coordinator for Meteorology, National Weather Service, 1325 East-West Hwy SSMC-2 15th Fl, Silver Spring, MD 20910, **Business Phone:** (301)427-8144.

WILLIAMSON, SAMUEL R
Lawyer. **Personal:** Born Nov 22, 1943, Ellaville, GA; son of Joseph S and Mittie M; married Barbara Ann Elliott; children: Patricia & Michael. **Educ:** Hampton Univ, BS, 1965; Seton Hall Univ, JD, 1975; Army Command & Gen Staff Col, graduated, 1982. **Career:** AT&T Bell Lab, elec engr, 1968-75, sr patent atty, 1976-95; Lucent Technols Inc, corp coun, 1995-. **Orgs:** Asn Black Lab Employees, 1970-85, Garden State Bar Asn, 1976-, Nat Bar Asn, 1976-, New York Urban League Inc, 1982-; bd mem, Nat Patent Law Asn, 1988-89, pres, 1989-91; New Jersey Wing Civil Air Patrol, 1983-; BEEP lectr; BPA Inc, The Alliance Inc, AUSA, Am Legion, YMCA, Phi Alpha Delta, Scabbard & Blade, Explorers; Prince Hall Mason. **Honors/Awds:** Electronics Asn Honor Award for Miliary Leadership; Award for Unselfish Devotion to ABLE Inc; Perseverance Award, OPP. **Military Serv:** USAR, lt col, 1965-93; Armed Forces Commendation. **Home Addr:** 17 Woodlawn Rd, Somerset, NJ 08873. **Business Addr:** Corporate Counsel, Lucent Technologies Inc, 600 Mountain Ave, Murray Hill, NJ 07974, **Business Phone:** (908)582-8500.

WILLIAMS-STANTON, DR. SONYA DENISE
Educator, consultant. **Personal:** Born May 31, 1963, Birmingham, AL; daughter of Sam L and Carolyn W; married Tom. **Educ:** Brown Univ, BA (hons) 1984; Univ Mich, Bus Sch, MBA (hons) 1986, PhD, 1994. **Career:** Irving Trust Co, account rep, 1986-88; Ohio State Univ, asst prof finance, 1993-2000; consult, JAT Analysis. **Orgs:** Pres, Brown Univ Chap, Alpha Kappa Alpha, 1982-83; Nat Black MBA Assoc; Fin Mgmt Assoc; vip, Univ Mich Black Bus Stud Asn; Am Finance Asn; Nat Econ Asn; St Philips Episcopal Church. **Honors/Awds:** Fel, Consortium Grad Study Mgt, 1984-86; Scholar, Nat Black MBA Assoc, 1985; Hon Soc Financial Mgt Assoc, 1985-87; Unisys Corp Doctoral Fel, 1989-92; Mich Merit Fel, 1991-94.

WILLIAMS-TAITT, PATRICIA ANN
School administrator, administrator. **Personal:** Born Jul 3, 1947, Toledo, OH; daughter of Charles Matthews and Nettie; married Arthur R, Apr 12, 1992; children: Jason C. **Educ:** Wayne State Univ, BS, elem educ, 1969, grad studies educ admin; Dale Carnegie Inst, effective speaking; Ctr Corp & Comm Relations, 1985; Leadership Detroit XII, 1990-91; IBM Leadership Develop, 1993. **Career:** Detroit Pub Sch Syst, 2nd grade teacher, 1969-70; Singer Career Syst, Detroit Job Corps, dir educ, 1972-86; Mercy Health Systs, dir external communs, 1986-89; Pub Relations consult, 1986-; Greater Detroit Chamber Comm, Detroit Compact, dep dir, 1989-; Advert & Specialty Markets, dir; City Connect Detroit, mkt & commun officer, currently. **Orgs:** Exec bd, Am Red Cross, 1994-; chairperson, Booker T Wash, assoc publicity, 1984-90; exec bd, Friends Southwest, 1990-; ed comt, Partners Tabloid, 1986-89;, vpres, Winship Community Coun, 1986-89; vpres, pub info,Am Cancer Soc, 1988-89; co-chair, Black Family Developt Inc, publicity chair, 1987-88; bd mem, Detroit Br NCP, 1997-00. **Honors/Awds:** Business Women of the Month, NW Area Business Asn, 1987; Services Plaque, Bus Asn, Am Cancer Soc, 1989; Spirit Detroit Award, City County, 1988; Booker T Wash, 1992-94; Honor for Chairperson of Principal & Educators Luncheon Booker T Wash; Citizen of the Week Award, WWJ Radio, 1994. **Business Addr:** Marketing & Communication Officer, City Connect Detroit, Third Fl 163 Madison Ave, Detroit, MI 48226, **Business Phone:** (313)887-6503.

WILLIAMS- WARREN, JANE E.
Government official. **Personal:** Born Jul 19, 1947, Paterson, NJ; daughter of John D and Mae J Jenkins. **Educ:** Passaic County Community Col; Paterson State Col; Seton Hall Univ; Rutgers Univ, Municipal clerk cert, intl municipal clerk cert. **Career:** City Paterson, City Clerk's Off, various secretarial titles, 1966-78; Paterson Planning Bd, comnr, 1971-72; City Paterson, dep city clerk, 1978-89, munic clerk, 1990-. **Orgs:** Recording secy, Municipal Clerks Asn Passaic County; New Jersey State Municipal Clerk's Asn; Intl Clerk's Asn; vice chairperson, Passaic County Mental Health Asn; treas, Municpal Clerk's Asn; New AME Zion Church, numerous positions; Nat Coun Negro Women; Nat Asn Advan Coloured People; bd trustees, St Joseph Hosp & Med Ctr; Fidelity Chapter 16 Order Easter Star. **Honors/Awds:** Special Award, New AME Zion Church, Pastor's Aide Club, Women's Gospel Chorus, certificate, Christian Seminar Award, 1985; Congress Award, 1989; Assembly Award, 1989; Senate Award, 1989; Conference Workers Club; New Jersey General Assembly, honored. **Business Addr:** Municipal Clerk, City Paterson, 155 Market St, Paterson, NJ 07505, **Business Phone:** (973)321-1310.*

WILLIAMS-WITHERSPOON, KIMMIKA L H
Writer, educator, playwright. **Personal:** Born Jan 7, 1959, Philadelphia, PA; daughter of Samuel S Hawes Jr and Lillian Yvonne Curry Hawes; children: Essence & Tenasha. **Educ:** Howard Univ, Wash, DC, BA, jour, 1980; Temple Univ, MFA, playwriting, Grad Cert, womens studies, Temple Univ, MA, anthrop, PhD, anthrop. **Career:** Philadelphia Tribune, Philadelphia, PA, reporter & columnist, 1984-86; Pa Prison Soc, Philadelphia, PA, instr, 1985-89; Bob Lott Prod, Philadelphia, PA, scriptwriter, 1986-89; WXPN-FM, Philadelphia, PA, arts host & producer, 1989-90; Village Arts Ctr, Philadelphia, PA, instr, 1990-; Walnut St Theatre, Philadelphia, PA, outreach instr & actress, 1990-; Temple Univ, Theatre Dept, post grad teaching fel, adj, 1996-2000, asst prof, lectr & head undergrad advising, 2000-; Published books: Negro Kinship to the Park, Halley's Comet, It Ain't Easy to be Different, God Made Men Brown, Selrahc Publication, 1982-90, Published Books: Envisioning a Sea of Dry Bones, 1994, Epic Memory: Places & Spaces I've Been, 1995, Signs of the Time: Culture Pop, Three-Goat Press, 1999, Darby, Pa, Spoken Word Poetry Compact Disc, Three Goat Press/Productions 2001, They Never Told Me Thered Be Days Like This, Three Goat Press, 2002, Brother Love, Three Goat Press/Productions, Darby, PA, 2005. **Orgs:** Future Fac fel, Anthrop Dept, Temple Univ; Int Womens League Peace & Freedom, 1988-; Nat Black Auth Tour, 1989-;Nat Black Storytellers, 1988-; Theater Asn Pa, 1994; Philadelphia Dramatist Ctr, 1993; Lila Wallace Creative Arts fel, Am Antiquarian Soc, 1995-96; Am Anthropolgist Asn, 1997-. **Honors/Awds:** American Poetry Center Grant, Teacher's Fellowship, 1990; Playwright's Fellowship, Theatre Asn Pa, 1990-91; Artist Grant, Philadelphia Neighborhood Arts Proj, 1990; Minneapolis Playwrights Ctr Exchange Grant, 1993; Writing Partnership Teachers Grant, 1995; Pew Charitable Trust Exchange Playwright with the Minneapolis Playwrights Ctr, 1996; Future Faculty Fellowship-Anthropology, 1996; Research Grant, Lila Wallace Creative Artists Grant, Am Antiquarian Soc,1996-97; Pew Charitable Trust Exchange Grant, Penumbra Theatre, Minneapolis, MN, 1996; PEW Charitable Table Trusts $50.000 Award in Script Writing, 2000; Independence Foundation Theater Communications Group Grant, 2001. **Special Achievements:** Author of over twenty plays, 9 volumes of poetry & has been a contribut-

ing writer to a host of anthologies & publications. **Business Addr:** Assistant Professor, Temple University, Theater Department, 207 Tomlinson Hall, Philadelphia, PA 19122, **Business Phone:** (215)204-8417.

WILLIAMSX, MAURECE JABARI. See WILLIAMS, MOE.

WILLIE, DR. CHARLES VERT
Educator. **Personal:** Born Oct 8, 1927, Dallas, TX; son of Carrie S and Louis J; married Mary Sue Conklin, Mar 31, 1962; children: Sarah S, Martin C & James T. **Educ:** Morehouse Col, BA, 1948; Atlanta Univ, MA, 1949; Syracuse Univ, PhD, 1957. **Career:** Syracuse Univ, from instr & asst prof to prof sociol, 1952-74, chmn, 1967-71, vpres, 1972-74; Upstate Med Ctr, Syracuse, NY Dept Preventive Med, instr, 1955-60; Pres Comt Delinquency Wash DC Proj, res dir, 1962-64; Harvard Med Sch, Dept Psychiat, vis lectr, 1966-67; Episcopal Divinity Sch, Cambridge, vis lectr, 1966-67; Harvard Univ, prof educ & urban studies, 1974-98; Harvard Univ, Charles William Eliot prof educ, 1998-2000; Harvard Univ, Charles William Eliot prof emer educ, 2000-. **Orgs:** Tech Adv Comt, Falk Fund; UNCF; pres, Eastern Sociol Soc; Am Sociol Asn; bd mem, Soc Sci Res Coun; hon trustee, Episcopal Div Sch; vpres, House Deputies, Gen Convention Episcopal Church USA; sr warden, Christ Episcopal Church, Cambridge, 1984-86; bd mem & chair, Dana McLean Greeley Found Peace & Justice; mem, President's Comn Mental Health, USA; Am Sociol Asn; Am Sociol Asn, vpres; Asn Black Sociologists; Am Sociol Asn; Am Educ Res Asn; Sociologists Women Soc; Soc Study Social Problems. **Honors/Awds:** Phi Beta Kappa, 1972; Distinguished Alumnus Award, Maxwell Sch Syracuse Univ, 1974; Nat Asn for Equal Opportunity in Higher Education Award, 1979; Male Hero, Ms Magazine 10th Anniversary Issue, 1982; Lee-Founders Award, Soc Study Social Problems, 1986; Distinguished Career Contribution Award, Comt Role & Status Minorities Am Educ Res Asn, 1990; Family of the Year Award, Int Inst Interracial Interaction of Families, Minneapolis, MN,1992; The Spirit of Public Service Award, Maxwell Sch Syracuse Univ, 1994; The Dubois-Johnson-Frazier Award, Amer Sociol Asn, 1994; The Robin Williams Distinguished Lecturership Award, Eastern Sociol0 Soc, 1994;Benjamin Mays Service Award, Morehouse Col, 1994; John La Farge Award, Fairfield Univ, 1995; Myer Center Outstanding Book in Human Rights Award for co-editing Mental Health, Racism and Sexism, 1996; Distinguished Career Award; Career of Distinguished Scholarship Award, Asn Black Sociologists, Am Sociol Asn, 2005; Outstanding Teacher Award, Harvard Univ, 2005; Honorary Degree, Berkeley Divinity School; Honorary Degree, Harvard University. **Special Achievements:** Author: over 30 books, over 150 articles or chapters in books; Books : A New Look at Black Families, 1976); The Education of African-Americans, 1991; Theories of Human Social Action, 1994; Mental Health, Racism and Sexism, 1995; Student Diversity, Choice, and School Improvement, 2002; A New Look at Black Families, 2003; The Black College Mystique, 2006; Grassroots Social Action, 2008. **Home Phone:** (978)369-2363. **Business Addr:** Charles William Eliot Professor Emeritus of Education, Harvard University, Graduate School of Education, Gutman Libr, 4th Fl Gutman 410, Cambridge, MA 02138, **Business Phone:** (617)495-4678.

WILLIFORD, STANLEY O.
Businessperson, publisher, editor. **Personal:** Born Jan 3, 1942, Little Rock, AR; son of Claude Theophilus and Mary Esther; married Corliss M, Sep 22, 1984; children: Steven D Woods, Nicole O Woods, Brian M & Brandon A. **Educ:** Calif State Univ, BA, jour, 1968. **Career:** Los Angeles Times, reporter, 1969-72; E Los Angeles Col, asst prof jour, 1970-71; Los Angeles Sentinel, reporter, 1972-75; Calif St Univ, asst prof jour, 1973-76; Entrepreneur Mag, ed-in-chief, 1975-76; Los AngelesHerald Examr, copy editor, 1975-76; Travel & Art Mag, ed-in-chief, 1975-76, co-publ, 1977-78; Ichthus Records/Productions, staff; Los Angeles Times, copy ed, 1976-93; Los Angeles City Col, jour instr, 1989-99; Crenshaw Christian Ctr, dir publ, 1993-94; Vision Publ, pres & founder, 1996-; Books: How the Blood Works. **Orgs:** Sigma Delta Chi, 1968; bd mem, Crenshaw Christian Ctr, 1991-95. **Honors/Awds:** Fel, Wash Jour Ctr, 1968; Nat Asn of Media Women Award, 1974; Award for General Excellence in Reporting, Michele Clark Found, Columbia Univ 1974. **Special Achievements:** Participated in a range of post graduate seminars, interviews and policy forums during fellowship studies at the WASHINGTON JOURNALISM CENTER, Washington, DC Interacted with Cabinet-level government officials and nationally known media experts. **Military Serv:** AUS sp-4 1964-66; Soldier of the Month Award.

WILLINGHAM, GLORIA J.
Educator, nurse. **Educ:** Regents Col, Univ State NY, BS; Univ Ark, MNSc; Claremont Grad Univ, PhD. **Career:** VA Med Ctr, Long Beach, CA, chief, Nursing Educ & Res; Calif State Univ, fac; Fielding Grad Inst, assoc dean, 2003-. **Orgs:** Founder, The Village Projects. **Military Serv:** USAR Nurse Corps, lt col. **Business Addr:** Associate Dean, Fielding Graduate Institute, School of Educational Leadership & Change, 2112 Santa Barbara St, Santa Barbara, CA 93105.*

WILLINGHAM, JAMES EDWARD
Association executive. **Personal:** Born Jun 15, 1948, Philadelphia, PA; son of Rubin and Ruth; married Dawn M, Dec 31, 1995; children: Lynette Wesley, Lynore, Andrea, Tiffany & James Jr. **Educ:** Philadelphia Community Col, AA, 1974; Temple Univ, studied Urban Affairs, 1975; Empire State Col New York Univ, BA, 1980. **Career:** New York City staff; Hartford, Connecticut staff; Scout Exec & Chief Exec Officer; Boy Scouts Am; Urban League Greater Hartford, pres/chief exec officer, currently. **Orgs:** Chair, Kappa Alpha Psi Frat, Youth Progs, 1990-; Greater Hartford Urban League, 1993-; Greater Hartford Chamber Com, 1993-; Sigma Pi Phi Frat, 1994-; past pres, bd dirs, Community Health Serv Inc, 1994-97; bd dirs, St Francis Hosp & Med Ctr, 1995-; adv bd, Capital Community Col, 1995-; Workforce Develop Bd, 1999; bd dir, Greek Letter Org Hartford; Capital Community Col; Salvation Army Advisory Bd; bd dir, Am Red Cross; Greater Hartford Convention & Visitors Bureau; Conn Fair Housing Ctr; Workforce Develop Bd; fel Am Leadership Forum; State Conn Task Force; Job Corps Ctr Community Relations Coun, Metro Hartford Regional Econ Alliance Bd; Trustee, Hartford Sch Bd, 2001-03; Hate Crimes Advisory Comm; Long Island Sound Fund Advisory Comm; Sovereign Bank New England Community Advisory Bd; bd dir, Channel 3 Kids Camp. **Honors/Awds:** William H. Gray's Outstanding Man of the Year Award, Bright Hope Baptist Church, 1971; Outstanding Service to All People Award, Four Chaplains Legion Hon, 1972; Community Service to Youth Award, New York Urban League, 1988; Achievement Award, Kappa Alpha Psi Frat Inc, 1991; AME Zion Church, Role Model for African American Males, 1992; Man of the Year Award, Shiloh Baptist Church, 1999; Whitney M Young Jr Leadership Award; The SANKOFA Award; WKND Radio Black History Celebration Award. **Home Addr:** 16 Cliffmount Dr, Bloomfield, CT 06002, **Home Phone:** (860)242-7945. **Business Addr:** President, Chief Executive Officer, Urban League of Greater Hartford, 140 Woodland Ave, Hartford, CT 06105, **Business Phone:** (860)527-0147.

WILLINGHAM, TYRONE
Football coach, football player. **Personal:** Born Dec 30, 1953, Kinston, NC; married Kim; children: Cassidy, Kelsey & Nathaniel. **Educ:** Univ Wash. **Career:** Mich State Univ, wide receiver, 1975-77, asst coach, 1977, 1982-82; Cent Mich Univ, asst coach, 1978-79; NC State Univ, asst coach, 1983-85; Rice Univ, asst coach, 1986-88; Stanford Univ, asst coach, 1989-91, head football coach, 1995-2001; Minne Vikings, asst coach, 1992-2004; Univ Notre Dame, head football coach, 2002-04; Univ Wash, head football coach, 2005-. **Orgs:** Bd trustees & vpres, pres, Am Football Coaches Asn, 2001-08. **Honors/Awds:** Sportsman of the Year, Sporting News, 2002; Coach of the Year, 2002. **Business Addr:** Head Football Coach, University of Washington, Intercollegiate Athletic Department, Graves Bldg, PO Box 351207, Seattle, WA 98195, **Business Phone:** (206)543-2223.

WILLINGHAM, VONCILE
Government official. **Personal:** Born Nov 9, 1935, Opp, AL; daughter of L K Lee and Ida Lee Liggins Lee; married Anderson Willingham Jr; children: Donna Marie & Doretta Monique. **Educ:** Ala State Univ, BS, 1957; Univ DC, MS, 1977; The Am Univ, MS, Personnel & Human Resources Mgt, 1987. **Career:** Greene Co Bd Educ, bus educ instr, 1957-58; UA Agency Int Develop, exec asst, 1961-69, employee dev specialist, 1970-77, equal employ mgr, 1978-. **Orgs:** Delta Sigma Theta Sor, 1955-; Sargent Memorial Presby Chancel Choir, 1975-; Southern Md Choral Soc, 1983-; mem bd dirs, Foreign Affairs Recreation Asn, 1985-; Interagency Comn Martin Luther King Fed Holiday Comm, 1986; mem bd dirs, Univ DC Sch Bus Educ; USAID Administrator's Adv Comn Women. **Honors/Awds:** Equal Employment Opportunity Award, US Agency Int Dev, 1977; Cert Community Outreach DC Public Sch, 1979-84; Superior Honor Award, US Agency Int Dev, 1981. **Business Addr:** EEO Manager, USAID, 21st St & Va Ave NW, Washington, DC 20523, **Business Phone:** (202)712-4810.

WILLIS, ANDREW
Executive director. **Personal:** Born Oct 5, 1938, Jamesville, NC; married Shirley; children: LaShirl, Anqileena. **Educ:** NC A&T State Univ, BS, 1964; Kent State Univ, MA, 1967; Univ NY, Buffalo. **Career:** Pub Welfare Dept Norfolk, VA, caseworker Summer, 1964; Kent State Univ, grad asst, 1964-67; State Univ NY, Buffalo, teaching asst, 1964-67; Health & Welfare Buffalo Urban League, assoc dir, 1967-68; Buffalo Urban League, dep dir, 1968-72; State Univ Col, Buffalo, pt instr, 1969-72; Buffalo Urban League, actg exec dir, 1972; Erie Community Col, asst prof, 1972-73; Urban League Onondaga County, exec dir, 1973-79. **Orgs:** Bd dirs, PEACE Inc; NY State Health Planning Adv Coun; bd dirs, Int Ctr Syracuse; adv Coun Equal Opportunity; Manpower Adv Planning Coun; Equal Opportunity Prog Comt; Educ Opportunity Ctr; exec coun, Nat Eastern Regional State; Nat Asn Advan Colored People. **Military Serv:** USAF, a1/c, 1956-60.

WILLIS, CECIL B.
Automotive executive. **Career:** Peninsula Pontiac, Inc, Torrance CA, chief exec officer & founder, 1979. **Business Addr:** Chief Executing officer, Founder, Peninsula Pontiac Inc, 2909 Pacific Coast Hwy, Torrance, CA 90505, **Business Phone:** (310)530-3954.

WILLIS, CHARLES L
Judge. **Personal:** Born Sep 11, 1926, New York, NY; married Judith Lounsbury; children: Lisa, Michael Elliott, Susan Elliott, Christopher & John Elliott. **Educ:** New York Univ, 1951; City Col New York, 1951; St John Univ Sch Law, LLB, 1955. **Career:** Monroe County Dist Atty Office, asst dist atty, 1967-68; Monroe County, pub defender, 1968-70; City Rochester, corp coun, 1970-71, city ct judge, 1971-72; McKay Comn, first dep coun, 1972; State New York, Family Ct, supervising judge, 1980-88, Supreme Ct Justice, 1989-96; Seventh Judicial Dist, admin judge, 1991; Law Firm Harris, Beach & Wilcox LLP, spec counsel; The Fla Acad Of Prof Mediators Inc, mediator, currently. **Orgs:** Trustee, Monroe County Bar Asn, 1970-72; adv, Fourth Judicial Dept, New York Adv common Law Guardians; Asn Family Ct Judges; dir, Urban League, Rochester Children's Convalescent Hosp, 1980-83, SPCC, 1981-83, Ctr Govt Res, 1981-84. **Military Serv:** USN, seaman 1st class, 2 yrs. **Business Addr:** Mediator, The Florida Academy of Professional Mediators Inc, 751 Pinella Bayway Suite 302, Tierra Verde, FL 33715.

WILLIS, FRANK B.
Government official, publisher. **Personal:** Born Mar 13, 1947, Cleveland, MS; son of Harry and Mattie; married Bobbie M Henderson; children: Oji-Camara Khari. **Educ:** Rochester Bus Inst, AA, 1968; Dyke Col, BS, 1971. **Career:** Communicade newspaper, founder, 1972-; City Urban Renewal Dept, family relocation aide, 1972-74; Okang Commun Corp, pres, 1973-; City Dept Soc Serv, eligibility examr, 1974; Communicade Newspaper, publisher & ed, 1981-; Rochester City Urban Renewal, 1972-74; County Monroe Dept Social Serv, 1974; Rochester City Sch Dist, sch bd mem, comnr, 1980-95. **Orgs:** Legis intern, Rapic Community Network Judicial Process Comn, 1977-78; Coalition Chap I Parents, 1978-; ed & writer, Horambee Parents Newsletter Chap I Prog, 1979-80; Nat Alliance Black Sch Educrs, 1980-; Caucus Black Sch Bd Mem, 1983-. **Honors/Awds:** Outstanding Personality, Afro-Am Soc, Dyke Col, 1971; Serv Award, Greater Rochester Tougaloo Col Alumni Asn Inc, 1983; Outstanding Serv, Rochester City Schs Dist Adv Coun Chap I, 1983; Serv Urban League Rochester, 1984. **Home Addr:** 67 Elba St, Rochester, NY 14608.

WILLIS, FREDERIC L.
Educator. **Personal:** Born May 14, 1937, Handley, WV; divorced. **Educ:** La City Col, AA, 1961; Calif State Univ, BS, 1970; Univ Calif, LosAngeles, grad study, 1971; Pepperdine Univ, attended 1973. **Career:** Los Angeles, dist atty, community affairs rep, investr, 1967-71; Los Angeles Sheriff, dep sheriff, 1964-67, community expert, 1960-64; W LosAngeles Col Admin Justice, instr, 1972-; SW Los Angeles Col Admin Justice Dept, coordr, 1973-; Los Angeles Dist Atty, supvr lt, 1971-93; CSAN/Nevada, Child Support Asst Network, dir, 1993-; Pre-Paid Legal Servs Inc, dir, vpres, independent assoc, currently; Emergency Travel Assurance Inc, dir mkt; Clark County, Southern Nev, Chamber Com, pres. **Orgs:** Chmn, Los Angeles Brotherhood Crusade Campaign, 1971; chmn, Sons Watts Ore Prog Adv Coun, 1972; Men Tomorrow; Nat Asn Adavan Colored People; NewFrontier Dem Club; bd mem, Rotary Int. **Military Serv:** USAF, airman first class, 1956-59.

WILLIS, GLADYS JANUARY
Educator. **Personal:** Born Feb 29, 1944, Jackson, MS; daughter of John January and Emily Young January; married A H Willis Jr; children: Juliet Christina & Michael Lamont. **Educ:** Jackson State Univ, BA, 1965; Bryn Mawr Col, Independent Study, 1966; Mich State Univ, MA, 1967; Princeton Univ, PhD, 1973; Lutheran Theol Sem, Philadelphia Pa, MDiv, 1996. **Career:** Cheyney State Univ, instr, Eng, 1967-68; Rider Col, instr, Eng, 1968-70; City Univ New York, asst prof, Eng, 1973-76; Pa Human Rel Comn, educ rep, 1976-77; Lincoln Univ, assoc prof, chair, 1977-84, prof, dean, Sch Humanities & Graduate Studies, 2002-; First Redemption Evangelical Church, asst pastor, 1992-; Bd Dirs, Arts Alliance Oxford.; Lincoln Univ, Dean Humanities & Graduate Studies, currently. **Orgs:** Founder, dir, Col Prep Tutorial, 1974; bd dir, Philadelphia Christian Acad, 1977-, Nat Coun Teachers Eng; reviewer, Middle States Asn. **Honors/Awds:** Woodrow Wilson Nat Fel, Woodrow Wilson Nat Fel Found, 1966-67; Princeton Univ Fel, Princeton Univ, 1970-73; Ordained Chaplain, 1988; Outstanding Young Women of America, 1978; author, Penalty Eve; John Milton & Divorce New York, Peter Lang, 1984; Lind back Distinguished Teachers Award, Lincoln Univ, 1984; Service Award, Lincoln Univ, 1992. **Special Achievements:** First Black American to earn a PhD in English from Princeton University. **Home Addr:** 232 Wiltshire Rd, Wynnewood, PA 19096-3333. **Business Addr:** Dean of Humanities & Graduate Studies, Lincoln University, Center for Graduate and Continuing Education Programs, Lincoln Plaza, 3020 Market St, Philadelphia, PA 19104, **Business Phone:** (215)387-2405.

WILLIS, JAMES EDWARD, III
Football player, football coach. **Personal:** Born Sep 2, 1972, Huntsville, AL; children: Jade Elise. **Educ:** Auburn Univ, attended 2003. **Career:** Football player (retired), football coach; Auburn Univ, linebacker, 1990-92, stud asst, 2001-02, defensive grad asst, 2003, 2006-; Green Bay Packers, linebacker, 1993-94; Philadelphia Eagles, 1996-98; Seattle Seahawks, 1999; Birmingham Thunderbolts, linebacker, 2001; Univ RI, linebacker, 2004-05; Temple Univ, athletics coach, 2005; Auburn Tigers, linebackers coach, 2006-; coach, Cotton Bowl, 2007. **Honors/Awds:** SEC Co-Defensive Freshman of the Year, 1990; Rookie of the Year, 1993; Most Valuable Player, 2001. **Business Addr:**

Linebackers Coach, Auburn Tigers, Beard Eaves Mem Coliseum 651 Roosevelt Dr, PO Box 351, Auburn, AL 36849, **Business Phone:** (334)844-4750.

WILLIS, JILL MICHELLE
Lawyer. **Personal:** Born Jan 4, 1952, Atlanta, GA; daughter of Louis Bell Willis Sr and Annette James Strickland; married Paul Hugh Brown, May 28, 1988; children: Bryant Alexander Brown. **Educ:** Wellesley Col, BA, 1973; Columbia Univ Sch Social Work, MS, 1975; Univ Chicago Law Sch, JD, 1984. **Career:** United Charities Chicago Family Serv Bur, caseworker III, 1975-79; Chapman & Cutler, assoc, 1984-86; Allstate Ins Co, asst coun, 1986-. **Orgs:** Waddell fel, Wellesley Col Study E Africa, 1972; Adv bd, Thresholds S, 1977-78; bd dirs, Howe Develop Ctr, 1984-86; Am Bar Asn, 1984-; Chicago Bar Asn, 1984-; Cook Co Bar Asn, 1984-. **Honors/Awds:** Henry R Luce Scholar Asia Internship, 1979-80; Chairmans Award, Allstate Ins Co, 1988. **Business Addr:** Assistant Counsel, Allstate Insurance Co, 8938 Forestview Rd, Evanston, IL 60062.

WILLIS, KATHI GRANT
Lawyer. **Personal:** Born Dec 2, 1959, Knoxville, TN; daughter of Lorenzo D Grant and Henrietta Arnold Grant; married Henry W, Oct 19, 1985; children: Elizabeth Danielle. **Educ:** Univ VA, BA, 1981; Univ Tenn Col Law, JD, 1984. **Career:** Provident Life & Accident Ins Co, Chattanooga, TN, mgr, contracts & claims, 1986-88, atty, 1988-89, asst coun, 1989, assoc coun, 1992-95; Blue Cross Blue Shield Tenn, sr coun, 1997; Healthsource Inc, Chattanooga, TN, coun, 1995-97; BlueCross & BlueShield Tenn, sr coun, 1997-, dir & chief employment coun, currently. **Orgs:** Alpha Kappa Alpha Sorority Inc; Chattonooga Chap Links Inc; Jr League Chattanooga; Grad Prof Opportunities Prog, 1981-84; Tenn Bar Asn. **Home Addr:** 308 Willow Glen Rd, Chattanooga, TN 37421-3205. **Business Addr:** Director, Chief Employment Counselor, BlueCross & BlueShield of Tennessee, 801 Pine St, Chattanooga, TN 37402-2556, **Business Phone:** (423)535-3618.

WILLIS, KEVIN ALVIN
Basketball player, businessperson. **Personal:** Born Sep 6, 1962, Los Angeles, CA. **Educ:** Jackson Community Col, attended 1981; Mich State Univ, fashion design, 1984. **Career:** Basketball player (retired), businessman; Atlanta Hawks, forward-ctr, 1984-94, 2004-05; Miami Heat, 1994-96; Golden State Warriors, 1996; Houston Rockets, 1997-98; Toronto Raptors, 1998-2001; Houston Rockets, 2001-02; San Antonio Suprs, forward-ctr, 2003-04; Dallas Mavericks, 2006-07; Willis & Walker, owner, currently. **Orgs:** Heal The World Found; Boys & Girls Club; Am Kidney Found. **Honors/Awds:** Most Improved Player award, 1992. **Special Achievements:** First round pick, No 1, NBA Draft, 1984; own clothing line, Kevin Willis for Black and White.

WILLIS, LEVY E
Executive. **Career:** Atlantic National Bank, Norfolk VA, chief executive, 1988. **Business Addr:** WPCE, 645 Church St Suite 400, Norfolk, VA 23510, **Business Phone:** (804)622-4600.

WILLIS, MIECHELLE ORCHID
Administrator. **Personal:** Born Feb 12, 1954, Lakewood, NJ; daughter of M Agnes Garland and Vernon. **Educ:** Grambling State Univ, Grambling, La, BS, 1976, MS, 1978. **Career:** Montclair State Col, Upper Montclair, NJ, head women's track coach, 1978-87; Temple Univ, Philadelphia, Pa, assoc dir athletics, 1987; Ohio State Univ, Dept Athletics, assoc dir, 1994-, sr woman adminr, currently. **Orgs:** Delta Sigma Theta Sorority Inc, 1975-78; Delta Psi Kappa Fraternity, 1976-78; chair, Field Hockey Comt, Atlantic 10 Conf, 1988-; Coun Col Womens Athletic Adminr, 1990-. **Military Serv:** USAF, staff sgt, 1983-89. **Business Addr:** Senior Women Administrator, Associate Director, Department of Athletics, Ohio State University, 227 St John Arena 410 Woody Hayes Dr, Columbus, OH 43210, **Business Phone:** (614)688-3280.

WILLIS, DR. ROSE W
Beautician, photographer. **Personal:** Born Jan 2, 1939, Columbus, GA; daughter of Christine Wright and Leonard Wright; divorced; children: Gwendolyn D Hunt & Sherry Ancrum. **Educ:** Nat Inst Cosmetology, BA, 1971, MA, 1974, PhD, 1978. **Career:** Lovely Lady Beauty Salon, Hollywood, FL, mgr & owner, 1967-; Orange Blossom Cosmetologists Asn, local pres unit 24, 1969-78; Orange Blossom Cosmetologists Asn, parade state chmn, 1970-80; Orange Blossom Cosmetologists Asn, state photographer, 1980; Nat Beauty Culturists League, chmn finance & registr, 1984-; Dillard High Sch, Ft Lauderdale, 1992-94; Columbus Times News Paper, freelance photographer, currently. **Orgs:** Pres, Fla State Nat Beauty Culturists' League, North Miami Beach, FL, 1978-94; mem, Nat Coun Negro Women, 1979-94; treas, Theta Nu Sigma, Mu chapter, 1983-92; fin secy, S Fla Bus Asn, 1988-93; mem, Dade County Sch Bd Cosmetology, 1988-94; co-chairman, Dade County Sch Cosmetology Adv Comt; vpres, Antioch Baptist Church Choir #1; mem, Nazareth Baptist Church. **Honors/Awds:** Woman of the Year, Theta Nu Sigma Sorority, 1984; Outstanding Service Award, Bahamian Cosmetologists Asn, 1989; Revlon Leadership Award, 1991; Cordelia G Johnson Pioneer Award, NBCL, 1991; No 1 for Thirty-Six Years, Outstanding Service & Dedication, Antioch Baptist Church & Choir, Miami; Outstanding Service, Fla Coun, Thela Nu Sigma, Mu-Chapter & Natl Beauty Culturist's, Miami. **Business Addr:** Freelance Photographer, Columbus Times Newspaper, PO Box 2845, Columbus, GA 31902-2845, **Business Phone:** (706)324-2404.

WILLOCK, DR. MARCELLE MONICA
Educator, dean (education). **Personal:** Born Mar 30, 1938, Georgetown, Guyana; son of George and Renee W. **Educ:** Col New Rochelle, BA, 1958; Howard Univ, MD, 1962; Columbia Univ, MA, 1982; Boston Univ, MBA, 1989. **Career:** Educator, Dean (retired); NY Univ Sch Med, asst prof, 1965-74; Columbia Univ Col Physicians & Surgeons, asst prof, 1978-82; Boston Univ Med Ctr, chief anesthesiol, 1982-98, asst provost for external affairs; Boston Univ Sch Medicine, prof & chmn, 1998; Charles R. Drew Univ Med & Sci, dean, 2002-05, prof psychiat & family med. **Orgs:** Pres, Louis & Marthe Deveaux Found, 1965; pres, Am Med Womens Asn Mass, 1985-86; pres, Mass Soc Anesthesiologists, 1986-87, 1987-89; deleg, Am Soc Anesthesiologists, 1986-94, dir, 1994-97; Asn Univ Anesthetists; sec/treasr, Soc Acad Anesthesia Chmn, 1989-91; Soc Acad Anesthesiol Chairs, pres, 1994-96; Med Found, Boston, MA, secy bd dirs, 1992-94; Col New Rochelle, trustee, 1978-82; Am Soc Anesthesiologists, bd, 1995-, asst secy, 1997-99; Alpha Omega Alpha; co-dir, UTHSCSA Nat Ctr Excellence Women's Health. **Honors/Awds:** Commencement Speaker Howard Univ Sch Med, 1982; Col New Rochelle, Medal. **Special Achievements:** First female Dean for the College of Medicine.

WILLOUGHBY, DR. SUSAN MELITA
School administrator. **Personal:** Born Nov 25, 1925; married; children: Gerald M & Juliette M. **Educ:** Atlantic Union Col, S Lancaster, Mass, BA, chem, 1956; Clark Univ Worcester, Mass, MA, educ, 1969; Harvard Univ, Cambridge, EdD, admin, 1972; Boston Univ, Sch Social Work, Mass, MSW, 1984; Boston Univ, Sch Med, MPH, 1985. **Career:** Worcester Found Exp Biol, sr res chemist, 1961-68; Ctr Urban Studies Harvard Univ, dir counseling serv, 1970-72; Mass Consumer Coun, Gov Sargent, gubernatorial appointee, 1973-75; Mass Pub Health Coun, Gov Dukakis, gubernatorial appointee, 1975-79; Atlantic Union Col, Dept Sociol & Social Work, prof educ & behav sci, 1972-, tenured prof & chmn, 1983-. **Orgs:** Phi Delta Kappa & Pi Lambda Theta, AAUP, 1972-; chmn, Health Task Force Mass State Consumer Coun, 1974-75; chmn, Centennial Comn Atlantic Union Col S Lancaster, Mass, 1978-82; mem bd trustees, Atlantic Union Col, 1986-; comnr, SDA Educ, W Africa, 1994. **Honors/Awds:** Scholar Clark Univ, Harvard Univ, 1968, 1971. **Special Achievements:** Several articles published in Atlantic Union Gleaner (local) 1974-78; Author, "The Go-Getter" Pacific Press Publishing Assoc Boise ID, 1985. **Home Phone:** (978)365-9782. **Business Addr:** Chairman, Professor of Education & Behavioral Sci, Atlantic Union College, Sociology & Social Work Department, PO Box 1000, South Lancaster, MA 01561, **Business Phone:** (978)368-2190.

WILLRICH, EMZY JAMES
Executive. **Personal:** Born Sep 16, 1959, Dallas, TX; son of Theodis Sr and Margie Crew. **Educ:** Univ Tex, Arlington, BBA, mkt, 1983; Tex Wesleyan Univ, Sch Law, JD, 1994. **Career:** Harte-Hanks Direct Mkt, sales consult, 1986-87; Advanced Telemarketing Corp, mkt agent, 1987; United Advertising, data mgmt supvr, 1987-88; Consolidated Freightways, Inc, acct mgr, 1988-99; The Willrich Scott Consulting Group Inc, dir, bus develop, 1999-; CLD Solutions Inc, dir mkt & bus develop, 2000; Arlington Independent Schl Dist, Substitute Teacher, 2001; Bruskin Audits & Surveys Worldwide, Mkt Researcher, 2001; US Small Bus Admin, Law Clerk, 2001; US Chamber Com, membership dir, 2002; Off Attorney Gen, Arlington, Tex, staff, currently. **Orgs:** Am Mkt Asn, 1982-87; Charter Mem, Metroplex Egyptian Hist Soc; Univ Tex Arlington Alumni Asn, Phonathon, 1985; Hands Across Am, 1986; Black Enterprise Prof Network Exchange, 1987; Nat Asn Advan Colored People, Grand Prairie, 1989; Dallas Urban League, 1989; African Am Men Endangered Species; NBA, 1990; Delta Theta Phi Int Law Fraternity; Tex Wesleyan Univ Stud Bar Asn; Nat Bar Asn. **Honors/Awds:** UTA Academic Achievement Award, 1981, 1982; UTA Alumni Leadership Scholar Acad Excellence & Campus Involvement, 1982; Jesse Jackson Delegate State Convention, 1988; West's Law & Tech Essay Winner, 1993. **Home Addr:** 705 Manning Rd, Grand Prairie, TX 75051, **Home Phone:** (972)660-5651. **Business Addr:** Director, The Willrich Scott Consulting Group Inc, 3700 Forums Dr Suite 106, PO Box 251247, Flower Mound, TX 75028-1849, **Business Phone:** (972)741-7539.

WILLRICH, PENNY
Judge, educator. **Personal:** Born Aug 12, 1954, Dallas, TX; daughter of Theodis and Margie; children: Amaya Maria. **Educ:** Univ Tex, Arlington, BA, polit sci, 1974, BA, hist, 1976; Antioch Sch Law, JD, 1982; Springfield Col, MS, 2001. **Career:** US Dist Ct, Phoenix; Fifth Circuit Ct Appeals; Ninth Circuit Ct Appeals; Reginald Heber Smith Community Law Fel, 1982-84; W Tex Legal Servs, managing atty, 1984-87; Community Legal Serv, litigation dir, 1987-92; Ariz Dept Econ Security, asst dir, 1992-94; Law Off Penny Willrich, priv pract, 1994-95; Superior Ct, Maricopa County, comnr, 1995-99; supr ct judge, 1999-05; Ariz State Univ, Col Law, adj prof, 2001; Phoenix Sch Law, assoc prof law & dir lawyering process, 2005-. **Orgs:** Alpha Kappa Alpha Sor; Phi Eta Sigma Honor Soc; Black Women's Task Force; Maricopa County Bar Asn; Nat Women Judges Asn; Thurgood Marshall Inn Court; Ariz Women Lawyers Asn; Hayzel B Daniels Bar Asn; Nat Asn Advan Colored People; Nat coun Negro Women; Phi Delta Phi Legal Frat; Parent Teacher Orgn; New Life Battered Women Shelter, bd mem, 1989-94; Supreme Court's Comn Minorities, 1990-00; adv bd, US Civil Rights Comn, 1991-98; bd mem, Friends Phoenix Pub Libr, 1992-94; Ariz Supreme Ct Domestic Violence Comm, 1992-96; vol, Maricopa County Modest Means Proj, 1994-95; orientation trainer, Ct Appointed Special Advocates, 1995-; cochair, ADES, Multi Ethnic Adv comm, 1997-98; chair, liaison to State Bar Bd of Governors, H B Daniels Bar Asn, Bar Issues Comm1998; Juvenile Div, presiding commissioner, 1998-99; Maricopa County Model Ct Comt, 1998-99; trainer, COLORBLIND Justice Conf, AZ Supreme Ct, 1998-99; Phoenix Violence Prev Initiative; State Bar Ariz Ed Bd, 1998-00; State Bar Ariz Ethics Comt; Phoenix Fire Dept Community Adv Bd; vol, Gilbert Jr High, Art Master's Program; Children's Voices; 1999 trainer, Ariz New Judge Orientation; minister & teacher, First New Life Missionary Baptist Church. **Honors/Awds:** Distinguished Service, HB Daniels Bar Assn, 1993; NCP Image Award, 1994; Leadership Award, Black Women's Taskforce, 1996; Outstanding African American Alumni, Univ Tex, Arlington, 1999; Trailblazer Award, 100 MNY & Women Lawyers, 2000; Phenomenal Woman Award, Ariz Asn Women Change, 2000; 100 Black Men Award; Roy Wilkins Award, NAACP, 2007. **Special Achievements:** Co-authored TX Young Lawyers Domestic Violence Help Manuel, 1985-86; video script on domestic violence, 1987-88; A Guide To Do It Yourself, AZ Default Divorce, 1988-89; assisted the Maricopa County Conciliation Court Services develop a domestic violence protocol for mediation of domestic relations cases, 1990; coordinated legal seminars with NAACP Community Legal Seminars and H B Daniels Bar Assn, 1990-92; assisted in developing grant proposal to ABA to fund program, 1990-92; State of AR Dept, consultant, 1992; participated in pilot project for detention mediation, 1995-97; participated in pilot project for assessment of cost of services, 1995-97; assisted in the development of a "Pro Per Self-Help Packet" for litigants in dependency cases, 1995-97; served as associated presiding commissioner, assisted in the development of orientation manual to train new judicial officers, liaison between the Dept of Economic Security and the Juvenile Court, 1996-97; SB1446, Get Tough on Juvenile Crime Initiative, statewide telecast, participant, 1998; Statewide Telecast Conf on Domestic Violence, participant, 1998-99; first Afr Amer woman appointed superior court judge by the governor of Ariz; Benchmark Legal Advocacy Awd, 2000; ordained American Baptist Churches USA, 2003. **Business Addr:** Associate Professor of Law, Director of Lawyering Process, Phoenix School of Law, 4041 N Central Ave Suite 100, Phoenix, AZ 85012, **Business Phone:** (602)682-6800.*

WILLRICH SCOTT, CANDACE YVETTE
Executive, president (organization), chief executive officer. **Personal:** Born Mar 26, 1965, Dallas, TX; daughter of Theodis and Margie; married Eugene, Jul 24, 1993. **Educ:** Univ Tex, Austin, TX, BS, math, 1988, MBA, finance & info systs, 1990. **Career:** Comshare Inc, consult, 1991-95; Willrich Scott Consult Group, founder,chief exec officer & pres, 1995-. **Orgs:** Nat Black MBA, 1990-; Tex Ex Alumni Asn, 1998-; Nat Asn Female Execs,1998-; Nat Asn Advan Colored People, 1998-; Women In Technol, 1999-; Data Mgt Asn, 1999-. **Honors/Awds:** North American Consultant of the Year, Comshare Inc, 1994; Member of the Year, Nat Black MBA Asn, Econ Comn, 1999. **Business Addr:** President, Chief Executive Officer, Willrich Scott Consulting Group, 3700 Forums Dr Suite 112, PO Box 251247, Flower Mound, TX 75028, **Business Phone:** (972)724-1725.

WILLS, DR. CORNELIA
School administrator. **Personal:** Born Jun 22, 1953, Eastaboga, AL; daughter of Willie Wills Jr and Rosa Lee Elston. **Educ:** Austin Peay State Univ, Clarksville, Tenn, BS, 1974; Tenn State Univ-,Nashville, Tenn, MEd, 1992, EdD, 1997. **Career:** Tenn State Univ, Nashville, Tenn, admin secy, 1974-77, 1979-81; Fisk Univ-,Nashville, Tenn, off mgr, 1981-84; Meharry Med Col, Nashville, gift acct coordr, 1984-88; Tenn Bd Regents, Nashville, Tenn, res analyst, 1988-89; Middle Tenn State Univ, Murfreesboro, Tenn, dir instnl res, currently. **Orgs:** Delta Sigma Theta Sorority Inc, 1973-; consult, Fac Res Comt, 1989-95;consult, Univ Planning Comt, 1989-; Asn Instnl Res, 1990-; elect, 19 Women Higher Educ Tenn, Tenn Asn Instnl Res, 1990-, pres, 1998-2000; Status Women Acad, 1991-; Task Force Performance Funding, 1991-; Exec Comn Instnl Effectiveness, 1992-; Southern Asn Instnl Res, 1996-; Phi Delta Kappa Int; Tenn State Univ Chap, vpres, 1998-99. **Honors/Awds:** Nat Beta Club, 1970; Outstanding Student Teacher Award, Austin Peay State Univ Ambassador, Austin Peay State Univ, 1978; Listed in PCSW, 2009. **Special Achievements:** First African American & first female director of institutional research at Middle Tennessee State. **Home Addr:** 765 McMurray Dr Suite C-7, Nashville, TN 37211, **Home Phone:** (615)333-0887. **Business Addr:** Director, Middle Tennessee State University, Office of Institutional Research, 153 Jones Hall, PO Box 140, Murfreesboro, TN 37132, **Business Phone:** (615)898-2854.

WILLS, DOROTHY
Nurse. **Personal:** Born Oct 17, 1942, Eastaboga, AL; daughter of Willie Jr and Rosa Lee. **Educ:** Webster Univ, BSN, 1998;

Covenant Theol Sem, MAC, 2001. **Career:** Barnes-Jewish Hosp, nurse, 1965-2001; Meier New Life Clinics, St Louis, counr, 2001-, therapist, currently. **Orgs:** Sigma Theta Tau Int Soc, 1998-. **Honors/Awds:** Certified, psychiatric & mental health nurse, 1994-; Nat Hon Soc, 1998. **Special Achievements:** Travelled to all seven continents, 1965-95. **Home Addr:** 1130 Martha Lane, St Louis, MO 63119-1145. **Business Addr:** Counselor/Therapist, Meier New Life Clinics, 9717 Landmark Pkway Dr Suite 208, St Louis, MO 63127, **Business Phone:** (314)849-2120.

WILLS, DR. JAMES WILLARD
Physician. **Personal:** Born Jan 23, 1933, Aquasco, MD; son of Rossie H and Clara Wright; married Waltine; children: Phyllis, John & Cecil. **Educ:** Morgan State Col, BS, 1954; Howard Univ, MD, 1961. **Career:** Glenn Dale Hosp, exec dir, 1973-77; Glenn Dale Hosp, chief, med serv; Pvt practice, physician, 1975-; chief med officer, Area "C" Chest Clinic (Washington D.C.), 1981-. **Orgs:** Alpha Phi Alpha, Medico-Chirurgical Soc, DC, Nat Med Asn. **Honors/Awds:** AUS, first lt, 1954-56. **Home Addr:** 11303 Earlston Dr, Mitchellville, MD 20721-2426, **Home Phone:** (301)464-3745. **Business Addr:** Physician, 14310 Old Marlboro Pke, Upper Marlboro, MD 20772, **Business Phone:** (301)627-1448.

WILMORE, GAYRAUD STEPHEN, JR.
Educator. **Personal:** Born Dec 20, 1921, Philadelphia, PA; son of Patricia Gardner (deceased); married Lee Wilson; children: Stephen, Jacques & Roberta Wilmore-Hurley. **Educ:** Lincoln Univ, BA, 1947; Lincoln Univ Theol Sem, BD, 1950; Temple Univ Sch Religion, 1952; Drew Theol Sem, 1963. **Career:** Educator (retired); 2nd Presbyterian Church West Chester, PA, pastor,1950-53; Mid-Atlantic Stud Christian Movement, regional secy, 1953-56; Pittsburgh Theol Sem, prof social ethics, 1960-63; United Presbyterian Coun Church & Race, exec dir, 1963-72; Boston Univ Sch Theol, prof soc ethics, 1972-74; Colgate Rochester Div Sch, ML King Jr prof, 1974-83; NY Theol Sem, MD IV Prog, dean & prof afro-am relig studies, 1983-87; Inter denominational Theol Ctr, distinguished vis scholar, 1986-87; United Theol Seminary, Dayton, Ohio, adj prof, 1995-98. **Orgs:** Am Soc Christian Ethics, 1961-78; bd mem, Faith & Order Comn, World Coun Church, 1973-89; Ecum Asn Third World Theol, 1976-; bd dir, Black Theol Project Inc, 1977-; consult, Eli Lilly Endowment, 1979-80; pres, Soc Study Black Relig, 1979-80; ed, J Info Technol Ctrs, 1989-94; founding mem, Nat Conf Black Churchmen; Am Theol Soc. **Honors/Awds:** DD, Lincoln Col, 1965; Bruce Klunder Award, Presbyterian Interracial Coun, 1968; DD, Tusculum Col, 1972. **Military Serv:** AUS, 92nd Infantry Div, sgt, 1943-46.

WILMOT, DAVID WINSTON
Educator, lawyer, businessperson. **Personal:** Born Apr 26, 1944, Panama, FL; son of David and Bertha; married Mary Elizabeth Mercer; children: Michele, Kristy & David II. **Educ:** Univ Ariz, BA, 1970; Georgetown Univ Law Ctr, JD, 1973. **Career:** Little Rock, asst city mgr, 1968-70; Dolphin Branton Stafford & Webber, legal asst, 1970-72; DC Proj Comm Legal Asst, dep dir, 1972-73; Georgetown Univ, asst dean, dir, 1973-92; Harmon & Wilmot, partner, 1992-; Georgetown Univ Law Ctr, res asst; OEO Legal Servs, intern; DC Convention Ctr Bd Dirs, gen coun; Hotel Assoc Wash DC, gen coun. **Orgs:** Pres, Stud Equality, 1967-68; vpres, GULC Legal Aid Soc, 1972-73; pres,Black Am Law Stud Assoc, 1972-73; adv bd, DC Bds & Comms Adv Bd Georgetown Today, 1973-76; DC Bar; PA Bar; US Supreme Ct Appeals; DC Ct Appeals; Supreme Ct PA; Assoc Am Law Schs; Law Sch Admin Coun; Am Bar Assoc; Trial Lawyers Assoc; Nat Bar Assoc; Nat Conf Black Lawyers; Alpha Kappa Psi; Lawyers Study Group; Potomac Fiscal Soc; Firemens & Policement Retirement Bd; mem bd dirs, Federal City Nat Bank, Wash Waterfront Restaurant Corp; mem bd govs, Georgetown Univ Alumni Assoc; mem bd dirs, Dist Cable vision Inc; Wash Tennis & Educ Found. **Honors/Awds:** Dean's List, 1967-70; Dean's Counselor Award, Univ AR, 1969; Outstanding Service Award, Georgetown Univ Stud Bar Assoc, 1971; Cert Merit DC Citz Better Ed, 1972; Jeffrey Crandall Award, 1972; WA Law Reptr Prize, 1973; Robert D L'Heureux Scholorship. **Military Serv:** USAF, E/5, 1963-67. **Business Addr:** Partner, Harmon & Wilmot LLP, 1010 Vermont Ave NW, Washington, DC 20005.

WILSON, ALVA L
Clergy. **Personal:** Born Nov 21, 1922, Lake City, SC; son of Malichi and Hattie Mayes; married Carrie Williams; children: Allesia Muldrow, Charles K & Benita F. **Educ:** Allen Univ, AB, 1949; Gammon Theol Sem, 1961. **Career:** Owner & farmer, 1950; freelance horticulturist, landscaper, 1979-; UMSC Conf, clergyman. **Orgs:** Barber Shaw AFB, 1949-75; vice chmn, Health Educ & Welfare Minister, 1972-78; secy, trustee bd, Florence County District third Sch Bd, 1974-91. **Honors/Awds:** Leadership Training Institute Award, SC Sch Bd Asn, 1975. **Military Serv:** AUS, pfc, 3 yrs. **Home Addr:** 1454 Eastland Ave, Kingstree, SC 29556-6036. *

WILSON, ANGELA BROWN
Government official. **Personal:** Born Mar 31, 1961, Detroit, MI; daughter of Bunnie Brown Sr (deceased) and Lillie M Brown; married Errol S, Feb 25, 1995. **Educ:** Wayne State Univ, BSW, 1984; MSW, 1988; Develop Training Inst, cert, 1989. **Career:** Warren/Conner Dev Coalition, prog dir, 1985-87, dep dir, 1987-94; City Detroit, exec asst mayor, 1994-. **Orgs:** Minister faith, Sacred Heart Church, 1982-; spokesperson,Save Our Spirit Coalition, 1986-93; chairperson, Dept Catholic Pastoral Alliance, 1992-; chairperson, Nat Community Rels Div Am Friends Serv Comt, 1993; Dominican High Sch Bd Assocs, 1994-; Am Friends Serv Comt, 1995-; NAACP; Wayne State Univ Alumni Asn; Knight & Ladies, St Peter Claver; Develop Practitioners, Develop Leadership Network. **Honors/Awds:** James E Wadsworth Jr Award; Achievement Award, Am Bus Women's Asn; Christopher Turner Eastside Community Leadership Award; Angela B Wilson Award, named in honor.

WILSON, BARBARA JEAN
Executive. **Personal:** Born Jun 5, 1940, Dallas, TX; married Porterfield (deceased); children: Porterfield Christopher. **Educ:** Prairie View A&M Col, BS, 1960-64; Gen Motors Inst Flint Mich, 1975; Hadley Dealer Acct Sch Royal Oak Mich, 1975; Reynolds & Reynolds Comput Sch Dayton Ohio, 1980. **Career:** TC Hassell Sch Dallas Tex, exec secy, 1964-73; Chrysler Corp Mound Rd Engine Detroit, bookkeeper, 1965-73; Porterfield Wilson Pontiac GMC Truck Mazda-Honda, exec secy, 1973-79; Mazda Honda, pres oper, 1979-84; Ferndale Honda, pres, 1984-; Porterfield's Marina Village, Detroit, Mich, pres, 1989-. **Orgs:** Pres, Carats Inc Detroit Chap Nat Club, 1969; women's Econ Club, 1975-; life mem, NAACP, 1975; Palmer Woods Asn, 1976; Am Imported Auto Dealers, 1979; Detroit Auto Dealers Asn, 1979; Negro Bus & Prof Women, 1979; Coalition 100 Black Women Detroit, 1980. **Honors/Awds:** Special Recognition Award, Carats Inc Detroit Chap, 1979; Woman of the Year, 1987; Michigan's Top 50 Business Owned & Operated by Women, Crain's Detroit Bus; Candice Award of Business. **Home Addr:** 19481 Gloucester, Detroit, MI 48203. **Business Addr:** President, Ferndale Honda, 21350 Woodward Ave, Ferndale, MI 48220-2542, **Business Phone:** (248)548-6300.

WILSON, BERNARD (RAPHAEL BERNARD WILSON)
Football player. **Personal:** Born Aug 17, 1970, Nashville, TN; married Roslyn; children: Khandi. **Educ:** Tenn State Univ. **Career:** Football player (Retired); Tampa Bay Buccaneers, defensive tackle, 1993-94; Ariz Cardinals, defensive tackle, 1994-98.

WILSON, DR. BLENDA JACQUELINE
School administrator. **Personal:** Born Jan 28, 1941, Perth Amboy, NJ; daughter of Horace Lawrence and Margaret Brogsdale; married Louis Fair Jr. **Educ:** Cedar Crest Col, BA, eng, 1962; Seton Hall Univ, MA, educ, 1965; Boston Col, PhD, higher educ admin, 1979. **Career:** Middlesex County Econ Opportunities Corp, New Brunswick, NJ, exec dir, 1968-69; Rutgers Univ, New Brunswick, NJ, asst provost, 1969-71, exec asst pres, 1969-72; Harvard Grad Sch Educ, Cambridge, MA, assoc dean admin, 1972-75, lectr educ, 1976-82, sr assoc dean, 1972-82; Independent Sector, Washington, DC, vpres, 1982-84; Colo Comn Higher Educ, Denver, CO, exec dir, 1984-88; Univ Mich-Dearborn, MI, chancellor, 1988-92; Calif St Univ, Northridge, pres, 1992-99; Fed Reserve Bank, chmn. **Orgs:** Chairperson, Am Asn Higher Educ, 1990-; bd dirs, Alpha Ctr, 1988-91; adv comm, Int Found Educ & Self-Help, 1986-; bd trustees, Boston Col; Found Ctr; bd trustees, Sammy Davis Jr Nat Liver Inst, 1989; exec bd, Detroit Area Boy Scouts Am; Detroit Chapter Nat Coalition 100 Black Women; Dearborn Rotary; Asn Governing Bds; United Way SE Mich, 1989; Women's Econ Club Detroit, 1989; bd dirs, Commonwealth Fund, 1981-; dir, James IrvineFound; trustee, J Paul Getty Trust; dir, Children's TV Workshop; pres & ceo, Nellie Mae Educ Found, 1999-2006; bd mem, Boston After Sch & Beyond, Boston Col, Federated Dorchester Neighborhood Houses, Medco Health Solutions & Partners Health Care Systs. **Honors/Awds:** Doctor of Educ, Eastern Mich Univ, 1990; Doctor of Laws, Rutgers Univ, 1989, Doctor of Humane Letters, Univ Detroit, 1989; Women on the Move Award, Renaissance Chapter of Links, 1989; Michigan Bell Living Dream Award, Michigan Bell, 1989; Distinguished Leader, Washtenaw Comm Col, 1990. **Special Achievements:** One of 100 Emerging Leaders in America, Higher Educ Change magazine, 1978, 90 for the 90's, Crain's Detroit Business Magazine, 1990. **Business Addr:** University President, Office of the President, California State University, 18111 Nordhoff St, Northridge, CA 91330.

WILSON, DR. BOBBY L
Educator. **Personal:** Born Sep 30, 1942, Columbus, MS; son of Lillie Coleman and Johnnie B; married Mary, Dec 22, 1966; children: Anthony, Melanie, Malissa & Melinda. **Educ:** Ala State Col, BS, chem, 1966; Southern Univ, MS, chem, 1972; Mich State Univ, PhD, chem, 1976. **Career:** Booker T Wash HS, instr, 1966-70; Jefferson Davis HS, instr, 1970-71; Mich State Univ, grad asst, 1971-76; Tex Southern Univ, asst prof, 1976-80, assoc prof, 1980-82; Exxon Res & Engineering, visiting prof, 1982-83; Tex Southern Univ, assoc prof, 1983-85, prof, 1985-, Col Arts & Sci, assoc dean, 1986-87, dept head, 1987-89, interim dean arts & sci, 1989-90, vpres, acad affairs, 1990-92, provost, 1992-94, prof, 1994, sr vice pres, acad affairs, currently, Distinguished prof, currently. **Orgs:** ACS; Beta Kappa Chi Honor Soc; KAP Frat; NAACP; Nat Geog Soc; Nat Org Prof Advan Black Chemists & Chem ENRs; Nat Urban League; Smithsonian Inst; Tex Acad Sci; Tex Asn Col Teachers; Tri-County Civic Asn; Tex Fac Asn; Forum Club Houston; Sigma Xi; Tex Inst Chemists; Am Inst Chemists, stud awards Comm, 1988; Sci Res Soc, 1988; Bylaws Comm, 1988; pres, Children Against Drugs & Drinking Inc. **Honors/Awds:** ROTC Gold Citation, 1967; Citizen of the Year Award, 1980, Audrey Logan Citizenship Award, 1988, The Briargate Comm; Community Serv Award, AKA Sorority, 1983; Appreciation Award, 1984, Outstanding Teacher Award, 1985, Nat Org Black Chemists & Chem Engineers.White House Initiative Faculty Award for Excellence in Sci & Tech, 1988; Graduate Brother of the Year Award, 1988, Service Award, 1988, Houston Alumni Chapter, Spotlight Award, KAP, Southwest Province, 1984; Researcher of the Year, Tex Southern Univ, 1988, Outstanding Teacher of the Year Award, Col Arts & Sci, 1989;, Showcase of Black Talent Award, Prog Coun, 1989; McCleary Teacher of the Year Award, 1989; Fellow, Am Inst Chemists, 1988; Albert Einstein World Award of Sci Diploma, 1987. **Special Achievements:** Author of over thirty scholarly manuscripts in national and international journals, co-author of General Chemistry Laboratory I Manual, Ginn Press, 1988, General Chemistry Laboratory II Manual, Ginn Press, 1989, two patents. **Home Phone:** (281)412-2621. **Business Addr:** Distinguished professor, Senior Vice President, Texas Southern University, Department of Chemistry, Rm SB 403L, Houston, TX 77004, **Business Phone:** (713)313-7133.

WILSON, BRYAN
Gospel singer. **Personal:** Born Nov 3, 1981, Danville, IL; son of Sheila Wilson and Lowell Briggs. **Educ:** Claflin Univ, BA, 2004. **Career:** Malaco Records, recording artist, 1994. Growing Up, 1998. **Orgs:** UNCF Pre-Alumni Coun, chaplin, 2002. **Honors/Awds:** Gospel Music Assn, Dove Award Nomination, for "Bryan's Songs," 1996; Don Jackson Productions, Stellar Awards, for "Bryan's Songs," 1996. **Special Achievements:** Albums: Bryan's Songs, Malaco Records, 1996; Growing Up, Malaco Records,1999. **Business Addr:** Gospel Singer, c/o Capital Entertainment, 217 Seaton Pl NE, Washington, DC 20002, **Business Phone:** (202)636-7028.

WILSON, CARL L.
Architect, clergy. **Personal:** Born Dec 24, 1921, Warren, OH; son of Michael Robert Wilson Sr and Georgia Russell Crawford; married Doris Hazel Bass; children: 1 son. **Educ:** Ohio State Univ, BS, 1951. **Career:** Wright-Patterson Area Off Dayton, proj engr, 1951-62; US Corps Engrs, architect; USACE Asmara, Ethiopia, asst rsch eng, 1962-66; Munsan-ni Korea second Inf Div, install plng officer, 1966-67; US Fed Bldg Canton, res engr, 1968-69; IRS Add Covington, KY, 1969-70; Baltimore Post Office, 1970-72; Cincinnati Bulk Mail Ctr, supervising staff of seventeen, 1972-75; OH Area Office Dayton, asst area engr, 1975-80; Montgomery Cty OH Bldg Reg Dept, dir, 1980-83; Mt Olive Baptist Church, Dayton, Ohio, assoc minister. **Orgs:** Reg arch State of OH, 1958-; imp officer, AEA Order Nobles Mystic Shrine, 1968-86; past master progress Lodge 85; past comdr in chief LD Easton Consistory 21; companion Johnson Chap 3 Columbus OH; past patron Lily of the Valley 55 Middletown OH; companion Solomon Johnson Coun 4; Sir Knight Boone Commandery 27; mem US Supreme Coun AASR North Jurisdiction; former nat dir Stud Aid for Boys of Prince Hall Shriners; Nat Asn Advan Colored People, Dayton Urban League; secy gen, USC AASR, NJ, 1975-83; imp potentate AEAONMS, 1984-86; archon, Sigma Bowle, Sigma Pi Phi Fraternity, 1986-; coordr, Minority Contractors Assistance Prog, Dayton, Ohio 1989-. **Honors/Awds:** highest rank black field official US Corps of Engrs; US Coun's Gold Medal Achievement Award, Meritorious Serv, Sovereign Grand Comdrs Award for Excellence; cited in Ebony Mag as one of 100 Most Influential Blacks in Am, 1985-86. **Special Achievements:** Only African Am grad Ohio State University School of Architect, 1919-51; First black to serve as deputy dir Dept of Pub Works State of OH, 1983-84. **Military Serv:** AUS, Sig Corps & Army Air Corps, WWII, 1942-46. *

WILSON, CARROLL LLOYD
Educator. **Personal:** Born Jul 9, 1937, Jamaica, NY; married Barbara Ellen Jones; children: Mark Lloyd, Eric Theodore & Ellen Clarice. **Educ:** Univ Maine, Orono, BA, 1962; Kean Col, NJ, MA, 1969; Rutgers Univ, Grad Studies. **Career:** Pub Health Educ State ME, asst to dir, 1962-63; Plainfield Pub Sch Plainfield NJ, teacher & asst track coach, 1963-69; Job Corps, Camp Kilmer NJ, res specialist 1966-67; Somerset Community Col & Annandale Youth Correctional Inst, Annandale NJ, coord spec prog, 1973-74; Raritan Valley Community Col, prof, prof emer, currently. **Orgs:** Bd dir, Somerset Comn Mental Health Asn, 1978-81; bd trustees, Correctional Inst Women, Clinton, NJ, 1978-82; NJ Asn Devel Educ, 1980-; coach, Hillsborough NJ Recreation Soccer, 1981-; Cub Master Pack, 1776; Boy Scouts Am, 1982-85; Nat Coun Black Am Affairs, 1983-; evaluator, Middle States Asn Cols & Univs, 1986-; chair, Paul Robeson Youth Achievement Award. **Honors/Awds:** Special Faculty Service Award, Somerset Community Col, 1975; Black Student Union Advisory Service Award, 1975-76; Special Faculty Service & Admin Award, 1976. **Business Addr:** Professor Emeritus, Raritan Valley Community College, 28 Lamington Rd, PO Box 3300, Somerville, MA 08876-1265, **Business Phone:** (908)526-1200.

WILSON, CASSANDRA
Singer. **Personal:** Born Dec 3, 1955, Jackson, MS; daughter of Herman B Fowlkes and Mary McDaniel; married Isaach de Bankole, Jan 1, 2000; married Anthony, Jan 1, 1981 (divorced 1983); children: Jeris. **Career:** Albums: Blue Light Til Dawn, New Moon Daughter; Blue Moon Rendezvous, 1998; Traveling Miles, 1999; Belly of the Sun, 2002; Sings Standards,2002; Glamoured, 2003; Thunderbird, 2006; Flims: Junior, singer, 1994; The Score, singer, 2001; songs: "Green Dolphin Street" & "You're About To Give In", 2001; "Time After Time", 2002; "Lost", 2005; "Thunderbird", 2006; "Loverly", 2008. **Orgs:** Alpha Kappa Alpha Sorority Inc. **Honors/Awds:** Female Jazz Vocalist of the Year, Down Beat mag, 1994-96; Grammy Award, Jazz Vocal, 1996; America's Best Singer, Time Mag, 2001; honorary doctorate in the Arts, Millsaps Col, 2003; Grammy Award, Best Jazz Vocal Album for Loverly, 2009. **Business Phone:** (212)786-8610.*

WILSON, CHANDRA DANETTE
Actor. **Personal:** Born Aug 27, 1969, Houston, TX; married; children: Joy, Serena & Michael. **Educ:** NY Univ, Tisch Sch Arts, BFA, drama, 1991; Lee Strasberg Theatre Inst. **Career:** Stage actor, 1975-; TV Actor, 1989-; Film Actor, 1993-; Films: Mad Dog & Glory, 1993; Philadelphia, 1993; Lone Star, 1996; Head of State, 2003; Strangers with Candy, 2005; TV series: "The Cosby Show", 1989; "Law &Order", 1992; "CBS School break Special", 1992; "Cosby", 2000; "Third Watch", 2001; "100 Centre Street", 2001; Bob Patterson, 2001; Sex & the City, 2002; "Queens Supreme", 2003; "Law & Order: Special Victims Unit", 2002-05; "The Sopranos", 2004; "Grey's Anatomy", 2005-09; A Single Woman, 2009; Frankie and Alice, 2009. **Honors/Awds:** Theatre World Award for Outstanding Debut Performance; Reel Stars of TexasAward, Houston Chap Women in Film TV, 2006; Screen Actors Guild Award,Outstanding Actress in a Drama Series: Grey's Anatomy, 2007; Screen ActorsGuild Award, Outstanding Cast in a Drama Series: Grey's Anatomy, 2007. **Business Addr:** Actress, c/o William Morris Agency Inc, 151 El Camino Dr, Beverly Hills, CA 90212, **Business Phone:** (310)859-4000.*

WILSON, CHARLES LEE, SR.
Executive. **Personal:** Born Oct 25, 1941, Atlanta, GA; son of William Fred Sr and Ethel Wilson; divorced; children: Charles Lee Jr & Angela Y. **Educ:** Bethune Cookman Col, BS, psychol; Temple Univ, MS, coun guid & admin; Rutgers Univ, educ admin. **Career:** Camden NJ Sch Syst, teacher, guid counr; Philadelphia Col Art, registr; Howard Univ, dir admis, Dept Educ, consult; Enterprises New Directions Inc, chief exec officer & pres. **Orgs:** Dist Multicultural Tourism Comt; State Md Minority Adv Comt. **Special Achievements:** Author of numerous reports and publications. **Business Phone:** (301)469-3301.

WILSON, DR. CHARLES Z., JR.
Educator. **Personal:** Born Apr 21, 1929, Greenville, MS; son of Charles Zachary and Ora Lee; married Doris (deceased); children: Charles Zachary, III, Joyce Lynne, Joanne Catherine & Gary Thomas; married Kelly Freeman, Apr 21, 1986; children: Amanda Fox & Walter Bremond. **Educ:** Univ Ill, BS, 1952, PhD, 1956; Carnegie Mellon Univ, 1961. **Career:** De Paul Univ, asst prof econs, 1959-61; State Univ New York, assoc prof bus, 1961-67, prof econs & bus, 1967-68; Educ Planning Prog, special asst adminr vice chancellor, 1968-70; Univ Calif Los Angeles, prof mgt & educ,1968-84, vice chancellor acad prog, 1985-87, prof emer, currently; CEO & pres, Cent News-Wave Publs, LA, 1987-93; pres, Czand Assocs, Pacific Palisades, Calif, 1994-; CEO, Wave Comt Newspapers, LA, 1997-. **Orgs:** AAAS; bd trustees, Teachers Inst & Annuity Asn Col Retirement Equities Fund, 1971-; pres adv coun, Minority Bus Enterprise, 1972-76; UNA Panel Advan US Japan Rels, 1972-; consult, Nat Inst Educ, Dept HEW, 1973-; Adv Bd Educ & Human Resources, The Rand Corp, 1972-; chmn, Bd Trustees, The Joint Cntgr Comm Studies, 1971-72; Los Angeles Co Mus Art, 1971-; bd dirs, Black Economic Res Ctr New York City, 1970-; Am Educ Res Asn; Inst Mgt Sci; Am Econs Asn; Am Asn Univ Profs. **Honors/Awds:** American Men of Science Recipient, Am Coun Educ, 1967-68; Jr C Outstanding Young Man of Year, 1965. **Home Addr:** 1053 Tellem Dr, Pacific Palisades, CA 90272. **Business Addr:** Professor Emeritus, University of California, 1147 Murphy Hall, Los Angeles, CA 90024-1436, **Business Phone:** (310)825-7906.

WILSON, CHARLIE
Singer. **Personal:** Born Jan 29, 1953, Tulsa, OK; son of Rev Oscar and Irma; married Mahin. **Career:** Albums: Magician Holiday, 1974; The Gap Band, 1977; The Gap Band II, 1979; The Gap Band III, 1980; The Gap Band IV, 1982; The Gap Band V, 1983; The Gap Band VI, 1985; The Gap Band VII, 1986; Straight from the Heart, 1987; Round Trip, 1989; You Turn My Life Around, 1992; Best of the Gap Band, 1994; Testimony, 1994; Ain't Nothin' but a Party, 1995; Bridging the Gap, 2000; Bridging The Gap, 2004; Charlie, Last Name Wilson, 2005; Magic, 2005. **Business Addr:** Recording artist, Innerscope Records, 2220 Colorado Ave, Santa Monica, CA 90404.

WILSON, CHRISTOPHER A
Journalist. **Personal:** Born Mar 22, 1961, Shelby, NC; married Gwendolyn, Aug 10, 1985; children: Evan & Grant. **Educ:** Winston Salem State Univ, bus admin, 1983. **Career:** Ebony Investor.com, ed; Wall Streetwise Newsletter, currently. **Orgs:** Regional pres, Cent NC Investors Coun. **Honors/Awds:** Investor of the Year, New Freedom Inv Group, 1991; Growth Stock of Year Winner, NAIC, 1992. **Special Achievements:** Publisher of 20 Most Commonly Asked Questions For Investment Clubs. **Business Phone:** 800-419-1318.

WILSON, CLARENCE A
Executive. **Personal:** Born Aug 27, 1943, Talladega, AL; son of Lara Montgomery Pruitt (deceased) and Philip Monroe (deceased); married Sue Carol Cottman, Jan 28, 1967; children: Brian & Eric. **Educ:** Ind Univ, Bloomington, Ind, BS, 1967, MBA, 1981. **Career:** Marathon Oil Co, Findlay, Ohio, sr planner, 1967-69; Du Pont Co, Wilmington, Del, bus dir, nylon staples, 1981-. **Orgs:** Kappa Alpha Psi Frat, 1965-; Fin Exec Inst, 1989-; Dean Bus Sch Adv Bd, Ind Univ, 1990-; bd dirs, Neighborhood House, 1990-. *

WILSON, CLARENCE S., JR.
Lawyer, educator. **Personal:** Born Oct 22, 1945, Brooklyn, NY; son of Clarence S Wilson Sr and Thelma Louise Richards; married Helena Chapellin Iribarren, Jan 26, 1972. **Educ:** Williams Col, BA, 1967; Foreign Service Inst US, attended 1969; Northwestern Univ, Sch Law, JD, 1974. **Career:** US Dept St, Caracas, Venezuela, third secy, vice coun, 1969-71; Friedman & Koven, assoc atty, 1974-76; United States Gypsum Co, legaldept, 1976-79; sole practitioner, 1979-81; Law Offices Jewel S Lafontant, partner, 1981-83; Chicago-Kent Col Law, adj prof, 1981-94; Boodell, Sears, Sugrue, Giambalvo & Crowley, assoc atty, 1983-84; pvt practr & coun, 1984-; Columbia Col, adj prof, 1996-2000. **Orgs:** Trustee, Chicago Symphony Orchestra, 1987-96; bd mbr, Implementation Cmsn The Lawyers Trust Fund Ill, 1983-85; Art Inst Chicago, Comm Twentieth Century Painting, Sculpture, Develop, 1989-, trustee, 1990-; Citizens Information Service Ill; bd mbr, The Harold Wash Found, 1989-92; bd mbr, Northwestern Univ Sch Law Alumni Asn; governing bd, Ill Arts Coun, panel, Established Regional Arts Inst; Ill representative, Arts Midwest; Chicago & Cook County Bar Asn; trustee, Merit Music Prog, 1991-96; Chicago dept Cultural Affairs, Mayor's Adv Bd; Sch the Art Inst Chicago, mem bd governors; Dept Music & Committee on the Visual Arts at the Univ Chicago, vis committee mem, 1992-; Ministry Culture, Republic Venezuela, special legal counsel; DuSable Mus African Am Hist; vchair, 1994-97, Jazz Mus Chicago. **Special Achievements:** Author, "Visual Arts and the Law," in Law and the Arts—Art and the Law, 1979; author of several copyright/art law articles.

WILSON, CLEO FRANCINE
Association executive, businessperson. **Personal:** Born May 7, 1943, Chicago, IL; daughter of Frances Page Watson and Cleo Chancey; children: David Patrice Silbar (deceased) & SuLyn Silbar. **Educ:** Univ Ill, Chicago, BA, 1976. **Career:** Playboy Enterprises Inc, supv, 1980-82, grants mgr, 1982-84, exec dir,1 984, dir pub affairs, 1989, vpres pub affairs; Playboy Found, exec dir; Intuit: Ctr for Intuitive & Outsider Art, pres, 2002-06, exec dir, currently. **Orgs:** Vpres, Donors Forum Chicago, 1986-88; secy, Chicago Women Philanthrophy, 1986-87, task force, Ill Interdisciplinary AIDS Adv Coun, 1986-87; pres, Emergency Loan Fund, 1987-89; chmn, Chicago Funders Concerned AIDS, 1989-99; founder, Intuit: Ctr for Intuitive & Outsider Art; adv coun, Chicago Dept Cult Affairs, 1988-90; pres, AIDS Found Chicago; vpres, Am Civil Liberties Union Ill; bd dirs, Nat Coalition Against Censorship, 1997-2000; Planned Parenthood, Chicago, 2000-. **Honors/Awds:** Kizzy Image Award, Black Woman Hall of Fame 1984; Chicago's Up & ComingDollars & Sense Magazine, 1985; Phenomenal Woman Award, Expo Today's Black Woman, 1997; Handy L Lindsey Jr Award, 2004; Edwin A. Rothschild Award, 2006. **Business Addr:** Executive Director, Intuit: The Center for Intuitive and Outsider Art, 756 N Milwaukee Ave, Chicago, IL 60622, **Business Phone:** (312)243-9088.

WILSON, DANTON THOMAS
Editor. **Personal:** Born Dec 21, 1958, Houston, TX; son of Thomas Henry and Ann Elizabeth Briscoe; married Janis Richard, May 17, 1981; children: SeKou J Wilson, Khari T Wilson & Ayanna I Wilson. **Educ:** Grambling State Univ, Grambling, BA, 1981; Wayne State Univ, JD, 1989. **Career:** Detroit Free Press, Detroit, reporter, 1981; Mich Chronicle, Detroit, reporter, 1982-86, exec ed, 1987; City Detroit Pub Info, Detroit, publicist, 1986-87. **Orgs:** Black Law Studs Asn, 1985-90; Black United Fund Annual Dinner Comt, 1989-90; chmn, Orchard's C's Serv Media Asn, 1990-; bd, Be the Best You Can Be Org, 1990-; Bd Rosa Parks Scholarship Fund, 1990-. **Honors/Awds:** James Wadsworth Community Serv Award, Fel Chapel United Church, 1987; 1st place Community Serv Award, 1986.

WILSON, DANYELL ELAINE
Military leader. **Personal:** Born Jul 16, 1974, Montgomery, AL; daughter of Shirley Wilson Rucks. **Educ:** Northern Va Community Col. **Career:** AUS military police officer, sargent, 1993-98; Walter Reed Army Med Ctr, med supply specialist, 1998-. **Special Achievements:** First African American female to receive the "Tomb Guard Identification Badge," its the second most least awarded military badge, 1997; first African American female guard at the Tomb of the Unknown Soldier. **Military Serv:** Army Achievement Medal, 1996; Tomb Guard Badge, 1997; Army Accomadation Medal; Good Conduct Medal. **Business Addr:** Sargent, HQCO WRAMC, Washington, DC 20307, **Business Phone:** (202)782-5991.

WILSON, DAVID
Founder (Originator). **Career:** HyLife Productions LLC, founder & dir, 1999-. **Business Addr:** Founder, Director, HyLife Productions LLC, 44 W 24th St, New York, NY 10010, **Business Phone:** (212)627-2650.*

WILSON, DR. DAVID
Educator. **Personal:** Born Nov 2, 1954, Thomaston, AL; son of Minnie and Henry. **Educ:** Tuskegee Univ, Tuskegee, Ala, BS, 1977, MS, 1979; Harvard Univ, Cambridge, MA, EdM, 1984, PhD, 1987. **Career:** Research & Development Inst Philadelphia, project dir, 1979-82; Ky State Univ, Frankfurt, Ky, exec asst, vpres bus affairs, 1984-85; Woodrow Wilson Nat Fel Found, Princeton, NJ, 1985-88; Rutgers Univ, Camden, NJ, assoc provost, 1988-94; Auburn Univ, vpres univ outreach, assoc provost, 1994-2006; Ayers and Assoc, consult; Univ Wis Col, chancellor, 2006-; Univ Wis Ext, chancellor, 2006-. **Orgs:** Bd dir, Afro-Am Historical & Cultural Museum, Philadelphia, PA, 1988-, Walt Whitman Asn, Camden, NJ, 1988-, Princeton Ballet, 1988-, Optimist Club Lower Bucks, Bensalem, Pa, 1986-91; mem, Alpha Phi Alpha Fraternity Inc, 1975-. **Honors/Awds:** Kellogg Fel, WK Kellogg Found, 1988-92; Woodrow Wilson Fel, Woodrow Wilson Nat Fel Found, 1984-85; One of America's Best & Brightest Young Bus & Prof Men, Dollars & Sense Magazine, 1987; Cert Appreciation, Governor Ala, 1987; Cert of Appreciation, Governor of Tenn, 1988; Legacy Award, Auburn Univ, 2005. **Special Achievements:** The first chancellor to lead two UW System institutions simultaneously. **Business Addr:** Chancellor, UW Colleges, 780 Regent St Suite 130, Madison, WI 53715-2635, **Business Phone:** (608)263-0476.

WILSON, DEBRA (DEBRA RENEE WILSON SKELETON)
Actor, comedian. **Personal:** Born Apr 26, 1962, New York, NY; married Cliff Skelton. **Educ:** Syracuse Univ. **Career:** Pre-School teacher, Sunnyside, NY; Films: Cracking Up, 1994; New Jersey Drive, 1995; Blue in the Face, 1995; Girl 6, 1996; Asylum, 1997; Soulmates, 1997; B.A.P.S, 1997; Grid lock'd,1997; Sleeping Together, 1997; Star Trek the Experience: The Klingon Encounter, 1998; Rubbernecking, 2000; Jane White Is Sick & Twisted, 2002; Skin Deep, 2003; Target, 2004; That's So Raven, 2004; Nine Lives, 2004; The Chosen OPre-School teacher, Sunnyside, NY; Films: Cracking Up, 1994; New Jersey Drive, 1995; Blue in the Face, 1995; Girl 6, 1996; Asylum, 1997; Soulmates, 1997; B.A. P.S, 1997; Grid lock'd,1997; Sleeping Together, 1997; Star Trek the Experience: The Klingon Encounter, 1998; Rubbernecking, 2000; Jane White Is Sick & Twisted, 2002; Skin Deep, 2003; Target, 2004; That's So Raven, 2004; Nine Lives, 2004; The Chosen One, 2004; CSI: Crime Scene Investigation, 2004; Knight to F4, 2005; Bringing Up BayBay, writer & actor, 2005; Rockin' Meera, 2006; Shut Up & Shoot!, 2006; Mandingo in a Box, 2006; Scary Movie 4, 2006; Whitepaddy, 2006; Danny Roane: First Time Director, 2006; The Adventures of Brer Rabbit, 2006; Cordially Invited, 2007; Super Sweet 16: The Movie, 2007; If I Had Known I Was a Genius, 2007; Cuttin Da Mustard, 2008; Friends & Lovers: The Ski Trip 2, 2008; TV series: "Uptown Comedy Club", 1992; "New York Undercover", 1995; "Mad TV", 1995-2007; "Girl 6", 1996; "Asylum", 1997; "Grid lock'd", 1997; "BAPS", 1997; "Soulmates", 1997;"Sleeping Together", 1997; "Star Trek: Deep Space Nine", 1998; "The MrPotato Head Show", 1998; "Family Guy", 2000-01; "The Proud Family",2002-03; "Clone High", 2002-03; "The Parkers", 2003; "Hawks & Handsaws", 2004; "CSI: Crime Scene Investigation", 2004-07; "Without a Trace", 2004; "That's So Raven", 2004; "I'm with Her", 2004, "Spa Day Afternoon", 2004; "You're Fired", 2005, "Studio House", 2005; "Second Time Around", 2005; "American Dad!", 2005, "Amazing Animal Inventions", 2005, "In Justice", 2006; City Girls, 2007; "Reno 911!", 2008; GSN Live. Co-host, currently. ne, 2004; CSI: Crime Scene Investigation, 2004; Knight to F4, 2005; Bringing Up BayBay, writer & actor, 2005; Rockin' Meera, 2006; Shut Up & Shoot!, 2006; Mandingo in a Box, 2006; Scary Movie 4, 2006; Whitepaddy, 2006; Danny Roane: First Time Director, 2006; The Adventures of Brer Rabbit, 2006; Cordially Invited, 2007; Super Sweet 16: The Movie, 2007; If I Had Known I Was a Genius, 2007; Cuttin Da Mustard, 2008; Friends & Lovers: The Ski Trip 2, 2008; TV series: "Uptown Comedy Club", 1992; "New York Undercover", 1995; "Mad TV", 1995-2007; "Girl 6", 1996; "Asylum", 1997; "Grid lock'd", 1997; "BAPS", 1997; "Soulmates", 1997;"Sleeping Together", 1997; "Star Trek: Deep Space Nine", 1998; "The MrPotato Head Show", 1998; "Family Guy", 2000-01; "The Proud Family",2002-03; "Clone High", 2002-03; "The Parkers", 2003; "Hawks & Handsaws", 2004; "CSI: Crime Scene Investigation", 2004-07; "Without a Trace", 2004; "That's So Raven", 2004; "I'm with Her", 2004, "Spa Day Afternoon", 2004; "You're Fired", 2005, "Studio House", 2005; "Second Time Around", 2005; "American Dad!", 2005, "Amazing Animal Inventions", 2005, "In Justice", 2006; City Girls, 2007; "Reno 911!", 2008; GSN Live. Co-host, currently. **Honors/Awds:** Audience Award, San Francisco Int

Lesbian & Gay Film Festival, 2003. **Special Achievements:** First African-American woman performer on "Mad TV", 1995. **Business Addr:** Actress, c/o William Morris Agency Inc, 1325 Avenue of the Americas, New York, NY 10019, **Business Phone:** (212)586-5100.*

WILSON, DEMOND
Evangelist, actor. **Personal:** Born Oct 13, 946 , Valdosta, GA. **Educ:** Hunter Col. **Career:** Sanford & Son, actor, 1972-77; Demond Wilson Ministries, evangelist; Films: All in the Family, 1971; The Organization, 1971; Mission: Impossible, 1971; Dealing: Or the Berkeley-to-Boston Forty-Brick Lost-Bag Blues, 1972; Sanford and Son, 1977; Baby, I'm Back, 1978; Full Moon High,1981; The Love Boat, 1981; The New Odd Couple, 1982; Me and the Kid, 1993; Hammerlock, 2000; Biography, 2000; American Soundtrack: Rhythm, Love and Soul, 2003; Praise the Lord, 2004; Girlfriends, 2005; Books: Grady D.Wilson and Avaneda D. Hobbs, 1998; The New Age Millennium: An Expose of Symbols, 1998; Slogans and Hidden Agendas, 1998; John Neuman Smith, 1999;Lil' Mowande, 1999; Mr. Fish Takes a Wife, 1999. "The O'Reilly Factor", playing Lynn's biological father, 2009.

WILSON, DR. DONALD
Dean (Education), physician. **Personal:** Born in Worcester, MA. **Educ:** Harvard Univ, attended; Tufts Univ, MD. **Career:** Univ Ill Med Sch, prof, chief gastroenterol; State Univ NY, Health Sci Ctr, Dept Med, prof & chmn; nat advocate, equality in healthcare & med educ; Univ Hosp, physician-in-chief; Kings Co Hosp Ctr, Brooklyn, physician-in-chief; Univ MD, Sch of Med, dean, 1991-2006, dir, currently, dean emeritus, currently. **Orgs:** Md Emergency Med Serv bd, 1993-; chmn, Md Health Care Comn, 1994-04; chmn, Asn Am Med Col, 2004; chmn, AAMC Coun Deans; Inst Med Nat Acad Sci. **Honors/Awds:** Frederick Douglass Award, Univ Md; Baltimore Urban League Whitney M Young Jr Humanitarian Award; Distinguished Black Marylander Award, Towson Univ; Herbert W Nickens Diversity Award, AAMC. **Special Achievements:** Fourth longest serving medical school dean in the US; First African-American dean at a predominantly white medical school. **Business Addr:** Dean Emeritus, University of Maryland, School of Medicine, 655 W Baltimore St 14-029 Bressler Res Bldg, Baltimore, MD 21201-1559, **Business Phone:** (410)706-7410.

WILSON, DONALD K, JR.
Lawyer. **Personal:** Born Mar 5, 1954, Lancaster, PA; son of Donald Sr and Gloria; married Lauren, Sep 3, 1977; children: Donald Ray, Tameka, Veronica & Matthew. **Educ:** Univ Southern Calif, BS, 1976; New York Law Sch, JD, 1979. **Career:** Mason & Sloane, assoc atty, 1979-83; Quincy Jones Productions, pres, 1984-89; Law Offices Johnnie L Cochran, counsel, 1992-2000; Law Offices Donald K Wilson, Jr, 2000-. **Orgs:** Nat Bar Asn; Black Entertainment & Sports Lawyers Asn; NAACP; trustee, First AME Church. **Honors/Awds:** Community Service Award, LA Entertainment Community; Outstanding Young Men Am. **Special Achievements:** Executive producer of Frank Sinatra documentary, Portrait of an Album; featured panelist for various entertainment and sports law symposiums; published "The Effect of Termination Rights on Buying and Selling Copyrights", The Los Angeles Daily Journal; "Settlements in the Entertainment Industry", published in Los Angeles Daily Journal; selected participant, Oxford Roundtable, Oxford university, Oxford, England. **Business Addr:** Attorney At Law, Law Offices of Donald K Wilson Jr, 4322 Wilshire Blvd Suite 1010, Los Angeles, CA 90010, **Business Phone:** (213)931-6200.

WILSON, DONALD P.
Association executive. **Career:** Improved Benevolent Protective Order Elks World, grand exalted ruler, 2003. *

WILSON, DR. DONELLA JOYCE
Educator, administrator. **Personal:** Born Jul 28, 1951, Milwaukee, WI; daughter of Paul Lawrence and Emily Frenchie Bailey-Wilson. **Educ:** Johnston Col, Redlands Univ, BA, 1973; Tex Southern Univ, MS, 1977; Purdue Univ, MS, 1979, PhD, 1981. **Career:** Wash Univ, res assoc, 1981; Harvard Sch Dent Med, assoc oral pathol, 1981-83; Radcliffe Col, Bunting fel, 1983-85; vis prof, Univ Mass, Boston, 1983-84; Meharry Med Col, asst prof, 1985-91, assoc prof, 1991-; Bio Career Ctr, columnist; Am Cancer Soc, dir Res Prom & Commun, currently. **Orgs:** AAAS, 1982-; Am Soc Cell Biol, 1983-; Harvard Health Prof Admis Comn, 1985; Fedn Am Socs Exp Biol, 1986-; Beta Kappa Chi; Beta Beta Beta; scientific prog dir, Dept Res, Am Cancer Soc. **Honors/Awds:** NSF & NIH First Award, 1986 & 1987; Woman of the Year, Compton, CA, 1987; Outstanding Women of the World, 1989. **Special Achievements:** The "Future Makers" Ebony Magazine, 1985; Invited to speak on genetic Enginering, British Broadcasting, 1990. **Home Addr:** 300 Cross Timbers Dr, Nashville, TN 37221. **Business Addr:** Director, Research Promotion & Communication, American Cancer Society, 1599 Clifton Rd, Atlanta, GA 30329, **Business Phone:** (404)329-7717.

WILSON, EARL LAWRENCE
Law enforcement officer, consultant. **Personal:** Born Jul 16, 1923, Philadelphia, PA; son of James R and Helen. **Educ:** Villanova Univ, criminal justice courses, attended 1973; PA State Univ,cert, 1970; St Joseph Univ, attended. **Career:** Law Enforment officer (retired), consultant; Philadelphia Prison Syst,corrections officer, sgt, lt, captain, dep warden, prison security coord,warden, 1951-79; corrections consult, currently; Pub Health Mgt Corp, The Bridge, bd dir, currently. **Orgs:** Examr, PA Civil Serv Comn, 1974-; PA Warden's Asn, 1978-; Am Correctional Asn, 1978-; consult & adv, Criminal Justice Syst; PA Prison Wardens Asn; pres, bd dir, Therapeut Ctr Fox Chase; Am Jail Asn; PA County Prison Wardens Asn. **Honors/Awds:** Lifetime Achievement Award, PA Prison Wardens Asn, 1993. **Special Achievements:** Article on crime published in Ebony Magazine, 1979. **Military Serv:** USAF, sgt, 1944-46; Good Conduct Medal; Asiatic Pacific Ribbon. **Business Addr:** Corrections Consultant, 700 Lower State Rd, Horsham, PA 19044, **Business Phone:** (215)542-6859.*

WILSON, ERNEST
Manager. **Personal:** Born Nov 4, 1936, New York, NY; son of Ernest and Bessie; married; children: Ernest Jr, Steven & Patricia. **Educ:** NY Univ, BA; cert, mediation/conflict resolution, 1997; Super Ctr, comput training, 1997. **Career:** Freight Liner Corp, personnel mgr, 1966-71; MBM Corp, personnel dir, 1971-72; TRW Corp, personnel admin, 1972-74; Commutronx Corp, personnel dir, 1974-75; City San Bernardino, dir affirmative action & community affairs, 1975-85, dir safety, community affairs, 1985-88, dir affirmative action, 1991-; Calif St Legis, field rep, 1989-90. **Orgs:** Vol, leg adv assembly man, 67th Dist St of Calif, 1979-80; Kiwanis Int; Mexican/Am Personnel Asn; Urban League; Nat Asn Advan Colored People; Am Soc Training & Develop; Kiwanis Club San Bernardino; bd mem, Black History Found; Econ Round Table; Westside Action Group; Calif Asn Affirmative Action Officers; Am Asn Affirmative Action; vpres, Easter Seal Soc. **Honors/Awds:** Outstanding Achievement, OSC Comn Org, 1975; Outstanding Achievement, JustX Club, 1976; Certificate of Outstanding Achievement, Mexican/Am Mgt Asn, 1978; Certificate of Outstanding Participation & Contributions, Calif Poly Univ, 1979; Certificate of Appreciation, Dr Martin Luther King Mem & Scholar Fund Inc, 1980; Good Will Ambassador, City of San Bernardino, 1982; Scroll of Honor, Omega Psi Phi Frat, 1983; Certificate of Achievement, San Bernardino Black History, 1983; We Serve Award, Highland Dist Lions Club; Commendation, Dept Fair Employment & Housing State, CA; Certificate of Achievement, Equal Employment Opportunity Comn; Certificate of Recognition, Civil rgency Mgt, 34th Senate Dist State, CA, 1990; Certificate of Recognition, Ruben S Ayala, Calif State Senator, 1990; Certificate of Award, Provisional Accelerated Learning Ctr, 1991; Certificate of Appreciation, San Bernardino Nat Forest, 1992; Certificate of Appreciation, Am Heart Asn, 1992; Certificate of Recognition, San Bernidino C C, 1992; Community Service Award, 1994; Certificate of Recognition, Nat Asn Advan Colored People, 1996. **Special Achievements:** Citation for Community Service, San Bernardino Light House of the Blind, 1982; Resolution by Mayor & Council City of San Bernardino Commending Leadership of the Affirmative Action Program. **Military Serv:** AUS, staff sargent, 1954-57.

WILSON, F LEON
Writer. **Personal:** Born Sep 20, 1953, Akron, OH. **Educ:** Ohio State Univ, BS, 1975, MBA, 1983. **Career:** Cent Control Systs, publ/prin writer; The Black Agenda, Regional coordr, 1983-; Code One Communs, prin agent, 1990-, sr proj mgr, currently. **Orgs:** Chmn, Ams Against Apartheid, 1985-87; Nat Black Wholistic Soc, 1989-; corresponding secy, bd mem, Nat Black Pub Soc; US Chess Fedn; founder, Chess Learn; nat dir, The Black Agenda; chairperson, Black Male Black Female Relationships. **Special Achievements:** Publs: The Black Agenda, Educating Blacks for Social, Political and Economic Development, Dorran Press 1983; Black Unity, Definition & Direction, CCS Press, 1985; The Black Woman, Ctr Black Economy, CCS Press, 1986; Emancipatory Psychol, CCS Press, 1990; Author: Dream and Wings, CCS Press, 1994, White Supremacy: Sources & Uses, CCS Press, 1995, The Net of My Conversations, Code One Communication, 2000; Black Pioneers of the Internet. **Business Addr:** Senior Project Manager, Code One Communications, PO Box 09726, Columbus, OH 43209-0726, **Business Phone:** (614)338-0321.

WILSON, FLOYD EDWARD, JR.
Government official, executive director. **Personal:** Born Nov 22, 1935, Lake Charles, LA; son of Floyd Edward Sr and Leada R; married Dorothy Lyons, Apr 9, 1988; children: J Keith & Tanya R Derryck M. **Educ:** Dillard Univ, BA, 1959. **Career:** Eastern HS, teacher, 1962-72; Hallmark Acad C Ctr, owner & admin, 1968-78; Glenarden MD, councilman vice mayor, 1969-74; Prince George's County Coun, councilman 1974; exec dir, Minority Bus Opportunities Comn, currently. **Orgs:** PG Bd Dir Social Serv 1976-; vice chrmn, NACO Criminal Justice Comn, 1983-; chrmn, COG Air Qual Comn, 1984; mem Alpha Phi Alpha Frat; life mem, Nat Asn Advan Colored People; Prince George's County Women's Comn. **Special Achievements:** First Black Elected to Prince George's County Counc, 1974. **Home Addr:** 8909 Pkwy, Cheverly, MD 20785, **Home Phone:** (301)341-1489. **Business Addr:** Director, Minority Business Development Division, 1400 McCormick Drive Suite 282, Largo, MD 20774, **Business Phone:** (301)883-6480.

WILSON, FRANK EDWARD
Association executive, publisher. **Personal:** Born Dec 5, 1940, Houston, TX; son of Wilson James and Samanther Gibbs Wilson; married Barbara Dedmon (died 1966); children: Tracey, Frank, Launi, Fawn, Christy & Gabrielle; married Philomina B. **Educ:** Southern Univ, Baton Rouge, La, 1959-60; Fuller Grad Sch Theol, 1978-81. **Career:** Specolite Music, Inc, self-employed; Black Am Response African Community, pres, 1984-94; New Dawn Publ, owner & publ, currently. **Orgs:** Pres, Fel W Inc, 1977-; secy, Destiny Inc, bd dirs; bd chmn, United Gospel Indust Coun; chmn, Home Ownership Made Easy; Black Am Response African Community. **Honors/Awds:** US Congress Award; Great Seal US States Am, 1986; RIAA, Song Writer/Record Producer Awards. **Special Achievements:** Author, 2 books, Harvest House Publishers; speaker at Family & Men's Conferences, churches, ect worldwide; host, Day Spring Annual Conf; host, McClaney Gospel Songfest; Awarded Doctorate of Divinity, Vision Intl Univ, 2003. **Home Addr:** 2435 Vista Laguna Terr, Pasadena, CA 91103. **Business Phone:** (626)398-7685.

WILSON, DR. FRANK FREDRICK, III
Physician. **Personal:** Born Jun 14, 1936, Oklahoma City, OK; son of Frank F Wilson III and Thelma Boyd; married Jacquelyn; children: Frank IV, Nathan, Yolanda & Coreen. **Educ:** Fisk Univ, BA, 1956; attended Univ Okla, OK; Howard Univ Sch Med, BA, 1961; Univ Mo, intern spec educ, Gen Hosp & Med Ctr, 1961-65. **Career:** Physician Obstet-Gynec; Univ Okla, Sch Med, clinical assoc prof, currently; pvt pract, currently. **Orgs:** Dir Bd, Park Comnr, 1971-74; Eastside YMCA, 1972-73; Collins Garden Housing Corp, 1972-74; Okla City Obstet-Gynec Soc, sec treas, 1973-74, exec bd, 1974-77, pres, 1975-76, vpres, 1976-77, pres, 1977-; Touchstone Montessori Sch, 1973-74; Okla County Med Soc, Okla State Med Asn, AMA, Nat Med Asn; dipl, Nat Bd Med Examiners; Am Fertility Soc; Am Bd Obstet-Gynec; fel, Am Col Obstet-Gynec; Central Asn Obstet-Gynec; chmn, admission bd, Univ Okla Sch Med; bd trustees, OU med ctr, 2005-. **Military Serv:** AUS, MC capt, 1965-67. **Home Addr:** 5408 N Stonewall Dr, Oklahoma City, OK 73111. **Business Addr:** Physician, 619 NW 23rd St, Oklahoma City, OK 73103, **Business Phone:** (405)528-2157.*

WILSON, GERALD STANLEY
Music arranger or orchestrator, composer, trumpet player. **Personal:** Born Sep 4, 1918, Shelby, MS; married Josefina Villasenor; children: Geraldine, Lillian, Nancy Jo & Anthony. **Educ:** Manassas high sch, trumpet; Cass Tech, Detroit. **Career:** Album: Royal Ste, 1948; Josefina, 1950; Blues for Yna Yna, 1962; Viva Tirado, 1963; Paco, 1964; El Viti, 1965; Carlos, 1966; Teotihuacan Ste, 1966; Col, 1968; Monterey Moods, 2007; Debut, Los Angeles Philharmonic Orch; trumpeter, arranger, composer, orchs Jimmie Lunceford, 1939-42; Count Basie, 1947-49; Duke Ellington, 1947-66; Hollywood Bowl, 1967; Music Ctr Los Angeles, 1968,San Fernando Valley State Col, Mus Dept, fac, 1969; Calif State Univ Northridge; Univ Calif, Los Angeles, fac; MAMA, composer, currently. **Orgs:** Partic Kongsberg Jazz Festival Norway, 1973; music dir, many TV shows; contributed orchestrations to Libr Ella Fitzgerald. **Honors/Awds:** Paul Robeson Award; William Grant Still Award; Jazz Educr Award, Jazz Soc, 1990; Jazz Arrangers Award, Los Angeles Jazz Soc, 1992. **Military Serv:** USN, 1942-44. **Business Addr:** Composer, MAMA Jazz, 12400 Ventura Blvd Suite 662, Studio City, CA 91604, **Business Phone:** (310)825-4321.

WILSON, DR. HARRISON B.
Educator. **Personal:** Born Apr 21, 1928, Amstead, NY; married Lucy; children: Benjamin, Harrison, John, Richard, Jennifer & Marquarite. **Educ:** Ky State Univ, BS; Ind Univ, MS, DHS. **Career:** Norfolk State Col, pres, 1975-; Fisk Univ, exec asst pres; Tenn State Univ, prof health & phys educ, dir coop educ; Jackson State Univ, prof, chmn dept health phys educ, 1960-67, head basketball coach, 1951-60. **Orgs:** Bd dir, Va Nat Bank; lay adv bd, DePaul Hosp; Va State Adv Coun Voc Educ; bd dir, Health Welfare Rec Planning Coun; Alpha Kappa Mu. **Honors/Awds:** KY State Univ; honoree, Dominion, 1997, "Male Most Likely to Succeed", "Most Scholarly Athlete", sr class.

WILSON, HAZEL FORROW SIMMONS
Educator. **Personal:** Born Jun 21, 1927, Houston, TX; daughter of Sam W and Summie Lee Whittington; married Jerrimiah (deceased); children: David Jerome & James (deceased); married Jesse L, Mar 16, 1991. **Educ:** Prairie View A&M Col, attended 1945-46; Tex So Univ, BA, 1954, MA, 1974. **Career:** Educator (retired); BH Grimes Elem Sch, teacher, 1954-59; J R Reynolds Elem Sch, teacher, 1959-68; Camp Fire Girls, field dir, 1960-68; Fort Worth Independant Pub Sch, Maude I Logan Elem, first Black coordr reading improv ctr, 1972-; G.W. Carver Elem. Sch, teacher, 1968-72; Springdale Elem Sch, Chap I resource teacher. **Orgs:** So reg dir, Amicae, 1960-64; charter mem, Houston League Negro Bus & Prof Women's Club, 1962-68; exec secy, Houston Classroom Teachers Asn, 1964-66; dir, Southern region Zeta Phi

Beta, 1965-72; nat trustee, Zeta Phi Beta, 1972-76; chmn, Zeta Phi Beta So Reg Exec Bd, 1972-78; charter & first vpres, Gr Ft Worth Area Negro Bus & Prof Women's Club, 1975-81; nat dir, Stork's Nest Proj Zeta Phi Beta, 1976-82; pres, Kappa Silhouettes, 1976-80; Tex State Teachers Asn; Tex Classroom Teacher's Asn; Ft Worth Classroom Teachers Asn; YWCA, YMCA; Golden life mem, Zeta Phi Beta; ruling elder, St Peter Presb Church, 1980-87; pres, Psi Zeta Chap Zeta Phi Beta Sor, 1981-; pres, Greater Ft Worth Area Negro Bus & Prof Women, 1981-84; sponsor, Zeta Amicae, 1981-; ruling elder, fin secy, St Mark Cumberland Presbyterian Church, 1986-; pres, Zeta Chapter, 1981-93. **Honors/Awds:** Outstanding Serv Award, Tex Southern Univ, 1962, 1963; Zeta of Year, 1964; Five Years Service Award, Zeta Amicae, 1965; Outstanding Service, Zeta Phi Beta, 1965-72; Southern Regional Zeta of Year, 1974; March Dimes Volume Service Award, 1974-75; First National Zeta Phi Beta Legacy Award, 1976; Lambda Zeta Service Award, 1984; Phi Beta Sigma Zeta of the Year, 1986; Psi Zeta's Zeta of the Year Award, 1987; Graduate Leadership Award, Phi Beta Sigma/Zeta Phi Beta, 1988; Citizen of the Year, Omega Psi Phi, 1996; Wind Beneath Our Wings Award, Phi Beta Sigma, 1997; 45 Years Extraordinary Service Award, ZPB, 1998; Phenom Woman Community Volunteer Award, ZPB, 1998; Outstanding Leadership Award, Bus & Prof Women, 2000; Outstanding Woman of Ft Worth Volunteer Award, Ft Worth Comn Status Women, 2000; Nat Volunteer Service Award, Nat Bus & Prof Women's Club, 2001; Ft Worth Citizen of the Month, 2001. **Home Addr:** 2801 Sarah Jane Lane, Fort Worth, TX 76119.

WILSON, DR. HELEN TOLSON
Executive. **Personal:** Born in New Franklin, MO; daughter of A A Tolson; married Jesse (deceased). **Educ:** Kans City Conserv Music, attended 4 yrs; Dale Carnegie Inst Charm & Voice, grad med tech; Tacome Warren; Mich Univ; Wayne State Univ, BA, Humanities, 1957; Urban Bible Col, DH Detroit, MI, 1984. **Career:** Executive (retired); KC Young Matrons, pres, founder, 1939; Detroit Soc Charm Sch, dir, 1973-; US Govt, accounting tech, 26 yrs; DSACE Coord Coun for the Arts, pres, founder. **Orgs:** Founder, ZONTA Bus & Prof Women's Club, 1944; presidency elder, ME Medical Conf, Kans City dist, 1954-; chmn, Cinerama in Fashions Ford's Auditorium, 1957; gen chrmn, dir, organizer, Alpha Theta Chap, 1960; gen chrmn, Detroit Urban League 4th Annual Gala Dinner Ball, 1968; chmn Nat Founders Day Gamma Phi Delta Sor 1969-; founder, pres, dance coordr Coun for the Arts, 1972-85; pres, founder, Youth Assembly of Detroit Urban League, 1973-78; bd trustees, Gamma Phi Delta Sor; gen chrmn & dir, Gamma Phi Delta Sor's Exec Staff; gen chrmn, dir publicity, N Region Gamma Phi Delta Sr Inc; nat boule chmn, Gamma Phi Delta Sor Inc; Wheatley Provident Hosp Aux; dir, Civic Fashion Show; supr, KC MO HS Press. **Honors/Awds:** Highest Award, The Detroit Zonta Club, 1939-46; Rose Pin Award, Gamma Phi Delta Sor Inc, 1971; The Gov Award token 27 yrs; 25 yr pin Detroit Urban League Guild; DHL, Wayne State Univ Detroit, MI, 1983; Picture Honor Roll National Urban League Inc, 1986; Honored at Urban League & Guild Annual Gala, 1986.

WILSON, HENRY, JR.
Executive. **Personal:** Born Nov 10, 1938, Taylor, TX; married Carrie L Twyman; children: Peggy Annette, Pamela Ann. **Educ:** Univ Cincinnati, AS Engr, 1968. **Career:** Cincinnati Water Work, engr tech, 1957-64; Kaizer Engrs, engr, 1964-68; Turner Construct Co, engr, 1968-71; Wilson & Asn Arch & Engrs, pres, 1971-. **Orgs:** Nat Soc Prof Engrs, 1968-; dir, Hamilton County State Bank, 1980-; trustee, Univ Cincinnati Found, 1981-; secy, zoning bd appeals silverton oH, 1980-; pastor, cornerstone missionary Baptist Church, 1984-; instr, Cornerstone Bible Inst, 1985; trustee, Greater Cincinnati C C, 1985-88. **Honors/Awds:** Minority Small Bus; Person of the Year, US Small Bus Admin, 1984. **Business Addr:** President, Wilson & Association Inc, 4439 Reading Rd, Cincinnati, OH 45229-1282, **Business Phone:** (513)641-2006.

WILSON, HUGH A.
Educator. **Personal:** Born Jun 20, 1940, Kingston, Jamaica; son of John and Ola. **Educ:** Howard Univ, BA, 1963; Fordham Univ Sch Social Serv, MSW, 1967; Adelphi Univ, DSW, 1995. **Career:** Inst Suburban Studies, dir, 1975-85; Adelphi Univ NY, prof & chair, prof emer, currently. **Orgs:** Dir, Welfare Tenants Coord Com Mineola NY, 1968-70; comt organizer, Comt Coord Coun Long Beach, NY, 1966-67; co-founder & sec, Alliance Minority Group Leaders Nassau-Suffolk, 1970; Yonkers Comt Action Prog, 1971-72; consult, Westchester Urban League, 1973; Addiction Serv Agency NY, 1973. **Special Achievements:** Awarded $45000 by N Shore Unitarian Ch to set up Inst for Suburban Studies at Adelphi Univ, 1973. **Business Addr:** Professor Emeritus, Adelphi University, Department of Political Science, PO Box 701, Garden City, NY 11530-0701, **Business Phone:** (516)877-4063.

WILSON, HUGHLYNE PERKINS
Educator. **Personal:** Born Jul 12, 1931, Louisville, KY; married Charles A; children: Stuart K. **Educ:** Howard Univ, BA, 1951; Univ Louisville, MEd, 1964. **Career:** Educator(retired); Louisville Public Schs, teacher, 1956-68; Univ Ky, coordr, 1968-70; Louisville Public Schs, Div Certificated Personnel, asst dir, 1970-72, dir, 1972-74; Ky Sch Dist, asst supr, dept empl personnel serv; Ky Secy St, dir, currently. **Orgs:** Nat Educ Asn; Ky Asn Sch Admin; Am Asn Sch Personnel; Am Ky Louisville Asn Childhood Educ; Urban League, Delta Sigma Theta Sorority; Phi Delta Kappa; Ky Asn Sch Supts; Western Ky Univ Bowling Green. **Special Achievements:** First Woman assistant superintendent in Louisville Public Schools.

WILSON, J RAY
Executive. **Personal:** Born Apr 16, 1937, Leesville, LA; son of Emmitt and Florence; married Dorothy Ellison, Jun 4, 1965; children: Taleia Appral & Marcus Ray. **Educ:** Tex Southern Univ, Houston, TX, BBA, 1965. **Career:** United Calif Bank, Los Angeles, CA, opers officer, 1965-67; Conoco Inc, Houston, TX, mgr, employee rels, 1967-93. **Orgs:** Bd mem, Houston Area Urban League, 1979-86; adv, Network Group, 1982-; Amigo De Ser, 1979-; vpres, Chase Wood Civic Club, 1980-82. **Military Serv:** USN, Petty Officer, 1956-60; Good Conduct Medal, Honor Recruit.

WILSON, JACI LAVERNE
Government official. **Personal:** Born Dec 9, 1961, Houston, TX; daughter of Mae Ola McKinley-Dogan. **Educ:** Tex Southern Univ, BA. **Career:** Clinton-Gore campaign, dem nat conv, 1996; US Senate, Carol Moseley-Braun; US Trade Rep, EOP; US Dept State, secy albright; Dem Nat Conv Comt, dep dir conv housing, dir con housing, currently. **Business Addr:** Director Convention Housing, Democratic National Convention Committee, 515 S Flower St 42nd Fl, Los Angeles, CA 90071.

WILSON, DR. JEFFREY R.
College teacher. **Personal:** Children: Rhonda, Roxanne & Rochelle. **Educ:** Univ West Indies, St Augustine, BA, math & econ, 1977; Iowa State Univ, Ames, IA, MS, statist, 1980, PhD, statist, 1984. **Career:** Iowa State Univ, Ames, IA, Dept Math, teaching asst, 1980?1983, Minority Stud Affairs, consult & dir tutorial serv, 1981-83, teaching asst, Statist Lab, Dept Statist, 1982 " 1983; Okla State Univ, Still water, OK, vis asst prof statist, 1983-84; Ariz State Univ, Tempe, AZ, Dept Decision & Info Syst, from asst to assoc prof statist, 1985-95, dir interdisciplinary prog statist, 1991-96, Sch Health & Admin Policy, assoc prof biostatistics,1994-2006; Ariz Grad Prog Pub Health, assoc prof biostatistics, 1998-99; Dept Econ, assoc prof biostatistics, 1996-; Ariz Col Pub Health, assoc prof biostatistics, 2000-; interim dir, Sch Health Admin & Policy, 2002-03; Sch Health Mgt & Policy, W P Carey Sch Bus, dir, 2003-06; Intercollegiate Athletics Brd, chair, 2004-; Univ Colo, assoc prof biostatistics, Dept Sci Health Admin, 1990-94; Charles Drew Univ Med & Sci, Los Angeles, CA, Dept Surg, adj prof surg, 1992-93, Drew Surg Res Group, Dept Surg, co-dir, 1993-96; Univ Ariz, Dept Family & Community Med, assoc prof, 1994-2000; Grad Interdisciplinary Progs, Grad Interdisciplinary Progs, assoc prof epidemiol, 2001-04, HAP Mel & Enid Zuckerman Col Pub Health, div dir & concentration dir, 2002-03; W. P. Carey Sch Business Dept Economics, assoc prof, biostatistics, currently. **Orgs:** Am Statist Assn, 1980; Royal Statist Soc, 1985; Am Pub Health Assn; Ariz Pub Health Assn; Biometrics Soc; WNAR; Biometrika. **Honors/Awds:** Open Mathematics Scholarship, Univ West Indies, 1974-77, Final Year Book Prize, Math & Econ, 1977; Certificate of Recognition, Stud Affairs, Iowa State Univ, 1981, Certificate of Appreciation, Minority Grad Stud, 1982,Distinguished Outstanding Service Award, Off Stud Affairs, 1983;Outstanding Graduate Faculty Teaching Award, Col Bus, Ariz State Univ,1985-, Outstanding Faculty Development Research Award, 1990-91, Faculty Research Development Award, 1991, MBA Faculty Achievement Award, 1991,Outstanding Professor Award, Chap Golden Key Nat Honor Soc, 1991, Off Stud Affairs, Significant Contributions to the Quality of Life Award, 1993; Outstanding Faculty Research Development Award, DIS, 1986-87; George Washington Carver Achievement Award, Iowa State Alumni Assn, 1995. **Business Addr:** Associate Professor of Biostatistics, Associate Professor of Statistics, Arizona State University, Department of Economics, BAC 600, PO Box 874506, Tempe, AZ 85287-4506, **Business Phone:** (480)965-5628.

WILSON, JERRY LEE, JR.
Football player. **Personal:** Born Jul 17, 1973, Alexandria, LA; children: Trittney, Tanner & Jerry III. **Educ:** Southern Univ, BS, rehab coun, 1994. **Career:** Miami Dolphins, defensive back, 1996-2000; New Orleans Saints, 2001-02; San Diego Chargers, 2002-05.

WILSON, JIMMIE L
State government official. **Career:** Lawyer, pvt pract; farmer; State Ark, rep; Phillips Co Br NAACP, pres, currently.

WILSON, JIMMY L
Law enforcement officer. **Personal:** Born Jan 1, 1946, Durham, NC. **Educ:** Am Univ, BS, admin justice, 1974. **Career:** Wash DC Police Dept, int affairs investr, 1968-86, dep chief, 1987-92; City Jackson, police chief, 1992-94; City Canton, MS, police chief, 1994-97; City Suffolk, Va, chief police, 1997-2001; Va State Univ, Dept Police & Pub Safety, chief police, 2003-. **Orgs:** Pres, NOBLE; Nat Org Black Law Enforcement Exec. **Military Serv:** USA, 1964-68. **Business Addr:** Chief Police Department of Police & Public Safety, Virginia State University, 1 Hayden Dr, Petersburg, VA 23806.

WILSON, JOE. **See WILSON, JOSEPH.**

WILSON, JOHN E.
Executive, accountant. **Personal:** Born Dec 9, 1932, Chicago, IL; son of Leroy and Carrie; married Velma J Brown; children: Ginger, Kelly. **Educ:** Northwestern Univ Sch Com, BS, 1954; CPA 1965. **Career:** Arthur J Wilson Cert Pub Accountants, acct, 1957-63; Ill Com Comn, auditor, 1963; Boweys Inc, gen acct, 1964; Capitol Food Indust Inc, treas, 1969; Bates Packaging Co, controller, 1969; Pub Bldg Comn, Chicago, IL, asst treas, currently; John E Wilson Ltd, pres, currently. **Orgs:** Amer Inst CPA; Ill Soc Cert Pub Accountants; Nat Asn Minority Cert Pub Accountants; Kappa Alpha Psi; Sigma Pi Phi; Trinity United Church Christ. **Honors/Awds:** Alumni National Award, 1996. **Special Achievements:** First African American to graduate from Northwestern Univ School of Commerce. **Military Serv:** USN, 1955-57. **Business Addr:** President, John E Wilson Ltd, 53 W Jackson Blvd Suite 1362, Chicago, IL 60604.

WILSON, JOHN T., JR. **See Obituaries section.**

WILSON, DR. JOHN W.
Administrator, educator. **Personal:** Born Jun 10, 1928, St Marys, GA; son of Albert and Ora; divorced; children: John Jr, Larry & Dwaughn. **Educ:** Albany State Col, BS, elem educ, 1951; Univ Akron, MA, educ admin, 1970, EdD, 1983. **Career:** Albany State Col, employee, 1951; Cleveland Pub Schs, elem teacher, 1957-69; Univ Akron, dir, Black Cult Ctr & Afro-Am Studies. **Orgs:** Nat Asn Advan Colored People, Omega Psi Phi, 1947-; overseas ext teacher, Univ Wis, (English), Korea, 1952; Phi Delta Kappa, 1970-; pres, Nat Black Alliance Grad Educ, 1972-; Higher Educ Comn, Nat Alliance Black Sch Educ, 1984-. **Honors/Awds:** Certificate & plaque, Martha Holden Jennings Scholar, 1966-67; Certificate, Reg Coun Int Educ, 1970-71, Ivory Coast & Lome, West Africa Workshop & Tour Lagos, Dakar, Benin, 1980. **Military Serv:** USAF, educ specialist, 1951-55. **Home Addr:** 11511 Martin Luther King Jr Dr, Cleveland, OH 44105.

WILSON, DR. JOHNNY LEAVERNE
Educator. **Personal:** Born Sep 17, 1954, Wilmington, NC; son of William E Wilson and Mary Wilson; children: Lynnezy Alorida Smith Wilson & Johnny Allen Smith Wilson. **Educ:** Winston Salem State Univ, BA, 1976; Cent Mo State Univ, MA, 1979; Atlanta Univ, Atlanta, GA, PhD, 1988. **Career:** Cent Mo State Univ, Warrensburg, MO, work study asst, 1976-78; Oper PUSH, Kans City, MO, assoc dir int affairs comn, 1978-80; Atlanta Univ, Atlanta, GA, work study asst, 1980-84; Morehouse Sch Med, Atlanta, GA, circulation asst, 1984-88; Atlanta Bd Educ, supply teacher, 1984-88; Clark Atlanta Univ, Atlanta, GA, asst prof, 1988-. **Orgs:** Nat Conf Black Polit Scientist, 1980-; pres, JW Mgt & Assoc, 1988-; bd dirs, Ment Health Asn Metro Atlanta Inc, 1989-90; Atlanta Employer Comn Atlanta Fields Serv Office, 1990-91; dir, internship prog, Clark Atlanta Univ, Dept Polit Sci. **Honors/Awds:** Nominated for the Governor's Awards in the Humanities, 1991; PEW Memorial Trust & Sears Fac Excellence Awards for Outstanding Undergraduate Teaching; Escalation of Tensions in Persian Gulf, Atlanta Voice, Sept 24, 1990; Black Politics in Atlanta: The Defeat of Andy Young, Atlanta Voice, Aug 1990; Going to War in the Gulf, Wilmington Journal, 1990; Book/Manuscript Reviewer for Urban Affairs and Waveland Press, 1990; PEW Mini Grant Clark Atlanta University, Research on black elderly mixing alcohol with prescription drugs to cure their physical ailments. **Home Phone:** (404)763-5072. **Business Addr:** Assistant Professor, Clark Atlanta University, Department Political Science, 240 James P Brawley Dr SW, Atlanta, GA 30311, **Business Phone:** (404)880-8245.

WILSON, JON
Executive. **Personal:** Born Sep 29, 1955, Canton, OH. **Educ:** Ohio Sch Broadcast Technique Cleveland, 1974. **Career:** WKNT Radio Kent OH, asst news dir, 1974; WHBC Radio, combo announcer & engr, 1974-76, prod spec, 1976-77, Black music dir, 1977-84; United Companies Life Ins Baton Rouge, regional dir, 1976-77; WHBC AM & FM, acct exec, res dir & co-op coordr. **Orgs:** Soc Broadcast Engrs, 1975; Black Music Asn, 1979; bd dir, Canton Black United Fund Pub Rels Div, 1979; bd dirs, Stark Co, Nat Asn Advan Colored People, 1980 & 1983; bd mem, Metrop Off Canton; Youth Comt, YMCA, youth coach; dir, Presenters Bur Com Div United Way. **Honors/Awds:** Outstanding, Teenagers Am Inc, 1973; Special Commendation, Stark Co, Nat Asn Advan Colored People, 1979 & 1982; Service Award, E Cent OH Easter Seals, 1979; Outstanding Young Man America Award, US Jaycees, 1980; Special Service Award, Canton Area Big Bros & Big Sisters, 1984-85; Certificate Satisfying Customer Needs, Ford Motor Mkt Inst. **Business Addr:** Account Executive, WHBC AM & FM, 550 Market Ave South, Canton, OH 44701, **Business Phone:** (216)456-7166.

WILSON, JONATHAN CHARLES
Artist, educator. **Personal:** Born Nov 4, 1949, Buffalo, NY; son of Jean Jimison and Jonathan C Wilson Sr; married Nan Withers-Wilson, Jun 24, 1978. **Educ:** Rosary Hill Col BFA, 1971; Univ Cincinnati, MA, 1972; Univ Wis, Madison, ABD, 1976; Northwestern Univ, MA, 1983; Daeman Col, BA. **Career:** Loyola

Univ, Chicago, prof theatre, 1976-; actor: Fraternity, The Death of Bessie Smith, Union Boys, Burning Bright; dir: Fraternity From the Miss Delta, A Raisin in the Sun, Jump for Joy. **Orgs:** Chmn bd, Playwrights' Ctr, Chicago, 1980-; Asn Theatre Higher Educ, 1981-; Ill Theatre Asn, 1985-; Soc Stage Dirs & Choreographers, 1991-. **Honors/Awds:** Best Director, Fraternity, Jeff Nomination-,Chicago, 1990; Chicago Tribune's, Chicagoan in the Arts Award, 1991; Best Director for From the Mississippi Delta, Helen Hayes Asn, 1991; Citation for work in professional theatre, Buffalo Common Coun, 1992; Joseph Jefferson Award for Direction of Two Trains Running, 2006. **Special Achievements:** Directed 3 Educational video's for Loyola University, Chicago, 1990-91; production of Dr Endesha Holland's, From the Mississippi Delta, taped for the New york Public Library Archives, 1991; production of Duke Ellington's, Jump for Joy, received national & international press coverage, 1991. **Home Addr:** 923 Wesley Ave, Evanston, IL 60202. **Business Phone:** (773)508-3838.

WILSON, JOSEPH (JOE WILSON)
Chief executive officer. **Career:** Integrated Packaging Corp, chief exec officer & co founder, chmn emer, currently. **Special Achievements:** Company is ranked 45 on Black Enterprise magazine's list of top 100 industrial and service companies, 1998. **Business Addr:** Chairman Emeritus, Integrated Packaging Corporation, 6400 Harper Ave, Detroit, MI 48211, **Business Phone:** (313)925-1800.

WILSON, DR. JOSEPH F.
Educator. **Personal:** Born Dec 2, 1951, Chicago, IL; son of Charles and Ida; married Maria Vazquez, May 6, 1984; children: Leslie. **Educ:** Columbia Univ, New York, BA, 1973, MA, 1975, MPhil, 1978, PhD, 1980; Harvard Univ, MDP prog, 1998. **Career:** Rutgers Univ, New Brunswick, NJ, asst prof, 1980-86; Brooklyn Col, Brooklyn, New York, assoc prof, 1986-94, Dept Polit Sci, prof, 1994-, Ctr Diversity & Multicultural Educ, dir, currently, Grad Ctr Worker Educ Prog, dept chairperson, dir, currently. **Orgs:** Exec comt, Black Fac & Staff Asn, 1987-95; dir, Brooklyn Col Multicultural Ctr, 1990-95. **Honors/Awds:** Distinguished Tow Professor of Political Science, 1993-95. **Special Achievements:** Author, Tearing Down the Color Bar, Columbia University Press, 1989, The Re-education of the American Working Class, Greenwood Press, 1990, Black Labor in America, Greenwood Press, 1986; International Encyclopedia of Revolution and Protest, assoc ed, 2009. **Home Addr:** 215 W 91st, New York, NY 10024. **Business Addr:** Professor, Brooklyn College, Department of Political Science, 3309 James Hall 2900 Bedford Ave, Brooklyn, NY 11210, **Business Phone:** (718)951-5997.

WILSON, JOSEPH HENRY, JR.
Dentist. **Personal:** Born Jan 29, 1966, Washington, DC; son of Frankie Jones and Joseph Henry Wilson Sr. **Educ:** St Louis Univ, BA, biol, 1987; Univ Ma, Baltimore, Col Dental Surgery, DDS, 1991. **Career:** St Elizabeth's Hosp, dental resident, 1991-92; Hamilton ctr, dentist, 1992-2000; Co Dental Assoc PC, dentist, scy, partner, 1992-2000; River Hill Dental Group, dentist, 2000-; pvt pract, dentist, currently. **Orgs:** Am Dental Asn, 1992-; Pa Dental Asn, 1992-00; Harrisburg Dental Soc, 1992-00; Md State Dental Asn, 2000-. **Home Addr:** 11087 Little Patuxent Pkwy, Columbia, MD 21044, **Home Phone:** (410)730-3323. **Business Addr:** Dentist, 5005 Signal Bell Lane Suite 101, Clarksville, MD 21029, **Business Phone:** (443)535-8940.

WILSON, JOY JOHNSON
Health services administrator, government official. **Personal:** Born Jul 12, 1954, Charleston, SC; daughter of Everett W and Martha L; married Ronald E; children: Devon & Trevon. **Educ:** Keene State Col NH, BS, 1976; Univ NC Chapel Hill, MRP, 1978. **Career:** Nat Conf State Leg, res assoc, 1978-79, staff assoc, 1979-82, sr staf assoc, 1982-83, staff dir, 1983-89, sr comm dir, health, 1990-96, dir, health comt & fed affairs coun, 1996-; Medicaid Commn, non voting mem; US Bipartisan Comn Comprehensive Health Care, prof staff mem, 1989-90. **Orgs:** Treas comn, 1982-83, Adv Neighborhood Comn; treas, Women & Health Round table, 1986-87; Women Govt Rels, 1986-; Am League Lobbyists, 1987-89. **Business Addr:** Director, National Conference of State Legislatures, 444 N Capitol St NW Suite 515, Washington, DC 20001, **Business Phone:** (202)624-5400.

WILSON, KEN
Executive. **Career:** Arista Rec; Columbia Rec, vp, black music prom, 1996; MCA Rec, pres, black music, 1996; J Rec, sr vpres prom, currently. **Orgs:** Bd mem, living legends found. **Business Phone:** (646)840-5600.

WILSON, KIM ADAIR
Lawyer. **Personal:** Born Sep 4, 1956, New York, NY; daughter of Walter (deceased) and Rosa J. **Educ:** Boston Col, BA, cum laude, 1978; Hofstra Univ Sch Law, JD, 1982. **Career:** New York City, Dept Invest, investigative atty, 1986-89; NY State Supreme Ct, ct atty, 1989-. **Orgs:** NY State Bar Asn, house deleg, 1994-96; pres, Metropolitan Black Bar Asn, 1994-96; bd gov, Nat Bar Asn, 1995-99. **Honors/Awds:** Nelson Mandela International Citizen of the Year Award, NY Asn Black Psychologists, 1994; Outstanding Bar Association Affiliate Chapter Award, Nat Bar Asn, 1995; Jane Matilda Bolin Award, Judicial Friends, 1996; Member of the Year, Women Lawyers Div, Nat Bar Asn, 1998. **Special Achievements:** Co-author: "Affirmative Action Can Help Create Tradition of Excellence," New York Law Journal, May 1995; "US Constitution and its Meaning to the Afa Ct," Nat Bar Assn Magazine, Volume 10, No 4, pp 3 & 30; Author of book review, Affirmative Action, Race & Am Values, published my book review, New York Law Journal, Jan 10, 1997. **Business Addr:** Attorney, New York State Supreme Court, Bronx Supreme Court, Rm 217 851 Grand Concourse, Bronx, NY 10451, **Business Phone:** (718)590-3956.

WILSON, LANCE HENRY
Banker, lawyer. **Personal:** Born Jul 5, 1948, New York, NY; son of William H and Ruth Thomas; married Deirdre Jean Jenkins; children: Jennifer Lee. **Educ:** Hunter Col, AB, 1969; Univ Pa Law Sch, JD, 1972. **Career:** Univ Pa Law Sch, legal writing teaching fel, 1971; Mudge Rose Guthrie & Alexander, atty, 1972-77; Equitable Life Assurance Soc US, assoc coun, 1977-81; US Dept Housing & Urban Develop, exec asst secy, 1981-84; New York City Housing Develop Corp, pres, 1984-86; Paine Webber Inc, first vpres, 1986-91; Pvt Bus Ventures & Pract Law, 1991-95; Greystone & Co, 1995-99; Ziegler & Co, sr vpres, co-dir, Housing Finance, 1999-2001; Am Property Financing Inc, sr vpres, 2001-. **Orgs:** NY State Bar Asn; Finance Comt NYS Repuban Party; vpres, NY Co Repuban Comn, 1984-90; pub mem, Admin Conf US, 1984-86; dir, Vis Nurse Serv NY, 1984-90; trustee, St Luke's Roosevelt Hosp Ctr, 1984-90; dir, Nat Housing Conf, 1986-93; Fed Nat Mortgage Asn Adv Coun, 1986-88; dir, Faith Ctr Community Develop, 2000-. **Honors/Awds:** Outstanding Leadership Award, Ill Coun Black Repubicans, 1982; Outstanding Leadership Award, NY State Coun Black Repubicans, 1982; Secretary Award Excellence, US Dept Housing & Urban Develop, 1984; Outstanding Pub Service Award, Nat Asn Home Builders, 1984; Exemplary Leadership Award, Nat Black Repubican Coun, 1984; Housing Man of the Year, Nat & NY Housing Conf, 1985; Humanitarian Award, Southern Brooklyn Comn, Org, 1985; Pvt Sector Initiative Commendation, White House, 1986. **Military Serv:** AUS, capt, 3 months duty 5 yrs reserves. **Home Addr:** 200 Riverside Blvd Suite 23 E, New York, NY 10069. **Business Addr:** Senior Vice President, American Property Financing Inc, 6 E 43rd St Fl 26, New York, NY 10017, **Business Phone:** (212)850-4200.

WILSON, DR. LAVAL S
School administrator. **Personal:** Born Nov 15, 1935, Jackson, TN; married Constance Ann; children: Laval Jr, Holly, Shawn & Nicole. **Educ:** Chicago Teachers Col, BEd, 1958; Univ Chicago, MA, 1962; Northwestern Univ, PhD, 1967. **Career:** Chicago Sch, teacher, counsr, 1958-64; Northwestern Univ Inst, asst dir, 1965 & 1966; Evanston, IL, asst prin, 1966-67, dir, integration inst & follow-up prog, 1967-70; Cent Sch Evanston, IL, prin, 1967-70; Philadelphia & Detroit Sch, supt's intern prog, 1970-71; Hempstead, NY, asst supt curric & instr, 1971-72 & 1973-74, acting supt schs, 1972-73; Berkeley, CA, supt schs, 1974-80; Rochester, NY, supt sch, 1980-85; Boston Pub Schs, Ma, supt sch, 1985-90; E Orange Sch Dist, supt, currently. **Orgs:** Am Asn Sch Admin; Asn Supvsn & Curric Develop; Kappa Alpha Psi Frat; Nat Asn Advan Colored People; Phi Delta Kappa; New York Coun Sch Dist Admin; League Women Voters; Adv Bd Girl Scouts Genesee Valley, 1984-; bd dirs, Rochester Area Found, 1984-; bd dirs, Ctr Govt Res Inc, 1984-; bd dir, Buffalo Br Fed Reserve Bank, NY, 1984-; bd dirs, Jr Achieve, Rochester 1983-; Otetiana Coun Exec Bd Boy Scouts Am, 1981-; bd trustees, Rochester Mus & Sci Ctr, 1981-; Rochester Rotary, 1981-; ed consult, Phi Delta Kappan publn Phi Delta Kappa, 1974-78; consult, NY Univ; Common PA Act 101 Western Reg; Am Asn Sch Admin; Race Deseg Inst Univ Pittsburgh; Nat Inst Educ; Nat Sch Bds Asn; Off Educ; Far West Lab, Los Angeles Conty Sch Dist, San Francisctate Univ; NY Sch Dist, New York City Sch Dist 12, Encyclopedia Brittanica. **Honors/Awds:** Appreciation Plaque, Phi Delta Kappa 1978; Resolution of Appreciation, Berkeley Bd Educ, 1980; Congressional Award, Cong Ronald Dellums; Legislative Resolution of Spec Publ Recognition and Commend, Assemblyman Elihu Harris & Sen Nicholas Petris 1980; Appreciation Plaque, Nat Conf Parent Involvement, 1981; Appreciation Plaque, Dist Adv Council to Chap 1 1982; Recognition Plaque, Berkeley Black principals 1980; Special Service Award, Rochester WEB DuBois Acad 1983; Community Service Award, Rochester Asn Black Communicators, 1983; Appreciation Award, Grad School Educ & Human Dev Univ Rochester 1984; Certification Appreciation, Mason Eureka Lodge No 36, 1984; Top Executive Educator Award, 1984; Certification of Recognition for contributions, Rochester community, United Church Ministry, 1985; Leadership Award, Rochester Chapter, Phi Delta Kappa 1985. **Special Achievements:** First Black superintendent of Boston's public school system. **Business Addr:** Superintendent, East Orange School District, 715 Pk Ave, East Orange, NJ 07017, **Business Phone:** (973)266-5757.

WILSON, LAWRENCE C.
Executive. **Personal:** Born May 16, 1932, Kansas City, KS; son of John R and Alfretta; divorced; children: Stacey Marie. **Educ:** LA Col; Certified Pub Housing Mgr, 1983. **Career:** exec (retired); Gen machinist, 1955-68; Greater KC Coun Religion & Race, proj dir, 1969-71; Human Resources Corp KC, MO, area coordr, 1963-69, dir, 1971-72; Shawnee County Community Asst & Action Inc, Topeka, Kans, exec dir, 1972-80; Nat Ctr Community Action Inc, exec dir, 1980-82; Topeka Housing Authority, dep dir, 1982-95. **Orgs:** Topeka Opt Club; Nat Assn Comn Develop; Lawrence C Wilson Assoc; chmn, KS Comn Civil Rights; advr, KS Sec Social Rehabilitation Series; Topeka-Shawnee Co Metro Planning Comn; League KS Municipalities Human Resources Comn; NAACP; Black Econ Union; KS Assn Comm Action; dir OEO; exec comn & bd dirs, Shawnee County Comn Asst & Action Inc; Shawnee County Coun Advocacy Aging. **Honors/Awds:** Urban Service Award; Alliance of Businessmen Jobs Award; Appreciation Award Black Economic Union. **Military Serv:** USN, 1949-53. *

WILSON, LEON E, JR.
Banker. **Personal:** Born Mar 12, 1945, Maine; son of Ollie H Taylor and Leon E Sr; married Sharon Clements, Jun 1970; children: Erika & Erin. **Educ:** Boston Univ, Boston, Ma, BS, 1975; Williams Col, Williamstown, MA, 1975; Univ Va, Charlottesville, Va, 1978; Harvard Bus Sch, Cambridge, Ma, PMD, 1986. **Career:** Shawmut Bank, Boston, MA, vpres, 1966-83; Bank Boston, Boston, Ma, sr vpres, 1983; Fleet Financial Group, exec vpres, 1992, regional mgr, sr vpres; Capital City Capital Group LLC, ceo, exec vpres & managing dir, currently; GMAC Residential, GMAC Mortgage, corp sr vpres & managing dir; Capital City Ventures, gen partner & investment mgr, currently. **Orgs:** Adv bd, Boston Univ, 1990-; chair, Roxbury Comn Col Found, 1990-; mem, Comn Mass Employee Inv & Ownership Comn, 1990-; pres, Am Inst Banking, 1982-83; commr, Plymouth Redevelopment, 1984; Harvard Univ Task Force, 1985; bd mem, Boston Ballet, 1994; Urban League Eastern Ma; United Negro Col Fund; Bell Found; Dimock Health Care; Fannie Mae's Regional Adv Bd. **Honors/Awds:** Black Achievement Award, YMCA; Professional Achievement Award, Boston Urban Bankers. **Military Serv:** Army Res, E4, 1966-72. **Home Addr:** 47 Old Farm Rd, Milton, MA 02186, **Home Phone:** (617)696-1590. **Business Addr:** Chief Executive Officer, Capital City Capital Group LLC, 1400 L St NW Suite 400, Washington, DC 20005.

WILSON, LEROY, JR.
Lawyer. **Personal:** Born Jun 16, 1939, Savannah, GA; son of Leroy Sr and Mary Louise (Frazier); married Helen Odum (divorced); children: Andrea; married Jane Marie Beaver; children: Jason, Christopher. **Educ:** Univ Vienna, Austria, 1960; Morehouse Col, BS, 1962; Univ Calif, Berkeley, MS, 1965, JD, 1968. **Career:** IBM, atty, 1968-72; Covington Grant Howard, atty, 1972; IBM, atty, 1972-74; Pvt pract, atty, 1974; Union Carbide Corp, atty, 1974-82; Pvt Pract, atty, 1982-. **Orgs:** Hon Woodrow Wilson Fel, 1962; dir, Asn Black Lawyers Westchester County Inc, 1978-, chmn, 1987-; gov mem, exec comn, Nat Bar Asn, 1979-80; Am Bar Asn; vpres, Nat Bar Asn; pub mem, NY State Banking Bd, 1983-87. **Honors/Awds:** Thayer Award, Civil Coun Sickle Cell Anemia Benefit, US Mil Acad; Personal Counsel to His Excellency, Godfrey Lukongwa Binaisa, Fifth Pres Repub Uganda. **Business Addr:** Attorney, Private Practice, 99 Court St Suite 2, White Plains, NY 10601-4264.*

WILSON, MADELAINE MAJETTE
Educator. **Personal:** Born Aug 23, 1920, Suffolk, VA; daughter of Junnie E and Lula O; married John A, Oct 28, 1961 (deceased); children: John H Bellamy, Madelaine B Johnson & James Allen (deceased). **Educ:** Elizabeth City State Univ, BS, 1940; Va State Univ, MS, 1962. **Career:** Camden County Schs, primary teacher, 1941-42; Southampton County Pub Schs, teacher, 1942-46; numerous teaching & educ acad positions, 1946-90; City of Suffolk, Dept of Parks & Recreation, senior citizens coordr, 1990. **Orgs:** Eucharistic minister, choir mem, trustee, St Mark's PE Church, 1975-93; former sr warden, chaplain, former pres, Pinochle Bugs Inc, Suffolk Chap; former basileus, AKA, Zeta Epsilon Omega Chap; charter mem, 1st pres, chaplain, reporter, Chums Club Suffolk, 1937-93; past worthy matron, tre, Nansemond Chap II 31 OES, PHA; bd pres, Tri-County Trust for Retarded Citizens, 1990-93; AARP, volunteer trainer, sre, Widowed Persons Serv, 1992-93; steering com, Golden Olympics, 1993. **Honors/Awds:** Dept Parks & Recreation; Outstanding Senior Citizen of the Year, 1985; Woman of the Year, Am Asn Univ Women; COT Service Plaque, NCP, 1992; Certificate of Service, Va Cooperative Extension Dept, 1993. **Home Addr:** 1115 Custis Rd, Suffolk, VA 23434. **Business Addr:** Senior Citizens Coordinator, Department of Parks and Recreation, City of Suffolk 301 N Main St, Suffolk, VA 23434, **Business Phone:** (804)925-6388.

WILSON, MARGARET BUSH
Lawyer, activist. **Personal:** Born Jan 30, 1919, St Louis, MO; daughter of James T Bush Sr and M Berenice Casey; divorced; children: Robert Edmund III. **Educ:** Talladega Col, BA (cum laude), 1940; Lincoln Univ Sch Law, LLB, 1943. **Career:** Rural Electrification Admin Dept Agr St Louis, legal atty, 1943-45; St Louis, pvt pract, 1947-65; asst atty gen MO, 1961-62; Mo Comm Serv & Continuing Educ, adminr, 1967-68, Legal Sv Cs Spec MO, 1965-67; Acting Dir St Louis, Model City Prog, dep dir, 1968-69; St Louis Lawyers Housing, asst dir, 1969-72; Coun Legal Educ Opportunity Inst St Louis Univ Sch Law, instr civil procedure, 1973; Wilson & Assocs, sr partner. **Orgs:** Fel, Juliette Derricotte, 1939-40; Mo Coun Criminal Justice, 1972-77; Vice chmn, Land Reutilization Aluth St Louis, 1975-77; treas, NAACP Nat Hous-

ing Corp; Arts & Educ Coun, St Louis; Lawyers Asn; ABA; NBA; Mo Bar Asn; Mound City Bar Asn; St Louis Bar Asn; Alpha Kappa Alpha; dir, Monsanto Co; trust, Mutual Life Ins Co NY; chmn nat bd, Nat Asn Advan Colored People, 1975-84; chmn bd trust, St Augustine's Col, 1986-88; chmn bd dir, Intergroup Corp, 1986-87; chmn bd trustees, Talladega Col, 1988-91. **Honors/Awds:** Recipient Bishops Award, Episcopal Diocese, MO, 1963; Honorary Degrees: Boston Univ, Wash Univ, Ala State Univ, St Paul's Col, Kenyon Col, Smith Col, Talladega Col; Pioneer Award, 1995; Dr Martin Luther King Jr State (MO), Celebration Comn Mo, 1995; Distinguished Lawyer Award, Bar Asn St Louis, 1997. **Business Addr:** Principal Attorney, Wilson & Associates, 4054 Lindell Blvd Suite 100, St Louis, MO 63108, **Business Phone:** (314)534-4400.

WILSON, MARGARET F
Librarian. **Personal:** Born Aug 8, 1932, Monroeville, AL; daughter of Leo and Carrie; married Willie C; children: Monica R Shular, Veronica E McCarthy, Danita Y Wooten, Constance K Harris & Willie C II. **Educ:** AL State Col, BS, 1953; Fla A&M Univ, Med, 1969; FL State Univ, MSLS 1972, AMD, 1979. **Career:** Rosenwald High Sch, secy & teacher, 1953-55; FL A&M Univ, librn 1963-. **Orgs:** Fla Libr Asn, 1972-, Spec Libr Asn, 1972-, Heroines Eastern Stars, 1979-; NAACP 1980-; Beta Phi Mu 1980-; Urban League 1980-; Am Libr Asn, 1983-; Am Col & Res Libr, 1983. **Honors/Awds:** Article "Zora Neale Hurston, Author & Folklorist," Negro History Bulletin 1982; "School Media Specialist Undergraduate Library Science Program," Journal Educ Media & Library Science 1986; "Selected Speeches of Florida A&M Univ, pres, 1987," unpublished. **Business Addr:** University Librarian, Florida A&M University, PO Box 164 BB Tech Ctr, Tallahassee, FL 32307, **Business Phone:** (904)599-3050.

WILSON, MARKLY
Administrator, executive director. **Personal:** Born Mar 30, 1947, Bridgetown, Barbados; married Gonul Mehmet; children: 2. **Educ:** St Clair Col, Ontario, Can; Adelphi Univ, NY. **Career:** Barbados Bd Tourism, recept & clerk, 1967-74, pub rel officer, 1974, sales rep, 1974-78, mgr, 1978-79; Skinner Sec Sch, bus Eng teacher, 1967-74; Ministry Civil Aviation, clerical officer, 1967; NY Univ, fac; consult; NY State Tourism, dir int mkt, currently; Int Inst Peace Through Tourism, chmn, mkt & prom, currently. **Orgs:** Photographic Soc Lindfield Sch, 1959-62; pres, Christ Church HS Debating Soc, 1963; sec Christ Church High Sch Old Scholars Assoc, 1967; Toastmasters Intl Bridgetown Chap, 1968; Graybar Toastmasters Club, 1974-; bd dir, CTA, 1981-82; chmn, Assembly Nat Tourist Office Rep NY, 1982-83; NY Skal Club; dir, Travel & Tourism Res Asn; bd adv, Tourism Dept New Sch Social Res. **Honors/Awds:** Awarded Cup for Most Outstanding Athlete of the Year, Lindfield Sch; Victor Ludorum, Athletics Christ Church High Sch; Tourism Dir of the Year, NY Based World Tourism Comt, 1984; Awarded Tourist Dir of the Year, World Travel Award Comt, 1984. **Business Addr:** Chairman of Marketing & Promotion, International Institute for Peace Through Tourism, 685 Cottage Club Rd Suite 13, Stowe, VT 05672, **Business Phone:** (802)253-2658.

WILSON, MARY
Singer. **Personal:** Born Mar 6, 1944, Greenville, MS; daughter of Sam and Johnnie Mae; married Pedro Ferrer, 1974 (divorced 1983); children: Turkessa, Pedro Antonio Jr, Rafael (deceased) & Willie. **Educ:** New York Univ, AA, 2001. **Career:** Mem Supremes, 1959-77; solo vocalist, 1979-; Albums with the Supremes: Meet the Supremes, 1963; A Bit of Liverpool, 1964; Where Did Our Love Go, 1965; Sing Country Western & Pop, 1965; More Hits By the Supremes, 1965; We Remember Sam Cooke, 1965; At the Copa, 1965; Merry Christmas, 1965; I Hear a Symphony, 1966; A Go-Go, 1966; Sing Holland-Dozier-Holland, 1967; Sing Rodgers & Heart, 1967; 70's Greatest Hits & Rare Classics, 1991; Supremes, 2000; Albums with Diana Ross & the Supremes: Greatest Hits Volumes I & II, 1967; Reflections, 1968; Love Child, 1968; Sing & Perform "Funny Girl,", 1968; Live at the Talk of the Town, 1968; Join the Temptations, 1968; TCB, 1968; Let the Sunshine In, 1969; Together, 1969; Cream of the Crop, 1969; On Broadway, 1969; Greatest Hits Vol 3, 1969; Farewell, 1970; Anthology, 1974; Great Songs & Performances, 1985; Motown Legends, 1985; Sing Motown, 1986; Solo: Mary Wilson, 1979; guest appearances: Love Lessons, 1992; Hold up the Light, 1987; Best of Diana Ross & the Supremes, Diana Ross & the Supremes, 1995; Soul Talkin', 1993; Billboard Top Dance Hits: 1976, 1976; River of Song: A Musical Journey, 1998. **Honors/Awds:** NAACP Image Award, Best Female Vocal Group, with the Supremes, 1972; Rock & Roll Hall of Fame, inducted with the Supremes, 1988; Hollywood Walk of Fame, inducted with the Supremes, 1994; Vocal Group Hall of Fame, inducted with the Supremes, 1998; Lifetime Achievement Award, Nat Found Woman. **Special Achievements:** Author: Dream Girl: My Life as a Supreme, St Martin's Press, 1986; Supreme Faith: Someday We'll Be Together, Harper Collins, 1990; Dreamgirl & Supreme Faith: My Life As A Supreme, Cooper Square Press, 2000. **Business Addr:** Singer, Mary Wilson Enterprises Inc, 2654 W Horizon Ridge Pkwy B-5 Suite 138, Henderson, NV 89052, **Business Phone:** (702)898-6721.

WILSON, MICHAEL
Basketball player. **Personal:** Born Jul 22, 1972. **Educ:** Univ Memphis, Tenn. **Career:** Basketball Player (Retired); Washington Bullet Rosters, 1983-84; Clevland Cavaliers, 1984-85; New Jersey Nets, 1984-87; Atlanta Hawks, 1986-87; Harlem Globetrotters, forward, 1996-01, univ memphais; World Record Basketball, CEO, currently. **Orgs:** Director, Headfirst Basketball, Founder & CEO, World Record Basketball. **Special Achievements:** Established a new Guiness Book of World Record for a slam dunk, 1996. *

WILSON, MITSY
Executive. **Personal:** Born in Georgetown, Guyana; children: Meisha & Alia. **Career:** WPIX-TV, NY, commercial coordr; NY Bd Educ, Coun & Spec Proj, dir; Times-Mirror Co, Leadership & Orgn Develop, vpres; Fox Entertainment Group, sr vp, diversity develop, currently. **Orgs:** Bd mem, Workplace Hollywood; bd mem, Univ Calif Los Angeles Med Ctr; NAACP; Nat Latino Media Coun; Asian Pac Am Coalition; Am Indians in Film & TV; bd mem, Kids in Sports, Los Angeles; Nat Asn Minority Media Exec. **Honors/Awds:** Phoenix Award, Minorities in Broadcasting Training Prog; Governors Award, NY Bd Educ; The President's Award, 16th Ann NAACP Theatre Awards, 2006. **Business Addr:** Senior Vice President, Diversity Development, FOX Entertainment Group, 1211 Ave of the Americas, New York, NY 10036-8799, **Business Phone:** (212)852-7111.

WILSON, MOOKIE
Sports manager, baseball player. **Personal:** Born Feb 9, 1956, Bamberg, SC; married Rosa; children: 3. **Educ:** Mercy Col, NY, attended 1996. **Career:** Baseball player (retired), sports manager; Jackson Generals, 1978; New York Mets, outfielder, 1980-89, coach, 1997-2002; Toronto Blue Jays, outfielder, 1989-91; Rookie League Kingsport Mets team, mgr; Brooklyn Cyclones, mgr, 2005. **Honors/Awds:** World Series Champion, 1986.

WILSON, NANCY
Singer, actor. **Personal:** Born Feb 20, 1937, Chillicothe, OH; daughter of Olden and Lillian (Ryan); married Rev Wiley Burton; children: Samanthia & Sheryl; married Kenneth C Dennis (divorced 1970); children: Kenneth. **Educ:** Cent State Col, teacher training prog, 1955. **Career:** Singer & actress; Rusty Bryant Band, singer, 1956; Midwest & Canada, singing tour, 1958; Capitol Rec, rec artist; EMI Rec, rec artist; Nippon Columbia Japan, rec artist; Interface Japan, rec artist; Epic Sony/CBS, rec artist; TV series: "Burke's Law", 1965; "I Spy", 1966; "Room 222", 1970; "Hawaii Five-O", 1970; "O'Hara, U.S. Treasury", 1972; "The Tonight Show Starring Johnny Carson", 1973; "Search", 1973; "The F.B. I.", 1973; "Police Story", 1974; "The Cosby Show", 1989; "The Sinbad Show", 1993;"The Parent 'Hood", 1995-97; "The Parkers", 2001; Films: The Killers,1964; The Big Score, 1983; The Meteor Man, 1993; Albums: Like in Love, 1960; Something Wonderful, 1960; The Swingin's Mutual, 1961; Nancy Wilson/ Cannonball Adderley, 1962; Hello Young Lovers, 1962; Broadway—My Way, 1963; Hollywood—My Way, 1963; Yesterday's Love Songs, 1963; Today, Tomorrow, Forever, 1964; How Glad I Am, 1964; The Nancy Wilson Show at the Coconut Grove, 1965; Nancy Wilson Today—My Way, 1965; Gentle Is My Love, 1965; From Broadway With Love, 1966; A Touch of Love Today, 1966; Tender Loving Care, 1966; Nancy—Naturally, 1966; Just for Now, 1967; Lush Life, 1967; Welcome to My Love, 1968; Easy, 1968; The Best of Nancy Wilson, 1968; Sound of Nancy Wilson, 1968; Nancy, 1969; Son of a Preacher Man, 1969; Close Up, 1969; Hurt So Bad, 1969; Can't Take My Eyes Off You, 1970; Now I'm a Woman, 1970; Double Play, 1971; Right to Love, 1971; I Know I Love Him, 1973; All in Love Is Fair, 1974; Come Get to This, 1975; This Mother's Daughter, 1976; I've Never Been to Me, 1977; Music on My Mind, 1978; Life, Love & Harmony, 1979; Take My Love, 1980; At My Best, 1981; Echoes of an Era, 1982; What's New, 1982; I'll Be a Song, 1984; (with R Lewis) The Two of Us, 1986; Keep You Satisfied, 1986; Forbidden Lover, 1987; Nancy Now!, 1990; With My Lover Beside Me, 1991; The Best of Nancy Wilson, 1992; (with G Washington) Next Exit, 1992; Color & Light, 1994; (with Boston Pops Orchestra) It Don't Mean a Thing, 1994; Joyful Christmas, 1994; Love, Nancy, 1994; (with Q Jones & others) Jook Joint, 1995; Spotlight on Nancy Wilson, 1995; Ballads, Blues & Big Bands, 1996; If I Had My Way, 1997; A Nancy Wilson Christmas, 2001; (with R Lewis-)Meant To Be, 2002; (with R Lewis) Simple Pleasures, 2003; R.S. V.P., 2004;Live From Las Vegas, 2005; Turned To Blue, 2006; Music for Lovers, 2007. **Orgs:** Presidential Coun Minority Bus Enterprises; Nat Asn Advan Colored People; Southern Christian Leadership Conf; chairperson, Oper PUSH; United Negro College Fund; Comt Kennedy Ctr Performing Arts. **Honors/Awds:** Numerous honors& awards including Paul Robeson Award, Urban League; Ruby Ring Award, Johnson & Johnson Co; 2 Emmy Awards; Black Book Award; Best Female Vocalist Award, Playboy, Downbeat Jazz Polls; Grammy for Best Rhythm & Blues Recording, 1964; Emmy for The Nancy Wilson Show; named Jazz Master, Nat Endowement Arts, 2004; UNCF Trumpet Award, 2005; Lifetime Achievement Award, NAACP; Oprah Winfrey's Legends Awaand rd; Grammy Award,2006. Best Jazz Vocal Album, 2007. **Business Phone:** (626)398-8179.*

WILSON, NATALIE
Music arranger or orchestrator, composer, singer. **Personal:** Born Jan 1, 1972?, Newark, NJ; daughter of Nathaniel Simmons and Johnnie Mae Simmons; married Joseph, 1993. **Career:** Sounds Of Praise Chorale, dir, 1992-; Flim: Kingdom Come, 2001; albums: Not the Same, 1996; Girl Director, 2000; The Good Life, 2004. **Home Addr:** 689 Sanford Ave, Newark, NJ 07106. **Business Addr:** Director, Sound of Praise Chorale, 662 S 18th St, Newark, NJ 07103.*

WILSON, NATARSHA JULIET
Salesperson. **Personal:** Born Oct 22, 1961, Atlanta, GA. **Educ:** Berry Col, BS, 1982. **Career:** Continental Distribr, sales consult; Soft Sheen Prod Inc, territorial sales merchandiser; Redken Labs Inc, dist sales mgr. **Home Addr:** 2795 Dodson Lee Dr, East Point, GA 30344. **Business Addr:** District Sales Manager, Redken Labs, 6625 Variel Ave, Canoga Park, CA 91303, **Business Phone:** (213)349-6563.

WILSON, NORMA JUNE. See DAVIS, NORMA JUNE.

WILSON, DR. OLLY W.
Educator, composer. **Personal:** Born Sep 7, 1937, St Louis, MO; son of Olly W Wilson Sr and Alma Grace Peoples; married Elouise Dolores Woods, Jun 27, 1959; children: Dawn Lynn & Kent Alan. **Educ:** Wash Univ, BM, 1959; Univ Ill, MM, hon 1960; Univ Iowa, PhD, 1964. **Career:** Musician with local jazz groups St Louis; played bass violin with St Louis Philharmonic Orchestra; St Louis Summer Chambers Players & Cedar Rapids Symphony Orch; Fla Agri & Mech Univ, educr; Oberlin Conservatory Music Univ Calif, educr; author compositions including chamber works, orchestral works & works electronic media; conducted num concerts contemporary music; orchestral compositions performed by major orchestras include Boston, Cleveland, San Francisco, St Louis, Houston, Oakland, Detroit Symphony Orchestras; Univ Calif Berkeley, pr music, asst chancellor, int affairs,prof & chair music, prof emer, currently. **Orgs:** Consult, Nat Endowment Arts, Nat Endowment Humanities; bd dir, Meet the Composer; Univ Calif, Berkeley, Young Musicians Prog; bd overseers, visiting comt Harvard Dept Music; ASCAP; NAACP; Nat Urban League; Alpha Phi Alpha; Sigma Pi Phi; World Affairs Coun; Inst Int Educ. **Honors/Awds:** Dartmouth Arts Council Prize, 1968; Boston Symphony, Orchestra & Fromm Found 1970; Guggenheim Fel, 1972-77; Oakland Symphony Orchestra, 1973; Award Outstanding Achievement in Music, Composition Am Acad Arts & Letters & Nat Inst Arts & Letters 1974; Nat Asn of negro Musicians Awd, 1974; Vstg Artist Am Acad, Rome, 1978; Nat Endowment Arts Comns Composition, 1976; Koussevitsky Found Comn, 1984; Houston Symphony Fanfare Comn, 1986. **Business Addr:** Professor Emeritus, Univsity of California, Berkeley, Department of Music, 104 Morrison Hall Suite 1200, Berkeley, CA 94720-1200, **Business Phone:** (510)642-2678.

WILSON, ORA BROWN
School administrator. **Personal:** Born in Austin, TX; children: Evelyn J Jones. **Educ:** Huston-Tillotson Col, BA, 1960; Prairie View Agri & Mech Univ, MEd, 1979; St Edwards Univ; Univ Tex, Austin. **Career:** Pub Sch, teacher, 1964-67; Austin Community Col, part-time instr, 1977-79; Huston-Tillotson Univ, teacher & admin asst, 1967-79, Title III coorr 1979-. **Orgs:** Austin-Travis Co MH-MR Adv Comt, 1981-86; Licensed Prof Counr, State Tex, 1983; vol, Austin Hospice 1983-; bd dir, Family EldeCare Inc, 1986; Alpha Kappa Alpha Sor. **Honors/Awds:** Special Serv Award, Huston-Tillotson Col, 1981. **Home Addr:** 1801 Loreto Dr, Austin, TX 78721. **Business Addr:** Title III Coordinator, Huston-Tillotson University, 900 Chicon St, Austin, TX 78702-2795, **Business Phone:** (512)505-3085.

WILSON, PATRICIA A.
Educator. **Personal:** Born Feb 1, 1948, Conway, SC. **Educ:** Univ Mich, BA, MA, Phd. **Career:** Univ MI, asst dir undergrad admis. **Orgs:** Black Faculty & Staff, Univ MI. **Business Addr:** 1220 SAB Univ of MI, Ann Arbor, MI 48104.

WILSON, DR. PATRICIA I (PATRICIA ISLES WILSON)
Educator. **Personal:** Born Jun 7, 1940, Belmont, NC; daughter of Hiawatha and Blondine Henderson; married Robert Erwin, Jun 17, 1961; children: Geoffrey Keith & Gary Stephen. **Educ:** NC A&T State Univ, Greensboro, NC, BS, bus educ, 1961; Univ Kent, Lexington, KY, MA, 1979, EdD, voc educ, 1984. **Career:** Educator (retired); Morris Township Jr High, Morristown, NJ, teacher, 1963-65; Roxbury High, Succasunna, NJ, teacher, 1965-67; Morris Hills Regional High, Rockaway, NJ, teacher, 1968-71; Cent High, Joliet, IL, teacher, 1972-73; Davenport West High Sch, Davenport, IA, teacher, 1974-77; Univ Ky, Lexington, KY, instr, 1979-81; Eastern Ky Univ, Richmond, KY, asst prof, 1981-85; Univ Ky, Col Educ, Lexington, KY, asst prof, 1985-92; Ala A&M Univ, Sch Bus, assoc prof. **Orgs:** Treas, Cent Ky Bus Edn Asn, 1986-87; awards chmn, Ky Bus Educ Asn, 1987; pres, Asn Records Mgrs Adminrs, 1987-88; pres, Delta Pi Epsilon, 1988-90, treas, Gamma Nu Chap, 1997-99, nat secy, 2002-03; secy/treas, Phi Delta Kappa, 1990-91, vpres, 1991-92; secy, Ala Bus Ed Asn, 1994-, pres elect, 1996-97; pres, Ala Bus Educr Asn, 1998-00; ed, Southern Bus Educ Asn, Newsletter, 1999-2000, pub rels comn, 1988-89; Nat Bus Educ Asn. **Honors/Awds:** President's Award, ARMA, 1986-87; Outstanding Researcher Award, Ala A & M Univ, Sch Bus, 1994; ABEA Bus Educators of the year, 2000. **Home Addr:** 105 McNaron Dr, Madison, WI 35758-8182.

WILSON, PATRICIA ISLES. See WILSON, DR. PATRICIA I.

WILSON, PRESTON JAMES
Baseball player. **Personal:** Born Jul 19, 1974, Bamberg, SC; son of Mookie Wilson; children: Taya. **Career:** NY Mets, 1998; Fla Marlins, 1998-02; Colo Rockies, 2003-05; Houston Astros, 2006; St Louis Cardinals, 2006-07; Long Island Ducks, 2009. **Orgs:** African Am Coun of Christian Clergy; Adopt-A-Classroom; Make-A-Wish Found; founder, Preston's Pride & Preston's Oper. **Honors/Awds:** Marlins 2001 All-Heart Award; Nat League RBI Leader Award, 2003; Rockies Good Guy Award, BBWAA, 2003. **Special Achievements:** Co-hosted the Fox Sports Net's "The Best Damn Sports Show Period". *

WILSON, RAPHAEL BERNARD. See WILSON, BERNARD.

WILSON, DR. RAY FLOYD
Educator. **Personal:** Born Feb 20, 1926, Giddings, TX; son of Fred; married Faye; children: Ray jr, Freddie, Roy & Mercedes. **Educ:** Huston Tillotson, BS, 1950; TX S Univ, MS, 1951; Univ Tex, PhD, 1953; TexaS Univ, JD, Law, 1973. **Career:** Educator (Retired); Univ Tex, Austin, res scientist, 1951-53; Tex S Univ, prof chem, 1972, grad & res adv; Houston Comm Col, part time instr chem, 1972. **Orgs:** Dir SE Tex, Sect Am Chem Soc, 1967-68, 1969-70; counr, SE TX Section Am Soc, 1968-69; vpres, SW Regional Meeting Am Chem Soc, 1955; Phi Alpha Delta Law Frat; Phi Beta Sigma Frat; Legislative Couns US Congresswoman; Supt Pilgram Congregational Ch; Comm Consult & Adv; pres, TSU-TACT Chapter; pres, PUC Credit Union. **Honors/Awds:** Acad Achievement Award, Huston-Tillotson Col, 1953; Beta Kappa Chi Achievement Awards, TSU, 1965; Faculty Forum Achievement Award, 1969; Faculty Forum Post Doctoral Cert Achievement TSU, 1970; Huston-Tillotson Alumni Asn Sci Achievement, 1971; Human Resource US, 1974. **Special Achievements:** Wilson was the first African American student to receive a Ph.D from the University of Texas at Austin in 1953. **Military Serv:** USN, petty officer, 1944-46. **Home Addr:** 3506 Arbor Ave, Houston, TX 77021.

WILSON, REINARD
Football player. **Personal:** Born Dec 17, 1973, Reinard, FL. **Educ:** Fla State Univ. **Career:** Football player (retired), coach; Cincinnati Bengals, linebacker, 1997-2002; Tampa Bay Buccaneers, 2003; Scouts Inc., currently.

WILSON, RITA P
Executive. **Personal:** Born Oct 4, 1946, Philadelphia, PA; daughter of Leroy Parker and Julia Phoenix Parker; married Harold, May 9, 1970; children: Marc Wilson. **Educ:** St Paul Col, Lawrenceville, VA, BS, educ, 1968; Temple Univ, Philadelphia, PA. **Career:** Children's Serv Inc, Philadelphia, PA, social worker, 1968-70; Dept Defense, Misawa, Japan, elem sch teacher, 1971-73; Allstate Ins Co, Northbrook, IL, sr vpres, 1974-94, sr vpres corp relations, 1996-98; Ameritech, Chicago, sr vpres of corp commun, 1994-96; Allstate Indemnity Co, pres, 1999-2000; Darden Restaurants, bd dir, currently. **Orgs:** Bd exec advs, Col Bus, Northern Ill Univ, 1988-; bd dirs, LeaderShape Inc, 1990-; pub rels comt, Nat Asn Independent Insurers, 1990-; trustee, Found Am Commun, 1990-; trustee, Nat Ctr Neighborhood Enterprise, 1991-. **Honors/Awds:** Twin Award, National YWCA, 1984; Top 100 Black Business & Professional Women, Dollars & Sense Mag, 1985; Dr Martin Luther King Jr Legacy Award, Boys & Girls Clubs, 1990. **Business Phone:** (407)245-4000.

WILSON, ROBERT
Football player. **Personal:** Born May 23, 1974, Tallahassee, FL. **Educ:** Fla A&M Univ. **Career:** Seattle Seahawks, wide receiver, 1998-99; New Orleans Saints, 2000-01.

WILSON, ROBERT H
Labor activist. **Personal:** Born in Columbia, SC; son of Alex and Marian M; married Elizabeth. **Educ:** Benedict Col, attended. **Career:** Butchers Union Greater New York & New Jersey Local 174, pres, currently. **Orgs:** Adv bd, Voc Ed New York City, 1969; exec bd, Coalition Black Trade Unionist, 1972; chmn, Politics, Civil Politics & Civil Rights Comm Tst, Calvary Baptist Church; life mem, Nat Asn Advan Colored People; exec counc, A Philip Randolph Leaders Tomorrow Scholar Fund Inc; adv counc, Benedict Col Alumni Asn Inc, New Jersey Chap; ex bd, New York State Coalition Black Trade Unionist; bd educ, New York City Youth Employ & Training Prog; bd trustees, Myopia Int Res Found Inc; chmn, bd trustees, UFCW Local 174 Health & Pension Funds; chmn, bd trustees, Commercial Health & Pension Funds; chmn, bd Trustees, Local 174 Retail Health & Pension Funds; bd trustees, Benedict Col. **Honors/Awds:** Deborah Hospital Founder's Award, 1978; Easter Seal Society Award, 1981; State Israel Bonds Award, 1984; ACRMD Humanitarian Award, 1985; United Way Award, 1990; Consumer Assembly Award, 1990; Proclamation, City New York, 1990; Comnr Plainfield Housing Authority, New Jersey; Proclamation, City Newark. **Business Addr:** President, UFCW Local 174, 540 W 48th St, New York, NY 10036, **Business Phone:** (212)307-7007.

WILSON, RONALD M
Association executive. **Personal:** Born Feb 19, 1949, Norfolk, VA; son of Guy and Wilhelmena Luster; married Katherine Stewart, Aug 30, 1986. **Educ:** Evergreen State Col, Olympia WA, BA, 1984; Baruch Col City Univ NY, MPA, 1985. **Career:** Metro Devel Coun, Tacoma WA, prog mgr, 1975-81; House Reps, Olympia, WA, legis asst, 1981-84; Nat League Cities, Wash, DC, spec asst exec dir, 1984-85; Commonwealth Pa, Harrisburg, PA, exec policy specialist, 1985; United Way Pa, dir pub policy, 1992, vpres pub policy, 1997. **Orgs:** Local pres, Omega Psi Phi Fraternity, 1969-; Nat Forum Black Pub Adminrs, 1984-; Int City Mgt Asn, 1985-88; Am Soc Pub Admn, 1986-88; vpres pub policy, Am Soc Asn Execs. **Honors/Awds:** Future Leader Award, NW Conf Black Public Off, 1982; masters fel, Nat Urban fel, 1984. **Special Achievements:** Author of poetry collection Reflections of Spring, 1987; author of monthly column "Status Quotes," 1989. **Military Serv:** AUS, E-6, 1970-75; highest ranking leadership graduate. **Business Addr:** Vice President Public Policy, United Way of Pennsylvania, 17 S Market Sq, Harrisburg, PA 17101, **Business Phone:** (717)238-7365.*

WILSON, RONALD RAY
Lawyer, president (organization). **Personal:** Born Sep 24, 1953, Galveston, TX; son of Carrie and Henry; married Treina; children: Erik & Colby. **Educ:** Univ Tex Plan II Prog, BS, 1977; Univ TX Law Sch, JD, 1988. **Career:** Comm on State Pension Sys, vice chmn; Sub comm on Energy Resources, chmn; Calendars Energy Resources & Finance Inst, com, 1976; House Rep 65th Session, state rep, 1976-77, 66th session, 1978-80, 67th session, 1980-81; Liquor Regulation 70th, 71st, 72nd Sessions, chmn; Fisher Gallagher & Lewis; Ron Wilson & Assocs, pres, currently. **Orgs:** Harris Co Coun Organ, 1976-80; liaison com, Comning Battleship USS TX, 1976; chmn, Select Comm Jr Col Funding, 1980. **Honors/Awds:** The Prairie View A&M Univ Centennial Distinguished Pub Service Award, Prairie View Bus Indus Cluster Group, 1978; Cert Appreciation Jerusalem Youth & Young Adults, 1978; 50 Future Leaders Am, Ebony Mag. **Business Addr:** President, Ron Wilson & Associates, 6371 Richmond Ave Suite 210, Houston, TX 77057.

WILSON, RUDOLPH GEORGE
Educator. **Personal:** Born Jun 17, 1935, River Rouge, MI; married Sandra Lavernn; children: Trent Duron, James Aaron, Dana Nicole & Amy Lynette. **Educ:** Los Angeles State Col, BA, 1962, MA, 1964; Wash Univ, PhD. **Career:** Juv Hall Col, counr, 1961-63; Claremont High Sch, eng dept chmn, 1964-69, master teacher eng, 1967-69; Second Educ, lectr, 1969-72; Southern Ill Univ, Dept Curriculum & Instruction, assoc prof, 1975-, Cult & Soc Diversity, asst provost, currently, vice chancellor acad affairs. **Orgs:** Pres, Nat Asn African Educ, 1970-71; pres, mem, Edwardsville Dist 7 Bd Educ, 1972-; pres fac Sen, Southern Ill Univ, 1975-76; Kappa Alpha Psi; founder & pres, Southern Ill Adoptive Parents Asn; bd mem, Sr Citizens Inc; bd mem, SW Ill Area Agency Aging; elected mem, Pres Search Com; SIUE; vpres, Business Affairs Search Com; coordr, Johnette Haley Scholarship Acad; pres, Piasa Healthcare; Paul Harris Fel, Rotary Int. **Honors/Awds:** Teaching Excellence Award, Southern Ill Univ, 1971; Art pub Harcourt-Brace, 1971; Great Teacher Award, 1974; Danforth Leadership Award, Danforth Fel; Kimmel Leadership Award; Martin Luther King Award; St Louis American Outstanding Educator Award; The Hudlin Award for Humanistic Teaching; named the Educator of the Year by the St. Louis American. **Special Achievements:** In Illinois, he was the first elected African American to serve on the Edwardsville School Board. **Military Serv:** USNAF, ASA spec four, 1957-60. **Business Addr:** Associate Professor, Assistant Provost, Southern Illinois University Edwardsville, PO Box 1122, Edwardsville, IL 62026, **Business Phone:** (618)650-2000.

WILSON, SANDRA E.
Educator, college teacher. **Personal:** Born Jun 13, 1944, Abington, PA; daughter of James O Walton and Frances Walton; married John H Wilson Jr; children: John III & Shawn. **Educ:** Cheyney Univ, BS, Educ, 1966; Montclair St Col, MS, Soc Sci, 1971; Beaver Col, MA Humanities w/a concentration Fine Arts, 1984; Temple Univ, PhD cand, educ, 1993-. **Career:** Abington Sch Dist, teacher, 1966-67, 1969-80; Endicott Sch Dist, teacher, 1967-68; mentally gifted prog, teacher, 1981-86; Abinton Sch Dist, teacher, 1986-99; Montgomery County Community Col, adj prof; Temple Univ, adj instr, currently. **Orgs:** Cheyney Alumni; NAACP; Abington Educ Asn; Nat Conf Artists; Alpha Kappa Alpha; Black Women's Educ Alliance, 1980-86; Prog dir, Comn Opportunity Coun, 1982-84; region rep, PSEA Minority Affairs Comn, 1984; pres, Montgomery County Chap; PA Asn Gifted Children; St rep, PSEA; NEA Nat Rep Assembly, 1986; secy, Am Asn Univ Women, 1986; vpres, Nat Chap, Coordr, youth Coun, NAACP, Willow Grove Branch; teacher testing comm PSEA Educ Testing Serv, 1987; pres-elect, Nat Chap, Black Women's Educ Alliance, 1988-; youth choir organist, Bethlehem Baptist Church; pres, Black Women's Educ Alliance National, 1991; NAACP Youth Director Eastern PA; NAACP, exec bd, WG Chap; dir, Sandra Wilson Dramatic Ensemble, 1995; charter mem, Phi Beta Omega Chapter, 1998. **Honors/Awds:** Phi Delta Scholar, 1962; Richard Humphrey's Scholar, 1962-66; Student Teacher of the Year, Cheyney Univ, 1966; Art Award, Jenkintown Festival Arts, 1980; vol serv, NAACP Youth Job Conf, 1983; Outstanding Service Dedication Award, Citizen Progress, 1983; Distinctive Service Award, BlackWomen's Educ Alliance, 1985; Black Women's Educ Alliance Leadership, 1986; NAACP Serv to Youth Award, 1988, 1999; Optimist of American Youth Service Award, 1989; poem published Poetic Voices Am, 1990; Nominated for Pennsylvania Teacher of the Year, 1995; BWEA Pres Award, 1993, BWEA, Mong Chapter, Newsletter Ed, 1993-; Temple Univ, Cooperating Teacher of the Year, 1999. **Special Achievements:** Play: We Are, Int Journal of Black Drama, 1995; ed, Antioch Baptist, News From the Pews; teacher, contrib, editor, Silver Burdett Science curric, second grade, 1992. **Home Addr:** 3106 Ori Place, Dresher, PA 19025. **Business Addr:** Professor, Montgomery County Community College, 340 Dekalbo Pike, Blue Bell, PA 19422.

WILSON, SHANICE
Singer. **Personal:** Born May 14, 1973, Pittsburgh, PA; daughter of Crystal; married Flex Alexander, Feb 1, 2000; children: Imani Shekinah & Elijah. **Career:** Albums: Discovery, 1987; Inner Child, 1991; 21 Ways To Grow, 1994; Shanice, 1999; Ultimate Collection, 1999; Every Woman Dreams, 2006; Grand' 88; The Collection, 2009. **Honors/Awds:** Winner, vocal category, Star Search, 1985; Golden Lion Award, BestInternational Artist, Ger, 1993; Special Jahruba Atkinson Award for Music,2005. *

WILSON, SHAWN-TA
Government official. **Personal:** Born Mar 31, 1967, Bridgeport, CT; daughter of Robert and Valerie Sterns; married Warren Wilson, Nov 20, 1993; children: Jordan Janae. **Educ:** Radford Univ, attended 1988; Northern Va Community Col, attended 1991; Millsborough Community Col, attended 1996. **Career:** Graphic Arts Show Co, show coordr, 1989-93; Tampa Conv Ctr, event coordr, 1994, sr conv serv mgr, asst dir convention serv, currently. **Special Achievements:** Published two articles in Tampa Bay Family Magazine, 1998. **Business Addr:** Assistant Director of Convention Services, Tampa Convention Center, 333 S Franklin St, Tampa, FL 33602, **Business Phone:** (813)274-7767.

WILSON, SHERMAN ARTHUR
School administrator. **Personal:** Born Nov 2, 1931, Crowley, LA; married; married Cozette Givens; children: Sherman Jr & Sherod Andrew. **Educ:** Leland Col, BS, 1952; Tuskegee Inst, MSEd, 1964; Univ Southwestern La, Masters, 1966. **Career:** Vet Night Sch, teacher, 1955-57; Carver High Sch, teacher, 1956-65; Ross High Sch, prin, 1965-70; Acadia Parish Sch Bd, supr sec educ, 1970-84, admin of fed prog, 1984-, Supvr Fed Prog, currently. **Orgs:** Pres, St Martin Parish Educ Asn, 1960-61; LIALO Dist III, 1969-70; La Asn Supvr & Consult, 1976-79; Acadia Admin Asn, 1980-81; chmn, Acadia Parish Comput Steering Comn, 1983-; treas, PA Fed Credit Union, 1970-; alderman City Crowley Ward Third Div B, 1982. **Honors/Awds:** Thirty two Degree Mason CF Ladd Lodge 48, 1982; 'Honorable Farmer of Year', Crowley High Future Farmers, 1974. **Military Serv:** AUS, pvt first class, 1952-54. **Home Addr:** 515 Ross Ave, Crowley, LA 70526. **Business Addr:** Supervisor of Federal Programs, Acadia Parish School Board, 2402 N Parkerson Ave, PO Box 309, Crowley, LA 70527, **Business Phone:** (337)783-3664 Ext 254.

WILSON, SIDNEY
Automotive executive, president (organization), chief executive officer. **Career:** Wilson Buick-Pontiac-GMC Truck Inc, pres & chief exec officer, currently. **Business Addr:** Chief Executive Officer, President, Wilson Buick-Pontiac-GMC Inc, 1639 US Hwy 45 Byp, Jackson, TN 38305-4413, **Business Phone:** (901)422-3426.*

WILSON, DR. SODONIA MAE
Educator. **Personal:** Born in Galveston, TX; daughter of Rev Jasper Moore and Willie Mae Reed Moore; married James, Mar 24, 1957; children: Demetrius D. **Educ:** French Hosp Sch Nursing, RN, 1957; San Francisco City Col, AS, 1961; San Francisco State Univ, BA, 1963, MA, 1965; Calif Sch Prof Psychology, PhD, 1973. **Career:** French Hosp SF CA, RN, 1956-57; Ft Miley Va Hosp SF CA, RN, 1957-60; SF Youth Guidance Ctr, counr, 1966, probation off, 1967; Off Econ Opportunities, head start analyst, 1968; SF Redevelop Agency, soc serv rep, 1969; Sequoia Union High Sch Dist, counseling coordr, 1969-72; Contra Costa Col, San Pablo, CA, counr, 1972-73, dir spec prog, 1973-83, dir spec prog & serv finance aid officer 1983-85, mgr instr & tech support serv, 1985-86, dir spec progs & serv, 1986-. **Orgs:** Pres, Calif Comn Col Admin, 1977-78; SF Bus & Prof Women's Club, 1978-; Black Women Polit Action, 1979-; Women Higher Educ Assoc, 1980-84; Nat Women's Polit Caucus 1981-86; vpres, SF Bd Educ, 1982-84, pres, 1986-88; Comnr, Calif Student Aid Comn, 1982-85; Bay Area Black Women United, 1982-84; student aid comn, 1982-85; pres, Contra Costa Community Col Dist Mgt Coun Exec Bd, 1992; Nat Asn Advan Colored People. **Honors/Awds:** Merit of Honor, Ernest Kay Hon Gen Ed Int Biography, 1973-; Certificate Distinguished Serv, San Francisco Unified Sch Dist Bd Edu, 1982-90; Certificate Outstanding Serv Rendered, San Francisco Alliance Black School Educrs, 1982-90; Cert Outstanding Serv, San Francisco African Am Hist & Cult Soc Inc, 1982-90; Cert Merit Form, Calif Community Col EOPS Assoc, 1985; Certificate of Appreciation, 1985; Cert Award, Marina Middle Sch, 1985; Certificate of Appreciation, Support Math Eng & Sci Achievement, 1986; Educational Acad Achievement Award, 1987; Cert Commendation, Nat Asn Negro Bus & Prof Women's Clubs Inc,

1987; Cert Award, 1989; Woman of the Year Award, 1989; Education Award, 1989. **Business Addr:** Director of Special Programs & Services, Contra Costa Colllege, 2600 Mission Bell Dr, San Pablo, CA 94806, **Business Phone:** (510)235-7800.

WILSON, SONALI BUSTAMANTE (Z SONALI BUSTAMANTE)
Lawyer. **Personal:** Born May 31, 1958, Cleveland, OH; daughter of H and F Joy Simmons John; married N Stephen II, Apr 12, 1991; children: Martine Celeste. **Educ:** Boston Univ, Boston, MA, BA, 1980; Harvard Univ, Boston, MA, govt studies, ALM, 1983; Georgetown Univ Law Ctr, WA, DC, JD, 1986. **Career:** Off Chief Compliance, DC, Dept Consumer & Regulatory Affairs, law clerk, 1984-86; Ohio Supreme Ct Justice, law clerk, 1987; Arter & Hadden, Cleveland, OH, assoc, 1986, litigation, 1988-94; Cleveland State Univ, chief legal coun & secy bd trustees, 1996-. **Orgs:** Am Bar Asn, Pre-Law Coun Com, Young Lawyers Div; bd trustees, Cleveland Bar Asn, Young Lawyer's Exec Coun, 1988-; corresp sec, Links Inc Cleveland; co-chair, Nat Trends, 1988-; bd trustees, Womenspace, 1988-91; Citizen's League Greater Cleveland, 1990-; Girlfriends Cleveland, 1990-; United Way, Govt Rels Comt, 1991-; pres, Cleveland Chap, The Links Inc; bd trustees, Cuyahoga Co Bd Mental Retardation & Develop Disabilities; legal advisor, Greater Cleveland Alumnae Chap, Delta Sigma Theta Sorority, Inc. **Honors/Awds:** Citation for Achievement in Organization and Leadership from Massachusetts House of Representatives, 1979; Citation in Recognition of Service in Recruiting Young Adults for Boston National Association for the Advancement of Colored People from Governor of King of Massachusetts, 1979. **Home Addr:** 1801 E 12th St Suite 1001, Cleveland, OH 44114, **Home Phone:** (216)621-3549. **Business Phone:** (216)687-3543.

WILSON, PROF. STANLEY CHARLES
Educator. **Personal:** Born Feb 2, 1947, Los Angeles, CA; son of Ernest Charles and Eleanor Mae Reid; married Jacquelyn Patricia Bellard; children: Jendayi Asabi. **Educ:** Chouinard Art Sch, 1965; Calif State Polytech Univ, Pomona, 1966; Calif State Univ, Los Angeles, Calif, 1967; Otis Art Inst, Los Angeles, Calif, BFA, 1969, MFA, 1971. **Career:** Jr Art Ctr, Los Angeles, Calif, instr, 1969-72; Southwestern Col, ChulaVista, Calif, asst prof, 1972-73; Otis Art Inst, Parsons Watts Towers, instr, 1981; Calif State Polytech Univ, Pomona, Calif, prof Visual Art, 1984-2002, prof emer, 2002-; Univ Art Gallery, dir. **Orgs:** Gallery cur dir, Calif State Polytech Univ, Pomona, Calif, 1975-85; planning & dir, Los Angeles Weave, Los Angeles Olympic Exhibit, 1984 planning bd, west coast black artist Exhib, 1976; Brand Art Ctr, Glendale, Calif; bd adv, Watts Towers Art Ctr, Los Bd artists, Brockman GalleryProd, Los Angeles, Calif, 1980-85; bd adv, Africa Quarter, Calif State Polytech Univ, 1984-85; awards panelist, New Genre Fel, Calif Arts Coun, Sacramento, Calif, 1989; bd adv, Latin Am Quarter, Calif Polytech Univ, Pomona, Calif, 1989; award panelist, sculpture, Calif Arts Coun, Sacramento, Calif, 1990; bd adv, gallery comt, Armony Art Cen, Pasadena, Calif, 1990-91; awards panelist, sculpture, Colo Coun Arts & Humanities, 1991; fel awards panelist, Ill Arts Coun, 1991-; chmn, City Pasadena, ArtsComn, 1997; nat develop comn, studio art, advan placement, Princeton, NJ; co-chair, sculputure panel, Col Art Asn, 1999; panel, Contemp Sculpture, Calif African Am Mus, 1999; chair, Pasadena Arts Comn, 1999-2000. **Honors/Awds:** Works publ Black Artist Art, Vol 2, Lewis & Waddy 1971, Afro-Am Artist, Boston Pub Libr, 1973; Nominated Fulbright Fel, West & East Africa, 1984-85; Vis Artist Residence Aberdeen, SD, 1975; Nat Endowment Art; Artist Residence, Studio Mus Harlem, NY, 1986-87; Meritorious & Prof Promise Award, Calif Polytech Univ, Pomona, Calif, 1986; Six African Am Artist, Calif State Univ, Dominquez Hills, Calif, 1989; Calif Art Rev, second ed, Chicago, Ill, 1989; Calif Art Rev, third ed Chicago, Ill, 1991; Two Man Exhibition, Sparc Gallery, Venice, Calif, 1990; One Man Exhibition, San Antonio Art Inst, San Antonio, Tex, 1992; Vis Artist, Univ Nevada-Las Vegas, 1990; Calif Polytech Univ, Pomona, Outstanding Pro, 1991; AP Rev Panel Princeton, New Jersey; Pasadena Arts Com, Visual Arts Award, 1998; Vis Artist & Grad Rev, Memphis Col Art, Memphis Tenn, 2001; Invited Lectr, Calif State Univ, North Ridge, Art Dept, 2001. **Special Achievements:** Curated selected art works Bakerfield Col Exhibition, Local, Space Gallery, Los Angeles, Calif, 1995; Appointed Arts Comn, City Pasadena, Calif; Calif Community Found, Brody fel, 1998; Artist Against the Spreadof Aids in Africia-Auction, 2001; co-curated Exhibition, "The Story is in the Telling," Armoney Center for the Arts, 2002; Two Man Exhibitional,"Method Meaning" Calif State Univ-Bakersfield, 2002. **Home Phone:** (323)256-2997. **Business Addr:** Professor Emeritus, California State Polytechnic University, 3801 W Temple Ave Bldg 13, Pomona, CA 91768, **Business Phone:** (909)869-7659.

WILSON, STEPHANIE Y.
Economist. **Personal:** Born Feb 16, 1952, Pittsburgh, PA. **Educ:** Goddard Col, BA 1973; State Univ NY, Stonybrook, MA 1975, PhD 1978. **Career:** Abt Assocs, Wash, DC, analyst, vpres & area mgr 1985-86, managing vpres 1987-92, group vpres int, 1992-. **Orgs:** Nat Econ Asn; Prof Serv Coun; US-Africa Bus Coun; Soc Int Develop; US-S Africa Bus Coun; US-Russian Bus Coun; Corp Coun Africa; Asn Women Develop. **Special Achievements:** 3rd woman to become a President of the Nat Econ Asn; recognized in the Who's Who among African Americans, The Inter Global Who's Who, Strathmores Who's Who, the Who's Who of Women Executives & Sterling Who's Who; published "A Different Vision: African American Economic Thought". **Business Addr:** Group Vice President - International, Abt Assoc Inc, 4800 Montgomery Lane Suite 600, Bethesda, MD 20814.

WILSON, THOMAS A, JR.
Banker. **Personal:** Born Sep 25, 1951, Baltimore, MD; son of Thomas A Sr and Margaret R Stokes; married Diane P Freeman, May 31, 1986; children: Cedric T & Dexter N. **Educ:** Morgan State Univ, BS, 1973. **Career:** Ind Bank Wash, comptroller currency, bank examiner, 1974-86, vpres, loan review officer, 1986-88, controller, sr vpres, 1988-, chief finance officer, currently. **Honors/Awds:** Award, Nat Bank, 2003. **Home Addr:** 1605 Tredegar Ave, Catonsville, MD 21228, **Home Phone:** (410)719-0119. **Business Addr:** Senior Vice President, Chief Finannce Officer, Industrial Bank of Washington, 4812 Ga Ave NW, Washington, DC 20011, **Business Phone:** (202)722-2000.

WILSON, TREVOR
Basketball player. **Personal:** Born Mar 16, 1968, Los Angeles, CA. **Educ:** Univ Calif, Los Angeles, CA, attended 1990. **Career:** Basketball player (retired); Atlanta Hawks, 1990-91; Los Angeles Lakers, 1994; Sacramento Kings, 1994-95; Philadelphia 76ers, forward, 1996; Turkey, 1998.

WILSON, VALERIE PETIT
Health services administrator, scientist, educator. **Personal:** Born Jan 24, 1950, New Orleans, LA; daughter of Alvin Joseph and Lorraine Kelly Petit; married Melvin; children: Daniel & Craig. **Educ:** Xavier Univ, BS, pre-med, chem, 1970; Johns Hopkins Univ, PhD, molecular biol, genetics, 1976. **Career:** Mt Sinai Hosp, Dept Human Genetics, researcher, 1976-77; Nat Inst Health, Lab Molecular Virol, NIAMDD, 1977-79; NIH, NHLBI, Lab Molecular Hemat, 1979-81; Sci Prog Admin, asst Diabetes Br, 1981-82, asst diabetes prog dir, 1982-83; NIH, asst div dir, Diabetes, Endocrinol & Metab, 1983-86; Cystic Fibrosis, prog dir, 1984-86; off asst secy Health, BioMed Res (NIH), desk Officer, 1986-88; NIH AIDS Policy Analyst, 1988-90, dir policy anal & coord, 1990-91, actg dir, 1992-93; Nat AIDS Prog Off, Howard Univ Sch Med, Dept Family & Community Med, adj appointment, 1994-97; Nat Acad Sci, Div Health Scis Policy, dir, 1993-97; CBR, dep dir, 1997-; Brown Univ, Leadership Alliance, exec dir, currently, Brown Univ Med Sch, clin assoc prof, 1998-, clin prof community health, currently. **Orgs:** Am Soc Biochemists & Molecular Biologists; adv bd, Jr League Wash, 1989-92; bd mem, 1993-96, vp bd, 1994-96, chmn bd, 1996-97, Nat Asn People AIDS. **Honors/Awds:** Exemplary Service Award, 1988, 1992; Award for Exceptional Achievement, Asst Sec Health, 1990; Special Recognition Group Awards, Off Asst Sec Health, 1991, 1993; Cert of Appreciation, US Surgeon Gen, 1992, 1993; Nat Acad Sci Award, 1995, 1997. **Special Achievements:** Research Publications include: co-author: "The Initiation of SV40 DNA Syntheseis in not Unique to the Replication Origin," Cell: Vol 20, pp 381-391, 1980; "The Roles of Simian Virus 40 Tumor Antigens in Transformation of Chinese Hamster Lung Cells: Studies with Double Mutants," Journal of Virology, 31: pp 597-607, 1979; "Lateral Phase Separation of Lipids in Plasma Membranes: Effect of Temperature on Mobility of Membrane Antigens," Science 184, pp 1183-1185, 1974; editor, Gender Differences in Susceptibility to Environmental Factors: "A Priority Assessment, 1998. National Academy Press," and other public policy reports of IOM/NAS; numerous other publications, interviews television interviews and reports. **Business Addr:** Executive Director, Clinical Professor of Community Health, Brown University, Leadership Alliance National Office, PO Box 1963, Providence, RI 02912-1963, **Business Phone:** (401)863-9892.

WILSON, VELMA J
Manager, president (organization). **Personal:** Born Aug 28, 1934, Chicago, IL; daughter of Joseph C and Rubye Therkeld; married John E, Jul 24, 1960; children: Ginger Renee & Kelly JoAnne. **Educ:** Chicago Teachers Col Chicago State Univ, BS, Educ0, 1958, masters degree, Educ, 1963. **Career:** Bd Educ, Chicago, primary teacher, 1958-68; Woodlawn Orgn, dir family focus, 1977; Chicago Urban League, consult young parents prog, 1979-83; Harold WAS for Mayor, scheduler, 1982-83; City Chicago, dir tourism, 1984-89; The Wilson GRP, pres, 1989-. **Orgs:** Delta Sigma Theta, 1958-; Bd mem, Oper Push, 1976-; bd mem, Dusable Museum Bd, 1977-85; mem, tres, secy, ETA Bd, 1978-83; pres, Women's Bd Chicago Urban League, 1985-87; sustaining mem, Univ Chicago Lying Hosp, 1979-; Jesse Owens FND, friend com chair, 1991-92; Links Inc, Windy City, chair, nat trends com, 1995-; pres, Parents Resource Inc. **Honors/Awds:** Operation Push, Salute to Excellence, Women's Delegation To Lebanon, 1979, Community Consciousness, 1977; Outstanding Service, Chicago Urban League, 1985; Woman of the Year, Norman LaHarry Scholarship Found, 1987; Outstanding Service, City of Chicago, 1989. **Home Addr:** 1031 E Hyde Pk 2nd Fl, Chicago, IL 60615, **Home Phone:** (773)752-6680.

WILSON, WALTER JAMES
Football player. **Personal:** Born Oct 6, 1966, Baltimore, MD. **Educ:** E Carolina Univ, criminal justice. **Career:** San Diego Chargers, wide receiver, 1990; Ohio Glory, wide receiver, 1992. **Honors/Awds:** Set E Carolina Univ rec with 91 receptions for 1670 yards & 16 touchdowns; hon mention all-Am, Sporting News.

WILSON, WESLEY CAMPBELL
Management consultant. **Personal:** Born Nov 29, 1931, Philadelphia, PA; son of Wesley and Emily; married Elaine Epps; children: Carl B, Wayne K, Michael K & Eric W. **Educ:** Morgan State Univ, BS, 1954; Col William & Mary, MEd, 1974, adv cert educ, 1978, EdD 1986. **Career:** Col William & Mary, asst pres, 1974-76; C & W Assoc Inc, vpres 1976-. **Orgs:** Newport News Dem Comn, 1974-; exec bd, First Dist Black Caucus, 1975-; pres, Alpha Alpha Chap Omega Psi Phi, 1975-76; chmn, Governors comn Adv Gov Va EEO, 1975-79; chmn sch bd, Newport News Va Pub Sch, 1977-; bd trustees, Peninsula United Way 1979-. **Honors/Awds:** Citizen of Year, Omega Psi Phi Newport News Va, 1977 & 78; Man of Year, Peninsula Negro Bus & Prof Women, 1979; Educ & Polit Strange Bedfellows, 1979. **Military Serv:** AUS, lt col, 1954-74; Legion of Merit, Vietnamese Cross, Bronze Star, Dist Flying Cross all, 1964-65. **Home Addr:** 3350 Spinnaker Way, Gloucester, VA 23061. **Business Addr:** Vice President, C & W Associates Inc, 825 Diligence Dr Suite 116, Newport News, VA 23606, **Business Phone:** (804)873-4735.

WILSON, DR. WILLIAM JULIUS
Sociologist, educator. **Personal:** Born Dec 20, 1935, Derry Township, PA; son of Pauline Bracy Wilson and Esco Wilson; married Beverly Huebner; children: Colleen, Lisa, Carter & Paula. **Educ:** Wilberforce Univ, BA, Sociol/Hist, 1958; Bowling Green State Univ, MA, Sociol/Hist, 1961; Wash State Univ, PhD, Sociol/Hist, 1966. **Career:** Univ Mass, Amherst, asst prof social, 1965-69, assoc prof social, 1969-71; Univ Chicago, asso prof social, 1972-75, prof social, 1975-80, chmn, Sociol Dept, 1978-81, 1984-87; Lucy Flower prof Urban Sociol, 1980-84; LucyFlower Distinguished serv prof, social, 1984-90, Lucy Flower Univ prof social & pub policy, 1990-96, Sch Pub Policy, Ctr Study Urban, dir, 1990-96; French-Am Found, vis prof, Am studies, Ecole des Hautes Etudes eng soc sci, Paris, 1989-90; Col de France, Paris, lectr, soc sci, 1990; Joblessness & Urban Res Prog, Malcolm Wiener Ctr Social Policy, dir, 1996-; Harvard Univ, Malcolm Wiener prof soc policy, prof Afro-Am studies, 1996-98, Lewis P & Linda L Geyser Univ prof, 1996-. **Orgs:** Chmn, res adv comn, Chicago Urban League, 1976-85; bd dirs, Soc Sci Res Coun, 1979-85; nat bd, A Philip Randolph Inst, 1981-; bd dirs, Chicago Urban League, 1983-97; nat bd, Inst Res Poverty, 1983-87; George M Pullman Found, 1986-93; Carnegie Coun on Adoloscent Devel, 1986-95; William TGrant Founds Comn Youth & Am Future, 1986-88; Ctr Budget & Policy Priorities, 1987-; Spencer Founf, 1987-96; bd dirs, Ctr Advan Study Behav Scis, 1988-2002; bd dirs, Russell Sage Found, 1989-98; bd trustees, Spelman Colm 1989-98; Nat Humanities Ctr, 1990-95; Consortium Soc Sci Asn, 1991-95; bd trustees, Bard Col, 1992-2001; trustee, Twentieth Century Fund, 1992-2001; bd, Manpower Demonstration Res Corp, 1993-; President's Comn White House Fel, 1994-2001; Bd, Public/Private Ventures, 1994-2002; President's Comn Nat Med Sci, Nat Sci Found, 1994-98; Adv bd, Ctr Pub Integrity, 1995-; Bd trustees, Wilberforce Univ, 1995-; Bd dir, Nat Urban League, 1995-98; Nat Acad Sci, Comt Sci, Engineering & Pub Policy, 1995-2001; bd adv, Frederick D Patterson Res Inst, 1996-; bd dirs, Policylink, 2000-; Scholar's Coun, Libr Cong, 2001; Bd trustees, Bard Col, 2001-; Bd gov, Levy Found Econ Inst, 2001-; AAAS. **Honors/Awds:** Received several honorary degrees from various Universities; Dr Humane Letters, Honoris Causa: Univ Mass, Amherst, 1982; MacArthur Prize Fellow, The John D and Catherine T MacArthur Found, 1987-92; Distinguished Alumnus Award, Washington State Univ, 1988; C Wright Mills Award for the truly disadvantaged, Soc Study of Soc Problems, 1988; North Central Sociological Asn Achievement Award, 1988; Washington Monthly's Annual Book Award, 1988; Dr of Laws Honoris Causa, Mt Holyoke Col, 1989, Marquette Univ, 1989; Dubois, Johnson, Frazier Award, Am Sociol Asn, 1990; New Sch Soc Res, 1991; Doctor of Humane Letters, Tulane Univ, Bard Col, John Jay ColCriminal Justice, 1992; Univ Penn, Southern Ill Univ, Edwardsville, 1993;Doctor of Laws, Honoris Causa, Northwestern Univ, 1993; Bowling GreenState Univ, State Univ NY, Binghamton, Princeton Univ, 1994; Frank ESeidman Distinguished Award in Political Economy, Rhodes Col, Memphis TN,1994; Doctor of Humane Letters, Honoris Causa, Haverford Col, 1995; MartinLuther King, Jr, Nat Award, 1998; Doctor of Laws, Clarion Univ, Penn, Colgate V Clark Univ, 1999, Bates Col, 1999; Doctor of Social Science, Northeastern Univ, 1999; Doctor Of Humane Letters, Macalester Col, St Paul, Ohio State Univ, Columbus, 2000; Occidental Col, Reusselars Polytechnic Inst, Lawrence Univ, 2001; Sidney Hillman Found Award; Winner of Talcot Parson Prize, 2003. **Special Achievements:** Receipient of National Medal of Science, 1998; Author of various books and articles. **Military Serv:** USY, spec 4 class, 1958-60; Meritorious Serv Awd 1960. **Business Addr:** Linda L Geyser University Professor, Harvard University, John F Kennedy School of Government, Malcolm Wiener Ctr Social Policy, 79 JF Kennedy St, Cambridge, MA 02138.

WILSON, REV. WILLIE FREDERICK (KWADWO I BOAFO)
Clergy, educator. **Personal:** Born Mar 8, 1944, Newport News, VA; son of Samuel B and Lovey E; married Mary Lewis, Sep 29,

1973; children: Anika, Kalilia, Bashiri & Hamani. **Educ:** Ohio Univ, BS, 1966; Howard Univ, Divinity Sch, MDiv, 1969; Doctoral Studies, 1969-71. **Career:** Union Temple Baptist Church, pastor, 1973-. **Honors/Awds:** 'Top 10 Most Valuable People in USA', USA Today, 1985; US Presidential Service Awd, 1997; 'One of 100 Model African American Churches in America.', Nat Congress Black Churchmen. **Special Achievements:** Publication, "The African American Wedding Manual"; Ordained as WOLOF priest in Gambia, West Africa, 1980; enstated as Ashanti subchief in Ghana, 1993. **Business Addr:** Pastor, Union Temple Baptist Church, 1225 W St SE, Washington, DC 20020, **Business Phone:** (202)678-8822.

WILSON, WILLIE MAE
Executive. **Personal:** Born Mar 18, 1942, Birmingham, AL; married William L; children: Bertrand LaMarr & Pelina. **Educ:** Knoxville Col, BA; Univ Minn, MA. **Career:** Minn St Comn Discrim, res clerk, 1964; St Paul Bpu Lib, asst librn, 1965-66; Urban League Comn, organizer proj, 1966-67; Econ Develop & Employ St Paul Urban League, actg dir, 1967; Urban Leag, housing dir, 1967-69; St Paul Urban Coal, housing & coord, 1969, ceo, 1972-74, pres, adminr dept; Twin Cities Met Coun, 1971. **Orgs:** Chmn bd comt, St Paul Housing & Redev Auth & Comn, 1972-76; co-chmn, Summit Univ, 1973; vpres, Urban N Non-prof Housing Corp, 1973; deleg, St Paul Dem Farm Labor, 1974; pres, Coun EXD Nat Urban Leag, 1980-82; chmn, Unit Way Coun Agency Dir; vpres, St Paul Ramsey Coun Agency Dir; bd dir, First Nat Bank St Paul; Cit Leag; bd dir, Comn Develop Corp; Oper 85 Planning Comn; Minn Met Orgn Displaced Women; tri-chmn, St Paul Publ Sch Sec Educ Adv Comm Desegrat; DST Sor; Iota Phi Lambda Bus & Prof Womens Sor; Am Soc Planning Off; Am Soc Pub Admin; St Paul Urban League; Nat Asn Advan Colored People. **Honors/Awds:** Samuel Ullman Scholar Award, 1960; Woodrow Wilson Enrichment Scholar, Col Univ, 1964.

WILSON, WILSON W
Military leader, real estate agent. **Personal:** Born May 31, 1942, Quachita Parish, LA; son of Phillip and Christel Jones; married Georgia Crawford, Mar 1963; children: Suzzon E, Ellen M, Warren M & Gladys C. **Educ:** Southern Univ, BA, 1964; McNeese State Univ; Roosevelt Univ; Univ Ky, grad study; Western Ky Univ, MPA, 1975; Northeast State Univ. **Career:** Military leader, Real estate agent (retired); AUS, min army off procurement; rep Vietnam joint US staff for military assistance, 1969-70, supply part officer 5H infantry div, Fort Polk, LA, 1978, 5th AUS hq staff off dep chief of staff ROTC, equal opportunity officer 5th infantry div, Ft Polk, LA, dep comn comdr Wertheim Military comn Wertheim Gery; Monroe City Sch Syst, sci teacher, 1989-91; self employed, Monroe, LA, real estate broker, 1988-; High Sch adminr, 1999-. **Orgs:** Minority Bus Asn, Alpha Phi Alpha Fraternity, 1963; YMCA, 1963; Asn AUS, 1965-73; Prince Hall Masonic, 1967; Office holder Hardin Co, Ky Br, Nat Asn Advan Colored People, 1973-75; Monroe Nat Asn Advan Colored People, Ouachita Br, 1988-. **Honors/Awds:** Numerous military decor; rec'd numerous commend for part in educ seminars MW U's; part in lecture series at these same MW Univs; numerous TV appearances disc the role of black soldier in AUS & black military hist; Legion of Merit Award, US Army, 1989. **Military Serv:** AUS, Lt col, 1964-89; numerous military awards.

WILSON-GEORGE, SYBIL
Football player, executive. **Career:** Miami Heat, Miami, FL, dir corp educ, spec asst to exec vpres, currently. **Honors/Awds:** Exemplary Partnership Award, Dade Co Pub Sch. **Business Addr:** Special Assistant to the Executive Vice President, Miami Heat, 1 SE 3rd Ave, Miami, FL 33131, **Business Phone:** (305)577-4328.

WILSON-SMITH, WILLIE ARRIE
Educator. **Personal:** Born Jan 12, 1929, Charlotte, NC; daughter of Booker T and Katie A Vance; married Jack, Aug 27, 1949 (deceased). **Educ:** Johnson C Smith Univ, BA, 1956; Western Reserve Univ, MEd. 1962. **Career:** Educator (retired); JB Iveys Millinery Shoe Repairing, 1951-54; Belks Shoe Repairing, 1954-57; Charlotte Mecklenburg Sch Syst, teacher, 1957-80. **Orgs:** Life Mem, NEA; life mem, NCAE; life mem, NCACT; Alpha Kappa Alpha Sor Inc; Mecklenburg County Dem Womens Club; deputy dir 9th Dist Dem Women, 1977-79; democratic candidate Charlotte City Coun Dist, 1997; NC Dem Exec Comt; Womens Forum NC; Charlotte BPC; past mem, Charlotte CRC, 1974-82; life mem, New Emmanuel Congregational United Church Christ; pastmem, Charlotte Mecklenburg NCCJ; PTA; Girl Scout Adv; Appt Study Comt Rel Between Prof Employ Asn & Sch Bd, 1973-75; apptd NC Adv Comt Teacher Educ, 1974-76; soror yr, AKA 1965; only black elected Mecklenburg Co Dem of Yr, 1977; bd trustees, Central Piedmont Community Col, 1979-87; volunteer off helper Charlotte Bus League, 1986, 1987; treas, New Emmanuel Congl UCC, 1989-97; chair 12th US Congressional District-NC, 1997-03; Governor appointee, NC Col Found bd trustees, 1997-; NC High Sch volunteer 1997-. **Honors/Awds:** Graduate Advisory Award, 1967; Oper Cir, 1966; Appreciation Award, Gamma Delta, 1965-74; Appreciation Award, Alpha Lambda Omega, 1965-74; Service & Plaque New Emmanuel Congregational UCC, 1987; Service & Plaque Central Piedmount Community Col, 1987. *

WILTZ, CHARLES J.
Dentist. **Personal:** Born Oct 18, 1934, New Orleans, LA; married Vivianne Carey (deceased); children: Charles Jr, Cary E. **Educ:** Xavier Univ, BS 1956; Howard Univ Sch Dent, DDS 1967. **Career:** MA Gen Hosp, asst hematologist, 1959-61; Am Polymer & Chem Corp, jr org chemist, 1962-63; Westside VA Hosp, staff dent, 1968-69; Mile Sq Health Ctr, Chicago staff dentist, 1970-71; Pvt Pract, dent, 1970-. **Orgs:** Consult Ill Dent Serv; Acad Gen Dent; Chicago Dent Soc; Ill State Dent Soc; Am Dent Asn, Nat Dent Asn; Chi Delta Mu; Lincoln Dent Soc; Billiken World Arts & Scis; Alpha Phi Alpha. **Honors/Awds:** City & state high sch basketball LA, 1952; Outstanding Merit of Achievement Va Hosp 1968. **Special Achievements:** Ten Best Dressed Black Men of Chicago, 1974, 1975, 1976. **Military Serv:** AUS sp 4 1957-59 1961-62. **Business Addr:** Dentist, 8701 S Racine Ave, Chicago, IL 60615.*

WILTZ, DR. PHILIP G, JR.
Physician. **Personal:** Born Jun 5, 1930, New Orleans, LA; married Barbara Allen; children: Teresa, Phyllis & Yvette. **Educ:** Savannah State Col, BS 1952; NY Univ, MA, 1956; Howard Univ, MD, 1968. **Career:** NY Pub Schs, teacher,1957-60; Wash DC Pub Schs, teacher, 1961-64; US Pub Health Serv, internship, 1968-69, resident orthop surg, 1969-73; Pvt Pract, physician orthop surg. **Orgs:** Alpha Phi Alpha Fraternity; Sigma Phi Fraternity; Phi Delta Kappa Hon Soc, NY Univ, 1957; Ga State Med Asn Inc; bd trustees, Morehouse Sch Med. **Military Serv:** AUS, corpl, 1952-54; USPHS, lt comdr, 1968-73. **Business Addr:** Physician, 285 Blvd NE Suite 110, Atlanta, GA 30312, **Business Phone:** (404)265-6701.*

WIMBERLEY, FRANK
Artist. **Personal:** Born Aug 31, 1926, Pleasantville, NJ; son of Frank Howell and Edythe Carolyn; married Juanita Olga, Dec 20, 1947; children: Walden. **Educ:** Howard Univ, attended, 2 yrs. **Career:** Exhibitions: African Am Mus, Charleston, NC, 1998; Different Directionsm Nese Alpan Gallery, Roslyn, NY, 1999; Then & Now, Ctr Gallery, Adelphi Univ, 2000; Omni Gallery, Uniondale, NY, 2001; Compositions Matter, June Kelly Gallery, New York, 2001; Gestures, Port Wash Libr Gallery, 2002; An Exhibition Hon Black Hist Month, Rensselaer Polytech Inst, Shelnutt Gallery, Troy, NY, 2002; Biennale Internazionale, Florence, Italy, 2003; artist, currently. **Orgs:** Bd mem, East Hampton Ctr Contemporary Art, 1986; panel mem, Selecting Artist & Art Work US Courthouse, Art-In-Archit Prog, Islip, NY, 1997. **Honors/Awds:** Pollock-Krasner Foundation Award, 1998; Best In Show, 36th Juried Exhib, Parrish Art Mus, South Hampton, NY. **Home Addr:** 9911 35th Ave, Corona, NY 11368. **Business Addr:** Artist, 9911 35th Ave, Corona, NY 11368, **Business Phone:** (718)335-3929.*

WIMBISH, C BETTE
Lawyer. **Personal:** Born Mar 24, 1924, Perry, FL; daughter of Tom Davis and Ola Mae Howard Davis; married Ralph Melvin, Nov 12, 1944 (deceased); children: Barbara Griffin, Ralph & Terence. **Educ:** Fla Agr & Mech Univ, BS, 1944, JD, 1967. **Career:** Fla Mem Col, instr, 1945-46; Pub Sch Syst, Hillsborough Co, instr, 1947-52; St Petersburg, gen law pract, 1968-73; City St Petersburg, city coun, 1969-71, vice-mayor, 1971-73; Fla Dept Com, dep secy; State Fla C & Families Dept, atty, currently. **Orgs:** League Women Voters; Am Arbitration Asn; pres, Caribe Export Mgt Co; legal adv, Delta Sigma Theta Sorority; Nat Coun Negro Women; bd dirs, Am Civil Libs Union; Nat Asn Advan Colored People; bd mem, S Regional Coun, Task Forces Southern Rural Dev & Econ Develop; Fla Bar Asn; Fla Gov Bar Asn; vpres, Dem Nat Comn; consult, CRS, Support Serv US Dept Justice & Off Contract Compliance Support Serv US Dept Labor; guest lectr, Univ S Fla; Am Bar Asn; NBA; adv coun, Factory-Built Housing; Comn Educ Outreach & Serv; Fla Dept Com & Employer-employee Rels Adv Coun; bd trustees, S Ctr Int Studies; comn, Dem Nat Comm; Fla A&M Univ Coun Advs; arbitrator, Labor Panel Fed Medication & Conciliation Serv, 1980-. **Honors/Awds:** Florida Women of District, 1974; Outstanding Woman in Governor Award, Orlando, FL, Chap Delta Sigma Theta Sorority, 1975. **Home Addr:** 7200 34th St S, St Petersburg, FL 33711-4932, **Home Phone:** (904)575-4560. **Business Addr:** Attorney, State of Florida Children & Families Department, 11351 Ulmerton Rd Fl 4, Largo, FL 34648, **Business Phone:** (727)588-3646.

WIMBUSH, FREDERICK BLAIR
Real estate executive. **Personal:** Born Jul 24, 1955, Halifax County, VA; son of Freddie B and Sue Carol Lovelace; married Jane Seay Wimbush, Jan 1, 1981. **Educ:** Univ Rochester, BA 1977; Univ Va, JD 1980; Duke Univ, Fuqua Sch Bus, Norfolk Southern Mgt Dev Prog, 1996; Advan Mgt Prog, Harvard Buss Sch, 2004. **Career:** Norfolk & Western Railway Co, atty, 1980-83; Norfolk Southern Corp, solicitor, 1983-85, asst gen solicitor, 1985-89, gen atty, 1989-96, gen solicitor, 1996-2000, gen coun, operations, 2000-02, sr gen coun, 2002-04, vpres, real estate, 2004-. **Orgs:** Am, Nat, VA, Old Dominion and Norfolk-Portsmouth Bar Asn; Asn Transportation Practitioners, VA State Bar; Roanoke Mus Fine Arts, 1981-, secy, 1982-84, vpres, 1984-86, pres, 1986-87; Legal Aid Soc Roanoke Valley, 1982-86; United Way Spec Study Agencies, 1983; Roanoke Co Transportation Safety Comn, 1984-85; Leadership Roanoke Valley, Roanoke Valley Chamber Com, 1984-85; Roanoke City Arts Comn, 1984-87; adv panel, VA Comn Arts Area III, 1985-87, Area VI Adv Panel, 1988-90; Nat bd dirs Big Brothers/Big Sisters Am, 1986-92; Western VA Found Arts & Sci, 1986-87; Am Red Cross, Tidewater 1990-93; Am Heart Asn, Tidewater 1990-92; pres, Va Comn Women & Minorities Legal Syst, 1992-93; bd dir, vpres, Va Law Found, 1994-95, pres, 1996-97; bd dirs, Va Symphony Orchestra; Univ Va Law Sch Alumni Coun; Univ Va Law Sch Bus Adv Coun; Va State Bar Prof Course Fac; bd gov, sect educ, Va State Bar,; fel Va Law Found; Civic Leadership Inst. **Business Addr:** Vice President, Norfolk Southern Corporation, 3 Commercial Pl, Norfolk, VA 23320, **Business Phone:** (757)629-2656.

WIMBUSH, GARY LYNN
College administrator. **Personal:** Born Oct 13, 1953, Warren, OH; married Aundra Diana Lewis; children: Brennan Jevon & Kyle Jameson. **Educ:** Oakwood Col, BA, 1975; Andrews Univ, MDiv, 1977; Western State Univ Sch Law, JD, 1984. **Career:** Allegheny W Conf SDA, sr clergymen, 1975-80; Southeastern Calif Conf SDA, sr Clergyman, 1980-84; Oakwood Col, dir admis & recruitment, 1984-. **Orgs:** Chaplain vol Orange County Hosp Syst, 1982-84; bus mgr, Viewpoint, A Theol Jour, 1983-85. **Honors/Awds:** Pastor of the Year Award, Allegheny W Conf SDA, 1979; Outstanding Young Men of America, 1986. **Business Addr:** Director, Oakwood College, Oakwood Rd, Huntsville, AL 35896.

WIMP, EDWARD LAWSON
Business owner. **Personal:** Born Feb 12, 1942, Chicago, IL. **Educ:** Roosevelt Univ, BS & BA, 1966. **Career:** DEW Rlty, vpres, broker, 1961-69; King Terco McDonald's Franchises, owner & operator. **Orgs:** Pres, Black McDonald's Operator's Asn, 1985; bd mem, Chicagoland McDonald's Operators Asn, 1985; exec bd mem, Nat Black McDonald's Operators Asn; bd mem & chmn, Wabash YMCA, 1985; bd Mgrs, Met YMCA'S, 1985; Sigma Pi Phi Frat, 1985. **Honors/Awds:** Nat Champion & World Speed Record Holder, Am Hot Rod Asn, 1963; Philanthropic World Community Islam, 1978; Outstanding Young Am US, 1979; James H Tilehman Award, YMCA, 1979. **Military Serv:** USNG, res, 1965-71.

WIMS, WARNER BARRY
Management consultant. **Personal:** Born Apr 1, 1945, Philadelphia, PA; son of Calvin and Minnie; married Greta F Clark, Oct 21, 2000; children: Leslie Wims & Richard Clark. **Educ:** Pa State Univ, BA, 1975; Columbia Univ, MA, 1979, MBA, 1981, PhD, 1982. **Career:** Hay Group, sr consult, 1980-84; Bank Boston, sr dir, 1984-87; WBW & Assoc, pres, 1987-; Bank Am, sr dir, 1995-99. **Special Achievements:** Provided Team & organization development for over 50 major corporations; Japanese, French, Spanish proficiency. **Business Addr:** President, WBW & Associates, 2449 Lake St, San Francisco, CA 94115, **Business Phone:** (415)387-4040.

WINANS, ANGELIQUE
Singer. **Personal:** Born Mar 4, 1968, Detroit, MI; daughter of David and Delores; married Cedric Caldwell. **Career:** Albums with Debbie Winans: "Angie & Debbie Winans", 1993; "Bold", 1998; Soloalbums: "Melodies of My Heart", 2001; "The Lord's Prayer", "Changing My Whole Life", "He Loves Me", "Lady Wisdom", "Roses Again" & "Come Go With Me"; Film: Follow the Star, actress, 2004. **Honors/Awds:** Grammy Awards; Soul Train Music Awards. **Special Achievements:** Book: What Manner of Love is This?: A Diary of God's Love in Times of Mourning, 2005; Co-author of the book, Never Alone; Nominated for a Grammy Award. **Business Phone:** (818)557-8200.*

WINANS, BEBE (BENJAMIN WINANS)
Gospel singer. **Personal:** Born in Detroit, MI; son of David Sr and Delores; married Debra Denise; children: Miya Destiny. **Career:** Vocalist, songwriter, producer, talk show host, actor; Gospel duo Mt Zion Church God & Christ, Detroit, MI; PTL Club, duo, 1982; Capitol Recs, duo; The Movement Group, currently; Film/tv appearances: The Gospel According to VH1; "Ebony & Jet Showcase", 1991; The Manchurian Candidate, 2004; "Sunday Best", 2007; Albums: Lord Lift Us Up, 1984; Be Be & Ce Ce Winans, 1987; Heaven, 1988; Different Lifestyles, 1991; First Christmas, 1993; Relationships, 1994; Greatest Hits, 1996; Be Be Winans, 1997; Love & Freedom, 2000; Live & Up Close, 2002; My Christmas Prayer, 2004; Dream, 2005; The Best Of Be Be & Ce Ce, 2006; Cherch, 2007; TBA, 2008; Singles: "Do You Feel Their Pain?", 1989; "All Of Me", 1996; "In Harm's Way", 1997; "Thank You", 1997; "Stay", 1997; "I Wanna Be The One", 1997; "Coming Back Home", 2000; "Stay With Me", 2000; "Jesus Children Of America", 2000; "Do You Know Him", 2002; "I Have A Dream", 2005; "Safe From Harm", 2005; "Love Me Anyway", 2005; "Broken Bridges", 2006; "I Don't Want To Be Wrong Today", 2007. **Honors/Awds:** Grammy Awards, Best Contemporary Soul Gospel Album, 1992; Dove Awards,Best Contemporary Gospel Recorded Song of the Year, 1998; Stellar Awards;NAACP Awards; Soul Train Award. **Special Achievements:** Stage appearances included Whitney Houston joining the duo to sing "LoveSaid Not So," 1989. **Business Addr:** Gospel Singer, TMG Records, 2000 Glenn Echo Rd Suite 104, Nashville, TN 37215.

WINANS, CECE (PRISCILLA WINANS LOVE)
Gospel singer. **Personal:** Born Oct 8, 1964, Detroit, MI; daughter of David Winans Sr and Delores Winans; married Alvin Love;

children: Alvin Love III & Ashley Love. **Career:** People That Love Club, gospel singer, 1982-85; brother BeBe Winans, gospel singer; albums as CeCe Winans, 1987; Heaven, 1988; Different Lifestyles, 1991; Relationships, 1994; Alone In His Presence, 1995; His Gift, 1998; Everlasting Love, 1998; Alabaster Box, 1999; CeCe Winans, 2001; Throne Room, 2003; Purified, 2005; beauty parlor, co-owner; Albums as BeBe & CeCe Winans: Lord Lift Us Up, 1985; BeBe & CeCe Winans, 1987; Heaven, 1988; Different Lifestyles, 1991; First Christmas, 1993; Relationships, 1994; Greatest Hits, 1996; Count on Me, 1996. **Honors/Awds:** Grammy Award, Best Contemporary Soul Gospel performance, 1987, 1989, 2006; Grammy Award, Best Contemporary Soul Gospel Album, 1991, 1995, 2001, 2006; Different Lifestyles, 1992; Female Vocalist of the Year, 1996 & 1997; Dove Award, Best Contemporary Gospel Recorded Song of the Year, 1998; Lifetime Achievement Award, 2007. **Special Achievements:** Author: On A Positive Note, 2000; Throne Room: Ushered Into the Presence of God, 2004; co-authored with Claire Cloninger. Always Sisters: Becoming the Princess You Were Created to Be, released on July 17, 2007. **Business Addr:** Gospel Singer, Pure-Springs Gospel, 5214 Maryland Way Suite 300, Brentwood, TN 37027, **Business Phone:** (615)371-1575.

WINANS, DEBBIE
Singer. **Personal:** Born Sep 3, 1972, Detroit, MI; daughter of David and Delores; married James Lowe. **Career:** LoweKey Entertainment, exec producer & owner, currently; Renee Image Agencies, owner; Albums: Angie & Debbie, 1993; Bold, 1997. **Special Achievements:** Has been in major magazines, newspapers, political arenas, and television mediums. **Business Phone:** (202)986-0693.*

WINANS, MARIO
Music producer, singer. **Personal:** Born in Orangeburg, SC; son of Marvin and Vickie. **Career:** Rec producer & vocalist; Album: Story of My Heart, Motown, 1997; Hurt NoMore, 2004; Love's Highway Bad Boy Records, song writer, producer & singer, currenlty. **Honors/Awds:** Grammy Award for Best Contempory R & B Album "Hurt No More", 2005; Image Award for Outstanding New Artist, 2005; Mobo Award for Best Song, 2004; Moo Award for Best Ringtone, 2004; Vibe Award for R&B Song of the Year, 2004. **Business Addr:** Producer, Singer, Bad Boy Records, 8 W 19th St, New York, NY 10036-4039, **Business Phone:** (212)741-7070.

WINANS, PASTOR MARVIN L
Singer, clergy. **Personal:** Born Mar 5, 1958, Detroit, MI; son of David and Delores; children: Mario, Marvin Jr & Josiah. **Career:** Albums: Introducing the Winans, 1981; Long Time Coming, 1983; Tomorrow, 1985; Let My People Go, 1986; Decisions, 1987; Live at Carnegie Hall, 1988; Return, 1990; Introducing Perfect Praise, solo, 1992; All Out, 1993; Heart & Soul, 1995; Don't Get God Started, starrer, 1987; Perfecting Church, pastor, currently; Marvin L Winans Acad Performing Arts, pres sch bd, currently. **Orgs:** I Care Int; Gospel group The Winans. **Honors/Awds:** Dove Award, Gospel Music Asn, 3 times; Stellar Award, Best Gospel Group, 8 times; 6 Grammy Awards. **Special Achievements:** Author of Marvin Winans: Image is Everything, 1996; foreword writer, Who's Who among African Americans, 9th ed, 1996. **Business Addr:** Pastor, Perfecting Church, 7616 E Nevada St, Detroit, MI 48234-3131, **Business Phone:** (313)365-3787.

WINANS, VICKIE (VIVIANE BOWMAN)
Gospel singer, business owner. **Personal:** Born Oct 18, 1953, Detroit, MI; daughter of Mattie; married Joe E McLemore, 2004; married Marvin (divorced 1995); children: Marvin Jr. **Career:** Albums: Be Encouraged, 1985; Total Victory, 1989; The Lady, 1991; The Best of All, 1991; Vicki Winans, 1995; Live in Detroit, 1997; Live In Detroit II, 1999; Share the Laughter, 1999; Feel the Passion, 1999; Best of Vickie Winans, 2002; Bringing It All Together, 2003; My Christmas Gift to You, 2004; Greatest Hits, 2005; Woman to Woman: Songs of Life, 2006; Happy Holidays from Vickie Winans, 2007; Singles: "Don't Throw Your Life Away", 1991; "Just When (featuring Marvin Winans)", 1992; "Work It Out", 1995; "Shake Yourself Loose", 2003; "It's Alright", 2006; "Special Day", 2007; The Winans, mem legendary gospel group; Viviane Inc, pres & owner, currently. **Honors/Awds:** Grammy-nominated gospel recording artist. **Business Phone:** (248)253-3203.*

WINBUSH, ANGELA
Singer, composer. **Personal:** Born Jun 26, 1954, St Louis, MO. **Educ:** Howard Univ, music educ. **Career:** Composer; Back-up vocalist Stevie Wonder, 1977-80; Rene & Angela duo, 1980-87; solo artist, 1987; songwriter & producer Isley Brothers, Lalah Hathaway, Klymaxx, Sheena Easton; Sharp, 1987; It's the Real Thing, 1989; Angela Winbush, 1994; composed: Gr& Theft Auto: Vice City, 2002; Album: Rene & Angela, 1980; Wall To Wall #15 Billboard Chart, 1981; Rise #33 Billboard Chart, 1983; Street Called Desire #5 Billboard Chart, 1985; The Best of Rene & Angela: Come My Way, 1996; A Street Called Desire & More, 1997; Classic Masters, 2002; Solo Albumns: Sharp #7 Billboard Chart, 1987; It's The Real Thing #12 Billboard Chart, 1989; Angela Winbush #11 Billboard Chart, 1994; Ultimate Collection, 2001; Greatest Love Songs, 2004. **Honors/Awds:** Soul Train Music Award Nomination, 1987.

WINBUSH, RAYMOND ARNOLD
Educator, administrator. **Personal:** Born Mar 31, 1948, Pittsburgh, PA; son of Harold and Dorothy; divorced; children: Omari, Sharifa & Faraji. **Educ:** Oakwood Col, BA, psychol, 1970; Univ Chicago, MS, psychol, 1973, PhD, psychol, 1976. **Career:** Oakwood Col, asst prof & chmn behav sci, 1973-77; Alabama A&M Univ, assoc prof, psychol, 1977-80; Vanderbilt Univ, asst prof human develop coun, 1980-84; United Press Int, vpres corp res, 1984-86; Vanderbilt Univ, asst provost, 1986-94; Johnson Black Cultural Ctr, Vanderbilt Univ, assoc prof human devel & dir, 1991-95; Encyclopaedia Africana Project, Accra, Ghana, West Africa, consult; Fisk Univ, Benjamin Hooks prof social justice, dir Race Relations Inst, 1995-2002; Inst Urban Res, Morgan State Univ, dir, currently. **Orgs:** Nat Coun Black Studies, treas & exec bd mem, 1992-; Asn Black Psychologists, 1992-; Am Psychol Asn, 1993-; Girl Scouts Am, 1993-; prof consult, Asn Black Culture Ctr; pres, Southern region; Encyclopaedia Africana Proj; grant writer; tech consult; ed bd, Jour Black Studies. **Honors/Awds:** 1990 MLK Award, Cleveland SCLC, 1990; Leader of Information Highway Technology, Ebony Mag. **Special Achievements:** Anxiety & Afrocentricity, Black Issues in Higher Educ, 1994. **Business Addr:** Director, Morgan State University, Institute for Urban Research, Rm D216 Montebello Complex 1700 E Cold Spring Lane, Baltimore, MD 21251, **Business Phone:** (443)885-4800.

WINCHESTER, KENNARD (KENNARD NORMAN WINCHESTER)
Basketball player. **Personal:** Born Sep 3, 1966, Chestertown, MD. **Educ:** Averett Univ. **Career:** Basketball Player (retired); Houston Rockets, 1991-92, 1993; NY Knickerbockers, 1992.

WINCHESTER, KENNARD NORMAN. **See WINCHESTER, KENNARD.**

WINDER, ALFRED M
Executive, transport worker. **Educ:** Allan Hancock Jr Col, AA, 1966; Rockhurst Col, BA, indust rel, 1969. **Career:** Kans City Area Transp Authority, mgr equal employ/minority bus enterprise, 1978-80; Saudi Pub Tranps Co, mgr admin personnel, 1981-82; ATB/Ryder Mgt Serv Co, Cincinnati, vpres/gen mgr, 1981-85; Bi-State Develop Agency, dep gen mgr admin, 1983-84; Suburban Bus/West Towns, gen mgr; Gary Pub Transp Corp, pres, gen mgr; Transp Kans City, Mo Sch Dist, assoc supt, 1991-96; City & Co San Francisco, Calif, dir recreation; Div Transp DC Pub Schs, gen mgr, 1999-2003. **Orgs:** COMTO, 1983-85; exec bd, Ind Transp Asn; policy comt mem, Northern Ind Regional Planning Comn; Gary Ind C C; exec vpres, COMTO Nat, 1986-; bd mem, Anderson Boys Club, 1986-; Nat Asn Intercollegiate Athletics. **Honors/Awds:** Volunteer of the Year, Boys Clubs Greater Kans City, 1977-79; Outstanding Citizen's Award, Black United Appeal, Mo, 1978; Contractor of the Year Award, MO-KS Contractors Asn, 1978; Volunteer of the Year Award, St Louis, Mo Sch Dist, 1984; Prestigious Presidents Award, 1986; Superintendent's Award of Excellence, DC Pub Schs, 2000. **Military Serv:** AUS, Canine Corp, pfc, 1962-64; Presidio of San Francisco. **Home Addr:** 5044 Call Pl SE, Washington, DC 20075.

WINDHAM, REVISH
Manager, writer. **Personal:** Born May 31, 1940, Panola, AL; son of Ike Sr and Lillie; married Janice Bowman, Sep 22, 1985. **Educ:** Morris Brown Col, Paine Col, BA, 1966; Old Dominion Col, attended 1967; New York City Col, 1963; New York Univ, New York, NY, MPA, 1989. **Career:** Manager (retired), writer; New York City Dept Soc Serv, caseworker, 1968-70; New York St Div Youth, youth counr, 1970-83, youth empl voc spec, 1984-90, New York St Div Human Rights, human rights specialist, 1990-2000; Black Forum Mag, ed chief, 1978-80; writing, 1999-; Book: I Wouldn't Take Nothing for My Journey. **Orgs:** Poetry ed, Black Forum Mag, 1975-77; bd mem, Black Caucus DFY Employees Inc, 1974-90; pres, Morris Brown Col Alumni Asn, 1978-82; charter mem, MLK, Jr Ctr Soc Change NY, 1978-, Support Group Minorities Criminal Justice, 1978; Am Correctional Asn; Nat Criminal Justice Asn; 369th Veteran's Asn Inc; Phi Beta Sigma Fratenity Inc; adv bd mem, Tip Prog, 1990-; Acad Am Poets; Nat Asn Advan Colored People; bd dir, Southeast Bronx Neighborhood Ctr Inc; bd dir, Quality Vending Serv Inc. **Honors/Awds:** Poet of Year, J Marks Press, 1972; Award of Appreciation, Black Caucus DFY Empl Inc, 1984, 1987; Editor's Choice Award, Nat Libr Poetry, 1989; Whos Who in US Writers, Editors & Poets, 1998; Whos Who In America, 2005. **Military Serv:** USN, petty ofc 3rd class, 1964-68. **Home Phone:** (914)923-4119.

WINDHAM, RHONDA
Sports manager, athletic director. **Career:** Los Angeles Sparks, WNBA, gen mgr, 1999; Los Angeles Summer Showcase, Womens Summer Basketball League, league dir, currently. **Special Achievements:** WNBA's first Black general manager. **Business Addr:** League Director, Los Angeles Summer Showcase, PO Box 561278, Los Angeles, CA 90056, **Business Phone:** (323)295-7690.

WINE, DONALD GARY
Automotive executive. **Personal:** Born Aug 16, 1951, Benton, AR; son of James (deceased) and Margaret; married Dorothy, Jun 1, 1974; children: Donald II & Steven Gary. **Educ:** Wayne State Univ, lib arts, 1984; Cent Mich Univ, MBA, 1986. **Career:** Gen Motor Corp, prod mgr, 1991-92, actg plant mgr, 1992-94, plant mgr, 1994-95, Cadillac/Luxury Car Div, plant mgr, 1995-, Pontiac Metal Ctr, GM Fabricating Div, plant mgr, currently. **Orgs:** Bd dirs, City Ypsilanti Mich Chamber Com, 1992-93; bd dirs, Arlington Ind Sch, 1994-95; bd dirs, Longhorn Coun, Boy Scouts Am, 1994-95, exec bd, Detroit Coun, 1996; bd dirs, City Arlington, Tex, Chamber Com, 1994-; adv bd, Wayne State Univ, 1997. **Home Addr:** 27185 Pembridge St, Farmington Hills, MI 48331, **Home Phone:** (248)426-6679. **Business Addr:** Plant Manager, General Motors Corporation, Pontiac Metal Center, 220 E Columbia Ave, Pontiac, MI 48340-2857, **Business Phone:** (248)857-0938.

WINEGLASS, HENRY
Pharmacist. **Personal:** Born Sep 11, 1938, Georgetown, SC; son of Johnnie and Albertha Drayton Hasbin; married Josephine Arkwright, May 28, 1965; children: Vincent Antonio (deceased) & Sheri LaDonna. **Educ:** Howard Univ, Wash DC, BS, 1962. **Career:** Fantle's Drugstore, Landover Md, pharmacist, 1965-90; Safeway Pharm, pharmacist, 1990-. **Orgs:** Am Pharmaceut Asn, 1965-; Nat Pharmaceut Asn, 1965-; DC Pharmaceut Asn, 1965-; sec, Lambda Chap, Chi Delta Mu, 1976-94; secy, meeting planner, Chi Delta Mu Inc Grand Chap, 1981-92; Md Pharmacists Asn, 1982-; Nat Coalition Black Meeting Planners, 1986-89; sergeant-at-arms, Howard Univ Alumni Club, 1988-89; grand pres elect, 1992-94, grand pres, 1994-96, Grand chap, Chi Delta Mu Fraternity. **Honors/Awds:** Cert Appreciation, Lambda Chap, Chi Delta Mu, 1973 & 1985; Citation Appreciation, Dart Drug Prof Servs Dept, 1980; Cert Appreciation, Langdon Sch PTA, 1981; Doctor Pharm, Md Pharmacists Asn, 1982; Man Year, Lambda Chap, Chi Delta Mu, 1986; Cert Appreciation, Howard Univ Col Pharm & Pharmaceut Scis, 1987; Grand Pres's Award, Chi Delta Mu Grand Chap, 1988; Man Year, Plymouth Congregational UCC Men's Club, 1988. **Military Serv:** AUS, SP-5, 1961-64; hon discharge, 1967. **Home Addr:** 1509 Evarts St NE, Washington, DC 20018-2017. **Business Addr:** Pharmacist, Safeway Pharmacy, 5545 Connecticut Ave NW, Washington, DC 20015, **Business Phone:** (202)364-0320.

WINFIELD, ARNOLD F
Executive. **Personal:** Born Sep 29, 1926, Chicago, IL; married Florence Frye; children: Michael A & Donna Winfield-Terry. **Educ:** Howard Univ, BS, 1949; Wayne State Univ, Grad Study, biochem, 1949-51. **Career:** Executive (retired); Ordinance Corp, chemist, 1952-59, biochemist, 1969-71; Abbott Labs, reg prod mgr, 1953-71, Admin Consumer Div, mgr regulatory affairs, 1971-83; 2nd Ward Evanston, alderman, 1963-77; Winfield & Assoc, consult, 1983; Colfield Foods Inc, corp secy, 1983. **Orgs:** Nat Asn Advan Colored People; Urban League; Alpha Phi Alpha; Evanston Neighbors at Work; bd mem, Victory Gardens Theater, 1979-. **Honors/Awds:** Youth Alliance Scholar, 1943; Jr Chamber of Commerce Man of the Year, 1964; Service Award Ebenezer Church, 1966. **Military Serv:** AUS, PFC, 1945-46; WWII Victory Medal.

WINFIELD, DAVID MARK
Baseball player, baseball executive. **Personal:** Born Oct 3, 1951, St Paul, MN; son of Frank and Arline; married Tonya Turner, Feb 18, 1988; children: Shanel, Arielle & David Mark II. **Educ:** Univ Minn, Pol Sci, 1970-73. **Career:** Baseball player (retired), Baseball executive; San Diego Padres, outfielder, 1973-80; New York Yankees, outfielder, 1981-88, 1990; Calif Angels, outfielder, 1990-91; Toronto Blue Jays, outfielder, 1992; Minnesota Twins, outfielder, 1993-94; Cleveland Indians, outfielder, 1995; FOX-TV, analyst; San Diego Padres, vpres & sr adv, 2002-. **Orgs:** Sponsor & founder, David M Winfield Found; Oxford Rec Ctr. **Honors/Awds:** Outstanding Col Athlete, Attucks Brooks Am Legion, 1972; Outstanding Community Service, Am Legion; Nat League All-Star Team, 1977-80; Golden Glove Award, 1979, 1980, 1982-85, 1987; Silver Slugger Award, 1981-85, 1992; Branch Rickey Award, 1992; Roberto Clemente Award, 1994; Baseball Hall of Fame, 2001; Col Baseball Hall of Fame, 2006. **Business Addr:** Vice President, Senior Advisor, San Diego Padres, PO Box 122000, San Diego, CA 92112-2000, **Business Phone:** (619)795-5000.

WINFIELD, ELAYNE HUNT
Counselor. **Personal:** Born Feb 9, 1925, Waco, TX; married Walter Lee; children: Daryl Lynn & Kevin Ren. **Educ:** Paul Quinn Col, BS, 1954; Univ Tex, MA, 1975; Cert Educ Admin, 1977. **Career:** Midland TX, teacher, 1955-56; Odessa L/LD res teacher, teacher; Big Springs TX, teacher, 1957-58; Spec Educ Dept, Odessa, elem counsr; Ector Co PubSch, elem counsr, 1977; testing & measurement, dir, 1984-. **Orgs:** Bd dir, NEA 1976-79; Tex St Teacher Asn, Human Rel Com, 1974-78; Tex Ed Agency Eval Team, 1976; adj instr, Univ Tex Permian Basin, 1975; Alpha Kappa Alpha Sor; Am Asn Univ Women; Delta Kappa Gamma Soc; First vpres Qepa Kappa Chap, 1976-79; Phi Delta Kappa Frat. **Honors/Awds:** Outstanding Elementary Teachers of America, 1973; Odessa Classroom Teachers HR Award, 1974; TSTA Hum Rel Award 1974; Child Dev Profl. **Business Addr:** Director, Ector Co Independent School District, PO Box 3912, Odessa, TX 79762.*

WINFIELD, DR. LINDA FITZGERALD
Educator. **Personal:** Born Dec 9, 1948, Wilmington, DE; daughter of William L Fitzgerald and Bertha Mason Fitzgerald (deceased); divorced; children: Kenneth Jr & David. **Educ:** Univ Del, BA (hons) 1975, MA, 1981, PhD 1982. **Career:** New Castle County Sch Dist Consortium, supvr res, 1982-85; Educ Testing Serv, NAEP vis scholar, 1985-86; Temple Univ, asst prof educ, 1986-89; Temple & Johns Hopkins Univs, Baltimore, MD, Ctr Study Effective Sching Disadvantaged Students; Univ Calif, Los angeles, Grad Sch Educ, vis prof, 1989-, CRESST, res staff, currently. **Orgs:** Am Educ Res Assoc, 1977-; Nat Coun Measurement Educ; Phi Delta Kapp; Am Psychol Asn. **Honors/Awds:** Woman of the Year in Research, Nat Asn Univ Women, 1984; Distinguished Alumni Gallery, Univ Del, 1984; Minority Res Fel, Rockefeller Found, 1987; AERA Palmer O Johnson Memorial Award, 1992; co-dir, Congressionally mandated fed contract spec strategies educating disadvantaged students, co-director. **Special Achievements:** Published numerous articles including "Teachers' Beliefs Towards At-Risk Students in Inner Urban Schools", The Urban Review, 1987; "Teachers' Estimates of Content Covered and First Grade Reading Achievement". Elementary School Journal, 1987. **Business Phone:** (310)206-1532.

WINFIELD, SUSAN REBECCA HOLMES
Judge. **Personal:** Born Jun 13, 1948, East Orange, NJ; daughter of Thomas S Holmes and Mildred L Holmes; children: Jessica L & Heather B. **Educ:** Univ Penn, BA, math, 1970; Boston Col Law Sch, JD, 1976. **Career:** Law Off Salim R Shakur, assoc atty, 1976-78; Dept Justice, Criminal Div, staff atty, 1978-79; US Atty Off, asst US atty, 1979-84; DC Super Ct, assoc judge, 1984-90, Family Div, dep presiding judge, 1990-94, assoc judge, sr judge, currently; George Washington Univ, adj prof; Coloumbia Law Sch, adj prof; Harvard Univ, Trial Advocacy Prog, fac; Georgetown Med Sch, Psychiat Dept, fac. **Orgs:** Mass Bar Asn, 1976; DC Bar Asn, 1978; Asst US Atty's Asn, 1979-; Women's Bar Asn DC, 1984-; Am Judges Asn, 1984-; Nat Asn Women Judges, 1984; bd dir, Bar Asn DC, currently. **Honors/Awds:** Spec Achievement Award, Off US Atty, 1983-84; DC CASA Award, 1993; Certificate of Recognition, DC Coalition Against Domestic Violence, 1996. **Special Achievements:** Judge Winfield has co-authored several articles and book chapters on various subjects involving law and religion. **Business Addr:** Senior Judge, Superior Court of District of Columbia, Moultrie Courthouse 500 Ind Ave NW, Washington, DC 20001, **Business Phone:** (202)879-1272.

WINFIELD, THALIA BEATRICE
Executive, chief executive officer, president (organization). **Personal:** Born Oct 17, 1924, Surry, VA. **Educ:** VA State Univ, BS, 1947. **Career:** Executive, Chief executive officer, president (retired); Storer Col Harpers Ferry, secy to pres, 1947-49; Morehouse Col Atlanta, secy tobursar, 1949-54; Columbia savings & Loan Asn, pres & ceo, 1974-92. **Orgs:** Dir, Carter Child Develop Ctr, 1976-; trustee, Citizens for Govt Res Bur, 1977-; Christ Presby Church elder, 1978-, treas 1984; trustee, Presbytery of Milwaukee, 1984.

WINFIELD, WILLIAM T
President (Organization). **Personal:** Born Oct 24, 1944, Baton Rouge, LA; son of Leander Winfield Sr and Alice Simmons Winfield; married Rita Gurney; children: William Gurney, Darlene Teresa & Paul Tyrone. **Educ:** Southern Univ, attended; La State Univ, attended. **Career:** WT & Assocs Inc, Eng Firm, chief exec officer & municipal planning & zoning comnr, pres, currently. **Orgs:** Pres, First Ward Voters League; pres, Mid-City Hist Cemetary Coalition; pres, Sweet Olive African Am Hist Cemetary. **Honors/Awds:** Hon Dist Atty, 1973. **Special Achievements:** First Baton Rougean to participate in a Southern Univ cooperative program with NASA at the Marshall Space Flight Center; first African American employed in engineering in the industrial complexes of LA. **Home Phone:** (225)344-7584. **Business Addr:** President, W T & Associates Inc, 2622 N St, Baton Rouge, LA 70802, **Business Phone:** (225)883-0822.

WINFREY, AUDREY THERESA
Nurse. **Personal:** Born in Houston, TX; daughter of Arthur W and E Agatha McIntyre; divorced; children: Jennifer Holland. **Educ:** Grant Hosp, dipl, 1962; DePaul Univ, BSN, 1969, MSN, 1973; Univ Ill Sch Pub Health, MPH, 1976. **Career:** Nurse (retired). Chicago Health Dept, nurse, 1963-66; USAID Vietnam Bur, nurse adv, 1966-68; One Mile Square Health Ctr, pub health nurse, 1968-70; Michael Reese Med Ctr Sch Nursing, instr 1970-73; Univ Ill Col Nursing, instr, 1973-74; Chicago City Col, asst prof, 1974-77; Va Westside Med Ctr, coordr adm amb care nursing, 1977; Vet Admin Hosp, Chicago, IL, nurse specialist hosp base home care, 1987-90; US Postal Serv, Chicago, IL, indust nurse, 1988-90; Univ Illinois, Col Nursing, Chicago, researcher, 1988-90; Halsted Terrace, Nursing Home, Chicago, IL, supvr, 1988-90; Amb Care Clinics, primary nurse surg serv, 1990. **Orgs:** Zeta Phi Beta; Am Nursing Asn; Nat League Nurse; Am Pub Health Asn; DePaul Univ Alumni Asn; Univ Ill Alumni Asn; bd mem, Plano Child Develop Ctr, 1978-; Variety Club Children Charities, 1980-; St James Cath Church, 1986-; mem comt, Women Achievement, 1987-; planning bd, VIA; Nat Black Nurses Asn. **Honors/Awds:** Civilian Govt Award; Medal of Achievement; Recog Award; Volunteer Service Award, Plano Child Develop Ctr, 1983; CAH-MCP Recognition Award, Ill Inst Technol, 1982. **Special Achievements:** published article: "Maximum Amount of Medication: How Much Is Too Much Injected into One Site" Nursing, July 1985; Published article w/ Dr Eva D Smith of U of I, College of Nursing "Church Based Hypertension Education Prgram," 1990. **Military Serv:** AUS Nurse Corp, Reserve, bird colonel, 1973-98, chief nurse of the 395th CSH (HUS). *

WINFREY, CHARLES EVERETT
Clergy, educator. **Personal:** Born Mar 6, 1935, Brighton, TN; married Ernestine. **Educ:** Lane Col, BA, 1961; Vanderbilt Univ, MDiv, 1964; Univ Tenn, MS, 1974. **Career:** Graham Chapel CME Church Savannah, 1958-61; W Jackson Circuit CME, 1961-64; Phillips Chapel CME Church Nashville, minister 1964-65; CME Church Nashville, minister Capers Mem 1965-; Metro Pub Sch Nashville, eng teacher, 1966; Phillips Chapel CME Church, pastor, 2001. **Orgs:** Ad Hoc Comt; Kappa Alpha Psi; Nat Educ Asn; Metrop Act Comn; MNEA; dean leadership training Nashville-Clarksville Dist CME Church. **Honors/Awds:** Rel Man of Yr, Kappa Alpha Psi, 1971; Good Conduct Award, USMC, 1954; chaplain St Sen, 1973; Hon Sgt-at-Arms, St Leg, 1974. **Military Serv:** USMC sgt 1950-54. **Business Addr:** 319 15 Ave N, Nashville, TN.

WINFREY, OPRAH
Television producer, entrepreneur, television talk show host. **Personal:** Born Jan 29, 1954, Kosciusko, MS; daughter of Vernon and Vernita Lee. **Educ:** Tenn State Univ, BA, speech, drama. **Career:** WVOL Radio Station, news reporter, 1971-72; WTVF-TV, reporter, newsanchorperson, 1973-76; WJZ-TV, news anchorperson, 1976-78, host morningtalk show "People Are Talking", 1978-83; WLS-TV, host talk show "AMChicago", 1984; Oprah Winfrey Show, host, 1985-, Nat syndication, 1986-;Harpo Prods, owner, producer, 1986-; Eccentric Restaurant, owner,currently; Oprah & Friends, owner, currently; host, supervising producer:series celebrity interview spec, including: "Oprah: Behind Scenes," 1992;ABC Aftersch Specs, 1991-93; host, exec producer: "Michael Jackson TalksTo Oprah, 90 Prime-Time Minutes With King Pop," 1993; films: Color Purple,actress, 1985; Native Son, actress, 1986; Ellen, actress, 1997; Beloved,actress, co-author, 1998; Our Friend, Martin, actress, 1999; Charlotte'sWeb, actress, 2006; The Great Debaters, 2007; Bee Movie, actress, 2007;co-author: "You Make Connection", 1997; "You Make Connection", home video,prod, host, 1997; Our Friend, Martin, 1999; Charlotte's Web, 2006; TV:"The Oprah Winfrey Show", 1986-2008; "The Women of Brewster Place",actress, 1989; "Brewster Place", actress, 1990; "Lincoln", actress, 1992;"ABC Afterschool Specials", 1993; "There are no Children Here", actress,1993; "Shades of a Single Protein", 1993; "Nine", 1992; "Overexposed",1992; "Before Women Had Wings", 1997; "The Wedding", 1998; "David & Lisa",1998; "Tuesdays with Morrie", 1999; "Amy & Isabelle", 2001; "Oprah Afterthe Show", 2002; "Entertainment Tonight", 2003-08; "Larry King Live",2003-07; "Their Eyes Were Watching God", 2005; "Emmanuel's Gift",narrator, 2005; "36th NAACP Image Awards", 2005; "Signe Chanel", 2005;"Late Show with David Letterman", 2005; "Corazon de..", 2005; "TheKennedy Center Honors: A Celebration of the Performing Arts", 2005;"Legends Ball", 2006; "Inside Edition", 2006; "The 2006 Black MovieAwards", 2006; "Rachael Ray", 2006; "Forbes Celebrity 100: Who MadeBank?", 2006; "The 60th Annual Tony Awards", 2006; "Legends Ball", 2006;"Showbiz Tonight", 2006; "Oprah Winfrey Presents: Mitch Album's For One More Day", 2007; "Building a Dream: The Oprah Winfrey Leadership Academy", 2007; "The Oprah Winfrey Oscar Special", 2007; "The Big Give", 2007; "Larry King Live: The Greatest Interviews", 2007; "Charlotte's Web: Some Voices", 2007; "Building a Dream: The Oprah Winfrey Leadership Academy", 2007; "Film '72", 2007; "Oprah's Roots: An African American Lives Special", 2007; "The Insider", 2008; "We Have a Dream", 2008; "Forbes 20 Richest Women in Entertainment", 2007; "Ocean's Thirteen", 2007; "Oprah Winfrey", 2007. **Orgs:** South Africa's Zulu Nation. **Honors/Awds:** Woman of Achievement Award, 1986; Emmy Award, Best Daytime Talk Show Host,1987, 1991, 1992, 1998; America's Hope Award, 1990; Industry Achievement Award, Broadcast Promotion Mkt Execs/Broadcast Design Asn, 1991; Broadcaster of the Year, Intl Radio & TV Soc, 1988; Image Awards, Nat Asn Advan Colored People, 1989-92; Entertainer of the Year Award, Nat Asn Advan Colored People, 1989; CEBA Awards, 1989-91; Academy Award & Golden Globe Award nominee, The Color Purple, 1985; Television Academy Hall of Fame; Daytime Emmy Awards, Lifetime Achievement Award, 1998; 50th Anniversary Gold Medal, Nat Book Awards, 1999; Bob Hope Humanitarian Award; Emmy Awards, 2002; Marian Anderson Award, 2003; Outstanding Community Service Award, Nat Urban League, 2003. **Special Achievements:** First black woman named to Forbes magazine's billionaire list, 2003; Publishes two magazines: O, The Oprah Magazine & O at Home; Richest African American of the 20th century; Named to the list of Greatest Chicagoans of the Century. **Home Addr:** 35 E Wacker Dr Suite 1782, Chicago, IL 60601, **Home Phone:** (312)591-9222. **Business Addr:** Owner, Producer & Actress, Harpo Productions, 110 N Carpenter St, Chicago, IL 60607-2101, **Business Phone:** (312)633-1000.

WING, PROF. ADRIEN KATHERINE
Educator. **Personal:** Born Aug 7, 1956, Oceanside, CA; daughter of Dr John E and Katherine P Wing; divorced; children: Willie, Brooks, Charles, Che & Nolan. **Educ:** Princeton Univ, AB, 1978; Univ Calif, Los Angeles, MA, 1979; Stanford Law Sch, JD, 1982. **Career:** Upward Bound, Univ Calif, Los Angeles, teacher & counr, 1979; Rosenfeld, Meyer & Susman, law clerk, 1980; United Nations, intern, 1981; Curtis,Mallet, et al, lawyer, 1982-86; Rabinowitz, Boudin, et al, lawyer, 1986-87; Univ Iowa Law Sch, prof law, 1987, Bessie Dutton Murray Prof & assoc dean fac develop, currently; Iowa-France, dir summer abroad prog, 2000-; Univ Mich Law Sch, vis prof, 2002. **Orgs:** Bd dirs, Nat Black Law Students Asn, 1981-82; Asn Black Princeton Alumni Bd, 1982-87; int chair, Nat Conf Black Lawyers, 1985-95; Palestine Human Rights Campaigns Bd, 1986-91; Am Soc Int Law Exec Coun, 1986-89, 1996-99, exec comt, 1998-99; Iowa City Foreign Rels Coun Bd, 1989-94; Transafrica Forum Scholars Coun, 1993-95; bd visitors, Stanford Law Sch, 1993-96; life mem, Coun Foreign Rel, 1993-; Iowa Peace Inst Bd, 1993-95; chair, Am Soc Int Law, Southern Africa Interest Group, 1994-95; Princeton Alumni Coun, 1996-2000; Int Third World Legal Studies Asn Bd, 1996-; Am Asn Law Schs Minority Sect Exec Comt, 1997-2002, chair, 2002; Princeton Comn Nominate Trustees, 1997-2000; Am Friends Serv Comn; Mid E Progs Bd, 1998-; Am Asn Law Schs Africa sect exec comn, 2000-; Princeton African Am Studies Adv Coun, 2000-; Princeton Exec Comn Alumni Coun, 2002-04; Am Bar Asn Law Sch Site Inspector, 2002-; Am Bar Asn; Am Br Int Law Asn; Nat Bar Asn; Soc Am Law Teachers; bd ed, Am Jour Comp Law; vpres, Am Soc Int Law, 2007-09; mem, Univ Iowa's interdisciplinary African Studies faculty. **Honors/Awds:** Numerous honors & awards including: Hope Stevens Award, Nat Conference Black Lawyers, 1988; Haywood Burns-Shanara Gilbert Award, 1997; Bessie Dutton Murray Distinguished Prof Law, 2001. **Special Achievements:** Over 90 publications including: editor, Global Critical Race Feminism: An International Reader, NYU, 2000; Critical Race Feminism: A Reader, NYU, Second Edition, 2003; Languages: French, Swahili, Portuguese. **Business Addr:** Bessie Dutton Murray Professor, Associate Dean for Faculty Development, The University of Iowa, College of Law, 410 Boyd Law Bldg, Iowa City, IA 52242-1113.

WING, THEODORE W
Executive, artist. **Personal:** Born Jul 12, 1948, Philadelphia, PA; son of Theodore W and Mardie Phillip; married Denise; children: Hillary Allen Theodore. **Educ:** Howard Univ, BA, 1970; Syracuse Univ, MS, 1972; Temple Univ, REL, 1981; George Wash Univ, MCPM, 1991; St Joseph's Univ, MS, 1997. **Career:** Executive (retired); White House, special asst vpres, 1970-71; Howard Univ, Wash, DC, special asst pres, 1971-72; Commonwealth Pa, Harrisburg, Pa, prin, 1972-74; City Philadelphia, Philadelphia, Pa, dir fed funding & youth prog, 1974-78; AT &T Fed Syst, 1978-91; City Philadelphia, dep comnr, 1991-92; Ray Commun, vpres; Prime Building Corp, dir; Theodore W Wing Productions, founder & prin, currently. **Orgs:** Pres, Howard Univ Alumni Club, 1978-81; pres, Philadelphia Sch Syst, Day Care Ctr, 1979-81; dir, Downtown Indust Sch, 1981-83; chmn, Boys & Girls Clubs, Philadelphia, 1989-91; dir, Tender Care Inc, Philadelphia, 1989-91; founder, Syracuse Challenger Newspaper; educ hon soc, Kappa Delta Pi; founder, Media Charter Sch K-7 grades. **Honors/Awds:** Outstanding Youth, John Wanamaker, 1970; Alumni Award, Howard Univ, 1986; Ben Franklin Award, Philadelphia Free Libr, 1987; Trustee Award, Bennet Col, 1988; President's Award, Univ Md, 1990. **Special Achievements:** Author, "Urban Education from the Bedlands to the Classroom;" Winner of numerous awards & fellowships, public speaker, involved with several movie and tv productions & author of many scholarly papers. **Business Addr:** Founder, Principal, Theodore W Wing Productions, 2412 N 54th St, Philadelphia, PA 19131, **Business Phone:** (215)477-6100.

WINGATE, DAVID GROVER STACEY
Basketball player. **Personal:** Born Dec 15, 1963, Baltimore, MD; married Tyra Holland; children: Howard senior Brandie Wingate, Bryce & Brittney. **Educ:** Georgetown Univ, attended. **Career:** Basketball player (retired); Philadelphia 76ers, guard forward, 1986-89; San Antonio Spurs, 1989-91; Washington Bullets, 1991; Charlotte Hornets, 1992-95; Seattle Supersonics, 1995-98; New York Knicks, 1999-2000; Seattle Super Sonics, 2001.

WINGATE, DR. JAMES G
President (Organization). **Educ:** Allen Univ, BS, chem & math; New York State Univ, MS, cert advan studies; Syracuse Univ, PhD, educ admin & supv. **Career:** Winston-Salem State Univ, exec asst to chancellor; of LeMoyne-Owen Col, TN, pres. *

WINGFIELD, DONTONIO
Basketball player. **Personal:** Born Jun 23, 1974, Albany, GA. **Educ:** Univ Cincinnati. **Career:** Basketball Player (retired); Seattle SuperSonics, forward, 1994-95; Portland TrailBlazers, forward, 1995-98; Toronto Raptors, 1995.

WINGFIELD, DR. HAROLD LLOYD
Educator. **Personal:** Born Sep 22, 1942, Danville, VA. **Educ:** Fisk Univ, BA, 1970; Univ Ore, MA, 1973, PhD, 1982. **Career:** Sonoma State Univ, vis asst prof, 1976-77; Tenn State Univ, vis asst prof,1977-78; Ariz State Univ, vis instr, 1979-80; Univ Rhode Island, vis asst prof, 1980-84; Kennesaw State Univ, Dept Polit Sci

& Int Affairs, from asst prof to assoc prof, 1985-98, prof, 1999-. **Orgs:** Am Polit Sci Asn; Western Polit Sci Asn; Southern Polit Sci Asn; Nat Conf Black Polit Scientists; Nat Asn Advan Colored People; Am Civil Liberties Union; Common Cause, People Am Way; Ga State Democratic Comm; elected, Polk Sch District Bd Educ. **Honors/Awds:** Philip Preston Community Leadership Award, Kennesaw State Univ, 2003. **Special Achievements:** Author with W Jones and A Nelson, "Black Ministers, Roles, Behavior, and Congregation Expectations," Western Journal of Black Studies, 1979;Author: "The Historical and Changing Role of the Black Church: The Social and Political Implication," Western Journal of Black Studies, 1988. **Military Serv:** AUS, 1967-69. **Business Addr:** Professor, Kennesaw State University, Department of Political Science & International Affairs, 1000 Chastain Rd SO 5046, Kennesaw, GA 30144-5591.

WINGO, A. GEORGE
Government official, air force officer. **Personal:** Born Dec 24, 1929, Detroit, MI; married Helen B Glassco; children: Alicia, Scott Andre. **Educ:** Ohio State Univ, attended 1957; Oakland Univ, attended 1970; Dept Defense Sch. **Career:** Defense Construct Supply Ctr, commodity mgr, 1960-64; Tank Automotive Mich, systs analyst, 1966-74; Wright Patterson Air Force Base, Ohio, country mgr, 1974-75; Eglin Air Force Base, Ohio, foreign mil sales mgr, 1976; USAF, prog mgr; Systs Eng & Mgt Co, support equip mgr. **Orgs:** Announcer, Mid Ohio Asn; Citizens Coun, 1968-72. **Honors/Awds:** Father of the Yr, New Haven Sch, 1973. **Military Serv:** AUS, corpl, 1951-54.

WINGO, ROBERT V
Executive. **Educ:** Univ Tex El Paso, BBA, 1973. **Career:** Sanders/Wingo Advert Inc, pres & chief exec officer, 1983-; Valcent Products Inc, bd dir; customer serv officer, asst nat sales mgr, vpres advt & sales. **Honors/Awds:** Gold Nugget Award, Univ Tex El Paso, Col Bus Admin, 2002. **Home Addr:** 1021 Los Jardines Circle, El Paso, TX 79912, **Home Phone:** (915)584-4000. **Business Addr:** President, Chief Executive Officer, Sanders/Wingo Advertising Inc., 221 N Kans Suite 900 9th Fl, El Paso, TX 79901, **Business Phone:** (915)533-9583.

WINLEY, DIANE LACEY
Hospital administrator, clergy, interior designer. **Personal:** Born in New York, NY; daughter of William and Esther Jackson; married Ronald. **Educ:** Univ Conn, Storrs, CT, BA, 1960; New York Theol Sem, MDIV, 1994. **Career:** Hunts Point Multi-Serv Compre Health Ctr, dir, 1968-70; City of New York, spl asst mayor, 1970-71; John Hay Whitney Ford Found, grantee, 1971-73; New York City Health Hosp Corp, asst pres, 1974-76; Sydenham Hosp, dir patient rels & vol serv, 1977-78; Radio Station WWRL AM, dir pub affairs, 1978-81; United Church of Spring Valley, assoc pastor, 1994-; Wellness Ctr, the Riverside Church, dir, 1996-; Spirit Landscapes & Interiors, pres. **Orgs:** Organizer, First Nat Conf Drug Abuse Policy Minority Leaders, 1972; John Hay Whitney Found, 1973-74; fel, Revson Found, 1981-82; bd dir, New York City Health Hosp Corp, 1982-; New York City exec dir, Physicians Social Responsibility, 1986-88; fel, Ellen Lurie Distinguished Serv, Community Serv Soc, 1988; founding mem, Asn Black Social Workers; candidate, State Leg. **Honors/Awds:** Twice Elected Dem Dist Leader.

WINN, CAROL DENISE
Television director, television producer. **Personal:** Born Mar 18, 1962, San Francisco, CA; daughter of Edward Jr and Mae Willie Baskins. **Educ:** SF State Univ, San Francisco, CA, 1980-83; Howard Univ, Wash, DC, BA, 1987. **Career:** WJLA TV Ch 7, Wash, DC, news asst, 1986-87; KBHK TV, San Francisco, CA, admn asst pres & insurance claims admn, 1987-88, assoc producer & dir, 1988-89, producer & dir, 1989-. **Orgs:** Recording secy, Bay Area Black Journalists Asn, 1989-90, scholar chair, 1990-91, prog chair, 1991-92. **Home Addr:** 2658 San Jose Ave, San Francisco, CA 94112-3027. **Business Addr:** Producer/Director, KBHK-TV, 650 California St 6th fl, San Francisco, CA 94108, **Business Phone:** (415)249-4444.

WINN, DWIGHT RANDOLPH. See WINN, RANDY.

WINN, JOAN T.
Lawyer, real estate agent. **Personal:** Born Apr 11, 1942, Dallas, TX; divorced; children: Elbert Ikoyi. **Educ:** Dillard Univ, BA, 1962; S Methodist Univ, JD, 1968. **Career:** Durham & Winn Dallas, atty, 1968-70; US Dept Labor & Off Solicitor, Dallas, trial atty, 1970-73; Fed Appeals Auth US Civil Serv Comn, asst appeals officer, 1973-75; Danas Co Ct Law No 2, judge, 1975-78; 191st St Judicial Dist Ct, judge, 1978-80; Honeymill & Gunn Realty Co Inc, pres. **Orgs:** St Bar TX, Am Bar Asn, Dallas Bar Asn, JL Turner Legeau Soc, Delta Sigma Theta, The Links Inc Dallas Chap. **Honors/Awds:** Woman of the Yr, Zeta Phi Beta, 1978; Women Helping Women Award, 1980; Women in Business, Iota Phi Lambda, 1986.

WINN, RANDY (DWIGHT RANDOLPH WINN)
Baseball player. **Personal:** Born Jun 9, 1974, Los Angeles, CA; son of Damon Buford. **Educ:** Santa Clara Univ. **Career:** Tampa Bay Devil Rays, 1998-02; Seattle Mariners, 2003-05; San

Francisco Giants, left wing & ctr-forward, 2006-09. **Honors/Awds:** All-WCC hons, 1995; All Star Selection, 2002; NBA Most Valuable Player, 2005. *

WINNINGHAM, HERMAN S., JR.
Baseball player. **Personal:** Born Dec 1, 1961, Orangeburg, SC; son of Rev Sr and Lucille Brizz; married Jane Moorman, Jan 20, 1990; children: Kevin A. **Educ:** S COT Col. **Career:** Baseball player (retired); New York Mets, Outfielder, 1984; Montreal Expos, 1984-88; Cincinnati Reds, 1988-91; Boston Red Sox, 1992. **Home Addr:** 1542 Belleville Rd, Orangeburg, SC 29115. *

WINSLOW, CLETA MERIS
City council member, government official. **Personal:** Born Jul 18, 1952, Rockford, IL. **Educ:** Tenn State Univ, BS Social Work, 1973; Atlanta Univ Sch Social Work, MS, 1975. **Career:** Vanderbilt Univ Res Ctr, psychotherapist social worker's aide, 1972-73; Atlanta Univ Sch Social Work, res asst, 1974; Morehouse Col Pub Rels, secy, 1975-76; Carrie Steele Pitts C's Home, chief social worker, 1976-79; Fulton Co Bd Comnr, admin asst; City Atlanta, Neighborhood Planning Unit, coordr; City Atlanta, Dist 4, city coun mem, currently. **Orgs:** Chair, West End Neighborhood Dev Inc, 1977-; Nat Assoc Neighborhoods; bd, Christian Coun Church, 1983-; W End Parents Action Youth Anti-Drug, 1985-; Nat treas, Delta Sigma Theta, 1985-; bd, Boatrock Family Serv Ctr; bd Ment Health Ment Retardation, 1985; Joel Chandler Harris Asn, 1986-; Brown HS PTSA Magnet Prog & Voc Adv Coun, 1986-; Black Women's Coalition, 1987-. **Honors/Awds:** Outstanding Young Women America, 1981, 1983; Citywide Neighborhood Service Award, Urban Life Asn, 1983; Movers & Shakers Atlanta Atlanta Const Newspaper, 1984; Outstanding Vol Service, EducAPPLE Corps; Award for Volume Service, HS PTSA, 1986; Certificate of Appreciation, Fulton Co Employees Asn. **Business Addr:** City Council Member, City of Atlanta, 55 Trinity Ave SW, Atlanta, GA 30303, **Business Phone:** (404)330-6047.

WINSLOW, KELLEN BOSWELL
Football player, football executive. **Personal:** Born Nov 5, 1957, St Louis, MO; married Katrina McKnight; children: Kellen II. **Educ:** Univ Mo, BS, coun psychol; Univ San Diego, LLB. **Career:** Football player (retired), Football executive; San Diego Chargers, tightend, 1979-87; Fox Sports Net, football announcer, 1998-; Cent State Univ, dir athletics & stud wellness, 2008-. **Orgs:** Comnr, Kellen Winslow Flag Football League, 1982; San Diego Police Deptres prog. **Honors/Awds:** All-Am; first team All-Pro, 1980-82; Most Valuable Player, Co-Pro Bowl, 1981; Offensive Player of the Game, Pro Bowl, 1981; Pro Football Hall Fame, 1995; Col Football Hall Fame, 2002; All-Time Team, Nat Football League 75th Anniversary . **Business Addr:** Director of Athletics and Student Wellness, Central State University, 1400 Brush Row Rd, PO Box 1004, Wilberforce, OH 45384, **Business Phone:** (937)376-6011.

WINSLOW, KENNETH PAUL
Investment banker. **Personal:** Born Jul 22, 1949, Chicago, IL; son of Eugene and Rose Rieras. **Educ:** Univ Ill, BA, 1971; Harvard Grad Sch Bus Admin, MBA, 1976; New York Univ, Advan Prof Cert, 1987. **Career:** Harvard Grad Sch Bus Admin, fac res asst; Fed Deposit Ins corp, asst examr, 1972-74; Harvard Univ, res asst, 1976-77; NY Chem Bank, Corp Finance Dept, vpres, 1978-87; Benefit Capital Southwest Inc, staff, 1988-89, pres, 1989-. **Orgs:** ESOP Asn, 1985-; Nat Ctr Employee Ownership, 1985-. **Business Phone:** (214)991-3767.

WINSLOW, REYNOLDS BAKER
Administrator. **Personal:** Born Jul 25, 1933, Auburn, NY; son of George M and Mary Baker; married Ovetra Russ; children: Reynolds, Danielle Winslow, Christopher & Ericka. **Educ:** Syracuse Univ, BID, 1961. **Career:** Administrator (retired); Thomas L Faul Assoc, Skaneateles NY, indust designer, 1962-63; Crouse Hinds Co, indust designer, 1963-69; Gen Elec Co, indust designer, 1969-75; Syracuse Univ, minority eng prog coord, 1976-83; Univ Mass Col Eng, dir Minority Eng Prog, 1983. **Orgs:** Allocation panel United Way Cent NY, 1980-82; bd dirs, Univ Mass Comn Collegiate Educ Blacks & Minorities, 1983-; bd dirs, Mass Pre-Eng Prog, 1984-; reg chair Nat Asn Minority Eng Prog Adminrs, 1985-86; nat treas Nat Asn Minority Eng Prog Admin, 1986-89; vpres, NAACP, 1989-91, pres, 1991-; Western Mass Coun, Girl Scouts Am, nomin comm, bd mem, 1994-98; bd mem, Roots Int, Univ Mass, 1993-; bd mem, Amherst Area Educ Alliance, 1994-; Human Rights Commission (Amherst). **Honors/Awds:** Achievement Recognition Award, United Way Cent NY, 1980; Silver Beaver Award, Boy Scouts Am, 1980; Service to Youth Award, YMCA, 1980; Syracuse Univ Advocacy Award, Off Minority Affairs, 1981; Dean's Award, 1987; Chancellor's Award, Community Service, 1997; MLK Community Award, 1997. **Military Serv:** AUS, artillery sgt, 2 yrs; Nat Defense Medal. **Home Addr:** 1040 N Pleasant St Suite 219, Amherst, MA 01002, **Home Phone:** (413)549-2770.

WINSTEAD, DR. VERNON A, SR.
Lawyer, executive, social worker. **Personal:** Born Sep 15, 1937, Roxboro, NC; married Claudette McFarland; children: Vernon Jr & Claudette. **Educ:** NC Central Univ, BS & BA, sociol & health

educ, LLB, 1962; Univ Ill, MSW, 1969, AM 1971, PhD, 1972. **Career:** NC Dept Pub Aid, social worker, 1962-63; NC Redevelop Comn, relocation & contract spec, 1963-65; US Labor Dept Manpower Admin, manpower devel specialist, 1965-83; VAW Indust Inc, labor rel specialist; consult; arbitrator; Winstead Rest & Convalescent Homes, Durham NC, co-owner. **Orgs:** Nat Asn Advan Colored People; Nat Educ Asn; Nat Conf Black Lawyers; Nat Bar Asn; SE Kiwanis, South Shore Ministerial Asn; Bravo Chap Chicago Lyric Opera, Male Affiliate; life mem Nat Coun Negro Women; life mem Alpha Phi Alpha; South Shore Community; Joint Negro Appeal; chair St Philip Neri Parish Sch Bd; pres, S Shore Econ Develop Community; found, exec co-dir, Connecting Link, McFarland-Winstead Conf Ctr; found, asst ed, Chicago S Shore Scene Newspaper. **Honors/Awds:** Outstanding Leadership Award, Danforth Found; Monarch Award for public service, Alpha Kappa Alpha, 1991. **Home Addr:** 7433 S Constance Ave, Chicago, IL 60649. **Business Addr:** Labor Relations Specialist, VAW Industries Inc, 7433 Constance, Chicago, IL 60649-3609, **Business Phone:** (773)643-0939.

WINSTON, BONNIE VERONICA
Journalist. **Personal:** Born Mar 13, 1957, Richmond, VA. **Educ:** Northwestern Univ, BSJ, 1978. **Career:** Southern Illinoisan, reporting intern, 1976; Richmond Va Times-Dispatch, reporting intern, 1977; Huntington WVa Advertiser, reporting intern, 1978; Richmond Va Times-Dispatch, reporter, 1979-86; Boston Globe, state house bur reporter, 1986-. **Orgs:** Minority journalist-in-residence, Tougaloo Col Am Soc Newspaper Eds, 1980; bd dir, Va Press Women Nat Fed Press Women, 1982-86; stringer, NY Times, 1983-86; bd dir, Richmond Chap Sigma Delta Chi, Soc Prof Journalists, 1983-86; planning comn, staff mem, Urban Jour Workshop, 1984-85; Nat Asn Black Journalists, 1985-; free-lance writer, Black Engr Mag, 1986-. **Honors/Awds:** National Achievement Award, Northwestern Univ, 1974; Alpha Lambda Delta Hon Soc, Northwestern Univ, 1975; Outstanding Young Women in America Award, 1982; Achievement Award, Miles W Conner Chap, Va Union, Univ Alumni Asn, 1982; First Place, Va Press Asn Writing Contest, VPA, 1983; United Press International Best Writing Award, United Press Int, VA, 1983. **Business Addr:** State House Bureau Reporter, The Boston Globe, 135 Morrissey Blvd, PO Box 55819, Boston, MA 02121.*

WINSTON, GEORGE B, III
Computer executive. **Personal:** Born Feb 16, 1943, Richmond, VA; son of George B Jr and Gertrude B. **Educ:** Hampton Inst, BS, 1965; Univ Del, MBA, 1972. **Career:** Wilmington Trust Co, 1968-72; GBW Inc, 1972-73; Del State Banking Comn, 1973-75; Bank Am Commercial Corp, vpres, 1975-82; GBW Int Comput Prod, pres, 1983-. **Orgs:** Pres, Wilmington Chap Hampton Alumni, 1987-98; secy, Monday Club, 1991-01; bd mem, Better Bus Bur, 1993-; Nu Upsilon Chap. **Honors/Awds:** MBE Service Award, Del Minority Business, 1985; Nu Upsilon Chapter of Omega Psi Phi, Entrepreneurship Award, 1987; Independence Blue Cross Vendor Excellence Award, 2000. **Business Addr:** President, GBW International Computer Products, PO Box 888, Wilmington, DE 19899, **Business Phone:** (302)658-1315.

WINSTON, HATTIE
Actor. **Personal:** Born Mar 3, 1945, Lexington, MS; married Harold Wheeler; children: Samantha. **Educ:** Howard Univ, grad; Group Theatre Workshop, New York. **Career:** Films: Uns et les autres, Les, 1981; Without a Trace, 1983; A Show of Force, 1990; Beverly Hills Cop III, 1994; Sunset Park, 1996; Jackie Brown, 1997; Meet the Deedles, 1998; Living Out Loud, 1998; The Rugrats The Movie (voice), 1998; Unbowed, 1999; True Crime, 1999; The Battle of Shaker Heights, 2003; Death dealer: A Documentary, 2004; TV series: "The Electric Company", 1973-77; Ann in Blue, 1974; Out to Lunch, 1974; "The DainCurse", 1978; Hollow Image, 1979; "3-2-1 Contact", 1980; Nurse, 1980; "Unset lesautres, Les", 1983; "Home front", 1991; "One Woman's Courage", 1994; "The Cherokee Kid", 1996; "Port Charles", 1997; "Becker", 1998-2004; "Port Charles", 1997; "To Tell the Truth", 2000; Scrubs, 2002-04; "My Old Man", 2002; "Chock Full O'Nuts", 2003; "Twas the Night", 2004; "With a Twist", 2005; Girlfriends, 2005; "Numb3rs", 2008; "The Game", 2008; "Cold Case", 2009. **Orgs:** Co-chairperson, AFTRA's Equal Employ Opportunities Comm. **Honors/Awds:** Hattie Winston Day, Nat Black Theater Festival NC, named in honor, 1993, 1997. **Business Addr:** Actress, Pakula/King & Associates, 9229 W Sunset Blvd Suite 315, Los Angeles, CA 90069, **Business Phone:** (310)281-4866.*

WINSTON, DR. HUBERT
Executive director, chemical engineer, educator. **Personal:** Born May 29, 1948, Washington, DC; son of Hubert and Helen Simmons Vincent. **Educ:** NC State Univ, BS, 1970, MS, 1973, PhD, chem eng, 1975. **Career:** NC State Univ, Dept Chem Eng, asst prof, 1975-77, Undergrad Admin, Dept Chem Eng, assoc prof chem eng, 1983-86, Col Eng, dir acad affairs, 1985-86; Exxon Prod Res Co, res specialist, 1977-83; NC State Univ, Biomanufacturing Training & Educ Ctr, exec asst dir, currently. **Orgs:** Am Inst Chem Engrs; Nat Org Prof Adv Black Chemists & Chem Engrs; Eng-in-Training State NC. **Military Serv:** USAR, capt, 1974. **Home Addr:** 4412 Seaforth Ct, Raleigh, NC 27606.

WINSTON, JANET E.
Commissioner. **Personal:** Born Feb 7, 1937, Morristown, NJ; married Shurney Winston II; children: Shurney III. **Career:** Ernes-

tine McClendon Agency, prof model, 1960-65; Belafonte Enterprises, secy & recpt, 1960-61; Music Corp Am, secy to vpres, 1961-62; Johnson Publicity Co, Ebony fashion fair model, 1963-64; Janet Winston Charm Sch, owner & dir, 1966-70; Winston's Taxi Serv, owner, 1970-72; Winston's Family Tree Bar Club, owner; Morristown Housing Authority, comnr, 1972-91. **Orgs:** Pres, Morris Co Urban League Guild, 1967-68; bd dir, Morristown Neighborhood House; vol, Morristown Memorial Hosp, 1975-76.

WINSTON, JEANNE WORLEY
School administrator. **Personal:** Born May 27, 1941, Washington, DC; daughter of Gordon Sr and Rosetta Curry; married Reuben Benjamin; children: Kimberly L, Kandace J, Kia L & Reuben B II. **Educ:** Dist Columbia Teachers Col, BS, elem educ, 1963; George Wash Univ, MA, elem admin, 1967; Univ Wash, DC & Maryland Univ, admin post masters, 1978. **Career:** Dist Columbia Pub Schs, teacher, 1963-67, grade chairperson, 1965-, supv instr, 1967-69, teacher, 1969-76, actg asst prin, 1976-77, staff devel co-ord, 1977-86, competence based curriculum comt chairperson, 1977, teacher, 1977-88, teacher's conv bldg coord, 1984, AIMS coord, 1985, residential supvry support prog, 1985, math, sci minorities prog, 1985, mentors prog, 1986; Dist Columbia Alliance Black Sch Educ, res comt mem, 1984-; Dist Columbia Pub Schs, Brightwood Elem, Wash, DC, asst prin, 1988. **Orgs:** Delta Sigma Theta, 1960-; PTA, 1963-; Gethsemane Baptist Church, 1966-; NAACP, 1969-; Geo Wash Alumni Asn, 1970-; Wash Teachers Union, 1970-; Urban League, 1975-; vol, Annual Toy Dr Brookland Sch, 1980-; Nat Coun Negro Women, 1980; Dist Columbia Asn Retarded Citizens, 1980-; Dist Columbia Govt Employees Recreation Asn, 1985-; congributor walk-a-thon participant, March Dimes, 1985-; vol, Dist Columbia Village, 1986-, c, 1986-; Dist Columbia Asn Supv Curric Develop, 1986-. **Honors/Awds:** Outstanding Teacher, Truesdell Elem Sch, 1975; Outstanding Teacher, Res Club Wash, DC, 1975; Exemplary Service, Region B, Dist Columbia Pub Schs, 1988. **Home Addr:** 1930 Kearney St NE, Washington, DC 20018, **Home Phone:** (202)635-8061.

WINSTON, JOHN H., JR.
Physician. **Personal:** Born Aug 7, 1928, Montgomery, AL; married Bertha Moore; children: Georgette, Joni Winston Canty, Diva Dotson, Terri. **Educ:** Ala State Univ, BS, 1949; Columbia Univ, MA, 1951; Meharry Med Col, MD, 1956. **Career:** Physician, pvt pract, currently. **Orgs:** Am Col Surgeons; Am Med Asn; Nat Med Asn; bd mem, Young Men's Christian Asn; Montogmery County Bd Educ; Red Cross. **Military Serv:** USAF. **Home Addr:** 1521 Robert Hatch Dr, Montgomery, AL 36106. **Business Addr:** Physician, Private Practice, 1156 Oak St, Montgomery, AL 36108.

WINSTON, LAMONTE
Sports manager. **Personal:** Born Apr 10, 1959, Oakland, CA; son of Henry C and Georgia R Winston; married Claire L, May 7, 1994; children: Cameron L & Alanah Nicole. **Educ:** Merritt Jr Col, 1977; Westminster Col, 1978; Long Beach City Col, AA,1980; San Francisco State Univ, BA, 1985. **Career:** Kaiser Engineers, fitness trainer, 1982-85; Albany High Sch, Albany, Calif; Westminster Col; Merritt Jr Col, asst football coach, 1982-84; San Francisco State Univ, asst football coach, 1986-89; Univ Nev, asst football coach, 1990-93; Atlanta Falcons, sr dir player develop; Kansas City Chiefs, dir Player develop, 1997-2006, exec dir player develop, 2006-. **Orgs:** The Youth Ftd, bd dir, 1996-; NFL Player Programs, adv comm, 1996-; Genesis Sci, spec adv, 1996-. **Honors/Awds:** San Francisco State Football Hall of Fame, San Francisco State Univ, 2000. **Business Addr:** Director of Player Development, Kansas City Chiefs, 1 Arrowhead Dr, Kansas City, MO 64129, **Business Phone:** (816)920-9300.

WINSTON, MARY A
Executive, chief financial officer. **Educ:** Univ Wis, Acct & Info Systs; Northwestern Univ, Kellogg Grad Sch Mgt, MBA. **Career:** Global Fin Opers Pharmaceut Bus, vpres, 2000-02; Pfizer & Arthur Andersen & Co, sr auditor; Warner-Lambert, sr fin mgt; Baxter Int, Biotech Div, dir bus develop & strategy; Visteon Corp, vpres & treas, 2002-03, vpres & controller, 2003-04; Scholastic Corp, exec vpres & chief fin officer, 2004-. **Special Achievements:** One of the 100 most influential people in finance by Treasury & Risk Mgt mag. **Business Addr:** Executive Vice President, Chief Financial Officer, Scholastic Corporation, 557 Broadway, New York, NY 10012, **Business Phone:** (212)343-6100.*

WINSTON, DR. MICHAEL RUSSELL
Educator. **Personal:** Born May 26, 1941, New York, NY; son of Charles Russell Winston and Jocelyn Anita Prem Das; married Judith A Marianno; children: Lisa M & Cynthia A. **Educ:** Howard Univ, BA, 1962; Univ Calif, MA, 1964, PhD, 1974. **Career:** Howard Univ, instr, 1964-66; Inst Serv Educ, exec asst & assoc dir, 1965-66; Educ Assoc Inc, educ consult, 1966-68; Langston Univ, develop consult, 1966-68; Howard Univ, asst dean liberal arts, 1968-69, dir reshist dept, 1972-73, vpres academic affairs, 1983-90; Moorland-Spingarn Res Ctr, dir, 1973-83; fel Woodrow Wilson Int Ctr Scholars-Smithsonian Inst, 1979-80; Alfred Harcourt Found, vpres, 1992-93, pres, 1993-. **Orgs:** Am Historical Asn; Asn Study Afro-Am Life & Hist; Orgn Am Historians; Nat Geog Soc; Soc Am Archivists; Phi Beta Kappa. **Special Achievements:** Co-author, Negro US; co-editor, Dict Am Negro Biography, Historical Judgements Reconsidered, 1988. **Business Addr:** President, Administration Bldg, Howard University, 2400 6 St NW, Washington, DC 20059, **Business Phone:** (202)806-6100.

WINSTON, DR. NEIL EMERSON
Physician, association executive, president (organization). **Career:** Pres, Chicago Med Soc; Ill Dept Pub Health & Human Servs, physician team leader; Ill State Med Soc, trustees; Chicago Med Soc, pres, currently. **Special Achievements:** The first African American elected President of Chicago Medical Society. **Business Addr:** President, Chicago Medical Society, 515 N Dearborn St Suite 1, Chicago, IL 60610, **Business Phone:** (312)670-2550.

WINSTON, SHERRY E
Diplomat, musician, broker. **Personal:** Born Feb 15, 1947, New York, NY. **Educ:** Howard Univ, BMus, 1968. **Career:** Flutist; Jazz Promotion, Columbia, dire; Arista, Grp & Elektra, dir; Rec Rotating Host: BET-TV'S "Jazz Cent" with Lou Rawls; Albums: Do It For Love, 1986; Love Madness; Love Is, 1991; Pepsi Cola, Coca Cola, Anheuser Busch, Nat Asn Advan Colored People LDI, AT&T, corp performances; Sherry Winston Enterprises, owner. **Orgs:** Nat Asn Market Developers, Black MBA's. **Honors/Awds:** Howard Univ Alumni Award, 1984; Grammy Nominee, 1991; Sally Award, 1991; Serwa Award 100 Black Women, 1993. **Special Achievements:** Honor of performing for two sitting presidents, for President & Mrs. Clinton, White House & former President George H Bush at the Waldorf Astoria Hotel in NYC; featured guest on the Today Show, "Emeril Live," and has co-hosted and performed on 8 shows for Bet TV.

WINT, ARTHUR VALENTINE NORIS
School administrator, college teacher. **Personal:** Born Oct 26, 1950, Kingston, Jamaica; son of Noris and Gwendolyn Nelson; married Carlotta Jo Bradley, Apr 3, 1971; children: Tsenia, Jhason, Llarehnn & Khirrah. **Educ:** Wash State Univ, Pullman, Wash, BA, 1973; Univ Wash Sch Law, Seattle, Wash, JD, 1976; Harvard Univ, Inst Educ Mgt, 1993. **Career:** Evergreen Legal Servs, Seattle, Wash, legal asst, 1976-77; City Seattle, Seattle, Wash, eo investr, 1977-79; Wash St Univ, Pullman, Wash, diraff action, 1979-86; Calif St Univ, Fresno, Fresno, Calif, asst pres, dir affirmative action, 1986-92; Calif St Univ, Fresno, exe asst pres, 1992-, assoc prof criminol, 1991, prof criminol, currently, coordr, Prace& Conflict Prog, currently. **Orgs:** Church Christ, 1975-; NAACP, 1976-; Pub Info Comt, 1988-90, dir Region X, 1985-86; Calif Asn AA Offrs, 1986-; bd mem, Golden Valley Girl Scouts, 1987-90; Cent Calif Employ, round table, 1989-; Acad Criminal Justice Scis, Am Asn Affirmative Action, dir Region IX, 1990-91. **Honors/Awds:** Senate Intern, Wash State Senate, 1972; Teaching Leadership Award, NAACP,Fresno, 1989; Pew Teaching Award, Univ Wash, 1989. **Home Phone:** (209)225-9955. **Business Addr:** Professor of Criminology, California State University at Fresno, Rm S2 136 5150 N Maple Ave, Fresno, CA 93740-0041, **Business Phone:** (559)278-7027.

WINTER, DARIA PORTRAY
Educator, government official. **Personal:** Born Sep 7, 1949, Washington, DC; daughter of James Michael Portray Jr and Susie Lillian Alston Portray; married Reginald C, Oct 6, 1973 (divorced); children: Michael Alan. **Educ:** Hampton Inst, BS, eng educ, 1972; Univ Va, MA, eng, 1973; George Washington Univ, PhD, 1989. **Career:** DC Off Bicentennial Progs, asst exec dir, 1975-76; Univ DC Coop Exten Prog, educ specialist, 1976-77; Univ DC, instr eng, 1977-97; Mayor DC, gen asst, 1992-95; Univ DC, asst prof eng, 1995-; Southeastern Univ, asst prof eng; Univ DC Lorton Col Prison Prog fac, 1998; Howard Univ, Dept Eng, Col Arts & Sci, lectr, currently. **Orgs:** Dist Statehood Comn, 1979-92; Alternate Nat Comt Woman; DC Dem State Comt, 1980-92; Nat Educ Asn Standing Comt Higher Educ, 1981-87; vice chair, DC Dem State Comt, 1984-92; Dem Nat Comt, 1984-92; deleg, Dem Convention, 1984, 1988 & 1992; Modern Lang Asn; Col Lang Asn; Nat Coun Teachers Eng; ed, Newsletter Nat Educ Asn Black Caucus 1987-89; Pub Defender Serv, comnr, 1987-; Pub Defender Serv Bd Trustees, 1988-92; vice chair, DNC Eastern Region Caucus, 1988-92; bd mem, DC Juv Justice Adv Group; bd mem, United Planning Orgn; pres Rank Comt, 1994; chairperson, Univ DC Advocacy Comt, 1996; chairperson, DC Juv Justice Adv Group, 1998-; chair, NE Coalition. **Honors/Awds:** Appreciation Award, Univ DC Stud Nat Educ Asn, 1984; Appreciation Award in Support of Public Education, Superintendent, Floretta McKenzie, 1983; Outstanding Service Award; Distinguished Public Service Award, 1994; Image Award, Univ ZC, Col Lib & Fine Arts, 1996; Reclaim Our Youth Award, Steering Comt DC, 1996, 1997; Outstanding Service Award, Lorton Prison Col Prog Stud Gov Asn. **Home Addr:** 1355 Underwood St NW, Washington, DC 20012, **Home Phone:** (202)882-5179. **Business Phone:** (202)806-6235.

WINTERS, DIANE
School principal. **Career:** Weisser Park Elem Sch, asst prin. *

WINTERS, JACKIE. **See WINTERS, JACQUELINE F.**

WINTERS, JACQUELINE F (JACKIE WINTERS)
Government official, executive, senator (u.s. federal government). **Personal:** Born Apr 15, 1936, Topeka, KS; daughter of Forrest V Jackson and Catherine L Green Jackson; married Marc P; children: Anthony, Marlon, William & Brian Mc Clain. **Career:** Portland Model Cities, vol coordr, 1967-68; Pac NW Bell, serv adv, 1968-69; Ore House Reps, staff, 1999-; State Ore, field mgr, 1969-70, prog exec, 1971-79, asst gov, 1979-, rep, 1999-2002, state sen, 2003-; Governor Vic Atiyeh, asst; Jackie's Ribs, pres. **Orgs:** State exec serv dir, Marion-Polk United Way, 1975; vpres & pres, Salem Br Nat Asn Advan Colored People, 1975-78; vpres, Salem Hum Rights Comn, 1975; campaign chair, United Way, 1981-82, pres, 1982-83; bd mem, Goodwill Indust Ore, 1991-; bd dir, Ore Col Ed Found Bd Trustees. **Honors/Awds:** Distinguished Service Award, City Salem, 1976-77; Presidential Award, Salem, Nat Asn Advan Colored People, 1977; Outstanding Community Service Award, United Way, 1979; Outstanding Leadership, Ore Woman Color, 1979; Martin Luther King Jr Community Service Award, Willamette Univ, 1990; Freshman of the Year, Nat Conf State Legis, 1999; Belka Koyuyomn Legislator Appreciation Award, 2003; Charles E Cannefax Legislative Award, Ore Disabilities Comn, 2003; Ore Health Care Achievement, Ore Health Forum, 2005; Ore Health Care Achievement, NOBEL & Women Leadership Inst, 2005. **Home Addr:** PM 1334676 Com SE, Salem, OR 97302. **Business Addr:** State Senator, State of Oregon, 900 Court St NE S-212, Salem, OR 97301, **Business Phone:** (503)986-1710.

WINTERS, JAMES
Executive, chief executive officer. **Educ:** Oregon State Univ, BS, 1986. **Career:** United Energy Inc, pres; United Energy Inc, chief exec officer, currently. **Business Phone:** (503)287-4000.*

WINTERS, JAMES ROBERT
Government official. **Personal:** Born Aug 26, 1937, Pittsburgh, PA; married Diane Herndon; children: Angela, Richard, Lisa & Ryan. **Educ:** Fayetteville State Univ, BS, 1965; Univ Pittsburgh, social work, 1972. **Career:** YMCA Prog Ctr Pittsburgh, caseworker, 1966-67, prog dir, 1967-70, exec dir, 1970-72; Old Fort & Kiwanis YMCA, Fort Wayne, IN, urban dir, 1972-78; Wayne Township Trustee's Off, trustee, 1978-90. **Orgs:** Adv comt mem, Univ Pittsburgh Learn Leisure Prog, 1967-70; organizer, Grambling-Morgan St Football Game, 1970; organizer, Pittsburgh Pirate Baseball Wives Benefit Pittsburgh, YMCA Capital Campaign Fund Dr, 1971; bd mem, Ind Criminal Justice Planning, 1980; bd mem, Ind St Black Assembly, 1980. **Honors/Awds:** Certificate of Commendation, Mayor's Off, 1979; Honorable Commander of the Garrison, 1979. **Military Serv:** USN, radarman, 2nd class, 1956-60; Good Conduct Medal. **Business Addr:** Staff, Chemical Waste Management of Indiana Inc, 4636 Adams Ctr Rd, Fort Wayne, IN 46806.

WINTERS, JAMES W
Executive. **Career:** United Energy Inc, pres & chief exec officer, currently. **Honors/Awds:** Honoree, Outstanding Alumni and Business Partners, Col Bus, Oregon State Univ. **Business Phone:** (503)287-4000.

WINTERS, KENNETH E.
Financial manager, real estate executive. **Personal:** Born Oct 22, 1959, Gonzales, TX; married Wendy C Gordon. **Educ:** St Mary's Univ, BA, finance; Golden Gate Univ, MA, finance. **Career:** United Serv Automobile Asn, financial reporting analyst, 1979-83; USAA Real Estate Co, real estate analyst, 1983; real estate asset mgr, 1983-87; Real Estate Acquisitions, 1987; Port San Francisco, dir real estate, 2002-; AEW Capital Mgt, prin. **Orgs:** Nat Asn Bus Economists; Am Finance Asn; tutor Eng & Reading, San Antonio Literacy Coun. **Home Addr:** 1924 Middlefield Rd, Redwood City, CA 94063-2241. **Business Addr:** Director of Real Estate, Port of San Francisco, Pier 1 The Embarcadero, San Francisco, CA 94111, **Business Phone:** (415)274-0400.

WINTERS, WENDY GLASGOW
School administrator. **Educ:** Cent Conn State Col, BS, elem educ, 1952; Columbia Univ, Sch Social Work, MS, psychol social work, 1954; Yale Univ, PhD, sociol, 1975. **Career:** Community Service Society, fel, 1952-54; Herrick House Bartlett, IL, dir girls unit, 1954; Community Serv Soc, NY, family caseworker & intake admin, 1954-65; Norwalk Bd Educ, social worker, 1965-68; Univ Conn, Sch Social Work, field instr, 1967-80, assoc prof, asst dean acad affairs, 1975-78; Atlanta Univ, Sch Social Work, field instr, 1970-71; Yale Univ, Child Study Ctr, chief social worker, 1968-75, instr, 1968-71, asst prof social work, 1971, fel, 1971-72, 1973-74, res assoc, 1975-82; Ethel B Morgan fel, 1972-73; Smith Col Northampton, adj assoc prof social work, assoc prof sociol & anthrop, dean, 1979-84; J Educ Studs Placed At Risk, assoc ed, currently; Howard Univ, emer prof urban sociol, currently; Baldwin King Sch Program, chief social worker. **Orgs:** Adv bd, Project Upward Bound Cherry Lawn Sch, 1966-68; adv comn, Norwalk Community Col, Educ Vocational Resource Ctr, 1967-68; Norwalk-Wilton Ed Proj, 1967-68; Greater New Haven Urban League, 1969-71; Am Asn Univ Women; Am Orthopsychiatric Asn; Am Sociol Asn; Black Analysis Inc; Nat Asn Social Workers; New Eng Deans Asn; New Eng Minority Women Admins; ed cultural adv comn, Yale Off Community Affairs Develop, 1974-75; Am Orthopsychiatric Asn; reg adv coun, 1975-78; bd dir, Leila Day Nurseries, 1975-78; sub-comt, community serv grants adv comn, Comn Higher Educ, 1976-77; chmn eval sub-comt, 1977-

78; Conn State, Dept C & Youth Servs; juv justice adv comt, Conn Justice Comn, 1977; bd corps, Northampton Inst Savings, 1979-, bd dir, 1977-80, exec comt, 1977-79; Ctr Res Educ Studs Placed At Risk, Johns Hopkins Univ; bd mem, Bd Managers Casey Family Serv, 1997-; bd mem, Annie E. Casey Found; bd mem, Black Women' s Agenda; bd mem, La State Bd Educ. **Honors/Awds:** Md Governor Citation, 1996. **Special Achievements:** Taped film on "Excellence", Gen Elect Corp, 1983; "The Practice of Social Work in Schools", workshop Baton Rouge, 1984; co-author, "The Practice of Social Work in Schools: An Ecological Perspective", Free Press or Macmillan; author, "African American Mothers and Urban Schools: The Power of Participation", Lexington Books.

WISDOM, DR. KIMBERLYDAWN
Educator, surgeon. **Personal:** Married Garth A Wisdom Sr; children: 3. **Educ:** Univ Mich Sch Pub Health, MD, 1982. **Career:** Henry Ford Hosp, emergency med physician, currently; Univ Mich Med Ctr, asst prof med educ, currently; Henry Ford Health Syst, Inst Multicultural Health, founder & dir, vpres community health, educ & wellness, 2007-; U.S. Dept Health & Human Serv Nat Inst Health Study, sect reviewer, 2002-04; Mich Dept Community Health, surgeon gen, 2003-; Univ Mich Sch Pub Health, Dept Health Behav & Health Educ, adj asst prof. **Orgs:** Founder & dir, African-Am Initiative Male Health Improv. **Honors/Awds:** Hon Doctorate, Morehouse Sch Med; Nat Sojourner Truth Meritorious Service Award, Nat Asn Negro Bus & Prof Women; received several awards from local communities. **Special Achievements:** The nation's - first state-level surgeon general.

WISE, C. ROGERS
Physician. **Personal:** Born Apr 8, 1930, Ft Worth, TX; married Margaret. **Educ:** Fisk Univ, BA; Univ de Lausanne, MD, PhD. **Career:** DePaul Hosp, 1971-75; Memorial Hosp, Dept Anesthesia, chief, 1972-74; Self-Employed, physician, 1985-. **Orgs:** Int Anesthesia Res Soc; Am Soc Anesthesiologists; mem bd trustee, 1968, vice chmn, 1973-77, chmn bd, 1974, Laramie Co Community Col. **Business Addr:** PO Box 1144, Cheyenne, WY 82602.

WISE, FRANK P.
Government official, executive director. **Personal:** Born Oct 28, 1942, Norfolk, VA; son of Frank P Wise Sr (deceased) and Marian C Williams; divorced; children: Terri Lynn, Dawne Shenette. **Educ:** BBA, 1965; MUA, 1972. **Career:** US Nat Stand Asn, res asst, 1966-67; Eastern Airlines, coordr, 1967-68; Prince Geo Co, admin asst, 1970-72; City Cincinnati, mgt analyst, 1972; asst to city mgr, 1973-74; City Savannah, asst city mgr, 1975-78; City E Cleveland, city mgr, 1979-83; City Dallas, admin finance, asst dir, 1984-87, Park & Recreation Bd, dir, 1987-. **Orgs:** Fel ICMA Urban, 1970; chmn, Minority Coalition, 1972-73; vpres at large, Financil Comt, Conf Planning Comn, 1973, 1975-76; vpres at-large, Am Soc Pub Admin, Conf Minority Pub Admin Sect Human Res Admin, 1978-79; Nat Develop Dir Asn; Nat Recreation & Park Asn, 1984-; Tex Recreation & Park Soc, 1984-; bd mem, Western Revenue Sources Mgt Sch, 1990-; Int City Mgt Asn; Ford Found. **Honors/Awds:** Citations, YMCA, 1973; Mayoral Proclamation, 1974; Award of Merit, Ohio Parks & Recreation Asn. **Special Achievements:** article "What Role for Minority Assistance? The Second Dilemma," Pub Mgmt Mag 1972; "The Art of Serving Two Masters," Pub Mgmt Mag 1975; "Toward Equity of Results Achieved One Approach," Pub Mgmt Mag 1976. **Military Serv:** USY, capt, 1968-72; Commendation Medal, 1969; Cross of Gallantry, 1970; Bronze Star, 1970; Staff Medal, 1970. **Business Addr:** Director, City Dallas, Dept Park Recreation Board, 1500 Marilla St Suite 6FN, Dallas, TX 75201.*

WISE, WILLIAM CLINTON, SR.
Manager. **Personal:** Born Jan 14, 1941, Steubenville, OH; son of Robert and Vivian Doggett; married Linda Rayam Wise (divorced 1988); children: Shawn, Sharon, Sandra, William Jr. **Educ:** Eastern Mich Univ, labor law; US Armed Forces Inst, bus admin; Washtenaw Community Col, psychol; Univ Mich Labor Sch. **Career:** City Ann Arbor, Ann Arbor, personnel dir, 1973-77; Ford Motor Co, Dearborn, spec prog coord, 1977-84; Martin Marietta Corp, Bethesda, mgr, mgt training, 1984-. **Orgs:** exec adv, Nat Technol Univ, 1991; Am Soc Training & Develop, 1984-. **Military Serv:** USAF, e-1, 1957-61.

WISE-HARRISON, PAMELA DORSEY
Pianist, composer. **Personal:** Born Jan 8, 1956, Steubenville, OH; daughter of Robert C and Eloise D; married Wendell Harrison, May 7, 1995. **Educ:** Univ Steubenville; Cuyahoga Community Col; Kent State Univ. **Career:** Jazz pianist & composer, 1980-; Albums: Songo Festividad, 1994; Wise Tells, 1995; Pamela Wise & the Afro Cuban Project I, 1999; Pamela Wise & the Afro Cuban Project II, 2000; Latin Wise, 2001; "Negre Con Leche, Black with Cream". **Orgs:** Exec dir, Rebirth Inc, 1983-; Detroit Fed Musicians Union, 2000-. **Honors/Awds:** Creative Artist Grant Award, Arts Serve MI, 1994, 1996, 1998, 2000. **Business Addr:** Pianist, Composer, 81 Chandler St, Detroit, MI 48202, **Business Phone:** (313)875-0289.

WISE-LOVE, KAREN A. See LOVE, KAREN ALLYCE.

WISHAM, CLAYBRON O
Executive. **Personal:** Born Dec 28, 1932, Newport, OH; son of Charlie and Willie; married Evelyn Bailey, Sep 4, 1964; children: Deshay Appling, Lorna & Karen. **Educ:** Philander Smith Col, BA, 1954; Univ Ark, MEd, 1963. **Career:** Executive (retired); AR Baptist Col, dir athletics, 1956-59; E End Boys Club, exec dir, 1957-59; Jones High Sch, guid counr, 1959-61; Union Com Bank, asst vpres personnel, 1970-72; Cleveland State Univ, affirmative action officer, 1972-74; personnel admin, 1974-83; Cleveland Elec Illuminating Co, gen mgr Operations, 1983-90; Centerior Energy Corp, mgr, training & develop, 1990. **Orgs:** Alpha Phi Alpha, 1952; Urban League Cleveland; Blacks Mgt, 1970-; Nat Asn Advan Colored People; Greater Cleveland Growth Asn; charter mem, Am Asn Blacks Energy; sr arbitrator, Cleveland Better Bus Bur; bd trustees, Ctr Rehab Serv, Miles Ahead Inc; Marymount Hosp Civic Adv Bd; United Way Servs Allocations Panel. **Special Achievements:** First Black Personnel Recruiter Corp Position, City Cleveland, Ohio, 1965; First Black Asst VP, Union Commerce Bank Personnel Dept, 1970; First Black Conf Chmn of EEO, Nat Sem for Edison Elec Inst, 1979; First Black Operations Manager at Cleveland Election Illuminating Co. **Military Serv:** AUS, pfc, 1954-56. *

WITCHER, VEROMAN D
Law enforcement officer. **Career:** OH State Hwy Patrol, field training officer, driving instr, police instr, background investr, state trooper, 1985. **Honors/Awds:** The Colonel Lynn Black Award of Excellence; Ohio Trooper's Caring Award; The Bellbrook Optimist Excellence in Law Enforcement Award; The Fairborn City Blue Coat Award of Excellence; presented with proclamation and Key to the City of Xenia, OH, Feb 1998. **Special Achievements:** First African American to receive the State Trooper of the Year Award, OH, 1997.

WITHERSPOON, ADDELLE
Artist. **Career:** Fiber Art by Rondell, artist, 2003-; Simply Art Inc, artist, currently. **Business Addr:** Artist, Fiber Art by Rondell, PO Box 656915, Fresh Meadows, NY 11365, **Business Phone:** (718)454-5189.*

WITHERSPOON, ANNIE C.
Educator. **Personal:** Born Oct 29, 1928, Bessemer, AL; daughter of Edward and Ethel Jones; married Willie George, Aug 17, 1959; children: Carole Lejuene & Yvas Lenese. **Educ:** WVa State Col, AB, Ed, 1951; Univ Ala, MA, Elem Ed, 1968. **Career:** Educator (retired); Jefferson County Sch Syst Birmingham, teacher social studies, until retirement; guidance counr, 1956-70; Tuscaloosa, teacher, 1952-56. **Orgs:** AL Ed Asn; Nat Ed Asn; Jefferson Co Ed Asn; NEA Minority Involvement Prog; coord, Dist VI, Jefferson Co Area Workshop Teachers; Jefferson Co Voice Teachers Ed; chairperson & deaconess, New Pilgrim Baptist Church, 1984; chairperson, constitution comt, Dunbar/Abram Alumni, 1986; dir, Volunteer Tutorial Prog, 1992; vpres, New Pilgrim Baptist Church Projects. **Honors/Awds:** Teacher of the Year, 1968; Teacher Recognition Awards, Ala Soc Studies Fair Dist & St, 1972-74; Outstanding Service to Children Green Valley Elementary Sch, Green Valley PTA, 1985; Outstanding Service Award, Center St Sch, 1986-87; Service Award, Blue & White Banquet, Dunbar/Abrams Alumni, 1987. **Special Achievements:** First African American to act as president of Jefferson County. **Home Addr:** 851 McCary St SW, Birmingham, AL 35211, **Home Phone:** (205)252-3066.

WITHERSPOON, AUDREY GOODWIN
School administrator. **Personal:** Born Aug 19, 1949, Greenwood, SC; daughter of Hudson and Essie Lue Chenault; children: Jacintha Dyan & Andre LaVern. **Educ:** Lander Univ, BA, sociol, 1971; Clemson Univ, MEd, admin & supv, 1975; Vanderbilt Univ, grad study, educ leadership, 1983. **Career:** McCormick County Sch Dist, teacher, 1971-72; GLEAMNS Head Start Prog, social worker, parent coordr, 1972-74, educ dir, 1974-75; GLEAMNS Human Resource Comn, child develop, founder & dir; Lander Univ, Lander Found Bd Trustees, mem, 2007-. **Orgs:** Nat Asn Educ Young C, 1975-93; vice chairperson, bd trustees, Greenwood Sch Dist, 50, 1977-93; chart mem, SC Child Develop Providers Inc, bd mem, 1978-96, pres, 1987; treas, Greenwood Br, Nat Asn Advan Colored People, 1979-96; vice chairperson, Gov Task Force, 1979-82; Negro Business & Prof Womens Club, 1981-87; Gov Riley's Ed Transition Team, 1983-84; proj coordr, Region V, SC Voices C, 1984-85; planning comn, Effective Schs, SC, 1985; Mt Moriah Baptist Church; State Adv Comt, Day Care Regulations, 1987-89; Lander Univ Class Agent, 1988-96; SC Pub Pvt Child Care Coun, 1990; Early Childhood Educ, Interagency Adv Comt, 1990-91; Nat Coun Negro Women, 1989-93; SC Sch Bds Asn, 1990, 1992. **Honors/Awds:** Female Citizen of the Year, 1982; Various State & Nat Community Awards, 1982-92; Distinguished Alumni Award, Lander Univ, 1989; Distinguished Service Award, Greenwood Rotary Int, 1993. **Business Addr:** Member, Lander University, Lander Foundation Board of Trustees, 320 Stanley Ave, Greenwood, SC 29649-2099, **Business Phone:** (864)388-8000.

WITHERSPOON, JOHN
Actor, comedian, television producer. **Personal:** Born Jan 27, 1942, Detroit, MI; married Angela Robinson, Jan 1, 1988; children: John David & Alexander. **Career:** Films: Kidnapped, 1986; Ratboy, 1986; Hollywood Shuffle, 1987; Bird, 1988;I'm Gonna Git You Sucka, 1988; Killer Tomatoes Strike Back!, 1990; House Party, 1990; The Five Heartbeats, 1991; Talkin' Dirty After Dark, 1991;Boomerang, 1992; The Meteor Man, 1993; Fatal Instinct, 1993; Vampire in Brooklyn, 1995; Friday, 1995; A Delicatessen Story, 1996; Fakin' Da Funk,1997; Sprung, 1997; High Frequency, 1998; Ride, 1998; Bulworth, 1998; I Got the Hook Up, 1998; Next Friday, 2000; Little Nicky, 2000; The Ladies Man, 2000; Friday After Next, 2002; Pryor Offenses, 2004; Soul Plane,2004; Little Man, 2006; After Sex, 2007; The Hustle, 2008. TV series: "The Incredible Hulk", 1978; "What's Happening!!", 1978; "Good Times", 1979; "Barnaby Jones", 1979; The Jazz Singer?, 1980; "WKRP in Cincinnati", 1982; "Hill Street Blues", 1982; "You Again?", 1986; "227", 1987; "What's Happening Now!", 1987; "Frank's Place",1987; "Amen", 1988; "L.A. Law", 1990; Sunday in Paris?, 1991; "Martin", 1993; Cosmic Slop, 1994; "The Fresh Prince of Bel-Air", 1994; "The Wayans Bros.", 1995-99; "Wayne head", 1996-97; "Living Single", 1997; "Happily Ever After: Fairy Tales for Every Child", 2000; "The Proud Family", 2003;"The Tracy Morgan Show", 2003-04; "Kim Possible", 2004; "Weekends at the DL", 2005; "The Boondocks", 2005-08; Thugaboo: A Miracle on D-Roc's Street, 2006; "The Super Rumble Mix show", 2008; exe prod, "John Witherspoon: You Got to Coordinate", 2008. **Business Addr:** Actor, c/o International Creative Management Inc, 8942 Wilshire Blvd, Beverly Hills, CA 90211, **Business Phone:** (310)550-4000.*

WITHERSPOON, NAOMI. See MADGETT, DR. NAOMI LONG.

WITHERSPOON, R. CAROLYN
Executive. **Personal:** Born in Detroit, MI; married William C Witherspoon; children: W Roger, L Courtney, David J. **Educ:** City Col NY, BS, 1951, MS, 1956. **Career:** Executive (retired); Town Hall NY, acct, 1945-48; Foreign Rels Libr, treas; Coun Foreign Rels Inc, asst treas & comptroller, 1952-87. **Orgs:** Nat financial secy, Nat Asn Negro Bus & Prof Women's Clubs Inc; Community Rel Bd; adjust com Teaneck; Kappa Delta Pi; Beta Alpha Psi. *

WITHERSPOON, SOPHIA
Basketball player. **Personal:** Born Jul 6, 1969, Fort Pierce, FL. **Educ:** Univ Fla, BS, rctrn ther, 1991. **Career:** Providencia Nyon, Switzerland, 1991-92; Hawthorne High Sch, asst coach, 1992-94; SPD Rouenm, france, 1994-95; FTC Budapest, Hungary, 1995-96; Galatasaray, Turkey, 1997-98; Ferencvarosi, Hungary, 1998-99; NY Liberty, guard, 1997-99; Portland Fire, 2000-01; Los Angeles Sparks, guard, 2002-03; Charlotte Sting, free agent, 2004-07. **Honors/Awds:** Italian All-Star, 1996 & 1997. *

WITHERSPOON, WILLIAM ROGER
Journalist. **Personal:** Born Mar 3, 1949, New York, NY; son of William C and Ruth C; married Cynthia O Bedford; children: Kir & Brie. **Educ:** Univ Mich, Ann Arbor, MI, 1966-67; Rider Col, Trenton, NJ, 1973; Rutgers Univ, Livingstone Col, New Brunswick, NJ, 1975; Fairleigh-Dickinson Univ (Edward Williams Col) Hackensack, NJ, Liberal Arts, 1976. **Career:** Star-Ledger, Newark, NJ, investment reporter, columnist, op-ed page, st house corresp, columnist senate, assembly, banking, transportation & agr, gen; assignment reporter, 1970-75; NY Daily News, Sunday assignment ed, NJ, health & environ reporter, Pasaic Cty reporter, New York City ed gen assignment reporter, 1975-79; The Atlanta Constitution, columnist, health & sci writer, 1979-82; Time Mag, SE Bur, Cable News Network, writer/producer; Black Enterprise Mag, Newsweek, GQ Mag, Fortune, Essence Mag, Nat Leader, freelance writer, 1982-85; Dallas Times Herald, ed bd, 1985-. **Orgs:** Atlanta African Film Soc, Nat Asn Black Journalists, Black Perspective, 1970-73; contributing ed, Essence Mag; ed adv bd, NAACP; Crisis Mag, 1979-80; Dallas-Fort Worth Asn Black Communicators. **Honors/Awds:** Special Citation, Reporting Awards Ed Writers Asn, 1982; First place Reg 5, Nat Asn Black Journalists, 1982; Nat Headliners Club Award for Consistently Outstanding Special/Feature Column Writing, 1981; Journ Acolade Award, Ga Conf on Social Welfare, 1981; First place energy series Media Award for Econ Understanding Series Amos Tuck Sch Bus Admin Dartmouth Col, 1980; First place outstanding news feature, Atlanta Asn Black Journalists, 1980; UPI Ga Newspaper Awards, Second place column writing, third place spot news coverage, Three Mile Island, 1979; Katie Award Best Ed Press Club Dallas, 1986; First Place Editorial Writing Tex Asn Press Managing Eds, 1987. **Special Achievements:** Author, "Martin Luther King Jr To The Mountaintop", Doubleday & Co, 1985. **Home Addr:** 2802 Dukeswood Dr, Garland, TX 75040. **Business Phone:** (214)720-6633.

WOFFORD, CHLOE ANTHONY. See MORRISON, TONI.

WOLFE, ALLEN, JR.
Nurse. **Career:** Wash Hosp Ctr, Medstar Health, clin supvr & chief flight nurse, currently. *

WOLFE, GEORGE C (GEORGE COSTELLO WOLFE)
Television producer, administrator, writer. **Personal:** Born Sep 23, 1954, Frankfort, KY; son of Costello Wolfe and Anna Lindsey. **Educ:** Pomona Col, BA, directing, 1976; New York Univ, MFA,

play writing, musical theatre, 1983. **Career:** Actor, Director, Writer, Producer; Actor: Fresh Kill, 1994, "Great Performances", 1991; "The Colored Museum", 1991TV Garden State, 2004; The Devil Wears Prada, 2006; Director: "Great Performances", 1991; "The Colored Museum", 1991; "Fires in the Mirror", 1993; "The WIN Awards", 2005; "Lackawanna Blues", 2005; Nights in Rodanthe, 2008; Self: The Papp Project, 2001; "Stage on Screen: The Topdog Diaries", 2002; The 58th Annual Tony Awards, 2004; Elaine Stritch at Liberty, 2004; "Broadway: The American Musical", 2004; 2006 Independent Spirit Awards, 2006; ShowBusiness: The Road to Broadway, 2007; Theater of War, 2008. **Orgs:** Artistic assoc, New York Shakespeare Festival, 1991-93; bd dirs, Young Playwrights Festival, 1992-93; exec coun, Dramatist Guild, 1992-93. **Honors/Awds:** Numerous honors and awards including Hull-Warriner Award, 1986; Obie Award, 1990; Dorothy Chandler Award, 1992; 2 Tony Award Nominations, 1992; Drama Desk Award, 1992; 2 Audelco Awards for Theatre, The George Oppenheimer; Newsday Award; The CBS/FDG New Play Award; The New York Univ Distinguished Alumni Award; The HBO/USA Playwrights Award; 9 Tony Award Nominations for Bring In Da Noise, Bring In Da Funk, 1996. **Special Achievements:** Publications: The Colored Museum, Grove Press Inc, 1988; Spunk TCG, 1991; Two By Wolfe, Fireside Theatre Inc, 1991; Jelly's Last Jam, Theatre Communications Group, 1993. **Business Addr:** Director, Home Box Office Inc., 1100 Ave of the Americas, New York, NY 10036, **Business Phone:** (212)512-1000.*

WOLFE, GEORGE COSTELLO. See WOLFE, GEORGE C.

WOLFE, DR. JOHN THOMAS
College administrator, chancellor (education). **Personal:** Born Feb 22, 1942, Jackson, MS; son of John and Jeanette; married; children: Wyatt, John T & David A. **Educ:** Chicago State Univ, BEd, 1964; Purdue Univ, MS, 1972, PhD, 1976. **Career:** Purdue Univ, mgr employee rels, 1975-77; Fayetteville State Univ, eng dept chair, 1977-79, div head humanities & fine arts, 1979-83, acad dean, 1983-85; Am Coun Educ, fel, 1982-83; Bowie State Univ, provost & vpres acad affairs; Ky State Univ, Frankfort, KY, pres; Univ Syst Md, assoc vice chancellor acad affairs, 2006-. **Orgs:** Pres, Black Caucus Nat Coun Teacher Eng, 1982-88; standing comn teacher, Prep Nat Coun Teachers Eng, 1984-87; bd dir, Bowie New Town Ctr Minority Adv Bd, 1985-; steering comt mem, Prince Georges Co, Md Univ High Sch, 1985-87; chair, adv bd, Prince Georges County, Md Entrepreneurial Develop Prog. **Honors/Awds:** Kappa Delta Pi Educ Honor Soc, 1972; hon mem Alpha Kappa Mu Honor Soc, 1983. **Business Phone:** (301)445-1917.

WOLFMAN, DR. BRUNETTA REID
School administrator. **Personal:** Born in Clarksdale, MS; married Burton I; children: Andrea C & Jeffrey Allen. **Educ:** Univ Calif, Berkeley, BA, 1957, MA, 1968, PhD, 1971; Boston Univ, DHL, 1983; N eastern Univ, DPed, 1983; Regis Col, DLaws, 1984; Suffolk Univ, DHL, 1985, Stonehill Col, 1985. **Career:** Univ Calif, Berkeley, teaching fel, 1969-71; Dartmouth Col, Calif coordr, 1971-72, asst dean fac & asst prof, 1972-74; Univ Mass, asst vpres, 1974-76; Wheelock Col Boston, acad dean, 1976-78; Mass Dept Educ, exec planner, 1978-82; Rox bury Community Col, pres, 1983-; George Wash Univ, assoc vpres Acad Affairs, 1990-91. **Orgs:** Prog dir, Young Women's Christian Asn, Oakland & Berkeley, CA, 1959-63; exec dir, Camp Fire Girls Berkeley, 1963-67; consult, Arthur D Little Inc, 1977-78; pres, New Eng Minority Women Admins, 1977-78; bd dir, Nat Ctr Higher Educ Mgt Systs, 1978-; bd dir, Boston Fenway Prog, 1979-; overseer, Boston Symphony Orchestra, 1984; Mus Fine Arts 1984; overseer, Stone Ctr, Wellesley Col; bd, Nat Conf Christians & Jews; bd, United States Trust Bank; bd, Boston Pvt Indust Coun; bd, Am Coun Educ; counr, Coun Educ Pub Health; urban comn, Am Asn Community & Jr Cols; Provice Town Coun, 2000. **Honors/Awds:** Nat Inst Educ grant Superwomen Study, 1978-79; "Roles", W minister Press, 1983. **Special Achievements:** Publ, two articles in black separatism & social reality, Pergamon Press, 1977; paper presented & publ, OECD, Paris, 1978; papers presented annual meeting, Am Educ Res Asn, 1980; author, 'Black Women in America: Social Science Perspectives', 1991. **Business Addr:** President, Roxbury Community College, 1234 Columbus Ave, Boston, MA 02119.

WOMACK, ANTHONY DARRELL. See WOMACK, TONY.

WOMACK, BOBBY DWAYNE
Singer, songwriter. **Personal:** Born Mar 4, 1944, Cleveland, OH; married Barbara Campbell; children: Vincent. **Career:** Gospel group, Womack Brothers, 1950s, renamed Valentinos, 1962 when they became back-up for Sam Cooke; guitarist, songwriter, vocalist for Ray Charles, Joe Tex, King Curtis, Aretha Franklin, Wilson Pickett; Albums: Fly Me to the Moon, 1968; My Prescription, 1969; The Womack "Live", 1970; Communication, 1971; Understanding, 1972; Across 110th Street, 1972; Facts of Life, 1973; Lookin' for a Love Again, 1974; Greatest Hits, 1975; I Don't Know What the World Is Coming To, 1975; I Can Understand It, 1975;Safety Zone, 1976; BW Goes C&W, 1976; Home Is Where the Heart Is, 1976; Pieces, 1977; Roads of Life, 1979; The Poet, 1981; The Poet II, 1984; So Many Rivers, 1985; Someday We'll All Be Free, 1985; Wo magic, 1986; Last Soul Man, 1987; Save The Children, 1989; Soul Seduction Supreme, 1994; Resurrection, 1994; Soul Sensation Live, 1998; Back to My Roots, 1998; Traditions, 1999; Christmas Album, 2000; Lookin' For a Love: The Best of 1968-76, 2003; Fly Me To The Moon/My Prescription on one CD, 2004; Understanding/Communication, 2004; Womack Live/The Safety Zone, 2004; Lookin' For A Love Again/BW Goes CW, 2004; Facts of Life/I Don't Know What the World Is Coming To, 2004; Post, 2006; Singles: "Lookin' For A Love",1962; "It's All Over Now", 1964; "Fly Me To The Moon", 1968; "What Is This", 1968; "How I Miss My Baby", 1969; "I Left My Heart in San Francisco", 1969; "It's Gonna Rain", 1969; "I'm Gonna Forget About You", 1969; "More Than I Can Stand", 1970; "Communication", 1971; "The Preacher(Part 2)/More Than I Can Stand", 1971; "Sweet Caroline (Good Times Never Seemed So Good)", 1972; "That's The Way I Feel About Cha", 1972; "Woman's Gotta Have It", 1972; "Across 110th Street", 1973; "Harry Hippie", 1973; "I'm Through Trying To Prove My Love To You", 1973; "Nobody Wants You When You're Down & Out", 1973; "Lookin' For A Love", 1974; "You're Welcome, Stop On By", 1974; "Check It Out", 1975; "It's All Over Now", 1975; "Daylight", 1976; "Where There's A Will, There's A Way", 1976; "Home Is Where The Heart Is", 1977; "Trust Your Heart", 1978; "How Could You Break My Heart", 1979; "Secrets", 1981; "If You Think You're Lonely Now", 1982; "Where Do We Go From Here", 1982; "It Takes a Lot of Strength to Say Goodbye", 1984; "Love Has Finally Come t Last", 1984; "I Wish He Didn't Trust Me So Much", 1985; "Let Me Kiss It Where It Hurts", 1985; "Someday We'll All Be Free", 1985; "(I Wanna) Make Love to You", 1986; "Save the Children", 1989; "I Wish I'd Never Met You", 1991; "California Dreamin' (re-release)", 2004. **Honors/Awds:** Youth Inspirational Award, 1975; Appreciation Award Walter Reed Army Med Ctr; several gold records. **Business Phone:** (310)553-3838.

WOMACK, CHRISTOPHER CLARENCE
Executive. **Personal:** Born Feb 26, 1958, Greenville, AL; son of Ruby Womack; married Sabrina Shannon; children: Shannon Ashley & Christopher Michael. **Educ:** Western Michigan Univ, BS, polit sci, 1979; American Univ, MPA, 1985. **Career:** US House Rep, legis aide Rep Leon E Panetta, 1979-84; Subcomt Personnel & Police, Comn House Adminr, staff dir, 1984-87; Ala Power Co, govt affairs rep, 1988-89, asst vpres pub affairs, 1989-91, dir community rels, 1991-93; vpres pub rels, 1993-95, sr vpres pub rels & corp serv, sr vpres & sr prod officer, currently. **Orgs:** Ala Ballet; exec dir, Ala Bus Charitable Trust Fund; chair, Alpha Phi Alpha Educ Found; treas, Birmingham Cult & Heritage Found, City Stages; Birmingham Community on Olympic Football; Bd Deacons, Sixth Ave Baptist Church. **Honors/Awds:** Silver Knight of Management Award, 1994. **Special Achievements:** Top 40 Under 40 Designation, Birmingham Business Journal, 1993; Leadership Birmingham, 1990. **Business Addr:** Senior Vice President, Senior Production Officer, Alabama Power Co, 600 N 18th St, PO Box 2641, Birmingham, AL 35291, **Business Phone:** 800-888-2726.

WOMACK, HENRY CORNELIUS
Educator. **Personal:** Born Feb 18, 1938, Grapeland, MS. **Educ:** Alcorn State Univ, BS, (summa cum laude), 1961; Wayne State Univ, MS, 1965, PhD 1974. **Career:** Harper Sch Nursing, dir basic sci, 1965-69; Ball St Univ, assoc prof physiol & health Sci, 1969-, teaching prof, currently. **Orgs:** Fel NDEA, 1970-74; Fedn Am Scientists, 1974-; Ind Acad Sci, 1974-; Human Biol Coun, 1974-; Am Civil Liberties Union, 1974-; AAAS, 1974-; Am Asn Univ Profs, 1974-. **Honors/Awds:** Scholar of Year, Omega Psi Phi Fraternity Inc, 1961; Excellence in Teaching Award, Ball State Univ, 1990. **Military Serv:** USAF, au/c, 1954-58. **Business Addr:** Associate Professor, Teaching Professor, Ball State University, Department of Physiology and Health Science, CL 325 Cooper Sci Bldg 2000 W Univ Ave, Muncie, IN 47306, **Business Phone:** (765)285-5961.

WOMACK, JOE NEAL, JR.
Executive. **Personal:** Born Oct 5, 1950, Mobile, AL; son of Joe N Sr and Annie Laura Brown Pressley; married Juliette F Womack (divorced 1986); children: Joe Neal Womack, III; married Mary B Womack, Dec 1991. **Educ:** St Paul's Col, Lawrenceville, BS, bus, 1972. **Career:** Metropolitan Life, Mobile, sales rep, 1972; Shell Chem, DuPont, Mobile, financial analyst, 1973-90; Prudential, Mobile, sales rep, 1990-95. **Orgs:** Alpha Phi Alpha Fraternity, 1972; comn chair, Mobile Area Mardi Gras Asn, 1987-; Mardi Gras Maskers, 1988-; chmn, African-Am Summit Steering Comt, 1989-. **Military Serv:** Marine Corps, maj, 1973-94. **Home Addr:** 2816 Westmoor Ct, Mobile, AL 36695, **Home Phone:** (251)666-5108.

WOMACK, REV. DR. JOHN H, SR.
Executive. **Personal:** Born Jul 8, 1944, Virginia; son of George and Elnora; married Bertha; children: Tonya, John Jr & Monica. **Educ:** Fisher Junior Col; Gordon-Conwell Theol Seminary, master relig educ, 1990, doctorate ministry, 2001. **Career:** Record Wagon, sales rep, 1967-70; McGarrahan Steel Erection, iron worker, 1970-77; Salem Fire Dept, Salem, firefighter, 1977-80; JJS Services/Peabody Paper, Peabody, founder & pres, chief exec officer, 1977-98; TJM Apparel, 1998-; Metropolitan Baptist Church, pastor; Warren Bancorp Inc, dir. **Orgs:** Pres, Black Corporate Pres New Eng; bd dir, Building Serv Contractors Asn Int, 1986; bd mem, Job for Youth, 1990-. **Honors/Awds:** Minority Advocate of the Year, US Small Bus Admin, 1984; Outstanding Services Small Bus, Boston Urban Bankers Forum James Ingram, 1984; Minority Small Bus Person Year, US Small Bus Admin; St. John's Baptist Church's Pastor Award, 1987; Black Corp Pres NEng Special Recognition Award, NAACP, 1988. **Military Serv:** USN, E-4, 1963-67. **Business Addr:** Pastor, Metropolitan Baptist Church, 393 Norfolk St, Dorchester, MA 02124-4024, **Business Phone:** (617)436-0479.

WOMACK, RICHARD
Executive, association executive. **Personal:** Born Nov 18, 1939, Danville, VA; son of Gilbert and Louise Patrick. **Career:** Am Fedn Labor-Congress Indust Orgn, Human Resources Develop Inst, asst dir, 1971, Dept Civil Rights, dir, 1986, asst to pres, 2003-. **Orgs:** Bd dirs, Nat Asn Advan Colored People; chair, Nat Bd Dirs Labor Comt; chmn bd, Nat Coalition Black Civic Participation; actg exec dir, Leadership Conf Civil Rights; bd mem, Fed Prison Indust. **Military Serv:** AUS, Fort Lee, Va, 1962. **Business Addr:** Assistant to the president, American Federation of Labor, Congress of Industrial Organizations, 815 16th St NW, Washington, DC 20006, **Business Phone:** (202)637-5000.*

WOMACK, STANLEY H. See Obituaries section.

WOMACK, TONY (ANTHONY DARRELL WOMACK)
Baseball player. **Personal:** Born Sep 25, 1969, Danville, VA; married Janet; children: Jessica & Alsander. **Educ:** Guilford Col, BA, 1992; Univ NC, MA, sports mgt. **Career:** Pittsburgh Pirates, infielder, 1993-98; Ariz Diamondbacks, 1999-03; Colo Rockies, 2003; Chicago Cubs, 2003-06; St Louis Cardinals, 2004; NY Yankees, 2005; Cincinnati Reds, 2006; Chicago Cubs, 2006; free agent, currently. **Orgs:** Founder, Stealing Hearts, Charlotte. **Honors/Awds:** NL All-Star Team, 1997; Clement Award, BBWAA, 1997. *

WOMBLE, JEFFERY MAURICE
Public relations executive. **Personal:** Born Apr 4, 1964, Fayetteville, NC; son of Charles Leo Sr and Corine McLean. **Educ:** Fayetteville State Univ, Fayetteville, NC, BA, English, 1986. **Career:** Fayetteville Observer, Fayetteville, NC, reporter & ed; Fayetteville State Univ, pub rels dir, currently. **Orgs:** Nat Asn Black Journalists, 1988-; ed Sphinx, Alpha Phi Alpha Fraternity, 1990-; Big Brothers Prog, 1990-; comm adv bd, Jr League Fayetteville; adv bd, Find-A-Friend; adv bd, Upward Bound, FSU; teen adv bd, Women's Ctr Fayetteville; bd dir, Fayetteville Scholar Pageant Assoc. **Honors/Awds:** Media Award, VFW Post 6018, 1987; Outstanding African-American Male Award, Alpha Kappa Alpha Sorority; Community Resource Specialist, Cumberland County Schs; Outstanding Journalist Award, Omar Ibyn Syiid; Community Service Award, Cumberland County Minority AIDS Speaker's Bur; 1st place, Profiles, NC Working Press; 1st place Profiles, 2nd place Fashion Writing, Teen Adv Bd, Women's Ctr Fayetteville, NC Working Press; Alpha Phi Alpha Man of Merit Award; Ashton Lilly Spirit Award, 2006. **Home Addr:** 629 Deep Creek Rd, Fayetteville, NC 28312. **Business Addr:** Public Relations Director, Fayetteville State University, Office of Public Relations, 1200 Murchison Road, Fayetteville, NC 28301-4298, **Business Phone:** (910)672-1474.

WOMBLE, LARRY W
School administrator, government official, educator. **Personal:** Born Jun 6, 1941, Winston-Salem, NC; son of Luchion and Dorothy Gwyn; married Lonnie Hamilton (divorced 1967). **Educ:** Winston-Salem State Univ, BS, 1963; Univ NC, cert, 1968; Univ NC, Greensboro, MEd, admin, 1975; Appalachian State Univ, EdS, admin, 1977. **Career:** Educator (retired), state rep; Winston-Salem/Forsyth County Sch, Diggs Intermediate, Winston-Salem, NC, dept chmn, instr, 1971-74; Wake Forest Univ, Winston-Salem, NC, supv, dir, 1974-75; Winston-Salem/Forsyth County Sch, Old Town Sch, Winston-Salem, NC, asst prin, 1975-86; Mineral Springs, Winston-Salem, WI, asst prin, 1986-89; Cook Mid Sch, asst prin, 1989-90, Kennedy Mid Sch, Winston-Salem, NC, asst prin, 1990-91; Paisley Mid Sch, Winston-Salem, NC, asst prin, 1992-93; NC House Rep, state rep, currently. **Orgs:** Pres, NC Black Elected Munic Off, 1985-90; Nat Asn Adv Colored People; Nat Black Caucus Local Elected Off, 1987-; Human Develop Policy Comt, 1989-; chmn, Community Develop Housing & Gen Govt Comt, 1989-; Pub Works Comt, 1989-. **Honors/Awds:** Young Educr of the Yr, 1964-65; R J Reynolds Scholar, R J Reynolds, 1971-72; Asst Prin of the Yr, 1980-81; Man of the Yr Award, Winston-Salem Chronicle Newspaper, 1985. **Special Achievements:** Ambassadors of Friendship Force, Europe & Kenya. **Home Addr:** 1294 Salem Lake Rd, Winston-Salem, NC 27107, **Home Phone:** (336)784-9373. **Business Phone:** (919)733-5777.

WONDER, STEVIE (STEVLAND HARDAWAY MORRIS)
Singer, songwriter. **Personal:** Born May 13, 1950, Saginaw, MI; son of Lula Mae Morris (deceased); married Kai Milla, Jan 1,

2001; children: Kailand & Mandla Kadjay Carl; married Syreeta Wright, 1971 (divorced 1972); children: Aisha, Keita Sawandi, Kwame, Sophia & Mumtaz Ekow. **Educ:** Mich Sch Blind, grad, 1968. **Career:** Performances Eng, Europe, Japan, Okinawa, Nigeria; TV: "Ed Sullivan"; "Mike Douglas"; "Tom Jones"; "Am Bandstand"; "Dinah Shore"; "Tony Bennett: An American Classic", 2006; Black Bull Music, founder & pres, 1970-; Wondirection Recs, founder & pres, 1972-; singer & songwriter & pianist, currently; Recordings: "The Ringer", writer, 2006; "Glory Road", writer, 2006; "Bobby", performer, 2006; Albums: Tribute to Uncle Ray, 1963; With A Song In My Heart, 1963; The Twelve-Year-Old-Genius, 1963; The Jazz Soul Of Little Stevie, 1963; Stevie At The Beach, 1964; Down To Earth, 1966; Uptight, 1966; Someday At Christmas, 1967; I Was Made To Love Her, 1967; Eivets Rednow, 1968; For Once In My Life, 1968; My Cherie Amour, 1969; Signed, Sealed And Delivered, 1970; Live In Person, 1970; Where I'm Coming From, 1971; Talking Book, 1972; Music Of My Mind, 1972; Innervisions, 1973; Fulfillingness' First Finale, 1974; Songs In The Key Of Life, 1976; Stevie Wonder's Journey Through The Secret Life Of Plants, 1979; The Woman In Red, 1984; In Square Circle, 1985; Characters, 1987; Jungle Fever, 1991; Natural Wonder, 1995; Conversation Peace, 1995; Song Review, 1996; At The Close Of a Century, 1999; Bamboozled, 2000; Hotter Than July, 2000; The Definitive Collection, 2002; Conception: An Interpretation of Stevie Wonder's Songs, 2003; A Time To Love, 2005. **Orgs:** Parent ambassador, Breithaupt Vocational Tech Ctr. **Honors/Awds:** Fifteen Grammy Awards; Songwriters Hall of Fame, 1982; Academic Award, 1984; Kennedy Ctr for the Performing Arts Award, 1999; Sammy Khan Lifetime Achievement Award, Songwriters Hall of Fame, 2002; George and Ira Gershwin Lifetime Achievement Award, 2002; Grammy Award, with Take 6 for Love's in Need of Love Today, 2003; Billboard Music Award, 2004; Michigan Walk of Fame, 2004. **Special Achievements:** Participant in numerous social projs, including the creation Martin Luther King Day Nat Holiday, AIDS awareness, anti-Apartheid demonstrations, and campaigns against drunk driving. **Business Addr:** Singer, Black Bull Record Company, 4616 Magnolia Blvd, Burbank, CA 91505, **Business Phone:** (323)877-8383.

WOOD, DR. A WILSON
Executive, clergy. **Personal:** Born Oct 13, 1919, Clinton, SC; son of Wilson and Annie Lee Duckett; married Gertrude M Burton, Sep 29, 1939; children: Verna M Wood Adams & Jesse Leon. **Educ:** Christian Bible Col & Seminary; BTh; Mdiv. **Career:** Kilrny Temple Baptist Church, pastor, 1947-54; Pilgirm Rest Bapt Church, 1947-51; Mt Zion Baptist Church, 1951-60; First Bapt Church, 1954-60; Missionary Kenya EA, 1981; Bethany Baptist Church, pastor, 1960-, sr pastor. **Orgs:** Pres, Winding Gulf Dist Sun Sch Conv, 1949-51; Nr N Side Fellowship Chs sec, 1962, pres, 1964; cor sec Cong Christian Ed, 1962-71; spokesman, Civ Rights Org Columbus 1966-69; exec sec, OH Baptist Gen Conv; sec WV Bd Evanglism; sec, Coal River Dist Asn; exec bd, WV Baptist St Conv; pres, Baptist Pastors Conf Columbus, 1970-78; asst dean Estn Union Dist Asn; judctry Metro Area Ch Bd Columbus; Bapt Minstrl All Columbus; Inter-denom Ministral All; Nat Bapt Conv USA Inc; NAACP, CLASP, Inst 1st Dist Women's Conv, 30 years; bursar EU Bible Sch; coord Columbus Baptist Simultaneous Revival, 1963-88; bd trustees, Ohio Coun Churches, 1990. **Honors/Awds:** OH Leadership Conf Plaque; Outstanding Leadership & Achievements, Ohio Bapt Gen Conv; Baptist Churches. **Special Achievements:** Special Recognitions & Hons because of work done in Bush country of Kenya. **Home Addr:** 2864 Ivanhoe Dr, Columbus, OH 43209. **Business Addr:** Senior Pastor, Bethany Baptist Church, 959 Bulen Ave, Columbus, OH 43206, **Business Phone:** (614)253-2931.

WOOD, ANTON VERNON
Executive. **Personal:** Born Jun 7, 1949, Washington, DC. **Educ:** Shepherd Col, BS, 1971; Montgomery Col, AA, 1969. **Career:** DC Office of Consumer Prot, community educ spec, serv area mgr; DC Power Inc, pub affairs dir; Wash Ecology Cen, prog dir; Wash Area Military & Draft Law Panel, couns. **Orgs:** Chmn, Neighborhood Community 6a; publ mem, DC Neighborhood Reinvestment Community; chmn, com on Employment prac; Metro Wash Planning & Housing Asn; past chmn, DC Statehood Party.

WOOD, BOB. See WOOD, R L.

WOOD, BRENDA BLACKMON
Television news anchorperson. **Personal:** Born Sep 8, 1955, Washington, DC; daughter of Alma Montgomery Blackmon and Henry Blackmon Jr; children: Kristen Brooke & Kandis Brittany. **Educ:** Oakwood Col, Huntsville, AL, 1975; Loma Linda Univ, Riverside CA, BA, Speech Commun & Mass Media, 1977. **Career:** WAAY-TV, Huntsville, AL, broadcaster, 1977-78; WSM-TV, Nashville, Tenn, gen assignment reporter, 1978; WAAY-TV, Huntsville, AL, news reporter, 1977-80; WMC-TV, Memphis, TN, news anchor & reporter, 1980-88; WAGA-TV, Atlanta, GA, news anchor & reporter, 1988-96; 11Alive News, anchor, 1997-. **Orgs:** Nat Acad TV Arts & Sci, 1989-; pres, Southern Soc Adventist Communrs, 1990-; Nat Asn Black Journalists, 1986-; Atlanta Asn Black Journalists; The Atlanta Press Club; Am Women Film. **Honors/Awds:** Gabriel Award of Merit, "Ramses the Great", The Catholic Denomination, 1986; Ace of Diamond Award, Women in Commun, GA, Chapter, 1990; Two Southern Regional Emmys, Best News Anchor; Four-Time Emmy Winner, Prime Time Spec; Emmy, Series Reporting; Emmy, News Team Coverage; GA Asn Broadcasters, News Personality of the Year, 1996; Phoenix Award, NAACP, 1998; Atlanta Asn Bloack Journalist Award, Documentary & Spec Reporting; Best Show Award, AABJ; 15 Emmy Awards. **Home Addr:** 8525 Sharpsburg Ct, Atlanta, GA, **Home Phone:** (770)703-6220. **Business Phone:** (404)892-1611.

WOOD, CURTIS A
Lawyer. **Personal:** Born Jul 31, 1942, Memphis, TN; son of Lou Lee and Curtis; married Claire O. **Educ:** Columbia Col, BA 1964; Columbia Law Sch, LLB, 1967. **Career:** Bedford Stuyvesant Restoration Corp, pres, 1977-82, gen coun, 1972-77; Wood, Williams, Rafalsky & Harris, managing partner, 1982; Wood, Rafalsky & Wood LLP, managing partner, currently. **Orgs:** NY Bar Assc; Ill Bar Asn; Dist Columbia Bar.

WOOD, DAISY M
Executive. **Educ:** SC State Univ. **Career:** Raytheon Systems Co, Global diversity & recruiting dir, currently. **Orgs:** Pres, Nat Pan-Hellenic Coun; bd dir, Urban League. **Honors/Awds:** Achievers Award, Nat Asn Advan Colored People, 1978; Citizen of the Year, Urban League, 1979; Undergraduate Award, 1980, Soror of the Year, 1976-82; Volunteer of the Year, 1983, Founders Day Award, 1983, Community Service Award, 1984, Delta; Outstanding Volunteer, 1986, Volunteer of the Yr, 1985, Community Achiever, 1984, Award Dinner Recognition, 1983, UNCF; Outstanding Prog Award, 1988, Presidential Award, 1987, Soror of the Year, 1987, Reclamation Award, 1984, Outstanding Soror, 1980, National Pan-Hellenic Coun; National Interfraternity Coun Achievement Award, 1992; NC A&T Univ Recruiting Award, 1995. **Home Addr:** PO Box 9507, Arlington, VA 22219.

WOOD, GARLAND E.
Investment banker, businessperson. **Personal:** Born Dec 29, 1943, New York, NY; children: Michelle, Cynthia & Scott. **Educ:** Columbia Col, AB, 1965; Columbia Bus Sch, MBA, 1972. **Career:** Goldman Sachs & Co, partner, 1972-94, ltd partner, 1994-. **Special Achievements:** First African American who was ever named partner at Goldman Sachs.

WOOD, HAROLD LEROY
Judge, lawyer. **Personal:** Born Dec 6, 1919, Bridgeport, CT; married Thelma Anne Cheatham; children: Gregory Lance & Laverne Jill Wertz. **Educ:** Lincoln Univ, AB, 1942; Cornell Univ Law Sch, JD, 1948; New York Univ Law Sch, LLM, 1952. **Career:** Westchester Co Bd Supers, super, 1957-67; NY Senate Albany, leg asst, 1964; Mt Vernon City Common Coun, alderman, 1968-69; Westchester Co, family ct judge, 1969-71; Westchester Co, co ct judge, 1971-74; Supreme Ct, NY, justice supreme ct, 1974-95; Kent Hazzard Wilson Conroy Verni & Freeman LLP, atty, currently. **Orgs:** Pres, NAACP Mt Vernon NY; bd dirs, Mt Vernon Hosp; bd dirs, Urban League White Plains NY. **Honors/Awds:** First African-American elected to public office in Westchester. **Military Serv:** USAF, 2d lt, 1942-46. **Home Addr:** 10 David Rd, Somers, NY 10589, **Home Phone:** (914)248-7579.

WOOD, JUANITA WALLACE
Administrator. **Personal:** Born Jun 30, 1928, Waycross, GA; divorced. **Educ:** Cent State Univ, BA; Northeastern IL Univ, Mass Inner City Studies; John Marshall Sch Law; Loyola Grad Sch Soc Work. **Career:** Cook Co Pub Aid, caseworker, 1952-53; Cook Co Juvenile Ct, probation officer, 1953-58; caseworker C div, 1958-64; Dept Human Resources Div Corrections Youth Serv, comn unit dir corrections soc work, 1969-; counseling youths & families involved in Correctional Syst; neighborhood worker comn youth welfare. **Orgs:** NASW Law Sor, 1958-61; Sensitivity Training Sessions & Seminars; managerial training with present agency, US Civil Serv Comn; Cook Co Comon Crim Justice. **Honors/Awds:** Recip Award, Develop Group Progs to deal with Youths & Families involved in Juvenile Justice Syst.

WOOD, LAWRENCE ALVIN
Ophthalmologist. **Personal:** Born Jan 5, 1949, New York, NY; son of Lillian Miller and Lawrence; married Yvette Marie Binns, Feb 5, 1983 (divorced); children: Aaron J Clark, Lawrence A, Alan R Clark & Seth P; married Vanessa Dale Smith, 1996. **Educ:** Hunter Col, BS, phys ther, 1972; Meharry Med Col, MD, 1979; Naval Hosp, San Diego, CA, ophthal residency, 1988. **Career:** Harlem Hosp, physical therapist, 1972-75; Howard Univ Hosp, intern, 1979-80; Pub Health Serv, gen practitioner, 1980-82; US Navy, flight surgeon, 1982-85; Millington Naval Hosp, dept head ophthal; Naval Hosp, Long Beach, CA, staff ophthalmologist; Naval Hosp, Okinawa, Opthal head, currently. **Orgs:** Acad Ophthal, 1985; Am Med Asn, 1986; Dramatist's Guild, 1986. **Honors/Awds:** Flight Surgeon of the Year, 1984. **Special Achievements:** Production of play "No Marks, Just Memories" 1986. **Military Serv:** USN, capt, 1991-; Navy Commendation Medal, 1983, 1991; Combat Action Ribbon, 1983; National Defense Ribbon, 1991; Meritorious Service Medal, 1999. **Business Phone:** (310)420-5397.

WOOD, LEIGH C
Executive. **Educ:** Williams Col, BA; New York Univ, MBA. **Career:** Cellular Communications Inc, chief exec officer; Air-Touch, chief exec officer, 1993-96; Cellular one, chief exec officer; NTL Inc, chief operating officer, 1996-2000; RealWinWin, chief operating officer, 2005-. **Business Addr:** Cheif Operating Officer, RealWinWin Inc., 1926 Arch St, Philadelphia, PA 19103, **Business Phone:** (215)732-4480.

WOOD, MARGARET BEATRICE
Government official. **Personal:** Born in Charleston, WV; daughter of John D and Ivory B; married Alvin B; children: Alvin B Jr, Irene B & Llewellyn. **Educ:** Howard Univ, BA, cum laude, 1934; Cent Conn State Univ, Elementary Educ, 1949; Univ Hartford, MEd, 1964; Bank St Col NY, NDEA Inst, 1969. **Career:** Hartford Pub Sch, teacher, 1948-60, reading consult, 1960-66, asst supvr reading & dir IRIT, 1966-75, coord reading & communiction arts, 1975-80; Town Bloomfield, Bloomfield, CT, town treas, 1987-90. **Orgs:** Dir, Summer Sch, 1974; Develop Lang Arts Generalist, 1972; pres, Community Assoc Reading Res, 1976; adj prof, Univ Hartford Seminar St Croix & St Thomas, 1978; Counman Town Bloomfield CT, 1969-75, dep mayor, 1974-75. **Honors/Awds:** Sojourner Truth Award, Nat Coun Negro Women, 1972; Distinguished Service Award, Hartford Chapter Delta Sigma Theta, 1981. **Home Addr:** 131 Wadhams Rd, Bloomfield, CT 06002.

WOOD, DR. MICHAEL H (MIKE WOOD)
Surgeon, physician. **Personal:** Born Mar 28, 1942, Dayton, OH; married Florentina Serquina; children: Mark, Anthony & Michael Jr. **Educ:** Ind Inst Tech, BS, 1968; Meharry Med Col, MD, 1972. **Career:** Westland Med Ctr, chief dept surg, 1984; Wayne State Univ Sch Med, Dept Surg, instr, 1977-78, clin asst prof, 1978-88, clin assoc prof, 1988-; Detroit Riverview Hosp, chief, dept surg; Cain-Wood Surgical Associates, physician; Harper Univ Hosp, Bariatric Surg Servs, dir, currently; Centers Obesity Related Illness, med dir & co-founder, currently; pvt pract, currently. **Orgs:** Chmn bd, Detroit Med Group, 1985-86; Am Soc Bariatric Surg; fel, Am Col Surgeons. **Honors/Awds:** Biomed Res Grant, 1979-80; Res Award Prog, 1980-81, Biomed Research Support Grant, 1981-82 Wayne State Univ; sponsor Frederick Coller Award, Am Col Surgeons, MI Chap, 1980; Theodore McGraw Clinical Faculty Teaching Award, Wayne State Univ Dept Surg, 1990; Obesity Surg, Best Author's Award, for "Marginal Ulcer After Gastric Bypass," 1998. **Special Achievements:** Co-author, "Marginal Ulcer After Gastric Bypass: A Prospective Three-Year Study of 173 Patients". **Military Serv:** USAF. **Home Phone:** (810)737-0749. **Business Phone:** (586)558-8435.

WOOD, MIKE. See WOOD, DR. MICHAEL H.

WOOD, OSIE LEON, III
Basketball player, government official. **Personal:** Born Mar 25, 1962, Columbia, SC; married; children: Ladera Ranch. **Educ:** Calif State Univ, Fullerton; Univ Ariz. **Career:** Basketball player (retired), refree; Philadelphia 76ers, 1984-86; Wash Bullets, 1986; NJ Nets, 1986-87; Atlanta Hawks, 1987-88; San Antonio Spurs, 1988; NJ Nets, 1989-90; Sacramento Kings, 1990-91; Nat Basketball Asn, referee, currently. **Orgs:** Nat Basketball Asn. **Honors/Awds:** Titan All-American. **Business Addr:** Referee, National Basketball Association, Olympic Tower, 645 5th Ave 15th Fl, New York, NY 10022-5986.*

WOOD, R L (BOB WOOD)
Executive. **Educ:** Univ Mich, BA, hist. **Career:** The Dow Chem Co; Crompton Corp, 2004-05; Jarden Corp, bd dir; Praxair, bd dir; Chemtura Corp, chmn, pres, ceo, 2005-. **Orgs:** Past chmn, Big Brothers/Big Sisters Am; treas, bd mem, exec comt, USA Gymnastics; vice chmn, Am Ch Coun. **Business Addr:** Chairman, President & Chief Executive Officer, Chemtura Corporation, 199 Benson Rd, Middlebury, CT 06749, **Business Phone:** (203)573-2000.*

WOOD, TOMMIE
Manager, basketball executive. **Career:** NBA, referee, currently. **Orgs:** Nat Basketball Referees Asn; Nat Asn Advan Colored People. **Business Addr:** Referee, National Basketball Association, 645 5th Ave 15th Fl, New York, NY 10022-5986, **Business Phone:** (212)826-7000.

WOOD, VIVIAN FRANCES
Librarian. **Personal:** Born Jan 28, 1945, Plainfield, NJ; daughter of L Cassell Sr and Sarah Frances. **Educ:** Howard Univ, BA, 1967; Catholic Univ, MA, 1969; Rutgers Univ, MLS, 1974. **Career:** DC Pub Schs, teacher, 1969-71; Prince Georges County, Md, Pub Libr, asst librn, 1971-73; Rutgers Univ, ref librn, asst prof, 1974-81; Hofstra Univ, colction develop librn, asst prof libr servs, asst prof emer, currently. **Orgs:** Nassau County Econ Opportunity Comn-92; New Jersey Libr Asn, Acad Libr Div, vpres, 1979-80; secy, exec bd mem, Asn Black Women in Higher Educ, Nassau/Suffolk Chap, 1994-97; vpres, Nassau City Libr Asn, Acad & Spec Libraries Div, 1993; Nassau County Libr Asn, Acad & Spec Libraries Div, pres, 1994. **Honors/Awds:** United Nations Fourth World Conf on Women/NGO Forum in Beijing, China, deleg, 1995; deleg, Res Librns Deleg to SAfrica, 1997. **Special Achievements:** Conf Paper, "Bibliographic Overview Harlem Renaissance," Nat Endowment for Humanities & Hofstra Univ; "Iceland" Read More

About It, vol 3 An Encyclopedia Information Sources on Hist Figures & Events, Pierian Press, 1989; Conf Paper "Colction Develop for Africana Studies," Assoc Col & Res Libraries, 1993; Panelist: Race, Gender & Academe, United Nations Fourth World Conf on Women NGO Forum, Beijing, China, 1995. **Home Addr:** 726 Center Dr, Baldwin, NY 11510. **Business Addr:** Assitent Professor Emerita, Hofstra University Axinn Library, 902c Axinn Libr, 123 Hofstra, Hempstead, NY 11550, **Business Phone:** (516)463-6431.

WOOD, HON. WILLIAM S
Lawyer, judge. **Personal:** Born Dec 3, 1926, Chicago, IL; married Rosita; children: William Jr & Eugene T. **Educ:** Univ Iowa, BA, 1947, LLD, 1950. **Career:** State Atty Off, asst atty, 1956-60; Pvt pract, 1960-83; Cook Co Cts, assoc judge, presiding judge, currently. **Orgs:** Chicago Bar Asn; Ill Judicial Coun; Ill Judges Asn. **Military Serv:** AUS, 1950-53. **Home Addr:** 4800 Chicago Beach Dr, Chicago, IL 60615. **Business Addr:** Presiding Judge, Circuit Court of Cook County, 2600 S Calif Ave, Chicago, IL 60608, **Business Phone:** (773)869-3160.

WOOD, WILLIAM VERNELL, SR.
Executive. **Personal:** Born Dec 23, 1936, Washington, DC; son of John and Amanda; married Sheila Peters; children: LaJuane, Andre & William Jr. **Educ:** Coalinga Jr Col, 1956; Univ Southern CA, BS, 1957-60. **Career:** Football player (retired), Coach, President; Green Bay Packers, Nat Football League, free safety, 1960-71; Philadelphia Bell WFL, head coach, 1976-77; Toronto Argonauts Football Team, asst coach, 1979-80, head coach, 1980-82; Willie Wood Mech Syst Inc, pres, 1983-. **Orgs:** Bd dir, Police Boys & Girls Club, 1984-. **Honors/Awds:** All-Pro 6 Yrs, Nat Football League, 1960-71; Pro-Bowl 8 yrs, Nat Football League, 1960-71; 5 World Championship Team Green Bay Packers, 1961-62, 1965-67; 1st two Superbowl Championship Teams, 1966-67; All 25 yrs Team NFL, 1982; National Football League Hall of Fame, 1989; Silver Anniversary Super Bowl All-Star Team. **Special Achievements:** First black head coach in professional football. **Business Addr:** Owner, President, Willie Wood Mechanical Systems, 7941 16th St NW, Washington, DC 20012, **Business Phone:** (202)746-3315.

WOODALL, DR. JOHN WESLEY
Physician. **Personal:** Born May 24, 1941, Cedartown, GA; son of Japheus P and Estherlena Harris; married Janet Carol Nunn; children: John Wesley Jr, Japheus Clay & Janita Carol. **Educ:** Ball State Univ, BS, med tech, 1959-64; St Johns Med Ctr, internship, med tech, 1964-65; Ind Univ Sch Med, MD, 1965-69; Whishard Memorial Hosp, rotating internship, 1969-70. **Career:** St Johns Hosp, chief Ob-Gyn, 1974, chief family pract, 1977; Bridges-Campbell-Woodall Med Corp, physician, owner; pvt pract, currently. **Orgs:** Diplo, Am Acad Family Pract; fel, Am Acad Family Pract, Aesculapian Med Soc, Am Med Dir Asn; Am Geriatric Soc; Nat Med Asn; Urban League; Friendship Baptist Church; life mem, NAACP. **Special Achievements:** First african american to establish a health clinic in anderson; First african american to become the president of staff in anderson community hospital. **Military Serv:** USAF, capt, 1970-72. **Business Addr:** Physician/Owner, Bridges Campbell Woodhall Medical Corporation, 1302 Madison Ave, Anderson, IN 46016, **Business Phone:** (317)644-3673.

WOODARD, DR. A. NEWTON
Physician. **Personal:** Born Aug 3, 1936, Selma, AL; married Bettye Davillier. **Educ:** Xavier Univ, New Orleans, BS, 1956; Meharry Med Col, Nashville, MD, 1960. **Career:** Cent Med Ctr, Los Angeles, co-owner & co-dir, 1970-; Kate Bitting Reynolds Mem Hosp, Winston-Salem, intern, 1960-61, 1962-66; Charlotte Community Hosp, resident, 1961-62; Portsmouth Naval Hosp, 1966-68; Dr Bassett Brown, partnership, 1968-. **Military Serv:** USN, lt comdr, 1966-68.

WOODARD, ALFRE
Actor. **Personal:** Born Nov 8, 1952, Tulsa, OK; daughter of Marion H Woodard and Constance; married Roderick Spencer; children: Duncan & Mavis. **Educ:** Boston Univ, BFA. **Career:** Films: Extremities, 1986; Scrooged, 1988; Grand Canyon, 1991; Passion Fish, 1992; The Gun in Betty Lou's Handbag, 1992; Heart & Souls, 1993; Crooklyn, 1994; How to Make an American Quilt, 1995; The Piano Lesson, 1995; Star Trek: First Contact, 1996; Primal Fear, 1996; Miss Firecracker, 1989; Miss Evers' Boys, 1997; Down in the Delta, co producer, 1998; Mumford, 1999; Love & Basketball, 2000; K-PAX, 2001; The Wild Thorn berrys Movie, 2002; The Singing Detective, 2003; The Core, 2003; Radio, 2003; A Wrinkle In Time, 2003; The Forgotten, 2004; Beauty Shop, 2005-006; Something New, 2006; Take the Lead, 2006; Pictures of Hollis Woods, 2007; Reach for Me, 2008; TV Series: "Tucker's Witch", 1982; "Hill Street Blues", 1983; "Sara", 1985; "L.A. Law", 1986; "St. Elsewhere", 1985-87;"Frasier", 1994; "The Practice", 2003; "Desperate Housewives", 2005. **Honors/Awds:** Miss KAY Chi Chap, Boston Univ 1974; Emmy Award, 1984-88, 1990, 1995, 1997-98, 2003, 2006; Golden Apple Award, Best new comer, 1984; Image Award Best Actress, NAACP, 1984; Independent Spirit Awards, 1993; Screen Actors Guild, Outstanding Actress in a TV Movie or Miniseries, The Piano Lesson, 1996; Emmy Award, Outstanding Lead Actress in a Miniseries or A Special, Miss Evers' Boys, 1997; Screen Actors Guild, Outstanding Actress in a TV Movie or Miniseries, Miss Evers' Boys, 1998; Golden Globe, Best Actress ina Mini, Miss Evers' Boys, 1998; Satellite Awards, 1998; Nominations:Academy ward, Best Supporting Actress, Cross Creek, 1984; Golden Globe,Best Supporting Actress, Passion Fish, 1993; Emmy Award, Outstanding Lead Actress in a Miniseries or Special, The Piano Lesson (Hallmark Hall of Fame, 1995; Women in Film Crystal Awards, 1995; Cable ACE Awards, 1997;Daytime Emmy Awards2001; Image Awards, 2004; Character and Morality in Entertainment Awards, 2005; Screen Actors Guild Awards, 2006; Black Reel Awards, 2007. **Special Achievements:** Oscar Award, nominee. **Business Addr:** Actress, Block-Korenbrat, 8271 Melrose Ave, Los Angeles, CA 90046, **Business Phone:** (323)655-0593.

WOODARD, DR. CHARLES JAMES
School administrator. **Personal:** Born Jun 9, 1945, Laurel, MS; married; children: Andrea, Craig, Ashley, Adeena & Ataya. **Educ:** Edinboro Univ PA, BS 1968; Wayne State Univ, MA 1972; Univ Mich, PhD 1975. **Career:** Univ Mich Flint, asst, asst dean spec proj 1973-75; Allegheny Col, assoc dean stud, 1975-82; Coppin State Col, dean stud serv, 1982-85; Ind Univ Northwest, dean stud serv, 1985-87; Savannah State Col, Stud Affairs, vpres dean, 1987-90; Cheyney Univ, Stud Affairs, vpres, appointed loaned exec, 1992; Kutztown Univ Penn, Student Affairs, vpres, dean, 1990-; coord Family Educ Rights & Privacy Act, currently. **Orgs:** Nat Asn Financial Aids Minority Stud, 1972-75; Am Personnel & Guidance Asn, 1975-; Non-White Concerns in Guidance, 1975-; Unity Inst Human Develop, 1976-80; Boy Scouts Am, 1977-82; race rels consult, Penn State Educ Asn, 1978-81; Am Higher Educ Asn, 1985-; Salvation Army, 1986. **Honors/Awds:** Kappa Delta Pi 1968; Black Achievers Award, presented by Black Opinion Magazine, 1991; fac, staff inductee, Phi Kappa Phi Honor Soc, Kutztown Univ, 1997. **Special Achievements:** Publication, "The Challenge of Your Life - A guide to help prepare students to get screened into higher education" 1974; co-author, paper, "A Comparative Study on Some Variables Related to Academic Success as perceived By Both Black and White Students" 1977; co-author, paper, "Enhancing the College Adjustment of Young Culturally Different Gifted Students" 1986. **Business Addr:** Vice President, Kutztown University, Department Student Services and Campus Life, 319 Stratton Administration Building, PO Box 730, Kutztown, PA 19530, **Business Phone:** (610)683-4020.

WOODARD, FREDRICK
School administrator, poet. **Personal:** Born Jan 29, 1939, Kingfisher, OK; son of Ralph Woodard and Rosetta Reed Bishop; widowed; married Barbara (died 1989); children: Jon & Jarilyn. **Educ:** Iowa Wesleyan Col, Mt Pleasant, BA, 1961; Univ Iowa, Iowa City, MA, 1972, PhD, 1976. **Career:** West High Sch, Davenport, IA, teacher, 1961-66; Black Hawk Community Col, Moline, IL, instr, 1967-69; Cornell Col, Mt Vernon, IA, instr, 1972-76; Univ Iowa, Iowa City, from instr to assoc prof, 1973-80, prof, currently, acting assoc dean fac, Off Acad Affairs, 1981-83, assoc dean fac, Off VPres Acad Affairs, 1983-90, assoc vpres Acad Affairs, 1990-, Mus Art, interim dir, 1990-92; Univ Calif, San Diego, vis assoc prof, 1980. **Orgs:** Chair session, Midwest Modern Lang Asn, 1970, 1972, 1973, 1977-79, 1981-83; chair session, Coun Col Compos, 1975, 1977, 1981, 1983, 1985; Am Libr Asn, 1980-; Modern Lang Asn, 1980-; chair session, Nat Coun Teachers Eng, 1985; comt mem, Big 10 Acad Personnel Officers, 1985; comt mem, Prof & Orgn Develop Network Higher Educ, 1985-. **Special Achievements:** Book : Reasons to Dream. Editor : True Poems, 1978; Love Songs and New Spirituals, 1980; Human Rights/Human Wrongs: Art and Social Change, 1986. **Home Addr:** 2905 Prairie du Chien Rd NE, Iowa City, IA 52240, **Home Phone:** (319)354-1498. **Business Addr:** Associate Vice President, Professor of English, Office of Academic Affairs, University of Iowa, 111 Jessup Hall, Iowa City, IA 52242, **Business Phone:** (319)335-0317.

WOODARD, KENNETH EMIL
Football player. **Personal:** Born Jan 22, 1960, Detroit, MI. **Educ:** Tuskegee Inst. **Career:** Football player (retired); Denver Broncos, linebacker, 1982-86; Post-season play, 1986: Pittsburgh Steelers, 1987; San Diego Chargers, linebacker, 1988-89.

WOODARD, LOIS MARIE
Systems analyst. **Personal:** Born in Porter, TX; married Laverne; children: Alesia Brewer, Erica Brewer & Cheryl Brewer. **Educ:** Los Angeles Trade Tech Col, AA, 1970; Cal Poly State Univ, San Luis Obispo, BS, 1975. **Career:** Cal Poly San Luis Obispo CA, data processor, 1972-76; Burroughs Corp, programmer, 1976-77; Long Beach Col Bus, instr, 1977-80; Nat Auto & Casualty Ins, syst analyst, 1980-. **Orgs:** Bus woman Esquire Cleaners, 1979-87; pres, Stewardess Bd 2 1st AME Ch, 1980-82; Nat auto co coord Youth Motivation Task Force, 1984-87; conductress Order Eastern Stars, 1985-86; corresponding sec Zeta Phi Beta Sor, 1986; Nat Asn Advan Colored People, 1986-87. **Honors/Awds:** Appreciation Award, 1st AME Church, Pasedena, CA, 1981. **Home Addr:** 804 W Figueroa Dr, Altadena, CA 91001. **Business Addr:** System Analyst, National Auto & Casualty Ins, 150 So Los Robles Suite 900, Pasadena, CA 91101, **Business Phone:** (818)577-0600.

WOODARD, LYNETTE
Basketball player, basketball coach, financial manager. **Personal:** Born Aug 12, 1959, Wichita, KS. **Educ:** Univ Kans, attended 1981. **Career:** Basketball player (retired), basketball coach (retired); Italy, 1987; japan, 1990-93; Cleveland Rockers, guard, 1997; Detroit Shock, 1998; New York City, stockbroker; univ kans, asst coach, 1999; MarianWashington, interim head coach, 2004; Kansas City, athletics dir, 1992-94; PFS Investments Incorporation, financial rep, 2004; A.G. Edwards & Sons Inc, Financial Consultant. currently. **Honors/Awds:** Wade Trophy, 1981; Broderick Cup; NCAA Top Five Award; GTE Academic Hall of Fame, 1992; Inducted in Basketball Hall of Fame, 2004; Inducted in Women's Basketball Hall of Fame, 2005. **Special Achievements:** First woman selected for the NCAA Top Five Award. *

WOODARD, RHONDA MARIE
Insurance executive. **Personal:** Born Jul 14, 1949, Kansas City, MO; daughter of Allen and Zelma; divorced; children: Nicole & Jeremy. **Educ:** George Williams Col, BS, 1971. **Career:** Allstate Ins Co, underwriting opers mgr, 1984, regional underwriting mgr, 1984-88, field support dir, 1988-90, personal lines dir, 1990-92, personal lines mkt dir, 1992-93, asst vp, 1993-95, vp, 1995-; underwriting vp, 1995-98, product vp, 1999-2002, vp policy, compliance & homeowners, 2002-. **Orgs:** Leadership Ill, 1997-; Neighborhood Housing Servs Am, bd dir, bd trustees, 1993-; Nat Black Womens Health Projects, 1988-. **Honors/Awds:** Chicago YMCA, Black & Hispanic Achievers; Dollars & Sense, Best and Brightest; YMCA of NY, Acad Women Achievers. **Business Addr:** Product Vice President, Product Operations, Allstate Insurance Co, 2775 Sanders Rd Suite E1N, Northbrook, IL 60062.

WOODARD, SAMUEL L.
Educator. **Personal:** Born May 26, 1930, Fairmont, WV; married Linda Waples; children: Mary Ellen, Charlene, Gail & Dana. **Educ:** Mansfield State Univ, BS, 1953; Canisius Col, MS, 1959; Lincoln Univ, Buffalo, EdD. **Career:** Buffalo & LA, teacher, 1954-66; Genesee-Humboldt Jr High Buffalo, vice prin, 1966-67; Temple Univ, asst prof educ, 1967-68; Philadelphia Sch Dist, dir prog implementation, 1968-70; Ill State Univ, assoc prof educ admin 1970-73; Howard Univ, prof educ admin, prof emer, currently. **Orgs:** Intl Asn Appl Soc Sci; Intl Transactional Analysis Asn; Phi Delta Kappa; Nat All Black Sch Educ; life mem, NAACP; life mem, Alpha Phi Alpha; founder, Naomi Woodard-Smoot Scholar. **Honors/Awds:** Distinguished Pennsylvania Educator, Pa Col Alumni Asn; Role Model for American Youth, Pa Col Alumni Asn. **Special Achievements:** First black student to receive the Phoenician Trophy, 1948; first African American at the State University of New York, Buffalo to receive a doctorate in educational administration, 1966; first black to teach on Educ TV in NY State, Buffalo, WNED-TV, 1961-62. **Business Addr:** Professor Emeritus, Howard University, 2400 Sixth St NW, Washington, DC 20059, **Business Phone:** (202)806-6100.

WOODBECK, FRANK RAYMOND
Media executive. **Personal:** Born Feb 2, 1947, Buffalo, NY; son of George and Avil; married Virginia Ann Carter; children: Harrison, Terry & Frank Raymond II. **Educ:** State Univ NY, Buffalo, BS, 1973. **Career:** Capital Cities Comm WKBW Radio, gen sales mgr, 1977-80, pres & gen mgr, 1980-84; Capital Cities Cable Inc, vpres advert, 1985-86; Post-Newsweek Cable Inc, advert vip, 1986-91; ABC Radio Networks, vip affiliate rel, 1992-2000; One Media Pl, sr vpres, radio, 2000-. **Orgs:** Omega Psi Phi Frat, 1976-; ticket chmn, Dunlop Pro Am Awards Dinner, 1979-84; vice chmn, chmn, Humboldt Br YMCA, 1979-84; Sigma Pi Phi Frat, 1981-; treas, ABC Radio Dir Affil Bd, 1983-84; pres, Buffalo Radio Asn, 1983-84. **Military Serv:** USAF, staff sgt, 1964-68; Air Force Commendation Medal, Nat Defense Medal, Vietnam Service Medal. **Business Addr:** Senior VP-Radio, One Media Place, 90 Pk Ave 10th Fl, New York, NY 10016, **Business Phone:** (212)297-1024.

WOODBURY, DAVID HENRY
Scientist. **Personal:** Born Mar 29, 1930, Camden, SC; son of David and Arline; married Margaret Jane Claytor; children: Arline E, Brenda L, Laura R, Kathryn L, Larry D, David H. **Educ:** Johnson C Smith Univ, BS, 1951; Va State Col, MS, 1952; Univ Mich, MD, 1961. **Career:** Atomic Energy Comn, biologist, 1955-57; Westland Med Ctr, dir, nuclear med, 1968-90; Univ Mich, asst prof, internal med, 1968-90; USPHS, dir, nuclear med, 1967-68. **Orgs:** Consult, FDA Radiopharmaceuticals Advisor, 1978-82, med officer, 1990-95, NRC Adv Comm, 1979-; vpres, Johnson C Smith Alumni Asn, 1978; bd regents, Am Col Nuclear Physicians, 1980-87; chief med staff, Wayne County Hosp, 1984-85; pres, club Johnson C Smith Univ, 1984; pres, Am Col Nuclear Physicians, 1987. **Honors/Awds:** Robert C Wood Scholar, Johnson C Smith Univ, 1950; fel, Am Col Nuclear Physicians, 1982. **Military Serv:** AUS, cpl; USPHS, lt col, 1961-68. *

WOODBURY, DR. MARGARET CLAYTOR
Physician. **Personal:** Born Oct 30, 1937, Roanoke, VA; daughter of John Bunyan Claytor Sr (deceased) and Roberta Morris Woodfin Claytor (deceased); married David Henry Woodbury Jr, Nov 30, 1968; children: David Henry III; married Lawrence DeWitt Young (divorced); children: Laura Ruth & Lawrence DeWitt Jr.

Educ: Mount Holyoke Col, AB, Cum Laude, 1958; Albany Med Col, Trustee Bio-Chem Award, 1960; Meharry Med Col, MD, Pediat Prize, 1962. **Career:** US Pub Health Serv Hosp, Staten Island NY, asst chief med/endo, 1967-68; US Pub Health Serv Hosp, Detroit MI, chief outpatient clin,1968-69; US Pub Health Serv Outpatient Clin, Detroit MI, med officer in charge, 1969-71; Univ Mich Med Sch, instr med endo, 1969-80, asst prof, 1980-90, HCOP proj dir, 1984-90, asst dean student & minority affairs, 1983-90, asst prof emer, currently. **Orgs:** Admis comm, Univ Mich Med Sch, 1978-83; chmn, ACAAP, Univ Mich Med Sch, 1983-91; chair steering comm., MLKCHC Series, 1984-85; nominating comm, bd alumnae, 1981-85, trustee, 1985-97, Mount Holyoke Col; pres, Alumnae Asn Mount Holyoke Col, 1994-97; co-chair precinct, Ann Arbor Democratic Party, 1972-73; parent rep, Eng Indust Support Prog, 1978-82; founding mem, Ann Arbor Alliance Achievement, 1981-89; volunteer various health related comts. **Honors/Awds:** Alpha Omega Alpha Hon Med Soc, Meharry Med Col, 1962; Alumnae Medal Hon, Mount Holyoke Col, 1983; diplo, Am Bd Internal Med, 1969; Dean's List, Albany & Meharry Med Col, 1959-62; 1st Biochemistry Award, Albany Med Col, 1959; Pediat Prize, Meharry Med Col, 1961; Outstanding Young Woman Am, 1967; Hon mem, Sigma Gamma Rho Sor Inc, Outstanding Woman for the 21st Century, 1986; Consortium Doctors Inc, 1993. **Special Achievements:** Publisher: has published numerous articles in field, "Quantitative Determination Cysteine in Salivary Amylase," Mt Holyoke Col, 1958; "Hypopituitarism in Current Therapy," WB Saunders Co, 1967; "Cushing's Syndrome in Infancy, A Case Complicated by Monilial Endocarditis," Am J Dis Child, 1971; "Three Generations Familial Turner Syndrome," Annals Int Med 1978; "Virilizing Syndrome Associated With Adrenocortical Adenoma Secreting Predominantly Testosterone," Am J Med 1979; "Hormones in Your Life From Childbearing (Or Not) to Menopause," Mt Holyoke Alumnae Quarterly 1980; "Scintigraphic Localization Ovarian Dysfunction," J Nuc Med, 1988. Co-author: Virginia Kaleidoscope: The Claytor Family of Roanoke & Some of its Kinships, from First Families of Virginia and Their Former Slaves, 1995. **Military Serv:** US Pub Health Serv, sr surgeon, 1961-71. **Business Addr:** Assitant Professor Emeritus, Department of Internal Medicine, 1500 E Med Cr Dr, Ann Arbor, MI 48109, **Business Phone:** (734)936-4340.

WOODEN, SHAWN ANTHONY
Football player, financial manager. **Personal:** Born Oct 23, 1973, Philadelphia, PA; married Marcia Charise Reeves, 2004. **Educ:** Notre Dame Univ, BS, comput sci. **Career:** Football player (retired); Miami Dolphins, safety, 1996-99, 2001-04; Chicago Bears, safety, 2000; Garrido & Wooden Wealth Mgt, financial mgt, currently. **Orgs:** Habitat for Humanity; Big Brothers & Big Sisters; Miami Dolphins Found; Broward Boys & Girls Club; Cystic Fibrosis Found; Prudential No Passing Zone; FAD orgn. **Honors/Awds:** Dolphins Community Serv Award, 1997. **Business Addr:** Financial Planner & Partner, Garrido and Wooden Wealth Management.*

WOODEN, TERRY
Football player, scout. **Personal:** Born Jan 14, 1967, Hartford, CT; married Cindy; children: Tea, Maya & Brock. **Educ:** Syracuse Univ, sociol. **Career:** Football player (retired), Scout; Seattle Seahawks, linebacker, 1990-96; Kansas City Chiefs, 1997; Oakland Raiders, 1998; Buffalo Bills, scout, 2003-06; New Orleans Saints, 2007-. **Honors/Awds:** All-Rookie Team, Football Digest, 1990; Ed Block Courage Award, 1992; Steve Largent Award, 1995. **Business Phone:** (716)648-1800.

WOODFOLK, JOSEPH O.
Educator. **Personal:** Born Mar 4, 1933, St Thomas, Virgin Islands of the United States; divorced. **Educ:** Morgan State Col, AB; NM Highlands Univ, ME, 1955; Morgan State Col, MA;Indian Culture Univ, Mysore, India, cert grad studies, 1973. **Career:** Baltimore County Bd Educ, chmn Social studies dept, 1969-; Baltimore Co Public Schs, teacher, 1955-; State Univ NJ, fac; NJ; Johns Hopkins Univ. **Orgs:** Develop, curric K-12 soc stud prog Baltimore county, 1969-; dir, Fulbright Alumni India summer stud prog; Teacher Asn, Baltimore County; Md State Teacher Asn; Nat Educ Asn; Phi Alpha Theta; Gamma Theta Upsilon; Am Hist Soc; Md Hist Soc; Org Am Historians; Soc Hist Educ; Nat Asn Advan Colored People; Friends Kenya; Asn Foreign Stud Alumni Asn; NM Highlands Univ; Phi Delta Kappa, John Hopkins Univ; eastern reg dir, publ Phi Beta Sigma Frat; Am Heart Asn Minority Comm Affairs; Phi Beta Sigma. **Honors/Awds:** Fulbright Fel, 1973; Special Recognition Award, Eta Omega chap Phi Alpha Theta. **Business Addr:** Faculty, Woodlawn Sr High School, 1801 Woodlawn Dr, Baltimore, MD 21207.

WOODFORD, JOHN NILES
Journalist, editor. **Personal:** Born Sep 24, 1941, Chicago, IL; son of Hackley E Woodford, MD and Mary Steele Woodford, MA; married Elizabeth Subeva Duffy Woodford, Jan 30, 1965; children: Duffy, Maize & Will. **Educ:** Harvard Univ, BA, Eng lit. magna cum laude, 1964, MA, 1968. **Career:** Ebony Mag, asst ed, 1967-68; Muhammad Speaks Newspaper, ed chief, 1968-72; Chicago Sun Times, copy ed, 1972-74; NY Times, copy ed nat desk, 1974-77; Ford Motor Co, Ford Times, sr ed, 1977-80; Univ MI, exec ed, 1981-2004; freelance writer & ed, currently; Mich today, exec ed. **Orgs:** Fac, Univ MI Asn Black Profs; essayist & reviewer, Black Scholar Jour. **Honors/Awds:** 3 Gold Medals & other Awards, Coun Advancement & Support Educ, 1984-86. **Special Achievements:** author: A Journey to Afghanistan, Freedomways, 1985; Messaging the Blackman, Voices From the Underground, Mica Press, 1992. **Home Addr:** 1922 Lorraine Pl, Ann Arbor, MI 48104.

WOODHOUSE, ENOCH O'DELL, II
Lawyer. **Personal:** Born Jan 14, 1927, Boston, MA. **Educ:** Yale Univ, attended 1952; Univ Paris France, jr yr, 1951; Yale Law Sch; Boston Univ Law Sch, LLB, 1955; Acad Int Law Peace Palace Hague Netherlands, 1960. **Career:** Pvt pract atty; US State Dept, diplomatic courier; City Boston, asst corp coun; Int French & German, pvt prac law; trial couns corp law. **Orgs:** Int Bar Assc; Boston Bar Asn; exec comt, Mass Trial Lawyers Asn; Yale Club of Boston; Reserve Officers Asn; Am Trial Lawyers Asn elected bd of Govs Yale, 1975; appointed Liaison Officer for AF Acad; Judge Adv Gen. **Military Serv:** WW II, lt col, AF Res.

WOODHOUSE, DR. JOHNNY BOYD
Clergy. **Personal:** Born Nov 9, 1945, Elizabeth City, NC; son of Charles and Helen; married Darlyn Blakeney; children: Yolanda, Johnny Jr, Fletcher & Touray. **Educ:** Elizabeth City State, BS, 1967; Shaw Divinity, MD, 1973; Va Sem, DD, 1983. **Career:** PW Moore High Sch, teacher, 1970; NC, Dept Corrections, instr, 1977; Johnston Tech Col, instr, 1978, dir human resources develop, currently; Women Correctional Ctr, Raleigh, NC, instr; Red Oak Grove Baptist Church, sr minister, 1980. **Orgs:** NAACP; MIZPAH Temple #66, Goldsboro, NC; Master Mason Prince Hall; Nat Bapt Conv Inc; treas, Smithfield Ministerial Conf; chmn bd, NC Child & Day Care Ctr; vpres, Smithfield Minister's Conf, 1975; vice moderator, Tar River Missionary Baptist Asn 1980; moderator, Tar River Asn, 1988. **Honors/Awds:** NAACP Award, 1970; Pastor of the year, 1972; Martin Luther King Jr Award, 1991. **Home Addr:** PO Box 2103, Smithfield, NC 27577. **Business Phone:** (919)209-2086.

WOODHOUSE, ROSSALIND YVONNE
Entrepreneur, manager, chief executive officer. **Personal:** Born Jun 7, 1940, Detroit, MI; daughter of Allen Venable and Pereditha Venable; married Donald; children: Joycelyn & Justin. **Educ:** Univ Wash, BA sociol, 1963; Univ Wash, MSW 1970, PhD, 1983. **Career:** Entrepreneur, manager, chief executive officer (Retired); New Careers Proj Seattle, prog cord guide consult, 1968; Seattle Housing Auth, comm org specialist, 1969-70; Central Area Motiv Prog Seattle, exec dir, 1971-73; Edmonds Community Col Lynnwood, instr cord, 1973-77; WA State Dept Licensing Olympia, dir, 1977-81; Rainier Ban corp, vpres employee rel, 1981-84; Urban League Metropolitan Seattle WA, pres & ceo, 1984-98; Woman Achievement, Women Commun, 1991; Custom Fit Productions inc, pres, 1998. **Orgs:** Alpha Kappa Alpha Sor, 1958; pres, Seattle Womens Commun, 1971-72,1975-76; bd mem, Seattle Pvt Indust Coun, 1986-98; brd trustees, Central Wash Univ, 1986-98; charter mem, brd, Natl Assn Minority Trusteeship Higher Educ, 1990. **Honors/Awds:** Natalie Skells Award, 1989; Alumni Legend, Univ Wash, 1987. **Special Achievements:** First female chief Motor Vehicle Dir in US or Canada; only black woman to direct a Cabinet Level Agency in Wash State.

WOODIE, HENRY L.
Engineer, clergy. **Personal:** Born Oct 24, 1940, Tallahassee, FL; son of Albert and Willie Mae Simmons Stephens; married Kathey Curry, Oct 20, 1990; children: Henry LaSean, Dorian Small, Aaron Jones & Travis Jones. **Educ:** Fla A&M Univ, BS, 1963; Stetson Univ, BBA, 1974; Rollins Col, MSM, 1979. **Career:** African Methodist Episcopal Church, minister, 1991-; Brevard Co Sch Syst Fla, teacher; RCA Patrick AFB Fla, mathematician; Auditor Gen Off Fla, auditor; Daytona Beach Community Col, internal auditor; Bell South, engr mgr. **Honors/Awds:** Keeper of peace, Omega Psi Phi Fraternity, 1990-91. **Home Addr:** 10 Hardee Circle N, Rockledge, FL 32955. **Business Addr:** Engineer, Clergyman, Bell South, 517 Hughlett Ave, Cocoa, FL 32922.

WOODING, DAVID JOSHUA
Physician. **Personal:** Born Apr 10, 1959, Cleveland, OH; married Karen Aline Rogers; children: Joshua David. **Educ:** Oakwood Col, BA, 1981; Meharry Med Col, MD, 1986. **Career:** Physician, currently. **Business Addr:** Physician, 5988 Via Loma, Riverside, CA 92506.

WOODLAND, DR. CALVIN EMMANUEL
President (organization), educator, school administrator. **Personal:** Born Nov 3, 1943, LaPlata, MD; son of Mildred and Philip H. **Educ:** Morgan State Univ, BS, 1965; Howard Univ, MA, 1970; Rutgers Univ, EdD,1975; Southern Calif Prof Studies, Psy D, 1997. **Career:** Md Dept Health & Ment Hygiene, music & rehab therapist, 1966-70; Essex County Col, counr/dir educ advisement, 1970-74; Morgan State Univ Sch Educ, dir teacher corps, assoc prof educ asst dean, 1974-81; Coppin State Col, dir spec serv, acting dean studies, 1981-82; Charles County Community Col, dean, 1982-86; Northern Va Community Col, dean, 1986; Daytona Beach Community Col, vpres stud develop; Bergen Community Col, vpres stud serv; Capital Community Col, pres, 2005-. **Orgs:** Evaluator, Mid States Asn Cols & Schs, 1979-; Am Psychol Asn; Am Asn Coun Develop; Am Asn Rehab Therapists; Nat Comn African-Am; lic ment health counr; Nat Bd Cert Counselors; pres, bd dirs, NCBAA. **Honors/Awds:** HEW Fel, US Dept Health, Educ Welfare, 1976; Innovations Coun Psychol Book Rev Jour Contemp Psychol, 1979; Outstanding Achievement Award & Community Service Award, Southern Md Chain Chap Links, 1986. **Home Addr:** 111 Mulberry St Renaissance Towers Suite 6D, Newark, NJ 07102. **Business Addr:** President, Capital Community College, 950 Main St, Hartford, CT 06103.

WOODLAND, STANLEY R
President (Organization). **Career:** SmithKline Beecham, dir; Communs Media Inc, pres & chief exec officer, currently. **Business Addr:** President, Chief Executive Officer, Communications Media Inc, 2200 Renaissance Blvd Suite 106, King of Prussia, PA 19406, **Business Phone:** (484)322-0880.

WOODLEY, ARTO
Chief executive officer. **Personal:** Born Aug 12, 1965, Tacoma, WA; son of Patricia E and Arto; married Yvette, Nov 30, 1991; children: 2. **Educ:** Bowling Green Univ, BS, jour, 1988, MA, col stud personnel, 1990. **Career:** Bowling Green State Univ, grad asst, 1988-90, asst vp, Univ relations, 1990-92; Wright State Univ, assoc dir corp found relation, 1992-94; dir advancement, Sch Med, 1994; Frontline Outreach Inc, pres, currently. **Orgs:** Dist comnr, Boy Scouts Am, 1994-95; emer mem, African Am Community Fund (Dayton Foundation); Fla's Comn on Marriage & Families; Orange County Fla Sch Readiness Coalition; the Gov Faith based Adv Comt; Mentoring Coalition, co-chair, 1994-95; Parity 2000, 1994-; Redeeming the Time Newsletter, ed; Visions Newsletter, ed, 1990. **Honors/Awds:** Presidential Service Award, Bowling Green State Univ, 1988, 1990. **Special Achievements:** Speech: Dr King & the Civil Rights Movement: Was it Just A Dream?, 1994; Speech: Dr Carter G Woodson, the Father of Black History, 1990. **Home Addr:** PO Box 547011, Orlando, FL 32854-7011. **Business Addr:** President, Frontline Outreach, 3000 CR Smith St, Orlando, FL 32805, **Business Phone:** (407)293-3000.

WOODRIDGE, WILSON JACK, JR.
Architect, administrator. **Personal:** Born Aug 29, 1950, East Orange, NJ; divorced. **Educ:** Essex City Col, AAS, 1970; Cornell Univ Col Arch, BA, 1975. **Career:** Bernard Johnson Inc, designer, 1976-77; Skidmore Owings & Merrill, designer, 1977-80; Welton Becket Assoc, proj designer, 1981; Grad Partnership, proj architect, 1981-85; Essex County Col, dir archit progs, 1983-2001; Woodridge & Ray Architects, 1985; Wilson Woodridge Architects, pres; Hillier Architecture, sr proj mgr, currently. **Orgs:** Official interviewer, Cornell Univ Alumni Sec Comn, 1975; chmn proj comn, Houston Community Design Ctr, 1978-80; sec exec comn, Houston Urban Bunch, 1979-80; chmn finance comn, Essex City Col Alumni Asn, 1982-84. **Honors/Awds:** Outstanding Alumni Award, Essex City Col, 1984; East Orange Merchants Award, 1987. **Home Phone:** (973)674-2412. **Business Addr:** Senior Project Manager, Hillier Architecture, 500 Alexander Pk, Princeton, NJ 08543-6395, **Business Phone:** (609)452-8888.

WOODRUFF, CHERYL
Editor, publisher. **Personal:** Daughter of Phy Stephens. **Career:** Cheryl Woodruff Communications LLC, owner, 2003-; Fawcett Books, staff; Ballantine Publishing Group, founding ed & assoc ed, vpres & exec ed, vpres & assoc publ. **Orgs:** Nat Coun Negro Woman Inc. **Honors/Awds:** Achievement Award, SISTAS MOVIN UP, 1996; Publishing Executive of the Year, Chicago's Black Book Fair, 1998.

WOODRUFF, JAMES W
Automotive executive. **Career:** Woodruff Oldsmobile Inc, Detroit, Mich, chief exec, 1988; Pochelon Lincoln-Mercury Inc, chief exec, 1988-. **Business Addr:** Chief Executive, Pochelon Lincoln Mercury, 5815 Bay Rd, Saginaw, MI 48604, **Business Phone:** (517)791-3000.

WOODRUFF, JEFFREY ROBERT
College teacher, educator. **Personal:** Born Jul 13, 1943, Pittsburgh, PA; son of Robert and Alyce Bailey; married Vickie Hamlin, Mar 21, 1970; children: Jennifer Ryan. **Educ:** Springfield Col, BS, 1966; New York Inst Tech, MBA, 1978. **Career:** KQV Radio Inc, dir res & develop, 1968-70; WLS Radio Inc, dir res, 1970-72; Elmhurst Col Mgt Prog, fac; Knoxville Col Sem Prog, vis prof; ABC AM Radio Sta, dir res & develop, 1972-77, dir sales & res, 1977-79; WDAI Radio, national sales mgr, 1979-80; N Central Col, asst prof, 1979-; Ill Bell Telephone Co, acct exec indust consult, 1980-83, mgr promos mkt staff, 1983-91, area mgr channel Opers, 1991-93, staff mgr, customer commun Opers, 1993-; Ameritech Sales Prom, dir, 1993-94; Computer Learning Ctr, lead instr, 1994-2001; DeVry Inst of Tech, instr, 1994-; Aurora Univ, adj prof, 1995; Northwood Univ; Lewis Univ, 2001; New York Inst Tech, adj fac; Col DuPage; Lincoln Technical Inst, instr & master trainer, asst exec dir, dir educ, 2003. **Orgs:** Radio TV Res Coun; Am Mkg Asn; Delta Mu Delta; Radio Advertising Bur; GOALS Com; Black Exec Exchange Prog; Nat Urban League Inc; Youth Motivation Task Force; consult, Network Programming Concepts Inc; indust adv, Arbitron Adv Coun Mensa Ltd. **Honors/**

Awds: Nat Alliance of Business Innovator Award, Am Res Bur, 1972; Black Achievers in Industry Award, Harlem YMCA, 1972; Amirtech Fel, Northwestern Univ, Inst Learning Servs, 1990. **Military Serv:** USMC, corpl, 1966-68. **Home Addr:** 4559 Normandy Dr, Lisle, IL 60532-1083. **Business Phone:** (630)637-4067.

WOODS, ALISON SCOTT
Executive, executive director. **Personal:** Born Jul 28, 1952, Chicago, IL; daughter of Eugene Scott and Erma; married Charles R, May 7, 1982; children: Jamel Scott, Jihan & Asia. **Educ:** Carleton Col, BA, 1994. **Career:** Int Bus Mach, staff, 1974-91; Arco Chem Co, mgr end user computing, 1992-96; Independence Blue Cross, sr dir, 1996-97; Philadelphia Coca-Cola Co, vpres info technol, chief info officer, 1998-2005; PepsiCo Inc, dir info technol strategy & bus intelligence, 2005-. **Orgs:** Bd mem, Urban League Philadelphia; bd mem, Girl Scouts SE Pa; Home & Sch Asn Philadelphia Creative. **Business Addr:** Director of Information Technology Strategy & Business Intelligence, PepsiCo Inc, 700 Anderson Hill Rd, Purchase, NY 10577, **Business Phone:** (914)253-2000.

WOODS, ALLIE, JR.
Educator, theatrical director, actor. **Personal:** Born Sep 28, 1940, Houston, TX; son of Allie Sr and Georgia Stewart; married Beverly (divorced); children: Allyson Beverly & Stewart Jordan. **Educ:** Tex Southern Univ, BA; Tenn State Univ, MS; New Sch, producing TV; NYUniv, film prod/writing film/TV; Ctr Media Arts, TV prod. **Career:** Woodswork Prod, producer & dir; Tony Award-winning Negro Ensemble Co,founding mem; Chelsea Theatre Ctr Brooklyn, Acad Music, actor & dir;LaMama Experimental Theatre Club NYC, dir residence; Univ Ibadan, teacherguest artist; Univ Wash, teacher guest artist; Brooklyn Col, teacher guestartist; Sunday Series NY Shakesphere Festival Pub Theatre, guest dir; NewFedn Theatre NYC, dir; State Univ NY Old Westbury, asst prof; Houston PubSchs, NYC Schs, teacher; PBS-TV, staging consult; Mich State Univ, visdir; Univ Conn, guest dir; Univ Pittsburgh, actg & dir credits; Film:Girlfight, 2000; Thirteen Conversations About One Thing, 2001; Bellclair Times, 2005; Sherry Baby, 2006; Heavy Petting, 2007; Be Kind Rewind, 2008. TV series: "Mother's Day", 2003; "Law & Order", 2003; "The Extra Man", 2001; "Blind Spot", 2006; "Law & Order: Criminal Intent" (2 episodes), 2001-06; "A New Light", 2006; "Six Degrees", 2006. **Orgs:** Actors Equity Asn; Screen Actors Guild; Am Fedn TV & Radio Artists.

WOODS, ANDRE VINCENT
Executive. **Personal:** Born Feb 21, 1947, Charleston, SC; son of Delbert Leon and Thelma Ruth; married Karen Lewis; children: Charity, Andre II & Meridith. **Educ:** Saint Augustine's Col, BA, 1975. **Career:** ACA State Ports Authority, ade analyst, 1975-80; Handyman Network Inc, pres & chief exec officer, 1981-; Interchange Inc, pres; COT Enterprise Tech Transition Team, pres, currently; HNI Ltd, pres, secy & treas, currently. **Orgs:** Vpres, Neighborhood Legal Servs Corp, 1977-; vpres, Eastside Bus Asn, 1989-; irb bd, Med Univ, 1990-; bd, Jr Achievement, 1990-; Sigma Pi Phi, Grand Blvd, 1990-; Trident 1000, 1990-91; vpres, Trident Chamber Com, 1991-92; bd vis, Charleston Southern Univ, 1991-. **Honors/Awds:** Outstanding Freedom Fighter Award, NCP, 1973; Outstanding Service Award, Nat Coun Negro Women, 1985; Minority Entrepreneur of the Year, US Small Bus Admin, 1988; Runner up to Small Business Person Award, US Small Bus Admin, 1988; Business Achievement Award. Alpha Phi Alpha, 1992. **Home Addr:** 236 Ashley Ave, Charleston, SC 29403, **Home Phone:** (843)722-4843. **Business Addr:** President, Secretary & Treasurer, HNI Ltd, 1120 Morrison Dr, Charleston, SC 29403-3111, **Business Phone:** (843)577-8252.

WOODS, ARLEIGH MADDOX
Judge. **Personal:** Born Aug 31, 1929, Los Angeles, CA; daughter of Benjamin and Ida L; married William T. **Educ:** Chapman Col, BA, 1949; Southwestern Univ Sch Law, LLB, 1952; Univ VA, LLM, 1983; Univ West Los Angeles, DDL, 1984. **Career:** Levy Koszdin & Woods, vpres, 1962-76; CA Ct Appeal, presiding justice; State Comn Judicial Performance, chair; Judge Los Angeles Super Ct, 1976-80; Gen Civil Trials Law & Motion, Settlements, family law & probate, 1977-80; Civil Trials & Settlement Judge; Supv Judge N Cent Dist, 1978-80; Admin Presiding Justice Ca Ct Appeal second Dist, 1984-87; Div Four, Presiding Justice, 1982-96. **Orgs:** Vpres, Const Rights Found, 1980-; bd dir, Cancer Res Found, 1983-; chmn bd trustees, Southwestern Univ Sch Law, 1986; Various bar Asns; Adv Bd, Bernard Witkin Inst; chair bd trustees, Southwestern Univ Sch Law. **Honors/Awds:** Woman of the Year Business & Professional Women, 1982; Justice of the Year, CA, 1983; Professional Woman of the Year, YMCA, 1984; Pioneer, Black Women Lawyers Asn, 1984; Silver Medallist Award, YMCA, 1984; LLD, Univ W Los Angeles, 1984; Life Commitment Award, Equal Opportunity League, 1985; Bernard Jefferson Award for Judicial Excellence, California Asn Black Lawyers, 1985; Outstanding Judicial Officer, Southwestern Univ Sch Law, 1987; Justice of the Year, Los Angeles Trial Lawyers, 1989; Appellate Justice of the Year, Los Angeles Trial Lawyers Asn, 1990; Alumna of the Year, Southwestern Univ, 1994; Hall of Fame Award, John M Langston, 1995; American Bar Association Award, 1995. **Business Addr:** Settlement judge, Mediator, c/o Deb Leathers, 675 S Westmoreland Ave, Los Angeles, CA 90005-3992, **Business Phone:** (213)738-6704.

WOODS, DR. BERNICE
Nurse, government official. **Personal:** Born Sep 27, 1924, Port Arthur, TX; married Melvin J; children: Melvin J Jr, Mary Jane, Jule Norman, Pernilla, Lewis, Kenneth Dale,Paulette, Dwight Clayton, Muriel Gale & Gregory Wayne. **Educ:** E Los Angeles Jr Col; Calif Sch & Nursing, BS, 1948; Univ Calif, Los Angeles, BS, behavioral sci, 1965; Calif State Univ Long Beach, MEd, 1968. **Career:** Nurse (retired); Los Angeles City Gen Hosp, nurse retired after 28 yrs service; Compton Unified Sch Dist, bd trustees mem. **Orgs:** Queen of Sheba Grand Chap OES, 1964; life mem, Nat Coun Negro Women, 1974; rep, Delegate Assembly, Calif Sch Bd Asn, 1975-83; mem bd of trustees, Compton Unified School Dist, 1975-; Union Baptist Church, Democratic Club of Compton; pres, Ladies Aux POP Warner Football; grand pres, Matron'sCoun OES; pres, Compton Union Coun; PTA Parent Teacher Asn; Willowbrook St Park; pres, vpres, Nat Coun Negro Women; juvenile protect chmn 33rd Dist PTA; Southeast Mental Health Liaison Comm; Nat Asn Advan Colored People Compton Chap. **Honors/Awds:** Helping All Children Nat School Bd Asn, 1978; 50 Year Serv Award, Parent Teacher Asn, 1978; Nat PTA Award, 1984; Woman of the Yr, 1970, 1975; TaskForce to Secure Funds for Compton Unified Sch Dist, 1974-75; Alternate Delto Dem Nat Conv NY, 1976; Inner City Challange; Nat Coun Negro Women Achievers Award; Youth Athletic Asn Award; Community Award Block Clubs; Fraternal Award, Order of the Eastern Star; Help All Agencies Dedicated Serv Award; Bethune Outstanding Achieve Award; Outstanding Church Serv Award; Outstanding Serv Award, Lt Gov Mervyn Dymally; Bronze Medal Award, Achievers Wash, DC; C of C Christmas Award; received numerous awards. **Special Achievements:** Co-author Book "I Am a Black Woman Who" 1976. **Home Addr:** 1515 W 166th St, Compton, CA 90220.

WOODS, BRYNDA
Executive, president (organization). **Career:** Career Advantage Personnel Serv, pres, currently. **Business Phone:** (909)466-9232.

WOODS, DR. CLIFTON
College administrator, educator. **Educ:** NC Cent Univ, BS, chem & math, 1966; NC State Univ, MS, PhD, chem. **Career:** Univ Tenn, fac, 1974, Dept Chem, prof & assoc vice chancellor inorg chem, 2003-. **Honors/Awds:** Outstanding Teaching Award.

WOODS, ELDRICK. See WOODS, TIGER.

WOODS, GENEVA HOLLOWAY
Nurse. **Personal:** Born Sep 16, 1930, Saluda, SC; daughter of Mattie Dozier and Zonnie; married Sylvania Webb Sr; children: Sylvania Jr & Sebrena. **Educ:** Grady Hosp Sch Nursing Atlanta, dipl, 1949; Dillard Univ Sch Anesthesia New Orleans LA, cert, 1957; Real Estate Cert - P.G. Comm. Col Largo, MD, 1983. **Career:** Nurse (retired); Grady Memorial Hosp Atlanta, pvt duty polio nurse, 1950-52; Grady Memorial Hosp, Atlanta, asst head nurse, 1952-54; Freedmen Hosp, Howard Univ, Wash, DC, staff nurse, 1955-57; DC Gen, staff nurse anesthetist, 1960-70; DC ANaA, pres, 1968-70; Providence Hosp, Wash, DC, chief nurse anesthetist, 1971-76; DC Lawyers Wives, parliamentarian, 1974-76; St Elizabeth Hosp, Wash, DC, chief nurse anesthetist, 1976-79; DC Gen Hosp, Wash, DC, staff nurse anesthetist, 1979-85; PG Co Lawyers Wives, parliamentarian. **Orgs:** Upper Room Bapt Ch Wash DC, 1961-; parliamentarian & charter Jack & Jills of PG Co Chap, 1973-75; chmn, Glenarden Inaugural Ball, 1979; chmn, Saluda Rosen Wald/Riverside Sch Alumni Asn; chmn, Grady Nurses Alumni Asn D.C; Va. Chapter; bd ethics, PG Co. **Honors/Awds:** Recipient mother of the year award, BSA Troop 1017, 1966; Certfied Parliamentarian Parliamentary Procecures, Chicago, IL, 1970; Continued Professional Excellence Award, Am Asn, Nurse, Chicago 1975&78; Outstanding Performance Award, St Elizabeth Hosp, Wash, DC, 1978. **Home Addr:** 7816 Fiske Ave, Glenarden, MD 20706.

WOODS, GEORGE W
Executive. **Educ:** BS, chem; MBA. **Career:** Combustion Engineering, lab technician & qual assurance mgr; Quali-Pro-Tech Servs, owner; USA Environ Mgt Inc, chief exec officer & owner, 1994-. **Honors/Awds:** Safety Award, AUS CEngr; Minority Enterprise Development Award, Small Bus Admin; Administrator's Award, Small Bus Admin.

WOODS, HENRY, JR.
Executive. **Personal:** Born May 10, 1954, Clarksdale, MS; son of Henry Neal and Estella Marie; children: John M Hite. **Educ:** Utica Jr Col, AA, 1974; Miss Valley State Univ, BA, 1976. **Career:** United CAL Bank, loan officer, 1977-79; Community Bank, bus develop officer, 1979-81; Crocker Nat Bank, bus develop officer, 1981-83; Golden State Financial, gen partner, 1983-84; Woods & ASC/CERS Group, 1984; Thermo Brique W, sr vpres, partner. **Orgs:** Challenger Boys & Girls Club, 1984-; bd trustee, Crossroad Arts Acad, 1989-; bd mem, Techn Health Career Sch, 1992-; steering comt, Beacon Hope Found, 1992-; Horace Mann Sch, One to One Team Mentoring Prog, 1993. **Honors/Awds:** Commendation Award, Mayor Tom Bradley, 1992; Recognition Award, Lt Gov Leo McCarthy, 1992; Recognition Award, State Senator Diane Watson, 1992.

WOODS, HORTENSE E.
Librarian. **Personal:** Born Mar 17, 1926, Malvern, AR; married Walter F; children: Marcia Laureen. **Educ:** Ark AM & N Col, Pine Bluff, BA, 1950; Catholic Univ Wash; Univ Calif Los Angeles; Pepperdine Univ; Univ Southern Calif. **Career:** Lincoln High Sch, Camden AR, sch librn, 1950-51; Vernon Br Lib, pub librn; Pine Bluff Pub Libr, librn, 1954-59; Wilmington Br Los Angeles Pub Libr, librn, 1961-65; Enterprise Sch Dist Los Angeles County, org librn, 1966-69; ed consult, Saturday Mag, 1979. **Orgs:** Dir, All City Emp Asn, Los Angeles, 1973-; secy, Cent Chamber Com, Los Angeles, 1973-; Am Film Inst; bd mem, Ctr Women Develop, Long Beach, CA. **Business Addr:** Branch Librarian, Vernon Branch Library, 4504 S Cent Ave, Los Angeles, CA 90011.

WOODS, JACCI
Executive. **Career:** Motor City Casino, commun mgr, dir pub rels & community affairs, currently. **Business Addr:** Director of Public Relations, Community Affairs, Motor City Casino, 2901 Grand River Ave, Detroit, MI 48201, **Business Phone:** (313)237-6714.*

WOODS, JACQUI
Executive. **Career:** BAM Local Develop Corp, community mem & chair.

WOODS, JEROME HARLAN
Football player. **Personal:** Born Mar 17, 1973, Memphis, TN; children: Jada & Dylan. **Educ:** Univ Memphis. **Career:** Football palyer (retired); Kans City Chiefs, defensive back, 1996-2005. **Honors/Awds:** One Time Pro Bowler Selection, 2003.

WOODS, KONDRIA YVETTE BLACK
Association executive. **Personal:** Born May 22, 1971, Fort Bragg, NC; daughter of Calhoun and Mary; married Fred W Jr, Aug 2, 1997. **Educ:** Howard Univ, BBA, 1993; Temple Univ, MBA, 1995. **Career:** Howard Univ, Bison Yearbook, bus mgr, 1991-93; Blackberry, retail sales assoc, 1994-95; Nations Bank, banking ctr mgr, 1995-97; Greenville Chamber Com, Small Bus Serv, mgr, 1997-2000; Talk Greenville Mag, writer, currently; Media Partners, managing dir, currently. **Orgs:** Golden Key Nat Honor Soc, 1989-; Delta Sigma Pi, 1991-; Beta Gamma Sigma Honor Soc, 1992-; comt mem, United Way Greenville Co, 1996-; bd vpres, YWCA Greenville, 1999-; Minority Women Bus, 1999-. **Business Addr:** Contributing Writer, Talk Greenville, 305 S Main St, PO Box 1688, Greenville, SC 29601, **Business Phone:** (864)298-4100.

WOODS, DR. MANUEL T
Educator. **Personal:** Born May 10, 1939, Kansas City, KS; son of Mable; married Wanda Emanuel; children: Susan & Daniel. **Educ:** Univ Minn, AA, 1968, BA, 1970, PhD, 1978; Univ Hartford, MEd, 1973. **Career:** Univ Minn, new careers prog counr, 1967-70, off admis & reg asst dir, 1970-85, off stud affairs asst vpres, 1985-86, educ stud affairs off dir, 1986-92; Turning Pt Inc, exec vpres. **Orgs:** Pres, Minn Counrs & Dirs, Minority Prog Asn; pres, Univ Asn Black Employ; prog chmn, Upper Midwest Asn Col Registrs & Admis Officers; prog convenor, Minn Counrs & Dir Minority Prog, Coun Disadvantaged Stud; comm mem, Minneapolis Comn Col Adv Bd; bd chmn, Hennepin Human Serv Network; Nat Black Alcoholism Coun, adv bd, chair, Minn Chap pres; Hennepin Co Mayor's Task Force Drug Abuse. **Honors/Awds:** Bush Fellowship Award, Bush Found, 1973; Outstanding Alumnus, Minneapolis Comn Col, 1986.

WOODS, MELVIN LEROY
Executive. **Personal:** Born May 10, 1938, Lexington, KY; married Elnora; children: Gregory & Alyssa. **Educ:** Jackson State Univ, BS, 1962; VA Hosp, cert 1962; Univ Ill, MS, 1967; Ind Univ-19Purdue Univ, Indianapolis, attended 1975. **Career:** Southern Wis Colony & Union Cp Training Sch, supr therapist, 1966-70; Wis Parks & Recreation, Univ Wis, consult, 1967; St Lukes Hosp, 1969-70; Marion Co Asn Retarded Citz, dior adult serv, 1970-73; Southern Ind Retardation Serv, 1972-73; Eli Lilly & Co, comm rel asso, mgr pub affairs; Lilly Endowment Inc, prog officer, 1973-77; Rubicon Pub Affairs, pres, currently. **Orgs:** Wis Parks & Rec Asn, 1966-73; Ind Asn Rehab Facilities; bd, Int Asn Rehab Facilities 1972-73; Nat Asn Retarded Citz, 1970-75; Am Asn Ment Deficiency, 1973-77; Kappa Alpha Psi; Alpha Kappa Mu, 1962; Medicare Coverage Adv Comt; White House Conf on Aging Policy Comt. **Honors/Awds:** Distd Hoosier citation Ind Gov Off, 1972; fellowship grant, Univ I 1965; publ, The Devel Pay Recreation Procedure in a Token Economy System; Mental Retardation 1971. **Military Serv:** AUS, sp 4, 1962-65.

WOODS, PHILIP WELLS
Composer, musician. **Personal:** Born Nov 2, 1931, Springfield, MA; son of Stanley and Clara Markley; married Jill Goodwin; children: Kim Parker, Baird Parker, Garth, Aimee, Allisen Trotter & Tracey Trotter; married Chan Parker (divorced). **Educ:** Saxophone Harvey La Rose; Juilliard Conserv, 1948-52. **Career:** Played with Dizzy Gillespie Band US Overseas 1965; played with

Quincy Jones Band on European tours 1959-61; played with Benny Goodman Band touring USSR 1962 & Monterey Jazz Festival 1962; rec artist; Phil Woods Quintet, leader; European Rhythm Machine based in Paris, 1968-73; Phil Woods Quartet (Now Quintet), 1974-; Phil Woods' Little Big Band 1987-; Celebration Of The Arts, founder, currently; Albums: All Bird's Children, 1990; Phil's Mood, 1990; Flowers for Hodges, 1991; An Affair to Remember, Evidence, 1993; Ornitology: Phil Salutes Bird, 1994; Our Monk, 1994; Alto Summit, 1995; Mile High Jazz, 1996; Celebration, 1997; Souvenirs, 1997; Just Friends, 1998; Porgy & Bess, 1999; Balladeer Supreme, 2001; The Solo Album, 2001; Americans Swinging in Paris, 2001; You & the Night & the Music, 2002; Live at the Montreux Jazz Festival, 2002; Thrill Is Gone,2003; This Is How I Feel About Quincy, 2004; Groovin' to Marty Paich (live), 2005; Phil Woods: A Life in E Flat (DVD), 2005. **Orgs:** Natl Assn Jazz Educators; Am Fedn Musicians; found & adv bd mem, Delaware Water Gap Celebration Of The Arts ("C. O.T.A." founded in 1978); co dir of COTA CampJazz; brd dir of the Al Cohn Memorial Jazz Collection (at East Stroudsburg University). **Honors/Awds:** New Star Award, 1956; Numerous honors and wards inculding New Star Award, Kennedy Center Living Legends in Jazz Award, Playboy Poll, Critics' Poll Winner, Readers' Poll Winner, Leonard Feather's Golden Feather Award, Grammy Awards, and Kennedy Center Living Legends in Jazz Award; Leonard Feather's Golden Feather Award (Phil Woods Quintet), 1985; Induction into the American Jazz Hall of Fame, 1994; Induction into Omicron Kappa Delta, 1997; Beacons in Jazz Award, 2001; Jazz Journalists Association Jazz Awards (Alto Saxophonist of the Year), 2005 - 2006; National Endowment for the Arts Jazz Master Fellowship: 2007; President's Merit Award from the Grammy Foundation, 2007; Kennedy Center Living Legends in Jazz Award, 2007; Governor's Awards for the Arts - Creative Community Award (with COTA), 2008; DePaul University Honorary Doctor of Humane Letters Degree, 2009. **Home Addr:** 154 Mountain Rd, Delaware Water Gap, PA 18327. **Business Addr:** Founder, Celebration of the Arts, PO Box 249, Delaware Water Gap, PA 18327, **Business Phone:** (570)424-2210.

WOODS, DR. ROBERT LOUIS
Dentist. **Personal:** Born Oct 24, 1947, Charlotte, NC; son of Clifton Woods Jr and Effie E; married Cynthia Dianne Hawkins; children: Sonja Nicole & Cheryl Lynnette. **Educ:** NC Central Univ, BS, Biol, 1969, MS, Biol, 1971; Univ NC, Sch Dentistry, DDS, 1977. **Career:** Duke Univ Med Ctr, res tech, 1969; NC Agr & Tech Univ, instr biol, 1971-73; pvt practice, 1977-90; Univ NC, Sch Dentistry, clinic instr, 1979-81; Orange Chatham Comprehensive Health Servs, lead staff dentist, 1982-89. **Orgs:** Am Dent Asn, 1977-, NC Dent Soc, 1977-, Old N State Dent Soc, 1977-; bd dir, fin comt, chair Person, Family Med Ctr, 1979-81; bd dir, facility comn, chair Person, Family Med Ctr, 1979-81; bd dir, Parents Adv Gifted Educ, 1982-83. **Home Addr:** 2242 Burlington Rd, Roxboro, NC 27574-9464, **Home Phone:** (336)599-0835. **Business Addr:** Dentist, PO Box 2500, Roxboro, NC 27509, **Business Phone:** (919)575-3070.

WOODS, SANDY. See WOODS, SANFORD L.

WOODS, SANFORD L (SANDY WOODS)
Automotive executive. **Career:** Brandon Dodge Inc, chief exec officer & prin; Sanford L Wood Enterprises Inc, pres, currently. **Orgs:** Greater Brandon Chamber Com. **Special Achievements:** Owner of Florida's largest African-American auto dealership; Ranked No 25 on Black Enterprise's list of top 100 auto dealers, 1994, ranked no 12, 1998; ranked No 5 on the BE Auto Dealer 100 list, Black Enterprise Mag, 2007. **Business Addr:** Preisdent, Sanford L Wood Enterprises Inc, 9207 Adamo Dr E, Tampa, FL 33619, **Business Phone:** (813)620-4300.

WOODS, SYLVIA (SYLVIA PRESSLEY)
Restaurateur, executive, cosmetics executive. **Personal:** Born Feb 2, 1926, Hemingway, SC; daughter of Van and Julia Pressley; married Herbert K Woods, Jan 18, 1944; children: Van, Bedelia, Kenneth, Crizette. **Educ:** La Robert Cosmetology Sch. **Career:** Sylvia's Restaurant, pres & owner, currently; Sylvia's Atlanta, owner, 1997-; Sylvia's Beauty Products & Sylvia's Express, owner, NY, 2001-. **Orgs:** Share Our Strength; City Meals on Wheels; Women's Roundtable. **Honors/Awds:** Woman of the Year Award, NAACP, 1978; Women's Day Award, Cert Appreciation, 1988; Bus Award, The Riverside Club, 1991; African American Award, Bus Award, 1990; Mayor NY City, Cert Appreciation, 1992; Lifetime Achievement Award, NY Metro Roundtable, 1993; Bus Award, The NY State Dept Econ Develop, 1994. **Special Achievements:** US Air Force, Cert Appreciation, 1989; US Army, Cert Appreciation, 1991; Sylvia's Soul Food Cookbook, William Morrow Co, 1992; Sylvia's Family Soul Food Cookbook, 1999. **Business Addr:** President, Owner, Sylvia's Restaurant, 328 Lenox Ave, New York, NY 10027, **Business Phone:** (212)996-0660.

WOODS, TIGER (ELDRICK WOODS)
Golfer. **Personal:** Born Dec 30, 1975, Long Beach, CA; son of Kultida and Earl D; married Elin Nordegren, May 5, 2004; children: Sam Alexis. **Educ:** Stanford Univ. **Career:** Prof golfer, 1996-. **Orgs:** Tiger Woods Found, 1996-; Tiger Woods Learning Ctr, 2006-. **Honors/Awds:** Player of the Year, Am Jr Golf Asn, 1991-92; Rolex, First Team All-American, 1991-92; Jr Golfer of the Year, Golfweek, 1991; Nat Junior Amateur Champion, US Golf Asn, 1991-92; Insurance Youth Golf Classic Champion, 1992; US Amateur Golf Championship, 1994; Champion, US Masters Golf Tournament, 1997, 2001-02, 2005; Player of the Year, PGA, 1997, 1999-03; Male Athlete of the Year, Asniated Press, 1997; Champion, Johnnie Walker Classic, 1998; Champion, BellSouth Classic, 1998; Champion, US PGA Championship, 1999; Champion, NEC Invitational, 1999; Co-champion, World Cup of Golf, 1999; PGA Championship, winner, 1999-00, 2006-07; Winner, US Open, 2000; Winner, British Open, 2000, 2005-06; Winner, NEC Invitational, 2001; Sportsman of the Year, 2001; Bay Hill Invitational Trophy, 2003. **Special Achievements:** First African American to win US Amateur Golf Championship; youngest person and first African American to win the US Masters Golf Tournament; mem of 1999 World Cup Team; 8-PGA Tour victories, 1999; Author: How I Play Golf, 2001; youngest person ever to win golf's 4 most prestigious events: PGA Championship, Masters, US Open, British Open; highest paid professional athlete in 2006; California Hall of Fame, 2007; He has been named Associated Press Male Athlete of the Year four times. **Business Phone:** (216)522-1200.

WOODS, WILBOURNE F
Association executive. **Personal:** Born May 7, 1935, Magee, MS; divorced. **Educ:** Roosevelt Univ, BA, 1972. **Career:** City Chicago, peace officer, currently. **Orgs:** Chmn, Midwest Reg, Nat Black Police Asn. **Honors/Awds:** Member of the Year, Midwest Reg, Nat Black Police Asn, 1986; Member of the Year, African-American Police League, 1991. **Home Addr:** 8155 S State St, Chicago, IL 60619-4719. **Business Addr:** Chairman, National Black Police Association, 8155 S State St, Chicago, IL 60619, **Business Phone:** (312)744-7969.

WOODS, WILLIE
President (Organization), executive director, association executive. **Career:** Digital Systs Res, founder, 1988-2001; Digital Systs Int Corp, pres & chief exec officer, 2001-03; Social & Sci Systs Inc, bd dirs, 2003-. **Military Serv:** USN. **Business Addr:** Board of Directors, Social & Scientific Systems Inc, 8757 Ga Ave 12th Fl, Silver Spring, MD 20910, **Business Phone:** (301)628-3000.

WOODS, WILLIE G
School administrator. **Personal:** Born Jan 1, 1943?, Yazoo City, MS; daughter of John Wesley Woods and Jessie Turner Woods (deceased). **Educ:** Shaw Univ, Raleigh, NC, BA Ed, 1965; Duke Univ, Durham, NC, MEd, 1968; Temple Univ, PA, attended; PA State Univ, attended; NY Univ, attended; Indi Univ Penn, Ind, PA, PhD Eng, 1995. **Career:** Berry O'Kelly Sch, lang arts teacher, 1965-67; Preston Sch, 5th grade teacher, 1967-69, adult educ teacher, 1968-69; Harrisburg Area Community Col, prof eng,educ 1969-, dir acad found prog, 1983-87, asst dean of Acad Found & Basic Educ Div, 1987-89, asst dean Soc Sci, Pub Servs & Basic Educ Div (SSPSBE), 1989-94, acting vpres, fac & instr, 1996-98, dean, SSPSBE Div, 1994-96, 1998; Chesapeake Col, dean, 1999-. **Orgs:** Bd mgr, Camp Curtin Branch, Harrisburg YMCA, 1971-79; rep coun 1972-, sec 1977-79, assoc educt, 1981-, PA Black Conf Higher Educ; exec bd, 1978-, coun chairperson, 1981-82, Western Reg Act 101 Dir Coun; bd dir, Alternative Rehab Comt Inc, 1978-; bd dir, 1979-, charter mem sec, 1981-82, treas, 1982-83, PA Asn Develop Educ; bd dir, 1981-, sec, 1984-85, Dauphin Residences Inc; bd adv, 1981-, chairperson, acting chairperson, bd sec,Youth Urban Serv Harrisburg, YMCA; inst rep, Nat Coun on Black Am Affairs Am Asn Comt & Jr Col 1983-. **Honors/Awds:** Certificate Merit, Community Serv, Harrisburg, 1971; Meritorious Faculty Contribution, Harrisburg, 1977; Outstanding Service Award, 1980-97, Central Regional Award, 1980, 1997, Penn Black Conf Higher Educ; Alpha Kappa Alpha Sor Outstanding Community Service Award, Harrisburg, 1983; Volunteer of the Year Award, YMCA Youth Urban Ser, 1983, 1997; Alpha Kappa Alpha Sor Basileus' Award for Excellence, Comn Chair, 1985; Administrative Staff Merit Award, Harrisburg Area Community Col, 1986; Outstanding Service Award, Black Student Union, Harrisburg Area Community Col, 1989; Outstanding contributions to Harrisburg Area Community Col & comm-at-large, HACC Minority Caucus, 1989; Alpha Kappa Mu Natl Hon Soc; Brooks Dickens Member Award in Education; Kellogg Fel in Expanding Leadership Diversity Pro, 1994-95. **Business Addr:** Dean, Chesapeake College, 1000 Col Cir, PO Box 8, Wye Mills, MD 21679, **Business Phone:** (410)822-5400 Ext 5847.

WOODS BADGER, MADELYNE
Publicist. **Personal:** Born Oct 10, 1965, Washington, DC; daughter of Lloyd Woods and Mary Kittrell; married L Michael; children: Montana Symone Woods Williams & Michael Bryce. **Educ:** Univ Md, Col Park, MD, BS, broadcast jour, 1986; Howard Univ, Wash, DC, MA, mass commun, 1987. **Career:** WHMM TV 32, Wash, DC, host, 1987-88; WJWJ TV 16, Beaufort, SC, news reporter, 1988-89; WCIV News 4, Charleston, SC, news reporter, 1989-90; Black Entertainment TV, Wash, DC, news anchor, 1990; freelance anchor/reporter, 1993-96; WJLA-TV, Wash, DC, news reporter, 1996-97; Walt Disney World, mkt & media rel, 1997-99; Fox/America's Health Network, host, news anchor, 1999; WCFB, news/community affairs dir, currently. **Orgs:** Nat Asn Black Journalists, 1987-; Wash Asn Black Journalists, 1987-; Nat Acad Arts & Scis, 1987-88. **Home Addr:** 9672 Camberley Cir, Orlando, FL 32836-5754. **Business Addr:** News/Community Affairs Director, WCFB, 4192 N John Young Pkwy, Orlando, FL 32804, **Business Phone:** (407)297-0945.

WOODS-BURWELL, CHARLOTTE ANN
Government official. **Personal:** Born Jan 7, 1932, Ft Wayne, IN; daughter of Beauford Williams and Josephine Gaines; married Lawrence Cornelius Burwell Sr, Jan 15, 1994; children: Beauford K, Brenda K Coleman, Parnell L Jr & Jeffry C. **Career:** Government official (retired); Peg Leg Bates Country Club, br mgr, 1976,asst mgr, 1980-86, off mgr 1987; Allen County Bd Voters Regist, Fort Wayne, Ind, chief dep, 1988. **Orgs:** Bd mem, Bd Ethics Kerhonkson, 1969-73; Ulster County Ment Health Asn,1970-76; chmn, Tower Rochester Dem Club, 1970-; Rondout Valley Sch Bd, 1983-87; New York State Sch Bd Legis Network, 1985-87; Prev Connection Community Drug & Alcohol Abuse; vice chmn, Allen County Dem Party, 1987-; secy, Lillian Jones Brown Club, 1988-; Ultra Art Club, 1988-. **Special Achievements:** Elected to Wayne Township Advisory Board, Mar 1992. **Home Addr:** 31 Northgate Dr, Albany, NY 12203.

WOODSON, AILEEN R
School administrator. **Personal:** Born Nov 27, 1927, East Chicago, IN; daughter of Jenese R and Gussie Smith Russell; married Edgar H, Jul 10, 1947; children: Adele H & Brett Denise. **Career:** School administrator (Retired); Dublin Ave Magnet Elementary Sch, prin, 1976-85; Los Angeles Unified Sch Dist, human resources div, interviewer. **Orgs:** Holman Methodist Church, 1952-; Delta Sigma Theta Sorority, 1953-; pres, Women Inc, 1962-64; founder/chmn, Coun Black Adminrs, 1971-79; Los Angeles City Comn Utilities & Transp, 1972-79; bd mem, PUSH, 1974-76; comnr, Los Angeles Comn Transp, 1979-84; comner, Los Angeles Social Serv Comn, 1984-; invited mem, Black Jewish Coalition, 1984; life mem, Nat Asn Advan Colored People; Urban League; SCLC; YMCA; Coun Black Adminrs Los Angeles. **Honors/Awds:** Red Cross Five Year Pin, 1960; LA Sentinel Newspaper Award, 1963; Nominee Sojourner Truth Award, Asn Negro Bus & Prof Women, 1963; PTA Sterling Pin Award, 112th St Sch PTA, Watts, 1969; Award Merit, Black Parents Watts, 1970; Freedom Foundation Award, 1970; Commendation Resolution, Calif State Assemblyman-Julian Dixon, 1973; Proclamation Unusual Service & Contributions, City Huntington Park, 1976; Ambassador of Good Will Award, 1977; Minerva Award, Delta Sigma Theta, 1977; Recognition of Unselfishness & Outstanding Award, Dublin Sch Parents, 1980; Tribute to Parents Ward, Mayor Thomas Bradley, 1980; Honorary PTA Service Award, Dublin Ave Sch PTA, 1980; Apple Award, 1981. **Home Addr:** 4561 Don Felipe Dr, Los Angeles, CA 90008.

WOODSON, ALFRED F
Banker. **Personal:** Born Feb 18, 1952, Georgetown, SC; son of Alfred F Sr and Zelda J; married Linda Washington, Dec 22, 1979. **Educ:** Princeton Univ, Princeton, NJ, BA, 1974. **Career:** Fidelity Bank, Philadelphia, PA, loan officer, 1974-78; First City, Tex, Houston, TX, vpres, 1978-89; First Am Metro Corp, McClean, VA, sr vpres, 1989; Chevy Chase Bank, sr vpres & chief credit officer, currently. **Business Addr:** Senior Vice President, Chief Credit Oofficer, Chevy Chase Bank, 4708 Bethesda Ave, Bethesda, MD 20814, **Business Phone:** (301)656-5402.

WOODSON, CHARLES
Football player. **Personal:** Born Oct 7, 1976, Fremont, OH. **Educ:** Univ Mich. **Career:** Oakland Raiders, defensive back, 1998-2005; Green Bay Packers, cornerback, 2006-. **Honors/Awds:** Big Ten Freshman of the Year, 1995; Mr. Football Award, 1994; Walter Camp Award, 1997; Heisman Trophy, 1997; Jim Thorpe Award, 1997; Chuck Bednarik Award, 1997; Defensive Rookie of Year, Nat football league, 1998; Pro Bowl, 1999-2001; Bronko Nagurski Trophy. **Special Achievements:** He is the only primarily defensive player to have won the Heisman Trophy. **Business Addr:** Corner Back, Green Bay Packers, Lambeau Field Atrium 1265 Lombardi Ave, PO Box 10628, Green Bay, WI 54304, **Business Phone:** (920)569-7500.

WOODSON, CHARLES R.
Health services administrator. **Personal:** Born Feb 22, 1942, Louisville, KY; married. **Educ:** Lincoln Univ, Mo, BS 1963; Univ Louisville, MSSW, 1969. **Career:** Smithfield Treatment Ctr, supt, 1969-70; Univ Louisville, dir off blackaffairs, 1971-74; Action Comn, dir neighbourhood orgn comn, 1970-71; Asn Cols Osteopathic Med, dir, 1974-79; Dept Health & Human Servs Pub Health Serv, proj dir, 1979-. **Orgs:** Nat Asn Black Social Workers, 1972-; Am Asn Higher Educ, 1973-; Am Pub Health Asn, 1974-; Kappa Alpha Psi. **Honors/Awds:** Unit Commendation, Pub Health Serv. **Special Achievements:** Public Health Service Citation. **Business Phone:** (301)594-4430.

WOODSON, CLEVELAND COLEMAN, III
Consultant, executive. **Personal:** Born Sep 5, 1946, Richmond, VA; son of Naomi Wilder and Cleveland C Jr; married Jannifer Eileen Vaughan, Oct 26, 1968; children: Cleveland C IV & Camille

C. **Educ:** Va Union Univ, BS, acct, 1970; Case Western Res Univ, MBA. **Career:** Ernst & Whinney, sr auditor, 1970-76; Marathon Oil Co, advan auditor, 1976-78, task force mem, 1978, advan acct analyst, 1979, sr acct analyst, 1979-80, supvr, 1980-83; Marathon Petroleum Co, mgr, 1983-86; Marathon Oil Co, mgr, 1987-99. **Orgs:** Bd dir, Nat Asn Black Accountants, 1971-73; Am Inst CPA's, 1973-; chairperson, acct personnel comt, Cleveland Chap, Ohio Soc CPA's, 1975; treas/auditor, Cleveland Jaycees, 1975-76; C Serv Adv Bd, 1975-76; treas, Wilson Vance Parent Teacher Org, 1981-83; Hampton Univ Indust Adv Cluster, 1982-99; Cent JH Parent Teacher Orgn, 1983-84; Am Asn Blacks Energy, 1983-99; treas, Findlay High Citizens Adv Comn, 1984-89; bd trustees, Hancock County Chap Am Red Cross; Multicultural Adv Comt, Univ Findlay. **Honors/Awds:** CPA, State Ohio, 1973. **Home Addr:** 4135 Starboard Shores Dr, Missouri City, TX 77459.

WOODSON, DARREN RAY
Football player, broadcaster. **Personal:** Born Apr 25, 1969, Phoenix, AZ. **Educ:** Ariz State Univ, BS, criminal justice. **Career:** Football player (retired), analyst; Dallas Cowboys, defensive back, 1992-2004; ESPN, analyst, currently. **Honors/Awds:** Pro Bowl, 1994, 1995, 1996, 1997, 1998; NFL Players Asn, Unsung Hero Award, 1997. **Business Addr:** Football Analyst, ESPN Television, ESPN Plz, Bristol, CT 06010, **Business Phone:** (860)766-2000.

WOODSON, JACQUELINE
Novelist. **Personal:** Born Feb 12, 1963, Columbus, OH; daughter of Mary Ann and Jack. **Career:** Goddard Col, MFA prog, assoc fac, 1993-95; Eugene Lang Col, assoc fac, 1994; Vermont Col, MFA Prog, assoc fac, 1996; Author: Last Summer With Maizon, 1990; The Dear One, 1991; Maizon At Blue Hill, 1992; Between Madison & Palmetto, 1993; The Book Chase, 1993; I Hadn't Meant To Tell You This, 1995; From The Notebooks of Malanin Sun, 1995; Autobiography of A Family Photo, 1995; A Way Out of No Way, 1996; The House You Pass On the Way, 1997; If you Come Softly, 1998; We Had A Picnic This Sunday Past, 1998; Lena, 1999; Miracle's Boys, 2000; Sweet, Sweet Memory, 2000; The Other Side, 2001; Hush, 2002; Our Gracie Aunt, 2002; Visiting Day, 2002. **Orgs:** Alpha Kappa Alpha. **Honors/Awds:** Granta, Fifty Best American Authors Under 40 Award, 1996; Kenyon Review Award, Lit Excellence Fiction, 1995; Honor Book Award, Coretta Scott King, 1995, 1996; Jane Addams Children's Book Award, 1995, 1996; Best Book Award, Publ's Weekly, 1994; Editor's Choice Award, Booklist; Best Book Award, Am Libr Asn; American Film Institute Award; Coretta Scott King Award, 2000; Los Angeles Times Book Award, 2000; Booklist Editor's Choice Award, 2001; Best Book Award, Child Mag, 2001; Best Book Award, Sch Libr Jour, 2001; Margaret A Edwards Award, 2006; Newbery Hon Medal, Asn Libr Serv C. **Business Addr:** c/o Charlotte Sheedy Literary Agency, 65 Bleecker St 12th Fl, New York, NY 10012.

WOODSON, JEFFREY ANTHONY
Government official. **Personal:** Born May 21, 1955, Baltimore, MD; son of Alfred C and Evelyn Trent; married Paula Mason; children: Jeffrey Jr, Devon. **Educ:** Va State Univ, BA, 1976; Va Commonwealth Univ, MPA, 1983. **Career:** Southside Va Training Ctr, social worker, 1976-78, asst prog mgr, 1978-83; Richmond City, budget & mgt analyst, 1983-85, sr budget analyst, 1985-91, strategic planning & budget dir. **Orgs:** Nat Jr Honor Soc, 1968; Omega Psi Phi, 1973; chmn, Membership Comt, Am Soc Pub Admin, 1983-; Conf Minority Pub Admin, 1983-; Nat Forum Black Pub Admin, 1983-; chap coun, Am Soc Pub Admin, 1985-87. **Honors/Awds:** Outstanding Academy Award, Va State Univ, 1972; Outstanding Young Man of America, Jaycees, 1983. **Special Achievements:** Productivity Analysis, Virginia Town & City Magazine, VA Municipal League, 1984. **Home Addr:** 10211 Duryea Dr, Richmond, VA 23235. **Business Addr:** Budget, Strategic Planning Director, City of Richmond, 900 E Broad St Rm 311, Richmond, VA 23219, **Business Phone:** (804)780-7913.

WOODSON, MIKE
Basketball player, basketball coach. **Personal:** Born Mar 24, 1958, Indianapolis, IN; married Terri Waters; children: Alexis & Mariah. **Educ:** Ind Univ, attended 1980. **Career:** Basketball player (retired), Basketball coach: NY Knicks, 1981; NJ Nets,1982; Kans City Kings, 1982-85; Sacramento Kings, 1986; Los Angeles Clippers, 1987-88; Houston Rockets, 1988-90; Cleveland Cavaliers, guard,1991; Toronto Raptors, scout, 1994-95; Milwaukee Bucks, asst coach,1996-99; Cleveland Cavaliers, asst coach, 1999-01; Philadelphia 76ers, asst coach, 2001-03; Detroit, asst coach; Atlanta Hawks, head coach, 2004-. **Honors/Awds:** Gold medal team, Pan Amer Games, 1979; All-American, 1979-80. **Business Addr:** Head Coach, Atlanta Hawks, Centennial Twr, 190 Marietta St NW, Atlanta, WI 30303, **Business Phone:** (404)827-3800.*

WOODSON, RODERIC L.
Lawyer. **Personal:** Born Aug 23, 1947, Philadelphia, PA; married Karen Smith; children: Roderic L. **Educ:** PA St Univ, BA, 1969; Howard Univ, JD, 1973. **Career:** Wdsn & Wdsn Attys & Coun Law, partner; SEC, atty adv corp finance, 1973-75, spec counr freedom info officer, 1976-79. **Orgs:** PA Bar Asn, 1973; St Bar Asn GA, 1974; DC Bar Asn, 1979; Nat Bar Asn; Am Bar Asn; Fed Bar Asn; Wash Bar Asn; Philadelphia Baraster's Asn; Gate City Bar Asn; correctional secy Wash Bar Asn, 1977-79, bd dir, 1977-, recording secy, 1979-; Delta Theta Phi Legal Frat; Kappa Alpha Psi Frat; Skull & Bones Soc. **Honors/Awds:** American Jurisprudence Award, 1972; outstanding alumini award, Hayes Senate Delta Theta Phi Legal Frat, 1974; Outstanding Young of America, 1980. **Business Addr:** Attorney & Counsellor at Law, Holland & Knight LLP, 2100 Pennsylvania Ave N W, Fourth Fl, Washington, DC 20037, **Business Phone:** (202)955-3000.

WOODSON, RODERICK KEVIN
Football player. **Personal:** Born Mar 10, 1965, Fort Wayne, IN; son of James and Linda Jo; married Nikki; children: 5. **Educ:** Purdue Univ, BS, criminal justice. **Career:** Football player (retired); Pittsburgh Steelers, corner back, 1987-96; San Francisco 49ers, corner back, 1997; Baltimore Ravens, corner back, 1998-2001; Oakland Raiders, corner back, 2002-04. **Honors/Awds:** NFL Defensive Player of the Year, Assoc Press, 1993; AFC Defensive Player of the Year, UPI, 1993; AFC Defensive Player of the Year, NFLPA, 1993,1994; Ed Block Courage Award, 1994; ranked number 22 on USA Today list of the 25 best NFL players of the past 25 years, 2007; elected to the Pro Football Hall of Fame, 2009. *

WOODSON, SHIRLEY A
Educator, artist. **Personal:** Born Mar 3, 1936, Pulaski, TN; daughter of Claude E and Celia Trotter; married Edsel Reid; children: Khari & Senghor. **Educ:** Wayne State Univ, BFA, 1958; Art Inst Chicago, grad study, 1960; Wayne State Univ, MA, 1965. **Career:** MacDowell Colony Fel, 1966; Forever Free Art African Am Women, 1962-80; Detroit Pub Schs, art supvr; Exhibitions, Childe Hassam Found NY, 1968; Arts Exended Gallery Detroit, 1969, Second World Festival African Cult Lagos Nigeria, 1977; Howard Univ, 1975; Pyramid Art Gallery, dir, 1979-80; Joslyn Mus Omaha NE, 1981; Your Heritage House Mus, 1984; "Share the Memories", Detroit Inst Arts, 1987; Conn Gallery, Marlborogh, Conn, 1989; Sherry Wash Gallery, 1989; Hughley Gallery, 1992; Corcoran Gallery Art, Wash, DC, 1993; Focus & Black Artists '88, Contemp Art Ctr, Cincinnati, Ohio. **Orgs:** Arts Extended Group, 1958-72; Nat Conf Artists, 1975-. **Honors/Awds:** NCA Award, 1977; Purchase Award, Toledo Art Comn, Toledo, OH, 1984; Creative Artists Grant, Mich Coun Arts, 1983, 1987; Creative Artists Grant, Detroit Coun Arts, 1987; Visual Arts Award, Mich Women's Found, 1988; Arts Achievement Award, Wayne State Univ Detroit, 1995; DIA Alain Locke Award, 1998.

WOODSON, THELMA L
Educator. **Personal:** Born in Rutherford County, TN; daughter of Johnny Evans Pate Sr (deceased) and Della Mae Jackson Pate (deceased); married Theodore B, Nov 12, 1955 (deceased); children: Kevan B. **Educ:** Wayne State Univ, Detroit MI, BEd, 1955, MEd, 1960. **Career:** Educator (retired); educational specialist at Univ of Mich, Ann Arbor Mich, Mich State Univ, Lansing MI, & Wayne State Univ, Detroit Mich; City Nashville TN, recreation leader, 1941-43; Fed Govt, Detroit Mich, statist clerk, 1943-44; City Detroit Mich, recreation leader, 1944-55; bd Educ, Detroit Mich, teacher, 1955-66, admin intern, 1966-68, asst prin, 1968-72, prin, 1972-86; T&T Industries Inc, corp dir, 1964-74, corp pres, 1974-79. **Orgs:** Mem & pres, Rho Sigma Chap, Sigma Gamma Rho, 1954-89; Wayne Univ Alumni, 1955-; bd chmn & pres, Am Bridge Asn, 1966-; Am Asn Univ Women, 1968-86; Nat Asn Elem Sch Prin, 1972-; Urban Prog Health, 1977-81; bd chmn, Kirwood Ment Health Ctr, 1979-; mem & pres, Wolverine Bridge Club, 1962-91. **Honors/Awds:** Citations, Detroit Bd Educ, 1963, Nat Educ, 1984, State Mich 1985, City Detroit 1985, City Nashville 1989. **Home Addr:** 2016 Glynn Ct, Detroit, MI 48206, **Home Phone:** (313)865-8921.

WOODS-WRIGHT, TOMICA
Executive. **Personal:** Born Jan 1, 1969?; married Eric (deceased); children: Christopher, Dominick & Daijah. **Career:** Clarence Avant, receptionist; Ruthless Records, pres & ceo, currently. **Business Addr:** President, Chief Executive Officer, Ruthless Records, 8201 W Third St, Los Angeles, CA 90048, **Business Phone:** (323)782-1888.

WOODWARD, AARON ALPHONSO, III
Executive. **Personal:** Married Joan J; children: Aaron A IV, Allen A, Kelvin & Darnell. **Career:** Citibank Opers Mgt, 1970-73; CUNY, Edgar Evers Col Seek Prog Fin Aid & Budget Officer; Var Ins Cos, licensed ins broker, 1975-83; Count Basie Enterprises, bus mgr, 1983-84, sec, treas, 1983-84, mgr, Count Basie Orchestra, 1983-, co-trustee, Diane Basie Trust, 1983-, ceo & co-execr, 1983-87; Diane Basie, co-guardian; Musicians Union Contractor, Entertainment Mgt, rec producer, currently; Christ Baptist Church, assoc minister, from asst to pastor, currently; Count Basie Enterprises Inc, ceo, currently. **Orgs:** Chmn, trustee bd Christ Baptist Church Coram, NY; life mem, Nat Asn Advan Colored People; past pres, Cent State Univ Metro Alumni Chapt; Omega Psi Phi Frat Nu Omicron Chap; Local 802 Musicians Union; Nat Alliance Bus Youth Motivation Task Force; consult & chair, Am Mgt Asn; 100 Blackmen New York, YCMSDG; chmn, deacon bd, NARAS, voting mem, bd dirs, Int Jazz Hall of Fame, Nat Jazz Serv Orgn. **Honors/Awds:** Harlem YMCA Black Achiever; US Presidential Commend Serv Others; Nat Alliance Bus Youth Motivation Task Force Chairperson Awards; Presidential Medal of Freedom, Pres Reagan; Basie Award Gov Kane, NJ; Numerous other awards worldwide. **Special Achievements:** Grammy 1984 for "88 Basie Street" Nat TV. **Business Phone:** (631)736-5587.

WOODY, JACKIE. **See WOODY, JACQUELINE BROWN.**

WOODY, JACQUELINE BROWN (JACKIE WOODY)
Government official. **Personal:** Born Oct 13, 1949, Nansemond County, VA; daughter of William and Ernestine Cowling; married Curtis, Sep 1974; children: Jonathan. **Educ:** Va Union Univ, Richmond, VA, BA, 1971; Rutgers Univ, New Brunswick, NJ,MLS, 1972. **Career:** Charles Taylor Pub Libr, Hampton, VA, librn, 1972-75; Prince George's County Mem Libr, MD, br mgr, 1975-89; Prince George's County Govt, MD, Off County Exec, sister county Rels coordr, 1989-90, Comn Children & Youth,educ coordr, 1990-92, Dept Family Serv, prog developer, 1992-94, proj mgr, currently; Prince George's County Coun, legis asst coun mem, Dorothy Bailey, Dist 7, sr staff advisor, 1994-99. **Orgs:** Bd mem, Big Sisters, Wash Metro Area, 1978-79; bd dirs, young adults serv dir, Am Libr Asn, 1983-86; acad selection bd, US Congmen Steny Hoyer,1985-; Alpha Kappa Alpha Sorority, Iota Gamma Omega Chap, 1988-; trustee,Greater Mount Nebo AME Church, 1991-; bd dirs, Bonnie Johns Children's Fund, 1992-. **Honors/Awds:** Proclamation, Outstanding Library Service, Prince George's County Coun,1987, Dept of Family Services Director's Award, 1994; Outstanding Educator, Black Dem Coun, 1989; Cornerstone Award, Bonnie Johns Children's Fund, 1994; Food & Friends Outstanding Volunteer, 2001; Community Service Award, J Franklin Bourne Bar Asn, 2002. **Home Addr:** 11323 Kettering Terr, Upper Marlboro, MD 20774. **Business Addr:** Project manager, Prince George's County Government, 14741 Gov Oden Bowie Dr, Upper Marlboro, MD 20772, **Business Phone:** (301)883-5985.

WOOLDRIDGE, DAVID
Executive. **Personal:** Born Dec 6, 1931, Chicago, IL; married Juana Natalie Hampton; children: David Juan, Samuel William & Gregg Wayne. **Educ:** Roosevelt Univ, Chicago, BS, Physics, 1961; Mass Inst Tech, MS, mgt sci, 1973. **Career:** Hughes Aircrft Co, design engr, 1961-68, mgr GED prog, 1968-72, prog mgr, 1973-74; LA City Col, instr, 1968-74; Motorola Inc, prog mgr, 1974-76, prod mgr, 1976-78, vpres & local sales commun & electronics; Motorola Univ, Partnership Ctr, corp vpres & dir, 1994; Mass Inst Technol Sloan Fel. **Orgs:** Alpha Kappa Alpha Sornity. **Honors/Awds:** Outstanding contrbution Youth Mtv tn Task Force, 1969; community serv award, Alpha Kappa Alpha Sornity, 1971; Outstanding serv & contrbution, Prairie View A&M Col, 1971; Alfred P Sloan Fel, Hughes Aircraft Co. **Military Serv:** USAF, a/1c, 1949-52.

WOOLLEY, HOWARD E
Executive. **Personal:** Married Gail. **Educ:** Syracuse Univ, BA, tv & radio; Johns Hopkins Univ, MS, mgt. **Career:** Nat Asn Broadcasters, vpres regulatory affairs; Bell Atlantic Corp, vpres wireless & int rels; Verizon Commun Inc, Fed Rels & State Pub Policy, vpres, sr vpres & dir, currently. **Orgs:** State Dept Communs & Info Policy Adv Comt; Fed Communs Comn; vpres, regulatory Affairs, Nat Asn Broadcasters; bd gov, Ford Theatre; bd dir, World Affairs Coun. **Business Addr:** Senior Vice President, Director, Verizon Communications Inc, 1095 Ave of The Americas, New York, NY 10036, **Business Phone:** (212)395-2121.*

WOOLLEY, PHYLLIS (PHYLLIS WOOLLEY-ROY)
Executive, marketing executive. **Educ:** Lincoln Univ. **Career:** Colgate-Palmolive Co, dir Af-Am mkt; AstraZeneca LP, dir consumer brand mkt & multicultural mkt; Patient Mktg Group Genentech Inc, Assoc Dir, currently. **Orgs:** ARF Minority Media Usage Adv Bd; Asn Nat Advertisers, ARF Minority Media Usage Adv Bd; Multicultural Mkt Comt; conf chair, Strategic Res Inst LLC; Bd Dirs, ARF, currently. **Business Addr:** Associate Director, Genentech Inc, Patient Marketing Group, 1 DNA Way, South San Francisco, CA 94080-4990, **Business Phone:** (650)225-1000.*

WOOLLEY-ROY, PHYLLIS. **See WOOLLEY, PHYLLIS.**

WOOLRIDGE, ORLANDO VERNADA
Basketball coach, basketball player. **Personal:** Born Dec 16, 1959, Bernice, LA. **Educ:** Notre Dame Univ, attended 1977. **Career:** Basketball player (retired), basketball coach; Chicago Bulls, 1981-86; NJ Nets, 1986-88; Los Angeles Lakers, 1989-90, coach, 1998-99; Denver Nuggets, 1990-91; Detroit Pistons, 1991-92, 1993; Milwaukee Bucks, 1992-92; Philadelphia 76ers, 1993-94; Benetton Treviso, Italy, 1994-95; Buckler Bologna, 1995-96; Houston Takers, head coach; Ariz Rhinos, head coach, 2008-09.

WOOTEN, CARL KENNETH
Newspaper executive, publishing executive. **Personal:** Born Oct 14, 1947, Chester, PA; son of Adam D and Hortensee E

Washington; married Barbra J Daniely; children: Tracy, Darryl. **Educ:** Univ Pittsburgh, BA, History, 1969, MAT, 1971; Fairleigh Dickinson, MBA, 1981. **Career:** The Wall St Journal, advertising sales rep, 1971-74, sr sales rep, 1975-83, dist sales mgr, 1984-90, southeast sales mgr, 1990-95; Atlanta Bus Chronicle, assoc publisher, 1995-98; Nat Acct Dir. **Orgs:** Sec Toast Masters Fairleigh Dickinson, 1980; Bus & Prof AA, 1981-83; Wash Ad Club; Youth Motivational Task Force, Xavier UNIV, 1992-98; Atlanta Ad Club, bd; Big Brother & Big Sister, Metro Atlanta, bd dirs, 1995-98; AM Cancer SOC, Atlanta Unit, bd dirs, 1995-98; Red Cross Disaster Relief Cabinet, 1996-98; Georgia Coun Econ Educ, bd dirs, 1995-98; Omega Psi Phi Fraternity, 1967; Community Found Metro Atlanta, bd dirs, 1997-98. **Honors/Awds:** Atlantans Who Made a Difference, 1992; Leadership Atlanta Class, 1997; 100 Black Men, Atlanta, 1997. *

WOOTEN, JOHN
Football executive, football player, business owner. **Personal:** Born Dec 5, 1936, Riverview, TX; married Beverly; married Juanita; children: Gina, Lynette & John David. **Educ:** Univ Colo, BS. **Career:** Cleveland Browns, guard, 1959-67; Addison Jr High Sch, 1960-63; Wash Redskins, guard, 1967-68; Pro Sports Advisors, player agent, 1973-75; Dallas Cowboys, scout, contract negotiator, player personnel, 1975-91, dir pro personnel, 1980-91; Nat Football League, dir player progs, 1991-92; Philadelphia Eagles, player personnel, 1992-93, vpres player personnel, 1994-97; Ravens, asst dir pro/col scouting, 1998-2001, consult-player personnel, 2001-04; Wooten Printing Inc, Dallas, Tex, pres, currently. **Orgs:** Bd dirs, Big Brothers, Cleveland, Ohio; City Planning Comn; Nat Minority Econ Develop Coun; chmn, Fritz Pollard Alliance. **Honors/Awds:** Hall of Fame, Tex Black Sports, 2002; William O Walker Community Excellence Honoree, 2002; Hall of Fame, Univ Colo, 2004. **Special Achievements:** One of the NFL's highest ranking African Am officials at the front-office level; Named to Cleveland Browns All-Time team, 1979. **Business Addr:** President, Wooten Printing Incorporated, 2772 W Commerce St, Dallas, TX 75212, **Business Phone:** (214)689-0707.

WOOTEN, PRISCILLA A
Association executive. **Personal:** Born Mar 31, 1936, Aiken, SC; daughter of James and Estella; married Joseph, 1954; children: Deborah M, Diana B & Donald T. **Educ:** NY Univ. **Career:** Family Worker, 1958-66; Head Start Prog, family asst, 1966; United Parents Asn, parent educ trainer, 1967; Brooklyn, educ asst, 1967-68, health nutritionist, 1968, educ asst trainer, 1968-69; Comn Liaison Worker, 1969-71; Off Educ & Info Serv, prin neighbourhood sch worker, 1971; Chancellors Action Ctr, pub rel dir; New York City Coun, E New York, Brooklyn councilwoman, 1982-2002. **Orgs:** Comn sch bd mem Dist 19k, 1967-; Evaluating Team Dist 19, 1969; vpres, New York City Sch Bd Asn, 1973-74, treas, 1974-;trust mem, Luth Hosp Brooklyn; Nat Asn Advan Colored People; first vpres, M S Douglas Soc; Bd Educ Employee; educ rep, Grace Baptist Church; vpres, Dist 19 Comm Sch Bd, 1973-; rep, Cent Bd Educ, 1973-; pres, E Brooklyn Civic Asn, 1973-; United Polit Club, 1974-. **Honors/Awds:** Local School Board Award, Dist 19k, 1968-70; Parents Teachers Association Award; Church Award, Grace Baptist Church Comn Work, 1972-74; Block Association Award, 1973-75; Commission School Board Award, 1973-75; Educator Award, 1974.

WORD, FLETCHER HENRY, JR.
School administrator. **Personal:** Born May 25, 1919, Petersburg, VA; son of Fletcher H Sr and Adelaide Penister; married Virginia Brown; children: Fletcher H III, Sharman Word Dennis. **Educ:** Va State Col, BS, 1940, MS, 1966; St John's Univ Law, attended 1945; Univ Md, attended 1960. **Career:** Eastern Sr High Sch, teacher & counr, 1960-66; Public Sch Wash DC, counr, 1966-68; Hine Jr High Sch, adminr, 1968-71; Kramer Jr High Sch, adminr, asst prin, 1971-78; Johnson Jr High Sch, adminr, 1978-79; Birney Sch, adminr, 1979-83. **Orgs:** Omega Psi Phi Frat, 1937-; St Gabriel Roman Cathc Church, 1960-; treas, DC Asn Sec Sch Principals, 1979-82; pres, DC Asn Sec Sch Principals, 1982-84; vol, Nat Mus Nat Hist; Ft Stevens Lions Club. **Honors/Awds:** Catholic Service Youth, 1964; Certification of Appreciation, Boy Scouts Am, 1965; Service Certification, DC Pub Schs, 1970; 3 plaques from schools served, 1981-84; Master Teacher Award, 1985. **Home Addr:** 53 Underwood Pl NW, Washington, DC 20012. *

WORD, DR. PARKER HOWELL
Physician. **Personal:** Born Jun 24, 1921, Petersburg, VA; children: Leslie, Parker & Lindsey. **Educ:** Va State Univ, BS, 1941; Howard Univ Med Sch, MD, 1944. **Career:** Human Develop Corp, med dir, 1964-66; Staff Mem, Deaconess Hosp, Homer G Phillips, Christian Hosp; Pvt Pract, physician; Wash univ, Sch med, Clinical Obstet & Gynec dept, Instr Emeritus, currently. **Orgs:** Life mem, NAACP; Urban League Local; Frontiers Inc. **Honors/Awds:** Mayor's Civic Award, 1969. **Military Serv:** AUSMC, capt, 1952-54. **Business Addr:** Instructor Emeritus, Clinical Obstetrics and Gynecology, Washington University, Department of Obstetrics and Gynecology, 660 S Euclid, Saint Louis, MO 63110, **Business Phone:** (314)362-7135.

WORDLAW, CLARENCE, JR.
Government official. **Personal:** Born Jan 28, 1937, Little Rock, AR; son of Thedora Shivers and Clarence Sr; married Pearlene Stegall; children: Zager, Derrick, Nicole & Thaddeus. **Educ:** Univ Iowa, BS, lib arts, 1959. **Career:** Beacon Neighborhood House, group work supvr, 1959-66; Circuit Ct Cook County, casework supvr, 1966-68; Chicago Urban League, dir w side off, 1969-70; Ill Bell Telephone Co, pub/personnel mgr, 1971-92; Youth Campus, 1994-95; Pro Care Ctr, facilitator, 1996-2000. **Orgs:** Bd dirs, Malcolm X Col Mid Mgt Intern Prog; brd managers, Dr Martin Luther King Jr Unit Chicago Boys & Girls Clubs; Chicago Urban Affairs Coun; brd dirs, Midwest Community Coun; Natl Assn Advan Colored People; adv brd, Career Training Inst Woodlawn Org Chicago; community develop brd, Off Spec Progs Univ Chicago; SCLC; Kappa Alpha Psi Frat Inc; Police Comn Rels Comt Maywood Human Rels Comn; brd dirs, Proviso E High Sch Booster Club, Maywood Chamber Com; bd mem, Austin Career Educ Ctr; brd dirs, St Joseph High Sch; Operation PUSH; Cook County Sch Dist 89, school bd mem, 1983-; brd dirs, Found Stud Athletes, 1990-. **Honors/Awds:** Outstanding Graduate Award, Crane High Sch, 1955; All Big Ten & Hon Mention All Am Basketball selection col, 1958-59; Black Achievers of Industry Award, Metro Chicago YMCA; Hall of Fame, Chicago Sports Found, 1982; Community Oscar Award, Midwest Community Coun; African American Male Image Award, Archbishop Lykes, OFM, 1995; Hall of Fame, Chicago Pub League Basketball Coaches Assn, 1999; Hall of Fame, Ill High Sch Basket ball Coaches Assn, 2000. **Military Serv:** AUS, First lt, 1959-68. **Business Addr:** School Board Member, Cook County School, District 89, 1133 S 8th Ave, Maywood, IL 60153.

WORFORD, CAROLYN KENNEDY
Broadcaster. **Personal:** Born Apr 6, 1949, Kansas City, MO; daughter of Lester and Sarah; married Thomas Worford Jr, Jan 28, 1984; children: Roger & Ashleigh. **Educ:** Metrop Jr Col, Kans City, Mo, attended 1967. **Career:** Southwestern Bell, Kans City, Mo, long distance operator, 1967; Hallmark Cards, Kans City, Mo, code analyst, 1968-74; KMBC-TV, Kans City, Mo, promotion asst, 1974-77; Allis-Chalmers, Kans City, Mo, personnel rec clerk, 1977; KSHB-TV, Kans City, Mo, prog dir, 1977-84; WJBK-TV, Southfield, Mich, prog mgr, 1984, dir opers, 1995, dir prog & audience develop, 1989-93, dir prog & audience develop, 1993, sta mgr, vpres, prog develop, 1995; My TV20, prog & news dir, ed, opers & prog mgr, currently. **Orgs:** Corp leader, Boys & Girls Club SE Mich, 1985-; BUF, 1986-; BART; alumni mem, Leadership Detroit, 1988-; lifetime mem, Nat Asn Advan Colored People, 1988-; bd mem, 1989-, chairperson, 1995, Nat Asn TV Prog Execs. **Honors/Awds:** Leadership Detroit, Detroit Chamber Com, 1987; Certificate of Appreciation, United Negro Col Fund, 1987; Certificate of Appreciation, Detroit Pub Schs, 1988; Outstanding Woman in Television, Top Management Award, Detroit Chap Am Women Radio & TV. **Special Achievements:** First African-American woman to head the National Association of Television Program Executives. **Business Addr:** Operations Manager, Program Manager, My TV20, 27777 Franklin Rd Suite 1220, PO Box 20, Southfield, MI 48037-0020, **Business Phone:** (248)355-2020.*

WORKMAN, ANTONIO F D
Executive. **Career:** Paracentral, pres & chief exec officer, currently. **Orgs:** Alpha Phi Alpha Fraternity.

WORKMAN, AURORA FELICE ANTONETTE
Educator. **Personal:** Born May 24, 1962, New York, NY; daughter of Earthalee LaBoard Layne and Rawle Workman (deceased); children: Jayden Taylor, Chykia Holliman & Cyer Layne. **Educ:** State Univ NY, Nassau Community Col, NY, AA, 1983; C.W. Post/Long Island Univ, Greenvale, NY, BS (hons), 1987. **Career:** NY News day, Melville, NY, ed asst, 1980-; Roosevelt Jr/Sr High Sch, Eng teacher, 1984-90; Here Comes the Dawn, Hempstead, NY, pres, 1991-; Nassau Community Col, Spec Proj, admin off; Title I Prog, educr, lectr, acad enrichment & comput tutor; Life Skills Appl Prog, prev specialist youth & young adults; 21st Century Commun Media, pres; The DAWN, publ, ed; NASSAU Community Col, asst dir human resources, currently. **Orgs:** Vice chairperson, Black Unity Day, NY, 1990, 1991; Tabernacle One Accord Deliverance Ctr Inc; educ dir, Harambee Ctr; victims rights advocate, Domestic Violence & C & Youth; transitional counr, Incarcerated Men & Women; exec admin, Million Man March, Local Organizing Comt Long Island. **Honors/Awds:** Jack Berland Award, Nassau Community Fedn Teachers, 1983; Entreprenuer of the Year Award, 1991-92; The NIA Award of Long Island, Community Service, 1994, 1995, 1996; Builder's Award, Million Women Found, 1998. **Home Addr:** 840 Northgate Dr, Uniondale, NY 11553-3020, **Home Phone:** (516)292-4698. **Business Addr:** Assistant to the Director/Human Resources, NASSAU Community College, Department of Human Resources, 1 Educ Dr Tower 702, Garden City, NY 11530-6793, **Business Phone:** (516)572-7759.

WORKMAN, HAYWOODE WILVON
Basketball executive, basketball player. **Personal:** Born Jan 23, 1966, Charlotte, NC; son of Charles Workman and Priscilla Funderburk Workman; married Nicole. **Educ:** Winston-Salem State Univ, attended 1985; Oral Roberts Univ, attended 1989. **Career:** Basketball player (retired), Basketball Official; Topeka Sizzlers, CBA, guard, 1989-90; Atlanta Hawks, 1989; Ill Express, CBA, 1990; Wash Bullets, 1990-91; Scavolini Pesaro, Italy, 1991-93; Ind Pacers, 1993-97; Milwaukee Bucks, 1998-99; Toronto Raptors, guard, 1999-2000; CBA, referee. **Orgs:** Big Brothers; 100 Black Men Indianapolis; Continental Basketball Asn. **Honors/Awds:** CBA All-Rookie Team, 1990.

WORMLEY, CYNTHIA L.
Educator, singer. **Personal:** Born Jan 15, 1953, Philadelphia, PA. **Educ:** Hartt Col Music, BM, music. **Career:** Philadelphia Bd Pub Educ, music teacher; Univ Hartford Spiritual Choir, soloist; Hartt Col Chamber Singers, soloist, 1970-74. **Orgs:** Pres, Epsilon Upsilon Chap Delta Sigma Theta Sor, 1973-74; Delta SigmaTheta Sor; Nat Coun Negro Women. **Honors/Awds:** Numerous awards for community service in field of music; Miss Ebony, PA,1974; Scholar Recipient for Study in Opera, Dept of Conservatory of Music, Hchschl Musik, Munich, Ger, 1979. **Special Achievements:** First black child soloist with Philadelphia Orchestra Age 9.

WORMLEY, DIANE-LOUISE LAMBERT
Educator. **Personal:** Born Apr 28, 1948, Hartford, CT; divorced. **Educ:** William Smith Col, BA 1970; Bryn Mawr Col, Summer Inst Women Higher Educ, attended 1989. **Career:** Mary Washington Col, admis coun, 1970-71; Wheaton Col, asst dir admis, 1971-73; Simmons Col, asst dir admis, 1973-74; Stanford Univ, asst dir liberal arts, 1974-76, dir, 1976-78; Fisk Univ, dir career planning, 1978-81; Atlanta Univ, dir corp assoc, 1981-84; Cornell Univ, Admin Mgt Inst, instr, 1993-95; Univ Penn, asst dir, 1984-88, dir product develop & mkt, 1988-94, dir process mgt, div finance, 1992-94, assoc treas, Community Housing, managing dir, currently. **Orgs:** Assoc mem, Nat Black MBA Asn, 1982-84; Southern Col Placement Asn, 1978-84; Vol in Pub Serv, 1991; pres, Alumnae Asn, Southern Smith Col, 1994-95. **Honors/Awds:** Individual Achievement National Black MBA Atlanta 1983; Alumnae Asn, Citation, 1989. **Home Addr:** 4805 Regent St, Philadelphia, PA 19143. **Business Addr:** Managing Director, Community Housing, Rm 6293 721 Franklin Bldg, Philadelphia, PA.

WORRELL, AUDREY MARTINY
Physician. **Personal:** Born Aug 12, 1935, Philadelphia, PA; daughter of Dorothy Rawley Martiny and Francis A Martiny; married Richard V; children: Philip, Amy. **Educ:** Meharry Med Col, MD, 1960; Fisk Univ, attended 1955; Whittier Col, attended 1956. **Career:** Physician (retired); Haverford State Hosp, chief Serv 1965-68; Univ Pa, Sch of Med, asst prof 1967; Erie County Mental Health Unit IV, Buffalo Psychiatric Ctr, chief 1970-74; VA Medical Ctr, Newington, CT, chief of psychiatry 1980-81; Univ of CT Sch of Med, asst prof of psychiatry, 1974-81, dir of div 1980-81, clinical prof of psychiatry, 1984-86; State of CT, commnsr of Mental Health 1981-86; Vista Sandia Hosp, CEO & medical dir 1986-87; Lovelace Medical Center, dir geriatric psychiatry, 1986-93; Univ of New Mexico, assoc prof, beginning 1986; St Joseph Medical Center, director geriatric services, 1993-02. **Orgs:** Am Psychiat Asn; CT State Psychiat Asn; Nat Asn Mental Health Prog; Am Pub Health Asn; Am Col Psychiat; Am bd Psychiat & Neurol. **Honors/Awds:** Diplomate Am Bd Psychiat & Neurol, 1970. *

WORRELL, KAYE SYDNELL
Nurse. **Personal:** Born Aug 18, 1952, Axton, VA; married Cleveland D. **Educ:** Petersburg Gen Hosp Sch Nursing, dipl, 1973; Hampton Inst, BS, nursing, 1975. **Career:** Petersburg Gen Hosp Sch Nursing, instr, 1975-78; Southside Community Col, part-time nursing instr, 1983; Poplar Springs Hosp, unit coordr. **Orgs:** Waverly Improv Asn, 1974-; secy, Sussex Co Red Cross, 1982-83; mem, Petersburg Gen Hosp Sch Nursing Alumnae, 1984-85; mem & elected WaverlyTown Coun, 1978-86. **Home Addr:** 8154 Beaverdam Rd, Waverly, VA 23890. **Business Addr:** Unit Coordinator, Poplar Springs Hospital, 350 Wagner Rd, Petersburg, VA 23805.

WORRELL, RICHARD VERNON
Physician, educator. **Personal:** Born Jun 4, 1931, Brooklyn, NY; son of Elaine and Elmer; married Audrey M; children: Philip & Amy. **Educ:** NY Univ, BA, 1952; Meharry Med Col, MD, 1958; State Univ NY, Buffalo, Affiliated Hosp, Residency Training Orthop Surg, 1964. **Career:** Univ Penn, instr Orthop Surg, 1968; Univ Conn Sch Med, Orthop Surg, from asst prof to assoc prof, 1968-83, Stud Affairs, asst dean, 1980-83; State Univ NY, Clin Surg, prof, 1983-86; Univ N Mex Med Ctr, prof orthop, 1986; Univ N Mex, Sch Med, Dept Orthop, prof & vice chair, 1997-2000, prof emer & vice chmn emer, currently. **Orgs:** Fel, Am Acad Orthop Surgeons, 1970-; fel, Am Col Surgeons, 1970-; Royal Soc Med, London, affiliate, 1973-; fel, Int Col Surgeons, 1981-; State Univ NY, Clin Surg, prof, 1983-86; dir, Dept Orthop Surg, Brookdale Hosp Med Ctr; Am Orthop Asn, 1990-; Acad Orthop Soc, 1991-. **Military Serv:** AUSR, capt, 1962-69. **Business Addr:** Professor Emeritus, Vice Chairman Emeritus, University of New Mexico Health Sciences Center, Department of Orthopaedics, 1 University of New Mexico, Albuquerque, NM 87131, **Business Phone:** (505)277-4107.

WORRELL, SCOTT P.
Surgeon. **Educ:** Harvard Univ, Cambridge, MD, 1990. **Career:** Montefiore Med Ctr, physician; Albert Einstein Hosp, Bronx, NY,

physician, 1990-91; Pvt pract, orthop surgeon, 1996-99; Montgomery Gen Hosp; Robinwood Orthop Specialty Ctr, physician, currently; Wash County Hosp, chief div Orthop surg & vice chief dept surg, currently. **Orgs:** Md Med Chirological Soc; American Orthop Sports Med Soc; Am Bd Orthop Surgeons; fel, Am Acad Orthop Surg; Am Col Surgeons. *

WORRILL, DR. CONRAD W
Educator, activist. **Personal:** Born Aug 15, 1941, Pasadena, CA; son of Walter Worrill and Anna Bell; married Talibah Collymore; children: Michelle, Femi, Sobenna & Aisha. **Educ:** George Williams Col, BS, 1968; Univ Chicago, MA, 1971; Univ Wisc, PhD, 1973. **Career:** Westside YMCA, prog dir, 1968; Northeastern Ill Univ, Carruthers Ctr Inner City Studies Educ, prog coordr & prof, 1976-, adv & dir, 2004-. **Orgs:** Task Force for Black Political Empowerment, co-founder, 1983; Nat Black United Front, chmn, 1985-; Ill Black United Fund, bd mem, 1985-; Kemetic Inst; Asn Study Classical African Civilizations; Temple African Community Chicago, bd mem; Nat Black Law Students Asn; econ develop comnr, Nat Coalition Blacks Reparations Am. **Honors/Awds:** AKA Monarch Awards; received numerous awards for community involvement. **Special Achievements:** Spec consult field opers for the hist Million Man March, 1995; presented the comn with a Declaration Genocide by the US Govt Against the Black Population in the US; weekly columnist, Chicago Defender, 1983-; writes the syndicated weekly column "Worrill's World,? which is widely read in African American newspapers across the country. **Military Serv:** AUS, specialist 4th class, 1962-64. **Business Phone:** (773)268-7500.

WORSHAIM, KEITH EUGENE
Law enforcement officer. **Personal:** Born Apr 17, 1960, Louisville, KY; son of John Henry Worsham Jr and Mary Lou; married Linda J Miller Worshaim, Feb 11, 1984; children: Bradford D & John W J. **Educ:** Kentucky State Univ, attended 1979. **Career:** Missi Univ Women, campus security officer, 1982-83; Columbus Police Dept, patrolman, 1983-88, narcotic agent, 1986-87, patrol corporal, 1988-92, patrol sgt, 1992-95, patrol lt, 1995-98, Comn Oriented Policing Enforcement, comdr, 1998, accreditation mgr, currently. **Orgs:** Col, Big Bros & Big Sisters Columbus, MS, 1983-87; Ala & MS Peace Officers Asn, 1989-; founder, Columbus Police Martial Arts, 1991-95; state rep state MS, World Police & Fire Games, 1991; Am Law Enforcement Trainers Asn, 1995; founder, Columbus Police Dept Athletics, 1996; Nat Orgn Black Law Enforcement Execs, 1998; Nat Black Police Officers Asn, 1998. **Honors/Awds:** House Reps State MS, House Resolution 52 Commending Efforts Comm Rels, 1996. **Special Achievements:** MidSouth Regional Police & Fire Games Medalist, Pistol & Martial Arts, 1995, 1996; Int Law Enforcement Games Medalist, Judo, Karate, and Tae Kwon Do, 1992, 1994; World Police & Fire Games Medalist, Karate, 1991, 1993. **Military Serv:** Army Nat Guard, KY & AL, pvt first class, 1979-82. **Business Addr:** Accreditation manager, Columbus Police Department, 120 Marconi Blvd, PO Box 1408, Columbus, MS 43215, **Business Phone:** (662)224-3500.

WORSHAM, JAMES E.
Labor activist, postmaster general. **Personal:** Born Jan 31, 1932, Chicago, IL; son of Adolphus E and Minnie L Smith; married Corrine Kelly Worsham, Jun 14, 1953 (died 1990); children: Valerie L, Vance E, Adrienne R. **Career:** Labor activist (retired); US Postal Serv, Chicago, IL, letter carrier, 1963-90, union steward, 1964-76, chief steward, 1976-78; Nat Asn Letter Carriers, Chicago Br 11, pres, 1978-95, dir retired mem, 1995-98; US Postal Serv, Wash, DC, nat trustee, 1980-94. **Orgs:** Amalgamated Bank Labor Coun, 1988-; chmn, Chicago Post Off Credit Union, 1986-; noble, Shriners, 1982-; Mason 32 degree, F&AM, Masonic, 1982-; Mason 3rd degree, F&AM, Masonic, 1959-; official bd, Emmanuel Baptist Church. **Special Achievements:** Union building named in honor of James E Worsham. **Military Serv:** USAF, S/sergent, 1949-53; Korean War, received several medals, 1952. *

WORSLEY, GEORGE IRA, JR.
Executive. **Personal:** Born Apr 3, 1927, Baltimore, MD; married Gloria M Morris; children: Mary Elizabeth Cunningham & Gayll Annette. **Educ:** Howard Univ, BSME, 1949. **Career:** Dollar Bltz Assocs, engr, 1959-64; Genl Engineering Asn, engr, 1949-59; George Ira Worsley Jr & Assocs, owner, 1964-. **Orgs:** Adv bd, United Comt Nat Bank; CEC; MW; ASHRAE; Nat Treatment Agency; BOCA; WBA; NFPA. **Military Serv:** USNR, smn third class, 1945-46, sargent, 1951-53. **Business Addr:** President, George Ira Worsley & Associates, 7705 Georgia Ave NW, Washington, DC 20011, **Business Phone:** (202)291-1666.

WORTH, CHARLES JOSEPH
Government official, chief executive officer, auditor. **Personal:** Born Jun 6, 1948, Raleigh, NC; son of James H and Rosa M; married Laurie Gray; children: Kellye N, Kimberlye N & Kourtnye N. **Educ:** NC A&T State Univ, BS acct, 1970; NC Cent Univ, MPA 1987. **Career:** Coopers & Lybrand, sr auditor, 1970-74; Gen Signal Corp, sr internal auditor, 1974-76; Bausch & Lomb, sr internal auditor, 1976-79; Soul City Co, dir finance, 1979-80; Charles J Worth & Assoc Inc, pres 1980-; Warren City, county mgr 1984; Vance Warren Comprehensive Health Plan Inc, chief exec officer. **Orgs:** Am Soc Pub Admin; Nat Forum Black Pub Admin; Nat Asn Black County Offs; Conf Minority Pub Admin; bd mem, NC City/Cty Mgmt Asn; Nat Asn City Admin; Omega Psi Phi Frat; former pres, Vance-Warren Chap SCLC; chmn, Kerr-Tar Pvt Indust Coun; Kerr Lake Bd Realtors; treas, Second Congional Dist Black Caucus; Warren County Polit Action Coun; NC A&T State Univ Alumni Assoc; Int City Mgmt Asn; NC Asn Minority Bus Inc; Nat Asn Advan Colored People; Soul City Rural Volunteer Fire Dept; Int City Mgt Asn. **Honors/Awds:** First Black Appointed Manager in State of NC, 1984; Certificate of Appreciation Boy's Clubs of America, 1978-79; Omega Man of the Year Zeta Alpha Chapter Omega Psi Phi 1983; Leadership Award, Kerr-Tar PIC, 1990; Distinguished Service Award, NABCO, 1990. **Home Addr:** 24 Macon Circle, PO Box 411, Manson, NC 27553.

WORTH, JANICE LORRAINE
Business owner, registered nurse. **Personal:** Born Apr 2, 1938, St Louis, MO; daughter of Oscar Eugene Farrar (deceased) and Beatrice Farrar; married J Quentin, May 4, 1963; children: Quentin E, Sean Shannon & Jason Evan. **Educ:** St Marys Hosp Sch Nursing, nursing dipl, 1962; Forest Park Community Col, AA, 1973; Wash Univ, 1990. **Career:** Prestige Products Co, secy & treas, 1982; St Mary's Health Ctr, registered nurse & supvr, 1991. **Orgs:** St Louis Minority Bus Develop Ctr, 1983; MENA, 1985; Black Nurses Asn; Nat Asn Advan Colored People; Million Women March Com St Louis; Zeta Phi Beta Soroity; League Women Voters. **Honors/Awds:** Volunteer of the Year, Mideast Agency Aging, 1994. **Home Addr:** 522 Holland Ave, Saint Louis, MO 63119, **Home Phone:** (314)963-9669.

WORTH, STEFANIE PATRICE
Journalist. **Personal:** Born Nov 8, 1962, St Louis, MO; daughter of Calvert Lee and Patrice Ann Dandridge; married Kevin Rene Gibbs, Nov 28, 1988 (divorced 1989); children: Denmark Sebastian Gibbs. **Educ:** Univ Mo, Columbia, MO, BA, 1985. **Career:** KBIA Radio, Columbia, MO, reporter, anchor, 1983-84; KOMU-TV, Columbia, MO, reporter, anchor, 1985; WJLB-FM Radio, Detroit, MI, reporter, anchor, 1985-86; Mich Chronicle, Detroit, MI, staff writer, 1987; Office Detroit City Councilman John Peoples, Detroit, MI, special projects consult, 1987-89; Wayne County Neighborhood Legal Servs Detroit St, Detroit, MI, law project admin consult, 1990; Mich Chronicle, Detroit, MI, staff writer, 1990-. **Special Achievements:** Writings under progress: "Where Souls Collide", (A completed work formerly titled Inkling. WC approx. 93,000), A contemporary paranormal romance; "Secrets to Tell", (A work in progress. Projected WC approx. 95,000), A contemporary paranormal romance. **Home Phone:** (248)893-4553. **Business Addr:** Staff Writer, Michigan Chronicle, 479 Ledyard St, Detroit, MI 48201, **Business Phone:** (313)963-5522.

WORTHAM, BARRON WINFRED
Football player. **Personal:** Born Nov 1, 1969, Fort Worth, TX; married Caledra, Feb 22, 1997. **Educ:** Univ Tex El-Paso. **Career:** Houston Oilers, linebacker, 1994-96; Tennessee Oilers, 1997-98; Tennessee Titans, 1999; Dallas Cowboys, 2000. **Honors/Awds:** Ed Block Courage Award, 1995.

WORTHAM, RUSSEAL
Educator. **Educ:** Sul Ross State Univ, BS, psychol, MEd, Coun. **Career:** Jarvis Christian Col, Career Mgt Serv, dir, adj prof & instr, currently. **Orgs:** Nat Asn Adv Colored People. **Business Addr:** Adjunct Professor, Instructor, Jarvis Christian College, PO Box 1470, Hawkins, TX 75765-1470, **Business Phone:** (903)769-5835.

WORTHEY, RICHARD E
Manager. **Personal:** Born Aug 11, 1934, Greensboro, NC; married Peggie J McTier. **Educ:** A&T St Univ, BSEE, 1960; USAF Inst Tech, MSSE, 1964; Ohio St Univ, PhD, training, 1969. **Career:** Manager (retired); USAF Aeronaut Syst Div, oper res analyst; ASD Wrght-Patterson AFB, elec engr, 1966-70, elec engr SEG, 1960-66; Supervisory Oper, res analyst, 1970-80; Oper Res Div, chief, 1980-86; Advan Syst Anal, dir, 1986-89. **Orgs:** Inst Elec & Electronics Engrs, 1964-; Dayton Area Chap, A&T St Univ Almn Asn, 1971-; chmn, ASD Incentive Awards Comn, 1972-78; AF Smelter Adv Group, 1975-78; past pres, mem, Fwy Golf Club, 1973-; Am Inst Aeronaut & Astronaut, 1976; Am Mgt Asn, 1975; DOD NASA Working Group Smelter Tech, 1976-78; one yr exec develop assignment Off Under Secy Def Res & Engr, 1979-80. **Honors/Awds:** Outstanding Performance Awards, 1968, 1971, 1972, 1973 & 1976; Letter Commend Performance, 1978; Outstanding Performance Awards, 1981-84, 1986-88; Meritorious Civilian Service Award, 1986; Outstanding Civilian Career Service Award, 1989. **Military Serv:** USN, rd1, 1953-57. **Home Addr:** 4738 Coulson Dr, Dayton, OH 45418, **Home Phone:** (937)263-9562.

WORTHY, DR. BARBARA ANN
Founder (Originator), educator. **Personal:** Born Nov 1, 1942, Thomaston, GA; daughter of Laura Bell Jones and S T. **Educ:** Morris Brown Col, Atlanta, GA, BA, 1964; Atlanta Univ, Atlanta, GA, MA, 1970; Tulane Univ, New Orleans, LA, PhD, 1983. **Career:** Camilla High Sch, Camilla, GA, social sci teacher, 1964-69; Southern Univ, New Orleans, LA, hist teacher, 1970-, social sci dept chair, Ctr African & African Am Studies, founder, 1989-, Col Arts & Soc Sci, interim dean, currently. **Orgs:** Southern Hist Asn, 1983-; Asn Study Afro-Am Life & Hist, 1984-85; Friends of Amistad, 1986-; bd dir, Soc Study Afro-LA & Hist, 1988-; New Orleans League Women Voters, 1988-; Delta Sigma Theta. **Honors/Awds:** Overdyke History Award, N La Hist Asn, 1981. **Special Achievements:** One of 14 participants selected from six inst higher educ in Louisiana to participate in six-week Intl Curriculum Seminar in Kenya & Tanzania, E Africa, summer, 1985. **Business Addr:** Interim Dean, Southern University at New Orleans, Department of Social Sciences, 6400 Press Dr, New Orleans, LA 70126, **Business Phone:** (504)286-5232.*

WORTHY, KYM
Judge, lawyer. **Personal:** Born 1956; children: 1. **Educ:** Univ Mich, polit sci & econ; Univ Notre Dame Law Sch, JD, 1984. **Career:** Wayne County, MI, asst prosecutor, 1984-94; Recorder's Ct, judge, 1994-; Wayne Co Circuit Ct, prosecutor, 2004-. **Orgs:** Am Bar Asn. **Honors/Awds:** State Bar of Michigan Honoree, 2007. **Special Achievements:** Successfully prosecuted the two Detroit police officers who were convicted of beating to death motorist, Malice Green, 1993; first African American & first woman to become Wayne County prosecutor, 2004. **Business Addr:** Prosecutor, Wayne County Circuit Court, 1441 St Antoine, 1200 Frank Murphy Hall of Justice, Detroit, MI 48226, **Business Phone:** (313)224-5777.

WORTHY, LARRY ELLIOTT (LARRY DOC ELLIOTT)
Radio host. **Personal:** Born Aug 18, 1953, Koziousko, MS; son of Allie B Carter and Saul T; children: Larry Jr & Sincerely. **Educ:** Career Acad Broadcasting, Milwaukee, Wis, 3rd Class FCC License, 1972. **Career:** WAWA, Milwaukee, Wis, announcer, pub serv dir & music dir, 1972-81; WOAK, Atlanta, Ga, announcer, 1981-82; WVEE, Atlanta, Ga, announcer, 1982-83; WJLB, Detroit, Mich, announcer, music dir, 1983-88; WHYT, Detroit, Mich, announcer, 1988-89; WGPR, host, currently; WJZZ, Detroit, Mich, announcer, promotion dir. **Honors/Awds:** Radio Announcer Yr, Metro Area Artists & Songwriters Asn, 1991; Big Mac Award, Best Announcer, Detroit News, 1986-88, 1990; Cert Merit, State Mich, 1987; First Honor Award, Best Radio Personality, Mich Lottery Black Music Month, 1986; Testimonial Resolution, Detroit City Coun, 1984. **Business Addr:** Host, WGPR, 3146 E Jefferson Ave, Detroit, MI 48207, **Business Phone:** (313)259-8862.

WORTHY, WILLIAM, JR.
Journalist, educator. **Personal:** Born Jul 7, 1921, Boston, MA; son of William Worthy and Mabel R Posey (deceased). **Educ:** Bates Col, BA, 1942; Harvard Univ, Nieman, Fel Jour, 1956-57. **Career:** Journalist, Educator (Retired); The Baltimore Afro-Am, foreign corresp & columnist, 1953-80; Boston Univ, Boston, MA, vis prof, 1974-79; Jour & Afro-Am Studies, Boston Univ, prof, 1974-79; Univ Mass, Boston, Ma, journalist residence, 1985-90; Howard Univ, Washington, DC, distinguished visiting prof. **Orgs:** Soc Nieman Fel; ACL. **Honors/Awds:** Journalism Award, MA Legis Black Caucus, 1988; Right-to-know & freedom info awards, Boston Press Club, Capital Press Club Lincoln Univ Mo; Louis M Lyons Award, Nieman Found, 2008. **Special Achievements:** Author of "The Rape of Our Neighborhoods" and Travelled to 58 countries, specializing in coverage of Third World revolutionary and neo-colonial issues.

WRENN, THOMAS H., III
Dentist. **Personal:** Born Oct 11, 1942, Mineola, TX; married Joel J Porter. **Educ:** Univ Mo, DDS, 1967; Univ Kansas City. **Career:** Dentist, pvt pract. **Orgs:** Nat Dental Soc, 1967; Am Dental Soc, 1970; Nat Asn Advanc Colored People, 1973; Soc Action Com Univ Mo Kansas City Dental Sch, 1974; past pres, Heart Am Dental Soc, 1974; Alpha Phi Alpha Frat; Jaycees Kansas City, 1975; Southern Christian Leadership Conf. **Business Addr:** Dentist, 2120 E 63rd St, Kansas City, MO 64130.*

WRICE, DAVID
Police officer. **Personal:** Born May 31, 1937, Lorain, OH; son of Johnnie and Savannah Wilson; divorced; children: Sharon Wrice Moore, Leonard Church, Barbara J. Wrice, Daniel, David. **Educ:** Lorain County Community Col, Lorain, OH, assoc police sci, 1972; Heidelburg Col, Tiffin, OH, BA, psychol, 1974. **Career:** Am Shipyard, Lorain, OH, foreman, 1963-66; Lorain County Community Col, instr; Lorain Police Dept, Lorain, OH, 1966-, jail warden, 1985-; Lorain Metrop Housing Authority, investr & resident asst watch coordr; OH Crime Prevention Asn, 1999. **Orgs:** Deleg, Nat Black Police Asn, 1986-; pres, Lorain Minority Police Asn, 1986-; comdr, Herman Daniels VFW Post 8226, 1988-; moderator, Concerned Citizens Lorain, 1989-; Buckeye Masonic Lodge; Al Lalim Temple; OH Crime Prevention Asn, 1999. **Honors/Awds:** Appreciation Award, Second Baptist Church, 1970; Appreciation Award, Herman Daniels VFW Post 8226, 1974; Buddy PoPPV Award, Lorain County Veterans Coun, 1975; Member of Year, Lorain County Minority Law Enforcement Asn, 1986; Outstanding Community Service, Shilow Baptist Church, 1986; Century Club Award, Nat Black Police Asn, 1986; Community Service Award, State Ohio Auditor's Off, 1986;

President Patrol Trainning Course, 1997. **Military Serv:** AUS, Spc 3rd class, 1954-57; received Good Conduct Medal, German Occupation Medal, Marksman Ribbon. *

WRICE, DR. SHELDON B
College teacher. **Personal:** Born Apr 9, 1966, Orangeburg, SC. **Educ:** SC State Univ, BA, 1988; Atlanta Univ, MLS, 1990; Univ Arkon, MA & MS, 1994, EdD, 1995. **Career:** Univ Akron, prof tech writing & compos, 2004-, Dept Assoc Studies, chair, currently. **Orgs:** Nat Alliance Black Educators; Ga Librn Asn, Ohio Librn & Media Asn. **Honors/Awds:** Named Young Man of Year, 1988. **Business Phone:** (330)972-6023.

WRICE, VINCENT J
Computer scientist, educator, business owner. **Personal:** Born Feb 20, 1963, Paterson, NJ; married Jun 29, 1991. **Educ:** Fla A&M Univ, BS, technol, 1986. **Career:** NJS Transit, syst analyst, 1986-88; Union Co Col, sr programmer analyst, adj instr, assoc prof, currently; Proper Gander, pres, currently. **Orgs:** Nat Soc Black Engrs; Kappa Alpha Psi; Nat Black Data Processing Asn; Black Filmmaker Found. **Business Addr:** Associate Professor, Union County College, H 105 Cranford Campus 1033 Springfield Ave, Cranford, NJ 07016, **Business Phone:** (908)497-4366.

WRIGHT, ALONZO GORDON
Executive. **Personal:** Born Jul 19, 1930, Cleveland, OH; married Patronella Ross; children: Cheryl, Joyce & Gordy. **Educ:** Hiram Col, BA, 1948; Western Reserve Univ, Cleveland, LLB, 1956. **Career:** Wright Dev Co, pres, 1975-; Cleveland, atty, 1957-58; Univ Euclid Urban Renewal Proj, dir, 1963-65; Midwest Area Econ Develop Admin, dir, 1965-67. **Orgs:** Pres, chmn, Econ Res Corp; pres, Bay Dist Motor Car Dealers; vpres, Venice C, 1974-; dir, Santa Monica Nat Conf Community & Justice. **Military Serv:** USN, 1948-55.

WRIGHT, ANTOINETTE D
Museum director. **Educ:** DePaul Univ, BS Bus; Mundelein Col, BS; Univ Colo, cert mus mgt. **Career:** DuSable Mus African Am Hist, pres, chief exec officer, currently. **Orgs:** Bd mem, Asn African Am Mus; bd mem, After Sch Matters; Arts Midwest Arts Admin Fel, Columbus Mus Art & Cin Mus Natural Hist. **Business Addr:** President, Chief Executive Officer, DuSable Museum African American History, The DuSable Museum, 740 E 56th Pl, Chicago, IL 60637, **Business Phone:** (773)947-0600.

WRIGHT, ARNOLD W., JR.
Executive. **Career:** CIGNA Corp, vpres contributions & civic affairs; CIGNA Found, exec dir, currently. **Orgs:** bd dirs, Susan G Komen Breast Cancer. **Business Addr:** Vice President, Executive Director, CIGNA Corporation, CIGNA Foundation, 1650 Mkt St, 1 Liberty Pl OL56A, Philadelphia, PA 19193-1540, **Business Phone:** (215)523-4000.*

WRIGHT, BENJAMIN HICKMAN
Association executive. **Personal:** Born Aug 5, 1923, Shreveport, LA; son of Nathan and Parthenia Hickman; married Jeanne Jason. **Educ:** Univ Cincinnati, BA, 1950, MA, 1951, DHL, 1971. **Career:** Associate executive (Retired); Johnson Pub Co, sales prom & merchandising mgr, 1952-66, sr vpres, dir, 1974; US Dept State, econ & polit reporting officer, 1952-53; Clairol Inc, mgr, urban affairs & ethnic develop, 1966-74; Black Media Inc, pres. **Orgs:** Bus coun, Nat Comn Black Churchmen; bd chmn, pres, NAMD, New York Chap, 1967-71; chmn, Action Comn Self-Determination, 1969-69; bd chmn, New York Unit Black Econ Union, 1970-71; Group Advert Progress, 1970-71; bd mem, John F Kennedy Memorial Libr Minorities, 1970-74; Nat ICBO, 1971-; bd ed, J Black Econ & Bus, Morehouse Col; bd mem, Sales Promo Exec Asn, 1971-72; exec dir, Nat Assault Illiteracy Program, 1980-. **Honors/Awds:** Media Workshop Award of Excellence, 1968; Alpha Phi Alpha Equitable Opportunity Award, 1969; Outstanding Black Businessman of Year, Black Africa Promotions, 1973; Distinguished Serv Educ, Phi Beta Sigma Fraternity, 1987; Baton for Progress Award for Distinguished Leadership, Nat Pan-Hellenic. **Special Achievements:** Pub "A Voyage of Awareness". **Military Serv:** USN, 1943-46.

WRIGHT, DR. C. T. ENUS
Educator. **Personal:** Born Oct 4, 1942, Social Circle, GA; married Mary Stevens, Aug 9, 1974. **Educ:** Ft Wayne State Univ, BS, 1964; Atlanta Univ, MA, 1967; Boston Univ, PhD, 1977; Mary Holmes Col, LHD, 2000. **Career:** Ga Pub Sch Social Circle, teacher, 1965-67; Morris Brown Col, faculty, 1967-73, div chmn, 1973-77; Eastern Wash Univ, prog dir asst provost, 1977-81; Talladega Col, vpres acad affairs, 1981-82; Cheyney Univ, pres, 1982-86; Fla Memorial Col, vpres acad affairs & provost, 1985-89; The Light of Hope Inst, chmn & founder, 2000; IFESH, chief executive officer & pres, 2001-04. **Orgs:** Dean pledgees, Phi Beta Sigma Ft Valley State, 1963-64; pres, Madison Bapt Sunday Sch & Training Union Congress, 1967-78; worshipful master, lt community Prince Hall Masons F & AM, 1973-75; del, Nat Dem Conv, 1980; Pub Broadcasting Commn State Wash; vpres, Cheney Lions Club; exec comn, Boy Scouts Am Philadelphia; Nat Asn Equal Opportunity Higher Educ; Am Hist Asn; Am Baptist Club; Am Asn Col & Univ; Asn Studt Afro-Am Life & Hist; Kiwanis Club Fountain Hills. **Honors/Awds:** Human Rels Scholar, Boston Univ, 1969-71; Phi Alpha Theta Hist Hon, Soc Boston Univ, 1971. **Special Achievements:** Book: A History of Black & Educ in Atlanta; Atlanta Hist Bull, 1977; pub Black History Week, A Time to Reflect & Eastern Wash Univ, 1979; The History of Black Historical Mythology, 1980.

WRIGHT, CARL JEFFREY
Publishing executive, lawyer. **Personal:** Born Nov 18, 1954; son of Alvin Sr (deceased) and Lottie Mae Thomas; married; children: Stephen, Amanda & Natalie. **Educ:** Fisk Univ, Nashville, TN, BA, 1975; Georgetown Univ, Wash, DC, JD, 1979; Columbia Univ, New York, NY, MBA, finance, 1982. **Career:** TransWorld Airlines, int tariff's analyst, 1976-80; Johnson & Johnson, int bus develop, 1982-84; Bristol-Myers Squibb, sr dir planning & admin, Corp Develop Dept, Consumer Health & Personal Care Groups, vpres corp develop, 1984-94; Urban Ministries Inc, pres & chief operating officer, currently. **Orgs:** Trustee, Black Student Fund, 1976-80; adj prof, Univ Evansville Grad Sch, 1986-89; trustee, Am Red Cross, SW Ind Chap, 1988-90; trustee, Circle Y Ranch, Bangor, MI; Am Bar Asn; Pen Bar; trustee, Payne Theol Sem; Am United Life; Christian Film & TV Comn; Evangelical Christian Publs Asn; Fuller Theol Sem; Urban Outreach Found. **Honors/ Awds:** Johnson & Johnson Leadership Award, Johnson & Johnson Co, 1980. **Special Achievements:** One of America's Best and Brightest Business and Professional Men, Dollars & Sense Magazine, 1989. **Business Addr:** President, Chief Operating Officer, Urban Ministries Inc, 1551 Regency Ct, Calumet City, IL 60409, **Business Phone:** (708)868-7100.

WRIGHT, CAROLYN ELAINE
Educator. **Personal:** Born Apr 22, 1951, Dayton, OH. **Educ:** Wright State Univ, BS, bus admin, 1973; MBA, 1978. **Career:** Bolinga Black Cultural Resources Ctr, asst dir, 1973-77, dir, 1977-81; Cent State Univ, asst prof; Materials Mgt, dir; Human Resources & Organisational devplop, exec dir; adjunct prof, Col Bus & Indust; Camp Fire USA Greater Dayton Area Coun, project adminr, currently. **Orgs:** Vpres, Day-Mont West Community Mental Health Ctr, 1984-85; first vpres, Mary Scott Nursing Ctr, 1984-85; chairperson, Citizen's Adv Coun, 1984-85; Mary Scott Nursing Ctr; Dayton Youth Golf Acad. **Honors/Awds:** Professional internship Cleveland Scholarship Foundation, 1983; graduate Black Leadership Program, Dayton Urban League, 1983-84; African American Award Excellence, Wright State Univ Alumni Asn, 2004. **Special Achievements:** Hosted Black Achievement on WAVI radio in Dayton. **Business Addr:** Project Administrator, Camp Fire USA Greater Dayton Area Council, 4301 Powell Rd, Dayton, OH 45424, **Business Phone:** (937)236-6115.

WRIGHT, CHARLES E.
Airline executive. **Personal:** Born Mar 1, 1946, Washington, DC; married Barbara H; children: Charles Wright Jr, Phillip. **Educ:** Howard Univ, attended 1969; workshops & seminars Xerox Prof Selling Skills; Negotiating Skills Seminar; Interpersonal Commun; Stress Mgt; Effective Presentations. **Career:** exec (retired); Eastern Air Lines Inc, ticket agent, 1969-76, sales rep, 1976-80, mgr market develop, 1980-83, mgr market develop & campus rep admin, beginning, 1983; Leon County Tourist Develop Coun, exec dir; Tallahassee Area Convention & Visitors Bur, pres, ceo. **Orgs:** Supvr Sr Citizens, Passport Staff; monitored Fulfillment House Strategic Mkt Systems; mem bd dirs, Miami Dade Trade & Tourism Comn; adv bd, World Inst Black Commun; Nat Asn Mkt Develop; bd mem, Inner City Dance Troupe; host & producer, contemporary talk show Black Kaleidoscope. **Honors/Awds:** US Army Outstanding Soldier, Combat Training Brigade, 1970. **Military Serv:** DC, Nat Guard, 1969-75; AUS. *

WRIGHT, CHARLES STEVENSON
Writer. **Personal:** Born Jun 4, 1932, New Franklin, MO; son of Stevenson and Dorothy Hughes. **Educ:** Lowney Handy's Writers Colony, Marshall, IL, attended. **Career:** Free-lance writer, currently; columnist, Village Voice; Novels: The Messenger, 1963; The Wig: A Mirror Image, 1966; Absolutely Nothing to Get Alarmed About, 1973. **Military Serv:** AUS, Korea, pvt, 1952-54. **Home Addr:** 308 E 8th St Suite 7I, New York, NY 10009, **Home Phone:** (212)260-6090.

WRIGHT, CHARLOTTE
Administrator. **Career:** Gary Community Sch Corp, high sch asst, prin; Dunbar-Pulaski Middle Sch, prin, currently; Roosevelt High Sch, prin, currently. **Business Addr:** Principal, Roosevelt High School, Gary Community School Corporation, 730 W 25th Ave, Gary, IN 46407, **Business Phone:** (219)881-1500.

WRIGHT, CLARENCE, SR.
Vice president (organization). **Career:** LIMRA International's Diversity Mkt Comt, chair, 2000-01; AXA Advisor, vpres, AXA Financial Inc, sr vpres opportunity mkt, currently. **Business Addr:** Senior Vice President of Opportunity Markets, AXA Advisors Inc, AXA Financial Inc, 1290 Avenue of the Americas, New York, NY 10104, **Business Phone:** (212)554-1234.

WRIGHT, CLINTON L. A.
Lawyer. **Personal:** Born Oct 24, 1951, Kingston, Jamaica; son of Clinton Wright and Jemima Webster; married Antoinette Green Wright, Aug 24, 1974; children: Nia, Challa, Calvin. **Career:** State Con, asst pub defender, 1977-79; CIGNA Corp, Kennedy & Sullivan, sr litigation coun, 1979-83; James, Turner & Wright, law partner, 1983-89; City New Haven, Con, asst corp coun, 1981-84, corp coun, 1990-91; Cooper, Liebowitz, Royster, Wright, law partner, 1990-91. **Orgs:** George Crawford Law Soc, 1976-91; bd mem, Am Cancer Soc, 1988-91; bd mem, Am Red Cross, 1989-91; United Way Greater New Haven, 1989-91; chair, Con Bar Asn Com Minority Participation, 1989-91; exec com, New Haven County Bar Asn, 1989-91.

WRIGHT, CRYSTAL ANDREA
Business owner, publisher. **Personal:** Born Jan 13, 1958, Los Angeles, CA; daughter of Sharon Lewis and Ray Morrow; married Michael Stradford, Mar 10, 1990 (divorced); married Bill Richardson, May 15, 2001. **Educ:** Seattle Univ, 1976-78; Fashion Inst Design & Merchandising, 1978-79; Univ Wash, 1979-81. **Career:** Xerox Corp, acct exec, 1982-85; Bobby Holland Photog, artist rep, 1985-86; Crystal Agency Inc, pres, 1986-, dir, currently; Set Pace Publ Group, owner, 1994-. **Orgs:** Womens Econ Develop Corp, 1994-; Nat Asn Women Bus Owners, 1996-; Women Inc, 1996-. **Honors/Awds:** Entrepreneur in Action, Womens Econ Dev Corp, 1998. **Special Achievements:** The Hair Makeup & Styling Career Guide, 1995, 1997; First Hold Magazine for freelance hair, makeup and fashion stylists, 1997-. **Business Addr:** President, Director, Crystal Agency Inc, 4237 Los Nietos Dr, Los Angeles, CA 90027-2911, **Business Phone:** (323)906-9600.

WRIGHT, DARLENE. See LOVE, DARLENE.

WRIGHT, DAWIN LYRON
Manager. **Personal:** Born Nov 24, 1951, Chicago, IL; son of Adell and Ruby L; married Carolyn; children: Dedra & Denita. **Educ:** Kennedy King Col, AAS, automotive, 1970; Chicago State Univ, BS, indust educ 1973, MS, occup educ, 1976. **Career:** Kennedy King Col, asst prof, 1971-76; GM Corp, Chevrolet Motor Div, area serv mgr, 1976-78, personnel coordr, 1978-80, asst serv mgr, 1981-85, zone serv mgr, 1986-88, acct mgr, 1988-90, br mkt mgr, 1990-93, zone mgr, 1993-94, asst regional mgr, 1994-96; dir, bus opers, 1996-2002; Dealer Integration, dir, 2002-05, Dealer Develop, exec dir, 2005; Gen Motors Corp, exec dir, currently. **Orgs:** Black Exec Forum; pres, 4 Us Investment. **Business Addr:** Executive Director, General Motors Corporation, Dealer Develpement, 100 Renaissance Ctr, PO Box 482 A06 C66, Detroit, MI 48265-1000, **Business Phone:** (313)667-9037.

WRIGHT, DEBORAH C.
President (Organization), chief executive officer, executive. **Personal:** Born Jan 1, 1958, Bennetsville, SC; daughter of Harry C. **Educ:** Radcliffe Col; Harvard Univ, MBA, JD, 1984. **Career:** New York City Housing Authority Bd, 1990-92; New York City Planning Comn, mem, 1992-94; Dept Housing Preserv & Develop, comnr, 1994-96; Upper Manhattan Empowerment Zone Develop Corp, pres & chief exec officer, 1996-99; Carver Bancorp, bd dirs; Carver Bancorp Inc, pres & chief exec officer, 1999-, chmn, 2005-; Carver Fed Savings Bank, pres & chief exec officer, 1999-, chmn, 2005-; bd dirs, Kraft Foods, currently. **Business Phone:** (212)876-4747.*

WRIGHT, DMITRI
School administrator, artist. **Personal:** Born Oct 17, 1948, Newark, NJ; son of John and Ruth; married Karen Shields; children: Odin. **Educ:** Newark Sch Fine Arts, cert, valedictorian, 1967-70; Cooper Union, 1972-74; NYACK Col, BS, org mgt, 1993. **Career:** Newark Sch Fine & Indust Arts, fine arts instr, 1971-81; Conn Inst Art, class drawing instr, 1971?81; painting & drawing instr, 1972?82; master fine art instr, 1983?94, dean, dir educ, 1994-2000, fine & applied art, dir spec progs; Brooklyn Mus Arts Sch, arts educr, 1972-82; Dmitri's Renaissance Workshops, founder, prin master fine artist & instr, 1982-. **Orgs:** Creative dir, Conn Inst Art, High Touch & High Tech Pigments Pixels Progs; artist residence, Hist Soc Greenwich, 2002-03, master instr, 2003-. **Honors/Awds:** Max Beckman Memorial Scholarship, 1970-71. **Special Achievements:** Received several awards including: First artist to hold Artist-in-Residence status at Bush-Holley historical site; Sound Shore Gallery, NY, 1986-87; One man images gallery, 1987; Greenwichs Newspaper & Greenwich News Newspaper, 1992-99. **Home Addr:** 106 Hunting Ridge Rd, Greenwich, CT 06831, **Home Phone:** (203)661-0105. **Business Addr:** Master artist & founder, Dmitri?s Renaissance Workshop, 106 Hunting Ridge Rd, Greenwich, CT 06831-3135, **Business Phone:** (203)661-0105.

WRIGHT, DR. EARL LEE
School administrator. **Personal:** Born Jul 5, 1941, Sinton, TX; son of Nola Beatrice Vaughn and Earilee; married Susan; children: Arlene, Darius, Adrian & Laura. **Educ:** St Mary's Univ, BA, 1965, MA, 1970; Univ Tex, Austin, doctoral fel, 1975,PhD, 1975. **Career:** San Antonio Independent Sch Dist, teacher, 1965-68; Swift & Co, mgt, 1968-70; San Antonio Col, prof & dean, 1970-82, vpres, 1982-95, full prof, psychol, 1995-; ES Wright Investments Inc, pres & chief exec officer. **Orgs:** Antioch Baptist Church, 1951-; vis prof, Prairie View A & M Univ, 1973-75;volunteer serv Northwest YMCA, 1973-78; natl consult, Nova

Univ, 1978-90; brd dir, San Antonio Boys Club Am, 1981-82; United Way Comn Adv Brd, 1981; consult Kelly AFT Mgt Org, 1982; mem, JCSPAT, 1982-86, TACUSPA; mem, Federal Exec Awards Panel, 1984-85; hon mem, Mayor's Martin Luther King Memorial Community, 1986; NCP; mem, Phi Delta Kappa; speaker, State & Natl Conferences & Convs. **Honors/Awds:** Honorarium, NY Univ, 1982. **Special Achievements:** Numerous publications in the area of educational administration. **Home Addr:** 100 Bikeway Lane, San Antonio, TX 78231-1401. **Business Addr:** Professor Psychology Department, San Antonio College, MLC 670 1300 San Pedro Ave, San Antonio, TX 78212, **Business Phone:** (210)476-1257.

WRIGHT, ERICA ABI. See BADU, ERYKAH.

WRIGHT, FALISHA
Basketball player. **Personal:** Born Jan 28, 1973; daughter of Brady. **Educ:** San Diego State Univ, BS, 1995. **Career:** Basketball player (retired), basketball coach; Portland Power, guard,1992-95; Portland State Univ, asst coach. **Honors/Awds:** Hon mention accolades, San Diego State Univ, 1993 & 1994; inducted Aztec Hall of Fame, 2002. *

WRIGHT, DR. FREDERICK DOUGLASS
College administrator. **Personal:** Born Aug 26, 1946, Columbia, GA; son of James Wright. **Educ:** Roosevelt Univ, BGS, 1972, MA, 1974; Princeton Univ, MA, 1982, PhD, 1982. **Career:** Princeton Univ, R R McCormick fel, 1977-78; Univ Notre Dame, asst prof, 1978-, dir black studies prog, 1983-, asst dean, 1986-, Dept Africana Studies, dir, currently; Roosevelt Univ, NDEA fel. **Orgs:** Evaluator NJ Dept Higher Educ, 1985-86; asst dir, Nat Endowment Humanities Inst Afro-Am Cult, 1987; Am Polit Sci Asn; Western Social Sci Asn; Southern Polit Sci Asn; Southwest Polit Sci Asn; Nat Conf Black Polit Scientists; Asn Study Afro-Am Life & Hist; Nat Asn Black Studies Prog; Ind Asn Historians. **Honors/Awds:** Frazier Thompson Faculty-Staff Award, 1984; "Afro-American Religious Studies for College Teachers," NEH, 1984; published scholarly articles on Black Politics in the American South. **Business Addr:** Assistant Dean, Director, University of Notre Dame, Department of Africana Studies, 327 O'Shaughnessy Hall, Notre Dame, IN 46556, **Business Phone:** (574)631-5628.

WRIGHT, GEOFFREY
Judge. **Educ:** Union Col, BA, 1971; Albany Law Sch, JD, 1975. **Career:** John L Edmonds, assoc, 1976-83; Seavey Fingerit Vogel Oziel & Skoller, assoc, 1984-90; Wright & Fingerit, partner, 1991-97; New York City Civil Ct, judge, 1998-. **Business Addr:** Judge, Civil Court Of The City of New York, New York County, 111 Ctr St, New York, NY 10013, **Business Phone:** (646)386-5706.

WRIGHT, GEORGE C.
Mayor, executive. **Personal:** Born Mar 9, 1932, Chesapeake City, MD; son of George C and Alice Brooks; married Mary Guy, Jul 21, 1953; children: Terun Palmer, George C III, Sharon & Lisa. **Educ:** Md State Col, BS, 1953. **Career:** Dover A&B, Dover DE, chief staffing, 1956-89; Town Smyrna DE, mayor, 1984-95; Del League Local Govt, exec dir, 1989-, pres, 1990-92. **Orgs:** Coun Police Training, DE, 1986-; vpres, steward bd, Bethel Am Church, 1987-; Kent Sussex Indust, 1987-; worshipful master, St John's Lodge 7; 33rd Degree Mason. **Honors/Awds:** Received DAPA Award, Distinguished Public Administration, St Del, 1994. **Military Serv:** AUS, E-5, 1952-54. **Home Addr:** 31 Locust St, Smyrna, DE 19977. **Business Addr:** Executive Director, Delaware League of Local Governments, PO Box 484, Dover, DE 19903-0484, **Business Phone:** (302)678-0991.

WRIGHT, DR. GEORGE C
Educator. **Personal:** Born in Lexington, KY. **Educ:** Univ Ky, BA, hist, MA, hist, DHL, 2004; Duke Univ, PhD, hist. **Career:** Univ Ky, asst prof, 1977-80; Univ Tex, Austin, asst prof, assoc prof, prof, vice provost undergrad educ, 1980-93; Duke Univ, Afro-Am Studies Prog, dir & vice provost, 1993-95; Univ Tex, Arlington, vpres acad affairs & provost, 1995-98, exec vpres acad affairs & provost, 1998-2002; Prairie View A&M Univ, pres, 2003-; Silver Spurs Centennial, teaching fel; Univ Tex, Lillian & Tom B Rhodes Centennial Teaching fel; Harvard Univ, Andrew W Mellon Faculty fel. **Orgs:** Bd dir, City Arlington Chamber Found; Med Ctr Arlington; Southern Hist Asn Prog Comt; Univ Ky Col Arts & Sci Adv Bd; Comn Col Southern Asn Col & Sch; Comn Advan Racial & Ethnic Equity Am Coun Educ & Tex Humanities. **Honors/Awds:** Jean Holloway Award, Univ Tex; Eyes of Texas Award; Outstanding Black Faculty Member, Kappa Alpha Psi Fraternity. **Special Achievements:** Author: A History of Blacks in Kentucky: In Pursuit of Equality, 1890-1980, Volume II; Racial Violence in Kentucky, 1865-1940: Lynchings, Mob Rule & Legal Lynchings; Life Behind a Veil: Blacks in Louisville, Kentucky, 1865-1930; biography, Robert Charles O'Hara Benjamin: A Forgotten Afro-American Leader; published numerous articles & chapters in books; co-dir: "Don't Let the Sun Go Down" & "Upon this Rock: The Black Church in Kentucky". **Business Addr:** President, Prairie View A&M University, PO Box 519, Prairie View, TX 77446-0519, **Business Phone:** (936)261-2111.*

WRIGHT, HOWARD GREGORY
Basketball player. **Personal:** Born Dec 20, 1967, San Diego, CA. **Educ:** Stanford Univ, attended 1989. **Career:** Atlanta Hawks, 1991; Orlando Magic, 1991, 1993; Dallas Mavericks, 1991.

WRIGHT, DR. JACKSON THOMAS
Physician, educator. **Personal:** Born Apr 28, 1944, Pittsburgh, PA; son of Jackson T Sr and Lillian Doak; married Mollie L Richardson, Sep 2, 1967; children: Adina. **Educ:** Ohio Wesleyan Univ, Delaware, BA, 1967; Univ Pittsburgh, Pittsburgh, MD, 1976, PhD, 1977. **Career:** Woodrow Wilson, Martin Luther King fel, 1971-73; Univ Mich, Ann Arbor, MI, residency internal med, 1977-80; Med Col Va, Va Commonwealth Univ, Richmond, VA, asst prof, 1980-86, assoc prof med & pharmacol, 1986-90; Case Western Res Univ, dir clin hypertension prog, 1990-, prof med, 1995-, Clin Res Ctr, prog dir, currently, Hypertension Sect, chief, currently. **Orgs:** Chmn, Va State Affil Hypertension Subcomt, Am Heart Asn, 1984-86; vice chmn, hypertension sci subsection, Am Soc Clin Pharmacol & Therapeutics, 1985-87; vpres, Richmond Med Soc, 1985-87; fel Am Physicians, 1987; Am Fed Clin Res; Am Col Physicians; chmn, Internal Med Sect, Nat Med Asn; exec comt mem, Old Dom State Med Soc; exec comt mem, Asn Black Cardiologists; pres, Black Educ Asn. **Honors/Awds:** Univ Pittsburgh Equalization Higher Education Fund Award, 1972-77; Certificate of Appreciation, Stud Nat Med Asn, MCV chap, 1982, 1984, 1985, 1986; Program Service Award, Am Heart Asn, 1986. **Military Serv:** USAF, capt, 1967-71. **Home Addr:** 2668 Wrenford Rd, Shaker Heights, OH 44122, **Home Phone:** (216)360-0348. **Business Addr:** Professor of Medicine, Program Director General Clinical Research Center, Case Western Reserve University, 11100 Euclid Ave, Cleveland, OH 44106-4982, **Business Phone:** (216)368-2000.

WRIGHT, JAMES CHRISTOPHER
Educator. **Personal:** Born Dec 25, 1918, Mecklenburg County, NC; married Annie B Smith. **Educ:** St Pauls Col, BS, 1953; Va State Col, MS, indust educ, 1976. **Career:** Mecklenburg Co Sch, masonry teacher. **Orgs:** Bd mem, Alpha Phi Alpha Fraternity; RC Yance Lodge 284 AF & AM; Nat Asn Advan Colored People; Southern Christian Leadership Conf; mem bd dir, Chase City Med Clin; Mecklenburg Educ Asn; Am Voc Asn; Nat Educ Asn; Town Coun; vice mayor, Chase City, VA. **Military Serv:** AUS, WW Ii. 3 yrs.

WRIGHT, JAMES E
Educator, college administrator. **Educ:** Va Union Univ, BS; Va State Univ, MED. **Career:** Richmond Pub Schs, sci instr; J Sargeant Reynolds Community Col, instr; Goochland County Pub Schs, sci instr & dept chair; Va Union Univ, asst prof; Univ Richmond, Col Arts & Sci, dir MSI, currently. **Special Achievements:** Recorded a series of vignettes on African-American inventors for broadcast on public radio. **Business Addr:** Director, University of Richmond, College of Arts & Sciences, 311 N Ct 28 Westhampton Way, Richmond, VA 23173, **Business Phone:** (804)289-8245.

WRIGHT, JAMES R
Clergy, librarian. **Personal:** Born May 12, 1941, Fayette, AL; son of Elvertis and Corine Henry; married Mary A Law; children: James jr, Coretta & Jason. **Educ:** Alabama State Univ, BS 1962; State Univ NY Geneseo, MLS, 1970; Union Inst Cincinnati, OH, PhD. **Career:** St Judes Educ Inst, Mont, AL, teacher, librn, 1962-66; Gary Pub Libr, Gary, IN, 1966-68; AL A&M Univ, Huntsville asst libr to libr, 1968-69; Rochester Pub Libr, dir, Phillis Wheatley Libr, 1969-88; pub Focus libr, 1968; Libr Jour, 1969; Col & Res librn, 1979; Wilson Libr Bull, 1971; Youth Adv Comn, Rochester Urban League, lectr & speaker probs librarianship; Progressive Church God Christ, pastor, 1981; Church of God in Christ Inc, bishop, currently. **Orgs:** Bd dir, Mont Neighborhood Ctr; Black Res Info Ctr; Black-O-Media; chmn, Black Caucus Am Libr Asn, 1973-74. **Home Phone:** (585)671-8344. **Business Addr:** Bishop, Church of God in Christ Inc, 384 Chili Ave, Rochester, TN 14611, **Business Phone:** (585)355-2823.

WRIGHT, JAMES W
Banker, chairperson. **Career:** Citizens Trust Bank, pres & chief exec officer; First Tuskegee Bank, pres, chief exec officer, chmn, currently. **Business Addr:** Chairman, First Tuskegee Bank, 301 N Elm St, Tuskegee, AL 36083, **Business Phone:** (334)727-2560.

WRIGHT, JANE C.
Surgeon, educator, endocrinologist. **Personal:** Born Nov 30, 1919, New York, NY; daughter of Louis and Corrine; married David D Jones; children: Jane, Alison. **Educ:** Smith Col, AB, 1942; NY Med Col, MD, 1945. **Career:** Surgeon (retired); Bellevue Hosp, asst resident internal med, 1945-46; Harlem Hosp, resident, 1947-48, chief resident, 1948, vis physician, 1949, head, Cancer Res Found, 1952; New York City Pub Schs, staff physician, 1949; vis phys consult, numerous hosp clins; NY Univ, assoc prof surg res, 1955; NY Univ Med Ctr, dir cancer chemother res & instr res therapy, 1955; Pres Comn Heart Disease, Cancer & Stroke, 1964; Univ NY Downstate Med Ctr, assoc dean prof, 1967-71; NY Med Col, prof of surg, head Cancer Chemother Dept & assoc dean, 1971-87. **Orgs:** Manhattan Coun State Community Human Rights; Nat Med Asn; Manhattan Cent Med Soc; Am Asn Cancer Res; NY Acad Sci; NY Co Med Soc; NY Cancer Soc; African Res Found; Am Cancer Soc; Am Asn Advan Sci; Sigma Xi; Medico-CARE; Am Soc Clin Oncol; Pres's Community Heart Disease; Alumni Asn Women's Med Col PA; NY Acad Med; Phys Manpower; Med Soc Col NY; NY State Woman's Coun NY State Dept Com; Smith Col Bd Trust; Am Asn Cancer Res; Nat Inst Health Med Sci Technol; Nat Inst Gen Med Scis; Alpha Kappa Alpha. **Honors/Awds:** Numerous publs in field; numerous awards, honors, special achievements, recognition. **Special Achievements:** First black assoc dean & prof, State Univ of NY Downstate Med Ctr, 1967; highest ranked African American woman at a nationally recognized medical institution, 1967; first woman president of the New York Cancer Society; publ many res papers on cancer chemother & led delegations of cancer res to Africa, China, Eastern Europe & Soviet Union.

WRIGHT, JEANNE JASON (JEANNE JASON)
Editor. **Personal:** Born Jun 24, 1934, Washington, DC; daughter of Robert S Sr (deceased) and Elizabeth Gaddis; married Benjamin Hickman, Oct 30, 1965; children: Benjamin Jr (deceased), Deborah, David & Patricia. **Educ:** Radcliffe Col, BA, 1956; Univ Chicago, MA, 1958. **Career:** Editor (retired); Psychiat social worker, var ment health facil, 1958-70; Black Media Inc, gen mgr, 1970-74, pres, 1974-75; Nat Black Monitor, exec ed, 1975-98, publ, 1977-98; Black Resources Inc, pres, 1975-98. **Orgs:** Nat Asn Media Women; Newswoman's Club NY; Nat Asn Social Workers; Alpha Kappa Alpha Sorority; Gamma Zeta Omega Chapter; Harvard Club NY; AAAS. **Honors/Awds:** Nat Asn Black Women Attorney Award, 1977; Second Annual Freedom's Journal Award, Journ Students & Faculty Univ DC, 1979; Metro Media Woman of the Year Award, NY Chap Nat Asn Media Women, 1984; Founders Award, 1986; Community Award, Am Red Cross Harlem Chapter, 1988. **Home Addr:** 1800 NW 187th St, Miami Gardens, FL 33056, **Home Phone:** (305)622-7233.

WRIGHT, JEFFERSON W.
Clergy, college teacher. **Personal:** Born Jul 24, 1935, Bluefield, WV. **Educ:** Marshall Univ, AB, 1959; Boston Univ Sch Theol, STB, 1963; Boston Univ Sch Theol, MDiv, 1973; Va State Col; WVa Univ Law Sch; WVa Univ Southern Calif. **Career:** Hebrew C Home, youth counr, 1959; Calvary Baptist Church, stud pastor, 1959-60; LA Pub Sch Syst, sch teacher, 1960-61; Tremont State Church, asst stud minister, 1961; Sheldon State Church, pastor, 1961-64; Second Baptist Church, Harrisburg, pastor, 1964-; Pa State Univ, fac, 1969-73. **Orgs:** Co-founder, OIC Harrisburg; Nat Baptist Church, Am Baptist Conv; Harrisburg Uptown Neighbors Together; adv comt, Pa Dept Health & Welfare; Urban Strat Comt Coun Christ; Nat Bd Black Churchmen; founder, First Black Sr Citizens Organ Cent Pa; bd mem, Nat Asn Adv Colored People; moderator, WITF-TV prog, A Time to Act; Urban Coalition & Black Coalition Harrisburg; Mayors Cits; adv comt chmn, Subcomt Housing; bd dirs, Family & C Serv; Tri-Co Planned Parenthood Asn; adv bd, Harrisburg Sch Dist. **Military Serv:** USAF. *

WRIGHT, REV. DR. JEREMIAH A, JR.
Clergy. **Personal:** Born Sep 22, 1941, Philadelphia, PA; son of Rev Jeremiah Wright Sr and Dr Mary Henderson; married Ramah; children: Janet Marie, Jeri Lynne, Mikul, Nathan & Jamila. **Educ:** Howard Univ, BA, 1968, MA, 1969; Univ Chicago Sch Divinity, MA, 1975; United Theol Sem, DMN, 1990. **Career:** Zion Church, interim pastor, 1968-69; Beth Eden Church, asst pastor, 1969-71; Am Asn Theol Schs, researcher, 1970-72; Rockefeller fel, 1970, 1972; Trinity United Church Christ, sr pastor, 1972-; Chicago Ctr Black Religious Studies, exec dir, 1974-75; Chicago Cluster Theol Schs, lectr 1975-77; United Theol Sem, prof, 1991-97; Sem Consortium Pastoral Educ, adj prof; Howard Univ, teaching asst fel. **Orgs:** Omega Psi Phi Frat, 1960-77; United Black Christians, 1972-; Black Clergy Caucus United Church Christ, 1972-; bd dir, Centes New Horizons, 1976-; Doric Lodge 77 F & AM, 1976-; Western Consistory 28, 1983-; bd dir, Malcolm X Col, Sch Nursing; bd dir, Off Church Soc; comnr, Comn Racial Justice; Ill Conf Churches; Urban League Ministerial Alliance; Ecumenical Strategy Comm; Ill Conf United Church Christ; Great Lakes Regional Task Force Churches Transitional Comn; Alpha Kappa Mu Honor Soc. **Honors/Awds:** Presidential Commendations LB Johnson. **Special Achievements:** Publications: "God Will Answer Prayer", "Jesus is His Name"; article publ "Urban Black Church Renewal" found in the "Signs of the Kingdom in the Secular City" edited by Helen Ujvarosy Chicago Covenant Press 1984. **Military Serv:** USMC, pfc, 1961-63; USN, home3, 1963-67. **Business Addr:** Senior Pastor, Trinity United Church of Christ, 400 W 95th St, Chicago, IL 60628, **Business Phone:** (773)962-5650.

WRIGHT, JOBY. See WRIGHT, JOSEPH A.

WRIGHT, DR. JOHN AARON
Educator. **Personal:** Born May 22, 1939, St Louis, MO; married Sylvia Henley; children: John Jr, David & Curtis. **Educ:** Harris Teachers Col, BA,1962; St Louis Univ, Med, 1968, PhD 1978; Atlanta Univ; Mo Univ; Teachers Col Columbia Univ. **Career:** Educator (retired); John Griscom Sch, prin 1965-70; Steger Jr High Sch, asst prin, 1970-73; Kinloch Sch Dist, supt, 1973-75; Ferguson-Florissant Sch Dist, asst supt comn relations, 1975-79; supt; St Louis Citizens Educ Task Force, exec dir 1977-79. **Orgs:** Sal Army del Int Corps Cadet Conf London, 1956; pres, Univ City Sch Bd, 1976; bd trustees & elected mem, St Louis Community Col, 1994-02; Phi Delta Kappa; Anniversary Club; Grace Meth Church; co-chair, St Louis CtrInt Rels; chmn, St Louis, Mo, Sene-

gal Sister Cities Comn; vice chmn, Mo Humanities Coun, 1998-2000, chmn, bd dir, currently. **Honors/Awds:** Man of the Year, Omega Psi Phi Fraternity, 1959, 1967; Danforth Leadership Fel, 1977; Fulbright Scholar, India, 1982; Service to Education Award, Harris-Stone State Col; St Louis Book Award; Julia Davis Award. **Special Achievements:** Author, Discovering African-American St Louis: A Guide to Historic Sites, Missouri Historical Society Press, 1994; Kinloch, Mo, 1999; University City2003; The Ville of St Louis, 2002. **Business Addr:** Board of Director, Missouri Humanities Council, 543 Hanley Industrial Ct Suite 201, St Louis, MO 63144-1905, **Business Phone:** (314)781-9660.

WRIGHT, JOSEPH A (JOBY WRIGHT)
Basketball player, basketball coach. **Personal:** Born Sep 5, 1950, Savannah, GA; married Cathy; children: Shay, Jenay, Cara, Joby III & Jesse. **Educ:** Ind Univ, BS, phys edcu, 1972. **Career:** Basketball player (retired), basketball coach; Seattle Supersonics, 1972-73; Memphis Tams, 1973-74; San Diego Sails, 1975-76; Va Squires, 1975-76; Ind Univ, asst basketball coach, 1980-90; Miami Univ, head basketball coach, 1990-93; Univ Wyo, head basketball coach, 1993; Cincinnati Stuff, coach; Harlem Globetrotters, coach, 2000; Ind Univ, coach, currently. **Orgs:** Select team comt, USA Basketball, 1993-96. **Honors/Awds:** Coach of the Year, Mid-Am Conf, 1992-93. **Business Addr:** Coach, Indiana University, 107 S Ind Ave, Bloomington, IN 47405, **Business Phone:** (812)855-3089.

WRIGHT, JOSEPH L
Pediatrician, educator. **Educ:** MD; MPH; FAAP. **Career:** Child Health Advocacy Inst, exec dir; State EMS Med Dir Pediat; Pediatrics Child Advocacy, vice chair; Children's Nat Med Ctr, Emergency Med & Prev & Community Health, fac, 1993-, assoc prof pediat, currently, Ctr Prehospital Pediat, med dir & founder, currently, minority recruitment officer, currently; George Washington Univ Sch Med, assoc prof pediat; Md Inst Emergency Med Serv Syst, State med dir. **Orgs:** Chair, Am Acad Pediat Comt Injury, Violence & Poison Prev; Delta Omega; adv bd, Inst Med; adv bd, Nat Asn Children's Hosps & Related Insts; adv bd, Am Acad Pediat. **Honors/Awds:** Recipient of many federal grants; Shining Star Award, Los Angeles-based Starlight Found. **Special Achievements:** Authored numerous scholarly publications, numerous broadcast and print media appearances and lectures widely to both professional and lay audiences. **Business Addr:** Medical Director, Childrens National Medical Center, 111 Michigan Ave NW, Washington, DC 20010-2970, **Business Phone:** (202)884-4177.

WRIGHT, DR. JOSEPH MALCOLM
School administrator, government official. **Personal:** Born Sep 27, 1944, Toomsboro, GA; son of Ed and May O Dixon; married Sheilah Delores Broome, Aug 10, 1967; children: Joseph Oliver, Tiffany Michele & Jennifer Nicole. **Educ:** Eastern Mich Univ, BS 1969; Wayne State Univ, JD 1974; Harvard Univ, edmgt dipl, 1983; Columbia State Univ, PhD, 1997. **Career:** GM-Buick, stat control asst, 1965-67; GM-Chev, sr acct, 1967-69; Univ Mich, suprv payroll, 1969-70, Col Arts Sci & Lett, admin mgr, 1970-72,dean stud affairs, 1973-88, chmn minority affaris, 1975-77; Detroit Col Bus, adj prof, 1975-77; United Motors Corp, pres, 1983-88; Wayne State Univ, adj prof, 1996; 36th Dist Ct, assoc judicial atty & chief dep ct adminr, 1988-; pvt pract, aaty, currently. **Orgs:** Bd dir, Washtenaw Co Black Contr & Tradesmen Asn, 1967-72; citizen rep,Oak Pk Urban Renewal Coun, 1969-74; pres, JM Wright & Asn Detroit, 1972-;pres, dir, Asn Urban Legal Ed, 1973-76; bd, Barrino Entertainment Corp,1973-79; adj prof, Wayne Cty Comt Col, 1975-; bd, Metamorphosis Inc NY,1975-79; New Detroit Inc MNY Bus Devel Comt, 1978-80; Am Arbitration Asn, 1979-; bd dir, Pink Ltd Allen Park MI, 1979-85; Am Bar Asn, NBA; Wolverine Bar Asn; bd, Inner-City Bus Improvement, Southeastern Mich Bus Devel Ctr;NCP; bd, Western Wayne & Oakland County Comt Housing Resource Bd, Fair Housing Ctr Detroit, 1985-88; bd, Worldwide Entertainment Ltd, 1991-; bd, E-W Airlines Inc, 1990-; partner, Pontchartrain Hotel Group LLC; bd dir,Cent City Investment Corp; Fla Bar Asn; Nat Asn Stud Personnel Adminrs. **Military Serv:** USF Res, 1966-70. **Business Addr:** Chief Deputy Court Administrator, 36th District Court, 421 Madison Av, Madison, MI 48226, **Business Phone:** (313)965-2788.

WRIGHT, JOYCE C.
Librarian, educator. **Personal:** Born Dec 17, 1951, Charleston, SC; daughter of Rhunette G Crawford. **Educ:** Voorhees Col, Denmark, SC, BA, 1973; Univ Mich, Ann Arbor, MI, AMLS, 1974; Univ Ill, Urbana, IL, CAS, 1986. **Career:** Trident Tech Col, Charleston, SC, ref/doc librn, 1974-76; Hampton Pub Libr, Hampton, VA, outreach librn, 1976-78; Memphis Pub Libr, Memphis, TN, head ref, 1978-80; Voorhees Col, Denmark, SC, admin librn, 1980-85; UnivIll, Urbana, IL, head undergrad libr & assoc prof libr admin, 1985-. **Orgs:** Am Libr Asn; Ill Libr Asn; Asn Col & Res Libr; Am Asn Univ profs; Am Asn Univ Women; AKA Sorority Inc; Libr Admin Mgt Sect; Staff Orgn Round table; Black Caucus Am Libr Asn; Am Cancer Soc; Midwest Fedn Libr Asn. **Honors/Awds:** Undergraduate Instructional Award for Outstanding Undergraduate Teaching, Univ Ill, Urbana, 1987. **Home Addr:** 4112 Amherst Dr, Champaign, IL 61822, **Home Phone:** (217)359-2748.

WRIGHT, DR. KATIE HARPER
Educator, journalist. **Personal:** Born Oct 5, 1923, Crawfordsville, AR; daughter of James Hale Harper and Connie Mary Locke Washington; married Marvin, Mar 21, 1952; children: Virginia Jordan. **Educ:** Univ Ill, AB, 1944, MEd, 1959; St Louis Univ, EdD, 1979. **Career:** E St Louis Pub Schs, elem teacher, 1944-57, spec educ teacher, 1957-65, media dir, 1966-71, spec educ dir, 1971-78, asst supt spec progs, 1978-79; St Louis Argus Newspaper, columnist, 1979, 1984-85, 1986-; Harris-Stowe State Col, assoc prof, 1980-99; St Louis Univ, learning specialist, 1989-; TLOD Crown Jour, nat ed, 1991-95, nat second vpres, 1996-; Harris-Stowe State Col, prof emer, 1999; Presidents Comn Excellence Spl Educ, mem, currently. **Orgs:** DST Sorority, 1949-; bd mem, United Way; past pres, E St Louis Libr Bd, 1964-81; past pres, Delta Pi Honor Soc, 1968-; past vice chmn, Ill Comn C, 1973-; MENSA, proctor 1973-; past pres, Phi Delta Kappa, 1976-; past pres, Pi Lambda Theta Hon Soc, 1978-; secy, E St Louis Election Bd, 1978-88; vice chmn, River Bluffs Girl Scout Coun, 1979-; assoc dir, Magna Bank Edgemont, 1981-; Girl Scout Nat Bd, 1981-84; bd mem, Ment Health; bd mem, Urban League; charter mem, Gateway Chap Links Inc, 1987-; pres, St Clair County Ment Health Bd, 1987-; regional vpres, Am Libr Trustees Asn, 1992-; exec comt, Urban League & United Way St Louis; organizer, Am Inst Parliamentarians, E St Louis Chap, 1992-; Ill Dept Corrections Sch Bd, 1993-; Educ Delegate S Africa, 1996; E St Louis Financial Adv Author, 1999-; President's Comn Excellence Spec Educ, 2001-. **Honors/Awds:** Woman of Achievement, St Louis Globe Dem Newspaper, 1974; First Place Prize, Author Chap Hist, DST Sorority 1979; Girl Scout Thanks Badge, River Bluffs Girl Scout Coun, 1982; Fel Study Peoples Rep China, 1983; Nat Hon Mem, Iota Phi Lambda Sorority Inc 1983-; Outstanding YWCA Alumnae, Univ Ill, 1984; Woman of the Year, St Clair County YWCA, 1987; Top Ladies of Distinction Inc, Nat Br, Nat Top Lady Distinction, 1988-, Vaskon High School Hall of Fame, Vashon High Sch-St Louis, 1989; World of Difference Award, World Difference Orgn, 1990; Phenomenal Woman Award, Spelman Col Alumni-St Louis, 1990; Leadership Award, 1991; Kimmel Award, 1991; St Cr County Ment Health Ctr Award, 1992; Media Award, 1992; ESL Business & Professional Women's Award, 1992; Distinguished Alumnus, Univ Ill, 1996; Ill Sr Hall of Fame, 1997; Ill Women Adminr Award, 1998; Urban League Award, 2002; Ill State Bd Educ Award, 2002; more than 100 other awards. **Home Addr:** 733 N 40 St, East St Louis, IL 62205. **Business Addr:** Columnist, The St Louis Argus Newspaper, 4595 Dr Martin Luther King Dr, St Louis, MO 63113, **Business Phone:** (314)531-1323.

WRIGHT, KEITH DEREK, SR.
Computer scientist, executive. **Personal:** Born Jun 2, 1953, Orange, NJ; son of Lola Hunt and Clarence Samuel Williams; divorced; children: Keisha, Keith & Khalid. **Educ:** Rutgers Univ, BA, 1979, MLA; Univ Md, MA, gen admin; Harvard Bus Sch, prog mgt develop. **Career:** Customer tech serv, vpres; MORNET-Plus Customer Care, customer care; MORNETPlus Tech Serv, vpres; Nabisco Brands, Inc., comput shift supvr; Hoffman-La Roche, Inc, sr comput ctr supvr; Port Authority NY & NJ, asst mgr comput oper; Fannie Mae Corp, dir comput oper, Regional Mgt & Housing Partnerships, vpres, 2001; Congressional Black Caucus Found Inc, exec vpres, 2007-. **Orgs:** Chairperson, BDPA Newsletter, 1983-85; pres, Black Data Processing Assoc, 1984-86; chmn, Parking Authority E Orange, 1984-; counr, YMCA Linkage Prog, 1985; bd dirs, Econ Develop E Orange, 1986-; chairperson, Pub Rels BDPA, 1987; chmn, E Orange Econ Develop, 1988-; dir, Tri-City Citizens Progress, 1988-. **Honors/Awds:** Scholastic Achievement Award, Essex League Vol Workers, 1971; YMCA Black Achievers Award, 1984. **Special Achievements:** Published "History of Jazz in Newark NJ 1938-70", 1981. **Business Addr:** Executive Vice President, Congressional Black Caucus Foundation Inc, 1720 Mass Ave NW, Washington, DC 20036, **Business Phone:** (202)263-2800.

WRIGHT, KENNY D.
Football player. **Personal:** Born Sep 14, 1977, Ruston, LA; children: DyQuon Roberts. **Educ:** Northwestern State Univ, LA, BS, physical educ. **Career:** Minn Vikings, defensive back, 1999-2001; Houston Texans, 2002-04;Jacksonville Jaguars, 2005; Wash Redskins, 2006; Cleveland Browns, 2007-08, free agent, currently.

WRIGHT, DR. LARRY L
Educator. **Personal:** Born Jun 20, 1954, Florida; son of Dennis Wright and Gertrude Robinson Wright. **Educ:** Chipola Jr Col, Marianna, Fla, AA, 1974; Fla State Univ, Tallahassee, Fla, BS, 1976, MS, 1978, PhD, 1980. **Career:** Fla House Representatives, Tallahassee, Fla, res asst, 1976; Fla State Univ, Tallahassee, Fla, res asst, 1977-78, teaching asst, 1978-80; Ctr Pub Affairs & Govt Serv, Tallahasse, Fla, consul, 1982-84; Fla A&M Univ, Tallahassee, Fla, assoc prof, poli sci & pub admin, 1988-; Andrew W Mellon fel, 1996. **Orgs:** Fla Polit Sci Asn; Am Soc Pub Admin; Ga Polit Sci Asn; Southern Polit Sci Asn; Asn Social & Behav; Pi Sigma Alpha; Nat Asn Advan Colored People; Scholarly Publ Comt; Univ Fac Senate. **Business Addr:** Associate Professor of Political Science, Public Administration, Florida A&M University, 410 Tucker Hall, Tallahassee, FL 32307, **Business Phone:** (850)599-3737.

WRIGHT, LINNEL N
School administrator. **Career:** Camden City Pub Schs, actg asst supt, Dept Prof Develop, dir, currently. **Business Addr:** Director, Acting Assistant Superintendent, Camden City Pub Schs, 201 N Front St 4th Fl, Camden, NJ 08102, **Business Phone:** (856)966-2436.

WRIGHT, LINWOOD CLINTON
Aeronautical engineer. **Personal:** Born Mar 24, 1919, Augusta, GA; son of Maria Wright and Leon Wright; married Ernestine Louise McIver; children: Linda Wright Moore, Linwood Jr. **Educ:** Wayne State Univ, BS, Aero Engr, 1944; Univ Cincinnati, MS, Aero Engr, 1960. **Career:** Aeronautical engineer (retired); Nat Adv Comt Aeronaut, aeronaut res scientist, 1943-56; Gen Elec Aircraft Engine Bus Gr, mgr adv compressor res, 1956-66, mgr, adv tech mktg, 1974-83; Garrett Ai Res Mfg Co, LA, chief aerodynamics, 1966-72; part-time security salesman, Putnam Financial, 1971-72; Pratt & Whitney Aircraft Co, asst gas turbine mgr, 1972-74; NASA, acting dir propulsion power & energy, 1983-85. **Orgs:** Am Inst Aeronaut & Astronaut, 1941-; Tech Mktg Soc Am, 1975; past chap pres, Sigma Pi Phi Prof Fraternity, Cincinnati, 1978-; Mayor's Task Force Zoning, Forest Park, OH, 1986; Econ Devel Comn, Forest Park, OH, 1986-. **Honors/Awds:** Distinguished Alumni Award, Wayne State Univ, 1958; guest lectr, Univ Tenn, Space Inst, 1974; Distinguished Alumni Award, Univ Cincinnati, 1984; auth/co-auth, 21 published tech papers, 1946-72. **Military Serv:** Army Air Corps, enlisted res, 1945-46. **Home Addr:** 303 Ironwood Cir, Elkins Park, PA 19027. *

WRIGHT, LORENZEN VERN-GAGNE
Basketball player. **Personal:** Born Nov 4, 1975, Memphis, TN; son of Herb; children: Lorenzen Jr. **Career:** Los Angeles Clippers, ctr-forward, 1996-99; Atlanta Hawks, 2000-01, 2006-08; Memphis Grizzlies, 2002-06; Sacramento Kings, 2008-. **Orgs:** Sierra Simone Wright Scholarship Fund, 2003-. **Honors/Awds:** Named Third Team All-Am, AP. **Special Achievements:** NBA Draft, First round pick, No 7, 1996. **Business Phone:** (916)928-0000.

WRIGHT, LOUIS DONNEL
Executive, football player, football coach. **Personal:** Born Jan 31, 1953, Gilmer, TX; son of Glover and Verbena; married Vicki; children: Summer Marie, Kyla Lynn & Evan Louis. **Educ:** San Jose State Univ, Bus Mgt. **Career:** Football player (retired), executive, football coach; Denver Broncos, cornerback, 1975-86; L Wright Enterprises, sec & tres, 1990; Rangeview High Sch, asst coach, currently; Mrachek Middle Sch, phys educ teacher, currently. **Orgs:** Conference Champ Track Team, 1973-74. **Honors/Awds:** Col All-Star Game, 1975; East-West Shrine Game, 1975; All-Coast Football Selection, 1975; Pro Bowl, 1977-79, 1983 & 1985; NEA All-Pro Team; Denver Broncos Team, capt, 1985-86; named All NFL by Sporting News and Pro Football Weekly; NFL Pro Football team, 1986; Denver Broncos Ring of Fame, 1993. **Business Phone:** (303)326-4258.

WRIGHT, LOYCE PIERCE
Government official, executive director. **Personal:** Born Dec 24, 1943, New Orleans, LA; daughter of Victoria Martin Pierce and Frank Pierce; married Louis Clifton Wright Jr, Feb 14, 1976; children: Kiana Tamika Wright. **Educ:** Southern Univ, Baton Rouge, LA, BS, 1965; Univ New Orleans, LA, MEd, 1976. **Career:** Orleans Parish Sch Bd, New Orleans, LA, fr/span teacher, 1965-76; New Orleans Sickle Cell Anemia Found, assoc dir, 1976-81; Communirep Inc, New Orleans, LA, mgt consult, 1980-86; Mayor's Off, City New Orleans, LA, dir, 1986-92; Excelth Inc, dir human resources, 1992-97; Southern Univ New Orleans, asst vice chancellor acad affairs, 1997-99; Governor's Off, La Comn Human Rights, exec dir, 1999-. **Orgs:** Past pres/founding mem, New Orleans Sickle Cell Anemia Found, 1972-76; campaign coordr state, local & presidential candidates, 1981-88; consult & mkt dir, Educ Jour SENGA; coordr, Martin Luther King Jr Fed Holiday Comn, New Orleans, LA, 1987-; vpres, bd dir, Ment Health Asn, New Orleans, LA, 1988; nominating comn, YWCA-USA, 1988-91; pres, bd dir, YWCA New Orleans, 1989-; planning comn, Agency Rels Comt; Admis/Growth Comt; United Way New Orleans, 1989-; Delta Sigma Theta Sorority Inc, New Orleans Alumnae Chap; founder, Phenomenal Women; bd dirs, YWCA USA, 1992-. **Honors/Awds:** Award for outstanding service, Gov La, 1986; Second Mile Award, Nat Asn Neighborhoods, 1987; Certificate of Merit, Mayor New Orleans, 1988; Role Model Award, YWCA New Orleans, 1989. **Home Addr:** 3945 Virgil Blvd, New Orleans, LA 70122. **Business Addr:** Executive Director, Governor, Louisiana Commission of Human Rights, 1001 N 23rd St Suite 262, Baton Rouge, LA 70802, **Business Phone:** (225)342-6969.

WRIGHT, MARILYN N
Entrepreneur, business owner. **Personal:** Born May 25, 1965, Philadelphia, PA; daughter of Willie and Rachel Bond; married Thomas, Nov 25, 1989; children: Marcello & Bianca. **Educ:** Elizabeth City State Univ, BA, 1987. **Career:** Allstate Insurance Co, sr staff claims rep, 1987-99; Marilyn's Fashions Inc, chief exec officer & found, 1994-. **Orgs:** New Castle County Chamber Com, 1999-; Wilmington Women Bus, 2000; Asn Image Consults Int; Nat Asn Female Execs. **Honors/Awds:** Image Consultant Certification, 2002. **Business Addr:** Chief Executive Officer, Marilyn's Fashions Inc, 100 W 10 th St Suite 1004, Wilmington, DE 19801, **Business Phone:** (302)366-0812.

WRIGHT, MARK ADRIAN
Executive, sales manager. **Personal:** Born Jan 29, 1957, Philadelphia, PA; son of Richard Wright and Vera Lennon; married Sheela, Feb 12, 1983; children: Kyle & Adrian. **Educ:** Drexel Univ, BSME, 1979; Wash Univ, MBA, 1990. **Career:** Monsanto, sales rep, 1979-83, ford motor develop mgr, 1983-86, world wide mkt mgr, 1986-87, regional sales mgr, 1987-90; Advan Elastomer Systems, auto mkt mgr Europe, 1990-93, sales mgr, Ger, 1993-94, dir, automotive, 1994-. **Orgs:** Soc Automotive Engrs, 1983-; bd dirs, Soc Plastic Engrs, 1994-95. **Special Achievements:** Lang Skills, French & German; Published in numerous plastic & Eng books; Presentations to SPE, SAE & Trade Groups. **Business Addr:** Director of Automotive, Advanced Elastomer Systems, 388 S Main St, Akron, OH 44331, **Business Phone:** (330)849-5000.

WRIGHT, MARVIN
Educator. **Personal:** Born May 20, 1917, Fulton, AL; son of Marvin and Almeda Falconer; married Katie Harper; children: Virginia Jordan. **Educ:** Xavier Univ, PhB, 1947; Univ Ill, EdM, 1962. **Career:** Educator (retired); Prof musician & drummer, 1940-50; E St Louis Pub Sch, elem teacher, 1948-65; E St Louis, 1965-79; Atty Gen's Off E St Louis, admin investr, 1980-84; Sch Dist, 1984. **Orgs:** Pres, E St Louis Prin Org; Phi Delta Kappa Ed, Ill Principal's Asn, Nat Elem Prin's Assoc 1974-76; chmn, bd trustees, State Community Col, 1977-84; alternate dele, 1976; Rep Nat Conv; Belleville Men's Rep Club; comm man, Boy Scout Troop; mem Ill Sr Citiznes Bd 1983; mem Civil Rights Comm E St Louis 1971-75; 4-H Youth Comt man 1971-; sch memhsip chmn E St Louis Branch, Nat Asn Advan Colored People; Ill Div United Way Bd 1984-; city chmn Am Cancer Soc, St Clair City Unit, 1976-77; Southern Ill Black Republican Coun; comdr Veterans Foreign Wars Post 3480, 1987-88; quartermaster, Veterans Foreign Wars Post 3480, 1988-. **Honors/Awds:** Meritorious Service Award, Am Cancer Soc, 1976; Outstanding Service Award, St Paul Church, 1976; Outstanding Service Award, E St Louis PTA, 1976; Board Member of the Year Award, United Way, 1983; East St Louis Criminal Justice Award, 1980; All State Commander, Veterans Foreign Wars, 1987. **Military Serv:** AUS, staff sgt, 1942-45; Overseas Serv Bar; Silver Battle Star; Good Conduct Medal; WW II Victory Medal. **Home Addr:** 733 N 40th St, East St Louis, IL 62205, **Home Phone:** (618)271-5174. *

WRIGHT, MELVIN
Dentist. **Career:** Pvt Pract, dentist, currently. **Orgs:** Secy, Tenn Dent Asn Found; Tenn Supreme Ct Comn; bd regents, Union Univ. **Business Addr:** Dentist, Private Practice, 340 N Hays Ave, Jackson, TN 38301.*

WRIGHT, MICHAEL
Actor. **Personal:** Born Apr 30, 1956, New York, NY; son of Alberta Wright; married Mitzie Lau (divorced 2000); children: 1. **Educ:** Lee Strasberg Theater. **Career:** Films: The Wanderers, 1979; Streamers, 1983; Bedtime Eyes, 1987; The Principal, 1987; The Five Heartbeats, 1991; Confessions of a Hitman, 1994; Sugar Hill, 1994; Confessions of a Hitman, 1994; The Cottonwood, 1996; Money Talks, 1997; Point Blank, 1998; Rage, 1999; Pinero, 2001; Downtown:A Street Tale, 2002; Light & the Sufferer, 2004; Downtown: A Street Tale, 2004; Coalition, 2004; The Interpreter, 2005; Raving, 2007; " hard Rock", 2007; "Before I self Destruct", 2009; TV movies: "We're Fighting Back", 1981; "Dream House", 1981; "Benny's Place", 1982; " V", 1983; "V: The Final Battle", 1984; "V", 1984-85; "The Laundromat", 1985; "Miami Vice", 1987; "Private Times", 1991; "Shake, Rattle & Roll: An American Love Story", 1999; "New York Undercover", 1996; "Oz", 2001-03. **Honors/Awds:** Volpi Cup Award for Best Actor, 1983. **Business Addr:** Actor, c/o Access Talent, 37 E 28th St Suite 500, New York, NY 10016, **Business Phone:** (212)331-9595.*

WRIGHT, MICHAEL L.
Lawyer. **Personal:** Born Jan 1, 1969. **Educ:** Univ Cincinnati, BS, mech eng, JD. **Career:** Gen Motors Corp, mfr engr; Cincinnati Pub Defenders Off, intern; Mich Bar Intellectual Property Firm, Harness, Dicker & Pierce, intern; Lexis-Nexis Corp, res reference atty; Wright & VanNoy LPA Inc, founder & atty, 2000-. **Orgs:** Ohio State Bar Asn; Thurgood Marshall Law Soc; African Am Chamber Com; AmTrial Lawyer Asn. **Honors/Awds:** Best Bachelor of the Year, EBONY, 2003. **Business Addr:** Attorney, Wright & VanNoy LPA Inc, 130 W Second St Suite 1600, Dayton, OH 45402, **Business Phone:** (937)222-7477.

WRIGHT, MILTON L., JR.
District court judge. **Personal:** Born in Miami, FL. **Educ:** Morehouse Col, BA, 1966; Boston Univ Law Sch, JD, 1971. **Career:** Roxbury Defenders, regional Supvr; Roxbury Dist Ct, first justice, 1999-. **Orgs:** lectr, Mass Continuing Legal Educ. **Business Addr:** First Justice, Boston Municipal Court, Roxbury Division, 85 Warren St, Roxbury, MA 02119, **Business Phone:** (617)427-7000.*

WRIGHT, N'BUSHE (BRUKLIN HARRIS)
Actor, television actor. **Personal:** Born Sep 20, 1970, New York, NY; daughter of Suleiman-Marim. **Educ:** Stella Adler's studio; The Alvin Ailey Sch; Stella Adler Conservatory; Martha Graham Sch Dance; Manhattan High Sch Performing Arts, New York, attended 1987. **Career:** Films include: Zebrahead, 1992; Fresh, 1994; Dead Presidents, 1995; Johns, 1996; A Woman Like That, 1997; His & Hers, 1997; Squeeze, 1997; Blade, 1998; Three Strikes, 2000; Civil Brand, 2002; MVP, 2003; He Say She Say But What Does GOD Say?, 2004; A Talent for Trouble, 2005; God's Forgotten House, 2005; Restraining Order, 2006; A Talent for Trouble, 2008; TV Series: "I'll Fly Away", 1992-93; "Am Gothic", 1995; "New York Undercover", 1996; "Swift Justice", 1996; "Close to Danger", 1997; "Third Watch", 1999; "UC: Undercover", 2001; "Widows", 2002; "The Award Show Awards Show", 2003; "Platinum", 2003, "Chappelle's Show", 2004. **Honors/Awds:** Won the recurring role of Claudia. **Business Addr:** Actress, Innovative Arts, 1505 Tenth St, Santa Monica, CA 90401, **Business Phone:** (310)656-5172.*

WRIGHT, PANDIT F
Vice president (Organization), executive. **Educ:** Univ Conn. **Career:** Aetna Corp; Salomon Brothers Inc, staff, 1981; Discovery Networks Asia, interim gen mgr; Discovery Commun Inc, Human Resouce & Admin, vpres, sr exec vpres, currently. **Orgs:** Discovery Channel Global Educ Partnership; Walter Kaitz Found Diversity Coun; bd mem, Boys & Girls Clubs Greater Wash; chmn, Silver Spring Town Ctr Inc; pres, Cable TV Human Resources Asn; bd mem, Women Cable & Telecommunications Found; pasr pres, Cable & Telecommunications Human Resources Asn. **Special Achievements:** Named to Discovery's Exec Comm, 1999, responsible for Discovery's nationally recognized LifeWorks at Discovery initiative, headed to South Africa to tour the Soweto Learning Center a product of the Discovery Channel Global Educational Partnership, keynote speaker, WICT Forum, 2003. **Business Addr:** Senior Executive Vice President, Discovery Communications Inc, Human Resources, Fl 5 7700 Wisconsin Ave, Bethesda, MD 20814, **Business Phone:** (301)986-1999.*

WRIGHT, RALPH EDWARD
Executive. **Personal:** Born Dec 29, 1950, Newark, NJ; married Sallie Riggins Williams; children: Galen & Garnel. **Career:** New York Stock Exchange, reporter, 1969-77; Carl H Pforzheimer & Co, clerk, stockbroker, 1977-89; Drexel Burnham, stockbroker, 1989-90; JJC Specialist Corp, stockbroker, 1990-95, Doley sec, vpres, 1995-96; W&P Securities, Inc., chair, ceo, 1996-; Exeter & Co, 1996-98; Stratatec LLC, exec dir, 1998-; AFC Partners, New York Stock Exchange Mkt, staff, 1998-99; Caria Group, exec vpres, 1999. **Orgs:** Bd mem, George Jr Republic; bd mem, The Clearpool Camps; Borkers United Youth Scholar Fund. **Honors/Awds:** Plaque, Tau Gamma Delta Sorority, 1991; Community Leader of the Year, Wheelchair Charities of New York, 1995. **Special Achievements:** First African Specialist in New York Stock Exchange, 1981; appeared in TV program "Profiles in Accomplishment", 1984; Profiled in Col textbook, Introduction to Business, Chap 19, 1987; Appeared in Business in a Changing World, 1991; One of the main subjects in Pictorial Songs of My People, A Life Magazine Publication, p 34, Feb 1992; First African-American & American dealer at the Johannesburg Stock Exchange in South Africa, 1995. **Home Addr:** 470 Sandford Ave, Newark, NJ 07106.

WRIGHT, RAYMOND LEROY, JR.
Dentist. **Personal:** Born May 7, 1950, Fort Dix, NJ; children: Raymond III. **Educ:** Univ Ill, attended 1970; Univ Ill Col Dent, DDS, 1974. **Career:** Cert Periodontics, 1974-76; Cermack Mem Hosp, staff dentist, 1975-84; Chicago Bd Health, dentist, 1976-77; Dr Clarence McNair, dentist periodontist, 1976-77; Dr Roger Berkley, dentist periodontist, 1977-80; McHarry Medical Col, asst prof, 1978-83; Univ Ill Col Dentist, asst prof,1977-85; self employed, 1980-. **Orgs:** Prog chmn, 1980-84, parliamentarian, 1984-85, treas, 1985-86, secy, 1986-87, Lincoln Dent Soc; scholar chmn, Nat Dent Asn, 1982; treas, Forum Evolution Progressive Arts; prog chmn, Kenwood Hyde Pk Br, Chicago Dental Soc, 1986-87. **Honors/Awds:** Nomination Outstanding Young Men of America, 1980; Service Award, Lincoln Dental Soc, 1982; Service Award, Nat Dent Soc, 1982.

WRIGHT, ROBERT A
Judge, lawyer. **Personal:** Born Dec 8, 1919, Chester, PA; son of E Courtlandt and Anne Davis; married Mary Maloney; children: Robert C. **Educ:** Lincoln Univ, BA, 1941; Temple Univ Sch Law, LLB, 1950. **Career:** Judge, lawyer (Retired); Chester, PA, atty, 1951-70; Del Co, Media, PA, asst dist atty, 1964-70, 32nd Judicial Dist PA, judge, 1970-89, sr judge (part-time), 1989-2003. **Orgs:** Del Co, PA & Am Bar Asn; Lawyers Club Del Co; PA Conf St Trial Judges; Am Judicature Soc; PA Coun Juv Ct Judges; Jud Inquiry & Rev Bd; Crime Comn Phil; Temple Law Alumni; Nat Asn Advan Colored People; IBPOE Women; Am Leg; VFW; Cent Rest Rec Club; past bd mgrs, W Branch YMCA; Meth Men; Frat Ord of Police; Women Penn Lodge, 19; Chester Youth League; Mag Asn Del Co Hon Awards; adv bd, Del Co Campus PA State Univ; Bunting Friendship Freedom House; Chester Sch Fund. **Honors/Awds:** Am Spirit Preserv Award, Del Co, PA, 1989; Donald J Orlowsky Mem Award, Delaware Co Bar Asn, 1989; First Ann Achievement Award, Deputies Club Elks IBPOE Women. **Military Serv:** AUS, first sgt, 1943-46.

WRIGHT, ROBERT COURTLANDT
Government official, judge. **Personal:** Born Nov 5, 1944, Chester, PA; son of Robert A and Mary; married Florence Fletcher; children: Josie & Robert Jr. **Educ:** George Washington Univ, BA, polit sci, 1966; Villanova Univ, law, 1969. **Career:** Self employed, atty, 1970-91; Penn Legislature, state rep, 1981-91; Ct Common Pleas Del Co, judge, 1992-2009. **Orgs:** Tau Epsilon Phi Soc Frat, 1963-; pres, Republican Coun Del County, 1977-91; exec Bd, Chester Br, NAACP, 1978-91; exec, Bd Nat Black Caucus State Legis, 1981-84; Penn Minority Bus Devel Authority, 1981-86; Penn Legis Black Caucus, 1981-91; treas, Penn Legis Black Caucus Found, 1982-91. **Home Addr:** 34 Rose Lane, Glen Mills, PA 19342.

WRIGHT, ROBERT L.
Association executive. **Personal:** Born Sep 23, 1917, Malvern, PA; married Beulah C; children: Robert L Jr. **Educ:** Lincoln Univ, BA, 1942; Temple Univ Law Sch. **Career:** Executive (retired); Social Security Admin, benefit authorizer. **Orgs:** Sec Malvern PTA Asn Malvern Pub Schs, 1957-59; sec Troop Com 7 Boy Scouts Am, 1960-61; sec Gr Valley High Gridiron Club, 1962-63; pres, Main Line Bh NAACP, 1964-89; vpres, Commission Act Bd Chester co, West Chester, 1968-71; vpres, UPAC, 1968; asst sec, Malvern Mun Authority, 1975-76; sec Mun, Auth 1977-79; vpres, Mal Mun Authority, 1980; life mem, NAACP Golden Heritage; past mem, Main Line Youth for Christ Com; PA State CNF. **Honors/Awds:** Legion Merit Chapel Four Chaplain Award; Isabelle Strickland Award, Main Line, 1981; PRS Award, 1989, Founders Award; Community Service Award, Main Line Bus & Prof Women, 1982. **Military Serv:** AUS, 1942-45. **Home Addr:** 62 Ruthland Ave, Malvern, PA 19355, **Home Phone:** (610)644-4669. *

WRIGHT, ROBERTA V. HUGHES
Lawyer. **Personal:** Born in Detroit, MI; daughter of Robert Greenidge; married Charles H Wright, Aug 19, 1989; children: Barbara, Wilbur B. **Educ:** Univ Mich, PhD, 1973; Wayne State Univ Law Sch, JD; Wayne State Univ, MEd. **Career:** Detroit Pub Sch, past sch social worker; Detroit Comn C & Youth, past dir; Shaw Col, past vpres Acad Affairs; County Pub Admin, practicing lawyer Mich Cts & admitted pract bar, DC & Supreme Ct USA; Lawrence, former prof; First Independence Nat Bank, inst organizer & dir; Charro Book Co Inc, vpres, currently. **Orgs:** Am Bar Asn; Mich Bar Asn; past mem Am & Mich Trial Lawyers Asn; Oakland County Bar Asn; Detroit Bar Asn; Wayne State Univ Law Alumni; Univ Mich Alumni Asn; AKA Sorority; life mem, Nat Asn Advan Colored Peopl; Renaissance Club; million dollar mem, Mus African Am Hist. **Honors/Awds:** NAACP Freedom Award; Harriet Tubman Award; Alpha Kappa Alpha Sorority Recognition Award; Quality Quintet Award Detroit Skyliner Mag. **Special Achievements:** Auth: LAY DOWN BODY : Living History in African American Cemeteries, Visible Ink, 1996. **Business Addr:** Vice President, Charro Book Co Inc, 29777 Telegraph Rd Suite 2500, Southfield, MI 48034.

WRIGHT, ROOSEVELT R., JR.
Educator. **Personal:** Born Jul 24, 1943, Elizabeth City, NC; son of Roosevelt R Sr and Lillie Mae Garrett. **Educ:** Elizabeth City State Univ, BS, 1964; NC Cent Univ, MA, 1969; Va State Univ, CGS, 1970; Syracuse Univ, Phd, 1993. **Career:** Elizabeth City State Univ, assoc dir ed media, 1968-69; DC State Col Dover, dir ed media, 1969-70; WNDR Radio Syracuse, announcer radio engr, 1970-72; Syracuse Univ, Doctoral fel, 1970-72, assoc prof, currently; NC Cent Univ, asst prof ed media, 1972-73; WDNC-AM/FM Durham, NC, announcer radio engr, 1972-73; WTNJ Radio, Trenton, NJ, gen mgr, 1973-74; WLLE Radio Raleigh, NC, prog dir, 1973-74; Nat Broadcasting Co, Radio Div WRC/WKYS Wash, acct exec, 1974-75; Howard Univ Wash, DC, adj prof, radio & TV,1974-75; SI Newhouse Sch Comm, assoc prof, radio/TV, 1975-; WOLF Radio Syracuse, NY, chief engr, 1980-84. **Orgs:** Historian Chi Pi Chap Omega Psi Phi Frat, 1975-95; radio com mem, Nat Asn Educ Broadcasters, 1976-80; adv, Nat Acad TV Arts & Scis Syracuse Chap, 1976-80; US naval liaison Officer, Syracuse Univ, 1981-; pub affairs Officer, Nat naval Officers Asn, 1983-85; chmn, Communs Comt, Am Heart Asn, NY, 1985-87; ceo, WJPZ-FM Syracuse, NY; steward AME Zion Church; pub affairs Officer, USN, Great Lakes Cruise, 1985-; commun comt, United Way Onondaga County, 1988-; bd mem, Hiawatha Coun Boy Scout Am, 1992-. **Honors/Awds:** Men's Day Award, Mt Lebanon AMEZ Ch Eliz City, 1974, 1997; Upward Bound Program Award, LeMoyne Col Syracuse, 1977; Ed Media & Speaker Award, NC Ed Media Asn, 1977; Nat Coun Negro Women Commun Award, 1984, 1994; Syracuse Univ Pan Hellenic Council Award, 1986, 1987, 1989, 1990; Outstanding Mass Media Teacher Award, 1987-91; Community Serv Award, Syracuse Univ, 1988; Keynote Speaker Award, Nat Asn Advan Colored People, Jefferson Co Chapter, Watertown, NY, 1989. **Military Serv:** AUS, sp/5, 1966-72; USNR, capt, 1992-; Soldier of the Quarter 32AADC AUS1967; Naval Achievement Medal, 1987, 1997; Naval Commendation Medal, 1992, 1993, 1995; USN Campus Liaison Officer of the Year, 1992. **Home Addr:** 310 W Matson Ave, Syracuse, NY 13205. **Business Addr:** Associate Professor, Syracuse University, 222 Waverly Ave, Syracuse, NY 13244, **Business Phone:** (315)443-1870.

WRIGHT, RUSSELL T.
Chief executive officer. **Educ:** Morehouse Col, BA; Keller Grad Sch, MBA; George Wash Univ Sch Bus & Pub Mgt. **Career:**

Dimensions Int Inc, chmn & chief exec officer, currently. **Orgs:** Norther Va Technol Coun; Fairfax Chamber Com; adv bd, Geroge Mason Univ Diversity. **Honors/Awds:** Entrepreneur of the year, Black Engr Year, 2005. **Business Phone:** (703)998-0098.*

WRIGHT, DR. SAMUEL LAMAR, SR.
School administrator. **Personal:** Born Jul 7, 1953, Boynton Beach, FL; son of Samuel Louis and Rovina Victoria Deal; children: Samuel Lamar Jr & Samaria Elizabeth. **Educ:** Univ Fla, BS, psychol, 1974, Med, 1975; Fla Atlantic Univ, pub admin, 1980-81; Univ S Fla, D.Ed, 1999. **Career:** PBC Bd Co Comnrs/Action Com, emp & personnel mgr, 1975-76, dir, Delray BchTAC, 1976-77, adm asst/planner, 1977-79, asst dir, 1979-84, head startdir, 1984-85; Boynton Beach FL, city councilman, 1981-85; Univ S Fla, Minority Stud Orgn, adv, 1985-86; Greater Tampa Urban League, Clerical/Word Processing Training Prog, ctr mgr, 1986-87; Univ S Fla, Multicult Admis, asst dir, 1987-2000, assoc dean stud relations & interim coordr, 2000-, Comt Black Affairs, chair, currently, dir multicultural affairs, currently. **Orgs:** Kappa Alpha Psi Frat Inc, 1972-; Fla Asn Comm Action, 1975-85; Fla Agr & Mech Univ Alumni Asn PBC, 1979-85; Univ Fla Alumni Asn, 1979-; City Boynton Beach Black Awareness Comm, 1981-85; bd dirs, Nat Black Caucus Local Elected Off, 1982-84; State Fla Comm Serv Block Grant Adv Comm, 1982-84; Fla Assoc Comm Rel Prof, 1982-84; bd dirs Southern County Drug Abuse Found, 1982-84; bd dir, Dem Black Caucus FL, 1982-84; Boynton Beach Kiwanis Sunrisers, 1982-85; bd mem, Selective Serv Syst, 1983-85; vpres, Fla Black Caucus Local Elected Officials 1983-85; vpres Comm Affairs Suncoast C of C 1983-85; elected Dem Exec Comm Palm Beach, 1983-85; GrBoynton Beach C C, 1983-85; Nat Asn Black Social Workers Inc, 1983-85; Fla Head Start Asn, 1984-85; chmn, Inter gov Rel Comm, 1984-85; chmn, Legmm Boynton/ Ocean Ridge Bd Realtors, 1984-85; 100 Black Men Tampa Inc,1988-89; Concerned Voters Coalition, 1991-; ambassador, Ctr Excellence Inc, 1988-; Tampa Male Club 1989-; Revealing Truth Ministries; Hillsborough Alliance Black Sch Educrs, 1993-; Hillsborough Co Children's Serv Adv Bd, 1993-; bd dir, Tampa Bay Conv & Visitors Bur, 1998-; Supt Sch Diversity Round table, 1999-; Tampa's Black Heritage Festival, 1999-; prog judge, Miss Am Scholar Pagent, 1999-; Children's Bd Hills borough Co, comm review team, 1999-; Afro-Am Men's HTH Forum, 2000-. **Honors/Awds:** Outstanding & Dedicated Service Award, Concerned Citizens Voter's League Boynton Beach, 1981; Citizen of the Yr, Omega Psi Phi Frat, 1982; Outstanding Civic Leadership Award, West boro Bus & Prof Women's Club of the Palm Beaches, 1983; participant Leadership Palm Beach County, 1984-85; Pole march's Award, Kappa Alpha Psi Frat, 1988-90; Outstanding Service Award Religion, 1988; Outstanding Service Award (Academic Affairs), Univ S Fla, 1988; Martin Luther King Jr Award, Outstanding Leadership, 1989; Community Service Award, 1989; State of Florida Notary Public. **Home Addr:** 3402 03 Pk Sq S, Tampa, FL 33613. **Business Addr:** Director, Associate Dean, University of South Florida, 4202 E Fowler Ave Ctr 246 SVC 1036, Tampa, FL 33620-6250, **Business Phone:** (813)974-5111.

WRIGHT, SARAH E
Writer. **Personal:** Born Dec 9, 1928, Wetipquin, MD; daughter of Willis Charles and Mary Amelia Moore; married Joseph G Kaye; children: Michael & Shelley. **Educ:** Howard Univ, attended 1945-49; Cheyney State Teachers Col, attended 1950-52; NY State Univ, Excelsior Col, Albany, BA, 1979; New Sch Social Res, various courses writing; Long Island Univ, C W Post Col. **Career:** Teacher, bookkeeper & office mgr; writer; Cert Poetry Therapist, 1986-; YMCA, The Writer's Voice, NY, teach fiction writing; Books: This Child's Gonna Live; Give Me a Child; A Philip Randolph: Integration Work Place, 1990. **Orgs:** Int Pen & Pen Am Ctr; Authors Guild; Authors League of Am; Harlem Writers Guild; Int Women's Writing Guild; Nat Asn Poetry Ther, Pen & Brush Inc; Nat Writers Union. **Honors/Awds:** Baltimore Sun Readability Award, This Child's Gonna Live, 1969; McDowell Colony fel, 1972 & 1973; NY State Creative Artists Public Service Award for Fiction & Novelist-Poet Award, Howard Univ's Inst Arts & Humanities' Second Nat Conf Afro-Am Writers, 1976; Silver Burdett Press/Simon & Schuster; Distinguished Writer Award, Middle Atlantic Writers Asn, 1988; Zora Neale Hurston Award, Zora Neale Hurston Soc, Morgan State Univ, 1990; Salisbury State Univ, Distinguished Contrib to Lit; Award renamed Sarah E Wright Graduate Paper Award; Enduring Contribs to the Life of the Guild, Harlem Writer's Guild, 1998; Outstanding Contribution to American Literature, Univ Md & Zora Neale Hurston Soc, 1999. **Home Addr:** 780 W End Ave Apt 1-D, New York, NY 10025. **Business Addr:** Author, Feminist Press at The City Univ of NY, 365 5th Ave, New York, NY 10016, **Business Phone:** (212)817-7925.

WRIGHT, SHARONE ADDARYL
Basketball player. **Personal:** Born Jan 30, 1973, Macon, GA. **Educ:** Clemson Univ. **Career:** Philadelphia 76ers, ctr-forward, 1995-96; Toronto Raptors, 1996-98; EiffelTowers 's-Hertogenbosch, currently.

WRIGHT, SHEENA
Administrator. **Personal:** Born in Bronx, NY; daughter of Debra Fraser-Howze; married Gregg Walker; children: 2. **Educ:** Columbia Col, attended 1990; Columbia Law Sch, BA, law, 1994. **Career:** New York Times Wash Bur, ed asst; law firm Wachtell, Lipton, Rosen & Katz, assoc, 1994-99; law firm Reboul, MacMurray, Hewitt, Maynard & Kristol, sr assoc, 1999-2000; Crave Technologies, gen counr & exec vpres; Abyssinian Develop Corp, chief operating officer, pres & chief exec officer, 2002-. **Orgs:** Numerous memberships including founding mem, Pan-African House; New York State Bar; Mayor Bloomberg's Neighborhood Investment Adv Panel; bd dir, Citizens Union Found. **Honors/ Awds:** Honored at Senator Hillary Rodham Clinton's African Am Heritage Celebration; Honored by the Ephesus Seventh Day Adventist Church at their Community Pride Day. **Business Addr:** President, Chief Executive Officer, Abyssinian Development Corporation, 4 W 125th St, New York, NY 10027, **Business Phone:** (212)368-4471.

WRIGHT, SORAYA M
Insurance executive, manager. **Personal:** Born Dec 24, 1961, Oakland, CA; married Karl, Jun 4, 1983; children: Dania & Deidre. **Educ:** Holy Names Col, BA, 1985. **Career:** Alexsis Risk Mgt, claim supvr; Clorox Co Found, East Oakland Youth Develop Ctr, claim mgr, corp risk mgr, currently. **Orgs:** Risk & Ins Mgt Soc; trustee, E Oakland Youth Develop Found; E Oakland Youth Develop Ctr; Assumption Sch Bd; bd trustee, Clorox Co Found. **Honors/Awds:** Outstanding Business & Professional Leader, Dollar & Sense, 1993; Adele Corvin Outstanding Agency Board Volunteer Award, United Way. **Home Addr:** 3656 La Mesa Dr, Hayward, CA 94542. **Business Addr:** Board of Trustee, The Clorox Company Foundation, 200 Frank Ogawa Plz, Oakland, CA 94612, **Business Phone:** (510)836-3223.

WRIGHT, STANLEY V. See Obituaries section.

WRIGHT, STEPHEN CALDWELL
Educator. **Personal:** Born Nov 11, 1946, Sanford, FL; son of Joseph Caldwell and Bernice I Wright. **Educ:** St Petersburg Jr Col, AA, 1967; Fla Atlantic Univ, BA, 1969; Atlanta Univ, MA, 1972; Ind Univ Pa, PhD, 1983. **Career:** Seminole County Sch Bd, teacher, 1969-70; Seminole Comm Col, prof, 1972-. **Orgs:** Gwendolyn Brooks Writers Asn Fla, founder & pres, 1987-; Revelry Poetry J, ed, 1987-; Zora Festival Arts & Humanities, nat planning comn, 1989-99; Boys & Girls Club, chmn, adv coun, 1993-96; Fla Div Cult Affairs Lit Orgn's Panel, panelist, 1996-98. **Honors/ Awds:** Distinguished Authors Series Award, Morgan State Univ, 1998; Illinois Salutes Award, Ill Poet Laureate, 1992; Gwendolyn Brooks Poetry Prize, 1984; First Superior Poet Award, Univ South Fla, 1969; SCC Foundation Faculty Excellence Award, 2002; Leadership Award, Nat Coun On Black Am Affairs, 2003. **Special Achievements:** First Statement, poetry collection, 1983; Poems In Movement, poetry collection, 1984; Making Symphony: New & Selected Poems, 1987; "Pearl" New Visions: Fiction by Florida Writers, 1989; Inheritance, poetry collection, 1992; Ed "On Gwendolyn Brooks: Reliant Contemplation," 1995; Co-ed, The Orlando Group & Friends, 2000. **Home Addr:** 127 Langston Dr, Sanford, FL 32771, **Home Phone:** (407)323-7184. **Business Addr:** Professor, Seminole Community Coll, English Department, 100 Weldon Blvd, Sanford, FL 32773-6199, **Business Phone:** (407)708-2063.

WRIGHT, TANYA
Entertainer, actor. **Personal:** Born in Bronx, NY. **Educ:** Vassar Col, independent writing. **Career:** Films: The Brothers, 2001; Ralph & Stanley, 2005; Ralph & Stanley, 2005; Angels Can't Help But Laugh, 2007; TV series: "The Cosby Show", 1986; "Professor Poopsnaggle", 1986; "Parker Lewis Can't Lose", 1991; "Beverly Hills, 90210", 1994; "Living Single", 1995; "Family Matters", 1995; "The Wayans Bros", 1996; "Buddies", 1996; "Mama Flora's Family", 1998; "Mutiny", 1999; "Moesha", 1999; "The District", 2000-01; "24", 2001-02; "NYPD Blue", 2002; "The Handler", 2003-04; "Strong Medicine", 2004; "ER", 2007; "Standoff", 2007; "To Love is to Worry", 2008; "Nothing but the Blood", 2009; "Shake and finger Prop", 2009; "Time Bomb", 2009; "True Blood", 2008-09. **Orgs:** Los Angeles Mission. **Business Addr:** Actress, c/o Schiowitz Connor Ankrum Wolf Inc, 1680 Vine St Suite 1016, Los Angeles, CA 90028, **Business Phone:** (323)463-8355.*

WRIGHT, TOBY LIN
Football player. **Personal:** Born Nov 19, 1970, Phoenix, AZ. **Educ:** Univ Nebr. **Career:** Football player (retired), Los Angeles Rams, 1994; St Louis Rams, defensive back, 1995-98; Washington Redskins, 1999. San Francisco Demons, 2001.

WRIGHT, VERLYN LAGLEN
Journalist. **Personal:** Born Aug 2, 1963, Saginaw, MI; daughter of Leeunice Calloway and Louis. **Educ:** Southern Univ, Baton Rouge, LA, BA, 1983; Univ Mo, Columbia, Mo, MA, 1986. **Career:** Dallas Times Herald, Dallas, Tex, reporter, 1987-88; Patriot Ledger, Quincy, Mass, copy ed, 1988. **Orgs:** Nat Asn Black Journalists, 1986-; Boston Asn Black Journalists, 1988-. **Home Phone:** (617)925-1090.

WRIGHT, VERNON S
Executive. **Career:** SFX Radio Networks, sr vpres, gen sales mgr; Am Urban Radio Networks, sr vpres sales, 2000-04, exec vpres sales & new bus develop, 2004-. **Business Phone:** (212)883-2106.

WRIGHT, WILL J
Executive, business owner, educator. **Personal:** Born Sep 9, 1950, Brooklyn, NY; son of Mildred and Gerard; married Patricia Ann, Feb 27, 1981; children: Patricia Antoinette. **Educ:** Fordham Univ, BA, commun, 1972; Columbia Univ, Grad Sch Jour, 1974. **Career:** CBS Network News, ed, writer & producer, 1972-80; Cable News Network, sr producer, 1980-84; KYW-TV, asst news dir, 1984-87; KRIV Fox TV News, vp & news dir, 1987-92; WWOR-TV, news dir, 1992-2002; BET Nightly News, exec producer, 2002-03; XS Momentum Ltd, pres news exec, 2003-; Will Wright Broadcast Found, founder, 2003-. **Orgs:** Bd dirs, Radio-Tv News Dir's Asn, 1993-98; bd trustees, Fordham Univ, 1995-98; chmn, bd dirs, Will J. Wright Broadcast Jour Coaching Found, 1997-. **Honors/Awds:** Emmy Awards Best Documentary, NATA Houston, Miami, 1989, 1990; Best Spot News, 1991; NATA NY Emmy Awards, Best Newscast, 1995, 1997; Best News Set, 1996; Nat Congress of Racial Equality Harmony Award, 1997; Edward R. Murrow Award, RTNDA, 1999; Kaiser Family Foundation Fellowship Award, 2003. **Special Achievements:** Art Exhibits: New York Art Expo, 1995; Ward Nasse Gallery, Soho, NY, 1994, 1996; "Because We Care," Art Exhibit, Morristown, NJ. **Business Addr:** Independent Broadcast & Television News Executive, Founder, XS Momentum Limited, 189 McNamara Rd, Wesley Hills, NY 10977-1022, **Business Phone:** (917)733-4867.

WRIGHT, WILLIAM A
Automotive executive, business owner. **Personal:** Born Apr 4, 1936, Kansas City, MO; son of Robert B and Madeline S; married Ceta D, Jul 21, 1961. **Educ:** Western Wash State, Bellingham WA, BEd, 1961. **Career:** Los Angeles Sch Dist, teacher, 1961-68; Pro Golf Tour, prof golfer, 1964-77; Pasadena Lincoln-Mercury, Pasadena, CA, owner, currently. **Orgs:** Black Ford Lincoln Mercury Dealers, 1978-; Nat Asn Advan Colored People, Pasadena Br. **Honors/Awds:** Man of Year, State of WA, 1959; Golf Champ, National Public Links, 1959; National Intercollegiate Champ, 1960; Man of Year, Seattle WA, 1960. **Military Serv:** Army National Guard, pvt, 1960-66. **Business Phone:** (818)793-0645.

WRIGHT, DR. WILSON, JR.
Educator, dentist. **Personal:** Born Apr 27, 1948, Prattville, AL; son of Wilson and Mary Debardelabon; married Malera Traylor, Aug 4, 1990; children: Ursula, Karla & Tray. **Educ:** Ala State Univ, Montgomery, AL, BA, 1969; Birmingham Southern Col, Birmingham, AL, 1970; Univ Ala, Birmingham, DMD, 1974; Army Command Gen Staff Col, 1989. **Career:** Fisk Univ, Nashville, TN, Biol, instr, 1969-70; Univ Ala, Sch Dent, Birmingham, AL, instr, 1974-77, from asst prof to assoc prof, 1977-93, prof dent, 1993-, dir, OD-OR-UC Clin, currently, dir, Stud Dent Health, currently, dir, Dent Assisting Prog, currently; 650th Med Det, commander, 1995; fel, Am Col Dentists, 2007. **Orgs:** Ala Dental Soc, 1975-; Nat Dental Asn, 1975-; Univ Ala Sch Denistry Alumni Asn, 1974-; Int Asn Dental Res, 1982-; Phi Phi Chap, Omicron Kappa Upsilon, Nat Dental Honor Soc, 1985-; Acad Gen Denistry, 1994-. **Honors/Awds:** International Col Denist Award, 1974; Miles College Community Award, Miles Col, 1979; Second place in competition, AADS meeting, Prod Dental Anatomy Videotape, 1983. **Special Achievements:** First African-Am stud and grad, Sch Dentistry, Univ Ala, Birmingham. **Military Serv:** AUS, col, 1977-; Medal Achievement Accommodation, 1990, Army Accommodation Medal, 1996. **Business Addr:** Professor, Restorative Dentistry, UAB Dental Group, School of Dentistry, 1919 7th Ave S Rm 521, Birmingham, AL 35294, **Business Phone:** (205)934-5234.

WRIGHT-BOTCHWEY, ROBERTA YVONNE
Lawyer, educator. **Personal:** Born Oct 9, 1946, York, SC. **Educ:** Fisk Univ, BA, 1967; Yale Univ, ISSP cert, 1966; Univ Mich, Sch AndrewIII, JD. **Career:** Pvt Pract; NC Cent Univ, Sch Law, asst prof corp counsel, Tanzania Legal Corp Dar, Salaam Tanzania; Zambia Ltd Lusaka Zambia, sr legal asst rural develop corp. **Orgs:** NC Asn Black Lawyers; Nat Bar Asn; Nat Conf Black Lawyers; SC & DC Bar Asn; hon mem, Delta Theta Phi; consult, EPA, 1976; lectr, Sci Jury Sel & Evidence Workshop; legal adv, Zambian Corp Del, Tel Aviv, Israel, 1971; Atty Gen Zambia Select Comt Investigate Railways, 1972; Delta Sigma Theta Sorority; consult, Women's Prison Group, 1975; consult, EPA Environ Litigation Workshop, 1976; NCBL Comn Invest Discrim Prac Law Schs, 1977; dir, Councon Legal Educ Opport Summer Inst, 1977; Phi Beta Kappa, 1967. **Honors/Awds:** Outstdg Young Women Am, 1976; Sydney P Raymond lectr, Jackson St Univ, 1977. **Business Addr:** Lawyer, 339 E Main, PO Box 10646, Rock Hill, SC 29730.

WYATT, ADDIE L
Government official, labor activist, clergy. **Personal:** Born Mar 8, 1924, Brookhaven, MS; daughter of Ambrose Cameron and Maggie; married Rev Claude S Wyatt Jr; children: Renaldo & Claude III. **Career:** Amalgamated Meat Cutters & Butcher Workmen N Am AFL-CIO, int vpres, dir womens affairs dept, 1941-54, int rep, 1968-74, dir women's affairs dept, 1974-78, dir human reights dept, 1978-, int vpres, 1976-; Wyatt Choral Ensemble, co found, 1944; UFCW-AFL-CIO, int vpres, 1979-84, personnel bd Chicago 1986-88; R.T.A. dir, exec vpres Emerita CLUW, 1988. **Orgs:** Int Adv Coun Amalgamated Meat Cutters & Butcher Workmen N Am

AFL-CIO Union Women; co-pastor & minister, Mus Vernon Park Church God Chicago; Social Ctr Inst Chicago Bd Ed;Protective Labor Legis Comn Pres Kennedy's Comn Status Women; labor adv, co-worker Dr Martin Luther King Jr, Dr Ralph D Abernathy, Rev Jesse L Jackson; Jewish Labor X Prog; adv & labor, Inst Labor Ed Roosevelt Univ; IL State AFL-CIO COPE Org; adv, Citizen Day Care; nat adv, Womens Org Church God; Coalition Black Trade Unionists; League Black Women; Nat coun, Negro Women; Chicago Urban League; Chicago Nat Asn Advan Colored People; vol, Youth & Community Serv Chicago Housing Auth; Delta Sigma Theta; co-chair, CBTA Woman; bd mem, PUSH. **Honors/Awds:** Distinguished Labor Leaders Award, League Black Women, Woodlawn Org 1975; One of Twelve Outstanding Women of Year, Time Mag, 1975; Women of the Year, Ladies Home J, 1977; Dr Martin Luther King Jr Labor Award, 1981; Outstanding Woman in Western Region, Iota Phi Lambda; Urban Ministries Inc Award; Outstanding Woman Ladies, Home Journal; Keeper of the Dream, Dr Martin Luther King Jr Ctr. **Special Achievements:** First female local union president of the United Packinghouse Food and Allied Workers; One of 100 Most Outstanding Black Am, Ebony Mag 1981-84; Citation, Ebony Mag, 1977. **Home Addr:** 8901 S Chappel, Chicago, IL 60617. **Business Addr:** Co-pastor, Vernon Park Church of God, 9011 S Stony Island, Chicago, IL 60617, **Business Phone:** (773)721-9011.

WYATT, ALFONSO
Executive. **Educ:** Howard Univ; Columbia Teacher Col; Ackerman Inst Family Therapy; NY Theol Sem. **Career:** NY Bd Educ, teacher & adminr; Valley Inc, dep exec dir; Fund City, NY, vpres, currently. **Orgs:** Adv bd, Black Leadership Comn AIDS; Correctional Asn & Osborne Asn; chairperson, Fountain Youth; Greater Allen Cathedral, NY. **Honors/Awds:** Lewis Hine Award, 1994; Community Hero, CBS-TV. *

WYATT, CLAUDE STELL, JR.
Clergy, founder (originator). **Personal:** Born Nov 14, 1921, Dallas, TX; married Addie Lorraine Cameron; children: Renaldo, Claude L. **Educ:** Wilson Col, attended 1955, Chicago Teachers Col, 1956, Chicago Bapt Inst, 1957; Urban Training Ctr for Christian Mission, cert, 1960; Roosevelt Univ Labor Dept, cert, 1974. **Career:** US PO, clerk, 1947-65; Vernon Park Ch of God, co pastor, reverend & co founder. **Orgs:** Consult Urban Ministries Anderson Coll IN 1978; consult for Ch Growth Com Anderson Coll 1979; bd mem Natl com of Black Churchmen 1975; bd mem & founder, Operation PUSH; dir, Ministerial Leadership Training Prog Southern Christian Leadership Conf. **Honors/Awds:** Outstanding Leadership in Religion Operation PUSH Chicago, 1973; Outstanding Bus & Prof Persons Blackbook Pubs Chicago, 1978; Hon DD Degree, Monrovia Univ, 1984. **Business Addr:** Co Founder, Pastor emeritus, Vernon Park Church of God, 7653 S Maryland Ave, Chicago, IL 60619.

WYATT, GAIL E.
Psychologist, educator. **Career:** Univ Calif Los Angeles AIDS Inst, assoc dir, currently; Univ Calif Los Angeles, prof psychiat & biobehavioral sci. **Honors/Awds:** Res Scientist Career Devel Awardee, NIMH. **Special Achievements:** Author: Stolen Women: Reclaiming Our Sexuality, Taking Back Our Lives; The first African-American woman to be licensed as a psychologist in the state of California.

WYATT, JULI
Executive. **Personal:** Born Jul 20, 1964. **Educ:** James Madison Univ, BA, polit sci; DC Sch Law, JD. **Career:** Jam Sports & Entertainment LLC, pres & ceo, founder, 1993-. **Orgs:** DC Law Rev. **Business Addr:** Founder, President & Chief Executive Officer, Jam Sports & Entertainment LLC, 13812 Amberfield Ct, Upper Marlboro, MD 20772, **Business Phone:** (301)627-3706.*

WYATT, LANCE EVERETT
Surgeon. **Personal:** Born Jan 19, 1967, Nashville, TN; son of Lewis and Gail. **Educ:** Howard Univ, BS, 1984-88; Univ Calif, Los Angeles Sch Med, MD, 1988-92; UCLA Med Ctr, Div Gen Surg, Resident, 1992-99; UCLA Div Plastic & Reconstructive Surg, Res Fellowship, 1994-97. **Career:** Nat Inst Health, summer res fellow, 1989; UCLA Med Ctr, internship, 1992-93, div gen surg, jr resident, 1993-94, Plastic & Reconstr Surg, sr res fellow, 1994-97, sr resident, 1997-98; Harvard Combined Plastic Surg Residency Training Prog, chief resident, 2003; pvt practitioner, currently. **Orgs:** Co-founder, Surgical Resident Forum, 1995; Am Col Surgeons, participant in the candidate group; William P Longmire Surg Soc; Soc Black Acad Surgeons; Nat Med Asn, Morestin Soc; Am Med Asn; The New Leaders, youth empowerment comm; Am Soc Bone & Mineral Res; co-founder, Health Relief Int. **Honors/Awds:** Best Basic Science Research, UCLA Div Plastic & Reconstr Surgery, 1996; Ralph Goldman Basic Research Award, UCLA Div Geriatric Med, 1996; Plastic Surg Educ Found, Lyndon Peer Fellow, 1996; Ebony Mag, 50 Leaders of Tomorrow, 1995; Individual National Research Service Award, Nat Inst Health, 1995-97; Ralph Goldman Basic Research Award, 1996; Lyndon Peer Fellowship, 1996; American Medical Association Foundation Leadership Award, 2003. **Special Achievements:** Plastic Surgery Educational Foundation Res Grant, 1995, 1997; Book chap "Lymphedema" in Grabb & Smith's Plastic Surgery, 1997; Book chap "Lymphedema & Tumors of the Lymphatics," 1997; Vascular Surgery: A Comprehensive Review, Nat Presentations and Peer Reviewed publication; mentor, Angel City Links, 1990, 1995-98; KACE-Radio, Sunday Morning Live, "Teen Sexuality," 1995. **Business Addr:** Surgeon, 8631 W 3rd St E Tower Suite 1125 E, Los Angeles, CA 90048, **Business Phone:** (310)360-7430.

WYATT, LORETTA
College administrator. **Career:** Bowie State Univ, Off Spec Proj, dir, 2001. *

WYATT, DR. RONALD MICHAEL
Physician, health services administrator. **Personal:** Born Mar 6, 1954, Selma, AL; son of Gladys and James; married Pamela, Jul 28, 1984; children: Michael, Scott & Christopher. **Educ:** Univ Ala, Birmingham, BS, 1976, MD, 1985. **Career:** St Louis Univ Sch Med, chief resident, 1987-88; St Louis Va Med Ctr, dir ER, 1988-89; Peoples Health Ctr, med dir, 1989-93; Central N Ala Health Servs, dir clinic servs, 1993-; Univ Ala, Birmingham Sch Med, asst dean. **Orgs:** Nat Asn Community Health Ctrs, chair health policy comn, 1993-94; US Pub Health Servs, assoc recruitor, 1990-; Nat Coordinating Comt Clinic Prevention Servs, advisor, 1992-. **Honors/Awds:** US Pub Health Servs, 'Special Recognition Award', 1992; US Nat Health Servs Corp, Exemplary Serv, 1992. **Military Serv:** AUS, capt, 1989-; Army Commendation, Desert Storm. **Home Addr:** 115 Lake Crest Dr, Madison, AL 35758. **Business Addr:** Physician, Huntsville Internal Medicine Associates, 250-220 Chateau Dr, Huntsville, AL 35801, **Business Phone:** (205)881-1989.

WYATT, S MARTIN, III (JAMAL ABDUL-KABIR)
Journalist. **Personal:** Born Jul 31, 1941, Memphis, TN; son of Nadine Bragg Poindexter and S Martin Wyatt II; married Joyce Hanson, Aug 17, 1990; children: Marcus, Sabriya, Jamila & Aisha. **Educ:** Vallejo Junior Col, Vallejo, Calif, 1956-60; Univ Wash, Seattle, Wash, 1960-62. **Career:** Journalist (retired); KYAC Radio, Seattle, Wash, sales mgr, 1966-72; KING-TV, Seattle, Wash, sports anchor/writer, 1972-76; WRC-TV, Wash, DC, sports anchor/writer, 1976-80; KGO-TV, San Francisco, Calif, sports anchor/writer, 1980-85; WMAR-TV, Baltimore, MD, sports anchor/writer, 1986-88; Black Entertainment TV, Wash, DC, producer/anchor/writer, 1986-89; KGO-TV, San Francisco, Calif, sports anchor/writer, 1989; ABC7 news, sports anchor. **Orgs:** Nat Asn Black Journalists, 1986-; Bay Area Black Journalists, 18981-. **Honors/Awds:** Emmy Award, "Bill Russell: A Man Alone," 1976; Access Award Finalist, "Voyage of Courage," 1987; Sigma Delta Chi Winner for Series, "Thoroughbred Breeding in MD," 1987; Martin Wyatt Day Declared in Seattle, WA, King County, May 27, 1976; 100 Black Men, Leaders in Action Award, 1994; Delta Sigma Theta Sorority, Image Awd for Journalism 1995; Omega Boys & Girls Club, Annual Street Soldier Award Winner, 1996; Vallejo Junior Col, Solano Col Athletic Hall of Fame, 1996; Calif Black Sports Hall of Fame, 1999; 100 Black News Community Service Award, 1999. **Military Serv:** AUS, corporal, Special Commendation for Service in Vietnam, 1964-66. **Home Addr:** 547 Merritt Ave, Oakland, CA 94610, **Home Phone:** (510)835-3460.

WYATT, WILLIAM N
Manager, chief executive officer. **Personal:** Born Oct 21, 1953, Canton, OH; son of Calvin W and Helen Hood; divorced; children: Chancelor & Shellie. **Educ:** Kent State Univ, bus admin, 1967-72. **Career:** A-WY Entertainment, pres, ceo, currently; Dick Clark Agency, Urban Contemporary Div, dir, currently. **Orgs:** Elks; Negro Oldtimers Baseball Hall of Fame. **Business Addr:** Director, Urban Contemporary Division, Dick Clark Agency, 3003 W Olive Ave, Burbank, CA 91505, **Business Phone:** (310)288-5716.

WYATT CUMMINGS MOORE, HON. THELMA LAVERNE
Judge. **Personal:** Born Jul 6, 1945, Amarillo, TX; daughter of James Odis Wyatt Sr and Annie Lavernia Lott Wyatt; married Luke C Moore (deceased); children: Khari Sekou Cummings & Ayanna Rashida Cummings. **Educ:** Univ Calif, BA, 1965; Ill Inst Tech Fel Psychodynamics, 1966; Emory Univ Sch Law, JD, 1971. **Career:** Bd Educ, City Chicago, teacher, 1965-67; Atlanta Urban League, field rep, 1967-69; Thelma Wyatt, atty, 1971-74; Ward & Wyatt, atty, 1974-77; Munic Ct Atlanta, judge, 1977-80; City Ct Atlanta, judge, 1980, State Ct Fulton County, judge, 1985-90, immediate post-chief judge, 1998-2000; Fulton County Super Ct, Ga, judge, currently. **Orgs:** Ga State Bar Asn, 1971-; Am Bar Asn; Nat Bar Asn; past chmn, Nat Judicial Coun; historian, Gate City Bar Asn, 1990-; Ga Asn Black Women Atty; Atlanta Bar Asn; Am Judicature Soc; Am Judges Asn; Phi Alpha Delta; Alpha Kappa Alpha; subscribing life mem, Nat Asn Advan Colored People; bd gov, Joint Ctr Polit Studies; bd trustees, Emory Univ; bd dirs, Nat Ctr State Conn, 1994-2000; Fulton Co Family Ct Proj, conceived & spearheaded, 1998. **Honors/Awds:** Distinguished Service, Nat Judicial Coun, 1982, 1983, 1986, 1988; Essence Award for Outstanding Contribution, Essence mag, 1982; Outstanding Jurist Award, Gate City Bar Asn, 1983; Outstanding Public Service Award, Ga Coalition Black Women Inc, 1984; Distinguished Alumni Award, Emory BLSA, 1986; Order of the Coif, Bryan Soc, Pi Delta Phi, Appellate Advocacy, Am Jurisprudence Awards in Comn Law, Mortgages & Admin Law, John Hay Whitney Fel, State Ill Fel, Nat Urban League Fel; Gate City Bar Asn Pres Award, 1990; Govt Award, Atlanta Bus League, 1990; Thurgood Marshall Award, 1991; Emory Medal, 1992; WSB Living Legend Award, 1992; Distinguished Alumni Award, Emory Law Sch, 1996; Woman of Vision Award, Atlanta Bus League, 1996-03; Emory Distinguished Law Alumni Award; Wiley Branton Award, NBA; Raymond Pare Alexander Award, NBA; US Chief Justice Award, 2001; Sojourner Truth Award, NBPW, 2002; Pinnacle Award, Delta Sigma Theta, 2003; Atlanta Bar Outstanding Jurist Award; Jondelle Johnson Legacy Award, Nat Asn Advan Colored People, 2004; Gate City Bar Judicial Section Legacy Award, 2005; Thurgood Marshall Award, Judicial Coun, Nat Bar Asn, 2006; Concerned Black Clergy President's Award, Georgia Legislative Black Caucus Pacesetter Award; Atlanta Business League Catalyst Award; numerous other awards. **Business Addr:** Judge, Fulton County Super Court, T4905 Justice Ctr Tower 185 Cent Ave SW, Atlanta, GA 30303, **Business Phone:** (404)730-4305.

WYCHE, KEITH
Executive. **Educ:** Cleveland State Univ, BA; Baldwin-Wallace College, MBA. **Career:** Pres, US Operations, Bitney Bowes Mgt Services;. **Honors/Awds:** Inductee, Martin Luther King Jr. International Board of Renaissance Leaders . *

WYCHE, LENNON DOUGLAS, JR.
Physician. **Personal:** Born Jul 13, 1946, Washington, DC; married Judith. **Educ:** Howard Univ, 1966; George Wash Univ, BS, 1969; Meharry Med Sch, MD, 1973. **Career:** USPHS, intern, 1973-74; USPHS Clin, gen med officer, 1974-46; Resd diagnostic radiology, 1976; Appling HealthCare Syst, physician, currently. **Orgs:** Alpha Phi Alpha Frat; Am Col Radiology; Nat Med Asn; jr mem, Am Roentgen Ray Soc; Eleven Black Men Liberty County. **Honors/Awds:** Personal Service Award, USPHS. **Military Serv:** USPHS, lt comdr, 1973-76. **Business Addr:** Physician, Appling HealthCare System, 163 E Tollison St, Baxley, GA 77030.

WYCHE, PAUL H
Executive. **Personal:** Born Oct 16, 1946, Miami, FL; son of Paul Howard and Gracie Thompson; married Louise Everett, Dec 11, 1971; children: Shaina Nicole & Kimberly Elise. **Educ:** Miami-Dade Jr Col; Univ Miami; Southeastern Univ, BS, pub admin; Univ Southern Calif & Southeastern Univ, grad study bus & pub. **Career:** Miami News, reporter, 1965-68; Econ Opportunity Prog Miami, dir pub affairs, 1968-70; WPLG-TV Miami, prog moderator, 1970-71; Fla Mem Col, pub rel dir, 1970-71; The Miami Times, assoc ed, 1970-71; US Rep Pepper (Dem-FL), legislative asst, 1971-73; Nat Black News Serv Inc, pres dir, 1972-84; US Rep Moakley, sr legislative asst, 1973-75; US Environ Protection Agency, assoc pub affairs dir, 1978-80, constituent develop & coord, 1977-78, exec asst pub affairs dir, 1975-77; E I du Pont de Nemours Co, pub affairs rep, 1980-82, pub affairs consult, 1982-88, pub affairs mgr, 1988-91; vpres, corp pub affairs & gov rel, 1991-93, dir, community rel & gov affairs; Safety-Kleen Corp, 1993-98; Whirlpool Corp, vpres, 1998; founder, principal & pres, Wyche & Associate, currently. **Orgs:** Life mem, NAACP; bd mem, Mt Vernon-Lee Enter Inc; Nat Urban League; PUSH; Sigma Delta Chi, 1968-; Nat Capital Press Clubs; Nat Young Demo Clubs; bd mem, Coun Catholic Laity; pres, Good Shepherd Parish Coun; Cong Staff Club; Admin Asst Asn; bd mem, S Fla Econ Opportunity Coun; Dade Co Drug Abuse Adv Bd; Jaycees; founding pres, bd, NW Miami Jaycees; vpres, United Blck Fedn Dade Co; pres, Fla Pub Affairs Dirs; bd mem, Black Coc; pres, Caths Shared Responsibility; pres, Good Shepherd Coun Laity; dir, Am Heart Asn, 1982-85; trustee, West End City Day Care Nursery, 1983-85; chmn, Brandywine Prof Asn, 1984-91; dir, Delaware Alliance Prof Women, 1984-86; pres, Civic Asn Surrey Park, 1985-86; dir, Boy Scouts Am, 1985-90; pres, Opportunity ter Inc, 1986-90; vice chmn, Govt Rel, bd dirs, United Way DE, 1987-90, chmn Govt Rel, United Way, 1987-89; dir, Ment Health Asn, 1988-90; dir, Layton Home Aged, 1988-90; trustee, Med Ctr Del Found, 1988-93; exec comt, Human Serv Partnership, 1989-91; dir, Del Community Investment Corp, 1989-91; bd dirs, Nat Asn Chem Recyclers, 1994-, vpres, 1995; Nat Asn Mfrs, Nat Pub Affairs Steering Comte, 1994-; pres, bd dir Nat Asn Chemical Recyclers, 1996-; bd dir, Pub Affairs Coun, 1997-; Conf Bd Corp Strategies Coun, 1997-; State Gov Rel Coun, 1995-. **Honors/Awds:** Awards reporting & broadcasting, 1964, 1967, 1968; Silver Knight Award, 1964; Superior Performance, US EPA, 1978; Outstanding Professionalism, Omega Psi Phi Fraternity, 1988; Outstanding Black Achiever Bus & Indus, YMCA, 1989; Outstanding Community Service, United Way Del, 1990. **Business Addr:** Founder, Principal, President, Wyche & Associates, 2920 Lowell Court, Casselberry, FL 32707.

WYCHE, DR. VERA ROWENA
School administrator. **Personal:** Born Feb 2, 1923, Rowus Run, PA; married Julian C (deceased); children: Evangeline. **Educ:** Cheyney State, BS, 1944; Howard Univ, MA, 1945; Univ Mich, PhD, 1974. **Career:** School Administrator (Retired). Detroit Pub Schs, teacher, 1949-63, admin princ, 1963-71; Univ Mich, lecturer educ & admin, 1971-74; Eastern Mich Univ, adjunct prof, Sch Housing, admin assoc to supt, 1976-87. **Orgs:** Bd mem, Bilalian Child Develop Ctr, 1977-82; bd mem, Univ Mich Women, Detroit

Chap 1, 1976-84; Nat Health & Safety Task Force, 1980-84; Internat Platform Assoc, 1980-; chr ed dev com, Nat Asn Negro Bus & Prof Woman, 1981-83; Detroit Woman's Forum, 1982-; Congressional Advisory Comm, 1983-. **Honors/Awds:** Excell in Leadership, BUF, 1980; Woman Excellency, NANBPW 1982; McKeesport High Sch Hall of Fame, 1994. **Home Addr:** 16 Foxwood Dr Suite BB, Morris Plains, NJ 07950-2650.

WYCLIFF, NOEL DON
Journalist. **Personal:** Born Dec 17, 1946, Liberty, TX; son of Wilbert A and Emily A; married Catherine A, Sep 25, 1982; children: Matthew William & Grant Erdmann. **Educ:** Univ Notre Dame, BA, 1969; Univ Chicago, 1969-70. **Career:** Chicago Sun-Times, reporter; The New York Times, ed writer, 1985-90; Chicago Tribune, dep ed page ed, 1990-91, ed page ed, 1991-2000, pub ed & columnist, 2000-. **Orgs:** Nat Asn Minority Media Execs, 1991-; Am Soc Newspaper Eds, 1991-; Nat Asn Black Journalists; ASNE Writing Awards Comt, 1995-97; Univ Notre Dame, Col Arts & Letters, adv coun, 1989-. **Honors/Awds:** Pulitzer Prize juror Finalist for the Pulitzer Prize for Ed Writing, 1996; Chicago Journalism Hall of Fame, Inductee, 1996; ASNE Distinguished Writing Award for Eds, 1997. **Special Achievements:** Contributor to Commonwealth Mag, 1990-. **Business Addr:** Public Editor, columnist, Chicago Tribune, 435 N Michigan Ave, Chicago, IL 60611, **Business Phone:** (312)227-3000.

WYKE, JOSEPH HENRY
Executive director. **Personal:** Born Jan 9, 1928, New York, NY; married Margaret Elaine Whiteman. **Educ:** City Col NYC, BSaS, 1949; NY Univ, MA, attended 1958. **Career:** Urban League Greater New Brunswick, exec dir, 1966-70; Urban Coalition Met Wilmington, DE, exec vpres, 1970-75; Col M Ed Dent NJ, asst adminr, 1975-76; Westchester Coalition Inc, exec dir, 1976-. **Orgs:** Bd mem, Afro-Am Cultural Found, 1977-; chmn bd dirs, Aspire Indust Inc, 1978-; Edges, 1978-; Julius A Thomas Soc, 1978; bd mem, Westchester Community Serv Coun, 1979-. **Honors/Awds:** Appreciation for Service Paul Robeson Award, Urban League Greater New Brunswick, 1980; Martin Luther King Jr Award, Greenburgh Community Ctr, 1980. **Business Addr:** Executive Director, Westchester Coalition Inc, 235 Main St, White Plains, NY 10601.

WYKLE, MAY LOUISE HINTON
Educator, dean (education), school administrator. **Personal:** Born Feb 11, 1934, Martins Ferry, OH; daughter of John R and Florence A Randall; married William Lenard; children: Andra Sims & Caron. **Educ:** Ruth Brant Sch Nursing, dipl RN, 1956; Western Reserve Col, Cleveland, BSN, 1962; Case Western Reserve Univ, MSN, psych nursing, 1969, PhD, educ, 1981. **Career:** Cleveland Psychiat Inst, staff nurse, head nurse, suprv, 1956-64, dir, nursing educ, 1964; Univ Hosp Cleveland, admin assoc; Ctr Aging & Health, dir, assoc dean community affairs; Res Psychiat Inst, MD Self-Style-compliance, NIA, black & white caregiver intervention, NIH; Case Western Reserve Univ, asst prof, psych nursing, 1975, prof chair person, dir psych nursing, adminr assoc, geront nursing, Frances Payne Bolton Sch Nursing, dean & Florence Cellar prof Geront Nursing, currently. **Orgs:** Clin nurse spec Fairhill Ment Health Ctr, 1970; nursing consult, Va Med Ctr, 1980-85; bd mem, Eliz Bryant Nursing Home, 1983; proj dir, Robert Wood Johnson Teaching Nursing Home; Res-Self Care among Elderly; chairperson res comm Margaret Hagner House Nursing Home; Prof Adv Bd-ARDA Org Cleveland OH; bd dir, Judson Retirement Ctr, 1989-; bd mem, Golden Age Ctr, Cleveland, 1991; ed bd, Generations Mag, 1991; Nat Panel Alzheimers Dis, 1992; Am Acad Nursing; Geront Soc Am. **Honors/Awds:** Alumni Award Martins Ferry, 1956; Sigma Theta Tau Nursing Hon Soc, 1966; Distinguished Teaching Award, FPB Sch Nursing, 1975; Merit Award Cleveland Coun Black Nurses, 1983; Geriatric Ment Health Academic Award, 1983-86, Cleveland Pacesetter Award, 1986; Distinguished Alumni Award- Frances Payne Bolton Sch Nursing, CWRU, 1986; Wykle, M & Dunkle R Decision Making Long Term Care, 1988; Florence Cellar Professorship Geront Nursing F P B Sch Nursing CWRU, 1989; John S Diekoff Teaching Excellence Award, CWRU, 1989; Distinguished Nurse Scholar, Lectr, Nat Ctr Nursing Res, 1991; Belle Sherwin Distinguished Nurse Award, 1992. **Special Achievements:** Coauthor of Stress & Health among the Elderly, 1992. **Home Addr:** 34552 Summerset Rd, Cleveland, OH 44139-5635. **Business Addr:** Dean, Florence Cellar Professor of Gerontological Nursing, Case Western Reserve University, Frances Payne Bolton School of Nursing, 2121 Abington Rd, Cleveland, OH 44106-4904, **Business Phone:** (216)368-2545.

WYLIE, ARTHUR
Chief executive officer. **Educ:** Univ NC, BS, Bus Admin, 1999. **Career:** Arthur Wylie Wealth Mgt Group, founder & chief exec officer, 1999-. **Honors/Awds:** Outstanding Young Alumnus Award, 2003; Charlotte Bus Journal's 2004 "40Under 40" winner. **Business Phone:** 877-211-1525.

WYLLIE, TONY
Executive. **Career:** Nat Football League team, media rels; Houston Texans, vpres commiserations, currently. **Business Phone:** (832)667-2000.*

WYMAN, DEVIN
Football player. **Personal:** Born Aug 29, 1973, East Palo Alto, CA; married Shelby McQueen; children: 5. **Educ:** Ky State Univ. **Career:** New England Patriots, defensive tackle, 1996-97; Kans City Chiefs, 2002; Arena Football League, San Jose Saber Cats, 2003-05; Arena Football League, Dallas Desperados, 2006-07; Utah Blaze, 2008. **Special Achievements:** Part of SaberCats team won Arena Bowl XVIII, 2006.

WYNN, ALBERT
Congressperson (U.S. federal government). **Personal:** Born Sep 10, 1951, Philadelphia, PA; married Gaines Clore; children: Meredith & Gabrielle. **Educ:** Univ Pittsburgh, BS, polit sci, 1973; Howard Univ, MS, pub admin, 1974; Georgetown Law Sch, JD, 1977. **Career:** Prince George's County Consumer Protection Comn, MD, dir, 1979-82; Albert R Wynn & Assocs, founder, 1982-; Md House Deleg, mem, 1983-87; Md State Senate, mem, 1987-93; US House Rep, 4th Cong Dist Md, congressman, 1992-. **Orgs:** Kappa Alpha Psi Fraternity; Dem Message Group; Dep Dem Whip; chmn, Cong Black Caucus Polit Action Comt; chair, Cong Black Caucus Task Force Campaign Finance Reform; Caucus Minority Bus Task Force; Maple Springs Baptist Church; Md Bar Asn. **Honors/Awds:** Award for Leadership, Small Business Admin, 2002. **Business Addr:** Congressman, United States House of Representatives, Maryland, 2470 Rayburn Bldg, Washington, DC 20515-2004, **Business Phone:** (202)225-8699.

WYNN, DR. CORDELL
College president. **Personal:** Born Feb 3, 1927, Eatonton, GA; married Annie Marie Lundy; children: 3. **Educ:** Boston Univ, AA; Fort Valley State Col, Ga, BS; SC State Univ, Med; Teachers Col, Columbus Univ, New York City, prof dipl; Univ Ga, EdS & PhD. **Career:** Stillman Col, Tuscaloosa, AL, pres, 1981-97, pres emer, 1997-; President's Round table Pres by Church, emer mem, 1997-; Univ Ala Syst, trustee emer, 1997-; Paul Harris Fel, Tuscaloosa Rotary Club, 1997-; Shelton State Community Col, fac, special asst to the pres. **Orgs:** Chmn, W Ala Chamber Com; UNCF Mem Inst; bd dirs, Nat Asn Equal Opportunity Higher Educ; Nat Collegiate Athletic Asn; Am Coun Educ. **Honors/Awds:** Hon degrees: Univ Ala, West Ala Univ, Alma Col, Alma Col, Stillman Col, Marion Mil Inst, Ala Agr & Mech Univ; Eleanor Roosevelt Human Relations Award, George Washington Univ; Outstanding Alumnus Award, Univ Ga, 1980; Col Administrator of the Year; Distinguished Leadership Award for Four-Year Cols and Universities; Citizen of the Year, Tuscaloosa Co, 1992; Educator of the Year Award, Martin Luther King Jr, Nat Southern Christian Leadership Conf; Higher Education Award, Presbyterian Church, 1996; Tuscaloosa County Civic Hall of Fame, 2002. **Business Addr:** President Emeritus, Stillman College, 3601 Stillman Blvd, Tuscaloosa, AL 35401, **Business Phone:** (205)349-4240.

WYNN, LAMETTA K
Mayor, nurse. **Personal:** Born in Galena, IL; married Thomas H Wynn (died 1996); children: 10. **Educ:** Graduate St Luke's Hosp Sch Nursing, Cedar Rapids, IA. **Career:** Nurse (retired), government official; Mercy Hosp, nurse; City Clinton, Iowa, mayor, currently. **Orgs:** Rotary Int; past trustee, Mt Clare Col; Nat Asn Advan Colored People; Bethel AME Church; hon mem, Delta Kappa Gamma Soc Int; Clinton Community Sch Bd; past chmn, Iowa Comn on the Status African-Am; bd dir, African Am Mus. **Honors/Awds:** Woman of Action, YWCA; Liberty Bell Award, Clinton County Bar Asn; hon doctorate degree, Teikyo-Marycrest Univ; St Ambrose Univ; Mt St Clare Col; Outstanding Citizen Award, Iowa Gov Branstad;; Inducted into Iowa African-Am Hall of Fame, Am NAACP fund Banquet, 2001; pres, Exec Bd Iowa League of cities, 2002. **Special Achievements:** First African-Am woman to be elected mayor in Iowa; Named by Newsweek Mag as one of 25 Most Dynamic Mayors in Am; To honor Lametta, Clinton city has named a street after her. **Business Addr:** Mayor, City of Clinton, PO Box 2958, Clinton, IA 52733, **Business Phone:** (563)242-2144.

WYNN, MALCOLM
Police officer. **Personal:** Born May 31, 1940, Greenville, MS; son of Harry and Roberta Hillard; married Billie Jean Moore, Feb 18, 1957; children: Caroline Ann, Anthony, Geraldine, Malcolm & Patrick Fitzgerald. **Educ:** MS Law Enforcement Training Acad, cert, 1969; LSU Law Enforcement Inst, cert, 1972; Delta State Univ, Cleveland, MS, 1974; FBI Nat Acad, Quantico, VA, cert, 1977. **Career:** Police officer (retired); US Gypsum, Greenville, MS, finishing dept, 1965-68; Greenville Police Dept, Greenville, MS, police officer, chief police, 1968-89; Greenville Pub Schs, Greenville, MS, student activities supvr. **Orgs:** Wa Boys Club, 1974-80; Greenville Chamber Com, 1987-89. **Honors/Awds:** Outstanding Serv, Elks Serene Lodge no 567, 1978; Outstanding Serv, Wash County Youth Ct, 1975; Community Serv Award, WDDT Radio Station, 1987; Safety Award, Loyal & Devoted Serv, Les Bonhur De Femmes, 1988; Civic Award, Kappa Tau Theta Sorority, 1988; Pub Serv Award, Star Bethlehem Church, 1988. *

WYNN, RENALDO
Football player. **Personal:** Born Sep 3, 1974, Chicago, IL. **Educ:** Univ Notre Dame, BS, sociol, 1996. **Career:** Jacksonville Jaguars, defensive tackle, 1997-2001; Wash Redskins, 2002-06, 2009-; New Orleans Saints, 2007; New York Giants, 2008. **Orgs:** Hon chmn, Cystic Fibrosis Found, Winner's Cir prog, 1999. **Business Phone:** (703)726-7000.

WYNN, SYLVIA J
Executive. **Personal:** Born Sep 30, 1941, New York, NY; daughter of Frank and Lucinda Townes. **Educ:** Hunter Col, City Univ New York, attended 1966-70; Simmons Middle Mgt Prog, Cert, 1979. **Career:** The Gillette Co, prod mgr, 1978-81; Int Playtex Inc, prod mgr, 1981-83; Johnson Prod Co Inc, group prod mgr, 1983-85, dir mkt, 1985-86, vpres mkt & sales, 1986-87; Women?s Bus Develop Ctr, bus counr, 1991-; SJW Enterprises, Chicago, IL, pres currently. **Orgs:** AMA; tutor Boston Half-Way House, 1978-81; founding mem & chairperson, Target Advertising Professionals. **Honors/Awds:** Boston Black Achiever Award, 1979. **Business Addr:** President, SJW Enterprises, 333 E Ontario St Suite 1302B, Chicago, IL 60611, **Business Phone:** (312)642-9720.

WYNN, DR. VALREE FLETCHER
Educator. **Personal:** Born May 9, 1922, Rockwall, TX; daughter of Will and Alice; widowed; children: Phail Jr & Michael David. **Educ:** Langston Univ, BA, 1943; Okla State Univ, MA, 1951, PhD, 1976. **Career:** Lawton Bd Educ, elem & high sch teacher, 1944-48, 1960-66; Cameron Univ, asst prof, assoc prof, prof, 1966-85, prof emer, 1985-. **Orgs:** AKA, 1942-; Phi Delta Kappa Hon Soc, 1973-; past cha basileus, Int Const Comn, 1978-82; Int Phi Kappa Phi Hon Soc, 1985-; past pres, Bd Regents Okla Cols, 1985-93; bd mem, US Sen David Boren's Found Excellence, 1985-; bd mem, Hospice, 1985-; adv coun, Okla Comn Status Women; hon mem, Awards Com, 1990-93; State Martin Luther King Jr Holiday CMS, 1992-; bd mem, Lawton Pub Schs Found, 1992-. **Honors/Awds:** Graduate Excellence Award, Okla State Univ, 1970-73; Professor Year, Lawton Coc, 1985; Outstanding Educator, DST, 1985; Valree F Wynn Scholar, Camon Univ, 1985-, Outstanding Service Award, 1993; Distinguished Alumnus, NAFEO, 1990; Woman Year, St John's Baptist Church, 1992; Outstanding Woman Comanche County, 1995; Faculty Hall Fame, Camon Univ, 1996; Oklahama Women's Hall Fame, 1996; Outstanding Educator in Humanities, Lawton Arts & Humanities Coun, 1998; Commission Service Award, Daughters Am Revolution, 1999. **Home Addr:** 6901 Sprucewood Dr, Lawton, OK 73505. **Business Addr:** Professor Emeritus, Cameron University, Department of English & Foreign Languages, 2800 W Gore Blvd, Lawton, OK 73505-6377, **Business Phone:** (580)581-2272.

WYNNE, DANA
Basketball player, basketball coach. **Personal:** Born Feb 2, 1975. **Educ:** Seton Hall Univ, BA, advert art & minor in socio, 1997. **Career:** Basket player (retired), basketball coach: Colorado Xplosion, forward, beginning, 1997; Sacramento Monarchs, forward, 2001; Washington Mystics, forward, 2004; Seton Hall Women's Basketball, asst coach; alma mater, asst coach; SHUPirates, asst coach, 2006-. **Honors/Awds:** Mention, three-time Kodak All-America Hon; inducted, Seton Hall Athletic Hall of Fame. *

WYNNE, DIANA S.
Executive. **Educ:** Spelman Col; Wright State Univ. **Career:** Blockbuster Inc, vpres & treas; Metromedia Restaurant Group, vpres & treas; CBRL Group Inc, sr vpres corp affairs, 2006-. **Orgs:** Am Dietetic Asn; chair, Women's Foodservice Forum. **Business Phone:** (615)443-9869.*

WYNNE, MARVELL
Baseball player. **Personal:** Born Dec 17, 1959, Chicago, IL; married; children: Marvell Wynne II. **Career:** Pittsburgh Pirates, outfielder, 1983-85; San Diego Padres, outfielder, 1986-89; Chicago Cubs, outfielder, 1989-90; Hanshin Tigers, Japanese Baseball League, 1990. **Honors/Awds:** Rookie of the Year, 1983.

WYNNS, CORYLISS LORRAINE
Journalist. **Personal:** Born Jan 17, 1958, St Louis, MO; daughter of Rufus Wynns and Helen De Wanda Foree. **Educ:** Ind Univ, BA, 1983. **Career:** WKXI-AM, Jackson, MS, chief reporter, 1982; AP radio network, Wash, DC, news clerk, 1984; KEEL-AM, Shreveport, LA, producer, reporter, anchor, 1984-85; KDKS-FM, Shreveport, LA, news dir, 1985; Sheridan Broadcasting Network, Pittsburgh, PA, freelance correspondent, 1985-87; WAWA-AM, Milwaukee, WI, news dir, 1985-87; WMAQ-AM, outside reporter, 1988-90, inside reporter, writer, 1990-92, ed, 1992; Morning Star Publicity Services, owner, currently. **Orgs:** Nat Asn Black Journalists, 1979-; co-founder, Indiana Univ Black Telecommunications Asn, 1980; vpres, Milwaukee Sec Nat Coun Negro Women, 1988. **Honors/Awds:** Image Award, Milwaukee, Wisconsin, Career Youth Development, 1986; Journalism Award, Radio Series, What About the Father, Nat Asn Black Journalists, 1987; InterNat Radio & Television Society, Col Conference, 1987; Nat Assn Black Journalists, InterNat Reporting, Radio Series, South Africa Referendum, 1992. **Business Addr:** Owner, Morning Star Publicity Services LLC, 1302 Chalfant St, South Bend, IN 46617, **Business Phone:** (574)210-3787.

WYNTER, LEON E
Journalist, writer. **Personal:** Born Aug 30, 1953, New York, NY; son of Sylvia Juredini and Rupert; divorced. **Educ:** Yale Univ, New Haven, CT, BA, Psychol, 1974; NY Univ, NY, MBA, Econs, 1979; NY Univ, NY, Jour, 1979-80. **Career:** Hanover Trust Corp, NY, lending officer corp banking, 1974-79; WA Post, WA, DC, staff writer, 1980-84; Wall St J, Dow Jones & Co, NY, staff

reporter, 1984-; Baruch Coll, City Univ NY, assoc prof Eng/jour, 1994-; Natl Public Radio, commentator "All Things Considered," 1993-; Random House Inc, author, currently. **Orgs:** Conv Comm, NY Asn of Black Journalists, 1989. **Honors/Awds:** Outstanding Communicator, Natl Black MBA Assn, 1992. **Home Addr:** 1354 College Ave, Bronx, NY 10456, **Home Phone:** (212)588-1759. **Business Addr:** Author, Random House Inc, 1745 Broadway Third Fl, New York, NY 10019, **Business Phone:** (212)572-6066.

WYRE, STANLEY MARCEL
Educator, school administrator. **Personal:** Born Mar 31, 1953, Detroit, MI; son of Nathaniel and Mervell; married Jerri Kailimai, 1988; children: Stanley III. **Educ:** Lawrence Inst Technol, BS, 1976; Detroit Col Law, JD, 1984. **Career:** Walbridge Aldinger Co, proj estimator, 1976-78; Palmer Smith Co, sr construction estimator & dir, 1979-83; Charfoos, Christensen & Archer PC, atty-at-law, 1984; Barton-Malow Co, construct mgr, 1984-87; prof photographer; Detroit Col Law, adj prof, 1985-; Lawrence Inst Technol, asst prof, 1985-; Detroit Pub Schs, asst supt, 1992; Chez Corp, consult, currently. **Orgs:** Arbitrator, Am Arbitrator Asn. **Business Addr:** Consultant, Chez Corp, Detroit, MI.

X

X, QUANELL (QUANELL RALPH EVANS)
Community activist. **Personal:** Born Dec 7, 1970, Los Angeles, CA; married Tabitha Stewart, Feb 26, 1998. **Career:** Mem, Nation of Islam; New Black Panther Party-Houston Chapter, info minister, currently. **Business Addr:** Information Minister, New Black Panther Party, 2428 Southmore, Houston, TX 77004, **Business Phone:** (281)472-5589.*

Y

YAMBA, DR. ZACHARY
Executive. **Educ:** Seton Hall Univ, BS, MS; Pacific States Univ, PhD; Brunel Univ, PhD. **Career:** Essex County Col, dir humanities, dean fac, dean liberal arts, pres, currently. **Orgs:** Trustee, Victoria Found; Newark Workforce Investment Bd; County Community Col Pres Asn NJ; New Community Corp Found, NJ Communities Sch; Int Youth Orgn; Nat Asn Advan Colored People. **Honors/Awds:** Ashby Award, 2005; Martin Luther King Jr Leadership Award, County of Essex, 2008; DHL, Seton Hall Univ. **Special Achievements:** Seton Hall University's Athletic Hall of Fame, 1980. **Business Addr:** President, Essex Coounty College, 303 Univ Ave, Newark, NJ 07102, **Business Phone:** (973)877-3022.

YANCEY, DR. ASA G, SR.
Physician, hospital administrator. **Personal:** Born Aug 19, 1916, Atlanta, GA; son of Arthur H and Daisy L Sherard; married Carolyn E Dunbar, Dec 28, 1944; children: Arthur H II, MD, Carolyn L, MD, Caren L Yancey-Covington & Asa G Jr, MD. **Educ:** Morehouse Col, BS, 1937; Univ Mich, MD, 1941. **Career:** Vet Admin Hosp, Tuskegee AL, chief surgeon, 1948-58; Hughes Spalding Hosp, chief surgeon, 1958-72; Grady Mem Hosp, med dir, 1972-89; Emory Univ Sch Med, assoc dean, 1972-89, prof surg emer; Ga Med Care Found Inc, assoc med dir, 1989-91; Morehouse Sch Med, clinical prof surg; Asa G Yancey Health Ctr, admin, currently. **Orgs:** Bd trustee, Ga Div Am Cancer Soc; fel, Am Col Surgeons; dipl, Am Bd Surg; ed bd, Jour of Nat Med Asn, 1960-80; Am Surg Asn; Southern Surg Asn; Atlanta Bd Educ, 1967-77; life mem, golden heritage mem, NAACP; Fulton-DeKalb Hosp Authority, the trustee body Grady Mem Hosp. **Honors/Awds:** Recipient, Distinguished Service Morehouse Col; 'Service Award', Atlanta Inquirer; Aven Cup; 'Hon Doctor of Science', Morehouse Col; 'Hon Doctor of Science', Howard Univ. **Special Achievements:** Author, "A Modification of the Swenson Operation for Congenital Megacolon," Journal of the Nat Med Asn, Sep 1952, published 10 years prior to Soave's publication of the same operation. **Military Serv:** USY, first lt, Med Corp, 1941. **Home Addr:** 2845 Engle Rd NW, Atlanta, GA 30318, **Home Phone:** (404)799-5045. **Business Addr:** Administrator, Asa G. Yancey Sr MD Health Center, 1247 Donald Lee Hollowell Pkwy, Atlanta, GA 30318-6657, **Business Phone:** (404)616-2265.

YANCEY, CAROLYN DUNBAR
Educator, school administrator. **Personal:** Born Feb 10, 1921, Detroit, MI; daughter of Henry S and Annie L Dye; married Asa G Yancey Sr, Dec 28, 1944; children: Arthur H II, Carolyn, Caren L Yancey-Covington & Asa G Jr. **Educ:** Wayne State Univ, BA, 1941, grad studies, 1942. **Career:** Educator, School Administrator (retired); Detroit Pub schs, teacher, 1941-48; Atlanta Bd Educ, Dist nine, at-large, 1982-97. **Orgs:** Spelman bd trustees, 1972-; Atlanta Bd Educ, Instruction Comt, chair, Personnel Comn, chair; Atlanta Pension Bd, Atl bd educ rep; PBA Bd, Atlanta bd edu rep; bd, Gate City Day Nursery Asn, Wesley Community Ctr; bd, Blue Star Camping Unlimited; bd, Nat Conf Christians & Jews, Ga Reg; bd, Atl Women's COC; NAACP; Atl Urban League; Delta Sigma Theta Sor; Engle Road Civic Asn, co-chair; League Women Voters; Atl Symphony Assocs; bd mem, Auxiliary Nat Med Asn; bd regents, Univ Ga Syst, 1985-02. **Honors/Awds:** Good Neighbor of the Year Award, Nat Conf Christians & Jews, 1972; Outstanding President, Frank L Stanton Sch PTA; WSB Radio, Leading Lady Day; Southern Bell, Calender Atl, Black Hist Honee, 1980-91; Mother of the Year, Atl Daily World, 1985; Educ Award for Outstanding Leadership & Community Enrichment, Tuskegee Airmen Inc, Atl Chap, 1993; Freedom Found Award, 1998. **Special Achievements:** City-wide PTA, All Citizens Voter Registration Drive, coordr; NAACP, Freedom Fund Effort, co-chair; MLK, Jr Ctr for Non-Violent Social Change, volunteer; GA Gov's Mansion, form guide; among first African-Am dep registrars, City-wide PTA; served eight yrs as capt, Atl Symphony Orchestra, Young People's Concerts; active participant, civil Rights Movement; NCCJ, served as African-Am rep for approx 100 progs; participated in numerous fundraising drives inckuding: March Dimes, United Appeal, Heart Fund, Am Cancer Soc, UNCF. **Home Addr:** 2845 Engle Rd NW, Atlanta, GA 30318-7216, **Home Phone:** (404)799-5045.

YANCEY, DR. CAROLYN LOIS
Physician, pediatrician. **Personal:** Born in Tuskegee, AL; daughter of Asa G Yancey Sr. **Educ:** Spelman Col, Atlanta Univ, BS, 1968-72; Univ Edinburgh Scotland, UK, attended 1972; Howard Univ Col Med, MD, 1976. **Career:** Univ Penn Childrens Hosp Philadelphia, resident, 1976-79, fel pediat rheumatol, 1979-81, instr pediat, 1980-81, clin asst prof pediatrics, 1981-82; Howard Univ Dept Pediat & Child Health, model pract, coordr, 1982-83, clin asst prof pediat, 1982-; Walter Reed Army Med Ctr, clin asst prof pediat, 1985-; George Wash Univ Sch Med, asst clin prof child health & develop, 1987; Ped Rheum, Kaiser Permanente, Mid Atlantic, dir, 1983-94; CIGNA Health Care, Mid Atlantic, assoc med dir, 1994-98, sr med dir, 1998-2000; Carolyn L Yancey LLC, pres; KPMG Consulting, Inc Health Care Practice, 2000-03; FDA/CDER, 2003-; pvt pract, currently. **Orgs:** Sect Rheumatol, Am Acad Pediat, 1983; diplo & fel, Am Acad Pediat, 1984; NMA & Am Rheumatism Asn, 1979; nominating comm., Sect Rheumatol, AAP, 1987; med adv comt, Arthritis Found, Wash Metropolitan Chap, 1990; exec comt, Sect Pediat Rheumatol, Am Acad Pediat, 1987-90; Jr League Wash, DC, 1990-93; chair, Section on Rheumatol, Am Acad Pediat, 1991-94. **Honors/Awds:** Department of Medical Award, Howard Univ Col Medicine, 1976; Distinguished Alumni Citation of the Year, Nat Asn Equal Opportunities Higher Educ, 1985; Professional Excellence Award, Kaiser Permanente Med Group, 1991. **Home Addr:** 10903 New Hampshire Ave, Silver Spring, MD 20910-2708, **Home Phone:** (301)585-6643. **Business Addr:** Physician, FDA, 9201 Corp Blvd HFD 550, Rockville, MD 20850, **Business Phone:** (301)827-2517.

YANCEY, CHARLES CALVIN
Government official. **Personal:** Born Dec 28, 1948, Boston, MA; son of Alice White and Howell T Sr; married Marzetta Morrissette; children: Charles, Derrick, Sharif & Ashley. **Educ:** Tufts Univ, BA, 1970; Harvard Univ, MPA, 1991. **Career:** Commonwealth,MA, dir,admin, 1977-79, Boston City Coun; Metro Area Planning Coun, dir finances 1979-82; CCY & Assoc, pres 1977-84; Legislative Branch City Govt, city coun, 1984-; Boston City Coun, Dist 4, councilman,currently; pres, Nat Black Caucus of Local Elected Off, 1999. **Orgs:** NAACP 1966-; Greater Roxbury Community Develop Corp, 1978-82; Transafrica1979-; Cod man Sq Community Develop Corp, 1981-83; former pres, Black Polit Task Force, 1982-83; Coastal Resources Adv Bd, 1983-; bd mem, Boston African-Am Nat Hist Site, Taxpayers Equity Alliance Mass, Roxbury YMCA, Boston Harbor Assocs; bd mem, Am Lung Asn, Boston, 1990-; bd mem, Amns Dem Action, 1991-; adv coun, Nat League Cities; pres, Nat Black Caucus Local Elected Officials, 1998-. **Honors/Awds:** Elected vpres, N Am Region Action Against Apartheid Community United Nations, 1984; Citizen of the Year, Omega Psi Phi, 1984; Meritorious Community Service Award, Kappa Alpha Psi, 1984; Passage Boston S Africa Divestment Legis City Coun, 1984. **Business Addr:** Councilman, Boston City Council, District 4, 1 City Hall Plz 5th Fl, Boston, MA 02201, **Business Phone:** (617)635-3131.

YANCEY, PRENTISS QUINCY
Lawyer. **Personal:** Born Aug 20, 1944, Atlanta, GA; son of Prentiss Q; divorced; children: Prentiss III, Cristian & Schuyler. **Educ:** Villanova Univ, BA, 1966; Emory Univ, JD, 1969. **Career:** Smith, Gambrell & Russell LLP, assoc, 1969-73, partner, 1973-94, Corp Sect, counsel, currently; Africom Telecommunications Ltd, pres & chief exec officer, 1994-98, dir, exec vpres & gen coun, 1998-2000. **Orgs:** Trustee, Clark Atlanta Univ, 1978-; Soc Int Bud Fels, 1986-; United Way Atlanta; Sears Found; Child Serv & Family Coun Serv; bd mem, Lovett Sch; Atlanta Ballet; Atlanta Chamber Com; Int Bus Coun; Gov Comn Higher Educ; dir, Southern Ctr Int Studies; Atlanta Charter Comn. **Military Serv:** AUS, lt, judge advocate gen corps, 1969-76. **Business Addr:** Counsel, Smith, Gambrell & Russell LLP, Corporate Section, 1230 Peachtree St NE Suite 3100, Atlanta, GA 30309, **Business Phone:** (404)815-3513.

YANCY, DR. DOROTHY COWSER
College president, educator, labor activist. **Personal:** Born Apr 18, 1944, Cherokee Cty, AL; daughter of Linnie Bell Covington and Howard; divorced; children: Yvonne. **Educ:** Johnson C Smith Univ, BA, History, 1964; Univ Mass, Amherst, MA 1965; Atlanta Univ, PhD, polit sci, 1978. **Career:** Albany State Col Albany, GA, instr, hist, 1965-67; Hampton Inst, Hampton VA, instr hist, 1967-69; Evanston Twp High Sch, teacher, 1969-71; Barat Col Lake Forest IL, dir black studies, 1971-72; Georgia Inst Tech, asst prof, 1972-78, assoc prof, 1978-88, prof, 1988-94; Johnson C Smith Univ, pres, 1994-2008. **Orgs:** Labor panel Am Arbitration Asn 1980; mediator, Mediation Res & Educ Proj, Northwestern Univ, 1988-; Arbitration Panel, Bd Regents State Univ Syst Fla & AFSCME, 1988-; chair women, Woman Power Comn, The Links, Inc,1990-94; bd trustees, Johnson C Smith Univ, 1991-94; Asn Study of Afro-Am Life & Hist; Indust Relations Res Asn; Soc Prof Dispute Resolutions; mem exec comt, Asn Soc & Behavioral Sci; So Pol Sci Asn; special master, Fla Pub Employees Relations Comn; bd mem, Asn Study of Afro-Am Life & History; Labor Arbitration Panel Fedn Mediation & Conciliation Serv; bd, Charlotte Coun; Charlotte Urban League; Metro Charlotte YMCA. **Honors/Awds:** Fulbright-Hayes Scholar, 1968; Distinguished Alumnus, Johnson C Smith Univ, 1981; People to People Delegation of Labor Experts, to Soviet Union & Europe, 1988, to London, Berlin, & Moscow, 1990; The Acad Polit & Social Sci Small Hural, Ulan Bator, Mongolia, lecturer and consultant, 1991; Nat Black Col Alumni Hall of Fame in Educ, inducted; named Black Issues of the 20th Century Educator; Lifetime Achievement Award, Asn of Social Change &Behavior Scientists; Maya Angelou Tribute to Achievement, UNCF; named Person of Prominance, Charlotte Post, 2000; Harold E Delaney Exemplary Educational Leadership Award, Am Asn Higher Educ, 2004; Old North State Award, State of North Carolina, 2005; Sisters Delany Honor Society Achievement Award, NC Women of Distinction, 2007; Horizon Award, Leadership Charlotte, 2007; William J Stanley Award, Ga Inst Technol, 2007; Women's History Hall of Fame, Nat Asn Negro Bus, 2008. **Special Achievements:** First female black president of Johnson C. Smith College; First female tobe elected President of the Central Intercollegiate Athletic Association;First African American to be promoted and tenured as a full professor at Georgia Tech. **Business Addr:** President, Johnson C Smith University, 100 Beatties Ford Rd, Charlotte, NC 28216, **Business Phone:** (704)378-1000.*

YANCY, EARL J
Executive. **Personal:** Children: 3. **Educ:** Southern Univ, BA, archit; Hoch Schule fur Bildende Kunste, advanced col study cert, 1970; Yale Univ, MCP, 1972; Harvard Univ, PhD, 1976. **Career:** Yale Univ, fac asst prof, 1972-75; Harvard Univ, grad sch design, Loeb fel, 1975; Yancy Minerals Inc, founder & pres, 1977-; Peak Electronics Inc, founder & pres, 1990-96; Yancy Van Clief Partners LLC, co-founder & managing dir, 1999-. **Orgs:** Dir, New Eng Minority Purchasing Coun, 1981; Young Pres? Orgn, 1986-93; World Pres? Orgn, 1993-; founder & chair, Black Young Pres? Orgn, 1994-; Beta Tau Boule Fraternal Group, 1998-; bd dirs, Ctr Bank; bd dirs, Middlesex Mutual Ins Co. **Honors/Awds:** Connecticut Business Person of the Year, Hartford Courant, 1989; Connecticut Minority Small Business Person of The Year, US Small Bus Admin. **Military Serv:** USMC, 1964-68. **Business Phone:** (203)397-5479.

YANCY, PROF. PRESTON MARTIN
Educator. **Personal:** Born Oct 18, 1938, Sylvester, GA; son of Preston Martin Yancy Sr and Margaret Elizabeth Robinson; married Marilyn Leonard; children: Robert James & Grace Elizabeth. **Educ:** Morehouse Col, BA, 1959; Univ Richmond, MH, 1968; Syracuse Univ, MSS, 1974, PhD, 1979. **Career:** Va Union Univ, prof, 1969, vpres acad affairs, 1994-97, Eng & Humanities, dept head, prof, currently; Richmond Free Press, columnist, 1992-94, 1997-2001. **Orgs:** Columnist, Richmond Afro-Am Newspaper, 1967-71, 1974-82; Asn Study Afro Am Life & Hist; Langston Hughes Soc, 1981-91. **Honors/Awds:** Doctoral Grants, Ford Found, 1973-75; Emory O Jackson Best Column Awards, 1975-78, 1980; Doctoral Grants, 1978-79, Post Doctoral Grants, 1981-84, United Negro Col Fund. **Special Achievements:** Author: The Afro-American Short Story: A Comprehensive, 1986. **Military Serv:** USAF, civilian supply clerk, 1959-61; US Dept Defense, civilian supply clerk, 1961-69. **Home Addr:** PO Box 25583, Richmond, VA 23260, **Home Phone:** (804)266-6168. **Business Addr:** Professor, Virginia Union University, Department of English and Humanities, 208 E Ellison Hall, Richmond, VA 23220-1711, **Business Phone:** (804)257-5757.

YANCY, DR. ROBERT JAMES
Educator. **Personal:** Born Mar 10, 1944, Tifton, GA; son of Preston Martin and Margaret Elizabeth Robinson; married Dorothy Cowser, Sep 8, 1967; children: Yvonne. **Educ:** Morehouse Col, Atlanta, GA, BA, 1964; Atlanta Univ, Atlanta, GA, MBA, 1967; Northwestern Univ, Evanston, IL, PhD, 1973. **Career:** Hampton Inst, Hampton, VA, asst prof, 1967-69; Atlanta Univ, Atlanta, GA, asst prof & assoc prof, 1971-82; Zebra Corp, Atlanta, GA, pres, 1972-82; W Ga Col Carrollton, GA, asst prof, 1982; Southern Tech Inst, Marietta, GA, prof, 1983-86; Southern Polytech State Univ, Marietta, GA, Sch Mgt, dean & prof, 1986-2000, prof, prof emer, currently. **Orgs:** Chairperson, Univ Syst Ga, Admin Comm Grad Work, 1990-91; chairperson, Univ Syst Ga, Acad Review Comm Bus Admin, Ft Valley State Col, 1989; chairperson, Annual Mem Campaign, Butler St YMCA, 1977; Leadership Cobb

Alumni asn; Leadership Atlanta Alumni asn; Soc Intl Business Fels; Acad Mgt; 100 Black Men Atlanta. **Honors/Awds:** Fed Govt Policy & Black Bus Enterprise-Ballinger, 1973; Black Georgian of The Year in Business, State Comm Hist Black Georgians, 1981; Living Legends In Black, Bi-Centennial Publ, Bailey Publ Co; Recipient of President Bush's Points of Light Award, 1988-91; Social Affairs Comm, 1989-90. **Business Addr:** Professor Emeritus, Southern Polytechnic State University, School of Management, 1100 S Marietta Pkwy, Marietta, GA 30060.

YANCYY, ROBERT
Entertainer, entrepreneur. **Personal:** Born Feb 13, 1971, St Thomas, VI; son of Keith and Lenora. **Educ:** Univ Mich, BMA, 1995. **Career:** CCS Inst Arts, teacher, 1996-98; Three y Entertainment, chief exec officer, currently. **Orgs:** Phi Mu Alpha, 1992. **Business Addr:** Chief Executive Officer, Three y Entertainment, 16203 Bentler, Detroit, MI 48219, **Business Phone:** (313)790-0924.

YARBORO, DR. THEODORE LEON
Physician. **Personal:** Born Feb 16, 1932, Rocky Mount, NC; married Deanna Marie Rose; children: Theodore L Jr, Deanna R & Theresa L. **Educ:** NC Cent Univ, BS, 1954, MS, 1956; Meharry Med Col, MD, 1963; Univ Pittsburgh Grad Sch Pub Health, MPH, 1979. **Career:** US Bureau Mines, chemist/anal & organic, 1956-59; Shenango Valley Campus Penn State Univ, lectr; Theodore L Yarboro MD Inc, family practitioner, 1965-. **Orgs:** Three publs J Organic Chem, J Chem, Eng Data, 1959-61; Nat Med Asn 1965-; Am Acad Family Physicians, 1965-; AMA, 1965-; mem/bd dirs Mercer Co Branch NAACP, 1965-; founder, Shenango Valley Urban League, 1968; bd dirs, Shenango Valley Urban League, 1968-78; founder/adv, Dr Maceo E Patterson Future Physician Soc, 1969-; charter diplo, Am Bd Family Pract, 1970-; charter fel, Am Acad Fam Pract, 1972-; mem bd trustees, Nat Urban League, 1973-78; Gov Adv Com on Multiple Health Screening, 1975-76; Gov's Com Health Educ, PA, 1975-76; life mem, NAACP, 1976-. **Honors/Awds:** Distinguished Service Award Midwestern PA Chap, Am Heart Asn, 1970 & 75; Distinguished Service Award, Shenango Valley Urban League, 1972; Man of the Year, Shenango Valley Jaycees, 1972; Community Service Award, Mercer Co Br, NAACP, 1976. **Military Serv:** USAF, airman 1/c, 1959. **Business Addr:** Family Practitioner, Theodore Leon Yarboro MD Incorporated, 755 Division St, Sharon, PA 16146, **Business Phone:** (724)346-4124.

YARBOROUGH, RICHARD A
Educator, writer. **Personal:** Born May 24, 1951, Philadelphia, PA; son of John W III and Yvonne K Newby; divorced. **Educ:** Mich State Univ, E Lansing, BA, 1973; Stanford Univ, PhD, 1980. **Career:** Stanford Univ, Whiting fel humanities, 1977-78; Univ Calif, Los Angeles, Dept Eng, asst prof, 1979-86, assoc prof, 1986-, African-Am Studies, fac res assoc, 1979-, dir, 1997-; Ford Found, postdoctoral fel, 1988-89. **Orgs:** Bd ed adv, Am Quarterly, 1987-91; nat coun, Am Studies Asn, 1988-91; mem ed bd, African Am Rev, 1989-; chair, Div Black Am Lit & Culture, Modern Lang Asn, 1989-90, exec comt; Calif Coun Humanities, 1992-96. **Honors/Awds:** US Presidential Scholar, 1969; Alumni Distinguished Scholars Award, Mich State Univ, 1969-73; Distinguished Teaching Award, Univ Calif, Los Angeles, 1987; Recognized as an Outstanding Faculty Member, African Stud Union, 1997. **Special Achievements:** Assoc gen editor, The Heath Anthology of American Literature, second ed, D C Heath, 1994, third ed, Houghton Mifflin, 1998; Published extensively on African American literature, & he is a literary historian who was one of the co-editors of the Norton Anthology of African American Literature. **Business Addr:** Associate Professor, University of California, Department of English, Humanities Bldg 201, Los Angeles, CA 90095-1530, **Business Phone:** (310)825-2914.

YARBRO, WILLIAM E., JR.
Business owner. **Career:** 95th & Columbus Prod, producer & co owner. **Business Addr:** Producer, Co Owner, 95th & Columbus Production Company, PO Box 2342, Venice, CA 90294-2342, **Business Phone:** (310)354-4002.

YARBROUGH, DELANO
School administrator. **Personal:** Born Sep 20, 1936, Thornton, AR; son of Roy and Sadie; married Samella O; children: Delano, Desiree & Darryl. **Educ:** Univ Ark Pine Bluff, BS; AZUSA Pacif Col, MA, 1973; Marquette Univ; Univ Calif Los Angeles; Univ San Francisco, doct; Pepperdine Univ, ABO. **Career:** School administrator (retired); E HS Lilbourn, teacher, 1961-63; US Navy, mathematician, 1963-65; Pasadena Unified Sch Dist, desegregation proj dir, 1967-77; Del Yarbrough & Assocs, consult, 1990; Eliot Middle Sch, prin, 1981-94. **Orgs:** Pres, Pasedena Branch, Nat Asn Advan Colored People, 2000; ASCD; CSCD; Am Polit Sci Asn; Phi Delta Kappa; Nat Asn Advan Colored People; Univ ArkPine Bluff Alumni Asn; Pasadena Educ Found; consult Afro-Am Educ Cult Ctr; consult Jet Propulsion Lab; vice chmn ESAA; Bd dir, Day One; BCDI; Calif State Math Framework Comt, 1984-86; pres & bd dir, Diversified Educ Serv, Inc, 1981. **Honors/Awds:** New Teacher of the Year Pasadena, 1964; Commendation in educ for serv rendered in reducing racial isolation; Pasadena & Altadena Branches; Nat Asn Advan Colored People, Community Serv Awards; Nat Parents of the Year Award, Tuskegee Univ, 1988; PTA Service Award, 1994; Commendation from Pres Clinton, 1995. **Military Serv:** USAF airman 1/c 1954-58. **Business Addr:** Pasadena, CA 91103.*

YARBROUGH, EARNEST. See Obituaries section.

YARBROUGH, KAREN
Government official, founder (originator), president (organization). **Educ:** Chicago State Univ, BA, bus admin; Northeastern Ill Univ, MA, inner city studies. **Career:** Hathaway Ins Agency, founder & pres; Maywood Chamber Com, pres, 8yrs; State Govt, state rep 7th dist, currently. **Orgs:** Bd mem, United Way Suburban Chicago; bd mem, Oak Park, YMCA; founder, Maywood's live theater; Maywood Youth Mentoring prog; supporter, various scholar progs. **Special Achievements:** Illinois House Joint Resolution 125, 2006. **Business Addr:** State Representative, Illinois, District 7, 292-S Stratton Off Bldg, Springfield, IL 62706, **Business Phone:** (217)782-8120.*

YARBROUGH, MAMIE LUELLA
Government official, real estate executive. **Personal:** Born Sep 19, 1941, Benton Harbor, MI; married Charles; children: Dawn Zoppi & Nyles Charles. **Educ:** Western Mich Univ, attended 1960. **Career:** NBD F&M Bank, banking, 1966-75; Berrien Homes Apts, housing mgr, 1975-81; River Terrace Apts, housing mgr, 1981-; Benton Harbor Area Sch Bd, vpres; Berrien County, Comnr, currently. **Orgs:** Bd mem, SW Mich Comn; bd mem, Mich Works Bd; vpres, Benton Harbor Libr Bd; Krasl Art Ctr Bd Directors; Scholarship Comt, New Territory Arts Asn; LoryAS Place Bd Dirs; CWCC Arts, Culture & Leisure Comt; Natural Sistas Literacy Soc. **Home Addr:** 1086 Monroe, Benton Harbor, MI 49022. **Business Addr:** Commissioner, Benton County, 701 Main St, St Joseph, MI 49085, **Business Phone:** (269)983-7111.

YARBROUGH, NANA CAMILLE
Educator, writer, singer. **Personal:** Born Jan 1, 1938?, Chicago, IL. **Career:** Dancer; City Col NY, prof African dance & diaspora; WWRL-AM, talk show host. **Honors/Awds:** 'Griot of the Year', Griot Society of NY, 1975; 'Woman of the Month, Essence', 1979; 'Coretta Scott King Award for Cornrows', 1979; 'Unity Award in Media', Lincoln Univ, 1982; 'Parents Choice Award for Summershine Queens', 1989. **Special Achievements:** Albums: The Iron Pot Cooker, 1975; Author: Cornrows (poems for children), 1979; The Shimmershine Queen (juvenile), 1989; Tamika & the Wisdom Rings (juvenile), 1994; Little Tree Growing in the Shade (juvenile), 1996. **Business Addr:** Actress, Poet, Activist, African American Traditions Workshop, 80 St Nicholas Ave Suite 4G, New York, NY 10026, **Business Phone:** (212)865-7460.*

YARBROUGH, PATRICIA NICHOLSON
Business owner. **Personal:** Born May 16, 1951, San Francisco, CA; daughter of Bernice; married Herbert, Jun 16, 1979; children: Kevin & Martin. **Educ:** Univ San Francisco, BA, 1973. **Career:** Blue World Travel, founder & pres, 1978-; Doris Easly Sch C, pres, currently. **Orgs:** UNCF, Our Festival Sea Prog. **Honors/Awds:** Best Travel Promotion, Travel Weekly, 1998; Top Producer Award, Royal Caribbean Cruise Line, 1994, 1995; Top 50 Producers, Travel Savers, 2000; Outstanding Support Award, Celebrity Cruise Lines, 1996. **Special Achievements:** Founded Festival at Sea African American Theme Cruises and Friends of Festival at Sea, African Americans Cruising the World. **Business Addr:** President, Blue World Travel, 50 First St Suite 411, San Francisco, CA 94105-2413, **Business Phone:** 800-466-2719.

YARBROUGH, ROBERT ELZY
Lawyer. **Personal:** Born Dec 16, 1929, Atlanta, GA. **Educ:** Boston Col, BSBA, 1951; Boston Univ, Law Sch, LLB 1958. **Career:** US Cust Serv, Dept Treas, sr impt specialist, 1975-; AUS & AUS Res, ret LTC FA, 1949-77; US Cust Serv, impt specialist, 1963-; atty law, 1961-; US Post Off, clerk, 1954-61; AUS, officer, 1951-54. **Orgs:** Bd trust, Boston Latin Sch Alumni Asn, 1980; Am Bar Asn; Mass Bar Asn; Prince Hall Grand Lodge F & AM, MA; Syria Temple No 31 AEAONMS. **Military Serv:** AUS, lt, 1949-77; Merit serv medal, AUS, 1977. **Business Addr:** Custom House, Boston, MA 02109.*

YARBROUGH, ROOSEVELT
Accountant. **Personal:** Born Jan 11, 1946, Pattison, MS. **Educ:** Chapman Col, attended 1968; Miss Valley State Univ, BS, 1973; John Marshall Law Sch, attended 1981; Am Mgt Asn Ctr, mgt develop cert, 1982. **Career:** Ernst & Ernst, staff acct, 1975; Bailey Meter Co, budget analyst, 1976; SW Miss Legal Serv, dir admin, 1982; First Entry Serv, acct; Claiborne City Sch, bd mem. **Orgs:** Claiborne City Bldg; Supvy & Curriculum Develop, Black Ed & Econ Proj; Nat Asn Advan Colored People; Miss Cult Arts Coalition; Claiborne City Family Reunion. **Military Serv:** USMC, cpr 3 yrs. **Home Addr:** 153 Pattison Tillman Rd, PO Box 141, Pattison, MS 39144, **Home Phone:** (601)437-4413. *

YARDE, PROF. RICHARD FOSTER
Educator, artist. **Personal:** Born Oct 29, 1939, Boston, MA; son of Edgar St Clair and Enid Foster; married Susan Donovan, Jul 8, 1967; children: Marcus & Owen. **Educ:** Boston Univ, BFA (cum laude), painting, 1962, MFA, painting, 1964. **Career:** Boston Univ, asst prof art, 1965-71; Wellesley Col, assoc prof art, 1971-76; Amherst Col, vis assoc prof, 1976-77; Mass Col Art, vis artist, 1977-79; Mt Holyoke Col, vis assoc prof art, 1980-81; Univ Mass, Boston, prof art, 1981-90; Mass Cult Coun, Mass Artist's fel, painting, 1985; Univ Mass, Amherst, prof art, 1990-. **Orgs:** Visual arts panelist, Mass Coun Art & Humanities, 1976-78; Acadian Nat Acad, 1984-; comn, Art-in-Architecture Prog Gen Serv Admin, Wash DC, 1989; bd overseers, Inst Contemp Art, Boston, Mass, 1991-. **Honors/Awds:** Blanche E Colman Award for Travel & Study in Nigeria, 1970; Arcadia Found Award for Painting, NY, 1975; fel Grant in Painting, Nat Endowment Arts, 1976; Childe Hassam Purchase, Am Acad Arts & Letters, NY, 1977, 1982, Academic Award, 1995; Henry W Ranger Fund Purchase, Nat Acad Design, NY, 1979, Adolph & Clara Obrig Prize, 1983; Chancellor's Award for Distinguished Scholar, Univ Mass, Boston, 1984, Distinguished Teaching Award, 1996-97, Samuel F Conti Faculty Fellowship Award, 2000; Alumni Award for Distinguished Contribution to the Arts, Boston Univ, 1987; Hon Doctor of Fine Arts, Mass Col Art, Boston, 1998; Commonwealth Award for Fine Art, 2002; honoree, Studio Mus Harlem, 2002; De Cordova Mus & Sculpture Park, 2003. **Special Achievements:** Paintings in Boston, 1950-2000, One person exhibit "Savoy" traveling to Studio Museum in Harlem, San Diego Museum, The Baltimore Museum, Studio Museum in Harlem, etc 1982-83, Galerie Tension Paris, 1986, Utah Museum of Arts, 1986, group exhibitions Metropolitan Museum of Art, Boston Museum of Fine Arts, Corcoran Gallery Washington DC, one person exhibits, Springfield Museum, 1987, Group, National Academy of Design, 1987, group exhibitions, Newport Art Museum, Newport, RI, 1990, "Mojo Hand," MA Coll of Art, Boston, Smith Coll Museum of Art, Northampton, MA, Studio Museum in Harlem, 1996-97, works on paper, New England Foundation for the Arts, Boston, MA, 1998, Smithsonian Inst; Anacostia Mus, 1999, New Museum of Contemporary Art, NY, 1999, group exhibitions, Spellman College Museum of Art, 2000, solo exhibitions, Ring Shout: An Installation Worchester Museum of Art, Worcester, MA, 2003; group exhibitions, Pulse, Art Healing and Transformation, Institute of Contemporary Art, Boston, MA, 2003, genetic expressions, Art After DWA, Heckscher Mus of Art, Huntington, NY, 2003. **Business Addr:** Professor of Art, University of Massachusetts, Department of Art, Architecture & Art History, Fine Arts Center E Clark Hall 151 Presidents Dr, OFC 1, Amherst, MA 01003-9330, **Business Phone:** (413)545-6972.

YARN, BARBARA LYNNE IVEY
Physician. **Personal:** Born in Knoxville, TN; daughter of Geraldine Celestine Harris and Boyd S (deceased); married Tyrone Von Yarn, 1963; children: Tiffany Nicole & Roan. **Educ:** Knoxville Col, BS, 1963; Univ Tenn, 1962-63; Univ Minn, MPH, 1969; Meharry Med Col, MD, 1973; Howard Univ Hosp, internship, 1974; Emory Univ Affiliated Hosps, anesthesiology residency, 1975-78; Univ Louis, anesthesiology fel, 1982-83. **Career:** Knoxville City Sch, sci teacher, 1963-64; Oak Ridge Nat Lab, res asst, 1964-67; Minn Head Start Prog, pub health educr & consult, 1968; Univ Minn Community Pub Health Care Ctr, stud health adv, 1968-69; Pub Health & Safety Admin, 1969; Greely Sch Dist Community Health Ctr, instr/pub health adv, 1969; Matthew Walker Health Care Ctr, 1972-73; Munich Military Hosp, physician, 1974-75; Grady Mem Hosp, anesthesiologist, 1975-78; US Pub Health Serv, sr surgeon, regional med consult; Dept Health & Human Serv, 1978-82; Cuban-Haitian Refugee Camp, chief med officer, 1981-82; Humana Hosp, Dept Anesthesiology & Dept Respiratory Therapy, chair & div head, 1982-91; Atlanta Outpatient Peachtree Dunwoody, anesthesiologist, 1991-; pvt pract, currently. **Orgs:** Am Med Asn; Nat Med Asn; Med Asn Ga; Knoxville Col Alumni Asn, 1963-; Alpha Kappa Alpha Sorority, Pi Alpha Omega chap; The Links, Buckhead Cascade City Chap, pres, 1995-01; Atlanta Symphony, bd dir, 1999-; Goodworks Int, co-sponsor, 1999-. **Honors/Awds:** Alpha Kappa Alpha Sorority, Acad Scholar Award, 1959-63; Pub Health Scholar Award, 1968-69; Jesse Smith Noyes Obstet & Gynec Fel, 1969-72; Sloan Found, Med Scholar Award, 1969-73; Univ Louis, Fel Anesthesiology, 1982-83; Pub Health Serv, Citation & Commendation Medal for Distinguished Serv, 1978-82; United States Pub Health Serv, Spec Assignment Ribbon Award, 1979; Habitat Humanity, Knoxville Chap, Plaque, 1992; Knoxville Col, Distinguished Alumnus Award, 1993; Int Yr of the Older Persons, 1999; selected one of 100 Most Powerful & Influential Women of Georgia, 2000. **Home Addr:** 111 Stonington Dr, Peachtree City, GA 30269. **Business Addr:** Physician, 1077 S Main St, Madison, GA 30650, **Business Phone:** (770)217-5111.

YATES, ANTHONY J.
Basketball coach, president (organization). **Personal:** Born Sep 15, 1937, Lawrenceburg, IN; married. **Educ:** Univ Cincinnati, BS, 1963. **Career:** Univ Ill, asst basketball coach, 1974-; Univ Cincinnati, asst basket ball coach, 1971-74; Cincin Royals Prof Basketball Team, part time scout, 1966-71; Fin Mgt Corp, salesman, 1968-71; Drake Mem Hosp, asst to admin, person, dir, 1966-68; Shillitos Dept Store, asst employ mgr, 1963-66; pres, TONY YATES CARING FOR KIDS FOUNDATION . **Orgs:** Nat Assn of Sec Deal; bd dir, Nat AAU Basktbl League; bd dir, Greater Cincin Jr Basketball Asn; former mem, Cincin Plan Parenthd; former mem, Cincin Sch Found; former mem, Baseball "Kid Gloves" game; former mem, Cincin Met AAU; Tom Shell Tony Yates TV Basketball Show WCPO TV, 1964; color caster, WKRC radio

broad of Univ of Cincin basketball games, 1970-71; sports banquet speaker, Coca Cola Btlg Co, 1963, 1964, 1965. **Special Achievements:** Univ of Cincin Basketball Team, NCAA Basketball Champ, 1961, 1962. **Military Serv:** USAF 1955-59.

YATES, LEROY LOUIS
Clergy. **Personal:** Born Dec 8, 1929, Terry, MS; son of Clarence and Mary Ella Summers (deceased); married Beverly Joanne Pannell, Dec 26, 1951; children: Sara Doreen, Jonathan Allen, Joyce Ellen, Mary Francis Coultman & LeRoy Louis Jr. **Educ:** Moody Bible Inst, Chicago, grad dipl, 1956; Chicago State Univ, BA, 1971, MS,1979; Detroit Bible Col, Hon Doctor Humanities, 1981. **Career:** Westlawn Gospel Chapel, Chicago, IL, sr pastor, 1957-; Hektoen Inst, Cook County Hosp, chief tech supvr, 1964-76; Chicago Medical Sch, microbiologist, 1968-79; Circle Youth Ranch, Bangor, MI, exec dir, 1978-80. **Orgs:** Exec bd mem, Leukemia Soc Am, 1961-80; exec bd mem, Int Mag Publ, 1967-80; draft bd mem, Local Bd 58, 1968-74; exec bd secy, PACE Inst, Cook County Jail Chicago, 1969-80; adv bd mem, Univ Ill Med Ctr, 1978-80; vol counr, Westside Hol Fam Ctr, 1978-80. **Military Serv:** AUS, sargent, 20 months; Korean Service Medal with 3 Bronze Camp Stars, Med Co 9th regiment, 1951; Unit Nat Serv Medal, Med Co 9th regiment, 1951; Combat Medal Badge, IOS Serv Bar, Med Co 9th regiment, 1051; Merit Serv Award, Ill selective Serv System, 1976. **Business Addr:** Senior Pastor, Westlawn Gospel Chapel, 2115 S St Louis, Chicago, IL 60623, **Business Phone:** (773)277-5482.

YATES, MARK
Vice president (Organization), banker, investment banker. **Personal:** Born Sep 15, 1966, Memphis, TN; son of Andres N and Mary F. **Educ:** Howard Univ, BA, 1988; Vanderbilt Univ, Owen Grad Sch Mgt, MBA, 1996. **Career:** First Tenn bank, vpres comm loan officer, 1989, sr vpres investor rels; US Rep Harold Ford Jr, chief staff; Morgan Keegan & Co, Memphis, investment banker; First Horizon Nat Corp, sr vpres, Financial Capital Mkt Div, sr vpres; Rice Financial Products Co, Memphis, managing dir, 2007-. **Orgs:** Howard Univ Alumni Asn, 1988-; bd mem, Boys Club, 1993-; keeper finance, Omega Psi Phi Frat, 1993-94. **Business Addr:** Managing Director, Rice Financial Products Company, 17 State St 40th Fl, New York, NY 10004, **Business Phone:** (212)908-9200.

YEARWOOD, DAVID MONROE, JR.
Executive. **Personal:** Born Nov 15, 1945; son of David M and Una U Holder; children: Edward, David III. **Educ:** Pace Univ, BBA, 1978; Keller Grad Sch Mgt, MBA, 1982, cert Human Resources, 1983. **Career:** Nat Broadcasting Co, NY, financial analyst, 1970-75, mgr budgets 1975-77; Nat Broadcasting Co, Chicago, mgr acct, 1977-80, dir finance & admin, 1980; WDRB-TV, Louisville, exec vpres, currently. **Orgs:** Leadership Louisville; Bingham Fels; Stage One; Louisville Sci Ctr; Hundred Black Men; Univ Louisville Int Servs Learning Prog. **Military Serv:** USN, Reserve petty officer 3rd, 1966-70.

YEARWOOD, REV. DR. KIRTLEY
Clergy. **Personal:** Born Oct 12, 1961, Barbados, West Indies. **Educ:** Tuskegee Inst, BS; Univ Okla; Univ Ark, Gen Theol Sem, MDiv; MD. **Career:** St Mary's, Wash, DC, rector; St Paul's, Wash, DC, 2004; Trinity Cathedral, Pittsburgh, PA, priest assoc; Grace Episcopal Church, vicar, 2007-. **Orgs:** Diocesan Comt Liturgy & Music. **Business Addr:** Vicar, Grace Episcopal Church, 98 Wentworth St, Charleston, SC 29401, **Business Phone:** (843)723-4575.

YEARY, JAMES E., SR.
Educator. **Personal:** Born Jul 7, 1917, Harrogate, TN; married Kathelene Toney; children: Glenna, Aaron, James, Jr, Brenda. **Educ:** Morristown Jr Col, 1941; Tenn State Univ, BS, 1954; Tuskegee Inst, MSEd, 1960. **Career:** Elem Sch Teaching, 1941-46; Burt High Sch, Clarksville, teacher, 1956-64; Edison High Sch, Gary, teacher, 1964-71; Knoxville Col, asst prof consult, 1969-72; Knoxville City Schs, teacher math dept chmn; Greenwood Annex Jr High Clarksville, prin. **Orgs:** St James Mason Lodge; Gen Elec fel, 1957; NSF, Austin Peay State Univ, 1962-63; Fisk Univ, 1959; Tenn State Univ, 1960; Ill Inst Tech, 1966; Univ Ill, 1968-69. **Honors/Awds:** Nat Sci Hon Soc Beta Kappa Chi; Nat Sci Acad Yr Inst 1959. **Special Achievements:** Author "War Inside"; column INFO weekly, 1968-69. **Military Serv:** AUS, 1942-45.

YELDELL, JOSEPH P.
Government official. **Personal:** Born Sep 9, 1932, Washington, DC; married Gladys Johnson; children: Gayle & Joi Lynn. **Educ:** DC Teacher Col, BS, math, 1957; Univ Pittsburgh, MEd, sec admin, 1961. **Career:** Government official (retired); Pgh Pub Sch, teacher, 1958-61; DC Pub Sch, teacher, 1961-62; Bureau Labor Stat, math stat, 1962-64; IBM Corp, mkt rep, 1964-70; DC City Coun, councilman, 1967-71; City WA DC, Dept Hum Res, dir, 1971-77, gen asst mayor, 1977-78; Automated Mgt Info Sys special asst city adm, 1979-83; Office Emergency Preparedness, dir, 1983-90; JPY Assoc Inc, pres, 1990-93; City WA DC, Human Res Develop, asst city admin & dir 1993-94; Dept Employ Serv, act dir & dir, 1993-96. **Orgs:** Nat Forum Black Pub Admin; Prince Hall Masons; Phi Beta Sigma Fraternity Inc; Nat Assn Advan Colored People; Nat Urban League; brd trustees, DC Pub Library; brd trustees, Wash Ctr Metrop Studies; brd of dirs, Reconstruction& Develop Corp; DC Comn Acad Facil; Sci Adv Comt, Wash Tech Inst; Pres Coun, Howard Univ; Pres Coun, Federal City Col; brd dirs, Wash Urban Coaltion; DC Pub Sch; Bi centennial Com; DC Citizens Better Pub Educ; brd mgrs, DC Cong PTAs; Am Soc Pub Admin; Natl Emergency Mgrs Assn; Natl Educ Assn; Am Academy Polit & Social Sci. **Honors/Awds:** Comm Service Award, Dupont Pk Civic Assn, 1972; Outstanding Award Fed Civic Assn, 1970; Distinguished service Award, Womens Dem Club, 1970; civil Service of Year Award, Nat AMVETS, 1975; listed Family, Blacks Ebony mag; Public Admin of the Year, Natl Forum Black Pub Admin, 1989. **Military Serv:** USAF, 1954-58. **Home Addr:** 1729 Verbena St NW, Washington, DC 20012.

YELDING, ERIC GIRARD
Baseball player. **Personal:** Born Feb 22, 1965, Montrose, AL. **Career:** Baseball player (retired), coach; Houston Astros, shortstop, 1989-92; Cincinnati Reds, shortstop, 1992; Chicago Cubs, shortstop, 1993; Fort Bend Texans, coach, currently.

YELITY, STEPHEN C
Executive. **Personal:** Born Oct 25, 1949, Littleton, NC; son of Stephen Jackson Yelity and Martha Ella Pitchford Yelity; married Matlyn Joyce Alston, Apr 22, 1973; children: Scott. **Educ:** Norfolk State Univ, Norfolk VA, BS, 1973. **Career:** Am Cynamid, Wayne NJ, acct, 1973-76; Johnson & Johnson, Chicapee & New Brunswick, sr acct & financial analyst, 1976-79; Johnson & Johnson Baby Products, Skillman NJ, acct mgr, 1979-84; Accurate Info Systs, S Plainfield NJ, pres & chief exec officer, 1984-; Creative Business Develop LLC, sr consult, currently. **Orgs:** NY/NJ Minority Purchasing Coun, 1986-; Black Data Processing Asn, 1987-; Int Network Unix Syst Uses, 1988-; Chamber Com, 1988-; NJ Brain Trust, 1989-; Nat Urban League, 1989-; Nat Asn Advan Colored People, 1989-. **Honors/Awds:** Minority Small Business Man of Year, Small Business Admin, 1987; Appreciation Award, Bell Commun Res, 1988; Appreciation Award, AT&T, 1988; Sponsor of Year, Black Date Processing Assoc, 1988/1990; Entrepreneur of the Year, YMCA, 1989. **Special Achievements:** Representative of minority small business in NJ for Grand Jury testimony concerning public opinion of Public Law 99-661, 1988; nominee for SBA Region II Man of Year, 1989; among top 100 black businesspersons recognized, Black Enterprise, 1989 & 1990; featured in Time magazine article on black executives, "Doing It for Themselves," June 1989. **Business Phone:** (973)257-9290.

YERBY, TAMI
Executive. **Career:** City Petersburg Blandford, dir park & leisure servs, currently. *

YERGAN, ERIC
Stockbroker. **Personal:** Born in Long Island, NY. **Educ:** Marist Col, Poughkeepsie, NY, BA; Harvard Bus Sch, MBA. **Career:** A G Becker, salesman; Paine Webber Group Inc, first vpres, sr vpres; The Yergan Agency, pres, currently. **Orgs:** Manhattan Chamber Com; CoachCougar Soccer Club. **Honors/Awds:** National Conference Award, Honor Ring. **Special Achievements:** One of 25 "Hottest Blacks on Wall Street" listed in Black Enterprise, October, 1992. **Business Phone:** (212)831-3100.*

YERGER, BEN
School administrator. **Personal:** Born Dec 8, 1931, Hope, AK; married Charlene A; children: Valerie B & Benjamin Jr. **Educ:** Philander Smith Col, BS, 1951; San Fran Univ, MA, 1969; Univ Calif, PhD, 1975. **Career:** Pub Sch Far West Educ Lab, sci educ res, 1955-68; Merritt & Col, admin asst pres, 1968-71; Grove St Col, pres, 1971; Merritt & Vista Col, dir comm serv, 1972-78; Vista Col, dean stud serv. **Orgs:** Bd dir, Berkeley Area Comn Found; vpres, Res Develop Ctr Soc Redes; chmn, Youth Employ Coun Berkeley, Calif; chapter mem, Asn Calif Comn Col Admin; Congregational Christian Church Coun Soc Action; CCJCA; NASPA; Am Asn Health Educ; Asn Advan Educ Res; NCCSCE; Alpha Kappa Mu Hon Soc; Phil Smith Col, 1949-50; Beta Kappa Chi Sci Hon Soc Phil Smith Col, 1949-50; Alpha Phi Alpha & Cum Laude Phil Smith Col, 1949-50. **Honors/Awds:** Outstanding educator in America higher education award, 1971; outstanding dissert award, Inst Res Plan Comn Calif Asn Community & Jr Col, 1976-77. **Military Serv:** AUS, 1956.

YIZAR, JAMES HORACE
Educator, school administrator. **Personal:** Born Aug 27, 1957, Los Angeles, CA; son of James H and Gladys Yizar. **Educ:** Idaho State Univ, BA, 1983, Master Coun, 1990. **Career:** Campbell Comm Therapy Ctr, recreation coordr, 1981-82; Upward Bound, asst dir, 1982-84; Idaho State Univ Student Support Serv, coordr, 1984-90, counr, learning supt, asst trio dir, 1990-94, trio dir, 1994-2000, asst dean, trio dir, 2000-; Idaho State Spec Olympics, game coordr, 1992-93. **Orgs:** Kappa Alpha Psi, 1977-; adv, Epsilon Theta Chap, 1984-; adv, Black Stud Alliance, 1984-86; bd dirs, Access Idaho, 1985-97, bd pres, 1988-92; NAACP, 1986-, local br pres, 1994-98; Phi Kappa Phi, 2000-; Rotary Club mem, 2001-; Kappa Delta Pi, 2002-. **Honors/Awds:** Outstanding Volunteer Access, Idaho Prog, 1986; Outstanding Speaker, Martin Luther King Day McCamon Sch Dist, 1986; Kappa Alpha Psi Western Province Chapter Advisor of the Year, 1997, 1998; KAP small chapter advisor of the year, 1999-00. **Business Addr:** TRiO Director, Idaho State University, TRiO Student Services, Museum Bldg Rm 312 921 S 8th Ave, Stop 8345, Pocatello, ID 83209-8345, **Business Phone:** (208)282-3242.

YO, YO (YOLANDA WHITAKER)
Actor, rap musician. **Personal:** Born Aug 4, 1971, Los Angeles, CA. **Career:** Rap musician & rec artist, 1990-; Tv: New York Undercover, 1995; Martin, 1993-95; Trials of Life, 1997; Films: 3 Strikes, 2000; Grand Theft Auto: San Andreas, 2004; Da Jammies, 2006; Waist Deep, 2006; Albums: Make Way for the Motherlode, 1991; Black Pearl. **Orgs:** Founder, Intelligent Black Woman's Coalition. **Business Addr:** Rap Singer, c/o E W Rec Am, 75 Rockefeller Plz Frnt, New York, NY 10019, **Business Phone:** (212)275-2500.

YOBA, ABDUL-MALIK KASHIE. See YOBA, MALIK.

YOBA, MALIK (ABDUL-MALIK KASHIE YOBA)
Actor, singer. **Personal:** Born Sep 17, 1967, Bronx, NY; son of Abdullah and Mahmoudah Lanier. **Educ:** HB Studio New York. **Career:** Films: Cool Runnings, 1993; Smoke, 1995; Blue in the Face, 1995; Copland, 1997; Ride, 1998; Harlem Aria, 1999; Oh Happy Day, 2004; Arrested Development, 2004; Oh Happy Day, 2004; The Days, 2004; Criminal, 2004; Kids in America, 2005; Slur, 2005; Girlfriends, 2005; Checkin' Out, 2006; They're Just My Friends, 2006; Why Did I Get Married?, 2007; Feel the Noise, 2007; Rockaway, 2007; TV appearances: "Law & Order,", 1994; "Where I Live"; "That's So Raven", 2006; "Thief", 2006; "Raines", 2007; CityKids Found, vpres, 1988-93; Nature Boy Enterprises, pres & chief exec officer, 1994-; Universal TV series, actor, "New York Undercover," 1994; TNT series, actor, "Bull", "Thief", 2005. **Orgs:** Bd mem, REACH, 1992-; adv, vpres, The CityKids Found, 1993; Childrens Peace Mem, 1994; comm mem, Hale House, 1995; Phi Beta Sigma Fraternity Inc. **Honors/Awds:** Image Award, 1996, 1997, 1998. **Special Achievements:** Co-musical dir, Emmy-Nominated tv show, "CityKids," 1992; Co-star, "New York Undercover," first television dramatic series starring actors of color during prime-time, 1994; Noted as one of 30 young artists under 30 who will change Am cult in the next 30 yrs, NY Times Mag, 1994; Creator, youth self-esteem prog, "Why are you on this Planet?" 1994.

YOHANNES, DANIEL W
Banker. **Personal:** Born in Ethiopia; married Saron; children: Tsedeye, Michael & Rebecca. **Educ:** Claremont McKenna Col, BS, econ; Pepperdine Univ, MBA. **Career:** US Bank, vice chmn; Colorado Nat Bank, pres & ceo; M&R Investments LLC, pres & ceo, currently. **Orgs:** Bd mem, Nat Jewish Med & Res Ctr, 1995, bd dir, currently; Denver Art Mus; Univ Med Sch; Proj CURE; former mem, Nat Bd Smithsonian Inst; former mem, Media One Group Inc. **Business Addr:** Board of Directors, National Jewish Medical and Research Center, 1400 Jackson St, Denver, CO 80206, **Business Phone:** (303)388-4461.

YORK, DR. RUSSEL HAROLD
Physician. **Personal:** Born May 6, 1952, Chicago, IL; married Yvonne Taylor; children: Damion, Renee & Marucs. **Educ:** Kalamazoo Col, BA, 1974; Howard Univ, MD, 1978. **Career:** Henry Ford Hosp, intern, resident, 1978-81; Wayne State Univ, fac mem, instr, 1984-86; pvt practice, 1986-. **Orgs:** Am Rheumatism Asn, 1986-, Mich Rheumatism Soc; assoc mem, Am Col Physicians. **Honors/Awds:** Dipl Am Bd Internal Med, 1982, Am Bd Rheumatology 1984; 'Minority Faculty Researh Award', Wayne State Univ, 1984-85, 1985-86; rheumatology fel, Wayne State Univ, 1982-84. **Home Addr:** 19625 Renfrew Rd, Detroit, MI 48221, **Home Phone:** (313)341-7009. **Business Phone:** (313)982-8330.

YORK, VINCENT
Musician, jazz musician. **Personal:** Born Jun 25, 1952, Jacksonville, FL; son of George and Lillie Evans; married Kathleen; children: Natasha & Cedric. **Educ:** Southern Univ, BA, 1974; Univ Mich, MA, 1976. **Career:** Vincent York's NY Force, founder, saxophonist, 1977-; Albums: Blending Forces, 1990; Ann Arbor Community High Sch, artist-in-residence, 1996-2000; Focusing the Vision, 1998; Vincent York's Jazzistry, founder, perfomer, 1999-. **Orgs:** Ann Arbor Fed Musicians; Detroit Fed Musicians; Am Fed Musicians. **Honors/Awds:** Best Soloist, Souther Univ; Outstanding Musician, Nat Educ Asn; Best Album, Metro Times, 1990. **Special Achievements:** Southern Universitys first jazz studies major. **Business Addr:** Founder, Performer, Vincent York's Jazzistry, 730 Miller Ave, PO Box 7146, Ann Arbor, MI 48103, **Business Phone:** (734)761-6024.

YOUNG, AHMEENAH
Executive. **Career:** Tourism & hospitality indust, Sr exec; Pa Convention Ctr Authority, pres & ceo, 2008; Philadelphia's Independence Visitor Ctr, gen mgr; Corp Diversity SearchWide, LLC, vpres; Sr vpres Sales & Mkt, Affirmative Action, dir; Sales & Marketing; Temple Univ, dir & vpres; Sch Tourism & Hospitality Mgt, currently. *

YOUNG, ALAN C (ALAN CLARE YOUNG)
Certified public accountant. **Personal:** Born Jan 16, 1953, Inkster, MI; son of Anderson and Sarah; married Colette Brooks, May 1,

1982; children: Aaron C, Adam C & Austen C. **Educ:** Mich State Univ, BA, 1976; Walsh Col, Masters Tax, 1985. **Career:** Deloitte Haskins & Sells, sr consult, 1977-81; Deloitte & Touche, sr consult, 1977-81; Keith Warlick & Co, mgr, 1981-83; Alan C Young & Assoc PC, pres, ceo, managing dir, 1983-; Fisher BodyOCoLivonia & Gen Motors Assembly Div, supvr acct. **Orgs:** Vpres, alumni founder, 1972-, Kappa Alpha Psi Fraternity; pres, Nat Asn Black Acct; Detroit Econ Club, 1990-; exec comm, Detroit Chamber Com, treas, bd dir, 1992-; pres, Booker T Wash Bus Asn, 1992-94, chmn bd, 1995-; adv, Fed Res Bd Chicago, 1999; Mich State Bd Acct, 2000-; bd dir, First Independence Bank; trustee bd, Henry Ford Hosp. **Honors/Awds:** Corp Achievement Award, Nat Asn Black Acct, 1987. **Special Achievements:** Frequent interviewee on tax matters, WDIV-TV News, Detroit News; one of Detroit's five emerging Black leaders, Greater Detroit Chamber Com, Detroiter Mag, 1993. **Home Addr:** 4253 Old Dominion Dr, West Bloomfield, MI 48323, **Home Phone:** (313)683-2865. **Business Addr:** Managing Director, President & CEO, Alan C Young & Assocs P.C, 2990 W Grand Blvd Suite 310, Detroit, MI 48202-3041, **Business Phone:** (313)873-7500.

YOUNG, ALAN CLARE. See YOUNG, ALAN C.

YOUNG, ALAN JOHN
Automotive executive. **Personal:** Born May 25, 1945, Chicago, IL; son of John M Young and Marion E Bradley Campbell; divorced; children: Jeffrey, Kimberly & Christopher. **Educ:** Univ Ill, BS, mkt, 1968. **Career:** AY Shell Serv Sta, owner, 1969-77; GM Dealer Develop Acad, trainee, 1977-79; Alan Young Pontiac Buick GMC, owner & pres, 1979-. **Orgs:** Bd mem, NE Motor Vehicle Licensing bd; Lincoln Found; Univ NE Found. **Honors/Awds:** Auto Dealer of the Year, Black Enterprise, 1993. **Business Addr:** Owner, President, Alan Young Pontiac Buick GMC, 7724 NE Loop 820, North Richland Hills, TX 76180, **Business Phone:** 877-554-8002.

YOUNG, ALBERT JAMES
Writer, publisher. **Personal:** Born May 31, 1939, Ocean Springs, MS; married Arlin. **Educ:** Univ Mich, attended 1961; Univ Calif, BA, spanish, 1969. **Career:** Loveletter, founder & ed, 1966-68; Wallace Stegner Writing fel, 1966; Nat Endowment Arts fel, 1968, 1969, 1975; Stanford Univ, Edward H Jones lecturer creative writing, 1969-76; Yardbird Publ Inc, ed, 1970-76; Laser Films, screenwriter, 1972; Stigwood Corp, screenwriter, 1972; Guggenheim fel, 1974; Nat Endowment Arts fel Creative Writing, 1974; Yardbird Wing Ed, co-publ, co-ed, 1975-; Verdon Prod, screenwriter, 1976; First Artists prod, screenwriter, 1976-77; Yardbird Lives, co-ed, 1978; Universal Studios, freelance writer, book publ & screenwriter, 1979-; Quilt, co-ed, 1980; Books: Dancing, 1969; Snakes, 1970; The Song Turning Back Into Itself, 1971; Who Is Angelina?, 1975; Geography of the Near Past, 1976; Sitting Pretty, 1976; Ask Me Now book, 1980; Bodies and Soul: Musical Memoirs, 1981. **Orgs:** E Bay Negro Hist Soc; Authors Guild; Authors League; Writers Guild Am; San Francisco Press Club. **Honors/Awds:** National Arts Council Awards, 1968-70; Joseph Henry Jackson Award, San Francisco Found, 1969; California Association of Teachers of English Special Award, 1973; Pushcart Prize, 1980; Before Columbus Foundation Award, 1982.

YOUNG, ALENE MARIE (PENNY)
Writer. **Personal:** Born Nov 18, 1952, Tuskegee, AL; daughter of Pleze and Laurae; divorced; children: Andre L Brooks. **Educ:** SF City Col, attended. **Career:** American Poultry, 1970; Pacific Bell Yellow Pages, administrative asst, 1970-2001; freelance writer, currently. **Honors/Awds:** Editors Choice Award, InterNat Library of Poetry, 1999-02. **Special Achievements:** Author: Survival The Will and the Way, 1999; Penny For Your Thoughts, volume one, 1999-02; Penny For Your Thoughts, volumes one and two, 2001. **Business Addr:** Author/Owner, The Will and the Way Pub Co, PO Box 347068, San Francisco, CA 94134-7075.

YOUNG, PROF. ALFRED
Educator, writer. **Personal:** Born Feb 21, 1946, New Orleans, LA; son of Mattie Rayno Young and Landry Young Sr; married Angela Marie Broussard, Aug 31, 1969; children: Tomara, Marcus, Malcolm & Miles Thurgood. **Educ:** La State Univ, New Orleans, LA, BA, 1970; Syracuse Univ, MA, 1972, PhD, 1977. **Career:** History & AFA Studies, vis prof, 1995-97; Syracuse Univ, lectr, Afro-Am studies, 1971, instr, hist, 1971-72, asst prof hist, 1972-82, assoc prof, hist, 1982-88; State Univ NY, Oswego; Colgate Univ, Hamilton, NY, A Lindsay O'Connor Chair, 1988-89; Georgia Southern Univ, assoc prof, hist, 1989-94, prof hist, 1994-, dir, African Studies prog, 1991. **Orgs:** Keeper finance, 1980-85, chap hist, 1988-89, Omega Psi Phi Frat Inc Chi Pi chapter; adjunct prof hist, Syracuse Univ & Univ College Auburn Correctional Facil prog, 1981-89; consult, fac adv, Nat Model OA Univ, Howard Univ, 1982-; bd mem, Friends of Syracuse Univ, Alumni Orgn, 1987-; bd, Nat Coun for Black Studies, 1992-; Acad Coun Univ Syst GEO Regents' Global Ctr, 1992-. **Honors/Awds:** Afro-Am Fellowship, Syracuse Univ 1970-72; National Fellow Fund Fellowship, 1975-76, 1976-77; Summer research grant, NY State Afro-Am Inst, 1987; certificate of appreciation, Howard Univ Model OA Univ, 1989; Certificate of Outstanding Service Award, The Nat Coun Black Studies Inc, 1994-96. **Special Achievements:** Contributor to Historical Dictionary of Civil Rights in the United States, 1992; Contributing Editor, African Home front; "Internationalizing the Curriculum: Africa and the Caribbean," Int Studies Asn Conference, Acapulco, Mexico, 1993; "Dr, Carter G Woodson's Legacy of Academic Excellence & Social Responsibility," "The African-American Response to Post-Reconstruction Conditions in the South, Birmingham, Alabama, February, 1993; Publisher of books and articles; Co-Author: Africana Studies: Past Present and Future. **Military Serv:** USN yeoman 3rd class 1965-67. **Home Addr:** 104 Merman Dr, DeWitt, NY 13214. **Business Addr:** Professor, Georgia Southern University, Department History, 1143 Forest Bldg, PO Box 8054, Statesboro, GA 30460-8054, **Business Phone:** (912)478-5835.

YOUNG, ANDRE RAMELLE. See DRE.

YOUNG, ANDREW
Association executive, mayor, chairperson. **Personal:** Born Mar 12, 1932, New Orleans, LA; son of Andrews J and Daisy Fuller; married Jean Childs, Jan 1, 1955 (died 1994); children: Andrea, Lisa, Paula & Andrew III; married Carolyn Watson, Jan 1, 1996. **Educ:** Howard Univ, BS, 1951; Hartford Theol Sem, BDiv, 1955. **Career:** United Church of Christ, pastor, 1955-57; Nat Coun Churches, assoc dir youth work, 1957-61; United Church Christ Christian Educ Prog, adminr,1961-64; Southern Christian Leadership Conf, staff mem, 1961-70; US House Rep, mem, 1972-76; United Nations, US ambassador, 1977-79; City Atlanta,mayor, 1982-90; Metro Atlanta Chamber Com, chmn, 1996; Atlanta Comn Olympic Games, co-chmn, currently; Law Int Inc, chmn, currently; Nat Coun Churches, NY, pres, currently. **Orgs:** Bd mem, Freedom House; co-chair, Good Works Int; dir, Drum Major Inst;Alpha Phi Alpha; Alpha Kappa Alpha. **Honors/Awds:** Pax-Christi Award, St John's Univ, 1970; Spingarn Medal; Presidential Medal of Freedom, 1981; Peace & Justice Award, Alpha Kappa Alpha, 1991; ROBIE Award, 1998; received numerous hon degrees chair, Southern Africa Enterprise Develop Fund. **Special Achievements:** First Black Congressman from Georgia since Jefferson Long; United States First African-American Ambassador to the United Nations. **Business Phone:** (404)396-8000.

YOUNG, ANGELA LYNN
Government official, consultant, founder (originator). **Personal:** Born Dec 1, 1968, Buffalo, NY; daughter of Charles and Carrie Phillips. **Educ:** Dillard Univ, BA, communs. **Career:** A Weight Life, consult & founder, 1994-; City New Orleans, communs & spec event coord, 1994-. **Orgs:** City New Orleans Gumbo Holiday Com, 1994-; Fr Quartee Festivals, 1995-; coord pub rels, Women Excellence, 1996-; dir pub rels, Full Gospel Baptist Church Fel, 1996-. **Honors/Awds:** Future Leader of Tomorrow, Johnson Publ Co, 1995. **Business Addr:** Communications, Special Events Chief Operating Officerrdinator, City of New Orleans Mayor, 1300 Perdido St Suite 2E10, New Orleans, LA 70112.

YOUNG, ARLENE H
Executive. **Personal:** Born in Orangeburg, SC; daughter of Louis Hanton and Nina Seaberry Hanton; married Eddie L, Dec 13, 1969; children: Eddie, Christopher & Patrick. **Educ:** Bennett Col, BS, 1968; St Joseph's Sch Med Tech, MT Cert, 1969; Oakland Col, ARDMS, 1983; Cent Mich Univ, MSA, 1989. **Career:** Georgetown Univ hosp, Med technologist, 1969; Walter Reed Army Med Ctr, Med technologist, 1971; Midwest Med Clin, diagnostic Med sonographer, 1983; Hanton Industries Inc, pres, 1984-. **Orgs:** Delta Sigma Theta, 1968-; Arts & Letters Comm, 1992-94; Michigan State Coun, Delta Sigma Theta, sec, 1992-94; Southfield Alumnae Chapter, immediate past pres & treas, 1990-94; Jack & Jill Oakland County Michigan Chapter, vpres, 1992-93; Nat Coun of Negro Women, 1986; Nat Asn of Women Bus Owners, 1987; Nat Asn for Female execs, 1992. **Honors/Awds:** State of Michigan, Top Forty Women Bus Owners, 1989; Negro Bus & Prof Women's Clubs Inc, Successful Entrepreneurs, 1989; State of Michigan, Top Fifty Women Business Owners, 1988; Cub Scout Pack 1676, Cubmaster, 1986. **Business Phone:** (313)272-7717.

YOUNG, ARTEE
Educator, college teacher. **Educ:** Southern Univ, BA, speech & theater, 1967; Eastern Mich Univ, MA, c theater, 1970; Univ Puget Sound Sch Law, JD, 1987; Univ Mich, PhD, speech commun & theater. **Career:** Wash State Supreme Ct, judicial clerk; US Forest Serv, consult; Southern Univ; Ind Univ; Univ Wash; Evergreen State Col, prof law & lit, currently. **Orgs:** Nat Ctr Minority Health & Health Disparities; NIH; Western Instnl Rev Bd; pres, St Edward Parish Coun; vol, Nat Asn Advan Colored People Acad Cult Technol Sci Olympics Youth. **Business Addr:** Professor, Evergreen State College, Tacoma Campus, 1210 6th Avenue, Tacoma, WA 98405, **Business Phone:** (360)867-3026.*

YOUNG, B ASHLEY
Journalist. **Personal:** Born in Danville, IL; daughter of Will Roy Smith and Annette Lewis Alexander; married G Steven, Aug 6, 1978; children: Jessica M. **Educ:** Ky State Univ, BA, journ, 1980; Cincinnati Bible Col & Sem, working towards master's degree in theol. **Career:** Am Cong Gov Ind Hyg, Cincinnati, OH, copy ed, 1986-87; Cincinnati, OH, freelance, 1990-; J News, Hamilton, OH, reporter & copy ed, 1988-. **Orgs:** Nat Asn Black Journ; Ohio Newspaper Women's Asn; Ohio Prof Writers. **Honors/Awds:** 'Journalism Award', Ohio Vet Med Asn, 1989. **Home Addr:** 707 Cloverdale Ave, Cincinnati, OH 45246. **Business Addr:** Journalist, Editorial, J News, 228 Ct St, Hamilton, OH 45011, **Business Phone:** (513)863-8200.

YOUNG, DR. BARBARA J.
Educator, college teacher. **Personal:** Born Nov 2, 1937, Muskogee, OK; daughter of Alonzo Dossett and Idessa Hammond Dossett; married Douglas Charles Jr; children: Crystal Marion Humphrey, Hammond George Bouldin & Danielle Humphrey. **Educ:** Calif State Univ, Sacramento, BA, psychol, 1977, MS, counsel, 1981, admin,1988. **Career:** Fresno State Univ, sec, 1967-69; Calif State Univ, Sacramento, exec asst pres, 1969-74, employ counr, 1974-77, financial aid officer, 1977-83, student affairs officer, asst dir, sch rels, 1983-86, asst adj prof, asst dean, 1986-90, assoc dean, acad affairs, Alumni Rels & Community Rels, Div Univ Advan, dir, Sch Bus & Pub Admin, univ adj prof, fac mem; Young Enterprises, chief exec officer & pres, 1983; CSU African American Initiative, consultant. **Orgs:** Sacramento Urban League, 1970-; WASFA, 1977-; Black Prof Asn; SPAC; Delta Sigma Theta Sorority, Nu Lambda Chap, 1977-; PACROW; Lambda Kappa Mu Sorority, basileus, 1990; bd mem, CAL-SOAP Adv Bd, 1991-; bd mem, Calif Respiratory Care, 1993; Leadership Calif, partic, 1994; pres, Pan African Doctoral Scholars Inc; United Way, Harbor City; bd mem, Nat Bd Respiratory Care; bd mem, Leadership Am, 1997. **Honors/Awds:** Nat Soror of the Year, Lambda Kappa Mu Sorority, 1996. **Home Addr:** 22640 Blue Teal Dr, Canyon Lake, CA 92587-6908. **Business Addr:** Chief Executive Officer, President, Young Enterprise, Peterley House Peterley Rd, Oxford OX4 2TZ, United Kingdom.

YOUNG, BRYANT COLBY
Football player. **Personal:** Born Jan 27, 1972, Chicago Heights, IL; married Kristin; children: Kai Marin. **Educ:** Univ Notre Dame, mktg. **Career:** Football player (retired); San Francisco 49ers, defensive tackle, 1994-2007; grad Asst, Univ Toledo, Notre Dame, 2009. **Honors/Awds:** Defensive Rookie of the Year, United Press Int, Nat Football League, 1994; Len Eshmont Award, 1996, 1998; Comeback Player of the Year, Nat Football League, 1999. **Special Achievements:** Holding one Super Bowl ring.

YOUNG, DR. CARLENE HERB
Psychologist, educator. **Personal:** Born in Selma, AL; divorced; children: Howard & Loren. **Educ:** Univ Detroit, MA, 1960; Wayne State Univ, Detroit, EdD 1967; Wright Inst Berkeley, CA, PhD, 1976. **Career:** Detroit Pub Sch, teacher, 1955-67; Univ Detroit, lectr, physiol dept,1966-69; Wayne State Univ, lectr, physiol dept, 1966-69; Natl Teacher Corp,team leader, 1966-67; Title III Lincoln Child Devel Ctr, proj dir, 1967; Oakland Co Community Col, dept chmn soc, 1968; San Jose State Univ, prof African Am Studies, 1969-92, prof emer, 1992-; San Jose Police Dept, consult, Law Enforcement Psychol Serv, psychol, 1985-97; mediator, 1998-; Carlene Young & Assoc, clin psychologist & forensic, currently; Mediation Consult, founder, currently. **Orgs:** Brd, Cath Social Serv, 1976-87; exec secy & chmn, Nat Coun Black Studies,1982-84; fel Am Col Forensic Examrs, 1996; Phi Kappa Phi Honor Soc; Alpha Kappa Alpha Sorority Inc; vpres, Calif Black Fac & Staff Assn, 1997;consult Psych, Assessment Pub Safety; adv comt, Calif State Personnel Brd Psychol; Am Psy Assn; Am Soc Clin Hypnosis Assn Black Psych; World Fedn Ment Health. **Honors/Awds:** Distinguished Alumna, Wayne State Univ, 1991. **Special Achievements:** Editor: "Black Experience analysis & synthesis" Leswing Press, 1972; traveled: Africa (Cameroon, Senegal, Ivory Coast, Ghana, Mali, Somalia,Egypt); Europe; Mexico; guest editor, Journal Negro Educ, 1984; co-editor: Out of the Revolution: African American Studies, The Development & Significance of A Discipline, Lexington Press, 2000. **Business Addr:** Clinical Psychologist, Carlene Young and Associates, 1550 S Winchester Blvd Suite 216, Campbell, CA 95008, **Business Phone:** (408)374-1884.

YOUNG, DR. CHARLES, JR.
School administrator. **Personal:** Born Aug 5, 1934, St Louis, MO; married Jessie Dolores Howell; children: Karen. **Educ:** Lincoln Univ, MO, BS Ed, 1957; Univ Ill, Med, 1962, EdD, 1972. **Career:** St Louis Pub Sch, teacher, 1957-66, from asst prin to prin, 1966-72; Urbana Comt Sch, prin, 1972-84; Joliet Pub Sch, asst supt 1984-. **Orgs:** Kappa Alpha Psi, 1952-; Phi Delta Kappa, 1964-; Am Assc Sch Adminr; Rotary Int, 1985; bd mem, Joliet Grade Schs Found Educ Excellence. **Honors/Awds:** Service Award, National Asn Secondary Sch Prin, 1966; Leadership Award, Champaign Co boys Club, 1978. **Military Serv:** AUSR, capt. **Home Addr:** 2650 Black Rd, Joliet, IL 60435. **Business Addr:** Assistant Superintendent, Joliet Public School, 420 N Raynor, Joliet, IL 60435, **Business Phone:** (815)740-3196.

YOUNG, CHARLES LEMUEL
Executive. **Personal:** Born Aug 27, 1931, Lauderdale County; married Doretha Connor (deceased); children: Charles L Jr, Dei-

dre, Arthur & Veldora. **Educ:** Tenn Agri & Indust Univ, BS, bus admin, 1951; Univ Denver, pub rels; Human Develop Inst. **Career:** Royal Oak Develop Co, pres; EF Young Jr Mfg, pres; Miss Legis, democratic rep, currently. **Orgs:** Exec comt & co-founder, Miss Action Progress; past bd mem, Inst Polit; life mem, Nat Asn Advan Colored People; past dir, Meridian Chamber Com; past dir, State Mutual Fed Savings & Loan. **Military Serv:** AUS sgt first class 2 yrs; Bronze Star; Good Conduct Medal; Korean Citation. **Home Addr:** 425 26th Ave, Meridian, MS 39301. **Business Addr:** Democratic Representative, Mississippi Legislature, Rm 205A-NC 400 High St, PO Box 1018, Jackson, MS 39215.

YOUNG, CHARLIE, JR.
Government official. **Personal:** Born Apr 28, 1928, Leary, GA; married Kathryn Robinson; children: Gail Y Smith, Aaron Lee & Valerie Y Pittman. **Educ:** Leary Sch. **Career:** Int Peoples Party, leader; City Councilman, currently. *

YOUNG, CLARENCE, III
Media executive. **Personal:** Born Apr 7, 1942, Dayton, OH; son of Louise McGee Young and Clarence Young Jr. **Educ:** Capital Univ, BA, 1979. **Career:** Playwright Theatre W Dayton Ohio, dir, 1968-82; Clarence Young III Prod, independent producer, TV prod, 1982-; Ellison Sr Citizen Ctr, dir. **Orgs:** Independent TV producer, Clarence Young III 1982-; pres, Clarence Young III Prod, 1981-; pres-publ, Young Sound Music BMI, 1981-; master mason Prince Hall Lodge Equity Lodge 121, 1983. **Honors/Awds:** I "Am A Young Lady", Playwright Musical Dayton Art Inst, 1981; Outstanding Independent producer & TV ed, 1984; Access 30 Dayton, Ohio, 1984; Parity 2000's Ten Top African Am Males, 1995. **Special Achievements:** Produced & wrote: The System, Black Love, Young Lady, Song of Memories Past, Bobby's Jacket, The Road to Brighton, Gooblegone; CD, Bow to the People; book of poems, I Want To Love In America; written 250 songs; performs one-man shows for schools, churches, univ & col; plays tenor sax & piano. **Military Serv:** USAF, a2c, 1961-65. **Home Addr:** 840 N Broadway St, Dayton, OH 45407, **Home Phone:** (937)224-7356. **Business Addr:** Director, Ellison Senior Citizen Center, 2412 W Third St, Dayton, OH 45417, **Business Phone:** (937)333-6606.

YOUNG, DR. COLEMAN MILTON, III
Physician. **Personal:** Born Nov 13, 1930, Louisville, KY; son of C Milton Young Jr and Hortense Houston Young; married Waltraud Schuessler, Jul 4, 1987; children: C Milton IV, Lloyd M & Christopher H. **Educ:** Univ Louisville, AB, 1952; Meharry Med Col, MD, 1961. **Career:** Louisville Genl Hosp, intern, 1961-62; St Joseph's Infirmary, res, 1962-65; Methadone Treatment Prog, founder & dir, 1968-72; Pvt Pract, physician internal med, currently. **Orgs:** Chmn bd mem, Park DuValle Neighborhood Health Ctr, 1966-69; Gov Young Kentuckian's Adv Comn, 1967-70; Louisville Jeffers on Co Air Pollution Ctrl Bd, 1968-77, chmn, 1968-72; Adv SSS, 1968-73; Hon Order KY Col, 1972; dir, Drug Abuse Prog River Region Ment Health Bd, 1972-73; med dir, Comm Hosp, 1972-75; consult, drug prog River Region Ment Health Bd, 1973-74; Govt Coun Alcohol & Drug Abuse, 1973; consult, Senate Com Juv Prob, 1973; Alpha Phi Alpha; AMA; life mem, NAACP; ed, bd chmn, Black Scene Mag, 1974-76; pres, Falls City Med Soc, 1982-85; Govs Oxycontin Task Force, 2001-; KY Med Asn, patient safety task force, 2001-03. **Honors/Awds:** Louisville Man of the Year Award, WHAS TV, 1970; Nat Adv Am Asn Med Asst, 1976-77; Distinguished Citizen Award, Key to City Mayor Harvey I Sloane, 1977. **Special Achievements:** First African Am undergraduate student at the Univ Louisville, 1950; first African Am med intern, Louisville Gen Hosp, 1961; first African Am med resident trained, pvt inst, KY, St. Joseph's Infirmary, Louisville, KY. **Military Serv:** AUS MC, corpl, 1952-54. **Business Addr:** Physician, 4001 Dutchmans Ln Suite 3C, Louisville, KY 40207-4735.

YOUNG, DMITRI DELL
Baseball player. **Personal:** Born Oct 11, 1973, Vicksburg, MS; son of Larry and Bonnie; married Rebecca; children: Owen. **Career:** St Louis Cardinals, infielder, 1996-97; Cincinnati Reds, 1998-2001; Detroit Tigers, 2002-06; Wash Nationals, 2007-. **Honors/Awds:** Two times All-Star selection, 2003, 2007; National League Comeback Player of the Year, 2007.

YOUNG, DONALD G
Founder (Originator). **Career:** Tennis In Motion Inc, founder, currently. **Business Addr:** Founder, Tennis In Motion, 1300 E 47th St, PO Box 161, Chicago, IL 60617, **Business Phone:** (773)768-5687.

YOUNG, E Y. See YOUNG, ERIC ORLANDO.

YOUNG, PROF. EDITH MAE
Educator. **Personal:** Born Oct 15, 1932, Denison, TX; daughter of Joe C Young Sr (deceased) and Pinkie Rambo Franklin (deceased). **Educ:** Tex Col, cert, sec sci, 1951; Lincoln Univ, MO, BSE, 1961, M.Ed, 1964; Univ Mont, CO, Ed.D, 1973. **Career:** Educator (retired); Lincoln Univ, sec & admin asst, libr, 1951-66; Educ & Ctr Res Social Behav, Univ Mont, CO, intern & voc teacher, 1973; Ctr Acad Develop UMSL, acting dir, 1977-80; Educ Bus Teacher Educ, instr & asst prof, 1966-70, 1973-77, 1980, acting assoc dean, 1993-94; Univ Mont, St.Louis, assoc prof educ; Univ Miss, St. Louis, chair educ studies, 1995-98. **Orgs:** Nat Bus Educ Asn, 1962-; AVA, 1966-; AAHE, 1967-; Alpha Sor, 1967; Delta Pi Epsilon, 1970-; Kappa Delta Pi, 1972-; Pi Lambda Theta, 1973-; Alpha Kappa edur examr, Nat Accrediting Comn Cosmetology Arts & Sci, 1985-; ed adv bd, Collegiate Press, 1989-90. **Honors/Awds:** EPDA Doctoral Fel Voc Educ, 1971-73; Summer Fac Res Fel UMSL, 1975; ACE Fel Acad Admin, 1979-80; Educator of the Year, 1994; Out standing Leadership in Higher Education, 1994.

YOUNG, EDWARD HIRAM
Meteorologist. **Personal:** Born Dec 10, 1950, Berkeley, CA; son of Edward Hiram Sr (deceased 1999) and Grace Jean King (deceased 1983); married Doris Kathleen Jackson, Nov 2, 1996. **Educ:** San Jose State Univ, BS Meteorol, 1973; 2 yrs grad work meteorol; N Harris Co Col, courses in mgt & bus, 1984; Delgado Community Col, courses comput, 1988. **Career:** Nat Weather Servs, meteorologist intern Portland, 1975-78; Riverside CA, agricult meteorologist, 1978-81; Ctr Weather Serv FAA Houston, aviation meteorologist, 1981-84; Nat Weather Serv Southern Region, prog mgr, 1981-87; Ft Worth Tex S Region, spec serv met, 1984-86; Nat Weather Serv, agri, forestry meteorologist, 1986-; Nat Oceanic & Atmospheric Admin, Nat Weather Serv Pac Region, Honolulu, Tech Serv Div, chief, 1988-, dep dir, currently. **Orgs:** Bd dirs, San Jose Chap Amer Red Cross 1970-72; Nat Col Stud Adv Coun Am Red Cross, 1971-72; black prog mgr, Nat Weather Serv Wrn Reg, 1978-81; bd dirs, Great Outdoors, 1980-81; AAAS, 1980; black prog mgr, Nat Weather Serv Srn Region 1981-; Am Meteorol Soc 1970-; bd, Women & Minorities Am Meteorol Soc 1985-87, chmn 1989-90; subcomt, Ft Worth United Way Allocations, 1986; consult, Sci, Math, Aeronautics, Res, Technol & Black Family, 1989; aux bd asst, Baha'i Faith Hawaiian Islands, 1988, staff; chair, subcomt, Hawaii Martin Luther King Jr Interim Comn, 1990-95; US China Peoples Friendship Asn, 1995-; Nat Spiritual Assembly Bahais Hawaiian Islands, 1997. **Honors/Awds:** Elks Leadership Award, Oakland CA Elks Club, 1968; EEO Award, Nat Oceanic & Atmospheric Admin, 1984; EEO Award, Dallas-Ft Worth Federal Exec Bd, 1986; Doer of Good Deeds Award, Hawaii Chap, B'Nai Brith, 1995; Outstanding Community Service Award, Honolulu-Pacific Federal Exec Bd, 1996. **Home Phone:** (808)262-1200. **Business Addr:** Deputy Director, National Oceanic & Atmospheric Administration, National Weather Service, 737 Bishop St Suite 2200, Honolulu, HI 96813-3213, **Business Phone:** (808)532-6412.

YOUNG, DR. ELIZABETH BELL
Consultant, public speaker, lecturer. **Personal:** Born Jul 2, 1929, Franklinton, NC; daughter of Joseph H (deceased) and Eulalia; married Charles A Jr, Nov 27, 1964. **Educ:** NC Cent Univ, BA, 1948, MA, 1950; Ohio State Univ, PhD, 1959. **Career:** Univ DC, Dept Speech Sci Comun & Eng, univ prof & chmn, 1949-84; Catholic Univ, grad sch prof, 1966-79; Barber Scotia Col, NC; Talladega Col, AL; Virg State Col; Ohio State Univ; Florida Agri & Mech Univ; Fayetteville State Univ, NC; Howard Univ, Wash DC; Univ Md, Eastern Shore; Princess Anne, MD; Congressional Staff Aide, 1980, 1987-91, Staff aide; US House of Reps Off Congressman Walter E Fauntroy, 1980, 1987-91; US State Dept promotion panelist, field reader & team reviewer, 1980-; Nati & Int Org & Univ, consult & lectr, 1981-; US Govt Off Educ, lectr & consult, 1981-87; Virg Brd of Audiology & Pathology, exec dir, currently. **Orgs:** Alpha Kappa Alpha Sor 1946-; bd mem, Pub Mem Assn, 1973-; brd dir, Handicapped Intervention Prog High Risk Infants Wash DC, 1978-87; brd dir, Wash Ctr Music Ther Clin; adv brd, Negro College Fund, 1979-82; Congressional Adv brd Educ, 1979-82; bd mem, Clin Cert Am Speech-L & H Assn, 1979-83; fel, Am Speech Lang Hearing Assn. **Honors/Awds:** Outstanding Alumni Award, Ohio State Univ, 1976; Pub: Journal Articles in Field of Communications & Made Over 450 Speeches in US. **Special Achievements:** First African to receive PhD in Speech Science; First African to obtain certification in Speech Pathology & Audiology; First African to obtain PhD from Ohio State Univ in communications & speech science; First certified speech & learning clinics in historically black colleges & universities. *

YOUNG, ERIC ORLANDO (E Y YOUNG)
Baseball player, media executive. **Personal:** Born May 18, 1967, New Brunswick, NJ; married MaLika Hakeem. **Educ:** Rutgers Univ, bus mgt, 1989. **Career:** Baseball player (retired), Media executive; Los Angeles Dodgers, infielder& outfielder, 1989-92, 1997-99; Colorado Rockies, infielder & outfielder, 1993-97; Chicago Cubs, infielder & outfielder, 2000-01; Milwaukee Brewers, infielder & outfielder, 2002-03; Tex Rangers, infielder, 2004 & 2006; San Diego Padres, pinch runner, 2005-06; ESPN, analyst, currently. **Honors/Awds:** Silver Slugger Award, 1996; Baseball team's Most Valuable Player, Rutgers Univ. **Business Addr:** Analyst, ESPN, ESPN Plz, Bristol, CT 06010, **Business Phone:** (860)766-2000.

YOUNG, ERNEST WESLEY
Baseball player, athletic coach. **Personal:** Born Jul 8, 1969, Chicago, IL. **Educ:** Lewis Univ. **Career:** Baseball player (retired), Athletic coach; Oakland Athletics, outfielder, 1994-97; Kansas City Royals, 1998; Ariz Diamondbacks, 1999; Yokohoma Bay Stars, 2002; Detroit Tigers, 2003; Cleveland Indians, 2004; Minor league, Cleveland Indians, 2005-07; Great Falls White Sox, hitting coach, currently; BASH Sports Acad, vis master instr, currently. **Special Achievements:** Olympic gold medal for the United States in the 2000. **Business Phone:** (773)588-2274.

YOUNG, F. CAMILLE
Manager. **Personal:** Born Sep 3, 1928, Boston, MA; married Dr Virgil J. **Educ:** Howard Univ, BS, 1949; Howard Univ, DDS, 1958; Univ MI, MPH, 1974. **Career:** Private Practice, Washington DC, 1962-; DC Dept of Public Health, dental officer, 1964-69; Comm Group Health Found, staff dentist, 1969-71; Howard Univ Col of Dentistry, asst prof; Comn Group Health Found, chief dental serv; American Found for Dental Health, bd trustee; Div Dental Health Bureau Health Resources Develop Dept HEW, consultant, 1971-74. **Orgs:** chmn, chmn, Social Com, 1966-70; exec sec, howard univ dental alumni asn, 1967-69; exec bd, 1967-69; Budget & Auditing Comn, 1968-70; secy, Dental Health Care Com, 1968; chmn, Speakers Bureau, 1968-72; Nat Dental Asn; pres, 1968-73; area dir Dentistry, Career Prog Recruit Com, 1968-73; chmn, protocol com, 1968, 1973; del, Lse Dels, 1969-73; nat dental asn am & dental asn liaison com, 1968-73; vpres, Robert T Freeman Dental Soc, 1970-72; chmn, Awards Com, 1970; DC Dental Soc; chmn, Table Clinic Com, 1970; chmn, travel com, 1970-73; am dental asn; american pub health asn; nat asn nNeighborhood health ctrs; asn american women dentists. **Honors/Awds:** President Award, Nat Dental Asn, 1969; special award, Nat Dental Asn, 1973. **Special Achievements:** first woman attain ofc mem Exec Bd 1966-72.

YOUNG, FLOYD ALEXANDER
Football player. **Personal:** Born Nov 23, 1975, New Orleans, LA; married Michelle; children: Ostin Giovanni. **Educ:** Tex A&M Univ Kingsville; Scottsdale Comm Col. **Career:** Tampa Bay Buccaneers, defensive back, 1997-2000; Orlando Predators, 2006-07. **Honors/Awds:** Rookie of the year, 1997.

YOUNG, GEORGE, JR.
Media executive, state government official. **Personal:** Born Oct 13, 1933, Gadsden, AL; children: Kathy Ann, Carrie Vernell Marie & Dorthy Louise. **Educ:** Lincoln Univ, MHS, 1984. **Career:** Harrisburg Glass Inc, affirm act coord, 1952-68; Toby Young Show, Echos of Glory, Jazz Today WKBO Radio, staff announcer, host, producer, 1965-71; Toby Young Enterprise, affirm act coord 1971-; TY Records, affirm act coord, 1971-72; Toby Young Show, Party Line, Echoes of Glory, Project People, WCMB Radio, comm rel spec 1971-; PN Civil Serv Comn, affirmative action, PR contract compliance coordr, currently; From Where I Sit, True Gospel, WTPA TV, writer producer, MC; WCMB-WMIX Echoes of Glory. **Orgs:** Life mem, Nat Asn Advan Colored People; mem bd, Camp Curtin YMCA, Harristown Community Complex; Tri-County March Dimes; chair person, 1976 Edgemont Fire House; pres, PA Chap Nat Assoc Radio & TV Artists; bd mem, Gaudinzia House; past co-chair person, Congress Affirm Action; past chmn, bd mgr, owners, Soulville & Jay Walking Records; bd mem, Nat Progressive Affirm Action Officers; mem, Daughin Cty Exec Comm Drug & Alcohol Inc, past master, dir PR Central; Chosen Friend Lodge 43 F&AM Prince Hall Club 21 Harrisburg PA. **Honors/Awds:** Gospel DJ of the Year; Meritorious Service Award. **Special Achievements:** Winner of two Glow Awards. **Military Serv:** AUS; USAR. **Home Addr:** 1726 N St, Harrisburg, PA 17103. **Business Addr:** Equal Opportunity, Contract Compliance Chief Operating Officerrdinator, PN Civil Serv Commission, Exec Offices, 320 Market St 4th Fl, PO Box 569, Harrisburg, PA 17108-0569.

YOUNG, IRA MASON
Lawyer. **Personal:** Born Sep 20, 1929, St Louis, MO; son of Nathan B and Mamie Mason; married Lillie. **Educ:** Oberlin Col, BA, 1951; WA Univ, JD, 1957. **Career:** Pvt Pract, atty, 1957-; Mo State Bd Law Examr, 1979-84; Young & Thompson, prin, currently. **Orgs:** Nat Bar Asn; Am Bar Asn; Am Trial Lawyers Asn; Lawyers Asn St Louis; St Louis Metro Bar Asn; pres, Mound City Bar Asn; bd dir, Legal Aid Soc, 1965-70; Family & C Serv Greater St Louis; adv coun, Legal Serv Corp Mo; bd dir, Girl Scout Coun St Louis. **Military Serv:** AUS, 1951-53. **Business Addr:** Principal, Young & Thompson, 509 Olive St Suite 1000, Saint Louis, MO 63101, **Business Phone:** (314)436-9603.

YOUNG, JAMES ARTHUR, III
Executive. **Personal:** Born Jan 6, 1945, Augusta, GA; son of James A Jr and Pauline Elim; married Felisa Perez (divorced);

children: Alvin Renato. **Educ:** Claflin Col, BA, 1967; Gable Sch Art Advert, cert, 1975. **Career:** Burke County Bd Educ Waynesboro, teacher, 1967; Montgomery County Bd Educ, Ailey, GA, teacher, 1967-68; CSRA Econ Opportunity Auth Inc, task force leader, 1970-71; Laney-Walker Mus Inc, Augusta, exec dir, 1976-; The Junction Inc, sr staff, Video Poker Industry, 1998; Early Intervention Prog Youth Inc, registered agent, 1998-2001. **Orgs:** Second Shilo Baptist Church, Augusta, 1957; Augusta Cultural Arts Asn, 1977-80; Nat Trust Hist Preservation, 1979-80; Augusta-Richmond Co Mus, 1979-80; Greater Augusta Arts Coun, 1980; judge, pub sch art contest Richmond Co Bd Educ, Augusta, 1980; Seven-Thirty Breakfast Club Columbia, SC, 1980. **Military Serv:** AUS, 1969-73. **Home Addr:** 938 Wrightsboro Rd, Augusta, GA 30901.

YOUNG, JAMES E
Banker. **Career:** Chase Manhttan Bank, NY, mgt trainee, 1971-72, Credit Audit Div, vp team mgr, human resource specialist, lending officer; City Nat Bank New Jersey, vp & chief com loan officer, 1989-90, svp gen admin & com loans, 1990-93; First Southern Bank, pres & ceo; Citizens Trust Bank, Atlanta, pres & chief exec officer, currently. **Orgs:** Nat Bankers Asn; bd dirs, YMCA. **Business Addr:** President, Chief Executive Officer, Citizens Trust Bank, 75 Piedmont Ave, PO Box 4485, Atlanta, GA 30303, **Business Phone:** (404)653-2800.

YOUNG, JAMES E.
Educator. **Personal:** Born Jan 18, 1926, Wheeling, WV; son of James E Young (deceased) and Edna (Thompson) Young. **Educ:** Howard Univ, BS, MS, 1949; Massachusetts Inst tech, MS, PhD, 1953; Harvard Univ, Div Med Sci, 1984-86. **Career:** Hampton Inst, instr physics, 1946-49; Gen Atomics, consult, 1957-58; Univ Minn, vis assoc prof, 1964; Sir Rudy Peierls Oxford, res asst, 1965-66; Harvard, vis res sci, 1978; Los Alamos Sci Lab, staff mem, 1956-59; Tufts Univ Med Sch, res assoc neuroscience dept anat & cell boil, 1986-; Massachusetts Inst tech, prof physics, 1970, prof emer physics, currently. **Orgs:** Am Physiol Soc, 1960-; Sigma Xi Hon Soc Massachusetts Inst tech, 1953; post-doctoral fel, Massachusetts Inst tech Acoustics Lab, 1953-55; Shell BP fell, Aeronaut Dept, Southampton, England, 1956; NAS-NRC Ford fel, Niels Bohr Inst, Copenhagen, 1961-62; pres, JEY Asn; chief oper officer, MHT Ltd; tech dir, CADEX; partner, Escutcheon Inc. **Honors/Awds:** US Patent no 4,564,798, 1986. **Business Addr:** Professor Emeritus of Physics, Massachusetts Institute of Technology, 77 massachusetts ave, Cambridge, MA 02139-4307, **Business Phone:** (617)253-1000.

YOUNG, DR. JAMES E., JR.
Lawyer. **Personal:** Born Jul 18, 1931, New Orleans, LA; married Eddie Mae Wilson; children: James, III, Adrienne & Darrin. **Educ:** Southern Univ, BA, 1958, Law Sch, JD, 1960. **Career:** Parish New Orleans, notary pub, 1962-; pvt pract atty, 1960-68; Va Reg Off, adjudicator, 1966-68; New Orleans Legal Asst Corp, neighborhood staff atty, 1968-69, sr staff atty, 1969-70, asst dir, 1970-71; atty & notary pub, 1971-. **Orgs:** La State Bar Asn; Am Bar Asn; Am Judicature Soc; Louis A Martinet Legal Soc; spec consult & guest lectr, Southern Univ New Orleans Evening Div; Poverty & Consumer Law Panelist & Symposium Partic Tulane Univ; pres & charter mem, Heritage Sq Develop Corp; pres & mem, Lake Area Pub Sch Improvement Asn; pres & officer, Edward Livingston Middle Sch; lifetime mem, Nat Bar Asn; Kappa Alpha Psi Frat; mem & former officer, Acad Pk Devel Asn; pres, New Orleans Pan-Hellenic Coun; gen coun & exec comt mem,Control City Econ Opportunity Corp. **Honors/Awds:** Gold Keys Awards, Nat Art Competition, Nat Scholastic, 1949 & 1950. **Special Achievements:** Graduate in top ten percent NCO Leadership & Motor Mechanics School, USMC; contribution & special features editor coll newspaper. **Military Serv:** USMC, 1951-54; Purple Heart Medal. **Business Phone:** (504)242-8181.

YOUNG, JAMES M., II
Marketing executive. **Personal:** Born Oct 29, 1946, Washington, DC; married Barbara Ann Johnson; children: Julie Elizabeth & Jason Michael. **Educ:** Fisk Univ, Nashville, BA, biol, 1968. **Career:** Xerox Corp, mkt rep, 1971-74; F Serv Bur Co, proj adminr educ, 1977-78; Serv Bur Co, Div Control Date Corp, mkt mgr, 1978-. **Orgs:** Alpha Phi Alpha Frat, 1965. **Military Serv:** AUS, cw2, 1968-71; Vietnam Aviation Medal. **Business Addr:** Marketing Manager, Service Bureau Co, 222 S Riverside Plz Suite 23, Chicago, IL 60606.

YOUNG, JIMMY RAY
Clergy. **Personal:** Born Apr 9, 1941, Natchitoches, LA; son of Booker T and Maggie; married Sylvia, Oct 7, 1962; children: Tarris, Linda, Lisa, LaShawn, John, Latrice, LaDonna. **Career:** Ford Motor Co, supv, 1965-95; Greater St John Baptist Church, pastor, currently. **Home Phone:** (313)836-4732. **Business Addr:** Pastor, Greater St John Baptist Church, 7433 Northfield St, Detroit, MI 48204, **Business Phone:** (313)895-7555.*

YOUNG, JONES. See YOUNG, TERRI JONES.

YOUNG, JOSEF A.
Psychotherapist, vice president (organization). **Personal:** Born Mar 24, 1941, Memphis, TN; married Dr Joyce Lynom Young; children: Jorald (deceased). **Educ:** Tenn State Univ, BS, 1962; Mich State Univ, Masters, attended 1967; Univ Tenn, Post Masters, attended 1972; Southern Ill Univ Carbondale, PhD, 1981. **Career:** Mason, 1974- ; Alpha Phi Alpha, vpres, 1980; Ctr Devel Growth, pres, 1980; Optimist Club Int, Comt Chmn, 1985. **Orgs:** bd dir, Int Coun Asn, 1970; pres, W Tenn Personnel & Guidance, 1972-73; Black Psychologist Asn, 1983; Asn Black Psychologist, 1984-; State Bd Regents " How to teach the hard to learn student"; Tenn Asn Counsel " Fetal Alcohol Syndrome and the Female Alcoholic" Am Asn Ethical Hypnosis. **Military Serv:** Air Force Reserve, 1958-60. **Home Addr:** 5131 Ravensworth Dr, Memphis, TN 38109. **Business Addr:** Senior Counselor, State Technical Institute, 5983 Macon Cove, Memphis, TN 38134.

YOUNG, JOSEPH, JR.
Government official. **Personal:** Married; children: 4. **Educ:** Mich State Univ, BA; Thomas M Cooley Law Sch; Western Mich Univ, grad prog, currently. **Career:** State Mich, house reps, 1978, senate, currently. **Orgs:** Nat Asn Advan Colored People; Knight Columbus; Nativity Lord parish. **Special Achievements:** Numerous awards. **Business Addr:** State Senator, State of Michigan, State Capitol Bldg, PO Box 30036, Lansing, MI 48909, **Business Phone:** (517)373-7346.

YOUNG, DR. JOYCE HOWELL
Physician. **Personal:** Born Mar 22, 1934, Cincinnati, OH; daughter of Lloyd Marion and Addiebelle Foster; married Coleman Milton Young III, Jun 25, 1960 (divorced); children: C Milton Young IV, Lloyd M Young & Christopher H Young. **Educ:** Fisk Univ, BA, Zoology, 1954; Womans Med Col Pa, MD, 1958; Miami Vly Hosp Dayton, OH, Cert Internship, 1959; Meharry Med Col, Hubbard Hosp, Cert Peds, 1960, Cert Int Med, 1961; Univ Louisville Chld Eval Ctr, Cert Growth & Develop, 1973. **Career:** Pvt Med Pract Louis, KY, 1961-67; Univ Louisville Child Eval Ctr, ped develop specialist, 1973-74; Park Duvalle Neighbourhood Health Ctr, med dir, 1974-76; KY Dept Human Resources, med consult, 1984-; Falls City Med Soc, pres, currently. **Orgs:** Alpha Kappa Alpha Sorority, 1952-, Falls City Med Soc, 1961-, Jefferson County Med Soc, 1962-, KY Med Asn, 1962-, Lou Links Inc, 1965-80; finan sec, 1980-, mem, 1973-, mem session, 1988-, Shawnee Presbyterian Church; Louis Bd Educ, 1971-74, chmn, 1974; bd mem, Lincoln Found, 1974-; dir, Continental Nat Bank KY, 1974-86; KY Human Rights Comn, 1983-; Am Med Asn; Syn Covenant Cabinet Ethnic Church Affairs, 1983-86; treas, KBPU 1983-; chmn, Comn Representation, 1985-86; Exec Coun Presbytery Louisville, 1986-91; bd mem, Jefferson City Med Soc Bus Bureau, 1990-. **Honors/Awds:** Appointment by gov KY Colonel, 1962; Comm Serv Award, Lou Links Inc, 1973-74, Alpha Kappa Alpha Sor, 1974, Zeta Phi Beta, 1975; diplomate, Am Bd Disability Consults, 1989-. **Special Achievements:** Series of articles on health, Black Scene Mag, 1975. **Home Addr:** 739 S Western Pkwy, Louisville, KY 40211, **Home Phone:** (502)776-9779. **Business Addr:** President, Falls City Medical Society, 739 S Wern Pkwy, Louisville, KY 40211, **Business Phone:** (502)595-4404 Ext 248.

YOUNG, KEVIN CURTIS
Track and field athlete, executive. **Personal:** Born Sep 16, 1966, Watts, CA; son of William Young and Betty Champion. **Educ:** Univ Calif, Los Angeles, BA, sociol, 1989. **Career:** Athlete (retired), Olympic track athlete; Flavours Co Inc; motivational speaker, currently. **Orgs:** Alpha Phi Alpha Frat Inc, 1987-. **Honors/Awds:** Male Athlete of the Year, Int Amateur Athlete Found, 1992; Athlete of the Year, Track & Field News, 1992; Harrison Dilliard Award, 1992; Jesse Owens Award, 1992; Male Athlete of the Year, USOC Track & Field, 1992; Olympic Games, Gold Medal, 400m Hurdles, 1992; ESPY Award.

YOUNG, KEVIN STACEY
Baseball player, athletic coach. **Personal:** Born Jun 16, 1969, Alpena, MI; married Kelly; children: Kaleb. **Educ:** Univ Southern Miss. **Career:** Baseball Player (Retired); Pittsburgh Pirates, infielder, 1992-95 & 1997-2003; Kansas City Royals,1996; Protege Sports Inc, dir & coach, currently. **Honors/Awds:** Clemente Award, 1997. **Business Addr:** Director, Coach, Protege Sports Inc., 9375 E Bell Rd Suite 201, Scottsdale, AZ 85260, **Business Phone:** (480)473-5888.

YOUNG, KORLEONE (SUNTINO KORLEONE YOUNG)
Basketball player. **Personal:** Born Dec 13, 1978, Wichita, KS. **Career:** Detroit Pistons, forward, 1998-99; Sichuan Panda; Richmond Rhythm, 1999-2000; LidoRose Roseto Basket, 2005-06; Beni HaSharon (Israel), 2006. **Honors/Awds:** Player of the Year, Vhinese Summer League (CBL), 2005; Champion, Chinese summer league, 2003. *

YOUNG, DR. LADONNA
Executive director. **Personal:** Born Dec 14, 1972, Demopolis, AL; daughter of Eugene B and Ella M. **Educ:** Christian Brothers Univ, BA, 1995; Univ Memphis, EdD, 2006. **Career:** SW Tenn Community Col, MAPS-GEAR-UP dir, Lib Studies & Educ, dept chair, currently. **Business Addr:** Department Chair, Southwest Tennessee Community College, 737 Union Ave Bldg A220, Memphis, TN 38103, **Business Phone:** (901)333-5350.

YOUNG, LARRY
Government official. **Personal:** Born Nov 25, 1949, Baltimore, MD; son of Mable Payne. **Educ:** Univ Md College Park, attended 1971. **Career:** Urban Environ Affairs Nat Off Izaak Walton League Am, dir, 1970-77; Young Beat Afro-Am Newspaper, former columnist, 1975-77; Md House Del, 1975-87; Ctr Urban Environ Studies, pres, 1977-82; Nat Black Caucus State Legislators, acitng exec dir, 1979-82; Md Gen Assembly 39th Legis Dist, chmn house environ matters comn, state sen, 1988-94; Exec Nominations Comt, chmn; Legislative Black Caucus, chmn; Senate Exec Nominations Comt, chmn; LY Group, chief exec officer; The Baltimore Times, radio host; Md Senate, 1988. **Orgs:** Chmn bd dirs, Citizen's Democratic Action Orgn, 1976; Baltimore Leadership; chmn, Md Health Convocation; chmn, Health Round table; Isaak Walton League Am; co-chmn, Md Conf Black Aged; legis adv Baltimore City Area Agency Aging; New Shiloh Baptist Church; Energy & Environ Study Conf; bd dirs, Univ Md Med Systems; bd dirs & founder, Black Health Study Group, 1990-; Delegate, Democratic Party Nat convention, 1996. **Honors/Awds:** Community Service Award, We Need Prayer Headquarters; Afro-American Newspaper Honor Roll Award, 1971; Distinguished Citizenship Award, State Md, 1972; Annual Award, Nat Asn Environmental Educ, 1976; Statesman Award, Baltimore Baptist Ministers' Conf, 1977; Legislator of the Year, 1978; Community Service Award, Gamma Chap Chi Eta Phi Sor Inc, 1979; MPHA Award, Md Pub Health Asn Your Support Health Legislation, 1980; Concerned Citizens Award, Am Cancer Soc Md State Div, 1980; Statesman Award, Bethel African Methodist Episcopal Church, 1980. *

YOUNG, LAWRENCE W, JR.
Administrator. **Personal:** Born Dec 30, 1942, Cleveland, OH; son of Lawrence W Sr and Maggie Fuggs; married Eddye (divorced 1989). **Educ:** Miami Univ, Oxford, BA, 1965, MEd, 1974. **Career:** Administrator (Retired); Cleveland Bd Educ, teacher Eng, 1965-69; Miami Univ, Oxford, dir minority affairs, 1969-82; Pa State Univ, Univ Park, PA, dir, Paul Robeson Cult Ctr, 1982-2004. **Orgs:** Alpha Phi Alpha, 1965; NAACP, 1969-; Nat Coun Black Studies, 1985; chair, steering comt, Asn Black Cultural Ctrs, 1989. **Honors/Awds:** Omicron Delta Kappa, ODK, 1989. **Special Achievements:** "Black Stud Leadership on Campus" in Hand Book Minority Stud Servs by Praxis Pubations, 1990; Columnist, Centre Daily Times, 1990-; Am Correspondent to "Afro Mart" Magazine, London, 1989-; Golden Key, 1992; "The Minority Cultural Ctr on White Campus," Cultural Pluralismon Campus, Am Col Personnel Asn, 1992. **Home Addr:** PO Box 251, State College, PA 16804, **Home Phone:** (814)234-1922.

YOUNG, LEE
Vice president (Organization), educator. **Educ:** Jackson State Univ, BS, MS. **Career:** Ind State Univ, assoc vpres enrollment serv; NC A&T State Univ, vice chancellor enrollment mgt & dir admis, currently.

YOUNG, LEE R
Law enforcement officer, executive. **Personal:** Born Jan 8, 1947, Del Rio, TX; son of Leroy and Abbylean A Ward Nunley; married Mary Sanchez; children: Anthony Lee & Kristen Marie. **Educ:** St Edwards Col, Austin, TX, 1973; Sam Houston State Univ, Huntsville, TX, 1973; Southwest Tex Jr Col, AA, 1973; Univ Tex, Austin, TX, BA, 1975. **Career:** Law Enforcement Officer (retired), executive; Nat Park Serv, Amistad Rec Area, Del Rio, TX, 1971-73; Tex Dept Pub Safety, Bryan, TX, trooper TX hwy patrol, 1975-77, Eagle Pass, TX, trooper TX hwy patrol, 1977-80, Del Rio, TX, trooper TX hwy patrol, 1980-88, San Antonio, TX, criminal intelligence investigator, 1988, Garland, TX, sgt TX ranger, 1988-, forensic hypnotist, 1994, comput forensics, 1995; Lee Young & Assoc, pres, currently. **Orgs:** Nat Hon Soc, SW Tex Jr Col, 1972; Nat Police Officers Asn, 1988-; Homocide Investr Tex, 1990-; Tex Police Asn, 1990; dir, Tex Asn Investigative Hypnosis, 1994; Seminole Indian Scout Cemetary Asn, 1990; dir region one, Tex Asn Licensed Investigator's; N Tex Pvt Investigator's Asn; Nat Coun Invest& Security Serv; Tex Rangers Asn; adv dir, Kiwanis Club McKinney Tex; ambassador, McKinney Tex Chamber Com; investigative hypnotist, Tex Comn Law Enforcement Officer Stand & Educ, master peace officer; process serv, Tex Supreme Ct; spec tex rang, Tex Dept Pub Safet, Pub Safety Comn. **Honors/Awds:** Trail Blazer Award, So Dallas Bus Women, 1989; Grand Marshal, Black Hist Parade, 1989. **Military Serv:** USN, petty officer, second class, 1966-70. **Business Addr:** President, Lee Young & Associates, PO Box 1932, McKinney, TX 75070, **Business Phone:** (972)548-1182.

YOUNG, LEON D
State government official. **Personal:** Born Jul 4, 1967. **Educ:** Univ Wis-Milwaukee. **Career:** Former police aide & police officer;

16th Assembly Dist, Milwaukee, WI, state rep, currently. **Orgs:** Numerous memberships including Dem Party; Harambee Ombudsman Proj; Milwaukee Police Asn; League Martin; House Peace; Nat Asn Advan Colored People; Urban League; Social Develop Comn Minority Male Forum Corrections; Nat Black Caucus State Legislators Task Force African Am Males; 100 Black Men; Milwaukee Metrop Fair Housing; Boy Scouts Am. **Business Addr:** State Representative, Wisconsin House of Representatives, 16th Assembly District, Rm 118 N State Capitol, PO Box 8952, Madison, WI 53708, **Business Phone:** (608)266-3786.

YOUNG, LIAS CARL
Lawyer. **Personal:** Born Nov 21, 1940, Big Sandy, TX; son of W L Young and Myrtle Davis; married Rose Breaux Young, Sep 20, 1943; children: Victor, Kimberly, Phyllis. **Educ:** Tyler Jr Col; Tex Southern Univ; Tex Southern Univ Law Sch, JD, 1965. **Career:** Lawyer (retired); Off Regional Coun US Dept HUD, atty advisor, 1968-76; Fed Nat Mortgage Asn, assoc regional counsel, 1976-97. **Orgs:** Fed Bar Asn; Tex Bar Asn; pres, Ft Worth Chap Fed Bar Asn, 1970-71; Nat Bar Asn. **Home Addr:** 4307 Star Dust Ln, Fort Worth, TX 76119. *

YOUNG, DR. LIONEL WESLEY
Pediatrician, radiologist. **Personal:** Born Mar 14, 1932, New Orleans, LA; son of Charles Henry and Ethel Johnson; married Florence Inez Brown, Jun 24, 1957; children: Tina I, Lionel T & Owen C. **Educ:** Benedictine Col, BS, 1953; Howard Univ Col Med, MD, 1957. **Career:** Univ Rochester NY, radiol resident, 1958-61; Univ Pittsburgh, PA, prof radiol & pediat, 1975-86; C's Med Ctr Akron, chmn radiol; Northeastern Ohio Univ Col Med, chmn radiol, 1986-91; Loma Linda Univ Med Ctr, head pediat radiol div & prof radiol, currently. **Orgs:** Pres, Soc Pediat Radiol, 1984-85; pres, Pittsburgh Roentgen Soc, 1985-86; pres, Akron Pediat Radiologists Inc, 1986-91; Sigma Pi Phi; Alpha Omega Alpha. **Honors/Awds:** Caffey Award, Soc Pediat Radiol, 1970; Distinguished Service Award, Howard Univ Col Med, 1987; Distinguished Alumnus Award, Howard Univ, 1989. **Military Serv:** USN, Med Corps, lt comdr, 1961-63. **Business Addr:** Professor, Head, Loma Linda University School of Medicine, Department of Radiology, Loma Linda, CA 92350.

YOUNG, MARGARET BUCKNER
Writer, educator. **Personal:** Born Jan 1, 1922?, Campbellsville, KY; daughter of Frank Buckner and Eva Buckner; married Whitney Young Jr (deceased); children: Marcia Cantarella & Lauren Casteel. **Educ:** Ky St Col, BA, eng & french, 1942; Univ Minn, MA, educ sychol, 1945. **Career:** Ky St Col, teacher; Atlanta Univ, Spelman Col, educ psychol; Books: Old Testament Modern Day: Journeys Black Saints, co-auth, 2001; First Book Am Negroes, The Picture Life Martin Luther King Jr, The Picture Life Ralph-Bunche, The Picture Life Thurgood Marshall. **Orgs:** Alt rep US, 28th Gen Assembly UN, 1973; Cult Exchange Prog, St Dept BurEduc & Cult Affairs, 1974; vis, Peoples Rep China; UNA-USA Nat Policy Panel, US-China Rels, 1979; bd visitors, US Mil Acad, 1979-81; Found Inc; bd dirs, Philip Morris; New York Life Ins Co; Pub Policy Comt Advert Coun; US Invests Serv, Whitney M Young Jr Libr; dir emer, Lincoln Ctr Performing Arts; Black Am Leaders chmn, Whitney M Young Jr Mem Found.

YOUNG, MARY E.
Educator. **Personal:** Born Jun 5, 1941, Harlan, KY. **Educ:** Detroit Bible Col, BRE, 1966; Eastern Ky Univ, BA, 1969, MA 1972; Univ Mich, ABD, 1973-75. **Career:** Eastern Ky Univ, counr, 1969-72; Univ Mich, coun, lab practi cum asst, 1973-74, grad teaching asst, 1974-75; Washtenaw Community Col, counr, 1975. **Orgs:** Nat Educ Asn, 1975; Mich Educ Asn, 1975; Washtenaw Community Col Educ Asn, 1975; Circle Y Ranch Camp, 1983-85; Nat Certified Career Counr, 1985; Nat Asn Advan Colored People, 1985; Nat Black Child Inc, 1985-86; Mich Community Col Counr Acad, 1990-91; Washtenaw Counr's Asn, 1992-93. **Honors/Awds:** Alumni of the Year, Detroit Bible Col, 1978; Outstanding Faculty Award, Wash tenaw Community Col, 1984. **Special Achievements:** Licd Prof Counr. **Home Addr:** 2827 Beechwood Dr, Ann Arbor, MI 48103, **Home Phone:** (313)434-2749.

YOUNG, DR. MICHAEL
Research scientist, educator. **Personal:** Born Mar 28, 1950, Muskogee, OK; son of Robert and Betty Brady; married Tamera Whitely, Mar 16, 1991; children: Betsy, Brandon, Bethany, Ricky & Devin. **Educ:** Bacone Col, AA, 1970; Southwest Baptist Univ, BA, 1972; Univ Ark, MEd, 1974; Tex A&M Univ, PhD, 1975. **Career:** Campbellsville Col, Campbellsville, KY, asst prof, 1975-78; Auburn Univ, Auburn, AL, asst prof, 1978-80; Univ Ark, prof health sci, Health Educ Proj Office, dir, currently, Univ prof health sci, currently. **Orgs:** Bd dirs, Soc Scientific Study Sexuality; founding mem, fel, Am Acad Health Behav; Am Sch Health Asn; Am Alliance Health, Physical Educ Recreation & Dance; Am Pub Health Asn. **Honors/Awds:** Dept Alumni Award for Res & Scholarly Productivity, Texas A&M, HPE Dept, 1980; Teaching Award, 1990, Outstanding Researcher, twice, Univ Ark, Col Educ; Distinguished Achievement in Research & Public Service Award, Univ Ark, Alumni Asn; SW Baptist Univ, Distinguished Contributions to Educ, 1990; Five US Dept Health & Human Servs Awards, Outstanding Work in Community Health Promotion; Exemplary Prog Award, Ctr Substance Abuse Prevention. **Special Achievements:** Authored more than 200 professional publications, most of them in the areas of drug education and human sexuality. **Business Addr:** Director, University Professor, University of Arkansas, Health Education Projects Office, 800 Hotz Hall HP 326A, Fayetteville, AR 72701, **Business Phone:** (479)575-4139.

YOUNG, DR. N LOUISE
Physician. **Personal:** Born Jun 7, 1910, Baltimore, MD; married William Spencer. **Educ:** Howard Univ, BS, 1927; Howard Univ, MD, 1930; Freedman's Hosp, Intern, 1930-31; Provident Hosp, Resident, 1940-45. **Career:** Physician (retired); Obstet-Gynec Practice, physician; S Baltimore Gen Hosp, visiting obstet; Gen N Charles Union Mem, assoc staff gynec, 1950-52; Provident Hosp, acting chief obstet asst, chief, Obstet exec comt, visiting staff & obstet-gynec, 1940-52; MD Training Sch Girls, staff physician, 1933-40; Mcculloh Planned Parenthood Clinic, clinician, 1935-42; Women Morgan State Col, physician, 1935-40; Douglas HS, 1936-69. **Orgs:** Chmn, First Aid & Evacuation Negro Women & Children Nat Emergency MD, Counc Def, 1941-; med adv comn, MD Planned Parenthood & March Dimes, 1969-71; AMA; NMA; Med & Chirurgical Faculty, MD; del, Baltimore County Med Asn, 1969-72; Monumental Med Soc; vpres, 1969-71; Am Fertility Soc; MD Obstet-Gynec Soc; Med Com Human Rights; life mem, Nat Asn Advan Colored People; IBPOE WAKA Sor; CORE; MD Com passage Abort Law; chmn com, Prevent Passage Steriliz Law; Afro-Am Hon Roll, 1947; Baltimore Howard Alumni, 1930; Philamathions, 1935 MD Hist Soc, 1975; AKA Heritage Servis-Woman Med, 1971.

YOUNG, DR. NANCY WILSON
Educator. **Personal:** Born May 1, 1943, Orangeburg, SC; married R Paul; children: Ryan Paul. **Educ:** Clafin Col, BS, 1965; SC State Col, attended 1966; George Peabody Col, attended 1968; Univ Miami, MEd, 1970; Barry Univ, grad courses. **Career:** Wateree Elem Sch Lugoff, SC, 3rd grade teacher, 1965-67; Ford Found fel, 1968-69; Univ Miami, grad adv, 1969-70, asst dir admis, 1970-80; Interval Int, personnel dir, 1980-83; Miami-Dade Comm Col, employment adv, 1983-91, fac, 1991-. **Orgs:** Consult, CEEB Summer Inst Col Bd, 1975-80; chmn, TOEFL Res Comm ETS, 1977-80; vice chmn, TOEFL Policy Coun ETS, 1977-80; exec comm, TOEFL Policy Coun ETS, 1977-80; life mem, Clafin Col Alumni Asn; consult, US State Dept Visits W Africa & Trinidad, 1979; adv bd, Epilepsy Found S FL, 1984-85; Comm Total Employment Comm, 1984-85; bd dir, Univ Miami Alumni, 1984-87; Dades Employ Handicapped Comm, 1984-; Dade County Chapter, Links; Jack & Jill Am; bd dirs, 11th judicial nominating comn, 1991-94; exec comm, Healthy People 1995, 2000. **Honors/Awds:** Alumni of the Year, Claflin Col, 1991; Outstanding Alumnus of Claflin Col, 1995. **Business Addr:** Faculty, Miami-Dade Community College, 11011 SW 104th St Bldg 6319, Miami, FL 33176-3393, **Business Phone:** (305)237-2178.

YOUNG, OLLIE L
Executive. **Personal:** Born Feb 8, 1948, Philadelphia, PA; daughter of Samuel B Sr and Mary Huggins; married Reginald B; children: Stephanie D. **Educ:** Tarkio Col, BA, 1970; Temple Univ, MBA, 1977. **Career:** Temple Univ Health Sci Ctr, asst personnel dir; Consolidated Rail Corp, personnel super; Ducat Assoc, consult; The New York Times Reg, employee rel mgr; Gannett Co Inc, human resources dir; Rutgers Univ, asst dir, personnel serv; Valic, financial planner, consult; N Philadelphia Health Syst, hr, dir, asst vpres, currently. **Orgs:** Am Mgt Asn, 1984-; volunteer, New Geth Bapt Church Tutorial Prog 1985-; prog chmn, Newspaper Personnel Rel Assocs, 1986-87; adv bd, Somerset YMCA, 1986-; mgt consult, Somerset United Way; CUPA, 1988-; Black MBA Asn; SHRM, 1998; Big Brother, Big Sister, 1998. **Honors/Awds:** Frank Tripp Award, Gannett Co, 1985; Tribute Women Industry Twin Somerset & Union, 1986; Delegate, People to People, 1993. **Business Addr:** HR Director, Assistant Vice President, North Philadelphia Health System, 8th W Girard Ave, Philadelphia, PA 19122, **Business Phone:** (215)787-2515.

YOUNG, PAMELA THORPE
Commissioner. **Personal:** Married Reuben F; children: 2. **Educ:** Univ NC, Chapel Hill, BA, 1980; NC Central Univ Sch Law, JD, 1985. **Career:** Travis County, Tx, asst dist atty & asst county atty; asst Gen, Coun Tex Ethics Comn; James E Pete Laney Tex House Representatives, coun for speaker; NC Off State Budget & Mgt, policy analyst; NC Indust Comn, dep comnr, 1996-2002, Legal Coun Dept Cult Resources, dep secy, comnr, 2003-04, vice chair, 2004-07, chair, 2007-. **Orgs:** NC State Bar; Tex State Bar; NC Bar Asn; NC Workers Compensation Sect NC Bar Asn; Wake County Bar Asn. **Business Addr:** Chair, North Carolina Industrial Commission, 4340 Mail Service Ctr, Raleigh, NC 27699-4340, **Business Phone:** (919)807-2500.

YOUNG, RAYMOND, JR.
Sales manager. **Personal:** Born Aug 22, 1960, Mobile, AL; son of Raymond and Tenner; married Lanie L Johnson. **Educ:** Ala A&M Univ, BS acct, 1982; Mt St Marys Col, MBA, 1989. **Career:** JC Penney Co, mgt trainee, 1981; Super Oil Co, jr acct, 1982; Int Bus Machine Corp, staff financial analyst, 1982-87; Mt Calvary Bapt Church, sunday sch instr, 1983-; Digital Equip Corp, financial planning mgr, 1988-92, sales mgr, 1992-. **Orgs:** Montgomery County Chap Nat Asn Advan Colored People, 1985-, Nat Black MBA Asn, 1987-. **Honors/Awds:** Delta Mu Delta Nat Honor Soc Bus Admin, 1982-; Outstanding Young Men Am, 1990. **Home Addr:** 11600 Whittier Rd, Mitchellville, MD 20721. **Business Addr:** Sales Manager, Digital Equipment Corporation, 6406 Ivy Lane, Greenbelt, MD 20770, **Business Phone:** (301)459-7900.

YOUNG, RICHARD EDWARD, JR.
Executive. **Personal:** Born Dec 30, 1941, Baltimore, MD; married Carol Emile Gette; children: Joyce Ann & Jeffrey Wendel. **Educ:** Univ Md, BA, 1971; Rutgers Univ, MCRP, 1973; Seton Hall Univ, JD, 1978. **Career:** Cty Baltimore Dept Housing & Community Develop, housing inspector, 1967-71; NJ Dept Community Affairs, 1971-72; Fed Govt US Dept HUD, urban planner, 1972-73; United Way Essex & W Hudson, Community Planning & Develop, assoc dir, 1973-74; City Newark, evltns chief, 1974-79; Econ Develop Planning, dir, 1979. **Orgs:** Pres, Centennial Commun Inc; pres, RE Young Assoc; pres, ARTEP Inc; bd trustee, NJ Neuro psychiatric Inst, 1977; bd trustee, vice pres Joint Conn Inc, 1976; Am Inst Planners Asn, 1970; 100 Black Men Inc, 1974; Am Soc Planning Officials, 1970; NJ Soc Prof Planners, 1973; NJ Prof Planner License, 1973. **Honors/Awds:** Outstanding Young Men of America, 1976; NJ St Dept Higher Educ Minority, Scholarship, 1974; Tri St Regional & Planning Comn, Fellowship in Urban Planning, 1971-73. **Military Serv:** AUS, major, 1964.

YOUNG, RICKEY DARNELL
Salesperson, football player. **Personal:** Born Dec 7, 1953, Mobile, AL; son of Nathanial Young and Deloris Echols; married Gloria Waterhouse, Jun 23, 1984; children: Micah Cole & Colby Darnell. **Educ:** Jackson State Col, BS, 1975. **Career:** San Diego Chargers, running back, 1975-77; Minn Vikings, running back, 1978-83; Edina Realty; Jeff Belzer's Todd Chevrolet, sales rep; Forest Lake Ford-Jeep & Eagle, Forest Lake Minn, sales rep; Eden Prairie Ford, sales rep; Courtesy Ford, vpres & dealer, currently. **Orgs:** Chmn, Heart & Lung Asn, 1981; C fund Viking, 1982. **Honors/Awds:** Pass Receiver Award, Viking's, 1978. **Home Phone:** (612)442-6162. **Business Addr:** Vice President, Dealer, Courtesy Ford, 3401 Coon Rapids Blvd, Coon Rapids, MN 55433, **Business Phone:** (612)427-1120.

YOUNG, RONALD R
School administrator. **Personal:** Born Nov 13, 1948, Chester, SC; son of Alberta Murphy and John W; married Jacqueline Marie Jackson, Nov 2, 1985; children: Jenelle Renee, Nicole Christine & Whitney Marie. **Educ:** Hampton Univ, Hampton, VA, BS, acct, 1971, Syracuse Univ, Syracuse, NY, MBA, 1975. **Career:** State Univ New York, Health Scie Ctr Syracuse, vpres pub gov affairs, 1998-. **Orgs:** Bd dirs, Grand Polemarch, Kappa Alpha Psi Fraternity Inc; bd, exec comt, Cent New York COT Found; bd, Inroads Upstate New York Inc; chmn, Coun Presidents Nat Pan Hellenic Coun. **Honors/Awds:** Fraternity Serv Awards, Kappa Alpha Psi Fraternity Inc, 1979-86; Community Serv Recognition, United Way Cent New York, 1988; Plaques, Certificates, Gifts, for speaking, Numerous Orgns. **Home Addr:** 6400 Randall Rd, Syracuse, NY 13214-2159, **Home Phone:** (315)446-1417. **Business Addr:** Vice President of Public & Government Affairs, SUNY Upstate Medical University, 750 EAdams St, Syracuse, NY 13210, **Business Phone:** (315)464-5476.

YOUNG, ROSE S.
Government official, army officer. **Personal:** Born Sep 18, 1943, Wadesboro, NC; daughter of Ethel R Sturdivant and Lester W Sturdivant (deceased); married Charles M Young, Sep 24, 1964; children: Robin, Charles M Jr. **Educ:** A&T Univ, attended 1960; Cortez Peters Bus Col, attended 1961. **Career:** Walter Reed Med Ctr, Army Med Dept, personnel spt, 1976-85; US Court Admin Off, retirement spt, personnel mgt spt, 1985-86; Navy Recruitment Command, pub affairs, mgt analyst; Dept Navy, utilities bus line team leader. **Orgs:** Fed Women, steering com, 1982-85, Fed Women, prog, 1987-; ITC, 1988; Sixth Church, deacon bd mem, ordained elder; NCP; Dist. **Honors/Awds:** Letter of Commendation, w/Silver Wreath, 1992, w/Plaque, 1993; Special Act Award, 1994; Civilian of the Yr.

YOUNG, SARAH DANIELS
Government official. **Personal:** Born Sep 25, 1926, Wetumpka, AL; daughter of Thomas Daniels II (deceased) and Novella Saxton Johnson (deceased); married Anderson Crutcher; children: Saundrea Shillingford & Alan Cla. **Educ:** Detroit Inst Com, Dipl Sec Sci, 1946; Wayne State Univ, 1964. **Career:** Rretired; Detroit Inst Com Bus Col, from sec to pres, 1946-48; Fed Govt, med sec, 1949-54; County Wayne, admin sec off mgr, labor rel anal, 1954-79. **Orgs:** St Clements Epis Chap, 1948-; bd canvassers, City Inkster, 1966-89; bddirs, Chateau Cherry Hill Housing Corp, 1973-89; comnr, Public Housing Auth, 1979-99; chairperson Friends of

the Library City Inkster, 1979-99; bd dirs, nat ed chief, nat tamias, trustee, Gamma Phi Delta Sor Inc;treas, Diocese MI ECW Exec Bd, 1983-91; bd dirs, NW Guid Clin, 1984-87; Top Ladies Distinction Inc; MI Metro Chap Exec Bd; Nat Coun Negro Women, YWCA, Nat Asn Advan Colored People; secy, Episcopal Diocese Mich Finance Comt, 1987-91. **Honors/Awds:** Pi Nu Tau Honor Award, Detroit Inst Com, 1946; first black female analyst Wayne Co MI; Outstanding Service Award, Nat Ed-in-chief Gamma Phi Delta Sor Inc, 1978; Outstanding Adult Comm Serv Award, Alpha Kappa Alpha, 1984; YWCA Service Award, 1991. **Home Addr:** 27164 Kitch Ave, Inkster, MI 48141.

YOUNG, SUNTINO KORLEONE. See YOUNG, KORLEONE.

YOUNG, TERRENCE ANTHONY
Banker. **Personal:** Born Feb 21, 1954, St Louis, MO; children: Terrence A Jr. **Educ:** Univ Ill, Champaign, BA, 1977, MBA, 1979; State Ill, CPA, 1980. **Career:** Inland Steel Co, finance, 1979-83; First Nat Bank Chicago, vpres, 1983-92; Peal Develop Co, pres, 1992-95; Fund Community Redevelop, develop specialist, 1993-95; Fannie Mae, regional exec dir, lead dir, currently. **Orgs:** Am Inst Cert Pub Accts; Alpha Phi Alpha Fraternity; bd pres, Covenant Develop Corp; bd mem, Hispanic Housing Develop Corp; bd mem, Black Pearl Gallery; Metro Bd, Chicago Urban League; founding mem, Network Real Estate Prof; life mem, Univ Ill Alumni Asn; Fed Nat Mortgage Asn. **Honors/Awds:** Outstanding Young Men of America, 1985. **Home Addr:** 4119 S Drexel Blvd, Chicago, IL 60653, **Home Phone:** (773)548-7607. **Business Addr:** Lead Director, Fannie Mae, 1 S Wacker Dr Suite 1300, Chicago, IL 60606, **Business Phone:** (312)368-8817.

YOUNG, TERRI JONES (JONES YOUNG)
School administrator, educator. **Personal:** Born May 11, 1957, Laurel, MS; daughter of Betty Jean Sanders Jones and Heywood Jones; married James Keith, Sep 6, 1986. **Educ:** Eastern Ill Univ, Charleston, Ill, BS, Bus, 1979; Ill Inst Tech, Chicago, Ill, MBA, 1989. **Career:** Ill Inst Tech, Chicago, Ill, dir, minority eng prog, 1980-87; Chicago State Univ, Chicago, Ill, dir, engineering studies, 1987-. **Orgs:** Nat Black MBA Asn; Phi Gamma Nu, 1977-; Nat Asn Advan Colored People, 1988-; NTA, 1989-; nat pres, Nat Asn Minority Eng Prog Advocates, 1992-94. **Honors/Awds:** Dr. Ronald McNair President Recognition Award, NTA, 1986; Special Recognition Award, Union Concerned Black Stud, 1986; Special Recognition Award, IIT Pre-Univ Prog, 1987; Award of Appreciation, Nat Soc Black Engrs, 1988; Region C Outstanding Prog Admin, NAMEPA, 1990; Nat Leadership Award, NAMEPA, 1995. **Business Addr:** Director of Engineering Studies Program, Chicago State University, Office of Engineering Studies, 9501 S King Dr, Chicago, IL 60628-1598, **Business Phone:** (773)995-2357.

YOUNG, THOMAS
Singer, educator. **Career:** Sarah Lawrence Col, prof music, currently; Albums: X: The Life & Times of Malcolm X; Tania - Anthony Davis; Blue Monday; Marco Polo; The Death of Klinghoffer; Too Hot to Handel; Black Christmas; A Star in the East; Cook Dixon & Young: Volume 1; Three Mo Tenors, 2001; William Bolcom's Songs of Innocence & Experience. **Special Achievements:** Appeared on Great Performances, PBS, 2001. **Business Addr:** Professor, Sarah Lawrence College, Department of Music, 1 Mead Way, Bronxville, NY 10708.

YOUNG, TOMMY SCOTT
Executive, founder (originator). **Personal:** Born Dec 13, 1943, Blair, SC; son of John Robert and Nancy Lee Thompson; children: Tamu Toliver & Lee Thompson Young. **Educ:** Calif State Univ, BA, 1968, post grad; LA Community Col, attended; Benedict Col, attended. **Career:** IBM Corp, customer eng, 1963-66; Raspberry Recordings, creative & performing artist, 1965-; Meat & Theatre Inc, founder, pres, 1969-72; Watts Writers Workshop, instr, 1969-71; Kitani Found Inc, exec dir, bd mem, founder, chmn bd, 1974-84; The Equitable Life Assurance Soc US, financial planner, 1984; SC Arts Comn, artist res; Lincoln Ctr Inst, Storyteller-in-Residence, currently; Lord Baltimore Press, printers asst. **Orgs:** NC Cult Arts Com, 1973; dir, Timia Enter, 1974; chmn, Educ Com Shel-Blair Fed Credit Union, 1974-75; Governors Int Yr, Child Com; Artistically Talented & Gifted Spcl Proj Adv Bd, 1977-; Mann-Simons Adv Comm, 1979-; SC Educ TV Adv Bd 1979-; Bro & Sisters Adv Bd, 1979-; Southern Arts Fed Prog Sel Comt, 1979-80; chmn, SC Arts Comn 5 yr Planning Com Richland Co, 1979-80; SC Arts Comn Adn Adv Com; treas SC Com Arts Agencies, 1979-; Govrs Cult Arts Com, 1979-; Govs Int Yr, Child Com; consult, Media Serv Nat Endow Arts, 1979-; Spoleto Midlands Comm, 1980; Nat Asn Life Underwriters, 1985-; Nat Asn Preserv & Perpetuation Storytelling, 1986-; Asn Bl Storytelling, 1987-; Toastmasters Int, 1987-; chmn, Christ Unity Columbia, 1988-, Youth Encouraged Succeed, 1989-; Columbia Youth Collaborative, 1989-; Southern Order Storytellers, SC Storytellers Guild; GA Coun Arts; Columbia C of C; Nat Lit Soc; Int Platform Asn; Gospel Music Workshop Am; Nat Entertainment Conf. **Honors/Awds:** Distinguished Performance Citation, The Equitable Financial Companies, 1988; Billings Educ Found Award. **Special Achievements:** Author of: "Black Blues & Shiny Songs" Red Clay Books 1977; Recipient "10 for the Future" Columbia Newspapers Inc, 1978; Tommy Scott Young Spins Magical Tales, Raspberry Recordings, 1985. **Military Serv:** USAF, 1960-63. **Business Addr:** Storyteller, Lincoln Center for the Performing Arts Inc, 70 Lincoln Ctr Plz, New York, NY 10023, **Business Phone:** (212)875-5000.

YOUNG, WALLACE L., JR.
Educator. **Personal:** Born Oct 5, 1931, New Orleans, LA; married Myra Narcisse. **Educ:** Loyola Univ; So Univ. **Career:** New Orleans Pub Libr, chmn bd, 1976-79; Sr Citizen Ctr, asst dir. **Orgs:** Pres & bd mem, Nat Asn Advan Colored People; exec sec, Knights Peter Claver; Dryades St YMCA; Free So Thtr; Nat Cath Conf for Inter racial Justice; LA State Lib Devel Com; coord, Cath Com Urban Ministry; Nat Office Black Catholics, Nat Black Lay Catholic Caucus. **Honors/Awds:** TX Farmworker Award Human Rights, 1977; Human Relation Catholic Award, 1978; Black Catholic Man of Vision, 1978; Dryades YMCA Man of the Year Award, 1979; NOBC Outstanding Service, 1980. **Military Serv:** Ordanance Corps, 1951-53. **Home Addr:** 4933 Madrid St, New Orleans, LA 70126, **Home Phone:** (504)282-6240. **Business Addr:** Assistant Director, Senior Citizen Center, 219 Loyola Ave, New Orleans, LA 70112.

YOUNG, DR. WALTER F
Consultant, dentist, general. **Personal:** Born Aug 18, 1934, New Orleans, LA; married Sonjia W; children: Tony Waller, Tonya Waller, Tammy & Nikki. **Educ:** Baldwin Wallace Col, BS, DDS, 1959; Howard Univ; Harvard Sch Bus, special prog, 1976. **Career:** Osaka Am Club Japan, consult; Am Comput Technol, Atlanta, consult; Gulfstream Aerospace, consult; Grady Healthcare, consult; Iberville Parish, Community Action; St Laudry Parish; St James Parish; St Helena Parish, dent dir; Datacon Int Inc; Health Mgt Decisions; Jamaica Community, dir; Nev State Penal Inst, 1964; Nev State Mental Hosp, dent dir, 1969; Young Int Develop Corp, pres & owner, 1975-; Pvt Pract, dentist, 1987-; Hon Consul Gen Liberia, 2003-04. **Orgs:** Southern Christian Leadership Conf; bd mem, Nat Asn Advan Colored People; bd mem, Fulton County Hosp Authority; bd trust, GA Econ Task Force; mem, GA Dent Asn; bd, Int Fel Prog; N Ga Dent Soc; Am Dent Asn; bd dir, 100 Black Men Atlanta Inc; bd trustees, Morris Brown Col. **Military Serv:** USN, dent officer, 1959. **Business Addr:** President, Owner, Young International Development Company, 2265 Cascade Rd SW, Atlanta, GA 30311-2801.

YOUNG, WATSON A.
Physician. **Personal:** Born Sep 27, 1915, Abbeville, SC; married Aundree Noretta Drisdale; children: Watson, Jr, Aundree, Jr, Ransom J, Leonard F, Anthony G. **Educ:** Univ Mich Med Sch, MD, 1942; Eastern Mich Univ. **Career:** Physician (retired); Homer G Phillips Hosp, St Louis, MO, intern; Pvt Pract, Physician, 1943-80. **Orgs:** Detroit Med Soc; Wolverine State Med Soc; Nat Med Asn; Wayne County & Mich State Med Socs; Am Med Asn; Am Soc & Abdominal Surgeons; life mem, Nat Asn Advan Colored People; life mem Alpha Phi Alpha Fraternity. **Military Serv:** USY, Major, 1954-56. *

YOUNG, WILLIAM
Executive. **Educ:** Calif State Univ, Long Beach, BS, bus admin. **Career:** Inroads Inc, pres & chief operating officer; A G Edwards & Sons Inc, staff; Buford Dickson Harper & Sparrow Inc, pres, chief operating officer, currently. **Orgs:** Bd mem, St Louis Empowerment Zone; chmn, Health & Safety Fair St Louis; pres & chmn invest comt, Buford, Dickson, Harper & Sparrow Inc Invest; bd dir, Dollar Gen Corp. **Business Phone:** (314)725-5445.

YOUNG, WILLIAM ALLEN
Actor, movie director. **Personal:** Born Jan 1, 1953?, Washington, DC. **Career:** Films: A Soldier's Story, 1984; Jagged Edge, 1985; Wisdom, 1986; Spies Inc, 1988; Lock Up, 1989; The Waterdance, 1992; Drop Squad, 1994; Almost Dead, 1994; Fear X, 2003; District 9, 2009; TV appearances: "Freedom Road", 1979; "The Jeffersons", 1980; "Fame", 1982; "Women of San Quentin", 1983; "Cagney &Lacey", 1983; "The Day After", 1983; "Victims for Victims: The Theresa Saldana Story", 1984; Boys in Blue, 1984; "Scarecrow & Mrs. King", 1985; "The Atlanta Child Murders", 1985; "Sins", 1986; "Outrage!", 1986; "Johnnie Mae Gibson: FBI", 1986; "Mariah", 1987; "The Twilight Zone",1987; 227, 1988; Amen, 1988; "Tour of Duty", 1988; "Knots Landing", 1989; "My Past Is My Own", 1989; "The Women of Brewster Place", 1989; "Cop Rock", 1990; Without Her Consent, 1990; "Without Her Consent", 1990; "Matlock", 1990-93; "Lies Before Kisses", 1991; "L.A. Law", 1991; "Knots Landing", 1992-93; "Matlock: The Vacation", 1992; "Simple Justice", 1993; "Home Improvement", 1993; "Sisters", 1993; "Renegade", 1993; I Can Make You Love Me, 1993; "The American Experience", 1993; "Diagnosis Murder", 1994; "Sweet Justice", 1994; "Babylon 5", 1994-95; "Serving in Silence: The Margarethe Cammermeyer Story", 1995; "Chicago Hope", 1995; "Fast Company", 1995; "Moesha", 1996-2001; "Murphy Brown", 1995; "Sister,Sister", 1998; "The Parkers", actor & dir, 2000-02; "Soul Food", 2001; "Any Day Now", 2001-02; "The Agency", 2003; "The District", 2003; "CSI:Miami", 2004-06; JAG, 2004; Fielder's Choice, 2005; Detective, 2005; "CSI:Crime Scene Investigation", 2005-07; "Commander in Chief", 2006; "Nip/Tuck", 2006; Murder 101, 2006; Primal Doubt, 2007; "Saving Grace", 2007; Depth Charge, 2008; "The Mentalist", 2008; "Navy NCIS: Naval Criminal Investigative Service", 2009. **Orgs:** Kappa Alpha Psi Fraternity. **Business Addr:** Actor, c/o Marc Bass Agency, 9255 Sunset Blvd Suite 727, Los Angeles, CA 90069, **Business Phone:** (310)278-1900.*

YOUNG, DR. WILLIAM FREDERICK, JR.
Physician. **Personal:** Born Aug 10, 1956, Cleveland, OH; son of William F Sr and Amy E; married Doris E, Sep 19, 1986; children: Lauren E. **Educ:** Dartmouth Col, BA, 1982; Cornell Univ Med Col, MD, 1982; Columbia Sch Pub Health, 1985. **Career:** Georgetown Univ Hosp, intern & gen surgery, 1982-83; Nat Health Serv Corps, gen med officer, 1983-85; Georgetown Univ Hosp, resident gen surg, 1985-86; Suburban Hosp, surg house officer, 1986-87; Temple Univ Hosp, resident neurosurg, 1987-92; Temple Univ Sch Med, assoc prof, 1992-2001; Mayo Clinic & Found Med Educ & Res, prof, currently. **Orgs:** Am Med Asn, 1992-; Congress Neurol Surgeons, 1992-; N Am Spine Soc, 1994-; Am Asn Neurol Surgeons, 1995-; Am Col Surgeons, 1996-; Nat Neuro Trauma Soc, 1997-; Cervical Spine Res Soc, 1998-; Int Soc Hypertension Blacks, 1999. **Honors/Awds:** Research Award, Paralyzed Veterans Am, 1996; Research Award, Cervical Spine Res Soc, 1996; Research Awd, N Am Spine Soci, 1996. **Special Achievements:** Numerous publications. **Business Addr:** Professor, Mayo Clinic and Foundation for Medical Education and Research, 200 First St SW, Rochester, MN 55905, **Business Phone:** (507)284-2511.

YOUNGBLOOD, DR. REV. JOHNNY RAY
Clergy. **Personal:** Born Jun 23, 1948, New Orleans, LA; son of Palmon and Ottie May; married Joyce Terrell; children: Johnny Jernell, Joel & Jason. **Educ:** Dillard Univ, LA BA, 1970; Colgate Rochester Divinity Sch, MDiv, 1973; United Theol Sem, Dayton, OH, DMin, 1990. **Career:** St Paul Community Baptist Church, sr pastor & exec organizer, currently. **Business Phone:** (718)257-1300.

YOUNGBLOOD, SHAY
Writer. **Personal:** Born Jan 1, 1959, Columbus, GA. **Educ:** Clark-Atlanta Univ, BA, 1981; Brown Univ, MFA, 1993. **Career:** Creative Writing Workshop Instr & Lectr var univs, 1987-; Peace Corps, Dominican Repub, agr info Officer; WETV, Atlanta, GA, pub info asst; Syracuse Community Writer's Proj, lectr; RI Adult Correctional Inst Women, playwrighting instr; Brown Univ, lectr; Wheaton Col, Col vis prof, 1995-97; Univ Miss, John & Renee Grisham Writer-in-Residence, 2002-03; New Sch Social Res, lectr, currently; Riverhead Books, author, currently; Plays: Communism Killed My Dog; Shakin' Mess Outta Misery, 1994; Talking Bones, 1994; Square Blues; Black Power Barbie in Hotel de Dream; fiction: Big Mama Stories, 1989; Novels: Soul Kiss, 1997; Black Girl in Paris, 2000. **Orgs:** Dramatists Guild; Authors Guild; Nat Writers Union; Writers Guild Am; Yaddo Artist's Colony. **Honors/Awds:** Best Playwright Award, Hollywood NAACP Theatre, 1991; Lorraine Hansberry Playwrighting Award, Kennedy Ctr Performing Arts, 1993; Edward Albee Honoree, Twenty-First-Century Playwrights Festival, 1993; Nat Theatre Award, 1995; Pushcart Prize, short story "Born with Religion"; John and Renee Grisham Writer in Residence, 2002; Sustained Achievement Award, New York Found Arts, 2005. **Home Addr:** PO Box 300772, Jamaica Plain, MA 02130.

YOUNGE, IDA
President (organization). **Career:** Jack & Jill Am Inc, pres, nat past pres. **Business Addr:** Past President, Jack & Jill of America Inc, 1930 17th St NW, Washington, DC 20009, **Business Phone:** (202)667-7010.

YOUNGE, RICHARD G
Lawyer. **Personal:** Born Aug 27, 1924, Kirkwood, MO; married Wyvetter H; children: Ruth, Torque, Margaret, Roland & Richard Jr. **Educ:** Univ Ill, BA, 1947; Lincoln Univ, LLB, 1953. **Career:** E St Louis IL, pract atty, currently; Forward Housing Corp, atty, 1973; Citizens Develop Corp, staff; Econ Develop Southern IL, engaged promotion. **Orgs:** Pres, Metro-East Bar Asn. **Honors/Awds:** Outstanding Legal Services to the Community Award, Mound City Bar Asn & Metro-East Bar Asn, 1982-84. **Special Achievements:** Developed Housing & Business Opportunities for Blacks in Southern Illinois. **Military Serv:** AUS, s sgt. **Business Addr:** Attorney, 1010 Martin Luther King Dr, East St Louis, IL 62201, **Business Phone:** (618)274-2177.

YOUNGER, CELIA DAVIS
Educator. **Personal:** Born Aug 24, 1939, Gretna, VA; married James Arthur; children: Felicia A & Terri E. **Educ:** VA State Univ, BS, 1970, MEd. **Career:** VA State Univ, prog coordr stud union, 1971-73, asst dir financial aid, 1973-75, bus devel specialist &

procurement officer, 1974-78; J Sargeant Reynolds Comm Col, adj fac sch bus, 1974-75; Ocean County Col, adj fac sch bus, 1982-83; Georgian Court Col, dir learning resource ctr, 1978-83, dir educ oppor fund prog, 1983-2005, dir stud support servs prog, currently. **Orgs:** Alpha Kappa Alpha Sor, 1968-, EOF Prof Asn, 1978-; chairperson, affirmative action comm workshop facilitator OC Adv Comm on Status Women, 1980-; exec bd mem, Ocean County Girl Scouts, 1983-; Am Asn Univ Women; NJ Asn Devel Educ; NJ Asn Stud Financial Aid Adminrs; Nat Asn Female Execs. **Honors/Awds:** Certificate of Appreciation, Toms River Regional Bd of Educ, 1984-85. **Business Addr:** Director, Georgian Court University, Student Support Services Program, 900 Lakewood Ave, Lakewood, NJ 08701, **Business Phone:** (732)364-2200.

YOUNGER, KENNETH C.
Automotive executive. **Personal:** Born in Missouri. **Career:** McDonnell Douglas Aircraft Corp CA, engr; Landmark Ford Fairfield, OH, owner, 1977-. **Orgs:** Founding mem, Black Ford Lincoln-Mercury Dealers Asn; pres, Nat Assoc Minority Automobile Dealers. **Business Addr:** Chief Excutive Officer, Landmark Ford Sales Inc, 5221 Dixie Hwy, Fairfield, OH 45014.

YOUNG-SALL, HAJAR
Physician. **Personal:** Born Jan 6, 1952, Asheville, NC; daughter of Gladys Young and Curtis; married El-Hadji Sall, May 21, 1995; children: Muhammad, Sulaiman & Khadijah. **Career:** Out Africa, owner, 1990-92; Int Massage Therapy Asn, certified massage therapist, 1992-. **Orgs:** Am Massage Therapy Asn, vpres, 1993-95; Sisters United Network, 1992-95; pres, Soc Against Subtle Racist Acts. **Honors/Awds:** Healing Arts Honoree, Int Masseuse Fed. **Home Addr:** 1650 Eastern Pkwy, Louisville, KY 40204. **Business Phone:** (502)458-7411.

YOUSSEF, SITAMON MUBARAKA
Publisher, writer. **Personal:** Born Nov 21, 1951, Greenwood, MS; daughter of Ellen Mae Dailey and Hurie Lee; divorced; children: Meahason Baldwin. **Educ:** Calif Univ, BA, 1987; William Carey Col, MEd, 1993. **Career:** Los Angeles Community Col, instr, 1989-90; Fla A&M Univ, instr, 1994-97; Tallahassee Communtiy Col, instr, 1997-99; Tillman Sims Communs, pres, 2000; Author: Mail From Jail: A Glimpse Into A Mother's Nightmare, 2001; Reflections: A Book of Poetry, 2001; Editor: Marcus Garvey: The FBI File, 2001. **Orgs:** Author's Guild, 1998-.

YUILL, ESSIE MCLEAN-HALL
Educator. **Personal:** Born Jan 31, 1923, Wise, NC; daughter of Edward and Lucy; married Lorenzo, Jun 12, 1965 (deceased); children: Lester Slade McLean. **Educ:** Shaw Univ, BA, 1946; Capital Univ, reading specialist cert, 1964; Ohio State Univ, MEd, 1970. **Career:** Educator (retired); Johnsonville High Sch, eng, 1950-55; Kent Elem, 1961-67; Franklin Middle Sch, 1967-70; Barrett Middle, coordr, supvr reading prog, 1971-77; Berry Middle Sch, reading, Commun, 1971-77; Briggs High Sch, reading, Commun skills, 1977-79; Cent High Sch, reading Commun skills, 1979-80; E High Sch, reading, commun skills, 1980-88. **Orgs:** Zeta Phi Beta; charter mem, Qual Sharing,; King Performing Arts; Friends Arts Cult Enrichment; Univ Women; Helen Jenkins Davis Scholar Award Group; Columbus Symphony Orchestra, east unit; Child Develop Coun; Martin Luther King Breakfast, hostess; charter mem, Qual Sharing. **Honors/Awds:** Miss Black Pageant, Les Ami Club, Judge, 1978; Quality of Sharing Recognition Award, 1981; Teacher of the Yr, 1986; Distinguish ServAward, Zeta Phi Beta, 1986-90; Serv Award, Columbus Pub Sch, 1988; Serv Award, Shiloh Baptist Church, 1989.

YUILLE, DR. BRUCE
Dentist. **Personal:** Born in New Jersey. **Career:** Saint Agnes Health Care Ctr, Catonsville, MD, dentist; Pvt pract, dentist, currently. **Orgs:** Pres, Univ Md Dent Sch, 2001; Am Dent Asn; Md Acad Gen Dent; pres, Baltimore City Dent Soc; pres, Alumni Asn; pres, Baltimore City Component Md; pres, Acad Gen Dent. **Honors/Awds:** Master dentist status, Md Acad Gen Dent, 1995; InterNat Honor Dental Organization, Pierre Fauchard Acad, 2001. **Special Achievements:** First African American to receive master dentist status from Maryland Academy of General Dentistry. **Home Phone:** (310)865-4811. **Business Addr:** Dentist, Private Practice, 5310 Old Ct Rd, Randallstown, MD 21133, **Business Phone:** (410)521-1888.

Z

ZACHARY, STEVEN W
Educator, government official. **Personal:** Born Apr 24, 1958, St Paul, MN; son of Percy J and Martha A; divorced; children: Steven Jr & James. **Educ:** Mankato State Univ, BS, 1981; Univ Minn Sch Law, JD, 1984. **Career:** City St Paul, human rights, 1984-92; William Mitchell Col Law, adj prof, 1989-92; State of Minn, diversity & equal opportunity dir, 1992-97; Brauer Law Offices, managing atty, currently. **Orgs:** Sch bd pres, St Peter Claver Sch, 1987-88; MN Minority Lawyer's Asn, 1987-93; pres, Nat Car Park St Paul Branch, 1990-93; bd mem, MCLU, 1990-93; criminal justice taskforce chairperson, Joint Relig Legis Coalition, 1991-92. **Honors/Awds:** Haines Distinguished Service Award, William Mitchell col Law, 1992. **Special Achievements:** What's In Store for Civil Rights in 1990. **Home Addr:** 1360 University Ave W 324, St Paul, MN 55104-4086, **Home Phone:** (612)510-0926. **Business Addr:** Managing Attorney, Brauer Law Offices, 16430 N Scottsdale Rd Suite 425, Phoenix, AZ 85254, **Business Phone:** (480)621-3535.

ZACHARY-PIKE, ANNIE R
Farmer. **Personal:** Born May 12, 1931, Marvell, AR; daughter of Cedel Davidson (deceased) and Carrie Davidson (deceased); married Lester Pike, Apr 10, 1977 (died 1997). **Educ:** Homer G Phillips Sch Nursing; St Christian Col, Hon PhD, 1972. **Career:** Farmer, owner & mgr; Marvell Sch Dist, chapter I parent coord, 1990-91. **Orgs:** Eastern Star; NAACP; AR Asn Colored Women; Phillips Co Extnsn Hmmkrs Coun; IPA; Ark Coun Human Rels; Ark Asn Crppld Inc; Wildlife Federation; EAME; Emergency Sch Asst Proj; Pta; 4-H; Farm Bureau; Farmers Home Admin; adv coun FHA; USDA Civil Rights Comn; Coun Aging; Fair Bd; Small Bus Asn; Nat Coun Christians & Jews; bd The Election Law Inst; Eastern Arkansas Mental Health; Delta Area Devel Inc; Workshop Inc; Rep, Ark St Com Farm; district deputy, Eastern Ark Order of Eastern Star. **Honors/Awds:** Family Year Award, 1959; 4-H Friendship, 1959; Home Demonstration Woman Year, 1965; Queens Womens Federated Club Inc 1969; Delg 1972 GOP Conv Wmn Yr, Alpha Kappa Alpha, 1971.

ZAKARI, TATA
Physician. **Educ:** Ahmadu Bello Univ, MD, 1986. **Career:** Henry Ford Health Syst, physician; Pvt Pract, currently. **Business Addr:** Physician, Private Practitioner, 20755 GREENFIELD, STE 1101, SOUTHFIELD, MI 48075, **Business Phone:** (248)569-7550.*

ZAMBRANA, DR. RAFAEL
Educator. **Personal:** Born May 26, 1931, Santa Isabel, Puerto Rico; married Laura E Alvarez; children: Gloria, Ralph (deceased), Aida, Magda, Wallace, Olga & Daphne. **Educ:** Catholic Univ PR, BA, hist, 1958; Hunter Col, 1962; Columbia Univ, psychol, 1965; MSW, 1974; City Univ New York, PhD, 1982. **Career:** Educator (retired); Bd Educ, NY, jr high sch teacher, 1958-62; Rabbi Jacob Joseph High Sch, teacher, 1962-65; Mobilization Youth, social worker, 1965-67; PR Community Develop Proj, dir training & block orgn prog, 1967-68; Lower E Side Manpower Neighborhood Serv Ctr, dir, 1968-69; Williamsburg Community Corp, exec dir, 1969-71; Community Develop Agency, asst comnr, 1971-74; Medgar Evers Col, City Univ NY, prof pub admin, 1974; City Univ NY, Social Sci Div, chairperson, 1982-89; City Univ NY, chairperson pub admin, 1990-95; City Univ NY, Sch Bus & Pub Admin, dean, 1995-98; City Univ NY, asst pres, 1998-2000. **Orgs:** Consult, Coney Island Community Corp, 1969-78; bd mem, Community Coun Greater New York, 1969-76; inst rep, Nat Asn Schs Penn, 1974-98; local sch bd mem, Dist 12 New York, 1975-85; consult, NY State Dept Corrections, 1976; adv bd mem, Mgt Adv Coun, US Dept Labor, Region II, 1980-82; pres, Coun PR & Hisp Orgn. **Honors/Awds:** Meritorious Service Award, Williamsburg Community Corp, 1971; Devotion to Children Award, Supvr Asn New York City Local Sch Bd Dist #12, 1977; Manpower Ed Grant, US Dept Labor, 1979-83; Outstanding Educator Award, Student's Coun Williamsburg Proj, 1980; various other awards, 1980-99. **Military Serv:** Honorable Discharge, 1950-55; Good Conduct Medal; Korean Serv Medal. **Home Addr:** 3600 Paseo Condado Levittown, Toa Baja, PR 00949-3015.

ZANDER, JESSIE MAE REASOR
School administrator. **Personal:** Born Jul 31, 1932, Inman, VA; married Johnny W. **Educ:** Berea Col, BA, Elem Educ, 1954; Univ Ariz, MA, elem educ, 1966, MA, counguid, 1976; Supvry & Admin Cert. **Career:** School administrator, educator (retired); Benham Elem High Sch, KY, teacher, 1954-58; Tucson Indian Training Sch, AZ, teacher, jr high, 1956-58; Tucson Unified Sch Dist, teacher, 1958-76; Tucson Unified Sch Dist, counr, 1976-79; Miles Explor Learning Ctr Tucson Unified Sch Dist, prin, 1979-80; Lin weaver Sch, Tucson Unified Sch Dist, prin, 1980-89. **Orgs:** Consult, Control Awareness Adminr Retreat, 1975-76; coordr poetry, Sch Ariz St Poetry Soc, 1977-80; bd mem, Pima Coun Community Serv, 1978-79; Educ Div Am Cancer Soc, 1975; Tamiochus Alpha Kappa Alpha Sor Eta Epsilon Omega Chap, 1976-81; vpres, Ariz St Poetry Soc, 1978; conf chair, Ariz St Poetry Soc, 1978-79; facilitator, Y's racial justice prog; coordr, Funeral Consumers Alliance Speakers Bur; prog chair & secy, State Poetry Soc. **Honors/Awds:** Outstanding Pres Coun Black Educr, 1978-79, 1979-80; Newspaper Article Open Educ Miles Exploratory Learning Ctr, 1980; The Phenomenal Woman Award Dinner, Univ Ariz Black Alumni. **Special Achievements:** First African-american to graduate from Berea College since the repeal of the Day Law. Works published in: Brush the Mind Gently, PEN Women, Appalachia Independent & other chap books. **Home Addr:** 5835 E Third St, Tucson, AZ 85711.

ZEALEY, SHARON JANINE
Lawyer. **Personal:** Born Aug 30, 1959, St Paul, MN; daughter of Marion Edward and Freddie Ward. **Educ:** Xavier Univ La, BS, 1981; Univ Cincinnati, JD, 1984. **Career:** Star Bank, corp trust adminr, 1984-86; UAW Legal Servs, atty, 1986-88; Manley, Burke & Lipton, assoc, 1988-90; Ohio Atty Gen, dep atty gen, 1990-94; Southern Judicial Dist Ohio, Asst US Atty, 1995-97; Univ Calif Col Law, adj prof law; US Atty, 1997-2001; Blank Rome LLP, partner, currently. **Orgs:** Am Bar Asn; Ohio Bar Asn; bd mem, Cincinnati Bar Asn; Fed Bar Asn; bd trustees, Legal Aid Soc, Cincinnati, 1987-92, secy, 1990-92; pres, Black Lawyer's Asn, Cincinnati, 1989-91; bd govs, Nat Bar Asn, 1989-91; City Cincinnati Equal Employment Opportunity Adv Review Bd, 1989-91; bd trustees, Cincinnati Bar Asn, 1990-94; City Cincinnati, Tall Stacks Comn, comnr, 1991-96; Mayor's Comn, Children, comnr, 1992-94; Greater Cincinnati Found Task Force, Affordable Home Ownership, 1992-93; Merit Selection Comt, US Sixth Circuit Ct Appeals, 1992-93; co-chair, Greater Cincinnati Minority Coun Prog, 2005; Legal Aid Soc; bd visitors, Univ Cincinnati Col Law. **Honors/Awds:** Member of the Year, Nat Bar Asn, Region VI, 1990; Nicholas Longworth Award, Univ Cincinnati, Col Law, 1997; Career Woman of Achievement, Cincinnati YWCA, 1998; Theodore M Berry Award, Cincinnati Chap, Nat Asn Advan Colored People, 1998; Black Woman of Courage Award, 1999; Political Awareness and Involvement Award, Delta Sigma Theta Sorority, Cincinnati Chap, 2000; Forward Together Award, US Atty's Off, Cincinnati Bar Asn & Cincinnati Black Lawyers Asn, 2000. **Business Addr:** Partner, Blank Rome LLP, 201 E 5th St Suite 1700 PNC Ctr, Cincinnati, OH 45202, **Business Phone:** (513)362-8700.*

ZEITLIN, JIDE J
Investment banker, executive. **Personal:** Born in Ibaden, Nigeria; son of Arnold and Marian. **Educ:** Amherst Col, AB, econ & eng magna cum laude, 1985; Harvard Univ, MBA, 1987. **Career:** Goldman Sachs & Co, summer assoc, 1983-86, assoc, 1987-91, vpres, 1991-96, sr investment banker, partner & managing dir, 1996; pvt investor. **Orgs:** Chmn, Bd Trustee, Amherst Col, 1993-; trustee, Milton Acad, 1996-; dir, Common Ground Community HDFC, 1996-; dir, Teach Am New York, 1997-; trustee, Montefiore Med Ctr, 1998-; Harvard Bus Sch Vis Comm; Playwrights Horizons & Common Ground Community; bd dirs, Affiliated Mgrs Group Inc, 2006; dir, Coach Inc. **Home Addr:** 147 W 15th St, New York, NY 10011. **Business Addr:** Board of Directors, Affiliated Managers Group Inc, 600 Hale St, Prides Crossing, MA 01965, **Business Phone:** (617)747-3300.

ZELIS, KAREN DEE
Lawyer. **Personal:** Born Oct 21, 1953, Washington, DC; daughter of Jeanne Rivoire; divorced; children: Jason Christopher, Erika Nikole. **Educ:** Univ Calif, BA, 1975; Armstrong Law Sch, JD, 1979. **Career:** Alameda County Family Ct Servs, secy, 1982-83; Contra Costa District Atty Off, dep dist atty, 1983-. **Orgs:** Calif State Bar Asn, 1982-; Calif Dist Atty Asn, 1983-; Charles Houston Bar Asn, 1990-; Am Bar Asn, 1990-; Contra Costa Bar Asn, 1990-. **Business Addr:** Deputy District Attorney, Contra Costa District Attorneys Office, 725 Court St 4th Fl, Martinez, CA 94553, **Business Phone:** (415)646-4500.

ZELLNER, HUNNDENS GUISEP. **See ZELLNER, PEPPI.**

ZELLNER, PEPPI (HUNNDENS GUISEP ZELLNER)
Football player. **Personal:** Born Mar 14, 1975, Forsyth, GA. **Educ:** Fort Valley State Univ. **Career:** Dallas Cowboys, defensive end, 1999-2002; Wash Redskins, 2003; Ariz Cardinals, defensive end, 2004.

ZEMAN, PAULA REDD
County government official. **Career:** Westchester County, Dept Human Resources, comnr, cur. **Orgs:** Vice chair, Westchester County Democratic Comt; Women Democrats Westchester; Democratic nat Conv & Electoral Col; Harriman Soc; Westchester Arts Coun; Downtown Musc Grace Church; bd dir, Empire State Pride Agenda. *

ZENO, MELVIN COLLINS
Judge. **Personal:** Born Jul 14, 1945, Jonesboro, LA; son of Ruth Doyle and Nathaniel Sr; married Margie Loud, Dec 27, 1967; children: Monica Lureen & Micah Collins. **Educ:** Southern Univ, BS, 1967; Loyola Univ S, JD, 1974. **Career:** Red Ball Motor Freight Co, dock worker, 1966; Iberville Parish, speech & hearing therapist, 1968; Jefferson Parish, spec educ teacher, 1968-75; atty law, 1974-92; Xavier Univ, bus law instr, 1986-88; Jefferson Parish, asst dist atty, 1975-92, 24th Judicial Dist Ct, division p, judge, 1992-. **Orgs:** Dir, La State Spec Olympics, 1969-; co-founder, vpres, bd dirs, Martin L King Jr Task Force, 1979-; int bd dirs, Omega Psi Phi Frat, 1983-90; adv bd, Hope Haven Madonna Manor Home Boys, 1984-; co-founder, pres, bd dirs, Jefferson Black Chamber Com Inc, 1989-92; bd dirs, March Dimes Birth Defects Found, 1991; life sustaining mem, NAACP; chmn, Jefferson Parish Econ Develop Comn, Bus Develop Expansion Adv Comt; Am Bar Asn; La State Bar Asn; Louis Martinet Legal Soc; Nat Bar Asn; Am Judges Asn; La Dist Judges Asn; Fourth & Fifth Circuit Judges Asn. **Honors/Awds:** Outstanding Community

Service Award, Kenner Kiwanis Club, 1979; Man of the Year Award, Omega Psi Phi Frat Inc, 1980-81, 1984, 1991, 1992; Outstanding Service Award, Jefferson Black Chamber Com Inc, 1989-91; Outstanding Service Award, Martin Luther King Jr Task Force Inc, 1991. **Special Achievements:** Elected international first vice grand basileus, Omega Psi Phi Fraternity, 1988; appointed Louisiana State Bar Association, attorney, arbitration board, 1991-92; Fourth National Conference on the Sexual Victimization of Children, lecturer; opened first African-American History Museum, Jefferson Parish, 1992; First black elected judge, 24th judicial district court, 1992. **Business Addr:** Judge, Jefferson Parish Courthouse, 24th Judicial District Court, 2nd & Derbigny St, Gretna, LA 70053, **Business Phone:** (504)364-3975.

ZENO, WILLIE D.
Executive. **Personal:** Born Mar 28, 1942, Dallas, TX. **Educ:** Univ OK, MSEE, 1972; Bus Bishop Col, MBA, 1968. **Career:** Hank Moore & Assoc; Goodyr Aerospace, personal dir; EOC US Dept Labor, dir; Eng & Design Eng Soc Am Leap, dir. **Orgs:** Urban Leg Nat Businessman. **Honors/Awds:** Goodyear, Weak Design Eng Month. **Military Serv:** USN, 1 lt.

ZIEGLER, DR. DHYANA
Educator, school administrator. **Personal:** Born May 5, 1949, New York, NY; daughter of Ernest and Alberta A Guy. **Educ:** Baruch Col CUNY, BA, BS (Cum Laude), 1981; Southern Ill Univ, Carbondale,MA, 1983, PhD, 1985. **Career:** Essence Mag, mkt researcher, 1972-75; Rosenfeld Sirowitz & Lawson,copywriter & radio producer, 1974-75; Patten & Guest Productions NY,regional mgr, 1976-79; WNEW TV, internship desk asst & production asst-;Seton Hall Univ, counr high sch studs, 1979-81; Baruch Col CUNY, Eng tutor& instr writing workshops, 1979-81; Westside Newspaper, reporter; CBS TV Network, production intern, 1980-81; Southern Ill Univ, Dept Radio &Television, lab instr, 1981-83; Jackson State Univ, dept Mass Commun, asstprof, 1984-85; Univ Tenn, Knoxville, dept Broadcasting, asst profbroadcasting, 1985-90, prof broadcasting, 1990-97, assoc dir diversityresources & educ serv; Fla A&M Univ, prof jour, 1997-, actg vpres res &dir, Univ Planning & Analysis, 2002-03, asst vpres instrnl technol & acadaffairs, currently. **Orgs:** Nat Pol Congress Black Women; Delta Sigma Theta Sor Inc; Phi Delta Kappa;Post Doctoral Acad Higher Educ, grad fel; Speech Comm Asn; Blacks in Communications Alliance; Nat Coun Negro Women Inc; Southern Ill Univ Alumni Asn; Metro Black Media Coalition Conf, 1984, Southern Ill Univ &Blacks Commun Alliance, 1985, Nat Black Media Coalition Conf, 1985; US Armed Forces Azores Portugal, speaker & consult, 1986; Kiwanis ClubKnoxville, 1988-; Southern Regional Develop Educ Proj Coordr, Delta Sigma Theta, 1988-; Women Commun, Inc, vpres develop, pres-elect, 1989, pres,1990-91; Soc Prof Journalists, 1988. **Honors/Awds:** Seek Scholar Awards Academic & Service, 1979-81; Baruch Col; Rita Leeds Service Award, 1981 Baruch Col; Sheldon Memorial Award Baruch Col, 1981; Scrippt-Howard Award Baruch Col, 1981; United Press Intl Outstanding Achievement Radio Documentary, 1982; Dept Radio & TV SIUC Outstanding Radio Production Award, 1982-83; Grad Dean's Doctoral Fel, 1983-84; Paul Robinson's Roby Scholar Award Black Affairs Council, 1984; Cert Merit Award, S Ill Univ Broadcasting Serv, 1984; Ebony Bachelorette, 1985; Seek Alumni Award Baruch Col, 1985; Outstanding Faculty Member of the Year, Col Communications, Univ Tenn, Knoxville, 1987-88; Chancellor's Citation Serv,Univ Tenn, Knoxville, 1988; State of Tenn Governor's Award for Outstanding Achievement, 1991; Consortium Doctors Award, 1991; Faculty Res Award,1992; Chancellor Citation Extraordinary Service, 1992; University's African-American Hall of Fame; '50 Most Important African-Americans', US Black Engineer & Information Technology magazine, 2003. **Special Achievements:** First African-American to be elected as President of the University of Tennessee-Knoxville Faculty Senate; Co-author: "Thunder and Silence: The Mass Media in Africa"; Several book chapters and journal articles; First African-American faculty member in the history of the University of Tennesse, Knoxville to serve as President of the Faculty Senate, 1995. **Business Addr:** Professor of Journalism, Florida Agricultural & Mechanical University, School of Journalism & Graphic Communication, 510 Orr Dr Suite 4003, Tallahassee, FL 32307, **Business Phone:** (850)599-3379.

ZIMMERMAN, EUGENE
Physician. **Personal:** Born Jul 7, 1947, Orangeburg, SC; married Sheila Beth Hughes; children: Brian, Monica. **Educ:** Jersey City State Col, BA, 1969; Howard Univ Med Sch, MD, 1973. **Career:** Harlem Hosp Ctr, intern, 1973-74; Howard Univ Hosp, resident, 1974-76; Stud Health Serv Gallanhet Col, actg med dir, 1977-81; SENAB, med dir, 1979-84; Dept Forensic Psychiatry, staff physician. **Orgs:** Med Soc DC, 1976-; NY Acad Scis 1984-. **Honors/Awds:** Board Certified Internist, Am Bd Internal Med, 1985. **Home Addr:** 4621 Sargent Rd NE, Washington, DC 20017. **Business Addr:** Staff Physician, Department of Forensic Psychiatry, 1905 E St SE Bldg 22, Washington, DC 20003.

ZIMMERMAN, MATTHEW AUGUSTUS
Clergy, military leader. **Personal:** Born Dec 9, 1941, Rock Hill, SC; son of Matthew Augustus and Alberta Loretta Brown; married Barbara Ann Boulware, Sep 5, 1964; children: Tina, Dana & Meridith. **Educ:** Benedict Col, BS, 1962; Duke Univ, MDiv, 1965; Long Island Univ, MSEd, 1975; AUS Command & Gen Staff Col; AUS War Col. **Career:** Hq, third infantry div, staff chaplain, 1980-82; Training Doctrine Command, dep staff chaplain, 1983-85; US Forces Command, command chaplain, 1985-89; USY, dep chief chaplains, 1989-90, chief chaplains, 1990-94; Vet Affairs Med Ctr, Dept Veterans Affairs Chaplain Serv, dir, 1994-98; First Baptist Church, Warrenton, VA, pastor, currently; Morris Col, campus pastor & instr; Idaho State Univ, campus pastor. **Orgs:** Military Chaplains Asn; Asn USY; bd gov, USO; Kiwanis Int; Opp Fraternity Inc; chair, bd visitors, Howard Univ Sch Divinity; bd dir, Coalition Spirit-filled Churches. **Honors/Awds:** Doctor of Humane Letters, Benedict Col, 1991; Roy Wilkins Meritorious Service Award, Nat Asn Advan Colored People, 1990; Distinguished Alumni Award, Duke Univ Divinity School, 1991; Black Hall of Fame, 1992. **Special Achievements:** Zimmerman became the first African-American student to graduate with a master of divinity degree from Duke University. First African director of the Dept of Veterans Affairs National Chaplains Center. In 1965, Chaplain Zimmerman became the first African-American to earn a Master of Science degree in Guidance and Counseling from Long Island University, Brooklyn, New York; first African-American to serve as Chief of Chaplains of any military service. **Military Serv:** AUS, major gen; Legion Merit, Bronze Star, 3 Meritorious Service Medals, Army Commendation Medal, Vietnam Honor Medal First Class; Dist Service Medal; The Defense Superior Service Medal; Legion of Merit. **Home Addr:** 2661 Centennial Ct, Alexandria, VA 22311-1303, **Home Phone:** (703)671-4833. **Business Addr:** Pastor, First Baptist Church, 39 Alexandria Pike, PO Box 189, Warrenton, VA 20188, **Business Phone:** (540)347-2775.

ZIMMERMAN, SAMUEL LEE
School administrator. **Personal:** Born Apr 28, 1923, Anderson, SC; son of William L and Corinne O Banks; married Blanche Carole Williams, May 30, 1946; children: Samuel Lee Jr. **Educ:** Benedict Col, AB, Elem Educ, 1962; Furman Univ, Grad Study, 1965, 1968; Univ Wash, attended 1973; Glassboro State Col, attended 1974. **Career:** Greenville Sch Dist, elem reading teacher, 1961-70; The Greenville Piedmont, news reporter, 1970-73; WFBC-TV, host, 1976-77; WFBC Radio, host, 1976-82; Sch Dist Greenville Co, dir sch & community rels, 1973-87; Partridge Assoc, consult. **Orgs:** Vice pres at large, Nat Sch Pub Rels Asn, 1979-81; SC Asn Sch Admin; Community Study Educ State SC; bd dir, SC Community Blind; bd dir, Goodwill Indus Upper SC; bd trustees, Springfield Baptist Church; pres, Rotary Club Pleasantburg, Greenville, SC, 1995-96. **Honors/Awds:** AP Award Sampling Attitudes of Young Blacks, 1969; William F Gaines Mem Award, 1971; Distinguished Service Award, City Greenville, 1974; Service Certificate Appreciation, United Way of Greenville, 1977; Certificate Appreciation, Nat Sch Pub Rels, 1976-77; Certificate Award, Greenville Co Human Rels, 1977-78; Jr Humanitarian Award, Whitney M Young, 1988; Outstanding Volunteer, United Negro Col Fund, 1989; The Eugene T Carothers Human Relations Award, Nat Sch Pub Rels Asn, 1991; SC Black Hall of Fame, 100 Black Men of South Carolina, 1997. **Military Serv:** AUS, T-5, 2 yrs. **Home Addr:** 6 Allendale Lane, PO Box 6535, Greenville, SC 29607.

ZIYAD, KARIM
President (Organization). **Career:** TYT Inc, pres. **Business Addr:** President, TYT Inc, 2808 Hidden Forest Ct, Atlanta, GA 30316, **Business Phone:** (404)569-1297.

ZOLA, NKENGE (TERESA KRISTINE NKENGE ZOLA BEAMON)
Broadcaster. **Personal:** Born Apr 11, 1954, Detroit, MI; daughter of Maya Beamon-Dean and Henry Edward Moscow Beamon. **Educ:** Univ Mich, Ann Arbor, MI, 1975; Rec Inst Det, E Detroit, MI, 1987; Wayne State Univ, Detroit, MI, 1977, 1989; Wayne County Community Col. **Career:** Tribe Mag, Detroit, MI, copy ed, 1976-77; WJLB AM/FM, Detroit, MI, continuity dir, 1977-78, news anchor, reporter, 1978-81; Christopher Pitts, Birmingham, MI, host, Jazzmasters: Keepers Flame, 1989-90; WDET-FM, Detroit, MI, producter, host, The Nkenge Zola Prog, 1982-, news anchor, reporter, 1990-; Arts & Soc, The Witness Mag, ed, 1995; Oakland Univ, fac, currently. **Orgs:** Project BAIT (Black Awareness TV), 1976-; Afrikan Libr Singers, 1989-; chair, Afrikan Child Enrichment Asn, 1989-; bd mem, Women's Justice Ctr, 1991-; bd mem, Creative Arts Collective, 1990-; forum coordr, Creative Community Artist Support Group, 1990-; Advocators, Nat Org Am Revolution, 1977-87; nat bd mem, Youth Coun Pres, Detroit; co-founder, U M Branch NAACP, 1970-76; James & Grace Lee Boggs Ctr Nuture Community Develop, 1996-; Casa de Unidad Cultural & Media Arts Ctr, bd; founding bd, Detroit Women's Coffee House, 1996-. **Honors/Awds:** Subject of tribute, "A Celebration of the Life of a Spiritual Warrior," Committee for Community Access to WDET, 1990; Exceptional Media Artist Award, Beatty & Asn, 1990; Outstanding Supporter of Jazz Artists, Success Academy of Fine Arts, 1985; Spirit of Detroit Award, City of Detroit, 1985; editor, Loving Them to Life, New Life Publishers, 1987; Miss NAACP Detroit, NAACP, 1970; Mich Asn Broadcasters First Place Award, Temple Confessions, Detroit Press Club Award, 1995; Asniated Press Award, 1992, 1995; Recipient Governor's Arts Award, 1995; Media Honor Roll, Arts Reporting; Recipient, Cultural Warrior Award, Societie Culturally Concerned. **Business Addr:** Faculty, Oakland University, 2200 N Squirrel Rd, Rochester Hills, MI 48309, **Business Phone:** (248)276-0450.

ZOLLAR, ALFRED
Executive. **Personal:** Born Jan 1, 1955?, Kansas City, MO; married Alicia Underwood; children: Al Jr & Keisha. **Educ:** Univ Calif San Diego, MA, appl math, 1976. **Career:** IBM, syst engr, 1977-86, corp staff mem, 1986-89, DB2 prod mgr, 1989-95, Software Group, lab mgr, 1995-96, Tivoli, sr vpres, 1996-98, 2004-, Ntwk Comput Software Div, gen mgr, 1998-2000, Lotus Develop Corp, pres & ceo, 2000-03, iSeries, gen mgr, 2003-. **Orgs:** Bd mem, Chubb Group Ins; co-chmn, IBM Black Family Tech Awareness; former bd mem, Alexian Bros Hosp Found; Harvard Univ, Kennedy Ctr Sch Govt, Ctr Bus & Govt, leadership coun. **Honors/Awds:** Named one of 50 Most Important African Americans in Technol, Black Money website, Soul Tech website, 2001; ranked # 15, Most Powerful Black Execs, Fortune, 2002. **Business Addr:** General Manager, IBM Corporation, 1 New Orchard Road, Armonk, NY 10504-1722, **Business Phone:** 888-839-9289.*

ZOLLAR, DORIS L.
Executive, educator. **Personal:** Born Dec 7, 1932, Little Rock, AR; married Lowell M, 1954; children: Nikki Michele & Lowell M Jr. **Educ:** Talladega Col, BA, 1951; Univ Calif, Grad Sch, MA, 1952; DePaul Univ, PostGrad, 1952-54, 1958-59. **Career:** Chicago Pub Sch, teacher, 1952-67; C Haven Residential Sch MultHandicapped C, found, org, sch dir, 1973-; Woodlawn Orgn, dir, 1974, dir develop, 1976; Independent Bull Newspaper, women's ed, 1976-77; Triad Consult Service, pres, 1977-. **Orgs:** Community leader, Mid-West Conf Pres Lyndon B Johnsons Community Equal Oppty, 1964; Chicago Urban League, 1965-, Lois R Lowe Womens Div UNCF, 1966-, Jackson Park Highlands Asn, 1966-; vpres, Bravo Chap Lyric Opera Chicago, 1966; chmn, Ebony Fashion Fair, 1968-69; corr sec Ill Childrens Home & Aid Soc, 1998-70; pub rel fund raising consult, Nat Med Asn Project, 1973-75; mem S Shore Community, 1974-; vpres, XXI bd Michael Reese Hosp, 1974-76; Cook Cty Welfare Serv Community, 1975-; Chicago Pub Sch Art Soc Chicago Art Inst, 1975-; org & coordr, Minority Constr Workers, 1975; adv Midwest Asn Sickle Cell Anemia, 1976-; adv, Black United Fund, 1976-; mem, Art Pub Places Bd, 1976-, The Coun Foreign Affaris, 1976; IntlVisitors Ctr, Bd, 1976-; dir, fung devel, The Woodlawn Org World Serv Counl Nat YWCA, 1976-. **Honors/Awds:** AKA Scholarship, competitive exam 1947; Exchange student from Talladega College to Cedar Crest College, 1948-49; Florina Lasker Fellowship Award, 1951; Will Rogers Meml Fellowship toward PhD in History, 1952; "Ed Motivation of the Culturally Disadvantaged Youth" Chicago Bd of Ed, 1958-60; National Medical Association Award, Womens Aux, 1966; The Pittsburgh Couriers National Ten Best Dressed, 1972-74; Honour Librarian of the Chicago Public Library City of Chicago, 1974; The Commercial Bread basket Association Award, 1975; Institute for Health Resources Devel Award, 1975; Oper PUSH Award, 1975, 76; Person of the Day Award, Radio Stations WAIT, WBEE, 1969, 76; Beatrice Caffrey Youth Services Inc, Annual Merit Award for Civic Achievement, 1976; Alpha Gamma Pi, Iota Phi Lambda Sor Bus & Professional Award, 1977; International Po Authority, dir Ill,1986-. **Special Achievements:** First black president of the United Nations Children's Fund Chicago. **Business Addr:** President, TRIAD Consulting Services, 6901 S Constance Ave, Chicago, IL 60637, **Business Phone:** (773)908-2928.

ZOLLAR, JAWOLE WILLA JO
Dancer, choreographer. **Personal:** Born Dec 21, 1950, Kansas City, MO; daughter of Alfred Jr and Dorothy Delores; children: Elizabeth Herron. **Educ:** Univ Miss, BA, dance, 1975; Fla State Univ, MFA, dance, 1979. **Career:** Fla State Univ, fac mem, 1977-80; Urban Bush Women dance troupe, founder & artistic dir, 1984-; NEA Choreography fel, 1992, 1993, 1994; Makato State Univ Worlds Thought prog, resident scholar, 1993-94; Univ Calif, Los Angeles, Dept Dance & Worlds Cult, Regents lectr, 1995-96; Ohio State Univ, guest teacher, 1996; Mass Inst Technol, Abramowitz Memorial Lectr, 1998; Fla State Univ, artist-in-residence & prof dance, 1997-. **Orgs:** Asn Am Cult; Int Asn Blacks Dance; founder, Urban Bush Women, 1984. **Honors/Awds:** NY Dance & Performance Award, 1992; Outstanding Alumni, Univ Miss, 1993; Capezio Award for outstanding achievement in dance, 1994; Alumna of the Year Award, Fla State Univ, 1997; Doris Duke Award, Am Dance Festival, 1997; New York Dance and Performance Award, A BESSIE, 2006; Martin Luther King Distinguished Service Award, Fl State Univ. **Special Achievements:** Was prominently featured in the PBS Documentary "Free to Dance", which chronicles the African American influence on modern dance. **Business Addr:** Founder, Urban Bush Women, 138 S Oxford St Suite 4B, Brooklyn, NY 11217, **Business Phone:** (718)398-4537.

ZOLLAR, NIKKI MICHELE

Lawyer, chief executive officer, president (organization). **Personal:** Born Jun 18, 1956, Chicago, IL; daughter of Doris Lowe and Lowell M; married William A von Hoene Jr, Jun 18, 1983; children: William Lowell von Hoene & Branden Tracey. **Educ:** Johns Hopkins Univ, Baltimore, MD, BA, 1977; Georgetown Univ Law Ctr, JD, 1980. **Career:** US Dist Ct Northern Dist Ill, judicial law clerk, 1980-81; Lafontant, Wilkins, Jones & Ware, Chicago, IL, assoc, 1981-83; Kirkland & Ellis, Chicago, IL, assoc, 1983-85; Chicago Bd Election Commissioners, chmn, 1987-90; Ill Dept Prof Regulation, dir, 1990-99; Gemini Electronics Inc, sr vpres & gen coun; Triad Consult Serv Inc, pres & chief exec officer, currently. **Orgs:** Co-chair, Telethon Night Event, UNCF, 1980-90; Chicago Comn Solidarity Southern Africa, 1986-; County Outreach Comn, Field Mus Natural Hist, 1987-90; alumni bd, Georgetown Univ Law Ctr, 1987-90; Lois R Lowe Women's Bd, UNCF, 1987-; chair educ comt, Chicago Archit Found Bd, 1987-90; Alpha Gamma Pi, 1987-; co-chair, Law Exploring Comn, Young Lawyers Sect Chicago Bar Asn, 1988-90; bd trustees, Woodland's Acad Sacred Heart, 1988-; Chicago Urban League, 1988-; County Youth Creative Learning Experience; trustee, Hektoen Inst Med; bd mem, Proj Explor; Chicago Heart Asn, Women's Coun. **Honors/Awds:** Certificate of Outstanding Achievement, Ill State Atty Appellate Serv Comn, 1981; Serv & Leadership Award, UNCF, 1983; Outstanding Young Professor, Chicago Urban Profs, 1985; Martin Luther King Award, Boy Scouts Am, 1989; African-Am Women's Achievement Award, Columbia Col, 1989; Kizzy Award, Revlon/Kizzy Found, 1989; David C Hilliard Award, Chicago Bar Asn, 1989; Youth Serv, Beatrice Caffrey, 1989; Achievement & Serv County Award, YMCA, 1991; Outstanding Achievement Award, YWCA. **Special Achievements:** One of 100 Outstanding Black Bus & Prof Women US, Dollars & Sense, 1988. **Business Addr:** Chief Executive Officer, President, Triad Consulting Services Inc, 10 S Riverside Plz Suite 810, Chicago, IL 60606, **Business Phone:** (312)863-2500.

ZOOK, KRISTAL BRENT

Writer, educator. **Personal:** Born in Los Angeles, CA. **Educ:** Univ Calif, Santa Barbara, BA, 1987; Univ Calif, Santa Cruz, PhD, 1994. **Career:** Univ Calif Santa Barbara, reader, 1986, acad adv & tutor, EOP/SAA Prog, 1986; Pvt Eng teacher, Madrid, Spain, 1986-87; Univ Calif Santa Cruz, tutor, Span lit & compos, 1988-89, instr 1990, Ctr Cult Studies, assoc, 1990-91, teacher's asst, 1991; Black Women Writers, teacher's asst, 1989; Univ Calif Irvine, Humanities Res Inst, resident scholar, 1993; Univ Calif Los Angeles, vis asst prof, African Am Studies, 1995-96; Murdoch Univ, Sch Humanities, vis lectr, 1996; Univ Nev, Reno, Spring, vis hilliard scholar, 1996; Washington Post, feature writer, arts/style section; Essence, Working Mother, contrib ed; New York Times Mag, feature writer; USA Weekend, features writer; Los Angeles Times Mag, features writer; LA Weekly, features writer; The Village Voice, features writer; Vibe, features writer; Essence, features writer; O: Oprah Mag, features writer; Calif State Univ Northridge, asst prof; Columbia Univ, Grad Sch Jour, assoc adj prof; Hofstra Univ, assoc prof jour, media studies & pub rels, currently. Books: Color by Fox: the Fox Network & the Revolution in Black Television, 1999; Black Women's Lives: Stories of Power & Pain, 2006. **Honors/Awds:** First Place Essay Winner, W.E.B. DuBois Writing Contest, Univ Calif Santa Barbara, 1986.

ZOW, JAMES ALLEN

Lawyer. **Educ:** Univ Fla Col Law, JD. **Career:** Savannah State Univ, chief legal officer, dir admin affairs, exec asst pres & legal coun, currently. **Orgs:** Am Asn State Col & Univ Millennium Leadership Initiative. **Honors/Awds:** Innovator Role Model Award, 2000; Healthcare Hero Award, 2002; E-Health & Technology Pacesetter Award, 2002. **Business Addr:** Executive Assistant to the President, Legal Counsel, Savannah State University, 3219 Col St, Savannah, GA 31404, **Business Phone:** (912)356-2507.

ZULU, ITIBARI M

Librarian, editor. **Personal:** Born Apr 24, 1953, Oakland, CA; married Simone N Koivogui, Aug 9, 1980; children: Akiba, Itibari Jr, Togba & Kadiatou. **Educ:** Merritt Col, Oakland, Calif, AA, 1974; Calif State Univ, Hayward, BA, 1976; San Jose State Univ, San Jose, Calif, MLS, 1989; Amen-Ra Theol Sem, Los Angeles, ThD, 1999. **Career:** Fresno Unified Sch Dist, Fresno, Calif, teacher, 1981-89; Calif State Univ, Fresno, Calif, lectr, 1988-89, ref librn, 1989-92; Univ Calif, Los Angeles, Ctr African-Am Studies, chief librn, 1992, dir & head librn, currently; The Journal Pan African Studies, founder & ed-in-chief, 1987-pres; Mesa Comm Coll, librn, 2006-pres. **Orgs:** African Diaspora Found; African Am Libr & Info Sci Asn; Former chair, African Am Studies, Black Caucus Am Libr Asn; Univ Calif Los Angeles Black Fac & Staff Asn; Am Libr Asn; founding provost, Amen-Ra Community Assembly Calif Inc; Asn Study Classical African Civilizations, 1995-; Librarians Sect Asn Col & REs Libr Am Libr Asn, 1996-99. **Honors/Awds:** Jomo Kenyatta Dedication Award, African Stud Union, Calif State Univ, Fresno, 1984; Outstanding Support & Guidance Faculty Award, Calif State Univ, Fresno, African Am Orgn Coun, 1991; co-founder, African Am Libr & Info Sci Asn, 1993. **Special Achievements:** Author, Ancient Kemetic Roots Library & Information Science, 1992-; Editor, Multicultural Review, African & African American Studies, 1993-; Co-Editor Lexicon African American Subject Headings, 1994; Contributing Editor: The Black Church Review, 1994; Author, Exploring the African Centered Paradigm: Discourse and Innovation in African World Community Studies, 1999. **Business Addr:** Librarian, UCLA Center for African American Studies, PO Box 951545, Los Angeles, CA 90095-1545.

Obituaries

ADAMS, ALBERT W.
Executive. **Personal:** Born Nov 22, 1948, Detroit, MI; died Dec 11, 2007, MO; son of Albert W Sr and Goldie I Davis; married Linda; children: Nichole Leahna, Albert III, Melanie Rachel & Kimberly Monet. **Educ:** Harris Teacher Col, St Louis, BA, 1970, post grad; Southern Ill Univ, MBA, 1974. **Career:** City St Louis, recreation supvr, 1968-70; St Louis Pub Sch, teacher, 1970-71; Magdala Found, counr, 1971-77; Seven-Up Co, personnel asst, 1971-74, EEO adminr 1974-77, mgr employ, 1977-79, mgr affirmative action, 1979-80, mgr indus Rels, 1981-83, mgr personnel progs & serv 1983-85, mgr personnel opers, 1985-89; Citi corp Mortgage Inc, Sales Div, asst vpres human resources, 1989-91; Lincoln Indust, vpres, human resources, 1991-95, vpres, human resources & qual, 1995. **Orgs:** ASPA, 1971-78; St Louis Indust Rels Asn, 1971-78; corp chmn, United Negro Col Fund, 1972; charter mem, St Louis EEO Group, 1974-76; comt mem, StLouis Univ Affirmative Action Comt, 1975-77; trustee, San Luis Hills subd1975-78; Mo Adv Comt Voc Placement, 1980-83; Kappa Alpha Psi; Antioch Baptist Church, St Louis MO; comnr, St Louis Civil Rights Enforcement Agency, 1988-91; mem bd dirs, United Way St Louis, 1989-92; mem bd dirs, Vanderschmidt Sch, 1989-97; develop coun mem, Habitat Humanity, 1996-98; trustee & deacon, Antioch Baptist Church; bd, AAIM, 1996; Gateway Purchasers for Health, 1996. **Honors/Awds:** Recognition for raising funds for United Negro Col Fund; Junior Achievement Scholarship, 1966; Eugene Nugent Business Innovation Award, 1999; Trio Achiever Award, 2000. **Home Addr:** 2331 Albion Pl, St Louis, MO 63104, **Home Phone:** (314)772-9244.

ADAMS, DR. CLARENCE LANCELOT, JR.
Educator, psychologist. **Personal:** Born in New York, NY; died Jan 1, 2008, New York, NY; son of Clarence Lancelot Sr and Ernesta Clarrisa Coppin Larier. **Educ:** Long Island Univ, BS, 1950; NY Univ, MA, 1952; Yeshiva Univ NY, EdD, 1973. **Career:** Pvt pract, NY State licensed clin psychologist, 1958; Hunter Col CUNY,psychologist, 1961-64; Bur Child Guid, New York Bd Ed, psychologist,1967-68; SEEK Prog, Hunter Col CUNY, psychologist, counr, 1968-70; NewYork Bd Ed, res consult, 1970-73; Bronx C C, CUNY, assoc prof, 1973; PaceUniv, Psychol Dept NY, adj prof, 1988. **Orgs:** Consult, Psychol Proj, 145, 1976, AMCRO Inc, 1977; comn educ & mental health, 100 Black Men, 1973; Harlem Cult Coun, Nat Assoc Blacks Concernedcriminal Justice, Col Pub Agency Prog Comt, US Civil Serv Comn, NY Psychol Asn, Am Psychol Asn, NY Soc Clin Psychol, Asn Black Psychol, Am Ortho Psychol Asn, Am Asn Mental Def, Am Soc Gp Psychol, Soc Study Gr Tensions,NEA, Prof Staff Cong. **Honors/Awds:** NY Perm Cert Sch Psychol, 1968; published A Study Factors Which Affect Acad Success Among SEEK Stud; NY Acad Scholar, 1946; diplomate, Am Acad Behav Med; Nat Regist Health Provider Psychol, 1975; fellow, Am Ortho psychiatric Asn, 1992. **Military Serv:** AUS. **Business Addr:** Adjunct Professor, Pace University, 1 Pace Plz, New York, NY 10038, **Business Phone:** (212)346-1200.

ALEXANDER, ROBERT I.
Social worker. **Personal:** Born Feb 17, 1913; died May 25, 2008, Nashville, TN; son of Israel and Frances; married J L Black; children: Arthur Harris Jr, Claudette E Douglas, Robert A & John Rodney. **Educ:** St Augustines Col, BA, 1943; Atlanta Univ, MA, 1948. **Career:** Buncombe Co, Welfare Dept, NC, child welfare caseworker, 1948-53; Guildord Co, NC, Welfare Dept, child welfare caseworker, 1953-65; A &T Col, Greensboro, soc worker; Proj Uplift, 1965-66; Meharry Med Col, chief soc worker, child develop clin, 1966-79. **Orgs:** Diamond Am Bridge Assn, 1976-77; coordr, Prev Serv Meharry Med Col Comn, 1975-79; past scout master & troup comt; chmn, PTA; chmn, Educ Comn; pres, Nat Asn Advancement Colored People; organizer & past chmn, Z Alexander Freedom Fund Ball; past pres, Middle Tennessee Chap,

Nat Asn Soc Work; past area rep, Nat Asn Soc Workers, TN; various community in connection with Baptist Church; Phi Beta Sigma; past pres, Nashville Duplicate Bridge Club; Emerald Soc Club; past vice chmn, Community Sch; governance bd, Community Mental Health Ctr, Meharry Med Col; Hadley Sr Ctr Bridge Club, Nashville, 1988; general chmn, ABAing Nat Tournament, Nashville, 1989; past pres, Men's Bridge Club. **Special Achievements:** Candidate 20th Councilman Dist Nashville, 1975,79; 19th Dist Rep, Metro Nashville Davidson Co, 1979. **Military Serv:** AUS, 1943-46. **Home Addr:** 2209 Morena St, Nashville, TN 37208, **Home Phone:** (615)329-9350.

ALLEN, BETTY.
Educator, opera singer. **Personal:** Born Mar 17, 1930, Campbell, OH; died Jul 22, 2009, Valhalla, NY; daughter of James Corr and Dora Catherine Mitchell; married Ritten Edward Lee III, Oct 17, 1953; children: Juliana Catherine Hogue & Anthony Edward. **Educ:** Wilberforce Univ, attended 1946; Hartford Sch Music, cert, 1953; BerkshireMusic Ctr; Wittenberg Univ, DHL, 1971; Union Col, PhD (music), 1981. **Career:** New York City Opera, 1954; Town Hall, 1958;Teatro Colon, Buenos Aires,Argentina, 1964; San Francisco Opera, 1966; Manhattan Sch Music, mem; CanOpera, 1971; New York City Opera, 1973-75; NC Sch Arts, teacher, 1978-87;Curtis Inst Music, teacher; Manhattan Sch Music, trustee, teacher; HarlemSch Arts, exec dir, Voice Dept, chair, 1979-92; pres emer, 1992. **Orgs:** NAACP; Hartford Music Club; Metro Opera Guild; Urban League; Am GuildMusic; Artists Equity; Am-Mus Nat Hist; AFTRA; Silvermine GuildArtists; Jeunesses Musicales; Gioventu Musicales; Unitarian UniversalistWomen's Fed; Student Sangverein Trondheim; Nat Negro Musicians Asn; bd mem& exec comt mem, Carnegie Hall; Nat Found Advan Arts; Arts & Bus Coun; AmArts Alliance; US Comt UNICEF; Manhattan Sch Music; trustee, Chamber MusicSoc Lincoln Ctr; New York City Adv Comt Cultural Affairs; Schomburg Comn;Harlem Arts Advocacy Coalition, co-chair. **Special Achievements:** Has appeared as soloist with world's leading orchestras & renownedconductors including: Bernstein, Casals, Dorati, Leinsdorf, Maazel-,Martinon, Munch, Ormandy, Ozawa, Pritchard, Solti, Steinberg, & Stokowski;regularly appears at the Marlboro, Casals, Tanglewood, & other musicfestivals; adjudicator vocal competitions: Metrop Opera Regionals, YoungConcert Artists, Oratorio Society, Can Women's Club, Natl Found Advan Arts& The Int Vocal Competition Herogenbosch.

ANDERSON, DR. MARCELLUS J., SR.
Executive. **Personal:** Born Jun 21, 1908, Anderson, SC; died Oct 10, 2004, Austin, TX; son of Edward Anderson; married Ada; children: Sandra Joy & Marcellus Jr. **Educ:** Ohio State Univ, AB; London Col Appl Sci Eng, doctor humane rel. **Career:** Livingstone Col, Samuel Huston Col, Huston-Tillotson Col, former teacher; Pan TX Mortgage Invest Co Austin, TX, pres, 1978-85; Great Nat Investment Co, currently. **Orgs:** Pres, bd chmn, 1989-, Fedn Masons World; dir comm, Natl Bank Austin; dir, United Mortgage Bankers Am Inc; pres, NatAlliance Black Orgs, 1980-; grand master, MW St Joseph Grand Lodge, 1978-95; mem, Littlefield Soc. **Honors/Awds:** St Andrew General Grand Masonic Cong AF & AM, Distinguished Meritorious Award; Outstanding Leadership & Community Service Award, The Seven-Up Company; BCL Citizenship Award, Ohio State Univ; Distinguished Service Award, Tex Church Ushers & United Political Orgs; Successful Businessman Award, Kappa Alpha Psi Fraternity; Emerson Marcee Award, NAACP; Distinguished Service Award, City Coun Austin TX; Achievement Award, TLOD; Outstanding Leadership

Award, District 13 AF & AM; Austin Area Brotherhood, Businessman Yr Award. **Special Achievements:** First African-American realtor in US.

ANDREWS, DR. ADOLPHUS.
Air force officer, educator. **Personal:** Born Jan 19, 1943, Tampa, FL; died Oct 27, 2008, Montgomery, OH; son of Willie L and Marjorie; married Ruby Nell Brownlee; children: Adolphus William & Dawn Ingliss. **Educ:** Howard Univ, BA, polit sci, 1964; Southern Ill Univ, Edwards ville, MS, polit sci, 1970; Ohio State Univ, PhD, polit sci, 1982; Harvard Inst Educ Mgt, grad, 1995. **Career:** Educator, Air Force Officer (retired); USAF Security Serv, flight comdr, 1965-67; USAF Scott AFB, Ill, Mil Airlift Command, spec security officer, 1967-70; USAF, Squadron Officer; Sch Air Univ Maxwell, AFB, AL, sect comdr & instr, 1970-73; USAF Nakhon Phanom RTAFB Thailand, intelligence analyst de commander pt, defense command briefing officer, 1973-74; Sec Air Force Legis Liaison, legis liaison officer, 1975; USAF Acad, Dept Polit Sci, instr & asst prof, 1974-76, asst prof personnel officer & dir, Am policy studies, 1979-81; Off Sec Air Force, policy anal & speech writer, 1984-85; USAF Acad Prep Sch, comdr, 1985-89; Atlantic Comt Col, exec dir budget &planning, 1989-93, dean admin & bus serv, 1989-97; Cent State Univ, exec vpres & chief financial officer, 1997-2004. **Orgs:** Air Force Asn, 1978-; Am Polit Sci Asn, 1978-; Nat Conf Black Polit Scientists, 1979-; Alpha Phi Alpha Fraternity, 1980; Nat Asn Col & Univ Bus Officers, 1989-; Soc Col Univ Planners, 1989-. **Honors/Awds:** Outstanding Chief Business Officer, Comt Col Bus Officers, NE Region, 1995-96. **Military Serv:** USAF, 1964-89; Distinguished Military Grad ROTC, 1964; Outstanding Unit Award Citation USAF, 1967 & 1973; Scott AFB Jr Officer Month USAF April, 1970; USAF Commendation Medal, 1970 & 1973, Joint Serv Commendation Medal,1974, Meritorious Serv Medal, 1984 & 1985; Legion Merit, 1989. **Home Addr:** 715 E Chip Shot Lane, Absecon, NJ 08201.

ANDREWS, JAMES F.
Educator. **Personal:** Born Oct 23, 1918, Council, NC; died Dec 27, 2000, Elizabethtown, NC; married Dollie Ellison; children: Audrey & Hal. **Educ:** Fayetteville State Univ, BS, 1949; NC A&T State Univ, attended 1961. **Career:** Plain View Elem Sch, prin. **Orgs:** Pres, Bladen Co Teacher Asn; pres, Southeastern Schoolmasters Orgn, 1975; secy, Kappa Rho Chapt, Omega Psi Phi Fraternity Inc; Div Prin; Fayetteville State Univ, Nat Alumni Asn; Lodge No 374, Prince Hall Masons, F&AM NC; Young Dem NC. **Home Addr:** PO Box 505, Elizabethtown, NC 28337.

ANDRIA, HALL. (ANDRIA LYNETTE HALL SIZEMORE)
President (organization). **Personal:** Born in Henderson, NC; died Jan 12, 2009; married Willie J Hall; children: Amber, Cameron & Chase. **Educ:** VA Univ, Lynchburg, Hon Doctorate. **Career:** Speak Easy Media Inc, pres. **Honors/Awds:** Emmy Award for Hosting, received numerous journalism awards. **Special Achievements:** Host radio program, The Walk at Work; Committed to Your Calling and Your Career; featured in Essence, Ebony, Jet, Precious Times.

ATKINS, DAVID. See SINBAD.

BAILEY, BEN E.
Educator. **Personal:** Born Nov 19, 1932, Durant, MS; died Jan 28, 2003, Jackson, MS. **Educ:** Jackson State Univ, BS; Northwestern Univ, MM, PhD. **Career:** Holmes County Training Sch, Durant, Miss, music teacher; Miss Indust Col, music teacher; Tougaloo Col, Dept Music, prof & chmn, consult pres, prof emer music.

Special Achievements: Nonfiction monographs: Constructing Classroom Tests in Music, Northbrook, Illinois: Whitehall Publishers, 1971; Kermit W. Holly, Sr.: The Unsung Hero, 1996; Numerous articles including "The Red Tops: The Orchestra that Covered theDelta.", Black Perspective in Music, Fall 1988; "Music in Slave Era Mississippi", The Journal of Mississippi History 54, February 1992; "The Minstrel Show in Mississippi.", The Journal of Mississippi History, 1995.

BATES, ELIAS. See DIDDLEY, BO.

BATHER, PAUL CHARLES.
Politician, counselor. **Personal:** Born Jun 30, 1947, Brooklyn, NY; died Feb 11, 2009, SAn Antonio, TX; son of Charles and Regina; married Coretta Waddell, Jun 7, 1969; children: Amir & Omar. **Educ:** Fairfield Univ, CT, BA, 1968; City Univ NY, MSW, 1970; Univ Louisville, KY, MBA, 1980. **Career:** Politician (retired), counselor; Jefferson County, Louisville, KY, treas, 1981-86; City Louisville, KY, alderman, 1986-2000; WJYL Radio, Louisville, KY, gen mgr, 1986-88; Urban Studies Inst, assoc dir, 1986-88; Louisville Commun, gen partner; Louisville Radio, ltd partner, 1988; Bather Group, Louisville, KY, pres, 1988; Best Bet Mag, Louisville, KY, pres; Bank Louisville, vpres, 1990-97; Ky State Legis, rep; Hoskins & Assoc LLC, Austin, TX, sr assoc. **Orgs:** Chmn, Economic Devel Comt; chmn, Affirmative Action Comt; mem bd dir, Downtown Devel Corp; life mem, Nat Asn Advan Colored People, Louisville; Louisville Chamber Com; Am Ctr Int Leadership. **Honors/Awds:** Eubank Tucker Award for Courage of Conviction, NAACP, 1984; Nat Alumnus ofthe Year, Am Ctr for Int Leadership, 1986; Outstanding leadership award,Am Ctr Int Leadership, 1987; Outstanding Achievement, Ky Alliance AgainstRacism, 1988; NAACP Freedom Award; Legislator of the Year, Ky HouseRepresentatives, 2001. **Home Addr:** 4706 Varble Ave, Louisville, KY 40211, **Home Phone:** (502)775-6982.

BATTLE, BERNARD J.
Executive. **Personal:** Born Jun 26, 1927, Memphis, TN; died Mar 6, 2009, Philadelphia, PA; son of Lewis (deceased) and Lenora Tolbert; married Corinne Stewart, Nov 4, 1985; children: Maureen B Prillerman, Aaron S, B J Jr, Edwin L & Michelle T. **Educ:** Pioneer Inst, Philadelphia, Pa, dipl, 1951; A&T State Univ, Greensboro, NC, advan spec; Am Savings & Loan League, cert Mgt Training, 1972. **Career:** Palmer Mem Inst, Sedalia NC, bus mgr, 1951-62; Am Fed Savings & Loan Asn, Greensboro NC, ceo & pres. **Orgs:** Pres & mem exec comt, Greensboro Citizens Asn, 1964; Greensboro Polit Action Comm, 1965; vice chmn, Greensboro War Mem Coliseum Comn, 1979-88; treas, 1962-84, pres, 1984-88, Nat Asn Advan Colored People, Greensborobr; treas, Nat Asn Advan Colored People State Conf, 1963-84; asst treas, Nat Asn Advan Colored People, Nat Office, 1979-85; bd dir, Nat Asn Advan Colored People, 1982-88. **Honors/Awds:** Service Award, NC St Nat Asn Advan Colored People, 1972; Service Award, Greensboro Branch Nat Asn Advan Colored People, 1972; Man of the Year, Region V Nat Asn Advan Colored People, 1976; Man of the Year, Greensboro Young Men's Club, 1976; Welterweight (amateur) Boxing Champion, Middle-Eastern Serv Conf AUS, Fort Meyers VA, 1987; Certificate, Youth Service Corp, Greensboro Br, 1984; Man of the Year, Greensboro Branch Nat Asn Advan Colored People, 1989. **Military Serv:** AUS, sgt, 1945-48; Marksman Medal, Peace Medal.

BAYLOR, ERNESTEIN WALKER.
Educator. **Personal:** Born May 26, 1926, McDonough, GA; died Jan 1, 2009, Baltimore, MD; married Solomon. **Educ:** Spelman Col, AB, 1949; Atlanta Univ, MA, 1953; Univ Edinburgh, 1958; Case Western Res Univ, PhD, 1964. **Career:** KY State Univ, 1954-55; Fort Valley State Col, instr, 1955-56; SC State Col, instr prof, 1956-65; Morgan State Univ, prof hist, 1965-98. **Orgs:** Am Hist Asn; Asn Study Afro Life & Hist; Soc Hist Asn; medieval acad pres Baltimore Chap Nat Alumnae Asn, Spelman Col Pub, "Disestablishment Ch Ireland", Jour Social Sci, 1960; "Age of Metternick a study in nonmenclature" exploration educ, 1962; "the influence of Lord Liverpool 1815-1827" Jour Higher Educ, 1967; "The Struggle Parliamentary Reform",1977; "The Black Woman" The Black Am Ref Book, 1976. **Special Achievements:** Books: The Black Woman in American Perspective & Struggle for the Reform of Parliament, 1977.

BIASSEY, DR. EARLE LAMBERT.
Physician. **Personal:** Born Jan 20, 1920, New Brunswick, NJ; died Nov 28, 2007, NJ; son of Earl Henry and Lillian Craig; married Marie Davis; children: Sharon, Earle Jr, Eric & Sandra. **Educ:** Upsala Col, AB, 1943; Howard Univ Sch Med, MD, 1947; Horace Racham Grad Sch, MS, 1953. **Career:** Ment Hyg Clinic, chief, 1955-60; Park City Hosp, attending staff, 1957; Woodfield C's Home, psychiat consult, 1957-62; Bridgeport Hosp, assoc attending, 1959-67, sr attending chief psychiat dept, 1968-76; Elmont Psychiat Inste, courtesy staff, 1969-75; Weslyan Univ, psychiat consult, 1970-; Whiting Forensic Inst, Middletown CT, psychiat consult, 1976-; St Vincent Hosp, sr attending physician; Pvt Pract. **Orgs:** Am Psychiat Asn; Am Acad Psycho anal; Soc Med Psycho anal; Fairfield Co Med Soc; CT Med Soc; Ment Hyg Asn Greater Bridgeport; Ment Health Coun; Stratford Rotary Club; Omega Psi Phi Fraternity; Bridgeport Ment Health Ctr, 1975; Fairfield Co Litch field Chap CT Psychiat Asn; CT Psychiat Asn; Bridgeport YMCA; Acad Educ Am Psychiat Asn; Social Issues Am Acad Psychoanal; Black Rock Cong Church; Soc Med Psycho anal; Prof Adv Comt Bridgeport Ment Health Asn; psychiat consult Bridgeport Educ Syst; Elm crest Psychiat Inst; consult Ment Health Serv & Afro-Am Inst Wesleyan Univ; Whiting Forensic Inst; Christian Med Soc; Am Psychiat Asn. **Honors/Awds:** Daniel Griffin Award, Bridgeport Mentl Health Asn. **Military Serv:** AUS, capt, 1953-55. **Home Addr:** 3300 Main St, Fairfield, CT 06614.

BLAND, ARTHUR HENRY.
Government official. **Personal:** Born Dec 1, 1923, Milledgeville, GA; died Jan 9, 2009, Reynoldsburg, OH; married Valerie Howard; children: Deborah, Stephanie & Angela. **Educ:** Ohio State Univ, BS, 1950; Cent Mich Univ, grad study; Indust Col Armed Forces, Air War Col, attended. **Career:** Government official (retired); USAF, Dept Defense, systs mgr, currently. **Orgs:** Mem Amer Logistics Asn; bd mem Comm Serv Corp; mem adv bd Columbus Parks & Recreation; mem adv bd Columbus Metro Parks Dist Adv Bd; bd mem Central Comm House; Bd Mem, Rotary Club. **Honors/Awds:** Meritorious Civilian Serv Award 1968; Ten Outstanding Personnel Defense Constr Supply Ctr 1972-75; inventor hand comput, 1968; Distinguished Career Award, 1990. **Special Achievements:** The first African-American member of the White hall-Bexley Club. **Military Serv:** USAF, flight officer.

BLAND, HEYWARD.
Executive. **Personal:** Born Oct 17, 1918, Tillatoba, MS; died Nov 25, 2004, Chicago, IL; married Maemell Fuller; children: Patricia & Ronald (deceased). **Educ:** Shiloh Seventh-Day Adventist Acad, attended 1937. **Career:** Furniture Dealer, Chicago 1943-48; Real Estate Investor, 1948; Shore Motel Corp, pres; 37th & Indiana Ave Bldg Inc, pres; Pacific Coast Bank, pres, chmn bd. **Orgs:** Precinct capt 2nd Ward Dem Orgn, 1962-68; co-sponsor Little League, 1969, 1970; bd dirs, Girls' Club San Diego, 1974-; bd dirs, PUSH Orgn San Diego; organizer, Pac Coast Bank, San Diego. **Honors/Awds:** Business Man of Year, Women's Club, San Diego. **Business Addr:** Chairman of the Board, Pacific Coast Bank, 5540 S Shore Dr, Chicago, IL 60637.

BLAYLOCK, DR. ENID VERONICA.
Educator, psychologist. **Personal:** Born Jan 24, 1925; died Jun 17, 2009, CA; married Lorenzo; children: Andre & Dellis. **Educ:** Loma Linda Univ, BSN, 1953; Univ Calif, Los Angeles, MS 1959; Univ Southern CA, PhD, 1966. **Career:** White Mem Hosp & St Vincent Hosp LA, staff nurse, 1953-59; LA City Sch Dist, health supvr, 1960-66; Prof Adv Bd, Charles Drew Post Grad Med Sch; Inst Intercultural Educ, dir, 1974; Calif State Univ, assoc prof, prof educ psychol, 1966, Lectr, UCLA Med Media Network, 1969-; prof emer educ psychol & admin, 1983-2009. **Orgs:** Women in Educ Leadership; Hon mem, Asn Women Educ, 1970; consult, Vet Admin Hosp, 1970-74; secy treas, Asn Black Col Faculty & Staff of Southern CA, 1972; Human Awareness Training Orange Co Personnel, 1974. **Honors/Awds:** Citation Distinguished Serv SDA, Sothern CA Conf Sch, 1965; Ed Assn Black, Col Faculty & Staff Southern CA Newsletter, 1972-74. **Special Achievements:** Author of "I am a black woman who.", "Living smart healthy and happy in a high-tech world". Author of article on drug abuse. **Business Addr:** Professor Emeritus, California State University, Department Education Psychology & Administration, 1250 Bellflower Blvd, Long Beach, CA 90840.

BOBO, ORLANDO.
Football player. **Personal:** Born Feb 9, 1974, West Point, MS; died May 14, 2007, Dallas, TX; son of debra bobo; children: Xavier, Anneshia & Kristen. **Educ:** E Miss CC, LA, Monroe. **Career:** Minn Vikings, guard, 1997-98, 2002; Cleveland Browns, 1999; Baltimore Ravens, 2000-01; Winnipeg Blue Bombers, offensive lineman, 2004. **Orgs:** Boys & Girls Club Minneapolis-Chicago Exchange Prog; Bobo's Kids, St Paul Area Learning Ctr. **Honors/Awds:** First Team All Independent Conf All Star Hons; Team's best offensive lineman, 1995.

BODDIE, DR. ARTHUR WALKER.
Physician. **Personal:** Born Apr 21, 1910, Forsyth, GA; died Jul 28, 2008; son of William Fisher and Luetta Sams; married Denise K Gray MD; children: Arthur W Jr. **Educ:** Atlanta Univ, AB, 1931; Meharry Med Col, MD, 1935. **Career:** Detroit Med & Surg Ctr, co-founder; Trinity Hosp, affil; Sidney Sumby Mem Hosp, affil; Edyth K Thomas Mem Hosp, affil; St Aubin Gen Hosp, affil; Kansas City Gen Hosp, intern; Frederick Douglas Hosp, intern; Burton Mercy Hosp, physician, currently. **Orgs:** Kappa Alpha Psi, 1933; Acad Family Pract, 1949, Mich State Med Soc, 1949, chmn, NMA, 1958-65; Am Soc Abdominal Surgeons, 1960, Pan Am Med Asn, 1968; exec comt mem, Acad Family Pract, 1973-77; Plymouth Cong Church; NAACP; examr, Selective Serv; Royal Acad Physicians; Nat Med Asn; fel Am Acad Family Med. **Honors/Awds:** Citation Pres Roosevelt, Truman, Harper Grace Hosp, St Joseph Mem Hosp, Detroit Mem Hosp. **Home Addr:** 1991 W Boston Blvd, Detroit, MI 48206. **Business Addr:** Physician, Burton Mercy Hospital, 271 Eliot, Detroit, MI 48202.

BOND, WILBERT.
Federal government official. **Personal:** Born Oct 21, 1925, Brownsville, TN; died Feb 4, 2007, TN; son of Hobson and Ethel Anderson; married LaVerne Love, Aug 24, 1946; children: Loretta, Wilbert Jr, Cordia & Thomas. **Educ:** Fisk Univ, Nashville, TN, BA, 1950; Middle Tenn State Univ, MA, 1965. **Career:** Federal government official (retired); Murfreesboro Schs, Murfressoboro, music inst, 1950-68; USN, Millington, equal employ, 1968-90; Memphis, pres. **Orgs:** Pres, Nat Asn Advan Colored People, 1978; Leadership Memphis, 1982; Fair Bd mem. **Honors/Awds:** Outstanding Federal Employee, 1987; Superior Civilian Serice Award, 1990. **Military Serv:** USN, 1943-46; Asiastic Pacific, Am Defence Ribbons, USN Res, 1947-85. **Home Addr:** 25 E Norwood Ave, Memphis, TN 38109, **Home Phone:** (901)774-1848.

BROWN, DR. GEORGE PHILIP.
Physician. **Personal:** Born Feb 8, 1920, Arlington, VA; died May 1, 1993, Columbia; married Phyllis Glazer; children: George Sabree, Rodney & Craig. **Educ:** Howard Univ, BS, 1940; Howard Univ Col Med, MD, 1944; Am Bd Pediat, dipl, 1953. **Career:** Pvt Pract, physician, 1947; Mark Twain Sch, psychiatrist, 1971-72; InstC, supt, 1972. **Orgs:** Am Bd Neurol & Psychiat, 1962. **Military Serv:** USAF, capt, 1951-53.

BROWN, JAMES.
Broadcaster, basketball player. **Personal:** Born Feb 25, 1951, Bethesda, MD; died Mar 1, 1978; married Dorothy; children: Katrina. **Educ:** Harvard Univ, Am Govt, attended 1973. **Career:** Basketball player (retired), broadcaster; Atlanta Hawks, basketball player; Wash Bullets, analyst; WTEM Radio, talk show host; WUSA-TV, sports anchor; WJLA-TV, sports anchor; WUSA-TV, sports anchor; CBS Sports, sportscaster; FOX Sports, sportscaster, "NHL Saturday"; HBO Sports, "Real Sports With Bryant Gumbel", corresp,; CBS, "NFL TODAY", host, 2006-, "NCAA Basketball", host; Sporting News Radio, host. **Orgs:** Marrow Found; Darrell Green's Youth Life Found; Ronnie Lott's All Stars Helping Kids; Fel Christian Athletes; Niemann Pick Disease Found. **Honors/Awds:** Two Sports Emmy Award, Best Studio host, FOX NFL SUNDAY; SportsHall of Fame, Harvard Univ; Sportscaster of the Year, Am Sportscaster Asn, 1999; Grant Hartley Diversity Award, Nat Marrow Donor Prog. **Business Phone:** (212)512-1000.

BROWN, JAMES H.
Chief executive officer, chairperson. **Personal:** Born Mar 16, 1935, Wake County, NC; died Oct 14, 2007, Raleigh, NC; married Geraldine G; children: Deborah C & James H Jr. **Career:** Raleigh Funeral Home, asst funeral dir, 1955-57; Salesman, 1957-58; 1st Nat Bank, bank mess, 1958-59; Wash Terr Apts, apt supt, 1958-59; J W Winters & Co, real estate sales mgr, 1961-66; Brown Realty Co LLC, chmn & chief exec officer 1966. **Orgs:** Chmn Polit Action Community; NAACP; Raleigh Citizens Asn; precinct chmn, Wake Co Dem Party; chmn trustee bd, chmn bldg community, chmn finance community, Ldc United Church Christ, 1972-73; chmn mayoral campaign. **Special Achievements:** First Black Mayor Elected in City of Raleigh, 1973.

BROWN, PAUL E. X.
Executive. **Personal:** Born Dec 20, 1910, Weir, MS; died Aug 2, 2007, Atlanta, GA; married Verna. **Educ:** Univ Minn, attended 1933; Columbia Col; Moody Bible Inst. **Career:** Prince Hall Masonic Rev, ed, 1947; WEAS Radio Sta, announcer; WEDR Radio Sta, chief announcer & news ed, AL, 1950; Nat Asn Market Devel Inc, exec dir, 1985; Atlanta Coca-Cola Bottling Co, sales & mkt, 1962-75; Radio WAOK, dir, news publ affairs, 1958-62; Ga Ed, Pittsburgh Courier, ed, mgr; Radio Sta WERD, prog dir, announcer. **Orgs:** Past pres, Atlanta Chapter, Nat Asn Market Develop; sr consult, chmn, Adv Coun, Triangle Asn; prince Hall mason Atlanta Emp Vol Merit Emp Asn; Shriner; Elk; Frontiers Int; Phi Beta Sigma; Imperial Dir; pub rels Shriners; pub Shriners Quarterly; radio news Ctr The Pyramid, 1946; bd mem, George Wash Carver Boys Club; bd mem, Goodwill Indust Atlanta; Enterprises Now; secy, Pledging Found; past pres, Adelphi Club; DeLeg Assembly UnitedWay; Task Force Youth Motivation; NAB. **Special Achievements:** First African American in Coca-Cola Bottling Co as sales in 1963.

BROWN, PAUL L.
Educator, dean (education). **Personal:** Born Feb 18, 1919, Anderson, SC; died Jan 13, 2009, Atlanta, GA; married Lorene S Byron; children: Pauletta B, Gloria J & Nanola K. **Educ:** Knoxville Col, BS, 1941, PhD, 1955; Univ Ill, MS, 1948. **Career:** Dean (retired); Southern Univ, instr biol, 1948-58; Fla A&M Univ, prof biol, 1958-59; Norfolk State Col, chmn, nat sci & math, 1958-74; Nat Sci Found, prog mgr, 1974, 1963-64; Atlanta Univ, prof biol, 1978; Clark Col, dean fac & instr, 1974-78; Atlanta Univ Sch Arts & Sci, dean. 1982-87. **Orgs:** Consult & sr prog, Asn Inst Serv Educ Soc, Sigma Xi; Beta Beta; Phi Sigma; Betta Kappa Chi; Phi Beta Sigma; Nat Inst Sci; Am Zoologists, Ill & VA Acad Sci; Inst Biol Sci; Am Micro Soc; J Hay Whitney Fel; Am Med Asn Fel. **Honors/Awds:** Published in Am Midland Natl & other learned j's. **Military Serv:** AUS, Europ theater opers, 1942-45.

BROWN, WILLIE B.
State government official. **Personal:** Born Jun 18, 1940, Anderson, SC; died Jan 5, 2009, Newark, NJ. **Educ:** SC State Col,

attended. **Career:** State NJ, assembly man, dist 29, 1973-89; real estate investment bus exec; NJ State Assembly, dean; NJ Off Legis Serv, NJ Bd Pub Utilities, mem. **Orgs:** Nat parliamentarian, Nat Black Caucus State Legislators; consult & adv, co-founder, S Ward New Dem Club; life mem, Nat Asn Advan Colored People; Wainwright Tri Block Asn; Coun State Govts; Grand Masonic Cong; AF & AM. **Honors/Awds:** Legislator of the Year, Nat Black Caucus State Legislator, 1983, co-recipient, Anheuser-Busch Annual Conf, 1989.

BROWNE, ROSCOE LEE.
Writer, actor, administrator. **Personal:** Born May 2, 1925, Woodbury, NJ; died Apr 11, 2007, Los Angeles, CA; son of Sylvanus and Lovie. **Educ:** Lincoln Univ; Middlebury Col; Columbia Univ. **Career:** Lincoln Univ, teacher french & lit; actor, writer, dir, narrator, currently; Films: The Connection, 1962; The Cool World, 1964; The Comedians, 1967; Uptight, 1968; Topaz, 1969; The Liberation of L.B. Jones, 1970; The Cowboys, 1972; The World's Greatest Athlete, 1973; Superfly, 1973; Black Like Me, 1974; Uptown Saturday Night, 1974; Logan's Run, 1976; Twilight's Last Gleaming, 1977; The Fifth Door; The Haunting of Harrington House; King; Legal Eagles; Unknown Powers; Jumping Jack Flash, 1986; The Mambo Kings, 1992; Naked in New York, 1993; Morgan's Ferry, 1999; numerous stage appearances since 1952 including: Julius Caesar, 1956; The Blacks, 1961; King Lear, 1962; The Winter's Tale, 1963; The Man Who Came to Dinner, 1966; The Dream on Monkey Mountain, 1970; AH & Is on the Gate, 1976-77; My One & Only, 1983; has appeared in many tv movies & as gueststar in continuing series including Space, Magnum PI, Barney Miller, Soap & The Cosby Show; Hamlet, 2000; Treasure Planet, 2002; Behind the Broken Words, 2003; Tales of a Fly on the Wall, 2004; "Will & Grace", 2004; "The Batman", 2005; Narrator: Babe, 1995; Babe: Pig in the City, 1998; "Static Shock", 2003; Tales of a Fly on the Wall, 2004; Garfield: A Tail of Two Kitties, 2006; Epic Movie, 2007. **Orgs:** Actor's Equity; Screen Actors Guild; Am Fedn TV & Radio Artists. **Honors/Awds:** Thousand Yard Indoors Track Champion, Amateur Athletic Union, 1949, 1951; Obie Award, Best Actor for Benito Cereno, 1965; Best Actor Los Angeles Drama Critics Award for The Dream on Monkey Mountain, 1970; Black Filmmakers Hall of Fame, 1977; Emmy Award, Best Actor in a Drama or Comedy Show, The Cosby Show, 1986; Named All-American Athlete Twice. **Business Phone:** (310)475-2111.

BROWN-WRIGHT, MARJORIE.
Educator, home economist. **Personal:** Born Jan 1, 1931, Little Rock, AR; died Jul 4, 2002; daughter of Norris brown and Verlea Stout Brown. **Educ:** DePaul Univ, PHB, 1956; Univ Il, MSW, 1961; Tulane Univ, advan stud cert, 1970; Ore State Univ, PhD, 1976. **Career:** St Elizabeth High Sch Chicago, 1956-57; Univ Chicago, proj secy, 1957-58; Ill Div Child Welfare Servs, child welfare worker, 1958-60; Cook County Dept Pub Welfare, various social work, 1958-66; Champaign Ill Pub Sch, sch & social worker, 1960-61; Lawndale Neighborhood Servs Chicago, social group worker, 1962-63; Univ Okla, asst prof Social Work, 1966-70; Tulsa Model Cities Prog, social planning team committeewoman, 1968-71; Community Serv Univ, OR, asst prof, 1970-77; Community Develop & Human Rel Serv Consult Mass Media & Minority Group Rel Conf, Tulsa, US Dept Justice, consult, 1970. **Orgs:** Assoc ed aurora, mag Sigma Gamma Rho, 1967-76; bd mem, Univ Asn Tulsa, 1970-71; pres, Lane Dist Nat & Asn Social Workers, 1971-72; pres, Lane County Ore Child Care Coun, 1973-74; nat bd mem & western reg campusc oord, Sigma Gamma Rho, 1974-76; chairperson, Ore Community Coordinated Child Care Coun, 1974-77. **Honors/Awds:** Central Regional Scholarship Award, Sigma Gamma Rho, 1955; Grad Study Scholarship Award, Cook County, Ill, 1959-61; Outstanding Young Women in America, 1965; citation mayor, Tulsa Contrib Model Cities Prg, 1970; Oregon Social Worker Year, 1973; Hall of Fame Educ Award Sigma Gamma Rho, 1974; Outstanding Human Service Profs America, 1974; Volunteer Service Award, Oregon Community Coord Child Care Coun, 1975.

BRYANT, CLARENCE.
Judge. **Personal:** Born Jun 13, 1928, Lewisville, AR; died May 27, 2008, Chicago, IL; son of Jehugh and Lucy Faulkner; married Doris L Hearns (deceased); children: Nelson T & Kevan L. **Educ:** Roosevelt Col, BA, 1953; Chicago Kent Col Law (ITT), LLB, 1956, JD, 1969. **Career:** Judge (retired) Clarence Bryan Wash & Durham, atty assoc, 1956-60; Wash Kennon Bryant & Hunter, atty partner, 1960-76; assoc appointed judge, 1976; Circuit Ct Cook County Ill, elected circuit ct judge, 1982. **Orgs:** First vpres, Cook County Bar Asn, 1970-72; pres, Cook County Bar Asn, 1973-74; mem Jud Coun, NBA, 1976-. **Honors/Awds:** Meritorious Serv Award, Cook Co Bar Asn, 1972. **Special Achievements:** Only African Am among first 9 mem Rev Bd, Ill Atty Diciplinary Syst, 1973-76. **Military Serv:** AUS, Lt, 4 years.

BRYANT, DR. HENRY C.
Pathologist. **Personal:** Born Feb 21, 1915, Birmingham, AL; died Apr 7, 2009; son of Myra Jones; married Barbara; children: Henry & Lisa. **Educ:** Talledega Col, BA, 1936; Univ Mich, MD, 1940, MS, 1947, PhD, 1949. **Career:** Pathologist (retired); Provident Hosp, Chicago, IL; Homer G Phillips Hos, St Louis, MO; St. Joseph Mercy Hosp, Ann Arbor, MI, pathologist, Physicians Clini-

cal Lab Co, dir pres; Univ Mich, res asst, res assoc, instr, lectr. **Orgs:** Nat Asn Advan Colored People, 1945; NY Acad Sci, 1948-; Washtenew Co Mich State Med Soc, 1949; Am Med Asn, 1949-; Nat Med Asn, 1949-; Am Soc ClinPathologists; Mich Soc Pathologists, 1949-; Dir, St Joseph Mercy Hosp,1958-64; dir, Peoples Community Hosp, 1958-64; dir, Merrywood Hosp, Herrick Memorial Hosp, 1958-82; Mich Asn Profs, 1976-; fel Col Am Pathologists; Ann Arbor Civic Forum; Alpha Phi Alpha fraternity. **Military Serv:** USAR, 1941-48. **Home Addr:** 1200 Earhart Rd, Ann Arbor, MI 48105-2768.

BULGER, LUCILLE O.
Executive. **Personal:** Born Sep 26, 1912; died Oct 6, 2007, New York, NY; married Robert; children: Neil & Kent. **Educ:** New Sch Social Res New York Cornell Univ Exten, 1968. **Career:** Executive (retired); Comm League W 159th St Inc, exec dir. **Orgs:** Pres, Community League of W 159th St, 1952-66; founder, Community League of W 159th St, 1952; pres, Coun Dist 6, 1954-56; vpres, United Parents Asn NY, 1957-61; mem, Neighborhood Clean-Up Campaign Comt, 1966-; bd mem, Wash Heights W Harlem Inwood Mental Health Coun, 1969-; bd mem, Cent Harlem Meals Wheels, 1972; chmn, Health Comn Off Neighborhood Govt; mem, Fed Grants Comn Addiction Serv Agency; Dist 6 Health Coun, 1973-75. **Honors/Awds:** Cert Pub Serv State NY, 1959; Nat Asn Media Women Inc Award, 1967; New York Dept Health Certificate of Merit, 1967, 1975.

BUSBY, JHERYL.
Executive, founder (originator), president (organization). **Personal:** Born May 5, 1949, Los Angeles, CA; died Nov 4, 2008, Malibu, CA; married; children: 3. **Educ:** Long Beach State Col. **Career:** A & M Recs, promotional worker, 1980-83; MCA Recs, from vpres to pres black music dept, 1984-88; Motown Recs Co, chief exec officer, 1988, pres; Mattel Toys, from inventory clerk to purchasing agent, new-toy coordr; Stax Recs, from regional prom rep to W Coast prom & mkt head; independent album promoter; Casablanca, promotional worker; Atlantic Recs, promotional worker; CBS Recs, promotional worker; DreamWorks Recs, exec; Def Soul Classics Recs, founder & pres, currently. **Orgs:** Chmn & founder, Nat Bank Los Angeles. **Honors/Awds:** Path of Excellence Award, Huston-Tillotson Col, 2001.

CARGILE, C. B., JR.
Labor relations manager. **Personal:** Born May 17, 1926, Bastrop, LA; died Aug 17, 2008, Richmond, VA. **Educ:** Rutgers State Univ, NJ, BA, polit sci, 1973; Rider Col, MA, mgt, 1980. **Career:** Manager (retired); NJ State Govt, adminr, 1966-70; Ocean Cty Col, asst dean bus, 1973. **Orgs:** Exec dir, Black Am, 1970-, Black Polit Orgn; life mem, Nat Asn Advan Colored People, Alpha Phi Alpha; Ocean City Col Speakers Bur. **Honors/Awds:** Disting Comm Serv Award, Concerned Citizens, 1970; Pol Awareness Award,Camden NJ Action Coun, 1979; Distinguished Service Award, Ocean City CETA Adv Coun. **Special Achievements:** First black elected dem municipal chairman Lakewood NJ; first black candcity freeholder Monmouth City NJ. **Military Serv:** AUS, cwo3, 1942-65; AUS Commendation Medal, 1959; Oak Leaf Clusters, 1963-64.

CARTER, JOHN E.
Singer. **Personal:** Born Jun 2, 1934; died Aug 21, 2009, Harvey, IL. **Career:** Albums: "There Is", 1968; "On Their Corner", 1992; "I Salute You", 1992; "Dreams of Contentment", 1993; "We Finally Meet", 1995; "Bring Back the Love: Classic Dells", 1996; "Last Love Letter", 1996; "I Touch a Dream/Whatever Turns", 1998.

CHAMBERS, FREDRICK.
Educator. **Personal:** Born Mar 28, 1928, Waterloo, IA; died Sep 6, 2008, Pine Bluff, AR; son of Viola Wilson; married Doris Foster (deceased); children: Ivie Cecilia & Fredrick Foster. **Educ:** Univ Ark Pine Bluff, BA, 1955; Univ AR, MEd, 1959; Ball State Univ, EdD, 1970. **Career:** R. AR Boy's Ind Sch, counr, 1955; Mound Bayou High Sch, soc sci teacher, 1955-57; Phelix High Sch, soc sci teacher, 1957-59; Univ AR Pine Bluff, assoc prof, 1959-71; Ball State Univ, teaching fellow History, 1967-70; Kent State Univ, assoc prof, prof emer. **Orgs:** Comnr, Ark Higher Educ, 1970; exec com, Ark Conf AAUP, 1965-67; state secy & bd mem, Ohio Am Civil Liberties. **Special Achievements:** Auth "Histories Black College" J Negro History, 1972; Black Higher Educ US Greenwood Press Inc, 1978. **Military Serv:** AUS, pfc, 1952-54. **Home Addr:** 2010 Carlton Dr, Kent, OH 44240.

CHURCH, ROBERT T., SR.
Government official. **Personal:** Born Sep 26, 1909, Athens, GA; died Dec 31, 2008, GA; son of Arthur and Pearl Billups; married Ruby Summers, Jun 26, 1938; children: Robert T Jr & Ruby A. **Educ:** Hampton Inst, BS, agr, 1934; Tuskegee Inst, MS, agr educ, 1958. **Career:** Wash Ga Bd Educ, asst prin & voc agr teacher, 1934-36; Millen Ga Bd Educ, prin & voc agr teacher, 1936-38; Jenkins County, county agent, 1938-46; Clarke County, county agent, 1946-48; Peach County Ft Valley, county agt(retired), 1948-69; Ft Valley State's ann Ham & Egg Show, head, 1949-66; Ft Valley, GA, city councilman, 1974-82, farmer, 1969-86; Church's Enterprises, mgr, 1969-89. **Orgs:** Lambda Phi Chap, Omega Psi

Phi; Ft Valley City Coun; chmn & bd dir, DivPeach County Family & C Servs; Deacon Bd Trinity Baptist Church; EpsilonSigma Phi, 1968; Grammatues Beta Chi Boule, 1984; appointed, Peach CityJurors Comn, 1986; pres, Cent Ga Chap, Hampton Univ Alumni Asn, 1985-;pres, Tabor Heights Community Club, 1986-; chmn bd, Peach County Family &C Servs, 1991-; chmn, Boule Found. **Honors/Awds:** Omega Man of the Year Award, 1968; Sponsored 4H winner of local/state & nat contest; Plaques for Distinguished Service, Ga Agr Ext Serv, 1969; Peach County Bd Comnrs, 1969; Silver Service Farmers Peach County, 1970; Omega Citizen of the Year Award, 1975; Man of the Year Award, Trinity Baptist Church, 1975; Public Service Award, 1980; Houston Stallworth Award for Outstanding Leadership, Citizens Ed Comn, 1982; Award for Outstanding Unselfish & Dedicated Service, S eastern Region Nat Hampton Alumni Asn Inc, 1986; Distinguished Service Award, Fort Valley State Univ, 1987; Certificate of Appreciation for Outstanding & Dedicated Service, Peach County, Div Family & C Serv, 1988; Fifty Year Award, Omega Psi Phi Fraternity, 1988; Bd Mem of the Year, Ga Welfare Asn, 1989; Man of the Year for Community Service, Trinity Baptist Church, 1990; Outstanding Service Award, Jenkins Co Alumni Asn, 1996; Distinguished Service Award, Peach County, Dept Family & C Serv Bd, 1996; History Maker Award, Chicago,2002; Outstanding 40-yr Service Award, Trinity Bapt Church, 2003; George Washington Carver Public Service Hall of Fame, inductee, 2003. **Special Achievements:** Selected to serve on the adv coun, Pres Ft Valley State Univ, 1996. **Home Addr:** 901 S Carver Dr, Fort Valley, GA 31030.

CLANCY, MAGALENE ALDOSHIA.
Government official. **Personal:** Born Jan 2, 1938, Midway, GA; children: Eric G, Delia A & Lorenzo K. **Educ:** Johnson C Smith Univ, 1957-59. **Career:** Government official (Retired); Liberty Elem Sch, sub teacher, 1962-65; Liberty Co, oeo worker, 1966-68; Ft Stewart GA, nurses asst, 1968-92; Midway City, mayor, pro-tem. **Orgs:** Fifth term, Counperson, Midway City, 1992; Usher bd, chmn youth group, Midway First Presby Church. **Honors/Awds:** Outstanding Award, Ft Stewart USAH, 1978; 15 Yrs Cert Ft Stewart USAH, 1983. **Home Addr:** PO Box 166, Midway, GA 31320.

CLARK, CAESAR A. W.
Clergy, evangelist. **Personal:** Born Dec 13, 1914, Shreveport, LA; died Jul 27, 2008, Dallas, TX; married Carolyn Elaine Bunche, Apr 16, 1987; children: Caesar Jr. **Educ:** Bishop Col, BA, BTh, LLD, DD. **Career:** Nat Baptist Conv USA Inc, vpres at large; Baptist Missionary & Educ Conv Tx, pres; Good St Baptist Church Dallas, pastor, currently; US postal Serv, sr post off bldg, currently; nationally known evangelist. **Orgs:** Bd dir, Nat Baptist Conv; numerous other church & civic groups. **Honors/Awds:** Recipient of numerous citations & awards; C.A.W. Clark Plaza in Dallas named in his Honour. **Business Addr:** Pastor, US Postal Serv, 1502 E Kiest Blvd, Dallas, TX 75216.

CLARK, DR. CHARLES WARFIELD.
Physician. **Personal:** Born Dec 6, 1917, Washington, DC; died Jan 1, 2006, Washington, DC; married Savanna Marie Vaughn. **Educ:** Univ Mich, BS, 1939; Howard Univ, MD, 1944; internship Freedman's Hosp, 1944. **Career:** Physician (retired); Sr attending urologist Howard Univ Hosp, Wash Hosp Ctr, C Nat Med Ctr Wash; Trinity Hosp, house physician, 1944-46; Howard Univ Sch Med, clin instr urol, 1946-52, clin asst prof urol, 1955-59, prof, 1960-97; Freedman's Hosp, chief resident urology, 1952-53. **Orgs:** Mid-Atlantic Sect Am Urologic Asn; Am Asn Clinical Urologists; Am Urol Asn; Nat Med Asn; Medico-Chirurgical Soc DC; Med Soc DC; Am Med Asn; Wash Urol Soc; Soc Internationale d'Urologie; fel Am Col Surgeons; Sigma Pi Phi Fraternity Epsilon Boule; Am Fertility Soc; Chi Delta Mu Fraternity; Friends Kennedy Ctr; Mus African Art; Pigskin Club Wash; Smithsonian Asn; Urban League; Nat Asn Advan Colored People; YMCA; Nat social dir Omega Psi Phi Frat; Plymouth Congregational Church; Wash Urol Asn, pres, 1984-85; life mem, 50 Year Club Am Med. **Honors/Awds:** W Dabney Jarman Teaching Award, Wash Hos Ctr; Georgetown Historic Club Award, 2000. **Special Achievements:** Author of three publications; National Museum of Women in the Arts, donor; Corcoran Gallery of Art, donor. **Military Serv:** AUS, med corps capt, 1953-55. **Home Addr:** 510 N St SW, Washington, DC 20024, **Home Phone:** (202)484-4536.

CLEVELAND, CLYDE.
Government official, politician. **Personal:** Born May 22, 1935, Detroit, MI; died Jun 3, 2009. **Educ:** Wayne State Univ. **Career:** Government official (retired), politician; public aid worker, 1958, 1960-64; Community Human Resources Develop, community serv mayor, 1965-68; Inner City Bus Improvement Forum, planner, 1968-70; Community Orgn, New Detroit Inc, specialist, 1970-71; Community Develop Div, New Detroit Inc, proj dir, 1971-73; Detroit City, councilman, 1974-01; vice chair, Mich Dem Party, 1977-79. **Orgs:** Mich Dem Party; Nacirema Club; Trade Union Leadership Coun; Mich Comt Law& Housing; Asn Study Negro Life & Hist; Asn Black Soc Workers; Booker T Washington Bus Asn; Adv Bd Black Caucus; Nat Asn Advan Colored People; Oper PUSH; 33 Degree Mason; Grand Exalted Ruler. **Honors/Awds:** Has received numerous service & community awards. **Special Achievements:** Delegate, Democratic National Convention, Michigan, 1980 & 1984. **Military Serv:** AUS, specialist 4th class, 1958-60. **Home Addr:** 6585 Hartford St, Detroit, MI 48210, **Home Phone:** (313)894-2658.

CLEVELAND, HATTYE M.
Counselor. **Personal:** Born Sep 22, 1911, Laurens, SC; died Jan 5, 2008, Mt Veron, NY; daughter of William Guy Johnson (deceased) and RosaLee Fuller Johnson (deceased); married John M, Aug 29, 1936 (deceased). **Educ:** Shaw Univ, BS, sci/home econs, 1935; NY Univ, post grad cert, Occup Therapy, 1956; Pace Univ, 1975; Westchester County Col, Fordham Univ, Lincoln Ctr, bus seminars, 1978, women polit II lobbying sem, 1978; Mary Mt Manhattan Col, blissymbolics, 1979. **Career:** Counselor (retired). Willowbrook St Sch, therapist, 1956-60; Beth Abraham Home, sr therapist, 1960-65; Monte-Mor Affil, asst supr occup therapy, 1965-72, supr occup therapy, 1973-76; Montefiore Hosp N Cent BxAffil, head occup therapy serv, 1976-77. **Orgs:** Charter mem Dist, Alpha Rho Chap Shaw Univ, 1934; Am Occup Therapy Asn, World Fedn Occup Therapists, 1956-93; S Side Res Asn, 1966-67; World Fed Occup Therapy, 1970-; pres, Westchester Co Nat Comn Women, life mem, 1970-; Women's Task Force, 1974-78; Am Biog Asn, 1977-; IFABI, 1979; ABIRA, 1980-; researcher no 370 Am Cancer Soc CPSII, 1982-86; League WomenVoters, 1985-; NY St & NY Dist OTA; Nat Alumni Asn & Alumni Club Shaw Univ; Grace Baptist Church, 1989; exec bd, chair, Scholar Fund; life mem, Mt Vernon Br Nat Asn Advan Colored People, 1988; comt mem, Home Health Care Mt Vernon NY Inc, 1988-; guild chair, Life mem's Guild NCW Inc, Westchester County Sect, 1985-; Democratic Nat Party, 1988-94; bd, Mt Vernon Home Health Care Qual Assurance Comn, 1993-; World Jewish Cong, dipl, 1994. **Honors/Awds:** Mary McLeod Bethune Centennial Award, NCW Inc, 1975; Outstanding Service, Montefiore Hosp & Med Ctr, 1976; Community Appreciation Award, Morrisania City Hosp Emp Coun, 1976; Alumni Achievement Award, Admin Community Leader & Humanitarian Shaw, Univ Nat Alumni Asn, 1976; Special Award, Loyalty Grace Baptist Church, 1979; Honourable Appt, Nat Adv Bd ABI, 1982; Certificate of Recognition as sustaining member, Democratic Nat Comn, 1982-; Appreciation Award for Service, Westcheser County, 1984; 5 yr & 10 yr Service Award, Montefiore Hosp & Med Ctr; 3 yr & 5yr Service Award, Beth Abraham Home; Citation for community service, United Way Mt Vernon, NY, 1985-; Mental Health Award, Westchester County, Dept Mental Health, 1985; Honorary Fellow, John F Kennedy Library, 1988-; Woman of the Year, Am Biog Inst, 1990, Presidential Seal of Honor, 1997; Half A Century Award, Univ, 1985; 3 Plaques, Appreciation of Contributions, Shaw University; Honor, Shaw Univ Elizah Shaw Club, 1991-93; Honorary Inductees inducted to the Senior Citizens Hall of Fame, Westchester County, NY County Exec, 1995; Distinguished Service Award, Westchester County Clerk, 1995; Certificate of Sponsorship, Andrus Found, 1994; Certificate, NY EasterSeals Soc. **Special Achievements:** Selected as Charter Member, "Americans for Change," Presidential TaskForce; Recipient of: The 52nd Presidential Inaugural, An American Reunion, 1993 Commemorative Invitation. **Home Addr:** 22 Union Ave, Mount Vernon, NY 10550-3511.

COFER, JAMES HENRY.
Funeral director. **Personal:** Born Mar 24, 1925, New York, NY; died Dec 1, 2007, Long Branch, NJ; married Marion D Willis; children: James H III & Linda S Hawkins. **Educ:** Amer Acad Mortuary Sci, 1961. **Career:** Ft Monmouth NJ, electronic tech, 1947-50; Long Br Police Dept, patrolman, 1951-60; Long Branch NJ, vpres city coun. **Orgs:** NJ State Funeral Dirs, 1964-73; owner-mgr, Cofer Mem Home, 1976; pres, Cofer-Willis Corp, 1976; dir, Cofer-Hawkins Funeral Home, 1981; bd mem, United Way, Red Bank Rotary Club, Cancer Soc, Second Baptist Church Long Br, Am Red Cross, Long Br Pub Health; vpres, Long Br City Coun; former trustee, PBA Local no 10. **Honors/Awds:** Lewis R Peet Award, NY, 1961; NY St Merit Cert, NY, 1961; Conf FS Examining Bd US, 1961; Nat Conf Christians & Jews. **Special Achievements:** First Black police officer to qualify for rank of SGT in Long Branch, NJ. **Military Serv:** AUS, corpl, 3 yrs. **Home Addr:** 149 Rockwell Ave, Long Branch, NJ 07740.

COLEMAN, DR. COLLIE.
School administrator. **Personal:** Died Oct 7, 2008; children: Kyle & connie. **Educ:** Shaw Univ, BA; Ohio State Univ, PhD. **Career:** Educator (deceased): Allen Univ, acad dean, pres, chancellor, 1984-94; Shorter Col, Little Rock, AR, staff; Shaw Univ, vpres acad affairs, 1994-99; Voorhees Col, chief acad officer, 1999-2002; Univ NC, Pembroke, NC, assoc vchanc outreach. **Orgs:** Vol, Peace Corps. **Honors/Awds:** Order Of Palmetto .

CONNOR, DR. ULYSSES J., JR.
Educator. **Personal:** Born Dec 13, 1948, New Orleans, LA; died Apr 15, 2008, Washington, DC; son of Estelle T and Ulysses J Connor. **Educ:** Adelphi Univ, BA, 1970; Syracuse Univ, JD, 1974. **Career:** Syracuse Univ, dir stud activities, 1974-82; Univ Md, asst vice chancellor, 1982-85, dir Intensive Educ Develop Prog, 1985-88; asst dean/Undergrad Studies, 1988-91, dir, Freshman Year Prog, 1991-92; Kutztown Univ, assoc prof/dir, educ outreach & retention progs, 1993-2007, dir, Upward Bound Math & Sci. **Orgs:** Bd dir, Syracuse Ctr Dispute Settlement, 1976-81; Allocations Comt, Wash, DC, United Way, 1986; NAACP; Zeta Beta Tau Nat Frat. **Honors/Awds:** Blue Book Greater, Syracuse Univ, 1981; Omicron Delta Kappa Hon Soc, 1986; Ctr Teaching Excellence, Univ Md, Teaching Excellence, 1991; Noel Levitz Retention Excellence Award, 1999. **Military Serv:** USAF capt. **Home Addr:** 1515, Washington, DC 20005.

CORBIE, DR. LEO A.
School administrator. **Personal:** Died Oct 1, 2007, Bronx, NY. **Educ:** Columbia Univ, Sch Social Work, DSW. **Career:** Bronx Community Col, pres; Medgar Evers Col, Brooklyn, NY, actg pres, vice chancellor; York Col, Stud Enrollment, provost, vpres acad affairs & dean. **Orgs:** Dir & chmn, Jazz Found Am.

COWAN, DR. JAMES R.
Physician, executive, president (organization). **Personal:** Born Oct 21, 1919, Washington, DC; died Feb 6, 1995, Sarasota, FL; married Juanita G; children: James Jr, Jay & Jill. **Educ:** Howard Univ, BS, 1939; Fisk Univ, MA, 1940; Meharry Med Col, MD, 1944. **Career:** Harlem Hosp, intern, 1944-45; Freedmen's Hosp, res, 1945-48; fel Howard Univ, 1948-50; pvt pract, 1953-70; Blue Cross & Blue Shield Greater NY, sr vpres; Health & Environ, asst secy defense, 1974-76; Off Asst Secy Defense, consult, 1974; NJ State Dept Health, comnr, 1970-74; United Hosps Med Ctr, pres & chief exec, 1977-88. **Orgs:** Am Med Asn; Am Col Prev Med; Essex Co Med Soc; Interns & Residents Asn; Am Asn Pub Health Phys; Am Asn Univ Profs; Acad Med NJ; Acad Med Wash, DC; Mental Health Asn Essex Co; Asn Mil Surg US; Am Hosp Asn; Am Pub Health Sci; Nat Cancer Adv Bd; Interagy Drug Rev Task Force White House Domestic Coun; Nat Comn Arthritis & Related Musculoskeletal Dis; Armed Forces Med& Policy Coun; Nat Coun Int Health; Strategical Coun Drug Abuse; Nat Adv Coun Alcohol Abuse; Nat Adv Mental Health Coun; Nat Adv Dental Res Coun; Nat Adv Allergy & Infect Dis Coun; Nat Arthrit Metab & Digestive Dis Adv Coun; Nat Adv Child Health & Human Develop Coun; Nat Adv Eye Coun; Nat Adv Gen Med Sci Coun; Nat Heart & Lung Coun; Nat Adv Neurol Dis & Stroke Coun; Nat Adv Res Researchers Coun; Sickle Cell Dis Adv Coun, Hyperten Info &Educ Adv Com; pres, Comn Mental Retardation. **Military Serv:** AUS, chief surg, battalion surgeon, 1950-53.

CRAWFORD, MARY GREER.
Educator. **Personal:** Born May 28, 1918, Marshall, TX; died Feb 6, 1995, Marshall, TX; daughter of Lucy Clark and Francis; divorced; children: Margaret & Cranford Jr. **Educ:** Wiley Col, BA, 1947; NMex Highland Univ, MA, 1953; East Tex State Univ, attended 1980; East Tex Baptist Univ, attended 1985. **Career:** Wiley Col, head dept bus, 1947-70, prof & advisor, dept admin bus educ; prof 1947-. **Orgs:** Coord, Div Social Sci & Bus, 1967-69; chmn, Dept Office Admin & Bus Educ, 1970-71, adv, 1972; Nat Alumni Asn Wiley Col; secy, Pi Omega Pi Nat Fraternity; Nat Coun, Uncf; secy chmn, Const Comm Pre-Alumn Act Nat Educ Asn; secy, Faculty Wiley Col; TX Bus Educ Asn; TX Cong Col, PTA, E TX Soc Cul Civ Educ Dev; asst juris, Conf Cent Jur; TX & Gulf Coast Confs; asst sec, Del Gen Conf UMC Charter; Nat Asn Negro Bus & Prof Women's Clubs Lectr; consult dir, workshops in fields; Am Asn Univ Profs; Region VIII TX Bus Educ Asn; Pi Omega Pi Nat Bus Teachers Honor Soc; Nat Bus Educ Asn; Mountain Plains Bus Educ Asn. **Honors/Awds:** Piper Prof, 1986; Woman of the Year, Zeta Phi Beta Sor; Alumnus of the Year, Pemberton HS Alumni Asn; Teacher of the Year, Dist VIII TBEA; Mrs MG Crawford Day, Wiley Col. **Special Achievements:** Elected & installed TX Black Womens Hall Fame; Outstanding Citizen of Marshall; Outstanding Educator of America; Leading Lady Business Civic & Political Marshall; cited in TV prods as Teacher of Excellence. **Business Addr:** Professor/Advisor, Wiley College, 711 Wiley Ave, Marshall, TX 75670, **Business Phone:** (214)938-8344.

DAVIS, LEON.
Executive. **Personal:** Born May 23, 1933, Chicago, IL; died Feb 17, 2009, Chicago, IL; son of Henry and Lillian; married Shirley Pickett, Oct 7, 1988; children: Leon Jr, Daryl, Terrence & Margo. **Educ:** Tenn Agr & Indust Univ, Nashville, attended 1953; Crane Jr Col, Chicago, attended 1955; Wilson Jr Col, Chicago, attended 1956. **Career:** Congressman Abner J Mikva, exec asst, 1969-71; Operation PUSH, nat exec dir, 1971-72; Congressman Ralph H Metcalfe, exec asst, 1972-73; Peoples Gas Light & Coke Co, admin off vpres, 1973, supt. **Orgs:** Chmn bd, Ill St Col & Univ 1973; higher educ bd, St Ill, 1977; Chicago Bd Educ, 1980; Univ Civil Serv Merit Bd, St Ill, 1975-77; Community Serv & Continuing Educ Prog, St Ill, 1977-79; bd mem, Afro-AmDu Sable Mus 1977. **Honors/Awds:** Numerous Published Articles 1971-76; Personal View Column, Chicago Sun-Times 1979; Chicago Sun-Times, Special Black History Month Section "The Political Legacy of Harold Washington" by Leon Davis 1988. **Military Serv:** AUS, pvt, 1953-55.

DAVIS, LOUIS GARLAND.
Educator, singer. **Personal:** Born Dec 10, 1923, Danville, VA; died Jul 21, 2009; son of Louis and Elizabeth. **Educ:** Oberlin Col Conserv, 1948; New Eng Conserv Music, BMus 1951; UnivFlorence, 1951; Boston Univ, MMus, 1955. **Career:** Newton Col Sacred Heart, instr, 1955-56; Phillips Acad & Bradford Jr Col, instr, 1956-61; Moses Brown Sch, dir music, 1961-68; Int Ferienkurse FurDeutshe Sprache & Germanistik, Salzburg, Austria, 1957; Cert Cum Laude, German Lang-Austrian Modern Europ Music Course; Univ Paris, Paris France, 1964; French Lang; Bryant Col, inst, 1969-70; Community Col, RI, profemer; Univ Rhode Island, summer dir poverty prog, 1968; Le Cercle FrancaisD'Amerique D'Ete L'Academic Int Nice, music dir, 1965; recitals include: Hist Music Hall, Cincinnati; Cincinnati Chamber Symphony Orchestra, soloist; Boston Univ Symphony Orchestra; Carnegie Hall; Basically Bach, baroque ensemble, bass soloist, 2000. **Orgs:** Chopin Club; Nat Asn Music Teachers; Taft Museum; RISD Museum; bd trustees, bass-baritone soloist, Young Peoples Symphony Orchestra. **Honors/Awds:** Honourable doctorate, Saengerfest Harvard Univ, 1967. **Special Achievements:** First African American to join the faculty at Phillips Andover Academy; Recital career continues since col retirement, 1988, including Music Mansion Recitals, Providence, Rhode Island. **Home Addr:** 100 Bowen St, Providence, RI 02906, **Home Phone:** (401)521-9067.

DAVIS, RAOUL A.
Consultant. **Personal:** Born Jul 4, 1931, Crewe, VA; died Feb 17, 2008, Richmond, VA; married Waunetta; children: Tierney, Rianna & Raoul Jr. **Educ:** Cent State Univ, BS, psychol, 1954; Columbia Univ, MA, personnel psychol, 1959. **Career:** Consultant (retired); Dept Pub Safety Pittsburgh, consult, 1966-67; OIC, Pittsburgh, Pa, exec dir, 1967-68; Wyandanch Pub Sch, comt rels consult, 1968-71; Manhasset Pub Sch Manhasset, com serv dir, 1971-74; Urban League Long Island, actg dir, 1974-75; Suffolk Co Youth Bur Suffolk Col Govt Riverhead NY, dep Dir, 1975-79; Gathering Beautiful People, exec dir, 1976; Davis & Davis Assoc/Cons, pres & sr consult, 1979; Amityville Inst Small Bus Res & Develop, pres; Ctr Life Planning & Career Develop, dir. **Orgs:** Bd dirs, Suffolk Community Co Col, 1969-71; bd dirs, Urban & League Ng Island, 1975-79; bd dirs, Nassau/Suffolk Health Syst Agency, 1976-78. **Honors/Awds:** Certificate of Appreciation, Wyandanch OEO Prog, Wyandanch Day Care Ctr,1977-78; Plaque for Outstanding Service, Urban League Long Island, 1977. **Special Achievements:** First Black to Attend Kiski Preperatory School. **Military Serv:** AUS, corpl, 1954-56. **Home Addr:** 133 Sunrise Hwy, Amityville, NY 11701.

DAVIS, SAMMY, JR.
Educator, mayor. **Personal:** Born Oct 2, 1930, Ferriday, LA; died Jan 1, 2006, LA; married Elizabeth A; children: Sammy III & Craig Fenton. **Educ:** Grambling State Univ, BS, 1954; Southern Univ, Baton Rouge, MA, 1967. **Career:** Breauybridge La, teacher, 1954-57; Ferriday La, 1957, bd vchmn, currently; Concordia Parish, prin, police juror, 1967-74; Concordia Parish Educ Asn, pres, 1971-73. **Orgs:** LEA-NEA; Kappa Alpha Psi; Nat Adv Asn Colored People; Helping Hand; Police Jury Asn; Educ Community States; Nat Asn Counties; Corcordia Parish Civil League; Stud Bar Asn; Jamadi Temple l7l (AEAONME Inc); Louis R Price Consistory 32 Prince Hall. **Honors/Awds:** Award for Outstanding Achievements in Politics; Special Award, LEA-NEA. **Military Serv:** AUS, sgt, 1951-53.

DEGRAFFENREIDT, ANDREW.
School administrator, writer. **Personal:** Born Mar 3, 1928, Kansas City, MO; died Feb 25, 2009, Fort Lauderdale, FL; married Eddie Pearl Black; children: Andrew, III, Fredi Grace & Carol. **Educ:** Tougaloo Col, BS, biol & chem; Pa State Univ, MS, zool, 1957. **Career:** Writer (Retired), School administrator; Broward & Co Sch Syst, asst admin; Dillard HS Ft Lauderdale, FL, biol teacher; Everglades Jr HS, teacher & chmn, sci dept; Broward Co ITV Ctr, develop taught spec prog, 1967-70, African Am Success Found. **Orgs:** CTA; FEA; BSAA; sch admin, Piper HS; elected Ft Lauderdale City Comn, 1973-79; Boy Scout Scoutmaster; neighbourhood scout comnr; Broward Co Charter Comn; United Way Broward Co; girl Scout Coun, Broward Co; Family Serv Agency; Project aging; chmn, Gold Coast League Cities; past chmn, NW Boys Club Adv Bd; past mem, City Comm Serv & Facil Bd; Broward Co Health & Planning Coun; Piney Grove Church. **Honors/Awds:** First African-American commissioner in Fort Lauderdale, Florida. **Special Achievements:** Auth, Grandpa the King; Ft Lauderdale city comn dedicated new bldg Andrew DeGraffenreidt Community Ctr; First African Am elected Ft Lauderdale City Comn.

DIDDLEY, BO. (ELIAS BATES)
Musician, actor. **Personal:** Born Dec 30, 1928, McComb, MS; died Jun 2, 2008, Archer, FL; son of Gussie McDaniel and Ethel Wilson; married Kay Reynolds, Jan 1, 1960 (divorced 1980); children: 2; married Ethel Smith, Jan 1, 1946 (divorced 1956); children: 2; married Louise Woolingham (divorced). **Career:** Musician & singer, recordings include: "Bo Diddly", "I'm a Man—Spell it M-A-N,"; "Who do you Love", "Say Man,"; "Mona,"; "Road Runner", "Hey Bo Diddley"; "Crackin' Up"; "Better Watch Yourself", 2005; TV series: "Thank Your Lucky Stars", 1965; "Golden Age of Rock'n'Roll", 1991; "E!True Hollywood Story", 1998; "So Weird", 2000; "According to Jim", 2003; "The Simpsons", 2007; films: Crush Proof, 1972; Trading Places, 1983; Eddie & the Cruisers II: Eddie Lives!, 1989; Rockula, 1990; Blues Brothers, 1998, 2000; Screamin' Jay Hawkins: I Put a Spell on Me, 2001; Rock at Fifty, 2003; 3-D Rocks, 2005; Cheat You Fair: The Story of Maxwell Street, 2006. **Honors/Awds:** Rock and Roll Hall of Fame; Guitar Player magazine, Editors Award for Lifetime Achievement, 1990; Pioneer in Entertainment Awd, Natl Assn of Black Owned Broadcasters, 2002.

DODDS, R. HARCOURT.
Lawyer, college teacher. **Personal:** Born Jan 11, 1938, New York, NY; died Jul 12, 2009, New Rochelle, NY; son of Reginald Alex-

ander (deceased) and Beryl Ianthe Archer (deceased); married Barbara Ann Arrington, Feb 14, 1965; children: Julian I, Jason S & Sarah C. **Educ:** Dartmouth Col, BA, 1958; Yale Law Sch, LLB, 1961. **Career:** Ministry Justice, Northern Nigeria, asst comnr native ct, 1961-63; US Atty Off, Southern Dist, NY, asst atty, 1963-66; Pfizer Inc, legal dept atty,1966-67; NY Police Dept, dep police comn legal matters, 1967-70; NY Law Dept, exec asst corp coun, 1970-73; Ford Found, prog officer, 1973-82; Champion Int Corp, dir corp responsibility prog, 1982-87; Kings County, Brooklyn, NY, exec asst dist atty, 1987-89; St Johns Univ, Jamaica, NY, assoc prof law, 1990-95. **Orgs:** Trustee, Dartmouth Col, 1973-83; New Rochelle Coun Arts, 1980; bd gov, Sound Shore Med Ctr Westchester, 1983-99; independent drug expert, Nat Basketball Asn & Nat Players Asn, 1984-87; vpres, Conn Bar Found, 1984-87; NY State Comn Crime Justice & Use Force, 1985-87; vice chair, bd trustees, NY Found, 1990-99; bd trustees, New Sch Univ, 1991; sr consult, Harlem Educ Activ Fund Inc, 1997-99; consult, Clark Phipps Harris Clark, NY, Rockefeller Found; NY State Organized Crime Task Force; Black Leadership Comn Aids; Phi Beta Kappa. **Honors/Awds:** Overseer, Amos Tuck Sch Bus Admin, 1974-80. **Military Serv:** NY, NG pe5, 3 months. **Home Phone:** (914)235-7144.

DOUGLAS, ARTHUR E.
School administrator. **Personal:** Born Apr 20, 1933, Camden, DE; died Oct 22, 2007, Falls, TX; married Rose Marie Stricklin; children: Daryl. **Educ:** Univ Md, BS, 1957; Tex A&M Univ, 1966; Tarleton, State Univ, MA, 1980. **Career:** Econ Opportunities Advan Corp, prog opers mgr, 1976-82; Tex St Tech Col, grants, dir, human resources, 1995; Marlin, Independant Sch Dist, city mgr. **Orgs:** Trustee & pres, Marlin Independant Sch Dist, 1979. **Military Serv:** USAF, maj, 1957-76; Meritorious Serv Medal, Air Force Commendation with 3Oak Leaf Clusters, 1957-76. **Home Addr:** 400 Bennett St, Marlin, TX 76661.

DOUGLAS, MANSFIELD, III.
Labor relations manager. **Personal:** Born Jun 28, 1930, Nashville, TN; died Mar 16, 2009, Nashville, TN; married Barbara Jean Baker; children: Camella Renee, Reginald Mansfield & Karen Rochelle. **Educ:** Tenn State Univ. **Career:** Western Elec, personnel officer; prev experience maintenance, acct, purchasing; Metropolitan County Coun, rep. **Orgs:** Exec Comn, Nashville Br NAACP, 1962-66; pres, Br NAACP, 1966-68; pres,Davidson Co Young Dem, 1967; VPres, Exec Bd, TN State Labor Coun, 1963-65; bd dirs, S St Comn Ctr; TN Adv Com US Comn Rights; Charter Mem, Metropolitan Co Coun, 1963-99; treasure, Metropolitan Govt . **Honors/Awds:** Merit Service, Nashville Urban League, 1972; Outstanding Recognition, CWA Local 3870, 1970; honouring 36 yrs serv mem Metropolitan Co Coun & for his outstanding dedication pub serv. **Special Achievements:** Served as a member of the council longer than any person in history. **Military Serv:** AUS, Korean Conflict.

DOWNES, DWIGHT.
Government official, executive. **Personal:** Born Apr 26, 1944, Detroit, MI; died Apr 15, 2007, Highland, MI; son of Milton; married Dieadra Ann; children: Damany. **Educ:** Ferris St Col, bus admin, 1966; Mich Lutheran Col, BA, bus admin, 1969; Univ Detroit, MBA. **Career:** Highland Park Community Col, adult educ instr, 1969-70; Chrysler Corp, admin trainee & indus rels rep, 1969-71, labor rels rep, 1971-72, laborrels personnel rep, 1972-74, safety admin, 1974-76; Allen Indus Inc, mgr personnel & labor rels, 1976-79; Highland Park Sch Dist, job placement counr, 1980-84; Wayne Co Intermediate Sch Dist, part-time mgr & placement specialist, 1980; Stroh Brewery Co, indust rel-personnel specialist, 1984-85; Mains Enterprises, 1985-89; City Highland Park, coun pres, currently. **Orgs:** Bd dirs, Highland Park Caucus Club; bd dirs, Chrysler Corp; Lions Club; bd dirs, Highland Park Men's Forum; life mem, Kappa Alpha Psi; bd dirs, Devco Inc; bd trustees, Highland Park Pension Fund; treas, Black Caucus; Nat League Cities; Black Nat Caucus Elected Off. **Special Achievements:** Ferris State Univ, varsity football & track scholar.

DUMMETT, CLIFTON ORRIN.
Educator. **Personal:** Born May 20, 1919, Georgetown, Guyana; married Lois Maxine Doyle. **Educ:** Roosevelt Univ, BS, 1941; N western Univ, DDS, 1941, MSD, 1942; Julius Rosenwald Fund Fel, Univ Mich, MPH, 1947. **Career:** Meharry Med Col, dept period ontology, prof & chmn, 1942-45, Dent educ, dean & dir, 1945-49, chmn dent & admin comt, 1942-47, Sch Dent, dean, 1947-49; Va Hosp, Tuskegee, AL, chief dent serv, 1949-65, assoc chief staff res & educ, 1962-65; Va Res Hosp Chicago, chief dent serv, 1965-66; Watts Neighborhood Health Ctr, dent dir, 1966-67; Univ Southern Calif, Sch Dent, Los Angeles, health ctr dir, 1967-68, Res Comn, chmn, 1968-70, dept community dent, prof & chmn, 1970, assoc dean extramural affairs, 1968, prof emer, currently. **Orgs:** Dipl, Am Bd Period ontology; dipl, Am Bd Oral Med; fel, AAAS; fel, Am Pub Health Asn; Am Col Dentists; Int Col Dentists; hon mem, Am Dent Asn; pres, Int Asn Dent Res, 1969-70; ed, Nat Dent Asn, 1953-75; Asn Emer Mil Surgeons US; Am Acad Dent Med; Acad Period ontology; Air Force Asn; Sigma Xi Omicron Kappa Upsilon Delta Omega; Sigma Pi Phi; Alpha Phi Alpha. **Honors/Awds:** Dentist of the Year Award, Nat Dent Asn, 1952. **Special Achievements:** Author of Charles Edwin Bentley: A Model for All Times (1983); Community Dentistry; Contributions to New Directions; The Hillenbrand Era: Organized Dentistry's Glanzperiode; Dental Education at Meharry Medical College: Origin and Odyssey (1993); Culture and Education in Dentistry at N western University (1994); and NDAII: The Story of America's Second National Dental Association (2000). **Military Serv:** USAF, 1955-57. **Business Addr:** Professor Emeritus, University of Southern California, School of Dental, 925 W 34th St, Los Angeles, CA 90089-0641.

DUNN, WILLIAM L.
Athletic coach, educator. **Personal:** Born Feb 11, 1919, Birmingham, AL; died Apr 18, 2007, Daytona Beach, AL; son of Levonia and Homer; married Greta L, Jun 1, 1965; children: Darryl, Michael & William Jr. **Educ:** Ala A&M Univ, BS, 1947; Kans State Col, MS, 1953; Fla State Univ, attended 1974. **Career:** Athletic coach, educator (retired); St John's Ben Franklin Sch, prin,1962-65; Bethune Cookman Col, assoc prof hist, 1967-88, track coach, 1982,golf coach, 1994-96. **Orgs:** Family Eagles. **Honors/Awds:** Winner, St Thomas Amateur Tournament, 1964; plaque, United Negro Col Fund, 1973; plaque, 1973, Leadership Award, 1987, Nat Asn Advan Colored People; The Christian Community Award, Mt Bethel Instnl Church, 1990; The Florence Roane & Anthony Hooks Mem, 1990, King of West side, 1989-91, West side Bus and Prof Asn; B-CC Research Grant, Paramaribo, Surinam, Social Sci Div, Bethune Cookman Col, 1982; Alabama A & M University Athletic Hall of Fame, inductee, 1993; numerous others. **Military Serv:** AUS, t5, 1943-46; Good Conduct Medal. **Home Addr:** 823 N Kottle Cir, Daytona Beach, FL 32114.

EARLEY, DR. STANLEY ARMSTEAD, JR.
Physician. **Personal:** Born Feb 12, 1919, Wellsville, OH; died Dec 7, 2007, Dayton, OH; married Charity Edna Adams (deceased); children: Stanley III & Judith Edna. **Educ:** Ohio State Univ, BA, 1941; Lafayette Col Easton PA, German 1942; Univ Zurich, MD, 1951. **Career:** Bordeaux, intern obstetrics & gynec; Jungian Inst; Kanton Hosp, intern pathology & pediatrics; Miami Valley Hosp, chief family prac; Dayton Pub Schs, sch physician; pvt practice, physician. **Orgs:** Am Arbitration Asn; Montg Co med Soc; OH St Med Soc; AMA; past pres, Gem City Med Soc; Nat Med Soc; chmn, Child Guidance Ctr, 1976; bd Drug & Alcohol; bd mem, Dayton Art Inst; Dayton Philharmonic Orch Soc; life mem, past bd mem, Nat Advan Asn Colored People; vpres, Comn Health & Welfare Coun; past bd mem, Health Planning Coun; past pres, Dayton Area Coun Serv; charter mem, Westmont Chap Optimist Int & Dayton Racquet Club; Sigma Pi Phi Boule'; Alpha Phi Alpha Frat; YMCA; May Co Comnr & Comn Citz; moderator St Health & Welfare Regional Meeting; bd mem, Dayton Com Boys Club; Alfred Adler Inst Dayton; Mont Co Soc & Cancer Ctr; Med Adv Com Planned Parenthood. **Military Serv:** USAF, tech sgt, 3 1/2 yrs.

EIKERENKOETTER, REV. DR. FREDERICK J.
Evangelist, preacher, founder (originator). **Personal:** Born Jun 1, 1935, Ridgeland, SC; died Jul 28, 2009, Los Angeles, CA; married Eula Mae Dent; children: Xavier Frederick III. **Educ:** Am Bible Col, ThB, 1956; DScL, 1971; PhD, 1969. **Career:** United Christian Evangelistic Asn, found & pres, 1962-; United Church Sci Living Inst, staff, 1969-; Rev Ike Found, staff, 1973-; Harvard Med Sch, Dept Psychiatry, preacher, vis lectr, 1973; Univ Ala, fac, 1975; Atlanta Univ Ctr, staff, 1975; Rice Univ, vis fac, 1977; Bible Way Church, asst pastor; United Church Jesus Christ for All People, founder; United Church Schs, founder & chancellor; Christ United Church, founder & pastor, currently. **Orgs:** Lifetime mem Nat Asn Advan Colored People. **Honors/Awds:** World Service Award For Outstanding Contributions to Mankind, Prince Hall Masons, 1975. **Military Serv:** USAF, chapl sect, 1956-58. **Business Addr:** Founder, Pastor, Christ United Church, 4140 Broadway, New York, NY 10033, **Business Phone:** (212)568-6700.

ELAM, DR. LLOYD C.
Educator, physician. **Personal:** Born Oct 27, 1928, Little Rock, AR; died Oct 4, 2008, IL; married Clara Carpenter; children: Gloria & Laurie. **Educ:** Roosevelt Univ, BS, 1950; Univ Wash, MD, 1957. **Career:** Univ Ill Hosp, internship, 1957-58; Univ Chicago, residency, 1958-61; Univ Chicago & Billing Hosp, instr psychiat, 1961; GW Hubbard Hosp, Dept psychiat, 1961-63; Meharry Med Col, prof, 1963-68, interim dean sch med, 1966-68, pres, 1968-81 & prof emer psychiat. **Honors/Awds:** American Business & Professional Leader of Year Award, Field of Medicine,1950-52; Hon Degrees DHL, Harvard Univ, 1974; DSc, St Lawrence Univ, 1974; DHL, Roosevelt Univ, 1974; DHL, Meharry Med Col, 1999; Eleanor Roosevelt Key, Roosevelt Univ; Citizen of Year, Omega Psi Phi. **Home Addr:** 710 Ledford Dr, Nashville, TN 37207.

ELLIGAN, REV. IRVIN, JR.
Clergy. **Personal:** Born Nov 24, 1915, Chattanooga, TN; died Jan 1, 2009, Miami, FL; son of Irvin Elligan McDonald Sr and Annie C Simmons; married Florence C Coston, Jun 23, 1945; children: Rachel A Clark & Irvin III. **Educ:** Knoxville Col, BS, 1938; Pittsburgh-Xenia Sem, MDiv, 1944; Union Theol SemVa, post grad 1966-67; Presby Inst Indust Rels, 1968; Columbia Theo Sem, attended 1972; Urban Training Ctr, Cert Org Devel, 1972, 1976. **Career:** Clergy (retired); Camden Acad, teacher, 1939-41; pastorates Va & Tenn, 1944-66; Knoxville Col, Bible instr, 1952; Presby Church US, assoc secy church & soc bd Christian educ, 1963-67; Lakeview Presby St Petersburg, assoc pastor, 1967-70; Columbia Theol Sem, vis instr, 1972; New Covenant Presby Church Miami, pastor; SFL Ctr Theol Studies, dir field educ, assoc prof Pastoral Ministries, assoc prof emer, 1991-2009; New Covenant Presby, 1985, pastor emer; Miami Shores Presby Church, parish assoc, 1993-; Fla Ctr Theol Studies, trustee emer. **Orgs:** Moderator Synod Fla PCUS, 1974; Stillman Col Bd; Fla Coun Churches, Fla Christian Migrant Ministry; moderator Everglades Presby PCUS, 1980; Synod Fla Mission Coun; Presby US Minority Mission Coun; bd mem, Presby Found; chmn, Racial/Ethnic Task Force, Presby Div Nat Mission; bd trustees, Presby Church USA Found; Greater Miami Religious Leaders Coalition; Miami Urban Coalition; Synod C Transition Com; chmn, Black Presby Proj Tropical Fla; Prog Comt Greater Miami Urban Coalition, 1986; chmn, Dade County Community Rels Bd, 1980-81; exec comm, Greater Miami Relig Leaders Coalition. **Honors/Awds:** Silver Beaver Award, BSA; Outstanding Citizen Award Richmond, VA, 1962; Key to the St Petersburg City, FL, 1970; Black Presbyterian Leadership Caucus Service Honors, 1973; Citizen of the Year, Award Omega Psi Phi Miami, 1979; Honors certificates by Metro-Dade County & Miami City; Florida National Peace Seekers Award, So Presbyterian Peace Fellowship,1981; Hon DD, Stillman Col, 1965; Hon DD, Florida Theological Ctr, 1991; Essie Silva Community Builder Award, 1992. **Special Achievements:** First Black Moderator Hanover Presbytery, VA, 1963. **Home Addr:** 8431 NW 12th Ave, Miami, FL 33150, **Home Phone:** (305)696-4085.

EVANS, CHUCK.
Football player. **Personal:** Born Apr 16, 1967, Augusta, GA; died Oct 12, 2008; married Etopia; children: Clarke. **Educ:** Clark Atlanta Univ. **Career:** Football player (retired); Minn Vikings, running back, 1993-98; Baltimore Ravens, 1999-00.

FAULKNER, GEANIE.
Entertainer, singer, television producer. **Personal:** Born Feb 10, 1939, Washington, DC; died Jan 1, 2008, Wahington, DC; daughter of Mildred James Faulkner and Ernest Faulkner; children: David Michel Dabney. **Educ:** Catholic Univ, BM, 1963, MM, 1964. **Career:** New Jersey Symphony, soloist, 1971; New York City Opera, Opera Theatre, soloist, 1972-78; Alvin Ailey Dance Theatre, soloist, 1973; Brooklyn Philharmonia Orchestra, soloist, 1976, 1979-82; New York Jazz Rep Orchestra, soloist, 1976, 1979, 1982; Harlem Opera Soc, prin soloist, 1969-; NY City Rep Opera Theatre, soloist, 1986; New York Found Arts, artist-in-residence; Harlem Cultural Coun, pres; Am Black Festival, Palermo Italy, producer, 1985-; Harlem Week in Madrid Spain, producer, 1989; NY Bd Educ, dir spec events & proj, currently; NY premiere, Gian-Carlo Menotti "Remembrances," soloist, 1990; Harlem Festival Orchestra, soloist, 1993; Concerto di Natale, Assisi, Italy, televised Eurovision, soloist, 1996. **Orgs:** Prod & dir, Dance mobile Proj, 1971-; Whitney Mus, 1977-84; pres, Harlem Performance Ctr, 1978-; Bellevue Hosp Art Adv Bd, 1978-84; music consult, Arts Humanities Proj, Teacher Corps Hunter Col, 1979-81; vpres, Fine Arts Fed; cultural consult, NY State Coun Arts, 1985-, New York City Dept Cultural Affairs, 1985, 1987. **Special Achievements:** First black member in the Whitney Museum; Critical Reviews, New York Times, New York Post, Village Voice, Chicago Daily News, Boston Globe, Houston Post, San Francisco Chronical, Amsterdam News, Am News, High Fidelity Musica America, Music Journal, Newsweek, Opera News. **Home Addr:** 317 W 98th St Apt 6BR, New York, NY 10025.

FELIOUS, ODETTA. **See HOLMES, ODETTA.**

FORD, DR. LUTHER L.
Educator. **Personal:** Born Dec 3, 1931, Florence, SC; died May 7, 2008; married Dr Willie B. **Educ:** Grambling State Univ, BS, 1961; Univ Iowa, MA, 1964; Univ Nebr, EdD, 1974. **Career:** Educator (retired); Carthage Ark, 1962-63; Tallulah La, teacher 1963-65; Davenport Iowa, special educ teacher, 1965-66; Evaluation Voc Rehab, Oakdale Iowa, teacher, 1966-67; Univ Nebr, vprof, 1971; Grambling State Univ, prof; Danforth, assoc prof, 1976-84. **Orgs:** Black Educr Coun Human Serv; Asn Study Afro-Am Life History; Kappa Delta Pi Honor Educ Soc; life mem, Phi Delta Kappa; Disabled Am Vet; bd dirs, Black Analysis NY, 1977; Nat Soc Study Educ; La Educ Asn; La PhilosophyEduc; La Educ Res Asn; life mem, Omega Psi Phi; Ford Found, 1973-74; TTT, 1971-73; Nat Advan Asn Colored People; nat Soc Study Educ; Important BlackMan; 1987; life mem, Grambling Alumni. **Military Serv:** AUS, army airborne sgt, 1951-58.

FORT, WILLIAM H.
Lawyer. **Personal:** Born Jul 18, 1915, Tuscumbia, AL; died Feb 22, 2009, Summit, OH; married Ruth Wilson; children: Gailmarie & W Howard Jr. **Educ:** Ohio State Univ, BS, 1940, JD, 1946; Univ Kans; Univ Wash. **Career:** Pvt pract, atty, 1947-; Ohio Bell Tel, dir; Goodyear Tire & Rubber Co, dir. **Orgs:** Pres, Frontiers Int Hon D Laws, Cent State Univ, 1969; chmn, Univ Akron, 1974-77; bd gov, Am eatl Red Cross, 1981-; pres, Blue coats Inc, 1983-;

chmn, Boys & Girls Clubs Summit County, OH, 1983-84; Exec bd, N Cent Asn Comn Higher Educ; Akron Ohio & Am Bar Asn; chmn, Akron Planning Comn; Am Judicature Soc; Nat Coun Juv Judges; Akron Barristers Club; Akron Law Libr Asn; bd trustees, Akron Area Coun BSA; vice chmn, bd trustees, chmn, Am Red Cross; pres, Akron Area C of C; Akron Gen Hosp; bd dir, First Nat Bank Akron; chmn, Akron City Planning Comn; pres, Akron Urban League; exec comt bd trustees, Akron Regional Develop Bd; exec comt bd trustees, Goals Greater Akron; bd trustees, Nat Alliance Bus Men; bd trustees, Akron Child Guid Ctr; Nat Asn Advan Colored People; pres, Frontiers Int; knight comnr, Repub Liberia. **Honors/Awds:** Peter Bommarito Award, 1969; Silver Beaver Award, BSA, 1971.

FOSTER, KEVIN CHRISTOPHER.
Baseball player. **Personal:** Born Jan 13, 1969, Evanston, IL; died Oct 11, 2008, Oklahama, OK. **Educ:** Kishwaukee Col. **Career:** Baseball player (deceased); Montreal Expos, 1988; Seattle Mariners, 1992;Philadelphia Phillies, pitcher, 1993; Chicago Cubs, pitcher, 1994-98;Cincinnati Reds, pitcher, 1998; Tex Rangers, pitcher, 2001.

FRANKLIN, DAVID M.
Executive, lawyer. **Personal:** Born Apr 27, 1943, Atlanta, GA; died Sep 7, 2008, Atlanta, GA; divorced; children: Kai, Cabral & Kali. **Educ:** Morehouse Col, BA 1964; Am Univ Law Sch, JD 1968. **Career:** Patterson Parks & Franklin, partner, 1972-75; David M Franklin & Assoc,pres, 1975; Roberta Flack, Richard Pryor, Cicely Tyson, Peabo Bryson, Miles Davis, mgr & atty, mgr invst couns; Franklin & Wilson Airport Concessions, founder, chief exec officer, chair, 1994; Nat Urban Coalition, consult. **Orgs:** Coop Assistance Fund; Rockefeller Bros Fund; Ford Found; Field Found; Nat Urban Coalition, 1968-70; Nat Minority Contractors Conf, 1969-73; Nat Bar Asn; Phi Alpha Delta Fraternity; bd dir, 20th Century Fund; bd dir, Emergency Black Land Found; bd dir, Penn Ctr; bd dir, Garland Foods; bd dir, WSOK Radio. **Honors/Awds:** Selected black professional of the Year, Black Enterprise Magazine, 1977;American Black Achievement Award in the Professions, Ebony Mag, 1979. **Special Achievements:** Only African American business licensed for more than one national retail franchise.

FRANKLIN, DR. JOHN HOPE.
Educator, historian. **Personal:** Born Jan 2, 1915, Rentiesville, OK; died Mar 25, 2009, Durham, NC; son of Buck Colbert and Mollie Parker; married Aurelia E Whittington; children: John Whittington. **Educ:** Fisk Univ, AB, 1935; Harvard Univ, AM, 1936, PhD, 1941. **Career:** Fisk Univ, hist instr 1936-37; St Augustine's Col, hist prof 1939-43; NC Col, Durham, hist prof 1943-47; Howard Univ, hist prof 1947-56; Brooklyn Col, chmn dept hist, 1956-64; Cambridge Univ, Pitt Prof Am Hist, 1962-63; Univ Chicago, prof Am hist, 1964-82, chmn hist dept, 1967-70; Duke Univ, James B Duke prof, hist, 1982-85, prof emer, 1985-2009; Duke Univ Law Sch, prof Legal hist, 1985-92, prof emer, 1992-2009. **Orgs:** Ed bd, Am Scholar, 1972-76;bd dirs, Salzburg Seminar Mus Sci & Indust; trustee, Chicago Symphony, 1976-80; bd trustees, Fisk Univ,1947-80; pres, Southern Hist Asn, 1969; pres, Am Studies Asn, 1969; AmHistorians, 1975; pres, Am Hist Asn, 1978-79; Asn Study Negro Life & Hist;Am Philos Soc; AAUP; senate, pres, 1973-76, Phi Beta Kappa; Phi Alpha Theta; DuSable Mus; chmn, advisory bd, President's Initiative on Race, 1997-98. **Honors/Awds:** Guggenheim Fel, 1950-51, 1973-74; Named to Oklahoma Hall of Fame, 1978; Sr Mellon Fellow, 1973-74; George Washington Williams, A Biography, 1985; Race and History: Selected Essays, 1938-88, 1990; John Hope FranklinPublications Prize of the American Studies Assn, inaugurated 1986;ClarenceHolte Literary Prize, 1986; Bunn Award, 1987; Haskins Lecturer, ACLS;Cleanth Brooks Medal, Fellowship of Southern Writers, 1989; honorarydegrees from numerous universities; Encyclopedia Britannica Gold MedalAward, 1990; University of North Carolina Medal, 1992; John CaldwellMedal, North Carolina Council on the Humanities, 1991; John Hope Franklin-Fellowship, Nat Humanities Center, Inaugerated, 1992; Charles FrankelMedal, 1993; The Color Line: Legacy for the Twenty-first Century, 1993;Jefferson Medal, 1993; NAACP Spingarn Medal, 1995; Bruce Catton Award, SocAm Historians, 1994; Cosmos Club Award, 1994; Sydney Hook Award, Phi BetaKappa Soc, 1994; Presidential Medal of Freedom, 1995; SmithsonBicentennial Award, 1997; Oklahoma Historians, Hall of Fame, 1996; Peggy VHelmerich, Distinguished Author Award, 1997; Johnson C Smith, Circle ofHonor Award, 1997; Booker T Washington, High School Hall of Fame, 1997;Lincoln Prize, awarded for excellence in Civil War Studies; John W. KlugePrize, 2006. **Special Achievements:** From Slavery to Freedom, 8th edition, 2000; Co-author: Land of the Free,1966; Illustrated History of Black Americans, 1970; Editor: Civil War Diary of James T Ayers, 1947, A Fool's Errand by Albion Tourgee, 1961, Army Life in a Black Regiment by Thomas Higginson, 1962, Color and Race, 1968, Reminiscences of an Active Life by John R Lynch, 1970, Black Leadersin the Twentieth Century with August Meier, 1982, Harlan Davidson'sAmerican History Series with Abraham Eisenstadt; Editor with John WFranklin: My Life and An Era: The Autobiography of Back Colbert Franklin,LSU Press, 1997; co-author, Runaway Slaves, 2000. Autobiography of Back Colbert Franklin," LSU Press, 1997; co-author, Runaway Slaves, 2000; Most recently he was the subject of the film First Person Singular: John Hope Franklin.

FRANKS, DR. JULIUS, JR.
Dentist. **Personal:** Born Sep 5, 1922, Macon, GA; died Nov 26, 2008, Grand Rapids, MI; son of Julius and Nellie Mae Solomon; children: Daryl, Cheryl, Bobby, Beverly A Grant & Fredrick. **Educ:** Univ Mich, BS, 1947, DDS, 1951. **Career:** Pvt practice dentist. **Orgs:** Exec comn, vpres, pres, 1951-87; Kent Co Dent Soc, 1951-92; Mich & Am Dent Assoc, 1951-96; trustee, Western Mich Univ, 1964-82; dir, Blvd Mem Med Ctr, 1974-84; trustee emer, Western Mich Univ, 1983; dir, United Way Kent Co, 1987-92. **Honors/Awds:** Mich Hall of Honor, Univ Mich, 1983.

FRAZIER, JOSEPH NORRIS, JR.
Police officer. **Personal:** Born Jul 5, 1925, New York, NY; died Mar 18, 2009, Atlantic City, NJ; son of Joseph and Hazel Washington; married Dolores Woodard, Jun 14, 1946; children: Toni Frazier Gilmore, Derek, Nicole & Wendy. **Educ:** Atlantic Comn Col, AA; Stockton Col, BA. **Career:** Police officer (retired); patrolman, 1954; sgt, 1970-74; capt, 1974-75; Atlantic City Police Dept, inspector police, 1975. **Orgs:** Nat Asn Advan Colored People; Sigma Chi Chi Frat; Police Benevolent Asn; Nat Conf Police Profs; NOBLE. **Honors/Awds:** William Sahl Mem Award, Law Enforcement, 1973; Legion of Honor, Outstanding Community Serv, Four Chaplains, 1990. **Military Serv:** USCG, seaman 1st class, 1942-46; Good Conduct, Victory, European Theatre.

FRENCH, GEORGE WESLEY, JR.
Educator. **Personal:** Born Jan 1, 1928?, Philadelphia, PA; died Aug 8, 2008, Philadelphia, PA; married Elene Johnson; children: Andrea Natasha & Geofrrey Wesley. **Educ:** Temple Univ, BS, Educ, MS, Educ, EdD, 1970. **Career:** Educator(retired); Sch Dist Philadelphia, dir, prin, teacher, 1952; Pa Susquehanna Sch Dist-,consult, 1969; Pennsauken Sch Dist, 1969; Fordham Univ, 1975; Kent State Univ, 1975; Dayton Sch Dist, 1975; McGraw-Hill Pub Soc Student Text, 1975-77; Pa State Dept Educ, 1970-77; Beaver Col, 1971; Fels Inst Govt, 1976. **Orgs:** Anti Defamation League, 1970-71; Pa State Dem Com, 1970-76; Am Acad Polit Sci; Am Hist Soc; Asn Curr Develop & Supv; Asn Black Leadership Educ; pres, Black Educ Forum; Law Educ & Part Adv Bd; Nat Hist Soc; Black Polit Forum; Nat Coun Soc Studies; Orgn Hist; Pa conf Black Basic Educ; pres, Bd Alice Rouse Donaldson Self-help Ctr; Big Brother Asn; pres, Christian StsMen's Club; pres, Bd Florence Crittenton Serv; secy, Bd Germantown Stevens Acad; exec bd, Nwest Nat Asn Advan Colored People; Soc Pa; United Way Rev Comt. **Honors/Awds:** Black Education Forum Award, 1970-71; OV Catto Elks Award; Educator of theYer, 1974; citation of honor Christian St YMCA, 1968; Government Award, 1974. **Military Serv:** USNA corp, 1946-47.

GALES, JAMES.
Government official. **Personal:** Born May 18, 1922, Jefferson, MS; died Dec 31, 2008, Fayette, MS; married Lucinda Perkins; children: Blanche, AC, Robert, Frank, Mary Ellen, Ronnie & Angela P. **Educ:** Jefferson Co Training Sch; Alcorn A&M Col, Cert, 1949. **Career:** Int Paper Co, safety dept, 1949; Town Fayette, mayor pro team city councilman, 1969-. **Orgs:** Bd dirs, Indl Pk City & County, 1969-; bd dirs, Adams Jefferson Franklin Caliborne Comn, 1969; bd dirs, Medgar Evers Comprehensive Health Clin, 1970; bd dirs, Unity Action Agency ARC, 1973-. **Honors/Awds:** Faithful worker award, NAACP, Jefferson County Chap, 1967; faithful worker award, AJFC Community Action Agency, 1979; faithful worker award, ARC Atlanta GA Chap, 1979. **Military Serv:** AUS, sgt.

GATES, AUDREY CASTINE.
Educator. **Personal:** Born Dec 9, 1937, Napoleonville, LA; died Apr 25, 2009, Jefferson, LA; married George M; children: George M & Geoffrey L. **Educ:** Dillard Univ, BA 1958; Dominican Col; Drake Univ; Loyola Univ. **Career:** Orleans Parish Sch Syst, teacher, dept hd, 1958-68; Urban League of Greater New Orleans, Carrollton Day Care Ctr, dir, First Scholar Classic,co-dir, Consumer Health Prog, dir, 1970-71; Central City Econ Opportunity Corp, training & techinal asst adv, 1971-72; Mayors Office of Consumer Affairs, asst dir; 1972-79; Off Manpower & Econ Develop, coordr of mayors summer youth prog, 1980-81; City of New Orleans & Civil Serv Dept, asst top sychometrician for developing exams, 1981-82; City of New Orleans, Pub Works, dir of residential parking, 1983-87; City Council Res Staff, prinanalyst & asst dir, 1987-94, interim dir, adminr to staff & other res activities, 1994; dir of res, 1996. **Orgs:** Fedl Consumer Resource Network; La Dairy Stabilization Bd; Better Bus Bur Arbitration Comt; La State Dept Edu, Consumer Edu Task Force; bd mem-,Family Serv Soc; WWL & WYES, consumer adv boards; Mater Dolorosa & St Augustine PTA; Band Parents Club; Palm Air Civic Asn, recording sec & pres-elect; Nat Forum of Black Pub Adminrs; Delta Sigma Theta Sorority;First United Methodist Church. **Honors/Awds:** YWCA Role Model, 1997; Women in Government Award, 1997.

GILMORE, EDWIN C.
Physician. **Personal:** Born Mar 27, 1931, New York, NY; died Oct 16, 2007, Maywood, NJ; married Dorothy; children: Pamela, Jonathan & Gregory. **Educ:** City Col NY, BS, 1952; State Univ NY, MD, 1956; Upstate Med Ctr. **Career:** Col Med & Dent NJ, chief serv dept radiol; Montefiore-Morrijania Affliation, assoc dir, 1964-75; Grasslands Hosp, asst dir, 1960-64; Am Bd Radiol, dipl. **Orgs:** Am Col Radiol; Am Trauma Soc; NY Roentgen Soc; Radiol Soc N Am Harlem Lions.

GORDON, ROBERT L.
Psychologist, consultant, president (organization). **Personal:** Born Jun 23, 1941, Lexington, KY; died Jun 8, 2007, Inkster, MI; married Mamie R Baker; children: Kimberly & Cedric. **Educ:** Edwards Waters Col, BS, 1964; Fla A&M Univ, 1965; Col Finger Lakes, MA, psychol, 1967. **Career:** Waycross, Ga, psychol teacher & baseball coach, 1964-65; New York Harlem Astronauts, pro basketball player, 1965-67; Ford Motor Co, labor rels, 1969-84; Premier Personnel Placement Consult Inc, pres, 1984-85. **Orgs:** Chmn, War Chest Comn Nat Assault Illiteracy, 1984-85; pres, Reagan's Task Force Pvt Sect, 1984-85; bd mem, Kappa Alpha Psi Found, 1984-85; former grand polemarch; co-chmn, Labor & Indust Comm, Nat Asn Advan Colored People, Ann Arbor Br, 1984-85. **Honors/Awds:** One Hundred Most Influential Blacks, 1982-85; received more than 40 awards throughout the US 1982-85; Hon Citizen's Award, Ky, 1983; Kentucky Coll State of Ky 1983; received more than 200 plaques & awards.

GOREE, JANIE GLYMPH.
Government official. **Personal:** Born Jan 24, 1921, Newberry, SC; died Jan 13, 2009, Mecklenburg, NC; daughter of Orlander Tobias and Chaney Hodges; married Charlie A (died 1997); children: Henry L Suber, Denice, Michael, Charles, Winifred Drumwright, Juanita & Darryl. **Educ:** Benedict Col, BS, 1948; Univ Colo, MBS, 1959; Univ SC; Univ WVa; Univ Notre Dame; SC State Col. **Career:** Government official (retired); Union County High Sch & Sims High Sch,teacher, 1948-81; Town Carlisle, judge, 1978-90, mayor, 1978-96. **Orgs:** Exec person, Dem Party, 1976-82; vice chairperson, SC Conf Black Mayors,1980-; treas, World Conf Mayors, 1984-89, bd dirs, 1989-; volunteer, comt person & Sunday sch teacher, Seekwell Baptist Church; Delta Sigma Theta Sorority; Alpha Kappa Mu Nat Hon Soc; secy, Grass root Rural Develop Adv Bd; rep, Nat Conf Black mayors Inter amer Travel Agents Soc Inc; Nat Conf Black Mayors, Japan, China, US, People Repub China; World Conf Mayor, Africa; historian, Nat Conf Black Mayors, 1989-96; historian, Black Women Caucus Nat Conf Black Mayors, 1990-96; pres, SC CNF Black Mayors, 1992-94; Union County Chamber Com, bd dirs; Clemson Extension Adv Comt, 1995. **Honors/Awds:** Special Tribute of Black Women Mayors, Nat Conf Black Mayors, 1983; Nation salutes 31 Black Female Mayors for Outstanding Political Achievement, Metrop Women Dem Club DC; Drum Major for Justice, Southern Christian Leadership Conf, 1984; Honourable Citizen Liberia, W Africa, 1984; Certificate of Award, Nat Alliance Bus, 1990; SC Comn Women, Pioneer Award, 1992; Southern Bell's SC African Am Hist Calendar, 1993; awarded 8continuing education units from Clark Atlanta University for participatingin the National Conference of Black Mayors, 1987-94; Nat Coun Negro Women, Bronx NY Sect, Aggressive & Distinguished Leadership Power with a Purpose, 1988; Union Alumni Chap SC State Col, Devoted serv leadership educ &mankind, 1989; Seekwell Baptist Church Award For service and dedication, 1993; Charles Ross Leadership Award for outstanding community service and leadership in the state of South Carolina, SC Conf Black Mayors, 1994; speaker at SC Schools, Bell South, 1998. **Special Achievements:** First elected African American female mayor of SC, SC Conf Black Mayors, 1980.

GREENFIELD, DR. WILLIAM RUSSELL, JR.
Physician. **Personal:** Born Sep 15, 1915, Williamsport, TN; died Nov 5, 1986; married Mae Rivers Ward; children: William R, Albert, Mae Helaine, Mary Jewel Howard, Theolya Louise & WilliamWard. **Educ:** Tenn State Univ, BS, 1938; Meharry Med Col, MD, 1949. **Career:** Physician, Pvt Prac, Tenn State, 1937-45, Dothan, AL, 1951. **Orgs:** Reviewer, Am Acad Famil Physicians, 1996-97.

GRIFFITH, MARK RICHARD.
Television producer. **Personal:** Born Apr 12, 1960, Brooklyn, NY; died Dec 18, 2008, Brooklyn, NY; son of Gloria E and Fitzroy Griffith (both deceased); married Lori Lynn Alfred, Jun 4, 1989. **Educ:** Columbia Univ, New York, BA, English literature, 1983; Emerson Col, Boston, MA, masters candidate, 1984. **Career:** WLVI-TV, Boston, MA, assignment editor, 1984-86; CBS News/ Radio, New York, NY, senior asst assignment editor, 1986-87; CBS News & TV, New York, NY, regional producer, 1987. **Orgs:** New York Assn of Black Journalists, 1986-; mem & Program Comm, Nat Assn of Black Journalists, 1989; mem, Writers Guild of Am, 1986; president CBS news division, CBS Black Enployees Assoc, 1990; mem, convention leader, New York Assoc of Black MBA's, currently; NAT ASN of Black Journalists, mem, 1988, bd mem, 1995; NAT Black MBA ASN, mem, 1991. **Honors/Awds:** New England Emmy NATAS, 1985; Leadership Award, United Negro College Fund, 1987; Positive Image Award, United Negro College Fund, 1989; Technical Director/Producer, United Negro College Fund, 1989; 45th Annual Dinner with President Bush, 1991; New York ASN of Black Journalists, Service Award, 1994. **Business Addr:** Regional Producer, CBS News, CBS Inc, 524 W 57th St, New York, NY 10019.

GRIGGS, JAMES CLIFTON, JR.
College administrator. **Personal:** Born Oct 24, 1930, Chicago, IL; died Oct 29, 2008, Chicago, IL; married Alice Rebecca Cox;

children: Eric James. **Educ:** Roosevelt Univ, BA, 1954; Ill St Teachers Col, MS, 1964; DePaul Univ, attended 1977. **Career:** Comm Youth Welfare City Chicago, asst dir, 1960-65; Chicago Comm Urban Opportunity, City Chicago, dir div training, 1965-68; Univ Ill, dir educ asst prog, 1968-77; Malcolm X Col, pres. **Orgs:** Mem exec comm, Metro Chicago Chap March Dimes, 1981-83; bd dir, Goodwill Indust, 1985; bd dir, Midwest Community Coun, 1985. **Honors/Awds:** Outstanding Leadership & Citizenship award, Dept of Human Service City Chicago, 1978; Human Relations Community, City Chicago, 1979. **Military Serv:** AUS, specialist 3rd class, 1954-57.

GRIGSBY, DR. MARGARET ELIZABETH.
Educator, physician. **Personal:** Born Jan 16, 1923, Prairie View, TX; died Jun 24, 2009, Washington, DC; daughter of John R and Lee Hankins. **Educ:** Prairie Veiw Col, BS, 1943; Univ Mich Med Sch, MD, 1948; Homer G Phillips Hosp, intern, 1949; Homer G Phillips, asst res med, 1950; Freedmen's Hosp, 1951; Univ London, Sch Hygiene & Tropical Med, DTM&H, 1963. **Career:** Educator; Physician (retired); Howard Univ Col Med, prof med, 1966, prof emer, currently; Howard Univ Col Med, admin asst assoc prof med lectr chief infectious diseases sect asst prof med instr med, 1952-62; Peace Corps, expert adv, 1964-; DCAsian Influenza Adv Comt, adv comt, 1957-58; DC Gen Hosp, attendphysician, 1958-; Mt Alto Va Hosp, 1958-64;consult, 1964-66; Freedmen'sHosp, phys, 1952-63; Univ Ibadan Nigeria, hon vis prof, 1967-68; HarvardMed Sch, teacher res fel, 1951-52; pvt pract physician. **Orgs:** Fel Am Col Phys; Am Med Asn; Nat Med Asn; Med Soc DC; Medico-Chirugical Soc DC; Sigma Xi; Sci Soc Howard Univ; Asn Former Interns & Res Freedmen's Hosp; Pasteur Med Reading Club; Alpha Epsilon Iota Med Sorority; Royal Soc Tropical Med & Hygiene; Am Soc Tropical Med & Hygiene; Nigerian Soc Health; Royal Soc Health; Royal Soc Med; Nat Geog Soc; Soc Med Asn; bd gov, Medico-Chirugical Soc, 1960-62; Howard Univ, Sigma Xi 1960-62; DC Citz Better Pub Educ; St Luke's Episcopical Church; Century Club-Bus & Prof Women's Club; Nat Asn Advan Colored People; Urban League; All-Saints Anglican Church, 1967-68; Ibadan Rec Club, 1967-68; Ibadan Motor Club, 1968; Alpha Kappa Alpha. **Honors/Awds:** Diplomate, Nat Bd Med Examrs 1949; Am Bd Internal Med 1956; numerous honors & publ; James D. Bruce Memorial Award, Distinguished Contributions in Preventive Medicine, 2004.

HALE, PHALE D.
State government official, clergy, executive director. **Personal:** Born Jul 16, 1915, Starksville, MS; died May 29, 2009, Columbus, OH; son of Church and Lee Ellen; married Cleo; children: Phale Jr, Janice Ellen, Marna A & Hilton Ingram. **Educ:** Morehouse Col, BA; Gammon Theol Sem, MDiv; Chapel Sch Theol, DDiv, 1948; Cincinnati Baptist Theol Sem, DD; Inter denominational Theol Sem, MDiv. **Career:** State Government Official, Clergy (retired); Baptist Church, pastor, 1940; Union Baptist Church, Ft Wayne, IN, pastor, 1950; Union Grove Baptist Church, Columbus, pastor, 1950-93; Ohio Dist 31, state rep, 1966-80; Dem Nat Comn, dep dir, 1968; Ohio Civil Rights Comn, chmn; Housing & Econ Coop Inc, dir; Columbus Area Anti-Poverty Coun. **Orgs:** Pres, Columbus Chap, Nat Asn Advan Colored People, 1950-60; chmn & bd mem, Am Baptist Theol Sem, 1957-83; dir, Soc Action Comn, Ohio Baptist Gen Conv, 1960-92; bd mem, United Negro Col Fund, 1966-; bd mem, CMACAO Econ Develop Corp, 1970; bd mem, Ohio Coun Churches, 1976; comt mem, Comn Poverty & Justice, Ohio Coun Churches, 1976; bd mem, Nat Bd Dirs, Oper PUSH, 1978; bd mem, J & L Elec Co, 1983; chmn, Health & Welfare Comn, Ohio Legis; chmn, Ohio Civil Rights Comn, 1983-87; Ohio Dem Comn, 1995; chmn, Human Resources; Nat Dem Comn, 1995; vpres, Columbus Urban Re develop Corp; vpres, Shiloh-Grove Corp; sem leader, Sem I, Nat Baptist USA Cong Pastors Div. **Honors/Awds:** Martin Luther King Humanitarian Award, Columbus Educ Asn, 1987; Inducted, Martin Luther King Jr Int Bd Preachers, Morehouse Col, 1992; Hon Citizenship, Mayors Miami, Fla & New Orleans LA; street named Phale D Hale Drive. **Home Addr:** 2480 Floribunda Dr, Columbus, OH 43209.

HAMILTON, AUBREY J.
State government official, executive, chief executive officer. **Personal:** Born Nov 2, 1927, Charleston, SC; died Jan 11, 2008, Princeton, NJ; son of William C and Rose Maud Langley; married Elsie Carpenter, Oct 1, 1949; children: Catherine H & Beverly H Chandler. **Educ:** St Georges, Kingston, Jamaica, 1936; Brooklyn Col, Brooklyn, NY, 1943. **Career:** Nat Maritime Union, New York, NY, 1956-70; Seafearers Intl Union, New York, NY, 1945-55; Southeastern Enterprises Inc, Groton, CT, chief exec officer, 1973; St CT, Groton, CT, harbor master, 1980. **Orgs:** Chmn, Groton City Dem, CT.

HAMILTON, DR. EDWIN.
Educator. **Personal:** Born Jul 24, 1936, Tuskegee, AL; died Dec 21, 2002, Bowie, MD; son of Everett and Julia Sullins; married Alberta Daniels, Aug 3, 1960; children: Michelle, Stanley, Gina & Carl. **Educ:** Tuskegee Univ, BS, 1960, MEd, 1963; The Ohio State Univ, PhD, 1973. **Career:** Macon Co Sch, dir, 1965-70; Opportunities Industrialization Ctr, exec dir, 1968; Ohio St Univ, res asst, 1971-73; Fla Intl Univ, prof, 1973-74; Howard Univ, prof, 1974, chmn educ admin & policy, 1997. **Orgs:** AAACE & ASTD, 1975-87; presidential asn, Tuskegee Univ, 1980-; Intl Asn, CAEO & ICA, 1984-87; res rep, Phi Delta Kappa, Howard Univ, 1986-87; adj prof, Univ DC, 1986; educ leader Prof, Seminar Consults, 1986; adj prof, OH St Univ, 1987; pres, Howard Univ, Phi Delta Kappa, 1989-89; elections judge, PG Bd Elections, Upper marlboro, MD, 1986-87; chief elections judge, 1988-95. **Honors/Awds:** Fulbright Scholar, CIES & USIA, 1982-83; Writer's Recognition Univ DC, 1984; Cert Appreciation, Phi Delta Gamma, Johns Hopkins Univ, 1986; Certificate Award, Phi Delta Kappa, Howard Univ, 1987-89; Distinguished Alumni Citation, Nat Asn Equal Opportunity Higher Educ & Tuskegee Univ, 1988; President's Award, Howard Univ, Phi Delta Kappa, 1989; designed study travel Hong Kong & China Tour, 1989; Alaska, 1994; Brazil, 1995; Greece & Turkey, 1997; Western Carribean & Mex, 1998. **Military Serv:** AUS, sp E-4, 1954-56; Good Conduct Medal, Hon Discharge, 1956; Active Army Res, 1956-63.

HAMPTON, EDWIN HARRELL.
Musician, educator. **Personal:** Born Feb 5, 1928, Jacksonville, TX; died Jul 21, 2009; son of Joe and Lela Barnett; married Rosalind, Jun 1, 1951 (deceased). **Educ:** Xavier Univ, attended 1952; Northwestern Univ, Vandercook Col. **Career:** Royal Dukes Rhythm Band, leader; 33rd Army Band, mem, 1940; St Augustine High Sch, band master, 1953; dir emer. **Orgs:** La Music Educrs Asn; NC Band Asn; Nat Band Asn; Musicians Union Local; Alpha Phi Omega; Phi Beta Mu; Mayors Adv Bd Mardi Gras, 1986; Lay adv bd, Josephite Fathers, 1987. **Honors/Awds:** Band Director of the Year, LA, 1967; Key to City, New Orleans, 1969; Doctor of Humane Letters, Baptist Christian Col, 1988; Father Hall Award,1992; Certificate of Appreciation, President Bill Clinton. **Military Serv:** Med Corps, sgt, 1946-49.

HARGROVE, DR. ANDREW.
Engineer, educator. **Personal:** Born Apr 1, 1922, Richmond, VA; died Sep 8, 2008; children: Andrea Marie. **Educ:** Hampton Inst, BS, 1950; City Col NY, BEE, 1966; NYU, MS, 1968; Pa State Univ, PhD, 1975. **Career:** NY Brd Educ, teacher, 1960-62; NY Transit Authority, elec engr, 1962-68; Pa State Univ, instr, 1972-74; Tuskegee Inst, prof, 1979-83; Andrew Hargrove Consult Eng, proprietor, 1986-; Hampton Univ, prof, 1983-87; Norfolk State Univ, prof, 1987-98. **Orgs:** Committeeman NY Co, 1966-70; Va Waste Mgt Bd, 1986-88; Power Eng Soc;Control Systs Soc; Inst Elec & Electronics Engrs; Nat Soc Prof Engrs; Am Soc Eng Educ; Nat Tech Assn; Alpha Kappa Mu; Omega Psi Phi; chair, Inst Elec & Electronics Engrs Va Coun; Eta Kappa Nu Elec Engineering Honor Soc. **Home Addr:** 446 Chapel St, Hampton, VA 23669, **Home Phone:** (757)722-8025.

HARRIS, DAVID L.
Advertising executive. **Personal:** Born Apr 26, 1952, Washington, DC; died Dec 23, 2008, Middle River, MD; son of Reuben T and Laura E Hart; married Sheila A Smith, Aug 27, 1983; children: David Jr & Todd. **Educ:** Boston Univ, Boston, Mass, BA, 1974; Univ NC, Chapel Hill, MBA, 1976. **Career:** Foote Cone & Belding, Chicago, Ill & New York, NY, acct exec, 1976-79; Ketchum Advert, Wash, DC, acct supvr, 1979-82; NY Ayer, New York, NY, vpres, acct supvr, 1982-85; Ogilvy & Mather, Atlanta, Ga, acct supvr, 1985-88; Lockhart & Pettus, New York, NY, sr vpres; Ogilvy & Mather New York, sr partner, multicultural media dir, currently.

HARRIS, E. LYNN. (EVERETTE LYNN HARRIS)
Writer, educator. **Personal:** Born Jun 20, 1955, Flint, MI; died Jul 23, 2009, Los Angeles, CA; son of Etta. **Educ:** Univ Ark, BA, jour, 1977; Southern Methodist Univ. **Career:** IBM, comput sales exec; AT&T, comput sales exec; Hewlett Packard, comput sales exec; Books: Invisible Life, self-published, 1992, Anchor Books, 1994; Just As I Am, Doubleday, 1994; And This Too Shall Pass, Doubleday, 1996; If This World Were Mine, Doubleday, 1997; Abide With Me, 1998; Not A Day Goes By, 2000; Any Way the Wind Blows, 2001; A Love of My Own, 2003; What Becomes of the Broken Hearted: A Memoir, 2004; I Say A Little Prayer, 2006; Basketball Jones, 2009; Univ Ark, Eng Dept, vis prof. **Orgs:** Founder, E Lynn Harris Better Days Found. **Honors/Awds:** Blackboard's Novel of the Year prize, 1996, 2002; James Baldwin Award for Lit Excellence, 1997; SBC Mag Brother of the Year in Lit; Harlem Y Mentor Award; Angel Award, Gay Men of African Descent; Citation of Distinguished Alumni, Univ Ark, 1999; Arkansas Black Hall of Fame, 2000; Sprague Todes Literary Award; Harvey Milk Hon Dipl; Silas Hunt Award for Outstanding Achievement, Univ Ark. **Special Achievements:** First African American male cheerleader of University of Arkansas; the first author to receive back-to-back honors and to receive the Blackboard Novel prize a record three times. **Business Addr:** Author, Doubleday & Co, 1540 Broadway, New York, NY 10036, **Business Phone:** (212)354-6500.

HARRIS, EVERETTE LYNN. **See HARRIS, E. LYNN.**

HAWKINS, DR. LAWRENCE C.
Educator, management consultant. **Personal:** Born Mar 20, 1919, Greenville, SC; died Apr 4, 2009, Cincinnati, OH; son of Wayman and Etta; married Earline Thompson; children: Lawrence Charles Jr & Wendel Earl. **Educ:** Univ Cincinnati, BA, hist, 1941, BEd, 1942, MEd, 1951, EdD, 1970, AA, hon,1970, Wilmington Col; Litt D, Cincinnati Tech Col; CLG Mt St Joseph, LHD. **Career:** Cert Sch Supt, elem & secy teacher, 1945-52, sch prin, dir 1952-67; Eastern Mich Univ, Ypsilanti, vis asst prof, 1955-60; Cincinnati Public Sch, asst supt, 1967-69; Univ Cincinnati, dean, 1969-75, vpres, 1975-77, sr vpres, 1977-84; Omni-Man Inc, pres, chief exec officer, 1981-98; LCH Resources, pres, 1996. **Orgs:** Cincinnati Asn, 1971-87; mem, Cincinnati Area Bd Fed Res Bank, 1977-83; bd trustees, C Home, 1978-87; bd dir, Bethesda Hosp Deaconess Asn, Cincinnati, 1980-90; co-chmn, Cincinnati Area Nat Conf community & Justice, 1980-87; bd dir, Wilmington Ohio Col, 1980-90, Inroads Cincinnati,1981-83; trustee, vice chair, Stud Loan Funding Corp, 1981-2000; vice chmn, Greater Cincinnati TV Ed Found, WCET-TV, 1983-86; life mem, Kappa Alpha Psi; adv bd, policy Cincinnati Coun World Affairs; bd dirs, Mount St oseph Col, 1989-93; bd dirs, Western-Southern Financial Group, 1990; bd trustees, Nat Underground RR Freedom Ctr, 1996; bd dir, Nat Underground Rd Mus; Sigma Pi Phi; Kappa Delta Pi; Phi Delta Kappa. **Honors/Awds:** Award of Merit, Cincinnati Area United Appeal, 1955, 1973; Certificate Presidents Council of Youth Opportunity, 1968; US Coc Urban Affairs Comm, 1977-78; Charles P Taft Gumption Award, 1984; Distinguished Service Award,1988; Great Living Cincinnatian Award, Greater Cincinnati Chamber Com,1989; Presidents Award, Public Relations Soc Am, Cincinnati Chap, 1995. **Military Serv:** USAAF, lt, Tuskegee Airman, 1943-45. **Home Phone:** (513)563-8387.

HAYES, ALVIN, JR.
Lawyer. **Personal:** Born Apr 11, 1932, Cedar Rapids, IA; died Apr 20, 2005, Tulsa, NY; married Julia Wilburn; children: Alvin Douglas III & Robert Ellis. **Educ:** BA, 1958; Univ Bsd Law Sch, BLegal Lang, 1961. **Career:** Pvt practice, lawyer, 1961-69; Woodbury Co, asst atty, 1964-69; Agrico Chem Co, labor & EEO coun; Wash St Human Rights Comn, dir, 1973-74; atty. **Orgs:** William Frank & Powell Consistory; Nat Advan Asn Colored People; Urban League; Share through Adoption; bd dir, Alvin Douglas Hayes III Corp; Citizens Task Force; Iowa Bar Asn; Sioux City Bar Asn; Okla Bar Asn; Fed Dist Ct N Dist OK. **Honors/Awds:** Award for outstanding performance, Gov Robert D Ray, 1973; Award Outstanding, Iowa Civil Rights Comn, 1977. **Military Serv:** AUS, sp3, 1953-55.

HAYES, DR. CHARLES LEONARD.
Educator. **Personal:** Born Dec 16, 1921, Baton Rouge, LA; died Mar 15, 2008, Greensboro, NC; married Bette Harris; children: Charles Jerome & Jaime. **Educ:** Leland Col, AB, 1947; Loyola Univ, EdM, 1949; Univ N Colo, EdD, 1958. **Career:** Chicago, teacher, 1948-49; NC A&T State Univ, instr, 1949-52, asst prof, 1952-56, prof, 1958-61, chmn, 1961-66; George Washington Univ, ace fel, 1966-67; US Off Educ HEW, chief, 1967-69; Albany State Col, pres, 1969-80; NC A&T State Univ, chmn, 1980, adj fac. **Orgs:** Am Asn Univ Profs; Asn Higher Educ; NEA; Phi Delta Kappa; Am Personnel & Guid Asn; Am Col Personnel Asn; Asn Counr Educators & Supvrs; NCPsychol Asn; Kappa Delta Pi; bd dir, Albany Urban League; Albany USO Coun; exec bd, Chehaw Coun Boy Scouts Am; Nat Conf Christian & Jews; YMCA; Citizens Adb Comt; Drug Action Coun, Vols to the Cts. **Military Serv:** USN, skd1c, 1942-46. **Home Addr:** 1915 Belcrest Dr, Greensboro, NC 27406.

HAYES, ISAAC LEE.
Singer, songwriter, actor. **Personal:** Born Aug 20, 1942, Covington, TN; died Aug 10, 2008; son of Isaac Sr and Eula; married Adjowa; children: 12. **Educ:** Manassas, attended 1962. **Career:** Singer, actor, musician; Various Gospel & Rhythm & Blues Group, singer; Various Nightclubs, pianist & saxophonist; Stax Rec, songwriter, 1962; Composer: Shaft, 1971; Albums: Hot Buttered Soul, 1969; ..to Be Continued, 1970; The Isaac Hayes Movement, 1970; Black Moses, 1971; Joy, 1973; Live at the Sahara Tahoe, 1973; Chocolate Chip, 1975; Don't Let Go, 1979; Singles: "Walk on By", 1969; "By the Time I Get to Phoenix", 1969; "Theme from Shaft", 1971; "Never Can Say Goodbye", 1971;"Do Your Thing", 1972; "Joy", 1973; "Don't Let Go", 1980; Filmography: Shaft, 1971; Soul in Cinema: Filming Shaft on Location, 1971; Save the Children, 1973; The Black Moses of Soul, 1973; Watt stax, 1973; Truck Turner, 1974; Three Tough Guys, 1974; It Seemed Like a Good Idea at the Time, 1975; Escape from New York, 1981; Counterforce, 1987; Dead Aim, 1987; I'm Gonna Git You Sucka, 1988; Fire, Ice & Dynamite, 1990; Guilty as Charged, 1991; Prime Target, 1991; Final Judgement, 1992; Deadly Exposure,1993; CB4, 1993; Posse, 1993; Robin Hood: Men in Tights, 1993; Oblivion, 1994; It Could Happen to You, 1994; Magic Island, 1995; The Fresh Prince of Bel-Air, 1995; Oblivion 2: Backlash, 1996; Orientation: A Scientology Information Film, 1996; Flipper, 1996; Ill town, 1996; Uncle Sam, 1997; Six Ways To Sunday, 1997; Blues Brothers 2000, 1998; Ninth Street, 1999; South Park: Bigger, Longer & Uncut, 1999; Dead Dog, 2000; Reindeer Games, 2000; Shaft, 2000; Dr. Dolittle 2, 2001; Chelsea Walls, 2001; Only the Strong Survive, 2002; Soulsville, 2003; Dodge City: A Spaghetto Western, 2004; Dream Warrior, 2004; Hustle & Flow, 2005; United, 2005; Return to Sleep away Camp, 2006; Soul Men, 2008; Stand, 2009; TV appearances: Rockford Files; A-Team; Film appearances: I'm Gonna Git You Sucka; Escape From New York;Posse, 1993; A Man Called Rage, 2002; Dodge City: A Spaghetto Western,Stargate SG-1, Dream Warrior,

2004; Return to Sleep away Camp, Hustle &Flow, United, 2005; Soul Men, 2008; Kill Switch, 2008; Return to Sleep away Camp, 2008. **Orgs:** Founder, Isaac Hayes Found. **Honors/Awds:** Oscar Award, Acad Motion Picture Arts & Sci, 1972; Grammy Award; inductee,Rock & Roll Hall of Fame, 2002; inductee, Songwriters Hall of Fame, 2005. **Special Achievements:** First African American composer to win an Oscar for Best Original Song, 1972; Author: Cooking with Heart & Soul, 2000; The Way to Happiness.

HENDERSON, DR. ROBBYE R.
Librarian. **Personal:** Born Nov 10, 1937, Morton, MS; died Oct 1, 2007, Ita Bena, MS; daughter of Robert Allen (deceased) and Aljuria Myers (deceased); children: Robreka Aljuria. **Educ:** Tougaloo S Christian Col, BA, 1960; Atlanta Univ, MSLS, 1968; S Ill Univ, PhD, 1976. **Career:** Patton Ln HS, head librn, 1960-66; Utica Jr Col, head librn, 1966-67; MS Valley State Univ, acquisitions librn, 1968-69; MS Valley State Univ, dir tech serv, 1969-72, univ librn, 1972-, dir. **Orgs:** Consult Office Health Resources Oppor, 1976-78; instr, S Ill Univ, Carbondale, 1976; consult, MS Asn Col Coun Study Accreditation, 1970; pres, Progressive Fac & Staff Women's Club, 1978-80; owner, partner, Itta Bena Nursey, 1978; fin secy, Alpha Kappa Omega, 1979. **Honors/Awds:** Fel, Libr Admin Develop Prog, 1973; Internship, Mellon ACRL Prog, 1974;Fel, Developing Leaders in Developing Insts, 1974-76; Fel cum laude, 1976. **Home Addr:** 14000 Hwy 82 W, PO Box 5042, Itta Bena, MS 38941, **Home Phone:** (601)254-7313.

HILL, OLIVER W., SR.
Lawyer. **Personal:** Born May 1, 1907, Richmond, VA; died Aug 5, 2007, Richmond City, VA; son of Olivia Lewis White-Hill and William Henry White II; married Beresenia Walker, Sep 5, 1934; children: Oliver W Jr. **Educ:** Howard Univ, AB 1931; Howard Univ Sch Law, JD 1933. **Career:** Lawyer (retired); Roanoke VA, lawyer 1934-36; Law Practice, 1939-61; FHA, asst to commr 1961-66; Hill Tucker & Marsh, attorney, 1966-98. **Orgs:** City Coun Richmond 1948-50; mem Pres Com on Gov Contracts, 1951-54; founder 1942, Old Dominion Bar Assn; chmn Legal Com VA St Conf NAACP, 1940-61; mem Richmond Dem Com, 1955-61, 1966-74; bd mem leg com NAACP; mem Urban League; mem bd VA Reg Med Prog; mem NBA Richmond Bar Assn & Old Dominion Bar Assn; mem Omega Psi Phi, Sigma Pi Phi; numerous other civicorgs; mem VA St Bar Discipl Bd 1977-82; mem VA St Bar Judiciary Comm, 1977-; former mem bd trustees St Paul's Coll; mem VA Bar Foundation 1985; pres Old Dominion Bar Assn Foundation 1985; fellow, Amer College of Trial Lawyers 1987-; mem, Omicrom Delta Kappa Honor Society 1989; mem, Comnon Constitution Rsion for Common wealth of VA, 1968-69; trustee, George C Marshall Foundation 1989-94; bd of dirs, Evolutionary Change Inc, 1990-. **Honors/Awds:** Chicago Defender Merit Awd 1948; Howard Univ Alumni Awd 1950; co-recipient Russwurm Awd natl Publ Assn 1952; Omega Man of the Yr Omega Psi Phi 1957; VA St Conf Award 1957, William Robert Ming Adv Awd 1980, NAACP; Lawyer of Yr NBA 1959; Democratic Party of Virginia Wm P Robinson Memorial Awd 1981; Brotherhood Citation Natl Conf of Christians & Jews 1982; Oliver W Hill Black Pre-Law Assn Univ of VA 1983; Richmond Amer Muslims Mission Ctr Pioneer Award 1984; NAACP Legal Defense and Educational Fund, Inc The Simple Justice Awd 1986; Honorary Doctor of Laws: St Paul's Coll 1979, VA St Univ 1982, Virginia Union Univ 1988; The Judicial Council of National Bar Assn Award 1979; The Charles H Houston Medallion of Merit, Washington Bar Assn 1976; Francis Ellis Rivers Award, NAACP Legal Defense anducational Fund 1976; Outstanding Contribution to the Legal System Award, Virginia Commission on Women and Minorities in the Legal System 1987; Hill-TuckerPublic Service Award, Richmond Bar Association, 1989; Doctor of Humane Letters, VA Commonwealth Univ, 1992; Honorary Doctor of Laws, Univ of Richmond, 1994, T C Williams Law School, The Williams A Green Award for Prof Excellence, 1991; Strong Men & Women Excellence in Leadership Award Virginia Power, North Carolina Power, 1992; Apex Museum, Atlanta GA, Tribute to Oliver W Hill for contribution to Brown vs Bd of Education, 1992; Senate of VA, Senate Resolution No 84, Commending Oliver W Hill, 1992; VA St Bar, Lewis F Powell, Jr, Pro Bono Award, 1992; VA Education Assn, Friend of Educ Award, 1992; VA St Conference-NAACP, Branches Hall of Fame, 1992; Governor L Douglas Wilder's Commission on Campaign Finance Reform, Government Accountability and Ethics, member, 1992; Richmond Branch NAACP, Outstanding Service Award, 1992; Mid-Atlantic Region Alpha Kappa Alpha Sorority, Inc. Citizen of the Year Award, 1993; Amer Bar Assn, Standing Comm on Lawyers' Public Service, Responsibility 1993 Pro Bono Publico Award, 1993, Opportunities for Minorities in the Profession, The Justice Thurgood Marshall Award, 1993; Natl Bar Assn, Wiley A Branton Symposium Award, 1993; Black Law Student Assn, established at Univ of Richmond, T C Williams Law School, The Oliver W Hill, Sr, Lecture Series, 1993; Co-recipient, City of Richmond First Annual Distinguished Citizen, Hill-Powell Award, 1994; Urban League of Greater Richmond, Lifetime Achievement Award, 1994; Coll of William & Mary, Marshall Wythe School of Law, Medal of Merit, 1994; Amer Bar Assn, Section on Individual Rights & Responsibilities, The Justice Thurgood Marshall Award, 1994; Black Law Student Assn, established at Mrarhsll-Wythe School of Law, Coll of William & Mary, Oliver W Hill Scholarship Fund, 1994; City of Roanoke, Distinguished Citizen Citation Proclamation declaring Feb 14, 1995 as Oliver W Hill Sr, Day, 1995; VA St bar, Secion on Criminal Law Harry L Carrico Professionalism Award, 1995; The Honorable Judges of the Juvenile & Domestic Relations Court & Richmond City Council designated the new Courthouse the Oliver Hill Courts Bldg, 1996; Presidential Medal of Freedom, 1999. **Military Serv:** AUS s/sgt 1943-45. **Home Addr:** 3108 Noble Ave, Richmond, VA 23222.

HILL, DR. RICHARD NATHANIEL.
School administrator. **Personal:** Born Nov 20, 1930, Port Chester, NY; died Dec 8, 1998, Kings, NY; son of Clarence J and Viola Stith; married Mayme Kathryn Hegwood; children: Richard H Jr, Lori S & Mark E. **Educ:** Univ Philippines, BA, 1959; Chapman Col, MA, 1969; Univ S Calif, EdD, 1977; Chaminade Univ Honolulu, MBA, 1984. **Career:** Pacific Air Forces, educ admn, 1970-72; Allan Hancock Col, dir, 1969-70; AUS Educ Ctr, NYAC & Fort Hamilton, acting educ serv officer, 1985-; Chaminade Univ Honolulu, dir, 1972-74; acting dean, 1974-77; acting asst dean, 1977-85. **Orgs:** Consult, Federally Employed Women, 1983; Am Asn Adult & Cont Ed, 1982, Waikiki Community Ctr, 1978; dir, Univ USC-HI Alumni, 1979-; World Affairs Forum HI, 1977-; pres, Kiwanis Int Waikiki, 1978-79. **Honors/Awds:** Outstanding Service Award, Phi Delta Kappa, Univ HA, 1984; Certificate of Appreciation, Federally Employed Women, WA, DC, 1983, Am Asn Adult & Cont Ed, San Antonio, TeX, 1982; Dist Press Award, Kiwanis Int CA, NV, HI Dist 1980; Certificate of Commendation, Alaska Adult Educ Asn, 1983; Outstanding Sustained Performance Award, Fort Hamilton, 1994; Certificate of Appreciation, Fort Hamilton, 1994. **Military Serv:** USAF, ret officer, commendation medal, 1969. **Business Addr:** Acting Education Services Officer, NY Area Command & Ft Hamilton, Brooklyn, NY 11252-5190.

HILLIARD, DR. ASA GRANT, III.
Educator. **Personal:** Born Aug 22, 1933, Galveston, TX; died Aug 13, 2007; married Patsy Jo; children: Asa IV, Robi Nsenga Bailey, Patricia Nefertari & Hakim Sequenenre. **Educ:** Univ Denver, BA, Psychol, 1955, MA, Counseling, 1961, Ed.D, Ed Psychol, 1963. **Career:** Denver Pub Schs, teacher, 1955-60; Univ Denver, teaching fel, 1960-63; San Francisco State Univ, prof, dean educ, 1963-83; Ga State Univ, disting prof educ, 1980, prof educ psychol, Prof Urban Educ. **Orgs:** Dir, Res Automated Serv Inc, 1970-72; consult testing African Hist Child Develop; bd dir, Nat Black Child Develop Inst, 1973-75, Am Asn Col Teacher Educ, 1974-76; Nat Asn Ed Young C, 1974; bd ethnic & minority affairs Am Psychol Asn, 1982-84; Study Classical African Civilizations. **Honors/Awds:** Nat Defense Ed Act Fel Univ Denver, 1960-63; Knight Commander of the Human Order of African Redemption, 1972; Disting Leadership Award, Asn Teacher Educ, 1983; Outstanding Scholar, Asn Black Psychol, 1984. **Military Serv:** Armored Infantry, 1st lt, 2 yrs.

HINES, LAURA M.
Psychologist, educator. **Personal:** Born Oct 29, 1922, Covington, VA; died May 29, 2009; married Dom Balducci. **Educ:** Va State Univ, BA; NY Univ, MA; Fordham Univ, PhD. **Career:** Byrd S Coler Metro Hosp, psychologist, 1960-65; Bd Educ NYC, psychologist, 1965-74, supvr psychologists, 1974-79; Columbia Univ, consult psychologist; Yeshiva Univ, Ferkauf Grad Sch Psychol, prof emer. **Orgs:** Fel Am Psychol Asn; pres, sch div, NYC Psychol Asn, 1983-84; Lexington Sch Deaf; Am Psychol Asn; Nat Asn Sch Psychologists; Soc Psychol Study Ethnic Minority Issues. **Home Addr:** 156 20 Riverside Dr W, New York, NY 10032.

HOLMES, ODETTA. (ODETTA FELIOUS)
Singer. **Personal:** Born Dec 31, 1930, Birmingham, AL; died Dec 2, 2008; daughter of Reuben and Flora Sanders; married Don Gordon, 1959 (divorced); married Gary Shead (divorced); married Iversen Minter, 1977. **Educ:** Los Angeles City Col, classical music & musical comedy. **Career:** Hollywood Turnabout Puppet Theatre, ensemble mem; Albums: Tin Angel, 1954; Sings Ballads & Blues, 1956; At the Gate of Horn, 1957; My Eyes Have Seen, 1959; Odetta & the Blues, 1962; It's a Mighty World, 1964; At Carnegie Hall, 1967; Odetta Sings the Blues, 1968; Yale Univ, Duke Ellington fel, 1972; Movin It On, 1987; Blues Everywhere I Go, 1999; Looking for a Home, 2002; Women in Emotion, 2002; Odetta, 2003; Films: Cinerama Holiday, 1955; William Faulkner's Sanctuary, 1961; The Autobiography of Miss Jane Pittman, 1974; TV series: "Lamp Onto My Feet", 1956; "Tonight with Belafonte", 1959; "Pure Oxygen", 2002. **Honors/Awds:** Sylvania Award for Excellence, 1959; Key to City of Birmingham, 1965; National Endowment for the Arts Medal of the Arts & Humanities, 1999; Visionary Award, Kennedy Ctr, Wash, 2004; Living Legend Award, Libr Cong, Wash, 2005; Lifetime Achievement Award, Winnipeg Folk Festival, 2006; Traditional Folk of the Year, Int Folk Alliance, 2007.

HUFF, WILLIAM.
Executive. **Personal:** Born Apr 10, 1920, Manchester, GA; died Dec 15, 2002; married Beatrice; children: Ronald, Cherie Fae & Brian. **Educ:** Youngstown Univ, BA, 1951; Ohio State Univ Mgt Develop Prog, Cert, 1968; Univ Pittsburgh, MSW, 1969; Training Course Mattatuck Col CT, Cert Housing Tech Training Course. **Career:** Youngstown Area Comm Action Coun, asso dir, 1965-70; Pearl St Neighborhood House, exec dir, 1970-73; Plymouth Urban Ctr, Louisville, exec dir. **Orgs:** Chmn, Commun Action Agency; CAC; Assoc Neighborhood Ctr Hagstrom House USMil Reservation, 1951-57; NAACP; Boys Work Comt, YMCA OH; Welf Rights Orgn Ohio; pres Prof, Group Workers Ohio; Stud Loan Com Conn; Mod Cities Adv on Recreation; adv Teen Parent Club; co-chmn, State Blk Polit Assembly KY;Black Social Workers Louisville; Equal Justice Info Ctr Bd Louisville;LEAP Bd Louisville, Urban Leage; THETA Omega Chap Omega PsiPhi; Russell Area Coun; adv comt, WLKY TV Louisville; Mayor's Human Rel Comn Ohio. **Honors/Awds:** Cert Ohio State Univ Mgt Develop Prog, 1968; Cert Housing Technician Course, 1969; Recipient Award, Freedom Inc A Native Son, Youngstown, OH,1971; Hon KY Col. **Military Serv:** USAF, 1944-45. **Home Addr:** Hwy 41 S, Manchester, GA 31816, **Home Phone:** (706)846-9178.

HUNT, JAMES, JR.
Executive. **Personal:** Born Oct 7, 1944, Hancock County, GA; died Dec 1, 1979; married. **Educ:** BS, 1968. **Career:** Baldwin Co Bd Educ, teacher, 1968-70; E Central Com Opportunity, deputy dir, vpres, 1985. **Orgs:** Chmn, Hancock Bd Ed; acting dir, Ogeechees Lakeview Mgt Co Inc; Hancock Co Chap Black Elected Officials; Dem Club. **Honors/Awds:** Alumni Award, Kappa Alpha Psi, 1971.

HUNT, SAMUEL D.
Manager. **Personal:** Born May 21, 1933, Fresno, CA; died Aug 1, 1979, Fresno, CA; married Ruby; children: Terry, Lanetta, Stanley, Steven & Brian. **Educ:** Fresno City Col, Working Toward Degree Pub Admin; 4 C's Col, attended 1956. **Career:** Fresno Redevelop Agency, sr relocation specialist. **Orgs:** Prince hall spec rep, Nat Urban Coal Conf, 1973; reg dir, Phi Beta Sigma Frat Inc; chmn, Fresno's Model Cities Ed Task Force; pres, Epsilon Delta Sigma Chap; pres, Phi Beta Sigma Frat Inc; pres, 20th Cent Golf Club; pubrel chmn, Western St Golf Asn; King Soloman Lodge; Mt Sinai Consistory; rep, Fresno City Schs Atlanta. **Honors/Awds:** Winner "Tray Award" Ach Ed & Cit Part. **Military Serv:** USAF, 1951-55. **Business Addr:** T W Patterson Bldg Suite 200, Fresno, CA 93728.

HUNTLEY, RICHARD FRANK.
Educator. **Personal:** Born Jan 25, 1926, Masury, OH; died May 8, 2008, Youngstown, OH; son of Joseph M and Ollie Guin Huntley; married Edith Marie Robinson; children: Dean, Lynn, Geoffrey, Steven & Donna Jean. **Educ:** Youngtown State Univ, BA; Univ Akron, MA. **Career:** City Youngstown, chief draftsman, 1964-65; Youngstown Planning Comm, res asst, 1966-70, assoc planner, 1970-71; Youngstown Demonstration Agency, sr planner, 1971; Youngstown Vindicator, dir comm rels, 1972-74; Youngs town State Univ, instr, 1974-92, admin emer. **Orgs:** Chmn bd, Buckeye Elks Youth Develop Ctr; bd mem, Mental Health & Mental Retardation; Soc Blind; Buckeye Review Publ Co; Mahoning County Selective Serv Bd; Vet Foreign Wars; Elks Lodge #73; Masons F & Am; Soc Planning Officials; Mayors Citizen Adv Com; dirs, McGuffey Comm Ctr Bd; Nat Asn Advan Colored People; trustee, Pub Libr Youngstown & Mahoning County, Ohio, 1979. **Military Serv:** AUS, 1944-45; USAF, 1945-48. **Business Addr:** Trustee, Public Library of Youngstown and Mahoning County, 305 Wick Ave, Youngstown, OH 44503.

HYDE, DR. WILLIAM R.
Educator, surgeon. **Personal:** Born Nov 9, 1923, St Paul, MN; died Mar 21, 2009; son of William M and Marie T; married Opal Brown; children: William R Jr, David J & Drew S. **Educ:** Howard Univ, BS (cum laude), 1944, MD, 1947. **Career:** Harlem Hosp, internship; Freedmen's Hosp, residency; Columbia Univ,1949-50; Harlem Hosp, 1952-53; Howard Univ, asst prof surg; Va Hosp, Wash,DC, Gen Hosp, Children's Hosp, Providence Hosp, sr attending surgeon; Howard Univ Col Med, surgeon; Wash Hosp Ctr, sr attending surgeon. **Orgs:** Dipl Am Bd Surg, 1953; Am Col Surgeons, 1958; Wash Acad Surg, 1974; DC Med Soc; fel Nat Med Asn; dipl, Nat Bd Med Examiners; Alpha Phi Alpha Frat; S eastern Surgical Asn; Sigma Pi Phi. **Honors/Awds:** Beta Kappa Chi, Kappa Pi Hon Soc. **Military Serv:** AUS, med corps capt, 1953-55.

HYTCHE, DR. WILLIAM P.
School administrator. **Personal:** Born Nov 28, 1927, Porter, OK; died Jul 15, 2007, Somerset, MD; married Deloris Juanita Cole; children: Pamelia, Jaqueta & William Jr. **Educ:** Langston Univ, BS, 1950; OK State Univ, MS 1958, EdD 1967; Oklahoma Univ; Oberlin Col, Ohio; Univ Wis, Madison; Univ Heidelberg, Germany. **Career:** School administrator (retired); Attucks Jr & Sr High Sch, teacher, 1952-55; Ponca City Sr High Sch, teacher, 1955-60; MD State Col, asst prof, 1960-66; Univ Md Eastern shore, instr math, chmn dept math, dean stud affairs, & chmn div Liberal Studies; acting chancellor, 1975, pres, 1976-97. **Orgs:** Past pres, Co-op Orgn Planning; bd dir, Princess Anne Area C C; Phi SigmaSoc; Alpha Phi Alpha; Holy Royal Arch Mason; Free & Accepted Mason; bddir, Nat Assoc Equal Opportunity Higher Educ; Mid-Delmarva YMCA, 1980-82; joint comn Agr R&D; bd dir, InterFuture; Agribus Promotion Coun; exec comn, Nat Assoc St Univs & Land-Grant Col; bd mem, Am Coun Educ; Pres's Adv Bd Historically Black Col & Univ; Secy, chmn, Interior's Adv Bd

Historically Black Col & Univ; chmn, Coun 1890 Pres & Chancellors; USDA & 1890 Task Force, co-chair; adv bd, Nat Aquarium; Dept Energy, Historically Black Col & Univ task group; Fed Aviation Admin, Airway Sci Task Force; Peninsula Regional Med Ctr, bd trustees; Del-Mar-Va, adv coun; Phi Delta Kappa; Phi Kappa Phi; sr assoc, Am Coun Higher Educ. **Honors/Awds:** Distinguished Alumni of the Year, Brochure 1980; Hall of Fame Inductee, Okla State Univ Alumni Asn, 1993; Thurgood Marshall Educ Achievement Award, 1992; George Wash Carver Pub Serv Hall Fame, Tuskegee Univ, 1994; honorary degrees: Fisk Univ; Wash Col; Univ Md Eastern Shore, Tuskegee Univ. **Special Achievements:** Author: Information Technology and the 1890 Land-Grant Colleges and Universities, Journal of Agricultural & Food Information, 1993; book chaptin A Century of Service, Land-Grant Colleges and Universities, 1890-1990, 1992; article, Historically Black Institutions Forge Linkages with African Nations; memoirs, Step by Step to the Top: The Saga of a President of aHistorically Black University. **Military Serv:** AUS 1950-52.

JACKSON, BOBBY L.
Government official, business owner. **Personal:** Born Feb 19, 1945, Fayetteville, NC; died Jan 9, 2008; married Gwendolyn; children: Martin & Marquisha. **Educ:** Essex Col Bus, sr acct; St Peter Col, acct. **Career:** Hudson Co Oper PUSH, chmn bd, 1978-81; Jersey City Cert Devel Corp, bd mem, 1981-; Jersey City Dem Organ, chmn; Comnr Ins, comm; City of Jersey, city coun pres, dem munic chmn; Urban Times News, owner. **Orgs:** Campaign mgr, Jesse Jackson, NJ; staff mem, Ken Gibson for Gov. **Honors/Awds:** Andrew Young Black Achievement Award, Lambda Omega Sor; Jesse Jackson Award, SC Chap Oper PUSH; Chap 1 Cent Parent Coun; Male of the Year, CETA Inc, Jersey City. **Home Addr:** 232 Wegman Pkwy, Jersey City, NJ 07305.

JACKSON, CHARLES ELLIS.
Government official. **Personal:** Born Jan 30, 1930, Tampa, FL; died Aug 8, 2005, Anchorage, AK; son of Ellis and Clara Yeoman; married Nellie Grace Smith, Dec 6, 1953; children: Donovan Renee & Ronald Eric. **Educ:** Clark Col Atlanta; Alaska Meth Univ, BS; Alaska Meth Univ. **Career:** Alaska Methodist Univ, assoc dean stud; Clinical Chem, chief, 1955-70; Alaska Stud Higher Educ Prog, counr, 1970-72; Prov & Anchorage Comn Hosp, consult, 1955-70; Matunuska Maid Dairy, bacteriologist; Alaska Native Serv Hosp, med technologist; Valley Hosp; Elemen dorf AFB Alaska Hosp, chief clinical chem; Alaska Methodist Univ, assoc dean stud; Alaska Pipe Line Co, personnel dir; Municipality Anchorage, personnel adminr, sanit supvr. **Orgs:** Nat Asn Stud Personnel Adminr; Am Asn Clinical Chemists; Alaska Soc Med Technologists; Pacific Asn Col Deans & Admis Officers; Technologists State Asn Guidance Counrs; past pres, Anchorage Rotary Club; past pres, Anchorage Toastmasters Club; bd mem, City Anchorage Human Rels Comn; bd dir, Lions Int; Omega Psi Phi Frat; World Affairs Coun; Am Cancer Soc; pres, Elem & Sec Sch PTA; bd dir, Kings Lake Mus Camp; house chmn, Anchorage Symphony; investigator Elmen dorf AFB EED Comn; vestryman St Marys Episcopal Ch; chmn, Worship & Parish Life Comt; scout master; cub scouts & BSA. **Honors/Awds:** Elks Oratorial Scholarship; Grand Union Palls bearers Lodge Scholarship, 1948; best dressed man, 1974. **Military Serv:** USAF, aviation cadet, 1952-55, lab officer, 1953-55.

JACKSON, REV. JAMES CONROY.
Clergy. **Personal:** Born May 9, 1913, Scranton, PA; died Apr 1, 1978, Norcross, GA; son of James and Ella Glascoe; married Daisy L Ledgister; children: Patricia Ann Cokley. **Educ:** Cheyney St Col, BS Educ, 1938; Philadelphia Divinity Sch, Mdiv, 1949; Univ South, MST, 1973. **Career:** Clergy (retired); St Philip's Episcol Church Dallas, 1949-56; St Philip's Episcol Church Little Rock, AR, 1956-62; Voorhees Col, chaplain 1962-80, asst prof, 1980; St Barnabus Epis Church, priest-in-charge, 1982-90. **Orgs:** Chmn bd, Urban League, 1960-62; bd mem, Tri-County Community Alcohol & Drug Abuse, 1973-80; officer, bd mem, Bamberg County mental Health, 1974-80; dean, col work Diocese, SC, 1978-80; exec bd, Mental Health Asn, SC, 1982-89. **Honors/Awds:** NAACP Cited, 1954; Big Brothers Dallas, 1956; Parent Teachers Asn, LittleRock, AR, 1962; Religious Education of Negro in SC prior to 1850, 1965; President Award, Voorhees Col, 1979. **Military Serv:** AUS, Corpl, 1942-45. **Home Addr:** 909 Aaron Dr, Columbia, SC 29203.

JACKSON, LEO EDWIN.
Educator. **Personal:** Born Dec 30, 1925, Springfield, MA; died May 27, 2009, New London, CT; son of Andrew J and Ethel Williams; married Barbara Lockwood; children: Reginald, Lionel T & Margo E. **Educ:** Tuskegee Inst, Tuskegee, AL, 1945; Mitchell Col, New London, Bus Admin, 1972. **Career:** Educator (retired); Gen Dynamics Corp, eng aid, 1958-68, suggestion analyst, 1968-70, shipyard placement rep, 1970-71, coordr job training, 1971-76, sr instr, 1976-80; Inst Cert Eng Techs, sr engr tech; City New London, CT, mayor, 1980-91. **Orgs:** Bd ed; Elec Boat Mgt Asn; Biracial Comn Metal Trades Coun; secy, treas, Re-develop Agency; advsy cap, Southeastern Reg Vocat Tech Sch; leading knight, Victory Leading Elks IBPOE W, 1970. **Special Achievements:** First Black Elected to the City of New London, 1975-77; First Black Mayor in New England. **Military Serv:** AAC, avia cadet, 1944-46.

JACKSON, PROF. LUTHER PORTER, JR.
Educator. **Personal:** Born Mar 7, 1925, Chicago, IL; died Apr 22, 2008, Bronx, NY; son of Luther P and Johnnella Frazer; married Nettie Lee; children: Luther P III & Lee Frazer (deceased). **Educ:** Va State Univ, BA, 1949; Columbia Univ Grad, Sch Jour, MS, 1951; Rutgers Univ, Ford Found Fellow, 1963; Columbia Univ, Russell Sage Fellow, 1968. **Career:** Educator (retired); NJ Record, 1949; NJ Herald News, 1949-50; Balt iAfro-Am, 1950; Chicago City News Bureau, 1951; The Newark News, 1951-58;The Wash Post, reporter, 1959-63; IBM News, Corp Headquarters Ed, ed, 1963-65; Communicating Res Urban Poor, cross-tell dir, 1965-67; Nat Advan Asn Colored People, assoc dir pub rel & assoc ed Crisis, 1968; Columbia Univ Grad Sch Jour, prof jour; prof emer, 1991. **Orgs:** Exec bd, Asn Study Afro-Am Life & Hist, 1964-74; pres, NY Br ASAALH, 1964-65; Omega Psi Phi Frat; NY Chap, Nat Asn Black Jour. **Honors/Awds:** Excellence in Teaching Award, 1991. **Special Achievements:** First black prof columbia's J-school. **Military Serv:** USMC, sgt, 1943-46.

JACKSON, MICHAEL JOSEPH.
Entertainer. **Personal:** Born Aug 29, 1958, Gary, IN; died Jun 25, 2009, Los Angeles, CA; son of Joseph and Katherine; married Lisa Marie Presley, May 26, 1994 (divorced 1996); married Debbie Rowe, Nov 15, 1996 (divorced 1999); children: Prince Michael Jr, Paris Michael Katherine & Prince Michael the Second. **Career:** Jackson Five, lead singer, 1968-75; The Jacksons, lead singer, 1975-90; solo artist; composer, singer; Music Videos: "Billie Jean", 1983; "Beat It", 1983; "Thriller", 1983; "Bad", 1987; "The Way You Make Me Feel", 1987; "Smooth Criminal", 1988; "Leave Me Alone", 1989; "Black or White", 1991; "Remember the time", 1992; "Scream", 1995; "Earth Song",1995; "Blood on the Dance Floor", 1997; "You Rock My World", 2001; Films: The Wiz, 1978; Captain EO, 1986; Moon walker, 1988; Ghosts, 1997; Men in Black II Cameo appearance), 2004; Miss Cast Away (Cameo appearance), 2004; Albums: Got to Be There, 1971; Ben, 1972; Music ande, 1973; Forever, Michael, 1975; Off the Wall, 1979; Thriller, 1982; Bad, 1987; Dangerous,1991; Hstory, 1995; Blood on the Dance Floor, 1997; Invincible, 2001; Number Ones, 2003; Songs: "Ben", 1972; "Don't Stop 'Till You Get Enough", 1979; "Rock with You", 1980; "Billie Jean", 1983; "Beat It", 1983; "Say Say Say" with Paul McCartney, 1983; "I Just Can't Stop Loving You", 1987; "Bad",1987; "The Way You Make Me Feel", 1987; "Man in the Mirror", 988; "Dirty Diana", 1988; "Black or White", 1991; "You Are Not Alone", 1995. **Orgs:** Founder, Heal the World Found, 1992. **Honors/Awds:** Male Vocalist of the Year, 1971; Jacksons ranked top in single-record sales, in album sales for new artists, 1970; group featured in animated cartoons on TV series, 1971; Gold & Platinum record awards; performed, Queen Elizabeth's Silver Jubilee, 1977; biggest selling solo album, Thriller, won 8 Grammy Awards, Album & Record of the Year, won over 140 Gold & Platinum Awards in 28 countries & 6 continents; 1985 recipient, ABAA Music Award for efforts to aid African famine victims, for conceiving and giving leadership to "USA for Africa" producing the album and video, We Are the World; Lifetime Achievement Award, Guinness Book Of World Records, 1993; Artist of the Decade Award, Popcorn Magazine, 1995; Favorite Male Vocalist, Popcorn Magazine Awards, 1997; Bob Fosse Award, 1997; Rock & Roll Hall of Fame, inductee, 1998, 2001; Diamond Award; 1999, 2006; Eighth Greatest Entertainer of the Past 50years, Entertainment Weekly, 1999; Lifetime Achievement Award, Namibian Premier Hage Geingob, 1999; World Music Awards, Best-Selling Male Artist of the Millenium, 2000; Charted thirteen number-one singles in the United States; has won more awards than any other artist. **Special Achievements:** Autobiography, Moonwalk, 1989; Appearances at the Super Bowl, 1993; Interviewed by Oprah Winfrey, February 10, 1993, first interview as an adult-viewed by numerous countries; Appearance at President Clinton's Inauguration Ceremonies, 1993; Record setting contract with Sony Music, 1991; First solo artist to generate four top ten hits on the Billboard charts on one album with "Off the Wall"; first artist to generate seven top ten hits (USA) on one album with "Thriller"; only artist in history to generate five #1 hits (USA) from one album with "Bad"; listed in Guinness Book of World Records, winner most awards ever (7) at American Music Awards, 1984; Biggest Selling Album Of All Time, Guiness Book Of World Records, with over 50 million copies sold worldwide; Greatest Audience, Guinness Book Of World Records, the highest-ever viewer ship was 133.4 million viewers watching the NBC transmission of Super Bowl XXVII on June 31, 1993; sold over 100 million singles and albums outside of the U.S; One of the 100 most important black people of the 20th century, Ebony Magazine, 1999. **Home Addr:** Neverland Ranch, Santa Ynez, CA 93460.

JAMES, ARMINTA SUSAN.
Educator. **Personal:** Born May 1, 1924, Erie, PA; died Mar 8, 2009, Mililani, HI; daughter of Leonard Martin and Alice Bowers Martin; married Walter R Jr, Jun 30, 1951. **Educ:** Fisk Univ, BA, 1946; Roosevelt Univ, MA, educ admin, 1965. **Career:** Educator (retired); Erie Co TB Asn, health educ worker, 1946-48; Chicago Welfare Dept, child placement worker, 1948-52; N Chicago Sch Dist 64, teacher, 1955-65, elem prin, 1965-86. **Orgs:** Life mem, past pres, Alpha Kappa Alpha Sorority Lake Co Chap, 1944; Sec & treas, Ill Principals Asn, 1965; Nat Asn Elem Sch Principals, 1965; Nat Alliance Black Sch Educators, 1977; bd mem, Lake Co Urban League; ASCD; Nat Asn Advan Colored People; vestry mem, Christ Episcopal Church; vestry & Christian educ coordr, St Timothy's Church, Aiea Hawaii; Am Asn Univ Women; Hawaii Chap, Links Inc, 1988; bd dirs, St Timothy's Child Care Ctr. **Honors/Awds:** Educator of the Yr, North Shore 12, 1975; Outstanding Woman of Lake County, Urban League, 1977; Outstanding Achievement Award, Omega Psi Phi Fraternity, 1978; Those Who Excell in Educ, Ill St Bd Educ, 1978; Outstanding Achievement Educ, Waukegan YWCA, 1981; Episcopal Diocese of Hawaii, honored for exemplary serv.

JAMES, TROY LEE.
State government official. **Personal:** Born Apr 18, 1924, Texarkana, TX; died Nov 1, 2007; son of Samuel and Anniebell Mack; married Alice G, Jul 3, 2003; married Betty Winslow, Dec 18, 1946 (divorced); children: Laura M. **Educ:** Fenn Col; Bethany Col; Western Reserve Col. **Career:** Government official (retired); Mkt Firm, Cleveland, owner; OH House Reps,10th Dist, laborer & union mem, legislator, 1967-98. **Orgs:** Bd mem, Margie Homes Mentally Retarded; Eliza Bryant Home Aged; dem exec com bd, Ohio State Legislators Soc; chmn, Comt Aging; pres, 5th Ward Dem Club; chmn, Econ Develop Comt; NCSL Comt Econ Develop; exec comt, Black Elected Democrats Ohio; Citizen's League; Consumer Protection Agency;Western Reserve Psychiatric Agency; Cleveland Asn C Learning Disabilities; sr mem, House Democratic Caucus; Ohio Legislative Black Caucus, 1995; Dem Exec Coun; Phyllis Wheatley Asn; Nat Conf St Legislators; Citizen's League; Consumer Protection Agency Cleveland; Ohio Adv Coun Aging. **Honors/Awds:** Legislator of the Year, OH House Reps; Outstanding Legislation to the Youth of Ohio, Ohio Educ Asn; Outstanding Legislation for Community Work,Champs Inc; Special Recognition for Community & Civic Work, Cleveland Bus League; ENA Award for Outstanding Services to Youth, Nat Asn Career Women; Special Appreciation, Nat Soc Social Workers; Senior Citizens Hall of Fame, 2006. **Military Serv:** AUS, 1943-46; Purple Heart.

JARMON, JAMES HENRY, JR.
School administrator. **Personal:** Born Jan 9, 1942, Sheffield, AL; died Jun 13, 2006, Dale, AL; son of James Jarmon Sr; married Lillie Watson; children: Elisa Ann, Monica Yvette & James Henry III. **Educ:** Ala State Univ, BS, 1965; Troy State Univ, MS, 1977. **Career:** DA Smith Jr High Sch, teacher 1965-70, asst prin, 1977-80, prin; Mixon Elem Sch, teacher, 1970-77; Flowers Elem Sch, prin, 1980-81. **Orgs:** Alpha Phi Alpha; Nat Educ Asn, 1965; ACSAS; Phi Delta Kappa,; chmn, Recrn Bd City Ozark; city Counman, City of Ozark; mem, Nat Middle Sch Asn; bd dirs, RSVP; bd dirs, Parents Anonymous; bd dirs, Ozark Chamber of Com; utilities bd, City of Ozark. **Honors/Awds:** Appreciation Award, Ozark Voters League, 1979; Man of the Yr, Ozark Voters League, 1980; Appreciation Award, Carroll High Sch, Ozark, 1983.

JEFFERSON, ANDREW L.
Lawyer. **Personal:** Born Aug 19, 1934, Dallas, TX; died Dec 8, 2008, Houston, TX; son of Andrew Jefferson and Bertha Jefferson; married Mary Brown; children: Andy & Martin. **Educ:** Tex Southern Univ, BA, 1956; Univ TX Sch Law, JD, 1959. **Career:** Washington & Jefferson, Attys at Law, prtnr, 1960-61; Bexar Co, asst-crim dist atty, 1961-62; US Atty, Western Dist TX, chief asst, 1962-67; Humble Oil & Ref Co, counr, 1968-71; Domestic Rel #2, Harris Co, judge, 1970-74; 208th Dist Ct, Harris Co, judge, 1974-75; Jefferson Sherman & Mims, pvt Pract, 1975-80; Jefferson & Mims, atty, 1980; atty, currently. **Orgs:** Houston Bar Asn; Houston Lawyers Asn; St Bar TX; Am Bar Asn; mem, Fed, Nat Bar Asn; Alpha Phi Alpha Frat Inc; Phi Alpha Delta Legal Frat, Tom Greener Chap; Nat Asn Advan Colored People; Pilgrim Cong United Ch Christ; Downtown Rotary Club, Houston; TX Breakfast Club; treas, 1st vpres, Houston Legal Found, 1973-74; bd dirs, pres, Houston Coun Human rels, 1974-75; Houston Area Urban League; Houston Bus Growth Corp; Gov's Drug Abuse Coun; bd mgrs, YMCA S Cent Br; Navigation Bank; former chmn, Federal Reserve Bank Dallas, Houston Br; Int Soc Barristers, 1996. **Honors/Awds:** Nat Torch Liberty Award, Anti-Defamation League 1974; Commission Service Award, LaRaza, 1974; Forward Times Comn Service Award, 1975; Charles A George Commission Service Award, 1975; Nat Commission Service Award, League United Latin Am Citizens, 1975. **Special Achievements:** Numerous guest speaker engagements; establishment of an endowment fortrial advocacy called the "Andrew L. Jefferson Endowment for Trial Advocacy" at Texas Southern University's Thurgood Marshall School of Lawin Houston, Texas. **Military Serv:** AUS, res capt. **Home Addr:** 3861 Palm, Houston, TX 77004. **Business Phone:** (713)227-7006.

JEFFERSON, JAMES E.
Government official, president (organization). **Personal:** Born Jul 22, 1922, Redlands, CA; died Aug 4, 2000, Yuma, AZ; married Pearl. **Career:** Yuma City Coun, mem, 1974-89. **Orgs:** Dir, Ariz Respiratory Disease Asn, 1971-75; adv comt, Ariz State Parks, 1984; pres, Nat Asn Advan Colored People, Yuma City. **Honors/Awds:** Man of the Year Yuma, 1973; Distinguish Service Award, Yuma Area Housing Opportunity, Yuma City, 1984. **Home Addr:** 200 S 10th Ave, Yuma, AZ 85364.

JENKINS, CYNTHIA.
State government official. **Personal:** Born Jul 21, 1924, Nashville, TN; died Jan 1, 2001; daughter of Maynie Burnley and Stephen A

Burnley; married Joseph D Jenkins Sr; children: Joseph D Jr. **Educ:** Univ Louisville, BA, hist & polit sci, 1945; Pratt Inst, MLS, libr sci, 1966; Columbia Univ, Post Grad. **Career:** State government official (retired); Brooklyn Pub Libr, librn, 1960-62; Queens Borough Pub Libr, librn, 1962-82; New York Assembly, legislator; Chairperson Assembly Sub-Comt Affirmative Action, 1985-86; Delegate, Gov Conf Libr, 1990; Delegate, White House Conf Libr, 1991. **Orgs:** Founder/chairperson, Social Concern Community Springfield Gardens Inc, 1969-82; Black Librarians, 1970-75; founder, Caucus Queens, 1976-; founder/chairperson, Social Concern Community Develop Agency, 1980-82; coun mem, Am Libr Asn Governing Body, 1982-; founder/chairperson, Social Concern Fed Credit Union, 1984-; Democratic State Comt. **Honors/Awds:** Community Service Award, Alpha Kappa Alpha Sorority, 1980; Distinguished Citizen Award, Friends Sr Citizens, 1982; Political Leadership Award, Queens Womens Polit Caucus, 1983; Outstanding Citizens Award, Opportunity Frat, 1984; Charter Member, AKA; Won, Sixth Term in the 29th Assembly Dist, 1992. **Home Addr:** 174-63 128 Ave, Jamaica, NY 11434.

JOHNSON, CLARISSA.
Artist, entrepreneur. **Personal:** Born Nov 14, 1913, Detroit, MI; died Mar 7, 2009, Detroit, MI; daughter of Bertha Bissell Cassey (deceased) and Alfred Cassey (deceased); married Alfred, Nov 25, 1960; children: Shirley Pembroke, Rodney Pearson, Laurence Pearson, Glenn Pearson,Charlotte Watson & Patricia Hall. **Career:** Clarissa's Creations, owner, 1978. **Honors/Awds:** Recognition Award, Negro Business & Professional Womens Club, 1989; Wayne County Community Service Award, 1985; First Place Award, North Rosedale Park Festival of Arts, 1990.

JOHNSON, ROY EDWARD.
Baseball player. **Personal:** Born Jun 27, 1959, Parkin, AR; died Jan 26, 2009. **Educ:** Tenn State Univ, Nashville, TN. **Career:** Baseball Player (retired); Montreal Expos, outfielder, 1984-85. **Honors/Awds:** Most Valuable Player; All-Star Squad, A New York Penn League; captured Expos minor league player of the month awards; Southern League Player of Week; Am Assn Battin Title, 1982.

JOHNSON, WENDELL NORMAN.
School administrator, military leader. **Personal:** Born Dec 20, 1933, Boston, MA; died Dec 7, 2006, Scottsdale, AZ; son of Oscar A and Ida M; married Helen L Underwood, Nov 15, 1958; children: Laura Lynn, Lois Underwood & Wendell Norman Jr. **Educ:** New Eng Col Pharm, Boston, MA, BS, 1955; US Naval Post grad Sch, Monterey, CA, cert, 1962; Nat War Col, Wash, DC, cert, 1975; Am Univ, Wash, DC, MA, 1976. **Career:** USN, USS Dahlgren, commanding officer, 1976-78; USS Jason, commandingofficer, 1979-82; Destroyer Squadron 35, commodore, 1982-83; Pentagon, dirres & develop, 1983-84, dir planning & programming logistics, 1984-87; US Naval Base, Charlotte, SC, commander, 1987-89; Mine Warfare Command, comdr, 1987-88; Coun Higher Educ, lectr, 1988; Boston Univ, MA, vpres & dean stud, 1989-2003. **Orgs:** US Naval Inst, 1980-; Govs Round table Literacy, 1988; consult, Coun Educ,1988; bd mem, YMCA; bd mem, Charleston Chamber Com; bd mem, United Way; pres, Boston Univ Charter Sch; Sigma Phi. **Honors/Awds:** Distinguished Leadership Award, Omega Phi Psi, 1988; Doctor of Letters,Col Charleston, 1989; Distinguished Leadership Award, YMCA SE Region,1989; Distinguished Service Award, Commonwealth Mass, 1989; Outstanding Alumni Award, Northeastern Univ, 1989; Legion of Merit; Meritorious Service Medal; Navy Commendation Medal; Navy Achievement Medal; Combat Action Ribbon, Order of Sikatuna (Phillippines). **Special Achievements:** Author: US Navy Minority Recruiting Guide, 1968; Communications Model for Integration of Blacks into the Navy, 1976.

JONES, DORINDA A.
Executive. **Personal:** Born May 27, 1926, Trenton, KY; died Oct 30, 2007; married John M; children: Dawna Lynn & John Jr. **Educ:** BA, 1953; Wayne State Univ, MSW, 1955. **Career:** Wayne St Univ, Sch Soc Work Detroit, asst prof, 1969-70; Mayor's Com, dir, office prog plann-res & eval, 1970, Human Resources Develop Detroit, exec dir, 1971-73; Human Resources Dept, from exec asst to dir, 1985. **Orgs:** Dept head, Soc Serv Head Start Detroit Pub Schs, 1966-68; dir, Overseas Proj, Nat Fed Settlements & Com Ctrs, New York City, 1964-66; prog supvr, bd dir, Gleiss Memorial Ctr, Protest Comn Serv, 1959-64; soc group worker & supv, Neighborhood Serv Org, 1955-58; princ soc planning & develop consult, City Detroit; Nat Asn Soc Workers; Nat Asn Black Soc Workers, Acad Cert Soc Workers; Am Sociol Pub Admin; Coun Minority Pub Admin; Delta Sigma Theta Sorority; Bethune Sect, Nat Coun Negro Woman.

JONES, ERNEST, SR.
Executive, tailor. **Personal:** Born Jul 20, 1923, Suffolk, VA; died Nov 14, 2006, New Haven, CT; married Mary Ann Mckoy; children: Brenda, Ernest, Wanda, Cheryl & Marc. **Educ:** St Paul's Col, Lawrenceville, VA. **Career:** Tailor (Retired), 1947-56; Riteway Cleaners & Tailors, owner. **Orgs:** St Luke's Epis Ch, 1949; bd dir Businessmen's Asn; Dixwell Community House; Dixwell Plaza Merchants Asn; 32 Deg Past Master Prince Hall Masons; pres Craftsmans Club; instr, tailoring Opportunities Industrialization Ctr, New Haven, CT; New Haven Black Elected Officials. **Military Serv:** AUS bandsman 1943-46.

JONES, REV. LEON C.
Clergy. **Personal:** Born Apr 16, 1919, Laurel, MS; died Oct 20, 2007, Pikesville, MD; married Rubye L Brown; children: Kathryn. **Educ:** BA, 1962; MSW, 1968; Am Baptist Sem W, ThD, 1984. **Career:** Second Baptist Church Everett WA, pastor, 1960-69; St Dept Pub Assistance, social caseworker, 1963-66; supr caseworkers & soc workers, 1968-69; Wash Baptist Conv, area minister, 1969-83; Seattle Pac Col, inst Black Am hist & cult, 1968-85; Bellevue Col, 1969; Seattle Community Col, 1971; Seattle Univ, 1970-; Martin Luther King Jr Mem Baptist Church, Renton, WA, pastor, 1978-99; Seattle Univ, adj prof, Theol & Relig, 1985-; Luther King Jr Mem Baptist Church, Renton, WA, pastor emer, 1999-. **Orgs:** SOIC, 1967-68; Nat Acad Soc Workers; Wash Asn Social Workers; chmn, pres Black United Clergy PAC NW, 1973-90. **Military Serv:** USN, cook 1st class, 1938-46. **Business Addr:** Pastor Emeritus, Martin Luther King Jr Mem Baptist Church, 4519 NE Tenth St, PO Box 2145, Renton, WA 98056, **Business Phone:** (425)255-1446.

JONES, LUCIUS.
Educator. **Personal:** Born Jun 16, 1918, Birmingham, AL; died Sep 25, 2008, Jefferson City, MO; married Vivian D; children: Vivian Eilene. **Educ:** Ala A&M, cert print, 1938; Lincoln Univ, BS, 1973; San Jose St, attended 1973. **Career:** Flashlight Herald Knoxville, linotype operator, 1937; Tulsa Art PrinterTulsa, shop foreman, 1939-48; OK Eagle Tulsa; Modern Litho-Print Co, Mo, linotype operator, 1973; Lincoln Univ, instr. **Orgs:** Danforth Assoc, 1963; seminar leader, Typographers Union, 1972-74; Int Graphic Arts Educ Asn; Am Voc Asn; deacon & minister, music Second Bapt Church, Jefferson City; chmn, Midwest Reg Selection Comt Danforth Assoc, 1973; Int comt nominate First Albert Schweitzer Prize, 1975; dir, Jefferson City Comm Male Chorus; Nat Asn Advan Colored People; Omega Psi Frat Inc; United Investment Club; Jefferson City Indust Develop Community. **Honors/Awds:** Board of Curators Award for Service, Lincoln Univ, 1973.

JONES, DR. WILLIAM JENIPHER.
Clergy. **Personal:** Born Oct 27, 1912, Spring Hill, MD; died Mar 31, 2005, Washington DC, DC; son of Richard Edward and Margret Sadie; married Pauline Payne; children: William Edward & William David. **Educ:** Cordoza Bus Sch, attended 1929; Tenn Christian Univ, BDiv, 1977; Univ Ill, Commissioners Training Inst, attended 1985; YMCA Local Community Col, BS,real estate; Moraine Valley Community Col, real estate broker/appraiser; Bibl Studies, cert. **Career:** Chicago Transit Authority, sta transp clerk, 1953-77; Village Robbins, village trustee, 1969-77; Ill Police & Fire Comt Bd, comnr chaplain, 1984; St John Community Church, pastor, 1985. **Orgs:** Agent, United Ins Co Am, 1953; village trustee, Village Robbins, 1969-77; chmn, S Suburban Mayors Planning Group, 1969-77; Gen broker, Universal Ins Agency, 1970; vpres, S Suburban Legal Aid, Harvey, IL, 1970; comdr, Robbins Memorial Post, 1281 Am Legion, 1975; spec dep, Pape Security Serv, 1977; debit mgr, Supreme Life Ins Co, 1978; Alpha Omega Masonic Lodge 121 Robbins, 1979; pres, Concerned Citizen Party Robbins, IL, 1981; secy, Village Robbins Fire & Police Comnr, 1983; chaplain, Ill Fire & Police Comnrs Asn, 1983-85. **Military Serv:** Quarter, master staff sgt, 1943-46; Good Conduct Medal; 3 Battle Stars; Medal of Honor. **Home Addr:** 3702 W 135th St, Robbins, IL 60472.

JOSEY, DR. E. J.
Educator. **Personal:** Born Jan 20, 1924, Norfolk, VA; died Jul 3, 2009, Washington, DC; son of Frances Bailey and Willie; married Dorothy Johnson (divorced); children: Amina. **Educ:** Howard Univ, BA, 1949; Columbia Univ, MA, 1950; State Univ NY Albany, MSLS, 1953; Shaw Univ, DHL, 1973; Univ Wisconsin, Milwaukee, DPS, 1987; NCCent Univ, Doctor Humanities, 1989; Clark Atlanta Univ, DLitt, 1995; Clarion Univ, DHL, 2001. **Career:** Columbia Univ, desk asst, 1950-52; NY Pub Libr Cent Br, tech asst grade 1,1952; NY State Libr, part-time asst, 1952-53; Free Libr Philadelphia,librn, 1953-54; Savannah State Col, instr social sci & hist, 1954-55,chief librn & assoc prof, 1959-66; Del State Col, dir libr, 1955-59; NYState Educ Dept, Bur acad & res libr, from assoc to chief, 1966-76; NYLibr, chief bur specialist libr serv, 1976-86; Univ Pittsburgh, Sch InfoSci, prof emer, 2009. **Orgs:** Am Civil Liberties Union, 1966; chmn, Prog Comn, Nat Asn Advan Colored People, 1972-82, pres, Albany Br, 1982-86; exec bd, Ala bd trustees, 1979-83; pres, Am Libr Asn, 1984-85; pres, Albany Br Asn Study Afro Am Life & Hist; Am Asn Univ Prof; Am Acad Polit & Social Sci; NY Libr Asn; Bd, dirs, Freedom Read Found; exec bd, Dist Am Libr Hist. **Honors/Awds:** National Office Award, Nat Asn Advan Colored People, 1965; Georgia Conference Award, Nat Asn Advan Colored People, 1966; Savannah State University Award, Savannah State Univ, 1967; Alabama Black Caucus Award, 1979; Distinguished Service in Librarianship, State Univ NY Albany, 1981; Distinguished Service Award, Libr Asn City Univ, 1982; DC Association School Librian Award, 1984; Africa Librarianship Award, Kenya Libr Asn, 1984; Martin Luther King Jr Award, 1984; New York Library Association Award, 1985; President Award, Nat Asn Advan Colored People, 1986; Equality Award, Am Libr Asn, 1991; Demco Award Distinguished Service Librarianship, Black Caucus ALA, 1994; Distinguished Service Award Librarianship, Penn Libr Asn, 1996; Alabama Washington Office Award, 1996; John Ames Humphrey Award, Forest Press & OOCLC, 1998; Honorary Membership Award, Am Libr Asn, 2002. **Special Achievements:** Author of numerous publications. **Military Serv:** AUS, 1943-46. **Home Addr:** 5 Bayard Rd, Pittsburgh, PA 15213-1905.

JULIAN, PERCY L., JR.
Lawyer. **Personal:** Born Aug 31, 1940, Chicago, IL; died Feb 24, 2008, Madison, WI; son of Percy Sr and Anna Johnson. **Educ:** Oberlin Col, BA, 1962; Univ Wisc, JD, 1966. **Career:** US Dept Housing & Urban Develop, consult; Wisc Spec Educ Mediation Syst, roster mediator; Julian, Olson & Lasker, sr partner; Pvt Pract, atty 1966; Julian & Assoc, atty. **Orgs:** Coop atty & spl coun; Am Civil Liberties Union; Ctr Const Rights; rep many civil rights groups; state bd, Am Civil Liberties, 1969-74; lectr, UnivWisc, 1970-77, 1979-80; City Study Com Judicial Orgn, 1971-72; chmn, Wisc State Personnel Bd, 1972-76; Wisc Coun Criminal Justice, 1972-80; Wisc State Bar; Fed Bar Western Dist Wisc, Eastern Dist WI; Southern Dist Ill, Cent Dist Ill; 5th, 7th, 8th, 9th, & 11th Circuit Ct Appeals; US Ct Appeals; DC & US Supreme Ct; ABA, Dane County Bar Asn; Nat Asn Criminal Defense Lawyers; Bar Asn 7th Fed Circuit; Am Soc Mag Photogr; Nat Press Photogr Asn; Prof Photogr Am; Employ Rel Study Comn, 1975-77; chmn, Wisc State Com US Commn Civil Rights, 1978-82; Nat Asn Advan Colored People; Am Civil Liberties Union; Fla Bd Bar Examiners. **Honors/Awds:** Member of the Year Award, Wisc Civil Liberties Union, 1972; Lawyer of the Year Award, Ctr Pub Representation, 1978; Robert Stone Memorial Service Award, 1979-80; Wisc Law Alumni Asn, Univ Wisc Law Sch, 1980; Fair Housing Advocate Award, Fair Housing Coun Dane Co, 1988.

KAUFMAN, MEL.
Administrator, football player. **Personal:** Born Feb 24, 1958, Los Angeles, CA; died Feb 7, 2009, Santa Margarita, CA. **Educ:** Calif Poly State Univ, BA, Social Serv, 1984. **Career:** Football player (retired), football coach; Wash Redskins, outside linebacker, 1981-88, personnel scout, 1990, scouting supvr; Blue Sky Co, asst Mgr, 1988-89; Cal Poly Athletics, asst coach, currently. **Honors/Awds:** Super Bowl, 1983-84, 1988; Cal Poly Athletics Hall of Fame, 1993.

KELLY, FLORIDA L.
Educator. **Personal:** Born Oct 13, 1920, Chesterfield, SC; died Oct 8, 2003, New York, NY; married George; children: Joyce Kelly Moore. **Educ:** Howard U, BA, 1938-44; NY U, MA 1953-54; CW Post, 1974. **Career:** Bd Educ New York City, reading specialist, 1975-; Libr Bd Educ New York City, teacher, 1962-75; Elem Bd Educ New York City, teacher, 1954-55. **Orgs:** Bd of dir porg chmn "Big Sisters"; Educ Action of Beta Omicron Chap, 1970-; fund raising chmn Nat Sorority of Phi Delta Kappa, 1970-; leadership com Black Trade Unionists AFL CIO, 1970-; mem Jamaica Br NAACP; chap leader PS 160 Queens, 1969-79; pres Social Serv Club Calvarty Bapt, 1975-; mem Delta Sigma Theta Inc Queens Alumnae. **Honors/Awds:** Chap Leader Award United Fedn of Tchrs, 1979; Article Pub Education Black Youth to Live in a Multi Racial Soc 1977; Article Pub "Bibliography of Black History-ednl Perspectives", 1975; Outstanding Serv Award Nat Sorority of Phi Delta Kappa Inc Beta Onicron Chap 1975; Community Serv Award & Negro Bus & Professional Women Jamaica Club 1968; Baisley Park Women's Business and Professional Award of The Sojourner Truth Award, 1984; Superintendent of the Calvary Baptist Church School, 1981-89; PS 160 Library named for Florida L Kelly of the Walter Francis Bishop Elementary School, 1990.

KENNEDY, MARVIN JAMES.
Manager. **Personal:** Born Apr 18, 1931, Ben Wheeler, TX; died Jan 8, 2008, San Antonio, TX; married Linzel Harmon; children: Wendolyn K Walker, Patrick A, Marva L & Angela M. **Educ:** Prairie View Agri & Mech Univ, BS, 1952; Univ Tex, San Antonio, MA, 1975. **Career:** Prairie View Agri & Mech Col, ROTC prof, 1966-69; Army Rep Vietnam, inspector gen adv dir, 1968-69; HQ 5th Army Ft Sam Houston, chief readiness oper officer, 1969-72, race rels officer, 1972-73; Bexar Co OIC, exec dir, 1974. **Orgs:** Exec dir, San Antonio Oppurtunies Industrialization Ctrs, 1975; past vpres, San Antonio Personnel & Mgt Asn, 1976; exec comt mem, United Negro Col Fund, 1976; rev comt mem, Metro Youth Org, 1978; Am Soc Training Develop, 1979; fund rev comt, United Way, 1979. **Honors/Awds:** Outstanding Performances Award, 1974-94; Appreciation Award, San Antonio Personnel & Mgt Asn, 1978; Community service Award, Nat Coun Negro Women Inc, 1979; Outstanding Performance Award, Kappa Alpha Psi, 1979. **Military Serv:** AUS, maj; Recipient of bronze star air & commendation medals, AUS,1960-66.

KINLOCH, JEROME.
City planner. **Personal:** Born Mar 28, 1943, Charleston, SC; died Jan 30, 2008, Charleston, SC. **Educ:** Col Charleston, broadcasting sch. **Career:** Community developer. **Orgs:** Charleston Coun, Shaws Boy Club; Grassroot Coalition; Nat Black Social Workers; Charleston Indust Educ Bd; Comt Against Racism & Political Repression; Charleston Lib Pty. **Honors/Awds:** Award for Political Action, Mu Alpha, 1976; Outstanding Young Man, CIEC.

KITT, EARTHA MAE.
Singer, actor. **Personal:** Born Jan 17, 1927, Columbia, SC; died Dec 25, 2008, Weston, CT; married John William; married Bill McDonald, Jan 1, 1960 (divorced 1965); children: Kitt Shapiro. **Career:** Katherine Dunham Dance Group, soloist 1948; Night Clubs France, Turkey, Greece, Egypt, New York City, Hollywood, Las Vegas, London, Stockholm, singer 1949-; Stage play Dr Faust Paris 1951, New Faces of 1952, Mrs Patterson 1954, Shinbone Alley 1957, Timbuktu 1978, performer; Motion pictures New Faces 1953, Accused 1957, Anna Lucasta 1958, Mark of the Hawk, St Louis Blues, Synanon 1965, Up the Chastity Belt 1971; Film: Casbah, 1948; New Faces, 1954; The Mark of the Hawk, 1958; St. Louis Blues, 1958; Anna Lucasta, 1959; Saint of Devil's Island, 1961; Uncle Tom's Cabin, 1965; All About People, 1967; Up the Chastity Belt, 1971; Friday Foster, 1975; All By Myself: The Eartha Kitt Story, 1983; The Serpent Warriors, 1985; The Pink Chiquitas, 1987; Dragonard, 1987; Master of Dragonard Hill, 1989; Erik the Viking, 1989; Living Doll, 1990; Ernest Scared Stupid, 1991; Boomerang, 1992; Fatal Instinct, 1993; Unzipped, 1995; Harriet the Spy, 1996; Ill Gotten Gains, 1997; I Woke Up Early the Day I Died, 1998; The Jungle Book: Mowgli's Story, 1998; The Emperor's New Groove, 2000; The Making & Meaning of We Are Family, 2002; The Sweat box, 2002; Anything But Love, 2002; Holes, 2003; On the One, 2005; Preaching to the Choir, 2005; The Emperor's New Groove 2: Kronk's New Groove, 2005; And Then Came Love, 2007; TV Series: "Feast of All Saints", 2001; "Santa Baby!", 2001; "My Life as a Teenage Robot", 2003; "The Emperor's New Sch?, 2006-08;Recording Artist; Star in the play, The Wizard of Oz, Wicked Witch of the West, 1998; play, Cinderella, 2000-01. **Honors/Awds:** Woman of the Year, Nat Asn Negro Musicians, 1968; Grammy Award; Daytime Emmy Award for Outstanding Performer in an Animated Program, 2008. **Special Achievements:** Author: Thursday's Child, 1956; A Tart Is Not A Sweet; Alone With Me; Confessions of A Sex Kitten; Ranked 89 on VH1's 100 Greatest Women of Rock N Roll; several command performances before the Queen of England; nominated twice for Broadway's Tony Award in 1978 & 2000.

LAMBERT, LECLAIR GRIER.
Consultant, state government official, writer. **Personal:** Born Feb 11, 1937, Miami, FL; died May 31, 2008, New york, NY; son of George F Lambert and Maggie Grier Lambert. **Educ:** Hampton Univ, BA, 1959; Harvard Univ, further study commun, 1959; Univ Munich, Germany, art hist, 1966; Grantsmanship Ctr-19 Prog Planning & Mgmt,cert, 1981; People Mgt MN, attended 1985. **Career:** Time-Life Books, writer & res, 1961-63; US Dependent Schs Overseas, teacher, 1964-65; Holt, Rinehart & Winston, biol ed, 1966-68; Faraday Press, ed translr russian & biol monographs, 1971-72; Nat Found March Dimes, pub rels writer, 1972; St Paul Urban League, asst to dir & comt officer, 1972-80, 1985-86; African-American Mus Art & Hist, dir, 1980-85; MN House Rep, Educ Prog, coordr & sergeant at arms, Officer of the House, 1987-96; Minn State House Rep, House Pub Info Off, dir, 1996-; Palestinian Legis Coun & Birzeit Univ Palestine, info & media consult, ARD & USAID, 1997. **Orgs:** Co-founder, Summit Univ Free Press, St Paul MN, 1974; bd mem, HEART, 1978-88; Dr Martin L King Jr Bust Comt Minn State Capitol, 1983; consult-,writer & designer, Black Hist Exhibits, 1984-94; bd mem, Twin Cities Cable Arts Consortium, 1984-86; bd mem, City Golden Valley Human Rights Comn, Black Hist Month Celebration 1981-88; Nat African-Am Mus Asn Exec Coun; Midwest Regional Rep, 1981-86; City St Paul Roy Wilkins Aud Dedication Comt, 1984; St Paul Urban League; co-chair, 75th annual meeting, 1999; chair, 2004; Urban League Volunteers, 1972-; St Paul Civic Ctr Authority,rep, City Public Arts, Oper & Personnel Comt, 1985-91; Am Smithsonian Exhibition, plan comt, 1996; vice chair, exec comt, bldg comt, 1991-97; bd mem, St Paul Conv Bur, 1990-92; MN Mus Am Art, task force comt, 1990-91, pres, 1993-94, chmn, 1994-95; Univ Minn, Archie Givens Sr African-Am Lit Found, 1990-; Dr Martin Luther King Jr State Holiday Celebration, 1987-94; bd mem, Col Visual Arts, 1997-; adv bd mem, YMCA Youth Govt, 1997-; comnr, St Paul Human Rights Comt, 1999-; Minn Landmarks, 2001-02; hon mem, Givens Found. **Honors/Awds:** St Paul Ministerial Alliance Award, 1974; Certificate of Appreciation,Univ Minn Black Stud, 1981; Minneapolis St Acad Appreciation Award, 1983; ed, Art Develop A Nigerian Perspective, 1984; Special Appreciation Award, Cult Awareness Roosevelt High Sch, 1985; Appreciation Award, Nat African Am Mus Asn, 1985; 50th Anniversary Guest Speaker & Awardee, Liberty Sq Tenant's Asn, Miami, FL, 1986; Volunteer Service Award, St Paul Urban League, 1988; USAID Palestinian Legislative Council Special Recognition, 1997; Special Recognition Award, Hubert H Humphrey Inst Int Fel Prog, 1998; Nat Information Staff Award, Nat Conf State Legislatures, 2003. **Special Achievements:** LeClair Grier Lambert Day, proclaimed in city of St Paul, Sept 29, 1997. **Military Serv:** AUS, first lt, 1959-61. **Home Addr:** 1111 Charlton, West St Paul, MN 55118. **Business Addr:** Director, Minnesota House of Representatives, Public Information Office, 100 Rev Dr Martin Luther King Jr Blvd, St Paul, MN 55155, **Business Phone:** (651)296-2146.

LANGFORD, DR. ANNA RIGGS.
Lawyer. **Personal:** Born Oct 27, 1917, Springfield, OH; died Sep 17, 2008; daughter of Arthur J Riggs and Alice; divorced; children: Lawrence W Jr. **Educ:** Roosevelt Univ, attended 1948; John Marshall Law Sch, LIB, JD, 1956. **Career:** Robinson Farmer & Langford, attorney, 1959-69; atty, pvt pract. **Orgs:** Nat Bar Asn, 1958-75; Pres Johnson's Conf, 1968; bd mem, Am Civil Liberties Union, 1970-71; delegate-at-large, Nat Dem Conv, 1972; Nat Asn Advan Colored People; Chicago Urban League; Chicago Chap Soutjern Christian Leadership Coun; founder, Pride Community Ctr; bd mem, Oper Breadbasket & PUSH; chmn, bd dir, IMPACT drug abuse prg; Sparling Comn; Ill Gov Olgilvie's Com Sr Citizens; Pres Nixon's Conf Aging, 1971; del, World Congress Peace Forces, Moscow, 1973; bd dir, Cook Co Bar Asn, 1973-75; invitee, Int Comm Inquiry Crimes Military Junta Chile, Helsinki, Finland, 1974. **Honors/Awds:** Mahatma Ghandi Centennial Greater Chicago Award, 1969; IOTA Bus Week Award, Alpha Chap, Iota Phi Lambda 1969; Interracial Justice & Brotherhood Award, 1970; Woman of Distiction, Etta Moten Civic & Educ Club, 1970;Civil Rights Award, Cook Co Bar Asn; Special Achievement Award, Cook CoBar Asn, 1971; James B Anderson Award for Outstanding Achievement,Montford Point Marine Asn 1971; Achievement Award, 7th Ward Ind Polit Orgn, 1971; Outstanding Service in Govt for human outstanding & equal justice in performance as Alderman, SCLS's Operation Breadbasket, 1971;Certificate Award, Int Travelers Asn, 1971; Am Friendship Club Award of Distinction, 1971; Testimonial Award, Afro-American Patrol men's Asn, 1971; WBEE Ro Community Award, 1971; Operation Bootstrap Award, 1971. **Special Achievements:** Anna R. Langford is the first black woman elected alderman in Chicago;first woman elected to the Chicago City Council. .

LARK, RAYMOND.
Artist, lecturer. **Personal:** Born Jun 16, 1939, Philadelphia, PA; died Sep 19, 2004, Los Angeles, CA; son of Thomas Crawford and Bertha Lark. **Educ:** Philadelphia Museum Sch Art, 1948-51; Los Angeles Trade Tech Col, 1961-62; Temple Univ Evening Col, BS, 1961; St Johns Night Col; Univ Colo, Boulder, LHD, 1985. **Career:** Museum & Gallery exhibitions: Libr Cong Wash, DC; Guggenheim Mus; Smithsonian Inst; Ava Dorog Galleries Los Angeles & Munich; LaGalerieMouffe Paris; Nader's Art Gallery Port-au-Prince, Haiti; Galleria d'Arte Caglairi Naples, Italy; Centre Int D-Art Contemporain Paris France; Accademia Italia Parma, Italy; Honolulu Acad Arts Hawaii; Mus African & African-Am Art & Antiquities Buffalo, NY; Portsmouth Mus VA; Calif Mus Sci & Indust Los Angeles; NJ State Mus Trenton; UCLA Ctr Afro-Am Studies LA; Stanford Univ Mus; Exec Mansion; Nelson A Rockefeller NY, vpres; Santa Barbara Mus CA; Univ Colo Mus Boulder; Utah Mus Fine Arts, Salt Lake City; Triton Mus Fine Arts, CA, Dickinson Univ N Dakota; Calif Mus African Hist & Cult Soc San Francisco; San Diego Museum CA; Mus African Am Art Santa Monica conjunction 1982 Nat Urban League Annual Conf; Gallery Vallombreuse Biarritz France; Smith-Mason Gallery Art Wash, DC; Phillip E Freed Gallery Art Chicago; Playboy Club Century City CA; Dalzell Harfield Galleries Ambassador Hotel Los Angeles; Diplomat Hotel Fla; Sheraton Park Hotel Wash, DC; Griffon's Light Gallery Denver, Co; Phoenix Art Gallery Atlanta, GA; Multi-Cult Arts Inst San Diego, CA; Lyzon Galleries Nashville, TN; Ames Art Galleries & Auctioneers Beverly Hills, Springfield Art Mus, MO, Wash County Mus Fine Arts, MD; Peninsula Fine Arts Ctr, VA; Greenville Mus Art, Inc, NC; African-Am Cult Ctr, NC St Univ, 1998-99; Alexandria Museum Art, Alexandria, Louisiana; NC St Univ, Raleigh; Hill Country Arts Found, Ingram Texas; Yerbu Buena Ctr Arts, San Francisco, 2000; Art Comns include work for "All in the Family"; "The Carol Burnett Show"; "Maude"; "Young & the Restless"; Univ City Studios Movie Land Wax Museum; Blue Cross Ins Co. **Orgs:** Nat Asn Advan Colored People; Int Platform Asn (IPA). **Honors/Awds:** Grants & Sponsors: Nat Endowment Arts, ARCO, Charles Schwab & Co., Inc, Mercedes-Benz, Am Express, Utah Endowment Arts, N Dakota coun arts, Smithsonian Inst, City Baltimore, MD, State NC, city Honolulu, Hawaii, City Atlanta, Ga Coors Beer Co, Colo Humanities Prog, stud Univ Colo; Dr Raymond Lark Day, State MD, named in honor, 1998. **Special Achievements:** A succession of citations, honors, salutes, commissions, advertising endorsements, headlined billings & Best-of-the-Show Cash Awards & Gold Medals, citations from Pres Jimmy Carter, Gerald Ford, Richard Nixon, Gov Jerry Brown of CA, & mayor Tom Bradley of LA, NAACP, over 50 "first" accomplishments, author & contributor to over 50 scholarly treatises on art, education, historical development of black Americans, which are used as textbooks translated & subscribed to by institutions & individuals in nearly every country of the world, lectured & debated at many museums, colleges & universities throughout the US, collections arranged include, Black Sculpturing Exhibition, Bowers Museum, Santa Ana, CA, 1969, Nine American Artists, Diplomat Hotel, Hollywood Beach, FL 1970, The Art of Bernard Wright, Pittsburgh City Hall Gallery, PA, 1990, The Art of Howard Marshall, Jr, Univ of Utah, Salt Lake City, 1993.

LAWRENCE, SANDRA.
Interior designer, architect. **Personal:** Born Jan 28, 1938, New York, NY; died Jan 29, 2006, New York, NY; daughter of George and Lossie; married Paul Evans Jr (divorced 1990). **Educ:** NY Sch Interior Design, BFA; Parsons, attended 1984. **Career:** Batakari Ltd, Ny, pres interior designer, 1973-81; Sandra Lawrence Assocs Inc, pres & dir. **Orgs:** Allied Bd Trade, 1980.

LEFLORE, DR. WILLIAM B.
Educator. **Personal:** Born Feb 22, 1930, Mobile, AL; died Dec 1, 1986, Atlanta, GA. **Educ:** St Augustine's Col, BS, 1950; Atlanta Univ, MS, 1952; Univ Southern Calif, MSc, 1961, PhD, 1965. **Career:** Bennett Col, instr biol, 1952-57; Spelman Col, asst prof biol, 1964, biol dept, prof & chmn; NC A&T Univ, vis prof biol, 1966; Col St Teresa, exchange prof biol, 1968-69. **Orgs:** Consul, Off Educ USPHS, 1968 1970-74; ad hoc consul, MBS Prog USPHS, 1975; consul, Kellogg Found Univ Ark, Pine Bluff, 1981; consul, Biol Dept Savannah State Col, 1984; Helminthological Soc Wash; Am Soc Parasitologist; Am Microscopical Soc; Am Soc Zoologists; Am Physiological Soc. **Honors/Awds:** Distinguished Scholar Award, United Negro Col Fund, 1982-83. **Special Achievements:** Published over 30 scientific articles in Journal of Parasitol and otherjournals. **Military Serv:** AUS, e-5, 2 yrs.

LEWIS, CHARLES GRANT.
Construction engineer. **Personal:** Born Mar 12, 1948, Los Angeles, CA; died Jan 20, 2008, Emeryville, CA. **Educ:** E Los Angeles Col, AA, 1973; Univ Souther Calif, BS, 1977. **Career:** John D Williams, draftsman, 1971-74; Charles Grant Orgn, prin, 1974-77; Benito Sinclair PE, engr, 1974-77; Am Inst Architects, asst vpres, 1977; Edward C Barker & Assoc, proj designer, 1977. **Orgs:** Assoc Urban Workshop, 1967-77, Alpha Phi Alpha Building Found, 1972-74; Alpha Phi Alpha Frat, 1971-73; stud rep, Nat Orgn Minority Architects, 1974-77; Design Ctr Planning & Architect Urban groups. **Honors/Awds:** Leadership Award, Am Soc Engrs & Architects, 1973; Commendation Order of Omega Hon Frat.

LIPSCOMBE, DR. WENDELL R.
Psychiatrist. **Personal:** Born Jun 9, 1920, Berkeley, CA; died May 6, 2004; divorced. **Educ:** San Diego State Col, AB, 1947; Univ CA, MD, 1951; Univ Mich, MPH, 1953. **Career:** Bur Chronic Dis, State Calif, Dept Pub Health, supvr, 1955-57; Div Alcoholic Rehab, sect chief, 1957-59, asst chief, 1959-61; Mendocino State Hosp, resident psychiat, 1961-64; Cowell Memorial Hosp, psychiat resident, 1964-65; Mendocino State Hosp, chief res, 1965-72; Gen Res Corp, prin consult/Study dir, 1972-73; Westside Community Mental Health Ctr, chief res, 1972-74; Drug Abuse Prog Berkeley Health Dept, chief clin serv, 1973-75; W Oakland Health Ctr, staff psychiat, 1974-; E Oakland Mental Health Ctr, consult med clin dir, 1975-; Source Inc Cons, exec dir, physician; pvt pract, psychiatrist. **Orgs:** N Calif Psychiat Soc; Pac Sociol Soc; AAAS; Pan Am Med Asn; Am Acad Polit & Social Sci; Am Med Soc Alcoholism; Am Therapeut Soc; Am Social Health Asn; Acad Psychosom Med; Bio feed back Res Soc; Int Coun Alcohol & Addictions; Am Soc Clinical Pharmacol & Therapeut; Black Psychiatrists N Calif; Calif Soc Treatment Alcoholism & Other Dependencies. **Honors/Awds:** Prin investigator "An Assessment of Alcoholism Serv Needs & Alcoholism Serv Utilization of CA Black Population". **Military Serv:** USAF, 1953-55.

LYMAN, WEBSTER S.
Lawyer. **Personal:** Born Sep 24, 1922, Columbus, OH; died Oct 14, 2008, Hilliard, OH; son of Webster S Sr and Madie A; married Marion E; children: Bonita L Logan & Alisa K. **Educ:** Ohio State Univ, BS, 1944, LLB, 1949, JD, 1949. **Career:** Pvt Pract atty, 1950; Ohio Civil Rights Comn, hearing examiner, 1970-78; Common Pleas Ct, chmn, med arbitration, 1982. **Orgs:** Pres, Mu Iota Chap Omega Psi Phi Fraternity, 1954-55; pres, Robert B Elliott Law Club, 1955-56; comdr, Am Legion 690, 1956; legal adv, Franklin Lodge Elks 203; charter mem, Lawyers Christian fel, 1966, pres, 1981; Parliamentarian Ohio Asn Black Attys, 1975; charter mem, Ohio Asn Black Atty, 1975; charter mem, Good Shepherd Baptist Church, 1976; nominating comt, Nat Bar Asn, 1977-78; legal adv, Past Exalted Rulers Coun Elks, 1978; vpres, Project Linden, 1980; pres, Second Community Bowling League, 1981-82; pres, Buckeye Bridge Club, 1982-84; pres, Inner City Lions Club, 1984-85; treas, Columbus Urban League; pres, Isabelle Ridgway Home Aged; vpres, Franklin County Forum, 1985-87. **Honors/Awds:** Fourty Year Pin, Omega Psi Phi Fraternity Inc, 1982; Family Award Second Baptist Church; Humanitarian Award, Gamma Phi Delta Sorority Inc, 1984; 50 Year Pin, Omega Psi Phi Frat Inc, 1992. **Military Serv:** AUS, S/Sgt, 1944-46; Chaplain Franklin County Forum, 1997; Secy Columbus Inner City Lions Club, 1986. **Home Addr:** 1620 E Broad St Suite 1005, Columbus, OH 43203, **Home Phone:** (614)252-4302.

LYNCH, DR. LILLIE RIDDICK.
Educator, college teacher. **Personal:** Born Sep 14, 1917, Gatesville, NC; died Apr 1, 2006; daughter of Lee and Rosa; divorced. **Educ:** Hampton Inst VA, BS, 1941; Univ MI, Ann Arbor, MPH, 1949; NY Univ, PhD, 1971. **Career:** Educator (retired); NC Public Schs, teachr sci & social studies, 1944-46; VA Pub Schs, teacher elem grades, 1947, teacher biol & chem, 1947-48; Portsmouth VA Pub Schs, teachng high sch & elem sch levels, 1951-57; NY City Pub Schs, health educ & testing, 1957-64, 1964-67; Jersey City State Col, asst prof health educ, 1964-69, assoc prof & co ordr comm health educ, 1969-76; Univ Mass, assoc prof pub health, 1972-73; Jersey City State Col, prof health sci, 1976-87; NC Cent Univ, adj prof, 1989; health educ & health prog planning, consult. **Orgs:** Fel Am Sch Health Asn; Am Alliance Health Phys Educ & Recreation; Royal Soc Health London; Am Fed Teachrs AFL-CIO, 1974-76; Am Public Health Asn; Am Asn Univ Profs; Nat Soc Public Health Educrs; Tri State Soc Pub Health Educrs; Const & Bylaws Comt, Am Sch Health Asn, 1968-72; dept rep Am Fed Trachers, AFL-CIO, 1974-78; SOPHE Ad Hoc Comt. **Honors/**

Awds: Alpha Kappa Alpha; Kappa Delta Pi Beta Pi Chapt; Pi Lambda Theta Rho Chap; Alpha Kappa Delta Mu Chap NY Univ Founder's Day Award, 1972; Zonta Club; Intl Inst of Jersey City & Bayonne NJ; Nat Found for Infantile Paralysis for study in Health Educ at Univ of MI Fellowship, 1948-49; Fellowship Found Field Study Public Health Educ, MI Kellogg Found; auth of many books & articles. **Home Addr:** 1725 Alfred St, Durham, NC 27713.

MACK, GORDON H.
Educator. **Personal:** Born Jul 1, 1927, Chicago, IL; died Sep 8, 2008, Princeton, NJ; son of W Howard Mack; married Kay Bell; children: Melissa, Michael, Margot & Matthew. **Educ:** Southern Univ, BA; New York Univ, MA. **Career:** Cent Atlantic Area Coun YMCA, asst dir 1964-67; Nat Bd YMCA, dir, 1967-69; Bank St Col Field Serv Div, chmn 1970; Leadership Resource Inc, sr assoc, 1970; YMCA USA, dir cult diversity, 1990; Am Humanics, dir, 1994; Univ Northern Iowa, admin staff. **Orgs:** YMCA Chicago Metro Asn, 1953-63; Am Counc Educ, 1970; Cent Atlantic Area Nat Coun; unit supr JOBS YMCA; youth dir, Hyde Pk; spec adv Tuckagee MIOTA Proj; instr & field supr, George Williams Col; Am Soc Training & Develop; Asn Prof YMCA & Whats New Recruiting; bd dirs, Am Montessori Soc. **Honors/Awds:** Human Relations Award, Nat Conf Christians & Jews. **Military Serv:** AUS, First lt, 1952-54.

MADISON, RICHARD.
Government official. **Personal:** Born Dec 6, 1932, Camden, AL; died Feb 13, 2009, Atlanta, GA; married Edith Sauhing Ho. **Educ:** Morehouse Col, BA, 1953; Univ Pa, MGA, 1958; Univ Pittsburgh, PhD. **Career:** Budget Bur Gov's Off Harrisburg, budget analyst, 1958-60; Gov's Off Harrisburg PA, adminstr asst to dir personnel, 1960-61; CARE Turkey, field rep, 1961-62; Peace Corps Colombia, assoc dir, 1962-63; CARE Honduras, asst dir, 1963-65; CARE Hong Kong, asst dir, 1965-68; CARE Malaysia, actg dir, 1967; CARE E Pakistan, dir, 1968; Nat Urban League Field Opers, asstdir, 1968-69; Nat Urban League Entrepreneurial Develop, nat dir, 1969-70; Inst Minority Bus Educ Howard Univ, exec dir, 1970-71; Gov's Off Adminr Pa, dir personnel, 1972. **Orgs:** Am Soc Pub Adminr; Int Personnel Mgt Asn; Nat Asn Advan Colored People; Foreign Policy Asn; Omega Psi Phi Fraternity; Black Polit Assembly. **Military Serv:** AUS, 1953-55.

MAHAN-POWELL, LENA.
Business owner, mayor, teacher. **Personal:** Born Dec 3, 1951, Myrlewood, AL; died Jan 19, 2004, Wilcox, AL; daughter of Buster and Anna Givan; married Willie Powell, Nov 22, 1978; children: Donyale Jones & Ricky Leyvahn Powell. **Educ:** Univ S Ala, Mobile, AL, attended 1971; Alabama State Univ, Montgomery, AL, BS, 1974, MEd, 1977; Univ Alabama Tuscaloosa, Tuscalossa, AL, attended 1978; Auburn Univ Montgomery, Montgomery AL, attended 1986. **Career:** Wilcox County Brd Educ, Camden, teacher, 1974-89; Talladega Deaf & Blind, Montgomery Ala, teacher, 1984-86; Town Yellow Bluff, Ala, coun mem, 1984-88, mayor, 1988; LMP Off & Sch Supply Co, founder, owner, currently. **Orgs:** Church secy, Arkadelphia Baptist Church, 1978; pres, Univ Brotherhood, 1980; Lewis Delight No 598 OES, 1982; brd dir, Wilcox Hum Res Dept, 1984; Prepared Cities Org, 1986; brd dir, Wilcox Educ Assn, 1987-89; Ala Conf Black Mayors, 1988; Natl Conf Black Mayors, 1988; Laws Comt, Cent High Sch PTO, 1988; vol, Fire Dept Assn, 1988, vpres, Wilcox Edn Assn, 1989; Wilcox Women Develop, 1990; Wilcox Develop Coun. **Honors/Awds:** Outstanding American Award. **Home Addr:** Rte 1, PO Box 198, Pine Hill, AL 36769.

MARTIN, WAYNE.
Automotive executive. **Personal:** Born Dec 31, 1949, Boston, MA; died Dec 19, 2008, San Jose, CA; son of Harry K and Helen N; married Millie Christmas, Jun 7, 1969; children: Charmaine, Shondalyn & Michael. **Career:** Weisenberger Motor Co, sales mgr, 1978-86; Bob Hoy's World Auto Mkt, gen sales mgr, 1986-89; Vision Ford Lincoln Mercury Inc, pres, owner, 1989. **Orgs:** Bd mem, NCP, Alamogordo Chap; Children Need Serv; Alamogordo Chamber Com; bd mem, Adult Basic Educ; bd dirs, Ford, Lincoln Mercury Minority Dealer. **Honors/Awds:** Governor's VIVA Award, NMex, 1995; Business of the Year Award, City Alamogordo, 1996. **Military Serv:** Army, e-4, 1970-71. **Business Addr:** President, Chief Executive Officer, Vision Ford Lincoln Mercury Inc, 1500 S White Sands Blvd, Alamogordo, NM 88310-7637, **Business Phone:** (505)434-4800.

MCCOY, GEORGE H.
Administrator. **Personal:** Born Dec 10, 1930, Philadelphia, PA; died Jan 23, 2008, Buffalo, NY; son of Clara J Palmer and James Ross; married Louise (deceased); children: Eva & Hassan. **Educ:** City Col NY, BA, 1970; Bernard Baruch Col, New York, MBA, 1973. **Career:** Albert Einstein Hosp, Bronx NY, from asst admin to sr asst admin, 1973-77; Kings County Hosp, Brooklyn, NY, dep dir, 1977-78; W County Med Ctr, Valhalla, NY, first dep comn, 1978-86; Erie County Med Ctr, Buffalo, NY, chief exec officer, 1986; Gov Juan Luis Hosp, St Croix, VI, chief exec officer, 1993. **Orgs:** Am Hosp Asn, 1970; Am Col Hosp Admin, 1972; adj prof, Marymount Col Terrytown, 1979-86; bd dir, West-Putnam March Dimes 1984-86; chmn bd dir, Congregations Concerned City Mt Vernon, 1983-86; pres, Nat Asn Pub Hosps, 1993; Greater Buffalo Chamber Com; Buffalo Urban League; exec bd, UnitedWay; Autistic Bd Buffalo; bd dirs, Buffalo Eye Bank; exec comn, Nat Asn Pub Hosps; Hosp Asn New York St; treas, Nat Pub Health & Hosps Inst. **Honors/Awds:** Community Serv Key Women Am, Upper Westchester, 1984; Professional of the Year, Buffalo Club, Nat Asn Negro Bus & Prof Women, 1988; Black Achievers Award, 1990. **Military Serv:** AUS, capt, 1951-59.

MCDONALD, DR. CURTIS W.
Educator. **Personal:** Born Jan 29, 1934, Cedar Creek, TX; died Apr 3, 2007, Harris, TX; son of Oscar and Virgie; married. **Educ:** Huston Tillotson Col, Austin, BS, 1955; Tex Southern Univ, MS, 1957; UnivTex, PhD, 1962. **Career:** Alcorn A&M Col, Lorman, MS, teacher, 1961-63; Ala State Univ, Montgomery, 1963-68; Southern Univ Baton Rouge, 1968-73; Tex Southern Univ, Houston, prof chem, 1973. **Orgs:** Am Chem Soc; Nat Inst Sci; Soc Applied Spectscpy; Soc Sigma Xi; TX AcadSci; Am Inst Chemists. **Honors/Awds:** Publications in Anal Chem, 1964, 1967, 1969, 1973, 1974; Mikrochim 1970,1972, 1974; 40 publications from 1964-90.

MCFARLAND, OLLIE FRANKLIN.
Educator. **Personal:** Born Oct 25, 1918, Jacksonville, FL; died Aug 10, 2009; married William A (deceased); children: William Michael. **Educ:** Spelman Col, BA, 1940; Wayne State Univ, MM, 1952. **Career:** Educator, (retired); Detroit Pub Schs, music teacher Cent High, 1958-67, supvr music educ, 1967-79, asst dir music educ, 1979-81, dir music educ, 1981. **Orgs:** John Hay Fel, Columbia Univ, 1965-66; life mem, Nat Asn Advan Colored People, 1979-; singer, Celeste Cole Opera Theatre; narrator, Detroit Symphony Det Pub Schs, Educ Concerts; concert/opera singer on radio/TV & St Joseph's Church; bd mem, Detroit Comm Music Sch; bd mem, Rackham Symphony Choir; Alpha Kappa Alpha Sor; Delta Kappa Gamma. **Honors/Awds:** Hon, Nat Asn Negro Musicians 1985; Educator's Achievement Award, Booker T Washington Bus Asn, 1983; Achievement Award, Omega Psi Phi Frat, 1977. **Special Achievements:** Auth music textbook, "Afro-America Sings" Det Pub Schools 1973, revised 1981.

MCGEE, ROSE N.
Association executive. **Personal:** Born Jan 23, 1921, Steubenville, OH; died Dec 21, 2001; widowed; children: Robert, John, Thaddeus & Patricia Williams. **Educ:** Steubenville Bus Col, attended 1947; Univ Steubenville. **Career:** Off City Steubenville, clerk treas, 1968-70; SSI OH Comn Aging, dir,1970-74; OH Comn Aging, area coordr, 1974-80. **Orgs:** Area ldr Cancer Soc; area ldr ARC; area ldr Comm Chest Rec; steward Phillips Chapel CME; past pres, life mem, exec bd NAACP; vpres, LeagueWomen Voters. **Honors/Awds:** Recipient Award Commendation & Recognition, WSTV-TV Inc, 1962; Outstanding Serv Award, OH Conf of NAACP, 1968; Cert of Commendation, Nat Coun Negro Women Inc, 1975; Certificate of Apppreciation Valued Contribution, Bus &Prof Women, 1976; Comm Award, City Steubenville, 1976. **Business Addr:** Area Coordinator, OH Department of Aging, 50 W Broad St 9th Fl, Columbus, OH 43266.

MCMILLAN, DR. WILLIAM ASBURY.
School administrator. **Personal:** Born Feb 29, 1920, Winnabow, NC; died Mar 14, 2009; son of James Calbert and Lydia Gore; married Mildred Newlin, Jun 3, 1950 (died 2001); children: Pamela Jackson, Paula Jones & William Jr. **Educ:** Johnson C Smith Univ, BA, 1942; Univ Mich, MA, 1945, PhD, 1954; Univ Pa,Col Loma Linda Calif; Harvard Univ. **Career:** Gatesville NC, teacher, 1942-44, 1946-47; Johnson C Smith Univ, asst dean instr, 1947-48; Pomeroy Pa, counr, 1948-49; Wiley Col, dir, 1949-58;Bethune-Cookman Col, acad dean, 1958-64, 1966-67; Rust Col, pres, 1967-93, pres emer, 1993. **Orgs:** Life mem, Nat Educ Asn; life mem, ATA; life mem, Alpha Phi Omega; lifemem, NAACP; MS Asn Col & Univ, pres, 1973-74; Boy Scouts Am, scoutmaster, 32 yrs; bd dir, Yocona Area Coun, 1980-; chair, life mem Comt, Marshall County NAACP, 1998-; secy, Holly Springs Tourism & Recreation Bur,1999-2001; chair, Holly Springs Comm Develop Corp, 1999-; chmn, Bd Educ NMS; Conf United Meth Ch; life mem, Omega Psi Phi; chmn, mem & visitation comt, bd dir, vice chair mem, UNCF; bd dir, Miss Methodist Hosp & RehabCtr; life mem, Phi Delta Kappa; chair, Marshall County Concerned Citizens Coalition; organizer & dir, Gentlemen Qual Club, 1995-2000; chair, bdtrustees, Alliance Healthcare Hosp. **Honors/Awds:** Hon LLD: Cornell Col, Johnson C Smith Univ, Bethune-Cookman Col, Mary Holmes Col, Rust Col; Silver Beaver Award, BSA, 1974; Exemplar Award, CIC,1997-98; 170 plaques & awards. **Military Serv:** USAF, 1945. **Home Addr:** 672 W Woodward Ave, Holly Springs, MS 38635, **Home Phone:** (662)551-1240.

MCNAIR, STEVE LATREAL.
Football player. **Personal:** Born Feb 14, 1973, Mt Olive, MS; died Jul 4, 2009, Nashville, TN; son of Lucille. **Educ:** Alcorn State Univ, phys educ. **Career:** Houston Oilers / Tennessee Oilers / Tennessee Titans, quaterback, 1995-2005; Baltimore Ravens, 2006-07. **Honors/Awds:** All-State & Super Prep All-Am hons; Walter Payton Award, 1994; Ed Block Courage Award, 1999; named in hon Steve McNair Day, Alcorn State Univ, 2000; NFL Most Valuable Player Award, Assoc Press, 2003.

MEANS, DR. CRAIG R.
Educator. **Personal:** Born Aug 16, 1922, Shreveport, LA; died Aug 25, 2007; children: Stephanie. **Educ:** Southern Univ, BS, 1950; Howard Univ, DDS, 1954; Ohio State Univ, MSc, 1963; Memorial Hosp Cancer, cert, 1964. **Career:** Educator (retired); Col Dent Howard Univ, from asst prof to assoc prof, 1961-70, dept chmn, 1968-70, assoc dean, 1970-81, Continuing Dent Educ, dir, 1982-85. **Orgs:** Community Dent Accreditation, 1982-85; Am Den Asn; Nat Dent Asn; Am Asn Dent Schs; Omicron Kappa Upsilon Dental Honor Soc. **Honors/Awds:** Fellow Louise C Ball Fellowship Fund, 1962-64; fel Am Col Dentists, 1971; Alumni Award, Howard Univ Col Dent, 1984. **Military Serv:** AUS, lt, 1941-46. **Home Addr:** 9823 Hedin Dr, Silver Spring, MD 20903.

MEHLINGER, KERMIT THORPE.
Psychiatrist. **Personal:** Born Jun 17, 1918, Washington, DC; died Jun 1, 1982; married Lillian L Pettiford; children: Dianne, Bonnie, Renee & Jill. **Educ:** Oberlin Col OH, AB, 1939; Howard Univ Med Sch, MD, 1950; Yale Univ, Post Grad Training 1953; Cook County Grad Sch Clinical Neurol, 1959. **Career:** Mental Health Ctr Chicago, sr psychiatrist, 1954-59; Circuit Ct Chgo, sr pshychiatrist, 1960-69; Martin King Neighbourhood Health Ctr Chicago, proj dir, 1969-71; Div Pshychiatry Cook County Hosp, dir, 1972-73; Pvt Prac; Chicago Med Sch, asso prof clinical pshychol, 1969-; Columbia Col, prof commun, 1973-; Div Vocational Rehab, psychol consult, 1967-; West Side Orgn, psychol consult, 1973-; Friendship Med Clinic, psychol consult,1974-; Rush Med Col, prof, 1976; Div Behav Sci & Psych oldynamic Med Jackson Park Hosp & Med Ctr Chicago, dir, 1978-. **Orgs:** Founder chmn, Image & Indentification, 1961-; pres, Coal Black Enterprise Inc, 1971-; Ill Dangerous Drug Adv Coun, 1966-73; Am Med Asn Comt Alcoholism, 1975-; Chicago Found Med Care, 1974-; Ill St Med Soc Comn Drugs & Hazards Substance, 1973-; bd dir, Gateway Houses Inc, 1971-; past pres, Cook Co Physician Asn, 1968-69; pres, S Side Br Chicago Med Soc,1970-; med adv com, Ill Criminol Soc; Ill Psychol Asn; Nat Rehab Asn; Am Veteran's Com; Kappa Alpha Psi. **Honors/Awds:** Recipient Fellow, Inst Med Chicago, 1970; fel, Am Psychol Asn, 1973; distinctive award, Am Med Asn, 1969; diplomate, Am Psychol Asn, 1961; author book "Coal Black & The Seven Dudes". **Military Serv:** AUS, capt med reserve ret, 1941-46. **Business Addr:** 7531 S Stoney Island Ave, Chicago, IL 60649.

MERCER, ARTHUR, SR.
Insurance agent, army officer. **Personal:** Born Mar 31, 1921, Pachuta, MS; died Apr 21, 2007, Cheyenne, WY; married Mildred Pugh; children: Arthur II, Lillian A & Lori A. **Educ:** Laramie County Community Col. **Career:** Army officer (retired), ins agent; AUS, 1942-47; USAF, 1947-74; Life Hosp Investment Ins, salesman, 1974-85. **Orgs:** Pres, Exchange Club Cheyenne, 1976-77; bd dir, Laramie County United Way, 1976-82; commander, Am Legion Carter Brown Post, 1977; life mem, Nat Coun On Aging, 1977; life mem, Air Force Asn, 1978; bd dir & treas, Laramie County Sch Dist 1 Bd Trustees, 1978-85, 1988-92; bd dir, WY Sch Bd Asn, 1980-82, 1992-96; pres, Rocky Mt Dist Exchange Clubs, 1981-82; vpres, Sch Bd Asn, 1983; vpres, WY Sch Bd Asn, 1984; WY Private Industry Coun, 1984-89;govt apptd mem, WY Community Col Comn, 1984-89; life mem, Air Force Sgt Asn, 1985; pres, WY Sch Bd Asn, 1985, 1986; Nat Sch Bds Asn Resolutions & Policy Comn, 1985; Nat Sch Bd Asn Delegate Assembly 1985, 1986; Cheyenne Rotary Club, 1987; life mem, Retired Enlisted Asn, 1987; Multicult Comn, Rocky Mountain Synod 1988; life mem, Am Legion, 1992. **Honors/Awds:** Service Medal; Korean Service Medal; w/1 Bronze Star; 3 Air Force Good Conduct Medal; 3 Bronze Star; 1 Silver Cluster; Air Force Commendation Medal; Air Force Missileman Badge; World War II Victory Medal; Army Good Conduct Medal; New Guinea Campaign Medal; Advanced Power Technol Off Medal. **Military Serv:** USAF, 31 yrs. **Home Addr:** 5131 Syracuse Rd, Cheyenne, WY 82009-4749.

MILLS, JOHN.
Entertainer, singer. **Personal:** Born Jan 1, 1956; died Jan 1, 1979, Morgan Field, KY. **Career:** Performances as "John and Donald Mills of the Mills Brothers", Copa Rm, Sands Hotel, Las Vegas, Fiesta Dinner Theater, San Diego, Carleton, Minneapolis; European tour including performance, Copenhagen, W Germany, Sweden & Eng; Albums: Cab Driver; Glow Worm; Lazy River; Yellow Bird; Basin Street Blues; Opus One; Paper Doll; Still-There's You. **Honors/Awds:** Grammy for Lifetime Achievement, 1998; The Vocal Group Hall of Fame, 1998. **Business Addr:** Singer, C/O BJR Public Relations, 11260 Overland Ave Suite 15 C, Culver City, CA 90230.

MIMS, CHRISTOPHER EDDIE.
Football player. **Personal:** Born Sep 29, 1970, Los Angeles, CA; died Oct 15, 2008, Los Angeles, CA; married Dina. **Educ:** Tenn Univ. **Career:** Football player (retired); San Diego Chargers, defensive tackle, 1992-96, 1998-99; Washington Redskins, 1997; Chicago Bears, 2000.

MOORE, CHARLIE W.
Consulting engineer. **Personal:** Born Feb 16, 1926, Chattanooga, TN; died Jan 14, 2007, Chattanooga, TN; son of Simon and Vallie Turner; married Elva M Stanley; children: Charlie W Jr & Kelli Noelle. **Educ:** Hampton Inst, BS 1950; Univ AL, 1951; Villanova

Univ, 1967-68; USAF Civil Eng Officer, dipl, 1957. **Career:** Civil Engineer (retired), Consultant; USA Corps Engr Anchorage Ala Dist, struc engr, 1951-52; AUS Corps Engrs N Atlantic Div, constr mgt engr, 1952-55; USAF New Castle Co Airport, constr mgt engr, 1955-57; USAF Fifth AF Ashiya & Tokyo, gen engr, 1957-58; Ankara Turkey USAFE HQ US LOG, maintenance engr, 1958-61; AUS Corps Engrs, civil engr, 1962, Civil Defense Support Br, civil engr, 1962-65, chief resident engr, support group, 1975-79; Eng Support Serv Corp, pres, 1981; FEMA NY, supvr civil engr; Eng Support, consult, currently. **Orgs:** Am Soc Civil Engrs; Soc Am Military Engrs; Penn Soc Prof Eng; Camphor United Meth Church; Nat Defense Exec Reserve, Frontiers Int. **Honors/Awds:** Letter of Appreciation, Yahata Labor Mgt Office; Outstanding Performance, New Eng Div USC E, 1976; Outstanding Commendation Defense Civil Preparation Agency, 1978. **Military Serv:** USN, MM3C, 1944-46.

MORRIS, KELSO B.
Educator. **Personal:** Born Feb 6, 1909, Beaumont, TX; died Jan 1, 1982, Washington, DC; married Marlene Isabella; children: Kenneth Bruce, Gregory Alfred, Karen Denise & Lisa Frances. **Educ:** Wiley Col, BS, 1930; Cornell Univ, MS, 1937, PhD, 1940. **Career:** Wiley Col, prof, 1940-46; Howard Univ, prof, 1946-77, dept head, 1965-69; Atlanta Univ, vis lectr, 1946, 1949, & 1951; NC Col, 1957-59; Air Force Inst Tech, Wright Patterson AFB, prof sect head, 1959-61; Howard Univ, chem dept head, 1965-69, emer prof. **Orgs:** Fel, Gen Educ Bd, 1936-37; Am Chem Soc; Nat Asn Res Sci Teaching; pres, D CInst Chemists, 1974-75; Alpha Phi Alpha Fraternity; Sigma Xi; Am Inst Chemists, fel; Tex Acad Sci; Wash Acad Sci, secy, 1977-78, gen chmn, Sci Achievement Awards Prog, 1974-78; AAAS. **Honors/Awds:** Distinguished Teaching Award, Wash Acad Sci, 1968; Cosmos Club of Wash, 1969; United Negro Col Fund Dreyfus Found, 1974-80.

MULDROW, JAMES CHRISTOPHER.
Educator, librarian. **Personal:** Born Dec 17, 1945, Washington, DC; died Jan 11, 2009, DC; son of James Walter and Josephine Cain. **Educ:** Inst African Studies, Univ Ghana, Legon, Accra, GH, 1971; Fed City Col, Wash, DC, BA, hist, 1973, MLS, 1975; Harvard Univ Grad Sch Educ, Cambridge, MA, 1987-88. **Career:** Dept Educ Govt US Virgin Islands, St Croix, VI, librn/media specialist, 1977-80; World Hunger Educ Serv, Wash, DC, cataloguer, 1984-86; Wash Metro Area Transit Authority, Facilities Maintenance Off, Wash, DC, tech librn, 1980-83; Wash Metro Area Transit Authority, Pub Affairs Off, Wash, DC, librn/pub info specialist, 1983-87; DC Pub Schs, Wash, DC, prog coordr, 1990, libr media specialist, 1994. **Orgs:** Am Libr Asn, 1980; Soc Intercult Educ Training & Res, 1981; Soc Int Develop, 1981; bd mem, Wash Chap Am Democratic Action (ADA), 1990. **Honors/Awds:** Harvard Grant, American Library Association, 1980. **Special Achievements:** Experiment in International Living, Semester in Ghana, 1971; The Contribution of the African-American Soldier in the US Military from the Colonial Period thru the Vietnam War Era: An Annotated bibliography, US Army Walter Reed Institute of Research, 1972; book review for The Information, Virgin Islands Bureau for Libraries, Museums and Archaeological Services, 1977-80. **Business Addr:** Library Media Specialist, DC Public Schools, 825 N Captol St NE, Washington, DC 20002-4210, **Business Phone:** (202)724-8618.

MUYUMBA, FRANCOIS N. (MUYUMBA WA NKONGOLA)
Educator. **Personal:** Born Dec 29, 1939, Luputa Kasai-orien, Democratic Republic of the Congo; died Feb 10, 2006; married Valentine Kanyinda; children: Walton M N & Muuka M K. **Educ:** David & Elkins Col Elkins, WV, BA, 1967; Portland State Univ, MS, 1970; Ind Univ, Bloomington, MA, PhD 1977. **Career:** Carfour des Jeunes, Kinshasa, Zaire, founder & dir, 1967; Usaid-Kinshasa, asst training officer, 1967-68; Univ Libre du Congo, asst prof/admin asst, 1968-69; Ind St Univ, asst prof, 1977, Dept African & African-American Studies, assoc prof; Great Lakes Res J, co-ed. **Orgs:** World Coun Curric & Instr, 1974-80; Int Peace Res Asn, 1975-80; consult, Inst World Order's Sch Progs, 1975-78; Peache Educ Coun, 1978-80; Nat Coun Black Studies 1976-80; founding pres, Pan-African Studies Asn; interim chair, All N Am Conf Congo. **Honors/Awds:** Soccer Letters & Trophies, Davis & Elkins Col, WV, 1963-67; Travel Grant, Int Peace Res Asn 1975; Consult, Grant Gilmore Sloane Presbyterian Ctr, 1975.

NEWMAN, DAVID, JR.
Musician. **Personal:** Born Feb 24, 1933, Corsicana, TX; died Jan 20, 2009, West Hurley, NY; married Karen; children: Terry, Andr, Cadino & Benji. **Educ:** Jarvis Christian Col, theol & music. **Career:** Ray Charles Band; Newmanism, leader, 1980; Muse Rec, rec artist, 1980; Fantasy Rec Co, rec artist, 1978-80; Warner Bros, rec artist, 1975-77; Atlantic Rec Inc, rec artist, 1959-74; Herbie Mann & Family Mann, sideman, 1970-71; Ray Charles Enterprises, sideman, 1954-64; BMI, writer & publ; Koko Pelli Rec, Inc, rec artist; Fathead: Ray Charles Presents "Fathead", 1959; Wide Open Spaces, 1960; Straight Ahead, 1962; Fathead Comes On, 1963; Bigger & Better, 1967; The Best of David Newman, 1968; The Weapon, 1969; The Many Facets of David 'Fathead' Newman, 1970; Lonely Avenue, 1971; Captain Buckles, 1972; Newmanism, 1973; Double Barreled Soul, 1973; Mr. Fathead, 1974; Front Money, 1975; Concrete Jungle, 1976; Keep the Dream Alive, 1977; Scratch My Back, 1978; Resurgence, 1980; Still Hard Times, 1981; Lone Star Legend, 1981; Retrun to the Wide Open Spaces, 1982; Back to Basics, 1987; Heads Up, 1987; Fire! Live at the Village Vanguard, 1990; Blue Head, 1990; Blue Greens & Beans, 1990; Blusiana Triangle, 1990; House of David, The David "Fathead" Newman Anthology, 1993; Mr. Gentle, Mr. Cool, 1994; Under A Woodstock Moon, 1995; It's Mr. Fathead, 1997; Chillin', 1999; Captain Buckles, 2000; Keep The Spirits Singing, 2001; Davey Blue, 2001; The Gift, 2003; Song for the New Man, 2004; I Remember Brother Ray, 2005; Cityscape, 2006; Life, 2007. **Orgs:** Nat Acad Recording Arts & Sci; Rhythm & Blues Soc. **Honors/Awds:** Down Beat Nomination, 1968-70; Outstand Musician ship, TX Jazz, 1970; Grammy Nomination, 1990; Pioneer Award, BMI, 1990; Pioneer Award, Rhythm & Blues Found, 1998. **Special Achievements:** Has appeared on many television shows including Saturday Night Live, David Sanborn's Night Music, David Letterman, and various featured news segments, appeared in Robert Altman's film Kansas City and did a national tour with the Kansas City Orchestra, for Verve Records.

NKONGOLA, MUYUMBA WA. See MUYUMBA, FRANCOIS N.

NORTHCROSS, DR. DAVID C.
Physician. **Personal:** Born Jan 29, 1917, Montgomery, AL; died Jan 12, 2009, Los Angeles, CA; son of David C Northcross and Daisy Hill; children: David, Michael, Gale, Gloria, Derrick & Grace. **Educ:** Meharry Med Col, attended 1944; Univ Pa, surg, 1957; Univ Detroit, attended. **Career:** Physician (Retired); Mercy Gen Hosp, admin, 1956-74; Gen practice, physician. **Orgs:** Mem Detroit Med Soc; Wayne County Med Soc; Nat Med Asn; Am Med Asn; Meharry Alumni Asn; Wolverine Med Asn; Mich St Med Asn; Booker T Wash Bus Asn; Detroit C C; UNA-USA; ACLU; Alpha Phi Alpha. **Military Serv:** AUS, 1943-45, 1953-55.

OWENS, KENNETH, JR.
Architect. **Personal:** Born May 23, 1939, Chattanooga, TN; died Mar 7, 2009, Birmingham, AL; son of Lydia A Owens and Kenneth Owens Sr; married Dannetta Kennon, Nov 24, 1989; children: Kevin L & Keith L. **Educ:** Tenn State Univ, BS, 1963; Birmingham Southern Col, MA, 1989. **Career:** US Corps Engineers, draftsman, 1963-65; Rust Engineers, draftsman, 1966-68; CH McCauley, architect, 1969-73; The Owens & Woods Partnership, PC, architect, pres, 1974. **Orgs:** Omega Psi Phi Fraternity, 1957; Leadership Birmingham, 1985; past pres, Vulcan Kiwanis Club, 1987; vpres, bd, Operation New Birmingham, 1987-90; bd mem, Metropolitan Development Bd, 1988; Newcomer Club, 1989; Sixth Avenue Baptist Church, deacon, 1989; chair, pres, Birmingham Jefferson Metro Chamber Com, 1992. **Honors/Awds:** Father of the Year, UNCF Birmingham, 1978; Boy Scouts of Am, SilverBeaver, 1982; Outstanding Engineer Alumni, Tenn St Univ, 1985; Outstanding Engineer Award, Engineers for Prof Develop, 1985. **Home Phone:** (205)322-6430. **Business Addr:** Architect, President, The Owens and Woods Partnership, PC, 214 N 24th St, Birmingham, AL 35203, **Business Phone:** (205)251-8426.

PALMER, DR. JAMES DIBBLE.
Physician. **Personal:** Born Oct 10, 1928, Sumter, SC; died Feb 6, 2009, Atlanta, GA; son of Edmund and Ellie Dibble; married Rose Martin; children: James Jr. **Educ:** Fisk Univ, attended 1949; Meharry Med Col, attended 1954. **Career:** Atlanta Life Ins Co, sr vpres & med dir; prv pract, physician, internal med, 1961. **Orgs:** Bd dir, Atlanta Life; trustee, AF & NB Herndon Found; trustee, Clark-Atlanta Univ & Gammon theol Sem; past pres, Atlanta Med Asn; GA St Med Asn; Nat Med Asn; Med Asn Atlanta; Med Asn GA; Am Med Asn; Med Asn Med Dirs; life mem, NAACP; Omega Psi Phi Frat; Kappa Boule, Sigma Pi Phi Frat; Warren United Meth Church Lay Leader; Atlanta Guardsmen. **Military Serv:** USAF, Maj. **Home Addr:** 1350 Niskey Lake Trail, Atlanta, GA 30331, **Home Phone:** (404)344-2880.

PARKS, GEORGE BROOKS.
Educator, consultant, lawyer. **Personal:** Born Feb 18, 1925, Lebanon, KY; died Sep 24, 2008, Los Angeles, CA; son of George W and Eleanor; children: Paula Lynn & William Earle. **Educ:** Howard Univ Sch Law, LLB, 1948; George Washington Univ Sch Law, LLM, 1949-51. **Career:** Coleman Parks & Washington Law Firm, attorney, 1948-60; Security Title InsCo, sr title officer, 1960-63; Mchts Title Co, Los Angeles, founder, pres, 1963-69; prof consult, 1963-73; Title Ins & Trust Co, Los Angeles, dirurban affairs, 1969-70; Housing Opportunity Ctr, Los Angeles, exec dir, 1970-73; LA City Councilman David Cunningham, spec asst, 1973-74; Summa Corp, Los Angeles, consult, 1978-84; Glendale Univ Sch Law, asst dean & prof law, 1979-80; Land Use & Polit Procedure, consult, 1984; George B Parks & Associates, owner & consult. **Orgs:** Ky Bar Asn; DC Bar Asn; Am Bar Asn; educ consult, Realty Bd; Calif Real Estate Advan Adv Comt; life mem, Southwest Music Symphony Asn; Realty Bd,C Mid-City; Luth Housing Corp; Los Angeles County Dist Attorney Adv Comt; Soc Am Law Teachers; founding dir, Calif Timeshare Owners Found; consult, Timeshare Mgt Corp; owner/pres, Parks Course Continuing Real Estate Educ, 1979; City Los Angeles Productivity, pres, currently. **Honors/Awds:** Special Service Award, Law Enforcement Coun, Washington, 1959; Man of Year, Nat Coun Bus & Prof Women, 1968; Special Citizens Testimonial Award, Los Angeles, 1969; Los Angeles City Council Award, 1969; Human Relation Award, Los Angeles, 1970; Man of Year, Crenshaw C, 1972; Recipient Certificiate of Appreciation, City Los Angeles, 1979; Association of Real Estate Brokers Award, 1980; National Society of Real Estate Appraisers Education Award, 1981; Distinguished Alumni Award, Howard Univ Alumni Club Southern Calif, 1982; numerous city/county/state awards and citations.

PATRICK, JULIUS, JR.
School administrator, mayor, school principal. **Personal:** Born May 16, 1938, Natchitoches, LA; son of Julius Patrick Sr and Ella Belle Wardsworth; married Beatrice M Jackson; children: Ronald, Karen, DiAnthia & Riqui. **Educ:** Dillard Univ, BA, 1966; Tuskegee Inst, MS, 1970. **Career:** Principal (retired); Rapide Parish Sch Brd, teacher, v princ & princ 1966-75;Reed Ave Ele Sch, teacher & prin; N Bayou; Town Boyce, LA, mayor. **Orgs:** Pres, Boyce Civic Improv League Inc; v chmn, Police Jury's Rehab Comt, 1977-80; Parishs Housing Auth Brd, 1978; chmn, Natl Conf Black Mayors; pres, Boyce Civic Improv League Inc; Rapides Parish Housing Auth, Rapides Area Planning Comn, Trade Mission Peoples Rep China, UMTA Rural Transp Mission Puerto Rico; pres, Rapides Assn Principals & Asst Principals. **Honors/Awds:** Hon Ambassador Goodwill, Exec Br State LA, 1980. **Special Achievements:** First Elected Mayor of Boyce. **Military Serv:** AUS, sp/4, 1961-64.

PATTERSON, CLARENCE J.
Executive, president (organization). **Personal:** Born Feb 23, 1925, Bogalusa, LA; died Aug 9, 2007, Antioch, CA; married; children: Clarence & Robert. **Educ:** S Fla State Univ, BA, 1949; Univ Calif, MA, 1951. **Career:** CJ Patterson Co, pres; Oakland CA, ins broker; Focus Cable TV Oakland, org chmn bd dir. **Orgs:** Mem bd dirs, Oakland RE Bd; pres & chmn bd dir, Golden St Bus League Oakland; mem exec comt & nat bd dir, Nat Bus League; vpres Regional 11 Nat Bus League; pres, Nat Mortgage Co; chmn bd, City Cent Econ Dev Corp; mem, Civic & Leg Comt Oakland RE Bd; mem, US dept Comt Nat Min Coun; bd dir, Peralta Col Dist Found; bd dir, Northwestern Title Co Inc; bd dir, New Oakland Comt; bd dir, Manpower Area Plan Coun; Bd dir, East Bay Bus & Prof Org; chmn bd dirs, Asn Real Prop Brok Inc; ex bd Nat Asn Advan Colored People Oakland Br; S Fla Bay Area Coun Boy Scouts; co-found & chmn E Oakland Ad-Hoc Com, Housing & Econ Dev; mem bd dir, Uplift Corp Oakland; Cooper AME Zion Ch; mem trst bd. **Honors/Awds:** Horace Sudduth Award, Nat Bus League, 1974; Merit award City of Oakland, 1972; Congress Award, econ dev City of Oakland, 1966.

PAXTON, GERTRUDE GARNES.
Dentist. **Personal:** Born Oct 9, 1931, Raleigh, NC; died Jan 20, 2009, Los Angeles, CA; married Lawrence; children: Lynn, Lori & Lawrence Jr. **Educ:** Howard Univ, BS, 1956, DDS, 1956; Univ Calif, Los Angles, attended 1966. **Career:** Dentist pvt prac; Pub Health, 1956-58, 1966-71; Howard Univ Col Dentistry, instr, 1956-58; Dept Health Serv Audits & Invests, med rev Sect, dent consult II; fel Howard Univ Col Dent; St Health Dept, dent consult. **Orgs:** Dental Adv Bd, S Central Multi-Serv & Child Develop Ctr; Alva C Garrott Dental Aux, 1966-68; Med Dental & Pharm Aux, 1968-70; pres, Cir Lets, 1973-75; Alain Lock High Sch 1976; Adv Coun Reachout Community Coun; Performing Arts Music Ctr; Omicron Kappa Upsilon Nat Dental Hon Soc; Beta Kappa Chi Sci Hon Soc; pres, Links Inc; Angel City Chap; pres, Jack & JillAm; Nat Dental Asn; Am Dental Asn; bd dir, YWCA LA. **Honors/Awds:** Outstanding Black Women Dentistry, Alpha Kappa Alpha Heritage Series; cited Nat Arthritis Found; Outstanding Link Angel City Chap; Outstanding Employee, Dept Health Serv, Med Rev Unit, 1994; dipl, Am Bd QualityAssurance & Utilization Rev Physicians.

PEAKE, EDWARD JAMES, JR.
Labor activist. **Personal:** Born Jan 19, 1933, Akron, OH; died Jun 1, 2009, Akron, OH; son of Edward J Peake Sr (deceased) and Minnie L (deceased); married Louise; children: Teresa E, Linda K & Kenneth T. **Educ:** Akron Univ, Fin, 1951-69. **Career:** Labor activist (retired); Goodyear Tire & Rubber Co, rubber worker-tire builder, 1950; US Dept Labor, team mgr, 1967-68; United Rubber Workers Int, field rep, spec rep, 1969-75, dir fair practices dept,1975-78, dir pension & ins dept, 1978-80, asst to pres, 1980, dir educ, 1980, dir fair practices, 1983, int representative. **Orgs:** Bd mem, Nat Urban League Akron, AIA Homes Inc; life mem, Alpha Phi Alpha Frat; Eta Tau Chap Akron; Nat Labor Comn NAACP, Nat Oper Comn, A Philip Randolph Inst; URW rep Leadership Conf on Civil Rights; bd mem, Akron Comm Serv Ctr & Urban League; nat bd mem, A Philip Randolph; state & local bd, APRI. **Military Serv:** USY, pfc, 1954-56. **Home Addr:** 481 Fernwood Dr, Akron, OH 44320-2353.

PETERS, DR. JAMES SEDALIA, II.
Educator, psychologist, administrator. **Personal:** Born May 11, 1917, Ashdown, AR; died Dec 12, 2008; son of Walter Lee Jack and Ardell Duckett Merritt; married Marie Ferguson, Jun 25, 1942 (deceased); children: James S III, Donna Marie & Kimberly C Bourne-Vanneck. **Educ:** Southern Univ Baton Rouge, BS; Hartford Seminary Found, MA; Ill Inst Technol, MS; Purdue Univ,

PhD. **Career:** Administrator (retired), Psychologist, Educator; US Naval Training Ctr, Great Lakes, Ill, teacher psychologist, 1942-45; Veterans Admin, clinical & coun psychologist, 1946-55; Springfield Col, dir & asst prof psychologist, 1955-56; Div Voc Rehab Ctr, adminr, 1956-81; Univ Hartford, adjunct prof; Pvt Pract, psychologist. **Orgs:** New England Bank & Trust Co, 1968; Am Automobile Asn, 1970; Alpha Phi Alpha Frat; Soc Sigma Xi; Sigma Pi Phi Frat; Episcopal Church. **Special Achievements:** Published numerous books. **Military Serv:** USN specialist teacher, first class, 1942-45. **Home Addr:** PO Box 431, Storrs, CT 06268.

POLITE, DR. CRAIG K., II.
Educator, psychologist. **Personal:** Born May 11, 1917, New York, AR; died Dec 12, 2008; married Cheryl Yvonne Bradford; children: Kimberly L, Craig K II & Adam. **Educ:** Univ Toledo, BA, 1969; Mich State Univ, MA, 1971, PhD, 1972; NY Univ, cert, 1983. **Career:** Mich State Univ, res asst ctr urban affairs, 1970-72; Econ Opportunity Planning Asn, Greater Toledo, employee, 1968-69; indust & clin psychol; State Univ New York, Stony Brook, asst prof, 1972-76; pvt pract, clin psychologist 1976-; Midtown Psychol Serv Inc, pres; Group Performance Assocs, clin & indust psychologist. **Orgs:** Am Psychol Asn; Asn Black Psychol; Omega Psi Phi; teaching fel, Mich State Univ, 1971-72; New York City Head Start, 1973; Metro Comn Mental Health Ctr, NY, 1974-; consult, Sch Dent Med State Univ New York, Stony Brook, 1974-. **Honors/Awds:** Dean's List, Univ Toledo, 1968. **Special Achievements:** Book: Children of the Dream: The Psychology of Black Success, co-auth,1992. **Military Serv:** AUS, capt, 1969-77. **Business Phone:** (732)384-2777.

POMARE, ELEO.
Artistic director, choreographer. **Personal:** Born Oct 20, 1937; died Aug 8, 2008, New York, NY. **Educ:** High Sch Performing Arts, New York, dipl. **Career:** First chairperson Am, 1958-62, second chairperson, European, toured Germany, Holland, Sweden, & Norway, 1962-64, Revival & expansion first chairperson, toured throughout US, Canada, Puerto Rico, West Indies, Australia & Italy, 1964; choreographed works for: Alvin Ailey Dance; Mar Ballet, chairperson; Dayton Contemporary Dance, chairperson; CleoParker-Robinson Dance, chairperson; Alpha & Omega Dance, chairperson; NatBallet Holland; Ballet instituttet, Oslo, Norway; Australian Contemporary Dance, chairperson; Ballet Palacio das Artes, Belo Horizonte, Brazil; Eleo Pomare Dance Co, artistic dir & founder, currently. **Orgs:** Exec planning comt, Int Asn Blacks Dance, 1992; bd adv, Am Dance Festival, 1992. **Honors/Awds:** John Hay Whitney European Fellowship, 1962-64; Guggenheim Fellowship Grant, 1973; TOR, Superior Artistry Award, 1983; Choreographer's Grants, Nat Endowment Arts, 1975, 1982, 1988, 1989; 1991-92, 1994-96; Jan, 7, 1987 proclaimed "Eleo Pomare Day" New York City; Outstanding Achievements in Dance Award, Int Conf Blacks Dance, 1994; Salute to Living Legends, AlphaOmega Theatrical Dance Co, 1993; Appreciation Award, John Dewey High Sch, 1999; Cert Recognition, Am Mus Natural Hist, 2001. **Home Addr:** 325 W 16th St, New York, NY 10011, **Home Phone:** (212)924-4628.

PRESTON, EDWARD LEE.
Musician. **Personal:** Born May 9, 1925, Dallas, TX; died Dec 1, 1993, New York, NY; son of Beulah Mae Williams Downs and Swanee Sr; divorced. **Educ:** UCLA, 1945-47; Wiley Col, 1941-42. **Career:** Count Basie Orchestra, trumpet player, 1963; Charles Mingus Sextex, trumpet player, 1963-66; NY Comm Young Audiences, band leader musician, 1975; Jazzmobile Inc, lectr instr, 1974-87. **Orgs:** Musicians Local 47, 1945; mason Thomas Waller Masonic Lodge, 1947; Hamptons Band, 1955-56; Musician Local, 802, 1962; Trumpet player Duke Ellington Orchestra, 1963, 1971-72, Archie Shepp Band, 1979; made recswith all bands except "All Am Brass Band". **Honors/Awds:** Russian Tour Duke Ellington Orchestra, 1971; Japan tour Chas Mingus Combo, 1970; African tour All Am Brass Band, 1964; Israel & European Tour Lionel Hampton Band, 1955.

PULLEY, PROF. CLYDE WILSON.
Educator, army officer. **Personal:** Born Sep 21, 1934, Spring Hope, NC; died May 5, 2007, San Antonio, TX; son of Madge Pulley and Zollie Pulley; children: Mary A, Sivalai & Jessie F. **Educ:** Culver-Stockton Col Canton MO, BS, 1973; Xavier Univ Cincinnati OH, MS, 1978. **Career:** Educator (retired); USAF, police admin, 1952-74; OH Dept Rehab & Correction, correction admin, 1974-77; NC Dept Correction, correction dir, 1977-79; Wilson Co Tech Inst, instr correction & social serv, 1979-81; Metro St Col, prof criminal justice & criminol, 1981-87; Ashland Univ, prof, criminal justice & sociol. **Orgs:** Consult, Am Corr Asn, 1979-81; spec corresp Afro-Am Newspapers, Balto, MD, 1979, bd dir, Comitis Crisis Ctr, 1983-84, CO, Prison Asn, 1984-87; Williams St Ctr; Nat Asn Blacks Criminal Justice; Nat Asn Human Serv Workers; Ohio Coun Criminal Justice Educ. **Honors/Awds:** Nat Asn Blacks Criminal Justice, 1982-91, Am Correctional Asn, 1977-89; Outstanding Educ Award, Goldsboro, NC, 1980; candidate, Lt Gov NC Demo Primary, 1980. **Military Serv:** AUS, USAF, master sgt, 1952-74; AFCM NDSM KSM VSM GCM UNSM, 1952-74. **Home Addr:** 111 Meadow Trail Dr, San Antonio, TX 78227.

RADCLIFFE, DR. AUBREY.
Educator. **Personal:** Born Aug 27, 1941, New York, NY; died Mar 27, 2009, East Lansing, MI; married Katherine; children: Rick & Deborah. **Educ:** Mich State Univ, BA, 1968, MA, 1972, PhD, psychol, 1975. **Career:** White Plaines Pub Sch, counr, 1962-63; Lansing Pub Sch, counr, 1966-74; Univ Mich, prof, 1974-75; Mich State Univ, trustee emer. **Orgs:** Young rep, Nat Comt, MI, 1966; state dir & adv, Mich Teenage Rep, 1967; adhoc rep, chmn, Human Rels, 1968; Mich Veteran Trust Fund, 1980; E Lansing Lions' Club, 1980; vice comdr, E Lansing Am Legion Post 205, 1980; bd trustees, Mich State Univ, 1980; rep cand, US Cong, 1980; Asn Gov Bd; Asn Admin & Higher Ed; Am Guid & Personnel Asn; prog dir, Am Legion Boys' State; Lansing Jaycees; Phi Delta Kappa; Greater Lansing Urban League; Delta Upsilon Int Fraternity. **Honors/Awds:** Outstanding Teacher of the Year Award, 1965; Mich Republican's Youth Award, 1966; Outstanding Young Man in Am, 1973.

REDD, M. PAUL, SR.
Publishing executive, businessperson. **Personal:** Born Aug 11, 1928, Martinsville, VA; died Jan 9, 2009; son of Lucy Martin and Peter; married Orial Banks, Sep 4, 1954; children: M Paul jr & Paula A. **Educ:** A&T Col, Greensboro, NC, 1953-55. **Career:** Floor Waxing Co, owner, 1955-66; Wechsler Coffee Co, salesman, sales mgr,1966-69; Mass Life Insurance Co, agent, 1972-74; Westchester-PutnamAffirmative Action Prog Inc, pres & chief operating officer, 1974; Westchester County Press, pres & publ, 1986; Westchester-Putman Affirmative Action Prog Inc, pres & chief operating officer. **Orgs:** Founding mem, Black Dem, Westchester, New York, 1966-; first vpres, NewYork State Conf, 1966-70, legis chmn, 1977; vice chmn, Rye City Dem Comt,1966; vice chmn, Westchester County Dem Comt, 1967; chmn Personnel Comt,Urban League Westchester, 1968-70; Task Force County Exec, WestchesterCoalition, 1968-70; bd dirs, United Way Westchester, 1970-86; mem, CounBlack Elected Democrats New York State, 1970, vpres, 1972; chmn, RegionIII, New York State Div Human Rights, 1985-88; first vice chmn, HudsonValley Econ Develo Dist, 1987, chmn, 1988; bd mem, Girl Scout CounWestchester-Putnam Inc; gubernatorial appointee, Col Coun State Univ NewYork; Nat Asn Advan Colored People. **Honors/Awds:** Eugene T Reed Award, New York State Nat Asn Advan Colored People, 1978. **Military Serv:** AUS, mgt, 1950-52.

REED, FLORINE.
Clergy. **Personal:** Born Dec 11, 1905, Turlton, OK; died Jan 27, 2001, Muncie, IN; married Eugene H. **Educ:** Boston, BTh, 1959. **Career:** Non-Denom Church, pastor; Temple Christ Churchs Inc, overseer; Dorchest, MA & San Antonio, Tex Churchs, pastor.

RIBBINS, GERTRUDE.
Singer, writer. **Personal:** Born Dec 28, 1924, Memphis, TN; died Feb 28, 2008, Cleveland, OH; daughter of James Pugh and Annie W Pugh; married John W (deceased); children: Anne Sylvia, John & Mark. **Educ:** Lmyn Col. **Career:** Detroit SS Asn, guest soloist; Greater Chicago SS Asn, guest soloist; Women Alv Ont Can, conf soloist; Faith at Work Ont, conf soloist; The Old Sta Chap Cleveland Singers, concerts, 1973-74; E Stanley Jones St James AME Church, ashrm soloist; USA & Can, speaking & singing tours; Nat Baptist Conv, Cong Christian Educ, fac emer. **Orgs:** Adv Comt Str Human Serv, 1974; bd mem, Wings Over Jordan, 1990-91; pres, Progressive Dist Women, Cleveland, 1977-81; bd trustees, Sunny Acres Skilled Nursing Care Facil, Cleveland, OH; Cleveland Fedn Community Planning; Calvary Hill Baptist Church. **Honors/Awds:** Sojourner Truth Award, NANBPWC-Cleveland, 1989; MTV Certificate of Commendation, 1988; Ebony Rose Tribute, 1990. **Special Achievements:** Soloist & Song Leader Women Alive; author of articles on Negro Music & Devotionals for Periodicals; featured in The Gospel Herald, Union Gospel Press, 1973, Clubdate Magazine, 1988.

RILEY, CLAYTON.
Writer, educator, journalist. **Personal:** Born May 23, 1935, Brooklyn, NY; died Oct 24, 2008, New York, NY; married Nancy; children: Hagar Lowine & Grayson. **Career:** Ebony, NY Times, The Liberator, Chicago Sun-Times & other publs, journalist; Fordham Univ Grad Sch Educ & Sarah Lawrence Col, teacher; performer tech theater film; Nothing But A Man, prod asst. **Orgs:** Drama Desk; Harlem Writers Guild.

ROBINSON, CARRIE C.
Educator. **Personal:** Born Apr 21, 1906, Madison County, MS; died May 25, 2008, Montgomery, AK; daughter of James S and Cordelia Julia; married Thomas L, Jun 12, 1935 (died 1989). **Educ:** Tougaloo Col, Tougaloo, MS, BA, 1931; Hampton Univ, Hampton, VA, BLS, 1932; Columbia Univ, NY, 1941; Univ Ill Urbana, IL, MLS, 1949, advan studies, 1955. **Career:** Educator (retired); W KY Indust Col, Paducah, KY, head librn, 1932-34; Avery Instm Charleston, SC, head librn, 1934-35; Tillotson Col, Austin, TX, head librn, 1935-37; Dorchester Acad, McIntosh, GA, head librn, 1938-40; Grambling Col, Grambling, LA, head librn, 1942-43; La Libr Comn, Scotlandville, LA, br libr supvr, 1943-45; Alcorn Col, Lorman, MS, head librn, 1945-46; Women's Fel; Ala St Univ & St Dept Educ, Montgomery, AL, asst prof, 1946-62; Purdue Univ, Lafayette, IN, assoc prof, summer, 1963-64; Ala St Dept Educ, Montgomery, AL, sch libr consult, 1946-72; Auburn Univ, Auburn, AL, assoc prof, 1972-75, prof, 1972-75. **Orgs:** First Cong Christian Church Montgomery, AL, 1946-; Am Libr Asn, 1946-; Am Asn Sch Librn, 1946-76; Ala Asn Sch Librns, 1947-75; Ala Libr Asn,1949-75; Ala A&M Univ, 1969; trustee, Freedom to Read Found, 1969-74; Ala Comn Accreditation Libr Schs; Stand Comn Am Asn Sch Librs; life mem, Nat Educ Asn; co-founder, Sch Libr Media; mem trustee bd, 1992-, chair mission & outreach comt, teacher church sch. **Honors/Awds:** Alabama Asn of School Librarians' Award; Distinguished Service, 1947-70; Alumnae of the Year Award; Tougaloo Col, 1970; Alpha Kappa Alpha Sorority Award for Courageous Pursuit and Accomplishments in Civil Rights, 1971; Black Caucus of ALA Award, 1974; Personalities of the South Award, 1976-77; Meritorious Service Award, Ala LAMP Workshops, 1979; Distinguished Service Award, Ala Libr Asn, 1980; Outstanding Service to Cause of Human Rights and Equal Justice, Certificate, Southern Poverty Law Ctr, 1990; Freedom to Read Foundation Award for School Library Administration, Libr Educr, Intellectual Freedom Advocate, Serv & Commitment, 1991. **Home Addr:** 155 Pinetree Dr, Montgomery, AL 36117.

ROHR, LEONARD CARL.
Executive. **Personal:** Born Sep 29, 1921, Kimball, WV; died Dec 4, 2008, Beaverton, OR; son of David and Irma; widowed; children: Ronald & Carol. **Educ:** Univ Denver, BS, ME, 1950. **Career:** Executive (retired); Koebig & Koebig Inc, chief mech engr, 1957-62; Leonard C Rohr Assocs, consult mech engr, owner, 1962-87; Co Los Angeles, comnr mech bd. **Orgs:** Am Soc Mech Engrs; Am Soc Heating Refrig & Air Conditioning Engr. **Honors/Awds:** Silver Star. **Military Serv:** AUS, 1st lt, 1942-46. **Home Addr:** 8350 SW Greenway Blvd, Beaverton, OR 97005, **Home Phone:** (503)643-0638.

SAMPLES, BENJAMIN NORRIS.
Judge. **Personal:** Born Aug 5, 1935, Baton Rouge, LA; died Mar 5, 2009, San Antonio, TX; married Tobortha M; children: Benjamin N II. **Educ:** Bishop Col, BA, pol sci, 1965; St Mary's Univ Sch Law, JD, 1970. **Career:** Bexar Co Legal Aid, staff atty, 1970-71, pvt practice, 1971-78; San Antonio Civil Serv Comn, chmn, 1975-78; Bexar Co Juvenile Dept, judicial referee, 1976-78; City San Antonio, municipal ct judge, 1978-81; Bexar Co Tx, judge, 1981. **Orgs:** Bars admitted to, St Bar Tex, 1970; US Dist Ct Western Dist Tex, 1972; US Ct Appeals 5th Cir, 1971; US Supreme Ct, 1973; San Antonio, Am Bar Asn; San Antonio Trial Lawyers Asn; Judicial Sect St Bar Tex. **Honors/Awds:** Delta Theta Phi Fraternity, 1969; bd dirs, Bexar Co Easter Seals, 1972; chmn trustee bd, St James AME Church, 1972; bd dirs, St Mary's Univ Alumni Asn, 1983.

SANDERS, WESLEY, JR.
Government official. **Personal:** Born Feb 7, 1933, Los Angeles; died Jan 1, 1992; married Benrice Jackson; children: Malinda Gale, Douglas Edward, Wesley III, Kenneth Wayne, Derlwyn Mark & Jeffery. **Educ:** Harbor Col, 1952. **Career:** Triple Qual Meats, founder, 1961; John Morrell Meat Co, salesman, 1966-71; City Compton, reserve police officer, city treas, 1973-92. **Orgs:** Compton C C; Negro Bus & Prof Mens Asn; BF Talbot No 8 Prince Hall Masons; welfare Planning Coun, Nat Municip Treas Asn; Calif Municip Treas Asn; Nat Asn Advan Colored People. **Honors/Awds:** Outstanding Salesman Award, John Morrell Meat Co, 1966-68; Outstanding Reserve Police Officer Award, 1974; Achievement Award, Model Cities; Outstanding Award Block Central. **Military Serv:** USAF, sgt, 1952-56.

SHANNON, REV. DAVID THOMAS.
School administrator, baptist clergy. **Personal:** Born Sep 26, 1933, Richmond, VA; died Mar 22, 2008, Atlanta, GA; married Shannon P Averett; children: Vernitia, Davine & David Jr. **Educ:** Va Union Univ, BA, 1954; Va Union Sch Relig, BD, 1957; Oberlin Grad Sch Theol, STM, 1959; Vanderbilt Univ, DMin, 1974; Univ Pittsburgh, PhD, 1975. **Career:** School administrator, pastor (retired); Fair Oaks Baptist Church, pastor, 1954-57; Antioch Baptist Church, stud asst, 1957-59; Oberlin Grad Sch Theol, grad asst, 1958-59; Va Union Univ, lectr, 1959-69; Va Union Univ, univ pastor, 1960-61; Ebenezer Baptist Church, pastor, 1960-69; Howard Univ, Div Sch, vis lectr, 1968; Am Baptist Bd Educ & Pub, dir, 1969-71; St Mary's Sem, vis prof, 1969-72; Bucknell Univ, prof & dir, 1971-72; Pittsburgh Presby Theol Sem, dean fac, 1972-79; Hartford Sem Found, Biblical Scholar prof biblical studies, 1979; Va Union Univ, pres, 1979-85; Inter denominational Theo Ctr, vpres acad affairs, 1985-91; Andover Newton Theol Sch, pres, 1991-94; Allen Univ, pres, 1993-97. **Orgs:** Chair, Baptist Task Force World Baptist Alliance Dialogue Secretariat Roman Catholic Church; Soc Biblical Lit; unit comt, Nat Coun Ch; comt theol concerns, Am Baptist Conv; coun comt, United Presby Church, USA; bd-dirs, First & Merchants Nat Bank Richmond; Baptist World Alliance; gen bd,Am Baptist Church, USA; Am Asn Higher Educ; Am Acad Relig, Richmond Rotary Club, Soc Biblical Lit, Soc Study Black Relig; broadcast series, Am Baptist Conv, 1973-74; scholar selection comt, Phillip Morris, New York, 1980-; bd dirs, Sovran Bank, Richmond, 1980-; bd dirs, Urban Training, Atlanta, 1985-; NAACP; Alpha Kappa Mu; Phi Beta Sigma. **Honors/Awds:** Man of the Year, NCCJ, 1981. **Special Achievements:** Numerous Publ: Theological Methodology & The Black Experience, The Future of Black Theol, 1977; The Old Testament Exper of Faith, Judson Press, 1977; Roots, Some Theol Reflections, J of Inter denom Sem, 1979. **Home Addr:** 3640 Rolling Green Rdg SW, Atlanta, GA 30331, **Home Phone:** (404)349-5097.

SIZEMORE, ANDRIA LYNETTE HALL. See ANDRIA, HALL.

SMITH, CONRAD P.
Political consultant, lawyer. **Personal:** Born Feb 15, 1932, Detroit, MI; died Oct 13, 2008, Washington, DC; son of Alfred and Minnie J; married Elsie May, Nov 27, 1957; children: Judy E & Conrad W. **Educ:** Howard Univ, BS, 1962, JD, 1969. **Career:** Danford fel, 1961; US Justice Dept, statistical analyst 1962; US Dept Labor, manpower res analyst, 1962-64; US Comn Civil Rights, soc sci analyst, 1964-66, asst gen coun, 1969-73; pvt pract law, 1979; polit consult. **Orgs:** Cand, DC City Coun, 1974; DC Bd Educ, 1976; pres, DC Bd Educ 1978; chmn, DC Parent-Child Ctr, Wash DC, 1980-85; chmn, Ward 1 Dem Community, WashDC; ACLU; Nat Asn Advan Colored People; Urban League; People's Involvement Corp; Civic Asn; DC Bar Asn. **Honors/Awds:** Falk Fellowship, Falk Found, 1962. **Military Serv:** AUS. **Home Addr:** 722 Fairmont St NW, Washington, DC 20001.

SMITH, EUGENE.
Executive. **Personal:** Born Sep 1, 1929, Miami, FL; died Sep 16, 2008, Miami, FL; married Josephine Scott; children: Michael & Milton Brown (foster). **Educ:** Fla A&M Univ, BS, 1958. **Career:** HUD, asst dir mgt, central dist dir. **Orgs:** Deacon, 1972; teacher, Sunday sch; bus mgr, Glendale Baptist Ch; NAHRO. **Military Serv:** AUS, pfc.

SMITH, JAMES DAVID.
Educator, artist. **Personal:** Born Jun 23, 1930, Monroe, LA; died Oct 5, 2008, Santa Barbara, CA; son of Ernest Leondrus and Sarah; married Ruth Johnson. **Educ:** Southern Univ, BA, 1952; Univ CA, 1954-55; Univ So CA, MFA, 1956; Chouinard ArtInst, 1962; CO Col, 1963; Univ OR, PhD, 1969. **Career:** So Univ, vis prof, 1954-55; Prairie View Col, instr, 1956-58; So Univ, asst prof, 1958-66; Santa Barbara HS, instr, 1966-67; Univ OR, vis asst prof, 1967-69; Univ CA, Dept Studio Art, prof, 1969, Dept Black Studies, chmn, 1969-73; Santa Barbara County Schs, consult, 1970, 1974, 1975; Univ CA, Santa Barbara, prof emer, currently. **Orgs:** Nat Art Educ Asn, 1963; Kappa Alpha Psi; Phi Delta Kappa; Nat Asn Advan Colored People; bd dir, Self Care Found Santa Barbara, 1974; bd dir, Children's Creative Proj Santa Barbara, 1975-84; pres, CA Art Educ Asn, 1975-77; co-orgnr, Spl Art Exhibition Hon Edmond Brown Jr, Governor St CA, 1975; pres, CA Art Educ Asn, 1977-79. **Honors/Awds:** Selected John Hay Whitney Fellow in the Humanities, 1963; exhibited in Dallas Mus of Art; Santa Barbara Mus Art, 1973; Award of Merit, CA Art Educ, 1983; Eugene J Grisby Jr Art Award, Natl Art Educ Assn, 1981; CA Art Educ of the Year, Nat Art Educ Assn, 1986; numerous shows in galleries throughout US; University Distinguished Professor Arts & Humanities, 1992-93. **Military Serv:** AUS, capt; Served in Korea.

SMITH, LOUIS.
Executive, government official. **Personal:** Born Nov 7, 1939, Ft Lauderdale, FL; died Jun 1, 1986, Somerset, NJ; married Bessie. **Educ:** Morgan St, BS, 1962; NYU, MA, 1970. **Career:** NYU Bellevue Hosp Ctr, liaison adminr, 1965-70; NYU Bellevue Hosp Ctr, asst liason adminr, 1968: Goldwater Memorial Hosp, asst adminr, 1970-71; NY Univ Med Ctr, asst adminr, 1968-71; Sydenham Hosp, assoc dir, 1971-73; Morrisania Hosp, assoc dir, 1973-74; NY Dept Mental Hygiene Kingsboro Psychiat Ctr, exec dir, 1974. **Orgs:** Nat Asn Health Exec; 100 Black Men NYC; NY City Comprehensive Health Comn; Asn Mental Health Adminr Assoc; adj prof, Long Island U; doctoral cand NYU Sch Pub Admin; examiner, NY St Dept Civil Serv Nat In Door Mile RelayTeam, 1959-61.

SMITH, DR. ROBERT.
Physician. **Personal:** Born Dec 20, 1937, Terry, MS; died Jul 1, 1987, Germantown, MD; married Otrie Hickerson; children: 4. **Educ:** Tougaloo Col, BA; Howard Univ, MD; Cook County Hosp Chicago, rotating internship; Univ TN; Harvard Univ; Univ MS. **Career:** Tuffs Univ Col Med, instr dept preventive med, 1967-69; Meharry Col, preceptor dept community & family med, area dir; Univ MS, Sch Family Med, part time asst prof; Univ IA, Col Med & Continuing Educ, preceptor; HindsGen Hosp, chief staff, 1989-90, MS Baptist Hosp, St Dominic-Jackson MemHosp; MS Family Health Ctr, dir; Univ MS, asst clin prof, 1975; Brown Univ, Sch Med, guest lectr, preceptor, asst prof, 1989, clin instr emer, currently; Cent MS Health Serv Inc, med dir, 1979; pvt pract, currently. **Orgs:** Charter bd, Jackson Urban League; founder, MS Com Human Rights; Am Cancer Soc MS Div; MS Med & Surg Asn; Am Med Asn; Nat Med Asn; MS Med Asn; charter dipl, Am Bd Family Pract; exec comt & deleg, MS St Med Asn, Cent Med Soc, AMA; bd dirs, memship chmn, Arts Alliance Jackson & Hinds County; former comnr, MS Health Care Comn; phys adv comt Child Health MS St Dept Health Jackson MS, 1987; chmn, Nat Adv Bd, Margaret Alexander Nat Res Ctr Study 20th Century African Am, Jackson St Univ, 1989; community adv bd, Bank MS, 1990; bd dir, MINACT Inc, 1991-92. **Honors/Awds:** First Solomon Carter Fuller Award, Black Psychiatrists Am; Physician Recognition Award, Am Med Asn, 1971; charter fel, Am Acad Family Physicians, 1972; Physician of the Year, MS Med & Surg Asn, 1974; Honorary LHD, Tougaloo Col, 1974; Distinguished Service Award, MS Med & Surg Asn, 1977; Man of the Year, Nat Coun Church of Christ Holiness, 1981; Outstanding Service, Nat Coun Negro Women, 1981; Outstanding Service Award, Jackson Links Inc, 1983; Expressions of Excellence Award, MS Cult Arts Coalition, 1984; Medgar Evers Award, MS NAACP Chap Freedom Awards Banquet, 1984; Disting Service Award, Nat Asn Med Minority Educators Southern Region, 1985; Health Service Award, Jackson Concerned Officers for Progress, 1986; Appreciation Award, Nat Caucus Black Aged, 1987; Role Model of the Year, Citizens High Sch Student Develop Fund Inc, 1987; National Citizen of the Year, Omega Psi Phi, 1990; Distinguished Community Service Award, MS State Med Asn, 1990. **Home Phone:** (601)948-4838.

STOVALL, MELODY S.
Executive director. **Personal:** Born Oct 13, 2008, Salem, VA; died Jul 31, 2009; daughter of Lewis J Stewart and Mildred Parker Stewart; married Ricardo, Jun 21, 1975; children: Ricardo C II & Raven C. **Educ:** Hampton Univ, Hampton, VA, BS, 1974. **Career:** Automobile Club Southern Calif, Inglewood, CA, field rep, 1976-82; Total Action Against Poverty, Roanoke, VA, job training dev specialist, 1984-85; Roanoke Redevelop & Housing Authority. **Orgs:** Community Awareness Coun Salem, 1985; The Links Inc, Roanoke Chap, 1988; Roanoke Arts Comn, 1989-93; bd mem, Nations Bank, Roanoke, 1990-93; The Moles, Inc, Roanoke Chap, 1994; pres, Harrison Mus African Am Culture, 2003; bd dir, Roanoke Adolescent Health Partnership. **Honors/Awds:** Honor Roll Awards, Automobile Club Southern Calif, 1979-81. **Special Achievements:** Producer of Black History Month project, WDBJ Channel 7, Roanoke VA, 1990; Girl Scouts, Woman Distinction, 1993.

STRAYHORN, EARL E.
Judge. **Personal:** Born Apr 24, 1918, Columbus, MS; died Jan 15, 2009, Chicago, IL; son of Earl E Strayhorn (deceased) and Minnie Lee Davis Strayhorn (deceased); married Lygia E Jackson, Aug 17, 1941; children: Donald R & Earlene E. **Educ:** Univ Ill, BA, 1941; DePaul Univ Col Law, JD, 1948. **Career:** Cook Co, asst states atty, 1948-52; City Chicago, civil serv commr, 1959-63; Met Sanitary Dist Gr Chicago, vpres bd trustees, 1963-70; Cook Co II circuit judge, 1970; Univ IL Dept Criminal Justice, adj prof, 1977-79; Northwestern Univ Sch Law, instr, 1977; Nat inst Trial Advocacy, instr, 1977-96; Nat Col Criminal Defense Attys, instr, 1980; Emory Univ Col Law, NITA, 1980; Nat Judicial Col, discussion leader, 1985; Benjamin Cardozo Sch Law, instr, NITA, 1987; Harvard Univ Col Law, instr trial advocacy, 1988-96; African Nat Mil Museum, asst curator, 2001; Loyola Univ Col Law NITA instr, 2001; Univ La Law, NITA instr, 2001; Hofstra Univ Law Sch, NITA instr, 2001; Office Spec Prosecutor, Cook County, 2002; Genson & Gillespie. **Orgs:** Parliamentarian Tuskegee Airmen Inc, 1985-94; Nat Asn Advan Colored People; vpres, Chicago Urban League; Kappa Alpha Psi; pres, PTA Howalton Day Sch; 6th Grace United Presbyterian Church; Comm Race & Relig United Presby Church USA; The Chicago Bar Found, currently. **Honors/Awds:** Earl B. Dickerson Award, 1994. **Military Serv:** AUS, 1st lt, 1941-46; IL Army Nat Guard, 1948-69, Lt col, 1968-69.

STROUD, HOWARD BURNETTE, SR.
School administrator. **Personal:** Born Mar 31, 1930, Athens, GA; died Mar 30, 2007; son of George E and Emma Flanigan; married Bettye Moore, Dec 16, 1989; children: Howard B Jr & Kesha D. **Educ:** Morehouse Col, BA, 1956; Atlanta Univ, MA, 1968; Univ Ga; Agnes Scott Col, Appalachian State Boone NC. **Career:** School administrator (retired); Union Inst, teacher, 1956; Burney Harris High Sch, teacher, 1956-63; Lyons Mid Sch, guid counr, asst prin teacher, 1963-65; Lyons Mid Sch, prin, 1965-78; Clark County Sch Dist, coord mid &sec sch, 1978-80; admin asst to supt, 1980-81, actg supt, 1981-82; assoc supt, 1981-92; ed bd, Am Mid Sch Educ J. **Orgs:** Bd dir, Ga Asn Educ Leaders, 1976-; polemarch, Elks; charter mem, Athens Area Opportunities Indust Ctr; bd dir, OIC, 1976-; chmn bd deacons, Mt Pleasant Baptist Church, 1980; Athens Coun Wellness, 1982-83; Prestigious Ga Prof Pract Comt, 1983-88; Ga Sec Comn, Southern Asn Col & Schs 1983-89; Hosp Auth Clarke Co, 1983-89; adv bd, Ga Coop Exten, 1990-92; bd dirs,Athen Regionaedical Ctr, 1991-97; chmn, Facil & Prog ARMC, 1991; chmn, Athens Regional Health Serv Inc, 1991-; bd dirs, Athens Tech Inst, 1991-; chair, Athens Regional Hosp Authority, 1992-93; Classic Ctr Authority1995-; Athens Tech Col Fedn; trustee, Ga Hosp, 1995-98; chair, Athens Regional Health Serv, 1998-; Bd dir, Ga Asn Educ Leaders; Prin Res & Info Ctr; ed bd, Ga Asn Middle Sch Prins Jour; Nat Educ Asn; pres, Ga Mid Sch Prin; exalted ruler, Classic City Elks Lodge; lay vpres, Athens-Clarke Cancer Soc; state bd, Cancer Soc; pres exec comt, Cancer Soc; Phi Delta Kappa; Kappa Alpha Psi; Mason; bd dir, Family Coun; chmn, Steering Comt, Union Baptist Inst Inc; bd dir, Clarke County Sch Dist, Fedn Excellence; Athens Revitalization Implementation Comn. **Honors/Awds:** Cert Appreciation, Athens Recreation Dept, 1975; Heritage Award, Optimist Int; Outstanding Educr Award, Lyons Fac, 1977; This is Your Life, Lyons Fac & Stud Body, 1977; Serv Award, Mosley Gospel Choir, 1977; Serv Award, Ga Asn Educ Leadership, 1977-79; Dedication & Serv Plaque, Lyons Fac & Stud Body; Outstanding Leadership, GA Asn Mid Sch Prin, 1978; Portrait Unveiled, Lyons Mid Sch, 1978; Serv Award, Citizens Group Athens, 1979; Outstanding Leadership Award, Clarke Cd Educ, 1981-82; Leadership Award, Phi Beta Sigma Fraternity, 1982; Mkt Place Achievement Award, Milledge Baptist Church, 1982; Outstanding Serv Award, Athens Tech Sch, 1982; Spec Recognition Award, 199 Percenters, 1982; Human Rels Award, Ga Asn Educs, 1983; W Judicial Circiut Liberty Bell Law Day Award, 1984; Outstanding Serv Award, Athens Ctr Recreation, 1984; Comn Serv Award, Athens Retired Teachers Asn, 1995; Retired Educr of the Year, GA Retired Teachers Asn, 1995; JW Fanning Humanitarian of the Year, 1996; Inspiration Award, Athens Coun Aging, 1999; Presidential Citation, Athens Breakfast Optimist Club; Cert Achievement, Kappa Alpha Psi Fraternity; Award Excellence, Pub Sch Admin Kappa Delta. **Military Serv:** USY, 1951-53; active res, 1953-59. **Home Addr:** 243 Deerhill Dr, Bogart, GA 30622, **Home Phone:** (404)353-7290.

STUBBS, LEVI. (TRAVIS STUBBS, JR.)
Singer, actor. **Personal:** Born Jun 6, 1936, Detroit, MI; died Oct 17, 2008, Detroit, MI; married Clineice, Jan 1, 1960; children: 5. **Career:** The Four Tops, mem, 1953-2000; Films: Little Shop of Horrors, voice, 1986; Celebrate the Dream: 50 Years of Ebony Magazine, 1996; Soulful Sixties, 2004; Motown: The Early Years, 2005; From the Heart: The Four Tops 50th Anniversary & Celebration, 2005; TV Series: "Captain N & the Adventures of Super Mario Bros 3," 1990; "Captain N & the New Super Mario World," 1991; Singles: "Baby I Need Your Loving," 1964; "Still Water," 1970; "Loco In Acapulco," 1988. **Honors/Awds:** Rock & Roll Hall of Fame, 1990.

STUBBS, TRAVIS, JR. See STUBBS, LEVI.

SUTTON, REV. MOSES.
Clergy. **Personal:** Born May 3, 1920, Morganfield, KY; died Jan 15, 2009, Louisville, KY; married Emma Lou Forbes; children: Ethel Pierce, Alvin, Berthenia Hall, Stanley & Stephanie. **Educ:** Lane Col, attended 1940; Louisville Munic Col, attended 1943; Eastern New Mexcio St Col, attended 1945; Univ Louisville, attended 1951. **Career:** Miles Chapel, pastor, 1939; Patterson Chapel, pastor, 1945; Muir Chapel, pastor, 1951; Louisville Dist, presiding elder, 1970; Christian Methodist Episcopal Church, mem, judicial coun, 1982-86; Lampkins Chapel Christian Methodist Episcopal, pastor, 1991-98. **Honors/Awds:** Citizen Award, Co Judge M McConnell, 1984; Christian Service Award, Brown Mem Church, 1984; Appreciation Award, Lanite Alumni, 1984; hon doct divinity, Great Theol Sem, Bowling Green.

SWAIN, ALICE M.
Educator. **Personal:** Born Feb 3, 1924, Oklahoma City, OK; died Jan 28, 2006, Oklahoma, OK; married Robert; children: Robert A. **Educ:** Famous Writer's Sch Westport, BS, 1946, ME, 1952. **Career:** Elem teacher, 1948-69; reading specialist, 1970-73; Langston Univ, asst prof, 1973-78; Univ Okla, grad teaching assoc, 1978-80; Sigma Gamma & Rho, org local chap. **Orgs:** Pres, vpres & secy; chmn bd, Youth Serv; vpres & secy, Nat Panhellenic Coun Inc; pres & owner, The Together Charm & Fashion Modeling Sch; owner & producer, Okla Hal Jackson's Miss US Talented Teen Pageant. **Honors/Awds:** Sowest Region Sigma of Yr, 1963; One of nation's ten outstanding women, 1967; local sigma of yr, 1970; congratulatory plaque local Omega Psi Phi, 1974; Soc columnist The Black Dispatch Weekly Grand Epistoleus Sigma Gamma Rho, 1974-76; Nat Pub Rel Chmn Sigma Gamma Rho, 1974-76; Sigma's Hall of Fame, 1974; award of merit, Nat Pan Hellenic Coun Inc, 1976; First gradanti basileus Sigam Gamma Rho Sor Inc, 1976-78; cert of merit for distinguished serv in Youth & Comm.

SWANSON, EDITH MAYS.
Educator. **Personal:** Born Jul 16, 1934, Detroit, MI; died Jan 1, 1989; married Charles; children: Kenneth & Charles II. **Educ:** Eastern Mich Univ, BS, 1970, MA, 1975. **Career:** Willow Run Community Sch, teacher; Willow Run Educ Asn, pres, 1972-75; Mich Educ Asn, vpres, 1977-83. **Orgs:** Pres, Ypsilanti Palm Leaf Club 1973-75; Delta Sigma Theta Sor Grad Chap; vice chairperson, Washtenaw Co Black Dem Caucus, 1974-77; bd dir, Mich Educ Asn, 1974-77; chairperson, Mich Educ Asn Minor Group & Task Force, 1975; vpres, elect Mich Educ Asn, 1977; chairperson, Coalition Against Parochaid, 1977-; NEA Del World Conf Orgn Teaching Prof Jakarta Indonesia, 1978; exec com, Mich Educ Asn; ctr reg coordr NEA Women's Caucus; Nat Alliance Black Sch Educrs; Mich Alliance Black Educrs; Coalition Labor Union Women; Nat Asn Advan Colored People. **Honors/Awds:** Outstanding women NEA educ award rep, 1976; maurine wyatt feminist award, Mich Educ Asn, 1978; One Of Most Influential Black Ed, Ebony Mag, 1980.

TARRY, ELLEN.
Writer. **Personal:** Born Sep 26, 1906, Birmingham, AL; died Sep 23, 2008, New York, NY; daughter of Eula and John Baber; divorced; children: Elizabeth & Tarry Patton. **Educ:** Ala State Univ; Bank St Col, NY; Fordham Univ Sch, Com, NY. **Career:** Journalist; Friendship House, NYC & Chicago, co-founder, 1929; Nat Catholic Comm Serv, staff mem; Support HUD, dir, 1958-76; Com Ctr Public Sch, dir, 1968; Comm Rel, St Charles Sch Fund, dir; Womens Activities NCCS-USO, dir. **Orgs:** Catholic Interracial CounCommr Black Ministry; Arch diocese of NY; Coalition of 100 Blk Women; Nat Asn Media Women Inc. **Honors/Awds:**

Author of Janie Bell, Garden City Pub, 1940; Hezekiah Horton, Viking, 1942; My Dog Rinty, Viking, 1946; The Runaway Elephant, Viking, 1950; The Third Door: The Autobiography of an Amer Negro Woman, McKay, 1955; Katharine Drexel: Friend of the Neglected, Farrar Straus, 1958; Martin de Porres: Saint of the New World, Vision Bks, 1963; Young Jim: The Early Years of James Weldon Johnson, Dodd, 1967; The Other Toussaint: A Modern Biog of Pierre Toussaint, a Post-Revolutionary Black, St Paul Editions, 1981. **Home Addr:** 65 W 96th St, New York, NY 10025.

TATUM, WILBERT A.
Executive, newspaper publisher. **Personal:** Born Jan 23, 1933, Durham, NC; died Feb 26, 2009, New York, NY; married Susan Kohn. **Educ:** Yale Univ, New Haven, Dr Humane Letters, 1988; Nat Urban Fel, 1972; Occidental Col, MA, 1972; Lincoln Univ, Pa, BA. **Career:** Milbank Frawley Urban Renewal Area City New York, exec dir, 1968-72; NY Amsterdam News, major stockholder, chmn, former publ, financier, 1972, chmn bd & publ emer, currently; Inner City Broadcasting Corp, major stockholder, 1972-80; Borough Manhattan City New York, dep pres, 1973-74; Health Ins Plan, vpres mkt; City New York, comnr, 1974-78; Stockholm Univ, instr. **Orgs:** Bd mgr, Sloane House YMCA, 1968-80; vpres, Educ Alliance, 1970-80; vice chmn bd, Col Human Serv, 1974-95; chmn bd, Tatum Kohn Assoc, 1979-80; asst comnr, dir community rels, Dept Bldgs; asst dir, Housing New York Urban Coalition; head, Mayor Beame's Apparel Off Planning & Develop; vpres mkt, Health Ins Plan New York. **Honors/Awds:** Citation of Merit, B'Nai B'rith, 1976; Achievement Award, Nat Asn Buying Off, 1976; Man of the Year, Am Jewish Cong, 1977; Man of the Year, Fashion Nat & Urban Fel; US Conf Mayors, Black Retail Action Group, 1977. **Military Serv:** USMC, corpl, 1951-54.

TAYLOR, CORA. (KOKO TAYLOR)
Musician, singer. **Personal:** Born Sep 28, 1935, Memphis, TN; died Jun 4, 2009; married Robert (deceased); children: Joyce Threatt. **Career:** Albums: I Got What It Takes, 1975; The Earthshaker, 1978; From the Heart of a Woman, 1981; Queen of the Blues, 1985; Live from Chicago: An Audience with the Queen 1987; Jump for Joy, 1990; Force of Nature, 1993; Royal Blue, 2000; Deluxe Edition, 2002; Old School, 2007; Singles: "Koko Taylor"; "Basic Soul"; "Southside Baby"; Actress: Wild at Heart, 1990; Blues Brothers 2000, 1998. **Honors/Awds:** Numerous awards including 8 Grammy Nominations & 24 W. C. Handy Awards. **Special Achievements:** Late Night with David Letterman, guest performance, 1988, performer in President inaugural event in 1989. **Business Addr:** Vocalist, Musician, c/o Alligator Records, PO Box 60234, Chicago, IL 60660, **Business Phone:** (773)973-7736.

TAYLOR, KOKO. See TAYLOR, CORA.

TAYLOR, RICHARD L.
Government official, mayor, chief executive officer. **Personal:** Born Jul 19, 1944, Richmond, VA; died Jul 31, 2009, Plainfield, NJ; married Gloria Jean McLendon; children: Richard Marcus II. **Educ:** Livingston Col Rutgers Univ, BA, 1971; Rutgers Univ, MA, 1974. **Career:** Grant Ave Community Ctr, pres & chief exec officer, 1976; City Plainfield, NJ, mayor, 1984. **Orgs:** Pres, Black Cult Asn Middlesex County Col, 1968; Plainfield Model Cities Coun, 1970; chmn, Plainfield Dem City Comn, 1975-76; pres, City Coun Plainfield, 1979, 1982-83; chmn, Union Co Employ Educ & Training Adv Coun, 1979-82; Plainfield Bd Sch Estimate, 1980, 1982-84; Community Church God; Rutgers Asn Planning Stud; ranking mem, Nat League Cities Comn & Econ Develop, Steering Comt; nat bd mem, Oper PUSH; Union Co Pvt Indust Coun; Nat Black Caucus Local Elected Officials; Plainfield Area Nat Asn Advan Colored People. **Honors/Awds:** Recognition Award Outstanding Leadership, Plainfield Clergy Asn, 1979; Outstanding Young Man of Am Award, Leadership & Except Comt Serv, 1980; Frederick Douglas Award, Civic Serv Black Cult & Hist Soc Union, 1983; Community Serv Award, NJ Black United Fund, 1984; Plainfield Babe Rugh Award, 1985; Community Serv Award, Community Church God; Plainfield Sci Ctr Award; Union Co Achievement Award, NJ Asn Black Social Workers; panelist, WNBC-TV First Tuesday; panelist, WNDT-TV Livingston Col. **Military Serv:** AUS, Sgt E-5, 1966-68; Bronze Star Valor; Purple Heart; Vietnam Combat Infantry man's Badge; Vietnam Serv Medal; All-Star Basketball & Football Post Teams Fort Dix, NJ & Fort Riley, KS.

TAYLOR, DR. THEODORE D.
School administrator. **Personal:** Born Mar 29, 1930, Ocala, FL; died Jan 1, 2008, Fort Lauderdale, FL; married Daisy R Curry; children: Tiffany, Tamila, Cedric, Theodore N & Patricia. **Educ:** Fla A&M Univ, BS, 1950, MS, 1956; Atlanta Univ, MS, 1962; Nova Univ, Ed.D,1972. **Career:** Marion Co Sch Dist, teacher, 1954, admin, 1958; Broward Co Sch Dist, counr, 1962, admin, 1963; Broward Community Col, dir spec serv, 1970-85, dir admis & col equity officer, 1985. **Orgs:** Desegregation counr, Univ Miami, 1972; Local Draft Bd 151, 1973; basileus, Omega Psi Phi Frat Zeta Chi Chap, 1976-78; pres, Kiwanis Club Cent Broward, 1978; exalted ruler, Elks Club, 1978; chmn, Equal Access/Equal Opprtunity Comn Broward Col Govt Employ, 1978-; Fac Task Force Supt Comn Pub Educ, Broward Co Sch; Broward Co Detention Adv Bd, Broward Bar Spec Comn. **Honors/Awds:** Omega Man of the Year, 1956, 1965 & 1976. **Military Serv:** USMC, sgt, 1950-53. **Home Addr:** 3860 NW 6th Pl, Fort Lauderdale, FL 33311.

THOMAS, CARL D.
Manager. **Personal:** Born May 13, 1950, Kansas City, MO; died Nov 19, 2008, Atlanta, GA; married Dana Morris. **Educ:** Univ Mass, Amherst, BS, 1973. **Career:** Off Minority Bus City Boston, bus develop specialist, 1978-81; Mass Dept Com & Develop, bus educ training dir, 1980-81; US Small Bus Admin, ace counselor, 1983; Contractor's Assoc Boston Inc, small bus develop coord, 1983. **Orgs:** ACE US Small Bus Admin, 1983; Nat Asn Advan Colored People, Boston Chap, 1984; Nat Asn Minority Contractors, 1984; Nat Bus Admin, 1984; steering comt, Mass Minority Bus Asst, 1985. **Honors/Awds:** Minority Advocate of Year, US Small Bus Admin, 1985; Minority Advocate of Year, Commonwealth MA, 1985.

THOMAS, ERMA LEE LYONS.
Government official, educator. **Personal:** Born Jul 7, 1928, Rentiesville, OK; died Aug 22, 2000; married Joe Elihue; children: Lee Wilbur, Dianna Kaye, Cheryl Lynn, Bonnie Sue & John Robert. **Educ:** Langston Univ, OK, BS, 1951; Northeastern State Col, OK, ME. **Career:** Government official (retired); St Thomas Primitive Baptist Church, treas, 1974-80; Alpha Epsilon Omega Chap Alpha Kappa Alpha Sor Inc, basileus, 1974-76; Local Langston Univ Alumni, secy, 1977-85; Langston's Reg Midwestern Conf, secy, 1980; State Dept OK, comn mem, 1984-85; Muskogee Sch, lang arts teacher; City Summit, mayor, trustee. **Orgs:** Democrat; Community Activist; Okla Educrs Asn; Am Asn Retired Persons. **Honors/Awds:** Received Key to the City from Mayor J Ford of Tuskegee, AL.

THOMAS, JOHN.
Manager. **Personal:** Born Sep 21, 1922, Meridian, LA; died Jan 4, 2006, Los Angeles, CA; son of Clifton and Sylvia; married Kathryn; children: Diane. **Career:** Manager (retired); Open novice amateur champion, 1938; AAU Feather Champion, 1939; Pacific Coast Golden Gloves, 1940; CA Lightweight Prof Champion, 1943-47; CA Athletic Comn, boxing ref; Four Roses Distillers Co, sales suprv; Athletic Comn, 2nd black referee; Four Roses Co House Seagrams, pub rels. **Military Serv:** AUS, pvt, 1945.

THOMAS, MARLA RENEE.
Executive, chief executive officer, president (organization). **Personal:** Born Apr 21, 1956, Weisbaden, Germany; died Mar 3, 2008, Oakton, VA; daughter of Carol Monroe and Laura Pedro; married Keith Gregory Barnes, Jun 4, 1988; children: Lindsay Carol Barnes & Laura Janice Barnes. **Educ:** Wellesley Col, BA, econ, 1978; Harvard Bus Sch, MBA, 1982. **Career:** Morgan Stanley, analyst, 1978-80; Drexel Burnham Lambert, investment banker, vpres corp finance, 1982-90; Am Shared Hosp Servs, pres corp develop, 1990-91, pres, 1991. **Orgs:** Equal Employment Opportunity Comn. **Home Addr:** 2041 Sacramento St, San Francisco, CA 94109.

THOMPSON, ERIC R.
Educator. **Personal:** Born Mar 23, 1941, Warren, OH; died Nov 27, 2005, Cuyahoga, OH. **Educ:** Hiram Col, BA. **Career:** Hiram Col, asst dir admin. **Orgs:** Reg rep Minority Ed Serv Asn. **Honors/Awds:** Outstanding College Athletic America, 1970-71. **Military Serv:** USMC.

THOMPSON, FLOYD.
Dentist. **Personal:** Born Aug 5, 1914, Houston, TX; died Jan 19, 1992; married Nellie Crawford; children: 6. **Educ:** Wiley Col, AB 1937; Howard, dds 1942; USC dntl sch, post grad 1964. **Career:** Dr of Dent Surg, self empl, 1985. **Orgs:** Ariz S Dent Soc; Nat Dent Asn; Am Dent Asn; Nat Asn Advan Colored People; trustee, Mt Calvary Bapt Ch; Urban League. **Honors/Awds:** Man of Yr Award, Tuscon Chap Nat Asn Advan Colored People, 1961; Alumni Award for Outstanding Contribution to Civic & Comn Act, 1971. **Special Achievements:** Tucson's first Black dentist. **Military Serv:** AUS, Dental Corps, first lt, 1942-46.

THORNTON, CLIFFORD E.
Educator. **Personal:** Born Sep 6, 1936, Philadelphia, PA; died Jan 1, 1989; widowed. **Educ:** Juiliard, BM, 1968; Manhattan Sch Mus, MM, 1971. **Career:** Black Arts Repertory Theatre Sch, 1965-66; NY Sch Music, 1966; NY City Pub Sch, teacher, 1967; Wesleyan Univ, asst prof of music, 1969; Jazz Composition Fel, 1972-73. **Orgs:** Founded & dir, prog in Afro-Am Mus; continuous activities as performer, composer & producer of concerts & recordings; Am Fed Mus jazz composer asn; pres, third world records; pres, third world mus; Broadcast mus Inc; kappa alpha psi. **Honors/Awds:** Recipient Nat Endowment for the Arts; NY St Council on the Arts Performance Grant. **Military Serv:** AUS, First lt, 1958-61.

TILDON, CHARLES G., JR.
Government official. **Personal:** Born Sep 10, 1926, Baltimore, MD; died Jan 1, 2007, Towson, MD; married Louise Smith. **Educ:** Morehouse Col; Morgan State Col; Johns Hopkins Univ, BS, 1954. **Career:** Government official (retired); Balt City PO, postal clerk, 1951-55; Balt Pub Sch, teacher head sci dept, 1955-64; Morgan St Col, coun, 1960-61; Provident Hosp Inc, asso dir, coordr, Neighborhood Health Ctr, 1968-71; Bio dynamics, consult off econ oppor, 1968-70; Dept Human Resources, asst secy community prog & admin, 1980; Community Col Baltimore, pres, 1982-86. **Orgs:** Adv, Club Balt; Am Col Hosp Admin; Nat Asn Health Serv Execs mem Large,past chmn Archdiocesan Urban Comn; adv bd, Advan Fed Savings & Loan, 1966; Am Cancer Soc; bd mem, mem exec comn, Citizens Planning & Housing Asn. **Honors/Awds:** Achievement Award, Archdiocesan Coun Cath men; Citizens Salute to Charles G Tildon Jr, 1969; Special Service Award, Urban Comn, Archdiocese Balt, 1972; Medical Staff Award, Provident Hosp, 1967.

TOLES, JAMES LAFAYETTE, JR.
Educator, dean (education). **Personal:** Born May 9, 1933, Monrovia, Liberia; died May 18, 2009, Fort Valley, GA; married Mattie Moore; children: Patricia Ann, Cynthia Annette & James Lafayette; married Barbara R Gallashaw; children: Celia Angeline & Jartu Gallashaw. **Educ:** Clark Col, BS, 1958; N Tex State Univ, MBA, 1962; Univ ND, PhD, 1970. **Career:** Liberian Govt Scholar, 1954-58; Miles Col, Birmingham, asst prof, 1958-59; Wiley Col Marshall, asst prof, 1960-62; Ft Valley State Col, Div Bus & Econs, prof & acct chmn, 1962-75; So fel fund grant, 1969-70; Albany State Col, prof bus admin, 1975-77; SC State Col, dean, 1977; Va State Univ, Sch Bus, dean, 1983. **Orgs:** Fel Ford Found, 1964; fel Repub Steel, 1964; regl exec comt, BSA, 1973; consult, Acad Admin, United Bd Col Develop; Am Acct Asn; Am Mgt Asn; Nat Bus Teacher Educ Asn; Am Voc Educ; Am Asn Col Schs Bus; Comn Real Estate Law & Policy Develop, Ga Bd Regents; Phi Omega Pi; Delta Pi Epsilon; Phi Beta Lambda Phi Delta Kappa; Alpha Phi Alpha; bd mem, Episcopalian Church; Mason; DBA Acad. **Honors/Awds:** Outstanding Serv Award, Ga Bus & Off Educ Asn, 1973.

TOTTEN, BERNICE E.
Manager, government official. **Personal:** Born Sep 1, 1921, Mississippi; died Jan 31, 2007; children: Othell, Adell, Bertrial, Mack C, Mildred Mitchell, Napolian Jr, Robert,Landon & Martha Jamison. **Educ:** Miss Ind Col, Holly Spring, MS, Teacher License, 1951; Tuskegee Inst AL, Early Childhood Ed, 1968; Rust Col, 1974. **Career:** Pub Sch, tchr, 1950-51; Head Start, tchr, 1964-75; Marshall Cty MS, city suprv, 1974-88. **Orgs:** NAACP, 1965-85. **Honors/Awds:** Shield MS Ind Col Holly Spring MS, 1975; Award, Inst Comn Serv, 1979-80; Shield Mid South Comn Org Tenn, 1980; Certtificate, MS Head Start Assoc.

TUCKER, PAUL, JR.
Consultant. **Personal:** Born Jun 15, 1943, Detroit, MI; died Feb 1, 1982; son of Paul Tucker Sr and Frances Kinney Tucker Williams; married Evelyn Virginia Reid; children: Kendrah, Kendall & Erika. **Educ:** Detroit Inst Tech, BSCE, 1971; Eastern Mich Univ, MBA, 1975. **Career:** Ayres Lewis Norris & May Inc, consult engr, 1970-76; Giffels & Assoc Inc, sr engr, 1976-78; Bechtel Power Corp, civil & site sr engr, 1978-79; Camp Dresser & McKee, sr engr & mgr, 1979-81; Eng Tucker & Assoc Inc, vpres & chief engr, 1981-84; Tucker Young Jackson Tull Inc, pres, chief exec officer, 1984, chmn bd dirs. **Orgs:** Dir, Detroit Chap Mich Soc Prof Engrs, 1986-89; Nat Soc Prof Engrs; Mich Water Environ Fedn; Am Soc Civil Engrs; dir, Consult Engrs Coun Mich, 1990-94; dir, Soc Am Military Engrs, 1986-89. **Honors/Awds:** Order of the Engineer, Ann Arbor MSPE, 1970; Outstanding Engineer Award, Pvt Pract Div Mich Soc Prof Engrs, 1993; Outstanding Civil Engineer Award, Am Soc Civil Engrs, Mich Sect, 1999; First Annual Felix A Anderson Image Award, Tucker Young Jackson Tull Inc, 2004. **Military Serv:** AUS, 1st lt, 3 yrs.

TURNER, JOHN B.
Educator. **Personal:** Born Feb 28, 1922, Ft Valley, GA; died Jan 30, 2009; son of Brister William and Virginia H Brown; married Marian Floredia Wilson; children: Marian Elizabeth & Charles Brister. **Educ:** Morehouse Col, BA, 1946; Case Western Res Univ, MSc, 1948, DSW, 1959. **Career:** Butler St YMCA, prog sec, 1948-50; Atlanta Univ, instr, 1950-52; Welfare Federation Field Serv Cleveland, dir, 1959-61; Case Western Res Univ, chmn community orgn sequence, 1957-67; Sch Appl Social Scis, dean, 1968-73; Ency Soc Work, ed, 1977; Univ NC Sch Social Work, Kenan prof, 1974, dean, 1981-93, prof emer, currently, dean emer, 1993. **Orgs:** Nat Urban League, 1966-71; Social Work Training Com, Nat Inst Mental Health, 1967-68; Nat Conf Soc Welfare; City Coun E Cleveland 1967-69; Mayor's Comn Commun Resources Cleveland, 1968-70; bd trustees, Cleveland Inst Art, 1970-74; Int Res Prog Cairo Egypt, 1974; sec, bd trust Chapel Hill YMCA 1986; bd trust, Coun Social Work Educ. **Military Serv:** USAF first lt, pilot, Tuskegee Airmen, 1943-45. **Home Addr:** 1703 Michaux Rd, Chapel Hill, NC 27514.

VARNER, JEWELL C.
Association executive. **Personal:** Born Apr 12, 1918, Tatums, OK; died Aug 23, 2008; daughter of Janie Lovejoy Carter and Joseph Carter; married Jimmy Lee (deceased); children: Jimmie Mae & Rose Marie. **Educ:** Langston Univ, BS; Kans St Teachers Col

Emporia, MS; Okla State Univ, Post Grad Studies. **Career:** Big Five Develop Found Head Start HEW, dir; Jewell's Ceramics & Gifts, owner, 1975; Tatums Ola Pub Sch, teacher, 28 yrs; Golden Acre Enterprizes, owner, dir. **Orgs:** Eastern Star; Delta Sigma Theta; vpres, Okla Asn C Under Six; Okla Educ Asn; life mem, NAACP; NTU, NAMPU, Nat Set Inc, Okla Chap Langston Alumnus Asn; Links Inc Okla City Chap; trustee, Jewell C Varner Trust. **Honors/Awds:** Black Voise Better Business Award, 1973; best dressed woman, Okla State Soul Bazaar, 1973; Outstanding Civic Serv Fed Club Women; Tatums Comn Action Agency Chmn War Poverty Gov's Adv Group; Inducted Okla Afro-Am Hall of Fame, 1984. **Home Phone:** (405)427-6666.

WALKER, JERRY EUCLID.
School administrator, chancellor (education). **Personal:** Born Sep 15, 1932, Statesbury, WV; died Jan 24, 2009, Sacramento, CA; married Patricia A; children: Faye L, Jonathan L & Sue L. **Educ:** Univ Md, ES, BA, 1958; Case-Western Res Univ, MSSA, 1962. **Career:** Ohio St Reformatory, Mansfield, dir soc serv, 1958; Sears Roebuck & Co, corp employ specialist, 1966-74, dir urban affairs; Los Rios Community Col Dist, vice chancellor-personnel, 1974; Lorain Co, OH, exec dir econ develop; Family Serv Asn, Mansfield, OH, actg dir. **Orgs:** Bd dirs, Urban League, Cuyahoga Co Red Cross, 1967; bd dirs, Half-way House Boys, 1968; bd dirs, Coun Blacks Am Affairs, 1979; Nat Asn Adv Colored People. **Military Serv:** USAF, a-1c, 1949-52.

WALKER, WILLIE M.
Engineer. **Personal:** Born Aug 18, 1929, Bessemer, AL; died Jul 15, 2007, GermanTown, WI; son of Johnnie and Annie Maimie Thompson; married Mae R Fulton, Apr 28, 1952; children: Patricia, Mark & Karen M Stokes. **Educ:** Marquette Univ, BEE, 1958; Univ Wis, MSEE, 1965. **Career:** Engineer (retired); AC Spark Plug Div GMC, devel tech, 1953-56, proj engr, 1956-60, engr supvr 1960-65; AC Electronics Div GMC, sr develop engr, 1965-71; Delco Electronics Corp, Oak Creek, WI, sr production engr, 1972-94; Walker Engineering, founder, 1995. **Orgs:** IEEE, since 1955, NSPE Wis Soc Prof Engrs, 1981; reg prof Engr, St Wis, 1963; Computer Sci Adv Bd, Milwaukee Area Tech Col, since 1982; pres, Potawatomi Area Counc, BSA, 1982-84; Nat Counc Boy Scouts Am; usher St Mary Catholic Church Men Falls, WI; chief camp inspector, Area 1 E Central Region, BSA; vpres program, Area One E Central Region, BSA, 1987-93; comnr, E Central Regional Boy Scouts Am Scout Jamboree, 1989; int comnr, Central Region Boy Scouts Am Scout Jamboree, 1993; chmn, Computer Sci Adv Bd, Milwaukee Area Tech Col, 1988-89; sr mem, Inst Ind Engrs, 1988; srmem, CASA Soc Manufacturing Engrs, 1989; certified systems integrator, Inst Ind Engrs, 1990; vpres, We Four Prog Inc, 1990-93; BSA, Central Region Bd, 1993; life mem, N Am Hunting Club; life mem, Nat Rifle Asn. **Honors/Awds:** GM Award for Excellence, Comn Act Delco Electronics, 1980; Man of the Year, Rotary Club Menomonee Falls, WI, 1983; Black Achiever Bus, Ind, YMCA Milwaukee, WI, 1984; Silver Antelope Award, E Central Region Boy Scouts Am, 1987; Silver Beaver Award, Potowatomi Area Council BSA, 1973; St Geo Award, Archdiocese, Milwaukee, 1975. **Military Serv:** USAF, Sgt, 1949-53. **Home Addr:** W153 N9646 Neptune Dr, Germantown, WI 53022.

WALLER, LOUIS E.
Executive, president (organization). **Personal:** Born Sep 10, 1928, Washington, PA; died Feb 20, 2009, Washington, PA; married Shirley James; children: Phyllis, Lorraine & Louis. **Educ:** W Pa Tech Inst, assoc, 1949; Univ Pittsburgh, 1960-65. **Career:** Plaster Prod Corp, mgr estimating, 1963; McAnallen Corp, staff, pres, 1963-86; Waller Corp, pres, 1986. **Orgs:** Pres, Kiwanis Club Wash Pa, 1970, United Way Wash Cty 1975; dir, first Fed Savings & Loan; pres, Interstate Contractors Supply; vpres, Pa St Contractors; pres, Master Builders Asn; trustee, Bd Deacons; treas, Nazareth Baptist Church; Nat Asn Advan Colored People. **Honors/Awds:** Layman of the Year award, 1964; Man of the Year, Jaycees, 1969; Hon Deg, Waynesburg Col, Waynesburg, Pa, 1985. **Home Addr:** 1035 Maple Ave, Washington, PA 15301.

WARD, ALBERT A.
Educator. **Personal:** Born Sep 20, 1929, Detroit, MI; died Jan 19, 2008, Westland, MI; son of Abe Waugh (deceased) and Mattie Smith (deceased); married Doris; children: Cheryl, David, Donald & Albert Michael. **Educ:** Wayne State Univ, BA, 1949, MEd, 1962; Univ Mich, EdD, 1971. **Career:** Educator (retired); Detroit Housing Comn, pub housing aide, 1955-57, 1950-53; Detroit Pub Schs, teacher, 1958-63; Mich Bell Tel Co, act commgr, 1965-66; Jackson Pub Schs, prin, 1966-71; Inkster Pub Schs, supt, 1972-75; Elliott Elem, Wayne-Westland Community Sch, prin. **Orgs:** Phi Delta Kappa; Am Asn Sch Admin; Mich Asn Sch Admin; Nat Asn Elem Sch Principals; Metro Detroit Soc Black Educ Admin; Nat Alliance Black Sch Educ; chmn, Westland Libr Bd; Am Asn Sch Adminr; Nat Acad School Exec; nat dir scouting ministries, CME Church, 1990-03; Professional Scouting visitor to Nigeria, 2000. **Honors/Awds:** Dr Albert A Ward Day, City of Westland, Mayor & City Council, 1989; District Award of Merit, 1987; The Harold Berry Senior Media Award; Silver Beaver Award, Boy Scouts Am, 1990; Best Script, "Listening for the Light", 2002. **Military Serv:** AUS, 2nd lt, 1953-55; AUS, capt, 1955-65. **Home Addr:** 36660 Avondale St, Westland, MI 48186-4060.

WARRICK, DELIA MAE. See WARWICK, DEE DEE.

WARWICK, DEE DEE. (DELIA MAE WARRICK)
Singer. **Personal:** Born Sep 25, 1945, Newark Heights, NJ; died Oct 18, 2008; daughter of Mancel and Lee Drinkard. **Career:** Singles: You're No Good, 1963; Do It With All Your Heart, 1965; We're Doing Fine, 1965; I Want To Be With You, 1966; I'm Gonna Make You Love Me, 1966; When Love Slips Away, 1967; That's Not Love, 1969; Ring of Bright Water, 1969; Foolish Fool, 1969; She Didn't Know, 1970; Cold Night In Georgia, 1970; Suspicious Minds, 1971; Get Out Of My Life, 1975. **Orgs:** New Hope Baptist Church Choir. **Business Addr:** Singer, Rhythm & Blues Foundation Inc, 1555 Connecticut Ave NW Suite 401, Washington, DC 20036-1124, **Business Phone:** (202)357-1654.

WASHINGTON, EDWARD.
Executive, business owner, chief executive officer. **Personal:** Born May 2, 1936, Pittsburgh, PA; died Aug 1, 1986; married Paula G; children: Felicia D, Teresa S, Jacquelyn R & Nicolas E. **Educ:** VA State Univ, Petersburg VA, BS, psychol, 1963; Univ Southern Calif, MBA, 1973. **Career:** Coca-Cola USA, acct exec, 1964-75; Uniworld Advert, acct supvr, 1975-79; Del Monto Corp, eastern div sales mgr, 1979-82; Mid-Atlantic Coca-Cola Bottling, gen mgr 1982-83; Edward Washington & Assocs Inc, owner, pres & ceo, 1992. **Orgs:** Nat Asn Mkt Develop, 1978-85; bd dir, Jr Achievement, 1982-85, Bowie St Col, 1983-85, Boys & Girls Club, 1983-85, WHMM Radio 1983-85; Prince George Chamber Com, 1983-85, Nat Bus League, 1985; life mem, Kappa Alpha Psi fraternity; 100 Black Men of Atlanta; bd mem, Atlanta Boys & Girls Clubs; Atlanta Tip-Off Club. **Honors/Awds:** Achievement Special Olympics, 1983,84; Achivement, Greater Wash Korean Asn, 1984; Outstanding Citizen, DC Dept Recognition 1984; PUSH Achievement Operation, PUSH, 1984; hon PhD, South eastern Univ. **Special Achievements:** First black General Manager of a sales center within the Coca-Cola system at the Capital Heights, Maryland Sales Center from 1981-82. **Military Serv:** USAF, airman 2c, 3 1/2 yrs.

WATERS, GARY STEVEN.
Basketball coach. **Personal:** Born in Highland Park, MI; died Aug 15, 1951; married Bernadette Amos; children: Sean & Seena. **Educ:** Ferris State Univ, BS, bus admin, 1975, BS, bus educ, 1978; Central Michigan, MA, educ admin, 1976. **Career:** Ferris State, Eastern Michigan, player, 1972-74, asst coach, 1974-95; Eastern Michigan, coach, 1989-93; Kent State, 1996-2001; Rutgers Univ, Scarlet Knights, assoc coach, 2001-06; Cleveland State Univ, head coach, 2006-. **Honors/Awds:** MAC Regular Season Championship, 2001; MAC Tournament Championship, 1999 & 2001; Horizon League Tournament Championship, 2009; MAC Coach of the Year, 1999 & 2000; Horizon League Coach of the Year, 2008. **Business Addr:** Head Basketball Coach, Cleveland State, 2121 Euclid Ave, Cleveland, OH 44115.

WATSON, GEORGETTE.
Association executive, state government official, executive director. **Personal:** Born Dec 9, 1943, Philadelphia, PA; died Aug 29, 2008, Baltimore, MD; daughter of Louise. **Educ:** Univ Mass, Boston, Legal degree, 1979, BA, 1980; Antioch Univ, MEd, 1981. **Career:** Dorchester Community News, writer, 1982 & 1983; Mass Comn Against Discrimination, investr; Roxbury Multi-Ser Anti-Crime, assoc mem, 1984; FIRST Inc, assoc mem, 1985; Parent's Discussion Support, founder, 1987; Mother's Against Drugs, co-founder, 1987; Drop A Dime Intelligence Data Inc, pres, co-founder, 1983; Governor's Alliance Against, Drugs, exec dir, currently. **Orgs:** Nat Asn Advan Colored People, 1987; assoc mem, United Front Against Crime Area B, 1987; bd mem, Boston Gr Legal Comn Liaison Prog; mediator, Boston Urban Ct Prog; Mayor's Anti-Creme Coun, 1989. **Honors/Awds:** Award, Mass Asn Afro-Am Police Inc, 1984; Appreciation, Shamnim Soc Mass, 1985; Community Service Award, Boston Br, Nat Asn Advan Colored People, 1985; Martin Luther King Award, Union Methodist Church, 1985; Distinguished Service Award, Eastern Region Alpha Phi Alpha Frat Inc, 1986; A Woman Meeting the Challenges of Time Award, Boston Chap Girlfriends Inc, 1986; Tribute to Women Award, Cambridge YWCA, 1986; Citizen of the Year Award, Kiwanis Club Roxbury, 1986; Community Service Award, Action Boston Community Develop, 1986; 100 Heroes Newsweek, 1986; 1987 Black Outstanding Women, Essence Mag, 1987; Sojourner Truth, Nat Asn Negro Bus & Prof Women's Club, 1989; President's Citation Vol Prog, 1989; FBI Award, 1990.

WATTS, WILSONYA RICHARDSON.
Funeral director, educator. **Personal:** Born Mar 10, 1934, Campbellsville, KY; died Dec 8, 2002; daughter of Reddie Roy and Henrietta Fisher; married Rudolph Franklin (deceased), Aug 13, 1957; children: Endraetta. **Educ:** KY Sch Mortuary Sci; KY State Univ, AB; Western KY Univ, MA. **Career:** EB Terry Elem Sch, math teacher; Campbellsville City Elem Sch, elem teacher; Taylor County Elem Sch, teacher; Glasgow Independent Schs, teacher grades 1-3; Watts Funeral Home (Black), mortician. **Orgs:** Kay Bledsoe BPW; Local Glasgow Jr Miss Pageant; Glasgow Urban Renewal & Community Develop Agency; Red Cross, chmn; Muscular Dystrophy; Easter Seals, capt; Glasgow Chamber Comn, Glasgow Beautification Comt, Glasgow Arts Comt; Barren County Literacy Coun, sec; Alpha Kappa Alpha Sorority, Anti Basileus grad chap, Omicron Sigma Omega, 1991. **Honors/Awds:** University Rank First, Western Ky Univ; Rotary Award, Campbellsville Rotary Club; Music Award, Ky BPW Orgn, Bus & Profes Women's Week; Woman of Achievement, Glasgow Kiwanis; Woman of Achievement, Kay Bledsoe BPW; Outstanding Teachers Award, Durham High Sch Alumni, 1987. **Home Addr:** 506 S Lewis St, Glasgow, KY 42141-2568.

WEBSTER, MARVIN NATHANIEL.
Basketball player. **Personal:** Born Apr 13, 1952, Baltimore, MD; died Apr 4, 2009, Tulsa, OK; married Maderia; children: Marvin Nathaniel II. **Educ:** Morgan State Univ. **Career:** Basketball player (retired); Denver Nuggets, 1975-77; Seattle SuperSonics,1977-78; New York Knicks, 1978-84; Milwaukee Bucks, 1986-87. **Orgs:** Founder, Galilee Baptist Church, Baltimore. **Honors/Awds:** Division II Player of the Year.

WHITE, DR. GEORGE.
Dentist. **Personal:** Born May 19, 1934, Houston County, GA; died Dec 30, 2005, Belle Glade, FL; son of Robert Sr and Lula Woolfolk; married Delores Foster; children: Terrilynn, George Jr & Miriam L. **Educ:** Fla A&M Univ, BA, 1956; Meharry Med Col, DDS, 1963; Veterans Admin, Tuskegee, AL, internship, 1964. **Career:** Retired: dentist Bell Glade, FL, Pvt pract. **Orgs:** Am Dental Asn, Nat Dental Asn, FL Dental Asn, Atlantic Coast Dist Soc, TLeroy Jefferson Med Soc, FL Med Dental Pharm Asn; Bell Glade C C; Deacon, St John 1st Baptist NCP; life mem, NAT Dental Asn; life mem, Am Dental Asn; life mem, FL Dental Asn. **Honors/Awds:** Oral Surgery Honor Student; Society Upper Tenth Meharry Med Col; Cert of Honor, Comt Serv FL A&M Univ Alumni Chap Palm Beach. **Special Achievements:** First Black dentist in western Palm Beach County. **Military Serv:** AUS, 1st lt, 1956-58.

WHITE, NATHANIEL B.
Executive, president (organization), manager. **Personal:** Born Sep 14, 1914, Hertford, NC; died Feb 22, 2009, Atlanta, GA; son of George White and Annie Wood White; married Elizabeth Jean Briscoe, Jun 21, 1941 (deceased); children: Nathaniel B Jr & Joseph M. **Educ:** Hampton Inst, BS, 1937. **Career:** Executive, resident, manager (retired); Serv Printing Co Inc, pres & gen mgr, 1939-83; Carolina Tribune, prod mgr, 1937-39. **Orgs:** Past pres, mem Exec Comt, Durham Bus & Prof Chain; Nat Bus League; Durham Cham Com; exec comt, Durham Com Affairs Black People; chmn trustees, WhiteRock Baptist Church; Scoutmaster, 1942-68; bd trustees, Durham TEC COT Col, 1963-95; chmn, Citizen Adv Comn Workable Prog Comn Improv, 1969-71. **Honors/Awds:** Man of Year, Durham Housewives League, 1953; Silver Beaver Award, BSA, 1953; NC Hamptonian of Year, 1956; City of Durham Recreation Award, 1958; Civic Award, Durham Comn Affairs Black People, 1971, 1989; Ann Serv Award, Durham Br NAACP, 1978; Nathaniel B White Building, Durham Tech Community Col, 1988.

WHITMAL, NATHANIEL.
Executive, certified public accountant, chief executive officer. **Personal:** Born Jul 28, 1937, Memphis, TN; died Aug 22, 2008, Chicago, IL; son of Eunice Crook and Nathaniel; married Yolanda Frances Pleasant; children: Nathaniel A & Angela M. **Educ:** Chicago City Col Wilson Br, AA, 1957; Loyola Univ Chicago, BSC, 1961, post grad studies. **Career:** Internal Revenue Ser Chicago, agent, 1962-69; Booz, Allen & Hamilton Inc, tax mgr, 1969-71; Mayfair Col, fac mem, 1971-72; Pvt Pract, CPA, 1971-77; Zenith Electronics Corp, mgr corp tax, 1977-87; Whitmal Oil Services; ceo, 1987; concurrent public accounting pract. **Orgs:** Tax Exec Inst, 1977-87; Am Inst CPA's, 1968; IL CPA Soc, 1971; ComInternal Rev Small Bus Adv Comt, 1975-76; Chicago Urban League; Nat Asn Advan Colored People; alt mem, Chicago Bd Educ City wide Adv Comt, 1977-78. **Military Serv:** Ill Nat Guard; AUS, res, Sp 4, 1961-67.

WHITTEN, DR. CHARLES F.
School administrator, educator. **Personal:** Born Feb 2, 1922, Wilmington, DE; died Aug 14, 2008, Detroit, MI; son of Tobias and Emma Carr; married Eloise Culmer; children: Lisa & Wanda. **Educ:** Univ Pa, BA, 1942; Meharry Med Col, MD, 1945; Univ Pa, Grad Sch, 1954. **Career:** Detroit Receiving Hosp, dir pediat, 1956-62; fel Buffalo Children's Hosp, 1956; Children's Hosp Mich, fel pediatric hemat, 1957; Wayne St Univ, instr & prof, 1962-70, Clin Res Ctr, dir, 1962-73, assoc dean curricular affairs, 1976-92, prof pediat, 1976-92, distinguished prof pediat, 1990-92, assoc dean special prog, 1992, distinguished prof pediat emer, 1992; Sickle Cell Ctr, Franklin lectr, Human Rels, 1972, dir, 1973-92; Georgetown Univ, Med Sch, Kennedy lectr, 1973. **Orgs:** Bd dir, Gerber Prod Co, 1972-92; pres, Nat Asn Sickle Cell Dis Inc, 1972-92; bd dir, Nat Bank Detroit Bancorp, 1988-93; pres emer, Nat Asn Sickle Cell Dis Inc, 1992; Am Acad Pediat; Am Fedn Clin Res; Am Pediat Soc; Am Soc Clin Nutrit; Am Soc Hemat Mid-West Soc Pediat Res; Soc PediatRes; Comt Nutrit Info, Nat Acad Sci; vpres, Am Blood Comn; chmn, TaskForce Personal Health Serv Workshop Mich Pub Health Statute Rev Proj; vice chmn, Pub Health Adv Coun St Mich; Adv Comt, Blood & Blood Pressure Resources, Nat Heart Lung & Blood Inst; Ad Hoc Comt S Hemoglobin pathies, Nat Acad Sci; Alpha Omega Alpha; Sigma

Xi; chmn, Genetics Dis Adv Comt, St Health Dept. **Honors/Awds:** Distinguished Achievement Award, Detroit Nat Asn Advan Colored People, 1972; Detroit Science Center Hall of Fame, 1987; Distinguished Service Award, Wayne State Univ, Sch Med, 1987; Distinguished Warrior Award, Detroit Urban League, 1990; L M Weiner Award, Wayne State Univ, Sch Med Alumni Asn, 1991; President's Cabinet Medallion, Univ Detroit Mercy, 1993; Distinguished Service Award, Nat Med Asn, 1997. **Military Serv:** AUS, Med Corp, capt, 1951-53.

WILKINS, DR. LEONA B.
Educator. **Personal:** Born Feb 9, 1922, Winston-Salem, NC; died Feb 19, 2007, Atlanta, GA; daughter of Lottie Gibson and Estridge H. **Educ:** NC Cent Univ, BA, 1941; Univ MI, MMus, 1944, PhD, 1971; Sorbonne Univ Paris, France, cert, 1968. **Career:** Raleigh NC, teacher, 1942-44; Bluefield St, 1944-45; Hampton Inst, 1945-48; Tenn St Univ, 1948-52; St Louis, teacher, 1952-55; Detroit, teacher, 1955-64; E MI Univ, fac, 1964-68; Temple Univ, fac, 1968-72; Northwestern Univ, assoc prof, assoc prof emer, 1988; Trinity Episcopal Church, Chicago, IL, Children's Music Educ, dir, 1990. **Orgs:** Mem Music Educ Conf; Int Soc Music Educr; Am Asn Univ Profs; Am Off Schulwerk Asn; Col Music Soc; Alpha Kappa Alpha; Bicentennial Commn MENC, 1974-76; Comn Rev Nat Teachers Exam Music Educ, 1974-75; consult, IL St Arts Plan; Comn Rev Music Objectives Nat Assessment Educ Progress Task Force; Role Arts Comm USOE; MENC; consult, Evanston Pub Sch Dist 65. **Honors/Awds:** Consult, Silver Burdett Music Series, 1970-71. **Special Achievements:** First African-American professor in the school of music at Northwestern.

WILLIAMS, JAMES E., JR.
Manager. **Personal:** Born Aug 28, 1936, Philadelphia, PA; died Jan 17, 2005, Scott, AZ; son of Gladys G Vincent; married Lois Collins; children: Karl, Robert & Renee. **Educ:** W Chester Univ, PA, BS, educ, 1959; Siena Col, MS, educ, 1968. **Career:** Battery A Second Rocket & Howitzer Bn 73 Artillery Germany, comnd gofficer, 1963-64; Mil Sci Siena Col, asst prof, 1965-68; 101st Airborne Div Vietnam, insp gen, 1968-69; Third Bn 26 Artillery, exec officer, 1970-71; CORDS Adv Team MACV Vietnam, oper adv, 1972; Armed Forces Examining Entrance Station Honolulu, comndg officer, 1973; Honolulu Dist Recruiting Command Honolulu, comndg officer, 1974-76; Dept Mil Sci Howard Univ, chmn & prof, 1976-79; Am Bar Asn, dir hr, 1989-93; Montgomery Ward & Co Inc, field personnel mgr, 1984-86, hq personnel mgr, 1986-89; Hershey Medical Ctr, mgr employment, 1994; Penn St Geisinger Health Syst, Milton S Hershey Med Ctr, Hershey, PA, oper mgr hr; Jim Williams & Assocs, prin, 1999. **Orgs:** Life mem, Alpha Phi Alpha; life mem, Nat Asn Advan Colored People; life mem, W Chester Univ Alumni Asn; Alpha Phi Alpha; life mem,

The Retired Officers Asn; Aircraft Owners & Pilots Asn; intl bd dir, US-TOO Intl Inc; co-chmn, Penn Prostate Cancer Coalition; Sigma Pi Phi Fraternity. **Honors/Awds:** Distinguished Alumni Award, W Chester Univ Alumni Asn, 1978; Anne Hines Allen Human Rights Award, The Main Line Br Nat Asn Advan Colored People, 1979; Certificate of Appreciation, Nat Asn Negro Bus & Prof Women's Clubs Inc, 2000. **Military Serv:** Fifth Training Battalion, Ft Sill OK, comndg officer, 1979-81; AUS Field Artillery Training Ctr Ft Sill OK exec ofcr 1981, dep comdr, 1982; HQ AUS Depot Syst Command Chambersburg PA, dir security plans & oper, 1983-84, col, 1984; Legion of Merit; Combat Infantry Badge; Bronze Star Medal, 1968, 1969, 1972; Air Medals Vietnam Cross of Gallantry with Bronze Star, 1968, 1972. **Home Addr:** 1089 Country Club Dr, Camp Hill, PA 17011-1049.

WILLIAMS, WILBERT.
Labor activist. **Personal:** Born Mar 30, 1924, Crockett, TX; died Jan 7, 2008, Houston, TX; married Theresa; children: Gentry, Raschelle, Keola, Lewis & Kimberly. **Educ:** Phillis Wheatley HS, diploma, 1942; TX Southern Univ, BS, 1952. **Career:** Retired: Intl Asn Machinist, pres, 1957-61; AFL-CIO, field rep, 1964-74; AFL-CIO Dept Org & Field Servs, asst dir, 1974-83; AFL-CIO Region IV, admin, 1983-86, dir, 1986-90. **Orgs:** Pres, AME Church TX Conf Laymen, 1972-73; life subscriber, NAACP 1974; Nat Bd A Philip Randolph Inst, 1974. **Honors/Awds:** Outstanding Laymen, TX Conf Laymen, 1983; William E Pollard TX State APhilip Randolph Inst, 1985. **Military Serv:** USN, BM 2 & C, 1943-45.

WILSON, JOHN T., JR.
Physician, school administrator, educator. **Personal:** Born Jun 2, 1924, Birmingham, AL; died Dec 15, 1993, Willingboro, NJ; son of John T Wilson and Rosalie Rush Wilson; married Artee F Young, Jun 21, 1980. **Educ:** Howard Univ, BS, cum laude, 1946; Columbia Univ, MD, 1950; Univ Cincinnati, ScD 1956. **Career:** Bur Occupational Health Santa Clara County Health Dept CA, chief, 1957-61; Lockheed A/C Corp CA, life sci adv, 1961-69; Stanford Univ, asst prof, Dept Comm & Prevent Med, 1969-71; Howard Univ, prof & chmn, Dept Comm Health Practice, 1971-74; Occupational Medicine Residency Prog, dir, 1977-87; Northwest Ctr Occupational Health & Safety, dir, 1977-87; Univ Wash, chmn & prof Dept Environmental Health, 1974-80, prof emer, 1992. **Orgs:** Armed Forces Epidemiol Bd, 1977; spec occupational med, Am Bd Preventive Med 1960; Washington Asn Black Health Care Providers; life mem, NAACP; dir Emerald City Bank, Seattle 1988-92. **Honors/Awds:** Naionall Scholarship Award, Howard Univ Alumni Asn, 1965. **Business Addr:** Professor Emeritus, University of Washington, Department of Environmental and Occupational Health Sciences, PO Box 357234, Seattle, WA 98195-7234, **Business Phone:** (206)543-6991.

WOMACK, STANLEY H.
Architect. **Personal:** Born Jul 8, 1930, Pittsburgh, PA; died Mar 19, 2009, Harrisburg, PA; married Winona; children: S Mathew, Deborah & Scott. **Educ:** Howard Univ, BArch, 1954. **Career:** Bellante & Clauss Archit & Engrs, St Thomas VI, asst office mgr, 1964-66; Edmund G Good & Partners Archit, job capt, 1964-66; Lawrie & Green Archit, archit, 1966-72; Murray/Womack Archit, partner 1972-76; Bender Royal Ebaugh Womack Inc Arch Engrs, princ, 1976-78; Stanley H Womack Assocs Arch, owner. **Orgs:** Am Ins Archit, PA Soc Archit; Omega Psi Phi; basileus Kappa Omega Chap, Harrisburg, PA; bd dir, Tri-Cty OIC; bd dir, Police Athletic League; NAACP; Urban league, St Paul Bapt Church; past comt chmn, Cub Pack 21; bd dir, Tri Cty Area YMCA; bd dir, Tri-Cty United Way; track & cross country team, Howard Univ; Harrisburg Tennis Team, Riverside Optimist Club, Harrisburg Rotary, Jaycees; bd dir, Nat Jr Tennis League; pres, Harrisburg Frontiers; Omega Psi Phi, Kappa Omega. **Honors/Awds:** Omega Man of the Year, 1975; 'Community Leaders of America Award'; Achievement Award Jaycees Int; Sports Achievement Award Pittsburgh Centennial. **Military Serv:** USAF, 1st lt. **Home Addr:** 1141 Colonial Club Dr, Harrisburg, PA 17112-1513.

WRIGHT, STANLEY V.
Educator, athletic coach. **Personal:** Born Aug 11, 1921, Englewood, NJ; died Nov 6, 1998; married Hazel; children: Stanley, Toni, Sandra & Tyran. **Educ:** Springfield Col, BS, 1949; Columbia Univ, MA, 1950; Univ Tex, grad study,1956; Ind Univ, 1968. **Career:** Calif State Univ, prof phys educ & head track coach; Mex City Olympic Games, asst track coach; US Olympic Track & Field Comt, appointed second time; US Olympic bd Dir for next quadrennial; Munich Olympic Games, sprint coach, 1972; dir athleteics, 1975; Nat Collegiate Ath Asn Recruit Comt, 1977; Int Olympic Acad, US Olympic Comt, 1977; Calif State Univ, emer prof phys educ, 1979. **Honors/Awds:** Recieved many honours & awards including "Award for excellence in History", National Track and Field Hall of Fame, 1993. **Special Achievements:** Published articles such as, "Techniques Related to Spring Racing", have appeared in leading athletic journals; participated in over 200 hs &college clinics.

YARBROUGH, EARNEST.
Magistrate. **Personal:** Born Mar 16, 1923, Buffalo, NY; died May 1, 1980; married Mary Holman. **Career:** MCAS, 1965-69; Ridgeland Clinic, supr trans, 1970; Beaufort Jasper Compre Health Serv Inc, magis, 1971-77. **Orgs:** Elke Lodge; VFW Lodge. **Military Serv:** USN, 1942-64.

Geographic Index

ALABAMA

Alexander City
Powers, Dr. Runas, Jr.

Andalusia
Carpenter, Lewis

Anniston
Banks, Manley E.
Owens, Nathaniel Davis
Trammell, William Rivers

Atmore
McBride, Ullysses
Shuford, Humphrey Lewis

Auburn
Willis, James Edward, III

Bay Minette
Thomas, Robert Lewis

Bayou La Batre
Benjamin, Dr. Regina M

Bessemer
McDowell, Benjamin A.
Patterson, Rev Clinton David
Underwood, Anthony
Wilson, Robert Stanley

Birmingham
Alexander, Wardine Towers
Anthony, Emory
Arrington, Richard, Jr.
Baker, Beverly Poole
Baldwin, Mitchell Cardell
Balton, Kirkwood R.
Barnes, Anthony L.
Blankenship, Eddie L.
Blankenship, Glenn Rayford
Boykin, Joel S.
Calhoun, Eric A
Campbell, Dr. Arthur Ree
Chambers, Harry
Champion, Jesse
Clemon, U. W.
Coker, Adeniyi Adetokunbo
Cook, Ralph D
Dale, Dr. Louis
Davis, Frank Allen
Davis, J Mason
Davis, Mike
Evans, Leon, Jr.
Flakes, Larry Joseph
Flood, Shearlene Davis
Grayson, Elsie Michelle
Griffin, Lula Bernice
Harrison, James C.
Hilliard, Earl Frederick
Howlett, Walter, Jr.
Ibelema, Dr. Minabere
Ivory, Carolyn Kay
James, Frank Samuel, III
Jenkins, Dr. Shirley Lymons
Johnson, Sarah Yvonne
Jones, Hon. Clyde Eugene

Kennon, Daniel, Jr.
Kincaid, Bernard
King, Lewis Henry
Lamar, Dr. Hattie G
Lucy Foster, Autherine
Mack, Roderick O
Martin-Ogunsola, Dellita Lillian
Matchett, Johnson
McCain, Ella Byrd
McGlothan, Ernest
McNair, Chris
McTier, Roselyn Jones
McWhorter, Grace Agee
Milner, Michael Edwin
Newton, Robert
Nixon, John William
Outlaw, Dr. Patricia Anne
Owens, Kenneth, Jr.
Pitt, Dr. Clifford Sinclair
Reese, Milous J.
Ricks, Albert William
Rivers, Valerie L
Sandridge, John Solomon
Scales, Jerome C.
Shepherd, Elmira
Sloan, Albert J. H., II
Smith, Sundra Shealey
Smitherman, Rodger M
Solomon, Donald L.
Spencer, Sharon A
Syler, M Rene
Taylor, Albert, Jr.
Terry, Roy
Thomas, Louphenia
Turner, Yvonne Williams
Vaughn, Audrey Smith
Ward, Dr. Perry W.
Watkins, Donald
White, Christine Larkin
Williams, W. Clyde
Witherspoon, Annie C.
Womack, Christopher Clarence
Wright, Dr. Wilson, Jr.

Brighton
Thomas, Dr. Jewel M

Camden
Johnson, Bobby JoJo
Pettway, Jo Celeste

Catherine
Hayes, Charles

Clanton
Agee, Bobby L.

Daphne
Wickware, Damon

Decatur
Butler, Tonia Paulette
Gilliam, Joel
Jacobs, Larry Ben
Ragland, Dr. Wylheme Harold

Dothan
Thomas, Althea Shannon Lawson

Enterprise
James, Peggi C
Pearce, Oveta W

Eutaw
Isaac, Earlean
Means, Donald Fitzgerald

Fairfield
Dennard, Gloria
Lloyd, Dr. Barbara Ann
Scott, Carstella H.

Florence
Brown, Dr. Alyce Doss
Davis, Dr. Ernestine
Davis, Dr. Ernestine Bady
Goldston, Bobby F
Hardy, Dorothy C.

Forkland
Branch, William McKinley
Isaac, Earlean

Gadsden
Thomas, Spencer
Turman, Robert L., Sr.

Greenville
Cook, James E.

Harvest
Gates, Jacquelyn Burch

Hayneville
Means, Elbert Lee

Helena
Baker, Beverly Poole

Homewood
Dennard, Gloria

Hoover
Kennon, Rozmond H

Hueytown
Grayson, Elsie Michelle
Terry, Lorene Jackson

Huntsville
Bradley, Jessie Mary
Campbell, Carlos, Sr.
Germany, Sylvia Marie Armstrong
Gill, Glenda Eloise
Grayson, George Welton
Hall, Lemanski
Henry-Fairhurst, Ellenae L
Hooker, Dr. Billie J.
Jones, Dr. Barbara Ann Posey
Lacy, Hugh Gale
Lacy, Walter
McCray, Dr. Roy Howard
Mitchell, Dolphus Burl
Montgomery, Dr. Oscar Lee
Moseley, Calvin Edwin, Jr.
Rainey, Timothy Mark
Rice, Horace Warren

Sheridan, Edna
Stanley, Thornton, Sr.
Stanmore, Dr. Roger Dale
Wimbush, Gary Lynn
Wyatt, Dr. Ronald Michael

Hurtsboro
Stovall-Tapley, Mary Kate

Irondale
Graham, James C, Jr.

Jacksonville
Brown, John Ollis
Green, James

Jemison
Reed, Eddie

Lafayette
Vester, Dr. Terry Y

Lanett
Crawley, Oscar Lewis

Letohatchee
Smith, Charles E, Sr.

Livingston
Jackson, Claude

Lower Peach Tree
Smith, Frank

Madison
Barkley, Mark E.
Reynolds, James W.
Stanmore, Dr. Roger Dale
Wyatt, Dr. Ronald Michael

Midfield
Frazier, Jordan

Mobile
Bivins, Sonja F
Boyd, Marvin
Brown, D Joan
Buskey, James E.
Campbell, Dr. Helen
Cooper, Jerome Gary
Crenshaw, Reginald Anthony
Dapremont, Delmont, Jr.
Figures, Thomas H
Hazzard, Dr. Terry Louis
Johnson, Clinton Lee
Kennedy, James E.
Lamar, Cleveland James
Madison, Yvonne Reed
Mitchell, Dr. Joseph Christopher, Sr.
Perry, Victoria
Porter, Charles William
Richardson, Frederick D
Sealls, Alan Ray
Smith, Elaine Marie
Taylor, Mary Quivers
Womack, Joe Neal, Jr.

Montevallo
Pearson, Clifton

Montgomery
Bailey, Richard
Bell, Dr. Katie Roberson

Bibb, Dr. T Clifford
Boggs, Nathaniel
Booth, Dr. Le-Quita
Boyd, Delores Rosetta
Bryson, Dr. Ralph J.
Buskey, John
Calhoun, Dorothy Eunice
Calhoun, Gregory Bernard
Carter, Billy L.
Christburg, Sheyann Webb
Colvin, Cedric B
Conley, Charles S.
Davis, Joan Y.
DeShields, Harrison F., Jr.
Finley, Dr. D. Linell, Sr.
Gaines, Mary E
Gamble, Oscar Charles
Gray, Fred David
Griffin, Gregory O
Hall, Dr. Ethel Harris
Harris, Dr. Willa Bing
Harris, Dr. William Hamilton
Holmes, Alvin Adolf
Johnson, Paul Edwin
Kennedy, Dr. Yvonne
Knight, John F., Jr.
Langford, Charles D.
Lee, Joe A.
Lloyd, Wanda
Long, Gerald Bernard
Mapp, Berbell
McClammy, Dr. Thad C
Means, Tyrone
Mitchell, Kelly Karnale
Moore, Dr. Archie Bradford, Jr.
Moore, Dr. Nathan
Myers, Dr. Jacqualine Desmona
Newton, Demetrius C
Norman, Georgette M.
Oglivie, Benjamin A.
Perdue, Rep. George, Jr.
Price, Charles
Pryor, Julius, Jr.
Reed, Joe Louis
Robinson, Carrie C.
Smiley, Dr. Emmett L
Smith, Jock Michael
Spears, Henry Albert
Thomas, James L
Thomas, Ora P
Thompson, Myron Herbert
Vaughn, Dr. Percy Joseph
Weiss, Joyce Lacey
Winston, John H., Jr.

Normal
Byrd, Dr. Taylor
Frazier, Leon
Jones, Dr. Barbara Ann Posey
Marbury, Carl Harris
McMillian, Marco W
Montgomery, Dr. Trent
Morrison, Richard David
Rice, Horace Warren
Toomer, Clarence

Northport
Culpepper, Lucy Nell
Davis, Joseph Solomon
Thomas, Frankie Taylor

Opelika
Lightfoote, William Edward, II

Pell City
Herd, Rev. John E
McGowan, Elsie Henderson

Pine Hill
Johnson, Bobby JoJo
Mahan-Powell, Lena

Prattville
Larkin, Dr. Byrdie A.

Prichard
Clark, William
Crenshaw, Reginald Anthony

Ridgeville
Adair, Charles, Jr.

Selma
Deese, Glenda
Hendricks, Dr. Constance Smith
Hunter, Rev. John Davidson
Jackson, Michael W
Reese, Rev. Frederick D
Robinson, Prof. Ella S.
Sanders, Hank

Sylacauga
McElrath-Frazier, Wanda Faith

Talladega
Franklin, Harold A.
Ponder, Dr. Henry

Troy
Osby, Parico Green

Tuscaloosa
Broomes, Lloyd Rudy
Colvin, Dr. William E
Culpepper, Lucy Nell
Delaney, John Paul
Fredd, Chester Arthur
Gray, Myrtle Edwards
Johnson, Dr. Rhoda E
Jones, Alma Wyatt
Lockett, James D.
McCrackin, Olympia H
Prewitt, Dr. Lena Voncille Burrell
Stinson, Constance Robinson
Whittaker, Sharon Elaine
Wynn, Dr. Cordell

Tuscumbia
Bailey, Bob Carl
Brown, Ouida Y.
Smith, Rev. Otis Benton, Jr.

Tuskegee
Biswas, Dr. Prosanto K.
Bowie, Dr. Walter C.
Capel, Wallace
Davis, Milton C.
Hardy, Charlie Edward
Henson, William Francis
Hodge, William Anthony
James, Advergus Dell
Jobe, Ben
Payton, Dr. Benjamin Franklin
Smith, Jock Michael
St Omer, Vincent V E
Thompson, Dr. Charles H.
Wright, James W

Tuskegee Institute
Biswas, Dr. Prosanto K.
Carter, Herbert E.
Carter, Howard Payne
Henderson, Dr. James Henry Meriwether
Louis, Dr. Suchet Lesperance
Mitchell, Noel C

Union Springs
Hodge, William Anthony

Uniontown
Turner, Leslie Ford

Wagarville
Dixon, Willie L.

York
Black, Lucius
Nixon, Rev. Felix Nathaniel

ALASKA

Anchorage
Andrews, Eleanor
Bailey-Thomas, Sheryl K.
Bolden, Clarence
Butler, Rex L
Davis, Bettye J
Greene, William
Patterson, Alonzo B., Jr.
Pendergraft, Michele M
Ray, Rev. Patricia Ann
Smith, Carol Barlow
Taylor, Sterling R
Tolan-Gamble, Janet Helen

Eagle River
Greene, William

Fairbanks
Dunlap King, Virgie M

Juneau
Davis, Bettye J
Henderson, Remond

Monticello
Campbell, Sandra

North Pole
Hunter, Rev. James Nathaniel, II

Palmer
Simton, Chester

Wasilla
Simton, Chester

ARIZONA

Benson
Gray, Earnest

Chandler
Ward, Arnette S.

Coolidge
Colbert, George Clifford

Flagstaff
Hannah, Melvin James
Johnson, Theodore L.
Locket, Arnold, Jr.

Fort Defiance
Gladney, Dr. Marcellious

Gilbert
Underwood, Paul L, Jr.

Glendale
Barnwell, Henry Lee
Beasley, Edward
Fuhr, Grant Scott
Jackson, William R
Reed, Joann
Travis, Geraldine

Lake Havasu City
Stone, Dolores June

Laveen
Minor, Willie

Mesa
Brouhard, Deborah Taliaferro
Fuller, Harold David
Jackson, Tomi L.
Merritt, Anthony Lewis

Orlando
Hill, Grant Henry

Paradise Valley
Green, Dr. Frederick Chapman

Phoenix
Andrews, Judis R
Avent, Jacques Myron

Beachem, Constance
Blackmon, Anthony Wayne
Blue, Gene C
Ceballos, Cedric Z.
Chapman, Samuel Milton
Clayton, Robert L
Culver, Rhonda
Davis, Major
Dumas, Richard
Edwards, John L.
Evans, Robert Oran
Gaines, Corey Yasuto
Gentry, Alvin
Gillom, Jennifer
Goode, Calvin C.
Green, A. C., Jr.
Grigsby, Jefferson Eugene
Groth, Chad
Hamilton, Art
Hardaway, Jerry David
Huff, Loretta Love
Jackson, Mannie L
Johnson, Kevin Maurice
Jones, Dr. Kenneth Leroy
Jordan, Steve Russell
Lowery, Carolyn T
Meridith, Denise Patricia
Miller, Tedd
Montague, Lee
Mosley, Bruce
Murrell, Adrian Bryan
Nelson, Doeg M.
Oliver, Jerry Alton
Pearson, Dr. Stanley E
Pettis, Bridget
Pitts, John Martin
Smith, Charles James, III
Stewart, Dr. Warren Hampton
Stoudemire, Amare Carsares
Watson, Genevieve
West, Mark Andre
Williams, Cody
Willrich, Penny
Zachary, Steven W

Phoenix
Edwards, Anthony

Scottsdale
Daurham, Ernest
Dodson, Selma L
Jackson, Karen Denise
Johnson, Geneva B.
Morrison, James W.
Reid, Dr. F. Theodore, Jr.
Sullivan, Leon Howard

Scottsdale,
Young, Kevin Stacey

Sierra Vista
Allen, George Mitchell
Buckhanan, Shawn L

Sun City
Sherman, Barbara J.

Surprise
Logan, George, III

Tempe
Bryant, Leon Serle
Campbell, Mark
Davis, Dr. Thomas Joseph
Edwards, John L.
Fitzgerald, Larry
Grigsby, Jefferson Eugene
Harris, Rubie J.
Harrison, Dr. Mernoy Edward
Hollin, Kenneth Ronald
Jackson, Karen Denise
Minor, Willie
Patterson, Cecil Booker, Jr.
Smith, A. Wade
Smith, Eugene DuBois
Stokes, Sheila Woods
Warren, Morrison Fulbright
Wilson, Dr. Jeffrey R.

Tucson
Bowens, Dr. Johnny Wesley
Burrows, Clare
Coleman Morris, Valerie Dickerson
Cooper, Dr. LaMoyne Mason
Davis, Richard

Erving, Julius Winfield
Fluellen, Velda Spaulding
Goodwin, Felix L.
Hopkins, Edward Charles
Hopkins, Dr. Gayle P.
Lander, Cressworth Caleb
Meade-Tollin, Dr. Linda C
Moore, Juliette R
Snowden, Fredrick
Todd, Charles O
Walker, Maurice Edward
Whaley, Dr. Joseph S
Wilber, Ida Belinda
Zander, Jessie Mae Reasor

Yuma
Jefferson, James E.

ARKANSAS

Arkadelphia
Shepherd, Dr. Lewis A
Smith, Virginia M.
Thomas, Eula Wiley
Thomas, Herman L.

Bentonville
Davis, Cora Bowie
Goodwin, Emerson
Lafayette, Excell, Jr.
Peterson, Coleman Hollis
Silver-Parker, Esther

Cherokee Village
Hollingsworth, John Alexander

Conway
Jones, Theodore

Cotton Plant
Babbs, Dr. Junious C., Sr.
Conley, Emmitt Jerome

Earle
Lewis, Ephron H.
Smith, Sherman, Sr.

Edmondson
Croft, Ira T

El Dorado
Gibson, Wayne Carlton
Sims, Pete
Van Hook, George Ellis

Fayetteville
Brazzell, Dr. Johnetta Cross
Brummer, Chauncey Eugene
Carter, Thomas
Dansby, Jesse L.
Lofton, Dr. Barbara
Morgan, Dr. Gordon D.
Young, Dr. Michael

Fordyce
Hartaway, Thomas N

Forrest City
Wilburn, Isaac G

Fort Smith
Fisher, George Carver

Gold River
Armistead, Milton

Hamburg
Morrison, Dr. Juan LaRue, Sr.

Helena
David, Geraldine R.

Hot Springs
Logan, Alphonso
Newman, Nathaniel

Jacksonville
Nellums, Michael Wayne

Jonesboro
Williams, Dr. Lonnie Ray

Lexa
David, Geraldine R.

Little Rock
Banks, Alicia
Bivens, Shelia Reneea

Bogard, Hazel Zinamon
Corrothers, Garry James
Evans, Dr. Grover Milton
Feaster, LaVerne Williams
Fitzhugh, B. Dewey
Fitzhugh, Kathryn Corrothers
Fletcher, Dr. Anthony M
Goldsby, W Dean, Sr.
Green, Thomas L
Hollingsworth, Perlesta A
Humphrey, Marion Andrew
Ibekwe, Lawrence Anene
Jewell, Jerry Donal
Johnson, J. Leon
Keaton, William T.
Lacey, Dr. Marian Glover
Means, Kevin Michael
Mitchell, Katherine Phillips
Moorehead, Eric K
Moss, Wilmar Burnett, Jr.
Owens, Jay R.
Petett, Freddye J Webb
Rayford, Phillip Leon
Scott, Dr. Julius S, Jr.
Smith, Judy Seriale
Tate, Sherman E
Tatum, Mildred Carthan
Taylor, Tommie W.
Thrasher, William Edward
Townsend, William Henry
Walker, Woodson DuBois
Ward, Lorene Howelton
Warren, Joyce Williams
White, Ralph L.
Williamson, Corliss Mondari

Magnolia
Gaylord, Ellihue, Sr.

Menifee
English, Clarence R.

Mineral Springs
Hendrix, Martha Raye

Monticello
Campbell, William Earl
Dupree, Sandra Kay

Newport
Sills, Gregory D.

North Little Rock
Blakely, Carolyn
Brookins, H. Hartford
Cooley, James F.
Goldsby, W Dean, Sr.
Hunter, Elza Harris
Ibekwe, Lawrence Anene
James, Frederick C.
Moses, Harold Webster
Pattillo, Joyce M

Pine Bluff
Daniels, Peter F.
Davis, Lawrence Arnette, Jr.
Early Lambert, Violet Theresa
Gilmore, John T
Henderson, Dr. Cortez V.
Johnson, Dr. Johnny B
Johnson, Dr. Vannette William
Kearney, Jesse L
Lewis, Therthenia Williams
McGee, Eva M
Roaf, Clifton G.
Roberts, Jacqueline Johnson
Roberts, Janice L
Sands, Jerry Leigh
Wilkins, Henry, III
Wilkins, Josetta Edwards

Sherrill
Edwards, Jean Curtis

State University
Smith, Charlie Calvin

Texarkana
Williams, Londell

Wabbaseka
Hall, Robert Johnson

Walnut Ridge
Gaines, Herschel Davis

West Memphis
McGee, Benjamin Lelon
Watkins, Lenice Jackie

CALIFORNIA
Baylor, Elgin Gay

APO
Person, Leslie Robin

Agoura Hills
Nichols, Crystal Faye
White, Jaleel Ahmed

Alameda
Brown, Willie
Cannon, Dr. Barbara E M
Davison, Jerone
Garrett, Darrell W
Jolivet, Linda Catherine
Lofton, James
Malliet, Schone
McPhail, Dr. Christine Johnson
Reaves, E. Fredericka M
Tucker, Norma Jean
Turner, Eric

Alta Loma
Okoye, Christian E

Altadena
Brown, Costello L.
Browne, Lee F.
Driver, Johnie M
Guy, Lygia Brown
Hines, Kingsley B
McMullins, Tommy
Smith, Bob
Streeter, Elwood James
Woodard, Lois Marie

Anaheim
Barnes, Milton, Jr.
Darke, Dr. Charles B
Hagan, Willie James
Honeycutt, Andrew E.
Hunter, Torii Kedar
Matthews, Gary Nathaniel, Jr.
Oliver, Darren Christopher

Antelope
Jackson, Mary

Antioch
Dubriel, Lisa M.

Apple Valley
Hurte, Leroy E.
Sanders, Augusta Swann

Arcadia
Cameron, Randolph W

Atascadero
London, Eddie

Azusa
Allen, John Henry

Bakersfield
Carson, Irma
Collier, Willye
Luster, Robert
Shaw, Mary Louise

Bakersfield, CA
Rooks, Sean Lester

Belmont
Dreyfuss, Joel P

Benicia
Lofton, Mellanese S

Berkeley
Allen, Robert L
Baker, LaVolia Ealy
Banks, Dr. William Maron
Basri, Gibor
Bayne, Henry G.
Bell, Theodore Joshua
Blackwell, David Harold
Blakely, Dr. Edward James
Burrows Dost, Janice H.

Carwell, Hattie V
Clarke, Greta Fields
Drummond, William Joe
Easter, Wilfred Otis, Jr.
Echols, Doris Brown
Edwards, Dr. Harry
Gifford, Dr. Bernard R.
Henry, Dr. Charles Patrick, III
Herring, Dr. Bernard Duane
Hintzen, Percy Claude
Holbert, Raymond
Irmagean, U.
Johnson, Prof. Stephanie Anne
Kirk-Duggan, Cheryl Ann
Laguerre, Michel S.
Lester, Dr. William Alexander
Lumbly, Carl
McGuire, Dr. Chester C., Jr.
Moore, Jane Bond
Morrison, Harry L.
Nelson, Ronald Duncan
Prelow, Arleigh
Reed, Ishmael Scott
Russell, Charlie L.
Satterfield, Floyd
Shack, William A.
Simmons, Kenneth H
Strait, George Alfred, Jr.
Sweet, Clifford C
Vaughn, Nora Belle
Walton, Carol Ann
Webb, Georgia Houston
Wilkerson, Prof. Margaret Buford
Williams, Dr. Carroll Burns, Jr.
Wilson, Dr. Olly W.
Word, Carl Oliver

Beverly Hills
Adams, Jan R.
Adams, John Oscar
Adams, Oleta
Albright, Gerald Anthony
Allen, Tina
Andrews, Tina
Beauvais, Garcelle
Beyer, Troy Yvette
Bonds, Barry Lamar
Boston, Gretha
Braugher, Andre
Carry, Julius J
Christian, William Leonard
Cooper, Barry Michael
Copage, Marc Diego
Creary, Ludlow Barrington
Curtis-Hall, Vondie
Davidson, Tommy
DeAnda, Peter
De'Leon, Lunden
Doug, Doug E.
Dutton, Charles S.
Epps, Omar Hashim
Ferrell, Tyra
Fields, Kim Victoria
Franks, Cree Summer
George, Jason Winston
Glover, Danny Lebern
Gossett, Louis Cameron, Jr.
Grier, David Alan
Hall, Delores
Hammond, Brandon La Ron
Harper, Hill
Harris, Steve
Haysbert, Dennis Dexter
Henderson, Barrington
Hill, Dule
Hooks, Kevin
Howard, Gregory Allen
Hudson, Jennifer Kate
Hughley, D L
Ice Cube
Jackson, La Toya Yvonne
Jackson, Samuel L
Kerr, Brook
Kingi, Henry Masao
Kravitz, Lenny
LaSalle, Eriq
Lindo, Delroy
Little Richard
McCoo, Marilyn
McDonald, Audra Ann
McGee, Vonetta
Meadows, Tim
Mitchell, Daryl
Moore, Dr. Oscar James, Jr.
Nicholas, Denise
Parker, Paula Jai
Payne, Freda Charcelia
Peete, Rodney
Perrineau, Harold, Jr.

Perry, Felton
Phifer, Mekhi
Pickens, James, Jr.
Pinkett Smith, Jada
Poitier, Sydney Tamiia
Pounder, C. C. H.
Prince-Bythewood, Gina
Randle, Theresa Ellen
Reese, Della
Reid, Christopher
Rhames, Ving
Rich, Matty
Richardson, Dr. Madison Franklin
Rivers, Johnny
Robinson, Matt
Robinson Peete, Holly
Rogers-Jone, Kelis
Savage, Janet Marie
Simmons, Henry Oswald, Jr.
Snipes, Wesley
St John, Kristoff
Story, Timothy Kevin
Studdard, Ruben
Sykes, Wanda
Tone-Loc
Trammel, Kimberly Elise
True, Rachel India
Tunie, Tamara
Tyson, Ron
Uggams, Leslie
Underwood, Blair
Vance, Courtney B
Vasquez, Joseph B.
Washington, Dr. Denzel
Wayans, Marlon
Westbrooks, Logan H.
Whitfield, Dondre T.
Whitfield, Lynn C.
Williams, Dick Anthony
Williams, Dr. Henry S
Williams, Michael Michele
Williams, Russell, II
Williams, Tonya Lee
Williams, Vanessa Lynne
Wilson, Chandra Danette
Witherspoon, John

Blythe
Clifford, Thomas E.

Bonita
Chapman, Dr. William Talbert
Russell, Wesley L.

Buena Park
White, Nan E.

Burbank
Barcliff, Melvin
Benet, Eric
Bowser, Yvette Denise Lee
Brady, Wayne Alfonzo
Campbell, Tevin Jermod
Campbell-Martin, Tisha
Cannon, Nick
Davis, Preston A
Day, Morris
De Veaux, Stuart Samuel
Dungey, Merrin
Eubanks, Kevin
Faison, Donald Adeosun
Gooding, Omar
Hickman, Frederick Douglass
Hill, Dule
Holmes, Robert Ernest
Johnson, Henry Wade
Johnson, R. Benjamin
Kinchen, Arif S.
Kirkland, Kenny David
Madison, Paula
Martin Chase, Debra
Mathis, Gregory
McNeal, Timothy Kyle
Robinson, Shaun
Simpson, Joyce Michelle
Sure, Al B.
Walker, Terry
Wheaton, Wendy E
White, Beverly Anita
White, Karyn
Wonder, Stevie
Wyatt, William N

Burlingame
Ali, Dr. Fatima
Bell, Theodore Joshua
Hall, Sydney Jay, III

Jones, Sinclair
Morse, Warren W.

Camarillo
Sawyer, William Gregory

Cambria
Harden, Marvin

Campbell
Young, Dr. Carlene Herb

Canoga Park
Allen, John Henry
McClure, Bryton Eric
Wilson, Natarsha Juliet

Canyon Lake
Young, Dr. Barbara J.

Carlsbad
Dimry, Charles Louis, III
Mills, Lois Terrell

Carson
Edney, Steve
Fontenot, Rev. Albert E., Jr.
Franklin, Costella M.
Hill, Deborah
Howard, Jules Joseph, Jr.
Jones, Cobi N'Gai
Mayberry, Patricia Marie
Robinson, Gill Doncelia
Turner, Franklin James
Walker, Charles

Century City
Patterson, Saladin K

Cerritos
Furlough, Joyce Lynn
Titus, LeRoy Robert

Chatsworth
Martin, Kevin

Chico
Epting, Marion

Chino Hills
Riddick, Eugene E

Chula Vista
Ferguson, Dr. Robert Lee, Sr.
Matthews, Dr. Merritt Stewart

Citrus Heights
Fulgham, Roietta Goodwin

Claremont
Fairchild, Halford H.
Jackson, Agnes Moreland
Lewis, Samella Sanders
McGee, Rev. Paula L.
Riddick, Eugene E

Coalinga
Russell, Beverly A.

Colton
Baker, Delbert Wayne
McKinney, Rev. Jesse Doyle

Commerce
Watts, Patricia L

Compton
Beauchamp, Patrick L.
Clegg, Legrand H
Cobbs, David E.
Cooper, Lois Louise
Crosbie, Ivan
Davis, Dr. Doris Ann
Dymally, Mervyn Malcolm
Edwards, Shirley
Filer, Kelvin Dean
Hart-Holifield, Emily B.
Henson, Charles A.
Hill, Betty J.
Hunn, Dorothy Fegan
Hunn, Myron Vernon
Patrick, Charles Namon, Jr.
Stewart, Ella

Viltz, Dr. Stanley
Woods, Dr. Bernice

Concord
Beals, Yvonne

Corona
Fowlkes, Nelson J

Corona Del Mar
Davis, Dr. Arthur David

Costa Mesa
McKayle, Donald Cohen

Culver City
Allen, Debbie
Diesel, Vin
Fanaka, Jamaa
Greene, Mary Ann
Harris, Fran
Hatchett, Glenda A.
Johnson, Rafer
Lang, Charles J.
McNeill, Cerves Todd
Mills, John
Roney, Raymond G
Snowden, Raymond C.
Solomon, Barbara J.
Stevens, John Theodore, Sr.
Walden, Barbara
Wayans, Damon
White, Jaleel Ahmed
Williams, Dr. Harriette F.

Culver city
Ralph, Sheryl Lee

Cupertino
Thompson, John W

Daly City
Ellis, Marilyn Pope
Lovelace, Onzalo Robert

Danville
Grigsby, Calvin Burchard
Merritt, Anthony Lewis

Davis
Major, Dr. Clarence
Ramey, Melvin R
Stewart, Dr. John Othneil

Diamond Bar
Davis, Dr. Brenda Lightsey-
  Hendricks
Davis, William R.

Downey
Gipson, Reve
Washington, Earl S.

Dublin
Barber, Dr. Janice Denise
Leonard, Jeffrey

East Palo Alto
Davis, Ronald
Satterwhite, Dr. Frank Joseph
Wilks, Gertrude

Edwards
Hedgley, David Rice, Jr.

El Cajon
Riggs, Hon. Elizabeth A

El Cerrito
McGowan, Thomas Randolph

El Segundo
Austin, Dr. Wanda M
Cleamons, James Mitchell
Dunn, W Paul
Hodges, Craig Anthony
McPherson, William H.
Perkins, Louvenia Black
Sampson, Dr. Henry Thomas
Shaw, Brian K
Toler, Penny

Elk Grove
Elmore, Dr. Ronn
Netters, Tyrone Homer

Emeryville
Bragg, Robert Henry, II
Brown, Richard Earl

Harrold, Lawrence A
Lyons, Dr. Laura Brown
Reed, Ishmael Scott

Encinitas
Alexander, Dr. Edward Cleve
McNeil, DeeDee

Encino
Anderson, Anthony
Mills, Donald
Milton, LeRoy

Enconia
McEachin, James

Escondido
Dunn, Jason
Gaffney, Michele Elizabeth
Lawhorn, Robert Martin

Fairfax
Campbell, Christopher Lundy

Fairfield
Roach, Deloris
Via, Thomas Henry

Foster City
Hall, Sydney Jay, III
Pitts, Dr. Vera L.
Smallwood, Dr. Catherine

Foullerton
Harvey, Michael P

Fremont
Byrd, Lewis E.
Jones, Dr. Vida Yvonne
Matthews, Denise
Thomson, J Peter

Fresno
Aldredge, Prof. James Earl
Avery, Jeromye Lee
Brown, Willie L.
Burns, Felton
Cheek, Donald Kato
Francis, Charles S L
Goodwin, Hugh Wesley
Hunt, Samuel D.
Johnson, Frank J., Sr.
Jones, Charlie
Jones, Ida M.
Kelley, Jack Albert
Kimber, Lesly H.
Neal, Lorenzo LaVon
Parks, James Edward
Small, Lily B.
Smith, William James
White, Paul Christopher
Wint, Arthur Valentine Noris

Fullerton
Cobb, Dr. Jewel Plummer
Hagan, Willie James
McFerrin, Sara Elizabeth Copper
Palmer, Robert L., II
Rycraw, Eugenia
Smith, Dr. Jesse Owens
Stokes, Julie Elena

Gardena
Bradford, Steven C
Campbell, Dr. Everett O.
Hale, Gene
Hines, Courtney
Johnson, Arthur L.
McClendon, Clarence E.
Sendaba, S. M.

Glendale
Flemming, Carolyn
Rippy, Rodney Allen
Treadwell, Tina McKinley

Glendora
Hammonds, Tom
Nance, Larry Donell

Granada Hills
Fox, Vivica A
Mance, John J.
McCraven, Carl Clarke

Greenbrae
Westray, Rev. Kenneth Maurice

Harbor City
Hardin, Eugene

Hayward
Andrews, Malachi
Ballard, Myrtle Ethel

Bowser, Benjamin Paul
Carmichael, Benjamin G.
Chuks-Orji, Austin
Franklin, Allen D.
Kitchen, Wayne Leroy
Lovett, Mack, Jr.
Pitts, Dr. Vera L.
Shepard, Linda Irene
White, Bryan
Wright, Soraya M

Hollywood
Beverly, Frankie
Cole, Natalie
Cumber, Victoria Lillian
Dozier, Lamont
Ephriam, Mablean
Evans, Faith Renee
Fann, Albert Louis
Lewis, Sarasvati Ananda
McFerrin, Bobby
Spencer, Tracie Monique
Washington, Kerry

Huntington Beach
Grooms, Dr. Henry Randall
Lathen, Deborah Ann
McCutcheon, Lawrence

Inglewood
Barrett, Dr. Ronald Keith
Benjamin, Rose Mary
Bennett, Mario Marcell
Brown, Deloris A
Childs, Joy
Davis, William Delford
Franklin, Kirk
Hankins, Hesterly G, III
Harper, Derek Ricardo
James, Charles Leslie
Kimble, Bettye Dorris
Matthews, Leonard Louis
Meshack, Lula M
Ormsby, William M
Reid, Benjamin F.
Seals, Shea
Slade, Karen E
Taylor, Eric Charles
Ulmer, Kenneth C., Bishop
Wiley, Maurice
Williams, Dr. Harvey Joseph
Williams, Dr. Herbert Lee
Williams, Homer LaVaughan

Irvine
Allen, Quincy L
Timm, Marion Eleanor
Williams, Harvey

Kensington
Major, Benjamin

La Jolla
Heineback, Barbara Taylor
Hutchinson, Dr. George
Reynolds, Dr. Edward
Ringgold, Faith
Troupe, Quincy Thomas, Jr.
Watson, Joseph W

La Mirada
Land, Chester C.
Nutt, Ambrose Benjamin

La Verne
Harrison, Boyd G, Jr.
Mosley, Shane

Laguna Beach
Blanton, Dain

Lake Forest
Addy, Tralance Obuama

Lake View Terrace
Carrington, Terri Lyne
Smith, William Fred

Lancaster
Hedgley, David Rice, Jr.
Robinson, Lawrence D.

Loma Linda
Young, Dr. Lionel Wesley

Lompoc
Rogers, Charles Leonard

Long Beach
Blaylock, Dr. Enid Veronica
Boston, Archie, Jr.

Clayton, James Henry
Dunn, George William
Dymally, Lynn V
Edwards, Oscar Lee
Johns, Jamie
Mitchell, Horace
Ono, Musashi
Person, Dr. Dawn Renee
Powell, Wilma D
Rains, Horace
Robinson, Jim C
Rosser, Dr. James M.
Stetson, Jeffrey P
Tillman, Dr. Talmadge Calvin, Jr.
Titus, LeRoy Robert
Williams, Dr. Betty Smith
Williams, Dr. Ora

Los Alamitos
Johnson, Joseph David
Peters, Samuel A.

Los Altos
Stewart, William

Los Altos, CA
Vaughters-Johnson, Cecilie A

Los Angeles
Adams, John Oscar
Alexander, Joseph Lee
Alexander, Josephine
Alexander, Theodore Thomas, Jr.
Allen, Byron
Allen, Walter R
Alston, Dr. Kathy Diane
Amos, John
Anderson, Bernadine M.
Anderson, Henry L N
Anderson, Michael Wayne
Arnold, Alton A., Jr.
Artope, William
Atkins, Pervis R., Jr.
Avant, Clarence
Babatunde, Obba
Bailey, Arthur
Bailey, Hiltron
Bailey, Lee
Bailey, Philip
Bain, Josie Gray
Bankhead, Patricia Ann
Baquet, Dean
Barnes, John B., Sr.
Barnes, Willie R.
Barrett, Dr. Ronald Keith
Barrois, Lyndon J.
Beach, Michael Anthony
Beasley, Jesse C.
Becker, Adolph Eric
Becker-Slaton, Dr. Nellie Frances
Bell, Charles A.
Bell, Darryl M.
Benton, Nelkane O
Benymon, Chico
Berry, Dr. Gordon L
Beverly, William C
Billings, Earl William
Billingslea, Monroe L.
Black, Dr. James Tillman
Black, Dr. Keith
Blake, Charles E
Blanding, Mary Rhonella
Boags, Charles D.
Boddie, Dr. Lewis F, Sr.
Bodison, Wolfgang
Boone, Eunetta
Borden, Harold F., Jr.
Bostic, Raphael W
Boston, Archie, Jr.
Bowdoin, Robert E.
Bowers, Mirion Perry
Brass, Reginald Stephen
Brenson, Verdel Lee
Brewer, Gregory Alan
Brisco-Hooks, Valerie Ann
Broadbent, Hydeia
Broderick, Johnson
Brooks, Golden A.
Brooks, Theodore Roosevelt, Jr.
Brown, Costello L.
Brown, Gilbert David, III
Brown, Joe
Brown, Jurutha
Bryant, John
Bryant, John Richard
Buckhalter, Emerson R.
Bunkley, Lonnie R
Burke, William Arthur
Burke, Yvonne Watson Brathwaite

Burroughs, Hugh Charles
Burton, Brent F.
Burton, Iola Brantley
Burton, Levar
Caddell, Phyllis
Calhoun, Monica
Callender, Ralph A.
Cannon, Reuben
Carroll, Diahann
Carroll, Lawrence William, III
Carroll, Raoul Lord
Charles, Ray
Charles, RuPaul Andre
Cheese, Pauline Staten
Chong, Rae Dawn
Clark-Hudson, Veronica L
Clayton, Ina Smiley
Cobb, Keith Hamilton
Cochran, Johnnie L., Jr.
Coleman, Gary Wayne
Coleman, Robert Earl, Jr.
Colley, Nathaniel S.
Collins, James Douglas
Collins, Kenneth L.
Cooper, Hon. Candace D
Cooper, Earl
Cooper, Michael Jerome
Corlette, Edith
Cornelius, Donald Cortez
Cox, Sandra
Crippens, David L.
Crockett, Ray
Curry, Mitchell L
Daniels, Jordan, Jr.
Daniels, Lemuel Lee
Davidson, Ezra C.
Davidson, Robert C., Jr.
Davis, Amos
Davis, Dr. John Albert
Davis, Richard C.
Davis, Viola
Davis-Carter, Holly
Dawson, Rosario
Dee, Ruby
DeFrantz, Anita L.
DeLilly, Mayo Ralph, III
Dent, Dr. Preston L.
de Passe, Suzanne
Diane, Glare
Dickerson, Ernest Roscoe
Dillard, Victoria
Dorn, Michael
Doss, Conya
Douglass, M Lorayne
Dourdan, Gary
Driver, Louie M., Jr.
Duke, George M.
Dummett, Clifton Orrin
Duncan, Michael Clarke
Dunn, W Paul
Durant, Karen
Eaton, Thelma Lucile
Edmonds, Kenneth
Edmonds, Tracey E.
Edwards, Ella Raino
Ellaraino
Ellis, Frederic L.
Ellis, Johnell A.
Eubanks, Dr. Rachel Amelia
Farquhar, Ralph R
Farrell, Cheryl Layne
Fergerson, Miriam N
Ferguson, Lloyd Noel
Finney, Sara Vernetta
Fishburne, Laurence John
Fleary, Kim
Fleming, Arthur Wallace
Fortier, Theodore T., Sr.
Foster, Ezola Broussard
Franklin, Floyd
G, Warren
Gant, Richard E.
Gault, Willie James
Gibbs, Marla
Gilchrist, Carlton Chester
Gillette, Dr. Lyra Stephanie
Givens, Robin
Glasco, Dr. Anita L.
Glover, Arthur Lewis, Jr.
Goddard, Rosalind Kent
Golson, Benny
Gonzaque, Ozie Bell
Good, Megan Monique
Goodson, James Abner, Jr.
Grant, Dr. Ellsworth R
Graves, Clifford Wayne
Grayson, Mel
Green, Geraldine D.

Greene, Dr. Charles Edward Clarence
Greene, Jehmu
Greene, Dr. Lionel Oliver
Greenfield, Mark Steven
Griffey, Dick
Griffin, Eddie
Griffith, Thomas Lee, Jr.
Guiton Hill, Bonnie
Guy, Jasmine
Hamilton, Lisa Gay
Hammer, M. C.
Hardin, Eugene
Harper, Sarah Elizabeth Grubbs
Harris, Lee
Harris, Thomas Walter
Harrison, Mya Marie
Harry, Jackee
Hart-Nibbrig, Harold C
Hartsfield, Arnett L., Jr.
Hathaway, Maggie Mae
Hawkins, Paulette
Hawkins, William Douglas
Hayes, Reginald
Haywood, Dr. L. Julian
Hazzard, Walter R., Jr.
Head, Helaine
Hendry, Gloria
Henry, Karl H.
Hill, Jacqueline R
Hill, Jimmy H.
Hill, Dr. Julius W.
Hill, Leo
Hillsman, Gerald C.
Holland, Brian
Holland, Edward, Jr.
Holman, Alvin T.
Holman, Doris Ann
Holmes, Rev. Zan W., Jr.
Holt, Deloris Lenette
Hooks, Brian
Hopkins, Bernard
Hord, Noel Edward
Howard, Joseph H.
Hubbard, James Madison, Jr.
Hudson, Elbert T.
Hunter, Gigi
Hunter, Kim L
Hunter, Lloyd Thomas
Hutchinson, Earl Ofari
Ighner, Benard T.
J., Ray
Jackson, Randy
James, Charles Leslie
Jefferson, Roland Spratlin, M.D.
Jemison, Aj D
Jenkins, Nedra
John, Dr. Mable
Johns, Stephen Arnold
Johnson, Anne-Marie
Johnson, Dr. Cage Saul
Johnson, Carl J.
Johnson, Henry Wade
Johnson, Lucien Love
Johnson, MaryAnn
Johnson, Patricia Duren
Johnson, Raymond L., Sr.
Johnson, William C.
Jones, Audrey Boswell
Jones, Carl
Jones, DeLisha Milton
Jones, Gary
Jones, Jill Marie
Jordan, Dr. Wilbert Cornelious
Keller, Dr. Edmond Joseph
Kendrick, Artis G.
King, Celes, III
King, Greg
King, Lewis M.
King, Regina
Klausner, Willette Murphy
Kyle, Genghis
Lachman, Dr. Ralph Steven
Laneuville, Eric Gerard
Lawson, John C, II
LeDay, John Austin
Lee, Clifton Valjean
Lee, Gloria A
Lee, Robinne
Lewis, Arthur A., Jr.
Lewis, Patricia
Lewis, Samella Sanders
Livingston, Joyce
Love, Faizon
Luck, Dr. Clyde Alexander, Jr.
Mack, John W.
MacLachlan, Janet A.
Mallory, George L, Jr.
Marshall, Consuelo B.

Martin, Carl E.
Martin, Duane
May, Charles W.
Mays, David
Mays, Dr. James Arthur
Mays, Dr. Vickie M
McBeth-Reynolds, Sandra Kay
McBride, Chi
McConnell, Dorothy Hughes
McCoo, Marilyn
McCormick, Larry William
McFarland, Roland C
McFarlin, Emma Daniels
McGehee, Maurice Edward
McGlover, Stephen Ledell
McIntosh, Walter Cordell
McKay, Patti Jo
McKinney, Jacob K.
McKnight, Brian
McNeal, Timothy Kyle
Mendes, Dr. Helen Althia
Mills, Doreen C
Mitchal, Saundra Marie
Mitchell-Kernan, Dr. Claudia Irene
Moore, Gwen
Moore, Shemar F.
Morgan, Debbi
Morgan, Meli'sa
Morgan, Stacey Evans
Morris, Greg
Morrow, Dion Griffith
Morton, Joe
Morton, Marilyn M
Moss, Winston
Muse, J Melvin
Nelson, Dr. H. Viscount
Nelson, Tanyka Shinell
Newcombe, Don
Nichols, Crystal Faye
Oliver, Pam
Orduna, Dr. Kenneth Maurice
Orticke, Leslie Ann
Osborne, Dr. Alfred E., Jr.
Outterbridge, John Wilfred
Owens, Curtis
Page, Murriel
Parker, Kai J
Parker, William Hayes, Jr.
Parks, Bernard C.
Parnell, Arnold W
Payton, Nolan H
Perez, Altagracia
Perry, Jean B.
Peters, Charles L, Jr.
Pharris, Chrystee
Phillips, Frank Edward
Pierce, Ponchitta A
Pinkney, Dove Savage
Pitcher, Capt. Frederick M A
Pittman, Marvin B.
Pitts, Gregory Philip
Polk, Don
Portee, Rev. Dr. Frank
Porter, Gloria Jean
Powe, Joseph S.
Pratt, Kyla Alissa
Preston, Dr. Michael B
Preston-Williams, Rodena
Purvis, Archie C.
Ramsey, David P.
Reed-Humes, Robi
Ribeiro, Alfonso
Richardson, Salli
Ridley-Thomas, Mark
Roberts, Angela Dorrean
Roberts, Dr. Terrence James
Robinson, Carl Cornell
Robinson, Dawn
Robinson, Rev. Fisher J
Rodman, John
Ross, Dr. Anthony Roger
Ross, Tracee Ellis
Rowell, Victoria Lynn
Ryan, Roz
Saint James, Synthia
Salley, John Thomas
Sanders, Joseph Stanley
Sanders, Melba T.
Sanford, Isabel G.
Savage, Dr. Edward W, Jr.
Savage, Janet Marie
Scott, Larry B.
Segar, Leslie
Shaw, Dr. Ann
Shepherd-Tarpley, Sherri
Shields, Dr. Clarence L
Shifflett, Lynne Carol
Shook, Patricia Louise
Shropshire, Thomas B.

Sinclair, Benito A
Singleton, Harold, III
Singleton, Robert
Smiley, Tavis
Smith, Ernest Howard
Smith, Kellita
Smothers, Ronald
Snead, Dr. Willie T, Sr.
Solomon, Barbara J.
Stafford-Odom, Trisha
Steptoe, Sonja
Stevens, Thomas Lorenzo, Jr.
Stewart, Horace W.
Streeter, Elwood James
Strother, Germaine D
Swinger, Hershel Kendell
Tate, Larenz
Taylor, Dr. Christopher Lenard
Taylor, Eric Charles
Taylor, Gerren
Taylor, Meshach
Taylor, Robert Derek
Teasley, Larkin
Tero, Lawrence
Terry, Adeline Helen
Thomason, Marsha
Tisdale, Wayman Lawrence
Tobin, Lauren
Toliver, Harold Eugene, Jr.
Torres, Gina
Toussaint, Lorraine
Tripplett, Larry
Tucker, Christopher
Tucker, Dr. M Belinda
Turman, Glynn
Turner-Givens, Ella Mae
Tweed, Andre R.
Union, Gabrielle M
Varner, Robert Lee, Sr.
Vaughn, Countess Danielle
Veals, Craig Elliott
VelJohnson, Reginald
Walker, Arman Kennis
Walker, Grover Pulliam
Ward, Lenwood E
Washington, Carl
Watkins, Ted
Watts, Patricia L
Wesson, Herman Jason, Jr.
Whitaker, William Thomas
White, Dr. Don Lee
Wiley, Maurice
Williams, Aaron
Williams, Bart H
Williams, David W.
Williams, Deniece
Williams, Gary C.
Williams, Hal
Williams, Harold Louis
Williams, Dr. Harriette F.
Williams, Dr. Herbert Lee
Williams, Joanne Louise
Williams, Malinda
Wilson, Dr. Charles Z., Jr.
Wilson, Donald K, Jr.
Wilson, Jaci Laverne
Wilson, Phill
Windham, Rhonda
Winston, Hattie
Woodard, Alfre
Woods, Arleigh Maddox
Woods, Hortense E.
Woodson, Aileen R
Woods-Wright, Tomica
Wright, Crystal Andrea
Wright, Tanya
Wyatt, Lance Everett, M.D.
Yarborough, Richard A
Young, William Allen
Zulu, Itibari M

Los Angelese
Johnson, Buena

Lynwood
Battle, Joe Turner
Buckhalter, Emerson R.
Paxton, Phyllis Ann
Savage, Dr. Edward W, Jr.
Sims, Dr. Edward Hackney

Manhattan Beach
Coleman, Dr. Sinclair B
Leal, Sharon

Marina Del Rey
Brown, Dr. Leroy Thomas
Glasco, Dr. Anita L.
Stetson, Jeffrey P

Martinez
Zelis, Karen Dee

Maywood
Richardson, Jerome

Menlo Park
Powell, Gen. Colin Luther
White, Billy Ray

Milpitas
Lewis, Anthony Harold, Jr.

Mira Loma
Prior, Anthony

Modesto
Snyder, George W

Moffett Field
Shawnee, Laura Ann

Monrovia
Smith, Bob
Watkins, Price I.

Montebello
Potter, Jamie

Moraga
Dawson Boyd, Dr. Candy

Moreno Valley
Bibbs, Charles

Mountain View
Drummond, David C.
Greene, Frank S

Mt Baldy
Walton, Dr. Edward D.

N Hollywood
Saadiq, Raphael

Napa
Swann, Eugene Merwyn
Weddington, Bill
Widener, Warren Hamilton

National City
Chapman, Dr. William Talbert

Newark
McSwain, Berah D

Newbury Park
Bland, Dr. Robert Arthur

Newport Beach
Oliver, Donald Byrd

Norco
Davis, Dr. Brenda Lightsey-Hendricks

North Hollywood
Sharp, Saundra

Northridge
Burke, Solomon
Daniels, Dr. Jean E.
Obinna, Dr. Eleazu S.
Ratcliffe, Alfonso F
Teruel, Lauren
Thomas, Nathaniel
Wilson, Dr. Blenda Jacqueline
Wright, Albert Walter, Jr.

Novato
King, William Frank
Nelson, Eileen F

Oakland
Adams, Stephan
Alexander, Rev. Cedric V
Allen, Carol Ward
Allen, Carole Geneva Ward
Armstrong, Saundra Brown
Ayers-Johnson, Darlene
Bailey, Didi Giselle, MD
Baker-Kelly, Dr. Beverly
Baranco, Gordon S.
Baskette, Ernest E., Jr.
Bennett, Patricia A.
Benton, Calvin B.

Berkley, Thomas Lucius
Blakely, Dr. Edward James
Brandford, Napoleon
Broach, S. Elizabeth Johnson
Brooks, Joseph
Broussard, Cheryl Denise
Brown, Fannie E. Garrett
Browne, Lee F.
Carter, Geoffrey Norton
Cartwright, Joan S.
Casper, Banjo
Cherry, Lee Otis
Clark, Claude Lockhart
Coaston, Shirley Ann Dumas
Cooper, Josephine H.
Davis, Cal Deleanor
Davis, Harold
Donaville, Vanessa
Easter, Wilfred Otis, Jr.
Fagbayi, Mutiu Olutoyin
Ford, Judith Donna
Ford, Dr. Marcella Woods
Freeman, Kenneth Donald
Gardner, Henry L.
Gilliam, Dorothy Butler
Gilmore, Carter C
Godbold, Donald Horace
Goodman, Harold
Grigsby, Jefferson Eugene, III
Guyton, Booker T.
Hall, Stanley H.
Hamilton, Wilbur Wyatt
Handy, John Richard
Harbin-Forte, Brenda F
Hargrave, Benjamin
Harkless-Webb, Mildred
Hawkins, Walter
Head, Dr. Laura Dean
Hebert, Stanley Paul
Herzfeld, Will Lawrence
Hewlett, Antoinette Payne
Hill, James H
Hopper, Dr. Cornelius Lenard
Jackson, Mabel I.
James, Frederick John
James, Gillette Oriel
Jensen, Marcus Christian
Johnson, Gene C.
Johnson, Walter Louis, Sr.
Johnson, Wayne J
Jones, Clara Stanton
Jones, Victoria Gene
Jones, Dr. Vida Yvonne
Joseph-McIntyre, Mary
Kitchen, Wayne Leroy
Lacy, Donald E., Jr.
Laird, Alan
League, Cheryl Perry
Lee, Barbara Jean
Lelaind, Detra Lynette
LeNoir, Michael A
Lewis, Diane
Lott, Juanita
Mann, Marcus Lashaun
Matthews, Rev. James Vernon, II
McGathon, Carrie M
McGhee, Walter Brownie
McMorris, Samuel Carter
Metoyer, Carl B.
Millner, Dianne Maxine
Mitchell, Charles, Jr.
Moore, Howard, Jr.
Moore, Jane Bond
Morgan, Michael
Morris, Dr. Frank Lorenzo, Sr.
Owes, Ray
Patterson, Charles Jerry
Patterson, William Benjamin
Pendergrass, Emma H
Reaves, E. Fredericka M
Reed, Dr. Rodney J
Richard, James L.
Sample, Herbert Allan
Seidenberg, Mark
Shaw, Melvin B
Smith, William Xavier
Spears, Stephanie
Staggers, Frank Eugene
Steele, Percy H., Jr.
Sterling, H. Dwight, Sr.
Sweet, Clifford C
Sylvester, Odell Howard, Jr.
Tanner, Craig
Taylor, Marie de Porres
Taylor, Martha
Taylor, Michael
Taylor, Dr. Scott Morris
Taylor, William Glenn
Thomas, Ron

Thomason, William, III
Watkins, Rosyln
Watson, Carole M.
Webber, Chris
Webster, William H
White, Donald R.
Williams, Barry Lawson
Williams, Benjamin Vernon
Williams, Carol H
Wray, Wendell Leonard
Wright, Soraya M
Wyatt, S Martin, III

Occidental
Snyder, George W

Oceanside
Hoye, Walter B., II

Ojai
Evans, Ernest

Orange
Agwunobi, Andrew C.
Caines, Ken
Moore, Evan Gregory
Ross, Ruthie M.
West, Dr. John Raymond

Orinda
Stokes, Carolyn Ashe
Swann, Eugene Merwyn

Oxnard
Pinkard, Bedford L

Pacific Palisades
Wilson, Dr. Charles Z., Jr.

Pacoima
Marshall, William Horace
McCraven, Carl Clarke

Palm Desert
Brown, William McKinley, Jr.
Nicholas, Brenda L.
Nicholas, Philip
Wade-Maltais, Dr. Joyce

Palm Springs
Beaver, Joseph T, Jr.

Palmdale
Ezozo, Agrippa O.

Palo Alto
Cadet, Ron
Fleming, June H.
Goss-Seeger, Debra A
Smith, Dr. Roulette William

Palto Alto
Green, Frank

Panorama City
Cargill, Sandra Morris
Howard, Wardell Mack

Pasadena
Alexander, James Eduard
Branch, Rochelle
Christian, William Leonard
Clark, Mario Sean
Crayton, Dr. James Edward
Gooden, Winston Earl
Hampton, Opal Jewell
Johnson, Charles Beverly
King, Dr. James, Jr.
Knight, Lynnon Jacob
Lesure, James
McKenna, Dr. George J.
Miller, Rev. Anthony Glenn
Pannell, William E
Reid, Joel Otto
Scott, Benjamin
Tunstel, Edward
Valentine, Diann
Wheaton, Frank Kahlil
Williams, Frank James
Wilson, Frank Edward
Woodard, Lois Marie
Yarbrough, Delano

Paso Robles
London, Eddie

Petaluma
Parks, Suzan-Lori

Piedmont
Martin, Hosea L

Pittsburg
Doss, LaRoy Samuel
Harrold, Lawrence A

Pollock Pines
Dunston, Shawon Donnell

Pomona
Walton, Dr. Edward D.
Wilson, Prof. Stanley Charles

Port Hueneme
Walker, Russell Dewitt

Poway
Templeton, Garry Lewis

Rancho Cordova
Gaines, Robert
Stone, Aubry L

Rancho Murieta
Embree, James Arlington, Jr.

Rancho Palos Verdes
White, Charles R.

Red Bluff
Price, Phillip G

Redding
Taylor, Arthur Duane

Redondo Beach
Fortune-Maginley, Lois J.

Redwood City
Brown, Reuben D
Goldsberry, Ronald Eugene
Hamilton, Dean
Winters, Kenneth E.

Redwood Shores
Archambeau, Shellye L.
Phillips, Charles E, Jr.

Represa
Fonville, Danny D

Richmond
Barnes, Matthew Molena
Bates, Nathaniel Rubin
Carroll, George D
Cash, Bettye Joyce
Cooper, Drucilla Hawkins
Jerkins, Jerry Gaines
Nelson, Ronald J
Tramiel, Kenneth Ray, Sr.
Watkins, Ira Donnell

Riverside
Anderson, Kathleen Wiley
Carson, Lois Montgomery
Curtis, James
Durant, Celeste Millicent
Hawkins-Russell, Hazel M.
Jackson, Dr. Ruth Moore
Sanders, Glenn Carlos
Teer, Wardene
Williams, Dr. Leona Clarice
Wooding, David Joshua

Rocklin
Bolton-Holifield, Ruthie

Rohnert Park
Webster, Niambi Dyanne

Roseville
Sherman, Thomas Oscar, Jr.

Sacramento
Abdelnaby, Alaa
Abdur-Rahim, Shareef
Adair, Gwen
Ambers, Monique
Banks, Loubertha May
Bannerman-Richter, Gabriel
Bond, James G.
Brooks, Suzanne R.

Brown, Leroy Bradford
Burrell, Garland, Jr.
Chappell, Ruth Rax
Clark, Dr. Fred Allen
Cooper, Joseph
Covin, Dr. David L.
Cullers, Samuel James
Davison, James, Jr.
Denmark, Robert Richard
Dodd, James C.
Farrell, Robert C.
Foster, Raunell H.
Fulgham, Roietta Goodwin
Gamble, Kevin Douglas
Garrett, Cain, Jr.
Goodrich, Linda S
Gorman, Bertha Gaffney
Gothard, Barbara Wheatley
Grayer, Jeffrey
Griffin, Ples Andrew
Harris, Arthur L
Hollis, Mary Lee
Hurdle, Hortense O McNeil
Jackson, Bobby
Jackson, Fred James, Sr.
Johnson, Raymond L
Jones, Asbury Paul
Kennedy, Callas Faye
Lawrence, Paul Frederic
Lawson, Herman A.
Lee, William H
Lever, Lafayette
Long, James L.
McGee, Adolphus Stewart
Millner, Dianne Maxine
Moore, Jellether Marie
Netters, Tyrone Homer
Nicholas, Gwendolyn Smith
Nowlin, Bettye J Isom
Peters, Kenneth Darryl
Pile, Michael David McKenzie
Pogue, Lester Clarence
Ramey, Felicenne H
Ransom, Gary Elliott
Raye, Vance Wallace
Riggins, Lester
Robinson, Carol Evonne
Robinson, Robert Love, Jr.
Ross, Adrian
Scott, Dr. Otis L
Scott, Windie Olivia
Shaw, Ferdinand
Simmons, Joseph
Simmons, Lionel J.
Smith, Heman Bernard
Somerville, Dr. Addison Wimbs
Tate, Lenore Artie
Theus, Reggie Wayne
Thompson, LaSalle, III
Vincent, Edward
Washington, Josie B.
Wayne, George Howard, Sr.

Sacramento,
Potter, Myrtle Stephens

Sacramento
Canson, Fannie Joanna

Salinas
Holt, Fred D

San Anselmo
Simmons, Stephen Lloyd

San Bernardino
Ervin, Kathryn
Frazier, Dan E., Sr.
Henry, Dr. Mildred M Dalton
Hobbs, John Daniel
Levister, Dr. Ernest Clayton
Martin, Prof. Carolyn Ann
McKinney, Rev. Jesse Doyle
Shelton, Jewell Vennerrie (Elvoid)

San Bruno
Bell, Sandra Watson

San Clemente
Hysaw, Guillermo Lark

San Diego
Alexander, Dr. Edward Cleve
Ard, Rev. Robert
Bailey, Eugene Ridgeway
Banks, Ellen
Bartley, Talmadge O.
Bennett, Michael

Brooks, Sidney Joseph
Bush, Lewis Fitzgerald
Carroll, Dr. Constance Marie
Chambers, Christopher J.
Coleman, Kenneth L.
Cornwell, Dr. JoAnne
Davis, Wendell
Dowd, Maria Denise
Evans, Vernon D.
Floyd, Cliff, Jr.
Fontenot-Jamerson, Berlinda
Forde, James Albert
Gordon, Winfield James, Sr.
Green, Ruth A.
Gwynn, Tony
Hales, Edward Everette
Harris, Arthur L
Hayes, Dr. Floyd Windom
Heineback, Barbara Taylor
Holmes, Richard Bernard
Hoston, Germaine A.
Hoye, Walter B.
Johnson, William E.
Joiner, Charles
Jones, Bernie
Jones, Napoleon A, Jr.
Lawrence, Elliott
Lloyd, Marcea Bland
Malone, Dr. Cleo
Matthews, Dr. Merritt Stewart
Matthews, Robert L.
McKinney, George Dallas
McQuater, Patricia A
Montgomery, Catherine Lewis
Morris, Major
Oyeshiku, Dr. Patricia Delores Worthy
Pinnock, Theodore A.
Powell, Richard Maurice
Riggs, Hon. Elizabeth A
Rollins, Lee Owen
Russell, Wesley L.
Smith, George Walker
Turner, Eric Scott
Washington, Todd Page
Wayne, Justine Washington
Weber, Dr. Shirley Nash
Williams, Cheryl L
Williams, Jamal
Williams, Dr. Lisa R.
Williams, Dr. Matthew Albert
Winfield, David Mark
Woodford, Hackley Elbridge
Younger, Paul Lawrence

San Fernando
Crouch, Andrae Edward

San Francisco
Adams, Eula L.
Ambeau, Karen M
Baker-Kelly, Dr. Beverly
Baltimore, Roslyn Lois
Belle, Charles E
Block, Carolyn B.
Booth, Anna Maria
Bostic, Harris, II
Boyd, Rev. J. Edgar
Brown, Dr. Amos Cleophilus
Brown, Bernice Baynes
Brown, Reuben D
Bryant, Anthony
Burks, Ellis Rena
Butler, Frederick Douglas
Cannon, H. LeRoy
Cannon, Tyrone Heath
Canson, Virna M.
Clark, Ralph H
Cobbs, Dr. Price Mashaw
Cochran, Todd S.
Coleman, Arthur H.
Collins, Charles Miller
Crisp, Sydney A.
Darke, Dr. Charles B
Davis, Belva
Davis, Morris E
Dearman, John Edward
Debas, Dr. Haile T.
Dewey, George
Evans, Cheryl Lynn
Evans, Patricia E.
Flowers, Dr. Loma Kaye
Ford, Nathaniel P
Gainer, Prof. John F
Gillette, Frankie Jacobs
Gomez, Jewelle L
Graves, Clifford Wayne
Guillory, Keven
Handy, John Richard

Hare, Julia Reed
Hare, Dr. Nathan
Harkless-Webb, Mildred
Head, Dr. Laura Dean
Henderson, Thelton Eugene
Hernandez, Aileen Clarke
Hewlett, Everett Augustus, Jr.
Hill, Patricia Liggins
Hooker, John Lee
Houston, Seawadon L
Jackson, Mattie J
Jackson, Oscar Jerome
Jeffers, Clifton R.
Johnson, Vaneese
Jones, Woodrow Harold
Jordan, Frederick E.
Kaslofsky, Thor
King, Alonzo B
King, Reginald F.
King, Dr. Talmadge Everett
Lane, John Henry
Marshall, Joseph Earl, Jr.
Marshall, Timothy H.
Mays, willie howard
McGhee, James Leon
McKinney-Johnson, Eloise
McKinnon, Darlene Lorraine
Medearis, Victor L
Minor, Jessica
Moore, Kevin
Morris, Effie Lee
Morris, Gertrude Elaine
Packer, ZZ
Pierce, William Dallas
Pogue, Brent Daryl
Richards, Johnetta Gladys
Robinson, Johnathan Prather
Rodgers, Barbara Lorraine
Saunders, Raymond
Scott, Timothy Van
Sewell, Edward C
Shepherd, Berisford
Simmons, Thelma M
Smith, Frederick D.
Smith, Robert Charles
Spears, Stephanie
Staples, Robert E.
Sweet, Lolita
Tatum, Carol Evora
Thomas, Marla Renee
Thurmond, Nate
Tipton, Dr. Dale Leo
Toler, Burl Abron
Tucker, Dr. Dorothy M.
Vaughns, Cleopatra
Walker, Ian Robin
Walker, Lisa
Walker, Phillip E.
Wallace, Arthur, Jr.
Ward, Doris Margaret
West, Dr. Gerald Ivan
Westbrook, Elouise
Williams, Rev. A Cecil
Williams, Barry Lawson
Wims, Warner Barry
Winn, Carol Denise
Winters, Kenneth E.
Yarbrough, Patricia Nicholson
Young, Alene Marie (Penny)
Young, Aner Ruth

San Franciso
Clay, Reuben Anderson, Jr.

San Gabriel
Sprewell, Latrell

San Jose
Beasley, Ulysses Christian, Jr.
Byrd, Dr. Marquita L.
Carr, Percy L.
DeLeon, Priscilla
Gordon, Dr. Joseph G
Grier, Mike
Harris, Anthony
Harris, Jay Terrence
Hyatt, Herman Wilbert, Sr.
Lacy, Aundrea
Martin, Edward Anthony
Nichols, Roy Calvin
Peters, Robert
Pichon, Rise Jones
Stuart, Reginald A
Stubblefield, Dana William

Terrell, Richard Warren
Walker, Dr. Ethel Pitts

San Juan Capistrano
Dixon, Raymond

San Leandro
Shedd, Kenny

San Luis Obispo
Whalum, Kirk

San Marcos
Blanks, Cecelia

San Mateo
Carson, Emmett D.

San Pablo
Daniels, Patricia Ann
Dawson Boyd, Dr. Candy
Wilson, Dr. Sodonia Mae

San Pedro
Brown, Gilbert David, III
Thomas, Matthew Manjusri, Jr.

San Rafael
Henry, Dr. Joseph Louis
Walden, Narada Michael

San Ramon
Wilkins, Rayford, Jr.

Santa Ana
Johnson, Theodore A.
Rhodes, Bessie M. L.
Thompson, Art

Santa Barbara
McMillan, Horace James
Oliver, Dr. Melvin L
Penn, Dr. Nolan E
Willingham, Gloria J.

Santa Clara
Barker, Roy
Hanks, Merton Edward
Harris, Walter Lee
Kirby, Terry Gayle
Price, Daryl
Shavers, Cheryl L.
Spikes, Takeo Gerard
Terrell, Richard Warren
Wilkins, Janice F
Williams, James Edward

Santa Clarita
Dash, Stacey Lauretta

Santa Cruz
Anthony, Dr. David Henry
Davis, Angela Yvonne
Hull, Akasha Gloria
Mayhew, Richard
Powell, Sis Paula Livers

Santa Monica
Arterbery, Vivian J.
Barnes, Stephen Darryl
Bryant, Joy
Fifty Cent
Jeffers, Eve
Jones, Richard Timothy
Jones, William Allen
Kweli, Talib
Lynn, Lonnie Rashid
Oliver, Bilal Sayeed
Porter, Arthur L.
Reddick, Lance
Slaughter, Atty. Fred L.
Smith, Howlett P.
Soulchild, Musiq
Thomas, Matthew Manjusri, Jr.
White, Maurice
Wilson, Charlie
Wright, N'Bushe

Santa Rosa
Mims, Robert Bradford
Troutt, Harry

Santa Ynez
Jackson, Michael Joseph

Sausalito
Times, Betty J.

Seaside
Carey, Pearl M.
Johnson, Prof. Stephanie Anne
Watson, Annie Mae

Sepulveda
Canty, Miriam Monroe

Sherman Oaks
Barber, Ornetta M
Blanks, Billy
Carroll, Diahann
Douglas, Suzzanne
Harvey, Steve
Jones, Samuel L., III
Lewis, Dawnn
Miller, Tangi
Snoop Dogg, U
Van Johnson, Rodney

Sierra Madre
Rush, Otis

Signal Hill
Templeton, Garry Lewis

Simi Valley
Anderson, Ronald Edward, Sr.
Arties, Walter Eugene, III

Solvang
Rideau, Iris

South Gate
Lara, Edison R, Sr.

South Lake Tahoe
Banner, Melvin Edward

South San Francisco
Churchwell, Caesar Alfred
Seymour, Cynthia Maria
Tipton, Dr. Dale Leo
Woolley, Phyllis

Stanford
Berry, Fredrick Joseph
Bond, Dr. Lloyd
Cordell, LaDoris Hazzard
Dawkins, Johnny Earl, Jr.
Ellington, Brenda Andrea
Gould, Prof. William Benjamin
Harris, Prof. Donald J
Rice, Dr. Condoleezza
Sowell, Thomas
Steele, Dr. Claude Mason
Steele, Dr. Shelby

Stockton
Hunt, Charles Amoes
Lorthridge, Dr. James E.
Merriweather, Michael Lamar
Nabors, Jesse Lee
Peters, Kenneth Darryl
Robinson, Robert Love, Jr.
White, Ralph

Studio City
Edwards, Ella Raino
Howard, Sherri
Isley, Ernie
Jennings, Dominique
Jones, Donna L.
Khali, Simbi
Knight-Pulliam, Keshia
Vinson, Chuck Rallen
Wilson, Gerald Stanley

Sunnyvale
Brooks, Gilbert
Dines, Steve
Greene, Frank S
Sherman, Thomas Oscar, Jr.
Smirni, Allan Desmond
Sutton, Mary A.

Sylmar
Baker, Althea
Brown, Reginald DeWayne

Tarzana
Imes, Mo'Nique

Templeton
Osibin, Willard S.

Thousand Oaks
Govan, Ronald M.
Reason, J Paul
Williams, Gregory M

Toluca Lake
Elder, Larry
Keymah, Crystal T

Torrance
Bryant-Howroyd, Janice
Davidson, Fletcher Vernon, Jr.
Grigsby, Alice Burns
Houze, Jeneice Carmel Wong
Howroyd, Janice Bryant
Hurd, Dr. James L P
Thompson, Sandra Ann
Willis, Cecil B.

Tracy
Dewberry-Williams, Madelina Denise
Lott, Ronald M
Powell, Charles Arthur
Waiters, Lloyd Winferd, Jr.

Turlock
Davenport, Calvin A.

Universal City
Ballard, Shareese Renee
Carroll, Rocky
Joseph, Lloyd Leroi
Miller, Lori E.
Peters, Charles L, Jr.
the Entertainer, Cedric

Upland
Jordan, Charles Wesley

Vacaville
Slade, Dr. John Benjamin

Valencia
Tyson, Andre

Vallejo
Brown, Lewis Frank
Brown, Robert Cephas, Sr.
Ealey, Mark E
Hicks, Foster
Johnson, Stafford Quincy
McGowan, Thomas Randolph
Watts, John E.

Van Nuys
Nicholas, Brenda L.

Vandenberg AFB
Rogers, Charles Leonard

Venice
Hines, Gregory Oliver
Yarbro, William E., Jr.

Venice Beach
Alston, Kwaku

Ventura
Pinkard, Bedford L

Visalia
Gillette, Dr. Lyra Stephanie

Walnut Creek
Bristow, Dr. Lonnie Robert
Curtis-Bauer, M Benay
McCovey, Willie Lee

West Covina
Harrison, Boyd G, Jr.

West Hills
Hyde, Dr. Maxine Deborrah

West Hollywood
Barnes, Ernie, Jr.
David, Keith
Houston, Cissy
Hubert, Janet Louise
Nunez, Miguel A
Simone, Nina
Stokes, Chris

Westlake Village
Graham, Odell

Whittier
Eaton, Thelma Lucile
Haynes, Ora Lee

Morris, Prof. Clifton
Peters, Samuel A.
Porter, Dr. Shikana Temille

Woodland Hills
Beasley, Arlene A
Jones, Gregory Allan
Nichols, Nichelle
Wayans, Shawn

Yorba Linda
Knight, Lynnon Jacob

illunois
Hill, Dr. Ray Allen

COLORADO

Aurora
Clark, Dr. Morris Shandell
Davis, Anthony R.
Hollins, Leroy
Love, James Ralph
Reed, Wilbur R
Taylor, Prof. Paul David

Boulder
Bailey, Sharon Brown
Bauduit, Harold S
Ellis, Clarence A
Flowers, William Harold, Jr.
Love, Dr. Eric
Nilon, Charles Hampton
Person, Waverly J.
Washington, Dr. Warren Morton

Broomfield
Auguste, Donna M.
Lowman, Carl D
Taylor, Dr. Kenneth Doyle

Colorado Springs
Armstrong Busby, Delia Bliss
Ashford, Evelyn
Bowen, Dr. Clotilde Dent
Bradshaw, Gerald Haywood
Clair, Areatha G.
Conway, Wallace Xavier, Sr.
Cottingham, Robert T., Jr.
Exum, Wade F
Flowers, Vonetta
Freeman, Kerlin
Guy, Mildred Dorothy
Hendrix, Deborah Lynne
Jackson, Kevin
James, Wynona Yvonne
Jones, Randy
Nengudi, Senga
Peterson, Lloyd
Rison, Dr. Faye
Shipp, Pamela Louise
Wilson, Deborah

Denver
Allen, Ty W
Ashby, Lucius Antone
Augmon, Stacey Orlando
Barefield, Ollie Delores
Bembry, Lawrence
Bolden, Charles E.
Boswell, Anthony O
Brewer, Gregory Alan
Bruton, Bertram A
Bryant, Russell Philip
Buckley, Victoria
Camby, Marcus D
Chambers, Olivia Marie
Cornell, Bob
Daniel, Wiley Young
Dantley, Adrian Delano
Deloach, Wendelin W.
Diallo
Easter, William H, III
Egins, Paul Carter
Gardner, Ava Maria
Garner, Velvia M
Gibson, Robert
Gill, Samuel A.
Glenn, Cecil E.
Greer, Dr. Robert O, Jr.
Groff, Peter Charles
Groff, Regina Coleen
Groff, Regis F.
Grove, Daniel
Hancock, Michael B
Harris, Freeman Cosmo

Harris-Diaw, Rosalind Juanita
Hickman, Thomas Carlyle
Hill, Glenallen
Holliman, David L
Hollins, Leroy
Holmes, Dr. Barbara J.
Iverson, Allen
Jackson, Franklin D. B.
Jackson, Gary Monroe
Jackson, Robert, Jr.
Johnson, Collis, Jr.
Jones, Raymond Dean
Jordan, Hon. Claudia J.
Lee, Tamela Jean
Lee-Eddie, Deborah
Love, Carolyn Diane
Lyle, Ron
Moland, Willie C.
Moore, Lewis Calvin
Mosley, Edna Wilson
Naves, Larry J
Person, Waverly J.
Phillips, Rev. Acen L.
Phillips, Dr. Earl W
Pippen, Scottie
Rabouin, E Michelle
Rhodes, Dr. Paula R
Rison, Dr. Faye
Robinson, Cleo Parker
Rollins, Ethel Eugenia
Rucker, Clyde
Sigur, Wanda Anne Alexander
Simpson, Diane Jeannette
Smith, William French
Stewart, Paul Wilbur
Strudwick, Lindsey H, Sr.
Tanner, Gloria Travis
Tappan, Dr. Major William
Tate, Valencia Faye
Taylor, Prof. Paul David
Terrell, David
Thomas, Robert Lee, IV
Walker, Dr. Gregory T S
Washington, Dr. Warren Morton
Webb, Joseph G
Webb, Wellington E.
Yohannes, Daniel W

Eaglewood
Conway, Curtis LaMont

Englewood
Bly, Dre'
Bradford, Ronnie
Burns, Keith Bernard
Burrows, Chelsye J
Geathers, Jumpy
Hebron, Vaughn Harlen
McGill, Lenny
McKyer, Timothy Bernard
Phifer, Roman Zubinsky
Robertson, Dewayne

Evergreen
Davis, Charles A

Fort Collins
Booker, Karen
Hiatt, Dana Sims

Golden
Brewer, Moses
Morgan-Smith, Sylvia
Oliver, Everett Ahmad

Greeley
George, Hermon, Jr.

Greenwood Village
Menogan, Annita M
Tate, Valencia Faye

Highlands Ranch
Kaiser, James Gordon

Littleton
Bell, Theron J.
Brown, Chad Everett

Lone Tree
Gary, Tim

Morrison
Griffith, Gary Alan

Parker
Lewis, Carl
Smith, Cedric Delon

Pueblo
Abebe, Teshome
Norwood, Dr. Tom

Onyejekwe, Dr. Chike Onyekachi
Poole, James F.
Wells, Dr. Elmer Eugene

Westminster
Daniels, Terry L
Langford, Jevon

CONNECTICUT

Ansonia
Smoot, Albertha Pearl

Bloomfield
Cassis, Glenn Albert
Coleman, Eric Dean
Craig, Brenda
Haye, Clifford S
Howard, Milton L.
Long, Jerry Wayne
Shaw, Dr. Spencer Gilbert
Willingham, James Edward
Wood, Margaret Beatrice

Branford
Brown, Derek Vernon

Bridgeport
Bellinger, George M.
Fewell, Richard
Harris, Jeanette
Hunter, Patrick J., Sr.
Morton, Margaret E.
Prestwidge-Bellinger, Barbara Elizabeth
Spear, E. Eugene

Bristol
Davis, Hubert Ira
Hasty, James Edward
Jackson, Tom
Johnson, Keyshawn
Mashburn, Jamal
Morgan, Joe
Peck, Carolyn
Scott, Stuart
Stewart, Bernard
Woodson, Darren Ray
Young, Eric Orlando

Brookfield
Gellineau, Victor Marcel

Brookfield Center
Stewart, Albert C.

Cheshire
Crawford, David
Ferguson, Shellie Alvin

Danbury
Furman, James B.
Rountree, Ella Jackson
Torian, Edward Torrence

East Hampton
States, Robert Arthur

East Hartford
Jones, Larry Wayne
Lewis, Robert Alvin

Fairfield
Biassey, Dr. Earle Lambert
Braden, Stanton Connell
Mazon, Larri Wayne
Merchant, John F
Tucker, Michael Kevin

Farmington
Hodge, Cynthia Elois
Morse, Dr. Laurence C

Gales Ferry
Waterman, Thelma M.

Glastonbury
Edmonds, Norman Douglas

Greenwich
Brown, Nancy Cofield
Campbell, Rogers Edward, III
Cox, Jesse L
Kwaku-Dongo, Francois

Stancell, Dr. Arnold Francis
Wright, Dmitri

Hamden
Burrell, Scott David
Cherry, Edward Earl
Hallums, Benjamin F.
Highsmith, Carlton L.
Mazon, Larri Wayne
Pearce, Richard Allen
Potts, Harold E.

Hartford
Arnold, Rudolph P
Bennett, Collin B.
Bibby, Deirdre L.
Billington, Clyde, Jr.
Booker, Carl Granger, Sr.
Borges, Saundra Kee
Carter, Dr. David G.
Cave, Perstein Ronald
Coleman, Eric Dean
Dyson, William Riley
Fisher, Rubin Ivan
Hales, William Roy
Henderson, Carl L, Jr.
Hendon, Lea Alpha
Hickmon, Ned
Hill, E.C.
Hodges, Dale
Hogan, Dr. James Carroll
Hoyt, Bishop Thomas L
Iloani, Gwendolyn Smith
Johnson, Wayne Lee
Jones, Carolyn
Martin, Arnold Lee, Jr.
Martin, Ionis Bracy
McFarlin, Kernaa D'Offert, Jr.
McLean, Dollie Clarice H
Monroe, James H.
Rawlins, Sedrick John
Roland, Jannon
Scott, R Lee
Simmons, Prof. John Emmett
Smith, Diane L
Smith, Gwendolyn Iloani
Spurlock-Evans, Karla Jeanne
Stewart, John B., Jr.
Strong, Marilyn Terry
Tate, Deanna
Thompson, Dr. Winston Edna
Warren, Annika Laurin
Waters, Willie Anthony
Whaley, Charles H
White, Paul Edward
Whitsett, James A, Jr.
Willingham, James Edward
Woodland, Dr. Calvin Emmanuel

Hatford
Simmons, Prof. John Emmett

Lakeville
Jamal, Ahmad

Manchester
Freeman, Diane S.
Hodgson-Brooks, Gloria J

Mansfield
Molette, Barbara J.

Marlborough
States, Robert Arthur

Meriden
Gooley, Charles E.

Middlebury
Wood, R L

Middletown
Pemberton, Dr. Gayle R.

Milford
Alexander, Sidney H., Jr.

Mystic
Davis, Luther Charles

New Britain
Baskerville, Dr. Charles Alexander
Collins, Constance Renee Wilson
Fox, Paulette
Head, Dena
Jones, Charles
Jones, Tebucky

Parker, Henry Ellsworth
Robinson, John E
Savage, Dr. Archie Bernard, Jr.
Scott, R Lee
Springer, George Chelston
Stewart-Copes, Michele Lynn

New Haven
Barber, James W.
Blassingame, John W.
Carby, Hazel V.
Carter, Stephen L
Comer, Dr. James Pierpont
Costen, Dr. Melva Wilson
Daniels, John C.
Days, Drew Saunders
Garner, Charles
Griffith, Dr. Ezra E H
Holley, Dr. Sandra Cavanaugh
Ince, Harold S.
Jaynes, Dr. Gerald David
Jones, Emma Pettway
Jones, James F.
Jones, William
Patton, Dr. Curtis Leverne
Robinson, Ann Garrett
Robinson, Charles E
Rogers, Victor Alvin
Shearin, Kimberly Maria
Slie, Samuel N
Stepto, Robert Burns
Thompson, Dr. Robert Farris
Watley, Margaret Seay

New London
Brown, Erroll M.
Gillis, Shirley J Barfield
Hammond, Ulysses Bernard
Hendricks, Barkley L.
Jennings, Bennie Alfred
McKissick, Mabel F. Rice
Pope, McCoy S
Waller, Eunice McLean

North Haven
Griffith, Dr. Ezra E H
Hogan, Dr. James Carroll

Norwalk
Brown, Otha N
Fearing, John T.
Foster, Pearl D.
Self, Frank Wesley
Walker, Vernon David
Wilson, Earl, Jr.

Old Lyme
Peagler, Owen Fair

Old Saybrook
Baker, Vin

Rocky Hill
Maule, Albert R

Shelton
Williamson, Keith

South Norwalk
Brown, Otha N
Burgess, Robert E., Sr.

South Windsor
Lewis, Robert Alvin

Southport
Clarke, Kenton

Stamford
Alexander, Preston Paul
Bassett, Angela
Battles, Sheryl Y
Bilson, Carole
Borges, Lynne MacFarlane
Christophe, Cleveland A
Foreman, S Beatrice
Fullwood, Emerson U
Gipson, Hayward R., Jr.
Gudger, Robert Harvey
James, Juanita T.
Johnson, Dr. Charles Edward
Johnson, Donna Alligood
Jones, Thomas Wade
Miles, Albert Benjamin
Murray, J Ralph
Nixon, James I, Jr.
Nixon, Patricia A.

Norcisse, Robbie, E. B.
Rozier, Gilbert Donald
Simmons, Ron
Starks, John Levell

Storrs
Bagley, Dr. Peter B E
Cazenave, Dr. Noel Anthony
Molette, Dr. Carlton Woodard
Peters, Dr. James Sedalia, II
Spivey, Dr. Donald
Taylor, Dr. Ronald Lewis

Stratford
Cromwell, Margaret M.
Merchant, John F

Suffield
Lanier, Jesse M, Sr.

Torrington
Lyons, A Bates

Trumbull
Huff, Louis Andrew

Uncasville
Locke-Mattox, Bernadette

Vernon
Lane, Eleanor Tyson

Vernon-Rockville
Johnson, Arthur Lyman
Johnson, Dr. Marie Love

W Hartford
Payne, Cecilia

Waterbury
Glass, Robert Davis
Mosley, Maurice B.
Snead, Dr. David Lowell
Thomas, Nina M

Waterford
Kimmons, Carl Eugene

West Hartford
Martin, Ionis Bracy
McLean, Rene
Price, JoAnn H
Reid, Pamela Trotman

West Haven
Chapman, Samuel Otha, Jr.
Holmes, Willie A.
Slie, Samuel N

Weston
Lauderback, Brenda Joyce

Westport
Hamer, Dr. Judith Ann

Willimantic
Bagley, Dr. Peter B E
Peagler, Owen Fair

Wilton
Parker, George Anthony
Trueheart, William E.

Windham
Terry, Dr. Angela Owen

Windsor
Freeman, Walter Eugene
Smith, Diane L

Windsor Locks
Thaxton, Judy Evette

Woodbridge
Cherry, Edward Earl

DELAWARE

Camden-Wyoming
Vernon, Easton D

Dover
Bradberry, Dr. Richard Paul
Brockington, Eugene Alfonzo

Coleman, Rudolph W.
Cotton, Joseph Craig
DeLauder, Dr. William B.
Goudy, Dr. Andrew James
Hardcastle, James C.
Harris, Winifred Clarke
Jones, Geraldine J.
Lavan, Alton
Laws, Dr. Ruth M.
Royster, Dr. Vivian Hall
Wardlaw, McKinley, Jr.
Wright, George C.

Laurel
Selby, Cora Norwood

Middletown
Showell, Hazel Jarmon

Milford
Fountain, William Stanley

Milton
Batten, Rev. Grace Ruth

New Castle
Gilliam, James H., Sr.
Rudd, James M.

Newark
Jones, James McCoy
Muhammad, Kevin
Newton, Dr. James Elwood
Seams, Francine Swann
Whittaker, Terry McKinley

Ocean View
Selby, Cora Norwood

Rehoboth Beach
McMillian, Frank L.

Selbyville
Stamps, Herman Franklin

Smyrna
Whaley, Wayne Edward
Wright, George C.

Washington
Tanter, Raymond

Wilmington
Alford, Haile Lorraine
Benefield, Michael Maurice, Jr.
Bolden, Stephanie T
Brown, Atlanta Thomas
Brown, Rodney W
Cannon, Eugene Nathaniel
Carey, Claire Lamar
Carey, Harmon Roderick
Davis, Lisa R
Ford, Evern D.
Gilliam, James H., Sr.
Gilliam, James H., Jr.
Holloway, Herman M., Sr.
King-Poynter, Marva
Mack, Sylvia Jenkins
Martin, Joshua Wesley
Mitchell, Charles E
Mobley, Dr. Joan Thompson
Mobley, Stacey J
Mosley, Elwood A
Nix, Theophilus Richard
Nix, Theophilus Richard, Jr.
Peters, Dr. Rev. Pamela Joan
Revelle, Robert, Sr.
Roberts, Harlan William, III
Rowe, Sr. Christa F
Sanders, Dr. Gwendolyn W.
Savage, Dennis James
Sleet, Gregory M
Sudler, Peggy
Taylor, Vernon Anthony
Wiggins, Leslie
Winston, George B, III
Wright, Marilyn N

DISTRICT OF COLUMBIA

Graham, Michael Angelo

Georgetown
Montgomery, Evangeline Juliet

NW Washington
Gaines, Brenda J.

South Washington
Smith, Lafayette Kenneth

Washington
Abney, Robert
Abraham, Tajama
Adair, Alvis V.
Adams, Alice Omega
Adams, Russell Lee
Adams Peck, Dr. Dorothy
Addison, James David
Adeyiga, Dr. Olanrewaju Muniru
Agurs, Donald Steele
Alexander, Clifford L., Jr.
Alexander, Dr. Lenora Cole
Alexander, Marcellus Winston
Alexander, Richard C.
Alexander-Whiting, Harriett
Alfonso, Pedro
Alford, Harry C.
Alice, Miller
Allen, Bernestine
Allen, Stanley M.
Allen, Willie B.
Amos, Donald E
Ampy, Dr. Franklin R.
Anderson, Arnett Artis
Anderson, Carl Edwin
Anderson, David Turpeau
Anderson, Donald L.
Anderson, Mary Elizabeth
Anthony, Jeffrey Conrad
Archer, Dr. Juanita A.
Arnez, Dr. Nancy L.
Arnwine, Barbara
Attaway, John David
Augustine, Hilton H
Auld, Albert Michael
Ausbrooks, Beth Nelson
Awkard, Linda Nanline
Bailey, Robin
Bailey, William H.
Baker, Maxine B
Baker, Willie L., Jr.
Ballance, Frank Winston, Jr.
Ballentine, Krim Menelik
Banks, George S.
Banks, Priscilla Sneed
Banks, Sharon P
Banks, Dr. Tazewell
Banner, Dr. William Augustus
Barber, Jesse B., Jr.
Barbour, Julia Watson
Barnes, Dr. Boisey O
Barnes, Melody
Barrett, Andrew
Barrett, Matthew Anderson
Baskerville, Lezli
Bates, Clayton Wilson, Jr.
Bates, Karen Grigsby
Battle, Thomas Cornell
Beal, Lisa Suzanne
Beard, Dr. Lillian McLean
Beckham, Edgar Frederick
Bell, Greg
Bell, Sheila Trice
Bellamy, Everett
Bellamy, Werten F W
Belser, Jason Daks
Benjamin, Dr. Tritobia Hayes
Bennett, Bobby
Bennett, Joyce Annette
Bennett, Kanya A
Bennett, Maybelle Taylor
Bernard, Michelle Denise
Bernard, Nesta Hyacinth
Berryman, Matilene S.
Best, Glenn
Bickerstaff, Cyndi L
Bins, Milton
Bishop, David Rudolph
Bishop, Sanford D
Black, Charlie J.
Black, Daniel L., Jr.
Black, Frederick Harrison
Blount, Sherri N
Boghassian, Skunder
Bond, Julian
Bond, Vernon
Booker, Johnnie Brooks
Bowers, George D
Bowles, Howard Roosevelt
Boyce, Dr. John G.
Boyd, George Arthur
Boyer, Spencer H
Boykin, A. Wade, Jr.

Marshall, Thurgood
Martin, Dr. Bertha M
Martin, Charles Howard
Martin, Curtis Jerome
Martin, Wisdom T
Mason, Dr. Donna S.
Mason, Hilda Howland M.
Matthews, Claude Lankford, Jr.
Maultsby, Dorothy M., Esq.
Mauney, Donald Wallace, Jr.
Mayes, McKinley
Mazique, Frances Margurite
McAllister, Singleton Beryl
McCants, Coolidge N.
McCloud, Thomas Henry
McCray, Maceo E.
McDonald, Herbert G
McDougall, Gay J
McGee, James M
McGee, James Madison
McGlowan, Angela
McHenry, Donald F.
McHenry, Mary Williamson
McIntosh, Simeon Charles
McKenzie, Floretta D
McLaren, Douglas Earl
McLaughlin, David
McQueen, Anjetta
McWilliams, James D
Meeks, Gregory Weldon
Mehreteab, Ghebre-Selassie
Menkiti, Bo
Mickelbury, Penny
Miles, Carlotta G.
Miller, E. Ethelbert
Miller, George Carroll, Jr.
Miller, James Arthur
Miller, Dr. Jeanne-Marie Anderson
Miller, Lawrence Edward
Mims, Beverly Carol
Mims, Oscar Lugrie
Miner, William Gerard
Mitchell, Brian Keith
Mitchell, Melvin Lester
Mitchell-Rankin, Zinora M
Mitchem, Dr. Arnold Levy
Moffitt, William B
Mohr, Diane Louise
Molock, Guizelous O
Moore, Barbara Crockett
Moore, Jerry A, Jr.
Moore, Minyon
Moose, George Edward
Moragne, Lenora, Ph.D.
Morris, Archie, III
Morris, Marlene C.
Mosee, Jean C.
Moses, Alice J.
Mudiku, Mary Esther
Muhammad, Askia
Muldrow, James Christopher
Murray, James Hamilton
Mutcherson, James Albertus
Myers, Dr. Ernest Ray
Myers, Frances Althea
Nabors, Rob
Nalls, Patricia
Nash, Curtis
Nash, Henry Gary
Neely, Henry Mason
Neil, Earl Albert
Nelson, Charles J
Newman, Constance Berry
Newsome, Steven Cameron
Niles, Prof. Lyndrey Arnaud
Nimmons, Dr. Julius F., Jr.
Norrell-Thomas, Sondra
Northern, Robert A.
Norton, Eleanor Holmes
Nunn, Robinson S.
Oates, Wanda Anita
O'Bryant, Constance Taylor
Ottley, Neville
Overton, Spencer
Owens, Bishop Alfred A, Jr.
Owens, Brigman
Owens, Curtis
Owens, David Kenneth
Owens, Kelly D
Owens, Robert Leon, III
Oyewole, Dr. Saundra Herndon
Page, Clarence
Page, John Sheridan
Palmer, Edgar Bernard
Palmer, Ronald DeWayne
Parker, Averette Mhoon
Parker, Vernon B
Parker-Sawyers, Paula
Parrott-Fonseca, Joan

Paschall, Jimmie Walton
Patterson, Barbara Ann
Patterson, Elizabeth Hayes
Payne, Donald M.
Payton, Carolyn Robertson
Peacock, Nicole
Peery, Benjamin Franklin, Jr.
Peoples, Alice Leigh
Perkins, Tony
Perry, June Carter
Peterson, Audrey Clinton
Peterson, Sushila Jane-Clinton
Petty, Dr. Rachel Monteith
Phillips, Dr. Frederick Brian
Phillips, Ralph Leonard
Pickrum, Michael
Pierce, Reuben G.
Pinkett, Harold Thomas
Pointer, Dr. Richard H
Polk, Dr. Lorna Marie
Pollard, Alfonso McInham
Pollard, Dr. Alton Brooks, III
Pollard, Dr. William Lawrence
Pope, Henry
Pope, James M.
Porter-Esmailpour, Carol
Poussaint-Hudson, Dr. Ann Ashmore
Powell, Georgette Seabrooke
Powell, Dr. Myrtis H
Price, Hugh Bernard
Pride, John L.
Prigmore, Kathryn Tyler
Prince, Richard Everett
Purnell, Marshall E
Quander, Esq. Rohulamin
Quarles, Herbert DuBois
Queen, Evelyn E Crawford
Quinn, Diane C
Quinton, Barbara Ann
Racine, Karl A
Raines, Franklin D.
Randolph, Laura B
Rankin, Dr. Edward Anthony
Rankin, Dr. Marc E.
Rankin, Michael L
Rashad, Johari Mahasin
Ray, David Bruce
Reagon, Dr. Bernice Johnson
Rearden, Sara B
Reason, Rebecca L
Reed-Miller, Rosemary E
Reid, Dr. Leslie Bancroft
Reid, Ronda Eunese
Reinhardt, John Edward
Remy, Donald M
Reynolds, Charles McKinley, Jr.
Rhoden, Dr. Richard Allan
Ricanek, Carolyn Wright
Rice, David Eugene, Jr.
Rice, Lois Dickson
Rice, Susan E.
Richardson, Laura
Richardson, Leroy
Richardson, Robert Eugene
Richmond, Jacqueline
Richmond, Rodney Welch
Rier, John Paul, Jr.
Risher, John Robert, Jr.
Roach, Prof. Hildred Elizabeth
Roane, Dr. Philip Ransom
Robbins, Warren
Roberson, F Alexis H
Roberts, James E.
Roberts, Talmadge
Robinson, Aubrey Eugene, Jr.
Robinson, Eugene Harold
Robinson, Harry G
Robinson, Dr. Luther Dabney
Robinson, Sandra Hawkins
Rogers, Desiree
Rogers, Elijah Baby
Rogers, Judith W
Rogers, Michael Charles
Ross, Frank Kenneth
Roux, Dr. Vincent J
Rowan, Carl Thomas
Rush, Bobby
Russell, Ernest
Ryan-White, Jewell
Saint-Louis, Rudolph Anthony
Sampson, Dr. Calvin Coolidge
Sanders, Rober LaFayette
Sanders, Robin Renee
Sargent, Virginia Hightower
Saunders, Edward Howard
Saunders, John Edward
Saunders, William Joseph
Savage, Dr. James Edward

Scales, Dr. Manderline Elizabeth Willis
Scales, Dr. Patricia Bowles
Schenck, Frederick A
Scott, David
Scott, Dr. Donald LaVern
Scott, Dr. Elsie L
Scott, Dr. Helen Madison Marie Pawne Kinard
Scott, Dr. Kenneth Richard
Scott, Nigel L.
Scott, Roland B.
Scott-Clayton, Patricia Ann
Secundy, Marian Gray
Shackelford, Lottie Holt
Shakoor, Dr. Waheedah Aqueelah
Shell, Theodore A.
Shiver, Jube
Shoffner, James Priest
Shopshire, Dr. James Maynard
Shuman, Jerome
Silva, Omega C. Logan
Simmons, Belva Tereshia
Simmons, Joseph Jacob, III
Simms, Dr. Margaret Constance
Simpkins, William Joseph
Sindler, Michael H.
Singleton, Harry M
Slater, Rodney E
Sloan, Edith Barksdale
Smith, Alfred J., Jr.
Smith, Anne Street
Smith, C Miles
Smith, Carol J
Smith, Charles Lebanon
Smith, Cleveland Emanuel
Smith, Conrad P.
Smith, Edith B
Smith, Dr. Edward Nathaniel, Jr.
Smith, Frank
Smith, Dr. J. Clay, Jr.
Smith, Janice Evon
Smith, John Raye
Smith, Joseph F.
Smith, Dr. Judith Moore
Smith, Lafayette Kenneth
Smith, Marietta Culbreath
Smith, Michael
Smith, Patricia Grace
Smith, Shirley LaVerne
Smith, Vida J
Smith, Rev. Dr. Wallace Charles
Smith-Smith, Peola
Snowden, Sylvia Frances
Sockwell, Oliver R, Jr.
Spann, Thomas
Spaulding, William Ridley
Spearman, Dr. Leonard Hall O
Speight, Eva B
Speights, Nathaniel H
Spriggs, William
Springer, George Chelston
Spurlock, Jeanne
Stafford, Derrick
Standard, Dr. Raymond Linwood
Stanton, Robert G
Stevens, Lisa Maria
Stewart, Bishop Imagene Bigham
Stewart, Jarvis Christopher
Stockton, Barbara Marshall
Stokes, Gerald Virgil
Stone, Reese J
Strudwick, Dr. Warren James, Sr.
Subryan, Carmen
Sullivan, Andrea D.
Sullivan, Emmet G
Sulton, John Dennis
Sutphen, Mona K.
Swygert, H. Patrick
Syphax, Dr. Burke
Tarver, Elking, Jr.
Tate, Grady Bernard
Tate, Sonsyrea
Tatem, Dr. Patricia Ann
Taylor, Arnold H.
Taylor, Charles Edward
Taylor, Charley R.
Taylor, Dr. Estelle Wormley
Taylor, Helen Hollingshed
Taylor, Orlando L
Taylor, William L.
Temple, Donald Melvin
Terrell, Mary Ann
Thaxton, June E
Thigpen, Donald A
Thomas, Arthur Lafayette, III
Thomas, Charles W
Thomas, Clarence
Thomas, Eunice S.

Thomas, James O.
Thomas, Joan McHenry Bates
Thomas, Juanita Ware
Thomas, Ralph Charles
Thompson, Daniel Joseph
Thompson, Jeffrey Earl
Thompson, John Robert
Thompson, Larry D
Thompson, Mozelle W
Thompson, Portia Wilson
Thomson, John, III
Thornell, Richard Paul
Thornton, Leslie
Thornton, Tracey
Tidwell, Billy Joe
Tilghman, Cyprian O
Titus-Dillon, Dr. Pauline Y
Totten, Dr. Herman Lavon
Touchstone, John E.
Towns, Edolphus
Towns, Eva Rose
Townsend, Dr. Nkechit Florence
Trapp-Dukes, Rosa Lee
Traylor, Prof. Eleanor W.
Trescott, Jacqueline Elaine
Trotter, Cortez
Trowell-Harris, Irene
Tucker, Karen
Turner, Leslie Marie
Turner, Willie
Turner Brown, Shadey K
Tutt, Lia S
Valentine, J. T.
Valien, Preston
Vanderpool, Eustace Arthur
Wagner, Annice
Walker, Angelina
Walker, Edwin L.
Walker, James
Walker, Kenneth R.
Walker, Dr. M Lucius
Wall, Tara
Wallace, C. Everett
Wallace, Paul Starett
Wallace, Peggy Mason
Walters, Curla Sybil
Walters, Frank E.
Walton, Dr. Tracy Matthew
Ware, Omego John Clinton
Warfield-Coppock, Nsenga
Warwick, Dee Dee
Washington, Adrienne Terrell
Washington, Robert Benjamin, Jr.
Washington, Shaunise A
Waters, Maxine
Waters, Neville R
Watkins, Mozelle Ellis
Watlington, Janet Berecia
Watson, Dr. Diane Edith
Watson, John Clifton
Watson, Karen Elizabeth
Watson, Theresa Lawhorn
Watts, Beverly L.
Watts, J. C., Jr.
Weaver, Reginald Lee
Webster, Charles
Welsing, Frances Cress
West, Dr. Togo Dennis, Jr.
West, William Lionel
Whisenton, Andre C.
Whitaker, Rosa
White, Evelyn M
White, Ida Margaret
Whitfield, Vantile E.
Whiting, Barbara E
Whitt, Dwight Reginald
Wicker, Dr. Marcia Sindos
Wilber, Margie Robinson
Wilbon, Joan Marie
Wilcox, Janice Horde
Wiles, Spencer H.
Wiley, Edward, III
Wiley, Ralph
Wilkinson, Dr. Robert Shaw, Jr.
Williams, Armstrong
Williams, Billy Myles
Williams, Dr. Charles Thomas
Williams, Deborah Ann
Williams, Debra D
Williams, Dr. E Faye
Williams, Eddie Nathan
Williams, Dr. Hubert
Williams, Dr. James Thomas
Williams, Juan
Williams, Karen Hastie
Williams, Larry C.
Williams, Dr. Melvin Walker
Williams, Ronald Lee
Williams, Dr. Shirley Yvonne

Williams, Stanley King
Williams, Stephanie V.
Williams, Dr. Sterling B., Jr.
Williams, Vernon Alvin
Williams, Wesley S
Williams, Wyatt Clifford
Williams-Bridgers, Jacquelyn L
Willingham, Voncile
Wilmot, David Winston
Wilson, Bryan
Wilson, Danyell Elaine
Wilson, Joy Johnson
Wilson, Leon E, Jr.
Wilson, Thomas A, Jr.
Wilson, Rev. Willie Frederick
Winder, Alfred M
Wineglass, Henry
Winfield, Susan Rebecca Holmes
Winston, Jeanne Worley
Winston, Dr. Michael Russell
Winter, Daria Portray
Womack, Richard
Wood, William Vernell, Sr.
Woodard, Samuel L.
Woodfork, Carolyn Amelia
Woodson, Roderic L.
Word, Fletcher Henry, Jr.
Worsley, George Ira, Jr.
Wright, Joseph L
Wright, Keith Derek, Sr.
Wynn, Albert
Yeldell, Joseph P.
Young, Charles Alexander
Younge, Ida
Zimmerman, Eugene

washington
Anderson, Dr. Bernard E.

FLORIDA

Apopka
Adams, Kattie Johnson
Harvey, Gerald

Arcadia
Hickson, Eugene, Sr.

Archer
Harris, Oscar L.

Avon Park
Cox, Dr. Arthur James, Sr.

Belle Glade
Atkinson, Regina Elizabeth
Grear, Dr. Effie Carter
Grear, William A.
Johns, Dr. Jackie C

Boca Raton
Barton, Wayne Darrell
Beamon, Bob
Eagan, Catherine B
Ferere, Dr. Gerard Alphonse
Grigsby, David P
Howard, Desmond Kevin
Ismail, Qadry Rahmadan
Sledge, Percy
Weatherspoon, Jimmy Lee

Boynton Beach
Bluford, Col. Guion Stewart
Clemons, Clarence

Bradenton
Early, Robert S.
Watkins, William, Jr.

Bushnell
Coney, Loraine Chapell

Cantonment
Seabrook, Rev. Bradley Maurice

Cape Coral
Ackord, Marie Mallory
Sawyer, William Gregory

Casselberry
Wyche, Paul H

Celebration
Johnson, Dorothy Turner
Lewis, Jim

Chapel Hill
Robinson, Steve

Clearwater
Harris, Calvin D.
Ingram, Valerie J.

Palm Harbor
McLean, Dr. Helen Virginia

Palmetto
Peterson, James

Palmetto Bay
Levermore, Dr. Monique A

Panama City
Kent, Melvin Floyd

Parkland
Miller, Dr. Dorsey Columbus, Jr.

Pembroke Pines
Chicoye, Etzer

Pensacola
Boyd, Charles Flynn
Canady, Dr. Alexa Irene
DaValt, Dorothy B.
Hixon, Mamie Webb
Hunter, Cecil Thomas
Ricard, Rev. John H
Smith, Darryl C.
Spence, Donald Dale

Plantation
Hansberry-Moore, Virginia T

Pompano Beach
Gillis, Theresa McKinzy
Jackson, Henry Ralph

Port Saint Lucie
McCraw, Tom

Port St Lucie
Doig, Elmo H.
LaBeach, Nicole Ann
Lewis, Richard John, Sr.

Quincy
Davis, Marva Alexis
Mitchell, Dean Lamont

Riviera Beach
Jones, James G.

Rockledge
Woodie, Henry L.

Royal Palm Beach
Branch Richards, Dr. Germaine Gail
Crutchfield-Baker, Verdenia

Saint Petersburg
Beane, Dorothea Annette

Sanford
Davis, H. Bernard
Simmons, Clayton Lloyd
Wright, Stephen Caldwell

Sarasota
Allen-Jones, Patricia Ann
Atkins, Fredd G
Daly, Marie Maynard
Mims, Dr. George L.
Owens, Geoffrey
Porter, Bishop Henry Lee

Sebring
Thomas-Richards, Jose Rodolfo

Silver Spring
Kern-Foxworth, Dr. Marilyn L.

Singer Island
Dunn, Linda Spradley

South Pasadena
Beane, Dorothea Annette

Spring Hill
Bradford, Charles Edward
Johnston, Wallace O.
Myers, Earl T.

St Augustine
Chase, Arnett C

St Petersburg
Blackshear, William
Brown, Delores Elaine

Cotman, Henry Earl
Davis, Goliath J., III
Downing, Alvin Joseph
Dunlap, Dr. Karen F Brown
Fry, Darrell
Goss, Theresa Carter
Green, Jacquez
Holmes, Litdell Melvin, Jr.
Jones, Theresa Diane
Lewis, Robert Edward
Peterman, Peggy M.
Reed, Sheila A
Swain, Robert J.
Wimbish, C Bette

Stuart
Carter, Daisy
Christie, James Albert
Gary, Tanisha
Hughes, Kori

Summerfield
Preston, Swanee H. T., Jr.

Sunrise
Dunn, Dax

Tallahassee
Abdullah, Samella Berry
Acosta Nesmith, Winifred L
Akbar, Dr. Na
Anderson, Gladys Peppers
Austin, Dr. Debra
Austin, Doris
Bolden, John Henry
Bryant, Pamela Bradley
Burnette, Dr. Ada Puryear
Bush, James, III
Carter, Dr. Lawrence
Clack, Doris H.
Close, Billy Ray
Close, Fran
Copeland, Emily America
Daggs, Leon
Davies, Marvin
Davis, Anita Louise
Dobson, Byron Eugene
Dozier, Richard K.
Drumming, Saundra T
Eaton, James Nathaniel, Sr.
Edney, Norris Allen, I
Elkins, Virgil Lynn
Fleming, Prof. Raymond Richard
Foster, Dr. William Patrick
Gayles-Felton, Dr. Anne Richardson
Gillum, Andrew D
Goodwin, Robert T., Sr.
Griffith, Elwin Jabez
Groomes, Dr. Freddie Lang
Hamilton, Dr. Franklin D.
Harris, Cynthia M.
Hatchett, Joseph Woodrow
Hemmingway, Dr. Beulah S.
Hooks, Mary Butler
Irvine, Dr. Carolyn Lenette
Irvine, Freeman Raymond, Jr.
Jackson, Edgar Newton
Jackson, Dr. Keith Hunter
Jeffers, Sheila B
Johnson, Walter Lee
Jones, Margaret B
Jones, William Ronald
Lawrence, John Edward
Lewis, Dr. Henry L., III
Logan, Willie Frank
Love, Edward A.
Marks, John
Martin, Evelyn B.
Metcalf, DaVinci Carver
Metcalf, Dr. Zubie West, Jr.
Mobley, Dr. Sybil Collins
Parker, Dr. Herbert Gerald
Perry, Dr. Aubrey M.
Quince, Peggy A.
Ravenell, William Hudson
Ridley, Dr. Alfred Dennis
Ritchie, Joe
Sapp, Lauren B
Scott, Levan Ralph
Session, Johnny Frank
Simmons, Joyce Hobson
Smith, Jeraldine Williams
Sorey, Hilmon S
Stiell, Phelicia D
Stith, Dr. Rep. Melvin Thomas
Taylor, Stacey Lorenzo
Thompson, Anita Favors
Wallace, Dr. Renee C
Wanton, Eva C.

Washington, Dr. Arthur Clover
Washington, Samuel, Jr.
Wesley, Nathaniel, Jr.
Williams, Dorothy P.
Wilson, Margaret F
Wright, Dr. Larry L
Ziegler, Dr. Dhyana

Tampa
Banks, Dr. Lula F.
Barber, Ronde
Barnett, Robert
Campbell, Carlos Cardozo
Cockburn, Alden George, Jr.
Collier, Troy
Collins, Corene
Daniels, Darrell
Dawson, Warren Hope
Dunn, Warrick De'Mon
Fry, Darrell
Galloway, Joey
Gibbons, Deveron M
Gordon, Garth
Griffin, Eurich Z.
Hammond, James A
Harris, Howard F.
Hendricks, Steven Aaron
Hilliard, Ike
Horton, Oscar J
Hubbard, Josephine Brodie
Jordan, Bettye Davis
Keys, Charlene
Lane, Curtis
Leftwich, Byron Antron
Mann, Richard
McClure, Fredrick H L
McGriff, Frederick Stanley
McKee, Clarence Vanzant
Miller, Gwendolyn Martin
Miller, Lesley James, Jr.
Mitchell, Robert Lee, Sr.
Monroe, Robert Alex
Morrow, W Derrick
Mosby, Carla Mane
Nichols, George
Quarles, Shelton Eugene
Reynolds, Ricky Scott
Rice, Simeon
Sanderlin, James B.
Saunders, Robert William, Sr., Ph.D.
Scrivens, John J
Smith, Freddie Alphonso
Smith, Dr. Walter L
Stewart, Carolyn House
Stokes, Rueben Martine
Stringer, Thomas Edward
Tate, Lars Jamel
Tokley, Joanna Nutter
Tribble, Israel, Jr.
(Cabrera) White, Eloise J.
Wilds, Jetie Boston, Jr.
Williams, Doug Lee
Wilson, Shawn-Ta
Woods, Sanford L
Wright, Dr. Samuel Lamar, Sr.

Temple Terrace
Stamps, Spurgeon Martin David

Tierra Verde
Willis, Charles L

University Park
Gladden, Brenda Winckler

Valrico
McFadden, Gregory L.

Vero Beach
Lindsay, Horace Augustin

Washington
Richardson, Dr. Lacy Franklin

Wauchula
Smith, Bobby Antonia

West Palm Beach
Clarke, Everee Jimerson
Crutchfield-Baker, Verdenia
Cunningham, T. J., Sr.
DuBose, Dr. Otelia
Hooks, Mary Butler
Jackson, Alvin B., Jr.
Jason, Henry Thomas
Johns, Dr. Jackie C

Perrin, David Thomas Perry
Turnquest, Sandra Close

Weston
McKnight, James

Wilmington
Rasheed, Howard S

Windermere
Kenoly, Ron
Reed, Andre Darnell
White, Alvin, Jr.

Winter Park
King, Shaun Earl
Reaves, Rev. Dr. Benjamin Franklin

GEORGIA

Acworth
Taylor, Charles E.

Albany
Adams, Willie, Jr.
Cribb, Juanita Sanders
Cutler, Donald
Hill, Prof. James Lee
Humphries, Charles, Jr.
Mayes, Helen M.
McLaughlin, LaVerne Laney
Pogue, Richard James
Reeves, Alan M
Sherrod, Rev. Charles M
Taylor, Dr. Robert, III
Wallace, Dr. Renee C

Alpharetta
Baylor, Helen
Belson, Jerry
Burges, Melvin E.
Claybrooks, John, Jr.
Judge, Dr. Paul Qantas

Americus
Ferguson, Ralph
McGrady, Eddie James
McLaughlin, LaVerne Laney
Paschal, Eloise Richardson
Smith, Rev. Elijah

Ashburn
King, Hodge

Athens
Allen, Walter R
Babb, Dr. Valerie M
Bell-Scott, Patricia
Bennett-Alexander, Dawn DeJuana
Blount, Larry Elisha
Boyd, Valerie
Boynton, Asa Terrell, Sr.
Castenell, Dr. Louis Anthony
Frasier, Mary Mack
Frett, La Keshia
Hill, Jennifer A
Jeffreys, John H
Locklin, James R.
Lyons, Charles H. S., Jr.
McBride, Frances E.
McKnight, Reginald
Miller, Dr. Ronald Baxter
Morrow, Dr. John Howard, Jr.
Nunnally, David H.
Parker, Dr. Keith Dwight
See, Dr. Letha A
Turner, Edward L
Williamson, Coy Colbert, Jr.

Atlanta
Adair, James E.
Aldridge, Dr. Delores Patricia
Alexander, William H.
Alfred, Dr. Dewitt C., Jr.
Anderson, Rev. Dr. Al H
Anderson, Garret Joseph
Anderson, Dr. Gloria L.
Anderson, James
Anderson, Kenny
Anderson, Shandon Rodriguez
Anderson, William
Arkansaw, Tim
Armour, Dr. Christopher E
Baety, Edward L.
Bailey, Dr. Randall Charles

Baird, Dr. Keith E.
Baker, Thurbert E.
Banks, Caroline Long
Banks, Jahshuwan-Jessean
Barkley, Charles Wade
Barnes, Paul Douglas
Barnett, Robert
Barr-Davenport, Leona
Batine, Rafael
Battiste, Audrey Elayne Quick
Belson, Jerry
Benham, Dr. Robert
Betha, Mason Durrell
Bethea, Edwin Ayers
Bibby, Mike
Bigham, Rita Lacy
Billings, Mac
Black, Charles E.
Blackburn, Benjamin Allan, II
Blackwell, Joey
Blackwell, Randolph Talmadge
Bolden, Dorothy Lee
Bolden, Wiley Speights
Bond, James G.
Bonds Staples, Gracie
Booker, Anne M
Boston, Thomas Danny
Boswell, Bennie
Bradley, M. Louise
Brandon, Jerome
Braxton, Toni
Brent, Charles Tyrone
Brice, Barbara
Bridgewater, Dr. Herbert Jeremiah, Jr.
Broadnax, Walter Doyce
Brooks, Tyrone L
Broomes, Melissa
Brown, Andrea
Brown, Evelyn Drewery
Brown, Marjorie M
Brown, Thomas Edison, Jr.
Brown, Dr. Uzee, Jr.
Brown, William Crews
Bryant, Gregory
Bryant, Precious
Bryant, Regina Lynn
Burgest, Rev. Dr. David Raymond
Burnett, Dr. Myra N
Burnett, Zaron Walter, Jr.
Burroughs, Baldwin Wesley
Bussey, Reuben T., Jr.
Butler, Johnnella E.
Butterfield, Torris Jerrel
Carpenter, Raymond Prince
Carter, Allen C.
Carter, Dr. Barbara Lillian
Carter, Dr. John H
Carter, Lawrence Edward, Sr.
Carter, Marva Griffin
Casterlow, Carolyn B
Chapman, David Anthony
Clement, William A., Jr.
Clement, William A.
Clemons, James Albert, III
Cole, Dr. Thomas Winston
Coleman, Michael Victor
Cone, Dr. Juanita Fletcher
Conwill, Giles
Cook, Tonya Denise
Cooper, Clarence
Cooper, Michael Gary
Costen, Dr. Melva Wilson
Couch, James W
Crawford, L. Marilyn
Crim, Alonzo A.
Croslan, John Arthur
Crump-Caine, Lynn
Crusoe-Ingram, Charlene
Culpepper, Louis S
Cunningham, Vernessa Smalls-Brantley
Daily, Lori Beard
Daniels, Frederick L., Jr.
Dash, Hugh M. H.
Davis, Dr. Edward L.
Davis, Erroll B., Jr.
Davis, Luella B
Davis, Dr. Marilyn Ann Cherry
Dean, James Edward
Dean, Vyvyan Ardena Coleman
Dejoie, Michael C
Delsarte, Louis
Donald, James E
Dorsey, Tredell
Dossman, Curley M., Jr.
Dottin, Roger Allen
Dryden, Charles Walter, Sr.
Duncan, Peggy

Belcher, Jacquelyn M.
Bellamy, Verdelle B.
Burroughs, Robert A
Bush, T W
Christie, Angella
Clark, William
Ferguson, Elliott LaRoy
Flowers, Runette
Grace, George H
Hale, Rev. Cynthia Lynnette
Harris, Archie Jerome
Keyes, Gwendolyn R
Kimbro, Dennis Paul
Lewis, Charles McArthur
Lindsay, Dr. Arturo
McKenzie, Miranda Mack
Moore, Dr. Harold Earl, Jr.
Murray, Albert R
Perrimon, Vivian Spence
Perry-Holston, Waltina D
Shackelford, William G
Shamsid-Deen, Waleed
Taylor, Kenneth Matthew
Vaughan, Gerald R.
Wheelan, Belle Smith
White, Raymond Rodney
Williams, Terry

Douglasville
Beasley, Victor Mario
Williams, Jean Carolyn

Duluth
McGuirt, Milford W

Dunwoody
Smith, Philip Gene

East Point
Birchette-Pierce, Cheryl L.
Duckett, Karen Irene
Godfrey, William R.
Harris, Archie Jerome
Izell, Booker T
Lucas, Earl S.
Walker, Dr. Mark Lamont
Wilson, Natarsha Juliet
Wright, J R

Ellaville
Goodwin, Dr. William Pierce, Jr.

Ellenwood
Odoms, Willie O.
Parks, Alfred G, Jr.
Sharpe, Dr. Audrey Howell

Evans
Karangu, David

Fairburn
Hall, Lt. Gen. James Reginald
Jordan, George Washington, Jr.
Ward, Sandra L

Fayetteville
Holley, John Clifton
Jones, Dr. Michael Andrea
Lee, Dr. Guy Milicon, Jr.
Matthews, Robert L
Minor, Emma Lucille
Osborne, Dr. William Reginald, Jr.

Flowery Branch
Clemmons, Dr. Sonya Summerour
Harrison, Bob
Mack, Rudy Eugene
Milloy, Lawyer
Smith, Jermaine
Thomas, Emmitt
Vick, Michael Dwayne

Forsyth
Campbell, Margie

Fort Valley
Carter, Dr. Judy L.
Church, Robert T., Sr.
Edwards, Claybon Jerome
Horton, Dollie Bea Dixon
Junior, Ester James, Jr.
Rutherford, Harold Phillip, III
Simmons, Julius Caesar, Sr.

Ft Valley
Harrison, Dr. Fred
Walker, Dr. Melvin E

Gainesville
Aikens-Young, Dr. Linda Lee

Georgetown
Kendrick, Tommy L.

Griffin
Phillips, Delores

Hampton
McMillan, Regina Ellis

Hapeville
Lucas, William S.
Patrick, Vincent Jerome

Hephzibah
Godbee, Thomasina D.

Homerville
Sherrod, Rev. Charles M

Jonesboro
Bell, Eldrin A.
Johnson, Kalanos Vontell
Ryan-White, Jewell

Junction City
Carter, Christopher Anthony

Kathleen
Pogue, Richard James

Kennesaw
Akinyemi, Dr. Nurudeen B
Collier, Julia Marie
Davis, Frank Allen
Ware, William
Wingfield, Dr. Harold Lloyd

LaGrange
Lewis, Frank Ross

Lake City
Grant, Ashley

Lawrenceville
Devers, Gail
Lawrence, Theresa A. B.

Lincolnton
Freeman, Denise

Lithia Springs
Collier, Dr. Millard James, Jr., MD

Lithonia
Daily, Byron
Edmondson, Jerome
King, Rev. Bernice Albertine
Long, Eddie L.
Moody, C David
Shakespeare, Easton Geoffrey
Smith, LaSalle, Sr.
Sulton, Dr. Jacqueline Rhoda
Thomas, Dr. Pamella D
Warren, Nagueyalti
Warren, Dr. Rueben Clifton

Mableton
Adams, Robert Eugene
Bellinger, Rev. Mary Anne Allen
Blake, B. David
Bryant, Gregory
Gary, Kathye J.

Macon
Braswell, Palmira
Byas, Dr. Ulysses S.
Dillard, Thelma Deloris
McGee, Sylvia Williams
Smith, Eddie D., Sr.
Vinson, Julius Ceasar
Wheeler, Chester A

Madison
Charis
Yarn, Barbara Lynne Ivey

Manchester
Carter, Christopher Anthony
Huff, William

Marietta
Adams, Dr. Howard Glen
Adams, Leonard E, Jr.

Baskett, Kenneth Gerald
Bronner, Sheila
Brown, Raymond Madison
Burton, Charles Howard, Jr.
Dean, Daniel R.
Jackson, Earl
Johnson, Marvin R, Jr.
Jordan, George Washington, Jr.
Mallory, James A
McWilliams, Dr. Alfred E.
Miller, George Carroll, Jr.
Moon, Walter D
Payne, Jacqueline LaVerne
Roberts, Dr. Rona Dominique
Robinson, Rev. Edsel F
See, Dr. Letha A
Smith, Beverly Evans
Smith, Robert W., Jr.
Thomas, Dr. Pamella D
Thompson, William L
Tuggle, Dorie C
Yancy, Dr. Robert James

Martinez
Johnson, George, Jr.

McDonough
Arnette, Evelyn

Metter
Whitaker, Mical Rozier

Midway
Clancy, Magalene Aldoshia
Miller-Holmes, Cheryl

Milledgeville
Griffin, Floyd Lee
Monroe, Annie Lucky
Taylor, Willie Marvin

Morrow
Baranco, Juanita P.
Burke, Rosetta Y
Cockerham, Peggy
Haynes, Dr. Brian Lee

Norcross
Thomas-Samuel, Kalin Normoet

Ocilla
Allen, Roscoe

Oliver
Brown, Justine Thomas

Palmetto
Smith, Tangela Nicole

Peachtree City
Yarn, Barbara Lynne Ivey

Pine Lake
Sumler Edmond, Janice L.

Powder Springs
Aziz, Samimah

Riceboro
McIver, John Douglas

Riverdale
Granger, Edwina C.

Rockmart
Billingslea, Edgar D.

Rome
Hill, Sandra Patricia
Reid, Duane L

Roswell
Darden, Calvin
Jamison, Isaac Terrell
Lottier, Patricia Ann

SW Atlanta,
Thomas, Ron

Savannah
Adams, Eugene Bruce
Ali, Maajid F.
Bass, James F
Bell, Joseph N.
Brantley, Daniel
Bynes, Frank Howard, Jr.

Clark, Dr. Irvin R.
Cooper, Curtis V.
Dawson, Shed, Jr.
Ford, Henry
Formey, Sylvester C
Freeman, Nelson R.
Gadsden, Eugene Hinson
Garrison, Esther F.
Jackson, Suzanne Fitzallen
Jamerson, John W
Jamerson, John William, Jr.
James, Robert Earl
Johnson, Lester B., III
Johnson, Dr. Otis Samuel
Jordan, Dr. Abbie H.
Jordan, Anne Knight
Martin, Clarence L.
Martin, Shedrick M., Jr.
Mathis, Frank
Milledge, Dr. Luetta Upshur
Mitchell, Bennie Robert, Jr.
Morse, John E
Oliver, Gary Dewayne
Reynolds, Viola J.
Riley, Shaunce R
Silver, Dr. Joseph Howard
Small, Israel G.
Thomas, Dr. Priscilla D
Walker, Herschel
Wallace, Thomas Albert
Whitaker, Von Frances
Wilfong, Henry T
Zow, James Allen

Smithville
Mitchell, Douglas

Smyrna
Edmonds, Bevelyn
Ewing, Steven R
Knight, Rev. Carolyn Ann

Sparta
Dixon, Jimmy
Ingram, Edith J.
Wiley, Leroy Sherman

St Simons Island
Ansa, Tina McElroy

Statesboro
Burden, Willie James
Grant, Dr. Wilmer, Jr.
Vaughan, Gerald R.
Young, Prof. Alfred

Stockbridge
Cain, Herman
Fields, Dr. Richard A., Sr.

Stone Mountain
Brown, John Baker, Jr.
Clark, Laron Jefferson
Coram, Willie Mae
Daniels, Frederick L, Jr.
Liverpool, Charles Eric
Patrick, Vincent Jerome
Shackelford, William G
Smith, Dr. Luther Edward
Smith, Philip Gene
Smith, Dr. Tommie
Staton, Canzetta Maria

Suwanee
Brandon, David Sherrod
Fountaine, Jamal
White, William Eugene
Wimberly, Marcus

Sylvania
Williams, Jesse

Temple
Beasley, Victor Mario

Thomasville
Fortson, Henry David, Jr.
Hardy-Hill, Edna Mae
McIver, Margaret Hill
Williams, Dr. Earl, Jr.

Thomson
Greene, Joseph David

Tifton
Daniel, Bertha
Graydon, Wasdon, Jr.

Tyrone
Bellamy, Ivory Gandy

Union City
Aaron, Henry Louis
Kennedy, Inga D.
Simmons, Isaac Tyrone

Valdosta
Brown, Dr. Ola M.
Roberts, Edgar
Williams, Dr. Lafayette W

Villa Rica
Morgan, Dr. Harry

Wadley
Charles, Lewis
Johnson, B. A.

Warner Robins
Canady-Laster, Rena Deloris

Washington
Challenor, Herschelle

Waycross
Adams, Samuel Levi, Sr.
Bonner, Theophulis W.
Bynum, Dr. Juanita
McCray, Christopher Columbus

Waynesboro
Griggs, James C.
Lodge, Herman

Whitesburg
Gamble, Robert Lewis

Winterville
Clifton, Dr. Ivery Dwight

Woodland
Carter, James

Woodstock
Daniel, James L.

HAWAII

Aiea
Richards, Leon

Honolulu
Ball, Richard Erwin
Carroll, Annie Haywood
Cartwright, Brenda Yvonne
Edwards, John W., Jr.
Jackson, Miles M.
Richards, Leon
Young, Edward Hiram

Kihei
Mabson, Glenn T

Lihue
King, LeRoy J.

Mililani
Smith, Dr. Richard Alfred

IDAHO

Boise
Livingston, Randy Anthony
Mercy, Leland, Jr.

Eagle
Spigner, Marcus E

Hailey
Purce, Dr. Thomas Les

Mountain Home
Montgomery, Robert E

Pocatello
Yizar, James Horace

ILLINOIS
Benjamin, Floyd
Stokes, Patrick

Abbott Park
Coleman James, Patricia Rea

Abbott Pk
Delaney, Dallas

Alton
Bartley, William Raymond

Argonne
Washington, Dr. Linda Phaire

Arlington Heights
Martin, Gwendolyn Rose
Phillips, W Thomas

Aurora
Edwards, Dr. Marvin E
McMillan, Robert Frank, Jr.
Wilkinson, Marie L

Belleville
Chalmers, Thelma Faye
Gregory, Most Rev. Wilton Daniel
LeCompte, Peggy Lewis
Lewis, Hon. Alexis Otis
McCaskill, Earle
Otis-Lewis, Alexis D
Thompson, Lloyd Earl
Wiley, Gerald Edward

Bellwood
Bailey, Ronald W

Bloomington
Jones, Gregory Wayne

Bolingbrook
Benford-Lee, Alyssia

Buffalo Grove
Dukes, Ronald

Burnham
Singleton, Rickey

Burr Ridge
Lue-Hing, Cecil

Cairo
Nelson, Harold E

Calumet City
Barry, Harriet S.
Muhammad, Wallace D.
Whitehurst, Steven Laroy
Wright, Carl Jeffrey

Carbondale
Bryson, Seymour L.
Calhoun, Thomas C
Guthrie, Robert V.
Jones, Jennie Y.
Price-Smith, Connie
Schumacher, Brockman
Shepherd, Benjamin Arthur
Stalls, Dr. M
Welch, Harvey

Carmel
Green, Dennis O.

Champaign
Clay, Ernest H., III.
Copeland, Robert M.
Cowan, Larine Yvonne
Dash, Leon DeCosta
Gibbs, Dr. Sandra E
Griggs, Dr. Mildred Barnes
Hunter, Richard C
Powell, Robert John
Singley, Yvonne Jean
Underwood, King James
Wright, Joyce C.

Charleston
Barnes, Quacy
Ridgeway, Dr. Bill Tom

Samuels, Annette Jacqueline
Smith-Surles, Dr. Carol Diann

Chicago
Abdullah, Dr. Larry Burley
Abdullah, Mustafa
Adair, Andrew A.
Adams, Dr. Carol Laurence
Adams, Sheila Mary
Akin, Ewen M., Jr.
Albert, Charles Gregory
Alexander, James Arthur
Allen, Mark
Allison, Verne
Amaker, Norman Carey
Anderson, Howard D.
Anderson, Richard Charles
Anthony-Perez, Dr. Bobbie M.
Argrett, Loretta Collins
Armster-Worrill, Cynthia Denise
Austin, Carrie M.
Bailey, Donn Fritz
Bailey, Duwain
Baines, Harold Douglas
Baiocchi, Regina Harris
Baird, Sr. Anita Price
Ball, William Batten
Banks, Jerry L.
Banks, Patricia
Barner, Sharon R
Barnett, Alfreda W. Duster
Barnett, Etta Moten
Barnett, William
Barney, Willie J
Barrow, Rev. Willie T.
Baskins, Lewis C.
Bateman, Paul E
Bell, Dr. Carl Compton
Bell, James A.
Belliny, Daniel S.
Bennett, Deborah Minor
Bennett, Ivy H.
Bennett, Lerone, Jr.
Benson, Sharon Marie
Berry, Leonidas H.
Bethel, Kathleen Evonne
Black, Leona R.
Blair, Chester Laughton Ellison
Bland, Heyward
Blanks, Wilhelmina E.
Blouin, Rose Louise
Boston, Dennis H
Boswell, Paul P.
Bowles, Barbara Landers
Bowman, Dr. James E.
Boyd, Hon William Stewart
Braden, Everette Arnold
Bradley, London M., Jr.
Braxton, Steve
Briggs, Carol J.
Bromery, Keith Marcel
Brooks, Delores Jean
Brooks, Gwendolyn
Brown, Abena Joan
Brown, Bartram S.
Brown, Clarice Ernestine
Brown, Constance Charlene
Brown, Geoffrey Franklin
Brown, Dr. Joan P.
Brown, Dr. Malore Ingrid
Brown, Michael
Brown, Milbert Orlando
Brown, Tony
Brown-Ellen, Kimi
Brownlee, Dr. Geraldine Daniels
Bruce, James C.
Bryant, Homer Hans
Bryant, Prof. Leroy
Bryant, Preston
Bryant, Robert E.
Bumpers, Katrina
Burke, Sterling
Burns, Diann
Burrell, Barbara
Burrell, Thomas J., Jr.
Burroughs, Dr. Margaret Taylor
Burrus, Clark
Butler, Jerome M.
Butler, Jerry
Butler, Joyce M
Bynoe, Peter CB
Byrd, Doris M.
Cage, Patrick B
Caldwell, Lewis A. H.
Campbell, James W.
Campbell, Wendell J.
Campbell, Zerrie D
Canady, Blanton Thandreus
Cannon, Dr. Charles Earl

Carey, Carnice
Carry, Rev. Helen Ward
Carter, Robert Henry
Carter, Dr. Warrick L.
Cash, Pamela J.
Chandler, Alton H
Chapman, Roslyn C.
Chappell, Kevin
Charleston, Gomez, Jr.
Chatman, Delle
Chatman, Donald Leveritt
Cheatham, Henry Boles
Chew, Cheryl
Chicago, Denovious Adolphus
Childs, Josie L.
Clark, Frank M
Clarke, Joseph Lance
Clay, Theodore Roosevelt, Jr.
Clay, Willie B.
Coleman, Cecil R.
Colemon, Rev. Dr. Johnnie
Collins, Annazette
Collins, Marva Delores Nettles
Collins, Rosecrain
Collins-Grant, Earlean
Colter, Cyrus J.
Comer, Dr. Marian Wilson
Compton, James W.
Conley, Mike
Conner, Steve
Cook, Keith Lynn
Cook, Rufus
Cooper, Warren
Corley-Blaney, Janice
Cotharn, Preston Sigmunde, Sr.
Cousins, William
Cross, Austin Devon
Cruthird, J Robert Lee
Dale, Robert J.
Daly, Ronald Edwin
Dames, Kathy W.
Damper, Ronald Eugene
Daniel, David L.
Daniel, Dr. Elnora
Danner, Margaret Essie
Davis, Barbara D
Davis, Danny K.
Davis, John Westley
Davis, Lucille H.
Davis, Monique Deon
Davis, Sonia
Dee, Merri
Dennard, Darryl W.
DePriest, Darryl Lawrence
Dickens, Jacoby
Dillard, Cecil R.
Dinizulu, Yao O
Dinkins, Traci
Dowell-Cerasoli, Patricia R
Downs, Crystal
Driskell, Claude Evans
Dugas, A Jeffrey Alan, Sr.
Dukes, Ronald
Dunn, Almeda Effie
Duster, Benjamin C., III
Dye, Jermaine Terrell
Eady, Lydia Davis
Earles, Dr. Rene Martin
Eatman, Joseph W
Eddy, Dr. Edward A.
Edwards, James Franklin
Edwards, Theodore Allen
Eichelberger, Brenda
English, Henry L
Epps, Edgar G.
Evans, Clay
Evans, Timothy C.
Evans, Webb
Ewell, Raymond W.
Farrakhan, Louis
Farrow, William McKnight, III
Felker, Joseph B.
Ferguson, Cecil
Ferguson, Fay
Ferguson, St Julian
Finch, G.A.
Finney, Leon D., Jr.
Flowers, D. Michelle
Floyd, Dr. Samuel A.
Forbes, Calvin
Ford, Ausbra
Foster, LaDoris J.
Francis, Cheryl Margaret
Francis, Ray William, Jr.
Fraser, Thomas Edwards
Frazier, Wynetta Artricia
Fredrick, Dr. Earl E
Freeman, Louis Lawrence
Freeman, Dr. Paul D.

Fuerst, Jean Stern
Gant, Phillip M, III
Gardner, Edward George
Gardner, Dr. Frank W.
Garnett, Marion Winston
Gaters, Dorothy L.
Gavin, Mary Ann
Gearring, Joel Kenneth
Geary, Clarence Butler
Gibson, Truman K., Jr.
Gilbert, Herman Cromwell
Golden, Marvin Darnell
Goodwin, Mercedier Cassandra de Freitas
Gordon, Milton A.
Gore, David L.
Goss, Frank, Jr.
Goss, William Epp
Grady, Walter E.
Graham, Stedman
Grant, Andre M.
Gray, Joanne S
Green, Anita Lorraine
Green, Dr. James L
Green, Larry A
Groomes, Emrett W.
Gurley, Annette Denise
Guy, Buddy
Hale, Kimberly Anice
Hall, Joel
Hamberlin, Dr. Emiel
Hamlar, Jocelyn B
Harlan, Emery King
Harper, Geraldine Seay
Harris, Nelson A.
Harth, Raymond Earl
Hartman, Hermene Demaris
Harvey-Byrd, Patricia Lynn
Hasson, Nicole Denise
Hasty, Keith A
Havis, Jeffrey Oscar
Hebert, Zenebework Teshome
Henton, George
Herring, Cedric
Hibbler, William J
Higgins, Ora A.
Higgins, Stann
Hill, Avery
Hill, Ellyn Askins
Hill, James, Jr.
Hilliard, Amy S
Hobson, Mellody
Hobson, Mellody L.
Hogu, Barbara J Jones
Holden, Aaron Charles
Holland, Louis A
Holland, Loys Marie
Hooper, Michele J
Horton, Andre
House, Michael A
Howard-Coleman, Billie Jean
Hubbard, Hon. Arnette Rhinehart
Hudson, Dianne Atkinson
Huggins, Larry
Hughes, Dr. Joyce A.
Hughes, Larry
Hunt, Richard Howard
Hunter, Bryan C.
Hunter, Dr. Mae M
Hunter, Norman L.
Hutchinson, Jerome
Hutt, Monroe L.
Irvin, Dennis J.
Isbell, James S.
Jackson, Angela
Jackson, Cheryle
Jackson, Donald J
Jackson, Jonathan
Jackson, Kevin Allen
Jackson, Larry Eugene
Jackson, Robert Andrew
Jackson, William Ed
James, Dr. Betty Nowlin
James, Darryl Farrar
James, Gerry M
Jarrett, Valerie B.
Jarrett, Vernon D.
Jenkins, Ella Louise
Jiggetts, Danny Marcellus
Johnson, Bennett J
Johnson, Costello O
Johnson, Eunice Walker
Johnson, Eunita E
Johnson, Evelyn F.
Johnson, George Ellis, Sr.
Johnson, Glenn T.
Johnson, Dr. Joseph Edward, Jr.
Johnson, Moria S.
Johnson, Randall Morris

Johnson, R.M.
Johnson, Robert Junius
Johnson, Waldo Emerson
Jolly, Marva Lee
Jones, Brent M.
Jones, Geri Duncan
Jones, Dr. Nina F.
Jones, Richmond Addison
Jones, Spencer
Jones, Theodore A.
Jones, Vivian R
Jones, Walter
Jones, Wilbert
Jor'dan, Jamilah R.
Jordan, Dr. Robert Howard, Jr.
Joseph, Anita Davis
Kent, Herb
Kimbrough, Robert L.
King, Earl B.
King, Gayle
King, Dr. Reatha Clark
Knott, Dr. Albert Paul
Knowling, Robert E, Jr.
Kunjufu, Jawanza
Latif, Naimah
Leavell, Dorothy R.
Leavy, Walter
Lee, Derrek Leon
LeFlore, Obie Laurence, Jr.
Lewis, Michael W
Lewis, Stephen Christopher
Lewis, Thomas P.
Lewis-Thornton, Rae
Lightfoot, Jean Harvey
Locke, Henry Daniel Jr.
Lott, Gay Lloyd
Love, Bob
Lowry, James Hamilton
Lowry, William E, Jr.
Lue-Hing, Cecil
Luster, Jory
Lyle, Freddrenna M
Lyons, Charlotte
Madhubuti, Haki R
Malveaux, Antoinette Marie
Manning, Blanche Marie
Marshall, Anita
Martin, Ephraim M.
Martin, LeRoy
Maryland, Mary Angela
Mason, B. J.
McClellan, Edward J.
McClelland, Marguerite Marie
McConner, Dorothy
McCoy, Wayne Anthony
McCrimon, Audrey L.
McCuiston, Dr. Stonewall, Jr.
McFarland, Claudette
McKinzie, Barbara A
McSween, Cirilo A.
McWhorter, Rosalynd D
Meek, Dr. Russell Charles
Mehlinger, Kermit Thorpe
Middlebrooks, Felicia
Miles, Dr. Norman Kenneth
Miller, Dr. Bernice Johnson
Miller, Marquis David
Miller, Robert, Jr.
Milliner, David M
Mitchell, William Grayson
Mohammad, Sandra B
Moore, Anthony Louis
Moore, David M
Moore, Johnny B
Moore, Trudy S
Moore, Winston E.
Moragne, Rudolph
Morris, Eugene
Moses, Milton E.
Moss, Tanya Jill
Mowatt, Oswald Victor
Muhammad, Ava
Muhammad, Shirley M.
Munis-Luster, Sonja
Munroe, Anthony E
Murphy, Clyde Everett
Muwakkil, Salim
Myers, Peter E.
Nash, Bob J.
Neal, Charlie
Neal, Langdon D
Neely, David E.
Neighbors, Dolores Maria
Nelson, Flora Sue
Newell, Daryl
Nipson, Herbert
Norfleet, Janet
Norment, Lynn A
Norris, LaVena M.

O, Fredrick William, Jr.
Obama, Barack
Onli, Turtel
Owens, James E, Jr.
Owens, Treka Elaine
Palmore, Roderick A
Parker, Jerry P.
Patin, Jude W. P.
Paul, Vera Maxine
Payne, Allison Griffin
Perry, Betty Hancock
Philpott, Ethel
Pinckney, Lewis, Jr.
Porter, Rev. Dr. Kwame John R.
Powell, Kemper O
Price, Cappy E.
Price, Ramon B.
Pride, Walter LaVon
Primo, Quintin, III
Pugh, Dr. Roderick Wellington
Pulley, Cassandra M.
Raab, Madeline Murphy
Randle, Wilma Jean-Elizabeth Emanuel
Rankin, Marlene Owens
Ransby, Barbara
Ransom, Leticia Buford
Reed, A.C.
Reed-Clark, Larita Diane
Reid, N Neville
Reid, Wilfred
Rhinehart, June Acie
Rhinehart, Vernon Morel
Rice, Judith Carol
Rice, Linda Johnson
Rice, William E.
Richardson, Odis Gene
Robbins, Millard D.
Roberson, Valerie R
Roberts, Robin
Roberts, Roy S.
Roberts-Smith, Debra
Robinson, Deanna Adell
Robinson, Johnathan Prather
Robinson, Renault Alvin
Robinson, Robin
Robinson, Ronnie W
Robinson, S Benton
Robinson-Ivy, Jacqueline
Rodgers, Carolyn Marie
Rogers, Desiree Glapion
Rogers, John W.
Roy, Jan S
Roy, Jasper K.
Royster, Don M, Sr.
Royster, Philip M
Russell, Milicent De
Ryan, Agnes C.
Sagers, Rudolph, Jr.
Salaam, Dr. Abdul
Salone, Marcus
Salter, Roger Franklin
Sampson, Rev. Dr. Albert Richard
Samuels, Ronald S
Satcher, Dr. Robert
Saunders, Vincent E
Sawyer, Roderick Terrence
Scott, Dr. Alice H
Scott, Col. Eugene Frederick
Scott, Michael W
Scott, Ruby Dianne
Scott-Heron, Gil
Seabrook, Lemuel, III
Seals, Theodore Hollis
Sengstacke, Myiti
Sherrell, Charles Ronald, II
Simmons, James Richard
Simmons, Willie
Simpson, Dr. Willa Jean
Sims-Davis, Edith R.
Singleton, Harold, III
Sizemore, Barbara A.
Skinner, Clementine Anna McConico
Skinner, Robert L, Jr.
Smith, Dr. Ann Elizabeth
Smith, Daniel H, Jr.
Smith, Dawn C F
Smith, Dolores J
Smith, Thelma J
Soliunas, Francine Stewart
Sosa, Samuel Peralta
South, Leslie Elaine
Spearman, Venita
Speights, John D.
Speller, Eugene Thurley

Spellman, Alonzo Robert
Spencer, Rozelle Jeffery
Staggers, Robin L
Starks, Robert Terry
Sterling, John
Stevens, Michelle
Stewart, Charles J
Stewart, Dr. Donald Mitchell
Stewart, William O.
Stratton-Morris, Madeline Robinson Morgan
Stringer, Nelson Howard, Jr.
Stroger, John Herman, Jr.
Sumner, Thomas Robert
Swiner, Dr. Connie, III
Taylor, Cora
Taylor, James
Taylor, Dr. Regina
Taylor, T Shawn
Temple, Herbert
Terrell, Dr. Melvin C
Thomas, Barbara Louise
Thomas, Charles Richard
Thomas, Raymond A
Thompson, Lowell Dennis
Thompson, Mark Randolph
Thompson, Richard Ellis
Thornton, Dr. John C
Thurman, Cedric Douglas
Tolliver, Rev. Joel
Tolliver, Dr. Richard Lamar
Travis, Dempsey J
Tribbett, Charles A., III
Trotter, Donne
Tucker, Robert L
Tyson, Lance C
Vance, William J., Sr.
Vertreace-Doody, Martha Modena
Wade, Joyce K
Walker, Albertina
Walker, Allene Marsha
Walker, Eugene Kevin
Walker, Lee H
Walters, Ronald L., Jr.
Walton, James Donald
Ward, Bill
Ward, Calvin
Ware, Dyahanne
Warmack, Gregory
Warmack, Kevin Lavon
Watkins, Judge Charles, Jr.
Watson, Clyniece Lois
Watson, Timothy S
Watt, Garland Wedderick
Watters, Linda A
Webb, Joseph
West, Donda C
Whack, Rita Coburn
Wheaton, Thelma Kirkpatrick
Wheeler, Lloyd G
Wheeler, Robyn Elaine
White, Deidre R
White, Jesse C.
White, John H
White, Lois Jean
White, Selma Stewart
Whiting, Leroy
Whiting, Willie
Whittler, Dr. Thomas
Whyte, Garrett
Wilder, Jason Barnard
Williams, Ann Claire
Williams, David S., Jr.
Williams, Edward Joseph
Williams, Elynor A
Williams, Fitzroy E
Williams, Frank J
Williams, Jeanette Marie
Williams, Jeffrey Lem
Williams, Ken
Williams, McGhee
Williams, Norman J
Williams, Philip B.
Williams, W Bill
Williams, Hon. Walter
Wilson, Cleo Francine
Wilson, John E.
Wilson, Velma J
Wilson, Willie James
Wiltz, Charles J.
Winbush, Clarence, Jr.
Winfrey, Oprah
Winstead, Dr. Vernon A, Sr.
Winston, Dr. Neil Emerson
Wood, Hon. William S
Woods, Jessie Anderson
Woods, Wilbourne F
Wright, Antoinette D
Wright, Rev. Dr. Jeremiah A, Jr.

W. Terri, Winston
Wyatt, Addie L
Wyatt, Claude Stell, Jr.
Wycliff, Noel Don
Wynn, Sylvia J
Wyrick, Floyd I.
Yates, LeRoy Louis
Young, Donald G
Young, James M., II
Young, Terrence Anthony
Young, Terri Jones
Zollar, Doris L.
Zollar, Nikki Michele

Chicago Heights
Abdullah, Dr. Larry Burley
Artis, Jennifer
McIntosh, Rhodina Covington
Owens, Rev. Zelba Rene

Chicago,
Ferguson, Renee

Country Club Hills
Knox, Marshall

Crete
Minor, DeWayne
Parker, Jacquelyn Heath

Danville
Blanden, Lee Ernest
Foulks Foster, Ivadale Marie

Darien
Heard, Georgina E

DeKalb
Bernoudy, Monique Rochelle
Daniel, Phillip T. K.
Thurman, Alfonzo
Williams, Dr. Eddie R
Williams, Prof. Edna C.
Young, Alfred F.

Decatur
Dobbins, Alphondus Milton
Ford, Deborah Lee

Deerfield
Cobb, Cynthia Joan
Gavin, James Raphael, III
Harrold, Jeffery Deland
Oglesby, Boris
Williams, Edward Ellis

Dekalb
Patton, Ricardo Maurice

Dolton
Lee, Dr. Gwendolyn B

Downers Grove
Nichols, Alfred Glen

East Moline
Edwards, Kenneth J.

East St Louis
Allen, Dr. Edna Rowery
Clayborne, Oneal
Dennis, Philip H.
Jackson, Willis Randell, II
Joyner-Kersee, Jackie
Mason, William E.
McGaughy, Will
Murphy, Della Mary
Officer, Carl Edward
Redmond, Eugene B.
Wharton, Milton S
Wright, Dr. Katie Harper
Wright, Marvin
Younge, Richard G

Edwardsville
Grist, Arthur L.
Haley, Prof. Johnetta Randolph
Hampton, Phillip Jewel
Smith, Joseph Edward
Wilson, Rudolph George

Elgin
Liautaud, Gregory
Liautaud, James

Vessup, Dr. Aaron Anthony

Elk Grove Township
Ward, Melissa

Evanston
Alexis, Dr. Marcus
Bethel, Kathleen Evonne
Binford, Henry C.
Byrdsong, Ricky
Cheeks, Carl L.
Curtis-Rivers, Susan Yvonne
Davis, Shani
Elam, Dr. Harry Penoy
Harris, Dr. Robert Allen
Hine, Darlene Clark
Hoyt, Bishop Thomas L
Jordan, Thurman
Lowe, Eugene Yerby
McMillan, Lemmon Columbus, II
Montgomery, Toni-Marie
Morton, Lorraine H
Osborne, Gwendolyn Eunice
Phillips, Bertrand D.
Phillips, Daniel P
Reynolds, Bruce Howard
Stewart, Jacqueline
Summers, Edna White
Taylor, Hycel B.
Warfield, William C.
Willis, Jill Michelle
Wilson, Jonathan Charles

Evergreen Park
Bernoudy, Monique Rochelle

Flossmoor
Ellis, Douglas, Jr.
Killingsworth Finley, Sandra Jean
Marsh, McAfee
Richmond, Delores Ruth
South, Leslie Elaine
Whack, Rita Coburn

Ford Heights
Beck, Saul L.

Forsyth
Moorehead, Thomas

Frankfort
Johnson, Eric G

Galesburg
Hord, Dr. Frederick Lee

Glenview
Roebuck-Hayden, Marcia
Winfield, Florence F.

Glenwood
Fentress, Shirley B.
Howard-Coleman, Billie Jean
Sutherland, Frankie

Grayslake
Northern, David A

Great Lakes
Davis, Sidney Louis

Gurnee
Larkin, Michael Todd

Hanover Park
Harrison, Delbert Eugene

Harvey
Barksdale, Chuck
Brown-Nash, JoAhn Weaver
Demonbreun, Thelma M
Junior, Marvin
Lee, Clara Marshall
McGill, Michael
Sherrell, Charles Ronald, II

Hazel Crest
Nichols, Alfred Glen

Highland Park
McCallum, Walter Edward

Hoffman Estates
Cwiklinski, Cheryl A
Lewis, Alwyn
Payton, Walter Jerry

Homewood
Banks, Ronald
Burleson, Dr. Helen L.
LaVeist, Wilbert Francisco

Hopkins Park
Runnels, Bernice M.

Jacksonville
Maye, Richard

Joliet
Bolden, Raymond A
Dukes, Carl R
Gavin, Mary Ann
Singleton, Isaac, Sr.
Young, Dr. Charles, Jr.

Kankakee
McCuiston, Dr. Stonewall, Jr.

Lake Forest
Graves, Roderick Lawrence
Hutchison, Dr. Peyton S.
Pace, Orlando Lamar
Smith, Lovie Lee
Sneed, Paula A

Lansing
Washington, Ben James, Jr.

Lisle
Allen, S Monique Nicole
Horton, Joann
Mass, Edna Elaine
Tucker-Allen, Sallie
Woodruff, Jeffrey Robert

Lockport
Blade-Tiggens, Denise Patricia

Lombard
Spooner, John C.

Long Grove
Johnson, Michael L
Martin, Charles Wesley

Lovejoy
Matthews, Dorothy

Lynwood
Reed, Dr. Charlotte

Macomb
Bracey, Willie Earl
Rutledge, Dr. Essie Manuel

Makanda
Shepherd, Benjamin Arthur

Marion
Stewart, Kebu

Matteson
Kirkland, Gwendolyn V
Sutton, Nathaniel K

Maywood
Brown, Joseph Davidson, Sr.
Morris, Leibert Wayne
Pratt, Melvin Lemar
Rodez, Andrew LaMarr
Rose, Bessie L
Sharpp, Nancy Charlene
Smith, Dolores J
Wordlaw, Clarence, Jr.

Melrose Park
McNelty, Harry

Milwaukee
Farley, William Horace, Jr.

Moline
Earl, Acie Boyd
Peters, Aulana Louise

Morton Grove
Croft, Norman F.

Mount Prospect
Brooks, Clyde Henry
Sayers, Gale Eugene

Mount Vernon
Kendrick, L John, Sr.

Naperville
Cousin, Rev. Philip R
Freeland, Russell L

Montgomery, Brian Walter
Perry, Gary W

Normal
Colvin, Dr. William E
Morris, Dr. Charles Edward, Jr.
Visor, Julia N.

Norridge
Washington, William

North Barrington
Shackelford, George Franklin

North Chicago
Brooks, Wadell, Sr.
Lampley, Dr. Edward Charles
Luther, Lucius Calvin
Newberry, Trudell McClelland
Robinson, Kenneth

Northbrook
Thomas, Isaac Daniel, Jr.
Woodard, Rhonda Marie

Northfield
McGuire, Kennard

O Fallon
Chalmers, Thelma Faye

Oak Brook
Canady, Blanton Thandreus
Coaxum, Harry Lee
Hill, Joseph Havord
Isaacs, Patricia
Mines, Raymond C
Rogers-Reece, Shirley
Watson, Daniel

Oak Park
Evans, Gregory James
Farley, William Horace, Jr.
Lee, Dr. Charlotte O.
Lucas, Dorothy J.
Maryland, Mary Angela
Nesbitt, Prexy-Rozell William
Robinet, Harriette Gillem
Strickland, R. James
Walton, James Donald

Olympia Fields
Burleson, Dr. Helen L.
Hicks-Bartlett, Sharon Theresa
Richmond, Delores Ruth
Scott, Col. Eugene Frederick

Oswego
Fregia, Ray, Sr.

Ottawa
Cunningham, Joy Virginia

Park Forest
Apea, Joseph Bennet Kyeremateng
Haney, Napoleon
Hicks-Bartlett, Sharon Theresa
Hill, Dr. Paul Gordon
Howard, Shirley M.
Simpson, Juanita H

Park Ridge
Cheeks, Darryl Lamont

Peoria
Garrett, Romeo Benjamin
Hendrix, Deborah Lynne
McDade, Joe Billy
Penelton, Barbara Spencer
Russell, Joseph D.

Prospect Heights
Leggette, Lemire

Richton Park
Martin, Myron C

River Forest
Johnson-Odim, Dr. Cheryl

River Grove
Latimer, Ina Pearl
Lee, Dr. Charlotte O.

Riverdale
Burton, William A
Sutherland, Frankie

Robbins
Clemons, Flenor
Dunn-Barker, Lillian Joyce

Haymore, Tyrone
Jones, Dr. William Jenipher

Rock Island
Mabry, Edward L

Rockford
Bell, Victory
Dotson-Williams, Henrietta
Gilbert, Eldridge H. E.
Lawson Roby, Kimberla
Palmer-Hildreth, Barbara Jean
Tyson, Cleveland Allen

Sherman
Smith, Gordon Allen

Skokie
Thomas, Hon. Mary Maxwell

South Holland
Perry, Rev. Joseph Nathaniel
Rockett, Damon Emerson

Springfield
Adams, Dr. Carol Laurence
Ali, Rasheedah Ziyadah
Anderson, Nathaniel
Ball-Reed, Patrice M.
Bowen, Richard, Jr.
Box, Charles
Forney, Mary Jane
Jones, Emil
King, Charles Abraham
Lawrence, Archie
Lee, Edwin Archibald
Logan, Willis Hubert
McNeil, Frank William
Moore, Arnold D.
Morrison, Dr. Juan LaRue, Sr.
Osby, Simeon B., Jr.
Rambo, Bettye R.
Shoultz, Rudolph Samuel
Singley, Elijah
Singley, Yvonne Jean
Trees, Candice D.
Veal, Howard Richard
White, Jesse C.
Williams, Annie
Yarbrough, Karen

St Anne
Haney, Napoleon
Wade, Casey, Jr.

University Park
Hulett, Rosemary D
Kennedy, Dr. Joyce S.

Urbana
Adams, Billie Morris Wright
Copeland, Robert M.
Eubanks, Robert A.
Gibbs, Dr. Sandra E
Ransom, Dr. Preston L
Robinson, Dr. Walker Lee
Summerville, Willie T
Thomas, Debi
Underwood, King James
Weissinger, Thomas
Williams, Willie James

Venice
Williams, Rev. John Henry

Villa Park
Glanville, Douglas Metunwa

Waukegan
Asma, Thomas M
Cook, Haney Judaea
Luther, Lucius Calvin
McCallum, Walter Edward
Thomas, Bette

Westchester
Cary, Rev. William Sterling
Hunter, Kimberly Alice

Westmont
Smith, Bruce L

Wheaton
Mass, Edna Elaine

Winnetka
Bridges, Ruby

Wood Dale
Porter, John T

Woodridge
Evans, Gregory James

chicago
Johnson, Ray

INDIANA

Anderson
Bridges, Dr. Alvin Leroy
Foggs, Edward L.
Morgan, Rev. Mary H Ethel
Simmons, Albert Bufort, Jr.
Steans, Edith Elizabeth
Williams, Donald Eugene
Woodall, Dr. John Wesley

Angola
Smith, Larry L

Bloomington
Baker, David Nathaniel
Burnim, Mellonee Victoria
Butler, Ernest Daniel
Chambliss, Alvin Odell, Jr.
Fletcher, Winona Lee
Garner, Dr. La Forrest Dean
Marshall, Dr. Edwin Cochran
Maultsby, Dr. Portia K
McCluskey, Audrey Thomas
McCluskey, John A
Pierce, Dr. Raymond O., Jr.
Taliaferro, Viola J.
Watts, Andre
Wiggins, William H., Jr.
Williams, Camilla Ella
Wright, Joseph A

Carmel
Smith, Dr. John Arthur

Columbus
Carter, Pamela Lynn
Trapp, Donald W.

Crown Point
Bradley, Hilbert L.
Clay, Rudolph

East Chicago
Florence, Johnny C.
Morris, Melvin
Randolph, Lonnie Marcus

Elkhart
Breckenridge, Franklin E., Sr.
Hill, Curtis T., Sr.

Evansville
Burton, Lana Doreen
Claybourne, Edward P.
Lawrence, Philip Martin
Malone, Michael Gregory
Miller, Mattie Sherryl
Moss, Estella Mae
Neal, Dr. Ira Tinsley

Fishers
Burris, Jeffrey Lamar

Fort Wayne
Adams, Dr. Verna May Shoecraft
Barksdale, Mary Frances
Brown, Priscilla
Connor, James Russell
Dobynes, Elizabeth
Edwards, Dr. Miles Stanley
Hunter, Rev. Sylvester
Jordan, Rev. Ternae T
Mizzell, William Clarence
Nolan, Daniel Kaye
Pressey, Junius Batten, Jr.
Scott, Levan Ralph
Stith, Hana L
Winters, James Robert

Gary
Bolling, Barbara
Boone, Clarence Wayne
Brown, Charles
Brundidge, Nancy Corinne
Carr, Sandra Jean Irons

Chambers, YJean S.
Clay, Rudolph
Comer, Jonathan
Comer, Zeke
Davidson, Dr. Charles Odell
Finn, John William
Fisher, Lloyd B.
Fisher, Shelley Marie
Freeland, Robert Lenward, Jr.
Freeman-Wilson, Karen Marie
Grimes, Douglas M.
Hamblin, Angela
Hawkins, Calvin D
Haywood, Roosevelt V., III
Ige, Dr. Dorothy
Ige, Dr. Dorothy W K
Irons, Sandra Jean
Johnson, Wallace Darnell
Jones, Bertha H.
Lowery, Robert O.
Millender, Dharathula H.
Morgan, Randall Collins, Sr.
Owens, Isaiah Hudson
Parrish, John Henry
Powers, Mamon M
Reed, Dr. Charlotte
Richards, Dr. Hilda
Smith, Vernon G
Stephens, Dr. Paul A
Taylor, Ruth Sloan
Wright, Charlotte

Goshen
Berry, Lee Roy

Granger
Calvin, Dr. Virginia Brown

Greencastle
Warren, Dr. Stanley

Hammond
Casanova, Dr. Gisele M
Chambers, YJean S.
Parrish, John Henry
Watkins, Dr. Walter J.

Highland
Cain, Nathaniel Z, Jr.

Huntingburg
Tollett, Dr. Charles Albert, Sr., M.D.

Indianapolis
Alexander, Vincent J.
Allen, Eugene, Jr.
Allen, Robert
Alloy, Dr. Valerie
Andrews, Carl R.
Artis, Anthony Joel
Bailey, Aaron Duane
Batties, Dr. Paul Terry
Bean, Walter Dempsey
Blackburn, Alpha C.
Blackmon, Robert James
Blair, Charles Michael
Boyd, Rozelle
Brewer, Webster L.
Brown, Andrew J.
Brown, Charles
Bryant, Jenkins, Jr.
Burroughs, Sammie Lee
Caldwell, James L
Carson, Julia M
Chowning, Frank Edmond
Clark, Rico Cornell
Clemons, Linda K
Coleman, Barbara Sims
Conner, Lester Allen
Crawford, William A.
Davis, Bennie L.
Downing, Stephen
Draper, Frederick Webster
Dungy, Tony
Faulk, Marshall William
Freeman-Wilson, Karen Marie
Gainer, Frank Edward
Gordon, Clifford Wesley
Gray, Moses W.
Haines, Charles Edward
Hanley, J Frank
Harkness, Jerry
Harris, Earl L.
Harris, Edward E.
Harrison, Calvin
Herrod, Jeff Sylvester
Hodge, Aleta S.
Hodges, Patricia Ann

Jackson, Darcy DeMille
Jeter-Johnson, Sheila Ann
Jones, Sam H, Sr.
Jones, William Edward
Journey, Lula Mae
Joyner, John Erwin
Keglar, Shelvy Haywood
Keith, Floyd A
King, Warren Earl
Lane, Johnny Lee
Lee, Nathaniel
Leek, Sandra D
Lewis, Cleveland Arthur
Little, Leone Bryson
Little, Monroe Henry
Lowe, Dr. Aubrey F.
Lyons, Lloyd Carson
Mays, William G
Mickey, Dr. Gordon Eugene
Miller, Mattie Sherryl
Mills, Alan Keith
Moore, Cleotha Franklin
Morrison, Dr. Gwendolyn Christine Caldwell
Newton, Pynkerton Dion
Oldham, Algie Sidney, Jr.
O'Neal, Jermaine
Owsley, Betty Joan
Powers, Clyde J
Rawls, Dr. George H
Rhea, Michael
Rhinehart, N Pete
Rice, Fredrick LeRoy
Robinson, Donald Lee
Robinson, Sherman
Rogers, Earline S
Ross, Dr. Edward
Ross, N. Rodney
Rucker, Dr. Robert D.
Rutledge, Philip J
Sam, Sheri
Scott, Julie
Scott, Dr. Leonard Stephen
Scott, Dr. Marvin Bailey
Shaw, Nancy H.
Shello, Kendel
Shields, Rev. Landrum Eugene
Slash, Joseph A
Smith, Dr. John Arthur
Smith, Vernon G
Spearman, Larna Kaye
Stevenson, Lillian
Stokes, Dr. Lillian Gatlin
Strong, Amanda L
Summers, Joseph W.
Tandy, Dr. Mary B
Taylor, Gilbert Leon
Thomas, Edward P.
Townsend, Mamie Lee Harrington
Walker-Smith, Rev. Dr. Angelique Keturah
Warren, Lamont
Watkins, Joseph Philip
Waugh, Judith Ritchie
Wells, Payton R.
Williams, Charles Richard
Williams, Vernice Louise
Williams-Dotson, Daryl

Kendallville
Driver, David E

Kokomo
Artis, Myrle Everett
Clarke, Theodore Henson

Marion
Casey, Joseph F
Marshall, Eric A
Pettiford, Quentin H.

Merrillville
Brown, Larry T.

Michigan City
Meriweather, Melvin, Jr.

Mishawaka
Williams, Theodore

Muncie
Booth, Lavaughn Venchael
Dowery, Mary
Foster, Bea Moten
Goodall, Hurley Charles
Greenwood, Dr. Charles H
Greenwood, Dr. Theresa M Winfrey
Kelley, Daniel, Jr.

Kumbula, Dr. Tendayi Sengerwe
Payne, Dr. June P
Womack, Henry Cornelius

Munster
Senegal, Charles

New Albany
Craft, E. Carrie

New Castle
Walker, William B

Noblesville
Hansen, Wendell Jay

North Vernon
Bass, Dr. Laurent

Notre Dame
Cleveland, Granville E.
Outlaw, Warren Gregory
Parmalee, Bernard A.
Wright, Dr. Frederick Douglass

Richmond
Patterson, Paul A
Sawyer, George Edward
Williams, Clyde

Shelbyville
Garrett, James Edward, Jr.

Sheridan
Daniels, Melvin J.

South Bend
Batteast, Robert V.
Calvin, Dr. Virginia Brown
Davis, Glen Anthony
Easton, Earnest Lee
Gilkey, William C.
Giloth-David, King R.
Hughes, Hollis Eugene, Jr.
Martin, Charles Edward, Sr.
Outlaw, Warren Gregory
Wynns, Corliss Lorraine

St Meinrad
Davis, Cyprian

Terre Haute
Conyers, Dr. James Ernest
Harrison, Angela
Howell, Laurence A.
Lyda, Wesley John
Martin, Mary E. Howell
Simpson-Taylor, Dr. Dorothy Marie

Valparaiso
Hatcher, Richard Gordon
Perry, Margaret

Vincennes
Summitt, Gazella Ann

West Lafayette
Blalock, Marion W.
Francisco, Joseph Salvadore
Martin, Kimberly Lynette
Mobley, Emily Ruth

IOWA

Scott, Melvina Brooks

Ames
Graham, Frederick Mitchell
Hunter, Dr. William Andrew
Perry, Leonard Douglas, Jr.

Ankeny
Howard, Glen

Cedar Falls
Kirkland-Holmes, Dr. Gloria

Cedar Rapids
Lipscomb, Darryl L.

Clinton
Wynn, LaMetta K

Clive
Crawford, James Maurice

Columbus
Evans, Dr. Donna Browder

Coralville
Berry, Venise

Davenport
Collins, James H.
Drew-Peeples, Brenda
Walker Williams, Hope Denise

Des Moines
Colston, Monroe James
Davis, Evelyn K.
Gentry, Nolden I., Jr.
Gilbert, Dr. Fred D.
Higgs, Mary Ann Spicer
Houston, Marsh S.
Jerrard, Paul
Maxwell, Roger Allan
McGhee, Odell G, II
Morris, Robert V
Nickerson, Don Carlos
Strickland, Dr. Frederick William, Jr.
Williams, Georgianna M

Dubuque
Jaycox, Mary Irine

Fort Dodge
Burleson, Jane Geneva

Grinnell
Gibel Mevorach, Katya

Indianola
Nichols, Dimaggio

Iowa City
Carter, Keith
Dungy, Dr. Claibourne I.
Hawkins, Dr. Benny F
Henry, Joseph King
Jones, Dr. Phillip Erskine
Mask, Susan L
McPherson, James Alan
Rodgers, Vincent G
Wing, Prof. Adrien Katherine
Woodard, Fredrick

Keokuk
Weldon, Ramon N.

Marshalltown
James, Dava Paulette

Mt Vernon
Monagan, Dr. Alfrieta Parks

Sioux City
Bluford, Grady L
Silva, Arthur P.

Waterloo
Abebe, Ruby
Anderson, Ruth Bluford
Cribbs, Williams Charles
Scott, Melvina Brooks
Weems, Vernon Eugene, Jr.

Waverly
Estes, Simon Lamont

West Burlington
Singletary, Reggie Leslie

West Des Moines
Greene, Franklin D
Saunders, Dr. Meredith Roy

KANSAS

Coffeyville
Price, Dr. Paul Sanford

Emporia
Bonner, Dr. Mary Winstead

Hesston
Cranford, Dr. Sharon Hill

Hutchinson
Crable, Dallas Eugene

Junction City
Dozier, Morris Cicero
Walker, Ronald Plezz

Kansas City
Beavers, Robert M.
Caruthers, Dr. Patricia Wayne

Criswell, Arthurine Denton
Dancy, William F.
Davis, James Parker
Freeman, Edward Anderson
Haley, David
Jenkins, Melvin Lemuel
Jerome, Dr. Norge Winifred
Jones, Herman Harvey, Jr.
Jones, Sherman Jarvis
Justice, Norman E.
Littlejohn, John B.
Manning, Brian
Meeks, Cordell David
Miller, Dr. Dennis Weldon
Parker, Maryland Mike
Smith, Edward Charles
Washington, Alonzo Lavert
Washington, Nancy Ann
White, Luther D.
Williams, Herbert C.

Lawrence
Criswell, Arthurine Denton
Gray-Little, Dr. Bernadette
Harris, William J
Manning, Daniel Ricardo
Sanders, Dr. Robert B
Tidwell, John Edgar
Vannaman, Madi T

Leavenworth
Moore-Stovall, Dr. Joyce

Leawood
Richie, Leroy C.

Manhattan
Dozier, Morris Cicero

Newton
Rogers, George

Olathe
Brogden, Robert, Jr.
Gray, Rev. Maceo

Overland Park
Claiborne, Lloyd R.
Shields, Will Herthie

Pittsburg
Hill, Dennis Odell

Salina
Parker, Maryland Mike

Shawnee
Jerome, Dr. Norge Winifred

Shawnee Mission
Summers, Loretta M

Topeka
Alexander, F S Jack
Barker, Pauline J.
Bolden, James Lee
Bonaparte, Norton Nathaniel
Bremby, Roderick LeMar
Bugg, Robert
Edwards, Horace Burton
Gardner, Cedric Boyer
Griffin, Ronald Charles
Henderson, Cheryl Brown
Henderson, Frank S, Jr.
Lewis, Wendell J.
Littlejohn, John B.
Love, Clarence C.
Otudeko, Adebisi Olusoga
Parks, Sherman A.
Rainbow-Earhart, Dr. Kathryn Adeline
Thompson, Joseph Allan

Wichita
Anderson, Eugene
Conley, Frankielieen
Evans, Kamiel Denise
Hayes, Graham Edmondson
Hutcherson, Bernice B R
Johnson, Thomas H
King, Clarence Maurice
McAfee, Charles Francis
McCray, Billy Quincy
Mitchell, Jacob Bill
Preston, Richard Clark
Tookes, Hansel, II
Vaughn, Mary Kathryn

Wesley, Clarence E.
Williams, T. Joyce

Winfield
Brooks, William P

KENTUCKY

Blye, Cecil A., Sr.
Martin, Cornelius A.

Ashland
Fryson, Sim E.

Barbourville
Daniels, Anthony Hawthorne

Berea
Baskin, Andrew Lewis
Olinger, David Y, Jr.

Bowling Green
Ardrey, Dr. Saundra Curry
Hardin, Dr. John Arthur
Jackson, Earl J.
Long, John Edward
Moxley, Frank O.

Clinton
Dillard, Howard Lee

Elizabethtown
Green, Larry W.
Robbins, Jessica Dowe

Florence
Spight, Benita L

Fort Knox
McGriggs-Jamison, Imogene

Frankfort
Banks, Ronald Trenton
Evans, William Clayton
Fleming, Dr. Juanita W.
Fletcher, Winona Lee
Gibson, Betty M.
Graham, Delores Metcalf
Jackson, Lee Arthur
Lambert, Charles H.
McDaniel, Karen Cotton
Rich, Isadore A
Ridgel, Dr. Gus Tolver
Smith, Andrew W.
Strickland-Hill, Dr. Marva Yvonne
Stuckey, Sheila Arnetta
Troupe, Dr. Marilyn Kay

Fulton
Dillard, Howard Lee

Georgetown
Mason, Luther Roscoe

Glasgow
Watts, Wilsonya Richardson

Highland Heights
Washington, Dr. Michael Harlan

Lexington
Bramwell, Dr. Fitzgerald Burton
Chance, Dr. Kenneth Bernard
Fakhrid-Deen, Nashid Abdullah
Fernandez-Smith, Wilhelmenia
Finn, Robert Green, Jr.
Forsythe, Hazel
Grundy, Chester
Harding, Roberta
Harley, Dr. Debra A.
Harris, Joseph John, III
Hildreth, Gladys Johnson
Holland, Robert
Jackson, Lee Arthur
Locke-Mattox, Bernadette
McCorvey, Dr. Everett D.
Olinger, David Y, Jr.
Smith, Andrew W.
Smith, Dr. Gerald Lamont
Stephens, Herman Alvin
Stout, Louis
Turner, Dr. William Hobert

Wilkinson, Doris
Williamson, Dr. Lionel

Louisville
Ali, Muhammad
Amos, Larry C.
Anderson, Carey Laine, Jr.
Anderson, Jay Rosamond
Aubespin, Mervin R.
Bateman, Michael Allen
Bather, Paul Charles
Baye, Betty Winston
Brown, Beverly J.
Burks, Juanita Pauline
Burse, Raymond Malcolm
Carter, Kenneth Gregory
Chenault, John
Coleman, James William
Daniels, C. Mackey
Davidson, Rudolph Douglas
Graham, Tecumseh Xavier
Griffith, Darrell Steven
Guyton, Sister Patsy
Hackett, Wilbur L
Hamilton, Edward N
Hart, Brenda G.
Hines, Carl R
Houston, Alice K.
Hudson, Dr. James Blaine
Jackson, Thelma Conley
Jones, Chester
Jones, Katherine Coleman
Jones, Dr. Yvonne Vivian
Lyles, Leonard E.
Majozo, Estella Conwill
Martin, Janice R.
McCarty, Walter Lee
McDonald, Larry Marvin
Meeks, Reginald Kline
Payne, Mitchell Howard
Pittman, Winston R., Sr.
Powers, Georgia M.
Richardson, Rhonda Karen
Roberts, Charles L.
Robinson, Jonathan N.
Robinson, Dr. Samuel
Sharp, Charles Louis
Smith, Robert W.
Summers, William E., IV
Taylor-Archer, Mordean
Thomas, Patrick Arnold
Troutman, Dr. Adewale
Turner, M Annette
Upshaw, Sam
Walker, Cynthia Bush
Washington, Patrice Clarke
White, Robert C
Williams, Harold L, Jr.
Young, Dr. Coleman Milton, III
Young, Herman A.
Young, Dr. Joyce Howell
Young-Sall, Hajar

Madisonville
Lowery, Michael Douglas

Midway
Bradley, Walter Thomas, Jr.

Morehead
Strider, Maurice William

Murray
Owens, Dr. Debbie A.

Nicholasville
Mensah, Nana

Paducah
Coleman, Robert A

Princeton
Moore, Allyn D

Prospect
Burse, Raymond Malcolm
Robbins, Jessica Dowe

Radcliff
Richard, Dr. Henri-Claude

Russellville
Hampton, Willie L.

Somerset
Wilson, Grant Paul, Jr.

Versailles
Fakhrid-Deen, Nashid Abdullah

LOUISIANA

Abbeville
Myles, Herbert John

Alexandria
Hines, J. Edward, Jr.
Larvadain, Edward
Metoyer, Rosia G

Angie
Ross, Emma Jean

Angola
Rideau, Wibert

Baker
Doomes, Dr. Earl

Bastrop
Hamlin, Arthur Henry
Loche, Lee Edward
Montgomery, Payne

Baton Rouge
Boddie, Gwendolyn M
Broome, Sharon Weston
Brown, Georgia W
Brown, Reginald Royce
Butler, Michael Keith
Calloway, Curtis A.
Carpenter, Barbara West
Chaney, Regmon A
Cobb, Dr. Thelma M.
Collins, Warren Eugene
Cummings, Roberta Spikes
Davidson, Dr. Kerry
Davis, Dr. Donald Fred
Davis, Lucille H.
Dawson, Dr. Alma
Delpit, Joseph A.
Dickens, Samuel
Dixon, Cheryl McKay
Doomes, Dr. Earl
Durant, Dr. Thomas James
Ellois, Edward R., Jr.
Evans, Mattie
Fields, Cleo
Frierson, Michael Anthony
George, Frankie
Green, Brenda Kay
Hall, David Anthony, Jr.
Hall, Robert Joseph
Hamer, Dr. Jaquator
Hardy, Timothy W
Haynes, John K.
Haynes, Leonard L., Jr.
Hayward, Olga Loretta Hines
Holden, Melvin Lee
Holt, Dr. Essie W.
Isadore, Harold W.
Jeffers, Ben L.
Johnson-Blount, Theresa
Jones, Johnnie Anderson
Kelly, Rev. Dr. Herman Osby
Kinchen, Dennis Ray
Lacour, Vanue B.
LaVergne, Luke Aldon
Lee, Dr. Allen Francis, Jr.
Lundy, Dr. Harold W
McNairy, Sidney A.
Mencer, Dr. Ernest James
Moch, Lawrence E.
Nelson, Otha Curtis
Nesbitt, Robin Anthony
Oliver, Robert Lee
Peoples, VerJanis Andrews
Perkins, Huel Davis
Perry, Emma Bradford
Pitcher, Freddie, Jr.
Prestage, James J.
Prestage, Dr. Jewel Limar
Prudhomme, Nellie Rose
Raby, Clyde T
Roberts, Dr. Jonathan
Stamper, Henry J.
Steptoe, Roosevelt
Stone, Jesse Nealand, Jr.
Tarver II, Dr. Leon R
Thomas, Arthur R
Turnley, Richard Dick, Jr.
Warner, Isiah Manuel
Wells, Roderick Arthur

Weston, Sharon
Williams, Dr. Karen Renee
Winfield, William T
Wright, Loyce Pierce

Belle Rose
Melancon, Norman

Bogalusa
Jenkins, Gayle Expose
Mims, Raymond Everett, Sr.

Bunkie
Sheppard, Stevenson Royrayson

Carville
Thomas, Alvin
Williams, Leslie J.

Crowley
Julian, John Tyrone
Wilson, Sherman Arthur

Eunice
Fields, Savoynne Morgan
Sergeant, Carra Susan
Thomas, Dr. Marvette Jeraldine

Franklinton
Martin, Rayfus
Tate, Matthew

Gonzales
Thomas, Irma

Grambling
Days, Rosetta Hill
Emmanuel, Dr. Tsegai
Gallot, Richard Joseph
Judson, Dr. Horace Augustus
Lee, Pauline W.
Smith, Arthur D.
Warner, Dr. Neari Francois

Greensburg
Paddio-Johnson, Dr. Eunice Alice
Payne, Jerry Oscar

Gretna
Madison, Dr. Romell J
Zeno, Melvin Collins

Harvey
Aramburo, Sophie Watts
Eziemefe, Godslove Ajenavi
Guidry, David
Mackie, Dr. Calvin

Hodge
Bradford, James Edward

Houma
Butler, Michael Keith

Jonesboro
Bradford, James Edward

Kenner
Ellis, Zachary L

Lafayette
Baranco, Raphael Alvin
Burns, Benjamin O.
Caillier, James Allen
Gaines, Ernest J.
Hegger, Wilber L
McZeal, Alfred, Sr.
Prudhomme, Nellie Rose
Thomas, Orlando

Lake Charles
Blackwell, Faye Brown
Cole, Charles Zhivaga
Miller, Dr. Andrea Lewis
Mims, Raymond Everett, Sr.
Shelton, Harold Tillman
St Mary, Joseph Jerome

Lake Providence
Frazier, Ray Jerrell

Lebeau
Labrie, Harrington
Taylor, Vanessa Gail

Lutcher
Jones, Nathaniel, Sr.

Mandeville
Ward, Keith Lamont

Mansfield
Patterson, Dessie Lee

Mansura
Cadoria, Sherian Grace

Marrero
Gumms, Emmanuel George, Sr.
Odom, Carla Morgan

Melville
Haynes, Willie C., III

Metairie
Bellamy, Jay
Guliford, Eric Andre
Hills, Keno
Jenkins, Trezelle Samuel
Johnson, Alonzo
Johnson, Tony
McKenzie, Michael
Pittman, Julian
Prioleau, Pierson
Sharper, Darren
Thomas, Hollis

Monroe
Garrett, Louis Henry
James, Eldridge M.
Jones, Charles D
Miller, Joseph Herman
Turner, Ervin

Natchitoches
Brossette, Alvin, Jr.
Johnson, Ben D.

New Iberia
Carrier, Clara L DeGay
Small, Stanley Joseph

New Orleans
Allen, Charles Edward
Bajoie, Diana E
Barnett, Helene
Barthelemy, Sidney John
Bashful, Dr. Emmett Wilfort
Birch, Willie
Bishop, Wesley T
Borders, Florence Edwards
Bouie, Joseph, Jr.
Bourgeois, Wardell R.
Braden, Henry E, IV
Breda, Malcolm J
Brister, Darryl Sylvester
Brown, Dr. Darlene Morgan
Brown, Debria M.
Brown, Winston D
Bruno, Michael B.
Burchell, Charles R.
Burns, Leonard L
Bynum, Horace Charles, Sr.
Caillier, James Allen
Carey, Addison, Jr.
Carter, Dr. James P.
Carter, Oscar Earl, Jr.
Carter, Troy A
Causey-Konate', Tammie
Charbonnet, Louis, III
Chase, Dooky, Jr.
Chigbu, Gibson Chuks
Coaxum, Henry L
Collins, Robert Frederick
Connor, George C., Jr.
Cook, Jeffrey
Copelin, Sherman Nathaniel
Craft, Sally-Ann Roberts
Dalferes, Edward R., Jr.
Davis, Jacklean Andrea
Doley, Ambassador Harold E
Dorsey, John L.
Duncan, Sandra Rhodes
Feltus, James, Jr.
Foster, Janice Martin
Francis, Dr. Norman C
Gibson, Antonio Marice
Glapion, Michael J
Goins, Richard Anthony
Gray, James Austin, II
Green, Hydia Lutrice
Hagan, Gwenael Stephane
Harris, Dr. Walter

Haydel, James V, Sr.
Hutchinson, James J., Jr.
Irons, Hon. Paulette R
Jackson, Greg Allen
James, Dr. Felix
Javery, Michael
Jefferson-Bullock, Jalila
Johnson, Bernette Joshua
Johnson, Jon D.
Jolly, Mary B
Jones, Michael B
Jordan, Eddie
Jordan, Eddie Jack, Sr
Kazi, Abdul-Khaliq Kuumba
Kelly, Marion Greenup
LeDoux, Jerome G
Lee, Dr. Silas, III
Lemelle, Ivan
Leonard, Catherine W.
Lewis, Michele
Loving, Rose
Loyd, Walter
Lundy, Larry
Marsalis, Jason
Massey, Janelle Renee
Mayfield, Curtis
McFarland, Arthur C
Misshore, Joseph O, Jr.
Montgomery, Willie Henry
Moore, Hazel Stamps
Mosley, Carolyn W
Nagin, C. Ray
Patnett, John Henry
Perkins, Thomas P.
Phillips, Rev. F Allison
Pittman, Keith B.
Powell, Bettye Boone
Richard, Alvin J.
Richmond, Rodney Welch
Robinson, Dr. Sandra Lawson
Roussell, Norman
Saulny, Cyril
Scott, Byron
Scott, John T, PhD
Shorty, Vernon James
Sigur, Wanda Anne Alexander
Simmons, Norbert
Smith, Norman Raymond
Stampley, Gilbert Elvin
St Etienne, Gregory Michael
Swanson, Charles
Taylor, Herman Daniel
Teamer, Dr. Charles C., Sr.
Towns, Sanna Nimtz
Verrett, Shannon L.
Vincent, Daniel Paul
Ward, Dr. Jerry Washington
Washington, Betty Lois
Washington, Robert Orlanda
Weather, Dr. Leonard, Jr.
Webb, Horace S
Wells, Barbara Jones
Wells, Bonzi
Wiley, Dr. Kenneth LeMoyne
Williams, Cassandra Faye
Williams, Rev. Ellis
Williams, Joseph E
Wilson, James Davis
Worthy, Dr. Barbara Ann
Wright, James A.
Wright, Loyce Pierce
Young, Angela Lynn
Young, Wallace L., Jr.
Zu-Bolton, Ahmos, II

NewOrleans
Bechet, Ronald

Opelousas
Climmons, Willie Mathew
Loeb, Charles P., Jr.
Richard, Dr. Arlene Castain

Plaquemine
Dawkins, Michael James
Dawson, Peter Edward

Pleasant Hill
Shannon, George A.

Rayne
Senegal, Nolton Joseph, Sr.

Ruston
Emmanuel, Dr. Tsegai
Malone, Karl Anthony

Shreveport
Abdul-Rahman, Tahira Sadiqa
Allen, Elbert E.

Aytch, Donald Melvin
Barnes, Dr. Leonard C.
Bennett, Lonnie M
Buggs, James
Christopher, John A.
Collier, Louis Malcolm
Dixon, Tom L.
Dyas, Patricia Ann
Epps, Dolzie C. B.
Farr, Herman
Hardy, Eursla Dickerson
Hayes, Albertine Brannum
Holt, Dr. Dorothy L Thomas
Holt, Dr. Essie W.
Holt, Dr. James Stokes, III
Holt, Jonathan Lamar
Huckaby, Hilry, III
Patton, Joyce Bradford
Pennywell, Phillip, Jr.
Phillips, June M J
Redden, Camille J
Simpkins, Cuthbert O.
Stewart, Carl E.
Tarver, Gregory Williams
Weather, Dr. Leonard, Jr.
Williams, Robert Lee

Slidell
Campbell, Otis Levy

St Martinville
Garrett, Aline M.

St Rose
Wiley, Dr. Kenneth LeMoyne

Sunset
Taylor, Vanessa Gail

Tallulah
Anthony, Leander Aldrich
Williams, Moses, Sr.

Thibodaux
Alexander, Ronald Algernon
Hypolite, Dr. Christine Collins
Jones, Dr. Leslie Faye
Williams-Hayes, Thea

West Monroe
Brown, Philip Rayfield, III
Martin, Dr. Rev. Lawrence Raymond

Zachary
Ransburg, Frank S.
Smith, Zachary

MAINE

Auburn
Rogers, Dr. Bernard Rousseau

Augusta
Dines, George B
Howard, Ray F.

Bangor
Burney, William D

Islesford
Bryan, Ashley F.

Lewiston
Jenkins, John

Old Town
Varner, James, Sr.

Portland
Talbot, Gerald Edgerton

MARYLAND
Dixon, John M.
Turner, Marvin Wentz

Aberdeen
Bruce, Carol Pitt

Aberdeen Proving Ground
Cannon, Paul L

Adelphi
Marshall, Pluria W.

Annapolis
Brown, Maxine J. Childress
Brown, Philip Lorenzo

Burnett, Dr. Calvin W.
Burton, Valorie
Cane, Rudolph C
DeGeneste, Henry Irving
Duncan, Charles Tignor
Gerald, William
Harrison, Hattie N.
Herndon, Craig Garris
Hoyle, Dr. Classie G.
Kelley, Dr. Delores G.
Logan, Lewis E
Marriott, Dr. Salima Siler
McFadden, Nathaniel James
Mosley, Elwood A
Powell, Robert Meaker
Raymond, Henry James, II
Scipio, Laurence Harold
Tose, Maurice B.

Arnold
Ballard, James M., Jr.
Fisher, E Carleton
Pounds, Dr. Augustine Wright

Baltimore
Adams, Curtis N.
Adams, Gregory Keith
Adams, Victorine Quille
Amory, Reginald L
Armstrong, Ernest W., Sr.
Arrington, Dr. Pamela Gray
Aziz, Kareem A
Baines, Henry T., Sr.
Banks, Saundra Elizabeth
Bell, Robert Mack
Boon, Ina M.
Boonieh, Obi Anthony
Bowie, Dr. Janice
Bridges, Leon
Brooks, Dunbar
Brown, Benjamin Leonard
Brown, Eddie C.
Brown, Marsha J.
Bryant, William Arnett, Jr.
Buckson, Toni Yvonne
Burnett, Sidney Obed
Butcher, Dr. Philip
Camp, Marva Jo
Carson, Dr. Benjamin Solomon
Carter, Vincent G
Chambers, Donald C.
Chester, Joseph A., Sr.
Cline, Dr. Eileen Tate
Collier, Dr. Eugenia W.
Colvin, Ernest J.
Conaway, Mary Ward Pindle
Cornish, Mae Golder
Crew, John L., Sr.
Curry, Rev. Michael Bruce
Daniel, Colene Yvonne
Daniels, Sidney
Davis, Clarence
Davis, John Alexander
Davis, Samuel C
Dean, Walter R
DeLoatch, Dr. Eugene
DeSousa, D. Jason
Dickson, Onias D, Jr.
Dixon, Ardena S
Dixon, Sheila
Dockery, Richard L.
Donaldson, Leon Matthew
Dorsey, Charles Henry, Jr.
Dorsey, Denise
Doxie, Marvin Leon
Draper, Dr. Edgar Daniel
Draper, Rev. Frances Murphy
Dupree, Edward A
Durant, Naomi C.
Ellis, Kenneth K
Emeagwali, Dale Brown
Felton, Leonard Ray
Fitchue, M. Anthony
Fitts, Leroy
Franklin, Dr. Renty Benjamin
Frazier-Ellison, Vicki L
Froe, Otis David
Funn, Courtney Harris
Gaddy, Beatrice
Gantt, Walter N.
Gardner, Dr. Bettye J.
Gibbs, Nathaniel K.
Gill, Roberta L.
Gill, Walter Harris
Goodwin, Stefan Cornelius
Goss, Linda
Graham, Richard A.
Gray, Dr. C. Vernon
Green, Lester L.

Green, Sam
Ham, Dr. Debra Newman
Hampton, Thomas Earle
Handy, Dr. Norman
Hardnett, Carolyn Judy
Hargrove, John R.
Harris, Noah Alan, Sr.
Harris, Vander E.
Harrison, Dr. Daphne Duval
Haskins, Joseph, Jr.
Hawthorne, Lucia Shelia
Hayden, Carla Diane
Hayes, Dr. Floyd Windom
Hayman, Warren C.
Haynes, Dr. James H.
Haysbert, Raymond Victor
Henderson, Dr. Lenneal Joseph
Hicks, Rev. Dr. Sherman G
Higginbotham, F. Michael
Hill, Thelma W.
Hoff, Nathaniel Hawthorne
Hollowell, Melvin Butch
Holt, John J.
Howard, Ellen D
Howard, Joseph Clemens
Howard, Leslie Carl
Hrabowski, Dr. Freeman Alphonsa, III
Hughes, Essie Meade
Hunt, Edward
Hynson, Carroll Henry, Jr.
Ike, Alice Denise
Johnson, Carroll Randolph, Jr.
Johnson, Edna DeCoursey
Johnson, John J
Johnson, Lorretta
Jones, Dr. Clifton Ralph
Jones, Susan Sutton
Josey, Leronia Arnetta
Jowers, Johnnie Edward, Sr.
King-Hammond, Dr. Leslie
Knight, Franklin W.
Lacy, Sam
Lansey, Yvonne F.
LaVeist, Dr. Thomas
Lawlah, Gloria Gary
Lawrence, Viola Poe
Lee, Michael Waring
Letson, Alfred, Jr.
Lindsay, Gwendolyn Ann Burns
Lokeman, Joseph R
Madison, Stanley D.
Malone, Rosemary C
Marshall, Rev. Paul M
Martin, Elmer P.
Martin, Dr. Joanne Mitchell
Martin, Dr. Richard Cornish
Massey, Jacquelene Sharp
Mathews, Gary C
Mathews, Keith E
Maynard, Valerie J
Maysa
McConnell, Catherine Allen
McConnell, Roland C
McDonald, Katrina Bell
McFadden, Nathaniel James
McKinney, Richard Ishmael
McLaughlin, Eurphan
McMillan, Douglas James
McPhail, Irving P.
Minion, Mia
Moore, Christine James
Moore, Lenny Edward
Murphy, Frances L
Musgrove, Margaret Wynkoop
Neal, Brandon
Neverdon-Morton, Dr. Cynthia
Nichols, David G
Noonan, Dr. Allan S.
Nwanna, Dr. Gladson I N
Oliver, John J., Jr.
Owens, Ronald C
Parker, James Thomas
Parker, Dr. Jeff, Sr.
Phillips, Dr. Glenn Owen
Pollard, William E.
Pratt, Joan M, CPA
Preston, Edward Michael
Proctor, William H
Quivers, William Wyatt, Sr.
Reed, Kwame Osei
Rice, Dr. Pamela Ann
Richardson, Dr. Earl Stanford
Richardson, Frank
Robertson, Karen A
Robinson, Anthony W
Robinson, Jeffrey
Rojas, Don
Roulhac, Dr. Edgar Edwin

Sands, Rosetta F
Saunders, Dr. Elijah
Savage, Dr. Vernon Thomas
Sheffey, Dr. Ruthe T.
Shinhoster, Earl
Simmons, Dr. Charles William
Simmons, Dr. Howard L
Simms, Stuart Oswald
Simon, Dr. Elaine
Sinkler, Dr. George
Smith, DeHaven L
Solomon, James Daniel
Stanley, Dr. Hilbert Dennis
Stansbury, Clayton Cresvell
Staton, Donna Hill
Staton, Kerry D
Stephenson, Allan Anthony
St Pierre, Dr. Maurice
Styles, Kathleen Ann
Suttle, Rhonda Kimberly
Taylor, Jeffery Charles
Taylor, Julius H
Terborg-Penn, Dr. Rosalyn M
Thaxton, June E
Theodore, Yvonne M.
Thomas, Jacqueline Marie
Thomas-Carter, Jean Cooper
Thompson, Garland Lee
Torain, Rev. Tony William
Turner, Richard M
Waddy, Walter James
Wade, Bruce L.
Walden, Dr. Emerson Coleman
Warren, Otis, Jr.
Watkins, Dr. Levi, Jr.
Weaver, Dr. Garland Rapheal, Jr.
Williams, Harold David
Williams, Henry R
Williams, Larry
Williams, Rev. Dr. Maceo Merton
Wilson, Dr. Donald
Winbush, Raymond Arnold
Woodfolk, Joseph O.

Balto
Thomas, Rev. Walter Scott

Bathesda
Penn, Audrey

Batlimore
Camper, Diane G

Bel Air
Brown, Jerome
Page, Rosemary Saxton

Beltsville
Blake, Peggy Jones
Hammond, Carol H.
Hammond, Dr. James Matthew
Subryan, Carmen
Wiley, Edward, III

Bethesda
Arties, Lucy Elvira Yvonne
Barham, Wilbur Stectson
Bell-Taylor, Wilhelmina
Bonham, Vence L
Branche, William C., Jr.
Dabney, David Hodges
Davenport, Chester C
Fleming, Patricia Stubbs
Floyd, Dr. Jeremiah
Fox, Richard K., Jr.
Freeman, Harold P.
Gilmore, Dr. Al Tony
Gooden, Linda
Gray, Brian Anton
Haile, Annette L
Hoyle, Dr. Classie G.
Jackson, Charles N., II
Javery, Michael
Jennings, Margaret Elaine
Johnson, Robert
Kington, Raynard S
May, James Shelby
McKee, Adam E
Pickrum, Lisa M.
Powell, Juan Herschel
Press, Dr. Harry Cody, Jr.
Ruffin, John
Sarreals, E. Don
Suneja, Sidney Kumar
Troutman, Porter Lee, Jr.
Wilson, Stephanie Y.

Woodson, Alfred F
Wright, Pandit F

Bowie
Ahoto, Yao
Anderson, Leon H.
Barfield, Dr. Rufus L.
Barham, Wilbur Stectson
Bolles, A Lynn
Boone, Dr. Zola Ernest
Bradberry, Dr. Richard Paul
Brandon, Dr. Ida Gillard
Brown, Agnes Marie
Chappelle, Edward H
Chew, Bettye L.
Clark, Vernon L.
Cunningham, Dr. William Dean
Davis, Thurman M, Sr.
Day, John H
Hall, Dr. Willie Green
Hammond, Carol H.
Hodge, Dr. Charles Mason
House, James E.
Johnson, G. R. Hovey
Mickle, Andrea Denise
Miller, Ingrid Fran Watson
Miller, Dr. M Sammye
Palmer, Edgar Bernard
Reid, Rubin J
Shakoor, Dr. Waheedah Aqueelah

Brentwood
Hall, Raymond A.
Parkinson, Nigel Morgan
Smith, Rev. Perry Anderson, III

Burtonsville
Covington, M. Stanley

California
Lancaster, John Graham

Camp Springs
Jackson, Ronald G
Pinkney, John Edward

Capitol Heights
Beard, Montgomery, Jr.
Dodson, Vivian M
Rogers, Norman
Tarver, Elking, Jr.
Turner, Marvin Wentz

Catonsville
Fullwood, Harlow, Jr.
Oden, Dr. Gloria (Catherine)
Wilson, Thomas A, Jr.

Cheltenham
Perkins, Bernice Perry

Cheverly
Raiford, Roger Lee
Wilson, Floyd Edward, Jr.

Chevy Chase
Gartrell, Bernadette A
Hudson, Anthony Webster
Jervay-Pendergrass, Dr. Debra
Mathis, Deborah F
Mitchell, Cranston J
Pinson, Margo Dean
Rayburn, Dr. Wendell Gilbert
Streeter, Denise Williams

Clarksville
Staton, Donna Hill
Staton, Kerry D
Wilson, Joseph Henry, Jr.

Clinton
Clark, Eligah Dane, Jr.
Feliciana, Dr. Jerrye Brown
Gant, Wanda Adele
Hubbard, Stanley
Johnson, Jacob Edwards, III
Jordan, Jacquelyn D.
Love, Lynnette Alicia
Parker, E Charmaine Roberts
Saint-Louis, Rudolph Anthony
Saunders, David J
Thompson, Linda Jo
Williams, Rev. Wilbert Lee

College Park
Bolles, A Lynn
Bonner, Alice Carol

Booth, Keith
Boyd, Dr. Vivian
Carroll, Charles H.
Dark, Lawrence Jerome
Davenport, Christian A.
Dill, Dr. Bonnie Thornton
Driskell, David C.
Fries, Sharon Lavonne
Gaston, Dr. Arnett W
Humphrey, Margo
Johnson, Dr. Martin Leroy
Johnson, Dr. Raymond Lewis
Kirkland, Sharon Elaine
Landry, L. Bartholomew
Lomax, Dervey A.
Montgomery, Dr. Edward B.
Moss, Alfred A
Scott, Marvin Wayne
Senbet, Prof. Lemma W
Valmon, Andrew Orlando
Walters, Ronald
Washington, Mary Helen

Columbia
Alexander, Dr. A Melvin
Ausbrooks, Beth Nelson
Boone, Dr. Zola Ernest
Braddock, Dr. Marilyn Eugenia
Brown, Shirley Ann Vining
Bruce, Preston, Jr.
Clifton, Lucille
Conaway, Samuel L
Hamilton, Dr. John Mark, Jr.
Harris, Dr. Marion Hopkins
Harrison, Dr. Daphne Duval
Hoff, Nathaniel Hawthorne
Howard, Ellen D
James, Dr. David Phillip
King, Ora Sterling
Ligon, Doris Hillian
Martin, Sylvia Cooke
Newsome, Dr. Clarence Geno
Nixon, Harold L
Pounds, Dr. Moses B
Smith, Alfred J., Jr.
Starks, Doris Nearror
Taylor, Patricia Tate
Thompson, Linda Jo
Walker, Betty Stevens
Ware, Charles Jerome
West, Dr. Herbert Lee, Jr.
Wilson, Joseph Henry, Jr.

Crownsville
McLaughlin, Brian P

Cumberland
Powell, Darrell Lee

Darnestown
Williams, Buck

Delmar
Harleston, Brigadier Gen. Robert Alonzo

District Heights
Doxie, Marvin Leon
Williams-Garner, Debra

Dundalk
Brooks, Dunbar

Edgewater
Whitby, Dr. Linda

Elkridge
Penha, Gail A.

Ellicott City
Brown, William T
Hightower, Herma J
Lee, Chandler Bancroft
West, Dr. Herbert Lee, Jr.
Williams, Robert B.

Fairmont Heights
Broadwater, Tommie, Jr.

Finksburg
Cortada, Dr. Rafael Leon

Forestville
Burse, Dr. Luther
Reid, Ronda Eunese
Turner, Evelyn Evon

Fort Washington
Avant, Albert A., II
Awkard, Linda Nanline

MASSA-CHUSETTS

Greenidge, James Ernest
Kendrick, Curtis L

Bedford
Hopkins, Perea M.

Belmont
Blakely, Allison
Greene, Gabrielle Elise

Boston
Alexander, Hon. Joyce London
Allen, Ray
Amiji, Hatim M.
Anderson, Norman
Angelou, Dr. Maya
Bailey, Prof. Gary
Batson, Ruth Marion
Beard, Charles Julian
Birchette-Pierce, Cheryl L.
Blakely, Allison
Bocage, Ronald J
Bolling, Bruce C.
Bolling, Carol Nicholson
Bowman, Jacquelynne Jeanette
Brown, Leonard
Brown, Rodger L, Jr.
Burnham, Margaret Ann
Burton, Ronald E.
Carey, Jennifer Davis
Carr, M L
Cash, Dr. James Ireland
Cassell, Samuel James
Chandler, Dana C., Jr.
Cofield, James E
Coleman, Audrey Rachelle
Coleman, Wanda
Collins, Tessil John
Crite, Allan Rohan
Daniel, Dr. Jessica Henderson
Davis, Arthur, Jr.
Davis, Marilynn A.
Davis, Willie J.
Diamond, Judith
Dilday, Hon. Judith Nelson
Dugger, Edward, III
Gaither, Barry
Garner, Grayce Scott
Gates, Otis A., III
Goodnight, Paul
Grimes, Calvin M., Jr.
Grimes, Darlene M C
Hall, David
Handy, Delores
Harris, John Everett
Harris, Leslie E.
Harrison-Sullivan, Jeanette LaVerne
Heard, Marian L
Henry, Brent Lee
Hilliard, Alicia Victoria
Ireland, Roderick Louis
Jacks, Ulysses
Jackson, Derrick Zane
Jackson, Isaiah Allen
Jackson, Dr. Reginald Leo
Jenkins-Scott, Jackie
Jobe, Shirley A.
Johnson, Beverley Ernestine
Jones, Clarence J., Jr.
Jones, Gayl
Kenney, James A
King, Sandra T.
Knight, Dr. Muriel Bernice
Knowles, Dr. Em Claire
Lee, M David, Jr.
Leoney, Antoinette E M
Lewis, Elma I.
Lewis, Ida Elizabeth
Lewis, Maurice
Lewis, Ramsey Emanuel
Lindsay, Reginald Carl
Mbere, Aggrey Mxolisi
McClain, James W.
McIntyre, Mildred J
Miller, Melvin B.
Moody, Cameron Dennis
Morgan-Welch, Beverly Ann
Morton, Karen Victoria
Moseley, Frances Kenney
Motley, J. Keith
Murphy, Michael McKay
Nelson, David S.
Nelson, Leon T.
Norris, Dr. Donna M
Overbea, Luix Virgil
Owens, William
Parham, Richelle
Parish, Robert
Parks, Paul

Patrick, Deval L
Peebles-Wilkins, Dr. Wilma Cecelia
Peoples, Florence W
Perkins, Frances J
Petty-Edwards, Lula Evelyn
Pierce, Paul
Pierce, Rudolph F
Poussaint, Dr. Alvin Francis
Prothrow-Stith, Deborah Boutin
Putnam, Glendora M
Rice, Jim
Rist, Susan E
Rivero, Marita
Roberts, Marcus
Roberts, Rev. Wesley A
Robinson, Jack E
Robinson, Dr. Malcolm Kenneth
Rushing, Byron D
Scanlan, Agnes Bundy
Settles, Darryl Stephen
Sherwood, Wallace Walter
Smith, Warren
Snowden, Gail
Soden, Richard Allan
Spicer, Kenneth, Sr.
Spruill, James Arthur
Stevens, Dr. Joyce West
Steward, Elaine Weddington
Stull, Donald L
Tarpley, Natasha Anastasia
Thomas, David Anthony
Thompson, Benjamin Franklin
Thompson, Jesse M.
Turner, Castellano Blanchet
Veney, Marguerite C
Venson, John E.
Walker, Adrian
Walker, Charles Ealy, Jr.
Walker, Joseph M., III
Wallace, Rasheed Abdul
Wallace-Benjamin, Joan
Walter, Mildred Pitts
Watkins, Dr. Michael Thomas
Weaver, Afaa Michael
White, Dr. Augustus A., III
White, Jo Jo
Wideman, John Edgar
Wiggs, Jonathan Louis
Wilson, John
Wilson, Sondra K.
Winston, Bonnie Veronica
Wolfman, Dr. Brunetta Reid
Yancey, Charles Calvin
Yarbrough, Robert Elzy

Bridgewater
Santos, Henry Joseph

Brighton
Harris, William Allen

Brockton
Thomas, John

Brookline
Christian, John L.
Cromwell, Adelaide M.
Fortune, Alvin V.
Price, Albert H
Traynham, Robert Lee

Broolkine
Russell, George A

Burlington
Hurd, Dr. Joseph Kindall

Cambridge
Amaker, Harold Tommy
Anderson, Perry L
Bailey, James W.
Barnett, Evelyn Brooks
Bennett, Robert A.
Bland, Bobby Blue
Brown, Emery N.
Brown, Rev. Jeffrey LeMonte
Castle, Keith L
Cator, Johnny
Clay, Phillip L.
Evans, David Lawrence
Farley, Dr. Jonathan David
Fuller, Arthur
Gaffney, Leslie Gale
Gates, Dr. Henry Louis
Gomes, Rev. Peter John
Guinier, Lani
Hamilton, Eugene Nolan
Harrington, Philip Leroy

Harris, Corey
Jackson, Marie O
Johnson, Willard Raymond
Jones, Frank S.
Kennedy, Randall
Ladd, Florence Cawthorne
Lee, Helen Elaine
Lightfoot, Dr. Sara Lawrence
Marsalis, Branford
McLurkin, James
Ogletree, Charles J
Patterson, Dr. Orlando Horace
Pickett, Cecil Bruce
Pierce, Dr. Chester Middlebrook
Plummer, Michael Justin
Redman, Joshua
Roberts, Louis Wright
Solomon, David
Thompson, Marcus Aurelius
Tucker, Clarence T.
Wilkins, David Brian
Williams, Dr. Clarence G.
Williams, Dr. Dwight
Williams, Dr. James H., Jr.
Williams, Dr. Preston N
Williams, Wayne Allan
Willie, Dr. Charles Vert
Wilson, Dr. William Julius
Young, James E.

Chestnut Hill
Araujo, Dr. Norman
Plummer, Michael Justin
Sarkodie-Mensah, Dr. Kwasi
Smith, Dr. Charles F.
Walters, Hubert Everett

Concord
Harrell, Oscar W., II

Danvers
Barron, Reginald

Dedham
Matory, Yvedt L

Dorchester
Jones, Victoria C.
Reynolds, Pamela Terese
Womack, Rev. Dr. John H, Sr.

Dorchester Center
Peoples, Florence W

Dover
Finley, Betty M

East Falmouth
McCane, Charlotte Antoinette

Fall River
Edwards, Wilbur Patterson, Jr.

Foxboro
Greenidge, James Ernest
Harrison, Rodney Scott
Moss, Randy
Sullivan, Jonathon
Tippett, Andre Bernard

Foxborough
Johnson, Pepper
Springs, Shawn

Framingham
Dyer, Dr. Charles Austen
Hendricks, Marvin B.
Lloyd, Rev. Dr. J Anthony

Gardner
Bell, Alberta Saffell

Gloucester
Fonvielle, William Harold

Groton
Gaskins, Louise Elizabeth

Hadley
Welburn, Ronald Garfield

Haverhill
Roberts, John Christopher

Holyoke
Scott, Anthony R

Hyde Park
Portis, Kattie Harmon

Jamaica Plain
Pierce, Dr. Chester Middlebrook
Scott, Dr. Deborah Ann
Youngblood, Shay

Lexington
Brannon, James R.
Long, James, Jr.

Lincoln
Marsalis, Delfeayo

Longmeadow
McFarlin, Kernaa D'Offert, Jr.

Lowell
Crayton, Samuel S.
Dorsey, Joseph A.
Roberts, Kay George
Scruggs, Allie W.
Thompson, Dr. Charles

Lynn
Long, James, Jr.

Malden
Phillips, Helen M.

Mansfield
Barros, Dana Bruce

Marion
McFadden, Samuel Wilton

Mashpee
Parnell, John V, III

Mattapan
Bispham, Frank L
Owens-Hicks, Shirley
Parks, Paul
Whitworth, Dr. E Leo, Jr.

Mattapoisett
Robinson, John L.

Medford
Anderson, Dr. Thomas Jefferson
Brown Knable, Bobbie Margaret
Gibson, Harris, Jr.
Norris, Lonnie H

Middleboro
Townsend, Murray Luke, Jr.

Middleton
Cousins, Frank, Jr.

Milton
Smith, Lawrence John, Jr.
Whitworth, Dr. E Leo, Jr.
Wilson, Leon E, Jr.

Newton
Morton, Karen Victoria
Peterson, Lloyd
Rist, Susan E
Simmons, Dr. Sylvia Q.
Thompson, Marcus Aurelius
Warren, Dr. Joseph David

Newton Center
Davis, Willie J.
Haymon, Alan
Howe, Prof. Ruth-Arlene W.

Newton Highlands
Turner, Castellano Blanchet

Newtonville
Whiteside, Larry

North Andover
Perryman, Robert

North Dartmouth
Hoagland, Everett H.
Martin, Baron H

North Easton
McClain, James W.

Northampton
Coleman, Trevor W
Daniel, Dr. Yvonne

Giddings, Paula Jane
Morris, Margaret Lindsay
Morris-Hale, Walter

Norton
Crutcher, Dr. Ronald Andrew

Oak Bluffs
Nix, Theophilus Richard, Jr.

Plymouth
Gregory, Richard Claxton
Hardeman, James Anthony

Prides Crossing
Zeitlin, Jide J

Quincy
Farrington, Thomas Alex
McDaniels, Warren E
Webster, Theodore E.

Randolph
Cannon, Edith H
Whitaker, Rev. Arthur L

Roxbury
Banks, Richard L.
Bolling, Bruce C.
Bullins, Ed
Bynoe, John Garvey
Carroll, Charlene O.
McGuire, Jean Mitchell
Merenivitch, Jarrow
Rickson, Gary Ames
Simmons, Dr. Sylvia Q.
Wright, Milton L., Jr.
Wyatt, Beatrice E.

Salem
Gerald, Arthur Thomas, Jr.
Leoney, Antoinette E M

Sharon
Edwards, Wilbur Patterson, Jr.
Johnson, Addie Collins
Walker, Charles Ealy, Jr.

Somerville
Wilson, Carroll Lloyd

South Hadley
McHenry, Mary Williamson

South Lancaster
Willoughby, Dr. Susan Melita

Springfield
Ali, Dr. Kamal Hassan
Copes, Ronald Adrian
Edmonds, Josephine E.
Edwards, Mattie Smith
Lanier, Jesse M, Sr.
Lee, Charles Gary, Sr.
Mapp, John Robert
McLean, Mary Cannon
Paige, Alvin
Smith, Elsie Mae
Smith, Dr. James Almer, Jr.

Stoughton
Bowman, Jacquelynne Jeanette

Sudbury
Harrell, Oscar W., II

Teaticket
Pena, Robert Bubba

Vineyard Haven
Clark, Doris
Hardman, Della Brown Taylor
Hayden, Robert C., Jr.
Tucker, Herbert E., Jr.

Wakefield
Roberts, Louis Wright

Waltham
Cash, Arlene Marie
McBride, Bryant

Watertown
Greene, Gabrielle Elise

Wellesley
Cudjoe, Dr. Selwyn Reginald
Hurd, Dr. Joseph Kindall

Martin, Dr. Tony
Norris, Dr. Donna M
Piper, Adrian Margaret Smith
Rich, Wilbur C
Rollins, Judith Ann

Wenham
Roberts, Rev. Wesley A

West Newton
Robinson, Dr. Malcolm Kenneth

Westboro
Byrd, George Edward

Westborough
Tucker, Clarence T.

Westfield
Ali, Dr. Kamal Hassan
Copes, Ronald Adrian

Weymouth
Nixon, James I, Jr.

Williamstown
Brown, Ernest Douglas

Winthrop
Freelon, Nnenna

Worcester
Hines, Deborah Harmon
LaBelle, Patti
Peace, Dr. G. Earl
Pope, Ruben Edward, III
Portis, Kattie Harmon

cambridge
Powell, Patricia

MICHIGAN
Arnold, John Russell, Jr.

Albion
Davis, Willie A.

Allen Park
Carter, Pat
Culpepper, Daunte
Gash, Samuel Lee, Jr.
Graves, John
Kelly, Brian
Rogers, Shaun
Salaam, Ephraim Mateen

Allendale
Haynes, Dr. Alphonso Worden
Hill, Mervin E., Jr.

Ann Arbor
Allen-Meares, Paula G
Anderson, James
Bates, Percy
Boyd, Melba Joyce
Brabson, Dr. Howard Victor
Bradley, James Howard, Jr.
Bryant, Dr. Bunyan I.
Bryant, Dr. Henry C.
Chaffers, James Alvin
Chivers, Gwendolyn Ann
Coleman-Burns, Dr. Patricia Wendolyn
Cooper, Robert N.
Cruse, Harold Wright
Cruzat, Dr. Gwendolyn S.
Deskins, Donald R., Jr.
Dulin, Joseph
Eaglin, Fulton B.
Eatman, Dr. Timothy K
Edwards, Alfred L
Elliott, Anthony Daniel
Evans, Dr. Billy Joe
Finney, Michael Anthony
Fuller, Almyra Oveta
Gibson, Ralph Milton
Hinton, Alfred Fontaine
Jackson, Dr. James Sidney
Jackson, Murray Earl
Johnson, Harold R.
Johnson, Henry
Johnson, Lemuel A.
Kilkenny, James H.
Lee, Dorothy A H
Lightfoot, Simone Danielle

Lockard, Jon Onye
McAfee, Leo C
Montague, Christina P
Moody, Charles David, Sr.
Neal, Dr. Homer Alfred
Northcross, Wilson Hill, Jr.
Parker, Dr. Walter Gee
Patterson, Willis Charles
Potts, Robert Lester
Shirley, George Irving
Simpson, John O
Thomas, Laurita
Thomas, Samuel Haynes, Jr.
Thompson, Bette Mae
Williams, Kevin A.
Williams, Dr. Melvin D
Williams, Dr. Trina Rachael
Williams, Wallace C
Wilson, Patricia A.
Woodbury, Dr. Margaret Claytor
Woodford, John Niles
York, Vincent
Young, Mary E.

Auburn Hills
Chapman, Dr. Gilbert Bryant
Curry, Michael
Dumars, Joe
Ford, Cheryl
Fountain, W. Frank
Goodwin, Donald Edward
Hunter, Lindsey Benson
Lartigue, Roland E
Lee, Larry Dwayne
Liberty, Marcus
Lindsey, Patrick O
Mahorn, Rick
Mallebay-Vacqueur Dem, Jean Pascal
Mason, John
McWilliams-Franklin, Taj
Moore, Herman Joseph
Nolan, Deanna
Powell, Elaine
Teasley, Nikki
Walker, Tracy A
Weiss, Leven C.

Battle Creek
Caudle, Anthony, Sr.
Hicks, Dr. Veronica Abena
McKinney, James Ray
Overton-Adkins, Dr. Betty Jean
Owens, Nathaniel Davis
Penn, Shelton C.
Stewart, Joseph M.

Bay City
Baker, Oscar Wilson
Littles, Dr. James Frederick, Jr.

Belleville
Cothorn, Marguerite Esters
Crawford, Margaret Ward

Benton Harbor
Cooke, Wilce L.
Ealy, Mary Newcomb
Madison, Shannon L
McKeller, Thomas Lee
Miller, Charles D, Jr.
Yarbrough, Mamie Luella

Berkley
Slaughter-Titus, Rev. Linda Jean

Berrien Springs
Warren, Dr. Joseph W
Watson, Dr. Janice

Beverly Hills
Brooks, Arkles Clarence, Jr.

Big Rapids
Gant, Raymond Leroy
Matthews, Dr. Gerald Eugene
Pilgrim, David

Bingham Farms
Bryant, N Z, Jr.
Tripp, Dr. Lucius Charles

Birmingham
Allen, Karen B.
Johnson, Dr. James Kenneth
Munday, Dr. Cheryl Casselberry

Bloomfield Hills
Anderson, Edwyna G.
Douglas, Walter Edmond

Hill, George Calvin
Jackson, James E., Sr.
Mullens, Delbert W
Pickard, Dr. William Frank
Simmons, Janice
Verbal, Claude A

Bloomfield Township
Parker, H Wallace

Boston
Robinson, Jeri

Brohman
Freeman, McKinley Howard, Sr.

Canton
Chappell, Michael James

Cassopolis
Underwood, Joseph M

Clarkston
Newton, Eric Christopher

Clinton
Shamberger, Jeffery L

Clinton Township
Hill, Bobby L
Miller, Sheila

Clio
Hatter, Henry

Comstock Park
McMorris, Michael Anthony

Dearborn
Armstrong, Walter
Bray, Leroy, Sr.
Bridgeman-Veal, Judy
Brown, Tony
Clarke, Benjamin Louis
Fields, Felicia J
Fowler, Bennie W
Frame, George J
Givens, Lawrence
Hazel, Darryl B.
Jensen, Dr. Ray M
Jones, Cloyzelle Karrelle
Jones, Mable Veneida
Laymon, Joe W.
Munson, Robert H
Procter, Harvey Thornton, Jr.
White, Richard Thomas

Dearborn Heights
Kennedy-Scott, Patricia

Detroit
Abraham, Jeanette
Adams, Dr. Charles Gilchrist
Adams, Deborah Ross
Adams, Katherine
Allen, Alex James, Jr.
Allen, Charles Edward
Allen, Chris
Allison, Vivian
Amderson, Gary
Anderson, Dr. Barbara Stewart Jenkins
Anderson, Derrick Rushon
Anderson, Nicholas Charles
Andrew, Milton
Anthony, Wendell
Archer, Dennis Wayne
Arrington, Robyn James, Jr.
Atchison, Leon H.
Atkins, Marylin E.
Austin, Richard H.
Ayala, Reginald P.
Bailey, Carol A
Barden, Don H.
Barrow, Thomas Joe
Baxter, Hon. Wendy Marie
Baylor, Margaret
Beatty, Christine
Beatty, Robert L.
Beckham, William J., Jr.
Beckles, Benita Harris
Bennett, George P.
Berger, Shirley A
Bing, Dave
Birru, Mulugetta
Blackwell, Arthur Brendhal, II
Blackwell-Hatcher, June E

Boddie, Dr. Arthur Walker
Boggs, Donald W
Boggs, Dr. Grace Lee
Bond, Alan D.
Bouldes, Ruth Irving
Boyce, Charles N
Bozeman, Catherine E.
Bradley, Vanesa Jones
Bradley, Wayne W
Brazelton, Edgar
Bridgeforth, Arthur Mac, Jr.
Bridgforth, Glinda
Brooks, Arkles Clarence, Jr.
Brooks, Rosemarie
Broughton, Christopher Leon
Brown, Dalton G
Brown, Helen E.
Brown, Joseph N
Brown, Venus
Bryant, Kathryn Ann
Bully-Cummings, Ella
Burke, Donna M
Burks, Darrell
Burrell, Hugh
Butler, Rosalind Marie
Byrd, Frederick E.
Cain, Waldo
Calloway, Laverne Fant
Campbell, Sandra Pace
Carpenter, Vivian L.
Carr, Virgil H.
Carter, Harriet LaShun
Carter, Lewis Winston
Carter, Ora Williams
Cartwright, Jonathan
Cason, David, Jr.
Catchings, Dr. Yvonne Parks
Cauthen, Richard L.
Caver, Carmen C Murphy
Chambers, Caroline
Chambers, Caroline E.
Chapman, Melvin
Chatman, Tyrone
Chestang, Dr. Leon Wilbert
Clay, Eric Lee
Clay Chambers, Juanita
Cleage, Albert B., Jr.
Clements, Walter H.
Clemons, Sandra L.
Clermont, Volna
Cleveland, Clyde
Cofield, Marvis
Cole, Andrea M
Coleman, DeeDee M.
Coleman, Donald
Coleman, Melissa Scott
Collins, Barbara-Rose
Collins, Carl
Colson, Lewis Arnold
Conner, Gail Patricia
Cook, Julian Abele
Cook, Ronald R
Cooper, Evelyn Kaye
Cothorn, John A
Cotman, Dr. Ivan Louis
Coulter, Phyllis A
Cox, Fr. Jesse
Craig, Carl
Craig, Rhonda Patricia
Crisp, Dr. Robert Carl, Jr.
Crosby, Mary
Cross, Haman
Daniels, Jesse
Davidson, Arthur B
Davis, Diane Lynn
Davis, Donald
Davis, Erellon Ben
Davis, H. Bernard
Davis, Marion Harris
Davis, Mary Agnes Miller
Davis, Robert Alan
Davis Anthony, Vernice
Day, Burnis Calvin
Dennard, Brazeal Wayne
Denning, Dr. Bernadine Newsom
DeRamus, Betty
Diggs, Deborah Dolsey
Dodd, Geralda
Dortch, Heyward
Doss, Lawrence Paul
Dotson, Hon. Norma Y
Douglas, Shannon
Dowell, Clyde Donald
Drain, Gershwin A
Drake, Maggie W.
Dulin, Robert O., Jr.
Dunbar, Joseph C.
Dunigan, Mayme O.
Dunmore, Gregory Charles

Duplessis, Harry Y.
Dykes, Marie Draper
Eagan, Emma Louise
Eason-Steele, Elaine
Edison, Joanne
Edwards, Dr. Abiyah, Jr.
Edwards, Esther Gordy
Edwards, Prentis
Evans, Elinor Elizabeth
Evans, Warren Cleage
Everett, Kay
Fair, Darwin
Farmer, Nancy
Fears, Harding, Jr.
Feemster, John Arthur
Ferrebee, Thomas G.
Fields, Dr. Dexter L.
Fields, M. Joan
Fields, Stanley
Fitzpatrick, Albert E.
Flack, Dr. John M.
Fobbs, Kevin
Ford, Geraldine Bledsoe
Forte, Linda Diane
Foster, Dr. Bellandra B.
Franklin, Eugene T., Jr.
Frazier, Greg
Freeman, V Diane
Frohman, Roland H.
Ganson, Wesley
Gardner, Harold
George, Alma Rose
Gibson, Cheryl Dianne
Gibson, JoAnn
Gibson, Kala
Gibson, Dr. Sarah L
Giles, Joe L
Givens, Leonard David
Goff, Pamela
Goodwin, Della McGraw
Graham, Charlene
Graves, Leslie Theresa
Green, Eddie L.
Green, Forrest F.
Green, John M.
Green, Lee
Green, Verna S
Griffin, Keith
Griffith, Vera Victoria
Guthrie, Michael J
Guyton, Louise Green
Hagood, Henry Barksdale
Hale, Dr. Janice Ellen
Hall, Perry Alonzo
Hall-Keith, Jacqueline Yvonne
Hamilton, Jonnie
Hamilton, Rainy, Jr.
Hankins, Dr. Andrew Jay
Harlan, Carmen
Harper, Laydell Wood
Harris, Harcourt Glenties
Harris, Dr. Joseph Benjamin
Harris, Joseph Preston
Harris, Dr. Marjorie Elizabeth
Harris, Ona C
Harris, Dr. Terea Donnelle
Harris, William Anthony
Harrison, Ernest Alexander
Harrison, Wendell Richard
Hartsfield, Judy
Harvey, Dana Colette
Hatcher, Lillian
Hathaway, Cynthia Gray
Haugabook, Terrence Randall
Hawkins, Robert B.
Hayden, Frank F.
Hayes-Giles, Joyce V.
Heath, Comer, III
Henderson, Angelo B
Hewitt, Ronald Jerome
Hill, George Calvin
Hill, George Hiram
Hines, Rosetta
Hinkle, Jackson Herbert
Hobson, Donald Lewis
Holbert, JoAnne
Holley, Jim
Holman, Forest H., Jr.
Hood, Aretha B.
Hood, Denise Page
Hood, Harold
Hoover, Jesse
Horton, Willie Wattison
Howard, Norman
Howell, Rachel
Howze, Dorothy J.

Davis, Bruce
Gladney, Rufus D

Kalamazoo
Brinn, Chauncey J.
Davis, Dr. Charles Alexander
Harvey, Raymond
Hudson, Dr. Roy Davage
Jones, Leander Corbin
Long, Monti M
Moore, Beverly
Payne, Vernon
Phillips, Dr. Romeo Eldridge
Smith, Isabelle R.
Walker, Dr. Lewis
Walker, Moses L
Washington, Dr. Earl Melvin
Washington, Dr. Von Hugo
White, Damon L.
Williams, Hon. Carolyn H
Williams, Sidney B., Jr.

Kentwood
Small, Isadore, III

Lansing
Brooks, James Taylor
Brown, Robert
Canady, Hortense Golden
Clarke, Hugh Barrington
Conley, James Sylvester
Cushingberry, George
Davis, Bruce
Davis, Dr. Willie
Dixon, Leonard Bill
Dunnings, Stuart
Ferguson, Joel I
Guthrie, Carlton Lyons
Hardman, Artina Tinsley
Haywood, Dwayne A.
Hood, Raymond W.
Jeff, Gloria Jean
Johnson, Georgia Anna Lewis
Jones, Dr. Lewis Arnold
Lang, Dr. Marvel
Leatherwood, Larry Lee
Lett, Gerald William
Lipscomb, Dr. Wanda Dean
McNeely, Matthew
Metcalf, Andrew Lee, Jr.
Morrison, Jacqueline
Norvell, Dr. Merritt J.
Price, Andrea R
Reide, Atty. Jerome L.
Richardson, Gilda Faye
Scott, Martha G.
Thomas, Samuel, III
Wallick, Ernest Herron
Waters, Mary D
Young, Joseph, Jr.

Lathrup Village
Abraham, Sharon L
Beckles, Benita Harris
Berry, Charles F, Jr.
Holliday, Prince E.
Thompson, Karen Ann

Lexington
Strong, Derek Lamar

Livonia
Fobbs, Kevin
Hill, Barbara A

Madison
Wright, Dr. Joseph Malcolm

Midland
Dorman, Linneaus C.
Peoples, Danita L

Milan
Bolden, Alfred, Jr.

Milwaukee
Bellegarde-Smith, Dr. Patrick

Monroe
Allen, Marva

Mount Clemens
Eddings, John R
Rickman, Dr. Lewis Daniel, Sr.

Mount Morris
Jackson, Gregory

Mount Pleasant
Baugh, Prof. Joyce A.
Hill, James L.

Sykes, William Richard
Toms-Robinson, Dolores C.

Mt Clemens
Hill, Bobby L

Muskegon
Cooper, Irmgard M
Pressley, Stephen, Jr.
Williams, John H.

Muskegon Heights
Terrell, John L
Wilkins, Rillastine Roberta

New Haven
Stone, Dolores June

Niles
Garba, Baba
Hamilton, Arthur Lee, Jr.
Watson, Dr. Elizabeth Darby

Northville
Sanders, Wendell Rowan

Novi
Conyers, Nathan G.
Ingram, Phillip M
Kellum, Anthony O
Lee, Aubrey Walter, Jr.
Richardson, Andra Virginia

Oak Park
Dill, Gregory
Mathews, Robert L
Oshiyoye, Dr. Emmanuel Adekunle, Sr.

Okemos
Barron, Wendell
Bouknight, Dr. Reynard Ronald

Orion Township
Guice, Rev. Gregory Charles

Owosso
Latimer, Frank Edward

Plymouth
Sturdivant, Col. Tadrial J

Pontiac
Brown, Hon. Christopher C
Carter, Anthony
Chambers, Pamela S
Crawford, Lawrence Douglas
Foley, Basil A., Sr.
Hatchett, Elbert
Hicks, Michael L
Johnson, Andre
Jones, Victor Tyrone
Kendall, Michelle Katrina
Langford, Denise Morris
Lee, Shalon D
Malone, Van Buren
McCree, Edward L.
McLemore, Thomas
Moore, Walter Louis
Morgan, Richard H., Jr.
Reeves, Julius Lee
Riggs, Harry L.
Uwaezuoke, Iheanyi
Wine, Donald Gary

Portage
Phillips, Dr. Romeo Eldridge

Redford
Lewis, Carmen Cortez
Stovall, Audrean

River Rouge
Miller, Doris Jean
Williams, Charles Earl

Rochester
Davis, Joseph
Gardiner, George L.
Gregory, Karl Dwight
Minor, Billy Joe
Wicker, Lisa J Lindsay

Rochester Hills
Lee, Larry Dwayne
Munson, Eddie Ray
Zola, Nkenge

Romulus
Martin, Lee
Pruitt, Rev. Eddie Jay Delano

Royal Oak
Shelby, Khadejah E.

SOUTHFIELD
Zakari, Tata

Saginaw
Barnes, Vivian Leigh
Clark, Leon Stanley
Coleman, Hurley J., Jr.
Colvin, Alonza James
Galloway, Lula Briggs
Gamble, Kenneth L.
Hall, David McKenzie
Jackson, Darnell
Leek, Everett Paul
Littles, Dr. James Frederick, Jr.
Nicholson, Gemma
Nix, Rick
Perry, LaVal
Pryor, Marvin C.
Quansah-Dankwa, Dr. Juliana Aba
Scott-Johnson, Roberta Virginia
Thompson, Hon. M T T
Thorns, Odail, Jr.
Wilson, James Paris
Woodruff, James W

Southfield
Addison, Caroline Elizabeth
Allen, Lecester L.
Anderson, William Gilchrist
Badger, Brenda Joyce
Ball, Brenda Louise
Benford, Edward A
Berry, Jay
Brown, Lomas, Jr.
Brown, Richard Osborne
Burgette, James M.
Cartwright, David G
Cole, Dorinda Clark
Coleman, Donald Alvin
Cox, Taylor H., Sr.
Cromer, Ronnie E, Jr.
Dortch, Heyward
Douglas, Walter Edmond
Dudley, Calmeze Henike, Jr.
Eagger, Jerome
Fletcher, Milton Eric
Flowers, Joyce E
Freeland, Shawn Ericka
Frierson, Nina
Gardner, LaMaurice Holbrook
Garvin-Leslie, Penola M
Grant, Ian
Graves, Ray Reynolds
Gray, Dr. E Delbert
Greene, Pamela
Hall Tyler, Delora
Hammond, Fred
Hawkins, Johnny L
Hill, Robert A.
Hogue, Leslie Denise
Hollowell, Melvin L.
Hope, Julius Caesar
Jackson, James E., Sr.
Jefferson-Ford, Charmain
Joe, Dr. Lonnie
Johnson, Gage
Johnson, Kimberly Lynn
Jones, Gus
Joseph, David E
Lartigue, Roland E
Lawrence, Brenda L.
Lawson, Debra Ann
Lewis, Carol J
Makupson, Amyre Ann Porter
McArthur, Dr. Barbara Jean
McKinney, Olivia Davene Ross
Moulton, Shirley
Norman, Clifford P
Orr, Marlett Jennifer
Parnell, William Cornellus, Jr.
Perry, Lowell Wesley, Jr.
Pope, Harold D
Revely, William
Robinson, Orlando
Rodgers, Horace J.
Shade, Dr. George H, Jr.
Smith, Denver Lester
Spand, Rev. Dr. Margot
Stewart, Bonita Coleman
Stewart, Loretta A
Stokes, Chuck

Taylor, Carol Ann
Thomas, Dr. Joseph Edward, Jr.
Trent, Jay Lester
Tupper, Leon E
Turner, Linda Darnell
Vaughn, Clarence B
Ward, Velma Lewis
Warden, George W
Washington, Gwendolyn
Worford, Carolyn Kennedy
Wright, Roberta V. Hughes

Southgate
McCammon, Marques
Poe, Fred J

Spring Arbor
Overton-Adkins, Dr. Betty Jean

St Joseph
Hawkins, Mary L
Yarbrough, Mamie Luella

Sterling Heights
Taylor, Herbert Charles

Thompsonville
Perry, Margaret

Trenton
Rodgers, Pamela E

Troy
Bowens, Gregory John
Caldwell, Ardis
Edwards, Verba L.
George, Pauline L
Irby, Mary
Johnson, Roy Lee
Lewis, Nicole
Moncrief, Sidney A.
O'Neal, Rodney
Preston, Franklin DeJuanette
Sanders, Barbara A.
Thomas, Joseph W.
Thompson, Karen Ann

University Center
Goodson, Dr. Martin L

Warren
Hill, Kenneth Randal
Lowe, Walter Edward, Jr.
McLaurin, Jasper Etienne
Spooner, Allan M.
Taylor, Sid E
Thomas, Terence A, Sr.

Washington
Gothard, Donald L.

Wayne
Mallett, Rosa Elizabeth Hunter

West Bloomfield
Anderson, Dr. Barbara Stewart Jenkins
Bryant, N Z, Jr.
Jackson, William Alvin
Lowe, Walter Edward, Jr.
Reed, Derryl L
Reeves, Julius Lee
Rhodes, Dr. Robert Shaw
Riley, Rosetta Margueritte
Trent, James E.
Walker, Rhonda
Young, Alan C

Westland
Bluford, James F
Ward, Albert A.

Wyandotte
Warren, James Kenneth

Wyoming
Smith, Marvin Preston

Ypsilanti
Abraham, Sharon L
Armstrong, Walter
Beatty, Charles Eugene, Sr.
Brown-Chappell, Betty L.
Clarke, Velma Greene
Edwards, Gerald Douglas
Fleming, Thomas A.
Golson, Leon

Hawkins, Dr. James
Horne-McGee, Patricia J
Jaggers, Garland
Jones, Dr. Toni Stokes
Martin, Sherman Theodore
McKanders, Kenneth Andre
Norris, Walter
Peoples, Alice Leigh
Peoples, Gregory Allan
Perry, Dr. Robert Lee
Robinson, Albert Arnold

MINNESOTA
McKinney, Billy

Bloomington
Lawrence, Thomas R, Jr.
Raphael, Bernard Joseph

Brooklyn Center
Watson, Perry, III

Brooklyn Park
Francis, Delma J

Burnsville
Posey, Dr. Edward W
Robinson, John G

Coon Rapids
Young, Rickey Darnell

Cottage Grove
Parham, Frederick Russell
Sergent, Ernest, Jr.

Eagan
Lane, Jeffrey D
Morton, Benjamin

Eden Prairie
Chapman, Sharon Jeanette
Daly, Ronald Edwin
Doleman, Christopher John
Fowler, Reggie
Harris, Jean Louise
Henderson, Keith Pernell
Lewis, Leo E
Robinson, Sam
Stringer, Korey
Williams, Pat

Edina
Jackson, Kevin L
Jam, Jimmy
Lewis, Terry
Smith, Dr. Henry Thomas
Warder, John Morgan

Ely
Brown, Mary Katherine

Forest Lake
Kemp, Leroy Percy

Golden Valley
Marsh, Donald Gene

Hopkins
Carr, Chris Dean

Maplewood
Barrett, Richard O.

Minneapolis
Alexander, Pamela Gayle
Baker, Jacqueline
Baker, Robert N.
Battle, Roxane
Belton, Y Marc
Benjamin, Michael
Brewer, Dr. Rose Marie
Bryant, Carl
Caldwell, George Theron, Sr.
Copeland, Richard Allen
Cunningham, William Michael
Davis, Michael James
Edwards, Ronald Alfred
Ellison, Keith
Francis, Delma J
Garnett, Kevin
Garrett, Dean
Hall, Hansel Crimiel
Henry, Daniel Joseph
Howell, Sharon Marie

James, Ronald
Johnson, Cyrus Edwin
McKinney, Billy
Minor, David M.
Moore, Cornell Leverette
Moore, Wenda Weekes
Myers, Dr. Samuel L
Neal, LaVelle E, III
Otieno-Ayim, Larban Allan
Pate, Alexs D
Peterson, Tony
Pinckney, Edward Lewis
Posey, Dr. Edward W
Richardson, Joseph
Robinson, Bunny
Robinson, James
Sims, Carl W
Smith, Dr. Henry Thomas
Snowden, Frank Walter
Southall, Geneva H.
Taylor, Kimberly Hayes
Terrell, Dorothy
Tuckson, Reed V
Walker, Antoine Devon
Warder, John Morgan
Watkins, Izear Carl
Whyte, Amelious N.
Wilderson, Dr. Frank B., Jr.
Williams, Theartrice T
Younger, Robert D.

Minnepolis
Pate, Alexs D
Taborn, Dr. John Marvin

Minnetonka
Snowden, Frank Walter

New Hope
Kinchlow, Ben

North Oaks
Myers, Dr. Samuel L

Oakdale
Lewis, Virginia Hill

Plymouth
Block, Dr. Leslie S.

Richfield
Thompson, John R

Robbinsdale
Eller, Carl L.

Rochester
Young, Dr. William Frederick, Jr., MD

Saint Paul
Dickson, Fred
Harris, Whitney G.
Lange, LaJune Thomas
Montgomery, Debbie

South Minneapolis
Lang, Dr. Marvel

St Cloud
Burnett, Bescye P.
Lehman, Dr. Christopher Paul
Tripp, Dr. Luke Samuel
Williams, Dr. Carolyn Ruth Armstrong

St Louis Park
Chapman, Sharon Jeanette

St Paul
Coleman, Melvin D.
El-Kati, Mahmoud
Garner, John W.
Harris, Duchess
Lambert, LeClair Grier
Lewis, Jeffrey Mark
Maxwell, Stephen Lloyd
Nicholson, Jessie R
Page, Hon. Alan Cedric
Parham, Frederick Russell
Troup, Elliott Vanbrugh
Waynewood, Dr. Freeman Lee
Wilderson, Thad

Williams, Kneely
Zachary, Steven W

West St Paul
Lambert, LeClair Grier

Woodbury
England, Dr. Rodney Wayne

MISSISSIPPI

Alcorn State
Williams, Dr. Malvin A, Sr.

Arcola
Harris, Clifton L.

Batesville
Herring, Larry Windell

Biloxi
Howze, Joseph Lawson
Mason, Gilbert Rutledge
Rhodeman, Clare M.
Ross, Cathye P
Stallworth, William Fred

Bolton
Thompson, Bennie G.

Brandon
Fletcher, Dr. Bettye Ward

Byhalia
Taylor, John L.

Canton
Blackmon, Barbara Martin
Blackmon, Edward
Esco, Fred, Jr.
Simmons, Shirley Davis
Williams, Jewel L

Clarksdale
Espy, Henry
Pride, William L., Jr.
Reed, Clara Taylor
Smith, Willie B

Cleveland
Evans, Ruthana Wilson
Lucas, Maurice F
Silas, Dennis Dean
Tolliver, Ned, Jr.
Washington, David Warren

Clinton
Nichols, Walter LaPlora

Columbia
Irvin, Regina Lynette
James, Sidney J.

Columbus
Brooks, Leroy
Shamwell, Joseph Melvin
Ward, Dr. James Dale
Worshaim, Keith Eugene

Como
Blakely, Charles

Crenshaw
Washington, James Lee, Sr.

Drew
Gough, Dr. Walter C
Tolliver, Ned, Jr.

Edwards
Pritchard, Daron

Ellisville
Jones, Joni Lou

Fayette
Bills, Johnny Bernard
Evers, James Charles
Guice, Leroy

Glendora
Thomas, Johnny B.

Greenville
Ayers-Elliott, Cindy
Cartlidge, Arthur J.

Goliday, Willie V.
Hall, Harold L
Hudson, Heather McTeer
Moore, Helen D S
Phillips, Earmia Jean
Pollard, Muriel Ransom
Smith Nelson, Dr. Dorothy J.

Greenwood
Williams, Jester C.

Gulfport
Abston, Nathaniel, Jr.

Hattiesburg
Adderton, Donald V
Aseme, Kate Nkoyeni, MD
Boykins, Ernest A.
Davis, James R.
Floyd, Vernon Clinton
Harris, Daisy
Lawrence, Charles
Stewart, Pearl

Hazlehurst
Hill, Annette Tillman

Hollandale
Brown, Hezekiah

Holly Springs
Beckley, Dr. David Lenard
Bell, Felix C.
DeBerry, Andre
Jones, Gwendolyn J
Lampley, Dr. Paul Clarence
Malone, Amanda Ella
McMillan, Dr. William Asbury
Smith, Dr. Nellie J.

Indianola
Matthews, Rev. David
Randle, Carver A

Itta Bena
Henderson, Dr. Robbye R.
Newsome, Dr. Moses, Jr.

Jackson
Ayers-Elliott, Cindy
Banks, Fred L.
Bell, Jimmy
Bell, Leon
Bennett, Patricia W
Byrd, Isaac, Jr.
Cameron, John E., Sr.
Cameron, Joseph A.
Catching-Kyles, Sharron Faye
Catchings, Howard Douglas
Clarke, Alyce Griffin
Collier-Wilson, Wanda
Coney, Melvene Lavon
Cox, Warren E.
Davis, Dr. Sheila Parham
Davis, Tyrone
Dilday, William Horace, Jr.
Dorsey, L. C.
Ellis, Tellis B., III
Espy, Michael
Ford, Barry W.
Gates, Jimmie Earl
Gibbs, Robert Lewis
Gordon, Lancaster
Hackett, Obra V.
Harden, Alice Varnado
Harvey, Clarie Collins
Haynes, Joe A
Haynes, Dr. Worth Edward
Hickerson Smith, Otrie B.
Hudson, Don R
Hunt, Betty Syble
James, Dr. Jimmie, Jr.
Johnson, David E.
Johnson, Linda Dianne
Johnson-Carson, Dr. Linda D
Jones, Chester Ray
Jones, Mavis N.
Jordan, David Lee
Lewis, Dr. Alvin
Little, Robert E
Livingston-Wilson, Karen E
Mack, Ally Faye
Macklin, Anderson D.
Magee, Sadie E.
Martin, Shirley
Mayes, Clinton, Jr.
May-Pittman, Ineva
McLemore, Leslie Burl

Melton, Frank E
Middleton, Rev. Dr. Richard Temple
Miller, Melvin Allen
Moreland-Young, Dr. Curtina
Myers, Dr. Lena Wright
Owens, George A.
Pennington, Jesse C
Peoples, Dr. John Arthur, Jr.
Polk, Richard A.
Presley, Oscar Glen
Reese, Viola Kathryn
Rigsby, Esther Martin
Sanders, Dr. Lou Helen
Shepherd, Malcolm Thomas
Shirley, Dr. Ollye Brown
Simon, Dr. Kenneth Bernard
Smith, Dr. Edgar Eugene
Smith, Hon. George S.
Stamps, Delores Bolden
Stewart, James A., III
Stringfellow, Eric DeVaughn
Teeuwissen, Pieter
Thompson, Rosie L
Thompson-Moore, Ann
Tingle, Lawrence May
Turner, Bennie L
Washington, Earlene
Watson, Jackie
Weary, Rev. Dolphus
Wheeler, Primus
White, Frankie Walton
Young, Charles Lemuel

Lamar
Allen, James Trinton

Lambert
Lyles, Marie Clark

Laurel
Mack, Melvin
Walker, Jimmy L

Lexington
Lewis, Hon. Jannie

Lorman
Shepphard, Dr. Charles Bernard
Williams, Robert Lee

Macon
Brooks, Richard Leonard

McComb
Bullock, Theodore

Meridian
Darden, Charles R.
Kornegay, Hobert
Little, Reuben R.
Young, Charles Lemuel

Metcalfe
Lindsey, S. L.

Mississippi State
Person, Dr. William Alfred
Uzoigwe, Dr. Godfrey N.

Moss Point
Carter, J B
Ellerby, William Mitchell
Elly, Andrew Jackie

Mound Bayou
Gough, Dr. Walter C
Johnson, Hermon M., Sr.

Natchez
Edney, Norris Allen, I
Jones, Chester Ray
Lewis, Charles Bady
Sanders, Larry Kyle
West, George Ferdinand, Jr.
West, Phillip Curtis

Oakland
Jones, Franklin D

Oxford
Edwards-Aschoff, Patricia Joann
Jackson, Hon. Ava Nicola

Pace
Washington, David Warren

Pascagoula
Davis, John Wesley, Sr.
Norvel, William Leonard
Owens, Cynthia Dean

Pattison
Yarbrough, Roosevelt

Pickens
Clarke, Henry Louis

Piney Woods
Beady, Dr. Charles H, Jr.

Port Gibson
Brandon, Carl Ray
Davis, Frank
Doss, Evan, Jr.
Noble, John Charles

Raymond
Harris, Clifton L.
Jenkins, Adam, Jr.

Ridgeland
Donelson, Tammie Dean

Rosedale
Trice, Juniper Yates

Ruleville
Edwards, Shirley Jean

Sardis
Blakely, Charles

Shelby
Gray, Robert Dean

Southaven
Roy, John Willie
Ware, Henry A, Jr.

Starkville
Campbell, Gertrude Sims
Person, Dr. William Alfred
Peters, Dr. Fenton
Ware, Dr. William Levi
Williams, Harold Edward

Stennis Space Center
Labat, Eric Martin

Summit
Williams, Doug
Williams, Melvin

Tougaloo
Fisher, Alma M
Hogan, Beverly Wade
Smith, Dr. Edgar Eugene

Tunica
Dunn, James Earl

Tupelo
Cook, Frederick Norman
Copeland, Russell Samoan
Lawless, Earl
Mabry, Mattie
Turner, Teresa Ann

University
Bell, Roseann P.
Crouther, Dr. Betty Jean

Utica
Cornelius, William Milton

Verona
Hill, Rufus S.

Vicksburg
Patrick, Isadore W
Rosenthal, Robert E
Winfield, James Eros

West Point
Potts, Sammie

Wiggins
Bills, Johnny Bernard

Woodville
Johnson, Charles E.
Tolliver, Thomas C., Jr.

MISSOURI

Blue Springs
Harris, Jasper William
Williams, Dr. Starks J

Bolivar
Junior, E J
Walker, Darnell Robert

Bridgeton
Coleman, Robert L

Caruthersville
Russell, Dorothy Delores

Chesterfield
Gillispie, William Henry
McKissack, Fredrick Lem, Sr.
Williams, Roland Lamar

Columbia
Ashford, L Jerome
Floyd, Dr. Elson S.
Hudson-Weems, Dr. Clenora
LeFlore, Lyah B
Morrison, Dr. K C
Strickland, Dr. Arvarh E
Thompson, Julius Eric
Watkins, Melvin

Florissant
Brooks, Joyce Renee Ward
Hines, Dr. William E
Huggins, Linda Johnson
Johnson, Dr. Ivory
McClure, Exal, Jr.
Newland, Dr. Zachary Jonas
Noah, Leroy Edward

Grandview
Bradley, Jesse J., Jr.
Jenkins, Melvin Lemuel

Hannibal
Crow, Hiawatha Moore
Duncan, Alice Geneva
Mallory, William Henry

Independence
Byrd, Edwin R.
Manning, Brian

Indianola
Matthews, Rev. David

Jefferson City
Boykins, Amber
Brent, David L.
Cook, Dr. Nathan Howard
Crouch, Robert Allen
Holland, Dr. Antonio Frederick
Myers, Victoria Christina
Parks, Dr. Arnold Grant
Pawley, Thomas D., III
Shelton, O L
Thompson, Rep. Betty Lou
Troupe, Charles Quincy

Kansas
Richardson, Munro Carmel

Kansas City
Bailey, Linda F
Bailey, Weltman D., Sr.
Baker, Gregory D.
Bell, Kendrell Alexander
Bivins, Edward Byron
Bolton, Wanda E.
Bryant, Dr. T. J.
Caro, Ralph M
Carter, James Earl, Jr.
Casey, Carey
Cleaver, Emanuel, II
Clemmons, Reginald C
Colding, Donna M.
Collins, Joanne Marcella
Cooper, Linda G
Dale, Virginia Marie
Davis, Leodis
Davis, Nigel S
Davis, Norma June
Diuguid, Lewis Walter
Dunson, Dr. Carrie Lee
Ellison, Nolen M
Eubanks, Eugene E.

Farmer, Ray
Franklin, Curtis U., Jr.
Gaitan, Fernando J., Jr.
Gibson, Elvis Sonny
Gonzalez, Tony
Harris, Kerri Gwinn
Henderson, Isaiah Hilkiah, Jr.
Hill, Julia H.
Hughes, Leonard S., Jr.
Hughes, Robert Danan
Jackson-Foy, Lucy Maye
Jenkins, Wanda Joyce
Johnson, Albert Lee, Sr.
Johnson, James S
Johnson, Ralph C
Jordan, Orchid I.
Kaiser, Inez Yeargan
Kee, Linda Cooper
Lester, George Lawrence
Mabin, Joseph E
Manuel, Louis Calvin
Martin, Samuel
McClinton, Curtis R., Jr.
McGruder, Aaron
Miller, Orlando Salmon
Moore, Derrick C.
Morris, Byron
Moten, Chauncey Donald
Myers, Rodney Demond
Myers, Sere Spaulding
Nash, Troy
Neal, LaVelle E, III
Powers, Ray
Reid, Robert Edward
Robinson, Dr. Genevieve
Robinson, Kenneth Eugene
Robinson, Verneda
Scott, Cornealious Socrates, Sr
Singleton, William Matthew
Smith, Cedric Delon
Spottsville, Clifford M.
Swift, Karen A.
Swift, Leroy V.
Taylor, Ellis Clarence, Sr.
Thomas, Derrick Vincent
Tunley, Naomi Louise
Turner, Sharon V
Walker, Dr. Sandra Venezia
Ward, Dedric Lamar
Washington, Alonzo Lavert
Washington, Lester Renez
Washington, William Montell
White, Frank, Jr.
Whitner, Donna K
Williams, George R
Winston, Lamonte
Wrenn, Thomas H., III

Liberty
Robinson, Dr. Cecelia Ann

Lilbourn
Clark, Theodore Lee

Manchester
Peoples, Veo

Maryland Heights
King, Hulas H
Steward, David L

Pagedale
Carter, Mary Louise

Pine Lawn
O'Kain, Roosevelt

Poplar Bluff
Arnold, Nancy

Rock Hill
Whitfield, Kennard O

Saint Louis
Anderson, Bishop Vinton Randolph
Banks, Richard Edward
Belancourt, Dunet Francois
Bentley, Herbert Dean
Bosley, Freeman Robertson, Jr.
Bouie, Dr. Merceline
Cahill, Clyde S., Jr.
Calhoun, Joshua Wesley
Calloway, DeVerne Lee
Calvert, Dr. Wilma Jean
Christian, Marion
Clay, William L.
Crawley, Darline
Daniels, Lincoln, Sr.

Dickson, Reginald D.
Diguid, Dr. Lincoln I.
Douthit, William E.
Dugas, Henry C.
Early, Ida H.
Freeman, Frankie M.
Freeman, Gregory Bruce
Garrett, Jacquelyn Brewer
Golden, Ronald Allen
Guerrero, Pedro
Gunnel, Joseph C., Sr.
Harper, David B.
Henderson, Leon C
Howard, Raymond
Jackson, Art Eugene, Sr.
Jackson, Ronald Lee
Johnson, Donn S
Jones, William Barnard
Kirkland, Prof. Jack A.
Lewis, Floyd Edward
Little, Leonard Antonio
Loveless, Theresa E
McClure, Exal, Jr.
McDaniel, Elizabeth
McGuffin, Dorothy Brown
Montgomery, George Louis, Jr.
Muhammad, Akbar A
Nelson, Edward O.
Newsome, Ruthie
Noble, John Pritchard
Norwood, Kimberly Jade
Orr, Clyde Hugh
Peay, Isaac Charles, Sr.
Perine, Martha Levingston
Peterson, Alphonse
Prophete, Beaumanoir
Pullman, Pam D.
Randolph, Dr. Bernard Clyde
Riley, Hon. Eve Montgomery
Roberts, Michael V.
Sanford, Mark
Saulsberry, Charles R.
Seay, Norman R
Shelton, Reuben Anderson
Smith, Wayman F, III
Smotherson, Rev. Melvin
Stamps, Lynman A., Sr.
Stevens, Sharon A
Stodghill, William
Taylor, Eugene Donaldson
Taylor, Theodore Roosevelt
Thompson, Anthony
Todd, Cynthia Jean
Trottman, Alphonso
Troupe-Frye, Betty Jean
Valley, Thomas James
Vickers, Eric Erfan
Walker-Thoth, Daphne LaVera
Wigfall, Samuel E.
Wiley, Gerald Edward
Wilson, Charles Stanley, Jr.
Woods-Miller, Jane Gamble
Word, Dr. Parker Howell
Worth, Janice Lorraine
Wright, Frederick Bennie
Young, Ira Mason

Springfield
Brown, Dr. O. Gilbert

St Charles
White, William E.

St Joseph
Nash, LeRoy T.

St Louis
Adams, Albert W.
Adkins, Leroy J
AkanDe, Benjamin Ola
Allen, Marcus
Atkins, Richard
Banks, Richard Edward
Bond, Leslie Fee
Bouie, Preston L
Brown, Lloyd
Bruce, Adriene Kay
Buckner, Quinn
Buford, James Henry
Burwell, Bryan Ellis
Calvin, Michael Byron
Carter, Paula J
Cheatham, Dr. Roy E.
Churchwell, Charles Darrett
Clay, William Lacy
Collins, William, Jr.
Cornelius, Charles Henry
Crim, Rodney
Crusto, Mitchell Ferdinand

Doggett, Dr. John Nelson
Early, Dr. Gerald
Ebo, Antona
Fowler, Dr. Queen Dunlap
Furr, Johnny, Jr.
Gates, Clifton W.
Gillespie, William G.
Givens, Dr. Henry, Jr.
Green, Darlene
Haley, Prof. Johnetta Randolph
Harper, Dr. Alphonza Vealvert, III
Harris, Dr. Zelema M.
Henderson, Ronald
Henry, Thomas
Hicks, Leon Nathaniel
Hite, Leon, III
Hudson, Keith
Jacob, John Edward
Littleton, Dr. Arthur C.
Logan, Lloyd
Mansfield, Andrew K.
McCutcheon, Lawrence
McFadden, Rev. Arthur B.
McKenzie, Miranda Mack
McRae, Harold Abraham
Morrow, Jesse
Nelson, Mary Elizabeth
Newsome, Ruthie
Pollard-Buckingham, Alice F
Shaw, Booker Thomas
Shelton, O L
Simmons, Kelvin
Smith, Ozzie
Swanigan, Jesse Calvin
Thompson, Rep. Betty Lou
Tillman, Dr. Mary AT
Toliver, Virginia F Dowsing
Walls, Melvin
Walton, Elbert Arthur, Jr.
Williams, Dr. Robert L
Wills, Dorothy
Wilson, Margaret Bush
Wright, Dr. John Aaron
Wright, Dr. Katie Harper

St Peters
Strawberry, Darryl Eugene

University City
Adams, Joseph Lee
Swanigan, Jesse Calvin

Velda Village
Williams, Lottie Mae

Warsaw
Ifill, Gwen

MONTANA

Bozeman
Stanley, Dr. Hilbert Dennis

Columbia
Williamson, Dr. Handy, Jr.

Emigrant
Morsell, Frederick Albert

Helena
Phelps, Constance Kay

Kansas City
Baker, Gregory D.
Casey, Rev. Carey Walden, Sr.
Cherry, Deron

Missoula
Griffith, Robert Otis

Saint Louis
Wead, Dr. Rodney Sam

St Louis
Murdock, Dr. Nathaniel H

NEBRASKA

Bellevue
Shoffner, Garnett Walter

Lincoln
Bowman, William Alton
Branker, Julian Michael

Crump, Arthel Eugene
Johnson, Frederick Douglass
McGee, Gloria Kesselle
Newkirk, Dr. Gwendolyn
Peterson, Harry W
Wallace, Ritchie Ray

Omaha
Atkins, Edna R.
Baker, Gail F.
Barnett, Dr. Alva P.
Coffey, Dr. Barbara Jordan
Ebong, Regina U
Foxall, Dr. Martha Jean
Gaines, Dr. Ray D.
Lintz, Frank D E
McGee, Waddell
Okhamafe, Imafedia
Pearson, Herman B.
Robinson, Alcurtis
Ross, Martha Erwin
Stewart, Freddie Mardrell
Thompson, John Andrew
Veland, Tony
Welch, Ashton Wesley

NEVADA

Henderson
Davis, Rev. Clifton Duncan
Langston, Dr. Esther J.
Shack, William Edward, Jr.
Wilson, Mary

Las Vegas
Amie, Gwen E
Babero, Dr. Bert Bell
Bell, Dr. Marion L
Brooks, Harry W, Jr.
Broughton, Christopher Leon
Clarke, Dr. Angela
Clarke, Raymond
Crawford, Cranford L., Jr.
Cunningham, Randall
Futch, Edward
Gates, Lee
Grant, Dr. Kingsley B
Guy, Addeliar Dell, III
Hatcher, Lizzie R
Higgins, Sean Marielle
Ita, Lawrence Eyo
Jackson, Kenya Love
Jarman, Patricia Morse
Johnson, Dorothy M
Langston, Dr. Esther J.
Lockette, Dr. Agnes Louise
Mack, Luther W, Jr.
Mayweather, Floyd
McCarrell, Clark Gabriel
McDaniels, Alfred F.
McGough, Robyn LaTrese
Miller, Donald Lesessne
Nelson, Debra J
Overstreet, Dr. Everett Louis
Pate, John W., Sr.
Patterson, Lloyd
Perry, Harold
Peterson, Alan Herbert
Rayford, Lee Edward
Soares, Bea T.
Thomas, Lacy L
Thomas, Samuel

New York
Steward, Emanuel

North Las Vegas
Bennett, Marion D.
Rhodes, John K

Reno
Berry, Ondra Lamon
Holloway, Jerry
Mack, Luther W, Jr.
McNeely, Charles E
Seals, Rupert Grant
Sneed, Paula A

Sparks
Hall, Dr. Jesse J.

NEW HAMPSHIRE

Hanover
Cook, William Wilburt
Hill, Errol Gaston

Lahr, Dr. Charles Dwight
Lewis, H. Ralph

Keene
Giles-Gee, Dr. Helen Foster

Manchester
Towns, Maxine Yvonne

Portsmouth
Hilson, Dr. Arthur Lee

NEW JERSEY
Chew, Vivian Scott
Harris, Jerome C., Jr.

Absecon
Andrews, Dr. Adolphus

Asbury Park
Jones, A. Lorraine

Atco
Gault, Marian Holness

Atlantic City
Clayton, Willie Burke, Jr.
Darkes, Leroy William
Griffin, Jean Thomas
Hopkins, Novellete O
LaSane, Joanna Emma
Mallette, Carol L
Milligan, Hugh D.
Norrell-Nance, Rosalind Elizabeth
Shabazz, Kaleem
Stewart, W. Douglas
Tyner, Damon G.

Avenel
Greenleaf, Louis E
Mohamed, Gerald R, Jr.

Basking Ridge
Jackson, Georgina
McCollum, Anita LaVerne
White, Joseph Councill

Bayonne
Cannon, Davita Louise Burgess
Hamill, Margaret Hudgens

Bayville
Gary, Melvin L

Belmar
Roper, Grace Trott

Bergenfield
Welch, John L.

Blackwood
Burton, Donald C.

Bloomfield
DeGeneste, Henry Irving
Fleetwood, Therez

Boonton
Miller, Rev. Kevin D

Bound Brook
Harris, Dale F.

Brick
Owens, Dr. Judith Myoli

Bridgeton
Hursey, James Samuel
Montgomery, Dr. Patricia Ann Felton

Brooklyn
Green, Sean Curtis

Burlington
Akins, Allen Clinton
Arnold, David

Caldwell
Hill, Dianne

Camden
Bryant, Wayne R
Butler, Dr. Rebecca Batts
Catlin, Robert A.

Drew, James Brown
Freeman, Ronald J.
Horton, Stella Jean
King, Rev. William L
Matthews, Jessie L.
Venable, Rev. Robert Charles
Wright, Linnel N

Cape May
Betty, Warren Randall

Cape May Court House
Richardson, George C

Chatham
Richardson, Charles Ronald

Cherry Hill
Brown, Joe
Foard, Frederick Carter
Grist, Ronald
Vann, Gregory Alvin
Walker, Dr. Manuel Lorenzo
Waters, William David

Cliffwood
Drake, Pauline Lilie

Clifton
Cornish, Jeannette Carter

Columbus
Brown, Roosevelt, Jr.

Cranford
Austin, Mary Jane
Wolfe, Deborah Cannon Partridge
Wrice, Vincent J

Dayton
Maynor, Vernon Perry

Dover
Jones, Benjamin E

Downtown Trenton
Williams, Jayson

E Rutherford
Overton, Douglas M.

East Brunswick
Johnson, Dr. Edward Elemuel

East Handover
Priestley, Marilyn

East Hanover
Mikell, Johnny

East Orange
Bowser, Hamilton Victor
Bowser, Robert Louis
Clark, Dr. James N.
Cooke, Thomas H, Jr.
Daniels, Joseph
Gibson, Althea
Giles, Althea B
Giles, William R.
Hudson, Cheryl Willis
James, Henry Grady, III
Jenkins, Joseph Walter
Jennings, Everett Joseph
Lambert, Joseph C.
Lewis, Aubrey C.
Muhammad, Marion
Peterson, Michelle Monica
Roberts, Paquita Hudson
Steed, Tyrone
Washington, Dr. James Edward
Wilson, Clarence Northon
Wilson, Dr. Laval S

East Rutherford
Armstrong, Darrell
Kidd, Jason Fredrick
Lee, Kurk
Massey, Robert Lee
McQuarters, Robert William, II
Miller, Corey
Toomer, Amani Askari
Way, Charles Christopher

Wooten, Tito
Young, Rodney Menard

Edison
Griffin, Bertha L.
McGuire, Paul M., Jr.

Egg Harbor Township
Norrell-Nance, Rosalind Elizabeth

Elizabeth
Smith, Frances C
Walker, Tanya Rosetta

Englewood
Brown, Arnold E.
Emeka, Mauris L P
Fay, Toni Georgette
Gallagher, Dr. Abisola Helen
Hadden, Eddie Raynord
Horne, Dr. Edwin Clay
Jenkins, Augustus G, Jr.
Loney, Carolyn Patricia
Perry, Richard
Polk, Dr. Gene-Ann
Taylor, Walter Scott

Englewood Cliffs
Holloway, Douglas V
Thomas-Graham, Pamela

Ewing
Collins, Elsie
Dickinson, Dr. Gloria Harper
Williams, Charles Mason, Jr.

Ewing Township
Muckelroy, William Lawrence

Fairton
Berry, Eric

Far Hills
Chapman-Minutello, Alice Mariah

Farmingdale
Oates, Caleb E.

Flemington
Gonzalez, Cambell

Fort Lee
Epperson, Sharon
Lester, Isaac
Rodriguez, Ruben

Fort Monmouth
Somerville, Patricia Dawn

Franklin Lakes
Haley, Earl Albert

Freehold
Hughes, George Vincent

Glassboro
Clark, Douglas L.
Ellis, Calvin H., III
James, Dr. Herman Delano
Moore, Oscar William
Robinson, Dr. Randall S
Sills, Marvin G.
Williams, Dr. Ora

Guttenberg
Johnson, Verdia Earline

Hackensack
Coleman, Chrisena Anne
Drakeford, Jack
Marshall, Rev. Calvin Bromley
Richardson, Louis M, Jr.

Hackettstown
Martin, Robert E.

Haddonfield
Bruner, Van B., Jr.

Hainesport
Austin, Dr. Ernest Augustus

Highland Park
Collier, Albert, III

Hillside
Ismial, Salaam Ibn
McGhee, Samuel T

Hoboken
Fairley, Juliette S

Ironia
Boschulte, Alfred F

Irvington
Brooks, Rosemary Bittings
Foreman, Lucille Elizabeth

Gatling, Chris Raymond
Stanley, Craig A
Williams, Junius W.

Jamesburg
Wiles, Joseph St. Clair

Jersey City
Diaz, F Louise
Estill, Dr. Ann H M
Gallagher, Dr. Abisola Helen
Harrold, Austin Leroy
Holmes, Carlton
Jackson, Bobby L.
Jones, Ben F
Latifah, Queen
Lawrence, Merlisa Evelyn
Littlejohn, Joseph Phillip
McMichael, Earlene Clarisse
Means, Dr. Fred E.
Mitchell, Judson, Jr.
Mosby, Carla Mane
Myers, Walter Dean
Patterson, Grace Limerick
Slade, Phoebe J.
Spears, Richard James
Sulton, Anne Thomas
Tolentino, Shirley A.

Jobstown
Fryar, Rev. Irving Dale, Sr.

Kendall Park
DeBerry, Virginia

Lakewood
Brown, Clarence William
Younger, Celia Davis

Lawnside
Cotton, Garner
Erving, John
Fisher, Joseph
Montgomery, Gregory B
Smith, Morris Leslie

Lawrenceville
Brooks, Carol Lorraine
Joyner, Rubin E
Turner, Shirley

Lincroft
Jones, Floresta Deloris
Scott, Hosie L

Long Branch
Cofer, James Henry
Stansbury, Kevin Bradley

Lyndhurst
Kennedy, Howard E.

Madison
Haynes, Ulric St Clair
Richardson, Charles Ronald

Magnolia
Lattany, Kristin Hunter

Mahwah
Davis, Diana L.
Johnson, Joseph
Pinn, Samuel J

Maplewood
Baugh, Edna Y
Bofill, Angela
Boyd, Robert Nathaniel, III
Brooks, Rosemary Bittings
Cooper, Daneen Ravenell
Holmes, Herbert
Phillips, Eric McLaren
Robbins, Leonard
Roper, Richard Walter
Slaton, Gwendolyn C
Spraggins, Dr. Stewart

Marlton
Bond, Cecil Walton
Jordan, J. St. Girard
Thomas, Linda

Mendham
Wright, Edward Lucius

Middletown
James, Alexander, Jr.

Monmouth Junction
Cherry, Theodore W

Monroe Township
Avery, James S

Montclair
Bolden, Dr. Theodore E.
Brown, Ronald Wellington
Curson, Theodore
Duncan, Stephan W.
Ewing, William James
Gill, Nia H
Griffith, John A.
Harris, James E.
McRae, Thomas W.
Millard, Dr. Thomas Lewis
Newman, Dr. Geoffrey W
Nunery, Dr. Leroy David, II
Scott, Donnell
Sharp, Jean Marie
Stone, Reese J
Tyson, Lorena E
Walker, Dr. George T.
Williams, Dr. Daniel Edwin

Montvale
Foster, Edward, Sr.

Moorestown
Armstead, Wilbert Edward, Jr.
Green, Joseph, Jr.
Waynes, Kathleen Yanes

Morris Plains
Lawson, Bruce B
Wyche, Dr. Vera Rowena

Morristown
Bettis, Anne Katherine
Crump, Wilbert S
Jones, James R
Montgomery, Ethel Constance

Murray Hill
Mitchell, Dr. James Winfield
Williamson, Samuel R

Neptune
Carter, Charles Michael

New Brunswick
Brooks, Avery Franklin
Clarke, Cheryl
Epps, C Roy
Gibson, Donald B.
Giles, Waldron H.
Grace, Dr. Marcellus
Hammond, Debra Lauren
Hinds, Lennox S
Khan, Dr. Ricardo M
Lambert, Benjamin Franklin
Nelson, Gilbert L.
Nurse, Richard A
Stevens, Dr. Maxwell McDew
Strickland, Dorothy S
Williams-Harris, Diane Beatrice

New Rochelle
McCormack, Edward G

Newark
Arbuckle, Ronald Lee
Banks, Cecil J.
Bateman, Celeste
Bettis, Anne Katherine
Branch, George
Brown, Dr. Diane R
Browne, Dr. Craig C.
Coleman, Claude M
Curvin, Robert
Daniels, A. Raiford
Davis, George B.
Davis, Harold Matthew
Denmark, Leon
Emmanuel, Anthony
Flagg, Dr. Eloise Alma William
George, Barbara
Gibson, Kenneth Allen
Grauer, Gladys Barker
Grundy, Dallas A
Hall, Lawrence H.
Hamilton, John Joslyn, Jr.
Harrison, James, Jr.
Holloway, Gerald
Holloway, Harris M.
Holt, Fred D

Houston, Dr. Whitney Elizabeth
Howard, M W
Jessie, Waymon Thomas
Johnson, Dr. Mark S.
Johnson, Robert L.
Johnson, Theodore Thomas
Kafele, Baruti Kwame
Lenix-Hooker, Catherine Jeanette
Lester, Betty J.
Marius, Kenneth Anthony
Marshall, Carter Lee
Maynor, Kevin Elliott
Mesa, Mayra L
Muldrow, Catherine
Petty, Oscar
Pinkett, Dr. Randal D
Prezeau, Louis E
Raines, Colden Douglas
Randolph, Leonard Washington
Rhines, Jesse Algeron
Robinson, Jeannette
Robinson, Jeffrey
Roper, Richard Walter
Slaton, Gwendolyn C
Smith-Gregory, Deborah P.
Smothers, Ronald Eric
Stancell, Dr. Dolores Wilson Pegram
Stenson, Lisa M.
Stephens, Doreen Y
Tate, Herbert Holmes
Terrell, Stanley E
Thomas, Philip S.
Thurman, Marjorie Ellen
Tucker, Donald
Walker, Dr. George T.
Walker, Karol Corbin
Williams, Kenneth Herbert
Wilson, Natalie
Woodland, Dr. Calvin Emmanuel
Wright, Ralph Edward
Yamba, Dr. Zachary

News Brunswick
Sneed, Michael

Newton
Fletcher, Sylvester James

North Bergen
Mayo, Harry D., III

North Brunswick
Richardson, Wayne Michael
Sims, Harold Rudolph
Thomas, Ralph Albert

Nutley
Gaither, Richard A
Reid, Malissie Laverne
Wainwright, Dr. Oliver O

Ocean
Phillips, Edward Alexander

Ocean City
Taylor, Prince Albert, Jr.

Orange
Jackson, Alfred Thomas

Palmyra
Flournoy, Valerie Rose
Linton, Sheila Lorraine

Paterson
Baker, Henry W., Sr.
Brown, Chauncey I., Jr.
Collins, Dr. Elliott
Davis, Anthony Eboney
Epps, Naomi Newby
Frazier, Shirley George
Garner, Dr. Mary E.
Gist, Jessie M. Gilbert
Harrington, Elaine Carolyn, Professor Emeritus
Harris, Juan
Harris, Thomas C.
Hicks, William H.
Howell, Robert L
Hutchinson, Ernest
Irving, Henry E, II
Kline, William M.
Lyde, Jeanette S
Nickerson, Willie Curtis
Rowe, Albert P

Williams, Ethel Jean
Williams- Warren, Jane E.

Pennington
Khatib, Dr. Syed Malik

Penns Grove
Pope, Rev. Courtney A

Pennsville
Bunche, Curtis J

Piscataway
Bethel, Dr. Leonard Leslie
Edwards, Michelle
Essien, Dr. Francine
Gordon-Dillard, Joan Yvonne
Jessup, Marsha Edwina
Johnson, Dr. Edward Elemuel
Mohamed, Gerald R, Jr.
Nelson, Jonathan P.
Nurse, Richard A
Phillips, Edward Martin
Richardson, Otis Alexander
Stringer, C Vivian
Wainwright, Dr. Oliver O

Plainfield
Allen, Clyde Cecil
Bethel, Dr. Leonard Leslie
Bright, Dr. Herbert L
Campbell, Dr. Milton Gray
Ganey, James Hobson
Graves, Dr. Jerrod Franklin
Horne, Westry Grover
Satchell, Elizabeth
Smith, Stanley G.
Williams, Dr. Daniel Edwin
Williamson, Ethel W

Pleasantville
Bryant, John G

Pomona
Reid-Merritt, Patricia Ann

Princeton
DeSouza, Ronald Kent
Dickerson, Janet Smith
Drewry, Henry Nathaniel
Gibson, Edward Lewis
Hope, Dr. Richard Oliver
Jackson, Eric Scott
Jordan, Stanley
Jordan, William Chester
Kennedy, Adrienne Lita
Lavizzo-Mourey, Risa Juanita
McRae, Ronald Edward
Morrison, Toni
Painter, Dr. Nell Irvin
Pearson, Marilyn Ruth
Peterson, Rocky Lee
Philander, Dr. S. George H.
Robinson, Clarence G.
Satterwhite, John H.
Schutz, Andrea Louise
Smith, Audrey S
Taylor, Howard Francis
Taylor, Dr. Patricia E.
Waller Shockley, Linda
West, Cornel
Woodridge, Wilson Jack, Jr.

Rahway
McDaniel, Dr. Adam Theodore
Southern, Herbert B.

Rancocas
Cogdell, D Parthenia

Randolph
Sandidge, Kanita Durice

Red Bank
Johnson, Theodore, Sr.

Ridgewood
Gray, Ronald A

River Vale
Brown, Dr. Lawrence S

Roseland
Giles-Alexander, Sharon
Powell, Arthur F

Roselle
Ford, Dr. Albert S.

Rutherford
Mangum, Ernestine Brewer

Salem
Johnson, Leon F.

Scotch Plains
Jackson, James Holmen

Secaucus
Baron, Neville A.
Blackmon, Brenda
De Graff, Jacques Andre
Rashad, Dr. Ahmad
Stewart, Alison
Wasow, Omar

Sewell
Barber, Hargrow Dexter
Davis, Russell Andre
Jackson, Harold Jerome

Short Hills
Burton, Ronald J
Evans, Gwendolyn

Shrewsbury
Sobers, Waynett A., Jr.

Sicklerville
King, Stanley Oscar

Somerdale
Gibson, John A

Somerset
Hinds, Lennox S
Horne, Semmion N
Mitchell, Dr. James Winfield
Williamson, Samuel R

Somerville
Gladwell, Malcolm
Stevens, Dr. Maxwell McDew

South Orange
Alexander, Walter Gilbert, II
Bowser, Lucius A
Boyer, Marcus Aurelius
Essoka, Gloria Corzen
Hall, Dr. Dolores Brown
Holmes, Dr. Louyco W
Jackson, Alfred Thomas
Marshall, Leonard Allen, Jr.
Peterson, Alan Herbert
Thorburn, Dr. Carolyn Coles

Springfield
Coleman, Rudy B.

Stratford
King, Stanley Oscar

Summit
Lassiter, James Edward, Jr.

Swedesboro
Gaither, Cornelius E.

Teaneck
Adair, Robert A.
Bond, George Clement
Browne, Robert Span
Glanville, Cecil E.
Hueston, Oliver David
Richardson, Wayne Michael
Richardson, William J.
Williams, John Alfred
Williams, Rasheda

Tinton Falls
Crocker, Clinton C
Foster, Alvin Garfield

Trenton
Carman, Edwin G.
Checole, Kassahun
Coy, John T
Eure, Jerry Holton, Sr.
Fitzgerald, Howard David
Fraser, Dr. Leon Allison
Gault, Marian Holness
Griffith, John A.

Hall, Kirkwood Marshal
Haqq, Khalida Ismail
Hopper, John Dowl, Jr.
LaGarde, Rev. Frederick H
Lewis, W Arthur
Palmer, Douglas Harold
Price, Pamela Anita
Pruitt, Dr. George Albert
Ravenell, Rev. Joseph Phillip
Robbins, Leonard
Sabree, Clarice S
Smith, LeRoi Matthew-Pierre, III
Steele, Tommy
Stubblefield, Jennye Lee Washington
Summerour-Perry, Lisa
Terry, Garland Benjamin
Thompson, Hon. Anne Elise
Thompson, William Henry

Union
Melton, Frank LeRoy
Robinson, Jeannette
Treadwell, David Merrill

Upper Montclair
Jones-Trent, Bernice R
Powell, Gayle Lett

Vauxhall
Gray, Christine

Vincentown
Green, Joseph, Jr.

Vineland
Gordon, Darrell R.

Voorhees
Montgomery, Dr. Patricia Ann Felton
Sanders, Steven LeRoy
Tucker, Dr. Wilbur Carey

Wayne
Barber, William, Jr.
Flint, Dr. Charley
Jones-Trent, Bernice R
McClean, Vernon E
Small, William
Waiguchu, Muruku

West Caldwell
Henderson, Henry F., Jr.
Henderson, Henry Fairfax, Jr.

West New York
Johnson, Sharon Reed

West Orange
Blakely, William H., Jr.
Cody, William L.
Connor, Herman P
Giles, Althea B
Giles, William R.
Jenkins, Joseph Walter
Lewis, James, Jr.
Marshall, David
Shepherd, Greta Dandridge
Tate, Herbert Holmes
Tucker, Sheryl Hilliard

West Paterson
Henderson, Henry Fairfax, Jr.

West Windsor
Campbell, Diane

Wharton
Groce, Rev. Herbert Monroe, Jr.

Whitehouse Station
Mckines, Charlotte

Williamstown
Buck, Ivory M., Jr.
Moore, Oscar William

Willingboro
Airall, Dr. Guillermo Evers
Bauldock, Gerald
Cogdell, D Parthenia
Harris, Dr. Jazmine A
Holland, J. Archibald
John, Anthony

Morris, Horace W
Saunders-Henderson, Martha M.

Woodbridge
Vertreace, Walter Charles

NEW MEXICO

Alamogordo
Martin, Wayne

Albuquerque
Ashanti, Keesha-Maria
Bradley, James George
Cartwright, Charles
Daly, Dr. Frederica Y
Graham, Rhea L
Ham, Darvin
Hoppes, Alice Faye
Jones, Dr. I. Gene
Okunor, Dr. Shiame
Siglar, Ricky Allan
Tomlinson, Mel Alexander
Worrell, Richard Vernon

Canoncito
Bowers, Theron. C.

Grants
Corley, Eddie B., Sr.
Gladney, Dr. Marcellious

Laguna
Bowers, Ava

Las Cruces
Allen, Samuel Washington
Boston, McKinley, Jr.
Clemmons, Clifford R.
Jenkins, Woodie R
Trotter, Andrew Leon

Los Alamos
Barefield, Dr. James E

Ramah
Murray, Dr. Thomas Azel, Sr.

Rochelle Park
White, Gary

Santa Fe
Sawyer, Alfred M.
Watson, Barbara
Watson, Leighton

Taos
Bagby, Rachel L.

NEW YORK

Bargonetti, Jill
Turner, Eugene
Violenus, Agnes A

AMHERST
Robinson, Edith

Albany
Alexander, Fritz W., II
Ballard, Allen Butler
Bowman, Joseph E.
Gaskin, Dr. Frances Christian
Hall, Lewis J.
Hansen, Stanley S., Jr.
Jones, Prof. Shirley Joan
Kane, Dr. Jacqueline Anne
Lee Sang, Sharon Nolan
McElroy, Dr. Lee A
Montgomery, Velmanette
Powell, Dr. Archie James
Wells-Merrick, Lorraine Roberta
Woods-Burwell, Charlotte Ann

Amherst
Granger, Dr. Carl Victor

Amityville
Brazier, William H.
Davis, Raoul A.
Taylor, DeForrest Walker

Ardsley
Bridgeman, Dexter Adrian
Lathan, Dr. William Edward

Armonk
Dungie, Ruth Spigner
Samuel, David
Zollar, Alfred

Arverne
Miller, Saundra C

Atlantic Highlands
Foster, James Hadlei

Auburn
Fletcher, Glen Edward

Baldwin
Wood, Vivian Frances

Baldwinsville
Harmon, M Larry
Morrow, Samuel P., Jr.

Bay Shore
McNeil, Freeman

Bayshore
Johnson, Cleveland, Jr.

Bayside
Martin, Patricia Elizabeth

Beacon
Carpenter, Ann M.

Bellport
Eleazer, George Robert, Jr.

Binghamton
Anderson-Butler, Carolyn
Bones, Ricky
Corprew, Wilbert E.
Graves, Denique
MacLean, Anita
Macon, Mark L
Span, Derrick L.
Summers, Dr. Rodger

Bobst
Komunyakaa, Yusef

Bohemia
Grandmaster Flash

Brentwood
Manning, Dr. Randolph H

Briarcliff Manor
Stewart, Raymond C

Brockport
James, Dr. Robert D.
Morgan, Clyde Alafiju

Bronx
Aviles, Dora
Baker-Parks, Sharon L
Belizaire-Spitzer, Julie
Beraki, Dr. Nailah G
Blair, Dr. Lacy Gordon
Blayton-Taylor, Betty
Blocker, Helen Powell
Brown, Anthony Maurice
Bruce, Raymond L.
Burns-Cooper, Ann
Clarke, Dr. Donald Dudley
Corinaldi, Austin
Cox, Keith
Diggs, Estella B.
Dudley-Washington, Loise
Dunbar, Anne Cynthia
Eastmond, Arlington Leon, Jr.
Ferguson, Derek Talmar
Fisher, Dr. Judith Danelle
Galiber, Joseph L.
Gidron, Richard D.
Grant, Claude DeWitt
Greene, Jerome Alexander
Hairston, Jerry Wayne, Jr.
Haywood, Spencer
Hester, Melvyn Francis
Hicks, Edith A.
Hudson, Frederick Bernard
Humphrey, Sonnie

Jackson, Karl Don
Jeter, Derek
Johnson, Charles Ronald, Sr.
Johnson, Robert T.
Lambert, Samuel Fredrick
Lee, Dr. Mildred Kimble
Lloyd, George Lussington
Maynard, Dr. Edward Samuel
McGee, Hansel Leslie
Morgan-Cato, Charlotte Theresa
Morisey, Patricia Garland
Palmer, Dr. Edward
Parris-Miller, June
Pugh, Dr. Clementine A.
Reid, Desiree Charese
Reid, Dr. Roberto Elliott
Richardson, Anthony W.
Robinson, Bishop William James
Ross, Regina D.
Samuels, Dr. Leslie Eugene
Simmelkjaer, Dr. Robert T
Simpson, Samuel G.
Small, Kenneth Lester
Stephens, Brooke Marilyn
Suite, Dr. Derek H
Taylor, Dr. Sandra Elaine
Taylor, William Edward
Thompson, Francesca
Thompson, Dr. Mavis Sarah
Thompson, Oswald
Travis, Jack
Valdes, Laura
Wansley, Lisa Payne
Warner, Ivan
White, William H.
Williams, Carolyn G
Williams, Patricia Anne
Wilson, Kim Adair
Wynter, Leon E

Bronxville
Kelley, William Melvin
Young, Thomas

Brooklyn
Abdul-Malik, Ahmed H.
Anderson, Madeline
Atkins, Thomas Irving
Bandele, Dr. Safiya
Behrmann, Serge T.
Bloomfield, Dr. Randall D.
Bobb-Semple, Crystal
Bowman, Joseph E.
Braithwaite, Mark Winston
Bramwell, Henry
Bramwell, Patricia Ann
Bryant-Mitchell, Ruth Harriet
Callender, Wilfred A.
Campbell, Tony
Carter, Robert Lee
Channer, Colin
Clarke, Yvette Diane
Collinet, Georges Andre
Coward, Onida Lavoneia
Criner, Clyde
Cummings, Aeon L
Daughtry, Herbert Daniel
Davidson, Arthur Turner
De Graff, Jacques Andre
Dennis, Dr. Rodney Howard
Douglass, Melvin Isadore
Eastmond, Joan Marcella
Edmond, Alfred Adam
Edwards, Audrey Marie
Edwards, Thomas Oliver
Esposito, Giancarlo
Evans-Tranumn, Shelia
Farrar, Moses
Farrow, Sallie A
Fierce, Milfred C.
Flateau, Dr. John
Folk, Dr. Frank Stewart
Francois, Theodore Victor
Franklin, Prestonia D.
Gabriel, Benjamin Moses
Gardner, Jackie Randolph
Garner, Nathan Warren
Gibel, Ronald L
Greene, Charles Rodgers
Greene, Clifton S.
Greenidge, Kevin C.
Greenwood, Monique
Hall, L Priscilla
Hastick, Roy A
Haywoode, M. Douglas
Hicks, Willie Lee
Higgins, Chester Archer, Jr.
Hightower, Edward Stewart
Hill, Dr. Richard Nathaniel

Hobson, Charles Blagrove
Hornburger, Jane M
Ingram, Gregory Lamont
Jackson, Dr. Edison O.
Jackson, Emory Napoleon
Jackson, Esther Cooper
Jackson, Pazel, Jr.
Jackson, Randolph
Johnson, Luther Mason, Jr.
Johnson, Michele
Johnson, Rita Falkener
Johnson, Robert H.
Johnson, Sheila Ann
Johnson, Sterling
Johnson, Vincent L
Jones, Vann Kinckle
Jones, William James
Keller, Mary Jean
Kelly, Ernece Beverly
Kernisant, Dr. Lesly
Kirby, Anthony T
Law, Robert Louis
Lee, Joie
Lee, William James Edwards, III
Leon, Jean G
Leon, Dr. Tania Justina
Lindo, J. Trevor
Majete, Dr. Clayton Aaron
Makau, Elena K
Malone, Maurice
Mandulo, Rhea
Marshall, Warren
Martin, Patricia Elizabeth
Maxwell, Dr. Marcella J.
McLaughlin, Dr. Andree Nicola
McMichael, Earlene Clarisse
Miles, Frederick Augustus
Millett, Knolly E.
Mister, Melvin Anthony
Monteiro, Dr. Thomas
Monteverdi, Mark Victor
Moore, Colin A.
Moore, Madeleine
Morancie, Horace L.
Morris, Celeste
Naylor, Gloria
Nelson, Novella C.
Nor, Genghis
Omolade, Barbara
Opoku, Evelyn
Owens, Victor Allen
Page, Willie F
Patton, Jean E
Perry, Richard
Pierre-Pierre, Garry
Price, Sr. Fred L
Primm, Benny J.
Primm, Dr. Beny Jene
Pugh, Robert William, Sr.
Reid-McQueen, Lynne Marguerite
Rico, Dr. Tracey
Rivers, Louis
Roberts, Edward A
Shaw, Theodore Michael
Singletary, Deborah Denise
Spradley, Frank Sanford
Steptoe, Javaka
Stroud, Milton
Taylor, Carol
Taylor, Rev. Gardner Calvin
Terry, Patricia S
Thomas, Dr. Lucille Cole
Thompson, Dr. Mark K
Townes, Hon. Sandra L.
Trent, Richard Darrell
Waldon, Hon. Alton Ronald, Jr.
Walker, Hezekiah
Wilks, James Lee
William, Thompson E.
Williams, Joseph B.
Williams, Prof. William Thomas
Wilson, Dr. Joseph F.
Zollar, Jawole Willa Jo

Brookville
Sylvester, Melvin R
Williams, Earl

Buffalo
Acker, Daniel R.
Amin, Karima
Arthur, George Kenneth
Bennett, William Donald
Brooks, Tilford Uthratese
Brown, Byron William
Brown, Ruben Pernell
Charles, Dr. Roderick Edward
Coles, Robert Traynham
Curtin, John T.

De Veaux, Alexis
Diji, Dr. Augustine Ebun
Durand, Henry J., Jr.
Easley, Brenda Vietta
Eve, Constance B.
Flemming, Carolyn
Fordham, Monroe
Glover, Diana M.
Grant Bishop, Ellen Elizabeth
Henderson, Stephen McKinley
Jones, Leeland Newton, Jr.
Kendrick, Joy A.
Kenyatta, Mary
Kirkland, Theodore
McDaniel, James Berkley, Jr.
McGrier, Jerry, Sr.
Merritt, Joseph, Jr.
Mitchell, Sharon L
Neal, Brenda Jean
Nickson, Sheila Joan
Noles, Eva M.
Peterson, Prof. Lorna Ingrid
Price, Prof. Alfred Douglas
Ryce, Sundra L
Sarmiento, Shirley Jean
Scales-Trent, Prof. Judy
Sconiers, Hon. Rose H
Scott, Hugh B
Sherrell, Rev. Calvin L
Sims, Barbara Merriweather
Smith, Bennett W., Sr.
Taylor, Dr. Henry Louis, Jr.
Tisdale, Prof. Celes

Cambria Heights
Benjamin, Arthur, Jr.
Boyd-Foy, Mary Louise
Reide, Saint Clair Eugene, Jr.
Southern, Eileen Jackson
Waldon, Hon. Alton Ronald, Jr.

Canaan
Sampson, Charles
Washington, Rose Wilburn

Canandaigua
Hill, Donna

Canton
Smith, Carson Eugene
Williams, Terri L.

Central Islip
Fillyaw, Leonard David

Chatham
Allen, Sanford

Chazy
Madison, Jacqueline Edwina

Claremont
Conrad, Cecilia Ann

Clifton Park
Ballard, Allen Butler
Bedell, Dr. Frederick Delano
Evans, Milton L.

Clinton
Johnson, C. Christine

Cooperstown
Beckett, Sydney A.
Irvin, Monford Merrill

Copiague
Hibbert, Dorothy Lasalle

Corning
Baity, Gail Owens
Truesdale, Dr. Carlton Maurice

Corona
Betty, Lisa C.
Heath, James E.
Jackson, Andrew Preston
Pease, Denise Louise
Wimberley, Frank

Cortland
Grantham, Prof. Regina
Peagler, Dr. Richard C
Smith, Keith Dryden

Croton on Hudson
Harris, Michele Roles
Van Liew, Donald H

DeWitt
Young, Prof. Alfred

Delmar
Thornton, Dr. Maurice

Dix Hills
Cave, Dr. Alfred Earl
Smith, Dr. Phillip M.

Douglaston
Jenkins, Dr. Herman Lee

East Elmhurst
Bolling, Deborah A
Grant-Bruce, Darlene Camille
Holloman, John L. S., Jr.
Jackson, Andrew Preston
Kaiser, Ernest Daniel
Lopez, Mary Gardner

East Patchogue
Washington, Herman A, Jr.

Elmhurst
Hicks, Henderson

Elmira
McGee, Dr. Joann
Trammer, Monte Irvin
Washington, Dr. Edith May Faulkner

Elmont
Chrichlow, Livingston L
Cobbs, Dr. Winston H B

Elmsford
Harris, Margaret R.
Jones, Yvonne De Marr
Ross, Winston A

Endicott
Johnson, Frederick E.

Fairport
Jackson, Fred H

Far Rockaway
Maple, Goldie M.

Farmingdale
Roberts, Roy J.

Flushing
Banks, Haywood Elliott
Brown, Emil Quincy
Byam, Milton S.
Coleman, Michael
Hammock, Edward R.
McRae, Brian Wesley
Randolph, Willie Larry
Tobias, Randolf A
Torrence-Thompson, Juanita Lee

Fredonia
Jordan, Robert

Freeport
Jenkins, Elizabeth Ameta
Smith, Hale
Watson, Prof. Denton L
Wilder, Mary A. H.

Fresh Meadows
Harper, Kendrick
Witherspoon, Addelle

Ft Drum
Rubio, Jacqueline

Garden City
Bellinger, Harold
Bennett-Murray, Judith
Dawson, Lumell Herbert
Harrison, Beverly E
James, Marquita L
Jenkins, Dr. Kenneth Vincent
Kimbrough-Lowe, Deborah
Lazard, Betty
Mills, Hughie E.
Paterson, Basil Alexander
Roberson, Gloria Grant

Vaughans, Kirkland Cornell
Wilson, Hugh A.
Workman, Aurora Felice Antonette

Germantown
Rollins, Walter Theodore

Glen Cove
Carroll, Robert F
Sylvester, Melvin R

Glen Oaks
Douglas, Ashanti Shequoiya

Glens Falls
Thomas, Roy L.

Great Bend
Jordan, John Wesley

Great Neck
Brown, Dr. Roy Hershel
Foskey, Carnell T.
Guilmenot, Richard Arthur
Murrain, Godfrey H
Tanksley, Ann Graves

Guilderland
James, Dr. Robert D.

Hamilton
Bryce-Laporte, Roy Simon

Harlem
Evans, Etu
Smith, Gregory Robeson, Sr.

Hauppauge
Anderson, Leslie Blake

Hempstead
Adams, Robert Hugo
Bonaparte, Lois Ann
Boone, Clinton Caldwell
Brown, Denise Sharon
Brown, Joyce
Clement, Anthony
Cross, Betty Jean
Cuffey, Chauncey Lawrence, Jr.
Harvey-Salaam, Dyane Michelle
Hunter, Deanna Lorraine
Lewis, Dr. Lloyd Alexander
Marshall, Rev. Calvin Bromley
Myers, L Leonard
Phears, William D.
Rainsford, Greta M.
Richardson, Tony
Robinson, Beverly Jean
Shipp, Etheleen R
Walters, George W
White, William Joseph
Wood, Vivian Frances

Henrietta
Byas, Thomas Haywood

High Falls
Staats, Dr. Florence Joan

Holliswood
Dye, Hon. Luther V

Huntington
Howard, Susan E

Huntington Station
Boozer, Emerson
Holmes, Cloyd James
Walker, Wesley Darcel

Inwood
Stanislaus, Rev. Gregory K

Ithaca
Curry, Dr. William Thomas
Dalton, Raymond Andrew
Harris, Robert L., Jr.
Hawthorne, Angel L.
Hill, Colin C
McClane, Prof. Kenneth Anderson, Jr.
Richardson, Roger Gerald
Smith, Keith Dryden

Sogah, Dr. Dotsevi Yao
Spencer, Dr. Michael Gregg

Jackson Heights
Eady, Kermit
Gordon, Claudia Lorraine

Jamaica
Alford, Thomas Earl
Allen, Gloria Marie
Bannerman, Alfred
Benjamin, Albert W.
Bennett, Debra Quinette
Blackwell, Dr. Milford
Brown, Sherman L.
Bryan, David Everett, Jr.
Burgie, Irving Louis
Carter, Etta F
Claytor, Charles E.
Cook, Ladda Banks
Copeland, Ray
Cormier, Lawrence J.
Couche, Ruby S.
Cright, Lotess Priestley
Curtis, Dr. James L
Dockett, Alfred B.
Duffoo, Dr. Frantz Michel
Ellis, Ernest W.
Faust, Naomi Flowe
Flake, Rev. Floyd H.
Fox, Thomas E, Jr.
Frazier, Adolphus Cornelious
Gaskin, Leonard O.
Goslee, Dr. Leonard Thomas
Greene, Dr. Beverly A
Hill, Arthur Burit
Holder, Reuben D.
Holmes, Carl
Jenkins, Cynthia
Jones, Annie Lee
Joy, Daniel Webster
Kennedy, Adrienne Lita
Ledee, Robert
Lewis, Daniel
Marshall, Lewis West, Jr.
McCarthy, Fred
Mitchell, Loften
Moore, Rev. Richard
Norris, Charles L, Sr.
Ray, Jacqueline Walker
Reid, Edith C.
Reide, Saint Clair Eugene, Jr.
Richardson, Ernest A.
Robinson, John F.
Satterfield, Patricia Polson
Shields, Rev. Del Pierce
Spradley, Frank Sanford
Taylor, Janice A.
Veal, Dr. Yvonnecris Smith
Vieira, Franklin
White, Howard A
Williams, Dr. Richard Lenwood

Jamestown
McDonald, Anita Dunlop
Peterson, Clarence Josephus
Taylor, Vivian A.
Thompson, Geraldine

Jeffersonville
Graham, Mariah

Jericho
Bailey, Kenetta
Fonrose, Dr. Harold Anthony

Kew Gardens
Moore, Emanuel A

Kingston
Ione, Carole

Lake Success
House, N Gerry

Laurelton
Holmes, Henry Sidney, III
Naphtali, Ashirah Sholomis

Lawrence
Davis, Brownie W

Loch Sheldrake
Howard, Dr. Mamie R

Long Island
Ebanks, Sylvan

Long Island City
Anderson, Avis Olivia
Bludson-Francis, Vernett Michelle

Fax, Elton C.
Harris, J. Robert, II
Washington, Herman A, Jr.

Mamaroneck
Rodney, Karl Basil

Massapequa
Jonas, Dr. Ernesto A
Quarles, Nancy L

Massapequa Park
Blake, Neil

Melville
Barfield, Deborah Denise
Howard, Susan E
Jonas, Dr. Ernesto A
Madison, Kristen Dorothy
Payne, Leslie

Middletown
Best, Rev. William Andrew

Mineola
Robbins, Alfred S.
Service, Russell Newton

Mohegan Lake
Harris-Jones, Yvonne

Monroe
Maynard, Dr. Edward Samuel

Mount Vernon
Bell, S. Aaron
Bozeman, Bruce L
Brown, Beatrice S.
Cleveland, Hattye M.
Dais, Larry
Dungie, Ruth Spigner
George, Constance P.
Mosley, Geraldine B.
Tarter, James H., Sr.

Mt Vernon
Robinson, Melvin P.
Scott, Osborne E.

New City
Marrs, Dr. Stella

New Hyde Pk
Skeene, Linell De-Silva

New Paltz
Butler, John Donald
Gonzalez, Anita Louise
Grant, James
Wade-Lewis, Margaret
Williams-Myers, Albert J

New Rochelle
Bankston, Archie M
Barksdale, Rosa Kittrell
Boddie, Daniel W.
Boyce, William M.
Branch, William Blackwell
Davis, Ossie
Edley, Christopher F., Sr.
Edwards, Theodore Unaldo
Goulbourne, Donald Samuel, Jr.
Hite, Nancy Ursula
Howard, Dr. John Robert
Kendrick, Carol Yvonne
Mardenborough, Leslie A.
Quarles, George R.
Quash, Rhonda
Rowe, Richard L.
Springer, Ashton, Jr.

New York
Abbott, Gregory
Abdul, Raoul
Abdullah-Musa, Omalawa
Abdus-Salaam, Sheila
Adams, Bennie
Adams, Betty Phillips
Adams, Dr. Clarence Lancelot, Jr.
Adams, Edward Robert
Adams, Nick
Adderley, Nathaniel
Addison, Adele
Adjaye, David
Adolph, Gerald Stephen
Aiken, William
Alexander, Khandi

Ali, Rashied
Allen, Alexander J.
Allen-Howard, Marquita W.
Alligood, Douglass Lacy
Alonzo, Jenny
Amado, Joseph S.
Ancrum, Alberta E.
Anderson, Granville Scott
Anderson, Harold A.
Anderson, Tony
Anderson, William A.
Andrews, Real
Anthony, Sterling
Armstrong, Janet
Armstrong, Reginald Donald, II
Armstrong, Robb
Arnold, Alison Joy
Arnold, Monica Denise
Arroyo, Prof. Martina
Ashford, John
Ashley, Dwayne
Atkins, Sharif
Ausby, Ellsworth Augustus
Austin, Joyce Phillips
Badu, Erykah
Baeza, Della Britton
Bailer, Bonnie Lynn
Bailey, Darlyne
Bain, Linda Valerie
Baker, Gwendolyn Calvert
Baker, Roland Charles
Baldwin, George R.
Ballard, Bruce Laine
Ballard, Dr. Harold Stanley
Balmer, Horace Dalton, Sr.
Bandele, Asha
Banks, Carlton Luther
Baraka, Imamu Amiri
Barber, Tiki
Barboza, Anthony
Bargonetti, Jill
Barnes, Joseph Nathan
Barnes, N Kurt
Barnett, Amy
Baron, Neville A.
Barr, LeRoy
Barzey, Dr. Raymond Clifford, II
Battle, Prof. Juan
Beal, Anne
Beal, Bernard
Beckford, Tyson Craig
Bell, Coby Erik
Bell, Derrick Albert
Bell, Gordon Philip
Bell, Raleigh Berton
Bell, Yvonne Lola
Bembry, Jerry E
Benjamin, Ronald
Bennett, Debra Quinette
Benoit, Edith B.
Benson, George
Bernard, Nicole A.
Berry, Philip Alfonso
Bertelsen, Phil
Biddle, Dr. Stanton F
Billingsley, Ray C.
Billops, Camille J.
Bisamunyu, Jeanette
Blackman, Cindy
Blair, Dr. Lacy Gordon
Blake, Grace
Bland, Ellen Taylor
Blaylock, Ronald E.
Blayton-Taylor, Betty
Bogle, Donald
Bond, George Clement
Bond, James Max
Bond, Max, Jr.
Booker, Marilyn F
Bostic, Viola W
Bouie, Simon Pinckney
Boyce, Joseph Nelson
Boyd, Gerald M
Boykin, Keith
Bradford, Gary C.
Bradley, Jeffrey
Bradley, Phillip Poole
Bragg, Joseph L.
Bridges, Sheila
Briscoe, Connie
Britton, Barbara
Britton, Dr. Carolyn B
Brokaw, Carol Ann
Brothers, Tony
Brown, Claudine K.
Brown, Clifton George
Brown, Courtney Coleridge
Brown, Denise Sharon
Brown, Harriett Baltimore

Brown, Dr. Joyce F.
Brown, Dr. Lawrence S
Brown, Lloyd Louis
Brown, Renee
Brown, Tony
Brownlee, Dennis J.
Bryant, Franklyn
Buckley, Gail Lumet
Buford, Howard
Bunkley, Anita Richmond
Burley, Dale S.
Burns, Jeff
Burns-Cooper, Ann
Busby, Everett C.
Butcher, Ernesto L.
Butler, John Gordon
Butler, Michael E
Butts, Calvin Otis
Butts, Dr. Hugh F
Byars, Keith Allan
Byrd, Joan Eda
Cadogan, Marjorie A.
Cage, Athena
Caines, Bruce Stuart
Caldwell, Benjamin
Callender, Leroy R.
Cameron, Randolph W
Campbell, George, Jr.
Campbell, Lloyd E
Campbell, Dr. Mary Schmidt
Campbell, Thomas W.
Candy, Dana
Cantarella, Marcia Y
Cantrell, Blu
Capers, Eliza Virginia
Capers, James, Jr.
Carey, Mariah
Carey, Patricia M
Carlton, Pamela Gean
Carreker, William, Jr.
Carroll, Edward Major
Carter, Nanette Carolyn
Carter, Robert Lee
Carter, Shawn Corey
Carter, Zachary Warren
Cave, Herbert G.
Channer, Colin
Chapman, Susan
Chapman, Tracy
Chapman-Minutello, Alice Mariah
Charity, Lawrence Everett
Charles, RuPaul Andre
Chenault, Kenneth I.
Cherot, Nicholas Maurice
Chisholm, June Faye
Chisholm, Samuel Jackson
Clark, Rosalind K.
Clarke, Richard V.
Clarke, Thomas P.
Clark-Sheard, Karen
Clash, Kevin
Clemendor, Dr. Anthony Arnold
Clemons, Earlie, Jr.
Clifton, Lucille
Cochran, Daniel Chester
Cohen, Gwen A
Cole, Harriette
Coleman, George Edward
Collins, Bernice Elaine
Colyer, Dr. Sheryl Lynn
Combs, Sean J
Concholar, Dan
Condren, Debra, PhD
Cone, Dr. James H.
Conner, Steve
Conwill, Houston Eugene
Cooper, J. California
Cooper-Gilstrap, Jocelyn
Cooper-Gilstrap, Jocelyn Andrea
Corbin, Sean
Cornwell, W. Don
Cortez, Jayne
Cose, Ellis
Cowell, Catherine
Coye, Dena E.
Crawford, Dan
Crews, Donald
Crider, Edward S., III
Cross, June Victoria
Crouch, Stanley
Cummings, Pat
Curry, Eddy
Curtis, Christopher Paul
Curtis, Dr. James L
Cylar, Keith
Dailey, Thelma
Dais, Larry
Daley-Meleschi, Valrine
Dalley, George Albert

Daniel, Samuel J
Daniels, Lee Louis
Dara, Olu
Dash, Damon
Dash, Darien
Davenport, Ronald R., Sr.
Davis, Alisha
Davis, Billy
Davis, Earl S.
Davis, Dr. Jewelnel
Davis, John Aubrey
Davis, Kery
Davis, Lisa E
Davis, Reuben K.
Dawkins, Stan Barrington Bancroft
Dawson, Ralph C
Dean, Diane D
DeBarge, Chico
de Jongh, Prof. James Laurence
Delany, Samuel Ray
Delice, Ronald
Dennis, Walter Decoster
Desert, Alex
Destine, Jean-Leon
DeVard, Jerri
Diggs, Taye
Dinkins, David N.
Dixon-Brown, Totlee
Dodson, Angela Pearl
Dodson, Howard, Jr.
Donald, Arnold Wayne
Dorsey, Herman Sherwood, Jr.
Dorsey, Sandra
Dotson, Howard
Dottin, Dr. Robert Philip
Dowdell, Dennis, Jr.
Du Bois, Nelson S. D'Andrea, Jr.
Dudley, Edward R.
Due, Tananarive
Dukes, Hazel Nell
Dukes, Dr. Walter L
Dumpson, Dr. James R.
Dunbar, Rockmond
Dure, Gerard
Duster, Troy
Dutton Brown, Marie
E-40, E
Eagle, Arnold Elliott
Ealy, Michael
Eastman, Eleanor Corinna
Eccles, Peter Wilson
Edmond, Alfred Adam
Edmonds, Terry
Edwards, Dennis, Jr.
Edwards, George R
Edwards, Leo Derek
Eikerenkoetter, Rev. Dr. Frederick J.
Ellington, Mercedes
Elliott, Joy
Elliott, Missy
Ellison, Carolyn
Emanuel, James Andrew
Ensley, Annette
Erskine, Kenneth F.
Evans, Albert
Evans, Hugh
Faison, Frankie R.
Fareed, Kamaal Ibn John
Farr, Llewellyn Goldstone
Farrell, Herman Denny
Faulkner, Geanie
Felton, James Edward, Jr.
Ferguson, Derek Talmar
Fernandez, Denise Burse
Ferrell, Rachelle
Files, Lolita
Fischer, Lisa
Fisher, Antwone Quenton
Flack, Roberta
Flatts, Barbara Ann
Fleming, Alicia DeLaMothe
Flemming, Dr. Charles Stephen
Fletcher, Robert E.
Ford, Wallace L
Fornay, Alfred R, Jr.
Forster, Jacqueline Gail
Fox, Thomas E, Jr.
Francis, Charles K.
Franklin, Don
Franklin, V. P.
Frazier, Audrey Lee
Frazier, Ramona Yancey
Frazier, Walt, Jr.
Freeman, Morgan Porterfield, Jr.
French, Howard W
Frost, Dr. Olivia Pleasants
Fudge, Ann Marie
Fuller, Curtis D.
Gadsden, Oronde Benjamin

Gaines, Adriane Theresa
Gaither, James W., Jr.
Garner, Melvin C
Garner, Nathan Warren
Garnett, Ronald Leon
Garrett, Denise Eileen
Gaston, Patrick Reginald
Gatling, Patricia Lynn
Gay, Alvin
Gayle-Thompson, Delores J.
Genet, Michael
Germany, Albert
Ghent, Henri Hermann
Gibel, Ronald L
Gibson, Nell Braxton
Gibson, Tyrese
Giles, Nancy
Gill, Prof. Jacqueline A.
Glenn, Wynola
Glover, Jonathan A
Gomez, Dr. Michael A
Goode, James Edward
Goode, Victor M.
Goodrich, Thelma E.
Gordon, Derek E.
Gordon, Helen A.
Gordon, Rufus Carl, Jr.
Goslee, Dr. Leonard Thomas
Grant, Denise
Graves, Denyce Antoinette
Graves, Earl G
Graves, John Clifford
Graves, Valerie Jo
Gray, Ronald A
Gray-Morgan, Dr. LaRuth H.
Grayson, Stanley Edward
Greaves, William
Green, Derek
Green, Lisa R.
Greene, Gregory A.
Greene, John Sullivan
Grey, Maurice E.
Grier, Johnny
Griffith, Mark Richard
Griffiths, Errol D.
Grigsby, David P
Grimes, Nikki
Guillebeaux, Tamara Elise
Guitano, Anton W.
Gumbel, Bryant Charles
Guy, Rosa Cuthbert
Hackney, L. Camille
Hadnott, Bennie L
Hageman, Hans Eric
Hall, Arsenio
Hall, Kim Felicia
Halliburton, Christopher
Hamilton, Charles Vernon
Hanes, Wendell L
Hankin, Noel Newton
Hanna, Roland
Hardison, Kadeem
Hardison, Ruth Inge
Harper, Arthur H
Harris, E. Lynn
Harris, John B., Jr.
Harris, Joseph R
Harris, Michael Wesley
Harty, Belford Donald, Jr.
Harvey, Errol Allen
Haskins, James S
Hatcher, Jeffrey French
Haywood, Gar Anthony
Heacock, Don Roland
Head, Edoris
Headley, Shari
Heavy D
Hence, Marie J.
Hermanuz, Ghislaine
Hewett, Howard
Hewitt, John H., Jr.
Hewitt, Vivian Ann Davidson
Higgins, Chester Archer, Jr.
Higginsen, Vy
Higginson, Vy
Hines, Laura M.
Hinton, Warren Miles
Hodges, Dr. David Julian
Holder, Geoffrey
Holder, Idalia
Holder, Laurence
Holliday-Hayes, Wilhelmina Evelyn
Hollinger, Reginald J
Holloman, John L. S., Jr.
Hopkins, John Orville
Horn, Shirley
Horne, Dr. Edwin Clay
Horne, June C
Horton, Clarence Michael

Houston, Allan Wade
Houston, W. Eugene
Howard, Norman Leroy
Howell, Robert J., Jr.
Hudlin, Reginald Alan
Hudson, Frederick Douglass
Huff, Janice Wages
Hull, Stephanie J
Hurd, David James
Hurse, Aubrey A.
Hutcherson, Dr. Hilda
Hyman, Earle
Ibrahim, Abdullah
Imbriano, Robert J.
Ingrum, Adrienne G
Innis, Roy Emile Alfredo
Jacko, Candice
Jackson, Beverly Anne
Jackson, Emory Napoleon
Jackson, Hal
Jackson, Pazel, Jr.
Jackson, Yvonne Ruth
Jackson-Bennett, Rosalind
Jacobs, Thomas Linwood
James, Alexander, Jr.
James, Letitia
Jamison, Judith Ann
Jarrett, Hobart Sidney
Ja Rule
Jasper, Kenji Nathaniel
Jeffers, Jack
Jefferson, David
Jeffries, Leonard
Jeffries, Dr. Rosalind R
Jemmott, Hensley B
Jenkins, Dr. Adelbert Howard
Jenkins, Augustus G, Jr.
Jenkins, Carol Ann
John, Daymond
Johnson, Herschel Lee
Johnson, Jeh Charles
Johnson, John Will
Johnson, Joseph
Johnson, Julie
Johnson, Patrice Doreen
Johnson, Patricia L
Johnson, R.M.
Johnson, Roy Steven
Johnson, Stephen A
Johnson, William L.
Johnson Cook, Suzan Denise
Jones, Dr. Billy Emanuel
Jones, David R
Jones, Delmos J.
Jones, Donell
Jones, Furman Madison, Jr.
Jones, Hank
Jones, Harold M.
Jones, Kimberly Denise
Jones, Nettie Pearl
Jones, Robert Wesley
Jones, Sarah
Jordan, Vernon Eulion
Joyner, Lauren Celeste
Kaalund, Sekou N
Kamau, Kwadwo Agymah
Kappner, Dr. Augusta Souza
Karpeh, Enid Juah Hildegard
Kashef, Ziba
Kearse, Amalya Lyle
Kellogg, Clark Clifton, Jr.
Kelly, R
Kemp, Emmerlyne Jane
Kendrick, Carol Yvonne
Kendrick, Curtis L
Kennedy, Teresa Kay-Aba
Keys, Alicia
King, Anita
King, B. B.
King, Brett
King, Cecilia D
King, Kelley A
King, Woodie, Jr.
Kirkland, Theodore
Kirwan, Roberta Claire
Kitt, Sandra Elaine
Knowles, Solange Piaget
Knuckles, Frankie
Knuckles, Kenneth J
Kodjoe, Boris
Land-Latta, Theresa E.
Lane, Nancy L
Lattimore, Kenny
Lawson, Bruce B
Lee, Consella Almetter
Lee, Dorothea
Lee, Felicia R.
Lee, Ritten Edward
Lee, Spike

Lee, William Thomas
Lenoir, Henry
Lenoir, Kip
LeNoire, Rosetta
Leonard, Sugar Ray
Levy, Valerie Lowe
Lew, Kim
Lewis, Byron E
Lewis, David Levering
Lewis, Dr. Delano Eugene
Lewis, Edward T.
Lewis, Emmanuel
Lewis, George E.
Lewis, Hylan Garnet
Lewis, Jenifer Jeanette
Lewis, Keri
Lewis, Wendy
Lewis, William Sylvester
Liles, Kevin
Lippman, Lois H.
Logan, Juan Leon
Logue-Kinder, Joan
London, Dr. Clement B G
Lopez, D Jacqueline
Louard, Agnes Anthony
Love, Darlene
Love, Mildred L.
Lowe, Jackie
Lucas, Raymond J.
Ludacris
Luke, Sherrill David
Luke, Hon. Sherrill David
Lynch, Hollis R.
Lynch, Loretta E
Mabrey, Vicki L
Mack, C.
Mack, Phyllis Green
Maitland, Tracey
Majete, Dr. Clayton Aaron
Mapp, Dr. Edward C.
Marbury, Stephon
Marchand, Inga
Mariner, Jonathan
Marsalis, Wynton
Marsh, Sandra M
Marshall, Ameila
Marshall, Jonnie Clanton
Martin, Jesse Lamont
Mason, Ronald Edward
Matthews, Candace S
Matthews, Dolores Evelyn
Matthews, Gregory J.
Mays, Leslie A
McAdams, David
McAlpine, Robert
McCannon, Dindga Fatima
McCrary, Michael
McCray, Darryl K
McDonald, Ella Seabrook
McFadden, Bernice L
McGee, Henry Wadsworth
McGuire, Raymond J.
McIntosh, James E.
McKenzie, Wilford Clifton
McKinney-Whetstone, Diane
Mcknight, Claude V., III
MC Lyte
McMillan, Rosalyn A.
McMillan, Terry L.
McPherson, David
McQuay, James Phillip
Mendes, Dr. Donna M
Mercado-Valdes, Frank Marcelino
Meriwether, Louise
Meriwether, Roy Dennis
Merritt Cummings, Annette
michael, b
Miller, Arthur J
Miller, Edith
Miller, Dr. Lamar Perry
Miller, Oliver O.
Mills, Joey Richard
Milner, Ron
Mindolovich, Monica Harris
Mitchell, Arthur
Mitchell, Bert Norman
Mitchell, Brian Stokes
Mitchell, Leona Pearl
Mixon, Veronica
Monet, Jerzee
Monroe, Earl
Monroe, Mary
Moody, Anne
Moore, Carman Leroy
Moore, Christopher Paul
Moorehead, Justin Leslie
Mordecai, David K A
Morgan, Tracy
Morgan-Murray, Joan

Morial, Dr. Marc
Morisey, Patricia Garland
Morning, John
Morris, Dr. Dolores Orinskia
Morris, Nathan Bartholomew
Morris, Valerie Coleman
Morris, Wanya
Morrison, Charles Edward
Morrison, Rick
Morrison, Yvonne Florant
Morston, Gary Scott
Morton, Patsy Jennings
Mos Def
Moutoussamy-Ashe, Jeanne
Muhammad, Ali Shaheed
Muhammad, Benjamin Chavis
Muhammad, Conrad
Murrain, Godfrey H
Murray, Albert L.
Murray, James P
Myers, Walter Dean
Namphy, Andre
Natta, Clayton Lyle
Neal, Elise
Neals, Felix
Nelly
Nelson, Novella C.
Nelson, Prince Rogers
Nelson, Tamara
Nelson-Holgate, Gail Evangelyn
Newkirk, Pamela
Newkirk, Thomas H.
Newman, Colleen A.
Nissel, Angela
Noble, Ronald K
Noguera, Dr. Pedro Antonio
Norris, Dr. James Ellsworth Chiles
Norwood, Brandy
Nunery, Dr. Leroy David, II
Nunes Kirby, Mizan Roberta Patricia
Nunn, Gregory
Nunn, Ronnie
Ofodile, Ferdinand Azikiwe
Ogilvie, Lana
Ogunlesi, Adebayo O
Oilver, Stephanie Stokes
Olugebefola, Dr. Ademola
ORee, Willie
Orlandersmith, Dael
Ortiz, Delia
Osborne, Gwendolyn Eunice
Owens, Andi
Owens, James Robert
Owens, Victor Allen
Page, Dr. Gregory Oliver
Paige, Dr. Roderick Raynor
Palmer, Stephanie
Palmer, Violet
Parham, Johnny Eugene, Jr.
Parker, Kellis E.
Parker, Lawrence Krisna
Parker Kodjoe, Nicole Ari
Parson, Richard Dean
Paterson, Basil Alexander
Paterson, David A
Patten, Edward Roy
Patterson, Raymond R.
Patton, Jean E
Patton, Leroy
Payne, Charles
Payne, Dr. N Joyce
Payton, Gary Dwayne
Pemberton, Priscilla Elizabeth
Penceal, Dr. Bernadette Whitley
Perry, Jeffery Stewart
Persip, Charles Lawrence
Peterson, Maurice
Petioni, Dr. Muriel M
Pettiford, Hasani
Phillips, Julian Martin
Phillips, Lionel Gary
Phillips, Mildred Evalyn
Pierce, Samuel R., Jr.
Pinkins, Tonya
Pinkney, Dr. Alphonso
Pittman, Dr. Sample Noel
Pitts, George Edward
Poe, Kirsten Noelle
Polite, Carlene Hatcher
Pomare, Eleo
Pool-Eckert, Marquita Jones
Porter, James H.
Porter, Karl Hampton
Preiskel, Barbara Scott
Preston, George Nelson
Prettyman, Quandra
Prevot, Rapheal M
Price, Kelly
Procope, Ernesta

Lyles, William K.
McCreary, Bill
Thomas, Charles Columbus
Vogel, Dr. Roberta Burrage

Stone Ridge
Reynolds, Milton L.

Stony Brook
Anderson, Edgar L.
Kennedy, Theodore Reginald
McKay, Karen Nimmons
Pindell, Howardena D
Roberts, Trish
Short, Kenneth L
Turner, W Burghardt

Suffern
Wilder, Cora White

Summit
Blair, George Ellis, Jr.

Sunnyside
Jerome, Joseph D

Syracuse
Barnett-Reyes, Saundra
Brown, Glenn Willard
Burgess, Dr. Norma J
Dunham, Clarence E.
Hardy, Kenneth
Ivey, Horace Spencer
Lee, Kermit J., Jr.
London, Dr. Harlan
Scruggs, Prof. Otey Matthew
Wells-Merrick, Lorraine Roberta
Wright, Roosevelt R., Jr.
Young, Ronald R

Tarrytown
Jackson, Freddie
Mills, Stephanie
Smith-Taylor, Rev. Donna Lyn
Whitely, Donald Harrison

Thiells
Street, Vivian Sue

Troy
Brown, Joeanna Hurston
Davis-Howard, Valerie V.
Dukes, Jerome Erwin
Jackson, Dr. Shirley Ann
Knowles, Dr. Eddie Ade
McCoy, James F.
Miller, Frederick A.

Uniondale
Workman, Aurora Felice Antonette

Utica
Mathis, David L
Taylor, Kimberly Hayes

Valhalla
Hewlett, Dr. Dial, Jr.
Mayo, Dr. Julia A
Whitely, Donald Harrison

Valley Cottage
Marr, Carmel Carrington
Marr, Warren, II

Valley Stream
Patterson, Gerald William
Robertson, Marilyn A

Vestal
Porter, Michael Anthony

Wantagh
Williams, Ada L.

Watertown
Fletcher, Glen Edward

Watkins Glen
Clifford, Thomas E.

Webster
Burns, Ursula M
Denson, Fred L

Howard, Darnley William
James, Dr. Herbert I

Wesley Hills
Wright, Will J

West Nyack
Dunbar, Harry B.

West Rochester
Johnson, Robert

Westbury
Evans, Alicia
Risbrook, Dr. Arthur Timothy

White Plains
Adams, Gregory Keith
Blake, James Riley
Brandon, Symra D
Bronz, Lois Gougis Taplin
Clark, Vincent W.
Duffy, Eugene Jones
English, Marion S.
Fowlkes, Nancy P
Frelow, Robert Dean
Grady-Smith, Mattie D
Grant, Claude DeWitt
Hooker, Olivia J
Jackson, Warren Garrison
King, Charles Abraham
Montgomery, Harry J.
Moody, William Dennis
Moses, MacDonald
Moss, Anni R.
Opoku, Evelyn
Parker, Barrington D, Jr.
Prince, Ernest S.
Reynolds, Grant
Riggs, Dr. Enrique A
Rubin, Chanda
Rutledge, Jennifer M
Salley, Lawrence C.
Simpson, Walter
Singletary, Inez M.
Spaulding, Lynette Victoria
Sudderth, William H.
Swiggett, Ernest L
West, Joseph King
Williams, Gayle Terese Taylor
Williams, Venus Ebone Starr
Wilson, Leroy, Jr.
Wyke, Joseph Henry

Williamsville
Howard, Robert Berry, Jr.

Wyandanch
Lewter, Andy C, Sr.

Yonkers
McLeod, Georgianna R.
Tolbert, Bruce Edward
West, Lena L

Yorktown Heights
Baylor, Sandra Johnson
Brooks, Norman Leon
Dean, Dr. Mark E
Ross, Winston A

Yorkville
Norris, William E.

NORTH CAROLINA

Mitchell, Carol Greene
Reuben, Dr. Lucy Jeanette
Steger, Dr. C Donald

Advance
Horne, Dr. Aaron

Ahoskie
Ruffin-Barnes, Wendy Yvette
Weaver, Joseph D.

Apex
Cunningham, Robert Shannon, Jr.

Asheville
Bowman, Dr. Janet Wilson
Harrell, Robert L.
Locke, Dr. Don C.

Thomas, Wade Hamilton, Sr.
Webb, Stanford

Bahama
Smith, Charles Edison

Bayboro
Bell, Kenneth M.

Bear Creek
Thompson, Rev. Carl Eugene

Belmont
Massey, Rev. Reginald Harold
Rann, Dr. Emery Louvelle

Bolton
Greene, Edith L

Burlington
Enoch, John D.
Freeman, Melinda Lyons
Leath, Verlyn Faye
Monroe, Charles Edward
Shanks, William Colemon, Jr.
Singletary, Reggie Leslie
Styles, Richard Wayne
Wade, Dr. Eugene Henry-Peter

Cary
Days, Bertram Maurice
Walls, Gen. George Hilton, Jr.

Chapel Hill
Banks, Ernest
Blake, John
Brooks, A. Russell
Brown, Dr. Frank
Campbell, Dr. Charles Everett
Daye, Charles Edward
Epps, Constance Arnettres
Evans, Slayton Alvin, Jr.
Grant, Ernest J
Harper, Curtis
Harris, Dr. Trudier
Horne, Gerald Charles
Jackson, Blyden
Johnson, Dr. Norris Brock
Lewis, James R.
Logan, Juan Leon
Long, Dr. Charles H.
Miller, Dr. Margaret Elizabeth Battle
Thompson, Donell
Turner, John B.
Wagoner, J Robert
Weaver, Garrett F.
Williams, John Earl

Chapell Hill
Thompson, Donell

Charlotte
Albright, Dr. Robert, Jr.
Alexander, Kelly Miller, Jr.
Artis, Katasha
Bickerstaff, Bernard Tyrone, Sr.
Bodrick, Leonard Eugene
Bogues, Tyrone Curtis
Bowser, Reginald
Bynum, Dr. Raleigh Wesley
Carpenter, Clarence E., Jr.
Carr, Roderich Marion
Carrier, Mark
Carruth, Rae Lamar
Cross, Dr. Oris Elizabeth Carter
Curry, Dell
Curtis, Mary C
Dunn, Traci
Evans, Carole Yvonne Mims
Ferguson, Roger W, Jr.
Flono, Fannie
Freeman, Brian M.
Gantt, Harvey Bernard
Garner, Edward, Jr.
Geiger, Kareem L.
Gist, Diane
Govan, Sandra Yvonne
Gray, Andrew Jackson
Greene, Dr. William Henry L
Grier, Arthur E., Jr.
Hackley, Dr. Lloyd Vincent
Harper, Joseph W
Harrington, Othella
Higgins, Roderick Dwayne
Hill, Esther P.
Hylton, Andrea Lamarr
Johns, Pollyanna
Johnson, Edmond R.

Johnson, J. Bernard
Johnson, Larry Demetric
Johnson, Robert L.
Johnson, Sam
Jones, Milton H., Jr.
Jordan, Michael
Kee, John P.
Kennedy, Ray C
King, Patricia E.
Leeper, Ronald James
LeGendre, Henri A
Lowery, Bobby G
Martin, Hoyle Henry
McCray, Almator Felecia
Means, Natrone Jermaine
Metcalf, Dr. Michael Richard
Mohammed, Nazr Tahiru
Muhammad, Muhsin, II
Newsome, Dr. Paula Renee
Nickerson, Hardy Otto
Nwagbaraocha, Joel O
Pinn, Dr. Melvin T, Jr.
Rayfield, Denise E
Ready, Stephanie
Rogers, Charles D
Shipman, Sheldon R.
Smith, Rodney Marc
Springs, Lenny F
Steger, Dr. C Donald
Stephenson, Dama F
Stone, Dwight
Taylor, Johnny C
Thomas, Dr. Herman Edward
Ware, Andre
Watt, Melvin L
Wheeler, Leonard Tyrone
Yancy, Dr. Dorothy Cowser

Clemmons
Hutton, Dr. Ronald I
Mitchell, Carol Greene

Clinton
Lane, Daphene Corbett

Columbia
Hill, Barbara Ann

Concord
Alston, Betty Bruner
Mathis, Robert Lee, Jr.
McLean, Dr. Mable Parker
Robinson, Harold Oscar
Steele, Tommy
Steele-Robinson, Alice Louise

Conover
Boyd, Kimberly
Ragland, Sherman Leon, II

Conway
Hunter, Howard Jacque

Dallas
Burris-Floyd, Pearl
Jaggers, George Henry

Davidson
Jackson, Rudy, Jr.

Durham
Ammons, Dr. James H.
Baker, Sharon Smith
Batchelor, Asbury Collins
Becote, Fohliette W
Belcher, Nathaniel L.
Bell, William Vaughn
Bond, John Percy, III
Bowden, Dr. Regina George
Brown, Furney Edward, Jr.
Bryant, R. Kelly
Bryant, Willa Coward
Caesar, Shirley
Carter, CDR James Harvey, Jr.
Chambers, Dr. Julius LeVonne
Chapman, Charles F.
Collins, Bert
Copeland, Betty Marable
Cox, Tyrone Y.
Dandy, Clarence L.
Davis, Brian Keith
Davis, Dr. Charles
Dawson, Dr. Robert Edward
Daye, Charles Edward
DeBracy, Warren
DeJarmon, Elva Pegues
Dempsey, Rev. Dr. Joseph Page
Eaves, Dr. Eugene

Edwards, Daniel
Fitch, Milton F
Fleming, Stanley Louis
Garrett, Nathan Taylor
George-Bowden, Dr. Regina
Grant, Augustus O
Hammond, Kenneth Ray
Harrell, Dr. Paula
Jackson, Jacquelyne Johnson
Jacobs, Danny Odell
Jacobs, Sylvia Marie
Johnson, Charles
Jones, Alice Eley
Joyner, Irving L
Joyner, Seth
Kenan, Randall G.
Kennedy, William J., III
King, Charles E.
Laisure, Sharon Emily Goode
Lattimore, Dr. Caroline Louise
Lawrence, William Wesley
Lewis, Dr. Meharry Hubbard
Lide, Dr. William Ernest
Lincoln, C. Eric
Lucas, Dr. John Harding
Lynch, Dr. Lillie Riddick
Lynch, Rev. Lorenzo A, Sr.
Lyons, Patrick Alan
Marsh, William A., Jr.
Marsh, William Andrew, III
McAdams, Robert L.
McClain, Dr. Paula Denice
McFadden, Cora
McMorris, Michael Anthony
Michaux, Eric Coates
Miller, Helen S.
Myers, Lewis Horace
Parrish, James Nathaniel
Patterson, Cecil Lloyd
Quick, George Kenneth
Raspberry, William J
Richmond, Tyronza R.
Riley, Liz
Rohadfox, Ronald Otto
Schooler, Dr. James Morse
Sellars, Harold Gerard
Shaw, William
Shields, Karen Bethea
Sloan, Maceo Archibald
Sloan, Maceo Kennedy
Smith, Charles Edison
Smith, Reginald Keith
Smith, William Gene
Spaulding, Jean Gaillard
Speed, James H, Jr.
Stanley, Carol Jones
Stephens, Brenda Wilson
Tuckett, LeRoy E
Vaughan, Rev. James Edward
Walker, Freeman, III
Watts, Charles Dewitt
Wells, Robert Benjamin, Jr.
White, Dr. Sandra LaVelle
Wiggins, Daphne Cordelia
Wiley, Ronald

Eden
Henry, I Patricia

Edenton
Hathaway, Anthony, Jr.
Perry, Rev. Jerald Isaac, Sr.
Taylor, James Elton

Elizabeth City
Burnim, Dr. Mickey L.
Cole, Edyth Bryant
Houston, Dr. Johnny L
Jenkins, Dr. Jimmy Raymond
Mitchell, Marian Bartlett
Taylor, James Elton

Elizabethtown
Andrews, James F.
McNeill-Huntley, Esther Mae

Elon
Ward, Frances Marie

Fair Bluff
Evans, Joe B.

Fayetteville
Andrews-McCall, Dr. Maxine Ram-
  seur
Coaxum, Callie B.
Curtis, Marvin Vernell
Goodson, Dr. Ernest Jerome

Harris, Marion Rex
Harris, Rex
Hedgepeth, Leonard
Isler, Marshall A., III
Johnson, Dr. Joyce Russell
Robinson, Dr. Joyce Russell
Womble, Jeffery Maurice

Fuquay Varina
Freeman, William M.

Garland
Brown, Mary Boykin

Garner
Sutton, Gloria W.

Gastonia
Latimer, Jennifer Ann

Goldsboro
Farmer, Hilda Wooten
Whitted, Earl, Jr.
Williams, Charles J., Sr.

Graham
Archibald, B. Milele

Grantsboro
Jones, Booker Tee, Sr.

Greensboro
Anderson, Joseph F.
Armstrong, J. Niel
Baber, Dr. Ceola Ross
Battle, Dr. Stanley F
Bender, Douglas Ray
Best-Whitaker, Vaughn
Bibbs, Patricia
Bowie, Oliver Wendell
Brewington, Thomas E., Jr.
Bright, Jean Marie
Carey, Dr. Phillip
Cole, Olen, Jr.
Davis, Arthur
Dennard, Dr. Turner Harrison
Dorsett, Dr. Katie Grays
Exum, Thurman McCoy
Fort, Dr. Edward B.
Franklin, Audrey Demps
Frye, Henry E.
Hackett, Barry Dean
Hairston, Otis L.
Harrigan, Rodney Emile
Hayes, Dr. Charles Leonard
Hicks, Dr. Arthur James
Johnson, Walter Thaniel, Jr.
Jones, Percy Elwood
Kilpatrick, Dr. George Roosevelt
Kirk, Dr. Sarah Virgo
Kirk, Wyatt D.
McLaughlin, John Belton
McMillan, James C.
Meadows, Lucile Smallwood
Monroe, Charles Edward
Moone, Wanda Renee
Murphy, Romallus O.
Parker, Karen Lynn
Patrick, Odessa R.
Player, Willa B.
Sampson, Robert R
Shelton, Ralph K
Simkins, George Christopher, Jr.
Smith, Obrie
Speight-Buford, Dr. Velma R
Spruill, Albert Westley
Stewart, Jewel Hope
Taylor, Natalie Manns
Tunstall, Richard Clayton
Vinson, Chuck Rallen
Whitaker, Von Frances
White, Booker Taliaferro
Williams, Dr. Lea E
Wooden, Ralph L.

Greenville
Carter, Edward Earl
Chestnut, Dr. Dennis Earl
Holsey, Dr. Lilla G.
Lewis, Lauretta Fields
Maye, Beatrice Carr Jones
Register, Dr. Jasper C.
Williams, Dorothy Daniel

Hampstead
Sidbury, Harold David

Havelock
Godette, Franklin Delano Roosevelt

Haw River
Williams, John Earl

Henderson
Henderson, Dr. Nannette S.
Johnson, Louise Mason

Hendersonville
Morgan-Cato, Charlotte Theresa

Hickory
Barrett, Iris Louise Killian

High Point
Andrews, Rev. Frazier L.
Brown, Robert Joe
Langford, John W.

Hillsborough
Stephens, Brenda Wilson

Huntersville
Snell, Johnna

Jacksonville
Woods, Almita

Kannapolis
Long, John Bennie
Nash, George T., III

Kernersville
Dudley, Joe Louis
Mathabane, Mark Johannes

Kinston
Dove, Dr. Shirley
Graham, George Washington

Kittrell
Faulcon, Dr. Gaddis J.

Landis
Taylor, Felicia Michelle

Laurinburg
Littlejohn, Samuel Gleason

Lenoir
Horton, Larkin, Jr.

Lewiston Woodville
Bond, Ollie P.

Lexington
Kindle, Archie

Liberty
Thompson, Rev. Carl Eugene

Louisburg
Othow, Helen Chavis

Magnolia
Becton, Rudolph

Manson
Worth, Charles Joseph

Matthews
Smith, Obrie

Maxton
Davis, Robert E.

Maysville
Frost, William Henry

Mebane
Cain, Frank

Monroe
Kersey, Elizabeth T.
Logan, Carolyn Green

Morrisville
McPherson, James R

Mt Olive
Jones, Leora Sam

Murfreesboro
Jones, Alice Eley

New Bern
Chenevert, Dr. Phillip Joseph
Frazier, Reginald Lee

Godette, Franklin Delano Roosevelt
Harmon, John H.
Raynor, Robert G

Newton
Boyd, Kimberly

Pinebluff
Capel, Felton Jeffrey

Powellsville
Coley, Donald Lee

Raeford
McPherson, Roosevelt

Raleigh
Allen, Dr. Brenda Foster
Andrews, James Edward
Arrington, Warren H., Jr.
Ball, Richard E.
Baskerville, Randolph
Beatty, Bryan E., Sr.
Beatty, Ozell Kakaskus
Birchette, Dr. William Ashby, III
Bishop, Ronald L.
Blow, Sarah Parsons
Blue, Daniel Terry
Boardley-Suber, Dr. Dianne
Burton, Leroy Melvin, Jr.
Carrington, Leon T., Jr.
Carter, Dr. James Harvey
Carter, Dr. Wilmoth Annette
Clark, Dr. Edward Depriest, Sr.
Clarke, James Alexander
Cook, Charles A
Dempsey, Rev. Dr. Joseph Page
Dorsett, Dr. Katie Grays
Edwards, John Wilson
Faulcon, Dr. Gaddis J.
Fields, Valerie K
Fountleory, Millicent
Gill, Rosa Underwood
Harris, Cynthia Julian
Hinton, Christopher Jerome
Holmes, Rev. James Arthur
Hunter, C. J.
Irving, Ophelia McAlpin
Jarrett, Gerald I, Sr.
Jones, Anthony Ward
Larkins, John Rodman
Lightner, Clarence E.
Lowe, Sidney Rochell
Lumpkin, Adrienne Kelly
Luten, Thomas Dee
McNeal, William R.
Michaux, Henry M
Moore, Lenard Duane
Newsome, Dr. Clarence Geno
Palmer, Elliott B., Sr.
Peebles, Allie Muse
Peebles-Wilkins, Dr. Wilma Cecelia
Pettis, Dr. Joyce Owens
Pickett, Rev. Henry B, Jr.
Pope, Mary Maude
Quigless, Dr. Milton Douglas, Jr.
Robinson, Dr. Prezell Russell
Scott, Quincy, Jr.
Shaw, Talbert Oscall
Silvey, Edward
Sims, Genevieve Constance
Smith, Carl William
Smith, Dr. James Almer, III
Spencer, Joan Moore
Stone, Chuck
Strachan, Lloyd Calvin, Jr.
Suber, Dianne Boardley
Sutton, Gloria W.
Sutton, William W., Jr.
Thomas, Dr. Herman Edward
Thompson, Dr. Cleon Franklyn
Trice, Trena
Wade, Beryl Elaine
Ward, Everett Blair
Watford-McKinney, Yvonne V
Webb, Harold H.
Wilkins, Kenneth C
Williams, George
Winston, Dr. Hubert
Young, Pamela Thorpe

Reidsville
Gordon, Ronald Eugene
Griggs, Harry Kindell, Sr.
Washington, Darryl McKenzie

Research Triangle Park
Johnson, Audreye Earle
Lewis, Aisha

Roaring River
Gilreath, Coot, Jr.

Rocky Mount
Gay, Helen Parker
Morgan, Hazel C Brown
Russell, Dian Bishop

Roxboro
Woods, Dr. Robert Louis

Salisbury
Cook, Elizabeth G
Freeman, Algeania Warren
Jenkins, Dr. Jimmy Raymond
Massey, Rev. Reginald Harold
Rountree, Louise M.

Sanford
Fisher, Dr. Judith Danelle

Seaboard
Broadnax, Melvin F.

Shannon
Goodman, Ruby Lene
McRae, Emmett N

Sharpsburg
Beasley, Annie Ruth

Shelby
Jones, Martha E.

Smithfield
Woodhouse, Dr. Johnny Boyd

Soul City
Crump, Janice Renae

Southern Pines
Thompson, Herman G
Turner-Forte, Diana
Wade, Kim Mache

Statesville
Foulks, Carl Alvin

Supply
Bryant, Jesse A
Gore, Joseph A.

Tarboro
Deloatch, Myrna Spencer
Summers, Retha

Thomasville
Booker, John, III
Waden, Fletcher Nathaniel, Jr.

Tillery
Grant, Gary Rudolph

Tobaccoville
Fauntroy, Rev. Walter Edward

Tryon
Carson, Warren Jason
Massey, Carrie Lee

Wadesboro
Little, Herman Kernel

Wagram
Gholston, Betty J.

Warrenton
Henderson, Dr. Nannette S.
Jervay, Paul Reginald, Jr.
Williams, Yarborough, Jr.

Washington
Perez, Lucille C., Dr.
Randolph, Louis T.

Weldon
Griffin, Dr. Ervin V
Shoffner, Clarence L

Whiteville
Jones, H Thomas

Whitsett
Tunstall, Richard Clayton

Wilkesboro
Gilreath, Coot, Jr.

Wilmington
Blanks, Delilah Bowen
Hairston, Raleigh Daniel

Moore, Katherine Bell
Waddell, Ruchadina LaDesiree

Wilson
Coleman, Avant Patrick
Ward, Rev. Melvin Fitzgerald, Sr.

Windsor
Cherry, Andrew Jackson, Jr.

Winston Salem
Hayes, Roland Harris
Jones, Lafayette Glenn

Winston-Salem
Bass, Marshall Brent
Bell, Winston Alonzo
Black, Veronica Correll
Brown, Clark S.
Burke, Vivian H.
Bush, Mary K.
Caldwell, Lisa Jeffries
Colston Barge, Gayle S
Crews, William Sylvester
Duren, Emma Thompson
Easley, Dr. Eddie V.
Eure, Herman Edward
Forrest-Carter, Dr. Audrey Faye
Hauser, Dr. Charlie Brady
Hedgley, David R.
Herrell, Dr. Astor Yeary
Hutton, Dr. Ronald I
Hymes, Jesse
Jackson, Felix W.
Jennings, Dr. Robert Ray
Johnson, Sheila Monroe
Lewis, Henry S., Jr.
McCarter, Ed
McEachern, D Hector
Miller, Ward Beecher
Murphy, Daniel Howard
Noisette, Ruffin N
Parker, Karen Lynn
Rann, Dr. Emery Louvelle
Sadler, Dr. Kenneth Marvin
Sadler, Dr. Wilbert L
Sandy Miller, Jones
Scales, Dr. Manderline Elizabeth
   Willis
Sprinkle-Hamlin, Sylvia Yvonne
Tate, David Kirk
Turner, Vivian Love
Turner, Dr. William Hobert
Wagner, David H.
Williams, Richard Lee
Womble, Larry W

Winton
Coley, Donald Lee

Yanceyville
Blackwell, Faiger Megrea

Zebulon
Vereen, Michael L

charlotte
Jackson, Dr. Arthur Roszell

NORTH DAKOTA

Fargo
Haney, Don

Grand Forks
Henderson-Nocho, Audrey J

Mullins
Reaves, Rev. Franklin Carlwell

OHIO
Phifer, B Janelle Butler

Akron
Arnold, Helen E.
Ashburn, Vivian Diane
Brown, Dr. Ronald Paul
Davidson, Hezekiah Miles
Demas, Dr. William F.
Evege, Walter L
Ferguson, Idell

Fowler, Ronald J.
Gladman, Charles R
Jones, Delores
Kennard, Patricia A.
King, Lawrence Patrick
Martin, Dr. Juanita K
McClain, Andrew Bradley
McClain, Shirla R.
McMillan, Jacqueline Marie
Morgan, Dolores Parker
Morgan, Eldridge Gates
Okantah, Mwatabu S
Parms, Edwin L.
Payne, Margaret Ralston
Peake, Edward James, Jr.
Pruitt, Michael
Roulhac, Joseph D.
Scruggs, Sylvia Ann
Silas-Butler, Jacqueline Ann
Sykes, Vernon Lee
Waterman, Jeffrey Trevor
Williams, Annalisa Stubbs
Williams, James R
Wright, Mark Adrian

Albany
Sharp, Dr. J Anthony

Alliance
Brown, Evelyn
Davison, Edward L.
Malone, Dr. Gloria S.

Ashtabula
Shelby, Dr. Reginald W

Athens
Childs, Dr. Francine C.
Crawley, Sylvia
Minor, Dale Michael
Myers, Dr. Lena Wright
Perdreau, Cornelia Whitener
Williams, Prof. Daniel Salu

Barberton
Berry, Archie Paul

Batavia
Doddy, Reginald Nathaniel
Warren, Clarence F

Beachwood
Banks, Andrew J.
Earls, Dr. Julian Manly
Holt, Donald H.
Leggon, Herman W.
Rice, Susie Leon
Romans, Ann
Williams, Barbara Ann

Berea
Brown, Gary Leroy
Cox, Bryan Keith
Henderson, Jerome Virgil
McGinest, Willie

Bidwell
Keels, James Dewey

Bluffton
Anderson, Fred

Bowling Green
Ford, Jack
Orr, Louis M.
Ribeau, Dr. Sidney
Scott, Dr. John Sherman
Skinner, Dr. Ewart C.
Taylor, Dr. Jack Alvin

Bratenahl
Chancellor, Carl Eugene

Brice
Gregory, Michael Samuel

Broadview Heights
Williams, Scott Christopher

Canton
Ball, John Calvin, Sr.
Bell, Yolanda Maria
Calhoun, Jack Johnson, Jr.
Gravely, Melvin J.
Johnson, William Edward
Mack, Charles L
McDaniels, Jeaneen J

McIlwain, Nadine Williams
Monroe, Kevin
Moore, Charles D.
Murphy, Vanessa
Nwa, Willia L Deadwyler
Pressley, DeLores
Robinson, R David, Sr.
Wilson, Jon

Centerville
Smith, Dr. Estus
Warren, Lee Alden

Chagrin Falls
Hunter, Frederick Douglas

Chicago
Holmes, E Selean

Chillicothe
McLaughlin, Benjamin Wayne

Cincinnati
Abercrumbie, Dr. Paul Eric
Allen, Herbert J.
Anderson, Dr. Carolyn
Anderson, Willie Aaron
Armstrong, Rich
Bates-Parker, Linda
Berry, Theodore M.
Bolden, Veronica Marie
Bond, Howard H.
Brown, Anthony
Brown, Herbert R
Bryant, Dr. Napoleon Adebola, Jr.
Burlew, Ann Kathleen
Caldwell, Dr. Esly Samuel
Carter, Troy A
Chapman, David Anthony
Colin, George H.
Collins, Dr. Patricia Hill
Cooper, Constance M.
Cooper, Emmett E., Jr.
Crawford, Betty Marilyn
Crew, Spencer R.
Cureton, Michael
Deane, Morgan R.
Dent, Gary Kever
Doddy, Reginald Nathaniel
Dunbar, Thomas Jerome
Edwards, Ruth McCalla
Elliott, Lori Karen
Eubanks, Dayna C
Felder, Ronald E.
Goodloe, Celestine Wilson
Gordon, Lois Jackson
Grant, Cheryl Dayne
Griffey, Ken, Sr.
Griffey, Ken, Jr.
Hall, Howard Ralph
Hatcher, William Augustus
Hayes, Jonathan Michael
Henderson, Theresa Crittenden
Hinton, Milton
Jackson, Dexter Lamar
James, Lawrence W
Jenkins, Roger J
Jones, Nathaniel R
Jones, William Lawless
Kearney, Esq. Eric Henderson
Keels, Paul C.
Keith, Hon. Damon Jerome
King, W James
Lee, Leron
Lightfoot, Simone Danielle
Logan-Tooson, Linda Ann
Maseru, Dr. Noble AW
McClain, William Andrew
McGoodwin, Dr. Roland C
McLean, Marquita Sheila McLarty
Meacham, Robert B.
Meadows, Cheryl R
Merchant, John Cruse
Merenivitch, Jarrow
Merriweather, Robert Eugene
Morton, William Stanley
Munoz, Anthony
Murray, Rev. J-Glenn
Nelson, Ramona M
Newberry, Cedric Charles
Norton, Dr. Aurelia Evangeline
Parham, Marjorie B.
Parker, David Gene
Patton, Rosezelia L.
Payne, Rod
Pleasant, Albert E, III
Pratt, Awadagin
Pryor, Chester Cornelius, II

Randolph, Thomas
Reed, Dr. Allene Wallace
Rivers, Clarence Rufus Joseph
Sawyer, Corey
Sells, Mamie Earl
Smiley, James Walker, Sr.
Smiley-Robertson, Carolyn
Spencer, Marian Alexander
Stallworth, Yolanda
Thompson, Sylvia Moore
Turner, Mark Anthony
Watts, Marsha
West, John Andrew
Wilbekin, Harvey E.
Williams, Marsha E
Williams, Otis
Williams, Stepfret
Wilson, Henry, Jr.
Young, B Ashley
Zealey, Sharon Janine
Zellars, Raymond Mark

Cleveland
Adams, H. Leslie
Adrine, Ronald Bruce
Arnold, Ethel N.
Atkins, Russell
Banks, Monica
Barrett, James A.
Bell, Rouzeberry, Jr.
Bernstein, Margaret Esther
Blackmon, Patricia Ann
Blount, Heidi Lynne
Boone, Alexandria Johnson
Braxton, Janice Lawrence
Brownlee, Wyatt China, III
Bryant, James W, Sr.
Bugg, Mayme Carol
Burke, Lillian W.
Burnley, Rev. Lawrence A Q
Burose, Renee
Bustamante, J W Andre
Butler, Annette Garner
Butterfield, Debra
Carson, John H., Jr.
Caviness, E. Theophilus
Chandler, Everett A.
Chandler, Dr. Mittie Olion
Chapman, Robert L., Sr.
Chatman, Anna Lee
Clark, Dr. Sanza Barbara
Clay, Cliff
Clouden, LaVerne C.
Copeland, Margot J.
Copeland, Dr. Ronald Louis
Crosby, James R
Crouther, Betty M.
Davidson, Lurlean G.
Dean, Willie B
Douglas, Dr. Janice Green
Duncan, Geneva
Dunnigan, Jerry
Earles, Dr. Julian
Earls, Dr. Julian Manly
Edwards, Dr. Robert Valentino
Ellis, J Delano, II
Fleming, Charles Walter
Floyd, Mark Stephen
Forbes, George L
Freeman, Dr. Lelabelle Christine
Fulwood, Sam
George, Allen
Goode, Bruce T
Graham, Donald
Greer, Thomas H.
Guffey, Edith A
Hale, Marna Amoretti
Hall, Brian Edward
Hardwick, Dr. Linda T.
Hawthorne, Nathaniel
Head, Edith
Hicks, Jimmie, Jr.
Huggins, Clarence L.
Hunter, David
James, LeBron
Jenkins, Edmond Thomas
Johnson, Andrew L., Jr.
Johnson, Dr. Henderson A, III
Jones, Peter Lawson
Jones, Sondra Michelle
Lairet, Dolores Person
Leaks, Emanuel, Jr.
Lee, Oliver B.
Lee, Shirley Freeman
Lockhart, Barbara H
Mackel, Dr. Audley Maurice
Madison, Robert P
Malone, Eugene William
Mayberry-Stewart, Melodie Irene

McClain, Jerome Gerald
Meaux, Ronald
Miller, Dr. Maposure T
Minter, Steven Alan
Moss, Rev. Otis, Jr.
Murphy, Dr. Donald Richard
Murray, Sylvester
Newsome, Ronald Wright
Ozanne, Dominic L.
Ozanne, Leroy
Parker, Anthony Michael
Parker, Irvin
Payden, Rev. Henry J, Sr.
Pinkney, Arnold R.
Pittman, Darryl E.
Pottinger, Albert A.
Powell, Doc
Prewitt, J Everett
Pruitt, Gregory Donald, Jr.
Rosemond, Dr. Manning Wyllard, Jr.
Rowan, Albert T.
Saffold, Shirley Strickland
Samuels, Marcia L.
Sanders, William E
Sharpe, Dr. Calvin William
Shaw, Alvia A.
Shumate, Glen
Smith, Barbara
Snow, Eric
Tipton-Martin, Toni
Tolliver, Stanley Eugene, Sr.
Vasser, Delphine Lynetta
Venable, Andrew Alexander, Jr.
Walker, Dorothea Bernice
Wallace, Ben
Walls, Gen. George Hilton, Jr.
Waters, Gary Steven
Weathers, Margaret A.
Webb, James Eugene
White, Frederic Paul, Jr.
Whitley, R. Joyce
Whitlow, Dr. Woodrow, Jr.
Willacy, Hazel M
Wilson, Dr. John W.
Wilson, Sonali Bustamante
Wright, Dr. Jackson Thomas
Wykle, May Louise Hinton

Cleveland Heights
Brown, Virgil E
Fraser, George C.
Gilbert, Albert C
Russell, Dr. Leonard Alonzo
Seaton, Dr. Shirley Smith
Storey, Robert D
Sutherland, Lynne
UmBayemake - Hayes, Linda

Columbus
Alexander, Dorothy Dexter
Allen, Jerry Ormes
Anglen, Reginald Charles
Barnes, Ronald Lewis
Barnes, Yolanda L.
Beatty, Otto, Jr.
Blackwell, John Kenneth
Booth, Charles E.
Boston, Dr. George David
Bowen, William F.
Boxill, John Hammond
Boyd, Terry A.
Bradley, Jennette B.
Brock, Lorraine
Brooks, Brian A.
Brown, Ralph H.
Brunson, Frank
Calloway-Moore, Doris
Charna, Daniel A.
Coleman, Michael Bennett
Corbin, Stampp W
Cortada, Dr. Rafael Leon
Craig, Elson L
Day, Donald K.
Dennis, Karen
Dillard, Wanda J
Dodson, William Alfred
Donald, Elvah T
Duncan, Robert M
Eiland, Mike
Evans, James L.
Evans, Liz
Fisher, Rev. David Andrew
Flowers, Michael E
Foster-Grear, Pamela
Frasier, Ralph Kennedy
Frazier, Frances Curtis
Freeman, Shirley Walker
Garraway, Michael Oliver
Garrison, Jewell K.

Gibbs, Jack Gilbert, Jr.
Gillespie, Avon E.
Gore, John Michel
Gramby, Shirley Ann
Greene, Dr. William Henry L
Griffin, Archie
Hairston, Rowena L.
Hale, Cleo Ingram
Hale, Dr. Frank Wilbur, Jr.
Hale, Hilton I
Hale, Phale D.
Hamlar, Dr. David Duffield, Sr.
Hardin, Marie D
Harris, Gene Thomas
Harris, Raymont LeShawn
Harris, Stanley Eugene
Hart, Phyllis D
Hayes, Eleanor Maxine
Haynes, Philip R
Hendricks, Leta
Hicks, Dr. Clayton Nathaniel
Hicks, William James
Holland, Robin W
Holloway, Ardith E
Hoover, Felix A
Hope, Marie H. Saunders
Humphrey, Howard John
Jackson, Dr. Benita Marie
Jackson, James Garfield
Jackson, Janet E.
Jewell, Curtis T
Johnson, William Theolious
Kirksey, M Janette
LaCour, Louis Bernard
Larken-Hicks, Patricia
Larkin, Michael Todd
Lemmie, Valerie A
Love, Lamar Vincent
Lundin-Hughes, Donna
Lyman, Webster S.
Maddox, Odinga Lawrence
Mallory, William L.
Marshall, Carl Leroy
McCall, Patricia
McDaniel, William T., Jr.
McGee, Rose N.
Merchant, James S, Jr.
Moore, Cynthia M
Moore, Floreese Naomi
Nelson, Dr. William Edward
Owens, Arley E., Jr.
Pailen, Donald
Patterson, Cheryl Ann
Payne, Debra K
Peal, Darryl Alan
Peal, Dr. Regina Randall
Pettigrew, Grady L., Jr.
Preston, Eugene Anthony
Pruitt-Logan, Dr. Anne Smith
Ransier, Frederick L
Redding, Gloria Ann
Reece, Guy L., II
Reed, Clarence Hammit, III
Revish, Jerry
Rhett, Michael L
Roberts, Margaret Mills
Robinson, S Yolanda
Rudd, Charlotte Johnson
Ruffin, Richard D.
Saunders, Jerry
Scott, Artie A.
Shipp, Dr. Melvin Douglas
Sims, Millicent Jeannine
Smallwood, Osborn Tucker
Smith, Janet Maria
Spencer, Larry Lee
Squire, Carole Renee
Stewart, Dr. Mac A.
Sullivan, Dr. Edward James
Sullivan, Ernest Lee
Tabb, Roosevelt
Thrower, Julius A.
Tolbert, Dr. Herman Andre
Tolbert, Lawrence J.
Trout, Nelson W.
Wade, William Carl
Weddington, Dr. Wilburn Harold, Sr.
West, Pheoris
White, Janice G
White, Kenneth Eugene, Sr.
Williams, James
Williams, Lucretia Murphy
Willis, Miechelle Orchid
Wilson, F Leon
Wood, Dr. A Wilson

Dayton
Adams, Lucinda Williams
Adams, Martha E. W.

Perkins, Edward Joseph
Williams, Norris Gerald

Okalahoma City
Holmes, Carl

Oklahoma
Lee, Forrest A, Sr.

Oklahoma City
Barclay, Carl Archie
Bedford, William
Benton, Leonard D
Berry, Major T., Jr.
Brown-Francisco, Teresa Elaine
Byrd, Camolia Alcorn
Gigger, Helen C.
Gigger, Nathaniel Jay
Greathouse, Jesse J, Jr.
Grigsby, Troy L
Hall, Melvin Curtis
Hardeman, Dr. Carole Hall
Henderson, Joyce Ann
Humphrey, Marian J
Jackson, Mattie Lee
Jackson, Walter Kinsley
Kirk, Leroy W.
Luper, Clara M.
McLeod, Dr. Michael Preston
McMurry, Dr. Kermit Roosevelt, Jr.
Miles-LaGrange, Vicki
Murrell, Hon. Sylvia Marilyn
Parks, Thelma Reece
Ponder-Nelson, Debra
Reed, Willis
Rogers, Dr. George
Sartin, Johnny Nelson, Jr.
Wharton, Ferdinand D, Jr.
Williams, Freddye Harper
Wilson, Dr. Frank Fredrick, III

Redbird
Billups, Mattie Lou

Spencer
Sloss, Minerva A.

Stillwater
Arnold, Lionel A.
Combs, Willa R.
Mitchell, Dr. Earl Douglass, Jr.

Tulsa
Anderson, Chester R.
Anderson, Elizabeth M
Andrews, Mark Althavean
Bryant, Hubert Hale
Bryant-Ellis, Paula D.
Butler, Roy
Cannon, Dr. Donnie E.
Chappelle, Thomas Oscar, Sr.
Clark, Major
Combs, Samuel, III
Cosby, Dr. William Henry
Evans, Leon Edward, Jr.
Goodwin, James Osby
Hopkins, Donald Ray
House, Kyla N
Hovell, Yvonne
Jeffrey, Charles James, Jr.
Johnson, Paul L.
Lacy, Edward J.
Lewis, Charles H.
Mathis, Johnny
Olds, Lydia Michelle
Payne-Nabors, Colleen J
Pearson, Bishop Carlton Demetrius
Pegues, Wennette West
Ragsdale, Charles Lea Chester
Sainte-Johnn, Don
Samuels, Everett Paul
Sanders, Hobart C.
Smith, Dr. Gregory Allen
Staten, Mark Eugene
Taylor, Dr. Thad, Jr.

OREGON

Ashland
Albers, Kenneth Lynn

Beaverton
DeBerry, Donna
Rohr, Leonard Carl
Smith, Wilson Washington, III

Thompson, John Robert
Way, Gary Darryl

Bend
Evers-Williams, Myrlie

Corvallis
Branch, Prof. Harrison
Gamble, Dr. Wilbert
Seals, Gerald

Eugene
Bradley, David Henry, Jr.
Campbell, Gary Lloyd
Carter, Dr. Lawrence Robert

Gresham
Parker, Clarence E

Portland
Benton, Phyllis Clora
Black, Gail
Borum, Regina A.
Brandon, Terrell
Britton, Elizabeth
Debnam, Chadwick Basil
Gainer, Prof. John F
Gatewood, Dr. Algie C.
Harrington, Denise Marion
Hartzog, Ernest E.
Heflin, John F.
Henry, Dr. Samuel Dudley
Jackson, Frederick Leon
Johnson, Olrick
Law-Driggins, Ellen T.
Leonard, Carolyn Marie
Mathabane, Mark Johannes
McCoy, Gladys
McMillan, Nate
Pickles, Patricia L.
Pool, Vera C
Spicer, Osker, Jr.
St John, Primus
Taylor, Michael Loeb
Temple, Dr. Jacqueline B
Toran, Kay Dean
Venable, Max

Salem
Bush, Charles Vernon
Carter, Margaret Louise
McCoy, William
Pelton, M. Lee
Winters, Jacqueline F

Stayton
McClain, William L

Troutdale
Henry, Dr. Samuel Dudley

West Linn
Hamilton, H J Belton
St John, Primus
Wilson, Edith N

PENNSYLVANIA
Hutchins, Francis L., Jr.
Jackson, Ricardo C

Abington
Brown, Tyrone W.

Aliquippa
Meade, Melvin C.
Smith, Eugene
Wallace, Ronald Wilfred

Allentown
Battle, Turner Charles, III
Bell, Ngozi O
Edwards, Lewis

Allison Park
Sessoms, Dr. Frank Eugene

Ambler
Vaughn, Dr. Alvin

Audubon
Vargus, Dr. Ione D.

Bala Cynwyd
Bishop, Dr. Alfred A.
Dyer-Goode, Pamela Theresa

Patterson, James
Reese, Ike

Berwyn
James, William

Bloomsburg
Bryan, Jesse A.

Blue Bell
Pegus, Cheryl
Wilson, Sandra E.

Braddock
Essiet, Dr. Evaleen Johnson

Bridgeville
Stewart, Dr. James Benjamin

Bryn Mawr
Collymore, Dr. Edward L.
Kirby, Nancy J

California
Kingdom, Roger Nona

Camp Hill
Williams, James E., Jr.

Chalfont
Lomax, Walter P.

Cheltenham
Harris, Dr. Dolores M.

Chester
Gaines, Ava Canda
Holmes, Leo S.
Leake, Willie Mae James
Nails, John Walker
Riley, William Scott

Cheyney
Arnold, Wallace C.
Eke, Kenoye Kelvin
Wilson, Wade

Clarion
Moore, Gary E

Claysville
Blount, Melvin Cornell

Coatesville
Johnson, Paul Lawrence
Middleton, Rose Nixon

Connellsville
Farmer, Dr. Robert Clarence

Coraopolis
Bullard, Keith
Smith, Dr. Earl Bradford

Courthouse
Bailey, Ronald W

Darby
Tyler, Robert James, Sr.

Delaware Water Gap
Woods, Philip Wells

Doylestown
Hill, Bennett David

Dresher
Wilson, Sandra E.

East Lansdowne
Emmons, Rayford E.

East Stroudsburg
Graham, Patricia
Sanders, Dr. Isaac Warren

Easton
Hay, Samuel Arthur
Holmes, Larry
Houston, William DeBoise
Jones, Alfredean
McCartney, John
Purdee, Nathan

Edinboro
Dillon, Aubrey
Pogue, Frank G., Jr.
Robinson, Curtis

Elkins Park
Evans, Therman E.
Wright, Linwood Clinton

Elkins Pk
Seale, Bobby

Enola
Gadsden, Rev. Dr. Nathaniel J

Erie
Cunningham, Don
Garibaldi, Dr. Antoine Michael
Summers, Dr. David Stewart
Trice, William B.

Gettysburg
Matthews, Harry Bradshaw

Gladwyne
Williams, Dyana

Glen Mills
Wright, Robert Courtlandt

Grantham
Burnley, Rev. Lawrence A Q

Greensburg
Johnson, Julia L.

Harrisburg
Ash, Richard Larry
Baldwin, Cynthia A.
Baxter, Nathan Dwight, D.Min.
Bostic, William C
Branche, Gilbert M.
Braxton, Harriet E.
Brooks, Rodney Norman
Cannon, Paul L
Chambers, Clarice Lorraine
Clark, Donald Lewis
Cummings, Cary, III
Gadsden, Rev. Dr. Nathaniel J
Gilmore, Charles Arthur
Gordon, Fannetta Nelson
Gumby, Dr. John Wesley
Hargrove, Trent
Johnson, Benjamin Washington
Love, Dr. George Hayward
Montgomery, William R.
Peguese, Charles R.
Preston, Joseph
Prioleau, Dr. Sara Nelliene
Raines, Timothy
Richards, Winston Ashton
Robinson, William
Roebuck, James Randolph
Rogers-Grundy, Ethel W.
Russell, Keith Bradley
Smalls, Charley Mae
Spigner, Dr. Donald Wayne
Thomas, Hon. W. Curtis
Utley, Richard Henry
Washington, LeAnna M
White, Scott A., Sr.
Wilson, Ronald M
Womack, Stanley H.
Young, George, Jr.

Haverford
Taylor, Karin

Hazleton
Harris, Dr. Arthur Leonard

Hershey
Bradley, Andrew Thomas, Sr.
Harvey, Dr. Harold A.
Mortel, Dr. Rodrigue

Horsham
Hill, Jeffrey Ronald
Wilson, Earl Lawrence

Imperial
Outlaw, Sitnotra

Jenkintown
Biagas, Edward D.
Smith, Rev. Dr. Robert Johnson

King Of Prussia
Foard, Frederick Carter

King of Prussia
Kinniebrew, Robert Lee
Thomas, Edward Arthur
Woodland, Stanley R

Kutztown
Westmoreland, Samuel Douglas
Woodard, Dr. Charles James

Lancaster
Williams, Hon. Louise Bernice

Langhorne
Miller, C Conrad, Jr.

Levittown
Jordan, Josephine E C

Lewistown
Carter, Ricardo, M.D.
Rogers, Dr. Bernard Rousseau

Lincoln
Pettaway, Charles

Lincoln Univ
Baxter, Kala Lynn

Lincoln University
Garcia, Dr. William Burres
Hunter Hayes, Tracey Joel
Nelson, Dr. Ivory V.
Pride, Rita McKinley
Rodgers, Joseph James, Jr.
Williams, Dr. Willie, Jr.

Lock Haven
Lynch, Robert D.

Malvern
Ali-Jackson, Kamil
Robbins, Carl Gregory Cuyjet
Wright, Robert L.

McKeesport
Hart, Barbara McCollum
Mason, Major Albert
Richardson, Dr. Lacy Franklin

Media
Brown, Dr. Glenn Arthur
Dennis, Edward S G, Jr.

Merion
Camp, Kimberly
Pierce, Kama B

Middletown
Gilpin, Clemmie Edward
Richards, Winston Ashton
Williams-Dovi, Joanna

Mill Hall
Lynch, Robert D.

Millersville
Hopkins, Leroy Taft
McNairy, Dr. Francine G.

Monreville
Jackson, Jaren

Monroeville
Mikell, Charles Donald
Wheeler, Shirley Y.

Newtown
Bernstine, Dr. Daniel O.

Norristown
Alexandre, Journel
Booker, Thurman D.
Davenport, Horace Alexander
Fair, Frank T.
Nelson, Cleopatra McClellan

North Wales
Bass, Dr. Herbert H.

Oberlin
Shepherd, Roosevelt Eugene

PHILADELPHIA
Carter, Fredrick Carter

Pennsylvania
Llewellyn, James Bruce

Petrolia
Lee, John C, III

Philadelphia
Ackridge, Florence Gateward
Adelekan, Tahira Gittens

Adom, Edwin Nii Amalai
Algotsson, Sharne
Ali, Shahrazad
Allen, Terrell Allison, III
Alston, Floyd William
Anderson, J Morris
Archie, Shirley Franklin
Asante, Kariamu Welsh
Asante, Dr. Molefi Kete
Ayers, Randy
Bailey, Curtis Darnell
Baker, Floyd Edward
Beach, George
Beckett, Charles Campbell
Bell, Thom R.
Benson, Rubin Author
Benton, George A.
Berry, Dr. Mary Frances
Bieniemy, Eric
Billue, Zana
Blockson, Charles LeRoy
Bogle, Robert W.
Bond, Cecil Walton
Bond, Gladys B.
Bond, Norman
Boozer, Darryl
Bradford, Andrea
Brand, Elton Tyron
Braxton, John Ledger
Brazington, Andrew Paul
Brooker, Moe Albert
Brown, Jamie Earl S
Brown, William H
Bullock, Samuel Carey
Bullock, Thurman Ruthe
Butts, Samantha F.
Cammack, Charles Lee, Jr.
Carr, Leonard G.
Cary, Lorene
Case, Arthur M.
Chandler, Allen Eugene
Chapman, Lee Manuel
Chappell, Emma Carolyn
Cheeks, Maurice Edward
Chisum, Gloria Twine
Clark, Della L
Clarke, Leon Edison
Clayton, Matthew D.
Coleman, William T, III
Collier-Thomas, Dr. Bettye
Collins, Sylvia Durnell
Coombs, Harry James
Cooper, Dr. Edward Sawyer
Cotton, Thomasenia
Crawford-Major, Toni
Crudup, Gwendolyn M
Dawkins, Brian Patrick
Days, Michael Irvin
Dennis, Andre L
Dickens, Helen Octavia
Dobson, Regina Louise
Dowkings, Wendy Lanell
Driver, Richard Sonny, Jr.
Drummond, David L., Sr.
Du Bose, Robert Earl, Jr.
Dunston, Walter T.
Dyson, Michael Eric
Echols, Alvin E
Edmunds, Dr. Walter Richard
Elcock, Dr. Claudius Adolphus Rufus
Ellis, Benjamin F., Jr.
Ellis, Dr. Leander Theodore, Jr.
Ellison, Keith
Erving, Julius Winfield
Evans, Dwight
Evans, Samuel London
Fattah, Chaka
Fattah, Falaka
Ferere, Dr. Gerard Alphonse
Ferguson, Valerie C
Fernandez, John Peter
Fields, Dr. Ewaugh Finney
Fields, Lynn M
Fontaine, John M.
Fordham, Cynthia Williams
Franklin, Oliver St Clair, Jr.
Frazier, Joe
Frazier-Lyde, Jacqui
Free, World B.
Frink Reed, Caroliese Ingrid
Gamble, Kenneth
Gilbert, Shirl E
Giles, James T.
Gilmore, Richard G.
Goode, Rev. W. Wilson
Goode, Hon. Wilson
Gordon, Levan
Gordon, Thomas
Goss, Clayton

Goss, Linda
Grant, John H., Sr.
Green, Clifford Scott
Gundy, Roy Nathaniel, Jr.
Hairston, Harold B.
Hall, Dr. Julia Glover
Hall, Tanya Evette
Hammond, Dr. Benjamin Franklin
Hancock, Gwendolyn Carter
Hansbury, Vivien H
Harper, Ronald J
Harper, Ruth B.
Harris, DeWitt O.
Harris, Douglas Allan
Haskins, Michael Kevin
Hawkins, Dr. Gene
Hill, William Randolph
Holloway, Hiliary H.
Holmes, William B
Holton, Priscilla Browne
Hopson, Harold Theodore
Huff, Leon Alexander
Hunt, Dr. Portia L
Hunter Hayes, Tracey Joel
Hyman, Mark J
Irvin, Milton M
Jackson, Burnett Lamar, Jr.
Jackson, Harold Jerome
Jackson, Paul L.
Jackson, Ricardo C
Jeff, DJ Jazzy
Jenkins, Lozelle DeLuz
Johnson, Ronald
Johnson, Walton Richard
Johnson, Willie F
Jolly, Elton
Jones, Esq. Ernest Edward
Jones, Dr. G Daniel
Jones, Ozro T., Jr.
Kamau, Mosi
Kennedy, William Thomas, Jr.
Kernodle, Obra Servesta, III
King, Billy
King, Julian F.
King, Robert Samuel
King, William Moses
Langston, Josephine Davidnell
Lassiter, Chad Dion
Leonard, Curtis Allen
Lewis, Karen A
Lewis, Dr. Samuel, Jr.
Link, Joyce Battle
Linton, Sheila Lorraine
Love, Edward Tyrone
Lynch, Dr. Rufus Sylvester
Maddox, Garry Lee
Manning, Dr. Eddie James
Mapp, Robert P
Marchand, Melanie Annette
Martin, I Maximillian
Mathis, Dr. Thaddeus P.
McBride, Ullysses
McClellan, Frank Madison
McCoy, James F.
McCrae, Larry C
McGill, Thomas L
McKee, Theodore A
McNabb, Donovan
McPherson, Rosalyn J
Merriweather, Barbara Christine
Miller, Horatio C.
Miller, William
Minyard, Handsel B.
Mitchell, Charles E
Moore, Acel
Moore, Richard Baxter
Moore, Robert Andrew
Mott, Stokes E, Jr.
Murray, Thomas W., Jr.
Myers, Andre
Myrick, Dr. Howard A.
Nichols, Rev. Edward K, Jr.
Nichols, Edwin J.
Nicholson, Alfred
Nuner, Dr. Lee
Odom, Vernon Lane, Jr.
Okore, Cynthia Ann
Oliver, Frank Louis
Padulo, Dr. Louis
Parks, Dr. Donald B
Paul, Wanda D, CPA
Payne, Ronnie E
Pennick, Janet
Perryman, Angelo R.
Peters, William Alfred
Pittman, Dr. Audrey Bullock
Poellnitz, Fred Douglas
Pratt, A Michael
Pryor, Malcolm D.

Quick, Mike
Ratliff, Theo Curtis
Reed, Esquire Jerrildine
Reed, Michael H
Reynolds-Brown, Blondell
Richardson, Henry J.
Riscoe, Romona A
Ritter, Thomas J.
Robinson, Charlotte L.
Robinson, Rev. Joseph
Roebuck, James Randolph
Rogers-Lomax, Dr. Alice Faye
Rouse, Donald E.
Russell, Keith Bradley
Scott, Syreeta
Seay, Dawn Christine
Shaw, Martini
Shelton, Ulysses
Simmons, Maurice Clyde
Simpson, Stephen Whittington
Smalls, Evelyn F
Smith, George Edmond
Smith, Dr. Marie Evans
Smith, Otis
Smith, Dr. Robert P., Jr.
Spencer, Prof. Margaret Beale
Staley, Kenneth Bernard
Stone, Daniel M.
Stubbs, Dr. George Winston
Swain-Cade McCoullum, Dr. Valarie Ena
Swainson, Sharon C.
Tann, Daniel J
Tasco, Marian B.
Taylor, Susan Charlene
Thomas, Dr. Harry Lee
Thompas, George Henry, Jr.
Thompson, Gloria Crawford
Thompson, Milt
Timmons, Bonita Terry
Tucker, Dr. Wilbur Carey
Tyree-Walker, Ida May
Vargus, Bill
Vargus, Dr. Ione D.
Waiters, Dr. Ann Gillis
Waites-Howard, Shirley Jean
Walker, Charles E
Walker, Dr. Manuel Lorenzo
Waller, Rev. Dr. Alyn Errick
Wansel, Dexter Gilman
Washington, Frank
Washington, Grover, Jr.
Washington, Paul M.
Washington, Ukee
Weaver, A. M.
Weddington, Dr. Wayne P, Jr.
Wells, Ira J. K., Jr.
Wilkie, Earl Augustus T
Williams, Dr. Anita Spencer
Williams, Hardy
Williams, Dr. Joseph Henry
Williams, Novella Stewart
Williams, Peyton
Williams, Randolph
Williams-Witherspoon, Kimmika L H
Willis, Gladys January
Wing, Theodore W
Wood, Leigh C
Wormley, Diane-Louise Lambert
Wright, Arnold W., Jr.
Wright, Charles
Wright, Grover Cleveland
Wynn, Prathia Hall
Young, Ollie L

Philipsburg
Johnson, Georgianna

Phoenixville
Osby, Gregory Thomas

Pittsbugh
Doss, Rod

Pittsburgh
Adams, Richard Melvin
Alexander, Livingston
Alexander, S Tyrone
Allen, Cheryl L
Anise, Ladun Oladunjoye E
Baldwin, Arthur L
Bartee, Kimera Anotchi
Batch, Charlie
Bates, William J
Bell, Paul, Jr.
Biggs, Dr. Shirley Ann
Bobonis, Regis Darrow, Jr.
Boyd, Marsha Foster

Brown, John C., Jr.
Brutus, Dr. Dennis Vincent
Bush, Esther L
Charlton, George N., Jr.
Clark, John Joseph
Conley, John A.
Conley, Martha Richards
Copeland, Kevon
Curry, Clarence F.
Curtis, Rev. Dr. William H.
Daniel, Jack L.
Davis, Dr. Larry Earl
Davis, Dr. Nathan Tate
Derricotte, Toi
Dunmore, Charlotte J.
Eskridge, Rev. John Clarence
Faison, Dr. Helen Smith
Farrior, James
Fortson, Elnora Agnes
French, Robert P.
Frye, Nadine Grace
Gist, Karen Wingfield
Gordon, Alexander H., II
Green, Dr. William Edward
Greene, Joe
Griggs, Anthony
Griggs, Judith Ralph
Hale, Edward Harned
Harris, Eugene Edward
Harris, Franco
Hayes, J Harold, Jr.
Horton, Raymond Anthony
Howard, Dr. Elizabeth Fitzgerald
Howard, Dr. Lawrence Cabot
Irvis, K. Leroy
Jefferies, Charlotte S.
Johnson, Hon. Justin Morris
Johnson, Livingstone M.
Jordan, Sandra D
Josey, Dr. E. J.
Kisner, Robert Garland
Lavelle, Robert R.
Lee, Tyronne T.
Lewis, Harold T
Lewis, James D
Lillie, Vernell A
Lucas Darby, Dr. Emma Turner
Lynch, Leon
Martin, Myron C
McClendon, Kellen
Miles, George L
Montgomery, Oliver R.
Moore, George Thomas
Nelson, Paul Donald
Nnaji, Bartholomew O
O'Neal, Stanley
Payne, Wilford Alexander
Poole, Marion L.
Quivers, Dr. Eric Stanley
Savage, William Arthur
Scales, Alice Marie
Scantlebury-White, Velma Patricia
Scruggs, Prof. Otey Matthew
Sessoms, Dr. Frank Eugene
Smith, Dr. Earl Bradford
Smith, Geraldine T
Spencer, Gregory Randall
Springer, Eric Winston
Stevens, Timothy S
Taylor, Carole Lillian
Tibbs, Hon. Edward A
Tomlin, Josephine D
Towns, Dr. Myron B, Jr.
Tucker, Weida G.
Uku, Eustace Oris
Waters, Brenda Joyce
Watkins, Charles Booker, Sr.
Weaver, Herbert C
Welch, Dr. Olga Michele
Williams, Wyatt Clifford
Wray, Wendell Leonard

Port Matilda
Asbury, William W

Pottsville
Delk, James F, Jr.
Harris, Dr. Arthur Leonard

Radnor
Butler, Oliver Richard

Reading
McCracken, Frank D

Rochester
Douglas, Elizabeth (Betty) Asche

Sewickley
Swann, Lynn Curtis

Sharon
Bataille, Jacques Albert
Yarboro, Dr. Theodore Leon

Shippenville
Shropshire, John Sherwin

Slippery Rock
Gaither, Dr. Thomas W
Polk, Prof. William C.

South Coatesville
Washington, John Calvin, III

State College
Henson, William L.
Patterson, Christine Ann
Young, Lawrence W, Jr.

Steelton
White, Scott A., Sr.

Swarthmore
Ellis, Dr. Leander Theodore, Jr.
James, Charles L.
Wood, Jerome H., Jr.

Uniontown
Gwynn, Florine Evayonne
Vaughns, Fred L

Univ park
Gunter, Laurie

University Park
Asbury, William W
Blake, Carl LeRoy
Harvell, Valeria Gomez
Henson, William L.
Jones, Jacqueline Valarie
Mayhew, Richard
Patterson, Christine Ann
Reed, Dr. Rodney J
Welmon, Vernis M

University Pk
Bowen, Dr. Blannie

Upper Darby
Brown, Dr. Glenn Arthur
Jasper, Lawrence E

Verona
Taliaferro, Cecil R.

Villanova
Christian, Theresa
James, William

Warminster
Johnson, Warren S.

Warrendale
Dixon, Dr. Louis Tennyson

Washington
Waller, Louis E.

Wayne
Harris, Douglas Allan

Wernersville
Spears, Angelena Elaine

West Chester
Black, Barbara Robinson
Guy, William I.
Meade, Alston B., Sr.
Ray, Dr. Judith Diana
Saddler, Elbert M
Sylvester, Dr. Patrick Joseph

West Mifflin
Essiet, Dr. Evaleen Johnson

Winfield
Valdes, Pedro H

Wyncote
Browne, Dr. Craig C.
Weddington, Dr. Wayne P, Jr.

Wynnewood
Willis, Gladys January

Wyomissing
Scott, Dr. Basil Y

Yardley
Greene, Gregory A.

Yeadon
Brown, Morgan Cornelius
Logan, Thomas W S, Sr.
Taylor, Roy Marcellus

York
Douglas, Joseph Francis

PUERTO RICO

Harrisburg
Mitchell, Stanley Henryk

Salinas
Alomar, Sandy

San Juan
Washington, Robert Benjamin, Jr.

Toa Baja
Zambrana, Dr. Rafael

RHODE ISLAND

Cranston
Morse, Barbara Lyn

East Providence
Coelho, Peter J.
Walker, Dr. Kenneth R.

Kingston
Davis, Luther Charles
Gilton, Dr. Donna L.
Johnson, Douglas H.
Lafayette, Bernard

Lincoln
Watkins Snead, Cheryl

Newport
Drummond, Thornton B., Jr.
Harper, Walter Edward

North Smithfield
Watkins, Cheryl L

Pawtucket
Wiggins, Daphne Cordelia

Providence
Addison, Terry Hunter, Jr.
Brandon, Barbara
Brown, Lawrence E.
Castro, George A
Cissoko, Alioune Badara
Davis, Louis Garland
Denniston, Prof. Dorothy L.
Gaines, Jo Eva
Harper, Michael Steven
Jones, Dr. Ferdinand Taylor
Lopes, William H.
Loury, Dr. Glenn Cartman
McDonald, Dr. Charles J.
Nichols, Charles Harold
O'Connor, Thomas F, Jr.
Rickman, Ray
Robinson, William Henry
Rose, Tricia
Santos, Edwin J
Simmons, Ruth J
Trotter, Lloyd G
Whitten, Thomas P
Wilson, Valerie Petit

West Greenwich
Alves, Paget L.

SOUTH CAROLINA

Aiken
Anderson, George Allen
Dunbar, Thomas Jerome
Hightower, Willar H

Allendale
Pinckney, James

Anderson
Anderson, Carl Edward
Floyd, Winston Cordell
Thompson, Dr. Beatrice R

Atlantic Beach
Montgomery, Joe Elliott

Beaufort
Grant, William W.
Morgan-Washington, Dr. Barbara

Bennettsville
McLeod, James S.

Bethune
Morgan, Leon M.

Blackville
Johnson, Carroll Jones
Morant, Mack Bernard

Bluffton
Brown, Dallas C, Jr.

Blythewood
Way, Dr. Curtis J.

Camden
Ruffner, Ray P.

Cayce
Simmons, Freddie Shelton Wayne

Charleston
Archie-Hudson, Marguerite
Blake, Alphonso R.
Blake, Dr. J. Herman
Davis-McFarland, Dr. E. Elise
Etheredge, James W.
Green, Lisa A
Johnson, Wilbur Eugene
Lewis, Rev. Theodore Radford
Little, General T.
Mack, Joan
Martin, Daniel E
Martin, Daniel Ezekiel
Martin, Montez Cornelius
Martin, Rosetta P
M- Middleton, Vertelle D
Moore, Fred Henderson
O'Neill, Anthony B., Sr.
Pickering, Robert Perry
Portee, Rev. Dr. Frank
Rashford, Dr. John Harvey
Seabrook, Juliette Theresa
Shealey, Richard W
Stanyard, Hermine P.
Woods, Andre Vincent
Yearwood, Rev. Dr. Kirtley

Cheraw
Reid, William J

Chester
Cutliff, John Wilson

Clemson
Craig, Starlett Russell
Crosby, Margaree Seawright
Thompson, Regina
Wiles, Leon E.

Clover
Campbell, Mary Allison

Cola
Lewis, Andre

Columbia
Adams, T. Patton
Aiken, Kimberly Clarice
Ards, Dr. Sheila Diann
Beasley, Dr. Paul Lee
Blackwell, Unita
Bracey, Henry J.
Brevard, Anthony
Brown, Franchot A
Brown, John E
Brown, LeRoy Ronald
Clyburn, James Emos
Cooper-Lewter, Rev. Dr. Nicholas
    Charles
Cromartie, Ernest W., II.

Crosby, Loretta
Dailey, Lenora Shell
Davis, James F.
Davis, Dr. Marianna White
Devine, Jamie
DiAna, DiAna
Dillihay, Tanya Clarkson
Everett, Percival L.
Feelings, Thomas
Felder, Loretta Kay
Flemming, Clente
Gilbert, Frank
Goodwin, Mac Arthur
Grant, Anthony T
Grant, Timothy Jerome
Hanley, Jerome Herman
Howell, Malqueen
Jackson, Rev. James Conroy
James, Joseph J
Johnson, Dinah
Johnson, I S Leevy
Johnson, Joseph A.
Joiner, Dr. Burnett
Lowman, Isom
Lynn, Louis B.
McLawhorn, James Thomas
McLean, Dennis Ray
Merritt Cummings, Annette
Miller, Richard Charles
Murphy, Charles William
Myers, Emma McGraw
Neal, Dr. Green Belton
Newborn, Dr. Odie Vernon, Jr.
Nichols, Elaine
Peay, Samuel
Pinckney, Clementa C.
Pride, Hemphill P, II
Prioleau, Peter Sylvester
Rhodes, Audrey B.
Richardson, Dr. Leo
Robinson, Eunice Primus
Rodgers, Dr. Augustus
Rowe, Marilyn Johnson
Salmond, Jasper
Scott, Juanita Simons
Scott, Robert L.
Simmons, Freddie Shelton Wayne
Smalls, O'Neal
Spain, Hiram, Jr.
Stephenson, Charles E, III
Swinton, Dr. David Holmes
Swinton, Sylvia P.
Waldo, Carol Dunn
Williams, Willie, Jr.

Conway
Lee, Dr. James E

Denmark
Henry, John Wesley, Jr.
Jones, Nancy Reed

Effingham
Canty, Ralph Waldo

Elgin
Givens-Little, Aurelio Dupriest

Filbert
Sanders, Dori

Florence
Adams, Lillian Louise T.
Beck, Roswell Nathaniel
Cooper, Ethel Thomas
Diggs, William P., Jr.
Gaines, John A., Sr.
Givens-Little, Aurelio Dupriest
Harley, Legrand

Fort Mill
Murphy, Dr. John Matthew, Jr.

Gray Court
Carter, John R.

Great Falls
Hall, John Robert

Greenville
Brewton, Dr. Butler E.
Channell, Eula L.
Corbitt, Dr. John H
Crosby, Dr. Willis Herman
Flemming, Lillian Brock
Golden, Louie
Jackson, Rusty
Kirby-Davis, Montanges

Mitchell, Theo W
Peden, S. T., Jr.
Reid, Janie Ellen
Talley, Michael Frank, Sr.
Whitney, William B
Woods, Kondria Yvette Black
Zimmerman, Samuel Lee

Greenville, SC
McGlockton, Chester

Greenwood
Witherspoon, Audrey Goodwin

Hardeeville
Riley, Shaunce R
Williams, Daniel Louis

Hilton Head Island
Butler, Marjorie Johnson
Driessen, Henry, Jr.
Harris, Dr. William Hamilton
Lightfoot, Dr. William P.

Hollywood
Holmes, Mary Brown

Johns Island
Rashford, Dr. John Harvey

Johnsonville
Tanner, James W., Jr.

Kingstree
Wilson, Alva L

Lancaster
Jeter, Delores DeAnn

Laurens
Coleman, Marian M.

Lexington
McLean, Dennis Ray

Little River
Williams, George L., Sr.

Loris
Watson, Fred D.

Lynchburg
Jefferson, Clifton

Manning
Jenkins, Barbara Williams

Marion
Cordery, Dr. Sara Brown

Mauldin
Cureton, Stewart Cleveland

McBee
Mack, Levorn

McClellanville
Smalls, Marcella E

McCormick
Gilchrist, Robertson

Moncks Corner
Mitchum, Dorothy M

Mount Pleasant
Brown, Angela Yvette

North Charleston
Bryant, Edward Joe, III
Pickering, Robert Perry

North Myrtle Beach
Sands, George M.
Sands, Prof. Mary Alice

Orangeburg
Abraham, Sinclair Reginald
Ball, Drexel Bernard
Booker, Jackie R
Brockington, Benjamin
Brunson, Debora Bradley
Byrd, Lumus, Jr.
Caldwell, Rossie Juanita Brower
Davis, Dr. Leroy
Evans, Arthur L.

Gore, Blinzy L.
Harris, Gil W.
Hickson, Dr. William F, Jr.
Hugine, Dr. Andrew, Jr.
Irogbe, Kema
James, Carrie Houser
Jenkins, Barbara Williams
Johnson, Carl Lee
Johnson, Charles H.
Johnson, Doris Elayne
Johnson, Dr. Vermelle Jamison
Jones, Dr. Marcus Earl
Keitt, Liz Zimmerman
Lewis, Kenneth Dwight
Luke, Dr. Learie B
Mack, Fred Clarence
Manning, Hubert Vernon
Martin, Frank C
McFadden, James L.
Middleton, Bernice Bryant
Nance, M. Maceo, Jr.
Simpson, Dr. John Randolph
Tisdale, Dr. Henry Nehemiah
Twiggs, Dr. Leo Franklin
Washington, Dr. Sarah M
Winningham, Herman S., Jr.

Pawleys Island
Manigault, Walter William

Pelzer
Reid, Janie Ellen

Pendleton
Morse, Annie Ruth W.

Plum Branch
Gilchrist, Robertson

Port Royal
Robinson, Henry

Rains
Johnson, Robert B.

Ravenel
Holmes, Mary Brown

Ridgeland
Garvin, Jonathan
Hicks, Doris Morrison

Rock Hill
Bethea, Mollie Ann
Copeland, Dr. Elaine Johnson
Douglas, John Daniel
Ervin, Deborah Green
Evans, Spofford L.
Goggins, Horace
Scurlock, Michael Lee
Sebhatu, Dr. Mesgun
Wright-Botchwey, Roberta Yvonne

Saint Stephen
Kennedy, Dr. Karel R

Seabrook
Kline, Joseph N.

Seneca
Martin, Amon Achilles, Jr.

Simpsonville
Floyd, James T.

Spartanburg
Allen, Ottis Eugene
Brooks, Bernard E
Carson, Warren Jason
Porter, John Henry
Talley, James Edward
Wiles, Leon E.

Springfield
Abraham, Sinclair Reginald

St Stephen
Ransom, Norman

Summerville
Johnson, T J
Washington, Arnic J.

Sumter
Blanding, Larry
Finney, Ernest A., Jr.
Gray, Ruben L.

Hardin, Henry E.
Mellette, David C.
Millican, Arthenia J. Bates
Pinkney, Willie
Richardson, Dr. Luns C
Sampson, Dorothy Vermelle
Thomas, Rev. Dr. Latta Roosevelt, Sr.
Weston, Larry Carlton

Walterboro
Thompson, Johnnie

Yonges Island
Fielding, Herbert Ulysses

SOUTH DAKOTA

Roslyn
Diggs, Lawrence J

TENNESSEE
Crowell, Dr. Bernard G.

Alcoa
Williams, Richard, Jr.

Blountville
Charlton, Rev. Charles Hayes

Bolivar
Hicks, Delphus Van, Jr.
Lake, Alfreeda Elizabeth

Brentwood
Armstrong, Vanessa Bell
Epps, Anna Cherrie
Howard, Anica
Howard, Samuel Houston
Scott, Veronica J.
Story, Charles Irvin
White, Katie Kinnard
Winans, CeCe

Brownsville
Bond, Cynthia Rawls
Rawls, William D., Sr.
Rawls Bond, Charles Cynthia

Chattanooga
Bell, James L., Jr.
Brown, Richard L.
Brown, Tommie Florence
Carter, Roland
Ebbe, Dr. Obi N I
Edwards, John Loyd, III
Henry, Alaric Anthony
Jackson, Dr. Horace
Jackson, Dr. Luke
Jewett, Katrina Ann
Jones, Carolyn G.
McCants, Dr. Jesse Lee, Sr.
McClure, Fredrick H L
McDaniel, Rev. Paul Anderson
Miller, James
Provost, Marsha Parks
Robinson, Clarence B.
Roddy, Howard W
Scruggs, Booker T., II
Stewart, Dr. William H.
Willis, Kathi Grant

Clarksville
Gachette, Louise Foston
Mock, James E

Clinton
Abif, Khafre Kujichagulia

Collierville
Duckett, Esq. Gregory Morris

Columbia
Hines, Dr. Morgan B

Cordova
Johnson, Dr. Fred D.
Royston, Evelyn Ross

Sessoms, Glenn D
Strickland, Herman William, Jr.

Corodova
Royston, Evelyn Ross

Covington
Bommer, Minnie L.
Rose, Shelvie, Sr.

Dyersburg
Biggs, Richard Lee
Jaycox, Mary Irine
Mitchell, George L

Franklin
Harris, Al Carl
Lownes-Jackson, Dr. Millicent Gray
Mills, Mary Elizabeth
Perry, Clifford, III
Venable, Abraham S

Gallatin
Malone, Dr. J. Deotha
Sherrill, Vanita Lytle

Gates
Nance, Booker Joe, Sr.

Goodlettsville
Boone, Dr. Carol Marie

Henderson
Saunders, Dr. Elizabeth Ann

Hendersonville
McClurkin, Donnie
Smallwood, Richard

Humboldt
Carr, Lenford
Coleman, Andrew Lee
Smith, James Russell

Jackson
Abernathy, Ronald Lee
Boone, Clarence Donald
Brown, Claudell, Jr.
Chambers, Alex A.
David, Arthur LaCurtiss
Dickerson, Dr. Warner Lee
Edwards, Dr. Nicole
Kirkendoll, Chester Arthur, II
McClure, Dr. Wesley Cornelious
Shaw, Dr. Willie G.
Wilson, Sidney
Wright, Melvin

Johnson City
Charlton, Rev. Charles Hayes

Jonesborough
McKinney, Ernest Lee, Sr.

Knoxville
Black, Harold A.
Booker, Robert Joseph
Bourne, Beal Vernon, II
Bowie, Stan L
Byas, William Herbert
Charles, Daedra
Conwill, William Louis
Davidson, Dr. Elvyn Verone
Felder-Hoehne, Felicia Harris
Ford, Lisa Denise
Franklin, Clarence Frederick
Gillespie, Bonita
Hall, Frances White
Hardy, Walter S. E.
Harrison, Faye Venetia
Hodges, Dr. Carolyn Richardson
Hodges, Dr. John O.
James-foster, Joy Lynne
Jones, Sherman J
Kindall, Dr. Alpha S.
Kindall, Dr. Luther Martin
LeVert, Francis E.
Lucas, Wilmer Francis, Jr.
Miller, Bubba
Owens, Jefferson Pleas
Peek, Marvin E.
Redmond, Dr. Jane Smith
Rollins, Avon William, Sr.

Russell, John Peterson
Tyson, John C

Lawrenceburg
Collier, Dr. Barbara

Lebanon
Burton-Shannon, Clarinda
Mitchell, Martha Mallard

Lexington
Reese, Viola Kathryn

Louisville
James, Wynona Yvonne

Madison
Butler, Washington Roosevelt, Jr.

Martin
Black, Frank S.
Parker, Dr. Henry H.

Maryville
Mosley, Tracey Ray

Memphis
Bailey, D'Army
Bates, Willie Earl
Berhe-Hunt, Annette
Bledsoe, Melvin
Bolton, Julian Taylor
Bond, Wilbert
Brooks, Todd Frederick
Brown, Kwame
Bryant, Anxious E.
Bufford, Edward Eugene
Burns, Calvin Louis
Carter, Patrick Henry
Chambliss, Prince C
Clark, LeRoy D.
Coleman, Harry Theodore
Coleman, Wisdom F
Davis, Bunny Coleman
Davis, Johnny Reginald
Davis, Rev. Tyrone Theophilus
Delk, Fannie M.
DeVaughn-Tidline, Donna Michelle
Dixon, Roscoe
Dorse, Earnestine Hunt
Duckett, Esq. Gregory Morris
Ford, Fred, Jr.
Ford, James W.
Ford, John Newton
Ford, Rev. Samuel Lee
Garrett, Cheryl Ann
Gholson, Dr. General James
Gholson, Robert L
Gilliam, Herman Arthur, Jr.
Gipson, Dr. Lovelace Preston, II
Green, Reuben H.
Harrell, H Steve
Harris, Dr. John H.
Harris, Loretta K
Haskins, Morice Lee, Jr.
Herenton, Dr. Willie W
Hooks, Frances Dancy
Hooks, Michael Anthony
Howard, Aubrey J
Howard, Osbie L
Hurd, William Charles
Jackson-Teal, Rita F.
Jamerson, Jerome Donnell
Jenkins, Charles E., Sr.
Johnican, Minerva Jane
Johnson, Betty Jo
Johnson, Cato, II
Johnson, Clinisson Anthony
Jones, Lorean Electa
Jones, Velma Lois
Jordan, Dr. Carolyne Lamar
Jordan, John Edward
Lawston, Marjorie Gray
Martin, Cortez Hezekiah
McKie, Aaron Fitzgerald
Melancon, Donald
Miles, Rachel Jean
Montgomery, Dwight Ray
Moore, Dr. Jossie A.
Morris, Herman
Neal, Joseph C., Jr.
Owens, Chandler D.
Parham, Brenda Joyce
Parker, Lee
Patterson, Bishop Gilbert Earl
Perry, Lee Charles, Jr.
Porter, David
Primous, Emma M.

Randolph, Zach
Rheams, Leonta
Robinson, George L.
Rodgers, Rev. Charles
Royal, James E.
Sessoms, Glenn D
Seymour, Laurence Darryl, M. D.
Shotwell, Ada Christena
Smith, Dr. Maxine Atkins
Smith, Vasco A.
Stansbury, Markhum L
Steib, James Terry
Stevens, Rochelle
Stockton, Clifford
Stoudmaire, Damon
Strickland, Herman William, Jr.
Strickland, Rodney
Talley, Curtiss J
Taylor, Harold Leon
Thompson, Dr. Theodis
Tieuel, Robert C. D.
Turner, Jesse H
Turner, Johnnie Rodgers
Venson, Clyde R
Walker, Felix Carr, Jr.
Walker, George Edward
Walker, Walter Lorenzo
Ward, Daniel
Watson, Ben
Webster, Niambi Dyanne
Westbrook, Joseph W., III
Wharton, A. C., Jr.
Williams, Eldredge M
Williams, Dr. Hugh Hermes
Williams, Roby S
Withers, Ernest C
Young, Josef A.
Young, Dr. LaDonna

Milan
David, Arthur LaCurtiss
Jenkins, Garey

Millington
Ford, Rev. Samuel Lee

Morristown
Hammock, Jimmy
Russell, John Peterson

Murfreesboro
Clark, Dr. Bertha Smith
Glanton, Lydia Jackson
Hare, Linda Paskett
McAdoo, Henry Allen
Pleas, John Roland
Wills, Dr. Cornelia

Nashville
Alexander, Robert I.
Allen, Dr. William Henry
Archer, Susie Coleman
Armstrong, Joe
Atchison, Dr. Calvin O.
Bacon, William Louis
Bailey, William R.
Baker, Dr. Houston Alfred, Jr.
Baldwin, Lewis V
Ballard, Dr. Billy Ray
Belton, Robert
Bernard, Harold O.
Bernard, Dr. Louis Joseph
Berry, Benjamin Donaldson
Birch, Adolpho A
Boone, Dr. Carol Marie
Boone, Dr. Robert L
Boyd, Theophilus B., III
Britton, John Henry
Brooks, Marcellus
Brown, Tommie Florence
Browner, Ross D
Byner, Earnest Alexander
Campbell, Dr. Otis, Jr.
Chatterjee, Lois Jordan
Claxton, Melvin L
Conley, James Monroe
Crenshaw, Waverly David
Crowell, Dr. Bernard G.
Davis, Herman E.
Dawson, Lake
DeBerry, Lois Marie
Del Pino, Jerome King
Dent, Carl Ashley
DeShields, Harrison F., Jr.
Dickerson, Prof. Dennis Clark
Driver, Rogers W.
Dudley, Charles Edward
Easley, Billy Harley

Elam, Dr. Lloyd C.
Elliott, Dr. Derek Wesley
Elliott, Irvin Wesley
Epps, Anna Cherrie
Felix, Dudley E.
Fielder, Dr. Fred Charles
Fort, Dr. Jane Geraldine
Foster, Dr. Henry Wendell, Jr.
George, Eddie
Giles, Henrietta
Guess, Francis S.
Hamberg, Dr. Marcelle R.
Hamby, Roscoe Jerome
Hampton, Dr. Robert L
Handy, William Talbot, Jr.
Harper, Thelma Marie
Hefner, Dr. James A
Henderson, Cheri Kaye
Hill, Dr. George C.
Hill, Henry, Jr.
Holmes, Robert L., Jr.
Horton, Dr. Carrell Peterson
Hull, Dr. George, Jr.
Humphries, Dr. Frederick S
Isibor, Edward Iroguehi
Jackson, Dr. Andrew
Jackson, Dr. Arthur James
Jackson, Clinton
Johnson, Charles William
Johnson, Ernest Kaye, III
Jones, Enoch
Jordan, Dr. Harold Willoughby
Junior-Spence, Samella E.
Kilcrease, Irvin Hugh, Jr.
Kimbrough, Charles Edward
Lawson, James M., Jr.
Lawson, Dr. William Daniel
Lee, Dr. Andre L
Lewis, Helen Middleton
Lillard, Kwame Leo
Lownes-Jackson, Dr. Millicent Gray
Luis, Dr. William
Mahone, Jeanine
Manson, Richard
Marshall, Anita
Martin, James Larence
Martin, Ruby Julene Wheeler
McGruder, Dr. Charles E.
McKissack, Leatrice Buchanan
McReynolds, Elaine A.
Mitchell, Edwin H., Sr.
Mobley, Eugenia L.
Moore, Samuel D.
Moses, Dr. Henry A.
Murray, Albert R
Murrell, Barbara Curry
Newhouse, Quentin
Nicholson, Aleathia Dolores
O'Leary, Hazel M
Patton, Princess E
Peterman, Leotis
Peters, Sheila Renee
Phillips, Theresa Lawrence
Poole, Tyrone
Ramsey, Freeman, Jr.
Richards, DeLeon Marie
Richardson, Elisha R
Ridley, Gregory D, Jr.
Ridley, Dr. May Alice
Riley, Dr. Wayne Joseph
Rogers, Dr. Decatur Braxton
Scott, Veronica J.
Shockley, Ann Allen
Shockley, Thomas Edward
Singleton, Chris
Smith, Dr. Jessie Carney
Story, Charles Irvin
Straight, Cathy A
Strong- Kimbrough, Dr. Blondell M
Temple, Edward Stanley
Towns, Dr. Myron B, Jr.
Traughber, Charles M.
Tropez-Sims, Susanne
Washington, Dr. Sandra Beatrice
Watson, Vernaline
White, Sharon Brown
Wiggins, Dr. Charles A
Williams, Dr. Johnny Wayne
Wills, Dr. Cornelia
Wilson, Dr. Donella Joyce
Winans, BeBe
Winfrey, Charles Everett
Wynn, Daniel Webster

Oak Ridge
Colston, Dr. Freddie C.
Lewis, Kenneth Dwight
Porter, Patrick A.

Shipe, Jamesetta Denise Holmes
Smith, Rufus Herman

Old Hickory
Finch, Dr. Janet M

Only
Campbell, Dr. Otis, Jr.

Pulaski
Brown, James Monroe

Rochester
Wright, James R

Rockwood
Barnes, Dr. Delorise Creecy

San Antonio
Warrick, Alan Everett

Smyrna
Williams, Dr. Johnny Wayne

South Nashville
McKenzie, Rev. Vashti

Springfield
Chatman, Melvin E.

Tallahassee
Hamilton, Leonard

Tennessee
Thomas, Dr. N Charles

Tullahoma
Duncan, Lynda J

Whiteville
Robertson, Evelyn Crawford

TEXAS
Ramirez, Richard M
Webb, Joe

Addison
Brown, Alvin
Pearson, Drew
Perkins, Sam Bruce

Allen
Cole, Mark

Amarillo
Patrick, Dr. Jennie R

Arlington
Anderson, Alfred Anthony
Coleman, Ronnald Dean
Connor, Dolores Lillie
Kitchen-Neal, Mary Kim
LeGrand, Bob Snake
Lofton, Kenneth
Smith-Croxton, Terri
Taylor, Dalmas A.

Austin
Adams, Edward B.
Allen, Cathy H.
Baker, Kimberley Renee
Baye, Prof. Lawrence James J
Belle, John Otis
Brewington, Donald Eugene
Bumphus, Dr. Walter Gayle
Butler, Dr. John Sibley
Canada, Benjamin Oleander
Craven, Judith
Crawford, Pam Scott
Delco, Wilhelmina R.
Doggett, John Nelson
Earvin, Larry L.
Evans, Akwasi Rozelle
Evans, Roxanne J
Freeman, Walter Eugene
Hanson, John L
Jefferson, Wallace B
Kennedy, Brenda Picola
Martin, Dr. Rosalee Ruth
McDaniel, Myra Atwell
McDaniel, Prof. Reuben R
McKee, Evelyn Palfrey
McMillan, Dr. Joseph Turner
McRoy, Dr. Ruth Gail

Means, Bertha E
Milburn, Glyn Curt
Moore, Etta R
Murphy, Harriet Louise M.
Nelson, Dr. Wanda Lee
Nesby, Donald Ray, Sr.
Overton, Volma Robert
Owens, Rissie Louise
Sanders, Deion Luwynn
Scott, Richard Eley
Sikes, Dr. Melvin Patterson
Sullivan, Dr. Allen R
Tucker, Geraldine Jenkins
Urdy, Dr. Charles E.
Ward, Nolan F
West, Royce Barry
White, Dr. Barbara Williams
Williams, Jerome D.
Williams, Sandra Roberts
Williams Davis, Edith G
Wilson, Ora Brown

Avery
Powell, Richard Maurice

Baytown
Hadnot, Thomas Edward
Piper, Elwood A
Stephens, David L.

Beaumont
Drake, Leonard
Flakes, Garland KaZell, I
Smith, Kevin Rey

Bedford
Merton, Joseph Lee

Belton
Demerson, Connie Marie

Bryan
Bell, Vivian

Canyon
Githiga, John Gatungu

Carrollton
Griggsby, Charles
Teague, George Theo

Carthage
Beck, Hershell P.

Cedar Park
Brown, Rubye Golsby
Morrison, Paul-David

China Spring
Richards, Jaime Augusto, III

College Station
Fletcher, James Andrew
Majors, Anthony Y
Miller, Warren F, Jr.
Rice, Dr. Mitchell F

Commerce
Talbot, David Arlington Roberts, Sr.

Conroe
Irvin, Charles Leslie

Corinth
Hendricks, Richard D

Corpus Christi
Carline, William Ralph
Gray, Valerie Hamilton
Gurley, Dr. Helen Ruth
Reed, Jake
Sanders, Dr. Woodrow Mac

Corsicana
Waters, Sylvia Ann

Crosby
Hayes, Elvin E.

Cypress
Copeland, Barry B

DFW Airport
Taylor, Gayland Wayne

Dallas
Alexander, Arika
Alexander, Drew W.

Allen, Billy R.
Allen-Rasheed, Jamal Randy
Archambeau, Shellye L.
Baisden, Michael
Banks, Jeffrey
Baraka, Larry
Bardwell, Rufus B., III
Beck, Arthello, Jr.
Bell, H. B.
Bell, Rosalind Nanette
Berry, Gemeral E., Jr.
Black, Albert, Jr.
Blackman, Rolando Antonio
Bolton, Terrell D.
Boutte, Rhonda
Bracken, Charles O.
Brannon, Deborah Dianne
Brashear, Berlaind Leander
Brown, Edward Lynn
Brown, Ellen Rochelle
Burns, Regina Lynn
Carter, Kenneth Wayne
Clark, Caesar A. W.
Cottrell, Comer J.
Cunningham, E Brice
Dampier, Erick Trevez
Darby, Castilla A., Jr.
Dartson, Dr. Myrna
Davis, Gregory T
Dick, George Albert
Edeler, Phyllis
Edwards O, Donna M
Ellis, Ladd
Emory, Emerson
Everett, Thomas Gregory
Farris, Deborah Ellison
Foutz, Samuel Theodore
Gates, Reginald
Glover, Clarence Ernest, Jr.
Gray, Carol Coleman
Gray, James Howard
Hammond, Ulysses S., Jr.
Hankins, Anthony Mark
Harris, Cornelia
Hendricks, Richard D
Hill, Hattie
Hill, Vonciel Jones
Hilliard, Delories, PhD
Hunter, Charles A
Hunter, Irby B.
Jackson, Brenda
Jackson, Janet Damita Jo
Jacques, Cornell
James, Eugenia H
Johnson, Marion T.
Joyner, Oscar Albert
Joyner, Tom
Kidd, Foster
Kirk, Ron
Kirven, Mythe Yuvette
Lacy, Versia Lindsay
Laday, Kerney
Lander, C Victor
Lander, Fred Leonard, III
Lane, Eddie Burgyone
Lawrie-Goodrich, Madeline
LeFebvre, Dale
Levermore, Jacqueline Maureen
Long, Leonard
Mason, Edward James
McCaa, John K
McClure, Frederick Donald
McElroy, Dr. Njoki
Miller, Kevin
Mincey, W. James, Jr.
Morris, Wayne Lee
Mumford, Jeffrey Carlton
Newhouse, Robert F
Nobles, Patricia Joyce
Norman, Bobby Don
Norman, Jessye
O'Banno, Donna Edwards
Oliver, Jesse Dean
Orr, Ray
Ortiz, Victor
Parker, Fred Lee Cecil
Phelps-Patterson, Lucy
Posey, John R
Powell, Dudley Vincent
Price, John Wiley
Pride, Charley Frank
Ray, Francis
Richards-Alexander, Billie J.
Richardson, Donna
Roberts, Dr. Alfred Lloyd
Robertson, Gertrude
Robinson, Dr. Harry, Jr.
Robinson, Malcolm
Robinson-Jacobs, Karen Denise

Rollins, Dr. Richard Albert
Rowe, Audrey
Ruffin, Herbert
Sanders, Patricia Roper
Shine, Theodis
Steele, Cleophas R., Jr.
Stewart, Edward L
Sulieman, Dr. Jamil
Sweets, Ellen Adrienne
Thompson, Frank William
Tinsley, Fred Leland, Jr.
Vasser, Delphine Lynetta
Wade, Norma Adams
Waits, Rev. Va Lita Francine
Ware, John
Washington, James A
Waters, Dianne E
Waters, Kathryn
Watkins, Craig
Watkins, Wynfred C
Wattley, Thomas Jefferson
White, Arthur W, Jr.
White, Mabel Meshach
Wiley, Aaron L
Wise, Frank P.
Wooten, John
Wright, Sylvester M.

DeSoto
Giddings, Helen
Sweatt, James L, III

Denison
Moore, Gary

Denton
Bower, Dr. Beverly L.
Jackson, Governor Eugene
Lawson, Erma J.
LeFlore, Dr. Larry
Terrell, Dr. Francis
Thibodeaux, Mary Shepherd
Totten, Dr. Herman Lavon
Wallace, Milton De
Washington, Roosevelt, Jr.
Wheeler, Dr. Maurice B.

Duncanville
Patterson, Sheron

El Paso
Daily, Dr. Maceo Crenshaw
Greer, Edward M
Johnson, Renard U
Wingo, Robert V
Young, John W.

Ennis
Coleman, Raymond Cato

Flower Mound
Willrich, Emzy James
Willrich Scott, Candace Yvette

Fort Worth
Austin, Jim
Bowman-Webb, Loetta
Briscoe, Leonard E.
Brooks, Marion Jackson
Brown, Jean Marie
Cary, Reby
DeSassure, Charles
Elliott, Monte Ray
Epps, Phillip Earl
Fretwell, Carl Quention, II
Greenwood, Edna Turner
Hardeman, Strotha E, Jr.
Heiskell, Michael Porter
Henderson, Australia Tarver
Higginbotham-Brooks, Renee
Jennings, Devoyd
Johnson, Erma Chansler
Johnson, Iola Vivian
Johnson, Mervil V.
Jones, Alphonzo James
Knight, Richard, Jr.
Knox-Benton, Shirley
Lister, Willa M
McCall, H. Carl
McEwing, Mitchell Dalton
McGregor, Rev. Miguel D
Mitchell, Huey P
Sims, Theophlous Aron
Standifer, Ben H.
Standifer, Lonnie Nathaniel
Sterling, Dr. Jeffrey Emery
Stewart, Dorothy Nell
Taylor, Gayland Wayne

Thompson, Glenda M
Ward, Nolan F
Wilson, Hazel Forrow Simmons
Young, Lias Carl

Forth Worth
Edmonds, Bobbie

Ft Worth
Davis, L. Clifford

Galveston
Gatson, Wilina Ione
Simmons, Annie Marie
Stanton, Janice D

Garland
Bogus, Dr. Houston, Jr.
Ward, Anna Elizabeth
White, Arthur W, Jr.
Witherspoon, William Roger

Georgetown
Swain, Dr. Ronald L
Wheeler, Beverly

Grand Prairie
Morris, Vivian Louise
Willrich, Emzy James

Greenville
Williams, Vernon R

Hawkins
Acrey, Autry
Caradine, Tracy
Hall, Delilah Ridley
Holmes, Dr. Lorene B
Wortham, Russeal

Hearne
McDaniel, Billy Ray

Helotes
Banks, Dr. Laura Nobles

Hempstead
Carter, Gwendolyn Burns
Singleton, Leroy, Sr.

Henderson
Waits, Rev. Va Lita Francine

Hidalgo
Canty, Chris

Houston
Adams, Dr. Elaine Parker
Adams, Melba K.
Adams, Samuel Clifford, Jr.
Alexander, Alma Duncan
Allen, Andrew A.
Anderson, Patricia Hebert
Andrews, Rawle
Banfield, Dr. Edison H
Barber, Shawn William
Barrington, Dr. Eugene L.
Barrows, Prof. Bryan H
Beard, James William
Belcher, Dr. Leon H.
Bell, Dr. Robert L.
Bishop, Verissa Rene
Blackwell, Dr. Harvel E.
Boney, J. Don
Bonner, Alice A.
Boze, U Lawrence
Bradley, Jack Carter
Bright, Willie S
Brittain, John C.
Brooks, Hunter O
Brown, Abner Bertrand
Brown-Guillory, Elizabeth
Buckner, William Pat
Buggage, Cynthia Marie
Bullock, James
Bunkley, Anita Richmond
Burrell, Leroy
Butler, Dr. Grace L., Ph.D.
Byears, Latasha
Caggins, Dr. Ruth Porter
Carter, Lenora
Celestine, Von C
Chase, Anthony R
Chase, John Saunders
Chase, Tony
Claye, Charlene Marette
Cooper, Cecil Celester

Coleman, Dr. Ronald Gerald
Cunningham, William L
Davis, France Albert
Davis, Grace E
Guillory, Dr. William A.
Holsey, Bernard
Ingram-Sampson, Barbara Jo
Jones, Curley C
Knight, Brevin
Samuels, Dr. Wilfred D

Sandy
Davis, Grace E

VERMONT

Burlington
Clemmons, Prof. Jackson Joshua
    Walter
McCrorey, Dr. H Lawrence
Reinhardt, John Edward
Sandoval, Dolores S.

Charlotte
Clemmons, Prof. Jackson Joshua
    Walter

Mendon
Wakefield, J. Alvin

Middlebury
Beatty, Martin Clarke

North Bennington
Dixon, William R.

Stowe
Wilson, Markly

VIRGINIA

Abingdon
Day, Eric Therander

Accomac
Cooper, Samuel H

Alexandria
Archer, Dr. Chalmers, Jr.
Barlow, William B.
Bell, Hubert Thomas
Booker, Vaughan P L
Brown, Jesse
Brown, Michael DeWayne
Burton, David Lloyd
Byrd, Brigadier Gen. Melvin L.
Carter, Dr. Gene Raymond
Collins, Cardiss H.
DeSandies, Dr. Kenneth Andre
Fields, William I, Jr.
Foster, Leonard H.
Gaither, Dr. Dorothy B
Garrett, James F.
Gaston, Mack Charles
Greene, Nelson E., Sr.
Harper, Bernice Catherine
Harris, Lee Andrew, II
Johnson, Mal
Jones, Cheryl Arleen
Jones, Horace F
Jordan, Carolyn D
Joyner, Claude C.
Lawrence, Merlisa Evelyn
Lee, Gerald Bruce
Lewis, Dr. Lloyd Alexander
Lockett, Alice Faye
Love, Jon
Lovett, Leonard
Mayden, Ruth Wyatt
McMillan, Wilton Vernon
McPherson, Rosalyn J
Morgan, Alice Johnson Parham
Prince, Richard Everett
Roye, Monica R Hargrove
Sievers, Eric Scott
Smith, James Charles
Thomas, Clarence
Thompson, Ronald Anthony
Tyler, Shirley Neizer

Weaver, Frank Cornell
Zimmerman, Matthew Augustus

Annandale
Archer, Dr. Chalmers, Jr.
Coates, Shelby L.
Murphy, Jeanne Claire Fuller

Arlington
Bell, William McKinley
Blount, Charlotte Renee
Brittain, Bradley Bernard, Jr.
Brown, Christine James
Brown, Michael DeWayne
Bruner, Denise
Carlyle, Shannia W
Coleman, Rodney Albert
Donahue, William T.
Ford, Sam
Gooden, C. Michael
Hardie, Robert L., Jr.
Hardnett, Carolyn Judy
Hazel, Janis D
Holman, Kwame Kent Allan
Houston, John R, III
Hutchison, Dr. Harry Greene
Jackson, Darrell Duane
Jones, Carmen
Lang-Jeter, Lula L
May, James Shelby
McCants, Dr. Odell
Miller, Marquis David
Moncure, Albert F.
Moore, Dr. Roscoe Michael
Neal, Eddie
Newman, William Thomas, Jr.
Pemberton-Heard, Danielle Marie
Penn, Tenesia Sharone
Perkins, Daniel T
Powell, Adam Clayton, III
Pualani, Gloria
Robinson, Crystal
Robinson, Eugene Harold
Rollins, Tree
Roye, Monica R Hargrove
Scott, Samuel
Sinnette, Dr. Calvin Herman
Sinnette, Elinor DesVerney
Smith, Carolyn Lee
Smith, Chester B.
Thomas, Brandy
Washington, Consuela M
Weaver, Frank Cornell
Wheat, Alan
White, E. Diane
White, Ida Margaret
Williams, Anthony A
Wood, Daisy M

Ashburn
Allen, Terry Thomas, Jr.
Campbell, Jesse
Ellard, Henry Austin
Fletcher, London Levi
Gaines, William Albert
Logan, Marc Anthony
Simmons, Edward
Williams, Michael D.

Ashland
Hite, Leon, III
Williams, John R.

Bedford
Brooks, Frank B.
Brooks, Robin C

Blacksburg
Campbell, Maia
Dixon, Dr. Benjamin
Giovanni, Nikki
Gray, Torrian
Sanders, Dr. Karen Eley
Warren, Herman Lecil

Boston
Leftwich, Willie L.

Bowling Green
Gibson, William M.

Boydton
McLaughlin, Dr. George W.

Bristol
Hairston, Jerry Wayne

Burke
Sylvas, Dr. Lionel B.

Centreville
Faulding, Juliette J.
Patton, Marvcus Raymond
Stafford, Earl W

Chantilly
Fergus, Joseph E
Fitzgerald-Mosely, Benita
McHenry, Emmit J
Mosley, Benita Fitzgerald

Charles City
Adkins, Iona W.

Charlottesville
Brown, Simon F.
Daniel, Wendy Palmer
Dove, Rita Frances
Garrett, Paul C
Harris, Paul Clinton, Sr.
Jones, Dr. Betty Jean Tolbert
Littlepage, Craig
Martin, Dr. Patrick M
Peck, Leontyne Clay
Rogers, David William
Scott, Prof. Charlotte Hanley
Scott, Dr. Nathan A, Jr.
Silva, Dr. Henry Andrew
Smith, Kevin L

Chesapeake
Barnard-Bailey, Wanda Arlene
Bryant-Shanklin, Dr. Mona Maree
Carroll, Dr. William
Green, Barbara Marie
Harrell, William Edwin
Isaac, Joseph William Alexander
Johnson, William A.
Jordan, George Lee, Jr.
McCall, Barbara Collins
Owens, Dr. Hugo Armstrong
Ozim, Dr. Francis Taino
Singleton, Dr. James LeRoy, Jr.
Taylor, Dr. Donald Fulton, Sr.
Walton, James Madison

Chester
Booker, Corliss Voncille
Eseonu, Dr. Dorothy N.

Chesterfield
Byrd, Arthur W

Clifton
Haston, Dr. Raymond Curtiss, Jr.

Clifton Forge
Goode, George Ray

Colonial Heights
Thigpen, Dr. Calvin Herritage

Culpeper
Hinton, Hortense Beck

Dale City
Bendy, Melinda

Danville
Harris, Charles Somerville
Jennings, Sylvesta Lee

Doswell
Tillman, Christine L.

Dumfries
Stallworth, Eddie, Jr.

Fairfax
Allen, Benjamin P., III
Boyer, James B.
Butler, Douthard Roosevelt
Dennis, Dr. Rutledge M.
Haynes, Farnese N
Johnson-Brown, Dr. Hazel Winfred
Lee, Kevin Brian
Lomax, Michael L.
Perry, Wayne D
Settles, Trudy Y
Siler, Brenda Claire
Whiting, Thomas J.

Wilkins, Roger Wood
Williams, Marcus Doyle

Fairfax County
Greaux, Cheryl Prejean

Fairfax Station
Bulls, Herman E.

Falls Church
Bonner, Alice Carol
Bridgewater, Albert Louis
Chatman-Driver, Patricia Ann
Fields, Faye F
Hairston, William
Lawson, Dawn M
Peguese, Herman A
Stansbury, Vernon Carver
Thomas, Dr. Lydia Waters

Farmville
Jones, Dr. Deneese LaKay
Miller, Erenest Eugene

Fort Belvoir
Ramsey, Donna Elaine

Fredericksburg
Davies, Rev. Lawrence A.
Farmer, James

Glasgow
Lyle, Roberta Branche Blacke

Glen Allen
Miller, Laurel Milton
Pierce, Dr. Gregory W

Gloucester
Honablue, Richard Riddick, M.D.
Wilson, Wesley Campbell

Great Falls
Gee, William Rowland, Jr.

Halifax
Gaines, Ava Canda

Hampton
Adeyiga, Dr. Adeyinka A.
Bontemps, Jacqueline Marie Fon-
    vielle
Braxton, Dr. Jean Bailey
Brown, Jennifer H.
Buchanan, Shonda T
Clark, Laron Jefferson
Darden, Dr. Christine Mann
Davis, Dr. Bertha Lane
Davy, Dr. Freddye Turner
Dawson, Martha E
Easter, Rufus Benjamin, Jr.
Gartrell, Luther R.
Hammond, Dr. Pamela V
Hargrove, Dr. Andrew
Harris, Dr. Carl Gordon
Harvey, Dr. William R.
Hendricks, Dr. Constance Smith
Hoffler, Dr. Richard Winfred, Jr.
Jamaludeen, Abdul Hamid
Jefferson, M. Ivory
Jenkins, Luther Neal
Johnson, Melvin Russell
Jones, Hon. Bonnie Louise
Jones, Edward Norman
Jones, Dr. Reginald L
Kerry, Leon G
Locke, Dr. Mamie Evelyn
McGhee, Nancy Bullock
Owens, Angle B., Jr.
Payne, Richelle Denise
Pleasant, Mae Barbee Boone
Porter, Michael LeRoy
Rolle, Jo-Ann
Scott, Jennifer J
Taylor, Joseph
Taylor, Wilford, Jr.
Thomas, Dr. Dennis
Wallace, George E
Ward, Albert M.
Watkins, James Darnell

Harrisonburg
Davis, Abraham
Gabbin, Dr. Alexander Lee
Gabbin, Dr. Joanne Veal

Jennings, Lillian Pegues
Toliver, George

Hayes
Evans, Dr. William E.

Haymarket
Curry, Major Gen. Jerry Ralph
Gravely, Samuel L., Jr.

Herndon
Davis, Howlie R
Johnson, James Walter
Lewis, Jimmy
Marks, Kenneth Hicks
Thompson, Warren M

Hopewell
Boone, Elwood Bernard, III
Edmonds, Campbell Ray

Keswick
Bates, George Albert

King George
Hughes, Isaac Sunny

Lawrenceville
Adesuyi, Dr. Sunday Adeniji
Satcher, Robert Lee
Waddell, John K.
Wilson, Connie Drake

Leesburg
Dixon, James Wallace Edwin, II

Lexington
Lewis, J B, Jr.
McCloud, Anece Faison

Lorton
Francis, Dr. E. Aracelis

Lynchburg
Mitchell, James H.
Whitehead, Andre

Manakin-Sabot
Groce, Rev. Herbert Monroe, Jr.

Manassas
Bowe-Quick, Marie
Byrd, Herbert Lawrence
Hinton, Hortense Beck
Jones, Jimmie Dene
Jones, Marcus Edmund
Leigh, Fredric H
Polk, Anthony Joseph

Martinsville
Knox, Wayne D. P.
Muse, William Brown

Mc Lean
White, Sylvia Kay

McLean
Allen, Benjamin P., III
Alston, Dr. Kathy Diane
Cooper, Barbara J
Govan, Reginald C
Hammond, Verle B
Jackson, Tonya Charisse
Johnson, Charles Bernard
Jones, Charisse Monsio
Malone, Claudine Berkeley
Metters, Dr. Samuel
Monroe, Bryan K
Powell, Adam Clayton, III
Pruitt-Logan, Dr. Anne Smith
Sechrest, Edward Amacker
Straight, Cathy A
Weaver, Gary W.
Wickham, DeWayne

Metairie
Schulters, Lance A.

Middleburg
Johnson, Sheila

Midlothian
Al-Mateen, Dr. K Bakeer
Smith, Shirley LaVerne
Thompson-Wright, Dr. Brenda Smith

Newport News
Allen, Charles Claybourne
Banks, Dwayne Martin

Burt, Carl Douglas
Davy, Dr. Freddye Turner
Dawkins, Wayne J
Harper, William Thomas, III
Holloman, Thaddeus Bailey
Kendall, Mark Acton Robertson
Mason, Felicia Lendonia
Price, Ray Anthony
Rattley, Jessie M.
Wilson, Wesley Campbell

Norfolk

Alexander, Otis Douglas
Alexander, Rosa M.
Ashby, Reginald W.
Barnard-Bailey, Wanda Arlene
Barnes, Anne T.
Barnes, Dr. Elsie M.
Bempong, Dr. Maxwell A
Braxton, Dr. Jean Bailey
Britt, L. D., MD, MPH
Brooks, Phillip Daniel
Bryant-Shanklin, Dr. Mona Maree
Byrd, Dr. Helen P Bessent
Cauthen-Bond, Cheryl G.
Chesley, Roger T
Clemons, Dr. Michael L
Cobb, Rev. Harold James, Jr.
Corprew, Charles Sumner, Jr.
Cotton, Joseph Craig
Crawley, George Claudius
Dandridge, Prof. Rita Bernice
Davenport, Dr. Carol A.
DeLoatch, Sandra
DeLoatch, Dr. Sandra J
Earl, Dr. Archie William
Fuller, William Henry, Jr.
Garnette, Dr. Booker Thomas
Isaac, Joseph William Alexander
Lane, George S., Jr.
Lewis, Dr. Brenda Neumon
Lewis, Jesse Cornelius
Lowe, Scott Miller
Marshall, Herbert A.
Mason, William Thomas, Jr.
McCall, Barbara Collins
McDemmond, Dr. Marie V
Miller, Yvonne Bond
Montgomery, Annette
Moore, Gregory B
Morris, Dr. Carole V.
Pope, Mirian Artis
Reid, Dr. Milton A.
Rodgers-Rose, LaFrances Audrey
Ryder, Dr. Georgia Atkins
Schexnider, Dr. Alvin J
Shakir, Dr. Adib Akmal
Spiva, Dr. Ulysses Van
Spurlock, Dr. James B
Strayhorn, Earl Carlton
Valentine, Herman E
Vernon-Chesley, Michele Joanne
Walker, Sterling Wilson
White-Parson, Willar F
Williams, Dr. Ira Joseph
Williams, Regina Vloyn-Kinchen
Willis, Levy E
Wimbush, Frederick Blair
Wynn, Gladys W

Oakton

Bowron, Eljay B
Davis, Nathaniel Alonzo
LeCesne, Alvarez

Painter

Ashby, Ernestine Arnold

Petersburg

Bailey, Dr. Gracie Massenberg
Buck, Dr. Judith Brooks
Carter, Dr. Joye Maureen
Crocker, Wayne Marcus
Dance, Hon. Rosalyn R.
Fleming, Bruce E.
Haughton, Dr. Ethel Norris
Hobbs, Dr. Alma Cobb
Moore, Eddie N., Jr.
Mosby, Dr. Carolyn Lewis
Odom, Stonewall
Reid, Daphne Etta Maxwell
Thigpen, Dr. Calvin Herritage
Toppin, Edgar Allan
White, Tytral T

Wilson, Jimmy L
Worrell, Kaye Sydnell

Portsmouth

Cooper, Iris N.
Daniels, Elizabeth
Edwards, Dr. Rondle E.
Holley, Dr. James W
Jenkins, Harry Lancaster
Jones, Helen Hampton
Lucas, L Louise
Moody, Eric Orlando
Morrison, Johnny Edward
Obayuwana, Alphonsus Osarobo
Randall, Marlene West
Smith, Rachel Norcom
Smith, Robert Lawrence, Sr.
Taylor, Almina
Wesley, Clemon Herbert, Jr.
White, Debra Y
Whitehurst, Charles Bernard, Sr.
Williamson, Carl Vance

Prince George

Poindexter, Gammiel Gray

Quantico

Carter, William Thomas, Jr.

Quinton

Green, Dr. Calvin Coolidge

Radford

Covington, Dr. H. Douglas

Reston

Ahart, Thomas I
Amprey, Walter G
Brown, Reginald L., Jr.
Cooke, William Branson
Gilliam, Arleen Fain
Haynes, Farnese N
Johnson, Johnnie Louis
Lawson, William R
Myricks, Dr. Noel
Reed, Kwame Osei
Watson, Joe

Richmond

Adiele, Dr. Moses Nkwachukwu
Al-Mateen, Dr. Cheryl Singleton
Barrett, Rev. Walter Carlin
Bass, Harry S.
Baugh, David
Benton, James Wilbert, Jr.
Beshah, Guenet
Billings, Cora Marie
Bledsoe, Carolyn E. Lewis
Boatwright, Joseph Weldon, III
Booker, Corliss Voncille
Boone, Dr. Elwood Bernard
Borum, Jennifer Lynn
Bowser, McEva R.
Branch, Je
Cameron, Wilburn Macio, Jr.
Carter, Gilbert Lino
Carver, Dr. Joanne
Conyers, Charles L.
Cooke, Leonard
Creighton-Zollar, Dr. Ann
Culbreath-Manly, Tongila M
Dance, Dr. Daryl Cumber
Davis, Esther Gregg
Davis, Glenn
Davis, Melvin Lloyd
Deese, Manuel
Dell, Willie J.
Dennis, Dr. Rutledge M.
Dixon, Leon Martin
Dixon, Valena Alice
Douglas, Willard H
Edwards, Antonio
Eggleston, Neverett A
Eseonu, Dr. Dorothy N.
Fowlkes, Doretha P
Grante, Jullian Irving
Gray, Earl Haddon
Harmon, Rhonda M
Harrell, Adam Nelson
Harris, Gladys Bailey
Harris, Kelly C.
Harris, Dr. Ruth Coles
Hassell, Leroy Rountree, Sr.
Herbert, Maj. Douglas A.
Hill, Oliver W., Sr.
James, Dr. Allix Bledsoe
Jamison, Birdie Hairston
Jefferson-Moss, Carolyn

Johnson, Jonathan F
Johnson, William Randolph
Jones, Michele Woods
Jones, William C.
Kennedy, Joseph J, Jr.
Khalfani, Salim
Lambert, Dr. Benjamin J., III
Lambert, Leonard W.
Latney, Harvey, Jr.
Leary, James E.
Madu, Anthony Chisaraokwu
Marsh, Sen. Henry L., III
Meadows, Richard H.
Miller, Yvonne Bond
Mitchell, Michelle Burton
Nelson, Mario
Newbold, Simeon Eugene, Sr.
Pickett, Donna A
Pinn, Dr. Melvin T, Jr.
Pruitt, Fr. Alonzo Clemons
Reed, Dr. Daisy Frye
Rhoades, Dr. Samuel Thomas
Roberts, Dr. Samuel Kelton
Robertson, Dr. Benjamin W
Robertson, Dolores W.
Saunders, Kim D
Simmons, Dr. S Dallas
Sims, Esau, Jr.
Smith, Voydee
Spencer, James R
Spurlock, Dr. James B
Taylor, Iris
Teekah, Dr. George Anthony
Thomas, Jacquelyn Small
Thomas, John Charles
Thornton, Frank J.
Townes, Clarence Lee, Jr.
Wallace, Helen Winfree-Peyton
Walston, Woodrow William
Weaver, Dr. John Arthur
West, Marilyn H.
West, Valerie Y
Whitaker-Braxton, Beverly, Dr.
Woodson, Jeffrey Anthony
Wright, James E
Yancy, Prof. Preston Martin

Roanoke

Adams, Paul Brown
Bolden, Aletha Simone
Boyd, Wilhemina Y.
Bruce, Antoinette Johnson
Burks, James William, Jr.
Cason, Joseph L.
Hamilton, Howard W
Taylor, Noel C.
Whitworth, Claudia Alexander

Salem

Pennix, James A

Sandston

Hill, Winfer L

Spotsylvania

Hatchett, William F.

Springfield

Adams, Theodore Adolphus, Jr.
Becton, Lt. Gen. Julius Wesley, Jr.
Eley, Randall Robbi
Forte, Johnie, Jr.
Frye, Robert Edward
Lawson, Dawn M
Ruffin, Paulette Francine
Sykes, Robert A
Tucker, Geraldine Coleman

St Stephens Church

Pollard, Percy Edward, Sr.

St Thomas

Alexis, Dr. Carlton Peter

Sterling

Green, Darrell
Hunigan, Col. Earl

Suffolk

Glover, Dr. Bernard Ellsworth
Hart, Ronald O.
Wilson, Madelaine Majette

Surry

Tunstall, June Rebecca

Tazewell

Garner, June Brown

Vienna

Ahart, Thomas I
Burrell, Judith Ann

Davis, William W
Glover, J. Calvin
Hayes, Edward
Iverson, Johnathan Lee
McClain, Andre
Reid-Coleman, Desma
Roane, Rev. Glenwood P, Sr.
Scott, Gilbert H, Sr.

Virginia Beach

Banks, June Skinner
Carroll, Dr. William
Corprew, Charles Sumner, Jr.
Dildy, Catherine Greene
Duke, Ruth White
Hamlin, Ernest Lee
Hoffler, Dr. Richard Winfred, Jr.
Reynolds, Charles McKinley, Jr.
Thomas, Dr. Dennis
Vernon-Chesley, Michele Joanne
White-Parson, Willar F
Wiggins, Joseph L.

Wakefield

Urquhart, James McCartha

Warrenton

Ruffner, Ray P.
Zimmerman, Matthew Augustus

Warsaw

Johns, Dr. Sonja Maria

Washington

Ellison, Pauline Allen

Waverly

Worrell, Kaye Sydnell

West Point

Reid, Miles Alvin

Williamsburg

Bryce, Dr. Herrington J
Charlton, Jack Fields
Pinson, Hermine Dolorez
Powell, Michael K
Rivers, Dr. Robert Joseph, Jr.
Sims, Prof. Ronald R
Stockton, Carlton A

Wise

Dawson, Bobby H

Woodbridge

Adams-Ender, Clara Leach
Carter, William Thomas, Jr.
Haston, Dr. Raymond Curtiss, Jr.

Woodford

West, William Lionel

Yorktown

Mason, Felicia Lendonia

WASHINGTON

Crockett-Ntonga, Noluthando

Arlington

Taylor, Henry F

Auburn

Neal, Sylvester

Bellevue

Barnes, Adia Oshun
Bennett, Dr. James L.
Johnson, Jerry L.
Strong, Mack
Taylor, Sterling R

Bellingham

Ford, Clyde W
Shropshire, Harry W.

Blaine

Smith, LeRoi Matthew-Pierre, III

Chehalis

Pope, Dr. Isaac S

District of Columbia

Terrell, Henry Matthew

Duvall

Rackley, Lurma M

Everett

Fitzpatrick, B Edward
Reggans, John B.

Issaquah

Anderson, James R., Jr.
King, Rev. Charles E.
Welch, Jesse Roy

Kirkland

Jones, Walter
McIntosh, Helen Young

Lynnwood

Brown, Marva Y

Mercer Island

Bailey, Mona Humphries
Thompson, Dr. Alvin J

Metro Area

Petersen, Arthur Everett, Jr.

Mill Creek

Donaldson, James Lee, III

Olympia

Belcher, Lewis, Jr.
Hawkins, Steven Wayne
Ingram, Winifred
Purce, Dr. Thomas Les

Port Townsend

Morgan, Robert Lee

Pullman

Anderson, Talmadge

Redmond

Gayle, Cruise
Rakestraw, Kyle Damon

Renton

Blake, J Paul
Franklin, Benjamin
Jones, Rev. Leon C.
Stokes, Eric

Seattle

Abe, Dr. Benjamin Omara A
Alex, Gregory K.
Anderson, Betty Keller
Bailey, Mona Humphries
Banks, Dr. James Albert
Bennett, Daina T
Bennette, Connie E.
Blake, J Paul
Branham, George, III
Brooks, Norward J
Byers, Susan M
Carmichael, Carole A
Cash, Swintayla Marie
Counts, Dr. George W.
Debro, Dr. Julius
Eason, Oscar, Jr.
Engram, Bobby
Farris, Hon. Jerome
Fearn, James E., Jr.
Fearn-Banks, Kathleen
Frye, Reginald Stanley
Gayton, Gary D.
Greene, Nathaniel D
Gunter, Laurie
Hailey, Priscilla W
Haynes, Sue Blood
Hill, Dr. James A, Sr.
Horne, Deborah Jean
Houston, Dr. Alice V.
Hubbard, Walter T.
Jackson, Arthur D., Jr.
Jackson, Tia
Johnson, Charles Richard
Johnson, Charles V.
Johnson, Shannon
Kennedy Franklin, Linda Cheryl
Kimbrough, Donna L
Knight, W H
Langford, Victor C., III
Large, Jerry D
Lawrence, Jacob A.
Lee, Vivian Booker
Leigh, James W., Jr.
Leonard, Gloria Jean
Leslie, Marsha R

Locke, Dr. Hubert G.
Lofton, Andrew James
Macklin, John W
Marshall, Donyell Lamar
Maxie, Peggy Joan
McConnell, Conrad
McElroy, Colleen J.
McGee, Henry W
Miles, Dr. Edward Lancelot
Miller, Constance Joan
Mitchell, Windell T
Mumford, Esther Hall
Newhouse, Millicent DeLaine
Osborne, Oliver Hilton
Pappillion, Glenda M
Peoples, John Derrick, Jr.
Priester, Julian Anthony
Purnell, Carolyn J
Reynolds, Andrew Buchanan
Rice, Dr. Constance Williams
Rice, Norman Blann
Riley, Teddy
Scott, Joseph Walter
Shaw, Dr. Spencer Gilbert
Sims, Ronald Cordell
Spigner, Dr. Clarence
Spratlen, Thaddeus H
Staton, Rhonda Bailey
Sunday, Delena
Sutton, Dr. Sharon Egretta
Swoopes-Jackson, Sheryl
Taylor, Dr. Quintard
Thompson, Dr. Alvin J
Toliver, Paul Allen
Washington, James W, Jr.
Williams, Clarence
Williams, Leroy Joseph
Willingham, Tyrone
Wilson, August
Wilson, John T., Jr.
Womack, William Martin

Spokane
Branch, Andre Jose
Givens, Rocelious
Roseman, Jennifer Eileen
Smith, James, Jr.

Tacoma
Anderson, Betty Keller
Baugh, Lynnette
Brown, Rev. Leo C
Davis, Alfred C., Sr.
Felder, Harvey
Fregia, Darrell Leon
Gilven, Hezekiah
Wesley, Barbara Ann
Young, Artee

Vashon
McGehee, Nan E

Washington
Lucas, Dr. C Payne
Owens, Robert Leon, III
Sims, Ronald Cordell

Washington DC
Simpson, Carole
Wharton, Dolores D
Wharton Boyd, Linda F.

WashingtonDC
Jackson, Tyoka

Yakima
Bohannon, Etdrick

WEST VIRGINIA

Beckley
Bradshaw, Doris Marion
Chambers, Madrith Bennett
Dobson, Helen Sutton
Motley, Dr. Ronald Clark
Scott, Albert Nelson
Seay, Lorraine King

Cannelton
Anderson, Louise Payne

Charleston
Carter, Phyllis Harden
Cox, Otis Graham, Jr.

Fowlkes, Nelson J
Griffin, Dr. Ervin Verome
James, Dr. Betty Harris
James, Charles H., III
James, Charles Howell, II
Lee, Ivin B
Martin, James Tyrone
Matthews, Virgil E.
Mitchell-Bateman, Mildred
Muhammad, James A
Shaw, Richard Gordon
Smoot, Carolyn Elizabeth
Tinsley, Dwane L

Dunbar
Griffin, Dr. Ervin Verome
Russell, James A., Jr.

Fairmont
Hinton, Gregory Tyrone
Taylor, Tyrone Curtis

Friday Harbor
White, Persia

Huntington
Carter, Philip W.
Henderson, Herbert H
Lawson, Robert L.
Redd, William L
Williams, Joseph Lee

Hurricane
Peters, Roscoe Hoffman, Jr.

Institute
Carter, Dr. Hazo William
Carter, Phyllis Harden
Garrett, Naomi M.
Giles, Charlotte Emma
Ledbetter, Charles Ted
Smoot, Carolyn Elizabeth
Thompson, Dr. Litchfield O

Keystone
Jackson, Aubrey N.

Lewisburg
Arbuckle, John Finley, Jr.

Morgantown
Brooks, Dr. Dana DeMarco
Cabbell, Edward Joseph
Gray, Kenneth D
Gwynn, Florine Evayonne
Howard, Dr. Elizabeth Fitzgerald

Oak Hill
Simms, Albert L

Parkersburg
Roberts, Cheryl Dornita Lynn

Philippi
Jones, Idus, Jr.
Redd, Thomasina A.

Shepherdstown
Roberts, Cheryl Dornita Lynn

Weirton
Jackson-Gillison, Esq. Helen L
Williams, Carletta Celeste

Welch
Stephens, Booker T

Wheeling
Lewis, Dr. Houston A.
Moore, John Wesley, Jr.
Smith, Andre Raphel

WISCONSIN

Atlanta
Woodson, Mike

Beloit
Knight, Walter R.

Brookfield
Jones, Fredrick E
Payne, Ulice, Jr.

Eau Claire
Taylor, Dr. Dale B

Germantown
Walker, Willie M.

Glendalee
McKinney, Venora Ware

Green Bay
Davis, Rob
Driver, Donald Jerome

Harris, Al
Henderson, William Terrelle
Highsmith, Alonzo Walter
Seale, Samuel Ricardo
Terrell, Patrick Christopher
Woodson, Charles

Kenosha
Brown, Jarvis Ardel
Shade, Dr. Barbara J.

Kewaunee
Qamar, Nadi Abu

La Crosse
Mitchem, Dr. John Clifford

Madison
Ally, Dr. Akbar F.
Bonds, Kevin Gregg
Davis, Richard
Dejoie, Carolyn Barnes Milanes
Evans, Patricia P
High, Freida
Hopkins, Dr. Dianne McAfee
Jones, Prof. James Edward
Lowery, Dr. Birl
Marrett, Dr. Cora B.
Nunnery, Willie James
Odom, John Yancy
Salter, Kwame S
Smith, Dr. Barbara Wheat
Turner, Robert Lloyd
Ward, Walter L., Jr.
Wilson, Dr. David
Wilson, Dr. Patricia I
Young, Leon D

Menomonee Falls
Olapo, Olaitan

Mequon
Bowie, Willette

Milwaukee
Aman, Mary Jo
Aman, Dr. Mohammed M.
Barrett, Sherman L.
Beach, Walter G., II
Bender, Barbara A
Bowie, Willette
Broussard, Leroy
Cameron, Michael Terrance
Carpenter, Joseph, II
Caulker, Ferne Yangyeitie
Clevert, Hon. Charles N.
Conyers, Nathan
Daniels, John W
Daniels-Carter, Valerie
Dunmore, Steve
Edmond, Paul Edward
Edwards, Genyne
Elam, Donna
Epps, Edgar G.
Evers, William Preston
Ford, Sarah Ann
Fuller, Dr. Howard L.
Granville, Billy
Harlan, Emery King
Hicks, Dr. Ingrid Diann
Holt, Kenneth Charles
Holt, Mikel
Hyler, Lora Lee
Jackson, Harold Baron, Jr.
Jamison, Lafayette
Johnson, Ben E.
Jones, Arthur L
Jones, James Bennett
Jones, Walter L.
Kane, Eugene A
Lockett, Sandra Bokamba
Matthis, James L., III
McLean, Zarah Gean
Murrell, Dr. Peter C
O'Flynn-Pattillo, Patricia
Olapo, Olaitan
Ologboni, Tejumola F.
Palmer, John A.
Parks, James Clinton
Parrish, Clarence R.
Perry, June Martin
Pollard, Dr. Diane S.
Prince, Joan Marie
Purnell, Mark W.
Riley, Glenn Pleasants
Ross, Lee Elbert
Sims, Deloris
Smith, Symuel Harold

Spence, Rev. Joseph Samuel, Sr.
Tate, Cornelius Astor
Thornton, Willie James, Jr.
Thurman, Alfonzo
Trotter, James
Tyson, Andre
Ward, Walter L., Jr.
Williams, George W., III
Williams, Virginia Walker
Wynn, Thomas Harold, Sr.

New Berlin
Nichols, Silas L.

Oak Creek
Bridgeman, Junior

Oshkosh
Hawkins, Dr. Muriel A.

Pleasant Prairie
Duerson, David R

Racine
Matthis, James L., III
Turner, Robert Lloyd

Strum
Majors, Richard G

Superior
Unaeze, Felix Eme

Thiensville
Dennis, Carolyn K

Wauwatosa
Purnell, Mark W.

West Allis
Brown, Gilbert Jesse

Whitewater
Hewing, Dr. Pernell Hayes
Jones, Dr. Lee

WYOMING

Cheyenne
Jeffrey, Ronnald James
Lavalais, Lester Joseph
Mercer, Arthur, Sr.
Mercer, Lillian Ann
Wise, C. Rogers

Newcastle
Simms, Albert L

Saratoga
Hendrix, Martha Raye

BAHAMAS

Nassau
Brown, Theophile Waldorf
Poitier, Sidney

BERMUDA

Hamilton
Swan, John William David

Paget Parish
Swan, John William David

BRAZIL

Rio de Janeiro
Atkins, Edmund E.

BULGARIA

Scafati
Smith, Stevin L

ALBERTA

Calgary
Davis, Shani
Iginla, Jarome

BRITISH COLUMBIA

Vancouver
Brown, Marcus James
Edwards, Blue

Edwards, Douglas
Johnson, Parker Collins
Lawrence, Ollie, Jr.
Mayberry, Lee
Mobley, Eric
Moten, Lawrence Edward, III
Newbill, Ivano Miguel

NOVA SCOTIA

Halifax
Anderson, Helen Louise

ONTARIO

Mississauga
James, Dr. Herbert I
Peterson, Oscar Emmanuel

Ottawa
Graham, Jeff Todd

St Catharines
Jenkins, Ferguson Arthur

Toronto
Jackson, Angela
Miller, Wade Thomas
Mitchell, Samuel E
Thomas, Frank Edward
Wells, Vernon
Williams, Jerome

Windsor
Nutt, Rev. Maurice Joseph

QUEBEC

Montreal
Porter, Dr. Arthur T
Sinclair, Michael Glenn
Tinsley, Lee Owen

Verdun
Thomas, Robert Charles

COTE D'IVOIRE

Abidjan
Dear, Alice

San Jose
Blue, Vida Rochelle, Jr.

DENMARK

Copenhagen
Burns, Ronald Melvin
Thigpen, Edmund Leonard

Copenhagen V
Thigpen, Edmund Leonard

FRANCE

Lamar, Jake V, Sr.

GERMANY

Hamburg
Laing, Edward A.

Jena
Davis, Mark Anthony

INDIA

Bangalore
Penn, Algernon H

Occupation Index

Accounting/Auditing (*See Also* **Management/ Administration— Accounting/Financial**)

Aiken, William
Allen, James H.
Allen, Philip C.
Anthony, Brenda Tucker
Arrington-Jones, Lorraine
Ashby, Lucius Antone
Bailey, Arthur
Baker, Darryl Brent, Sr.
Ball, Brenda Louise
Ball, William Batten
Barnett, Teddy
Barr, LeRoy
Becote, Fohliette W
Bell, Theodore Joshua
Benjamin, Ronald
Bennett, Joyce Annette
Benson, Sharon Marie
Berry, Charles F, Jr.
Billings, Mac
Bowers, Mirion Perry
Boyd, Thomas
Branch, Je
Brown, Clarice Ernestine
Brown, Dalton G
Brown, Lawrence E.
Bryant-Ellis, Paula D.
Bullard, Edward A., Jr.
Burks, Darrell
Burton, David Lloyd
Bynes, Glenn Kenneth
Carpenter, Raymond Prince
Carpenter, Vivian L.
Cheeks, Darryl Lamont
Clark, Sheila Wheatley
Cook, Frank Robert, Jr.
Copeland, Barry B
Cox, J. Linloy
Cox, Taylor H., Sr.
Cox, Tyrone Y.
Crim, Rodney
Culver, Rhonda
Davis, Cal Deleanor
Davis, Rev. Tyrone Theophilus
Davis, Dr. William L.
Dickerson, Tyrone Edward
Drennen, Gordon
Easton, Richard James
Ebong, Regina U
Echols, Doris Brown
Evans, Vernon D.
Finney, Michael Anthony
Fisher, George Carver
Flint, Mary Frances
Flynn, H Welton
Frazier, Greg
Gabbin, Dr. Alexander Lee
Gainey, Leonard Dennis, II
Gant, Wanda Adele
Garnier, Thomas Joseph
Garrett, Nathan Taylor
Gates, Otis A., III
Gill, Rosa Underwood
Gillespie, Bonita
Gore, John Michel
Gray, Andrew Jackson

Gray, Earl Haddon
Green, Dennis O.
Greene, Gregory A.
Griffin, Bobby L.
Guitano, Anton W.
Hadnott, Bennie L
Hall, Hansel Crimiel
Hambrick, Harold E., Jr.
Hampton, Randall C.
Harper, Mary L.
Harris, Robert Eugene Peyton
Hill, James, Jr.
Holmes, Richard Bernard
Huff, Lula Lunsford
Hymes, Jesse
Isaacs-Lowe, Arlene Elizabeth
Jackson, Harold Leonard, Jr.
Jackson, Larron Deonne
Jeffers, Grady Rommel
Jeter, Clifton B
Johnson, Ralph C
Jordan, Thurman
Joseph, Abraham
Keffers, Jamie L
Keller, Mary Jean
Law, M Eprevel
Lee, William Thomas
Levychin, Richard
Lewis, Arthur A., Jr.
Lewis, Jim
Liverpool, Charles Eric
Lokeman, Joseph R
Long, Gerald Bernard
Lowe, Martha P.
Martin, William R.
Matthews, Gregory J.
McEachern, D Hector
McGuirt, Milford W
McHenry, Donald F.
McKinzie, Barbara A
McMillian, Josie
McReynolds, Elaine A.
Mercado-Valdes, Frank Marcelino
Mitchell, Bert Norman
Mitchell, Judson, Jr.
Mohamed, Gerald R, Jr.
Moore, Alfred
Moore, Dr. Charles W
Newkirk, Thomas H.
Norman, Wallace
Pappillion, Glenda M
Patterson, Cheryl Ann
Pearson, Ramona Henderson
Phifer, B Janelle Butler
Ransom, Leticia Buford
Robinson, Robert Love, Jr.
Self, Frank Wesley
Session, Johnny Frank
Shepherd, Elmira
Simmons, Joyce Hobson
Slash, Joseph A
Smith, Eugene
Stamps, Leon Preist
Stewart, Ronald Patrick
Swanigan, Jesse Calvin
Tate, Matthew
Taylor, Kenneth Matthew
Thomas, Ralph Albert
Thompson, Karen Ann
Thorpe, Earl Howard

Tillman, Dr. Talmadge Calvin, Jr.
Titus, Robert P
Turner, Mark Anthony
Walls, Gen. George Hilton, Jr.
Watson, Chester N.
Wattley, Thomas Jefferson
Whitmal, Nathaniel
Wilfong, Henry T
Williams, Harold L, Jr.
Williams, Leroy Joseph
Williams, Morris
Wilson, John E.
Witherspoon, R. Carolyn
Yarbrough, Roosevelt

Acting

Adams, Jonathan, III
Adams, Nick
Albers, Kenneth Lynn
Alexander, Flex
Alexander, Khandi
Alice, Mary
Allen, Debbie
Amos, John
Anderson, Anthony
Andrews, Mark Althavean
Andrews, Real
Atkins, Erica
Atkins, Sharif
Avery, James L.
Babatunde, Obba
Badu, Erykah
Baker, Shaun
Banks, Tyra Lynne
Bassett, Angela
Beach, Michael Anthony
Beauvais, Garcelle
Belafonte, Harry
Belafonte, Shari
Bell, Coby Erik
Bell, Darryl M.
Benymon, Chico
Berry, Dr. Gordon L
Berry, Halle M
Billings, Cora Marie
Billings, Earl William
Blackwood, Ronald A.
Blacque, Taurean
Blake, Grace
Bledsoe, Br. James L
Boatman, Michael Patrick
Bodison, Wolfgang
Boston, Gretha
Boutte, Rhonda
Bow Wow, Lil
Brady, Wayne Alfonzo
Braugher, Andre
Bridges, Todd Anthony
Brooks, Golden A.
Broughton, Christopher Leon
Brown, Jim
Browne, Roscoe Lee
Bryant, Joy
Burton, Levar
Busia, Akosua Cyamama
Calhoun, Monica
Calloway, Vanessa Bell
Campbell, Maia
Campbell, Tevin Jermod
Campbell-Martin, Tisha

Cannon, Nick
Carroll, Diahann
Carroll, Rocky
Carry, Julius J
Carson, Lisa Nicole
Carter, Shawn Corey
Chappelle, Dave
Charles, RuPaul Andre
Cheadle, Don
Chestnut, Morris L.
Chong, Rae Dawn
Christian, William Leonard
Clark, Rosalind K.
Clay, Stanley Bennett
Cobb, Keith Hamilton
Cole, Natalie
Coleman, Gary Wayne
Coles, Kimberley
Cook, Victor Trent
Copage, Marc Diego
Cosby, Camille Olivia Hanks
Cosby, Dr. William Henry
Cowden, Michael E.
Curry, Mark G.
Curtis-Hall, Vondie
Dash, Stacey Lauretta
David, Geraldine R.
Davis, Guy
Davis, Robert E.
Davis, Sammy, Jr.
Davis, Viola
Dawson, Rosario
Day, Morris
DeAnda, Peter
Dee, Ruby
De'Leon, Lunden
Denton, Sandi
Desert, Alex
Desselle, Natalie
Devine, Loretta
Diesel, Vin
Digga, Rah
Diggs, Taye
Dillard, Victoria
Divins, Charles
Dorn, Michael
Doug, Doug E.
Douglas, Ashanti Shequoiya
Douglas, Suzzanne
Dourdan, Gary
Duke, Bill
Dunbar, Rockmond
Duncan, Michael Clarke
Dungey, Merrin
Dutton, Charles S.
Ealy, Michael
Edwards, Ella Raino
Elmore, Dr. Ronn
Epps, Omar Hashim
Esposito, Giancarlo
Evans, Faith Renee
Faison, Donald Adeosun
Faison, Frankie R.
Fann, Albert Louis
Fareed, Kamaal Ibn John
Fernandez, Peter Jay
Ferrell, Tyra
Fields, Kim Victoria
Fingaz, Sticky
Fishburne, Laurence John

Fox, Vivica A
Foxx, Jamie
Franklin, Aretha Louise
Franklin, Don
Franklin, Kirk
Franks, Cree Summer
Freeman, Albert Cornelius, Jr.
Freeman, Morgan Porterfield, Jr.
Freeman, Yausmenda
Gaines, Mary E
Gant, Richard E.
Garrett, Denise Eileen
Gault, Willie James
Genet, Michael
George, Jason Winston
Gibbs, Marla
Giles, Nancy
Ginuwine
Givens, Robin
Glass, Erecka Tiffany
Glass, Ronald E.
Glover, Danny Lebern
Glover, Savion
Goldberg, Whoopi
Good, Megan Monique
Gooding, Cuba
Gooding, Omar
Gordon, Rufus Carl, Jr.
Gossett, Louis Cameron, Jr.
Gray, Macy
Grier, David Alan
Grier, Pamela S.
Griffin, Eddie
Guillaume, Robert
Guy, Jasmine
Hagler, Marvelous Marvin
Hall, Arsenio
Hall, Delores
Hall, Regina
Hamilton, Lisa Gay
Hamilton, Lynn
Hammond, Brandon La Ron
Hampton, Kym
Hardison, Kadeem
Harper, Hill
Harris, Jeanette
Harris, Shawntae
Harris, Steve
Harrison, Mya Marie
Harry, Jackee
Harvey, Steve
Hatchette, Matt
Hayes, Isaac
Hayes, Reginald
Haysbert, Dennis Dexter
Headley, Heather
Headley, Shari
Hemsley, Sherman Alexander
Henderson, Stephen McKinley
Hendry, Gloria
Henson, Darrin Dewitt
Hill, Dule
Hill-Marley, Lauryn Noelle
Holden, Michelle Y
Holder, Geoffrey
Holliday, Jennifer
Hooks, Brian
Hooks, Kevin
Hopkins, Telma
Horne, Lena Mary Calhoun

Horsford, Anna Maria
Houston, Dr. Whitney Elizabeth
Howard, Sherri
Hubert, Janet Louise
Hudson, Ernie
Hudson, Jennifer Kate
Hughley, D L
Hunter, Gigi
Hyman, Earle
Ice Cube
Ice-T
Imes, Mo'Nique
Jackson, Janet Damita Jo
Jackson, Mel
Jackson, Millie
Jackson, Randy
Jackson, Samuel L
James, Hawthorne
Jennings, Dominique
Johnson, Anne-Marie
Johnson, Beverly
Johnson, Dwayne Douglas
Jones, Grace
Jones, James Earl
Jones, Jill Marie
Jones, Kimberly Denise
Jones, Maxine
Jones, Orlando
Jones, Quincy Delight, III
Jones, Richard Timothy
Jones, Samuel L., III
Jones, Tamala
Joyce, Ella
Kennedy-Overton, Jayne
Kerr, Brook
Keymah, Crystal T
Khali, Simbi
Kimble, Bo
Kinchen, Arif S.
King, Regina
Kingi, Henry Masao
Kitt, Eartha Mae
Knight-Pulliam, Keshia
Knowles, Beyonce
Knowles, Solange Piaget
Kodjoe, Boris
Kotto, Yaphet
LaBelle, Patti
Laine, Cleo
Lane, Eric, III
Laneuville, Eric Gerard
Lange, Ted W.
Langhart Cohen, Janet
LaSalle, Eriq
Lateef, Dr. Yusef
Lathan, Sanaa
Latifah, Queen
Lawrence, Martin
Leal, Sharon
Lee, Joie
Lee, Malcolm D
Lee, Robinne
Lemmons, Kasi
Leonard, Sugar Ray
Lesure, James
Lewis, Dawnn
Lewis, Emmanuel
Lewis, Jenifer Jeanette
Lindo, Delroy
Long, Nia
Love, Darlene
Love, Faizon
Lowe, Jackie
Lumbly, Carl
Lynn, Lonnie Rashid
Mac, Bernie
MacLachlan, Janet A.
Marshall, Ameila
Marshall, Donald James
Martin, Christopher
Martin, Duane
Martin, Jesse Lamont
Matthews, Denise
McBride, Chi
McClure, Bryton Eric
McCoo, Marilyn
McDonald, Audra Ann
McEachin, James
McGee, Vonetta
McGill, Michele Nicole Johnson
McNeill, Cerves Todd
Meadows, Tim
Merkerson, Sharon Epatha
Miller, Percy Robert
Miller, Tangi
Mills, Stephanie
Mitchell, Brian Stokes
Mitchell, Daryl
Mitchell, Donald Michael

Moore, Christopher Paul
Moore, Juanita
Moore, Kenya
Moore, Melba
Moore, Samuel D.
Moore, Shemar F.
Morgan, Debbi
Morgan, Tracy
Morris, Garrett Gonzalez
Morsell, Frederick Albert
Morton, Joe
Mos Def
Moseka, Aminata
Moss, Anni R.
Murphy, Eddie
Nash, Niecy
Neal, Elise
Nelson, Prince Rogers
Nicholas, Denise
Nichols, Nichelle
Norwood, Brandy
Nunes Kirby, Mizan Roberta Patricia
Nunez, Miguel A
Okino, Elizabeth Anna
O'Neal, Shaquille Rashaun
Owens, Geoffrey
Page, Harrison Eugene
Parker, Paula Jai
Parker, Ray, Jr.
Parker Kodjoe, Nicole Ari
Parsons, Karyn
Patton, Antwan Andre
Payne, Allen
Payne, Freda Charcelia
Payton-Noble, JoMarie
Pena, Robert Bubba
Perrineau, Harold, Jr.
Perry, Felton
Pharris, Chrystee
Phifer, Mekhi
Pickens, James, Jr.
Pinkett Smith, Jada
Pinkins, Tonya
Plummer, Glenn
Poitier, Sidney
Poitier, Sydney Tamiia
Pounder, C. C. H.
Pratt, Kyla Alissa
Purdee, Nathan
Ralph, Sheryl Lee
Ramsey, David P.
Randle, Theresa Ellen
Rashad, Phylicia
Reddick, Lance
Redman, R
Reese, Della
Reid, Christopher
Reid, Daphne Etta Maxwell
Reid, Tim
Reuben, Gloria
Reynolds, James
Rhames, Ving
Rhymes, Busta
Ribeiro, Alfonso
Richards, Jaime Augusto, III
Richardson, LaTanya
Richardson, Salli
Ridley, John
Rippy, Rodney Allen
Robinson, Charles S
Robinson, Dawn
Robinson, Shaun
Robinson, Wendy Raquel
Robinson Peete, Holly
Rochon, Lela
Rock, Chris
Rodman, Dennis Keith
Rogers, Dr. George
Rose, Anika Noni
Ross, Diana
Ross, Tracee Ellis
Ross, Tracey
Roundtree, Richard
Rowell, Victoria Lynn
Rowland, Kelly Trene
Rudolph, Maya Khabira
Russ, Timothy Darrell
Scott, Jill
Scott, Larry B.
Scott, Seret
Scott, Stuart
Segar, Leslie
Sharp, Saundra
Shepherd, Berisford
Shepherd-Tarpley, Sherri
Simmons, Henry Oswald, Jr.
Simpson, O. J.
Sinbad
Smith, Anna Deavere

Smith, Chelsi
Smith, Clifford
Smith, Kellita
Smith, Will
Snipes, Wesley
Spruill, James Arthur
Starr, Fredro
Stickney, Phyllis Yvonne
St John, Kristoff
St Patrick, Matthew
Studdard, Ruben
Sullivan, Dr. J. Christopher
Sure, Al B.
Sweat, Keith
Sykes, Wanda
Symone, Raven
Tate, Larenz
Taylor, Gerren
Taylor, Lawrence Julius
Taylor, Meshach
Taylor, Dr. Regina
Taylor, Tamara
Taylor, William Edward
Tero, Lawrence
Terry, Saunders
the Entertainer, Cedric
Thomas, Philip Michael
Thomas, Rozonda
Thomason, Marsha
Todd, Beverly
Tone-Loc
Torres, Gina
Torry, Guy
Toussaint, Lorraine
Townsend, Robert
Trammel, Kimberly Elise
Tresvant, Ralph E.
True, Rachel India
Tucker, Christopher
Tunie, Tamara
Turman, Glynn
Tyson, Mike
Uggams, Leslie
Underwood, Blair
Union, Gabrielle M
Vance, Courtney B
Van Johnson, Rodney
Van Peebles, Mario
Van Peebles, Melvin
Vaughn, Countess Danielle
Velez, Lauren
VelJohnson, Reginald
Vereen, Ben Augustus
Vincent, Irving H.
Voorhies, Lark
Walbey, Theodosia Emma Draher
Walden, Barbara
Walker, Jimmie
Ward, Douglas Turner
Warfield, Marsha
Warner, Malcolm-Jamal
Warren, Michael
Washington, Dr. Denzel
Washington, Isaiah, IV
Washington, Keith
Washington, Kerry
Washington, Leroy
Washington, Ukee
Washington, Dr. Von Hugo
Watkins, Tionne
Watts, Rolanda
Wayans, Damon
Wayans, Keenen Ivory
Wayans, Marlon
Wayans, Shawn
Weathers, Carl
Webb, Veronica Lynn
Whitaker, Forest
White, Jahidi
White, Jaleel Ahmed
White, Michael Jai
White, Persia
Whitfield, Dondre T.
Whitfield, Lynn C.
Williams, Alyson
Williams, Billy Dee
Williams, Cynda
Williams, Dick Anthony
Williams, Hal
Williams, Malinda
Williams, Michael Michele
Williams, Montel
Williams, Samm-Art
Williams, Saul
Williams, Serena
Williams, Tonya Lee
Williams, Vanessa A.
Williams, Vanessa Lynne
Williams, Vesta

Williamson, Mykelti
Wilson, Chandra Danette
Wilson, Debra
Wilson, Demond
Wilson, Jonathan Charles
Wilson, Nancy
Winfrey, Oprah
Winston, Hattie
Witherspoon, John
Wolfe, George C
Womack, Bobby Dwayne
Woodard, Alfre
Woods, Allie, Jr.
Wright, Michael
Wright, N'Bushe
Wright, Tanya
Yoba, Malik
Young, William Allen

Activism, Political/Civil/ Social Rights

Abebe, Ruby
Ali, Dr. Kamal Hassan
Ali, Rasheedah Ziyadah
Allen, George Mitchell
Allen, Mark
Anthony, Wendell
Ardrey, Dr. Saundra Curry
Ashhurst-Watson, Carmen
Ashton, Vivian Christina R.
Bailey, Doris Jones
Barfield, Clementine
Barnes, Paul Douglas
Bell, George
Bell, Theron J.
Bennett, Debra Quinette
Bennett, Delores
Bennett, Marion D.
Berry, Reginald Francis
Billingsley, Andrew
Bland, Glenn W
Boggs, Dr. Grace Lee
Bolden, Dorothy Lee
Bommer, Minnie L.
Borges, Lynne MacFarlane
Bowman, Phillip Jess
Bracey, John Henry, Jr.
Bradley, Melvin LeRoy
Brazile, Donna L.
Breeding, Carl L.
Bridges, Ruby
Broadbent, Hydeia
Brown, Dr. Amos Cleophilus
Brown, Jim
Brown, Joseph Samuel
Brown, Zora Kramer
Brown-Wright, Flonzie B
Brutus, Dr. Dennis Vincent
Bryant, John
Burgess, Robert E., Sr.
Butts, Calvin Otis
Cafritz, Peggy Cooper
Campbell, Melanie L
Captain, Myrtle L
Childs, Josie L.
Ciccolo, Angela
Clayton, Eva
Cole, Charles Zhivaga
Coleman-Burns, Dr. Patricia Wen-
dolyn
Collins, Clifford Jacob
Colson, Lewis Arnold
Cosby, Camille Olivia Hanks
Dabney, David Hodges
Daniels, Richard D.
Daniels, Ron D.
Daughtry, Herbert Daniel
Dauphin, Borel C.
Davenport, Christian A.
Dejoie, Michael C
Demerson, Connie Marie
DiAna, DiAna
Dickson, Onias D, Jr.
Dorsett, Mary Alice
Doxie, Marvin Leon
Dulin, Joseph
Dunigan, Mayme O.
Dyer, Bernard Joel
Eason, Oscar, Jr.
Easton, Earnest Lee
Ebo, Antona
Edelman, Marian Wright
Edwards, Horace Burton
English, William E
Eure, Jerry Holton, Sr.
Evans, Akwasi Rozelle
Evers-Williams, Myrlie
Flack, William Patrick
Fletcher, Louisa Adaline

Fletcher, Robert E.
Francis, Livingston S
Gaines, Robert
Galloway, Lula Briggs
Goodson, Frances Elizabeth
Graham, James C, Jr.
Greely, M Gasby
Green, Geraldine D.
Greene, Jehmu
Greene, Sarah Moore
Gregory, Richard Claxton
Grier, Rosey
Griffin, Virgil
Groff, Regis F.
Guyton, Tyree
Hall, Kathryn Louise
Hamilton, Aubrey J.
Hammond, John B., III
Hare, Julia Reed
Harris, Daisy
Harris, Tricia R
Harvey, Jacqueline V.
Hayden, Carla Diane
Hayes, Dennis Courtland
Head, Dr. Laura Dean
Henderson, Wade
Henderson-Nocho, Audrey J
Hernandez, Aileen Clarke
Hill, Anita Faye
Hillman, Gracia
Hodges, Virgil Hall
Holman, Karriem Malik
Holmes, Mary Brown
Hooks, Frances Dancy
Hope, Julius Caesar
Hutchins, Rev. Markel
Ige, Dr. Dorothy W K
Irby, Galven
Isaac, Telesforo Alexander
Ivy, James E
Jackson, Dorothy R., J.D.
Jackson, Rev. Jesse Louis
Jackson, Michael Joseph
Jennings, Bernard Waylon-Handel
Johnson, Dr. Arthur J.
Johnson, Georgianna
Jones, David R.
Jones, Hardi Liddell
Jones, Johnnie Anderson
Jones, Yvonne De Marr
Joyner, Irving L
Kee, Marsha Goodwin
Kelly, John Paul
Khalfani, Salim
King, Earl B.
Kline, William M.
Lanier, Shelby, Jr.
Lassiter, Chad Dion
Lewis, Tom
Lillard, Kwame Leo
Lipscomb, Darryl L.
Lofton, Ernest
Logan, Warren E
Lowery, Carolyn T
Lucy Foster, Autherine
Mack, John W.
Malone, Dr. Cleo
Marshall, Pluria W.
Matthews, Virgil E.
McCane, Charlotte Antoinette
McFadden, Ernest
McIntosh, Rhodina Covington
Meeks, Reginald Kline
Mfume, Kweisi
Miller, Dr. Dennis Weldon
Milner, Thirman L.
Mitchell, Robert Lee, Sr.
Mitchell, Theo W
Moody, Anne
Morrison, Jacqueline
Moss, James Edward
Murphy, Laura W.
Nails, John Walker
Nalls, Patricia
Newman, Miller Maurice
Nickson, Sheila Joan
Nix, Roscoe Russa
Odom, Stonewall
Osborne, Gwendolyn Eunice
Owens, Dr. Hugo Armstrong
Perez, Altagracia
Powell, Addie Scott
Ransby, Barbara
Richards, William Earl
Richardson, George C
Richie, Winston Henry
Riggins, Lester
Riley, William Scott
Roberts, Janice L

Burnett, Calvin Waller
Burns, Ronald Melvin
Burroughs, Dr. Margaret Taylor
Cade, Walter, III
Camp, Kimberly
Carter, Allen D.
Carter, JoAnne Williams
Carter, Nanette Carolyn
Carter, Ora Williams
Catchings, Dr. Yvonne Parks
Clark, Claude Lockhart
Clark, Edward
Clay, Cliff
Clements, Walter H.
Collins, Paul
Conway, Wallace Xavier, Sr.
Cook, Jeffrey
Coppedge, Arthur L
Cortor, Eldzier
Dabbs, Henry Erven
Daniel, Mary Reed
Davis, Donald
Delsarte, Louis
DePillars, Murry Norman
Dixon, William R.
Dotson, Philip Randolph
Edmonds, Josephine E.
Edmunds, Allan L.
Ferguson, Dr. Robert Lee, Sr.
Fleming, Patricia Stubbs
Flores, Joseph R
Gibbs, Nathaniel K.
Gilchriest, Lorenzo
Gilliam, Sam, Jr.
Goodnight, Paul
Granger, Edwina C.
Grauer, Gladys Barker
Green, Jonathan
Greenfield, Mark Steven
Guyton, Tyree
Hampton, Phillip Jewel
Harden, Marvin
High, Freida
Jackson, Oliver L
Jackson, Suzanne Fitzallen
Johnson, John
Johnson, Luther E
Johnson, Timothy Julius, Jr.
Jones, Ben F
Jones, Richmond Addison
Knox, Simmie
Laird, Alan
Lark, Raymond
Lewis, Samella Sanders
Lindsay, Dr. Arturo
Locke, Donald
Martin, Ionis Bracy
Mayhew, Richard
McCullough, Geraldine
McMillan, Douglas James
McMillan, James C.
Merritt, Eleanor L
Mitchell, Dean Lamont
Mitchell, Rhonda Alma
Morrison, Prof. Keith Anthony
Norman, Bobby Don
Norwood, Dr. Tom
Olugebefola, Dr. Ademola
Onli, Turtel
Owens, Wallace, Jr.
Padgett, James A
Pajaud, William E, Jr.
Pindell, Howardena D
Pitts, George Edward
Rickson, Gary Ames
Ringgold, Faith
Robinson, Prof. Ella S.
Rogers, Charles D
Saint James, Synthia
Sandoval, Dolores S.
Saunders, Raymond
Sherman, C A
Simpson, Merton Daniel
Singletary, Deborah Denise
Smythe, Victor N.
Snowden, Sylvia Frances
Talley, Rev. Clarence
Tanksley, Ann Graves
Tomlinson, Dr. Robert
Twiggs, Dr. Leo Franklin
Walker, Kara
Walker, Larry Moore
Warmack, Gregory
Watkins, Ira Donnell
West, Pheoris
Whyte, Garrett
Wilkie, Earl Augustus T
Williams, Katherine
Williams, Prof. William Thomas

Wilson, Sandra E.
Woodson, Shirley A
Wright, Dmitri
Yarde, Prof. Richard Foster

Art, Visual—Sculpting

Allen, Tina
Anderson, William
Auld, Albert Michael
Battle, Turner Charles, III
Billington, Clyde, Jr.
Birch, Willie
Blayton-Taylor, Betty
Burroughs, Dr. Margaret Taylor
Carter, Allen D.
Catlett, Elizabeth
Chase-Riboud, Dr. Barbara DeWayne
Clark, Edward
Conwill, Houston Eugene
Cook, Jeffrey
Davidson, Earnest Jefferson
Douglas, Elizabeth (Betty) Asche
Foreman, Doyle
Guyton, Tyree
Hamilton, Edward N
Hardison, Ruth Inge
Harris, William Joseph, II
Hodgson-Brooks, Gloria J
Hubbard, Calvin L
Hunt, Richard Howard
Johnson, Prof. Stephanie Anne
Locke, Donald
Maynard, Valerie J
McCullough, Geraldine
McMillan, Douglas James
McMillan, James C.
Meeks, Larry Gillette
Montgomery, Evangeline Juliet
Nengudi, Senga
Owens, Wallace, Jr.
Padgett, James A
Pugh, Robert William, Sr.
Puryear, Martin
Scroggins, Bobby
Sherman, C A
Simms, Carroll Harris
Snowden, Gilda
Talley, Rev. Clarence
Warmack, Gregory
Williams, Prof. William Thomas
Wilson, Prof. Stanley Charles
Wimberley, Frank

Art, Visual—Not Elsewhere Classified

Adams, John Oscar
Allain, Stephanie
Allen, Tina
Anderson, William
Asma, Thomas M
Ausby, Ellsworth Augustus
Bechet, Ronald
Bell, Ngozi O
Benjamin, Dr. Tritobia Hayes
Bernard, Donald L
Billingsley, Ray C.
Billington, Clyde, Jr.
Bontemps, Jacqueline Marie Fonvielle
Brailsford, Marvin D.
Brandon, Barbara
Bright, Alfred Lee
Brown, Kay B.
Byrd, Joan Eda
Carter, Ora Williams
Carter, Yvonne P.
Catchings, Dr. Yvonne Parks
Catlett, Elizabeth
Claye, Charlene Marette
Conway, Curtis LaMont
Cortor, Eldzier
Crouther, Dr. Betty Jean
Curtis-Rivers, Susan Yvonne
Dalton, Raymond Andrew
Dash, Julie
Davis, Dr. Donald Fred
Diggs, Lawrence J
Douglas, Elizabeth (Betty) Asche
Dunnigan, Jerry
Edmonds, Josephine E.
Epting, Marion
Franklin, Prestonia D.
Gilliam, Sam, Jr.
Gittens, Anthony Edgar
Goodwin, Mac Arthur
Green, Jonathan
Harrison, Pearl Lewis
Hendricks, Barkley L.

Hilton, Stanley William, Jr.
Hogu, Barbara J Jones
Holmes, E Selean
Humphrey, Margo
Imhotep, Akbar
Ingram, Gregory Lamont
Irmagean, U.
Jackson, Earl
Jackson, Dr. Reginald Leo
Johnson, Benjamin Earl
Johnson, Clarissa
Johnson, Rita Falkener
Johnson, Prof. Stephanie Anne
Jones, Grace
Jones-Henderson, Napoleon
Kamau, Mosi
Kent, Herb
King-Hammond, Dr. Leslie
Ligon, Doris Hillian
Mayo, Barry Alan
McCane, Charlotte Antoinette
McCray, Almator Felecia
McElrath-Frazier, Wanda Faith
McGruder, Aaron
Mercer, Valerie June
Miller-Lewis, S Jill
Mills, Joey Richard
Moody, Dominique Faye
Morgan-Welch, Beverly Ann
Mudiku, Mary Esther
Nelson, Eileen F
Nengudi, Senga
Newton, Dr. James Elwood
Nixon, Norm Ellard
Owens, Andi
Parham, Dashton Daniel
Patterson, Curtis Ray
Patton, Leroy
Pearson, Clifton
Pinckney, Stanley
Pindell, Howardena D
Piper, Adrian Margaret Smith
Powell, Georgette Seabrooke
Raab, Madeline Murphy
Richardson, Frank
Rico, Dr. Tracey
Robinson, Anthony W
Robinson, John E
Robinson, Jontyle Theresa
Rogers, Shaun
Saar, Betye Irene
Sandridge, John Solomon
Sherman, C A
Simms, Carroll Harris
Simpson, Lorna
Sprout, Francis Allen
Staats, Dr. Florence Joan
Stallings, Henry E
Stewart, Jacqueline
Styles, Freddie L.
Temple, Herbert
Tessema, Tesfaye
Thomas, Matthew Manjusri, Jr.
Thompson, Lowell Dennis
Todd, Charles O
Walker, George Edward
Weaver, A. M.
Webb, Veronica Lynn
White, Clarence Dean
Whitfield, Jenenne
Williams, Prof. Daniel Salu
Wilson, Dr. Helen Tolson

Association Management

Adair, Andrew A.
Adams, Gregory Keith
Adams, Sheila J
Adams, V Toni
Addams, Robert David
Addison, Caroline Elizabeth
Aldridge, Karen Beth
Alexander, Harry Toussaint
Alexander, Vic
Alford, Brenda
Ali, Rasheedah Ziyadah
Allen, Dr. Edna Rowery
Allen, Terrell Allison, III
Ambrose, Ethel L.
Anderson, Doreatha Madison
Anderson, Elizabeth M
Anderson, J Morris
Anderson, Michael Wayne
Anderson, Nicholas Charles
Anderson, Perry L
Andrews, Carl R.
Anthony, Wendell
Aramburo, Sophie Watts
Bailey, Doris Jones
Bain, Linda Valerie

Baines, Dr. Tyrone Randolph
Banks, Waldo R., Sr.
Barefield, Ollie Delores
Barrow, Rev. Willie T.
Bates, Barbara Ann
Bates, Clayton Wilson, Jr.
Battle, Mark G.
Battle, Maurice Tazwell
Baugh, Florence Ellen
Beal, Lisa Suzanne
Beasley, Arlene A
Beckett, Justin F.
Bell, H. B.
Bell, Lawrence F.
Bell, Thom R.
Bernard, Nicole A.
Bettis, Anne Katherine
Billups, Mattie Lou
Bingham, Rebecca Josephine
Bishop, Cecil
Blanks, Wilhelmina E.
Bofill, Angela
Bogle, Robert W.
Bolden, Betty A.
Bolden, Dorothy Lee
Bolton, Julian Taylor
Bostic, Viola W
Bramble, Peter W. D.
Braxton, Harriet E.
Brooks, Carol
Brown, Annie Gibson
Brown, Bettye Jean
Brown, Claudell, Jr.
Brown, Dr. Joan P.
Brown, Dr. Malore Ingrid
Brown, William J.
Brown, Zora Kramer
Brown-Ellen, Kimi
Bryant, Carl
Bryant, Jesse A
Bryant, R. Kelly
Buford, James Henry
Bulger, Lucille O.
Bullock, Thurman Ruthe
Bumpers, Katrina
Bunte, Doris
Burgess, Dwight A.
Burrell, Judith Ann
Burton, William A
Bush, Lenoris
Callaway, Dwight W
Campbell, James W.
Campbell, Melanie L
Cannon, Edith H
Carey, Audrey L.
Cargile, C. B., Jr.
Carpenter, Barbara West
Carroll, Sally G.
Carson, Emmett D.
Carter, Gilbert Lino
Carter, Martin Joseph
Carter, Rubin
Cassis, Glenn Albert
Celestine, Von C
Chaney, Alphonse
Cherry, Lee Otis
Cherry, Robert Lee
Clark, Jesse B., III
Clemons, Linda K
Clingman, Kevin Loren
Coleman, Veronica F
Collins, Constance Renee Wilson
Collins, Rosecrain
Connor, Dolores Lillie
Cook, Ronald R
Cooper, William B.
Craven, Judith
Crawford, Jayne Suzanne
Cright, Lotess Priestley
Cromartie, Eugene Rufus
Crouther, Melvin S., Jr.
Cummings, James C., Jr.
Curvin, Robert
Cuyjet, Cynthia K.
Dailey, Quintin
Daniel, Mary Reed
Davis, Dr. John Albert
Davis, Milton C.
Davis, Norman Emanuel
Davis, Patricia C.
Davis, Preston Augustus
Davis, Ronald R.
Dean, Diane D
Dean, Willie B
Debnam, Chadwick Basil
Delaney, Willi
Delpit, Lisa Denise
de Passe, Suzanne
DePriest, Darryl Lawrence

Dickerson, Ralph
Dismuke, Mary Eunice
Dorsey, Harold Aaron
Dorsey, Herman Sherwood, Jr.
Dorsey, Sandra
Dossman, Curley M, Jr.
Douglas, Walter Edmond
Drake, Pauline Lilie
Drew, Thelma Lucille
Driggriss, Daphne Bernice Sutherland
Duncan, Geneva
Easley, Brenda Vietta
Eason-Steele, Elaine
Ecton, Virgil E.
Edeler, Phyllis
Edelman, Marian Wright
Edwards, John Loyd, III
Edwards, Tamra
Edwards-Aschoff, Patricia Joann
Eichelberger, Brenda
Elliott, John
Ellis, P. J.
Ellison, Bob
Emeka, Mauris L P
English, Alex
English, Henry L
Epps, C Roy
Epps, Dolzie C. B.
Evans, Amos James
Evans, Samuel London
Evans, Webb
Fair, Talmadge Willard
Farmer, Clarence
Fattah, Falaka
Felder, Ronald E.
Fields, William I, Jr.
Fisher, Shelley Marie
Flamer, John H
Flanagan, Elizabeth
Fletcher, Patricia Louise
Floyd, Dr. Jeremiah
Ford, Aileen W.
Ford, Kenneth A.
Ford, William L., Jr.
Foster, James H.
Foster, Jylla Moore
Fowler, Dr. Queen Dunlap
Foxx, Laura R.
Francis, Cheryl Margaret
Francis, Livingston S
Francis, Patrick John
Franklin, Eugene T., Jr.
Frazier, Eufaula Smith
Freeman, Kerlin
French, George Wesley, Jr.
Frisby, H. Russell, Jr.
Fudge, Marcia L
Fufuka, Tika NY
Futrell, Dr. Mary Alice Hatwood
Gaither, Israel L
Gales, James
Garrett, Cheryl Ann
Garrison, Esther F.
George, Alma Rose
George, Frankie
Gibbs, Dr. Sandra E
Glaude, Stephen A
Golden, Joyce Marie
Goodman, George D
Goodwin, Robert Kerr
Gordon, Claudia Lorraine
Goss, William Epp
Grace, George H
Graham, James C., Jr.
Graham, Scottie
Grant, Ashley
Gray, Derwin Lamont
Gray, Dr. E Delbert
Gray, William Herbert, III
Greaux, Cheryl Prejean
Griffey, Dick
Guiton Hill, Bonnie
Gunter, Laurie
Hambrick, Harold E., Jr.
Hamlar, Portia Yvonne Trenholm
Hardy, Dr. Freeman
Hargrave, Thomas Burkhardt, Jr.
Harper, Laydell Wood
Harris, Caspa L, Jr.
Harris, James Alexander
Harris, Lester L.
Harris, Ona C
Harris, Robert Eugene Peyton
Hasan, Aqeel Khatib
Haskins, William J.
Hasson, Nicole Denise
Hayes, Richard C.
Head, Edith

Heard, Georgina E
Hegger, Wilber L
Height, Dr. Dorothy I.
Henderson, Cheri Kaye
Henderson, Wade
Hendrix, Deborah Lynne
Herman, Alexis Margaret
Hill, Barbara A
Hill, Cynthia D
Hill, Mary Alice
Hill, Robert A.
Hill, Robert Lewis
Hill, Velma Murphy
Hillman, Gracia
Hillsman, Gerald C.
Hodges, Helene
Hodges, Virgil Hall
Holland, Louis A
Holliman, Argie N
Hollis, Mary Lee
Holman, Karriem Malik
Hooks, Frances Dancy
Hoover, Theressa
Hopkins, Perea M.
Horton, Stella Jean
Howard, Anica
Howard, Ellen D
Howard, Norman Leroy
Howell, Robert J., Jr.
Huff, William
Huffman, Rufus C.
Huggins, Hosiah, Jr.
Hughes, Hollis Eugene, Jr.
Hunter, Cecelia Corbin
Hunter, Dr. Mae M
Hurst, Beverly J.
Hutchinson, Jerome
Hutchinson, Louise Daniel
Ismial, Salaam Ibn
Jackson, Charles N., II
Jackson, Cheryle
Jackson, Deborah Byard Campbell
Jackson, Hiram
Jackson, Rev. Jesse Louis
Jackson, Jonathan
Jackson, Karen Eubanks
Jackson, Keith M.
Jackson, Leo Edwin
Jackson, Lillian
Jackson, Mattie J
Jackson, Norman A.
Jackson, Robert E.
Jackson, Ronald G
Jackson-Bennett, Rosalind
James, Dr. Betty Harris
Jefferson-Jenkins, Carolyn
Jennings, Bennie Alfred
Jeter, Clifton B
Jobe, Ben
Johnson, Dr. Arthur J.
Johnson, Bill Wade
Johnson, Cleveland, Jr.
Johnson, Frank J., Jr.
Johnson, Geneva B.
Johnson, Esq. Harry E, Sr.
Johnson, John J
Johnson, Marjorie Lynn
Johnson, Mervil V.
Johnson, Dr. Shirley B
Johnston, Henry Bruce
Jolly, Elton
Jones, Alexander R.
Jones, Booker Tee, Sr.
Jones, Esq. Ernest Edward
Jones, Francis R
Jones, Geri Duncan
Jones, Johnnie Anderson
Jones, Monique
Jones, Richard Julius
Jones, Rosemary M
Jones, Thomas Wade
Jordan, Frederick E.
Jordan, J Paul
Jordan, Marjorie W.
Jordan, Patricia Carter
Jordan, Vernon Eulion
Joseph, James Alfred
Keith, Luther
Kelley, William E.
Kennedy, Ray C
Kennedy, Teresa Kay-Aba
Kenny, James A
Kidd, Herbert, Jr.
King, Dexter
King, Ruby E.
King, William Carl
Kington, Raynard S
Kinloch, Jerome
Kispert, Dorothy Lee

Knight, Sammy D., Jr.
Knight, Walter R.
Knox, Marshall
LaCour, Nathaniel Hawthorne
Ladd, Florence Cawthorne
Lafayette, Bernard
Lanier, Horatio Axel
Lawrence, Edward
Lawrence, Elliott
Lawrence, John Edward
Lawyer, Vivian
Lee, Margaret S
Lee, Oliver B.
Lee, Shirley Freeman
LeGrand, Yvette Marie
Leigh, Fredric H
Levy, Valerie Lowe
Lewis, Dr. Bettye Davis
Lewis, Lillian J.
Lightfoot, Jean Drew
Little, Reuben R.
Locket, Arnold, Jr.
Love, Roosevelt Sam
Lowery, Carolyn T
Lytle, Marilyn Mercedes
Mack, John W.
Mackey, John
Maddox, Julius A
Madhubuti, Haki R
Mallette, Carol L
Malveaux, Antoinette Marie
Marrs, Dr. Stella
Marsh, Alphonso Howard
Marshall, Joseph Earl, Jr.
Marshall, Pluria W.
Martin, Dr. Annie B.
Martin, Arnold Lee, Jr.
Martin, Hosea L
Martin, Dr. Rev. Lawrence Raymond
Mason, Dr. Cheryl Annette
Mayes, McKinley
May-Pittman, Ineva
McClinton, Curtis R., Jr.
McCloud, Thomas Henry
McClung, Willie David
McGoodwin, Dr. Roland C
McGuire, Jean Mitchell
McLean, Dollie Clarice H
McRoy, Dr. Ruth Gail
Meaux, Ronald
Merritt, William T
Mesa, Mayra L
Metoyer, Rosia G
Metters, Dr. Samuel
Meyers, Dr. Rose M.
Miller, Rev. Anthony Glenn
Miller, Frank Lee, Jr.
Miller, Rev. Kevin D
Miller, Marquis David
Miller, William Nathaniel
Miller-Pope, Consuelo Roberta
Millett, Ricardo A.
Milner, Thirman L.
Milton, LeRoy
Mims, Marjorie Joyce
Mims, Rhonda
Mincey, W. James, Jr.
Minter, Steven Alan
Minter, Wilbert Douglas, Sr.
Mitchell, William Grayson
Mitchem, Dr. Arnold Levy
Moore, Cleotha Franklin
Moore, Evelyn K.
Morrison, Jacqueline
Moseley, Frances Kenney
Moss, Tanya Jill
Muhammad, Akbar A
Muhammad, Benjamin Chavis
Muhammad, Shirley M.
Murphy, Laura W.
Murray, Edna McClain
Nabors, Jesse Lee
Nelson, Larry
Nelson, Richard Y., Jr.
Newbille, Cynthia
Nix, Rick
Nixon, James Melvin
Norman, Moses C
Northern, David A
O'Banner-Owens, Jeanette
O'Brien, Mary Nell
Ohene-Fremprong, Kwaku
Orticke, Leslie Ann
Owens, Kelly D
Palmer, Elliott B., Sr.
Palmer, Stephanie
Parker, Anthony L
Parker, Bernard F., Jr.
Parker, Dr. William C, Jr.

Patterson, Barbara Ann
Pearson, Jesse S.
Peeples, Audrey Rone
Pender, Mel
Perkins, John M.
Peterson, Alan Herbert
Phifer, B Janelle Butler
Phillips, Frances Caldwell
Philpott, Ethel
Pickrum, Michael
Polk, Richard A.
Porter, Michael LeRoy
Pounds, Dr. Augustine Wright
Preston, Eugene Anthony
Price, Brenda G
Price, Hugh Bernard
Pride, John L.
Priestley, Marilyn
Rasheed, Fred
Rayford, Brenda L.
Reed, Joe Louis
Reynolds, James F.
Rhea, Michael
Rhodes, Audrey B.
Rhodes, Jacob A
Richardson, Linda Waters
Richardson, Timothy L
Ritter, Thomas J.
Rivers, Dorothy
Roach, Lee
Robinson, Albert M.
Robinson, Denauvo M.
Robinson, George Ali
Robinson, Jack E
Robinson, Kenneth Eugene
Robinson, Renault Alvin
Rodgers-Rose, LaFrances Audrey
Rodriguez, Doris L.
Romans, Ann
Roscoe, Wilma J.
Roshell, Pamela P
Rowe, Jimmy L.
Runnels, Bernice M.
Sampson, Dr. Calvin Coolidge
Sanders, Lina
Sandler, Joan D
Sandy Miller, Jones
Saulny, Cyril
Saunders, John Edward
Saunders, William Joseph
Sawyer, Alfred M.
Scales, Robert L.
Scott, Albert Nelson
Scott, Dr. Mary Shy
Scott, Michael W
Seale, Bobby
Sellers, Walter G.
Shamwell, Ronald L
Shaw, Melvin B
Shepphard, Dr. Charles Bernard
Shields, Vincent O.
Simmelkjaer, Dr. Robert T
Simmons, James Richard
Simmons, Shirley Davis
Simpson-Watson, Dr. Ora Lee
Singleton, Isaac, Sr.
Singleton, Robert
Small, Israel G.
Small, William
Smith, Dr. Alonzo Nelson
Smith, Beverly Evans
Smith, Debbie A.
Smith, Dr. Estus
Smith, Gwendolyn Iloani
Smith, Dr. Jane E
Smith, John Raye
Smith, Lafayette Kenneth
Smith, Marie F
Smith, Marzell
Smith, Dr. Maxine Atkins
Smith, Shirley LaVerne
Sneed, Michael
Spand, Rev. Dr. Margot
Spears Jones, Patricia Kay
Springs, Lenny F
Stanley, Dr. Hilbert Dennis
Stanton, Robert G
Starks, John Levell
Staten, Everett R
Stepp, Marc
Sterling, Dr. Jeffrey Emery
Stevens, Reatha J.
Stevens, Timothy S
Stewart, Diana Brown
Stinson, Donald R
Stockton, Clifford
Stone, Aubry L
Streeter, Denise Williams
Stubblefield, Raymond M.

Sylvester, Odell Howard, Jr.
Taliaferro, George
Tasco, Marian B.
Taylor, Carl
Taylor, Marie de Porres
Taylor, Vivian A.
Thomas, Barbara Louise
Thomas, Bette
Thomas, Eunice S.
Thomas, Hollis
Thomas, Johnny B.
Thomas-Williams, Gloria M.
Thompson, Rep. Betty Lou
Thompson, Linda Jo
Thompson-Moore, Ann
Thomson, Alice G
Thornton, Osie M.
Thorpe, Wesley Lee, Sr.
Thurston, Charles Sparks
Timberlake, John Paul
Todman, Terence Alphonso
Tokley, Joanna Nutter
Townsend, Dr. Nkechit Florence
Traylor, Dr. Horace Jerome
Tripp, Dr. Luke Samuel
Trueheart, William E.
Tucker, Paul, Jr.
Tukufu, Darryl S
Turner, Bennie L
Turner, Ervin
Turner, Johnnie Rodgers
Veal, Howard Richard
Vieira, Franklin
Vinson, Nathan
Walker, Eugene Kevin
Walker, Lula Aquillia
Walker, Tanya Rosetta
Walker, Dr. William Sonny
Wall, Tara
Walsh, Everald J.
Ward, Bill
Ward, Haskell G
Ware, Charles Jerome
Washington, Carl
Washington, Jacquelin Edwards
Washington, Rudy
Watson, Carole M.
Watson, Dennis Rahiim
Watson, Joann Nichols
Weathers, Margaret A.
Wesley, Clarence E.
White, Robert L.
White, William T., III
Whitfield, Jenenne
Wilber, Margie Robinson
Wiley, Margaret Z. Richardson
Williams, Dr. Ann E A
Williams, Carol H
Williams, Eddie Nathan
Williams, Geneva J.
Williams, Herman
Williams, James E., Jr.
Williams, Kenneth Herbert
Williams, Dr. Lea E
Williams, Novella Stewart
Williams, Reginald T.
Williams, Ruby Mai
Willis, Andrew
Wilson, Cleo Francine
Wilson, Donald P.
Winston, Dr. Neil Emerson
Woodhouse, Rossalind Yvonne
Woods, Willie
Wooldridge, David
Worth, Janice Lorraine
Wright, Clarence, Sr.
Wright, Robert L.
Wyke, Joseph Henry
Young, Wallace L., Jr.

Astronomy
See **Physics/Astronomy**

Athletics
See **Sports—Amateur;
Sports—Professional/
Semiprofessional; Sports—Not
Elsewhere Classified; Sports
Coaching/Training/ Managing/
Officiating**

Auditing
See **Accounting/Auditing**

Automobile Industry
See **Manufacturing—Motor
Vehicles; Retail Trade—Motor

Vehicles, Parts, and Services;
Wholesale Trade—Motor
Vehicles and Parts**

Aviation
See **Airline Industry**

Banking/Financial Services
Adams, Cecil Ray
Aikens, Alexander E
Allen, Benjamin P., III
Anderson, James
Anderson, Dr. Marcellus J., Sr.
Andrews, George G., III
Arbuckle, John Finley, Jr.
Arnold, Rudolph P
Arrington, Lloyd M., Jr.
Ashburn, Vivian Diane
Avery-Blair, Lorraine
Backstrom, Don
Baker, Darryl Brent, Sr.
Baltimore, Roslyn Lois
Baptista, Howard
Baranco, Juanita P.
Barkley, Mark E.
Barnes, N Kurt
Baskette, Ernest E., Jr.
Bates, Yasmin T.
Batties, Thomas L.
Battle, Jacqueline
Beal, Bernard
Becote, Fohliette W
Bell, Gordon Philip
Bell, Joseph N.
Bell, Karl I.
Bell, Melvyn Clarence
Belmear, Horace Edward
Bennett, Joyce Annette
Benson, Sharon Marie
Bernard, Nesta Hyacinth
Biggins, J Veronica
Bland, Edward
Blount, Heidi Lynne
Bludson-Francis, Vernett Michelle
Booker, Simeon S.
Boswell, Bennie
Bowie, Dr. Walter C.
Bowman, Dr. James E.
Boyd, Kimberly
Boyd, Marvin
Braddock, Carol T
Bradshaw, Wayne-Kent
Brandford, Napoleon
Bridgeman, Donald Earl
Brigham, Freddie M
Brimmer, Dr. Andrew Felton
Brooks, Don Locellus
Brown, Eddie C.
Brown, John C., Jr.
Brown, John Mitchell, Sr.
Brown, Joyce
Brown, Kwame R
Brown, Reuben D
Brown, Rose Denise
Brown, Todd
Brown, Todd C.
Brown-Harris, Ann
Bryant, Kathryn Ann
Bryant-Ellis, Paula D.
Bryant-Reid, Johanne
Buford, Wesley R.
Burgin, Bruce L
Burrus, Clark
Burton, Barbara Ann
Bush, Mary K.
Carlton, Pamela Gean
Carpenter, Clarence E., Jr.
Carpenter, Lewis
Carr, Roderich Marion
Carroll, Raoul Lord
Carter, Kevin Antony
Caudle, Anthony, Sr.
Chambers, Caroline E.
Chapman, Nathan A
Chappell, Emma Carolyn
Chatterjee, Lois Jordan
Chavis, Omega Rochelle
Chivis, Martin Lewis
Christophe, Cleveland A
Clark, Walter L
Clay, Timothy Byron
Clingman, Kevin Loren
Cochran, Daniel Chester
Cole, Deborah A.
Coleman, Cecil R.
Coleman, Columbus E., Jr.
Coles, John Edward
Cook, Frederick Norman

Cook, Rufus
Coombs, Fletcher
Corley, Leslie M
Cornwell, W. Don
Counts, Allen W
Cowans, Alvin Jeffrey
Crews, William Sylvester
Cummings, Aeon L
Cunningham, William Michael
Curry, Levy Henry
Curtis-Bauer, M Benay
Dale, Bryant
Daniels, Frederick L., Jr.
Daniels, LeGree Sylvia
Davidson, Lurlean G.
Davidson, Rick Bernard
Davis, Alfred C., Sr.
Davis, Bruce
Davis, Denice Faye
Davis, Nigel S
Davis, Sonia
DeGeneste, Henry Irving
Derricotte, C. Bruce
Dewey, George
Dickens, Jacoby
Dickson, Reginald D.
Disher, Spencer C, III
Dixon, Richard Nathaniel
Doig, Elmo H.
Dolby, Edward C.
Doley, Ambassador Harold E
Dudley, Eunice Mosley
Dugger, Edward, III
Dunmore, Lawrence A., Jr.
Eagan, Catherine B
Easton, Richard James
Eley, Randall Robbi
Ellis, Ernest W.
Ellis, Rodney
Elmore, Stephen A, Sr.
Evans, Charlotte A.
Evans, Cheryl Lynn
Evans, Leon Edward, Jr.
Ewing, Samuel Daniel
Farmer, Hilda Wooten
Farrell, Cheryl Layne
Ferguson, Johnnie Nathaniel
Ferguson, Roger W, Jr.
Fields, Samuel Bennie
Fierce, Hughlyn F.
Fisher, Ronald L, Sr.
Flemming, Clente
Flood, Eugene, Jr.
Flores, Leo
Follmer, Paul L
Forde, Fraser Philip, Jr.
Forte, Linda Diane
Foster, William K.
Fowler, James Daniel, Jr.
Frasier, Ralph Kennedy
Garrett, James Edward, Jr.
Garrison-Corbin, Patricia Ann
Gary, Howard V
Gibbs, William Lee
Gibson, Kala
Glenn, Diane
Grady, Walter E.
Graham, Donald
Graves, Clifford Wayne
Gray, Ronald A
Grayson, Derek L., II
Grayson, Stanley Edward
Green, Anita Lorraine
Green, Dennis O.
Green, Ernest G.
Green, Gloria J
Green, Hydia Lutrice
Greene, Frank S
Greer, Baunita
Gregg, Lucius Perry, Jr.
Grigsby, Calvin Burchard
Grigsby, David P
Grisham, Arnold T.
Grist, Ronald
Guyton, Louise Green
Haddon, James Francis
Hamer, Dr. Judith Ann
Hamilton, John M
Hamlar, Jocelyn B
Hammonds, Alfred
Hannah, Mosie R.
Harrington, Gerald E
Harris, Jeanette G.
Harris, Nathaniel C., Jr.
Harris, Stanley Eugene
Harrison, Delbert Eugene
Hart, Ronald O.
Harvey, Richard R
Haskins, Joseph, Jr.

Haskins, Morice Lee, Jr.
Hatchett, Paul Andrew
Hayden, William Hughes
Heard, Blanche Denise
Hedgepeth, Leonard
Henley, Vernard W.
Herndon, Phillip George
Hill, Henry, Jr.
Hobson, Mellody L.
Hodge, Aleta S.
Hodge, Norris
Holloman, Thaddeus Bailey
Holloway, Harris M.
Holmes, Richard Bernard
Houston, Seawadon L.
Howard, Linwood E.
Howard, Osbie L
Hudson, Elbert T.
Hudson, Paul C.
Hughes, Robert Danan
Hull, Everson Warren
Humphrey, Marian J
Hunt, Eugene
Hunter, Bryan C.
Hutchinson, James J., Jr.
Irvin, Dennis J.
Irvin, Milton M
Jackson, Pazel, Jr.
Jackson, Sandra Stevens
James, Robert Earl
Jeffers, Grady Rommel
Jenkins, Carlton J.
Jennings, Sylvesta Lee
Johnson, Alexander Hamilton
Johnson, Cleveland, Jr.
Johnson, David E.
Johnson, Donna Alligood
Johnson, Ernest L.
Johnson, Mitchell A
Johnson, Dr. Pompie Louis, Jr.
Johnson, Stephen L
Johnson, William C.
Johnson, William T
Jones, Leora Sam
Jones, Shalley A
Jordan, Carolyn D
Jordan, Emma Coleman
Joseph-McIntyre, Mary
Joyner, Lauren Celeste
Kaalund, Sekou H
Kea, Arleas Upton
Kelly, John Paul
King, Colbert I
Kirkland, Gwendolyn V
Knight, W H
Lambert, Joseph C.
Lanier, Willie
Lansey, Yvonne F.
Lavelle, Robert R.
Law, M Eprevel
Laymon, Heather R
Lazard, Betty
Lee, Aubrey Walter, Jr.
Lee, E Jacques
Lee, John M
Lee, John Robert E.
Leigh, Fredric H
Lemon, Ann
Lewis, Andre
Lewis, Michael W
Lewis, Thomas P.
Lewis, Willard C
Linyard, Richard
London, Gloria D.
Loney, Carolyn Patricia
Long, Steffan
Loving, James Leslie
Lowery, Donald Elliott
Lyons, Lamar Andrew
Lyons, Patrick Alan
Mack, C.
Maitland, Tracey
Malone, Claudine Berkeley
Manley, Bill
Mariel, Serafin
Martin, Charles Howard
Martin, I Maximillian
Mausi, Shahida Andrea
Mayes, Doris Miriam
McBeth-Reynolds, Sandra Kay
McClure, Fredrick H L
McDonald, Alden J
McEachern, D Hector
McLin, Lena Johnson
McMullins, Tommy
McQueen, Kevin Paige
McReynolds, Elaine A.
Miller, George Carroll, Jr.
Miller, James

Miller, Ward Beecher
Milner, Michael Edwin
Mitchell, Carlton S
Montgomery, George Louis, Jr.
Moorehead, Justin Leslie
Mordecai, David K A
Morris, Vivian Louise
Morris, William Howard
Moses, Edwin
Mosley, Edna Wilson
Mosley, Elwood A
Mullings, Paul
Myles, Wilbert
Naphtali, Ashirah Sholomis
Nash, Bob J.
Neal, Mario Lanza
Newell, Daryl
Newsome, Ronald Wright
Newton, Ernest E., II
Nichols, George
Oliver, Kenneth Nathaniel
Ourlicht, David E.
Owens, Mercy P
Parker, George Anthony
Patterson, Rev Clinton David
Patterson, Ronald E
Pearce, Richard Allen
Pearson, Michael Novel
Pease, Denise Louise
Pendergraft, Michele M
Penn, Dr. Suzanne Y.
Perine, Martha Levingston
Perkins, Charles Windell
Perry, Clifford, III
Perry-Mason, Gail F
Phillips, Wilburn R.
Pierson, Kathryn A
Plummer, Milton
Poole, James F.
Pope, Mirian Artis
Powell, Arthur F
Powell, Kemper O
Powell, Kenneth Alasandro
Powell, Richard Maurice
Prestwidge-Bellinger, Barbara
  Elizabeth
Prezeau, Louis E
Price, JoAnn H
Prioleau, Peter Sylvester
Prout, Patrick M
Pryor, Malcolm D.
Purnell, Mark W.
Quick, George Kenneth
Raines, Franklin D.
Ramirez, Richard M
Remy, Donald M
Rice, Edward A.
Rice, Emmett J.
Rice, Norman Blann
Richards, George
Riggs, Dr. Enrique A
Robinson, Virgil, Jr.
Robinson-Ivy, Jacqueline
Rodgers, Horace J.
Rodgers, Napoleon
Rodman, Michael Worthington
Rogers, John W.
Roland, Benautrice, Jr.
Ross, Cathye P
Roundfield, Danny Thomas
Royster, Don M, Sr.
Rucker, Alston Louis
Russell, George Alton, Jr.
Sanders, Steven LeRoy
Saunders, Kim D
Savage, Frank
Scott, Prof. Charlotte Hanley
Scott, James Henry
Scott, Joseph M
Seidenberg, Mark
Sellars, Harold Gerard
Shealey, Richard W
Simmons, Craig, Sr.
Simmons, Norbert
Simmons, Willie
Sims-Person, LeAnn Michelle
Singleton, Harold, III
Sloan, Maceo Kennedy
Small, Eric
Smith, Debbie A.
Smith, Estella W
Smith, Stanley G.
Smith, Thelma J
Smith, Voydee
Smith, William Gene
Smith, William Xavier
Snowden, Gail
Sobers, Waynett A., Jr.
Spaulding, Aaron Lowery

Speed, James H, Jr.
Spencer, Anthony Lawrence
Spencer, Donald Andrew
Spooner, Richard C.
Stahnke, William E.
Stamper, Henry J.
Staten, Mark Eugene
Stephens, Brooke Marilyn
Stephenson, Dama F
St Etienne, Gregory Michael
Stewart, Raymond C
Stith, Antoinette Freeman
Stokes, Bunny
Strickland, Herman William, Jr.
Sudarkasa, Michael Eric Mabogunje
Sullivan, Ernest Lee
Sutton, Wilma Jean
Sweat, Sheila Diane
Tate, Brett Andre
Taylor, Sterling R
Thomas, Earle Frederick
Thomas, Ralph Albert
Thornton, Wayne T
Thurman, Cedric Douglas
Tidwell, Isaiah
Tomlin, Josephine D
Toon, Albert L.
Tucker, James F.
Turner, Jesse, Jr.
Turner, Jesse H
Turnipseed, Carl Wendell
Turpin, Mel Harrison
Utendahl, John O
Van Amson, George Louis
Vaughan, Gerald R.
Wade, Joyce K
Walker, Arman Kennis
Walker, John Leslie
Ward, Calvin
Warder, John Morgan
Washington, Ada Catherine
Washington, William
Waters, John W
Watson, Daniel
Watson, Theresa Lawhorn
Watters, Linda A
Wheat, James Weldon, Jr.
White, Edward Clarence
Whitfield, Alphonso
Wiggins, Paul R
Wilcox, Thaddeus
Wilkes, Jamaal
Wilkins, Herbert Priestly
Williams, Christopher J
Williams, E Thomas
Williams, Edward Joseph
Williams, Joseph Barbour
Williams, Joseph Lee
Williams Boyd, Sheila Anne
Willis, Levy E
Wilson, Lance Henry
Wilson, Leon E, Jr.
Wilson, Thomas A, Jr.
Winslow, Kenneth Paul
Winters, Kenneth E.
Wood, Garland E.
Woodson, Alfred F
Wright, Deborah C.
Wright, James W
Yates, Mark
Yohannes, Daniel W
Young, James E
Young, Terrence Anthony
Young, Tommy Scott

Biochemistry

Bargonetti, Jill
Clarke, Dr. Donald Dudley
Daley, Thelma Thomas
Daly, Dr. Frederica Y
Davis, Leodis
Dyce, Barbara J.
Gamble, Dr. Wilbert
Harris, Dr. Don Navarro
Hogan, Dr. James Carroll
Hopson, Kevin M
Jones, George H.
Mitchell, Dr. Earl Douglass, Jr.
Pointer, Dr. Richard H
Sanders, Dr. Robert B
Schooler, Dr. James Morse
Scott, Dr. Kenneth Richard
Smith, Dr. Edgar Eugene
Sudbury, Leslie G.
Ward, Velma Lewis

Washington, Dr. Linda Phaire
West, William Lionel

Biology/Microbiology

Ampy, Dr. Franklin R.
Babero, Dr. Bert Bell
Bargonetti, Jill
Bass, Harry S.
Cameron, Joseph A.
Christopher, John A.
Cobb, Dr. Jewel Plummer
Coleman, James William
Comer, Dr. Marian Wilson
Cook, Dr. Nathan Howard
Craft, Dr. Thomas J
Dave, Alfonzo, Jr.
Dottin, Dr. Robert Philip
Emeagwali, Dale Brown
Essien, Dr. Francine
Eure, Herman Edward
Foster, Alvin Garfield
Foster, Lloyd L
Fuller, Almyra Oveta
Hammond, Dr. Benjamin Franklin
Harris, Dr. Geraldine E.
Harris, Dr. Mary Styles
Henderson, Dr. Nannette S.
Hendricks, Marvin B.
Hogan, Dr. James Carroll
Hollingsworth, John Alexander
Holt, Dr. James Stokes, III
Hopkins, Thomas Franklin
Hull, Dr. George, Jr.
Jackson, Earl, Jr.
Jackson, Dr. Julius Hamilton
Jay, Dr. James M.
Johnson, Dr. Charles Edward
Jones, George H.
Leak, Prof. Lee Virn
LeFlore, Dr. William B.
Love, Dr. George Hayward
Madu, Anthony Chisaraokwu
Meade, Alston B., Sr.
Miller, Anna M.
Nance, Jesse J., Jr.
Parker, Charles McCrae
Parson, Willie L.
Patton, Dr. Curtis Leverne
Pickett, Cecil Bruce
Porter, Dr. Clarence A.
Salters, Dr. Charles Robert
Sanders, Dr. Robert B
Taylor, Dr. Welton Ivan
Watkins, Dr. Michael Thomas
Wells, Roderick Arthur

Botany

Haugstad, May Katheryn
Hicks, Dr. Arthur James
Hill, Dr. Ray Allen
Hodge, William Anthony
Warren, Herman Lecil

Building/Construction (*See Also* **Retail Trade— Building/Construction Materials; Wholesale Trade—Building/ Construction Materials**)

Adams, Leonard E, Jr.
Apea, Joseph Bennet Kyeremateng
Argrette, Joseph
Bates, William J
Batteast, Robert V.
Bell, Robert Wesley
Bolling, Bruce C.
Bowser, Hamilton Victor
Brown, Raymond Madison
Brown, Rodney W
Brown, Wesley Anthony
Burges, Melvin E.
Burks, Juanita Pauline
Bynam, Sawyer Lee, III
Byrd, Lumus, Jr.
Cargile, William, III
Carter, Thomas, II
Carter, Thomas Allen
Cason, Joseph L.
Chapman, Cleveland M.
Chigbu, Gibson Chuks
Coleman, John H.
Coles, John Edward
Cooke, Thomas H, Jr.
Cooper, Albert, Sr.
Copeland, Richard Allen
Cotton, Garner
Davis, Frank Allen
Davis, Melvin Lloyd
Davis, Ronald

James, Gillette Oriel
James, Rev. William M.
Jefferson, Austin, Jr.
Jeffries, Dr. Rosalind R
Jemison, Rev. Dr. Theodore Judson
Jerkins, Jerry Gaines
Jerome, Joseph D
Johnson, Clinton Lee
Johnson, Cynthia
Johnson, James H.
Johnson, Dr. Leroy
Johnson, Paul Edwin
Johnson, Willie
Johnson Cook, Suzan Denise
Jones, Albert Allen
Jones, Enoch
Jones, Dr. Lawrence N.
Jones, Rev. Leon C.
Jones, Ozro T., Jr.
Jones, Rev. Robert Earl
Jones, Spencer
Jones, Vernon A., Jr.
Jones, Dr. William Jenipher
Jones, Dr. William O.
Jordan, Charles Wesley
Jordan, John Wesley
Jordan, Rev. Ternae T
Joyner, Claude C.
Kee, John P.
Kelly, Rev. Dr. Herman Osby
Kelly, James Clement
Kenoly, Ron
Kimbrough, Charles Edward
Kinchlow, Ben
King, Rev. Bernice Albertine
Kirk-Duggan, Cheryl Ann
Knight, Rev. Carolyn Ann
LaGarde, Rev. Frederick H
Lane, William Keith
Langford, Victor C., III
Lawson, James M., Jr.
Lemmons, Herbert Michael
Lewis, Dr. Alvin
Lewis, Harold T
Lewis, Henry S., Jr.
Lewis, Kenneth Dwight
Lewis, Dr. Lloyd Alexander
Lewis, Robert Louis
Lewis, Rev. Theodore Radford
Lindsey, S. L.
Liverpool, Herman Oswald
Lloyd, Rev. Dr. J Anthony
Long, Eddie L.
Lovett, Leonard
Lowe, Eugene Yerby
Lowery, Rev. Dr. Joseph E.
Luther, Lucius Calvin
Lynch, Rev. Lorenzo A, Sr.
Mack, Charles Richard
Madison, Samuel C.
Manley, John Ruffin
Marshall, Anita
Marshall, Rev. Calvin Bromley
Martin, Edward
Martin, James Tyrone
Martin, Dr. Rev. Lawrence Raymond
Martin, Dr. Richard Cornish
Mason, Luther Roscoe
Massey, James Earl
Mayes, Clinton, Jr.
McCall, H. Carl
McClendon, Clarence E.
McGuire, Raymond J.
McKenzie, Rev. Vashti
McKinney, Jacob K.
McMillan, Dr. Mae F.
McNeal, Rev. John Alex
McNeill, Cerves Todd
McNorriell, Mozell M.
McPhatter, Thomas H.
McWhorter, Grace Agee
Medford, Isabel
Mickle, Andrea Denise
Middleton, Rev. Dr. Richard Temple
Miles, Rachel Jean
Mims, Raymond Everett, Sr.
Minus, Homer Wellington
Mitchell, Rev. Dr. Ella Pearson
Mitchell, Sadie Stridiron
Montague, Nelson C.
Montgomery, Dwight Ray
Montgomery, James C.
Moore, Helen D S
Moore, Oscar William
Morgan, Rev. Mary H Ethel
Morrison, Dr. Juan LaRue, Sr.
Muhammad, Benjamin Chavis
Murray, Cecil Leonard
Murray, Thomas W., Jr.

Nabors, Michael C.R.
Napoleon, Harry Nelson
Neighbors, Dolores Maria
Nelms, Ommie Lee
Nelson, Otha Curtis
Newbold, Simeon Eugene, Sr.
Newman, Nathaniel
Newsome, Rev. Burnell
Newsome, Dr. Clarence Geno
Nicholson, Aleathia Dolores
Nixon, Rev. Felix Nathaniel
Notice, Rev. Guy Symour
Oates, Caleb E.
O'Hara, Leon P
Okunor, Dr. Shiame
Oliver, Donald Byrd
Ollison, Ruth Allen
O'Neal, Rev. Eddie S
Outlaw, Dr. Patricia Anne
Owens, Chandler D.
Paddio-Johnson, Dr. Eunice Alice
Pannell, William E
Parker, Matthew
Parrish, John Henry
Patrick, Charles Namon, Jr.
Patterson, Alonzo B., Jr.
Patterson, Rev Clinton David
Patterson, Bishop Gilbert Earl
Pearson, Bishop Carlton Demetrius
Pearson, Herman B.
Perkins, Dr. James Connelle
Perry, Rev. Jerald Isaac, Sr.
Pinder, Nelson W.
Poindexter, Charles L. L.
Pollard, Dr. Alton Brooks, III
Portee, Rev. Dr. Frank
Porter, Ellis Nathaniel
Porter, Bishop Henry Lee
Porter, Rev. Dr. Kwame John R.
Powell-Jackson, Dr. Rev. Bernice
Price, Dr. Joseph L.
Pruitt, Fr. Alonzo Clemons
Pruitt, Rev. Eddie Jay Delano
Pulliam, Betty E
Rambison, Dr. Amar B
Rasberry, Robert Eugene
Ratliff, Joe Samuel
Redd, Albert Carter, Sr.
Reed, Florine
Reed, Kwame Osei
Reid, Dr. Milton A.
Ricard, Rev. John H
Richardson, Dr. Lacy Franklin
Richardson, Louis M, Jr.
Roane, Rev. Glenwood P, Sr.
Robertson, Dr. Benjamin W
Robinson, Rev. Edsel F
Robinson, Frank J.
Robinson, Rev. Joseph
Rogers, Rev. Dr. Oscar Allan
Rogers, Victor Alvin
Rollins, Dr. Richard Albert
Rowe, Dr. Nansi Irene
Roye, Monica R Hargrove
Rucker, Raleigh
Sanders, James William
Sandidge, Dr. Oneal C
Scott, Dr. Leonard Stephen
Shaw, Martini
Sheard, Rev. John Drew
Shields, Rev. Landrum Eugene
Shipley, Rev. Anthony J
Shopshire, Dr. James Maynard
Simpson, Samuel G.
Singleton, Harold Douglas
Sloan, Edith Barksdale
Smith, Rev. Elijah
Smith, George Walker
Smith, Gregory Robeson, Sr.
Smith, Harold Gregory
Smith, J. Alfred, Sr.
Smith, Dr. Luther Edward
Smith, Paul
Smith, Rev. Dr. Wallace Charles
Snead, Dr. Willie T, Sr.
Spann, Paul Ronald
Speaks, Ruben L.
Stamps, Lynman A., Sr.
Steele, Tommy
Stewart, Dr. Warren Hampton
Stewart, Dr. William H.
Stotts, Valmon D.
Suggs, William Albert
Sutton, Gloria W.
Swain, Dr. Ronald L
Swiggett, Ernest L
Talley, Rev. Clarence
Taylor, Hycel B.
Taylor, Martha

Thomas, James Samuel
Thomas, Rev. Walter Scott
Thompson, Rev. Carl Eugene
Timmons-Toney, Rev. Deborah Denise
Tolliver, Rev. Joel
Tolliver, Dr. Richard Lamar
Torain, Rev. Tony William
Tottress, Richard Edward
Trice, Juniper Yates
Tuggle, Rev. Reginald
Turman, Kevin
Turner, Eugene
Tyner, Charles R.
Underwood, King James
Vaughan, Rev. James Edward
Venable, Rev. Robert Charles
Vivian, Cordy Tindell
Waits, Rev. Va Lita Francine
Warner, Edward L.
Washington, Emery, Sr.
Washington, Rev. Henry L
Washington, Johnnie M.
Weathers, J. Leroy
Weathersby, Joseph Brewster
Weaver, William Courtsworthy, II
Webb, Joe
White, Woodie W
Wiggins, Daphne Cordelia
Wiggins, William H., Jr.
Wiley, Herley Wesley
Williams, Rev. A Cecil
Williams, Charles J., Sr.
Williams, Curtis Cortez
Williams, Deborah Brown
Williams, Dr. Earl, Jr.
Williams, Dr. Eddie R
Williams, Rev. Ellis
Williams, Rev. Dr. Maceo Merton
Williams, Reginald Clark
Wilson, Alva L.
Wilson, Carl L.
Wilson, Demond
Winfrey, Charles Everett
Winley, Diane Lacey
Woodhouse, Dr. Johnny Boyd
Woodward, Aaron Alphonso, III
Wright, James R
Wright, Jefferson W.
Wyatt, Claude Stell, Jr.
Yates, LeRoy Louis
Zimmerman, Matthew Augustus

Clergy—Not Elsewhere Classified

Alex, Gregory K.
Anderson, Derrick Rushon
Andrews, Rev. Frazier L.
Anthony, Wendell
Ard, Rev. Robert
Ashe, Clifford
Bagley, Stanley B.
Barry, Rev. Richard L.M.
Baxter, Frederick Denard
Baxter, Nathan Dwight, D.Min.
Beckwith, Rev. Dr. Michael Bernard
Bell, Christopher
Bennett, Gordon D.
Blake, Charles E
Blake, Jennifer Lynn
Boddie, Rev. James R
Booker, Vaughan P L
Boyd, Rev. J. Edgar
Boyd, Hon William Stewart
Bradford, Charles Edward
Bradford-Eaton, Zee
Brister, Darryl Sylvester
Brown, Rev. Greggory Lee
Brown, Rev. Jeffrey LeMonte
Brown, Richard S., Jr.
Browning, Jo Ann
Bryant, Gregory
Buckhanan, Shawn L
Burgest, Rev. Dr. David Raymond
Burnley, Rev. Lawrence A Q
Calbert, Rev. William Edward, Sr.
Carry, Rev. Helen Ward
Casey, Rev. Carey Walden, Sr.
Cheek, Donald Kato
Cheeks, Darryl Lamont
Chrichlow, Livingston L
Christie, Angella
Cobbs, Harvey, Jr.
Cohea, Fr. Victor
Coleman, DeeDee M.
Colemon, Rev. Dr. Johnnie
Conaway, Mary Ward Pindle
Cox, Fr. Jesse
Cross, William Howard

Curry, Rev. Victor Tyrone
Curtis, Rev. Dr. William H.
Davis, Alfred C., Sr.
Davis, Rev. Willie Floyd, Jr.
Delk, Yvonne V
Dudley, Charles Edward
DuPree, Prof. Sherry Sherrod
Durant, Naomi C.
Durham, Rev. Eddie L, Sr.
Eason, Rev. Gregory V
Edwards, Dr. Abiyah, Jr.
Eikerenkoetter, Rev. Dr. Frederick J.
Ellis, J Delano, II
Elly, Andrew Jackie
Flakes, Garland KaZell, I
Fletcher, Terrell Antoine
Geyer, Edward B, Jr.
Giloth-David, King R.
Gordon, Sherman A
Green, Sterling
Groce, Rev. Herbert Monroe, Jr.
Guyton, Sister Patsy
Hagler, Graylan S.
Handy, Dr. Norman
Harley, Philip A.
Harris, Rev. H. Franklin, II
Harvey, William James, III
Hawkins, Walter
Heyward, Isaac
Hill, Dr. James A, Sr.
Hill, Rev. Dr. Robert Lee
Howell, William B
Hunter, Rev. James Nathaniel, II
Hunter, Rev. Sylvester
Hutchins, Rev. Markel
Jackson, Rev. James Conroy
Jackson, Rev. Jesse Louis
Jackson, Wiley, Jr.
Jacobs, Rev. Gregory Alexander
Jenkins, Kenneth Joe
John, Dr. Mable
Johnson, Carroll Randolph, Jr.
Jones, Ammia W.
Jones, Benjamin A
Jones, Frank Benson
Jones, Dr. G Daniel
Jones, Dr. Michael Andrea
Jones, Vernon A., Jr.
Kelly, Leontine T C
King, Rev. Barbara Lewis
King, Rev. Charles E.
Knight, Rev. Carolyn Ann
Lawless, Earl
Layne, Steven
Logan, Thomas W S, Sr.
Manigo, George F, Jr.
Marable, Rev. Dr. June Morehead
Marbury, Donald Lee
Massey, Rev. Reginald Harold
Matthews, Rev. David
Matthews, Denise
McCall, Rev. Emmanuel Lemuel, Sr.
McClearn, Billie
McCloud, Rev. J Oscar
McDaniel, Charles William
McDaniel, Rev. Paul Anderson
McFall, Mary
McGowan, Thomas Randolph
McKelpin, Joseph P.
McKinney, Rev. Jesse Doyle
McKinney, Norma J.
Medearis, Victor L
Miles, Dr. Norman Kenneth
Miller, Rev. Kevin D
Mills, Rev. Dr. Larry Glenn
Mitchell, Bennie Robert, Jr.
Mitchell, Rev. Dr. Ella Pearson
Montgomery, Dwight Ray
Moore, Helen D S
Moore, Jerry A, Jr.
Moss, Rev. Otis, Jr.
Nathan, Rev. Timothy Eric
Nixon, Otis Junior
Noisette, Ruffin N
Norris, Charles L, Sr.
Nutt, Rev. Maurice Joseph
Ogunde, Adeyemi
Owens, Lynda Gayle
Owens, Rev. Zelba Rene
Parris, Rev. Alvin, III
Payden, Rev. Henry J, Sr.
Perez, Altagracia
Perrin, David Thomas Perry
Perry, Joseph James
Perry, Rev. Joseph Nathaniel
Phillips, Rev. F Allison
Pogue, Richard James
Polk, Rev. Dr. Robert L
Pope, Rev. Courtney A

Porter, Rev. Dr. Glen Eugene
Powell, Rev. Grady Wilson, Sr.
Powell, Joseph T
Ragland, Dr. Wylheme Harold
Rainey, Timothy Mark
Rates, Rev. Norman M
Rice, Rev. Allen Troy
Rodgers, Rev. Charles
Ross, Rev. Ralph M
Sampson, Rev. Dr. Albert Richard
Sanders, Rev. Dr. Cheryl J
Sanders, William E
Scott, Rev. Otis, Sr.
Scott, Quincy, Jr.
Shannon, Sylvester Lorenzo
Sharpton, Rev. Alfred Charles
Sheffield, Rev. Horace L
Sherrod, Rev. Charles M
Shields, Rev. Del Pierce
Shuttlesworth, Fred L
Simms, Albert L
Simon, Lonnie A
Singleton, Rickey
Sinkford, Rev. William George
Slaughter-Titus, Rev. Linda Jean
Smith, Bishop Alfred M
Smith, Rev. Conrad Warren
Smith, Eddie D., Sr.
Smith, Rev. Otis Benton, Jr.
Smith, Rev. Perry Anderson, III
Smith, Rev. Reginald Edward
Smith, Rev. Robert, Jr.
Smith, Rev. Dr. Robert Johnson
Smith-Taylor, Rev. Donna Lyn
Smotherson, Rev. Melvin
Soaries, Rev. Dr. DeForest Blake, Jr.
Springer, Lloyd Livingstone
Stanislaus, Rev. Gregory K
Stephens, Rev. Shaheerah
Stevenson, Jerome Pritchard, Sr.
Stewart, Bishop Imagene Bigham
Styles, Richard Wayne
Sullivan, Jack, Jr.
Summerville, Willie T
Sutton, Rev. Moses
Talbert, Melvin George
Taylor, Rev. Gardner Calvin
Tomlinson, Mel Alexander
Vance, William J., Sr.
Walker, Charles E
Walker, Hezekiah
Walker, Rev. Wyatt Tee
Walker-Smith, Rev. Dr. Angelique Keturah
Waller, Rev. Dr. Alyn Errick
Walls, Fredric T
Ward, Rev. Melvin Fitzgerald, Sr.
Warren, Annika Laurin
Watkins, Joseph Philip
Weary, Rev. Dolphus
Webb, Rev. William
Westray, Rev. Kenneth Maurice
Whalum, Rev. Kenneth Twigg
Whatley, Ennis
Williams, Rev. A Cecil
Williams, Dr. Ira Joseph
Williams, Rev. John Henry
Williams, Dr. John L
Williams, Londell
Williams, Rev. Wilbert Lee
Wood, Dr. A Wilson
Wright, Rev. Dr. Jeremiah A, Jr.
Yearwood, Rev. Dr. Kirtley
Young, Jimmy Ray
Youngblood, Dr. Rev. Johnny Ray

Community Service

Aiken, Kimberly Clarice
Ali, Rasheedah Ziyadah
Alomar, Sandy
Anderson, Patricia Hebert
Andrews, Phillip
Austin, Joyce Phillips
Bacoate, Matthew, Jr.
Bacon, Charlotte Meade
Badger, Brenda Joyce
Bailey, Doris Jones
Bailey, Ronald W
Barnes, Martin G.
Baugh, Florence Ellen
Belizaire-Spitzer, Julie
Bellamy, Verdelle B.
Belmear, Horace Edward
Bennett, Debra Quinette
Bennett, Marion D.
Bernard, Michelle Denise
Block, Dr. Leslie S.
Bommer, Minnie L.
Booker, Robert Joseph

Christian, Eric Oliver, Jr.
Clark, Dr. Sanza Barbara
Clayton, Eva
Close, Billy Ray
Clyne, John Rennel
Cole, Patricia A
Cole Carey, Wilhemina
Coleman, Barbara Sims
Coleman, Dr. Sinclair B
Collins, Lenora W.
Colston Barge, Gayle S
Conway, Wallace Xavier, Sr.
Cook, Charles A
Cook, Levi
Cook, William Wilburt
Cooke, Dr. Paul Phillips
Cooke, Thomas H, Jr.
Cooley, Keith Winston
Cooper, Earl
Cooper, Irmgard M
Cooper, Linda G
Cormier, Lawrence J.
Cornish, Betty W.
Cotman, Dr. Ivan Louis
Countee, Thomas Hilaire
Craft, Dr. Thomas J
Crawford, Vanella Alise
Crocker, Clinton C
Croft, Wardell C.
Cross, Dr. Oris Elizabeth Carter
Cruzat, Dr. Gwendolyn S.
Curry, Major Gen. Jerry Ralph
Cuyjet, Aloysius Baxter
Cuyjet, Cynthia K.
Daniel, James L.
Danzy, Patricia Lynn
Davis, Arthur
Davis, Charles
Davis, Charles A
Davis, Esther Gregg
Davis, Luther Charles
Davis, Major
Davis, Raoul A.
Dawson, Martha E
Dawson Boyd, Dr. Candy
Dean, Diane D
Debnam, Chadwick Basil
Dember, Jean Wilkins
Dessaso-Gordon, Janice Marie
Diane, Mamadi
Dismuke, Leroy
Dixon, Arrington Liggins
Dixon, Diane L.
Dolphin, Derrick
Donawa, Dr. Maria Elena
Dorsey, Ivory
Dortch, Heyward
Douglas, Shannon
Downs, Crystal
Drennen, Gordon
Dukes, Ronald
Duster, Benjamin C., III
Edwards, Horace Burton
Edwards, Monique Marie
Edwards, Oscar Lee
Elliott, J. Russell
Ellis, Douglas, Jr.
Ellison, Nolen M
Eure, Jerry Holton, Sr.
Evans, Dr. Billy Joe
Evans, Dr. Grover Milton
Evans, Milton L.
Evans, Ruthana Wilson
Evans, Warren Cleage
Evans, Dr. William E.
Ewing, Samuel Daniel
Fagbayi, Mutiu Olutoyin
Fauntroy, Rev. Walter Edward
Fay, Toni Georgette
Fergerson, Miriam N
Ferguson, Dr. Robert Lee, Sr.
Ferrell, Rosie E.
Fields, Stanley
Flagg, Dr. Eloise Alma William
Fletcher, Dr. Bettye Ward
Flournoy, Valerie Rose
Floyd, Dr. Samuel A.
Fobbs, Kevin
Fonvielle, William Harold
Ford, Florida Morehead
Francis, Cheryl Margaret
Francis, Henry Minton
Francis, Livingston S
Fraser, George C.
Frazier, Shirley George
Frost, Dr. Olivia Pleasants
Frye, Reginald Stanley
Gainer, Prof. John F
Garrett, Darrell W

Gayles, Dr. Joseph Nathan Webster
Gibson, Elvis Sonny
Gibson, JoAnn
Giles, Althea B
Gillespie, Marcia A.
Gillespie, Dr. Rena Harrell
Gillette, Frankie Jacobs
Gillispie, William Henry
Gilmore, Dr. Robert McKinley, Sr.
Gipson, Reve
Glass, Virginia M.
Godbold, Donald Horace
Gooden, Cherry Ross
Goodman, Dr. James Arthur
Goodwin, Mac Arthur
Gordon, Robert L.
Grace, Horace R
Grant, Claude DeWitt
Gravenberg, Eric Von
Graves, Clifford Wayne
Gray-Little, Dr. Bernadette
Greaux, Cheryl Prejean
Green, Dr. Calvin Coolidge
Green, Lee
Green, Saul A.
Gregory, Michael Samuel
Griffey, Ken, Sr.
Griffin, Dr. Betty Sue
Grigsby, Calvin Burchard
Guillory, Linda Semien
Guilmenot, Richard Arthur
Gunter, Laurie
Hadnott, Bennie L
Hagan, Gwenael Stephane
Hale, Marna Amoretti
Hale, Phale Dophis
Hammond, Dr. James Matthew
Hampton, Dr. Delon
Harrell, Andre
Harrell, Oscar W., II
Harrington, Denise Marion
Harris, Archie Jerome
Harris, Gladys Bailey
Harris, J. Robert, II
Harris, James G., Jr.
Harris, Dr. Mary Styles
Harris, Vernon Joseph
Haskins, Michael Kevin
Hawkins, Mary L
Haynes, Sue Blood
Haynes, Ulric St Clair
Head, Samuel
Henderson, Dr. Lenneal Joseph
Hendrix, Deborah Lynne
Henry, Dr. Charles E.
Herring, Marsha K Church
Hicks, Eleanor
High, Claude, Jr.
Hill, Hattie
Hogan, Edwin B.
Holland, Robert
Holliday, Dr. Gayle
Holman, Alvin T.
Holmes, Willie A.
Holmes, Wilma K.
Holton, Priscilla Browne
Horton, Joann
Horton, Larkin, Jr.
Howard, Dr. Lawrence Cabot
Howze, Karen Aileen
Huff, Loretta Love
Hunt, Dr. Portia L
Hunter, Teola P.
Hutchins, Rev. Markel
Hutchison, Dr. Peyton S.
Hyler, Lora Lee
Ingram, Phillip M
Ingram, William B.
Irons, Hon. Paulette R
Jackson, Darcy DeMille
Jackson, Emory Napoleon
Jackson, Warren Garrison
Jefferson, Andrea Green
Jefferson-Jenkins, Carolyn
Johnson, Addie Collins
Johnson, Brent E.
Johnson, Carl Earld
Johnson, Charles
Johnson, Cleveland, Jr.
Johnson, Frank J., Jr.
Johnson, Dr. Fred D.
Johnson, Kenneth L.
Johnson, Dr. Tommie Ulmer
Johnston, Wallace O.
Jones, Alice Eley
Jones, Carolyn G.
Jones, Jimmie Dene
Jones, Lester C
Jones, Sherman J

Jones-Grimes, Dr. Mable Christine
Jordan, J. St. Girard
Joseph, Abraham
Kee, Linda Cooper
Kilson, Martin Luther, Jr.
King, Jeanne Faith
King, Lewis Henry
King, Reginald F.
Kirby-Davis, Montages
Kispert, Dorothy Lee
Knott, Dr. Albert Paul
Kondwani, Kofi Anum
Kunjufu, Jawanza
Laday, Kerney
Lambert, LeClair Grier
LaSane, Joanna Emma
Lattimer, Robert L.
Lawrence, John Edward
Leace, Donal Richard
Lee, Tamela Jean
Leeke, John F.
Lester, Nina Mack
Levermore, Dr. Monique A
Lewis, Arthur W
Lewis, Dr. Delano Eugene
Lewis, Reta Jo
Lewis, William M., Jr.
Livingston-White, Dr. Deborah J H
Locke, Dr. Don C.
Lockhart, Barbara H
Long, Jerry Wayne
Lynn, Louis B.
Lyons, A Bates
Lyons, Dr. Laura Brown
Mabrey, Harold Leon
Majete, Dr. Clayton Aaron
Mallory, Glenn Oliver, Jr.
Malone, Claudine Berkeley
Mance, John J.
Mardenborough, Leslie A.
Marshall, David
Marshall, Timothy H.
Martin, Myron C
Matthews, Robert L.
Maxie, Peggy Joan
McCabe, Jewell Jackson
McCullers, Eugene
McHenry, Emmit J
McIntosh, Rhodina Covington
McKenzie, Reginald
McLaughlin, Dr. Andree Nicola
McLean, Marquita Sheila McLarty
McLurkin, James
McNeely, Charles E
McWhorter, Sharon Louise
Mendez, Hugh B.
Merritt, Wendy Warren
Merriweather, Robert Eugene
Miller, Arthur J
Miller, Evelyn B
Miller, George Carroll, Jr.
Miller, Saundra C
Miller, William
Mills, Capt. Mary Lee
Minor, Jessica
Moone, Wanda Renee
Moore, Charlie W.
Moore, Christine James
Moore, Lenny Edward
Moorehead, Bobbie Wooten
Morisey, Patricia Garland
Morman, Alvin
Morris, Bernard Alexander
Morris, Effie Lee
Morris, Horace W
Morris, Robert V
Morrison, James W.
Morse, Mildred S
Morse, Dr. Oliver
Moss, James Edward
Moss, Robert C., Jr.
Moss, Tanya Jill
Moyo, Yvette Jackson
Murray, Dr. Thomas Azel, Sr.
Nash, Henry Gary
Nellum, Albert L.
Nelson, Gilbert L.
Nelson, Ramona M
Newhouse, Quentin
Nix, Rick
Norman, Georgette M.
Odom, John Yancy
Olapo, Olaitan
O'Leary, Hazel R
Orticke, Leslie Ann
Owens, Dr. Hugo Armstrong
Owens, Dr. Judith Myoli
Owens, Lynda Gayle
Parker, James L.

Parker, Dr. Stephen A.
Parker, Vernon B
Parsons, Philip I
Patterson, Lloyd
Patterson, Lydia R
Pattillo, Joyce M
Patton, Jean E
Patton, Rosezelia L.
Payne, Osborne Allen
Peal, Darryl Alan
Peal, Dr. Regina Randall
Pearson, Clifton
Pearson, Marilyn Ruth
Pearson, Preston James
Penn, Tenesia Sharone
Peoples, Harrison Promis, Jr.
Perkins, Frances J
Perry, Jeffery Stewart
Perry, June Martin
Perry, Leonard Douglas, Jr.
Perry-Mason, Gail F
Person, Earle G.
Petersen, Arthur Everett, Jr.
Peterson, Coleman Hollis
Phillips, Edward Martin
Pitts, Dr. Vera L.
Pleas, John Roland
Polk, Eugene Steven S, Sr.
Ponder, Dr. Henry
Poole, Dr. Rachel Irene
Porter, Charles William
Porter, Ellis Nathaniel
Powell, Gayle Lett
Powell, Kenneth Alasandro
Pruitt-Logan, Dr. Anne Smith
Ray, James R, III
Reed, Clarence Hammit, III
Rembert, Dr. Emma White
Reynolds, Andrew Buchanan
Rhodes, John K
Rice, Dr. Mitchell F
Richards-Alexander, Billie J.
Richardson, Ernest A.
Richardson, Munro Carmel
Riddick, Eugene E
Riscoe, Romona A
Ritchie, Dr. Louise Reid
Roberson, Lawrence R
Roberts, Jacqueline Johnson
Robertson, Charles E, Jr.
Robinson, Charlotte L.
Robinson, Jeffrey
Robinson, Sherman
Robinson, Verneda
Robison, Louis
Rogers, Earline S
Rohadfox, Ronald Otto
Russell, Herman Jerome
Rutledge, Jennifer M
Salmond, Jasper
Sampson, Ronald Alvin
Samuels, Annette Jacqueline
Samuels, Charlotte
Samuels, Dr. Leslie Eugene
Samuels, Robert J
Sanders, Glenn Carlos
Sanders, Patricia Roper
Sanderson, Randy Chris
Sandoval, Dolores S.
Sands, George M.
Sargent, Virginia Hightower
Saunders, Doris E.
Scaggs, Dr. Edward W.
Scott, Benjamin
Scott, Gilbert H, Sr.
Scott, Melvina Brooks
Scott, Ruth Elaine Holland
Segree, E Ramone
Shack, William Edward, Jr.
Shackelford, William G
Shanks, Wilhelmina Byrd
Sharp, Dr. J Anthony
Shaw, Melvin B
Shaw, Dr. Spencer Gilbert
Shepherd, Malcolm Thomas
Sherrod, Rev. Charles M
Shields-Jones, Esther L M
Shropshire, Harry W.
Simms, Robert H
Simons, Renee V H
Sims, Genevieve Constance
Sims, Prof. Ronald R
Small, Kenneth Lester
Smith, Carolyn Lee
Smith, Conrad P.
Smith, Dolores J
Smith, Dr. Edgar Eugene
Smith, Lafayette Kenneth
Smith, Morris Leslie

Smith, Shirley Hunter
Smith, Symuel Harold
Smith, William Fred
Sobers, Waynett A., Jr.
Spurlock, Dorothy A
Stamps, Delores Bolden
Stanley, LaNett
Stanton, Robert G
Steele, Carolyn Odom
Stewart, John B., Jr.
Stewart-Copes, Michele Lynn
Stickney, Janice L.
St Omer, Vincent V E
Stovall, Audrean
Streeter, Denise Williams
Strong- Kimbrough, Dr. Blondell M
Strozier, Yvonne Iglehart
Sudarkasa, Michael Eric Mabogunje
Sulieman, Dr. Jamil
Sullivan, Dr. Allen R
Summers, Dr. David Stewart
Summers, Loretta M
Swain, Michael B.
Swanigan, Jesse Calvin
Tate, Lenore Artie
Taylor, Charles Edward
Taylor, Gilbert Leon
Taylor, Sterling R
Taylor, Dr. Welton Ivan
Thomas, David Anthony
Thomas, Franklin A
Thomas, Dr. Jewel M
Thomas, Dr. Lucille Cole
Thomas, Roderick
Thompson, Geraldine
Todman, Terence Alphonso
Tramiel, Kenneth Ray, Sr.
Trent, James E.
Tribbett, Charles A., III
Troutman, Dr. Adewale
Tucker, Dr. Dorothy M.
Turner, Bailey W.
Turner, M Annette
Turner, Dr. William Hobert
Turner-Forte, Diana
Tyner, Regina Lisa
Tyree-Walker, Ida May
Uku, Eustace Oris
Vernon, Easton D
Waden, Fletcher Nathaniel, Jr.
Wakefield, J. Alvin
Walker, Willie M.
Walker Williams, Hope Denise
Wallace, Ritchie Ray
Ward, Daniel
Ward, Haskell G
Ware, Omego John Clinton
Warfield-Coppock, Nsenga
Warren, Beth I
Washington, Dr. Edith May Faulkner
Waterman, Jeffrey Trevor
Watkins, Shirley R
Watson, Aaron
Watson, Daniel
Watts, Patricia L
Weaver, Frank Cornell
Weaver, George Leon-Paul
West, Lena L
Weston, Sharon
Wharton Boyd, Linda F.
Wheat, Alan
White, Jesse C.
White, Nan E.
White, Yolanda Simmons
Whitehead, Arch Sylvester
Wilkins, Allen Henry
Wilkins, Charles O
Wilkins, Thomas A.
Williams, Barry Lawson
Williams, Dr. Betty Smith
Williams, Dr. Carolyn Ruth Arm-
strong
Williams, Charles C
Williams, Clarence
Williams, Dr. Lisa R.
Williams, Dr. Patricia Hill
Williams, Wayne Allan
Williams-Garner, Debra
Williamson, Dr. Handy, Jr.
Williams-Stanton, Dr. Sonya Denise
Willrich Scott, Candace Yvette
Wilson, Hugh A.
Wilson, Wesley Campbell
Witherspoon, Audrey Goodwin
Woodson, Cleveland Coleman, III
Woodson, Shirley A
Wordlaw, Clarence, Jr.

White-Hunt, Debra Jean
Zollar, Jawole Willa Jo

Dentistry

Abdullah, Dr. Larry Burley
Adams, Curtis N.
Adams, Lehman D., Jr.
Adams, Melba K.
Aikens, Dr. Chester Alfronza
Airall, Dr. Guillermo Evers
Alexander, Walter Gilbert, II
Allen, Herman, Dr.
Allen, Dr. William Henry
Anderson, Arnett Artis
Arbuckle Alston, Pamela Susan
Ayers, George Waldon, Jr.
Baaqee, Susanne Inez
Bacon, Albert S.
Badger, Dr. Leonard Michael
Bailey, Weltman D., Sr.
Baker, Floyd Edward
Ballard, Dr. Billy Ray
Ballard, Walter W.
Baranco, Raphael Alvin
Barber, Hargrow Dexter
Barber, Dr. Janice Denise
Baskins, Lewis C.
Bell, Rouzeberry, Jr.
Bishop, Clarence
Black, Gail
Black, Dr. James Tillman
Blackburn, Benjamin Allan, II
Bluitt, Juliann Stephanie
Bolden, Raymond A
Boone, Melanie Lynn
Boston, Dr. George David
Boston, Dr. Horace Oscar
Braddock, Dr. Marilyn Eugenia
Braithwaite, Gordon L.
Braithwaite, Mark Winston
Braynon, Dr. Edward J
Bronson, Dr. Fred James
Brown, Dr. Glenn Arthur
Brown, Dr. James Harvey
Brown Bryant, Jacqueline D.
Bryant, William Jesse
Buckner, Dr. James L
Caldwell, Dr. Sandra Ishmael
Calhoun, Dr. Noah Robert
Cameron, Wilburn Macio, Jr.
Campbell, Dr. Charles Everett
Case, Arthur M.
Cashin, John
Chance, Dr. Kenneth Bernard
Chappelle, Edward H
Cheek, Robert Benjamin, III
Cheeks, Carl L.
Chowning, Frank Edmond
Churchwell, Caesar Alfred
Clark, Dr. James N.
Clark, Dr. Morris Shandell
Coffee, Lawrence Winston
Coleman, Harry Theodore
Coleman, Wisdom F
Collins, Bobby L
Colvin, Ernest J.
Contee, Dr. Carolyn Ann
Cook, Dr. Henry Lee, Sr.
Cook, Wallace Jeffery
Cornwall, Dr. Shirley M.
Cox, Dr. Georgetta Manning
Cox, Dr. Wendell
Craig, Frederick A.
Crawford, Lawrence Douglas
Cryer, Linkston T.
Daniels, Elizabeth
Darke, Dr. Charles B
Dawkins, Stan Barrington Bancroft
Deane, Morgan R.
Derricotte, Eugene Andrew
Dickey, Leonel
Driskell, Claude Evans
Dunston, Walter T.
Eagan, Emma Louise
Effort, Dr. Edmund D
Epps, Constance Arnettres
Farrow, Harold Frank
Felder, Loretta Kay
Fielder, Dr. Fred Charles
Flanagan, T Earl, Jr.
Flowers, Sally A.
Ford, Dr. Albert S.
Ford, Robert Blackman
Fortier, Theodore T., Sr.
Fortson, Henry David, Jr.
Franks, Dr. Julius, Jr.
Frohman, Roland H.
Gaither, Cornelius E.
Ganey, James Hobson

Garner, Dr. La Forrest Dean
Garnette, Dr. Booker Thomas
Gates, Dr. Paul Edward
Gipson, Dr. Lovelace Preston, II
Glover, Dr. Bernard Ellsworth
Goggins, Horace
Goodson, Dr. Ernest Jerome
Graves, Dr. Jerrod Franklin
Hairston, Eddison R, Jr.
Hall, David Anthony, Jr.
Hall, Dr. Willie Green
Hamilton, Dr. John Mark, Jr.
Hamlar, Dr. David Duffield, Sr.
Hammond, Melvin Alan Ray, Jr.
Hardeman, Strotha E, Jr.
Harper, Dr. Alphonza Vealvert, III
Harper, Robert Lee
Harris, Horatio Preston
Harris, Dr. Joseph Benjamin
Harrison, Nancy Gannaway
Haston, Dr. Raymond Curtiss, Jr.
Hawkins, Dr. Benny F
Hawkins, Mary L
Haynes, Dr. Walter Wesley
Herring, Larry Windell
Hickson, Sherman Ruben
Hickson, Dr. William F, Jr.
Hines, Dr. Morgan B
Hines, Wiley Earl
Hodge, Cynthia Elois
Holley, Dr. James W
Holloway, Dr. Nathaniel Overton, Jr.
Holmes, Dr. Louyco W
Horne, Dr. Edwin Clay
Hubbard, James Madison, Jr.
Hunn, Myron Vernon
Hunter, Irby B.
Hutton, Dr. Ronald I
Ince, Harold S.
Jackson, Aubrey N.
Jackson, Burnett Lamar, Jr.
Jackson, Dr. Luke
Jamerson, John W
Jefferson, Horace Lee
Jenkins, Harry Lancaster
Johns, Dr. Jackie C
Johnson, Charles Lee
Johnson, Collis, Jr.
Johnson, Dr. Henderson A, III
Johnston, Charlene B.
Jones, Roscoe T., Jr.
Jones, Theodore Cornelius
Jordan, George Lee, Jr.
Jordan, John Edward
Jordan, Joy A
Kimbrough, Robert L.
Kirkland-Briscoe, Gail Alicia
Lane, George S., Jr.
Lassiter, James Edward, Jr.
Lee, Dr. James E
Lewis, Dr. Houston A.
Lewis, James R.
Lockhart, Dr. Robert W
Maddox, Elton Preston, Jr.
Martin, Amon Achilles, Jr.
Martin, Dr. Bertha M
Martin, Blanche
Martin, Harold B.
Martin, James Larence
Martin, Paul W.
Martin, Russell F.
Maupin, Dr. John E
Mays, David
McCray, Dr. Roy Howard
McDaniel, Dr. Adam Theodore
McGoodwin, Dr. Roland C
McLeod, Dr. Michael Preston
McNeely, Charles E
Means, Dr. Craig R.
Means, Donald Fitzgerald
Miller, Dr. Maposure T
Minus, Homer Wellington
Mitchell, Dr. Byron Lynwood
Mitchell, Orrin Dwight
Mobley, Eugenia L.
Moody, William Dennis
Morgan, Dr. John Paul
Morgan-Washington, Dr. Barbara
Murphy, Dr. John Matthew, Jr.
Murray, James Hamilton
Murrell, Dr. Peter C
Myers, Sere Spaulding
Norman, P. Roosevelt
O'Connor, Dr. Rodney Earl
O'Hara, Leon P
Otieno-Ayim, Larban Allan
Owens, Dr. Charles Clinton
Owens, Dr. Hugo Armstrong
Owens, Jay R.

Page, Dr. Gregory Oliver
Paxton, Gertrude Garnes
Perkins, Robert E. L.
Person, Earle G.
Peterson, Alphonse
Pierre, Dr. Dallas
Pittman, Marvin B.
Poindexter, Dr. Zeb F
Powell, William
Powell, Dr. William O
Prioleau, Dr. Sara Nelliene
Quansah-Dankwa, Dr. Juliana Aba
Raines, Colden Douglas
Rawlins, Sedrick John
Reynolds, Bruce Howard
Richardson, Anthony W.
Richardson, Elisha R
Richie, Winston Henry
Riggs, Dr. Enrique A
Rivers, Dr. Robert Joseph, Jr.
Rodney, Dr. Martin Hurtus
Rosemond, Dr. Manning Wyllard, Jr.
Russell, Dr. Leonard Alonzo
Sadler, Dr. Kenneth Marvin
Salaam, Dr. Abdul
Scales, Jerome C.
Scott, Dr. Leonard Stephen
Simpkins, Cuthbert O.
Singh, Dr. Rajendra P
Smiley, Dr. Emmett L
Smith, Joseph Edward
Smith, Vasco A.
Spence, Donald Dale
Streeter, Elwood James
Sullivan, Dr. Edward James
Tappan, Dr. Major William
Taylor, Dr. Christopher Lenard
Taylor, Dr. Robert, III
Terry, Garland Benjamin
Thompson, Floyd
Thompson, James W.
Trice, William B.
Tutt, Dr. Walter Cornelius
Wareham, Alton L.
Watkins, James Darnell
Waynewood, Dr. Freeman Lee
Weaver, Dr. Garland Rapheal, Jr.
Webb, Dr. Harvey
Webster, Charles
White, Artis Andre
White, Dr. George
Whitworth, Dr. E Leo, Jr.
Williams, Dr. Harvey Joseph
Williams, Hayward J
Williams, Henry R
Williams, Dr. John L
Williams, Dr. Lafayette W
Williams, Dr. Richard Lenwood
Wilson, Joseph Henry, Jr.
Wiltz, Charles J.
Woods, Dr. Robert Louis
Worrell, Scott P., M.D.
Wrenn, Thomas H., III
Wright, Raymond LeRoy, Jr.
Young, F. Camille
Young, Dr. Walter F
Yuille, Dr. Bruce

Directing/Producing
(Performing Arts)

Albers, Kenneth Lynn
Allen, Debbie
Amderson, Gary
Anderson, Madeline
Arties, Walter Eugene, III
Billings, Cora Marie
Billington, Clyde, Jr.
Billops, Camille J.
Bolling, Deborah A
Boone, Eunetta
Bowser, Yvette Denise Lee
Branch, William Blackwell
Brown, Dr. Joan P.
Brown, Reginald DeWayne
Browne, Roscoe Lee
Burnett, Zaron Walter, Jr.
Burton, Levar
Caines, Bruce Stuart
Cannon, Reuben
Cheatham, Henry Boles
Clay, Stanley Bennett
Coker, Adeniyi Adetokunbo
Coleman, Elizabeth Sheppard
Collie, Kelsey E
Collins, Bernice Elaine
Collins, Tessil John
Combs, Sean J
Cosby, Dr. William Henry
Crawford, Deborah Collins

Crudup, Gwendolyn M
Curtis-Hall, Vondie
Daniels, Lee Louis
Dash, Julie
de Passe, Suzanne
Destine, Jean-Leon
Dickerson, Ernest Roscoe
Diesel, Vin
Dorn, Michael
Dunmore, Gregory Charles
Dutton, Charles S.
Eason-Steele, Elaine
Ellington, Mercedes
Eskridge, Rev. John Clarence
Fales, Susan
Fanaka, Jamaa
Faulkner, Geanie
Flake, Nancy Aline
Fletcher, Winona Lee
Frazier, Cliff
Freisen, Gil
Gamble, Kenneth
Gates, Prof. Thomas Michael
Giles, Henrietta
Glover, Danny Lebern
Gonzalez, Anita Louise
Gramby, Shirley Ann
Gray, F Gary
Greaves, William
Guillaume, Robert
Haddock, Mable J.
Halliburton, Christopher
Hardison, Kadeem
Harris, Helen B.
Harris, Thomas Walter
Harrison, Paul Carter
Head, Helaine
Hendry, Gloria
Hicklin, Fannie
Higginson, Vy
Holder, Geoffrey
Hooks, Kevin
Horsford, Anna Maria
Hudlin, Reginald Alan
Hudson, Dianne Atkinson
Hudson, Frederick Bernard
Hughes, Albert
Hughes, Allen
Hurte, Leroy E.
Imhotep, Akbar
Ione, Carole
Jam, Jimmy
Jessup, Gayle Louise
Johnson, Charles Floyd
Johnson, Prof. Stephanie Anne
Joyner, Lemuel Martin
Khan, Dr. Ricardo M
King, Woodie, Jr.
Klausner, Willette Murphy
Knight, Gladys Maria
Knowles, Beyonce
Knuckles, Frankie
Kotto, Yaphet
Lane, Charles
Laneuville, Eric Gerard
Lange, Ted W.
Lathan, Dr. William Edward
Lee, Damon
Lee, Spike
LeFlore, Lyah B
Lemmons, Kasi
Lipscombe, Margaret Ann
Livingston-White, Dr. Deborah J H
MacLachlan, Janet A.
Martin, Darnell
Martin, Jesse Lamont
Martin Chase, Debra
McCord, LaNissa Renee
McHenry, Douglas
McKayle, Donald Cohen
McKee, Adam E
McNeill, Cerves Todd
Meek, Dr. Russell Charles
Merritt, Wendy Warren
Mitchell, Arthur
Morgan, Stacey Evans
Morton, Joe
Moseka, Aminata
Nelson, Novella C.
Nelson, Prince Rogers
Newman, Dr. Geoffrey W
Nicholas, Denise
Nurse, Richard A
Page, Harrison Eugene
Palcy, Euzhan
Parsons, Karyn
Patterson, Saladin K
Pawley, Thomas D., III
Peoples, Dottie

Phifer, Mekhi
Poitier, Sidney
Prelow, Arleigh
Preston-Williams, Rodena
Prince-Bythewood, Gina
Purdee, Nathan
Reed-Humes, Robi
Reid, Tim
Rhames, Ving
Ribeiro, Alfonso
Rich, Matty
Riley, Teddy
Rivera, Lance
Rock, Chris
Rodgers, Nile Gregory
Russ, Timothy Darrell
Ryan-White, Jewell
Sarmiento, Shirley Jean
Schultz, Michael A
Scott, Seret
Sharp, Saundra
Shivers, P Derrick
Simmons, Russell
Singleton, John
Snipes, Lolita Walker
Springer, Ashton, Jr.
Stokes, Chris
Story, Timothy Kevin
Sykes, Wanda
Talbert, Ted
Taylor, Almina
Thomas, Lorna E
Thomas, Nathaniel
Thomas, Philip S.
Tillman, George, Jr.
Todd, Beverly
Townsend, Robert
Treadwell, Tina McKinley
Tunie, Tamara
Turner-Forte, Diana
Van Peebles, Mario
Vincent, Irving H.
Vinson, Chuck Rallen
Wade, Kim Mache
Wagoner, J Robert
Walker, Charles
Wallace, Linda Skye
Ward, Douglas Turner
Warren, Michael
Washington, Dr. Von Hugo
Wayans, Keenen Ivory
Wayans, Shawn
West, Valerie Y
Whitaker, Mical Rozier
Wilkerson, Prof. Margaret Buford
Williams, Dick Anthony
Wilson, Jonathan Charles
Winfrey, Oprah
Wolfe, George C
Woods, Allie, Jr.
Young, Clarence, III
Young, William Allen

Ecology

Crisp, Dr. Robert Carl, Jr.
Hoyte, James Sterling
Lillard, Kwame Leo
Malcom, Dr. Shirley Mahaley
Marsh, Sandra M
Meridith, Denise Patricia
Mesiah, Raymond N.
Nelson, Edward O.
Williams, Howard Copeland

Economics

Alford, Harry C.
Anderson, Dr. Carol Byrd
Anise, Ladun Oladunjoye E
Bailey, Thomas R., Jr.
Bell, Elmer A.
Bostic, Raphael W
Brown-Wright, Marjorie
Butler, John Gordon
Clifton, Dr. Ivery Dwight
Conrad, Cecilia Ann
Davie, Damon Jonathon
Flood, Eugene, Jr.
Foreman, S Beatrice
Gloster, Jesse E.
Gregory, Karl Dwight
Harris, Prof. Donald J
Jaynes, Dr. Gerald David
King, Dr. Arthur Thomas
Lemuwa, Ike Emmanuel
Loury, Dr. Glenn Cartman
Love, Carolyn Diane
Mordecai, David K A
Myers, Samuel L, Sr.
Myers, Dr. Samuel L
O'Neal, Raymond W, Sr.

Brown, Costello L.
Brown, Dallas C, Jr.
Brown, Dr. Darlene Morgan
Brown, Emery N.
Brown, Emma Jean Mitchell
Brown, Dr. Frank
Brown, Furney Edward, Jr.
Brown, George Houston
Brown, Dr. James Harvey
Brown, Jerome
Brown, John Andrew
Brown, Dr. Joyce F.
Brown, Dr. Milton F
Brown, Mortimer
Brown, Dr. O. Gilbert
Brown, Dr. Ola M.
Brown, Otha N
Brown, Paul L.
Brown, Paula Evie
Brown, Hon. Robert Lee
Brown, Ronald Edward
Brown, Dr. Ronald Paul
Brown, Ronald Wellington
Brown, Tommie Florence
Brown, Dr. Walter E
Brown, Dr. William, Jr.
Brown, William T
Brown-Chappell, Betty L.
Browne, Lee F.
Brown-Guillory, Elizabeth
Brownlee, Dr. Geraldine Daniels
Brown-Wright, Marjorie
Bruce, James C.
Brummer, Chauncey Eugene
Brutus, Dr. Dennis Vincent
Bryant, Anxious E.
Bryant, Dr. Bunyan I.
Bryant, Dr. Henry C.
Bryant, Leon Serle
Bryant, Prof. Leroy
Bryant, Dr. Napoleon Adebola, Jr.
Bryant, Willa Coward
Bryant, William Jesse
Bryce-Laporte, Roy Simon
Bryson, Dr. Ralph J.
Bryson, Seymour L.
Buchanan, Shonda T
Buck, Ivory M., Jr.
Buckner, William Pat
Bugg, Dr. George Wendell
Bullard, Edward A., Jr.
Bullins, Ed
Bullock, Alice Gresham
Bullock, James
Bumphus, Dr. Walter Gayle
Burchell, Charles R.
Burgess, Dr. Norma J
Burgest, Rev. Dr. David Raymond
Burgett, Dr. Paul Joseph
Burkeen, Ernest Wisdom
Burlew, Ann Kathleen
Burnett, Calvin Waller
Burnett, Dr. Myra N
Burnim, Mellonee Victoria
Burnley, Rev. Lawrence A Q
Burrell, Kenneth Earl
Burroughs, Joan
Burroughs, Dr. Margaret Taylor
Burroughs, Dr. Todd Steven
Burton, Iola Brantley
Butcher, Dr. Philip
Butler, Douthard Roosevelt
Butler, Dr. John Sibley
Butler, Johnnella E.
Butler, Marjorie Johnson
Butler, Dr. Rebecca Batts
Butler, Tonia Paulette
Butler, Washington Roosevelt, Jr.
Byrd, Albert Alexander
Byrd, Arthur W
Byrd, Dr. Helen P Bessent
Byrd, Joseph Keys
Byrd, Katie W.
Byrd, Dr. Marquita L.
Caesar, Dr. Lael O.
Caesar, Lois
Caggins, Dr. Ruth Porter
Cain, Rudolph Alexander
Caldwell, Dr. Cleo Howard
Caldwell, Marion Milford, Jr.
Calhoun, Fred Steverson
Calhoun, Thomas C
Callender, Dr. Clive Orville
Calvert, Dr. Wilma Jean
Cameron, Joseph A.
Cameron, Mary Evelyn
Cameron, Ulysses
Campbell, Dr. Arthur Ree
Campbell, Diane

Campbell, Dr. Everett O.
Campbell, Gary Lloyd
Campbell, Dr. Mary Schmidt
Campbell, Dr. Otis, Jr.
Campbell, Zerrie D
Canady, Dr. Alexa Irene
Cannon, Dr. Joseph Nevel
Cannon, Rev. Dr. Katie Geneva
Canson, Fannie Joanna
Cantarella, Marcia Y
Carby, Hazel V.
Carey, Addison, Jr.
Carey, Dr. Phillip
Carmichael, Benjamin G.
Carpenter, Barbara West
Carpenter, Carl Anthony
Carpenter, Vivian L.
Carroll, Dr. William
Carson, Dr. Benjamin Solomon
Carson, Warren Jason
Carter, Alphonse H.
Carter, Dr. Barbara Lillian
Carter, Dr. David G.
Carter, Dr. Joye Maureen
Carter, Dr. Judy L.
Carter, Dr. Lawrence
Carter, Lawrence Edward, Sr.
Carter, Dr. Lawrence Robert
Carter, Dr. Marion Elizabeth
Carter, Marva Griffin
Carter, Nanette Carolyn
Carter, Philip W.
Carter, Dr. Raymond Gene, Sr.
Carter, Robert Louis, Jr.
Carter, Robert Thompson
Carter, Roland
Carter, Thomas
Carter, Troy A
Carter, Dr. Warrick L.
Carter, Yvonne P.
Cartwright, Brenda Yvonne
Cary, Reby
Casanova, Dr. Gisele M
Cash, Dr. James Ireland
Cashin, Sheryll D.
Castenell, Dr. Louis Anthony
Caswell, Rosell R
Cathey, Leon Dennison
Caulker, Ferne Yangyeitie
Cave, Perstein Ronald
Cavin, Dr. Alonzo C.
Cayou, Nontsizi Kirton
Cazenave, Dr. Noel Anthony
Chaffers, James Alvin
Chambers, Fredrick
Chambers, Van B.
Chambliss, Alvin Odell, Jr.
Chandler, James Phillip
Chandler, Dr. Mittie Olion
Chaney, Regmon A
Channer, Colin
Chapman, Dr. George Wallace, Jr.
Chapman, Dr. Gilbert Bryant
Chappell, Michael James
Charles, Bernard L.
Charlton, Rev. Charles Hayes
Chase, Anthony R
Chase, Tony
Chavis, Theodore R.
Cheek, Donald Kato
Cheek, Donna Marie
Cheek, Dr. James Edward
Cheek, King Virgil, Jr.
Chenault, John
Chennault, Dr. Madelyn
Chestang, Dr. Leon Wilbert
Chestnut, Dr. Dennis Earl
Childs, Dr. Francine C.
Childs, Oliver Bernard
Chivers, Gwendolyn Ann
Christburg, Sheyann Webb
Chunn, Dr. Jay Carrington
Cissoko, Alioune Badara
Clark, Dr. Bertha Smith
Clark, Dr. Charles Warfield
Clark, Dr. Claude Lockhart
Clark, Dr. Edward Depriest, Sr.
Clark, Dr. Irvin R.
Clark, Laron Jefferson
Clark, Dr. Lawrence M
Clark, Linda Day
Clark, Dr. Morris Shandell
Clark, Dr. Sanza Barbara
Clark, Savanna M. Vaughn
Clarke, Dr. Donald Dudley
Clarke, Joy Adele Long
Clemendor, Dr. Anthony Arnold
Clemmons, Prof. Jackson Joshua
Walter

Clifton, Lucille
Clinkscales, Jerry A.
Clinkscales, Rev. Dr. Marcia J
Close, Billy Ray
Close, Fran
Coatie, Robert Mason
Cobb, Dr. Thelma M.
Cofield, Dr. Elizabeth Bias
Cole, Edyth Bryant
Cole, Olen, Jr.
Cole, Dr. Thomas Winston
Coleman, Dr. Don Edwin
Coleman, Dr. Edwin Leon, II
Coleman, Gilbert Irving
Coleman, Dr. Ronald Gerald
Coleman, Warren B.
Coleman, Wisdom F
Coleman-Burns, Dr. Patricia Wen-
dolyn
Coles, Robert Traynham
Collie, Kelsey E
Collier, Dr. Eugenia W.
Collier, Julia Marie
Collier, Willye
Collier-Mills, Cheryl
Collier-Thomas, Dr. Bettye
Collins, Dr. Elliott
Collins, Elsie
Collins, James Douglas
Collins, Dr. Joann Ruth
Collins, Dr. Patricia Hill
Collins, Dr. Paul V.
Collins, Robert Frederick
Colston, Dr. Freddie C.
Colvin, Dr. William E
Comer, Dr. James Pierpont
Comer, Dr. Marian Wilson
Cone, Dr. James H.
Conley, John A.
Conrad, Cecilia Ann
Contee, Dr. Carolyn Ann
Conwill, Giles
Conwill, William Louis
Conyers, Dr. James Ernest
Cook, Dr. Nathan Howard
Cook, Tonya Denise
Cook, William Wilburt
Cooper, Constance M.
Cooper, Dr. Edward Sawyer
Cooper, Ernest, Jr.
Cooper, Iris N.
Cooper, Joseph
Cooper, Julius
Cooper, Dr. Marva W
Cooper, Ronald
Cooper-Lewter, Rev. Dr. Nicholas
Charles
Copeland, Dr. Elaine Johnson
Copeland, Leon L
Coppedge, Arthur L
Corbett, Dr. Doris R
Cordell, LaDoris Hazzard
Corley, Dr. Charles J.
Cornish, Mae Golder
Cornwell, Dr. JoAnne
Corprew, Wilbert E.
Cortada, Dr. Rafael Leon
Costen, Dr. Melva Wilson
Cotman, Henry Earl
Cottle, Christopher
Cottrol, Robert James
Coulon, Burnel Elton
Coursey, Dr. Leon N
Courtney, Dr. Cassandra Hill
Covin, Dr. David L.
Cowell, Catherine
Cox, Dr. Arthur James, Sr.
Cox, Dr. Georgetta Manning
Craig, Elson L
Craig, Starlett Russell
Crawford, Mary Greer
Creighton-Zollar, Dr. Ann
Crenshaw, Reginald Anthony
Crocker, Clinton C
Crocker, Cyril L.
Cromwell, Adelaide M.
Crosby, Dr. Edward Warren
Crosby, Margaree Seawright
Cross, Dr. Dolores E.
Cross, Dr. Oris Elizabeth Carter
Crouther, Dr. Betty Jean
Crumpton, Dr. Lesia
Crusto, Mitchell Ferdinand
Crutchfield, James N
Cruthird, J Robert Lee
Cruz, Dr. Iluminado Angeles
Cruzat, Dr. Gwendolyn S.
Cudjoe, Dr. Selwyn Reginald
Cummings, Dr. Jay R.

Cunningham, Dr. James J.
Cunningham, Paul Raymond Gold-
wyn
Cunningham, Dr. William Dean
Curry, Dr. James
Curry, Sadye Beatryce
Curry, Dr. William Thomas
Curtis, Dr. James L
Curvin, Robert
Daily, Dr. Maceo Crenshaw
Dale, Clamma Churita
Daley, Thelma Thomas
Dalley, George Albert
Dalton, Raymond Andrew
Daly, Dr. Frederica Y
Damper, Ronald Eugene
Dandridge, Prof. Rita Bernice
Dandy, Clarence L.
Daniel, Griselda
Daniel, Simmie Childrey
Daniels, A. Raiford
Daniels, Geraldine L.
Daniels, Dr. Jean E.
Daniels, William James
Dansby, Jesse L.
Darden, Dr. Joseph S., Jr.
Dark, Lawrence Jerome
Dark, Okianer Christian
Dartson, Dr. Myrna
Dash, Leon DeCosta
Dates, Jannette Lake
Dauway, Lois McCullough
Dave, Alfonzo, Jr.
Davenport, Calvin A.
Davenport, Dr. Carol A.
Davenport, Christian A.
David, Arthur LaCurtiss
Davidson, Earnest Jefferson
Davidson, Dr. Elvyn Verone
Davidson, Ezra C.
Davis, Abraham
Davis, Angela Yvonne
Davis, Dr. Arthur David
Davis, Dr. Bertha Lane
Davis, Dr. Carrie L Filer
Davis, Denice Faye
Davis, Diana L.
Davis, Donald
Davis, Earl S.
Davis, Dr. Edward L.
Davis, Dr. Elaine Carsley
Davis, Dr. Ernestine
Davis, Dr. Ernestine Bady
Davis, Erroll B., Jr.
Davis, Etheldra S.
Davis, France Albert
Davis, Gene A.
Davis, George B.
Davis, Goliath J., III
Davis, Jean E.
Davis, Dr. Jewelnel
Davis, Joan Y.
Davis, Dr. John Albert
Davis, Johnetta Garner
Davis, Joseph Solomon
Davis, Dr. Katie Campbell
Davis, Lance Roosevelt
Davis, Lelia Kasenia
Davis, Leodis
Davis, Louis Garland
Davis, Dr. Marianna White
Davis, Dr. Marilyn Ann Cherry
Davis, Myrtle A.
Davis, Dr. Nathan Tate
Davis, Robert N
Davis, Russell Andre
Davis, Dr. Sheila Parham
Davis, William Hayes, Sr.
Davis, William R.
Davis, Dr. Willie
Davis, Willis H.
Davis-Haley, Dr. Rachel T
Davis-McFarland, Dr. E. Elise
Davy, Dr. Freddye Turner
Davy, Gloria
Dawkins, Miller J.
Dawkins, Stan Barrington Bancroft
Dawkins, Tammy C.
Dawson, Dr. Alma
Dawson, Dr. B. W.
Dawson, Michael C
Dawson, Shed, Jr.
Dawson Boyd, Dr. Candy
Days, Drew Saunders
Days, Rosetta Hill
Dean, Diane D
Dean, Walter R
DeBerry, Lois Marie
DeCarava, Roy Rudolph

DeCosta-Willis, Dr. Miriam
Dejoie, Carolyn Barnes Milanes
de Jongh, Prof. James Laurence
DeLauder, Dr. William B.
Delco, Wilhelmina R.
DeLeon-Jones, Frank A., Jr.
DeLoatch, Dr. Sandra J
Delpit, Lisa Denise
Delsarte, Louis
Demby, Prof. William E.
Dempsey, Rev. Dr. Joseph Page
Dennard, Brazeal Wayne
Dennis, Hugo, Jr.
Dennis, Dr. Rutledge M.
Denniston, Prof. Dorothy L.
Dent, David
Dent, Dr. Preston L.
DePillars, Murry Norman
Derricotte, Eugene Andrew
Derricotte, Toi
DeSassure, Charles
De Veaux, Alexis
Devine, Frank E.
Dickerson, Dr. Bette Jeanne
Dickerson, Prof. Dennis Clark
Dickerson, Lowell Dwight
Dickerson, Ron, Sr.
Dickinson, Dr. Gloria Harper
Dickson, Dr. Charlie Jones
Diggs, William P., Jr.
Dill, Dr. Bonnie Thornton
Dillard, Dr. Martin Gregory
Dinkins, David N.
Diuguid, Dr. Lincoln I.
Dixon, Dr. Armendia P.
Dixon, Dr. Benjamin
Dixon, Cheryl McKay
Dixon, Dr. Ruth F.
Dixon, William R.
Dobard, Raymond G
Dodson, Howard, Jr.
Dodson, Dr. Jualynne E.
Doggett, John Nelson
Donaldson, Leon Matthew
Donaldson, Shawn Riva
Donegan, Charles Edward
Doomes, Dr. Earl
Dorsey, Dr. Carolyn Ann
Dorsey, L. C.
Dottin, Dr. Robert Philip
Douglas, Elizabeth (Betty) Asche
Douglas, Herbert P., Jr.
Douglas, James Matthew
Douglas, Dr. Janice Green
Douglas, Joseph Francis
Douglas, Samuel Horace
Douglass, M Lorayne
Dove, Dr. Pearlie C.
Dove, Rita Frances
Dowdy, Dr. Joanne Kilgour
Dowery, Mary
Downie, Dr. Winsome Angela
Downing, Dr. John William, Jr.
Downs, Crystal
Draper, Dr. Edgar Daniel
Draper, Frederick Webster
Drewry, Cecelia Hodges
Driskell, David C.
Drumming, Saundra T
Drummond, William Joe
Dube, Thomas M T
Dudley-Washington, Loise
Dugas, A Jeffrey Alan, Sr.
Dummett, Clifton Orrin
Dumpson, Dr. James R.
Duncan, Marvin E.
Dungy, Dr. Claibourne I.
Dunlap, Dr. Karen F Brown
Dunmore, Charlotte J.
Dunn, Marvin
Dunn, William L.
Dunston, Walter T.
Dupree, David H.
DuPree, Kia
DuPree, Prof. Sherry Sherrod
Durand, Henry J., Jr.
Durant, Celeste Millicent
Durham, Dr. Joseph Thomas
Durr, Marlese
Duster, Troy
Dyce, Barbara J.
Dykes, DeWitt S.
Dymally, Lynn V
Dyson, Michael Eric
Eady, Cornelius
Ealy, Mary Newcomb
Earl, Dr. Archie William
Earls, Dr. Julian Manly
Early, Dr. Gerald

Maultsby, Rev. Dr. Sylvester
Maxey, Dr. Randall W
Maxwell, Dr. Marcella J.
May, Dr. Gary Stephen
May, James F.
Mayden, Ruth Wyatt
Mayes, Helen M.
Maynard, Dr. Edward Samuel
Maynard, Valerie J
Mayo, James Wellington
Mays, Dr. James Arthur
Mays, Dr. Vickie M
Mazon, Larri Wayne
McAdoo, Dr. Harriette P
McAdoo, Henry Allen
McAfee, Leo C
McAndrew, Anne E Battle
McArthur, Dr. Barbara Jean
McBride, Frances E.
McCall, Barbara Collins
McCarrell, Clark Gabriel
McCartney, John
McClain, Dr. Paula Denice
McClain, William Andrew
McClane, Prof. Kenneth Anderson, Jr.
McClean, Vernon E
McClearn, Billie
McClellan, Frank Madison
McClelland, Marguerite Marie
McClendon, Clarence E.
McClendon, Kellen
McClomb, George E.
McCloud, Aaron C.
McCloud, Anece Faison
McClure, Donald Leon, Sr.
McCluskey, Audrey Thomas
McCluskey, John A
McCorvey, Dr. Everett D.
McCrorey, Dr. M Lawrence
McCummings, Dr. LeVerne
McDaniel, Prof. Reuben R
McDaniels, Alfred F.
McDemmond, Dr. Marie V
McDonald, Dr. Curtis W.
McDonald, Jon Franklin
McDonald, Katrina Bell
McElroy, Dr. Lee A
McElvane, Pamela Anne
McFadden, Rev. Arthur B.
McFarlin, Emma Daniels
McFerrin, Sara Elizabeth Copper
McGee, Henry W
McGee, Dr. Joann
McGehee, Nan E
McGhee, Samuel T
McGinnis, James W.
McGlothan, Ernest
McGregor, Edna M.
McGuire, Dr. Chester C., Jr.
McGuire, Cyril A.
McHenry, Mary Williamson
McIlwain, Nadine Williams
McIntosh, Dr. Frankie L.
McIntosh, James E.
McIntyre, Dianne Ruth
McKanders, Kenneth Andre
McKandes, Dorothy Dell
McKayle, Donald Cohen
McKee, Adam E
McKenna, Dr. George J.
McKenzie, Reginald
McKinney, Alma Swilley
McKinney, Ernest Lee, Sr.
McKinney, George Dallas
McKinney, Rufus William
McKinney-Whetstone, Diane
McKinnon, Isaiah
Mckissack, Cheryl Mayberry
McKnight, Reginald
McLaughlin, Dr. Andree Nicola
McLaughlin, Dr. George W.
McLaughlin, Jacquelyn Snow
McLaughlin, LaVerne Laney
McLaughlin, Megan E.
McLaurin, Jasper Etienne
McLean, Dr. Helen Virginia
McLean, Dr. Mable Parker
McLemore, Leslie Burl
McMillan, Douglas James
McMillan, Jacqueline Marie
McMillan, Dr. William Asbury
McMillian, Frank L.
McMorris, Michael Anthony
McNeal, William R.
McNeil, Dr. Ogretta V.
McPhail, Sharon M
McReynolds, Elaine A.

McWilliams, Dr. Alfred E.
Meade-Tollin, Dr. Linda C
Meadows, Cheryl R
Means, Bertha E
Means, Dr. Craig R.
Means, Donald Fitzgerald
Mell, Patricia
Melton, Bryant
Mendez, Hugh B.
Merideth, Charles Waymond
Meridith, Denise Patricia
Meriwether, Roy Dennis
Merritt Cummings, Annette
Merriweather, Barbara Christine
Mesa, Mayra L
Metcalf, Dr. Zubie West, Jr.
Mickens, Dr. Ronald Elbert
Middleton, John Allen
Middleton, Phillip
Middleton, Rev. Dr. Richard Temple
Milburn, Dr. Corinne M.
Miles, Carlotta G.
Miles, Dr. Edward Lancelot
Miles, Frank J W
Miles, Dr. Norman Kenneth
Miles, Rachel Jean
Millard, Dr. Thomas Lewis
Milledge, Dr. Luetta Upshur
Millender, Mallory Kimerling
Miller, Dr. Andrea Lewis
Miller, Anna M.
Miller, Dr. Bernice Johnson
Miller, Dr. Dorsey Columbus, Jr.
Miller, E. Ethelbert
Miller, Horatio C.
Miller, Ingrid Fran Watson
Miller, Jacqueline Elizabeth
Miller, James Arthur
Miller, Dr. Jeanne-Marie Anderson
Miller, Louise T.
Miller, Dr. M Sammye
Miller, Dr. Margaret Greer
Miller, Richard Charles
Miller, Dr. Ronald Baxter
Miller, Russell L., Jr.
Miller, Tedd
Miller, Dr. Telly Hugh
Miller, Warren F, Jr.
Miller, Yvonne Bond
Miller-Jones, Dr. Dalton
Miller-Reid, Dora Alma
Millican, Arthenia J. Bates
Mimms, Dr. Maxine Buie
Mims, Beverly Carol
Mims, Dr. George L.
Minor, Billy Joe
Minor, Dale Michael
Minter, Thomas Kendall
Mitchell, Dr. Earl Douglass, Jr.
Mitchell, Rev. Dr. Henry Heywood
Mitchell, Joann
Mitchell, Sharon L
Mitchell, Theo W
Mitchell-Kernan, Dr. Claudia Irene
Mitchem-Davis, Anne
M- Middleton, Vertelle D
Moaney, Eric R.
Mobley, Emily Ruth
Mobley, Eugenia L.
Mobley, Dr. Sybil Collins
Mock, James E
Molette, Dr. Carlton Woodard
Molette-Ogden, Carla
Monagan, Dr. Alfrieta Parks
Monroe, Annie Lucky
Monteiro, Dr. Thomas
Monteith, Dr. Henry C.
Montgomery, Dr. Clyde, Jr.
Montgomery, Toni-Marie
Moody, Charles David, Sr.
Moore, Alice Evelyn
Moore, Annie Jewell
Moore, Dr. Archie Bradford, Jr.
Moore, Beverly
Moore, Dr. Jean E.
Moore, Jerry A, Jr.
Moore, Dr. Jossie A.
Moore, Juliette R
Moore, Larry Louis
Moore, Lenard Duane
Moore, Dr. Nathan
Moore, Oscar William
Moore, Dr. Quincy L
Moore, Robert F
Mooring, Dr. Kittye D.
Moo-Young, Louise L.
Moreland, Dr. Lois Baldwin
Moreland-Young, Dr. Curtina
Morgan, Dr. Gordon D.

Morgan, Dr. Harry
Morgan, Hazel C Brown
Morgan, Jane Hale
Morgan-Cato, Charlotte Theresa
Morial, Sybil Haydel
Morisey, Patricia Garland
Morris, Bernard Alexander
Morris, Dr. Carole V.
Morris, Prof. Clifton
Morris, Dr. Dolores Orinskia
Morris, Effie Lee
Morris, Dr. Frank Lorenzo, Sr.
Morris, Kelso B.
Morris, Leibert Wayne
Morris, Margaret Lindsay
Morris, Stanley E., Jr.
Morris, William Howard
Morrison, Dr. Juan LaRue, Sr.
Morrison, Dr. K C
Morrison, Prof. Keith Anthony
Morrison, Toni
Morrow, Dr. John Howard, Jr.
Morse, Dr. Oliver
Mortimer, Delores M.
Morton, Rev. Charles E
Moseka, Aminata
Mosely, Dr. Kenneth
Moses, Harold Webster
Moses, Dr. Henry A.
Mosley, Carolyn W
Mosley, Marie Oleatha
Mosley, Walter
Moss, Alfred A
Moss, Robert C., Jr.
Murdock, Dr. Nathaniel H
Murray, Albert L.
Murray, James Hamilton
Murray, Dr. Mabel Lake
Murray, Thomas W., Jr.
Musgrove, Margaret Wynkoop
Muwakkil, Salim
Muyumba, Francois N.
Mwamba, Zuberi I
Myers, Dr. Jacqualine Desmona
Myers, Dr. Lena Wright
Myers, Samuel L, Sr.
Myers, Dr. Samuel L
Myrick, Dr. Howard A.
Myricks, Dr. Noel
Nabors, Michael C.R.
Nagan, Winston Percival
Nance, Jesse J., Jr.
Natta, Clayton Lyle
Neal, Dr. Homer Alfred
Neal-Barnett, Angela M.
Neavon, Joseph Roy
Neely, David E.
Nelson, Dr. Ivory V.
Nelson, Dr. Wanda Lee
Nelson, Dr. William Edward
Nelson-Holgate, Gail Evangelyn
Nengudi, Senga
NeSmith, Kimblin E
Nettleford, Hon. Rex Milton
Neverdon-Morton, Dr. Cynthia
Newell, Virginia K.
Newhouse, Quentin
Newkirk, Dr. Gwendolyn
Newkirk, Pamela
Newman, Dr. Geoffrey W
Newsome, Dr. Clarence Geno
Newsome, Dr. Moses, Jr.
Newsome, Ruthie
Newton, Jacqueline L.
Newton, Dr. James Elwood
Newton, Oliver A., Jr.
Neyland, Leedell Wallace
Nichols, Charles Harold
Nichols, David G
Nichols, Dr. Owen D.
Nicholson, Gemma
Nicholson, Lawrence E
Niles, Prof. Lyndrey Arnaud
Nixon, Harold L
Nnaji, Bartholomew O
Nnolim, Charles E.
Noble, John Charles
Noble, Ronald K
Noguera, Dr. Pedro Antonio
Noles, Eva M.
Norman, Georgette M.
Norman, Dr. William H
Norris, Dr. Donna M
Norris, Lonnie H
Northcross, Deborah Ametra
Northcross, Wilson Hill, Jr.
Northern, Robert A.
Norton, Dr. Aurelia Evangeline
Norton, Eleanor Holmes

Norwood, Kimberly Jade
Nowlin, Bettye J Isom
Nunnally, David H.
Nurse, Richard A
Nwagbaraocha, Joel O
Nwanna, Dr. Gladson I N
Obinna, Dr. Eleazu S.
Ogletree, Charles J
Ojumu, Ayodele
Okantah, Mwatabu S
Okhamafe, Imafedia
Okunor, Dr. Shiame
Oliver, Dr. Melvin L
Ollee, Mildred W.
Omolade, Barbara
Orduna, Dr. Kenneth Maurice
Osakwe, Prof. Christopher
Osborne, Dr. Alfred E., Jr.
Osby, Parico Green
Othow, Helen Chavis
Overstreet, Morris L
Overton, Spencer
Owens, Andi
Owens, Charles Edward
Owens, Dr. Debbie A.
Owens, Dr. Jerry Sue
Owens, Dr. Joan Murrell
Owens, Dr. Judith Myoli
Owens, Wallace, Jr.
Oxley, Dr. Leo Lionel
Oyewole, Dr. Saundra Herndon
Packer, ZZ
Padgett, James A
Padulo, Dr. Louis
Page, Willie F
Paige, Alvin
Painter, Dr. Nell Irvin
Palmer, Edgar Bernard
Palmer, Robert L., II
Palmer, Ronald DeWayne
Pannell, William E
Parham, Brenda Joyce
Parham, Johnny Eugene, Jr.
Parker, Dr. Henry H.
Parker, Jacquelyn Heath
Parker, Dr. Keith Dwight
Parker, Dr. Stephen A.
Parks, Dr. Arnold Grant
Parks, George Brooks
Parks, Thelma Reece
Parson, Willie L.
Paschal, Eloise Richardson
Paschal, Trisa Long
Pate, Alexs D
Patrick, Odessa R.
Patterson, Christine Ann
Patterson, Dr. Elizabeth Ann
Patterson, Elizabeth Hayes
Patterson, Evelynne
Patterson, Grace Limerick
Patterson, Lydia R
Patterson, Dr. Orlando Horace
Patterson, Willis Charles
Pattillo, Roland A
Patton, Dr. Curtis Leverne
Paul, Dr. Alvin
Payne, Jerry Oscar
Payne, Leslie
Payton, Albert Levern
Peace, Dr. G. Earl
Peagler, Owen Fair
Pearson, Clifton
Peck, Leontyne Clay
Peebles, Allie Muse
Peebles-Wilkins, Dr. Wilma Cecelia
Peek, Booker C.
Peery, Benjamin Franklin, Jr.
Pemberton, Dr. Gayle R.
Penceal, Dr. Bernadette Whitley
Penn, Dr. Nolan E
Peoples, Dr. Gerald C
Peoples, VerJanis Andrews
Perkins, Edward Joseph
Perkins, Frances J
Perkins, Huel Davis
Perry, Dr. Aubrey M.
Perry, Leonard Douglas, Jr.
Perry, Dr. Patsy Brewington
Perry, Richard
Perry, Dr. Robert Lee
Perry, Wayne D
Persip, Charles Lawrence
Person, Dr. Dawn Renee
Person, Dr. William Alfred
Persons, W Ray
Peters, Dr. James Sedalia, II
Peters, Samuel A.
Petersen, Eileen Ramona
Peterson, Alphonse

Peterson, Prof. Lorna Ingrid
Petett, Freddye J Webb
Petioni, Dr. Muriel M
Pettaway, Charles
Pettis, Dr. Joyce Owens
Petty, Dr. Rachel Monteith
Petty-Edwards, Lula Evelyn
Phelps, Constance Kay
Phillip, Dr. Michael John
Phillips, Edward Martin
Phillips, Dr. Glenn Owen
Phillips, Dr. James Lawrence
Phillips, June M J
Phillips, Dr. Romeo Eldridge
Pickens Glass, Ernestine W. McCoy
Pickett, Rev. Henry B, Jr.
Pierce, Dr. Chester Middlebrook
Pierce, Cynthia Straker
Pierce, Dr. Raymond O., Jr.
Pierce, Walter J
Pile, Michael David McKenzie
Pilgrim, David
Pinado, Alan E., Sr.
Pindell, Howardena D
Pinkard, Dr. Deloris Elaine
Pinkney, Jerry
Pinn, Samuel J
Pinson, Hermine Dolorez
Piper, Adrian Margaret Smith
Piper, Dr. W Archibald
Pitcher, Freddie, Jr.
Pittman, Dr. Audrey Bullock
Pittman, Dr. Sample Noel
Pitts, Dr. Vera L.
Plummer, Michael Justin
Plumpp, Sterling Dominic
Pogue, Frank G., Jr.
Pointer, Dr. Richard H
Polite, Dr. Craig K., II
Polk, Dr. Gene-Ann
Polk, Prof. William C.
Pollard, Dr. Alton Brooks, III
Pollard, Dr. Diane S.
Pollard, Dr. William Lawrence
Ponder, Eunice Wilson
Pope, Derrick Alexander
Porter, Charles William
Porter, Dr. Clarence A.
Porter, Dr. John W
Porter, Karl Hampton
Portlock, Dr. Carver A.
Poussaint, Dr. Alvin Francis
Powell, Dudley Vincent
Powell, Patricia
Powell, Sis Paula Livers
Prather, Jeffrey Lynn
Prather, Susan Louise
Pratt, Awadagin
Press, Dr. Harry Cody, Jr.
Prestage, Dr. Jewel Limar
Preston, George Nelson
Preston, Dr. Michael B
Prettyman, Quandra
Prewitt, Dr. Lena Voncille Burrell
Prezeau, Dr. Maryse
Price, Prof. Alfred Douglas
Price, Sr. Fred L
Price, John Elwood
Price, Ray Anthony
Priest, Dr. Marlon L
Priester, Julian Anthony
Prigmore, Kathryn Tyler
Primous, Emma M.
Primus-Cotton, Dr. Bobbie J
Pringle, Nell Rene
Proctor, William H
Prothro, Dr. Johnnie Watts
Prothrow-Stith, Deborah Boutin
Prudhomme, Nellie Rose
Pruitt, Dr. George Albert
Pruitt-Logan, Dr. Anne Smith
Pugh, Dr. Clementine A.
Pugh, Dr. Roderick Wellington
Pulley, Prof. Clyde Wilson
Purce, Dr. Thomas Les
Puryear, Dr. Alvin Nelson
Queen, Evelyn E Crawford
Quigless, Dr. Milton Douglas, Jr.
Quinton, Barbara Ann
Rabouin, E Michelle
Raby, Clyde T
Radcliffe, Dr. Aubrey
Rambison, Dr. Amar B
Ramey, Felicenne H
Ramey, Melvin R
Rampersad, Arnold
Ramseur, Andre William
Randall, Ann Knight
Randall, Dr. Queen Franklin

Randolph, Robert Lee
Ransby, Barbara
Ransom, Lillie
Ransom, Dr. Preston L
Rasheed, Howard S
Rashford, Dr. John Harvey
Raspberry, William J
Rates, Rev. Norman M
Ravenell, Mildred
Ravenell, William Hudson
Ray, Jacqueline Walker
Ray, Dr. Judith Diana
Ray, Prof. William Benjamin
Reagon, Dr. Bernice Johnson
Reaves, Rev. Dr. Benjamin Franklin
Redmond, Eugene B.
Reed, Dr. Allene Wallace
Reed, Dr. Charlotte
Reed, Dr. Daisy Frye
Reed, Ishmael Scott
Reed, Dr. James W
Reed, Jasper Percell
Reed, Michael H
Reed, Dr. Rodney J
Reese, Mamie Bynes
Register, Dr. Jasper C.
Reid, Dr. F. Theodore, Jr.
Reid, Irvin D
Reid, Joel Otto
Reid, Dr. Leslie Bancroft
Reid, Pamela Trotman
Reid, Dr. Roberto Elliott
Reide, Atty. Jerome L.
Reid-Merritt, Patricia Ann
Reinhardt, John Edward
Rembert, Dr. Emma White
Render, Arlene
Reuben, Dr. Lucy J
Reuben, Dr. Lucy Jeanette
Revis, Dr. Nathaniel W
Reynolds, Dr. Edward
Reynolds, Mel
Rhines, Jesse Algeron
Rhodes, Dr. Paula R
Rice, Dr. Condoleezza
Rice, Horace Warren
Rice, Dr. Louise Allen
Rice, Dr. Mitchell F
Rice, Dr. Pamela Ann
Rich, Wilbur C
Richard, Alvin J.
Richards, Johnetta Gladys
Richards, Leon
Richards, Winston Ashton
Richardson, Andra Virginia
Richardson, Elisha R
Richardson, Henry J.
Richie, Dr. Beth E.
Ridgeway, Dr. Bill Tom
Ridley, Dr. Alfred Dennis
Rife, Anita
Riggins, Lester
Rigsby, Esther Martin
Riley, Clayton
Riley, Liz
Riley, Shaunce R
Ringgold, Faith
Rison, Dr. Faye
Ritchie, Joe
Ritchie, Dr. Louise Reid
Rivers, Louis
Rivers, Dr. Robert Joseph, Jr.
Roach, Prof. Hildred Elizabeth
Roane, Dr. Philip Ransom
Roberson, Gloria Grant
Roberts, Bryndis Wynette
Roberts, Kay George
Roberts, Kim
Roberts, Marcus
Roberts, Roy J.
Roberts, Dr. Terrence James
Robertson, Dr. Benjamin W
Robertson, Quincy L.
Robeson, Paul, Jr.
Robinson, Dr. Andrew
Robinson, Ann Garrett
Robinson, Carrie C.
Robinson, Dr. Cecelia Ann
Robinson, Charles E
Robinson, Curtis
Robinson, Edward A.
Robinson, Eunice Primus
Robinson, Frank J.
Robinson, Dr. Genevieve
Robinson, Jeffrey
Robinson, Jim C
Robinson, Jontyle Theresa
Robinson, Dr. Joyce Russell
Robinson, Dr. Kitty Kidd

Robinson, Dr. Luther Dabney
Robinson, Dr. Letha A
Robinson, Dr. Malcolm Kenneth
Robinson, Dr. Milton J
Robinson, Dr. Prezell Russell
Robinson, Dr. Randall S
Robinson, Dr. Randall S.
Robinson, Dr. Rufus E
Robinson, Dr. Samuel
Robinson, Dr. Walker Lee
Rockett, Damon Emerson
Rodgers, Dr. Augustus
Rodgers, Carolyn Marie
Rodgers, Vincent G
Rodriguez, Argelia Velez
Rogers, Charles D
Rogers-Lomax, Dr. Alice Faye
Rollins, Judith Ann
Rollins, Dr. Richard Albert
Rose, Alvin W.
Rose, Tricia
Ross, Dr. Anthony Roger
Ross, Dr. Catherine Laverne
Ross, Dr. Denise Elizabeth
Ross, Lee Elbert
Ross, Rev. Ralph M
Rosser, Dr. James M.
Rosser, Samuel Blanton
Rotan, Dr. Constance S.
Roulhac, Dr. Nellie Gordon
Rouse, Jacqueline Anne
Royster, Philip M
Rushing, Byron D
Russell, Charlie L.
Russell, George A
Russell, James A., Jr.
Russell, Joseph J.
Rutledge, Dr. Essie Manuel
Ryan-White, Jewell
Saddler, Elbert M
Sadler, Dr. Wilbert L
Saffold, Oscar E.
Salmon, Dr. Jaslin Uriah
Samkange, Tommie Marie
Sampson, Dr. Calvin Coolidge
Samuels, Annette Jacqueline
Samuels, Dr. Wilfred D
Sanchez, Dr. Sonia Benita
Sanders, Rev. Dr. Cheryl J
Sanders, Dr. Gwendolyn W.
Sanders, Dr. Karen Eley
Sanders, Larry Kyle
Sanders, Dr. Lou Helen
Sanders, Dr. Robert B
Sanders, Dr. Woodrow Mac
Sandidge, Dr. Oneal C
Sandoval, Dolores S.
Sands, George M.
Sands, Prof. Mary Alice
Santos, Henry Joseph
Sapp, Lauren B
Sarkodie-Mensah, Dr. Kwasi
Satchell, Elizabeth
Satchell, Ernest R
Satcher, Robert Lee
Saunders, Dr. Elijah
Saunders, Dr. Elizabeth Ann
Saunders, Raymond
Savage, Dr. Edward W, Jr.
Savage, Horace Christopher
Savage, Dr. Vernon Thomas
Sawyer, William Gregory
Scales, Alice Marie
Scales, Jerome C.
Scales, Dr. Manderline Elizabeth
  Willis
Scales-Trent, Prof. Judy
Scarborough, Charles S.
Schooler, Dr. James Morse
Scott, Prof. Charlotte Hanley
Scott, Dr. Elsie L
Scott, Dr. Gloria Dean Randle
Scott, Dr. Helen Madison Marie
  Pawne Kinard
Scott, Dr. Hugh J.
Scott, Dr. John Sherman
Scott, Joseph Walter
Scott, Marvin Wayne
Scott, Dr. Mona Vaughn
Scott, Dr. Otis L
Scott, Portia Alexandria
Scott, Veronica J.
Scrivens, John J
Scroggins, Bobby
Scruggs, Cleorah J.
Scruggs, Prof. Otey Matthew
Seals, Rupert Grant
Sealy, Joan Rice
Seaton, Sandra Cecelia
Seaton, Dr. Shirley Smith

Sebhatu, Dr. Mesgun
See, Dr. Letha A
Senbet, Prof. Lemma W
Sergeant, Carra Susan
Sessoms, Allen Lee
Sevillian, Clarence Marvin
Shade, Dr. Barbara J.
Shamwell, Ronald L
Shange, Ntozake
Sharp, Charles Louis
Sharp, Dr. J Anthony
Sharpe, Dr. Calvin William
Shaw, Dr. Ann
Shaw, Booker Thomas
Shaw, Ferdinand
Shaw, Dr. Spencer Gilbert
Shaw, Theodore Michael
Sheffey, Dr. Ruthe T.
Shepherd, Benjamin Arthur
Shepherd, Dr. Lewis A
Shepherd, Roosevelt Eugene
Sherwood, Wallace Walter
Shields, Dr. Clarence L
Shine, Theodis
Shipp, Etheleen R
Shipp, Howard J., Jr.
Shipp, Dr. Melvin Douglas
Shirley, George Irving
Shockley, Ann Allen
Shopshire, Dr. James Maynard
Short, Kenneth L
Shorty, Vernon James
Shotwell, Ada Christena
Showell, Hazel Jarmon
Shuford, Humphrey Lewis
Sikes, Dr. Melvin Patterson
Siler, Dr. Joyce B
Silver, Dr. Joseph Howard
Simmons, Annie Marie
Simmons, Dr. Howard L
Simmons, Prof. John Emmett
Simmons, Kenneth H
Simmons, Dr. S Dallas
Simmons, Dr. Sylvia Q.
Simms, Carroll Harris
Simpkins, J. Edward
Simpson, Dr. John Randolph
Simpson, Dr. Willa Jean
Simpson-Taylor, Dr. Dorothy Marie
Sims, Genevieve Constance
Sims, Prof. Ronald R
Singh, Dr. Rajendra P
Singleton, Leroy, Sr.
Sinkler, Dr. George
Sinnette, Elinor DesVerney
Skinner, Byron R
Skinner, Dr. Ewart C.
Slade, Phoebe J.
Slaughter, Atty. Fred L.
Slaughter, Dr. John Brooks
Slaughter-Defoe, Dr. Diana T.
Slie, Samuel N
Small, Dr. Clara Louise
Small, Lily B.
Smalls, O'Neal
Smallwood, Dr. Catherine
Smith, Dr. Albert E
Smith, Alfred J., Jr.
Smith, Alphonso Lehman
Smith, Andrew W.
Smith, Dr. Ann Elizabeth
Smith, Arthur D.
Smith, Audrey S
Smith, Dr. Barbara Wheat
Smith, Carol J
Smith, Charles Edison
Smith, Dr. Charles F.
Smith, Dr. Charles U.
Smith, Charlie Calvin
Smith, Darryl C.
Smith, Dolores J
Smith, Dr. Donald Hugh
Smith, Dr. Edgar Eugene
Smith, Dr. Edward Nathaniel, Jr.
Smith, Dr. Eleanor Jane
Smith, George Edmond
Smith, Dr. Gerald Lamont
Smith, Geraldine T
Smith, Heman Bernard
Smith, Howlett P.
Smith, Dr. J. Clay, Jr.
Smith, Dr. James Almer, Jr.
Smith, James David
Smith, Dr. Jesse Owens
Smith, Dr. Jessie Carney
Smith, Dr. Joanne Hamlin
Smith, Dr. John Arthur
Smith, John L, Jr.
Smith, Dr. Joshua L.

Smith, Dr. Judith Moore
Smith, Keith Dryden
Smith, LeRoi Matthew-Pierre, III
Smith, Dr. Luther Edward
Smith, Mary Levi
Smith, Dr. Nellie J.
Smith, Paul
Smith, Philip Gene
Smith, Dr. Phillip M.
Smith, Dr. Quentin Ted
Smith, Reginald D
Smith, Robert Charles
Smith, Robert London
Smith, Dr. Robert P., Jr.
Smith, Dr. Roland Blair
Smith, Dr. Roulette William
Smith, Shirley Hunter
Smith, Vernon G
Smith, Virginia M.
Smith, Dr. Walter L
Smitherman, Carole
Smitherman, Dr. Geneva
Smith Nelson, Dr. Dorothy J.
Snowden, Frank Walter
Snowden, Gilda
Snowden, Sylvia Frances
Sockwell, Oliver R, Jr.
Sogah, Dr. Dotsevi Yao
Soliunas, Francine Stewart
Solomon, Barbara J.
Somerville, Dr. Addison Wimbs
Sommerville, Joseph C.
Southerland, Ellease
Southern, Joseph
Southgate, Martha
Sowell, Thomas
Spaulding, Jean Gaillard
Spears, Henry Albert
Spears Jones, Patricia Kay
Speiginer, Gertha
Spence, Rev. Joseph Samuel, Sr.
Spencer, Prof. Margaret Beale
Spencer, Dr. Michael Gregg
Spigner, Dr. Clarence
Spikes, Dr. Delores R.
Spiva, Dr. Ulysses Van
Sprauve, Dr. Gilbert A.
Sprout, Francis Allen
Spruill, James Arthur
Stalls, Dr. M
Stamps, Spurgeon Martin David
Stancell, Dr. Arnold Francis
Stanley, Carol Jones
Stansbury, Clayton Cresvell
Staples, Robert E.
Starks, Robert Terry
Steele, Dr. Claude Mason
Steele, Ruby L
Steele, Dr. Shelby
Stent, Madelon Delany
Stephens, E. Delores B.
Stepto, Robert Burns
Stetson, Jeffrey P
Stevens, Althea Williams
Stevens, George Edward
Stevens, Dr. Joyce West
Stevens, Dr. Maxwell McDew
Stevenson, Bryan A
Stevenson, Russell A.
Stewart, Dr. Bess
Stewart, Dr. Donald Mitchell
Stewart, Dr. Elizabeth Pierce
Stewart, Ella
Stewart, Jacqueline
Stewart, Dr. James Benjamin
Stewart, Dr. John Othneil
Stewart, Dr. Mac A.
Stewart, Pearl
Stewart, Dr. William H.
Stinson, Joseph McLester
Stith, Dr. Rep. Melvin Thomas
St John, Primus
Stockman, Dr. Ida J
Stodghill, Dr. Ronald
Stokes, Gerald Virgil
Stokes, Julie Elena
Stokes, Dr. Lillian Gatlin
Stokes, Shereitte Charles
St Omer, Vincent V E
Stone, Chuck
St Pierre, Dr. Maurice
Strickland, Dorothy S
Stripling, Dr. Luther
Strother, Germaine D
Stubblefield, Jennye Lee Washington
Stull, Virginia Elizabeth
Styles, Kathleen Ann
Suber, Dianne Boardley
Subryan, Carmen

Suggs, Dr. Robert Chinelo
Sullivan, Dr. Allen R
Sullivan, Dr. J. Christopher
Sullivan, Zola Jiles
Sulton, Anne Thomas
Sumler Edmond, Janice L.
Summers, Loretta M
Suneja, Sidney Kumar
Sutton, Dianne Floyd
Sutton, Dr. Sharon Egretta
Sutton, Dr. William Wallace
Swan, Dr. George W., III
Swan, L. Alex
Swann, Eugene Merwyn
Swindell, Dr. Warren C.
Sykes, Vernon Lee
Sykes, William Richard
Sylvas, Dr. Lionel B.
Sylvester, Melvin R
Sylvester, Dr. Patrick Joseph
Syphax, Dr. Burke
Taborn, Dr. John Marvin
Talbot, Gerald Edgerton
Talbot, Theodore A.
Talley, Michael Frank, Sr.
Talley, William B
Tanner, James W., Jr.
Tanner, Tyrone
Tanter, Raymond
Tarter, Roger Powell, M.D.
Tarver, Marie Nero
Tate, Dr. James A.
Tatum, Dr. Beverly Daniel
Tatum, James
Taylor, Arnold H.
Taylor, Carole Lillian
Taylor, Dr. Charles E
Taylor, Dr. Dale B
Taylor, Dr. David Vassar
Taylor, Edward Walter
Taylor, Dr. Estelle Wormley
Taylor, Dr. Henry Louis, Jr.
Taylor, Howard Francis
Taylor, Hycel B.
Taylor, Jerome
Taylor, Joseph
Taylor, Julius H
Taylor, Mary Quivers
Taylor, Michael Loeb
Taylor, Orlando L
Taylor, Prof. Paul David
Taylor, Dr. Quintard
Taylor, Dr. Robert, III
Taylor, Dr. Ronald Lewis
Taylor, Stuart A.
Taylor, William L
Taylor-Thompson, Dr. Betty E
Teasley, Ronald
Tei, Dr. Ebo
Temple, Edward Stanley
Temple, Dr. Jacqueline B
Terborg-Penn, Dr. Rosalyn M
Terrell, Dr. Francis
Terrell, Francis D'Arcy
Terrell, Mary Ann
Terrell, Dr. Melvin C
Terrell, Robert L.
Teruel, Lauren
Thelwell, Michael M Ekwueme
Thigpen, Edmund Leonard
Thomas, Althea Shannon Lawson
Thomas, Carl Alan
Thomas, Charles Columbus
Thomas, David
Thomas, David Anthony
Thomas, Dr. Dennis
Thomas, Eula Wiley
Thomas, Gerald Eustis
Thomas, Dr. Harry Lee
Thomas, Dr. Herman Edward
Thomas, Jacquelyn Small
Thomas, James Samuel
Thomas, Jane Roscoe, PhD
Thomas, Joyce Carol
Thomas, Kendall
Thomas, Rev. Dr. Latta Roosevelt,
  Sr.
Thomas, Dr. Lucille Cole
Thomas, Mary A.
Thomas, Matthew Manjusri, Jr.
Thomas, Maxine Suzanne
Thomas, Nathaniel
Thomas, Nina M
Thomas, Dr. Pamella D
Thomas, Robert Lewis
Thomas, Rodolfo Rudy
Thomas, Stephen
Thomas-Carter, Jean Cooper
Thompson, Betty Taylor

Thompson, Dr. Charles
Thompson, Francesca
Thompson, Dr. Joseph Earl, Sr.
Thompson, Dr. Litchfield O
Thompson, Marcus Aurelius
Thompson, Regina
Thompson, Dr. Robert Farris
Thompson, Dr. Sidney A
Thompson, Sylvia Moore
Thompson, Dr. Winston Edna
Thomson, Gerald Edmund
Thomson, Dr. Thelma B
Thorburn, Dr. Carolyn Coles
Thornell, Richard Paul
Thornton, Clifford E.
Thornton, Dozier W.
Thornton, Dr. Maurice
Thurman, Alfonzo
Thurston, Dr. Paul E.
Tidwell, John Edgar
Tildon, Charles G., Jr.
Tillis, Dr. Frederick C.
Tillman, Dr. Talmadge Calvin, Jr.
Tipton, Dr. Dale Leo
Tisdale, Prof. Celes
Titus-Dillon, Dr. Pauline Y
Tobias, Randolf A
Tolbert, Dr. Herman Andre
Tolbert, Jacquelyn C.
Tolbert, Odie Henderson, Jr.
Toler, Burl Abron
Tolliver, Dr. Richard Lamar
Tomlinson, Dr. Robert
Torrence-Thompson, Juanita Lee
Tottress, Richard Edward
Towns, Sanna Nimtz
Traylor, Prof. Eleanor W.
Traylor, Dr. Horace Jerome
Treadwell, David Merrill
Trent, Richard Darrell
Trice, William B.
Trimiar, Dr. J. Sinclair
Tripp, Dr. Luke Samuel
Tropez-Sims, Susanne
Trottman, Charles Henry
Troupe, Dr. Marilyn Kay
Troupe, Quincy Thomas, Jr.
Troutman, Dr. Adewale
Troutman, Porter Lee, Jr.
Tucker, Dr. Dorothy M.
Tucker, Dr. M Belinda
Tucker, Norma Jean
Tuckson, Reed V
Tufon, Chris
Tukufu, Darryl S
Turnbull, Dr. Charles Wesley
Turner, Castellano Blanchet
Turner, Dr. Doris J.
Turner, Geneva
Turner, Jean Taylor
Turner, Dr. Moses
Turner, W Burghardt
Turner, Dr. William Hobert
Turner, Winston E.
Turner-Givens, Ella Mae
Twigg, Dr. Lewis Harold
Twiggs, Dr. Leo Franklin
Tyler, Rev. Gerald DeForest
Unaeze, Felix Eme
Uzoigwe, Dr. Godfrey N.
Valdes, Pedro H
Vance, Dr. Irvin E
Van Trece, Jackson C.
Varner, James, Sr.
Varner, Dr. Nellie M.
Vaughans, Kirkland Cornell
Vaughn, Janice S
Vereen-Gordon, Dr. Mary Alice
Vernon, Alexander
Verrett, Shannon L.
Vertreace-Doody, Martha Modena
Vessup, Dr. Aaron Anthony
Via, Thomas Henry
Vick-Williams, Dr. Marian Lee
Violenus, Agnes A
Vogel, Dr. Roberta Burrage
Wade, Achille Melvin
Wade, Dr. Joseph Downey
Wade, William Carl
Wade-Gayles, Dr. Gloria Jean
Wade-Lewis, Margaret
Wade-Maltais, Dr. Joyce
Wafer, Deborah
Waiguchu, Muruku
Walden, Dr. Robert Edison
Walker, Annie Mae
Walker, Charles
Walker, Charles Ealy, Jr.
Walker, Cynthia Bush

Walker, Dr. Ethel Pitts
Walker, Dr. Gregory T S
Walker, Dr. Kenneth R.
Walker, Larry Moore
Walker, Dr. LeRoy Tashreau
Walker, Dr. Lewis
Walker, Margie
Walker, Dr. Sandra Venezia
Walker, Dr. Sheila Suzanne
Walker, Stanley Michael
Walker, Valaida Smith
Walker, Wilbur P.
Wallace, John M., Jr.
Wallace, Milton De
Wallace, Dr. Renee C
Walls, Gen. George Hilton, Jr.
Walter, Dr. John C.
Walters, Curla Sybil
Walters, Hubert Everett
Walters, Marc Anton
Walters, Ronald
Walton, Dr. Edward D.
Walton, Hanes
Walton, Dr. Harriett J.
Walton, R Keith
Ward, Arnette S.
Ward, Daniel
Ward, Dr. James Dale
Ward, Dr. Jerry Washington
Ward, Dr. Perry W.
Ward, Velma Lewis
Wardlaw, McKinley, Jr.
Ware, Dr. Gilbert
Ware, Dr. William Levi
Warner, Isiah Manuel
Warren, Herman Lecil
Warren, Dr. Joseph David
Warren, Dr. Joseph W
Warren, Nagueyalti
Warren, Dr. Stanley
Washington, Dr. Earl Melvin
Washington, Gladys J.
Washington, James Lee, Sr.
Washington, Joseph R., Jr.
Washington, Josie B.
Washington, Dr. Linda Phaire
Washington, Mary Helen
Washington, Dr. Michael Harlan
Washington, Oscar D
Washington, Roosevelt, Jr.
Washington, Dr. Sandra Beatrice
Washington, Dr. Sarah M
Washington, Dr. Thomas
Washington, Dr. Von Hugo
Waters, John W
Watkins, Dr. Charles B
Watkins, Dr. Levi, Jr.
Watson, Dr. Bernard C.
Watson, Dennis Rahiim
Watson, Dr. Elizabeth Darby
Watson, Genevieve
Watson, Dr. Janice
Watson, John Clifton
Watson, Joseph W
Watts, Dr. Anne Wimbush
Watts, Dr. Roberta Ogletree
Wead, Dr. Rodney Sam
Weaver, Afaa Michael
Weaver, Dr. John Arthur
Weaver, Reginald Lee
Weaver, William Courtsworthy, II
Webb, Dr. Harvey
Webb, Melvin Richard
Weber, Dr. Shirley Nash
Webster, Niambi Dyanne
Weddington, Bill
Weddington, Dr. Rachel Thomas
Weddington, Dr. Wilburn Harold, Sr.
Weiss, Joyce Lacey
Welburn, Ronald Garfield
Welch, Ashton Wesley
Welch, Harvey
Welch, Dr. Olga Michele
Wells, Patrick Roland
Welmon, Vernis M
West, Cornel
West, George Ferdinand, Jr.
West, Dr. Herbert Lee, Jr.
West, Dr. John Raymond
West, Pheoris
West, Valerie Y
West, William Lionel
Westmoreland, Samuel Douglas
Whaley, Edward I
Wharton, A. C., Jr.
Wharton Boyd, Linda F.
Wheelan, Belle Smith
Whitaker, Mical Rozier
White, Dr. Augustus A., III

White, Dr. Barbara Williams
White, Clayton Cecil
White, Dr. Don Lee
White, Frederic Paul, Jr.
White, Howard A
White, Katie Kinnard
White, Dr. Keith L.
White, Marilyn Elaine
White, Paul Edward
White, Dr. Sandra LaVelle
White, Sharon Brown
White, Dr. Tommie Lee
White, Yolanda Simmons
Whitehurst, Steven Laroy
Whitely, Donald Harrison
White-Parson, Willar F
Whiting, Albert Nathaniel
Whitten, Dr. Charles F.
Whittington, Dr. Harrison DeWayne
Whittler, Dr. Thomas
Whyte, Garrett
Wideman, John Edgar
Wiggins, Joseph L.
Wiggins, William H., Jr.
Wilder, Cora White
Wilderson, Dr. Frank B., Jr.
Wiles, Leon E.
Wiley, John D., Jr.
Wilkerson, Prof. Margaret Buford
Wilkins, Allen Henry
Wilkins, David Brian
Wilkins, Josetta Edwards
Wilkins, Dr. Leona B.
Wilkins, Roger Wood
Wilkinson, Donald Charles
Wilkinson, Dr. Doris
Williams, Arnette L.
Williams, Dr. Audrey
Williams, Benjamin Vernon
Williams, Dr. Betty Smith
Williams, Camilla Ella
Williams, Carolyn G
Williams, Dr. Carolyn Ruth Armstrong
Williams, Dr. Carroll Burns, Jr.
Williams, Cody
Williams, Prof. Daniel Salu
Williams, Donald H.
Williams, Dorothy Daniel
Williams, Dorothy P.
Williams, Dr. Dwight
Williams, Earl
Williams, Prof. Edna C.
Williams, Dr. Ella O.
Williams, Dr. Euphemia Goodlow
Williams, Frank James
Williams, Gary C.
Williams, George L., Sr.
Williams, Gregory Howard
Williams, Heather Andrea
Williams, Dr. Helen Elizabeth
Williams, Dr. Henry P
Williams, Dr. Hugh Hermes
Williams, Dr. James H., Jr.
Williams, Dr. James Hiawatha
Williams, Dr. James Thomas
Williams, Dr. Jamye Coleman
Williams, Jean Carolyn
Williams, Jeanette Marie
Williams, Jerome D.
Williams, John Alfred
Williams, Juan
Williams, Larry
Williams, Dr. Lisa R.
Williams, Lorece P.
Williams, Dr. Malvin A, Sr.
Williams, Marcus Doyle
Williams, Dr. McDonald
Williams, Dr. Melvin D
Williams, Naomi B
Williams, Norris Gerald
Williams, Dr. Oliver J
Williams, Dr. Ora
Williams, Dr. Preston N
Williams, Robert H.
Williams, Dr. Robert L
Williams, Sandra Roberts
Williams, Dr. Scott W.
Williams, Dr. Sterling B., Jr.
Williams, T. Joyce
Williams, Dr. Trina Rachael
Williams, W. Clyde
Williams, Rev. Wilbert Lee
Williams, Prof. William Thomas
Williams, Dr. Willie, Jr.
Williams, Dr. Willie Elbert
Williams, Willie L
Williams, Willie LaVern
Williams, Prof. Yvonne Carter

Williams-Green, Joyce F.
Williams-Hayes, Thea
Williams-Myers, Albert J
Williamson, Ethel W
Williamson, Dr. Handy, Jr.
Williams-Stanton, Dr. Sonya Denise
Williams-Taitt, Patricia Ann
Williams-Witherspoon, Kimmika L H
Willie, Dr. Charles Vert
Willis, Gladys January
Willock, Dr. Marcelle Monica
Willoughby, Dr. Susan Melita
Wills, Dr. Cornelia
Wilmore, Gayraud Stephen, Jr.
Wilmot, David Winston
Wilson, Dr. Blenda Jacqueline
Wilson, Dr. Bobby L
Wilson, Carroll Lloyd
Wilson, Dr. Charles Z., Jr.
Wilson, Clarence S., Jr.
Wilson, Dr. David
Wilson, Dr. Donald
Wilson, Dr. Donella Joyce
Wilson, Hugh A.
Wilson, Hughlyne Perkins
Wilson, Dr. Jeffrey R.
Wilson, John T., Jr.
Wilson, Dr. John W.
Wilson, Dr. Johnny Leaverne
Wilson, Jonathan Charles
Wilson, Dr. Joseph F.
Wilson, Patricia A.
Wilson, Dr. Patricia I
Wilson, Rudolph George
Wilson, Sandra E.
Wilson, Prof. Stanley Charles
Wilson, Dr. William Julius
Winbush, Raymond Arnold
Winfield, Dr. Linda Fitzgerald
Wing, Prof. Adrien Katherine
Wingfield, Dr. Harold Lloyd
Winslow, Reynolds Baker
Winston, Dr. Hubert
Winston, Dr. Michael Russell
Wint, Arthur Valentine Noris
Winter, Daria Portray
Winters, Wendy Glasgow
Womack, Henry Cornelius
Woodard, Fredrick
Woodard, Samuel L.
Woodland, Dr. Calvin Emmanuel
Woodruff, Jeffrey Robert
Woods, Allie, Jr.
Woods, Dr. Clifton
Woods, Willie G
Woodson, Shirley A
Wormley, Diane-Louise Lambert
Worrell, Richard Vernon
Worrill, Dr. Conrad W
Wortham, Russeal
Worthy, Dr. Barbara Ann
Worthy, William, Jr.
Wrice, David
Wrice, Dr. Sheldon B
Wrice, Vincent J
Wright, Dmitri
Wright, Dr. Earl Lee
Wright, Dr. Frederick Douglass
Wright, Dr. George C
Wright, Dr. Jackson Thomas
Wright, James E
Wright, Jane C.
Wright, Dr. John Aaron
Wright, Joyce C.
Wright, Dr. Katie Harper
Wright, Dr. Larry L
Wright, Roosevelt R., Jr.
Wright, Stephen Caldwell
Wright, Dr. Wilson, Jr.
Wright-Botchwey, Roberta Yvonne
Wykle, May Louise Hinton
Wyre, Stanley Marcel
Yamba, Dr. Zachary
Yancey, Dr. Carolyn Lois
Yancy, Dr. Dorothy Cowser
Yancy, Prof. Preston Martin
Yarborough, Richard A
Yarde, Prof. Richard Foster
Yizar, James Horace
Young, Prof. Alfred
Young, Dr. Edith Mae
Young, Dr. Elizabeth Bell
Young, F. Camille
Young, James E.
Young, Lee
Young, Margaret Buckner
Young, Dr. Michael
Young, Dr. Nancy Wilson

Young, Thomas
Zachary, Steven W
Zambrana, Dr. Rafael
Ziegler, Dr. Dhyana
Zollar, Jawole Willa Jo
Zook, Kristal Brent
Zulu, Itibari M

Education—Elementary/Secondary

Abebe, Ruby
Abney, Robert
Ackord, Marie Mallory
Adams, Lillian Louise T.
Adams, Robert Hugo
Adams, Dr. Verna May Shoecraft
Aikens-Young, Dr. Linda Lee
Aldridge, Allen Ray
Alexander, Dorothy Dexter
Alexander, Vincent J.
Allen, Walter R
Alston, Betty Bruner
Amin, Karima
Anders, Richard H.
Anderson, Mary Elizabeth
Anderson, S. A.
Andrew, Milton
Andrews, James F.
Arkhurst, Joyce Cooper
Armstrong Busby, Delia Bliss
Arties, Lucy Elvira Yvonne
Atchison, Lillian Elizabeth
Atkinson, Curtis L.
Aviles, Dora
Bailey, Dr. Adrienne Yvonne
Baker, Henry W., Sr.
Baker, Jacqueline
Banks, Dwayne Martin
Banks, June Skinner
Barefield, Morris
Barnes, Diane
Barnes, Vivian Leigh
Baskett, Kenneth Gerald
Beady, Dr. Charles H, Jr.
Bean, Bobby Gene
Beasley, Annie Ruth
Becker, Adolph Eric
Bell, Charles Smith
Bell, George
Bell, Kenneth M.
Benning, Dr. Emma Bowman
Benson, Lillian
Benson, Rubin Author
Bing, Rubell M.
Bins, Milton
Birchette, Dr. William Ashby, III
Block, Dr. Leslie S.
Bond, Ronald A
Booth, Anna Maria
Bouie, Dr. Merceline
Bowe-Quick, Marie
Boyd, Evelyn Shipps
Bradley, William B.
Bradshaw, Doris Marion
Breeding, Carl L.
Bronz, Lois Gougis Taplin
Brooks, James Taylor
Brooks, Norman Leon
Brooks, Rosemary Bittings
Brown, Bernice Baynes
Brown, Carolyn M
Brown, Conella Coulter
Brown, Emma Jean Mitchell
Brown, James Marion
Brown, Jennifer H.
Brown, Justine Thomas
Brown, Malcolm McCleod
Brown, Michael DeWayne
Brown, Otha N
Brown, Philip Lorenzo
Brown, Rubye Golsby
Brown, Yolanda B
Bryant, Regina Lynn
Buck, Dr. Judith Brooks
Buckhanan, Shawn L
Burks, James William, Jr.
Burnette, Dr. Ada Puryear
Burroughs, Dr. Margaret Taylor
Burton, Lana Doreen
Buskey, James E.
Butler, Kathleen Jean
Butts, Janie Pressley
Byas, Dr. Ulysses S.
Campbell, Alma Porter
Campbell, Margie
Campbell, Mary Allison
Carey, Carnice
Carlisle, James Edward, Jr.
Carpenter, Ann M.

1453

Education—Not Elsewhere Classified

Educational Administration

Blake, James G.
Blake, Rev. William J
Blakely, Carolyn
Bland, Dr. Robert Arthur
Blanks, Cecelia
Blaylock, Ronald E.
Bledsoe, Tempestt
Block, Carolyn B.
Block, Dr. Leslie S.
Bobbitt, Leroy
Bobino, Dr. Rita Florencia
Boddie, Daniel W.
Bolden, Betty A.
Bolden, Dr. Theodore E.
Bolden, Wiley Speights
Bolton, Linda Burnes
Bond, Cecil Walton
Bond, George Clement
Bonds, Kathleen
Bonner, Anthony
Booker, Corliss Voncille
Boone, Ronald Bruce
Borom, Lawrence H.
Bouldes, Charlene
Boulware, Fay D.
Bowen, George Walter
Bowen, Dr. Raymond Cobb
Bowen, Richard, Jr.
Bowens, Dr. Johnny Wesley
Bowles, James Harold, Sr.
Bowman, Dr. James E.
Boyce, Robert
Boyd, George Arthur
Boyd, Marsha Foster
Boyd, Muriel Isabel Belton
Boyd, Dr. Vivian
Boyer, James B.
Bracey, Willie Earl
Brady, Julio A.
Bramwell, Dr. Fitzgerald Burton
Branch, Prof. Harrison
Branche, William C., Jr.
Brandon, Dr. Ida Gillard
Brangman, H Alan
Bransford, Paris
Brasey, Henry L.
Braswell, Palmira
Braxton, Dr. Jean Bailey
Brazil, Robert D.
Brazzell, Dr. Johnetta Cross
Briggs, Carol J.
Brinkley, Norman, Jr.
Brinn, Chauncey J.
Britt, Paul D., Jr.
Britton, Elizabeth
Britton, John Henry
Broach, S. Elizabeth Johnson
Brock, Annette
Brockett, Charles A.
Bromery, Randolph Wilson
Bronson, Oswald P.
Brooks, Dr. Carolyn Branch
Brooks, Dr. Henry Marcellus
Brooks, Norman Leon
Brooks, Patrick, Jr.
Brooks, Suzanne R.
Brossette, Alvin, Jr.
Brown, Agnes Marie
Brown, Bernice Baynes
Brown, Bertrand James
Brown, Carol Ann
Brown, Conella Coulter
Brown, Constance Young
Brown, Emma Jean Mitchell
Brown, Evelyn Drewery
Brown, Dr. Frank
Brown, Rev. Greggory Lee
Brown, Jennifer H.
Brown, John Andrew
Brown, Joyce
Brown, Dr. Julius Ray
Brown, Kimberly
Brown, Leonard
Brown, LeRoy
Brown, Dr. Lucille M.
Brown, Marva Y
Brown, Mary Boykin
Brown, Dr. Milton F
Brown, Morse L.
Brown, Dr. O. Gilbert
Brown, Paul L.
Brown, Richard L
Brown, Dr. Ronald Paul
Brown, Dr. Roscoe C.
Brown, Rubye Golsby
Brown, Simon F.
Brown, Wesley Anthony
Brown, Winston D
Browne, Dr. Craig C.

Browne, Lee F.
Brownlee, Dr. Geraldine Daniels
Bruner, Van B., Jr.
Brunson, Debora Bradley
Bryan, Dr. Curtis E.
Bryan, T.J.
Bryant, Castell Vaughn
Bryant, Faye B.
Bryant, Pamela Bradley
Bryant, Preston
Bryce, Dr. Herrington J
Bryson, Seymour L.
Buford, James A
Buie, Dr. Sampson, Jr.
Bullock, Byron F
Bumphus, Dr. Walter Gayle
Bunch, Lonnie G., III
Bunte, Doris
Bunyon, Ronald S.
Burgett, Dr. Paul Joseph
Burkette, Dr. Tyrone L.
Burnett, Dr. Calvin W.
Burnette, Dr. Ada Puryear
Burnim, Dr. Mickey L.
Burnley, Kenneth
Burns, Felton
Burns, Jesse L
Burrows Dost, Janice H.
Burton, Lana Doreen
Butler, Eugene Thaddeus, Jr.
Butler, Marjorie Johnson
Butler, Dr. Rebecca Batts
Butler, Rosalind Marie
Byars, Dr. Lauretta F
Byas, Dr. Ulysses S.
Byas, William Herbert
Byrd, Camolia Alcorn
Byrd, Edwin R.
Byrd, Joseph Keys
Byrd, Lanier
Byrd, Dr. Taylor
Cabbil, Lila
Cade, Harold Edward
Caillier, James Allen
Cain, Rudolph Alexander
Calhoun, Cecelia C.
Calvin, Dr. Virginia Brown
Cameron, Joseph A.
Campbell, Alma Porter
Campbell, William Earl
Campbell, Zerrie D
Canada, Benjamin Oleander
Canady, Hortense Golden
Cannon, Dr. Barbara E M
Cannon, Dr. Charles Earl
Carby, Hazel V.
Carey, Jennifer Davis
Carey, Patricia M
Carpenter, Barbara West
Carpenter, Carl Anthony
Carper, Gloria G.
Carreathers, Kevin R
Carreker, William, Jr.
Carroll, Dr. Constance Marie
Carry, Rev. Helen Ward
Carter, Alphonse H.
Carter, Dr. Arthur Michael
Carter, Dr. Barbara Lillian
Carter, Dr. David G.
Carter, Etta F
Carter, Dr. Gene Raymond
Carter, Dr. Hazo William
Carter, Herbert E.
Carter, Dr. James Edward, III
Carter, Dr. James P.
Carter, JoAnne Williams
Carter, Lamore Joseph
Carter, Dr. Lawrence
Carter, Philip W.
Carter, Stephen L
Carter, Dr. Warrick L.
Carter, William Beverly
Cartlidge, Arthur J.
Caruthers, Dr. Patricia Wayne
Carver, Dr. Joanne
Cash-Rhodes, Winifred E.
Cason, Udell
Cassis, Glenn Albert
Castenell, Dr. Louis Anthony
Cavin, Dr. Alonzo C.
Cayou, Nontsizi Kirton
Challenor, Herschelle
Chambers, Clarice Lorraine
Chance, Dr. Kenneth Bernard
Chapman, Melvin
Charles, Bernard L.
Chatman, Melvin E.
Chatman, Ronald Dean
Chatmon, Linda Carol

Chavous, Barney Lewis
Chavous, Mildred L.
Cheatham, Dr. Roy E.
Cheek, Dr. James Edward
Cherry, Robert Lee
Chestang, Dr. Leon Wilbert
Chew, Bettye L.
Churchwell, Charles Darrett
Clansy, Cheryl D.
Clark, Dr. Bertha Smith
Clark, Douglas L.
Clark, Irma
Clark, Dr. Irvin R.
Clark, Joe Louis
Clark, Laron Jefferson
Clark, Dr. Lawrence M
Clark, Leon Stanley
Clark, Vincent W.
Clarke, Cheryl
Clark-Hudson, Veronica L
Clark-Thomas, Eleanor M.
Clay, Dr. Camille Alfreda
Clay, Rev. Julius C.
Clay, Ross Collins
Clayton, Dr. Constance Elaine
Clemmons, Reginald C
Clemons, Dr. Michael L
Clemons, Thomasina
Clifton, Dr. Ivery Dwight
Cline, Dr. Eileen Tate
Clouden, LaVerne C.
Cobb, Dr. Jewel Plummer
Cobbs, David E.
Coffey, Dr. Barbara Jordan
Cogdell, D Parthenia
Coker, Adeniyi Adetokunbo
Colbert, Benjamin James
Cole, Edyth Bryant
Cole, Dr. Johnnetta Betsch
Cole, Olen, Jr.
Cole, Dr. Thomas Winston
Coleman, April Howard
Coleman, Audrey Rachelle
Coleman, Dr. Collie
Coleman, Dr. Don Edwin
Coleman, Gilbert Irving
Coleman, Lemon, Jr.
Coleman, Melissa Scott
Coleman, Dr. Ronald Gerald
Coleman, Wisdom F
Coles, Dr. Anna Bailey
Collier, Clarence Marie
Collier, Troy
Collier-Thomas, Dr. Bettye
Collins, Clifford Jacob
Collins, Dorothy Lee
Collymore, Dr. Edward L.
Colvin, Dr. William E
Comer, Dr. James Pierpont
Comer, Dr. Norman David
Cone, Dr. Cecil Wayne
Connor, Dr. Ulysses J., Jr.
Conyers, Charles L.
Cook, Dr. Nathan Howard
Cook, Dr. Samuel DuBois
Cooke, Nellie
Cooke, Dr. Paul Phillips
Cooper, Bobby G.
Cooper, Josephine H.
Copeland, Dr. Elaine Johnson
Copeland, Robert S
Coram, Willie Mae
Corbie, Dr. Leo A.
Cose, Ellis
Cotton, Joseph Craig
Courtney, Dr. Cassandra Hill
Cousins, Althea L.
Covington, Dr. H. Douglas
Cowan, Larine Yvonne
Craft, Dr. Thomas J
Craig, Starlett Russell
Crawford, Dr. Carl M.
Crawford, Ella Mae
Crayton, Dr. James Edward
Crew, John L., Sr.
Crew, Rudolph F.
Cright, Lotess Priestley
Crisp, Dr. Robert Carl, Jr.
Cromwell, Adelaide M.
Crosby, Dr. Edward Warren
Cross, Dr. Dolores E.
Crowell, Dr. Bernard G.
Crutcher, Dr. Ronald Andrew
Cummings, Frances McArthur
Cummings, Dr. Jay R.
Cunningham, Dr. James J.
Cureton, Stewart Cleveland
Dailey, Thelma
Dais, Larry

Dale, Clamma Churita
Dale, Robert J.
Dames, Kathy W.
Daniel, Bertha
Daniel, Dr. Elnora
Daniel, Simmie Childrey
Daniels, A. Raiford
Daniels, Patricia Ann
Daniels, Terry L
Dansby, Jesse L.
Darity, William A.
Dates, Jannette Lake
Davenport, C. Dennis
Davenport, Calvin A.
Davidson, Dr. Kerry
Davis, Anthony Eboney
Davis, Arthur, Jr.
Davis, Dr. Bertha Lane
Davis, Dr. Earlean
Davis, Dr. Edward L.
Davis, Dr. Gloria-Jeanne
Davis, J Mason
Davis, Johnetta Garner
Davis, Dr. Larry Earl
Davis, Norma June
Davis, Warren B
Davis, Dr. Wiley M.
Davis, Dr. William
Davy, Dr. Freddye Turner
Dawson, Dr. B. W.
Dawson, Horace Greeley
Dawson, Dr. Lawrence E
Dawson, Leonard Ervin
Dawson, Martha E
Dawson, Sidney L., Jr.
Dawson Boyd, Dr. Candy
Days, Rosetta Hill
Dean, Clara Russell
Dean, Vyvyan Ardena Coleman
Dean, Walter R
Debas, Dr. Haile T.
Debro, Dr. Julius
DeGraffenreidt, Andrew
DeLauder, Dr. William B.
Delco, Dr. Exalton Alfonso, Jr.
Delk, Oliver Rahn
DeLoatch, Dr. Eugene
DeLoatch, Dr. Sandra J
Denning, Dr. Bernadine Newsom
Denning, Joe William
Dennis, Dr. Evie Garrett
Dent, Gary Kever
DeNye, Blaine A.
DePillars, Murry Norman
Deskins, Donald R., Jr.
DeSousa, D. Jason
Diaz, F Louise
Dickerson, Harvey G, Jr.
Dickerson, Janet Smith
Dickinson, Dr. Gloria Harper
Dill, Gregory
Dillard, Dr. Martin Gregory
Dillenberger, R. Jean
Dillon, Aubrey
Dilworth, Dr. Mary Elizabeth
Dismuke, Leroy
Dixon, Dr. Armendia P.
Dixon, Dr. Benjamin
Dixon, Margaret A
Dixon, Dr. Ruth F.
Dixon, Tom L.
Dobbs, Dr. John Wesley
Dodson, Dr. Jualynne E.
Dotson, Philip Randolph
Douglas, Arthur E.
Douglas, Harry E., III
Douglas, Samuel Horace
Douglass, Melvin Isadore
Dove, Dr. Pearlie C.
Downing, Dr. Beverly
Downing, Stephen
Dozier, Richard K.
Draper, Dr. Edgar Daniel
Draper, Frederick Webster
Drewry, Cecelia Hodges
Drewry, Henry Nathaniel
Dual, Peter A.
Duke, Ruth White
Dulin, Joseph
Dummett, Clifton Orrin
Dungy, Dr. Claibourne I.
Dungy, Madgetta Thornton
Dunnigan, Jerry
Dunson, Dr. Carrie Lee
Durand, Henry J., Jr.
Durham, Dr. Joseph Thomas
Duster, Troy
Duvall, Henry F
Eady, Mary E

Early, Ida H.
Early Lambert, Violet Theresa
Earvin, Larry L.
Easley, Charles F., Sr.
Easter, Rufus Benjamin, Jr.
Easter, Wilfred Otis, Jr.
Eaton, Minetta Gaylor
Echols, Mary Ann
Edelin, Kenneth C
Edney, Norris Allen, I
Edwards, Dr. Marvin E
Edwards, Dr. Miles Stanley
Edwards, Robert
Edwards, Dr. Robert Valentino
Edwards, Shirley
Edwards, Thomas Oliver
Elam, Donna
Elam, Dr. Lloyd C.
Ellis, Calvin H., III
Ellis, Dr. Edward V.
Ellis, Dr. George Washington
English, Leontene Roberson
English, Dr. Richard Allyn
Engs, Robert Francis
Epperson, David E.
Epps, Anna Cherrie
Epps, Charles Harry, Jr.
Epps, Dolzie C. B.
Ervin, Deborah Green
Espree, Allen James
Ethridge, Dr. Robert Wylie
Eubanks, Eugene E.
Evans, Arthur L.
Evans, David Lawrence
Evans, Dr. Donna Browder
Evans, Dr. Eva L
Evans, Dr. Jack
Evans, Kamiel Denise
Evans, Ruthana Wilson
Evans, Dr. William E.
Eve, Christina M.
Evege, Walter L
Ewers, Dr. James Benjamin
Fair, Frank T.
Faison, Dr. Helen Smith
Fakhrid-Deen, Nashid Abdullah
Farris, Dr. Alicia Renee
Farris, Dr. Vera King
Faucett, Barbara J.
Faulk, Estelle A.
Faulkner, Geanie
Favors, Steve Alexander
Feaster, LaVerne Williams
Feliciana, Dr. Jerrye Brown
Ferguson, Joel I
Fielder, Dr. Fred Charles
Fields, Brenda Joyce
Fields, Dr. Dexter L.
Fields, Dr. Ewaugh Finney
Finch, Dr. Janet M
Finn, John William
Fisher, E Carleton
Fitchue, M. Anthony
Flamer, John H
Flateau, Dr. John
Fleming, George
Fleming, Quince D., Sr.
Fletcher, Patricia Louise
Flood, Shearlene Davis
Floyd, Dr. Jeremiah
Floyd, Dr. Samuel A.
Floyd, Vircher B.
Fluker, Dr. Walter Earl
Fomufod, Dr. Antoine Kofi
Foote, Yvonne
Ford, Aileen W.
Ford, Donald A.
Ford, Dr. Robert L
Fort, Dr. Edward B.
Fort, Dr. Jane Geraldine
Foster, Delores Jackson
Foster, Dr. Henry Wendell, Jr.
Foster, Dr. Rosebud Lightbourn
Foster, Dr. William Patrick
Fowler, John D.
Fowler, Dr. Queen Dunlap
Francis, Charles K.
Francis, Charles S L
Francis, Gilbert H.
Francis, Dr. Norman C
Franklin, Allen D.
Franklin, Audrey Demps
Franklin, Bernard W.
Franklin, Dr. Herman
Franklin, Dr. Robert Michael
Fraser, Dr. Leon Allison
Frazier, Adolphus Cornelius
Frazier, Leon
Freeman, Albert Cornelius, Jr.

Lawson, Robert L.
Lawson, Dr. William Daniel
Lawyer, Vivian
Leak, Virginia Nell
Leavell, Dorothy R.
Leavell, Dr. Walter F.
Lechebo, Dr. Semie
LeCompte, Peggy Lewis
Lede, Naomi W
Lee, Dr. Andre L
Lee, Clara Marshall
Lee, Gerald E.
Lee, Dr. Guy Milicon, Jr.
Lee, LaVerne C.
Lee, Dr. Mildred Kimble
Lee, Oliver B.
LeFlore, Dr. William B.
Leflores, George O., Jr.
Leggette, Violet Olevia Brown
LeMelle, Tilden J.
Leonard, Curtis Allen
Leonard, Dr. Walter J.
Levermore, Claudette Madge
Lewis, Almera P.
Lewis, Dr. Brenda Neumon
Lewis, Earl
Lewis, Dr. Felton Edwin
Lewis, Dr. Henry L., III
Lewis, Jesse Cornelius
Lewis, Jesse J.
Lewis, Dr. Lloyd Alexander
Lewis, Lyn Etta
Lewis, Dr. Margaret W
Lewis, Dr. Shirley A R
Lide, Dr. William Ernest
Lipscomb, Dr. Wanda Dean
Little, Herman Kernel
Littlejohn, Joseph Phillip
Littlejohn, Samuel Gleason
Livingston-White, Dr. Deborah J H
Locke, Dr. Hubert G.
Locke, Dr. Mamie Evelyn
Lockhart, Dr. Verdree, Sr.
Lomax, Michael L.
Long, James Alexander
Lorthridge, Dr. James E.
Louis, Dr. Suchet Lesperance
Love, Dr. Barbara J.
Love, Edward Tyrone
Love, Dr. George Hayward
Lovett, Mack, Jr.
Lownes-Jackson, Dr. Millicent Gray
Lucas, Gerald Robert
Lucas, Dr. John Harding
Lucas, Willie Lee
Lucas Darby, Dr. Emma Turner
Luckey, Dr. Evelyn F.
Lundy, Dr. Harold W
Luten, Thomas Dee
Lyde, Jeanette S
Lyles, Dewayne
Lynch, Dr. Rufus Sylvester
Lyons, Dr. James E.
Mabrey, Prof. Marsha Eve
Mabry, Edward L
Mack, Ally Faye
Mack, Dr. Astrid Karona
Mack, Gordon H.
Mack, Sylvia Jenkins
Mahan-Powell, Lena
Malone, Dr. Cleo
Malone, Eugene William
Malone, Dr. J. Deotha
Malone, Sandra Dorsey
Manley, Dr. Audrey Forbes
Mann, Dr. Marion
Manning, Dr. Eddie James
Manning, Jane A.
Manning, Dr. Jean Bell
Manning, Dr. Randolph H
Mapp, Dr. Edward C.
Marable, Rev. Dr. June Morehead
Marshall, Dr. Edwin Cochran
Martin, Dr. Edward Williford
Martin, Dr. Joanne Mitchell
Martin, Kimberly Lynette
Martin, Lee
Martin, Shirley
Mask, Susan L
Mason, Rev. Herman Skip
Massey, Jacquelene Sharp
Massey, James Earl
Massey, Rev. Reginald Harold
Mathews, George
Matthews, Dorothy
Matthews, Harry Bradshaw
Matthews, Dr. Hewitt W.
Matthews, Leonard Louis
Matthews, Robert L.

Maupin, Dr. John E
Maxwell, Dr. Marcella J.
Mayden, Ruth Wyatt
Mayes, McKinley
Mayo, Blanche Irene
Mays, Dr. William O
Mazon, Larri Wayne
McAdoo, Dr. Harriette P
McBride, Frances E.
McCants, Keith
McClain, Andrew Bradley
McCloud, Aaron C.
McClurkin, Johnson Thomas
McCoy, Dr. Walter D.
McCurdy, Dr. Brenda Wright
McDaniel, James Berkley, Jr.
McDaniel, Karen Cotton
McDaniels, Jeaneen J
McDaniels, Warren E
McDemmond, Dr. Marie V
McElroy, Dr. Njoki
McFadden, Samuel Wilton
McFerrin, Sara Elizabeth Copper
McGee, Eva M
McGee, Sylvia Williams
McGehee, Nan E
McGowan, Elsie Henderson
McGowan, Thomas Randolph
McGregor, Edna M.
McGriff, Dr. Deborah M.
McGuirt, Milford W
McIntosh, James E.
McIntosh, Levi H., Jr.
McIntyre, Dianne Ruth
McKissick, Mabel F. Rice
McMillan, Jacqueline Marie
McMillan, Dr. Joseph Turner
McMurry, Dr. Kermit Roosevelt, Jr.
McMurry, Merley Lee
McNary, Oscar Lee
McPhail, Dr. Christine Johnson
McPhail, Sharon M
McRae, Ronald Edward
McTyre, Robert Earl, Sr.
Meacham, Robert B.
Means, Dr. Fred E.
Mease, Quentin R.
Meeks, Reginald Kline
Meeks, Stephen Abayomi Obadele
Melancon, Norman
Meridith, Denise Patricia
Metcalf, Dr. Zubie West, Jr.
Metoyer, Carl B.
Mickins, Andel Watkins
Mickle, Andrea Denise
Miles, Carlotta G.
Miles, Dr. E. W.
Miller, Dr. Andrea Lewis
Miller, Doris Jean
Miller, Ernest Eugene
Miller, Dr. M Sammye
Miller, Dr. Margaret Greer
Miller, Marquis David
Miller, Mattie Sherryl
Miller, Melvin Allen
Miller-Holmes, Cheryl
Mims, Dr. George L.
Minor, Willie
Mitchell, Connie R Cohn
Mitchell, Horace
Mitchell, Joann
Mitchell, Dr. Judy Lynn
Mitchell, Dr. Julius P
Mitchell, Katherine Phillips
Mitchell, Dr. Robert L.
Mitchell, Tex Dwayne
Mitchell-Kernan, Dr. Claudia Irene
Mitchem, Dr. Arnold Levy
Mitchem, Dr. John Clifford
M- Middleton, Vertelle D
Mobley, Dr. Sybil Collins
Mohr, Dr. Paul B., Sr.
Moland, Willie C.
Monroe, Charles Edward
Montgomery, Dr. Edward B.
Montgomery, Dr. Patricia Ann Felton
Montgomery, Dr. Trent
Moore, Alice Evelyn
Moore, Dr. Archie Bradford, Jr.
Moore, Beverly
Moore, Christine James
Moore, Eddie N., Jr.
Moore, Evia Briggs
Moore, Floreese Naomi
Moore, Gary E
Moore, Juliette R
Moore, Larry Louis
Moore, Dr. Nathan
Moore, Dr. Quincy L

Moore, Rodney Gregory
Moorehead, Eric K
Moreland, Dr. Lois Baldwin
Moreland-Young, Dr. Curtina
Morris, Bernard Alexander
Morris, Dr. Charles Edward, Jr.
Morris, Dr. Dolores Orinskia
Morris, Ernest Roland
Morris, Dr. Frank Lorenzo, Sr.
Morris, Major
Morris, Stanley E., Jr.
Morrison, Dr. Gwendolyn Christine
  Caldwell
Morrison, Dr. Juan LaRue, Sr.
Morrison, Prof. Keith Anthony
Morrison, Pearl Patty
Morrison, Richard David
Mortel, Dr. Rodrigue
Mortimer, Delores M.
Morton, Lorraine H
Mosby, Dr. Carolyn Lewis
Mosely, Dr. Kenneth
Moses, Dr. Henry A.
Moses, Yolanda T.
Moss, Wilmar Burnett, Jr.
Mullett, Dr. Donald L.
Murdock, Patricia Green
Murphy, Margaret Humphries
Murray, Sylvester
Murray, Dr. Thomas Azel, Sr.
Murrell, Barbara Curry
Muse, Dr. Willie L
Myers, Dr. Ernest Ray
Myers, Samuel L, Sr.
Myrick, Bismarck
Nayman, Robbie L.
Neal, Dr. Ira Tinsley
Nelson, Dr. H. Viscount
Nelson, Dr. Ivory V.
Nelson, Dr. Wanda Lee
Neufville, Dr. Mortimer H
Newberry, Trudell McClelland
Newkirk, Dr. Gwendolyn
Newkirk, Thomas H.
Newlin, Dr. Rufus K
Newsome, Dr. Emanuel T.
Neyland, Leedell Wallace
Nichols, Dr. Owen D.
Nicholson, Alfred
Nickson, Sheila Joan
Nimmons, Dr. Julius F., Jr.
N'Namdi, Carmen Ann
Noble, John Charles
Nolan, Daniel Kaye
Noonan, Dr. Allan S.
Norrell-Nance, Rosalind Elizabeth
Norrell-Thomas, Sondra
Norris, Lonnie H
Norvell, Dr. Merritt J.
Norwood, Dr. Tom
Nunery, Dr. Leroy David, II
Nunnally, David H.
Nwagbaraocha, Joel O
O'Bryant, Beverly J.
Oden, Walter Eugene
Okunor, Dr. Shiame
Oldham, Algie Sidney, Jr.
O'Leary, Hazel M
Oliver, Gary Dewayne
Oliver, Jesse Dean
Omolade, Barbara
O'Neale, Sondra
Ortiz, Delia
Osborne, Dr. Alfred E., Jr.
Outlaw, Warren Gregory
Overton-Adkins, Dr. Betty Jean
Owens, Robert Leon, III
Paddio-Johnson, Dr. Eunice Alice
Padulo, Dr. Louis
Paige, Dr. Roderick Raynor
Palmer, Elliott B., Sr.
Palmer, Noel D.
Parham, James B.
Parker, Dr. Herbert Gerald
Parker, Jacquelyn Heath
Parker, Paul E
Parks, Dr. Arnold Grant
Parks, Thelma Reece
Paschal, Trisa Long
Paschal, Trisa Long
Paschal, Willie L.
Pates, Harold
Patrick, Julius, Jr.
Patrick, Dr. Opal Lee Young
Patterson, Cecil Lloyd
Patterson, Evelynne
Patterson, Joan Delores
Patton, Joyce Bradford
Payne, Margaret Ralston

Payne, Mitchell Howard
Payne, Dr. N Joyce
Payne, Vernon
Payton, Dr. Benjamin Franklin
Peagler, Dr. Richard C
Peal, Dr. Regina Randall
Pegues, Robert L., Jr.
Pegues, Wennette West
Peguese, Charles R.
Pendleton, Bertha Mae Ousley
Pendleton, Florence Howard
Penelton, Barbara Spencer
Penn, Dr. Nolan E
Pennington, Leenette Morse
Pennix, James A
Pennywell, Phillip, Jr.
Peoples, Dr. Gerald C
Peoples, Gregory Allan
Peoples, Dr. John Arthur, Jr.
Peoples, Joyce P.
Peoples, Dr. L Kimberly
Peoples, Sesser R.
Peoples, VerJanis Andrews
Perdreau, Cornelia Whitener
Perdue, Rep. George, Jr.
Perdue, Wiley A
Perine, James L.
Perkins, Myla Levy
Perry, Dr. Aubrey M.
Perry, Dr. Patsy Brewington
Perry, Dr. Robert Lee
Peters, Dr. Fenton
Peterson, Lloyd
Pettigrew, Dr. L Eudora
Petty, Jervie Scott
Petty-Edwards, Lula Evelyn
Peyton, Jasper E.
Phelps, Constance Kay
Phillip, Dr. Michael John
Phillips, Frances Caldwell
Phillips, June M J
Pierre, Dr. Percy Anthony
Pinkard, Dr. Deloris Elaine
Pinkney, Arnold R.
Pinson, Margo Dean
Pitt, Dr. Clifford Sinclair
Pittman, Dr. Sample Noel
Pleasant, Albert E, III
Pleasant, Mae Barbee Boone
Pleasants, Charles Wrenn
Poellnitz, Fred Douglas
Pogue, Frank G., Jr.
Poindexter, Charles L. L.
Polk, Dr. Lorna Marie
Polk, Rev. Dr. Robert L
Pollard, Raymond J.
Ponder, Dr. Henry
Poole, Dillard M.
Poole, Dr. Rachel Irene
Porche-Burke, Lisa
Porter, Bishop Henry Lee
Portlock, Dr. Carver A.
Potts, Sammie
Pounds, Dr. Augustine Wright
Pounds, Dr. Moses B
Powell, Dr. Archie James
Powell, Dr. Myrtis H
Powell, Sis Paula Livers
Prater, Dr. Oscar L
Pratt, Alexander Thomas
Pratt, Mable
Prestage, James J.
Prestage, Dr. Jewel Limar
Price, Glenda Delores
Price, Dr. Paul Sanford
Primous, Emma M.
Prothrow-Stith, Deborah Boutin
Provost, Marsha Parks
Pruitt, Dr. George Albert
Pruitt-Logan, Dr. Anne Smith
Purce, Dr. Thomas Les
Pyles, J. A.
Rambo, Bettye R.
Rampersad, Arnold
Ramsey, Henry, Jr.
Randle, Lucious A.
Ransburg, Frank S.
Ransom, Lillie
Rauch, Doreen E.
Ray, Andrew
Rayburn, Dr. Wendell Gilbert
Rayford, Lee Edward
Reaves, Rev. Dr. Benjamin Franklin
Reaves, Ginevera N.
Reavis, John William
Reddick, Alzo Jackson
Redding, Gloria Ann
Redmond, Dr. Jane Smith
Reed, Dr. Allene Wallace

Reed, Dr. Charlotte
Reed, Dr. James W
Reed, Joann
Reed, Dr. Rodney J
Reed, Dr. Vincent Emory
Reid, Irvin D
Reid, Janie Ellen
Renick, James C.
Rhoades, Dr. Samuel Thomas
Ribeau, Dr. Sidney
Rice, Dr. Constance Williams
Richard, Alvin J.
Richards, Dr. Hilda
Richards, LaVerne W.
Richards, Leon
Richardson, DeRutha Gardner
Richardson, Dr. Earl Stanford
Richardson, Dr. Luns C
Richardson, Mary Margaret
Richardson, Odis Gene
Richardson, Roger Gerald
Ridgel, Dr. Gus Tolver
Ridley, Dr. May Alice
Rigsby, Esther Martin
Riley, Dorothy Winbush
Rivers, Vernon Frederick
Robbins, Herman C.
Roberson, Valerie R
Roberts, Dr. Alfred Lloyd
Roberts, Edward A
Roberts, Grady H., Jr.
Roberts, Paquita Hudson
Roberts, Roy J.
Robertson, Evelyn Crawford
Robertson, Quindonell S.
Robinson, Alfreda P.
Robinson, Dr. Andrew
Robinson, Prof. Ella S.
Robinson, Eunice Primus
Robinson, Harry G
Robinson, Jeannette
Robinson, Dr. Prezell Russell
Robinson, S Yolanda
Robinson, Dr. Samuel
Robinson, Thelma Maniece
Robison, Louis
Rochester, Dr. Mattilyn T
Rockett, Damon Emerson
Rodgers, Dr. Augustus
Rodgers, Shirley Marie
Rodriguez, Argelia Velez
Rogers, Dr. Decatur Braxton
Rogers, George
Rogers, Esq. Joyce Q
Rogers, Rev. Dr. Oscar Allan
Roney, Raymond G
Roper, Bobby L.
Roscoe, Wilma J.
Ross, Emma Jean
Rosser, Dr. James M.
Ross-Lee, Barbara
Roulhac, Dr. Edgar Edwin
Roulhac, Dr. Nellie Gordon
Roussell, Norman
Royster, Philip M
Rudd, Charlotte Johnson
Ruffin, Paulette Francine
Runnels, Bernice M.
Russell, Dian Bishop
Russell, James A., Jr.
Russell, John Peterson
Russell, Milicent De
Rutherford, Harold Phillip, III
Salmond, Jasper
Salters, Dr. Charles Robert
Samuel, Lois S.
Sanders, Dr. Gwendolyn W.
Sanders, Dr. Isaac Warren
Sanders, Dr. Karen Eley
Sanders, Dr. Lou Helen
Sanders, Dr. Robert B
Sands, Prof. Mary Alice
Sands, Rosetta F
Sardin, James
Satcher, Robert Lee
Saunders, Dr. Elizabeth Ann
Saunders-Henderson, Martha M.
Savage, Dr. Archie Bernard, Jr.
Savage, William Arthur
Sawyers, Dorret E
Saxton, Paul Christopher
Schexnider, Dr. Alvin J
Scott, Dr. Basil Y
Scott, Hosie L
Scott, Dr. Julius S, Jr.
Scott, Dr. Marvin Bailey
Scott, Dr. Mona Vaughn
Scott, Quincy, Jr.
Scott, Veronica J.

Electronics
See **Computer Science—Programming/Software Development; Computer Science—Systems Analysis/Design; Computer Science—Not Elsewhere Classified; Engineering—Electrical/Electronics; Retail Trade—Electrical/Electronics Products; Wholesale Trade—Electrical/Electronics Products**

Engineering—Aerospace

Spooner, Richard Edward
Taylor, Julius H
Voldase, Iva Sneed
Walker, Willie M.
Weaver, Frank Cornell
West, Dr. Togo Dennis, Jr.
Whitehead, James T, Jr.
Whitlow, Dr. Woodrow, Jr.
Wilkins, Dr. Roger L
Wright, Linwood Clinton
Zeno, Willie D.

Engineering—Chemical
Adeyiga, Dr. Adeyinka A.
Bauldock, Gerald
Canty, George
Coleman James, Patricia Rea
Edwards, Dr. Robert Valentino
Evans, Milton L.
Frazier, Julie A
Howard, Donald R.
Jacobs, Larry Ben
Levister, Dr. Ernest Clayton
Mallory, Glenn Oliver, Jr.
Marchand, Melanie Annette
Oyekan, Dr. Soni Olufemi
Patrick, Dr. Jennie R
Stancell, Dr. Arnold Francis
Tufon, Chris
Wilson, Dr. Ray Floyd
Winston, Dr. Hubert

Engineering—Civil
Amory, Reginald L
Apea, Joseph Bennet Kyeremateng
Atkins, Richard
Bass, Joseph Frank
Bell, James L., Jr.
Bowser, Hamilton Victor
Bowser, McEva R.
Bowser, Robert Louis
Cooper, Lois Louise
Cotton, Garner
Davis, James Edgar
Davis, Leonard Harry
Davis, Lester E.
DeHart, Henry R.
Emeagwali, Philip
Ford, Kenneth A.
Gray, Valerie Hamilton
Hicks, William L.
Humphrey, Howard John
Jackson, John
Jackson, Larry Eugene
Jeffries, Freddie L.
Jordan, Frederick E.
Kennedy, Nathelyne Archie
Kidd, Charles C
Madison Polk, Sharon L
McGee, Waddell
Olapo, Olaitan
Overstreet, Dr. Everett Louis
Patin, Jude W. P.
Powers, Mamon M
Ramey, Melvin R
Rohadfox, Ronald Otto
Russell, Michael
Sinclair, Benito A
Staley, Kenneth Bernard
Taylor, Gayland Wayne
Weaver, Herbert C
White, Charles R.
Winfield, William T

Engineering—Electrical/Electronics
Adkins, Rodney C
Alwan, Mansour
Anderson, Kenneth Richard
Asom, Moses T.
Bagley, Gregory P.
Baylor, Sandra Johnson
Bell, Ngozi O
Blalock, Marion W.
Boutte, Ernest John
Bray, Leroy, Sr.
Brunson, Frank
Burkett, Gale E.
Byrd, Herbert Lawrence
Carter, Norman L
Clarke, Bryan Christopher
Cooper, Daneen Ravenell
Darkes, Leroy William
Dean, Dr. Mark E
Demby, James E.
Douglas, Joseph Francis
Driver, Johnie M
Ellis, Johnell A.
Esogbue, Augustine O.

Fleming, David Aaron
Floyd, Vernon Clinton
Garrett, Cain, Jr.
Gothard, Donald L.
Graham, Odell
Gray, Rev. Maceo
Green, Lester L.
Gundy, Roy Nathaniel, Jr.
Hardie, Robert L., Jr.
Hargrove, Dr. Andrew
Harris, Dr. Gary Lynn
Harris, Vernon Joseph
Herndon, Harold Thomas, Sr.
Johnson, Earl
Johnson, Frederick E.
Jordan, B Delano
Keyser, Dr. George F
King, Reginald F.
Knight, Lynnon Jacob
Lartigue, Roland E
Lawrence, Rodell
Leaphart, Eldridge
Lewis, Aisha
Mabson, Glenn T
Mallebay-Vacqueur Dem, Jean Pascal
Marius, Kenneth Anthony
May, Dr. Gary Stephen
McAfee, Leo C
McDonald, William Emory
McLaurin, Jasper Etienne
Mitchell, Jacob Bill
Montague, Nelson C.
Monteith, Dr. Henry C.
Nelson, Edward O.
Owens, David Kenneth
Padulo, Dr. Louis
Parham, Frederick Russell
Pinkett, Dr. Randal D
Ransom, Dr. Preston L
Rodgers, William M., Jr.
Rogers, Charles Leonard
Rose, Bessie L
Sanders, Rober LaFayette
Shelton, Roy Cresswell, Jr.
Sherman, Thomas Oscar, Jr.
Smith, Roger Leroy
Spencer, Dr. Michael Gregg
Strachan, Lloyd Calvin, Jr.
Stricklin, James
Taylor, Ellis Clarence, Sr.
Taylor, Dr. Kenneth Doyle
Taylor, Miles Edward
Thaxton, June E
Thompson, Dr. Charles
Turner, Allen H.
Vereen, Michael L
Vivians, Nathaniel Roosevelt
Waddell, Theodore R.
Wallace, Richard Warner
Washington, Darryl McKenzie
Waters, William L.
White, William Joseph
Williams, Cheryl L
Williamson, Samuel R
Worthey, Richard E

Engineering—Industrial
Behrmann, Serge T.
Blackmon, Anthony Wayne
Boyce, Charles N
Clarke, Charlotte
Crumpton, Dr. Lesia
Esogbue, Augustine O.
Hatter, Henry
Hightower, Willar H
James, John A
James, Wynona Yvonne
Jenkins, Woodie R
King, Hulas H
Lewis, Cleveland Arthur
Lillard, Kwame Leo
Mills, Lois Terrell
Mitchell, Jacob Bill
Moody, Cameron Dennis
Nnaji, Bartholomew O
Rakestraw, Kyle Damon
Reeves, Julius Lee
Russell, Wesley L.
Spencer, Brenda L
Ware, Albert M
Winfield, William T

Engineering—Mechanical
Barnes, Matthew Molena
Barton, Rhonda L
Boyd, Gwendolyn Elizabeth
Bryant, William Henry, Jr.
Butler, John O.

Dorsey, Herman Sherwood, Jr.
Godbolt, Ricky Charles
Hull, Bernard S., Sr.
Johnson, Carl Elliott
Johnston, Wallace O.
King, Lawrence Patrick
Marshall, Donald James
McCarrell, Clark Gabriel
Parker, Paul E
Parnell, Arnold W
Pitts, Brenda S
Pogue, Brent Daryl
Porter, Michael Anthony
Reeves, Julius Lee
Riddick, Eugene E
Rohr, Leonard Carl
Scantling, Wayne Lamar
Smith, Brian R
Taylor, Edward Walter
Thompson, Dr. Charles
Verbal, Claude A
Via, Thomas Henry
Walker, Dr. M Lucius
Ware, Albert M
Watkins, Dr. Charles B
Williams, Dr. James H., Jr.

Engineering—Metallurgical/Ceramic/Materials
Bragg, Joseph L.
Bragg, Robert Henry, II
Cane, Rudolph C
Chapman, Dr. Gilbert Bryant
Crossley, Dr. Frank Alphonso
Dixon, Dr. Louis Tennyson
Evans, Dr. Billy Joe
McClendon, Raymond
Mitchell, Dr. James Winfield
Phillips, Edward Martin

Engineering—Nuclear
Johnson, Lonnie G.
Jupiter, Clyde Peter
LeVert, Francis E.
Lewis, Kenneth Dwight
Pogue, Brent Daryl
Williams, Dr. Dwight

Engineering—Petroleum
Avery, James S
Coshburn, Henry S., Jr.
Douglas, Nicholas
Granville, William, Jr.
Grimes, Darlene M C
Hightower, Stephen Lamar
Kirklin, Dr. Perry William
Landers, Naaman Garnett
Oyekan, Dr. Soni Olufemi
Riddick, Eugene E

Engineering—Not Elsewhere Classified
Ambeau, Karen M
Armstead, Wilbert Edward, Jr.
Bayliss, Jocelyn Kelly
Betty, Lisa C.
Bland, Heyward
Bowser, McEva R.
Bray, Leroy, Sr.
Brooks, John S.
Cadet, Ron
Callender, Leroy R.
Cooley, Keith Winston
Crutcher, Sihon Heath
Davis, Leonard Harry
Davis, Nathaniel Alonzo
Dawkins, Michael James
Dixon, Dr. Louis Tennyson
Eason, Oscar, Jr.
Ferguson, Sherlon Lee
Finn, Robert Green, Jr.
Fleming, David Aaron
Gaither, James W., Jr.
Gartrell, Luther R.
Gay, Eddie C.
Gee, William Rowland, Jr.
Goodwin, Donald Edward
Gothard, Donald L.
Griffin, Floyd Lee
Griffin, Michael D.
Grooms, Dr. Henry Randall
Hannaham, Fred
Haynes, Philip R
Hill, Robert J., Jr.
Hooker, Douglas Randolf
Jackson, Karen Denise
Jackson, Richard H.

James, Anthony R
Javery, Michael
Jenkins, Woodie R
Johnson, Marvin R
Kennedy, Nathelyne Archie
Kidd, Charles C
Lue-Hing, Cecil
Mabrey, Ernest L
Madison, Shannon L
Martin, Montez Cornelius
McCuiston, Frederick Douglass, Jr.
Metters, Dr. Samuel
Morgan, Robert
Munson, Robert H
Murray, Gary S., Sr.
Neal, Curtis Emerson, Jr.
Owan, Dr. Ransome E
Pattman, Virgil Thomas, Sr.
Pollard, Muriel Ransom
Porter, John T
Rakestraw, Kyle Damon
Ratcliffe, Alfonso F
Ray, Dr. Judith Diana
Richardson, Alfred Lloyd
Rucks, Alfred J
Sanders, Barbara A.
Sanders, Dr. Woodrow Mac
Sawyer, Deborah M.
Sigur, Wanda Anne Alexander
Snell, Joan Yvonne Ervin
Snowden, Phillip Ray
Stallworth, Oscar B
Sutton, Mary A.
Taylor, Dr. Kenneth Doyle
Trueblood, Vera J
Tucker, Paul, Jr.
Turner, Franklin James
Underwood, Anthony
Walker, Willie M.
Webster, Theodore E.
Wilhoit, Carl H.
Winfield, William T
Woodie, Henry L.

Entertainment/Recreation—Not Elsewhere Classified (*See Also* Acting; Dance/Choreography; Directing/Producing (Performing Arts); Music—Composing/Songwriting; Music—Conducting/Directing; Music—Instrumental; Music—Vocal; Music—Not Elsewhere Classified; Sports—Amateur; Sports—Professional/Semiprofessional; Sports—Not Elsewhere Classified)
Ali, Laila
Allotey, Victor
Amin, Karima
Anderson, Bernadine M.
Anderson, Tony
Ashhurst-Watson, Carmen
Atkins, Pervis R., Jr.
Avant, Clarence
Bailey, Kenetta
Bailey, Thurl Lee
Bateman, Celeste
Bell, Ricky
Bellamy, Bill
Bertelsen, Phil
Blanc, Eric Anthony-Hawkins
Bobbitt, Leroy
Bowser, Kyle D
Bowser, Yvette Denise Lee
Boyd, Wilhemina Y.
Broderick, Johnson
Broughton, Christopher Leon
Brown, Dr. Joan P.
Brown, Lomas, Jr.
Brown, Reginald DeWayne
Brown, Ronald Wellington
Brown, Tony
Brown, William T
Buchanan, Raymond Louis
Burke, Kirkland R.
Carpenter, Vivian L.
Carter, Daisy
Carter, Regina
Chappelle, Dave
Charles, RuPaul Andre
Clark, Linda Day
Clarke, Priscilla
Clash, Kevin

Cole, Dorinda Clark
Copage, Marc Diego
Copeland, Misty
Cosby, Camille Olivia Hanks
Cosby, Dr. William Henry
Cumber, Victoria Lillian
Cummings, Terry
Dawson, Horace G
DeBarge, Chico
Douglas, Elizabeth (Betty) Asche
Duke, Bill
Dunlap, Ericka
Dupri, Jermaine
Durant-Paige, Beverly
Eckstine, Ed
Ellaraino
Emerson, Melinda
Ervin, Kathryn
Evans, Gregory James
Fay, Toni Georgette
Fearn-Banks, Kathleen
Fernandez-Smith, Wilhelmenia
Fox, Rick
Friday, Jeff
Goldberg, Whoopi
Goodrich, Linda S
Gordon, Derek E.
Gray, F Gary
Greaves, McLean
Greene, Dr. Dennis
Gregory, Richard Claxton
Griffey, Dick
Hagins, Ogbonna
Hall, Aaron
Hardwick, Gary C
Harrell, Andre
Harris, Joyce
Harris, Dr. MaryAnn
Harris, Tricia R
Harvey, Kenneth Ray
Hatcher, Jeffrey French
Hayes, Isaac Lee
Hayes, Laura
Haymon, Alan
Hopson, Harold Theodore
Iverson, Johnathan Lee
J., Ray
Jackson, Eugene D.
Jackson, Tomi L.
James, Hawthorne
James, Toni-Leslie
Jamison, Judith Ann
Jeter, Clifton B
Johnson, Charles Floyd
Johnson, Henry Wade
Jolley, Willie
Jones, Donna L.
Jones, Gary
Jones, Roy
Karpeh, Enid Juah Hildegard
Kilgore, Twanna Debbie
King, Brett
King, Gayle
Lacy, Donald E., Jr.
Lauren, Green
Lawrence, Elliott
Lee, Debra Louise
Lewis, Charles Henry
Love, Darlene
Mac, Bernie
MacLachlan, Janet A.
Mahoney, Dwayne
Martin, Cheryl
Martin Chase, Debra
Mashburn, Jamal
McElvane, Pamela Anne
McGill, Michael
McHenry, Douglas
McKayle, Donald Cohen
Medina, Benny
Miller, Tangi
Moore, Juliette R
Moore, Shemar F.
Morgan, Dolores Parker
Morris, Garrett Gonzalez
Mumford, Thaddeus Quentin
Nellums, Michael Wayne
Nelson, Novella C.
Nichols, Nichelle
Okino, Elizabeth Anna
Parker, James L.
Pinkney, Rose Catherine
Pressley, DeLores
Prince-Bythewood, Gina
Reid, Daphne Etta Maxwell
Richards, DeLeon Marie
Richardson, Lita Renee, Esq.
Richardson, Timothy L
Riggins, Jean

Robinson, Wendy Raquel
Robinson Peete, Holly
Roker, Albert Lincoln
Rolle, Janet
Ruffin, John Walter
Sabree, Clarice S
Savage, Janet Marie
Shaw, Dr. Spencer Gilbert
Simmons, Juanita
Simpson, Donnie
Slocumb, Jonathan
Sneed, Gregory J
Tamia
Taylor, Tenisha Nicole
Terry, Saunders
Timbaland
Treadwell, Tina McKinley
Varner, Dr. Nellie M.
Walden, Narada Michael
Walker, Chester
Watson, Dennis Rahiim
Wayans, Marlon
Wheaton, Frank Kahlil
Williams, Armstrong
Williams, Judith Byrd
Wilson, Madelaine Majette
Wilson, Mitsy
Wing, Theodore W
Wolfe, George C
Woodward, Aaron Alphonso, III

Fashion Design

Aiken, Kimberly Clarice
Banks, Jeffrey
Barkley, Rufus, Jr.
Barnwell, Andre
Bates, Barbara Ann
Beckford, Tyson Craig
Blake, Jennifer Lynn
Burrows, Stephen
Carter, Ruth E.
Collins, Cornell
Dean, Angela
Devers, Gail
Dunmore, Gregory Charles
Fleetwood, Therez
Fuller, Jack Lewis
Grayson, Mel
Green, Derek
Haggins, Jon
Hankins, Anthony Mark
Hilton, Stanley William, Jr.
Hunter, Gigi
Kani, Karl
King, Shaka C
Kirby, Anthony T
Kodjoe, Boris
Lars, Byron
Lockett, Bradford R.
Malone, Maurice
McCray, Darryl K
McGee, Benjamin Lelon
michael, b
Miller-Lewis, S Jill
Moore, Annie Jewell
Morgan, Rose
Nedd, Cathy
Ogilvie, Lana
Patton, Jean E
Perkins, Louvenia Black
Ralph, Sheryl Lee
Revish, Danielle A
Rohe, Bernie
Simmons, Kimora Lee
Smith, Dorothy O.
Smith, Wilson Washington, III
Snell, Johnna
Steele, Lawrence
Stubblefield, Michael Jerome
White, Sylvia Kay
Williams, Serena

Financial Services
See **Banking/Financial
Services; Management/
Administration—Accounting/
Financial**

Fire Prevention and
Control
Alfred, Rayfield
Blackshear, William
Brown, Carrye Burley
Brown, Thomas Edison, Jr.
Burton, Brent F.
Davie, Timothy M
Douglas, Joe, Jr.
Dyas, Patricia Ann

Edmonds, Curtis
Gladman, Charles R
Graham, Charlene
Hairston, Harold B.
Hart, Noel A.
Jackson, Frank Donald
Johnson, George, Jr.
Kimbrew, Joseph D.
Love, J. Gregory
Neal, Sylvester
Parker, G John, Sr.
Spaulding, Romeo Orlando
Stewart, John B., Jr.
Tatem, Dr. Patricia Ann
Thomas, Reginald Maurice
Trotter, Cortez
Watkins, Harold D, Sr.
Wester, Richard Clark
Williams, Charles Earl

Food and Beverage
Industry
See **Manufacturing—Food/
Beverages; Restaurant/Food
Service Industry; Retail
Trade—Food and Beverages;
Wholesale Trade—Food and
Beverages**

Foreign Service
Boldridge, George
Carson, Johnnie
Carter, William Beverly
Cooper, Dr. LaMoyne Mason
Davis, Robert N
Flemming, Dr. Charles Stephen
Fox, Richard K., Jr.
Hewan, Clinton George
Jones, Dr. William Bowdoin
LeMelle, Tilden J.
Mack, John L.
Moose, George Edward
Perkins, Edward Joseph
Perry, June Carter
Reinhardt, John Edward
Render, Arlene
Spriggs, Edward J
Todman, Terence Alphonso
Williams, Elvira Felton

Forestry/Forest Industries
Burse, Dr. Luther
Dixon, Ora Wright
Gaines, Mary E
Jackson, Charles N., II
Keene, Sharon C.
Wilds, Jetie Boston, Jr.
Williams, Dr. Carroll Burns, Jr.

Funeral Service
See **Mortuary Services**

Gallery/Museum
Administration/Education
Aviles, Dora
Bibby, Deirdre L.
Bolden, Aletha Simone
Booker, John, III
Brown, Joseph Clifton
Burroughs, Dr. Margaret Taylor
Burton, Brent F.
Cabbell, Edward Joseph
Camp, Kimberly
Campbell, Dr. Mary Schmidt
Conway, Wallace Xavier, Sr.
Conwill, Kinshasha
Crew, Spencer R.
Crocker, Clinton C
Cruz, Patricia
Davis, Dr. Willie
Driskell, David C.
Felton, Zora Martin, Emerita
Fleming, John Emory
Gaither, Barry
Ghent, Henri Hermann
Gilliam, Sam, Jr.
Halfacre, Frank Edward
Hall, Robert L
Haymore, Tyrone
High, Freida
Hodges, Dr. David Julian
Houston, Willie Lewis
Jackson, Earl, Jr.
Jeffries, Dr. Rosalind R
John, Daymond
Johnson, Patricia Anita
Kelley, Jack Albert

Ligon, Doris Hillian
Mack, Dr. Deborah Lynn
Martin, Frank C
Montgomery, Evangeline Juliet
Moore, Dr. Marian J.
Morgan-Welch, Beverly Ann
Newman, Constance Berry
Newsome, Steven Cameron
Nichols, Elaine
N'Namdi, George Richard
Palmer, Elliott B., Sr.
Parrish, Maurice Drue
Peerman-Pledger, Vernese Dianne
Pierce, Aaronetta Hamilton
Pilgrim, David
Pindell, Howardena D
Porter, Michael LeRoy
Robinson, Dr. Harry, Jr.
Saunders-Henderson, Martha M.
Shifflett, Lynne Carol
Sims, Lowery Stokes
Smythe, Victor N.
Stewart, Paul Wilbur
Stewart, Raymond C
Stewart, Ruth Ann
Stith, Hana L
Taylor, Dr. Cledie Collins
Taylor, Gilbert Leon
Walker, Roslyn Adele
Ward, Doris Margaret
Washington, Sherry Ann
Williams, Kathryn
Williamson, Ethel W
Young, James Arthur, III

Geography
Jones, Dr. Marcus Earl
King, Thomas Lawrence

Geology/Geophysics
Baskerville, Dr. Charles Alexander
Bromery, Randolph Wilson
Brown, Charles Edward
Norman, Bobby Don
Owens, Dr. Joan Murrell
Person, Waverly J.
Thomas, Sherri Booker
Underwood, Maude Esther
Williams Davis, Edith G

Geophysics
See **Geology/Geophysics**

Government Service
(Elected or Appointed)/
Government Administra-
tion—City
Ackridge, Florence Gateward
Adams, Floyd, Jr.
Adams, Joseph Lee
Adams, T. Patton
Adams, Willie, Jr.
Alexander, F S Jack
Allen, Carol Ward
Allen, Charles Claybourne
Allen, Dozier T., Jr.
Allison, Vivian
Anderson, Mary Elizabeth
Archer, Dennis Wayne
Archer, Trudy DunCombe
Arrington, Judge Marvin S., Sr.
Arrington, Richard, Jr.
Arthur, George Kenneth
Ashton, Vivian Christina R.
Askew, Bonny Lamar
Atkins, Edmund E.
Atkins, Fredd G
Austin, Carrie M.
Avent, Jacques Myron
Ayers, Hon. Timothy F.
Ayers-Johnson, Darlene
Bacon, Randall C.
Badger, Lloyd, Jr.
Badgett, Edward
Bailey, Duwain
Bailey, Harry Augustine, Jr.
Bajoie, Diana E
Baker, Sharon Smith
Baldwin, Olivia McNair
Bankett, William Daniel
Banks, Caroline Long
Banks, Priscilla Sneed
Barnes, Martin G.
Barnes, Thomas V.
Barry, Marion Shepilov
Barthelemy, Sidney John
Bass, Joseph Frank
Bather, Paul Charles

Battle, Joe Turner
Beal Bagneris, Michele Christine
Beasley, Annie Ruth
Beasley, Edward
Beatty, Christine
Beck, Hershell P.
Beck, Saul L.
Belardo de O, Lilliana
Bell, Elmer A.
Bell, George
Bell, Lawrence A.
Bell, Michael P
Bell, Winston Alonzo
Bell, Yvonne Lola
Bellamy, Angela Robinson
Belton, Sharon Sayles
Bennett, Arthur T
Bennett, Marion D.
Berry, Philip Alfonso
Best, John T.
Bethea, Gregory Austin
Bing, Dave
Birru, Mulugetta
Black, Lucius
Blackshear, William
Blackwell, Arthur Brendhal, II
Blackwell, Faiger Megrea
Blackwell, Robert B.
Blackwell, Unita
Blackwell-Hatcher, June E
Blanding, Larry
Blanford, Colvin
Bledsoe, Carolyn E. Lewis
Blocker, Tyree C
Boggs McDonald, Lynette Maria
Bolden, Stephanie T
Bolles, A Lynn
Bolling, Deborah A
Bonaparte, Lois Ann
Bonaparte, Norton Nathaniel
Bond, Michael Julian
Bond, Ronald A
Boone, Clarence Wayne
Boozer, Emerson
Borges, Saundra Kee
Bowser, Robert Louis
Box, Charles
Boyd, Gwendolyn Viola
Boykin, A. Wade, Jr.
Bradford, Steven C
Bradley, Jennette B.
Branche, Gilbert M.
Brandon, Symra D
Bridgeman, Donald Earl
Bronz, Lois Gougis Taplin
Brooks, Alvin Lee
Broussard, Arnold Anthony
Brown, Charles
Brown, Constance Charlene
Brown, Evelyn
Brown, Evelyn Drewery
Brown, James Marion
Brown, Joseph Davidson, Sr.
Brown, Julius J.
Brown, Jurutha
Brown, Justine Thomas
Brown, LeRoy
Brown, Marjorie M
Brown, Maxine J. Childress
Brown, Nancy Cofield
Brown, Otha N
Brown, Stanley Donovan
Brown, Willie Lewis
Brownridge, J Paul
Bryant, Donnie L.
Bryant, Teresena Wise
Bryant, Vivian
Buggage, Cynthia Marie
Burden, Pennie L.
Burke, Vivian H.
Burkeen, Ernest Wisdom
Burleson, Jane Geneva
Burrell, George Reed, Jr.
Burrell, Judith Ann
Burris, Chuck
Burts, Ezunial
Butler, Keith Andre
Butler, Pinkney L.
Cadogan, Marjorie A.
Caldwell, John Edward
Campbell, Mary Delois
Campbell, Dr. Mary Schmidt
Campbell, William
Canady-Laster, Rena Deloris
Carey, Carnice
Carman, Edwin G.
Carpenter, Lewis
Carr, Lenford
Carroll, Raoul Lord

Carter, Edward Earl
Carter, James
Carter, John R.
Carter, Judy Sharon
Carter, Mary Louise
Cates, Hon. Sidney Hayward, IV
Charlton, George N., Jr.
Cheatham, Betty L.
Cheatham, Linda Moye
Childs, Josie L.
Christian, John L.
Christie, James Albert
Claiborne, Lloyd R.
Clark, Augusta Alexander
Clark, Irma
Clark, Leon Stanley
Clarke, Yvette Diane
Clay, William L.
Cleaver, Emanuel, II
Clemons, Sandra L.
Cleveland, Clyde
Cobb, Ethel Washington
Cobb, Rev. Harold
Cofer, James Henry
Cole Carey, Wilhemina
Coleman, Avant Patrick
Coleman, Lemon, Jr.
Coleman, Michael Bennett
Coleman, Michael Victor
Coleman, Robert A
Colvin, Alonza James
Comer, Jonathan
Conaway, Mary Ward Pindle
Conner, Marcia Lynne
Cooke, Wilce L.
Cooper, Cardell
Cooper, Maudine R
Copeland, Kevon
Couch, James W
Cousins, William
Cox, Otis Graham, Jr.
Cox, Tyrone Y.
Crawford, Lawrence Douglas
Crawford, Vanessa Reese
Crawley, Darline
Crawley, George Claudius
Crenshaw, Waverly David
Crockett, George W., III
Cromartie, Ernest W., II.
Cropp, Dwight Sheffery
Currie, Jackie L.
Dance, Hon. Rosalyn R.
Daniels, Jesse
Daniels, John C.
Daniels, Preston
Dantley, Adrian Delano
Darnell, Edward Buddy
Davenport, Dr. Lawrence Franklin
Davidson, Alphonzo Lowell, Sr.
Davidson, Robert C., Jr.
Davidson, Rudolph Douglas
Davis, Arthur
Davis, Danny K.
Davis, Harold
Davis, L. Clifford
Davis, Lelia Kasenia
Davis, Robert Alan
Davis, Ronald
Davis, Sammy, Jr.
Dawkins, Miller J.
DeBerry, Andre
Deese, Manuel
DeHart, Henry R.
Dell, Willie J.
Denning, Joe William
Devereueawax, John L., III
Didlick, Wells S.
Dillard, Howard Lee
Dillard, Thelma Deloris
Dinkins, David N.
Dixon, Ardena S
Dixon, Richard Clay
Dixon, Sheila
Dobbins, Lucille R.
Doby, Allen E
Dodson, Vivian M
Donahue, William T.
Donegan, Charles Edward
Dotson-Williams, Henrietta
Douglass, Melvin Isadore
Dowell, Clyde Donald
Dowell-Cerasoli, Patricia R
Downes, Dwight
Drake, Pauline Lilie
Drakeford, Jack
Drew-Peeples, Brenda
Driessen, Henry, Jr.
Duckett, Esq. Gregory Morris
Dudley, Juanita C.

Dukes, Hazel Nell
Dumas, Karen Marie
Dumpson, Dr. James R.
Dunn-Barker, Lillian Joyce
Dupree, Edward A
Dymally, Mervyn Malcolm
Eddings, John R
Edwards, Luther Howard
Edwards, Shirley Jean
Edwards, Tamra
Elder, Geraldine H.
Ellis, Clarence Jack
Ellis, Rodney
Ellison, David Lee
Esco, Fred, Jr.
Espy, Henry
Etheredge, James W.
Evaige, Wanda Jo
Evans, Elinor Elizabeth
Evans, Dr. Grover Milton
Evans, Joe B.
Everett, Charles Roosevelt
Evers, James Charles
Fattah, Chaka
Feaster, Bruce Sullivan
Fields, C. Virginia
Fitzgerald, Howard David
Flake, Rev. Floyd H.
Fleming, June H.
Flemming, Lillian Brock
Fontayne, K. Nicole
Ford, Aileen W.
Ford, Harold Eugene
Ford, Jack
Ford, Johnny
Ford, Wallace L
Foster, Dr. E. C.
Foxworth, Derrick
Francis, James L.
Francisco, Anthony M.
Franklin, Shirley Clarke
Frazier, Dan E., Sr.
Frost, William Henry
Gaines, Cassandra Jean
Gaines, Paul Laurence
Gallot, Richard Joseph
Gamble, Kenneth L.
Gantt, Harvey Bernard
Gardner, Henry L.
Garner, Lon L.
Garner, Dr. Mary E.
Garrett, Paul C
Gates, Audrey Castine
Gates, Reginald
Gay, Helen Parker
Gayles, Franklin Johnson
Gentry, LaMar Duane
Gibson, Kenneth Allen
Gibson, Paul, Jr.
Gill, Nia H
Givens, E. Terrian
Givins, Abe, Jr.
Gonzaque, Ozie Bell
Goode, Calvin C.
Goode, Hon. Wilson
Goodwin, Dr. Jesse Francis
Gordon, Bertha Comer
Gordon, Charles D.
Goree, Janie Glymph
Grace, Bobbie H
Gray, Robert Dean
Gray, Valerie Hamilton
Green, Darlene
Green, Forrest F.
Green, Thomas L
Greene, Dr. Charles Edward Clarence
Griffin, Floyd Lee
Griffin, Percy Lee
Hairston, Rowena L.
Haley, David
Hall, Anthony W., Jr.
Hall, Katie Beatrice
Hall, Robert L.
Hall, Tracee K
Hamilton, Phanuel J.
Hamilton, Wilbur Wyatt
Hamlin, Arthur Henry
Hammond, Dr. W Rodney
Hampton, Thomas Earle
Haney, Napoleon
Harmon, Clarence
Harrell, William Edwin
Harris, Clifton L.
Harris, Jerome C., Jr.
Harris, Juan
Harris, Melvin
Harris, Roosevelt
Harrold, Austin Leroy

Harvey, Gerald
Hatcher, Richard Gordon
Hayden, Frank F.
Hayes, Jim
Head, Raymond, Jr.
Henderson, Hon. Erma L.
Henderson, Ronald
Herman, Kathleen Virgil
Hewitt, Ronald Jerome
Hewlett, Antoinette Payne
Hill, Betty J.
Hill, Gilbert R.
Hill, James O.
Hill, Jimmy H.
Hill, Mary Alice
Hilliard, Patsy Jo
Hines, Alice Williams
Hines, Carl R
Holden, Hon. Nate
Holder, Reuben D.
Holland, Loys Marie
Holliday-Hayes, Wilhelmina Evelyn
Hollowell, Kenneth Lawrence
Hoover, Jesse
Hopkins, Novellete O
Horton, Dollie Bea Dixon
Howard, Osbie L
Hubbard, Hon. Arnette Rhinehart
Hudson, William Thomas
Huger, James E., Sr.
Hughes, Mamie F.
Hunt, Jeffrey C.
Hursey, James Samuel
Hutchins, Jan Darwin
Jackson, Alvin B., Jr.
Jackson, Arthur Howard
Jackson, Bobby L.
Jackson, Charles Ellis
Jackson, Frank Donald
Jackson, James Garfield
Jackson, John
Jackson, John H.
Jackson, Leo Edwin
Jackson, Pamela J.
Jackson, Richard E., Jr.
Jacobs, Hazel A.
James, Eugenia H
James, Sharpe
James, Stephen Elisha
Jarmon, James Henry, Jr.
Jarrett, Valerie B.
Jeffers, Ben L.
Jefferson, James E.
Jefferson, Robert R.
Jefferson, Hon. William Jennings
Jenkins, Andrew
Jenkins, John
Jenkins, Woodie R
Johnson, Arthur T
Johnson, Ben E.
Johnson, Cleveland, Jr.
Johnson, Clinton Lee
Johnson, Harvey
Johnson, Leon F.
Johnson, Marlene E.
Johnson, Phyllis Campbell
Johnson, R. Benjamin
Johnson, Sarah H.
Johnson, Walter Louis, Sr.
Johnson, Wilhelmina Lashaun
Johnson, William A
Jones, Anthony, Jr.
Jones, Clarence J., Jr.
Jones, Sen. Emanuel Davie
Jones, Frank
Jones, Lawrence W.
Jones, Leeland Newton, Jr.
Jones, Nathaniel, Sr.
Jones, Patricia Yvonne
Jones, Stanley Bernard
Jones, Theresa Diane
Jones, Viola
Jordan, David Lee
Jordan, Patricia Carter
Kaslofsky, Thor
Keels, James Dewey
Kelly, James Johnson
Kelly, Marion Greenup
Kennedy, Hon. Willie B.
Kenney, Walter T.
Kincaid, Bernard
King, Ceola
King, Howard O., Sr.
Kirk, Ron
Kirven, Mythe Yuvette
Knight, Walter R.
Knuckles, Kenneth J
Laisure, Sharon Emily Goode
Lander, Cressworth Caleb

Lane, Allan C
Langham, John M.
Larkins, Elijah Pat
Lawrence, Brenda L.
Lawson, William R
LeCesne, Terrel M
Lee, Aaron
Lee, Edward S.
Lee, Howard N.
Lemmie, Valerie A
Lewis, Diane
Lewis, Karen A
Lewis, Ronald C.
Lindsey, S. L.
Lipscomb, Darryl L.
Locke, Henry Daniel Jr.
Locke, Dr. Mamie Evelyn
Lomax, Dervey A.
Lovelace, Dean Alan
Lucas, Earl S.
Lucas, Maurice F
Lyle, Roberta Branche Blacke
Lyles, Marie Clark
Mack, John L.
Mack, Levorn
Mahan-Powell, Lena
Makokha, James A N
Marsh, Sen. Henry L., III
Martin, Hoyle Henry
Martin, Janice R.
Martin, Shedrick M., Jr.
Mathis, Robert Lee, Jr.
Matthews, Virgil E.
McCrackin, Olympia H
McCray, Christopher Columbus
McEachern-Ulmer, Sylvia L
McEachin, James
McFadden, Cora
McFadden, Samuel Wilton
McGee, Adolphus Stewart
McGhee, Samuel T
McGlover, Stephen Ledell
McIver, John Douglas
McIver, Margaret Hill
McKinney, Cynthia Ann
McLean, Dr. John Alfred, Jr.
McNeil, Frank William
McRae, Emmett N
Meeks, Reginald Kline
Meeks, Willis Gene
Melton, Frank E
Michaux, Henry M
Middlebrooks, Felicia
Miller, Gwendolyn Martin
Mills, Mary Elizabeth
Mitchell, Quitman J.
Monroe, Kevin
Monson, Angela Zoe
Montgomery, Debbie
Montgomery, Joe Elliott
Montgomery, Payne
Moore, Katherine Bell
Morancie, Horace L.
Morgan, Joseph C.
Morial, Dr. Marc
Morrison, Robert B., Jr.
Morrow, Charles G, III
Morton, Lorraine H
Mosley, Elwood A
Moss, Estella Mae
Moss, Tanya Jill
Moss, Wayne B
Murray, Sylvester
Murrell, Hon. Sylvia Marilyn
Nagin, C. Ray
Neal, Richard
Nelson, Flora Sue
Nelson, Mary Elizabeth
Nesbitt, Prexy-Rozell William
Netters, Tyrone Homer
Newman, Kenneth J.
Newton, James Douglas, Jr.
Noah, Leroy Edward
Noble, John Pritchard
Norris, Walter
O, Fredrick William, Jr.
Odom, Darryl Eugene
Officer, Carl Edward
Oliver, Jerry Alton
Oliver, Kenneth Nathaniel
Owens, Major R
Palmer, Douglas Harold
Pappillion, Glenda M
Parker, Stafford W
Parker-Robinson, D LaVerne
Parker-Sawyers, Paula
Parks, Bernard C.
Parks, Thelma Reece
Parrish, John Henry

Parrish, Maurice Drue
Patrick, Julius, Jr.
Patrick, Lawrence Clarence, Jr.
Patterson, Dessie Lee
Patterson, William Benjamin
Patton, Robert
Paul, John F.
Payne, James Edward
Pearson, Herman B.
Petersen, Eileen Ramona
Peterson, Gerard M.
Peterson, Rocky Lee
Pierce, Abe, III
Pittman, Keith B.
Porter, Linsey
Portis, Kattie Harmon
Pounds, Elaine
Powell, Debra A
Prewitt, Al Bert
Price, John Wiley
Pritchard, Daron
Quander, Esq. Rohulamin
Quarles, Nancy L
Raab, Madeline Murphy
Ramseur, Isabelle R
Randall, Marlene West
Randolph, Lonnie Marcus
Rangel, Charles Bernard
Reese, Rev. Frederick D
Reid, Duane L
Reynolds-Brown, Blondell
Ricanek, Carolyn Wright
Rice, Judith Carol
Rice, Dr. Pamela Ann
Richards, William Earl
Richardson, Frederick D
Richardson, Gilda Faye
Richardson, Rhonda Karen
Richmond, Myrian Patricia
Riley, Dr. Wayne Joseph
Rivers, Valerie L
Roane, Rev. Glenwood P, Sr.
Roberts, Charles L.
Robinson, Henry
Robinson, Kenneth
Robinson, William
Robinson, William Earl
Rogers, Gwendolyn H
Rose, Shelvie, Sr.
Ruffin, Ronald R.
Rundles, James Isaiah
Rush, Bobby
Samples, Jared Lanier
Samuels, Dr. Leslie Eugene
Sanders, Archie, Jr.
Sanders, Robin Renee
Sanders, Wesley, Jr.
Santos, Mathies Joseph
Saunders, William
Scott, Carstella H.
Scott-Johnson, Roberta Virginia
Scruggs-Leftwich, Yvonne
Seabrooks, Nettie Harris
Seabrooks-Edwards, Marilyn S.
Session, Johnny Frank
Shabazz, Kaleem
Shakoor, Adam Adib
Shakoor, Dr. Waheedah Aqueelah
Shanks, James A
Sharpp, Nancy Charlene
Shelby, Khadejah E.
Shepherd, Veronika Y
Sheppard, Stevenson Royrayson
Shoemaker, Veronica Sapp
Simms, James Edward
Simpkins, Cuthbert O.
Sinclair, Benito A
Sindler, Michael H.
Singleton, James Milton
Singleton, Leroy, Sr.
Sloan, Edith Barksdale
Smallwood, William Lee
Smiley-Robertson, Carolyn
Smith, Carol Barlow
Smith, Dorothy O.
Smith, Frank
Smith, Dr. J. Clay, Jr.
Smith, Joseph F.
Smith, Juanita
Smith, Shirley Hunter
Smith, Toni Colette
Smith, Vernel Hap
Spaulding, William Ridley
Spencer, Marian Alexander
Spurlock, Dorothy A
Stanley, Ellis M., Sr.
Stanley, Woodrow
Stapleton, Marylyn A
Starks, Rick

Stent, Nicole M
Stewart, Charles J
Stewart, Dorothy Nell
Stewart, John B., Jr.
Stewart, Mae E
Stewart, Tylitha Helen
Stewart, W. Douglas
Stockard, Betsy
Stovall-Tapley, Mary Kate
Stubblefield, Jennye Lee Washington
Sullivan, Martha Adams
Summers, William E., IV
Talley, James Edward
Tarver, Gregory Williams
Tarver, Marie Nero
Tasco, Marian B.
Taylor, Marie de Porres
Taylor, Norman Eugene
Taylor, Richard L.
Teer, Wardeen
Terrell, Robert E.
Terry, Frank W.
Thomas, Erma Lee Lyons
Thomas, Dr. Joseph Edward, Jr.
Thompson, Aaron A
Thompson, Benjamin Franklin
Thompson, Rep. Betty Lou
Thompson, Hon. Bobby E.
Thompson, Johnnie
Thompson, William C., Jr.
Tillery, Dwight
Tinsley-Talabi, Alberta
Toby, William, Jr.
Todd, William S
Todman, Jureen Francis
Townsend, Murray Luke, Jr.
Travis, Geraldine
Trice, Juniper Yates
Truitt, Kevin
Turner, Melvin E.
Tyson, Edward Charles
Vaughn, Mary Kathryn
Vereen, Nathaniel
Wade, Beryl Elaine
Wade, Casey, Jr.
Wainwright, Gloria Bessie
Walker, Willie Leroy
Walls, Melvin
Ward, Anna Elizabeth
Ward, Doris Margaret
Ward, Everett Blair
Ware, John
Washington, Arnic J.
Washington, David Warren
Washington, Rev. Henry L
Washington, James Lee, Sr.
Waters, Mary D
Waters, William David
Watkins, Mozelle Ellis
Watt, Melvin L
Watts, John E.
Way, Dr. Curtis J.
Webb, Wellington E.
Wells, Billy Gene
Wesson, Cleo
Westbrooks, Phil
Wester, Richard Clark
Weston, Sharon
Wharton Boyd, Linda F.
Wheat, Alan
Wheeler, Dr. Maurice B.
White, Billy Ray
White, Debra Y
White, James Matthew, Jr.
White, Michael Reed
Whitfield, Kennard O
Whiting, Leroy
Wiggins, Lillian Cooper
Wilkins, Rillastine Roberta
William, Thompson E.
Williams, Anthony A
Williams, Cody
Williams, Dr. Earl, Jr.
Williams, Herman, Jr.
Williams, Jason Harold
Williams, Londell
Williams, Regina Vloyn-Kinchen
Williams, Reginald Clark
Williams, Robert L
Williams, Rodney Elliott
Williams, Ronald
Williams, Wayne Allan
Williams, Willie L
Williams- Warren, Jane E.
Wilson, Lawrence C.
Winston, Janet E.
Winter, Daria Portray
Wise, Frank P.
Womble, Larry W

Howard, Raymond
Hudson, Heather McTeer
Hudson, Merry C.
Hughes, Vincent J
Hunter, Teola P.
Hynson, Carroll Henry, Jr.
Jacks, Ulysses
Jackson, Alphonse
Jackson, Darnell
Jackson, Johnny, Jr.
Jackson, Lee Arthur
Jackson, Sandra Stevens
James, Kay Coles
James, Troy Lee
Jeff, Gloria Jean
Jefferson-Moss, Carolyn
Jenkins, John
Johnson, Bennett J
Johnson, Cleveland, Jr.
Johnson, Clinton Lee
Johnson, F. Raymond
Johnson, Jon D.
Johnson, Julia L.
Johnson, Hon. Justin Morris
Johnson, Paul Edwin
Johnson, Phyllis Mercedes
Johnson, Willie F
Jones, Charles D
Jones, Chester Ray
Jones, Christine Miller
Jones, Daryl L.
Jones, Emil
Jones, Gaynelle Griffin
Jones, Marilyn Elaine
Jones, Peter Lawson
Josey, Leronia Arnetta
Kane, Dr. Jacqueline Anne
Kelley, Dr. Delores G.
Kelley, Jack Albert
Kennedy, Sandra Denise
Kennedy, Dr. Yvonne
Keyes, Gwendolyn R
Kilpatrick, Carolyn Cheeks
Kilpatrick, Hon. Kwame M
Kindall, Dr. Luther Martin
King, Martin Luther, III
Lambert, Dr. Benjamin J., III
Lambert, LeClair Grier
Lawlah, Gloria Gary
Lawrence, Archie
Lawson, Herman A.
League, Cheryl Perry
Lee, Ivin S
Leek, Sandra D
LeFlore, Dr. Larry
Lewis, James B.
Lima, George Silva
Linton, Gordon J.
Long, Gerald Bernard
Lucas, David Eugene
Lyons, A Bates
Mallory, William L.
Malry, Lenton
Mann, Thomas J.
Mansfield, Andrew K.
Marable, Herman, Jr.
Marriott, Dr. Salima Siler
Marsh, Ben Franklin
Marshall, Charlene Jennings
Marshall, John W
McClain-Thomas, Dorothy Mae
McClendon, Ruth Jones
McCrimon, Audrey L.
McFadden, Nathaniel James
McNair, Chris
McRipley, G. Whitney
Meadows, Richard H.
Meek, Carrie P
Meeks, Perker L., Jr.
Melton, Bryant
Metcalf, Andrew Lee, Jr.
Michel, Harriet Richardson
Miller, Yvonne Bond
Mitchell, Brenda K.
Mitchell, Cranston J
Mitchell, Theo W
Montgomery, Velmanette
Moore, Eddie N., Jr.
Morgan, Alisha Thomas
Morse, John E
Morton, Margaret E.
Murphy, Margaret Humphries
Murphy, Raymond M.
Murray, Kay L.
Myers, Lewis Horace
Napolean, Benny Nelson
Neal, Sylvester
Nelson, Charles J
Nicholas, Gwendolyn Smith

Norwood, Calvin Coolidge
Nunnery, Willie James
Oliver, Jesse Dean
Owens, Arley E., Jr.
Owens, Lynda Gayle
Owens, Rissie Louise
Owens, William
Owens-Hicks, Shirley
Paterson, David A
Patterson, Kay
Payne, Debra K
Payne, Mitchell Howard
Pease, Denise Louise
Pelote, Dorothy B
Pendleton, Florence Howard
Perdue, Rep. George, Jr.
Peters, Kenneth Darryl
Pickering, Robert Perry
Pickett, Donna A
Pinckney, Clementa C.
Plummer, Ora Beatrice
Powers, Georgia M.
Preston, Joseph
Pulliam, Betty E
Putnam, Glendora M
Quince, Kevin
Ragsdale, Paul B.
Ramey, Adele Marie
Randolph, Lonnie Marcus
Raye, Vance Wallace
Rayford, Lee Edward
Reddick, Alzo Jackson
Reynolds, Mel
Reynolds, Nanette Lee
Rhodes, Hon. C Adrienne
Rice, William E.
Richardson, Dr. Leo
Rickman, Ray
Ridley, Dr. May Alice
Riley, Antonio
Roberts, Gregory G
Roberts, Jacqueline Johnson
Roberts, Janice L
Robinson, Dr. Prezell Russell
Roebuck, James Randolph
Rogers, Earline S
Rogers, Ormer, Jr.
Ross, Dr. Catherine Laverne
Rushing, Byron D
Sabree, Clarice S
Sanders, Hank
Savage, Dennis James
Scott, Albert J
Scott, David
Scott, Portia Alexandria
Scott, Samuel
Scott, Windie Olivia
Scruggs-Leftwich, Yvonne
Seavers, Clarence W.
Settles, Trudy Y
Sewell, Isiah Obediah
Shelton, O L
Shelton, Ulysses
Shepphard, Dr. Charles Bernard
Simmons, Kelvin
Simms, Stuart Oswald
Simpkins, Cuthbert O.
Sims, Millicent Jeannine
Singleton, Leroy, Sr.
Smith, Diane L
Smith, Judy Seriale
Smith, Robert London
Smith, Vernon G
Smitherman, Carole
Smitherman, Rodger M
Smyre, Calvin
Spencer, Anthony Lawrence
Spicer, Kenneth, Sr.
Spigner, Marcus E
Spruce, Kenneth L
Stallings, Henry E
Stallworth, Alma G.
Stanley, Craig A
Stanley, LaNett
Steele, Michael S.
Strozier, Yvonne Iglehart
Sykes, Vernon Lee
Tabor, Lillie Montague
Tanner, Gloria Travis
Tarver, Gregory Williams
Tate, Lenore Artie
Taylor, David Richard, III
Thigpen, Donald A
Thomas, Alvin
Thomas, Cheryl T
Thomas, Edith Peete
Thomas, James L
Thomas, Mable
Thomas, Hon. W. Curtis

Thompson, Bennie G.
Tollett, Dr. Charles Albert, Sr., M.D.
Townsend, Leonard
Traughber, Charles M.
Travis, Geraldine
Trotter, Donne
Troupe, Charles Quincy
Troupe, Dr. Marilyn Kay
Turnbull, Dr. Charles Wesley
Turner-Forte, Diana
Vann, Albert
Vaughn, Ed
Vernon, Alexander
Vincent, Edward
Von Mike McGhee, Daedra Anita
Waldon, Hon. Alton Ronald, Jr.
Walker, Carolyn
Walker, Charles W
Walker, Edwin L.
Walker, Dr. Howard Kent
Wallick, Ernest Herron
Walton, Elbert Arthur, Jr.
Wansley, Lisa Payne
Ward, Walter L., Jr.
Warren, Joyce Williams
Washington, LeAnna M
Waters, Kathryn
Watson, Dr. Diane Edith
Watt, Garland Wedderick
Watts, Beverly L.
Watts, J. C., Jr.
Webb, Harold H.
Wells, Roderick Arthur
Wesson, Herman Jason, Jr.
West, Phillip Curtis
West, Royce Barry
Wheeler, Heaster
Whipper, Hon. Lucille Simmons
Whisenton, Andre C.
White, Ida Margaret
White, Michael Reed
Wilder, Lawrence Douglas
Wilkerson, Hon. Dianne
Williams, Ada L.
Williams, Hardy
Williams, James
Williams, Hon. Louise Bernice
Wilson, Jimmie L
Wilson, Kim Adair
Wilson, Ronald Ray
Winters, Jacqueline F
Winters, James Robert
Wright, James Christopher
Young, George, Jr.
Young, Joseph, Jr.
Young, Larry
Young, Lee R
Zealey, Sharon Janine
Zollar, Nikki Michele

Government Service (Elected or Appointed)/ Government Administration—Federal

Anderson, Dr. Bernard E.
Anderson, Carl Edwin
Argrett, Loretta Collins
Baker, Shana V
Batine, Rafael
Bell, Theron J.
Bennett, Marian C
Best, Jennings H
Biggins, J Veronica
Bishop, Sanford D
Bishop, Verissa Rene
Bond, Wilbert
Booker, Johnnie Brooks
Bowman, William Alton
Bradley, Jeffrey
Breeding, Carl L.
Broadwater, Tommie, Jr.
Brown, Carrye Burley
Brown, Kwame R
Brown, Lee Patrick
Brown, Ralph Benjamin
Bruce, Carol Pitt
Bryant, Clarence W.
Buchanan, Calvin D.
Burke, Brian
Burroughs, John Andrew
Burse, Dr. Luther
Butterfield, G.K.
Calbert, Roosevelt
Campbell, Gertrude Sims
Cannon, Calvin Curtis
Carson, Andre
Carter, Zachary Warren
Charlton, George N., Jr.
Christian-Christensen, Donna-Marie

Cole Carey, Wilhemina
Collier, Dr. Barbara
Collins, LaVerne Vines
Cook, Joyce Mitchell
Cook, Julian Abele
Cooper, Jerome Gary
Cooper, Dr. LaMoyne Mason
Copeland, Barry B
Coram, Willie Mae
Corley-Saunders, Angela Rose
Counts, Dr. George W.
Cox, Warren E.
Crockett, Delores Loraine
Crosse, Rev. St George Idris Bryon, III
Curtis, Christopher Paul
Dandy, Clarence L.
Daniels, Joseph
Davis, John Alexander
Davis, Marilynn A.
Davis, Marion Harris
Davis, Ruth A.
Davis, Thurman M, Sr.
Davis, William E., Sr.
Dawson, Horace Greeley
Days, Drew Saunders
Dellums, Leola Higgs
Derryck, Vivian Lowery
Dillenberger, R. Jean
Druitt, Atty. Beverly F
Early, James Counts
Edmonds, Terry
Edwards, Donna
Edwards, Theodore Thomas
Elders, Dr. M. Joycelyn
Elmore Archer, Dr. Joyce A.
English, Kenneth
Enoch, Hollace J.
Evaige, Wanda Jo
Farmer, Sharon
Ferguson, Roger W, Jr.
Fields, Earl Grayson
Foster, Clyde
Fowler, William E
Fox, Richard K., Jr.
Franks, Gary A.
Frye, Robert Edward
Gaffney, Thomas Daniel
Gavin, Mary Ann
Gipson, Francis E., Sr.
Govan, Reginald C
Gray, Donnee L
Greaux, Cheryl Prejean
Green, Deborah Kennon
Griffin, Ples Andrew
Haley, George Williford Boyce
Hamilton, H J Belton
Hammond, Dr. W Rodney
Hardy-Hill, Edna Mae
Hargrave, Charles William
Harper, Bernice Catherine
Harris, DeWitt O.
Harris, Dr. Geraldine E.
Hart, Noel A.
Hastings, Alcee Lamar
Henderson, James H.
Hensley, Willie L.
Hibbler, William J
Hicks, Eleanor
Hill, Randal Thrill
Hobson, Robert R.
Holder, Eric, Jr.
Holder, Eric H
Holmes, James Franklin
Hoover, Jesse
Howard, Ray F.
Irby, Galven
Irving, Clarence Larry, Jr.
Jackson, Alphonso
Jackson, Franklin D. B.
Jackson, Jesse L., Jr.
Jackson, Lisa P.
Jackson-Lee, Sheila
James, Wynona Yvonne
Jerome, Dr. Norge Winifred
Johnson, Cleveland, Jr.
Johnson, Elaine McDowell
Johnson, Hank
Johnson, Lloyd A.
Johnson, Robert
Jones, Annie Lee
Jones, Hardi Liddell
Jones, Lorean Electa
Jones, Meredith J
Jones, Napoleon A, Jr.
Jones, Randy Kane
Jones-Smith, Jacqueline
Josey, Leronia Arnetta
Kaiser-Dark, Phyllis E

Kea, Arleas Upton
Kennard, William Earl
King, Frederick L.
King, William Charles
Labat, Eric Martin
Lang-Jeter, Lula L
Langston-Jackson, Wilmetta Ann Smith
Latimer, Allie B.
Lavizzo-Mourey, Risa Juanita
Lawless, Earl
Lawson, Dawn M
Lee, Sheila Jackson
Lee, Sheila Jackson
Lee, Vivian Booker
LeFlore, Dr. Larry
Lewis, John R.
Lewis, John Robert
Lightfoot, Jean Drew
Little, Irene Pruitt
Littlejohn, John B.
Lockett, Alice Faye
Lucas, Gerald Robert
Lucas, Dr. William
Madison, Richard
Majette, Denise
Mansfield, W. Ed
Marbury, Martha G.
Marshall, Thurgood
Mayes, Nathaniel H., Jr.
McIntosh, James E.
McMorris, Jacqueline Williams
McReynolds, Elaine A.
Medford, Isabel
Meriweather, Melvin, Jr.
Miller, Lorraine
Mills, Cheryl
Moore, Johnnie Adolph
Moore, Dr. Roscoe Michael
Morgan, Fletcher
Morris, Archie, III
Morrison, Trudi Michelle
Myrick, Bismarck
Nabors, Rob
Napper, Hyacinthe T.
Newman, William Thomas, Jr.
Newton, James Douglas, Jr.
Nichols, Sylvia A.
Norris, LaVena M.
Norton, Edward Worthington
O'Banno, Donna Edwards
O'Bryant, Constance Taylor
Osborne, Ernest L.
Parrott-Fonseca, Joan
Patrick, Deval L
Perry, June Carter
Pittman, Darryl E.
Polk, Dr. Lorna Marie
Powell, Gen. Colin Luther
Raines, Franklin D.
Ramseur, Andre William
Reid, Dr. Clarice Wills
Remy, Donald M
Reynolds, James W.
Rice, Emmett J.
Rice, Susan
Richardson, Laura
Roberts, Edgar
Roberts, Dr. Esther Pearl
Robinson, Dr. Prezell Russell
Robinson, William Andrew
Rollins, Avon William, Sr.
Saint-Louis, Rudolph Anthony
Satcher, Dr. David
Saulter, Gilbert John
Schoonover, Brenda Brown
Scott, David
Scott, Robert Cortez
Scott-Clayton, Patricia Ann
Scruggs, Sylvia Ann
Scruggs-Leftwich, Yvonne
Shannon, Hon. John William
Sharpless, Mattie R
Shippy, John D
Sleet, Gregory M
Smith, Charles Lebanon
Smith, Chester B.
Smith, Gregory Robeson, Sr.
Smith, Lila
Smith, Robert London
Smith, Rufus Herman
Solomon, David
Spigner, Marcus E
Spriggs, Edward J
Stephenson, Allan Anthony
Stewart, Ruth Ann
Stiell, Phelicia D
Stith, Charles Richard
Stokes, Louis

Strautmanis, Mike
Sutton, Dr. Ozell
Taylor, Daisy Curry
Taylor, Gayland Wayne
Taylor, Patricia Tate
Terry, Frank W.
Thomas, Carol M.
Thomas, Edith Peete
Thomas, Eunice S.
Thomas, James O.
Thompas, George Henry, Jr.
Thompson, Mozelle W
Thornell, Paul Nolan Diallo
Thornton, Leslie
Thornton, Tracey
Tolan-Gamble, Janet Helen
Townsend, Wardell C
Tribble, Huerta Cassius
Turner, Winston E.
Turner, Yvonne Williams
Tyler, Cheryl Lynnett
Vinson, Rosalind Rowena
Wallace, C. Everett
Walton, Reggie Barnett
Warmly, Leon
Warren, Dr. Rueben Clifton
Washington, Consuela M
Washington, Lester Renez
Watlington, Janet Berecia
Webb, Wilma J.
West, Dr. Togo Dennis, Jr.
Whisenton, Andre C.
White, Evelyn M
Wilber, Margie Robinson
Wilcher, Shirley J
Wiley, Leroy Sherman
Wilkins, Thomas A.
Williams, Ann Claire
Williams, Deborah Ann
Williams, Debra D
Williams, Howard Copeland
Williams, Paul
Williams, Vernon Alvin
Williams-Bridgers, Jacquelyn L
Woodson, Charles R.
Wright, Robert Courtlandt
Young, Rose S.

Government Service (Elected or Appointed)/ Government Administration—Not Elsewhere Classified (*See Also* **Judiciary**)

Abramson, John J., Jr.
Adams, Dr. Carol Laurence
Aldridge, Karen Beth
Alexander, Cornelia
Allen, James Trinton
Allen-Howard, Marquita W.
Ancrum, Alberta E.
Anderson, Marva Jean
Bailey, Linda F
Ballentine, Krim Menelik
Baltimore, Ambassador Richard Lewis, III
Baylor, Emmett Robert, Jr.
Bell, Hubert Thomas
Bell, Victory
Bell, William McKinley
Benefield, Michael Maurice, Jr.
Benham, Dr. Robert
Black, Barry C.
Blankenship, Glenn Rayford
Bohannan-Sheppard, Barbara
Bolen, David B
Bond, James G.
Booker, Johnnie Brooks
Bremby, Roderick LeMar
Broadnax, Walter Doyce
Brown, Carroll Elizabeth
Brown, Claudell, Jr.
Brown, Joseph Davidson, Sr.
Brown, Joseph Samuel
Brown, Lester J
Brown, Hon. Robert Lee
Brownridge, J Paul
Bugg, Robert
Bullock, Thurman Ruthe
Burt, Carl Douglas
Butler-Bush, Tonia
Calhoun, Eric A
Captain, Myrtle L
Carson, Johnnie
Carthan, Eddie James
Cave, Perstein Ronald
Chapman, David Anthony
Chappell, Michael James
Chatman, Jacob L.

Clancy, Magalene Aldoshia
Clarke, Anne-Marie
Clayborne, Oneal
Clyburn, James Emos
Collins, Annazette
Collins, Corene
Collins, Leroy Anthony, Jr.
Croft, Ira T
Crutchfield-Baker, Verdenia
Cummings, Elijah E
Davis, Christine R.
Davis, Clarence
Davis, John W., III
Davis, Thurman M, Sr.
Demeritte, Dr. Edwin T.
Dennis, Dr. Evie Garrett
Dessaso-Gordon, Janice Marie
Dorn, Roosevelt F
Douglas, Nicholas
DuBois, Joshua
Durham, Rev. Eddie L, Sr.
Dyas, Patricia Ann
Eaglin, Ruth
Edmonds, Curtis
Edwards, Theodore Unaldo
Elam, Harriet
Fagin, Darryl Hall
Fields, Rear Adm. Evelyn Juanita
Fobbs, Kevin
Foster, Ezola Broussard
Gamble, Robert Lewis
Gardner, Walter
Giles, Althea B
Gill, Roberta L.
Gillis, Theresa McKinzy
Gladman, Charles R
Green, Alexander N
Greenleaf, Louis E
Grigsby, Alice Burns
Groff, Peter Charles
Grooms-Curington, Talbert Lawrence, Sr.
Hampton, Thomas Earle
Haralson, Larry L
Harris, Elihu Mason
Harris, Robert F.
Hawkins, Walter L
Hayes, Elvin E.
Haynes, Dr. Leonard L
Haynes, Willie C., III
Head, Samuel
Hearne, Earl
Henderson, Remond
Hicks, Doris Morrison
Hightower, Herma J
Holley, Dr. James W
Holmes, Mary Brown
Hood, Nicholas
Horne-McGee, Patricia J
Howard, Calvin Johnson
Hunter, Cecelia Corbin
Isaac, Tameika
Ivery, James A
Jenkins, Andrew James
Jenkins, Cynthia
Jennings, Bernard Waylon-Handel
Johnson, Jared Modell
Johnson, Richard Howard
Jones, Gerald Winfield
Jones, Prof. James Edward
Jones, Patricia Yvonne
Jones, Willie
Jordan, Anne Knight
Joyner, Claude C.
Kee, Marsha Goodwin
Kelly, Dr. John Russell
Kilpatrick, Robert Paul
Kimbrough, Kenneth R
King, Rev. Bernice Albertine
King, John Thomas
Lawson, Lawyer
Lay, Clorius L.
Leatherwood, Larry Lee
Lee, Barbara Jean
Lee, Vivian O
Leeper, Ronald James
Lima, George Silva
Lindsay, Gwendolyn Ann Burns
Lofton, Andrew James
Lowe, Hazel Marie
Mack, Gladys Walker
Makokha, James A N
Malone, Amanda Ella
Marchant, Ann Walker
Marrow-Mooring, Barbara A
May, Floyd O
McGlowan, Angela
McLaughlin, Brian P
McLemore, Nelson, Jr.

Meadows, Cheryl R
Meek, Kendrick B
Meeks, Gregory Weldon
Miles, Steen
Mitchell, Douglas
Montague, Christina P
Moore, Gwen
Moore, Walter Louis
Morgan, Fletcher
Morse, Mildred S
Moses, Charles T
Murray, Dr. Thomas Azel, Sr.
Nelson, Charles J
Nelson, Mary Elizabeth
Newman, Paul Dean
Newton, James Douglas, Jr.
Nibbs, Alphonse, Sr.
Norrell-Nance, Rosalind Elizabeth
Obama, Barack
O'Leary, Hazel R
Palmer, Ronald DeWayne
Payne, Donald M.
Payne, William D
Peacock, Nicole
Perkins, Bernice Perry
Perry, Betty Hancock
Pinkard, Bedford L
Pinkney, Dr. Betty Kathryn
Pogue, Richard James
Pratt, Joan M, CPA
Quinn, Diane C
Rand, Cynthia
Reeves, John E
Reeves, Martha Rose
Rhodes, John K
Rice, Susie Leon
Richardson, Louis M, Jr.
Rivers, Valerie L
Robinson, Kenneth
Robinson, William
Robinson, William Peters, Jr.
Roper, Richard Walter
Sailor, Elroy
Saxton, Paul Christopher
Scott, Anthony R
Scott, Dr. Beverly Angela
Scott, Dr. Donald LaVern
Scott, Melvina Brooks
Scott, Ruth Elaine Holland
Seals, Gerald
Shivers, S. Michael
Simmons, Joseph Jacob, III
Simpson, Samuel G.
Slater, Rodney E
Smiley, James Walker, Sr.
Smith, Bobby Antonia
Smith, James Russell
Smith, Janet K
Smith, Shirley LaVerne
Smithers, Priscilla Jane
Soaries, Rev. Dr. DeForest Blake, Jr.
Solomon, David
Spencer, Collins
Stallworth, Ann
Stanton, Janice D
Stanton, Robert G
Steger, Dr. C Donald
Sterling, H. Dwight, Sr.
Stevens, Patricia Ann
Stewart, Jarvis Christopher
Talbot, Gerald Edgerton
Tarver, Elking, Jr.
Tayari, Kabili
Taylor, Felicia Michelle
Taylor, Paul
Teague, Gladys Peters
Thomas, Joan McHenry Bates
Thomas, Roy L.
Thomas, Samuel, III
Thomas, Wilbon
Thompson, Gloria Crawford
Thompson, Portia Wilson
Tibbs, Hon. Edward A
Towns, Edolphus
Trotter, Andrew Leon
Troupe-Frye, Betty Jean
Turner, Leslie Marie
Turner, Sharon V
Tyler, Robert James, Sr.
Wallace, Peggy Mason
Ware, Jewel C
Washington, John Calvin, III
Waters, Maxine
Watkins, Shirley R
Watson, Georgena
Webber, William Stuart
White, Robert C
Wiley-Pickett, Gloria
Wilkins, Kenneth C

Williams, Charles C
Williams, Charles Earl
Williams, Earl West
Williams, Enoch H.
Williams, Joe H.
Williams, Dr. Leon Lawson
Williams, Margaret Ann
Williams, Ronald Lee
Williamson, Carl Vance
Williamson, Samuel P
Willingham, Voncile
Wilson, Angela Brown
Wilson, Jaci Laverne
Wilson, Joy Johnson
Windham, Revish
Woods-Burwell, Charlotte Ann
Wordlaw, Clarence, Jr.
Wright, Loyce Pierce
Wynn, Albert
Young, Leon D
Young, Sarah Daniels

Graphic Design
See **Art, Visual—Commercial Art/Graphic Design**

Health Care—Not Elsewhere Classified (*See Also* **Chiropractic; Dentistry; Health Services Administration; Medicine—specific categories, e.g. Medicine—Anesthesiology; Nursing; Nutrition; Optometry; Pharmacy; Podiatry**)

Abdul-Malik, Dr. Ibrahim
Ali-Jackson, Kamil
Anderson, Howard D.
Barnes, Melody
Bellamy, Ivory Gandy
Benjamin, Donald S.
Bernard, Harold O.
Best, Jennings H
Bracey, Willie Earl
Brice, Barbara
Brown, Dr. J. Theodore, Jr.
Brown, Marsha J.
Buckner, William Pat
Burks, Juanita Pauline
Calhoun, Dr. Thomas
Cash, Bettye Joyce
Chivers, Gwendolyn Ann
Cooper, Almeta E
Cooper, Gary T.
Copeland, Betty Marable
Copeland, Terrilyn Denise
Copelin, Sherman Nathaniel
Davis, Myrtle Hilliard
Davis, Sidney Louis
De Loatch, Raven L.
Dorsey, Joseph A.
Dotson, Hon. Norma Y
Dual, Peter A.
Durham, C. Shelby
Fleming, Arthur Wallace
Fort, Dr. Jane Geraldine
Fowlkes, Nelson J
Francois, Emmanuel Saturnin
Freeman, Melinda Lyons
Gramby, Shirley Ann
Gray, Carol Coleman
Gresham, Darryl Wayne
Hall-Turner, Deborah
Hamberg, Dr. Marcelle R.
Harkins-Carter, Dr. Rosemary Knighton
Harrison, Roscoe Conklin, Jr.
Hatter, Henry
Hawkins, Dr. Muriel A.
Heard, Georgina E
Holland, Ethel M
Hollingsworth, John Alexander
Horne, June Merideth
Hudson, Dr. Roy Davage
Jackson, Lurline Bradley
Johnson, Cynthia L. M.
Johnson, Ernest Kaye, III
Johnson, Patricia Duren
Jones, Dr. Edward
Jones, Ervin Edward
Jones, Dr. Kenneth Leroy
Lane, Daphene Corbett
Lucas, John Harding, II
Martin, Dr. Rosalee Ruth
Maseru, Dr. Noble AW
McArthur, Dr. Barbara Jean

McGough, Robyn LaTrese
Mikell, Charles Donald
Mikell, Johnny
Miller, Lawrence A., Jr.
Mims, Robert Bradford
Morrison, James W.
Morse, Mildred S
Norris, Dr. James Ellsworth Chiles
Northern, Gabriel O.
Parker, Dr. Walter Gee
Pegues, Francine
Pinkney, Dove Savage
Powell, C. Clayton
Price, Glenda Delores
Ragland, Dr. Wylheme Harold
Robertson, Marilyn A
Roulhac, Dr. Edgar Edwin
Sands, Prof. Mary Alice
Scott, Syreeta
Seams, Francine Swann
Shorty, Vernon James
Sinnette, Dr. Calvin Herman
Smalls, Dr. Jacquelyn Elaine
Smith, Rev. Conrad Warren
Smith, Tommie M
Steele, Joyce Yvonne
Stovall-Tapley, Mary Kate
Street, Vivian Sue
Taylor, Dr. Dale B
Taylor, Prof. Paul David
Teague, Robert
Thomas-Richardson, Dr. Valerie Jean
Timmons, Bonita Terry
Walker, Moses L
Walters, Frank E.
Watson, Milton H
Welch, Lolita
Wigfall, Samuel E.
Wiggins, Dr. Charles A
Williams, Dr. Melvin Walker
Wilson, Joy Johnson
Winston, John H., Jr.
Wolfe, Allen, Jr.

Health Services Administration

Adair, Robert A.
Adiele, Dr. Moses Nkwachukwu
Agwunobi, Andrew C.
Alexander, Wardine Towers
Alexis, Dr. Carlton Peter
Allen, Herbert J.
Allen, Percy
Arrington, Harold Mitchell
Avery, Byllye Y
Bacon, Dr. Gloria Jackson
Ball, Clarence M.
Barksdale, Rosa Kittrell
Bassard, Yvonne Brooks
Baugh, Reginald F.
Bell, Rouzeberry, Jr.
Bellamy, Ivory Gandy
Belton, C Ronald
Benjamin, Donald S.
Boaz, Valerie A
Bonner, Della M.
Bowers, Mirion Perry
Branch, Dr. Geraldine Burton
Brandon, Jerome
Brannon, James R.
Braynon, Dr. Edward J
Brooks, Phillip Daniel
Brooks, Todd Frederick
Brooks, William P
Brown, A. Sue
Brown, Dr. Glenn Arthur
Brown, Dr. Walter E
Brown, Zora Kramer
Bryant, William Arnett, Jr.
Burrows, Clare
Butler, Michael Keith
Caison, Thelma Jann
Campbell, Dr. Charles Everett
Campbell, Emmett Earle
Camphor, Michael Gerard
Cantrell, Forrest Daniel
Capel, Wallace
Caro, Ralph M
Carper, Gloria G.
Carson, Regina M. E.
Carter, Jandra D.
Carter, Oscar Earl, Jr.
Carter, Tracy L
Chastang, Mark J.
Christian, Cora LeEthel
Christian, John L.
Clark, John Joseph
Clarke, Leon Edison
Clayton, Lloyd E

Cleveland, Hattye M.
Clifton, Rosalind Maria
Cochran, Dr. James David, Jr.
Combs, Dr. Julius V
Copeland, Dr. Ronald Louis
Couch, James W
Cowan, Dr. James R.
Craft, Dr. Thomas J
Craig, Frederick A.
Crawford, Brenita
Culpepper, Lucy Nell
Dandy, Dr. Roscoe Greer
Daniel, Colene Yvonne
Daniel, Samuel J
Darity, Janki Evangelia
Dash, Hugh M. H.
Davis, Adrianne
Davis, Brownie W
Davis, Myrtle Hilliard
Davis Anthony, Vernice
Delphin, Dr. Jacques Mercier
DeVaughn-Tidline, Donna Michelle
Dillard, Wanda J
Dorsey, L. C.
Duckett, Esq. Gregory Morris
Dumpson, Dr. James R.
Dunn, Marvin
Dunston, Walter T.
Earls, Dr. Julian Manly
Edwards, John W., Jr.
Edwards, Lonnie
Eller, Carl L.
Ellis, O. Herbert, Sr.
Epps, Charles Harry, Jr.
Evans, Therman E.
Fields, Dr. Richard A., Sr.
Forde, James Albert
Frazier, Wynetta Artricia
Fregia, Darrell Leon
Furlough, Joyce Lynn
Garner, John W.
Garrett, Kathryn
Gaston, Dr. Marilyn Hughes
Gates, Nina Jane
Gates, Dr. Paul Edward
Gatson, Wilina Ione
George, Alma Rose
Gilmore, Edwin C.
Gladney, Dr. Marcellious
Goodson, Leroy Beverly
Goodwin, Dr. Jesse Francis
Goodwin, Norma J.
Goulbourne, Donald Samuel, Jr.
Greene, Horace F.
Grist, Arthur L.
Hall, Evelyn Alice
Hall, Kathryn Louise
Ham-Ying, J. Michael
Hannah, Hubert H., Sr.
Harper, Walter Edward
Harvey, Jacqueline V.
Hayes, Edward
Heard, Georgina E
Heineback, Barbara Taylor
Henry, Brent Lee
Herring, Marsha K Church
Hill, Jacqueline R
Hill, Rufus S.
Hogan, Dr. James Carroll
Holland, Loys Marie
Holt, Maude R
Hopper, Dr. Cornelius Lenard
Howard, Osbie L
Howard, Samuel Houston
Howard, Shirley M.
Hoyle, Dr. Classie G.
Humphries, Charles, Jr.
Hunn, Dorothy Fegan
Ince, Harold S.
Jackson, Lurline Bradley
Jenkins-Scott, Jackie
Johnson, Cleveland, Jr.
Johnson, Elaine McDowell
Johnson, Ernest Kaye, III
Johnson, Dr. James Kenneth
Johnson, Robert
Johnson-Brown, Dr. Hazel Winfred
Johnson-Carson, Dr. Linda D
Jones, Dr. Billy Emanuel
Jones, Sondra Michelle
Jordan, Thurman
Jordan, Dr. Wilbert Cornelious
Kelly, Thomas, Jr.
King, Edgar Lee
King, John L.
King, Dr. Rosalyn Cain
King, Dr. Talmadge Everett
Kirchhofer, Dr. Wilma Ardine Lyghtner

Lavizzo-Mourey, Risa Juanita
Lee, Dr. Andre L
Lee, Vivian Booker
Lee, Vivian O
Leon, Jean G
Lewis, Alonzo Todd
Lewis, Polly Meriwether
Lewis, Therthenia Williams
Logan, Lloyd
Mabson, Glenn T
Mack, Wilhelmena
Mackay, Leo S, Jr.
Malone, Dr. Cleo
Manley, Dr. Audrey Forbes
Marion, Dr. Phillip Jordan
Mark, Richard
Marsh, Donald Gene
Martin, Lee
Martin, Wanda C.
Maseru, Dr. Noble AW
Mayberry-Stewart, Melodie Irene
McCabe, Jewell Jackson
McCants, Dr. Odell
McCraven, Carl Clarke
McCraven, Marcus R.
McDonald, Mark T.
McGregor, Edna M.
McLeod, James S.
McMillan, Jacqueline Marie
McWhorter, Rosalynd D
Meeks, Perker L., Jr.
Menzies, Dr. Barbara A
Metcalf, Dr. Zubie West, Jr.
Metoyer, Carl B.
Mills, Capt. Mary Lee
Mobley, Dr. Joan Thompson
Moone, Wanda Renee
Moore, Alfred
Moore, Lois Jean
Morgan, Alice Johnson Parham
Moten, Emmett S, Jr.
Munroe, Anthony E
Murray, James Hamilton
Myers, Dr. Woodrow Augustus, Jr.
Noble, John Pritchard
Osborne, Dr. William Reginald, Jr.
Owens, Rev. Zelba Rene
Parham Hopson, Rear Adm. Deborah L.
Parker, Henry Ellsworth
Patterson-Townsend, Margaret M.
Payne, Jerry Oscar
Peoples, Florence W
Persaud, Inder
Peters, Kenneth Darryl
Pinckney, Lewis, Jr.
Pinkney, Dove Savage
Pinn, Dr. Melvin T, Jr.
Plummer, Ora Beatrice
Polk, Dr. Gene-Ann
Poole, Dr. Rachel Irene
Porter, Lionel
Pounds, Dr. Moses B
Price, Andrea R
Priest, Dr. Marlon L
Primm, Dr. Beny Jene
Reed, Clara Taylor
Reed, Dr. Theresa Greene
Riley, Dr. Wayne Joseph
Risbrook, Dr. Arthur Timothy
Roberts, Cheryl Dornita Lynn
Roberts, Dr. Jonathan
Robertson, Evelyn Crawford
Robinson, Robert G
Robinson, Thomas Donald
Roddy, Howard W
Rosser, Dr. James M.
Rowan, Michael Terrance
Ruffin, John
Rutledge, Dr. William Lyman
Sadler, Dr. Kenneth Marvin
Sampson, Marva W
Sanders, Sally Ruth
Sanford, Mark
Savage, Dr. Archie Bernard, Jr.
Scrivens, John J
Simpson, Dr. Dazelle Dean
Singletary, Inez M.
Sinnette, Dr. Calvin Herman
Smith, Gloria Dawn
Smith, Dr. Gloria Richardson
Smith, Dr. Quentin Ted
Smith, Sundra Shealey
Stent, Nicole M
Story, Otis L
Street, Vivian Sue
Strickland, Dr. Frederick William, Jr.
Strong, Amanda L
Sullivan, Dr. Louis Wade

Tappan, Dr. Major William
Taylor, Prof. Paul David
Thomas, Edward S.
Thomas, Marla Renee
Thomas, Dr. Pamella D
Thompson, Dr. Theodis
Tingle, Lawrence May
Towns, Dr. Myron B, Jr.
Turner, Jean Taylor
Veal, Dr. Yvonnecris Smith
Walker, Allene Marsha
Walker, Dr. Mark Lamont
Warren, Dr. Rueben Clifton
Washington, Dr. James Edward
Watson, Anne
Webb, Dr. Harvey
Webb, Linnette
Webb, Shelia J
Wesley, Nathaniel, Jr.
Wheeler, Primus
White-Perkins, Denise M
Williams, Jason Harold
Wilson, Dr. Donald
Worrell, Audrey Martiny
Wyatt, Dr. Ronald Michael
Yancey, Dr. Asa G, Sr., M.D.
Yarbrough, Earnest

History
Anthony, Dr. David Henry
Bailey, Richard
Ballard, Allen Butler
Binford, Henry C.
Bond, Julian
Bracey, Henry J.
Bracey, John Henry, Jr.
Brooks, Rosemary Bittings
Brown, Courtney Coleridge
Brown, Rev. Jeffrey LeMonte
Brown, John Mitchell, Sr.
Cabbell, Edward Joseph
Callum, Agnes Kane
Carey, Harmon Roderick
Carpenter, William Arthur
Claye, Charlene Marette
Coleman, Dr. Ronald Gerald
Connor, Dolores Lillie
Crew, Spencer R.
Crosby, Dr. Edward Warren
David, Arthur LaCurtiss
Dember, Jean Wilkins
Dickerson, Prof. Dennis Clark
Drewry, Henry Nathaniel
DuPree, Prof. Sherry Sherrod
Edwards, John Loyd, III
Ekechi, Felix K.
Ford, Dr. Marcella Woods
Franklin, Dr. John Hope
Galloway, Lula Briggs
Gilmore, Dr. Al Tony
Goodwin, Maria Rose
Green, John M.
Ham, Dr. Debra Newman
Hamilton, Roy L.
Hardin, Dr. John Arthur
Harding, Vincent
Harris, Francis C
Harris, Michael Wesley
Hayden, Robert C., Jr.
Holland, Dr. Antonio Frederick
Holmes, E Selean
Holmes, Rev. James Arthur
Hopson, Kevin M
Houston, Willie Lewis
Hudson, Dr. James Blaine
Jacobs, Sylvia Marie
Jefferson, Alphine Wade
Jones, Alice Eley
Jones, Dr. Edward Louis
Jordan, William Chester
King-Hammond, Dr. Leslie
Knight, Franklin W.
Lee, Clara Marshall
Ligon, Doris Hillian
Lockett, James D.
Martin, Sylvia Cooke
Matthews, Christy
Matthews, Vincent Edward
Miller, Dr. M Sammye
Moore, Dr. Marian J.
Morse, Annie Ruth W.
Moss, Alfred A
Mumford, Esther Hall
Neverdon-Morton, Dr. Cynthia
Painter, Dr. Nell Irvin
Patterson, Dr. Orlando Horace
Phillips, Dr. Glenn Owen
Pinkney, Enid C.
Pitre, Merline

Ransby, Barbara
Reynolds, Dr. Edward
Roberts, Rev. Wesley A
Robinson, Dr. Genevieve
Rouse, Jacqueline Anne
Rushing, Byron D
Saunders, Doris E.
Scruggs, Prof. Otey Matthew
Sinkler, Dr. George
Smith, Dr. Gerald Lamont
Strickland, Dr. Arvarh E
Sumler Edmond, Janice L.
Taylor, Dr. Henry Louis, Jr.
Terborg-Penn, Dr. Rosalyn M
Thomas, Robert James
Troupe, Dr. Marilyn Kay
Washington, Dr. Michael Harlan
Welch, Ashton Wesley
Williams, Dr. Carolyn Ruth Armstrong
Williams, Kathryn
Winston, Dr. Michael Russell
Wright, Dmitri

Horticulture
See **Landscape/Horticultural Services**

Hotel/Motel Industry
Alexander, Larry
Ash, Richard Larry
Bright, Kirk
Broadwater, Tommie, Jr.
Carter, Harriet LaShun
Childs, Oliver Bernard
Corley, Todd L.
Dean, Curtis
DeLeon, Priscilla
Deramus, Bill R.
Dixon, John M.
Edwards, Daniel
Eggleston, Neverett A
Harmon, James F., Sr.
Hudson, Lester Darnell
Isom, Eddie
Jenkins, Ozella
King, Lewis Henry
Littlejohn, Bill C.
Porcher, Robert, III
Robinson, Deanna Adell
Roy, Jan S
Shelton, John W
Walker, Eugene Kevin
Watson, Barbara
White, Alvin, Jr.

Industrial Design
Bates, William J
Charity, Lawrence Everett
Charles, Lewis
Ellis, Michael G.
Morris, Earl Scott
Winslow, Reynolds Baker

Information Science
See **Library/Information Science**

Insurance
Alexander, Willie
Anderson, Abbie H.
Anderson, Ronald Edward, Sr.
Anderson, Tony
Anderson Janniere, Iona Lucille
Ashby, Reginald W.
Ayers, Hon. Timothy F.
Bailey, Clarence Walter
Baker, LaVolia Ealy
Baker, Roland Charles
Balton, Kirkwood R.
Batchelor, Asbury Collins
Bates, Willie Earl
Bell, William Jerry
Bennett, Ivy H.
Bluford, James F
Bonaparte, Dr. Tony Hillary
Bowie, Willette
Brannen, James H., III
Britton, Theodore R
Brown, Abner Bertrand
Brown, D Joan
Brown, Herbert R
Brown, Sherman L.
Brown, Virgil E
Bryant, R. Kelly
Bryce, Dr. Herrington J
Buggs, James
Burges, Melvin E.

Caldwell, John Edward
Campbell, Otis Levy
Carter, Lemorie, Jr.
Carter, Robert Henry
Catchings, Howard Douglas
Chaney, Alphonse
Clifton, Rosalind Maria
Cockrell, Mechera Ann
Collins, Robert
Copes, Ronald Adrian
Crawford, James Maurice
Creuzot, Cheryl D.
Croft, Wardell C.
Cunningham, David S., Jr.
Dance, Dr. Daryl Cumber
Davis, Dr. Brenda Lightsey-Hendricks
Davis, Brownie W
Davis, Darlene Rose
Demeritte, Dr. Edwin T.
Dennis, James Carlos
DeVaughn-Tidline, Donna Michelle
Dillard, Dr. Melvin Rubin
Dixon, Dr. Benjamin
Dixon, Isaiah, Jr.
Dozier, Morris, Sr.
Duncan, Sandra Rhodes
Duncan, Verdell
Easley, Jacqueline Ruth
Elliott, Cathy
Esco, Fred, Jr.
Evans, Leon, Jr.
Fields, Stanley
Fontayne, K. Nicole
Forster, Jacqueline Gail
Gaines, Richard Kendall
Gholson, Robert L
Givens, Lawrence
Givins, Abe, Jr.
Glapion, Michael J
Golden, Arthur Ivanhoe
Golden, Ronald Allen
Gomez, Dennis Craig
Goodrich, Thelma E.
Hale, Hilton I
Hall, Pamela Vanessa
Handwerk, Jana D.
Hardy, Charlie Edward
Harper, Bernice Catherine
Harris, Joseph Preston
Harrison, Delbert Eugene
Haugstad, May Katheryn
Haydel, James V, Sr.
Haywood, Roosevelt V., III
Herndon, Gloria E.
Hicks, Willie Lee
Holmes, Willie A.
Hopkins, William A
Houston, Ivan J
Howard, Leon W., Jr.
Howell, Gerald T
Hunter, Rev. John Davidson
Hurst, Rodney Lawrence
Jackson, Dwayne Adrian
Jackson, James E., Sr.
James, Charles Leslie
Jenkins, Joseph Walter
Johnson, Ben D.
Johnson, Cleveland, Jr.
Johnson, Hermon M., Sr.
Johnson, John
Johnson, Patricia Duren
Jones, Gregory Allan
Jones, Gregory Wayne
Jones, Leonard Warren
Jones, Thomas Wade
Kendrick, Carol Yvonne
Kennedy, William J., III
King, Charles Abraham
King, Josephine
Knight, W H
Leigh, Fredric H
Livingston-Wilson, Karen E
Lomax, Michael Wilkins
Lyons, Robert P.
Mack, Daniel J
Marsh, McAfee
Martin, Reddrick Linwood
Mauney, Donald Wallace, Jr.
McFerrin, Bobby
McGinnis, Robert Lawrence
McGrier, Jerry, Sr.
McReynolds, Elaine A.
Mercer, Arthur, Sr.
Merritt, Willette T.
Miller, Donald Lesessne
Miller, Joseph Herman
Misshore, Joseph O, Jr.
Morris, Joe

Morse, Mildred S
Moses, Milton E.
Murphy, Charles William
Murray, J Ralph
Myers, Andre
Nelms, Ommie Lee
Obi, James E.
Olawumi, Bertha Ann
Orr, Dr. Dorothy J
Owens, James E, Jr.
Palmer, Douglas Harold
Palmer, Dr. James Dibble
Parrish, James Nathaniel
Parsons, Philip I
Patterson, James
Pegues, Francine
Pemberton, David Melbert
Peoples, Erskine L.
Pinkett, Allen Jerome
Pocknett, Lawrence Wendell
Porter, Linsey
Procope, Ernesta
Rawls, Mark Anthony
Rawls Bond, Charles Cynthia
Rivers, Alfred J.
Roberts, Cecilia
Robinson, Alcurtis
Rogers-Grundy, Ethel W.
Ruffin-Barnes, Wendy Yvette
Ruffner, Ray P.
Salter, Roger Franklin
Scott, Artie A.
Scott, Hubert R.
Shakespeare, Easton Geoffrey
Shell, Theodore A.
Simms, William E.
Slaughter-Titus, Rev. Linda Jean
Smith, Dr. Ann Elizabeth
Smith, Denver Lester
Smith, James Russell
Snowden, Raymond C.
Sockwell, Oliver R, Jr.
Solomon, Donald L.
Spears, Henry Albert
Steed, Tyrone
Stewart, James A., III
Stith, Antoinette Freeman
St Mary, Joseph Jerome
Taylor, Carol Ann
Teasley, Larkin
Thomas, Edward Arthur
Thomas, Isaac Daniel, Jr.
Thompson, Rev. Carl Eugene
Thompson, Joseph Isaac
Tinsley, Dwane L.
Trammell, William Rivers
Turnbull, Horace Hollins
Veney, Marguerite C
Vincent, Daniel Paul
Walker, Laneuville V
Walker, Solomon W., II
Walters, George W
Warden, George W
Ware, William
Waters, John W
Watson, Milton H
Webb, Dr. Harvey
White, Arthur W, Jr.
Wilkes, Jamaal
Williams, Annalisa Stubbs
Williams, Charlotte Leola
Williams, Eldredge M
Williams, Herman
Wilson, Rita P
Woodard, Rhonda Marie
Woodson, Roderic L.
Woodward, Aaron Alphonso, III
Wright, Soraya M

Interior Design
Bridges, Sheila
Carter, Vincent G
Charity, Lawrence Everett
Duckett, Karen Irene
Gainer, Prof. John F
Hubbard, Lawrence Ray
Johnson, Costello O
Johnson, Edward M
Lawrence, Sandra
Merritt, Wendy Warren
Reid, Malissie Laverne
Robinson, Joseph William
Stull, Donald L

Travis, Jack
Wilder, Jason Barnard

Interpretation
See **Translation/Interpretation**

Journalism—Broadcast
Adams, Katherine
Agurs, Donald Steele
Alexander, Marcellus Winston
Anglen, Reginald Charles
Bailey, Lee
Bates, Karen Grigsby
Bell, Harold Kevin
Bennett, Dr. Sybril M.
Berry, Halle M
Berry, Ondra Lamon
Black, Charles E.
Blackmon, Brenda
Blanton, Dain
Blount, Charlotte Renee
Bobonis, Regis Darrow, Jr.
Boykin, Keith
Brewington, Rudolph W
Bridgeforth, Arthur Mac, Jr.
Bridgewater, Dr. Herbert Jeremiah, Jr.
Bromery, Keith Marcel
Brown, Angela Yvette
Brown, Paul E. X.
Brown-Francisco, Teresa Elaine
Bundles, A'Lelia
Burns, Diann
Burns, Regina Lynn
Burose, Renee
Burwell, Bryan Ellis
Carroll, Lawrence William, III
Casey, Frank Leslie
Castleberry, Edward J.
Christian, Spencer
Coleman Morris, Valerie Dickerson
Costa, Annie Bell Harris
Covington, Kim Ann
Coward, Onida Lavoneia
Crockett-Ntonga, Noluthando
Cross, June Victoria
Cunningham, Malena Ann
Curwood, Stephen Thomas
Daniels, Kysa
Davis, Alisha
Davis, Barbara D
Dee, Merri
Dember, Jean Wilkins
Dennard, Darryl W.
Dickerson, Thomas L, Jr.
Dorsey, Sandra
Drummond, William Joe
Dyer, Joe, Jr.
Edwards, Delores A.
Elder, Larry
Ellison, Bob
Estes-Sumpter, Sidmel Karen
Evans, James L.
Ferguson, Renee
Ford, Sam
French, MaryAnn
Gill, Rev. Laverne McCain
Gillum, Andrew D
Gite, Lloyd Anthony
Gordon, Ed
Green, Barbara Marie
Greer, Karyn Lynette
Griffith, Mark Richard
Guillory, Keven
Gumbel, Bryant Charles
Gumbel, Greg
Hampton, Cheryl Imelda
Handy, Delores
Haney, Don Lee
Hanson, John L
Harlan, Carmen
Harris, Gil W.
Harrison-Sullivan, Jeanette LaVerne
Hayes, J Harold, Jr.
Hayward, Dr. Jacqueline C
Hedgspeth, Adrienne Cassandra
Heyward, Isaac
Hilliard, Alicia Victoria
Holman, Kwame Kent Allan
Holt, Melonie R
Horne, Deborah Jean
Hughes, Catherine Liggins
Hunter-Gault, Charlayne
Ifill, Gwen
Ingram, Valerie J.
Izrael, Jimi
Jenkins, Carol Ann
Jessup, Gayle Louise
Jiggetts, Danny Marcellus

Johnson, Charles Bernard
Johnson, Donn S
Johnson, Iola Vivian
Johnson, John
Johnson, Patrice Doreen
Johnson, Vinnie
Jones, Leander Corbin
Jones, Marsha Regina
Jones, Star
Jones, Victoria C.
Jordan, Dr. Robert Howard, Jr.
Kaigler-Reese, Marie Madeleine
Kennedy Franklin, Linda Cheryl
Kennedy-Overton, Jayne
Keyes, Alan L.
King, Emery C
King, Gayle
Lane, Janis Olene
Langhart Cohen, Janet
Lawson, Debra Ann
Lee, Consella Almetter
Lewis, Maurice
Lomax, Janet E
Love, Thomas Clifford
Lowry, Donna Shirlynn (Reid)
Mabrey, Vicki L
Mack, Joan
Madison, Eddie L, Jr.
Madison, Paula
Makupson, Amyre Ann Porter
Martin, Carol
Martin, Robert E.
Martin, Wisdom T
Massey, Selma Redd
Mathis, Deborah F
McCovey, Willie Lee
McCreary, Bill
McCree, Edward L.
McGee, Rose N.
McMichael, Earlene Clarisse
McTyre, Robert Earl, Sr.
Mickelbury, Penny
Miles, Steen
Moore, Cynthia M
Moore, Dr. Jean E.
Morris, Valerie Coleman
Morse, Barbara Lyn
Nelson, Debra J
Newsome, Elisa C
Ollison, Ruth Allen
Owens, Dr. Debbie A.
Parker, E Charmaine Roberts
Parker, Maryland Mike
Peoples, John Derrick, Jr.
Petty, Bob
Phillips, Julian Martin
Poindexter, Malcolm P
Pool-Eckert, Marquita Jones
Powell, Darrell Lee
Pressley, Condace L
Quarles, Norma R.
Randolph-Jasmine, Carol Davis
Revish, Jerry
Rice, Horace Warren
Rideau, Wibert
Ridenhour, Carlton Douglas
Riley, Glenn Pleasants
Roberts, Deborah
Roberts, Robin
Roberts, Troy
Robinson, Angela Yvonne
Robinson, Carol Evonne
Robinson, Shaun
Rodgers, Barbara Lorraine
Rodgers, Johnathan A.
Rojas, Don
Romans, Ann
Sample, William Amos
Santiago, Roberto
Sartin, Johnny Nelson, Jr.
Saunders, John P
Scafe, Judith Arlene
Scott, Portia Alexandria
Sealls, Alan Ray
Shaw, Bernard
Shearin, Kimberly Maria
Shifflett, Lynne Carol
Simpson, Carole
Slade, Karen E
Smiley, Tavis
Smith, Greg
Smith, Dr. Ian
Smith, Philip Gene
Smith, Steven Delano
Smothers, Ronald Eric
Snyder, George W
South, Wesley W.
Steptoe, Sonja
Stevens, Sharon A

Stovall, Stanley V.
Strait, George Alfred, Jr.
Stricklin, James
Sutton, Percy E.
Sykes, William Richard
Taylor, Carol
Thompson, DeHaven Leslie
Todd, Cynthia Jean
Tucker, Sheryl Hilliard
Turner, Bennie L
Tyree, Omar
Vincent, Marjorie Judith
Wagoner, J Robert
Walker, Kenneth R.
Warmly, Leon
Washington, Adrienne Terrell
Washington, Robin
Waters, Brenda Joyce
Watson, Ben
Weston, Sharon
Wheaton, Wendy E
Whitaker, William Thomas
White, Beverly Anita
White, Deidre V.
Wickham, DeWayne
Wilkins, Betty
Williams, Rev. Dr. Clarence Earl
Williams, Gayle Terese Taylor
Williams, Jeffrey Lem
Williams, Jewel L
Williams, Juan
Williams, Margo E
Williams, Montel
Witherspoon, William Roger
Wood, Brenda Blackmon
Woods Badger, Madelyne
Worthy, William, Jr.
Wright, Carl Jeffrey
Wright, Verlyn LaGlen
Wright, Will J
Wyatt, S Martin, III
Wynns, Coryliss Lorraine
Wynter, Leon E
Ziegler, Dr. Dhyana

Journalism— Photojournalism (*See Also* Photography)
Bailey, Hiltron
Banks, Marguerita C.
Barboza, Anthony
Brown, Milbert Orlando
Burton, Cheryl
Davis, Clarence
Easley, Billy Harley
Higgins, Chester Archer, Jr.
Johnson, Charles Bernard
Johnson, Paul L.
Locke, Henry Daniel Jr.
Marshall, Eric A
McCray, Christopher Columbus
Perry, Rita Eggleton
Ramsey, Freeman, Jr.
Sartin, Johnny Nelson, Jr.
Scott, Charles E
Stricklin, James
Tarry, Ellen
Townes, Hon. Sandra L.
Upshaw, Sam
White, Constance C. R.
White, John H
Wiggs, Jonathan Louis
Williams, Sherman

Journalism—Print (*See Also* Writing/Editing— Nonfiction)
Adams, Robert Hugo
Adams, Samuel Levi, Jr.
Alexander, James Brett
Allen, Robert L
Allen-Jones, Patricia Ann
Anderson, Betty Keller
Anderson, Monroe
Andrews, Sharony S
Anglen, Reginald Charles
Ansa, Tina McElroy
Armstrong, Reginald Donald, II
Aubespin, Mervin R.
Bailey-Thomas, Sheryl K.
Baker, Delbert Wayne
Ballentine, Krim Menelik
Barboza, Steven Alan
Barfield, Deborah Denise
Bates, Karen Grigsby
Beckham, Barry Earl
Bellinger, Luther Garic
Bembry, Jerry E

Bennett-Alexander, Dawn DeJuana
Benson, Wanda Miller
Benyard, William B
Bernstein, Margaret Esther
Berry, Gemeral E., Jr.
Blackshear, William
Bogus, Dr. S. Diane Adamz
Bonds Staples, Gracie
Bonner, Alice A.
Booker, John, III
Boone, Frederick Oliver
Boone, Raymond Harold, Sr.
Bradford, Equilla Forrest
Britt, Donna
Brooks, Rodney Alan
Brooks, Rosemary Bittings
Brown, Clifton George
Brown, Geoffrey Franklin
Brown, Hardy
Brown, Jamie Foster
Brown, Jean Marie
Brown, Joseph Clifton
Brown, Warren Aloysius
Burley, Dale S.
Burns, Calvin Louis
Burns, Regina Lynn
Burroughs, Dr. Todd Steven
Cain, Herman
Camper, Diane G
Carmichael, Carole A
Carpenter, William Arthur
Carter, Kelly Elizabeth
Channer, Colin
Chavous, Mildred L.
Claxton, Melvin L
Clayton, Janet Theresa
Clemons, James Albert, III
Coleman, Chrisena Anne
Coleman, Trevor W
Cooper, Kenneth Joseph
Cose, Ellis
Cox, Corine
Cox, Jesse L
Cumber, Victoria Lillian
Curtis, Mary C
Daniels, David Herbert, Jr.
Daniels, Earl Hodges
Daniels, Kysa
Davenport, Reginald
Davis, Reginald Francis
Davis, Samuel C
Dawkins, Wayne J
Days, Michael Irvin
Dejoie, Carolyn Barnes Milanes
Dejoie, Michael C
Delaney, John Paul
Dember, Jean Wilkins
DeRamus, Betty
Diuguid, Lewis Walter
Dobson, Byron Eugene
Dodson, Angela Pearl
Draper, Rev. Frances Murphy
Dreyfuss, Joel P
Due, Tananarive
Dunlap, Dr. Karen F Brown
Dunmore, Gregory Charles
Durant, Celeste Millicent
Dyer, Bernard Joel
Edmond, Alfred Adam
Edwards, Audrey Marie
Egiebor, Sharon E.
Elliott, Joy
Evans, Akwasi Rozelle
Evanzz, Karl Anderson
Fearn-Banks, Kathleen
Fitchue, M. Anthony
Fitzpatrick, Albert E.
Flono, Fannie
Fluker, Elayne M
Francis, Delma J
French, Howard W
Fry, Darrell
Fugett, Jean Schloss, Jr.
Fulwood, Sam
Garrett Harshaw, Karla
Gaston, Patricia Elaine
Gates, Jimmie Earl
Gill, Rev. Laverne McCain
Gillespie, Marcia A.
Gilliam, Dorothy Butler
Giloth-David, King R.
Givhan, Robin Deneen
Gladwell, Malcolm
Glover, Chester Artis
Goodwin, Martin David
Grant, Claude DeWitt
Gray, Karen G
Green, Barbara Marie
Green, John M.
Green, Lisa R.

Greenwood, Edna Turner
Greer, Thomas H.
Guiton Hill, Bonnie
Hardnett, Carolyn Judy
Harris, Jay Terrence
Harris, Lee
Harris, Peter J.
Hartman, Hermene Demaris
Harvin, Alvin
Haygood, Wil
Henderson, Angelo B
Hiatt, Dietrah
Hill, Jennifer A
Hilliard, William Arthur
Hite, Nancy Ursula
Hodge, Aleta S.
Holloway, Ardith E
Holsendolph, Ernest
Holt, Mikel
Hoover, Felix A
House, Michael A
Hoye, Walter B.
Hudson, Don R
Hunter-Gault, Charlayne
Ibelema, Dr. Minabere
Israel, Mae H
Izell, Booker T
Izrael, Jimi
Jackson, Darcy DeMille
Jackson, Derrick Zane
Jackson, Esther Cooper
Jackson, Gordon Martin, Jr.
Jackson, Harold Jerome
Jackson, Prof. Luther Porter, Jr.
Jackson, Robert, Jr.
James, Venita Hawthorne
Jefferson, Margo
Jeffries, Fran M
Jeter-Johnson, Sheila Ann
Johnson, Kerry Gerard
Johnson, Rita Falkener
Johnson, Roy Steven
Johnson-Crosby, Deborah A.
Johnston, Ernest
Jones, Bernie
Jones, Charisse Monsio
Jones, Floresta Deloris
Jones, Jacqueline Valarie
Kane, Eugene A
Kashif, Ghayth Nur
Kazi, Abdul-Khaliq Kuumba
Keith, Luther
Kelly, Ernece Beverly
King, Colbert I
Kirwan, Roberta Claire
Knight, Athelia Wilhelmenia
Kumbula, Dr. Tendayi Sengerwe
Lacey, Marc Steven
Lacy-Pendleton, Stevie A
Large, Jerry D
Lawrence, James Franklin
Leavell, Dorothy R.
Lee, Felicia R.
Leigh, Fredric H
Leslie, Marsha R
Levermore, Jacqueline Maureen
Lewis, Janice Lynn
Lewis, Matthew
Lewis, Melanie
Lipscomb, Curtis Alexander
Lister, Valerie Lynn
Lloyd, Wanda
Locke, Henry Daniel Jr.
Love, Karen Allyce
Madison, Paula
Mallory, James A
Mason, Felicia Lendonia
McCall, Nathan
McClean, Vernon E
McConnell, Dorothy Hughes
McDaniel, Robert Anthony
McDaniel, Sharon A.
McElroy, Dr. Lee A
McGee, William Torre
McGill, Thomas L
McLaren, Douglas Earl
McWhorter, Grace Agee
Mickelbury, Penny
Miller, Dr. Andrea Lewis
Mixon, Veronica
Molaire, Michel Frantz
Monroe, Bryan K
Moore, Acel
Moore, Carman Leroy
Moore, Trudy S
Muhammad, Askia
Murray, Virgie W.
Nelson, Jill
Newkirk, Pamela

Nipson, Herbert
O'Flynn-Pattillo, Patricia
Oglesby, Joe
Overbea, Luix Virgil
Owens, Keith Alan
Page, Clarence
Parker, E Charmaine Roberts
Parker, Karen Lynn
Patton, Princess E
Payne, Leslie
Pierce, Ponchitta A
Pitts, George Edward
Porter, Charles William
Porter, Bishop Henry Lee
Preston, Edward Michael
Prince, Richard Everett
Quarles, Herbert DuBois
Raspberry, William J
Rawls, Mark Anthony
Redd, Orial Anne
Reed, Sheila A
Reed, Dr. Vincent Emory
Reynolds, Pamela Terese
Richardson, Eddie Price, Jr.
Rideau, Wibert
Riley, Clayton
Ritchie, Joe
Ritchie, Dr. Louise Reid
Robeson, Paul, Jr.
Robinson, Sharon
Robinson-Jacobs, Karen Denise
Rodgers, Carolyn Marie
Rodney, Karl Basil
Russell, Sandra Anita
Russell-McCloud, Patricia
Sample, Herbert Allan
Sanders, Rhonda Sheree
Scott, Col. Eugene Frederick
Seals, Rupert Grant
Seals, Theodore Hollis
Shannon, Marian L H
Shelton, Charles E
Shipe, Jamesetta Denise Holmes
Shipp, Etheleen R
Shiver, Jube
Simmons, Belva Tereshia
Sims, Calvin Gene
Sims, Carl W
Smith, Danyel
Smith, Douglas M
Smythe, Victor N.
Spears, Angelena Elaine
Spicer, Osker, Jr.
Stevens, Michelle
Stickney, William Homer
Stone, Chuck
Straight, Cathy A
Stuart, Reginald A
Sutton, Clyde A., Sr.
Sutton, William W., Jr.
Tandy, Dr. Mary B
Tate, Eleanora Elaine
Tate, Greg
Tate, Sonsyrea
Taylor, Iris
Taylor, Kimberly Hayes
Taylor, Susan L.
Taylor, T Shawn
Teasley, Marie R.
Terrell, Robert L.
Terrell, Stanley E
Thomas, Jacqueline Marie
Thomas, Ron
Thompson, Art
Thompson, DeHaven Leslie
Thompson, Garland Lee
Tipton-Martin, Toni
Todd, Cynthia Jean
Tomlinson, Randolph R.
Trammer, Monte Irvin
Trescott, Jacqueline Elaine
Tucker, Cynthia Anne
Tucker, Geraldine Coleman
Vernon-Chesley, Michele Joanne
Wade, Kim Mache
Wade, Norma Adams
Walker, Douglas F.
Walker, James Zell, II
Ward, Frances Marie
Ware, Janis L
Washington, James A
Washington, Robin
Waters, Sylvia Ann
Watkins, Aretha La Anna
Watkins, Joseph Philip
Watson, Prof. Denton L
Watson, Joann Nichols
Watson, John Clifton
Weathersbee, Tonyaa Jeanine

Webb, Veronica Lynn
Wesley, Herman Eugene, III
Weston, Martin V
Whack, Rita Coburn
Wheeler, Robyn Elaine
Wheeler, Dr. Susie Weems
White, George Gregory
White, Jack E
White, John Clinton
White, Margarette Paulyne Morgan
Wickham, DeWayne
Wiley, Edward, III
Wilkins, Betty
Wilkins, Roger Wood
Williams, Armstrong
Williams, Dr. Jamye Coleman
Williams, Dr. McDonald
Winston, Bonnie Veronica
Womble, Jeffery Maurice
Woodford, John Niles
Workman, Aurora Felice Antonette
Wright, Carl Jeffrey
Wright, Jeanne Jason
Wright, Dr. Katie Harper
Yancy, Prof. Preston Martin
Young, B Ashley
Zola, Nkenge

Journalism—Not Elsewhere Classified

Alexander, Vincent J.
Allen, Dr. Harriette Insignares
Anderson Janniere, Iona Lucille
Ashley-Ward, Amelia
Austin, Lucius Stanley
Baker, Kimberley Renee
Bennett-Alexander, Dawn DeJuana
Berry, Venise
Billops, Camille J.
Blackmon, Brenda
Booker, Simeon S.
Bowens, Gregory John
Bradford, Gary C.
Brandford, Napoleon
Britton, John Henry
Brooks, Clyde Henry
Browder, Anne Elna
Cobb, Delmarie L.
Coleman, Robert Earl, Jr.
Cook, Elizabeth G
Cooper, Barry Michael
Curtis-Rivers, Susan Yvonne
Dash, Leon DeCosta
Dowkings, Wendy Lanell
Drummond, William Joe
Effort, Elaine
Eubanks, Dayna C
Evans, Alicia
Fields, Valerie K
Fletcher, Robert E.
Ghent, Henri Hermann
Hornsby, Dr. Alton, Jr.
Jackson, Gordon Martin, Jr.
Jackson, Janine Michele
Jackson, Warren Garrison
Kern-Foxworth, Dr. Marilyn L.
Kluge, Pamela Hollie
Knight, Dr. Muriel Bernice
Madison, Eddie L, Jr.
Mathis, Deborah F
Merritt, Joseph, Jr.
Meyers, Lisa Anne-Marie
Middlebrooks, Felicia
Owens, Cynthia Dean
Randle, Wilma Jean-Elizabeth Emanuel
Roberts, Tara Lynette
Routte-Gomez, Eneid G
Smith, Monica LaVonne
Smith-Gregory, Deborah P.
Stewart, Alison
Stewart, Mae E
Stewart, Pearl
Stone, Reese J
Sullivan, Lencola
Tipton-Martin, Toni
Traynham, Robert Lee
Tucker, Dr. Dorothy M.
Vernon-Chesley, Michele Joanne
Way, Dr. Curtis J.
Williams, Benjamin Vernon
Wilson, Christopher A
Worrill, Dr. Conrad W
Zook, Kristal Brent

Judiciary

Abdus-Salaam, Sheila
Adams, John Oscar
Adrine, Ronald Bruce

Alexander, Harry Toussaint
Alexander, Hon. Joyce London
Alexander, Pamela Gayle
Allen, Alex James, Jr.
Allen, Cheryl L
Allen-Rasheed, Jamal Randy
Anderson, David Turpeau
Anthony, Emory
Archer, Trudy DunCombe
Argrett, Loretta Collins
Armstrong, Joan Bernard
Armstrong, Saundra Brown
Arrington, Judge Marvin S., Sr.
Atkins, Marylin E.
Baety, Hon. Wendy Marie
Bailey, D'Army
Baker, Althea
Banks, Patricia
Baranco, Gordon S.
Baskerville, Lezli
Baxter, Hon. Wendy Marie
Baylor, Margaret
Bell, Robert Mack
Bennett, Al
Bennett, Patricia A.
Benton, George A.
Benton, James Wilbert, Jr.
Birch, Adolpho A
Bishop, Ronald L.
Bivins, Edward Byron
Blackwell, Willie
Blackwell-Hatcher, June E
Bledsoe, Tempestt
Bledsoe, William
Blye, Cecil A., Sr.
Boyd, Delores Rosetta
Braden, Everette Arnold
Bradley, Vanesa Jones
Bramwell, Henry
Braxton, John Ledger
Brewer, Webster L.
Brock, Gerald
Brown, George Henry, Jr.
Brown, Helen E.
Brown, Irma Jean
Brown, Janice Rogers
Brown, Joe
Bruce, Raymond L.
Bryant, Clarence
Bugg, Mayme Carol
Burke, Lillian W.
Burnett, Arthur Louis
Burrell, Garland, Jr.
Byrd, Isaac, Jr.
Byrd, Jerry Stewart
Calvin, Michael Byron
Campbell, Calvin C.
Canady, Herman G., Jr.
Card, Larry D
Carroll, George D
Carroll, Sally G.
Carson, Curtis C., Jr.
Carter, Robert Lee
Cartwright, Joan S.
Chenevert-Bragg, Irma J.
Clark, Tama Myers
Clarke, Anne-Marie
Clemon, U. W.
Clevert, Hon. Charles N.
Coleman, Claude M
Coleman, Rudy B.
Coleman, Veronica F
Collins, Daisy G.
Collins, Jeffrey G
Collins, Robert Frederick
Connally, C Ellen
Cook, Julian Abele
Cook, Ralph D
Cooley, Wendy
Cooper, Hon. Candace D
Cooper, Clarence
Cooper, Evelyn Kaye
Cousins, William
Craig, Rhonda Patricia
Crider, Edward S., III
Crockett, George W., III
Cross, Denise L.
Culpepper, Dellie L.
Curtin, John T.
Curtis, James
Daniel, Wiley Young
Davenport, Horace Alexander
Davis, Arnor S.
Davis, L. Clifford
Davis, Lawrence Arnette, Jr.
Davis, Michael James
Davis, Reuben K.
Davis, Susan D
Dearman, John Edward

Delaney, Duane B.
Dilday, Hon. Judith Nelson
Donald, Dr. Bernice Bouie
Dorn, Roosevelt F
Dorse, Earnestine Hunt
Doss, Hon. Theresa
Dotson, Hon. Norma Y
Douglas, Willard H
Douglass, Hon. Lewis Lloyd
Drain, Gershwin A
Drake, Maggie W.
Dunn, Reginald Arthur
Dye, Hon. Luther V
Edwards, Dennis, Jr.
Edwards, Harry Thomas
Edwards, Prentis
Edwards, Raymond
Edwards, Wilbur Patterson, Jr.
Edwards O, Donna M
Elam, Harry Justin
Ephriam, Mablean
Evans, Carole Yvonne Mims
Farmer, Nancy
Farris, Hon. Jerome
Figures, Thomas H
Finney, Ernest A., Jr.
Floyd, Marquette L.
Ford, Judith Donna
Fordham, Cynthia Williams
Foskey, Carnell T.
Fowler, William E
Franklin, Robert Vernon, Jr.
Freeman, Ronald J.
Freeman-Wilson, Karen Marie
Frye, Henry E.
Gaines, Clarence L.
Gaitan, Fernando J., Jr.
Garner, Edward, Jr.
Gartin, Claudia L.
Gibbs, Robert Lewis
Gibson, Benjamin F.
Gibson, Reginald Walker
Giles, James T.
Gilmore, Vanessa D
Glover, Don Edward
Gordon, Levan
Goree, Janie Glymph
Grant, Cheryl Dayne
Grante, Jullian Irving
Graves, Ray Reynolds
Green, Alexander N
Greene-Thapedi, Dr. Llwellyn L.
Greenlee, Peter Anthony
Grimes, Douglas M.
Guice, Leroy
Hall, L Priscilla
Hall, Sophia H.
Hamilton, Arthur N.
Hamilton, Eugene Nolan
Hamilton, H J Belton
Harbin-Forte, Brenda F
Harper, Sara J.
Harris, Alonzo
Harris, Barbara Ann
Harris, Leodis
Hassell, Leroy Rountree, Sr.
Hatchett, Glenda A.
Hathaway, Cynthia Gray
Hatter, Terry J
Haynes, William J., Jr.
Hazelwood, Hon. Harry, Jr.
Henderson, Thelton Eugene
Hibbler, William J
Hicks, Maryellen
Hill, Reuben Benjamin
Hill, Vonciel Jones
Hobson, Donald Lewis
Hollingsworth, Perlesta A
Holt, Leo E
Hood, Denise Page
Hood, Harold
Howard, Raymond
Hoyt, Hon. Kenneth M
Humphrey, Marion Andrew
Humphries, Paula G
Ingram, Edith J.
Ireland, Roderick Louis
Irons, Hon. Paulette R
Jackson, Arthur D., Jr.
Jackson, Carol E
Jackson, Darnell
Jackson, Giles B
Jackson, Harold Baron, Jr.
Jackson, Janet E.
Jackson, Marie O
Jackson, Michael W
Jackson, Randolph
James, Letitia
Jamison, Birdie Hairston

Labor Relations

See **Labor Union Administration; Management/ Administration—Personnel/ Training/Labor Relations**

Labor Union Administration

Landscape/Horticultural Services

Law Enforcement

Smith, Marvin Preston
Stafford, Don
Stalling, Ronald Eugene
Stephen, Joyce
Stone, Dwight
Sturdivant, Col. Tadrial J
Swain, James H
Sylvester, Odell Howard, Jr.
Tate, Earnest L
Taylor, Benjamin Garland
Taylor, Vanessa Gail
Taylor, Vernon Anthony
Thomas, Fred
Thomas, Dr. Joseph Edward, Jr.
Thomas, Nina M
Thomas, Robert Lewis
Thomas, Rodolfo Rudy
Thompas, George Henry, Jr.
Tillmon, Joey
Tucker, Dr. Dorothy M.
Turner, Eddie William
Turner, Melvin E.
Underwood, Joseph M
Veals, Craig Elliott
Wade, Casey, Jr.
Waith, Eldridge
Walker, May
Ward, Christopher Evan
Washington, Leonard
Watford-McKinney, Yvonne V
Watson, Jackie
Wearing, Melvin H
Weldon, Ramon N.
White, Lt. Gen. June Joyce
Williams, Rev. Ellis
Williams, Dr. Hubert
Williams, Leonard
Williams, Moses, Sr.
Williams, Rodney Elliott
Williams, Willie L
Wilson, Jimmy L
Winfield, Susan Rebecca Holmes
Witcher, Veroman D
Worshaim, Keith Eugene
Wrice, David
Wynn, Malcolm
Young, Lee R

Law/Legal Services

Acosta Nesmith, Winifred L
Adams, Deborah Ross
Adams, Edward Robert
Adams, Gregory Albert
Adams, John Oscar
Addams, Robert David
Ahmad, Jadwaa
Aikens, Dr. Chester Alfronza
Albert, Charles Gregory
Alexander, Clifford L., Jr.
Alexander, James, Jr.
Alexander, James Eduard
Ali-Jackson, Kamil
Allen, George Mitchell
Allen, Jerry Ormes
Allen, W George
Al'Uqdah, William Mujahid
Amos, Donald E
Anderson, George Allen
Anderson, Leslie Blake
Anderson, Louise Payne
Anderson, Richard Charles
Andrews, Judis R
Archibald, B. Milele
Armano, Kwadwo J.
Armistead, Milton
Arnelle, Hugh Jesse
Arnold, Alison Joy
Arnold, Rudolph P
Arnwine, Barbara
Atkins, Edna R.
Atkins, Thomas Irving
Audain, Linz
Austin, Joyce Phillips
Awkard, Linda Nanline
Baker, Althea
Baker, Beverly Poole
Baker, Thurbert E.
Baker-Kelly, Dr. Beverly
Baldwin, Cynthia A.
Baldwin, George R.
Ball, Richard E.
Ball-Reed, Patrice M.
Baltimore, Ambassador Richard
  Lewis, III
Banks, Cecil J.
Banks, Fred L.
Banks, Haywood Elliott
Banks, Patricia
Banks, Richard Edward

Banks, Sharon P
Bankston, Archie M
Barber, Vaughn J
Barksdale, Leonard N
Barley, Tracy Hicks
Barnes, Joseph Nathan
Barnes, Stephen Darryl
Barnes, William L.
Barnes, Willie R.
Barnes, Yolanda L.
Barton, Rhonda L
Barzey, Dr. Raymond Clifford, II
Baskerville, Randolph
Bass, James F
Bateman, Paul E
Bates, Arthur Verdi
Batine, Rafael
Batts, Alicia
Bauduit, Harold S
Baugh, Edna Y
Beal Bagneris, Michele Christine
Beamon, Arthur Leon
Beane, Dorothea Annette
Beard, James William
Beasley, Ulysses Christian, Jr.
Beasley, Victor Mario
Beatty, Otto, Jr.
Bell, Napoleon A.
Bell, Sheila Trice
Bell, William A.
Bellamy, Everett
Bellamy, Werten F W
Belton, Robert
Bennett, Arthur T
Bennett, Kanya A
Bennett, Patricia A.
Benton, James Wilbert, Jr.
Berkley, Dr. Constance E Gresham
Bernstine, Dr. Daniel O.
Berry, Lee Roy
Berry, LeRoy
Beshah, Guenet
Besson, Paul Smith
Best, Jennings H
Bishop, Wesley T
Bivins, Cynthia Glass
Bivins, Demetrius
Bivins, Sonja F
Black, Dr. Lee Roy
Blackmon, Barbara Martin
Blackmon, Edward
Blackmon, Patricia Ann
Blade-Tiggens, Denise Patricia
Blair, Chester Laughton Ellison
Blount, Sherri N
Blue, Daniel Terry
Bocage, Ronald J
Boddie, Dr. Arthur Walker
Bolden, Clarence
Bolden, Frank Augustus
Bolton, Julian Taylor
Booker, James E.
Booth, Dr. Le-Quita
Borum, Jennifer Lynn
Bostic, James Edward, Jr.
Bourne, Judith Louise
Bowers, Gwendolyn
Bowling, Lysia Huntington
Bowman, Jacquelynne Jeanette
Boykin, Keith
Boze, U Lawrence
Bozeman, Bruce L
Bracey, Willie Earl
Braden, Everette Arnold
Braden, Henry E, IV
Bradford, Martina Lewis
Brady, Charles A
Brady, Julio A.
Branton, Leo, Jr.
Braxton, John Ledger
Breckenridge, Franklin E., Sr.
Brent, Charles Tyrone
Brooke, Edward William
Brooks, Rosemary Bittings
Brown, Bartram S.
Brown, Hon. Christopher C
Brown, Claudine K.
Brown, Denise J.
Brown, Dwayne Marc
Brown, Franchot A
Brown, Dr. Glenn Arthur
Brown, Irma Jean
Brown, Jamie Earl S
Brown, Janice Rogers
Brown, Jasper C., Jr.
Brown, John E
Brown, Joseph N
Brown, Lewis Frank
Brown, Ouida Y.

Brown, Ronald Wellington
Brown, Virgil E
Brown, William H
Brown, Willie Lewis
Brownlee, Wyatt China, III
Brummer, Chauncey Eugene
Bryan, David Everett, Jr.
Bryant, Andrea Pair
Bryant, Hubert Hale
Bryant, Regina Lynn
Bryant, Wayne R
Bryson, Cheryl Blackwell
Buchanan, Calvin D.
Buchanan, Sam H
Bugg, Mayme Carol
Bullock, J Jerome
Bullock, James
Bully-Cummings, Ella
Burke, Yvonne Watson Brathwaite
Burnham, Margaret Ann
Burns, Benjamin O.
Burris, Roland W
Burroughs, Robert A
Burse, Raymond Malcolm
Burt, Carl Douglas
Bush, Nathaniel
Bussey, Reuben T., Jr.
Butler, Annette Garner
Butler, Frederick Douglas
Butler, Jerome M.
Butler, Patrick Hampton
Butler, Rex L
Butterfield, Torris Jerrel
Bynoe, John Garvey
Byrd, Isaac, Jr.
Byrd, Jerry Stewart
Cadogan, Marjorie A.
Cage, Patrick B
Cain, Frank Edward, Jr.
Cain, Robert R, Jr.
Cain, Simon Lawrence
Caldwell, James E.
Caldwell, Lisa Jeffries
Callender, Carl O.
Callender, Wilfred A.
Calvin, Michael Byron
Camp, Marva Jo
Campbell, Christopher Lundy
Carlisle, James Edward, Jr.
Carpenter, Raymond Prince
Carroll, James S
Carroll, Raoul Lord
Carter, Billy L.
Carter, Geoffrey Norton
Carter, Phyllis Harden
Carter, Thomas, II
Carter, Zachary Warren
Cason, Marilynn Jean
Chambers, John Curry, Jr.
Chambers, Dr. Julius LeVonne
Chambliss, Alvin Odell, Jr.
Chambliss, Prince C
Chancellor, Carl Eugene
Chandler, Everett A.
Chandler, James Phillip
Chapman, David Anthony
Chase, Anthony R
Cheek, King Virgil, Jr.
Chenault, Kenneth I.
Cherot, Nicholas Maurice
Chicago, Denovious Adolphus
Childs, Joy
Childs, Winston
Ciccolo, Angela
Clark, Augusta Alexander
Clark, Eligah Dane, Jr.
Clarke, Hugh Barrington
Clay, Eric Lee
Clay, William Lacy
Clayton, Matthew D.
Clayton, Theaoseus T.
Clegg, Legrand H
Clements, Walter H.
Cloud, W. Eric
Clyne, John Rennel
Coar, David H.
Cohen, Vincent H
Cole, James O
Cole, Ransey Guy, Jr.
Coleman, April Howard
Coleman, Claude M
Coleman, Eric Dean
Coleman, Michael Bennett
Coleman, Michael Victor
Coleman, William T., Jr.
Coleman James, Patricia Rea
Collins, Daisy G.
Collins, Kenneth L.
Collins, Robert Frederick

Colvin, Cedric B
Conley, Charles S.
Conley, John A.
Conley, Martha Richards
Cook, Frank Robert, Jr.
Cook, Ronald R
Cook, Rufus
Cooper, Almeta E
Cooper, Clarence
Cooper, Drucilla Hawkins
Cooper, Gordon R., II
Cooper, Joseph
Cooper, Julius
Corlette, Edith
Cormier, Rufus
Cornish, Jeannette Carter
Corrothers, Garry James
Cothorn, John A
Countee, Thomas Hilaire
Cousins, William
Cox, Sandra Hicks
Cox, Warren E.
Crenshaw, Waverly David
Cromartie, Ernest W., II.
Cromer, Ronnie E, Jr.
Crosby, Fred Charles
Cross, Denise L.
Cruise, Warren Michael
Crump, Arthel Eugene
Crusto, Mitchell Ferdinand
Cunningham, Courtney
Cunningham, E Brice
Cunningham, Joy Virginia
Cunningham, T. J., Sr.
Curry, Levy Henry
Curtis, James
Daggs, Leon
Dalferes, Edward R., Jr.
Dalley, George Albert
Daniels, Earl Hodges
Daniels, John W
Darden, Anthony Kojo
Darden, Christopher Allen
Darden, Edwin Carley
Dark, Lawrence Jerome
Davenport, Horace Alexander
Davidson-Harger, Joan Carole
Davis, Alfred C., Sr.
Davis, Artur
Davis, Denise
Davis, Dr. Doris Ann
Davis, Dupree Daniel
Davis, Dr. Elaine Carsley
Davis, John Wesley
Davis, Lawrence Arnette, Jr.
Davis, Lisa E
Davis, Marva Alexis
Davis, Milton C.
Davis, Morris E
Davis, Nathan W., Jr.
Davis, Robert N
Davis, Willie J.
Davison, Edward L.
Dawson, Horace G
Dawson, Ralph C
Dawson, Warren Hope
Daye, Charles Edward
Days, Drew Saunders
DeGraffenreidt, James H
Dellums, Leola Higgs
Deloach, Wendelin W.
Dennis, Andre L
Dennis, Edward S G, Jr.
Denson, Fred L
DePriest, Darryl Lawrence
DeWitt, Franklin Roosevelt
Dillard, June White
Dixon, Yvonne T
Dodds, R. Harcourt
Donald, Dr. Bernice Bouie
Donald, James E
Donegan, Charles Edward
Dorse, Earnestine Hunt
Dorsey, Elbert
Dorsey, John L.
Dotson, Albert E., Jr.
Douglas, Carl E
Douglas, James Matthew
Drew, Stephen Richard
Drew-Peeples, Brenda
Druitt, Atty. Beverly F
Duckett, Esq. Gregory Morris
Dudley, Godfrey D.
Dukes, Dr. Walter L
Duncan, Robert M
Dunn, Almeda Effie
Dunnings, Stuart
Dupree, David H.
Eaglin, Fulton B.

Earley, Keith H.
Echols, Alvin E
Edmonds, Bobbie
Edmonds, Lisa I.
Edmunds, David L., Jr.
Edwards, Carl Ray, II
Edwards, Donald Philip
Edwards, Ruth McCalla
Edwards, Dr. Sylvia
Edwards, Wilbur Patterson, Jr.
Edwards O, Donna M
Elam, Harry Justin
El-Amin, Sa'ad
Elder, Larry
Elliott, Darrell Stanley, Sr.
Elliott, Lori Karen
Ellis, Rodney
Elmore, Ernest Eric
Ephriam, Mablean
Epps, Phillip Earl
Espy, Michael
Evans, Carole Yvonne Mims
Evans, Dorsey
Evans, Dr. LeRoy W.
Evans, Timothy C.
Evans, Warren Cleage
Everett, Cynthia A
Everett, J Richard
Everett, Ralph B
Ewing, William James
Fain, Constance Frisby
Farley, William Horace, Jr.
Farris, Deborah Ellison
Farrow, Sallie A
Fearn, James E., Jr.
Feaster, Bruce Sullivan
Fields, Inez C.
Figures, Thomas H
Filer, Kelvin Dean
Finch, Gregory Martin
Finlayson, Arnold Robert
Fisher, Lloyd B.
Fitch, Harrison Arnold
Fitzhugh, Kathryn Corrothers
Flatts, Barbara Ann
Fletcher, Robert E.
Flowers, Michael E
Flowers, Michael E
Flowers, Ralph L.
Flowers, William Harold, Jr.
Floyd, Mark Stephen
Forbes, George L
Ford, Wallace L
Fordham, Cynthia Williams
Foreman, Peggy E
Forster, Jacqueline Gail
Fort, William H.
Fortson, Walter Lewis
Foster, Gladys M.
Foster, Janice Martin
Foutz, Samuel Theodore
Fox, Thomas E, Jr.
Franklin, David M.
Fraser, Thomas Edwards
Frasier, Ralph Kennedy
Frazer, Victor O
Frazier-Lyde, Jacqui
Freeman, Frankie M.
Freeman-Wilson, Karen Marie
Frisby, H. Russell, Jr.
Fudge, Marcia L
Fugett, Jean Schloss, Jr.
Gaines, John A., Sr.
Gaither, Richard A
Galloway, Lula Briggs
Gardner, Cedric Boyer
Garland, John William
Garner, Melvin T
Garnett, Ronald Leon
Garrett, Nathan Taylor
Gartrell, Bernadette A
Gary, Sekou
Gary, Tanisha
Gary, Willie E.
Gatling, Joseph Theodore
Gatling, Patricia Lynn
Gayton, Gary D.
Gentry, Nolden I., Jr.
George, Allen
Geraldo, Manuel Robert
Gibbs, Jack Gilbert, Jr.
Gibbs, Robert Lewis
Gibson, Warren Arnold
Gigger, Helen C.
Gigger, Nathaniel Jay
Gilford, Vera E
Gill, Roberta L.
Gilliam, Robert M., Sr.
Gillum, Roderick D.

Moseley Braun, Carol Elizabeth
Mosley, Maurice B.
Mott, Stokes E, Jr.
Muckelroy, William Lawrence
Muhammad, Ava
Munday, Reuben A
Murphy, Clyde Everett
Murphy, Dr. Donald Richard
Murphy, Ira H.
Murphy, Romallus O.
Murrain, Godfrey H
Myatt, Hon. Gordon J
Myricks, Dr. Noel
Nabrit, James M
Nails, John Walker
Nance, Frederick R
Naphtali, Ashirah Sholomis
Napoleon, Benny Nelson
Nash, Curtis
Neal, Langdon D
Neals, Felix
Neely, David E.
Neely, Henry Mason
Nelson, Gilbert L.
Nelson, Harold E
Nelson, Otha Curtis
Nelson, Ricky Lee
Nelson, Ronald Duncan
Nesbitt, Robin Anthony
NeSmith, Kimblin E
Newell, Kathleen W
Newhouse, Millicent DeLaine
Newton, Andrew E., Jr.
Newton, Demetrius C
Newton, Robert
Nicholson, Jessie R
Nickerson, Don Carlos
Nix, Theophilus Richard
Nix, Theophilus Richard, Jr.
Nobles, Patricia Joyce
Northcross, Wilson Hill, Jr.
Northern, Christina Ann
Norville, Erleigh
Norwood, Kimberly Jade
Nunnery, Willie James
O'Banno, Donna Edwards
O'Connor, Thomas F, Jr.
Ogletree, Charles J
Ogletree, John D, Jr.
Ogunlesi, Adebayo O
Olinger, David Y, Jr.
Oliver, Jesse Dean
Oliver-Simon, Gloria Craig
O'Neal, Raymond W, Sr.
O'Neill, Anthony B., Sr.
Ormsby, William M
Ortique, Revius Oliver, Jr.
Oshiyoye, Dr. Emmanuel Adekunle, Sr.
Otis-Lewis, Alexis D
Owens, Ronald C
Ozanne, Dominic L.
Page, Rosemary Saxton
Pailen, Donald
Palmore, Roderick A
Parker, H Wallace
Parker, Jerry P.
Parker, Joseph Caiaphas, Jr.
Parker, Vernon B
Parks, Bernard
Parks, Edward Y
Parks, George Brooks
Parks, James Edward
Parms, Edwin L.
Parrish, Alex L.
Paschall, Evita Arneda
Paterson, Basil Alexander
Patrick, Deval L
Patrick, Lawrence Clarence, Jr.
Patterson, Cecil Booker, Jr.
Patterson, Elizabeth Hayes
Patterson, Michael Duane
Patterson, Pickens Andrew
Payne, Jacqueline LaVerne
Payne, James Edward
Payne, Ulice, Jr.
Payton, Jeff
Payton, Nolan H
Peay, Samuel
Peek, Gail Lenore
Pemberton-Heard, Danielle Marie
Pendergrass, Emma H
Pennington, Jesse C
Peoples, Veo
Persons, W Ray
Peters, Aulana Louise
Peters, Samuel A.
Peterson, Rocky Lee
Pettigrew, Grady L., Jr.

Phillips, Frank Edward
Pierce, Cynthia Straker
Pierce, Hon. Lawrence Warren
Pierce, Rudolph F
Pierson, Kathryn A
Pinkney, Dr. Betty Kathryn
Pittman, Darryl E.
Pitts, Cornelius
Pitts, Donald Franklin
Pitts, Ronald James, Sr.
Plummer, Matthew W, Sr.
Poindexter, Gammiel Gray
Pollard-Buckingham, Alice F
Pope, Derrick Alexander
Pope, Harold D
Pope, Ruben Edward, III
Porter, Edward Melvin
Posey, Bruce Keith
Posten, William S
Poston, Carl
Poston, Carl C, Jr.
Poston, Kevin D
Pottinger, Albert A.
Powell, Darlene Wright
Pratt, A Michael
Prevot, Rapheal M
Pride, Hemphill P, II
Pride, Walter LaVon
Prioleau, Oscar Eugene
Procter, Harvey Thornton, Jr.
Pryor, Calvin Caffey
Pullen-Brown, Stephanie D
Purnell, Carolyn J
Putnam, Glendora M
Quander, Esq. Rohulamin
Rabouin, E Michelle
Racine, Karl A
Ramey, Adele Marie
Randle, Carver A
Randolph, Lonnie Marcus
Randolph-Jasmine, Carol Davis
Rangel, Charles Bernard
Ransier, Frederick L
Rauch, Doreen E.
Raven, Ricky A
Ravenell, William Hudson
Rawls, Raleigh Richard
Ray, Rosalind Rosemary
Raye, Vance Wallace
Raynor, Robert G
Rearden, Sara B
Redd, William L
Reed, Esquire Jerrildine
Reed, Gregory J.
Reed, Kimberley Del Rio
Reed, Kwame Osei
Reed, Michael H
Reid, Dr. Inez Smith
Reid, N Neville
Reide, Atty. Jerome L.
Reid-McQueen, Lynne Marguerite
Remy, Donald M
Renfroe, Iona Antoinette
Rhinehart, June Acie
Rhodes, Dr. Paula R
Rice, Florence
Rice, Fredrick LeRoy
Rice, Judith Carol
Richardson, Andra Virginia
Richardson, Ralph H
Richardson, Rhonda Karen
Richardson, Robert Eugene
Richardson, Wayne Michael
Richie, Leroy C.
Risher, John Robert, Jr.
Rist, Susan E
Rivera, Eddy
Roane, Rev. Glenwood P, Sr.
Robbins, Kevin F
Roberts, Bryndis Wynette
Roberts, Edward A
Robinson, Carl Cornell
Robinson, Edward Ashton
Robinson, Jack, Jr.
Robinson, Learthon Steven, Sr.
Robinson, Malcolm
Robinson, Maurice C
Robinson, Dr. Randall S.
Robinson, Rosalyn Karen
Robinson, Sandra Hawkins
Rodgers, Horace J.
Rogers, John W, Sr.
Rogers, Judith W
Ross, Kevin Arnold
Rotan, Dr. Constance S.
Roulhac, Hon. Roy L.
Roundtree, Dovey
Rowe, Dr. Nansi Irene
Roye, Monica R Hargrove

Ryan, Agnes C.
Saint-Louis, Rudolph Anthony
Salone, Marcus
Sampson, Thomas Gatewood
Samuels, Ronald S
Sanders, Hank
Sanders, Joseph Stanley
Saulsberry, Charles R.
Savage, Janet Marie
Sawyer, George Edward
Sawyer, Roderick Terrence
Scales-Trent, Prof. Judy
Schmoke, Kurt Lidell
Scott, Hugh B
Scott, Judith Sugg
Scott, Nigel L.
Scott, Windie Olivia
Scott-Clayton, Patricia Ann
Scurry, Fred L
Selby, Myra C
Sellers, Jacqueline H
Senegal, Nolton Joseph, Sr.
Seraile, Janette Grey
Seymour, Barbara L.
Shakoor, Adam Adib
Sharpe, Dr. Calvin William
Shaw, Charles Alexander
Shaw, Curtis Mitchell
Shaw, Theodore Michael
Shelton, Reuben Anderson
Sherwood, O Peter
Sherwood, Wallace Walter
Shields, Karen Bethea
Silas-Butler, Jacqueline Ann
Simmelkjaer, Dr. Robert T
Simmons, Clayton Lloyd
Simmons, Esmeralda
Simmons, Geraldine Crossley
Simms, Stuart Oswald
Simpson, Stephen Whittington
Sims, Genevieve Constance
Sinclair, Clayton
Singleton, Harry M
Slater, Rodney E
Slaughter, Atty. Fred L.
Sleet, Gregory M
Smalls, O'Neal
Smirni, Allan Desmond
Smith, Charles Edison
Smith, Conrad P.
Smith, DeHaven L
Smith, H Russell
Smith, Harold Teliaferro
Smith, Heman Bernard
Smith, Dr. J. Clay, Jr.
Smith, J Thomas
Smith, Jeraldine Williams
Smith, Jock Michael
Smith, Stanley G.
Smith, William James
Smitherman, Rodger M
Soden, Richard Allan
Soliunas, Francine Stewart
Sowell, Myzell
Spain, Hiram, Jr.
Spaulding, Lynette Victoria
Speights, Nathaniel H
Spence, Rev. Joseph Samuel, Sr.
Springer, Eric Winston
Squire, Carole Renee
Stampley, Gilbert Elvin
Stancell, Dr. Dolores Wilson Pegram
Stanley, Carol Jones
Staton, Donna Hill
Staton, Kerry D
Stearns Miller, Camille Louise
Stephens, Cynthia Diane
Stewart, Carolyn House
Stewart, John Ogden
Stiell, Phelicia D
Stokes, Louis
Stone, William T
Storey, Robert D
Sudarkasa, Michael Eric Mabogunje
Sulton, Anne Thomas
Sumler Edmond, Janice L.
Sumner, Thomas Robert
Sutton, Norma J.
Swain, James H
Swann, Eugene Merwyn
Swanson, Charles
Sweet, Clifford C
Talley, Michael Frank, Sr.
Tann, Daniel J
Tate, David Kirk
Tate, Herbert Holmes
Taylor, Carol Ann
Taylor, Charles Edward
Taylor, David Richard, III

Taylor, Eartha Lynn
Taylor, Eric Charles
Taylor, Janice A.
Taylor, Jeffery Charles
Taylor, Johnny C
Taylor, Dr. Patricia E.
Taylor, Wilford, Jr.
Taylor, William L.
Teeuwissen, Pieter
Telfair, Brian Kraig
Temple, Donald Melvin
Terrell, Francis D'Arcy
Terrell, Henry Matthew
Terrell, Mary Ann
Terrell, Reginald V.
Terry, Adeline Helen
Thigpen, Dr. Calvin Herritage
Thigpen, Donald A
Thomas, Dermond Edwin
Thomas, Edward Arthur
Thomas, Franklin A
Thomas, James O.
Thomas, Kendall
Thomas, Maureen A.
Thomas, Samuel Haynes, Jr.
Thomas, Terence A, Sr.
Thompson, Daniel Joseph
Thompson, Herman G
Thompson, Larry D
Thompson, Hon. M T, Jr.
Thompson, Hon. William Coleridge, Sr.
Thompson, William L
Thornton, Leslie
Thorpe, Josephine Horsley
Tibbs, Hon. Edward A
Tillman, Paula Sellars
Tinsley, Dwane L
Tinsley, Fred Leland, Jr.
Todd, Thomas N.
Tolliver, Stanley Eugene, Sr.
Toote, Gloria E. A.
Townsend, P A
Travis, Benjamin
Trumbo, George William
Tucker, Geraldine Jenkins
Tucker, Karen
Tucker, Michael Kevin
Tucker, Robert L
Tucker, Walter Rayford
Tuffin, Paul Jonathan
Turner, Leslie Marie
Turner, Reginald M
Turner Brown, Shadey K
Tyson, Lance C
Uku, Eustace Oris
Underwood, Arthur C.
Valentine, J. T.
Vance, Lawrence N.
Van Hook, George Ellis
Van Lierop, Robert F
Vaughters-Johnson, Cecilie A
Veals, Craig Elliott
Venson, Clyde R
Vertreace, Walter Charles
Vickers, Eric Erfan
Vinson, Rosalind Rowena
Waddell, Ruchadina LaDesiree
Wade, Beryl Elaine
Wagner, David H.
Waits, Rev. Va Lita Francine
Walker, Betty Stevens
Walker, Charles Ealy, Jr.
Walker, Charles H
Walker, Grover Pulliam
Walker, Karol Corbin
Walker, Stanley Michael
Walker, Tanya Rosetta
Walker, Woodson DuBois
Wallace, C. Everett
Wallace, Paul Starett
Walton, Elbert Arthur, Jr.
Ward, Christopher Evan
Ward, Keith Lamont
Ward, Nolan F
Ward, Ronald R
Ward, Sandra L
Ware, Charles Jerome
Ware, Dyahanne
Ware, R David
Wareham, Roger
Warrick, Alan Everett
Washington, Betty Lois
Washington, Consuela M
Washington, Craig Anthony
Washington, Mickey Lynn
Washington, Robert Benjamin, Jr.
Washington, Roosevelt, Jr.
Washington, Valdemar Luther

Watford-McKinney, Yvonne V
Watkins, Craig
Watkins, Donald
Watkins, Rosyln
Watson, Aaron
Watson, Solomon B
Watson, Theresa Lawhorn
Watt, Garland Wedderick
Way, Gary Darryl
Webb, Joseph G
Weber, Daniel
Webster, Lesley Douglass
Webster, William H
Webster, Winston Roosevelt
Weeks, Deborah Redd
Weems, Vernon Eugene, Jr.
Wells, Ira J. K., Jr.
Wells, Theodore V, Jr.
West, George Ferdinand, Jr.
West, John Andrew
West, Royce Barry
West, Dr. Togo Dennis, Jr.
Weston, Larry Carlton
Wharton, A. C., Jr.
Wheaton, Frank Kahlil
White, D. Richard
White, Frankie Walton
White, Frederic Paul, Jr.
White, Howard A
White, Janice G
White, Richard Thomas
Whiting, Barbara E
Whiting, Willie
Whitted, Earl, Jr.
Wickliff, Aloysius M., Sr.
Wilber, Ida Belinda
Wilbon, Joan Marie
Wilcher, Shirley J
Wilder, Kurt
Wiley, Aaron L
Wiley, Fletcher Houston
Wilkins, David Brian
Willacy, Hazel M
Williams, Alexander, Jr.
Williams, Annalisa Stubbs
Williams, Bart H
Williams, Charles E
Williams, Clyde
Williams, Dr. E Faye
Williams, Gary C.
Williams, Gregory Howard
Williams, James R
Williams, Junius W.
Williams, Karen Hastie
Williams, Larry C.
Williams, Paul S
Williams, Paul T
Williams, Philip B.
Williams, Randolph
Williams, Robert B.
Williams, Ronald Charles
Williams, Sandra K.
Williams, Sidney B., Jr.
Williams, Vernon Alvin
Williams, Wesley S
Williams, Yvonne LaVerne
Williamson, Samuel R
Willis, Frederic L.
Willis, Jill Michelle
Willis, Kathi Grant
Willrich, Emzy James
Willrich, Penny
Wilson, Clarence S., Jr.
Wilson, Donald K, Jr.
Wilson, Kim Adair
Wilson, Lance Henry
Wilson, Margaret Bush
Wilson, Sonali Bustamante
Wimbish, C Bette
Wing, Prof. Adrien Katherine
Winstead, Dr. Vernon A, Sr.
Wood, Curtis A
Wood, Hon. William S
Woodhouse, Enoch O'Dell, II
Worthy, Kym
Wright, Clinton L. A.
Wright, Geoffrey
Wright, Dr. Joseph Malcolm
Wright, Michael L.
Wright, Robert A
Wright, Roberta V. Hughes
Wright-Botchwey, Roberta Yvonne
Yancey, Prentiss Quincy
Yarbrough, Robert Elzy
Young, Andrew
Young, Ira Mason
Young, Dr. James E., Jr.
Young, Lias Carl
Younge, Richard G

Zachary, Steven W
Zealey, Sharon Janine
Zelis, Karen Dee
Zollar, Nikki Michele

Library/Information Science

Abif, Khafre Kujichagulia
Adams, Dr. Elaine Parker
Alexander, Otis Douglas
Alford, Thomas Earl
Allen, Ottis Eugene
Aman, Dr. Mohammed M.
Anderson, Barbara Louise
Arkhurst, Joyce Cooper
Armstrong, Evelyn Walker
Ashford, Mary E
Atchison, Lillian Elizabeth
Avery, Charles E
Axam, John Arthur
Barnes, Fannie Burrell
Battle, Thomas Cornell
Bean, Bobby Gene
Beane, Patricia Jean
Bell, Dr. Katie Roberson
Benning, Dr. Emma Bowman
Bethel, Kathleen Evonne
Bickham, Dr. Luzine B.
Birchette-Pierce, Cheryl L.
Birtha, Jessie M.
Blake, Peggy Jones
Bogger, Dr. Tommy
Bond, Dr. Louis Grant
Bowens, Dr. Johnny Wesley
Boyce, William M.
Boyd, Barbara Jean
Bradberry, Dr. Richard Paul
Brown, Atlanta Thomas
Brown, Freddiemae Eugenia
Brown, Dr. Malore Ingrid
Burnett, Bescye P.
Butler, Kathleen Jean
Byrd, Joan Eda
Calhoun, Dorothy Eunice
Cameron, Ulysses
Campbell, Sandra
Cannon, Tyrone Heath
Carter, Darline Louretha
Cash, Pamela J.
Chisum, Gloria Twine
Clark, Laron Jefferson
Clark, Patricia Ann
Clayton, Minnie H.
Cleveland, Granville E.
Coaston, Shirley Ann Dumas
Conner, Dr. Laban Calvin
Cooke, Anna L
Craft, Dr. Guy Calvin
Crayton, Dr. James Edward
Crocker, Wayne Marcus
Cruzat, Dr. Gwendolyn S.
Culpepper, Betty M
Cunningham, Dr. William Dean
Curtis, Jean Trawick
Daniel, Celia G
Davis, Bunny Coleman
Davis, Denyvetta
Dupree, Sandra Kay
DuPree, Prof. Sherry Sherrod
Ellis, Elizabeth G.
Estes, Elaine Rose Graham
Fancher, Dr. Evelyn Pitts
Felder-Hoehne, Felicia Harris
Fillyaw, Leonard David
Fisher, Alma M
Fisher, Edith Maureen
Fitzhugh, Kathryn Corrothers
Freeman, Shirley Walker
Fuller, Gloria A
Gardiner, George L.
Gay, Birdie Spivey
Gill, Prof. Jacqueline A.
Gilton, Dr. Donna L.
Gleason, Dr. Eliza Veleria Atkins
Goddard, Rosalind Kent
Grant, Dr. George C
Gray, Beverly A
Gray, Donnee L
Grigsby, Alice Burns
Guilford, Diane Patton
Gunn, Arthur Clinton
Hale, Kimberly Anice
Ham, Dr. Debra Newman
Hardnett, Carolyn Judy
Hardy, Eursla Dickerson
Hargrave, Charles William
Harris, Loretta K
Harris, Thomas Walter
Hart, Mildred

Harvell, Valeria Gomez
Hawkins, Ernestine L
Hayden, Carla Diane
Hayward, Olga Loretta Hines
Henderson, Dr. Robbye R.
Hendricks, Leta
Hernandez, Mary N
Hewitt, Vivian Ann Davidson
Hicks, Doris Askew
Hinson, Ann J.
Holley, Sharon Yvonne
Hopkins, Dr. Dianne McAfee
Howard, Dr. Elizabeth Fitzgerald
Hunt, Charles Amoes
Hunter Hayes, Tracey Joel
Hylton, Andrea Lamarr
Irving, Ophelia McAlpin
Isadore, Harold W.
Jackson, Andrew Preston
Jackson, Miles M.
Jackson, Dr. Ruth Moore
James, Olive C. R.
James, Stephen Elisha
Jefferson, Karen L.
Jefferson, Marcia D.
Jenkins, Dr. Althea H.
Jenkins, Barbara Williams
Jenkins, Cynthia
Jobe, Shirley A.
Johnson, Doris Elayne
Johnson, Dorothy Turner
Johnson, Sheila Ann
Johnson, Sheila Monroe
Johnson, Shirley
Johnson-Blount, Theresa
Jolivet, Linda Catherine
Jones, Clara Stanton
Jones, Curley C
Jones, Gwendolyn J
Jones, Helen Hampton
Jones-Trent, Bernice R
Josey, Dr. E. J.
Kendrick, Curtis L
King, Thomas Lawrence
Kitt, Sandra Elaine
Knowles, Dr. Em Claire
Langston-Jackson, Wilmetta Ann Smith
Lee, Pauline W.
Leonard, Gloria Jean
Lewis, Billie Jean
Livingston, Joyce
Lockett, Sandra Bokamba
Lockley-Myles, Barbara J
Lucas, Willie Lee
Mack, Phyllis Green
Madison, Jacqueline Edwina
Mangum, Ernestine Brewer
Marks, Rose M.
Marshall, Anita
Martin, Rosetta P
Maye, Richard
McCain, Ella Byrd
McCoy, James F.
McCrackin, Olympia H
McCray, Melvin
McDaniel, Karen Cotton
McKeller, Thomas Lee
McKinney, Venora Ware
McKinney, Wade H
McKitt, Willie, Jr.
McLaughlin, LaVerne Laney
McLaughlin, Megan E.
McPherson, James Alan
McTyre, Robert Earl, Sr.
Metcalf, DaVinci Carver
Middleton, Ernest J.
Miles, Ruby A Branch
Miller, Constance Joan
Miller, Erenest Eugene
Miller, Jacqueline Elizabeth
Miller, Dr. Jake C
Miller, Robert, Jr.
Miller-Holmes, Cheryl
Mobley, Emily Ruth
Mohammad, Sandra B
Mohr, Diane Louise
Moore, Christopher Paul
Moore, Evia Briggs
Moore, Hazel Stamps
Moore, M Elizabeth Gibbs
Morgan, Jane Hale
Morris, Effie Lee
Morrison, Samuel F.
Mothershed, Spaesio W
Muldrow, James Christopher
Murphy, Paula Christine
Ojumu, Ayodele
Page, John Sheridan

Patterson, Grace Limerick
Peguese, Charles R.
Perry, Emma Bradford
Peterson, Prof. Lorna Ingrid
Powell, Addie Scott
Price, Pamela Anita
Price, Dr. Paul Sanford
Ramsey, Donna Elaine
Randall, Ann Knight
Reese, Gregory Lamarr
Riley, Barbara P
Roberson, Gloria Grant
Robertson, Karen A
Robinson, Carol W.
Robinson, Carrie C.
Robinson-Walker, Mary P.
Roney, Raymond G
Royster, Dr. Vivian Hall
Russell, Beverly A.
Sapp, Lauren B
Sarkodie-Mensah, Dr. Kwasi
Scott, Dr. Alice H
Seunagal, Deborah Evans
Shaw, Dr. Spencer Gilbert
Shockley, Ann Allen
Simton, Chester
Singley, Elijah
Sinnette, Elinor DesVerney
Slaton, Gwendolyn C
Smith, Dr. Jessie Carney
Smith-Epps, E. Paulette
Smythe, Victor N.
Spradling, Mary Elizabeth Mace
Sprinkle-Hamlin, Sylvia Yvonne
Staley, Valeria Howard
Stallworth, Ann
Stephens, Brenda Wilson
Stewart, Ruth Ann
Stinson, Linda
Strong- Kimbrough, Dr. Blondell M
Stuckey, Sheila Arnetta
Sutton, Gloria W.
Swift, Linda Denise
Sylvester, Melvin R
Terry, Patricia S
Thomas, Frankie Taylor
Thomas, Dr. Lucille Cole
Thomas, Maurice McKenzie
Thompson, Bette Mae
Tolbert, Odie Henderson, Jr.
Toliver, Virginia F Dowsing
Toomer, Clarence
Totten, Dr. Herman Lavon
Towns, Rose Mary
Turner, Diane Young
UmBayemake - Hayes, Linda
Unaeze, Felix Eme
Venable, Andrew Alexander, Jr.
Walters, Mary Dawson
Weissinger, Thomas
Whitner, Donna K
Williams, Ethel Langley
Williams, Dr. Helen Elizabeth
Williams, Wallace C
Wilson, Margaret F
Wood, Vivian Frances
Woods, Hortense E.
Woody, Jacqueline Brown
Wright, James R
Wright, Joyce C.
Young, Wallace L., Jr.
Zulu, Itibari M

Management/ Administration— Accounting/Financial (See Also **Accounting/Auditing**)

Adams, Don L.
Adams, Kathy J
Aiken, William
Ali, Grace L.
Allen, Bernestine
Anderson, George A.
Anthony, Brenda Tucker
Armstrong, Kevin
Ashby, Lucius Antone
Ayers-Elliott, Cindy
Ball, Brenda Louise
Barkley, Mark E.
Bassett, Dennis
Batties, Thomas L.
Benham, Dr. Robert
Bludson-Francis, Vernett Michelle
Boland, D Steven
Bolden, Juran
Boschulte, Alfred F
Bouknight, Dr. Reynard Ronald
Bowie, Oliver Wendell
Braddock, Carol T

Bridgforth, Glinda
Brown, Constance Young
Brown, Todd
Bryant-Reid, Johanne
Burges, Melvin E.
Burke, Olga Pickering
Campbell, Carlos Cardozo
Campbell, Sandra Pace
Carswell, Gloria Nadine Sherman
Carter, Norman L
Cave, Perstein Ronald
Chambers, Harry
Chapman, Lee Manuel
Chappell, Emma Carolyn
Chism, Harolyn B.
Chivis, Martin Lewis
Clark, John Joseph
Clark, Walter L
Clayton, Robert L
Cohen, Gwen A
Cooper, Barbara J
Coulter, Phyllis A
Cox, Taylor H., Sr.
Craig-Rudd, Joan
Creuzot, Cheryl D.
Crim, Rodney
Crutchfield-Baker, Verdenia
Daniels, Lemuel Lee
Davenport, C. Dennis
Davis, Harold R.
Davis, Rev. Tyrone Theophilus
Dear, Alice
Dennis, Carolyn K
Dickerson, Harvey G, Jr.
Ealy, Mary Newcomb
Edgerton, Brenda Evans
Eley, Randall Robbi
Elmore, Stephen A, Sr.
Faulding, Juliette J.
Fentress, Shirley B.
Fierce, Hughlyn F.
Fletcher, James Andrew
Forde, Fraser Philip, Jr.
Francisco, Anthony M.
Frazier-Ellison, Vicki L
Gaines, Crystal Monique
Garnier, Thomas Joseph
Gholson, Robert L
Gillespie, Bonita
Godfrey, William R.
Gonzalez, Cambell
Gordon, Alexander H., II
Gore, James Anthony
Grady, Walter E.
Green, Jarvis R
Greene, Gregory A.
Griffin, Virgil
Guitano, Anton W.
Hall, David McKenzie
Hall, Ira D.
Hall, Pamela Vanessa
Hammock, Jimmy
Haralson, Larry L
Harper, David B.
Harris, Douglas Allan
Harris, John H.
Harris, Robert Eugene Peyton
Harvey, Richard R
Hawes, Bernadine Tinner
Hawkins, Dr. Gene
Heflin, Marrion
Henderson, Remond
Henton, George
Howard, Osbie L
Hudson, Paul C.
Huff, Lula Lunsford
Humphrey, Marian J
Hunter, Kimberly Alice
Isaacs-Lowe, Arlene Elizabeth
Jackson, Harold Leonard, Jr.
Jackson, Tonya Charisse
Jenkins, Carlton J.
Johnson, Wallace Darnell
Jones, Shalley A
Jordan, Thurman
Kelley, William E.
Kellum, Anthony O
Kelso-Watson, Angela M.
Kirkland, Gwendolyn V
Lander, Cressworth Caleb
Law, M Eprevel
Lemon, Ann
Lemuwa, Ike Emmanuel
Lewis, Jeffrey Mark
Lewis, William M., Jr.
Liverpool, Charles Eric
Lockett, Kevin
Lokeman, Joseph R
Lowman, Carl D

Mack, Fred Clarence
Madison Polk, Sharon L
Mariel, Serafin
May, Floyd O
Mayo, Harry D., III
McClomb, George E.
McDonald, Alden J
McGuirt, Milford W
McKinzie, Barbara A
McPhatter, Thomas H.
McQueen, Kevin Paige
Mensah, E. Kwaku
Micks, Deitra Handy
Milner, Michael Edwin
Milton, LeRoy
Mitchell, Joanne
Mohamed, Gerald R, Jr.
Moore, Dr. Charles W
Moses, Milton E.
Mosley, Edna Wilson
Nanula, Richard D
Naphtali, Ashirah Sholomis
Neal, Joseph C., Jr.
Nelson, Ricky Lee
Nunn, John
Ogden, Christopher A.
Oliver, Everett Ahmad
Parnell, William Cornellus, Jr.
Patterson, Cheryl Ann
Paul, Wanda D, CPA
Pearson, Jesse S.
Pearson, Ramona Henderson
Pendergraft, Michele M
Pressey, Junius Batten, Jr.
Prioleau, Peter Sylvester
Quick, George Kenneth
Reed-Clark, Larita Diane
Reid, Desiree Charese
Reynolds, Sandra Michele
Rhinehart, N Pete
Richards, William Earl
Roberson, Lawrence R
Rollins, Avon William, Sr.
Ross, Frank Kenneth
Sandidge, Kanita Durice
Santos, Edwin J
Saunders, Vincent E
Scanlan, Agnes Bundy
Scott, Judith Sugg
Segree, E Ramone
Senbet, Prof. Lemma W
Sharp, Charles Louis
Sherman, Barbara J
Shoemaker, Veronica Sapp
Shropshire, Harry W.
Simmons, Willie
Sims, Deloris
Small, Eric
Smith, Chester B.
Smith, Lawrence John, Jr.
Stahnke, William E.
Stamper, Henry J.
Stanley, Dr. Hilbert Dennis
Stephenson, Dama F
Stewart, Raymond C
Stokes, Bunny
Streeter, Denise Williams
Teamer, Dr. Charles C., Sr.
Thompson, Jeffrey Earl
Thompson, Karen Ann
Thompson, Sylvia Moore
Titus, LeRoy Robert
Torian, Edward Torrence
Trapp, Donald W.
Travis, Tracey T.
Turner, Jesse H
Turner, Marvin Wentz
Turnipseed, Carl Wendell
Tyson, Ron
Vance, Tommie Rowan
Vest, Donald Seymour
Wade, Joyce K
Wade, William Carl
Walker, John Leslie
Walker, Willie Leroy
Wallace, John A.
Warfield, Robert N
Warren, Roland C
Watson, Timothy S
Webb, James O
White, Clarence Dean
Whitehead, David William
Wilkes, Reggie Wayman
Wilkins, Janice F
Williams, James
Williams, Jan
Williams Boyd, Sheila Anne
Wooden, Shawn Anthony
Woodson, Alfred F

Woodson, Jeffrey Anthony
Wright, Soraya M
Yates, Mark
Young, Alan C
Young, Ollie L

Management/ Administration— Advertising/Marketing/ Public Relations (*See Also* Advertising/Promotion)

Abrams, Kenneth Rodney
Adams, Edward B.
Alexander, Arika
Alexander, Dawn
Allen, Charles Edward
Allen, Clyde Cecil
Allen, Quincy L
Allston, Thomas Gray, III
Anderson, Rev. Dr. Al H
Anderson, Harold A.
Anderson, James
Anderson, Rosaland Guidry
Archambeau, Shellye L.
Arnold, Ethel N.
Ashburn, Vivian Diane
Ashton, Vivian Christina R.
Atchison, Leon H.
Atkins, Fredd G
Avery, James S
Bailey, Myrtle Lucille
Baker, Gregory D.
Baker, Kimberley Renee
Ball, Drexel Bernard
Banfield, Anne L.
Banks, Beatrice
Barber, Ornetta M
Bateman, Celeste
Bates, Willie Earl
Beach, Walter G., II
Beckett, Evette Olga
Bell, Rosalind Nanette
Bennett, Ivy H.
Berry, Gemeral E., Jr.
Bisamunyu, Jeanette
Black, Don Gene
Blake, Dr. J. Herman
Block, Dr. Leslie S.
Booker, Anne M
Boon, Ina M.
Bostic, Viola W
Boston, Dennis H
Boyce, Joseph Nelson
Bradford, Martina Lewis
Britton, John Henry
Brown, Ralph Benjamin
Brown, Sharon Marjorie Revels
Brown, Tony
Brown-Francisco, Teresa Elaine
Buckhanan, Dorothy Wilson
Bullins, Ed
Burke, William Arthur
Burns, Jeff
Caldwell, Marion Milford, Jr.
Cameron, Randolph W
Campbell, Rogers Edward, III
Caraway, Yolanda H
Carey, Claire Lamar
Carroll, Robert F
Carson, Regina M. E.
Carter, Kenneth Gregory
Carter, Kenneth Wayne
Chambers, Caroline E.
Chapman, Sharon Jeanette
Chess, Eva
Clarke, Everee Jimerson
Claybrooks, John, Jr.
Clayton, Robert L
Clemons, John Gregory
Cobbin, W. Frank, Jr.
Colbert, Virgis W.
Coleman, Don
Collins, Tessil John
Colston Barge, Gayle S
Cotton, Joseph Craig
Crombaugh, Hallie
Cross-McClam, Deloris Nmi
Cureton, John Porter
Daily, Lori Beard
Davis, Charles
Davis, Howlie R
Davis, Walter Paul
Davis-Carter, Holly
Dilday, William Horace, Jr.
Dinkins, Traci
Dixon, John Frederick
Donald, Arnold Wayne
Dottin, Roger Allen

Dowd, Maria Denise
Doxie, Marvin Leon
Draper, Rev. Frances Murphy
Dukes, Ofield
Durant-Paige, Beverly
Duvall, Henry F
Eady, Lydia Davis
Earl, Acie Boyd
Easley, Dr. Eddie V.
Edwards, Oscar Lee
Edwards, Ronald Wayne
Emmanuel, Anthony
Evans, Alicia
Evans, Elinor Elizabeth
Farrow, William McKnight, III
Fears, Harding, Jr.
Fernandez, John Peter
Fields, Lynn M
Flowers, D. Michelle
Fontenot-Jamerson, Berlinda
Gaffney, Leslie Gale
Gaines, Adriane Theresa
Gayle, Cruise
Gayles, Dr. Joseph Nathan Webster
Gellineau, Victor Marcel
George, Pauline L
Giles, Althea B
Giles, Terri Lynnette
Gipson, Reve
Givens, Joshua Edmond
Gordon, Bruce S.
Graham, Stedman
Graves, Valerie Jo
Greaves, McLean
Gregory, Robert Alphonso
Griffiths, Errol D.
Guilmenot, Richard Arthur
Hackney, L. Camille
Hall, Fred, III
Hankin, Noel Newton
Hanson, John L
Harris, Michele Roles
Harrison, Ronald E.
Harrison, Roscoe Conklin, Jr.
Hatcher, Jeffrey French
Hawkins, James C.
Herring, Leonard
Herring, Marsha K Church
Herring, William F.
Hill, James H
Hill, Jeffrey Ronald
Hilliard, Amy S
Holmes, Carlton
Hopkinson, Mark I
Horton, Carl E.
Horton, Dollie Bea Dixon
House, James E.
Hudson, Frederick Bernard
Hunter, Kim L
Hutchins, Jan Darwin
Jackson, Mary
Jackson, Reggie Martinez
Jackson, Rusty
Jackson Robinson, Tracy Camille
James, Lawrence W
Jasper, Lawrence E
Jaycox, Mary Irine
Jemmott, Hensley B
Jenkins, Bobby G
Jenkins, John
Johns, Michael Earl
Johnson, Cleveland, Jr.
Johnson, Cyrus Edwin
Johnson, Donna Alligood
Johnson, Joseph David
Johnson, Juliana Cornish
Johnson, Verdia Earline
Johnson, Wayne Alan
Jones, Bob
Jones, Delores
Jones, Jake
Jones, Marsha Regina
Jones, Nathaniel Jamal
Jones, Victoria Gene
Kerry, Leon G
King, Greg
King, Gwendolyn Stewart
King, Lawrence Patrick
King, Marcellus, Jr.
Knox, George L
Latimer, Chris
LaVelle, Avis
Lawson, Bruce B
Leggett, Renee
Leigh, Fredric H
Lenix-Hooker, Catherine Jeanette
Lewis, Byron E
Lewis, Karen A
Lewis, Robert Alvin

Lewis, Stephen Christopher
Livingston-White, Dr. Deborah J H
Locklin, James R.
London, Denise
Love, Karen Allyce
Lucas, Victoria
Lyle, Percy H., Jr.
Mahone, Jeanine
Majors, Mattie Carolyn
Marshall, Eric A
Marshall, H Jean
Martin, Gertrude S
Martin, Hosea L
Massey, Ardrey Yvonne
Matthis, James L., III
McAfee, Flo
McDonald, Herbert G
McKenzie, Miranda Mack
Mckines, Charlotte
McNeil, Robert Lawrence
McPherson, James R
McPherson, Rosalyn J
McWhorter, Grace Agee
Meridith, Denise Patricia
Merritt Cummings, Annette
Miller, Kevin
Mills, Doreen C
Mitchal, Saundra Marie
Mitchell, Carol Greene
Mitchell, Martha Mallard
Moore, Anthony Louis
Moore, Johnnie Adolph
Morton, Patsy Jennings
Mosby, Carolyn Elizabeth
Moss, Anni R.
Moss, Wayne B
Moyo, Yvette Jackson
Mudd, Louis L.
Murdock, Patricia Green
Myers, Dr. Ernest Ray
Nelson, Mario
Newman, Paul Dean
Norman, Clifford P
Pandya, Harish C.
Parham, Marjorie B.
Passmore, Juanita Carter
Pearson, Preston James
Pena, Robert Bubba
Penn, Algernon H
Penn, Mindell Lewis
Perez, Anna
Perry, Marc Aubrey
Perry, Pam Elaine
Pinkett, Allen Jerome
Poe, Kirsten Noelle
Ponder-Nelson, Debra
Pounds, Elaine
Powell, Kenneth Alasandro
Powell, Robert John
Price, George Baker
Proctor, Earl D.
Pualani, Gloria
Purvis, Archie C.
Reece, Steven
Reed, Dr. Vincent Emory
Reynolds, Barbara A
Rhodes, Hon. C Adrienne
Rhodes, Jeanne
Richardson, Valerie K.
Robinson, Johnathan Prather
Rochester, Geof
Rogers, Desiree Glapion
Rogers-Reece, Shirley
Roseman, Jennifer Eileen
Ross, Cathye P
Roux, Dr. Vincent J
Sagers, Rudolph, Jr.
Salmond, Jasper
Sanders, Jasmine
Sargent, Virginia Hightower
Sayers, Gale Eugene
Scott, Werner Ferdinand
Sewell, Luther Joseph
Shackelford, George Franklin
Sharpton, Denise
Shepard, Beverly Renee
Shipe, Jamesetta Denise Holmes
Short, Leslie
Shumate, Glen
Siler, Brenda Claire
Simmons, Maurice Clyde
Simmons-Edelstein, Dee
Simons, Eglon E
Simons, Renee V H
Smalls, Diedre A
Smith, Dawn C F
Smith, Gregory Robeson, Sr.
Smith, Patricia Grace
Smith-Gaston, Linda Ann

Snow, Kimberly
Sobers, Waynett A., Jr.
Spears, Sandra Calvette
Spraggins, Dr. Stewart
Spratlen, Thaddeus H
Spurlock, Dr. James B
Steans, Edith Elizabeth
Stephens, Doreen Y
Stevens, Rochelle
Stewart, Bonita Coleman
Stewart, Edward L
Stith, Antoinette Freeman
Stone, Harold Anthony
Sykes, William Richard
Tassie, Robert V.
Taylor, Edgar R
Taylor, Tommie W.
Tennant, Melvin, II
Thompson, Glenda M
Thompson, Gloria Crawford
Thurmond, Nate
Triche, Arthur
Utley, Richard Henry
Wagoner, J Robert
Walker, Felix Carr, Jr.
Walker, Freeman, III
Walker, Tracy A
Waters, Paul Eugene, Jr.
Waugh, Judith Ritchie
Weaver, Frank Cornell
West, Denise Joyner
West, Dr. Togo Dennis, Jr.
Wheeler, Robyn Elaine
White, James Louis, Jr.
Whitney, Rosalyn L
Whittler, Dr. Thomas
Williams, Armstrong
Williams, Gayle Terese Taylor
Williams, Lloyd L
Williams, Rasheda
Williams, Richard Lee
Williams, Rosa B.
Williams, Terrie Michelle
Wilson, F Leon
Wingo, Robert V
Winley, Diane Lacey
Womack, Christopher Clarence
Wood, Anton Vernon
Woodruff, Jeffrey Robert
Woods, Kondria Yvette Black
Woolley, Phyllis
Wright, Benjamin Hickman
Wright, Mark Adrian
Wyatt, William N
Wyche, Paul H
Young, James M., II
Young, Ronald R

Management/Administration—Computer Systems/ Data Processing

Adams, Stephan
Adkins, Rodney C
Ahart, Thomas I
Anderson, Fred
Baldwin, Carolyn H.
Ball, Roger
Bond, Elroy
Brasey, Henry L.
Brockington, Donella P
Brockington, Eugene Alfonzo
Bryant, Regina Lynn
Cargill, Sandra Morris
Carter, Charles Michael
Collins, Calvin Lewis
Cooper, Daneen Ravenell
Cooper, William B.
Corbin, Stampp W
Davis, Denyvetta
Doxie, Marvin Leon
Franklin, Martha Lois
Gore, Cedric J
Gragg, Lauren Andrea
Grant, Claude DeWitt
Gray, Christine
Greene, Jerry Louis
Hall, David McKenzie
Handy, Lillian B.
Hannah, Johnnie, Jr.
Heard, Blanche Denise
Hughes, Isaac Sunny
Hylton, Taft H.
Ingram, Phillip M
Jacobs, Patricia Dianne
Jacques, Cornell
James, Donna Anita
Johns, Marie C.
Johnson, William Paul
Jordan, George Washington, Jr.

Kinsey, Bernard W.
Kline, Joseph N.
Lawes, Verna
Lawrence, Rodell
Lewis, Richard John, Sr.
Lewis, Dr. Samuel, Jr.
Logans, Renee
Malliet, Schone
Mayo, James Wellington
Miller, Arthur J
Moran, George H
Morris, Carolyn G
Moseley-Davis, Barbara M.
Moss, Anni R.
Perry, Lee Charles, Jr.
Powell, Kenneth Alasandro
Rice, Lois Dickson
Ridgeway, William C.
Rodman, John
Rowe, Audrey
Saunders, Vincent E
Sherrod, Ezra Cornell
Shipe, Jamesetta Denise Holmes
Smith, James Charles
Swain, Michael B.
Terrell, Dorothy
Terrell, Richard Warren
Turner, Yvonne Williams
Wade, Brent James
Walker, Vernon David

Management/ Administration— Consultation/Analysis (*See Also* Consulting)

Adams, Edward B.
Adolph, Gerald Stephen
Ahart, Thomas I
Alexander, Clifford L., Jr.
Alexander, Dr. Lenora Cole
Allen, Billy R.
Allen, George Mitchell
Aman, Dr. Mohammed M.
Amos, Kent B.
Backus, Bradley
Baldwin, Carolyn H.
Banks, Charlie
Barnes, Martin G.
Battle, Turner Charles, III
Baylor, Sandra Johnson
Bell, William Jerry
Bembry, Lawrence
Bennett, Deborah Minor
Best, Jennings H
Bethea, Edwin Ayers
Billings-Harris, Lenora
Black, Charles E.
Black, Frederick Harrison
Blackmon, Joyce McAnulty
Blackwell, Faye Brown
Block, Dr. Leslie S.
Bonaparte, Dr. Tony Hillary
Brailsford, Marvin D.
Braxton, John Ledger
Brewer, Moses
Britton, Theodore R
Broussard, Cheryl Denise
Brown, Arnold E.
Brown, Bernice Baynes
Brown, John Mitchell, Sr.
Brown, Sherman L.
Bullard, Edward A., Jr.
Bunyon, Ronald S.
Butler, John Gordon
Byrd, Arthur W
Campbell, Sandra Pace
Carey, Carnice
Cargill, Sandra Morris
Christian, John L.
Clark, John Joseph
Cole, Patricia A
Coleman, Rodney Albert
Collins, Joanne Marcella
Cooper, Earl
Cooper, Walter
Curry, Clarence F.
Cuyjet, Aloysius Baxter
Dalferes, Edward R., Jr.
Daniel, Jack L.
Daniels, William James
Danzy, Patricia Lynn
Davis, Clarence A.
Davis, Erroll B., Jr.
Davis, Luther Charles
Dawson, Shed, Jr.
Deese, Manuel
Dent, Richard Lamar
Dickson, Reginald D.
Diggs, Lawrence J

Management/Administration—General

Bunyon, Ronald S.
Burd, Steven A
Burges, Melvin E.
Burke, Donna M
Burley, Jack L
Burnett, Dr. Myra N
Burns, Jesse L
Burns, Leonard L
Burns, Tommie
Burns, Ursula M
Burris-Floyd, Pearl
Burroughs, Hugh Charles
Burrows, Chelsye J
Busby, Jheryl
Bush, Charles Vernon
Bush, Esther L
Bush, Nathaniel
Bush, Patricia
Butcher, Ernesto L.
Butler, Eugene Thaddeus, Jr.
Butler, Joyce M
Butler, Oliver Richard
Butler, Pinkney L.
Byers, Susan M
Byrd, Lewis E.
Byrd, Lumus, Jr.
Cabbil, Lila
Cadet, Ron
Caillier, James Allen
Cain, Herman
Cain, Robert R, Jr.
Caldwell, Ardis
Calhoun, Essie Lee
Callaway, Dwight W
Camp, Marva Jo
Campbell, Carlos, Sr.
Campbell, George, Jr.
Campbell, Maia
Campbell, Melanie L
Canady, Blanton Thandreus
Cane, Rudolph C
Cannon, Reuben
Caradine, Tracy
Carey, Wayne E
Carlo, Nelson
Carroll, Charlene O.
Carroll, Dr. Natalie L
Carroll, Robert F
Carroll, Rodney
Carson, Irma
Carter, Arlington W., Jr.
Carter, Cecilia K.
Carter, Fredrick Carter
Carter, Harriet LaShun
Carter, Kenneth Wayne
Carter, Robert Thompson
Carter, Roda Ward
Carter, Shawn Corey
Carter, Troy A
Cartwright, Jonathan
Casey, Carey
Casey, Rev. Carey Walden, Sr.
Cash, Lisa
Cason, Joseph L.
Casselberry, James Arthur
Castle, Keith L
Castro, George A
Caswell, Rosell R
Cator, Johnny
Chambers, Chris
Chambers, Olivia Marie
Chaney, Matthew
Channell, Eula L.
Chapman, Samuel Otha, Jr.
Chapman, Willie R
Chappelle, Joseph C
Chargois, James M
Charlton, George N., Jr.
Charna, Daniel A.
Chase, Anthony R
Chase, Arnett C
Chase, Tony
Chastine, Robert
Chatman, Tyrone
Chenault, Kenneth I.
Chennault, Dr. Madelyn
Cherry, Edward Earl
Chew, Cheryl
Chew, Vivian Scott
Chigbu, Gibson Chuks
Childs, Joy
Childs, Winston
Chisholm, Samuel Jackson
Chriss, Henry Thomas
Christian, Dolly Lewis
Christian, John L.
Chuks-Orji, Austin
Clark, Mario Sean
Clark, Ralph H

Clark, Walter H.
Clark, William
Clark Diggs, Joetta
Clarke, Raymond
Clay, Timothy Byron
Clay Chambers, Juanita
Clayton, Lloyd E
Clemons, Alois Ricardo
Clemons, Sandra L.
Clinkscales, Keith
Clowney, Audrey E
Coakley, HM
Coaston, Shirley Ann Dumas
Coaxum, Harry Lee
Cobb, Cynthia Joan
Cofield, Marvis
Cohen, Gwen A
Colbert, Virgis W.
Cole, Andrea M
Coleman, Derrick D.
Coleman, Frankie Lynn
Coleman, Leonard
Coleman, Robert L
Collier-Wilson, Wanda
Collins, Dorothy
Collins, Lenora W.
Colston Barge, Gayle S
Combs, Samuel, III
Combs, Sean J
Compton, Charletta Rogers
Conaway, Samuel L
Conley, Mike
Connor, Dolores Lillie
Connor, Herman P
Conyers, Jean L.
Cook, Keith Lynn
Cook, Ladda Banks
Cook, Levi
Cook, Dr. Samuel DuBois
Coombs, Harry James
Cooper, Barbara J
Cooper, Barry
Cooper, Margaret J
Cooper, Merrill Pittman
Corbi, Lana E.
Corley, Eddie B., Sr.
Cormier, Lawrence J.
Cornelius, Charles Henry
Cottrell, Comer J.
Coulter, Phyllis A
Counts, Allen W
Cousin, Ertharin
Covington, Dr. H. Douglas
Covington, Tarriel
Cox, Sandra
Crawford, Curtis J.
Crawford, HR
Crawford, Jayne Suzanne
Crawford, Pam Scott
Crawford, Vanella Alise
Crawford-Major, Toni
Crosbie, Ivan
Crosby, James R
Crosby, Dr. Willis Herman
Crump, Janice Renae
Crump-Caine, Lynn
Crusoe-Ingram, Charlene
Crutchfield, James N
Cunningham, Randall
Cunningham, William
Curry, Charles H
Daggs, Leon
Daily, Lori Beard
Daley-Meleschi, Valrine
Daly, Ronald Edwin
Dames, Sabrina A.
Dandridge, Prof. Rita Bernice
Daniels, A. Raiford
Daniels, Darrell
Daniels, Greg
Daniels, John W
Daniels, Willie L
Daniels-Carter, Valerie
Darden, Anthony Kojo
Darden, Calvin
Darden, Edwin Carley
Dash, Darien
Dates, Jannette Lake
Davenport, Chester C
Davidson, Arthur B
Davidson, Hezekiah Miles
Davie, Damon Jonathon
Davis, Agnes Maria
Davis, Algenita Scott
Davis, Donald Gene
Davis, George Nelson, Jr.
Davis, Glenn
Davis, Herman E.
Davis, Julia H.

Davis, Kery
Davis, Dr. Leroy
Davis, Major
Davis, Marie H.
Davis, Mary Agnes Miller
Davis, Preston Augustus
Davis, Ronald
Davis, Ronald Weston
Davis, Stacey H
Davis, William W
Davis-Howard, Valerie V.
Davis Steed, Stacey D.
Dawson, Bobby H
Dawson, Harold A., Sr.
Days, Bertram Maurice
Dean, Terrance
DeBerry, Donna
DeGeneste, Henry Irving
De Graff, Jacques Andre
DeGraffenreidt, James H
DeJesus, Edward
Dejoie, Michael C
Delaney, Wilma I.
DeLauder, Dr. William B.
De'Leon, Lunden
DeLoatch, Sandra
Delpit, Joseph A.
Denmark, Leon
Dennard, Gloria
Dennis, Hugo, Jr.
Dennis, James Carlos
Dennis, Michael A.
Dennis, Shirley M
Denson, Andre B.
Dent, Dr. Preston L.
de Passe, Suzanne
Derbigny, Rhoda L
DeShields, Delino Lamont
DeVard, Jerri
Devine, Jamie
DeVore Mitchell, Ophelia
DiAna, DiAna
Dick, George Albert
Dickens, Samuel
Dickerson, Dr. Bette Jeanne
Dickerson, Eric Demetric
Dickerson, Ralph
Dickson, Fred
Diggs, Christian Emanuel
Diggs, Deborah Dolsey
Dildy, Catherine Greene
Dines, Steve
Dinizulu, Yao O
Dixon, Arrington Liggins
Dixon, Diane L.
Dixon, Julius B.
Dixon, Leonard Bill
Dixon, Valena Alice
Doan, Lurita
Doanes-Bergin, Sharyn F
Dodd, Geralda
Doig, Elmo H.
Dotson, Howard
Dove, Dr. Shirley
Dowdy, James H
Drake, Lawrence M, II
Drakeford, Jack
Drummond, David C.
Dual, J. Fred, Jr.
Dubriel, Lisa M.
Dudley, Joe Louis
Duhaney, Trevor
Dukes, Carl R
Dukes, Hazel Nell
Dukes, Ofield
Dukes, Dr. Walter L
Duncan, Peggy
Duncan, Sandra Rhodes
Dunn, Almeda Effie
Dunn, Traci
Dupri, Jermaine
Durand, Winsley, Jr.
Duster, Benjamin C, IV
Dyer, Bernard Joel
Dymally, Mervyn Malcolm
Eady, Kermit
Earl, Acie Boyd
Earles, Dr. Julian
Earls, Dr. Julian Manly
Easley, Kenny Mason, Jr.
Easter, William H, III
Eastmond, Arlington Leon, Jr.
Eatman, Janice A
Eatman, Joseph W
Echols, Alvin E
Echols, James Albert
Eckstine, Ed
Edison, Joanne
Edmond, Paul Edward

Edmondson, Jerome
Edmunds, Allan L.
Edwards, Genyne
Edwards, George R
Edwards, Gerald Douglas
Edwards, Horace Burton
Edwards, Monica
Edwards, Preston Joseph
Edwards, Renia
Edwards, Theodore Allen
Eggleston, Neverett A
Elder, Larry
Elizey, Chris William
Eller, Carl L.
Ellington, E David
Elliott, J. Russell
Elliott, Sharon Lomax
Ellis, Douglas, Jr.
Ellis, Ladd
El Wilson, Barbara
English, Henry L
English, William E
Enoch, John D.
Ensley, Annette
Epps, Evern Cooper
Epps, George Allen, Jr.
Esquerre, Jean Roland
Eure, Dexter D, Sr.
Evans, Etu
Evans, Gwendolyn
Evans, Hugh
Evans, Dr. Jack
Evans, James L.
Evans, Milton L.
Ewing, Steven R
Exum, Thurman McCoy
Ezozo, Agrippa O.
Faison, Derek E.
Faison, Eugene M
Fancher, Dr. Evelyn Pitts
Farmer, Forest Jackson, Sr.
Farrell, Samuel D.
Farrington, Thomas Alex
Farrow, Sallie A
Farrow, William McKnight, III
Fay, Toni Georgette
Fergus, Joseph E
Ferguson, Derek Talmar
Ferguson, Fay
Ferguson, Idell
Ferguson, Ralph
Ferguson, Sherlon Lee
Fernandez, Tony
Ferrer, Jose
Fields, Faye F
Fields, William I, Jr.
Finney, Karen
Finney, Michael Anthony
Fisher, Edith Maureen
Fitzgerald, Howard David
Fitzpatrick, B Edward
Fleming, Alicia DeLaMothe
Fleming, Ellis T.
Fleming, John Emory
Fletcher, Dr. Bettye Ward
Fletcher, Glen Edward
Fletcher, James Andrew
Flint, Mary Frances
Floyd, Vernon Clinton
Fluker, Philip A.
Fobbs, Kevin
Ford, Antoinette
Ford, Henry
Foreman, Joyce Blacknall
Foreman, Peggy E
Formey, Sylvester C
Forte, Patrick
Foster, Dr. Bellandra B.
Foster, Deborah
Foster, Edward, Sr.
Foushee, Prevost Vest
Fowler, Reggie
Fox, Paulette
Frame, George J
Francis, Gilbert H.
Francis, Livingston S
Franklin, Clarence Frederick
Franklin, Harold A.
Franklin, Dr. Lance Stonestreet
Franklin, Oliver St Clair, Jr.
Franklin, Prestonia D.
Frasier, Ralph Kennedy
Frazier, Jordan
Frazier-Ellison, Vicki L
Freeland, Russell L
Freeland, Shawn Ericka
Freeman, Walter Eugene
Freeman, Yausmenda
Freisen, Gil

Friday, Jeff
Frye, Thomas John
Fufuka, Tika NY
Fugett, Jean Schloss, Jr.
Fuller, William Henry, Jr.
Fullwood, Emerson U
Gaines, Brenda J.
Gaines, Crystal Monique
Gainey, Leonard Dennis, II
Gallot, Richard Joseph
Galloway, Joey
Gamble, G. Arlivia Babbage
Gambrell, Donna J
Gant, Phillip M, III
Garba, Baba
Gardner, Edward George
Gardner, Harold
Gardner, Loman Ronald
Garner, Nathan Warren
Garrett, Darrell W
Garrett, Louis Henry
Garrett, Paul C
Garrett, Ruby Grant
Gartrell, Bernadette A
Gary, Howard V
Gary, Willie E.
Gaston, Linda Saulsby
Gay, Alvin
Gee, William Rowland, Jr.
Gellineau, Victor Marcel
Gibel, Ronald L
Gibson, Kala
Gibson, Nell Braxton
Gibson, Tyrese
Giles, Joe L
Gill, Walter Harris
Gilliam, Herman Arthur, Jr.
Gilmore, Dr. Robert McKinley, Sr.
Gipson, Hayward R., Jr.
Givens, Dr. Henry, Jr.
Givens, Larry
Glenn, Patricia Campbell
Glover, Hamilton
Glover, Kevin Bernard
Glover, Robert G
Godfrey, Randall Euralentris
Golden, Joyce Marie
Goldston, Bobby F
Goldston, Nathaniel R., III
Goliday, Willie V.
Goode, Bruce T
Goode, Rev. W. Wilson
Goode, Willie K.
Gooden, C. Michael
Gooden, Linda
Goodman, Harold
Goodwin, Donald Edward
Gordon, Garth
Gorman, Bertha Gaffney
Gotti, Irv
Grace, George H
Grady, Glenn G
Graham, James C, Jr.
Graham, Stedman
Grant, Anthony T
Grant, Dr. Ellsworth R
Grant, Gary Rudolph
Grantham, Charles
Granville, Billy
Graves, Allene
Graves, Valerie Jo
Gray, Dr. E Delbert
Gray, Harold B.
Gray, Moses W.
Greaves, William
Green, Darrell
Green, Darryl Lynn
Green, Dennis
Green, Harold
Green, Hugh
Green, Hydia Lutrice
Green, Ruth A.
Green, Sean Curtis
Green, Sterling
Green-Campbell, Deardra Delores
Greene, Franklin D
Greene, Gabrielle Elise
Greene, Maurice
Greene, Nathaniel D
Greenfield, Mark Steven
Greenwood, Monique
Greer, Cherie
Grier, John K
Griffey, Dick
Griffin, Archie
Griffin, Bertha L.
Griffith, Darrell Steven
Grigsby, Calvin Burchard
Grimes, Calvin M., Jr.

Grissom, Marquis Dean
Groce, Rev. Herbert Monroe, Jr.
Groff, Regis F.
Guillebeaux, Tamara Elise
Gunnings, Dr. Thomas S.
Guthrie, Carlton Lyons
Guy, Buddy
Gwynn, Florine Evayonne
Haber, Lois
Hackett, Wilbur L
Haile, Annette L
Hailstock, Shirley
Hale, Marna Amoretti
Hall, Brian Edward
Hall, Everett
Hall, Frances White
Hall, Hansel Crimiel
Hall, Lt. Gen. James Reginald
Hall, Robert L
Hall, Stanley H.
Hamilton, Darryl Quinn
Hamilton, Dean
Hamilton, Howard W
Hamlar, Jocelyn B
Hamlin, David W.
Hamm, Paula
Hammond, James A
Hammond, Verle B
Hampton, Randall C.
Hancock, Herbie
Handwerk, Jana D.
Handy, Lillian B.
Hankins, Anthony Mark
Hardin, Marie D
Harding, John Edward
Harding, Michael S
Hardman, Artina Tinsley
Hargrett, James T., Jr.
Harkness, Jerry
Harper, Earl
Harper, T Errol
Harrell, H Steve
Harrell, Oscar W., II
Harris, Barbara Clemente
Harris, Carla Ann
Harris, Carol R
Harris, Caspa L., Jr.
Harris, Corey Lamont
Harris, Dale F.
Harris, David
Harris, Earl L.
Harris, Franco
Harris, J. Robert, II
Harris, John J.
Harris, Dr. Joseph Benjamin
Harris, Marcelite J.
Harris, Marion Rex
Harris, Dr. Mary Styles
Harris, Ramon
Harris, Raymont LeShawn
Harris, Robert L.
Harris, Steve
Harris, Thomas C.
Harris, Tricia R
Harris, Dr. William Hamilton
Harris-Diaw, Rosalind Juanita
Harris-Ebohon, Dr. Altheria Thyra
Harrison, Charles
Harrison, Dr. Roderick
Hartaway, Thomas N
Hartsfield, Judy
Harvey, Maurice Reginald
Harvey, Michael P
Hastick, Roy A
Hasty, Keith A
Havis, Jeffrey Oscar
Hawk, Charles Nathaniel, III
Hawkins, Ernestine L
Hawkins, James C.
Hawkins, La-Van
Hawkins, Paulette
Hayes-Jordan, Margaret
Haynes, Joe A
Haysbert, Raymond Victor
Haywood, Dwayne A.
Haywood, George Weaver
Hazel, Janis D
Head, Helaine
Heard, Marian L
Henderson, Cheryl Brown
Henderson, Frank S, Jr.
Henderson, William Avery
Hendon, Lea Alpha
Hendricks, Steven Aaron
Henley, Carl R
Henry, Alaric Anthony
Henry-Fairhurst, Ellenae L
Henson, Daniel Phillip, III
Herbert, Adam W

Herrington, Perry Lee
Hickman, Elnor B G
Hicks, Dr. Clayton Nathaniel
Hicks, Jimmie, Jr.
Hicks, Dr. Veronica Abena
Hicks-Bartlett, Sharon Theresa
High, Claude, Jr.
Highsmith, Carlton L.
Hightower, Herma J
Hightower, Stephen Lamar
Hill, Arthur Burit
Hill, Barbara A
Hill, Colin C
Hill, Cynthia D
Hill, Deborah
Hill, Frederick W
Hill, George Hiram
Hill, James, Jr.
Hill, Jesse, Jr.
Hill, Marvin Lewis
Hill, Robert K.
Hilliard, Amy S
Hipkins, Conrad
Hodge, Ernest M
Hodges, Virgil Hall
Hogges, Ralph
Holland, Robert
Holley, Sharon Yvonne
Holliman, David L
Hollinger, Reginald J
Holloway, Ardith E
Holloway, Douglas V
Holmes, Arthur
Holmes, E Selean
Holmes, Larry
Holmes, Robert Kathrone, Jr.
Holyfield, Evander
Hooker, Douglas Randolf
Hooper, Michele J
Hopkins, Edward Charles
Hord, Noel Edward
Hornbuckle, Napoleon
Horton, Carl E.
Horton, Willie Wattison
House, Kyla N
Houston, Allan Wade
Hovell, Yvonne
Howard, Anica
Howard, Aubrey J
Howard, Ellen D
Howard, Jules Joseph, Jr.
Howard, Leslie Carl
Howard, Ray F.
Howell, Amaziah, III
Howell, Chester Thomas
Howell, Rachel
Howlett, Walter, Jr.
Hubbard, Paul Leonard
Hubbard, Reginald T.
Hudson, Elbert T.
Hudson, Paul C.
Huger, Raymond A
Huggins, Linda Johnson
Huggins-Williams, Dr. Nedra
Hughes, Catherine Liggins
Hughes, George Vincent
Hughes, Kori
Hughley, Stephanie
Hull, Stephanie J
Humphrey, Sonnie
Hunt, Edward
Hunter, Edwina Earle
Hunter, Kim L
Hurd, Bridget G.
Hutchins, Lawrence G., Sr.
Hyde, Dr. Maxine Deborrah
Hyler, Lora Lee
Hyman, Mark J
Ingram, Kevin
Ingram, Phillip M
Ingram, William B.
Ingrum, Adrienne G
Innis, Roy Emile Alfredo
Irvin, Dennis J.
Isaacs, Patricia
Isler, Marshall A., III
Ismial, Salaam Ibn
Jackson, Arthur Howard
Jackson, Beverly Anne
Jackson, Brenda
Jackson, Donald J
Jackson, Dr. Edison O.
Jackson, Elijah
Jackson, Emory Napoleon
Jackson, George
Jackson, Gerald E.
Jackson, Dr. Horace
Jackson, Inez Austin
Jackson, Kenya Love

Jackson, Mannie L
Jackson, Marcus
Jackson, Mary
Jackson, Ronald G
Jackson, Tonya Charisse
Jackson, William Alvin
Jackson, William Ed
Jackson, William R
Jackson, Yvonne Ruth
Jacob, John Edward
Jacobs, Dr. Daniel Wesley, Sr.
Jacques, Cornell
James, Anthony R
James, Dr. Betty Nowlin
James, Charles Howell, II
James, Clarence L., Jr.
James, John A
James, Joseph J
James, Kevin Porter
James, Ronald
Jamison, Isaac Terrell
Javery, Michael
Jean, Kymberly
Jefferson, Andrea Green
Jefferson, Clifton
Jefferson, Gary Scott
Jefferson, Linda
Jefferson, Shawn
Jemison, Aj D
Jenifer, Dr. Franklyn Green
Jenkins, Jim
Jenkins, Melvin Lemuel
Jenkins, Monica
Jennings, Devoyd
Jensen, Dr. Ray M
John, Anthony
Johnson, Arthur E
Johnson, Barry
Johnson, Bennett J
Johnson, Carl Earld
Johnson, Charles E.
Johnson, Cheryl P.
Johnson, Clarissa
Johnson, Cleveland, Jr.
Johnson, Costello O
Johnson, Davis
Johnson, Eunita E
Johnson, Fran
Johnson, Frank J., Sr.
Johnson, George Ellis, Sr.
Johnson, Jean
Johnson, Joan B.
Johnson, John
Johnson, Jon D.
Johnson, Jonathan F
Johnson, Julia L.
Johnson, Juliana Cornish
Johnson, Kimberly Lynn
Johnson, Dr. Marie Love
Johnson, Mark A
Johnson, Marvin R, Jr.
Johnson, Ralph C
Johnson, Robert
Johnson, Robert E
Johnson, Robert L.
Johnson, Roy Lee
Johnson, Sheila
Johnson, T J
Johnson, Walter Thaniel, Jr.
Johnson, Wayne Lee
Johnson, Wendell L., Jr.
Johnson, William Randolph
Johnson, Willie F
Jolley, Samuel Delanor
Jones, A. Lorraine
Jones, Aaron Delmas
Jones, Albert C.
Jones, Anthony Ward
Jones, Benjamin A
Jones, Benjamin E
Jones, Booker Tee, Sr.
Jones, David L
Jones, David R.
Jones, Elaine R
Jones, Esq. Ernest Edward
Jones, Francis R
Jones, Gregory Allan
Jones, Gregory Wayne
Jones, Gus
Jones, Horace F
Jones, Ingrid Saunders
Jones, James R
Jones, Larry Wayne
Jones, Lester C
Jones, Mable Veneida
Jones, Michelle
Jones, Milton H., Jr.
Jones, Nathaniel Jamal
Jones, Phillip Madison

Jones, Theresa C
Jones, Vivian R
Jordan, Dr. Carolyne Lamar
Jordan, Dr. Dedra R
Jordan, George Washington, Jr.
Jordan, J Paul
Jordan, Thurman
Jordan, Vernon Eulion
Joseph, David E
Joseph, Lloyd Leroi
Joseph-McIntyre, Mary
Jowers, Johnnie Edward, Sr.
Joyner-Kersee, Jackie
Kaiser, James Gordon
Keith, Dr. Leroy, Jr.
Kendrick, L John, Sr.
Kennard, William Earl
Kennedy, Rev. James E
Kennedy, Marvin James
Kennedy, Sandra Denise
Kennon, Rozmond H
Kent, Melvin Floyd
Kilimanjaro, John Marshall
Kinchen, Arif S.
Kindall, Dr. Alpha S.
King, Dexter
King, Hulas H
King, Dr. James, Jr.
King, Dr. Reatha Clark
Kinsey, Bernard W.
Kirby-Davis, Montanges
Kirchhofer, Dr. Wilma Ardine Lyghtner
Kirksey, M Janette
Klausner, Willette Murphy
Knight, Gladys Maria
Knott, May
Knowles, Sudani
Knowling, Robert E, Jr.
Knox, Wayne Harrison
Kornegay, William F
Kunes, Ken R.
Kyles, Dwain Johann
LaBeach, Nicole Ann
Labrie, Harrington
Lacey, Dr. Marian Glover
Lacy, Aundrea
Lacy, Venus
Laday, Kerney
Lafayette, Excell, Jr.
Laird, Alan
Lander, C Victor
Lander, Cressworth Caleb
Landry, Dolores Branche
Lane, Curtis
Langford, Daria
Lanier, Jesse M, Sr.
Larken Hicks, Patricia
LaSane, Joanna Emma
Latimer, Frank Edward
Lauderback, Brenda Joyce
Lavergneau, Rene L.
Law, M Eprevel
Law, Robert Louis
Lawal, Kase Lukman
Lawrence, Dr. Barbara Ann
Lawrence, Philip Martin
Lawrence, Philip Martin
Lawrence, Philip Martin
Lawrie-Goodrich, Madeline
Lawson, Anthony Eugene, Sr.
Lawson, Charles H, III
Lawson, Jennifer Karen
Laymon, Joe W.
Leath, Verlyn Faye
Leavell, Dorothy R.
LeCesne, Alvarez
Lee, Aubrey Walter, Sr.
Lee, Charles Gary, Sr.
Lee, E Jacques
Lee, Forrest A, Sr.
Lee, Fred D, Jr.
Lee, Jefferi K
Lee, Leron
Lee, M David, Jr.
Lee, Margaret S
Lee, Ritten Edward
Lee, Robert Emile
Lee, William H
Leeke, John F.
Leeper, Ronald James
LeFebvre, Dale
LeFebvre, Dale
LeGendre, Henri A
LeGrand, Bob Snake
Leigh, Fredric H
Lelaind, Detra Lynette
Leonard, Sugar Ray
Lester, George Lawrence

Levell, Edward, Jr.
Lewellen, Michael Elliott
Lewis, Arthur W
Lewis, Charles Michael
Lewis, Ephron H.
Lewis, Loida Nicolas
Lewis, Ora Lee
Lewis, Terry
Lewis, Tom
Lewis, W Arthur
Lewis-Kemp, Jacqueline
Lewis-Thornton, Rae
Lewter, Andy C, Sr.
Liautaud, James
Liggins, Alfred, III
Liles, Kevin
Lindsay, Horace Augustin
Lindsey, Patrick O
Linton, Gordon J.
Lister, Willa M
Locke, Henry Daniel Jr.
Lockhart, Barbara H
Lockhart, Keith E
Lofton, Michael
Logan, Harold James
Logan, Lewis E
Logan-Tooson, Linda Ann
London, Eddie
Long, James, Jr.
Long, Steffan
Lott, Ronald M
Louis, Joseph
Love, Carolyn Diane
Love, James Ralph
Loveless, Theresa E
Lowe, Dr. Aubrey F.
Lowe, Walter Edward, Jr.
Lowery, Rev. Dr. Joseph E.
Lowery-Jeter, Renecia Yvonne
Lowman, Carl D
Lowry, James Hamilton
Lowry, William E, Jr.
Lozada, De Juana
Lucas, L Louise
Lundy, Dr. Harold W
Lundy, Larry
Luster, Jory
Luster, Robert
Lynch, Leon
Lyons, Dr. James E.
Lyons, Lamar Andrew
Lythcott, Janice Logue
Lytle, Marilyn Mercedes
Mack, C.
Mack, Dr. Deborah L
Mack, Nate
Mack, Roderick O
Mackie, Timothy
MacLean, Anita
Madhubuti, Haki R
Madison, William Edward
Majors, Anthony Y
Malbroue, Joseph, Jr.
Malcom, Dr. Shirley Mahaley
Maldon, Alphonso, Jr.
Mallebay-Vacqueur Dem, Jean Pascal
Malone, Maurice
Manlove, Benson
Manney, William A.
Mapp, Robert P
Mariner, Jonathan
Marr, Carmel Carrington
Marsh, Alphonso Howard
Marshall, Eric A
Marshall, Julyette Matthews
Marshall, Pluria William, Jr.
Martin, Charles Wesley
Martin, DeWayne
Martin, Frank T
Martin, Dr. Joanne Mitchell
Martin, Joshua Wesley
Martin, Walter L
Martin Chase, Debra
Mason, Ronald Edward
Massenburg, Kedar
Matchett, Johnson
Mathew, Knowles
Mathews, Gary C
Mathews, Keith E
Mathis, David L
Mathis, Kevin
Matthews, Candace S
Mauney, Donald Wallace, Jr.
Maxie, Peggy Joan
Maxwell, Bertha Lyons
Mays, William G
McBride, Bryant
McCain, Ella Byrd

McCammon, Marques
McCants, Dr. Jesse Lee, Sr.
McClammy, Dr. Thad C
McClendon, Raymond
McClure, Dr. Wesley Cornelious
McCluskey, Audrey Thomas
McCord, LaNissa Renee
McCoy, George H.
McCrae, Larry C
McDaniel, Elizabeth
McDonald, Ella Seabrook
McDonald, Herbert G
McDonald, Jeffrey Bernard
McDonald, Larry Marvin
McDonald, Timothy
McDuffie, Deborah
McElvane, Pamela Anne
McFarland, Ollie Franklin
McFarland, Roland C
McGee, Col. Charles Edward
McGee, Henry Wadsworth
McGee, James M
McGee, Rev. Paula L.
McGhee, Georgia Mae
McGlover, Stephen Ledell
McGuire, Jean Mitchell
McHenry, Douglas
McHenry, Emmit J
McHenry, Dr. James O
McIlwain, Toni
McIntosh, Helen Young
McIntosh, Marc
McIntosh, Rhodina Covington
McKenzie, Eli, Jr.
McKinney, Samuel Berry
McKissack, Leatrice Buchanan
McLaughlin, Benjamin Wayne
McLaughlin, Katye H
McLawhorn, James Thomas
McLean, Dennis Ray
McLean, Marquita Sheila McLarty
McLemore, Andrew G
McLeod, Dr. Gustavus A.
McMillan, Robert Frank, Jr.
McMillian, Marco W
McNeal, Timothy Kyle
McNeil, Randy
McPherson, David
McRae, Ronald Edward
McWhorter, Rosalynd D
McZeal, Alfred, Sr.
McZier, Arthur
Means, Bertha E
Meeks, Willis Gene
Meggett, David Lee
Melendez-Rinehart, Carmen M.
Menkiti, Bo
Menogan, Annita M
Merenivitch, Jarrow
Merritt, Anthony Lewis
Mesiah, Raymond N.
Meyers, Ishmael Alexander
Michael, Dr. Charlene Belton
Michel, Harriet Richardson
Mickens, Maxine
Mickle, Andrea Denise
Miles, Albert Benjamin
Miles, George L
Miller, C Conrad, Jr.
Miller, Charles D, Jr.
Miller, Doris Jean
Miller, George Carroll, Jr.
Miller, Dr. Margaret Elizabeth Battle
Miller, Oliver O.
Miller, Tedd
Milliner, David M
Mills, Alan Keith
Mims, Terrence
Minyard, Handsel B.
Mister, Melvin Anthony
Mitchell, Bert Norman
Mitchell, Roderick Bernard
Mitchell, Sally Ruth
Mitchum, Dorothy M
Moncrief, Sidney A.
Moncrieffe, Peter
Monk, Art
Monroe, Anthony E
Monroe, Robert Alex
Montgomery, Catherine Lewis
Moody, C David
Moody, Charles David, Sr.
Moore, Allyn D
Moore, Barbara Crockett
Moore, Cornell Leverette
Moore, David M
Moore, Gary
Moore, Herman Joseph
Moore, Jerry A, Jr.

Moore, John Wesley, Jr.
Moore, Minyon
Moore, Wenda Weekes
Moore-Poole, Jessica Care
Moragne, Lenora, Ph.D.
Morgan, Rose
Morgan, Stanley Douglas
Morgan-Smith, Sylvia
Morial, Dr. Marc
Morning, John
Morris, Carolyn G
Morris, Dr. Charles Edward, Jr.
Morris, Eugene
Morris, Horace W
Morris, John P, III
Morrison, Charles Edward
Morrow, Jesse
Morrow, W Derrick
Morse, Dr. Laurence C
Morse, Dr. Oliver
Morton, Marilyn M
Moses, Edwin
Mosley, Benita Fitzgerald
Mosley, Christopher D
Moss, Tanya Jill
Motley, David Lynn
Muckelroy, William Lawrence
Muhammad, Marion
Mullens, Delbert W
Mullins, Jarrett R
Munson, Cheryl Denise
Munson, Eddie Ray
Murphy, Daniel Howard
Murphy, Dr. John Matthew, Jr.
Murphy, Michael McKay
Murray, Gary S., Sr.
Murray, James P
Myers, Dr. Ernest Ray
Myers, L Leonard
Myers, Walter Dean
Myles, Wilbert
Nalls, Patricia
Nanula, Richard D
Nash, Henry Gary
Naylor, Gloria
Neal, Brandon
Neal, Brenda Jean
Neal, Frederic Douglas
Neal, Lorenzo LaVon
Nearn, Arnold Dorsey, Jr.
Neizer, Meredith Ann
Nellums, Michael Wayne
Neloms, Henry
Nelson, Charles J
Nelson, Debra J
Nelson, Jonathan P.
Nelson, Ronald Duncan
Nelson, Ronald J
Nelson, Dr. Wanda Jean
Newberry, Cedric Charles
Newell, Daryl
Newkirk, Thomas H.
Newsome, Ronald Wright
Newton, Gen. Lloyd W
Nibbs, Alphonse, Sr.
Nicco-Annan, Lionel, Clipper Int
    Corp
Nightingale-Hawkins, Monica R
Nixon, Rev. Felix Nathaniel
Nixon, Harold L
Nixon, James I, Jr.
Nixon, Norm Ellard
Noble, John Pritchard
Norman, Bobby Don
Norman, James H
Norman, William Stanley
Norrell-Nance, Rosalind Elizabeth
Norris, Fred Arthur, Jr.
Norris, William E.
Norvell, Dr. Merritt J.
Nowlin, Frankie L
Nunn, John
Nwagbaraocha, Joel O
Oben, Roman Dissake
Odom, Clifton Lewis
Odom, Melanie
Odom, Stonewall
Officer, Carl Edward
O'Flynn-Pattillo, Patricia
Oglesby, Boris
Ogunlesi, Adebayo O
Ohuche, Emeka
Oliver, Al
O'Neal, Malinda King
O'Neal, Rodney
O'Neal, Stanley
Ono, Musashi
Orduna, Dr. Kenneth Maurice
Orr, Ray

Osborne, Gwendolyn Eunice
Owens, Brigman
Owens, Curtis
Owens, Isaiah Hudson
Owens, James E, Jr.
Owens, Mercy P
Owens, Treka Elaine
Owens, Wallace, Jr.
Ozanne, Leroy
Paddio-Johnson, Dr. Eunice Alice
Pailen, Donald
Palmer, Dr. Annette
Palms, Sylvia J
Parham, Richelle
Parker, George Anthony
Parker, Kai J
Parker, Stafford W
Parker, Thomas Edwin, III
Parker, Dr. William C, Jr.
Parkinson, Nigel Morgan
Parks, James Clinton
Parks, Kenneth
Parnell, Arnold W
Parnell, John V, III
Parrish, James Nathaniel
Parrish, Maurice Drue
Parson, Richard Dean
Parsons, Philip I
Paschall, Jimmie Walton
Patnett, John Henry
Patrick, Charles Namon, Jr.
Patrick, Dr. Jennie R
Patterson, Clarence J.
Patterson, Gerald William
Patterson, Lloyd
Patterson, Michael Duane
Patterson, Pickens Andrew
Pattillo, Joyce M
Paul, Wanda D, CPA
Payne, Ronnie E
Payne, Ulice, Jr.
Payne-Nabors, Colleen J
Peal, Darryl Alan
Pearce, Oveta W
Pearson, Drew
Pearson, Michael Novel
Peck, Leontyne Clay
Peebles, Daniel Percy
Peete, Calvin
Penha, Gail A.
Penn, James T, Jr.
Peoples, Alice Leigh
Peoples, Danita L
Peoples, Harrison Promis, Jr.
Perez, Anna
Perry, Betty Hancock
Perry, Clifford, III
Perry, Eugene Calvin, Jr.
Perry, Rev. Jerald Isaac, Sr.
Perry, LaVal
Perry, Lee Charles, Jr.
Perry, Lowell Wesley, Jr.
Perryman, Angelo R.
Peters, Aulana Louise
Peters, Charles L, Jr.
Peters, Dr. Rev. Pamela Joan
Petersen, Allan Ernest
Peterson, Gerard M.
Petett, Freddye J Webb
Phillips, Charles E, Jr.
Phillips, Daniel P
Phillips, Edward Alexander
Phillips, Eric McLaren
Phillips, Rev. F Allison
Phillips, W Thomas
Pickard, Vivian
Pickard, Dr. William Frank
Pickett, Donna A
Pickrum, Lisa M.
Pierre, Jennifer Casey
Pierson, Derron
Pierson, Randy
Pinckney, Andrew Morgan, Jr.
Pinkney, Arnold R.
Pinkney, John Edward
Pinkney, Rose Catherine
Pittman, Darryl E.
Pitts, Meagan R
Plunkett, Raphael Hildan
Poe, Alfred
Poe, Fred J
Pogue, D Eric
Pollard, Percy Edward, Sr.
Porter, Edward Melvin
Porter, John T
Porter, Dr. John W
Porter, Michael C

Porter, Dr. Shikana Temille
Portis, Kattie Harmon
Posey, Deborah
Posey, John R
Potter, Jamie
Potter, Myrtle Stephens
Powell, Adam Clayton, III
Powell, Bettye Boone
Powell, Gen. Colin Luther
Powell, Juan Herschel
Powell, Michael K
Powell, Wayne Hugh
Powell, Wilma D
Powell-Jackson, Dr. Rev. Bernice
Powers, Ray
Prather, Jeffrey Lynn
Preston, Eugene Anthony
Price, JoAnn H
Price, Phillip G
Pride, J. Thomas
Prince-Bythewood, Gina
Prioleau, Oscar Eugene
Prioleau, Dr. Sara Nelliene
Prior, Anthony
Prothro, Gerald Dennis
Pruitt, Michael
Pryor, Malcolm D.
Pugh, Mary E
Puryear, Dr. Alvin Nelson
Quarles, Nancy L
Ramsey, Jerome Capistrano
Randall, Dr. Queen Franklin
Randle, Berdine Caronell
Rankin, Marlene Owens
Rann, Dr. Emery Louvelle
Rasheed, Fred
Raveling, George Henry
Raven, Ricky A
Reagon, Dr. Bernice Johnson
Reason, J Paul
Reaves, Rev. Dr. Benjamin Franklin
Redd, M. Paul, Sr.
Reddrick, Mark A
Redmond, DeVera Yvonne
Redon, Leonard Eugene
Reed, Cordell
Reeves, Brenda
Reeves, Julius Lee
Reeves, Michael Stanley
Reid, Pamela Trotman
Reid, William J
Reid-McQueen, Lynne Marguerite
Renford, Edward
Reyes, Ricardo A.
Reynolds, Charles McKinley, Jr.
Reynolds, James
Reynolds, Ricky Scott
Rhodes, Edward Thomas, Sr.
Rhodes, Gerald
Rhone, Sylvia M
Rice, Edward A.
Rice, J Donald, Jr.
Rice, Linda Johnson
Richards, William Earl
Richards-Alexander, Billie J.
Richardson, Albert Dion
Richardson, Joseph
Richardson, Dr. Leo
Richardson, Leon
Richardson, Linda Waters
Richardson, Munro Carmel
Richardson, Otis Alexander
Richardson, Timothy L
Richardson, Valerie K.
Rideau, Iris
Ridenour, Lionel
Riggins, Jean
Riggs, Dr. Enrique A
Riley, Rosetta Marguritte
Risbrook, Dr. Arthur Timothy
Riscoe, Romona A
Rivera, Lance
Robbins, Carl Gregory Cuyjet
Roberson, F Alexis H
Roberts, Angela Dorrean
Roberts, Lillian
Roberts, Michael V.
Robertson, Charles E, Jr.
Robertson, Oscar Palmer
Robinson, Anthony W
Robinson, Beverly Jean
Robinson, Cleo Parker
Robinson, Harold Oscar
Robinson, Dr. Harry, Jr.
Robinson, James Edward
Robinson, Dr. JaMuir Michelle
Robinson, Jeffrey
Robinson, John E
Robinson, John F.

Robinson, John M.
Robinson, Malcolm S
Robinson, Melvin P.
Robinson, Myron Frederick
Robinson, Nina
Robinson, Patricia
Robinson, Ronnie W
Robinson, Sherman
Robinson, Smokey
Robinson, Will
Rodgers, Johnathan A.
Rodgers, Pamela E
Rodman, Dennis Keith
Rodman, John
Rodriguez, Ruben
Rogers, John W.
Rogers, Esq. Joyce Q
Rogers, Ormer, Jr.
Rogers-Reece, Shirley
Rohadfox, Ronald Otto
Rojas, Don
Romain, Pierre R
Rose, Jalen
Ross, William R
Rowe, Marilyn Johnson
Roy, John Willie
Royster, Don M, Sr.
Rozier, Gilbert Donald
Rucker, Clyde
Ruffin, John H
Ruffin, John Walter
Russell, Charlie L.
Russell, Jerome
Russell, Mark
Russell, Michael
Russell, Wesley L.
Rutledge, Jennifer M
Ryan, Marsha Ann
Ryce, Sundra L
Salaam, Abdel R
Salter, Kwame S
Samara, Noah Azmi
Sampson, Marva W
Samuel, Antoinette Allison
Samuels, Bryan
Samuels, Everett Paul
Samuels, Dr. Leslie Eugene
Samuels, Robert J
Sanderson, Randy Chris
Sarreals, E. Don
Satterwhite, Dr. Frank Joseph
Saunders, David J
Saunders, William Joseph
Savage, Frank
Scales, Dr. Patricia Bowles
Schmoke, Kurt Lidell
Scott, Donnell
Scott, Gilbert H, Sr.
Scott, Marian Alexis
Scott, Michael W
Scott, R Lee
Scott, Robert Jerome
Scott, Stephen L
Scribner, Arthur Gerald, Jr.
Seabrooks, Nettie Harris
Searcy, Lillie
Seavers, Clarence W.
Seay, Dawn Christine
Seele, Pernessa C.
Self, Frank Wesley
Sergeant, Carra Susan
Sergent, Ernest, Jr.
Sessoms, Glenn D
Settles, Trudy Y
Sewell, Edward C
Sewell, Luther Joseph
Seymore, Stanley
Shack, William Edward, Jr.
Shackelford, George Franklin
Shackelford, Lottie Holt
Shamsid-Deen, Waleed
Shaw, Carl Bernard
Shead, Ken
Shealey, Richard W
Shelton, Charles E
Shelton, Harvey William
Shelton, Helen C
Shelton, Joseph B, Jr.
Shepherd, Malcolm Thomas
Shepherd, Veronika Y
Sherrell, Charles Ronald, II
Shields, Cydney Robin
Shields-Jones, Esther L M
Shirley, Dr. Ollye Brown
Shivers, P Derrick
Shivers, S. Michael
Short, Leslie
Shumate, Glen
Simeus, Dumas M

Management/Administration—Operations/Maintenance

Carson, Regina M. E.
Carter, Charles Michael
Chenault, Kenneth I.
Clark, Frank M
Coaxum, Henry L
Cochran, Edward G.
Colbert, Virgis W.
Cooke, Thomas H, Jr.
Crawford, David
Crump, Wilbert S
Curry, Charles H
Davis, Preston A
Donald, Arnold Wayne
Dorsey, Herman Sherwood, Jr.
Dortch, Heyward
Elly, Andrew Jackie
Evans, Leon, Jr.
Fowler, Bennie W
Gladney, Rufus D
Glen, Ulysses, Jr.
Griffin, Bertha L.
Griffin, Michael D.
Guthrie, Michael J
Haile, Annette L
Harding, Michael S
Hardy, Michael Leander
Harrold, Lawrence A
Hayes-Giles, Joyce V.
Holliman, David L
Hunigan, Col. Earl
Jackson, Frank
Johnson, Dr. Charles Edward
Johnson, Fran
Johnson, Miriam B.
Jordan, Carolyn D
Jordan, Steve Russell
King, Kelley A
Knight, Suge
Leigh, Fredric H
Lewis, Ronald N
Louis, Joseph
Lowry, James E.
Lozada, De Juana
Martin, George Alexander, Jr.
Martin, Walter L
Martin, William R.
Meriwether, Louise
Miller, George Carroll, Jr.
Monteverdi, Mark Victor
Moore, Rick
Mosley, Elwood A
Murrell, Adrian Bryan
Nearn, Arnold Dorsey, Jr.
Neizer, Meredith Ann
Nicholas, Philip
Petersen, Frank Emmanuel, Jr.
Pitchford, Gerard Spencer
Reed, Cordell
Reeves, Julius Lee
Rogers, Charles Leonard
Rogers, Elijah Baby
Rogers, George
Rogers-Reece, Shirley
Sanders, Laura Green
Schenck, Frederick A
Shavers, Cheryl L.
Smith, Aubrey Carl
Smithers, Priscilla Jane
Springs, Lenny F
Sterling, John
Taylor, Charles E.
Taylor, Lorenzo James, Jr.
Taylor, Natalie Manns
Ukabam, Innocent O.
Verbal, Claude A
Wade, Unav Opal
Walker, Russell Dewitt
Washington, Shaunise A
Watkins, Price I.
Weissinger, Thomas
Welburn, Edward Thomas, Jr.
Wesley, Clemon Herbert, Jr.
White, Winifred Viaria
Whitfield, Robert
Williams, Barbara Ann
Williams, Edward Ellis
Williams, Stanley King
Wright, Sheena
Young, William

Management/Administration—Personnel/Training/Labor Relations

Adams, Albert W.
Adderly, T. C., Jr.
Albright, William Dudley
Alexander, Preston Paul
Allen, Billy R.

Arrington, Dr. Pamela Gray
Bailey, Antoinette M.
Bailey, Ronald W
Baity, Gail Owens
Banks, Paula A.
Barksdale, Mary Frances
Barnes, Diane
Barrett, Iris Louise Killian
Baskerville, Penelope Anne
Bates, George Albert
Beckles, Benita Harris
Bell, Sandra Watson
Berry, Paul Lawrence
Berry, Philip Alfonso
Besson, Paul Smith
Black, Frederick Harrison
Black, Veronica Correll
Blackmon, Joyce McAnulty
Blackmon, Mosetta Whitaker
Blakely, Dr. Edward James
Block, Dr. Leslie S.
Bolden, Frank Augustus
Bolling, Bruce C.
Boyd, Rozelle
Boyd, Theophilus B., III
Bridgeman, Donald Earl
Brooks, Wadell, Sr.
Browder, Anne Elna
Brown, A. David
Brown, Booker T
Brown, Jurutha
Bruce, Carol Pitt
Bryant-Reid, Johanne
Burges, Melvin E.
Burrows Dost, Janice H.
Caldwell, George Theron, Sr.
Caldwell, John Edward
Caldwell, Lisa Jeffries
Cammack, Charles Lee, Jr.
Canty, Otis Andrew
Carter, Jandra D.
Carter, Judy Sharon
Carter, Patrick Henry
Cason, Marilynn Jean
Cates, Hon. Sidney Hayward, IV
Chalmers, Thelma Faye
Champion, James A
Chandler, Effie L.
Chapman-Minutello, Alice Mariah
Chappell, Ruth Rax
Cissoko, Alioune Badara
Clark, Della L
Clark, James Irving, Jr.
Clarke, Benjamin Louis
Cockerham, Haven Earl
Collins, James H.
Colyer, Dr. Sheryl Lynn
Cooper, Linda G
Copes, Ronald Adrian
Cornell, Bob
Cox, M. Maurice
Crawley, Oscar Lewis
Cribb, Juanita Sanders
Crosse, Rev. St George Idris Bryon, III
Crowder, Wayne L
Crusoe-Ingram, Charlene
Cureton, John Porter
Cuyjet, Aloysius Baxter
Davis, Brownie W
Davis, Dr. Gloria-Jeanne
Dean, Diane D
Deloatch, Myrna Spencer
Dent, Gary Kever
Dewberry-Williams, Madelina Denise
Dickson, Daryl M.
Doanes-Bergin, Sharyn F
Dominic, Irwing
Dorman, Hattie Lawrence
Dorsey, Herman Sherwood, Jr.
Dortch, Heyward
Dotson, Betty Lou
Douglas, Mae Alice
Douglas, Mansfield, III
Dowdell, Dennis, Jr.
Downes, Dwight
Dumars, Joe
Dungie, Ruth Spigner
Dunn, Ross
Eagle, Arnold Elliott
Early, Robert S.
Edwards, Bessie Regina
Edwards, Verba L.
Enders, Murvin S
Evans, Gwendolyn
Ferrell, Rosie E.
Fields, Felicia J
Fisher, Rubin Ivan

Fitzpatrick, Albert E.
Fleming, Alicia DeLaMothe
Flemming, Lillian Brock
Fletcher, Milton Eric
Ford, Evern D.
Ford, Hilda Eileen
Foster, Jylla Moore
Francis, Dr. E. Aracelis
Franklin, Clarence Frederick
Frazier, Ramona Yancey
Gaskin, Jeanine
Gaston, Linda Saulsby
Gaston, Mack Charles
Gibson, JoAnn
Giles, Terri Lynnette
Glover, Diana M.
Gomez, Dennis Craig
Gordon-Dillard, Joan Yvonne
Grant, Nathaniel
Gray, Brian Anton
Greaux, Cheryl Prejean
Greene, Cecil M
Gudger, Robert Harvey
Guillory, Linda Semien
Gurley, Dr. Helen Ruth
Hall, Terry
Hamer, Dr. Judith Ann
Hardeman, James Anthony
Harmon, M Larry
Harrington, Denise Marion
Harris, Al Carl
Harris, Eugene Edward
Harris, Joseph Elliot, II
Harris, Robert D.
Harris, Robert Eugene Peyton
Harris-Jones, Yvonne
Harrison, Shirley Dindy
Hatchett, William F.
Hawkins, Dr. Lawrence C.
Hawkins, William Douglas
Hawthorne, Kenneth L.
Hayes-Giles, Joyce V.
Haywood, Hiram H., Jr.
Heard, Georgina E
Higgins, Ora A.
Hightower, Michael
Hill, Alfred
Hill, James H
Hill, Leo
Holman, Forest H., Jr.
Holmes, Michael R
Holt, Donald H.
Hopson, Melvin Clarence
Horton, Lemuel Leonard
Howroyd, Janice Bryant
Huff, Loretta Love
Hunigan, Col. Earl
Isaac, Brian Wayne
Jackson, Alfred Thomas
Jackson, Dwayne Adrian
Jackson, Frank
Jackson, James E., Sr.
Jackson, Kevin Allen
Jackson, Yvonne Ruth
James, Donna Anita
James, Dr. Herbert I
James, Peggi C
Jenkins, Joseph Walter
Jenkins, Monica
Johnson, Alvin Roscoe
Johnson, Cleveland, Jr.
Johnson, Michael
Johnson, Milton D.
Johnson, Vaneese
Johnson, Warren S.
Jolly, Mary B
Jones, Dorinda A.
Jones, Lemuel B.
Jones, Ronald Lyman
Jones, Willie
Jordan, Dr. Dedra R
Jordan, John Wesley
Kee, Linda Cooper
Kellogg, George Earl
Killingsworth Finley, Sandra Jean
Kimbrough, Donna L
King, Howard O., Sr.
King, John L
Lane, Nancy L
Lawrence, Ollie, Jr.
Lawrence, Thomas R, Jr.
Lawson, Herman A.
Lee, Kevin Brian
Leigh, Fredric H
Leonard, Gloria Jean
Lewis, Floyd Edward
Lewis, Henry S., Jr.
Lewis, Dr. Meharry Hubbard
Lister, David Alfred

Lister, Willa M
Little, Irene Pruitt
Mackey, John
Mahone, Barbara J.
Marbury, Martha G.
Mardenborough, Leslie A.
Marsh, Ben Franklin
Martin, Sylvia Cooke
Mason, William E.
Mays, Leslie A
McGuire, Raymond J.
McIntosh, Rhodina Covington
Merritt Cummings, Annette
Miller, Frederick A.
Miller, George Carroll, Jr.
Miller, Saundra C
Mills, Rev. Dr. Larry Glenn
Mims, Raymond Everett, Sr.
Mitchell, LeMonte Felton
Moore, Cleotha Franklin
Moragne, Maurice S.
Morrow, Laverne
Moss, Nikki
Newman, Constance Berry
Nunn, John
Oliver-Simon, Gloria Craig
Orr, Clyde Hugh
Osborne, Clayton Henriquez
Patton, Jean E
Pearson, Marilyn Ruth
Peterson, Coleman Hollis
Pickett, Donna A
Polk, Eugene Steven S, Sr.
Pope, Ruben Edward, III
Porter, Gloria Jean
Powell, Bettye Boone
Powell, Kenneth Alasandro
Powell, Robert John
Powers, Clyde J
Procter, Harvey Thornton, Jr.
Reynolds, Andrew Buchanan
Richardson, Joseph
Richardson, Ralph H
Robinson, Jeannette
Robinson, John G
Robinson, Renault Alvin
Robinson, Ronnie W
Robinson, Wendy Raquel
Rogers-Reece, Shirley
Rosenthal, Robert E
Ryan-White, Jewell
Sandidge, Kanita Durice
Saunders, John Edward
Saunders, Vincent E
Savage, Dr. James Edward
Schutz, Andrea Louise
Scott, Dr. Helen Madison Marie Pawne Kinard
Scott, Ruby Dianne
Shawnee, Laura Ann
Shelton, Charles E
Shepard, Linda Irene
Simms, Robert H
Smith, Dolores J
Smith, James, Jr.
Smith, William Fred
Smoot, Carolyn Elizabeth
Somerville, Patricia Dawn
Spearman, Larna Kaye
Spencer, Brenda L
Spencer, Gregory Randall
Spicer, Kenneth, Sr.
Spurlock, Langley Augustine
Staggers, Robin L
Steele, Warren Bell, II
Story, Charles Irvin
Suggs, Dr. Robert Chinelo
Sullivan, Ernest Lee
Summers, Loretta M
Sutton, Dianne Floyd
Swain, James H
Tabb, Roosevelt
Taylor, Johnny C
Taylor, Mildred E. Crosby
Thomas, Samuel
Thomas-Williams, Jovita
Thompson, Jesse M.
Thomson, Cynthia Bramlett
Toliver, Virginia F Dowsing
Turner, Linda Darnell
Turner, Vivian Love
Turnley, Richard Dick, Jr.
Turnquest, Sandra Close
Vannaman, Madi T
Vertreace, Walter Charles
Walker, Tracy A
Walker, Dr. William Sonny
Ward, Lenwood E
Warren, Beth I

Warren, James Kenneth
Washington, David Warren
Washington, Jacqueline Ann
Webb, Joseph
Wells-Davis, Dr. Margie Elaine
White, Alvin, Jr.
Wilds, Jetie Boston, Jr.
Wilkins, Charles O
Willacy, Hazel M
Williams, Annalisa Stubbs
Williams, Dr. Felton Carl
Williams, Harold David
Williams, James
Williams, James E., Jr.
Williams, Janice L.
Williams, Karen Elaine
Williams, Stanley King
Wims, Warner Barry
Wise, William Clinton, Sr.
Womack, Joe Neal, Jr.
Woods, Andre Vincent
Young, Dr. Nancy Wilson
Young, Ollie L

Management/Administration—Purchasing

Armstrong, William F.
Banks, Charlie
Banks, Dr. Lula F.
Brannon, Deborah Dianne
Brown, Tony
Camphor, Michael Gerard
Carey, Carnice
Cargill, Sandra Morris
Clarke, Charlotte
Connor, Dolores Lillie
Corbett, Dr. Alexander E., III
Edwards, Lewis
Fleming, Vernon Cornelius
Freeman, Walter Eugene
Gibson, Wayne Carlton
Hayes-Giles, Joyce V.
Horne, June C
Jackson, Audrey Nabors
Johnson, Wendy Robin
Keitt, Liz Zimmerman
Knott, May
London, Roberta Levy
Marshall, Betty J
Mercer-Pryor, Diana
Merchant, James S, Jr.
Olds, Lydia Michelle
Payne, Ronnie E
Reynolds, James W.
Richardson, Johnny L.
Sheridan, Edna
Smith, Lafayette Kenneth
Strudwick, Lindsey H, Sr.
Sutton, James Carter
Welch, Lolita

Management/Administration—Sales

Alexander, Kelly Miller, Jr.
Anderson, Dr. Marcellus J., Sr.
Baker, Gregory D.
Bankston, Archie M
Barrett, Matthew Anderson
Bassett, Dennis
Baugh, Howard L.
Bell, Vivian
Benton, Phyllis Clora
Birtha, Jessie M.
Bisamunyu, Jeanette
Brooks, Arkles Clarence, Jr.
Brown, Gilbert David, III
Bryant, Franklyn
Burton, Ronald J
Carey, Pearl M.
Chapman, Roslyn C.
Claybrooks, John, Jr.
Clemmons, Dr. Sonya Summerour
Conley, James Sylvester
Cornell, Bob
Coshburn, Henry S., Jr.
Curry, Thomas Lee, Sr.
Daniel, James L.
Daniels, Cecil Tyrone
Davis, Frank
Davis, H. Bernard
DeLeon, Priscilla
Derbigny, Rhoda L
Dorsey, Ivory
Earles, Dr. Rene Martin
Enders, Murvin S
Evans, Elinor Elizabeth
Evers, William Preston
Faison, Sharon Gail
Ferguson, St Julian

Forde, Fraser Philip, Jr.
George, Pauline L
Gresham, Darryl Wayne
Griffiths, Errol D.
Harris, Marion Rex
Harris, Stanley Eugene
Harvey, Sandi
Hawkins, Robert B.
Herron, Bruce Wayne
Holloway, Ardith E
Jackson, Kevin L
Jackson, William Alvin
Jackson, William Ed
James, Gerry M
Johns, Stephen Arnold
Johnson, Mark A
Jones, William Barnard
King, Lawrence C.
Lacy, Donald E., Jr.
Lamar, William
Lawson, Bruce B
Lewis, Robert Alvin
Lindsay, Eddie H S
Marshall, H Jean
Moragne, Maurice S.
Neal, Joseph C., Jr.
Nelson, Kim
Norman, Clifford P
Patrick, Vincent Jerome
Perry, Gary W
Phillips, Basil Oliphant
Pierce, Aaronetta Hamilton
Pillow, Vanita J.
Ray, Rev. Patricia Ann
Ray, Walter I
Reed, Clarence Hammit, III
Richmond, Delores Ruth
Robbins, Carl Gregory Cuyjet
Robinson, Renault Alvin
Rogers, Desiree Glapion
Rogers-Grundy, Ethel W.
Salter, Kwame S
Scott, Jacob Reginald
Seay, Dawn Christine
Small, Isadore, III
Stevens, Barrington
Stokes, Rueben Martine
Tate, Adolphus
Temple, Oney D.
Thurman, Cedric Douglas
Wade, Brent James
Walton, James Donald
Warden, George W
Washington, Lorenza Benard
Waterman, Jeffrey Trevor
West, Bruce Alan
White, James Louis, Jr.
Wiley, Forrest Parks
Wilkinson, Raymond M
Williams, Edward Ellis
Willrich, Emzy James
Wilson, Barbara Jean
Wimbush, Frederick Blair
Woodbeck, Frank Raymond
Woodruff, Jeffrey Robert
Wooten, Carl Kenneth
Wynn, Sylvia J
Young, Raymond, Jr.
Young, Rickey Darnell

Management/Administration—Not Elsewhere Classified (*See Also* Association Management; Educational Administration; Health Services Administration; Labor Union Administration; Sports Coaching/ Training/ Managing/ Officiating)

Abdur-Rahim, Shareef
Abernathy, Ralph David
Adams, Katherine
Adams, Leon
Adams-Ender, Clara Leach
Adkins, William
Alexander, Billye J.
Alexander, Derrick Scott
Alfonso, Pedro
Alice, Miller
Allen, Martha
Allen, Roscoe
Allen, Dr. Winston Earle
Amado, Joseph S.
Amaro, Ruben, Sr.
Anderson, Amelia Veronica
Anderson, Helen Louise
Anderson, Michael Wayne

Anderson, Tyfini Chence
Andrews, Donnovan
Apea, Joseph Bennet Kyeremateng
Ards, Dr. Sheila Diann
Arnold, Clarence Edward, Jr.
Arnold, Wallace C.
Arterbery, Vivian J.
Atchison, Dr. Calvin O.
Bacon, Charlotte Meade
Baker, Gregory D.
Baldwin, Mitchell Cardell
Banton, Linda Wheeler
Barnes, Milton, Jr.
Barnett, Ken
Barnett, Robert
Barr-Bracy, Adrian
Barr-Davenport, Leona
Barry, Harriet S.
Baskerville, Lezli
Bass, Marshall Brent
Bassey, Morgan
Baxter, A. D.
Beard, Darryl H., CPP, C
Beavers, Nathan Howard, Jr.
Bell, Greg
Bell, Harold Kevin
Bell, Leon
Bell, Dr. Marion L
Bell, Ngozi O
Bell, William Vaughn
Bell-Taylor, Wilhelmina
Benford, Edward A
Benjamin, Michael
Bennett, Delora
Benton, Adrienne R.
Benton, Leonard D
Bernard, Sharon Elaine
Berry, Eric
Berryman, Matilene S.
Bibbs, Charles
Bibbs-Sanders, Angelia
Bilson, Carole
Bingham, Porter
Birdine, Steven T
Black, Albert, Jr.
Blackburn, Alpha C.
Blackwell, Joey
Blackwell, Patricia A
Blake, B. David
Bland, Larcine
Blanks, Billy
Blaylock, Ronald E.
Blocker, Tyree C
Blue, Gene C
Bluford, Grady L
Boggan, Daniel, Jr.
Boggs, Donald W
Bolden, Barbaranette T.
Bonds, Kathleen
Booker, Marilyn F
Booth, George Edwin
Borden, Harold F., Jr.
Bost, Fred M.
Bostic, William C
Boswell, Anthony O
Bowles, Barbara Landers
Boyer, Charles E.
Bradford, Andrea
Bradford, Charles Edward
Brewer, Dr. Arthelia J
Brewer, Moses
Bronner, Bernard
Brooks, Carl
Brooks, Sheila Dean
Brothers, Al
Broussard-Simmons, Vanessa
Brown, Alver Haynes
Brown, Alvin
Brown, Carlton E.
Brown, Courtney Coleridge
Brown, Derrick Leslie
Brown, Heather M.
Brown, James H.
Brown, Joe
Brown, Lloyd
Brown, Mary Katherine
Brown, Paul, Jr.
Brown, Paul E. X.
Brown, Robert J., III
Brown, Ronald Wellington
Brown, Dr. Roscoe C.
Brown, Sheila R.
Brown, Virgil E
Brown-Dickerson, Tonia
Browner, Ross D
Bruce, Adriene Kay
Bryant, R. Kelly
Bugg, Robert
Burke, Gary Lamont

Burke, Sterling
Burns, Tommie
Burris, Bertram Ray
Butler, Eula M.
Butler, Patrick Hampton
Butler, Washington Roosevelt, Jr.
Butts, Carlyle A.
Byrd, Alice Turner
Cain, Ruby
Caldwell, Barry H
Calhoun, Gregory Bernard
Calhoun, Kevin
Campbell, Lloyd E
Canty, George
Carroll, Beverly A
Carson, Lois Montgomery
Carter, Vincent G
Carwell, Hattie V
Cash, Bettye Joyce
Chastang, Mark J.
Cheek, Donald Kato
Chicoye, Etzer
Clark, Shirley Lorraine
Clarke, Cheryl
Clarke, Raymond
Clarke, Richard V.
Clements, Fr. George H.
Clingman, Kevin Loren
Clyburn, John B
Cofield, James E
Cole, Harriette
Cole, Mark
Coleman, Faye
Coleman, Kenneth L.
Colin, Kathleen
Collins, Carl
Collins, James H.
Collins, Rodney
Colston, Dr. Wanda M
Compton, James W.
Concholar, Dan
Conyers, Nathan G.
Cook, Robert
Cooper, Larry B
Cooper-Farrow, Valerie
Corley-Blaney, Janice
Coward, Onida Lavoneia
Cox, Keith
Cranford, Dr. Sharon Hill
Crawford, Odel
Crawford, Rainey
Criswell, Arthurine Denton
Crocker, David
Crockett, William F.
Crosby, Loretta
Crosby, Mary
Cross-McClam, Deloris Nmi
Crump, Benjamin L
Crutchfield, Lisa
Culbreath-Manly, Tongila M
Culpepper, Louis S
Cunningham, Don
Custis, Andrea L.
Cwiklinski, Cheryl A
Cyrus-Albritton, Sylvia
Daniel, Martha
Daniels, C. Mackey
Dansby, Jesse L.
Daurham, Ernest
Davis, Adrian
Davis, Agnes Maria
Davis, Anita Louise
Davis, Diane Lynn
Davis, Donald W.
Davis, Frederick D.
Davis, Leon
Davis, William Delford
Debro, Joseph Rollins
DeCosta, Herbert Alexander, Jr.
Delaney, Dallas
Dellums, Ronald V
Diggs, Lawrence J
Dines, George B
Dorsey, Joseph A.
Dottin, Roger Allen
Douglas, Walter Edmond
Duffy, Eugene Jones
Dumas, Karen Marie
Dunn, Dax
Dure, Gerard
Easter, Dr. Marilyn
Edmond, Alfred Adam
Evans, Charlotte A.
Fann, Albert Louis
Felker, Joseph B.
Fernandes, Mary A
Fields, William I, Jr.
Finney, Leon D., Jr.
Fitzgerald-Mosely, Benita

Fontenot, Rev. Albert E., Jr.
Ford, Nathaniel P
Foreman, Doyle
Forster, Cecil R., Jr.
Free, Vicky L
Freeman, V Diane
Fudge, Ann Marie
Galloway, Lula Briggs
Gates, Jacquelyn Burch
Gatling, Chris Raymond
Gibbons, Deveron M
Gilbert, Albert C
Gilford, Vera E
Gill, Dr. Wanda Eileen
Gillis, Theresa McKinzy
Glanville, Douglas Metunwa
Glover, Jonathan A
Goff, Wilhelmina Delores
Goldsberry, Ronald Eugene
Golson, Leon
Gordon, Dr. Joseph G
Graham, Ladell
Grant, Ian
Grante, Jullian Irving
Grayson, John N.
Green, Anita Lorraine
Green, Jarvis R
Green, Larry A
Green, Lester L.
Greene, Frank S
Gregory, Most Rev. Wilton Daniel
Griffin, Bertha L
Griffin, Dr. Betty Sue
Griffin Golden, Dr. Cecilia
Grooms, Dr. Henry Randall
Gudger, Robert Harvey
Guffey, Edith A
Guyton, Louise Green
Hair, Princell
Haley, Damon L
Halfacre, Frank Edward
Hall, Eddie, Jr.
Hall, Kathryn Louise
Hall, Ronald
Hall, Sharon
Hall Tyler, Delora
Hampton, Frank, Sr.
Hancock, Michael B
Hankins, Benjamin B., Jr.
Hannah-Jones, Beverly K
Hare, Julia Reed
Harris, Anthony
Harris, Charles Cornelius
Harris, Cynthia Julian
Harris, David L.
Harris, John, III
Harris, John J.
Harrison, Angela
Harrison, Dr. Robert Walker
Harvey, Dana Colette
Hawthorne, Angel L.
Henderson, Dr. John L.
Hendricks, Jon
Hendrix, Ida
Henry, Dr. Joseph Louis
Herndon, Gloria E.
Heyward, Isaac
Hicks, William L.
Higginbotham, Eve Juliet
Higgs, Frederick C.
Hill, Dr. James A, Sr.
Hilton, Tanya
Hines, Alice Williams
Hines, Courtney
Hodges, Lillian Bernice
Hogan, William E., II
Holland, Spencer H
Hollingsworth, Alfred Delano
Hollins, Leroy
Horne, Marvin L. R., Jr.
Horne, Semmion N
Hubbard, Stanley
Hunt, James, Jr.
Hunt, Samuel D.
Hunter, Clarence Henry
Irvin, Regina Lynette
Jackson, Hal
Jackson, Hiram
Jackson, Rusty
Jeff, DJ Jazzy
Jefferies, Mary
Jefferson, Patricia Ann
Jeffries, Freddie L.
Jenkins, Andrew
Jenkins-Scott, Jackie
Johns, Jamie
Johnson, Beverley Ernestine
Johnson, Clark W
Johnson, Earvin

Johnson, Eunice Walker
Johnson, J. Bernard
Johnson, Jay
Johnson, Jerry L.
Johnson, Joshua
Johnson, Dr. Otis Samuel
Johnson, Renard U
Johnson, Robert Junius
Johnson, Ronald Cornelius
Jones, Cynthia R.
Jones, Duane L.
Jones, H Thomas
Jones, Harold M.
Jones, K. C.
Jones, Nolan E
Jordan, Bettye Davis
Joyner, Tom
Junior, E J
Keglar, Shelvy Haywood
Kellman, Denis Elliott
Kent, Deborah Stewart
Kimbrough, Ted D.
King, Clarence Maurice
King, Dr. James, Jr.
King, W James
Kirby-Davis, Montanges
Knight, Richard, Jr.
Kountze, Vallery J
Lancaster, Ronny B.
Lane, Jerome
Langford, Debra Lynn
Lartigue, Roland E
Latimore, Gail
Lavalais, Lester Joseph
Lawrence, Lonnie R
Leaks, Emanuel, Jr.
Lee, Milton B
Lee, Shalon D
Lee, W. Randolph
Lee-Eddie, Deborah
Leffall, LaSalle D
Leigh, Fredric H
Leonard, Donis
Lester, Isaac
Leverette, Dr. Michelle A
Lewis, Dr. Delano Eugene
Lewis, Edward
Lewis, James R.
Lewis, Jim
Lewis, Jimmy
Lewis, Kirk
Lewis, Lemuel E.
Lewis, Nicole
Lewis, Patricia
Lewis, Richard Allen
Lewis, Vickie J.
Little, Robert E
Logan, Willis Hubert
Logue-Kinder, Joan
London, Dr. Harlan
Long, James Alexander
Lowery, Bobby G
Lucas, Rubye
Lundin-Hughes, Donna
Luney, Percy R
Lyons, Robert P.
Madison, Paula
Manager, Vada O.
Manney, William A.
Marchand, Melanie Annette
Mathews, Lawrence Talbert
McClenic, Patricia Dickson
McCoo, Marilyn
McDaniel, Charles William
McKinnon, Darlene Lorraine
Mckissack, Cheryl Mayberry
McLaren, Douglas Earl
McLean, Rene
McMurry, Dr. Kermit Roosevelt, Jr.
Mease, Quentin R.
Merriweather, Michael Lamar
Millner, Dianne Maxine
Minter, Wilbert Douglas, Sr.
Minyard, Handsel B.
Mitchell, Charles, Jr.
Mobley, Stacey J
Moon, Walter D
Moore, Ralph G
Morris, Wanya
Muhammad, Dr. Tiy-E
Murphy, John H, III
Muse, J Melvin
Nicholas, Bob
Nicholson, Gemma
Nivens, Beatryce Thomasinia
Nixon, James I, Jr.
Noel, Gerald T, Sr.
Norman, James H
Packer, Daniel Fredric, Jr.

Page, John Sheridan
Parham, Johnny Eugene, Jr.
Parker, Harry
Parker-Sawyers, Paula
Parks, Paul
Patton, Jean E
Payne, Debra K
Peerman-Pledger, Vernese Dianne
Penn-Atkins, Barbara A.
Perdreau, Cornelia Whitener
Perkins, Daniel T
Perryman, Lavonia Lauren
Phillips, Rev. Acen L.
Pierson, Kathryn A
Pinkney, William D
Pitts, Brenda S
Porter, Gloria Jean
Powell, Georgette Seabrooke
Powell-Jackson, Dr. Rev. Bernice
Pressley, DeLores
Price, George Baker
Pritchard, Robert Starling, II
Pualani, Gloria
Rankin, Sheila
Rashad, Johari Mahasin
Rayfield, Denise E
Reeves, Louise
Rice, Simeon
Richardson, Lita Renee, Esq.
Rison, Dr. Faye
Roebuck, Gerard Francis
Roshell, Win C
Rowe, Richard L.
Scott, Dr. Gloria Dean Randle
Scott, Dr. Helen Madison Marie Pawne Kinard
Scott, Larry B.
Sewell, Eugene P
Seymour, Cynthia Maria
Sharp, James Alfred
Shatteen, Westina Matthews
Silver-Parker, Esther
Simmons, James, Jr.
Simpson, Dr. Willa Jean
Simpson-Mitchell, Sandra
Sims, John Leonard
Singleton, Kathryn T
Small, Kenneth Lester
Smith, Bob
Smith, Dr. Jane E
Smith, Vida J
Smith, Wayne Franklin
Smith-Epps, E. Paulette
Spain, Hiram, Jr.
Spigner, Marcus E
Springer, Ashton, Jr.
Steed, Tyrone
Stephens, David L.
Steward, Elaine Weddington
Stokes, Herb
Stokes, Patrick
Stovall, Melody S.
Strong, Amanda L
Sudler, Peggy
Swiggett, Ernest L
Syler, M Rene
Talley, Dianne W
Talley, Sarah
Taylor, Tyrone Curtis
Terry, Patricia S
Thomas, Brandy
Thomas, Carl D.
Thomas, Doris
Thomas, John
Thomas, John Charles
Thomas, Josephine
Thomas, Judith
Thomas, Laurita
Thomas, Dr. N Charles
Thomason, William, III
Thompson, Anthony
Thompson, Gail L.
Thornton, Cornelius
Thornton, Otis J.
Thornton, Willie James, Jr.
Tibbs, Hon. Edward A
Torrence, Gwen
Townsend, Ronald
Tramiel, Kenneth Ray, Sr.
Trowell-Harris, Irene
Turley, Louis Edward
Turnquest, Sandra Close
Valentine, Diann
Villarosa, Clara
Wade, James Nathaniel
Walker, Rhonda
Walker, Russell Dewitt
Walls, Fredric T
Warder, John Morgan

Washington, Betty Lois
Washington, Rose Wilburn
Washington, Wendy
Wasow, Omar
Watkins, William, Jr.
Watson, Annie Mae
Watson, Joe
Watts, Marsha
Webb, Reginald
Webb, Stanford
Weiss, Leven C.
Wheeler, Beverly
White, Jo Jo
White, Paul Christopher
Whitehurst, Steven Laroy
Whitlow, Dr. Woodrow, Jr.
Wilkinson, Marie L
Williams, Audrean
Williams, Billy Myles
Williams, Donald Eugene
Williams, George R
Williams, Harvey
Williams, Dr. John L
Williams, W Bill
Williamson, Henry M
Williamson, Keith
Wilson, Henry, Jr.
Wilson, J Ray
Winters, James W
Witherspoon, Addelle
Womack, Richard
Wood, Daisy M
Woodland, Stanley R
Woods, Alison Scott
Woods, Jacqui
Woods, Willie
Wooten, Priscilla A
Wrice, David
Wright, Antoinette D
Wright, Carolyn Elaine
Wright, Crystal Andrea
Wright, Dmitri
Wright, Roberta V. Hughes
Wyche, Keith
Young, Clarence, III
Younge, Ida
Zeitlin, Jide J

Manufacturing—Apparel

Asma, Thomas M
Delice, Ronald
Hall, Harold L
Jones, Carl
Jones, Ernest, Sr.
Jones, Nancy Reed
Jordan, Michael
McCray, Darryl K
michael, b
Miller-Lewis, S Jill
Olugebefola, Dr. Ademola
Polk, Don
Powell, Gayle Lett
Shead, Ken
Terry, Roy
Washington, Ben James, Jr.
Watson, Mary Elaine

Manufacturing— Chemicals and Allied Products

Allen, Eugene, Jr.
Carey, Claire Lamar
Eggleston, Neverett A
Harris, Thomas C.
Haskins, James W., Jr.
Herring, William F.
Hill, George Hiram
Jones, Victoria Gene
King, Lawrence Patrick
Knight, Richard, Jr.
Lewis, Virginia Hill
Matthews, Virgil E.
McMillian, Frank L.
Robertson, Andre Levett
Tucker, Clarence T.

Manufacturing—Drugs and Toiletries

Allen, Eugene, Jr.
Campbell, Carlos, Sr.
Cannon, Chapman Roosevelt, Jr.
Cannon, Dr. Donnie E.
Carter, Edward Earl
Cottrell, Comer J.
Elliott, J. Russell
Foard, Frederick Carter
Givens, Joshua Edmond
Grayson, Jennifer A

James, Gerry M
Johnson, Dr. Charles Edward
Johnson, George Ellis, Sr.
Johnson, Joan B.
Roche, Joyce M
Steele, Joyce Yvonne
Washington, Ben James, Jr.
White, Joseph Councill
Wilson, Natarsha Juliet
Woods, Melvin LeRoy
Woods, Sylvia
Wright, Mark Adrian

Manufacturing— Electrical/Electronics Products

Blackburn, Benjamin Allan, II
Bush, Patricia
Butts, Carlyle A.
Douglass, Robert Lee
Farmer, Forest Jackson, Sr.
Fletcher, James Andrew
Gaffney, Leslie Gale
Gordon, Dr. Joseph G
Gray, Robert Dean
Hall, Harold L
Handy, Lillian B.
Harris, Vernon Joseph
Henderson, Henry Fairfax, Jr.
Hill, Alfred
King, Warren Earl
Lewis, Aisha
Phillips, Jerry P
Pride, William L., Jr.
Wesley, Clemon Herbert, Jr.
Whitlow, Barbara Wheeler

Manufacturing—Food/ Beverages

Abel, Renaul N.
Adams, Albert W.
Andrews, William Phillip
Belton, Y Marc
Brown, L. Don
Burley, Jack L
Carter, Kenneth Gregory
Dames, Sabrina A.
David, George F., III
Davis, Theodis C.
Diggs, Lawrence J
Donald, Arnold Wayne
Edgerton, Brenda Evans
Ferguson, Valerie C
Foushee, Prevost Vest
Gordon, Ronald Eugene
Harris, Charles Cornelius
Haysbert, Raymond Victor
Henry, I Patricia
Jackson, Rusty
Johnson, Eric G
Johnson, Ray
Jones, Wilbert
Lewis, George Ralph
Llewellyn, James Bruce
Morrison, Charles Edward
Palmore, Roderick A
Parker, Claude A.
Parnell, John V, III
Poe, Alfred
Robichaux, Jolyn H.
Scott, Jacob Reginald
Simeus, Dumas M
Smith, Barbara
Sneed, Paula A
Stevens, Barrington
Stewart, Joseph M.
Ware, Carl H.

Manufacturing— Furniture/Fixtures

Dowdy, James H
McQuay, James Phillip

Manufacturing— Industrial/Commercial Machinery

Buford, William Ken M., III
Clardy, William J.
Collins, James H.
Daily, Byron
Eastmond, Arlington Leon, Jr.
Guidry, David
Jennings, Bennie Alfred
Lee, Forrest A, Sr.
McLean, Dennis Ray
Trapp, Donald W.

Wattley, Thomas Jefferson

Manufacturing— Metalworking Industries

Bing, Dave
Byrd, Lumus, Jr.
Carlo, Nelson
Ford, Vernon N.
Guidry, David
Horton, Willie Wattison
Hughes, Johnnie Lee
Newman, Miller Maurice
Snoddy, Anthony L
Sullivan, Ernest Lee
Taylor, Herbert Charles
Tupper, Leon E

Manufacturing—Motor Vehicles

Anderson, Joseph B., Jr.
Bridgeman-Veal, Judy
Clifford, Thomas E.
Crawford, Lawrence Douglas
Curtis, Christopher Paul
Davidson, Fletcher Vernon, Jr.
Davis, Harold R.
Dixon, Dr. Louis Tennyson
Edwards, Gerald Douglas
Edwards, Verba L.
Ellis, Michael G.
Embry, Wayne Richard
Evers, William Preston
Farmer, Forest Jackson, Sr.
Fears, Harding, Jr.
Fletcher, Milton Eric
Fowler, Bennie W
Frame, George J
Frost, William Henry
Goldsberry, Ronald Eugene
Goodwin, Donald Edward
Hall, Alfonzo Louis
Hall, Elliott Sawyer
Herring, William F.
Howard, Norman
Hunter, Clarence Henry
Irby, Mary
Jensen, Dr. Ray M
Jensen, Renaldo Mario
Jones, Sen. Emanuel Davie
Jones, Jake
Kent, Deborah Stewart
Kornegay, William F
Latimer, Frank Edward
Lewis, W Howard
McLaughlin, LaVerne Laney
Merchant, James S, Jr.
Mullens, Delbert W
Newman, Paul Dean
Nixon, James I, Jr.
Perry, Gary W
Pickard, Vivian
Preston, Franklin DeJuanette
Proctor, Earl D.
Reeves, Julius Lee
Richie, Leroy C.
Sanders, Barbara A.
Stevens, Warren Sherwood
Thorns, Odail, Jr.
Turner, Harry Glenn
Verbal, Claude A
Welburn, Edward Thomas, Jr.

Manufacturing—Paper and Allied Products

Bryant, Clarence W.
Erving, John
Foreman, Joyce Blacknall
Kendrick, L John, Sr.
McIver, Margaret Hill
Tunstall, Richard Clayton
Wilson, Joseph
Worth, Janice Lorraine

Manufacturing—Textile Mill Products

Crawley, Oscar Lewis
Parker, Harry
Patton, Marvcus Raymond
Thornton, Cora Ann Barringer

Manufacturing—Not Elsewhere Classified

Addy, Tralance Obuama
Bates, Robert E., Jr.
Clyburn, John B
Davis, Herman E.
Days, Bertram Maurice
El Wilson, Barbara

Fields, Stanley
Greene, Clifton S.
Hall, Harold L
Hill, Rufus S.
Hogan, William E., II
Jackson, Dwayne Adrian
Kennedy, Howard E.
King, Hulas H
King, William Frank
Knott, Dr. Albert Paul
Knox, George L
Lewis, George Ralph
Long, James, Jr.
Lovelace, John C.
Marshall, Jonnie Clanton
Mathew, Knowles
McLaughlin, Benjamin Wayne
McLean, Dennis Ray
Melton, Frank E
Osborne, Clayton Henriquez
Pitts, Brenda S
Reddick, Mark A
Rush, Sonya C
Smith, Wilson Washington, III
Stone, Reese J
Thomas, Roy L.
Waddy, Jude
Woods, Henry, Jr.
Worth, Janice Lorraine
Young, Charles Lemuel

Marketing
See **Advertising/Promotion; Management/Administration— Advertising/Marketing/Public Relations**

Mathematics

Black, Lucius
Brown, Furney Edward, Jr.
Cash-Rhodes, Winifred E.
Dale, Clamma Churita
Earl, Dr. Archie William
Emeagwali, Philip
Fillyaw, Leonard David
Hedgley, David Rice, Jr.
Houston, Dr. Johnny L
Howell, Amaziah, III
Hughes, Isaac Sunny
Johnson, Dr. Martin Leroy
Johnson, Dr. Raymond Lewis
Jordan, Patricia
King, Calvin E.
King, Dr. John Q. Taylor, Sr.
Lahr, Dr. Charles Dwight
Mabson, Glenn T
McAdoo, Henry Allen
McLaurin, Jasper Etienne
Mickens, Dr. Ronald Elbert
Monteith, Dr. Henry C.
Morton, Norman
Porter, Bishop Henry Lee
Richards, Winston Ashton
Samuels, Charlotte
Thomas, Dr. Ronald F.
Tisdale, Dr. Henry Nehemiah
Vance, Dr. Irvin E
Wallace, Milton De
Waller, Eunice McLean
Walton, Dr. Harriett J.
Williams, Dr. Willie Elbert

Medicine—Anesthesiology

Brown, Emery N.
Clark, Dr. Morris Shandell
Dickey, Bernestine D.
Lord, Clyde Ormond
Nichols, David G
Primm, Dr. Beny Jene
Yarn, Barbara Lynne Ivey

Medicine—Cardiology

Anderson, Arnett Artis
Banks, Dr. Tazewell
Barnes, Dr. Boisey O
Batties, Dr. Paul Terry
Belton, C Ronald
Charleston, Gomez, Jr.
Cooper, Dr. Edward Sawyer
Cutliff, John Wilson
Daniels, Curtis A.
Ellis, Tellis B., III
Ferdinand, Dr. Keith C
Fletcher, Dr. Anthony M
Fontaine, John M.
Gibson, Harris, Jr.
Grant, Augustus O
Haywood, Dr. L. Julian

Kemp, Emmerlyne Jane
Kenoly, Bingo
Kenoly, Samuel
Keys, Alicia
Kimble, Bettye Dorris
Lasley, Phelbert Quincy, III
Lateef, Dr. Yusef
Latifah, Queen
Lee, William James Edwards, III
Leon, Dr. Tania Justina
Lewis, Dawnn
Lewis, George E.
Lewis, Ramsey Emanuel
Livingston-White, Dr. Deborah J H
Mahal, Taj
Marsalis, Delfeayo
Marsalis, Ellis, Jr.
Martin, Christopher
May, Dickey R.
Mayfield, JoAnn H O
McCrary, Michael
McFall, Mary
McGill, Michele Nicole Johnson
McKissack, Perri Alette
McKnight, Brian
McLean, Rene
MC Lyte
McNeil, DeeDee
McNeil, Ernest Duke
McNeill, Cerves Todd
Moore, Carman Leroy
Moore, Kermit
Morgan, Meli'sa
Mumford, Jeffrey Carlton
Najee, J.
Nelson, Prince Rogers
Newman, David, Jr.
Nicholas, Brenda L.
Nicholas, Philip
Norton, Cheryl Week
Osby, Patricia Roberta
Ousley, Harold Lomax
Owens, James Robert
Parker, Lawrence Krisna
Parker, Ray, Jr.
Parris, Rev. Alvin, III
Pate, John W., Sr.
Patterson, Willis Charles
Patton, Antwan Andre
Preston, Edward Lee
Price, John Elwood
Priester, Julian Anthony
Pritchard, Robert Starling, II
Qamar, Nadi Abu
Reeves, Dianne
Reid, Antonio
Richards, DeLeon Marie
Richie, Lionel Brockman, Jr.
Riley, Teddy
Rivera, Maxwell
Roach, Maxwell Lemeul
Rodgers, Carolyn Marie
Rodgers, Nile Gregory
Rogers-Jone, Kelis
Rollins, Walter Theodore
Roper, Deidre
Rudd-Moore, Dorothy
Rushen, Patrice Louise
Russell, George A
Sabree, Clarice S
Scott, Jill
Scott-Heron, Gil
Shamborguer, Naima
Shepherd, Berisford
Simpson, India Arie
Simpson, Valerie
Smith, Hale
Smith, Howlett P.
Smith, James Todd
Smith, Will
Staton, Canzetta Maria
Stone, Angie
Sure, Al B.
Tatum, James
Taylor, William Edward
Thomas, Irma
Thomas, Joe Lewis
Thomas, Robert Charles
Tillis, Dr. Frederick C.
Tisdale, Wayman Lawrence
Too Short, a
Turner, Tina
Tyner, Alfred McCoy
Tyson, Ron
Walbey, Theodosia Emma Draher
Walker, Dr. George T.
Walker, Dr. Gregory T S
Walker, Jimmie
Walters, Ronald L., Jr.

Wansel, Dexter Gilman
Washington, Keith
Waters, Crystal
White, Dr. Don Lee
White, Karyn
White, Maurice
Williams, Deniece
Williams, Saul
Wilson, Bryan
Wilson, Charlie
Wilson, Frank Edward
Wilson, Gerald Stanley
Wilson, Natalie
Wilson, Dr. Olly W.
Wilson, Shanice
Winans, CeCe
Winbush, Angela
Woods, Philip Wells

Music—Conducting/Directing
Alexander, Otis Douglas
Anderson, Fred
Anderson, Dr. Thomas Jefferson
Atkins, Dr. Carl J
Bagley, Dr. Peter B E
Baker, David Nathaniel
Berry, Reginald Francis
Betha, Mason Durrell
Blake, Jennifer Lynn
Brice, Percy A., Jr.
Brooks, Norman Leon
Burnim, Mellonee Victoria
Carr, Kurt
Carter, Roland
Christian, Eric Oliver, Jr.
Clansy, Cheryl D.
Costen, Dr. Melva Wilson
Curtis, Marvin Vernell
Davis, Hon. Arrie W.
Davis, Louis Garland
Dennard, Brazeal Wayne
DePreist, James Anderson
Dixon, William R.
Dunner, Dr. Leslie Byron
Edmonds, Kenneth
Elliott, Anthony Daniel
Eubanks, Kevin
Fears, Emery Lewis, Jr.
Felder, Harvey
Fischer, William S.
Foster, Dr. William Patrick
Freeman, Dr. Paul D.
Gainer, Prof. John F
Hampton, Edwin Harrell
Harris, Dr. Carl Gordon
Harris, Dr. Robert Allen
Harris, Dr. Walter
Harvey, Raymond
Hill, Rev. Dr. Robert Lee
Holland, Brian
Hunt, Darrold Victor
Hurte, Leroy E.
Jackson, Isaiah Allen
Jeffers, Jack
Jones, Harold M.
Jones, Quincy Delight
Kimble, Bettye Dorris
Kirk-Duggan, Cheryl Ann
Kyle, Genghis
Lane, Johnny Lee
Lawhorn, John B.
Lee, William James Edwards, III
Leon, Dr. Tania Justina
Mabrey, Prof. Marsha Eve
Mobley, Charles Lamar
Moore, Carman Leroy
Moore, Kermit
Morgan, Michael
Morris, Nathan Bartholomew
Ousley, Harold Lomax
Pate, John W., Sr.
Pollard, Alfonso McInham
Porter, Karl Hampton
Preston-Williams, Rodena
Roberts, Kay George
Rushen, Patrice Louise
Smith, Andre Raphel
Smith, Howlett P.
Stripling, Dr. Luther
Walden, Narada Michael
Walker, Charles E
Ward, Calvin Edouard
Ward, Daniel
Waters, Willie Anthony
White, Clayton Cecil

White, Dr. Don Lee
Wilson, Natalie

Music—Instrumental
Adams, Armenta Estella
Albright, Gerald Anthony
Ali, Rashied
Allen, Sanford
Arties, Walter Eugene, III
Austin, Dallas
Ayers, Roy
Bates, Arthur Verdi
Benoit, Edith B.
Benson, George
Benson, Hayward J., Jr.
Berry, Chuck
Black, Dr. Malcolm Mazique
Blake, Carl LeRoy
Bond, Wilbert
Bradley, Hilbert L.
Brice, Percy A., Jr.
Broach, S. Elizabeth Johnson
Brooks, Avery Franklin
Brown, Tyrone W.
Burrell, Kenneth Earl
Burton-Lyles, Blanche
Cade, Walter, III
Campbell, Thomas W.
Carrington, Terri Lyne
Chapman, Tracy
Christie, Angella
Clarke, Stanley Marvin
Clemons, Clarence
Clouden, LaVerne C.
Coleman, George Edward
Collins, Bootsy
Cray, Robert
Crutcher, Dr. Ronald Andrew
Curson, Theodore
Dara, Olu
Davis, Dr. Arthur David
Davis, Guy
Dickerson, Lowell Dwight
Diddley, Bo
Dixon, William R.
Dozier, Morris Cicero
Duke, George M.
Elliott, Anthony Daniel
Ellis, Ernest W.
Eubanks, Kevin
Eubanks, Dr. Rachel Amelia
Fears, Emery Lewis, Jr.
Foster, Dr. Frank B., III
Foster, Dr. William Patrick
Fuller, Curtis D.
Gaines, Grady
Garner, Charles
Gholson, Dr. General James
Giles, Charlotte Emma
Gill, Samuel A.
Graham, Larry, Jr.
Hampton, Edwin Harrell
Hancock, Herbie
Handy, John Richard
Hanna, Cassandra H.
Harris, Corey
Harris, Shawntae
Heath, James E.
Hence, Marie J.
Holder, Laurence
Hunter, Edwina Earle
Hurd, David James
Hurd, Dr. James L P
Hurst, Robert
Ibrahim, Abdullah
Isley, Ernie
Isley, Marvin
Jamal, Ahmad
James, Dr. Jimmie, Jr.
Jean, Nelust Wyclef
Jeffers, Jack
Jones, Hank
Jones, Quincy Delight
Jordan, Robert
Jordan, Robert A.
Jordan, Stanley
Kemp, Emmerlyne Jane
Kennedy, Prof. Matthew W.
Keys, Alicia
King, B. B.
King, Clarence Maurice
Kyle, Genghis
Lane, Johnny Lee
Lasley, Phelbert Quincy, III
Lawrence, Azar Malcolm
Lee, William James Edwards, III
Lewis, Ramsey Emanuel
Majors, Jeff
Marsalis, Branford

Marsalis, Ellis, Jr.
Marsalis, Jason
Marsalis, Wynton
McBride, James
McElrath-Frazier, Wanda Faith
McGill, Michele Nicole Johnson
McNeill, Cerves Todd
Mencer, Dr. Ernest James
Miller, Horatio C.
Montgomery, Toni-Marie
Moore, Johnny B
Moore, Kevin
Morgan, Clyde Alafiju
Najee, J.
Nelson-Holgate, Gail Evangelyn
Northern, Robert A.
Osby, Gregory Thomas
Owens, James Robert
Parham, Frederick Russell
Payton, Nicholas
Pettaway, Charles
Petty, Oscar
Pilot, Ann Hobson
Pollard, Alfonso McInham
Pratt, Awadagin
Preston, Edward Lee
Priester, Julian Anthony
Pritchard, Robert Starling, II
Qamar, Nadi Abu
Redman, Joshua
Reid, Vernon
Rene, Althea
Riley, Teddy
Roach, Maxwell Lemeul
Roberts, Marcus
Robinson, Melvin P.
Rush, Otis
Rushen, Patrice Louise
Sabree, Clarice S
Sample, Joe
Santos, Henry Joseph
Shepherd, Berisford
Smallwood, Richard
Smith, Hale
Smith, Howlett P.
Smith, John L, Jr.
Stevenson, Russell A.
Summer, Donna
Swindell, Dr. Warren C.
Tate, Grady Bernard
Terry, Clark
Terry, Saunders
Thigpen, Edmund Leonard
Thompson, Marcus Aurelius
Tisdale, Wayman Lawrence
Tolliver, Charles
Turner-Givens, Ella Mae
Tyner, Alfred McCoy
Walker, Dr. Gregory T S
Walker-Slocum, Frances
Walters, Ronald L., Jr.
Walton, Dr. Ortiz Montaigne
Wansel, Dexter Gilman
Watts, Andre
Whalum, Kirk
White, Maurice
Wilkins, Dr. Leona B.
Williams, Earl
Williams, Junius W.
Williams, Larry
Wilson, Gerald Stanley
Winston, Sherry E
Wonder, Stevie
Woods, Philip Wells
Yancyy, Robert
York, Vincent

Music—Vocal
Abdul, Raoul
Adams, Oleta
Adams, Yolanda
Addison, Adele
Albert, Donnie Ray
Alexander, Dorothy Dexter
Ali, Tatyana Marisol
Allah, Rakim
Allen, Betty
Allison, Verne
Alston, Gerald
Archer, Michael Eugene
Armstrong, Vanessa Bell
Arnold, David
Arnold, Monica Denise
Arroyo, Prof. Martina
Ashford, Nickolas
Atkins, Erica
Atkins, Tina
Austin, Patti
Badu, Erykah

Bailey, Philip
Baker, Anita
Ballard, Shareese Renee
Barcliff, Melvin
Barksdale, Chuck
Battle, Kathleen
Baylor, Helen
Belafonte, Harry
Bell, Ricky
Belle, John Otis
Benson, George
Benymon, Chico
Berry, Benjamin Donaldson
Berry, Chuck
Beverly, Creigs C.
Beverly, Frankie
Blake, Jennifer Lynn
Bland, Bobby Blue
Blige, Mary J.
Blow, Kurtis
Bodrick, Leonard Eugene
Bow Wow, Lil
Braxton, Toni
Brooks, Avery Franklin
Brown, Bobby
Brown, Dr. Uzee, Jr.
Bryson, Peabo
Burke, Solomon
Butler, Jerry
Cade, Walter, III
Caesar, Shirley
Cage, Athena
Campbell, Tevin Jermod
Cantrell, Blu
Carey, Mariah
Carrington, Terri Lyne
Carroll, Diahann
Carter, John E.
Chapman, Tracy
Christian, Eric Oliver, Jr.
Clark, Rosalind K.
Clark-Sheard, Karen
Clouden, LaVerne C.
Cole, Natalie
Collins, Bootsy
Combs, Sean J
Cook, Victor Trent
Costen, Dr. Melva Wilson
Crouch, Andrae Edward
Cummings, Terry
Davis, Billy
Davis, Clarence A.
Davis, Rev. Clifton Duncan
Davis, Guy
Davis, Louis Garland
Davy, Gloria
Day, Morris
DeBarge, El
Denton, Sandi
Desert, Alex
DeVoe, Ronald Boyd, Jr.
Diddley, Bo
Digga, Rah
Dixon, Rodrick
Dobbs, Mattiwilda
Domino, Fats
Douglas, Ashanti Shequoiya
Douglas, Elizabeth (Betty) Asche
Douglas, Suzzanne
Downing, Will
Dre
Easton, Earnest Lee
Elliott, Missy
Ellis, Terry Lynn
Estes, Simon Lamont
Estill, Dr. Ann H M
Evans, Ernest
Evans, Faith Renee
Falana, Lola
Faulkner, Geanie
Fifty Cent
Fischer, Lisa
Flack, Roberta
Franklin, Aretha Louise
Franklin, Kirk
Freelon, Nnenna
G, Warren
Gainer, Prof. John F
Gamble, Kenneth
Garrett, Denise Eileen
Gary, Kathye J.
Gaynor, Gloria
Gill, Johnny
Ginuwine
Gist, Carole Anne-Marie
Golson, Benny
Grandmaster Flash
Graves, Denyce Antoinette
Gray, Macy
Green, Al

Music—Not Elsewhere Classified

Nursing

Sanders, Sally Ruth
Sands, Rosetta F
Shaw, Ferdinand
Starks, Doris Nearror
Steele, Ruby L
Stevenson, Lillian
Stewart, Dr. Bess
Stokes, Dr. Lillian Gatlin
Strong, Amanda L
Taylor, Carol
Thomas, Mary A.
Thompson, Geraldine
Thompson, Regina
Troupe-Frye, Betty Jean
Tunley, Naomi Louise
Turner, Geneva
Wheeler, Shirley Y.
Whitaker, Von Frances
White, Christine Larkin
White-Parson, Willar F
Williams, Dr. Betty Smith
Williams, Dorothy Daniel
Wills, Dorothy
Winfrey, Audrey Theresa
Woods, Dr. Bernice
Woods, Geneva Holloway
Worrell, Kaye Sydnell
Worth, Janice Lorraine
Wykle, May Louise Hinton
Wynn, LaMetta K

Nutrition
Barber, Hargrow Dexter
Brown, Lillie Richard
Davis, Ronald R.
Ford, Nancy Howard
Forsythe, Hazel
Gaffney, Michele Elizabeth
Jerome, Dr. Norge Winifred
Johnson, Addie Collins
Lockett, Alice Faye
Osby, Parico Green
Ross, Martha Erwin
Shields-Jones, Esther L M

Oceanography
Labat, Eric Martin

Optometry
Beasley, Jesse C.
Bynum, Dr. Raleigh Wesley
Coates, Janice E.
Hicks, Dr. Clayton Nathaniel
Howard, Keith L.
Jackson, Felix W.
Johnson, Linda Dianne
Lambert, Dr. Benjamin J., III
Marshall, Dr. Edwin Cochran
Newsome, Dr. Paula Renee
Powell, C. Clayton
Saunders, Dr. Meredith Roy
Shipp, Dr. Melvin Douglas
Troup, Elliott Vanbrugh
Washington, Dr. James Edward
Williams, John R.

Personnel Management
See **Management/
Administration—Personnel/
Training/Labor Relations**

Pharmacology
Coram, Willie Mae
Draine, Michael
Stickney, Janice L.
West, William Lionel

Pharmacy
Beasley, Dr. Eula Daniel
Bynum, Horace Charles, Sr.
Carey, Wayne E
Dawkins, Tammy C.
Frazier, Regina Jollivette
Grace, Dr. Marcellus
Harper, Curtis
Harrison, James, Jr.
Hebert, Zenebework Teshome
Hills, James Bricky
Jeter, Delores DeAnn
Kendall, Michelle Katrina
King, Dr. Rosalyn Cain
Ladson, Dr. Louis Fitzgerald
Logan, Lloyd
Mims, Beverly Carol
Sampson, Robert R
Scott, Dr. Kenneth Richard
Sims, Theophlous Aron

Williams, Edward Ellis
Wineglass, Henry

Philanthropy
Adams, Betty Phillips
Block, Dr. Leslie S.
Burton-Lyles, Blanche
Carson, Emmett D.
Dean, Diane D
Edwards, Claudia L.
Epps, Evern Cooper
Gordon, Alexander H., II
Groff, Regis F.
Lowry, William E, Jr.
Martin, Jesse Lamont
McFadden, Ernest
McIlwain, Nadine Williams
Millines Dziko, Trish
Moore, Annie Jewell
Petett, Freddye J Webb
Ray, Rev. Patricia Ann
Segree, E Ramone
Sheppard, Donald
Small, Kenneth Lester
Sockwell, Oliver R, Jr.
Stanley, Donna Jones
Stewart, Ruth Ann
Turner, Vivian Love
Wharton, Dr. Clifton Reginald, Jr.
Widener, Warren Hamilton
Wilkerson, Prof. Margaret Buford
Williams, Dr. Everett Belvin
Williams-Taitt, Patricia Ann
Wilson, Ronald M
Woodley, Arto

Photography (See Also Journalism—Photojournalism)
Alston, Kwaku
Barboza, Anthony
Bland, Heyward
Brown, Ernest Douglas
Caines, Bruce Stuart
Daniel, Mary Reed
DeCarava, Roy Rudolph
Farmer, Sharon
Fournier, Collette V.
Grant, Claude DeWitt
Hardison, Ruth Inge
Henderson, Leroy W., Jr.
Herndon, Craig Garris
Higgins, Chester Archer, Jr.
Hinton, Christopher Jerome
Holloway, Joaquin Miller, Jr.
Johnson, Joshua
Jones, Brent M.
Julian, Percy L., Jr.
Lewis, Matthew
Marshall, Eric A
Marshall, Pluria W.
McNair, Chris
Moore, Lenard Duane
Morgan, Monica Alise
Morris, Major
Moutoussamy-Ashe, Jeanne
Parker, Maryland Mike
Pitts, George Edward
Posey, John R
Powell, Clarence Dean, Sr.
Purdee, Nathan
Ramsey, Freeman, Jr.
Reide, Saint Clair Eugene, Jr.
Sandoval, Dolores S.
Sherman, Edward Forrester
Teasley, Ronald
White, Kenneth Eugene, Sr.
Williams, Clarence
Williams, Prof. Daniel Salu

Physics/Astronomy
Basri, Gibor
Bragg, Robert Henry, II
Bransford, Paris
Calbert, Roosevelt
Campbell, George, Jr.
Carruthers, Dr. George Robert
Carwell, Hattie V
Chapman, Dr. Gilbert Bryant
Crutcher, Sihon Heath
Day, John H
Godbee, Thomasina D.
Govan, Ronald M.
Hargraves, Col. William Frederick, II
Harris, Dr. Bernard A.
Jackson, Dr. Keith Hunter
Jackson, Dr. Shirley Ann
Johnson, Dr. Anthony Michael

Jupiter, Clyde Peter
Lewis, Dr. Lonzy James
McGowan, Anna-Maria
Mickens, Dr. Ronald Elbert
Mickey, Dr. Gordon Eugene
Noel, Gerald T, Sr.
Peery, Benjamin Franklin, Jr.
Rodgers, Vincent G
Sebhatu, Dr. Mesgun
Sergent, Ernest, Jr.
Sessoms, Allen Lee
Taylor, Julius H

Physiology
Ball, Wilfred R.
Bond, Vernon
Diji, Dr. Augustine Ebun
Dunbar, Joseph C.
Elcock, Dr. Claudius Adolphus Rufus
Franklin, Dr. Renty Benjamin
Hopkins, Thomas Franklin
McGruder, Dr. Charles E.
Simmons, Prof. John Emmett
Wash, David Keane
Weddington, Dr. Wilburn Harold, Sr.
White-Perkins, Denise M
Winston, Dr. Neil Emerson

Podiatry
Brown, Bernice H.
Harris, John Clifton
Martin, Edward Anthony
Nelson, Nathaniel W.
Newland, Dr. Zachary Jonas
Singleton, Dr. James LeRoy, Jr.
Turner, George R.

Political Rights Activism
See **Activism, Political/Civil/
Social Rights**

Political Science
Bailey, Harry Augustine, Jr.
Bishop, Sanford D
Brooks, Rosemary Bittings
Brown, Ronald Edward
Callender, Lucinda R.
Carey, Addison, Jr.
Carter, William Beverly
Clemons, Dr. Michael L
Colston, Dr. Freddie C.
Daniels, Terry L
Davis, Dr. Doris Ann
Davis, John Alexander
Davis, Dr. Marilyn Ann Cherry
Dember, Jean Wilkins
De Veaux, Stuart Samuel
Downie, Dr. Winsome Angela
Easton, Earnest Lee
Eke, Kenoye Kelvin
Flemming, Dr. Charles Stephen
Fogam, Margaret Hanorah
Gill, Nia H
Greene, Jehmu
Hall, Dr. Jarvis
Harris, Duchess
Henry, Dr. Charles Patrick, III
Herman, Alexis Margaret
Hudspeth, Gregory Charles
Irogbe, Kema
Jackson, Dorothy R., J.D.
Jacobs, Hazel A.
Johnson, Cleveland, Jr.
Johnson, Willard Raymond
Keller, Dr. Edmond Joseph
Larkin, Dr. Byrdie A.
Lee, Dr. Margaret Carol
Lee, Dr. Silas, III
Lewis, Dr. Angela K.
Lightfoot, Simone Danielle
Maddox-Simms, Margaret Johnnetta
Marsh, Dr. Pearl-Alice
Mathis, Walter Lee
Matthews, Mary Joan
McClain, Dr. Paula Denice
McIntosh, James E.
Meeks, Reginald Kline
Miller, James Arthur
Moreland, Dr. Lois Baldwin
Morris, Celeste
Morrison, James W.
Onwudiwe, Ebere C
Rice, Dr. Mitchell F
Schexnider, Dr. Alvin J
Sessoms, Allen Lee
Silver, Dr. Joseph Howard
Smith, Robert Charles
Smith, Robert London

Spruce, Kenneth L
Stallings, Henry E
Starks, Robert Terry
Strickland-Hill, Dr. Marva Yvonne
Tanter, Raymond
Tolliver, Ned, Jr.
Walton, Hanes
Ward, Everett Blair
Ward, Dr. James Dale
White, Yolanda Simmons
Wilson, Hugh A.
Wingfield, Dr. Harold Lloyd
Wright, Dr. Larry L

Printing
See **Publishing/Printing**

Producing/Directing (Performing Arts)
See **Directing/Producing (Performing Arts)**

Promotion
See **Advertising/Promotion**

Psychology
Abdullah, Samella Berry
Abston, Nathaniel, Jr.
Adair, Alvis V.
Adams, Dr. Clarence Lancelot, Jr.
Adams, Jean Tucker
Akbar, Dr. Na
Alloy, Dr. Valerie
Anderson, Dr. James Alan
Andrews, James E.
Andrews, William Pernell
Anthony-Perez, Dr. Bobbie M.
Appleby-Young, Sadye Pearl
Atkinson, Eugenia Calwise
Barrett, Dr. Ronald Keith
Bates, Percy
Bell, Dr. Robert L.
Berry, Fredrick Joseph
Block, Carolyn B.
Bobbitt, Leroy
Bowman, Joseph E.
Boyd, Julia A
Boyd, Melba Joyce
Boykin, A. Wade, Jr.
Brown, Beatrice S.
Brown, Dr. Joyce F.
Brown, Mortimer
Burdette, LaVere Elaine
Burlew, Ann Kathleen
Burnett, Dr. Myra N
Burns, Felton
Byrd, Katie W.
Carey, Patricia M
Carrington, Christine H.
Carter, Allen C.
Carter, Lamore Joseph
Casanova, Dr. Gisele M
Chisholm, June Faye
Chisum, Gloria Twine
Cissoko, Alioune Badara
Clark, Dr. Fred Allen
Coleman, Melvin D.
Collins-Eaglin, Dr. Jan Theresa
Colyer, Dr. Sheryl Lynn
Conwill, William Louis
Copeland, Betty Marable
Courtney, Dr. Cassandra Hill
Dalton, Raymond Andrew
Daniel, Dr. Jessica Henderson
Dartson, Dr. Myrna
Davis, Hon. Arrie W.
Davis, Dr. Arthur David
Davis, Lance Roosevelt
Dember, Jean Wilkins
Dent, Dr. Preston L.
Doss, Dr. Juanita King
Dunn, Marvin
Early, Robert S.
Edwards, Thomas Oliver
Eleazer, George Robert, Jr.
Ferguson, Dr. Robert Lee, Sr.
Frazier, Leon
Freeman, Kimberley Edelin
Fresh, Edith McCullough
Gallagher, Dr. Abisola Helen
Gary, Melvin L
Gaston, Dr. Arnett W
Gibbs, Dr. Jewelle Taylor
Gilbert, Christopher
Gray-Little, Dr. Bernadette
Greene, Dr. Beverly A
Griffin, Jean Thomas
Hall, Addie June

Hall, Dr. Julia Glover
Hammond, Dr. W Rodney
Hardy-Hill, Edna Mae
Hare, Dr. Nathan
Harper, William Thomas, III
Harris, Jasper William
Heard, Georgina E
Henderson, Virginia Ruth McKinney
Hicks, Dr. Ingrid Diann
Hines, Laura M.
Holland, Spencer H
Holmes, Dorothy E
Holt, Dr. Edwin J.
Hooker, Olivia J
Horton, Dr. Carrell Peterson
Hunt, Dr. Portia L
Ifalase, Dr. Olusegen
Jackson, Dr. Anna Mae
Jackson, Dr. Hermoine Prestine
Jackson, Dr. James Sidney
Jeffrey, Ronnald James
Jenkins, Dr. Adelbert Howard
Jenkins, Louis E
Jennings, Lillian Pegues
Johnson, William L.
Jones, Annie Lee
Jones, Arnold Pearson
Jones, Dr. Ferdinand Taylor
Jones, James McCoy
Jordan, Patricia
Keglar, Shelvy Haywood
Kindall, Dr. Luther Martin
Kirkland, Sharon Elaine
Leek, Sandra D
Leland, Joyce F.
Levermore, Dr. Monique A
Lopez, D Jacqueline
Lyles, William K.
Majors, Richard G
Malone, Rosemary C
Martin, Dr. Juanita K
Maynard, Dr. Edward Samuel
Mays, Dr. Vickie M
Mays, William, Jr.
McGee, Gloria Kesselle
McGehee, Nan E
Miller-Jones, Dr. Dalton
Mills, Doreen C
Minor, Jessica
Mitchell, Sharon L
Morris, Dr. Dolores Orinskia
Munday, Dr. Cheryl Casselberry
Murfree, Dr. Joshua, Jr.
Myers, Dr. Ernest Ray
Neal-Barnett, Angela M.
Newhouse, Quentin
Nichols, Edwin J.
Norton, Dr. Aurelia Evangeline
Outlaw, Dr. Patricia Anne
Payne, Dr. June P
Payne, Margaret Ralston
Pennywell, Phillip, Jr.
Perry, Dr. Aubrey M.
Peters, Dr. James Sedalia, II
Peters, Dr. Rev. Pamela Joan
Peters, Sheila Renee
Petrick, PhD, Jane Allen
Petty, Dr. Rachel Monteith
Pierce, William Dallas
Plummer, Dr. Diane Loretta
Polite, Dr. Craig K., II
Porche-Burke, Lisa
Poussaint-Hudson, Dr. Ann Ashmore
Pugh, Dr. Roderick Wellington
Ray, Jacqueline Walker
Roberts, Dr. Terrence James
Robinson, Jane Alexander
Ruffin, Janice E.
Saddler, Elbert M
Savage, Horace Christopher
Savage, Dr. James Edward
Shell, Dr. Juanita
Shipp, Pamela Louise
Sikes, Dr. Melvin Patterson
Smith, Dr. James Almer, III
Smith, Dr. Marie Evans
Somerville, Dr. Addison Wimbs
Spencer, Prof. Margaret Beale
Stokes, Julie Elena
Suite, Dr. Derek H
Taborn, Dr. John Marvin
Tate, Lenore Artie
Tatum, Dr. Beverly Daniel
Taylor, Dr. Sandra Elaine
Terrell, Dr. Francis
Thomas, John Henderson, III
Thompson, Dr. Beatrice R
Thornton, Dozier W.
Tucker, Leota Marie
Tucker, Dr. M Belinda

Tucker, Dr. Samuel Joseph
Turner, Castellano Blanchet
Vaughans, Kirkland Cornell
Vogel, Dr. Roberta Burrage
Warfield-Coppock, Nsenga
Wells-Davis, Dr. Margie Elaine
West, Dr. Gerald Ivan
Whitaker, Von Frances
White, Dr. Tommie Lee
Whitney, Dr. W Monty
Wilderson, Dr. Frank B., Jr.
Wilderson, Thad
Williams, Dr. Daniel Edwin
Williams, Dr. Everett Belvin
Williams, Willie S
Wilson, Dr. Sodonia Mae
Winfield, Dr. Linda Fitzgerald
Workman, Aurora Felice Antonette
Wyatt, Gail E.
Young, Dr. Carlene Herb
Young, Josef A.

Public Administration
See **Government Service (Elected or Appointed)/ Government Administration— City; Government Service (Elected or Appointed)/ Government Administration— County; Government Service (Elected or Appointed)/ Government Administration— State; Government Service (Elected or Appointed)/ Government Administration— Federal; Government Service (Elected or Appointed)/ Government Administration— Not Elsewhere Classified**

Public Utilities
Adderly, T. C., Jr.
Ambeau, Karen M
Anthony, Bernard Winston
Barney, Lemuel Jackson
Baugh, Lynnette
Blackmon, Edward
Bryant, Anthony
Crutchfield, Lisa
Daniels, Alfred Claude Wynder
DeGraffenreidt, James H
Doby, Allen E
Dorsey, Herman Sherwood, Jr.
Enders, Murvin S
Flint, Mary Frances
Fontenot-Jamerson, Berlinda
Gladney, Rufus D
Goss-Seeger, Debra A
Grantley, Robert Clark
Griffith, John A.
Harrell, William Edwin
Harris, Robert L.
Hayes-Giles, Joyce V.
Horton, Dollie Bea Dixon
Jackson, Brenda
Jennings, Devoyd
Jones, Delores
King, Gwendolyn Stewart
Lofton, Andrew James
Loyd, Walter
Lucas, Victoria
Manlove, Benson
McCarrell, Clark Gabriel
McCraw, Tom
McKinney, Samuel Berry
McPherson, James R
McZier, Arthur
Moore, Gregory B
Moore, Ronald
Morris, Herman
Penn, Mindell Lewis
Rogers, Alfred R
Roland, Benautrice, Jr.
Rollins, Lee Owen
Tate, Sherman E
Taylor, Andre Jerome
Taylor, S Martin
Thaxton, June E
Thomas, Samuel
Tufon, Chris
Turner, George Cordell, II
Urdy, Dr. Charles E.
Wagoner, J Robert
Ware, Irene Johnson
Washington, Earlene
Washington, Nancy Ann
Watkins, William, Jr.

Watts, Patricia L
Whitehead, David William
Williams, James

Publishing/Printing
Abebe, Ruby
Adams, Floyd, Jr.
Adams, Robert Hugo
Allen, S Monique Nicole
Bailey, Harry Augustine, Jr.
Bailey-Thomas, Sheryl K.
Ball, Jane Lee
Baquet, Dean
Barrett, Audra
Bauldock, Gerald
Beckham, Barry Earl
Bell, Alberta Saffell
Benson, Wanda Miller
Black, David Eugene, Sr.
Blair, George Ellis, Jr.
Blunt, Madelyne Bowen
Bobb-Semple, Crystal
Booker, Michael
Bowens, Gregory John
Boyd, Terry A.
Bridgeman, Dexter Adrian
Bronner, Bernard
Bronner, Sheila
Brown, Barbara Ann
Buckner, Floyd
Burns, Jeff
Burns-Cooper, Ann
Burton, Ronald J
Carter, Lenora
Carter, Stephen L
Chandler, Alton H
Chappell, Kevin
Checole, Kassahun
Cherry, Lee Otis
Cole, Harriette
Conyers, Nathan
Cortez, Jayne
Crosby, James R
Cross-White, Agnes
Daly, Ronald Edwin
DeVore Mitchell, Ophelia
Doss, Rod
Drew, Kenneth R.
Driver, David E
Driver, Richard Sonny, Jr.
Ducksworth, Marilyn Jacoby
Dunn, Linda Spradley
DuPree, Prof. Sherry Sherrod
Dutton Brown, Marie
Eady, Lydia Davis
Earl, Dr. Archie William
Easter, Eric Kevin
Edmonds, Tracey E.
Edwards, Audrey Marie
Edwards, Claudia L.
Edwards, Preston Joseph
English, Dr. Perry T., Jr.
Enoch, John D.
Erving, John
Eubanks, W Ralph
Fairley, Juliette S
Farrar, Moses
Felder, Loretta Kay
Ferguson, Dr. Robert Lee, Sr.
Fischer, William S.
Foard, Frederick Carter
Fornay, Alfred R, Jr.
Foster, Dr. Frank B., III
Fraser, George C.
Frazier, Shirley George
Gant, Crystal M.
Glover, Robert G
Grant, Dr. George C
Grant, Ian
Graves, Earl G.
Graves, Earl G
Gray, Wilfred Douglas
Green, Pha M
Guy-Sheftall, Beverly
Hailey, Priscilla W
Hansford, Louise Todd
Harris, Charles F.
Harris, Peter J.
Harris-Diaw, Rosalind Juanita
Hartman, Hermene Demaris
Hines, Courtney
Holt, Deloris Lenette
House, Michael A
Hudson, Cheryl Willis
Hurte, Leroy E.
Jackson, Karen Denise
James, Juanita T.
Jenkins, Frank Shockley
Jervay, Paul Reginald, Jr.

John, Dr. Mable
Johnson, Eunice Walker
Johnson, Frank J., Sr.
Johnson, R. Benjamin
Joseph, Raymond Alcide
Kafele, Baruti Kwame
Kearney, Esq. Eric Henderson
Kearse, Gregory Sashi
Kelly, Dr. John Russell
Kilimanjaro, John Marshall
Latif, Naimah
Lawson Roby, Kimberla
Lee, Debra Louise
Lee, William H
Lewis, Edward
Lewis, Edward T.
Lewis, Ida Elizabeth
Lewis, James D
Logan, Dr. John C.
Lottier, Patricia Ann
Love, Ruth Burnett
Lovick, Calvin L
Mack, Donald J
Marr, Warren, II
Maxwell, Roger Allan
McClure, Exal, Jr.
McClure, Frederick Donald
McElroy, Dr. Lee A
McKnight, Reginald
McLaughlin, Katye H
McPherson, Rosalyn J
McWright, Carter C
Messiah-Jiles, Sonceria
Meyer, Alton J
Millender, Mallory Kimerling
Minor, Tracey L
Moore-Poole, Jessica Care
Moragne, Lenora, Ph.D.
Morant, Mack Bernard
Morgan, Dr. Harry
Morris, Celeste
Mumford, Esther Hall
Nichols, Alfred Glen
Norment, Lynn A
O'Flynn-Pattillo, Patricia
Oliver, John J., Jr.
Onli, Turtel
Paschall, Evita Arneda
Pemberton-Heard, Danielle Marie
Perry, Pam Elaine
Perry, Rita Eggleton
Peters, William Alfred
Pierce, Ponchitta A
Porter, Charles William
Posey, John R
Powell, Charles Arthur
Randolph, Laura B
Rawls, Mark Anthony
Ray, Walter I
Redd, M. Paul, Sr.
Reid, Dr. Milton A.
Rhinehart, June Acie
Rhodes, Jeanne
Rice, Linda Johnson
Richardson, Eddie Price, Jr.
Robinson, Beverly Jean
Robinson, Nina
Roebuck-Hayden, Marcia
Roney, Raymond G
Russell, Mark
Samuel, Jasper H
Scott, Alexis
Scott, Marian Alexis
Shelton, Charles E
Shepphard, Dr. Charles Bernard
Smith, Dr. Charles U.
Smith, Clarence O.
Smith, Janet Maria
Smith, John B., Sr.
Smith, Norman Raymond
Sockwell, Oliver R, Jr.
Spight, Benita L
Sterling, H. Dwight, Sr.
Stewart, Ruth Ann
Tandy, Dr. Mary B
Tarpley, Natasha Anastasia
Tatum, Elinor Ruth
Tatum, Wilbert A.
Taylor, Susan L.
Thompson, Dr. Charles H.
Thompson, Derrick
Tomlinson, Randolph R.
Trammer, Monte Irvin
Turner, Yvonne Williams
Vest, Donald Seymour
Vest, Hilda Freeman
Ware, Janis L
Ware, William
Washington, Alonzo Lavert

Washington, James A
Wells, Billy Gene
Wesley, Herman Eugene, III
Whitworth, Claudia Alexander
Williams, Eddie Nathan
Williams, John Alfred
Williford, Stanley O.
Willis, Frank B.
Wilmore, Gayraud Stephen, Jr.
Wilson, F Leon
Wilson, Frank Edward
Winston, Dr. Michael Russell
Woodruff, Cheryl
Woods, Kondria Yvette Black
Wooten, Carl Kenneth
Workman, Aurora Felice Antonette
Worth, Janice Lorraine
Wright, Carl Jeffrey
Wright, Crystal Andrea
Young, Albert James
Youssef, Sitamon Mubaraka

Radio Broadcasting Industry
Anderson, Kernie L.
Arnold, John Russell, Jr.
Bailey, Lee
Baisden, Michael
Bambaataa, Afrika
Banks, Alicia
Banks, Carl E.
Beach, Walter G., II
Benham, Dr. Robert
Blake, Neil
Brown, Floyd A.
Brown, Larry, Jr.
Brown, Sharon Marjorie Revels
Brownlee, Dennis J.
Brunson, Dorothy Edwards
Burley, Dale S.
Bush, Lewis Fitzgerald
Butler, Clary Kent
Carter, Robert T.
Chideya, Farai
Chretien, Gladys M.
Cole, Lydia
Collinet, Georges Andre
Covington, Tarriel
Cox, Dr. Wendell
Curry, Rev. Victor Tyrone
Davis, Gregory T
Davis, Nathaniel Alonzo
Davis, William Delford
Dodson, Selma L
Ellis, LaPhonso Darnell
Evans, Liz
Finley, Skip
Fletcher, Cliff
Freeland, Shawn Ericka
Gaines, Adriane Theresa
Germany, Albert
Gilliam, Herman Arthur, Jr.
Golightly, Lena Mills
Graham, Jeff Todd
Green, Verna S
Hampton, Cheryl Imelda
Harris, Daisy
Harvey, Linda Joy
Hickson, Dr. William F, Jr.
Hines, Rosetta
Hodgins, James William
Hopson, Harold Theodore
Horton, Dollie Bea Dixon
Howard, Samuel Houston
Jackson, Gordon Martin, Jr.
Jackson, Hal
Jackson, Keith Jerome
Jones, Robert Bernard
Joyner, Oscar Albert
Joyner, Tom
Kennard, Patricia A.
Law, Robert Louis
Lee, Aubrey Walter, Jr.
Logan, Dr. John C.
Majors, Jeff
Marshall, Pluria William, Jr.
Mason, John
Mathews, Keith E
Mayo, Barry Alan
McGee, Rose N.
McKee, Lonette
McKinney, Billy
Miles, George L
Moncrieffe, Peter
Moss, Anni R.
Muhammad, James A
Myrick, Dr. Howard A.
Nightingale-Hawkins, Monica R
Rawls, Mark Anthony

Reese, Ike
Rivero, Marita
Robinson, Eugene Keefe
Royster, Scott Robert
Sainte-Johnn, Don
Satchell, Elizabeth
Segar, Leslie
Sherrell, Charles Ronald, II
Shields, Rev. Del Pierce
Simpson, Donnie
Smith, C Miles
Smith, Charles Henry, III
Smith, Darryl C.
Smith, J Thomas
Smith, Dr. Judith Moore
South, Wesley W.
Spruill, Robert I.
Stewart, Ryan
Sutton, Percy E.
Sutton, Pierre Monte
Talley, James Edward
Tigger, Big
Wagoner, J Robert
Wansley, Lisa Payne
Ward, Sandra L
Ware, Andre
Waters, Neville R
Wheaton, Frank Kahlil
White, Deidre R
Williams, Alfred Hamilton
Williams, Charlene J.
Wilson, Jon
Winley, Diane Lacey
Woodbeck, Frank Raymond
Worthy, Larry Elliott
Wynns, Coryliss Lorraine
Zola, Nkenge

Real Estate
Abdul-Rahman, Tahira Sadiqa
Allen, Charles Edward
Allen, James H.
Anderson, Dr. Marcellus J., Sr.
Arbuckle, Ronald Lee
Armstrong, Ernest W., Sr.
Baker, LaVolia Ealy
Bates, William J
Bauldock, Gerald
Billingsley, Ray C.
Bingham, Rebecca Josephine
Blanden, Lee Ernest
Bonaparte, Dr. Tony Hillary
Booker, Simeon S.
Brandt, Lillian B.
Bridgforth, Walter, Jr.
Brisco, Gayle
Briscoe, Leonard E.
Brooks, John S.
Brown, Arnold E.
Brown, Franchot A
Brown, John Mitchell, Sr.
Brown, Julius J.
Brown, Rodger L, Jr.
Brown, Willie B.
Bryant, Anxious E.
Bulls, Herman E.
Bunkley, Lonnie R
Burges, Melvin E.
Burleson, Dr. Helen L.
Burrell, Barbara
Burrell, Leroy
Bynoe, John Garvey
Calhoun, Eric A
Campbell, Bobby Lamar
Carey, Vince
Carter, James
Carter, Lemorie, Jr.
Carter, William Beverly
Charlton, George N., Jr.
Chicago, Denovious Adolphus
Christian, John L.
Church, Robert T., Sr.
Clark, Douglas L.
Cofield, James E
Collins, Charles Miller
Collins, Rosecrain
Conley, Charles S.
Cook, Rashard
Cooke, Thomas H, Jr.
Cornwall, Dr. Shirley M.
Crawford, HR
Crawley, Darline
Daniels, A. Raiford
DaValt, Dorothy B.
Devine, Jamie
DeVoe, Ronald Boyd, Jr.
Donald, Elvah T
Dotson, Albert E., Jr.
Dowdy, James H

Dunigan, Mayme O.
Dyer-Goode, Pamela Theresa
Edwards, Hon. Al E.
Edwards, Bessie Regina
Ferguson, Idell
Ferguson, Joel I
Fields, Stanley
Fisher, Shelley Marie
Fletcher, Louisa Adaline
Fowlkes, Doretha P
Franks, Gary A.
Garner, June Brown
Goodrich, Thelma E.
Green, Gloria J
Green, Walter
Greer, Edward M
Hackett, Barry Dean
Hagood, Henry Barksdale
Hall, Morris B
Harps, William S.
Harris, Clifton L.
Harvey, Richard Clemont, Jr.
Henderson, Gerald
Hill, Alfred
Hill, Rev. Dr. Robert Lee
Hilton, Stanley William, Jr.
Hines, Carl R
Hodge, Norris
Hooks, Dr. James Byron, Jr.
Hooks, Michael Anthony
Horton, Lemuel Leonard
Huggins, Linda Johnson
Hymes, Jesse
Isler, Marshall A., III
Jackson, Gerald Milton
Jarrett, Valerie B.
Jefferson, Patricia Ann
Jennings, Everett Joseph
Johnson, Addie Collins
Johnson, Cleveland, Jr.
Johnson, Joyce Colleen
Johnson, Rev. William Smith
Jones, Robert Wesley
Jones, Theresa Mitchell
Jordan, Bettye Davis
Kellum, Anthony O
Kimbrough, Charles Edward
King, Richard L.
Kinniebrew, Robert Lee
LaCour, Louis Bernard
Lavelle, Robert R.
Law, M Eprevel
Lawrence, Philip Martin
Lively, Ira J.
London, Dr. Edward Charles
Maddox, Jack H.
Martin, Reddrick Linwood
Martin, Shedrick M., Jr.
Martin, Wayne
McGhee, James Leon
McKissack, Leatrice Buchanan
McLaurin, Daniel Washington
Mehreteab, Ghebre-Selassie
Melendez-Rhinehart, Carmen M.
Michaux, Henry M
Michel, Harriet Richardson
Miller, George Carroll, Jr.
Miller, William
Mingo, Pauline Hylton
Montgomery, George Louis, Jr.
Morris, Joe
Morrow, Phillip Henry
Motley, David Lynn
Naphtali, Ashirah Sholomis
Nelson, Ramona M
Newhouse, Robert F
Norris, LaVena M.
Oliver, Louis
Parks, George Brooks
Peer, Wilbur Tyrone
Penn, Algernon H
Perry, Rev. Jerald Isaac, Sr.
Peters, Charles L., Jr.
Phillips, Daniel P
Pierson, Kathryn A
Pinado, Alan E., Sr.
Powell, Kenneth Alasandro
Prewitt, J Everett
Ragland, Sherman Leon, II
Recasner, Eldridge David
Reece, Steven
Reed, Beatrice M.
Reed, Gregory J.
Reid, Malissie Laverne
Reid, Rubin J
Richie, Winston Henry
Richmond, Delores Ruth
Rivera, Eddy
Robinson, Rev. Edsel F

Robinson, James L
Robinson, William
Ruffner, Ray P.
Russell, Dr. Leonard Alonzo
Satchell, Elizabeth
Scott, Charles E
Scott, Hattie Bell
Scott, Stephen L
Seabrook, Juliette Theresa
Sewell, Edward C
Shows, Mark D
Singleton, Harry M
Slaughter, Atty. Fred L.
Smith, Bruce Bernard
Somerset, Leo L., Jr.
Spears, Richard James
Steward, Lowell C.
Stewart, John B., Jr.
Stewart, W. Douglas
Stinson, Constance Robinson
Stith, Antoinette Freeman
Stone, Reese J
Strong- Kimbrough, Dr. Blondell M
Sutton, Wilma Jean
Tanner, Gloria Travis
Taylor, Anderson
Teer, Wardeen
Thomas, Samuel Haynes, Jr.
Thompson, Rev. Carl Eugene
Thornton, Dr. John C
Thornton, Wayne T
Toon, Albert L.
Travis, Dempsey J
Turner, Ervin
Turner, Lana
Tyler, Robert James, Sr.
Tyree-Walker, Ida May
Varner, Dr. Nellie M.
Vaughn, Mo
Wallace, Charles Leslie
Wallace, Helen Winfree-Peyton
Wamble, Carl DeEllis
Ware, Dyahanne
Warren, Otis, Jr.
Wash, Glenn Edward
Watkins, Lottie Heywood
Whisenton, Andre C.
White, Mabel Meshach
White, Wendell F
Williams, Enoch H
Williams, Frank J
Williams, Leslie J.
Williams, Raleigh R.
Williams, Willie, Jr.
Williamson, Carl Vance
Winn, Joan T.
Winslow, Cleta Meris
Winters, Kenneth E.
Woods, Geneva Holloway
Wright, Dr. Samuel Lamar, Sr.
Yarbrough, Mamie Luella
Young, Terrence Anthony

Regional Planning
See **Urban/Regional Planning**

Religion
See **Clergy—Catholic;
Clergy—Moslem/Muslim;
Clergy—Protestant; Clergy—
Not Elsewhere Classified**

Restaurant/Food Service Industry (*See Also* **Retail Trade—Food and Beverages**)
Ash, Richard Larry
Bailey, William H.
Beavers, Robert M.
Bell, Yvonne Lola
Blackwell, Unita
Blount, Corie Kasoun
Braxton, Steve
Brown, Doris
Burrell, Leroy
Cain, Herman
Chase, Dooky, Jr.
Clark, Gary C.
Coaxum, Harry Lee
Coleman, Dennis
Creuzot, Percy P.
Dawson, Horace G
Duerson, David R
Ferguson, Valerie C
Fletcher, Sylvester James
Gaines, Brenda J.
Garrett, Louis Henry
Gay, Helen Parker

Goldston, Nathaniel R., III
Gonzalez, Tony
Hamilton, Aubrey J.
Haysbert, Raymond Victor
Hill, Joseph Havord
Hollins, Leroy
Hoskins, Michele
Jackson, Yvonne Ruth
Jones, Wilbert
Kelly, Ida B.
Kwaku-Dongo, Francois
Lee, Otis K
Lockhart, Eugene
Lundy, Larry
Malcolm, Catherine
Malcolm, Desmond
May, Dickey R.
McCovey, Willie Lee
McRae, Emmett N
McTeer, George Calvin
Mines, Raymond C
Mingo, Pauline Hylton
Parker, David Gene
Pickard, Dr. William Frank
Rivers, Johnny
Rogers-Reece, Shirley
Samuelsson, Marcus
Settles, Darryl Stephen
Shelton, John W
Simmons, Stephen Lloyd
Smith, Ozzie
Smith, Zachary
Smothers, Ronald
Sosa, Samuel Peralta
Stephenson, Charles E, III
Taylor, Frank
Taylor, Frank Anthony
Thompson, Warren M
Thurmond, Nate
Toon, Albert L.
Watkins, Rolanda Rowe
Williamson, Carlton
Winters, Jacqueline F
Woods, Sylvia

Retail Trade—Apparel and Accessories
Blake, Jennifer Lynn
Brown-Harris, Ann
Burrell, Leroy
Duncan, Joan A.
Eggleston, Neverett A
Fleetwood, Therez
Foster-Grear, Pamela
Franklin, David M.
Gwynn, Florine Evayonne
Hankins, Anthony Mark
Harkness, Jerry
Horne, June C
Hudson, Dr. Jerome William
King, Shaka C
Lett, Gerald William
McBride, Frances E.
McCray, Darryl K
Moore, Annie Jewell
Reed-Miller, Rosemary E
Reid, Daphne Etta Maxwell
Sanders, Glenn Carlos
Sherrod, Ezra Cornell
Sockwell, Oliver R., Jr.
Stocks, Eleanor Louise
Taylor, Karin
Taylor, Tommie W.
Washington, Ben James, Jr.
Waters, Dianne E

Retail Trade—Building/ Construction Materials
Coleman, James William
Ellis, Zachary L
Hale, Gene
Henry-Fairhurst, Ellenae L
Knox, William Robert
Law, M Eprevel
Thomas, Sirr Daniel

Retail Trade—Drugs and Toiletries
Bronner, Bernard
Burgess, Dr. Norma J
Bynum, Horace Charles, Sr.
Clarke, Joseph Lance
Gaskin, Dr. Frances Christian
Monday, Sabrina Goodwin
Potter, Myrtle Stephens

Pratt, Dr. Ruth Jones
Ruffin, John Walter

Retail Trade—Electrical/ Electronics Products
Brown, Leander A
Foreman, Joyce Blacknall
Harvey, Maurice Reginald
McGlover, Stephen Ledell
Pride, William L., Jr.
Ramsey, Walter S.
Rand, A. Barry
Robie, Clarence W.

Retail Trade—Food and Beverages
Anderson, Alfred Anthony
Anderson, Eugene
Billue, Zana
Bullock, Theodore
Calhoun, Gregory Bernard
Clarke, Priscilla
Diggs, Lawrence J
Dunham, Robert
Fluellen, Velda Spaulding
Goss, Tom
Grayson, Mel
Greene, Clifton S.
Haysbert, Raymond Victor
Heard, Lonear Windham
Hopson, Melvin Clarence
Hunt, Edward
Mack, Luther W, Jr.
Merchant, James S, Jr.
Milner, Thirman L.
Murray, Edna McClain
Nelson, Mario
Ruffin, John Walter
Shaw, Carl Bernard
Singleton, Rickey
Skipper, Clarence
Taylor, Natalie Manns
Walker, Herschel
Webb, Joe
Wimp, Edward Lawson

Retail Trade—Furniture/ Home Furnishings
Castle, Keith L
Clark, Robert G.
Crosby, Fred McClellen
Davis, Charles A
Dean, Daniel R.
Foreman, Joyce Blacknall
France, Frederick Doug, Jr.
Grier, John K
Johnson, Costello O
Johnson, Eunita E
Marshall, Julyette Matthews
McQuay, James Phillip
Merritt, Wendy Warren

Retail Trade—General Merchandise
Brown, A. David
Coleman, Robert L
Davis, Cora Bowie
Hendricks, Richard D
LeDay, John Austin
McGee, Sherry
McGhee, James Leon
Moran, Joyce E
Ruffin, John Walter
Shakespeare, Easton Geoffrey
Waters, Dianne E
Watkins, Wynfred C
White, Claude Esley

Retail Trade—Hardware
Banks, Ronald
Sutton, Clyde A., Sr.
Williams, Joe H.

Retail Trade—Motor Vehicles, Parts, and Services
Aaron, Henry Louis
Armstrong, William
Bankston, Charles E.
Baranco, Gregory T.
Baranco, Juanita P.
Barnett, Carl L
Barron, Reginald
Barron, Wendell
Beckford, Orville
Bennett, Lonnie M
Beyer, Troy Yvette

Boyland, Dorian Scott
Bradley, James George
Brogden, Robert, Jr.
Brown, John, Jr.
Brown, Larry T.
Bullard, Keith
Bunche, Curtis J
Cabell, Enos M
Cain, Nathaniel Z, Jr.
Callaway, Louis Marshall, Jr.
Carter, Will J.
Carthen, John, Jr.
Chargois, James M
Chuks-Orji, Austin
Cockerham, Peggy
Conyers, Nathan G.
Corley, Eddie B., Sr.
Davis, Richard O.
Delk, James F, Jr.
Dillard, Howard Lee
Doss, LaRoy Samuel
Douglas, Walter Edmond
Dukes, Carl R
Early, Ezzard Dale
Edgar, Jacqueline L.
Eggleston, Neverett A
Falkner, Bobbie E.
Farr, Melvin, Sr.
Fletcher, Glen Edward
Frazier, Jordan
Fregia, Ray, Sr.
Frink, Samuel H.
Fryson, Sim E.
Gatewood, Dr. Algie C.
Gordon, Darrell R.
Grace, Princeston
Hall, Ronald
Harper, T Errol
Harrell, Charles H
Harrison, Boyd G, Jr.
Hatcher, Robert L
Hayes, Elvin E.
Hill, Robert A.
Hines, Jimmie
Hodge, Ernest M
Horton, Oscar J
Hughes, George Vincent
Hysaw, Guillermo Lark
Jackson, Clarence A
Jackson, Gregory
Johnson, Albert William, Sr.
Johnson, Hester
Johnson, Robert
Johnson, Sam
Johnson, T J
Jones, Fredrick E
Jones, James B
Jones, James V
Jones, Lester C
Jones, Theresa C
Karangu, David
Kemp, Leroy Percy
Kindle, Archie
Lee, Chandler Bancroft
Lewis, Clarence K
Lloyd, Phil Andrew
Long, Monti M
Majors, Anthony Y
Mallisham, Joseph W.
Martin, Wayne
Matthews, Irving J.
McClain, William L
McClammy, Dr. Thad C
Mitchell, Emmitt W.
Mitchell, George L
Mitchell, James H.
Montgomery, Robert E
Moore, Allyn D
Moore, Jesse A
Newberry, Cedric Charles
Nichols, Dimaggio
Norris, William E.
O'Neal, Rodney
Parker, Clarence E
Perry, LaVal
Piper, Elwood A
Price, Phillip G
Reeves, Alan M
Reid, Duane L
Roberts, John Christopher
Roberts, Roy S.
Rodgers, Pamela E
Roy, John Willie
Rutledge, George
Shamberger, Jeffery L
Shaw, Henry
Sutton, Charles W.
Sutton, Nathaniel K
Swain, Hamp, Jr.
Taylor, Henry F

Hill, Robert Bernard
Hines, Dr. Charles A.
Hope, Dr. Richard Oliver
Hunter, Charles A
Jackson, Esther Cooper
Jackson, Jacquelyne Johnson
James, Dr. Herman Delano
Jones, Dr. Marcus Earl
Jordan, Patricia Carter
Kirk, Dr. Sarah Virgo
Landry, L. Bartholomew
LaVeist, Dr. Thomas
Lee, Dr. Silas, III
Majete, Dr. Clayton Aaron
Marrett, Dr. Cora B.
Mayo, Dr. Julia A
McDonald, Katrina Bell
Montgomery, Annette
Morgan, Dr. Gordon D.
Noguera, Dr. Pedro Antonio
Oliver, Dr. Melvin L
Parker, Dr. Keith Dwight
Parks, Dr. Arnold Grant
Plummer, Michael Justin
Reed, Kathleen Rand
Register, Dr. Jasper C.
Robinson, Dr. Prezell Russell
Rodgers-Rose, LaFrances Audrey
Rogers, Victor Alvin
Rollins, Judith Ann
Rutledge, Dr. Essie Manuel
Salmon, Dr. Jaslin Uriah
Scott, Joseph Walter
Scott, Dr. Marvin Bailey
Slade, Phoebe J.
Smith, Dr. Charles U.
Stamps, Spurgeon Martin David
Temple, Edward Stanley
Thompson, Dr. Litchfield O
Walton, Dr. Ortiz Montaigne
Wead, Dr. Rodney Sam
Weathers, Margaret A.
West, Dr. Herbert Lee, Jr.
Westmoreland, Samuel Douglas
Williams, Dr. Clarence G.
Willie, Dr. Charles Vert
Wilson, Dr. William Julius

Sports—Amateur

Burnett, Calvin Waller
Burrell, Leroy
Campbell, Christopher Lundy
Carey, Pearl M.
Claiborne, Loretta
Conley, Mike
Cross-Battle, Tara
Dawes, Dominique Margaux
DeFrantz, Anita L.
Devers, Gail
Drake, Leonard
Finn, Michelle
Flowers, Vonetta
Forrest, Vernon
Foster, Gregory
Free, Kenneth A.
Hall, Darnell
Hines, Garrett
Jackson, Kevin
Jenkins, Chip
Johnson, Georgia Anna Lewis
Johnson, Michael
Johnson, Rafer
Jones, Randy
Kemp, Leroy Percy
Kingdom, Roger Nona
Lofton, Michael
Miller, Inger
Mitchell, Dennis Allen
Montgomery, Tim
Pipkins, Robert Erik
Powell, Mike
Scott, Marvin Wayne
Stevens, Rochelle
Torrence, Gwen
Valmon, Andrew Orlando
Washington, Anthony
Wilson, Danyell Elaine

Sports—Professional/
Semiprofessional

Aaron, Henry Louis
Abdul-Jabbar, Kareem
Abdullah, Rabih Fard
Abdul-Rauf, Mahmoud
Abdul-Wahad, Tariq
Abdur-Rahim, Shareef
Abraham, Clifton Eugene
Abraham, Donnie
Abraham, Tajama

Abrams, Kevin R.
Adams, Don L.
Adams, Flozell
Adams, Sam Aaron
Adams, Vashone LaVey
Adderley, Herb Anthony
Addison, Rafael
Agee, Thomas Lee
Agnew, Raymond Mitchell, Jr.
Aguirre, Mark Anthony
Ahanotu, Chidi Obioma
Aldridge, Allen Ray
Aldridge, Markita
Alexander, Brent
Alexander, Charles Fred, Jr.
Alexander, Cory Lynn
Alexander, Derrick L.
Alexander, Derrick Scott
Alexander, Gary Roberts
Alexander, Liyongo Patrise
Alexander, Willie
Alford, Brian Wayne
Ali, Laila
Ali, Muhammad
Allen, James
Allen, Larry Christopher, Sr.
Allen, Marcus LeMarr
Allen, Ray
Allen, Taje LaQayne
Allen, Tremayne
Allen, Will D.
Allensworth, Jermaine LaMont
Allotey, Victor
Alomar, Roberto
Alomar, Sandy
Alston, Derrick Samuel
Ambers, Monique
Ambrose, Ashley Avery
Anders, Kimble Lynard
Anderson, Alfred Anthony
Anderson, Antonio
Anderson, Darren Hunter
Anderson, Derek
Anderson, Eddie Lee, Jr.
Anderson, Garret Joseph
Anderson, Gary Wayne
Anderson, Gregory Wayne
Anderson, Jamal
Anderson, Keisha
Anderson, Kenny
Anderson, Marlon Ordell
Anderson, Nick
Anderson, Richard Darnoll
Anderson, Ronald Gene
Anderson, Shandon Rodriguez
Anderson, Steve
Anderson, Willie Aaron
Anderson, Willie Lee, Jr.
Andrade, Mery
Andujar, Joaquin
Anthony, Eric Todd
Anthony, Gregory C
Anthony, Reidel Clarence
Archambeau, Lester Milward, III
Archibald, Nathaniel
Armstead, Jessie Willard
Armstrong, B. J.
Armstrong, Bruce Charles
Armstrong, Darrell
Armstrong, Tyji
Arnold, Jahine Amid
Artest, Ronald William, Jr.
Ashford, Evelyn
Ashmore, Darryl Allan
Aska, Joseph
Askew, Vincent Jerome
Askins, Keith Bernard
Atkins, James
Attles, Alvin A., Jr.
Atwater, Stephen Dennis
Augmon, Stacey Orlando
Austin, Isaac Edward
Austin, Raymond Demont
Autry, Darnell
Aycock, Angela Lynnette
Bailey, Carlton Wilson
Bailey, Robert Martin Luther
Bailey, Thurl Lee
Baines, Harold Douglas
Baker, Dusty
Baker, Myron Tobias
Baker, Vin
Baldwin, James, Jr.
Ball, Jerry Lee
Ballard, Gregory
Banks, Carl E.
Banks, Chris
Banks, Ernest
Banks, Gene

Banks, Tony
Banks, Willie Anthony
Bankston, Michael Kane
Barber, Michael Lenard
Barber, Ronde
Barber, Shawn William
Barber, Tiki
Barkley, Charles Wade
Barlow, Reggie Devon
Barnes, Adia Oshun
Barnes, Johnnie Darnell
Barnes, Lionel, Jr.
Barnes, Quacy
Barnett, Fred Lee
Barney, Lemuel Jackson
Barros, Dana Bruce
Barrow, Micheal Colvin
Bartee, Kimera Anotchi
Basil, Richard
Bass, Anthony
Bass, Kevin Charles
Batch, Charlie
Bates, Mario Doniel
Bates, Michael Dion
Batiste, Kim
Battie, Tony
Bautista, Danny
Baxter, Frederick Denard
Baylor, Elgin Gay
Bayne, Chris
Beard, Butch
Beasley, Aaron Bruce
Beasley, Frederick Jerome
Beasley, Jamar
Beck, Corey Laveon
Beckles, Ian Harold
Bell, Derek Nathaniel
Bell, George Antonio
Bell, Kendrell Alexander
Bell, Myron Corey
Bell, Ricky
Bellamy, Jay
Belle, Albert Jojuan
Belser, Jason Daks
Benjamin, Arthur, Jr.
Benjamin, Corey Dwight
Bennett, Brandon
Bennett, Cornelius O'landa
Bennett, Donnell, Jr.
Bennett, Edgar, III
Bennett, Michael
Bennett, Michael
Bennett, Tommy
Bennett, Tony Lydell
Benoit, David
Benson, Darren
Berry, Bertand Demond
Berry, Jay
Berry, Latin
Best, Travis Eric
Bettis, Jerome Abram
Beverly, Eric
Biakabutuka, Tim
Bibby, Mike
Billups, Chauncey
Bing, Dave
Bishop, Blaine Elwood
Bivins, Jimmy
Blackburn, Charles Miligan, II
Blackman, Rolando Antonio
Blackmon, Roosevelt, III
Blackshear, Jeffery Leon
Blades, Bennie
Blaise, Kerlin
Blake, James Riley
Blake, Jeff
Blake, John
Blanks, Delilah Bowen
Blanton, Dain
Blanton, James B., III
Blaylock, Dr. Enid Veronica
Blaylock, Mookie
Blevins, Tony
Blount, Corie Kasoun
Blue, Octavia
Blue, Vida Rochelle, Jr.
Bly, Dre'
Bobo, Orlando
Bol, Manute
Bolden, Juran
Bolen, David B
Bolton-Holifield, Ruthie
Bonds, Barry Lamar
Bones, Ricky
Bonilla, Bobby
Bonner, Alice Carol
Bonner, Anthony
Booker, Karen
Booker, Michael

Booker, Vaughn Jamel
Boose, Dorian
Booth, Keith
Boozer, Emerson
Bosley, Freeman Robertson, Jr.
Bosley, Thad
Boston, Archie, Jr.
Boston, David Byron
Bouie, Tony Vanderson
Boulware, Peter Nicholas
Boutte, Marc Anthony
Bowden, Joseph Tarrod
Bowdoin, Robert E.
Bowe, Riddick
Bowen, Bruce
Bowens, Timothy L.
Bowie, Larry Darnell, Jr.
Bownes, Fabien Alfranso
Boyd, Delores Rosetta
Boyd, Tommie
Boykins, Earl
Brackens, Tony Lynn, Jr.
Bradford, Corey Lamon
Bradford, Paul
Bradford, Ronnie
Bradley, Milton
Bradley, Phillip Poole
Branch, Calvin
Brand, Elton Tyron
Brandon, Terrell
Branham, George, III
Brantley, Clifford
Brashear, Donald
Braxton, Janice Lawrence
Braxton, Tyrone Scott
Breaux, Timothy
Brewer, Jim
Bridgeman, Junior
Bridges, Bill
Brigance, O J
Briggs, Greg
Brisby, Vincent Cole
Briscoe, Marlin
Brisco-Hooks, Valerie Ann
Bromell, Lorenzo
Bronson, Robert Zack
Brooks, Aaron Lafette
Brooks, Barrett
Brooks, Derrick Dewan
Brooks, James Robert
Brooks, Macey
Broughton, Luther Rashard
Broussard, Steven
Brown, Adrian Demond
Brown, Chad Everett
Brown, Chucky
Brown, Cindy
Brown, Cornell Desmond
Brown, Corwin Alan
Brown, Cyron
Brown, Dee
Brown, Derek Darnell
Brown, Derek Vernon
Brown, Dermal
Brown, Emil Quincy
Brown, Eric Jon
Brown, Gary Leroy
Brown, Gates
Brown, Gerald
Brown, Gilbert Jesse
Brown, J. B.
Brown, James
Brown, James Lamont
Brown, Jamie Shepard
Brown, Jarvis Ardel
Brown, Kwame
Brown, Larry, Jr.
Brown, Lomas, Jr.
Brown, Michael
Brown, Na Orlando
Brown, Omar
Brown, P J
Brown, Randy
Brown, Ray, Jr.
Brown, Reggie
Brown, Reuben
Brown, Roosevelt Lawayne
Brown, Ruben Pernell
Brown, Rushia
Brown, Tarrik Jumaan
Brown, Timothy Donell
Brown, Troy
Brown, Willie
Browne, Jerry
Browner, Joey Matthew
Browner, Ross D
Browning, John
Bruce, Aundray
Bruce, Isaac Isidore

Brunson, Rick Daniel
Bryant, Junior
Bryant, Kobe B
Bryant, Mark
Buchanan, Raymond Louis
Buckley, Marcus Wayne
Buckley, Terrell
Buckner, Brentson Andre
Buford, Damon Jackson
Bullett, Vicky
Burgess, James
Burgess, Linda
Burnett, A. J.
Burnett, Robert Barry
Burns, Keith Bernard
Burns, Lamont
Burras, Alisa
Burrell, Scott David
Burris, Jeffrey Lamar
Burroughs, Tim
Burton, Kendrick
Bush, Devin M.
Bush, Homer Giles
Bush, Lewis Fitzgerald
Butler, Duane
Butler, LeRoy
Butler, Mitchell Leon
Butts, Marion Stevenson, Jr.
Byars, Keith Allan
Byears, Latasha
Byner, Earnest Alexander
Bynum, Kenneth Bernard
Byrd, George Edward
Byrd, Isaac
Cabell, Enos M
Caffey, Jason Andre
Cage, Michael Jerome
Cain, Joseph Harrison, Jr.
Caldwell, Adrian Bernard
Caldwell, Mike Isaiah
Calloway, Christopher Fitzpatrick
Cambridge, Dexter
Camby, Marcus D
Cameron, Michael Terrance
Campbell, Edna
Campbell, Elden
Campbell, Lamar
Campbell, Michele
Campbell, Dr. Milton Gray
Campbell, Tony
Cannida, James Thomas, II
Canty, Chris
Carpenter, Ronald
Carr, Chris Dean
Carr, Corey Jermaine
Carr, Kenneth Alan
Carr, M L
Carr, William
Carrier, Mark Anthony
Carroll, Joe Barry
Carswell, Dwayne
Carter, Butch
Carter, Chris
Carter, Cris
Carter, Dale Lavelle
Carter, Joseph Chris
Carter, Kevin Louis
Carter, Ki-Jana
Carter, Marty LaVincent
Carter, Nigea
Carter, Pat
Carter, Perry Lynn
Carter, Quincy
Carter, Rubin
Carter, Thomas, II
Carter, Thomas, III
Carter, Tony A.
Carter, Vince
Cartwright, Bill
Carver, Shante
Cash, Swintayla Marie
Cassell, Samuel James
Cato, Kelvin T.
Causwell, Duane
Ceballos, Cedric Z.
Cedeno, Cesar
Centers, Larry Eugene
Chamberlain, Byron Daniel
Chamberlain, Wesley Polk
Chambers, Christopher J.
Chancey, Robert Dewayne
Chandler, Tyson
Chaney, Donald Ray
Chase, Sonia
Chavous, Corey
Cheaney, Calbert N
Cheeks, Maurice Edward
Cherry, Deron
Cherry, Je'Rod L.

Chester, Larry
Childress, Randolph
Childs, Chris
Christie, Douglas Dale
Clancy, Sam, Jr.
Clark, David Earl
Clark, Gary C.
Clark, Keon Arian
Clark, Tony
Clark, Willie Calvin, Jr.
Clark Diggs, Joetta
Clarke, Charlotte
Clay, Willie James
Clayborn, Ray Dewayne
Clayton, Royce Spencer
Clement, Anthony
Clemons, Charlie Fitzgerald
Clemons, Duane
Closs, Keith Mitchell, Jr.
Coakley, William Dexter
Coates, Ben Terrence
Cobb, Reginald John
Cobbins, Lyron Duryea
Cofer, Michael Lynn
Coffey, Richard Lee
Coghill, George
Coleman, Benjamin Leon
Coleman, Derrick D.
Coleman, Marco Darnell
Coleman, Marcus
Coleman, Monte
Coleman, Quincy
Coleman, Ronnald Dean
Coles, Bimbo
Coles, Darnell
Colleton, Katrina
Collier, Louis Keith
Collins, Andre Pierre
Collins, Calvin Lewis
Collins, James
Collins, Mark Anthony
Collins, Mo
Collons, Ferric Jason
Colon, Harry
Congreaves, Andrea
Connell, Albert Gene Anthony
Conner, Lester Allen
Conway, Curtis LaMont
Cook, Anthony Andrew
Cook, Rashard
Cook, Toi Fitzgerald
Cooper, Cecil Celester
Cooper, Cynthia
Cooper, Duane
Copeland, Horace Nathaniel
Copeland, John
Copeland, Russell Samoan
Corbin, Tyrone Kennedy
Coryatt, Quentin John
Cotton, James
Cowart, Sam
Cox, Bryan Keith
Cox, Ronald
Craig, Dameyune Vashon
Craver, Aaron LeRenze
Crawford, Keith
Crawford, Vernon
Crawley, Sylvia
Crittenden, Ray
Crockett, Henri
Crockett, Ray
Crockett, Zack
Croel, Michael
Cross, Howard
Cross-Battle, Tara
Crowell, Germane L.
Crumpler, Carlester T., Jr.
Cullors, Derrick Shane
Culpepper, Daunte
Cummings, Midre Almeric
Cummings, Terry
Cunningham, Randall
Cunningham, Rick
Cunningham, William
Cureton, Earl
Curry, Dell
Curry, Eddy
Curry, Eric Felece
Curry, Michael
Custis, Ace
Dampier, Erick Trevez
Danenberg, Sophia
Daniel, Eugene, Jr.
Daniel, Wendy Palmer
Daniels, Antonio Robert
Daniels, Jerome Alvonne
Daniels, LeShun Darnell
Daniels, Lloyd

Daniels, Melvin J.
Daniels, Phillip Bernard
Daniels, Richard Bernard
Darby, Matthew Lamont
Dar Dar, Kirby David
Darkins, Christopher Oji
Darling, Helen Marie
Darling, James Jackson
Davidds-Garrido, Norbert
Davidson, Cleatus Lavon
Davis, Alonzo J
Davis, Anthony D.
Davis, Antone Eugene
Davis, Antonio Lee
Davis, Ben Jerome
Davis, Brian Keith
Davis, Charles
Davis, Chili
Davis, Cyprian
Davis, Dale
Davis, Donald Earl, Jr.
Davis, Emanual
Davis, Erellon Ben
Davis, Eric Keith
Davis, Eric Wayne
Davis, Hubert Ira
Davis, Isaac
Davis, John
Davis, Johnny Reginald
Davis, Latina
Davis, Mark Anthony
Davis, Pernell
Davis, Reuben Cordell
Davis, Ricky
Davis, Rob
Davis, Ronald Weston
Davis, Shani
Davis, Stephen
Davis, Terrell
Davis, Travis Horace
Davis, Troy
Davis, Tyrone
Davis, Walter Paul
Davis, Wendell
Davis, William Augusta, III
Davis, Willie Clark
Davis-Wrightsil, Clarissa
Dawkins, Brian Patrick
Dawkins, Darryl
Dawkins, Johnny Earl, Jr.
Dawkins, Sean Russell
Dawsey, Lawrence Leneir
Dawson, Andre Nolan
Dawson, Lake
Day, Terry
Day, Todd Fitzgerald
Deese, Derrick Lynn, Sr.
Dehere, Terry
Dele, Bison
DeLeon, Jose
Delk, Tony Lorenzo
Denson, Autry
Denson, Damon
Dent, Richard Lamar
Denton, Timothy Jerome, Sr.
DeShields, Delino Lamont
Dickerson, Eric Demetric
Dickerson, Michael
Dillon, Corey
Dimry, Charles Louis, III
Dishman, Cris Edward
Dixon, Diane L.
Dixon, Ernest
Dixon, Gerald Scott
Dixon, Ronnie Christopher
Dixon, Tamecka Michelle
Dodge, Dedrick Allen
Dogins, Kevin Ray
Donaldson, James Lee, III
Dorrell, Karl
Dorsett, Anthony Drew, Jr.
Dorsett, Tony Drew
Dotson, Earl Christopher
Douglas, Hugh Lamont
Douglas, James
Douglas, Omar
Douglas, Sherman
Douglass, Maurice Gerrard
Drake, Jerry
Drakeford, Tyronne James
Drayton, Troy Anthony
Drew, Larry Donelle
Drexler, Clyde
Driessen, Daniel
Driver, Donald Jerome
Dudley, Rickey D.
Duerson, David R
Duff, Jamal Edwin
Dulaney, Michael Faulkerson

Dumars, Joe
Dumas, Michael Dion
Dumas, Tony
Dumas, Troy
Duncan, Jamie
Duncan, Tim
Dungy, Tony
Dunn, David
Dunn, Jason
Dunn, Warrick De'Mon
Dunston, Shawon Donnell
Duper, Mark Super
Durham, Leon
Durham, Ray
Dye, Ernest Thaddeus
Dye, Jermaine Terrell
Earl, Acie Boyd
Early, Quinn Remar
Easler, Michael Anthony
Easley, Damion
Easley, Kenny Mason, Jr.
Edmunds, Ferrell
Edney, Tyus Dwayne
Edwards, Anthony
Edwards, Antonio
Edwards, Antuan
Edwards, Dixon Voldean, III
Edwards, Donnie
Edwards, Herman Lee
Edwards, Kevin Durell
Edwards, Michelle
Edwards, Robert Lee
Edwards, Teresa
Edwards, Tonya
Egins, Paul Carter
Eisley, Howard Jonathan
Elewonibi, Mohammed Thomas
    David
Elie, Mario Antoine
Elliott, Sean Michael
Ellis, Dale
Ellis, Greg
Ellis, LaPhonso Darnell
Ellison, Jerry Ernest
Ellison, Pervis
Elliss, Luther
Ellsworth, Percy Daniel, III
Emanuel, Bert Tyrone
Embry, Wayne Richard
Emmons, Carlos
England, Eric Jevon
English, Albert J.
English, Stephen
Engram, Bobby
Enis, Curtis
Enis, Shalonda
Epps, Phillip Earl
Erving, Julius Winfield
Ethridge, Raymond Arthur, Jr.
Evans, Chuck
Evans, Donald Lee
Evans, Douglas Edwards
Evans, Josh
Evans, Lee
Evans, Leomont Dozier
Evans, Mike
Everett, Carl Edward, III
Everett, Thomas Gregory
Ewing, Patrick Aloysius
Fair, Terry
Fann, Chad Fitzgerald
Farmer, Ray
Farr, D'Marco Marcellus
Farrior, James
Faulk, Marshall William
Feaster, Allison
Ferguson, Jason
Ferguson, Jason
Fernandez, Tony
Ferrell, Duane
Fielder, Cecil Grant
Fields, Kenneth Henry
Fields, Mark Lee
Figures, Deon Juniel
Finley, Michael H
Finnie, Roger L., Sr.
Fisher, Derek Lamar
Fitzgerald, Larry
Fleming, Vern
Fletcher, London Levi
Fletcher, Terrell Antoine
Flowers, Lethon, III
Floyd, Chris
Floyd, Cliff, Jr.
Floyd, Eric Augustus
Floyd, Malcolm
Floyd, William Ali
Flynn, H Welton
Foley, Steve

Folston, James Edward
Fontenot, Albert Paul
Fonville, Chad Everette
Footman, Dan Ellis, Jr.
Forbes, Marlon
Ford, Cheryl
Ford, Henry
Ford, Kisha
Ford, Stacey
Foreman, George Edward
Forrest, Vernon
Forte, Patrick
Fortson, Danny
Foster, George Arthur
Foster, Gregory Clinton
Foster, Kevin Christopher
Foster, Toni
Fox, Rick
Foyle, Adonal David
Franco, Julio Cesar
Frank, Tellis Joseph
Frazier, Joe
Frazier, Walt, Jr.
Frazier-Lyde, Jacqui
Free, World B.
Freeman, Antonio Michael
Freeman, Lauretta
Frett, La Keshia
Fryar, Rev. Irving Dale, Sr.
Fugett, Jean Schloss, Jr.
Fuhr, Grant Scott
Fuller, Corey
Fuller, Randy Lamar
Fuller, William Henry, Jr.
Funderburke, Lawrence Damon
Gadsden, Oronde Benjamin
Gaffney, Derrick Tyrone
Gaines, Corey Yasuto
Gaiter, Tony
Gaither, Katryna
Galbraith, Scott
Galbreath, Harry Curtis
Galloway, Joey
Gamble, Oscar Charles
Gandy, Wayne Lamar
Gant, Ronald Edwin
Gant, Travesa
Garbey, Barbaro
Gardener, Daryl Ronald
Gardner, Barry Allan
Garner, Charlie, III
Garner, Chris
Garnes, Sam Aaron
Garnett, Kevin
Garrett, Dean
Garrison-Jackson, Zina Lynna
Gash, Samuel Lee, Jr.
Gaskins, Percell
Gatling, Chris Raymond
Gault, Willie James
Geary, Reggie
George, Eddie
George, Ronald
George, Tate Claude
Gerald, Dr. Melvin Douglas
German, Jammi
Gervin, George
Gibbs, Kevin Casey
Gibson, Damon
Gibson, Derrick Lamont
Gibson, Oliver Donnovan
Gibson, Robert
Gilbert, Sean
Gildon, Jason Larue
Gilkey, Bernard
Gill, Kendall Cedric
Gilliam, Armen Louis
Gilliam, Frank Delano
Gillom, Jennifer
Gipson, Charles, Jr.
Givens, Reginald Alonzo
Glanville, Douglas Metunwa
Glass, Gerald Damon
Glass, Virginia M.
Glenn, Aaron DeVon
Glenn, Tarik
Glenn, Terry Tyree
Glover, Andrew Lee
Glover, Kevin Bernard
Glover, La
Godfrey, Randall Euralentris
Goldwire, Anthony
Gomes, Wayne Maurice
Gonzalez, Tony
Gooch, Jeffrey Lance
Gooden, Dwight Eugene
Goodson, Adrienne M.
Goodwin, Curtis LaMar
Goodwin, Thomas Jones

Gordon, Alexander H., II
Gordon, Bridgette
Gordon, Darrien X. Jamal
Gordon, Dwayne K.
Gordon, Lancaster
Gordon, Thomas
Graham, DeMingo
Graham, Gregory Lawrence
Graham, Jeff Todd
Graham, Paul
Graham, Scottie
Grant, Brian Wade
Grant, Harvey
Grant, Horace Junior
Grant, Stephen Mitchell
Grantham, Charles
Granville, Billy
Graves, Denique
Gray, Carlton Patrick
Gray, Derwin Lamont
Gray, Earnest
Gray, Ed
Gray, Jerry
Gray, Johnnie Lee
Gray, Mel
Gray, Torrian
Green, A. C., Jr.
Green, Ahman
Green, Darrell
Green, Harold
Green, Hugh
Green, Jacquez
Green, Litterial
Green, Rickey
Green, Robert David
Green, Roy
Green, Scarborough
Green, Sean Curtis
Green, Sidney
Green, Victor Bernard
Green, Willie Aaron
Greene, Joe
Greene, Maurice
Greene, Willie Louis
Greenwood, David Kasim
Greer, Cherie
Greer, Donovan Orlando
Greer, Harold Everett
Grier, Marrio Darnell
Grier, Mike
Griffey, Ken, Jr.
Griffin, Leonard James, Jr.
Griffith, Darrell Steven
Griffith, Howard Thomas
Griffith, Robert Otis
Griffith, Yolanda Yvette
Griggs, Anthony
Grissom, Marquis Dean
Groce, Clifton Allen
Guynes, Thomas V.
Guyton, Wanda
Guzman, Juan Andres Correa
Gwynn, Tony
Hackett, Barry Dean
Hackman, Luther Gean
Hagler, Marvelous Marvin
Hagood, Jay
Hairston, Jerry Wayne
Hairston, Jerry Wayne, Jr.
Hakim, Az-zahir
Haley, Charles Lewis
Hall, Albert
Hall, Dana Eric
Hall, Lamont
Hall, Lemanski
Ham, Darvin
Hambrick, Darren
Hamer, Steve
Hamilton, Bobby
Hamilton, Darryl Quinn
Hamilton, Harry Edwin
Hamilton, Michael Antonio
Hamilton, Ruffin, III
Hamiter, Uhuru
Hammonds, Jeffrey Bryan
Hammonds, Tom
Hampton, Kym
Hampton, Rodney
Hancock, Darrin
Hand, Jon Thomas
Hand, Norman
Hanspard, Byron Courtenay, Sr.
Hardaway, Anfernee Deon
Hardaway, Timothy Duane
Harden, Cedric
Hardmon, Lady
Hardy, Darryl Gerrod
Hardy, Kevin Lamont
Harkey, Michael Anthony

Harper, Dwayne Anthony
Harper, Ronald
Harper, Terry Joe
Harper, Tommy
Harrington, Othella
Harris, Al
Harris, Al Carl
Harris, Bernardo Jamaine
Harris, Corey Lamont
Harris, Derrick
Harris, Fran
Harris, Franco
Harris, Jackie Bernard
Harris, James
Harris, Jonathan Cecil
Harris, Leonard Anthony
Harris, Lucious H
Harris, M. L.
Harris, Pep
Harris, Raymont LeShawn
Harris, Reggie
Harris, Robert Lee
Harris, Dr. Sarah Elizabeth
Harris, Sean Eugene
Harris, Walter Lee
Harrison, Alvin
Harrison, Calvin
Harrison, Chris
Harrison, Lisa Darlene
Harrison, Marvin Daniel
Harrison, Rodney Scott
Hartley, Frank
Harvey, Antonio
Harvey, Kenneth Ray
Harvey, Richard Clemont, Jr.
Hasselbach, Harald
Hastings, Andre Orlando
Hasty, James Edward
Hatcher, William Augustus
Hatchette, Matt
Hawkins, Artrell, Jr.
Hawkins, Courtney Tyrone, Jr.
Hawkins, Hersey R., Jr.
Hawkins, LaTroy
Hawkins, Michael
Hayden, Aaron Chautezz
Hayes, Charles Dewayne
Hayes, Chris
Hayes, Donald Ross, Jr.
Hayes, Elvin E.
Hayes, Jonathan Michael
Hayes, Melvin Anthony
Hayes, Mercury
Haynes, Michael David
Haywood, Spencer
Head, Dena
Heard, Gar
Heard, Herman Willie, Jr.
Hearns, Thomas
Hearst, Gerald Garrison
Hegamin, George
Hempstead, Hessley James, II
Hemsley, Nate
Henderson, Alan Lybrooks
Henderson, Cedric Earl
Henderson, Gerald
Henderson, Jerome Virgil
Henderson, Rickey Henley
Henderson, Tracy
Henderson, William Terrelle
Henry, Herman
Herndon, Larry Lee
Hewitt, Chris
Hicks, Eric David
Hicks, Foster
Hicks, Jessie Yvette
Hicks, Michael
Hicks, Robert
Hicks, Skip
Higgins, Sean Marielle
Highsmith, Alonzo Walter
Hill, Bruce Edward
Hill, Calvin G.
Hill, Eric
Hill, Glenallen
Hill, Grant Henry
Hill, Gregory LaMonte
Hill, Kenneth Wade
Hill, Randal Thrill
Hill, Raymond
Hill, Tyrone
Hilliard, Ike
Hilliard, Randy
Hinson, Roy Manus
Hitchcock, Jimmy Davis, Jr.
Hoard, Leroy
Hobbs, Daryl Ray
Hodge, Donald Jerome
Hodges, Craig Anthony

Hodgins, James William
Holbert, Ray Arthur, III
Holcombe, Robert
Holdsclaw, Chamique
Holland, Darius
Holland-Corn, Kedra
Holliday, Vonnie
Hollier, Dwight Leon, Jr.
Hollins, Lionel Eugene
Holmes, Clayton Antwan
Holmes, Darick
Holmes, Earl
Holmes, Jerry
Holmes, Kenny
Holmes, Larry
Holmes, Lester
Holmes, Priest Anthony
Holsey, Bernard
Holt, Leroy
Holt, Torry Jabar
Holyfield, Evander
Honeycutt, Jerald DeWayne
Hopkins, Bernard
Hopkins, Bradley D.
Hopkins, Wes
Horn, Joseph
Horne, Tony Tremaine
Horry, Robert Keith
Horton, Andre
Horton, Andreana Suki
Horton, Raymond Anthony
Horton, Willie Wattison
Houston, Allan Wade
Houston, Bobby
Houston, Kenneth Ray
Howard, Brian
Howard, Desmond Kevin
Howard, Juwan Antonio
Howard, Stephen
Howard, Ty
Hubbard, Philip Gregory
Hubbard, Trent
Huckaby, Malcolm
Hudson, Charles Lynn
Hudson, Christopher Resherd
Hudson, Troy
Hughes, Larry
Hughes, Mark
Hughes, Robert Danan
Hughes, Tyrone Christopher
Humphrey, Robert Charles
Humphries, Jay
Hundon, James Henry
Hunt, Cletidus
Hunter, Brian Lee
Hunter, Brian Ronald
Hunter, C. J.
Hunter, Lindsey Benson
Hunter, Tony Wayne
Hunter, Torii Kedar
Huskey, Butch
Hutson, Tony
Iginla, Jarome
Ingram, Garey
Ingram, Stephen Anthony
Irvin, Ken
Irvin, Michael Jerome
Irvin, Monford Merrill
Irvin, Sedrick
Irving, Terry Duane
Ismail, Qadry Rahmadan
Ismail, Raghib Ramadian
Israel, Steven Douglas
Iverson, Allen
Ivery, Eddie Lee
Jackson, Bo
Jackson, Bobby
Jackson, Charles Richard, Jr.
Jackson, Damian Jacques
Jackson, Dexter Lamar
Jackson, Grady O'Neal
Jackson, Grant Dwight
Jackson, Greg Allen
Jackson, Jaren
Jackson, Jim
Jackson, John
Jackson, Larron Deonne
Jackson, Mark A.
Jackson, Michael Ray
Jackson, Randell
Jackson, Raymond DeWayne
Jackson, Reggie Martinez
Jackson, Rickey Anderson
Jackson, Roy Lee
Jackson, Stanley Leon
Jackson, Steven Wayne
Jackson, Tammy
Jackson, Terry
Jackson, Tia

Jackson, Tyoka
Jackson, Waverly Arthur, Jr.
Jackson, Willie Bernard, Jr.
Jacobs, Regina
Jacobs, Tim
Jacox, Kendyl
Jacquet, Nate
James, Dion
James, Henry Charles
James, Jerome Keith
James, LeBron
James, Tory Steven
Jamison, Antawn Cortez
Jamison, George R., Jr.
Jasper, Edward Videl
Jeffcoat, James Wilson
Jefferies, Greg Lemont
Jefferson, Greg Benton
Jefferson, Reggie
Jefferson, Shawn
Jeffries, Greg
Jells, Dietrich
Jenkins, Billy Leon, Jr.
Jenkins, DeRon Charles
Jenkins, James
Jenkins, Melvin
Jensen, Marcus Christian
Jeter, Derek
Jett, James
Joe, William (Billy)
Johns, Pollyanna
Johnson, Adrienne
Johnson, Albert James
Johnson, Anthony Mark
Johnson, Anthony Scott
Johnson, Avery
Johnson, Charles Edward, Jr.
Johnson, Charles Everett
Johnson, Darrius Dashome
Johnson, Dave
Johnson, Dwayne Douglas
Johnson, Earvin
Johnson, Edward Arnet
Johnson, Ellis Bernard
Johnson, Ervin, Jr.
Johnson, Ezra Ray
Johnson, Frank
Johnson, Jimmie
Johnson, Joe T.
Johnson, Kelley Antonio
Johnson, Kevin Maurice
Johnson, Keyshawn
Johnson, Lance
Johnson, Larry Demetric
Johnson, LaTonya
Johnson, Leslie
Johnson, Lonnie Demetrius
Johnson, Mamie Peanut
Johnson, Melvin Carlton, III
Johnson, Niesa
Johnson, Olrick
Johnson, Pepper
Johnson, Raylee Terrell
Johnson, Ron
Johnson, Roy Edward
Johnson, Shannon
Johnson, Tiffani Tamara
Johnson, Tre
Johnson, Troy Dwan
Johnson, Vickie Annette
Johnson, Vinnie
Johnson, Wallace Darnell
Johnson, William Arthur
Johnson, William Edward
Johnson, William Leon
Johnstone, Lance
Joiner, Charles
Jones, Aaron Delmas
Jones, Andruw Rudolf
Jones, Bobby M.
Jones, Brian Keith
Jones, Caldwell
Jones, Cedric
Jones, Charles Gadget
Jones, Charles Rahmel
Jones, Charlie
Jones, Chris
Jones, Christopher Todd
Jones, Clarence Thomas
Jones, Cobi N'Gai
Jones, Damon
Jones, Damon Darron
Jones, DeLisha Milton
Jones, Dontae' Antijuaine
Jones, Eddie Charles
Jones, Edward Lee
Jones, Ernest Lee
Jones, Freddie
Jones, Gary DeWayne

Jones, Greg
Jones, Grover William, Jr.
Jones, Henry Louis
Jones, Jacque Dewayne
Jones, James Alfie
Jones, Jimmie Sims
Jones, K. C.
Jones, Lenoy
Jones, Marcus Edward
Jones, Marion
Jones, Markeysia Donta
Jones, Marvin Maurice
Jones, Merlakia Kenyatta
Jones, Michael Anthony
Jones, Michael David
Jones, Popeye
Jones, Reggie
Jones, Robert Lee
Jones, Rodrek Edward
Jones, Roger Carver
Jones, Rondell Tony
Jones, Roy
Jones, Samuel
Jones, Selwyn Aldridge
Jones, Tebucky
Jones, Tony Edward
Jones, Walter
Jordan, Andrew
Jordan, Brian O'Neil
Jordan, Darin Godfrey
Jordan, Eddie
Jordan, Kevin
Jordan, Michael
Jordan, Randy Loment
Jordan, Reggie
Jordan, Richard
Jordan, Ricky
Jordan, Steve Russell
Joseph, Kerry
Joyner, Seth
Joyner-Kersee, Jackie
Junior, E J
Justice, David Christopher
Kalu, Ndukwe Dike
Kapler, Gabe
Kazadi, Muadianvita Matt
Kellogg, Clark Clifton, Jr.
Kelly, Brian
Kelly, Joseph Winston, Jr.
Kelly, Michael Raymond
Kemp, Shawn T.
Kenlaw, Jessie
Kennedy, Cortez
Kennedy, Lincoln
Kennison, Eddie Joseph, III
Kerner, Marlon Lavelle
Kersey, Jerome
Keys, Randolph
Kidd, Jason Fredrick
Kidd, Warren Lynn
Killens, Terry Deleon
Kimble, Bo
King, Albert
King, Bernard
King, Gerard
King, Jimmy Hal
King, Ray
King, Shaun Earl
King, Shawn
King, Stacey
Kinnebrew, Larry D.
Kirkland, Levon
Kittles, Kerry
Knight, Brevin
Knight, Negele Oscar
Knight, Sammy D., Jr.
Knight, Thomas Lorenzo
Knox, William Robert
Koonce, George
Kroon, Marc Jason
Lacy, Venus
Lake, Carnell Augustino
Lamb, Monica
Land, Daniel
Landreaux, Kenneth Francis
Landrum, Tito
Lane, Jerome
Lang, Andrew Charles
Lang, Antonio
Lang, Kenard
Langford, Jevon
Langham, Antonio
Lanier, Rob
Lanier, Willie
Lankford, Raymond Lewis
Larkin, Barry Louis
Lassiter, Kwamie
Latham, Christopher Joseph
Lathon, Lamar Lavantha

Lauderdale, Priest
Lavan, Alton
Law, Tajuan E.
Lawrence, Philip Martin
Lawson, Jason
Lawton, Matthew, III
Leavell, Allen Frazier
Lee, Amp
Lee, Carl
Lee, Derrek Leon
Lee, Mark Anthony
Lee, Shawn Swaboda
Leftwich, Byron Antron
Legette, Tyrone
Lemon, Meadowlark
Lenard, Voshon Kelan
Lennon, Patrick Orlando
Lennox, Betty
Leonard, Jeffrey
Leonard, Sugar Ray
Leslie, Lisa Deshaun
Lester, Bill
Lester, George Lawrence
Lester, Tim Lee
Levens, Dorsey
Lever, Lafayette
Levingston, Bashir
Lewis, Albert Ray
Lewis, Carl
Lewis, Darren Joel
Lewis, Jermaine Edward
Lewis, Martin
Lewis, Marvin
Lewis, Mo
Lewis, Rashard Quovon
Lewis, Raymond Anthony
Lewis, Roderick Albert
Lewis, Ronald Alexander
Lewis, Steve Earl
Lewis, Thomas
Lincoln, Jeremy Arlo
Linton, Jonathan C.
Lippett, Ronnie Leon
Lipps, Louis Adam
Lister, Alton Lavelle
Little, Leonard Antonio
Livingston, Randy Anthony
Lloyd, Gregory Lenard
Lloyd, Lewis Kevin
Lockett, Kevin
Lockhart, Eugene
Lofton, James
Lofton, Kenneth
Lofton, Steven Lynn
Logan, Ernest Edward, II
Logan, James
Lombard, George Paul
Long, Grant Andrew
Long, John Eddie
Long, Terrence Deon
Lott, Ronnie
Louchiey, Corey
Loud, Kamil Kassan
Loville, Derek Kevin
Lowe, Sidney Rochell
Lowery, Michael
Lowery, Terrell
Lucas, Raymond J.
Lue, Tyronn Jamar
Lyght, Todd William
Lyle, Keith Allen
Lyle, Ron
Lyles, Lester Everett
Lynch, Eric
Lynch, George DeWitt
Lynn, Anthony Ray
Mack, Kevin
Mack, Shane Lee
Mack, Tremain
Mackey, John
Mackey, Malcolm
Macon, Mark L
Maddox, Garry Lee
Maddox, Mark Anthony
Madison, Samuel Adolfus, Jr.
Madlock, Bill, Jr.
Magee, Wendell Errol, Jr.
Mahomes, Patrick Lavon
Mahorn, Rick
Malone, Karl Anthony
Malone, Moses Eugene
Mann, Charles
Manning, Daniel Ricardo
Manning, Sharon
Manuel, Jerry
Manuel, Lionel
Mapp, Rhonda
Marbury, Stephon
Marion, Brock Elliot

Marion, Fred D
Marsh, Doug
Marsh, Michael Lawrence
Marshall, Anthony Dewayne
Marshall, Donyell Lamar
Marshall, Henry H.
Marshall, Leonard Allen, Jr.
Marshall, Marvin
Marshall, Wilber Buddyhia
Martin, Albert Lee
Martin, Curtis
Martin, Danyel Cecil
Martin, Darrick
Martin, Emanuel C.
Martin, George Dwight
Martin, Steven Albert
Martin, Tony Derrick
Martin, Wayne
Martinez, Ralph
Martinez, Ramon Jaime
Marts, Lonnie, Jr.
Marve, Eugene Raymond
Mashburn, Jamal
Mason, Anthony
Mason, Eddie Lee
Massenburg, Tony Arnel
Mathis, Dedric
Mathis, Kevin
Matthews, Gary Nathaniel, Jr.
Matthews, Vincent Edward
Maxey, Marlon Lee
Maxwell, Anita
Maxwell, Vernon
May, Derrick Brant
May, Mark Eric
Mayberry, Jermane Timothy
Mayberry, Tony
Mayers, Jamal David
Mayes, Alonzo
Mayes, Derrick
Mays, David
Mays, Kivuusama
Mays, Travis Cortez
Mays, willie howard
McAdoo, Bob
McAfee, Fred Lee
McBride, Tod Anthony
McBurrows, Gerald
McCants, Keith
McCarthy, Gregory O'Neil
McCarty, Walter Lee
McClendon, Lloyd Glenn
McClendon, Moses C.
McCleon, Dexter Keith
McCleskey, J. J.
McCloud, George Aaron
McCloud, Tyrus Kamall
McCombs, Tony
McCormack, Hurvin
McCorvey, Kez
McCoy, Anthony Bernard
McCoy, Jelani Marwan
McCracken, Quinton Antoine
McCrary, Fred Demetrius
McCraw, Tom
McCray, Nikki
McCrimmon, Nicky
McCutcheon, Lawrence
McDaniel, Edward
McDaniel, Emmanuel
McDaniel, Randall Cornell
McDaniel, Terrence Lee
McDaniel, William T., Jr.
McDaniel, Xavier Maurice
McDonald, Darnell Ali
McDonald, Donzell
McDonald, Jason Adam
McDonald, Dr. R. Timothy
McDonald, Ramos
McDonald, Ricardo Milton
McDonald, Timothy
McDyess, Antonio Keithflen
McElroy, Charles Dwayne, Sr.
McElroy, Leeland
McElroy, Raymond Edward
McFarland, Anthony Darelle
McGarity, Wane
McGee, Buford Lamar
McGee, Eva M
McGee, Pamela
McGee, Rev. Paula L.
McGee, Timothy Dwayne
McGee, Tony
McGee, Willie Dean
McGill, Lenny
McGinest, Willie
McGlockton, Chester
McGrady, Tracy
McGrew, Reggie

McGriff, Frederick Stanley
McInnis, Jeff Lemans
McIver, Everett
McKandes, Darnell Damon
McKenzie, Keith
McKenzie, Michael
McKey, Derrick Wayne
McKie, Aaron Fitzgerald
McKinnon, Ronald
McKnight, James
McLemore, Mark Tremell
McLeod, Kevin
McLeod, Roshown
McMillan, Nate
McMillan, Regina Ellis
McMillian, Mark
McMillon, Billy
McNabb, Donovan
McNair, Steve LaTreal
McNeal, Don
McNeely, Carol J.
McNeil, Freeman
McNeil, Lori Michelle
McNeil, Ryan Darrell
McPhail, Irving P.
McPhail, Jerris
McQuarters, Robert William, II
McRae, Harold Abraham
McSwain, Rodney
McSween, Cirilo A.
McWilliams, Johnny
McWilliams-Franklin, Taj
Means, Natrone Jermaine
Mee, LaFarrell Darnell
Meggett, David Lee
Mendenhall, John Rufus
Menefee, Juan F.
Mercer, Ronald Eugene
Merriweather, Michael Lamar
Metcalf, Eric Quinn
Mickell, Darren
Mickens, William Ray
Middleton, Frank, Jr.
Milbourne, Lawrence William
Milburn, Glyn Curt
Millender, Dharathula H.
Miller, Anthony
Miller, Bubba
Miller, Fred Junior, Jr.
Miller, Jamir Malik
Miller, Lawrence Anthony
Miller, Nate
Miller, Oliver J
Miller, Reginald Wayne
Miller, Robert Laverne
Miller, Wade Thomas
Milliard, Ralph Gregory
Milligan, Randall Andre
Milloy, Lawyer
Mills, Alan Bernard
Mills, Christopher Lemonte
Mills, Ernie
Mills, John Henry
Mills, Terry Richard
Milstead, Roderick Leon, Jr.
Mims, Christopher Eddie
Mincy, Charles Anthony
Miner, Harold
Minor, DeWayne
Minor, Greg Magado
Minter, Barry Antoine
Minter, Michael Christopher
Mitchell, Basil Mucktar
Mitchell, Brandon
Mitchell, Brian Keith
Mitchell, Keith
Mitchell, Mike Anthony
Mitchell, Robert C.
Mitchell, Samuel E
Mitchell, Shannon Lamont
Mix, Bryant Lee
Mixon, Kenny
Mobley, John Ulysses
Mobley, Singor A.
Mohammed, Nazr Tahiru
Molden, Alex M.
Moncrief, Sidney A.
Monroe, Earl
Montgomery, Joseph
Montgomery, Monty
Moon, Warren
Moore, Damon E.
Moore, Derrick C.
Moore, Herman Joseph
Moore, Jerald Christopher
Moore, John Brian
Moore, Kerwin Lamar
Moore, Larry Maceo
Moore, Lenny Edward

Moore, Nathaniel
Moore, Penny
Moore, Rob
Moore, Ronald
Moore, Will H., III
Moorer, Michael
Morgan, Stanley Douglas
Morman, Alvin
Morris, Christopher Vernard
Morris, Jamie Walter
Morris, Joe
Morris, Laticia
Morris, Wayne Lee
Morrow, Harold, Jr.
Morton, Johnnie James, Jr.
Moseby, Lloyd Anthony
Moses, Edwin
Mosley, Shane
Moss, Eric
Moss, Randy
Moss, Winston
Moss, Zefross
Moulds, Eric Shannon
Mourning, Alonzo
Mouton, James Raleigh
Mouton, Lyle Joseph
Mowatt, John
Muhammad, Muhsin, II
Mullen, Roderick
Mumphrey, Jerry Wayne
Munoz, Anthony
Murdock, Eric Lloyd
Murphy, Calvin Jerome
Murray, Calvin D.
Murray, Eddie Clarence
Murray, Lamond Maurice
Murray, Tracy Lamont
Murrell, Adrian Bryan
Mutombo, Dikembe
Myers, Michael
Myers, Peter E.
Myles, DeShone J.
Myles, Toby
Naeole, Chris
Nails, Jamie Marcellus
Nance, Larry Donell
Nash, Marcus DeLando
Nathan, Tony Curtis
Nattiel, Ricky Rennard
Ndiaye, Makhtar Vincent
Ndiaye-Diatta, Astou
Neal, Frederic Douglas
Neal, Lorenzo LaVon
Nelson, Darrin Milo
Newfield, Marc Alexander
Newman, Anthony
Newman, John Sylvester
Newman, Terence
Newsome, Ozzie, Jr.
Newsome, Vincent Karl
Newton, Nate
Nicholson, Tina
Nickerson, Hardy Otto
Nixon, Norm Ellard
Nixon, Otis Junior
Nolan, Deanna
Norman, Kenneth Darnel
Northern, Gabriel O.
Norton, Kenneth Howard
Nunn, Ronnie
Nunnally, Jonathon Keith
Oakley, Charles
O'Bannon, Charles Edward
O'Bannon, Edward Charles, Jr.
Oben, Roman Dissake
Odom, Clifton Lewis
Odomes, Nathaniel Bernard
Ogbogu, Eric O.
Ogden, Jonathan Phillip
Oglivie, Benjamin A.
Okino, Elizabeth Anna
Okoye, Christian E
Olajuwon, Hakeem Abdul
Oldham, Christopher Martin
Oldham, Jawann
O Leary, Troy Franklin
Oliver, Al
Oliver, Brian Darnell
Oliver, Darren Christopher
Oliver, Louis
Oliver, Winslow Paul
Olowokandi, Michael
O'Neal, Jermaine
O'Neal, Leslie Cornelius
O'Neal, Shaquille Rashaun
Outlaw, Charles
Outlaw, John
Overton, Douglas M.
Owens, Billy Eugene

Owens, Brigman
Owens, Isaiah Hudson
Owens, Rich Darryl
Owens, Terrell Eldorado
Oxendine, Kenneth
Pace, Orlando Lamar
Pack, Robert John
Paddio, Gerald
Page, Murriel
Page, Solomon
Paige, Stephone
Palmer, David Lee
Parish, Robert
Parker, Anthony
Parker, Anthony
Parker, Anthony Michael
Parker, David Gene
Parker, De
Parker, Riddick
Parker, Vaughn Antoine
Parmalee, Bernard A.
Parrish, Tony
Paschal, Tia
Pathon, Jerome
Patten, David
Patterson, Andrae Malone
Patterson, Ruben Nathaniel
Patton, Joseph
Patton, Marvcus Raymond
Paul, Tito
Payne, Kenneth Victor
Payton, Gary Dwayne
Payton, Jarrett
Peebles, Daniel Percy
Peeler, Anthony Eugene
Peete, Calvin
Peete, Rodney
Pegram, Erric Demont
Pelshak, Troy
Pena, Robert Bubba
Pena, Tony
Pendleton, Terry Lee
Penn, Christopher Anthony
Perkins, Sam Bruce
Perry, Darren
Perry, Edwardccc
Perry, Elliott
Perry, Marlo
Perry, Michael Dean
Perry, Timothy D
Perry, Wilmont
Perryman, Robert
Person, Chuck Connors
Person, Robert Alan
Person, Wesley Lavon
Peterson, Tony
Pettis, Bridget
Pettis, Gary George
Phifer, Roman Zubinsky
Phillips, Anthony Dwayne
Phillips, Tari Lynn
Philyaw, Dino
Pickens, Carl McNally
Pierce, Aaron
Pierce, Paul
Pierce, Ricky Charles
Pinckney, Edward Lewis
Pinkett, Allen Jerome
Pippen, Scottie
Pittman, Dr. Audrey Bullock
Pittman, Kavika Charles
Pittman, Michael
Pleasant, Anthony Devon
Pless, Willie
Pollard, Marcus LaJuan
Polynice, Olden
Poole, Tyrone
Porcher, Robert, III
Porter, Rufus
Porter, Terry
Posey, Jeff
Potts, Roosevelt Bernard
Pounds, Darryl Lamont
Powell, Carl
Powell, Craig
Powell, Dante
Powell, Elaine
Powell, Marvin, Jr.
Powell, Renee
Preston, Roell
Price, Marcus
Pride, Curtis John
Pringle, Mike
Prioleau, Pierson
Prior, Anthony
Pritchard, Michael Robert
Pritchett, Kelvin Bratodd
Pritchett, Stanley Jerome
Pruitt, Gregory Donald, Jr.

Pruitt, James Boubias
Pruitt, Michael
Pryce, Trevor
Purnell, Lovett
Purvis, Andre
Quarles, Shelton Eugene
Quick, Mike
Raines, Timothy
Ramsey, Jerome Capistrano
Randle, John
Randolph, Zach
Ransom, Derrick
Rasby, Walter Herbert
Rathman, Thomas Dean
Ratliff, Theo Curtis
Ray, Johnny
Rayford, Floyd Kinnard
Recasner, Eldridge David
Redmon, Kendrick Anthony
Redus, Gary Eugene
Reed, Andre Darnell
Reed, Brandy
Reed, Jake
Reed, Willis
Reese, Albert
Reese, Ike
Reese, Izell
Reese, Pokey
Reeves, Carl
Reeves, Khalid
Reid, Don
Reid, J. R.
Reid, Robert
Reid, Tracy
Relaford, Desi
Renfro, Melvin Lacy
Reynolds, Jerry
Reynolds, R. J.
Reynolds, Ricky Scott
Rheams, Leonta
Rhett, Errict Undra
Rhodes, Arthur Lee, Jr.
Rhodes, Karl Derrick
Rhodes, Rodrick
Ribbs, William Theodore, Jr.
Rice, Rev. Allen Troy
Rice, Glen A.
Rice, Jerry Lee
Rice, Ronald
Rice, Simeon
Richard, Stanley Palmer
Richardson, Clint Dewitt, Jr.
Richardson, Damien
Richardson, Gloster V.
Richardson, Jerome
Richardson, Tony
Richmond, Mitch
Ricks, Mikhael
Rider, Isaiah
Riggs, Gerald Antonio
Rijo, Jose Antonio
Riley, Eric
Riley, Victor Allan
Rison, Andre Previn
Rivers, Mickey
Rivers, Ronald Leroy
Roaf, William Layton
Robbins, Austin Dion
Roberts, Bip
Roberts, Brett
Roberts, Nyree
Roberts, Ray
Roberts, William Harold
Robertson, Andre Levett
Robertson, Dewayne
Robertson, Marcus Aaron
Robertson, Oscar Palmer
Robinson, Chris
Robinson, Clifford Ralph
Robinson, Crystal
Robinson, Damien Dion
Robinson, David Maurice
Robinson, Eddie Joseph, Jr.
Robinson, Eugene Keefe
Robinson, Frank
Robinson, Glenn A
Robinson, Larry
Robinson, Marcus
Robinson, R David, Sr.
Robinson, Rumeal James
Rodgers, Derrick Andre
Rodman, Dennis Keith
Rogers, Carlos Deon
Rogers, Charles
Rogers, Chris
Rogers, Rodney Ray
Rogers, Roy
Rogers, Sam
Rolison, Nate

McCutcheon, Lawrence
McDaniel, Emmanuel
McDaniels, Alfred F.
McDonald, Timothy
McElrath-Frazier, Wanda Faith
McElroy, Dr. Njoki
McGee, Willie Dean
McGill, Lenny
McGlockton, Chester
McKandes, Darnell Damon
McKandes, Dorothy Dell
McKenzie, Keith
McKie, Aaron Fitzgerald
McKinney, Billy
McKnight, James
McLeod, Kevin
McLeod, Roshown
McMillan, Nate
McNorton, Bruce Edward
McRae, Harold Abraham
Mendez, Hugh B.
Merriweather, Michael Lamar
Middleton, Frank, Jr.
Miller, Cheryl De Ann
Mills, Ernie
Mills, John Henry
Mills, Steve
Mitchell, Robert C.
Mitchell, Samuel E
Monk, Art
Moore, Derrick C.
Moore, Oscar William
Moore, Yolanda
Moorman, Clinton R
Morgan, Joe
Morgan, Wayne
Mosley, Benita Fitzgerald
Moss, Winston
Mouton, James Raleigh
Murray, Tracy Lamont
Myles, William
Napper, Hyacinthe T.
Nathan, Tony Curtis
Natt, Kenny
Nelson, Darrin Milo
Newsome, Ozzie, Jr.
Newsome, Vincent Karl
Nichols, Crystal Faye
Nickerson, Hardy Otto
Norrell-Thomas, Sondra
Norton, Kenneth Howard
Norvell, Dr. Merritt J.
Nunn, Ronnie
Oates, Wanda Anita
Ogden, Jonathan Phillip
Orr, Louis M.
Outlaw, John
Oxendine, Kenneth
Palmer, Violet
Paris, William H.
Parker, Charlie
Parker, David Gene
Parmalee, Bernard A.
Patterson, Paul
Patton, Ricardo Maurice
Payne, Kenneth Victor
Payne, Vernon
Peay, Francis
Peck, Carolyn
Pegram, Erric Demont
Pender, Mel
Perry, Gerald
Perry, Wilmont
Perryman, Robert
Person, Chuck Connors
Pettis, Gary George
Phillips, Theresa Lawrence
Pippen, Scottie
Pitts, Lee H.
Polynice, Olden
Porter, Terry
Pressey, Paul Matthew
Prince, Andrew Lee
Pritchett, Stanley Jerome
Raines, Timothy
Randolph, Willie Larry
Rathman, Thomas Dean
Raveling, George Henry
Ray, Dr. Judith Diana
Ready, Stephanie
Reed, Willis
Renfro, Melvin Lacy
Respert, Shawn Christopher
Rhett, Errict Undra
Rhodes, Ray
Rice, Jim
Richardson, Gloster V.
Richardson, Jerome
Richardson, Leroy

Richardson, Nolan
Richmond, Mitch
Rijo, Jose Antonio
Riley, Kenneth J.
Rivers, Glenn Anton
Roberts, Cheryl Dornita Lynn
Roberts, Ray
Roberts, Trish
Roberts, William Harold
Robertson, Andre Levett
Robinson, Eugene Keefe
Robinson, Frank
Robinson, Sharon
Robinson, Steve
Robinson, Will
Rollins, Tree
Romain, Pierre R
Rooks, Sean Lester
Ross, Adrian
Royal, Donald
Rush, Eddie F.
Russell, Bill
Rycraw, Eugenia
Sampson, Kelvin
Sands, Jerry Leigh
Scott, Brent
Scott, Byron
Scott, Melvina Brooks
Scott, Olympia Ranee
Scurlock, Michael Lee
Seale, Samuel Ricardo
Searcy, Leon, Jr.
Shell, Arthur
Sherman, Ray
Shields, Dr. Clarence L
Shipp, Howard J., Jr.
Shuler, Adrienne
Siglar, Ricky Allan
Silas, Paul Theron
Simien, Tracy Anthony
Simmons, Bob
Simmons, Juanita
Simon, Matt
Simon, Miles Julian
Simpkins, LuBara Dixon
Sinclair, Michael Glenn
Singleton, Kenneth Wayne
Smith, Cedric Delon
Smith, Eugene DuBois
Smith, Larry
Smith, Lovie Lee
Smith, Michael
Smith, Otis
Smith, Otis Fitzgerald
Smith, Robert Scott
Smith, Rodney Stacey
Smith, Tarik
Smith, Tubby
Solomon, Jimmie Lee
Sparrow, Rory Darnell
Spencer, Jimmy
Stafford, Derrick
Stafford-Odom, Trisha
Staley, Dawn
Steward, Emanuel
Stewart, Rayna Cottrell, II
Still, Valerie
Stokes, Eric
Stout, Louis
Strickland, R. James
Strickland, Rodney
Stringer, C Vivian
Strong, Marilyn Terry
Strong, Otis Reginald
Stubblefield, Dana William
Taylor, Charley R.
Taylor, Joseph
Taylor, Vanessa Gail
Teague, George Theo
Temple, Edward Stanley
Theus, Reggie Wayne
Thomas, Blair
Thomas, Dr. Dennis
Thomas, Isiah Lord
Thomas, Jim
Thomas, John
Thomas, Orlando
Thompson, David O'Neil
Thompson, John Robert
Thompson, Milt
Thompson, Rhonda Denise
Thompson, Ronald Anthony
Thomson, John, III
Threatt, Sedale Eugene
Timpson, Michael Dwain
Toler, Penny
Toliver, George
Tovar, Steven Eric
Trapp, James

Tremitiere, Chantel
Tribble, Keith
Trice, Trena
Truvillion, Wendy
Turner, Robert, Jr.
Unseld, Wes
Upshaw, Willie Clay
Ussery, Terdema Lamar
Valmon, Andrew Orlando
Vanover, Tamarick
Veland, Tony
Venable, Max
Walker, Darnell Robert
Walker, Darrell
Walker, Dr. LeRoy Tashreau
Walker-Gibbs, Shirley Ann
Ward, Charlie
Ward, Dedric Lamar
Ware, R David
Washington, Coquese
Washington, Marian
Washington, Rudy
Washington, Todd Page
Washington, Tom
Waters, Gary Steven
Watkins, Melvin
Watson, Perry
Watson, Robert Jose
Weathers, Andre
West, Mark Andre
Westbrook, Peter Jonathan
Wheatley, Tyrone
Wheaton, Frank Kahlil
Wheeler, Theodore Stanley
Whigham, Larry Jerome
Whitaker, Pernell
White, Rory Wilbur
White, Dr. Tommie Lee
White, Tytral T
Wiley, Morlon David
Wilkens, Leonard Randolph
Wilkins, Jacques Dominique
Williams, Billy Leo
Williams, Bobby
Williams, Buck
Williams, Doug Lee
Williams, Fred
Williams, George
Williams, Herb E.
Williams, Herb L.
Williams, Ken
Williams, Monty
Williams, Willie James
Williams, Willie LaVern
Williamson, Corliss Mondari
Willingham, Tyrone
Willis, James Edward, III
Wilson, Mookie
Wilson-George, Sybil
Windham, Rhonda
Winslow, Kellen Boswell
Winston, Lamonte
Winters, James Robert
Wood, Osie Leon, III
Wood, Tommie
Wood, William Vernell, Sr.
Wooden, Terry
Woodson, Mike
Wooldridge, Orlando Vernada
Wright, Joseph A
Wright, Stanley V.
Wynne, Dana
Yates, Anthony J.

Statistics

Andrews, Nelson Montgomery
Brown, Charles Edward
Earl, Dr. Archie William
Ebbe, Dr. Obi N I
Freeman, Kimberley Edelin
Guffey, Edith A
Harris, Dr. John H.
Newhouse, Quentin
Richards, Winston Ashton
Smith, Dr. Roulette William
Stokes, Julie Elena
Wilson, Dr. Jeffrey R.

Telegraph Industry
See **Telephone/Telegraph Industry**

Telephone/Telegraph Industry

Adams, Eula L.
Banks, Perry L
Bolling, Deborah A
Bradford, James Edward

Brown, Arnold E.
Campbell, Blanch
Carter, Dr. John H
Clark-Taylor, Kristin
Cochran, Edward G.
Cooper, Larry B
Cooper, Robert N.
Daniel, Jack L.
Dunham, Clarence E.
Dyer, Joe, Jr.
Edwards, Theodore Allen
Elliott, Monte Ray
Fernandez, John Peter
Gordon, Garth
Grayson, Byron J., Sr.
Grier, Johnny
Heyward-Garner, Ilene Patricia
Hite, Nancy Ursula
Hodges, Patricia Ann
Honore, Stephan LeRoy
Jackson, Dr. Shirley Ann
Jeter, Joseph C., Jr.
Lewis, Charles McArthur
Love, Jon
Lumpkin, Adrienne Kelly
Mateen, Malik Abdul
Miller, Dr. Andrea Lewis
Montgomery, Ethel Constance
Morris, Bernard Alexander
Nobles, Patricia Joyce
Norfleet, Janet
Owens, Victor Allen
Pinkney, John Edward
Ransom, Leticia Buford
Reed, Derryl L
Salaam, Dr. Abdul
Savage, Dr. James Edward
Simmons, Thelma M
Smith, Anthony Edward
Spurlock, Dr. James B
Stockton, Carlton A
Stovall, Audrean
Summers, Retha
Walker, Vernon David
Washington, William Montell
Wells, Robert Benjamin, Jr.
Wesley, Clemon Herbert, Jr.
Whaley, Charles H
Williams, Vernice Louise
Wing, Theodore W

Television/Cable Broadcasting Industry

Abdullah, Talib
Abney, Robert
Alfonso, Pedro
Allen, Marcus LeMarr
Anderson, Bernadine M.
Anderson, Jamal
Arnold, John Russell, Jr.
Bailey, Thurl Lee
Bailey, William H.
Baldwin, Louis J
Barden, Don H.
Battle, Roxane
Bell, Victory
Bellamy, Bill
Berry, Ondra Lamon
Blackwell, Faye Brown
Boatwright, Cynthia
Bolling, Carol Nicholson
Boston, McKinley, Jr.
Bowser, Kyle D
Brady, Wayne Alfonzo
Brittain, Bradley Bernard, Jr.
Brooks, Sheila Dean
Brown, Ellen Rochelle
Brown, James
Brownlee, Jack M
Bryant, Damon K
Burnett, David Lawrence
Burwell, Bryan Ellis
Cafritz, Peggy Cooper
Cannon, Reuben
Castro, George A
Charles, RuPaul Andre
Christian, Spencer
Clayton, Xernona
Cole, Lydia
Collinet, Georges Andre
Collins, Tessil John
Cooley, Wendy
Cornelius, Donald Cortez
Cornwell, W. Don
Coye, Dena E.
Craft, Sally-Ann Roberts
Crippens, David L.
Crockett, Ray
Crombaugh, Hallie

Cross, Howard
Culbreath-Manly, Tongila M
Davis, Frederick D.
Davis, Preston A
Davis, Terrell
Dejoie, Michael C
Denson, Fred L
Dorsey, Sandra
Drexler, Clyde
Dyer, Joe, Jr.
Easter, Eric Kevin
Edwards, Delores A.
Eiland, Mike
Elliott, Sean Michael
Estes-Sumpter, Sidmel Karen
Evans, Liz
Ferguson, Joel I
Ferguson, Renee
Flake, Nancy Aline
Fortune-Maginley, Lois J.
Fox, Charles Washington
Gaines, Adriane Theresa
Gaines, Mary E
George, Eddie
George, Pauline L
Gibbs, Karen Patricia
Gordon, Alexander H., II
Gordon-Dillard, Joan Yvonne
Grandberry, Nikki
Gray, Derwin Lamont
Green, Roy
Greer, Karyn Lynette
Griffith, Howard Thomas
Griffith, Mark Richard
Griffith, Robert Otis
Guitano, Anton W.
Gumbel, Bryant Charles
Guynes, Thomas V.
Hagan, Gwenael Stephane
Haggins, Jon
Hall, Arsenio
Hammons, William, II
Haney, Don Lee
Hankins, Anthony Mark
Harrell, Andre
Harris, Fran
Hasty, James Edward
Hawthorne, Angel L.
Hayes, Eleanor Maxine
Hayward, Ann Stewart
Hayward, Dr. Jacqueline C
Hazel, Janis D
Henderson, Eddie L.
Henderson, Gerald
Herman, Kathleen Virgil
Hickman, Frederick Douglass
Hill, Mervin E., Jr.
Hobson, Charles Blagrove
Holden, Michelle Y
Horton, Dollie Bea Dixon
Howard, Gregory Allen
Howard, Samuel Houston
Hudson, Dianne Atkinson
Huff, Janice Wages
Jackson, Beverly Anne
Jackson, Beverly Joyce
Jackson, Donald J
Jackson, Eugene D.
Jackson, Randy
Jackson, Tomi L.
Jaycox, Mary Irine
Jenkins, Carol Ann
Jessup, Gayle Louise
Johnson, Dennis
Johnson, Henry Wade
Johnson, Iola Vivian
Johnson, Jay
Johnson, Luther E
Johnson, MaryAnn
Jones, Bob
Jones, Cheryl Arleen
Jones, Jill Marie
Jones, Marcus Edmund
Jones, Star
Jones, Victoria C.
Karpeh, Enid Juah Hildegard
Kellogg, Clark Clifton, Jr.
Kennard, Patricia A.
Kerr, Brook
Kinchlow, Ben
LaMotte, Jean Moore
LaVeist, Wilbert Francisco
Lawson, Debra Ann
Lawson, Jennifer Karen
LeCompte, Peggy Lewis
Lee, Jefferi K
LeFlore, Lyah B
Levy, Victor Miles, Jr.
Lewis, Byron E

Lewis, Maurice
Lewis, Ronald Stephen
Lewis, Sarasvati Ananda
Love, Thomas Clifford
Lowry, William E, Jr.
Lucas, Raymond J.
Mann, Charles
Marbury, Donald Lee
Marshall, Patricia Prescott
Marshburn, Everett Lee
Martin, Carol
Matchett, Johnson
Mathews, Keith E
Matthews, Claude Lankford, Jr.
May, Mark Eric
McCaa, Mark Eric
McCree, Edward L.
McEwen, Mark
McEwing, Mitchell Dalton
McFarland, Roland C
McGee, Henry Wadsworth
McGinest, Willie
McGlowan, Angela
McKee, Clarence Vanzant
McKee, Lonette
McNeill, Cerves Todd
Miles, George L
Miller, Bubba
Miller, E. Ethelbert
Miller, Dr. Lamar Perry
Mitchell, Brian Keith
Mohamed, Gerald R, Jr.
Montgomery, Joseph
Moore, Cynthia M
Moore, Gregory B
Morgan, Joe
Morgan, Stacey Evans
Moss, Anni R.
Murphy, Calvin Jerome
Murray, James P
Myles, Stan, Jr.
Myrick, Dr. Howard A.
Neal, Charlie
Newman, Anthony
Newton, Nate
Nightingale-Hawkins, Monica R
Ogilvie, Lana
Oliver, Pam
Ollison, Ruth Allen
Owens, Dr. Debbie A.
Palmer, Darlene Tolbert
Parker, William Hayes, Jr.
Payne, Allison Griffin
Peete, Rodney
Perkins, Tony
Phillips, Julian Martin
Phillips, Lionel Gary
Pippen, Scottie
Pool-Eckert, Marquita Jones
Posey, Deborah
Pounds, Elaine
Poussaint, Renee Francine
Powell, Adam Clayton, III
Prelow, Arleigh
Price, Ray Anthony
Purvis, Archie C.
Quick, Mike
Rashad, Dr. Ahmad
Ready, Stephanie
Revish, Jerry
Rich, Betty
Rickman, Ray
Riley, Glenn Pleasants
Rivero, Marita
Roberts, Bip
Roberts, Kim
Robinson, John L.
Robinson, Johnathan Prather
Robinson, Robin
Rodgers, Johnathan A.
Rogers, David William
Roker, Albert Lincoln
Rolle, Janet
Rose, Jalen
Russell, Sandra Anita
Ryan-White, Jewell
Sapp, Warren Carlos
Satchell, Elizabeth
Scafe, Judith Arlene
Scott, Robert Jerome
Scott, Samuel
Sharpe, Shannon
Sharper, Darren
Simmons-Edelstein, Dee
Simons, Eglon E
Simpson, Donnie
Singleton, Kenneth Wayne
Small, Sydney L.
Smith, Barbara

Smith, Gerald Wayne
Smith, Nick
Smith, Vinson Robert
Stewart, Alison
Stewart, Bernard
Stokes, Chris
Stokes, Jerel Jamal
Strong, Mack
Swainson, Sharon C.
Syler, M Rene
Talbert, Ted
Taylor, Aaron Matthew
Taylor, Ellis Clarence, Sr.
Terrell, Donna
Thomas, Arthur Lafayette, III
Thomas, Terence
Thomas-Samuel, Kalin Normoet
Thoms, Donald H
Timpson, Michael Dwain
Tobin, Lauren
Townsend, Ronald
Vargus, Bill
Vaughan, Rev. James Edward
Vincent, Irving H.
Wagoner, J Robert
Walker, Mary L
Walker, Rhonda
Wallace, John
Warfield, Robert N
Washington, Carl Douglas
Washington, Dante Deneen
Washington, Dr. Edith May Faulkner
Washington, Ukee
Waters, Brenda Joyce
Waters, Paul Eugene, Jr.
Watson, Ben
Watson, Karen Elizabeth
Watson, Leighton
Watts, Rolanda
Waugh, Judith Ritchie
Webb, Spud
Whack, Rita Coburn
Whitsett, James A, Jr.
Williams, Armon Abdule
Williams, Charlene J.
Williams, Jayson
Williams, Joanne Louise
Williams, Montel
Winfrey, Oprah
Winn, Carol Denise
Woodbeck, Frank Raymond
Woodson, Darren Ray
Worford, Carolyn Kennedy
Wright, Pandit F
Yearwood, David Monroe, Jr.
Young, Eric Orlando
Zola, Nkenge

Translation/Interpretation
Hodges, Patricia Ann
Jackson, William Ed

Transportation/Moving Services
Aiken, William
Allen, Bernestine
Allen, Stanley M.
Atkinson, Eugenia Calwise
Baker, Robert N.
Barnes, Ronald Lewis
Black, Dr. Billy Charleston
Bledsoe, Melvin
Branker, Julian Michael
Brazil, Robert D.
Brown, Edward Lynn
Buckson, Toni Yvonne
Burts, Ezunial
Butler, Roy
Carter, Will J.
Cooke, Thomas H, Jr.
Copeland, Richard Allen
Curry, Major Gen. Jerry Ralph
DeLibero, Shirley A.
Diane, Mamadi
Duncan, Sandra Rhodes
Farmer, Clarence
Ferguson, Elliott LaRoy
Ferguson, Sherlon Lee
Fisher, George Carver
Frazier, Joe
Gabriel, Benjamin Moses
Garrett, Melvin Alboy
George, Edward
Griffith, John A.
Gulley, Wilson
Hall, Brian Edward
Harris, Archie Jerome
Hart, Christopher Alvin
Henry, I Patricia

Heyward-Garner, Ilene Patricia
Hogan, Carolyn Ann
Hunter, John W.
Jackson, Fred H
Jones, Frank Benson
Jordan, Josephine E C
Kennard, Patricia A.
Lee, John Robert E.
Leigh, Fredric H
Lewis, Robert Alvin
Lewis, Dr. Samuel, Jr.
Medford, Isabel
Mohamed, Gerald R, Jr.
Moore, David Bernard, II
Morris, John P, III
Newhouse, Robert F
Norwood, William R.
Petersen, Arthur Everett, Jr.
Robinson, Albert Arnold
Scott, Dr. Beverly Angela
Sigler, I. Garland
Smith, LeRoi Matthew-Pierre, III
Stewart, Ronald Patrick
Stokes, Rueben Martine
Taylor, Martha
Thomas, Charles W
Tyree, Patricia Grey
White, Gary Leon
Williams, Bruce E.
Williams, Dr. Lisa R.

Travel Industry
Bailey, Myrtle Lucille
Bledsoe, Melvin
Bridgewater, Dr. Herbert Jeremiah, Jr.
Burns, Leonard L
Campbell, Blanch
Campbell, Franklyn D.
Davis, Adrianne
Davis, Agnes Maria
Dildy, Catherine Greene
Gardner, Ava Maria
Gray, Ronald A
Grimsley, Ethelyne
Hall, Tanya Evette
Heard, Georgina E
Houston, Wade
Jackson, Darcy DeMille
Jackson, Mary
Mingo, Pauline Hylton
Muhammad, Akbar A
Norman, William Stanley
Pitcher, Capt. Frederick M A
Quick, R Edward
Robinson, Malcolm
Rochester, Geof
Saunders, Barbara Ann
Spencer, Brenda L
Strong, Otis Reginald
Taylor, Valerie Charmayne
Walker, Eugene Kevin
Wilson, Charles Lee, Sr.
Wilson, Markly
Yarbrough, Patricia Nicholson

Urban/Regional Planning
Allen, Charles Claybourne
Arbuckle, John Finley, Jr.
Armstead, Ron E.
Bennett, Maybelle Taylor
Best, John T.
Black, Dr. Malcolm Mazique
Blayton-Taylor, Betty
Bridges, Leon
Brooks, Dunbar
Brown, Norman E.
Campbell, Wendell J.
Cason, David, Jr.
Coleman, Hurley J., Jr.
Colston, Monroe James
Compton, James W.
Cooper, Ernest, Jr.
Daniels, A. Raiford
Davis, Anita Louise
Davis, William E., Sr.
Dowell-Cerasoli, Patricia R
Dubose, Cullen Lanier
Dye, Clinton Elworth, Jr.
Earvin, Larry L.
Garner, Thomas L.
Gilliam, James H., Sr.
Griggs, John W.
Grigsby, Jefferson Eugene, III
Grigsby, Troy L
Harris, Dr. William McKinley
Hernandez, Aileen Clarke
Hill, Robert Bernard
Holder, Reuben D.

Jeff, Gloria Jean
Johnson, Kalanos Vontell
Johnson, Ronald Cornelius
Knight, Leonard G.
Knox, Wayne D. P.
Lane, Allan C
Lang, Dr. Marvel
Lee, Dr. Silas, III
Lillard, Kwame Leo
Lindsey, Jerome W.
Maith, Sheila Francine
McGuire, Cyril A.
Meeks, Reginald Kline
Millett, Ricardo A.
Mock, James E
Morrison, Jacqueline
Price, Prof. Alfred Douglas
Robinson, Joseph William
Ross, Dr. Catherine Laverne
Russell, Jackson
Schmiegelow, Toni D
Scruggs-Leftwich, Yvonne
Shepherd, Malcolm Thomas
Smith, Diane L
Stull, Donald L.
Wescott, Abraham
Williams, Harold Louis
Williams, Reginald Clark
Williams, Roy Levy

Veterinary Medicine
Adams, Eugene William
Christie, James Albert
Foster, Alvin Garfield
Kimbrough, Charles Edward
Lee, Dr. Allen Francis, Jr.
Moore, Dr. Roscoe Michael
Myers, Bernard Samuel
Parker, Charles McCrae
Presley, Oscar Glen
Raby, Clyde T
St Omer, Vincent V E

Wholesale Trade—Apparel, Piece Goods, and Notions
Brandon, Carl Ray
Clarke, Charlotte
Foster-Grear, Pamela
Jackson, Willis Randell, II
Lauderback, Brenda Joyce
Liggins, W Anthony
McQueen, Anjetta
Mohamed, Gerald R, Jr.
Robinson, Ronnie W
Sockwell, Oliver R, Jr.
Thornton, Cora Ann Barringer

Wholesale Trade—Building/Construction Materials
Davis, Frank Allen
Dean, Daniel R.

Wholesale Trade—Chemicals and Allied Products
Coshburn, Henry S., Jr.
Harrison, Charles
Mays, William G
Williams, Joseph Lee

Wholesale Trade—Drugs and Toiletries
Bethea, Edwin Ayers
Clarke, Greta Fields
Daurham, Ernest
Dudley, Joe Louis
Pratt, Dr. Ruth Jones
Williams, Dr. E Faye
Williams, Paul S

Wholesale Trade—Electrical/Electronics Products
Davis, Frank Allen
Handy, Lillian B.
Turner, Robert Lloyd

Wholesale Trade—Food and Beverages
Beauchamp, Patrick L.
Carter, Chester C.
Diggs, Lawrence J
Duerson, David R
Gates, Clifton W.
Goss, Tom

Harvey, Dr. William R.
Henry, I Patricia
James, Charles Howell, II
Johnson, Eric G
Lara, Edison R, Sr.
Locklin, James R.
McCain, Ella Byrd
McCoy, Jessie Haynes
Price, Judith
Richardson, Johnny L.
Robinson, R David, Sr.
Thompson, Albert N.
White, Ralph L.
Woods, Alison Scott

Wholesale Trade—Hardware
Thornton, Willie James, Jr.
Worth, Janice Lorraine

Wholesale Trade—Industrial Machinery, Equipment, and Supplies
Anderson, Alfred Anthony
Lewis, Robert Alvin
Moody, Harold L.
Morrison, Paul-David
Oliver, Everett Ahmad
Thornton, Willie James, Jr.

Wholesale Trade—Motor Vehicles and Parts
Addison, James David
Brown, Larry T.
Davidson, Fletcher Vernon, Jr.
Dixon, Raymond
Durden, Earnel
Hovell, Yvonne
Hysaw, Guillermo Lark
Lee, Fred D, Jr.
Lewis-Kemp, Jacqueline
Munson, Robert H
Statham, Carl
Wright, Dawin Lyron

Wholesale Trade—Paper and Allied Products
Gray, Wilfred Douglas
Thornton, Willie James, Jr.
Williams, Joseph Lee

Wholesale Trade—Not Elsewhere Classified
Apea, Joseph Bennet Kyeremateng
Arrington, Warren H., Jr.
Benjamin, Floyd
Bennett, Courtney Ajaye
Black, Walter Weldon, Jr.
Cowden, Michael E.
Honore, Stephan LeRoy
Howell, Amaziah, III
Lewis, Michele
Love, Lamar Vincent
McGhee, Georgia Mae
McMillan, Rosalyn A.
Richardson, Otis Alexander
Seals, George E.
Tate, Brett Andre
Taylor, Lorenzo James, Jr.
Thornton, Willie James, Jr.
Turner, Robert Lloyd
Williams, Joseph Lee
Young, Arlene H

Writing/Editing—Fiction
Alexander, Dr. Estella Conwill
Angelou, Dr. Maya
Ansa, Tina McElroy
Austin, Dr. Bobby William
Avery, Charles E
Bailey, Richard
Baiocchi, Regina Harris
Baraka, Imamu Amiri
Bates, Karen Grigsby
Bauldock, Gerald
Becker-Slaton, Dr. Nellie Frances
Beckham, Barry Earl
Bell, Jimmy
Billingsley, Ray C.
Bradley, Andrew Thomas, Sr.
Bradley, David Henry, Jr.
Branch, Otis Linwood
Bright, Jean Marie
Brown, Kay B.
Brown, Margery Wheeler
Bryan, Ashley F.
Buchanan, Shonda T

Bullins, Ed
Bunkley, Anita Richmond
Burnett, Zaron Walter, Jr.
Burroughs, Dr. Margaret Taylor
Cary, Lorene
Channer, Colin
Chase-Riboud, Dr. Barbara DeWayne
Cleage, Pearl Michelle
Coleman, Wanda
Collier, Dr. Eugenia W.
Cooper, J. California
Covin, Dr. David L.
Cummings, Pat
Curtis, Christopher Paul
Danticat, Edwidge
Davis, Gene A.
Dawson Boyd, Dr. Candy
DeBerry, Virginia
DeGraffenreidt, Andrew
Delany, Samuel Ray
Demby, Prof. William E.
DeRamus, Betty
De Veaux, Alexis
Dickey, Eric Jerome
Draper, Sharon Mills
Due, Tananarive
Evans, Mari
Fewell, Richard
Files, Lolita
Flournoy, Valerie Rose
Forbes, Calvin
Fortune, Dr. Gwendoline Y.
Fry, Darrell
Fuller, Charles
Gaines, Ernest J.
Gates, Dr. Henry Louis
Golden, Marita
Gomez, Jewelle L
Goss, Linda
Greenlee, Sam
Grimes, Nikki
Guy, Rosa Cuthbert
Hairston, William
Hale, Marna Amoretti
Halliburton, Warren J.
Hansen, Joyce Viola
Harris, E. Lynn
Hayes, Teddy
Haywood, Gar Anthony
Herron, Carolivia
Hill, Donna
Hogue, Leslie Denise
Ione, Carole
Jackson, Darcy DeMille
Jackson, Garnet Nelson
Jasper, Kenji Nathaniel
Johnson, Charles Richard
Johnson, Dorothy Turner
Johnson, Georgia Anna Lewis
Johnson, Mathew
Johnson, R.M.
Jones, Gayl
Kamau, Kwadwo Agymah
Kenan, Randall G.
Keymah, Crystal T
Kincaid, Jamaica
King-Gamble, Marcia
Kitt, Sandra Elaine
Kuykendall, Dr. Crystal Arlene
Ladd, Florence Cawthorne
Lamar, Jake V, Sr.
Large, Jerry D
Larkin, Dr. Byrdie A.
Lattany, Kristin Hunter
Lawson Roby, Kimberla
Lee, Andrea
Lee, Helen Elaine
Lee, William James Edwards, III
Leeke, Madelyn Cheryl
Lester, Julius
Levermore, Jacqueline Maureen
Little, Benilde Elease
Lockhart, Zelda
London, Dr. Clement B G
Major, Dr. Clarence
Malone, James Hiram
Marshall, Paule Burke
Mason, Felicia Lendonia
Massaquoi, Hans Jurgen
Massey, Brandon
Mathis, Sharon Bell
McArthur, Dr. Barbara Jean
McCluskey, John A
McElroy, Colleen J.
McElroy, George A.
McElvane, Pamela Anne
McFadden, Bernice L
McKee, Evelyn Palfrey
McMillan, Terry L.

McMillan, Dr. William Asbury
McWilliams-Franklin, Taj
Meriwether, Louise
Meriwether, Roy Dennis
Mickelbury, Penny
Millican, Arthenia J. Bates
Mindolovich, Monica Harris
Mitchell, Sharon L
Mixon, Veronica
Monroe, Mary
Moody, Anne
Morrison, Toni
Mosley, Walter
Murray, Albert L.
Myers, Walter Dean
Naylor, Gloria
Packer, ZZ
Patterson, Dr. Orlando Horace
Patton, Princess E
Perry, Richard
Pettis, Dr. Joyce Owens
Pinson, Hermine Dolorez
Powell, Charles Arthur
Powell, Patricia
Prewitt, J Everett
Randall, Alice
Ray, Francis
Richardson, Odis Gene
Ringgold, Faith
Robinet, Harriette Gillem
Robinson, Prof. Ella S.
Russell, Sandra Anita
Saint James, Synthia
Sampson, Dr. Henry Thomas
Sanders, Dori
Sandoval, Dolores S.
Santiago, Roberto
Scott-Heron, Gil
Smith, Barbara
Steptoe, Javaka
Stewart, Dr. John Othneil
Tademy, Lalita
Tarry, Ellen
Tate, Eleanora Elaine
Thelwell, Michael M Ekwueme
Thomas, Joyce Carol
Vanzant, Dr. Rev. Iyanla
Wade, Brent James
Walker, Alice Malsenior
Walker, Margie
Walter, Mildred Pitts
Watkins, Lenice Jackie
Welsing, Frances Cress
Wesley, Valerie Wilson
Whack, Rita Coburn
Whitfield, Van
Wideman, John Edgar
Wilkinson, Brenda
Woodson, Jacqueline
Worth, Stefanie Patrice
Wright, Sarah E
Young, Albert James

Writing/Editing—Nonfiction (*See Also* Journalism—Print)

Abdul, Raoul
Ali, Shahrazad
Allen, Robert L
Allen, S Monique Nicole
Allen, Samuel Washington
Aman, Dr. Mohammed M.
Anderson, Harold A.
Anderson, Talmadge
Angelou, Dr. Maya
Araujo, Dr. Norman
Archer, Dr. Chalmers, Jr.
Aremu, Aduke
Audain, Linz
Babb, Dr. Valerie M
Baldwin, Lewis V
Ballentine, Krim Menelik
Bandele, Asha
Banks, Dr. James Albert
Barboza, Anthony
Barboza, Steven Alan
Bates, George Albert
Bates, Karen Grigsby
Bauldock, Gerald
Becker-Slaton, Dr. Nellie Frances
Beckham, Barry Earl
Bell, Derrick Albert
Bellinger, Rev. Mary Anne Allen
Bennett, Robert A.
Bogle, Donald
Bouldes, Charlene
Boulware, Fay D.
Bowman, Dr. James E.
Boyd, Julia A

Boykin, Keith
Bradley, Andrew Thomas, Sr.
Bradley, David Henry, Jr.
Brown, Jamie Foster
Brown, Philip Lorenzo
Brown, Ralph Benjamin
Browne, Roscoe Lee
Bryant, R. Kelly
Buckley, Gail Lumet
Bundles, A'Lelia
Butcher, Dr. Philip
Butler, Washington Roosevelt, Jr.
Caines, Bruce Stuart
Canady-Laster, Rena Deloris
Carter, Dr. Wilmoth Annette
Cary, Lorene
Chavous, Mildred L.
Chideya, Farai
Coles, Kimberley
Cook, Joyce Mitchell
Cooper-Lewter, Rev. Dr. Nicholas Charles
Crews, Donald
Curwood, Stephen Thomas
Dabbs, Henry Erven
Davis, Dr. Arthur David
Davis, Belva
Davis, Gene A.
DeCosta-Willis, Dr. Miriam
DeGraffenreidt, Andrew
Derricotte, Toi
De Veaux, Alexis
Dickerson, Dr. Bette Jeanne
DuPree, Prof. Sherry Sherrod
Dyson, Michael Eric
Early, Dr. Gerald
Eubanks, W Ralph
Evanzz, Karl Anderson
Evers-Williams, Myrlie
Fairley, Juliette S
Fanaka, Jamaa
Fisher, Antwone Quenton
Fisher, Edith Maureen
Ford, Clyde W
Francis, Henry Minton
Fraser, George C.
Frazier, Shirley George
French, MaryAnn
Fulwood, Sam
Gates, Dr. Henry Louis
Gibson, Donald B.
Giddings, Paula Jane
Gill, Rev. Laverne McCain
Gill, Dr. Troy D.
Gillespie, Marcia A.
Gilmore, Dr. Al Tony
Githiga, John Gatungu
Golightly, Lena Mills
Goodman, Ruby Lene
Green-Campbell, Deardra Delores
Greenwood, Monique
Greenwood, Dr. Theresa M Winfrey
Grosvenor, VertaMae
Guy, Rosa Cuthbert
Guy-Sheftall, Beverly
Hall, Addie June
Halliburton, Warren J.
Hamilton, Dr. Paul L.
Hansen, Joyce Viola
Harris, Eddy Louis
Harris, Francis C
Harris, Dr. Trudier
Harris, William J
Haskins, James W., Jr.
Hayden, Robert C., Jr.
Hogue, Leslie Denise
Holt, Deloris Lenette
Hoover, Felix A
Hudson, Dr. Theodore R.
Huger, James E., Sr.
Hutchinson, Earl Ofari
Hyman, Mark J
Ingrum, Adrienne G
Ione, Carole
Jackson, Darcy DeMille
Jackson, Garnet Nelson
Jackson, Gordon Martin, Jr.
Jackson, Harold Jerome
Jackson, La Toya Yvonne
Jakes, Bishop Thomas Dexter
Jellerette deJongh, Monique Evadne
Johnson, Georgia Anna Lewis
Johnson, Mathew
Jones, Dr. Edward Louis
Jones, Nettie Pearl
Jones-Wilson, Faustine Clarisse
Kaiser, Ernest Daniel
Kashif, Ghayth Nur
Keyes, Alan L.

Kimbro, Dennis Paul
Kimbrough, Marjorie L.
Kincaid, Jamaica
Kitt, Sandra Elaine
Kotto, Yaphet
Kunjufu, Jawanza
Kuykendall, Dr. Crystal Arlene
Larkin, Dr. Byrdie A.
LaVeist, Dr. Thomas
Lawrence, Merlisa Evelyn
Lee, Andrea
Lee, William James Edwards, III
Leeke, Madelyn Cheryl
Lester, Julius
Lewis, David Levering
Lewis, Janice Lynn
Liverpool, Charles Eric
London, Dr. Clement B G
Long, Prof. Richard A.
Madhubuti, Haki R
Mandulo, Rhea
Mapp, Dr. Edward C.
Marr, Warren, II
Marriott, Michel
Marrs, Dr. Stella
Martin, Gertrude S
Mathabane, Mark Johannes
Matthews, Dr. Gerald Eugene
McCall, Nathan
McCray, Billy Quincy
McElroy, Colleen J.
McKee, Adam E
McKinney-Johnson, Eloise
McKissack, Fredrick Lem, Sr.
McKissack, Patricia Carwell
McMorris, Michael Anthony
Meek, Dr. Russell Charles
Meriwether, Louise
Meriwether, Roy Dennis
Miller, E. Ethelbert
Millican, Arthenia J. Bates
Mindolovich, Monica Harris
Moody, Anne
Moore, Lenard Duane
Moorehead, Eric K
Morris, Robert V
Morrow, Dr. John Howard, Jr.
Moss, Anni R.
Mumford, Esther Hall
Murray, Albert L.
Murray, Virgie W.
Musgrove, Margaret Wynkoop
Myers, Dr. Ernest Ray
Nelson, Jill
Nettleford, Hon. Rex Milton
Neverdon-Morton, Dr. Cynthia
Nivens, Beatryce Thomasinia
Nnolim, Charles E.
Noles, Eva M.
Othow, Helen Chavis
Page, Clarence
Patton, Jean E
Pawley, Thomas D., III
Pearson, Bishop Carlton Demetrius
Pemberton, Dr. Gayle R.
Perkins, Myla Levy
Perry, Margaret
Pinson, Hermine Dolorez
Porter, Bishop Henry Lee
Porter, Michael LeRoy
Powell, Adam Clayton, III
Prelow, Arleigh
Rackley, Lurma M
Ralph, Sheryl Lee
Ransby, Barbara
Redmond, Eugene B.
Reid-Merritt, Patricia Ann
Ribbins, Gertrude
Richardson, Odis Gene
Ridenhour, Carlton Douglas
Riley, Dorothy Winbush
Roberts, Tara Lynette
Rodney, Dr. Martin Hurtus
Rollins, Judith Ann
Russell, Sandra Anita
Saint James, Synthia
Sandoval, Dolores S.
Sarkodie-Mensah, Dr. Kwasi
Saunders, Doris E.
Scruggs-Leftwich, Yvonne
Seals, Theodore Hollis
Sharp, Saundra
Shields, Cydney Robin
Shockley, Ann Allen
Small, Kenneth Lester
Smith, Dr. Charles U.
Smith, Dr. Dorothy Louise White
Smith, Dr. Jessie Carney
Sowell, Thomas

Steele, Dr. Shelby
Stephens, Brooke Marilyn
Stepto, Robert Burns
Stewart, Ella
Stewart, Dr. John Othneil
Strayhorn, Lloyd
Sullivan, Andrea D.
Talbot, Gerald Edgerton
Tarry, Ellen
Taulbert, Clifton LeMoure
Taylor, Mildred D
Thelwell, Michael M Ekwueme
Thomas, Ron
Thomas-Graham, Pamela
Tollett, Dr. Charles Albert, Sr., M.D.
Travis, Dempsey J
Tyson, Asha
Van Peebles, Melvin
Vanzant, Dr. Rev. Iyanla
Wade, Unav Opal
Wade-Maltais, Dr. Joyce
Walker, Alice Malsenior
Walker, Dr. Sheila Suzanne
Walter, Mildred Pitts
Washington, Robin
Washington, Rudy
Watkins, Lenice Jackie
Watson, Prof. Denton L
Weaver, A. M.
West, Cornel
White, Constance C. R.
Wilkins, Roger Wood
Williams, Ethel Langley
Williams, John Alfred
Williams, Kathryn
Williams-Myers, Albert J
Wilson, F Leon
Wilson, Dr. Joseph F.
Witherspoon, William Roger
Woodhouse, Rossalind Yvonne
Wright, Carl Jeffrey
Wyatt, Gail E.
Wycliff, Noel Don
Wynter, Leon E
Young, Alene Marie (Penny)
Young, B Ashley
Youssef, Sitamon Mubaraka

Writing/Editing—Plays, Screenplays, TV Scripts

Abney, Robert
Angelou, Dr. Maya
Aremu, Aduke
Baraka, Imamu Amiri
Bauldock, Gerald
Beckham, Barry Earl
Benson, James Russell
Bertelsen, Phil
Blake, Jennifer Lynn
Bradley, Andrew Thomas, Sr.
Bradley, David Henry, Jr.
Branch, Otis Linwood
Branch, William Blackwell
Brown-Guillory, Elizabeth
Bullins, Ed
Burns, Khephra
Caldwell, Benjamin
Chenault, John
Clark, Dr. Fred Allen
Clark-Taylor, Kristin
Clay, Stanley Bennett
Cleage, Pearl Michelle
Coleman, Wanda
Coles, Kimberley
Colley, Nathaniel S.
Collie, Kelsey E
Collins, Tessil John
Cooper, Barry Michael
Cooper, J. California
Cowden, Michael E.
de Jongh, Prof. James Laurence
Dickey, Eric Jerome
Diesel, Vin
Easton, Earnest Lee
Evans, Mari
Fales, Susan
Fernandez, Denise Burse
Fewell, Richard
Fisher, Antwone Quenton
Franklin, J E
Fuller, Charles
Genet, Michael
Gomez, Jewelle L
Goss, Clayton
Greaves, William
Greene, Dr. Dennis
Hairston, William
Hamilton, Arthur Lee, Jr.
Hardwick, Gary C